FLYING BOATS
& AMPHIBIANS
SINCE 1945

FLYING BOATS & AMPHIBIANS
SINCE 1945

David Oliver

Airlife
England

Copyright © David Oliver 1987

First published 1987
by Airlife Publishing Ltd.

Oliver, David
    Flying boats and amphibians since 1945.
    1. Seaplanes —— History
    I. Title
    629.133'347'0904   TL684

    ISBN 0-906393-83-3

Printed in England by Livesey Ltd., Shrewsbury.

Airlife Publishing Ltd.

7 St. John's Hill, Shrewsbury, England.

CONTENTS

ACKNOWLEDGEMENTS

I would like to thank the many individuals and companies who have given their generous assistance during the preparation of this book by offering personal recollections, information and photographs, with particular thanks to the following: Giorgio Apostolo, Hubert Bolzinger, Patrick Crean, Antoine Givaudon, Rick Grant, Stuart Haig, Donald McGregor, Alain Pelletier, Wim H. Schoenmaker, J. A. Vlasto, Ron Paquet of Canadair Ltd., Christy Graham and the crews of Chalk's International Airlines, and last, but not least, Lois Lovisolo, Grumman's Corporate Historian, who has patiently and promptly dealt with my numerous queries over the past five years.

INTRODUCTION

For many, the 'Golden Age' of the flying boat began and ended in the 1930s when Imperial Airways flew the privileged few to exotic destinations on the Empire, and later North American routes in great luxury aboard a fleet of majestic Short 'C' Class boats. However, fewer than five hundred flying boats of all types, both commercial and military, were manufactured between 1930 and 1939, while almost 8,000 left the world's production lines during the subsequent six years of World War Two. Following the undoubted success of the flying boat in wartime, many saw no reason why it should not dominate commercial flying in peacetime, but they were to be proved wrong.

Due in part to the fact that the reliability and economy of landplanes had improved dramatically during the war years, and that by 1945 there was an abundance of airports with long paved runways all over the globe, again products of wartime expansion, the commercial flying boat, which required difficult to maintain and expensive marine terminals, quickly lost favour with the airlines, if not the public, and they rapidly became regarded by them as relics of a bygone age. The case for the flying boat was not helped by the fact that few leading aircraft manufacturers were willing to risk the high costs of developing new types using up-to-date technology for a dwindling civil market, or without extensive backing from governments for military versions. Therefore only civil conversions of wartime designs were available to compete with the latest breed of post-war landplane airliners.

The only flying boats available to commercial operators in the immediate post-war period were civil conversions of the wartime Short Sunderland maritime reconnaissance flying boat such as G-BJHS, the last airworthy survivor of its type. Built as a Sunderland III in 1944 for the RAF, and later the Royal New Zealand Air Force, this flying boat was subsequently bought, and civilised, by Ansett Airways of Australia in 1963. Eleven years later it was sold to Antilles Air Boats in the US Virgin Isles before being acquired by Edward Hulton in 1981, returning to the UK a year later when it flew into the Pool of London and then on to Calshot. It currently operates from the Medway at Chatham. (D. Oliver)

Model of the Saro Dutchess, a projected 74-seat flying boat powered by six Goblin turbojets of the mid-1950s that got no further than the drawing board despite having a superior performance to that of the Comet I.

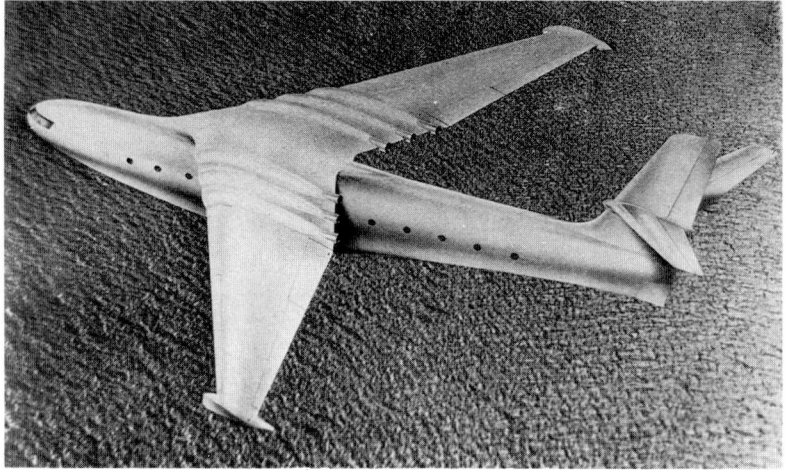

Opposite:

Saro Princess G-ALUN, the only example to fly of three built, all of which had been scrapped by 1967 without being given a chance to prove their worth. (Saunder Roe via J. Stroud)

The majestic but unfortunate Saro Princess which first flew in August 1952 having been ordered by the Ministry of Supply for BOAC, which ceased flying boat operations two years earlier. (Saunder Roe via J. Stroud)

One of the few exceptions was the unfortunate Saunders Roe Princess that had been built for the Ministry of Supply to BOAC specifications in 1952 but was destined to fail from the formidable combination of lack of suitable engines and becoming politically unfashionable. Despite a number of serious commercial bids following BOAC's rejection of the £8 million 150-ton eight-engine flying boat, from Don Bennett of British South American Airways and Eoin Mekie of Aquila Airways amongst others, the three completed Saro Princesses were cocooned 'to be available to RAF Transport Command in time of emergency'. When that time came, during the 1956 Suez crisis, the conflict was over long before the flying boats, which were each capable of carrying up to 200 troops, could be made ready and they remained in open storage at Calshot until 1967 when they were unceremoniously scrapped. The flight controls from these magnificent flying boats ended up in the flight-deck of SRN4 cross-Channel hovercraft! Despite these setbacks, Saunders Roe still firmly believed that there was a healthy future for the flying boat in the UK and had persisted with the design of the even more advanced Saro Dutchess, a promising 74-seat six-jet commercial flying boat, that could travel faster than the Comet I and at a fare of only one penny (1953 — 1d) per passenger mile, but this, along with a number of projected turboprop replacements for the RAF's ageing Sunderland, ultimately came to nothing and the company withdrew from the aviation business at the end of the 1960s.

Following the failure of Short Bros' own Sunderland replacement, the Shetland, in 1947, the disbanding of BOAC's flying boat fleet in 1950 and, more importantly, the Ministerial statement made in the House of Commons in 1954 that 'The Government have considered the future of the flying boat and have decided that it would not be justifiable to undertake the development of a new flying boat for military purposes', Britain's leading 'boat manufacturer' turned its back on the flying boat.

However, in the United States the military continued to support the flying boat concept and such experienced marine aircraft manufacturers as Martin and Grumman were taking full advantage of the new technologies that had recently become available to develop a new breed of post-war flying boats and amphibians. But even here there were a number of very expensive casualties, including Howard Hughes' gigantic $40 million H3 Hercules, known as the 'Spruce Goose', which made a very brief maiden flight in 1947 and was promptly consigned to permanent storage by its unpredictable designer. Two more costly failures of the 1950s, both in money and lives, were the US Navy's revolutionary jet-powered Martin Seamaster long range mine-laying and reconnaissance flying boat and turboprop Convair Tradewind military transport, both of which had the misfortune of being designed ahead of the then known technology.

At the same time, behind the Iron Curtain, disappointing performances of a number of jet-powered maritime reconnaissance flying boats designed by the Soviet Union's most experienced flying boat designer, Georgii Beriev, failed to justify large scale production, while a twin-engine ten-seat commercial amphibian in the Mallard category, the Chyetverikov TA-1, was produced for Aeroflot in 1948, but as with BOAC and the Princess, its design bureau fell from political favour and further production of the amphibian was subsequently cancelled.

Meanwhile, France had built a number of giant six-engined passenger flying boats during the immediate post-war period, in particular the Sud-Est SE 200 and Latécoère 631, both of which were pre-war designs and destined to enjoy very short careers with Air France before being broken up.

In spite of such expensive and often spectacular failures, many of them having nothing to do with the basic design of the aircraft, it may come as a surprise to learn that some 1,700 multi-engined military and commercial flying boats and amphibians have been built since 1945, plus another 2,000-plus single engine types, such as the Republic Seabee and Lake Buccaneer, along with countless floatplane conversions.

There are currently approximately 350 multi-engined types operating throughout the world undertaking such specialised roles as that of search and rescue and maritime reconnaissance with several air forces and navies, the commercial transport of passengers and cargo in isolated areas, oceanographic research and, of increasing importance, fighting forest fires.

The development of the reliable and economical turboprop engine in recent years has led to a new lease of life for the flying boat and amphibian. Not only are existing piston engine types having their lives extended, as well as range and payload, by being retrofitted with compact lightweight turboprop power-plants, but the turboprop has encouraged new designs that will be able to compete on favourable terms with contemporary landplane designs in both cost and performance, while retaining the unique capability of operating from either land or water.

The following chapters will attempt to describe eleven major multi-engined flying boats and amphibians that have been produced by seven different countries since 1945, and to look at some of the exciting new marine aircraft projects that are currently being developed in West Germany, Italy and Japan. Although some of the featured aircraft were produced in relatively small numbers, all operated commercially or served with regular military units, and many will continue to do so well into the 21st century.

CHAPTER ONE
THE GRUMMAN MALLARD

During the Second World War the Grumman Aircraft Corp of Bethpage, New York, had built up an enviable reputation for producing a line of tough and powerful Navy fighter aircraft, such as the Wildcat, Hellcat and Bearcat, that had captured the public's imagination by helping to defeat the Japanese in a series of classic Pacific carrier battles.

However, one of the company's first products had been a single-engined utility amphibian, the J2 Duck, which was designed by Grover Loening for the US Navy in 1933. This was soon followed by Grumman's first twin-engined amphibian, the rugged six/seven-seat G-21 Goose that flew for the first time in June 1937. Three years later a four-seat twin, the G-44 Widgeon, virtually a scaled-down Goose, also went into production at the company's

Bethpage plant near New York. The initial, and continuing success, of these two amphibians, many of which are still flying almost half a century later, can be attributed largely to the simplicity of their design and the strength of their construction. Both the Goose and Widgeon were originally conceived as executive 'yachts' for wealthy sportsmen and adventurers, but both were destined to see extensive wartime, and post-war, service with the air arms of more that a dozen countries including the US Navy and Coast Guard, the RAF and the Royal Navy, and France's Naval air arm.

Mallard NC2947 was the tenth built, being operated by Grumman as a demonstrator before being sold to the magazine Popular Mechanics in 1947. (Grumman)

With the end of hostilities in sight, Grumman's amphibian design team, led by William T. Schwendler and Gordon Israel, set about developing the well-proven Goose/Widgeon theme by producing a large twin-engined ten-seat commercial transport amphibian.

The result was the G-73 Mallard that first flew in April 1946 with Frederick C. Rowley at the controls. The attractive, well-proportioned high-wing amphibian, powered by two 600 hp Pratt & Whitney R-1340-S3H1 Wasp radial engines, featured a modern tricycle undercarriage and extra fuel tanks fitted in the wing floats. The new amphibian suffered few teething troubles and the first customer aircraft left the Bethpage production line in September 1947, although the type was not fully certified for another year. Grumman had pinned its hopes on a large worldwide market, thought at the time to be in access of 250, for the small amphibious passenger airliner, but they had not taken into account the large numbers of cheap war surplus transports that flooded the market in the late 1940s, including many ex-military Gooses and Widgeons, and with a price tag of between $100,000 and $125,000, were disappointed at selling only 59 when production ceased in 1951.

The second ex-Shell Mallard to be sold to the Indonesian Police in 1963, P2011, seen here at Hong Kong's Kai Tak airport, was converted to turboprops in 1971 and is currently operated by Chalks International Airline in Miami. (L. Callaghan)

In the event, most of the 26 Mallards delivered during the first full year of production were purchased by large corporations for use by company executives, Ford, General Motors and Christian Dior were all early Mallard customers while the amphibian also sold steadily to the oil companies including Texaco, which operated four for nearly thirty years, and Shell, which purchased a total of five between 1948 and 1951. Two were acquired by the Superior Oil Company in 1947, one of which was involved in a fatal crash in London two years later. The Dior aircraft, although registered to the company's New York office, spent much of its time in Europe flying the rich and famous, such as the Aga Khan, to social hotspots in Britain and on the Continent and was to be seen at Croydon Airport on a number of occasions in the mid-1950s on Derby Day or during Ascot week.

A few were acquired by magazines and newspapers, one belonging to the *New York Daily News* being used to film the sinking of the Italian luxury liner, the *Andrea Doria,* in 1954. Yet another was sold to Twentieth Century-Fox Films in Hollywood.

Grumman's prototype Mallard, NX41824, seen against the New York skyline. This aircraft first flew in April 1946 and was later sold in Canada where it was destroyed in a crash in December 1951. (Grumman)

N2947, seen without floats when owned by Bower Rolling Bearing Co in the 1960s, became the first Turbo Mallard conversion in 1968. It is currently operated by Virgin Island Seaplane Shuttle. (Air Britain)

Mallard F7 was delivered to the Royal Egyptian Air Force in March 1949 but was little used before being scrapped at Cairo seventeen years later.

A number of Grumman Mallards wer purchased by other aircraft manufacturers Sikorsky, Boeing, Aero Commander and Canadai amongst them, and the latter company was t incorporate a number of Grumman's desig philosophies when it produced its own amphibiou aircraft in 1967. Few in fact, were initiall purchased by airlines although Pacific Wester Airlines of Vancouver, BC, acquired three in 1954 which continued to operate in Canada with th airline and its successors until the early 1980s. Nitt Airlines of Tokyo purchased five in the same yea while another was used by Air Tahiti to fl passengers between Bora Bora and Papeete durin the late 1950s. An ex-Shell Mallard also carrie fare-paying passengers in the Pacific when it wa operated briefly by Trans Australia Airlines in 196 and later with Air Pacific, based in Fiji, from 196 to 1971.

Apart from becoming a popular form of luxur transport for a number of wealthy individual many of whom had previously owned a Goose or Widgeon, various members of Royalty and Head of State used the Mallard at one time or another. I June 1948, Prince Bernhard of the Netherlands fle one of the Shell Mallards from Amsterdam Airpor while the aircraft was on its delivery flight to th Dutch East Indies (Indonesia), and was reported t have been keen to acquire one for the Netherland Royal Flight. Egypt's King Farouk ordered tw Mallards in 1949. These luxuriously appointe amphibians, registered *F7* and *F8,* were used by th Egyptian Royal Flight until Farouk fled th country in 1952 after which they were taken over b the Egyptian Air Force and stripped of their Roya trappings, but were seldom used before bein scrapped in the late 1960s. Queen Elizabeth an Prince Philip flew in a BC Airlines Mallard fror Kamloops to Pennash Lake in British Columbi during their 1959 Royal Tour of Canada. In 1974 Mallard was acquired for Gabon's Presidenti Flight but was destroyed in a crash in the Atlant off the coast of Gabon less than a year later — th President was not aboard.

However, the worst period for Mallard accident was 1954/55 when no less than four were lost. On of these occurred in January 1954 when the Unio Producing Co's Mallard crashed near Shrevepor Louisiana, while returning from a hunting tri killing all on aboard including Tom Braniff, th founder of Braniff Airways. The major cause c this, and a large proportion of other Mallard accidents, was icing, since the aircraft's floats and wingtips lacked de-icers. Many of the aircraft operated in northern Canada and Alaska where, during the exceptionally cold winters, ice was liable to build up on these parts, which in turn created extra drag. As the piston-engined Mallard was considered by some to be somewhat under-powered, this condition resulted in the loss of several aircraft. The only major crash to a passenger-carrying aircraft occurred in February 1964 when a Nitto Airlines Mallard crashed en route to Tokyo after losing power on take-off from Osaka.

However it was the advent of the compact turboprop engine, and in particular the small but powerful Pratt & Whitney PT6, that gave the ageing Mallard a new lease of life in the late 1960s. The moving force behind the conversion was not the manufacturer, but a former bush pilot called Fred Frakes, who had owned a Mallard for some time but was less than impressed with its single engine performance, or lack of it. Encouraged by Ray Peterson, president of Wein Consolidated Airlines of Alaska, Frakes replaced the Mallard's R-1340 piston engines with 680 shp PT6A-27 turboprops and overnight the Mallard was transformed into the world's only turboprop-powered commercial amphibian.

The Turbo Mallard was an unqualified success. The all-up weight was increased by a ton, range, with a full passenger load and baggage, almost doubled, economical cruising speed increased by twenty per cent and direct operating costs reduced. Additional benefits were derived from the slightly increased angle of the PT6 installation combined

The second Mallard to be delivered to the REAF, F8, in August 1949 was used by King Farouk's Royal Flight before he was forced to abdicate in 1952. (Grumman)

Built in January 1949, N51151 was converted to turboprops in 1981 and is currently operated by Chalks in whose Fort Lauderdale maintenance facility it is seen here undergoing a major check. (D. Oliver)

with the fitting of a smaller diameter propeller which gave greater tip clearance when on the water and thus less spray and water ingestion so reducing turbine corrosion. As an added bonus the Turbo Mallard was also better balanced both in the air and on the water. Short take-offs in the Beta mode took only 300 ft (91m) of water. All these improvements were very attractive to the feeder airline market, the one that the Mallard had been originally designed for, but there was one disadvantage — the high price of conversion: some $800,000!

However, Frakes completed the first of thirteen conversions to date at his base at Angwin California in 1971, although most were carried out at Frakes Aviation's present base at Cleburn Lake Texas, all of which had extra de-icing equipment fitted as an additional safety feature. The majority were re-engined with the 715 shp Pratt & Whitney Canada PT6A-34 turboprops.

Meanwhile the twenty-year-old Mallard had lost its 'playboy' image as executive examples were sold off to more down-to-earth industrial corporations during the 1960s, such as the Freeport Sulpher Co of New Orleans and the Utah Mining Co of Invercargill, New Zealand. Early in 1960, a Mallard belonging to the Canadian aerial survey company Spartan Air Services, made a 23,000-mile (37,000km) round trip from Toronto to Mahé in the Seychelles, where it undertook an extensive photo survey of the island group. A unique feature of the Spartan aircraft was the positioning of a watertight camera hatch in the hull aft of the step on the centre line. Two of Shell's aircraft were sold to the Indonesian Police Force in 1963 after fifteen years of continuous service with the oil company in Indonesia and New Guinea, and in the same year the first Mallard to be operated and registered in the United Kingdom was purchased by Dennis Ferranti Ltd of Bangor, Wales.

This aircraft was bought from the Quebec Dep of Transport & Communication and delivered to Starways Ltd at Speke (Liverpool) in September 1962, who overhauled the amphibian and fitted it with an executive interior. Registered G-ASCS, the Mallard was based in Manchester from where it was mainly used to fly Mr Dennis Ferranti to his properties in Scotland and France. In 1967 Captain Donald 'Mac' McGregor, a Canadian ex-BOAC flying boat pilot, was employed to fly the Mallard and has some fond memories of the amphibian.

'I liked the Mallard. It was reliable and handled well in the air and on the water. Taxying in cross winds was no problem thanks to the tricycle undercarriage whereas its predecessor, the Goose with its tail wheel undercarriage was a real handful. Most of the flights were to Scotland where Mr Ferranti had a large estate at Mallaig on the West Coast opposite the Isle of Skye. I used to fly the Mallard from Manchester to RAF Valley on Anglesey to pick up Mr Ferranti, often with family or friends. We flew the 250 miles [400km] to Mallaig following the West Coast, sometimes landing at Tiree en route. We landed on Loch Morar, the western end of which was bordered by the road to Mallaig, some two miles away, and the aircraft would be moored in the Loch while Mr Ferranti took his party on hunting or fishing trips. Occasionally I would fly around the area looking for "flunk holes" — emergency landing sites.

'I also flew the Mallard to Jersey via Southampton on one occasion, and more than once to Biarritz, where Mr Ferranti owned another property and kept his yacht. The longest flight I made in the Mallard was to Coruña in Spain when we cleared customs in Bilbao after the short flights from Bordeaux and Biarritz. The aircraft was full of heavy equipment including HF, ILS and Decca, but as Mr Ferranti had said that, as he bought the Mallard to be able to see what he was flying over he did not want to fly in the clouds, so the navaids were seldom used. Mr Ferranti also had the habit of filling the aircraft with vast amounts of luggage on these trips which, when added to the weight of all the navigational equipment, made it close to the limit on occasions although we never operated out of any restricted areas. Loch Morar was nearly ten miles long and there was plenty of room at Manchester and Valley. In between trips I often practised water landings on the Menai Straits which divided Anglesey from the mainland. Sometimes Mr Ferranti's helicopter pilot came along for the ride.'

The ex-Dior Mallard was converted to turboprops in 1973 and sold by Air BC in 1983 to Air Whitsunday in Australia, as VH-JAW, currently operated by Helicopter Resources in the same country. (L. Callaghan)

One of Chalks International Airways Grumman Turbo Mallards approaching the airline's flying boat base on Watson Island, Miami, Florida, in November 1986. (D. Oliver)

Three of Chalks four Turbo Mallards at Watson Island, Miami, in November 1986. (D. Oliver)

Antilles Air Boats Piston Mallard N1208 at St Croix in 1981 before it was acquired by Chalks and converted to turboprops and currently operated by Chalks. (K. Sissons). *See above.*

At the beginning of 1968 the Mallard was sold and after a period, during which time it was rumoured to have been used for gun-running to Biafra, it was eventually acquired by Chalk's International Airline of Miami in 1972. Chalk's was one of the oldest airlines in the US, having been formed on 1 June 1919 as Chalk's Flying Service, using Curtiss HS-2L flying boats. The airline's early passengers included bootleggers, Prohibition having been introduced in January 1919, and mobsters, such as Al Capone who lived on nearby Star Island. The airline, which has been flying much the same route network since it started, from Watson Island, Miami, to islands in the Bahamas, began to supplement, and ultimately replace, its fleet of Gooses and Widgeons with Mallards during the late 1960s. By 1974 the airline operated six Mallards, one of which was hi-jacked to Cuba in March 1972 but returned undamaged although the pilot, Captain James Cothron, was shot and wounded during the incident.

In the same year Antilles Air Boats, founded by the veteran flying boat pilot Captain Charles Blair in 1964, added four Mallards to its varied fleet of Goose and Widgeon amphibians, and Sandringham, Sunderland and Vought-Sikorsky VS-44A flying boats, flying between San Juan and the US Virgin Isles.

In the late 1970s, a Mallard starred in the Australian Television series entitled *Bailey's Bird* about an Australian boy whose father was a Mallard pilot flying for a charter company existing on a shoestring budget in Malaysia. During the making of the series, which was extensively shown in Australasia, Britain and the United States, the US registered Mallard *N83781*, thought to be an ex-Shell aircraft, was based in Singapore.

By the end of 1986, no less than a third of all Mallards built, including all of the turbo versions, were still in active service with airlines as far apart as Canada and Australia. Currently the largest Mallard operator is the Virgin Islands Seaplane Shuttle that took over Antilles Air Boat routes after the airline folded following Captain Blair's fatal accident in a Goose in 1979. VISS operates a fleet of five fifteen-passenger Piston Mallards and seven seventeen-passenger Turbo Mallards flying high-frequency commuter services connecting St Thomas and St Croix in the US Virgin Islands, with Tortola in the British Virgin Islands and San Juan, Puerto Rico. Unfortunately, the airline suffered its first fatal accident on 28 November 1986 when a Piston Mallard N60455, the oldest still flying — number four off the production line built in October 1946 — lost power in one engine during take-off from St Croix and crashed into the sea off

A privately owned Mallard, N168W, seen at Miami in 1976.
(Air Britain)

The ex-Ferranti Mallard seen here at St Croix in the US Virgin Islands in 1981 operated by Antilles Air Boats as N7356, and is currently operated by that airline's successor Virgin Island Seaplane Shuttle. (K Sissons)

Protestant Cay. One passenger was drowned and thirteen injured.

Chalk's International Airlines have operated four Turbo Mallards since 1979 flying nine scheduled round-trip flights per day out of Watson Island, Miami, and Fort Lauderdale to Paradise Island, Nassau, Bimini and Cat Cay in the Bahamas, one of which was seen in millions of homes every week on the credits of another TV series, *Miami Vice*. Nearly all of Chalk's Mallard crews are younger than the aircraft they fly, having come to the airline with a commercial rating before being sent to Jack Brown's Seaplane Base in Florida to convert to a Twin Seabee amphibian before becoming a Mallard co-pilot. The Turbo Mallard is considered by its pilots as a 'hot ship', being responsive, manoeuvrable and fast. It cruises at 160 knots and the extra power has to be handled with respect, especially during take-off when too much power too quickly can lead to porpoising. The Chalk's aircraft have little in the way of navaids but are fitted with dual instrument panels for the two-man crew. However, they have proved popular with both the airline, since the time between overhauls of the PT6s has recently been increased to 5,000 hours, and with their passengers, average Mallard passenger loads being a healthy 85 per cent.

For many of its passengers, a flight in a Chalk's Mallard is their first and, probably, only flight in a flying boat. Seated in narrow, non-reclining but comfortable plastic-covered seats, facing two electric fans at the front of the cabin, the experience of taxying down the ramp on Watson Island and into the water to be surrounded by yachts, motor cruisers and luxury liners that are for ever entering and leaving the busy Port of Miami, is a memorable one. As soon as the pilot reaches a clear stretch of water leading out to sea the throttles are opened and the view from the windows is immediately obscured by a wall of water until the Mallard is up on its step, then the slap of the water on the hull

CF-UOT, an ex-Nordair Turbo Mallard owned by Maclad Enterprises of Ottawa seen at Northolt in June 1985 en route to Islay in Scotland. (I. Cave)

Mallard N2980 was used by its manufacturer as a utility aircraft before being sold to Texaco.

suddenly ceases as the amphibian begins a leisurely climb on an easterly heading. The Mallard settles down to a 160 knot cruise flying between 1,000 and 2,500 ft (305 and 760m) according to the weather for the sixty-mile (96km) flight to the closest of the Bahama islands, Bimini. Twenty minutes later the aircraft begins its descent to the island. Heading straight for water in an aircraft, with no runway in view, can be disconcerting for those more used to travelling in wide-bodied jets, as does the rush of water that seems to engulf the Mallard as it alights. For most passengers it is an unforgettable experience.

A second Florida-based commuter airline, Walkers International, also operate a Piston Mallard from Fort Lauderdale. On the other side of the globe, the colourfully named flying boat operator, Air Whitsunday, runs sightseeing and charter flights along Australia's Great Barrier Reef from Hardy Lagoon in Queensland, with a Piston Mallard, while Helicopter Resources of Adelaide operate an ex-Air BC Turbo Mallard on charter services in support of mineral research and gas exploration. A second ex-Air BC Turbo Mallard owned by Maclad Enterprises of Ottawa was based on the Island of Islay in the Inner Hebrides for three months during the summer of 1985 flying well-to-do North American fishermen around Scotland.

So, some forty years after the maiden flight of its durable Mallard, Grumman's original concept of an amphibious feeder-liner seems to have been proved correct and is one being closely studied by a number of European manufacturers who may produce a replacement for the Mallard by the time it reaches its half century.

Grumman G-73 Mallard

Accommodation: Crew: 2
Passengers: 10
Power Plants: Two 600 hp Pratt & Whitney R-1340-S3H1 Wasp nine-cylinder radials
Dimensions: Wingspan: 66 ft 8 in (20.32 m)
Length: 48 ft 4 in (14.73 m)
Height: 18 ft 9 in (5.7 m)
Wing area: 444 sq ft (41.3 m²)
Weights: Empty: 9,350 lb (4,241 kg)
Average: 12,750 lb (5,783 kg)
Performance: Max speed: 215 mph (346 km/h)
Cruising speed: 180 mph (290 km/h)
Range: 730 miles (1,175 km)

Grumman G-73T Turbo Mallard

Accommodation: Crew: 2
Passengers: 15
Power Plants: Two 715 shp Pratt & Whitney Canada PT6A-34 Turboprops
Dimensions: Wingspan: 66 ft 8 in (20.32 m)
Length: 48 ft 4 in (14.73 m)
Height: 18 ft 9 in (5.7 m)
Wing area: 444 sq ft (41.3 m²)
Weights: Empty: 8,500 lb (3,855 kg)
Average: 14,000 lb (6,350 kg)
Performance: Max speed: 225 mph (362 km/h)
Cruising speed: 200 mph (322 km/h)
Range: 1,065 miles (1,714 km)

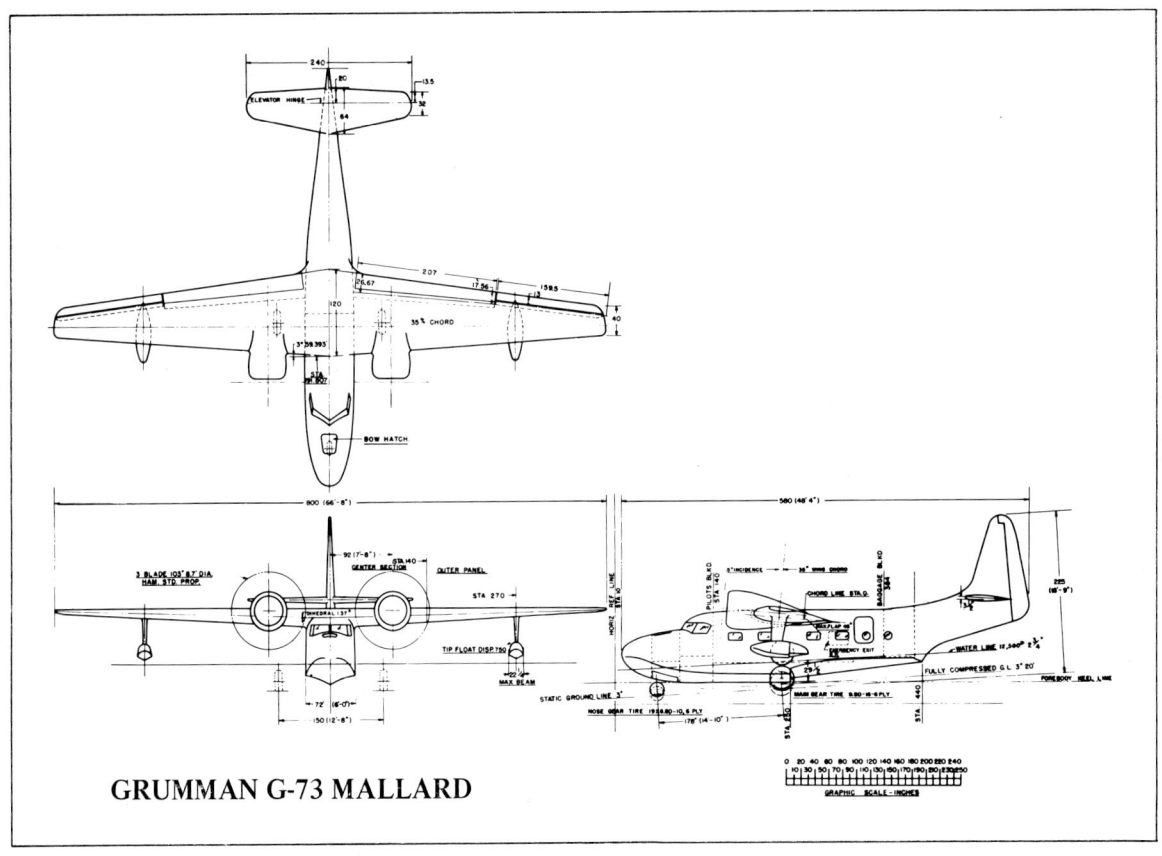

GRUMMAN G-73 MALLARD

CHAPTER TWO
THE SHORT SOLENT

In April 1945 the Short Seaford, a more powerful and heavily armed derivative of Short's classic wartime flying boat, the Sunderland, made its first flight from Rochester. Short Brothers were at the time Britain's most experienced commercial flying boat manufacturer, having produced their first, the twin-engined biplane Calcutta, in 1926; this had been followed by the luxurious 'C' Class 'Empire' boats built for Imperial Airways in the 1930s, and they in turn were the forerunners of the even more famous long-range Maritime Reconnaissance Sunderland that served with the RAF's Coastal Command throughout the Second World War and for many years after.

However, the Second World War was almost over in April 1945 and BOAC was looking for a replacement for its fleet of pre-war 'C' Class flying boats, few of which had survived the war, and for its converted Sunderlands (known in the Corporation as Hythes), so the second production Seaford was loaned to BOAC in 1946 for evaluation as a commercial transport. As a result of these trials the Corporation ordered twelve civilianised Seafords, known as the Short S45 Solent 2, to be named *Salisbury, Scarborough, Southampton, Somerset, Sark, Scapa, Severn, Solway, Salcombe, Stornoway,* *Sussex* and *Southsea,* while the six of the Seafords so far produced for the RAF, but which with the end of hostilities had already been declared surplus to requirements, were converted to Solent 3 commercial transports. These were named *City of London, City of Cardiff, City of Belfast, City of Liverpool, Singapore* and *Sydney.* The first BOAC Solent 2, *G-AHIL,* powered by two 1,690 hp Bristol Hercules 637 radial engines, was launched at Rochester on 11 November 1947, while the third, *G-AHIN,* was christened *Southampton* on the occasion of the opening of BOAC's new marine air terminal at Berth 50 in the Old Docks at Southampton on 14 April 1948. This could accommodate two flying boats at the end of a 1,000 ft (300m) pier. In September 1948, the second BOAC Solent, *G-AHIM Scarborough,* made an impressive public debut at the first SBAC air show at Farnborough when Captain Alcock put the big boat through its paces at low level and more often than not using only two of the four engines.

BOAC Solent 2 G-AHIY, Southsea, was the last to be launched, on 8 April 1948, and the last flying boat to be built at Rochester. (Charles E. Brown)

Short's production line of Solent 2 flying boats for BOAC at Rochester in 1947 with G-AHIO, Somerset, in the foreground. (Shorts)

The Corporation's pilots had nothing but praise for the flying boat and, apart from the loss of a number of wing floats during take-offs and landings, which led to the struts being moved outboard and strengthened, the Solent had a relatively trouble-free entry into service. However, following route-proving flights to Australia, BOAC decided that the London to Sydney route, which between 1948 and 1950 was flown by the Sandringham (a civilised Sunderland 3), would be taken over by Lockheed Constellations. This was in order to compete with same type operated by Qantas which took $4\frac{1}{2}$ days instead of the Solents' $10\frac{1}{2}$ days, and left the flying boats to operate the South African service.

The BOAC Solents seated 34 passengers in some comfort on two decks. A spiral staircase connected the decks, the upper being fitted with a cocktail bar, lounge, stewards' compartment and galley, while the lower deck was divided into three passenger cabins with a promenade, dressing rooms and lavatories. A crew of seven was normally carried.

Something of the experience of flying Flight BA103/115, the Springbok route, by Solent in the early post-war years can be gained from a BOAC press release of the time.

'The service is operated by BOAC's No 4 line with the new 35-ton Short Solent aircraft — the largest British commercial flying boat used so far — which began on 4 May 1948, when a twice-weekly service was introduced increasing later to a frequency of three per week, in each direction. It leaves from the new BOAC marine air terminal at Southampton and is flown by the Solent which accommodates 34 passengers.

'The flight leaves Southampton on Tuesday and is due in Johannesburg on Friday morning. The route and flying times for each day's journey on the outward flight are approximately as follows:

	Hours	Miles
Southampton — Augusta (Sicily)	6½	1,260
Augusta — Luxor via Cairo	7	1,360
Luxor — Port Bell via Khartoum	10	1,752
Port Bell — Victoria Falls	7	1,340
Victoria Falls — Vaaldam FB Terminal (Jo'burg)	4	640

BOAC Solent 2 G-AHIY, Southsea, was the last to be launched, on 8 April 1948, and the last flying boat to be built at Rochester. (Charles E. Brown)

BOAC's Solent 2 G-AHIN, Southampton, was launched in January 1947 but not christened until April 1948 at the inauguration of BOAC's new marine terminal at Southampton. (Shorts)

The fifth BOAC Solent 2 G-AHIR, Sark, also launched in January 1947, retired in November 1950. (Shorts)

'Night stops are made at Augusta, Luxor, Port Bell and Victoria Falls. On the return journey there are night stops at Victoria Falls, Port Bell, Cairo and Augusta. A refuelling stop is made at Cairo on the outward flight and at Khartoum in each direction. There is no call at Luxor on the return journey. Alternative landing facilities for the service are available near Lusaka, capital of Northern Rhodesia, and on the southern end of Lake Victoria, on the northern journey. The alternative alighting area for the Jo'burg terminal at Vaaldam will be Lourenco-Marques.

'From the UK to Khartoum, the route is already well known. Mainly it is the same as the pre-war Imperial Airways flying boat service to South Africa, as far as Port Bell, although various intermediate stops made by the "C" Class flying boats are now omitted, and Augusta is a new point of call. After Port Bell, the old route follows the coast from Mombasa to Durban; the new one goes across Tanganyika and Northern and Southern Rhodesia to Jo'burg. It is the later stages of the journey, indeed, that are of special interest, as for the first time flying boats are making regular use of the central African system of rivers and lakes, altogether some 2,000 miles [3,200 km], the longest section being from Port Bell to Victoria Falls.

'The passenger begins these later stages of the flight with the attractions of historic Luxor fresh in the mind. Luxor, in the Nile valley, is a noted tourist attraction and was originally an Arab settlement on the site of the ruins of the great city of Thebes. After Luxor and Khartoum the air journey continues to Port Bell, flying boat landing point on the northern shores of Lake Victoria Nyanza, and facilities, including a restaurant, will be available for passengers in transit. Passengers will overnight at Kampala, seven miles [11 km] to the north-west. On the next leg of the journey, passengers are treated to the unique view of the mighty spectacle that is the Victoria Falls by the thunderous roar which can be heard for many miles; from the air passengers can first see in the far distance what appears to be a little plume of spray above a vast green African forest — a sight which alone is an excellent guide to the flying boat's alighting area. An alternative alighting area at Kafue is only used when flying boats are unable to alight at Victoria Falls due to weather or other reasons.

'The Johannesburg terminal at Vaaldam is on the Vaal River. Vaaldam was constructed to store water for the domestic and industrial needs of the City of Johannesburg and the Reef.

'Between Vaaldam and Jo'burg, a distance of 58 miles [93 km], passengers are carried by an airport coach in two hours. No internal air services operate to Vaaldam but Jo'burg is connected by air to the chief centres in South Africa, Portuguese West

BOAC Solent 2 G-AHIU, Solway, launched in February 1948, seen here taking-off from Southampton water. (BA)

The ex-BOAC Solent 3 G-AKNU was acquired by Aquila Airways in December 1951. (Shorts)

The same aircraft seen at Capri on the inaugural flight from Southampton on 3 June 1954. The aircraft was lost on 15 November 1957 when it crashed near Chessel on the Isle of Wight while en route from Southampton to Lisbon, with the loss of 35 lives. (J. Stroud)

Africa [Angola], the Rhodesias and Nyasaland, as well as with most of the main cities of the world.'

Although the BOAC flying boats no longer flew to Australasia, Shorts' first export order for the Solent was placed by Tasman Empire Airways Ltd (TEAL) of New Zealand which ordered five long-range Solent 4s powered by the more powerful 2,040 hp Bristol Hercules 733 to replace its fleet of Short Sandringhams, civilianised Sunderlands, in 1949. In May of that year, TEAL's flagship, *ZK-AML*, was christened *Aotearoa II* by Princess Elizabeth at Belfast, where Solent production had been transferred when the Rochester line closed. The airline flew its first scheduled Solent service, to Fiji, in June 1950, the fare for the $7\frac{1}{2}$-hour flight being £31. On 3 October 1950 TEAL's second 45-seater Solent, *Ararangi*, took off from Evans Bay to launch a three times a week Wellington to Sydney service in addition to its five flights each week from Auckland to Sydney. The single fare for both routes cost £28 with a £50 return fare. Two months later a Wellington to Chatham Islands route was inaugurated. However, by 1950 BOAC had reconsidered its flying boat operations in light of the increasing costs and competition from landplane operations. Back in 1947 the Corporation's Annual Report had complained that marine airports and flying boat passengers' overnight accommodation was costing £1,150,000 a year, and by 1949 some 900 staff were employed at the Corporation's flying boat headquarters at Hythe. At the beginning of 1950 BOAC announced that flying boat operations would begin to be phased out during the next two years. However, on 3 November 1950, services abruptly ceased with Solent *G-AHIO Somerset* leaving Southampton's Berth 50 for the last time, bound for South Africa. Most of the three-year-old Solent fleet was subsequently scrapped at Hamsworthy or Belfast.

This decision had far-reaching consequences for Britain's flying boat manufacturers, bringing to an end not only of any further Solent sales (a total of 23 having been produced), but the ambitious Saro Princess programme that had been built to BOAC's specifications, and ultimately leading to the demise of flying boat production in the United Kingdom.

Meanwhile, in New Zealand and the South Pacific, TEAL's Solents were enjoying something of an Indian summer as landplanes took over the world's international services. Having taken delivery of its fifth Solent in September 1951, which was in fact an ex-BOAC Mark 3, TEAL established the famous 'Coral Route' in December 1951. Fortnightly flights from Auckland to Suva, Aitutaki (Cook Islands) and Tahiti were initially inaugurated while the route was extended to include Satapaula (Western Samoa) in October 1952, and Tonga in March 1953.

During 1953, TEAL's flagship *ZK-AML Aotearoa II* (which is Maori for 'Land of the Long White Cloud'), carried Queen Elizabeth and Prince Philip on their tour of New Zealand. However, a little over a year later TEAL had replaced the Solents with DC6s on both the New Zealand to Sydney routes and the landplanes took over the Fiji flights by the end of June 1954, although the flying boats continued to operate between Suva-Satapaula-Aitutaki and Tahiti and between Suva and Tonga.

At the same time Trans Oceanic Airways had been operating a flying boat service from Sydney's ~~ose~~ Bay Water Airport since 1947, initially with a ~~et~~ of Hythes and, later, three ex-BOAC Solents. ~~he~~ airline's first Solent 3, *G-AKNO City of ~~ondon~~*, was lost during its delivery flight to ~~ustralia~~ when it crashed on take-off from ~~Marsaxlokk~~ Bay, Malta, in January 1951. It was ~~arrying~~ 39 passengers on the flight from Belfast to ~~ydney~~ but the crew and all but one of the ~~assengers~~ were fortunate to be rescued by RAF ~~unches~~. A replacement, another Mark 3 named *~~tar~~ of Papua,* ex-*G-AKNP City of Cardiff,* arrived ~~n~~ Australia three months later and had been joined

BOAC's first Solent 3 G-AKNO, City of London, seen on the Thames on the occasion of the 30th anniversary of British Air Transport, in May 1949. Following the end of BOAC's flying boat operations, the flying boat was sold to Trans Oceanic Airways but sank on take-off from Malta during its delivery flight to Australia in January 1951. (Shorts)

TEAL's first Solent 4 ZK-AML, Aotearoa II, was christened by Princess Elizabeth at Belfast on 26 May 1949, seen here on a pre-delivery test-flight. (Shorts)

Opposite:

TEAL's third Solent 4 ZK-AMN, Awatere, was launched from Belfast in October 1949 seen here on a test-flight soon after in company with its little brother, the Short Sealand amphibian. (Charles E. Brown)

by two more 'Starliners' by October 1951. The airline, which was partly owned by the Clan Shipping Line, was operating twice-weekly Solent flights between Sydney and Port Moresby, and four services a week from Sydney to Hobart by the end of the year. However, less than a year later, following the loss of a second Solent, *VH-TOC Star of Hobart,* after hitting a dredger on take-off in October 1951, the resignation of the airline's founder, Captain Brian Monkton, in March 1952 and increasing competition from Qantas, TOA went into liquidation listing amongst its assets two Solents valued at £110,000.

The following April, Captain Monkton formed South Pacific Airlines in partnership with Captain Fred Barnes, and purchased the two TOA Solents to operate a weekly service between Honolulu and Tahiti via a refuelling stop on Christmas Island. However the new venture, backed by a large US corporation, was experiencing delays from both the US authorities in Honolulu and the British on Christmas Island, and services had still not begun by the time a third Solent, *G-AKNT,* ex-BOAC *Singapore,* joined *N9946F* and *N9945F* at San Francisco in November 1955 where they awaited FAA certification.

Cut-away of a Trans Empire Airways Ltd (TEAL) Solent 4.
(Shorts)

Following the demise of BOAC's flying boat fleet, its facilities at Southampton had been taken over by Aquila Airways Ltd, which was formed in 1948 by Wing Commander Barry Aikman. Aquila's fleet of ex-BOAC Hythes, civil conversions of the Sunderland, had taken part in the Berlin airlift and flown charters to such diverse destinations as Karachi and the Falkland Islands. However, in 1949 the airline took an important step forward when it was granted approval to operate a scheduled weekly service from Southampton to the island of Madeira. Aquila acquired an ex-BOAC Solent 3, *G-AKNU Sydney,* in December 1951, and this enabled the route to be extended to Las Palmas in the Canary Islands. The airline was fortunate to have the use of excellent flying boat facilities at Funchal Bay, Madeira, and Las Palmas as well as Cabo Ruivo, Lisbon, which was used as a refuelling stop on the northbound journey, and the service was increased to twice weekly in 1952 with a return fare of £59.10s. The Solent was also used for trooping flights to Singapore carrying 53 Servicemen and their families, the upper deck bar having been removed to make room for the extra seats; it also undertook a number of charters to the 1952 Olympic Games at Helsinki. In June 1953, *Sydney* flew a series of sightseeing flights, at £10 a time, over the Fleet assembled off Spithead for the Royal Review following the Queen's Coronation.

The year 1953 was to be an eventful one for the airline, beginning with the loss of two of its three Hythes in January, and ending with it being taken over by the British Aviation Services Group in April. Wing Commander Aikman continued as Managing Director under the Group's Chairman, Mr Eoin C. Mekie, one of whose first moves was to make an unsuccessful bid (reputed to be £1 million each) for the three Saro Princess flying boats that remained cocooned at Southampton. In the event Aquila acquired a second Solent, the Seaford originally evaluated and later used as a crew trainer by BOAC. The airline undertook the conversion to a 42-seat Solent at its engineering base at Hamble and the new aircraft, registered *G-ANAJ* and named *City of Funchal,* entered service on 21 May 1954 when it flew a proving flight direct to Capri with the singer Gracie Fields amongst the forty passengers. Scheduled flights to the isle began on 3 June, taking some seven hours for the 1,300-mile (2,090 km) journey. This included a 1½-hour refuelling stop at Marseille, during which the passengers were treated to a five-course meal, before continuing to Capri's Marine Grande harbour passing over Elba, Corsica and Sardinia en route. The Solent cruised at some 200 mph (320 km/h) at a height between 7,000 and 9,000 ft (2,133 and 2,743 m). The return fare was £66.

The Capri route was just one of many applied for by the new management. Others included an all-freight service to Australia and in July 1954 Aquila's Chief Pilot, Captain Doug Pearson, commanded *G-ANAJ* on a proving flight to Hong Kong. However, an engine failure resulted in the flight being abandoned at Saigon on 7 August and the aircraft finally returning to Southampton on 16 September after two engine changes. Neither of these routes were taken up. At the end of the year Aquila purchased two of TEAL's recently retired Solent 4s, *Aotearoa II* and *Awatere,* which were re-registered *G-AOBL* and *G-ANYI* respectively.

Ex-BOAC Solent 3 at Belfast in 1951, still with UK registration G-AKNP, prior to its delivery to Trans Oceanic Airways. (Shorts)

Captain Doug Pearson, Aquila's Chief Pilot, knew all marks of the Solent and remembers it with affection.

'A most beautiful flying boat, very light on the controls. So light in fact that they were counter-balanced to introduce some feel into them. It had a larger turning circle on the water than either the Sunderland or Sandringham due to its physical size but this presented no real problems to the experienced Solent pilot.

'Her only real problem was a cross-wind take-off (as with most large flying boats). Each pilot developed his own technique for this manoeuvre and I seem to have favoured running along the swell, trying to ignore the wind if possible. The cross-wind take-off, of course, depended on the length of the swell, wind direction and restrictions on take-off direction, if any. As you will appreciate, power was brought up on the out-of-wind engines, leading with the outer to counteract swing and to keep the take-off run as straight as possible; at the same time trying to counteract the "weathercocking" effect inherent in all large flying boats. Also, the wind had to be kept from lifting the into-wind wing and consequently dragging the opposite float in the water. Engine torque effect would also play a part, either aiding or hindering the take-off depending on the wind direction.

'The Mks 2 and 3 were basically the same to handle while flying. BOAC, however, had problems with the hydrodynamic qualities of the Mk 2. It seems the wingtip float clearance was insufficient at its 78,000 lb [35,380 kg] take-off weight. The Solent 2s were taken out of service for a short period in 1948 and their floats were repositioned eighteen inches [45cm] forward and 87 inches [2.2 m] outboard; they were also more robustly mounted on two pairs of inclined struts, eliminating the need for spanwise wire bracing. This modification was incorporated into the Mks 3 and 4 during construction.

'I believe BOAC also had problems with vibration through the airframe in the early days. This was eventually traced to the engines which still had the Sunderland characteristic of pointing slightly outwards and upwards from the line of flight. Apparently the propeller manufacturers (de Havilland) did not realise this and the props on early Solents only had a very short life, about sixty hours I believe. The engines themselves also underwent some modification. BOAC used the Hercules 637, 1,690 hp, fourteen-cylinder radial. By the time I flew them in service with Aquila (although I did fly one BOAC boat, *G-AHIO,* to get the type on my licence), the Solent 2s and 3s they used were fitted with the Hercules 637V. I believe that this was something to do with the master rods which were now opposed in a V rather than diagonally. This again was to cut down the vibration.

'The Mark 4 Solent was a completely different flying boat. TEAL had laid down some very stringent specifications. The more powerful 2,040 hp Hercules 733s were fitted so that they pointed in line of flight. This put all the power where it was required and cut down on the built-in drag the engines of the 2 and 3 created. These Solents were fast and smooth and had a greater range than the earlier marks. I recall being on a trooping charter out of Cyprus with one of the 4s, while a colleague was using a Mk 3, and I overhauled the Mk 3 in flight and beat her back to Southampton by quite a margin. The avionics fit, to use a modern term, was also much better in the Mk 4, one of the items I recall having fitted as standard was an electronic auto-pilot.'

By the time the two Solent 4s had joined Aquila's fleet, the airline had been granted approval to operate weekly non-stop flights to Genoa and Santa Margherita on the Italian Riviera and, by the end of the year, a fortnightly non-stop flight to Las Palmas (a distance of 1,600 miles [2,575 km]), was added to the network.

In April 1956 *G-ANYI* damaged a float on landing at Genoa, while a month later Wing Commander Aikman resigned from the company and was replaced by Air Commodore G. J. Powell.

Following mounting tension in the Middle East during the year, Aquila's Solents were involved in the evacuation of hundreds of British civilians from the Suez Canal zone in August, using the old flying-boat base at Fanara on Egypt's Great Bitter Lake and taking most of the evacuees first to Malta and then on to Southampton. During this time it was reported that the British Forces had seriously considered reactivating the stored Saro Princess flying boats, but as it was estimated that it would take at least six months to get them into the air the idea was not pursued.

Weeks later, Solent *G-ANAJ* was damaged beyond repair during a storm on 26 September while moored at Santa Margherita. The port wing collapsed when it was beached and after being written off all salvable parts were removed and

Halcyon, one of only two surviving Short Solents, is owned by the Grant brothers who hope to rebuild it to an airworthy condition at their base at Richmond, California. The Solent 3, N9946F, ex-BOAC G-AKNP City of Cardiff, ex-TOA VH-TOB Star of Papua, ex-SPAL and Howard Hughes.

Opposite
The spacious flight deck of the ex-BOAC Solent 3, G-AKNP City of Cardiff, preserved at Richmond, California, on the edge of San Francisco Bay. The 40-year-old flying boat, now christened 'Halcyon', was developed from the famous Sunderland and its owner, Rick Grant, plans to restore the Solent to flying condition to become a flying oceanographic research laboratory. (D. Oliver)

One of only two surviving examples of Shorts last pure flying boat, the Solent, Halcyon has been stored at Richmond looking out over the waters of San Francisco Bay for nearly twenty years. (D. Oliver)

returned to England as spares. Despite the setbacks, Aquila's flying boats carried a record number of passengers in 1956, some 16,500, and had reasonable hope of doing even better in 1957.

In January Aquila was granted what was potentially its most lucrative holiday route, to Majorca, but in May *G-ANYI* was holed while taxying out of Pollensa Bay. Although it flew back to Hamble after temporary repairs on the island, it was to remain out of action for nearly a year. Meanwhile, the airline's route network was continuing to grow with the addition of a weekly inclusive-tour contract to Montreux on Lake Geneva commencing in June, and another to fly Club Méditerranée holiday-makers from Marseille to Sicily and Corfu. To cope with expanding demand, Aquila acquired a fifth Solent, *G-AHIN*, named *Southampton,* a Mk 2 that had been laid up at Belfast since being withdrawn from BOAC service. Unfortunately, before the year was out, Aquila lost yet another Solent in what was to be one of the world's worst flying boat accidents.

On the evening of 15 November, Solent *G-AKNU,* named *Sydney,* took off from Southampton bound for Madeira with fifty passengers and eight crew aboard under the command of Captain F. Eltis. Soon after reporting engine trouble and that it was returning to Southampton, *Sydney* crashed into a hill near Shalcombe on the Isle of Wight with the loss of 43 passengers and all of the crew. The subsequent Board of Enquiry found no conclusive cause for the accident other than the fact that both starboard engines had stopped while the port engines were at full power at the time of impact.

Left with only two serviceable Solents, Aquila was forced to reduce some of its services during 1958, but it was the fact that there was no modern replacement in sight for the ageing and over-

Solent 3 N9946F, now preserved at Richmond, California named Halcyon, seen at Honolulu, Hawaii, in 1954/5 while on route proving flights with South Pacific Air Lines. (via R. Grant)

orked flying boats that brought the British viation Services Group to the inevitable decision concentrate its resources on Aquila's sister line, Britavia, which was equipped with modern essurised Hermes landplanes. So, on September , Solent *G-ANYI Awateri,* left Berth 50 for adeira to become the last passenger-carrying ing boat to leave Southampton. The following y the airline ceased operations.

A month later South Pacific Air Lines went into quidation following the British government's cision to use the Christmas Island area as an omic bomb testing range, having never operated Solents. All three were put into storage in San ancisco until they were purchased by the centric millionaire and erstwhile flying boat nstructor, Howard Hughes. There they remained r another nine years before being secretly moved ross San Francisco Bay to Richmond and sold to scrap dealer.

Meanwhile, Aquila's three surviving Solents re ferried to Portugal, having been sold to a new ing boat airline, ARTOP (Aero Topografica SA) operate a Lisbon to Madeira service. However, lowing the loss of one of ARTOP's two ilianised Martin Mariner flying boats on a oving flight to Madeira in November 1958, mmanded by an ex-Aquila Captain, Jim oadbent, the airline folded leaving the once oud Solents to rot away on the banks of the river gus.

Against all the trends, one Solent continued to rn its keep by carrying fare-paying passengers til September 1960 when TEAL's last flying boat, *A-AMO Aranui,* flew back to Auckland from hiti bringing New Zealand's flying boat erations in the Pacific finally to an end. *Aranui* is w on display at Auckland's Museum of ansport and Technology, but it is not the only e of its breed to survive.

Short S45A Solent 2

Accommodation:	Crew: 3-7
	Passengers: 34
Power Plants:	Four 1,690 hp Bristol Hercules 637 fourteen-cylinder radials
Dimensions:	Wingspan: 112 ft 9½ in (34.37 m)
	Length: 88 ft 7 in (27 m)
	Height: 34 ft 3¼ in (10.44 m)
	Wing area: 1,687 sq ft (157 m²)
Weights:	Empty: 47,760 lb (21,664 kg)
	Average: 78,000 lb (35,381 kg)
Performance:	Max speed: 273 mph (439 km/h)
	Cruising speed: 244 mph (392 km/h)
	Range: 1,800 miles (2,896 km)

Short S45A Solent 4

Accommodation:	Crew: 3-7
	Passengers: 42-50
Power Plants:	Four 2,040 hp Bristol Hercules 733 fourteen-cylinder radials
Dimensions:	Wingspan: 112 ft 9½ in (34.37 m)
	Length: 88 ft 7 in (27 m)
	Height: 34 ft 3 ¼ in (10.44 m)
	Wing area: 1,687 sq ft (157 m²)
Weights:	Empty: 47,760 lb (21,664 kg)
	Average: 78,000 lb (35,381 kg)
Performance:	Max speed: 276 mph (444 km/h)
	Cruising speed: 251 mph (404 km/h)
	Range: 2,200 miles (3,540 km)

One of the ex-Howard Hughes aircraft was saved from the scrapman's torch by an American marine biologist, Rick Grant, and his US Navy engineer brother Randy, who paid $50,000 for the ex-BOAC Solent 3, *G-AKNP City of Cardiff* in 1976. They lived in it for two years, the luxuriously appointed interior having remained virtually intact throughout its years of storage. During this period the flying boat became a pre-war Pan Am Clipper for an appearance in Steven Spielburg's film *Raiders of the Lost Ark.*

The brothers' aim is to restore the Solent, re-christened *Halcyon,* to flying condition and put it back to work with an interior that could be readily adapted to oceanographic research or for carrying passengers. Rick Grant and his colleagues have done a lot of preparatory work on the Solent and have obtained a large quantity of spare Hercules engines and components, but plan to begin serious restoration only when sufficient funds are available to do the job professionally. Meanwhile, the brothers' venture is being encouraged by many flying boat enthusiasts around the world including ex-BOAC, Aquila and TOA aircrew and engineers who have banded together in a group calling themselves the 'Friends of Halcyon', all with the avowed intention of seeing the last of the 'big boats' once again slicing through the water and lifting majestically into the air.

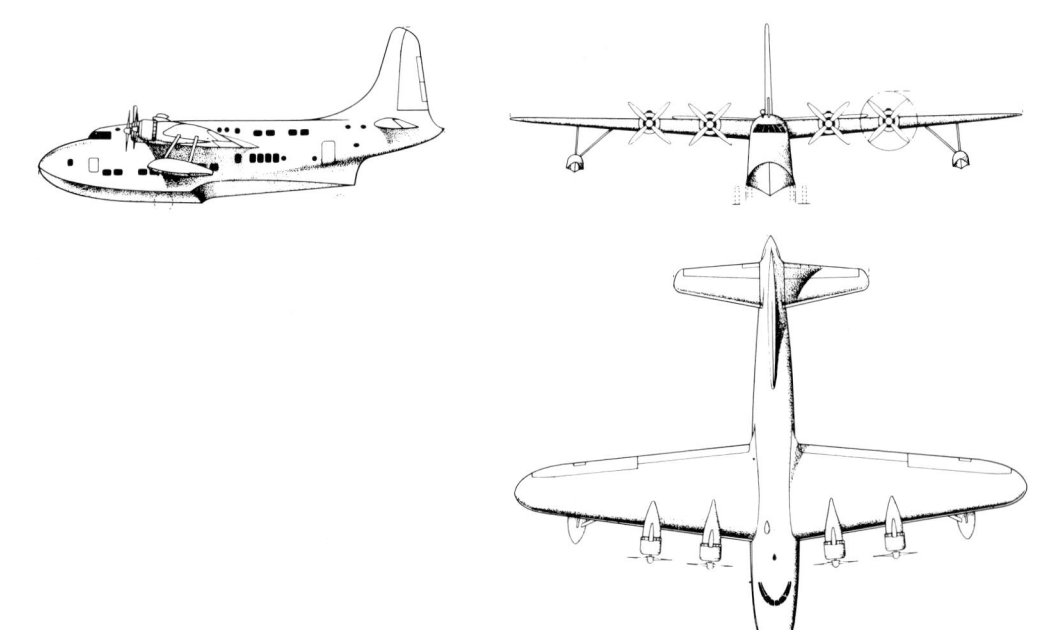

CHAPTER THREE
THE BERIEV Be-6

Surprisingly, especially in view of its vast coastline, the Soviet Union was alone amongst the major combatants of World War Two not to have produced a large long-range maritime patrol bomber flying boat. The standard reconnaissance flying boat of the Soviet Navy (AVMF) between 1939 and 1945 was a five-man single-engined 'boat of wooden construction designed in 1931 by G. M. Beriev, the MBR-2.

Georgii Mikhailovich Beriev had joined the Soviet design bureau headed by the French designer Paul-Aime Richard in 1928, before being rapidly promoted to the post of chief seaplane designer with the Central Aviatrust bureau in Moscow only two years later. During this time he became responsible for the licence production of the Italian Savoia Marchetti SM-62 at a new flying boat factory at Taganrog, near Rostov on the Azov Sea, as the MBR-4, while at the same time working on his own design which would would ultimately become the MBR-2. More than 1,500 of the short-range MBR-2s were built, including a number of a six-passenger commercial version, before it was superseded in production for a brief period by the medium-range twin-engined MDR-6 in 1941.

Just before the outbreak of the Second World War, the Soviet Union had purchased a number of modern American flying boats including a Sikorsky S-43, a Martin 156 (an enlarged development of the pre-war Martin 130 Clipper) and three Consolidated 28 flying boats (the forerunner of the PBY Catalina), along with licence production rights for the latter. Large numbers of licence-built Catalinas were produced at Taganrog from 1939, under the designation GST, and the type, later joined by 138 PNB-1 and 48 PBY-6A Consolidated Catalinas supplied under Lend-Lease agreements, became the Soviet Naval air arm's main long range maritime patrol bomber and subsequently served alongside the MBR-2, later redesignated the Beriev Be-4, well into the 1950s when they became known in the West by their NATO codenames of 'Mop' and 'Mug' respectively.

A Beriev Be-6 being launched giving a good view of the twin cannon in the tail turret and the stores carrier mounted under the engine nacelle. (via W. Schoenmaker)

At the end of World War Two, the entire Sovi[et] development of flying boats was concentrated in [G.] M. Beriev's bureau, now reinstated at Taganr[og] which had been closed down in 1941 whe[n] threatened by the advancing German force[s.] Priority was given to the design and development [of] a modern long-range maritime patrol an[d] reconnaissance flying boat. However, the first pos[t-]war design to appear from the bureau was a singl[e-]engined eight-seat utility amphibian in t[he] Grumman Goose category which failed to atta[in] quantity production.

All Beriev's designs possessed excelle[nt] hydrodynamic qualities and, having learne[d] valuable lessons about modern all-met[al] construction techniques by studying the import[ed] American flying boats, he designed the prototype [of] what was to be one of the most advanced Sovi[et] aircraft to attain production in the immediate pos[t-]war period. With the simple designation of LL-1[43] ('Letayushchaya Lodka' being Russian for flyi[ng] boat), the large gull-winged aircraft, powered [by] two 2,000 hp Shvetsov ASh-72 eighteen-cylind[er] radials, first took to the air from Krasnoyarsk [in] June 1947. Initially it was thought to be a straig[ht] copy of the Martin Mariner which had been the [US] Navy's standard wartime maritime patrol flyi[ng] boat, but this was not the case. Apart from [a] similarity in size, gull-wing configuration and twi[n] tail layout, the Beriev design, with its longer re[ar] planning bottom, swept-back leading edge to t[he] wings and wing floats fitted on two slim unbrac[ed] struts, was aerodynamically and hydrodynamica[lly] more efficient. The flying boat was fitted with du[al] controls, an autopilot and extensive de-icing ai[ds] including heated leading edges and windscreen[s,] with alcohol sprays for the propeller blades. T[he] spacious Soviet flying boat carried a crew of sev[en] and featured a defensive armament of six 12.7 m[m] cannon in nose, dorsal and tail turrets, while up [to] 8,000 lb (3,629 kg) of mines, depth charges, bom[bs] or torpedoes could be carried on wing pylons.

A production Beriev Be-6 (Madge), the Soviet Union's first post-war, and most successful, long-range maritime reconnaissance flying boat. (via R. Ruffle)

Three Beriev Be-6 flying boats on beaching gear at a Soviet Naval airbase, the machine in the foreground running up its 2,400 hp A Sh-73 radials. (via W. Schoenmaker)

Following thorough testing of the flying bo[at] over a two-year period by the manufacturer and t[he] State Trials organisation at Taganrog an[d] Sevastopol, a production version of the LL-143 w[as] ordered under the designation Be-6, the first [of] which flew in February 1949 with the veteran Beri[ev] test pilot, M. I. Tsepilov, at the controls.

The production Beriev Be-6 differed from the prototype in a number of respects. These included being powered by the more powerful 2,300 hp ASh-73TK engines driving four-bladed V-3BA-5 propellers, having a re-designed bow that eliminated the nose cannon, and being fitted with short bow spray fences to each side of the nose to reduce spray. A retractable radome was installed in the hull aft of the single step and a retractable magnetic anomaly detector (MAD) stinger extended from the extreme tail below the remotely-controlled rear barbette which was fitted with a 23 mm N2-23 cannon. The similarly-armed dorsal barbette was retained, as were the underwing weapons pylons mounted outboard of the engine nacelles enabling the Be-6 to carry various bomb loads of up to 8,800 lb.

Deliveries to the Aviatsiya Voenno Morskikh Flota (AVMF) began during the latter half of 1950 when the Be-6 was issued to the Soviet Baltic, Black Sea and Northern Fleets as their principal anti-submarine aircraft, and it soon gained an excellent reputation as being a tough and reliable boat that stood up well to the harsh conditions of the northern latitudes in which it operated, where its excellent de-icing systems were of vital importance.

With a maximum speed of 258 mph at 7,875 ft (415 km/h at 2,400 m), the Be-6 had a maximum range of 3,045 miles (4,900 km) when cruising at 210 mph (338 km/h). For long patrols, the Beriev flying boat was capable of remaining airborne for more than sixteen hours and provision was made for the accommodation of a four-man relief crew, in addition to the normal crew of eight. Despite the long-ranging missions and the relatively large numbers in service, the Be-6 seldom came in contact with Western air forces or navies and it was not until 1953 that the type was allocated the codename 'Madge' by NATO Forces.

More than 300 Be-6s were produced at Taganrog between 1949 and 1955, during which time the flying boat undertook a number of varied tasks whilst serving with the Soviet Naval Air Fleet. Apart from its primary role of long-range maritime reconnaissance, the Beriev flying boats undertook submarine co-operation missions, weather patrol and troop and cargo transport flights (it was capable of carrying forty fully armed troops).

A small number of Beriev Be-6s appeared in Aeroflot colours in the mid-1950s, operating passenger and cargo flights from Moscow Khimski Reservoir.

During their long operational life with the AVMF, the flying boats were progressively updated with the installation of the latest avionics and anti-submarine warfare equipment and the NR-23 cannon. They were also retrofitted with auxiliary power units and a stores carrier mounted under each nacelle. Following their withdrawal from front-line duties during the 1960s, when they were largely relegated to fishery protection patrols and second line operations, all defensive armament was removed. However, the last Be-6s were not retired by the Soviet Navy until the early 1970s.

A rare in-flight shot of a late production Beriev Be-6 (Madge) giving a clear view of the extended ventral 'dustbin' radome in the hull and wingtip sensors. This example has had the original cannon-armed dorsal barbette replaced by an astrodome.

The LL-143, which served as the prototype for the Beriev Be-6, seen taking off on an early test-flight cutting cleanly through the water.

Beriev had produced a potential replacement for the Be-6 as early as 1950 by the simple expedient of fitting a new wing to a Be-6 airframe and replacing the four piston engines with two jet engines. Known as the Be R-1, the world's first multi-engined flying boat featured an elongated planing bottom forward of the step, a single fin with a high-mounted tailplane, an offset bubble canopy and a straight gull-wing on which were mounted two 6,040 lb thrust Klimov VK-1 centrifugal-flow turbojets. The jet flying boat attained an impressive speed of 478 mph (769 km/h) during trials, but as the more economical and virtually trouble-free Be-6 was then entering service in large numbers, development of the Be R-1 was abandoned by 1952, but not before being allocated the codename 'Mole' by NATO.

At the end of the 1950s, just prior to the breakdown in relations between the Soviet Union and the Republic of China, some twenty ex-Soviet Naval Aviation Beriev Be-6 flying boats were acquired by China's Aviation of the People's Navy (APN). Thirty-five years later, a dozen survivors are used for maritime reconnaissance, anti-submarine warfare and transport duties, and following China's unsuccessful bid to purchase a number of Japanese Shin Meiwa US-1 ASW/SAR amphibians in the 1970s, the veteran Soviet boats are likely to remain in operation until they are replaced by the four-engined Harbin PS-5, an amphibian designed and built in China, which made its maiden flight in 1986.

The only example of Beriev's capable piston engine flying boat known to survive in the Soviet Union was mounted on a pedestal in 1976 looking out over the Barents Sea near Severomorsk/Murmansk, the main base of the Soviet Northern Fleet.

The prototype of the Beriev Be-6, LL-143, which was launched in September 1947 and test flown for two years at Taganrog and Sevastopol. (via W. Schoenmaker)

Beriev Be-6 (Madge)

Accommodation:	Crew: 8
Power Plants:	Two 2,400 hp Shvetsov ASh-73 radials
Dimensions:	Wingspan: 108 ft 2½ in (33 m)
	Length: 77 ft 3½ in (23.56 m)
	Height: 25 ft 0½ in (7.6 m)
	Wing area: 1,292 sq ft (120 m²)
Weights:	Empty: 41,419 lb (18,788 kg)
	Average: 63,933 lb (29,000 kg)
Performance:	Max speed: 258 mph (415 km/h)
	Patrol speed: 175 mph (280 km/h)
	Range: 3,045 miles (4,900 km)
	Max endurance: 16 hr

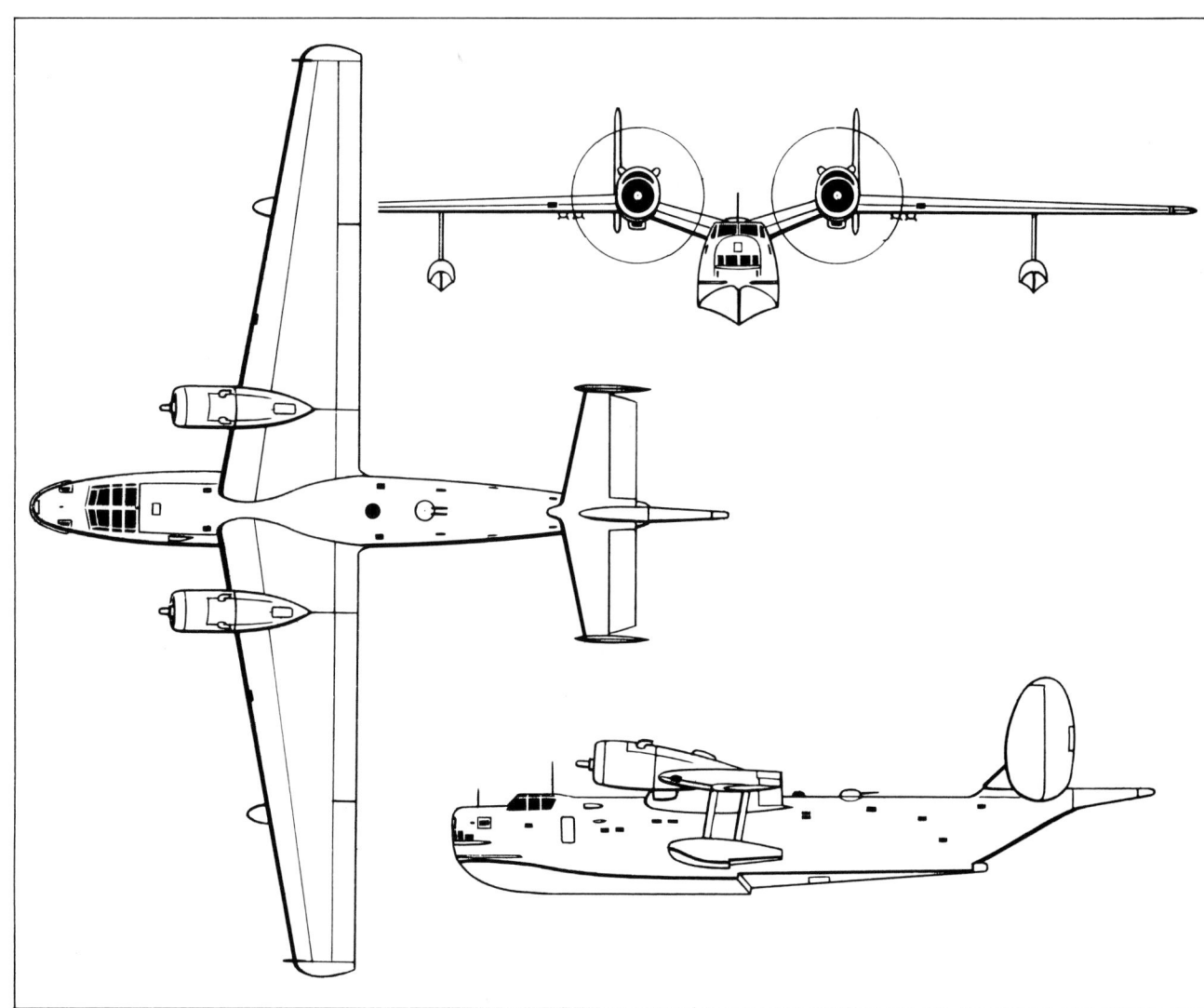

CHAPTER FOUR
THE GRUMMAN ALBATROSS

Responding to a United States Navy requirement for a utility amphibian to replace its fleet of ageing PBY Catalinas and J3F Gooses, Grumman produced what might at first sight appear to be a beefed-up version of their commercial Mallard. However, the prototype G-64 Albatross, which flew for the first time on 24 October 1947, incorporated many improvements to both its hydrodynamic and aerodynamic shape that reduced drag and improved performance on water and in the air.

Although it retained the now traditional Grumman high-wing, twin-engine layout with a conventional two-step hull and tricycle undercarriage, it was considerably larger and more powerful than the Mallard. Powered by two 1,425 hp Wright R-1820-76A nine-cylinder Cyclone radial engines, the Albatross had a wingspan of 80 ft (24.38 m) and weighed more than twice as much as its predecessor. The tricycle undercarriage, which looked complicated and fragile, proved to be exceptionally strong and well able to cope with all that it was subjected to over the years in operations in all parts of the globe.

A MATS SA-16A Albatross showing underwing fuel tanks and aerials. (USAF)

A USAF SA-16A Albatross of the first production batch delivered in 1950. (Grumman)

An early USAF SA-16A belonging to the Air Rescue Service of the Military Air Transport Service (MATS) during a practice rescue in calm seas. (Grumman)

The prototype, which had flown nearly a year behind schedule, was the first of two ordered by the US Navy and carried the designation, XJR2F-1. In May 1948, in the same month that the second naval aircraft took to the air, the newly created US Air Force, successor to the US Army Air Force, and which had considerable funds at its disposal, placed an order for 52 Albatrosses, designated SA-16A, to be used in the search and rescue role. The first was delivered in July 1949. The US Navy placed an initial order for thirteen aircraft, six utility transports (designated UF-1A), five dual-control training versions (the UF-1T), which were used as flying classrooms at the Annapolis Naval Academy, and two UF-1Ls for use in the Arctic and Antarctic. A further seventeen were purchased by the US Coast Guard for air-sea rescue duties under the designation UF-1G, the first of which was received in March 1952.

The Albatross was designed to operate from 4-6 ft (1.2-1.8 m) waves, but on many occasions it was to operate into and out of much heavier seas, especially with the use of jet-assisted take-off (JATO). Four JATO units, attached to the main access door in the port side of the rear fuselage, and the emergency door of the starboard side, delivered 1,000 lb (454 kg) of thrust for fifteen seconds and could reduce the take-off length by up to forty per cent. Reversible-pitch propellers helped to make the Albatross exceptionally manoeuvrable on the water, a particularly useful characteristic for the air-sea rescue role in which it was to gain universal recognition with the USAF during the Korean War. The first USAF SA-16As, serving with the Air Rescue Service of the Military Air Transport Service (MATS), had been rushed out to the front-line base of Taegu, forty miles north of Pusan, within a month of the outbreak of hostilities, and only seven days later the type made its first rescue. During the conflict two Groups of SA-16s, the 2nd and 3rd, based at Wonsan, Seoul, Taegu and, for a time, Cho-do Island (which was fifty miles [eighty km] north of the 38th Parallel), were subsequently responsible for the rescue of some 900 downed

A MATS SA-16A Albatross. (Grumman)

airmen during the four-year conflict, many of them from behind enemy lines and under fire from communist forces. Typical of USAF SA-16 missions was the rescue of an F-51 Mustang pilot in June 1951 by Lieutenant J. Najarian who put down his Albatross on the Taedong River near Kyomipo under intense enemy fire and at night to snatch the downed pilot to safety. A little over a year later, another SA-16A rescued Major Frederick Blesse, at the time the USAF's leading Sabre ace, after he had been shot down over the Yellow Sea.

In the air-sea rescue role, the SA-16A carried a crew of five, pilot, co-pilot, radio operator, navigator and medical technician, with seating for up to ten passengers, although as many as 25 have been carried on more than one occasion. Three inflatable rafts were carried along with medical supplies, fresh water and a hot plate. As an ambulance aircraft it could be fitted with eleven stretchers with room for at least one attendant. One of the few criticisms levelled at the Albatross was that, in common with other Grumman amphibians, it sat low in the water and in rough seas the rear passenger hatch, which had a door that lowered to make a platform, often took in considerable amounts of water.

A US Navy HU-16C Albatross, an SAR aircraft attached to the Patrol Force of the Seventh Fleet. (J. Gradidge)

Apart from the many epic rescues undertaken by US Air Force Albatrosses in and around Korea, men were not the only things to be plucked out of the sea from under the nose of the enemy. In July 1952 an early example MiG-15 was shot down in the sea near the mouth of the Yalu River in north-east Korea and recovered by the Royal Navy, with an SA-16A being involved in the race to retrieve parts of the communist jet, the first to fall into the hands of the UN Forces. During the conflict the Albatross proved it could operate in all weathers, heavy seas, and over long distances, with rugged reliability that won fulsome praise from both flight and maintenance crews alike. When fitted with two 300 US-gallon long-range drop tanks, the Albatross was able to stay airborne for at least 22 hours, and as it was capable of being refuelled at sea, the main restriction to its endurance was crew fatigue. Although the SA-16 was relatively spacious and comfortable for the crew on long flights, it was notoriously noisy and a large box of cotton wool for the ears was an essential piece of equipment on the flight deck.

Even before the Korean War was over, the SA-16 was proving its worth in peacetime missions in various parts of the world. In February 1953, exceptionally high tides in the North Sea led to disastrous flooding in Holland and six SA-16As of the 66th ARS based at Manston and the 68th ARS at Burtonwood joined others from Wiesbaden, Germany, to play a major part in the rescue and relief of flood victims.

The following year two Philippine-based SA-16As took part in a typical peacetime mission that would enhance their excellent wartime reputation. In July 1954, a Cathay Pacific DC4, en route from Bangkok to Hong Kong, was shot down without warning by two communist Chinese Lavochkin La-9 fighters outside Chinese airspace near Hainan Island. Nine of the passengers and crew were killed outright in the attack but nine others managed to get into a life-raft, not knowing whether their brief SOS radio call had been picked up before the DC4 hit the water. Luckily it had and a message reached Clark Field in Manila, stating only that a commercial aircraft was missing, and two SA-16s of the 31st Air Rescue Squadron were launched to search an area nearly 700 miles (1,125 km) away.

The prototype USAF triphibian, in fact the first production SA-16A, fitted with a skid to the bottom of the hull and wing-float skis to enable it to land on snow and ice as well as land and water. (Grumman)

Meanwhile, the survivors had been sighted by a pair of RAF Hornets based at Hong Kong which led an RAF Sunderland flying boat to the scene. However, by this time the raft had drifted into a small bay close to Timboas Island and the Sunderland was unable to land due to the high waves and restricted landing area. Meanwhile the communists were threatening to shoot down any military aircraft if they approached the area, but having come so far, and pin-pointed the survivors, Captain Jack Woodyard put his Albatross down in the heavy swell using reversible propellers to bring it to a stop between the crests while a French Privateer circled overhead to give warning of any attack from the mainland and to guide him to the life-raft. Having picked a relatively smooth stretch of water some 2½ miles (4 km) away, it took the Albatross over an hour to taxy to the raft. After taking on board the nine survivors, one of whom died within minutes of being rescued, the SA-16A managed to take off in the heavy swell with the use of JATO and flew them to Hong Kong to complete the journey they had begun nearly 24 hours earlier.

An early production US Navy UF-1 finished in dark blue overall with yellow wingtips and floats. (Grumman)

The interior of a USCG UF-1G Albatross showing the navigator's position. (USCG)

The Kriegs marine's second UF-2 Albatross taking-off from water. (Kriegsmarine)

Two years later another USAF SA-16A broke some kind of record when it was called out to search for a B-26 Invader that was reported missing over the South China Seas. After spotting one of its crew in the water being kept afloat in heavy seas by nothing more than his Mae West, the pilot decided to attempt a landing before losing sight of the survivor. After landing safely in the heavy swell and rescuing the injured crewman, the state of the sea precluded any possibility of a take-off, even with the use of JATO, so the pilot was left with no alternative but to taxy back to his base at Okinawa in Japan — 98 miles (158 km) away.

By now, Grumman's amphibian was in demand from many overseas air forces and ultimately, more than 100 Albatrosses were to see service with no less that nineteen different countries, many supplied as the result of mutual defence assistance programmes (MDAP). One of the first European countries to benefit from such an aid programme was Spain which asked the USAF to organise an air-sea rescue service on the same lines as its own, when it took delivery of five SA-16As in September 1954.

The Albatross was nothing if not versatile, undertaking such varied tasks, apart from SAR, as hauling VIPs, troops and cargo, but in 1955 it became a commercial airliner for the first time. In 1947, Micronesia, made up of 96 inhabited islands in the Pacific including the Marshall Islands, the Caroline Islands and the Marianas, all former Japanese colonies, became a Trust Territory administered by the USA for the United Nations. The American authorities formed Transocean Airlines in 1955 equipped with three early production ex-USAF SA-16A Albatrosses. Based at Guam, the amphibians registered *N9942-4F,* flew regular services to Yap, Truk, Koror, Ponape and Majoiro. However, after three years of operations the airline faced bankruptcy proceedings and in 1960 the contract, and two of the SA-16s, were taken over by Pan American Airways. The Albatross operations were limited to daylight hours and a qualified engineer flew on each service as there were no maintenance facilities at most ports of call.

One of six Grumman UF-2 Albatross amphibians delivered to the Japanese Maritime Self Defence Force (JMSDF) in 1961, later converted into a G-111 and currently flying with Chalks International Airline in Florida. (Grumman)

On 16 January 1956, an improved Albatross, designated SA-16B, took to the air from Bethpage for the first time. The main difference between the A and B versions was in the wing, with the latter having the span increased by 16 ft 8 in (5 m), cambered wing leading-edges instead of wingtip slots, larger ailerons and new high pressure de-icing boots. The area of both the fin and the rudder were also increased. Drag was reduced by fitting many of the numerous antennae that had sprouted from the SA-16A's wing and cabin roof over the years, under flush mountings or internally. The wing-mounted floats were moved outboard 70 in (1.77 m) which improved stability and manoeuvrability in the water. As a result of these changes, single engine climb rate and cruising speed were increased, while the stalling speed was reduced from 70 to 64 knots. Range was increased from 2,683 miles to 3,282 miles (4,317 to 5,280 km).

An ex-USAF SA-16B transferred to the US Coast Guard in 1962 finished in the red and white Coast Guard finish of the period. (Grumman)

An Indonesian Naval Aviation SA-16A SAR amphibian, one of twelve delivered in 1957 some of which are still in operation thirty years later. (Grumman)

These improvements were incorporated in all aircraft leaving the production lines from mid-1950 onwards and many A models still in service were progressively updated. The total number of SA-16s ordered by the USAF, for use with the Military Air Transport Service (MATS) Air Rescue Service, later the Military Airlift Command (MAC), the Aerospace Rescue and Recovery Service (ARRS), Strategic Air Command (SAC), Tactical Air Command, Pacific Air Forces, Air Force Reserve and the Air National Guard, was 305 although some of these were later transferred to other air arms under mutual assistance programmes.

Following the Sino-American Defence pact of 1955, Nationalist China, later Taiwan, received a dozen Albatross amphibians for search and rescue and maritime patrol tasks, although at the height of the Quemoy and Matsu Islands' crisis in 1958, Nationalist SA-16s undertook a number of clandestine flights to pick up agents who had been spying on the mainland, from junks in the South China Seas.

Other SA-16 operators in the Far East included Japan, one of whose aircraft was later fitted with four engines and used as a test machine for the Shin Meiwa flying boat in December 1962. Three of the amphibians belonging to No 12 Squadron of the Pakistan Air Force were involved in a massive search for the crew of an RAF Javelin which went missing during a transit flight over East Bengal in February 1961. Apart from the Albatrosses, the search was joined by RAF Hastings, Shackletons and a civilian Goose. One of the missing crewmen was eventually spotted close to a narrow waterway having spent three days in the jungle after ejecting. However, the river was too small for an Albatross to attempt a landing so its crew had to be content with acting as a guide for the smaller Goose which made a successful landing and picked up the navigator, who was suffering from nothing worse than exhaustion and exposure. The pilot was never found. Later the Pakistan Air Force SA-16As were involved in the short, but bloody, Indo-Pakistan wars of September 1965 and December 1971.

Chalks G-111 Albatross taking off in the Miami Harbour entrance passing luxury cruise liners. (D. Oliver)

In Europe, in addition to Spain, the SA-16 Albatross was delivered to the air forces of Portugal and Italy, as well as the newly created West German Navy, the Kriegsmarine, which operated eight aircraft fitted with enlarged tail surfaces. The Royal Canadian Air Force also took delivery of ten aircraft fitted with Canadian-built 1,525 hp Wright R-1820-82 engines and modified undercarriages, designated the CSR-110.

An ex-US Navy HU-16C Albatross, N9722C, bought by its ex-crew Chief, Dennis Buehn who restored it to its original colours and won the Best Seaplane Award at Oshkosh 86. (P. Coggan)

A total of 127 SA-16s was modified to give it triphibious capabilities for operations on snow and ice during the mid-1950s. A hydraulically retractable hull-skid, 12 in wide and 15 ft in length (3005 cm x 4.57 m) with a shock-absorbing strut fitted to the end, fitted into a recess in the front hull while small shock-absorbing swivelling skids were attached to the floats. Although the kit considerably enhanced the aircraft's operational capabilities, it added some 675 lb (306 kg) to its overall weight with a resulting penalty to the payload.

Two US Navy UF-1L triphibians were assigned to Air Development Squadron Six, VX-6, in 1956 to take part in Operation 'Deep Freeze', the most ambitious Antarctic exploration and research programme to be undertaken by the United States at that date. Operation 'Deep Freeze' was a lead-up to the 1957/8 International Geophysical Year during which scientists from the USA, USSR, Britain, France, Australia and New Zealand took part, all supported to a large extent from the air. The UF-1L Albatrosses were held in readiness to rescue crews having to ditch in the icy waters off the Antarctic coastline.

N693S is one of two ex-USN HU-16s rebuilt by Grumman for the Smithsonian Institution of Washington DC in 1980. The two Albatrosses are currently used for oceanographic research by the Institution's Marine Systems Laboratory. (Grumman)

The VII Brigada of the Argentine Air Force operated three Grumman HU-16B Albatross search and rescue amphibians from Moron BAM, Buenos Aires until 1981. (via J. J. Halley)

Back in 1948 the US Navy had studied the possibility of using the Albatross in the Anti-Submarine Warfare (ASW) role but dropped the idea after trials of a PF-1A (Patrol Aircraft) version later the same year. However, in 1961, eighteen SA-16Bs were built as ASW aircraft for the Royal Norwegian Air Force, plus seven for Spain and two trials aircraft for the USAF and USN. The ASW amphibians, the last of more than 460 Grumman Albatrosses to be manufactured during twelve years of production, were fitted with new longer range radar with a wider sweep, magnetic airborne detection equipment with a rear-mounted retractable MAD boom, sonobuoy receiver equipment, plus sonobuoys (launched from a pod attached to the JATO supports on the rear hatch), electronic counter-measures equipment, marine marker and sound signal depth charges. Attack equipment included Mk 43/1 torpedoes, Mk 54/2 or Mk 101 depth bombs, the Aero 101 Zuni rocket packs or 5-in HVAR rockets. The Aero 65 bomb rack, which was standard equipment on the amphibian, could carry a 2,000 lb (907 kg) weapon load while up to 600 lb (272 kg) of stores could be carried under each wing, and a searchlight was fitted under the starboard wing. They were also fitted with engines uprated to 1,525 hp. One of the Norwegian ASW aircraft, which served with 330 and 333 Squadrons, appeared at the 1962 Paris Air Show. When the amphibians were replaced by P-3B Orions in 1969 the surviving Norwegian Air Force SA-16Bs were passed on to Chile and Greece.

A MATS Grumman SA-16B Albatross circa 1958. (Grumman)

A privately owned ex-USAF Grumman HU-16B Albatross, registered N3398F, seen at Fort Lauderdale airport in Florida in November 1986. (D. Oliver)

The last USAF SA-16A to leave the production line, Albatross 7255 was subsequently modified to 'B' specifications before being transferred to the US Coast Guard in the early 1960s. (Grumman)

Following the rationalisation of designations by the US Forces in 1962, USAF SA-16A/Bs became the HU-16A/Bs, those for Antarctic service were LU-16Cs and dual-control trainers became TU-16Cs. The US Coast Guard followed suit with its 34 UF-1/2Gs all becoming known as HU-16Es.

The same year a number of International Records were established by the Grumman Albatross, including a speed over 1,000 km (625 miles) of 231.96 mph (373.22 km/h) set by a US Coast Guard HU-16E piloted by Commander Wallace C. Dahlgren on 13 August, and an altitude record of 29,475 ft (8,984 m) by a US Navy UF-2 on 11 September 1962. The following year the USAF responded by setting a speed record with a HU-16B, carrying a 5,000 kg (11,025 lb) payload, of 153.65 mph (247.22 km/h), and an altitude record, carrying the same weight, of 19,747 ft (6,019 m). An outright altitude record for an Albatross, of 32,883 ft (10,023 m) with no payload, was not established until 4 July 1973, by Lieutenant Colonel Charles H. Manning, USAF.

By the beginning of 1964 there were six USAF Air Rescue Squadrons equipped with the HU-16B: the 33rd ARS at Naha AFB, Okinawa, Japan; the 41st ARS at Hamilton AFB, California, USA; the 48th ARS at Elgin AFB, Florida, USA; the 54th ARS at Goose AFB, Labrador, Canada; the 55th ARS at Kindley AFB, Bermuda; and the 58th ARS at Wheelus AFB, Libya. There were also five Reserve Units, each with four HU-16Bs.

However, the Albatross was about to become a front-line aircraft again with the escalation of hostilities in South-East Asia during the early 1960s.

A Chalks Albatross being turned around at the airline's base on Watson Island, Miami. (D. Oliver)

By June 1964, a detachment of four HU-16Bs, belonging to the 31st ARS, had arrived at Da Nang, South Vietnam, and two more from the 33rd ARS were stationed over the Thai border at Korat RTAFB. For nearly eighteen months, an HU-16B would remain airborne over the Gulf of Tonkin from sunrise to sunset, during which time the amphibians were credited with some fifty rescues, many under Vietcong fire. Typical was the rescue of the CO of US Navy Squadron VF-154 who had ejected from his Phantom and was picked up in the water near Bock Island, which had been his target, by an HU-16B after 45 hours in the water. Another rescue almost exactly a year later was not so successful. An HU-16B was destroyed and two of its crew killed by a mortar while landing close to Hon Me Island attempting to pick up a Phantom crew. The surviving Albatross crewmen along with the two Phantom crew were eventually rescued by a Navy SH-3A helicopter. Helicopters, such as the air-refuellable HH-3 'Jolly Green Giant', began to replace the ageing amphibians in Vietnam from 1966 although they continued to give valuable service until the end of the conflict, acting as radio relay stations for the helicopters during rescues, undertaking CASEVAC flights and coastal patrols.

PANAM's Clipper 'Duck' N9944F, one of two Grumman SA-16B Albatross amphibians operated by PANAM in the US Trust Territories of Micronesia from July 1960, seen here at Ponape in the Caroline Islands shortly before its last flight in the Pacific in May 1968. The PANAM Albatrosses were transferred to Mahe in the Seychelles in support of a US tracking station before finally retiring in December 1971. (PANAM)

The prototype Grumman G-111 N112FB, an ex-JMSDF UF-2, first flew as such in 1979 and entered service with Chalks International in Florida in 1982. It is seen flying along the Miami coastline. (Grumman)

One of Chalks four G-111 Albatrosses, the 30-seater N120FB, undergoing routine maintenance at the airline's Florida base at Fort Lauderdale airport in November 1986. (D. Oliver)

The 33rd ARS HU-16Bs also operated in Laos from 1964 to '66, losing at least one aircraft to enemy ground fire. To prolong the life of the Albatross in US service, Fairchild-Hiller Aircraft had received a $700,000 contract in 1964 to update 26 HU-16s at the company's facility at St Augustine, Florida, where the Albatross was destined to return some fifteen years later.

The 1970s were the twilight years of the Albatross in US military service but the aircraft was being looked at seriously by the civil sector of the market. Apart from operating with the quasi-military Transocean Airlines in the late 1950s, the HU-16 had been extensively used as a medium transport by the US National Guard, including some Special Operations Squadrons, the US Marine Corps and the US Navy (the latter operating a number of VIP HU-16Ds on behalf of Naval attachés in northern Europe, which were maintained at RAF Mildenhall during the late 1960s).

In 1971, a team from Grumman Aircraft Corporation, headed by Henry E. Prew, Deputy Director, Advanced Concepts, undertook a $50,000, four-month feasibility study of waterborne commuter operations in the New York/Long Island area using a projected four turboprop-engined Super Albatross. The Super Albatross, powered by Pratt & Whitney PT-6s, could carry 36 passengers on short-haul routes, taking off and landing in less than 2,500 ft (760 m) of water. Meanwhile, in February 1970, the Conroy Aircraft Corp of Santa Barbara, California, had flown the first Turbo Albatross powered by two ex-Viscount 700 Rolls Royce Dart 510 turboprops. The price of conversion was $150,000. However, nothing came of either of these promising projects and it would be another ten years before a commercial Albatross became a reality.

In 1974 the last USAF HU-16B, serving in Kodiak, Alaska, was withdrawn from service, and in September 1976 the US Navy's last HU-16D flew from Guantanamo Bay, Cuba, to honourable retirement in the Naval Aviation Museum at NAS Pensacola. The only HU-16s still in operation in the United States at the end of the decade were some 25 HU-16Es belonging to the US Coast Guard, where the amphibian was affectionately known as the 'Goat'. Apart from the original 34 acquired in the mid-1950s, 55 more had been transferred from USAF stocks, and had given excellent and reliable service undertaking medium-range rescue missions from a dozen bases as far apart as Alaska and Puerto Rico. However, by the end of the 1970s the HU-16s, which, due to their age were banned from making water landings except in dire emergencies (such as double engine failure), were restricted to fishery protection and oil slick surveillance duties. For this they had been fitted out with the latest state-of-the-art electronic detection equipment including SLAR (Side Looking Airborne Radar) infrared sensors, ultraviolet scanners and microwave detectors. The US Coast Guard's final flying boat operation was flown by HU-16E N7250 from Cape Cod, Massachusetts, close to its birthplace, on 10 March 1983. In the meantime the last of the European Albatrosses to be used for search and rescue, the Italian Air Force's SA-16A belonging to the 84th and 85th Gruppos, had been withdrawn from their Rome-Ciampino base.

Royal Canadian Air Force CRS-110 Albatross 9303, one of ten obtained in 1960 and used by the Air Transport Command's extensive search and rescue organisation. (P. Beaver)

Nevertheless, at the end of 1986, there were more than fifty of these durable amphibians still operating with some seven air forces and navies around the world. The largest fleet belongs to the Greek Air Force which operates twelve ex-Norwegian Air Force ASW HU-16Bs. Flown by Air Force crews of 353 *Moira Nautikis Synergasias* based at Elefsis, near Athens, the Albatrosses have been fitted with British mission avionics including EC Super Searcher radar, IFF, GEC Marconi apads sonics processing suite, and AD3400 radios and are expected to continue in service well into the 90s. Mexico, one of six South American countries, Argentina, Brazil, Chile, Venezuela and Peru were the others that have used HU-16s at one time or the other, continues to use a dozen HU-16Bs in the anti-drug smuggling and SAR role. The Far East remains an Albatross stronghold, with examples still serving with the Philippine and Taiwan Air Forces, and the navies of Thailand and Indonesia. Remarkably, Grumman received their latest order for the Albatross in 1985 when the Royal Malaysian Air Force ordered two amphibians as troop and staff transports to be used between the many small islands that make up Malaysia. These aircraft were selected from some forty retired Albatrosses held in long-term storage at the US Military Aircraft Storage and Disposition Centre at Davis-Monthan AFB, Arizona, and overhauled by Grummans.

Following renewed interest in a commercial commuter version of the Albatross, by the giant US hotel company, Resorts International (the owners of Chalk's International Airline, that already operated a fleet of Turbo Mallards), Grumman looked at a number of recently retired HU-16s stored at Davis-Monthan AFB with the aim of re-manufacturing those in the best condition.

The second UF-1G to be delivered to the US Coast Guard in 1951, this aircraft was based at St Petersburg, Florida, and crashed in the Gulf of Mexico on 5 March 1967 while responding to a vessel in distress in bad weather. All six on board were killed. (USCG)

One of eight ex-Norwegian HU-16B (ASW) Albatrosses currently serving with 353 Moira of Greece's Helliniki Aeroporia at Elefsis near Athens. (HAF)

The work was carried out by the Grumman facility at St Augustine, Florida, where fifteen years earlier, when owned by Fairchild-Hiller, USAF HU-16s had been overhauled and updated. Airframe and engines were disassembled and thoroughly examined. Detail design changes were put into effect, new equipment installed and, as required, parts repaired, rebuilt or replaced. The extensive conversion included the replacement of aluminium cap strips on the wing centre section box beams with titanium cap strips, treatment of the airframe with modern anti-corrosion materials and the powerplants completely rebuilt. All engines were certified to zero time and protected by a two shot fire control system. New stainless steel oil tanks were installed. A nickel-cadmium battery aided self-starting system was also fitted as was an auto-feather system, while the reverse-pitch controls were upgraded. All control surfaces were re-covered with Ceconite coating. Much needed flight deck soundproofing and crew seating was improved, avionics and electronics were replaced with the latest state-of-the-art solid state units, with an overall saving of nearly a ton in weight. The passenger cabin was fitted out for 28 to 30 passengers and a flight attendant, fully carpeted and soundproofed with individual light and ventilation controls. Other improvements included the installation of new emergency exits, extra baggage space and, last but not least, a modern toilet. The G-111 Albatross began flight testing on 13 February 1979, completed FAA certification in July 1980 and made an appearance at the 1982 Paris Air Show with a price tag or $3.3 million.

At that time Grumman were studying two further developments of the G-111, the water bomber and yet another turboprop conversion. In the former role, the G-111 has stiff competition from the Canadair CL-215 which, although marginally more expensive, is capable of picking up 12,000 lb (5,443 kg) of water, compared with 10,000 lb (4,536 kg) by the Albatross. Both use a similar scoop system that enables twin-internal tanks to be filled in seconds while skimming over the surface of a lake or sheltered sea.

Although Resorts International had originally looked at the General Electric CT7, Grumman's projected Turbo G-111 was based on using a pair of Garrett TPE331-15UAR ('marinized') turboprop engines rated at 1,645 shp with Dowty Rotol four bladed propellers. Airframe modification would be limited to enlarged rudder, tail span and wingtips. It was anticipated that the Turbo G-111 would show significant increases in take-off weight, cruising speed and range and although it was announced that HU-16s of the Greek and Mexican navies might be re-engined with turboprops, none have been converted to date.

Meanwhile, a total of thirteen Albatrosses were re-manufactured by Grumman at St Augustine to G-111 standards for Resorts International, six of which were put into commercial service with Chalk's International Airlines, the majority being low-time ex-Japanese Maritime Self Defence Force HU-16s with up-rated R1820-82 engines, to fly the airline's high-density routes between Miami and the Bahamas. By the end of 1986, four of the G-111 remained in service with Chalk's, two 28-seaters one 30-seater fitted with lightweight interior, and a en-seat 'Corporate' aircraft used for flying Resorts International VIP guests to the company's casinos in Nassau. The Albatrosses are popular with Chalk's pilots, typical of whom is 35-year-old Captain Roger Nair who was born in Bombay and has been flying with the airline for the past six years. The Albatross is very stable in the air and on the water. It can handle rough water much better than the Mallards and although it does not have an autopilot, our longest flight is only one hour, and it can be easily trimmed to fly straight and level. It is a comfortable aircraft although noisy by today's standards. The up-rated engines are near their power limit on take-off and have to be treated sympathetically. When it's hot and heavy, the Albatross requires quite a long take-off run but a very short landing run using the reverse props. On scheduled flights we have a load factor of about 75 per cent in the high season — which is between December and April — but we also carry a lot of cargo at thirty cents a pound. Charter flights are regularly flown with the Albatross. The only problem with the aircraft is the high amount of maintenance required to keep them on line, especially with the engines. The time between overhauls is only about 1,500 hours.'

Grumman has also converted a number of other ex-military Albatrosses in the past few years, although not to the G-111 standard. One was purchased by Pelita Air Services in Indonesia and used for offshore oil-support work with the state-owned Pertamina oil company, while another Indonesian airline, Dirgantara Air Service (DAS), operates an ex-Indonesian Navy UF-2 on charter flights out of Jakarta.

Two more Grumman overhauled ex-USN aircraft were acquired by the Marine Systems Laboratory of the Smithsonian Institute in 1980 for use in oceanographic research. These amphibians were specially modified with sophisticated communications and navigation equipment, a depth finder and domed observation windows for aerial photography.

A USCG UG-2G with a wider span and taller fin. (Grumman)

A line-up of eight of the eighteen HU-16B (ASW) built for the Royal Norwegian Air Force in 1962. Serving with 330 and 333 Squadrons of the RNAF the amphibians were fitted with underwing weapons stores stations and enlarged nose radome. (Grumman)

Grumman HU-16A Albatross

Accommodation: Crew: 6
Power Plants: Two 1,425 hp Wright R-1820-76A nine-cylinder radials
Dimensions: Wingspan: 80 ft (24.38 m)
Length: 60 ft 8 in (18.5 m)
Height: 24 ft 10 in (7.57 m)
Wing area: 833 sq ft (77.5 m²)
Weights: Empty: 20,100 lb (9,117 kg)
Average: 33,000 lb (14,969 kg)
Performance: Max speed: 245 mph (394 km/h)
Patrol speed: 225 mph (362 km/h)
Range: 2,683 miles (4,317 km)

Grumman HU-16B Albatross

Accommodation: Crew: 6
Power Plants: Two 1,425 hp Wright R-1820-76A nine-cylinder radials
Dimensions: Wingspan: 96 ft 8 in (29.46 m)
Length: 62 ft 10 in (19.15 m)
Height: 25 ft 10 in (7.87 m)
Wing area: 1,035 sq ft (96.25 m²)
Weights: Empty: 22,883 lb (10,380 kg)
Average: 37,500 lb (17,010 kg)
Performance: Max speed: 236 mph (380 km/h)
Patrol speed: 224 mph (360 km/h)
Range: 3, 281 miles (5,279 km)

The two Royal Malaysian Air Force Albatrosses were purchased to support off-shore garrisons and military installations situated on the many islands that make up Malaysia. The two aircraft were air-ferried to Kuala Lumpur from Grumman's St Augustine facility in Florida early in 1986 and managed to average 145 knots during the flight, which took two weeks. Both are operated by No 2 Squadron based at Kuala Lumpur (Simpang) Air Base and fitted to take 28 passengers, although they can be adapted to carry cargo in the rear compartment or fitted with fewer seats in a VIP role. The two Albatrosses are finished in the latest RMAF three-tone grey low-visibility scheme.

A number of ex-military HU-16s have been privately converted for use by charter companies and individuals in North and South America. One of the oldest, a 33-year-old ex-Spanish Air Force SA-16A, was flown back to the United States in April 1986, via Dublin, Gatwick and the Channel Islands (when it briefly appeared on the British register as *G-BMDW*, the only one of its type to do so), where the owner plans to use it for hunting and fishing trips in British Columbia. Another ex-military HU-16C, registered *N9722C*, was rebuilt by its owner Dennis Buehn who had flown the same aircraft when they both served in the US Navy, to become a regular performer on the US air show circuit resplendent in the US Navy colours that won it the Best Seaplane Award at Oshkosh '86.

It is now forty years since the last of Grumman's classic boats first took to the air and it is set to rival the DC3 as one of aviation's great survivors, which carries on earning a living long after its contemporaries have faded into history.

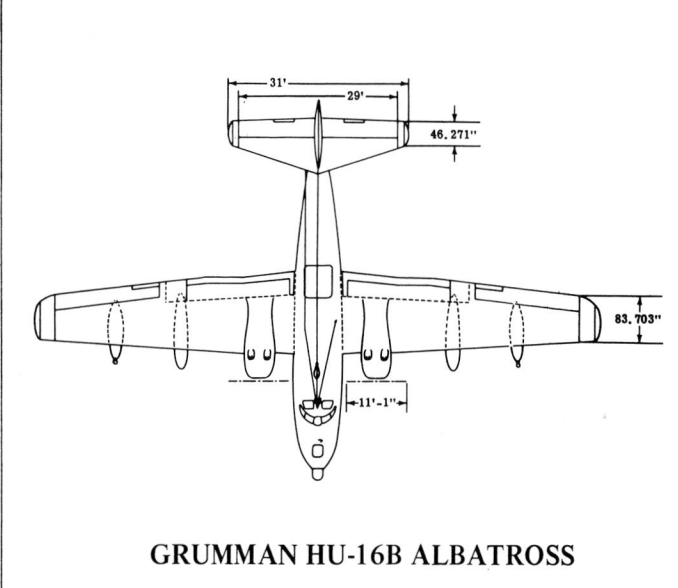

GRUMMAN HU-16B ALBATROSS

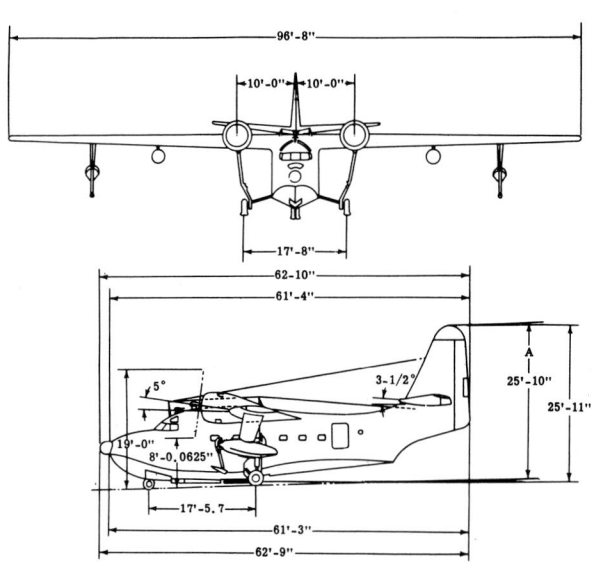

CHAPTER FIVE
THE SHORT SEALAND

On 22 January 1948 an attractive all-metal twin-engined flying boat took to the air for the first time from Belfast Lough. It was the prototype of what was to be Short Brothers' last flying boat, the Short SA6 Sealand designed by C. P. T. Lipscomb. The five to seven-seater, powered by two de Havilland Gypsy Queen inline engines, resembled a scaled-down version of the Solent, and was designed to break into a market that up to that time had been the preserve of the Grumman family of small amphibians, namely the rugged Goose and its smaller brother, the Widgeon.

After two short flights as a flying boat in the hands of Harold Piper, the Sealand prototype, *G-AIVX,* was fitted with a mainwheel undercarriage that retracted into the sides of the fuselage plus a retracting tailwheel, and was flown for the first time as an amphibian by Tom Brooke-Smith on 19 January 1948, making its first public appearance as

such at the 1948 SBAC Show which was the first to be held at Farnborough.

However, early flight trials were to reveal a number of serious problems which included those of high interference drag, low speed throttle sensitivity, and engine overheating in certain conditions. In an effort to cure these faults, the engine position was lowered in the Sealand's high wing, smaller diameter three-bladed propellers fitted and the oil coolers moved from the top of the engine nacelles to the leading edges of the wings. At the same time the planing surfaces were modified to reduce the Sealand's tendency to porpoise during take off.

G-AKLM in Short Brothers livery prior to leaving on a sales demonstration tour of Scandinavia in October 1949, but it was to crash in Norway on 15 October with the loss of three crew. (Shorts)

The prototype of Short Brothers' Sealand, G-AIVX, with the engines in the original above-the-wing position, seen on step taking-off from Belfast Lough. Britain's only post-war amphibian first flew as a flying boat on 22 January 1948. (Shorts)

The SA6 was granted a full certificate of Airworthiness on 28 July 1949 and three days later the first production aircraft, *G-AKLM,* was flown in the first King's Cup Air Race to be held for eleven years, at Elmdon (Birmingham), by Tom Brooke-Smith at an average speed of 169 mph (272 km/h), but only managed to finish in twelfth place.

The first sales of the type were announced in September 1949 when the initial one of three ordered by British West Indian Airways, *VP-TBA,* appeared at the Farnborough Air Show in the airline's colours. Immediately after Farnborough, *G-AKLM* left for an extensive sales tour of Scandinavia, but on 15 October this aircraft crashed on high ground in bad weather near Lindesnes, Norway, killing all three members of the crew.

The third production Sealand, *G-AKLO,* then became the company's European and North African demonstrator, while *G-AKLP,* which was to have become British West Indian Airways' first aircraft, set out on a comprehensive sales tour of South and North America following the cancellation of the BWIA order after a series of unsatisfactory sea trials in the West Indies. During its flights around the Americas, *G-AKLP* visited, amongst other countries, Argentina, where it was enthusiastically received by the military but, due to the country's political and financial turmoil, no order was forthcoming, Chile, the Bahamas, the United States and Canada were also visited and when the Sealand landed at Montreal in January 1952, it had spent 350 hours in the air flying a total of 50,000 miles (80,450 km) with no major mechanical problems — but no orders either.

It was here that the Sealand was acquired, at a very reasonable price, by the experienced flying boat pilot and later TV personality, Hughie Green, on behalf of Lambert Brothers of London who were to operate it for the Greek shipping tycoon, Aristotle Onassis. Onassis, who thought that he was getting a Mallard, was disappointed when told by Green that the Sealand was not capable of flying non-stop from Lake Geneva to Croydon with a full load. Hughie Green, who was to fly the Lambert amphibian for almost a year, had the distinction of flying the world's top shipping magnates, Onassis and his brother-in-law Niarchos, together in *G-AKLP* on more than one occasion. However, he was less than complimentary about the Sealand's performance, especially on water. His view was shared by pilots of the Marine Aircraft Experimental Establishment at Felixstowe who evaluated the Sealand for the air-sea rescue role at the end of 1951. The MAEE examiners criticised the amphibian's high take-off and landing speeds on water, and its alarming swing to starboard during take-off from calm waters.

The first British post-war commercial aircraft to be sold to the United States was this Sealand that was purchased by the Christian & Missionary Alliance of New York which operated in Indonesia as PK-CMA from 1950 to 1953 when it was abandoned following a forced landing in Java. (Shorts)

One of three Sealands ordered by British West Indian Airways, VP-TBB, being flown with one propeller feathered. The BWIA order was subsequently cancelled and this aircraft, registered was sold to JAT at YU-CFJ. (Shorts)

One of a pair of Sealand flying boats, LN-SUH, operated by the Norwegian airline Vestlandske Luftfartselskap (VLS) at its base at Bergen in 1953. (J. Stroud)

As a result of these trials the Sealand's wingspan was increased by thirty inches (76.2 cm) and wing fences were fitted in an attempt to reduce the stalling speed. The take-off swing was practically cured by the combination of reducing overall weight by some 330 lb (150 kg), modifying the hull shape to increase buoyancy, and the fitting of a small asymetric fin to the rear of the planing surface.

Meanwhile, Short Bros had sold a Sealand to Captain Al Lewis of the Christian and Missionary Alliance of New York — the first British post-war commercial aircraft to be sold to the United States. This aircraft was shipped direct to Djakarta, Indonesia, in December 1950 where it soon began operations with CMA from Trandjoengselor, registered *PK-CMA*. Although it was an unmodified aircraft, the Sealand performed well in difficult conditions before it was forced down during a tropical thunderstorm in an inaccessible part of Java where it had to be abandoned in February 1953. A replacement, the 24th and last production Sealand, was purchased by CMA in November 1953, registered *JZ-PTA*. This aircraft was based in Hollandia, New Guinea, from where it was flown into the remote Baliem Valley, regularly using a lake 10,000 ft (3,000 m) above sea level as one of its alighting points. But it too was lost, this time with all on board including Captain Lewis, when it crashed into a mountain on 10 May 1955 while flying from Eidenburg to Baliem.

Meanwhile, following *G-AKLO*'s European and North African sales tour, two Sealands were sold in Norway, two in Yugoslavia and another in Egypt. In May 1951, a Sealand 1M was purchased by Vestlandske Luftfartselskap of Bergen, Norway, registered *LN-SUH,* which was joined by *LN-SUF* a year later. These two aircraft were operated as pure flying boats, known as the Sealand 3, and with the weight saved from the removal of the undercarriage they were able to carry eight passengers and their baggage between Bergen, Alesund and Trondheim. After years of trouble-free service in harsh climatic conditions, the Norwegian Sealands were sold to a Swedish charter company in 1960 but scrapped two years later.

In September 1951 two Sealand 1Fs, *YU-CFJ* and *-CFK,* were flown to Zagreb to begin an Adriatic coastal service with Jugoslovenski Aerotransport (JAT). These two aircraft were later transferred to the Yugoslav Air Force with which they served until the early 1960s.

The sole Sealand 1G was sold to Ahmed Abboud Pasha, a Director of the Egyptian Khedivial Shipping Line, and was very much a luxury yacht. Named *Nadia,* the Sealand featured dual controls, extra fuel tanks, air-conditioning, hide upholstery for six passengers, a built-in wine cabinet, book case, and a forward toilet.

However, the largest commercial operator of the Sealand was the Shell Petroleum Co which added three of Short's amphibians to its large and varied worldwide fleet of aircraft, the first of which, *VR-UDS,* was purchased in October 1952 for use in the Borneo oilfields. Two years later the company acquired the much travelled ex-Lambert Bros aircraft, which was also based in the Far East as *VR-UDV.* A third, registered *YV-P-AEG,* operated from Lake Maracaibo in Venezuela and all three proved to be capable and reliable performers in the often inhospitable conditions in which they operated.

Three Sealands, delivered during 1951 were, top to bottom, G-AKLV to Ralli Bros., of London for service in East Pakistan, and YU-CFJ and 'CFK to Jugoslavenski Aero Transport of Belgrade (JAT). (Shorts)

The luxuriously equipped Sealand, SU-AHY, sold to His Excellency Ahmed Abboud Pasha, director of the Khedivial Mail Line of Cairo. Named 'Nadia', the Egyptian Sealand was returned to Shorts at Belfast in August 1986 where it is hoped that it will be rebuilt to an airworthy condition. (Shorts)

One of Shell's three Sealands, VR-UDV, seen here at Croydon airport in November 1957, was the ex-Short Bros demonstrator G-AKLP. It is fitted with the skeg forward of the tail wheel which improved stability on water take-offs.

Short's most successful marketplace for their small amphibian was to be the Indian sub-continent where more than half of all the 24 Sealands produced were to operate. The first of these was a 1G, *G-AKLV,* bought by Ralli Brothers of London in 1952 for use in the company's Bengal jute plantations. The Sealand arrived in Dacca in May 1952 re-registered *AP-AFM* and named *Pegasus.* J. A. Vlasto, an inspector with Ralli Bros, was a frequent passenger in the aircraft and recalls it well.

'The machine was used for inspections and contact with our various plantations in the jute growing area of East Pakistan with its innumerable rivers where transport was almost solely by boat. Railways were few and far between and roads almost non-existent. An inspection visit to one of our more distant premises by cabin launch might have needed three or four days whereas it could be accomplished in less than a morning by air.

'The aircraft was kept and serviced at Dacca airport close to our headquarters at Narainganj where our pilot, a fellow called Rumbelow, was based. It had a toilet, four quite comfortable seats in the cabin, and there was always a spare seat next to the pilot in the cockpit. Apart from Dacca the only other airport in the area was Chittagong which was used in preference to the very busy stretch of river fronting our premises there. Otherwise calls at all our jute stations necessitated river landings and take-offs. Although the rivers were normally wide and afforded sufficient straight stretches, there were often problems with numerous river craft which made landings and take-offs quite exciting. If there were some near misses there were fortunately no accidents.

'I seem to remember that the aircraft cost about £35,000 which was a lot of money in those days. In general it did its job well. Mechanical troubles were minor. It could have done with a bit more power. With a full load, take-off from Dacca or Chittagong seemed to require quite a stretch of runway, perhaps as much as that needed by a Dakota which was the plane used on the Calcutta-Dacca-Chittagong service. And river take-offs seemed endless.'

Nevertheless, *Pegasus* gave good reliable service to the company until October 1957 when it returned to Rochester and was withdrawn from use.

Two other Sealands were based at Dacca at the same time as *Pegasus,* these being two 1Ns that were purchased by the government of East Pakistan in December 1952 for use by the East Bengal Transport Commission. Registered *AP-AGB* and '*C,* the two amphibians were seldom used before one was damaged beyond repair when a hangar roof collapsed on it following a severe storm soon after its delivery to Dacca. The second Sealand was scrapped in 1962 due to 'non-utilisation for want of pilots and spare parts'. Also, according to the records this aircraft had flown only 54 hours of familiarisation and check flights during ten years in Pakistan.

However, the recently formed air component of the Indian Navy became the Short Sealand's best customer when a contract was signed in 1953 for a total of ten aircraft. Designated the Sealand 1L, the Indian Navy aircraft differed in many respects from the commercial types built to date. They were fitted with uprated Gipsy Queen 70/4 engines, constant-

One of the ten Sealand ILs, INS-105, that were purchased by the newly formed Indian Navy in 1953. These amphibians had up-rated engines, extra fuel tanks and observation windows, and served with Fleet Requirements Unit for nearly ten years.(Shorts)

peed propellers, dual controls and long-range fuel anks to give up to six hours' endurance. The first ircraft, *INS-101,* left Rochester for Cochin on 13 anuary 1953, piloted by Ray Gough and C. C. Tubby) Dash. The same crew would ferry all ten ealands, the last of which was delivered to India in November 1953. The Sealands served with the ndian Navy's Fleet Requirements Unit based at NS Dabolin at Goa where they operated for nearly en years as liaison and training aircraft. During his time they were flown by many of the Indian avy's top pilots including Commander A. rakash who was to become the CO of the service's rst Sea Harrier squadron some twenty years later.

While many pilots who flew the Sealand praised ome of its features such as the design, layout and xcellent visibility of the cockpit, low noise levels nd, by the standards of its day, comfort, along ith the reversible pitch propellers that eased water axying, they also complained of its lack of power nd endurance especially with a full load. Had the ealand been produced to the Indian Navy's pecifications from the outset, or better still, had ne proposed Mark 2 powered by Alvis Leonides adial engines been put into production, Short rothers' last 'boat' may well have sold in greater umbers and still have been active today. As it is, nd thanks to its rugged overall construction, three xamples of the type have survived.

One of the two Yugoslav Air Force Sealands, No *0662*, still existed at the end of 1986, albeit in less than perfect condition, and has been earmarked for preservation in the projected Air Force Museum at Belgrade, while an Indian Navy example, *INS-105*, has been kept in open storage at Cochin awaiting for funds to be made available for its rebuild as another museum exhibit. Of most interest is the ex-Egyptian Sealand, *SU-AHY,* which, after limited use during the 1950s, was sold to the Saudi Arabian Air Force that used it for Red Sea SAR duties based at Jeddah. After a relatively short service life with the fledgling Saudi Air Force, the Sealand remained in open storage at the Old Jeddah Airport until it was discovered by an American Overseas National Airways pilot, Captain Rick Skala, who purchased it in 1975 with the intention of rebuilding it to airworthy condition after shipping it back to the United States. However, three years later he donated the partially rebuilt amphibian to the New England Air Museum of Windsor Lock, Connecticut, which in turn put it up for sale in 1984. It has since been acquired by the Ulster Transport Museum and the Sealand was returned to its birthplace at Belfast in August 1986 where it will be made fully airworthy by a team of past and present Short Bros personnel. The plan is to add it to the growing number of flying boats and amphibians that have recently joined the British air show circuit, so after an absence of nearly forty years, the graceful shape of the Sealand amphibian may well be seen again in the skies over England as a welcome reminder of Short Brothers', and Britain's, last flying boat.

Accommodation:	Crew: 2
	Passengers: 5 - 7
Power Plants:	Two 340 hp de Havilland
	Gipsy Queen 70-3 six-cylinder
	engines
Dimensions:	Wingspan: 61 ft 6 in (18.74 m)
	Length: 42 ft 2 in (12.85 m)
	Height: 15 ft (4.57 m)
	Wing area: 359 sq ft (33.4 m²)
Weights:	Empty: 7,065 lb (3,204 kg)
	Average: 9,100 lb (4,128 kb)
Performance:	Max speed: 187 mph (300 km/h)
	Cruising speed: 176 mph (283 km/h)
	Range: 525 miles (845 km)

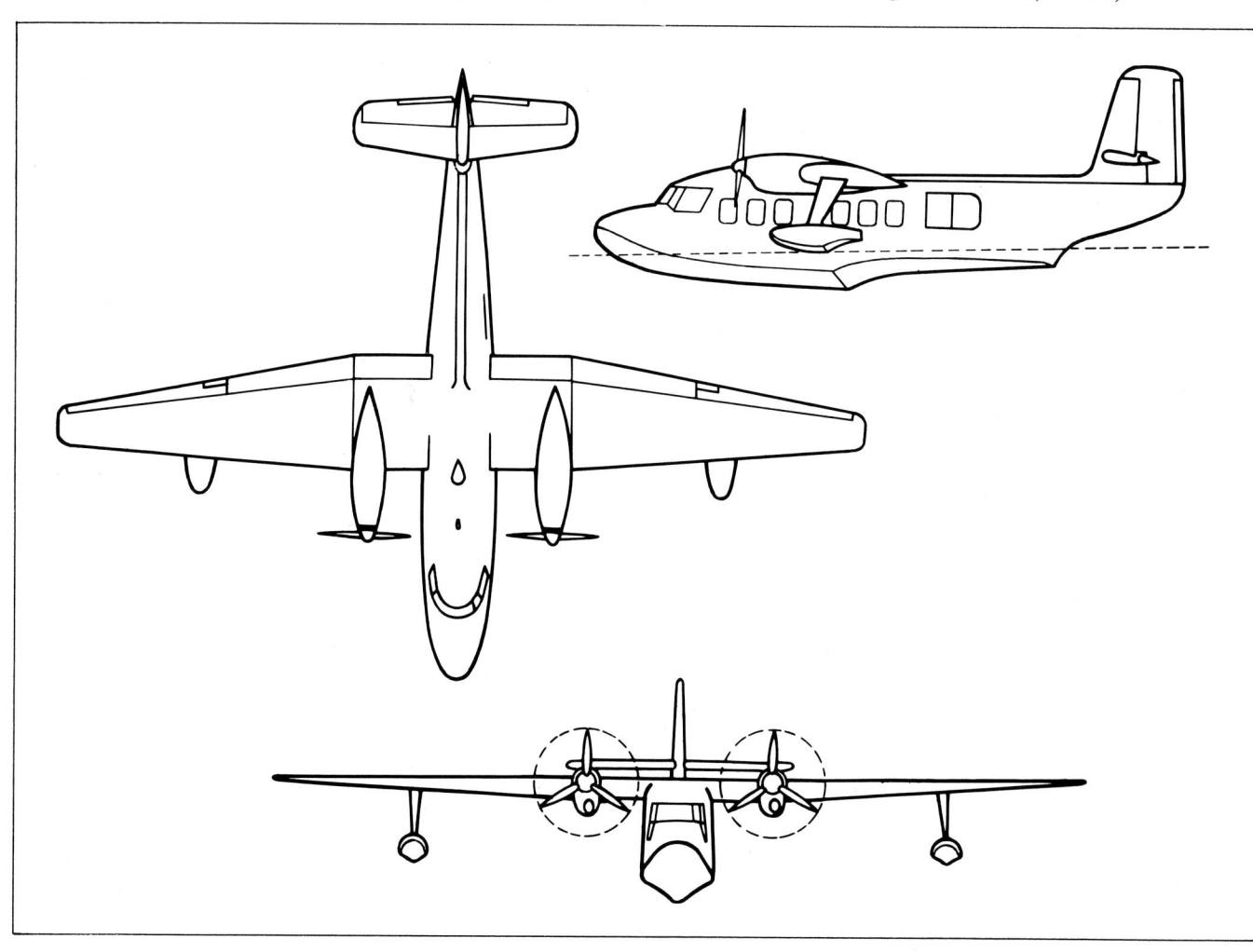

CHAPTER SIX
THE PIAGGIO P136

Six months after the first flight of Short's light amphibian, yet another small twin boat took to the air for the first time when the Italian Piaggo P136 was flown from Genoa on 29 August 1948 with Nicolo Lana at the controls.

Rinaldo Piaggio had been building seaplanes and flying boats since 1915 when the company started licence production of the French Schreck FBA. Ten years later another foreign design, the German Dornier Wal flying boat, was being assembled on the Finale Ligure production line, many of them powered by Piaggio-built Jupiter engines, while a futuristic, but unsuccessful, Piaggio-Pegna Pc7 hydrofoil project was designed for the 1929 Schneider Trophy race. During World War Two Piaggio built more than 200 CANT Z506 bomber-reconnaissance seaplanes, a number of which continued to serve with the post-war Italian Air Force in an air-sea rescue role until the early 1950s.

During the immediate post-war period, when Piaggio was kept solvent by producing Vespa scooters, Ing Alberto Faraboschi, under the supervision of Professor Giovanni Casiraghi, designed a neat gull-winged, twin-engined five-seat amphibian. Piaggio was another company that anticipated a large market for a small sporting amphibian, but although the smooth lines of the P136 were much admired when it appeared at the 1949 Paris Air Show, orders were slow in coming.

A Piaggio P136F, M 80007, belonging to the 84th Group at its base at Vigna di Valle. Note the cargo hatch and split flaps. (Aeronautica Militare)

The first flying boat to be produced by Rinaldo Piaggio was the French Schreck FBA built under licence from 1915. (D. Oliver)

The first Piaggio P136L to be delivered to the Aeronautica Militare, MM 80076, fresh from the factory. Note the revised engine intakes and the small recess in the hull forward of the tail wheel. (via G. Apostolo)

The prototype, which was given one of the first 'personalised' registrations — *I-PIAG* — featured a single-step planing bottom, slightly swept-back gull wing, and wingtip floats mounted on single streamlined struts. The smoothly finished monocoque hull of all-metal construction was wide enough to accommodate five people, in two single front seats and a bench seat for three in the rear, in comfort in an extensively glazed cabin, while the mainwheels retracted neatly into the fuselage sides and the tailwheel was raised upwards to fit behind the tail step. A novel feature of the Piaggio P136 was the high mounted pusher engine layout. Two 215 hp Franklin 6A8-215-B9F six-cylinder engines driving two-bladed airscrews gave the P136 a maximum speed of 181 mph (291 km/h), but a limited range, with five on board, of only 373 miles (600 km).

The pusher engines, raised above the cabin by the gull-wing, kept the propellers behind the passenger cabin to give a quiet and vibration-free ride. To help to establish production of the amphibian in view of the lack of firm orders, and to enable the Aeronautica Militare to establish an efficient low-cost air-sea rescue service, the Italian Government placed an order for fifteen Piaggio P136s after extensive testing of the second prototype. The first 'military' aircraft, designated the P136F, was in fact the fourth to leave the Finale Ligure production line, and although the amphibian had few vices, either in the water or the air, and proved popular with the Italian Air Force crews, the additional military payload of radios and basic air-sea rescue equipment reduced endurance to less than two hours. The Piaggio P136F, fitted with an extra observation window in the forward-opening cabin doors, was operated by the 84th Group based at Vigna di Valle on the shores of Lake Braccianco, some twenty miles north-west of Rome, for air-sea rescue and communications duties.

One of the few orginal Franklin-engined versions to be sold to the civil market, and the second to be built, *I-ALCE*, was purchased by King Farouk of Egypt in October 1949 when it joined his fleet of Royal Egyptian Air Force-operated Mallard amphibians as *SU-AHM*. The Piaggio was used for King Farouk's frequent travels to the South of France and was in fact out of the country when he was toppled from power by a military coup in July 1952.

Despite the Piaggio's limited range, Mauro Lualdi and Leonardo Bonzi managed to establish a number of Class 3 FAI records for amphibians in March 1950, while the third P136, *I-FIMA*, took part in a number of air races in the early 1950s. In an effort to improve the performance of the P136 and make it more attractive to civil operators, the prototype was fitted with a pair of 260 hp Lycoming GO-435-C2 flat-six engines, and was certified in July 1953. The only external differences between two versions were an enlarged fin and rudder, to cope with the extra power, slightly re-profiled engine nacelles and the fitting of three-blade constant-speed Hartzall propellers. The first production deliveries of the Lycoming-engined version, known as the P136L, powered by Piaggio-built GO-480-B1A6s developing 270 hp, began in 1955. Meanwhile, the re-engined prototype, *I-PIAG*, was used by the Marchesa Carina Negrone in ine 1954 to establish an international Class 3 record for amphibians by flying non-stop from Brescia to Luxor, a total distance of 1,856 miles (2,986 km), in 13 hours 34 minutes. The production Piaggio P136L had a cruising speed of 167 mph (269 km/h) and a maximum range of 1,056 miles (1,700 km) which made it a much more attractive aircraft to potential amphibian customers, both military and civil.

In July 1956 the Italian Air Force ordered eight examples of the new version to supplement the remaining P136Fs, three of which had been written off following accidents, all of which occurred on land, and a number of commercial airtaxi operators' initial interest was translated into firm orders. Typical of these was Dagens Nyheter of Sweden which purchased a P136L, *SE-CDE,* in July 1956. Based at Bromma, Stockholm, the Piaggio flew a daily service to Nordmaling, a distance of some 120 miles (193 km) to the north, flown via Sweden's rugged west coast. Operating close to the Arctic Circle, where the temperature could fall to minus forty degrees centigrade in winter, the aircraft performed reliably in the hostile conditions for a number of years before being sold to another Swedish charter company.

Olympic Airways Piaggio P136L, SX-BDB, originally purchased by Lambert Bros of London registered G-APNY in 1958, and was written off in Greece following a wheels-up landing at Elefsis in 1972 after an eventful career as Aristotle Onassis's personal aircraft. (via J. J. Halley)

P136L-1, N160EG one of more than two dozen Trekker Royal Gulls that were on the US Register during the 1970s. (Air Britain)

In August 1958 the small Naples-based aerota▮ company, Alisud, purchased a re-engined P136, ▮ *FIMA,* to operate regular services betwee▮ Capodichino, Salerno and Ischia. Meanwhile t▮ first P136L to appear on the British register, *▮ AOFN,* was acquired in Belfast by Lambert Bros ▮ July 1954 to replace the Short Sealand amphibi▮ that the company had operated for the Gree▮ shipping magnate Aristotle Onassis. Although t▮ Piaggio was maintained at Croydon Airport, ▮ spent much of its time in Monaco, which w▮ Onassis' business base at the time, flying the Gree▮ tycoon, his family, friends and business associat▮ to his yacht *Christina,* a $4 million conversion of ▮ ex-Canadian frigate that had deck space for sever▮ speedboats, a hydrofoil — and two amphibians ▮

Following the type's American certification ▮ September 1956, a P136L, *N220A,* undertook ▮ extensive sales tour of the United States duri▮ which one of the amphibians was ordered by ▮ American machine-tool magnate from Milwauke▮ Francis J. Trecker. He was so impressed with h▮ acquisition that he formed a company, the Roy▮ Aircraft Corporation, to import and market t▮ Piaggio P136, to be known as the Trecker Gull, ▮ North America. He saw the main market bei▮ wealthy sportsmen and airtaxi companies th▮ could make use of the many lakes and inla▮ waterways that abounded in northern and coast▮ areas of the United States and Canada. The aircra▮ were shipped unpainted and with only basic cab▮ furnishings. US-produced instrumentation a▮ accessories were fitted at Milwaukee along with t▮ customer's choice of radios and avionics. With ▮ full production line at Finale Ligure, of both ci▮ and military P136Ls, Piaggio had begun to study▮ number of flying boat projects in 1955 including▮ forty-passenger multi-purpose amphibian power▮ by two Napier Nomad turboprops, but it was at t▮ Paris Air Show of 1957 that the compan▮ announced that funds had been granted by t▮ Italian Ministry of Defence for the construction of▮ prototype boat designated the P155. Models of ▮ less than four different versions of this large twi▮ engined flying boat, which closely resembled t▮ Martin Marlin in size and configuration, we▮ shown at the Paris Salon. They were the P15▮ SAM-1 and 2 air-sea rescue and anti-submari▮ warfare amphibians powered by two 1,800 hp Pra▮ & Whitney R-2800 engines, and the P155-S nav▮ reconnaissance and P155-CT commerci▮ transport, both of which were to be turbopro▮ powered. Work on the first piston-engine▮ prototype commenced in July 1957, the sam▮ month that saw the first flight of the Piaggio P166▮ landplane development of the P136.

In March 1958, an ex-Aeronautica Milita▮ P136L registered *I-GULL,* one of at least thre▮ military boats that appeared in civil markings whe▮ taking part in air races, made an extensive sales to▮ of Great Britain during which it made a series ▮ water landings on the rivers Medway, Dee an▮ Mersey, resulting in at least one sale when Lambe▮ Bros acquired a second amphibian, *G-APNY,* ▮ behalf of Aristotle Onassis. By this time Onass▮ had acquired Olympic Airways and the Piaggio w▮ transferred to the airline, registered *SX-BDB.* It w▮ still used as Onassis' private aircraft and spe▮ much of its time flying to and from his yac▮

ristina in Monaco, Nice or Rome. In September
59, the aircraft played a central part in the
ebrated marital feud between Onassis and his
·e Tina. During this period, the amphibian, and
Italian pilot Angelo Pirotti, was kept busy flying
assis around Europe for clandestine meetings
h the international opera singer Maria Callas, or
rsuing Tina Onassis to Paris after she walked out
him taking their children with her. However, by
>0, more than a dozen P136s had been sold in the
ited States and Canada, most of them through
· Royal Aircraft Corp, including two which
;an operations with Lake Tahoe Airlines in 1957
ing seasonal services between San Francisco and
· holiday resorts of Clear Lake and Lake Tahoe.
e Trecker Royal Gull cost $25,000, which
luded customs clearance, US certification and
ivery charges. The cost of the radio and avionic
· supplied to the customer's specification, was
ra. However, in response to Trecker's request for
· even more powerful version, which the US
npany considered would have excellent sales
tential in North America, the factory fitted an ex-
litary P136L with two 340 hp Lycoming GSO-
·)-B1C6 engines in 1959. The production version,
wn as the P136L-2, differed little externally
m its predecessor except for a straight dorsal fin
1 a different three-bladed propeller. However,
ne sold in the United States by Trecker, which
·re marketed as the Royal Super Gull 200, were
ed with a small bow spray dam. The increased
wer of the P136L-2 enabled the amphibian to
ry an extra 400 lb (181 kg) payload, or two
>ple at a squeeze, and cruise at 190 mph (306
/h) for more then 900 miles (1,450 km). The cost
the basic Royal Super Gull 200 was $89,925.

An abandoned Piaggio P136L-1 amphibian, N40031, marketed
in the United States as the Trecker Royal Gull, seen 'resting' at
Orange County airport, California, in November 1986. (D. Oliver)

An immaculate Trecker Royal Super Gull 200, N1449Z, a Piaggio P136L-2 amphibian fitted with 340 hp Lycoming engines, at Fort Lauderdale airport, Florida, in November 1986 carrying an oceanographic research instrument pod under the port wing. (D. Oliver)

Meanwhile, Piaggio continued to export their amphibian in small numbers, with sales to Pakistan and Hong Kong being recorded in the early 1960s. The first, a P136L registered *AP-ALV*, was delivered to the Director General of the East Pakistan Rifles in 1960, and a year later it was joined by an L-2, *AP-AOH*, for use by the Governor of East Pakistan. As with the Short Sealands sold to Pakistan some years earlier, the Italian boats saw little use before being abandoned following the independence of East Pakistan as Bangladesh in 1971. Another Piaggio P136L-2, *VR-HFP*, was sold to Macau Air Transport in March 1961, to operate a high frequency service between Hong Kong and the Portuguese colony of Macau on the Chinese mainland for two years until a more competitive hydrofoil service took over the forty-mile route. In 1963 the aircraft was sold to a charter company in Portuguese Timor but by 1970, it appeared on the Australian register as *VH-BJP*, having been acquired by the small airline, Dolphinair. The Piaggio started a flying boat service in 1974 flying the 100 mile route between Townsville, in North Queensland, to Cape Richards, a holiday resort on Hinchinbrook Island, but was involved in an accident during take-off from the sea near the island early the following year. Although the aircraft was recovered from shallow waters, it was damaged beyond economical repair and Dolphinair ceased operations while the Piaggio was put on static display at the Townsville Museum.

In Canada, Piaggio P136Ls were used by Eastern Provincial Airways in Newfoundland and Time Air Ltd of Alberta for a period during the mid-1960s. In the meantime, by the middle of 1961, the surviving P136s operated by the 84th Group based at Vigna di Valle had been replaced by the American Grumman SA-16 Albatross amphibian, that was to become the Aeronautica Militare's principal SAR aircraft for the next twenty years, and not the stillborn P155-SAM1 which had been cancelled before the first aircraft could take to the air. The reason for abandoning the ambitious P155 project was a combination of the availability of relatively inexpensive MDAP Albatrosses plus the high development cost for what, at the time, seemed to the Italian government to be a dying market for large flying boats. However, a number of the Piaggio P136s were retained by the Aeronautica Militare, serving as trainers and liaison aircraft with the 140th Squadron until the end of the decade.

In 1964, Aristotle Onassis bought the four hundred acre island of Skorpios off the coast of Ithaca some 150 miles (240 km) west of Athens. This island 'retreat' had few roads and no airstrip so Olympic Airways invested in a second Piaggio P136, an L-2 equipped with full airways avionics, to be available to ferry the airline's boss to his island. Another Greek shipping magnate to appreciate the stylish Italian amphibian was Stavros Livanos who resided at St Moritz in Switzerland. The Livanos P136L-2, *HB-EMG,* was registered to one of the tycoon's many companies called Aztec Airlines.

However, after nearly twenty years of continuous production, the 63rd and final P136 amphibian left the line at Finale Ligure in 1967, but it was yet to hit the headlines of the world's press.

An Aeronautica Militare Piaggio 136L at Vigna di Valle photographed with Lake Braccianco as a backdrop.
(Aeronautica Militare)

In 1971, Olympic Airways formed a subsidiary to operate light aircraft and helicopters on charter, air-taxi and flying-training duties. The company, known as Olympic Aviation, was run by Aristotle Onassis' son Alexander who, despite being unable to fulfil his ambition by becoming a commercial pilot due to defective eyesight, was a proficient private pilot able to fly all the types in the company's fixed-wing fleet, including the Piaggio P136Ls. The amphibians were available for charter at $1.27 per kilometre, or $330 per hour, but were seldom hired as at least one was kept on constant standby for use by Onassis senior. One of the problems of operating amphibians in the 1970s was that experienced flying boat captains were few and far between, but Olympic Airways were lucky enough to have a very experienced man within its own ranks to fill the vacancy following the purchase of the second P136.

The pilot concerned was the Canadian Donald McGregor who had flown Short 'C' Class boats, Hythes, Hermes and Comets with BOAC prior to joining the Greek airline as a Boeing 727 Captain. In 1967 he had flown Dennis Ferranti's Grumman Mallard amphibian so was well used to the whims of VIP passengers. However, soon after he took over the position in 1972, the original P136L, *SX-BDB,* made a wheels-up landing at a Greek Air Force base. Although damage to the hull was superficial, it was found to be suffering from terminal internal corrosion so the amphibian which could boast of having carried most of Europe's, and Hollywood's, rich and famous amongst its passengers during the previous fourteen years, was subsequently written off. However, Captain McGregor was to fly Olympic Aviation's P136L-2, *SX-BDC,* on numerous occasions for nearly a year. Most of the flights were between Athens and Skorpios carrying Onassis or his new wife, Jackie, plus frequent trips to Corfu, Crete and Mekanos with family friends.

Captain 'Mac' McGregor remembers this time with mixed feelings.

'Despite being called out at all times of the day and night, Onassis was no problem. The only time we had words was when he was in a hurry to get out of the aircraft before I had a chance to turn it round on the ramp at Skorpios. I told him to wait as it was dangerous to get out and walk towards the rear of the aircraft — straight into the propellers. The aircraft handled well on the water and the large engined version had a reasonable performance and was easy to fly. Much of the time was spent looking for suitable water landing areas because there was lack of anchorage available around many of the islands, the water being too deep and the shores too steep to taxy on to.

'I always got on well with Alexander who was an extremely capable pilot although he did not think much of the Piaggio. He was going to replace it with a helicopter as soon as possible. However, in January 1973 Onassis announced that he was taking the *Christina* on a cruise to Miami and the West Indies and wanted to take the Piaggio on board, but as I was grounded following an eye operation, an American pilot, Donald McClusker, was brought over to be checked out on the aircraft. On 22 January 1973, McClusker arrived at Athens and Alexander decided to get the check over

Piaggio P136L SE-CDE was purchased by the Swedish operator Dagens Nyheter in 1956 and later sold to SLF, also based at Bromma, Stockholm, carried fare-paying passengers in the harsh conditions of northern Sweden for many years without incident. (J. Gradidge)

An early US registered P136L-1, N222A, that was marketed in North America by the Trekker Corporation as the Royal Gull (J. Stroud)

Piaggio P136L, MM 80080, of 140th Squadron based at Vigna di Valle differed from the earlier military model (see below) in a number of respects including a taller fin, three bladed propellers and a revised nacelle to house the more powerful Lycoming engines. (Aeronautica Militare)

Another view of P136F MM 80007 at Vigna di Valle with Lake Braccianco in the background showing the extra observation windows in the cabin door. (Aeronautica Militare)

traight away. I just happened to be there at the irport at the time and he asked me if I would like to ome along for the ride. After briefing the new ilot, we walked out to the aircraft and discovered hat we had not brought a check list, but as Alexander and I had written the L-2's check list etween us, this was no problem. McClusker taxied ut seated in the left-hand seat with Alexander on is right, I was in the back. We stopped at the olding point while a Boeing 727 took off, and aving received take-off clearance from the tower e lined up and began our take-off run. Almost as oon as the wheels had left the ground we did a harp turn to the right and that's about as much as I emember until I woke up in hospital.'

The Piaggio's right wingtip had hit the ground nd the aircraft cartwheeled along the runway efore coming to rest extensively damaged, but not n fire. McClusker and McGregor were badly jured but not critical. Alexander Onassis suffered assive head injuries and died 24 hours later. The rash hit the world's headlines along with ccusations of sabotage by persons unknown and ilot error by McClusker. In fact, after a number of parate and lengthy investigations, which ventually exonerated the two surviving pilots from ny blame, the cause of the crash was given as an correctly installed control column which reversed e controls. Captain McGregor, amongst others, as convinced that reversed controls would have een spotted in Alexander's pre-flight check, uring which the control column movement is seen 'full and free', and that the most likely reason for e accident was 'wake turbulence'. This was used by following the Boeing 727's take-off too osely, and flying into the turbulent air stirred up y the accelerating airliner.

Whatever the true reason for the accident, it had been conclusively proved that the Piaggio had not suffered any mechanical or structural failure. In fact the amphibian had a very good safety record and was extremely well constructed. Twenty years after the last P136 was manufactured, about ten examples remain airworthy in the United States and Canada where they are considered by their pilots as something akin to a vintage Ferrari of the air. A number of the ex-Aeronautica Militare P136L amphibians were sold off to private flyers including two that joined the Varese Seaplane club based at Lake Como. One of them, *MM800082,* which appeared on the civil register as *I-FRLV* in June 1964, was damaged beyond repair after hitting submerged debris in 1976. However, this aircraft is currently under restoration by a group of enthusiasts at Milan's Bresso airfield while no less than three military Piaggios, a P136F and two P136Ls, are held in storage at the Italian Air Force Museum housed, appropriately, on the site of the old flying boat base at Vigna di Valle. Although Piaggio has not produced another flying boat design, a turboprop version of the P166 landplane is still in production at Genoa, while two other Italian aerospace companies are currently studying amphibious aircraft projects for the 1990s.

Piaggio P136F

Accommodation:	Crew: 2
Power Plants:	Two 215 hp Franklin 6A8-215-B9F six-cylinder engines
Dimensions:	Wingspan: 43 ft (13.1 m)
	Length: 35 ft 5 in (10.79 m)
	Height: 11 ft 2 in (3.4 m)
	Wing area: 250 sq ft (23.25 m²)
Weights:	Empty: 4,200 lb (1,905 kg)
	Average: 5,500 lb (2,495 kg)
Performance:	Max speed: 175 mph (282 km/h)
	Cruising speed: 149 mph (240 km/h)
	Range: 770 miles (1,239 km)

Piaggio P136L-1

Accommodation:	Crew: 5
Power Plants:	Two 270 hp Lycoming GO-480-B six-cylinder engines
Dimensions:	Wingspan: 44 ft 4¾ in (13.53 m)
	Length: 35 ft 5 in (10.79 m)
	Height: 12 ft 7 in (3.83 m)
	Wing area: 270.2 sq ft (25 m²)
Weights:	Empty: 4,400 lb (1,996 kg)
	Average: 5,996 lb (2,720 kg)
Performance:	Max speed: 183 mph (294 km/h)
	Cruising speed: 167 mph (269 km/h)
	Range: 1,056 miles (1,700 km)

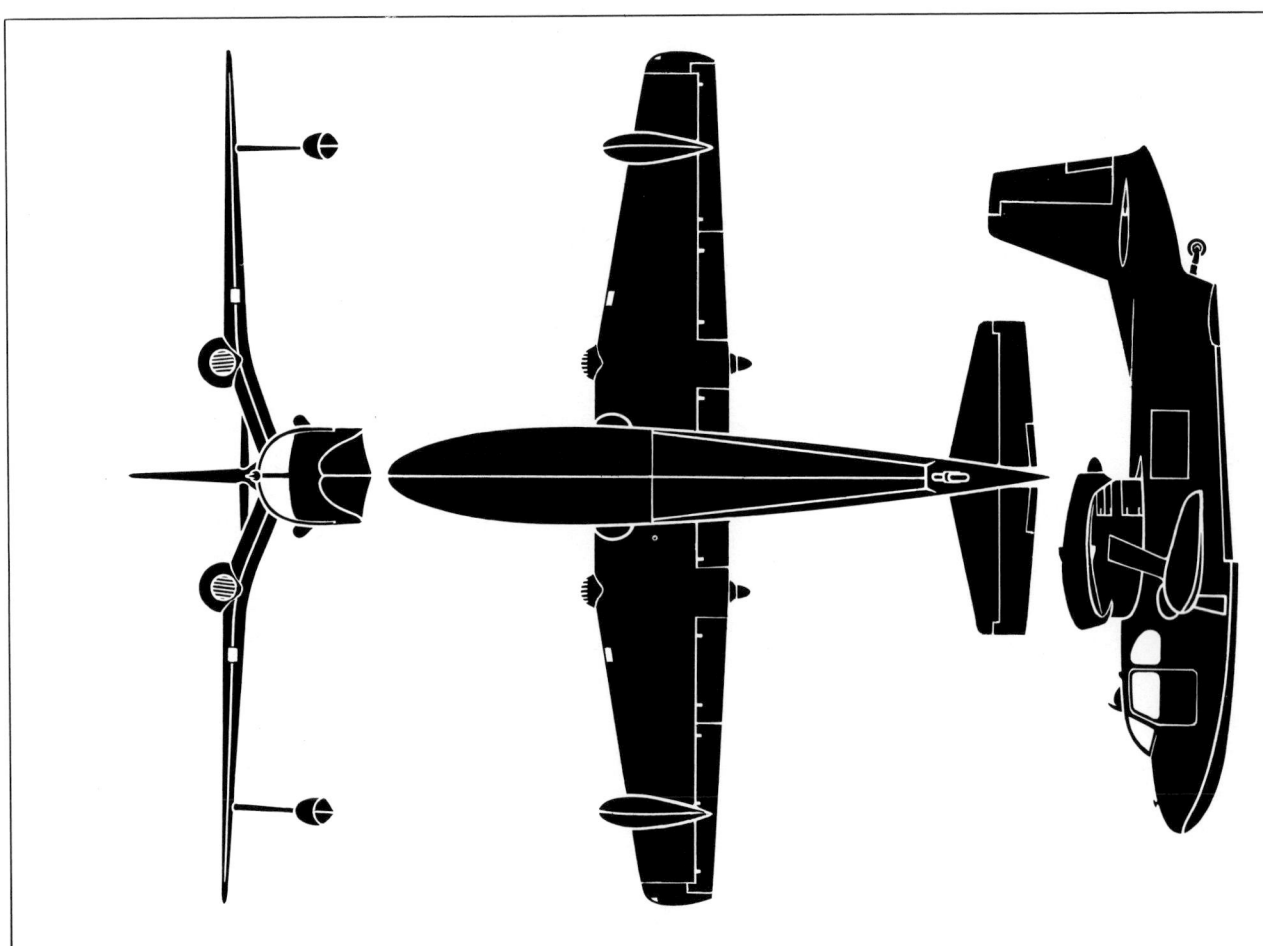

CHAPTER SEVEN
THE NORD NOROIT

What was to become the swansong of French flying boat design, the SNCAN Noroit, took to the air for the first time at Le Havre in January 1949. The Société Nationale de Construction du Nord (SNCAN) had been formed in 1937 with the acquisition of the Breguet factory at Le Havre, where derivatives of the Short Calcutta flying boat, known as the Breguet 521 Bizerte, had been produced for the French Navy under licence since 1931. At the same time the new company took over the former CAMS flying boat plant at Sartrouville near Paris to give it additional expertise in flying boat production.

After the German occupation of France in 1940, the company's factories turned out an assortment of German designs for use by the Luftwaffe and Vichy government. These included 46 Dornier Do 24T flying boats that were produced at Sartrouville, many of which were transferred to the French Navy following the German withdrawal in 1944. A further batch of 24 CAMS-built Do 24s were ordered by the French Navy in 1945, these subsequently serving with Escadrilles 20S and 30S in the transport and air-sea rescue roles. The SNCAN Noroit was originally conceived to replace both the Do 24 and the PBY-5A Catalina maritime reconnaissance amphibian that equipped a number of Flottilles of the Aéronavale (French naval air arm) in the late 1940s.

The Noroit was an all-metal twin-engined triple-tailed amphibian flying boat with an extensively glazed nose, and a retractable tailwheel undercarriage. The two-step hull was almost identical to that of the pre-war Potez-CAMS 141, the hulls of which had been produced at Le Havre in 1939, and the non-retractable wing floats were attached to N struts. No spray suppressing bow chime or water rudder were fitted.

The first production Noroit, 06, showing the heavy undercarriage assembly, large diameter radome, high bow and revised nose glazing. (via A. Givaudon)

The Gnôme-Rhône powered SNCAN Noroit prototype, the N 1400-01 flying boat, F-WFDL, took off from Le Havre for the first time on 6 January 1949. (Musee de l'Air)

Although Nord had recall to its predeccessor's wealth of experience in the production of flying boats, the Noroit was the company's first amphibian design. The only other amphibians to be built in France since the end of the war were forty Grumman Widgeons built under licence by the Société de Constructions Aéro-Navales as the SCAN-30 at the same time as the Noroit. Encouraged by the French government, which was anxious to re-establish France's aero industry, and saw the Noroit as rekindling the country's long tradition of producing impressive flying boats while at the same time providing the Aéronavale with the basis for a low cost air-sea rescue and maritime reconnaissance organisation in a similar way to that which the Italian government was attempting with the Piaggio P136.

However, from the beginning the Noroit design contained a number of inherent flaws, some of which were never to be fully cured. Three important factors managed to conspire against the ultimate success of the amphibian, principally engines, materials and weight, all of which related directly or indirectly to France's limited post-war financial resources.

The first major problem facing the designers was the choice of engines. It was reported that the original project had been designed around the powerful Bristol Centaurus radial engine that was used to power the Hawker Sea Fury naval fighter and the Airspeed Ambassador airliner, but this was rejected on the grounds of it being too powerful and too expensive. With France's chronic lack of foreign exchange, the questions of which engine to use had to be answered by what was available and affordable at the time. One type of powerplant that was both, was the 1,600 hp Gnôme-Rhône 14R25 fourteen-cylinder radial air-cooled engine of pre-war design, earlier versions of which powered the biplane Bizerte flying boat, and it was this engine that was chosen to power the first Noroit prototype, the N 1400-01 registered *F-WFDL,* which flew as a pure flying boat on 6 January 1949. The first amphibian, N 1401-02 *F-WFKU,* flew from Le Havre on 6 August 1949 powered by 1,540 hp Bristol Hercules 100 radials. As the amphibious version was seriously overweight even before it took to the air for the first time, the Hercules were rejected as being underpowered and too expensive. However, it is difficult to understand why the Noroit was not fitted with the 2,090 hp Hercules 738 that was then being produced in France under licence for the company's very successful twin-engined Nord Noratlas military transport aircraft, the prototype of which had made its first flight only a month after the first Noroit, also powered by Gnôme-Rhône 14R25 radials.

However, in an attempt to solve the power problem, a third Noroit, N 1402-03, flown on 23 January 1950, was powered by yet another type of power plant, the 2,070 hp Arsenal 12H twelve-cylinder inverted vee engine. The Arsenal was in fact the German Junkers Jumo 213A, another pre-war design that was manufactured in France during World War Two, and being both available and affordable was ultimately chosen to power all subsequent production aircraft as well as the fourth pre-production aircraft, N 1402-04 registered *F-WFRP.* A fifth development Noroit, N 1401-05

The first gull-winged SNCAN N 1400-01 Noroit flying boat, F-WFDL, flying over Le Havre in 1949. (via A. Givaudon)

A Noroit of Escadrille 53S, the Aéronavale's Flying Boat Pilots School at Karouba, over North Africa in 1954. (via D. Oliver)

own in September 1950, was for some inexplicable eason the second to be powered by the already ejected Bristol Hercules 100. In the meantime, a roduction batch of twenty aircraft had been laid own at Le Havre for the Aéronavale.

Initial flight trials of the Noroits at Le Havre roceeded without incident. In the air the mphibian handled well and performed within esign tolerances although the aircraft required a onsiderable length of runway to get airborne. On he water, it was hydrodynamically efficient, eaworthy and simple to manoeuvre.

However, various components and systems, ncluding propellers, hydraulics, hatches and wheels, were found to have a number of basic esign faults, most of which manifested themselves uring early trials. While the Arsenal engine had he required power range and proved to be xtremely reliable, difficulties were experienced vith the three-bladed Ratier propellers that tended o overrun at full throttle, making not only an larming amount of noise but a mess of the eduction gear. The only course of action that could lleviate this condition, apart from redesigning the ropellers, was to recommend that revs should be ncreased only very gradually.

The first pre-production Noroit powered by the Arsenal engines was N 1402-03 which flew on 23 January 1950. (via A. Givaudon)

Nord Noroit N 1402-03 was used for radar and radio trials with the Centre d'Essais en Vol (CEV) at Bretigny. Note the large diameter radome above the cockpit, small tail-wheel doors and lack of rear turret. (via D. Oliver)

A certain amount of redesign was necessary after the discovery that hydraulic fluid from two different systems was feeding into a single hose, and during take-off on an early test flight, water pressure forced open the weapons aiming and photography panel in the front turret, which happened to be hinged inwards — luckily without serious damage to the aircraft or its crew. These particular defects were able to be corrected before the initial production aircraft left the factory. However, the Noroit's most serious defect that showed up at a very early stage of its development was the design and construction of the undercarriage main wheel units. Not only was the whole undercarriage unit excessively heavy and bulky, thus requiring a lot of power to raise and lower it, but the main wheels were made from dural and magnesium which oxidised when in contact with sea water. Again, the answer to this particular problem was to place a restriction on the use of the component rather than to replace it. Therefore it was recommended that the undercarriage should not be lowered when the aircraft was in the water, which in reality meant that the Noroit could not taxy out of the water on to a slipway, and thus it ceased to be a practical amphibian. In October 1950, Noroits 03 and 04 were flown to Bretigny for official radar and radio trials with the CEV (Centre d'Essais en Vol, the Air Ministry's organisation that tested new military aircraft), while acceptance trials continued with Aéronavale pilots at Melun situated to the south of Paris. These were, however, not without mishap and one aircraft was damaged during night landing tests in November 1950. At the subsequent enquiry, the Aéronavale pilot was found to be not sufficiently experienced at making water landings at night, when height above water is difficult to judge accurately, and the heavy landing caused the Noroit to porpoise resulting in damage to the amphibian's nose and one of the stabilising floats. In January 1951 Captain Corvette Arangnol, whose experience of piloting flying boats dated back to the 1930s, was put in command of the Aéronavale's ERC (Escadrille de Réception et Convoyage — Receipt and Delivery unit) at Melun, a move which appreciably speeded up the aircraft's acceptance trials. On 25 January SNCAN test pilot Claude Chautemps, son of the pre-war minister Camille Chautemps, flew Noroit No 6 from Melun to Marseille's Marignane airport in 3 hours 15 minutes and subsequently carried out a number of successful water operations on Lake Berre before returning to Melun on 28 January in a flight time of 3 hours 45 minutes to conclude the type's most successful series of tests to date.

At this time, the Noroit's ultimate role in the Aéronavale had still not been clearly defined although production aircraft were beginning to arrive at the Navy's ERC at Melun for acceptance by the Service at the rate of one a month. For example, Noroit 06 was accepted by the Navy after a flight of 4 hours 20 minutes on 1 March 1951, and a second flight of no less than eight hours from Melun on 28 March. Noroit 07 was in the hands of the ERC in April 1951 but was not accepted until 4 September. Following a series of test flights, 07 was returned to Melun for modifications after which it flew to Le Havre to make a water landing on 29 August. It was eventually issued to Flottille 5F at

ann-Bihoue a week later. By the end of 1951 the
nth Noroit was at the ERC while No 19 was
ccepted by the Aéronavale on 30 May 1952 after 6
ours' 10 minutes' flying.

The Noroit became operational with Flottille 5F
t Lann-Bihoue on 1 August 1951 in the maritime
econnaissance and air-sea rescue roles. In service
ne Noroit had a defensive armament of six 20 mm
annon, two each in the nose, dorsal and tail
ositions. Bomb bays in the engine nacelles carried
n assortment of anti-submarine warfare stores
icluding six 250 lb (113 kg) bombs, sonar buoys
nd depth charges, while eight rocket projectiles
ould be carried on paired brackets on the forward
art of the hull. The Noroit had a range of 1,500
iiles (2,413 km) at a cruising speed of 128 mph (206
m/h) and a maximum endurance of twelve hours,
ut this was seldom put to the test in service. The
nit's work-up was a slow one due to the protracted
elivery of accepted aircraft and the numerous
iechanical problems that it suffered, some trivial
nd others serious. Most related to the
ndercarriage, the weight of which made the
ircraft underpowered and slow to take off with a
ıll load, and with it being unable to be operated in
ater, made launching and beaching a long and
omplicated affair that could only be carried out at
ertain ports. The low quality of the materials used
ı its construction was another limiting factor to the
mphibian's operational capabilities, as was the
ntiquated equipment carried on board.

An early production Noroit ground running its Arsenal engines.
Note the leading edge wing fences and extended flap hinges and
rear turret. (via A. Givaudon)

The first amphibious Noroit, and the second to fly, was the
Bristol Hercules powered N 1401-02, F-WFKU. First flown on 6
August 1949, N 1401-02 differed from the first prototype by
having an increased tailplane span and fewer glazed panels in the
nose. (via A. Givaudon)

In-flight shot of Noroit No 24 belonging to Escadrille 33S, with nose mounted radar and underwing pylons. (ECPA)

In-flight shot of the second pre-production Nord Noroit N 1402-04, F-WFRP. (Nord)

Michel Pompard was a Noroit radio engineer with Flottille 5F. 'The radio was of pre-war design with push-in plugs like those of an old-fashioned telephone exchange. It was also of a similar size and weight. I was one of five crew on board "5F.5" piloted by Lieutenant de Vaisseau Turq which broke up after porpoising on landing in the sea off Brest on 21 May 1952 — luckily no one was seriously hurt but the aircraft was a write-off.'

Soon after that accident a second Aéronavale Noroit was destroyed by fire on the ground at Lann-Bihoue, again with no casualties. Yet another Noroit was lost when it crashed into high ground near Privas on 12 December 1952 during a test flight from Marignane to Melun with a factory crew aboard. All five SNCAN technicians were killed.

Soon after the last Noroit was delivered in March 1953, the last four production aircraft had a modified nose to take the radar that had previously been fitted in a large one-metre-diameter radome above the co-pilot's position. Flottille 5F was disbanded and its aircraft transferred to Flottille 26F at Mureaux in June 1953. At the same time the Aéronavale decided to relegate the Noroit to training and second line duties. It was also decided that in an effort to save weight and improve performance, its guns, and the troublesome undercarriage would be removed. In this form, the Noroit flying boat served briefly with Escadrille 33S, and for a longer period with Escadrille 53S, the flying boat pilots' school at Karouba. However some were delivered to North Africa as amphibians including No 21 which flew from Mureaux to Sidi Ahmet in Tunisia in 5 hours 20 minutes on 24 June 1953, only to return to Mureaux two days later to have its undercarriage removed. Service aircraft were modified over a period of eighteen months, as and when they were made available by their units.

Claude Bellendy, a pilot with 53S at the time, considered the Noroit 'flying boat' to be a much improved aircraft over the Noroit 'amphibie'. 'It flew well enough, with or without wheels. It was stable in the air and manoeuvrable in the water but although the climb out was markedly improved without wheels, along with its single engine performance — previously it did not have one — it still required a long take off run.'

During 1954, Noroit 08 was returned to the factory where it was taken apart and a number of faults detected, including one of metal fatigue in the wing flap hinge. Ironically, before SNCAN'S report on its findings was completed, a Noroit of Escadrille 53S, piloted by L. V. Mignot, crashed while landing at Karouba on 2 November 1954. The only survivor of the seven-man crew was Maxime Chaussery who, despite serious injuries, recovered well enough to become an Aéronavale helicopter pilot. Failure of a flap hinge was diagnosed as the cause of the accident, one that signalled the deathknell of the unfortunate Noroit.

One of Escadrille 53S Noroits that has had its troublesome retractable undercarriage removed, on beaching gear at St Mandrier near Toulon in 1954. (via D. Oliver)

Nord N1402 Noroit

Accommodation: Crew: 7

Power Plants: Two 2,070 hp SFEC-MAS Arsenal 12H twelve-cylinder inverted-vee engines

Dimensions: Wingspan: 103 ft 8 in (31.6 m)
Length: 72 ft 3½ in (22 m)
Height: 22 ft 5½ in (6.84 m)
Wing area: 1,076 sq ft (100 m²)

Weights: Empty: 31,431 lb (14,257 kg)
Average: 45,947 lb (20,841 kg)

Performance: Max speed: 230 mph (370 km/h)
Patrol speed: 128 mph (206 km/h)
Patrol range: 1,553 miles (2,500 km)
Ferry range: 2,610 miles (4,200 km)
Max endurance: 12 hr 6 min

In less than a year, the Aéronavale's last and only post-war flying boat had been withdrawn from operational service and most of them ended their days on the scrapheap. A few examples survived as ground instruction airframes, one of which, believed to be the last surviving example, was finally destroyed by one of France's worst natural disasters. The Noroit was kept at St Raphael in the South of France and used by Escadrille 20S, the Aéronavale's test squadron. On the night of 2 December, a giant dam at Malpasset high above the town of Frejus burst and flooded the Frejus/St Raphael area causing much loss of life and a great deal of destruction. However, it was reported that two people being swept towards the sea by a torrent of mud and water at St Raphael, managed to hang on to the Noroit as the old flying boat involuntarily took to the water for the last time. It finally came to rest in a car park on the edge of the airfield but was badly damaged and subsequently consigned to the scrapheap in the clear up that followed in the wake of the disaster.

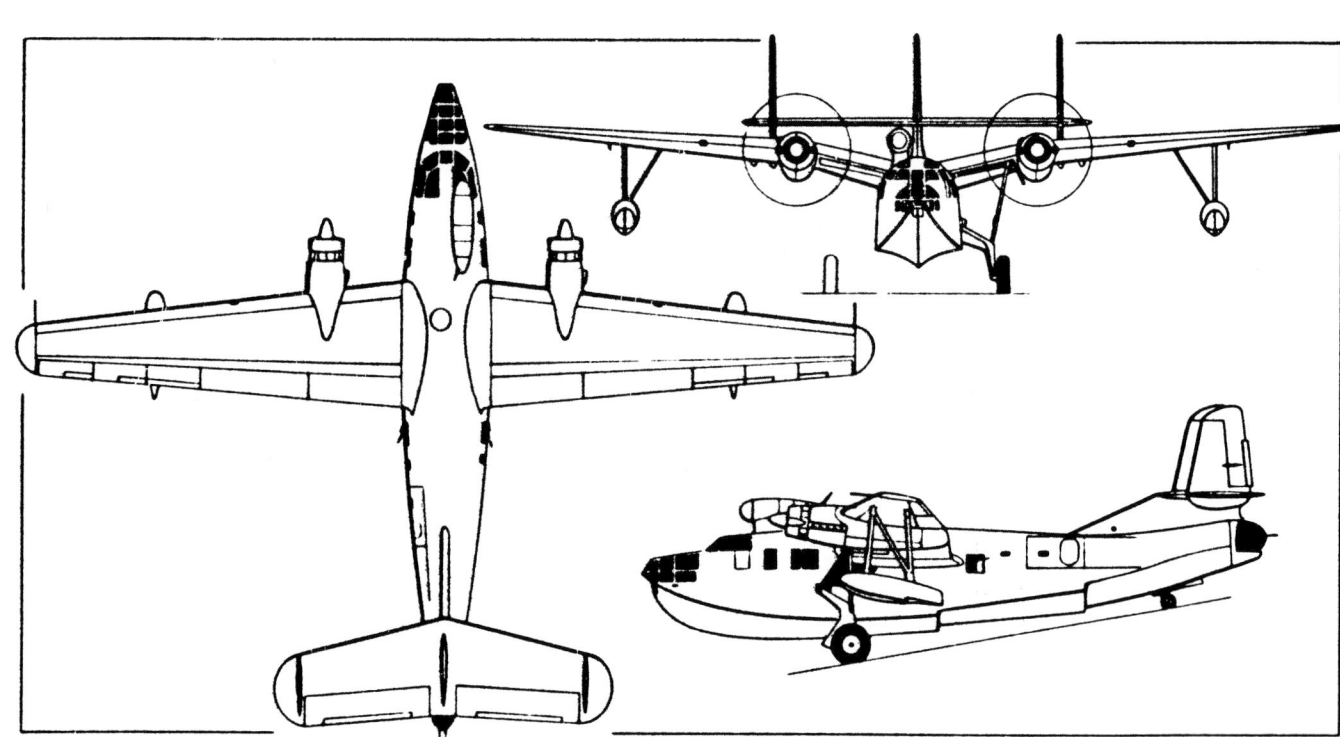

CHAPTER EIGHT
THE MARTIN MARLIN

In June 1951, what was to become America's last operational flying boat, the twin-engined Martin M-237, took off from the water at Middle River, Maryland. In many respects the flying boat's manufacturer, the Glenn L. Martin Company of America had paralleled that of Short Brothers in England. Glenn Luther Martin built his first aircraft, a pusher biplane fitted with floats, in 1909 and two years later it flew from Balboa, California, to Catalina Island, a distance of 34 miles (55 km). In July 1913, Martin entered and flew a development of his original floatplane in a race for flying boats from Chicago to Detroit, via Lakes Michigan and Huron, but was forced to retire following delays due to bad weather. However, it was after his now thriving company had moved to Baltimore, Maryland, in 1926, where excellent seaplane facilities were available all year round, that Martin began to build flying boats in any numbers. The first large flying boats to be built at the new factory in the early 1930s were 55 PM-1 and PM-2 twin-engined biplane designs based on the Naval Aircraft Factory's PN-12.

However, it was following Pan American Airways' specification for a commercial flying boat capable of carrying four crew and 300 lb of mail over 2,500 miles, that the Martin company designed what was to become one of the best known pre-war passenger flying boats, the M-130. Three of the giant, four-engined long range boats, capable of seating up to 41 passengers (the first of which flew on 30 December 1934), were ordered by Pan American, named the *China, Philippine* and *Hawaii Clippers*. On 11 November 1935, one of the airline's M-130s inaugurated the world's first scheduled trans-Pacific passenger service. A larger development of the M-130, the 53-seat M-156, was built for the Soviet Union in 1937 and subsequently operated by Aeroflot on the 1,700-mile (2,735 km) route across the Sea of Okhotsk between Vladivostock and Petropavlovsk in Siberia during World War Two.

In-flight shot of a rare unarmed P5M-2G Marlin, the first of only four delivered to the US Coast Guard in 1956. The -2G 1312 was assigned to USCG Station, Elizabeth City, North Carolina, for long range air-sea rescue work and decommissioned in December 1960 before being delivered to the US Navy as a training aircraft. (USCG)

One of seven unarmed Martin P5M-1G Marlin flying boats ordered by the US Coast Guard in 1952 for long-range air sea rescue duties. This aircraft, 1285, operated from the US Coast Guard Air Station at St Petersburg, Florida. (USCG)

In-flight shot of a P5M-2 Marlin belonging Aéronavale's Flotille 27F based at Daker in West Africa during the early 1960s. (ECPA)

The design for a twin-engine medium-range maritime reconnaissance bomber flying boat known as the M-162, also appeared in 1937 and was promptly ordered off the drawing board by the US Navy. The aircraft, named the Mariner, first flew in February 1939 under the designation XPBM-1 with deliveries of production PBM-1s commencing the following year. More than 1,300 Martin PBM Mariners of all versions, including 36 PBM-5A amphibians, were produced in ten years of production, serving with the US Navy in the Atlantic and Pacific theatres throughout the Second World War, and later during the Korean conflict. Martin also produced a small number of the giant M-170, the largest operational flying boat built, between 1942 and 1945. The four-engined JRM-1 Mars, with a wingspan of 200 ft (61 m), was originally designed as a long-range maritime reconnaissance bomber in 1941, but subsequently was used by the US Navy to fly cargo, or up to 300 men, on scheduled 2,400-mile (3,860 km) flights between NAS Alameda near San Francisco California, and Honolulu in the late 1940s and early '50s. After retiring from military service in 1956 having transported more than 200,000 passengers without a single mishap, three of the surviving Mars were converted to fire-fighting water-bombers for Forest Industries Flying Tankers Limited of Vancouver, Canada, two of which are still in operation more than thirty years later.

At the end of the war, the US Navy decided to continue to support maritime reconnaissance flying boat operations and in June 1946 awarded the Martin Company a contract to produce a prototype of a flying boat to replace the Mariner. That prototype, first flown on 4 May 1948, was in fact an extensively modified Mariner, designated XP5M-1, featuring a new and more efficient, single step hull with a higher beam-to-length ratio, and revised nose and tail turrets.

In July 1950 the US Navy placed an order for 25 P5M-1s, to be known as the Marlin, the first of which flew on 22 June 1951. The production P5M was to all intents and purposes a completely new design. Whilst it retained the gull-wing configuration of its predecessor, it was powered by two Wright R-3350-30WA radial engines rated at 3,250 hp, and featured a substantially longer and deeper hull, a bulbous radome nose housing a 5 ft 6 in (167 cm) diameter APS-80 search radar dish, raised flight deck and a single fin. Stabilising wing floats were fitted on single streamline pylons braced with an inverted V strut, and a unique Martin designed 'Hydroflap', which opened to 65 degrees to act as a landing brake and turning aid on the water, was fitted in each side of the hull. The P5M-1 Martin carried a normal crew of eight, two pilots, a navigator, radio operator, three search radar operators and a tactical co-ordinator (TACCO). Bomb bays built into the lower portion of each engine nacelle were capable of carrying a total of four 2,000 lb (907 kg) bombs or four 2,156 lb (978 kg) torpedoes, up to eight 1,000 lb (454 kg) bombs or mines, or a combination of sonobuoys and depth charges, while five-inch rocket projectiles and anti-personnel bombs could be carried on underwing racks. The only defensive armament carried by the P5M-1 was a twin 20 mm cannon in a remotely controlled radar-operated rear turret.

The first US Navy P5M-1s, which had a maximum speed of 246 mph (396 km/h) and an endurance of twenty hours patrolling at 150 mph (240 km/h), were delivered to Patrol Squadron VP-4 on 23 April 1952 at Norfolk, Virginia, while VP-9 based at San Diego, California, became the first West Coast squadron to replace its Mariners with the new flying boat exactly one year later.

At the end of the year, US Navy Marlins began to supplement the ageing Mariners in the Far East, flying long-range patrol missions along the Korean coast searching for North Korean shipping and communist infiltration boats landing agents in South Korea. They also flew long-range air-sea rescue missions in support of US Navy Task Force 77. Amongst the first Marlin squadrons to take part in the blockade of North Korea in 1953 was VP-56 when a formation of eight of its flying boats flew across the Pacific, island hopping from California to Iwakuni in Japan.

The crew of a US Coast Guard P5M-1G Marlin flying boat based at Elizabeth City, North Carolina, sprint to their aircraft to carry out a search and rescue mission over the Atlantic. (USCG)

An SP-5B Marlin flying boat of VP-40 flying low over a junk in the waters off South Vietnam in August 1965 during 'Operation Market Time'. (US Navy)

A P5M-1 Marlin of Patrol Squadron VP-46, in blue and white colour scheme, seen during a training exercise in 1961 firing two 2″ SCAR rockets. (US Navy)

In September 1953, the first three of seven Marlins, stripped of any armament, ordered by the United States Coast Guard and designated P5M-1G, were delivered to the US Coast Guard Air Station at St Petersburg, Florida. Equipped to operate in a long-range air-sea rescue role, the P5M-1Gs gave seaplane protection to shipping and small craft in the Gulf of Mexico, Caribbean and Atlantic offshore areas of the southern states of America. On one occasion, four seamen were rescued by a USCG Marlin no less than 1,150 miles (1,850 km) out at sea.

However, even before the first P5M-1 had entered service with the US Navy, Martin had undertaken a considerable redesign of the Marlin and an improved model, designated P5M-2, took to the air for the first time on 29 April 1954. Apart from being fitted with updated ASW equipment which included an AN/ASQ-8 Magnetic Anomaly Detection (MAD) device, and revised crew accommodation, the P5M-2 featured a high-mounted T-type tailplane to increase aerodynamic efficiency while reducing weight, and a lower bow chine line to reduce spray height. The MAD 'stinger' was fitted at the top of the tailplane and a directable 130 million candle-power carbon arc searchlight was attached to the starboard wing tip. More powerful Wright R-3350-32W radial engines developing 3,450 hp were installed, along with additional internal fuel tankage and there was also provision for a jettisonable 670-gallon tank in each weapons bay giving the P5M-2 a maximum speed of 251 mph (404 km/h) and a ferry range of over 3,000 miles (4,827 km). The first of the improved Marlins was delivered to Patrol Squadron VP-47 at Alameda, California, in June 1954.

A total of 121 P5M-1s had been completed when production was phased out at the end of 1954, by which time the Marlin equipped eight US Navy Patrol Squadrons, one of which had paid a rare visit to England earlier that year. In July 1954, P5M-1s of VP-44 took part in the Anglo-American exercise 'Dividend' operating from the flying boat support tender USS *Currituck* anchored off Plymouth. The Marlins flew to British waters from Norfolk, Virginia, via the Naval Air Station at Bermuda, and a number of the squadron's aircraft were refuelled in the open sea from the submarine-oiler USS *Guavina*.

In the mid-1950s, the Marlin was the world's most powerfully equipped anti-submarine patrol aircraft and was proving to be a popular boat with

Opposite
Forward section of a SP-5B Marlin preserved at NAS Pensecola showing the deep hull, large radome, high cockpit and underwing weapons pylons. (D. Oliver)

its crews, who appreciated the power-controls and efficient autopilot, especially during the long fatigue-inducing patrols flown low and slow, 1,000 (305 m) at between 150 and 180 mph (240 and 290 km/h), over the Atlantic and Pacific Oceans. As was to be expected, Martin's latest flying boat proved to be a useful performer on the water as was graphically shown in public when a P5M-1, of VP-44 from NAS Norfolk, became a star turn of the Canadian National Air Show at Toronto in June 1955 by demonstrating a series of dramatic retarded landings on Lake Ontario using reverse propellers and hydroflaps.

Most of the US Navy's Marlin-equipped patrol squadrons were based at Norfolk, Virginia, and Jacksonville, Florida, on the East Coast, and Alameda and San Diego, California, on the West Coast, with Pacific units being regularly deployed on six-month tours to the Philippines or Japan. At the beginning of 1956, VP-42, equipped with P5M-1s, changed home ports from Alameda to Sangley Point in the Philippines, while six months later the US Navy's last Martin PBM Mariners belonging to VP-50, based at Iwakuni, Japan, which had operated alongside RAF Sunderlands during the Korean War, were replaced by brand new P5M-2 Marlins.

The US Navy's last operational Martin SP-5B Marlin, no 5533, which belonged to Patrol Squadron VP-40 made its final flight at NAS North Field, San Diego, in November 1967 marking the end of the US Navy's seaplane operations. (D. Oliver)

By 1953, Glenn L. Martin had retired from the company he founded forty years earlier and he died in December 1955 but not before seeing the world's most advanced flying boat, built by his company, the four-jet swept-wing XP6M-1 SeaMaster, take to the air. Designed as a minelayer and maritime reconnaissance aircraft for the US Navy, the 650 mph (1,046 km/h) pressurised SeaMaster was logged with problems from the beginning and following the loss of two prototypes and the escalating costs of production aircraft, the programme was finally cancelled in 1959 after only four P6M-2 flying boats had been completed.

Above and overleaf:
A Martin SP-5B Marlin flying boat on beaching gear preserved at the Naval Aviation Museum at NAS Pensecola in November 1986. (D. Oliver)

A Beriev Be-12 'Mail', Russia's standard medium range anti-submarine warfare aircraft. Examples of the turboprop powered amphibian of the Soviet Navy's Pacific Fleet operate from Cam Rahn Bay and Da Nang in Vietnam some twenty years after the US Navy's last flying boat, the Martin Marlin, was based in the area.

In 1957, the Glenn L. Martin Co had been awarded a contract to modernise eighty P5M-1s, with improvements to the power plants, installation of new electronic equipment permitting the detection of submerged submarines, and the introduction of an improved magnetic anomaly detector (MAD). The new equipment included 'Jezebel', a search-detection system using sonobuoys in the water, 'Julie', a localisation system which furnished range data, and AIDS (Aircraft Integrated Display System) which filtered and computed data fed to it from the other systems. To accommodate the new equipment, the Marlin grew a large hump on the rear of the flight deck roof along with a curious cylindrical fairing attached to the top of the fin which housed the MAD sensing head. The modernisation programme was completed by the end of 1958 by which time P5M Marlin-equipped front-line US Navy squadrons had peaked at twelve (VP-31, 34, 40, 42, 44, 45, 46, 47, 48, 49, 50 and 56).

In February 1959, ten P5M-2s were supplied to France under the Military Assistance Programme by the United States, to become the first Marlins to be supplied to a country outside America. They were delivered to the Aéronavale's Flottille 27F based at Dakar in West Africa to replace the veteran Short Sunderland MR5 flying boats that had been in service with the unit, originally No 343 Free French Squadron, since 1943. The Marlins, which were identical to those in service with the US Navy, were obviously a great advance over their predecessors in equipment and comfort, but many of the French Navy pilots were less than enthusiastic about the new boat. Whereas the Sunderland had a reputation for durability, ease of maintenance and reliability, the Marlin was packed with heavy complicated systems that required a lot of maintenance and initially suffered from a relatively low serviceability rate.

An early production Martin P5M-1 Marlin belonging to Patrol Squadron VP-44 using a rubber U dock alongside USS Ashland. (US Navy)

Hosing down a P5M-2 Marlin of VP-42 at Sangeley Point in the Philippines after a patrol over the South China Seas in October 1956. (USN)

Claude Delauney was posted to Flottille 27F in 1961 as a young pilot and remembers the big American boat well. 'I was sent to NAS Norfolk Virginia, for my training on the Marlin before joining one of the twelve crews of Flottille 27F at Dakar. The flying boat was well built, easy to fly with the power controls making it very manoeuvrable for its size, although it was almost impossible to fly without them. The Marlin was able to land and taxy in high seas, up to four metres being flown on and off the water at a neutral attitude whereas the Sunderland flew nose up. The engines were reliable but the aircraft was crammed full of too much heavy and complicated equipment that used a vast amount of power to operate, and if an engine failed the systems had to be shut down in order to save the remaining engine, especially in the hot and humid weather we frequently experienced off the west coast of Africa. After every patrol which lasted between fourteen and seventeen hours it had to be beached and thoroughly washed down with fresh water.

'Although routine servicing was carried out at Dakar, heavy maintenance was carried out at St Mandrier near Toulon, a flight of about eleven hours. We also made regular visits to Brest. In 1963 I converted to the P-2 Neptune.' Ten years later Captain Delauney joined France's Sécurité Civile to fly Canadair CL-215 amphibian water-bombers.

However, US Navy Lieutenant Commander James S. Christensen and his crew had nothing but praise for the Marlin's strength and durability after taxying nearly 200 miles (320 km) on only one engine following an emergency landing on the sea off Florida. Their aircraft, a P5M-2 belonging to VP-45 based at NAS Bermuda, had taken off from Jacksonville, Florida, on a routine patrol over the Atlantic when the port engine failed some 200 miles from the Florida coastline. Having suffered no obvious damage following its heavy single-engine landing in high seas, the Marlin's crew decided to attempt to taxy home. The flying boat's painfully slow progress was continually monitored by US Navy Neptunes and Constellations from the air and Navy tugs, Coast Guard cutters and a passenger liner, the *Ocean Monarch*, on the sea until the Marlin finally arrived none the worse for wear off Mayport, Florida, after nearly 24 hours on the water.

A different period of potential danger for Marlin crews came later the same year, this time in Far East waters when the men of VP-40 flew the Formosa Strait Patrol from their temporary base at Sangley Point in the Philippines for six months during the Quemoy/Matsu crisis of 1959 and earned themselves the Armed Forces Expeditionary Medal for their work.

At the end of 1959, the Martin company was awarded a second contract to update the Marlin, this time for 28 early production P5M-2s to be updated to the same specification as the 75 P5M-1 Marlins modernised the previous year. The same new equipment was being installed in undelivered Marlins before they left the factory. In addition to the installation of the latest ASW equipment, the P5M-2s had a pod fitted under the port wing housing a camera for recording damage to targets during day or night operations. With the prospect of current orders for the P5M-2 being completed by the end of the year, the Martin Company made a big effort during 1960 to sell the flying boat abroad. Having failed to interest the Australians, who had operated Mariners for a short period in the early 1950s and who were looking for a replacement for the RAAF's Lincoln MR30, the company reported sales to two of its neighbours in the Pacific. The first was New Zealand which announced its intention to purchase six Marlins to replace the Royal New Zealand Air Force's fleet of veteran Short Sunderland GR5 flying boats operated by No 5 Squadron based at Lauthala Bay in the Fiji Islands. The Sunderlands and US Navy Marlins based at Sangley Point were regular participants in numerous SEATO exercises in the late 1950s. Japan also announced an intention to purchase six Marlins to supplement the Maritime Self-Defence Force's fleet of Neptunes and replace its Grumman UF-1 Albatross SAR amphibians. The deal would also provide for the licence production of at least thirty P5M-2 Marlins to begin in 1963. Meanwhile, the last of 117 P5M-2 Marlins, which included four P5M-2Ms for the US Coast Guard and the ten Aéronavale flying boats, was delivered on 20 December 1960, a few days after the last of the 28 modified aircraft had been completed, so ending thirty years of flying boat production at the Baltimore plant.

Two P-5B Marlins of VP-42 with the veteran Seaplane Tender, USS Currituck, at Seadrome Anchorage, Santa Catalina, off the coast of Long Beach, California, in June 1963. (US Navy)

An SP-5B Marlin of VP-40 on step in Cam Ranh Bay, South Vietnam, in July 1967. VP-40 was the last flying boat squadron deployed to South East Asia and the last US Navy unit to operate flying boats when the Marlins were replaced by P-3 Orion landplanes by the end of 1967. (US Navy)

A P-5B Marlin fitted with a General Electric J85 Turbojet in the tail in place of the rear turret during trials with the Naval Air Test Centre (NATC) at NAS Patuxent River, Maryland, in 1966. (J. Gradidge)

Early in 1962 the US Navy, along with the USAF, changed the designation of all its aircraft, with the result that the P5M-1 and 2 became the P-5A and B. The modified versions were changed to SP-5A and B, and a small number of unmodified aircraft used for training were known as the TP-5A.

Although the Marlin continued to give valuable service with the US and French Navies, with a number of Florida-based P-5Bs becoming involved in the United States blockade of Cuba in October/November 1962 when US Navy patrol aircraft monitored the return of Soviet missiles to Russia, they were slowly giving way to land-based maritime patrol and anti-submarine aircraft. By September 1964, only five West Coast-based US Navy squadrons continued to fly the Martin flying boats; VP-40, 42, 47, 48 and 50, the last Atlantic P-5 Squadron, VP-40, having replaced its Marlins with Lockheed P-3A Orions by the end of 1964, while the Aéronavale's Flottille 27F disbanded at the end of 1965 and its P-5Bs were flown to NAS Norfolk for storage.

Another example of the landplane's relentless advance over the flying boat, both technically and economically, was illustrated by the Royal New Zealand Air Force's failure to confirm its order for six Marlins, choosing instead the Lockheed P-3A Orion to replace the long-serving Sunderlands. The final blow to the Marlin's export hopes was struck by Japan which also failed to place a firm order for the American flying boat. Having carried out a thorough technical evaluation of the type and an in-depth study of how it was put together prior to entering into an agreement to manufacture the P-5 in Japan under licence, the Japanese government decided to support its own emerging aero industry by placing an order with Shin Meiwa to produce an indigenously designed flying boat, that many considered to be a high-technology development of the Marlin, fitted with a high-lift wing and four turboprop engines.

However, on the eve of its retirement from the US Navy, the Marlin found itself involved in a full-scale shooting war with the escalation of hostilities in South-East Asia. From May 1965, detachments from P-5 squadrons based at Sangley Point in the Philippines took part in Operation 'Market Time' during which the flying boats patrolled the Gulf of Tonkin, from South Cambodia to the 17th Parallel, watching out for communist cargo ships supplying North Vietnam and communist junks attempting to smuggle arms and ammunition to the Vietcong in South Vietnam, as well as being tasked with locating any Soviet or Chinese submarines that may have been in the area.

The SP-5Bs, belonging to one of the three remaining Marlin squadrons, operated from the US Navy's last operational flying boat tender, USS *Salisbury Sound,* anchored in Cam Ranh Bay off the coast of South Vietnam some 300 miles (480 km) south of the Demilitarised Zone. These flying boats carried additional surveillance equipment and were armed with underwing rockets, including two-inch SCAR as well as five-inch RPs and provision was made for .50 machine-guns to be mounted on a number of the hatches, which were manned by up to eleven crew. The two 20 mm cannon originally fitted in the rear turret had been replaced by additional ASW gear during the modernisation programme five years earlier.

In an effort to improve the SP-5B Marlin's performance with the ever-increasing demand for extra payload, and to extend its operational life, the US Navy considered retrofitting the flying boats with a single General Electric 2,400 lb thrust J85-GE-J2 turbojet installed in the rear fuselage. Although a modified aircraft was successfully flown and tested in 1966, the US government did not consider it to be sufficiently cost-effective to modify the dwindling numbers of Marlins still in front-line service.

In May 1966, SP-5Bs of VP-47 took part in the type's last SEATO exercise at the end of their operational tour in South Vietnam. The Philippines were the venue for exercise 'Sea Imp' in which RAF Shackleton MR2s of 205 Squadron and RAAF P-2H Neptunes of 12 Squadron took part. In February 1967, VP-40 begun the last deployment of an operational flying boat squadron of the US Navy when it returned to Sangley Point. The last patrol by a SP-5B over South Vietnam waters was flown on 11 April and by June of that year most of the Marlins had been flown to Japan where they were broken up for scrap. Ironically, during the same period the Royal New Zealand Air Force was retiring the last of its Short Sunderland flying boats which, only a few years earlier, it had planned to replace with the Marlin.

A P-5B Marlin of VP-40 leads a formation of a Short Sunderland GR.5 belonging to No 5 Squadron Royal New Zealand Air Force, (foreground) and a Lockheed P2V-7 Neptune of No 10 Squadron Royal Australian Air Force, background) during SEATO's 'Operation Sea Serpent' in the South China Seas in June 1963. (RNZAF)

One of VP-40's Marlins, No 5533, made the long flight back across the Pacific to the United States, and NAS North Field, San Diego, in particular to take part in a final flypast over the base in November 1967 marking not only the last flight of the last Martin flying boat, but the end of 56 years of continuous US Navy seaplane operations. This particular aircraft was later to become the sole surviving example of its type to be preserved when it was put on display at the Naval Air Museum at NAS Pensecola, Florida.

To show its affection for the flying boat, VP-40 adopted the nickname the 'Fighting Marlins' and had the symbol of a Marlin — the fish — painted on the fin of the P-3 Orions when the squadron converted to the new type in January 1968, a motif that has been retained on all VP-40's subsequent aircraft.

Just ten days before the Martin P-5 Marlin made its last flight in California, Japan's Shin Meiwa SS-2 flying boat made its first flight at Kobe.

Martin P5M-1 Marlin

Accommodation:	Crew: 8
Power Plants:	Two 3,250 hp Wright R-3350-36WA Turbo Compound eighteen-cylinder radials
Dimensions:	Wingspan: 118 ft 2¼ in (36 m) Length: 94 ft 11 in (28.93 m) Height: 38 ft 8½ (11.8 m) Wing area: 1406.33 sq ft (130.79 m²)
Weights:	Empty: 47,686 lb (21,630 kg) Average: 73,488 lb (33,334 kg)
Performance:	Max speed: 246 mph (396 km/h) Patrol speed: 150 mph (241 km/h) ASW range: 2,000 miles (3,218 km) Ferry range: 3,000 miles (4,827 km)

Martin P-5B Marlin

Accommodation:	Crew: 10
Power Plants:	Two 3,450 hp Wright R-3350-32W Turbo Compound eighteen-cylinder radials
Dimensions:	Wingspan: 118 ft 2¼ in (36 m) Length: 100 ft 7¼ in (30.66 m) Height: 32 ft 8½ in (10 m) Wing area: 1,406.33 sq ft (130.79 m²)
Weights:	Empty: 50,485 lb (22,900 kg) Average: 76,635 lb (34,761 kg)
Performance:	Max speed: 251 mph (404 km/h) Patrol speed: 150-180 mph (240-290 km/h) ASW range: 2,050 miles (3,300 km) Ferry range: 3,100 miles (5,000 km)

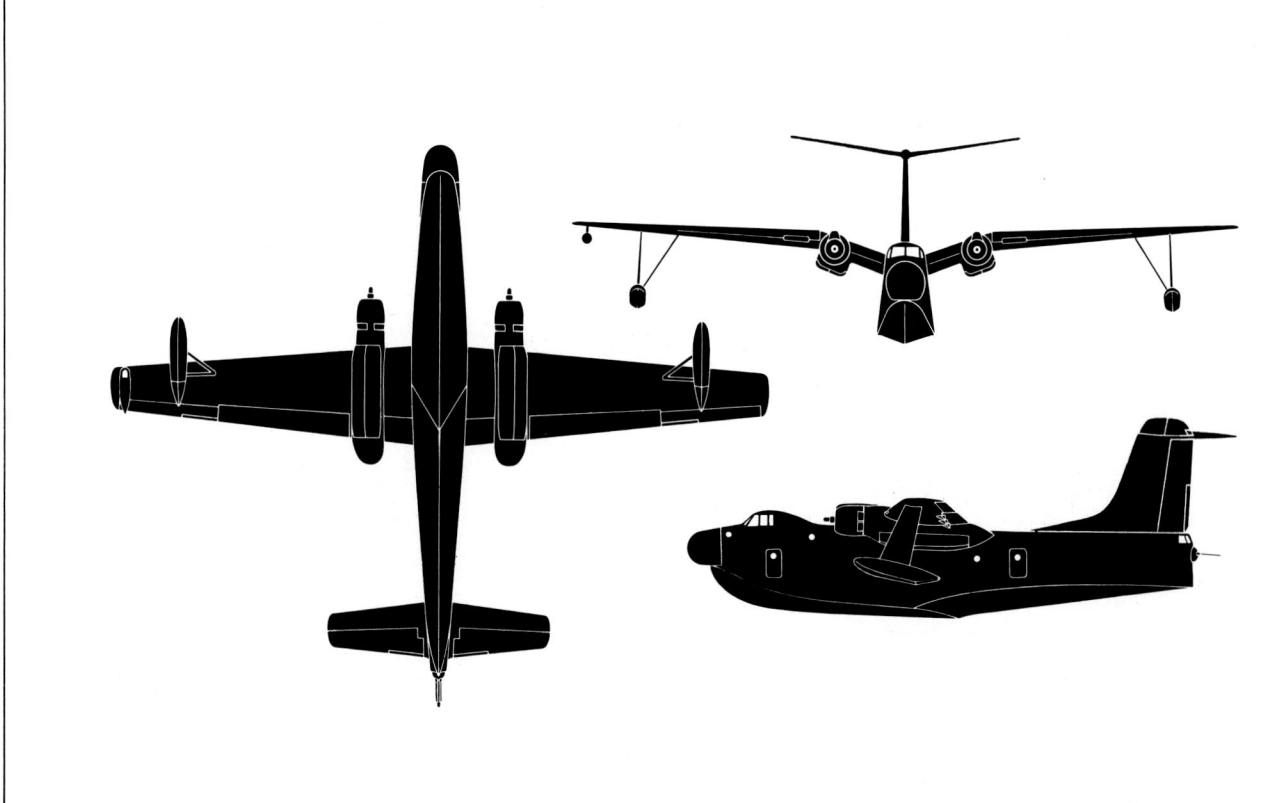

CHAPTER NINE
THE BERIEV Be-12

By the end of the 1950s, flying boat development in the West, both military and commercial, had virtually come to a halt. However, this was not the case in the Soviet Union and Western observers were somewhat taken aback when no less than two new multi-engine military flying boats made an unexpected appearance at the 1961 Aviation Day Flypast at Tushimo Airport, Moscow. Both were products of the Soviet design bureau headed by the world's most prolific post-war flying boat designer, Georgii Mikhailovich Beriev.

In view of the recent cancellation of America's advanced jet-powered Martin SeaMaster in 1959, it was all the more surprising that no less than four swept-wing twin-jet Beriev Be-10 flying boats took part in the Tushimo Air Display of 1961, by which time it was claimed to be already in service with Russia's Naval Air Fleet as a long-range maritime reconnaissance flying boat. The Be-10, NATO code-name 'Mallow', was an obvious development of Beriev's first jet-powered design the Be-8 but had an advanced hull design, featuring a relatively long and narrow planing bottom in order to reduce hydrodynamic and aerodynamic drag, a deep single-step, fifty-degree swept wings with a pronounced anhedral, and fixed wingtip floats attached to short solid pylons.

An early production Beriev Be-12 'Mail', no 53, on step showing a clean wake created by the excellent hydrodynamic design of Beriev's hulls. (via W. Schoenmaker)

Beriev Be-12, no 31, showing its amphibious capabilities as it taxies out of the water on to a slipway at its base.
(via W. Schoenmaker)

A Beriev Be-12, no 78, assigned to the Soviet Navy's Northern Fleet taxies out of a AV-MF base at Murmansk past a preserved example of its predecessor, the Beriev Be-6 'Madge' flying boat.

The shoulder-mounted engines were two 14,330 lb thrust Type Lyulka AL-7PB turbojets giving the large boat, which had a wingspan of 82 ft (25 m) and a length of 108 ft (33 m), a reasonable preformance if the impressive series of FAI-recognised records for water-borne aircraft that the type established soon after its first appearance at Tushimo were anything to go by. On 7 August 1961, pilot Nikolai Andrievsky with a navigator and radio-operator on board, averaged 566.69 mph (911.8 km/h) over a straight course of 15-25 km (9-15 miles), and Gueorgui Bourianov and his crew established no less than twelve records in nine days beginning on 3 September. These included a 544.2 mph (875.6 km/h) speed record with an 11,023 lb (5,000 kg) payload over a 1,000-km (620 mile) closed-circuit course, and altitude records of 49,088 ft (14,962 m) without payload, 46,135 ft (14,062 m) with a five-ton payload, 41,775 ft (12,733 m) with a ten-ton payload and 39,360 ft (11,997 m) with a payload of fifteen tons.

Despite its record-breaking performances, the Be-10 was limited in range and weapons capacity. The Mallow's defensive armament comprised a pair of 23 mm cannon in a radar-directed, but manned, tail turret, while its offensive loads were restricted, not by weight, but by what could be carried on underwing racks, the Be-10 having no bomb bays in the hull or engine nacelles. Doubts about the aircraft's capacity for operating in open waters were strengthened by the number of pronounced boundary layer-fences on the wings, wide bow chine (to protect engine intakes from spray), and strakes on the sides of the rear hull to protect the Be-10's gun turret. The small size of the non-retractable water rubber was further indication of the difficulty of manoeuvring on the water at low speeds. After its dramatic public debut in 1961, little was heard of the Be-10 in service, although a Soviet postage stamp was issued in 1965 depicting one of the jet flying boats in Aeroflot livery, and it was assumed that it met a similar fate to that of the Martin SeaMaster with only a few being issued to a trial unit of the AV-MF.

The second Beriev design to make its debut at the 1961 Tushimo show was almost ignored by the Western Press who saw the Be-10 as the star performer, being described merely as a turboprop conversion of the Beriev Be-6 'Madge'. However, this description was far from accurate although it would be another six years before the type was shown to Western observers in detail at the USSR's 50th Anniversary Air Display at Moscow's Domodedovo airport in 1967 when three production Beriev Be-12s made an appearance. It was then revealed that the Be-12 was a completely new amphibious design, the first amphibian designed from the Beriev bureau to be put into quantity production at Taganrog, that had flown for the first time in February 1959 and entered service with the AV-MF in 1964.

The overall configuration of the Be-12, codename 'Mail', was at first sight similar to that of its piston-engined predecessor with the familiar narrow high-gull wing (from which it derived its Russian name of 'Tchaika' or Seagull), and twin fin dihedral tailplane. Non-retractable wingtip floats were attached to a single streamlined pylon and mounted at the elbow of each wing was a 4,190 shp Ivchenko AI-20D turboprop engine. The compact but spacious hull housed a crew of five or six,

The Soviet Navy's Beriev Be-12 was first revealed to the West in 1967 when two of the ASW amphibians, nos 52 and 56, appeared at the USSR's 50th Anniversary Air Display at Moscow's Domodedovo airport in 1967. The pair are seen here taxying at Domodedovo giving a good view of the pronounced gull-wing, high-mounted Ivchenko turboprops and thimble radome mounted in the nose. (via W. Schoenmaker)

An in-flight view of Beriev Be-12, no 80, showing the type's deep V hull, pronounced step, kink in the rear hull — possibly a launch tube, and the water rudder. (Kriegsmarine)

Another early production Be-12, with the thin Magnetic Anomaly Detection (MAD) boom extended from the rear fuselage, low over its base in Northern Russia. (via W. Schoenmaker)

including pilot, co-pilot, radio operator, electronics operator and one or two ASW sensor operators, according to its tasking. The Be-12's glazed observation and weapons aiming and navigation station in the nose with its radar 'proboscis' is almost identical to that of late production versions of France's Nord Noroit amphibian. The relatively simple, for an amphibian, mainwheel units fold neatly upwards into the fuselage sides in line with the leading edge of the wing, while the tailwheel retracts up into the rear stern beneath the MAD stinger closed by two doors. These doors can act as water rudders although there is also a small skeg at the end of the hull.

The traditional defensive gun turrets on most Beriev 'boats were replaced by an observation astrodome in the dorsal position and a magnetic anomaly detection (MAD) extension protruding fifteen feet (406 m) from the rear fuselage. The sharp planing surface was almost identical to that of the Be-10, although considerably shorter in overall length, and with a shallower single step than that of the jet boat. A Be-10-type bow dam was also fitted to the amphibian, which has a lip fitted to the edge of the hull acting as an additional spray suppressor. The rear strake of the Be-10 was deleted from the Be-12. Weapons, such as torpedoes, depth charges and sonobuoys, are carried in an internal unpressurised bay with watertight doors to the rear of the step, and bombs, guided anti-submarine missiles or rockets can be carried on two pylons beneath each wing outboard of the engines. The Beriev Be-12 is capable of carrying a total weapons-load in excess of 11,000 lb (5,000 kg). Sonobuoys, markers and flares can be launched at sea level through a number of unpressurised launch tubes. The amphibian is able to alight on calm water to search with its own on-board sonar equipment to supplement the air-dropped sonobuoys. Weapons and various stores can be loaded via side hatches in the rear of the hull while the Be-12 is on the water. An auxiliary power unit is fitted behind the trailing edge of the port wing, the exhaust of which can be used to heat the leading edges of the tail. It is comprehensively equipped with navaids and no less than four radar altimeters.

By the time the Be-12 had made its second public appearance, Beriev's 'Tchaika' had already established a string of officially-recognised international altitude records in the FAI class C3 Group II for turboprop-powered amphibians. In October 1964 a Be-12 piloted by Captain M. I. Mikhailov, and his crew of two, attained six records including an altitude of 39,977 ft (12,185 m) without payload, an altitude of 37,290 ft (11,366 m) with payloads of 2,205 and 4,409 lb (1,000 and 2,000 kg), 30,682 ft (9,352 m) with a 22,046 lb (10,000 kg) payload and 6,560 ft with a maximum payload of 22,266 lb (10,100 kg). The Be-12 has a maximum speed of 378 mph (608 km/h) and a maximum range of 2,485 miles (4,000 km) at 199 mph (320 km/h).

A pair of Beriev Be-12 'Tchaika' amphibians at an AV-MF air base giving a good view of the MAD boom, tailwheel assembly and starboard rear access hatch. (via R. Ruffle)

A Beriev Be-12 'Mail', no 17, seen over a Soviet warship. Note larger diameter MAD boom which is white tipped as is the radome. (via W. Schoenmaker)

By 1965 the Be-12 had become the AV-MF's standard medium-range maritime patrol and reconnaissance aircraft serving with the Baltic, Black Sea and Northern Fleets flying from bases on the shores of the Baltic and Black Seas and in the Kola peninsula. Beriev's amphibian soon built up a reputation that rivalled its predecessor's for being a reliable and rugged 'boat with excellent on the water characteristics. Being amphibious, the Be-12 could operate all the year round in places such as the Arctic, and under conditions that kept the earlier Beriev flying boats restricted to their ice-free bases.

In 1968, it was announced that a Beriev Be-12 had broken more FAI records for amphibians, this time for speed. On 24 April, the aircraft established a C3 Group II 310.6-mile (500 km) closed-circuit speed record of 343 mph (552 km/h), and two days later established a similar record in the C2 Group II for flying boats of 351 mph (565 km/h). The latter is thought to have been established by a specially modified flying boat variant with the undercarriage removed. However, it was not only in the field of record breaking that the Beriev Be-12 was coming to prominence. From 1968, the AV-MF operated a detachment of Be-12s from an Egyptian Air Force base for the surveillance of the US 6th Fleet in the Mediterranean. The aircraft, the first Be-12s to operate outside the Soviet Union, were crewed by Soviet personnel although the aircraft appeared in Egyptian Air Force camouflage schemes and carried Egyptian insignia. The detachments continued until 1972 when all Soviet military personnel were expelled by President Anwar Sadat following the Six-Day War with Israel.

By the early 1970s, the last of more than 200 Beriev Be-12 amphibians had been completed at the Taganrog flying boat factory and the type had become the largest amphibian flying boat then currently in military service anywhere in the world, the Soviet Union being the only major power to operate flying boats in front-line service. In the mid-1980s some 95 Be-12 'Seagulls' continue to fly anti-submarine patrols although they are largely restricted to coastal reconnaissance of up to 250 miles (400 km) radius, not because of their age, but by the relatively low power of their A304 search and mapping radar, although a few are reported to have been fitted with more powerful surveillance radars, tail-warning and passive receivers, and an Early Warning variant is also known to be in limited service.

Not only is it retained by the AV-FM's Northern Fleet, covering Norway and Sweden, and the Baltic Fleet covering Denmark for coastal patrol, anti-ship, ASW and ELINT duties, but it has been reported that up to a dozen Be-12s are operating from Cam Rahn Bay in Vietnam, the old hunting grounds of US Navy Marlin flying boats twenty years earlier, where they patrol the South China Sea watching for elements of the US Navy's Pacific Fleets based in the Philippines. Although the amphibians are in Vietnam People's Air Force markings, it is thought that they are flown by Soviet crews detached to the Far East as had been the case in Egypt fifteen years earlier. The 'Tchaika' has also been used to carry out a series of geophysical surveys in Siberia.

Be-12 'Tchaika' or Seagull, no 88, over the Baltic giving an excellent view of the wide bow chine, high mounted engines and crewman in the rear astradome. Also to be seen is a new panel forward of the mainwheel covers and the remnants of camouflage of the same pattern as previously seen on Be-12s operating in Egypt in the late 1960s. (Swedish Air Force)

An in-flight shot of an AV-MF Beriev Be-12, no 20, on patrol over the Baltic Sea. The light coloured patch behind the number is the auxiliary power unit (APU) outlet. (Swedish Air Force)

In the meantime the Be-12 has continued to break records, including those for speed over a 100 km (62 mile) closed circuit in the classes for amphibians, at 371.2 mph (597.3 km/h) and 370.7 mph (596.4 km/h) respectively, set by Captain G. Efimov and his crew on 19 April 1976, while Captain V. Svyatoshnyuk established an altitude record for amphibians of 30,715 ft (9,362 m) on 3 May 1976. To date Beriev's amphibian holds no less than forty — or all the available FAI turboprop amphibian and flying boat class records — the most recent of which was set in 1983.

An unusual view of Beriev Be-12, no 41, over the Baltic Sea showing the partial camouflage pattern on the fuselage. (Swedish Air Force)

Beriev Be-12 ('Mail') Specification

Accommodation: Crew: 5/6
Power Plants: Two 4,190 shp Ivchenko AI-20D turboprops
Dimensions: Wingspan: 97 ft 6 in (29.7 m)
Length: 99 ft 0 in (30.17 m)
Height: 22 ft 11½ in (7 m)
Wing area: 1,130.25 sq ft (105 m²)
Weights: Empty: 39,680 lb (18,000 kg)
Average: 64,925 lb (29,164 kg)
Performance: Max speed: 378 mph (608 km/h)
Patrol speed: 199 mph (320 km/h)
Patrol range: 2,485 miles (4,000 km)
Ferry range: 3,250 (5,230 km)
Max endurance: 15 hr

It is perhaps ironic that the Soviet naval air force's second choice has turned out to be such a success, for a flying boat, and in retrospect it may have been a mistake not to keep the Be-12 in production longer and develop it to take an advanced radar, the latest electronic surveillance equipment and the latest state-of-the-art turboprop engines, as there is yet no obvious replacement for the long serving Beriev.

Although one example of the Be-12 'Tchaika' is already on display at the Soviet Air Force Museum at Morimo, near Moscow, many others are destined to soldier on into the 21st century in the search and rescue, submarine and warship co-operation, transport and fishery protection roles, and it will be interesting to see if the Beriev Design Bureau will ever design another water-borne aircraft to succeed it.

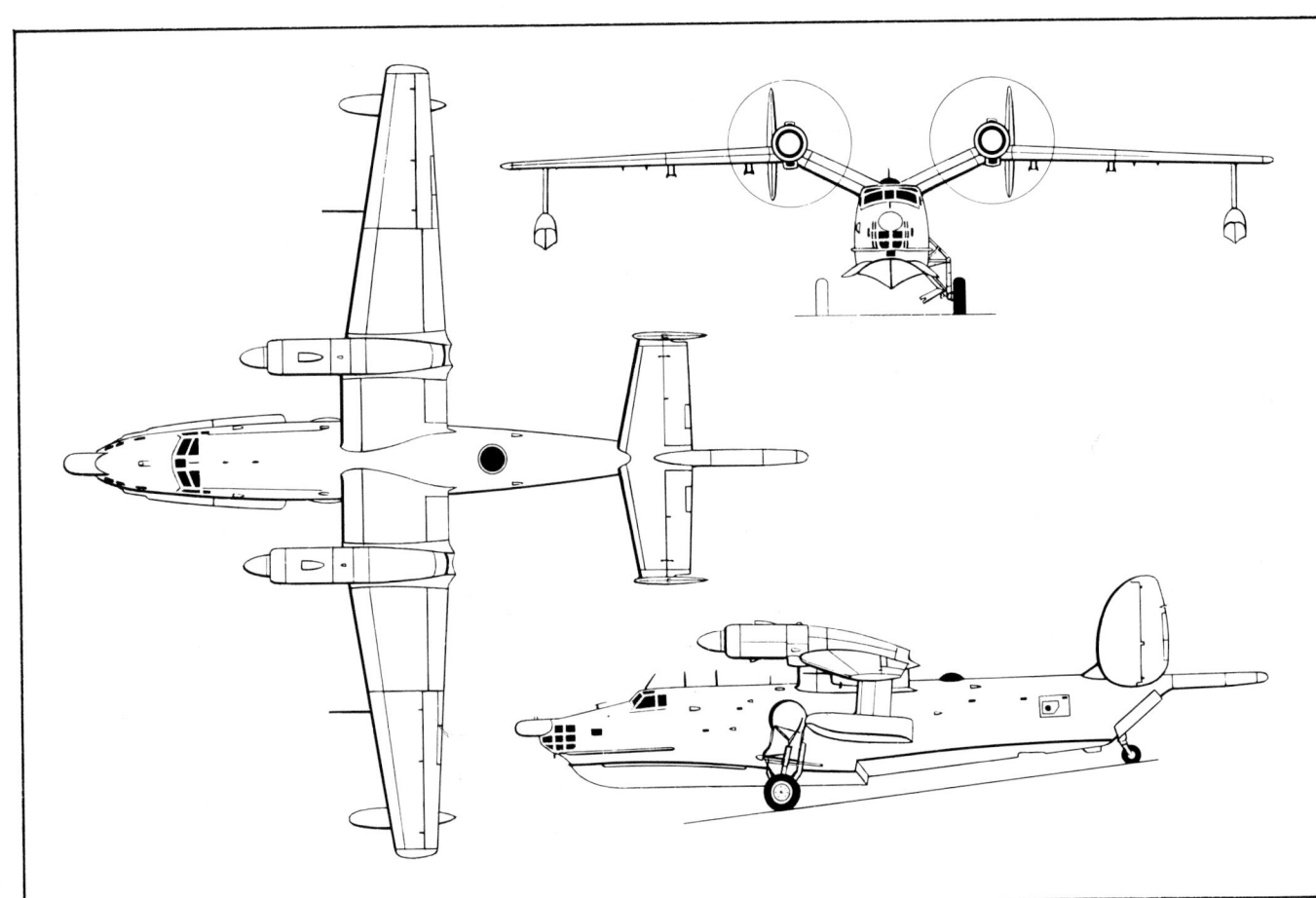

CHAPTER TEN
THE CANADAIR CL-215

The first flight of what was to become the world's most successful post-war commercial amphibious flying boat — the Canadair CL-215 — took place on 23 October 1967. The CL-215 was designed specifically to a Canadian requirement for a modern fire-fighting water-bomber to replace an ageing fleet of diverse ex-World War Two veterans that were kept busy in many Canadian Provinces during the summer months fighting devastating forest fires which every year were proving more and more costly to forest industry — the country's largest industry — and Canada's economy.

On 9 December 1963, the Forest Fire Protection Committee of Canada's National Research Council, made up of senior fire-fighting officers from each of Canada's Provinces, representatives of the Federal Government and Canadian industry,

met in Ottawa to agree on a common requirement for a water-bomber amphibian. The specification that they came up with was very detailed and called for a twin-engined amphibious aircraft able to scoop between 800 and 1,500 gallons of water from a mile-long lake without coming to a halt. Take-off distance to fifty feet (15 m) was to be no more than 3,000 ft (914 m), cruising speed between 140-150 knots and stalling speed 60-70 knots. It was also to have excellent visibility from the cockpit, an endurance of four hours, be stressed to + 3g and capable of being readily adaptable to other roles in order to make it economically viable.

Sécurité Civile CL-215 F-ZBBV makes a low level approach to a lake where it will refill its tanks. (D. Oliver)

In-flight shot of Sécurité Civile CL-215 showing the crew in the cockpit mounted close to the nose giving them an excellent view forward and below. (D. Oliver)

One of Sécurité Civile's fleet of Canadair CL-215 amphibians, F-ZBBV on fire-patrol over south west France. (D. Oliver)

Canadair, which was looking for a new produc in the mid-1960s, responded to the requiremen with enthusiasm and embarked on a comprehensiv market research programme, the results of whic would dictate the aircraft's ultimate layout.

The company had been formed in 1944 to tak over and develop the Canadian Vickers aircra factory at Carterville near Montreal, where 37 amphibious versions of the PBY-5A Catalina known in Canada as the Canso, were produce between April 1943 and May 1945, thus giving th company a thorough grounding in the complexitie of producing amphibious aircraft.

The first water-bomber configuration studied b the company was the CL-204, a twin-engined twin boom floatplane, the fuselage pod of which ha little room for more than a cockpit and a 1,200 gallon water tank, but this was discarded as bein too specialised and unsuitable for use in other role such as transport or crop spraying. The first CL-21 layout was a twin-engined flying boat with parasol wing, blister cockpit and T-tail, and whil this could have been a useful sprayer, it was agai too small to be a practical transport.

Each of these designs was submitted to th National Research Committee for approval and was as a result of its recommendations that the CL 215's configuration was significantly revisec Following extensive computer analysis of its fire fighting profile, 800 hours of water-tank testing, th initial 200 hours in Convair's tank at San Diego and 1,100 hours of wind tunnel testing, the projec received design approval and production go-ahea on 1 February 1966.

The final CL-215 configuration was conventional twin-engine amphibian with a gros weight of 41,500 lb (18,824 kg) able to carry 1,20 gallons of water or pesticide in two removable tank carried internally in a spacious cabin. The engine were mounted high on top of a one-piece cantileve wing, to keep the propellers out of the spray, whic in turn was bolted to the top of the fuselage. single wide chord wing flap helped to reduce th stalling speed of 66 knots. The tailplane wa positioned midway up a tall swept-back fin and th non-retractable wingtip floats were fitted to shor solid pylons. The single-step hull and advance planing bottom were designed to give a low wate impact load and minimise hull weight, combine with excellent high speed planing efficiency. Th CL-215 could operate in wave heights of up to 6. feet (1.65 m) and swell lengths of sixty feet (18 m). had excellent water handling characteristics with turning radius in calm water of less than fifty fee (15 m). An efficient bow chine reduced spray t engines, control surfaces and the windscreen. Th amphibian's robust tricycle undercarriag mainwheels retracted up into the hull sides beneat the wings, leaving the low profile tyred whee exposed to the slipstream, the designers havin sacrificed low drag for rugged simplicity. The twin nose wheel arrangement was short legged bu equally robust.

Initially, no less than five engine alternatives ha been studied including the turbo-compounded an uncompounded versions of the Wright R-13350 the Pratt & Whitney R-2800 Twin Wasp, and Rolls Royce Dart R. Da. 10 and Allison 501 turboprops

The two turboprop engines were rejected due to low acceleration and high operating costs and eventually the 2,100 hp R-2800-CA3 eighteen-cylinder radial, driving a Hamilton Standard constant-speed three-bladed propeller, was chosen on the grounds of proven reliability, low cost, required power output, ease of maintenance and the fact that it was manufactured by United Aircraft of Canada at Quebec. Ground power was provided by an air-cooled petrol engine mounted in the rear fuselage. The CL-215 had maximum cruising speed of 193 mph (310 km/h) and a normal range of 1,150 miles (1,850 km), with a ferry range of nearly 2,000 miles (3,200 km). Provision was made for a two-man crew on the flight deck and the basic navigation fit included dual ADF, dual VOR/ILS with marker beacon, a gyro-magnetic compass and standby compass. An ATC transponder and emergency location transmitter were also fitted along with dual VHF radio and single VHF/FM.

CL-215 C-GKDN was delivered to the Italian Air Ministry in July 1982 to become 15-51. (Canadair)

A Series 1 production CL-215 delivered to the government of Quebec in January 1971, on step about to lift off the water. (Canadair)

Two Canadair CL-215 SAR amphibians were delivered to the Royal Thai Navy in 1978. Based at U-Tapao they are also used for coastal patrol. (Canadair)

Yugoslavia's Air Force operates the CL-215 amphibian on firefighting, oil pollution control and SAR missions. No 225 was delivered in December 1981 but lost on the 11 July 1986 with three crew. (Canadair)

The Canadair's fire-fighting installatio consisted of the two internal tanks located each si of the fuselage amidships, comprising a removab glass fibre section above the floor and a low portion formed by a permanent hull structure. T floor of each tank incorporated a hinged do which was opened by gravity and clos hydraulically. Two hydraulically extended ar retracted probes, designed by Fields of Canad mounted behind the step, scooped water into t tanks as the aircraft skimmed the surface of a lake or coastal water of at least five feet (1.5 m) depth. The probes were lowered on approach, ar full power was applied immediately after touc down and maintained during the scoop. When t content indicators in the flight deck showed that t tanks were full, the probes were retracted and t aircraft lifted off. The total distance required, fro a height of fifty feet (15 m) on approach to fifty fe during climb out, was 3,940 ft (1,200 m) with water-borne distance of 1,850 ft (564 m). T normal speed for scooping was 82.6 mph (1. km/h) and scooping time about ten seconds. T Canadair's generous rudder area ensured th directional stability was maintained even whe scooping in high wind and wave conditions. T two water doors could be opened simultaneously individually. The drop pattern was controlled varying speed, altitude and release sequence. Drop could be made at speeds between 100 and 150 m (160 and 240 km/h) at heights from 100 ft to 150 (30 to 45 m). With both doors opened together, t 1,200-gallon water 'bomb' could be dropped in le than a second to cover a ground area approximately 280 ft by 65 ft (85 by 20 m) whi would receive a density of at least one litre per t square feet. When the doors opened consecutive the area covered was approximately 465 by 40 (140 by 12 m). Fires in residential areas we attacked at low level, enabling the 'bomb' to brea down the roof of a burning building to soak t interior, or from a greater height to create a hea rainfall effect to contain the outbreak in a heavi built-up area. Oil fires could be controlled dropping a foam liquid mixed with water. The C 215 was designed to fight fires for over four hou without refuelling. Its excellent low speed handlir characteristics and outstanding visibility from t cockpit set high in the nose minimised crew fatig while allowing consistently accurate drops to made in adverse conditions.

Strength, durability, and the minimum of maintenance requirements, had been achieved by the use of conventional materials and well-proven components in the production of a rugged structure extensively protected by the latest anti-corrosion materials. An initial production batch of thirty CL-215 amphibians was laid down in June 1966 against launch orders of twenty from the government of the province of Quebec, which at the time operated a fleet of Canso amphibians on fire-fighting duties, and ten from the French government for its Protection Civile service.

The 83rd production CL-215 amphibian in special colours to coincide with the announcement in May 1983 that the Canadian Federal Government would purchase an additional 20 aircraft for Provincial governments. (Canadair)

A CL-215 of Spain's Ejercito del Aire 432 Escuadron, 432-14, dropping chemical foaming agents on a forest fire near Valencia. (Canadair)

Two Sécurité Civile CL-215 water-bombers return to Marignane after a fire patrol over southern France. (D. Oliver)

The prototype Canadair CL-215, registered *CF-FEU-X, (FEU* being French for fire) made its first flight from Carterville Airport on 23 October 1967 with the amphibian making its first water take-off on 2 May 1968. Problems with stall characteristics and directional stability were overcome by redesigning the wingtips and increasing the height of the fin above the tailplane, but although Canadair's amphibian was certified by the Canadian Department of Transport and the US Federal Aviation Administration in March and May 1969, Quebec's provincial government was not satisfied with the performance of the engines and refused to accept delivery of the CL-215 despite the fact that France took delivery of its own first aircraft in May 1969. It was almost a year before Quebec accepted its the CL-215, by which time the order had been reduced to fifteen. However, the Protection Civile subsequently bought two additional aircraft off the original production run, including the prototype which was to have been Quebec's first aircraft, while another two were sold to Spain's Ministry of Agriculture and one to the Greek government.

The CL-215 was an immediate success in the role for which it had been designed, that of fighting fires. It proved to be twice as effective as the PBY Canso that had been previously operated by both the Province of Quebec and France's Protection Civile, not only by carrying a larger load of water more reliably than the veteran Cansos during Canada's fire season (which stretches from April to October), but by its ability to carry cargo during the winter months when fire-fighting aircraft had previously been put into storage. During the winter of 1971, five CL-215s lifted 600 tons of bulky equipment in support of Quebec's James Bay Hydro Project during a thirty-day period. Six months later, four of the same aircraft, with two Cansos in support, fought a fire that was threatening to engulf the town of Val d'Or situated 260 miles north-west of Montreal. In two hours the six amphibians dropped a total of 33 tons or water to halt the fire at the outskirts of the town.

In the meantime, the European CL-215s were earning their keep with France's paramilitary organisation, the Protection Civile. Ten of the amphibians had been delivered by the start of the 1970 fire season, and they were to fight fires in every month of their first full year of operations, while the two Spanish aircraft made almost 4,000 drops between March 1971 and September 1972. In the twelve months to August 1972, 28 CL-215s dropped a total of 38,000 loads — 228,000 tons of water.

In November 1973, a Canadair CL-215 was loaned to the Swaziland government and was operated on fire-fighting duties by a local aviation company, General Air. To permit the operation of water bombers across the frontier with South Africa, Avex Air of Rand, South Africa, hoped to enter into an agreement with General Air by which they would purchase at least two CL-215s between them. However, nothing came of this particular project and the first deliveries of a second production batch of twenty CL-215s were made to the Spanish Air Force against a follow-on order for eight CL-215Bs.

The CL-215B was primarily a search and rescue (SAR) version which featured a nose-mounted

erry AN/AVQ-21 weather and search radar, a
HF transceiver and UVF/VHF homer plus,
ME, while a radio altimeter was added to the
sic avionics fit. The Spanish aircraft carried a
ew of six, comprising pilot, co-pilot, flight
gineer, navigator and two observers. An
tensive de-icing system was fitted as well as
med observation windows, a galley, toilet and
commodation for nine stretchers and three
lking patients. The Spanish CL-215B provided
R facilities in the Mediterranean and around the
anary Islands, being capable of ten hours'
durance with $7\frac{1}{2}$ hours on station 450 miles (725
n) from base flying at 2,000 ft (600 m) and 150
ph (240 km/h). All the CL-215s of the second and
bsequent production batches were fitted with
proved R-2800-2AH engines, extra fuel tanks,
e GPU relocated in the rear of the starboard
celle and the gross weight for water take-off
creased to 37,700 lb (17,100 kg). Other deliveries
om the second batch included an additional seven

Greece, three more to France (one of which
placed an aircraft written off in 1971) and one
ch to the Provincial governments of Manitoba
d Ontario, although the latter did not take
livery until 1983.

Meanwhile, the Canadair CL-215's reputation as
fire-fighter was strengthened by a series of
pressive performances such as the Quebec
rcraft that created an all-time record in 1975 for
e number of drops in one hour with an amazing
tal of 31 — one drop every 1 minute 55 seconds!
the same year, France's Protection Civile was
ked by the Lebanese government to base two of
Canadairs at Beirut Airport during the summer

Two of France's Sécurité Civile Canadair CL-215 water-bombers at their base at Marseille's Marignane airport. The amphibian in the foreground, F-ZBAR, was the first to be delivered to France in June 1969. (D. Oliver)

The fifth Canadair CL-215 to fly was CF-PQJ seen dropping 5,500 litres of water on to a forest fire through two doors in the hull. This aircraft was delivered to France's Protection Civile in July 1970. (Canadair)

CL-215 scooping 6 tons of water into its internal tanks while skimming across the surface of a lake at 70 knots. CF-TXE was delivered to the government of Quebec in March 1971. (Canadair)

months, but in April 1975, just as the aircraft wer preparing to leave Marseille, civil war broke out i Lebanon and the request was cancelled. Two year later, two Canadian CL-215s were loaned to th Los Angeles authorities to fight fires in souther California and, although they had a spectacula success in saving a number of houses in the Laure Canyon suburb of Los Angeles from an out control bush fire, the abundance of cheap e military bombers and freighters that have bee converted to fire-fighting aircraft in California an Arizona meant that no sales of the CL-215 have ye been made to the United States.

Yet another repeat order from Spain, this tim for seven dual purpose fire-fighter/SAR CL-215 prompted a third production batch of fiftee aircraft to be put in hand in 1977. The aircraft wer essentially the same as those of the second serie apart for a modified scoop which maintained th time taken to fill the tanks at ten seconds bu reduced the scooping distance to around 1,600 (488 m). In 1978 Greece increased its order to eleve while Canadair made its first CL-215 sale to the Fa East when two SAR versions were purchased by th Royal Thai Navy to be based at Bangkok. (Thes aircraft, incidentally, were the first of their type n to be delivered in overall orange/yellow colou scheme.) In February 1979, the first of two 26-sea CL-215Cs was delivered to the Venezuela operator CVG Ferrominera Orinocco CA. Th 215C was a utility transport version that coul carry up to 32 passengers while retaining the fire fighting capability, although the Greek Air Forc has carried as many as 39 troops in its CL-215s. Th Venezuelan amphibians, which were also fitte with ten passenger windows, a toilet and galle were used to transport mining personnel to remot parts of the country and provide fire protection fo the company's plantations in south-we Venezuela.

In an effort to increase CL-215 sales in Sout America, one of Canadair's demonstrators wa based at San Carlos de Bariloche in Argentina fo several weeks at the beginning of 1981. Operating i conjunction with the Instituto Forestal Naciona Argentina, the CL-215 made no fewer than 40 water drops to help fight more than thirty fires mostly in grasslands and forests of a large nationa park, resulting in a great deal of enthusiasti comments but, as with the Short Sealand amphibian thirty years earlier, no orders.

At the same time Canadair was laying down fourth production batch at its new 300,000 sq f factory at Dorval International Airport, situate four miles south-west of Cartierville where spac was required for production of the company's CL 601 Challenger corporate jet. Customers for th fifteen CL-215s of this series, completed i December 1983, included the Province of Ontario Greece and Spain, which ordered their second twelfth, and eighteenth aircraft respectively. Ne customers were Italy, with an order for two, and th Yugoslavian government which ordered four dua role aircraft. These were water bombers fitted wit a lightweight integrated spray similar to that use by two of the Quebec Canadairs. The system use the amphibian's internal tanks and is operated by single motor-pump assembly powered by th aircraft's hydraulic system. The fluids are pumpe to the full-span spray booms attached to the underside of the wing by quick-release fasteners. Chemicals from the two tanks can be mixed and flow rate varied, all of which can be controlled from the flight deck.

The Quebec government spraying aircraft are used in the battle against the destructive spruce budworm and can deliver up to eighty gallons of pesticide per minute in swath widths, using the cross-wind drift techniques, of up to 1,600 ft (488 m) to cover as much as 11,000 acres (4,455 hectares) in one mission. The Yugoslav aircraft, based at Zadar on the Adriatic coast, are capable of spraying both pesticides and oil dispersants. When applying the latter, only the inner section of the spray boom is used. For this task, flow rates of up to 214 US gallons per minute are suitable to enable 16.6 acres (6.7 hectares) of contaminated area to be treated on each mission. The Litton LTN-51 inertial navigation system ensures accurate spraying swaths. The Yugoslavian aircraft retained their full fire-fighting capability and in fact it was one of these that made an amazing 225 drops in one day soon after its delivery in 1982, establishing a record for one aircraft, of any type, in one day that to date has not been broken. Unfortunately, another of the Yugoslav aircraft, No 225, was lost on 11 September 1984 when it crashed into the sea whilst scooping off Zadar, killing its three-man crew. A replacement, the fifth CL-215 to be ordered by Yugoslavia, was delivered in 1986.

Sécurité Civile Canadair CL-215, F-ZBBH, at Marignane in 1985. (D. Oliver)

Two 26-seat Canadair CL-215 amphibians were delivered to CVG Ferriminera Orinocco CA in Venezuala in 1979. YV-O-CFO-5 retains its firefighting capability. (Canadair)

15 Stormo CL-215, 15-51 flying over St. Peter's in Rome in June 1986. (Aeronautica Militare)

By the early 1980s, no fewer than five Mediterranean countries had purchased a total of 52 CL-215s, with Spain being the largest customer having received nineteen aircraft between 1970 and 1984. Spain's first two aircraft were based at Getafe near Madrid and initially attached to Esc 803, an SAR unit equipped with HU-16 Albatross amphibians. In March 1970 the Canadairs took part in the type's first SAR mission, searching for survivors of a cargo ship that had sunk in the Atlantic off Santiago. Two months later the Spanish CL-215s fought their first fire at Galizia and their performance during the following year prompted the Spanish government to order enough aircraft to equip a new squadron, Esc 404, which was formed at Torrejon airport, near Madrid, in January 1973. The Canadair was designated UD-13 (utility amphibian-13) by the Spanish Air Force and in March 1975 two were loaned to Esc 802 based in the Canary Islands while the unit's ageing HU-16 Albatrosses were grounded with mechanical problems.

However, a number of the CL-215s were to be lost during fire-fighting operations in Spain. In September 1976, UD-13/7 crashed into Mount Xiabre near Vigo in north-west Spain with the loss of two crew, and on 7 March 1977, UD-13/9 hit a submerged rock while landing in rough water at Fuenterrabia and had to be abandoned, though with no less of life. A month later UD-13/8 crashed while scooping in the sea off Valencia and although the amphibian quickly capsized and sunk, the two crew were picked up suffering only minor injuries.

In March 1980, the CL-215s replaced the Spanish Air Force HU-16 amphibians in the SAR role and a new Group was formed, Gruppo 43, comprising two squadrons, 431 and 432, each equipped with seven UD-13 aircraft and 21 two-man crews. During the summer months, the Group's aircraft are detached to a number of high risk areas around the country including Santiago, Reus, Palma de Mallorca, Valencia and Jerez. By this time Spain's national aircraft company, CASA, had become a major sub-contractor of CL-215 components and was responsible for heavy servicing of the Spanish Air Force's fleet.

The Group's first loss occurred on 12 October 1980 when UD-13/13 crashed while fighting a fire near Alicante. The amphibian was attempting to land on a small reservoir when the pilot lost control and the aircraft crashed into trees close to a dam above the lake. Although it broke up on impact the Canadair did not catch fire and the co-pilot, although gravely injured, survived. Yet another was lost during a training flight on 2 March 1982, UD-13/2 crashing into a lake near Cuenca and sinking after experiencing an engine failure during take-off.

In spite of the many hazards of fighting fires from the air, the Spanish CL-215s have made a total of 98,115 drops — 580 million litres of water — in fifteen years, and between 1 July and 15 August 1985, a detachment of two aircraft made a total of 730 drops on 114 fires in the Manises-Valencia area alone.

The CL-215's first operator in Europe, or anywhere else, however, was France's Protection Civile which was originally formed in 1954 as part of the Paris Fire Service with a fleet of Bell 47 helicopters. By the 1960s, the organisation had

Aeronautica Militare Canadair CL-215 15-52, one of four belonging to 15 Stormo, about to alight on Lake Villeta Barrea in September 1985. (Aeronautica Militare)

some thirty Alouette III helicopters based at eighteen locations around the country, mainly in coastal or mountainous regions, to carry out missions such as search and rescue, casualty evacuation, flood and disaster relief and fire control. In 1963, a fixed-wing Air Group was formed initially equipped with two Canso Catalina water-bombers, although a further five were purchased by 1969. The amphibians proved an ideal weapon against the devasting forest fires that broke out in the South of France during the hot summer months, often in areas totally inaccessible to ground fire-fighting units. The experience with the Cansos led the Protection Civile (renamed Sécurité Civile in 1975) to become a launch customer for the Canadair CL-215 which incorporated many design features specified by the French. A total of fifteen was subsequently delivered to the Air Group's fixed-wing base at Marseille's Marignane Airport starting in 1969, and soon earned the fulsome praise of the crews who appreciated the amphibian's rugged and dependable qualities that were ideally suited to the very specialised and demanding role of aerial fire-fighting.

Although the Sécurité Civile is not a military unit, all the Air Group's 46 fixed-wing pilots are ex-Aéronavale with at least fifteen years' experience

A view of the Canadair CL-215's sturdy wing and short wing-float pylon from the interior of Sécurité Civile CL-215 F-ZBBJ. (D. Oliver)

The CL-215 amphibian assembly line in Canadair's Plant 3 at Dorval, Quebec, in 1985. (Canadair)

and a minimum of 3,000 hours in command. Typical of the Group's pilots is Captain Hubert Bolzinger, a 52-year-old ex-Naval pilot whose log-book entries include the Lancaster, Neptune, Crusader and Etendard, and who joined the Sécurité Civile in 1971.

'The Canadair is a suberb fire-fighting aircraft. It is strong, manoeuvrable and reliable. With its ability to scoop water from lakes and reservoirs — there are sixteen in our area that we are permitted to use — and of course the sea, it enables us to reach any outbreak within twenty minutes from receiving the call at Marignane. Two airfields in our sector, Le Luc and Calvi, are equipped with water tanks, and two more at Ales and Aubenas have supplies of retardant with which we can refill our tanks in about $1\frac{1}{2}$ minutes if necessary. Four Canadairs are detached every year to Ajaccio in Corsica between July and the beginning of October. At least two aircraft are dispatched to any reported outbreak by the regional control centre at Valabre. Our high risk season lasts from May to October and the number of missions we fly increases every year. The work is long and hard. When we are on duty, we remain on standby from dawn to dusk. Each crew is responsible for refuelling and refilling his aircraft at the end of every mission. When not reacting to alerts, we fly four-hour patrols, always in pairs, during which we practise scooping from lakes en route which is done with the co-operation of the local fire department who send out a boat to clear the water of tourists and floating debris.

'When fighting fires for real, drops are made from a height of thirty metres on a target that more often than not is partly obscured by smoke from an aircraft that is being thrown around by heat turbulence. The worst fires usually occur high in the hills and are fanned by the 'Mistral' which can blow at anything up to 60 mph (100 km/h). Without an autopilot or power-controls, the Canadair is a heavy aircraft to fly and manoeuvre in confined spaces. On a typical summer's day the temperature in the flight deck can reach forty degrees centigrade and that is before we get over a fire. With its high tail the Canadair can prove tricky to taxy in high cross winds on land but there are few problems with it on the water. So far we have lost four Canadairs and their crews. Since 1980 the government have been buying converted DC6 airliners and Tracker anti-submarine aircraft as water-bombers because they are cheap, but being landplanes they have to return to base after every drop to refill their tanks and they cannot operate when the Mistral is full strength. We have lost two of the four DC6s, half the fleet, in three years. We want more CL-215s which can do the job of three or four of the other aircraft.'

By the end of 1984, Italy's Civil Defence Ministry had increased its order for Canadair CL-215s to four. The amphibians were purchased on behalf of the Ministry of Agriculture and Forests to supplement the Italian Air Force's C-130 Hercules and Aeritalia G222 cargo aircraft that could be fitted with temporary fire-fighting systems. The CL-215s were based at Rome's Ciampino Airport and operated by a government-financed civilian unit, on the same lines as France's Sécurité Civile, with four Canadian pilots and twelve Italians (mostly ex-HU-16 pilots) on strength. The first two rcraft carried the civil registrations *I-CFSQ* and *-FSR*('CFS' standing for Corpo Forestale dello tato).

In 1984, it was decided that the Aeronautica Militare should take over the operational responsibility of the unit and a new Group, Gruppo 4, was formed within the Air Force's 15 Stormo, or Wing, already based at Ciampino and equipped with HH-3F SAR helicopters. The pilots were drawn from various units within the Aeronautica Militare and the first sixteen arrived at the base in March 1984 to be instructed by the Canadians. The Group's first fire-fighting operations were flown by combined crews. By the end of 1985, the four Canadairs were officially assigned to the Air Force and numbered *15-51* to *15-54* although they are still maintained by Italy's national airline Alitalia.

Lieutenant Colonel Roberto Bologna, commander of the 15 Stormo, describes the CL-15's role in Italy. 'The plans are utilised mainly for water-bombing and training, occasionally for passenger transport. We operate both from the sea and inland lakes of which there are few that are large enough for our use.

'Two aircraft are placed on alert all the year long and three during the fire season. There are three stages of alert: Blue — take off in three hours; yellow — take off in one hour; and Red — take off in fifteen minutes. The Red alert is very difficult to maintain with a piston-engined plane, so we have to re-heat the engines and the oil.

'Luckily, up to now we have not had any serious accidents, the worst incident being when one of the planes began taking on water through a crack in the fuselage near the landing gear recess during a scoop on Lake Albano. The plane was repaired on the lake and a week later was back on duty.'

In the meantime, the Canadian government had announced in 1983, that due to the continuing and mounting losses to Canada's $23 billion forest industry (an average fire season in Canada being 6,700 fires, while in the previous five years 3½ times more trees were burned than harvested), it was sponsoring an ambitious programme to purchase an additional seventeen Canadair CL-215 water bombers for existing provincial operators. Under the co-operative federal/provincial government scheme, Ontario's fleet is being increased to nine aircraft while Quebec, Alberta, Newfoundland and Saskatchewan each received two, Manitoba one and the Yukon and Northwest Territories four. In June 1986, Conair Aviation Ltd of Abbotsford, BC, was awarded a five-year contract to operate the northern province's four aircraft.

In May 1986, the Greek government placed an order for three more CL-215s which are operated by 355 Moire based at Elevsis, west of Athens. This unit has lost two only of its Canadairs since 1973, although a third was badly damaged following an emergency landing in the Gulf of Salonika on 17 January 1986. By the end of 1986, a total of 111 Canadair CL-215s had been sold to eight countries on four continents and, with current production at 1.5 aircraft per month, only three would be available for delivery during 1987, while the company was confident of further sales to new customers including Turkey, Portugal and possibly China, where Canadair has a sub-assembly plant at Xi'an, in the near future.

A line-up of Sécurité Civile CL-215 water-bombers at Marignane at dusk. (D. Oliver)

F-ZBBV skimming across Lake Salvetat in southern France. (D. Oliver)

Canadair CL-215

Accommodation:	Crew: 3-6
Power Plants:	Two 2,100 hp Pratt & Whitney R-2800-83 eighteen-cylinder radials
Dimensions:	Wingspan: 93 ft 10 in (28.6 m) Length: 65 ft 0½ in (19.82 m) Height: 29 ft 5½ in (8.98 m) Wing area: 1,080 sq ft (100.4 m²)
Weights:	Empty: 26,810 lb (12,161 kg) Average: 43,497 lb (19,730 kg)
Performance:	Max speed: 218 mph (350 km/h) Cruising speed: 181 mph (290 km/h) Patrol speed: 133 mph (214 km/h) (SAR version) Max range: 1,300 miles (2,092 km) Max endurance: 9 hr 45 min (SAR version)

Continuing CL-215 developments have included a drop pattern modification kit and an onboard foam injection system. Field trials of the foam system were concluded in Europe in 1985. The foam concentrate is injected into the water tanks in small quantities as the aircraft scoops its water load. However, the most important CL-215 development to date was announced soon after Canadair was taken over by Bombardier Inc, a major Canadian manufacturer of mass transit vehicles. In November 1986, following long and detailed engineering studies and market assessments, the Canadair CL-215 Turboprop was launched. The CL-215T programme not only covers the production of a new series of amphibians powered by the 2,000 shp Pratt & Whitney Canada PW100-37 turboprop engine, but the supply of retrofit kits, with a choice of two engines — the PW 100-47 and -37 — to existing users, all of which should ensure a long and healthy production life of Canada's very specialised, but invaluable, amphibious flying boat.

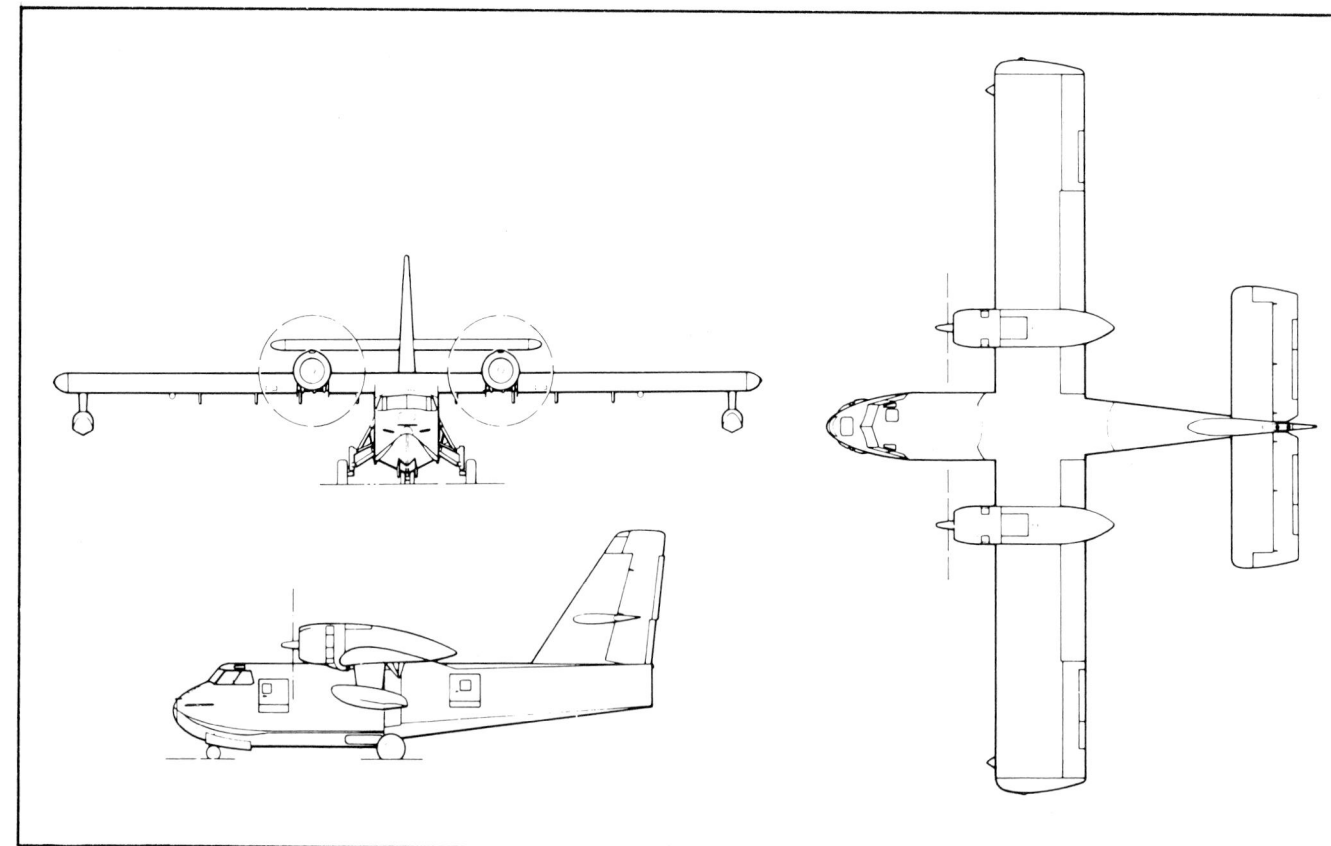

CHAPTER ELEVEN
THE SHIN MEIWA PS-1/US-1

When Shin Meiwa's SS-2 flying boat took to the air for the first time at Kobe on 29 October 1967, it was the first aircraft to be built by the Japanese company. However, the four-turboprop-powered flying boat could trace its origins back to what is arguably the best maritime reconnaissance flying boat to be produced by any country during the Second World War, the Kawanishi Type 2.

The giant four-engined Kawanishi H8K2, codenamed by the allies 'Emily', had a wingspan of 124 ft 8 in (38 m), carried a crew of ten, was armed with five 20 mm cannon and four 7.7 mm machine-guns, and had a maximum speed of 290 mph (466 km/h) with an impressive range of nearly 4,500 miles (7,240 km).

The Kawanishi Aircraft Company had become the Shin Meiwa Industry Company Ltd in 1949 when it was permitted to re-establish itself in the aviation business by overhauling US military and commercial aircraft based in Japan. Three years later Japan was allowed to resume aircraft manufacture and Shin Meiwa were awarded a research and development contract for a maritime reconnaissance flying boat following a series of feasibility studies of such an aircraft by the Japanese Maritime Self-Defence Force (JMSDF).

A Shin Meiwa US-1 SAR amphibian, 9072, belonging to 71st Squadron of the JMSDF, differs from the PS-1 flying boat by having larger wheel bulges, bow chine and extra domed observation windows. The large radome, high mounted flight deck and 'T' tail is reminiscent of the US Navy's last operational flying boat, the Martin P-5 Marlin. (JMSDF)

An in-flight shot of Shin Meiwa US-1A, 9076, flying over low clouds and rough seas. Note the dorsal fin-mounted loudspeaker in the centre of the yellow SAR stripe. (JMSDF)

The rescue crew of a 71st Squadron Shin Meiwa US-1A, 9076, practice with the amphibian's outboard motor-powered inflatable dinghy in a moderate swell. (JMSDF)

An ex-JMSDF Grumman UF-2 Albatross amphibian was used as the basis for a $\frac{3}{4}$ scale model of the proposed aircraft, known as the UF-XS. Apart from being fitted with two additional 600 hp Pratt & Whitney R-1340-AN-1 engines supplementing the Albatross' normal pair of 1,425 hp Wright R-1820 radials, a third type of engine, a 1,250 shp General Electric T58-GE-6 turbine, was fitted in the hull to provide blown-air over the control surfaces to give added lift. The UF-XS, which also featured a modified planing bottom and revised tailplane, flew for the first time on 20 December 1962.

Five years of research and development using high technology hydrodynamic developments pioneered, and largely financed by, Shin Meiwa resulted in a large deep-hulled, high-winged flying boat, designed by Dr Shizuo Kikuhara and built at the company's factories at Itami and Konan, that had more than a passing resemblance to the Kawanishi 'Emily'. However, on closer examination, the one bore little relationship to the other apart from its basic configuration. The SS-2 was powered by four 2,850 hp General Electric T64-1H1-10 turboprop engines, built under licence in Japan by Ishikawajima-Harima Heavy Industries Co Ltd, driving Hamilton Standard 63E60-15 three-blade constant-speed reversible pitch propellers. The same engine was used to power the Japanese-built P-2J Turbo Neptune maritime and anti-submarine patrol landplane.

Shin Meiwa had designed the SS-2 from the outset as a short take-off and landing (STOL) flying boat and to this end its 110 ft (33.5 m) wing, mounted high on the shoulders, bristled with high-lift leading edge slats, spoilers, and 'blown' continuous trailing edge flaps. The large all-metal T tail unit also featured leading edge slats with 'blown' rudder and elevators to improve handling at low speeds.

A Ishikawajima-built 1,400 hp General Electric T58-1H1-10-M1 gas turbine engine, fitted in the wing centre-section, provided the air for the boundary layer control system as well as acting as a conventional auxiliary power unit for engine starting, air conditioning, the pneumatic system and the generator. The deep fuselage is of all metal semi-monocoque construction with a deep V-shaped single-step planing bottom with a conventional bow spray chine and a novel spray suppressor groove running around the bow to the propeller line which minimised spray by ducting water from the bows to eject it horizontally further along the hull sides.

The large nose radome and high mounted cockpit are reminiscent of the Martin Marlin which had been studied in depth as a possible candidate for being produced under licence but was eventually rejected by the Japanese ten years previously. Although the SS-2 was a pure flying boat, it was fitted with a single-wheel retractable beaching gear which enabled it to be launched and beached from a slipway under its own power, thus simplifying servicing and maintenance. Perhaps surprisingly for such an unconventional design, the Shin Meiwa did not feature retractable wing floats but relied on a very conventional multi-strutted arrangement.

A Shin Meiwa US-1A, 9078, belonging to the 71st Squadron coming into land at Iwakuni. (JMSDF)

A Shin Meiwa PS-1 ASW flying boat, 5813, belonging to the 31st Squadron of the JMSDF, standing on its integral beaching gear at the 31st Air Group's airbase at Iwakuni. (via J. J. Halley)

A Shin Meiwa PS-1, 5821, about to alight on the water at Iwakuni with its water-flaps, mounted in the sides of the hull at the base of the red 'beware of the propellers' line, in an open position. (Shin Meiwa)

Having completed initial rough water tests in th Kii Straits, the prototype was delivered to the 51s Flight Test Squadron of the JMSDF in April 196 to be followed three months later by the first pre production SS-2 which flew on 14 June. Durin; lengthy and comprehensive development trials with the squadron, a series of successful take-offs an landings were made in seas with wave heights of up to thirteen feet. In ten-foot waves with a headwind of 25 knots, the flying boat became airborne in only twelve seconds and 260 ft (80 m) of water and satisfactorily proved that it was capable o operating from the open sea in the North Wester Pacific Ocean for 65 per cent of the year.

While the trials continued, presentations were made to the US, Canadian and Venezuela governments, with the latter seriously considering purchase of the flying boat subject to satisfactor financing. However, this could not be agreed, but a a result of the trials, the JMSDF ordered a total o fourteen production SS-1 ASW flying boat powered by the more powerful 3,060 hp T6 turboprop, to be designated PS-1, the first of which was delivered to the 31st Squadron of the 31st Ai Group at Iwakuni on 1 March 1974.

Having been impressed with the high standard o seaworthiness of the SS-2, the JMSDF made i known that it would be interested in an amphibiou search and rescue version to replace its squadron o fifteen-year-old Grumman UF-2 Albatros amphibians based on the southern island o Ohmura. The project gained powerful suppor from the Japanese fishing industry and in 1970 the US Navy made a detailed study of this version, bu no decision was made to acquire the type.

Meanwhile the company had been actively promoting a pressurised commercial flying boa capable of carrying up to 69 passengers over range of up to 930 nautical miles. In 1971, the Grumman Aircraft Corporation seriously considered building under licence a 100-passenger commuter version that would cruise at 250 knots and take off and land in less than 2,000 ft (609 m) of water. However, the high initial cost of the civil Shin Meiwa plus the lack of permanent maritime facilities capable o handling such a large 'boat, effectively killed off the project before it could fly.

An amphibious version, the SS-2A, did fly on 1 October 1974, though. As the only major difference between the flying boat and the amphibian, apar from internal equipment, was the addition of a 11 f 8 in (3.5 m) wide-track retractable undercarriage in place of the integral beaching gear, the first amphibian to fly was also the first production aircraft, and by the end of the year it had been joined by the second and third to form the nucleus of the 71st Squadron of the 31st Air Group which was commissioned at Iwakuni in July 1976. At the same time as placing the order for the three US-1s the JMSDF also approved the purchase of nine additional PS-1 flying boats to form a second unit the 32nd Squadron, to be commissioned in 1975.

In its anti-submarine warfare (ASW) form, the PS-1 has a crew of twelve, comprising pilot, co-pilot and flight engineer on the flight deck, while a navigator, radio operator, two sonar operators radar and MAD operators and a tactical co ordinator are accommodated in the tactical compartment aft of the flight deck and forward o he crew rest-room, plus two observers. On the lower deck is a galley, equipment storage, mainwheel bay and two main fuel tanks. The PS-1 is equipped with a full anti-submarine warfare avionics including electronic counter-measures (ECM) and magnetic anomaly detector (MAD) plus 'dipping sonar', while external armament consists of four homing torpedoes, or four 330 lb (150 kg) anti-submarine bombs carried in two underwing pods mounted between each pair of engine nacelles, plus two wingtip launchers for six five-inch HVAR rockets.

On a typical ASW patrol, the PS-1 can remain on station for nearly eight hours cruising at 175 knots at a height of 8,000 ft (2,440 m) using two engines, and has a maximum endurance of fifteen hours. It is capable of being refuelled in the air or on the sea from a ship.

At the end of 1980, Admiral Tsugio Yada, chief of the JMSDF, announced that no more PS-1s were to be procured as the ASW role performed by the flying boat would in future be fulfilled by the P-3C Orion, and the 31st Squadron took delivery of its 23rd and last Shin Meiwa PS-1 in February 1981 (ironically only six months after the last surviving example of its predecessor, the Kawanishi 'Emily', was returned to Japan from the United States, where it had been stored at the NAS Norfolk, Va, since the end of World War Two, to be put on public display at the Museum of Maritime Science in Tokyo).

An in-flight shot of the Shin Meiwa SS-2, the prototype of the Japanese Maritime Self Defence Force's ASW flying boat, the PS-1. Note the high-lift leading edge slats and magnetic anomaly detection (MAD) stinger mounted at the top of the 'T' tailplane. (Shin Meiwa)

Shin Meiwa US-1, 9072, in service with the 71st Rescue Squadron based at Iwakuni. (A. Heape)

Although the PS-1 has proved to be reliable and relatively mechanically trouble-free in service, it has two disadvantages. The first is its restricted range, with a full payload of less than 1,500 miles (2,400 km), although it is capable of being refuelled at sea or off the many small islands that abound in Japanese waters. The second is that its unique (for a flying boat) STOL capabilities have led to the loss of a number of PS-1s, caused mainly by pilot error. The JMSDF had operated numerous types of amphibians, including the Catalina, Goose and Albatross, since it was established in 1952 and consequently had built up a cadre of experienced marine aircraft pilots. However, the Shin Meiwa was a generation apart from these earlier types, and to land a 32-ton flying boat in sea state 5 — rough sea, waves eight to thirteen feet high (2.4 to 3.9 m) — at a speed of only 45 knots, calls for not only cool judgement but a clear understanding of all its sophisticated high-lift systems. Although a total of six PS-1s had been lost by the end of 1984, not all of them resulted from water operations. For example, on 17 May 1978 the twelth production PS-1 5812, hit some trees on the crest of a hill at Kochi, Shikoku, some 450 miles (725 km) south-west of Tokyo, while en route from Iwakuni to investigate an unidentified submarine off Kochi. All thirteen crew were killed. Then on 26 April 1983 another 5802, crashed during an air show at Yamaguchi while making a low-level pass which resulted in the death of nine crew and the serious injury of five more. Yet another 5803, one of a five ship formation, crashed into the sea 15 miles (25 km) east of Matsuyama after a mid-air collision during a turn, on 27 February 1984, killing all twelve aboard. Following this last accident, all PS-1s and US-1s were temporarily grounded but no obvious mechanical fault was found by the subsequent board of enquiry and the accident was attributed to pilot error. Due to the type's high rate of loss, the second PS-1 unit was never formed.

Six of the JMSDF 31st Squadron's Shin Meiwa PS-1 flying boats standing on their retractable beaching gear at Iwakuni airbase.

Shin Meiwa US-1, 9072, with the tail-markings of the 51st Operational Training Squadron in 1975. (A. Watanabe)

Nevertheless, sixteen surviving Shin Meiwa maritime patrol flying boat, (the first to be delivered having been retired in June 1986 having flown a total of 5,400 hours) continue to carry out round-the-clock operations with the JMSDF in 1987, albeit supplementing a growing fleet of Japanese-built Lockheed P-3C land-based ASW aircraft. With its ability of landing on water to check out sightings, either visual or on radar, the US-1 has an advantage over its land-based rivals and this was graphically illustrated during the intensive searches that took place in Japanese waters for debris and bodies following the shooting down of the Korean Airlines 747 by Soviet fighters over the Sea of Okhotsk in July 1983. During this massive search, the Shin Meiwa flying boats operated alongside their amphibious SAR relatives. By the end of 1986, the 71st Squadron had a total of ten US-1s on strength, which had been produced at the rate of one every two years since 1980, with another due to be delivered during 1987. In the SAR role, the US-1 normally carries a crew of eight comprising pilot, co-pilot, flight engineer, navigator, radar operator, radio/telex operator and two observers. The crew can be augmented by two to three air medics or rescue divers as required. There is canvas seating for up to twenty survivors or space for twelve stretcher cases. For medevac flights, a total of 36 stretchers can be carried plus up to five medical attendants. The US-1 is fitted with Sutton AN/APS-80N nose-mounted search radar and the navigation equipment includes Loran A and C, and Doppler radar. An HPN-101B wave-measuring height meter provides an accurate indicator of sea conditions when landing on water.

A Shin Meiwa US-1A SAR amphibian of the 71st Squadron, 9078, tests its uprated Ishikawajima-built General Electric T64-IHI-10J turboprops at Gifu in October 1983. (A. Heape)

The comprehensive rescue kit carried on boa[r]
includes a marker launcher, parachute flar[e]
rescue line launcher, camera and gyrosco[p]
binoculars, two droppable life-raft containe[rs]
three lifebuoys, portable ladder, inflatable ran[p]
and a six-man inflatable dinghy with outboa[rd]
motor and transceiver. A rescue hoist is fitted abo[ve]
the rear rescue hatch, which has a sliding upp[er]
door that may be opened at speeds up to 138 m[ph]
(222 km/h), and through which the floating ramp [is]
deployed. Aft of the door is a fin-mount[ed]
loadspeaker which can be used to communica[te]
with survivors or rescue crews in the water.

The 71st Squadron's first rescue occurred with[in]
two weeks of its formation when a US-1 took [an]
injured seaman off a Greek merchant ship lying 3[50]
miles (563 km) off the Japanese coast and, by 198[4]
seven aircraft had been responsible for the saving [of]
some 170 lives, six of which were picked up mo[re]
than 1,000 miles (1,600 km) from Iwakuni. As [a]
matter of course, one of the amphibians is regular[ly]
detached to the tiny island of Iwo Jima, situat[ed]
nearly 800 miles (1,300 km) south-east of Iwaku[ni]
which is largely barren except for an 8,000 ft (2,4[40]
m) runway, while a permanent detachment of thr[ee]
US-1s has been based at Atsugi on the shores [of]
Tokyo Bay since 1981.

A typical US-1 search and rescue mission enta[ils]
an outbound flight to the search area of up to 1,0[00]
miles (1,600 km) flying between 10 and 15,000[ ]
(3,000-4,500 m) at a speed of 230 knots, while t[he]
search pattern in the area, at which a six-hour loit[er]
is possible at a distance of 690 miles (1,110 km) [or]
2½ hours at 1,150 miles (1,850 km), is flown at 1,0[00]
ft (300 m) and at a speed of 175 knots using only tw[o]
engines. For a water landing at maximum weig[ht]
(94,800 lb 143,000 kg), fifty per cent flap, wi[th]
boundary layer control on, is used to give a landir[g]
speed of 64 knots using 950 ft (290 m) of water. [At]
the lower weight of 79,400 lb (36,016 kg), sixty p[er]
cent flap and BLC on reduces speed and distance [to]
55 knots and 720 ft (220 m).

Commander Sukehiro Ohya, Commandi[ng]
Officer of the 71st Air Rescue Squadron, explai[ns]
the different rescue methods employed by the US[-1]
crews. 'At the rescue scene, we drop various resc[ue]
kits to the airmen or seamen in distress. Then if s[ea]
conditions permit, we land and implement one [of]
three rescue techniques.

'The first, after a water landing, we dispatch a[n]
outboard motor boat with rescue scuba divers an[d]
medical crew on board to pick up the survivors. T[he]
boat has a nine-person capacity.

'The second, after a water landing, one scu[ba]
diver attached to a lifeline dives into the sea an[d]
then swims to the survivor to pick him up.

'The third, we use the lifeline launcher. After t[he]
water landing, we launch a lifeline at the survivor[']
lifeboat to pick them up.'

Apart from taking part in actual rescue missio[ns]
the US-1s frequently act as a relay for other vessel[s]
such as ships on call to another in distress, an[d]
assist by dropping life-rafts or ferrying medic[al]
personnel and supplies to isolated communities o[r]
isolated islands without an airstrip as well as flyin[g]
out emergency patients to mainland hospitals.

None of the US-1 amphibians, which a[re]
maintained by Aircraft Maintenance Squadron 3[1]
at Iwakuni along with the PS-1 flying boats, hav[e]

The first Shin Meiwa SS-2 STOL flying boat, 5801, taking off
from Kobe in 1971 with the aid of its sophisticated 'blown' flaps
and tailplane. This aircraft was later converted into a water-
bomber capable of scooping and dropping 8 tons of water.
(Shin Meiwa)

en lost to date, and the last four to be delivered
re fitted with the more powerful T64 turboprops
ed at 3,490 hp and known as US-1As. Already
ssessing a STOL capability that enables it to
erate from 2,500 ft (760 m) airstrips, the
reased power has added to the amphibian's
xibility and the aircraft now undertakes a
mber of varied roles including those of fishery
otection patrols, pollution monitoring and ship
upply. Stripped of its SAR equipment, the US-1
capable of carrying up to 115 troops.
Apart from Shin Meiwa's projected commercial
ssenger/cargo transport versions of the SS-2A, a
ter bomber version of the flying boat has been
veloped for Japan's National Fire Protection
ard with the capability of scooping up water
ile skimming the surface of rivers, lakes and
eltered seas for airborne fire-fighting operations.
e first PS-1 prototype was converted to a large
pacity water bomber, making its first flight as
ch on 17 May 1976, able to carry eight tons of
ter, although the tanks have been designed to
uble this capacity. Using a similar scooping
tem to that used on the Canadair CL-215, the
-1 fire-bomber was designed to cope with large
es caused by earthquakes in metropolitan areas
well as forest and brush fires, ship fires and blazes
oil refineries. However, the comparatively small
oduction runs of these complex aircraft make
em very expensive to purchase and no orders for
s version have materialised to date, although it is
t inconceivable that converted ex-JMSDF Shin
eiwa PS-1s might be used to replace the Canadian
et of veteran Martin Mars fire-fighting flying
ats by the end of the century.

The first Shin Meiwa US-1 SAR amphibian, 9071, which flew for
the first time in October 1974, is assigned to the 71st Squadron of
the 31st Air Group based at Iwakuni, seen here taxiing in
choppy seas. (JMSDF)

There may be a potential market for retired Shin Meiwas in the civil sector following a bid for the recently retired first production PS-1 flying boat by a group of British pilots and aviation specialists in August 1986, who plan to operate a flying boat service between Britain and the British island of St Helena in the South Atlantic. The group, called the St Helena Aviation Development Group, plans to run a scheduled fortnightly service to St Helena, amongst other destinations, a distance of 5,000 miles (8,000 km). The island has no airstrip and its 5,000 inhabitants rely on a British government subsidised cargo ship calling four times a year for transport, essential supplies and contact with the outside world. The only threat to this ambitious venture is that the Japanese government has yet to make up its mind as to whether it is able to approve the sale of a military aircraft, albeit without its ASW equipment, to a commercial group.

Although a number of countries have shown interest in acquiring the US-1 (the People's Republic of China making an in-depth study of the amphibian in 1975, for example), no firm orders have been placed, cost again being the main factor. Apart from the possibility of further one-off orders from the JMSDF, total production of the Shin Meiwa boats is thus unlikely to exceed forty aircraft.

Shin Meiwa have made a bold attempt to take flying boat/amphibian technology into the 21st century, and although in retrospect it may have been wrong to concentrate on a large ASW aircraft, it is to be hoped that the wealth of experience that the company has built up since embarking on its flying boat programme will not be wasted in the future.

Shin Meiwa PS-1

Accommodation:	Crew: 10
Power Plants:	Four 3,060 ehp Ishikawajima-built General Electric T64-1H1-10E turboprops
Dimensions:	Wingspan: 108 ft 9 in (33.15 m)
	Length: 109 ft 9 in (33.45 m)
	Height: 31 ft 10½ in (9.7 m)
	Wing area: 1,462 sq ft (136 m²)
Weights:	Empty: 56,218 lb (25,500 kg)
	Average: 99,208 lb (45,000 kg)
Performance:	Max speed: 340 mph (547 km/h)
	Patrol speed: 266 mph (428 km/h)
	Patrol range: 1,347 miles (2,167 km)
	Ferry range: 2,948 miles (4,743 km)

Shin Meiwa US-1A

Accommodation:	Crew: 9-12
Power Plants:	Four 3,490 ehp Ishikawajima-built General Electric T64-1H1-10J turboprops
Dimensions:	Wingspan: 108 ft 9 in (33.15 m)
	Length: 109 ft 9 in (33.45 m)
	Height: 32 ft 7½ in (9.94 m)
	Wing area: 1,462 sq ft (136 m²)
Weights:	Empty: 51,400 lb (23,315 kg)
	Average: 99,208 lb (45,000 kg)
Performance:	Max speed: 324 mph (521 km/h)
	Patrol speed: 266 mph (428 km/h)
	Max range: 2,371 miles (3,815 km)

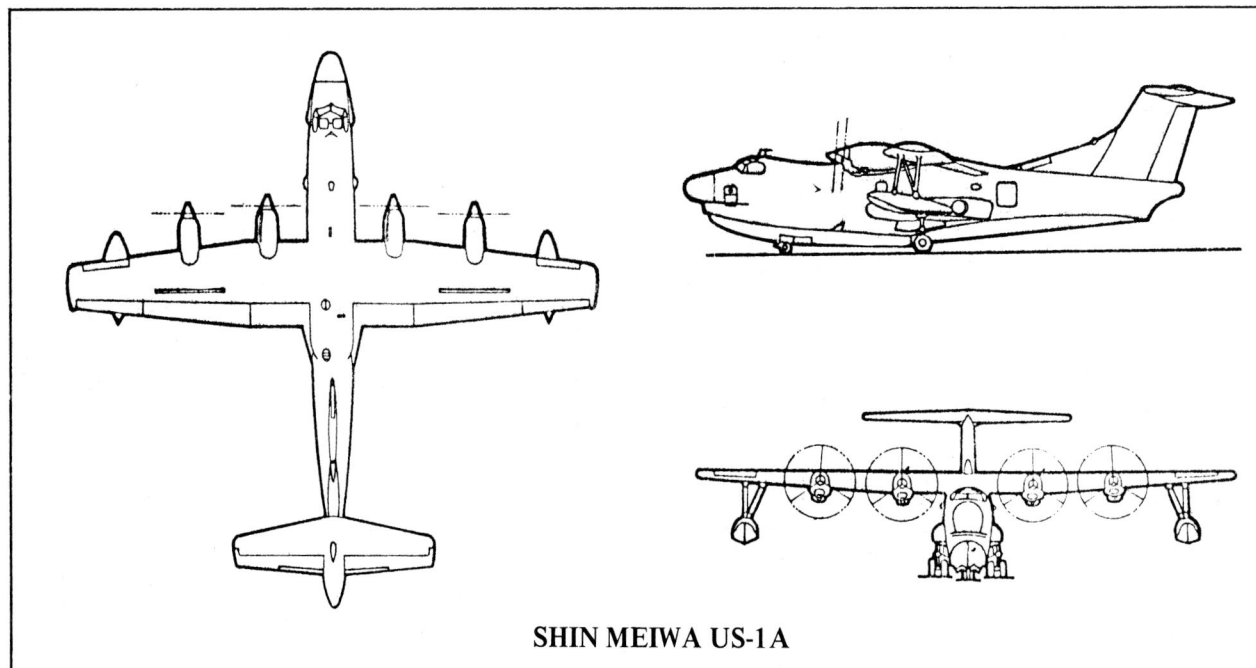

SHIN MEIWA US-1A

CHAPTER TWELVE
THE FUTURE

By the beginning of the 1980s only two nations remained actively involved in the manufacture of multi-engined amphibious flying boats, Canada and Japan, although single-engined types, such as the Lake Buccaneer, were still being produced in the USA.

Although the United States' principal marine aircraft manufacturer, Grumman, had not produced an amphibian for nearly thirty years, the company continued to maintain an Advanced Concepts Division that carried out studies of the latest developments in waterborne operations. These included the projected four-turboprop Super Albatross and the possible licence production of a commercial version of the Shin Meiwa PX-S flying boat in the 1970s, while in 1979, the Grumman Corporation announced that it was studying the possible manufacture of a high-productivity twin-engine commercial amphibian for the 1980s known as 'Design 711'.

The Grumman Design 711 offered a number of power plant options including the Continental GTS10-520 and Lycoming TIGD-540 piston engines, the AiResearch TPE-331, Lycoming LTP-101 and the P&W PT6A-10 turboprops. A corrosion-resistant glass fibre hull, whose lines resembled that of the Mallard, plus retractable tricycle undercarriage and wingtip floats would be fitted. With a projected wing-span of 59 ft (18 m), length of 39 ft (11.9 m) and height of 16 ft (4.9 m), the 8,000 lb (3,629 kg) aircraft could accommodate nine passengers and a pilot and cruise at 200 mph (322 km/h), putting it firmly in the Goose category. Configured for cargo, the 711 could carry a payload of up to 1,675 lb (760 kg), while range was to be between 250 and 900 miles (400-1,450 km) depending on the load. Wind tunnel tests confirmed analytical predictions of the 711's performance and flying qualities.

In 1979, the Grumman Corporation announced a new amphibian project, 'Design 711' which was planned to replace the numerous Grumman Gooses, Widgeons and Mallards in the 1980s. However the project progressed no further than wind-tunnel models as illustrated. (Grumman)

Grumman showed preliminary studies of four designs to amphibian pilots, owners, operators and maintenance experts throughout the United States, Canada and the Caribbean before settling on the final high-wing, twin-engined design. The 'Design 711' incorporated the latest lighter and stronger corrosion-resistant materials, improved avionics and power plants, more efficient aircraft interiors and improved handling qualities, both in the air and on the water. For one reason or another, possibly due to the fact that more than 100 Widgeons, Gooses and Mallards were still commercially active in the 1980s, 'Design 711' progressed no further than a wind tunnel model.

Another experienced flying boat manufacturer who has retained an active interest in marine aircraft over the years is Dornier GmbH of Munich. At the 30th Paris Salon of 1973, the German manufacturer had displayed a model of the Dornier Do 72, a turboprop-powered search and rescue amphibian development of the pre-war Do 24 flying boat. In 1981 the company won a DM 36 million contract from the Federal German Ministry of Research and Technology for a three-year research and development programme to study the design of a new amphibious flying boat.

Various systems and project studies relating to amphibian flying boats had been made by Dornier over the past years based on experience of their earlier designs including the Do 15 Wal, the Do 18 and in particular the Do 24. The Dornier Do 24, which was orginally developed for the Dutch government in 1938, had demonstrated outstanding seaworthiness on countless air-sea rescue missions with the Luftwaffe during World War Two and with the Spanish Air Force (which operated Do 24T-3 flying boats from Puerto Pollensa in Majorca on SAR duties until the early 1970s). It was one of the ex-Spanish aircraft that was chosen to be the basis of a research prototype for the contract, designated the Do 24 TT (Technology Testbed). The aims and objects of the programme were to test improved high-seas capability for the Do 24 TT compared with presently known flying boats; operational flexibility deriving from the amphibian configuration; improved STOL characteristics; improvements to performance and economy compared with earlier amphibians; an advanced technology wing of simple construction to reduce manufacturing costs; and up-to-date turboprop engines for operations at sea.

The definition phase for the Do 24 TT amphibian Technology Testbed began in April 1979 and was completed in June 1980. The likely roles for a new-technology amphibian had been established as those of maritime surveillance, search and rescue, passenger and cargo transportation, oceanographic research, water bombing and casualty evacuation.

The results of the extensive design studies led to the test aircraft's eventual configuration. With the exception of the original Do 24 hull and twin-finned tailplane, the TT's major design features consisted of a strutted cabane-type high-wing monoplane with a rectangular new Technology Wing with triangular tips similar to that designed for the Dornier Do 228 commuter airliner. Power was provided by three 1,125 shp P&W PT6A-45B turboprops in place of the original 1,000 hp BMW

radials. Stabilisation on the water was provided by sponsons adapted from the original design while they and the V-shaped bow and flat hull underside with two steps was covered with glass fibre panels to evaluate corrosion resistance. A retractable tricycle undercarriage, taken from the Dornier Do 31E (an experimental military vertical take off [VTOL] tactical transport dating back to the mid-1960s), was fitted to the flying boat. The Do 24 TT was completed at the end of March 1983 and following a series of tests and taxying trials, the first flight took place at Dornier's Oberpfaffenhofen airfield on the evening of 25 April.

That first flight, which lasted more than one hour, was made by Dornier Chief Test Pilot Dieter Thomas and his co-pilot Meinhard Feuersenger and went off without a hitch. During the next sixteen months the Dornier Technology Testbed carried out a series of detailed test flights which included 85 hours of landing tests, approximately twenty hours of inland seas testing and some fifteen hours of high seas trials in the Baltic. At the conclusion of the programme, during which the aircraft performed faultlessly throughout, no immediate decision was reached as to the commercial viability of putting a high-technology flying boat into production. The market forecast for such an aircraft was estimated to be 350, but an amphibious version of the high-wing Do-228 landplane may be considered in the future.

One of the driving forces behind Dornier GmbH until his retirement, was Professor Dipl-Ing Claudius Dornier, a long-time proponent of the flying boat, who had also been considering the feasibility of producing a modern flying boat using the latest technology. At the 1983 Paris Air Show, 68-year-old Claudius Dornier unveiled his latest design, the Seastar, that bore more than a passing resemblance to the pre-war Dornier Wal flying boat. The Seastar was a twin-engined lightweight ten-passenger amphibian with STOL capability, a cruising speed of 200 mph (320 km/h) and a range of 700 (1,125 km) miles — very similar in specification and performance to Grumman's 'Design 711'. However, the Seastar differed from the American design in a number of respects. It was to be very much lighter in weight, due to extensive use of composite materials in the hull — the strength of which would make it capable of operating from grass, water, snow and ice — and its two 500 shp Pratt & Whitney Canada PT6A-11 turboprops driving three-bladed constant speed propellers were fitted in tandem, similar to the pre-war Claudius Dornier-designed Wal and Do 18. The main panels of the high-mounted wing were standard Dornier Do 27 components, and stability on water was provided by Dornier-type sponsons into which the main-wheels of the tricycle undercarriage retracted. It also featured a large upward-hinging freight loading door in the aft portside of the hull.

To prove that his design was practicable, Claudius Dornier built a ⅕th scale model of the Seastar which was used for preliminary testing on Lake Constance. These trials proved successful enough for him to begin the construction of a full-scale Seastar prototype in the latter part of 1983. This was assembled in a Lufthansa hangar at Hamburg Airport by half a dozen airline technicians working under the supervision of four C. Dornier GmbH personnel and was completed in less than a year. The Seastar's first flight took place on 17 August 1984 and went without problem. Flight testing continued on schedule and water-handling trials, carried out in the Baltic Sea near Kiel, were completed by February 1985. At this time certification was envisaged by the end of 1986 with full scale production commencing the following year.

The centreline thrust concept of the tandem-mounted PT6 turboprops gave the amphibian excellent directional stability in the air and on the water while the combination of the high-lift wing with fixed leading-edge slots and large-area trailing-edge flaps enabled the Seastar to achieve its projected STOL performance with ease.

Although much smaller than the Do 24 TT, the Seastar was aimed at similar roles, namely cargo and passenger transport, maritime surveillance, search and rescue, casualty evacuation, oceanographic research and offshore patrol, for which it had been estimated that there would be a world market for some 300 in the first ten years of production.

On the eve of the Seastar's first public appearance at the 1985 Paris Air Show, Claudius Dornier announced that construction of a second, and larger, prototype, with a maximum take-off weight increased from 8,855 lb to 9,240 lb (4,016 to 4,190 kg) and seating for twelve passengers, was to begin in the New Year — so confirming the initial confidence that its designer had had in the new amphibian. However, the first prototype had already suffered a heavy landing while en route to the Paris Air Show, which restricted its flying programme, and six weeks later on 24 July 1985, the Seastar was damaged beyond repair due to pilot error when it landed on Lake Constantine near Friedrichshafen with its wheels down.

Although this was a severe setback to the programme, Professor Dornier was able to confirm that construction of the second prototype had begun at Dornier's Oberpfaffenhofen airfield by April of 1986 but only two months later the Seastar project suffered a second, and potentially more serious blow, with the sudden death of the veteran designer who was the moving force behind the venture. Not only was the whole future of the Seastar put in jeopardy but the flying boat had lost one of its most passionate supporters, a man who had continued to advocate the use of boats of various sizes capable of undertaking many diverse roles — such as a giant 1,000-ton flying boat powered by ten turbojets using special pre-fabricated docking facilities to support NATO forces in Europe.

However, the project was taken over by Claudius Dornier's two sons, Camilo and Conrado, and final assembly of the second prototype, which featured an all new glass and carbon fibre composite wing, the largest ever built, continued around the clock at Oberpfaffenhofen. The all-composite Seastar made its maiden flight in April 1987 in the hands of company' chief test pilot, Alfred Lauf.

Another veteran designer whose ideas on the future of the flying boat were closely akin to those of Professor Dornier's but seen from the other side of the Iron Curtain, was Georgii Mikhailovich

Following his retirement from Dornier GmbH, the designer of the original Do 24, Professor Dipl-Ing Claudius Dornier announced the development of a light utility amphibious flying boat, the Seastar. The ten-seat amphibian, built largely of composite materials, was powered by two PT6A turboprops fitted in tandem and was assembled in a Lufthansa hangar at Hamburg and flew for the first time on 17 August 1984.

When the Spanish Air Force retired the last of its 1944 vintage Dornier Do 24T-3 air-sea rescue flying boats in 1971, one of them was used as the basis for Dornier's high-technology amphibian test-bed, the Do 24TT, while another, the one illustrated, was presented to the RAF Museum at Hendon. (D. Oliver)

Beriev who announced as long ago as the mid-1960s plans for a long-range flying boat weighing roughly four times as much as a Boeing B-52 bomber and carrying no less than two thousand passengers/troops. However the Soviet Union has until recently always lagged behind the West in the design and manufacture of large turbojets and powerful commercial turbofans needed in particular to power wide-bodied airliners and freighter, thus preventing Beriev's flying boat projects from progressing any further than the drawing board. In 1967 the Beriev bureau designed its first landplane for more than thirty years, the Be-30, a short-range commercial feederliner, but despite the fact that no flying boat has been produced in the Soviet Union since the last Be-12 was completed in the mid-1970s, it would not be inconceivable that a new Beriev flying boat, possibly an amphibious development of the existing turboprop landplane, may make an appearance before the end of the century.

Meanwhile two such landplane development concepts are being studied actively in Italy. In March 1982, the SIAI-Marchetti company, which had a long tradition of flying boat construction dating back to the 1920s, announced that an amphibious version of its Canguro (Kangaroo) feeder liner, the S700 Cormorano (Cormorant) was under consideration. The company's SF600TP Canguro is a light general utility transport that has accommodation for a crew of two and nine passengers but will be available in a variety of internal options ranging from a maritime surveillance variant through an aeromedical version that could accommodate four stretcher patients and two medical attendants to a military transport version able to carry twelve paratroops. It is powered by two 420 shp Allison 250-B17C turboprops giving it a cruising speed of 190 mph (305 km/h) and a normal range of 982 miles (1,580 km). The S700 amphibian would incorporate the wings, tailplane and upper fuselage of the SF600 landplane with a Kevlar and carbon-fibre reinforced hull built on to the bottom while the engines, which would be two 580 hp Alfa Romeo AR 318 turboprops, would be installed above the wing rather than below it as on the landplane. The SF600 has small winglets into which the undercarriage retracts and these could be easily extended to form Dornier-type stabilising sponsons. The amphibious Cormorano would be able to carry out similar tasks to the Canguro plus those of fire-fighting and SAR. The extra power provided by the Alfa Romeo turboprops would more than compensate for the additional weight of the composite hull bottom, to put the S700 in direct competition with the Dornier Seastar. However, since SIAI-Marchetti became a subsidiary of Agusta SpA, the project has been slowed down but as there is obviously a substantial world market, predicted by SIAI-Marchetti in 1983 to be 430 in fifteen years for a ten to twelve passenger twin turboprop amphibian, that it can only be a matter of time before construction of a prototype S700 begins in earnest.

The second of the current Italian studies is a much more ambitious venture that is an offshoot of the Franco/Italian ATR 42 regional airliner. This aircraft was developed jointly by Aérospatiale of France and Aeritalia of Italy on a fifty/fifty basis.

he fifty-seat commuter airliner, powered by two ,800 hp Pratt & Whitney Canada PW120 urboprops enabling it to cruise at 320 mph (515 m/h) over a range of 1,094 miles (1,760 km), first lew in the summer of 1985, with deliveries to Italy's ational airline, Alitalia, beginning a year later. As vith the SIAI-Marchetti SF-600TP, military ransport and maritime patrol variants of the andplane are being developed.

A study of the feasibility of producing an mphibious version was announced by Aeritalia in November 1985. Known as the AIT 460, it would be . wholly Italian development to be constructed in xactly the same way as the proposed Cormorano mphibian — by attaching a composite planing 'ottom on to the existing fuselage, extending the undercarriage bulges to form stabilising sponsons, etaining the landplane's tailplane and fitting a pair f uprated PW120 turboprops high on the existing ving. A large proportion of the latter is already onstructed of corrosive-resistant carbon-fibre and Kevlar materials. Aeritalia forecast the market for uch an amphibian, provisionally planned to seat ıp to 46 passengers, as being between fifty and a undred based on a fifteen-year production cycle. It emains to be seen whether the sophisticated AIT 460 can be produced at a realistic price that ommercial operators could afford.

Aeritalia will also have to take into account the ompetition that will undoubtedly come from Canadair which plans to have its own turboprop-owered amphibian in full production by the late .980s, well before any proposed launch date of the AIT 460.

Having decided to go ahead with the CL-215T programme in November 1986, Canadair wasted 10 time in spelling out the advantages of the urboprop version of their proven CL-215 over the current piston engine version, as well as any ootential competitors in the same class. According o Canadair's market research, the demand for modern amphibians in the latter part of the 20th century is strengthening due to their operating ersatility compared with land-based aircraft, oerformance and cost advantage over large ıelicopters and low infrastructure costs of ransport systems by the use of inexpensive ımphiports.

The Canadian company's own market forecast or the CL-215T is for between 180 and 200 sales in he first fifteen years, a figure that does not take into ıccount any future sales of the piston version. The hree key markets identified for the new aircraft emain civil and environmental protection, which ncludes fire-fighting, aerial spraying, SAR and naritime reconnaissance; defence, for ASV, ASW ınd special forces transport; and transport, commercial passenger and cargo transport.

Two variants of the Pratt & Whitney Canada PW 20 turboprop, both rated at 2,000 shp, are offered ıs power plants for the CL-215T. The 100/47 version would meet current requirements of most North American and European operators, while the 100/37 'hot and high' model would be an option for Asian and Latin American countries. Turboprop retrofit kits would be available to existing piston CL-215 operators from 1989. The airframe of the CL-215T would remain virtually unchanged from the current production series, ıpart from an enlarged fin and rudder, but would

The Dornier Do 24TT used the hull of an ex-Spanish Air Force Do 24T-3, with a New Technology Wing (TNT) similar to that used for the Do 228 light regional airliner, revised stabilization sponsons and tricyle undercarriage while three 1,125 shp Pratt & Whitney Canada PT6A-45B turboprops replaced the original 1,000 hp BMW radial powerplants. (Dornier)

After more than a year of flight trials and high-sea trials in the Baltic Sea, the Dornier Do 24TT seen here taking off from the water at Kiel, retired for the second time. Despite the successful outcome of the programme no decision has yet been made by Dornier to develop a production version of the amphibian (Dornier)

feature improved corrosion resistance, improved cockpit controls and instrumentation, and a steerable nosewheel. Limited power controls, colour weather radar, Omega navigation system, larger capacity water tanks and air conditioning would be optional extras.

Performance improvements over the piston version projected for the CL-215T are impressive: 37 per cent more payload, 33 per cent more speed and 32 per cent more range, while the figures for fire-fighting missions are even better. In ten seconds, the CL-215T will scoop more than 1,400 US gallons of water and, with fifteen per cent less circuit time, average drops can be increased to more than seven per hour. Since the amphibian would be capable of working fires for nearly five hours without refuelling, total mission drops could be as many as 33 without a pause. The turboprop fire-fighting aircraft will feature drop pattern modifications and drop door sequencing to improve productivity.

Maritime reconnaissance and SAR variants will have underwing hardpoints and pylons for long-range fuel tanks, stores and other payloads, and with the turboprop's extra power and reverse pitch propellers, which will shorten take-off and landing distances on water, the CL-215T should be able to operate on a year-round basis for 96 per cent of the time in the Mediterranean, 86 per cent of the time in the Bay of Biscay and 80 per cent of the time in the Atlantic.

The CL-215T will also be more efficient at moving people and cargo — the equivalent of 35 passengers or 6,600 lb (3,000 kg) of cargo — up to 1,000 miles (1,600 km) with full fuel reserves. It is designed to climb more quickly to an economic cruising height giving the 'T' a long-range cruising speed of nearly 200 mph (320 km/h), all of which adds up to an attractive package for the commercial operator, and by the date of the programme launch the manufacturer reported serious initial interest from a number of European airlines, in Italy and Holland in particular.

The proposed CL-215T programme schedule is for the first prototype to fly in May 1988, with certification a year later and the first customer delivery in April 1989, at a provisional (1985) price of US $7.75 million. Planned delivery rate of new aircraft, and retrofit kits, is between one and 2.2 per month according to demand. France, Spain and the Provisional government of Quebec who, at the time of writing, operate 58 piston CL-215 amphibians between them, have been identified as launch customers. With a proven airframe, reliable fuel-efficient state-of-the-art turboprops, a serious commitment to long-term support and development, and a healthy record of satisfied customers, the turboprop development of Canadair's versatile amphibian would seem to quarantee the survival of the species for the foreseeable future.

One of only two other companies still building flying boats in the late 1980s, apart from Canadair, is the Japanese manufacturer, Shin Meiwa. For the past ten years the Shin Meiwa Industry Co Ltd, in conjunction with the Society of Japanese Aerospace Companies, has been carrying out studies into the possibility of developing a new transportation system using amphibious aircraft.

An artist's impression of a military variant of the Canadair CL-215T amphibian to be powered by two P&W PW100 turboprops to give additional speed, payload and endurance. (Canadair)

he ultimate goal of this ambitious project is to
pen routes to isolated islands and regional cities
hich are off the major air routes, and where the
onstruction of conventional airports would be
ifficult and prohibitively expensive.

The Japanese Agency of Industrial Science and
echnology has been carrying out a technological
ssessment to determine the social impact of
mplementing such a system while Shin Meiwa have
repared designs for a number of new flying boat
rojects which would become an integral part of
uch a system, in order to capitalise on its expertise
n this field. Four of these concepts were a thirty-to
fty-passenger jet-powered amphibious feeder-
ner, a 250-seat and a 400-seat amphibians
owered by four turbofans and, shades of Georgii
eriev and Claudius Dornier, a giant 1,200-seat
ong-haul commercial flying boat. The most
dvanced of these projects is the amphibious
eeder-liner, known as the SS-X, which has reached
he point where wind-tunnel testing has begun and
etailed specifications released.

These are for a STOL amphibian with a
aximum take-off weight of 17½ tons equipped to
arry a crew of three (pilot, co-pilot and flight
ttendant) and forty passengers. It would be
owered by two advanced turbofans of about 8,000
(3,630 kg) thrust, such as the General Electric
F34 or Avco Lycoming ALF 502, positioned high
nd forward on a straight wing that utilises USB
pper surface blowing) flaps on the trailing edge,
poilers and high-lift leading-edge flaps. The
ailplane is T-mounted to be clear of the jet exhaust
nd water spray and all tail control surfaces are
ouble hinged. Stabilising wing floats would be
on-retractable for simplicity as well as cost and
eight saving.

With emphasis being placed on low development
osts, the structure would be conventional although
omposite components would be used to some
xtent. Empty weight would be 25,005 lb (11,342
g), maximum take-off weight 38,588 lb (17,500
g), economical cruising speed 348 mph (560
m/h), range with forty passengers to be 510 miles
820 km) with a maximum range of 1,195 miles
1,923 km). The SS-X amphibian's take-off run on
ater would be 886 ft (270 m) while the landing run
n water would be no more than 689 ft (210 m). It
hould be able to operate in a wave height of five
eet (1.5 m) (sea state 3). Again, the Shin Meiwa SS-
is planned to undertake the tasks that have now
ecome identified as those being particularly
pplicable to the modern flying boat concept,
hich apart from transporting passengers and
argo, include search and rescue, maritime
urveillance, oceanographic research, etc.

However, the Japanese studies of a new
mphibious Air Transport System go much further
han any other embarked upon in the last 25 years.
hin Meiwa's SS-X is only one component of the
ompany's overall concept that encompasses the
o-operation of all manufacturers who have any
nterest in the future of flying boat operations. In
ugust 1985, the Japanese government invited
rumman and Canadair to join Shin Meiwa's SS-X
roject, the research programme having already
een joined by Dornier and the Indonesian State
erospace company Nuritanio, in the hope that
uch an aircraft may become an international

An artist's impression of the projected Shin Meiwa SS-X, a 40-
passenger jet-powered STOL amphibious feeder-liner which is
under study by Dornier and the Indonesian aerospace company,
Nurtanio.

An artist's impression of Canadair's commercial turboprop-
powered development of its successful CL-215 amphibian due to
make its first flight in May 1988. (Canadair)

The Seastar CD2, a 14-seat light utility amphibian with a corrosion resistant composite hull and one-piece glassfibre wing, made its first water take-off at Kiel on 20 May 1987. (Claudius Dornier GmbH)

collaborative venture with guaranteed sales in at least five countries. Shin Meiwa forecasts a total market for amphibians over the next fifteen years of between 800 and 1,000, mainly in the transport role, which may seem over-optimistic but the most important aspect of the Japanese Amphibious Air Transport System is not the aircraft but the infrastructure in which they operate and the use of inexpensive amphiports.

Over the past forty years, commercial flying boat operations have failed largely because of the lack of, or the expense of, landing facilities for marine aircraft. Unless a practical answer is found to these problems they will fail again in the future. Canadair and Shin Meiwa, in particular, are actively promoting the establishment of low cost amphiports with integrated Air Traffic Control systems and navigation aids. These include beacons, precise sea state measuring equipment, compact microwave landing systems (MLS) to increase the flying boats' all-weather capabilities and, perhaps one of the most important features, night operations. Landing a flying boat on water at night, particularly in flat calm conditions when height is especially difficult to judge accurately using the Mk 1 eyeball, has in the past been something only attempted in emergencies. With the advent of the latest state-of-the-art altimeters that give precise readings down to the last foot, and with the development of laser lighting that can be simply moved to point downwind by remote control from an amphiport, it will become no more difficult than landing on a tarmac runway.

Bad weather and darkness have in the past severely limited flying boat operations, both commercial and military. Costly overnight stops on BOAC's flying routes were one of the main reasons put forward by the corporation for ceasing flying boat operations in 1950. Future amphibious passenger and cargo operators should be able to fly to and from amphiports throughout the hours of darkness unhindered by noise restrictions and traffic delays, while fire-fighting aircraft could continue their battle against major outbreaks around the clock.

The Japanese market study for a future generation of flying boats is based on the assumption that there are no geographical locations where they could not operate. Apart from the traditional flying boat strongholds of Malaysia, Indonesia and the West Indies which consist mainly of dozens of small islands, few of which have airstrips, and the west coasts of Canada and Alaska, the confines of large urban cities in the United States, Canada and Europe are also seen to be potential operating areas and amphiport sites. The development of inner city centre STOLports, many built on redundant dock sites such as those in London, Rotterdam and New York, most of which are surrounded by areas of unused waterways that were designed for commercial marine craft, has already shown the way. Where there have been objections from local inhabitants to city centre STOLports, as in London, on the grounds of noise and safety, amphibious aircraft operating from the water would significantly reduce these two factors. Also, by using both land and water runways, the STOLport's utilisation could be increased and cost reduced.

Apart from the British plan to open a flying boat service to the island of St Helena in the South Atlantic, using civilianised Shin Meiwa PS-1s, there are still a number of islands in the Mediterranean, Adriatic and Aegean which are popular tourist centres but have no airfields. These include Formentera in the Balearics, Elba, Capri — which has featured on a number of flying boat routes in the past — and a large percentage of the Greek islands.

Japan has both remote islands, which are frequently subject to natural disasters ranging from hurricanes to earthquakes, the results of which often require rapid response by air from relief organisations, and powerful environmental opposition to the construction of new airports. The opening of Tokyo's new Narita airport was delayed for several years by violent demonstrations, and constant high profile security is required to guard it against possible disruption of services by the same demonstrators. Faced with such determined opposition, along with the ever-increasing cost of land required for even a modest local airport and the government's severe noise restrictions over built-up areas, Japan's study of an alternative air transport system using amphibious aircraft is one of increasing importance.

Japan's monolithic neighbour, the People's Republic of China, surprised the aviation world by announcing at the end of 1986 that it had designed and built a large maritime reconnaissance and ASW amphibian to replace its ageing fleet of Soviet built Beriev Be-6 flying boats.

The Harbin PS-5's deep hull, which resembles the Shin Meiwa PS-1, has a glazed nose surrounding the large radome and twin fins and rudders similar to that of the Beriev Be-12. The wings and powerplants, four 4,200 shp Wojiang WJ-5s, Chinese copies of the Soviet Ivchenco AI-20 turboprops that power the Be-12, are based on those of the Antonov AN-12 heavy transport which is produced in China as the Shaanxi Y-8. The initial production batch of ten PS-5s which features fixed stabilising floats attached to 'V' struts and a Shin Meiwa inspired single-wheel retractable beaching gear, has a wing span of some 125 ft making it the largest flying boat since the handsome but troubled Convair Tradewind of the 1950s and its development will be watched with interest.

In the meantime, while the amphibian's fire-fighting role will continue to expand, oil and gas exploration is on the decline and the amphibious flying boat, with its greater payload and range, may well replace the expensive helicopter as the prime oil support craft in many parts of the world in the near future. At the same time, as more and more countries extend the Exclusive Economic Zone (EEZ) around their coasts, the market for inshore maritime patrol aircraft has increased sharply while at the same time the cost of long range ASW and MR aircraft has become prohibitive to all but the super-powers. Canadair took advantage of this situation by offering a MR/SAR version of the CL-15 and the turboprop development of the Canadian amphibian looks set to increase its share of this growing market.

As for the future of the military flying boat, given the recent emphasis on the development of runway denial weapons, by both the East and West, and the

The one-piece composite wing of the second Claudius Dornier Seastar prototype, the largest made to date, being tested to the equivalent of 90,000 hr at the IABG Ottobrunn test centre.
(Claudius Dornier)

outbreaks of serious conflicts in remote areas far away from North America or Europe (such as the South Atlantic and, to a lesser extent, the Seychelles and New Caledonia), the giant troop transport flying boats envisioned by Georgii Beriev, Claudius Dornier and Shizuo Kikuhara may yet become a reality. It is more likely, though, that the main defence applications of the amphibious flying boat will remain those of maritime reconnaissance, anti-submarine warfare and special forces transport.

The following announcement was published in the aviation press by one prominent flying boat manufacturer:

'The modern flying boat can operate from any natural stretch of water, in any weather that a landplane can cope with. Its runways and taxy-tracks are free — and bomb-proof. And while landplane size is already nearly at the feasible limit, due to prohibitive runway costs, the flying boat can be as big as military and operational requirements demand. Its runways will still be at hand. Its base facilities will still be available at a fraction of the cost of a landplane layout.

'It will be able to refuel and re-arm from ships in the open ocean, in conditions hitherto impossible.

'Its flexibility is unchallenged. The squadron of tomorrow (it should be today), equipped with its own flying maintenance men, its own inflatable sectional pontoons, could take off, fly to the other side of the world, establish its own base and operate independently. This same flexibility could be applied to the immediate transport of troops to almost any area where armed aid is urgent. Servicing is relatively easy, with new and up-to-date methods. The flying boat has no heavy undercarriage mechanism and needs to come out of the water only occasionally. Routine maintenance can be done afloat.

'What is your verdict? Do you think we are wise to neglect this fine defensive weapon?'

The manufacturer was Saunders Roe, and the date of the announcement 1956. Since that date the flying boat has survived, if not flourished, but its true worth is only now being recognised and the type's development over the next forty years will ensure the preservation of the species.

$275.00

W9-BDM-175

06-27156

THE BIG BOOK

OF LIBRARY GRANT MONEY

2006

Profiles of Private and Corporate Foundations
and Direct Corporate Givers Receptive
to Library Grant Proposals

PREPARED BY

Taft®

FOR THE

American Library Association

AMERICAN LIBRARY ASSOCIATION
Chicago   2006

The Big Book of Library Grant Money, 2006

LIBRARY OF CONGRESS CATALOGING-IN-PUBLICATION DATA

ISBN 0-8389-3558-3
ISSN 1086-0568

Printed in the United States of America
10 9 8 7 6 5 4 3 2 1

The Big Book of Library Grant Money 2006 provides detailed descriptive profiles of nearly 2,400 philanthropic programs in the United States—programs associated with private foundations, corporate foundations, and corporate direct givers. All of the funders in this directory have either made grants to libraries within the last few reporting periods or have listed libraries as a typical recipient category on their questionnaires returned to Taft. *The Big Book* provides fund raisers and researchers with quick and convenient access to important information on the major U.S. funding organizations supporting libraries.

The Big Book of Library Grant Money includes current data on over 1,730 of the top private foundations, those with assets or grant distributions of at least $100,000. Interfiled with these major private foundations are 515 corporate foundations and nearly 120 hard-to-find direct corporate givers. Collectively, the funders profiled in this edition awarded nearly $11.7 billion during their most recent reporting period to support libraries and other nonprofit organizations.

The directory excludes funders that do not accept unsolicited requests for funds and those funders that give to only preselected recipients. All of the funders included will consider unsolicited proposals.

Content and Arrangement

The funders are arranged alphabetically by the name of the foundation or by the name of the corporation sponsoring the foundation or direct giving program. Foundations named after family members are listed alphabetically by family name. For instance, the Theodore H. Barth Foundation appears alphabetically under "Barth." For corporation names and corporate foundations that are personal names, the user is advised to located a company first by surname, and if unsuccessful, to try the first element in the name.

Giving profiles are as detailed as permitted by the information available. Contents of a profile can include:

- Foundation name or sponsoring company name and corporate foundation name, if applicable
- Corporate contact information

- Corporate profile information—financial figures, number of employees, parent company, former name(s), SIC(s), Fortune rank, EIN, operating locations, and subsidiary companies
- Giving contact information
- Foundation profiles information—year founded, organization type, giving location(s), and grant types
- Financial summary
- Typical recipients
- Application procedures
- Foundation/corporate officials
- Grants lists and analysis

Method of Compilation

The Big Book of Library Grant Money 2006 consists of giving profiles that are compiled for Taft's *Corporate Giving Directory* and *Foundation Reporter*. Profiles are selected that support libraries and library services. Foundation profiles are updated annually and are based on the most recent Form 990-PF available from the IRS, as well as the foundation's annual reports, grants lists, guidelines, questionnaire responses, and telephone interviews. Profiles of corporate direct-giving programs are based on information provided directly by the companies, press releases, telephone interviews, standard business publications, and data uncovered in extensive surveys of publication in the field.

Indexes

Five indexes allow users to quickly locate information presented in the profiles.

Funders by Headquarters State—Lists foundations and corporations alphabetically by the state of their primary location. Within each state, foundation and corporation names are listed in alphabetical order.

Funders by Operating Locations—Arranges corporations by the states of the major operating locations. Within each state, company names are listed in alphabetical order.

Library Recipients by State—Organizes grants given to libraries and other library-related projects by the state in which the library and/or project is located. Within each state, grants are listed in alphabetical order. When more than one grant has been given to the same organization, such as the New York Public Library, individual grants are listed in descending order by the grant amount.

Officers and Directors by Name—Lists officers, trustees, managers, staff, and contact people in alphabetical order with the name of the funder.

Master Index—Lists in alphabetical order the private foundations, corporate foundations, and corporate direct-giving programs profiled in this directory and includes the page number on which the profile appears. Also listed are former names of funders, as well as parent company names for corporate foundation/direct-giving programs. These citations also include the page number of the profile in which this information is located.

Comments and Suggestions Welcome

We encourage your comments and suggestions on how future editions of *The Big Book of Library Grant Money* may be enhanced to meet your prospecting needs. Please submit comments to:

Thomson Gale
27500 Drake Rd.
Farmington Hills, MI 48331-3535
Phone: (248) 699-4253
Toll-free: (800) 347-4253
Fax: (248) 699-8069
URL: www.gale.com

or

Editorial Director
ALA Editions
50 E. Huron St.
Chicago, IL 60611
www.alastore.ala.org

Members, trustees, and other library professionals often contact the Development Office at the American Library Association (ALA) to ask, "Where do I find funders for library initiatives, cultural programs, or building campaigns?" *The Big Book of Library Grant Money 2006* goes a long way toward answering this question. It's a unique resource for anyone seeking financial support for library-related initiatives, programs, or services.

Since the recent economic downturn across the country, competition among nonprofits for scarce resources has become fierce. Now more than ever, library fund-raisers must act strategically. *The Big Book of Library Grant Money* will help you focus on the most probable sources for success.

The Big Book is superior to other sources in two important ways. First, it provides a depth of information about a breadth of sources not found in a single directory devoted to library funding. Second, it includes untapped resources—organizations that have indicated an interest in funding libraries—as well as those private foundations, corporate foundations, and corporate direct-givers that have funded libraries in the past.

Getting Started

Before consulting *The Big Book*, you should have a clear understanding of the program or service that you are trying to fund. Boil the program description down to the essentials in a one-to-two-page synopsis that highlights the goals of your program. *The Big Book* will then be a valuable tool for matching the goals of your program to the goals of the funding agencies.

Once you select a list of potential funders, check with your library staff and trustees to determine if anyone has a contact at any of those foundations. It's always better to have a contact within a foundation than to cold call. However, you can certainly move ahead even if you do not know anyone at the foundation by contacting its program officers or other appropriate people. A program officer will be able to communicate the foundation's level of interest based on your program synopsis.

After you have identified a potential funding source, your relationship with that foundation's program officer becomes critical. The program officer is responsible for seeking excellent initiatives and programs to fund on behalf of the foundation. Foundations want to make a good investment when they fund programs. Therefore, you must work together with the program officer as you proceed to find funding for your program. The importance of developing a rapport with the foundation program officer cannot be overestimated. The funding process must be a positive experience for both your library and the foundation.

Making Your Case

You must be able to give program officers information that will help them present your project to their foundation boards. State the specifics in terms that will resonate with the funder—avoid library jargon. Following are some statistics that should help the program officer prepare a case on your behalf. Look for additional statistics or other documentation specific to your library or the community you serve to reinforce your case.

General Library Statistics

- Americans go to school, public, and academic libraries more than twice as often as they go to the movies.
- Reference librarians in the nation's public and academic libraries answer more than seven million questions weekly. Standing single file, the line of questioners would stretch from Boston to San Francisco.
- Federal spending on libraries annually is only 54 cents per person.
- A 2002 poll conducted by the American Library Association found that 91 percent of respondents expect libraries to be needed in the future, despite the increased availability of information via the Internet.

Public Library Statistics

- There are more public libraries than McDonald's in the United States—a total of more than 16,500, including branches.
- Americans spend more than three times as much on salty snacks as they do on public libraries.
- Americans check out an average of more than six library books a year. They spend $25.25 a year for the public library—much less than the average cost of one hardcover book.

- Public libraries are the number-one point of online access for people without Internet connections at home, school, or work.
- 95 percent of public libraries provide public access to the Internet.

School Library Statistics

- Research shows that the highest-achieving students attend schools with good library media centers.
- Americans spend seven times as much money on home video games ($7 billon) as they do on school library materials for their children ($1 billion).
- School library media centers spend an average of $7 per child for books—less than half the average cost of one hardcover school library book.
- Students visit school library media centers almost 1.5 billion times during the school year—about one-and-a-half times the number of visits to state and national parks.

Academic Library Statistics

- Academic librarians answer 97 million reference questions each year, almost three times the attendance at college football games.
- College libraries receive less than 3 cents of every dollar spent on higher education.

SOURCES: Quotable Facts about America's Libraries (Chicago: American Library Association Public Information Office, 2002); http://www.ala.org/Source/quotablefact.pdf. Falling through the Net (National Telecommunications and Information Administration, 2000); http://www.ntia.doc.gov/ntiahome/digitaldivide/.

Finalizing and Publicizing Your Grant

Once you receive your grant, review your agreement with the funder carefully. This is a legally binding document that outlines the expectations of each party in the relationship. If changes are necessary during the implementation phase, these must be communicated to and negotiated with the funder both in person and in writing. Because the agreement is legally binding, you should consult legal counsel to review the terms, as well. Counsel can suggest wording when there is some disagreement over terms.

Be sure to utilize as many publicity avenues as you have available. Remember public service announcements and the new opportunities that the Web provides. Recognizing the support of your donors is a wonderful tool in building long-term relationships. There are many ways to acknowledge your donors while getting the most out of public relations opportunities for your library and library initiatives. Check with your funder for specific guidelines on press releases.

Using ALA Inititatives to Leverage Local Support

In 2005 ALA adopted Ahead to 2010, a five-year initiative to position libraries and librarians for the twenty-first century. Be sure to put the weight of the national organization goals behind your initiatives. For instance, ALA has identified five key action areas: diversity, education and continuous learning, equity of access, intellectual freedom, and twenty-first-century literacy. In order to achieve these goals, ALA leaders have adopted the following goal statements:

- ALA and its members are the leading advocates for libraries and the library profession.
- Through its leadership, ALA ensures the highest quality graduate and continuing education opportunities for librarians and library staff.
- ALA plays a key role in the formulation of national and international policies and standards that affect library and information services.
- ALA is a leader in recruiting and developing a highly qualified and diverse library work force.
- Members receive outstanding value for their ALA membership.
- ALA is an inclusive, effectively governed, well-managed, and financially strong organization.

Among the initial steps in achieving these goals is the national Campaign for America's Libraries. Up-to-date information on the campaign and other useful data for your proposals are available from the ALA Public Information Office (http://www.ala.org/).

For additional resources on library fund-raising from ALA Editions, visit the ALA online store: http://www.alastore.ala.org.

We wish you luck as you pursue funding for your program. As always, we welcome input for future editions of this book.

Susan Roman
Director, Development Office (2000–2005)
American Library Association

ATLANTA TECHNICAL COLLEGE
Library/Media Services
1560 Metropolitan Pkwy., SW
Atlanta, Georgia 30310

Arrangement of Giving Profiles

Giving profiles are arranged alphabetically by the name of the foundation or by the sponsoring company name in the case of corporate foundations and corporate direct-giving programs.

If a giving profile is for a corporate foundation, such as Boeing Corporation/The Boeing Corporation Charitable Trust, the profile has two headings—one for information on the corporation and another for information on the foundation. Giving profiles for private foundations and corporate direct-giving programs have only one profile heading.

Data Elements

Data elements for each type of profile vary. The abbreviated entry shown below illustrates the standard data elements that a giving profile can contain, depending on the nature of the profile—private foundation, corporate foundation, or corporate direct-giving program. Numbered items in the sample are explained in the corresponding numbered paragraphs below.

❙1❙ XYZ Stores
❙2❙ *Company Headquarters*
700 Haywood Rd.
Greenville, SC 29607
Phone: (555) 392-2000
Fax: (555) 392-3000
E-mail: info@xyz.com
URL: http://www.xyz.com
❙3❙ *Company Description*
Founded: 1902
Ticker: XYZ
Exchange: NYSE
Former Name: Archer Inc.
Revenue: US$4 billion (2002)
Profit: US$2 billion (2002)
Employees: 5,000 (2002)
Fortune Rank: 200, per FORTUNE Magazine's list of 500 Largest U.S. Corporations (2003)
SIC(s): 5555 Department stores
❙4❙ Operation Locations
CA: XYZ Limited, Los Angeles, San Diego; CT: XYZ Limited, New Haven; ME: XYZ Limited, Bangor; Australia: XYZ Limited, Sydney
❙5❙ Nonmonetary Support
Value: $9,000,000 (2002); $4,000,000 (2001)
Type: Donated Products
Note: Product donations are directed primarily to organizations that support overseas educational programs.
❙6❙ XYZ Foundation
❙7❙ *Giving Contact*

Emmit Roman, Executive Director
555 Haywood Rd., Ste. 200
Greenville, SC 29607
Phone: (555) 297-3203
Email: eroman@xyz.com
❙8❙ *Foundation Description*
Founded: 1944
EIN: 551127710
Organization Type: Corporate Foundation
Giving Locations: headquarters and operating communities
Grant Types: General Support, Project, and Research
Note: Employee matching gift ratio: 2 to 1 for contributions over $25 to colleges and universities, up to $2,000 annually; 1 to 1 for gifts to hospitals and cultural institutions, up to $500 annually.
❙9❙ *Donor Information*
Founder: Margaret Burns
❙10❙ *Financial Summary*
Total Giving: $1,800,000 (2003 approx.); $1,752,934 (2002); $1,493,082 (2001); $1,271,427 (2000)
Giving Analysis: Giving for 2002 includes: foundation ($1,715,434); foundation grants to United Way ($37,500).
Assets: $13,974,021 (2002); $12,675,142 (2001); $13,058,376 (2000)
Gifts Received: $242,355 (2002); $224,794 (2001); $99,749 (2000).
Note: Contributions are received from various XYZ Stores.
❙11❙ *Typical Recipients*
Arts & Humanities: Arts Centers, Art Institutes, Ballet, Community Arts, Historic Preservation, Libraries, Museums/Galleries, Music, Opera, Performing Arts, Public Broadcasting, Theater
Education: Afterschool/Enrichment Programs, Agricultural Education, Arts/Humanities Education, Colleges and Universities
Environment: Resource Conservation, Wildlife Protection
Health: Cancer, Hospitals, Medical Research, Nursing Services
Social Services: YMCA/YMHA/YWCA/YWHA
❙12❙ *Application Procedures*
Initial Contact: Initial contact should be made by letter.
Application Requirements: Proposals should include a summary statement and background information, names of board members, a copy of annual budget and most recent Form 990, the specific monetary amount requested, a budget listing how the funds will be spent, and a copy of the organization's IRS tax-exempt letter.
Deadlines: None.
Review Process: Proposals must be received at least four weeks prior to the month in which the request is to be reviewed.
Evaluative Criteria: Priority is given to organizations serving XYZ employees.
Decision Notification: Final decisions are usually made within eight to ten weeks of receipt.
❙13❙ *Restrictions*
Does not support individuals, political or lobbying groups, or religious organizations for sectarian purposes.
❙14❙ *Additional Information*
XYZ Stores acquired ACME Products in 1999.
Publications: Annual Report; Guidelines
❙15❙ *Corporate Officials*
John C. Belk: chairman B. Charlotte, NC 1920. ED Davidson College (1943). PRIM CORP EMPL chairman: Belk Stores Services Inc.

CORP AFFIL director: Lowes Home Centers Inc.; chairman: Parks-Belk Co. Northern Virginia; vice president: Leggett Realty South Boston Virginia; director: Lowes Companies; chairman: Charlotte Belk Inc.; director: Coca-Cola Bottling Co. Consolidated; director: Brothers Investment Co.; director: Chaparral Steel Co.

Montgomery Burns: pres B. Springfield, IL 1900. ED Henderson Univ (1922). PRIM CORP EMPL pres: XYZ Stores Services Inc. CORP AFFIL director: Lowes Home Center Inc.; vice president: Parks-Belk Co. Northern Virginia

Foundation Officials
John A. Kuhne: director
Emmit Roman: executive director
Kate M. Simpson: director

∎16∎ *Grants Analysis*
Disclosure Period: 2002
Total Grants: $1,715,434
Number of Grants: 158
Average Grant: $7,742*
Highest Grant: $500,000
Typical Range: $5,000-$100,000
*Average grant figure excludes highest grant.

∎17∎ *Recent Grants*
Note: Grants derived from 2002 Form 990.
Library-Related

75,000	New York Public Library, New York, NY—Utopia Exhibition
50,000	Columbia University Avery Library

General

500,000	QRS Communications, Boston, MA— toward capital campaign
200,000	Southern Maine Museum of Art, Freeport, ME—toward a new satellite building
175,000	Vermont Artist Visions, Burlington, VT— to support annual programs
50,000	Historical MA—toward capital campaign
25,000	Converse College, Spartanburg, SC— toward capital campaign
15,000	University of South Carolina Lancaster, Lancaster, SC
10,000	Highlands Land Trust—for wetlands preservation projects
10,000	Greenville Free Medical Clinic, Greenville, SC
10,000	Presbyterian Hospital, Charlotte, NC
5,000	Pickens County YMCA, Easley, SC

Description of Numbered Elements

∎1∎ *Company Name.*

∎2∎ *Company Headquarters:* The address, phone, fax, e-mail, and URL for the sponsoring corporation's headquarters locations, when available.

∎3∎ *Company Description:* Includes financial and other statistical information as reported in the April 14, 2003, issue of *Fortune* magazine (Time, Inc., New York, NY), and several corporate databases available on-line. If the sponsoring company is a subsidiary of or affiliated with another company, this information is listed under **Parent Company. Revenue/sales, profits, number of employees, Fortune rank,** and **SIC(s)** as reported by the company or major business publications, give a capsule look at the financial health and business interests of the profiled company. The entry may also include former name(s), ticker symbol, and stock exchange information for the company. Corporate giving levels are closely tied to a company's sales and profits: the more profitable a company, the greater its philanthropic potential. Many companies base

their giving on a percentage of pretax profits, typically 0.5 percent to 2.5 percent, but occasionally as high as 5 percent. Fortune rank is a classic indicator of how a company compares to its peers. The number of employees also provides a quick measure of a company's size, and corporate programs are usually interested in seeing charitable contributions affect the largest number of corporate employees. Fortune rank, as well as company sales, profits, and number of employees are given where available. SIC information helps identify corporations with a special interest in a particular activity due to the nature of their business.

∎4∎ *Operating Locations:* Company business typically revolves around corporate headquarters and operating locations, and charitable giving information reflects this orientation. Headquarters information is indexed in the index to *Funders by Headquarters State.* Operating locations are indexed in the *Funders by Operating Locations* index. The names and locations of the company's U.S. subsidiaries are also included when available. A company's field of business or marketing orientation often influences its charitable objectives.

∎5∎ *Nonmonetary Support:* Notes the types and amounts of nonmonetary support offered, such as cause-related marketing and promotion, donated equipment, donated products, in-kind services, loaned employees, loaned executives, and workplace solicitation. Also includes the value of such support and whom to contact, if available.

∎6∎ *Foundation Name.*

∎7∎ *Giving Contact:* The name of the person responsible for answering inquiries and receiving grant applications for the foundation, as well as the individual's title, organization name, mailing address, telephone number, fax number, e-mail, and URL, when available.

∎8∎ *Foundation Description:* Listed here is general information about the foundation, such as year **Founded,** its **Employer Identification Number (EIN)**—the unique nine-digit number assigned to a philanthropic institution by the Internal Revenue Service—**Organization Type, Giving Locations,** and **Grant Types.** Foundations are grouped into four general categories (or **Organization Type**): **Family, General Purpose, Institutional,** or **Special Purpose. Grant Types** lists the financial support typically offered by the foundation using nineteen standard categories ranging from award to seed money. **Giving Locations** indicates the geographic preference for disbursing funds as reported by the foundation or based on analysis of grant lists. Users should review the index to *Funders by Headquarters State* and the *Library Recipients by State* index to gain a greater understanding of a foundation's geographic giving interests. The **Note** section offers any other relevant information pertaining to Grant Types or employee matching gift programs.

∎9∎ *Donor Information:* Contains background information on the donor, his or her family members or spouses, the sources of their wealth or businesses, or their other philanthropies. The specific interests of foundations are frequently oriented toward the philanthropic, business, educational, vocational, religious, political, or social interests of their donors.

▌10▌ *Financial Summary:* For corporate foundations and direct-giving programs, lists giving figures for the three most recent years available, as reported by the company. Also includes information on the scope of the program, including whether the company gives directly, through a foundation, or both. If the company has a foundation, this section lists foundation assets and any gifts the foundation received for the three most recent years available. Use this information to qualify a corporation according to its giving potential and to spot trends in its overall corporate giving. For private foundations, lists the three most current figures of market value of a foundation's assets, along with figures for overall giving (both actual and projected) for at least the three most recent years available. The gifts received category reports, by year, the dollar amount of donations given to a foundation. The source of a gift is explained in the **Financial Note**, when the information is available. Use the information in the Financial Summary to rate foundations according to their financial potential and giving trends.

▌11▌ *Typical Recipients:* Presents an inventory of the types of nonprofit causes that a foundation or direct-giving program most frequently supports, using 215 standard recipient categories under nine broad categories: Arts & Humanities, Civic & Public Affairs, Education, Environment, Health, International, Religion, Science, and Social Services. This section is designed to catalog the kinds of activities supported, rather than indicate priority. A complete list of the 215 recipient organization types, arranged under the 9 major categories, is available on page xv.

▌12▌ *Application Procedures:* **Initial Contact, Application Requirement,** and **Deadlines** outline the preferred methods of contacting the company, meeting requirements for proposals, and sending requests within specific time frames, respectively. **Review Process, Evaluative Criteria,** and **Decision Notification** describe the decision-making process foundations or companies follow when reviewing requests, including procedures, the criteria upon which requests are evaluated, and when decisions are made.

▌13▌ *Restrictions:* A brief description of restrictions on eligibility, or types of programs, campaigns, or organizations that are not funded.

▌14▌ *Additional Information:* Reports additional procedures, significant changes in the status of the foundation or company, or policies that could influence solicitation efforts. The **Publications** section lists any printed material provided by the foundation or giving program.

▌15▌ *Corporate Officials:* Provides biographical information on principal corporate officers and contributions program officers, directors, or trustees. When available, includes year and place of birth, education (school, program, degree, and year of graduation), current employment, corporate affiliations, nonprofit affiliations, and club affiliations. This background biographical information helps nonprofits discover connections to development teams and boards of directors, as well as uncover opportunities to cultivate relationships with these decision makers.

Foundation Officials: Provides biographical information on principal foundation officers (usually the chairman, vice chairman, president, vice president, and chief executive officer). When available, includes year and place of birth, education (school, program, degree, and year of graduation), current employment, corporate affiliations, nonprofit affiliations, and club affiliations. This background biographical information helps nonprofits discover connections to development teams and boards of directors, as well as uncover opportunities to cultivate relationships with these decision makers.

▌16▌ *Grants Analysis:* An analytical section which calculates **Total Grants, Number of Grants, Average Grant, Highest Grant,** and **Typical Range.** The **Disclosure Period** indicates the year (actual or fiscal) from which the analytical information was derived. The **Note** contains information on large grants that may skew the average, or any other relevant information pertaining to the grants analysis.

▌17▌ *Recent Grants:* When available, provides a listing of top library-related grants and a general listing of the top 10 recently awarded grants from the following categories: Arts & Humanities, Civic & Public Affairs, Education, Environment, Health, International, Religion, Science, and Social Services. Grants are listed in descending order based on dollar amount. The **Note** at the top of this section indicates the year of the Recent Grants listings.

Abbreviations

A

&	And
AA	Associate of Arts
AB	Arts, Bachelor of
acct	accountant
admin	administration, administrative, administrator
adv	advisor, advisory
AFB	Air Force Base
Aff	Affairs
affil	affiliation
AG	Aktiengesellschaft
Am	America, American
AM	Arts, Master of
Apt	Apartment
APO	Army Post Office
archt	architect
Assn	Association
Assoc(s)	Associate(s), Associated
asst	assistant
atty	attorney
Ave	Avenue

B

b	born
BA	Bachelor of Arts
BBA	Bachelor of Business Administration
bd	board
BD	Bachelor of Divinity
BE	Bachelor of Engineering
BFT	Bachelor of Foreign Trade
Bldg	Building
Blvd	Boulevard
Bros	Brothers
BS	Bachelor of Science
BSChE	Bachelor of Science in Chemical Engineering
BSME	Bachelor of Science in Mechanical Engineering
Bur	Bureau
Bus	Business

C

c/o	care of
CC	Country Club
ceo	chief executive officer
cfo	chief financial officer
Chap	Chapter
Chem	Chemical, Chemist, Chemistry
chmn	chairman
chp	chairperson
chwm	chairwoman
Co	Company
Coll	College
comm	committee
commn	commission
commnr	commissioner
Commun	Communication(s), Community
comptr	comptroller
Conf	Conference
Confed	Confederation
Cong	Congress
Consult	Consultant, Consulting
contr	controller
coo	chief operating officer
Coop	Cooperating, Cooperative, Cooperaton
Corp	Corporate, Corporation
Counc	Council
couns	counsel, counseling, counselor
CPA	Certified Public Accountant
Ct	Court
Ctr	Center, Centre
curr	current
cust	customer

D

DB	Divinity, Bachelor of
del	delegate
Dem	Democrat
dep	deputy
Dept	Department
Devel	Development
dir	director
Distr	Distributor, Distribution, Distributing
Div	Division
don	donor
Dr	Doctor
Dr	Drive

E

E	East
Econ	Economic, Economics
Ed	Education, Educational, Educated
EIN	Employer Identification Number

empl	employment
Engg	Engineering
engr	engineer
exec	executive
Expy	Expressway

F

f/b/o	for the benefit of
Fdn	Foundation
fdr	founder
Fed	Federal, Federation, Federated
Fin	Finance, Financial
Fl	Floor
FPO	Fleet Post Office
Ft	Fort
Fwy	Freeway

G

GC	Golf Club
gen	general
gov	governing, governor
govt	government
grad	graduate

H

hon	honorable, honorary
Hosp	Hospital
Hwy	Highway

I

Inc	Incorporated
Indus	Industrial, Industries, Industry
Ins	Insurance
Inst	Institute, Institution
Intl	International

J

JD	Juris Doctor
Jr	Junior

L

Legis	Legislation, Legislative, Legislator
LLB	Laws, Bachelor of
LLD	Laws, Doctor of

Ln	Lane
LP	Limited Partnership
Ltd	Limited

M

MA	Master of Arts
MBA	Master of Business Administration
Med	Medical
mem	member
Meml	Memorial
Metro	Metropolitan
Mfg	Manufacturing
Mfr	Manufacturer
Mgmt	Management
mgr	manager
misc	miscellaneous
Mktg	Marketing
Mng	Managing
MS	Master of Science
Mt	Mount
Mus	Museum

N

N	North
NAACP	National Association for the Advancement of Colored People
N. Ap.	Not Applicable
N. Av	Not Available
Natl	National
NE	North East
No	Number
nonpr	nonprofit
NW	North West

O

off	office, officer
oper	operating, operations
Org	Organization

P

per	personnel
PhB	Philosophy, Bachelor of
PhD	Philosophy, Doctor of

phil	philanthropic
Pk	Park
Pke	Pike
Pkwy	Parkway
Pl	Place
Plz	Plaza
PO	Post Office
Polytech	Polytechnic, Polytechnical
pres	president
prin	principal
prof	professor
Prov	Province, Provincial
Pt	Point
Pte	Pointe
Ptnr	Partner
pub(s)	publication(s)
pub	public
pub(s)	published, publisher, publishing
Pvt	Private

R

Rd	Road
RD	Rural Delivery
rehab	rehabilitation
rel	religious, religion
rels	relations
rep	representative
Repbl	Republican
Res	Research, Researcher
ret	retired
RFD	Rural Free Delivery
Rm	Room
RR	railroad
RR	Rural Route
Rte	Route
RY	Railway

S

S	South
SB	Science, Bachelor of
Sch	School
SE	South East
secy	secretary
sen	senator
SM	Science, Master of
Soc	Society
Sq	Square
Sr	Senior

SR	Star/State Route
St	Saint, State, Street
Sta	Station
Ste	Sainte, Suite
Sub(s)	Subsidiary(ies)
supt	superintendent
supvr	supervisor
Svc(s)	Service(s)
SW	South West
Sys	System(s)

T

Tech	Technological, Technical, Technology
Tel &Tel	Telephone and Telegraph
Terr	Terrace
Tpke	Turnpike
treas	treasurer
trust	trustee

U

Un	United
Univ	University
US	United States
u/w/o	under the will of

V

vchmn	vice chairman
vp	vice president

W

W	West

Y

YC	Yacht Club
YMCA	Young Men's Christian Association
YMHA	Young Men's Hebrew Association
YWCA	Young Women's Christian Association
YWHA	Young Women's Hebrew Association

Nonprofit Recipient Categories and Organization Types

Arts & Humanities ❚ Art History, Art Appreciation, Arts Associations & Councils, Arts Centers, Arts Festivals, Art Funds, Arts Institutes, Arts Outreach, Ballet, Community Arts, Dance, Ethnic & Folk Art, Film & Video, Historic Preservation, History & Archeology, Libraries, Literary Arts, Museums/Galleries, Music, Opera, Performing Arts, Public Broadcasting, Theater, Visual Arts

Civic & Public Affairs ❚ African American Affairs, Asian American Affairs, Botanical Gardens/Parks, Business/Free Enterprise, Chambers of Commerce, Civil Rights, Clubs, Community Foundations, Economic Development, Economic Policy, Employment/Job Training, Ethnic Organizations, First Amendment Issues, Gay/Lesbian Issues, Hispanic Affairs, Housing, Inner-City Development, Law & Justice, Legal Aid, Minority Business, Municipalities/Towns, Native American Affairs, Nonprofit Management, Parades/Festivals, Philanthropic Organizations, Professional/Trade Associations, Public Policy, Rural Affairs, Safety, Urban/Community Affairs, Women's Affairs, Zoos/Aquariums

Education ❚ Afterschool Enrichment Programs, Agricultural Education, Arts/Humanities Education, Business Education, Business-School Partnerships, Colleges & Universities, Community/Junior Colleges, Continuing Education, Economic Education, Education Associations, Education Funds, Education Reform, Elementary Education (private), Elementary Education (public), Engineering Education, Environmental Education, Faculty Development, Gifted & Talented Programs, Health & Physical Education, International Exchange, International Studies, Journalism/Media Education, Leadership Training, Legal Education, Literacy, Medical Education, Minority Education, Preschool Education, Private Education (precollege), Public Volunteerism, Science/Mathematics Education, Secondary Education (private), Secondary Education (public), Social Sciences Education, Special Education, Student Aid, Vocational/Technical Education

Environment ❚ Air/Water Quality, Energy, Forestry, Protection, Research, Resource Conservation, Sanitary Systems, Watershed, Wildlife Protection

Health ❚ Adolescent Health Issues, AIDS/HIV, Alzheimer's Disease, Arthritis, Cancer, Children's Health/Hospitals, Clinics/Medical Centers, Diabetes, Emergency/Ambulance Services, Eyes/Blindness, Geriatric Health, Health Funds, Health Organizations, Health Policy/Cost Containment, Heart, Home-Care Services, Hospices, Hospitals, Hospitals (university affiliated), Kidney, Long-Term Care, Medical Rehabilitation, Medical Research, Medical Training, Mental Health, Multiple Sclerosis, Nursing Services, Nutrition, Outpatient Health Care, Prenatal Health Issues, Preventive Medicine/Wellness Organizations, Public Health, Research/Studies Institutes, Respiratory, Single-Disease Health Associations, Speech & Hearing, Transplant Networks/Donor Banks, Trauma Treatment

International ❚ Foreign Arts Organizations, Foreign Education Institutions, Health Care/Hospitals, Human Rights International Affairs, International Development, International Environmental Issues, International Law, International Organizations, International Peace & Security Issues, International Relations, International Relief Efforts, Missionary/Religious Activities, Trade

Religion ❚ Bible Study/Translation, Churches, Dioceses, Jewish Causes, Ministries, Missionary Activities (domestic), Religious Organizations, Religious Welfare, Seminaries, Social/Policy Issues, Synagogues/Temples

Science ❚ Observatories/Planetariums, Science Exhibits/Fairs, Scientific Institutes, Scientific Organizations

Social Services ❚ Animal Protection, At-Risk Youth, Big Brother/Big Sister, Camps, Child Abuse, Child Welfare, Community Centers, Community Service Organizations, Counseling, Crime Prevention, Day Care, Delinquency/Criminal Rehabilitation, Domestic Violence, Emergency Relief, Family Planning, Family Services, Food & Clothing Distribution, Homes People With Disabilities, Recreation & Athletics, Refugees Assistance, Scouts, Senior Services, Sexual Abuse, United Funds/United Way, Veterans, Volunteer Services, YMCA/YMHA/YWCA/YWHA, Youth Organizations

1ST SOURCE CORP.

Company Headquarters
100 N. Michigan Street
South Bend, IN 46601
Phone: (219)235-2000
Fax: (219)235-2882
Web: http://www.1stsource.com

Company Description
Founded: 1971
Ticker: SRCE
Exchange: NASDAQ
Assets: US$3.409 billion (2002)
Employees: 1220 (2003)
SIC(s): 6022 State Commercial Banks.

Operating Locations
First Source Corp. (IN--South Bend)

First Source Foundation

Giving Contact
Mary Sonneborn, Trust Officer
Care of First Source Bank
PO Box 1602
South Bend, IN 46601
Phone: (219)235-2790
Fax: (219)235-2771

Alternate Contact
Lee Morton
1st Source Bank
PO Box 1602
South Bend, IN 46601

Description
Founded: 1952
EIN: 356034211
Organization Type: Corporate Foundation
Giving Locations: IN
Grant Types: General Support, Scholarship.

Donor Information
Founder: First Source Bank Charitable Trust

Financial Summary
Total Giving: $685,516 (2002); $620,708 (2001)
Giving Analysis: Giving for 2002 includes: foundation ($2,721,367)
Assets: $15,074,573 (2002); $15,024,448 (2001)
Gifts Received: $249,421 (2001); $700,000 (1999); $951,907 (1998). Note: In 1999, contributions were received from First Source Bank.

Typical Recipients
Arts & Humanities: Arts Centers, Arts Funds, Arts & Humanities-General, Historic Preservation, History & Archaeology, Libraries, Museums/Galleries, Music, Performing Arts, Public Broadcasting
Civic & Public Affairs: Botanical Gardens/Parks, Business/Free Enterprise, Chambers of Commerce, Clubs, Community Foundations, Economic Development, Economic Policy, Ethnic Organizations, Civic & Public Affairs-General, Housing, Inner-City Development, Minority Business, Municipalities/Towns, Parades/Festivals, Safety, Urban & Community Affairs
Education: Afterschool/Enrichment Programs, Arts/Humanities Education, Business Education, Colleges & Universities, Community & Junior Colleges, Economic Education, Education Associations, Education Funds, Elementary Education (Private), Engineering/Technological Education, Education-General, International Exchange, International Studies, Medical Education, Private Education (Precollege), Public Education (Precollege), Religious Education, Science/Mathematics Education, Secondary Education (Private), Secondary Education (Public), Student Aid
Environment: Environment-General
Health: Alzheimer's Disease, Cancer, Children's Health/Hospitals, Diabetes, Emergency/Ambulance Services, Health Funds, Health Organizations, Home-Care Services, Hospices, Hospitals, Kidney, Mental Health, Nursing Services, Preventive Medicine/Wellness Organizations, Public Health
Religion: Bible Study/Translation, Churches, Religion-General, Jewish Causes, Religious Organizations, Religious Welfare
Social Services: Animal Protection, Big Brothers/Big Sisters, Camps, Child Abuse, Community Service Organizations, Crime Prevention, Delinquency & Criminal Rehabilitation, Emergency Relief, Family Planning, Family Services, Food/Clothing Distribution, Homes, People with Disabilities, Recreation & Athletics, Shelters/Homelessness, Social Services-General, Substance Abuse, United Funds/United Ways, Volunteer Services, YMCA/YWCA/YMHA/YWHA, Youth Organizations

Application Procedures
Initial Contact: Submit a written request.
Application Requirements: Requests should include a written statement of purpose concerning grant request.
Deadlines: None.

Corporate Officials
Christopher J. Murphy, III: president, chief executive officer, director B Washington, DC 1946. ED University of Notre Dame BA (1968); University of Virginia JD (1971); Harvard University Graduate School of Business Administration MBA (1973). PRIM CORP EMPL president, chief executive officer, director: First Source Corp. CORP AFFIL director: Trust Corp. Mortgage Inc.; director: Quality Dining Inc.; director: Titan Holding; director: Comair Inc.; director: Omega Health System; chairman: 1st Source Industry Inc.; chairman, chief executive officer: 1st Source Bank; chairman: 1st Source Capital Corp. NONPR AFFIL member: Virginia Bar Association; international board director, member: Young Presidents' Organization; member: Saint Joseph County Bar Association; advisory council: Notre Dame College Arts and Letters; member: Robert Morris Associates; director, chairman: National Association Publically Traded Companies; member: National Association Securities Dealers; member: National Association Business Economists; member: Indiana Bar Association; chairman: Medical Education Foundation; member: American Bankers Association; member: American Bar Association.

Foundation Officials
Harry Gerber: director
Christopher J. Murphy, III: director (see above)

Grants Analysis
Disclosure Period: calendar year ending 2002
Total Grants: $685,516*
Number of Grants: 70
Average Grant: $6,718*
Highest Grant: $222,000
Lowest Grant: $50
Typical Range: $1,000 to $5,000
***Note:** Average grant figure excludes highest grant.

Recent Grants
Note: Grants derived from 2003 Form 990.

Library-Related
5,000	St. Joseph County Public Library, South Bend, IN

General
200,000	Indiana University Scholarship Foundation, South Bend, IN
100,000	Memorial Hospital, South Bend, IN
100,000	Northern Indiana Education Foundation, South Bend, IN
50,000	Bethel College, South Bend, IN
50,000	Logan Industries, South Bend, IN
50,000	Niles Buchanan YMCA, Niles, MI
25,000	Alzheimer's Services of Northern Indiana, South Bend, IN
25,000	Indiana Chamber of Commerce Foundation, South Bend, IN
14,000	Independent Colleges of Indiana, Indianapolis, IN
14,000	South Bend Symphony Orchestra Association, South Bend, IN

ABBOTT LABORATORIES

Company Headquarters
100 Abbott Park Road
Abbott Park, IL 60064-2500
Phone: (847)936-1000
Fax: (847)937-1511
Web: http://www.abbott.com

Company Description
Founded: 1900
Ticker: ABT
Exchange: NYSE
Revenue: US$20.473 billion (2004)
Profit: US$3.235 billion (2004)
Employees: 71819 (2003)
Fortune Rank: 100, per FORTUNE Magazine's list of 500 Largest U.S. Corporations (2004).
SIC(s): 2833 Medicinals & Botanicals, 2834 Pharmaceutical Preparations, 2844 Toilet Preparations, 3841 Surgical & Medical Instruments.

Operating Locations
Abbott Ambulatory Infusion Systems (CA--San Diego); Abbott Critical Care Systems (CA--Morgan Hill; UT--Salt Lake City); Abbott Diagnostics (CA--Santa Clara); Abbott Laboratories (KS--McPherson; NJ--Fairfield; NY--Buffalo; NC--Laurinburg, Rocky Mount; OH--Ashland; TX--Austin, Irving); Abbott Laboratories Hematology Operations, Inc. (MA--Bedford); Ross Products (AZ--Casa Grande; MI--Sturgis; OH--Columbus; VA--Altavista); Tap Pharmaceuticals (IL--Deerfield)

Nonmonetary Support
Value: $100,000,000 (2001 approx); $1,850,000 (2000)
Type: Donated Products
Note: Product donations are directed primarily to organizations that support overseas health care programs and disaster relief efforts.

Abbott Laboratories Fund

Giving Contact
Cindy Schwab, Vice President
Abbott Laboratories Fund
Dept. 379, Building AP6D
100 Abbott Park Road
Abbott Park, IL 60064-6048
Phone: (847)937-7075
Fax: (847)935-5051
Web: http://abbott.com/citizenship/citizenship.cfm

Description
Founded: 1951
EIN: 366069793
Organization Type: Corporate Foundation
Giving Locations: headquarters and operating communities; United Kingdom; Puerto Rico
Grant Types: Employee Matching Gifts, General Support, Research.
Note: Employee matching gift ratio: 1 to 1 for elementary and secondary schools and higher education; public broadcasting; foundations (meeting criteria); and hospitals. Contact Rhonda Rudolph, Matching Grant Coordinator.

Donor Information
Founder: Abbott Laboratories

Financial Summary
Total Giving: $21,324,242 (2003); $16,948,001 (2002); $15,547,595 (2001)
Giving Analysis: Giving for 2002 includes: foundation matching gifts ($2,318,982); foundation grants to United Way ($3,008,261).
Assets: $142,352,142 (2003); $85,723,978 (2002); $130,249,818 (2001)
Gifts Received: $47,905,520 (2003); $6,917,177 (2002); $12,015,796 (2001). Note: In 2002 and 2003, contributions were received from Abbott Laboratories. In 2001, contributions were received from Miles White ($5,268), Phil and Sandra Tobin ($5,341), and Abbott Laboratories ($12,000,000).

Typical Recipients
Arts & Humanities: Arts Institutes, Ballet, Community Arts, Dance, Arts & Humanities-General, Historic Preservation, History & Archaeology, Libraries, Museums/Galleries, Music, Opera, Performing Arts, Public Broadcasting, Theater
Civic & Public Affairs: Botanical Gardens/Parks, Clubs, Community Foundations, Economic Development, Economic Policy, Civic & Public Affairs-General, Hispanic Affairs, Housing, Law & Justice, Professional & Trade Associations, Public Policy, Rural Affairs, Safety, Urban & Community Affairs, Women's Affairs, Zoos/Aquariums
Education: Afterschool/Enrichment Programs, Business Education, Colleges & Universities, Community & Junior Colleges, Continuing Education, Education Associations, Education Funds, Engineering/Technological Education, Health & Physical Education, Legal Education, Medical Education, Minority Education, Private Education (Precollege), Public Education (Precollege), Religious Education, Science/Mathematics Education, Student Aid, Vocational & Technical Education
Environment: Forestry, Environment-General
Health: AIDS/HIV, Cancer, Children's Health/Hospitals, Clinics/Medical Centers, Diabetes, Emergency/Ambulance Services, Health-General, Geriatric Health, Health Funds, Health Organizations, Heart, Hospices, Hospitals, Hospitals (University Affiliated), Kidney, Medical Rehabilitation, Medical Research, Medical Training, Nursing Services, Nutrition, Public Health, Research/Studies Institutes, Single-Disease Health Associations
International: Health Care/Hospitals, International Development

Religion: Religious Welfare, Seminaries
Science: Observatories & Planetariums, Science Museums, Scientific Centers & Institutes, Scientific Research
Social Services: Child Welfare, Community Centers, Community Service Organizations, Day Care, Delinquency & Criminal Rehabilitation, Domestic Violence, Emergency Relief, Family Services, People with Disabilities, Refugee Assistance, Scouts, Sexual Abuse, Shelters/Homelessness, Substance Abuse, United Funds/United Ways, Veterans, Volunteer Services, YMCA/YWCA/YMHA/YWHA, Youth Organizations

Application Procedures
Initial Contact: Send a written request.
Application Requirements: Include a description of organization's mission; geographic area served; description of project, outlining needs and goals; amount requested; budget information; copy of 501(c)(3) tax-exempt letter; most recent audited financial statement; annual report and other supporting materials; and list of current supporters and donors.
Deadlines: None; contributions committee meets continuously throughout the year.
Evaluative Criteria: Priority is given to organizations serving communities in which Abbott has significant operations or employees; organizations whose activities support professions in health care fields related to Abbott's primary areas of operation; institutions of higher learning which benefit the health care industry and its employees. The fund's primary areas of interest are human health and welfare and higher education. Also of interest are secondary education, elementary education, culture, the arts, and civic activities.
Decision Notification: Final decisions are usually made within eight weeks of receipt.

Restrictions
Does not award grants to individuals, political or lobbying groups, or religious organizations for sectarian purposes; purely social organizations; symposia or conferences; memberships; or business-related purposes. Does not support dinners, special events, ticket purchases, meetings, marketing sponsorships, or goodwill advertising.

Additional Information
The fund gives preference to requests for one-time contributions and for programmatic and operating purposes; multiyear and capital requests are considered as exceptions.
Abbott Laboratories Fund is supported by contributions from Abbott Laboratories employees, retirees, and the corporation.
Publications: Abbott Laboratories Fund Contributions Policy; Annual Report

Corporate Officials
Miles D. White: chairman, chief executive officer B Minneapolis, MN March 10, 1955. ED Stanford University BS (1978); Stanford University MBA (1980). PRIM CORP EMPL chairman, chief executive officer: Abbott Laboratories. CORP AFFIL director: Nasdaq Stock Market Inc.; director: Pharmaceutical Research & Manufacturers of America. NONPR AFFIL trustee: Field Museum; trustee: Joffrey Ballet; chairman: Executives' Club of Chicago; deputy chairman: Federal Reserve Bank of Chicago; director: Art Institute of Chicago; director: Culver Educational Foundation.

Foundation Officials
Catherine V. Babington: president, director
Cindy A. Schwab: vice president
Carol A. Sebesta: treasurer
Brian J. Smith: secretary B 1951. ED Bradley University BA (1973); University of Michigan JD (1976). CORP AFFIL senior vice president: Hospira Inc. NONPR AFFIL member: American Bar Association; member: Illinois Bar Association.
Thomas M. Wascoe: director B October 10, 1946.

ED University of Wisconsin BA; University of Wisconsin MBA.
Miles D. White: director (see above)

Grants Analysis
Disclosure Period: calendar year ending 2003
Total Grants: $15,917,652*
Number of Grants: 890 (approx)
Average Grant: $5,481*
Highest Grant: $11,045,000
Lowest Grant: $100
Typical Range: $1,000 to $10,000
*****Note:** Giving excludes matching gifts and United Way. Average grant figure excludes highest grant.

Recent Grants
Note: Grants derived from 2003 Form 990.
General

11,045,000	Axios Foundation, Cleveland, OH
1,150,000	International HIV/AIDS Alliance, Brighton United Kingdom
838,844	United Way of Lake County, Gurnee, IL
300,000	Stanford University, Stanford, CA
242,442	United Way, Columbus, OH
227,324	United Way, San Juan, PR
225,000	Baylor College of Medicine, Houston, TX
219,000	Joffrey Ballet, Chicago, IL
210,000	Museum of Science and Industry, Chicago, IL
200,000	Northwestern University, Evanston, IL

ABC INC.

Company Headquarters
77 W. 66th St.
New York, NY 10023-6298
Web: http://www.abc.go.com

Company Description
Former Name: Capital Cities/ABC.
Employees: 20,200
SIC(s): 2711 Newspapers, 2731 Book Publishing, 4832 Radio Broadcasting Stations, 4833 Television Broadcasting Stations.

Operating Locations
ABC (CA--Los Angeles, San Francisco; CO--Englewood; CT--Bristol, Groton, Guilford, Mystic, North Haven, West Hartford; IL--Belleville, Cahokia, Carol Stream, Chicago, Highland, Lombard, O'Fallon; MA--Marshfield; MI--Pontiac; MN--Minneapolis; MO--Clayton, St. Louis; NY--Astoria; NC--Durham, Greensboro; OH--Cleveland; OR--Albany, Ashland, Cottage Grove, Newport, Portland, Sandy, Springfield; PA--Radnor, Wilkes-Barre; RI--Providence, Wakefield; TX--Dallas, Houston; WA--Spokane)

ABC Broadcasting Foundation, Inc.

Giving Contact
Bernadette Longford, Manager of Corporate Communications
77 West 66th Street, 6th Floor
New York, NY 10023
Phone: (212)456-7011
Fax: (212)456-7909

Alternate Contact
Andrew Jackson, Vice President, Corporate Affairs

Description
Founded: 1975
EIN: 237443020
Organization Type: Corporate Foundation

Former Name: Capital Cities/ABC Foundation.
Former Name: ABC Foundation.
Giving Locations: headquarters and operating communities.
Grant Types: Employee Matching Gifts, Fellowship, General Support, Scholarship.

Financial Summary

Total Giving: $300,000 (2003); $2,400,875 (2002); $2,931,076 (2001). Note: Contributes through corporate direct giving program only.
Giving Analysis: Giving for 2002 includes: foundation grants to United Way ($7,500); foundation scholarships ($85,000); foundation ($2,308,375)
Assets: $104,470 (2003); $284,295 (2001)
Gifts Received: $504,084 (2002); $6,000,000 (2001); $3,000,000 (1999). Note: In 2002, contributions were received from ABC, Inc.

Typical Recipients

Arts & Humanities: Arts Associations & Councils, Arts Centers, Arts Festivals, Arts Funds, Ballet, Dance, Ethnic & Folk Arts, Film & Video, Arts & Humanities-General, Historic Preservation, History & Archaeology, Libraries, Museums/Galleries, Performing Arts, Public Broadcasting, Theater
Civic & Public Affairs: African American Affairs, Botanical Gardens/Parks, Business/Free Enterprise, Chambers of Commerce, Clubs, Community Foundations, Economic Development, Employment/Job Training, First Amendment Issues, Civic & Public Affairs-General, Hispanic Affairs, Housing, Minority Business, Municipalities/Towns, Philanthropic Organizations, Professional & Trade Associations, Public Policy, Safety, Urban & Community Affairs, Women's Affairs
Education: Arts/Humanities Education, Business Education, Colleges & Universities, Education Funds, Education Reform, Engineering/Technological Education, Education-General, Gifted & Talented Programs, Journalism/Media Education, Leadership Training, Legal Education, Literacy, Medical Education, Minority Education, Private Education (Precollege), Public Education (Precollege), Secondary Education (Public), Student Aid
Environment: Environment-General, Wildlife Protection
Health: AIDS/HIV, Cancer, Children's Health/Hospitals, Clinics/Medical Centers, Health Organizations, Heart, Hospitals, Hospitals (University Affiliated), Medical Research, Medical Training, Single-Disease Health Associations, Transplant Networks/Donor Banks
International: Foreign Arts Organizations, International Affairs, International Relief Efforts
Religion: Jewish Causes, Religious Welfare
Science: Science Museums
Social Services: At-Risk Youth, Camps, Child Abuse, Child Welfare, Community Service Organizations, Family Services, Food/Clothing Distribution, Homes, People with Disabilities, Recreation & Athletics, Scouts, Senior Services, Substance Abuse, Volunteer Services, YMCA/YWCA/YMHA/YWHA, Youth Organizations

Application Procedures

Initial Contact: Send a brief letter or proposal on the organization's letterhead.
Application Requirements: Include a description of organization; amount requested; purpose of funds sought; recently audited financial statement; proof of tax-exempt status.
Deadlines: None.
Decision Notification: Decisions are generally made on a quarterly basis.

Restrictions

Does not make contributions to individuals.

Corporate Officials

Daniel Barnett Burke: director vice president B Albany, NY 1929. ED University of Vermont AB (1950);

Harvard University MBA (1955). CORP AFFIL director: Washington Post Co.; director: Rohm & Haas Co.; director: Darden Restaurants Inc.; director: Morgan Stanley Group Inc.; director: Consolidated Rail Corp.; director: Capital Cities/ABC Inc.; director: Conrail Inc. NONPR AFFIL director: Partnership Drug Free America; trustee: Presbyterian Hospital; chairman: International Executive Service Corps; director: American Film Institute.
Ronald J. Doerfler: senior vice president, chief financial officer B Jersey City, NJ 1941. ED Fairleigh Dickinson University BS (1965); Fairleigh Dickinson University MBA (1973). PRIM CORP EMPL senior vice president, chief financial officer: Capital Cities ABC Inc. ADD CORP EMPL senior vice president: American Broadcasting Companies; director, vice president: ABC News Inc.; vice president. chief financial officer: Hearst Corp.; vice president: WABC-AM Radio Inc. NONPR AFFIL member: Institute Newspaper Financial Executives; member: International Radio & Television Society; member: American Institute CPAs; member: Broadcast Financial Management Association.
Philip Richeson Farnsworth: secretary B New Orleans, LA 1941. ED Washington & Lee University BA (1964); Tulane University JD (1967); New York University LLM (1968). PRIM CORP EMPL secretary: ABC, Inc. ADD CORP EMPL secretary: ABC Holding Co. Inc.; secretary, director: ABC News Inc.; secretary: TV Connection Inc. CLUB AFFIL University Club.
Michael Patrick Mallardi: senior vice president B New York, NY 1934. ED University of Notre Dame BA (1956). PRIM CORP EMPL senior vice president: ABC.

Foundation Officials

Alan N. Braverman: vice president
Griffith W. Foxley: president
James Hanford: assistant treasurer
Bernadette Williams Longford: manager corporate giving
Marsha Reed: secretary
Laurie Younger: vice president
John W. Zucker: assistant secretary

Grants Analysis

Disclosure Period: calendar year ending 2003
Total Grants: $300,000
Number of Grants: 2
Highest Grant: $200,000
Lowest Grant: $100,000

Recent Grants

Note: Grants derived from 2001 Form 990.

Library-Related

25,000	New York Public Library, New York, NY

General

200,000	Academy of Television Arts & Sciences Foundation, North Hollywood, CA
100,000	New York University School of Medicine, New York, NY
90,000	Museum of Television and Radio, New York, NY
83,333	Little League Baseball Incorporated, Williamsport, PA
75,000	Lincoln Center for the Performing Arts/Consolidated Corporate Fund, New York, NY
75,000	National Fish and Wildlife Foundation Inc., Washington, DC
65,000	West Side YMCA of Greater New York, New York, NY
50,000	Columbia University/Graduate School of Journalism, New York, NY
50,000	Communities in Schools, Alexandria, VA
50,000	Inner-City Scholarship Fund, New York, NY

ABELL FOUNDATION

Giving Contact

Robert C. Embry, Jr., President
111 South Calvert Street, Suite 2300
Baltimore, MD 21202
Phone: (410)547-1300
Fax: (410)539-6579
E-mail: abell@abell.org
Web: http://www.abell.org

Description

Founded: 1953
EIN: 526036106
Organization Type: General Purpose Foundation
Giving Locations: MD: Baltimore
Grant Types: Challenge, Employee Matching Gifts, Endowment, General Support, Loan, Matching, Project, Research, Scholarship, Seed Money.

Donor Information

Founder: Established in 1953 by the late Harry C. Black, then chairman of A. S. Abell Company, publisher of the Baltimore Sun papers. Formerly known as the A. S. Abell Company Foundation, the Abell Foundation is dedicated to improving the quality of life for the citizens of Maryland. Mr. Black believed it was important "to give something back to the community in such a way that was deemed to be wise and helpful."

Financial Summary

Total Giving: $9,097,486 (2003); $9,776,846 (2002); $10,907,163 (2001)
Giving Analysis: Giving for 2001 includes: foundation scholarships ($748,338)
Assets: $208,873,380 (2003); $177,561,737 (2002); $237,925,990 (2001)

Typical Recipients

Arts & Humanities: Arts Associations & Councils, Arts Centers, Arts Festivals, Arts Funds, Arts Institutes, Arts Outreach, Dance, Ethnic & Folk Arts, Arts & Humanities-General, Historic Preservation, Libraries, Literary Arts, Music, Opera, Performing Arts, Theater, Visual Arts
Civic & Public Affairs: African American Affairs, Botanical Gardens/Parks, Business/Free Enterprise, Civil Rights, Community Foundations, Economic Development, Employment/Job Training, Civic & Public Affairs-General, Housing, Inner-City Development, Law & Justice, Legal Aid, Public Policy, Safety, Urban & Community Affairs, Women's Affairs, Zoos/Aquariums
Education: Arts/Humanities Education, Business-School Partnerships, Colleges & Universities, Education Associations, Education Funds, Education Reform, Elementary Education (Private), Elementary Education (Public), Environmental Education, Faculty Development, Education-General, International Studies, Leadership Training, Legal Education, Literacy, Medical Education, Minority Education, Private Education (Precollege), Public Education (Precollege), Science/Mathematics Education, Secondary Education (Private), Secondary Education (Public), Social Sciences Education, Special Education, Student Aid, Vocational & Technical Education
Environment: Air/Water Quality, Environment-General, Protection, Resource Conservation
Health: Clinics/Medical Centers, Eyes/Blindness, Health-General, Health Policy/Cost Containment, Health Organizations, Mental Health, Nutrition, Preventive Medicine/Wellness Organizations
International: International Affairs, International Organizations
Religion: Churches, Dioceses, Religion-General, Ministries, Religious Welfare
Science: Science-General, Scientific Centers & Institutes
Social Services: Child Welfare, Community Centers,

Community Service Organizations, Crime Prevention, Delinquency & Criminal Rehabilitation, Domestic Violence, Family Planning, Family Services, Food/Clothing Distribution, People with Disabilities, Recreation & Athletics, Scouts, Senior Services, Shelters/Homelessness, Substance Abuse, United Funds/United Ways, Youth Organizations

Application Procedures

Initial Contact: Requests for grants should be initiated by a one or two page letter, describing the mission, scope of the activities, a summary of the project with its goals and objectives, and amount requested. Applicants will be asked to submit a formal and detailed application if the board is interested in the preliminary proposal.

Application Requirements: Along with the formal application form, each applicant should include one copy of the following information: a copy of latest IRS determination letter of tax-exempt status; most recent audited financial statement and current operating budget; projected operating budget for each year funding is requested; list of names and professional affiliations of current board; and any other pertinent supporting materials.

Deadlines: January 1 for consideration by the board in February, March 1 for consideration in April, May 1 for consideration in June, August 1 for consideration in September, September 1 for consideration in October, and November 1 for consideration in December.

Review Process: The board usually makes a determination on proposals within a week of the bi-monthly meetings. In essence, the foundation encourages applications that show promise of having a substantial impact on the beneficiaries and the organization's growth and stability. It also seeks applications for grants that provide creative responses to pressing community needs, demonstrate potential for stimulating new sources of financial support, and strengthen the operational base to ensure more effective and efficient delivery of services for those in need.

Notes: Unless initiated by a trustee, communications with individual trustees regarding proposals are discouraged and will not be helpful. However, the staff welcomes inquiries regarding the grant-making process and specific questions about individual proposals.

A site visit may be requested after the full proposal has been received and acknowledged.

Restrictions

The foundation does not provide funds for individuals, sponsorships, deficit financing, annual sustaining funds, plans, or travel. The foundation does not fund housing projects, hospitals or medical research. It prefers to award grants on a one-time basis, but may make multi-year grants in exceptional cases. If a request is declined, the applicant should wait one year before submitting another proposal.

Grantees must submit post-grant report.

Additional Information

The foundation reports that it also sponsors conferences, seminars, and workshops. On occasion, the foundation requests applications from organizations and initiates its own programs; the foundation also commissions studies to determine community needs.

Publications: Annual Report; Policies and Guidelines; Application Form; Newsletters

Foundation Officials

William Shepherdson Abell, Jr.: trustee B Washington, DC 1943. ED Boston College AB (1963); University of Fribourg (1964); Harvard University MPA (1965); Georgetown University JD (1970). PRIM CORP EMPL partner: Furey, Doolan & Abell.

Gary Black, Jr.: chairman, trustee B 1942. PRIM CORP EMPL co-owner, publisher: Ski Racing Magazine. CORP AFFIL publ: Ski Show Daily.

George Lloyd Bunting, Jr.: trustee B Baltimore, MD 1940. PRIM CORP EMPL president, chief executive

officer: Bunting Management Group. CORP AFFIL director: Mercantile Safe Deposit Trust Co.; director: USF&G Corp.; director: Crown Central Petroleum Corp.

Ann LaFarge Culman: vice president

Robert C. Embry, Jr.: president, trustee

Robert Garrett: trustee B Morristown, NJ 1937. ED Princeton University AB (1959); Harvard University MBA (1965). PRIM CORP EMPL president: Robert Garrett & Sons Inc. CORP AFFIL president: AdMedia Corp.; director: Mickelberry Communication Inc. CLUB AFFIL River New York Club; University New York Club; Nantucket Yacht Club; Piping Rock Club; Knickerbocker New York Club.

Jaqueline Hrabowski: trustee

Frances Murray Keenan: vice president finance

Sally J. Michel: trustee PRIM NONPR EMPL secretary, director: Maryland Zoological Society. CORP AFFIL trustee: Michel Real Estate. NONPR AFFIL secretary, director: Baltimore Zoo.

Eileen O'Rourke: treasurer

Walter Sondheim, Jr.: trustee

Esthel Summerfield: secretary

Grants Analysis

Disclosure Period: calendar year ending 2003
Total Grants: $9,097,486
Number of Grants: 166
Average Grant: $54,804
Highest Grant: $578,600
Lowest Grant: $200
Typical Range: $25,000 to $75,000

Recent Grants

Note: Grants derived from 2002 Form 990.
General

592,930	Ingenuity Project, Baltimore, MD
500,000	Baltimore Center for the Performing Arts, Baltimore, MD
500,000	Baraka School, Baltimore, MD
350,000	Baltimore Police Foundation, Baltimore, MD
350,000	Center for Fathers, Families and Workforce Development, Baltimore, MD
336,500	Baltimore City Healthy Start, Baltimore, MD
225,000	Baltimore Police Foundation, Baltimore, MD
200,000	Open Gates, Baltimore, MD
187,900	Harford-Belair Community Mental Health Center, Baltimore, MD
180,000	Parks & People Foundation, Baltimore, MD

ABELL-HANGER FOUNDATION

Giving Contact

David L. Smith, Executive Director
PO Box 430
Midland, TX 79702
Phone: (432)684-6655
Fax: (432)684-4474
E-mail: ahf@abell-hanger.org
Web: http://www.abell-hanger.org

Description

Founded: 1954
EIN: 756020781
Organization Type: General Purpose Foundation
Giving Locations: TX
Grant Types: Capital, Challenge, Conference/Seminar, Employee Matching Gifts, General Support, Matching, Multiyear/Continuing Support, Operating Expenses, Project.

Donor Information

Founder: Established in Texas in 1954 by George Thomas Abell and his wife, Gladys Hanger Abell.

"Mr. Abell was born in Wakeeney, KS. While attending Colorado A&M (now Colorado State University), he was a member of Gamma Omega, an honorary fraternity, and Sigma Alpha Epsilon, a social fraternity. He graduated with degrees in civil and irrigation engineering and mechanical engineering. In 1927, he moved to Midland, TX, where he trained himself as a geologist and entered the petroleum business as an independent oil operator.

"In addition to his professional endeavors, Mr. Abell was active in many civic, community, cultural, social, educational, and historical activities. He devoted much time to the Boy Scouts of America, serving in various capacities in the Buffalo Trail Council. He led the capital fund campaign which secured the 6,000-acre camp in the Davis mountains. For his service to the Boy Scouts, he was awarded the highest recognition of the Boy Scouts, the Silver Beaver Award.

"While serving as a director of the Midland Chamber of Commerce, Mr. Abell originated the idea for the Permian Basin Petroleum Museum, Library and Hall of Fame. He spent much time and effort collecting antique oil field equipment now displayed on the museum's grounds. Many of the oil paintings of historical events which are on display in the museum were researched by Mr. Abell and commissioned by the Abell-Hanger Foundation.

"In 1939, he married Gladys Hanger of Ft. Worth, TX, the daughter of a pioneer Tarrant County family. She graduated from Paschal High School and attended Texas Christian University and the University of Texas at Austin. Throughout her life, Mrs. Abell was an active champion of civic and cultural causes, contributing her time, talents, energy, and financial resources. An avid American patriot, she was a member of the National Society of Colonial Dames of America, and the Daughters of the American Revolution." 1995 Annual Report

Financial Summary

Total Giving: $6,169,055 (fiscal year ending June 30, 2004); $7,309,582 (fiscal 2003); $7,200,000 (fiscal 2002 approx)

Giving Analysis: Giving for fiscal 2003 includes: foundation matching gifts ($92,147); foundation grants to United Way ($456,565); fiscal 2001: foundation matching gifts ($90,187).

Assets: $145,034,202 (fiscal 2004); $130,829,470 (fiscal 2003); $130,000,000 (fiscal 2002 approx)

Typical Recipients

Arts & Humanities: Arts Associations & Councils, Dance, Historic Preservation, History & Archaeology, Libraries, Literary Arts, Museums/Galleries, Music, Theater

Civic & Public Affairs: Botanical Gardens/Parks, Business/Free Enterprise, Community Foundations, Economic Development, Employment/Job Training, Hispanic Affairs, Housing, Law & Justice, Municipalities/Towns, Philanthropic Organizations, Professional & Trade Associations, Public Policy, Safety, Urban & Community Affairs

Education: Afterschool/Enrichment Programs, Agricultural Education, Colleges & Universities, Community & Junior Colleges, Education Associations, Education Funds, Elementary Education (Public), Engineering/Technological Education, Faculty Development, Education-General, Legal Education, Literacy, Medical Education, Minority Education, Private Education (Precollege), Public Education (Precollege), Science/Mathematics Education, Social Sciences Education, Special Education, Student Aid, Vocational & Technical Education

Environment: Environment-General, Research, Resource Conservation

Health: AIDS/HIV, Alzheimer's Disease, Cancer, Children's Health/Hospitals, Diabetes, Emergency/Ambulance Services, Eyes/Blindness, Health Funds,

Health Organizations, Hospices, Hospitals, Hospitals (University Affiliated), Medical Rehabilitation, Medical Research, Medical Training, Mental Health, Multiple Sclerosis, Nursing Services, Public Health, Single-Disease Health Associations
International: Health Care/Hospitals, Missionary/Religious Activities
Religion: Ministries, Religious Organizations, Religious Welfare, Seminaries
Science: Observatories & Planetariums, Scientific Organizations, Scientific Research
Social Services: At-Risk Youth, Camps, Child Abuse, Child Welfare, Community Centers, Community Service Organizations, Counseling, Crime Prevention, Day Care, Delinquency & Criminal Rehabilitation, Domestic Violence, Emergency Relief, Family Planning, Family Services, Food/Clothing Distribution, Homes, People with Disabilities, Recreation & Athletics, Scouts, Senior Services, Sexual Abuse, Shelters/Homelessness, Substance Abuse, United Funds/United Ways, Veterans, YMCA/YWCA/YMHA/YWHA, Youth Organizations

Application Procedures

Initial Contact: If applicant has never received funding from the Abell-Hanger Foundation, initial contact should be by letter requesting a pre-proposal questionnaire. Upon return of the questionnaire, the trustees will review the request to determine whether it warrants a complete proposal. A full application form will then be sent to the applicant.
Application Requirements: Application should be submitted on the original forms supplied by the foundation. These forms should include the grant affidavit, institutional profile, grant request summary, current year operating budget and current fiscal year budget comparison, staff salaries and benefits, and contributions analysis. The applicant will also be asked to supply the organization's latest audited financial statement. The grant request summary is comprised of five components and serves as a condensation of the detailed proposal: summary statement of request, statement of need, methodology statement, evaluation of project statement, and future funding needs.
Deadlines: Applications will be accepted during the month prior to the trustee meetings in August, November, February, and May. Applicants are strongly encouraged to submit the application as early as possible.
Review Process: Trustee meetings are held in September, December, March, and June. Applicants will be notified within a week after the trustee meeting.
Notes: Please do not make attachments to or bind application forms for presentation; presentations to the trustees are not permitted. Applicants may, at their option, submit any additional proposal information, which will be summarized by foundation staff for the trustees and included with the required application forms.

Restrictions

Specific criteria for awarding a grant include: the organization seeking a grant should be located in Texas or have significant operations in, or provide material benefits to the citizens of, Texas; the applicant must have IRS 501(c)(3) status; and the foundation generally will not contribute to private foundations as defined in Internal Revenue Code 509.
The foundation does not fund loans, grants, scholarships, or fellowships for individual students. Block scholarship grants are made only to institutions of higher education located within Texas. The foundation generally limits its educational grants to institutions of higher education, including religious institutions. Applicants must seek funding for the same proposal from various sources, as sole sponsorship of programs is rarely undertaken. Grants are made without any commitment for future support of operations or specific projects. Unsuccessful proposals may not be resubmitted for at least 12 months.

Additional Information

Publications: Annual Report; Guidelines; Application Form; Pre-Proposal Questionnaire

Foundation Officials

Herbert L. Cartwright, III: secretary, treasurer, comptroller
Arlen L. Edgar: trustee
Jerome M. Fullinwider: trustee PRIM CORP EMPL president: VF - Russia Inc.
Tevis Herd: president, trustee
Robert C. Leibrock: trustee CORP AFFIL director: Elcor Corp.
Clarence Scharbauer, III: trustee
David L. Smith: executive director, trustee
James I. Trott: trustee
Lester Van Pelt, Jr.: vice president, trustee
Charles M. Younger, MD: trustee

Grants Analysis

Disclosure Period: fiscal year ending June 30, 2003
Total Grants: $6,760,870*
Number of Grants: 281
Average Grant: $19,503*
Highest Grant: $1,300,000
Typical Range: $5,000 to $50,000
*Note:** Giving excludes matching gifts; United Way. Average grant figure excludes highest grant.

Recent Grants

Note: Grants derived from fiscal 2003 Form 990.
Library-Related
| 33,334 | Canyon Library Inc., Canyon, TX -- towards construction of new library |
General
1,300,000	Permian Basin Petroleum Museum, Library and Hall of Fame, Midland, TX -- towards gift of paintings to museum
450,000	Texas Interscholastic League Foundation, Austin, TX -- towards annual scholarships
400,000	Midland College, Midland, TX -- towards consolidated scholarship fund
362,682	Permian Basin Petroleum Museum Library and Hall of Fame, Midland, TX -- towards transportation wing project
250,000	Permian Basin Petroleum Museum Library and Hall of Fame, Midland, TX -- towards transportation wing project
170,000	United Way of Midland Inc., Midland, TX
150,000	Boy Scouts of America Buffalo Trail Council Inc., Midland, TX -- towards purchase of land
120,000	United Way of Midland Inc., Midland, TX
100,000	George W Bush Childhood Home, Midland, TX
100,000	Midland Children's Rehabilitation Center, Midland, TX

ABERCROMBIE FOUNDATION

Giving Contact

John Backer, General Manager
PO Box 68
Versailles, KY 40383
Phone: (859)873-4477

Alternate Contact

Josephine E. Abercrombie, President

Description

Founded: 1950
EIN: 760229183
Organization Type: Family Foundation
Giving Locations: KY

Grant Types: Department, General Support, Operating Expenses, Project.

Donor Information

Founder: Established in Texas in 1950 with funds donated by James S. Abercrombie, an independent oil man from the Houston area who died in 1975. Mr. Abercrombie founded J. S. Abercrombie Minerals, which discovered oil in Texas and Louisiana. The company is still privately owned. He also founded the Cameron Iron Works, a manufacturer of aerospace products and oil production equipment. Abercrombie's only daughter, Josephine Abercrombie, is the president of the foundation.
In May of 1988, the J. S. Abercrombie Foundation distributed all of its assets and liabilities to the Abercrombie Foundation and the Robinson Foundation, 70% and 30% respectively.

Financial Summary

Total Giving: $1,290,600 (2001)
Assets: $5,989,804 (2001)

Typical Recipients

Arts & Humanities: Arts & Humanities-General, History & Archaeology, Libraries, Museums/Galleries, Music, Public Broadcasting, Theater, Visual Arts
Civic & Public Affairs: Botanical Gardens/Parks, Clubs, Civic & Public Affairs-General, Housing, Urban & Community Affairs, Women's Affairs
Education: Arts/Humanities Education, Colleges & Universities, Education Funds, Elementary Education (Private), Elementary Education (Public), Engineering/Technological Education, Education-General, International Exchange, Leadership Training, Literacy, Medical Education, Private Education (Precollege), Public Education (Precollege), Student Aid
Environment: Environment-General, Resource Conservation, Wildlife Protection
Health: Cancer, Children's Health/Hospitals, Clinics/Medical Centers, Diabetes, Geriatric Health, Health Organizations, Medical Research, Mental Health, Prenatal Health Issues, Research/Studies Institutes, Speech & Hearing
Social Services: Animal Protection, At-Risk Youth, Big Brothers/Big Sisters, Child Welfare, Crime Prevention, Domestic Violence, Emergency Relief, Family Planning, Food/Clothing Distribution, People with Disabilities, Recreation & Athletics, Senior Services, Social Services-General, Special Olympics, Substance Abuse

Application Procedures

Initial Contact: 501(c)(3) organizations are invited to send one copy of a proposal.
Deadlines: May15 and November15.

Additional Information

Publications: Guidelines

Foundation Officials

Josephine E. Abercrombie: donor, president, trustee B Kingston, Jamaica 1926. PRIM CORP EMPL president: Josephine E. Abercrombie Interests. CORP AFFIL president: Pine Oak Stud Inc.

Grants Analysis

Disclosure Period: calendar year ending 2001
Total Grants: $1,290,600
Number of Grants: 30
Average Grant: $19,624*
Highest Grant: $250,000
Lowest Grant: $500
Typical Range: $5,000 to $40,000 and $100,000 to $150,000
*Note:** Average grant figure excludes two highest grants totaling $521,310.

Recent Grants

Note: Grants derived from 2002 Form 990.

General

200,000	University of Kentucky, College of Fine Arts, Lexington, KY
100,000	Cornell University Medical College, New York, NY
100,000	National Center on Addiction and Substance Abuse at Columbia University, New York, NY
100,000	Sanders-Brown Center on Aging, Lexington, KY
100,000	Texas A & M Foundation, Texas A & M College-Veterinary Medicine, College Station, TX
100,000	Texas Children's Hospital, Houston, TX
100,000	University of Kentucky Equine Research, Lexington, KY
75,000	University of Kentucky, College of Medicine, Lexington, KY
30,000	Baylor College of Medicine, Houston, TX
10,000	Pine Manor College, Chestnut Hill, MA

TALBERT AND LEOTA ABRAMS FOUNDATION

Giving Contact
Joe C. Foster, Jr., Secretary & Director
PO Box 27337
Lansing, MI 48909
Phone: (517)706-0000

Description
Founded: 1960
EIN: 386082194
Organization Type: Private Foundation
Giving Locations: MI: Lansing central
Grant Types: Endowment, General Support.

Donor Information
Founder: the late Leota Abrams, Talbert Abrams

Financial Summary
Total Giving: $403,165 (2001)
Giving Analysis: Giving for 2001 includes: foundation grants to United Way ($5,000)
Assets: $9,757,838 (2001)
Gifts Received: $2,358,812 (1992). Note: In fiscal 1992, contributions were received from Talbert Abrams Trust.

Typical Recipients
Arts & Humanities: History & Archaeology, Libraries, Museums/Galleries
Civic & Public Affairs: Clubs, Civic & Public Affairs-General, Philanthropic Organizations
Education: Colleges & Universities, Community & Junior Colleges, Engineering/Technological Education, Education-General, Literacy, Public Education (Precollege), Special Education
International: Foreign Educational Institutions
Science: Scientific Organizations
Social Services: Community Service Organizations, Counseling, Substance Abuse, United Funds/United Ways, Youth Organizations

Application Procedures
Initial Contact: Send a brief letter of inquiry, not more than two pages. Include proof of tax-exempt status.
Application Requirements: Include description of organization, amount requested, purpose of funds sought, and proof of tax-exempt status.
Deadlines: June 30.

Restrictions
Limited to scientific and educational purposes in central MI.

Additional Information
Publications: Annual Report

Foundation Officials
Kyle C. Abbott: director
Barbara J. Brown: president, director
Craig C. Brown: treasurer, director
Joe C. Foster, Jr.: secretary, director B Lansing, MI 1925. ED Wabash College (1943-1944); University of Michigan JD (1949). PRIM CORP EMPL partner: Fraser, Trebilcock, Davis & Foster. NONPR AFFIL member: Phi Gamma Delta; member: Rotary; member: Phi Beta Kappa; member: International Academy Estate & Trust Law; fellow: Michigan Bar Foundation; fellow: American College Trust & Estate Counsel; member: Florida Bar Association; fellow: American College Tax Counsel; member: American Bar Association; fellow: American Bar Foundation.
Shane A. Patzer: director
Tiffany L. Patzer: director
Thomas M. Schafer: vice president, director

Grants Analysis
Disclosure Period: calendar year ending 2001
Total Grants: $398,165*
Number of Grants: 13
Average Grant: $8,560*
Highest Grant: $174,000
Lowest Grant: $2,500
Typical Range: $5,000 to $20,000
*Note: Giving excludes United Way. Average grant figure excludes two highest grants($304,000).

Recent Grants
Note: Grants derived from 2002 Form 990.
Library-Related

179,500	Library of Michigan Foundation, Lansing, MI

General

110,000	Utica Community Schools Foundation, Utica, MI
54,895	Michigan Historical Center Foundation, Detroit, MI
20,000	Starr Commonwealth, Albion, MI
10,000	Junior Achievement, Lansing, MI
10,000	Michigan Industrial and Technology Education Society, Brown City, MI
9,000	Friends of Historic Meridian
8,000	Ingham County Genealogical Society, Mason, MI
7,000	International Geographic Information Foundation, Waverly, OH
6,000	Lansing Community College Foundation, Lansing, MI
5,000	Capital Area United Way, Lansing, MI

ACF INDUSTRIES

Company Headquarters
620 N 2nd St.
St. Charles, MO 63301-5418
Web: http://www.acfindustries.com

Company Description
Employees: 1,548
SIC(s): 3700 Transportation Equipment, 4700 Transportation Services, 6700 Holding & Other Investment Offices.

ACF Foundation

Giving Contact
Nancy Collins, Manager, Treasure Operations
620 North Second Street
St. Charles, MO 63301-2081
Phone: (636)940-5101
Fax: (314)940-5109

Description
EIN: 136085065
Organization Type: Corporate Foundation
Giving Locations: MO
Grant Types: General Support, Matching.

Financial Summary
Total Giving: $35,955 (fiscal year ending April 30, 2005); $43,223 (fiscal 2001)
Giving Analysis: Giving for fiscal 2004 includes: foundation matching gifts ($1,655); fiscal 2001: foundation matching gifts ($4,010)
Assets: $586,604 (fiscal 2004); $676,908 (fiscal 2001)

Typical Recipients
Arts & Humanities: Arts & Humanities-General, Libraries, Museums/Galleries, Music, Public Broadcasting
Civic & Public Affairs: Clubs, Economic Development, Employment/Job Training, Civic & Public Affairs-General, Municipalities/Towns
Education: Business Education, Colleges & Universities, Community & Junior Colleges, Engineering/Technological Education, Education-General, Private Education (Precollege), Religious Education, Special Education, Student Aid, Vocational & Technical Education
Health: Alzheimer's Disease, Children's Health/Hospitals, Emergency/Ambulance Services, Health Funds, Hospitals, Mental Health
Religion: Jewish Causes, Religious Organizations, Religious Welfare
Social Services: At-Risk Youth, Child Welfare, Community Centers, Community Service Organizations, Day Care, Emergency Relief, Food/Clothing Distribution, Homes, People with Disabilities, Scouts, Shelters/Homelessness, Substance Abuse, YMCA/YWCA/YMHA/YWHA, Youth Organizations

Application Procedures
Initial Contact: The foundation has no formal grant application procedure or application form.
Deadlines: None.

Restrictions
Grants are not made to individuals.

Additional Information
Publications: Contributions Guidelines Sheet

Corporate Officials
James C. Bates: vice president, chief financial officer B Saint Louis, MO 1951. ED University of Missouri (1973). PRIM CORP EMPL vice president, chief financial officer: ACF Industries. CORP AFFIL director: Campbell Chemicals; director: Trail Ltd.; vice president: ACF Industries Subs.
Carl Celian Icahn: owner, chairman, director B Queens, NY 1936. ED New York University School of Medicine; Princeton University BA (1957). PRIM CORP EMPL owner, chairman, director: Icahn & Co. CORP AFFIL chairman: XO Communications Inc.; chairman: Stratosphere Corp.; chairman, president, chief executive officer: Trans World Airlines; Samsonite Corp.; chairman, chief executive officer: Starfire Holding Corp.; president: Riverdale Investors Corp., Inc.; president: Foxfield Thoroughbreds Inc.; chairman, president: Icahn Holding Corp.; director: Fairchild Corp.; chairman: Bayswater Realty & Capital; director: Cadus Corp.; chairman: American RE Holdings LP. NONPR AFFIL Jewish Guild for the Blind Inc.
Robert J. Mitchell: treasurer PRIM CORP EMPL treasurer: ACF Industries.
James J. Unger: vice chairman, chief executive officer PRIM CORP EMPL vice chairman, chief executive officer: ACF Industries.
Roger D. Wynkoop: president B Oakland, CA 1948. ED Western Maryland College (1970). PRIM CORP

EMPL president: ACF Industries. NONPR AFFIL member: National Freight Traffic Association.

Foundation Officials
Gail Golden: secretary
Carl Celian Icahn: president (see above)
Alfred D. Kingsley: vice president

Grants Analysis
Disclosure Period: fiscal year ending April 30, 2004
Total Grants: $34,300*
Number of Grants: 35
Average Grant: $980
Highest Grant: $3,000
Lowest Grant: $250
Typical Range: $500 to $2,000
*Note: Giving excludes matching gifts.

Recent Grants
Note: Grants derived from fiscal 2004 Form 990.
General

3,000	Ranken Technical Institute, St. Louis, MO
2,000	National Alliance for the Mentally Ill, St. Louis, MO
1,500	Mosaics, St. Charles, MO
1,000	American Red Cross, St. Louis, MO
1,000	Boone Center Workshop Inc., St. Charles, MO
1,000	Boys Hope, St. Louis, MO
1,000	Central Institute for the Deaf, St. Louis, MO
1,000	Children's Home Society, St. Louis, MO
1,000	Covenant House, St. Louis, MO
1,000	DARE, St. Charles, MO

ACHELIS FOUNDATION

Giving Contact
Joseph S. Dolan, Secretary & Executive Director
Morris & McVeigh
767 3rd Avenue, 4th Floor
New York, NY 10017-2023
Phone: (212)644-0322
Fax: (212)759-6510
E-mail: main@achelis-bodman-fnds.org
Web: http://fdncenter.org/grantmaker/achelis-bodman

Description
Founded: 1940
EIN: 136022018
Organization Type: General Purpose Foundation
Giving Locations: NY: New York
Grant Types: Capital, Conference/Seminar, Emergency, Employee Matching Gifts, General Support, Matching.

Donor Information
Founder: Established in 1940 with funds donated by the late Elisabeth Achelis, who was born in 1880 in Brooklyn Heights and was active in many social and charitable causes until her death in 1974. The Achelis Foundation is affiliated with the Bodman Foundation, and it reports that they share some officers.

Financial Summary
Total Giving: $2,885,000 (2003); $1,665,000 (2002); $1,919,100 (2001)
Giving Analysis: Giving for 2001 includes: foundation matching gifts ($180,600)
Assets: $31,226,295 (2002); $37,866,499 (2001)
Gifts Received: $11,000 (2002); $26,000 (1999); $3,080,005 (1998). Note: In 1999 and 2002, contributions were received from the residuary beneficiary of the Elizabeth Achelis Trust. Gifts represent remainder trusts in 1998.

Typical Recipients
Arts & Humanities: Arts Outreach, Ballet, Dance, Ethnic & Folk Arts, Arts & Humanities-General, Historic Preservation, History & Archaeology, Libraries, Museums/Galleries, Music, Opera, Performing Arts, Public Broadcasting, Theater
Civic & Public Affairs: African American Affairs, Asian American Affairs, Botanical Gardens/Parks, Business/Free Enterprise, Clubs, Community Foundations, Economic Development, Employment/Job Training, Ethnic Organizations, Civic & Public Affairs-General, Housing, Inner-City Development, Law & Justice, Nonprofit Management, Philanthropic Organizations, Public Policy, Urban & Community Affairs, Women's Affairs, Zoos/Aquariums
Education: Afterschool/Enrichment Programs, Arts/Humanities Education, Business Education, Business-School Partnerships, Colleges & Universities, Education Associations, Education Funds, Education Reform, Elementary Education (Private), Elementary Education (Public), Environmental Education, Faculty Development, Education-General, Legal Education, Literacy, Medical Education, Minority Education, Preschool Education, Private Education (Precollege), Public Education (Precollege), Social Sciences Education, Special Education, Student Aid
Environment: Air/Water Quality, Environment-General, Protection, Resource Conservation, Wildlife Protection
Health: AIDS/HIV, Alzheimer's Disease, Cancer, Children's Health/Hospitals, Clinics/Medical Centers, Emergency/Ambulance Services, Eyes/Blindness, Health-General, Health Funds, Health Organizations, Hospitals, Hospitals (University Affiliated), Medical Rehabilitation, Medical Research, Medical Training, Mental Health, Nursing Services, Outpatient Health Care, Public Health, Speech & Hearing, Transplant Networks/Donor Banks
International: Foreign Arts Organizations, Health Care/Hospitals, International Development, International Relations, International Relief Efforts
Religion: Churches, Religion-General, Jewish Causes, Ministries, Religious Organizations, Religious Welfare, Social/Policy Issues
Science: Science Museums, Scientific Centers & Institutes, Scientific Labs, Scientific Research
Social Services: Animal Protection, At-Risk Youth, Big Brothers/Big Sisters, Child Welfare, Community Centers, Community Service Organizations, Counseling, Day Care, Domestic Violence, Emergency Relief, Family Planning, Family Services, Food/Clothing Distribution, People with Disabilities, Recreation & Athletics, Refugee Assistance, Scouts, Senior Services, Sexual Abuse, Shelters/Homelessness, Social Services-General, Substance Abuse, Volunteer Services, YMCA/YWCA/YMHA/YWHA, Youth Organizations

Application Procedures
Initial Contact: Grant requests should be forwarded by letter, one copy only, with the signature of an appropriate officer. Organizations with which the foundation may not be familiar should include a statement of history and purpose for which funds are sought and financial data for both the organization and the proposal itself, along with proof of tax-exempt status.
Deadlines: None.
Review Process: The foundation's board meets in May, September, and December, and holds special meetings whenever warranted. The trustees review all requests for funds from staff recommendations and make all decisions on grant applications. Organizations requesting support must be aware that the foundation can respond affirmatively to only a small number of the many applications received each year.

Restrictions
The foundation's activities are primarily centered in greater NY under the current program. Grants are usually not authorized for travel, publications, films, or conferences. The foundation does not directly engage in research or experimental projects. The foundation does not make loans nor does it make grants to individuals.

Additional Information
Publications: Biennial Report; Guidelines

Foundation Officials
Horace I. Crary, Jr.: treasurer
Anthony Drexel Duke, Sr.: trustee B New York, NY July 28, 1918. ED Princeton University (1941). NONPR AFFIL chairman, president, founder: Boys Harbor.
Peter Frelinghuysen: vice president, trustee ED Princeton University (1963); Yale University (1968). PRIM CORP EMPL attorney: Morris & McVeigh. CORP AFFIL secretary: K O A Holdings Inc.

Grants Analysis
Disclosure Period: calendar year ending 2003
Total Grants: $2,885,000
Number of Grants: 93
Average Grant: $31,022
Highest Grant: $100,000
Lowest Grant: $5,000
Typical Range: $10,000 to $50,000

Recent Grants
Note: Grants derived from 2002 Form 990.
General

150,000	Rockefeller University, New York, NY -- research on immunization strategies to prevent infectious diseases by developing new vaccines
75,000	Manhattan Institute for Policy Research, New York, NY -- fellowship for David Gratzer
65,000	Foundation for Education Reform and Accountability, Clifton Park, NY
50,000	Baruch College, New York, NY -- research, editing and oversight of monographs regarding welfare policy by Jason Turner
50,000	Boy Scouts of America, Greater New York Councils, New York, NY -- support of Scout reach program
50,000	Civic Builders Inc., New York, NY -- start-up expenses
50,000	Corporation for Educational Radio and Television, New York, NY
50,000	Explore Charter School, Brooklyn, NY -- start-up and renovation expense for new charter school
50,000	Girl Scout Council of Greater New York Inc., New York, NY -- women with wings program
50,000	Girls Educational & Mentoring Services, New York, NY

ANNA KEESLING ACKERMAN TRUST

Giving Contact
Philip Devries
c/o U.S. Bank National Association
6 S. Tejon St., Suite 300
Colorado Springs, CO 80903
Phone: (719)630-4200

Description
Founded: 1963
EIN: 846032046
Organization Type: Private Foundation
Giving Locations: CO
Grant Types: Endowment, General Support.

Financial Summary

Total Giving: $433,203 (2004); $454,977 (2001)
Giving Analysis: Giving for 2004 includes: foundation scholarships ($10,916) 2001: foundation scholarships ($3,477)
Assets: $8,966,020 (2004); $9,197,260 (2001)

Typical Recipients

Arts & Humanities: Arts Outreach, Libraries, Museums/Galleries, Performing Arts, Theater
Civic & Public Affairs: Community Foundations, Civic & Public Affairs-General, Housing, Urban & Community Affairs, Zoos/Aquariums
Education: Business Education, Colleges & Universities, Education Associations, Education Funds, Education-General, Public Education (Precollege), Social Sciences Education, Student Aid
Environment: Resource Conservation
Health: Children's Health/Hospitals, Diabetes, Emergency/Ambulance Services, Heart, Home-Care Services, Hospices, Mental Health, Multiple Sclerosis, Prenatal Health Issues, Single-Disease Health Associations
Religion: Churches, Ministries, Religious Welfare, Synagogues/Temples
Social Services: Animal Protection, Community Centers, Community Service Organizations, Day Care, Domestic Violence, Family Services, Food/Clothing Distribution, People with Disabilities, Recreation & Athletics, Scouts, Senior Services, Social Services-General, YMCA/YWCA/YMHA/YWHA, Youth Organizations

Application Procedures

Initial Contact: Send a brief letter of inquiry.
Application Requirements: Include purpose of funds sought and proof of tax-exempt status.
Deadlines: None.

Restrictions

Does not provide grants to individuals.

Additional Information

Trust(s): U.S. Bank

Grants Analysis

Disclosure Period: calendar year ending 2004
Total Grants: $422,287*
Number of Grants: 51
Average Grant: $6,446*
Highest Grant: $100,000
Lowest Grant: $1,000
Typical Range: $1,000 to $10,000
*Note: Giving excludes scholarships. Average grant figure excludes highest grant.

Recent Grants

Note: Grants derived from 2001 Form 990.

General

102,000	Pro Rodeo Hall of Fame, Colorado Springs, CO
50,000	Bust Rodeo Foundation, Colorado Springs, CO
35,000	Cheyenne Mountain Zoo, Colorado Springs, CO
30,000	US Olympic Committee, Colorado Springs, CO
25,000	American Heart Association Pikes Peak Chapter, Colorado Springs, CO
25,000	YMCA of Pikes Peak Region, Colorado Springs, CO
15,000	Boys and Girls Club of Larimer County, Ft. Collins, CO
15,000	Salvation Army, Colorado Springs, CO
12,500	Nature Conservancy, Boulder, CO
10,000	Al Kaly Temple, Pueblo, CO

ACME-MCCRARY CORP./SAPONA MANUFACTURING CO.

Company Headquarters

PO Box 1287
Asheboro, NC 27204
Web: http://www.saponamfg.com

Company Description

Employees: 900
SIC(s): 2200 Textile Mill Products.

Acme-McCrary and Sapona Foundation

Giving Contact

Fred M. Kearns, Jr., President
PO Box 1287
Asheboro, NC 27204
Phone: (336)625-2161

Description

EIN: 566047739
Organization Type: Corporate Foundation
Giving Locations: NC: Randolph County
Grant Types: Capital, General Support, Scholarship.

Financial Summary

Total Giving: $33,950 (2003). Note: 1997 and 2000 Giving includes United Way ($16,000).
Giving Analysis: Giving for 2003 includes: foundation grants to United Way ($16,000)
Assets: $1,176,835 (2003)
Gifts Received: $39,525 (2000); $50,000 (1998); $50,000 (1997). Note: In 1998, contributions were received from Sapona Manufacturing Co. ($50,000).

Typical Recipients

Arts & Humanities: Arts Associations & Councils, Arts & Humanities-General, Libraries, Museums/Galleries, Music
Civic & Public Affairs: Chambers of Commerce, Clubs, Employment/Job Training, Civic & Public Affairs-General, Housing, Inner-City Development, Professional & Trade Associations, Safety, Zoos/Aquariums
Education: Colleges & Universities, Community & Junior Colleges, Education-General, Health & Physical Education, Medical Education, Minority Education, Preschool Education, Private Education (Precollege), Public Education (Precollege)
Health: Alzheimer's Disease, Cancer, Children's Health/Hospitals, Clinics/Medical Centers, Diabetes, Emergency/Ambulance Services, Health-General, Health Organizations, Hospices, Hospitals, Hospitals (University Affiliated), Medical Rehabilitation, Nursing Services, Public Health
Religion: Churches, Religion-General, Religious Organizations
Social Services: Community Centers, Community Service Organizations, Recreation & Athletics, Scouts, Senior Services, Social Services-General, United Funds/United Ways, YMCA/YWCA/YMHA/YWHA, Youth Organizations

Application Procedures

Initial Contact: Send a letter.
Application Requirements: Include purpose of funds sought and the scope of the organization's activities. If the funds are requested for a regular purpose or activity, a description of the purpose or activity should be included.
Deadlines: December 1.

Restrictions

Does not support individuals or political or lobbying groups.

Corporate Officials

Charles W. McCrary, Jr.: chairman, chief executive officer, director PRIM CORP EMPL chairman, chief executive officer, director: Acme-McCrary Corp.
Bruce T. Patram: chief financial officer PRIM CORP EMPL chief financial officer: Acme-McCrary Corp.
William H. Redding, Jr.: president, director PRIM CORP EMPL president, director: Acme-McCrary Corp.
John O. H. Toledano: vice chairman, secretary, director PRIM CORP EMPL vice chairman, secretary, director: Acme-McCrary Corp.

Foundation Officials

Fred M. Kearns, Jr.: president
C. W. McCrary, III: director
Charles W. McCrary, Jr.: vice president (see above)
Bruce T. Patram: secretary, treasurer (see above)
S. Steele Redding: vice president
William H. Redding, Jr.: vice president (see above)
John O. H. Toledano: vice president (see above)
John O.H. Toledano, Jr.: director

Grants Analysis

Disclosure Period: calendar year ending 2003
Total Grants: $17,950*
Number of Grants: 14
Average Grant: $1,282
Highest Grant: $4,000
Lowest Grant: $100
Typical Range: $300 to $2,000
*Note: Giving excludes United Way.

Recent Grants

Note: Grants derived from 2001 Form 990.
General

16,000	United Way of Randolph County, Elkins, WV -- annual fund
6,250	Boy Scouts of America Old North State Council, Greensboro, NC -- park renovation
2,500	Regional Consolidated Services -- annual fund
1,500	North Carolina Zoological Society, NC -- annual fund
1,250	Randolph-Asheboro YMCA, Asheboro, NC -- annual fund
1,000	American Cancer Society, Wallingford, CT -- annual fund
1,000	Asheboro City School Systems, Asheboro, NC -- scholarship
1,000	East Side Improvement Association, Asheboro, NC -- School Renovation Project
1,000	George Washington Carver Community Enrichment Center, Asheboro, NC -- building fund
1,000	Greensboro Symphony Orchestra, Greensboro, NC -- annual fund

ACUSHNET FOUNDATION

Giving Contact

R. William Blasdale, Foundation Manager
Acushnet Foundation
PO Box 1498
Mattapoisett, MA 02739
Phone: (508)758-6159
Fax: (508)758-8960
E-mail: seamark@ma.ultranet.com

Description

EIN: 046032197
Organization Type: Private Foundation
Giving Locations: MA: New Bedford

Grant Types: Capital, Emergency, General Support, Multiyear/Continuing Support, Scholarship, Seed Money.

Donor Information
Founder: Established by Acushnet Co.

Financial Summary
Total Giving: $510,500 (fiscal year ending June 30, 2001)
Giving Analysis: Giving for fiscal 2001 includes: foundation grants to United Way ($107,000)
Assets: $9,733,868 (fiscal 2001)

Typical Recipients
Arts & Humanities: Arts Associations & Councils, Community Arts, Historic Preservation, History & Archaeology, Libraries, Museums/Galleries, Music, Public Broadcasting, Theater
Civic & Public Affairs: Civil Rights, Community Foundations, Economic Policy, Civic & Public Affairs-General, Law & Justice, Legal Aid, Philanthropic Organizations, Public Policy, Urban & Community Affairs
Education: Business Education, Colleges & Universities, Economic Education, Education Funds, Engineering/Technological Education, Education-General, International Exchange, Minority Education, Public Education (Precollege), Science/Mathematics Education, Secondary Education (Private), Secondary Education (Public), Special Education, Student Aid
Environment: Environment-General
Health: Children's Health/Hospitals, Clinics/Medical Centers, Health Funds, Health Organizations, Hospitals, Medical Rehabilitation, Nursing Services, Public Health
Religion: Churches, Religious Organizations, Religious Welfare
Science: Science Exhibits & Fairs
Social Services: Animal Protection, Child Welfare, Community Centers, Community Service Organizations, Day Care, Family Services, Scouts, Substance Abuse, United Funds/United Ways, YMCA/YWCA/YMHA/YWHA, Youth Organizations

Application Procedures
Initial Contact: Send a brief letter of inquiry.
Application Requirements: amount desired, purpose of funds sought, and other pertinent information
Deadlines: None.
Review Process: The board meets when required and notifies applicants within four to six weeks after receipt of letter.

Restrictions
The foundation does not support endowments, operating expenses, or matching gifts. Grants are made in the New Bedford area unless a project receives specific board approval.

Additional Information
The foundation favors organizations with no other means of support. Grant seekers currently receiving government aid are not encouraged to apply.
The Acushnet Co. was the original donor to the Acushnet Foundation. It is currently not involved with administering the foundation.

Foundation Officials
William Blasdale: trustee
Bill Blazedale: trustee
Robert S. Dubiel: trustee PRIM CORP EMPL executive vice president: Acushnet Co. CORP AFFIL president, chief executive officer: Cobra Golf Inc.; president: Titleist Foot-Joy Worldwide.
Grame L. Flanders: trustee
Glenn Johnson: trustee PRIM CORP EMPL vice president: Woburn National Bank Corp.
Edward Powers: foundation managing, trustee
Carl Ribeiro: trustee
Robert Vanz: trustee

Thomas C. Weaver: trustee
Richard B. Young: trustee
William Young: trustee B New Bedford, MA 1943. ED University of Massachusetts, Amherst (1969); Boston University JD (1981). PRIM CORP EMPL vice president, fiduciary tax counsel: Boston Safe Deposit & Trust Co. NONPR AFFIL member: American Bar Association.

Grants Analysis
Disclosure Period: fiscal year ending June 30, 2001
Total Grants: $403,500*
Number of Grants: 59
Average Grant: $6,839
Highest Grant: $50,000
Typical Range: $1,000 to $20,000
*Note: Giving excludes United Way.

Recent Grants
Note: Grants derived from fiscal 2002 Form 990.
General

95,000	United Way of New Bedford, Inc., New Bedford, MA
50,000	Boys and Girls Club of New Bedford, New Bedford, MA
25,000	Community Foundation, New Bedford, MA
25,000	New Bedford Child and Family Service, New Bedford, MA
22,000	Old Dartmouth Historical Society, New Bedford, MA
20,000	Boys and Girls Club of New Bedford, New Bedford, MA
20,000	Dennison Memorial Community Center, New Bedford, MA
20,000	St. Luke's Hospital, New Bedford, MA
15,000	YMCA New Bedford, New Bedford, MA
10,000	Animal Rescue League, New Bedford, MA

CHARLES E. AND CAROLINE J. ADAMS TRUST

Giving Contact
Sharon M. Driscoll, Executive Account Manager
Charles E. and Caroline J. Adams Trust
Care of Fleet National Bank Boston
PO Box Box 6767
Providence, RI 02940
Phone: (617)434-5669
Fax: (617)434-7567

Description
Founded: 1955
EIN: 046011995
Organization Type: Private Foundation
Giving Locations: MA: Boston
Grant Types: Capital, General Support.

Donor Information
Founder: the late Charles E. and Caroline J. Adams

Financial Summary
Total Giving: $537,362 (fiscal year ending May 31, 2004); $148,911 (fiscal 2001)
Assets: $13,751,481 (fiscal 2004); $15,683,700 (fiscal 2001)

Typical Recipients
Arts & Humanities: Libraries, Museums/Galleries, Music
Civic & Public Affairs: African American Affairs, Business/Free Enterprise, Economic Development, Employment/Job Training, Civic & Public Affairs-General, Hispanic Affairs, Nonprofit Management,

Philanthropic Organizations, Urban & Community Affairs
Education: Colleges & Universities, Education Reform, Engineering/Technological Education, Education-General, Medical Education, Public Education (Precollege), School Volunteerism, Science/Mathematics Education
Science: Science Museums
Social Services: At-Risk Youth, Camps, Child Abuse, Child Welfare, Community Centers, Community Service Organizations, Day Care, Family Services, Youth Organizations

Application Procedures
Initial Contact: Send full proposal.
Application Requirements: Include a description of organization, amount requested, purpose of funds sought, recently audited financial statement, and proof of tax-exempt status.
Deadlines: None.
Review Process: Board meets in March, June, September, and December.

Additional Information
Trust(s): Fleet Natl Bank Boston

Grants Analysis
Disclosure Period: fiscal year ending May 31, 2004
Total Grants: $537,362
Number of Grants: 10
Average Grant: $25,000*
Highest Grant: $131,181
Lowest Grant: $5,000
Typical Range: $5,000 to $50,000
*Note: Average grant figure excludes three highest grants ($362,362).

Recent Grants
Note: Grants derived from 2001 Form 990.
General

165,258	Massachusetts Institute of Technology, Cambridge, MA
165,257	Harvard Medical School, Cambridge, MA
75,000	Center for Women and Enterprise, Boston, MA
30,000	Boston Plan for Excellence, Boston, MA
30,000	Career Connections Collaborative, Boston, MA
29,996	Mt. Auburn Associates
20,000	Tri-City Community Action Program, Malden, MA
15,000	Dorchester Bay Economic Development Corp, Dorchester, MA
10,000	Latino Parents Association, Boston, MA
10,000	Suited for Success, Miami, FL

ADC TELECOMMUNICATIONS

Company Headquarters
13625 Technology Drive
Eden Prairie, MN 55344-2252
Web: http://www.adc.com

Company Description
Employees: 2,900
SIC(s): 3600 Electronic & Other Electrical Equipment.

Operating Locations
ADC Telecommunications (MN--Minneapolis)

Nonmonetary Support
Type: Donated Equipment; Donated Products; In-kind Services

Giving Contact

Sandra Larson, Manager, Contributions & Community Relations
PO Box 1101
Minneapolis, MN 55440-1101
Phone: (952)946-3113
Fax: (952)946-3292

Description

Organization Type: Corporate Giving Program
Giving Locations: principally near operating locations and to national organizations.
Grant Types: Capital, Emergency, General Support, Operating Expenses, Seed Money.

Financial Summary

Total Giving: Company does not disclose contributions figures.

Typical Recipients

Arts & Humanities: Arts Appreciation, Arts Associations & Councils, Arts Centers, Arts Institutes, Ballet, Community Arts, Dance, Ethnic & Folk Arts, Arts & Humanities-General, Libraries, Museums/Galleries, Music, Opera, Performing Arts, Public Broadcasting, Theater, Visual Arts
Civic & Public Affairs: African American Affairs, Asian American Affairs, Botanical Gardens/Parks, Business/Free Enterprise, Civil Rights, Economic Development, Economic Policy, Employment/Job Training, Ethnic Organizations, Civic & Public Affairs-General, Housing, Inner-City Development, Minority Business, Native American Affairs, Nonprofit Management, Philanthropic Organizations, Public Policy, Urban & Community Affairs, Women's Affairs, Zoos/Aquariums
Education: Afterschool/Enrichment Programs, Arts/Humanities Education, Business Education, Business-School Partnerships, Colleges & Universities, Community & Junior Colleges, Continuing Education, Economic Education, Education Funds, Elementary Education (Public), Engineering/Technological Education, Education-General, Legal Education, Literacy, Minority Education, Preschool Education, Public Education (Precollege), Science/Mathematics Education, Secondary Education (Public), Special Education, Vocational & Technical Education
Environment: Environment-General
Health: Adolescent Health Issues, Clinics/Medical Centers, Health-General, Medical Rehabilitation, Medical Research, Mental Health, Public Health
International: Human Rights, International Affairs, International Relations
Science: Science-General, Science Exhibits & Fairs, Science Museums, Scientific Centers & Institutes, Scientific Labs, Scientific Organizations, Scientific Research
Social Services: At-Risk Youth, Camps, Child Welfare, Community Centers, Community Service Organizations, Counseling, Day Care, Delinquency & Criminal Rehabilitation, Domestic Violence, Emergency Relief, Family Services, Food/Clothing Distribution, Homes, People with Disabilities, Recreation & Athletics, Refugee Assistance, Senior Services, Sexual Abuse, Shelters/Homelessness, Social Services-General, Substance Abuse, United Funds/United Ways, Volunteer Services, Youth Organizations

Application Procedures

Initial Contact: Send a brief letter of inquiry and a full proposal.
Application Requirements: Include a description of organization, amount requested, purpose of funds sought, recently audited financial statement, and proof of tax-exempt status. Also include a list of the board of directors.

Restrictions

Does not support political or lobbying groups or religious organizations for sectarian purposes.

Corporate Officials

J. A. Blanchard, III: chairman, chief executive officer B 1942. ED Princeton University BA (1965); Massachusetts Institute of Technology MS (1978). PRIM CORP EMPL chairman: ADC Telecommunications.
Robert E. Switz: president, chief executive officer PRIM CORP EMPL president, chief executive officer: ADC Telecommunications ADD CORP EMPL treasurer: ADC Systems Integration Inc.

Grants Analysis

Typical Range: $1,000 to $2,500

DIANA S. ADELSON TRUST

Giving Contact

Edward B. Corcoran
31 America's Cup Ave.
Newport, RI 02840
Phone: (401)847-0872

Description

Founded: 1993
EIN: 050466295
Organization Type: Private Foundation
Giving Locations: RI
Grant Types: General Support.

Financial Summary

Total Giving: $49,700 (2004); $49,000 (2001)
Assets: $607,433 (2004); $700,375 (2001)
Gifts Received: $9,246 (1994); $83,178 (1993); $686,188 (1992). Note: In 1994, contributions were received from the estate of Diana Adelson.

Typical Recipients

Arts & Humanities: Libraries, Music, Public Broadcasting
Civic & Public Affairs: African American Affairs, Civic & Public Affairs-General, Legal Aid, Safety, Urban & Community Affairs
Education: Public Education (Precollege)
Health: Emergency/Ambulance Services, Hospitals, Nursing Services
Religion: Religion-General, Jewish Causes, Religious Organizations, Religious Welfare, Synagogues/Temples
Social Services: Camps, Community Service Organizations, Crime Prevention, Domestic Violence, Family Services, Food/Clothing Distribution, People with Disabilities, Social Services-General, Youth Organizations

Application Procedures

Initial Contact: Send a brief letter of inquiry.
Application Requirements: Include a description of organization and constituents served, general organizational materials, proof of tax-exempt status, and purpose of funds sought.
Deadlines: None.

Restrictions

Supports only 501(c)(3) organizations. No grants are made to individuals.

Foundation Officials

Edwin S. Gozonsky: trustee
Jeffrey J. Teitz: trustee

Grants Analysis

Disclosure Period: calendar year ending 2004
Total Grants: $49,700
Number of Grants: 13
Average Grant: $3,823
Highest Grant: $10,000

Lowest Grant: $1,000
Typical Range: $1,000 to $5,000

Recent Grants

Note: Grants derived from 2001 Form 990.
Library-Related

1,500	Ruth Woolf Adelson Medical Library Fund, Newport, RI

General

10,000	New Visions of Newport County, Newport, RI
10,000	Newport Hospital Foundation, Newport, RI
5,000	Boys and Girls Club of Newport County, Inc, Newport, RI
3,000	Martin Luther King Center, Newport, RI
2,500	Camp Ruggles Rhode Island, Newport, RI
2,500	Child and Family Services, Newport, RI
2,500	Congregation Jesuat Israel, Newport, RI
2,500	Justice Assistance, Providence, RI
2,500	Rhode Island Legal Services, Providence, RI
2,000	Thompson Middle School, Newport, RI

LEO ADLER TRUST

Giving Contact

Marlyn Norquist, Trust Officer
c/o U.S. National Association Bank
PO Box 3168
Portland, OR 97208-3168
Phone: (503)275-4327
E-mail: teresa.ingram@usbank.com
Web: http://www.leoadler.com

Description

Founded: 1995
EIN: 936289087
Organization Type: Private Foundation
Giving Locations: OR: Baker County
Grant Types: General Support, Scholarship.

Financial Summary

Total Giving: $1,072,296 (2002); $1,315,801 (2001)
Giving Analysis: Giving for 2002 includes: foundation scholarships ($719,264)
Assets: $21,881,719 (2002); $25,592,850 (2001)
Gifts Received: $50 (2002); $150 (2001); $29,300 (2000). Note: Contributions were received from the estate of Leo Adler.

Typical Recipients

Arts & Humanities: History & Archaeology, Libraries, Museums/Galleries, Performing Arts
Civic & Public Affairs: Botanical Gardens/Parks, Employment/Job Training, Civic & Public Affairs-General, Municipalities/Towns, Urban & Community Affairs
Education: Colleges & Universities, Public Education (Precollege), Student Aid
Environment: Environment-General
Health: Clinics/Medical Centers, Emergency/Ambulance Services, Health Organizations, Hospitals
Religion: Religious Welfare
Social Services: Community Centers, Domestic Violence, Family Services, Recreation & Athletics, YMCA/YWCA/YMHA/YWHA

Application Procedures

Initial Contact: Request application form.
Deadlines: October 1 for Community Fund applications, April 1 for first time scholarship applications, March 1 for scholarship renewals.

Restrictions

Grants are not made to support individuals, religious organizations for sectarian purposes, political or lobbying groups, or organizations outside operating areas.

Additional Information

The foundation gives through two funds: a Community Grants fund, with a grant range of $300 to $75,000 and a scholarship fund, with a range of $600 to $5,000. The foundation awards scholarships to students who are graduates of high schools in Baker County, OR, or North Poweder High School in Union County, OR. In addition, the Leo Adler Community Fund was created for the purpose of awarding grants to tax-exempt organizations in the Baker County, OR, area.

Trust(s): US Natl Bank OR

Grants Analysis

Disclosure Period: calendar year ending 2002
Total Grants: $353,032*
Number of Grants: 52
Average Grant: $5,942*
Highest Grant: $50,000
Lowest Grant: $300
Typical Range: $1,000 to $10,000
*Note: Giving excludes scholarships. Average grant figure excludes highest grant.

Recent Grants

Note: Grants derived from 2001 Form 990.
General

127,180	Eastern Oregon University, La Grande, OR -- scholarship/education
100,000	Partnership II, Baker City, OR
100,000	St. Elizabeth Health Care Foundation, Baker City, OR
71,783	Oregon State University, Corvallis, OR -- scholarship/education
50,000	Baker Sports Complex, Baker, OR -- to build phase III
47,390	Blue MT Community College, Pendleton, OR -- scholarship/education
38,500	University of Oregon, Eugene, OR -- scholarship/education
34,950	University of Idaho, Moscow, ID -- scholarship and education
34,650	Boise State University, Boise, ID -- scholarship/education
30,000	City of Baker City, Baker City, OR

ADOBE SYSTEMS

Company Headquarters

345 Park Avenue
San Jose, CA 95110-2704
Web: http://www.adobe.com

Company Description

Founded: 1982
Ticker: ADBE
Exchange: NASDAQ
Former Name: Aldus Corp.
Revenue: US$1.164 billion (2002)
Employees: 3341 (2002)
SIC(s): 7300 Business Services.

Operating Locations

Adobe Systems (WA--Seattle)

Nonmonetary Support

Type: Donated Products; In-kind Services

Giving Contact

345 Park Avenue
San Jose, CA 95110

Phone: (408)536-6528
Fax: (408)537-6313
Web: http://www.adobe.com/aboutadobe/philanthropy/main.html

Alternate Contact

Phone: (401)536-3993

Description

Organization Type: Corporate Giving Program
Giving Locations: CA: Seattle/King County, San Francisco Bay area, San Jose, Silicon Valley
Grant Types: Award, Capital, Emergency, General Support, Operating Expenses, Project.

Financial Summary

Total Giving: Company does not disclose contributions figures.

Typical Recipients

Arts & Humanities: Arts Appreciation, Arts Centers, Arts Funds, Arts Outreach, Ballet, Community Arts, Dance, Arts & Humanities-General, Libraries, Literary Arts, Museums/Galleries, Music, Performing Arts, Public Broadcasting, Theater, Visual Arts
Civic & Public Affairs: Botanical Gardens/Parks, Community Foundations, Employment/Job Training, Ethnic Organizations, Civic & Public Affairs-General, Housing, Inner-City Development, Native American Affairs, Nonprofit Management, Women's Affairs, Zoos/Aquariums
Education: Afterschool/Enrichment Programs, Arts/Humanities Education, Business Education, Business-School Partnerships, Faculty Development, Education-General, Literacy, Minority Education, Preschool Education
Environment: Air/Water Quality, Resource Conservation, Wildlife Protection
Health: Adolescent Health Issues, AIDS/HIV, Alzheimer's Disease, Arthritis, Cancer, Children's Health/Hospitals, Diabetes, Eyes/Blindness, Health-General, Heart, Hospices
Science: Science-General, Science Exhibits & Fairs, Science Museums, Scientific Research
Social Services: Animal Protection, At-Risk Youth, Child Welfare, Community Centers, Counseling, Delinquency & Criminal Rehabilitation, Domestic Violence, Family Services, Food/Clothing Distribution, People with Disabilities, Recreation & Athletics, Sexual Abuse, Shelters/Homelessness, Social Services-General, United Funds/United Ways, Volunteer Services, Youth Organizations

Application Procedures

Initial Contact: Send postcard with address, call 408/536-3993, or consult the Web site.

Restrictions

Does not support individuals, religious organizations for sectarian purposes, political or lobbying groups, organizations outside operating areas, or organizations which unlawfully discrimate against any kind of person.

Corporate Officials

Bruce Chizen: president, chief executive officer, director B 1955. ED Brooklyn College BS. PRIM CORP EMPL president, chief executive officer, director: Adobe Systems Inc.
Charles Matthew Geschke: co-chairman B Cleveland, OH 1939. ED Carnegie Mellon University PhD; Xavier University AB (1962); Xavier University MS (1963). PRIM CORP EMPL co-chairman: Adobe Systems. NONPR AFFIL member: Math Association America; member: National Academy Engineers; member: Association Computer Math.
Dr. John E. Warnock: co-chairman, chief technology officer B Salt Lake City, UT 1940. ED University of Utah BS (1961); University of Utah MS (1964); University of Utah PhD (1969). PRIM CORP EMPL co-chairman, chief technology officer: Adobe Systems Inc. CORP AFFIL director: Netscape Communica-

tions Corp.; director: Red Brick Systems; Evans Sutherland Computer Corp.:. NONPR AFFIL member: NAE; chairman: Tech Museum Innovation; member entrepreneurial board advisory committee: American Film Institute.

Grants Analysis

Typical Range: $3,000 to $30,000

AHMANSON FOUNDATION

Giving Contact

Lee E. Walcott, Jr., Vice President & Managing Director
9215 Wilshire Boulevard
Beverly Hills, CA 90210
Phone: (310)278-0770
Fax: (310)278-4581

Description

Founded: 1952
EIN: 956089998
Organization Type: Family Foundation
Grant Types: Capital, Challenge, Emergency, Endowment, General Support, Matching, Operating Expenses, Project, Scholarship, Seed Money.

Donor Information

Founder: Established in 1952 in California as an independent foundation with funds donated by the late Howard F. Ahmanson and his wife, the late Dorothy G. Sullivan. Other donors include William H. Ahmanson and Robert H. Ahmanson, both nephews.

A graduate of the University of Southern California, Howard Ahmanson built an extensive financial empire consisting primarily of savings and loan associations and insurance companies. A noted philanthropist, yachtsman, and art collector, Howard Ahmanson served on the boards of the Los Angeles County Museum of Art, University of Southern California, Kennedy Center for the Performing Arts, and California Museum of Science and Industry.

Financial Summary

Total Giving: $32,233,345 (fiscal year ending October 31, 2003); $30,063,706 (fiscal 2002); $29,443,705 (fiscal 2001)
Assets: $832,146,389 (fiscal 2003); $715,170,664 (fiscal 2002); $785,613,165 (fiscal 2001)
Gifts Received: $61,330,500 (fiscal 1999); $69,863 (fiscal 1997)

Typical Recipients

Arts & Humanities: Arts Appreciation, Arts Centers, Arts Funds, Arts Institutes, Arts Outreach, Ballet, Dance, Ethnic & Folk Arts, Film & Video, Arts & Humanities-General, Historic Preservation, History & Archaeology, Libraries, Literary Arts, Museums/Galleries, Music, Opera, Performing Arts, Public Broadcasting, Theater, Visual Arts
Civic & Public Affairs: African American Affairs, Botanical Gardens/Parks, Civil Rights, Clubs, Economic Development, Economic Policy, Employment/Job Training, Civic & Public Affairs-General, Hispanic Affairs, Housing, Law & Justice, Legal Aid, Nonprofit Management, Parades/Festivals, Philanthropic Organizations, Public Policy, Safety, Urban & Community Affairs, Zoos/Aquariums
Education: Arts/Humanities Education, Business Education, Colleges & Universities, Education Associations, Education Funds, Education Reform, Elementary Education (Private), Elementary Education (Public), Engineering/Technological Education, Faculty Development, Education-General, Health & Physical Education, International Studies, Journalism/Media Education, Leadership Training, Legal Education, Literacy, Medical Education, Minority Education, Preschool Education, Private Education

(Precollege), Public Education (Precollege), School Volunteerism, Science/Mathematics Education, Secondary Education (Private), Social Sciences Education, Special Education, Student Aid, Vocational & Technical Education

Environment: Air/Water Quality, Environment-General, Resource Conservation, Wildlife Protection

Health: Adolescent Health Issues, AIDS/HIV, Alzheimer's Disease, Cancer, Children's Health/Hospitals, Clinics/Medical Centers, Emergency/Ambulance Services, Eyes/Blindness, Health Funds, Health Organizations, Heart, Hospitals, Long-Term Care, Medical Research, Mental Health, Multiple Sclerosis, Nursing Services, Outpatient Health Care, Prenatal Health Issues, Public Health, Research/Studies Institutes, Single-Disease Health Associations, Speech & Hearing, Trauma Treatment

International: Foreign Arts Organizations, Foreign Educational Institutions, Health Care/Hospitals, International Development, International Environmental Issues, International Peace & Security Issues, Missionary/Religious Activities

Religion: Churches, Dioceses, Jewish Causes, Religious Organizations, Religious Welfare, Social/Policy Issues, Synagogues/Temples

Science: Science-General, Observatories & Planetariums, Science Museums, Scientific Centers & Institutes, Scientific Organizations, Scientific Research

Social Services: Animal Protection, At-Risk Youth, Child Abuse, Child Welfare, Community Centers, Community Service Organizations, Counseling, Crime Prevention, Day Care, Delinquency & Criminal Rehabilitation, Domestic Violence, Emergency Relief, Family Planning, Family Services, Food/Clothing Distribution, Homes, People with Disabilities, Recreation & Athletics, Senior Services, Shelters/Homelessness, Substance Abuse, Volunteer Services, YMCA/YWCA/YMHA/YWHA, Youth Organizations

Application Procedures

Initial Contact: Applicants should review a copy of the foundation's annual report and guidelines before sending in a proposal. After determining that a proposal matches the foundation's interests, a brief proposal or letter of inquiry should be sent to the managing director.

Application Requirements: Applicants should describe the purpose of the organization, its background, project, and overall funding plan. Also include current annual budget, project budget, amount requested, list of other available sources of support, audited financial statement, a copy of 501(c)(3) tax-exempt status letter, and a list of the organization's governing board and officers.

Deadlines: None.

Review Process: After reviewing proposals, the foundation may request additional information or an interview. Notification generally occurs within 30 to 60 days; written responses will be sent promptly to those not likely to qualify, to that they may proceed in their search for funding. Others who may qualify will be notified so that a full proposal can be submitted for further consideration.

The foundation evaluates the quality of the program and the organization. Organizations must be well-managed, fiscally sound, have a developed history, and maintain a record of program integrity. Requests for capital support are considered most often after there is clear and assured evidence that the goal of the campaign is going to be achieved and that such will be accomplished within a reasonable time period.

Restrictions

Generally, no grants are made to individuals, or for endowed chairs, annual campaigns, fellowships or exchange programs, continuing support, deficit financing, professorships, internships, individual scholarships, conferences, exhibits, films or video production, or loans.

The foundation generally does not fund organizations which make grants to others, religious organizations for sectarian or propagation of faith purposes, traveling exhibits, performance underwriting, seminars, workshops, studies, surveys, general research and development, operational support of regional and national charities, or political advocacy.

Additional Information

Publications: Annual Report; Guidelines

Foundation Officials

Howard Fieldstead Ahmanson, Jr.: trustee NONPR AFFIL director: California Independent Business PAC.

Robert H. Ahmanson: president, trustee B 1927. CORP AFFIL director: Home Savings of America FSB. NONPR AFFIL trustee: UCLA Brain Mapping Medical Research Organization.

William H. Ahmanson: vice president, trustee B Omaha, NE 1925. ED University of California, Los Angeles BS (1950). NONPR AFFIL director: International Shooting Sport Park; director: Los Angeles Police Historical Society.

Lloyd E. Cotsen: trustee B Boston, MA 1929. ED Princeton University BA (1950); Harvard University MBA (1957). NONPR AFFIL trustee: American School of Classical Studies at Athens.

Lloyd Edward Cotsen: trustee B Boston, MA 1929. ED Princeton University BA (1950); Harvard University MBA (1957). PRIM CORP EMPL chairman, chief executive officer, director: Neutrogena Corp. NONPR AFFIL trustee: American School of Classical Studies at Athens.

Robert M. DeKruif: trustee B 1919. PRIM CORP EMPL vice chairman, director: H.F. Ahmanson & Co. CORP AFFIL director vice chairman: Home Savings of America FSB.

Robert F. Erburu: trustee B Ventura, CA 1930. ED University of Southern California BA (1952); Harvard University JD (1955). CORP AFFIL director: Marsh & McLennan Companies Inc. NONPR AFFIL trustee: National Gallery Art; director: Pacific Council on International Policy; life director: Independent Colleges Southern California; member: American Bar Association; chairman board trustee: H.E. Huntington Library Art Gallery.

Karen A. Hoffman: secretary

Kristen K. O'Connor: chief financial officer, treasurer NONPR AFFIL member: Toastmasters.

Leonard E. Walcott, Jr.: vice president, managing director NONPR AFFIL member: Colorado Art Association.

Grants Analysis

Disclosure Period: fiscal year ending October 31, 2003

Total Grants: $32,233,345

Number of Grants: 460 (approx)

Average Grant: $52,161*

Highest Grant: $2,500,000

Lowest Grant: $1,000

Typical Range: $10,000 to $100,000

***Note:** Average grant figure excludes five highest grants ($8,500,000).

Recent Grants

Note: Grants derived from 2003 Form 990.

Library-Related

500,000	Henry E. Huntington Library & Art Gallery, San Marino, CA
500,000	Henry E. Huntington Library & Art Gallery, San Marino, CA

General

2,500,000	Friends of the Observatory, Los Angeles, CA
2,500,000	University of Southern California, Los Angeles, CA
1,500,000	California Science Center Foundation, Los Angeles, CA
1,000,000	UCLA Foundation, Los Angeles, CA
1,000,000	University of Southern California, Los Angeles, CA
800,000	Museum Associates, Los Angeles, CA
700,000	Museum Associates, Los Angeles, CA
500,000	Archdiocese of Los Angeles, Los Angeles, CA
500,000	Archdiocese of Los Angeles, Los Angeles, CA
500,000	Autry National Center of the American West, Los Angeles, CA

CLAUDE W. AND DOLLY AHRENS FOUNDATION

Giving Contact

Claude W. Ahrens, Trustee
Claude W. and Dolly Ahrens Foundation
PO Box 284
Grinnell, IA 50112
E-mail: info@ahrensfamilyfoundation.org
Web: http://www.ahrensfamilyfoundation.org

Description

Founded: 1994
EIN: 421413842
Organization Type: Private Foundation
Giving Locations: CA; IA

Donor Information

Founder: Established in 1994 by Claude W. Ahrens.

Financial Summary

Total Giving: $1,131,783 (fiscal year ending October 31, 2004)

Gifts Received: $12,805 (fiscal 1996); $6,630,782 (fiscal 1994). Note: In fiscal 1996, contributions were received from Claude W. Ahrens.

Typical Recipients

Arts & Humanities: Arts Associations & Councils, Libraries

Civic & Public Affairs: Philanthropic Organizations, Safety

Education: Agricultural Education

Health: Clinics/Medical Centers

Social Services: Family Services, Recreation & Athletics

Application Procedures

Initial Contact: Send a brief letter of inquiry.
Deadlines: None.

Foundation Officials

Chad Ahrens: trustee
Claude W. Ahrens: trustee
John Ahrens: trustee
Richard Ahrens: trustee
David Clay: trustee
Randy Juhl: trustee
Dick Muckler: trustee

Grants Analysis

Disclosure Period: fiscal year ending October 31, 2004

Total Grants: $1,131,783

Number of Grants: 25

Average Grant: $8,945*

Highest Grant: $500,000

Lowest Grant: $500

Typical Range: $1,000 to $20,000

***Note:** Average grant figure excludes three highest grants ($935,000).

Recent Grants

Note: Grants derived from 1996 Form 990.

Library-Related

25,000	Stewart Library, Grinnell, IA -- automation of library equipment

General

150,000	Ahrens Family Center, Grinnell, IA -- facility addition

100,000	Grinnell Regional Medical Center, Grinnell, IA -- for plaza construction
5,000	Grinnell Area Arts Council, Grinnell, IA -- fundraising for the arts
3,333	Grinnell Volunteer Fire Department, Grinnell, IA -- for rescue truck
2,500	Iowa 4-H Foundation, Ames, IA -- renovation of 4-H Center

AIR FRANCE

Company Headquarters

142 W. 55th St., Fl. 2
New York, NY 10019
Web: http://www.airfrance.com/us

Company Description

Employees: 850
SIC(s): 4500 Transportation by Air.
Parent Company: Groupe Air France, 45 Rue de Paris, Roissy, Charles de Gaulle, France

Operating Locations

Air France (Southwestern Region) (FL--Miami; TX--Houston); Air France (U.S. Pacific Region) (CA--Los Angeles)

Nonmonetary Support

Type: Donated Products

Giving Contact

125 W. 55th St.
New York, NY 10019-3300
Phone: (212)830-4000

Description

Organization Type: Corporate Giving Program
Giving Locations: CA: Los Angeles, San Francisco; DC; FL: Miami; MA: Boston; NY: New York; PA: Philadelphia; TX: Houston generally near "gateway" cities from which Air France flies to Europe.

Typical Recipients

Arts & Humanities: Dance, Historic Preservation, Libraries, Museums/Galleries, Music, Performing Arts, Public Broadcasting, Theater
Civic & Public Affairs: Professional & Trade Associations
Education: International Studies
Health: Hospitals, Medical Research, Single-Disease Health Associations
International: International Relations
Religion: Religious Organizations
Science: Scientific Organizations
Social Services: Child Welfare

Application Procedures

Initial Contact: Initial letter may be submitted at any time to the nearest Air France local sales office. While applications are accepted throughout the year, fall is generally best for funding during the following year. Include a description of organization, number of tickets requested, purpose for which tickets are sought, and the type and level of exposure (advertisements, press releases, etc.) which Air France will gain from making the contribution.

Restrictions

While Air France has no set restrictions on its giving, the company generally prefers to support those organizations whose image is compatible with its own.

Additional Information

Compagnie Nationale Air France in Paris has its own contributions program.

AIR PRODUCTS AND CHEMICALS INC.

Company Headquarters

Allentown, PA
Web: http://www.airproducts.com/maxx

Company Description

Founded: 1940
Ticker: APD
Exchange: NYSE
Revenue: US$7.411 billion (2004)
Profit: US$604.1 million (2004)
Employees: 18500 (2003)
Fortune Rank: 281, per FORTUNE Magazine's list of 500 Largest U.S. Corporations (2004).
SIC(s): 2813 Industrial Gases, 2819 Industrial Inorganic Chemicals Nec, 2873 Nitrogenous Fertilizers, 3443 Fabricated Plate Work--Boiler Shops.

Operating Locations

Air Products & Chemicals, Inc. (AL--Aliceville, Burkville, Decatur, Flomaton, Theodore; AZ--Chandler, Phoenix, Tempe; AR--Fayetteville, Fort Smith, Little Rock, Magnolia; CA--City of Industry, Concord, Fountain Valley, Huntington Beach, Mountain View, Newport Beach, Pleasanton, Sacramento, San Marcos, Santa Clara, Stockton; CO--Denver, Fort Collins; CT--West Hartford; DC--Washington; FL--Fort Walton Beach, Longwood, Miami, Orlando, Pace, Pensacola, Tallahassee; GA--Albany, Atlanta, Conyers, Dalton; IL--Chicago, Granite City, Hennepin, Lisle, Marion, Springfield, Tuscola; IN--Chesterton, Terre Haute; IA--Davenport, Des Moines, Sioux City; KS--Fort Scott, Liberal; KY--Ashland, Louisville, Paducah; LA--Baton Rouge, Convent, Geismar, Monroe, St. Gabriel; MD--Baltimore, Calverton, Elkton, Hyattsville, Salisbury; MA--Hopkinton, Hudson, Marlborough; MI--Saginaw; MS--Greenwood, Southaven; MO--Earth City, Kingsville, Palmyra; NE--Grand Island, Lincoln, Omaha; NJ--Camden, Dayton, Edison, Paulsboro; NM--Rio Rancho; NY--East Fishkill, Glenmont, Latham, New Windsor; NC--Asheville, Durham, Greensboro, Laurinburg, Reidsville; OH--Baltimore, Cincinnati, Cleveland, Columbus, Middletown; OK--Oklahoma City, Pryor; OR--Eugene, Gresham, Salem, Tualatin; PA--Creighton, Leetsdale, Lyndora, Tamaqua, Wilkes-Barre; SC--Columbia, Florence, Greenville, Taylors; TN--Dyersburg, Kingsport, Knoxville, Memphis; TX--Austin, Dallas, Deer Park, Gruven, Iraan, Irving, La Porte, Midlothian; UT--Centerville; VA--Chester, Hampton, Lynchburg, Roanoke; WA--Puyallup, Renton; WV--Apple Grove, Proctor, Weirton; WI--Green Bay, Oak Creek, Waukesha)

Nonmonetary Support

Type: Donated Equipment; Donated Products; In-kind Services; Loaned Employees; Loaned Executives; Workplace Solicitation
Volunteer Programs: Seventy percent of employees volunteer in community activities. Volunteerism is encouraged and recognized by the company, but it does not have a formal volunteer program.
Contact: Marta Boulos Gabriel, Manager, Community Relations & Philanthropy
Air Products & Chemicals, Inc.
7201 Hamilton Blvd.
Allentown, PA 18195-1501

E-mail: gabriemb@apci.com

Corporate Officials

Robert C. Iversen: chief operating officer PRIM CORP EMPL chief operating officer: Air France U.S.A.

Grants Analysis

Typical Range: $1,000 to $2,500

Air Products Foundation

Giving Contact

T. J. Holt, President
7201 Hamilton Boulevard
Allentown, PA 18195-1501
Phone: (610)481-4453
Fax: (610)481-6642
Web: http://www.airproducts.com/social_responsibilities/

Description

EIN: 232130928
Organization Type: Corporate Foundation
Giving Locations: headquarters and select operating communities.
Grant Types: Award, Capital, Emergency, Employee Matching Gifts, General Support, Matching, Multiyear/Continuing Support, Operating Expenses, Project.
Note: Matching gifts are for higher education, arts and cultural organizations. Employee matching gift ratio: 1 to 1 for gifts to accredited colleges and universities, up to $5,000. Employee matching gift ratio: 2 to 1 for gifts to arts groups, up to $2,000.

Financial Summary

Total Giving: $11,820 (fiscal year ending September 30, 2003); $3,042,317 (fiscal 2002); $3,220,117 (fiscal 2001)
Giving Analysis: Giving for fiscal 2001 includes: foundation scholarships ($21,500); foundation grants to United Way ($87,345); foundation matching gifts ($1,435,336); foundation ($1,675,936)
Assets: $5,895,266 (fiscal 2003); $146,858 (fiscal 2002); $2,800,289 (fiscal 2001)
Gifts Received: $358,278 (fiscal 2003); $13,237,500 (fiscal 1994). Note: In 1994, contributions were received from Prodair Corporation.

Typical Recipients

Arts & Humanities: Arts Festivals, Arts Funds, Community Arts, Dance, Historic Preservation, Libraries, Museums/Galleries, Music, Opera, Performing Arts, Public Broadcasting, Theater
Civic & Public Affairs: Botanical Gardens/Parks, Business/Free Enterprise, Civil Rights, Economic Development, Economic Policy, Employment/Job Training, Civic & Public Affairs-General, Housing, Municipalities/Towns, Nonprofit Management, Philanthropic Organizations, Public Policy, Safety, Urban & Community Affairs, Women's Affairs
Education: Arts/Humanities Education, Business Education, Colleges & Universities, Continuing Education, Economic Education, Education Associations, Education Funds, Education Reform, Engineering/Technological Education, Environmental Education, Education-General, Legal Education, Literacy, Medical Education, Minority Education, Religious Education, Science/Mathematics Education, Vocational & Technical Education
Environment: Air/Water Quality, Environment-General, Resource Conservation
Health: Cancer, Children's Health/Hospitals, Emergency/Ambulance Services, Health Organizations, Heart, Multiple Sclerosis, Nutrition, Single-Disease Health Associations
International: International Peace & Security Issues
Religion: Religious Welfare
Science: Science Exhibits & Fairs
Social Services: Child Welfare, Community Service Organizations, Counseling, Day Care, Delinquency & Criminal Rehabilitation, Domestic Violence, Emergency Relief, Family Services, Food/Clothing Distribution, Homes, People with Disabilities, Recreation & Athletics, Scouts, Senior Services, Shelters/Homelessness, Substance Abuse, United Funds/

United Ways, Volunteer Services, Youth Organizations

Application Procedures

Initial Contact: Submit a written request on organization's letterhead.

Application Requirements: Include information on the purpose and background of the organization, including a list of its board of directors; amount requested; planned use of the contribution, including short- and long-term goals and when and how results will be evaluated; statement of community needs that the organization is addressing; time frame for the project; copy of the organizations Articles of Incorporation and By-Laws; current operating budget; list of current contributions or commitments received; and follow-up evaluation of contribution impact. Applicants must include a copy of the organization's IRS tax-exempt determination letter. Requests for funding for greater Lehigh Valley/Allentown, PA organizations should be submitted to Marta Boulos Gabriel, Manager of Community Relations and Philanthropy, at the company's Allentown address. For requests outside of this area, submit requests to the nearest Air Products location.

Deadlines: None.

Review Process: Requests are screened by contributions officer, then the committee reviews for approval or denial.

Evaluative Criteria: Committee examines benefit to Air Products community, need, population served, and funding sources.

Decision Notification: Requests are generally processed within 60 days.

Restrictions

Does not support fraternal organizations, labor groups, service clubs, individuals, operating funds for member agencies of the United Way, political or lobbying groups, religious organizations, or veterans organizations.

Additional Information

Company has participated in public/private ventures to rehabilitate abandoned and condemned properties in Allentown, PA.

Corporate Officials

John P. Jones, III: chairman, president, chief executive officer B November 09, 1950. ED Villanova University BSChE (1972). PRIM CORP EMPL chairman, president, chief executive officer: Air Products and Chemicals, Inc.

John R. Owings: vice president, chief financial officer ED Northern Illinois University BS (1971); Northern Illinois University MBA (1976). PRIM CORP EMPL vice president, chief financial officer: Air Products and Chemicals, Inc.

Foundation Officials

W. D. Brown: chairman, trustee
D. L. Geist: assistant secretary
D. H. Green: vice president
Timothy J. Holt: president
L. C. Minella: trustee
P. E. Puck: vice president, treasurer, trustee
K. G. Wright: secretary

Grants Analysis

Disclosure Period: fiscal year ending September 30, 2003
Total Grants: $11,820
Number of Grants: 32
Average Grant: $369
Highest Grant: $2,000
Lowest Grant: $50
Typical Range: $100 to $500

Recent Grants

Note: Grants derived from fiscal 2003 Form 990.
General

2,500	Carnegie Mellon University, Pittsburgh, PA
2,000	Association of Graduates of the US Military Academy, West Point, NY
1,400	Lehigh University, Bethlehem, PA
1,000	Saint Louis Symphony Orchestra, St. Louis, MO
500	Agnes Scott College, Decatur, GA
500	City College Fund, New York, NY
500	University of Florida Foundation Inc., Gainesville, FL
350	Allentown Art Museum, Allentown, PA
300	Friends of Public Road, Wilmington, NC
250	Golden Gate University (GGU), San Francisco, CA

AK STEEL HOLDING CORP.

Company Headquarters

703 Curtis St.
Middletown, OH 45043
Phone: (513)425-5000
Fax: (513)425-2676
Web: http://www.aksteel.com

Company Description

Founded: 1994
Ticker: AKS
Exchange: NYSE
Acquired: ARMCO (1999).
Revenue: US$5.243 billion (2004)
Profit: US$238.4 million (2004)
Employees: 10300 (2003)
Fortune Rank: 376, per FORTUNE Magazine's list of 500 Largest U.S. Corporations (2004).

Nonmonetary Support

Type: Workplace Solicitation
Volunteer Programs: The foundation gives volunteer support donations to community organizations where employees volunteer their time and services.

AK Steel Foundation

Giving Contact

Alan McCoy, Executive Director
703 Curtis Street
Middletown, OH 45043
Phone: (513)425-2991
Fax: (513)425-5683

Description

Founded: 1990
EIN: 311284344
Organization Type: Corporate Foundation
Formed by Merger of: Armco Inc. (1999).
Giving Locations: operating locations.
Grant Types: Award, Employee Matching Gifts, General Support, Matching, Scholarship.
Note: Employee matching gift ratio: 1 to 1 for educational and cultural institutions.

Donor Information

Founder: Established in 1990 by Armco, Inc., and Kawasaki Steel Investments.

Financial Summary

Total Giving: $1,106,093 (2003); $1,276,129 (2002); $1,145,300 (2001). Note: Contributes through foundation only.
Assets: $16,168,690 (2003); $14,450,013 (2002); $17,374,380 (2001)
Gifts Received: $145,000 (2003); $229,500 (2002); $1,000,000 (1995). Note: Contributions were received from Armco, Inc., Kawasaki Steel Investments, Inc, Armco Steel Co., L.P. and Breed, Abbott & Morgan.

Typical Recipients

Arts & Humanities: Arts Associations & Councils, Arts Centers, Arts Festivals, Arts Institutes, Community Arts, Dance, Film & Video, Historic Preservation, History & Archaeology, Libraries, Museums/Galleries, Music, Opera, Performing Arts, Public Broadcasting, Theater

Civic & Public Affairs: Business/Free Enterprise, Chambers of Commerce, Clubs, Community Foundations, Civic & Public Affairs-General, Housing, Law & Justice, Parades/Festivals, Philanthropic Organizations, Public Policy, Rural Affairs, Safety, Urban & Community Affairs

Education: Afterschool/Enrichment Programs, Business Education, Colleges & Universities, Economic Education, Education Associations, Education Funds, Engineering/Technological Education, Education-General, International Studies, Public Education (Precollege), Special Education, Student Aid

Environment: Air/Water Quality, Wildlife Protection

Health: Cancer, Clinics/Medical Centers, Emergency/Ambulance Services, Health Funds, Health Organizations, Heart, Hospices, Hospitals, Public Health, Single-Disease Health Associations

International: Foreign Arts Organizations

Religion: Religious Welfare

Social Services: Child Abuse, Child Welfare, Community Service Organizations, Crime Prevention, Domestic Violence, Emergency Relief, Family Services, Food/Clothing Distribution, Homes, People with Disabilities, Recreation & Athletics, Scouts, Senior Services, Shelters/Homelessness, Social Services-General, Substance Abuse, United Funds/United Ways, Veterans, YMCA/YWCA/YMHA/YWHA, Youth Organizations

Application Procedures

Initial Contact: Send a brief letter of inquiry.
Application Requirements: Include a description of organization, amount requested, project description, and proof of tax-exempt status.
Deadlines: None for matching grants; November 30 for scholarship.
Notes: For scholarship or matching grant programs, applicants can request application forms, which include specific criteria for each program.

Additional Information

In 1995, the company reported it changed its name from Armco Steel Company to AK Steel Corporation. The foundation has also undergone a name change; it is now called the AK Steel Foundation. Kawasaki owns approximately 15-16% of AK Steel Corp.'s stock.

AK Steel announced, its merger with Armco Inc. would take effect September 30, 1999. As a result of the merger, the business and operations of Armco will be conducted by and in the name of AK Steel. Armco shares will cease to trade on the New York Stock Exchange as of close of business on September 30, 1999.

Publications: Application Forms; Sons and Daughters of Alaska Steel Corporate Employees Scholarship Program; Employee Matching Gift Program Informational Brochure

Corporate Officials

Michael T. Adams: senior vice president ED Ohio State University BSME (1981). PRIM CORP EMPL senior vice president: AK Steel Holding Corp.

Brian T. Coughlin: corporate manager government affairs PRIM CORP EMPL corporate manager government affairs: AK Steel Holding Corp.

Brenda S. Harmon: vice president human resources PRIM CORP EMPL vice president human resources: AK Steel Holding Corp.

Alan H. McCoy: vice president public affairs PRIM CORP EMPL vice president public affairs: AK Steel Holding Corp.

James L. Wainscott: chief executive officer B 1957. ED Ball State University BS (1979); University of

Notre Dame MBA (1982). PRIM CORP EMPL chief executive officer: AK Steel Holding Corp.

Foundation Officials

Rebecca Appenzeller: assistant secretary
Al Ferrara: trustee
David Horn: trustee
John Kaloski: trustee
Greg Kuzma: treasurer
Alan H. McCoy: executive director (see above)
Joe Plye: secretary
James L. Wainscott: chairman (see above)

Grants Analysis

Disclosure Period: calendar year ending 2003
Total Grants: $453,498*
Number of Grants: 16
Average Grant: $28,345
Highest Grant: $65,000
Lowest Grant: $1,500
Typical Range: $5,000 to $40,000
*Note: Giving excludes matching gifts; scholarship; United Way.

Recent Grants

Note: Grants derived from 2003 Form 990.

General

319,000	Middletown Community Foundation, Middletown, OH
125,000	Mid-Miami Healthcare Foundation, Middletown, OH
93,446	United Way, Middletown, CT
85,000	United Way, Hamilton, OH
65,000	SHIELD
65,000	S.H.I.E.L.D
46,723	Middletown United Way, Middletown, OH
46,723	United Way, Alexandria, VA
36,500	Boyd County United Way, Ashland, KY
35,000	United Way, Mansfield, OH

AKC FUND

Giving Contact

Ann Brownell-Sloane, Administrator
67A E. 77th St.
New York, NY 10021
Phone: (212)737-1011

Description

Founded: 1955
EIN: 136091321
Organization Type: Private Foundation
Giving Locations: CT; DC; NY: nationally.
Grant Types: Capital, General Support, Multiyear/Continuing Support, Professorship.

Donor Information

Founder: members of the Childs and Lawrence families

Financial Summary

Total Giving: $289,000 (2003); $225,500 (2001)
Giving Analysis: Giving for 2003 includes: foundation grants to United Way ($1,000); 2001: foundation grants to United Way ($6,000)
Assets: $5,388,500 (2003); $5,927,377 (2001)
Gifts Received: $92,768 (1994). Note: In 1994, contributions were received from the Vannie Hamblet Trust.

Typical Recipients

Arts & Humanities: Arts Festivals, Ballet, Historic Preservation, History & Archaeology, Libraries, Literary Arts, Museums/Galleries, Music, Performing Arts, Public Broadcasting, Theater
Civic & Public Affairs: Community Foundations, Economic Development, Civic & Public Affairs-General, Professional & Trade Associations, Rural

Affairs, Urban & Community Affairs, Women's Affairs
Education: Arts/Humanities Education, Colleges & Universities, Education-General, International Studies, Minority Education, Preschool Education, Private Education (Precollege), Public Education (Precollege), Religious Education, Social Sciences Education
Environment: Forestry, Environment-General, Resource Conservation, Wildlife Protection
Health: AIDS/HIV, Clinics/Medical Centers, Health-General, Health Organizations, Hospitals, Medical Research, Mental Health, Prenatal Health Issues, Single-Disease Health Associations
International: Foreign Educational Institutions, International Affairs, International Development, International Environmental Issues, International Organizations
Religion: Churches, Religion-General
Science: Science Museums, Scientific Research
Social Services: Camps, Child Welfare, Community Service Organizations, Family Planning, Recreation & Athletics, Refugee Assistance, Senior Services, Social Services-General, United Funds/United Ways, YMCA/YWCA/YMHA/YWHA, Youth Organizations

Application Procedures

Initial Contact: Send a brief letter of inquiry. Foundation will decide if a full proposal should be submitted.
Deadlines: None.

Restrictions

Emphasis is on education, conservation and preservation, and health and welfare in the Northeast.

Additional Information

Publications: Annual Report

Foundation Officials

Alice Childs Anderson: vice president
Hope S. Childs: director
John D. Childs: treasurer

Grants Analysis

Disclosure Period: calendar year ending 2003
Total Grants: $288,000*
Number of Grants: 50
Average Grant: $5,760
Highest Grant: $25,000
Lowest Grant: $500
Typical Range: $1,000 to $10,000
*Note: Giving excludes United Way.

Recent Grants

Note: Grants derived from 2001 Form 990.

Library-Related

5,000	Norfolk Library, Norfolk, CT

General

25,000	Geer Foundation, North Canaan, CT
15,000	Phillips Exeter Academy, Exeter, NH
15,000	Student Conservation Association, Charlestown, NJ
15,000	Watertown Cooperative Nursery School, Watertown, MA
14,000	Bard College, East Brunswick, NJ -- Clemenete course in the humanities
10,000	American Farmland Trust, Washington, DC
10,000	Committee to Protect Journalists, New York, NY
10,000	Emory University, Atlanta, GA
10,000	Farm School, Athol, MA
5,000	American Near East Refugee Aid, Washington, DC

AKZO NOBEL CHEMICALS

Company Headquarters

300 S. Riverside Plaza
Chicago, IL 60606
Web: http://www.akzonobelusa.com

Company Description

Former Name: Akzo America.
Employees: 9,000
SIC(s): 2833 Medicinals & Botanicals, 2834 Pharmaceutical Preparations, 2899 Chemical Preparations Nec, 6719 Holding Companies Nec.
Parent Company: Akzo Nobel N.V., Velperweg 76, PO Box 9300, Arnhem, Netherlands

Operating Locations

Akzo Chemicals Inc. (NJ--New Brunswick; NY--Burt; TX--Pasadena; WI--Janesville); Akzo Coatings (GA--Atlanta, Baxley; IL--Zion; KY--Louisville; MI--Troy; MS--Clinton; OH--Columbus, Springfield); Akzo Dreeland (CO--Denver); Akzo Electronics Materials Co. (CO--Colorado Springs); Akzo Engineering Plastics (NJ--Neshanic Station); Akzo LanChem Corp. (IL--East St. Louis); Akzo Nobel Chemicals (AL--Birmingham; CA--Los Angeles; CO--Colorado Springs, Denver; GA--Baxley, Norcross; IL--Addison, Chicago, Morton Grove; KY--Louisville; MI--Manistee; NJ--Neshanic Station, New Brunswick, West Orange; NY--New York; NC--Asheville, High Point; OH--Akron, Columbus; OK--Oklahoma City; TN--Rockwood; TX--Pasadena; WI--Janesville); Akzo Nobel Fibers Inc. (NC--Asheville); Akzo Nobel Fortafil Fibers Inc. (TN--Rockwood); Akzo Resins & Vehicles (IL--Addison); Diosynth, Inc. (IL--Chicago); Eka Chemicals North America (GA--Marietta); Fostafil Fibers (TN--Rockwood); Harshaw Filtrol (OH--Solon); Intervet America, Inc. (DE--Millsboro); Organon Inc. (NJ--West Orange); Organon Teknika Corp. (NC--Durham); Pharmaceutical Basics Inc. (CO--Denver; IL--Chicago); Sikkens Aerospace Finishers (CA--Torrance); Sikkens Car Refinishes (CA--Torrance)

Giving Contact

Robin Hall, Gen. Counsel
300 S. Riverside Plz.
Chicago, IL 60606
Phone: (312)906-7500
Fax: (312)906-7680

Description

Organization Type: Corporate Giving Program
Giving Locations: headquarters and operating communities.
Grant Types: Capital, Employee Matching Gifts, Fellowship, Matching, Scholarship.

Donor Information

Founder: Akzo America

Typical Recipients

Arts & Humanities: Community Arts, Arts & Humanities-General, Libraries, Music, Opera, Public Broadcasting
Civic & Public Affairs: Chambers of Commerce, Economic Development, Law & Justice, Philanthropic Organizations, Public Policy, Safety, Urban & Community Affairs
Education: Colleges & Universities, Community & Junior Colleges, Economic Education, Education Associations, Education-General, International Exchange, Minority Education, Science/Mathematics Education, Special Education, Vocational & Technical Education
Environment: Environment-General
Health: AIDS/HIV, Clinics/Medical Centers, Emergency/Ambulance Services, Health Organizations, Heart, Hospitals, Single-Disease Health Associations
Social Services: Child Welfare, Community Service

Organizations, United Funds/United Ways, Youth Organizations

Application Procedures
Initial Contact: The foundation has no formal grant application procedure or application form.
Deadlines: None.

Restrictions
Program does not support fraternal, political, or religious organizations. Goodwill advertising is handled by the advertising department.

Additional Information
Akzo Nobel handles contributions for other U.S. subsidiaries of Akzo NV, including Akzo Nobel Chemicals.

Grants Analysis
Typical Range: $500 to $1,000

Alabama Power Co.

Company Headquarters
2046 Patton Chapel Rd.
Birmingham, AL 35216
Web: http://www.alapower.com

Company Description
Employees: 6,865
SIC(s): 4911 Electric Services.
Parent Company: Southern Co., Atlanta, GA, United States

Operating Locations
Alabama Power Co. (AL--Abbeville, Alexander City, Aliceville, Asheville, Ashford, Ashland, Atmore, Auburn, Bankhead Dam, Bay Minette, Bayou La Batre, Blountsville, Bouldin Dam, Brewton, Butler, Carbon Hill, Centerville, Childersburg, Citronelle, Clayton, Columbia, Dadeville, Daleville, Dora, East Jefferson, Enterprise, Eufaula, Flomaton, Florala, Fort Deposit, Gadsden, Gardendale, Georgiana, Goodwater, Greensboro, Greenville, Haleyville, Hamilton, Harris Dam, Headland, Henry Dam, Holt Dam, Jackson, Jacksonville, Jordan Dam, Lay Dam, Leeds, Lineville, Logan Martin Dam, Marion, Martin Dam, Miller, Mobile, Monroeville, Montevallo, Montgomery, Ozark, Parrish, Pell City, Phenix City, Plant Chickasaw, Plant Farley, Plant Gadsen, Plant Gaston, Plant Greene County, Prattville, Prichard, Reform, Saraland, Selma, Smith Dam, Sylacauga, Theodore, Thomasville, Thurlow Dam, Tuscaloosa, Valley, Wedwee, Weiss Dam, West Jefferson, Winfield, Yates Dam)

Nonmonetary Support
Type: In-kind Services; Loaned Employees; Workplace Solicitation
Note: Co. reports that nonmonetary support is limited.

Alabama Power Foundation

Giving Contact
William B. Johnson, President
Alabama Power Foundation
600 N. 18th Street
Birmingham, AL 35291-0011
Phone: (205)257-2508
Fax: (205)257-1860
Note: Proposals should be sent to the manager of the nearest Alabama Power Business Office.

Description
Founded: 1990
EIN: 570901832
Organization Type: Corporate Foundation
Giving Locations: headquarters and operating communities.
Grant Types: Capital, Employee Matching Gifts, Endowment, General Support, Matching, Multiyear/Continuing Support, Operating Expenses, Project, Research, Scholarship, Seed Money.
Note: Employee matching gift ratio: 1 to 1 up to $2,000 per calendar year.

Financial Summary
Total Giving: $6,466,482 (2003); $7,382,827 (2002); $8,224,218 (2001). Note: Contributes through corporate direct giving program and foundation. 1997 Giving includes foundation. 1996 Giving includes scholarship ($246,850); matching gifts ($85,782).
Giving Analysis: Giving for 2002 includes: foundation scholarships ($461,204); foundation grants to United Way ($925,854); foundation ($5,995,769)
Assets: $135,336,072 (2003); $119,824,835 (2002); $136,510,166 (2001)
Gifts Received: $41,877 (2003); $560,718 (2002); $513,760 (2001). Note: In 2003, contributions were received from Alabama Power Service Org - Eastern ($5,000), Alabama Power Service Org - Western ($5,000), Alabama Power Service Org - Southeast ($5,000), and other individual donors. In 2002, contributions were received from Alabama Power Service Org - State ($75,000), Alabama Power Service Org - Western ($5,000), Camp ASCCA ($75,000), Elmer Harris ($200,000), Hoover City Schools Foundation ($45,000) and other corporate, foundation, and individual donors. In 2001, contributions were received from Alabama Power Service Organization-State ($75,000), Alabama Power Service Organization-Eastern ($5,000), Alabama Power Service Organization-Southeast ($5,000), Alabama Power Service Organization-Western ($5,000), Camp ASCCA ($75,000), Robert O. Finley, III Foundation ($6,000), Michael D. Garrett ($5,000), Hoover City Schools Foundation, Inc. ($35,000), William B. Hutchins ($50,000), Charles D. McCrary ($100,000), Alan Martin ($5,000), Mike Scott ($10,000), Steve R. Spencer ($50,00), and J.J. Thomley ($50,000). The foundation receives funds from Alabama Power Co., APSO, Birmingham Urban, E.B. Harris, and Robert O'Finley Foundation.

Typical Recipients
Arts & Humanities: Arts Associations & Councils, Arts Centers, Arts Festivals, Arts Funds, Community Arts, Dance, Arts & Humanities-General, Historic Preservation, History & Archaeology, Libraries, Museums/Galleries, Music, Performing Arts, Public Broadcasting, Theater, Visual Arts
Civic & Public Affairs: African American Affairs, Botanical Gardens/Parks, Business/Free Enterprise, Chambers of Commerce, Civil Rights, Clubs, Community Foundations, Economic Development, Civic & Public Affairs-General, Housing, Municipalities/Towns, Parades/Festivals, Professional & Trade Associations, Public Policy, Safety, Urban & Community Affairs, Women's Affairs, Zoos/Aquariums
Education: Business Education, Colleges & Universities, Community & Junior Colleges, Education Funds, Education Reform, Elementary Education (Private), Engineering/Technological Education, Environmental Education, Education-General, Literacy, Minority Education, Preschool Education, Private Education (Precollege), Public Education (Precollege), Science/Mathematics Education, Special Education, Student Aid
Environment: Environment-General, Resource Conservation
Health: Cancer, Children's Health/Hospitals, Clinics/Medical Centers, Diabetes, Eyes/Blindness, Health Organizations, Heart, Hospices, Medical Rehabilitation, Mental Health, Single-Disease Health Associations

International: International Relief Efforts
Religion: Jewish Causes, Ministries, Missionary Activities (Domestic), Religious Welfare
Science: Science Exhibits & Fairs, Science Museums, Scientific Labs
Social Services: Camps, Child Welfare, Community Centers, Community Service Organizations, Delinquency & Criminal Rehabilitation, Family Services, Food/Clothing Distribution, People with Disabilities, Scouts, Senior Services, Shelters/Homelessness, Substance Abuse, United Funds/United Ways, Veterans, Volunteer Services, YMCA/YWCA/YMHA/YWHA, Youth Organizations

Application Procedures
Initial Contact: Send a letter no longer than four pages. For scholarships, request application form.
Application Requirements: Include a description of organization, and its mission; previous support from foundation; projects goals and objectives; need project is trying to meet; expected results of project; key staff members, including those directly involved in project; list of board of directors; amount requested; description of use and evidence of need; how results will be measured; how project may be used by others; how project will be sustained once foundation's funding is gone; sources of other support; recently audited financial statements; and proof of tax-exempt status. For scholarships, include letters of recommendation, academic record, and test scores.
Deadlines: None.
Review Process: Manager at local plant will review request and decide whether or not to refer it to the foundation with a recommendation. Foundation will review forwarded proposals and make the final decision.
Evaluative Criteria: Preference is given to programs that have a long-term effect, can be replicated, and respond to issues that concern the customers, employees, and shareholders of Alabama Power Co.; provide opportunities for achievement and leadership to youth, minorities, and elderly; support community development; promote understanding of public issues; identify new programs which can adapt to other communities; or stimulate giving by other organizations. Scholarship applicants are evaluated on prior academic performance; recommendations from instructors or other individuals not related to applicant; leadership ability as evidenced by extra-curricular activities; and performance on either SAT Test, ACT Test, or other equivalent test.
Decision Notification: Six to eight weeks after application is received.

Restrictions
Does not support individuals, religious organizations for sectarian purposes, political or lobbying groups, or organizations which lack 501(c)(3) status.
Also does not fund organizations which discriminate on the basis of race, color, creed, gender, or national origin or operating expenses which duplicate United Way funding (capital or special project funding will be considered).

Additional Information
Publications: Charitable Giving Pamphlet; Foundation Annual Report

Corporate Officials
Art P. Beattie: vice president, secretary, treasurer B Pittsburgh, PA 1954. ED University of Tennessee BS (1975); University of Alabama MBA (1979). PRIM CORP EMPL vice president, secretary, treasurer: Alabama Power Co. ADD CORP EMPL secretary: Southern Electric Generating Co. NONPR AFFIL director: Alabama School of Fine Arts Foundation.
James H. Miller, III: senior vice president

Foundation Officials
Art P. Beattie: treasurer, director (see above)
Robert Holmes, Jr.: chairman ED Alabama A&M

University BA. NONPR AFFIL director: Josephson Institute of Ethics; trustee: Samford University; director: Boy Scouts of America; director: Ethics Officer Associate; director: Birmingham Urban League; director: Birmingham YMCA; trustee: Birmingham Southern Colorado.

Robin A. Hurst: director

William Bruce Hutchins, III: director B Tuscaloosa, AL 1943. PRIM CORP EMPL executive vice president, chief financial officer: Alabama Power Co. CORP AFFIL director: Southern Electric Generating Co. NONPR AFFIL member: National Association Accountants; member: National Management Association; member: Financial Executives Institute; member: Micron Delta Epsilon; member: Beta Alpha Psi; member: Beta Gamma Sigma; member:.

William B. Johnson: president, director NONPR AFFIL trustee: Southeastern Council of Foundations.

Richard S. King: assistant treasurer

C. Alan Martin: director Birmingham Regional Chamber of Commerce NONPR AFFIL director:.

Charles D. McCrary: director Auburn University NONPR AFFIL trustee:.

Rodney O. Mundy: director

Michael D. Scott: director

Steve R. Spencer: director Birmingham Regional Chamber of Commerce NONPR AFFIL director:.

Jerry L. Stewart: director

Kay I. Worley: assistant secretary

William E. Zales, Jr.: secretary

Grants Analysis

Disclosure Period: calendar year ending 2003
Total Grants: $5,412,846*
Number of Grants: 1,300 (approx)
Average Grant: $4,163
Highest Grant: $367,000
Lowest Grant: $50
Typical Range: $1,000 to $5,000 and $10,000 to $100,000
*Note: Giving excludes United Way and scholarships.

Recent Grants

Note: Grants derived from 2003 Form 990.
General

367,000	Birmingham Urban Revitalization Partnership Inc., Birmingham, AL
175,000	United Way of Central Alabama Inc., Birmingham, AL
150,000	Board of Trustees of the University of Alabama, Tuscaloosa, AL
100,000	Alabama Children's Hospital Foundation, Birmingham, AL
100,000	Alabama Institute for Deaf and Blind Foundation Inc., Talladega, AL
100,000	Alabama Shakespeare Festival Inc., Montgomery, AL
100,000	Dexter Avenue King Memorial Foundation Inc., Montgomery, AL
100,000	Rotary Club of Birmingham Foundation, Birmingham, AL
100,000	United Way of Southwest Alabama Inc., Mobile, AL
100,000	University of South Alabama, Mobile, AL -- towards endowed scholarship

ALAVI FOUNDATION

Giving Contact

Dr. Mohammad Geramian, President
500 Fifth Avenue, Suite 3900
New York, NY 10110
Phone: (212)944-8333
Fax: (212)921-0325
Web: http://www.alavifoundation.org

Description

Founded: 1973
EIN: 237345978
Organization Type: General Purpose Foundation
Giving Locations: nationally.
Grant Types: Endowment, Multiyear/Continuing Support, Project.

Donor Information

Founder: Incorporated in 1973 by Bank Melli of Iran.

Financial Summary

Total Giving: $1,765,799 (fiscal year ending March 31, 2002); $994,868 (fiscal 2001). Note: The figure for 1999 includes $60,838 in nonmonetary support in the form of publicaton and book distributions to educational institutions.
Giving Analysis: Giving for fiscal 2002 includes: foundation grants to United Way ($3000)
Assets: $85,045,636 (fiscal 2002); $82,555,915 (fiscal 2001)
Gifts Received: $12,981 (fiscal 2002); $14,573 (fiscal 2001); $14,850 (fiscal 2000)

Typical Recipients

Arts & Humanities: Libraries, Public Broadcasting
Civic & Public Affairs: African American Affairs, Ethnic Organizations, Civic & Public Affairs-General, Safety, Women's Affairs
Education: Agricultural Education, Arts/Humanities Education, Colleges & Universities, Community & Junior Colleges, Elementary Education (Private), Education-General, International Exchange, International Studies, Medical Education, Private Education (Precollege), Religious Education, Science/Mathematics Education
Environment: Air/Water Quality
Health: Arthritis, Cancer, Children's Health/Hospitals, Eyes/Blindness, Health Organizations, Heart, Hospitals, Multiple Sclerosis, Single-Disease Health Associations, Transplant Networks/Donor Banks
International: Foreign Educational Institutions, International-General, Health Care/Hospitals, International Organizations, International Peace & Security Issues, International Relief Efforts, Missionary/Religious Activities
Religion: Religion-General, Religious Organizations, Religious Welfare, Seminaries
Science: Scientific Organizations
Social Services: Community Centers, Community Service Organizations, Emergency Relief, People with Disabilities, Shelters/Homelessness, United Funds/United Ways

Application Procedures

Initial Contact: The foundation has no formal application form. Send a letter of inquiry.
Deadlines: None.

Additional Information

The foundation owns four centers in New York, Maryland, Texas, and California that are utilized as educational/religious centers and are open free of charge to all interested parties.

As part of its educational purpose, the foundation operates Saturday Schools in New York and New Jersey for teaching Islamic religion and Middle Eastern languages and cultures. The programs can be utilized by all interested parties.

Foundation Officials

Hoshang Ahmadi: director
Alireza Ebrahimi: secretary
Mohammad Geramian: president
Mehdi Hodjat: director
Abbas Mirakhor: director, treasurer
Mohammad Pirayandeh: director

Grants Analysis

Disclosure Period: fiscal year ending March 31, 2002
Total Grants: $1,762,799*
Number of Grants: 52
Average Grant: $30,207*
Highest Grant: $192,000
Lowest Grant: $100
Typical Range: $5,000 to $50,000
*Note: Giving excludes United Way. Average grant figure excludes highest grant.

Recent Grants

Note: Grants derived from 2002 Form 990.
General

192,000	Jafaria Association of Connecticut Inc., CT
125,000	Shia Lthna Asheri Jamaat of Pennsylvania, PA
123,000	Razi School, Woodside, NY
115,800	Brooklyn Mosque, Brooklyn, NY
105,000	Zainabia Nonprofit, Inc.
100,000	New York State World Trade Center Relief Fund, New York, NY
71,930	Islamic Institute of New York, Woodside, NY
65,000	Islamic Center of America, Portland, OR
64,980	Islamic Education Center, Tampa, FL
62,379	Anjuman-e Haideri

ALBERTSON'S INC.

Company Headquarters

250 E. Parkcenter Blvd.
Boise, ID 83726
Web: http://www.albertsons.com

Company Description

Founded: 1939
Ticker: ABS
Exchange: NYSE
Acquired: American Stores (1999).
Revenue: US$40.052 billion (2004)
Profit: US$444 million (2004)
Employees: 200000 (2003)
Fortune Rank: 35, per FORTUNE Magazine's list of 500 Largest U.S. Corporations (2004).
SIC(s): 5411 Grocery Stores, 5912 Drug Stores & Proprietary Stores.

Operating Locations

Acme Markets Inc. (PA--Malvern); Albertson's Drug Stores (AZ--Scottsdale); Albertson's Inc. (AR--Hot Springs, Texarkana; CA--Brea, Rocklin; CO--Aurora; OK--Tulsa; OR--Portland; TN--Memphis; TX--Katy, San Antonio; WA--Bellevue); Jewel Food Store (IL--Melrose Park); Max Food & Drug Division (ID--Boise); Osco Drug (AR--Fort Smith); Rx America (UT--Salt Lake City); Sav-on Drugs (CA--Buena Park); Yarnell Ice Cream Co. (AR--Searcy)
Note: Operates in 37 states.

Nonmonetary Support

Type: Cause-related Marketing & Promotion; Donated Products; In-kind Services
Volunteer Programs: The company sponsors the Warren E. McCain Community Volunteer Award. The program annually recognizes employees for volunteer efforts, donating $500 in the name of ten grand award winners to the charity of his/her choice. The company also selects an award winner from each of its operating divisions and donates $250 to each winner's charity of choice.

Giving Contact

Brandy Robbins, Marketing Specialist
250 Park Ctr. Boulevard
Boise, ID 83706

Phone: (208)395-4900
Fax: (208)395-6110

Description

Organization Type: Corporate Giving Program
Giving Locations: headquarters and operating communities.
Grant Types: Award, Capital, Conference/Seminar, Emergency, Employee Matching Gifts, Endowment, General Support, Matching, Multiyear/Continuing Support.
Note: Employee matching gift ratio: 1 to 1 for higher education only, up to $1000.

Financial Summary

Total Giving: $83,768,000 (2004 approx); $78,353,000 (2003); $65,000,000 (2002)
Assets: $115,211,000 (2002)

Typical Recipients

Arts & Humanities: Arts Appreciation, Arts Centers, Community Arts, Historic Preservation, Libraries, Music, Opera, Performing Arts, Public Broadcasting
Education: Business Education, Colleges & Universities, Community & Junior Colleges, Economic Education, Elementary Education (Private), Minority Education
Health: Emergency/Ambulance Services, Geriatric Health, Hospitals, Medical Rehabilitation, Mental Health, Public Health
Social Services: Child Welfare, Community Centers, Community Service Organizations, Emergency Relief, Food/Clothing Distribution, Senior Services, Shelters/Homelessness, Substance Abuse, United Funds/United Ways, Youth Organizations

Application Procedures

Initial Contact: Submit a full written proposal on the applicant organization's letterhead.
Application Requirements: Proposals should include a cover letter, narrative, and attachments. The cover letter should include a proposal summary and amount requested, and must be signed by the organization's executive director or president. The narrative section should be no longer than five pages, and must include agency information, including a brief a description of organization (history, mission, goals, and objectives), overview of current programs/activities and accomplishments, a description of organization of organizational structure, board/staff responsibilities and level of volunteer involvement, and description of agency affiliation with public agencies; information on the purpose of the grant, including a statement of need, description of constituency served and benefits to constituents, program goals, measurable objectives, program activities planned to accomplish goals (specify whether activities are new or ongoing), timetable for implementation, list of any other organizations participating in the program, list of names and qualifications of key staff members and volunteers responsible for the project, and project budget; and answers to the following questions relating to project evaluation: What results are expected during the funding period? How will success be defined and measured? How will the project's results be used and disseminated? The following attachments must be included with the proposal: board of directors list including occupations, community affiliations, committee assignments, and criteria for board selection; finances including current annual operating budget with summary of itemized revenues and expenses, funding sources for the organization with listing of past major contributions and amounts, anticipated future funding sources, and recently audited financial statement; annual report; and proof of tax-exempt status.
Deadlines: None.
Evaluative Criteria: Present an identifiable community need, tax-exempt status, efficient and effective administration, plentiful volunteer support, serves large population, programs have long-term effects, employee participation, participants encouraged to be self-sufficient, wide community support.
Decision Notification: Company responds to proposals in writing within six to eight weeks.

Restrictions

Does not support religious organizations for sectarian purposes, or political or lobbying groups.

Additional Information

In community fund drives, company generally contributes on a pro rata basis, figuring the number of Albertson's employees as a percentage of private employment in the area.
Publications: Contributions Policy and Procedures

Corporate Officials

Renee Bergquist: vice president investor relations
Lawrence R. Johnston: chairman, chief executive officer, director B Corning, NY August 29, 1948. ED Stetson University BA (1972). PRIM CORP EMPL chairman, chief executive officer, director: Albertson's Inc. Food Marketing Institute NONPR AFFIL director:; director: World Food Forum.

Giving Program Officials

Renee Bergquist: director investor relations (see above)
John G. Danielson: vice president, treasurer PRIM CORP EMPL vice president, treasurer: Albertson's Inc.

Grants Analysis

Disclosure Period: calendar year ending 2001
Total Grants: $34,000,000 (approx)*
*Note: Giving excludes money donated through the Albertson's Community Partners Card program.

ALCOA INC.

Company Headquarters

Pittsburgh, PA
Web: http://www.alcoa.com

Company Description

Founded: 1888
Ticker: AA
Exchange: NYSE
Former Name: Aluminum Co. of America;
Acquired: Reynolds Metals (2000); Cordant Technologies (2000).
Revenue: US$23.96 billion (2004)
Profit: US$1.31 billion (2004)
Employees: 120000 (2003)
Fortune Rank: 79, per FORTUNE Magazine's list of 500 Largest U.S. Corporations (2004).
SIC(s): 2819 Industrial Inorganic Chemicals Nec, 3334 Primary Aluminum, 3353 Aluminum Sheet, Plate & Foil, 3354 Aluminum Extruded Products.

Operating Locations

Alcoa Automotive (OH--Northwood; PA); Alcoa Closure Systems International, Inc. (IN--Crawfordsville); Alcoa Extrusions, Inc. (AR--Magnolia; GA--Fairburn; MS--Hernando); Alcoa Inc. (AL--Cullman; AR--Russellville; CA--Irvine, Visalia; CO--Englewood; FL--Fort Meade; GA--Norcross; IL--Danville, Princeville; IN--Evansville, Lafayette, Richmond; IA--Davenport; KY--Hawesville; LA--Baton Rouge, Vidalia; MI--Southfield; MS--Houston, Olive Branch; MO--St. Louis; NY--Massena; OH--Barberton, Chillicothe, Cleveland, Lima, Sidney, Warren; PA--Lebanon, Leetsdale, Pittsburgh; SC--Gaffney; TN--Elizabethton, Nashville; TX--Dennison, Denton, Rockdale, San Antonio; VA--Stuarts Draft; WA--Auburn)

Alcoa Foundation

Giving Contact

Kathleen W. Buechel, President
Alcoa Foundation
201 Isabella Street
Pittsburgh, PA 15212-5858
Phone: (412)553-2348
Fax: (412)553-4532
Web: http://www.alcoa.com/site/community/homepage/community.asp

Alternate Contact

PO Box 185
Pittsburgh, PA 15230-9897
Phone: (412)553-4761

Description

Founded: 1952
EIN: 251128857
Organization Type: Corporate Foundation
Giving Locations: principally near operating locations and to national organizations.
Grant Types: Award, Capital, Challenge, Conference/Seminar, Emergency, Employee Matching Gifts, Fellowship, General Support, Matching, Multiyear/Continuing Support, Research, Scholarship, Seed Money.
Note: Employee matching gift ratio: 2 to 1 for higher education.

Financial Summary

Total Giving: $14,970,191 (2003); $17,216,813 (2002); $21,326,190 (2001). Note: Contributes through foundation only.
Assets: $453,096,351 (2003); $391,868,847 (2002); $409,678,168 (2001)
Gifts Received: $1,000,000 (2003); $500,000 (2001); $500,000 (2000). Note: Contributions are received from Alcoa World Alumina.

Typical Recipients

Arts & Humanities: Arts Associations & Councils, Arts Centers, Arts Festivals, Arts Funds, Arts Institutes, Ballet, Community Arts, Dance, Arts & Humanities-General, Historic Preservation, History & Archaeology, Libraries, Literary Arts, Museums/Galleries, Music, Opera, Performing Arts, Public Broadcasting, Theater, Visual Arts
Civic & Public Affairs: African American Affairs, Botanical Gardens/Parks, Business/Free Enterprise, Chambers of Commerce, Civil Rights, Community Foundations, Economic Development, Economic Policy, Employment/Job Training, Civic & Public Affairs-General, Hispanic Affairs, Housing, Inner-City Development, Law & Justice, Legal Aid, Municipalities/Towns, Parades/Festivals, Philanthropic Organizations, Professional & Trade Associations, Public Policy, Safety, Urban & Community Affairs, Women's Affairs, Zoos/Aquariums
Education: Afterschool/Enrichment Programs, Agricultural Education, Arts/Humanities Education, Business Education, Business-School Partnerships, Colleges & Universities, Community & Junior Colleges, Economic Education, Education Associations, Education Funds, Education Reform, Elementary Education (Private), Engineering/Technological Education, Faculty Development, Education-General, Gifted & Talented Programs, International Exchange, International Studies, Journalism/Media Education, Leadership Training, Legal Education, Literacy, Medical Education, Minority Education, Preschool Education, Private Education (Precollege), Public Education (Precollege), Science/Mathematics Education, Student Aid, Vocational & Technical Education
Environment: Environment-General, Protection, Resource Conservation
Health: AIDS/HIV, Cancer, Children's Health/Hospitals, Clinics/Medical Centers, Emergency/Ambulance Services, Health-General, Geriatric Health, Health Policy/Cost Containment, Health

Funds, Health Organizations, Heart, Hospices, Hospitals, Medical Rehabilitation, Medical Research, Medical Training, Mental Health, Prenatal Health Issues, Public Health, Single-Disease Health Associations, Speech & Hearing
International: Foreign Arts Organizations, Foreign Educational Institutions, International-General, Health Care/Hospitals, International Development, International Environmental Issues, International Organizations, International Peace & Security Issues, International Relations, International Relief Efforts, Missionary/Religious Activities, Trade
Religion: Churches, Jewish Causes, Religious Organizations, Religious Welfare, Seminaries
Science: Science Exhibits & Fairs, Science Museums, Scientific Organizations
Social Services: At-Risk Youth, Big Brothers/Big Sisters, Child Welfare, Community Centers, Community Service Organizations, Counseling, Day Care, Delinquency & Criminal Rehabilitation, Domestic Violence, Emergency Relief, Family Planning, Family Services, Food/Clothing Distribution, Homes, People with Disabilities, Recreation & Athletics, Senior Services, Shelters/Homelessness, Social Services-General, Special Olympics, Substance Abuse, United Funds/United Ways, Volunteer Services, YMCA/YWCA/YMHA/YWHA, Youth Organizations

Application Procedures

Initial Contact: Organizations should contact the Alcoa facility nearest them, and the facility will make a recommendation to the foundation for grant awards. Though not encouraged, unsolicited requests may be sent directly to the foundation in the form of a two-page letter.
Application Requirements: Include description of specific project, purpose and objective, procedure to be followed (for research requests), amount requested, budget information, list of other corporate and foundation donors; recently audited financial statement; and proof of tax-exempt status.
Deadlines: None; requests acknowledged upon receipt.
Evaluative Criteria: Compatibility with foundation's five Areas of Excellence, serves area where company operates and has employees.
Decision Notification: Foundation directors usually meet bi-monthly.
Notes: Applicants are encouraged to contact the management of the local Alcoa facility. Management at the local facility will then make recommendations for grant awards to the foundation. National and international organizations should contact Alcoa Foundation in Pittsburgh directly.

Restrictions

In general, foundation does not fund the following: projects outside the area of operation of Alcoa plant or office locations; endowment funds, deficit reduction, or operating reserves; hospital capital campaigns (unless the hospital can present a comprehensive area analysis which justifies, regionally rather than on an individual institutional basis, the need for the capital improvement); individuals (except for the scholarship program for relatives of Alcoa employees); organizations and programs designed to influences legislation or promote political candidates; religious organizations for sectarian purposes; tickets, tables, souvenir programs, advertising, fundraising dinners, golf outings, and the like for benefit purposes, trips, tours or student exchange programs, documentaries, or videos. The foundation only funds organizations classified as public charities and tax-exempt per Section 501(c)(3) of the Internal Revenue Code.

Additional Information

Alcoa merged with Alumax Inc. in 1998.
Recommendations from local Alcoa personnel are important in determining awards.

The foundation reports a growing interest in international giving; international grants tripled between 1993 and 1996.
The Reynolds Metals Company Foundation merged into the Alcoa Foundation February 1, 2001.
The Cordant Technologies Foundation merged into the Alcoa Foundation May 1, 2002.
Publications: Foundation Annual Report
Trust(s): Mellon Bank, N.A.

Corporate Officials

Richard Lawrence Fischer: executive vice president, chairman counsel B Pittsburgh, PA 1936. ED University of Pittsburgh AB (1958); University of Pittsburgh JD (1961); Georgetown University LLM (1965). PRIM CORP EMPL executive vice president, chairman counsel: Alcoa Inc. ADD CORP EMPL president: Alcoa International Holdings Co. NONPR AFFIL trustee: Equal Rights Alliance; chairman: University Pittsburgh Medical Center.

Foundation Officials

Ricardo E. Belda: director B 1945.
Kathleen W. Buechel: president, treasurer, director B 1955. ED Harvard University MPA (1988). NONPR AFFIL president: Grantmakers of Western Pennsylvania; vice president: The Winchester Thurston School.
Richard B. Kelson: director B Pittsburgh, PA 1946. ED University of Pennsylvania BA (1968); University of Pittsburgh JD (1972). PRIM CORP EMPL executive vice president, chief financial officer: Aluminum Co. of America ADD CORP EMPL executive vice president, chief financial officer: Alcoa Inc. CORP AFFIL member: MeadWestvaco Corp.; director: PNC Financial Services. NONPR AFFIL member: Private Sector Councils; director: University Pittsburgh Law School Board Visitors; member: Pennsylvania Economic League; member: Financial Executives Institute Officers Conference Group; director: Pennsylvania Business Roundtable; member: American Corp. Counsel Association; member: Financial Executives Institute; member: American Bar Association.
William E. Leahey, Jr.: director B 1950.
Velma Montelro-Tribble: secretary
Renata Camargo Nascimento: director NONPR AFFIL chairman: Instituto Cultural E Filantropico Alcoa.
Barry C. Owens: director
G. John Pizzey: director NONPR AFFIL director: International Aluminum Institute; chairman: Ivanhoe Grammar School.
Richard L. (Jake) Siewert: director

Grants Analysis

Disclosure Period: calendar year ending 2003
Total Grants: $14,223,301*
Number of Grants: 1,782 (approx)
Average Grant: $7,982 (approx)
Highest Grant: $250,000 (approx)
Lowest Grant: $50
Typical Range: $500 to $25,000
*Note: Giving excludes scholarships.

Recent Grants

Note: Grants derived from 2003 Form 990.
General
215,000	Share Our Strength, Washington, DC
166,666	Conservation Student Association, Charlestown, NH
100,000	Historical Society of Western Pennsylvania, Pittsburgh, PA
100,000	Population Services International, Washington, DC
90,000	Exchange Fellowships Eisenhower, Philadelphia, PA
83,334	Fund for Public Schools Inc., New York, NY
80,000	Women's Center & Shelter of Greater Pittsburgh, Pittsburgh, PA
77,800	Youth Alive Inc., Louisville, KY
60,000	Partnership / White Pine Compass Foundation, Muskegon, MI
58,300	Youth Alive Inc., Louisville, KY

ALCON LABORATORIES INC.

Company Headquarters
Fort Worth, TX
Web: http://www.alconlabs.com

Company Description
Employees: 5,037 (1999)
SIC(s): 2834 Pharmaceutical Preparations, 3841 Surgical & Medical Instruments, 3851 Ophthalmic Goods.

Operating Locations
Alcon Laboratories, Inc. (MD--Elkridge; PA--Sinking Spring; TX--Fort Worth); Alcon Pharma (TX--Fort Worth); Alcon Surgical (TX--Fort Worth); Alcon Systems (TX--Fort Worth)

Nonmonetary Support
Value: $15,000,000 (2000); $10,000,000 (1998)
Type: Donated Equipment; Donated Products
Contact: Winona Edwards, Manager Humanitarian Services
Note: Co. provides nonmonetary support. Products are donated to vision care specialists participating in medical mission trips.

Alcon Foundation

Giving Contact
Winona Edwards, Chairman
Alcon Foundation
6201 South Freeway
Ft. Worth, TX 76134-2099
Phone: (817)293-0450
Fax: (817)568-7000
Web: http://www.alconlabs.com

Description
Founded: 1962
EIN: 756034736
Organization Type: Corporate Foundation
Giving Locations: TX: Ft. Worth nationally.
Grant Types: General Support, Scholarship.

Donor Information
Founder: Alcon Laboratories, Inc.

Financial Summary
Total Giving: $1,398,981 (2002); $1,177,981 (2001).
Note: Contributes through corporate direct giving program and foundation.
Assets: $13,008 (2002); $8,903 (2001)
Gifts Received: $1,398,000 (2002); $1,184,750 (2001); $622,000 (2000). Note: The foundation receives donations from Alcon Laboratories, Inc.

Typical Recipients
Arts & Humanities: Arts Associations & Councils, Arts Outreach, Ballet, Libraries, Museums/Galleries, Music, Opera, Performing Arts, Public Broadcasting, Theater
Civic & Public Affairs: African American Affairs, Business/Free Enterprise, Clubs, Civic & Public Affairs-General, Hispanic Affairs, Philanthropic Organizations, Urban & Community Affairs, Women's Affairs, Zoos/Aquariums
Education: Afterschool/Enrichment Programs, Business Education, Colleges & Universities, Community & Junior Colleges, Education Associations, Education-General, Health & Physical Education, Medical

Education, Minority Education, Private Education (Precollege), Public Education (Precollege), Science/Mathematics Education, Secondary Education (Private), Secondary Education (Public), Student Aid
Health: Cancer, Children's Health/Hospitals, Clinics/Medical Centers, Emergency/Ambulance Services, Eyes/Blindness, Health Funds, Health Organizations, Hospitals, Hospitals (University Affiliated), Medical Research, Mental Health, Prenatal Health Issues, Public Health, Single-Disease Health Associations, Transplant Networks/Donor Banks
International: Foreign Educational Institutions, Health Care/Hospitals, International Affairs, International Peace & Security Issues
Religion: Ministries, Religious Welfare, Seminaries
Science: Science-General, Science Museums
Social Services: Camps, Child Welfare, Community Centers, Community Service Organizations, Counseling, Emergency Relief, Family Services, Food/Clothing Distribution, Homes, People with Disabilities, Shelters/Homelessness, Social Services-General, United Funds/United Ways, YMCA/YWCA/YMHA/YWHA, Youth Organizations

Application Procedures

Initial Contact: Submit a letter or proposal.
Application Requirements: Include a description of organization; amount requested; purpose of funds sought; a copy of budget or annual financial report indicating sources of funding and how funds are distributed; and proof of tax-exempt status.
Deadlines: None.
Decision Notification: Decisions are announced bimonthly.

Restrictions

Alcon limits contributions to education and research institutions within Alcon's areas of specialization: ophthalmology, optometry, and vision care. Funding is available for support of community-based activities in areas where Alcon has a facility.

Corporate Officials

C. Allen Baker: executive vice presidento B 1942. PRIM CORP EMPL executive vice president: Alcon Laboratories, Inc.
Timothy R. G. Sear: president, chief executive officer B 1937. ED Manchester University (1962). PRIM CORP EMPL president, chief executive officer: Alcon Laboratories, Inc. CORP AFFIL president: Alcon Puerto Rico Inc.

Foundation Officials

Mary Dulle: co-chairman PRIM CORP EMPL director professional relations: Alcon Laboratories, Inc.
J. Hiddeman: trustee
Fred Pettinato: trustee
Timothy R. G. Sear: trustee (see above)
John Alexander Walters: co-chairman B Philadelphia, PA 1938. ED Wagner College BA (1960). PRIM CORP EMPL corporate vice president human resources: Alcon Laboratories, Inc.

Grants Analysis

Disclosure Period: calendar year ending 2002
Total Grants: $1,383,731*
Number of Grants: 236
Average Grant: $4,203*
Highest Grant: $250,000
Lowest Grant: $150
Typical Range: $150 to $25,000
*Note: Giving excludes scholarship; United Way. Average grant figure excludes two highest grants ($400,000).

Recent Grants

Note: Grants derived from 2003 Form 990.
General
250,000	American Society of Cataract and Refractive Surgery Foundation, Fairfax, VA
150,000	Los Angeles Eye Institute, Los Angeles, CA
100,000	Orbis International, New York, NY
50,000	American Academy of Ophthalmology, San Francisco, CA
50,000	Cook Children and Medical Center, Ft. Worth, TX
50,000	New York Eye and Ear Infirmary, New York, NY
41,646	Texas Christian University, Ft. Worth, TX
25,000	Ford Henry Health Care System, Detroit, MI
25,000	Fort Worth Symphony, Ft. Worth, TX
25,000	Glaucoma Foundation, New York, NY

GEORGE I. ALDEN TRUST

Giving Contact

Susan B. Woodbury, Chairman & Trustee
370 Main St., 12th Fl.
Worcester, MA 01608
Phone: (508)798-8621
Fax: (508)791-6454
E-mail: trustees@aldentrust.org
Web: http://www.aldentrust.org

Description

Founded: 1912
EIN: 046023784
Organization Type: General Purpose Foundation
Giving Locations: MA: Worcester New England area.
Grant Types: Capital, Endowment, General Support, Project, Scholarship.
Note: Foundation makes restricted endowments primarily for scholarships and not for operating support.

Donor Information

Founder: Established in 1912 in Massachusetts by Mr. George I. Alden, a creative academic innovator who taught mechanical engineering at Worcester Polytechnic Institute for 28 years, served as a trustee of the institute and the Worcester Boys' Trade School, and was a leading member of the Worcester School Committee. Mr. Alden was an inventor; co-founder, president, and chairman of the Norton Company; and the founder and director of America's second hydraulic laboratory. When he died in 1926 at the age of 83, his shares of the Norton Company were bequeathed to the trust.

Financial Summary

Total Giving: $6,227,000 (2003); $8,167,500 (2001)
Assets: $163,521,781 (2003); $159,683,000 (2001)

Typical Recipients

Arts & Humanities: Arts Centers, Historic Preservation, History & Archaeology, Libraries, Museums/Galleries, Music, Public Broadcasting
Civic & Public Affairs: Botanical Gardens/Parks, Clubs, Community Foundations, Employment/Job Training, Civic & Public Affairs-General, Professional & Trade Associations
Education: Arts/Humanities Education, Business-School Partnerships, Colleges & Universities, Community & Junior Colleges, Continuing Education, Education Associations, Education Funds, Education Reform, Engineering/Technological Education, Faculty Development, Education-General, Legal Education, Medical Education, Minority Education, Private Education (Precollege), Religious Education, Science/Mathematics Education, Secondary Education (Private), Secondary Education (Public), Special Education, Student Aid, Vocational & Technical Education
Environment: Environment-General, Resource Conservation
Health: Clinics/Medical Centers, Emergency/Ambulance Services, Health Funds, Health Organizations, Medical Research

Science: Science Museums, Scientific Centers & Institutes, Scientific Research
Social Services: Child Welfare, Community Service Organizations, Emergency Relief, Family Planning, Family Services, YMCA/YWCA/YMHA/YWHA, Youth Organizations

Application Procedures

Initial Contact: Send a request in letter form.
Application Requirements: Requests for funding should include a budget, list goals to be achieved, reasons the applicant is well suited to receive funding, explanation of how applicant's goals fit within existing activities of the foundation, evidence of 501(c)(3) tax-exempt status, an annual report, list of trustees and their other affiliations, and an audited financial statement. Applications must be signed by the organization's chief executive officer. See website for additional details.
Deadlines: None.
Review Process: The trustees meet bimonthly to review applications.
Notes: Proposals should be made in a reasonably brief narrative form with an appropriate budget with enrollment and financial trends in recent years.

Restrictions

No grants are made to individuals or tax-supported institutions. A three year gap applies between grants to any one recipient. The foundation primarily supports preselected organizations.

Additional Information

If grants are given outside the Worcester area, they are only to independent colleges and universities in the United States.
Publications: Annual Report; Guidelines

Foundation Officials

James E. Collins: treasurer, trustee
Warner S. Fletcher: secretary, trustee B Worcester, MA 1945. ED Williams College BA (1967); Boston University JD (1973). PRIM CORP EMPL treasurer: Fletcher, Tilton & Whipple PC. CORP AFFIL director: Wyman-Gordon Co.
Richard P. Traina: vice chairman, trustee
Susan B. Woodbury: chairman, trustee

Grants Analysis

Disclosure Period: calendar year ending 2003
Total Grants: $6,227,000
Number of Grants: 61
Average Grant: $86,898*
Highest Grant: $600,000
Lowest Grant: $5,000
Typical Range: $25,000 to $100,000
*Note: Average grant figure excludes two highest grants ($1,100,000).

Recent Grants

Note: Grants derived from 2003 Form 990.
Library-Related
250,000	American Antiquarian Society, Worcester, MA

General
600,000	Manufacturing Assistance Foundation Vocational School, Worcester, MA
500,000	UMASS Memorial Foundation, Worcester, MA
300,000	Boys and Girls Club of Worcester, Worcester, MA
250,000	Clark University, Worcester, MA
250,000	Clark University, Worcester, MA
150,000	Barnard College, New York, NY
150,000	Emerson College, Boston, MA
150,000	Wellesley College, Wellesley, MA
150,000	WICN, Worcester, MA
140,000	Babson College, Babson Park, MA

JOHN W. ALDEN TRUST

Giving Contact
Amy F. Sahler, Trust Officer
c/o U.S. Trust Co.
225 Franklin Street
Boston, MA 02110
Phone: (617)897-3209

Description
Founded: 1986
EIN: 222719727
Organization Type: Private Foundation
Giving Locations: MA
Grant Types: General Support, Project, Research, Seed Money.

Donor Information
Founder: the late Priscilla Alden

Financial Summary
Total Giving: $460,215 (fiscal year ending September 30, 2003); $699,107 (fiscal 2001)
Assets: $9,830,887 (fiscal 2003); $10,919,461 (fiscal 2001)
Gifts Received: $10,957 (fiscal 1996); $2,584 (fiscal 1992)

Typical Recipients
Arts & Humanities: Arts Associations & Councils, Arts Funds, Arts Institutes, Museums/Galleries, Music
Civic & Public Affairs: Civic & Public Affairs-General, Philanthropic Organizations
Education: Afterschool/Enrichment Programs, Arts/Humanities Education, Colleges & Universities, Leadership Training, Literacy, Medical Education, Private Education (Precollege), Public Education (Precollege), Religious Education, Science/Mathematics Education, Special Education, Vocational & Technical Education
Health: Adolescent Health Issues, Cancer, Children's Health/Hospitals, Clinics/Medical Centers, Eyes/Blindness, Health Organizations, Hospices, Hospitals, Medical Rehabilitation, Medical Research, Mental Health, Prenatal Health Issues, Single-Disease Health Associations
Religion: Religious Welfare
Social Services: At-Risk Youth, Camps, Child Abuse, Child Welfare, Community Service Organizations, Day Care, Delinquency & Criminal Rehabilitation, Family Services, Homes, People with Disabilities, Recreation & Athletics, Youth Organizations

Application Procedures
Initial Contact: Send a brief letter of inquiry.
Application Requirements: Include a description of organization and purpose of funds sought.
Deadlines: None.

Additional Information
Publications: Application Guidelines
Trust(s): State Street Bank & Trust Co

Foundation Officials
William B. Tyler: trustee

Grants Analysis
Disclosure Period: fiscal year ending September 30, 2003
Total Grants: $460,215
Number of Grants: 29
Average Grant: $14,115*
Highest Grant: $65,000
Lowest Grant: $176
Typical Range: $10,000 to $20,000
***Note:** Average grant figure excludes highest grant.

Recent Grants
Note: Grants derived from fiscal 2000 Form 990.

General

40,000	Associated Day Care Services, Boston, MA -- Building Block Campaign
35,000	McLean Hospital, Belmont, MA -- risk and residency longitudinal study
35,000	Perkins School for the Blind, Watertown, MA -- Toy Lending Library
29,880	Salem State College, Salem, MA -- Computer Literacy Program
25,741	Massachusetts General Hospital, Boston, MA -- support project to prevent ongoing prenatal alcohol damage
25,582	Franciscan Children's Hospital, Boston, MA -- Library Resource Center
25,000	American Academy of Arts and Sciences, Cambridge, MA -- support active girls initiative project
25,000	CAST, Boston, MA -- consortium on universal design for learning
25,000	Margaret Gifford School, Inc. -- building renovations
25,000	Massachusetts General Hospital, Boston, MA -- pediatric study

TOM S. AND MARYE KATE ALDRIDGE CHARITABLE AND EDUCATIONAL TRUST

Giving Contact
Robert S. Aldridge, Director
3035 Northwest 63rd, Suite 207N
Oklahoma City, OK 73116-3606
Phone: (405)840-9916

Description
Founded: 1996
EIN: 731484075
Organization Type: Private Foundation
Giving Locations: headquarters and operating communities.
Grant Types: General Support.

Financial Summary
Total Giving: $86,038 (fiscal year ending June 30, 2004); $174,364 (fiscal 2001)
Assets: $3,186,210 (fiscal 2004); $3,695,722 (fiscal 2001)
Gifts Received: $26,197 (fiscal 1999); $1,901,693 (fiscal 1997). Note: In fiscal 1997, contributions were received from the Tom S. Aldridge Trust.

Typical Recipients
Arts & Humanities: Libraries
Civic & Public Affairs: Law & Justice
Education: Colleges & Universities, Education-General, International Exchange, Public Education (Precollege), Secondary Education (Public)
International: International-General
Religion: Bible Study/Translation, Churches, Ministries
Social Services: Crime Prevention, Food/Clothing Distribution, People with Disabilities, Recreation & Athletics, Social Services-General

Application Procedures
Initial Contact: Send a brief letter of inquiry.
Application Requirements: Include a description of organization proof of tax-exempt status, name and qualifications of the person responsible for the funds, statement of goals and purpose of the program and number of people who will benefit, staff required and their qualifications, itemized budget, amount requested, purpose of funds sought, and other sources of funding.
Deadlines: None.

Restrictions
Requests are not accepted for facility construction or repair, retirement of debt, funding of day to day operations, utilities or other overhead, or fund raising activities.

Foundation Officials
Kimberly F. Aldridge: director
Laverne R. Aldridge: director
M. L. Aldridge: director
Robert S. Aldridge: director
Tom S. Aldridge, II: director
Barbara Foerster: director
Mickie Beth Smith: director

Grants Analysis
Disclosure Period: fiscal year ending June 30, 2004
Total Grants: $86,038
Number of Grants: 14
Average Grant: $5,080*
Highest Grant: $20,000
Lowest Grant: $138
Typical Range: $1,000 to $10,000
***Note:** Average grant figure excludes highest grant.

Recent Grants
Note: Grants derived from fiscal 2001 Form 990.
Library-Related

10,000	Lone Oak Area Public Library, Lone Oak, TX
10,000	Navarre Public Library, Navarre, FL

General

20,000	National Institute on Development Delays, Shawnee, OK
17,000	Regional Food Bank of Oklahoma, Oklahoma City, OK
10,000	Crown Center Church, Moore, OK
10,000	Donna Nigh Foundation, Oklahoma City, OK
10,000	Hand Up Ministries, Oklahoma City, OK
10,000	International Student Outreach, Arlington, TX
8,400	University of Central Oklahoma, Edmond, OK
8,000	University of Oklahoma, Norman, OK
7,500	Oklahoma State University, Stillwater, OK
7,275	First Baptist Church of Newalla, Newalla, OK

MARGARET ALEXANDER EDWARDS TRUST

Giving Contact
Julian L. Lapides
2 Hamill Rd., Suite 332
Baltimore, MD 21210
Phone: (410)752-4518

Description
Founded: 1989
EIN: 526389629
Organization Type: Private Foundation
Giving Locations: IL: Chicago; MD: Baltimore
Grant Types: General Support.

Financial Summary
Total Giving: $34,400 (2003); $29,941 (2001)
Assets: $916,000 (2003); $1,017,562 (2001)
Gifts Received: $4,974 (2001); $650 (2000); $500 (1998). Note: In 1998, contributions were received from C. M. Clapp.

Typical Recipients
Arts & Humanities: Arts Festivals, Libraries, Literary Arts, Theater
Education: Colleges & Universities, Elementary Ed-

ucation (Private), Literacy, Private Education (Precollege), Religious Education, Secondary Education (Private), Secondary Education (Public)
Social Services: Family Services

Application Procedures

Initial Contact: The foundation has no formal grant application procedure or application form.
Deadlines: None.

Restrictions

Emphasis is on programs that promote reading among young adults.

Foundation Officials

Anna A. Curry: trustee
Ray M. Fry: trustee
Sara Siebert: trustee emeritus

Grants Analysis

Disclosure Period: calendar year ending 2003
Total Grants: $34,400
Number of Grants: 5
Highest Grant: $15,000
Lowest Grant: $3,800
Typical Range: $3,000 to $5,000

Recent Grants

Note: Grants derived from 2003 Form 990.
Library-Related

15,000	Enoch Pratt Free Library Teen Reading -- to promote reading among young adults
7,750	American Library Association, Chicago, IL -- to promote reading among young adults

General

4,050	Eastern Middle School, Silver Spring, MD -- to promote reading among young adults
3,800	Casey Family Services, Baltimore, MD -- to promote reading among young adults
3,800	Western High School, Baltimore, MD -- to promote reading among young adults

JOSEPH ALEXANDER FOUNDATION

Giving Contact

Robert M. Weintraub, President & Director
400 Madison Avenue, Suite 906
New York, NY 10017
Phone: (212)355-3688

Description

Founded: 1960
EIN: 510175951
Organization Type: General Purpose Foundation
Giving Locations: NY: New York nationally.
Grant Types: Capital, Conference/Seminar, Endowment, General Support, Project, Research, Scholarship.

Donor Information

Founder: Established in 1960 by the late Joseph Alexander.

Financial Summary

Total Giving: $613,500 (fiscal year ending October 31, 2001)
Assets: $17,399,960 (fiscal 2001)

Typical Recipients

Arts & Humanities: Arts Centers, Arts Festivals, Arts Institutes, Dance, Historic Preservation, History & Archaeology, Libraries, Museums/Galleries, Music, Performing Arts, Public Broadcasting, Visual Arts
Civic & Public Affairs: Clubs, Community Founda-

tions, Ethnic Organizations, Civic & Public Affairs-General, Philanthropic Organizations, Urban & Community Affairs, Women's Affairs
Education: Afterschool/Enrichment Programs, Arts/Humanities Education, Business Education, Colleges & Universities, Education Funds, Elementary Education (Private), Faculty Development, Education-General, Gifted & Talented Programs, Legal Education, Literacy, Medical Education, Private Education (Precollege), Religious Education, Science/Mathematics Education, Special Education, Student Aid
Environment: Environment-General
Health: AIDS/HIV, Alzheimer's Disease, Cancer, Children's Health/Hospitals, Clinics/Medical Centers, Diabetes, Emergency/Ambulance Services, Eyes/Blindness, Health-General, Geriatric Health, Health Funds, Health Organizations, Hospices, Hospitals, Kidney, Long-Term Care, Medical Rehabilitation, Medical Research, Mental Health, Multiple Sclerosis, Nursing Services, Single-Disease Health Associations, Transplant Networks/Donor Banks, Trauma Treatment
International: Foreign Arts Organizations, Foreign Educational Institutions, Health Care/Hospitals, International Organizations, International Peace & Security Issues, International Relations, Missionary/Religious Activities
Religion: Religion-General, Jewish Causes, Religious Organizations, Religious Welfare, Seminaries, Synagogues/Temples
Science: Science Museums
Social Services: At-Risk Youth, Child Welfare, Community Service Organizations, Day Care, Family Planning, Family Services, Homes, People with Disabilities, Recreation & Athletics, Senior Services, Social Services-General, Substance Abuse, United Funds/United Ways, Youth Organizations

Application Procedures

Initial Contact: The foundation requests applications be made in writing.
Deadlines: None.
Review Process: The board meets on a regular basis.

Restrictions

Grants are not made to individuals.

Additional Information

Publications: Financial Statement
Trust(s): John Alexander Foundation

Foundation Officials

Arthur S. Alfert: vice president, director
Harvey A. Mackler: director PRIM CORP EMPL executive vice president: Gibraltar Corp. America.
Helen Mackler: secretary, director
Robert M. Weintraub: president, director

Grants Analysis

Disclosure Period: fiscal year ending October 31, 2001
Total Grants: $613,500*
Number of Grants: 52
Average Grant: $11,480*
Highest Grant: $50,000
Lowest Grant: $1,000
Typical Range: $5,000 to $20,000
***Note:** Giving excludes scholarships.

Recent Grants

Note: Grants derived from 2002 Form 990.
General

50,000	Bar Ilan University, New York, NY -- towards program for legal aid advocacy in family law.
35,000	University of Pennsylvania, Philadelphia, PA -- towards Computer Science program
30,000	Genesis Foundation, Staten Island, NY -- towards Auditorium in Beit Shemesh

30,000	Western Wall Heritage Foundation, New York, NY -- excavation and museum
25,000	ALS Association of Greater Philadelphia, Philadelphia, PA -- towards Scott A. Mackler assistive technology program
25,000	Salk Institute, San Diego, CA -- for research in nerve cell development
25,000	UAHC Camp Harlam, Philadelphia, PA -- towards Health Center in Camp Harlam
15,000	Dorot, New York, NY -- towards unrestricted contribution
15,000	Jewish Braille Institute, New York, NY -- towards unrestricted contribution
15,000	Long Island Jewish Children's Health Network, Great Neck, NY -- for comprehensive tertiary care satellite network

ROBERT D. AND CATHERINE R. ALEXANDER FOUNDATION

Giving Contact

R. Denny Alexander, Investment Counselor & Trustee
4200 S. Hulen St., Suite 617
Ft. Worth, TX 76109-4913
Phone: (817)731-1317

Description

Founded: 1962
EIN: 756012124
Organization Type: Private Foundation
Giving Locations: TX: Tarrant County, Fort Worth
Grant Types: General Support.

Donor Information

Founder: R. D. Alexander Trust

Financial Summary

Total Giving: $289,906 (2003)
Giving Analysis: Giving for 2003 includes: foundation grants to United Way ($10,000)
Assets: $5,280,560 (2003)
Gifts Received: $144,063 (1999); $75,000 (1995); $27,604 (1994). Note: In 1996 and 1999, contributions were received from Catherine R. Alexander.

Typical Recipients

Arts & Humanities: Arts Associations & Councils, Ballet, Community Arts, Dance, Libraries, Museums/Galleries, Music, Opera, Performing Arts, Public Broadcasting
Civic & Public Affairs: Clubs, Civic & Public Affairs-General, Housing, Philanthropic Organizations
Education: Business Education, Colleges & Universities, Education-General, Private Education (Precollege), Student Aid
Health: AIDS/HIV, Children's Health/Hospitals, Clinics/Medical Centers, Eyes/Blindness, Health Organizations, Hospitals, Medical Research, Research/Studies Institutes, Single-Disease Health Associations
Religion: Churches, Jewish Causes, Missionary Activities (Domestic), Religious Organizations, Religious Welfare, Social/Policy Issues
Science: Science Museums
Social Services: Camps, Child Welfare, Community Service Organizations, Day Care, Food/Clothing Distribution, People with Disabilities, Shelters/Homelessness, Substance Abuse, United Funds/United Ways, YMCA/YWCA/YMHA/YWHA, Youth Organizations

Application Procedures

Initial Contact: Send a brief letter of inquiry.
Deadlines: None.

Restrictions
Does not support individuals.

Foundation Officials
R. Denny Alexander: trustee PRIM CORP EMPL owner: R. Denny Alexander & Co. CORP AFFIL director: TNP Enterprises Inc.; director: Texas-New Mexico Power Co. NONPR AFFIL director: Cook Childrens Medical Center.

Grants Analysis
Disclosure Period: calendar year ending 2003
Total Grants: $279,906*
Number of Grants: 21
Average Grant: $9,745*
Highest Grant: $85,000
Lowest Grant: $100
Typical Range: $1,000 to $15,000
*Note: Giving excludes United Way. Average grant figure excludes highest grant.

Recent Grants
Note: Grants derived from 2001 Form 990.
General

77,000	Cook Children's Medical Center, Ft. Worth, TX
52,100	University Christian Church, Ft. Worth, TX
50,000	Camp Carter YMCA, Ft. Worth, TX
42,000	Fort Worth Dallas Ballet, Ft. Worth, TX
25,000	Union Gospel Mission, Ft. Worth, TX
10,000	Texas Christian University, Ft. Worth, TX
10,000	United Way of Metro Tarrant County, Ft. Worth, TX
7,500	Prevent Blindness Texas, Ft. Worth, TX
5,000	Fort Worth Opera, Ft. Worth, TX
2,500	American Fund Raising Professionals, Ft. Worth, TX

WALTER ALEXANDER FOUNDATION

Giving Contact
Stanley F. Staples, Jr., Secretary
PO Box 2137
Wausau, WI 54402-2137
Phone: (715)845-4556

Description
Founded: 1952
EIN: 396044635
Organization Type: Private Foundation
Giving Locations: WI
Grant Types: Capital, Emergency, General Support.

Donor Information
Founder: the late Ruth Alexander, the late Anne M. Alexander

Financial Summary
Total Giving: $179,333 (fiscal year ending November 30, 2003)
Giving Analysis: Giving for fiscal 2003 includes: foundation grants to United Way ($2,500)
Assets: $3,622,378 (fiscal 2003)

Typical Recipients
Arts & Humanities: Arts Associations & Councils, Arts Centers, Community Arts, Historic Preservation, History & Archaeology, Libraries, Museums/Galleries, Opera, Performing Arts, Public Broadcasting, Theater
Civic & Public Affairs: Botanical Gardens/Parks, Chambers of Commerce, Community Foundations, Economic Development, Civic & Public Affairs-General, Legal Aid, Municipalities/Towns
Education: Business Education, Colleges & Univer-

sities, Education Funds, Education-General, Gifted & Talented Programs, Medical Education, Preschool Education, Private Education (Precollege), Secondary Education (Private), Secondary Education (Public), Student Aid, Vocational & Technical Education
Environment: Air/Water Quality, Environment-General, Resource Conservation, Wildlife Protection
Health: Eyes/Blindness, Health Organizations
International: International Development, International Environmental Issues
Religion: Religious Welfare
Social Services: Animal Protection, Camps, Community Service Organizations, Counseling, People with Disabilities, Scouts, Social Services-General, Special Olympics, United Funds/United Ways, YMCA/YWCA/YMHA/YWHA, Youth Organizations

Application Procedures
Initial Contact: applications should spell out the activity or capital need for which support is requested.
Application Requirements: Include other sources of funding, proof of tax-exempt status, evaluation procedures, and a commitment to provide any contemplated future sources of income.
Deadlines: None.

Restrictions
Does not support individuals.

Foundation Officials
Nancy Anne Cordaro: director
Jean A. Koskinen: director
Walter Koskinen: vice president, director
Alexander Reichl: president, director

Grants Analysis
Disclosure Period: fiscal year ending November 30, 2003
Total Grants: $176,833*
Number of Grants: 29
Average Grant: $4,530*
Highest Grant: $50,000
Lowest Grant: $300
Typical Range: $1,000 to $10,000
*Note: Giving excludes United Way. Average grant figure excludes highest grant.

Recent Grants
Note: Grants derived from fiscal 2001 Form 990.

Library-Related

10,000	Marathon County Public Library Foundation, Wausau, WI -- humanities challenge

General

33,334	Grand Theater Foundation, Inc., Wausau, WI -- arts block
33,333	Grand Theater Foundation, Inc., Wausau, WI -- arts block
10,000	Lawrence University, Appleton, WI -- environment studied
10,000	Theda Clark Medical Center Foundation, Inc., Neenah, WI -- trauma helicopter
10,000	Wisconsin Public Broadcasting Foundation, Milwaukee, WI -- public television
9,100	Town of Plum Lake, Sayner, WI -- tennis court repair
7,500	Friends of Mead McMillan Association, Inc., Marshfield, WI -- education building
7,500	Lincoln County Humane Society, Inc., Merrill, WI -- cat cages
7,500	Marathon County Historical Society, Wausau, WI -- heating costs increase
6,000	Wisconsin Public Broadcasting Foundation, Milwaukee, WI -- public radio

ALEXANDER STEWART MD FOUNDATION TRUST

Giving Contact
Arnold Johnsen, Trust Officer
c/o Mellon Bank NA
PO Box 185
Pittsburgh, PA 15230
Phone: (215)553-2295

Description
Founded: 1981
EIN: 236732616
Organization Type: Private Foundation
Former Name: Stewart Alexander Foundation (2002).
Giving Locations: PA: Cumberland County, Franklin County, Fulton County, Perry County, Shippensburg County
Grant Types: General Support, Scholarship.

Financial Summary
Total Giving: $310,953 (fiscal year ending June 30, 2004); $374,788 (fiscal 2001)
Giving Analysis: Giving for fiscal 2001 includes: foundation grants to United Way ($2,543)
Assets: $7,300,376 (fiscal 2004); $8,039,095 (fiscal 2001)
Gifts Received: $41,224 (fiscal 1997); $188 (fiscal 1993). Note: In fiscal 1997, contributions were received from Jane Stewart.

Typical Recipients
Arts & Humanities: Arts Associations & Councils, History & Archaeology, Libraries, Music
Civic & Public Affairs: Civic & Public Affairs-General, Housing, Law & Justice, Legal Aid, Rural Affairs, Safety, Women's Affairs
Education: Agricultural Education, Education-General
Environment: Resource Conservation
Health: Cancer, Emergency/Ambulance Services, Home-Care Services, Mental Health, Public Health
Religion: Religious Welfare
Social Services: Animal Protection, Domestic Violence, Family Services, People with Disabilities, Recreation & Athletics, Scouts, Senior Services, Shelters/Homelessness, YMCA/YWCA/YMHA/YWHA

Application Procedures
Initial Contact: Send a brief letter of inquiry.
Application Requirements: Include a description of organization, amount requested, purpose of funds sought, recently audited financial statement, and proof of tax-exempt status.
Deadlines: April 1.

Additional Information
Trust(s): Mellon Bank NA

Grants Analysis
Disclosure Period: fiscal year ending June 30, 2004
Total Grants: $310,953
Number of Grants: 52
Average Grant: $5,980
Highest Grant: $20,000
Lowest Grant: $1,000
Typical Range: $1,000 to $10,000

Recent Grants
Note: Grants derived from fiscal 2001 Form 990.
Library-Related

10,000	Franklin County Library System, PA

General

20,000	Lutheran Home Care Services, Chambersburg, PA
20,000	Salvation Army, Chambersburg, PA
20,000	Shippensburg Area Recreation and Parks Department, Shippensburg, PA

16,152	Shook Home for the Aged, Chambersburg, PA
15,000	Agape Residential Ministries & Services, PA
14,000	Buchanan Valley Volunteer Fire Department, Philadelphia, PA
13,500	Quincy United Methodist Home, Quincy, PA
12,000	Cumberland Valley Mental Health Center, PA
12,000	Manito Inc., PA
10,000	Bendersville Community Fire Department, Philadelphia, PA

ALLEGHENY FOUNDATION

Giving Contact

Mathew A. Groll, Executive Director
One Oxford Center
301 Grant Street, Suite 3900
Pittsburgh, PA 15219-6401
Phone: (412)392-2900
Web: http://www.scaife.com

Description

Founded: 1953
EIN: 256012303
Organization Type: General Purpose Foundation
Giving Locations: PA: including western Pennsylvania
Grant Types: General Support, Project.

Donor Information

Founder: Established in 1953 by Richard Mellon Scaife, the Allegheny Foundation makes grants mainly for the benefit of Pittsburgh and western Pennsylvania. Richard Scaife is the son of Sarah Mellon Scaife, and great grandson of Judge Thomas Mellon, founder of Mellon Bank.

Financial Summary

Total Giving: $1,360,300 (2003); $1,594,600 (2002)
Assets: $38,862,681 (2003); $32,189,890 (2002); $40,398,096 (2001)
Gifts Received: $681,250 (1999); $130,375 (1993); $1,156,250 (1992). Note: The foundation received contributions in the form of stock from Richard M. Scaife.

Typical Recipients

Arts & Humanities: Arts Associations & Councils, Historic Preservation, History & Archaeology, Libraries, Museums/Galleries, Music, Opera, Public Broadcasting, Theater
Civic & Public Affairs: Botanical Gardens/Parks, Business/Free Enterprise, Clubs, Economic Development, Economic Policy, Employment/Job Training, Civic & Public Affairs-General, Housing, Inner-City Development, Legal Aid, Municipalities/Towns, Nonprofit Management, Philanthropic Organizations, Professional & Trade Associations, Public Policy, Urban & Community Affairs
Education: Colleges & Universities, Economic Education, Education Associations, Education Funds, Education Reform, Elementary Education (Private), Environmental Education, Education-General, Leadership Training, Literacy, Medical Education, Private Education (Precollege), Public Education (Precollege), Science/Mathematics Education, Special Education, Student Aid
Environment: Air/Water Quality, Environment-General, Resource Conservation, Watershed
Health: Cancer
International: Health Care/Hospitals
Religion: Churches, Dioceses, Ministries, Religious Welfare
Science: Scientific Centers & Institutes, Scientific Organizations

Social Services: Animal Protection, Camps, Child Welfare, Community Centers, Community Service Organizations, Counseling, Crime Prevention, Emergency Relief, Family Planning, Food/Clothing Distribution, People with Disabilities, Recreation & Athletics, Senior Services, Social Services-General, Youth Organizations

Application Procedures

Initial Contact: Letter, signed by the organization's president or authorized representative. The letter should be approved by the organization's board of directors.
Application Requirements: Concise description of the specific project for which funds are sought, annual budget for the project and the organization, latest audited financial statement and annual report, list of board of directors, and proof of tax-exempt status. The foundation may request additional information.
Deadlines: December, for following year.
Review Process: The annual meeting is held in December. Proposals are accepted throughout the year, and will be acted upon as soon as possible.

Restrictions

The foundation does not make grants to individuals, or for endowments, scholarships, or fellowships.

Additional Information

Publications: Annual Report; Guidelines

Foundation Officials

Ralph H. Goettler: trustee B 1929. ED University of Pittsburgh (1957). PRIM CORP EMPL president: Goettler Associates Inc.
Doris O'Donnell: trustee
Margaret R. Scaife: trustee
Richard Mellon Scaife: chairman, trustee B Pittsburgh, PA 1932. ED Yale University (1950-1951); University of Pittsburgh BA (1957). PRIM CORP EMPL owner, chairman, publisher: Tribune Review Publishing Co. CORP AFFIL chairman, director: T-R Printing & Publishing Co.; chairman, publisher, director: Tribune Review; partner: 301 Capital Mall Associates; chairman, director: Standard Observer Newspaper.
George A. Weymouth: trustee PRIM NONPR EMPL chairman, director: Brandywine Conservancy Inc. NONPR AFFIL chairman, director: Brandywine River Museum; chairman, director: Environment Management Center.
Arthur P. Ziegler, Jr.: trustee B Pittsburgh, PA 1937. ED University of Pittsburgh BA (1958); University of Pittsburgh MA (1959); Union Theological Seminary (1960); Case Western Reserve University (1961). PRIM NONPR EMPL president, director: Pittsburgh History & Landmarks. CORP AFFIL director: Steel Heritage Corp. NONPR AFFIL trustee emeritus: Washington National Trust; member, board advisors: Waterfront Center; director: Pittsburgh Partnership Neighborhood Development; trustee: Walden Trust; director: Allegheny County Chamber of Commerce; trustee: Historic Houses America. CLUB AFFIL City Club.

Grants Analysis

Disclosure Period: calendar year ending 2003
Total Grants: $1,360,300*
Number of Grants: 35
Average Grant: $28,244*
Highest Grant: $400,000
Lowest Grant: $1,000
Typical Range: $10,000 to $50,000
***Note:** Average grant figure excludes highest grant.

Recent Grants

Note: Grants derived from 2002 Form 990.
Library-Related
75,000	Nantucket Athenaeum, Nantucket, PA

General
100,000	Allegheny Institute for Public Policy, Pittsburgh, PA
100,000	Pittsburgh Parks Conservancy, Pittsburgh, PA
100,000	River City Brass Band, Pittsburgh, PA
90,000	Lincoln Institute of Public Opinion Research Inc., Harrisburg, PA
80,000	Boys & Girls Clubs of Western Pennsylvania, Pittsburgh, PA -- summer program
60,000	Pittsburgh History and Landmarks Foundation, Pittsburgh, PA -- construction of Homestead Borough building
58,500	Braddock's Field Historical Society, Braddock, PA -- towards archive project and capital support
55,000	Children Requiring a Caring Kommunity, Garden Grove, CA
50,000	Center for the Study of Popular Culture, Los Angeles, CA -- project support
50,000	Extra Mile Education Foundation Inc., Pittsburgh, PA -- operating support

NIBS AND EDNA ALLEN FOUNDATION

Giving Contact

Robert C. Lucas, Trustee
Nibs and Edna Allen Foundation
PO Box 250
Miles City, MT 59301
Phone: (406)232-3620

Description

Founded: 1993
EIN: 810480143
Organization Type: Private Foundation
Grant Types: General Support.

Financial Summary

Total Giving: $128,232 (fiscal year ending June 30, 2001)
Giving Analysis: Giving for fiscal 2001 includes: foundation scholarships ($22,312)
Assets: $2,719,633 (fiscal 2001)
Gifts Received: $1,500,000 (fiscal 2001); $750,000 (fiscal 1993). Note: In fiscal 2001, contributions were received from the late Edna Allen. In fiscal 1993, contributions were received from Edna R. Allen.

Typical Recipients

Arts & Humanities: Arts Centers, History & Archaeology, Libraries, Music
Civic & Public Affairs: Community Foundations, Civic & Public Affairs-General, Housing, Parades/Festivals, Safety
Education: Community & Junior Colleges, Education-General, Public Education (Precollege), Secondary Education (Public), Student Aid
Health: Clinics/Medical Centers, Emergency/Ambulance Services, Mental Health
Religion: Religious Organizations
Social Services: At-Risk Youth, Recreation & Athletics, Senior Services, Youth Organizations

Application Procedures

Initial Contact: Send a brief letter of inquiry.
Application Requirements: Inlcude a description of organization, purpose of funds sought, and proof of tax-exempt status.
Deadlines: None. Requests should be made at least two weeks in advance of need.

Restrictions

Contributions are limited to southeastern MT.

Foundation Officials

Edna R. Allen: president
Nancy D. Larsen: secretary, treasurer
Robert C. Lucas: vice president

Grants Analysis

Disclosure Period: fiscal year ending June 30, 2001
Total Grants: $105,920*
Number of Grants: 29
Average Grant: $3,652
Highest Grant: $20,000
Typical Range: $1,000 to $15,000
*Note: Giving excludes scholarships.

Recent Grants

Note: Grants derived from fiscal 2001 Form 990.
Library-Related
10,000   Miles City Public Library, Miles City, NY
General
20,000   Miles City School District 1, Miles City, MT -- playground equipment
15,000   Parenting Education in East Montana, Miles City, MT
10,000   Miles City Hockey Association, Miles City, MT -- sprinkler system for building
7,500   Miles City School District 1, Miles City, MT -- school bleachers
6,000   Custer County Education Foundation, Miles City, MT -- scholarship fund
5,942   Miles Community College, Miles City, MT -- basketball team
5,000   Custer County High School, Miles City, MT
5,000   Fairgrounds Improvements, Miles City, MT
5,000   Kent Ewalt Fund, Miles City, MT
5,000   Veterans Administration Medical Center Redevelopment Project, Miles City, MT

ALLIANT ENERGY CORP.

Company Headquarters

4902 N. Biltmore Ln.
Madison, WI 53718-2132
Web: http://www.alliant-energy.com

Company Description

Ticker: LNT
Exchange: NYSE
Assets: US$2.777 billion (2001)
Employees: 8943 (2003)
SIC(s): 4911 Electric Services, 4924 Natural Gas Distribution, 4941 Water Supply.

Operating Locations

Wisconsin Power & Light Co. (WI, Madison)

Alliant Energy Foundation, Inc.

Giving Contact

JoAnn Healy, Foundation Administrator
Alliant Energy Foundation
4902 North Biltmore Ln.
PO Box 77007
Madison, WI 53701-1007
Phone: (608)458-3311
Fax: (608)283-6991
E-mail: customercare@alliantenergy.com
Web: http://alliantenergy.com/community/charity.htm
Note: Contact for Wisconsin applications.

Alternate Contact

Jean Bjorseth
Alliant Energy Foundation
200 First Street SE
Cedar Rapids, IA 52401
Note: Contact for Iowa, Minnesota, and Illinois applications.

Description

EIN: 391444065
Organization Type: Corporate Foundation
Former Name: Wisconsin Power & Light Foundation, Inc..
Giving Locations: IL: company operating locations; IA; MN; WI: near headquarters and service areas (central and south central Wisconsin)
Grant Types: Capital, Employee Matching Gifts, General Support.
Note: Employee matching gift ratio: 1 to 1.

Financial Summary

Total Giving: $2,151,766 (2002); $2,660,932 (2001)
Assets: $23,923,318 (2002); $27,912,636 (2001)
Gifts Received: $1,200,000 (2002); $2,948,250 (1999); $1,200,000 (1997). Note: In 2000 contributions were received from Wisconsin Power & Light Co. and Interstate Power & Light Co.

Typical Recipients

Arts & Humanities: Arts Associations & Councils, Arts Centers, Arts Festivals, Community Arts, Historic Preservation, History & Archaeology, Libraries, Museums/Galleries, Music, Performing Arts, Public Broadcasting, Theater
Civic & Public Affairs: African American Affairs, Botanical Gardens/Parks, Business/Free Enterprise, Clubs, Community Foundations, Economic Development, Economic Policy, Employment/Job Training, Civic & Public Affairs-General, Housing, Municipalities/Towns, Parades/Festivals, Professional & Trade Associations, Safety, Urban & Community Affairs
Education: Afterschool/Enrichment Programs, Arts/Humanities Education, Business Education, Colleges & Universities, Community & Junior Colleges, Education Funds, Engineering/Technological Education, Education-General, Leadership Training, Preschool Education, Private Education (Precollege), Student Aid, Vocational & Technical Education
Environment: Environment-General
Health: Cancer, Children's Health/Hospitals, Clinics/Medical Centers, Emergency/Ambulance Services, Health Funds, Health Organizations, Hospitals, Nursing Services, Public Health, Single-Disease Health Associations
Religion: Religious Welfare
Science: Science-General, Science Museums, Scientific Centers & Institutes
Social Services: At-Risk Youth, Child Welfare, Community Centers, Community Service Organizations, Emergency Relief, Family Services, Food/Clothing Distribution, People with Disabilities, Scouts, Senior Services, Shelters/Homelessness, Social Services-General, United Funds/United Ways, YMCA/YWCA/YMHA/YWHA, Youth Organizations

Application Procedures

Initial Contact: Contact the foundation to obtain an Application for Funding form. An Application may be downloaded from the foundation Web site.
Application Requirements: A completed application form must be submitted with a narrative relating to specific topics listed on the application form.
Deadlines: December 1 for funding in the following year.
Review Process: During the review process, the foundation may request additional information or conduct a site visit.
Decision Notification: Grant notification letters are sent in the first quarter of each year.

Restrictions

The foundation focuses on program grants and will not accept proposals for capital projects. The foundation does not provide grants for individuals; ads in programs, door prizes, raffle tickets, dinner tables, golf outings, or sponsorships of organized sports teams or activities; religious, fraternal or social clubs; endowments; registration fees for fundraising events such as walk-a-thons, runs, or travel funds for tours or tournaments; or books, magazines, or professional journal articles. Applicants must be classified as 501(c)(3) tax-exempt.

Additional Information

In 1998, WPL Holdings, the parent company of Wisconsin Power and Light Co., was involved in a three-way merger along with IES Industries and Interstate Power Co. The three companies formed Alliant Energy Corporation. Wisconsin Power and Light Co. is now a subsidiary of Alliant Energy Corporation.

Corporate Officials

Erroll Brown Davis, Jr.: chairman, president, chief executive officer B Pittsburgh, PA August 05, 1944. ED Carnegie Mellon University BSEE (1965); University of Chicago MBA (1967). PRIM CORP EMPL chairman, president, chief executive officer: Alliant Energy Corp.; president, chief executive officer, director: Interstate Energy Corp. ADD CORP EMPL chief executive officer: Wisconsin Power & Light Co. CORP AFFIL chief executive officer: Wisconsin Power & Light Co.; director: Sentry Insurance Co.; chief executive officer: Interstate Power Co.; director: PP&G Industries Inc.; chairman: Heartland Development Corp.; chief executive officer: IES Utilities; chief executive officer: Alliant Industries Inc.; director: BP Amoco Corp. NONPR AFFIL director: Wisconsin Manufacturing & Commerce; director: Wisconsin Utilities Association; member: Selective Service Board; director: Edison Electric Institute; director: Electric Power Research Institute; trustee: Carnegie Mellon University; director: Competitive Wisconsin; member: Association of Edison Illuminating Companies; member: American Gas Association; member: American Society Corporate Executives; member: American Association Blacks Energy.

Foundation Officials

Edward M. Gleason: secretary-treasurer
Jo Ann Healy: administrator
James E. Hoffman: director
John O. Larsen: director
Steven F. Price: assistant treasurer
Eliot G. Protsch: director
Diane H. Ramsey: vice president
Barbara J. Swan: director
Carol Toussaint: Interim executive director

Grants Analysis

Disclosure Period: calendar year ending 2002
Total Grants: $2,151,766*
Number of Grants: 1,806
Average Grant: $1,191
Highest Grant: $100,000
Lowest Grant: $50
Typical Range: $1,500 to $30,000
*Note: Giving includes matching gifts, scholarship, United Way.

Recent Grants

Note: Grants derived from 2003 Form 990.
Library-Related
1,500   Garrett Memorial Library, Moulton, IA
General
117,466   United Way of Dane County, Madison, WI
101,960   United Way of East Central Iowa, Cedar Rapids, IA
58,530   Scholarship America, St. Peter, MN -- towards scholarship of children of employees
33,735   United Way of Dane County, Madison, WI
33,333   City of Cedar Rapids, Cedar Rapids, IA -- towards theatre renovation
33,333   Science Station, Cedar Rapids, IA
30,525   United Way of Dane County, Madison, WI
27,500   Dubuque County Historical Society, Dubuque, IA
25,000   University of Wisconsin Foundation, Madison, WI
23,113   Dubuque Area United Way, Dubuque, IA

ALLIANZ LIFE INSURANCE COMPANY OF NORTH AMERICA

Company Headquarters
5701 Golden Hill Dr.
Minneapolis, MN 55416
Web: http://www.allianzlife.com

Company Description
Founded: 1896
Assets: US$25.498 billion (2001)
SIC(s): 6311 Life Insurance.
Parent Company: Allianz AG, Koniginstrasse 28, Munich, Germany

Operating Locations
Allianz Life Insurance Company of North America (TX--Dallas); Allianz Underwriters Insurance Co. (CA--Burbank)

Nonmonetary Support
Type: Loaned Employees; Workplace Solicitation

Giving Contact
Laura Juergens, Senior Charitable Giving specialist
5701 Golden Hills Drive
Minneapolis, MN 55416
Phone: (763)765-6500
Fax: (763)765-7299
E-mail: Laura_Juergens@allianzlife.com
Web: http://www.allianzlife.com/allianzcommunity/

Description
Organization Type: Corporate Giving Program
Giving Locations: near headquarters only.
Grant Types: Capital, General Support, Matching.

Financial Summary
Total Giving: $1,500,000 (2005 approx); $1,200,000 (2004)

Typical Recipients
Arts & Humanities: Libraries, Museums/Galleries, Music
Civic & Public Affairs: Economic Development, Housing, Urban & Community Affairs
Education: Colleges & Universities, Economic Education, Education Funds
Health: Health Organizations, Heart, Hospitals
Religion: Churches, Religious Organizations
Social Services: People with Disabilities, Scouts, United Funds/United Ways, YMCA/YWCA/YMHA/YWHA, Youth Organizations

Application Procedures
Initial Contact: Send a brief letter of inquiry and a full proposal. Include a description of organization, amount requested, and purpose of funds sought. It is best to apply by the end of the third quarter, as the review board meets in the fall.

Restrictions
Company does not support individuals, political or lobbying groups, or religious organizations for sectarian purposes.

Additional Information
According to Allianz of America, Inc., each local office administers independent contributions programs, with Allianz Life's being the largest. Local offices decide on recipients and support levels, with nonmonetary support such as loaned employees included in programs.

Corporate Officials
Edward J. Bonachi: senior vice president, treasurer, chief financial officer PRIM CORP EMPL senior vice president, treasurer, chief financial officer: Allianz Life Insurance Co. North America.

Giving Program Officials
Julie Wall: Asst. VP Corp. Mktg.

Grants Analysis
Typical Range: $1,000 to $2,500

ALLMERICA FINANCIAL CORP.

Company Headquarters
Worcester, MA
Web: http://www.allmerica.com

Company Description
Founded: 1995
Ticker: AFC
Exchange: NYSE
Former Name: State Mutual Life Assurance Co.; Hanover Insurance Co.
Revenue: US$3.263 billion (2003)
Profit: US$86.9 million (2003)
Employees: 4700 (2003)
SIC(s): 6726 Investment Offices Nec.

Operating Locations
Allmerica Financial Corp. (MA--Worcester)
Note: Operates offices in 22 states and the District of Columbia.

Nonmonetary Support
Type: Donated Equipment; In-kind Services; Loaned Executives; Workplace Solicitation
Volunteer Programs: The company sponsors a Volunteer Incentive Program.

Allmerica Financial Charitable Foundation, Inc.

Giving Contact
Michael Buckley, President
Allmerica Financial Charitable Foundation
440 Lincoln Street
Worcester, MA 01653
Phone: (508)855-4660
Fax: (508)855-6332

Description
Founded: 1991
EIN: 043105650
Organization Type: Corporate Foundation
Giving Locations: MA: Boston, Worcester; MI
Grant Types: Employee Matching Gifts, General Support.

Financial Summary
Total Giving: $942,697 (2002); $1,093,249 (2001). Note: Contributes through corporate direct giving program and foundation.
Giving Analysis: Giving for 2001 includes: foundation matching gifts ($121,760); foundation grants to United Way ($296,454); foundation ($675,035)
Assets: $3,783,787 (2002); $4,623,615 (2001)
Gifts Received: $990,248 (2002); $104,198 (2000); $125,100 (1999). Note: Foundation receives contributions from the First Allmerica Financial Life Insurance Company, the Hanover Insurance Company, and Citizens Insurance Company of America.

Typical Recipients
Arts & Humanities: Arts Associations & Councils, Arts Festivals, Arts Outreach, Arts & Humanities-General, History & Archaeology, Libraries, Museums/Galleries, Music, Opera, Performing Arts, Theater
Civic & Public Affairs: Botanical Gardens/Parks, Business/Free Enterprise, Clubs, Community Foundations, Economic Development, Employment/Job Training, Civic & Public Affairs-General, Hispanic Affairs, Housing, Inner-City Development, Law & Justice, Legal Aid, Municipalities/Towns, Parades/Festivals, Philanthropic Organizations, Professional & Trade Associations, Public Policy, Safety, Urban & Community Affairs, Women's Affairs
Education: Afterschool/Enrichment Programs, Arts/Humanities Education, Business Education, Business-School Partnerships, Colleges & Universities, Community & Junior Colleges, Education Associations, Education Funds, Education Reform, Engineering/Technological Education, Faculty Development, Education-General, Leadership Training, Medical Education, Preschool Education, Private Education (Precollege), Public Education (Precollege), Religious Education, School Volunteerism, Secondary Education (Private), Student Aid
Environment: Environment-General, Resource Conservation
Health: AIDS/HIV, Cancer, Children's Health/Hospitals, Clinics/Medical Centers, Diabetes, Emergency/Ambulance Services, Eyes/Blindness, Health-General, Health Organizations, Heart, Hospitals, Hospitals (University Affiliated), Medical Research, Nursing Services, Public Health, Single-Disease Health Associations
Religion: Religious Welfare
Science: Scientific Centers & Institutes
Social Services: Big Brothers/Big Sisters, Camps, Child Abuse, Child Welfare, Community Centers, Community Service Organizations, Day Care, Domestic Violence, Family Services, Food/Clothing Distribution, Recreation & Athletics, Scouts, Senior Services, Sexual Abuse, Shelters/Homelessness, Social Services-General, Special Olympics, Substance Abuse, United Funds/United Ways, Volunteer Services, YMCA/YWCA/YMHA/YWHA, Youth Organizations

Application Procedures
Initial Contact: Send a brief letter of inquiry.
Application Requirements: The foundation has no formal application policy. Include a description of organization, amount requested, purpose of funds sought, audited financial statement, and proof of tax-exempt status.
Deadlines: None.

Restrictions
The foundation's efforts focus primarily on giving in Worcester, MA.

Corporate Officials
John Francis O'Brien, Jr.: president, chief executive officer B Brockton, MA 1943. ED Harvard College (1965); Harvard University MBA (1968). PRIM CORP EMPL president, chief executive officer: Allmerica Financial Corp. CORP AFFIL director: State Mutual Life Assurance Co.; director: TJX Co. Inc.; chairman: Hanover Insurance Co. Inc.; member, executive committee: Massachusetts Capital Resource Co.; director: First Allmerica Life Insurance Co.; president,ceo: First Allmerica Financial Life Insurance Co.; chairman: Citizens Insurance Co. of America; director: Cabot Corp.; chief executive officer, director, president: Citizens Corp.; president, chief executive officer: Allmerica Financial Corp.; president, chief executive officer, director: Allmerica Property & Casualty Companies Inc.; director: Abiomed Inc.; president: Allamerica Financial Life Insurance and Annuity Co. NONPR AFFIL director: Life Insurance Association of Massachusetts; trustee: Worcester Polytech Institute; visitors committee board overseers: Harvard College; director: American Council Life Insurance; executive committee: Harvard Alumni Association.

Foundation Officials
Bruce C. Anderson: vice president, director
Michael Buckley: president, director
Laura Gobron: treasurer
Joseph W. MacDougall, Jr.: director, clerk

Grants Analysis
Disclosure Period: calendar year ending 2002
Total Grants: $526,605*
Number of Grants: 89
Average Grant: $5,917
Highest Grant: $50,000
Lowest Grant: $50
Typical Range: $1,000 to $20,000
*Note: Giving excludes matching gifts; scholarship; United Way.

Recent Grants
Note: Grants derived from 2003 Form 990.
General

50,000	United Way of Livingston County, Howell, MI
47,500	United Way of Central Massachusetts, Worcester, MA
47,500	United Way of Central Massachusetts, Worcester, MA
47,500	United Way of Central Massachusetts, Worcester, MA
30,000	Student Leadership Services Inc., Waterford, MI
20,000	Worcester Public Schools, Worcester, MA
15,000	Mass Insight Education, Boston, MA
15,000	Park Spirit of Worcester Inc., Worcester, MA
13,800	Roy Western Scholarship Foundation, Worcester, MA
10,000	Central Mass Housing, Worcester, MA

ALLYN FOUNDATION

Giving Contact
Meg O'Connell, Executive Director
PO Box 22
Skaneateles, NY 13152
Phone: (315)685-9427

Description
Founded: 1958
EIN: 156017723
Organization Type: Private Foundation
Giving Locations: NY: Cayuga County, Onondaga County
Grant Types: Capital, Fellowship, General Support, Research, Scholarship.

Donor Information
Founder: the late William N. Allyn, William G. Allyn, Welch Allyn, Inc.

Financial Summary
Total Giving: $506,000 (2003); $522,444 (2001)
Giving Analysis: Giving for 2003 includes: foundation scholarships ($27,000); 2001: foundation scholarships ($23,000)
Assets: $11,231,020 (2003); $11,157,063 (2001)
Gifts Received: $506,968 (2003); $100,000 (2000); $200,000 (1999). Note: In 2003, contributions were received from William Allyn. In 1995, 1999, and 2000, contributions were received from Welch Allyn.

Typical Recipients
Arts & Humanities: Historic Preservation, Libraries, Museums/Galleries, Music, Performing Arts, Public Broadcasting, Theater
Civic & Public Affairs: African American Affairs, Botanical Gardens/Parks, Chambers of Commerce, Community Foundations, Economic Development, Employment/Job Training, Ethnic Organizations, Civic & Public Affairs-General, Housing, Native American Affairs, Public Policy, Safety, Urban & Community Affairs, Zoos/Aquariums
Education: Colleges & Universities, Community & Junior Colleges, Education Funds, Literacy, Minority Education, Preschool Education, Private Education (Precollege), Public Education (Precollege), Special Education, Student Aid
Health: Alzheimer's Disease, Cancer, Children's Health/Hospitals, Clinics/Medical Centers, Emergency/Ambulance Services, Health Organizations, Hospices, Hospitals, Hospitals (University Affiliated), Long-Term Care, Medical Research, Research/Studies Institutes, Single-Disease Health Associations
International: Missionary/Religious Activities
Religion: Churches, Religious Welfare
Science: Science Museums, Scientific Centers & Institutes
Social Services: Big Brothers/Big Sisters, Camps, Child Welfare, Community Service Organizations, Counseling, Day Care, Family Planning, Family Services, Food/Clothing Distribution, People with Disabilities, Recreation & Athletics, Scouts, Sexual Abuse, Shelters/Homelessness, Social Services-General, Substance Abuse, YMCA/YWCA/YMHA/YWHA, Youth Organizations

Application Procedures
Initial Contact: Return completed application with proof of tax-exempt status, a list of board members, and recently audited financial statement.
Deadlines: None.

Additional Information
Publications: Application Guidelines

Foundation Officials
Amy Allyn: director
David Allyn: director
Dawn N. Allyn: director
Eric R. Allyn: director
Janet J. Allyn: secretary
Lew F. Allyn: vice president B 1941.
Scott Allyn: director
William G. Allyn: hon officer
Tanya Dillon: honorary director
Tasha Given: hon director
Donald Nelson: advisory
Margaret Mary O'Connell: executive director
Elsa A. Soderberg: treasurer
Jon Soderberg: director
Libby Soderberg: director
Peer Soderberg: director
Peter Soderberg: director
Wilbur L. Townsend: director
Charles S. Tracy: director
Sonya Weinfeld: director

Grants Analysis
Disclosure Period: calendar year ending 2003
Total Grants: $479,000*
Number of Grants: 55
Average Grant: $7,944*
Highest Grant: $50,000
Lowest Grant: $500
Typical Range: $1,000 to $15,000
*Note: Giving excludes scholarships. Average grant figure excludes highest grant.

Recent Grants
Note: Grants derived from 2001 Form 990.
Library-Related

28,500	Skaneateles Library Association, Skaneateles, NY -- for operating support

General

29,000	Matthew House, Chicago, IL -- for capital improvements
29,000	New York Police and Fire Widows and Orphans Fund, New York, NY -- for 9/11 support
25,000	Native American Service Agency, Syracuse, NY -- for operating support
24,750	East Hill Family Medicine, Auburn, NY -- for school based dental programs
20,000	Hospice of the Finger Lakes, Finger Lakes, NY -- for capital improvements
19,000	Skaneateles Recreational Charitable Trust, Skaneateles, NY -- for capital project
18,900	Cuyaga Boy Scouts, Auburn, NY -- for operating support
15,000	Alzheimer's Disease of Central New York, Syracuse, NY -- for Respite Program
15,000	Auburn YMCA, Auburn, NY -- for capital improvements
15,000	Crouse Health Foundation, Syracuse, NY -- for capital improvements

ELEANORA ALMS TRUST

Giving Contact
Heidi Jark, Trust Officer
c/o Fifth Third Bank, Department 00864
38 Fountain Square Plaza
Cincinnati, OH 45263
Phone: (513)534-4397

Description
Founded: 1939
EIN: 316019723
Organization Type: Private Foundation
Giving Locations: OH: Cincinnati
Grant Types: Capital, General Support, Seed Money.

Donor Information
Founder: the late Eleanora Alms

Financial Summary
Total Giving: $206,000 (fiscal year ending September 30, 2004). Note: Fiscal 1997 Giving includes United Way ($6,760).
Assets: $3,244,365 (fiscal 2004)

Typical Recipients
Arts & Humanities: Arts Associations & Councils, Arts Centers, Arts Festivals, Arts Funds, Arts Institutes, Ballet, Dance, Arts & Humanities-General, Historic Preservation, History & Archaeology, Museums/Galleries, Music, Opera, Performing Arts, Public Broadcasting
Civic & Public Affairs: Botanical Gardens/Parks, Parades/Festivals, Urban & Community Affairs
Education: Education-General, Public Education (Precollege)
Environment: Environment-General, Resource Conservation
Health: Alzheimer's Disease
Religion: Churches
Social Services: Community Centers, Family Planning, Family Services, United Funds/United Ways, YMCA/YWCA/YMHA/YWHA, Youth Organizations

Application Procedures
Initial Contact: Request application.
Deadlines: February 10, May 10, August 10, and November 10.

Restrictions
Does not support individuals, religious organizations for sectarian purposes, or political or lobbying groups.

Additional Information
Publications: Annual Report; Application Form
Trust(s): Fifth Third Bank

Grants Analysis

Disclosure Period: fiscal year ending September 30, 2004
Total Grants: $206,000
Number of Grants: 9
Average Grant: $19,500*
Highest Grant: $50,000
Lowest Grant: $5,000
Typical Range: $10,000 to $25,000
*Note:** Average grant figure excludes highest grant.

Recent Grants

Note: Grants derived from fiscal 2004 Form 990.
General

50,000	National Underground Railroad Freedom Center, Cincinnati, OH
41,000	Taft Museum of Art, Cincinnati, OH
25,000	Cincinnati May Festival, Cincinnati, OH
25,000	Cincinnati Opera Association, Cincinnati, OH
25,000	Fine Arts Fund, Cincinnati, OH
15,000	YMCA of Greater Cincinnati, Cincinnati, OH
10,000	CET, Cincinnati, OH
10,000	Cincinnati Arts Association, Cincinnati, OH
5,000	Hillside Trust, Cincinnati, OH

BEN J. ALTHEIMER CHARITABLE FOUNDATION

Giving Contact

John S. Selig, President, Secretary & Treasurer
425 W. Capitol Ave., Ste. 1800
Little Rock, AR 72201
Phone: (318)797-2163

Description

Founded: 1995
EIN: 710769229
Organization Type: Private Foundation
Grant Types: General Support.

Financial Summary

Total Giving: $429,792 (2003); $617,286 (2001)
Assets: $3,061,201 (2003); $4,399,952 (2001)
Gifts Received: $93 (1998); $2,023,065 (1996).
Note: In 1996, contributions were received from the Ben J. Altheimer Foundation ($2,018,367); miscellaneous contributions of less than $5,000 each also were received.

Typical Recipients

Arts & Humanities: Arts Centers
Civic & Public Affairs: Civic & Public Affairs-General, Municipalities/Towns
Education: Colleges & Universities, Education Funds, Education-General, Legal Education, Medical Education, Private Education (Precollege)
Health: Cancer, Children's Health/Hospitals
Religion: Religion-General
Social Services: Scouts

Application Procedures

Initial Contact: Send a brief letter of inquiry.

Foundation Officials

William H. Bowen: vice president, assistant secretary
John S. Selig: president, secretary, treasurer
Michael J. Selig: vice president

Grants Analysis

Disclosure Period: calendar year ending 2003
Total Grants: $429,792

Number of Grants: 8
Highest Grant: $101,130
Lowest Grant: $1,735

Recent Grants

Note: Grants derived from 2003 Form 990.
General

101,130	Arkansas Children's Hospital, Little Rock, AR
100,000	Florence Crittenton Services Inc., Charlotte, NC
77,062	City of Altheimer, Altheimer, AR
50,000	University of Arkansas Medical School Foundation
43,000	Hendrix College, Conway, AR -- Altheimer-Hendrix college minority advancement program
41,865	Pathway to College Program -- for pathway to college program in Altheimer
15,000	Arts and Science Center for Southeast Arkansas, Pine Bluff, AR -- for expansion of its school tour programs
1,735	Quapaw Area Boy Scouts, Little Rock, AR

ALTMAN FOUNDATION

Giving Contact

Karen L. Rosa, Vice President & Executive Director
521 Fifth Ave., 35th Fl.
New York, NY 10175-3599
Phone: (212)682-0970
Web: http://fdncenter.org/grantmaker/altman/

Description

Founded: 1913
EIN: 131623879
Organization Type: General Purpose Foundation
Giving Locations: NY: focusing on the five boroughs of New York City
Grant Types: General Support, Project.

Donor Information

Founder: Established in 1913 in New York under the will of Benjamin Altman, the founder of the B. Altman & Company department store, who bequeathed his ownership of the company to the foundation to support charitable and educational institutions in New York.
Since its earliest days, the foundation has reflected Mr. Altman's own philanthropic concern for social service, healthcare, educational and cultural institutions and organizations.

Financial Summary

Total Giving: $10,530,636 (2003); $11,061,540 (2002)
Giving Analysis: Giving for 2003 includes: foundation matching gifts ($77,502); foundation grants to United Way ($100,000); 2002: foundation matching gifts ($84,540); foundation scholarships ($110,000); foundation grants to United Way ($150,000)
Assets: $234,733,151 (2003); $205,477,151 (2002)

Typical Recipients

Arts & Humanities: Arts Associations & Councils, Arts Outreach, Historic Preservation, History & Archaeology, Libraries, Museums/Galleries, Music, Performing Arts, Theater, Visual Arts
Civic & Public Affairs: Asian American Affairs, Botanical Gardens/Parks, Business/Free Enterprise, Community Foundations, Economic Development, Employment/Job Training, Ethnic Organizations, Civic & Public Affairs-General, Housing, Law & Justice, Legal Aid, Nonprofit Management, Philanthropic Organizations, Safety, Urban & Community Affairs, Women's Affairs, Zoos/Aquariums
Education: Afterschool/Enrichment Programs, Arts/

Humanities Education, Colleges & Universities, Continuing Education, Education Funds, Elementary Education (Private), Environmental Education, Faculty Development, Education-General, Legal Education, Literacy, Medical Education, Minority Education, Private Education (Precollege), Religious Education, Science/Mathematics Education, Special Education, Student Aid
Environment: Air/Water Quality, Environment-General, Resource Conservation, Wildlife Protection
Health: AIDS/HIV, Cancer, Children's Health/Hospitals, Clinics/Medical Centers, Emergency/Ambulance Services, Eyes/Blindness, Geriatric Health, Health Policy/Cost Containment, Health Funds, Health Organizations, Home-Care Services, Hospitals, Mental Health, Nursing Services, Outpatient Health Care, Prenatal Health Issues, Preventive Medicine/Wellness Organizations, Public Health
Religion: Dioceses, Jewish Causes, Religious Organizations, Religious Welfare, Seminaries
Science: Science Museums, Scientific Centers & Institutes
Social Services: At-Risk Youth, Big Brothers/Big Sisters, Child Abuse, Child Welfare, Community Centers, Community Service Organizations, Day Care, Delinquency & Criminal Rehabilitation, Domestic Violence, Emergency Relief, Family Services, Food/Clothing Distribution, People with Disabilities, Recreation & Athletics, Refugee Assistance, Senior Services, Shelters/Homelessness, Social Services-General, United Funds/United Ways, YMCA/YWCA/YMHA/YWHA, Youth Organizations

Application Procedures

Initial Contact: Submit grant requests in letter form, not exceeding five pages.
Application Requirements: Applicants must describe the project for which funds are being solicited, include a copy of 501(c)(3) most recent audited financial statement, project and organization budgets, a list of major corporate and foundation supporters with amounts, and a list of officers or trustees and their affiliations.
Deadlines: None.
Notes: The Altman Foundation accepts, but does not require, the New York area common grant application form.

Restrictions

No grants are made to individuals. As a general rule, the foundation does not fund bricks and mortar or the purchase of capital equipment. Grant requests from outside the State of New York are generally not considered for funding.

Additional Information

The foundation occasionally initiates discretionary grants and offers ongoing support to organizations that have received previous funding.
Publications: General Guidelines; Application Procedure Brochure; Application Form; Annual Report

Foundation Officials

James M. Burke: trustee
Thomas C. Burke: trustee emeritus
John P. Casey: treasurer B NY 1945. ED City University of New York Bernard M. Baruch College (1971). CORP AFFIL director: Energy Tech International Corp. NONPR AFFIL vice chairman, director: Saint Agnes Hospital; treasurer: Union League; trustee: Franciscan Services.
Bernard Finkelstein: trustee B New York, NY 1930. ED New York University BA (1951); Yale University LLB (1954). PRIM CORP EMPL partner: Paul, Weiss, Rifkind, Wharton & Garrison. NONPR AFFIL member wills trusts advisory committee: Practicing Law Institute; member: Yale Law School Association; member: Phi Beta Kappa; member: Order Coif; member: Phi Alpha Delta; member: New York State Bar Association; member: Association Bar New York City; member: New York Bar Foundation; fellow: American College Trust & Estate Counsel; member: American

Bar Association. CLUB AFFIL Elmwood Country Club.
Anna M. Johnson: administrative assistant
Sharon B. King: trustee, assistant secretary
Justine Koch: accountant
Kate Liebman: program officer
Nina B. Mogilnik: senior program officer
Jane B. O'Connell: president, trustee B New York, NY 1941. ED Manhattanville College BA (1963); New York University MA (1968). PRIM NONPR EMPL school administrator: Convent of Sacred Heart. NONPR AFFIL chairwoman devel committee: Network of Sacred Heart Schools; director: Saint Aloysius Educational Clinic; member: Case Commission Committees; director: City Harvest.
Karen L. Rosa: vice president, executive director
Doriann Sama: administrative assistant
Maurice A. Selinger, Jr.: trustee
Julia V. Shea: secretary, trustee
John W. Townsend, IV: vice president, trustee NONPR AFFIL assistant executive director, assistant secretary: Boettcher Foundation.
Patricia J. Volland: trustee ED Ottawa University; San Diego State University MSW; Loyola College MBA (1981). PRIM NONPR EMPL senior vice president administration finance: New York Academy Medicine. NONPR AFFIL member: National Association Social Workers; director: Planned Parenthood New York; Council Social Work Education; member: Health Care Executive Forum.

Grants Analysis

Disclosure Period: calendar year ending 2003
Total Grants: $10,353,134*
Number of Grants: 162
Average Grant: $60,395*
Highest Grant: $390,000
Lowest Grant: $2,500
Typical Range: $25,000 to $100,000
***Note:** Giving excludes matching gifts and United Way. Average grant figure excludes two highest grants ($690,000).

Recent Grants

Note: Grants derived from 2003 Form 990.
Library-Related
200,000	Queens Library Foundation, New York, NY
150,000	New York Public Library, New York, NY

General
390,000	Saint Vincent Catholic Medical Centers of New York, New York, NY
300,000	The Graduate Center, New York, NY
300,000	New York Botanical Garden, NY
225,000	Saint Nicholas Neighborhood Preservation Corporation, Brooklyn, NY
200,000	Literacy Assistance Center Inc., New York, NY
175,000	New York Medical College, New York, NY
175,000	Notre Dame School, New York, NY
158,000	United Hospital Fund, New York, NY
150,000	Literacy Assistance Center, New York, NY
145,000	Children's Aid society, New York, NY

MAURICE AMADO FOUNDATION

Giving Contact

Pam Kaizer, Executive Director
3940 Laurel Canyon Boulevard, Suite 809
Studio City, CA 91604
Phone: (818)980-9190
Fax: (818)980-9190
Web: http://www.mauriceamadofdn.org

Description

Founded: 1961
EIN: 956041700
Organization Type: Family Foundation
Giving Locations: CA: Los Angeles; NY: New York
Grant Types: General Support, Project.
Note: Grants also include program and publishing awards.

Donor Information

Founder: Incorporated in 1961 by the late Maurice Amado.

Financial Summary

Total Giving: $1,500,000 (fiscal year ending November 30, 2003 approx); $1,500,000 (fiscal 2002); $1,840,235 (fiscal 2001)
Assets: $30,000,000 (fiscal 2003 approx); $30,000,000 (fiscal 2002); $36,360,759 (fiscal 2001)

Typical Recipients

Arts & Humanities: Arts Centers, Arts Outreach, Ballet, Dance, Ethnic & Folk Arts, Arts & Humanities-General, Historic Preservation, History & Archaeology, Libraries, Literary Arts, Museums/Galleries, Music, Opera, Public Broadcasting, Visual Arts
Civic & Public Affairs: Community Foundations, Ethnic Organizations, Civic & Public Affairs-General, Philanthropic Organizations, Safety, Women's Affairs
Education: Arts/Humanities Education, Colleges & Universities, Education Associations, Education Funds, Education-General, International Exchange, International Studies, Legal Education, Medical Education, Preschool Education, Private Education (Precollege), Public Education (Precollege), Religious Education, Social Sciences Education
Health: Cancer, Children's Health/Hospitals, Clinics/Medical Centers, Emergency/Ambulance Services, Geriatric Health, Health Organizations, Hospitals, Hospitals (University Affiliated), Long-Term Care, Mental Health, Multiple Sclerosis
International: Foreign Arts Organizations, Foreign Educational Institutions, Health Care/Hospitals, International Relief Efforts, Missionary/Religious Activities
Religion: Jewish Causes, Religious Organizations, Synagogues/Temples
Social Services: Animal Protection, Camps, Community Centers, Community Service Organizations, Domestic Violence, Family Services, Recreation & Athletics, Senior Services, Social Services-General, United Funds/United Ways, YMCA/YWCA/YMHA/YWHA

Application Procedures

Initial Contact: Initial inquiry should be by letter. Application and procedures will be made available if the foundation would like a full proposal.
Application Requirements: Letters of request should include an overview of the request; a project description, including activities, timeline, staff, intended audience, and desired outcomes; a budget with projected costs, amount requested from the foundation, and additional funding sources; background information including the applicant's history, mission, goals and objectives, as well as financial statements; proof of non-profit status, including proof of tax exempt 501(c)(3) status; and an evaluation statement of how the progress and success of the program will be measured.
Deadlines: February 15 and August 15.
Review Process: The board meets twice a year, in the fall and the spring, at which time funding decisions are made.

Restrictions

Grants are not made to individuals.

Additional Information

Publications: Guidelines

Foundation Officials

Bernice Amado: vice president, secretary, director
Ralph A. Amado: director
Ralph D. Amado: director ED Stanford University BA (1954); Oxford University PhD (1957). PRIM NONPR EMPL professor: University of Pennsylvania. CORP AFFIL consultant: Los Alamos Science Lab. NONPR AFFIL member: American Association Advancement Science; fellow: American Physics Society.
Renee T. Kaplan: director
Stella Amado Lavis: director
Elaine L. Lindheim: president
Joyce G. Miller: executive director
Regina Amado Tarica: vice president, cfo, director
Samuel R. Tarica: vice president, director

Grants Analysis

Disclosure Period: fiscal year ending November 30, 2001
Total Grants: $1,836,767
Number of Grants: 108
Average Grant: $14,175*
Highest Grant: $100,000
Typical Range: $500 to $100,000
***Note:** Average grant figure excludes highest grant.

Recent Grants

Note: Grants derived from fiscal 2002 Form 990.
General
400,845	Jewish Community Foundation, Los Angeles, CA
100,000	USC School of Dentistry, Los Angeles, CA
75,000	Regents of the University of California, Oakland, CA
70,000	University of Pennsylvania, Philadelphia, PA
68,000	Opera Company of Philadelphia, Philadelphia, PA
50,000	Foundation for Jewish Camping, New York, NY
50,000	Martha's Vineyard Hospital, Oak Bluffs, MA
50,000	Martha's Vineyard Hospital, Oak Bluffs, MA
50,000	USC Casden Institute, Los Angeles, CA
45,000	AFS Intercultural Program, New York, NY

THE AMBROSE MONELL FOUNDATION

Giving Contact

George Rowe, Jr., President
1 Rockefeller Plaza, Suite 301
New York, NY 10020
Phone: (212)586-0700
Fax: (212)245-1863
E-mail: info@monellvetlesen.org
Web: http://www.monellvetlesen.org/monell/default.htm

Description

Founded: 1952
EIN: 131982683
Organization Type: General Purpose Foundation
Giving Locations: NY: New York metropolitan area nationally.
Grant Types: Capital, Endowment, General Support, Multiyear/Continuing Support, Research.

Donor Information

Founder: The Ambrose Monell Foundation was established in 1952. Funds for its incorporation were donated by Mrs. Maude Monell Vetlesen. Ambrose Monell, who died in 1921, served as president of International Nickel Company.

Financial Summary

Total Giving: $10,302,500 (2003); $10,472,500 (2002); $11,177,500 (2001)
Assets: $221,389,294 (2003); $197,154,217 (2002); $217,722,530 (2001)

Typical Recipients

Arts & Humanities: Arts Funds, Ballet, Dance, Libraries, Museums/Galleries, Music, Opera, Performing Arts, Public Broadcasting, Theater
Civic & Public Affairs: Botanical Gardens/Parks, Economic Development, Employment/Job Training, Civic & Public Affairs-General, Legal Aid, Public Policy
Education: Arts/Humanities Education, Colleges & Universities, Education Associations, Education Funds, Education-General, Health & Physical Education, Literacy, Medical Education, Minority Education, Private Education (Precollege), Public Education (Precollege), Religious Education, Science/Mathematics Education, Secondary Education (Private), Social Sciences Education
Environment: Resource Conservation
Health: AIDS/HIV, Alzheimer's Disease, Arthritis, Cancer, Children's Health/Hospitals, Clinics/Medical Centers, Emergency/Ambulance Services, Eyes/Blindness, Health-General, Geriatric Health, Health Funds, Hospitals, Hospitals (University Affiliated), Medical Rehabilitation, Medical Research, Mental Health, Public Health, Research/Studies Institutes, Respiratory, Speech & Hearing
International: Health Care/Hospitals, International Peace & Security Issues, International Relief Efforts
Religion: Churches, Jewish Causes
Science: Science Museums, Scientific Centers & Institutes, Scientific Research
Social Services: Animal Protection, Child Welfare, Delinquency & Criminal Rehabilitation, Homes, Scouts, YMCA/YWCA/YMHA/YWHA, Youth Organizations

Application Procedures

Initial Contact: Send a brief letter to the foundation.
Application Requirements: Letters should include an outline of the proposed project, explain the reason funding is needed and be addressed to the president of the foundation.
Deadlines: December.
Review Process: The board meets on December 1.

Foundation Officials

Gary Beauchamp: director
Eugene P. Grisanti: director
Joseph T. C. Hart: treasurer
Ambrose K. Monell: director
Maurizio J. Morello: secretary, assistant treasurer, director
Laura Naus: secretary

Grants Analysis

Disclosure Period: calendar year ending 2003
Total Grants: $10,302,500
Number of Grants: 147
Average Grant: $62,948*
Highest Grant: $675,000
Lowest Grant: $2,500
Typical Range: $25,000 to $150,000
*Note: Average grant figure excludes two highest grants ($1,175,000).

Recent Grants

Note: Grants derived from 2003 Form 990.
Library-Related
100,000	New York Public Library, New York, NY
100,000	Pierpont Morgan Library, New York, NY

General
675,000	Monell Chemical Senses Center, Philadelphia, PA
500,000	Brookdale University Hospital and Medical Center, Brooklyn, NY -- for renovation and expansion of emergency department
500,000	Harvard School of Public Health, Boston, MA
350,000	Institute for Advanced Study, Princeton, NJ -- towards schools of Natural Science and Mathematics
350,000	Massachusetts General Hospital, Boston, MA -- towards detection and treatment of cancer
300,000	American Museum of Natural History, New York, NY
300,000	Educational Broadcasting Company
250,000	Metropolitan Opera Association, New York, NY
250,000	New York Botanical Garden, Bronx, NY -- towards Plant Genomics Program
200,000	Hospital for Special Surgery, New York, NY

AMCAST INDUSTRIAL CORP.

Company Headquarters

PO Box 98
Dayton, OH 45401
Web: http://www.amcast.com

Company Description

Founded: 1869
Ticker: AIZ
Exchange: NYSE
Revenue: US$423.9 million (2003)
Employees: 4040 (2003)
SIC(s): 3354 Aluminum Extruded Products, 3363 Aluminum Die-Castings, 3366 Copper Foundries, 3400 Fabricated Metal Products.

Operating Locations

Amcast Industrial Corp. (AL--Anniston; AR--Fayetteville; IN--Elkhart, Franklin, Gas City, Geneva, Richmond; MI--Southfield; OH--Wapakoneta; PA--Washington; WI--Cedarburg)
Note: Includes division and plant locations.

Amcast Industrial Foundation

Giving Contact

Samuel Rees, Secretary
Amcast Industrial Foundation
7887 Washington Village Dr.
Dayton, OH 45459
Phone: (937)291-7023

Description

EIN: 316016458
Organization Type: Corporate Foundation
Giving Locations: OH: Dayton
Grant Types: Capital, Challenge, Emergency, Employee Matching Gifts, Multiyear/Continuing Support, Project, Research, Scholarship.

Financial Summary

Total Giving: $24,195 (fiscal year ending August 31, 2004); $85,610 (fiscal 2001)
Giving Analysis: Giving for fiscal 2004 includes: foundation grants to United Way ($5,000); foundation scholarships ($13,720); fiscal 2001: foundation grants to United Way ($16,500); foundation scholarships ($19,500)
Assets: $157,620 (fiscal 2004); $346,045 (fiscal 2001)
Gifts Received: $150,000 (fiscal 1998); $150,000 (fiscal 1996); $100,000 (fiscal 1995). Note: In 1998, contributions were received from Amcast Industrial Corp.

Typical Recipients

Arts & Humanities: Arts Associations & Councils, Arts Centers, Arts Funds, Arts Institutes, Ballet, Arts & Humanities-General, Historic Preservation, History & Archaeology, Libraries, Performing Arts, Theater
Civic & Public Affairs: African American Affairs, Botanical Gardens/Parks, Chambers of Commerce, Community Foundations, Economic Development, Civic & Public Affairs-General, Housing, Inner-City Development, Parades/Festivals, Professional & Trade Associations, Public Policy, Safety, Urban & Community Affairs, Women's Affairs
Education: Business Education, Colleges & Universities, Community & Junior Colleges, Education Funds, Education Reform, Engineering/Technological Education, Education-General, International Studies, Minority Education, Public Education (Precollege), Science/Mathematics Education, Secondary Education (Public), Student Aid
Environment: Resource Conservation
Health: AIDS/HIV, Alzheimer's Disease, Cancer, Children's Health/Hospitals, Health-General, Health Organizations, Heart, Hospices, Hospitals, Medical Research, Prenatal Health Issues
Social Services: Community Centers, Community Service Organizations, Crime Prevention, Emergency Relief, Family Planning, Family Services, Recreation & Athletics, Scouts, Senior Services, Shelters/Homelessness, Social Services-General, United Funds/United Ways, YMCA/YWCA/YMHA/YWHA, Youth Organizations

Application Procedures

Initial Contact: Send a brief letter of inquiry and a full proposal.
Application Requirements: Include a description of organization, amount requested, purpose of funds sought, and proof of tax-exempt status.
Deadlines: None. Requests are processed quarterly in November, February, May, and August.

Restrictions

Does not support individuals, religious organizations for sectarian purposes, political or lobbying groups, organizations outside operating areas, hospitals, organizations receiving support from the United Way, or schools, except in certain situations.

Additional Information

The company sponsors Amcast Engineering Scholarships through the Ohio Foundation of Independent Colleges.
Publications: Operating Guidelines; Matching Gift Program Guidelines

Corporate Officials

Denis G. Daly: secretary financial, chief financial officer PRIM CORP EMPL secretary: Amcast Industrial Corp. ADD CORP EMPL secretary: Elkhart Products Corp.; secretary: Wheeltek Inc.
John Henry Shuey: chairman, president, chief executive officer, director B Monroe, MI 1946. ED University of Michigan BS (1968); University of Michigan MBA (1970). PRIM CORP EMPL chairman, president, chief executive officer, director: Amcast Industrial Corp. ADD CORP EMPL president: Amcast & Elkhart Industries Products; president: Speedline North America Inc.; president: Wheeltek Inc. CORP AFFIL director: Cooper Tire & Rubber Co. NONPR AFFIL trustee: Ohio Foundation of Industries College; director: Wright State University Indiana; member: Financial Executives Institute; trustee: Dayton Ballet.
Douglas D. Watts: vice president financial, chief financial officer PRIM CORP EMPL vice president financial, chief financial officer: Amcast Industrial Corp.

Foundation Officials

Michael R. Higgins: treasurer
Byron O. Pond, Jr.: president

Grants Analysis

Disclosure Period: fiscal year ending August 31, 2004
Total Grants: $5,475*
Number of Grants: 7
Average Grant: $782
Highest Grant: $2,000
Lowest Grant: $100
Typical Range: $500 to $2,000
*Note: Giving excludes scholarships; United Way.

Recent Grants

Note: Grants derived from 2004 Form 990.
General

13,720	National Merit Scholarship, Evanston, IL
5,000	United Way of Greater Dayton, Dayton, OH
2,000	Arcadia University, Glenside, PA
1,375	Thunderbird Graduate School, Glendale, AZ
800	University of Iowa, Ames, IA
500	DePaul University, Chicago, IL
500	FEF
100	University of Illinois, Chicago, IL
100	University of Michigan, Ann Arbor, MI
100	Xavier University, Cincinnati, OH

AMCORE FINANCIAL INC.

Company Headquarters

501 7th Street
Rockford, IL 61104
Web: http://www.amcore.com

Company Description

Founded: 1982
Ticker: AMFI
Exchange: NASDAQ
Assets: US$4.522 billion (2002)
Employees: 1491 (2003)

AMCORE Foundation

Giving Contact

James S. Waddell, President
AMCORE Bank Foundation
501 7th St., PO Box 1537
Rockford, IL 61110
Phone: (815)968-2241
Fax: (815)961-7530
Web: http://www.amcore.com

Description

EIN: 366042947
Organization Type: Corporate Foundation
Giving Locations: IL: Rockford including surrounding communities
Grant Types: Capital, General Support.

Financial Summary

Total Giving: $382,250 (2003); $251,075 (2002); $289,775 (2001)
Giving Analysis: Giving for 2002 includes: foundation grants to United Way ($85,000); 2001: foundation grants to United Way ($80,000); foundation ($209,775)
Assets: $636,016 (2003); $491,898 (2002); $151,284 (2001)
Gifts Received: $420,020 (2003); $658,992 (2002); $319,700 (2001). Note: Contributions were received from Amcore Investment Group NA.

Typical Recipients

Arts & Humanities: Arts Associations & Councils, Arts Festivals, Dance, Arts & Humanities-General, Historic Preservation, Libraries, Literary Arts, Muse-ums/Galleries, Music, Performing Arts, Public Broadcasting, Theater
Civic & Public Affairs: African American Affairs, Botanical Gardens/Parks, Business/Free Enterprise, Chambers of Commerce, Clubs, Community Foundations, Economic Development, Employment/Job Training, Civic & Public Affairs-General, Hispanic Affairs, Housing, Inner-City Development, Minority Business, Municipalities/Towns, Parades/Festivals, Philanthropic Organizations, Public Policy, Rural Affairs, Safety, Urban & Community Affairs, Women's Affairs
Education: Afterschool/Enrichment Programs, Business Education, Colleges & Universities, Community & Junior Colleges, Economic Education, Education Funds, Education-General, Gifted & Talented Programs, Health & Physical Education, Literacy, Medical Education, Minority Education, Preschool Education, Private Education (Precollege), Public Education (Precollege), Science/Mathematics Education, Secondary Education (Private), Secondary Education (Public), Special Education, Student Aid
Environment: Environment-General
Health: AIDS/HIV, Alzheimer's Disease, Cancer, Clinics/Medical Centers, Emergency/Ambulance Services, Health-General, Health Funds, Health Organizations, Hospices, Hospitals, Long-Term Care, Medical Rehabilitation, Mental Health, Nursing Services, Nutrition, Public Health, Single-Disease Health Associations
Religion: Jewish Causes, Ministries, Religious Welfare
Science: Science Museums
Social Services: Child Abuse, Child Welfare, Community Centers, Community Service Organizations, Counseling, Crime Prevention, Day Care, Delinquency & Criminal Rehabilitation, Domestic Violence, Emergency Relief, Family Services, Food/Clothing Distribution, Homes, People with Disabilities, Recreation & Athletics, Scouts, Senior Services, Sexual Abuse, Shelters/Homelessness, Social Services-General, Substance Abuse, United Funds/United Ways, Veterans, Volunteer Services, YMCA/YWCA/YMHA/YWHA, Youth Organizations

Application Procedures

Initial Contact: Submit a written request for funding.
Application Requirements: Include name and a description of organization, number of members, amount requested, purpose of funds sought, federal tax status, a list of officers and board members, most recent annual report, operating budget for last two years, a statement as to how the organization benefits the community, and a list of general sources of funds.
Deadlines: None.
Evaluative Criteria: Perceived effectiveness of the organization within the community and the benefit that the community will derive from AMCORE Bank Foundation support.

Restrictions

Does not support individuals, religious organizations for sectarian purposes, political or lobbying groups, organizations outside operating areas, or loans of any kind.

Corporate Officials

Charles E. Gagnier: chairman, chief executive officer, director PRIM CORP EMPL chairman: AMCORE Bank Rockford.
John Hecht: chief financial officer PRIM CORP EMPL chief financial officer: AMCORE Bank Rockford.
James Warsaw: president, chief executive officer, director PRIM CORP EMPL president, chief executive officer, director: AMCORE Bank Rockford.

Foundation Officials

Robert A. Doyle: director
Kenneth Edge: director
Bruce Lammers: director
Joseph McGougan: director
David W. Miles: director
Richard D. Nordolf: director
Michael Tulley: director
James S. Waddell: president, director
Diana M. Ward: secretary, director

Grants Analysis

Disclosure Period: calendar year ending 2003
Total Grants: $292,250*
Number of Grants: 41
Average Grant: $6,056*
Highest Grant: $50,000
Lowest Grant: $500
Typical Range: $1,000 to $10,000
*Note: Giving excludes United Way. Average grant figure excludes highest grant.

Recent Grants

Note: Grants derived from 2003 Form 990.

General

90,000	United Way of Rock River Valley, Rockford, IL
50,000	Junior Golf Association of Greater Rockford (JGAGR), Rockford, IL
36,000	YMCA of Rock River Valley, Rockford, IL
30,000	Swedish American Medical Foundation, Rockford, IL
15,000	Burpee Museum of Natural History, Rockford, IL
15,000	Rosecrance Foundation, Rockford, IL
12,500	Illinois Growth Enterprises, Rockford, IL
11,000	Rockford Memorial Development Foundation, Rockford, IL
10,000	Crusader Clinic, Rockford, IL
10,000	Lifescape Community Service, Rockford, IL

AMEREN CORP.

Company Headquarters

St. Louis, MO
Web: http://www.ameren.com

Company Description

Ticker: AEE
Exchange: OTC
Former Name: Union Electric Co.
Revenue: US$5.16 billion (2004)
Profit: US$530 million (2004)
Employees: 7650 (2003)
Fortune Rank: 380, per FORTUNE Magazine's list of 500 Largest U.S. Corporations (2004).
SIC(s): 4931 Electric & Other Services Combined.

Operating Locations

Ameren Corp. (MO--Cape Girardeau, Jefferson City); Ameren Corp. (MO--St. Louis)

Nonmonetary Support

Value: $96,312 (1998)
Type: Cause-related Marketing & Promotion; Donated Equipment; Donated Products
Volunteer Programs: Ameren Helping Hands where employees and their families volunteer. VIP/TEAMS Program in which small grants ($50-$500) are given to nonprofits for which Ameren employees volunteer. The company also supports the "Ameren Helping Hands" program which involves group volunteer projects at local nonprofit organizations.

Ameren Corp. Charitable Trust

Giving Contact

Otis Cowan, Manager, Community Relations
Ameren Corporate
PO Box 66149, Mail Code 100
St. Louis, MO 63166-6149
Phone: (314)554-4740
Fax: (314)554-2888
E-mail: ocowan@ameren.com
Web: http://www.ameren.com/community/adc_com_homepage.asp
Note: for nonprofits in the St. Louis, MO area

Alternate Contact

Public Affairs
AmerenCIPS
607 East Adams Street, C1301
Springfield, IL 62739
Note: for nonprofits in the Springfield, IL area

Description

EIN: 436022693
Organization Type: Corporate Foundation
Giving Locations: IL: Peoria, Springfield; MO: St. Louis the company's local district offices.
Grant Types: Award, Capital, Conference/Seminar, Emergency, Employee Matching Gifts, General Support, Multiyear/Continuing Support, Project, Scholarship.
Note: Employee matching gift ratio: 1 to 1 between $10 and $500 annually per employee, for accredited colleges and universities only.

Financial Summary

Total Giving: $2,567,964 (2003); $2,442,972 (2002); $2,548,344 (2001)
Assets: $8,663,206 (2003); $8,150,143 (2002); $10,281,558 (2001)
Gifts Received: $3,000,000 (2003); $5,000,000 (2000). Note: Contributions are received from Ameren Corp.

Typical Recipients

Arts & Humanities: Arts Associations & Councils, Arts Centers, Arts Festivals, Arts Funds, Arts Institutes, Community Arts, Dance, Arts & Humanities-General, Historic Preservation, History & Archaeology, Libraries, Museums/Galleries, Music, Opera, Performing Arts, Public Broadcasting, Theater, Visual Arts
Civic & Public Affairs: African American Affairs, Botanical Gardens/Parks, Chambers of Commerce, Community Foundations, Economic Development, Ethnic Organizations, Civic & Public Affairs-General, Housing, Inner-City Development, Public Policy, Safety, Urban & Community Affairs, Zoos/Aquariums
Education: Afterschool/Enrichment Programs, Arts/Humanities Education, Business Education, Colleges & Universities, Community & Junior Colleges, Economic Education, Education Funds, Education Reform, Elementary Education (Private), Engineering/Technological Education, Education-General, Minority Education, Private Education (Precollege), Public Education (Precollege), Science/Mathematics Education, Secondary Education (Private), Social Sciences Education, Student Aid, Vocational & Technical Education
Environment: Forestry, Environment-General
Health: AIDS/HIV, Children's Health/Hospitals, Clinics/Medical Centers, Emergency/Ambulance Services, Health Funds, Health Organizations, Hospitals, Multiple Sclerosis
Religion: Dioceses, Jewish Causes, Ministries, Religious Organizations, Religious Welfare
Science: Observatories & Planetariums, Scientific Centers & Institutes
Social Services: Child Welfare, Community Centers, Community Service Organizations, Counseling, Delinquency & Criminal Rehabilitation, Domestic Violence, Emergency Relief, Family Services, Food/Clothing Distribution, Homes, People with Disabilities, Recreation & Athletics, Scouts, Senior Services, Shelters/Homelessness, United Funds/United Ways, Volunteer Services, YMCA/YWCA/YMHA/YWHA, Youth Organizations

Application Procedures

Initial Contact: Send a letter or proposal on organization's letterhead.
Application Requirements: Include an explanation of project for which funds are requested, along with projected outcomes, statement of organization's mission and how project fits organization's purpose; current status of fundraising for project and end goal; organization's current board-approved operating budget, and audited financial statements; specific amount requested; proof of tax-exempt status; and roster of organization's governing board and staff.
Deadlines: None.
Review Process: Proposals reviewed by contributions committee. Requests for contributions exceeding $10,000 are reviewed and approved by the contributions committee of the Ameren board of directors; contributions of less than $10,000 are awarded directly by the AmerenUE or AmerenCIPS.
Evaluative Criteria: Determining factors include the location of organization in area in which company operates; conformity to company's priorities; overall benefit to community; qualifications, including management experience, of individuals who administer program; total level of support sought by organization throughout community and prospects for obtaining that support; Ameren's current operating situation and priorities relative to overall amount available for contributions.
Decision Notification: Two to three months after bi-annual meeting.
Notes: Outside the Saint Louis, MO; Springfield, IL; and Peoria, IL areas, request should be sent to AmerenUE, AmerenCIPS, or AmerenCILCO local district offices.

Restrictions

Does not support individuals; political, fraternal, veterans', religious organizations; or social or similar groups.
The company never contributes electric or natural gas service.

Additional Information

Ameren was formed at the end of 1997 as the result of the merger of Union Electric Co. and Central Illinois Public Service Co.
Grantees must submit reports indicating project results.
Items of salvage from company stock are sometimes donated to nonprofit organizations, including utility poles, office furnishings, and other surplus items. Organizations receiving such material must arrange pickup. Same general policies and procedures prevail as with monetary contributions. monetary contributions. monetary contributions. monetary contributions.
Publications: Community Report; Giving Guidelines; Annual Report
Trust(s): Bank of America, NA

Corporate Officials

Susan M. Bell: senior supervisor-corporate communicationslic Policy PRIM CORP EMPL senior supervisor-corporate communications: Ameren Corp.
J. Kay Smith: vice president, Corp. Communications/Public Policy

Foundation Officials

Susan M. Bell: senior supervisor-corporate communications (see above)

Grants Analysis

Disclosure Period: calendar year ending 2003
Total Grants: $1,365,140*
Number of Grants: 39
Average Grant: $30,662*
Highest Grant: $200,000
Lowest Grant: $7,000
Typical Range: $5,000 to $25,000
*Note: Giving excludes matching gifts, scholarships, and United Way. Average grant figure excludes highest grant.

Recent Grants

Note: Grants derived from 2003 Form 990.
General
926,500	United Way, St. Louis, MO
200,000	Saint Louis Zoo, St. Louis, MO -- toward penguin and puffin coast lighting
100,000	Regional Housing & Community Development Alliance, St. Louis, MO
100,000	University of Illinois, Springfield, IL -- toward ameren professor of business and Government
72,000	Arts & Education Council of St. Louis, St. Louis, MO
70,000	United Way of Illinois Inc., Springfield, IL -- toward Ameren Cips Dollar More program
50,000	Cardinal Ritter College Preparatory High School, St. Louis, MO
50,000	Forest Park Forever, St. Louis, MO
50,000	Illinois State Museum society, Springfield, IL -- funding for shark attack exhibit
50,000	Missouri Historical Society, St. Louis, MO -- funding for Jefferson memorial building lighting

AMERICAN CENTURY COMPANIES INC.

Company Headquarters

4500 Main St., Ste. 1500
Kansas City, MO 64111
Web: http://www.americancentury.com

Company Description

Founded: 1958
Former Name: Twentieth Century Mutual Funds.
Operating Revenue: US$877 million (2002)
Employees: 1800 (2003)
SIC(s): 6211 Security Brokers & Dealers, 6282 Investment Advice.

American Century Companies Foundation

Giving Contact

Mary Jo Browne
4500 Main Street
Kansas City, MO 64111
Phone: (816)531-5575
E-mail: communityinvestments@americancentury.com
Web: http://www.americancentury.com/welcome/community.jsp

Description

Founded: 2000
EIN: 431881225
Organization Type: Corporate Foundation
Giving Locations: CA: Mountain View; MO: Kansas City; NY: New York
Grant Types: Capital, General Support, Operating Expenses, Research.

Financial Summary

Total Giving: $1,281,600 (2003); $1,034,300 (2002); $376,475 (2001)

Giving Analysis: Giving for 2001 includes: foundation grants to United Way ($13,600)

Assets: $4,311,618 (2003); $1,227,538 (2002); $2,592,479 (2001)

Gifts Received: $3,845,110 (2003); $918 (2002); $1,000,000 (2001). Note: Contributions were received from American Century Companies.

Typical Recipients

Arts & Humanities: Arts Associations & Councils, Arts Centers, Arts Festivals, Arts Funds, Arts Institutes, Ballet, Dance, Ethnic & Folk Arts, Historic Preservation, Libraries, Museums/Galleries, Music, Public Broadcasting, Theater, Visual Arts

Civic & Public Affairs: Community Foundations, Civic & Public Affairs-General, Housing, Inner-City Development, Safety, Urban & Community Affairs, Women's Affairs, Zoos/Aquariums

Education: Afterschool/Enrichment Programs, Arts/Humanities Education, Business Education, Economic Education, Education Funds, Education-General, Leadership Training, Science/Mathematics Education, Special Education, Student Aid

Health: AIDS/HIV, Alzheimer's Disease, Children's Health/Hospitals, Clinics/Medical Centers, Health Organizations, Medical Rehabilitation, Medical Research, Mental Health, Nursing Services, Preventive Medicine/Wellness Organizations

Religion: Jewish Causes, Religious Welfare

Social Services: Animal Protection, At-Risk Youth, Child Welfare, Community Centers, Community Service Organizations, Counseling, Domestic Violence, Family Services, Food/Clothing Distribution, People with Disabilities, Recreation & Athletics, Shelters/Homelessness, United Funds/United Ways, Volunteer Services, YMCA/YWCA/YMHA/YWHA, Youth Organizations

Application Procedures

Initial Contact: Submit written proposal that includes a mission statement, brief financial report, copy of the 501(c)3 determination letter, list of board members and officers, and description and budget of the program for which you are seeking support.

Application Requirements: No formal application.

Deadlines: September 1 for projects considered for the following year.

Additional Information

Foundation concentrates on four broad areas for funding.

Arts for professional visual and performing arts organizations and educational outreach programs.

Education for innovative financial education programs and programs to support unique education opportunities.

Civic issues for neighborhood support and business and economic development.

Health and human services for programs that support the elderly, youth, disadvantaged or handicapped and medical research.

Foundation Officials

Robert T. Jackson: treasurer, director
William M. Lyons: president, director
Wendy B. Welte: secretary
Jon W. Zindel: vice president, director

Grants Analysis

Disclosure Period: calendar year ending 2003
Total Grants: $1,141,500*
Number of Grants: 169
Average Grant: $6,348*
Highest Grant: $75,000
Lowest Grant: $500
Typical Range: $1,000 to $10,000
*Note: Giving excludes United Way. Average grant figure excludes highest grant.

Recent Grants

Note: Grants derived from 2003 Form 990.
General

130,000	Heart of America United Way, Kansas City, MO
75,000	Friends of the Zoo, Kansas City, MO
55,000	Truman Medical Center Behavioral Health Network, Kansas City, MO
50,000	Liberty Memorial Association, Kansas City, MO
50,000	Ronald McDonald House Charities, Kansas City, MO -- towards plaza prazz benefit
50,000	Ronald McDonald House Charities, Kansas City, MO
50,000	Salvation Army, Kansas City, MO
35,000	Coterie Theatre, Kansas City, MO -- towards dramatic AIDS education project
35,000	Kansas City Young Audiences, Kansas City, MO
25,000	Charter School Partnership Fund, Kansas City, MO

AMERICAN FIDELITY ASSURANCE CO.

Company Headquarters

2000 N. Classen Blvd., Ste 226A
Oklahoma City, OK 73106
Web: http://www.afadvantage.com

Company Description

Employees: 1,100

American Fidelity Corp. Founders Fund

Giving Contact

Joella Ramsey, Secretary
2000 Classen Center
PO Box 25523
Oklahoma City, OK 73125
Phone: (405)523-5008
Fax: (405)523-5421

Description

EIN: 731236059
Organization Type: Corporate Foundation
Giving Locations: OK
Grant Types: General Support.

Financial Summary

Total Giving: $244,126 (2003); $233,977 (2001). Note: Contributes through corporate direct giving program and foundation.

Assets: $4,165,659 (2003); $4,171,933 (2001)

Gifts Received: $98,279 (2003); $5,722 (1994); $200,000 (1993). Note: In 2003, contributions were received from American Fidelity Assurance Co. In fiscal 1994, contributions were received from Lenice B. Cameron 1980 Trust for William M. Cameron; Lenice B. Cameron 1980 Trust for Lynda L. Cameron; C. W. Cameron 1980 Trust for William M. Cameron; C. W. Cameron 1980 Trust for Lynda L. Cameron ($907 each); and Jo Carol Cameron 1980 Trust for William M. Cameron and Jo Carol Cameron 1980 Trust for Lynda L. Cameron ($1,047 each).

Typical Recipients

Arts & Humanities: Arts Associations & Councils, Arts Festivals, Arts Funds, Arts Institutes, Arts Outreach, Ballet, Dance, Historic Preservation, History & Archaeology, Libraries, Museums/Galleries, Music, Performing Arts, Public Broadcasting, Theater

Civic & Public Affairs: Botanical Gardens/Parks, Clubs, Community Foundations, Economic Development, Employment/Job Training, Civic & Public Affairs-General, Housing, Municipalities/Towns, Native American Affairs, Nonprofit Management, Philanthropic Organizations, Public Policy, Urban & Community Affairs, Women's Affairs, Zoos/Aquariums

Education: Afterschool/Enrichment Programs, Business Education, Colleges & Universities, Community & Junior Colleges, Economic Education, Education Funds, Faculty Development, Education-General, Leadership Training, Literacy, Private Education (Precollege), Public Education (Precollege), Religious Education, Science/Mathematics Education, Social Sciences Education

Environment: Environment-General, Protection, Resource Conservation

Health: AIDS/HIV, Arthritis, Cancer, Children's Health/Hospitals, Clinics/Medical Centers, Emergency/Ambulance Services, Health Funds, Health Organizations, Heart, Home-Care Services, Hospitals, Hospitals (University Affiliated), Medical Rehabilitation, Prenatal Health Issues, Single-Disease Health Associations

International: International Development, International Relief Efforts

Religion: Churches, Ministries, Religious Organizations, Religious Welfare

Science: Science Museums, Scientific Centers & Institutes

Social Services: Big Brothers/Big Sisters, Child Abuse, Child Welfare, Community Service Organizations, Emergency Relief, Family Services, Food/Clothing Distribution, People with Disabilities, Recreation & Athletics, Scouts, Shelters/Homelessness, Social Services-General, Substance Abuse, United Funds/United Ways, Veterans, YMCA/YWCA/YMHA/YWHA, Youth Organizations

Application Procedures

Initial Contact: Submit a letter requesting application form.

Restrictions

The foundation does not support organizations that are not classified as 501(c)(3) tax-exempt by the IRS. No donations are made for propaganda or political purposes, or to any organization that discriminates on the basis of race, color, national origin, sex, or physical disability.

Corporate Officials

Brett Browman: assistant vice president PRIM CORP EMPL assistant vice president: American Fidelity Corp.

William E. Durrett: senior chairman B 1930. ED University of Oklahoma. PRIM CORP EMPL senior chairman: American Fidelity Corp. CORP AFFIL director: OGE Energy Corp.

John Rex: president B 1933. PRIM CORP EMPL president: American Fidelity Corp. CORP AFFIL president, chief operating officer: American Fidelity Assurance Co.; president: American Fidelity Securities.

Foundation Officials

William M. Cambrom: president
JoElla Ramsey: secretary
John Rex: treasurer (see above)

Grants Analysis

Disclosure Period: calendar year ending 2003
Total Grants: $172,842*
Number of Grants: 133
Average Grant: $1,300
Highest Grant: $18,000
Lowest Grant: $25
Typical Range: $500 to $5,000
*Note: Giving excludes United Way.

Recent Grants

Note: Grants derived from 2003 Form 990.

Library-Related

2,220	Library Endowment Trust Metropolitan Library System, Oklahoma City, OK

General

71,284	United Way, Oklahoma City, OK
18,000	Westminster Presbyterian Church, Oklahoma City, OK
14,460	Allied Arts Foundation, Oklahoma City, OK
10,025	Oklahoma City Public School Foundation, Oklahoma City, OK
7,600	Oklahoma City Philharmonic Orchestra, Oklahoma City, OK
7,100	Ballet Oklahoma Nutcracker, Oklahoma City, OK
6,930	Ballet Oklahoma, Oklahoma City, OK
6,690	OU Foundation Inc., Norman, OK
6,675	OKC Museum of Art, Oklahoma City, OK
5,600	Last Frontier Council Boy Scouts of America, Oklahoma City, OK

AMERICAN GENERAL FINANCE

Company Headquarters

Evansville, IN
Web: http://www.agfinance.com

Company Description

Former Name: Credithrift Financial.
Employees: 6,500
SIC(s): 6141 Personal Credit Institutions, 6411 Insurance Agents, Brokers & Service.

Operating Locations

American General Finance (AZ--Tucson; CA--Van Nuys; KY--Dawson Springs, Providence; MT--Bozeman; NJ--Brick, Millville, Pleasantville; PA--Thorndale; TN--Dickson, Tullahoma; WY--Casper)
Note: Operates offices in 42 states.

Nonmonetary Support

Volunteer Programs: The company's Community Spirit Awards program recognizes employees who demonstrate outstanding volunteer service. Award recipients designate $2,500 grants to the organizations they serve.

American General Finance Foundation

Giving Contact

Michelle Dixon, Community Relations Coordinator
American General Finance Corp.
601 Northwest Second Street
PO Box 59
Evansville, IN 47701-0059
Phone: (812)468-5620
Fax: (812)468-5682
Web: http://www.agc.com/agfg2000/agfgweb.nsf

Alternate Contact

8600 University Boulevard
Evansville, IN 47712
Note: Inquiries regarding scholarships should be directed to the University of Southern Indiana, Vice President for Student Affairs.

Description

Founded: 1958
EIN: 356042566
Organization Type: Corporate Foundation
Giving Locations: IN: Evansville including tri-state area
Grant Types: General Support, Matching, Scholarship.

Note: Employee matching gift ratio: 2:1 for employee gifts to institutions of higher education and public broadcasting under the auspices of a university or college; 1:1 for employee gifts to United Way.

Donor Information

Founder: American General Finance, Inc., and subsidiaries

Financial Summary

Total Giving: $457,525 (2002); $446,124 (2001).
Note: Contributes through foundation only.
Assets: $91,449 (2002); $73,361 (2001)
Gifts Received: $475,000 (2002); $425,000 (2001); $400,000 (2000). Note: In 2002, 2001, 2000, 1999 and 1998, contributions were received from American General Finance, Inc. and its subsidiaries.

Typical Recipients

Arts & Humanities: Arts Associations & Councils, Dance, Historic Preservation, Libraries, Museums/Galleries, Music, Public Broadcasting, Theater
Civic & Public Affairs: Botanical Gardens/Parks, Business/Free Enterprise, Clubs, Community Foundations, Economic Development, Civic & Public Affairs-General, Housing, Inner-City Development, Municipalities/Towns, Parades/Festivals, Safety, Urban & Community Affairs
Education: Agricultural Education, Business Education, Colleges & Universities, Education Funds, Education-General, Literacy, Private Education (Precollege), Public Education (Precollege), Secondary Education (Public), Student Aid
Health: AIDS/HIV, Alzheimer's Disease, Arthritis, Cancer, Children's Health/Hospitals, Diabetes, Emergency/Ambulance Services, Heart, Hospices, Hospitals, Medical Rehabilitation, Medical Research, Mental Health, Prenatal Health Issues, Single-Disease Health Associations
Religion: Religious Organizations, Religious Welfare
Science: Science-General, Science Museums
Social Services: Big Brothers/Big Sisters, Community Service Organizations, Day Care, Domestic Violence, Emergency Relief, Family Services, Food/Clothing Distribution, People with Disabilities, Recreation & Athletics, Scouts, Senior Services, Shelters/Homelessness, Special Olympics, Substance Abuse, United Funds/United Ways, Volunteer Services, YMCA/YWCA/YMHA/YWHA, Youth Organizations

Application Procedures

Initial Contact: Proposals for grants should be made in writing; request application form for scholarships.
Application Requirements: Grant proposals should include the name of the person making the request; a description of organization, including objectives, activities, accomplishments, and geographic scope; purpose of funds sought; amount requested; current budget; list of the names and business or professional affiliations of the organization's officers and board of directors or trustees; proof of tax-exempt status; and contact name, address, and telephone number for the organization. support continue to be consistent with its exempt status as established in the determination letter; current audited financial statement; other community organizations providing similar service/project/activity; amount of funds requested; and the name(s) and qualifications of person(s) administering funds support continue to be consistent with its exempt status as established in the determination letter; current audited financial statement; other community organizations providing similar service/project/activity; amount of funds requested; and the name(s) and qualifications of person(s) administering funds
Deadlines: March 1 for scholarships; None for grant proposals.
Review Process: Committee of senior management personnel reviews proposals each quarter, and notifies potential grantees of their decision.

Restrictions

Grants are not made to organizations without 501(c)(3) status; United Way agencies; veterans, labor, religious, political, fraternal, or external athletic groups, except when such groups provided needed benefits or services to the community at large; national organizations; private foundations; individuals; hospitals, unless it is a teaching institution; and international organizations.

Corporate Officials

Frederick Wallace Geissinger: president, vice chairman, chief executive officer B Huntington, PA 1945. ED Dartmouth College AB (1967); University of Chicago MBA (1969). PRIM CORP EMPL president, chief executive officer: American General Finance Inc. ADD CORP EMPL president, chief executive officer: American General Consumer Lending. NONPR AFFIL member: Real Estate Board New York; member: Urban Land Institute. CLUB AFFIL member: Pelham Country Club.

Foundation Officials

Frederick Wallace Geissinger: president (see above)

Grants Analysis

Disclosure Period: calendar year ending 2002
Total Grants: $172,225*
Number of Grants: 20 (approx)
Average Grant: $8,611
Highest Grant: $26,100
Lowest Grant: $1,000
Typical Range: $1,000 to $15,500
*Note: Giving excludes matching gifts, scholarship, and United Way.

Recent Grants

Note: Grants derived from 2003 Form 990.

General

18,000	Evansville Museum of Arts & Science, Evansville, IN
16,000	Evansville Philharmonic Orchestra, Evansville, IN
15,000	Signature Learning Center, Evansville, IN
15,000	YMCA of South Indiana, Evansville, IN
10,000	Carver Community Organization, Evansville, IN
10,000	IVY Tech, Evansville, IN
10,000	University of Evansville, Evansville, IN
5,000	Downtown Evansville Inc., Evansville, IN
5,000	University of Southern Indiana, Evansville, IN
3,000	Evansville Dance Theatre & School, Evansville, IN

AMERICAN HONDA MOTOR COMPANY INC.

Company Headquarters

1919 Torrance Boulevard
Torrance, CA 90501-2746
Phone: (310)783-2000
Fax: (310)783-2110
Web: http://www.honda.com

Company Description

Employees: 13,774
SIC(s): 3711 Motor Vehicles & Car Bodies, 3714 Motor Vehicle Parts & Accessories, 3751 Motorcycles, Bicycles & Parts, 5012 Automobiles & Other Motor Vehicles.
Parent Company: Honda Motor Company Ltd., 1-1, 2-chome, Minami-Aoyama, Minato-ku, Tokyo, Japan

Operating Locations

American Honda Finance Corp. (CA--San Ramon, Torrance; GA--Roswell; MA--Longmeadow); American Honda Mid-Atlantic (VA--Richmond); American Honda Motor Co. (CA--Stockton, Torrance; GA--Alpharetta; JA--Davenport; MI--Ann Arbor; OH--Troy; OR--Portland); American Honda Motor Co., Inc. (CA--Richmond); Calhac, Inc. (CA--Anaheim); Celina Aluminum Precision Tech (OH--Celina); Honda of America Manufacturing (OH--Marysville); Honda of America Manufacturing Inc. (OH--East Liberty); Honda Lock (OH--Marysville); Honda Lock American (AL--Selma); Honda North America (CA--Torrance); Honda North America Inc. (CA--Torrance; DC--Washington; MI--Detroit); Honda Power Equipment Manufacturing (NC--Swepsonville); Honda Power Products (ID--Idaho Falls); Honda R&D North America (CA--Torrance); Honda Trading America Corp. (CA--Torrance); Honda Transmissions of America (OH--Russells Point); Indiana Precision Technology (IN--Greenfield); KTH Parts Industries Inc. (OH--St. Paris)

Nonmonetary Support

Volunteer Programs: The company has a commitment to participate actively in community service and encourages employees to play an active role in the community.

American Honda Foundation

Giving Contact

Kathryn Carey, Foundation Manager
American Honda Foundation
1919 Torrance Boulevard
Torrance, CA 90501
Phone: (310)781-4090
Fax: (310)781-4270
Web: http://hondacorporate.com/community/index.html?subsection=foundation

Alternate Contact

Corporate Community Relations Division
American Honda Motor Co.
1919 Torrance Boulevard
Torrance, CA 90501
Phone: (310)783-2000

Description

EIN: 953924667
Organization Type: Corporate Foundation
Giving Locations: nationally.
Grant Types: Challenge, Fellowship, General Support, Matching, Multiyear/Continuing Support, Operating Expenses, Project, Scholarship, Seed Money.

Financial Summary

Total Giving: $958,698 (fiscal year ending March 31, 2003); $1,587,744 (fiscal 2002); $1,486,436 (fiscal 2001). Note: Contributes through corporate direct giving program and foundation.
Giving Analysis: Giving for fiscal 2001 includes: foundation scholarships ($20,000); foundation ($1,466,436)
Assets: $24,763,284 (fiscal 2003); $28,782,457 (fiscal 2002); $28,942,715 (fiscal 2001)
Gifts Received: $1,000,000 (fiscal 2003); $1,000,000 (fiscal 2002); $1,000,000 (fiscal 2001). Note: Contributions were received from American Honda Motor Co., Inc.

Typical Recipients

Arts & Humanities: Libraries, Museums/Galleries, Public Broadcasting
Civic & Public Affairs: Employment/Job Training, Law & Justice, Public Policy, Zoos/Aquariums
Education: Afterschool/Enrichment Programs, Colleges & Universities, Community & Junior Colleges, Economic Education, Education Reform, Elementary Education (Private), Elementary Education (Public), Engineering/Technological Education, Environmental Education, Education-General, Gifted & Talented Programs, Health & Physical Education, Leadership Training, Literacy, Medical Education, Minority Education, Preschool Education, Private Education (Precollege), Public Education (Precollege), Science/Mathematics Education, Secondary Education (Public), Special Education, Student Aid, Vocational & Technical Education
Environment: Environment-General, Resource Conservation, Wildlife Protection
Health: Health Funds
International: International Organizations
Science: Science Museums, Scientific Centers & Institutes, Scientific Organizations, Scientific Research
Social Services: Child Abuse, Community Service Organizations, Delinquency & Criminal Rehabilitation, Food/Clothing Distribution, People with Disabilities, Volunteer Services, Youth Organizations

Application Procedures

Initial Contact: Request application form, then send full proposal.
Application Requirements: Include statement of organization's purpose; description of program for which grant is requested; proof of tax-exempt status; copy of most recent Form 990; list of board of directors and a resolution from the board that authorizes request; copy of organization's current budget with comparisons to previous budget and with significant changes reconciled; two most recently audited financial statements; list of current contributions with amounts for each; three- to five-year plan for organization; proposed budget utilizing the grant funds requested with line item detail; and supporting materials.
Deadlines: Applications must be received by November 1 for grants awarded February 1, February 1 for grants awarded May 1, May 1 for grants awarded August 1, and August 1 for grants awarded November 1.
Review Process: In the first month of the quarter, grants are evaluated and approximately 10% of proposals continue in the review process; in the second month, a site visit is conducted; board of directors meets at the end of each quarter to make final decisions on proposals.
Evaluative Criteria: Board looks for proposals that are imaginative, creative, youthful, scientific, humanistic, innovative, and forward thinking; also considered in funding are programs that are: national in scope, broad, soundly managed, financially sound and have a high potential for success, a low degree of duplication of effort, an urgency of need (not merely financial), and a minimal risk for venture capital investment.
Decision Notification: Those applications that do not pass the first review will be notified immediately of the disposition of their proposals. Proposals that go through a full board review will receive notification of the board's decision after the appropriate board meeting in January, April, July, or October.
Notes: Grant applications can be requested in writing at above address. Mark the request Attn: Grant Application Request, and include a self-addressed, stamped envelope. For direct corporate contributions, send a letter of inquiry to Community Relations Department at American Honda Motor Co. No application form is required.

Restrictions

The foundation does not support individuals; for-profit organizations; small, local, community and/or regional projects; scholarships; loans for small businesses; advocacy; foreign exchange programs; sponsorships, conferences, or seminars; veterans or fraternal organizations; labor groups; service club activities; propaganda statements; arts and culture; health, social, or welfare issues; research papers; medical and/or educational research; disaster relief; annual fund drives; corporate memberships; trips or tours; direct support of churches, religious groups, or sectarian organizations; attempts to influence legislation; advertising in charitable publications; hospital operating funds; private foundations; beauty or talent contests; groups serving special interests of their constituencies; marathon-type fundraising; political organizations, programs, campaigns, or candidates; dinners or special events; or organizations outside the United States. Also does not make grants considered to be in the company's self-interest. Organizations should not submit an application more than once in a 12-month period; repeat requests are not considered in the same year. In addition, the foundation does not make gifts or donations of any Honda products for any purpose.

Additional Information

In 1993, company announced a ten-year, $40 million commitment to establish a special alternative secondary school and teacher development center-- Eagle Rock School and Professional Development Center, in Estes Park, CO. This school operates independently of the foundation.
Also, Honda of America Manufacturing Co., a subsidiary of American Honda Motor Co., gives through the Honda of America Foundation.
Publications: Policy Statement; Grant Application Form; Guidelines; Newsletter

Corporate Officials

Koichi Kondo: chief executive officer, director B 1946. PRIM CORP EMPL chief executive officer, director: American Honda Motor Co. Inc.

Foundation Officials

Kathryn Ann Carey: foundation manager B Los Angeles, CA 1949. ED California State University BA (1971). NONPR AFFIL member: Public Relations Society America; member: Southern California Association Philanthropy; member: Ninety-Nines; member: Ocicats International; member: Humane Society U.S.; member: Los Angeles Society Prevention Cruelty Animals; member: Elsa Wild Animal Appeal; member: Greenpeace; member: American Quarter Horse Association; member: Council Foundations; member: Aircraft Owners & Pilots Association; member: American Humane Association; director: Advocates Nursing Home Reform; president: Affinity Group Japanese Philanthropy. CLUB AFFIL mem: Advertising Los Angeles Club.
Kent Dellinger: director
Abrahm Dent: director
Lou Juneman: director
Gary Kessler: vice president
Tom Ross: secretary, treasurer
Hiroshi Soda: president
Wade Terry: director
Jeanette Tomikawa: director

Grants Analysis

Disclosure Period: fiscal year ending March 31, 2003
Total Grants: $958,698
Number of Grants: 17
Average Grant: $56,394
Highest Grant: $99,400
Lowest Grant: $10,000
Typical Range: $25,000 to $75,000

Recent Grants

Note: Grants derived from 2004 Form 990.
General

100,000	Reading is Rundamental Inc., Washington, DC
87,732	Earthspan, Baltimore, MD
80,000	College Summit, Washington, DC
75,000	Association of Science Technology Centers Inc., Washington, DC
75,000	College Bound, Cerritos, CA
75,000	Jumpstart, Boston, MA

75,000	KISS Institute for Practical Robotics, Norman, OK
75,000	Science Service, Washington, DC
74,976	YouthBuild USA, Somerville, MA
69,080	University of Georgia, Aiken, SC

AMERICAN OPTICAL CORP.

Company Headquarters
Greenwich, CT

Company Description
Employees: 2,000
SIC(s): 2200 Textile Mill Products, 3000 Rubber & Miscellaneous Plastics Products, 3800 Instruments & Related Products, 5000 Wholesale Trade--Durable Goods.

Operating Locations
American Optical Corp. (MA--Southbridge)

American Optical Foundation

Giving Contact
Gary Bridgeman, Director
14 Mechanic St.
Southbridge, MA 01550
Phone: (508)765-7085

Description
EIN: 046028058
Organization Type: Corporate Foundation
Giving Locations: MA
Grant Types: Employee Matching Gifts, General Support, Scholarship.

Financial Summary
Total Giving: $51,335 (2004); $58,782 (2001)
Giving Analysis: Giving for 2004 includes: foundation grants to United Way ($2,000); foundation scholarships ($31,385); 2001: foundation grants to United Way ($2,000); foundation scholarships ($52,441)
Assets: $1,478,958 (2004); $1,607,142 (2001)
Gifts Received: $18,316 (1995); $25,000 (1994); $26,895 (1993). Note: In 1995, contributions were received from the G. B. Wells Foundation.

Typical Recipients
Arts & Humanities: Arts Centers, Historic Preservation, History & Archaeology, Libraries, Music, Theater
Civic & Public Affairs: Employment/Job Training, Civic & Public Affairs-General, Municipalities/Towns
Education: Colleges & Universities, Community & Junior Colleges, Economic Education, Education Funds, Engineering/Technological Education, Faculty Development, Education-General, International Exchange, Legal Education, Preschool Education, Private Education (Precollege), Public Education (Precollege), Science/Mathematics Education, Secondary Education (Public), Student Aid
Health: Children's Health/Hospitals, Health Organizations, Prenatal Health Issues
International: Health Care/Hospitals
Religion: Religious Welfare
Social Services: Camps, Child Welfare, Scouts, United Funds/United Ways, Youth Organizations

Application Procedures
Initial Contact: Send a formal letter of application, two letters of recommendation, transcripts, SAT scores, and an essay on career objective.
Deadlines: April 25.

Restrictions
Loans and scholarships are for children of American Optical employees only.

Corporate Officials
Maurice Cunnisse: chairman, president chief financial officer, director PRIM CORP EMPL chairman, president: Am Optical Corp.
John W. Van Dyke: senior vice president, chief financial officer, director B New York, NY 1942. ED Drexel University; Princeton University (1965). PRIM CORP EMPL senior vice president, chief financial officer, director: American Optical Corp. CORP AFFIL senior vice president, chief financial officer, director: Radiac Abrasives; senior vice president, chief financial officer, director: M & R Industries. NONPR AFFIL member: Financial Executives Institute.

Foundation Officials
Gary Bridgeman: director
Allen Skott: director
John W. Van Dyke: director (see above)

Grants Analysis
Disclosure Period: calendar year ending 2004
Total Grants: $17,950*
Number of Grants: 5
Highest Grant: $10,000
Lowest Grant: $200
*Note: Giving excludes scholarships; United Way.

Recent Grants
Note: Grants derived from 2004 Form 990.
Library-Related
10,000	Chariton Public Library, Chariton, IA
5,000	Joshua Hyde Library, Sturbridge, MA

General
2,500	Old Sturbridge Village, Sturbridge, MA
2,000	United Way
250	Kans for Kids Tri-Community
200	Girls Scouts of Montachusett, Worcester, MA

AMERICAN STANDARD INC.

Company Headquarters
1 Centennial Ave.
Piscataway, NJ 08855-6820
Web: http://www.americanstandard.com

Company Description
Ticker: ASD
Exchange: OTC
Revenue: US$9.508 billion (2004)
Profit: US$313.4 million (2004)
Employees: 38,000
Fortune Rank: 238, per FORTUNE Magazine's list of 500 Largest U.S. Corporations (2004).
SIC(s): 3261 Vitreous Plumbing Fixtures, 3431 Metal Sanitary Ware, 3432 Plumbing Fixtures Fittings & Trim, 3585 Refrigeration & Heating Equipment.

Operating Locations
American Standard Inc. (IL--Skokie; KY--Paintsville; NV--Las Vegas; NJ--Piscataway, Trenton; NC--Greensboro; OH--Tiffin; VA--Arlington); American Standard Medical Systems (NY--New York); Societe Trane (WI--Golbey Cedex); Trane Co. (TX--Tyler; WI--La Crosse); Worldwide Applied Systems (WI--La Crosse)

American Standard Foundation

Giving Contact
G. Peter D'Aloia, President
American Standard Foundation
One Centennial Avenue
Piscataway, NJ 08855-6820
Phone: (732)980-6000
Fax: (732)980-6121

Description
EIN: 256018911
Organization Type: Corporate Foundation
Giving Locations: headquarters and operating communities.
Grant Types: Employee Matching Gifts, General Support, Scholarship.

Financial Summary
Total Giving: $1,627,155 (2003); $1,903,859 (2002); $2,297,132 (2001). Note: Contributes through foundation only.
Giving Analysis: Giving for 2001 includes: foundation scholarships ($51,420); foundation matching gifts ($506,415); foundation ($657,504); foundation grants to United Way ($1,081,793)
Assets: $2,039,888 (2003); $1,204,462 (2002); $5,786,941 (2001)
Gifts Received: $22,999 (1999). Note: In 1999, contributions were received from American Standard Inc.

Typical Recipients
Arts & Humanities: Arts Associations & Councils, Arts Funds, Dance, Libraries, Museums/Galleries, Performing Arts
Civic & Public Affairs: Business/Free Enterprise, Clubs, Community Foundations, Economic Policy, Employment/Job Training, Civic & Public Affairs-General, Housing, Law & Justice, Legal Aid, Philanthropic Organizations, Professional & Trade Associations
Education: Afterschool/Enrichment Programs, Agricultural Education, Business Education, Colleges & Universities, Economic Education, Education Funds, Education Reform, Environmental Education, Education-General, International Exchange, Private Education (Precollege), Public Education (Precollege), Religious Education, Secondary Education (Private), Secondary Education (Public), Student Aid, Vocational & Technical Education
Environment: Energy
Health: Emergency/Ambulance Services, Heart, Preventive Medicine/Wellness Organizations, Single-Disease Health Associations
International: Foreign Educational Institutions, International Affairs, International Development, International Relations
Religion: Religious Organizations, Religious Welfare
Science: Scientific Centers & Institutes
Social Services: Animal Protection, Community Service Organizations, Emergency Relief, People with Disabilities, Social Services-General, Substance Abuse, United Funds/United Ways, YMCA/YWCA/YMHA/YWHA

Application Procedures
Initial Contact: Send a brief letter.
Application Requirements: Include purpose, history, and scope of organization; amount requested; purpose for which funds are sought; recently audited financial statement; and proof of tax-exempt status.
Deadlines: None.

Corporate Officials
Fred A. Allardyce: senior vice president chairman, chief financial officerl B Rahway, NJ 1941. ED Yale University BA (1963); University of Chicago Graduate School of Business Administration MBA (1965). PRIM CORP EMPL senior vice president, chairman,

chief financial officer: American Standard Inc. ADD CORP EMPL senior vice president: Diasorin Inc.

Adrian B. Deshotel: vice president human resources PRIM CORP EMPL vice president human resources: American Standard Companies Inc.

Horst Hinrichs: vice chairman, director B 1933. ED University of Stuttgart (1958). PRIM CORP EMPL vice chairman, director: American Standard Inc.

Richard A. Kalaher: vice president, secretary, general counsel B Milwaukee, WI 1940. ED Union College AB (1962); Northwestern University JD (1965). PRIM CORP EMPL vice president, secretary, general counsel: American Standard Inc. NONPR AFFIL chairman, legal officer: Conference Board; member: International Bar Association; member: American Bar Association; member: Association Bar New York City.

Foundation Officials

Lawrence B. Costello: vice president, director
G. Peter D'Aloia: president, director
Marilyn Gargano: assistant treasurer
Mary Jane Mahoney: assistant secretary
R. Scott Massengil: vice president, director
J. Paul McGrath: vice president, director

Grants Analysis

Disclosure Period: calendar year ending 2003
Total Grants: $278,050*
Number of Grants: 10
Average Grant: $8,672*
Highest Grant: $200,000
Lowest Grant: $200
Typical Range: $1,000 to $10,000
*Note: Giving excludes matching gifts, scholarships, and United Way. Average grant figure excludes highest grant.

Recent Grants

Note: Grants derived from 2003 Form 990.

General

820,111	United Way, Alexandria, VA
200,000	American Supply Association Education Foundation, Chicago, IL
77,914	United Way, Alexandria, VA
30,000	Eisenhower Exchange Fellowships, Philadelphia, PA
25,000	American Society of Heating, Refrigerating and Air-Conditioning Engineers Foundation, Atlanta, GA
15,803	National Merit Scholarship Corporation, Evanston, IL
10,000	New Jersey Performing Arts Center, Newark, NJ
5,000	United Fund for Arts and Humanities
3,967	United Way, Alexandria, VA
3,000	Coulee Region Humane Society, Onalaska, WI

AMERITAS LIFE INSURANCE CORP.

Company Headquarters

Lincoln, NE
Phone: 800-745-6665
Web: http://www.ameritas.com

Company Description

Employees: 800
SIC(s): 6311 Life Insurance, 6321 Accident & Health Insurance, 6324 Hospital & Medical Service Plans.

Ameritas Charitable Foundation

Giving Contact

Lawrence J. Arth, Secretary, Treasurer, & Director
5900 "O" Street
Lincoln, NE 68510
Phone: (402)467-7706
Fax: (402)467-7939

Description

Founded: 1985
EIN: 363428705
Organization Type: Corporate Foundation
Giving Locations: NE: Lincoln
Grant Types: Capital, General Support, Multiyear/Continuing Support, Professorship, Project, Research.

Donor Information

Founder: Ameritas Life Insurance Corp.

Financial Summary

Total Giving: $339,850 (2003); $404,015 (2002); $427,425 (2001)
Giving Analysis: Giving for 2001 includes: foundation grants to United Way ($225); foundation scholarships ($10,000); foundation ($417,200)
Assets: $7,452,904 (2003); $6,722,091 (2002); $7,179,188 (2001)
Gifts Received: $202,119 (2003); $177,375 (2002); $101,167 (2001). Note: Contributions were received from Ameritas Life Insurance Corp.

Typical Recipients

Arts & Humanities: Arts Associations & Councils, Arts Centers, Arts Funds, Ballet, Dance, Ethnic & Folk Arts, Film & Video, Historic Preservation, History & Archaeology, Libraries, Museums/Galleries, Music, Performing Arts, Public Broadcasting, Theater
Civic & Public Affairs: Botanical Gardens/Parks, Clubs, Community Foundations, Economic Development, Economic Policy, Employment/Job Training, Civic & Public Affairs-General, Housing, Inner-City Development, Legal Aid, Parades/Festivals, Philanthropic Organizations, Professional & Trade Associations, Urban & Community Affairs, Women's Affairs
Education: Afterschool/Enrichment Programs, Business Education, Colleges & Universities, Continuing Education, Economic Education, Education Associations, Education Funds, Faculty Development, Education-General, Health & Physical Education, Leadership Training, Medical Education, Minority Education, Private Education (Precollege), Public Education (Precollege), Religious Education, Science/Mathematics Education, Secondary Education (Private), Special Education, Student Aid
Environment: Environment-General, Research, Resource Conservation, Wildlife Protection
Health: AIDS/HIV, Cancer, Children's Health/Hospitals, Clinics/Medical Centers, Emergency/Ambulance Services, Health Funds, Health Organizations, Hospitals, Medical Research, Multiple Sclerosis, Public Health, Research/Studies Institutes, Single-Disease Health Associations, Transplant Networks/Donor Banks
Religion: Religious Organizations, Religious Welfare
Science: Science Museums, Scientific Centers & Institutes
Social Services: Animal Protection, At-Risk Youth, Big Brothers/Big Sisters, Child Abuse, Child Welfare, Community Service Organizations, Counseling, Domestic Violence, Emergency Relief, Family Services, Food/Clothing Distribution, Homes, People with Disabilities, Recreation & Athletics, Scouts, Senior Services, Social Services-General, Special Olympics, Substance Abuse, United Funds/United Ways, YMCA/YWCA/YMHA/YWHA, Youth Organizations

Application Procedures

Initial Contact: Send a written application.
Application Requirements: Include agency name, principal address, phone number, and names of the board of directors and officers; agency purpose; current financial statement, including an analysis of support, revenue, and expenses; balance sheet and statement of changes in retained earnings/fund balances; proposed budget, including sources of funds and analysis of expenses; the organization's tax status; and amount requested and intended use.
Deadlines: None.
Evaluative Criteria: Preference is given to local charitable organizations. Funding requests for the support of hospitals, athletic activities, religious associations, and public activities will be closely reviewed.
Notes: Additional information may be requested as necessary.

Restrictions

Does not support individuals, religious organizations for sectarian purposes, political or lobbying groups, or organizations that require a major portion of budget for administration and solicitation.

Corporate Officials

Kenneth C. Louis: president, chief operating officer, director chief financial officer B Pittsburgh, PA 1938. ED Pennsylvania State University (1961). PRIM CORP EMPL president, chief operating officer, director: Ameritas Life Insurance Corp. CORP AFFIL director: Pathmark Assurance Co.; director: Veritas Corp.; director: Lincoln Gateway Shopping Center Inc.; executive vice president, director: Ameritas Variable Life Insurance Co.; director: First Ameritas Life Insurance Co. New York; senior vice president, director: Ameritas Investment Corp.; director: Ameritas Managed Dental Plan Inc.; vice president, director: AMAI Corp.; director: Ameritas Investment Advisors Inc.

JoAnn M. Martin: senior vice president, partner, chief financial officer B Plainview, NE 1954. ED University of Nebraska (1975); Colorado State University (1982). PRIM CORP EMPL senior vice president, partner, chief financial officer: Ameritas Life Insurance Corp. ADD CORP EMPL senior vice president, chief financial officer, corporate treasurer: Ameritas Acacia Mutual Holding Co.; chief financial officer, director: Ameritas Managed Dental Plan. CORP AFFIL director, controller: Lincoln Gateway Shopping Center Inc.; compt, director: Pathmark Assurance Co.; comptroller, director: Ameritas Variable Life Insurance Co.; vice president, controller: First Ameritas Life Insurance Corp.; director: Acacia National Life; comptroller: Ameritas Marketing Group. NONPR AFFIL member: American Institute CPAs; fellow, member: Life Management Institute.

Foundation Officials

Jim Abel: president, director
Lawrence Joseph Arth: secretary, treasurer, director B Lincoln, NE 1943. ED University of Nebraska BBA (1965); University of Nebraska MA (1969). ADD CORP EMPL chairman, president, chief executive officer: AMAL Corp.; chief executive officer: Ameritas Acacia Mutual Holding Co.; chief executive officer: Ameritas Holding Co. NONPR AFFIL member: Lincoln Chamber of Commerce; member: Omaha/Lincoln Society; member: Financial Analysts Federation. CLUB AFFIL Lincoln Country Club.
JoAnn M. Martin: controller (see above)

Grants Analysis

Disclosure Period: calendar year ending 2003
Total Grants: $339,850
Number of Grants: 70
Average Grant: $4,855
Highest Grant: $30,000
Lowest Grant: $250
Typical Range: $1,000 to $10,000

Recent Grants

Note: Grants derived from 2003 Form 990.
General

30,000	University of Nebraska Lincoln, Lincoln, NE
25,000	Boy Scouts of America, Walton, NE
22,000	Nebraska Wesleyan University, Lincoln, NE -- towards great teaching program
20,000	Missouri River Basin Lewis and Clark, Lincoln, NE -- towards capital campaign education center
20,000	YMCA of Lincoln, Lincoln, NE
10,400	University of Nebraska Foundation, Lincoln, NE -- towards actuarial science fund
10,000	BryanLGH Foundation, Lincoln, NE
10,000	Lincoln Parks and Recreation Foundation, Lincoln, NE -- towards sunken gardens renovation
10,000	Nebraska Community Foundation, Lincoln, NE -- towards rural community improvements program
10,000	Nebraska Wesleyan University, Lincoln, NE -- towards faculty fellowship fund

AMERUS GROUP CO.

Company Headquarters

611 5th Ave.
Des Moines, IA 50309
Web: http://www.amerus.com

Company Description

Founded: 1996
Ticker: AMH
Exchange: NYSE
Former Name: American Mutual Life Insurance Co., Central Companies.
Assets: US$20.293 billion (2002)
Employees: 1113 (2003)
SIC(s): 6311 Life Insurance.

Nonmonetary Support

Type: Donated Equipment; In-kind Services; Loaned Employees; Loaned Executives
Note: Co. provides nonmonetary support.

AmerUs Group Charitable Foundation

Giving Contact

Jonna LaToure, Assistant Director
AmerUs Group Charitable Foundation
699 Walnut Street, 20th Fl.
Des Moines, IA 50309
Phone: (515)557-3910
Fax: (515)283-3269
Web: http://www.amerus.com/about/community.html

Description

EIN: 421431745
Organization Type: Corporate Foundation
Giving Locations: IA
Grant Types: Employee Matching Gifts, General Support.
Note: Employee matching gifts have a $500 maximum.

Financial Summary

Total Giving: $618,226 (2002); $577,895 (2001).
Note: Contributes through corporate direct giving program only.
Giving Analysis: Giving for 2001 includes: foundation grants to United Way ($225,956)
Assets: $5,105,188 (2002); $6,571,849 (2001)

Typical Recipients

Arts & Humanities: Arts Associations & Councils, Arts Centers, Arts Festivals, Arts Funds, Community Arts, Arts & Humanities-General, Historic Preservation, Libraries, Museums/Galleries, Music, Opera, Performing Arts, Theater
Civic & Public Affairs: Business/Free Enterprise, Community Foundations, Economic Development, Civic & Public Affairs-General, Housing, Professional & Trade Associations, Urban & Community Affairs, Women's Affairs, Zoos/Aquariums
Education: Business-School Partnerships, Colleges & Universities, Community & Junior Colleges, Economic Education, Education Funds, Education-General, Gifted & Talented Programs, Private Education (Precollege), Public Education (Precollege), Science/Mathematics Education, Secondary Education (Private)
Environment: Air/Water Quality, Environment-General, Protection
Health: Health-General, Hospices
Religion: Ministries
Science: Scientific Centers & Institutes, Scientific Research
Social Services: Animal Protection, Child Welfare, Community Centers, Community Service Organizations, Counseling, Day Care, Emergency Relief, Family Services, Food/Clothing Distribution, Homes, Shelters/Homelessness, Social Services-General, Substance Abuse, United Funds/United Ways, Volunteer Services, YMCA/YWCA/YMHA/YWHA, Youth Organizations

Application Procedures

Initial Contact: See website for guidelines and application form.
Application Requirements: Include itemized budget reflecting current and anticipated funds (this should include sources of income, contributions received to date, any fundraising expenses, and other expected expenses; recently audited financial statement; proof of tax-exempt status; list of other funding sources approached for support; background information on the sponsoring organization, goals, geographic scope, number of paid employees, total salary expense, and size of volunteer involvement); names and affiliations of officers and board of directors; and amount requested.
Deadlines: March 31 and June 30.
Review Process: Board meetings are generally held three or four times annually.
Notes: Grantees are required to submit annual reports.

Restrictions

Does not support athletes or athletic groups; conference or seminar attendance; courtesy advertising; endowments; fellowships; festival participation; fraternal organizations; hospitals or health care facilities; individuals; individual K-8 schools; organizations, projects, or programs outside the U.S. or whose activities are mainly international; organizations redistributing funds to separate, independent tax-exempt groups (except United Way and independent college funds); political parties, campaigns or candidates, partisan political organizations; private foundations; sectarian, religious, and denominational organizations; social organizations; trade, industry, and professional associations; United Way organizations seeking funds for operating expenses of United Way-funded programs; veterans groups.

Additional Information

Program areas and priorities are United Way, Education, Health and Human Services, Arts and Culture, Civic and Community Programs, and Children At Risk. Company reports that it underwent a merger and a name change in January 1995. Formerly Central Companies, it was known as the American Mutual Life Insurance Company, now known as the AmerUS Group.
Publications: Annual Report

Corporate Officials

Roger Kay Brooks: chairman, director B Clarion, IA 1937. ED University of Iowa BA (1959). PRIM CORP EMPL chairman: AmerUS Group. CORP AFFIL chairman: Amer US Savings Bank; chairman: Central Life Assurance Co. NONPR AFFIL member: Phi Beta Kappa; fellow: Society Actuaries; member: Greater Des Moines Chamber of Commerce; member: Iowa Insurance Hall Fame. CLUB AFFIL Actuaries Des Moines Club; Des Moines Club.
Tom Godlasky: executive vice president, chief investment officer B Tyrone, PA 1955. ED Indiana University of Pennsylvania (1977); University of Pittsburgh (1979). PRIM CORP EMPL executive vice president, chief investment officer: AmerUS Life Holdings Inc.
Sam Charles Kalainov: chairman, president, chief executive officer B Steele, ND 1930. ED North Dakota State University BS (1956); American College Life Underwriters (1966). PRIM CORP EMPL chairman, president, chief executive officer: AmerUS Group. CORP AFFIL director: Bankers Trust Co.; director: Des Moines International Airport; director: AmerUS Life Insurance Co.; chairman: American Mutual Holding Corp.; officer: AmerUS Life Holdings Inc. NONPR AFFIL member: Greater Des Moines Chamber of Commerce; member: National Association Life Underwriters; trustee: Drake University; member: American Legion; chairman: Corporate International Trade; director: American Council Life Insurance. CLUB AFFIL Rotary Club.
Gary McPhail: president emeritus PRIM CORP EMPL president emeritus: AmerUS Group.
Michael E. Sproule: chief financial officer, director PRIM CORP EMPL chief financial officer, director: Central Life Assurance Co.

Giving Program Officials

Ted W. Wheat: PRIM CORP EMPL director committee relations: AmerUS Group.

Foundation Officials

Roger Kay Brooks: president, director (see above)
Victor Daley: executive vice president, director
Tom Godlasky: executive vice president, director (see above)
James Smallenberger: secretary
Melinda Urion: treasurer

Grants Analysis

Disclosure Period: calendar year ending 2002
Total Grants: $386,260*
Number of Grants: 90
Average Grant: $4,292
Highest Grant: $25,000
Lowest Grant: $50
Typical Range: $100 to $10,000
*Note: Giving excludes scholarship and United Way.

Recent Grants

Note: Grants derived from 2003 Form 990.
Library-Related

1,500	Public Library of Des Moines Foundation, Des Moines, IA -- towards education

General

231,466	United Way of Central Iowa, Des Moines, IA
25,000	Civic Center of Greater Des Moines, Des Moines, IA
25,000	Dowling High School, Des Moines, IA
25,000	Grays Lake Park Care of Greater Des Moines Community Foundation, Des Moines, IA
25,000	Greater Des Moines Community Foundation, Des Moines, IA
25,000	Hope Ministries, Des Moines, IA
21,135	Des Moines Public Schools, Des Moines, IA
21,000	Des Moines Arts Festival, Des Moines, IA

| 20,000 | Des Moines Art Center, Des Moines, IA |
| 15,000 | Belin Blank International Center for Gifted & Talented Development, Iowa City, IA |

AMETEK INC.

Company Headquarters
Paoli, PA
Web: http://www.ametek.com

Company Description
Founded: 1930
Ticker: AME
Exchange: NYSE
Revenue: US$1.04 billion (2002)
Employees: 7800 (2003)
SIC(s): 3316 Cold-Finishing of Steel Shapes, 3621 Motors & Generators, 3823 Process Control Instruments, 3829 Measuring & Controlling Devices Nec.

Operating Locations
AMETEK Dixson (CO--Grand Junction); AMETEK, Inc. (CA--Costa Mesa; CT--Wallingford; DE--Wilmington; FL--Largo; IL--West Chicago; OH--Kent; PA--Eighty-Four, Feasterville, Horsham, Nesquehoning, Pittsburgh, Sellersville; WA--Redmond); AMETEK Process & Analytical Instruments (DE--Newarkphy); AMETEK Rotron Industrial Products (NY--Saugerties); AMETEK Rotron Mil-Aero Products (NY--Woodstock); AMETEK Sensor Technology (MI--Clawson); AMETEK Test & Calibration Instruments (NY--Kew Gardens)

AMETEK Foundation

Giving Contact
Kathryn E. Londra, Secretary, Treasurer
AMETEK Foundation
37 North Valley Road, Bldg. 4
PO Box 1764
Paoli, PA 19301-0801
Phone: (610)647-2121

Description
Founded: 1960
EIN: 136095939
Organization Type: Corporate Foundation
Giving Locations: headquarters and operating communities; nationally.
Grant Types: General Support, Research.

Financial Summary
Total Giving: $1,011,196 (2003); $874,415 (2002); $1,087,655 (2001). Note: Contributes through foundation only.
Giving Analysis: Giving for 2001 includes: foundation scholarships ($34,750); foundation grants to United Way ($161,103); foundation ($891,802)
Assets: $7,037,073 (2003); $6,911,528 (2002); $7,623,478 (2001)
Gifts Received: $650,100 (1996); $650,000 (1995); $650,000 (1994). Note: The foundation receives contributions from AMETEK, Inc.

Typical Recipients
Arts & Humanities: Arts Centers, Arts Funds, Ballet, Dance, Ethnic & Folk Arts, Arts & Humanities-General, Historic Preservation, History & Archaeology, Libraries, Museums/Galleries, Music
Civic & Public Affairs: Botanical Gardens/Parks, Economic Development, Ethnic Organizations, Civic & Public Affairs-General, Housing, Minority Business, Municipalities/Towns, Professional & Trade Associations, Safety, Urban & Community Affairs, Women's Affairs, Zoos/Aquariums
Education: Business Education, Colleges & Univer-

sities, Community & Junior Colleges, Education Associations, Education Funds, Elementary Education (Private), Engineering/Technological Education, Education-General, International Exchange, Legal Education, Literacy, Medical Education, Private Education (Precollege), Public Education (Precollege), Science/Mathematics Education, Secondary Education (Public), Student Aid, Vocational & Technical Education
Environment: Environment-General, Resource Conservation, Wildlife Protection
Health: Cancer, Clinics/Medical Centers, Diabetes, Emergency/Ambulance Services, Health Funds, Health Organizations, Hospitals, Medical Rehabilitation, Medical Research, Mental Health, Preventive Medicine/Wellness Organizations, Public Health, Single-Disease Health Associations
International: International Affairs
Religion: Jewish Causes, Ministries
Science: Science-General, Science Museums, Scientific Centers & Institutes
Social Services: At-Risk Youth, Child Welfare, Community Service Organizations, Family Services, Food/Clothing Distribution, Homes, People with Disabilities, Scouts, Senior Services, Shelters/Homelessness, Social Services-General, United Funds/United Ways, YMCA/YWCA/YMHA/YWHA, Youth Organizations

Application Procedures
Initial Contact: Submit brief letter or proposal.
Application Requirements: Submit a description of organization, amount requested, purpose of funds sought, recently audited financial statement, and proof of tax-exempt status.
Deadlines: None.

Restrictions
The foundation does not support political or lobbying groups.

Corporate Officials
Frank S. Hermance: chairman, chief executive officer, director B December 29, 1948. ED Rochester Institute Technology BSEE (1971); Rochester Institute Technology MSEE (1973). PRIM CORP EMPL president, chief executive officer, director: AMETEK, Inc.

Foundation Officials
Helmut N. Friedlaender: director CORP AFFIL director: Ametek Inc.
Frank S. Hermance: president, director (see above)

Grants Analysis
Disclosure Period: calendar year ending 2003
Total Grants: $848,303*
Number of Grants: 63
Average Grant: $9,831*
Highest Grant: $127,609
Lowest Grant: $1,000
Typical Range: $5,000 to $25,000
*Note: Giving excludes United Way and scholarships. Average grant figure excludes two highest grants ($248,601).

Recent Grants
Note: Grants derived from 2003 Form 990.
Library-Related
| 14,000 | Free Library of Philadelphia Foundation, Philadelphia, PA |
| 10,000 | New York Public Library, New York, NY |
General
127,609	Binghamton School District, Binghamton, NY
120,992	Rochester School District, Rochester, MN
60,133	Science Explorer Inc.
50,000	Eagles Youth Partnership, Philadelphia, PA
35,755	United Way of Southeastern Pennsylvania, Philadelphia, PA

30,100	National Merit Scholarship Corporation, Evanston, IL
30,000	Paoli Memorial Hospital, Paoli, PA
25,000	Central Park Conservancy, New York, NY
25,000	Cornell Cooperative Extension of Broome County, Binghamton, NY
25,000	Sloan Kettering Cancer Center, New York, NY

AMGEN INC.

Company Headquarters
Houston, TX
Web: http://www.amgen.com

Company Description
Ticker: AMGN
Exchange: AMEX
Revenue: US$10.55 billion (2004)
Profit: US$2.363 billion (2004)
Employees: 4,594 (1999)
Fortune Rank: 212, per FORTUNE Magazine's list of 500 Largest U.S. Corporations (2004).
SIC(s): 5122 Drugs, Proprietaries & Sundries.

Operating Locations
Amgen, Inc. (CA--Newbury Park; CO--Boulder, Longmont; DC--Washington; KY--Louisville; PR--Juncos)

Nonmonetary Support
Type: Donated Equipment; Donated Products
Volunteer Programs: The Amgen Staff Community Involvement Program (SCIP) makes the services of Amgen staff available to nonprofit organizations or needy individuals for community improvement.

Amgen Foundation

Giving Contact
Elizabeth Malkerson, President and Chief Executive Officer
The Amgen Foundation
One Amgen Center Drive
Thousand Oaks, CA 91320-1799
Phone: (805)447-1000
Web: http://www.amgen.com/community/

Description
Founded: 1991
EIN: 770252898
Organization Type: Corporate Foundation
Giving Locations: headquarters; nationally.
Grant Types: Employee Matching Gifts, General Support, Matching, Research, Scholarship.
Note: Employee matching gift ratio: 1 to 1 from $50 to $20,000.

Financial Summary
Total Giving: $10,897,549 (2003); $7,700,927 (2002); $5,591,606 (2001). Note: Contributes through corporate direct giving program and foundation.
Giving Analysis: Giving for 2001 includes: foundation grants to United Way ($80,944)
Assets: $111,463,413 (2003); $70,986,889 (2002); $28,506,637 (2001)
Gifts Received: $50,000,000 (2003); $50,000,000 (2002); $5,000,000 (2001). Note: Contributions are received from Amgen, Inc.

Typical Recipients
Arts & Humanities: Arts Associations & Councils, Arts & Humanities-General, Historic Preservation, History & Archaeology, Libraries, Museums/Galleries, Music
Civic & Public Affairs: Asian American Affairs, Bo-

tanical Gardens/Parks, Community Foundations, Employment/Job Training, Gay/Lesbian Issues, Civic & Public Affairs-General, Hispanic Affairs, Housing, Law & Justice, Parades/Festivals, Public Policy, Safety, Zoos/Aquariums

Education: Business Education, Colleges & Universities, Economic Education, Education Funds, Education Reform, Elementary Education (Private), Elementary Education (Public), Engineering/Technological Education, Education-General, Literacy, Medical Education, Private Education (Precollege), Public Education (Precollege), Science/Mathematics Education, Secondary Education (Public), Student Aid, Vocational & Technical Education

Environment: Air/Water Quality, Environment-General, Resource Conservation

Health: AIDS/HIV, Alzheimer's Disease, Cancer, Children's Health/Hospitals, Clinics/Medical Centers, Emergency/Ambulance Services, Health-General, Health Organizations, Heart, Hospices, Hospitals, Medical Research, Preventive Medicine/Wellness Organizations, Public Health, Single-Disease Health Associations

International: Health Care/Hospitals, International Environmental Issues, International Relief Efforts

Religion: Jewish Causes, Religious Welfare

Science: Science Museums, Scientific Centers & Institutes

Social Services: At-Risk Youth, Child Abuse, Child Welfare, Community Service Organizations, Day Care, Family Services, Homes, People with Disabilities, Recreation & Athletics, Scouts, Senior Services, Shelters/Homelessness, Social Services-General, United Funds/United Ways, YMCA/YWCA/YMHA/YWHA, Youth Organizations

Application Procedures

Initial Contact: Send a one- to two-page written request.

Application Requirements: The foundation recommends that applicants provide organizational information, a description of the grant request, and documentation. Organization information should include name and address or organization; contact person's name, title, and telephone number; background of the organization; and the target population and geographic area served by the organization. Grant information should include purpose of funds sought and amount requested; project description, including objectives, target population, needs to be addressed, planned activities, staff qualifications and timetable; and allocation of funds requested and percentage of funds spent on administrative expenses. Documentation should include proof of tax-exempt status; current list of corporate funders and amounts of grants; organization's brochure (if available); and current financial statement and budget report.

Deadlines: None; requests for grants must be received at least 90 days prior to desired distribution date.

Review Process: Both the foundation committee and the corporate contribution committee meet quarterly to evaluate proposals.

Notes: All requests should be submitted to the Foundation. If the request is not appropriate for the Foundation, the request will be forwarded to the appropriate corporate contribution committee.

Restrictions

Does not support alumni drives or teacher organizations; construction or building improvements; capital campaigns; city/municipal/federal government departments; endowments and foundations; individuals or scholarships; charitable dinners or sporting events; labor unions; municipal or for-profit hospitals; religious, political, fraternal, service or veterans organizations; professional sports events or athletes; civic organizations that do not serve the areas in which Amgen is located.

Additional Information

Company has established a series of programs that provide its products, including Epogen and Neupogen, to medically needy patients with no insurance or with limited financial resources.

Company's commitment to education extends beyond basic science and the local community to include users of its products. Company also provides educational programs and tools to assist the medical community to better understand its products.

Company also sponsors an annual Teacher Excellence Award.

Company also sponsors an annual Teacher Excellence Award.

Corporate Officials

Kathryn E. Falberg: senior vice president finance, chief financial officer ED University of California, Los Angeles MBA (1981). PRIM CORP EMPL senior vice president finance, chief financial officer: Amgen, Inc.

Kevin W. Sharer: president, chief executive officer ED United States Naval Academy BS (1970); University of Pittsburgh MBA (1982). PRIM CORP EMPL president, chief executive officer: Amgen Inc.

Foundation Officials

Jackie Crouse: director
Karen Daniels: director
Marie Kennedy: chief executive officer, president
Jean Lim: vice president
Sally Mcleish: director
Richard D. Nanula: director
Andrea Robinson: assistant secretary
Barry Schehr: chief financial officer

Grants Analysis

Disclosure Period: calendar year ending 2003
Total Grants: $7,106,828*
Number of Grants: 81
Average Grant: $64,643*
Highest Grant: $1,000,000
Lowest Grant: $100
Typical Range: $50 to $10,000
*Note: Giving excludes matching gifts and scholarships. Average grant figure excludes two highest grants ($2,000,000).

Recent Grants

Note: Grants derived from 2001 Form 990.
General

800,000	New York Times 9-11 Neediest Cases Fund, New York, NY
520,681	American Red Cross, Ventura, CA
400,000	University of Washington, Seattle, WA
303,400	National History Museum of Los Angeles County Foundation, Los Angeles, CA
300,000	EMS Fund Greater New York Hospital Foundation, New York, NY
250,000	Los Angeles Philharmonic, Los Angeles, CA -- Walt Disney Concert Hall
150,000	New York City Fire Safety Foundation, New York, NY
150,000	New York City Police Foundation, New York, NY
100,000	Survivors Fund of the Community Foundation, Washington, DC
80,944	United Way Ventura County, Ventura, CA

AMP Inc.

Company Headquarters

Harrisburg, PA
Web: http://www.amp.com

Company Description

Employees: 40,000
SIC(s): 3423 Hand & Edge Tools Nec, 3629 Electrical Industrial Apparatus Nec, 3643 Current-Carrying Wir-

ing Devices, 3678 Electronic Connectors.
Parent Company: Tyco International Ltd., 1 Tyco Park, Exeter, NH, United States

Operating Locations

AMP Inc. (CA--Palo Alto; IL--Itasca; IN--Carmel; MI--Comstock Park, Troy; NC--Charlotte, Greensboro, Lowell, Winston-Salem; OR--Sherwood; PA--East Berlin, Jacobus, Loganville, Manheim, Selinsgrove, Seven Valleys, Shrewsbury, Tower City, Williamstown; VA--Harrisonburg, Mount Sidney); AMP Packaging & Carroll Touch Systems Division (TX--Round Rock); M/A-Com Division (MA--Lowell); Madison Cable Corp. (MA--Worcester); Precision Interconnect Division (OR--Portland)

Nonmonetary Support

Type: Donated Equipment; Donated Products
Volunteer Programs: After employees complete 100 hours of volunteer services in a calendar year with a nonprofit organization, the Dollars for Doers program will authorize a $250 contribution from the Foundation to that organization. This is a yearly maximum of $2,000 to one eligible organization.
Note: Nonmonetary support is provided by the company.

Tyco Electronics Foundation

Giving Contact

Harris T. Booker, Jr., Assistant Chairman
Tyco Electronics Corp.
PO Box 3608, M/S 176-42
Harrisburg, PA 17105-3608
Phone: (717)592-4869
Fax: (717)592-3043
E-mail: mjrakocz@tycoelectronics.com
Web: http://www.tycoelectronics.com/about/foundation

Description

EIN: 232022928
Organization Type: Corporate Foundation
Former Name: AMP Foundation (2002).
Giving Locations: NC: Triad; PA: central Pennsylvania; VA headquarters and operating communities.
Grant Types: Employee Matching Gifts, Multiyear/Continuing Support.
Note: Employee matching gift ratio: 2 to 1 for education, for the first $100 of employee gift, then 1 to 1 up to maximum of $5,000. Employee education matching gift program contributes to accredited secondary schools, colleges and universities.

Financial Summary

Total Giving: $1,106,803 (2003); $1,196,084 (2002); $1,150,937 (2001)
Assets: $16,125,221 (2003); $15,108,726 (2002); $18,490,755 (2001)

Typical Recipients

Arts & Humanities: Arts Associations & Councils, Arts Centers, Arts Funds, Ballet, Arts & Humanities-General, Libraries, Museums/Galleries, Music, Opera, Performing Arts, Public Broadcasting, Theater

Civic & Public Affairs: African American Affairs, Business/Free Enterprise, Civil Rights, Clubs, Economic Development, Employment/Job Training, Civic & Public Affairs-General, Hispanic Affairs, Housing, Minority Business, Municipalities/Towns, Professional & Trade Associations, Safety, Urban & Community Affairs

Education: Afterschool/Enrichment Programs, Business Education, Colleges & Universities, Community & Junior Colleges, Education Associations, Education Funds, Education Reform, Elementary Education (Private), Elementary Education (Public), Engineering/Technological Education, Environmental Education, Education-General, Literacy, Medical Education, Minority Education, Private Education (Precollege), Public Education (Precollege), School Volunteerism, Science/Mathematics Education, Secondary Education (Private), Special Education, Vocational & Technical Education

Environment: Environment-General

Health: Cancer, Children's Health/Hospitals, Clinics/Medical Centers, Emergency/Ambulance Services, Health-General, Health Organizations, Hospices, Hospitals, Mental Health, Single-Disease Health Associations

International: International Relations

Religion: Ministries

Science: Science-General, Science Museums, Scientific Centers & Institutes

Social Services: Big Brothers/Big Sisters, Child Abuse, Child Welfare, Community Centers, Community Service Organizations, Crime Prevention, Family Services, Food/Clothing Distribution, People with Disabilities, Recreation & Athletics, Scouts, Shelters/Homelessness, Social Services-General, Substance Abuse, United Funds/United Ways, YMCA/YWCA/YMHA/YWHA, Youth Organizations

Application Procedures

Initial Contact: Send a brief letter or proposal.

Application Requirements: Provide a description of organization and its purposes; description of the project, including costs, proposed budget, and source of funding; list of board members; proof of IRS section 501(c)(3) status; most recent IRS Form 990.

Deadlines: None. Applications are accepted throughout the year and decisions are made on a quarterly basis; the majority of grants are budgeted in the first quarter of the year.

Evaluative Criteria: Preference is given to organizations where Tyco Electronics employees volunteer; organizations must be 501(c)(3) non-profit, and operate within geographic areas where Tyco Electronics has employees; organizations should support Tyco's corporate objectives in education, community development, and arts and culture.

Notes: Requests for over $2,500 must answer specific questions on the foundation's application for corporate contributions.

Restrictions

Foundation does not support organizations in geographic areas where Tyco Electronics has few or no employees; individuals; private foundations; national organizations; general operating needs of United Way agencies; service clubs; social, labor, or veterans organizations; political campaigns; organizations or programs that pose a potential conflict of interest for Tyco Electronics; organizations that discriminate based on race, religion, color, nationality, age, sex, physical or mental conditions, veteran status or marital status; programs of churches or religious organizations with the exception of nondenominational programs such as food banks, youth centers or nonsectarian education programs.

Foundation may not support courtesy advertising; testimonial or fund-raising dinners, loans or investments; capital campaigns or other fund-raising of national organizations.

Additional Information

Grant recipients must submit a final report which evaluates the results of the funded program.

Grants Analysis

Disclosure Period: calendar year ending 2003
Total Grants: $774,687*
Number of Grants: 325
Average Grant: $2,384
Highest Grant: $100,675
Lowest Grant: $50
Typical Range: $250 to $10,000
***Note:** Giving excludes United Way.

Recent Grants

Note: Grants derived from 2003 Form 990.
General

100,675	Massachusetts Institute of Technology, Cambridge, MA
65,000	Penn State Harrisburg, Middletown, PA
57,311	United Way, Lynchburg, VA
54,417	United Way, Enola, PA
50,605	United Way, San Francisco, CA
50,000	University of California, Berkeley, CA
50,000	University of California, Davis, CA
40,000	Mathcounts Foundation, Alexandria, VA
40,000	National Engineers Week Foundation, Alexandria, VA
35,000	Opportunities Industrialization, Harrisburg, PA

AMR CORP.

Company Headquarters

4333 Amon Carter Blvd.
Fort Worth, TX 76155
Web: http://www.amrcorp.com

Company Description

Ticker: AMR
Exchange: OTC
Revenue: US$18.645 billion (2004)
Profit: (US$761 million) (2004)
Employees: 92,000
Fortune Rank: 119, per FORTUNE Magazine's list of 500 Largest U.S. Corporations (2004).
SIC(s): 4512 Air Transportation--Scheduled, 6719 Holding Companies Nec.

Operating Locations

American Eagle Airlines Inc. (TX--Fort Worth); AMR Corp. (TX--Fort Worth); AMR Investment Service Inc. (TX--Fort Worth)

Nonmonetary Support

Type: Donated Products; In-kind Services
Volunteer Programs: Company reports that no formal volunteer program exists, other than a volunteer recycling program aboard flights and in offices.
Note: Sales Department provides in-kind services for nonprofits. Company also donates travel vouchers to organizations.

AMR/American Airlines Foundation

Giving Contact

Kathy Anderson
PO Box 619616
Mail Drop 5656
Dallas, TX 75261-9616
Phone: (817)967-1597
Web: http://www.amrcorp.com/corpinfo.htm

Description

EIN: 762086656
Organization Type: Corporate Foundation
Giving Locations: nationally and internationally.
Grant Types: General Support, Scholarship.

Financial Summary

Total Giving: $207,730 (2002); $780,169 (2001)
Assets: $1,053,489 (2002); $1,213,126 (2001)
Gifts Received: $287,110 (2002); $276,565 (2001); $292,098 (2000). Note: In 2001 and 2002, contributions were received from Flagship Charities. In 1999, contributions were received from Flagship Charities ($274,948) and Chicago Charities ($2,225).

Typical Recipients

Arts & Humanities: Arts Associations & Councils, Arts Centers, Community Arts, Historic Preservation, History & Archaeology, Libraries, Museums/Galleries, Music, Opera, Performing Arts, Public Broadcasting, Theater

Civic & Public Affairs: African American Affairs, Botanical Gardens/Parks, Business/Free Enterprise, Civil Rights, Clubs, Community Foundations, Employment/Job Training, Civic & Public Affairs-General, Hispanic Affairs, Law & Justice, Legal Aid, Minority Business, Municipalities/Towns, Nonprofit Management, Parades/Festivals, Philanthropic Organizations, Professional & Trade Associations, Public Policy, Safety, Urban & Community Affairs, Women's Affairs, Zoos/Aquariums

Education: Arts/Humanities Education, Business Education, Colleges & Universities, Education Reform, Education-General, Leadership Training, Medical Education, Minority Education, Private Education (Precollege), Public Education (Precollege), Religious Education, School Volunteerism, Science/Mathematics Education, Secondary Education (Public), Special Education, Student Aid

Environment: Resource Conservation

Health: AIDS/HIV, Cancer, Children's Health/Hospitals, Clinics/Medical Centers, Diabetes, Emergency/Ambulance Services, Eyes/Blindness, Health Funds, Health Organizations, Heart, Hospitals, Hospitals (University Affiliated), Kidney, Medical Research, Multiple Sclerosis, Public Health, Single-Disease Health Associations, Transplant Networks/Donor Banks

International: Foreign Educational Institutions, Human Rights, International Relations, International Relief Efforts

Religion: Churches, Jewish Causes, Religious Organizations, Religious Welfare

Science: Science Museums

Social Services: At-Risk Youth, Big Brothers/Big Sisters, Child Abuse, Child Welfare, Community Service Organizations, Counseling, Crime Prevention, Emergency Relief, Family Planning, Family Services, Food/Clothing Distribution, People with Disabilities, Recreation & Athletics, Scouts, Senior Services, Shelters/Homelessness, Social Services-General, Substance Abuse, United Funds/United Ways, Volunteer Services, YMCA/YWCA/YMHA/YWHA, Youth Organizations

Application Procedures

Initial Contact: Send a brief letter or proposal.

Application Requirements: Proposals should include contact name, mailing address, phone number, and e-mail address; a description of organization, including overall structure, purpose, and objectives; a list of officers and key staff members; a list of board members and their professional affiliations; amount requested; purpose of funds sought, including objectives, project purpose, and population served; specific reasons why AMR/American Airlines would be an appropriate donor; project budget, including breakout of costs and sources of funding (both committed and expected); size and demographic information about the population to be served; project timetable; methods of evaluating project success; proof of tax-exempt status and a copy of the organization's certification as a 501(c)(3) charitable organization, or preferably the organization's 509(a)(1), (2), or (3); recently audited financial statement; primary funding sources, including United Way; detailed description of how the Foundation's grant will be acknowledged; and any additional support materials.

Deadlines: None.

Decision Notification: Notice of a decision or request for more information is usually sent within two months of receipt of proposal.

Notes: Foundation requests that organizations contact foundation administrator only.

Restrictions

Does not contribute to the support of organizations lacking proof of 501(c)(3) tax-exempt status; endowments; annual operating support fund drives; organizations that discriminate on the basis of race, religion, sex or national origin; religious, fraternal, social or veterans' organizations; political or partisan organizations established to influence legislation or specific elections; individuals; organizations receiving support from United Way drives; basic academic or scientific research; athletic events or sponsorships; or social functions or advertising in commemorative journals, yearbooks or special event publications.

Additional Information

In 2003, the AMR/American Airlines Foundation announced that it had suspended all cash grants due to the financial crisis in the airline industry. Currently, only requests for air transportation will be considered, albeit on a limited basis. The Foundation intends to resume giving when the industry outlook improves.

The American Airlines AAdvantage frequent traveler program sponsors the Miles for Kids in Need program, which provides travel assistance for children facing medical emergencies or requesting special wishes and up to two parents or guardians.

Corporate Officials

Gerard J. Arpey: president, chief executive officer ED University of Texas BBA (1980); University of Texas MBA (1982). PRIM CORP EMPL president, chief executive officer: AMR Corp.
James Beer: chief financial officer PRIM CORP EMPL chief financial officer: AMR Corp.

Foundation Officials

Kathy Andersen: administrator
Gerard J. Arpey: treasurer, director (see above)

Grants Analysis

Disclosure Period: calendar year ending 2002
Total Grants: $184,000*
Number of Grants: 6
Average Grant: $30,666
Highest Grant: $45,000
Lowest Grant: $1,000
*Note: Giving excludes scholarship.

Recent Grants

Note: Grants derived from 2003 Form 990.
General
45,000	Eisner Pediatric & Family Medical Center, Dallas, TX
45,000	Friends of Child Advocates, Monterey Park, CA
45,000	Ronald McDonald House Charities, Los Angeles, CA
45,000	Volunteer League of the San Fernando Valley, Arlington, TX
23,730	National Merit Scholarship Corporation, Evanston, IL
3,000	Dallas Symphony Association, Dallas, TX
1,000	Leukemia & Lymphoma Society, Dallas, TX
500	Boy Scouts of America, Sunnyside, NY

ANDERSEN CORP.

Company Headquarters

100 4th Ave., N
Bayport, MN 55003
Web: http://www.andersencorp.com

Company Description

Revenue: US$1.8 billion (2001)
Employees: 8000 (2003)
SIC(s): 2431 Millwork.

Operating Locations

Andersen Corp. (WI--St. Croix)

Bayport Foundation of Andersen Corporation

Giving Contact

Chloette Haley, Grants Consultant
Bayport Foundation
White Pine Building
342 Fifth Ave. North
Bayport, MN 55003
Phone: (651)439-1557
Fax: (651)439-9480
E-mail: chloettehaley@scenicriver.org
Web: http://www.scenicriver.org

Alternate Contact

Phone: 888-439-9508

Description

EIN: 416020912
Organization Type: Corporate Foundation
Former Name: Bayport Foundation.
Giving Locations: MN: East Metro area, Washington County; WI: Barron County, Burnett County, Dunn County, Pierce County, Polk County, St. Croix County
Grant Types: Capital, Emergency, General Support, Project.

Financial Summary

Total Giving: $1,931,500 (fiscal year ending November 30, 2003); $2,043,050 (fiscal 2002); $2,069,535 (fiscal 2001). Note: Contributes through corporate direct giving program and foundation.
Assets: $41,897,866 (fiscal 2003); $38,569,272 (fiscal 2002); $42,837,830 (fiscal 2001)
Gifts Received: $500,000 (fiscal 2003); $1,000,000 (fiscal 2002); $250,000 (fiscal 2001). Note: Contributions were received from the Andersen Corporation.

Typical Recipients

Arts & Humanities: Arts Centers, Arts Institutes, Arts & Humanities-General, Historic Preservation, History & Archaeology, Libraries, Museums/Galleries, Music, Performing Arts, Public Broadcasting, Theater
Civic & Public Affairs: African American Affairs, Asian American Affairs, Business/Free Enterprise, Civil Rights, Clubs, Community Foundations, Economic Development, Economic Policy, Employment/Job Training, Civic & Public Affairs-General, Housing, Inner-City Development, Legal Aid, Municipalities/Towns, Philanthropic Organizations, Professional & Trade Associations, Public Policy, Safety, Urban & Community Affairs, Zoos/Aquariums
Education: Arts/Humanities Education, Colleges & Universities, Economic Education, Education Associations, Education Funds, Elementary Education (Private), Elementary Education (Public), Engineering/Technological Education, Education-General, Minority Education, Preschool Education, Private Education (Precollege), Public Education (Precollege), Religious Education, Science/Mathematics Education, Special Education, Student Aid, Vocational & Technical Education
Environment: Energy, Environment-General, Resource Conservation, Wildlife Protection
Health: Cancer, Children's Health/Hospitals, Clinics/Medical Centers, Emergency/Ambulance Services, Eyes/Blindness, Health Funds, Health Organizations, Hospitals, Kidney, Medical Rehabilitation, Medical Research, Public Health, Single-Disease Health Associations, Speech & Hearing
International: International Peace & Security Issues
Religion: Churches, Jewish Causes, Religious Organizations, Religious Welfare
Science: Science Museums
Social Services: Animal Protection, At-Risk Youth,

Camps, Child Welfare, Community Centers, Community Service Organizations, Emergency Relief, Family Planning, Family Services, Food/Clothing Distribution, Homes, People with Disabilities, Recreation & Athletics, Refugee Assistance, Scouts, Senior Services, Substance Abuse, United Funds/United Ways, Veterans, Volunteer Services, YMCA/YWCA/YMHA/YWHA, Youth Organizations

Application Procedures

Initial Contact: Call the foundation to request guidelines.
Application Requirements: Submit a full written proposal.
Deadlines: None.

Foundation Officials

D. L. Garofalo: director
J. E. Humphrey: director
M. O. Johnson: director
M. E. McDonough: director
Keith D. Olson: secretary, treasurer
J. D. Piepel: director
W. Pat Riley: director

Grants Analysis

Disclosure Period: fiscal year ending November 30, 2003
Total Grants: $1,878,000*
Number of Grants: 142
Average Grant: $11,986*
Highest Grant: $100,000
Lowest Grant: $250
Typical Range: $1,000 to $20,000
*Note: Giving excludes United Way. Average grant figure excludes two highest grants ($200,000).

Recent Grants

Note: Grants derived from fiscal 2003 Form 990.
Library-Related
47,500	Bayport Public Library, Bayport, MN

General
100,000	Twin Cities Habitat for Humanity Inc., Minneapolis, MN
100,000	Twin Cities Habitat for Humanity Inc., Minneapolis, MN
100,000	Washington County Association for Senior Citizens, Washington, DC
68,000	Indianhead Scouting/BSA, St. Paul, MN
60,000	American Red Cross, Washington, DC
55,000	Girl Scout Council of Saint Croix Valley, St. Paul, MN
50,000	Courage Center, Minneapolis, MN
50,000	Family Means, Stillwater, MN
50,000	Independent School District 834, Stillwater, MN
50,000	Saint Croix Area United Way, Stillwater, MN

ANDERSEN FOUNDATION

Giving Contact

Mary Gillstrom, Assistant Secretary & Director
Andersen Corp.
100 4th Avenue, North
Bayport, MN 55003-1096
Phone: (651)642-5150
Fax: (651)430-5537

Alternate Contact

Gregory L. Benson, Treasurer, Director
Phone: (651)439-5195
Fax: (651)439-4027

Description

Founded: 1959
EIN: 416020920
Organization Type: General Purpose Foundation

Giving Locations: MN: nationally.
Grant Types: General Support.

Donor Information

Founder: Incorporated in Minnesota in 1959 by the late Fred C. Andersen, who was a director and former president of Andersen Corporation, a producer of wood and vinyl-clad windows and door units. His wife, Katherine B. Andersen, has made several contributions to the foundation.

Financial Summary

Total Giving: $25,098,716 (2003); $24,799,655 (2002); $22,175,600 (2001)
Giving Analysis: Giving for 2003 includes: foundation grants to United Way ($35,000)
Assets: $551,654,682 (2003); $463,698,178 (2002); $440,540,979 (2001)

Typical Recipients

Arts & Humanities: Arts Centers, Arts Funds, Arts Institutes, Historic Preservation, Libraries, Museums/Galleries, Music, Opera, Performing Arts, Public Broadcasting, Theater
Civic & Public Affairs: Botanical Gardens/Parks, Economic Development, Civic & Public Affairs-General, Housing, Minority Business, Municipalities/Towns, Professional & Trade Associations, Public Policy, Safety, Urban & Community Affairs, Zoos/Aquariums
Education: Arts/Humanities Education, Colleges & Universities, Community & Junior Colleges, Education Funds, Elementary Education (Private), Faculty Development, Education-General, Minority Education, Private Education (Precollege), Public Education (Precollege), Religious Education, Science/Mathematics Education, Secondary Education (Public), Special Education, Student Aid
Environment: Air/Water Quality
Health: Cancer, Children's Health/Hospitals, Clinics/Medical Centers, Emergency/Ambulance Services, Eyes/Blindness, Health Funds, Health Organizations, Heart, Hospices, Hospitals, Kidney, Medical Research, Mental Health, Research/Studies Institutes, Single-Disease Health Associations
International: Foreign Educational Institutions, Health Care/Hospitals
Religion: Churches, Ministries, Religious Organizations, Religious Welfare, Seminaries
Science: Science Museums
Social Services: Animal Protection, Child Welfare, Community Centers, Community Service Organizations, Domestic Violence, Emergency Relief, Family Services, Food/Clothing Distribution, Homes, People with Disabilities, Recreation & Athletics, Scouts, Senior Services, Social Services-General, Substance Abuse, United Funds/United Ways, Volunteer Services, YMCA/YWCA/YMHA/YWHA, Youth Organizations

Application Procedures

Initial Contact: The foundation has no formal application requirements or procedures. Prospective applicants should send a letter to the foundation.
Application Requirements: The letter should describe the organization and the project for which funds are sought.
Deadlines: None.

Restrictions

Grants are not given to colleges that receive federal aid.

Foundation Officials

Gregory L. Benson: director, treasurer PRIM CORP EMPL president: First State Bank of Bayport.
Mary Gillstrom: assistant secretary, director
George O. Hoel: director
Alan H. Johnson: director, vice president B 1932. PRIM CORP EMPL secretary: Andersen Corp.
Jerold W. Wulf: director, president CORP AFFIL chairman: Dashwood Industries Ltd.; president: R.

Laflamme & Freres Inc.; president, chief executive officer, chairman board of directors: Andersen Corporate.

Grants Analysis

Disclosure Period: calendar year ending 2003
Total Grants: $25,063,716*
Number of Grants: 188
Average Grant: $94,676*
Highest Grant: $2,500,000
Lowest Grant: $2,000
Typical Range: $25,000 to $200,000
*Note: Giving excludes United Way. Average grant figure excludes five highest grants ($7,738,000).

Recent Grants

Note: Grants derived from 2003 Form 990.
General
2,500,000	Croixdale Residence & Apartments, MN
1,608,000	Boy Scouts of America Indianhead Council, St. Paul, MN
1,275,000	Salvation Army, Alexandria, VA
1,230,000	Gillette Childrens Hospital, St. Paul, MN
1,125,000	Childrens Hospitals and Clinics Foundation, St. Paul, MN
512,000	Minnesota Opera, Minneapolis, MN
350,000	American Red Cross, Washington, DC
300,000	Arcola Mills Historic Foundation, Stillwater, MN
254,000	Minnesota Historical Society, St. Paul, MN
250,000	Alice Lloyd College, Pippa Passes, KY

HUGH J. ANDERSEN FOUNDATION

Giving Contact

Brad Kruse, Program Officer
342 Fifth Ave. N.
Bayport, MN 55003-0204
Phone: (651)439-1557
Fax: (651)439-9480
E-mail: hjafdn@srinc.biz
Web: http://www.scenicriver.org/hja/index.html

Description

Founded: 1962
EIN: 416020914
Organization Type: Family Foundation
Giving Locations: MN: St. Paul (secondary focus), St. Croix Valley St. Croix Valley also covers WI; WI: Pierce County, Polk County, St. Croix County
Grant Types: Capital, General Support, Operating Expenses, Project.

Donor Information

Founder: The foundation was established in 1962. Although the foundation began as "a general charitable fund, its resources are now focused primarily on the geographic area surrounding Bayport, Minnesota and western Wisconsin."

Financial Summary

Total Giving: $2,610,162 (fiscal year ending February 28, 2003); $2,076,024 (fiscal 2002); $2,050,889 (fiscal 2001)
Giving Analysis: Giving for fiscal 2003 includes: foundation grants to United Way ($21,000); fiscal 2001: foundation grants to United Way ($68,300)
Assets: $65,233,103 (fiscal 2003); $47,771,866 (fiscal 2002); $49,467,715 (fiscal 2001)
Gifts Received: $805,566 (fiscal 1995)

Typical Recipients

Arts & Humanities: Arts Centers, Arts Institutes, Arts Outreach, Film & Video, Arts & Humanities-General, Historic Preservation, History & Archaeology, Libraries, Museums/Galleries, Performing Arts, Public Broadcasting, Theater
Civic & Public Affairs: Business/Free Enterprise, Community Foundations, Economic Development, Employment/Job Training, Civic & Public Affairs-General, Hispanic Affairs, Housing, Municipalities/Towns, Native American Affairs, Nonprofit Management, Professional & Trade Associations, Public Policy, Safety, Urban & Community Affairs, Women's Affairs, Zoos/Aquariums
Education: Arts/Humanities Education, Colleges & Universities, Education Funds, Elementary Education (Private), Elementary Education (Public), Environmental Education, Faculty Development, Education-General, Health & Physical Education, Literacy, Private Education (Precollege), Public Education (Precollege), Religious Education, Science/Mathematics Education, Social Sciences Education, Special Education, Student Aid, Vocational & Technical Education
Environment: Environment-General, Wildlife Protection
Health: AIDS/HIV, Cancer, Children's Health/Hospitals, Clinics/Medical Centers, Diabetes, Emergency/Ambulance Services, Health Organizations, Hospitals, Medical Rehabilitation, Medical Research, Mental Health, Preventive Medicine/Wellness Organizations, Single-Disease Health Associations
International: International Relief Efforts, Missionary/Religious Activities
Religion: Churches, Ministries, Religious Organizations, Religious Welfare, Seminaries
Science: Science Museums
Social Services: Child Welfare, Community Service Organizations, Counseling, Day Care, Domestic Violence, Emergency Relief, Family Planning, Family Services, Food/Clothing Distribution, Homes, People with Disabilities, Recreation & Athletics, Scouts, Senior Services, Sexual Abuse, Social Services-General, Substance Abuse, United Funds/United Ways, Volunteer Services, YMCA/YWCA/YMHA/YWHA, Youth Organizations

Application Procedures

Initial Contact: Prospective applicants should contact the foundation to request guidelines, questionnaire, and a grant proposal checklist. Letters of inquiry are also welcomed by the foundation.
Application Requirements: Applicants must supply the following material: a completed questionnaire; copy of a recent Section 501(c)(3) tax determination letter; copy of the most recent IRS Form 990 or audit; copy of the organization's current budget and project budget; listing of past, current, and pending support; brief history of the organization; description of mission and programs; description of results achieved by organization; detailed project description if special funding is sought; summary of qualifications of key staff; and a list of board members and their affiliations. The materials should be unbound. Proposals should be limited to 10 pages excluding attachments.
Deadlines: The foundation reports that deadlines are March 15, June 15, September 15, and November 15.
Review Process: Grant requests are administered by Scenic River, Inc., Stillwater, MN, and all grant decisions are made by the foundation's board of directors.
Decision Notification: Applicants will be notified within four week of the deadline. Final decisions will be mailed within 2-3 weeks of board meeting.
Notes: Applications faxed will not be considered. The foundation requests that grant applicants do not send videos.

Restrictions

The foundation only responds to personalized requests, not to mass appeals or generic solicitations. The foundation stresses that it is conscious of the environment and does not want proposals to be bound or placed in folders or other casings.

The foundation reports that it does not make loans and does not provide grants or scholarships to individuals. It does not provide grants for lobbying activities, fund-raising dinners and events, or travel. The foundation does not generally consider the following types of organizations and programs for funding: agencies/divisions/councils/programs that have counterparts in St. Paul or the St. Croix Valley; athletic teams; business/economics education; child care centers; civic action groups; immigration/refugee issues and programs; independent media productions; political/voter education; private schools; and religious institutions. The foundation will not generally fund the entire budget for a project, but prefers to be part of an effort that is supported by a number of sources. Major endowment and capital requests are given a low priority.

Additional Information

The foundation accepts the Minnesota Common Grant Application Form.
Publications: Annual Report; Application Guidelines; Application Form; Grant Proposal Checklist

Foundation Officials

Christine E. Andersen: vice president CORP AFFIL director: Andersen Corp.
Sarah J. Andersen: president PRIM CORP EMPL chairman board: Andersen Corp. CORP AFFIL director: Andersen Corp.
Lisa W. Copeland: director
William H. Rubenstein: secretary, treasurer
Stephen S. Wolfson: director

Grants Analysis

Disclosure Period: fiscal year ending February 28, 2003
Total Grants: $2,589,162*
Number of Grants: 213
Average Grant: $10,375*
Highest Grant: $200,000
Lowest Grant: $500
Typical Range: $1,000 to $20,000
***Note:** Giving excludes United Way. Average grant figure excludes two highest grants ($400,000).

Recent Grants

Note: Grants derived from fiscal 2004 Form 990.

Library-Related
75,000	City of Stillwater Public Library, Stillwater, MN -- towards capital campaign

General
200,000	Croxidale, Bayport, MN -- towards capital campaign
200,000	Twin Cities Habitat for Humanity, Minneapolis, MN -- towards Double the Homes and Double the Hope Campaign
125,000	Family Means, Stillwater, MN -- towards capital campaign
100,000	Guthrie Theatre Foundation, Minneapolis, MN -- towards capital campaign
100,000	Neighborhood House, St. Paul, MN -- towards capital campaign
70,000	National Youth Leadership Council, St. Paul, MN -- towards Minnesota youth foundation
59,675	Community Volunteer Service and Senior Centers, Stillwater, MN -- towards Bayport senior center
50,000	Como Zoo and Conservatory Society, St. Paul, MN -- towards capital campaign
50,000	Courage Center, Golden Valley, MN -- towards "imagine the Possibilities" a campaign for courage
50,000	Ronald McDonald House Charities, Minneapolis, MN -- towards capital support

JOHN W. ANDERSON FOUNDATION

Giving Contact
William N. Vinovich, Vice Chairman
402 Wall Street
Valparaiso, IN 46383
Phone: (219)462-4611

Description
Founded: 1967
EIN: 356070695
Organization Type: General Purpose Foundation
Giving Locations: IL: funds some organizations in Northeastern Illinois; IN
Grant Types: Capital, General Support, Operating Expenses, Research.

Donor Information
Founder: Established in Indiana in 1967 with funds donated by the late John W. Anderson, an inventor and president of Anderson Company, a manufacturer of automobile accessories.

Financial Summary
Total Giving: $8,212,301 (2003); $9,234,410 (2002); $10,100,000 (2001 approx)
Giving Analysis: Giving for 2003 includes: foundation grants to United Way ($550,000); 2002: foundation scholarships ($94,400) foundation grants to United Way ($600,000)
Assets: $179,452,019 (2003); $164,163,971 (2002); $205,494,000 (2001 approx)

Typical Recipients
Arts & Humanities: History & Archaeology, Libraries, Opera, Public Broadcasting
Civic & Public Affairs: Community Foundations, Economic Development, Employment/Job Training, Civic & Public Affairs-General, Housing, Law & Justice, Legal Aid, Municipalities/Towns, Philanthropic Organizations, Public Policy, Urban & Community Affairs
Education: Business-School Partnerships, Colleges & Universities, Continuing Education, Economic Education, Education Associations, Education Funds, Engineering/Technological Education, Education-General, Legal Education, Medical Education, Minority Education, Preschool Education, Private Education (Precollege), Religious Education, Special Education, Student Aid, Vocational & Technical Education
Health: Cancer, Children's Health/Hospitals, Clinics/Medical Centers, Emergency/Ambulance Services, Health Organizations, Heart, Hospices, Medical Rehabilitation, Mental Health, Nursing Services, Public Health, Research/Studies Institutes, Single-Disease Health Associations
Religion: Churches, Dioceses, Religion-General, Jewish Causes, Missionary Activities (Domestic), Religious Organizations, Religious Welfare
Science: Science Museums
Social Services: At-Risk Youth, Child Welfare, Community Service Organizations, Counseling, Delinquency & Criminal Rehabilitation, Domestic Violence, Emergency Relief, Family Planning, Family Services, Food/Clothing Distribution, Homes, People with Disabilities, Scouts, United Funds/United Ways, YMCA/YWCA/YMHA/YWHA, Youth Organizations

Application Procedures
Initial Contact: Submit an application.
Application Requirements: Proposals should include the organization's purpose; amount requested; planned use for the grant; list of officers and board of directors; current financial statement and budget (audit and annual report, if available); and proof of tax-exempt status.
Deadlines: None.
Review Process: Grants are awarded in February, April, June, August, October, and December. To be considered at a specific meeting, an application must be received by the 20th day of the month preceding the meeting.
Decision Notification: Applicants will be advised of the status of their requests in writing approximately two to four weeks after the meeting of the Trustees.
Notes: Applications will not be accepted by fax. Applicants should not call regarding the status of their application.

Restrictions
No grants are made to individuals, businesses, for fund raising events advertising, start-up costs, endowment funds, deficit financing, or loans. Applicants must be public charities classified as 501 (c)(3) nonprofits.

Additional Information
Recipients of grants must acknowledge receipt of grants within 30 days.
Organizations may submit an application once in a twelve-month period.
Grants are generally limited to organizations which have been in existence for at least two years, demonstrated service to their community, and received public support. Requests from outside northwest Indiana must state how program or services will benefit northwest Indiana and its residents. Indiana and its residents. Indiana and its residents. Indiana and its residents. Indiana and its residents.
Publications: Brochure; Guidelines

Foundation Officials
Charles W. Conover: trustee
William L. Staehle: trustee
William N. Vinovich: vice chairman, trustee
Bruce W. Wargo: secretary, treasurer B East Chicago, IN 1938. PRIM CORP EMPL chief financial officer: Nyloncraft.
Wilfred G. Wilkins: chairman, trustee

Grants Analysis
Disclosure Period: calendar year ending 2003
Total Grants: $7,662,301*
Number of Grants: 280
Average Grant: $17,027*
Highest Grant: $1,910,776
Lowest Grant: $500
Typical Range: $5,000 to $50,000
***Note:** Giving excludes United Way. Average grant figure excludes two highest grants ($2,928,726).

Recent Grants
Note: Grants derived from 2003 Form 990.

General
1,910,776	Boys & Girls Clubs of Northwest Indiana Inc., Gary, IN
1,017,950	Boys & Girls Clubs of Porter County Inc., Valparaiso, IN
450,000	Lake Area United Way Inc., Griffith, IN
225,000	Purdue University, West Lafayette, IN
200,000	Independent Colleges of Indiana Foundation, Indianapolis, IN
150,000	Cerebral Palsy of Northwest Indiana Inc., Hobart, IN
150,000	Indiana University Foundation, Bloomington, IN
150,000	Purdue University Calumet, Hammond, IN
125,000	Indiana University Northwest, Gary, IN
120,000	Northwest Indiana Public Broadcasting Inc., Merrillville, IN

L. P. AND TERESA ANDERSON FOUNDATION

Giving Contact

Sandra K. Anderson, President
L. P. and Teresa Anderson Foundation
PO Box 190
Miles City, MT 59301-0190
Phone: (406)232-3920

Description

Founded: 1993
EIN: 810479060
Organization Type: Private Foundation
Grant Types: General Support, Scholarship.

Financial Summary

Total Giving: $592,493 (fiscal year ending June 30, 2004); $52,950 (fiscal 2001)
Giving Analysis: Giving for fiscal 2001 includes: foundation scholarships ($2,000)
Assets: $565,065 (fiscal 2004); $1,239,268 (fiscal 2001)
Gifts Received: $500,000 (fiscal 1994); $500,000 (fiscal 1993). Note: In fiscal 1994, contributions were received from L. P. Anderson.

Typical Recipients

Arts & Humanities: Arts Centers, History & Archaeology, Libraries
Civic & Public Affairs: Economic Development, Civic & Public Affairs-General, Housing, Municipalities/Towns, Parades/Festivals, Philanthropic Organizations
Education: Agricultural Education, Community & Junior Colleges, Education-General, Private Education (Precollege), Science/Mathematics Education
Health: Cancer, Children's Health/Hospitals
Religion: Religious Organizations, Religious Welfare
Social Services: At-Risk Youth, Big Brothers/Big Sisters, Child Welfare, Community Service Organizations, Domestic Violence, Food/Clothing Distribution, Recreation & Athletics, Scouts, Senior Services, Social Services-General, Substance Abuse, Volunteer Services

Application Procedures

Initial Contact: Send a brief letter of inquiry.
Application Requirements: Include a description of organization, amount requested, purpose of funds sought, recently audited financial statement, and proof of tax-exempt status.
Deadlines: March 1 and September 1.

Restrictions

Preference is given to Miles City and Custer County, MT.

Foundation Officials

Sandra K. Anderson: president

Grants Analysis

Disclosure Period: fiscal year ending June 30, 2004
Total Grants: $592,493
Number of Grants: 6
Highest Grant: $576,493
Lowest Grant: $500
Typical Range: $3,000 to $5,000

Recent Grants

Note: Grants derived from fiscal 2004 Form 990.
General

576,493	LP and Teresa Anderson Family Fund, Helena, MT
5,000	Livingston Center for Art and Culture, Livingston, MT -- for new special project documentary film
5,000	Parents Let's Unite for Kids, Billings, MT -- for expansion to Custer County
3,000	County of Custer, Miles City, MT -- for new program family treatment court
2,500	Miles City Area Economic Development Council, Miles City, MT
500	Central Montana Youth Mentoring Program, Lewistown, MT

M. D. ANDERSON FOUNDATION

Giving Contact

Toloria Allen, Grants Administrator
PO Box 2558
Houston, TX 77252-8037
Phone: (713)216-5348
Fax: (713)216-2119

Description

Founded: 1936
EIN: 746035669
Organization Type: General Purpose Foundation
Giving Locations: TX: Harris County, Houston and metropolitan area
Grant Types: Capital, General Support, Project, Research.

Donor Information

Founder: Established in 1936 to institutionalize the philanthropy of Monroe D. Anderson, a founder of Anderson, Clayton & Co., Houston cotton merchants. Mr. Anderson, who died in 1939, intended the foundation to continue to reflect his interests after his death, although he gave the trustees wide latitude in the choice of funding recipients.

Financial Summary

Total Giving: $6,128,677 (2002)
Assets: $123,103,750 (2002)
Gifts Received: $18,050 (1992)

Typical Recipients

Arts & Humanities: Ballet, History & Archaeology, Libraries, Museums/Galleries, Music, Opera, Performing Arts, Theater
Civic & Public Affairs: Botanical Gardens/Parks, Community Foundations, Economic Development, Economic Policy, Employment/Job Training, Civic & Public Affairs-General, Hispanic Affairs, Housing, Law & Justice, Legal Aid, Minority Business, Urban & Community Affairs, Women's Affairs, Zoos/Aquariums
Education: Business Education, Colleges & Universities, Education Associations, Education Funds, Education Reform, Elementary Education (Private), Elementary Education (Public), Faculty Development, Education-General, International Exchange, Legal Education, Literacy, Medical Education, Minority Education, Private Education (Precollege), Public Education (Precollege), Religious Education, Science/Mathematics Education, Secondary Education (Private), Social Sciences Education, Special Education, Student Aid, Vocational & Technical Education
Health: Adolescent Health Issues, Cancer, Children's Health/Hospitals, Clinics/Medical Centers, Emergency/Ambulance Services, Eyes/Blindness, Health-General, Geriatric Health, Health Policy/Cost Containment, Health Funds, Health Organizations, Heart, Hospices, Hospitals, Hospitals (University Affiliated), Medical Rehabilitation, Medical Research, Mental Health, Nursing Services, Prenatal Health Issues, Public Health, Research/Studies Institutes, Single-Disease Health Associations, Transplant Networks/Donor Banks
International: Foreign Educational Institutions
Religion: Bible Study/Translation, Churches, Dioceses, Jewish Causes, Religious Welfare, Social/Policy Issues
Science: Science Museums, Scientific Centers & Institutes
Social Services: Animal Protection, At-Risk Youth, Camps, Child Abuse, Child Welfare, Community Centers, Community Service Organizations, Delinquency & Criminal Rehabilitation, Emergency Relief, Family Planning, Family Services, Homes, People with Disabilities, Recreation & Athletics, Scouts, Senior Services, Shelters/Homelessness, Substance Abuse, YMCA/YWCA/YMHA/YWHA, Youth Organizations

Application Procedures

Initial Contact: Applicants should send a brief letter describing the proposed project, along with an original and four copies of the full proposal. If applying for a matching grant, indicate other sources of funding.
Application Requirements: With the cover letter, include the amount needed and proof of tax-exempt status. If the project falls within the foundation's scope of interest, further information may be requested.
Deadlines: None. Board meetings are held on the third Tuesday of each month. Applications should be received a month prior to the meeting to be considered.
Review Process: The foundation reports that it responds to all proposals by letter detailing whether the application has been approved or denied.

Additional Information

On January 1, 2003, the M.D. Anderson Foundation (EIN:74-6035699) was converted form a trust under Texas state law into a nonprofit corporation (EIN:30-0129656). The new corporation has inherited the assets, carryovers, filing requirements, and distribution requirements of the foundation. The entity's name remains unchanged, and the operations of the foundation have continued uninterrupted.

Foundation Officials

Uriel E. Dutton: trustee B Hamilton, TX 1930. ED Howard Payne University (1946-1948); Baylor University LLB (1951). PRIM CORP EMPL partner: Fulbright & Jaworski. CORP AFFIL director: Energy Ventures; director: Grey Wolf Drilling. NONPR AFFIL member: Texas Bar Association; member: Texas Bar Foundation; member: Houston Bar Association; member: Phi Delta Phi; member: American Bar Association; member: American Bar Foundation.
Gibson Gayle, Jr.: president, trustee B Waco, TX 1926. ED Baylor University LLB (1950); Baylor University AB (1950). CORP AFFIL director: Daniel Industries Inc. NONPR AFFIL fellow: Texas Bar Foundation; adj professor: University Texas Law School; member: Texas Bar Association; member: Houston Chamber of Commerce; board governors: Leon Jaworski Foundation; trustee: Baylor College Medicine; member: Houston Bar Association; fellow: American Bar Foundation; member: American Bar Association.
Charles W. Hall: trustee B Dallas, TX 1930. ED University of the South BA (1951); Southern Methodist University JD (1954). PRIM CORP EMPL senior partner, attorney: Fulbright & Jaworski. CORP AFFIL assistant vice chairman: Friedman Industries Inc. NONPR AFFIL member: State Bar Texas; director: Texas Medical Center; trustee: Institute Religion; member: International Bar Association; member: Dallas Bar Association; member: Houston Bar Association; member: American College Tax Counsel; member: American Law Institute; member, chairman national conf lawyers & CPAs: American Bar Association; fellow: American Bar Foundation. CLUB AFFIL River Oaks Country Club; Metro Club; member: Petroleum Club; Coronado Club; Houston City Club.
Ann Trotter: secretary-treasurer
Jack T. Trotter: vice president, trustee CORP AFFIL director: First Interstate Bank Texas.

Grants Analysis

Disclosure Period: calendar year ending 2002
Total Grants: $6,128,677

Number of Grants: 149
Average Grant: $41,132
Highest Grant: $200,000
Typical Range: $5,000 to $50,000

Recent Grants

Note: Grants derived from 2002 Form 990.
General

200,000	Pyramid Community -- for comprehensive wellness center
200,000	Rice University, Houston, TX -- to history building renovation campaign
200,000	Southwestern Legal Foundation, Plano, TX -- for new headquarters building
200,000	University of Houston, Houston, TX -- for expansion of library
200,000	University of Texas, Richardson, TX -- to nursing and bio-medical science building
150,000	University of Texas School of Law, TX -- for faculty exchange program
135,000	Houston Grand Opera Association, Houston, TX
135,000	Houston Symphony Society, Houston, TX
100,000	Annunciation Orthodox School, Houston, TX -- to construction of middle school wing
100,000	Baylor College of Medicine, Houston, TX -- for experimental therapeutics center

ANDERSON FOUNDATION (NY)

Giving Contact

E. William Whittaker, Treasurer & Trustee
Chemung Canal Trust Co.
c/o Chemung Canal Trust Co.
PO Box 1522
Elmira, NY 14902
Phone: (607)737-3711

Description

Founded: 1960
EIN: 166024689
Organization Type: Private Foundation
Giving Locations: NY: Elmira
Grant Types: General Support, Operating Expenses, Scholarship.

Donor Information

Founder: Jane G. Anderson, the late Douglas G. Anderson

Financial Summary

Total Giving: $145,993 (fiscal year ending April 30, 2004); $206,240 (fiscal 2001)
Giving Analysis: Giving for fiscal 2001 includes: foundation grants to United Way ($13,650)
Assets: $3,194,351 (fiscal 2004); $3,884,217 (fiscal 2001)

Typical Recipients

Arts & Humanities: Community Arts, Historic Preservation, History & Archaeology, Libraries, Museums/Galleries, Music, Opera, Performing Arts, Public Broadcasting
Civic & Public Affairs: Community Foundations, Employment/Job Training, Housing, Urban & Community Affairs
Education: Arts/Humanities Education, Business Education, Colleges & Universities, Economic Education, Gifted & Talented Programs, Literacy, Preschool Education
Environment: Environment-General, Resource Conservation
Health: Clinics/Medical Centers, Heart, Hospitals, Long-Term Care, Multiple Sclerosis, Nursing Services

Religion: Religious Welfare
Social Services: Animal Protection, Camps, Child Welfare, Community Centers, Community Service Organizations, Food/Clothing Distribution, People with Disabilities, Recreation & Athletics, Senior Services, Substance Abuse, United Funds/United Ways, Volunteer Services, YMCA/YWCA/YMHA/YWHA, Youth Organizations

Foundation Officials

Elizabeth T. Dalrymple: trustee
Clover M. Drinkwater: assistant secretary, trustee
Paul Greenlee, Jr.: vice president, trustee
J. Philip Hunter: secretary, trustee
Jane G. Joralemon: president, trustee
Edwin P. Marosek: trustee
Margaret B. Streeter: trustee
E. William Whittaker: treasurer, trustee
Jeanne Whittaker Word: trustee

Grants Analysis

Disclosure Period: fiscal year ending April 30, 2004
Total Grants: $145,993
Number of Grants: 26
Average Grant: $5,615
Highest Grant: $13,073
Lowest Grant: $500
Typical Range: $1,000 to $10,000

Recent Grants

Note: Grants derived from fiscal 2001 Form 990.
Library-Related

20,000	Steele Memorial Library, Elmira, NY -- A. Marshall Lowman and Charles A. Winding Material Fund

General

20,000	Community Foundation of the Elmira-Corning Area, Elmira, NY -- S. Roberts Rose Youth Fund Endowment
15,000	Arnot Ogden Medical Center Foundation, Elmira, NY -- CT simulation and planning system package
15,000	Glove House, Elmira, NY -- renovation and consolidation of administrative offices
15,000	St. Joseph's Hospital, Elmira, NY -- bed and mattresses
13,650	United Way of the Southern Tier, Elmira, NY
13,000	Clemens Center for Performing Arts, Elmira, NY -- operating expenses
12,000	Peace by Piece, Inc., Elmira, NY -- operating expense
10,000	Community Foundation of the Elmira-Corning Area, Elmira, NY -- Kenneth A. Tifft/Robert T. Jones Field Experience Fund
10,000	Spencer Van Etten Community Services Corporation, Van Etten, NY -- medical center
10,000	Tanglewood Community Nature Center, Elmira, NY -- capital campaign

ANDERSONS INC.

Company Headquarters

480 W. Dussel Dr.
Maumee, OH 43537
Web: http://www.andersonsinc.com

Company Description

Founded: 1947
Ticker: ANDE
Exchange: NASDAQ
Former Name: The Andersons.
Revenue: US$984.6 million (2001)
Employees: 2888 (2003)
SIC(s): 0119 Cash Grains Nec, 5153 Grain & Field

Beans, 5191 Farm Supplies, 7389 Business Services Nec.

Operating Locations

Andersons Inc. (IN--Poneto; MI--Albion; OH--Bryan, Maumee, Toledo)

Anderson Foundation

Giving Contact

Fredi Heywood, Foundation Services Administrator
608 Madison Avenue, Suite 1540
Toledo, OH 43604
Phone: (419)243-1706

Description

EIN: 346528868
Organization Type: Corporate Foundation
Giving Locations: headquarters and operating communities, including plant locations.
Grant Types: Capital, Employee Matching Gifts, General Support, Project, Scholarship, Seed Money.
Note: Employee matching gift ratio: 1 to 1.

Financial Summary

Total Giving: $392,317 (2003); $348,500 (2002); $286,737 (2001). Note: Contributes through corporate direct giving program and foundation.
Giving Analysis: Giving for 2002 includes: foundation grants to United Way ($116,650); 2001: foundation grants to United Way ($158,052)
Assets: $4,308,569 (2003); $3,959,505 (2002); $4,559,996 (2001)
Gifts Received: $305,000 (2002); $25,000 (2001); $50 (2000). Note: Contributions were received from The Andersons, Inc.

Typical Recipients

Arts & Humanities: Arts Associations & Councils, Arts Centers, Arts & Humanities-General, Historic Preservation, History & Archaeology, Libraries, Museums/Galleries, Music, Opera, Performing Arts, Public Broadcasting, Theater
Civic & Public Affairs: African American Affairs, Botanical Gardens/Parks, Business/Free Enterprise, Clubs, Community Foundations, Economic Development, Economic Policy, Employment/Job Training, Civic & Public Affairs-General, Housing, Municipalities/Towns, Parades/Festivals, Philanthropic Organizations, Public Policy, Rural Affairs, Safety, Urban & Community Affairs, Zoos/Aquariums
Education: Afterschool/Enrichment Programs, Agricultural Education, Business Education, Colleges & Universities, Community & Junior Colleges, Education Associations, Education Funds, Education Reform, Education-General, Literacy, Minority Education, Private Education (Precollege), Public Education (Precollege), Science/Mathematics Education, Secondary Education (Private), Secondary Education (Public), Student Aid, Vocational & Technical Education
Environment: Environment-General, Protection, Resource Conservation, Wildlife Protection
Health: Clinics/Medical Centers, Diabetes, Emergency/Ambulance Services, Eyes/Blindness, Health Organizations, Hospices, Hospitals, Medical Research, Mental Health, Nursing Services, Preventive Medicine/Wellness Organizations, Single-Disease Health Associations
Religion: Churches, Dioceses, Jewish Causes, Ministries, Religious Organizations, Religious Welfare
Science: Scientific Centers & Institutes, Scientific Organizations, Scientific Research
Social Services: Animal Protection, At-Risk Youth, Camps, Child Welfare, Community Centers, Community Service Organizations, Day Care, Emergency Relief, Family Services, Food/Clothing Distribution, People with Disabilities, Recreation & Athletics, Refugee Assistance, Scouts, Senior Services, Shelters/

Homelessness, Social Services-General, United Funds/United Ways, YMCA/YWCA/YMHA/YWHA, Youth Organizations

Application Procedures

Initial Contact: Send written application, of not more than five pages.
Application Requirements: Include amount requested; purpose of funds sought; description of the organization, with organization's purpose and objectives; need the project intends to address; the need the project will address, and geographical area and population to be served; timetable for the project; name(s) and qualifications of the person who will administer the grant; telephone number of an appropriate contact person; how the success of the project will be evaluated; recently audited financial statements; proof of tax-exempt status; organizational budget for the current year showing anticipated expenses and income by sources (if the request is for a capital drive or specific project, also include a budget showing expenses and income for the drive/project); list of officers and directors; and list of major donors within the past 12 months.
Deadlines: At least three weeks before quarterly board meetings, which are in March, June, September, and December.

Restrictions

Does not support individuals, endowment funds, church building or operating funds, or building or operating funds for elementary schools.
The foundation generally does not serve as major or sole funder of projects.

Additional Information

The foundation's major donor is The Andersons, Inc., but the foundation reports that its activities are separate. The company does offer a very limited amount of direct giving in its headquarters area.

Corporate Officials

Thomas Harold Anderson: chairman, director B Toledo, OH 1924. ED Michigan State University BS (1966). PRIM CORP EMPL director: The Andersons Inc. ADD NONPR EMPL president, director: International Center Preservation Wild Animals. CLUB AFFIL Rotary Club.

Foundation Officials

Charles W. Anderson: trustee B Detroit, MI 1931. ED Michigan School of Mines (1953). PRIM CORP EMPL chairman, president: Anderson Tool Sales Inc. CORP AFFIL chairman: ATD Tools Corp. NONPR AFFIL member: Fraternal Order Eagles.
Jeffrey W. Anderson: trustee
Matthew C. Anderson: trustee
Richard M. Anderson: trustee
Richard P. Anderson: trustee
Thomas Harold Anderson: chairman, trustee (see above)
Dale W. Fallat: trustee
John P. Kraus: trustee
Brian F. Peterson: vice president, treasurer

Grants Analysis

Disclosure Period: calendar year ending 2003
Total Grants: $257,317*
Number of Grants: 81
Average Grant: $2,175*
Highest Grant: $83,333
Lowest Grant: $100
Typical Range: $500 to $5,000
*Note: Giving excludes United Way. Average grant figure excludes highest grant.

Recent Grants

Note: Grants derived from 2003 Form 990.
Library-Related
2,000	Evergreen Community Library, Metamora, OH

General
83,333	Catholic Diocese of Toledo, Toledo, OH
75,000	United Way of Greater Toledo, Toledo, OH
25,000	Notre Dame Academy, Toledo, OH
16,667	Central Catholic High School, Toledo, OH
16,667	St Francis De Sales High School, Toledo, OH
15,000	Toledo Symphony Orchestra, Toledo, OH
13,400	United Way of Franklin County, Columbus, OH
10,000	Adopt America Network, Toledo, OH
10,000	Ohio Historical Society, Columbus, OH
9,250	United Way of Cass County, Logansport, IN

FRANK G. ANDRES CHARITABLE TRUST

Giving Contact

David Myer, Trustee
Frank G. Andres Charitable Trust
c/o First Bank of Tomah
PO Box 753
Tomah, WI 54660
Phone: (608)372-2131

Description

EIN: 510172405
Organization Type: Private Foundation
Giving Locations: WI: Tomah
Grant Types: General Support.

Financial Summary

Total Giving: $82,782 (fiscal year ending June 30, 2004); $113,846 (fiscal 2001)
Assets: $2,823,841 (fiscal 2004); $2,973,381 (fiscal 2001)

Typical Recipients

Arts & Humanities: History & Archaeology, Libraries, Music
Civic & Public Affairs: Botanical Gardens/Parks, Clubs, Employment/Job Training, Civic & Public Affairs-General, Municipalities/Towns, Rural Affairs, Safety, Urban & Community Affairs
Education: Education Funds, Education-General, Public Education (Precollege), Science/Mathematics Education, Vocational & Technical Education
Environment: Environment-General
Health: Emergency/Ambulance Services, Hospices, Hospitals
Social Services: Child Welfare, Community Service Organizations, Recreation & Athletics, Senior Services, Shelters/Homelessness, Substance Abuse, Youth Organizations

Application Procedures

Initial Contact: Application form required.
Deadlines: May15.

Foundation Officials

Jay Charmichael: trustee
Roxana O'Connor: trustee, treasurer
Raymond E. Paulis: trustee

Grants Analysis

Disclosure Period: fiscal year ending June 30, 2004
Total Grants: $82,782
Number of Grants: 19
Average Grant: $4,357
Highest Grant: $11,800
Lowest Grant: $500
Typical Range: $1,000 to $8,500

Recent Grants

Note: Grants derived from fiscal 2001 Form 990.

Library-Related
3,660	Tomah Public Library, Tomah, WI -- air conditioning for computer room

General
22,000	Tomah Area School District, Tomah, WI -- portable platforms and staging and defibrillator
15,000	Tomah Memorial Hospital, Tomah, WI -- ultrasound for obstetrics and cart for surgical patients
10,000	Boys and Girls Club
10,000	Tomah Memorial Hospital, Tomah, WI -- hospice touch
9,000	Western Wisconsin Technical College, La Crosse, WI -- for laptop computers for Tomah
5,584	City of Tomah Fire Department, Tomah, WI -- skid unit for brush truck
5,000	City of Tomah Senior Board, Tomah, WI -- to establish center
5,000	Monroe County Agriculture Society -- toward parking lot project
4,000	Tomah Concert Association, Tomah, WI -- to sponsor a concert
3,750	City of Tomah Ambulance Service, Tomah, WI -- purchase portable suction units

ANDREWS FOUNDATION

Giving Contact

Laura Baxter-Heuer, President & Trustee
13111 Shaker Sq., Suite 208
Cleveland, OH 44120
Phone: (216)751-2115

Description

Founded: 1951
EIN: 346515110
Organization Type: Private Foundation
Giving Locations: OH: including northeastern Ohio
Grant Types: Capital, Endowment, General Support.

Donor Information

Founder: the late Mrs. Matthew Andrews

Financial Summary

Total Giving: $532,300 (2003)
Assets: $9,424,508 (2003)

Typical Recipients

Arts & Humanities: Arts Centers, Arts Outreach, Ballet, Community Arts, Arts & Humanities-General, Libraries, Museums/Galleries, Music, Performing Arts, Theater
Civic & Public Affairs: Economic Development, Employment/Job Training, Civic & Public Affairs-General, Law & Justice, Municipalities/Towns, Nonprofit Management, Parades/Festivals, Urban & Community Affairs, Women's Affairs
Education: Arts/Humanities Education, Colleges & Universities, Education Funds, Environmental Education, Faculty Development, Education-General, Medical Education, Minority Education, Private Education (Precollege), Public Education (Precollege), Religious Education, Secondary Education (Private), Secondary Education (Public), Special Education, Student Aid
Health: AIDS/HIV, Cancer, Children's Health/Hospitals, Clinics/Medical Centers, Diabetes, Emergency/Ambulance Services, Health Organizations, Heart, Hospitals (University Affiliated), Medical Rehabilitation, Mental Health, Nursing Services, Research/Studies Institutes, Transplant Networks/Donor Banks
Religion: Ministries, Religious Organizations, Religious Welfare, Seminaries
Science: Science Museums
Social Services: At-Risk Youth, Camps, Child Wel-

fare, Community Service Organizations, Day Care, Delinquency & Criminal Rehabilitation, Domestic Violence, People with Disabilities, Substance Abuse, Veterans, Youth Organizations

Application Procedures
Initial Contact: Send a brief letter of inquiry.
Application Requirements: Include a description of organization, purpose of funds sought, and proof of tax-exempt status.
Deadlines: None.

Foundation Officials
James Howard Dempsey, Jr.: secretary, trustee B Cleveland, OH October 18, 1916. ED Yale University BA (1938); Yale University LLB (1941). PRIM CORP EMPL general partner: Squire, Sanders & Dempsey. NONPR AFFIL member: Ohio Bar Association; trustee: University Hospitals; member: Cleveland Bar Association; member: American Bar Association. CLUB AFFIL Union Club; Pepper Pike Club; Tavern Club; Chagrin Valley Hunt Club; Kirtland Country Club.
Laura Baxter Heuer: president, trustee

Grants Analysis
Disclosure Period: calendar year ending 2003
Total Grants: $532,300
Number of Grants: 21
Average Grant: $25,348
Highest Grant: $55,000
Lowest Grant: $1,500
Typical Range: $10,000 to $50,000

Recent Grants
Note: Grants derived from 2001 Form 990.
General
50,000	University Hospitals, Cleveland, OH
40,000	Ratner School, Lyndhurst, OH
35,000	Desert Rehabilitation Services, Inc., Desert Hot Springs, CA
35,000	Hanna Perkins Center, Cleveland, OH
35,000	Hathaway Brown School, Shaker Heights, OH
35,000	Minority Organ Tissue Transplant Education Program (MOTTEP), Washington, DC
34,000	Julie Billiart School, Cleveland, OH
30,000	Great Lakes Theater Festival, Cleveland, OH
25,000	Free Clinic of Greater Cleveland, Cleveland, OH
25,000	Horizon Activities Center, North Olmsted, OH

ANDREWS MCMEEL UNIVERSAL

Company Headquarters
4520 Main St., Ste. 700
Kansas City, MO 64111
Phone: (816)932-6606
Web: http://www.amuniversal.com

Company Description
Revenue: US$130 million (2001)
Employees: 200 (2001)

Andrews McMeel Universal Foundation

Giving Contact
Kathleen W. Andrews, Vice President & Secretary
4520 Main St., Suite 700
Kansas City, MO 64111

Phone: (816)932-6700
Fax: (816)531-5323
E-mail: kandrews@amuniversal.com

Description
Founded: 1991
EIN: 431570308
Organization Type: Corporate Foundation
Giving Locations: KS; MO, Kansas City metropolitan area: nationally.
Grant Types: General Support.

Donor Information
Founder: Established in 1991 by the United Press Syndicate.

Financial Summary
Total Giving: $288,005 (2003); $301,403 (2002); $309,786 (2001)
Assets: $4,603,488 (2003); $4,360,090 (2002); $4,916,268 (2001)
Gifts Received: $12,937 (2001); $23,357 (2000); $28,717 (1999). Note: In 2001, contributions were received from Starbucks ($11,437) and Kathleen Andrews ($1,500). In 1999, contributions were received from Starbucks.

Typical Recipients
Arts & Humanities: Arts Associations & Councils, Arts Festivals, Arts Institutes, Ballet, Arts & Humanities-General, Libraries, Literary Arts, Museums/Galleries, Music, Opera, Theater
Civic & Public Affairs: Clubs, Ethnic Organizations, Civic & Public Affairs-General, Housing, Philanthropic Organizations, Professional & Trade Associations, Public Policy, Urban & Community Affairs, Women's Affairs, Zoos/Aquariums
Education: Colleges & Universities, Education Funds, Education-General, Gifted & Talented Programs, Journalism/Media Education, Literacy, Private Education (Precollege), Public Education (Precollege), Religious Education, Secondary Education (Private), Secondary Education (Public), Student Aid, Vocational & Technical Education
Health: AIDS/HIV, Cancer, Clinics/Medical Centers, Health Funds, Health Organizations, Kidney, Medical Research, Nursing Services, Prenatal Health Issues, Single-Disease Health Associations
International: Foreign Arts Organizations, Human Rights, International Environmental Issues
Religion: Jewish Causes, Religious Organizations, Religious Welfare, Seminaries
Science: Science Museums
Social Services: Child Welfare, Community Centers, Community Service Organizations, Domestic Violence, Emergency Relief, People with Disabilities, Substance Abuse, United Funds/United Ways, Youth Organizations

Application Procedures
Initial Contact: The foundation has no formal grant application procedure or application form.
Application Requirements: Include information that would support the request.
Deadlines: None.

Foundation Officials
Hugh T. Andrews: director
James C. Andrews: director
Kathleen W. Andrews: vice president, secretary ED College of Notre Dame BS (1959); University of Notre Dame MS (1962). PRIM CORP EMPL chief executive officer: Andrews McMeel Publishing ADD CORP EMPL vice chairman: Andrews McMeel Universal. NONPR AFFIL trustee: Notre Dame Colleges; trustee: University Notre Dame; member: Newspaper Features Council; director: NCCJ; member: Newspaper Cartoonists Society; member: Catholic Charities; member: Malta Federation Association; trustee: Avila College; member: American Booksellers Association; trustee: Association of Governing Boards of Colleges and Universities.

Elena Fallon: director
Thomas I. Gill: assistant secretary
John T. Howard: director
Ole C. Jenson: director
Bridget J. McMeel: director
John Paul McMeel: president, treasurer B South Bend, IN 1936. ED University of Notre Dame BS (1957). PRIM CORP EMPL chairman: Andrews McMeel Publishing. CORP AFFIL director: Universal/Belo Productions; president: Universal Press Syndicate. NONPR AFFIL member: Sovereign Military Order Malta; member advisory council: University Notre Dame Institute Church Life; director: Newspaper Features Council; member: International Press Institute; chairman, director: National Catholic Reporter; co-founder: Christmas October Kansas City; member: Fed Association USA; director: Christmas April USA.
Susan S. McMeel: director
Suzanne E. McMeel Glynn: director
Maureen McMeel Jackoboice: director
Dr. Jeffrey F. Rayport: director
Eugene Leslie Roberts, Jr.: director B Goldsboro, NC 1932. ED Mars Hill Junior College AA (1950-1952); University of North Carolina BA (1952-1954); Colby College LLD (1989). PRIM CORP EMPL managing editor: New York Times Co. NONPR AFFIL member: North Caroliana Society; member: Society Professional Journalists; member: Cosmos Club; board advisors: Center Foreign Journalists; vice chairman: Commission to Protect Journalists; member: American Society Newspaper Editors; director: Arthur Burns Fellowship; member: American Antiquarian Society; international board: American Commission International Press Institute.
Thomas N. Thornton: director

Grants Analysis
Disclosure Period: calendar year ending 2003
Total Grants: $273,972*
Number of Grants: 153
Average Grant: $1,333*
Highest Grant: $71,432
Lowest Grant: $50
Typical Range: $50 to $10,000
*Note: Giving excludes matching gifts. Average grant figure excludes highest grant.

Recent Grants
Note: Grants derived from 2003 Form 990.
Library-Related
3,000	Harry S. Truman Library Institute, Independence, MO

General
71,432	University of Notre Dame, Notre Dame, IN
10,000	Christmas in October, Kansas City, MO
10,000	International Press Institute, Allentown, PA
9,500	Cartoon Art Museum, San Francisco, CA
7,500	Donnelly College, Kansas City, KS
7,000	Catholic Charities, Kansas City, KS
6,000	Catholic Charities, Kansas City, MO
6,000	UJA Federation, New York, NY
5,000	Avila University, Kansas City, MO
5,000	Central City School Fund, Kansas City, MO

ANHEUSER-BUSCH COMPANIES INC.

Company Headquarters
St. Louis, MO
Web: http://www.anheuser-busch.com

Company Description
Founded: 1852
Ticker: BUD

Exchange: NYSE
Revenue: US$14.934 billion (2004)
Profit: US$2.24 billion (2004)
Employees: 23316 (2003)
Fortune Rank: 139, per FORTUNE Magazine's list of 500 Largest U.S. Corporations (2004).
SIC(s): 2046 Wet Corn Milling, 2051 Bread, Cake & Related Products, 2082 Malt Beverages, 6719 Holding Companies Nec.

Operating Locations

Anheuser-Busch Companies, Inc. (AR--Jonesboro; CA--Carson, Fairfield, Los Angeles, San Diego, Sylmar, Stockton, Visalia; CO--Denver, Fort Collins, Windsor; FL--Gainesville, Orlando, Tampa, Winter Haven; GA--Cartersville; ID--Idaho Falls; IL--Chicago; LA--New Orleans; MA--Boston; MN--Clearbrook, Moorhead; MO--Arnold, St. Louis; NH--Merrimack; NJ--Newark; NY--Baldwinsville, Newburgh; OH--Aurora, Columbus; OK--Oklahoma City; PA--Langhorne, York; TN--Fayetteville; TX--Houston; VA--Williamsburg; WI--Fort Atkinson, Manitowoc)

Nonmonetary Support

Type: Donated Products
Volunteer Programs: Through the Anheuser-Busch Employee Volunteer Grant Program, the company supports and recognizes its employees who actively volunteer their time and talents to nonprofit organizations by making grants to these organizations for unusual or special projects. An Employee Matching Gifts Program for educational institutions is also offered through the company's charitable foundation.
Note: The company has donated cans of fresh drinking water to victims of natural disasters.

✓ Anheuser-Busch Foundation

Giving Contact

Jayne Nicholson, Specialist, Charitable Contributions
Anheuser-Busch Companies
USBank
PO Box 387, FL-TW-16IT
St. Louis, MO 63166-0587
Phone: (314)418-2168
Fax: (314)577-3251

Alternate Contact

Specialist, Charitable Contributions
Anheuser-Busch Companies
One Busch Place
St. Louis, MO 63118-1852
Phone: (314)577-2453

Description

Founded: 1975
EIN: 510168084
Organization Type: Corporate Foundation
Giving Locations: principally near operating locations and to national organizations.
Grant Types: Capital, Employee Matching Gifts, General Support.

Donor Information

Founder: Anheuser-Busch Co.

Financial Summary

Total Giving: $16,609,421 (2003); $17,576,658 (2002); $19,140,827 (2001). Note: Contributes through corporate direct giving program and foundation.
Assets: $40,311,916 (2003); $28,139,664 (2002); $40,062,047 (2001).
Gifts Received: $20,000,000 (2003); $10,016,918 (2002); $543,000 (2001). Note: In 2003, contributions were received from Anheuser-Busch Companies, Inc.

Typical Recipients

Arts & Humanities: Arts Associations & Councils, Arts Centers, Arts Funds, Community Arts, Film & Video, Historic Preservation, History & Archaeology, Libraries, Museums/Galleries, Music, Performing Arts, Public Broadcasting, Theater
Civic & Public Affairs: African American Affairs, Botanical Gardens/Parks, Civil Rights, Clubs, Community Foundations, Economic Development, Economic Policy, Employment/Job Training, Civic & Public Affairs-General, Hispanic Affairs, Housing, Law & Justice, Public Policy, Rural Affairs, Urban & Community Affairs, Women's Affairs, Zoos/Aquariums
Education: Agricultural Education, Arts/Humanities Education, Business Education, Colleges & Universities, Community & Junior Colleges, Continuing Education, Education Funds, Education Reform, Engineering/Technological Education, Education-General, Health & Physical Education, International Exchange, Legal Education, Literacy, Medical Education, Minority Education, Private Education (Precollege), Public Education (Precollege), Science/Mathematics Education, Secondary Education (Private), Secondary Education (Public), Special Education, Student Aid, Vocational & Technical Education
Environment: Air/Water Quality, Environment-General, Resource Conservation, Wildlife Protection
Health: AIDS/HIV, Alzheimer's Disease, Cancer, Children's Health/Hospitals, Emergency/Ambulance Services, Health Policy/Cost Containment, Health Funds, Health Organizations, Heart, Hospitals, Medical Research, Public Health, Single-Disease Health Associations
International: Foreign Educational Institutions
Religion: Dioceses, Religion-General, Jewish Causes, Religious Organizations, Religious Welfare, Seminaries
Science: Science Museums, Scientific Centers & Institutes, Scientific Organizations, Scientific Research
Social Services: At-Risk Youth, Child Welfare, Community Service Organizations, Counseling, Delinquency & Criminal Rehabilitation, Emergency Relief, Family Services, Food/Clothing Distribution, People with Disabilities, Recreation & Athletics, Scouts, Senior Services, Shelters/Homelessness, Social Services-General, Substance Abuse, United Funds/United Ways, Volunteer Services, YMCA/YWCA/YMHA/YWHA, Youth Organizations

Application Procedures

Initial Contact: Write or call to request guidelines form.
Application Requirements: The guidelines request the official name of your organization, complete mailing address, phone number, brief general a description of organization of organization's purpose and major activities; purpose of funds sought, including the amount requested and total project budget; dates and amounts of any previous grants received from Anheuser-Busch; whether the applicant is a United Way member agency; and whether the organization has a permanent liquor license. The following items should be attached to the proposal: most recent audited financial statement, current operating budget, apartment (or other materials summarizing programs), list of current board of directors and their affiliations, list of current corporate contributors, IRS letter of tax-exempt certification, do not include videos with proposal.
Deadlines: None.
Evaluative Criteria: Program areas focus on education, health care and human services, minorities and youth, cultural enrichment, and environmental protection in communities where Anheuser-Busch and its subsidiaries operate major facilities and where its employees and their families live and work.
Decision Notification: Review takes approximately six to eight weeks.
Notes: The foundation does not accept videos submitted with proposals.

Restrictions

Does not support organizations that are not designated tax-exempt by the IRS, aid to individualss, political candidates or organizations, religious organizations, organizations with limited constituency such as fraternal or social groups, athletic organizations, or operating funds for hospitals.

Additional Information

As the world's largest brewer, Anheuser-Busch works to encourage responsible drinking among adults who choose to drink and to fight alcohol abuse, drunk driving, and underage drinking. Anheuser-Busch is a major supporter of alcohol education efforts on college campuses, including the BACHUS (Boost Alcohol Consciousness Concerning the Health of University Students) peer-education network, the National Collegiate Athletic Association Foundation's "Choices" grant program, "TIPS for the University" program, and National Collegiate Alcohol Awareness Week.

The company's Busch Gardens and Sea World parks care for endangered and threatened species, such as manatees. The Sea World Parks are known for their rescue and rehabilitation programs. The Anheuser-Busch Theme Parks also support "A Pledge and a Promise" environmental awards program. Established in 1993, the program is held in cooperation with national conservation organizations to honor outstanding efforts of school groups that have made positive contributions to the environment. It offers 13 awards totaling $100,000. The company sponsors an innovative urban beautification program, Operation Brightside, in 12 communities where its breweries are located. The program is based on a public/private partnership designed to involve citizens in cleaning up their cities and, more importantly, in keeping them clean.
Publications: Guidelines; Application Form

Corporate Officials

August Adolphus Busch, III: chairman, chief executive officer, director B Saint Louis, MO 1937. ED University of Arizona (1957-1958); Siebel Institute of Technology (1960-1961). PRIM CORP EMPL chairman, president, director: Anheuser-Busch Companies, Inc. ADD CORP EMPL chairman, chief executive officer, director: Anheuser-Busch Inc. CORP AFFIL director: Emerson Electric Co.; director: SBC Community Inc. CLUB AFFIL Log Cabin Club; Saint Louis Country Club.
Patrick T. Stokes: president, chief executive officer, director B 1943. PRIM CORP EMPL vice president, group executive: Anheuser-Busch Companies, Inc. ADD CORP EMPL president: Anheuser-Busch Inc. CORP AFFIL director: Ameren Corp.; director: US Bancorp.

Giving Program Officials

August Adolphus Busch, III: trustee (see above)

Foundation Officials

JoBeth Goode Brown: director B Oakdale, LA 1950. ED Tulane University Newcomb College BA (1972); Washington University JD (1979). ADD CORP EMPL vice president, secretary: Anheuser-Busch Inc. NONPR AFFIL member: Missouri Womens Forum; member: Order Coif; secretary: International Womens Forum; member: Missouri Bar Association; member: American Society of Corporate Secretaries; member: Bar Association Metropolitan Saint Louis; member: American Bar Association. CLUB AFFIL Algonquin Golf Club.
August Adolphus Busch, III: director (see above)
John E. Jacob: director CORP AFFIL director: Coca-Cola Enterprises Inc.; director: Morgan Stanley.

Grants Analysis

Disclosure Period: calendar year ending 2003
Total Grants: $15,615,043*
Number of Grants: 289

Average Grant: $50,747*
Highest Grant: $1,000,000
Lowest Grant: $25
Typical Range: $5,000 to $75,000
Note: Giving excludes scholarship, matching gifts, and United Way. Average grant figure excludes highest grant.

Recent Grants

Note: Grants derived from 2003 Form 990.
General

1,575,000	United Way of Greater St. Louis, St. Louis, MO
500,000	Saint Louis University, St. Louis, MO
333,334	Washington University, St. Louis, MO
275,862	Boy Scouts of America, Irving, TX
200,000	Dillard University, New Orleans, LA
200,000	National Urban League Inc., New York, NY
200,000	Whidbey Island Films, Van Nuys, CA
125,000	Atlanta Historical Society Inc., Atlanta, GA
125,000	Local Initiatives Support Corp., New York, NY
100,000	Boston College, Chestnut Hill, MA

ANNENBERG FOUNDATION

Giving Contact

Dr. Gail C. Levin, Executive Director
St. Davids Center, Suite A-200
150 Radnor-Chester Road
St. Davids, PA 19087
Phone: (610)341-9066
Fax: (610)964-8688
E-mail: info@annenbergfoundation.org
Web: http://www.annenbergfoundation.org

Description

Founded: 1989
EIN: 236257083
Organization Type: General Purpose Foundation
Giving Locations: nationally.
Grant Types: General Support, Project, Seed Money.
Note: The foundation also provides program grants.

Donor Information

Founder: Founder Walter H. Annenberg is the son of Moses Annenberg, who owned the Philadelphia Inquirer and the Daily Racing Form. Walter Annenberg took over the family business in 1940 and launched the very successful TV Guide in 1953. In 1970, he sold the Philadelphia Inquirer to Knight Ridder. Mr. Annenberg sold his other publications to Rupert Murdoch in 1988 for $3 billion. He is an avid art collector, and owns one of the most coveted art collections in the country. The Annenberg Foundation is the successor corporation to the Annenberg School at Radnor, PA, established in 1958. Mr. Annenberg is also the sole trustee of several Annenberg family trusts, including the J.A. Hooker Charitable Trust, the Evelyn A.J. Hall Charitable Trust, the Lita Hazen Charitable Trust, the Esther Simon Charitable Trust, the Polly Annenberg Levee Charitable Trusts, and the Harriett Ames Charitable Trust. He also served as president of the corporate-sponsored M.L. Annenberg Foundation, which has ceased operations. Mr. Annenberg has also been involved in several private philanthropic pursuits. In 1958, he founded and endowed the Annenberg School for Communication, a graduate school at the University of Pennsylvania. He also endowed the Annenberg School for Communication at the University of Southern California, and the Washington Program in Communications Policy Studies of Northwestern University. The Annenberg Foundation

provides ongoing support to each of these institutions. Mr. Annenberg has also donated a library and a residence to his alma mater, the Peddie School; in 1983, the school received $12 million. He has given $3 million to the University of Pennsylvania for a performing arts center, $8 million to the University of California, and $10 million to the Annenberg Center for Health Sciences, part of a subsidiary of the Eisenhower Medical Center. Mr. Annenberg has also given major gifts to the Episcopal Academy in Philadelphia, the State of Israel, the Metropolitan Museum of Art, and the Desert Museum in Palm Springs, which he built. In 1993, Mr. Annenberg made several major gifts from his foundation, including a gift to the University of Pennsylvania to endow the Annenberg School for Communication and to establish a Center for Public Policy; a gift to the University of Southern California to establish the Annenberg Center for Communication; a contribution to the Peddie School for an endowment and scholarships; and a gift to Colonial Williamsburg Foundation for an education center, museum, and library. In 1989, he told a Washington Post reporter that "Richard Nixon gave me the greatest honor of my life." In 1968, Nixon appointed Annenberg as Ambassador to the Court of St. James and he served in Great Britain until 1974. The former ambassador remains close to many prominent Republicans, as well as the Royal Family.

Financial Summary

Total Giving: $192,070,571 (fiscal year ending June 30, 2003); $355,021,336 (fiscal 2002); $136,895,959 (fiscal 2001)
Giving Analysis: Giving for fiscal 2003 includes: foundation grants to United Way ($2,560,000)
Assets: $2,676,000,851 (fiscal 2003); $2,354,837,085 (fiscal 2002); $2,932,205,767 (fiscal 2001)
Gifts Received: $387,562,634 (fiscal 2003); $548,509 (fiscal 1992). Note: In fiscal 2003, contributions were received from the estate of Walter H. Annenberg.

Typical Recipients

Arts & Humanities: Arts Appreciation, Arts Associations & Councils, Arts Centers, Arts Funds, Arts Institutes, Film & Video, Historic Preservation, History & Archaeology, Libraries, Museums/Galleries, Music, Opera, Performing Arts, Public Broadcasting, Theater
Civic & Public Affairs: Business/Free Enterprise, Community Foundations, First Amendment Issues, Civic & Public Affairs-General, Housing, Inner-City Development, Legal Aid, Municipalities/Towns, Nonprofit Management, Philanthropic Organizations, Professional & Trade Associations, Public Policy, Rural Affairs, Urban & Community Affairs
Education: Afterschool/Enrichment Programs, Arts/Humanities Education, Colleges & Universities, Community & Junior Colleges, Continuing Education, Education Associations, Education Funds, Education Reform, Elementary Education (Public), Environmental Education, Faculty Development, Education-General, International Studies, Journalism/Media Education, Legal Education, Literacy, Medical Education, Minority Education, Preschool Education, Private Education (Precollege), Public Education (Precollege), Religious Education, Science/Mathematics Education, Vocational & Technical Education
Environment: Environment-General, Resource Conservation, Wildlife Protection
Health: Cancer, Children's Health/Hospitals, Clinics/Medical Centers, Emergency/Ambulance Services, Health Funds, Health Organizations, Hospitals, Medical Research, Mental Health, Nursing Services, Preventive Medicine/Wellness Organizations, Public Health, Research/Studies Institutes
International: Foreign Arts Organizations, Foreign Educational Institutions, International Affairs, International Development, International Environmental Issues, International Organizations, International Rela-

tions, Missionary/Religious Activities
Religion: Churches, Dioceses, Jewish Causes, Ministries, Missionary Activities (Domestic), Religious Organizations, Religious Welfare, Social/Policy Issues, Synagogues/Temples
Science: Science Museums, Scientific Centers & Institutes, Scientific Organizations
Social Services: Animal Protection, Child Welfare, Community Service Organizations, Crime Prevention, Family Planning, Family Services, People with Disabilities, Recreation & Athletics, Scouts, Substance Abuse, United Funds/United Ways, Volunteer Services, Youth Organizations

Application Procedures

Initial Contact: Applicants should submit a brief letter of inquiry.
Application Requirements: Letters should include a brief statement of the need for funds and sufficient factual information to enable the foundation's staff to determine whether or not the application falls within the foundations areas of preferred interest or warrants consideration. If a formal proposal is then requested, it should contain a cover letter providing a brief a description of organization, the proposed project, and the amount requested. This proposal should also include background information on the organization, a full description of the proposed project with evidence of its need, an outline for carrying out the project, an evaluation plan, biographical information about the person implementing the program, and principal affiliations of any directors or trustees. In the proposal, a detailed program budget showing sources of funding, a statement concerning plans for continuing support following the foundation's grant, a financial statement, the organization's operating budget during the years of the project, documentation that the organization's board of directors supports the project, and a copy of the organization's exemption letter. Also, advised to consult the Internet site.
Deadlines: None.
Review Process: Following submission of both the letter of inquiry and the full proposal, the review process is generally prompt, but may take up to six months. All grants are approved by the foundation's advisory committee.
A project's contribution to long-term K-12 school reform carries weight, as do fiscal soundness, realistic prospects for future support, and a detailed project budget.
Notes: Applicants should not send a full proposal without preliminary inquiry.

Restrictions

The foundation reports that it does not support individuals, basic research, capital campaigns, construction projects, or operating expenses and is unwilling to offer long-term support of an organization or activity. The foundation does not directly or indirectly support candidates for political office or influence legislation.

Additional Information

The Annenberg Fund, which was established by Walter Annenberg in 1951, has merged with the Annenberg Foundation.
New requests from previously funded organizations will normally be reviewed only after the expiration of the foundation's first grant.
Award recipients are expected to comply with conditions set forth in grant award letters. Challenge grant recipients, working with an independent evaluator, are also responsible for undertaking their own evaluation and documentation. A national assessment of the Annenberg Challenge's impact will be conducted separately. Challenge grants generally cover a period of five years and are tied to progress.
Publications: Guidelines

Foundation Officials

Leonore A. Annenberg: president, chairman, director ED Stanford University BA. NONPR AFFIL trustee: Philadelphia Museum Art; trustee emeritus: University Pennsylvania; honorary trustee: Palm Springs Desert Museum; managing director: Metropolitan Opera Association; member trustee council: National Gallery Art; trustee emeritus: Metropolitan Museum Art; member: Distinguished Daughters Pennsylvania; honorary trustee: Louisiana Music Center; member: Council of American Ambassadors; honorary president: American Friends of the British Museum; member: Committee Preservation White House; member: Academy of Music Committee.

Wallis Annenberg: vice president ED Pine Manor College (1959). NONPR AFFIL honorary member: USC Annenberg School for Communication; director: Young Musicians Foundation; honorary member: UCSB Center for Film, Television and New Media; director: Los Angeles Philharmonic Association; trustee emeritus: Pine Manor College; trustee: Entertainment Industries Council Inc.

Lauren Bon: trustee
Dr. Gail C. Levin: executive director
Dr. Gillian Norris-Szanto: senior program officer
Charles Annenberg Weingarten: trustee
Gregory Annenberg Weingarten: trustee NONPR AFFIL board of directors: University Pennsylvania Museum of Archaeology and Anthropology.

Grants Analysis

Disclosure Period: fiscal year ending June 30, 2003
Total Grants: $189,510,571*
Number of Grants: 571
Average Grant: $320,912*
Highest Grant: $6,590,564
Lowest Grant: $100
Typical Range: $50,000 to $500,000
*Note: Giving excludes United Way. Average grant figure excludes highest grant.

Recent Grants

Note: Grants derived from fiscal 2003 Form 990.

Library-Related

1,500,000 Richard Nixon Library & Birthplace Foundation, Yorba Linda, CA -- towards Annenberg Court

1,000,000 George Bush Presidential Library Foundation, College Station, TX -- fund for The Leonore and Walter Annenberg Presidential Conference Center

1,000,000 William J. Clinton Presidential Foundation, Little Rock, AR -- fund for William J. Clinton Presidential Library

General

13,500,000 Corporation for Public Broadcasting, Washington, DC -- fund for Annenberg/CPB channel

6,590,564 South Florida Annenberg Challenge Inc., Davie, FL -- towards Annenberg Challenge for School Reform program

5,000,000 National Constitution Center, Philadelphia, PA

5,000,000 Philadelphia Foundation, Philadelphia, PA

5,000,000 Philadelphia Museum of Art, Philadelphia, PA

5,000,000 Philadelphia Orchestra Association, Philadelphia, PA -- fund for Walter and Leonore Annenberg Music Director Chair

5,000,000 Public Education Network, Washington, DC -- towards LEF expansion and policy/practice change

5,000,000 Trustees of the University of Pennsylvania, Philadelphia, PA -- fund for the Institute for Adolescent Risk Communication

4,000,000 Eisenhower Medical Center, Rancho Mirage, CA -- towards expansion program

3,334,000 Museum Associates, Los Angeles, CA -- fund for Wallis Annenberg Directorship

ANSCHUTZ FAMILY FOUNDATION

Giving Contact

Sue Anschutz-Rodgers, President
555 17th Street, Suite 2400
Denver, CO 80202
Phone: (303)293-2338
Fax: (303)299-1235
E-mail: info@anschutzfamilyfoundation.org
Web: http://www.anschutzfamilyfoundation.org

Description

Founded: 1982
EIN: 742132676
Organization Type: Family Foundation
Giving Locations: CO
Grant Types: General Support, Project.

Donor Information

Founder: Established in 1982. The donors are Fred B. Anschutz, Marian Pfister Anschutz, Sue Anschutz-Rodgers, and Philip F. Anschutz. Sue Anschutz-Rodgers is primarily responsible for the overall governance of the foundation's philanthropic giving.
Fred and Marian Pfister Anschutz endowed the foundation as a result of their many years of gas and oil, real estate, and livestock ventures. The foundation continues to receive contributions from family members to supplement the annual grant making capacity.

Financial Summary

Total Giving: $1,998,221 (fiscal year ending November 30, 2004); $1,788,260 (fiscal 2002); $1,680,430 (fiscal 2001)
Assets: $40,753,155 (fiscal 2002); $42,524,820 (fiscal 2001)
Gifts Received: $12,007,339 (fiscal 1997); $2,214,750 (fiscal 1996); $390,000 (fiscal 1995).
Note: In fiscal 1997, contributions were received from Fred B. Anschutz Trust and other contributors.

Typical Recipients

Arts & Humanities: Arts Outreach, Ethnic & Folk Arts, Historic Preservation, History & Archaeology, Libraries, Museums/Galleries, Opera, Public Broadcasting

Civic & Public Affairs: African American Affairs, Asian American Affairs, Botanical Gardens/Parks, Community Foundations, Economic Development, Employment/Job Training, Civic & Public Affairs-General, Hispanic Affairs, Housing, Legal Aid, Municipalities/Towns, Native American Affairs, Nonprofit Management, Professional & Trade Associations, Rural Affairs, Urban & Community Affairs, Women's Affairs, Zoos/Aquariums

Education: Afterschool/Enrichment Programs, Arts/Humanities Education, Business Education, Colleges & Universities, Continuing Education, Education Funds, Education Reform, Elementary Education (Private), Elementary Education (Public), Education-General, Leadership Training, Literacy, Minority Education, Private Education (Precollege), Public Education (Precollege), Science/Mathematics Education, Social Sciences Education, Special Education, Student Aid

Environment: Environment-General

Health: AIDS/HIV, Alzheimer's Disease, Cancer, Children's Health/Hospitals, Clinics/Medical Centers, Emergency/Ambulance Services, Geriatric Health, Health Organizations, Heart, Home-Care Services, Hospices, Hospitals, Medical Rehabilitation, Medical Research, Mental Health, Multiple Sclerosis, Nursing Services, Preventive Medicine/Wellness Organizations, Public Health, Research/Studies Institutes, Single-Disease Health Associations, Trauma Treatment

International: Health Care/Hospitals, International Relief Efforts

Religion: Dioceses, Religion-General, Ministries, Religious Organizations, Religious Welfare, Social/

Policy Issues
Science: Science Museums
Social Services: At-Risk Youth, Big Brothers/Big Sisters, Camps, Child Welfare, Community Centers, Community Service Organizations, Counseling, Crime Prevention, Domestic Violence, Family Planning, Family Services, Food/Clothing Distribution, Homes, People with Disabilities, Recreation & Athletics, Scouts, Senior Services, Shelters/Homelessness, Social Services-General, Substance Abuse, Volunteer Services, Youth Organizations

Application Procedures

Initial Contact: Request application guidelines or submit a proposal using the Colorado Common Grant Application.

Application Requirements: Proposals should include a summary of the applicant organization, including the organization's name, address, telephone and fax numbers, email and Web addresses, name of executive director, contact person, amount requested, brief description of request, and signature of chief administrator; organizational information, including mission, purpose, and brief statement of goals, a brief history of organization, summary of the organization's activities, including community/client engagement efforts, and description of the role of volunteers; purpose of grant, including expanded description of goals and measurable objectives, plans for cooperation with other organizations, funding strategies, statement of need and project scope, planned activities and administration, and timetable; evaluation efforts, including anticipated outcomes, how they will be measured, and organization's evaluation capacity. Attachments should include proof of tax-exempt status, list of key personnel and qualifications, current and future organizational budget, project budget, audited financial statements, list of major contributors, roster of board of directors with affiliations, anti-discrimination statement, and any other material that might be helpful.

Deadlines: Proposals are due January 15 and August 1.

Review Process: Foundation acknowledges the receipt of all proposals; only one proposal per year per organization will be reviewed. Proposals are reviewed semi-annually. Upon review of the application letter, a foundation staff member may request further information. All applicants will be notified whether their requests were denied or granted in writing soon after the May 1 and December 1 semi-annual meetings.

Evaluative Criteria: Alignment with the mission and interests of the Foundation; clearly presented proposal; solid financial sustainability plan; committed board of directors who make financial contributions to the organization; strong volunteer participation; community buy-in; solid effort to engage in the community and/or participants in program development; effective and inspired leadership; an eye on the future that reflects recognition of potential impacts on and opportunities for the organization; geographic location and focus.

Notes: Faxes and emails are not acceptable for transmitting a proposal.

Restrictions

The foundation generally does not support individuals, programs outside of Colorado, graduate or postgraduate research, religious organizations for religious purposes, special events or promotions, candidates for political office, endowments, debt reduction, multi-year grants, or capital campaigns.

Additional Information

The Anschutz Family Foundation receives many requests from very qualified and capable non-profit organizations. Although they provide grants to over 200 Colorado non-profit organizations each year, they cannot be counted on as a sustained giver. In order to be fair in distributing grants, they instituted the "two year rule" in 1990, asking that an organization which receives funding from the Anschutz Family Foundation for two successive years to take one year off before reapplying.

Publications: Annual Report; Guidelines

Foundation Officials

Sue Anschutz-Rodgers: donor, president, trustee B 1933. NONPR AFFIL director: Up with People.
Elizabeth Anschutz Brown: trustee
Melinda A. Rodgers Couzens: trustee
Sarah Anschutz Hunt: trustee
Melissa A. Rodgers Padgett: trustee
Jeff W. Pryor: assistant executive director
Robert S. Rich, Esq.: vice president, secretary, assistant treasurer, trustee B New York, NY 1938. ED Harvard University (1961); Yale University (1965). PRIM CORP EMPL partner: Davis, Graham & Stubbs. NONPR AFFIL member: International Bar Association; adjunct faculty: University Denver; Denver World Affairs Council; member: Colorado Bar Association; member: Colorado International Trade Advisory Council; sponsor: American Tax Policy Institute; member: American Bar Association. CLUB AFFIL Yale Club; Mile High Club; Cactus Club; Denver Club.
Susan E. Rodgers Drumm: program ofr, trustee
Susan A. Spindler: treasurer

Grants Analysis

Disclosure Period: fiscal year ending November 30, 2004
Total Grants: $1,998,221
Number of Grants: 351
Average Grant: $5,693
Highest Grant: $50,000
Lowest Grant: $1,000
Typical Range: $2,500 to $10,000

Recent Grants

Note: Grants derived from fiscal 2002 Form 990.

General

25,000	Wichita State University Foundation, Wichita, KS -- fund Hugh Braley scholarship
20,000	Community Resource Center, Denver, CO -- scholarships for Leadership and Management programs
20,000	Greater Denver Neighborhood Partnership, Denver, CO -- support the opportunity for neighborhood representatives in metro Denver to make decisions for local projects
20,000	Rocky Mountain Public Broadcasting Network Inc., Denver, CO -- support LIFE WISE, a program for seniors
15,000	Habitat for Humanity of Colorado, Denver, CO -- provide supportive services to Habitat affiliates across the state
10,000	Care and Share Inc., Colorado Springs, CO -- support for food bank
10,000	Colorado Northwestern Community College Foundation, Rangely, CO -- to help update equipment for dental hygiene program
10,000	Historic Denver Inc., Denver, CO -- operating support for Faith Action programs
10,000	Metro Denver Black Church Initiative, Denver, CO -- strengthen the capacity of Denver area black churches
10,000	Northeast Denver Housing Center, Denver, CO -- provide support to low and moderate income families in purchasing homes

RONALD M. ANSIN FOUNDATION

Giving Contact
Ronald M. Ansin, Trustee
1 Main St.
Leominster, MA 01453
Phone: (978)543-0463

Description
Founded: 1984
EIN: 042786469
Organization Type: Private Foundation
Giving Locations: DC; MA; NY
Grant Types: Emergency, General Support, Project.

Donor Information
Founder: Ronald M. Ansin

Financial Summary
Total Giving: $1,402,154 (fiscal year ending November 30, 2004); $985,112 (fiscal 2001). Note: Contributes through foundation only.
Giving Analysis: Giving for fiscal 2004 includes: foundation grants to United Way ($61,300); fiscal 2001: foundation grants to United Way ($10,500)
Assets: $10,282,748 (fiscal 2004); $13,454,122 (fiscal 2001)
Gifts Received: $271,632 (fiscal 2000); $1,400,000 (fiscal 1993); $3,941,484 (fiscal 1992). Note: In fiscal 1993 and 2000, contributions were received from Ronald M. Ansin.

Typical Recipients
Arts & Humanities: Arts Funds, Community Arts, Arts & Humanities-General, History & Archaeology, Libraries, Museums/Galleries, Music, Performing Arts, Theater
Civic & Public Affairs: Chambers of Commerce, Civil Rights, Clubs, Community Foundations, Gay/Lesbian Issues, Civic & Public Affairs-General, Legal Aid, Municipalities/Towns, Parades/Festivals, Public Policy, Urban & Community Affairs
Education: Colleges & Universities, Community & Junior Colleges, Education Reform, Faculty Development, International Exchange, Legal Education, Private Education (Precollege), Vocational & Technical Education
Environment: Air/Water Quality, Environment-General, Resource Conservation, Watershed
Health: AIDS/HIV, Children's Health/Hospitals, Clinics/Medical Centers, Emergency/Ambulance Services, Hospitals, Mental Health, Single-Disease Health Associations
International: International-General, International Environmental Issues, International Organizations, International Peace & Security Issues, International Relations, International Relief Efforts, Missionary/Religious Activities
Religion: Churches, Jewish Causes, Religious Organizations, Religious Welfare, Synagogues/Temples
Science: Scientific Labs
Social Services: At-Risk Youth, Child Welfare, Community Service Organizations, Domestic Violence, Family Planning, Family Services, People with Disabilities, Recreation & Athletics, Scouts, Senior Services, Social Services-General, Special Olympics, Substance Abuse, United Funds/United Ways, Veterans, Youth Organizations

Application Procedures
Initial Contact: Send brief letter describing program.
Application Requirements: Include purpose of funds sought, recently audited financial statement, and proof of 501 (c) (3) status.
Deadlines: None.

Foundation Officials
Ronald M. Ansin: trustee B Worcester, MA 1934. ED Harvard University BA (1955); Yale University JD

(1958). PRIM CORP EMPL chairman, treasurer, director: L.B. Evans & Son Co. CORP AFFIL chairman: Merchants National Bank; director, president: Cleghorn Shoe Corp.; director: Cole-Haan; chairman: Anwelt Corp.; chairman: America Footwear Corp.; chairman: Ansewn Shoe Corp. NONPR AFFIL trustee: Fitchburg Saint College; trustee: Leominster Hospital; trustee: Fitchburg Art Museum; trustee: Applewild School.

Grants Analysis
Disclosure Period: fiscal year ending November 30, 2004
Total Grants: $1,340,854*
Number of Grants: 91
Average Grant: $12,257*
Highest Grant: $150,000
Lowest Grant: $100
Typical Range: $1,000 to $25,000
*Note: Giving excludes United Way. Average grant figure excludes two highest grants ($250,000).

Recent Grants
Note: Grants derived from fiscal 2001 Form 990.
General
100,000	GLSEN, New York, NY
50,000	American Civil Liberties Union Foundation, Boston, MA
50,000	Fenway Community Health Center, Boston, MA
50,000	Spanish American Center, Leominster, MA
50,000	Victory Foundation, Washington, DC
30,000	ARC Foundation, Washington, DC
30,000	New Israel Fund, Chestnut Hill, MA
25,000	AIDS Action Committee, Boston, MA
25,000	Fitchburg Art Museum, Fitchburg, MA
25,000	Yeshiva Achei Tmimin, Worcester, MA

ANTHEM INC.

Company Headquarters
120 Monument Circle
Indianapolis, IN 46204
Web: http://www.anthem.com

Company Description
Ticker: ATH
Exchange: NYSE
Former Name: Anthem Insurance Co. (2001);
Acquired: Southeastern Mutual Insurance (1993); Community Mutual Insurance Co. (1995).
Revenue: US$16.771 billion (2003)
Profit: US$774.3 million (2002)
Employees: 20130 (2003)
SIC(s): 6311 Life Insurance, 6321 Accident & Health Insurance.

Anthem Foundation, Inc.

Giving Contact
Vicki Perkins, Executive Director
Anthem Foundation
120 Monument Circle
Indianapolis, IN 46204
Phone: 800-563-5465
Note: Contact and mailing address for applications.

Alternate Contact
Anthem Foundation
9901 Linn Station Road
Louisville, KY 40223
Phone: (502)423-2331
Note: Foundation's official address

Description
Founded: 1990
EIN: 611191499
Organization Type: Corporate Foundation
Giving Locations: KY
Grant Types: Employee Matching Gifts, General Support, Project.

Donor Information
Founder: Blue Cross and Blue Shield of Kentucky, Southeastern Mutual Insurance Co.

Financial Summary
Total Giving: $456,970 (2003); $199,515 (2002); $221,447 (2001). Note: Contributes through foundation only.
Giving Analysis: Giving for 2002 includes: foundation grants to United Way ($120,065)
Assets: $6,669,714 (2003); $6,355,694 (2002); $6,578,320 (2001).
Gifts Received: $12,000 (2003); $12,000 (2002); $12,000 (2001). Note: Contributions were received from SpectraCare.

Typical Recipients
Arts & Humanities: Arts Festivals, Arts Funds, Ballet, History & Archaeology, Libraries, Museums/Galleries, Music, Opera, Public Broadcasting, Theater
Civic & Public Affairs: African American Affairs, Botanical Gardens/Parks, Business/Free Enterprise, Community Foundations, Economic Development, Civic & Public Affairs-General, Municipalities/Towns, Professional & Trade Associations, Public Policy, Urban & Community Affairs, Women's Affairs
Education: Arts/Humanities Education, Business Education, Colleges & Universities, Community & Junior Colleges, Economic Education, Education Associations, Education Funds, Education Reform, Education-General, Leadership Training, Medical Education, Minority Education, Preschool Education, Private Education (Precollege), Public Education (Precollege), Religious Education, Secondary Education (Private), Secondary Education (Public), Special Education, Student Aid
Environment: Environment-General, Resource Conservation
Health: AIDS/HIV, Cancer, Children's Health/Hospitals, Clinics/Medical Centers, Diabetes, Emergency/Ambulance Services, Health-General, Health Organizations, Heart, Hospitals, Medical Rehabilitation, Multiple Sclerosis, Nursing Services, Prenatal Health Issues, Preventive Medicine/Wellness Organizations, Public Health, Respiratory, Single-Disease Health Associations, Trauma Treatment
Religion: Dioceses, Religious Organizations, Religious Welfare
Science: Scientific Centers & Institutes
Social Services: At-Risk Youth, Camps, Child Abuse, Child Welfare, Community Service Organizations, Food/Clothing Distribution, Scouts, Senior Services, Special Olympics, Substance Abuse, United Funds/United Ways, YMCA/YWCA/YMHA/YWHA

Application Procedures
Initial Contact: Request application form.
Deadlines: None.

Corporate Officials
Larry G. Glasscock: chairman, chief executive officer chief medical officer
Samuel R. Nussbaum, MD: executive vice president, chief medical officer
Michael L. Smith: executive vice president, chief financial officer

Foundation Officials
David R. Frick: president, director PRIM CORP EMPL executive vice president, chief administrative officer: Anthem Insurance Companies. CORP AFFIL officer: Anthem Companies Inc.; officer: Anthem Life Insurance Co.
Larry G. Glasscock: director (see above)
George Martin: treasurer
Nancy L. Purcell: secretary PRIM CORP EMPL secretary: Anthem Companies Inc. CORP AFFIL secretary: Anthem Health Indiana; secretary: Anthem Insurance Companies.
Michael L. Smith: director (see above)

Grants Analysis
Disclosure Period: calendar year ending 2003
Total Grants: $171,189*
Number of Grants: 20
Average Grant: $6,642*
Highest Grant: $45,000
Lowest Grant: $25
Typical Range: $1,000 to $10,000
*Note: Giving excludes United Way. Average grant figure excludes highest grant.

Recent Grants
Note: Grants derived from 2003 Form 990.
General

107,866	Metro United Way, Louisville, KY
96,052	Warren County United Way, Warren, VA
70,893	United Way, Cincinnati, OH
45,000	Greater Louisville Foundation, Louisville, KY -- towards economic development
40,000	Louisville Deaf Oral School, Louisville, KY
25,000	Hudson Institute, Washington, DC -- towards education
13,500	American Association of Diabetes Educators, Education and Research Foundation, Chicago, IL
13,489	United Way, Youngstown, OH
10,000	Health Kentucky, Louisville, KY -- towards health education
10,000	Local Initiatives Support Corporation, Washington, DC

AOL TIME WARNER

Company Headquarters
75 Rockefeller Plaza
New York, NY 10019
Phone: (212)484-8000
Fax: (212)489-6183
Web: http://www.aoltimewarner.com

Company Description
Founded: 1985
Ticker: AOL
Exchange: NYSE
Acquired: Time Warner (2001);
Former Name: America Online (AOL) (2001);
Acquired: Time Warner Entertainment Co..
Revenue: US$42.869 billion (2004)
Profit: US$3.364 billion (2004)
Employees: 91250 (2003)
Fortune Rank: 32, per FORTUNE Magazine's list of 500 Largest U.S. Corporations (2004).
Parent Company: AOL Time Warner, 75 Rockefeller Plaza, New York, NY, United States

Time Warner Foundation, Inc.

Giving Contact
22000 AOL Way
Dulles, VA 20166-9323
Phone: (703)265-2282
Web: http://www.timewarner.com/corp/citizenship/education/index.html

Description
EIN: 541886827
Organization Type: Corporate Foundation
Also Known As: AOL Foundation.
Former Name: Time Warner Foundation.
Former Name: AOL Time Warner Foundation (2003).
Giving Locations: nationally.
Grant Types: Capital, Employee Matching Gifts, General Support.

Financial Summary
Total Giving: $7,241,900 (2003); $6,366,757 (2002 approx); $4,223,324 (2001)
Assets: $3,165,152 (2003); $2,660,422 (2001)
Gifts Received: $9,292,892 (2003); $4,551,645 (2001); $5,728,971 (2000). Note: In 2001 and 2003, contributions were received from AOL Time Warner ($4,551,645). In 2000, contributions were received from AOL, Inc. ($5,718,971) and Ikon Office Solutions ($10,000). In 1999, contributions were received from AOL.

Typical Recipients
Arts & Humanities: Arts Associations & Councils, Film & Video, Arts & Humanities-General, History & Archaeology, Libraries, Museums/Galleries, Music, Public Broadcasting
Civic & Public Affairs: African American Affairs, Asian American Affairs, Business/Free Enterprise, Community Foundations, Economic Development, Ethnic Organizations, Civic & Public Affairs-General, Minority Business, Municipalities/Towns, Native American Affairs, Nonprofit Management, Philanthropic Organizations, Urban & Community Affairs, Zoos/Aquariums
Education: Colleges & Universities, Education Associations, Education Funds, Elementary Education (Public), Education-General, Journalism/Media Education, Literacy, Medical Education, Private Education (Precollege), Public Education (Precollege), Science/Mathematics Education, Secondary Education (Private), Secondary Education (Public), Special Education, Vocational & Technical Education
Health: Cancer, Children's Health/Hospitals, Health-General, Health Organizations, Public Health, Transplant Networks/Donor Banks
International: Foreign Educational Institutions, International Peace & Security Issues
Religion: Ministries, Religious Welfare
Science: Science Museums
Social Services: Community Service Organizations, Counseling, People with Disabilities, Senior Services, Social Services-General, United Funds/United Ways, Youth Organizations

Application Procedures
Initial Contact: Telephone requests are not accepted.
Application Requirements: Include organization name and address; brief history; mission statement; contact's name, title, phone number, and e-mail address; amount requested; project start and end dates; project description and evaluation process; other partners working on the project; any additional project funding from other sources; description of how the project fits into one of the four priority areas; project audience; and project budget.
Deadlines: None.
Review Process: Proposals are reviewed throughout the year. Allow 8 to 12 weeks for a response.
Evaluative Criteria: Organizations must have a well-defined purpose which is within the foundation's scope of giving, namely the four key priorities: Equipping Kids for the 21st Century; Extending Internet Benefits to All; Engaging Communities in the Arts; and Empowering Citizens and Civic Participation. They should have a national focus and should be a good strategic partner.

Restrictions

As a general rule, the foundation does not fund unsolicited proposals except under very special circumstances. However, organizations who believe they have an exceptional proposal that falls within the foundation's priorities may submit a request.

AOL Time Warner does not consider funding the following: organizations that do not have 501(c)(3) tax-exempt status; individuals; political, labor, religious or fraternal organizations; amateur or professional sports groups; publications of books or the production of films and music; capital fund drives; or organizations whose missions fall outside the four focus areas.

Additional Information

Time Warner, Inc. and America Online, Inc. merged to form AOL Time Warner, Inc. TW Foundation will dispose of all assets to AOL Time Warner Foundation, Inc. pursuant to the merger.

Corporate Officials

Stephen M. Case: chairman B August 21, 1958. ED Williams College BA (1980). PRIM CORP EMPL chairman: AOL Time Warner Inc.

Foundation Officials

Katherine Bushkin: president, director ED Purdue University BA. NONPR AFFIL co-founder: Stargazer Group; board member: Wolf Trap National Park; board member: International Women's Media Foundation; board member: Share Our Strength.
Stephen M. Case: director (see above)
Michele M. Cavataio: executive director
Gary Credle: director
Brian S. Keys: secretary
Kenneth B. Lerer: director
Henry McGee: director
Kenneth J. Novack: director
Richard D. Parsons: chairman, president
Lisa Quiroz: director
Sylvia Rhone: director
Thomas M. Rutledge: director
Michel C. Sacconaghi: treasurer
George Vradenburg, III: director
Andrey Weil: director

Grants Analysis

Disclosure Period: calendar year ending 2003
Total Grants: $7,241,900
Number of Grants: 1,238
Average Grant: $4,934
Highest Grant: $300,000
Lowest Grant: $10
Typical Range: $500 to $2,000 and $1,503 to $93,321

Recent Grants

Note: Grants derived from 2003 Form 990.
General

50,000	Youth Radio, Berkeley, CA -- education and literacy
5,000	Youth Welfare, Alexandria, VA
1,000	Zoo Atlanta, Atlanta, GA -- education and literacy

AON CORP.

Company Headquarters

200 E. Randolph
Chicago, IL 60601
Web: http://www.aon.com

Company Description

Founded: 1979
Ticker: AOC
Exchange: NYSE
Revenue: US$10.205 billion (2004)

Profit: US$546 million (2004)
Employees: 54000 (2003)
Fortune Rank: 218, per FORTUNE Magazine's list of 500 Largest U.S. Corporations (2004).
SIC(s): 6411 Insurance Agents, Brokers & Service, 6719 Holding Companies Nec.

Operating Locations

Aon Corp. (MD--Owings Mills; NJ--Lyndhurst; TN--Nashville; TX--Dallas)

Aon Foundation

Giving Contact

Carolyn E. Labutka, Executive Director
AON Foundation
200 East Randolph Street
Chicago, IL 60601
Phone: (312)381-3549
Fax: (312)701-4533

Description

EIN: 363337340
Organization Type: Corporate Foundation
Giving Locations: internationally; operating locations.
Grant Types: Award, Capital, Challenge, Department, Employee Matching Gifts, Endowment, General Support, Operating Expenses, Research.
Note: Employee matching gift ratio: 1 to 1.

Financial Summary

Total Giving: $8,447,538 (2003); $6,482,559 (2002); $5,704,663 (2001). Note: Contributes through foundation only.
Giving Analysis: Giving for 2002 includes: foundation grants to United Way ($571,465); foundation matching gifts ($796,386).
Assets: $705,798 (2003); $521,434 (2002); $654,966 (2001)
Gifts Received: $8,386,414 (2003); $6,424,663 (2002); $4,748,729 (2001). Note: Contributions were received from AON Corporation and its subsidiaries.

Typical Recipients

Arts & Humanities: Arts Associations & Councils, Arts Centers, Arts Festivals, Arts Funds, Arts Institutes, Dance, Film & Video, Historic Preservation, History & Archaeology, Libraries, Museums/Galleries, Music, Opera, Performing Arts, Public Broadcasting, Theater
Civic & Public Affairs: Botanical Gardens/Parks, Business/Free Enterprise, Chambers of Commerce, Civil Rights, Clubs, Community Foundations, Economic Development, Economic Policy, Employment/Job Training, Ethnic Organizations, Civic & Public Affairs-General, Hispanic Affairs, Law & Justice, Municipalities/Towns, Parades/Festivals, Philanthropic Organizations, Public Policy, Safety, Urban & Community Affairs, Women's Affairs, Zoos/Aquariums
Education: Afterschool/Enrichment Programs, Arts/Humanities Education, Business Education, Business-School Partnerships, Colleges & Universities, Education Associations, Education Funds, Elementary Education (Private), Elementary Education (Public), Faculty Development, Education-General, Health & Physical Education, Legal Education, Preschool Education, Private Education (Precollege), Public Education (Precollege), Religious Education, Science/Mathematics Education, Secondary Education (Private), Student Aid
Environment: Environment-General, Protection, Resource Conservation
Health: AIDS/HIV, Alzheimer's Disease, Cancer, Children's Health/Hospitals, Clinics/Medical Centers, Diabetes, Emergency/Ambulance Services, Health Funds, Hospitals, Hospitals (University Affiliated), Medical Rehabilitation, Medical Research, Multiple Sclerosis, Single-Disease Health Associations
International: Foreign Educational Institutions, International-General, International Affairs, International Organizations, International Relations, International Relief Efforts
Religion: Churches, Dioceses, Jewish Causes, Religious Organizations, Religious Welfare
Science: Science Museums, Scientific Centers & Institutes
Social Services: At-Risk Youth, Child Welfare, Community Centers, Community Service Organizations, Counseling, Crime Prevention, Food/Clothing Distribution, Homes, People with Disabilities, Recreation & Athletics, Refugee Assistance, Scouts, Senior Services, Substance Abuse, United Funds/United Ways, Volunteer Services, YMCA/YWCA/YMHA/YWHA, Youth Organizations

Application Procedures

Initial Contact: Send a letter or proposal.
Application Requirements: Provide name, address, phone number of organization, and name of executive director; one paragraph description of organization; description of project, including specific objectives, evidence of need, proof that program would not duplicate existing services, and history of organization with such projects; amount requested and purpose of request; list of other potential funding sources and amounts; description of the greatest challenges facing organization in the next two or three years, and evaluation of organization's strengths and weaknesses; list of current contributors and amounts; proof of 501(c)(3) status, and annual report.
Deadlines: None.

Restrictions

Grants are not made to individuals or political organizations. Awards are restricted to charitable, educational (excluding the operation of a secondary educational institution or vocational school, and scientific organizations that qualify as: a) exempt organizations under the 1954 Internal Revenue Code Section 501 (c)(3) (or the corresponding provisions of any future United States revenue law), or (b) organizations described in the 1954 Internal Revenue Code Section 509 (a)(1),(2), or (3) (or the corresponding provisions of any United States revenue law).

Additional Information

AON Corporation was formerly Combined International Corporation. The AON Foundation was formerly the Combined International Foundation.
Publications: Foundation Annual Report

Corporate Officials

Daniel T. Cox: chairman vice president, chief counsel, director B 1946. ED University of North Carolina (1968); Vanderbilt University MA (1971). PRIM CORP EMPL chairman: Aon Corp.
Harvey Norman Medvin: executive vice president, treasurer, chief financial officer B Chicago, IL 1936. ED University of Illinois BS (1958). PRIM CORP EMPL executive vice president, treasurer, chief financial officer: Aon Corp. CORP AFFIL director: Ryan Insurance Group DE; president, treasurer, director: Ryan Warranty Services; director: Combined Insurance Co.
Patrick G. Ryan: chairman, president, chief executive officer B Milwaukee, WI 1937. ED Northwestern University BS (1959). PRIM CORP EMPL chairman, president, chief executive officer: Aon Corp. CORP AFFIL director: Tribune Co.; president: Ryan Properties Inc.; director: Sears, Roebuck & Co.; president: Ryan Companies United States Inc.; chairman, director: Pat Ryan & Associates; president: Ryan Builders Inc.; director: Combined Insurance Co.; director: AON Risk Services Companies; officer: AON Warranty Group; chairman: AON Group Inc. NONPR AFFIL trustee: Northwestern University; trustee: Rush-Presbyterian-Saint Lukes Medical Center; trustee: Field Museum Natural History.
Raymond Inwood Skilling: executive vice president, chief counsel, director B Enniskillen, United Kingdom 1939. ED Queens University LLB (1961);

University of Chicago JD (1962). PRIM CORP EMPL executive vice president, chief counsel, director: Aon Corp. CORP AFFIL executive vice president, chief couns, director: Combined Insurance Co. NONPR AFFIL member: Chicago Bar Association; member: Illinois Bar Association; member: American Bar Association. CLUB AFFIL Racquet Club Chicago; City London Club; Economic Club; Chicago Club; Carlton Club London; Casino Club.

Foundation Officials

Kevann M. Cooke: corp secretary
Lester B. Knight: chairman, director
Carolyn E. Labutka: vice president, executive director
R. Eden Martin: chairman, director
Andrew James McKenna: director B Chicago, IL 1929. ED University of Notre Dame BS (1951); DePaul University JD (1954). PRIM CORP EMPL chairman, president, chief executive officer: Schwarz Paper Co. CORP AFFIL director: Skyline Corp.; director: Tribune Co.; director: McDonald's Corp.; director: First Chicago NBD Corp.; director: First National Bank Chicago; director: Children's Memorial Hospital; director: Dean Foods Co.; director: Chicago Bears Football Club; director: Chicago National League Baseball Club; director: AON Corp. NONPR AFFIL chairman board trustees: Museum Science & Industry; chairman board trustees: University Notre Dame; director: Catholic Charities Chicago; director: Childrens Memorial Medical Center.
Harvey Norman Medvin: treasurer (see above)
Patrick G. Ryan, Jr.: director
Patrick G. Ryan: president, director (see above)
Raymond Inwood Skilling: director (see above)

Grants Analysis

Disclosure Period: calendar year ending 2003
Total Grants: $6,673,555*
Number of Grants: 400 (approx)
Average Grant: $16,684
Highest Grant: $500,000
Lowest Grant: $100
Typical Range: $5,000 to $30,000
*Note: Giving excludes matching gifts and United Way.

Recent Grants

Note: Grants derived from 2003 Form 990.
General

500,000	Chicago Symphony and Lyric Opera Facilities Fund, Chicago, IL
200,000	Millennium Park Inc., Chicago, IL
200,000	University of Chicago Arthur Quern Memorial Fund, Chicago, IL
165,400	Boys and Girls Clubs, Chicago, IL
150,000	Chicago Symphony Orchestra, Chicago, IL
125,000	Northwestern University, Evanston, IL
121,524	American Friends of Versailles, Chicago, IL
100,000	Archdiocese of Chicago Big Shoulders Fund, Chicago, IL
100,000	Homan Square Community Center Foundation, Chicago, IL
100,000	Providence Saint Mel School, Chicago, IL

APPELBAUM-KAHN FOUNDATION

Giving Contact

Carol G. Emerling
201 Ocean Avenue, Apt. 1510B
Santa Monica, CA 90402

Description

Founded: 1999
EIN: 957043271

Organization Type: Private Foundation
Grant Types: General Support.

Financial Summary

Total Giving: $46,500 (fiscal year ending October 31, 2004); $37,250 (fiscal 2001)
Assets: $1,182,506 (fiscal 2004); $1,055,998 (fiscal 2001)
Gifts Received: $460 (fiscal 1999); $1,234,410 (fiscal 1998). Note: In 1998, contributions were received from the Estate of Beatrice A. Kahn.

Typical Recipients

Arts & Humanities: Arts Centers, Arts & Humanities-General, Performing Arts, Public Broadcasting
Civic & Public Affairs: Civic & Public Affairs-General, Law & Justice
Health: Clinics/Medical Centers, Health Policy/Cost Containment, Hospices, Mental Health
International: Human Rights
Religion: Synagogues/Temples
Social Services: People with Disabilities

Application Procedures

Initial Contact: Send a brief letter of inquiry.
Application Requirements: Include a description of organization.
Deadlines: None.

Foundation Officials

Carol G. Emerling: co trustee
Keith S. Emerling: co trustee
Susan C. Emerling: co trustee

Grants Analysis

Disclosure Period: fiscal year ending October 31, 2004
Total Grants: $46,500
Number of Grants: 9
Highest Grant: $10,000
Lowest Grant: $1,000

Recent Grants

Note: Grants derived from 2004 Form 990.
General

10,000	Inner City Arts, Los Angeles, CA -- to adopt-a-teacher
10,000	Montefiore, Bronx, NY
10,000	Site Santa Fe, Santa Fe, NM
4,000	Mass MoCA, North Adams, MA
3,500	Southern Poverty Law Center, Montgomery, MA
3,000	Austen Riggs Center, Stockbridge, MA -- towards patient aid Directors' fund
3,000	HospiceCare in the Berkshire, Pittsfield, MA
2,000	United Cerebral Palsy, Washington, DC
1,000	Berkshire Community Radio Alliance, Great Barrington, MA

SCOTT B. AND ANNIE P. APPLEBY TRUST

Giving Contact

Christine A. Butler
c/o Suntrust Bank
PO Box 2018
Sarasota, FL 34230
Phone: (941)951-3324

Description

Founded: 1948
EIN: 526334302
Organization Type: Private Foundation
Giving Locations: DC; FL; GA
Grant Types: General Support.

Financial Summary

Total Giving: $222,187 (2003); $283,298 (2002); $322,000 (2001)
Assets: $4,716,239 (2003); $4,367,610 (2002); $5,476,631 (2001)

Typical Recipients

Arts & Humanities: Arts Institutes, Ballet, Community Arts, Libraries, Museums/Galleries, Music, Performing Arts, Theater
Civic & Public Affairs: Community Foundations, Civic & Public Affairs-General, Housing
Education: Arts/Humanities Education, Colleges & Universities, Environmental Education, Education-General, Minority Education, Private Education (Precollege), Secondary Education (Private), Secondary Education (Public), Special Education
Environment: Environment-General
Health: Cancer, Children's Health/Hospitals, Emergency/Ambulance Services, Health Organizations, Hospices, Hospitals, Mental Health, Multiple Sclerosis, Prenatal Health Issues
Social Services: Child Abuse, Child Welfare, Community Service Organizations, Day Care, Family Services, Food/Clothing Distribution, People with Disabilities, Senior Services, Shelters/Homelessness, Volunteer Services, Youth Organizations

Application Procedures

Initial Contact: Send a brief letter of inquiry.
Application Requirements: Include a description of organization, amount requested, proof of tax-exempt status.
Deadlines: None.

Restrictions

The foundation does not support individuals.

Foundation Officials

Benjamin N. Colby: trustee
F. Jordan Colby: trustee
Sarah Rob Colby Pierce: trustee

Grants Analysis

Disclosure Period: calendar year ending 2003
Total Grants: $222,187
Number of Grants: 26
Average Grant: $6,887*
Highest Grant: $50,000
Lowest Grant: $1,000
Typical Range: $1,000 to $10,000
*Note: Average grant figure excludes highest grant.

Recent Grants

Note: Grants derived from 2001 Form 990.
Library-Related

20,000	Augusta Richmond Public Library
20,000	Augusta Richmond Public Library
5,000	Rye Free Reading Room, Rye, NY

General

40,000	Anthropologist 's Fund Legacy
35,000	Gallaudet University, Washington, DC
35,000	New College Endowment Fund, Sarasota, FL
30,000	Girls, Inc.
20,000	Anthropologist 's Fund Legacy
20,000	Putney School, Putney, VT
15,000	Northern Wings, Portland, ME
15,000	Planned Parenthood of Asheville, Asheville, NC
11,000	Center for Preventive Psychology
10,000	Black Student Fund, Washington, DC

APPLETON PAPERS INC.

Company Headquarters

825 E. Wisconsin Ave.
Appleton, WI 54912-0359

Web: http://www.appletonideas.com

Company Description
Founded: 1907
Employees: 1400 (2003)
SIC(s): 2672 Coated & Laminated Paper Nec, 2679 Converted Paper Products Nec.
Parent Company: Arjo Wiggins Appleton Ltd., St. Clement House, Alencon Link, Basingstoke, United Kingdom
Parent Revenue: US$4,927,700,000 (2001)

Operating Locations
Appleton Papers Inc. (GA--Atlanta; IA--Davenport; KS--Kansas City; KY--Florence; NY--Albany, Newton Falls; OH--West Carrollton; OR--Portland; PA--Harrisburg; WI--Combined Locks); Appleton Papers International (PA--Roaring Spring); Appleton Papers-Locks Mills (WI--Combined Locks); Appleton Papers-Portage Plant (WI--Portage); Appleton Papers-Spring Mill (PA--Roaring Spring)

Nonmonetary Support
Type: Donated Equipment; Donated Products
Contact: Billy Van Den Brandt, Staff Public Relations Representative

Giving Contact
Donna Kolb, Contribution Committee
825 East Wisconsin Avenue
PO Box 359
Appleton, WI 54912
Phone: (920)991-7448
Fax: (920)991-7258
E-mail: dkolb@appletonideas.com

Description
Organization Type: Corporate Giving Program
Giving Locations: OH: Dayton; PA: Roaring Spring; WI: Appleton headquarters and operating communities.
Grant Types: Award, Capital, Employee Matching Gifts, General Support, Multiyear/Continuing Support, Project, Scholarship.
Note: Employee matching gift ratio: 1 to 1 for education only.

Financial Summary
Total Giving: $800,000 (2002 approx); $800,000 (2001). Note: Contributes through corporate direct giving program only. Giving includes nonmonetary support.

Typical Recipients
Arts & Humanities: Arts Associations & Councils, Libraries, Museums/Galleries, Music, Performing Arts, Visual Arts
Civic & Public Affairs: Business/Free Enterprise
Education: Colleges & Universities, Economic Education, Engineering/Technological Education, Faculty Development, Minority Education, Science/Mathematics Education, Student Aid
Environment: Environment-General
Health: Single-Disease Health Associations
Social Services: Child Welfare, Community Service Organizations, Counseling, Domestic Violence, Emergency Relief, Food/Clothing Distribution, People with Disabilities, Recreation & Athletics, Senior Services, Shelters/Homelessness, Substance Abuse, United Funds/United Ways, Youth Organizations

Application Procedures
Initial Contact: Send a brief letter of inquiry and proposal.
Application Requirements: Include a description of organization, amount requested, purpose of funds sought, recently audited financial statement, proof of tax-exempt status, number of people benefiting from the project, and extent of Appleton employees' involvement.
Deadlines: None.

Restrictions
The company does not consider funding for the following: dinners or special events, goodwill advertising, member agencies of united funds, individuals, hospitals, fraternal organizations, political or lobbying groups, religious organizations for sectarian purposes, or groups whose agendas differ from the goals of the company.

Giving Program Officials
Dennis N. Hultgren: director B Milwaukee, WI 1946. ED University of Wisconsin (1969); University of Wisconsin (1973). PRIM CORP EMPL director environmental & public affairs: Appleton Papers Inc. CORP AFFIL director: Norwest Bank. NONPR AFFIL member: Rotary International.

Grants Analysis
Typical Range: $5,000 to $10,000

MARIAN MEAKER APTECKAR FOUNDATION

Giving Contact
Care of Chase Bank of TX, NA
PO Box 140
El Paso, TX 79980-0001
Phone: (915)546-6515

Description
Founded: 1997
EIN: 742060589
Organization Type: Private Foundation
Grant Types: General Support.

Financial Summary
Total Giving: $129,446 (fiscal year ending May 31, 2001)
Assets: $2,336,513 (fiscal 2001)

Typical Recipients
Arts & Humanities: Libraries, Museums/Galleries, Music
Education: Colleges & Universities, Education-General
Religion: Jewish Causes

Additional Information
Trust(s): Chase Bank of TX NA

Grants Analysis
Disclosure Period: fiscal year ending May 31, 2001
Total Grants: $129,446
Number of Grants: 6
Highest Grant: $45,489
Lowest Grant: $7,767

Recent Grants
Note: Grants derived from 2001 Form 990.
Library-Related

7,767	El Paso Public Library, El Paso, TX	

General

45,489	El Paso Symphony, El Paso, TX	
35,889	National Jewish Medical and Research Center	
24,767	El Paso Museum of Art, El Paso, TX	
7,767	American Association University, New York, NY	
7,767	Delta Kappa Gamma Educational	

MARY ALICE ARAKELIAN FOUNDATION

Giving Contact
John H. Pramberg, Jr., Trustee
PO Box 510
Newburyport, MA 01950
Phone: (617)346-4000

Description
Founded: 1966
EIN: 046155695
Organization Type: Private Foundation
Grant Types: General Support.

Financial Summary
Total Giving: $345,000 (2001)
Giving Analysis: Giving for 2001 includes: foundation grants to United Way ($25,000)
Assets: $7,439,569 (2001)

Typical Recipients
Arts & Humanities: Arts Associations & Councils, Arts Funds, Community Arts, Historic Preservation, History & Archaeology, Libraries, Museums/Galleries, Public Broadcasting, Theater
Civic & Public Affairs: Botanical Gardens/Parks, Civic & Public Affairs-General, Municipalities/Towns, Safety, Urban & Community Affairs
Education: Colleges & Universities, Education-General, Special Education
Environment: Environment-General
Health: Health Organizations, Hospitals, Prenatal Health Issues
Religion: Churches, Religious Organizations, Religious Welfare, Synagogues/Temples
Social Services: Community Service Organizations, Recreation & Athletics, United Funds/United Ways, YMCA/YWCA/YMHA/YWHA

Application Procedures
Deadlines: September 15.

Additional Information
Trust(s): Fleet Bank MA NA

Foundation Officials
Rose M. Marshall: co-trustee
Donald D. Mitchell: co-trustee
John H. Pramberg, Jr.: co-trustee
Charles P. Richmond: co-trustee
Mark Welch: co-trustee

Grants Analysis
Disclosure Period: calendar year ending 2001
Total Grants: $320,000*
Number of Grants: 9
Average Grant: $35,556
Highest Grant: $50,000
Lowest Grant: $10,000
Typical Range: $25,000 to $50,000
*Note: Giving excludes United Way.

Recent Grants
Note: Grants derived from 2002 Form 990.
General

75,000	Newburyport YWCA, East Bridgewater, MA	
50,000	First Religious Society	
40,000	Society for Arts and Humanities	
30,000	New Hampshire Public Television, Durham, NH	
30,000	Newburyport Education and Business Coalition, Newburyport, MA	
27,000	Pettingill House	
25,000	Anna Jacques Community Health, Newburyport, MA	
25,000	Newburyport Youth Soccer Association, Newburyport, MA	

25,000   United Way of Merrick Valley, Inc., Lawrence, MA

ARATA BROTHERS TRUST

Giving Contact
4061 Marsalla Court
Sacramento, CA 95820
Phone: (916)451-5358

Description
Founded: 1976
EIN: 237204615
Organization Type: Private Foundation
Giving Locations: CA
Grant Types: General Support.

Financial Summary
Total Giving: $500,639 (2001)
Assets: $7,517,924 (2001)
Gifts Received: $4,193,959 (1996)

Typical Recipients
Arts & Humanities: Ballet, Historic Preservation, History & Archaeology, Libraries, Museums/Galleries, Music, Opera, Performing Arts, Public Broadcasting, Theater
Civic & Public Affairs: Clubs, Community Foundations, Employment/Job Training, Civic & Public Affairs-General, Housing, Inner-City Development, Municipalities/Towns, Public Policy, Safety
Education: Business Education, Colleges & Universities, Elementary Education (Private), Elementary Education (Public), Legal Education, Literacy, Private Education (Precollege), Public Education (Precollege), Religious Education, Science/Mathematics Education, Secondary Education (Private)
Health: AIDS/HIV, Arthritis, Cancer, Children's Health/Hospitals, Diabetes, Emergency/Ambulance Services, Health Funds, Health Organizations, Hospitals, Medical Research, Research/Studies Institutes, Respiratory, Single-Disease Health Associations, Speech & Hearing
International: Foreign Educational Institutions
Religion: Churches, Religion-General, Jewish Causes, Ministries, Religious Organizations, Religious Welfare
Social Services: At-Risk Youth, Child Abuse, Child Welfare, Community Service Organizations, Domestic Violence, Family Services, Food/Clothing Distribution, Homes, People with Disabilities, Scouts, Senior Services, Special Olympics, Volunteer Services, YMCA/YWCA/YMHA/YWHA, Youth Organizations

Application Procedures
Initial Contact: Send a brief letter of inquiry.
Application Requirements: Include proof of tax-exempt status and description of program or project.
Deadlines: None.

Foundation Officials
Francis B. Dillon: trustee
Janette Lavezzo: trustee
Renato R. Parenti: trustee
Mark Sewell: trustee

Grants Analysis
Disclosure Period: calendar year ending 2001
Total Grants: $500,639
Number of Grants: 66
Average Grant: $6,932*
Highest Grant: $50,074
Lowest Grant: $750
Typical Range: $2,500 to $15,000
*Note: Average grant figure excludes highest grant.

Recent Grants
Note: Grants derived from 2002 Form 990.

General

45,000   Children's Receiving Home, Sacramento, CA
40,000   Mercy Hospital Foundation, Rancho Cordova, CA
30,000   Boy Scouts of America, Sacramento, CA
25,000   Boys and Girls Club, Sacramento, CA
20,000   KVIE Channel 6, Sacramento, CA
18,876   YMCA Sacramento, Sacramento, CA
15,000   Junior Achievement, Sacramento, CA
15,000   Sacramento Children's Home and Family Unit, Sacramento, CA
15,000   Salk Institute, San Diego, CA
15,000   Sutter Hospital Foundation, Sacramento, CA

ARCA FOUNDATION

Giving Contact
Donna F. Edwards, Executive Director
1308 19th St., NW
Washington, DC 20036
Phone: (202)822-9193
Fax: (202)785-1446
E-mail: grants@arcafoundation.org
Web: http://www.arcafoundation.org

Alternate Contact
Jeanne Mathison

Description
Founded: 1952
EIN: 132751798
Organization Type: General Purpose Foundation
Giving Locations: nationally.
Grant Types: Conference/Seminar, General Support, Matching, Multiyear/Continuing Support, Project.

Donor Information
Founder: Nancy Susan Reynolds founded the Arca Foundation, formerly known as the Nancy Reynolds Bagley Foundation, in 1952. By this time she had been active in philanthropy for over two decades. Her main concern was population control, because she felt overpopulation would hinder the standard of living worldwide. Until her death in 1985, she focused on hunger, human and civil rights, peace, a safe and healthy environment, and solar energy. This reflected her belief that ecological soundness is necessary to provide a place where people can create the opportunities to raise their own standard of living.
Nancy Susan Reynolds was the daughter of the late R. J. Reynolds, founder of the R. J. Reynolds Tobacco Company. She was the honorary chairman of the Z. Smith Reynolds Foundation and the vice president of the Sapelo Island Research Foundation.

Financial Summary
Total Giving: $2,404,705 (2003); $2,900,000 (2002 approx); $2,900,000 (2001)
Assets: $59,002,894 (2003); $73,000,000 (2002)

Typical Recipients
Arts & Humanities: Ethnic & Folk Arts, Film & Video, Museums/Galleries, Performing Arts, Theater
Civic & Public Affairs: African American Affairs, Civil Rights, Community Foundations, Economic Development, Economic Policy, Employment/Job Training, Ethnic Organizations, First Amendment Issues, Civic & Public Affairs-General, Hispanic Affairs, Law & Justice, Philanthropic Organizations, Public Policy, Rural Affairs, Safety, Urban & Community Affairs, Women's Affairs
Education: Colleges & Universities, Education Funds, Education-General, International Exchange, International Studies, Journalism/Media Education, Leadership Training, Legal Education, Literacy, Medical Education
Environment: Environment-General, Resource Conservation
Health: Clinics/Medical Centers, Health Policy/Cost Containment
International: Foreign Arts Organizations, Foreign Educational Institutions, Health Care/Hospitals, Human Rights, International Affairs, International Development, International Environmental Issues, International Organizations, International Peace & Security Issues, International Relations, International Relief Efforts, Missionary/Religious Activities, Trade
Religion: Churches, Ministries, Religious Organizations, Religious Welfare
Social Services: Child Abuse, Child Welfare, Community Service Organizations, Family Planning, Food/Clothing Distribution, Refugee Assistance, Substance Abuse

Application Procedures
Initial Contact: The foundation has no formal grant application procedure or application form. Send a clear, concise proposal (one copy).
Application Requirements: The proposal should include a cover letter that describes the project in a brief paragraph, states its total cost, and requests a specific grant amount. It should be signed by the Executive Director and/or Project Director. The proposal should also contain a one page summary, separate from the body of the proposal, highlighting the project's purposes and goals. Include a proposal narrative, of no more than ten pages, that summarizes the policy issue addressed; presents the organization's approach to the problem and specific goals, and provides background on the organization 's history, current range of activities and qualifications for carrying out the project. Organizational information should include short bios or resumes of the project staff and a list of the Board of Directors including affiliations. Also submit financial information including a list of all past Arca grants (year, amount, and project); a list of all grants received for the current year (amount, source, and project), the total organizational budget for the current and previous fiscal year; a list of project grants received in the current year (amount and source), a line-item project budget of income and expense;, and a list of potential funding sources for the project (amounts and contact persons). In addition, submit current IRS documents confirming the organization's status as both tax-exempt (501(c)(3)) and publicly supported (509(a)).
Deadlines: April 1 for the June board meeting; October 1 for the December board meeting.
Review Process: Applicants will receive a postcard acknowledging receipt of their proposal, and the foundation will request further information as needed. Applicants will be informed of the board's decision shortly after the board meets. If an applicant's proposal falls outside guidelines, it will be notified in writing within a month of submission.
Notes: Proposals received via fax will not be considered.

Restrictions
The foundation does not fund direct social services, scholarship funds, scholarly research, individuals, government programs, capital projects/endowments, or groups outside the U.S.

Additional Information
All grantees must submit a narrative and financial progress report prior to submitting additional funding requests. Deadlines for such a report are stipulated in the Grant Agreement that every grantee must sign.
Publications: Annual Report; Grantmaking Guidelines

Foundation Officials
Nancy R. Bagley: vice president, director
Nicole Bagley: director
Smith Bagley: president PRIM CORP EMPL president: Smith Bagley Inc. NONPR AFFIL trustee: Ken-

nedy Center for the Performing Arts; secretary: The Sapelo Foundation.

Ellsworth Culver: director B Seattle, WA 1927. ED Asbury College BA (1949). PRIM CORP EMPL senior vice president: Mercy Corp.s International. CORP AFFIL president: Culver Stowell Inc. NONPR AFFIL chairman: ProTem Foundation; co-founder: Sports Ambs International People-to-People Program; founder: Oregon Inter-Religious Committee Peace in Middle East; board member: Global Action; director: Mercy Corps Europe.

Donna F. Edwards: executive director

Mary E. King: secretary, director B Crump, TN 1937. PRIM CORP EMPL vice president benefits development & training, secretary: Cummings.

Mike Lux: director

Janet Shenk: director

Eric Sklar: treasurer, director B 1962. ED University of California at Berkeley (1984); London School of Economics (1985-1986). PRIM CORP EMPL president: Burrito Brothers Inc.

Margery Tabankin: director

Grants Analysis

Disclosure Period: calendar year ending 2003
Total Grants: $2,404,705
Number of Grants: 59
Average Grant: $40,758
Highest Grant: $104,200
Lowest Grant: $1,000
Typical Range: $20,000 to $50,000

Recent Grants

Note: Grants derived from 2002 Form 990.
General

125,000	Pebble of Faith Network, Brooklyn, NY -- for a new campaign to abolish sweatshops and child labor
100,000	Institute for Media Analysis, New York, NY
75,000	Center for Public Interest, Los Angeles, CA -- to support and promote regulatory reforms to make corporations accountable to the public
75,000	Georgetown University, Washington, DC -- for the construction project to continue public education work on reforms in the implementation of capital punishment
75,000	Institute for America's Future, Washington, DC
75,000	Medical Education Cooperation with Cuba, Atlanta, GA -- for operational support in its endeavors to bridge the US and Cuban medical communities
75,000	National Security Archive Fund, Washington, DC -- for its work on accountability for the US involvement in western hemispheric policy issues
75,000	Proteus Fund, Amherst, MA -- for the Piper Fund to promote and nurture state campaign reform efforts
75,000	Public Justice Foundation, Austin, TX -- to support work organizing former workers and shareholders of corporations involved in accounting scandals to tell their stories to the public
75,000	USAction Education Fund, Washington, DC

ARCADIA FOUNDATION

Giving Contact

Marilyn L. Steinbright, President
105 East Logan Street
Norristown, PA 19401-3060
Phone: (610)275-8460
Fax: (610)275-8460

Description

Founded: 1964
EIN: 236399772
Organization Type: Family Foundation
Giving Locations: PA: zip codes 18000 to 19800
Grant Types: Capital, Endowment, General Support.
Note: Scholarships are for higher education only-not personally, only to the School.

Donor Information

Founder: Established in 1964 by the late Edith C. Steinbright, and Marilyn Lee Steinbright.

Financial Summary

Total Giving: $7,290,659 (fiscal year ending September 30, 2003); $8,000,000 (fiscal 2002 approx); $7,955,744 (fiscal 2001 approx)
Assets: $5,556,238 (fiscal 2003); $50,000,000 (fiscal 2002 approx); $49,733,968 (fiscal 2001)
Gifts Received: $22,958 (fiscal 1999); $1,000 (fiscal 1996); $4,389,124 (fiscal 1995). Note: Contributions were received from the estate of Edith C. Steinbright.

Typical Recipients

Arts & Humanities: Arts Associations & Councils, Arts Centers, Arts Festivals, Arts Institutes, Arts Outreach, Ballet, Community Arts, Ethnic & Folk Arts, Arts & Humanities-General, Historic Preservation, History & Archaeology, Libraries, Museums/Galleries, Music, Performing Arts, Public Broadcasting, Theater
Civic & Public Affairs: Botanical Gardens/Parks, Clubs, Community Foundations, Economic Development, Ethnic Organizations, Civic & Public Affairs-General, Hispanic Affairs, Housing, Law & Justice, Legal Aid, Philanthropic Organizations, Safety, Urban & Community Affairs, Women's Affairs, Zoos/Aquariums
Education: Arts/Humanities Education, Colleges & Universities, Community & Junior Colleges, Education Associations, Education Funds, Engineering/Technological Education, Education-General, Literacy, Medical Education, Private Education (Precollege), Religious Education, Secondary Education (Private), Special Education, Student Aid
Environment: Air/Water Quality, Environment-General, Protection, Resource Conservation, Wildlife Protection
Health: Arthritis, Children's Health/Hospitals, Clinics/Medical Centers, Diabetes, Emergency/Ambulance Services, Health Funds, Health Organizations, Hospices, Hospitals, Hospitals (University Affiliated), Long-Term Care, Mental Health, Nursing Services, Research/Studies Institutes, Single-Disease Health Associations
International: International Organizations, International Relations
Religion: Churches, Jewish Causes, Ministries, Religious Organizations, Religious Welfare, Seminaries
Science: Science Museums, Scientific Centers & Institutes, Scientific Organizations
Social Services: Animal Protection, Camps, Child Welfare, Community Centers, Community Service Organizations, Crime Prevention, Day Care, Emergency Relief, Food/Clothing Distribution, People with Disabilities, Recreation & Athletics, Senior Services, Volunteer Services, YMCA/YWCA/YMHA/YWHA, Youth Organizations

Application Procedures

Initial Contact: Applicants should submit a succinct letter of proposal, no longer than two pages, to the foundation.
Application Requirements: The letter should include a brief history and purpose of organization, the amount of funding requested, how funds will be spent, and proof of the organization's tax-exempt status.
Deadlines: Proposals are accepted only between September 1 and November 1 for the following calendar year.

Review Process: The board meets in December. Notification is usually given within one month.
Notes: The foundation will discard applications that include any extra material, such as brochures, a board of directors list, or treasurer's report.

Restrictions

Grants are not made for, fellowships, conferences, publications, demonstration projects, deficit financing, dinners, special events, fraternal organizations, multi-year grants, political or lobbying groups, or goodwill advertising. New proposals are limited to organizations residing in Pennsylvania within zip codes 18-19800. Grants are not made to individuals.

Additional Information

When requesting a grant for the first time, don't ask for a large amount ($20,000 or more), it will be thrown out immediately.
Publications: Guidelines

Foundation Officials

Tanya Hashorva: vice president
Harvey S. Shipley Miller: treasurer B Philadelphia, PA 1948. ED Swarthmore College MBA (1970); Harvard University JD (1973). NONPR AFFIL trustee: University Pennsylvania; board overseers: University Pennsylvania School Nursing; trustee: Philadelphia Museum Art; member: Union League; member: Phi Sigma Kappa; member: Philadelphia Art Alliance; member: Metropolitan Museum Art; trustee: National Gallery Art; member: Collections Comm Historical Society; member: Library College; member: Association Bar New York City; member: Athenaeum Association; member: American Bar Association; member: American Philosophical Society. CLUB AFFIL Harvard Club; Swarthmore Club.
David P. Sandler: secretary B 1935. PRIM CORP EMPL president: Dreslin Co. Inc. CORP AFFIL certified public accountant: Norristown Brick Inc.
Marilyn L. Steinbright: president

Grants Analysis

Disclosure Period: fiscal year ending September 30, 2003
Total Grants: $7,290,659
Number of Grants: 222
Average Grant: $19,864*
Highest Grant: $500,000
Lowest Grant: $500
Typical Range: $5,000 to $40,000
*Note: Average grant figure excludes six highest grants ($3,000,000).

Recent Grants

Note: Grants derived from fiscal 2003 Form 990.
Library-Related

50,000	Library Company of Philadelphia, Philadelphia, PA
25,000	Free Library of Philadelphia, Philadelphia, PA

General

500,000	Arcadia University, Glenside, PA
500,000	Cedar Crest College, Allentown, PA
500,000	Lancaster Theological Seminary, Lancaster, PA
500,000	Montgomery Hospital Foundation, Norristown, PA
500,000	Pennsylvania Academy of Fine Arts, Philadelphia, PA
500,000	Ursinus College, Collegeville, PA
300,000	Philadelphia Museum of Art, Philadelphia, PA
250,000	Pennsylvania Se Conference of the United Church of Christ, Collegeville, PA
150,000	Hancock Fire Company, Norristown, PA
150,000	University of Pennsylvania Nursing School, Philadelphia, PA

ADRIAN AND JESSIE ARCHBOLD CHARITABLE TRUST

Giving Contact

Myra Mahon, Director
c/o J.P. Morgan Chase Bank
1211 Ave. of the Americas, 34th Fl.
New York, NY 10036
Phone: (212)789-4156

Description

Founded: 1976
EIN: 510179829
Organization Type: General Purpose Foundation
Giving Locations: NY: eastern United States
Grant Types: Conference/Seminar, General Support, Multiyear/Continuing Support.

Donor Information

Founder: Established in 1976 by the late Mrs. Adrian Archbold.

Financial Summary

Total Giving: $1,568,000 (fiscal year ending November 30, 2002); $1,791,000 (fiscal 2001)
Assets: $28,912,373 (fiscal 2002); $33,986,070 (fiscal 2001)

Typical Recipients

Arts & Humanities: Arts Associations & Councils, Arts Funds, Arts Institutes, Ballet, Dance, Arts & Humanities-General, Historic Preservation, Libraries, Museums/Galleries, Music, Opera, Performing Arts, Theater
Civic & Public Affairs: African American Affairs, Botanical Gardens/Parks, Business/Free Enterprise, Community Foundations, Employment/Job Training, Ethnic Organizations, Civic & Public Affairs-General, Hispanic Affairs, Housing, Legal Aid, Philanthropic Organizations, Public Policy, Safety, Urban & Community Affairs, Women's Affairs
Education: Arts/Humanities Education, Business-School Partnerships, Colleges & Universities, Education Associations, Education Funds, Education Reform, Environmental Education, Education-General, Health & Physical Education, Legal Education, Medical Education, Private Education (Precollege), Public Education (Precollege), Religious Education, Secondary Education (Public), Special Education, Student Aid
Environment: Environment-General, Protection, Research, Resource Conservation, Wildlife Protection
Health: AIDS/HIV, Cancer, Children's Health/Hospitals, Clinics/Medical Centers, Emergency/Ambulance Services, Health-General, Health Funds, Health Organizations, Hospitals, Hospitals (University Affiliated), Medical Rehabilitation, Medical Research, Mental Health, Prenatal Health Issues, Public Health, Single-Disease Health Associations
International: Health Care/Hospitals, International Environmental Issues, International Peace & Security Issues, International Relations
Religion: Churches, Dioceses, Religion-General, Religious Organizations, Religious Welfare, Seminaries
Science: Scientific Centers & Institutes, Scientific Labs, Scientific Research
Social Services: At-Risk Youth, Big Brothers/Big Sisters, Camps, Child Welfare, Community Service Organizations, Day Care, Family Planning, Family Services, Homes, People with Disabilities, Recreation & Athletics, Scouts, Shelters/Homelessness, Social Services-General, Substance Abuse, United Funds/United Ways, YMCA/YWCA/YMHA/YWHA, Youth Organizations

Application Procedures

Initial Contact: The trust has no formal grant procedure or grant application form.
Deadlines: None.
Review Process: Grants are made throughout the tax year.

Restrictions

The trust makes grants only to organizations that are tax-exempt under IRS tax laws. Grants are made for general charitable purposes with emphasis on medical programs and research. No grants are made to individuals, or for endowment funds, scholarships, fellowships, building funds, or loans.

Additional Information

The trust reports that Chase Manhattan Bank acts as a corporate trustee.
Particular consideration may be given to programs associated with the Archbold Memorial Hospital at the trustee's discretion.
Publications: Program Policy Statement

Foundation Officials

Arthur Joseph Mahon: trustee B New York, NY 1934. ED Manhattan College BA (1955); New York University JD (1958). PRIM CORP EMPL counsel: McDermott, Will & Emery. NONPR AFFIL member: New York State Bar Association; member committee trustee & estate gift plans: Rockefeller University; trustee: Manhattan College; member: Florida Bar Association; trustee: Inner City Scholarship Fund; member: District of Columbia Bar Association; chairman board overseers: Cornell University Medicine College; counselor: Ira W De Camp Foundation; vice president, director: Catholic Communal Fund; chairman planned giving committee: Archdiocese New York; member: Association Bar New York City; director: American Skin Association.

Grants Analysis

Disclosure Period: fiscal year ending November 30, 2002
Total Grants: $1,568,000
Number of Grants: 97
Average Grant: $8,521*
Highest Grant: $750,000
Lowest Grant: $1,000
Typical Range: $5,000 to $25,000
*Note: Average grant figure excludes highest grant.

Recent Grants

Note: Grants derived from fiscal 2002 Form 990.
General

750,000	Archbold Memorial Hospital, Thomasville, GA
75,000	Alvin Ailey Dance Foundation Inc., New York, NY
30,000	New York Weill Cornell Medical Center, New York, NY
25,000	Mountainside Foundation, Canaan, CT
25,000	Providence Health Services Foundation, New York, NY
20,000	God's Love We Deliver, New York, NY
15,000	Alvin Ailey Dance Foundation Inc., New York, NY
15,000	Calvary Hospital, Bronx, NY
15,000	Mountainside Foundation, Canaan, CT
15,000	New York City Ballet, New York, NY

ARCHER-DANIELS-MIDLAND CO.

Company Headquarters

Decatur, IL
Web: http://www.admworld.com

Company Description

Founded: 1923
Ticker: ADM
Exchange: NYSE
Revenue: US$36.151 billion (2004)
Profit: US$494.7 million (2004)
Employees: 25000 (2003)
Fortune Rank: 44, per FORTUNE Magazine's list of 500 Largest U.S. Corporations (2004).
SIC(s): 2041 Flour & Other Grain Mill Products, 2045 Prepared Flour Mixes & Doughs, 2046 Wet Corn Milling, 2074 Cottonseed Oil Mills.

Operating Locations

ADM Animal Health & Nutrition (NC--Dunn); ADM Arkady Products (IN--Olathe); ADM Bio Products Division (IL--Decatur); ADM Cocoa Division (IL--Decatur); ADM Corn Processing Division (IL--Decatur); ADM/Country Mark (IL--Decatur); ADM Export Co. (IL--Decatur); ADM Growmark (IA--Cedar Rapids); ADM Investor Service Inc. (IL--Chicago); ADM Milling Co. (KS--Overland Park); Agri-Sales Inc. (MI--Saginaw); Agrinational Insurance Co. (IL--Decatur); American River Transportation (IL--Decatur); Archer-Daniels-Midland Shipping (IL--Decatur); Benson-Quinn Co. (MN--Minneapolis); Collingwood Grain Inc. (KS--Hutchinson); Gooch Foods Inc. (NE--Lincoln); Hickory Point Bank & Trust Co. (IL--Decatur); Iowa Interstate Railroad (IA--Iowa City); Moorman's Inc. (IL--Quincy); Southern Cellulose Products (TN--Chattanooga); Southern Cotton Oil Co. (IL--Decatur); Tabor Grain Co. (IL--Macon)

Nonmonetary Support

Value: $3,000,000 (2000)
Type: Donated Equipment; Donated Products
Contact: Larry, senior vice president
Note: Cunningham

Archer-Daniels-Midland Foundation

Giving Contact

Brian F. Peterson, Vice President & Treasurer
Archer-Daniels-Midland Foundation
4666 Faries Parkway
PO Box 1470
Decatur, IL 62525
Phone: (217)424-5957
Fax: (217)424-5581
Web: http://www.admworld.com
Note: Telephone inquiries are strongly discouraged. A contact person is not listed.

Description

Founded: 1953
EIN: 416023126
Organization Type: Corporate Foundation
Giving Locations: nationally, principally near operating locations and to national organizations.
Grant Types: Capital, Employee Matching Gifts, General Support, Matching, Multiyear/Continuing Support.
Note: Employee matching gift ratio: 1 to 1, up to $2,000 annually per recipient per employee.

Financial Summary

Total Giving: $1,565,836 (fiscal year ending June 31, 2004); $4,542,254 (fiscal 2003); $2,600,000 (fiscal 2002 approx). Note: Contributes through foundation only.
Giving Analysis: Giving for fiscal 2003 includes: foundation matching gifts ($918,867); fiscal 2002: foundation (approx $2,600,000); fiscal 2001: foundation matching gifts ($806,188); foundation ($1,575,206)
Assets: $1,057 (fiscal 2004); $1,543,742 (fiscal 2003); $112,150 (fiscal 2001)
Gifts Received: $6,000,000 (fiscal 2003);

$2,600,000 (fiscal 2002 approx); $2,400,000 (fiscal 2001). Note: Contributions were received from Archer-Daniels-Midland Company.

Typical Recipients

Arts & Humanities: Arts Associations & Councils, Arts Centers, Arts Festivals, Arts Funds, Arts Institutes, Ethnic & Folk Arts, Historic Preservation, History & Archaeology, Libraries, Museums/Galleries, Music, Opera, Performing Arts, Public Broadcasting, Theater

Civic & Public Affairs: African American Affairs, Business/Free Enterprise, Civil Rights, Clubs, Community Foundations, Economic Development, Economic Policy, Civic & Public Affairs-General, Hispanic Affairs, Law & Justice, Legal Aid, Native American Affairs, Philanthropic Organizations, Professional & Trade Associations, Public Policy, Rural Affairs, Safety, Urban & Community Affairs, Women's Affairs, Zoos/Aquariums

Education: Agricultural Education, Arts/Humanities Education, Business Education, Colleges & Universities, Community & Junior Colleges, Economic Education, Education Associations, Education Funds, Engineering/Technological Education, Faculty Development, Education-General, Health & Physical Education, International Exchange, International Studies, Legal Education, Medical Education, Minority Education, Private Education (Precollege), Public Education (Precollege), Religious Education, Science/Mathematics Education, Secondary Education (Private), Student Aid, Vocational & Technical Education

Environment: Forestry, Environment-General, Resource Conservation, Wildlife Protection

Health: Cancer, Children's Health/Hospitals, Emergency/Ambulance Services, Health Organizations, Heart, Hospices, Hospitals, Mental Health, Prenatal Health Issues

International: Foreign Educational Institutions, Health Care/Hospitals, Human Rights, International Affairs, International Development, International Environmental Issues, International Organizations, International Peace & Security Issues, International Relations, International Relief Efforts, Missionary/Religious Activities, Trade

Religion: Churches, Religion-General, Jewish Causes, Missionary Activities (Domestic), Religious Organizations, Religious Welfare

Science: Science-General, Science Museums, Scientific Centers & Institutes

Social Services: Camps, Child Welfare, Community Service Organizations, Day Care, Delinquency & Criminal Rehabilitation, Emergency Relief, Family Planning, Family Services, Food/Clothing Distribution, People with Disabilities, Recreation & Athletics, Scouts, Senior Services, Shelters/Homelessness, Social Services-General, Substance Abuse, United Funds/United Ways, Volunteer Services, YMCA/YWCA/YMHA/YWHA, Youth Organizations

Application Procedures

Initial Contact: Send a brief letter or proposal.
Application Requirements: Include a description of organization, amount requested, purpose of funds sought, recently audited financial statement, and proof of tax-exempt status.
Deadlines: April 30 for consideration in planned giving for following fiscal year, July 1 to June 30.
Notes: The foundation does not accept phone inquiries.

Restrictions

Grants are not made to individuals.
Generally does not give to united funds except in the form of matching gifts.

Corporate Officials

G. Allen Andreas: chairman, chief executive officer B June 22, 1943. ED Valparaiso University BA (1965); Valparaiso University JD (1968). PRIM CORP EMPL chairman, chief executive officer: Ar-

cher Daniels Midland Co.
Richard P. Reising: senior vice president, general counsel, secretary B 1944. ED Stanford University BA; University of Missouri JD (1969). PRIM CORP EMPL senior vice president, general counsel, secretary: Archer-Daniels-Midland Co. ADD CORP EMPL president: Agrinational Insurance Co.; secretary: Coeval Inc. CORP AFFIL director: Hickory Point Bank & Trust.

Foundation Officials

G. Allen Andreas: director (see above)
M. H. Carter: director
D. J. Schmalz: president
D. J. Smith: vice president, secretary
G. Webb: director

Grants Analysis

Disclosure Period: fiscal year ending June 31, 2004
Total Grants: $603,521*
Number of Grants: 31
Average Grant: $16,784*
Highest Grant: $100,000
Lowest Grant: $100
Typical Range: $5,000 to $30,000
*Note: Giving excludes matching gifts; United Way. Average grant figure excludes highest grant.

Recent Grants

Note: Grants derived from 2004 Form 990.
General

100,000	Minnesota Historical Society, St. Paul, MN
67,120	Community Foundation of Decatur and Macon County, Decatur, IL
65,000	United Way of Decatur & Macon County, Decatur, IL
50,000	American Red Cross, Washington, DC
50,000	Anti Defamation League of B'nai B'rith Canada
50,000	Dakota Wesleyan University, Mitchell, SD
50,000	Greater Y Capital Campaign, Providence, RI
50,000	Little Theatre on the Square
25,000	Association of Illinois Soil & Water Conservation
25,000	Robertson Charter School

NORMAN ARCHIBALD CHARITABLE FOUNDATION

Giving Contact

Chuck Viele, Vice President, Trust Officer
Norman Archibald Charitable Foundation
c/o Wells Fargo Bank
PO Box 21927
Seattle, WA 98111
Phone: (206)292-3533

Description

Founded: 1976
EIN: 911098014
Organization Type: Private Foundation
Giving Locations: WA: Puget Sound region
Grant Types: Capital, General Support, Project, Research.

Donor Information

Founder: the late Norman Archibald

Financial Summary

Total Giving: $436,700 (fiscal year ending September 30, 2004); $582,100 (fiscal 2001). Note: Giving includes scholarship, United Way.
Giving Analysis: Giving for fiscal 2004 includes:

foundation grants to United Way ($45,000); fiscal 2001: foundation grants to United Way ($75,000)
Assets: $9,036,908 (fiscal 2004); $9,638,406 (fiscal 2001)
Gifts Received: $2,730 (fiscal 1997)

Typical Recipients

Arts & Humanities: Arts Associations & Councils, Arts Centers, Ballet, Dance, Historic Preservation, History & Archaeology, Libraries, Museums/Galleries, Music, Opera, Performing Arts, Theater

Civic & Public Affairs: Botanical Gardens/Parks, Chambers of Commerce, Clubs, Economic Development, Employment/Job Training, Civic & Public Affairs-General, Housing, Municipalities/Towns, Safety, Urban & Community Affairs, Women's Affairs, Zoos/Aquariums

Education: Arts/Humanities Education, Business Education, Colleges & Universities, Community & Junior Colleges, Education Funds, Education Reform, Education-General, Leadership Training, Legal Education, Literacy, Private Education (Precollege), Public Education (Precollege), Religious Education, Secondary Education (Private), Secondary Education (Public), Special Education, Vocational & Technical Education

Environment: Air/Water Quality, Environment-General, Resource Conservation

Health: AIDS/HIV, Alzheimer's Disease, Arthritis, Cancer, Children's Health/Hospitals, Clinics/Medical Centers, Emergency/Ambulance Services, Health Organizations, Hospitals, Medical Rehabilitation, Medical Research, Mental Health, Nursing Services, Research/Studies Institutes, Single-Disease Health Associations, Transplant Networks/Donor Banks

International: International Environmental Issues, International Organizations

Religion: Churches, Dioceses, Jewish Causes, Religious Welfare

Science: Science Museums, Scientific Centers & Institutes

Social Services: Animal Protection, At-Risk Youth, Child Welfare, Community Centers, Community Service Organizations, Counseling, Day Care, Domestic Violence, Food/Clothing Distribution, Homes, People with Disabilities, Scouts, Senior Services, Substance Abuse, United Funds/United Ways, Volunteer Services, YMCA/YWCA/YMHA/YWHA, Youth Organizations

Application Procedures

Initial Contact: Applications should be submitted in the form of a letter signed by the chairman of the board, president, or chief operating officer of the organization.
Application Requirements: Include name and address of organization, list of board of directors with principal affiliations, a description of organization, amount requested, list of other funding sources, description of project and what it is designed to achieve, detailed budget for project, location of project and people expected to benefit from it, name of person in charge of the project, financial statements for the past two years, and proof of tax-exempt status.
Deadlines: None.

Restrictions

Does not support individuals, religious organizations, or governmental organizations.

Additional Information

Foundation emphasizes one-time, tangible needs rather than operational or programmatic proposals.
Publications: Annual Report; Application Guidelines
Trust(s): Wells Fargo Bank

Foundation Officials

Robert L. Gerth: adv
Shan J. Mullin: adv B Bellingham, WA 1934. ED University of Washington BS (1956); University of Washington JD (1958). PRIM CORP EMPL partner: Perkins Cole. NONPR AFFIL trustee: University

Washington Law School Foundation; member: Washington State Bar Association; chairman: United Way King County Endowment Fund; member: Seattle International Tax Roundtable; member: Seattle-King County Bar Association; Rotary; co-founder, vice chairman: Seattle Alliance Education; Phi Delta Phi; Phi Gamma Delta; member, director: Fred Hutchinson Cancer Research Center; member: Intl Bar Association; member: Greater Seattle Chamber of Commerce; member, director: American Red Cross; Beta Gamma Sigma; member: American Bar Association. CLUB AFFIL Seattle Tennis Club; Broadmoor Golf Club; Rainier Club.

Stuart H. Prestrud: adv ED University of Washington (1946); Pacific Coast Banking School (1955). CORP AFFIL vice president, director: Aldarra Management Co.; consult: First Interstate Bank Washington.

Grants Analysis

Disclosure Period: fiscal year ending September 30, 2004
Total Grants: $391,700*
Number of Grants: 72
Average Grant: $5,440
Highest Grant: $25,000
Lowest Grant: $1,000
Typical Range: $1,000 to $10,000
***Note:** Giving excludes United Way.

Recent Grants

Note: Grants derived from fiscal 2000 Form 990.
General

40,000	Seattle Art Museum, Seattle, WA
30,000	Puget Sound Blood Center, Seattle, WA
30,000	Seattle Foundation for United Way Gates Foundation, Seattle, WA
25,000	United Way of King County, Seattle, WA
20,000	Museum of Flight, Seattle, WA
20,000	Seattle Opera Association, Seattle, WA
15,000	Pacific Northwest Ballet, Seattle, WA
10,000	Corporate Council for the Arts, Seattle, WA
10,000	Henry Gallery Association, Seattle, WA
10,000	Independent Colleges of Washington, Seattle, WA

ARGUILD FOUNDATION

Giving Contact

Arthur G. Connolly, Jr., Secretary
1007 N. Orange Street
Wilmington, DE 19801
Phone: (302)658-9141

Description

Founded: 1959
EIN: 516016487
Organization Type: Private Foundation
Giving Locations: DE: Wilmington Northeastern United States.
Grant Types: Capital, General Support.

Donor Information

Founder: Arthur G. Connolly, Sr.

Financial Summary

Total Giving: $323,000 (2003); $695,206 (2001)
Assets: $7,187,470 (2003); $7,352,679 (2001)
Gifts Received: $146,850 (1995); $123,188 (1994); $37,009 (1993). Note: In 1995, contributions were received from Arthur G. Connolly, Sr.

Typical Recipients

Arts & Humanities: Libraries, Music, Public Broadcasting
Civic & Public Affairs: Community Foundations, Employment/Job Training, Civic & Public Affairs-General, Public Policy

Education: Colleges & Universities, Engineering/Technological Education, Education-General, Health & Physical Education, Legal Education, Minority Education, Private Education (Precollege), Secondary Education (Private)
Environment: Environment-General, Resource Conservation
Health: Cancer, Children's Health/Hospitals, Clinics/Medical Centers, Hospices
International: International Relief Efforts
Religion: Dioceses, Religion-General, Jewish Causes, Ministries, Religious Organizations, Religious Welfare
Social Services: Child Welfare, Community Service Organizations, Family Planning, Family Services, Substance Abuse, United Funds/United Ways

Application Procedures

Initial Contact: Send a brief letter of inquiry. Additional materials may be sent at the requesting organization's discretion.
Deadlines: None.

Restrictions

Contributions are made to IRC 501(c)(3) organizations which have demonstrated through past performance a proven excellence and successful accomplishment of objectives. Grants are not made to individuals.

Foundation Officials

Mary Connolly Braun: president
Arthur G. Connolly, Jr.: secretary
Thomas A. Connolly, Esq.: treasurer

Grants Analysis

Disclosure Period: calendar year ending 2003
Total Grants: $323,000
Number of Grants: 87
Average Grant: $2,718*
Highest Grant: $46,000
Lowest Grant: $1,000
Typical Range: $1,000 to $5,000
***Note:** Average grant figure excludes two highest grants ($92,000).

Recent Grants

Note: Grants derived from 2003 Form 990.
General

46,000	Arguild Foundation Boston
46,000	Arguild Foundation West
25,000	Princeton University, Princeton, NJ
10,000	Christ or Chaos Inc.
10,000	St. Mary Conference
10,000	University of Pennsylvania, Philadelphia, PA
5,500	Salvation Army
5,000	Ava Maria School of Law
5,000	Children & Families First, Wilmington, DE
5,000	National Adoption Center, DE

ARGYLE FOUNDATION

Giving Contact

Margo Marbut, President
200 Concord Plaza, Suite 700
San Antonio, TX 78216-6941
Phone: (210)822-3100
Fax: (210)828-7300

Description

Founded: 1997
EIN: 742815647
Organization Type: Private Foundation
Giving Locations: GA; NY; TX
Grant Types: General Support.

Financial Summary

Total Giving: $81,620 (2003); $146,900 (2001)
Giving Analysis: Giving for 2001 includes: foundation grants to United Way ($20,000)
Assets: $1,760,612 (2003); $1,664,726 (2001)
Gifts Received: $54,526 (2003); $11,000 (2001); $102,900 (1998). Note: In 2001 and 2003, contributions were received from Robert and Margo Marbut.

Typical Recipients

Arts & Humanities: Dance, Libraries, Museums/Galleries, Music, Public Broadcasting
Civic & Public Affairs: Community Foundations, Ethnic Organizations, Civic & Public Affairs-General, Public Policy
Education: Business Education, Colleges & Universities, Education Funds, International Studies, Preschool Education, Private Education (Precollege), Religious Education, Science/Mathematics Education
Environment: Environment-General
Health: Cancer, Emergency/Ambulance Services, Health Organizations
International: Foreign Educational Institutions, International Organizations
Religion: Jewish Causes, Synagogues/Temples
Science: Scientific Centers & Institutes
Social Services: Emergency Relief, Family Planning, Substance Abuse, United Funds/United Ways, YMCA/YWCA/YMHA/YWHA, Youth Organizations

Application Procedures

Initial Contact: The foundation has no formal grant application procedure or application form.
Application Requirements: Provide proof of tax-exempt status.
Deadlines: December 31 for contributions made the following year.

Foundation Officials

Joann Bennett: treasurer
Margo Marbut: president
Mike Marbut: director
Robert Marbut: chairman
Patricia Meyer: secretary

Grants Analysis

Disclosure Period: calendar year ending 2003
Total Grants: $81,620
Number of Grants: 16
Average Grant: $3,759*
Highest Grant: $25,240
Lowest Grant: $250
Typical Range: $1,000 to $5,000
***Note:** Average grant figure excludes highest grant.

Recent Grants

Note: Grants derived from 2003 Form 990.

General

25,240	Hewitt School, New York, NY
11,100	Temple Beth - El, San Antonio, TX
10,000	Campus of the San Antonio Jewish Community, San Antonio, TX
10,000	Partners of '63, New Haven, CT
5,000	American Red Cross, San Antonio, TX
5,000	Cancer Therapy and Research Center, San Antonio, TX
5,000	St. Mary's University, San Antonio, TX
2,700	Middle East Form, Philadelphia, PA
2,000	St. Andrews College, Bronxville, NY
1,000	Georgia Tech Foundation Inc., Atlanta, GA

ARGYROS FOUNDATION

Giving Contact
Daniel Russo, Trustee
949 S. Coast Dr., Suite 600
Costa Mesa, CA 92626
Phone: (714)481-5000
Fax: (714)481-5000

Description
Founded: 1979
EIN: 953421867
Organization Type: Private Foundation
Giving Locations: CA
Grant Types: Capital, Project.

Donor Information
Founder: the Argyros Charitable Trusts

Financial Summary
Gifts Received: $535,870 (fiscal year ending July 31, 2000); $1,525,715 (fiscal 1999); $274,075 (fiscal 1998). Note: In fiscal 2000, contributions were received from Argyros Charitable Trust 4 ($309,000) and George L. Argyros ($226,870). In fiscal 1999, contributions were received from Argyros Charitable Trust No. 4. ($315,000), Georgeh Argyros ($1,294,983) and GLA Foundation ($5,732).

Typical Recipients
Arts & Humanities: Arts Associations & Councils, Arts Centers, Arts Funds, Ballet, Arts & Humanities-General, Historic Preservation, History & Archaeology, Libraries, Museums/Galleries, Music, Opera, Performing Arts, Public Broadcasting, Theater
Civic & Public Affairs: Clubs, Economic Development, Economic Policy, Civic & Public Affairs-General, Hispanic Affairs, Philanthropic Organizations, Professional & Trade Associations, Public Policy, Safety, Urban & Community Affairs, Women's Affairs, Zoos/Aquariums
Education: Business Education, Colleges & Universities, Education Funds, Education-General, International Studies, Student Aid, Vocational & Technical Education
Environment: Air/Water Quality, Resource Conservation, Wildlife Protection
Health: AIDS/HIV, Cancer, Children's Health/Hospitals, Clinics/Medical Centers, Diabetes, Emergency/Ambulance Services, Eyes/Blindness, Health Organizations, Hospitals, Medical Research, Preventive Medicine/Wellness Organizations, Public Health, Single-Disease Health Associations, Trauma Treatment
International: International-General, International Affairs, International Peace & Security Issues, International Relief Efforts
Religion: Churches, Dioceses, Religion-General, Jewish Causes, Religious Organizations, Religious Welfare, Social/Policy Issues
Science: Science Museums, Scientific Centers & Institutes, Scientific Labs, Scientific Organizations
Social Services: Big Brothers/Big Sisters, Child Abuse, Child Welfare, Community Service Organizations, Domestic Violence, Food/Clothing Distribution, Homes, People with Disabilities, Recreation & Athletics, Scouts, Senior Services, Substance Abuse, United Funds/United Ways, Volunteer Services, YMCA/YWCA/YMHA/YWHA, Youth Organizations

Application Procedures
Initial Contact: Send a brief letter of inquiry.
Application Requirements: a description of organization, purpose of funds sought, proof of tax-exempt status, and federal identification number.
Deadlines: June 1.

Restrictions
Grants are typically awarded for special projects and situations.

Foundation Officials
Julie A. Argyros: president, trustee
Carol Campbell: director
Warren Finley: trustee
Charles E. Packard: trustee

Grants Analysis
Disclosure Period: fiscal year ending July 31, 2000
Total Grants: $3,019,323
Number of Grants: 77
Average Grant: $19,673*
Highest Grant: $1,524,200
Lowest Grant: $250
Typical Range: $5,000 to $50,000
***Note:** Average grant excludes highest grant.

Recent Grants
Note: Grants derived from 2002 Form 990.
General

1,205,000	South Coast Repertory Theater, Costa Mesa, CA
1,059,800	Chapman University, Orange, CA
200,000	Horatio Alger Association of Distinguished Americans, Alexandria, VA
198,600	Vaanda S.A., Madrid Spain
160,000	Doheny Eye Institute, Los Angeles, CA
100,000	Sage Hill School, Newport Beach, CA
51,500	Orange County Council, Boy Scouts of America, Costa Mesa, CA
50,500	Orange County Performing Arts Center, Costa Mesa, CA
50,000	Center for Strategic and International Studies (CSIS), Washington, DC
50,000	Crystal Cathedral, Garden Grove, CA

BEN H. AND GLADYS ARKELIAN FOUNDATION

Giving Contact
Richard G. McBurnie, Jr., President
PO Box 1825
Bakersfield, CA 93303
Phone: (661)873-0360
Fax: (661)873-0362

Description
Founded: 1959
EIN: 956103223
Organization Type: Private Foundation
Giving Locations: CA
Grant Types: Capital, General Support.

Financial Summary
Total Giving: $129,833 (2003); $153,407 (2001)
Assets: $4,374,539 (2003); $3,703,026 (2001)

Typical Recipients
Arts & Humanities: Historic Preservation, History & Archaeology, Libraries, Museums/Galleries, Music, Opera, Public Broadcasting, Theater
Civic & Public Affairs: Clubs, Civic & Public Affairs-General, Legal Aid, Native American Affairs, Rural Affairs
Education: Colleges & Universities, Community & Junior Colleges, Education-General, Legal Education, Preschool Education, Private Education (Precollege), Public Education (Precollege), Secondary Education (Private), Secondary Education (Public)
Environment: Environment-General
Health: Arthritis, Cancer, Children's Health/Hospitals, Clinics/Medical Centers, Emergency/Ambulance Services, Health Funds, Health Organizations, Hospices, Hospitals, Multiple Sclerosis, Single-Disease Health Associations, Transplant Networks/Donor Banks
International: Health Care/Hospitals
Religion: Churches, Religion-General, Religious Organizations, Religious Welfare
Social Services: At-Risk Youth, Child Welfare, Community Service Organizations, Counseling, Crime Prevention, Domestic Violence, Family Services, Homes, People with Disabilities, Recreation & Athletics, Shelters/Homelessness, Social Services-General, Substance Abuse, United Funds/United Ways, Youth Organizations

Application Procedures
Initial Contact: Send a brief letter of inquiry.
Application Requirements: Include a description of program.
Deadlines: None.

Restrictions
Generally, grants are limited to Kern County, CA.

Foundation Officials
Richard G. McBurnie: president, director
Mary C. Means: bookkeeper

Grants Analysis
Disclosure Period: calendar year ending 2003
Total Grants: $129,833
Number of Grants: 27
Average Grant: $3,712*
Highest Grant: $33,320
Lowest Grant: $179
Typical Range: $1,000 to $5,000
***Note:** Average grant figure excludes highest grant.

Recent Grants
Note: Grants derived from 2001 Form 990.
General

20,000	Hoffman Hospice, Bakersfield, CA -- capital improvements
20,000	Houchin Blood Bank, Bakersfield, CA -- capital improvements
10,000	California State University, Bakersfield, CA -- capital improvements
10,000	Friends of Mercy Foundation, Bakersfield, CA -- capital improvements
9,800	Emanuel Medical Center, Turlock, CA -- capital improvements
8,300	Bright Beginnings, Bakersfield, CA -- capital improvements
8,000	Bakersfield Homeless Center, Bakersfield, CA -- capital improvements
8,000	Garces Memorial High School, San Francisco, CA -- capital improvements
7,500	Boys and Girls Club, Bakersfield, CA -- capital improvements
6,000	South Fork School and Community, Weldon, CA -- capital improvements

ARKELL HALL FOUNDATION

Giving Contact
Joseph A. Santangelo, Vice President, Treasurer, Administrator
68 Front Street
PO Box 240
Canajoharie, NY 13317-0240
Phone: (518)673-5417
Fax: (518)673-5493

Description
Founded: 1948
EIN: 141343077
Organization Type: General Purpose Foundation
Giving Locations: NY: Western Montgomery County
Grant Types: Award, Capital, Challenge, Endowment, General Support, Matching, Seed Money.

Donor Information
Founder: Established in 1948 by the late Mrs. F. E. Barbour.

Financial Summary
Total Giving: $1,489,400 (fiscal year ending November 30, 2003); $600,000 (fiscal 2002 approx); $1,212,395 (fiscal 2001). Note: Fiscal 1997 Giving includes scholarship ($33,000).
Giving Analysis: Giving for fiscal 2003 includes: foundation grants to United Way ($20,000); foundation scholarships ($70,000); fiscal 2001: foundation scholarships ($27,000); foundation grants to United Way ($30,000)
Assets: $54,350,720 (fiscal 2003); $57,181,711 (fiscal 2001)
Gifts Received: $950 (fiscal 1997)

Typical Recipients
Arts & Humanities: Arts Centers, Ballet, Historic Preservation, History & Archaeology, Libraries, Museums/Galleries, Music, Public Broadcasting, Theater
Civic & Public Affairs: Botanical Gardens/Parks, Clubs, Community Foundations, Economic Development, Civic & Public Affairs-General, Housing, Legal Aid, Municipalities/Towns, Philanthropic Organizations, Rural Affairs, Safety, Urban & Community Affairs
Education: Colleges & Universities, Community & Junior Colleges, Education Funds, Engineering/Technological Education, Environmental Education, Education-General, Health & Physical Education, International Exchange, Legal Education, Literacy, Medical Education, Minority Education, Private Education (Precollege), Public Education (Precollege), Religious Education, Science/Mathematics Education, Secondary Education (Public), Student Aid
Health: Alzheimer's Disease, Cancer, Children's Health/Hospitals, Clinics/Medical Centers, Diabetes, Emergency/Ambulance Services, Health-General, Health Funds, Health Organizations, Heart, Hospices, Hospitals, Long-Term Care, Medical Research, Nursing Services, Outpatient Health Care, Prenatal Health Issues, Single-Disease Health Associations
International: International Development, International Relief Efforts
Religion: Churches, Ministries, Religious Organizations, Religious Welfare
Social Services: Animal Protection, Big Brothers/Big Sisters, Community Centers, Community Service Organizations, Counseling, Crime Prevention, Domestic Violence, Emergency Relief, Family Services, Food/Clothing Distribution, People with Disabilities, Recreation & Athletics, Scouts, Senior Services, Substance Abuse, United Funds/United Ways, YMCA/YWCA/YMHA/YWHA, Youth Organizations

Application Procedures
Initial Contact: Applications should be sent in a maximum 3 page narrative format with financial statements. Deadline is September 15.
Application Requirements: Grant proposals should include a one- to three-page statement describing, in order: how the project will significantly impact the target community; a description of organization, its staff, its goals, the problem to be addressed, how the proposal addresses the problem; and the funding amount requested. Also include documentation providing financial background on the organization and the proposal, including overall expense and revenue budgets and other funding sources; and an official IRS determination letter documenting the organization's tax-exempt status.
Deadlines: Applications are accepted between August 15 and October 1. Request received between November and May will be denied or returned for later re-submission.
Review Process: Preliminary review of requests is performed upon receipt. Results are forwarded to the

applicant within one month. Qualifying requests are then reviewed and acted upon by the foundation's trustees around November 1, with notification and distribution (if awarded) by November 30.
Notes: Visits to the foundation are scheduled only when requested by foundation personnel.

Restrictions
Grants or loans are not made to individuals or to organizations for the express use or benefit of any individual. Grant are made on a single year basis only. No pledges, multiple year commitments, or loans are made. The foundation does not fund operating expenses or wages. Grants limited to Western Montgomery County, NY only.

Additional Information
The foundation is not currently seeking new funding opportunities.
Preferred projects will demonstrate significant volunteer support and have well-defined time periods or will become self-funding after a start-up period.
Publications: Grant Program Guidelines

Foundation Officials
Joyce G. Dresser: trustee
Frances L. Howard: assistant secretary, trustee
Ferdinand C. Kaiser: vice president, secretary, trustee
Joseph A. Santangelo: vice president, treasurer B Norristown, PA 1954. ED Drexel University (1977). PRIM CORP EMPL chief financial officer, secretary, treasurer: FPA Corp. CORP AFFIL vice president: Orleans Construction Corp.; treasurer: Orleans Corp.
Edward W. Shineman, Jr.: president, trustee B Canajoharie, NY April 09, 1915. ED Cornell University AB (1937). CORP AFFIL board director: Fenimore Asset Management; director: Taconic Farms Inc. NONPR AFFIL member: Financial Executives Institute; member: Institute of Management Accountants; member emeritus council: Cornell University.
Charles J. Tallent: trustee
Robert H. Wille: vice president, trustee
Charles E. Wright: trustee B 1942. PRIM CORP EMPL president: W W Custom Clad Inc.

Grants Analysis
Disclosure Period: fiscal year ending November 30, 2003
Total Grants: $1,399,400*
Number of Grants: 53
Average Grant: $7,681*
Highest Grant: $1,000,000
Lowest Grant: $200
Typical Range: $1,000 to $15,000
*Note: Giving excludes scholarship and United Way. Average grants excludes highest grant.

Recent Grants
Note: Grants derived from fiscal 2003 Form 990.
Library-Related

1,000,000	Canajoharie Library and Art Gallery, Canajoharie, NY -- towards capital project
15,000	Canajoharie Library and Art Gallery, Canajoharie, NY -- operating support
2,000	Fort Plain Free Library, Ft. Plain, NY -- towards programs for children

General

75,000	St. Mary's Hospital Foundation, Amsterdam, NY -- provide new emergency care facility
50,000	Canajoharie Central School, Canajoharie, NY -- student scholarships
50,000	Village of Canajoharie, Canajoharie, NY -- assist village improvement projects
25,000	Canajoharie Community Youth Center, Canajoharie, NY -- towards operation and sidewalk repairs
20,000	College of Human Ecology, Ithaca, NY -- towards program support
20,000	Mountain Valley Hospice, Gloversville, NY -- for hospice care facility
20,000	United Way of Montgomery County Inc., Amsterdam, NY -- to assist annual campaign
15,000	Little Falls Hospital, NY -- purchase Anesthesia machine
12,500	Twin Rivers Council Boy Scouts of America, Albany, NY -- towards Woodworth lake operation
10,000	American Red Cross, Albany, NY -- towards disaster services

ARNOLD FUND

Giving Contact
John C. Sawyer, Executive Director
1201 W. Peachtree St., Suite 4200
Atlanta, GA 30309
Phone: (404)881-7886

Description
Founded: 1952
EIN: 586032079
Organization Type: Private Foundation
Giving Locations: GA
Grant Types: General Support.

Donor Information
Founder: Florence Arnold

Financial Summary
Total Giving: $914,280 (2003); $1,266,673 (2001)
Assets: $19,346,332 (2003); $23,946,331 (2001)
Gifts Received: $5,029,894 (1992)

Typical Recipients
Arts & Humanities: Ballet, Community Arts, Libraries, Museums/Galleries, Music
Civic & Public Affairs: Clubs, Community Foundations, Civic & Public Affairs-General, Municipalities/Towns, Public Policy, Urban & Community Affairs
Education: Colleges & Universities, Engineering/Technological Education, Literacy, Private Education (Precollege), Public Education (Precollege), Secondary Education (Public), Special Education, Student Aid
Environment: Wildlife Protection
Health: Hospices, Hospitals
Religion: Churches, Religious Welfare
Social Services: Community Service Organizations, People with Disabilities, Recreation & Athletics, Scouts, Special Olympics, United Funds/United Ways, YMCA/YWCA/YMHA/YWHA, Youth Organizations

Application Procedures
Initial Contact: Send a brief letter of inquiry.
Application Requirements: Describe program or project, include purpose of funds sought, area to be served, budget, and other pertinent information.
Deadlines: None.

Foundation Officials
Robert F. Fowler, III: trustee
David A. Newman: trustee
John C. Sawyer: executive director
Frank B. Turner: trustee

Grants Analysis
Disclosure Period: calendar year ending 2003
Total Grants: $914,280*
Typical Range: $5,000 to $25,000
*Note: No grants list available for 2003.

Recent Grants
Note: Grants derived from 2000 Form 990.

General

200,000	YMCA
165,000	First United Methodist Church, Williamsport, PA
155,150	City of Covington
150,000	Georgia Wildlife Federation, Conyers, GA
120,000	Newton County Public Facilities
70,560	Oxford College, Oxford, GA
70,000	Project Adventure
50,000	Oxford College, Oxford, GA
45,000	Covington Kiwanis Charitable Trust
42,000	Concert Association of Florida, Miami Beach, FL

JOHN ARRILLAGA FOUNDATION

Giving Contact

John Arrillaga, Director
2560 Mission College Blvd., Suite 101
Santa Clara, CA 95054
Phone: (408)980-0130
Fax: (408)988-4893

Description

Founded: 1978
EIN: 942460896
Organization Type: Private Foundation
Giving Locations: CA
Grant Types: Capital, General Support, Scholarship.

Donor Information

Founder: John Arrillaga

Financial Summary

Total Giving: $1,022,454 (fiscal year ending September 30, 2004); $331,224 (fiscal 2001)
Assets: $23,025,449 (fiscal 2004); $17,685,488 (fiscal 2001)
Gifts Received: $600,000 (fiscal 2004); $827,853 (fiscal 2000); $3,965,000 (fiscal 1994). Note: In fiscal 2004, the Center for Jewish Campus Life Inc. In fiscal 2000, contributions were received from Arrillaga Family Trust. In fiscal 1994, contributions were received from John Arrillaga.

Typical Recipients

Arts & Humanities: Arts Associations & Councils, Arts Centers, Arts Institutes, Dance, Arts & Humanities-General, Historic Preservation, Libraries, Museums/Galleries, Music, Public Broadcasting, Theater, Visual Arts
Civic & Public Affairs: Botanical Gardens/Parks, Clubs, Community Foundations, Employment/Job Training, Civic & Public Affairs-General, Law & Justice, Legal Aid, Municipalities/Towns, Parades/Festivals, Philanthropic Organizations, Safety, Urban & Community Affairs
Education: Arts/Humanities Education, Colleges & Universities, Continuing Education, Education Associations, Education Funds, Education Reform, Education-General, Private Education (Precollege), Public Education (Precollege), Secondary Education (Private), Secondary Education (Public), Student Aid
Environment: Environment-General
Health: Arthritis, Children's Health/Hospitals, Eyes/Blindness, Health Funds, Heart, Hospices, Hospitals, Hospitals (University Affiliated), Medical Research
International: Health Care/Hospitals
Religion: Bible Study/Translation, Churches, Ministries, Religious Welfare
Science: Science Museums
Social Services: At-Risk Youth, Child Welfare, Community Service Organizations, Counseling, Crime Prevention, Family Services, Food/Clothing Distribution, People with Disabilities, Recreation & Athletics, Scouts, Senior Services, Volunteer Services, YMCA/YWCA/YMHA/YWHA, Youth Organizations

Application Procedures

Application Requirements: Send a brief letter of inquiry. with any applicable brochures.
Deadlines: –None.

Foundation Officials

John Arrillaga, Jr.: treasurer, director
John Arrillaga: president, director B 1938. ED Stanford University. CORP AFFIL director: Morrison Knudsen Delaware Corp.; director: Morrison Knudsen Ohio Corp.
Laura Arrillaga: secretary, director

Grants Analysis

Disclosure Period: fiscal year ending September 30, 2004
Total Grants: $1,022,454
Number of Grants: 22
Average Grant: $13,163*
Highest Grant: $659,192
Lowest Grant: $79
Typical Range: $1,000 to $20,000
*Note: Average grant figure excludes two highest grants ($759,192).

Recent Grants

Note: Grants derived from fiscal 2004 Form 990.
General

659,192	Stanford University Hospital, Stanford, CA
100,000	California Family Foundation, Palo Alto, CA
50,000	Washington Hospital Healthcare, Fremont, CA
46,800	Mid-Peninsula High School, Menlo Park, CA
25,000	Bellarmine College Preparatory, San Jose, CA
25,000	Project Contact, Round Rock, TX
23,483	Palo Alto Junior Museum, Palo Alto, CA
15,000	Community Foundation of Silicon Valley, San Jose, CA
10,000	Ecumenical Hunger Project, East Palo Alto, CA
10,000	William and Flora Hewlett Foundation, Menlo Park, CA

ARRONSON FOUNDATION

Giving Contact

Joseph C. Kohn, President & Treasurer
One South Broad Street, Suite 2100
Philadelphia, PA 19107-3389
Phone: (215)238-1700

Description

Founded: 1957
EIN: 236259604
Organization Type: Private Foundation
Giving Locations: PA: Philadelphia
Grant Types: Endowment, General Support, Research, Scholarship, Seed Money.

Donor Information

Founder: the late Gertrude Arronson

Financial Summary

Total Giving: $190,710 (fiscal year ending October 31, 2004); $554,585 (fiscal 2001)
Giving Analysis: Giving for fiscal 2004 includes: foundation grants to United Way ($5,500); fiscal 2001: foundation grants to United Way ($8,000).
Assets: $5,122,180 (fiscal 2004); $5,694,064 (fiscal 2001)
Gifts Received: $1,500 (fiscal 1998)

Typical Recipients

Arts & Humanities: Arts Associations & Councils, Arts Outreach, Arts & Humanities-General, Historic Preservation, History & Archaeology, Libraries, Museums/Galleries, Music, Opera, Performing Arts, Theater
Civic & Public Affairs: Botanical Gardens/Parks, Employment/Job Training, Civic & Public Affairs-General, Legal Aid, Municipalities/Towns, Philanthropic Organizations, Public Policy, Urban & Community Affairs, Women's Affairs, Zoos/Aquariums
Education: Arts/Humanities Education, Colleges & Universities, Continuing Education, Faculty Development, Education-General, Legal Education, Literacy, Medical Education, Private Education (Precollege), Religious Education, Secondary Education (Private), Special Education, Student Aid, Vocational & Technical Education
Environment: Air/Water Quality, Resource Conservation
Health: Alzheimer's Disease, Cancer, Geriatric Health, Health Organizations, Home-Care Services, Hospices, Hospitals, Medical Rehabilitation, Medical Research, Nursing Services, Single-Disease Health Associations, Trauma Treatment
International: Foreign Arts Organizations, International Relief Efforts, Missionary/Religious Activities
Religion: Churches, Dioceses, Jewish Causes, Religious Organizations, Religious Welfare
Science: Scientific Centers & Institutes
Social Services: Child Welfare, Community Centers, Community Service Organizations, Day Care, Family Planning, Family Services, Homes, People with Disabilities, Recreation & Athletics, Shelters/Homelessness, United Funds/United Ways, YMCA/YWCA/YMHA/YWHA, Youth Organizations

Application Procedures

Initial Contact: Send a brief letter of inquiry.
Application Requirements: Include information on the nature of the organization and its work.
Deadlines: None.

Foundation Officials

Amy Goldberg: vice president
Edith Kohn: vice president, secretary
Ellen Kohn: vice president
Joseph C. Kohn: president, treasurer

Grants Analysis

Disclosure Period: fiscal year ending October 31, 2004
Total Grants: $188,210*
Number of Grants: 13
Average Grant: $7,351*
Highest Grant: $100,000
Lowest Grant: $210
Typical Range: $1,000 to $20,000
*Note: Giving excludes United Way. Average grant figure excludes highest grant.

Recent Grants

Note: Grants derived from 2004 Form 990.
General

100,000	Cumberland College, Williamsburg, KY
25,000	University of Pennsylvania Law School, Philadelphia, PA
10,000	Arden Theatre Company, Philadelphia, PA
10,000	Children's Literacy Initiative, Philadelphia, PA
10,000	Madlyn and Leonard Abramson Center for Jewish Life, North Wales, PA
5,000	Community Women's Education Project, Philadelphia, PA
5,000	Jewish Community Centers of Greater Philadelphia, Philadelphia, PA
5,000	John Bartram Association, Philadelphia, PA
5,000	Lantern Theater Company, Philadelphia, PA

5,000   White - William Scholars, Philadelphia, PA

ASH CHARITABLE CORP.

Giving Contact
John T. Pollano, Treasurer & Trustee
Ash Charitable Corp.
871 Turnpike St.
North Andover, MA 01845-6105
Phone: (978)683-6700

Description
Founded: 1990
EIN: 222994115
Organization Type: Private Foundation
Giving Locations: MA: North Andover
Grant Types: General Support.

Financial Summary
Total Giving: $7,500 (2003)
Assets: $1,160,235 (2003)

Typical Recipients
Arts & Humanities: Libraries
Civic & Public Affairs: Community Foundations, Civic & Public Affairs-General, Municipalities/Towns, Parades/Festivals, Urban & Community Affairs, Women's Affairs
Education: Colleges & Universities, Education-General, Legal Education, Private Education (Precollege), Secondary Education (Private)
Health: Cancer, Children's Health/Hospitals, Hospitals
International: International Relief Efforts
Religion: Churches, Religion-General, Jewish Causes, Religious Welfare, Synagogues/Temples
Social Services: Child Welfare, Community Centers, Community Service Organizations, Family Services, Recreation & Athletics, Scouts, Social Services-General, Substance Abuse, YMCA/YWCA/YMHA/YWHA, Youth Organizations

Application Procedures
Initial Contact: Send a brief letter of inquiry.
Deadlines: None.

Restrictions
Does not support individuals, religious organizations for sectarian purposes, political or lobbying groups, or organizations outside operating areas.

Foundation Officials
Donald A. George: clerk, trustee
Robert H. Goldstein: president, trustee
John T. Pollano, Esq.: treasurer, trustee

Grants Analysis
Disclosure Period: calendar year ending 2003
Total Grants: $7,500
Number of Grants: 3
Highest Grant: $5,000
Lowest Grant: $1,000
Typical Range: $1,000 to $5,000

Recent Grants
Note: Grants derived from 2001 Form 990.
General
5,000   Essex County Community Foundation, Essex, MA
5,000   Town of North Andover, Andover, MA
1,000   Holy Family Hospital, Methuen, MA

STANLEY P. AND BLANCHE E. ASH FOUNDATION

Giving Contact
Stanley P. Ash, President
PO Box 310
Greenville, MI 48838-0310
Phone: (616)754-5693

Description
Founded: 1992
EIN: 382966745
Organization Type: Private Foundation
Giving Locations: MI
Grant Types: General Support, Scholarship.

Financial Summary
Total Giving: $171,930 (2003); $213,799 (2001)
Giving Analysis: Giving for 2003 includes: foundation scholarships ($93,895); 2001: foundation scholarships ($65,978)
Assets: $3,236,900 (2003); $3,398,795 (2001)
Gifts Received: $100,000 (2003); $265,000 (2000); $800,000 (1999). Note: In 2003, contributions were received from Stanley P. Ash. In 1995, 1999 and 2000, contributions were received from Stanley and Blanche Ash ($306,000).

Typical Recipients
Arts & Humanities: Libraries, Literary Arts
Civic & Public Affairs: Botanical Gardens/Parks, Clubs, Community Foundations
Education: Colleges & Universities, Community & Junior Colleges, Engineering/Technological Education, Education-General, Private Education (Precollege), Special Education, Student Aid
Health: Cancer, Single-Disease Health Associations
Religion: Churches, Religion-General
Social Services: Camps, Community Centers, Special Olympics

Application Procedures
Initial Contact: Request application form for scholarship program.
Deadlines: None.

Additional Information
Provides scholarships to students in the Montcalm County, MI, area who show financial need and have satisfactory grades.

Foundation Officials
Blanche E. Ash: vice president
Jennifer K. Ash: director
Stanley P. Ash: president

Grants Analysis
Disclosure Period: calendar year ending 2003
Total Grants: $78,035*
Number of Grants: 34
Average Grant: $406*
Highest Grant: $40,000
Lowest Grant: $25
Typical Range: $100 to $1,000
*Note: Giving excludes scholarships. Average grant figure excludes two highest grants ($65,050).

Recent Grants
Note: Grants derived from 2001 Form 990.
Library-Related
8,000   White Pine Library
General
100,000   Montcalm Community College Foundation, Montcalm, WV
20,000   Greenville Area Community Center
9,000   St. Paul's Lutheran Church
3,500   Faith Lutheran

1,500   Central Michigan University, Mt. Pleasant, MI -- scholarship
1,500   Grand Valley State University, Allendale, MI -- scholarship
1,500   Kalamazoo College, Kalamazoo, MI -- scholarship
1,500   Michigan State University, East Lansing, MI -- scholarship
1,400   Central Michigan University, Mt. Pleasant, MI -- scholarship
1,301   Montcalm Community College Foundation, Montcalm, WV -- scholarship

ASHTABULA FOUNDATION

Giving Contact
Gary Ensign
Ashtabula Foundation
510 W. 44th St.
Ashtabula, OH 44004
Phone: (440)992-6818

Description
Founded: 1922
EIN: 346538130
Organization Type: Private Foundation
Giving Locations: OH: Ashtabula
Grant Types: General Support, Scholarship.

Financial Summary
Total Giving: $729,554 (2003)
Giving Analysis: Giving for 2003 includes: foundation scholarships ($3,000); foundation grants to United Way ($60,000)
Assets: $16,467,576 (2003)
Gifts Received: $74,046 (2003); $397,320 (2000); $8,396 (1998). Note: In 2003, contributions were received from Zonta-Kahne. In 1998, contributions were received from Jefferson United Methodist Church ($5,000), Thurgood Marshall Family Resource Center ($2,946) and two others. In 1996, contributions were received from the Jefferson United Methodist Church.

Typical Recipients
Arts & Humanities: Arts Centers, Ballet, History & Archaeology, Libraries, Music
Civic & Public Affairs: Botanical Gardens/Parks, Chambers of Commerce, Economic Development, Civic & Public Affairs-General, Housing, Inner-City Development, Urban & Community Affairs
Education: Agricultural Education, Colleges & Universities, Education Reform, Elementary Education (Public), Faculty Development, Education-General, Leadership Training, Private Education (Precollege), Public Education (Precollege), School Volunteerism, Science/Mathematics Education, Secondary Education (Private), Secondary Education (Public), Special Education, Student Aid
Environment: Environment-General, Resource Conservation
Health: Alzheimer's Disease, Cancer, Clinics/Medical Centers, Emergency/Ambulance Services, Heart, Prenatal Health Issues, Speech & Hearing
Religion: Bible Study/Translation, Churches, Ministries, Religious Organizations, Religious Welfare
Social Services: Big Brothers/Big Sisters, Camps, Child Welfare, Community Centers, Community Service Organizations, Family Planning, People with Disabilities, Recreation & Athletics, United Funds/United Ways, Volunteer Services, YMCA/YWCA/YMHA/YWHA

Application Procedures
Initial Contact: Request application form for either grant or scholarship award.
Deadlines: February 1, May 1, August 1, and November 1. Scholarship deadline is May 1.

Additional Information

Provides scholarships to Ashtabula, OH, residents and to Ashtabula County High School football letter winners.
Publications: Application Form

Foundation Officials

Wilbur L. Anderson: trustee
Roy H. Bean: trustee
Dr. Jerome R. Brockway: trustee
Eleanor A. Jammal: secretary, treasurer
Glen W. Warner: trustee
Barbara P. Wiese: trustee

Grants Analysis

Disclosure Period: calendar year ending 2003
Total Grants: $666,554*
Number of Grants: 47
Average Grant: $10,944*
Highest Grant: $65,000
Lowest Grant: $200
Typical Range: $5,000 to $20,000
*Note: Giving excludes United Way and scholarship. Average grant figure excludes three highest grants ($185,000).

Recent Grants

Note: Grants derived from 2003 Form 990.
General

65,000	Ashtabula County Metroparks Foundation, Ashtabula, OH
60,000	Civic Development Corporation, Ashtabula, OH -- for payment of five-year pledge
60,000	Messiah Lutheran Church, Cincinnati, OH -- for roof repairs and Washington elementary playground
60,000	United Way of Ashtabula, Ashtabula, OH
50,000	Ashtabula County Medical Center, Ashtabula, OH -- for partial payment of pledge
36,000	Second Congregational Church, Attleboro, MA -- for Amistad visit and overrun
33,522	Ashtabula County Medical Center, Ashtabula, OH -- for income distribution
30,000	St. Paul's Lutheran Church, Fulton, MD -- for building addition
28,559	Ashtabula County Board of MR/DD, Ashtabula, OH -- for Ida Green fund distribution & defibrillator
22,204	YMCA, Columbus, OH -- for income distribution

ASPLUNDH FOUNDATION

Giving Contact

Edward K. Asplundh, President
708 Blair Mill Rd.
Willow Grove, PA 19090
Phone: (215)784-4200

Description

Founded: 1953
EIN: 236297246
Organization Type: Private Foundation
Giving Locations: OR; PA; WV
Grant Types: Emergency, Endowment, General Support, Multiyear/Continuing Support, Project.

Donor Information

Founder: the late Carl H. Asplundh, Lester Asplundh

Financial Summary

Total Giving: $799,500 (2003); $636,000 (2001)
Assets: $16,185,199 (2003); $14,005,679 (2001)
Gifts Received: $70,000 (2003); $100,000 (2001); $100,500 (2000). Note: Contributions were received from Asplundh Tree Expert Co.

Typical Recipients

Arts & Humanities: Arts Centers, Historic Preservation, History & Archaeology, Libraries, Museums/Galleries, Music, Performing Arts, Visual Arts
Civic & Public Affairs: Botanical Gardens/Parks, Clubs, Employment/Job Training, Civic & Public Affairs-General, Rural Affairs, Safety, Zoos/Aquariums
Education: Colleges & Universities, Elementary Education (Public), Environmental Education, Education-General, Private Education (Precollege), Religious Education, Student Aid
Environment: Environment-General, Resource Conservation
Health: AIDS/HIV, Cancer, Clinics/Medical Centers, Emergency/Ambulance Services, Health Organizations, Hospitals
International: Foreign Educational Institutions, Health Care/Hospitals, International Environmental Issues
Religion: Churches, Religious Organizations
Science: Science Museums, Scientific Organizations
Social Services: At-Risk Youth, Child Welfare, Community Service Organizations, People with Disabilities, Recreation & Athletics, United Funds/United Ways, Youth Organizations

Application Procedures

Initial Contact: Send a brief letter of inquiry.
Application Requirements: Include a description of organization, amount requested, and purpose of funds sought.
Deadlines: None.

Foundation Officials

Christopher B. Asplundh: vice president, director B 1939. CORP AFFIL Asplundh Motor Co. Inc.; director: Utility Pole Technologies Inc.; director: Asplundh Construction Corp.; American Lighting Signalization; director: Asplundh Buick GMC Trucks.
Edward K. Asplundh: president

Grants Analysis

Disclosure Period: calendar year ending 2003
Total Grants: $799,500
Number of Grants: 110
Average Grant: $4,435*
Highest Grant: $125,000
Lowest Grant: $250
Typical Range: $1,000 to $10,000
*Note: Average grant figure excludes three highest grants ($325,000).

Recent Grants

Note: Grants derived from 2001 Form 990.

General

150,000	Bryn Athyn Church School, Bryn Athyn, PA -- for church school
100,000	Academy of the New Church Campaign 2000, Bryn Athyn, PA -- for building fund
100,000	Swedenborg Foundation, Chester, PA -- for publishing new edition of Swedenborg writings
50,000	Abington Memorial Hospital Foundation, Abington, PA -- for endowed nursing scholarship
25,000	Carmel Church School, Waterloo, ON Canada -- for expansion
25,000	Doylestown Hospital, Doylestown, PA -- pledge for cardiac unit
25,000	Holy Redeemer Hospital, Meadowbrook, PA -- pledge
25,000	Pittsburgh New Church School, Pittsburgh, PA
10,000	Abington Art Center, Jenkintown, PA
10,000	Academy of the New Church, Bryn Athyn, PA -- for campaign 2000

✳ ASSURANT

Company Headquarters

One Chase Manhattan Plaza
New York, NY 10005
Phone: (212)859-7000
Web: http://www.assurant.com

Company Description

Former Name: Amev Holdings; Fortis, Inc..
Revenue: US$7.403 billion (2004)
Profit: US$350.6 million (2004)
Employees: 6,000
Fortune Rank: 282, per FORTUNE Magazine's list of 500 Largest U.S. Corporations (2004).
SIC(s): 6211 Security Brokers & Dealers, 6719 Holding Companies Nec.
Parent Company: Fortis, Rue Royale 20, Brussels, Belgium

Operating Locations

American Security Group (GA--Atlanta); First Fortis Life Insurance Co. (NY--Syracuse); Fortis (NY--New York); Fortis Benefits Insurance Co. (AZ--Phoenix; CA--El Segundo, Sacramento, San Diego, San Francisco, Santa Ana; CO--Englewood; FL--Coral Gables, Tampa; GA--Atlanta; IL--Oakbrook Terrace; KS--Overland Park; MD--Annapolis; MA--Westborough; MI--Grand Rapids, Troy; MN--Minneapolis; MO--Kansas City, St. Louis; NJ--Parsippany; NY--New York, Pittsford; NC--Charlotte; OH--Cincinnati, North Olmsted; OR--Portland; PA--Bala-Cynwyd, Pittsburgh; TX--Austin, Dallas, Houston, Memphis; WI--Waukesha); Fortis Family (GA--Atlanta); Fortis Financial Group (MN--Woodbury); Fortis Health (WI--Milwaukee); Fortis Long Term Care (WI--Milwaukee)

Fortis Foundation

Giving Contact

Jackie Gentile, Directory
1 Chase Manhattan Plaza, 41st Floor
New York, NY 10005
Phone: (212)859-7000
Fax: (212)859-7010
E-mail: Joanie.Marquette@us.fortis.com
Web: http://www.fortisfoundation.com

Description

Founded: 1982
EIN: 133156497
Organization Type: Corporate Foundation
Giving Locations: NY: nationally health-related organizations.
Grant Types: Award, Employee Matching Gifts, General Support, Matching, Scholarship.

Donor Information

Founder: AMEV Holdings

Financial Summary

Total Giving: $318,866 (2002); $368,439 (2001). Note: Contributes through foundation only.
Giving Analysis: Giving for 2002 includes: foundation grants to United Way ($33,390); foundation matching gifts ($74,176); foundation scholarships ($150,750)
Assets: $662,514 (2002); $1,010,405 (2001)
Gifts Received: $5,236 (2002); $244 (2001); $1,000,000 (2000). Note: In fiscal 1999, 2000, and 2002, contributions were received from Fortis Benefits Insurance Company.

Typical Recipients

Arts & Humanities: Arts Centers, Arts & Humanities-General, Libraries, Museums/Galleries, Music
Civic & Public Affairs: Civic & Public Affairs-General, Parades/Festivals, Philanthropic Organizations

Education: Arts/Humanities Education, Business Education, Colleges & Universities, Education Funds, Engineering/Technological Education, Education-General, Legal Education, Medical Education, Private Education (Precollege), Public Education (Precollege), Religious Education, Student Aid
Health: AIDS/HIV, Cancer, Children's Health/Hospitals, Emergency/Ambulance Services, Multiple Sclerosis, Single-Disease Health Associations, Transplant Networks/Donor Banks
International: Health Care/Hospitals
Religion: Jewish Causes, Ministries
Social Services: Child Welfare, Community Centers, Community Service Organizations, Domestic Violence, Emergency Relief, Family Planning, Food/Clothing Distribution, Recreation & Athletics, Shelters/Homelessness, Social Services-General, Special Olympics, United Funds/United Ways, Volunteer Services, Youth Organizations

Application Procedures

Initial Contact: Request application form for scholarships, for employees' children only.
Application Requirements: For other requests, send a brief letter of inquiry; include a description of organization, amount requested, purpose of funds sought, and proof of tax-exempt status.
Deadlines: None.
Evaluative Criteria: Scholarship grants are based on the following criteria: prior academic performance, performance on tests designed to measure scholastic abilities and aptitudes, at least two recommendations from instructors, and conclusions from a personal interview as to motivation, character, ability and performance.

Restrictions

Fortis Inc. does not consider the following for charitable contributions: individuals, goodwill advertising, political or lobbying groups, religious organizations for sectarian purposes, or organizations outside NY operating area.

Corporate Officials

Jon Kerry Clayton: president, chief executive officer B Cincinnati, OH 1945. ED Georgia Institute of Technology BIE (1968); Harvard University MBA (1970). PRIM CORP EMPL president, chief executive officer: Fortis Inc.

Foundation Officials

Jon Kerry Clayton: trustee (see above)
Robert B. Pollock: trustee

Grants Analysis

Disclosure Period: calendar year ending 2002
Total Grants: $60,550*
Number of Grants: 27
Average Grant: $1,560*
Highest Grant: $20,000
Lowest Grant: $50
Typical Range: $500 to $3,000
*Note: Giving excludes matching gifts, scholarship, United Way. Average grant figure excludes highest grant.

Recent Grants

Note: Grants derived from 2003 Form 990.
General

25,137	United Way of New York City, New York, NY
17,710	United Way, New York, NY
15,198	United Way, New York, NY
13,910	United Way, New York, NY
13,681	Great American Bake Sale
5,000	New York Cares, New York, NY
5,000	Woodruff Arts Center, Atlanta, GA
2,500	Georgia Tech Foundation Inc., Atlanta, GA
2,500	Hartwick College, Oneonta, NY
2,500	Kent Place School

AT&T CORP.

Company Headquarters

New York, NY
Web: http://www.att.com

Company Description

Founded: 1885
Ticker: T
Exchange: NYSE
Acquired: MediaOne (2000).
Revenue: US$30.537 billion (2004)
Profit: (US$6.469 billion) (2004)
Employees: 71000 (2003)
Fortune Rank: 56, per FORTUNE Magazine's list of 500 Largest U.S. Corporations (2004).
SIC(s): 4812 Radiotelephone Communications, 4813 Telephone Communications Except Radiotelephone, 4899 Communications Services Nec.

Operating Locations

ACC Corp. (NY--Rochester); Associated Group (PA--Pittsburgh); At Home Corp. (CA--Redwood City); AT&T Alascam Inc. (AK--Anchorage); AT&T Broadband, LLC (CO--Englewood); AT&T CampusWide Access Solutions Inc. (AZ--Phoenix); AT&T Communication Inc. (NJ--Basking Ridge); AT&T Global Network Services (NJ--Florham Park); AT&T Internet Services (NJ--Bridgewater); AT&T Latin America Corp. (FL--Coral Gables); AT&T Local Service (NJ--Dayton); AT&T Solutions Inc. (NJ--Florham Park); Concert (VA--Reston); Four Media Computer (CA--Burbank); GRC International Inc. (VA--Vienna); Kearns-Tribune Corp. (UT--Salt Lake City); Liberty Digital (NY--New York); Liberty Media Group (CO--Englewood); Management Consulting & Research (VA--McLean); MediaOne Group Inc. (CO--Englewood); Net 2 Phone, Inc. (NJ--Hackensack); Wireless Group (WA--Redmond)

Nonmonetary Support

Value: $23,700,000 (2002)
Type: Cause-related Marketing & Promotion; Donated Products; In-kind Services; Loaned Employees; Loaned Executives
Volunteer Programs: Supports the AT&T CARES program, which makes grants to organizations where employees volunteer, and the Telephone Pioneers of America, a volunteer service organization. In 2002, product and service donations were contributed primarily in the form of free cable and broadband service donated to elementary and secondary schools through the former AT&T Broadband (now part of Comcast) and pre-paid calling cards from AT&T Consumer.
Contact: Jo-Ann Greene, Director, AT&T University Equipment Donation Program
Note: Co. does not accept unsolicited requests for nonmonetary support.

AT&T Foundation

Giving Contact

Vivian Nero, Operations & Local Grants
32 Avenue of the Americas
New York, NY 10013
Phone: (212)387-6557
Fax: (212)387-5098
Web: http://www.att.com/foundation

Description

EIN: 133166495
Organization Type: Corporate Foundation
Giving Locations: headquarters and operating communities; nationally and internationally.
Grant Types: Award, Conference/Seminar, Emergency, Employee Matching Gifts, Fellowship, Matching, Multiyear/Continuing Support, Operating Expenses, Project.

Note: Employee matching gift ratio: 1 to 1 for tax-deductible gifts to higher education and cultural institutions with grants from $25 to $10,000 and a maximum of $50,000 per organization. Foundation also sponsors the AT&T Cares program to provide grants to organisation where employees volunteer at least 50 hours of time.

Financial Summary

Total Giving: $18,228,630 (2003); $39,509,769 (2002); $44,196,080 (2001). Note: Contributes through corporate direct giving program and foundation. 1998 Giving includes foundation.
Assets: $28,453,835 (2003); $12,312,917 (2002); $48,824,236 (2001)
Gifts Received: $40,415,000 (2003); $25,199,987 (2001); $36,326,104 (2000). Note: In 2003, contributions were received from AT&T Corp.

Typical Recipients

Arts & Humanities: Arts Associations & Councils, Arts Centers, Arts Festivals, Arts Funds, Arts Institutes, Ballet, Dance, Historic Preservation, History & Archaeology, Libraries, Museums/Galleries, Music, Opera, Performing Arts, Theater, Visual Arts
Civic & Public Affairs: African American Affairs, Asian American Affairs, Botanical Gardens/Parks, Civil Rights, Community Foundations, Economic Development, Economic Policy, Employment/Job Training, Civic & Public Affairs-General, Hispanic Affairs, Housing, Inner-City Development, Minority Business, Nonprofit Management, Professional & Trade Associations, Public Policy, Urban & Community Affairs, Women's Affairs
Education: Arts/Humanities Education, Business Education, Colleges & Universities, Education Associations, Education Funds, Education Reform, Elementary Education (Public), Engineering/Technological Education, Faculty Development, Education-General, International Exchange, International Studies, Leadership Training, Legal Education, Literacy, Medical Education, Minority Education, Preschool Education, Public Education (Precollege), Science/Mathematics Education, Secondary Education (Public), Social Sciences Education, Special Education, Student Aid, Vocational & Technical Education
Environment: Environment-General, Wildlife Protection
Health: AIDS/HIV, Children's Health/Hospitals, Emergency/Ambulance Services, Health Policy/Cost Containment, Hospitals, Speech & Hearing
International: Foreign Arts Organizations, Foreign Educational Institutions, International Affairs, International Relations, International Relief Efforts
Science: Science Museums, Scientific Centers & Institutes
Social Services: Child Welfare, Community Service Organizations, Day Care, Emergency Relief, Family Services, People with Disabilities, Recreation & Athletics, Substance Abuse, United Funds/United Ways, Youth Organizations

Application Procedures

Initial Contact: Write for guidelines and application form, then send brief letter with completed application.
Application Requirements: Include brief history of the organization and description of mission; statement relating purpose to interests and priorities of foundation; detailed description of purpose for which grant is sought and amount requested; operating and/or project budget for current year showing anticipated sources of revenue and expenses (if project support sought, include a detailed budget for the project); and proof of 501(c)(3) status.
Deadlines: None.
Review Process: Staff members make recommendations to board of trustees.
Evaluative Criteria: Grants focus on cities and regions with large concentrations of AT&T employees and business operations, with the majority of funds supporting U.S.-based institutions. Organizations

must be nonsectarian and nondenominational to receive support; organizations must seek to advance AT&T's goals of promoting diversity and equal opportunity, and that programs will be open and accessible to all segments of society. Grants are awarded in the following program areas: education, civic & community service, and arts and culture through such programs as: AT&T Learning Network grants, direct grants, employee-directed grants, AT&T Cares program, AT&T Employee Matching Gifts Program; arts and cultures programs include AT&T: On Stage, AT&T:NEAT. enhance the quality of life in communities where AT&T employees live and work; utilize technology in inventive ways; or involve employee volunteers.

Decision Notification: Trustees meet monthly.

Notes: For U.S.-based national organizations, apply to foundation. For local projects, apply to Regional Contributions Manager in area; contact information is included in guidelines.

Restrictions

Foundation does not make grants to individuals; organizations whose chief purpose is to influence legislation or to participate or intervene in political campaigns on behalf of or against any candidate for public office, endowments or memorials, construction or renovation projects, sports teams or any sports-related activity or competition even if it addresses our program interests, and fund-raising events or advertising. The Civic & Community Service Program does not support organizations that channel the funds received to third parties, organizations formed to combat specific diseases, medical research, programs to reduce deficits, alcohol-abuse and substance-abuse treatment programs, and programs to alleviate homelessness. The Arts & Culture Program generally does not support student or amateur groups; arts education programs; individual artists; artistic training or scholarships; film and media productions; competitions; arts programs designed primarily for rehabilitation or therapy; public radio and television stations for unrestricted purposes, equipment acquisition or program underwriting; science museums or science/technology exhibitions, except through the AT&T NEAT initiative, and the purchase of equipment.

Additional Information

Guidelines may be obtained by either calling (212) 387-4868, or sending a fax message to (212) 387-4906.

Guidelines include extensive restrictions by program area, and should be carefully reviewed before submitting a request.

The company's nonmonetary support program provides AT&T computer laboratories to selected colleges and universities. This is an invitational program not open to unsolicited requests.

Regional contributions offices for organizations outside the U.S. are as follows:

For organizations in Australia, China, India, Indonesia, Japan, Philippines, South Korea, Taiwan, and Thailand, contact AT&T Asia/Pacific Inc., Shell Tower, Times Sq., 1 Matheson St., 30th Fl., Causeway Bay, Hong Kong, 011-852-2-506-5051.

For organizations in France, contact AT&T France SA, Tour Horizon, 52 quai de Dion-Bouton, 92806 Puteaux, Cedex, France, 011-33-1-4767-4709.

For organizations in Germany, contact AT&T Deutschland, Eschersheimer Landstrasse 14, D-60322, Frankfurt, Germany, 011-49-69-153-06-431.

For organizations in Italy, The Netherlands, Poland, South Africa, and Spain, contact AT&T Communications Service SA, Chaussee de Wavre 1943, B-1160 Brussels, Belgium.

For organizations in Russia, contact AT&T CIS Ltd., Toko Tower,11th Fl., 6, Krasnopresnenskaya, 123242 Moscow, Russia, 011-7-095-974-1462.

For organizations in the United Kingdom, contact AT&T England, Norfolk House, 31 St. James' Sq., London, SW1 4JR, United Kingdom, 011-44-171-925-8116.

For organizations in Canada, c/o AT&T Canada, 320 Front St. West, 17th Fl., Toronto, Ontario, Canada M5V 3B6, 416-204-2908.

For organizations in Argentina, Brazil, Chile, Colombia, Mexico, Puerto Rico, and Venezuela, contact AT&T, 233 Ponce de Leon Blvd., Rm. 941-10, Coral Gables, FL 33134, 305-569-3753.

Publications: Foundation Report; Guidelines

Corporate Officials

C. Michael Armstrong: chairman, chief executive officer, director B Detroit, MI October 18, 1938. ED Miami University BS (1961); Dartmouth College (1976). PRIM CORP EMPL chairman, chief executive officer, director: AT&T Corp. CORP AFFIL director: Citigroup Inc.; chief executive officer: Comcast Corp. NONPR AFFIL vice chairman: Sabriyas Castle Fun Foundation; member supervisory board: Thyssen-Bornemisza Group; member: National Security Telecommunications Advisory Committee; chairman: President's Export Council; trustee: Johns Hopkins University; member business advisory council: Miami University Ohio; chairman advisory board: Johns Hopkins School Medicine; member: Defense Policy Advisory Committee Trade; member: General Motors President Council; visiting professor:; member: Council Foreign Relations. CLUB AFFIL member: Alfalfa Club.

Harold W. Burlingame: executive vice president wireless group B Zanesville, OH. PRIM CORP EMPL executive vice president wireless group: AT&T Corp. CORP AFFIL chairman: ORC Worldwide. NONPR AFFIL director: Tucson Electric Power Co..

David W. Dorman: chairman, chief executive officer ED Georgia Institute of Technology BA. PRIM CORP EMPL president, director: AT&T Corp. CORP AFFIL director: Scientific-Atlanta Inc.; director: YUM! Brands Inc. NONPR AFFIL trustee: Georgia Tech Foundation; trustee: Woodruff Arts Center; trustee: Episcopal High School.

Richard J. Martin: executive vice president public relations employee communications ED Ohio State University BS. PRIM CORP EMPL executive vice president public relations employee communications: AT&T Corp.

John D. Zeglis: chairman and chief executive officer wireless group B 1948. ED Harvard Law School JD; University of Illinois BA. PRIM CORP EMPL chairman and chief executive officer wireless group: AT&T Corp. CORP AFFIL director: Helmerich & Payne Inc.; director: State Farm Mutual Automobile Insurance Co.; director: Georgia-Pacific Corp..

Foundation Officials

Dana Bonanno-Regelski: associate IR manager
Sandy Colon: executive secretary
David P. Condit: trustee
Alicia Fonseca: executive secretary
Mirian Graddick-Weir: trustee
R. Reed Harrison, III: trustee
Lucy Jackson: support
Marie Juliano: executive secretary
James Kirby: local grants manager
David Krantz: trustee
Fanny LaScala: executive secretary
Barbara Peda: trustee
Marilyn Reznick: executive director ED University of Illinois MA; University of Kansas BA.
Bob Schauer: trustee
Gloria Shuler: financial grants manager
Ann B. Sullivan: executive secretary
Mitzi Vaimberg: secretary ED Clemson University BS (1980).
Connie Weaver: president

Grants Analysis

Disclosure Period: calendar year ending 2003
Total Grants: $13,949,720*
Number of Grants: 840
Average Grant: $16,607
Highest Grant: $500,000
Lowest Grant: $450

Typical Range: $1,000 to $50,000
*Note: Giving excludes matching gifts, scholarships, fellowships, United Way, and foundation related expenses.

Recent Grants

Note: Grants derived from 2003 Form 990.
Library-Related

100,000	Library of Congress, Washington, DC -- sponsoring 2003 national book festival

General

625,000	United Way of Tri-State, New York, NY
500,000	United Way of Tri-State, New York, NY
444,400	Women in Engineering Programs and Advocates Network, Hoboken, NJ -- seventh cohort of ALFP students
375,000	Stevens Institute of Technology, Hoboken, NJ -- for management course revision
323,100	Women in Engineering Programs and Advocates Network, Hoboken, NJ -- eighth cohort of ALFP students
300,000	National Board for Professional Teaching Standards, Arlington, TX -- digital library project
250,000	National Park Foundation, Washington, DC -- independence day celebrations
250,000	National Underground Railroad Freedom Center, Cincinnati, OH -- for kiosks exhibiting American freedom and slavery
250,000	New Jersey Performing Arts Center, Newark, NJ -- for AT&T premier artist series up to June 2005
200,000	Carnegie Hall, New York, NY -- setting up an institute for music education

AT&T NATIONAL PRO-AM YOUTH FUND

Giving Contact

Carmel C. Martin, Jr., Secretary & Treasurer
490 Calle Principal
PO Box 112
Monterey, CA 93940
Phone: (831)375-3151

Description

Founded: 1963
EIN: 946050251
Organization Type: Private Foundation
Giving Locations: CA: Monterey County, Santa Cruz County
Grant Types: Capital, General Support, Scholarship.

Donor Information

Founder: The late Bing Crosby.

Financial Summary

Total Giving: $463,225 (fiscal year ending June 30, 2003); $489,625 (fiscal 2002); $358,650 (fiscal 2001)
Giving Analysis: Giving for fiscal 2001 includes: foundation scholarships ($15,000)
Assets: $79,463 (fiscal 2003); $195,289 (fiscal 2002); $286,789 (fiscal 2001)
Gifts Received: $388,025 (fiscal 2003); $414,614 (fiscal 2002); $502,165 (fiscal 2001). Note: Contributions were received from AT&T Pro-Am Golf Tournament.

Typical Recipients

Arts & Humanities: Arts Associations & Councils, Arts Centers, Arts Outreach, Community Arts, History & Archaeology, Museums/Galleries, Music, Theater
Civic & Public Affairs: Ethnic Organizations, Civic & Public Affairs-General, Housing, Safety, Urban & Community Affairs, Women's Affairs, Zoos/Aquariums

Education: Arts/Humanities Education, Colleges & Universities, Environmental Education, Education-General, International Studies, Journalism/Media Education, Leadership Training, Legal Education, Private Education (Precollege), Public Education (Precollege), Science/Mathematics Education, Secondary Education (Private), Secondary Education (Public), Student Aid

Environment: Environment-General

Health: Health Organizations, Hospitals

International: International Peace & Security Issues, International Relations

Religion: Churches, Religious Organizations, Religious Welfare

Social Services: Big Brothers/Big Sisters, Camps, Child Welfare, Community Service Organizations, Counseling, Domestic Violence, Family Planning, People with Disabilities, Recreation & Athletics, Scouts, Special Olympics, United Funds/United Ways, Youth Organizations

Application Procedures

Initial Contact: full proposal

Application Requirements: Include a description of organization, amount requested, purpose of funds sought, recently audited financial statement, proof of tax-exempt status, and other sources of funding.

Deadlines: None.

Restrictions

Does not support individuals.

Foundation Officials

Daniel Albert: trustee
Peter J. Coniglio: trustee
Peter Cutino: trustee
Nancy Durein: trustee
Jack Holt: trustee
Carmel C. Martin, Jr.: secretary, treasurer
Frank Thacker: chairman
Daniel Tibitts: trustee
Murray C. Vout: trustee

Grants Analysis

Disclosure Period: fiscal year ending June 30, 2003
Total Grants: $463,225*
Typical Range: $1,000 to $5,000
*Note: No grants list available for 2003.

Recent Grants

Note: Grants derived from fiscal 2000 Form 990.

General

21,000	Monterey Peninsula College, Monterey, CA
7,500	Lyceum of Monterey County, Monterey, CA
6,000	Carmel Bach Festival, Carmel, CA
5,000	Barracuda Aquatics, Monterey, CA
5,000	Big Brothers Big Sisters of Monterey, Monterey, CA
5,000	California State University Monterey Bay, Seaside, CA
5,000	California Women's Amateur Championship Association, Pebble Beach, CA
5,000	Carmel Unified School District, Carmel, CA
5,000	Carmel Valley Little League, Carmel Valley, CA
5,000	Carmel Valley Village Improvement, Carmel Valley, CA

ATHERTON FAMILY FOUNDATION

Giving Contact

Lissa Schiff, Private Foundation Services Officer
Care of Hawaii Community Foundation

1164 Bishop Street, Suite 800
Honolulu, HI 96813
Phone: (808)566-5524
Fax: (808)521-6286
E-mail: foundations@hcf-hawaii.org
Web:
http://www.hawaiicommunityfoundation.org/atherton
Note: Toll free: 888-731-3863.

Description

Founded: 1976
EIN: 510175971
Organization Type: General Purpose Foundation
Giving Locations: HI
Grant Types: Capital, General Support, Matching, Multiyear/Continuing Support, Project, Scholarship.
Note: The foundation also makes program grants.

Donor Information

Founder: Established in 1975 to continue the charitable work of the original donor and trustees of the Juliette M. Atherton Trust, established in 1915. Juliette M. Atherton was the daughter of pioneer American missionaries in Hawaii. Her husband, Joseph Ballard Atherton, was the son-in-law of Samuel Northrup Castle, the president of Castle and Cooke. Mrs. Atherton entrusted her estate to three of her children, Charles H. Atherton, Mary A. Richards, and Frank C. Atherton, to continue the charitable work in which she was interested. In 1976, the assets of her trust, as well as the assets of the Frank C. Atherton Trust, which had provided support for charitable organizations since 1935, were transferred to the Atherton Family Foundation. The charitable giving patterns of both original trusts were similar through the years. Consolidation of the two trusts was carried out to provide more efficient administration, greater flexibility in foundation policies, and greater protection and growth of the investment assets. It also permitted an increase in the number of members and directors for a broader representation of charitable interests.

Financial Summary

Total Giving: $5,119,068 (2002); $4,800,075 (2001)
Giving Analysis: Giving for 2002 includes: foundation scholarships ($60,000); foundation grants to United Way ($284,600); 2001: foundation scholarships ($149,175); foundation grants to United Way ($277,800)
Assets: $82,069,269 (2002); $99,600,900 (2001)

Typical Recipients

Arts & Humanities: Arts Associations & Councils, Arts Centers, Arts Funds, Arts Institutes, Arts Outreach, Ballet, Community Arts, Dance, Arts & Humanities-General, Historic Preservation, History & Archaeology, Libraries, Museums/Galleries, Music, Opera, Performing Arts, Public Broadcasting, Theater, Visual Arts

Civic & Public Affairs: Asian American Affairs, Botanical Gardens/Parks, Business/Free Enterprise, Community Foundations, Economic Development, Employment/Job Training, Civic & Public Affairs-General, Hispanic Affairs, Housing, Legal Aid, Public Policy, Rural Affairs, Safety, Urban & Community Affairs, Zoos/Aquariums

Education: Afterschool/Enrichment Programs, Arts/Humanities Education, Business Education, Colleges & Universities, Education Associations, Education Funds, Elementary Education (Private), Faculty Development, Education-General, Gifted & Talented Programs, International Exchange, International Studies, Literacy, Medical Education, Preschool Education, Private Education (Precollege), Public Education (Precollege), Religious Education, Science/Mathematics Education, Secondary Education (Private), Secondary Education (Public), Social Sciences Education, Special Education, Student Aid

Environment: Environment-General, Protection, Resource Conservation

Health: Cancer, Children's Health/Hospitals, Clinics/Medical Centers, Emergency/Ambulance Services,

Geriatric Health, Health Funds, Health Organizations, Hospices, Hospitals, Long-Term Care, Medical Rehabilitation, Medical Research, Medical Training, Mental Health, Nursing Services, Prenatal Health Issues

International: International Affairs, International Environmental Issues, International Organizations

Religion: Churches, Dioceses, Religion-General, Ministries, Religious Organizations, Religious Welfare

Science: Science Museums, Scientific Centers & Institutes, Scientific Organizations, Scientific Research

Social Services: Animal Protection, At-Risk Youth, Big Brothers/Big Sisters, Camps, Child Welfare, Community Centers, Community Service Organizations, Counseling, Crime Prevention, Delinquency & Criminal Rehabilitation, Domestic Violence, Emergency Relief, Family Planning, Family Services, Food/Clothing Distribution, Homes, People with Disabilities, Recreation & Athletics, Scouts, Senior Services, Shelters/Homelessness, Substance Abuse, United Funds/United Ways, Veterans, Volunteer Services, YMCA/YWCA/YMHA/YWHA, Youth Organizations

Application Procedures

Initial Contact: Applicants should send a written proposal to the foundation. Guidelines are different for requests for automation equipment and scholarships; contact the foundation for more information.

Application Requirements: The initial proposal should include one, unbound copy, of the following: a description of organization including its history, mission and leadership; brief description of the population to be served or benefited by the project and the approximate size; the need or opportunity for which the proposed activity is a response or solution; project objectives and summary of the activities to be funded; amount requested, duration of time funds will be needed, and anticipated sources of support when foundation funding ceases; method used to determine effectiveness of funded project; information about the organization's staff, including those responsible for the program/project; name and phone number of contact persons; expense budget and revenue plan for the total project budget indicating categories of sources and amounts; a one- or two-page summary of the proposal; and a list of the board of directors, including occupations and affiliation and a statement of board involvement and functions within the organization. Additional materials that must be included are signatures of the presiding officer of the board and the executive director indicating that the board and chief staff person approve of the proposal; IRS determination letter; and the organization's Charter and Bylaws, current annual operating budget, and most recently completed financial statements.

Deadlines: December 1, February 1, April 1, August 1, October 1.

Review Process: If an organization wishes to have its request considered at a particular meeting, its proposal must be received by the first of the month two months prior to the month in which there is a meeting. Meetings are scheduled on the third Wednesday of February, April, June, August, October, and December.

Restrictions

Grants are made only to tax-exempt organizations whose projects or programs will benefit the people of Hawaii. The foundation does not usually support requests for annual operating support, organizations which have already received a grant in the same calendar year, including a grant for automation equipment (exceptions, see "collaborative project"), individuals, with the exception of the Juliette M. Atherton Scholarship Funds, loans, grants for endowment funds, private foundations. The foundation does not award grants for political or lobbying groups. Requests from individual Departments of Education school and organizations intending to redistribute the grant to other beneficiaries (regranting) are not accepted. The University of Hawaii is awarded a grant each year to be expended at the president's discretion, therefore, no other proposals will be accepted from the university for that year, as this considered the universities annual grant.

Additional Information

Any organization receiving a grant from the foundation will be required to submit a brief report summarizing the outcome of the project and a fiscal accounting of the grant expenditures as soon as the operating period for which the funds were used is completed.
Publications: Annual Report; Grant Guidelines; Scholarship Guidelines
Trust(s): Bank of Hawaii

Foundation Officials

Frank C. Atherton: vice president, treasurer, director
Judith Dawson: vice president, secretary, director B Honolulu, HI 1939. ED Wellesley College (1957-1959); University of California BA (1962); University of Hawaii MA (1977). PRIM NONPR EMPL vice president, treasurer: Punahou School. NONPR AFFIL trustee: Oriental Art Society; director: University California Alumni Association; trustee: Hawaiian Mission Childrens Society; member: Hawaii Society Fund-Raising Executive. CLUB AFFIL Oahu Country Club.
Patricia R. Giles: vice president, director
Robert Richards Midkiff: president, director B Honolulu, HI September 24, 1920. ED Yale University BA (1942); Harvard University AMP (1962). PRIM CORP EMPL chairman, director: American Trust Co. Hawaii PRIM NONPR EMPL chief executive officer, president: American Financial Services. CORP AFFIL director: Persis Corp. NONPR AFFIL member: Profit Sharing Research Foundation; director: Small Business Council America; member: Phi Beta Kappa; member, director: Profit Sharing Council America; director: Hawaii Visitors Bureau; member, board directors: Lahaina Restoration Foundation; treasurer, director: Hawaii Community Foundation; director: Hawaii Theatre Center; director: Downtown Improvement Association; director: Good Beginnings Alliance; member: Council Foundations. CLUB AFFIL Pacific Club; Waialae Country Club; Oahu Country Club.
Paul F. Morgan: vice president, director
Joan H. Rohlfing: vice president, director

Grants Analysis

Disclosure Period: calendar year ending 2002
Total Grants: $4,774,468*
Number of Grants: 270
Average Grant: $17,683
Highest Grant: $200,000
Lowest Grant: $1,000
Typical Range: $5,000 to $40,000
***Note:** Giving excludes United Way and scholarships.

Recent Grants

Note: Grants derived from 2002 Form 990.
General
260,000	Aloha United Way, Honolulu, HI -- towards annual campaign
200,000	Mid-Pacific Institute, Honolulu, HI -- fund for Technology Learning Complex
200,000	Punahou School, Honolulu, HI -- towards middle school project
200,000	YMCA of Honolulu, Honolulu, HI -- towards Reaching for Tomorrow capital campaign
150,000	Iolani School, Honolulu, HI -- towards Building Futures capital campaign
150,000	La Pietra, Honolulu, HI -- towards capital campaign
100,000	Bishop Museum, Honolulu, HI -- towards science learning center
100,000	Hawaii Mission Children's Society, Honolulu, HI -- towards preservation of the Chamberlain House at Mission Houses Museum

85,000	Good Beginnings Alliance, Honolulu, HI -- general assistance
75,000	Hanahauoli School, Honolulu, HI -- towards capital campaign

LEBURTA ATHERTON FOUNDATION

Giving Contact

c/o Pacific Century Trust
PO Box 3170
Honolulu, HI 96802-3170
Phone: (808)538-4472

Description

Founded: 1998
EIN: 943260209
Organization Type: Private Foundation
Giving Locations: CA; CO; HI
Grant Types: General Support.

Financial Summary

Total Giving: $371,100 (2003); $291,000 (2001)
Assets: $9,453,767 (2003); $6,024,320 (2001)
Gifts Received: $1,151,000 (2003). Note: In 2003, contributions were received from Leburta Atherton Trust.

Typical Recipients

Arts & Humanities: Arts Centers, Libraries, Theater
Civic & Public Affairs: Clubs, Civic & Public Affairs-General, Philanthropic Organizations
Education: Colleges & Universities, Preschool Education, Private Education (Precollege)
Environment: Wildlife Protection
Health: Hospitals
Religion: Religious Welfare
Social Services: Child Welfare, Emergency Relief

Additional Information

Trust(s): Bank of Hawaii

Foundation Officials

Frank C. Atherton, II: secretary, director
Leburta G. Atherton: president, director
Balbi A. Brooks: treasurer, director
Marjory A. Newell: vice president, director

Grants Analysis

Disclosure Period: calendar year ending 2003
Total Grants: $371,100
Number of Grants: 14
Average Grant: $14,258*
Highest Grant: $100,000
Lowest Grant: $1,000
Typical Range: $1,000 to $25,000
***Note:** Average grant figure excludes two highest grants ($200,000).

Recent Grants

Note: Grants derived from 2003 Form 990.
Library-Related
10,000	Long Beach Public Library Foundation, Long Beach, CA

General
100,000	Hanahauoli School, Honolulu, HI
100,000	Mid-Pacific Institute, Honolulu, HI
50,000	Hawaii Preparatory Academy, Kamuela, HI
50,000	Punahou School, Honolulu, HI -- for capital campaign
20,000	KCAA Pre-Schools of Hawaii, Honolulu, HI
10,000	American Red Cross, Honolulu, HI
10,000	Dolphin Institute, Honolulu, HI
5,000	Long Beach Day Nursery, Long Beach, CA

5,000	Long Beach Public Charitable Foundation, Long Beach, CA

ATKINSON FOUNDATION

Giving Contact

Elizabeth H. Curtis, Administrator & Director
1720 South Amphlett Blvd.
Suite 100
San Mateo, CA 94402
Phone: (650)357-1101
Fax: (650)357-1101
E-mail: atkinfdn@aol.com

Description

Founded: 1939
EIN: 946075613
Organization Type: General Purpose Foundation
Giving Locations: CA: San Mateo County United States-based international organizations serving Latin America; United States-based international organizations serving the Caribbean.
Grant Types: Capital, General Support, Project, Seed Money.

Donor Information

Founder: Established in 1939 by George H. Atkinson (1905-1978) and his wife Mildred M. Atkinson (1904-1967). George Atkinson, along with his father, co-founded the international construction firm, Guy F. Atkinson Company. He made numerous trips, often accompanied by his wife, to under-developed and developing countries throughout the world. The Atkinsons' "first-hand awareness of the problems of third-world countries and their wish to help the people of these countries created in the foundation a pattern for giving that serves human needs and contributes to the self-esteem and independence of individuals, families, and communities in the developing areas of the world."
George and Mildred made significant contributions to their community in San Mateo County and the San Francisco Bay area. They were leaders in many social service organizations and were actively involved in the Methodist Church, locally, regionally, and nationally.
The value of education, learned while the Atkinsons were both undergraduates at Willamette University in Salem, OR, guides present grants to secondary education, community colleges, and selected universities and black colleges.

Financial Summary

Total Giving: $740,000 (2003); $733,907 (2002); $634,290 (2001)
Assets: $14,437,183 (2002); $15,761,391 (2001)

Typical Recipients

Arts & Humanities: History & Archaeology, Libraries, Museums/Galleries, Public Broadcasting
Civic & Public Affairs: Asian American Affairs, Botanical Gardens/Parks, Business/Free Enterprise, Civil Rights, Community Foundations, Economic Development, Economic Policy, Employment/Job Training, Gay/Lesbian Issues, Civic & Public Affairs-General, Hispanic Affairs, Law & Justice, Legal Aid, Municipalities/Towns, Nonprofit Management, Urban & Community Affairs, Women's Affairs
Education: Afterschool/Enrichment Programs, Colleges & Universities, Community & Junior Colleges, Education Associations, Education Reform, Education-General, International Studies, Literacy, Minority Education, Preschool Education, Private Education (Precollege), Public Education (Precollege), Religious Education, Secondary Education (Public), Student Aid
Environment: Forestry, Environment-General, Protection, Resource Conservation

Health: AIDS/HIV, Alzheimer's Disease, Children's Health/Hospitals, Clinics/Medical Centers, Eyes/Blindness, Health-General, Geriatric Health, Health Funds, Health Organizations, Heart, Hospitals, Long-Term Care, Medical Rehabilitation, Medical Research, Mental Health, Public Health
International: Foreign Educational Institutions, International-General, Health Care/Hospitals, International Development, International Environmental Issues, International Organizations, International Peace & Security Issues, International Relief Efforts, Missionary/Religious Activities
Religion: Bible Study/Translation, Churches, Ministries, Missionary Activities (Domestic), Religious Welfare
Science: Scientific Centers & Institutes
Social Services: At-Risk Youth, Big Brothers/Big Sisters, Child Welfare, Community Centers, Community Service Organizations, Counseling, Crime Prevention, Day Care, Delinquency & Criminal Rehabilitation, Domestic Violence, Emergency Relief, Family Planning, Family Services, Food/Clothing Distribution, Homes, People with Disabilities, Recreation & Athletics, Refugee Assistance, Senior Services, Shelters/Homelessness, Social Services-General, Substance Abuse, Volunteer Services, YMCA/YWCA/YMHA/YWHA, Youth Organizations

Application Procedures

Initial Contact: Phone to ascertain whether the proposal is within foundation guidelines and to request application materials. Applications should be submitted in writing.
Application Requirements: Completed foundation coversheet, the organization's name, address, and telephone number, along with the names of the organization's president, executive director, and person to be contacted in connection with the proposal; names and affiliations of officers and directors; brief history and statement of current activities and goals of the organization; description of the proposed program demonstrating the need to be met, population to be served, specific objectives, resources to be applied, description of staff and its qualifications, anticipated outcome, and method of evaluation; program budget with projected income and expenses over a specific period of time, as well as a financial statement for the organization; other sources of funding; copy of IRS letter of tax exemption; and any supplementary information which may significantly strengthen the application.
Deadlines: February 1, May 1, August 1, and November 1.
Review Process: The directors meet quarterly, usually in March, June, September, and December, with distribution committees meeting more frequently. Applicants can expect prompt notification once a decision has been reached. The foundation typically does not meet with grantseekers, and communication with individual foundation directors is discouraged; however, the staff does try to respond to telephone inquiries, and the staff will make occasional site visits and/or meet with grantseekers as necessary to complete or clarify information contained in a grant request.
Evaluative Criteria: Requests are generally viewed more favorably if they are for specific, innovative, and/or non-repetitive purposes. If the project is to continue for an indeterminate period, it is important that the organization indicate future funding plans. Additional positive factors include needs which are not likely to be fully satisfied from other sources, demonstration of cooperation with other donors or agencies, and indication of community support.
Notes: Normally, an applicant will not receive more than one grant per year.

Restrictions

The foundation does not fund grants, scholarships, or loans to individuals; organizations which do not have proof of current tax-exempt status; doctoral study or research; organizations chartered outside the U.S.; fundraising events; media presentations; annual campaigns; sports groups; national or statewide umbrella organizations; grants designed to influence legislation; or travel to conferences or events.

Additional Information

Publications: Annual Report; Guidelines; Proposal Cover Sheet

Foundation Officials

Duane E. Atkinson: president, director B 1927. ED Stanford University BSEE (1951). PRIM CORP EMPL director: Guy F. Atkinson Co. California. CORP AFFIL vice president: Guy F. Atkinson Co. NV; president, general manager: Atkinson Dynamics Co.
Ray N. Atkinson: vice president, director B Portland, OR 1929. ED Stanford University BA (1950). PRIM CORP EMPL director, vice chairman: Guy F. Atkinson Co. California.
James R. Avedisian: director
Elizabeth H. Curtis: director, admin
Thomas J. Henderson: vice president, director B 1931. ED Massachusetts Institute of Technology BS; Massachusetts Institute of Technology MS (1954). PRIM CORP EMPL chairman, president, chief executive officer: Guy F. Atkinson Co. California.
John E. Herrell: treasurer, assistant secretary
James C. Ingwersen: secretary, assistant treasurer, director
Linda L. Lanier: director
Lawrence A. Wright: director

Grants Analysis

Disclosure Period: calendar year ending 2002
Total Grants: $733,907*
Number of Grants: 110
Average Grant: $6,672
Highest Grant: $40,000
Lowest Grant: $2,000
Typical Range: $4,000 to $10,000
Note: Grants analysis provided by foundation.

Recent Grants

Note: Grants derived from 2002 Form 990.

General

40,000	Boys & Girls Club, San Mateo, CA -- towards capital campaign of Bayshore Community Center
20,000	Coastside Adult Day Health Center/Senior Coastsiders, Half Moon Bay, CA -- towards Coastside Center for independent living
20,000	Samaritan House, San Mateo, CA -- towards operating support for homeless shelter
12,500	St. Vincent de Paul Society, San Mateo, CA -- towards capital campaign for multiservice center in South San Francisco
10,000	AIDS Prevention Action Network Inc., Redwood City, CA -- towards San Mateo County - syringe exchange program
10,000	Community Association for Rehabilitation, Palo Alto, CA -- towards training of home respite companions
10,000	Fundacion Adelante, Miami, FL -- for rural micro credit groups, Honduras
10,000	International Development Exchange, San Francisco, CA -- towards grassroots development in Chiapas, Mexico
10,000	International Institute of San Francisco, San Francisco, CA -- towards domestic violence program for immigrant families
10,000	National Economic Development and Law Center, Oakland, CA -- towards transition funding of tenants center project

ATRAN FOUNDATION, INC.

Giving Contact

Diane Fischer, Secretary
23-25 East 21st Street, 3rd Floor
New York, NY 10010
Phone: (212)505-9677

Description

Founded: 1945
EIN: 135566548
Organization Type: General Purpose Foundation
Giving Locations: NY
Grant Types: Conference/Seminar, Emergency, Endowment, Fellowship, General Support, Loan, Multiyear/Continuing Support, Operating Expenses, Project, Research, Scholarship, Seed Money.

Donor Information

Founder: Incorporated in 1945 by the late Frank Z. Atran.

Financial Summary

Total Giving: $591,083 (fiscal year ending November 30, 2001)
Assets: $17,078,090 (fiscal 2001)
Gifts Received: $500 (fiscal 1999); $5,000 (fiscal 1996)

Typical Recipients

Arts & Humanities: Arts Associations & Councils, Arts Centers, Arts Funds, Historic Preservation, History & Archaeology, Libraries, Museums/Galleries, Performing Arts, Public Broadcasting, Theater
Civic & Public Affairs: African American Affairs, Botanical Gardens/Parks, Economic Policy, Employment/Job Training, Ethnic Organizations, Civic & Public Affairs-General, Law & Justice, Philanthropic Organizations, Professional & Trade Associations, Public Policy, Women's Affairs, Zoos/Aquariums
Education: Colleges & Universities, Education Funds, Education Reform, Elementary Education (Private), Education-General, International Studies, Medical Education, Minority Education, Religious Education, Social Sciences Education
Environment: Environment-General
Health: Clinics/Medical Centers, Emergency/Ambulance Services, Eyes/Blindness, Geriatric Health, Hospitals, Hospitals (University Affiliated), Long-Term Care, Medical Research, Research/Studies Institutes
International: Foreign Educational Institutions, Human Rights, International Peace & Security Issues, International Relations, International Relief Efforts, Missionary/Religious Activities
Religion: Jewish Causes, Religious Organizations, Religious Welfare, Seminaries, Synagogues/Temples
Social Services: Child Welfare, Community Service Organizations, Homes, People with Disabilities, Senior Services, Special Olympics, United Funds/United Ways, Youth Organizations

Application Procedures

Initial Contact: Send proposals in the form of an informal letter.
Application Requirements: Proposals should include the nature of the project; its objectives including its significance and usefulness; a program or plan for achieving the objectives; estimate time to carry out the program; itemized budget showing the total cost of the project, any contributions by the applicant or others, and the amount requested from the foundation; is the project expected to continue following the achievement of its objectives and what kind of continued financial support will be required; a list of expected sources. Applicants should include whether the results of the project will be disseminated and how, and a copy of the ruling granting federal tax exemption

pursuant to section 501 (c)(3).
Deadlines: September 30.
Decision Notification: Only grant recipients will be notified of decisions.

Restrictions

No grants are made to individuals. Only proposals from tax-exempt public organizations will be considered.

Additional Information

Recipients are expected to forward periodic progress reports, and upon termination of the project, to submit a final report detailing the statements of disbursements. Funds not expended are required to be returned to the foundation.
Publications: Application Guidelines

Foundation Officials

Diane Fischer: corporate secretary
Dr. George Kessler Fraenkel: treasurer B Deal, NJ 1921. ED Harvard University BA (1942); Cornell University PhD (1949). NONPR AFFIL member: Phi Kappa Phi; member: Sigma Xi; member: Phi Beta Kappa; dean emeritus: Columbia University; fellow: International Electron Spin Resonance Society; fellow: American Physics Society; member: Association Graduate Schools; fellow: American Association Advancement Science; fellow: American Chemical Society.
William Stern: vice president, director NONPR AFFIL director: Forward Association.

Grants Analysis

Disclosure Period: fiscal year ending November 30, 2001
Total Grants: $591,083
Number of Grants: 33
Average Grant: $17,912
Highest Grant: $107,408
Lowest Grant: $250
Typical Range: $5,000 to $25,000

Recent Grants

Note: Grants derived from fiscal 2002 Form 990.
Library-Related
3,500	New York Public Library, New York, NY

General
107,407	Jewish Labor Committee, New York, NY
90,000	YIVO Institute for Jewish Research, New York, NY
52,000	Columbia University, New York, NY
45,798	Congress for Jewish Culture, New York, NY
45,000	Albert Einstein College of Medicine of Yeshiva University, Bronx, NY
35,000	Foundation of University of Medicine & Dentistry of New Jersey, Stratford, NJ
28,000	Brandeis University, Waltham, MA
24,747	Relief Committee of the General Jewish Workers' Union of Poland Inc.
15,000	Folksbiene Yiddish Theater, New York, NY
15,000	UJA/Federation of New York, New York, NY

AUBURN FOUNDRY

Company Headquarters

1537 W. Auburn Dr.
Auburn, IN 46706

Company Description

Employees: 615
SIC(s): 3300 Primary Metal Industries.

Operating Locations

Auburn Foundry (IN--Auburn)

Auburn Foundry Foundation

Giving Contact

James Westerfield
National City Bank of Indiana
PO Box 110
Ft. Wayne, IN 46801
Phone: (219)461-7126

Description

EIN: 356019220
Organization Type: Corporate Foundation
Giving Locations: headquarters area only.
Grant Types: General Support, Scholarship.

Donor Information

Founder: Auburn Foundry

Financial Summary

Gifts Received: $250,000 (fiscal year ending February 28, 1997); $50,000 (fiscal 1995); $550,000 (fiscal 1994). Note: In 1997, contributions were received from Auburn Foundry.

Typical Recipients

Arts & Humanities: Arts Associations & Councils, Arts & Humanities-General, Libraries, Music
Civic & Public Affairs: Economic Development, Civic & Public Affairs-General, Housing
Education: Business Education, Colleges & Universities, Education Funds, Literacy, Private Education (Precollege), Public Education (Precollege), Science/Mathematics Education
Health: Prenatal Health Issues
Religion: Religious Welfare
Social Services: Food/Clothing Distribution, People with Disabilities, Scouts, Social Services-General, United Funds/United Ways, YMCA/YWCA/YMHA/YWHA

Application Procedures

Initial Contact: The foundation requests applications be made in writing.
Application Requirements: Include purpose of funds sought and proof of tax-exempt status.
Deadlines: None.

Restrictions

Scholarships are limited to Dekalb High School graduates enrolled in a four year accredited school.

Additional Information

Publications: Scholarship application form.
Trust(s): Fort Wayne Natl Bank

Corporate Officials

David Fink: president financial PRIM CORP EMPL president: Auburn Foundry.
William E. Fink: chairman PRIM CORP EMPL chairman: Auburn Foundry.
John Neiger: vice president financial PRIM CORP EMPL vice president financial: Auburn Foundry.

Foundation Officials

Walt Bienz: trustee
William E. Fink: trustee (see above)

Grants Analysis

Disclosure Period: fiscal year ending February 28, 2000
Total Grants: $37,000*
Number of Grants: 13
Average Grant: $1,500*
Highest Grant: $19,000
Lowest Grant: $500
Typical Range: $500 to $5,000
*Note: Giving excludes scholarships; United Way. Average grant figure excludes highest grant.

Recent Grants

Note: Grants derived from fiscal 2002 Form 990.
General
19,000	Independent Colleges of Indiana, Indianapolis, IN
9,000	United Way De Kalb County, Auburn, IN
5,000	Hillsdale College, Hillsdale, MI
4,000	Tri-State University, Angola, IN
3,000	De Kalb County Habitat for Humanity, Auburn, IN
2,800	Junior Achievement De Kalb County, Auburn, IN
2,500	Youth for Christ, Auburn, IN
2,200	Saint Francis College, Loretto, PA
2,000	Fort Wayne Philharmonic, Ft. Wayne, IN
1,500	Arts United of Greater Fort Wayne, Ft. Wayne, IN

AUDUBON STATE BANK

Company Headquarters

315 Broadway St.
Audubon, IA 50025

Audubon State Bank Charitable Foundation

Giving Contact

Brett Irlmeier, President & Director
Audubon State Bank
Audubon, IA 50025
Phone: (712)563-2644
Fax: (712)563-3654

Description

EIN: 421366431
Organization Type: Corporate Foundation
Giving Locations: IA
Grant Types: General Support.

Financial Summary

Total Giving: $38,330 (2004)
Assets: $20,008 (2004)
Gifts Received: $24,000 (2004); $22,000 (2000); $22,000 (1999). Note: Contributions were received from Audubon State Bank.

Typical Recipients

Arts & Humanities: Arts Centers, History & Archaeology, Libraries, Museums/Galleries, Music, Performing Arts, Public Broadcasting
Civic & Public Affairs: Botanical Gardens/Parks, Business/Free Enterprise, Civil Rights, Clubs, Economic Development, Civic & Public Affairs-General, Legal Aid, Municipalities/Towns, Parades/Festivals, Rural Affairs, Safety, Urban & Community Affairs, Women's Affairs
Education: Agricultural Education, Colleges & Universities, Education Funds, Education-General, International Exchange, Public Education (Precollege), Secondary Education (Private), Secondary Education (Public), Student Aid
Environment: Environment-General
Health: Cancer, Diabetes, Emergency/Ambulance Services, Heart, Hospitals, Single-Disease Health Associations, Transplant Networks/Donor Banks
Religion: Churches, Religious Organizations, Religious Welfare
Science: Scientific Centers & Institutes
Social Services: Community Service Organizations, Crime Prevention, Emergency Relief, Family Planning, Family Services, Homes, People with Disabilities, Recreation & Athletics, Scouts, Senior Services, Special Olympics, Substance Abuse, Veterans

Application Procedures

Initial Contact: Send a brief letter of inquiry with an explanation of the purpose of funds sought.
Deadlines: None.

Corporate Officials

Louis Venteicher: chairman, president, chief executive officer PRIM CORP EMPL chairman, president, chief executive officer: Audubon State Bank.

Foundation Officials

Mary Garst: director
William C. Hess: vice president, director PRIM CORP EMPL chief executive officer: Iowa Savings Bank.
John C. Parrott, Jr.: director

Grants Analysis

Disclosure Period: calendar year ending 2004
Total Grants: $38,330
Number of Grants: 39
Average Grant: $811*
Highest Grant: $7,500
Lowest Grant: $25
Typical Range: $100 to $2,000
Note: Average grant figure excludes highest grant.

Recent Grants

Note: Grants derived from 2001 Form 990.
Library-Related

1,375	Audubon Public Library, Audubon, IA

General

2,231	United Methodist Church, Audubon, IA
2,000	Audubon County Hospital Foundation, Audubon, IA
1,035	Friends of Iowa Public Television, Johnston, IA
1,000	Audubon Community School, Audubon, IA
1,000	Audubon Sports Boosters, Audubon, IA
1,000	Friendship Home, Audubon, IA
1,000	WOI, Ames, IA
970	Our Saviour's Lutheran Church, Audubon, IA
850	Hamlin Lutheran Church, Hamlin, IA
600	Cystic Fibrosis Foundation, Urbandale, IA

CHARLES J. AND BURTON S. AUGUST FAMILY FOUNDATION

Giving Contact

Burton August, Sr., Trustee
Charles J. and Burton S. August Family Foundation
200 Holleder Parkway
Rochester, NY 14615
Phone: (716)647-6400
Note: Ext. 315

Description

Founded: 1989
EIN: 161355601
Organization Type: Private Foundation
Giving Locations: Monroe County.
Grant Types: Capital, Emergency, Project, Scholarship.

Donor Information

Founder: Charles J. August, Burton S. August

Financial Summary

Gifts Received: $6,170 (fiscal year ending June 30, 1997); $81,187 (fiscal 1995); $331,271 (fiscal 1994).
Note: In fiscal 1995, contributions were received from

Charles J. August ($79,175) and Burton S. August ($2,012).

Typical Recipients

Arts & Humanities: Libraries, Museums/Galleries, Public Broadcasting, Theater
Civic & Public Affairs: Community Foundations, Employment/Job Training, Civic & Public Affairs-General, Housing, Public Policy, Urban & Community Affairs, Zoos/Aquariums
Education: Afterschool/Enrichment Programs, Arts/Humanities Education, Colleges & Universities, Continuing Education, Engineering/Technological Education, Education-General, Legal Education, Medical Education, Private Education (Precollege), Special Education
Health: Adolescent Health Issues, Alzheimer's Disease, Clinics/Medical Centers, Diabetes, Emergency/Ambulance Services, Health-General, Heart, Medical Rehabilitation, Mental Health, Nursing Services
Religion: Religion-General, Jewish Causes, Religious Welfare, Synagogues/Temples
Science: Science Museums
Social Services: Animal Protection, Camps, Child Welfare, Community Centers, Community Service Organizations, Crime Prevention, Day Care, Domestic Violence, Emergency Relief, Family Planning, Family Services, Food/Clothing Distribution, People with Disabilities, Recreation & Athletics, Scouts, Senior Services, Shelters/Homelessness, United Funds/United Ways, YMCA/YWCA/YMHA/YWHA

Application Procedures

Initial Contact: Send a full proposal.
Application Requirements: Include a description of organization, amount requested, purpose of funds sought, recently audited financial statement, and proof of tax-exempt status.
Deadlines: None. The board meets semi-annually.

Restrictions

Grants are not made to individuals. or for ongoing support.

Foundation Officials

Andrew August: trustee B 1966. PRIM CORP EMPL president: Alternative Sports Inc.
Burton S. August, Sr.: trustee
Charles J. August: trustee
Jan Lise August: trustee
Jean B. August: trustee
John W. August: trustee
Robert W. August: trustee
Cortland L. Brovitz: trustee
Susan Eastwood: trustee
Andrew M. Greenstein: trustee
August Mafreci: trustee
David Mitchell: trustee

Grants Analysis

Disclosure Period: fiscal year ending June 30, 1999
Total Grants: $149,296*
Number of Grants: 47
Average Grant: $2,267*
Highest Grant: $45,000
Typical Range: $200 to $5,000
Note: Giving excludes United Way. Average grant excludes highest grant.

Recent Grants

Note: Grants derived from fiscal 2002 Form 990.
Library-Related

3,000	Rundel Library Foundation, Rochester, NY

General

30,000	Park Ridge Foundation, Rochester, NY
21,000	Boy Scouts of America, Rochester, NY
16,000	United Way of Greater Rochester, Rochester, NY
12,500	Al Sigle Center Partner Agencies, Rochester, NY
12,500	Boy Scouts of America, Rochester, NY

10,000	Community Place of Rochester, Rochester, NY
7,500	Hillside Children's Center, Rochester, NY
5,000	Foodlink, Rochester, NY
5,000	Hope Hall, Rochester, NY
5,000	Rochester Children's Nursery, Rochester, NY

AUTRY FOUNDATION

Giving Contact

Jacqueline Autry, President
4383 Colfax Avenue
Studio City, CA 91604
Phone: (818)752-7770
Fax: (818)752-7779

Description

Founded: 1974
EIN: 237433359
Organization Type: General Purpose Foundation
Giving Locations: CA: including southern California; MN: Eden Prairie; WY: Jackson Hole
Grant Types: General Support.

Donor Information

Founder: Established in 1974 by former actor and radio entertainer Gene Autry, who starred in more than 80 western movies and wrote more than 200 songs.

Financial Summary

Total Giving: $1,000,000 (2003 approx); $1,305,143 (2002)
Assets: $18,000,000 (2003 approx); $17,413,659 (2002)

Typical Recipients

Arts & Humanities: Arts Associations & Councils, Arts Centers, Arts Funds, Arts Institutes, Ethnic & Folk Arts, Film & Video, Arts & Humanities-General, Historic Preservation, History & Archaeology, Libraries, Museums/Galleries, Music, Opera, Public Broadcasting, Theater
Civic & Public Affairs: African American Affairs, Botanical Gardens/Parks, Business/Free Enterprise, Clubs, Employment/Job Training, Civic & Public Affairs-General, Hispanic Affairs, Professional & Trade Associations, Public Policy, Urban & Community Affairs, Women's Affairs, Zoos/Aquariums
Education: Arts/Humanities Education, Business Education, Colleges & Universities, Education Reform, School Volunteerism, Student Aid
Environment: Energy, Forestry, Environment-General
Health: Alzheimer's Disease, Cancer, Children's Health/Hospitals, Clinics/Medical Centers, Diabetes, Eyes/Blindness, Health-General, Health Organizations, Heart, Hospices, Hospitals, Medical Research, Prenatal Health Issues, Public Health, Research/Studies Institutes, Respiratory, Single-Disease Health Associations, Speech & Hearing
International: Human Rights, International Affairs, International Organizations, International Relations, International Relief Efforts
Religion: Jewish Causes, Religious Organizations, Religious Welfare, Social/Policy Issues
Science: Science Museums, Scientific Centers & Institutes
Social Services: At-Risk Youth, Child Abuse, Child Welfare, Community Service Organizations, Counseling, Crime Prevention, Delinquency & Criminal Rehabilitation, Domestic Violence, Family Services, Food/Clothing Distribution, People with Disabilities, Recreation & Athletics, Scouts, Shelters/Homelessness, Substance Abuse, United Funds/United Ways, Volunteer Services, YMCA/YWCA/YMHA/YWHA, Youth Organizations

Application Procedures

Initial Contact: Prospective applicants should send a brief letter of inquiry on organization letterhead.
Application Requirements: Applicants should include IRS 501 (c)(3) confirmation.
Deadlines: None.

Foundation Officials

Jacqueline Autry: vice president, director NONPR AFFIL president: Gene Autry Museum of Western Heritage.
Karla Buhlman: vice president music and film
Maxine Hansen: director
Stanley Schneider: treasurer, director NONPR AFFIL vice president, treasurer: Gene Autry Museum of Western Heritage.

Grants Analysis

Disclosure Period: calendar year ending 2002
Total Grants: $1,305,143
Number of Grants: 29
Average Grant: $45,004*
Highest Grant: $1,001,397
Lowest Grant: $250
Typical Range: $2,500 to $50,000
***Note:** Average grant figure excludes highest grant.

Recent Grants

Note: Grants derived from 2002 Form 990.
General

1,001,397	Autry Museum of Western Heritage, Los Angeles, CA
100,000	P.A.T.H., Los Angeles, CA
50,000	Provident St. Joseph Hospital, Burbank, CA
28,746	Tempe Sports Authority Trust, Tempe, AZ
25,000	Los Angeles Sheriff's Star, Burbank, CA
11,000	Doheny Eye Institute, Los Angeles, CA
10,000	June Ebensteiner Hospice Foundation, Los Angeles, CA
10,000	KCET - TV, Los Angeles, CA
10,000	Ueberroth Family Foundation, Laguna Beach, CA
10,000	William H. Parker Los Angeles Police Foundation, Los Angeles, CA

MILTON AND SALLY AVERY ARTS FOUNDATION

Giving Contact

March Avery Cavanaugh, Trustee
Milton and Sally Avery Arts Foundation
300 Central Park W.
New York, NY 10024
Phone: (212)595-7338
Fax: (212)595-2840

Description

EIN: 133093638
Organization Type: Private Foundation
Giving Locations: NY: New England states.
Grant Types: General Support.

Donor Information

Founder: Sally M. Avery

Financial Summary

Total Giving: $420,693 (2003)
Assets: $4,473,829 (2003)
Gifts Received: $636,005 (2000). Note: In 2000, contributions were received from Sally Avery.

Typical Recipients

Arts & Humanities: Arts Associations & Councils, Arts Centers, Arts Festivals, Arts Funds, Arts Institutes, Community Arts, Dance, Arts & Humanities-General, Historic Preservation, Libraries, Literary Arts, Museums/Galleries, Music, Opera, Public Broadcasting, Theater, Visual Arts
Civic & Public Affairs: Civic & Public Affairs-General, Women's Affairs
Education: Arts/Humanities Education, Colleges & Universities, Education Reform, Engineering/Technological Education, Private Education (Precollege), Special Education
Environment: Environment-General
International: Foreign Educational Institutions
Religion: Seminaries
Social Services: At-Risk Youth, Community Service Organizations, People with Disabilities

Application Procedures

Initial Contact: Send a brief letter of inquiry and a full proposal.
Application Requirements: Include a description of organization of organization, amount requested, recently audited financial statement, proof of tax-exempt status, and purpose of funds sought.
Deadlines: None.

Restrictions

Awards are restricted to art education and the further development of artists.

Foundation Officials

March A. Cavanaugh: trustee
Philip Cavanaugh: trustee
Sean Avery Cavanaugh: trustee
Harvey Shipley Miller: trustee

Grants Analysis

Disclosure Period: calendar year ending 2003
Total Grants: $420,693
Number of Grants: 110
Average Grant: $3,824
Highest Grant: $30,000
Lowest Grant: $1,000
Typical Range: $1,000 to $5,000

Recent Grants

Note: Grants derived from 2003 Form 990.
General

30,000	Pitzer College, Claremont, CA
22,000	New York Studio School, New York, NY
19,000	Yaddo, NY
17,000	Purchase College, Purchase, NY
15,000	Bard College, Red Hook, NY
15,000	Bard College, Red Hook, NY
10,000	Bard College, Red Hook, NY
10,000	John Richardson Fund
10,000	Skowhegan School of Painting and Sculpture, Skowhegan, ME
7,000	Down Under the Manhattan Bridge Overpass Arts Center, Brooklyn, NY

AVISTA CORP.

Company Headquarters

Spokane, WA
Web: http://www.avistacorp.com

Company Description

Founded: 1889
Ticker: AVA
Exchange: NYSE
Former Name: Washington Water Power Co. (WWP).
Assets: US$4.037 billion (2001)
Employees: 1450 (2003)
SIC(s): 4931 Electric & Other Services Combined.

Operating Locations

Washington Water Power Co. (ID--Bonners Ferry, Coeur D Alene, Kellogg, Lewiston, Orofino, Post Falls, Sandpoint; OR--Ashland, Klamath Falls, La Grande, Medford, Roseburg; WA--Colfax, Colville, Othello, Pullman)

Nonmonetary Support

Type: Donated Equipment; In-kind Services; Loaned Employees

Giving Contact

Debbie Simock, Communications & Community Investment Manager
PO Box 3727
Spokane, WA 99220
Phone: (509)495-8031
Fax: (509)495-4000
E-mail: debbie.simock@avistacorp.com
Web: http://www.avistafoundation.org

Description

Organization Type: Corporate Giving Program
Giving Locations: ID: Northern Idaho service area; WA: Eastern Washington service area, northern Idaho, as well as Sanders County, Montana and South Lake Tahoe, California
Grant Types: General Support, Matching, Multiyear/Continuing Support, Project.

Financial Summary

Total Giving: $680,000 (2004 approx); $680,000 (2003); $735,000 (2002). Note: Contributes through corporate direct giving program only.
Assets: $2,500,000 (2003 approx); $2,000,000 (2002)

Typical Recipients

Arts & Humanities: Arts & Humanities-General, Libraries, Museums/Galleries, Performing Arts, Public Broadcasting, Theater
Civic & Public Affairs: Civic & Public Affairs-General, Safety, Women's Affairs
Education: Colleges & Universities, Community & Junior Colleges, Economic Education, Elementary Education (Private), Engineering/Technological Education, Faculty Development, Minority Education, Public Education (Precollege)
Environment: Environment-General
Social Services: Community Service Organizations, Senior Services, United Funds/United Ways, Youth Organizations

Application Procedures

Initial Contact: Requests must be submitted in writing.
Application Requirements: Include a brief summary of the organization including date of establishment, history, mission statement, and objectives; copy of IRS letter designating the organization's 501(c)(3) status; current financial statement; list of board of directors and key staff; a brief overview of the program/project for which funding is requested including purpose, targeted population, evaluation strategies, anticipated results, budget, other organizations providing support, and timeline; and current or past corporate involvement, if any, in the organization or program, including employee volunteers, board members, etc.
Deadlines: None.
Review Process: Proposals reviewed by corporate contributions committee.
Evaluative Criteria: Organizations must be tax-exempt and must provide documentation confirming 501(c)(3) status; be located within areas where company operates; show evidence of sound fiscal policies and responsible financial management; have a competent, knowledgeable, and broad-based board of directors with policy-making authority that represents the organization and its members; show a method to evaluate the results of the proposed proj-

ect; describe collaborative efforts, if applicable, with similar programs/providers and show the project does not represent an unnecessary duplication of effort; and be relevant to company's business interests.
Decision Notification: Requests in excess of $5,000 are reviewed quarterly in February, May, August, and November; requests under $5,000 are usually processed within 30 days.
Notes: Applicants outside Spokane are encouraged to submit requests to regional offices. Contact headquarters for further information. Special attention is given to organizations and programs that serve a large number of people, have long-term benefits, include the company's employees, have broad community support, and are consistent with Avista Corp.'s business interests.

Restrictions

Generally does not contribute to individuals, team or extra-curricular school events, tournament fund raisers, trips or tours, churches or other religious organizations, organizations that discriminate for any reason, endowments or foundations, or hospital or patient care institution operating funds.
Restricts giving to eastern Washington and northern Idaho.

Additional Information

Priority is given to requests that demonstrate partnerships and cooperative efforts between organizations and agencies and which directly benefit people within areas where company conducts business.
Publications: Contributions Guidelines

Corporate Officials

Gary G. Ely: chairman, president, chief executive officer B October 08, 1947. ED Brigham Young University BS (1983). PRIM CORP EMPL chairman, president, chief executive officer: Avista Corp.
Malyn K. Malquist: senior vice president, chief financial officer B Artesia, CA 1952. ED Brigham Young University (1976); Brigham Young University (1978). PRIM CORP EMPL senior vice president, chief financial officer: Avista Corp. CORP AFFIL director: Headwaters Inc.

Giving Program Officials

Debbie Simock: manager community relations

Grants Analysis

Disclosure Period: calendar year ending 2002
Total Grants: $735,000
Number of Grants: 450
Average Grant: $1,000
Highest Grant: $15,000
Lowest Grant: $100
Typical Range: $500 to $1,000

AVON PRODUCTS INC.

Company Headquarters

New York, NY
Web: http://www.avon.com

Company Description

Founded: 1886
Ticker: AVP
Exchange: NYSE
Revenue: US$7.747 billion (2004)
Profit: US$846.1 million (2004)
Employees: 45900 (2003)
Fortune Rank: 278, per FORTUNE Magazine's list of 500 Largest U.S. Corporations (2004).
SIC(s): 2844 Toilet Preparations, 3961 Costume Jewelry, 5122 Drugs, Proprietaries & Sundries.

Operating Locations

Avon Products, Inc. (CA--Pasadena, Santa Monica; DE--Newark; IL--Glenview, Morton Grove; NY--New York, Rye; OH--Springdale)

Nonmonetary Support

Type: Donated Equipment; Donated Products; In-kind Services
Note: Products are distributed through a partnership with Gifts In Kind.

Avon Products Foundation, Inc.

Giving Contact

Mary P. Quinn, Assistant Secretary & Director
Avon Products Foundation, Inc.
1345 Avenue of the Americas
New York, NY 10105-0196
Phone: (212)282-5517
Fax: (212)282-6049
E-mail: avon.foundation@avon.com
Web: http://www.avoncompany.com/women/

Description

Founded: 1955
EIN: 136128447
Organization Type: Corporate Foundation
Giving Locations: headquarters and operating communities.
Grant Types: Capital, Challenge, Employee Matching Gifts, Matching, Multiyear/Continuing Support, Scholarship.
Note: The foundation matches Avon associate donations to charitable arts, health, educational, and community and social service organizations through its Matching Gifts Program. Employee matching gift ratio: 1:1 up to $5,000 annually per associate.

Donor Information

Founder: Avon Products

Financial Summary

Total Giving: $49,353,930 (2003); $31,502,065 (2002); $39,602,732 (2001). Note: Contributes through foundation only.
Giving Analysis: Giving for 2001 includes: foundation matching gifts ($238,100); foundation scholarships ($466,335); foundation ($38,898,297)
Assets: $77,450,080 (2003); $103,650,842 (2002); $59,103,671 (2001)
Gifts Received: $49,449,161 (2003); $149,403,302 (2002); $101,146,340 (2001). Note: In 2003, contributions were received from Avon Products, Inc. ($21,878,950). In 2002, contributions were received from Avon Products, Inc. In 1999, contributions were received from Avon Breast Cancer 3-Day ($16,431,436) and Avon Products, Inc. ($5,714,488).

Typical Recipients

Arts & Humanities: Arts Associations & Councils, Arts Centers, Arts Festivals, Arts Funds, Arts Institutes, Arts Outreach, Community Arts, Dance, Ethnic & Folk Arts, Libraries, Museums/Galleries, Music, Opera, Performing Arts, Public Broadcasting, Theater
Civic & Public Affairs: African American Affairs, Asian American Affairs, Business/Free Enterprise, Chambers of Commerce, Civil Rights, Clubs, Economic Development, Economic Policy, Employment/Job Training, Civic & Public Affairs-General, Hispanic Affairs, Law & Justice, Legal Aid, Native American Affairs, Nonprofit Management, Philanthropic Organizations, Professional & Trade Associations, Public Policy, Rural Affairs, Safety, Urban & Community Affairs, Women's Affairs, Zoos/Aquariums
Education: Afterschool/Enrichment Programs, Arts/Humanities Education, Business Education, Colleges & Universities, Community & Junior Colleges, Eco-

nomic Education, Education Associations, Education Funds, Environmental Education, Education-General, International Exchange, Leadership Training, Literacy, Medical Education, Minority Education, Science/Mathematics Education, Special Education, Student Aid
Environment: Environment-General, Wildlife Protection
Health: Cancer, Children's Health/Hospitals, Clinics/Medical Centers, Emergency/Ambulance Services, Health-General, Health Funds, Health Organizations, Hospices, Hospitals, Medical Rehabilitation, Medical Research, Mental Health, Outpatient Health Care, Prenatal Health Issues, Preventive Medicine/Wellness Organizations, Single-Disease Health Associations
International: Foreign Educational Institutions, Health Care/Hospitals, International Development, International Organizations, International Relief Efforts
Religion: Religious Welfare
Science: Science Museums, Scientific Centers & Institutes
Social Services: Animal Protection, At-Risk Youth, Big Brothers/Big Sisters, Child Abuse, Child Welfare, Community Centers, Community Service Organizations, Delinquency & Criminal Rehabilitation, Domestic Violence, Family Services, Food/Clothing Distribution, People with Disabilities, Recreation & Athletics, Refugee Assistance, Scouts, Senior Services, Shelters/Homelessness, Social Services-General, Special Olympics, Substance Abuse, United Funds/United Ways, Volunteer Services, YMCA/YWCA/YMHA/YWHA, Youth Organizations

Application Procedures

Initial Contact: Applicants for Economic Opportunity for Women and Girls funding are encouraged to submit a one-page preliminary application letter. Applicants for scholarships should contact foundation for an application packet. Non-profit, community-based breast health programs wishing to request funding from the Avon Breast Care Fund should contact The Avon Breast Care Fund, 505 Eighth Ave. Suite 2001, New York, NY 10018-6505; telephone: (212) 244-5368; fax: (212) 695-3081; web site: www.avonbreastcare.org.
Application Requirements: Preliminary application letters should include the name, address, telephone number and IRS tax-exempt classification of the organization; a description of organization, including objectives and programs; amount requested, and its proposed use.
Deadlines: None.
Review Process: Preliminary requests for funding are reviewed as they are received.
Evaluative Criteria: Requests asking the foundation to fund a portion of the project will generally receive greater priority than one asking the foundation to be the sole monetary source.
Decision Notification: Responses to preliminary requests generally occurs within 60 days. The foundation will notify the applicant if a formal proposal is needed.
Notes: Preliminary inquiries by telephone or letter are accepted if the applicant has questions regarding funding priorities.

Restrictions

The Foundation does not support individuals; political or lobbying groups; religious, fraternal, or veteran organizations; fundraising events; memberships; journal advertisements; or organizations that discriminate in any way inconsistent with national equal opportunity policies.

Additional Information

Avon sponsors worldwide programs that focus on women's concerns, primarily through cause-related marketing programs. Since 1992, Avon and its sales representatives in the U.S., U.K., Canada, Mexico, Venezuela, the Philippines, and other countries have spearheaded a grass-roots breast cancer awareness campaign to educate women about the importance of early detection and to improve access to mammography exams and breast cancer education. Money raised through the sale of products supports community-based programs worldwide. The company has established a Worldwide Fund for Women's Health, which addresses breast cancer efforts, as well as such other health-related issues as AIDS in Thailand and elder care in Japan, and emotional and financial support for mothers in need in Germany. The company also has awards programs that recognize women's achievements in many fields in Avon countries around the world. The foundation, which has traditionally limited support to U.S. organizations, is expanding its support of women worldwide. Working in partnership with Avon Russia, the foundation agreed to underwrite a series of events in Russia on behalf of Magee Womancare International. Affiliated with the Magee-Women's Hospital of Pittsburgh, PA, this organization seeks to improve the quality of healthcare for women around the world. The first event was a wellness festival held in Moscow in March 1997. Avon also supports research into alternatives to the use of animal testing in new product development. To strengthen its Global Supplier Code of Conduct, Avon in 1997 implemented a certification and monitoring program to ensure that all suppliers meet and conform to the code. According to the 1996 annual report, "Together with other major corporations and with the guidance of the Council on Economic Priorities, Avon is working to create cooperative certification and monitoring programs that will aid in endorsing those suppliers who meet the agreed-upon criteria."

The Avon Women of Enterprise Awards program is a partnership between Avon Products, Inc. and the U.S. Small Business administration. The program recognizes and honors women entrepreneurs who have overcome personal and professional challenges or have exhibited exceptional entrepreneurial skills.

Publications: Information and Guidelines Brochure

Corporate Officials

Andrea Jung: chairman, chief executive officer B Toronto, ON Canada 1959. ED Princeton University BA (1979). PRIM CORP EMPL chairman, chief executive officer: Avon Products Inc. CORP AFFIL director: CE Co. NONPR AFFIL trustee: Cosmetic, Toiletry & Frangrance Association; chairman: New York Presbyterian Hospital Board.

Foundation Officials

Brian Connolly: vice president, director
Robert Corti: treasurer, director
Jill Kanin-Lovers: vice president, director
Carol Kurzig: vice president, director
Mary Quinn: assistant secretary, director
Thomas Sarakatsannis: secretary, legal counsel, director
Kathleen Walas: president, director

Grants Analysis

Disclosure Period: calendar year ending 2003
Total Grants: $48,254,098*
Number of Grants: 126
Average Grant: $108,255*
Highest Grant: $6,569,656
Lowest Grant: $1,000
Typical Range: $1,000 to $20,000 and $2,000,000 to $10,000,000
*Note: Giving excludes matching gifts and scholarships. Average grant figure excludes ten highest grants ($35,696,529).

Recent Grants

Note: Grants derived from 2003 Form 990.
General
6,569,656 Cicatelli Associates Inc., New York, NY -- to provide breast cancer education and access to low or no cost screening services to underserved women

5,827,767 Sidney Kimmel Comprehensive Cancer Center at Johns Hopkins Medical Center, Baltimore, MD -- to set up the Avon Foundation Comprehensive Breast Center
4,675,000 Cicatelli Associates Inc., New York, NY -- to fund the community based breast cancer outreach and education programs
3,890,188 National Cancer Institute, Rockville, MD
3,705,650 Center for Disease Control and Prevention Foundation, Atlanta, GA -- towards Avon-CDC mobile access program that provides breast cancer screening to medically underserved women
3,000,000 Cancer Care Inc., New York, NY -- towards AVONCares financial assistance program
3,000,000 Robert H Lurie Comprehensive Cancer Center of Northwestern University, Chicago, IL
2,028,268 UCSF Comprehensive Cancer Center and San Francisco General Hospital, San Francisco, CA -- towards research in breast cancer biology
2,000,000 Massachusetts General Hospital/Harvard Comprehensive Cancer Center, Boston, MA -- for research in breast cancer, genetics and clinical care for underserved women and set up of "Avon Foundation Breast Imaging Center"
1,000,000 Intrepid Museum Foundation, New York, NY -- towards the Intrepid fallen heroes fund

AYLWARD FAMILY FOUNDATION

Giving Contact

E. W. Aylward, President
PO Box 409
Neenah, WI 54957-0409
Phone: (920)722-0901

Description

Founded: 1953
EIN: 396042143
Organization Type: Private Foundation
Former Name: Neenah Foundry Foundation (1998).
Giving Locations: FL: Palm Beach, West Palm Beach; WI
Grant Types: Capital, General Support, Multiyear/Continuing Support, Operating Expenses.

Donor Information

Founder: Neenah Foundry Co.

Financial Summary

Total Giving: $349,500 (2001)
Giving Analysis: Giving for 2001 includes: foundation grants to United Way ($25,000)
Assets: $4,147,412 (2001)
Gifts Received: $250,000 (1996). Note: In 1996, contributions were received from the Neenah Foundry Co.

Typical Recipients

Arts & Humanities: Arts Associations & Councils, Arts Centers, Ballet, Arts & Humanities-General, History & Archaeology, Libraries, Museums/Galleries, Public Broadcasting, Visual Arts
Civic & Public Affairs: Business/Free Enterprise, Clubs, Economic Development, Civic & Public Affairs-General, Philanthropic Organizations, Safety, Urban & Community Affairs
Education: Business Education, Colleges & Universities, Education Funds, Engineering/Technological Education, Education-General, Private Education (Precollege), Secondary Education (Private), Student

Aid, Vocational & Technical Education
Health: Cancer, Children's Health/Hospitals, Health-General, Nursing Services, Single-Disease Health Associations
International: International Environmental Issues
Religion: Churches, Religion-General, Religious Welfare
Social Services: Community Service Organizations, Domestic Violence, People with Disabilities, Social Services-General, Substance Abuse, United Funds/United Ways, YMCA/YWCA/YMHA/YWHA, Youth Organizations

Application Procedures

Initial Contact: Send a letter of request detailing need.
Deadlines: October 31.

Restrictions

Does not make grants to individuals. Most of the foundation's grants are made to preselected organizations.

Foundation Officials

A. A. Aylward: vice president PRIM CORP EMPL director: Neenah Transport Inc.
E. W. Aylward: president
R. J. Aylward: director

Grants Analysis

Disclosure Period: calendar year ending 2001
Total Grants: $324,500*
Number of Grants: 20
Average Grant: $11,026*
Highest Grant: $115,000
Lowest Grant: $1,000
Typical Range: $2,000 to $15,000
*Note: Giving excludes United Way. Average grant figure excludes highest grant.

Recent Grants

Note: Grants derived from 2001 Form 990.
Library-Related
25,000 Neenah Public Library, Neenah, WI
General
450,000 Rawhide Boys Ranch, New London, WI
25,000 United Way Fox Cities, Menasha, WI
20,000 Goodwill Industries, WI
20,000 United Community Services, Neenah, WI
15,000 Lawrence University, Appleton, WI
15,000 Rawhide Boys Ranch, New London, WI
15,000 Ripon College, Ripon, WI
10,000 ALS Association, Woodland Hills, CA
10,000 Norton Museum of Art, West Palm Beach, FL
10,000 Wayland Academy, Beaver Dam, WI

AYRES FOUNDATION

Giving Contact

John E.D. Peacock, President & Director
5610 West 82nd Street
Indianapolis, IN 46278
Phone: (317)872-5400

Description

Founded: 1944
EIN: 356018437
Organization Type: Private Foundation
Giving Locations: IN: Indianapolis
Grant Types: Capital, General Support, Operating Expenses, Project.

Donor Information

Founder: L.S. Ayres & Co., the late Theodore B. Griffith, Mrs. Theodore B. Griffith

Typical Recipients

Arts & Humanities: Art History, Arts Institutes, Historic Preservation, History & Archaeology, Libraries, Museums/Galleries, Music, Theater

Civic & Public Affairs: Botanical Gardens/Parks, Community Foundations, Employment/Job Training, Civic & Public Affairs-General, Municipalities/Towns, Zoos/Aquariums

Education: Colleges & Universities, Education Associations, Education Funds, Engineering/Technological Education, Education-General, Medical Education, Private Education (Precollege), Public Education (Precollege), Special Education

Environment: Resource Conservation

Health: Cancer, Clinics/Medical Centers, Health Organizations, Home-Care Services, Hospitals, Long-Term Care, Nursing Services, Public Health, Single-Disease Health Associations

International: Foreign Arts Organizations

Religion: Churches, Religious Welfare

Social Services: Animal Protection, Big Brothers/Big Sisters, Child Welfare, Community Service Organizations, Day Care, Family Planning, Family Services, Food/Clothing Distribution, Homes, People with Disabilities, Scouts, Senior Services, Shelters/Homelessness, Social Services-General, Special Olympics, Substance Abuse, United Funds/United Ways, Volunteer Services, YMCA/YWCA/YMHA/YWHA, Youth Organizations

Application Procedures

Initial Contact: Send brief proposal including name, address, telephone number, financial data, and information on current sources of funding.

Application Requirements: Include a description of organization, amount requested, purpose of funds sought, recently audited financial statement, and proof of tax-exempt status.

Deadlines: None.

Restrictions

Does not support individuals, religious organizations for sectarian purposes, political or lobbying groups, or organizations outside operating areas.

Foundation Officials

David S. Evans: director

Alvin C. Fernandes, Jr.: secretary, director

John E. D. Peacock: president, director

John E. D. Peacock, Jr.: vice president, treasurer, director

William J. Stout: assistant secretary, treasurer B Bloomington, IN December 14, 1914. ED Indiana University AB (1937). CORP AFFIL president, director: Citizens Gas & Coke Utility. NONPR AFFIL director: Saint Richards Day School; director: Saint Vincent Hospital; member: Indianapolis Personnel Association; member: National Retail Merchants Association; member: Indianapolis Chamber of Commerce; member: Indianapolis Merchants Association; president, director: Flanner House.

Bert M. Wilboith: director

Grants Analysis

Disclosure Period: calendar year ending 2000

Total Grants: $230,010*

Number of Grants: 49

Average Grant: $3,294*

Highest Grant: $42,000

Lowest Grant: $200

Typical Range: $500 to $10,000

*Note: Giving excludes United Way. Average grant figure excludes two highest grants ($75,200).

Recent Grants

Note: Grants derived from 2002 Form 990.

Library-Related

10,075	Indianapolis Marion County Library, Indianapolis, IN -- capital fund

General

20,000	Indiana State Museum, Indianapolis, IN -- capital building fund
18,000	Martin University, Indianapolis, IN -- operating fund
15,000	Charles A. Tindley School, Indianapolis, IN -- operating fund
9,500	Eiteljorg Museum, Indianapolis, IN -- operating fund
7,500	United Way, Indianapolis, IN -- operating fund
7,000	Bosma Industries, Indianapolis, IN -- operating fund
5,500	Executive Service Corps, Indianapolis, IN -- operating fund
5,000	Cathedral High School, Indianapolis, IN -- capital fund
5,000	Clarian Health Partners, Indianapolis, IN -- operating fund
5,000	Gleaners Food Bank, Indianapolis, IN -- operating fund

AZADOUTIOUN FOUNDATION

Giving Contact

Carolyn G. Mugar, Trustee
c/o Gravestar
1 Broadway
Cambridge, MA 02142
Phone: (617)492-4118
Fax: (617)492-4118

Description

Founded: 1985

EIN: 042876245

Organization Type: Private Foundation

Giving Locations: MA

Grant Types: General Support, Project.

Donor Information

Founder: Carolyn G. Mugar

Financial Summary

Total Giving: $609,402 (2003)

Assets: $3,388,233 (2003)

Gifts Received: $151,233 (1999); $45,000 (1996); $153,000 (1995). Note: In 1999 and 1996, contributions were received from Carolyn G. Mugar.

Typical Recipients

Arts & Humanities: Arts Associations & Councils, Historic Preservation

Civic & Public Affairs: Economic Development, Employment/Job Training, Ethnic Organizations, Civic & Public Affairs-General, Public Policy, Urban & Community Affairs, Women's Affairs

Education: Arts/Humanities Education, Business Education, Colleges & Universities, Continuing Education, Education Funds, Elementary Education (Private), Education-General, International Studies, Private Education (Precollege), Social Sciences Education

Environment: Air/Water Quality, Environment-General

Health: Children's Health/Hospitals, Health Policy/Cost Containment, Health Funds

International: Health Care/Hospitals, Human Rights, International Relief Efforts

Religion: Churches, Religious Organizations, Religious Welfare

Social Services: Child Welfare, Community Service Organizations, Day Care, Recreation & Athletics, Youth Organizations

Application Procedures

Initial Contact: Send a brief letter of inquiry describing program or project.

Deadlines: None.

Foundation Officials

Janet Corpus: trustee

Carolyn G. Mugar: trustee

Sidney Peck: trustee

Sharryn Ross: trustee

Grants Analysis

Disclosure Period: calendar year ending 2003

Total Grants: $609,402

Number of Grants: 6

Highest Grant: $537,012

Lowest Grant: $10,000

Typical Range: $10,000 to $20,000

Recent Grants

Note: Grants derived from 2001 Form 990.

General

72,000	Armenian Assembly of America, Washington, DC
50,000	ANI, Washington, DC
35,000	Country Road, Inc., Arlington, MA
25,000	Texans United Education Fund, Houston, TX
20,000	Ani and Narod Memorial Fund, New York, NY
20,000	Institute for Local Self-Reliance, Minneapolis, MN
10,000	Project Save, Watertown, MA
10,000	Southwest Writers Collection, San Marcos, TX
5,000	Land and Culture Organization, New York, NY
2,000	Armenian Library and Museum of America, Watertown, MA

MARY REYNOLDS BABCOCK FOUNDATION

Giving Contact

Gayle Williams, Executive Director
2920 Reynolda Road
Winston-Salem, NC 27106-5123
Phone: (336)748-9222
Fax: (336)777-0095
E-mail: info@mrbf.org
Web: http://www.mrbf.org

Description

Founded: 1953

EIN: 560690140

Organization Type: Family Foundation

Giving Locations: Southeastern United States.

Grant Types: Award, General Support, Loan, Multi-year/Continuing Support, Seed Money.

Note: Awards organizational development grants.

Donor Information

Founder: Incorporated in North Carolina in 1953 with funds donated by the late Mrs. Mary Reynolds Babcock and Charles H. Babcock. Mary Reynolds was one of four children of R.J. Reynolds, of R.J. Reynolds Tobacco Company.

Financial Summary

Total Giving: $5,624,294 (2003); $4,815,334 (2002)

Assets: $142,282,378 (2003); $108,875,545 (2002)

Gifts Received: $10,350,000 (2003); $6,782,109 (2002). Note: In 2002 and 2003, contributions were received from the estate of Betsy Babcock.

Typical Recipients

Arts & Humanities: Arts Centers, Arts Funds, Community Arts, Film & Video, History & Archaeology, Museums/Galleries, Performing Arts, Public Broadcasting

Civic & Public Affairs: African American Affairs, Business/Free Enterprise, Civil Rights, Clubs, Community Foundations, Economic Development, Economic Policy, Employment/Job Training, First Amendment Issues, Civic & Public Affairs-General, Hispanic Affairs, Housing, Law & Justice, Legal Aid, Minority Business, Nonprofit Management, Philanthropic Organizations, Public Policy, Rural Affairs, Safety, Urban & Community Affairs, Women's Affairs

Education: Colleges & Universities, Continuing Education, Economic Education, Education Funds, Education Reform, Elementary Education (Private), Faculty Development, Education-General, Leadership Training, Literacy, Preschool Education, Public Education (Precollege), Student Aid

Environment: Air/Water Quality, Environment-General, Protection, Resource Conservation, Sanitary Systems, Wildlife Protection

Health: Emergency/Ambulance Services, Health Organizations, Hospitals, Nutrition

International: Human Rights, International Peace & Security Issues, International Relations

Religion: Religion-General, Ministries, Religious Organizations, Religious Welfare

Social Services: Child Welfare, Community Centers, Community Service Organizations, Crime Prevention, Day Care, Delinquency & Criminal Rehabilitation, Family Planning, Family Services, Food/Clothing Distribution, Recreation & Athletics, Volunteer Services, Youth Organizations

Application Procedures

Initial Contact: Call or write foundation for grant application for the Organizational Development program.

Application Requirements: Information needed for two-page Organizational Development Grant Application includes the following: organization's name, contact name, address, phone, and e-mail; description of organization; list of board members including race and gender of each member; list of staff with title, including volunteers if half-time or greater; proof of tax-exempt status; and financial information. Additional information needed for the second part of application form includes the following: description of organization's mission and how it ties to the foundation's goals; description of current activities; definition of organization's current constituency; report on evaluation methods; account of organization's greatest accomplishments and difficult challenges; summary of organization's five-year vision; a description of organization's development work plan; amount of grant request; a cover letter signed by board chair or executive director, and a one page budget.

Deadlines: March 1 and August 1. Applicants can see guidelines and updated information on the foundation's website. Prospective applicants should call the foundation before submitting a letter of request.

Restrictions

Grants are not made to individuals. No grants for international programs, nor for construction.

Additional Information

The foundation reports that it is affiliated with the Z. Smith Reynolds Foundation, Winston-Salem, NC. The foundations share some directors.

Program-related investments are made on a selective basis when a loan is a more appropriate use of the foundation's funds than a grant.

Publications: Annual Report; Guidelines; Application Form

Foundation Officials

Bruce M. Babcock: director
Victoria Creed: director

David Dodson: secretary, director
Akosua Barthwell Evans: director
Wayne Flynt: director
Nathaniel Irvin, II: president, director
Wendy S. Johnson: director
Sandra H. Mikush: assistant director
Barbara B. Millhouse: vice president, director
Katharine Reynolds Mountcastle: director B Greenwich, CT 1963. ED Williams College BA (1985). PRIM CORP EMPL associate producer: CBS News. NONPR AFFIL volunteer: Greater District of Columbia Cares.
Kenneth F. Mountcastle, III: director
Laura Lewis Mountcastle: treasurer, director ED Trinity College BA (1978); Yale University MBA (1984). PRIM CORP EMPL vice president planning & investor relations: CMS Energy Corp.
Mary Mountcastle: director NONPR AFFIL assistant director: Center Community Self-Help; director: Tides Indiana Inc.; director: Boggs Rural Life Center; director: Center Community Change.
Gayle Williams: executive director
Carol Prejean Zippert: director

Grants Analysis

Disclosure Period: calendar year ending 2003
Total Grants: $5,624,294
Number of Grants: 159
Average Grant: $28,635*
Highest Grant: $1,100,000
Lowest Grant: $1,000
Typical Range: $10,000 to $50,000
*Note: Average grant figure excludes highest grant.

Recent Grants

Note: Grants derived from 2003 Form 990.
General

1,100,000	Reynolda House Museum of American Art, Winston-Salem, NC -- funds for Betsy Babcock endowment
300,000	MDC Inc., Chapel Hill, NC -- for enterprise and asset development
250,000	Reynolda House Museum of American Art, Winston-Salem, NC -- for capital campaign
200,000	Center for Economic Options, Charleston, WV -- for enterprise and asset development
120,500	Mcauley Institute, Raleigh, NC
95,500	Reynolda House Museum of American Art, Winston-Salem, NC
75,000	Cobb Microenterprise Council, Kennesaw, GA -- for enterprise and asset development
75,000	Five Rivers Community Development Corporation, Georgetown, SC -- for enterprise and asset development
75,000	Greater Birmingham Ministries, Birmingham, AL
75,000	Lightstone Foundation and Community Development Corporation, Moyers, WV -- for enterprise and asset development

PAUL AND EDITH BABSON FOUNDATION

Giving Contact

Elizabeth D. Nichols, Grant Administrator
c/o Nichols and Pratt
50 Congress St., Suite 832
Boston, MA 02109
Phone: (617)523-8368
Fax: (617)523-8949
E-mail: pebabsonfdn@babsonfoundations.org
Web: http://www.babsonfoundations.org

Description

Founded: 1957
EIN: 046037891
Organization Type: Private Foundation
Giving Locations: MA: Greater Boston
Grant Types: Capital, General Support, Project.

Donor Information

Founder: the late Paul T. Babson

Financial Summary

Total Giving: $533,248 (2004); $648,543 (2001)
Giving Analysis: Giving for 2004 includes: foundation grants to United Way ($20,000); 2001: foundation grants to United Way ($20,000)
Assets: $12,442,323 (2004); $13,166,051 (2001)

Typical Recipients

Arts & Humanities: History & Archaeology, Libraries, Museums/Galleries, Music, Opera, Performing Arts, Public Broadcasting, Theater

Civic & Public Affairs: African American Affairs, Business/Free Enterprise, Community Foundations, Economic Development, Employment/Job Training, Gay/Lesbian Issues, Civic & Public Affairs-General, Hispanic Affairs, Municipalities/Towns, Native American Affairs, Nonprofit Management, Philanthropic Organizations, Public Policy, Urban & Community Affairs, Women's Affairs

Education: Arts/Humanities Education, Business Education, Colleges & Universities, Education Associations, Engineering/Technological Education, Faculty Development, Education-General, Leadership Training, Medical Education, Minority Education, Private Education (Precollege), Public Education (Precollege), Science/Mathematics Education, Secondary Education (Private), Student Aid

Environment: Air/Water Quality, Environment-General, Resource Conservation

Health: AIDS/HIV, Hospitals, Medical Research, Mental Health, Public Health

International: Foreign Arts Organizations, Human Rights, International Relief Efforts

Religion: Churches, Religious Organizations, Religious Welfare

Science: Science Museums

Social Services: At-Risk Youth, Child Welfare, Community Centers, Community Service Organizations, Crime Prevention, Family Planning, Family Services, Food/Clothing Distribution, Homes, People with Disabilities, Sexual Abuse, Shelters/Homelessness, United Funds/United Ways, YMCA/YWCA/YMHA/YWHA, Youth Organizations

Application Procedures

Initial Contact: Submit two copies of a two-page concept letter and a completed Concept Letter Summary Sheet. The Summary Sheet may be downloaded from the foundation's web site.

Deadlines: April 1 and September 25 for concept letters.

Review Process: The board of trustees review concept letters and invite a limited number of applicants to submit full proposals.

Decision Notification: The board of trustees meets in late May and early December to consider proposals. Decisions are generally communicated to applicants within six weeks of each meeting.

Restrictions

The foundation does not support individuals, films, videos, conferences, fundraising, or donor cultivation events.

Additional Information

Foundation accepts the Common Grant Application of the National Network of Grantmakers for full proposals.
Publications: Guidelines

Foundation Officials

James A. Babson: trustee
Katherine L. Babson: trustee
James R. Nichols: trustee

Grants Analysis

Disclosure Period: calendar year ending 2004
Total Grants: $513,248*
Number of Grants: 81
Average Grant: $6,336
Highest Grant: $26,000
Lowest Grant: $1,000
Typical Range: $1,000 to $10,000
*Note: Giving excludes United Way.

Recent Grants

Note: Grants derived from 2001 Form 990.
General

25,000	MACDC Community Business Network
25,000	Trustees of Phillips Academy, Andover, MA
20,000	Associated Grantmakers, Boston, MA
20,000	Newton Wellesley Hospital, Wellesley, MA
20,000	United Way of Massachusetts Bay, Boston, MA
20,000	YMCA of Greater Boston, Boston, MA
15,000	AIDS Action Committee, Boston, MA
15,000	Boston Partners in Education, Boston, MA
15,000	Center for Women and Enterprise, Boston, MA
15,000	Island Alliance, Boston, MA

BEATRICE AND ROY BACKUS FOUNDATION

Giving Contact

Inge T. Stephens, President
536B Heritage Hills
Somers, NY 10589
Phone: (914)277-3024

Description

Founded: 1988
EIN: 133442922
Organization Type: Private Foundation
Giving Locations: CA; MA
Grant Types: Department, General Support, Multi-year/Continuing Support, Research.

Financial Summary

Total Giving: $45,000 (2003); $87,500 (2002 approx); $145,290 (2001)
Assets: $1,594,194 (2003); $1,691,893 (2001)

Typical Recipients

Arts & Humanities: Libraries
Education: Afterschool/Enrichment Programs, Education-General, Health & Physical Education, Medical Education, Preschool Education, Science/Mathematics Education
Health: AIDS/HIV, Children's Health/Hospitals, Health Organizations, Hospitals, Medical Rehabilitation, Medical Research, Research/Studies Institutes, Single-Disease Health Associations, Transplant Networks/Donor Banks
Social Services: Child Welfare, Community Service Organizations, Counseling, Day Care, Scouts, Shelters/Homelessness

Application Procedures

Initial Contact: The foundation reports that applications should be submitted in written form detailing the purpose for which the funds will be used.
Deadlines: None.

Restrictions

Grants are limited to programs in the areas of medical research, education, and science.

Foundation Officials

Adolf Haasen: director
Christopher H. Stephens: secretary, director
Inge T. Stephens: treasurer, president

Grants Analysis

Disclosure Period: calendar year ending 2003
Total Grants: $45,000
Number of Grants: 1

Recent Grants

Note: Grants derived from 2001 Form 990.
General

85,290	Massachusetts General Hospital - Harvard Medical School, Charlestown, MA -- research into pain causation and treatment arising from post-herpetic neuralgia pain
20,000	Massachusetts General Hospital - Harvard Medical School, Charlestown, MA -- funding for the establishment of The Center for Shingles and Post Herpetic Neuralgia
20,000	Parkinson's Institute, Sunnyvale, CA -- for three-year study of the role of Alfa-Synuclein in Parkinson's Disease
20,000	Salk Institute, San Diego, CA -- for Gene Chip Workstation to determine gene function in Parkinson's disease

BACON FAMILY FOUNDATION

Giving Contact

Staci Adelman
c/o Wells Fargo Bank
PO Box 4010
Grand Junction, CO 81502
Phone: (970)243-1611
Fax: (970)242-1066

Description

Founded: 1978
EIN: 841269589
Organization Type: Private Foundation
Former Name: E. L. and Oma Bacon Foundation.
Giving Locations: CO
Grant Types: General Support.

Donor Information

Founder: the late E. L. Bacon, the late Oma Bacon

Financial Summary

Total Giving: $528,265 (fiscal year ending August 31, 2004)
Giving Analysis: Giving for fiscal 2004 includes: foundation grants to United Way ($22,000)
Assets: $12,273,761 (fiscal 2004)

Typical Recipients

Arts & Humanities: Arts Associations & Councils, Arts Centers, History & Archaeology, Libraries, Museums/Galleries, Music, Public Broadcasting, Theater
Civic & Public Affairs: Chambers of Commerce, Civil Rights, Economic Development, Civic & Public Affairs-General, Housing, Municipalities/Towns, Nonprofit Management, Philanthropic Organizations, Safety, Urban & Community Affairs, Women's Affairs, Zoos/Aquariums
Education: Colleges & Universities, Education Funds, Journalism/Media Education, Preschool Education, Religious Education, Student Aid

Environment: Environment-General
Health: AIDS/HIV, Children's Health/Hospitals, Clinics/Medical Centers, Eyes/Blindness, Hospitals, Medical Rehabilitation, Mental Health, Public Health
Religion: Churches, Religious Organizations, Religious Welfare
Social Services: Child Welfare, Community Service Organizations, Domestic Violence, Food/Clothing Distribution, People with Disabilities, Senior Services, Substance Abuse, United Funds/United Ways, Volunteer Services, Youth Organizations

Application Procedures

Initial Contact: Send a brief letter of inquiry describing program.
Deadlines: None.

Restrictions

Does not support individuals.

Additional Information

Publications: Application Guidelines

Foundation Officials

Herbert L. Bacon: director
Laura May Bacon: director
Patrick A. Gormley: director

Grants Analysis

Disclosure Period: fiscal year ending August 31, 2004
Total Grants: $506,265*
Number of Grants: 48
Average Grant: $9,531*
Highest Grant: $58,288
Lowest Grant: $250
Typical Range: $1,000 to $20,000
*Note: Giving excludes United Way. Average grant figure excludes highest grant.

Recent Grants

Note: Grants derived from 2004 Form 990.
General

58,288	Mesa State College Foundation, Grand Junction, CO
30,000	Children's Hospital, Denver, CO
25,000	Blue Sage Center, Paonia, CO
25,000	Catholic Outreach, Grand Junction, CO
25,000	ILIFF School, Denver, CO
25,000	WCCF Grand Valley Housing Initiatives, Grand Junction, CO
25,000	Wisconsin Chamber of Commerce Foundation, Grand Junction, CO
22,000	United Way, Grand Junction, CO
20,000	Family Health West, Fruita, CO
20,000	Housing Resources of Western Colorado, Grand Junction, CO

ROSE M. BADGELEY RESIDUARY CHARITABLE TRUST

Giving Contact

Roberta Grossman, Vice President
Care of HSBC Bank, USA
140 Broadway, 11th Fl.
New York, NY 10005
Phone: 800-975-4722
Fax: (212)658-7790

Description

Founded: 1977
EIN: 136744781
Organization Type: General Purpose Foundation
Former Name: Rose M. Badgeley Charitable Trust.
Giving Locations: NY
Grant Types: General Support, Research.

Donor Information

Founder: Established in 1977 through the will of the late Rose M. Badgeley.

Financial Summary

Gifts Received: $111,388 (fiscal year ending October 1, 1999); $109,984 (fiscal 1997); $250,379 (fiscal 1995). Note: In 1999, contributions were received from the Rose M. Badgeley Annuity Trust.

Typical Recipients

Arts & Humanities: Film & Video, Libraries, Museums/Galleries, Music, Opera, Performing Arts, Theater

Civic & Public Affairs: Botanical Gardens/Parks, Clubs, Employment/Job Training, Civic & Public Affairs-General, Hispanic Affairs, Housing, Women's Affairs

Education: Arts/Humanities Education, Colleges & Universities, Education-General, Literacy, Minority Education, Preschool Education, Private Education (Precollege), Public Education (Precollege), School Volunteerism, Science/Mathematics Education, Student Aid, Vocational & Technical Education

Environment: Air/Water Quality, Resource Conservation

Health: AIDS/HIV, Alzheimer's Disease, Cancer, Children's Health/Hospitals, Clinics/Medical Centers, Emergency/Ambulance Services, Eyes/Blindness, Geriatric Health, Health Organizations, Heart, Hospitals, Hospitals (University Affiliated), Medical Rehabilitation, Medical Research, Mental Health, Nursing Services, Prenatal Health Issues, Single-Disease Health Associations, Transplant Networks/Donor Banks

International: Health Care/Hospitals

Religion: Churches, Dioceses, Jewish Causes, Ministries, Religious Welfare

Social Services: At-Risk Youth, Camps, Child Welfare, Community Centers, Community Service Organizations, Counseling, Family Services, Food/Clothing Distribution, Homes, People with Disabilities, Scouts, Senior Services, Shelters/Homelessness, Substance Abuse, Veterans, Volunteer Services, YMCA/YWCA/YMHA/YWHA, Youth Organizations

Application Procedures

Initial Contact: Letters of inquiry should be directed to the chairman of the trust's grants committee at HSBC.

Application Requirements: Requests should include current financial statements, list of board members and patrons, operating budget, and proof of tax-exempt status.

Deadlines: Applications must be postmarked no earlier than December 1 and no later than March 15.

Additional Information

Publications: Guidelines; Application Form
Trust(s): HSBC Bank USA

Foundation Officials

Roberta Grossman: vice president

Grants Analysis

Disclosure Period: fiscal year ending October 1, 1999
Total Grants: $1,128,648
Number of Grants: 46
Average Grant: $24,536
Highest Grant: $65,000
Lowest Grant: $2,500
Typical Range: $5,000 to $30,000

Recent Grants

Note: Grants derived from fiscal 2000 Form 990.
General

75,000	New York Presbyterian Hospital, New York, NY -- to support programs in research and teaching in Pediatric Cardiology
50,000	Alzheimer's Association, New York, NY -- to help extend and expand the efforts of the New York City Chapter
50,000	Make-A-Wish Foundation, New York, NY -- to support the cost of funding one wish for a critically ill child
50,000	Mount Sinai Medical Center, New York, NY -- support for the clinical development of combination cytotoxic differentiation therapy of colon cancer and prostate cancer
46,000	Carnegie Hall Society, New York, NY -- for the Family Concert Series
46,000	Metropolitan Opera Guild, New York, NY -- to help provide some New York area schools with an affordable and effective opera education program
45,000	New York City Opera, New York, NY
45,000	Skin Cancer Foundation, New York, NY -- to prepare the vaccine needed for the trial and to cover part of the cost of the assays
42,000	AMFAR, Los Angeles, CA -- to research various possible vaccines for treatment of HIV
35,000	Lincoln Center Theater, New York, NY -- to support the audience development and education project

BADGER METER INC.

Company Headquarters

Milwaukee, WI
Web: http://www.badgermeter.com

Company Description

Founded: 1905
Ticker: BMI
Exchange: AMEX
Revenue: US$138.5 million (2001)
Employees: 1065 (2003)
SIC(s): 3823 Process Control Instruments, 3824 Fluid Meters & Counting Devices.

Operating Locations

Badger Meter, Inc. (AZ--Rio Rico; OK--Tulsa)

Badger Meter Foundation

Giving Contact

Beth McCallister, Secretary
4545 West Brown Deer Road
Milwaukee, WI 53223
Phone: (414)371-5704
Fax: (414)371-5956

Description

EIN: 396043635
Organization Type: Corporate Foundation
Giving Locations: WI: Milwaukee
Grant Types: General Support.

Financial Summary

Total Giving: $149,495 (2003); $165,219 (2002); $410,108 (2001)
Giving Analysis: Giving for 2001 includes: foundation scholarships ($6,000); foundation grants to United Way ($92,250); foundation ($311,858)
Assets: $1,786,214 (2003); $1,603,472 (2002); $1,763,808 (2001)
Gifts Received: $100,000 (2003); $100,000 (2002); $106,000 (2001). Note: Contributions were received from Badger Meter, Inc.

Typical Recipients

Arts & Humanities: Arts Festivals, Arts Institutes, Ballet, Dance, Film & Video, Arts & Humanities-General, Historic Preservation, Libraries, Museums/Galleries, Music, Opera, Performing Arts, Theater

Civic & Public Affairs: Botanical Gardens/Parks, Clubs, Community Foundations, Economic Development, Employment/Job Training, Civic & Public Affairs-General, Hispanic Affairs, Housing, Law & Justice, Minority Business, Municipalities/Towns, Nonprofit Management, Parades/Festivals, Philanthropic Organizations, Public Policy, Rural Affairs, Urban & Community Affairs, Zoos/Aquariums

Education: Arts/Humanities Education, Business Education, Business-School Partnerships, Colleges & Universities, Education Funds, Elementary Education (Private), Engineering/Technological Education, Faculty Development, Education-General, Health & Physical Education, Leadership Training, Literacy, Medical Education, Minority Education, Preschool Education, Private Education (Precollege), Public Education (Precollege), Religious Education, Science/Mathematics Education, Secondary Education (Private), Secondary Education (Public), Student Aid

Environment: Environment-General, Protection, Resource Conservation

Health: Arthritis, Cancer, Diabetes, Health Funds, Health Organizations, Heart, Hospitals, Medical Research, Mental Health, Preventive Medicine/Wellness Organizations, Public Health, Single-Disease Health Associations, Speech & Hearing, Transplant Networks/Donor Banks

Religion: Religious Welfare, Seminaries

Science: Science Exhibits & Fairs, Science Museums

Social Services: Animal Protection, Child Abuse, Child Welfare, Community Centers, Community Service Organizations, Day Care, Delinquency & Criminal Rehabilitation, Domestic Violence, Family Services, Food/Clothing Distribution, Homes, People with Disabilities, Recreation & Athletics, Scouts, Shelters/Homelessness, Social Services-General, Substance Abuse, United Funds/United Ways, YMCA/YWCA/YMHA/YWHA, Youth Organizations

Application Procedures

Initial Contact: Send a brief letter of inquiry on organization's letterhead.

Application Requirements: Information should include purpose of funds sought; amount requested; and an attached copy of an IRS 501(c)(3) determination letter.

Deadlines: None.

Decision Notification: Board meets in April, August, and December.

Additional Information

RES Grants are awarded solely to charitable, scientific, literary, or educational organizations.

Corporate Officials

Ronald H. Dix: vice president administration & human resources B 1944. ED University of Wisconsin BS (1969). PRIM CORP EMPL vice president administration & human resources: Badger Meter, Inc.

Richard A. Meeusen: vice president, chief financial officer, treasurer B 1954. ED University of Wisconsin, Whitewater BS (1976). PRIM CORP EMPL vice president, chief financial officer, treasurer: Badger Meter, Inc.

James O. Wright: chairman, director B Milwaukee, WI 1921. ED Yale University BS (1944). PRIM CORP EMPL chairman, director: Badger Meter, Inc. CORP AFFIL director: Northwestern Mutual Life Insurance Co.; director: Wisconsin Natural Gas Co.; director: Marshall & Ilsley Corp.; director: Grede Foundries Inc.; director: Marshall & Ilsley Bank; director: Becor Western Inc.

Foundation Officials

John P. Biever: treasurer

Peter Wayne Bruce: director B Rome, NY 1945. ED University of Wisconsin BA (1967); University of Chicago JD (1970). PRIM CORP EMPL executive vice president chief compliance officer general: Northwest Mutual Life Insurance Co. NONPR AFFIL member: Village Shorewood Community Development Association; member: Wisconsin Bar Association; chairman, director: Saint Marys Hill Hospital Curative Foundation; member: American Law Institute; member: Milwaukee Bar Association; director: Alverno College.

Ronald H. Dix: vice president, director (see above)

Richard S. Gallagher: director B Minot, ND 1942. ED Northwestern University BSBA (1964); Harvard University JD (1967). NONPR AFFIL member: Memorial Park Committee; director: United Performing Arts Fund; fellow: American Law Institute; director: Donors Forum Wisconsin; fellow: American College Tax Counsel; fellow: American College Trust & Estate Counsel; member: American Bar Association.

Beth M. McCallister: secretary

Barbara M. Wiley: director

James O. Wright: president, director (see above)

Grants Analysis

Disclosure Period: calendar year ending 2003
Total Grants: $145,770*
Number of Grants: 71
Average Grant: $2,053
Highest Grant: $10,000
Lowest Grant: $50
Typical Range: $500 to $5,000
*Note: Giving excludes matching gifts and scholarships.

Recent Grants

Note: Grants derived from 2003 Form 990.
General

8,000	Alverno College, Milwaukee, WI
5,000	Boy Scouts of America, Milwaukee, WI
5,000	Community Memorial Foundation, Milwaukee, WI
5,000	Dominican High School, Milwaukee, WI
5,000	Goodwill Industries, Milwaukee, WI
5,000	Health Education Center, Milwaukee, WI
5,000	Messmer High School, Milwaukee, WI
3,000	Milwaukee Achiever Program, Milwaukee, WI
2,500	Blood Center Research Foundation, Milwaukee, WI
2,500	Brookfield Academy, Brookfield, WI

LOUIS W. AND DOLPHA BAEHR FOUNDATION

Giving Contact

Carl F. Gump
c/o Team Bank
PO Box 369
Paola, KS 66071
Phone: (913)294-4311

Description

Founded: 1967
EIN: 486129741
Organization Type: Private Foundation
Giving Locations: MO: Kansas City
Grant Types: Capital, Endowment, Project, Research, Seed Money.

Donor Information

Founder: the late L. W. Baehr, the late Dolpha Baehr

Financial Summary

Total Giving: $244,808 (fiscal year ending April 30, 2004); $362,808 (fiscal 2001)
Giving Analysis: Giving for fiscal 2004 includes: foundation grants to United Way ($3,000); fiscal 2001: foundation grants to United Way ($3,000)
Assets: $4,778,228 (fiscal 2004); $5,740,131 (fiscal 2001)

Typical Recipients

Arts & Humanities: Arts Centers, Historic Preservation, History & Archaeology, Libraries, Museums/Galleries, Music

Civic & Public Affairs: Botanical Gardens/Parks, Civic & Public Affairs-General, Municipalities/Towns, Parades/Festivals, Safety, Urban & Community Affairs

Education: Arts/Humanities Education, Colleges & Universities, Community & Junior Colleges, Continuing Education, Education-General, Minority Education, Private Education (Precollege), Public Education (Precollege), Secondary Education (Public)

Health: Children's Health/Hospitals, Clinics/Medical Centers, Health Organizations, Hospitals, Mental Health, Nutrition

International: International Relations

Social Services: Child Welfare, Community Service Organizations, People with Disabilities, Recreation & Athletics, Scouts, United Funds/United Ways, Youth Organizations

Application Procedures

Initial Contact: Send a brief letter of inquiry.

Application Requirements: Include a description of organization, amount requested, purpose of funds sought, recently audited financial statement, and proof of tax-exempt status.

Deadlines: Meetings are scheduled for January, April, August, and October.

Review Process: Proposals must be received at least four weeks prior to the month in which the request is to be reviewed.

Restrictions

Does not support individuals or provide funds for advertising.

Additional Information

Publications: Application Guidelines
Trust(s): Team Bank

Grants Analysis

Disclosure Period: fiscal year ending April 30, 2004
Total Grants: $241,808*
Number of Grants: 26
Average Grant: $7,330*
Highest Grant: $58,570
Lowest Grant: $1,000
Typical Range: $5,000 to $10,000
*Note: Giving excludes United Way. Average grant figure excludes highest grant.

Recent Grants

Note: Grants derived from fiscal 2004 Form 990.
General

58,570	Unified School District 368, Paola, KS
27,150	Unified School District 368, Paola, KS -- for Paola high school wireless and mobile computer lab
25,000	Lakemary Endowment Association, Paola, KS
13,377	Osawatomie Fire Department, Osawatomie, KS
11,635	Miami County Swan River Museum, Paola, KS
10,000	Paola Youth Friends, Paola, KS
10,000	University of Kansas Medical Center, Kansas City, KS
8,000	Paola Babe Ruth Baseball, Paola, KS
8,000	Paola Little League, Paola, KS
7,200	Paola Madrigal Singers, Paola, KS

CHARLES M. BAIR FAMILY TRUST

Giving Contact

c/o U.S. Bank NA
303 N. Broadway
PO Box 30678
Billings, MT 59115-0678
Phone: (406)657-8083

Description

Founded: 1994
EIN: 816075761
Organization Type: Private Foundation
Giving Locations: MT
Grant Types: General Support.

Donor Information

Founder: Established in 1994 by Alberta M. Bair.

Financial Summary

Total Giving: $945,607 (fiscal year ending April 30, 2004); $476,133 (fiscal 2001)
Assets: $64,800,723 (fiscal 2004); $51,905,874 (fiscal 2001)
Gifts Received: $3,007,545 (fiscal 2004); $1,100,097 (fiscal 2001); $250,022 (fiscal 2000). Note: In 2000, 2001, and 2004, contributions were received from Bair Ranch Foundation. In fiscal 1996 and 1997, contributions were received from the estate of Alberta M. Bair.

Typical Recipients

Arts & Humanities: Arts Centers, Arts Outreach, Arts & Humanities-General, Historic Preservation, History & Archaeology, Libraries, Literary Arts, Museums/Galleries, Music, Public Broadcasting, Theater

Civic & Public Affairs: Botanical Gardens/Parks, Business/Free Enterprise, Civic & Public Affairs-General, Safety, Zoos/Aquariums

Education: Colleges & Universities, Private Education (Precollege), Public Education (Precollege)

Environment: Environment-General

Health: AIDS/HIV, Clinics/Medical Centers, Emergency/Ambulance Services, Mental Health

Religion: Ministries, Religious Welfare

Social Services: Community Service Organizations, Day Care, Domestic Violence, Family Services, Food/Clothing Distribution, Recreation & Athletics, Scouts, Senior Services, YMCA/YWCA/YMHA/YWHA, Youth Organizations

Application Procedures

Initial Contact: Send a brief letter requesting application form.
Deadlines: March 1.

Additional Information

Trust(s): U.S. Bank NA

Grants Analysis

Disclosure Period: fiscal year ending April 30, 2004
Total Grants: $945,607
Number of Grants: 38
Average Grant: $22,584*
Highest Grant: $110,000
Lowest Grant: $2,500
Typical Range: $5,000 to $40,000
*Note: Average grant figure excludes highest grant.

Recent Grants

Note: Grants derived from fiscal 2004 Form 990.
General

110,000	Harlowton Arena Projects, Harlowton, MT
85,200	Yellowstone Art Museum, Billings, MT
80,000	Alberta Bair Theater, Billings, MT
55,000	Billings Symphony Society, Billings, MT
50,000	Boys & Girls Club of Billing and Yellowstone County, Billings, MT

42,000	Mountainview Medical Center Inc., White Sulphur Springs, MT
40,000	YWCA of Billings Inc., Billings, MT
38,680	Upper Musselshell Historical Society, Harlowton, MT
30,000	Billings Food Bank Inc., Billings, MT
30,000	Head Start Inc., Billings, MT

BAIRD BROTHERS CO. FOUNDATION

Giving Contact
Donna Auten
c/o Huntington Trust Co. NA
41 S. High St.
Columbus, OH 43216
Phone: (614)480-5453

Description
EIN: 316194844
Organization Type: Private Foundation
Giving Locations: OH: Nelsonville
Grant Types: General Support.

Financial Summary
Total Giving: $106,793 (fiscal year ending June 30, 2004); $169,561 (fiscal 2001)
Assets: $3,848,613 (fiscal 2004); $3,988,811 (fiscal 2001)

Typical Recipients
Arts & Humanities: Arts Centers, Arts Festivals, Ballet, Arts & Humanities-General, Historic Preservation, History & Archaeology, Libraries, Museums/Galleries, Music, Opera, Performing Arts, Theater
Civic & Public Affairs: Botanical Gardens/Parks, Economic Development, Civic & Public Affairs-General, Municipalities/Towns, Urban & Community Affairs
Education: Colleges & Universities, Economic Education, Engineering/Technological Education, Education-General, Preschool Education, Public Education (Precollege), Science/Mathematics Education
Environment: Environment-General
Health: Children's Health/Hospitals, Diabetes, Eyes/Blindness, Hospitals, Long-Term Care, Transplant Networks/Donor Banks
Religion: Churches, Religious Welfare
Social Services: Animal Protection, Camps, Community Service Organizations, Emergency Relief, Family Services, Food/Clothing Distribution, Recreation & Athletics, Scouts, United Funds/United Ways, YMCA/YWCA/YMHA/YWHA, Youth Organizations

Application Procedures
Initial Contact: The foundation has no formal grant application procedure or application form.
Deadlines: None.

Additional Information
The foundation is no longer associated with the Baird Brothers Co.
Trust(s): Huntington National Bank

Foundation Officials
David S. Fraedrich: director
Jane E. Harmony: director
Wilbert W. Warren, Jr.: director

Grants Analysis
Disclosure Period: fiscal year ending June 30, 2004
Total Grants: $106,793
Number of Grants: 5
Highest Grant: $79,100
Lowest Grant: $4,000
Typical Range: $4,000 to $11,500

Recent Grants
Note: Grants derived from fiscal 2001 Form 990.
Library-Related

5,000	Milwaukee Public Library, Milwaukee, WI

General

80,000	United Way, Milwaukee, WI
47,500	United Performing Arts Fund, Milwaukee, WI
20,182	Wisconsin Council on Economic Education, Milwaukee, WI
18,600	Boys and Girls Clubs of Greater Milwaukee, Milwaukee, WI
17,500	Florida Council on Economic Education, Tampa, FL
15,000	Florida Orchestra, Tampa, FL
15,000	Marquette Center for Family Business, Marquette, WI
15,000	Miller Park Gala
15,000	Outward Bound Inc., Garrison, NY
15,000	Wisconsin Technical College Foundation, Waunakee, WI

BAIRD FOUNDATION

Giving Contact
Catherine F. Schweitzer, Manager
Ellicott Station
PO Box 1210
Buffalo, NY 14205
Phone: (716)883-2429

Description
Founded: 1947
EIN: 166023080
Organization Type: Private Foundation
Giving Locations: NY: Western New York
Grant Types: General Support.

Donor Information
Founder: the late Flora M. Baird, the late Frank B. Baird, Jr., the late Cameron Baird, the late William C. Baird

Financial Summary
Total Giving: $665,763 (2003); $659,461 (2001)
Giving Analysis: Giving for 2003 includes: foundation grants to United Way ($4,000)
Assets: $11,356,672 (2003); $11,127,368 (2001)

Typical Recipients
Arts & Humanities: Arts Funds, Arts Institutes, Arts & Humanities-General, Historic Preservation, History & Archaeology, Libraries, Museums/Galleries, Music, Opera, Performing Arts, Public Broadcasting, Theater
Civic & Public Affairs: Botanical Gardens/Parks, Community Foundations, Economic Development, Ethnic Organizations, Civic & Public Affairs-General, Housing, Municipalities/Towns, Parades/Festivals, Professional & Trade Associations, Urban & Community Affairs, Zoos/Aquariums
Education: Arts/Humanities Education, Colleges & Universities, Engineering/Technological Education, Environmental Education, Literacy, Private Education (Precollege), Secondary Education (Private), Special Education
Environment: Air/Water Quality, Environment-General, Resource Conservation, Wildlife Protection
Health: Arthritis, Children's Health/Hospitals, Clinics/Medical Centers, Eyes/Blindness, Health Funds, Health Organizations, Hospices, Hospitals, Medical Research, Multiple Sclerosis, Public Health, Speech & Hearing
International: Foreign Educational Institutions, International Organizations
Religion: Churches
Science: Science Museums
Social Services: Animal Protection, Camps, Community Service Organizations, Food/Clothing Distribution, Homes, People with Disabilities, Recreation & Athletics, Senior Services, Social Services-General, Substance Abuse, United Funds/United Ways, Youth Organizations

Application Procedures
Initial Contact: The foundation requests applications be made in writing and include amount requested, purpose of funds sought, proof of tax-exempt status, recently audited financial statement, and a list of board members. The application must be signed by a person receiving no compensation from the organization.
Deadlines: None.

Restrictions
Prefers to award grants in the western New York area.

Foundation Officials
Arthur W. Cryer: trustee
Robert James Armstrong Irwin: trustee B Buffalo, NY 1927. ED Colgate University BA (1949); University of Buffalo (1949-1950); Babson College Institute of Finance (1952-1953). CORP AFFIL member advisory board: Manufacturers & Traders; director: Niagara Share Corp.; director, deputy chairman: ASA Ltd.; member advisory board: First Empire State Corp. NONPR AFFIL trustee: Saint Barnabas College Fund Inc.; director: University Cape Town Fund Inc.; trustee: Old Ft Niagara Association; trustee: Ridley College Scholarship Fund Inc.; director: Hauptman Woodward Medical Research Institute; trustee: Library Foundation Buffalo Erie County. CLUB AFFIL Saturn Club; University Club; Mid-Day Club; Royal Canadian Yacht Club; Buffalo Canoe Club.
William Baird Irwin: trustee
Catherine F. Schweitzer: foundation manager

Grants Analysis
Disclosure Period: calendar year ending 2003
Total Grants: $661,763*
Number of Grants: 201
Average Grant: $3,292
Highest Grant: $40,000
Lowest Grant: $90
Typical Range: $1,000 to $5,000
*Note: Giving excludes United Way.

Recent Grants
Note: Grants derived from 2001 Form 990.
General

25,000	Old Fort Niagara Association, Youngstown, NY
22,000	Boys and Girls Club of Buffalo, Buffalo, NY
20,000	Boys and Girls Club of Buffalo, Buffalo, NY
20,000	Hauptman-Woodward Medical Research Institute, Buffalo, NY
16,500	Theodore Roosevelt Inaugural Historic Site, Buffalo, NY
15,000	Buffalo Green Fund, Buffalo, NY
12,500	Irish Classical Theater, Buffalo, NY
11,370	Tapestry Charter School, Buffalo, NY
10,000	Buffalo State College Foundation, Buffalo, NY
10,000	Canisius College, Buffalo, NY

DEXTER F. AND DOROTHY H. BAKER FOUNDATION

Giving Contact
Dexter F. Baker, Trustee, Chairman
c/o Air Products & Chemicals Inc.

7201 Hamilton Blvd.
Allentown, PA 18195-1501
Phone: (610)481-7357

Description
Founded: 1988
EIN: 232453230
Organization Type: Private Foundation
Giving Locations: FL: Collier; PA: Lehigh Valley
Grant Types: General Support.

Donor Information
Founder: Dexter F. and Dorothy H. Baker

Financial Summary
Total Giving: $732,950 (2003)
Giving Analysis: Giving for 2003 includes: foundation scholarships ($82,500)
Assets: $15,967,869 (2003)
Gifts Received: $452,577 (2000); $601,780 (1998); $389,358 (1996). Note: In 1998 and 2000, contributions were received from Dexter F. Baker.

Typical Recipients
Arts & Humanities: Arts Associations & Councils, Arts Festivals, Ballet, Community Arts, Dance, Historic Preservation, History & Archaeology, Libraries, Museums/Galleries, Music, Opera, Performing Arts, Public Broadcasting, Theater
Civic & Public Affairs: Public Policy, Safety, Urban & Community Affairs, Women's Affairs
Education: Arts/Humanities Education, Colleges & Universities, Engineering/Technological Education, Education-General, Literacy, Private Education (Precollege), Student Aid
Environment: Resource Conservation
Health: Health Funds, Medical Rehabilitation, Prenatal Health Issues
Religion: Churches, Religious Welfare
Science: Science Museums
Social Services: Child Welfare, Community Centers, Food/Clothing Distribution, People with Disabilities, Recreation & Athletics, Scouts, Senior Services, Shelters/Homelessness, United Funds/United Ways, Volunteer Services, YMCA/YWCA/YMHA/YWHA, Youth Organizations

Application Procedures
Initial Contact: Request application form.
Deadlines: Deadline for letter of intent is March 15. Application deadline is July 1.

Additional Information
Trust(s): Mellon Bank NA

Foundation Officials
Dexter Farrington Baker: chairman B Worcester, MA 1927. ED Lehigh University BS (1950); Lehigh University MBA (1957). CORP AFFIL director: AMP Inc. NONPR AFFIL member: National Association Manufacturers; member: Theta Chi; trustee: Harry C. and Mary M. Trexler Foundation; board associates: Muhlenberg College; member: AICHE; member: American Management Association.
Dorothy H. Baker: trustee

Grants Analysis
Disclosure Period: calendar year ending 2003
Total Grants: $650,450*
Number of Grants: 43
Average Grant: $9,386*
Highest Grant: $100,000
Lowest Grant: $250
Typical Range: $1,000 to $20,000
*Note: Giving excludes scholarships. Average grant excludes three highest grants ($275,000).

Recent Grants
Note: Grants derived from 2001 Form 990.
General

102,628	Lehigh University, Bethlehem, PA -- Baker Hall
100,000	Muhlenberg College, Allentown, PA -- Baker theatre
79,030	Lehigh Valley Hospital, Allentown, PA -- ICU research
57,000	First Presbyterian Church of Allentown, Allentown, PA -- religious outreach
50,000	First Presbyterian Church of Allentown, Allentown, PA -- Sixth Street Shelter
40,000	Lehigh University, Bethlehem, PA -- Baker scholars
30,000	Muhlenberg College, Allentown, PA -- guest artists
20,000	Baum School of Art, Allentown, PA -- artist in residence
20,000	Muhlenberg College, Allentown, PA -- Baker scholars
15,075	First Presbyterian Church, Bonita Springs, FL -- radio ministry

R. C. BAKER FOUNDATION

Giving Contact
Frank L. Scott, Chairman
PO Box 6150
Orange, CA 92863-6150
Phone: (714)750-8987

Description
Founded: 1952
EIN: 951742283
Organization Type: General Purpose Foundation
Giving Locations: western US.
Grant Types: General Support, Operating Expenses, Research, Scholarship.

Donor Information
Founder: Established in 1952 by the late R. C. Baker Sr., the foundation takes a broad-based approach to philanthropy. Mr. Baker founded Baker International Corp. (now known as Baker Hughes), a supplier of oilfield tools and services. Because his work was centered in California and in oil-producing and mining areas, many of the foundation's grants are awarded to organizations in those locations.

Financial Summary
Total Giving: $1,200,000 (2003 approx); $1,275,425 (2002)
Assets: $33,000,000 (2003 approx); $28,887,915 (2002)
Gifts Received: $600,000 (1994); $590,000 (1993); $565,000 (1992)

Typical Recipients
Arts & Humanities: Ballet, History & Archaeology, Libraries, Literary Arts, Museums/Galleries, Music, Performing Arts, Public Broadcasting, Theater
Civic & Public Affairs: Botanical Gardens/Parks, Business/Free Enterprise, Chambers of Commerce, Civil Rights, Clubs, Community Foundations, Economic Policy, Employment/Job Training, Civic & Public Affairs-General, Hispanic Affairs, Law & Justice, Legal Aid, Parades/Festivals, Public Policy, Rural Affairs, Safety, Urban & Community Affairs
Education: Arts/Humanities Education, Business Education, Business-School Partnerships, Colleges & Universities, Engineering/Technological Education, Education-General, Private Education (Precollege), Public Education (Precollege), Science/Mathematics Education, Secondary Education (Private), Secondary Education (Public), Special Education, Student Aid
Environment: Resource Conservation
Health: Cancer, Children's Health/Hospitals, Clinics/Medical Centers, Emergency/Ambulance Services, Eyes/Blindness, Health Organizations, Hospitals, Medical Rehabilitation, Medical Research, Mental Health, Multiple Sclerosis, Nursing Services, Preventive Medicine/Wellness Organizations, Research/Studies Institutes, Single-Disease Health Associations, Speech & Hearing
International: International Peace & Security Issues
Religion: Churches, Jewish Causes, Missionary Activities (Domestic), Religious Organizations, Religious Welfare
Science: Scientific Centers & Institutes
Social Services: Big Brothers/Big Sisters, Camps, Child Welfare, Community Centers, Community Service Organizations, Day Care, Delinquency & Criminal Rehabilitation, Domestic Violence, Family Services, Food/Clothing Distribution, People with Disabilities, Recreation & Athletics, Senior Services, Shelters/Homelessness, Social Services-General, Substance Abuse, United Funds/United Ways, Volunteer Services, YMCA/YWCA/YMHA/YWHA, Youth Organizations

Application Procedures
Initial Contact: There are no formal application procedures. Applicants should mail a letter to the foundation.
Application Requirements: Include a description of the proposed project and anticipated results, a recently audited financial statement, amount requested, and a listing of other sources of support. Applicants should also include proof of tax-exempt status (if not listed in the IRS Cumulative List of Tax Exempt Organizations).
Deadlines: Applications should be received by May 1 and October 1.
Review Process: No interviews are conducted.

Restrictions
The foundation does not make grants to individuals or to political or lobbying groups. It also does not grant funds for endowments, loans, or capital projects of tax-supported institutions. No grants are made to organizations in the Eastern U.S.

Foundation Officials
Kenneth Dale: trustee
James H. Hickey: trustee
Frank L. Scott: chairman board trustees B Houston, TX 1915. ED University of Houston (1934).
James J. Shelton: trustee B Mayfield, KY 1916. PRIM CORP EMPL senior vice president, director: Baker International Corp. CORP AFFIL director: Epic Microwave Inc.; director: Tetra Tech Inc.
Ronald G. Turner: vice chairman board trustees B Houston, TX 1936. ED University of Houston (1958); University of Houston (1967). PRIM CORP EMPL vice president: Baker Hughes Inc.

Grants Analysis
Disclosure Period: calendar year ending 2002
Total Grants: $1,275,425
Number of Grants: 88
Average Grant: $12,131*
Highest Grant: $220,000
Lowest Grant: $275
Typical Range: $1,000 to $50,000
*Note: Average grant figure excludes highest grant.

Recent Grants
Note: Grants derived from 2002 Form 990.
General

220,000	Presbyterian Intercommunity Hospital Foundation, Whittier, CA
100,000	St. Anne School, Laguna Niguel, CA
100,000	St. Paul Lutheran Church
66,500	Help for Brain Injured Children, La Habra, CA
50,000	Cedars Sinai Medical Center, Los Angeles, CA
50,000	St. Francis of Assisi School
45,000	Los Ayudantes de Naranja
40,000	Speech and Language Development Center, Buena Park, CA

30,000   YMCA Orange County, Tustin, CA
25,000   Anaheim Memorial Medical Center, Anaheim, CA

WILLIAM G. BAKER, JR. MEMORIAL FUND

Giving Contact
Melissa Warlow
Latrobe Building, 9th Floor
2 East Read Street
Baltimore, MD 21202
Phone: (410)332-4171
Fax: (410)837-4701

Description
Founded: 1964
EIN: 526057178
Organization Type: General Purpose Foundation
Giving Locations: MD: Baltimore
Grant Types: Capital, Endowment, General Support, Matching, Multiyear/Continuing Support, Project.

Donor Information
Founder: The fund was established in Maryland in 1964.

Financial Summary
Total Giving: $1,785,204 (2002); $1,963,800 (2001)
Giving Analysis: Giving for 2002 includes: foundation grants to United Way ($95,000)
Assets: $24,640,062 (2002); $30,840,690 (2001)

Typical Recipients
Arts & Humanities: Arts Associations & Councils, Arts Centers, Arts Festivals, Arts Funds, Arts Institutes, Arts Outreach, Dance, Arts & Humanities-General, Historic Preservation, History & Archaeology, Libraries, Museums/Galleries, Music, Opera, Performing Arts, Public Broadcasting, Theater
Civic & Public Affairs: African American Affairs, Botanical Gardens/Parks, Community Foundations, Economic Development, Employment/Job Training, Civic & Public Affairs-General, Housing, Law & Justice, Legal Aid, Nonprofit Management, Parades/Festivals, Philanthropic Organizations, Urban & Community Affairs, Women's Affairs, Zoos/Aquariums
Education: Arts/Humanities Education, Business Education, Colleges & Universities, Community & Junior Colleges, Education Funds, Education Reform, Education-General, Health & Physical Education, Literacy, Minority Education, Private Education (Precollege), Public Education (Precollege), Secondary Education (Private), Special Education, Student Aid
Environment: Resource Conservation
Health: Children's Health/Hospitals, Clinics/Medical Centers, Emergency/Ambulance Services, Eyes/Blindness, Health-General, Health Funds, Health Organizations, Heart, Hospices, Hospitals, Medical Research, Mental Health, Public Health, Speech & Hearing
Religion: Churches, Religion-General, Jewish Causes, Ministries, Religious Organizations, Religious Welfare, Synagogues/Temples
Science: Science-General, Scientific Centers & Institutes, Scientific Research
Social Services: Child Abuse, Child Welfare, Community Centers, Community Service Organizations, Counseling, Crime Prevention, Day Care, Delinquency & Criminal Rehabilitation, Family Services, Food/Clothing Distribution, Homes, People with Disabilities, Recreation & Athletics, Scouts, Senior Services, Shelters/Homelessness, Social Services-General, Special Olympics, Substance Abuse, United Funds/United Ways, Volunteer Services, YMCA/YWCA/YMHA/YWHA, Youth Organizations

Application Procedures
Initial Contact: The foundation requests applications be made in writing.
Application Requirements: Applicants should submit five copies of a written proposal that includes a cover letter with proposal summary and amount requested; proposal narrative should include agency information including history, mission, goals, programs, future plans, organizational structure, and affiliations; detailed information concerning the purpose of the grant, including goals and objectives; need to be addressed, and activities planned to accomplish goals; and how progress will be evaluated. Attachments should include a list of the board of directors and officers, project budget, list of current donors to the proposed project, financial reports, and the copy of organization's tax-exempt letter.
Deadlines: February 1, May 1, August 1 and November 1.
Review Process: The review board usually meets four times a year and its decisions are made within three months.
Notes: The fund accepts The Association of Baltimore Area Grantmakers' Grant Application Format. The foundation requests that only organizations described in IRS sections 509(a)(1)(2) and 170(b)(1)(vii) apply.

Restrictions
No grants are made to individuals, or for loans, deficit financing, or annual campaigns. The Fund does not normally make grants for continuing operating support.

Additional Information
Grants for unique and socially significant purposes are encouraged by the Fund; educational concerns are given priority over general welfare projects.
Publications: Application Guidelines

Foundation Officials
Timothy D. Armbruster: governor PRIM NONPR EMPL president, director: Baltimore Community Foundation.
Connie Imboden: governor
J. Marshall Reid: governor, chair PRIM CORP EMPL president: Mercantile Bankshares Corp.
Walter Sondheim, Jr.: governor

Grants Analysis
Disclosure Period: calendar year ending 2002
Total Grants: $1,690,204*
Number of Grants: 124*
Average Grant: $13,631
Highest Grant: $100,000
Lowest Grant: $1,000
Typical Range: $5,000 to $25,000
*Note: Giving excludes United Way.

Recent Grants
Note: Grants derived from 2002 Form 990.
Library-Related
25,000   Enoch Pratt Free Library, Baltimore, MD
General
100,000   Baltimore Community Foundation (FEES), Baltimore, MD
55,000   United Way of Central Maryland, Baltimore, MD
50,000   Baltimore Center for the Performing Arts, Baltimore, MD
50,000   Baltimore Museum of Art, Baltimore, MD
50,000   Fells Point Creative Alliance, Baltimore, MD
40,000   Baltimore Opera Company, Baltimore, MD
40,000   United Way of Central Maryland, Baltimore, MD
35,000   Baltimore Symphony Orchestra, Baltimore, MD
25,000   Baltimore Community Foundation, Baltimore, MD

25,000   Episcopal Social Ministries, Baltimore, MD

CLAYTON BAKER TRUST

Giving Contact
John B. Powell, Jr., Trustee
2 East Read Street, Suite 100
Baltimore, MD 21202
Phone: (410)837-3555

Description
Founded: 1960
EIN: 526054237
Organization Type: Private Foundation
Giving Locations: MD: Baltimore
Grant Types: General Support, Operating Expenses, Project, Seed Money.

Donor Information
Founder: Julia C. Baker

Financial Summary
Total Giving: $1,459,550 (2004); $668,750 (2001)
Giving Analysis: Giving for 2001 includes: foundation grants to United Way ($5,000)
Assets: $34,878,050 (2004); $36,161,552 (2001)
Gifts Received: $24,243,984 (2001); $502,425 (1998); $202,675 (1994). Note: In 2001, contributions were received from the estate of Julia C. Baker. In 1998, contributions were received from Julia C. Baker.

Typical Recipients
Arts & Humanities: Libraries, Museums/Galleries, Opera, Public Broadcasting
Civic & Public Affairs: Botanical Gardens/Parks, Civil Rights, Clubs, Community Foundations, Economic Development, Employment/Job Training, Civic & Public Affairs-General, Housing, Law & Justice, Legal Aid, Parades/Festivals, Philanthropic Organizations, Public Policy, Urban & Community Affairs
Education: Colleges & Universities, Education Funds, Education Reform, Environmental Education, Education-General, Literacy, Private Education (Precollege), Science/Mathematics Education, Student Aid
Environment: Air/Water Quality, Environment-General, Protection, Resource Conservation, Wildlife Protection
Health: AIDS/HIV, Clinics/Medical Centers, Diabetes, Emergency/Ambulance Services, Health Organizations, Medical Research, Medical Training, Mental Health
International: International Peace & Security Issues
Religion: Churches, Jewish Causes, Ministries, Religious Organizations, Religious Welfare
Science: Scientific Centers & Institutes
Social Services: At-Risk Youth, Big Brothers/Big Sisters, Child Abuse, Child Welfare, Community Centers, Community Service Organizations, Family Planning, Family Services, Food/Clothing Distribution, Homes, People with Disabilities, Recreation & Athletics, Scouts, Senior Services, Shelters/Homelessness, Substance Abuse, United Funds/United Ways, Youth Organizations

Application Procedures
Initial Contact: Send letter requesting application form and guidelines.
Application Requirements: Applications should include a cover letter and narrative as described in the foundation's guidelines. The following attachments are required: a list of the organization's board of directors, including occupations and/or community affiliations, board committee assignments, and criteria for board selection; financial information, including the organization's current annual operating budget,

funding sources for the organization (major past contributors and anticipated funding sources), recently audited financial statement, and list of other foundations to which the proposal has been submitted; an annual report (if available); examples of current relevant newspaper/magazine articles or reviews about the organization's program (if available); and proof of tax-exempt status.

Deadlines: April 5, August 5, and December 5.

Restrictions

The majority of the grants are made within the Baltimore area and seek to aid the disadvantaged through results-oriented projects with an emphasis on children's needs. Grants made outside the Baltimore area are usually limited to organizations concerned with environmental protection, population control, arms control, and nuclear disarmament.

Additional Information

Publications: Application Guidelines

Foundation Officials

William C. Baker: trustee
John B. Powell, Jr.: trustee

Grants Analysis

Disclosure Period: calendar year ending 2004
Total Grants: $1,459,550
Number of Grants: 72
Average Grant: $19,501*
Highest Grant: $75,000*
Lowest Grant: $1,500
Typical Range: $5,000 to $30,000
***Note:** Average grant figure excludes highest grant.

Recent Grants

Note: Grants derived from 2001 Form 990.

Library-Related

50,000   Village Learning Place, Inc., Baltimore, MD -- for community development and capital campaign

20,000   Enoch Pratt Free Library, Baltimore, MD -- for youth development, After-School Program at Roland Park Public School

General

60,000   Bryn Mawr School, Baltimore, MD -- for education, Julia C. Baker chair in Environmental Studies

40,000   Baltimore Community Foundation, Baltimore, MD -- for community development, Baltimore Police Foundation

35,000   Chesapeake Bay Foundation, Annapolis, MD -- for environment and Baltimore City Education Program

30,000   Fund for Educational Excellence, Baltimore, MD -- for education "Achievement First" in Baltimore public schools

25,000   Baltimore Community Foundation, Baltimore, MD -- for youth program, PAL centers and Summer Programs

25,000   Baltimore Community Foundation, Baltimore, MD -- for youth programs and A-teams

25,000   Catholic Relief Services, Baltimore, MD

25,000   Kennedy Krieger Institute, Baltimore, MD -- for health care

25,000   Shepherd's Clinic, Baltimore, MD -- for health care, endowment and relocation

20,000   American Civil Liberties Union Foundation of Maryland, Baltimore, MD -- for education and state funding for Baltimore Public Schools

GEORGE F. BAKER TRUST

Giving Contact

Ms. Rocio Suarez, Executive Director
477 Madison Avenue, Suite 1650
New York, NY 10022
Phone: (212)755-1890
Fax: (212)319-6316

Description

Founded: 1937
EIN: 136056818
Organization Type: Family Foundation
Giving Locations: NY: New York Nationally.
Grant Types: General Support, Professorship.

Donor Information

Founder: Established in 1937 by the late George F. Baker, chairman of the First National Bank of New York.

Financial Summary

Total Giving: $2,184,650 (2002)
Giving Analysis: Giving for 2002 includes: foundation scholarships ($8,400)
Assets: $14,302,677 (2002)

Typical Recipients

Arts & Humanities: Arts Appreciation, Arts Centers, Ballet, Historic Preservation, History & Archaeology, Libraries, Museums/Galleries, Music, Opera, Performing Arts, Theater
Civic & Public Affairs: Civil Rights, Clubs, Community Foundations, Economic Development, Employment/Job Training, Civic & Public Affairs-General, Legal Aid, Philanthropic Organizations, Public Policy, Safety, Urban & Community Affairs, Women's Affairs, Zoos/Aquariums
Education: Arts/Humanities Education, Business Education, Colleges & Universities, Community & Junior Colleges, Education Funds, Elementary Education (Private), Elementary Education (Public), Engineering/Technological Education, Environmental Education, Faculty Development, Education-General, Health & Physical Education, International Studies, Literacy, Medical Education, Minority Education, Private Education (Precollege), Public Education (Precollege), Religious Education, Science/Mathematics Education, Secondary Education (Private), Social Sciences Education, Special Education, Student Aid
Environment: Air/Water Quality, Environment-General, Protection, Resource Conservation, Wildlife Protection
Health: AIDS/HIV, Cancer, Children's Health/Hospitals, Clinics/Medical Centers, Diabetes, Emergency/Ambulance Services, Health-General, Health Organizations, Heart, Hospices, Hospitals, Hospitals (University Affiliated), Medical Rehabilitation, Medical Research, Prenatal Health Issues, Public Health
International: Health Care/Hospitals, Human Rights, International Environmental Issues, International Relations, International Relief Efforts, Missionary/Religious Activities
Religion: Churches, Ministries, Religious Organizations, Religious Welfare
Science: Scientific Labs, Scientific Research
Social Services: Animal Protection, At-Risk Youth, Camps, Child Welfare, Community Centers, Community Service Organizations, Counseling, Crime Prevention, Family Planning, Family Services, People with Disabilities, Recreation & Athletics, Senior Services, Social Services-General, Substance Abuse, YMCA/YWCA/YMHA/YWHA, Youth Organizations

Application Procedures

Initial Contact: Applicants should send a brief description of the proposed project. There is no formal application form.
Application Requirements: The initial letter should

outline the proposed project, include the amount requested, list other sources of funding, and be signed by an authorized officer. Only the original copy of the application needs to be submitted.
Deadlines: None.
Review Process: Board meetings are held in June and November. Notification of grant approval occurs within six months following proposal receipt. No notice is sent to those applicants who do not receive funding.

Restrictions

No grants are made to individuals, or for scholarships, capital or endowment funds, fellowships, loans, or special projects.

Additional Information

Citibank, N.A. is listed as a corporate trustee of the foundation.
Publications: Annual Report
Trust(s): Citibank N.A.

Foundation Officials

Anthony K. Baker: trustee
George F. Baker, III: trustee B 1939. ED Harvard University AB (1961); Harvard University MBA (1964). PRIM CORP EMPL general partner: Baker New York Securities ADD CORP EMPL managing partner: Cambridge Capital Fund; chief executive officer, chairman: Whitehall Corp.
Kane K. Baker: trustee
Rocio Suarez: executive director

Grants Analysis

Disclosure Period: calendar year ending 2002
Total Grants: $2,176,250*
Number of Grants: 46
Average Grant: $27,470*
Highest Grant: $450,000
Lowest Grant: $1,600
Typical Range: $10,000 to $50,000
***Note:** Giving excludes scholarships. Average grant figure excludes five highest grants ($1,050,000).

Recent Grants

Note: Grants derived from 2002 Form 990.

Library-Related

25,000   Company of the Redwood Library and Athenaeum, Newport, RI -- general assistance

General

450,000   Harvard University, Cambridge, MA -- general assistance

300,000   New York Hospital-Cornell Medical, NY -- general assistance

100,000   Drexel University, Philadelphia, PA -- towards restoration & renovation

100,000   Nantucket Historical Association, Nantucket, MA -- towards construction of new building

100,000   Sea Education, Woods Hole, MA -- towards capital campaign

85,000   Palm Beach Zoo at Dreher Park, West Palm Beach, FL -- general assistance

80,000   Palm Beach Day School, Palm Beach, FL -- general assistance

70,000   Academy of the Palm Beaches, West Palm Beach, FL -- general assistance

70,000   YMCA of the Palm Beaches, Boca Raton, FL -- general assistance

62,500   Greenville Baker Boys & Girls Club, Greenville, NC -- towards capital campaign

BAKEWELL CORP.

Company Headquarters
7800 Forsyth Blvd.
St. Louis, MO 63105

Company Description
Employees: 25

Operating Locations
Bakewell Corp. (MO--St. Louis)

Edward L. Bakewell, Jr. Family Foundation

Giving Contact
Richard W. Meier, Director & Secretary
7800 Forsyth Boulevard, 8th Floor
St. Louis, MO 63105
Phone: (314)862-5555
Fax: (314)862-5076

Description
Founded: 1987
EIN: 431434313
Organization Type: Corporate Foundation
Giving Locations: AR; CA; CO; IL; MD; MO; NM; VA
Grant Types: Emergency, General Support, Operating Expenses, Research.

Donor Information
Founder: Edward L. Bakewell, Jr., Edward L. Bakewell III, Bakewell Corp.

Financial Summary
Total Giving: $24,500 (2003); $23,835 (2001)
Giving Analysis: Giving for 2003 includes: foundation grants to United Way ($500)
Assets: $1,012,234 (2003); $467,311 (2001)
Gifts Received: $580,000 (2003). Note: In 2003, contributions were received from Edward L. Bakewell III.

Typical Recipients
Arts & Humanities: Arts Outreach, Historic Preservation, History & Archaeology, Libraries, Museums/Galleries, Public Broadcasting
Civic & Public Affairs: Botanical Gardens/Parks, Economic Policy, Civic & Public Affairs-General, Public Policy, Zoos/Aquariums
Education: Arts/Humanities Education, Colleges & Universities, Continuing Education, Education-General, International Studies, Private Education (Precollege)
Environment: Research, Resource Conservation
Health: Cancer, Children's Health/Hospitals, Emergency/Ambulance Services, Geriatric Health, Long-Term Care, Medical Research, Multiple Sclerosis, Public Health, Speech & Hearing
International: Health Care/Hospitals, International Relief Efforts, Missionary/Religious Activities
Religion: Churches, Religion-General, Religious Organizations, Religious Welfare
Science: Science Museums, Scientific Centers & Institutes
Social Services: Child Welfare, Counseling, Day Care, People with Disabilities, Scouts, Substance Abuse, United Funds/United Ways

Application Procedures
Initial Contact: Send written application.
Application Requirements: Applications should include explanation of the merits of the specific request complete with supporting literature.
Deadlines: Applications are accepted between September 1 and November 30.

Additional Information
Publications: Application Guidelines

Corporate Officials
Edward L. Bakewell, III: chairman, chief executive officer PRIM CORP EMPL chairman, chief executive officer: Bakewell Corp.
Thomas J. Bannister, Jr.: president PRIM CORP EMPL president: Bakewell Corp. ADD CORP EMPL president: Bakewell Investment Co.
Ron Horak: controller PRIM CORP EMPL controller: Bakewell Corp.

Foundation Officials
Edward L. Bakewell, III: president, director (see above)
Richard W. Meier: director, secretary

Grants Analysis
Disclosure Period: calendar year ending 2003
Total Grants: $24,000*
Number of Grants: 39
Average Grant: $615
Highest Grant: $2,500
Lowest Grant: $100
Typical Range: $100 to $1,000
*Note: Giving excludes United Way.

Recent Grants
Note: Grants derived from 2001 Form 990.
Library-Related
1,000	Friends of the Saint Louis Public Library, St. Louis, MO -- operating funds

General
2,500	Ashoka, Arlington, VA -- for operating funds
1,500	American Red Cross Armed Forces Emergency Services, Falls Church, VA -- public education, emergency relief and blood services
1,500	St. Louis Children's Hospital, St. Louis, MO -- research/general operating funds
1,375	St. Louis Zoo, St. Louis, MO -- operating funds
1,360	St. Louis Science Center Foundation, St. Louis, MO -- operating funds
1,000	Cardinal Glennon Children's Hospital, St. Louis, MO -- operating funds
1,000	Central Institute for the Deaf, St. Louis, MO -- education/services for the deaf
1,000	Enterprise Mentors International, St. Louis, MO -- for operating funds
1,000	Environic Foundation International, Inc., Chevy Chase, MD -- for operating funds
1,000	Heifer International, Little Rock, AR -- for operating funds

FRED BALDWIN MEMORIAL FOUNDATION

Giving Contact
Janis Reischmann, Grants Administrator
c/o Hawaii Community Foundation
1164 Bishop St., Suite 800
Honolulu, HI 96813
Phone: (808)566-5570
Fax: (808)521-6286

Description
Founded: 1910
EIN: 990075264
Organization Type: Private Foundation
Giving Locations: HI: Maui County
Grant Types: Capital, General Support, Project.

Donor Information
Founder: the late Fred Baldwin, members of the Baldwin family

Financial Summary
Total Giving: $286,110 (2004); $327,500 (2001).
Note: 1997 Giving includes United Way ($5,016).
Assets: $5,512,685 (2004); $6,162,045 (2001)

Typical Recipients
Arts & Humanities: Arts Associations & Councils, Arts Centers, Community Arts, Dance, Arts & Humanities-General, History & Archaeology, Libraries, Museums/Galleries, Music, Opera, Performing Arts, Public Broadcasting, Theater, Visual Arts
Civic & Public Affairs: Botanical Gardens/Parks, Clubs, Community Foundations, Economic Development, Economic Policy, Employment/Job Training, Civic & Public Affairs-General, Law & Justice, Legal Aid, Parades/Festivals, Professional & Trade Associations, Urban & Community Affairs, Women's Affairs
Education: Arts/Humanities Education, Environmental Education, Education-General, Literacy, Private Education (Precollege), Secondary Education (Public), Special Education
Environment: Environment-General, Resource Conservation
Health: AIDS/HIV, Cancer, Children's Health/Hospitals, Clinics/Medical Centers, Diabetes, Health Organizations, Hospices, Hospitals, Medical Rehabilitation, Nutrition, Single-Disease Health Associations
International: International Affairs, International Relations
Religion: Churches, Dioceses, Ministries, Religious Organizations, Religious Welfare
Social Services: Animal Protection, At-Risk Youth, Big Brothers/Big Sisters, Child Welfare, Community Centers, Community Service Organizations, Crime Prevention, Emergency Relief, Family Planning, Family Services, Food/Clothing Distribution, People with Disabilities, Scouts, United Funds/United Ways, Volunteer Services, YMCA/YWCA/YMHA/YWHA, Youth Organizations

Application Procedures
Initial Contact: Send cover letter and full proposal.
Application Requirements: Include a description of organization, amount requested, purpose of funds sought, recently audited financial statement, and proof of tax-exempt status. Also evaluation methods.
Deadlines: January 2 and May 1.

Restrictions
Does not support individuals, political or lobbying groups, or organizations outside operating areas.

Foundation Officials
John C. Baldwin: treasurer, trustee B 1937. PRIM CORP EMPL treasurer: HNJ2 Inc. CORP AFFIL officer: Walker Industries Ltd.
Shaun L. Lyons: vice president, assistant secretary, trustee
Elizabeth Norcross: trustee
Wendy Rice Peterson: trustee
Claire C. Sanford: trustee
Mary Cameron Sanford: trustee B 1930. PRIM CORP EMPL chairman: Maui Land & Pineapple Co. CORP AFFIL pub: Maui News; chairman: Maui Publishing Co. Ltd.; director: Haleakala Ranch Co.; director: Kapalua Land Co. Ltd.
Emily B. Young: trustee

Grants Analysis
Disclosure Period: calendar year ending 2004
Total Grants: $286,110
Number of Grants: 42
Average Grant: $6,812
Highest Grant: $23,000
Lowest Grant: $2,000
Typical Range: $2,500 to $10,000

Recent Grants

Note: Grants derived from 2004 Form 990.
General

23,000	Maui Arts & Cultural Center, Kahului, HI -- for education complex renovation, reconfiguration and expansion
12,000	Makawao Union Church, Paia, HI
12,000	Maui AIDS Foundation, Wailuku, HI -- for volunteer services program
12,000	Seabury Hall, Makawao, HI
10,000	Catholic Charities, Honolulu, HI -- towards financial advocacy for seniors on Maui
10,000	Haleakala School, Kula, HI -- for expansion of early childhood education program
10,000	J. Walter Cameron Center, Wailuku, HI -- for infant and childcare facility
10,000	Maui Coastal Preservation Inc., Wailuku, HI -- for involving community in the Waihee Preserve
10,000	Maui Family YMCA, Kahului, HI -- for Kalakupua Community Playground - Maui Community playground project
10,000	Planned Parenthood of Hawaii, Honolulu, HI -- for Maui Clinic fund development

L. G. BALFOUR FOUNDATION

Giving Contact

Kerry H. Sullivan, Director, Grants
Care of Fleet National Bank
100 Federal St.
Mail Code: MABOFO7B
Boston, MA 02110
Phone: (781)346-2484
Fax: (781)346-2495

Alternate Contact

Christine Feeney
Phone: (617)346-2479

Description

Founded: 1973
EIN: 222751372
Organization Type: General Purpose Foundation
Giving Locations: MA: New England area.
Grant Types: Capital, General Support, Scholarship.

Donor Information

Founder: Lloyd G. Balfour (d.1978) founded and was the sole owner of the L. G. Balfour Company, producer of class rings and fraternity pins. After Mr. Balfour's death in 1973, the company was managed for a number of years by the Bank of New England, first as executor of L. G. Balfour's estate, and then as trustee of the L. G. Balfour Foundation, which was established in 1973. The company was sold in 1983, but the foundation retains a significant financial interest.

Financial Summary

Total Giving: $4,459,500 (2004); $5,021,000 (2003); $5,958,600 (2002)
Giving Analysis: Giving for 2004 includes: foundation scholarships ($513,000)
Assets: $95,187,781 (2004); $86,387,534 (2003); $105,102,977 (2002)

Typical Recipients

Arts & Humanities: Libraries
Education: Colleges & Universities, Education Associations, Education Funds, Minority Education, Public Education (Precollege), Student Aid
Health: Hospitals
Social Services: Day Care

Application Procedures

Initial Contact: Applicants should submit a letter of intent to the trustee for review and response before a formal grant proposal is prepared.
Application Requirements: The letter should describe the nature and objective of the program to be funded and include a list of the organization's board members or trustees along with the names and qualifications of officers and staff; evidence of tax-exempt status; detailed budget for the projects; Form 990 and audited financial statement for the most recent fiscal year; statement of other sources of funding, both private and public; and a statement of agreement to report on the results of the project and on the expenditure of grant funds.
Deadlines: Proposals should be submitted by January 31 for consideration in the spring, or by July 31 for consideration in the fall.
Review Process: The foundation's distribution committee usually meets twice each year, in the spring and fall.

Restrictions

No grants are made to individuals or private foundations. Grant proposals for capital projects such as construction, renovation, or equipment purchase will be considered, but will be given less priority.

Additional Information

Fleet Investment Management is listed as corporate trustee for the foundation.
Publications: Grant Application Procedures

Foundation Officials

Kerry H. Sullivan: trustee officer, director grant making PRIM CORP EMPL vice president: Fleet Investment Services.

Grants Analysis

Disclosure Period: calendar year ending 2004
Total Grants: $3,946,500*
Number of Grants: 58
Average Grant: $57,348*
Highest Grant: $435,000
Lowest Grant: $5,000
Typical Range: $25,000 to $100,000
*Note: Giving excludes scholarships. Average grant figure excludes two highest grants ($735,000).

BALL BROTHERS FOUNDATION

Giving Contact

Douglas A. Bakken, Executive Director
222 South Mulberry
PO Box 1408
Muncie, IN 47308
Phone: (765)741-5500
Fax: (765)741-5518
E-mail: ballfoundation@yahoo.com

Description

Founded: 1926
EIN: 350882856
Organization Type: Family Foundation
Giving Locations: IN: East Central Indiana, Muncie
Grant Types: Capital, General Support, Operating Expenses, Project.

Donor Information

Founder: Established in 1926 by Edmund B. Ball, Frank C. Ball, Lucius L. Ball, and William A. Ball, all of whom are deceased. The estate of Edmund B. Ball provided the foundation's initial endowment, with securities valued at about $3.5 million. His brothers subsequently donated additional money and securities to augment the foundation's assets. The foundation is affiliated with the George and Frances Ball Foundation. Edmund Burke Ball was one of the founders of the Ball Brothers Company, which grew over the years to become the Ball Corporation, a large and diversified manufacturer whose best-known product is the Ball glass preserving jar.

Financial Summary

Total Giving: $4,870,200 (2003); $4,650,000 (2002 approx); $4,473,142 (2001). Note: The 2001 total giving figure includes a non-cash contribution made to the Ball State University Art Museum valued at $1,223,263.
Giving Analysis: Giving for 2003 includes: foundation grants to United Way ($103,550); 2001: foundation grants to United Way ($88,500)
Assets: $118,648,591 (2003); $112,979,404 (2001)
Gifts Received: $1,100,000 (2000); $5,000 (1992). Note: In 2000, contributions were received from the estate of Edmund F. Ball.

Typical Recipients

Arts & Humanities: Arts Associations & Councils, Arts Centers, Arts Funds, Arts Outreach, Arts & Humanities-General, Historic Preservation, History & Archaeology, Libraries, Museums/Galleries, Music, Public Broadcasting, Theater, Visual Arts
Civic & Public Affairs: Botanical Gardens/Parks, Clubs, Community Foundations, Economic Development, Civic & Public Affairs-General, Housing, Municipalities/Towns, Nonprofit Management, Parades/Festivals, Philanthropic Organizations, Public Policy, Rural Affairs, Urban & Community Affairs
Education: Afterschool/Enrichment Programs, Arts/Humanities Education, Business Education, Business-School Partnerships, Colleges & Universities, Economic Education, Education Associations, Education Funds, Elementary Education (Public), Engineering/Technological Education, Education-General, International Exchange, International Studies, Journalism/Media Education, Literacy, Private Education (Precollege), Public Education (Precollege), Science/Mathematics Education, Secondary Education (Public), Special Education, Student Aid
Environment: Environment-General, Protection, Resource Conservation
Health: AIDS/HIV, Children's Health/Hospitals, Diabetes, Health Funds, Health Organizations, Heart, Hospitals, Medical Rehabilitation, Preventive Medicine/Wellness Organizations, Public Health
Religion: Churches, Ministries, Religious Organizations, Religious Welfare
Social Services: Animal Protection, Big Brothers/Big Sisters, Community Centers, Community Service Organizations, Day Care, Family Services, People with Disabilities, Recreation & Athletics, Scouts, Social Services-General, Special Olympics, United Funds/United Ways, Volunteer Services, YMCA/YWCA/YMHA/YWHA, Youth Organizations

Application Procedures

Initial Contact: Grant seekers can approach the foundation in one of three ways: send a preliminary proposal, and ask for an initial reaction in thirty days; send a complete proposal; or ask for a personal visit to discuss a potential grant request with the Executive Director.
Application Requirements: A preliminary proposal should be one to two pages (not including the cover letter) and include a description of idea; need; who will do the work; and what the project will cost. A complete proposal should be two to five pages (not including cover letter) and include a succinct description of request; an outline; reason for need; when it will be accomplished; who will undertake work; a program budget; an organization budget; evaluation procedures including who will be responsible for evaluation; and an IRS not-for-profit determination letter.
Deadlines: None, but foundation prefers that proposals be submitted between February and May.
Review Process: The grants committee and board

of directors review grant applications at committee and board meetings during the year. Grant making takes place April through December each year.

Restrictions

The foundation does not fund individuals, booster organizations, direct scholarships to individuals, or services which the community-at-large should underwrite (e.g. roads, buses, etc.).

Additional Information

The foundation reports that, in addition to grant making, it also offers proposal writing assistance and conducts seminars and workshops.
Publications: Application Guidelines; General Information

Foundation Officials

Douglas Adair Bakken: executive director B Breckenridge, MN 1939. ED North Dakota State University BS (1961); University of Nebraska MA (1967). NONPR AFFIL fellow: Society American Archivists; member: Sports and Hobby Development Group Inc.; member: Minnesota Cultural Foundation; member: Muncie Rotary Club; president: Indiana Donors Alliance Foundation; president: Indiana Dunes Alliance Foundation; member: Independent Colleges Indiana.
Frank E. Ball: vice president, director B 1938. PRIM CORP EMPL president: Minnetrista Corp. CORP AFFIL president: B B & S Properties Inc.
William M. Bracken: director B 1942. ED Carleton College BA (1963); University of Michigan MBA (1965). PRIM CORP EMPL chairman: Northco Corp. CORP AFFIL Northco Investment Group Inc.; Northco Minerals Inc.; Northco Financial Corp.
John Wesley Fisher: chairman, president B Walland, TN July 15, 1915. ED University of Tennessee BS (1938); Harvard University MBA (1942). PRIM CORP EMPL chairman emeritus: Ball Corp. CORP AFFIL director: Minnetrista Corp.; president: Nature's Catch Inc.; president: Fisher Properties Indiana; director: Kindel Furniture Co.; chairman: CID Partners LP; president: Cardinal Health Systems; chairman: CID Equity Partners; director: America National Trust & Investment Co.; partner: Blackwood & Nichols Corp. NONPR AFFIL member: Muncie Chamber of Commerce; member, director: National Association Manufacturers; member: Indiana Academy; member: Indiana Chamber of Commerce; member: Glass Packaging Institute; member: Grocery Manufacturer Association; member: Delta Tau Delta; chairman board directors: Ball Memorial Hospital; member: Conference Board. CLUB AFFIL Royal Poinciana Country Club; Skyline Club; Rotary Club; Naples National Golf Club; Naples Yacht Club; Muncie Club; Delaware Country Club; Indianapolis Athletic Club; Columbia Club.
Douglas J. Foy: treasurer, assistant secretary, director PRIM CORP EMPL secretary, director: Pri Pak Inc.
Nancy Keilty: director
Judith F. Oetinger: director
William L. Skinner: secretary, director
Terry L. Walker: director

Grants Analysis

Disclosure Period: calendar year ending 2003
Total Grants: $4,766,670*
Number of Grants: 37
Average Grant: $36,826*
Highest Grant: $2,354,298
Lowest Grant: $100
Typical Range: $5,000 to $50,000
*Note: Giving excludes United Way. Average grant figure excludes two highest grants ($3,477,763).

Recent Grants

Note: Grants derived from 2003 Form 990.
Library-Related
7,500   Jay County Public Library, Portland, IN

General
2,354,298   Minnetrista Cultural Foundation, Muncie, IN
242,500   Ball State University Foundation, Muncie, IN
225,000   Community Alliance to Promote Education, Muncie, IN
143,000   Delaware Greenways, Wilmington, DE
132,900   YMCA, Muncie, IN
103,550   United Way of Delaware County, Muncie, IN
60,000   Ball Memorial Hospital Foundation, Muncie, IN
50,000   DePauw University, Greencastle, IN
50,000   Independent Colleges of Indiana Foundation, Indianapolis, IN
50,000   Unitarian Universalist Church, Muncie, IN

GEORGE AND FRANCES BALL FOUNDATION

Giving Contact

Joyce M. Beck, Administrative Assistant
PO Box 1408
Muncie, IN 47308
Phone: (765)741-5500
Fax: (317)741-5518
E-mail: jjpcuis@iquest.net

Description

Founded: 1937
EIN: 356033917
Organization Type: General Purpose Foundation
Giving Locations: IN: Delaware County, East Central Indiana, Muncie
Grant Types: Capital, Challenge, Conference/Seminar, General Support, Loan, Multiyear/Continuing Support, Operating Expenses, Project.

Donor Information

Founder: Established in 1937 by the late George A. Ball.

Financial Summary

Total Giving: $4,492,233 (2003); $4,185,643 (2002); $4,548,500 (2001)
Assets: $95,401,782 (2003); $88,350,165 (2002)

Typical Recipients

Arts & Humanities: Arts Associations & Councils, Arts Centers, Arts Festivals, Arts Funds, Arts Institutes, Arts Outreach, Film & Video, Historic Preservation, History & Archaeology, Libraries, Museums/Galleries, Music, Public Broadcasting, Theater, Visual Arts
Civic & Public Affairs: Botanical Gardens/Parks, Clubs, Community Foundations, Economic Development, Civic & Public Affairs-General, Housing, Municipalities/Towns, Parades/Festivals, Philanthropic Organizations, Safety, Urban & Community Affairs
Education: Afterschool/Enrichment Programs, Arts/Humanities Education, Business Education, Colleges & Universities, Economic Education, Education Funds, Education Reform, Environmental Education, Faculty Development, Education-General, Leadership Training, Medical Education, Minority Education, Public Education (Precollege), Science/Mathematics Education, Secondary Education (Public), Student Aid, Vocational & Technical Education
Environment: Air/Water Quality, Environment-General, Protection, Resource Conservation, Watershed
Health: Children's Health/Hospitals, Emergency/Ambulance Services, Health Funds, Health Organizations, Hospitals, Medical Rehabilitation, Medical Research
Religion: Ministries, Religious Welfare

Social Services: Big Brothers/Big Sisters, Child Welfare, Community Centers, Community Service Organizations, Crime Prevention, Day Care, Emergency Relief, Family Planning, Family Services, Food/Clothing Distribution, People with Disabilities, Recreation & Athletics, Scouts, Special Olympics, Substance Abuse, United Funds/United Ways, Volunteer Services, YMCA/YWCA/YMHA/YWHA, Youth Organizations

Application Procedures

Initial Contact: Applications should be addressed to the administrative assistant of the foundation.
Application Requirements: Applications should include a complete description of the project, budget, time frame, amount requested and brief rationale, and a copy of the organization's IRS tax exemption letter.
Deadlines: None.
Notes: Grants for operational expenses and budget emergencies are seldom made.

Restrictions

The foundation does not make grants to individuals.

Foundation Officials

Stefan Stolen Anderson: director B Madison, WI 1934. ED Harvard University AB (1956); University of Chicago MBA (1960). PRIM CORP EMPL chairman, chief executive officer: First Merchants Corp. CORP AFFIL director: DE Advancement Corp.; director: Maxon Corp. CLUB AFFIL Rotary Club.
Joyce M. Beck: administrative assistant
Frank A. Bracken: president, director B 1934. PRIM CORP EMPL attorney: Bingham, Summers, Welsh & Spilman ADD CORP EMPL under secretary: Department Interior. CORP AFFIL director: Ball Corp.; chairman: Ball InCon Glass Packaging Corp.
Douglas J. Foy: treasurer, director PRIM CORP EMPL secretary, director: Pri Pak Inc.
Joan McKee: secretary, director
John H. Moll: director
John J. Pruis: executive vice president, director B Borculo, MI 1923. ED Western Michigan University BS (1947); Northwestern University MA (1949); Northwestern University PhD (1951). NONPR AFFIL member: Speech Community Association; director: United Way Delaware County; member: Omicron Delta Kappa; member: Phi Delta Kappa; director: Muncie Symphony Association; director: North Central Association; member: Muncie Chamber of Commerce; director: Big Brothers/Big Sisters; director: Indiana Legal Foundation; chairman, director: Ball Memorial Hospital; member: Beta Gamma Sigma; member: American Association Higher Education. CLUB AFFIL Rotary Club; Blue Key Club.
Robert M. Smitson: director B 1936. ED Purdue University BSME (1958). PRIM CORP EMPL chief executive officer: Maxon Corp. CORP AFFIL director: Dalton Foundries Inc.; vice chairman: First Merchants Bank NA.

Grants Analysis

Disclosure Period: calendar year ending 2003
Total Grants: $4,492,233
Number of Grants: 54
Average Grant: $28,741*
Highest Grant: $1,026,460
Lowest Grant: $1,500
Typical Range: $5,000 to $50,000
*Note: Average grant figure excludes three highest grants ($3,026,460).

Recent Grants

Note: Grants derived from 2003 Form 990.
General
1,026,460   Minnetrista Cultural Foundation Inc., Muncie, IN -- fund for Oakhurst gardens
1,000,000   Ball State University Foundation, Muncie, IN -- fund for capital campaign
1,000,000   BMH Foundation Inc., Muncie, IN -- fund for graduate medical education

225,000	Community Alliance to Promote Education, Muncie, IN -- fund for early reading program
145,000	United Way of Delaware County Inc., Muncie, IN
142,900	Community Arts & Building Foundation, Muncie, IN -- fund for community civic center-elevator and fire alarm
75,000	Family Services of Delaware County Inc., Muncie, IN -- fund for passage way project
60,000	Leelanau Conservancy, Leland, MI -- fund for capital campaign
60,000	Nature Conservancy, Indianapolis, IN -- fund for saving Indiana's last great places campaign
50,000	BMH Foundation Inc., MUncie, IN -- fund for the cancer center

BALLET MAKERS

Company Headquarters
20-10 Maple Avenue
Fair Lawn, NJ 07410
Web: http://www.balletmakers.com

Company Description
Employees: 600
SIC(s): 2200 Textile Mill Products, 3100 Leather & Leather Products.

Operating Locations
Ballet Makers (NJ--Totowa)

Capezio/Ballet Makers Dance Foundation

Giving Contact
Jane Remer, Grants & Program Director
Capezio/Ballet Makers Dance Foundation
1 Campus Road
Totowa, NJ 07512
Phone: (973)595-9000
Fax: (973)595-0341

Description
Founded: 1953
EIN: 136161198
Organization Type: Corporate Foundation
Giving Locations: nationally.
Grant Types: Award, General Support, Project.

Financial Summary
Total Giving: $110,000 (2003)
Assets: $36,429 (2003)
Gifts Received: $100,000 (2003); $100,000 (1999); $100,000 (1998). Note: Contributions were received from Ballet Makers.

Typical Recipients
Arts & Humanities: Arts Associations & Councils, Arts Centers, Arts Funds, Arts Outreach, Dance, Film & Video, Arts & Humanities-General, Libraries, Music, Performing Arts, Public Broadcasting, Theater
Civic & Public Affairs: Employment/Job Training, Civic & Public Affairs-General
Education: Arts/Humanities Education, Colleges & Universities, Education-General
Religion: Churches

Application Procedures
Initial Contact: Send letter requesting application and cover sheet/form.
Application Requirements: In addition to cover sheet/form and application, applicants must provide an audited financial statement, proof of tax-exempt status, a list of the board of directors, and other sources of support.
Deadlines: None.

Restrictions
Does not support individuals, religious organizations for sectarian purposes, political or lobbying groups, or organizations outside operating areas.

Additional Information
Grants are limited to service organizations engaged in the promotion of dance in America. Cover sheet/form must accompany application. Company also sponsors the Capezio Dance Award, which is given at the discretion of the trustees and not open for application.

Corporate Officials
Anthony Giacoio: chief executive officer, director PRIM CORP EMPL chief executive officer, director: Ballet Makers.
Nick Terlizzi, Jr.: chairman, director PRIM CORP EMPL chairman, director: Ballet Makers.

Foundation Officials
Anthony Giacoio: president (see above)
Donald Terlizzi: treasurer PRIM CORP EMPL vice chairman: Ballet Makers.
Nick Terlizzi, Jr.: vice president (see above)

Grants Analysis
Disclosure Period: calendar year ending 2003
Total Grants: $110,000
Number of Grants: 67
Average Grant: $1,385*
Highest Grant: $10,000
Lowest Grant: $1,000
Typical Range: $1,000 to $4,000
*Note: Average grant excludes two highest grants ($20,000).

Recent Grants
Note: Grants derived from 2001 Form 990.
General

10,000	Dancing in the Streets, New York, NY
5,000	American Dance Guild, New York, NY
4,000	Florida State Dance Association, Miami, FL
3,250	John Harms Center for the Arts, Englewood, NJ
2,750	Dance Notation Bureau, New York, NY
2,250	Orchestra of St. Luke's, New York, NY
1,500	New York Foundation for Arts, New York, NY
1,000	Dallas Dance Council, Dallas, TX
1,000	Dance Critics Association, New York, NY
1,000	Dance Theater Workshop, New York, NY

BALTIMORE EQUITY SOCIETY

Company Headquarters
Baltimore, MD

Company Description
Employees: 10

Baltimore Equitable Insurance Foundation

Giving Contact
Sharon V. Woodward, President, Chief Executive Officer
100 North Charles Street
S-640
Baltimore, MD 21201
Phone: (410)727-1794
Fax: (410)539-1073

Description
EIN: 521645633
Organization Type: Corporate Foundation
Giving Locations: MD
Grant Types: General Support.

Financial Summary
Total Giving: $111,475 (2003); $162,720 (2002); $207,500 (2001)
Giving Analysis: Giving for 2001 includes: foundation grants to United Way ($50,000)
Assets: $4,752,717 (2003); $3,937,150 (2002); $4,396,453 (2001)
Gifts Received: $100 (2003); $305,920 (2001); $611,919 (1999). Note: In 1998, 1999, 2001, and 2003, contributions were received from Baltimore Equitable Society.

Typical Recipients
Arts & Humanities: Libraries, Museums/Galleries, Public Broadcasting
Civic & Public Affairs: Community Foundations, Housing, Philanthropic Organizations, Safety, Urban & Community Affairs
Education: Religious Education, Student Aid
Religion: Jewish Causes, Religious Welfare
Social Services: Crime Prevention, Recreation & Athletics, United Funds/United Ways

Application Procedures
Initial Contact: The foundation has no formal grant application procedure or application form.
Deadlines: Jan 1, April 1, July 1, and October 1.

Restrictions
Foundation supports Maryland area organizations only.

Corporate Officials
Stephen J. Bernhardt: chairman, president, chief executive officer, chief financial officer PRIM CORP EMPL chairman, president, chief executive officer, chief financial officer: Balt Equity Soc.

Foundation Officials
Richard O. Berndt: director
Stephen J. Bernhardt: president, treasurer (see above)
Anthony L. Brennan: director
George L. Bunting: director
M. Jenkins Cromwell, Jr.: director CORP AFFIL director: Provident Bank of Maryland; director: Provident Bankshares Corp.
Edward A. Crooke: director B 1938. ED University of Maryland BS (1968); Loyola College MBA (1971). CORP AFFIL director: First Maryland Bancorp; director: First National Bank Maryland Inc.; director: Constellation Energy Group Inc.; chairman: BGE Energy Projects & Services; chairman: BGE Home Products & Services Inc.
Edward K. Dunn, Jr.: director
Juliet Eurich: director
George B. Hess, Jr.: director
Howard D. Jones, III: secretary
Judy J. Mohraz: director
Betsy Nelson: director
Philip J. Raub: director
James S. Riepe: director
Sharon V. Woodward: president, treasurer

Grants Analysis
Disclosure Period: calendar year ending 2003
Total Grants: $56,475*
Number of Grants: 7
Average Grant: $8,068
Highest Grant: $20,275
Lowest Grant: $1,200

Typical Range: $5,000 to $10,000
***Note:** Giving excludes United Way.

Recent Grants

Note: Grants derived from 2003 Form 990.
Library-Related
7,500	Enoch Pratt Free Library, Baltimore, MD -- for family place program

General
55,000	United Way of Central Maryland, Baltimore, MD -- to provide charitable and educational programs
20,275	Fire Museum of Maryland, Lutherville, MD -- for educational outreach coordinator and fire safety house instructor metropolitan school market
10,000	Institute for Christian and Jewish Studies, Baltimore, MD -- ICJS high school genesis project
7,500	Enterprise Foundation, Baltimore, MD -- for Maryland re-entry partnership initiative
5,000	B&O Railroad Museum, Baltimore, MD -- to conserve and restore artifacts
5,000	WBAL Radio Kids Campaign, Baltimore, MD -- general contribution to aid the children in the Baltimore area
1,200	Association of Baltimore Area Grantmakers, Baltimore, MD -- to promote philanthropy in Baltimore area

JOHN ERNEST BAMBERGER AND RUTH ELEANOR BAMBERGER MEMORIAL FOUNDATION

Giving Contact

Eleanor Roser, Chairman
136 South Main Street, Suite 418
Salt Lake City, UT 84101-1690
Phone: (801)364-2045
Fax: (801)322-5284

Description

Founded: 1947
EIN: 876116540
Organization Type: Private Foundation
Giving Locations: UT: Salt Lake City
Grant Types: General Support, Loan, Multiyear/Continuing Support, Operating Expenses, Scholarship.

Donor Information

Founder: Established in 1947 by Ernest Bamberger, the late Eleanor F. Bamberger.

Financial Summary

Total Giving: $849,494 (2003); $995,857 (2001)
Giving Analysis: Giving for 2003 includes: foundation scholarships ($129,744).
Assets: $23,566,819 (2003); $25,892,584 (2001)

Typical Recipients

Arts & Humanities: Community Arts, Film & Video, History & Archaeology, Libraries, Museums/Galleries, Performing Arts, Public Broadcasting, Theater
Civic & Public Affairs: Asian American Affairs, Botanical Gardens/Parks, Clubs, Economic Development, Gay/Lesbian Issues, Civic & Public Affairs-General, Housing, Law & Justice, Legal Aid, Municipalities/Towns, Native American Affairs, Public Policy, Safety, Urban & Community Affairs
Education: Afterschool/Enrichment Programs, Business Education, Colleges & Universities, Community & Junior Colleges, Elementary Education (Public),

Education-General, International Exchange, Legal Education, Literacy, Medical Education, Private Education (Precollege), Public Education (Precollege), Science/Mathematics Education, Secondary Education (Private), Secondary Education (Public), Social Sciences Education, Special Education
Environment: Environment-General, Resource Conservation
Health: Alzheimer's Disease, Cancer, Children's Health/Hospitals, Clinics/Medical Centers, Emergency/Ambulance Services, Eyes/Blindness, Health-General, Health Organizations, Hospices, Hospitals, Long-Term Care, Mental Health, Multiple Sclerosis, Nursing Services, Preventive Medicine/Wellness Organizations, Public Health, Respiratory, Single-Disease Health Associations
Religion: Churches, Jewish Causes, Religious Organizations, Religious Welfare
Science: Science Museums
Social Services: Child Abuse, Child Welfare, Community Service Organizations, Counseling, Crime Prevention, Day Care, Domestic Violence, Family Planning, Family Services, Food/Clothing Distribution, Homes, People with Disabilities, Recreation & Athletics, Sexual Abuse, Shelters/Homelessness, Social Services-General, Special Olympics, Substance Abuse, United Funds/United Ways, YMCA/YWCA/YMHA/YWHA, Youth Organizations

Application Procedures

Initial Contact: Send a brief letter of inquiry., 6 copies, with copies of 501c3 and 3 copies of last audit.
Deadlines: Each year in January.

Additional Information

Provides undergraduate scholarships for student nurses.

Foundation Officials

Clarence Bamberger, Jr.: mem
Julie Barrett: member
Clark P. Giles: member
Carol Olwell: member
Eleanor Roser: chairman, member

Grants Analysis

Disclosure Period: calendar year ending 2003
Total Grants: $719,750*
Number of Grants: 75
Average Grant: $9,597
Highest Grant: $20,000
Lowest Grant: $1,000
Typical Range: $5,000 to $20,000
***Note:** Giving excludes scholarships.

Recent Grants

Note: Grants derived from 2003 Form 990.
General
20,000	YWCA, Washington, DC
10,000	American Indian Services, Sioux Falls, SD
10,000	And Justice for All, Washington, DC
10,000	Children's Service Society of Utah, Salt Lake City, UT
10,000	Neighborhood House, Seattle, WA
10,000	Utah Youth Village, Salt Lake City, UT
10,000	Wasatch Academy, Mt. Pleasant, UT
10,000	YMCA, Salt Lake City, UT
8,000	Road Home
7,000	Utah Valley State College, Orem, UT

BANDAI AMERICA INC.

Company Headquarters

5551 Katella Ave.
Cypress, CA 90630
Web: http://www.bandai.com

Company Description

Employees: 22
SIC(s): 5000 Wholesale Trade--Durable Goods.
Parent Company: Bandai Company Ltd., 5-4 Komagata 2-chome, Taito-ku, Tokyo, Japan

Bandai Foundation

Giving Contact

Alison Miller, Contributions Advisor
Bandai Foundation
c/o The Carmen Group
1299 Pennsylvania Ave. NW, Eighth Fl.
Washington, DC 20004
Web: http://www.bandai.com/about/bandai_foundation.html

Alternate Contact

5551 Katella Avenue
Cypress, CA 90630
Phone: (714)816-9500

Description

Founded: 1994
EIN: 330655933
Organization Type: Corporate Foundation
Giving Locations: CA: nationally.
Grant Types: General Support.

Financial Summary

Total Giving: $342,500 (2003); $345,995 (2002); $352,995 (2001)
Assets: $10,148,151 (2003); $10,188,606 (2002); $10,024,855 (2001)

Typical Recipients

Arts & Humanities: Film & Video, Libraries, Museums/Galleries, Performing Arts, Public Broadcasting
Civic & Public Affairs: Civil Rights, Civic & Public Affairs-General, Professional & Trade Associations
Education: Afterschool/Enrichment Programs, Arts/Humanities Education, Colleges & Universities, Education-General, Medical Education, Private Education (Precollege), Student Aid
Health: AIDS/HIV, Arthritis, Cancer, Children's Health/Hospitals, Clinics/Medical Centers, Hospitals (University Affiliated), Medical Research, Single-Disease Health Associations
International: Human Rights, International Organizations, International Relief Efforts
Science: Scientific Centers & Institutes
Social Services: Big Brothers/Big Sisters, Child Welfare, Community Service Organizations, Family Services, Food/Clothing Distribution, Substance Abuse

Application Procedures

Initial Contact: Send a brief letter of inquiry.
Application Requirements: Include a description of organization, amount requested, purpose of funds sought, and proof of tax-exempt status.
Deadlines: None.

Restrictions

Grants are not made to individuals, religious organizations for sectarian purposes, or political or lobbying groups.

Corporate Officials

Steve Grimes: chief financial officer, president, chief executive officer PRIM CORP EMPL chief financial officer: Bandai America.
Paul Nojima: chairman, president, chief executive officer PRIM CORP EMPL chairman, president, chief executive officer: Bandai America.

Foundation Officials

Seiichi Takeuchi: secretary, treasurer
Masaaki Tsuji: chairman, president

Grants Analysis

Disclosure Period: calendar year ending 2003
Total Grants: $342,500
Number of Grants: 7
Highest Grant: $150,000
Lowest Grant: $10,000
Typical Range: $35,000 to $70,000

Recent Grants

Note: Grants derived from 2003 Form 990.

General

150,000	Elizabeth Glaser Pediatric AIDS Foundation, Santa Monica, CA -- for assistance to children with AIDS
70,000	Toys "R" US Children's Fund Inc., New York, NY -- for benefit children with AIDS
47,500	Starlight Children's Foundation International, Los Angeles, CA -- for benefit of sick children
35,000	St. Jude Children's Research Hospital, Memphis, TN
15,000	Children's Health Fund, New York, NY -- for providing medical care for children
15,000	Los Angeles Team Mentoring Inc., Los Angeles, CA -- to assist with after-school mentoring programs
10,000	Otis College, Los Angeles, CA -- to support school's scholarship fund

BANK OF AMERICA CORP.

Company Headquarters

Bank of America Corporation Center
100 N. Tryon St.
Charlotte, NC 28255
Phone: 888-279-3457
Fax: (704)386-6699
Web: http://www.bankofamerica.com

Company Description

Founded: 1998
Ticker: BAC
Exchange: NYSE
Former Name: BankAmerica Corp. (1999);
Acquired: NationsBank (1998).
Revenue: US$63.324 billion (2004)
Profit: US$14.143 billion (2004)
Employees: 133549 (2003)
Fortune Rank: 18, per FORTUNE Magazine's list of 500 Largest U.S. Corporations (2004).
SIC(s): 6021 National Commercial Banks, 6712 Bank Holding Companies.

Nonmonetary Support

Type: Cause-related Marketing & Promotion; Donated Equipment; Loaned Employees
Volunteer Programs: The company sponsors the Volunteer Time for Schools program, which allows each full-time associate to volunteer at a public or private school for up to two hours of paid time per week. The company also sponsors a Volunteer Grants Program. If an associate volunteers 50 or more hours at a nonprofit organization in a calendar year, Bank of America donates $250 to that organization in the associates name; the donation is increased to $500 for those who volunteer 100 or more hours. In addition, the company maintains the Team Bank of America Volunteer Network, which provides volunteer opportunities for Bank of America associates wishing to get involved in any of the approximately 3,000 volunteer events the company sponsors each year.

Bank of America Foundation

Giving Contact

Paula J. Fraher, Corporate Initiatives Executive
100 North Tryon Street
NC1-007-16-19
Charlotte, NC 28255-0001
Phone: (704)388-3183
Web: http://www.bankofamerica.com/foundation

Alternate Contact

401 North Tryon Street
NC1-021-02-20
Charlotte, NC 28255
Phone: (704)386-5659

Description

EIN: 582429625
Organization Type: Corporate Foundation
Giving Locations: headquarters and operating communities, except in Washington State.
Grant Types: Capital, General Support, Project, Seed Money.
Note: Foundation matches gifts. Employee matching gift ratio: 1 to 1, for gifts from $25 to $5,000.

Financial Summary

Total Giving: $108,000,000 (2004 approx); $76,513,808 (2003); $72,663,964 (2002). Note: Contributes through corporate direct giving program and foundation.
Assets: $2,255,903 (2003); $2,022,151 (2002); $2,933,072 (2001)
Gifts Received: $75,854,274 (2003); $72,304,000 (2002); $86,323,627 (2001). Note: In 2002 and 2003, contributions were received from Bank of America, N.A. In 2001, contributions were received from Bank of America, N.A. ($84,553,481) and Cassella Trust ($1,770,146). In 1994, gifts were received from BankAmerica Corp. and Seafirst Bank Matching Gifts Program.

Typical Recipients

Arts & Humanities: Arts Appreciation, Arts Associations & Councils, Arts Centers, Arts Festivals, Arts Funds, Arts Institutes, Ballet, Community Arts, Ethnic & Folk Arts, Historic Preservation, Libraries, Museums/Galleries, Music, Opera, Performing Arts, Public Broadcasting, Theater
Civic & Public Affairs: Asian American Affairs, Botanical Gardens/Parks, Business/Free Enterprise, Chambers of Commerce, Civil Rights, Community Foundations, Economic Development, Employment/Job Training, Civic & Public Affairs-General, Hispanic Affairs, Housing, Legal Aid, Minority Business, Native American Affairs, Nonprofit Management, Professional & Trade Associations, Public Policy, Rural Affairs, Urban & Community Affairs, Women's Affairs, Zoos/Aquariums
Education: Afterschool/Enrichment Programs, Agricultural Education, Business Education, Colleges & Universities, Community & Junior Colleges, Economic Education, Education Funds, Education Reform, Elementary Education (Private), Engineering/Technological Education, Environmental Education, Faculty Development, Education-General, Health & Physical Education, International Exchange, International Studies, Leadership Training, Medical Education, Minority Education, Preschool Education, Public Education (Precollege), Science/Mathematics Education, Special Education, Student Aid
Environment: Environment-General, Research, Resource Conservation, Wildlife Protection
Health: Children's Health/Hospitals, Clinics/Medical Centers, Emergency/Ambulance Services, Health Funds, Health Organizations, Hospitals, Medical Research, Prenatal Health Issues
International: International Environmental Issues, International Relations

Religion: Dioceses
Science: Science Museums, Scientific Centers & Institutes
Social Services: Big Brothers/Big Sisters, Child Abuse, Child Welfare, Community Service Organizations, Emergency Relief, Family Services, Food/Clothing Distribution, People with Disabilities, Refugee Assistance, Shelters/Homelessness, Substance Abuse, United Funds/United Ways, YMCA/YWCA/YMHA/YWHA, Youth Organizations

Application Procedures

Initial Contact: Send a brief letter of inquiry or obtain application form from the foundation's web site.
Application Requirements: Information should include: purpose of funds sought; correct mailing address, name and phone number of contact person; amount requested; brief statement of mission; copy of IRS letter of designation; current list of board members with affiliations; operating budget and project budget if applicable; population and geographic area served; list of sources and amounts of other funding obtained, pledged or requested for this purpose; and financial information for the previous two years, with an audited financial statement, if available.
Deadlines: None.
Evaluative Criteria: Organizations must demonstrate fiscal and administrative stability, good management policies and practices, and the ability to produce a budget and organizational financial statement.
Decision Notification: Decisions regarding funding requests are ongoing. All requests will be reviewed in a competitive process.

Restrictions

Generally not receptive to individuals, organizations without 501(c)(3) public charity status, memorial campaigns, fund-raising events, political activities, religious organizations for sectarian purposes, research, athletic events and programs, endowment campaigns, advertising, member agencies of united funds, book or film or video projects, public or private education (K-12), disease advocacy organizations, or organizations that discriminate on the basis of age, culture, race, gender, or sexual orientation.

Additional Information

In 1992, BankAmerica Corp. and BankAmerica Foundation acquired, respectively, Security Pacific Corp. and Security Pacific Foundation and related entities, Security Pacific Foundation Northwest and Security Pacific Bank Arizona Foundation. The foundations associated with Security Pacific completely dissolved; the giving program for BankAmerica Corp. and its subsidiaries continues to be contained completely within BankAmerica Foundation.
BankAmerica Corp. and NationsBank have merged to create Bank of America.

Corporate Officials

Kenneth D. Lewis: chairman, president, chief executive officer B Meridian, MS April 09, 1947. ED Georgia State University BS (1969). PRIM CORP EMPL chairman, president, chief executive officer: Bank of America Corp. NONPR AFFIL past chairman: National Urban League; director: United Way of Central Carolinas Inc.; director: Homeownership Education and Counseling Institute; member: Committee to Encourage Corporate Philanthropy; member: Financial Services Roundtable.

Foundation Officials

Catherine P. Bessant: trustee B Jackson, MI. ED University of Michigan BS. NONPR AFFIL director: Children's Theatre of Charlotte; trustee: Enterprise Foundation; director: Blue Cross Blue Shield of Florida; chairman: Charlotte Chamber of Commerce.
Paula J. Fraher: vice chairman, secretary
Gary S. Williams: treasurer, director

Grants Analysis

Disclosure Period: calendar year ending 2003
Total Grants: $54,329,033*
Number of Grants: 17,623 (approx)
Average Grant: $3,082
Highest Grant: $1,450,000
Lowest Grant: $25
Typical Range: $1,000 to $25,000
*Note: Giving excludes matching gifts, scholarships, and United Way.

Recent Grants

Note: Grants derived from 2003 Form 990.
General

550,000	United Way of Metro Chicago, Chicago, IL
405,514	United Way of North East Florida, Jacksonville, FL
320,013	United Way of North East Florida, Jacksonville, FL
300,000	United Way of Metro Atlanta, Atlanta, GA
260,000	United Way of Orange County, Irvine, CA
200,000	Center for Scholarship Administration Inc., Taylors, SC
200,000	Georgia State University Foundation Inc., Atlanta, GA
200,000	Georgia State University Foundation Inc., Atlanta, GA
175,000	United Way of New York City - Neighborhood Community, New York, NY
141,856	United Way of Miami-Dade, Miami, FL

THE BANK OF GREENE COUNTY

Company Headquarters

302 Main St.
Catskill, NY 12414
Web: http://www.thebankofgreenecounty.com

Company Description

Founded: 1889
Parent Company: Greene County Bancorp Inc., PO Box 470, Catskill, NY, United States

Bank of Greene County Charitable Foundation

Giving Contact

Michelle M. Plummer, Chief Financial Officer
425 Main Street
Catskill, NY 12414-1300
Phone: (518)943-3700
Web: http://www.thebankofgreenecounty.com/Charitable.htm

Description

Founded: 1999
EIN: 141810419
Organization Type: Corporate Foundation
Giving Locations: , NY

Donor Information

Founder: The Bank of Greene County established the Bank of Greene County Charitable Foundation in 1998 in connection with the bank's conversion from a mutual to stock organization.

Financial Summary

Total Giving: $26,500 (fiscal year ending 0, 2002); $20,100 (fiscal 2001)
Assets: $752,094 (fiscal 2002); $516,217 (fiscal 2001)

Typical Recipients

Arts & Humanities: Museums/Galleries
Civic & Public Affairs: Housing
Science: Scientific Centers & Institutes
Social Services: Animal Protection, Food/Clothing Distribution, Social Services-General, YMCA/YWCA/YMHA/YWHA

Application Procedures

Initial Contact: Requests for grants of $1,000 or less should be submitted in writing to a Bank of Greene County retail branch. Requests for grants of more than $1,000 should be submitted to the Bank's operations office using the New York/New Jersey Area Common Grant Application form.
Application Requirements: Requests for $1,000 or less should include a cover letter on the applicant organization's letterhead detailing the amount requested; purpose of funds sought; and the name, address and telephone number of the contact person. Include a brief description of the organization's purpose, history and forward outlook. Attachments must include a copy of the organization's operating budget for the current and preceding years; a list of the organization's officers and directors; proof of tax-exempt status; and a list of other current sources of financial support, including the purpose and amount received from each. If the organization has previously applied for funding from Bank of Greene County Charitable Foundation, list the dates and amounts of any previous grants received and any applications to the foundation that were not granted.
Requests for more than $1,000 may obtain a copy of the New York/New Jersey Area Common Grant Application form at http://www.nyrag.org.
Deadlines: Requests for funding should be submitted between December 1 and January 15.
Decision Notification: The foundation typically processes applications within 90 days of the close of the application period.
Notes: Generally, the maximum amount that may be requested is $2,500. An organization may submit only one application per foundation fiscal year.

Restrictions

The foundation does not ordinarily support individuals; candidates for political office; religious organizations; sectarian activities; seminars, conferences, or endowments; or activities that would benefit The Bank of Greene County.

Foundation Officials

Bruce P. Egger: secretary
Walter H. Ingalls: director
David H. Jenkins, DVM: director
Raphael Klein: director
Dennis R. O'Grady: director
John M. Olivett: treasurer
Michelle M. Plummer: chief financial officer
Paul Slutzky: director
Martin C. Smith: director
J. Bruce Whittaker: president

Grants Analysis

Total Grants: $26,500
Number of Grants: 18
Average Grant: $1,472
Highest Grant: $2,500
Lowest Grant: $500
Typical Range: $1,000 to $2,500

Recent Grants

Note: Grants derived from fiscal 2002 Form 990.
General

2,500	Community Action of Green County, Inc, Catskill, NY -- senior companion volunteers program
2,500	Mountain Top Arboretum, Tannersville, NY -- computer and software
2,000	Catskill Mountain Foundation, Hunter, NY -- 2002 programming plan
2,000	Catskill Mountain Housing Development Corp, Catskill, NY -- 1st time homebuyer workshops for low/moderate income
2,000	Hunter Foundation, Inc., Hunter, NY -- signage
1,500	Capital District YMCA, Troy, NY -- youth campaign
1,500	Michael J Quill Irish Cultural & Sports Center, East Durham, NY -- support Irish arts week
1,500	St. Patrick's Academy, Catskill, NY -- strategic plan for future viability in community
1,000	Albany County Rural Housing Alliance, Inc., Voorheesville, NY -- 0% loans to low income homeowners
1,000	All Arts Matter, Greenville, NY -- improve and expand programs

BANK OF NEW YORK

Company Headquarters

New York, NY
Web: http://www.bankofny.com

Company Description

Founded: 1968
Ticker: BK
Exchange: NYSE
Former Name: Bank of New York Company, Inc.
Revenue: US$7.144 billion (2004)
Profit: US$1.44 billion (2004)
Employees: 22091 (2003)
Fortune Rank: 293, per FORTUNE Magazine's list of 500 Largest U.S. Corporations (2004).
SIC(s): 6022 State Commercial Banks, 6712 Bank Holding Companies.

Operating Locations

Bank of New York Co., Inc. (MO--St. Louis; NY--Harrison; TX--Irving; WI--Milwaukee); BNY Financial (Holdings) Ltd. (IL--London); BNY International Financial Corp. (NY--New York); CTC Illinois Trust Co. (IL--Chicago)

Giving Contact

Pat Bicket, Vice President and Secretary
1 Wall St.
38th Floor
New York, NY 10286
Phone: (212)635-1787
Fax: (212)635-1269

Description

Organization Type: Corporate Giving Program
Giving Locations: DE; NJ; NY
Grant Types: Award, Capital, Conference/Seminar, Emergency, Employee Matching Gifts, Endowment, Fellowship, General Support, Multiyear/Continuing Support.
Note: Employee matching gift ratio: 1 to 1.

Financial Summary

Total Giving: Contributes through corporate direct giving program only.

Typical Recipients

Arts & Humanities: Arts Appreciation, Arts Associations & Councils, Arts Centers, Historic Preservation, Libraries, Literary Arts, Museums/Galleries, Music, Opera, Performing Arts, Public Broadcasting
Civic & Public Affairs: Business/Free Enterprise, Civil Rights, Economic Development, Housing, Zoos/Aquariums
Education: Education Associations, Elementary Education (Private), Minority Education, Private Education (Precollege)
Environment: Environment-General

Health: Health Organizations, Hospitals, Nursing Services, Single-Disease Health Associations
Social Services: Child Welfare, Community Service Organizations, Family Services, Shelters/Homelessness, Substance Abuse, United Funds/United Ways, Volunteer Services, Youth Organizations

Application Procedures

Initial Contact: letter with proposal attached
Application Requirements: goals and financial statement for organization and project; tax identification number
Deadlines: None, but prefers to receive proposals in the fall
Notes: Regional branches have discretionary budgets for contributions to local nonprofits. The headquarters office handles requests from statewide groups.

Restrictions

Company does not support religious or political organizations or individuals.

Additional Information

Majority of recipients are organizations the company traditionally supports, though policy does not restrict first-time requests.

Corporate Officials

Alan Richard Griffith: vice chairman, chief executive officer, director B Mineola, NY 1941. ED Lafayette College BA (1964); City University of New York MBA (1971). PRIM CORP EMPL vice chairman: Bank of New York Co., Inc. CORP AFFIL vice chairman: Bank New York Co. Inc. NONPR AFFIL trustee: Chesapeake Bay Foundation; trustee: Lafayette College; trustee: Amyotrophic Lateral Sclerosis Association. CLUB AFFIL University Club New York; Marco Polo Club.
Thomas A. Renyi: chairman, chief executive officer, director B Passaic, NJ 1946. ED Rutgers University BA (1967); Rutgers University MBA (1968). PRIM CORP EMPL president, chief executive officer, director: Bank of New York Co., Inc. CORP AFFIL president, director: Bank New York Co. Inc.; chairman: BNY Mortgage Co. Inc.

Grants Analysis

Typical Range: $1,000 to $10,000

BANKATLANTIC BANCORP

Company Headquarters

Fort Lauderdale, FL
Web: http://www.bankatlantic.com

Company Description

Founded: 1952
Ticker: BBX
Exchange: NYSE
Assets: US$4.015 billion (2001)
Employees: 2547 (2003)
SIC(s): 6035 Federal Savings Institutions, 6712 Bank Holding Companies.

BankAtlantic Foundation

Giving Contact

Shelley Levan-Margolis, Executive Director
2100 W. Cypress Creek Rd.
Ft. Lauderdale, FL 33309
Phone: (954)940-5058
Web: http://www.bankatlantic.com/communityinvestment/bafoundation.asp

Alternate Contact

PO Box 8608
Ft. Lauderdale, FL 33310
Phone: (954)760-5458

Description

Founded: 1994
EIN: 650499150
Organization Type: Corporate Foundation
Giving Locations: FL: Southern Florida
Grant Types: Emergency, General Support, Operating Expenses, Project.

Financial Summary

Total Giving: $364,530 (2003); $344,470 (2002); $330,725 (2001)
Giving Analysis: Giving for 2001 includes: foundation ($330,725)
Assets: $1,556,884 (2003); $1,193,731 (2002); $1,071,246 (2001)
Gifts Received: $600,000 (2003); $500,154 (2002); $950 (2001). Note: Contributions were received from BankAtlantic.

Typical Recipients

Arts & Humanities: Arts Associations & Councils, Arts Centers, Arts Funds, Arts Institutes, Arts Outreach, Ballet, Dance, Ethnic & Folk Arts, Film & Video, Arts & Humanities-General, History & Archaeology, Libraries, Museums/Galleries, Music, Opera, Performing Arts, Public Broadcasting, Theater
Civic & Public Affairs: African American Affairs, Business/Free Enterprise, Civil Rights, Community Foundations, Economic Development, Civic & Public Affairs-General, Hispanic Affairs, Housing, Law & Justice, Municipalities/Towns, Nonprofit Management, Professional & Trade Associations, Public Policy, Safety, Urban & Community Affairs, Women's Affairs
Education: Afterschool/Enrichment Programs, Arts/Humanities Education, Business Education, Business-School Partnerships, Colleges & Universities, Community & Junior Colleges, Economic Education, Education Funds, Education Reform, Education-General, Leadership Training, Legal Education, Minority Education, Public Education (Precollege), Science/Mathematics Education, Student Aid
Health: AIDS/HIV, Emergency/Ambulance Services, Mental Health, Prenatal Health Issues
International: Human Rights
Religion: Jewish Causes, Religious Welfare
Science: Science Museums
Social Services: At-Risk Youth, Child Abuse, Child Welfare, Community Centers, Community Service Organizations, Day Care, Domestic Violence, Emergency Relief, Family Services, Food/Clothing Distribution, Homes, People with Disabilities, Scouts, Senior Services, Shelters/Homelessness, Social Services-General, Substance Abuse, United Funds/United Ways, Volunteer Services, YMCA/YWCA/YMHA/YWHA, Youth Organizations

Application Procedures

Initial Contact: Submit typewritten proposal on organization's letterhead.
Application Requirements: Include the name, address, telephone number of organization; name of the director; brief history of organization; project description, including problem, need, or issue to be addressed; anticipated benefits; total amount requested; dates of proposed project; operating and project budgets; actual and prospective sources of income for the project, including amounts; project director's name, address, and telephone number (if different); project location; proof of tax-exempt status; copy of charitable solicitation license; list of board members and their affiliations; list of any funding received from BankAtlantic during the same calendar year; and the signature of the executive director acknowledging application.
Deadlines: Applications must be received between February 15 and October 1.
Review Process: Applications are generally reviewed within 60 to 90 days.

Restrictions

Does not support social functions or sporting events; religious organizations; capital, building, or endowment campaigns; individuals, purchase of ad space; fundraising events; funds for travel expenses; hospitals, medical research, or national health organizations; K-12 schools; organizations without 501(c)3 status; political or lobbying organizations; programs or organizations operating outside of Florida; or school athletic teams, cheerleading squads, bands, choirs, etc. The foundation will not fund an organization twice in one calendar year or for more than three consecutive years.

Additional Information

Support goes to education, human services, arts, civic organizations, public policy, economic development, and affordable housing.

Corporate Officials

Alan Levan: chairman, president, chief executive officer PRIM CORP EMPL chairman, president, chief executive officer: BankAtlantic Bancorp.

Foundation Officials

Alan Levan: president, trustee (see above)
Shelley Levan Margolis: secretary, trustee
Lewis Saricea: treasurer, trustee

Grants Analysis

Disclosure Period: calendar year ending 2003
Total Grants: $364,530
Number of Grants: 156
Average Grant: $2,337
Highest Grant: $25,000
Lowest Grant: $500
Typical Range: $1,000 to $5,000

Recent Grants

Note: Grants derived from 2003 Form 990.
Library-Related

3,780	Broward Public Library Foundation Inc., Ft. Lauderdale, FL

General

25,000	Broward Community College Foundation, Ft. Lauderdale, FL
10,000	Florida Grand Opera Inc., Miami, FL
10,000	Junior Achievement of the Palm Beaches Inc., West Palm Beach, FL
5,000	Broward Education Foundation Inc., Ft. Lauderdale, FL
5,000	Florida Grand Opera Inc., Miami, FL
5,000	Leadership Broward Foundation Inc., Ft. Lauderdale, FL -- for economic development
5,000	Local Initiatives Support Corporation, Miami, FL -- for economic development
5,000	Museum of Discovery and Science Inc., Ft. Lauderdale, FL
5,000	Tampa Bay Partnership Regional Research & Educational Foundation, Tampa Bay, FL
5,000	Young at Art of Broward Inc., Davie, FL

BANTA CORP.

Company Headquarters

Menasha, WI
Web: http://www.banta.com

Company Description

Founded: 1901
Ticker: BN
Exchange: NYSE

Revenue: US$1.366 billion (2002)
Employees: 8300 (2003)
SIC(s): 2732 Book Printing, 2752 Commercial Printing--Lithographic, 2759 Commercial Printing Nec, 7336 Commercial Art & Graphic Design.

Operating Locations
Banta Book Group (TN--Johnson City; UT--Spanish Fork; VA--Harrisonburg; WA--Kent; WI--Appleton, Green Bay, Kaukauna, Menasha); Banta Catalog Group (MN--Maple Grove, St. Paul); Banta Corp. (CA--Rialto; MN--Long Prairie; MO--Liberty; OH--Greenfield; WI--Milwaukee, Neenah, Plover); Banta Ventures, Inc. (WI--Plover)

Banta Corp. Foundation

Giving Contact
Frank W. Rudolph, President
Banta Corp. Foundation
PO Box 8003
Menasha, WI 54952-8003
Phone: (920)751-7777
Fax: (920)751-7790

Description
Founded: 1953
EIN: 396050779
Organization Type: Corporate Foundation
Giving Locations: WI: operating locations.
Grant Types: Award, Capital, Employee Matching Gifts, General Support, Multiyear/Continuing Support.
Note: The foundation matches Banta Corp. employee gifts to institutions of higher learning; alumni funds, foundations, or associations; hospitals; and cultural organizations.

Donor Information
Founder: Banta Corp.

Financial Summary
Total Giving: $619,605 (2002); $569,237 (2001). Note: Contributes through corporate direct giving program and foundation.
Giving Analysis: Giving for 2001 includes: foundation matching gifts ($12,579); foundation scholarships ($77,500); foundation ($479,158)
Assets: $226,540 (2003); $29,821 (2001)
Gifts Received: $753,625 (2003); $596,500 (2002); $600,000 (2001). Note: Contributions were received from the Banta Corp.

Typical Recipients
Arts & Humanities: Arts Centers, Arts & Humanities-General, Historic Preservation, History & Archaeology, Libraries, Museums/Galleries, Music, Performing Arts, Public Broadcasting, Theater, Visual Arts
Civic & Public Affairs: Botanical Gardens/Parks, Business/Free Enterprise, Chambers of Commerce, Community Foundations, Economic Development, Civic & Public Affairs-General, Housing, Municipalities/Towns, Parades/Festivals, Public Policy, Safety, Urban & Community Affairs
Education: Afterschool/Enrichment Programs, Arts/Humanities Education, Business Education, Colleges & Universities, Education Associations, Education Funds, Engineering/Technological Education, Education-General, Gifted & Talented Programs, International Studies, Journalism/Media Education, Literacy, Medical Education, Minority Education, Preschool Education, Private Education (Precollege), Science/Mathematics Education, Secondary Education (Private), Student Aid, Vocational & Technical Education
Environment: Environment-General, Protection, Resource Conservation
Health: AIDS/HIV, Cancer, Children's Health/Hospitals, Clinics/Medical Centers, Emergency/Ambulance Services, Health Funds, Heart, Hospitals, Mental Health, Nursing Services, Preventive Medicine/Wellness Organizations
Religion: Religious Organizations, Religious Welfare
Social Services: At-Risk Youth, Big Brothers/Big Sisters, Child Welfare, Community Service Organizations, Counseling, Domestic Violence, Emergency Relief, Family Services, Food/Clothing Distribution, People with Disabilities, Recreation & Athletics, Scouts, Social Services-General, Substance Abuse, United Funds/United Ways, YMCA/YWCA/YMHA/YWHA, Youth Organizations

Application Procedures
Initial Contact: Send a brief letter of inquiry.
Application Requirements: Include a description of organization, amount requested, purpose of funds sought, recently audited financial statement, and proof of tax exempt status.
Deadlines: November 1.
Decision Notification: The board meets twice annually, in the spring and fall.

Corporate Officials
Donald David Belcher: chairman, president, chief executive officer, director B Kansas City, MO 1938. ED Dartmouth College BA (1960); Stanford University MBA (1964). PRIM CORP EMPL chairman, president, chief executive officer, director: Banta Corp. CORP AFFIL chairman: Packaging Fulfillment Specialists; director: Fellowes Manufacturing Co.; director: Hunt Manufacturing Co. NONPR AFFIL trustee: Lawrence University.
Gerald A. Henseler: executive vice president, chief financial officer, director B Marshfield, WI 1940. ED University of Wisconsin, Madison BS (1962). PRIM CORP EMPL executive vice president, chief financial officer, director: Banta Corp. CORP AFFIL director: First National Bancshares Corp.; vice president: Tidi Products Inc.; director: Banta Healthcare Products Inc.

Foundation Officials
Ronald D. Kneezel: treasurer
Robert T. Michel: secretary
Frank W. Rudolph: president
Stephanie A. Streeter: vice president

Grants Analysis
Disclosure Period: calendar year ending 2003
Total Grants: $396,028*
Number of Grants: 73
Average Grant: $4,285*
Highest Grant: $87,500
Lowest Grant: $125
Typical Range: $1,000 to $10,000
*Note: Giving excludes matching gifts; scholarships. Average grant figure excludes highest grant.

Recent Grants
Note: Grants derived from 2003 Form 990.

General
100,000	Citizen's Scholarship Foundation
87,500	Fox Cities Performing Arts Centre, Appleton, WI
62,500	Elisha D. Smith Public Library, Menasha, WI
25,000	Fox Cities Kurgan Sister City Conference, Appleton, WI
15,000	Neenah YMCA, Neenah, WI
15,000	Wisconsin Foundation for Independent College, Milwaukee, WI
15,000	Wisconsin Public Broadcasting Foundation Inc., Madison, WI
12,500	Theda Clark Medical Centre Foundation, Neenah, WI
10,000	Community Foundation, WI
10,000	University of Wisconsin Stout, WI

ROBERT BARD FOUNDATION

Giving Contact
Pat Kling, Trust Officer
Robert Bard Foundation
Care of Mellon Bank NA
PO Box 7236, AIM 193 0224
Philadelphia, PA 19101-7236
Phone: (215)553-3208

Description
Founded: 1988
EIN: 236806099
Organization Type: Private Foundation
Giving Locations: PA: Royersford
Grant Types: General Support.

Donor Information
Founder: the late Agnes Cook Bard

Financial Summary
Total Giving: $25,000 (fiscal year ending June 30, 2001)
Assets: $4,313,448 (fiscal 2001)

Typical Recipients
Arts & Humanities: History & Archaeology, Libraries, Music
Civic & Public Affairs: Clubs, Community Foundations, Economic Development, Civic & Public Affairs-General, Urban & Community Affairs, Zoos/Aquariums
Education: Arts/Humanities Education, Colleges & Universities, Private Education (Precollege), Public Education (Precollege)
Environment: Environment-General
Health: Children's Health/Hospitals, Emergency/Ambulance Services, Nursing Services
Social Services: Child Welfare, Community Centers, Community Service Organizations, Counseling, Family Services, Food/Clothing Distribution, People with Disabilities, Senior Services, United Funds/United Ways, Volunteer Services, YMCA/YWCA/YMHA/YWHA, Youth Organizations

Application Procedures
Initial Contact: Send a brief letter of inquiry.
Application Requirements: Include a description of organization, total cost, name of contact person, and IRS determination letter.
Deadlines: April 1.

Restrictions
Preference is first given to charities in Royersford, PA, after which any worthy charities will be considered.

Additional Information
Trust(s): Mellon Bank NA

Foundation Officials
Norman E. Donoghue, II: trustee B Coatesville, PA 1944. ED Williams College BA (1966); Duke University JD (1969). PRIM CORP EMPL partner: Dechert Price & Rhoads. NONPR AFFIL legal counselor, director: International Visitors Council Philadelphia; trustee, legal counselor, corporate secretary: Princess Grace Foundation; member: American Bar Association; fellow: International Academy Trust & Estate Lawyers.

Grants Analysis
Disclosure Period: fiscal year ending June 30, 2001
Total Grants: $25,000
Number of Grants: 1

Recent Grants
Note: Grants derived from fiscal 2001 Form 990.

General

25,000	Spring-Ford Area Historical Society, Spring-Ford, PA

BARDEN PRECISION BEARINGS

Company Headquarters

200 Park Ave.
Danbury, CT 06813
Web: http://www.bardenbearings.com

Company Description

Employees: 850
SIC(s): 3469 Metal Stampings Nec, 3562 Ball & Roller Bearings, 3568 Power Transmission Equipment Nec.

Operating Locations

Barden Corp. (CT--Winsted); Winsted Precision Ball Co. (CT--Winsted)

Barden Foundation, Inc.

Giving Contact

Thomas F. Loughman, Treasurer, Secretary, & Trustee
1146 Barnum Avenue
Bridgeport, CT 06610
Phone: (203)336-7531
Fax: (203)336-6440

Alternate Contact

Scholarship Committee
Barden Foundation, Inc.
200 Park Avenue
Danbury, CT 06810
Phone: (203)744-2211
Note: Application address for scholarships.

Description

Founded: 1959
EIN: 066054855
Organization Type: Corporate Foundation
Giving Locations: CT: Bridgeport, Danbury, Winsted
Grant Types: General Support, Scholarship.

Donor Information

Founder: The Barden Corp.

Financial Summary

Total Giving: $270,500 (fiscal year ending October 31, 2003); $316,675 (fiscal 2002); $361,500 (fiscal 2001). Note: Contributes through foundation only.
Giving Analysis: Giving for fiscal 2002 includes: foundation scholarships ($62,250); foundation grants to United Way ($80,000); fiscal 2001: foundation scholarships ($54,500); foundation grants to United Way ($90,000); foundation ($217,000)
Assets: $5,857,168 (fiscal 2003); $5,699,375 (fiscal 2002); $6,209,743 (fiscal 2001)
Gifts Received: $8,000 (fiscal 1992). Note: Contributions were received from the Barden Corp.

Typical Recipients

Arts & Humanities: Arts Centers, Libraries, Museums/Galleries, Music, Theater
Civic & Public Affairs: African American Affairs, Civil Rights, Clubs, Civic & Public Affairs-General, Municipalities/Towns, Parades/Festivals, Professional & Trade Associations, Safety, Urban & Community Affairs, Zoos/Aquariums
Education: Business Education, Colleges & Universities, Community & Junior Colleges, Economic Education, Education Funds, Engineering/Technological Education, Education-General, Private Education (Precollege), Public Education (Precollege), Science/Mathematics Education, Student Aid, Vocational & Technical Education
Health: AIDS/HIV, Cancer, Children's Health/Hospitals, Clinics/Medical Centers, Emergency/Ambulance Services, Health Funds, Health Organizations, Hospices, Hospitals, Medical Rehabilitation, Mental Health, Nursing Services, Preventive Medicine/Wellness Organizations, Single-Disease Health Associations
Religion: Religious Organizations, Religious Welfare
Science: Science Exhibits & Fairs, Science Museums, Scientific Organizations
Social Services: Child Welfare, Community Centers, Community Service Organizations, Day Care, Emergency Relief, Family Services, Homes, People with Disabilities, Recreation & Athletics, Scouts, Social Services-General, Special Olympics, United Funds/United Ways, Volunteer Services, YMCA/YWCA/YMHA/YWHA, Youth Organizations

Application Procedures

Initial Contact: Send a letter of request for grants; request an application for scholarships.
Application Requirements: Requests should include a description of organization, goals and requirements, amount requested, purpose of grant, recent financial statement, and copy of IRS determination letter.
Deadlines: By January for grant award in following year; March 31 for scholarships.
Decision Notification: Trustees meet in February.

Restrictions

Most scholarships are restricted to children of employees of the Barden Corp.
Organizations must be tax-exempt charities.

Additional Information

Publications: Informational Brochure

Corporate Officials

John Emling: vice president B 1956. ED Saint Bonaventure University BBA Marketing. PRIM CORP EMPL vice president: Barden Corp.

Foundation Officials

Robert H. Buch: president, trustee
Robert M. Davis: trustee PRIM CORP EMPL vice president: Barden Corp.
Jeannine Frink: trustee
Thomas F. Loughman: secretary, treasurer, trustee
Robert P. Moore: trustee B 1924. CORP AFFIL president: Lacey Manufacturing Co. Division.
Stanley Noss: trustee

Grants Analysis

Disclosure Period: fiscal year ending October 31, 2003
Total Grants: $145,000*
Number of Grants: 38
Average Grant: $2,139*
Highest Grant: $34,000
Lowest Grant: $425
Typical Range: $1,000 to $5,000
*Note: Giving excludes scholarships; United Way. Average grant figure excludes two highest grants ($68,000).

Recent Grants

Note: Grants derived from 2003 Form 990.
General

40,000	United Way of Northern Fairfield County, Danbury, CT
34,000	Bridgeport Hospital, Bridgeport, CT
34,000	Danbury Hospital Development Foundation Inc., Danbury, CT
16,000	United Way of Northwest Connecticut Inc., Winsted, CT
15,000	United Way of Eastern Fairfield County, Bridgeport, CT
10,000	Ability Beyond Disability, Brookfield, CT
7,000	American Cancer Society, Wilton, CT
5,000	Winsted Area Childcare Center Inc., Winsted, CT
4,000	Hanahoe Children's Clinic, Danbury, CT
4,000	MCCA, Danbury, CT

BARDES CORP.

Company Headquarters

Cincinnati, OH

Company Description

Employees: 700
SIC(s): 3451 Screw Machine Products, 3643 Current-Carrying Wiring Devices.

Bardes Fund

Giving Contact

Rebecca Autry
Bardes Fund
4730 Madison Road
Cincinnati, OH 45227-1426
Phone: (513)533-6228
Fax: (513)871-4084
E-mail: rautry@ilsco.com

Description

Founded: 1955
EIN: 316036206
Organization Type: Corporate Foundation
Giving Locations: OH: Cincinnati
Grant Types: General Support.

Financial Summary

Total Giving: $77,495 (2003). Note: Contributes through corporate direct giving program and foundation. Giving includes foundation. 1996 Giving includes foundation ($144,545); United Way ($28,000).
Giving Analysis: Giving for 2003 includes: foundation grants to United Way ($7,500); foundation scholarships ($9,000)
Assets: $1,633,743 (2003)
Gifts Received: $600,000 (1999 approx); $150,000 (1996); $215,000 (1995). Note: Contributions were received from Bardes Corp.

Typical Recipients

Arts & Humanities: Arts Associations & Councils, Arts Centers, Arts Funds, Community Arts, Historic Preservation, History & Archaeology, Libraries, Museums/Galleries, Music, Opera, Performing Arts, Public Broadcasting, Theater
Civic & Public Affairs: Botanical Gardens/Parks, Clubs, Employment/Job Training, Civic & Public Affairs-General, Philanthropic Organizations, Public Policy, Urban & Community Affairs, Zoos/Aquariums
Education: Business Education, Colleges & Universities, Education Associations, Education Funds, Elementary Education (Public), Education-General, Private Education (Precollege), Student Aid, Vocational & Technical Education
Environment: Environment-General, Resource Conservation
Health: AIDS/HIV, Alzheimer's Disease, Cancer, Children's Health/Hospitals, Emergency/Ambulance Services, Eyes/Blindness, Heart, Hospices, Hospitals, Medical Rehabilitation, Medical Research, Preventive Medicine/Wellness Organizations, Public Health, Single-Disease Health Associations
International: Foreign Arts Organizations, International Affairs
Religion: Churches, Religious Organizations, Religious Welfare
Social Services: Animal Protection, Camps, Child

Welfare, Community Service Organizations, Family Planning, Family Services, Recreation & Athletics, Social Services-General, United Funds/United Ways, Youth Organizations

Application Procedures
Initial Contact: Written request
Deadlines: None.

Corporate Officials
Merrilyn B. Bardes: president B 1945. PRIM CORP EMPL president: Bardes Corp.
Brittain B. Cudlip: chairman B 1948. PRIM CORP EMPL chairman: Bardes Corp. CORP AFFIL president: WRB Inc.; chairman: Walnut Hill Properties Inc.; vice president: Kentucky Connector Corp.; president: New Horizons Madonna Hall; vice president: Ilsco Corp. NONPR AFFIL trustee: Tufts University.
David J. FitzGibbon: president, chief executive officer B 1944. ED Thomas More College (1965). PRIM CORP EMPL president, chief executive officer: Bardes Corp. CORP AFFIL chief operating officer: Ilsco Corp.; president: Kentucky Connector Corp.
J. E. Valentine: chief financial officer PRIM CORP EMPL chief financial officer: Bardes Corp.

Foundation Officials
Rebecca Autry: secretary, treasurer
Merrilyn B. Bardes: president (see above)

Grants Analysis
Disclosure Period: calendar year ending 2003
Total Grants: $60,995*
Number of Grants: 38
Average Grant: $1,605
Highest Grant: $13,000
Lowest Grant: $60
Typical Range: $100 to $3,000
*Note: Giving excludes scholarships; United Way.

Recent Grants
Note: Grants derived from 2001 Form 990.
General

21,000	Lawrenceville School, Lawrenceville, NJ
15,000	National Gallery of Art, Washington, DC
10,000	Boston College, Chestnut Hill, MA
10,000	Jefferson Scholars Program, Charlottesville, VA
9,226	Riverbend Music Center, Riverbend, NJ
7,500	Fine Arts Fund, Cincinnati, OH
6,500	Cincinnati Symphony Orchestra, Cincinnati, OH
5,850	Society of Four Arts, Palm Beach, FL
5,000	NESF, Rosslyn, VA
4,200	Preservation Foundation, Palm Beach, FL

HOLLIS AND HELEN BARIGHT FOUNDATION

Giving Contact
Thomas V. Van Robays, Contact
6015 Northwest Radial Highway
Omaha, NE 68104
Phone: (402)554-4792

Description
Founded: 1995
EIN: 470789577
Organization Type: Private Foundation
Giving Locations: NE: Omaha
Grant Types: General Support, Scholarship.

Donor Information
Founder: Established in 1995 by the late Hollis Baright.

Financial Summary
Total Giving: $411,500 (2003); $401,000 (2001)
Giving Analysis: Giving for 2003 includes: foundation scholarships ($1,500); 2001: foundation scholarships ($1,000)
Assets: $4,466,863 (2004); $5,264,638 (2001)
Gifts Received: $4,556,340 (1995)

Typical Recipients
Arts & Humanities: Museums/Galleries
Civic & Public Affairs: Botanical Gardens/Parks, Zoos/Aquariums
Education: Colleges & Universities, Education Funds, Student Aid
Environment: Protection
Social Services: Crime Prevention, Shelters/Homelessness

Application Procedures
Initial Contact: Send a brief letter of inquiry.
Application Requirements: Include a description of organization, amount requested, and purpose of funds sought.
Deadlines: None.

Restrictions
Donations are not usually made for current operating expenses.

Additional Information
Trust(s): Great Western Bank

Foundation Officials
Ralph W. Palmer: co-trustee
Nick R. Taylor: co-trustee

Grants Analysis
Disclosure Period: calendar year ending 2004
Total Grants: $410,000*
Number of Grants: 4
Highest Grant: $225,000
Lowest Grant: $50,000
*Note: Giving excludes scholarships.

Recent Grants
Note: Grants derived from 2003 Form 990.
General

225,000	Omaha Zoo Foundation, Omaha, NE
85,000	Fontenelle Nature Association, Bellevue, NE -- for sense of place
50,000	Sienna/Francis House, Omaha, NE -- towards capital campaign
50,000	University of Nebraska Foundation, Omaha, NE
1,500	UNO Office of Financial Aid, Omaha, NE -- for scholarship

COETA AND DONALD R. BARKER FOUNDATION

Giving Contact
Nancy G. Harris, Executive Administrator
PO Box 936
Rancho Mirage, CA 92270
Phone: (760)324-2656
Fax: (760)321-8662

Description
Founded: 1977
EIN: 930698411
Organization Type: Private Foundation
Giving Locations: CA; OR
Grant Types: General Support, Operating Expenses.

Donor Information
Founder: Donald R. Barker

Financial Summary
Total Giving: $294,650 (fiscal year ending November 30, 2001)
Giving Analysis: Giving for fiscal 2001 includes: foundation grants to United Way ($16,000)
Assets: $5,924,505 (fiscal 2001)

Typical Recipients
Arts & Humanities: Arts Associations & Councils, Arts Centers, Arts Funds, Ballet, Museums/Galleries, Music, Opera, Performing Arts, Theater
Civic & Public Affairs: Botanical Gardens/Parks, Civic & Public Affairs-General, Urban & Community Affairs, Women's Affairs, Zoos/Aquariums
Education: Arts/Humanities Education, Business Education, Colleges & Universities, Community & Junior Colleges, Education Funds, Environmental Education, Faculty Development, International Studies, Private Education (Precollege), Science/Mathematics Education, Secondary Education (Private), Secondary Education (Public), Student Aid, Vocational & Technical Education
Environment: Air/Water Quality, Environment-General
Health: AIDS/HIV, Arthritis, Cancer, Children's Health/Hospitals, Clinics/Medical Centers, Diabetes, Emergency/Ambulance Services, Heart, Hospices, Hospitals, Long-Term Care, Medical Research, Mental Health, Preventive Medicine/Wellness Organizations, Research/Studies Institutes, Single-Disease Health Associations
Religion: Churches, Religious Welfare
Science: Scientific Centers & Institutes
Social Services: Animal Protection, At-Risk Youth, Child Welfare, Community Service Organizations, Crime Prevention, Family Planning, Family Services, Homes, People with Disabilities, Recreation & Athletics, Scouts, Senior Services, Shelters/Homelessness, United Funds/United Ways, Youth Organizations

Application Procedures
Initial Contact: Submit a letter requesting a grant application form.
Application Requirements: Initial letters of request should be submitted on the requesting organization's stationery (or including complete organization contact information if on plain paper) and should be signed by either the president or, with board approval, by its executive director (a trust may have a trustee or authorized executive director sign the letter). The letter should contain a brief description of the project or program; why it is a community priority need; total amount of funding that will be required for the project or program; amount requested; a copy of the organization's IRS tax exemption approval and non-private foundation status determination; and a statement from an officer, trustee, or other authoritative person that the 501(c)(3) and 509(a) status has not been revoked and that the present operation of the applicant organization and its current sources of support are consistent with that status.
Deadlines: None for initial letters of request. Full applications must be submitted prior to the May or October meeting to receive spring or fall consideration.
Review Process: The foundation will review the initial letter of request and will forward an application form to applicants that meet the requirements of the foundation.

Additional Information
Publications: Application Guidelines; Application Form

Foundation Officials
Coeta Barker: trustee
John D. Brennan: trustee
Vernon Gleaves: trustee
John R. Lamb: trustee
Joseph A. Moore: trustee

Dana Newquist: trustee
Jim Richards: trustee

Grants Analysis

Disclosure Period: fiscal year ending November 30, 2001
Total Grants: $278,650*
Number of Grants: 64
Average Grant: $3,629*
Highest Grant: $50,000
Lowest Grant: $325
Typical Range: $1,000 to $5,000
*Note: Giving excludes United Way. Average grant figure excludes highest grant.

Recent Grants

Note: Grants derived from fiscal 2002 Form 990.
General

30,000	University of Oregon Development Fund, Eugene, OR -- towards expansion of the Museum of Art
25,000	Friends of the Cultural Center, Palm Desert, CA -- for endowment fund
10,000	Desert AIDS Project, Palm Springs, CA -- for volunteer room
10,000	United Way of Santa Barbara County, Santa Barbara, CA -- for Fun in Sun Program
10,000	University of Oregon Development Fund, Eugene, OR -- towards expansion of the Museum of Art
7,500	Friends of the Cultural Center, Palm Desert, CA -- for the facilities committee study
5,000	Arthritis Foundation, Palm Desert, CA
5,000	Brentwood Symphony Orchestra, Brentwood, CA -- for John Lamb
5,000	Children's Museum of the Desert, Rancho Mirage, CA -- for the Early Childhood Educational Program
5,000	College of the Desert Foundation, Palm Desert, CA -- for Work Study Scholarship Program

BARKER FOUNDATION INC.

Giving Contact

Allan M. Barker, Treasurer & Trustee
Barker Foundation Inc
PO Box 328
Nashua, NH 03061-0328
Phone: (603)889-1763

Description

Founded: 1954
EIN: 026005885
Organization Type: Private Foundation
Giving Locations: DC; ME; MA; NH
Grant Types: Emergency, General Support.

Donor Information

Founder: the late Walter Barker, Irene L. Barker

Financial Summary

Total Giving: $209,476 (2004); $292,786 (2001)
Assets: $5,208,018 (2004); $6,097,009 (2001)

Typical Recipients

Arts & Humanities: Historic Preservation, History & Archaeology, Libraries, Public Broadcasting
Civic & Public Affairs: Community Foundations, Employment/Job Training, Civic & Public Affairs-General, Municipalities/Towns, Safety, Urban & Community Affairs
Education: Colleges & Universities, Elementary Education (Private), Education-General, Private Educa-

tion (Precollege)
Environment: Environment-General
Health: Arthritis, Cancer, Children's Health/Hospitals, Clinics/Medical Centers, Diabetes, Emergency/Ambulance Services, Eyes/Blindness, Heart, Hospices, Hospitals, Medical Research, Multiple Sclerosis, Nursing Services, Respiratory, Single-Disease Health Associations, Trauma Treatment
Religion: Churches
Social Services: Animal Protection, Big Brothers/Big Sisters, Child Welfare, Community Service Organizations, Crime Prevention, Day Care, Domestic Violence, Family Services, Food/Clothing Distribution, People with Disabilities, Scouts, Senior Services, Shelters/Homelessness, Special Olympics, United Funds/United Ways, YMCA/YWCA/YMHA/YWHA, Youth Organizations

Application Procedures

Initial Contact: Submit a one-page concept paper.
Application Requirements: Include a description of organization, amount requested, purpose of funds sought, proof of tax-exempt status.
Deadlines: None.
Notes: Due to the volume of applications, individual replies to requests are not possible. Phone inquiries are not accepted.

Restrictions

Does not support individuals, political or lobbying groups, or non tax-exempt organizations. No restrictions by geographical areas, but the majority of requests are from New Hampshire organizations.

Additional Information

Provides scholarships to students demonstrating financial need.

Foundation Officials

Anne M. April: trustee
Allan M. Barker: treasurer, trustee
Dorothy A. Barker: trustee
Douglas M. Barker: secretary
Elizabeth M. Bucknam: president, trustee
Carol A. Larouche: assistant treasurer
Edward P. Moran, Jr.: trustee
Susan B. Moran: vice president, trustee
Sidney F. Thaxter: clerk

Grants Analysis

Disclosure Period: calendar year ending 2004
Total Grants: $209,476
Number of Grants: 51
Average Grant: $3,486*
Highest Grant: $35,160
Lowest Grant: $500
Typical Range: $1,000 to $5,000
*Note: Average grant figure excludes highest grant.

Recent Grants

Note: Grants derived from 2001 Form 990.
General

52,053	Lahey Clinic, Burlington, MA
25,000	American Red Cross Disaster Relief Fund, Washington, DC
15,000	Community Hospice House, Merrimack, NH
12,250	Boy and Girls Club of Greater Nashua, Nashua, NH
12,000	New Hampton School, New Hampton, NH
10,000	Dexter Historical Society, Dexter, ME
10,000	Nashua Soup Kitchen & Shelter, Inc., Nashua, NH
10,000	St. Joseph Community Services, Merrimack, NH
8,000	Colby College, Waterville, ME
6,000	New Hampshire Association for the Blind, Concord, NH

J.M.R. BARKER FOUNDATION

Giving Contact

Care of Rothstein, Kass & Co. PC
1350 Ave. of the Americas
New York, NY 10019

Description

Founded: 1968
EIN: 136268289
Organization Type: Private Foundation
Giving Locations: MA: Boston; NY: New York
Grant Types: Capital, Endowment, General Support, Multiyear/Continuing Support, Operating Expenses, Project, Research.

Donor Information

Founder: the late James M. Barker, the late Margaret R. Barker, Robert R. Barker

Financial Summary

Total Giving: $1,817,035 (2003)
Assets: $42,871,666 (2003)
Gifts Received: $2,308,573 (2003). Note: In 2003, contributions were received from Robert R. Barker Trust.

Typical Recipients

Arts & Humanities: Community Arts, Libraries, Literary Arts, Museums/Galleries, Music, Performing Arts, Public Broadcasting
Civic & Public Affairs: Civic & Public Affairs-General, Housing, Nonprofit Management, Philanthropic Organizations, Public Policy, Urban & Community Affairs
Education: Colleges & Universities, Continuing Education, Engineering/Technological Education, Education-General, Gifted & Talented Programs, International Studies, Legal Education, Minority Education, Private Education (Precollege), Public Education (Precollege), School Volunteerism, Vocational & Technical Education
Environment: Environment-General, Resource Conservation, Wildlife Protection
Health: Clinics/Medical Centers, Health Funds, Health Organizations, Home-Care Services, Hospitals, Multiple Sclerosis
International: Foreign Arts Organizations, International Environmental Issues, International Relations, International Relief Efforts
Religion: Churches, Jewish Causes, Religious Organizations
Science: Science Museums, Scientific Centers & Institutes, Scientific Labs
Social Services: Child Welfare, Community Service Organizations, Crime Prevention, Family Planning, Family Services, People with Disabilities, Refugee Assistance, Senior Services, Social Services-General, United Funds/United Ways, Volunteer Services, Youth Organizations

Application Procedures

Initial Contact: Before sending a formal grant proposal, submit a preliminary letter of inquiry.
Application Requirements: Briefly describe the programs of the sponsoring organizations. Indicate amount requested and what will be accomplished as a result of the grant.
Deadlines: November 1.

Restrictions

Primarily supports preselected organizations.

Foundation Officials

James R. Barker: vice president, director B Cleveland, OH 1935. ED Columbia University BA (1957); Harvard University MBA (1963). PRIM CORP EMPL founder, vice chairman, co-owner: Mormac Marine Group. CORP AFFIL director: Pittston Co.; chairman:

Lakes Shipping Co.; vice chairman: Moran Towing Co.; chairman: Interlake Holding Co.; chairman, director, president: Interlake Steamship Co.; trustee: Eastern Enterprises; director: GTE Corp. NONPR AFFIL vice chairman, trustee: Stamford Hospital.

Margaret Barker Clark: director, president

Robert P. Conner: treasurer, assistant secretary, director B New Bedford, MA 1948. ED Boston College BS (1970); Pace University MS (1977). PRIM CORP EMPL senior vice president: J&W Seligman & Co. CORP AFFIL director: CRB Broadcasting Corp. NONPR AFFIL member: Beta Gamma Sigma; member: New York Saint Society CPA's; member: American Institute of CPA's; member: Alpha Sigma Nu.

John W. Holman, Jr.: director PRIM CORP EMPL managing director: Triak Services Corp.

Maureen A. Hopkins: secretary, admin

Richard D. Kahn: director B New York, NY 1931. ED Harvard University AB (1952); Harvard University JD (1955). PRIM CORP EMPL counsel: Debevoise & Plimpton. NONPR AFFIL member: New York City Bar Association; member: Phi Beta Kappa; director: JMR Barker Foundation; member: Montauk Citizens Advisory Committee; director: Concerned Citizens Montauk; director: Group South Fork. CLUB AFFIL Harvard Club.

Grants Analysis

Disclosure Period: calendar year ending 2003
Total Grants: $1,817,035
Number of Grants: 27
Average Grant: $23,081*
Highest Grant: $1,000,000
Lowest Grant: $1,000
Typical Range: $5,000 to $50,000
*Note: Average grant figure excludes two highest grants ($1,240,000).

Recent Grants

Note: Grants derived from 2003 Form 990.
General

1,000,000	Harvard University, Cambridge, MA
240,000	Massachusetts Institute of Technology, Cambridge, MA
113,250	Child Inc., Wilmington, DE
100,000	Amazon Conservation Team, Arlington, VA
60,000	Connecticut Friends School, Wilton, CT
50,000	Theban Mapping Project, Cairo Egypt
40,000	Bridge Fund of New York Inc., New York, NY
35,000	Missionary Servants of St. Anthony, San Antonio, TX
25,000	Amyotrophic Lateral Sclerosis, Calabasas Hills, CA
25,000	Manhattan Institute for Policy Research Inc., New York, NY

BARKER WELFARE FOUNDATION

Giving Contact

Sarane H. Ross, President & Director
PO Box 2
Glen Head, NY 11545
Phone: (516)759-5592
Fax: (516)759-5497
E-mail: barkersmd@aol.com
Web: http://www.barkerwelfare.org

Description

Founded: 1934
EIN: 366018526
Organization Type: General Purpose Foundation
Giving Locations: IL: Chicago; IN: Michigan City; NY: New York
Grant Types: Capital, General Support, Loan, Operating Expenses, Project, Research.

Donor Information

Founder: Established in 1934 by the late Catherine B. Hickox, whose daughter, Mrs. Walter L. Ross II, is the current president. In addition, five relatives are also active in the foundation's activities.

Financial Summary

Total Giving: $2,423,600 (fiscal year ending September 30, 2003); $2,992,705 (fiscal 2002); $2,627,607 (fiscal 2001)
Giving Analysis: Giving for fiscal 2002 includes: foundation matching gifts ($44,135)
Assets: $53,522,827 (fiscal 2003); $48,622,609 (fiscal 2002); $60,278,364 (fiscal 2001)

Typical Recipients

Arts & Humanities: Arts Centers, Arts Institutes, Arts Outreach, Ballet, Ethnic & Folk Arts, Arts & Humanities-General, Historic Preservation, History & Archaeology, Libraries, Museums/Galleries, Music, Opera, Performing Arts, Public Broadcasting, Theater
Civic & Public Affairs: Botanical Gardens/Parks, Economic Development, Employment/Job Training, Gay/Lesbian Issues, Civic & Public Affairs-General, Hispanic Affairs, Inner-City Development, Legal Aid, Nonprofit Management, Philanthropic Organizations, Urban & Community Affairs, Zoos/Aquariums
Education: Afterschool/Enrichment Programs, Arts/Humanities Education, Colleges & Universities, Education Reform, Elementary Education (Public), Environmental Education, Education-General, Health & Physical Education, Literacy, Minority Education, Preschool Education, Private Education (Precollege)
Environment: Forestry, Environment-General, Resource Conservation, Wildlife Protection
Health: Adolescent Health Issues, AIDS/HIV, Cancer, Children's Health/Hospitals, Clinics/Medical Centers, Emergency/Ambulance Services, Health Funds, Health Organizations, Heart, Home-Care Services, Hospitals, Long-Term Care, Medical Rehabilitation, Medical Training, Mental Health, Nursing Services, Nutrition, Outpatient Health Care, Prenatal Health Issues, Public Health
International: International Environmental Issues
Religion: Dioceses, Religious Organizations, Religious Welfare
Science: Science Museums, Scientific Labs, Scientific Research
Social Services: At-Risk Youth, Big Brothers/Big Sisters, Camps, Child Abuse, Child Welfare, Community Centers, Community Service Organizations, Crime Prevention, Day Care, Delinquency & Criminal Rehabilitation, Domestic Violence, Emergency Relief, Family Planning, Family Services, Food/Clothing Distribution, People with Disabilities, Recreation & Athletics, Scouts, Senior Services, Shelters/Homelessness, Social Services-General, Substance Abuse, United Funds/United Ways, Volunteer Services, YMCA/YWCA/YMHA/YWHA, Youth Organizations

Application Procedures

Initial Contact: To apply, a brief two- to three-page letter or telephone call is suggested, describing the organization and the request for which funds are being sought.
Application Requirements: A budget and evidence of tax-exempt status should be included with the letter of inquiry. If the request falls within the current scope of the foundation's interests, the applicant will be asked to submit an application and supply additional information as required.
Deadlines: The foundation requires that completed applications be submitted by February 1 for May board meeting, and by August 1 for November board meeting.
Review Process: Applicants may be notified during the process that funds are not available. Organizations who receive approval for a grant will receive the funds approximately six weeks after the directors meet.

Notes: Organizations in the Michigan City, IN, area must also send an additional copy of complete proposal to Thomas P. McCormick, First Citizens Bank, PO Box 800, Michigan City, IN 46360.

Restrictions

As a general rule, the foundation will not consider support for individual scholarships or fellowships; costs of fund-raising campaigns; endowments; conferences; seminars; conduit organizations; medical research; scientific research; national education, health, or welfare funds; grants to operating foundations; institutions of higher education, private elementary or secondary schools; professional schools or trade organizations; or films.

No grants are made for lobbying or legislative activities, or for start-up organizations, emergency funds, or deficit financing. The foundation also does not accept unsolicited applications for grants in the Chicago, IL, area. the Chicago, IL, area.

Additional Information

The foundation will not accept more than one proposal within a 12-month period.
The foundation suggests submitting completed proposals at least a month before the official deadline so that site visits can be made in a timely matter.
Publications: Application Form; Checklist; Annual Report (including Guidelines)

Foundation Officials

Katrina H. Becker: vice president, secretary, director
Diane Curtis: director
Susan M. DeMaio: assistant secretary, assistant director
Danielle A. Hickox: director
John B. Hickox: director
Mary Lou Linnen: director
Alline Matheson: director
Thomas P. McCormick: treasurer, director
Sarane R. O'Connor: director
Alexander B. Ross: director
Sarane H. Ross: president, director

Grants Analysis

Disclosure Period: fiscal year ending September 30, 2003
Total Grants: $2,423,600
Number of Grants: 225
Average Grant: $10,772
Highest Grant: $100,000
Lowest Grant: $500
Typical Range: $5,000 to $20,000

Recent Grants

Note: Grants derived from fiscal 2003 Form 990.
Library-Related

20,000	New York Public Library, New York, NY
15,000	Chicago Public Library Foundation, Chicago, IL

General

50,000	Carnegie Hall Society Inc., New York, NY
50,000	Field Museum of Natural History, Chicago, IL
50,000	Metropolitan Opera Association, New York, NY
50,000	Yale University Art Gallery, New Haven, CT
45,000	Friends of Barker Civic Center Inc., Michigan City, IN
37,000	Rehabilitation Institute Foundation, Chicago, IL
30,000	Boy's Club of New York, New York, NY
30,000	Chicago Commons Association, Chicago, IL
26,826	Palm Beach County Association for Retarded Citizens, River Beach, FL
25,000	Center for Arts Education, New York, NY

BARNES FOUNDATION

Giving Contact
Sally A. O'Connor, Vice President & Executive Director
PO Box 315
East Hartland, CT 06027-0315
Phone: (860)653-0462
E-mail: barnesfd@erols.com

Description
Founded: 1945
EIN: 066037160
Organization Type: Private Foundation
Giving Locations: CT
Grant Types: Conference/Seminar, Project, Scholarship, Seed Money.

Donor Information
Founder: Carlyle F. Barnes, Aurelia B. Bristow, Louise B. Adams, the late Myrtle I. Barnes, the late Fuller F. Barnes

Financial Summary
Total Giving: $244,000 (2002)
Assets: $7,223,809 (2002)
Gifts Received: $200 (1998); $300 (1993); $36,000 (1992)

Typical Recipients
Arts & Humanities: Arts Centers, Arts Outreach, Dance, Libraries, Literary Arts, Museums/Galleries, Music, Performing Arts, Public Broadcasting, Theater
Civic & Public Affairs: Botanical Gardens/Parks, Community Foundations, Zoos/Aquariums
Education: Afterschool/Enrichment Programs, Arts/Humanities Education, Colleges & Universities, Education Associations, Education Funds, Elementary Education (Public), Engineering/Technological Education, Environmental Education, Faculty Development, Education-General, Gifted & Talented Programs, International Exchange, International Studies, Leadership Training, Minority Education, Private Education (Precollege), Public Education (Precollege), Science/Mathematics Education, Special Education, Student Aid
Environment: Environment-General
Religion: Churches
Science: Science Museums, Scientific Centers & Institutes
Social Services: Camps, Child Welfare, Community Service Organizations, Family Services, People with Disabilities, Scouts, YMCA/YWCA/YMHA/YWHA, Youth Organizations

Application Procedures
Initial Contact: Send a letter of inquiry requesting application guidelines.
Application Requirements: Include a description of organization, amount requested, purpose of funds sought, recently audited financial statement, and proof of tax-exempt status.
Deadlines: Apply 6 to 12 months in advance.
Notes: Foundation accepts the Common Application Form of the Connecticut Council on Philanthropy.

Restrictions
Limited to federally tax-exempt nonprofit organizations relating to precollegiate education in Connecticut.

Additional Information
Publications: Annual Report (including Application Guidelines)

Foundation Officials
Louise B. Adams: trustee
Carlyle Fuller Barnes: president B Bristol, CT 1924. ED Wesleyan University AB (1948). CORP AFFIL director: Travelers Life & Annuity Co.; director: United Bank & Trust Co.; director: Travelers Insurance Companies; director: Travelers Insurance Co.; director: Travelers Corp.; director: Travelers Indemnity Co. North America. NONPR AFFIL director: Institute Living; trustee: New England Colleges Fund; president: Bristol Hospital Development Foundation.
Elliott B. Bristow: treasurer
Joan B. Flynn: secretary
Sally A. O'Connor: vice president, executive director

Grants Analysis
Disclosure Period: calendar year ending 2002
Total Grants: $244,000
Number of Grants: 31
Average Grant: $7,871
Highest Grant: $20,000
Lowest Grant: $2,500
Typical Range: $2,000 to $10,000

Recent Grants
Note: Grants derived from 2002 Form 990.
General
20,000	MacDuffie School, Springfield, MA -- for improving the technology resources at the school
20,000	Walks Foundation, Simsbury, CT -- for Scholarship Program
15,000	Lake Champlain Maritime Museum, Vergennes, VT -- for Champlain Discovery Program
15,000	Main Street Community Foundation, Bristol, CT -- for a special fund in honor of Hap Barnes
15,000	Walnut Hill School, Natick, MA -- to establish a special fund in honor of Louise B. Adams
10,000	Maritime Aquarium, Norwalk, CT -- for Harbor Seal Census Study
10,000	Science Center of Connecticut, West Hartford, CT -- for collaborative environmental education program
10,000	Teachers College Columbia University, New York, NY -- for the Private School Leadership Program
10,000	University of Hartford, Hartford, CT -- for educational main street - a tutoring program
9,000	New Haven Ecology Project, New Haven, CT -- support for the agricultural, science and environmental education programs

BARNES GROUP INC.

Company Headquarters
123 Main Street
PO Box 489
Bristol, CT 06011-0489
Phone: (860)583-7070
Fax: (860)589-7466
Web: http://www.barnesgroupinc.com

Company Description
Founded: 1857
Ticker: B
Exchange: NYSE
Revenue: US$784 million (2002)
Employees: 6026 (2003)
SIC(s): 3465 Automotive Stampings, 3493 Steel Springs Except Wire, 3495 Wire Springs, 3496 Miscellaneous Fabricated Wire Products.

Operating Locations
Barnes Group Inc. (CA--Gardena; CT--East Windsor, Windsor; GA--Norcross; IL--Rockford; MI--Lansing, Saline, Ypsilanti; MS--Meridian; NJ--Edison; NY--Syracuse; OH--Cleveland, Dayton; PA--Corry; TN--Memphis; TX--Arlington, Dallas; UT--Ogden; WA--Auburn; WI--Milwaukee, New Berlin)

Barnes Group Foundation Inc.

Giving Contact
Thomas Barnes, Secretary
123 Main Street
PO Box 489
Bristol, CT 06011-0489
Phone: (860)583-7070
Fax: (860)589-7466

Alternate Contact
Scholarship Application Contact
Citizen Scholarship Foundation of America
1505 Riverview Road
PO Box 297
St. Peter, MN 56082
Phone: (603)627-3870

Description
EIN: 237339727
Organization Type: Corporate Foundation
Giving Locations: operating communities.
Grant Types: General Support, Scholarship.

Financial Summary
Total Giving: $821,755 (2003); $775,913 (2002); $670,933 (2001). Note: Contributes through foundation only.
Giving Analysis: Giving for 2002 includes: foundation grants to United Way ($89,764); foundation scholarships ($218,472); 2001: foundation grants to United Way ($60,699); foundation scholarships ($151,050); foundation ($459,184)
Assets: $955,369 (2003); $1,183,670 (2002); $1,748,961 (2001)
Gifts Received: $400,005 (2003); $397,775 (2002); $500,000 (1998). Note: Contributions were received from Barnes Group Inc.

Typical Recipients
Arts & Humanities: Arts Associations & Councils, Arts Centers, Arts Festivals, Community Arts, Dance, Historic Preservation, Libraries, Museums/Galleries, Music, Opera, Performing Arts, Public Broadcasting, Theater
Civic & Public Affairs: African American Affairs, Clubs, Community Foundations, Economic Development, Civic & Public Affairs-General, Housing, Law & Justice, Legal Aid, Minority Business, Municipalities/Towns, Professional & Trade Associations, Public Policy, Safety, Urban & Community Affairs, Zoos/Aquariums
Education: Afterschool/Enrichment Programs, Business Education, Business-School Partnerships, Colleges & Universities, Community & Junior Colleges, Economic Education, Education Funds, Elementary Education (Private), Elementary Education (Public), Engineering/Technological Education, Environmental Education, Education-General, Leadership Training, Minority Education, Private Education (Precollege), Public Education (Precollege), Religious Education, Science/Mathematics Education, Secondary Education (Private), Special Education, Student Aid, Vocational & Technical Education
Environment: Air/Water Quality, Environment-General
Health: Cancer, Children's Health/Hospitals, Clinics/Medical Centers, Emergency/Ambulance Services, Health Funds, Hospitals, Medical Research, Single-Disease Health Associations, Trauma Treatment
International: International Relief Efforts
Religion: Religious Organizations
Science: Science Museums
Social Services: Big Brothers/Big Sisters, Child Welfare, Community Service Organizations, Crime Prevention, Family Services, Homes, People with Disabilities, Recreation & Athletics, Scouts, Senior Services, Special Olympics, Substance Abuse, Unit-

ed Funds/United Ways, YMCA/YWCA/YMHA/
YWHA, Youth Organizations

Application Procedures
Initial Contact: Write or call an operating division of
the company requesting application form.
Application Requirements: State purpose, history
of organization, describe project, annual itemized
budget, project budget, foundation and corporate donors, and 501(c)(3) exemption letter.
Deadlines: March 1.
Decision Notification: Board meets four times per
year.

Restrictions
To be an eligible candidate for the scholarship grant,
applicants must be a child of either a current Barnes
Group employee in the US or Canada who has
worked for the company at least one year by the application deadline, or a retired employee.
The foundation does not support political or lobbying
efforts.

Additional Information
Publications: Contributions Policy; Guidelines

Corporate Officials
Thomas O. Barnes: board chairmans B 1949. PRIM
CORP EMPL board chairman: Barnes Group Inc.
CORP AFFIL chairman: Chapman Machine Co. Inc.
John Edward Besser: senior vice president finance
& law B Iowa City, IA 1942. ED University of Rochester AB (1964); Northwestern University JD (1967).
PRIM CORP EMPL senior vice president finance &
law: Barnes Group Inc. NONPR AFFIL member: Missouri Bar Association; board electors: Wadsworth
Atheneum; member: American Bar Association; director: Greater Hartford Arts Council.
Edmund Mogford Carpenter: president, chief executive officer B Lodi, CA December 28, 1941. ED University of Michigan BS (1963); University of Michigan
MBA (1964). PRIM CORP EMPL president, chief executive officer: Barnes Group Inc. CORP AFFIL di-
rector: Electroglas Inc.; director: ChevronTexaco Inc.;
director: Dana Corp.; director: Campbell Soup Co.
NONPR AFFIL director: Junior Achievement; mem-
ber: Machinery & Allied Products Institute.
John J. Locher: vice president, treasurer B 1944. ED
Fordham University BA (1966); New York University
Leonard N. Stern School of Business MBA (1971).
PRIM CORP EMPL vice president, treasurer: Barnes
Group Inc.

Foundation Officials
John R. Arrington: director
Thomas O. Barnes: secretary, director (see above)
Edmund Mogford Carpenter: president, director
(see above)
William C. Denninger: vice president
Signe S. Gates: director

Grants Analysis
Disclosure Period: calendar year ending 2003
Total Grants: $453,882*
Number of Grants: 334
Average Grant: $1,359
Highest Grant: $25,000
Lowest Grant: $6
Typical Range: $300 to $3,000
*Note: Giving excludes United Way and scholar-
ships.

Recent Grants
Note: Grants derived from 2003 Form 990.
Library-Related
5,000	Farmington Library, Farmington, CT

General
139,044	Citizens' Scholarship Foundation of Ad-ministation, Minneapolis, MN
139,044	Citizens' Scholarship Foundation of America, Minneapolis, MN
66,992	United Way, Bristol, CT

25,000	Bristol Hospital Development Founda-tion, Bristol, CT
15,000	Bushnell, Hartford, CT
12,500	Connecticut Children's Hospital Center, Hartford, CT
12,000	Greater Hartford Arts Center, Hartford, CT
11,000	Greater Hartford Jaycees Foundation, Hartford, CT
10,000	Connecticut Public Broadcasting Inc., Hartford, CT
10,000	Connecticut Public Broadcasting Inc., Hartford, CT

BARRA FOUNDATION

Giving Contact
William Harral, III, President & Director
The Barra Foundation, Inc.
8200 Flourtown Avenue, Suite 12
Wyndmoor, PA 19038-7976
Phone: (215)836-1030
Fax: (215)836-1033

Description
Founded: 1963
EIN: 236277885
Organization Type: General Purpose Foundation
Giving Locations: PA: Philadelphia
Grant Types: Conference/Seminar, General Sup-
port, Matching, Project, Research, Seed Money.

Donor Information
Founder: Established in 1963 by Robert L. McNeil
Jr., who currently serves as chairman and treasurer
of the foundation.

Financial Summary
Total Giving: $2,141,031 (2002); $2,294,000 (2001)
Giving Analysis: Giving for 2002 includes: founda-
tion grants to United Way ($13,500)
Assets: $43,391,140 (2002); $50,692,059 (2001)
Gifts Received: $1,003 (2000); $5,034,000 (1997).
Note: In 1997, contributions were received from Rob-
ert L. McNeil, Jr.

Typical Recipients
Arts & Humanities: Arts Associations & Councils,
Arts Centers, Arts Funds, Arts Institutes, Ballet, Com-
munity Arts, Dance, Ethnic & Folk Arts, Historic Pres-
ervation, History & Archaeology, Libraries, Literary
Arts, Museums/Galleries, Opera, Performing Arts,
Public Broadcasting, Theater
Civic & Public Affairs: Botanical Gardens/Parks,
Business/Free Enterprise, Chambers of Commerce,
Civil Rights, Clubs, Community Foundations, Eco-
nomic Development, Employment/Job Training, First
Amendment Issues, Civic & Public Affairs-General,
Hispanic Affairs, Housing, Philanthropic Organiza-
tions, Professional & Trade Associations, Public Poli-
cy, Urban & Community Affairs, Women's Affairs,
Zoos/Aquariums
Education: Afterschool/Enrichment Programs, Arts/
Humanities Education, Colleges & Universities, Com-
munity & Junior Colleges, Economic Education, Edu-
cation Associations, Education Reform, Education-
General, Health & Physical Education, Leadership
Training, Literacy, Medical Education, Minority Education, Private Education (Precollege), Religious Education, Science/Mathematics Education, Social Sciences Education
Environment: Air/Water Quality, Environment-
General, Resource Conservation, Watershed
Health: Alzheimer's Disease, Cancer, Children's
Health/Hospitals, Clinics/Medical Centers, Emergen-
cy/Ambulance Services, Health-General, Health Organizations, Home-Care Services, Hospices, Hospitals, Hospitals (University Affiliated), Long-Term

Care, Medical Rehabilitation, Medical Research, Pre-
ventive Medicine/Wellness Organizations, Public
Health, Single-Disease Health Associations
International: Foreign Arts Organizations, Foreign
Educational Institutions, International Relations, In-
ternational Relief Efforts
Religion: Churches, Religion-General, Jewish
Causes, Religious Organizations, Religious Welfare
Science: Science-General, Scientific Centers & Insti-
tutes, Scientific Research
Social Services: Animal Protection, At-Risk Youth,
Child Welfare, Community Service Organizations,
Day Care, Emergency Relief, Family Planning, Fami-
ly Services, Food/Clothing Distribution, Homes, Peo-
ple with Disabilities, Scouts, Senior Services, Shel-
ters/Homelessness, Social Services-General, United
Funds/United Ways, Volunteer Services, Youth Or-
ganizations

Application Procedures
Initial Contact: Send in a preliminary letter not exceeding two pages.
Application Requirements: The preliminary letter
should serve as request for funding, summarizing the
objectives and significance of the project; the methodology; qualifications of the investigator; estimated
timetable; project budget and other sources of support; the organization's history and goals; listing of officers and directors; and a copy of the IRS tax-
exemption ruling. If the letter indicates that the project
may fall within the foundation's interest, a formal application will be sent.
Deadlines: None.
Review Process: Upon receipt, the project will be
submitted to the foundation's advisors for evaluation
and recommendation to the board of directors. The
board meets in November, and as appropriate. The
evaluation process may take three to six months. Applicants will be notified of a final decision.

Restrictions
Most grants are restricted to the greater Philadelphia
community. The foundation does not provide support
for ongoing operating expenses, budget deficits, endowment or capital campaigns (including construction, equipment, renovation, or repairs), publications,
exhibitions or catalogues, international programs and
institutions, or individual scholarships or fellowships.

Additional Information
Publications: Guidelines; Application Form; Program Policy Statement

Foundation Officials
Harry E. Cerino: director
Frank R. Donahue, Jr.: secretary, director
Robert Paul Hauptfuhrer: director B Philadelphia,
PA 1931. ED Princeton University BA (1953); Har-
vard University Graduate School of Business Administration MBA (1957). PRIM CORP EMPL chairman,
chief executive officer, director: Oryx Energy Co.
CORP AFFIL director: Quaker Chemical Corp.
NONPR AFFIL trustee: Princeton University; chair-
man board advisors: University Pennsylvania Cancer
Center; member: National Petroleum Council; mem-
ber: Natural Gas Supply Association; member, board
governors: Dallas Symphony Association; member:
National Association Manufacturers; member: Con-
ference Board; member: American Petroleum Insti-
tute; director: American Productivity & Quality Control
Center. CLUB AFFIL Union League Club; Philadel-
phia Country Club; Pine Valley Golf Club; Merion
Cricket Club.
Herman R. Hutchinson: vice president, director
Victoria M. Levine: director
Joanna M. Lewis: director
Collin F. McNeil: director
Robert L. McNeil, Jr.: president, treasurer, director
CORP AFFIL director: Arrow International Inc.
Seymour S. Preston, III: director
Lowell S. Thomas, Jr.: director

Grants Analysis

Disclosure Period: calendar year ending 2002
Total Grants: $2,127,531*
Number of Grants: 263
Average Grant: $4,789*
Highest Grant: $500,000
Lowest Grant: $1,000
Typical Range: $1,000 to $25,000 and $50,000 to $70,000
*****Note:** Giving excludes United Way. Average grant figure excludes four highest grants ($785,640).

Recent Grants

Note: Grants derived from 2002 Form 990.
Library-Related

49,000	Athenaeum of Philadelphia, Philadelphia, PA -- Retroconversion Project
10,000	Athenaeum of Philadelphia, Philadelphia, PA -- William Birch Catalogue
7,500	Athenaeum of Philadelphia, Philadelphia, PA

General

500,000	Trustees of University of Pennsylvania, Philadelphia, PA -- MCEAS
125,000	Academy of Music of Philadelphia, Philadelphia, PA -- capital campaign
85,640	Drexel University, Philadelphia, PA -- digitize costume collection
75,000	American Philosophical Society, Philadelphia, PA -- Carter Fellows
75,000	Metropolitan Career Center, Philadelphia, PA -- STRIVE Program
69,172	Historical Society of Pennsylvania, Philadelphia, PA -- retrospective conversion
56,950	Germantown Academy, Ft. Washington, PA -- distance learning
55,422	Academy of Natural Sciences of Philadelphia, Philadelphia, PA -- electronic data delivery
50,000	Children's Literacy Initiative, Philadelphia, PA -- classroom training
47,100	WHYY-TV 12, Philadelphia, PA -- Thomas Eakins documentary

BARRINGTON FOUNDATION

Giving Contact

David Strassler, President
Barrington Foundation
PO Box 750
Great Barrington, MA 01230
Phone: (914)285-9393

Description

Founded: 1978
EIN: 132930849
Organization Type: Private Foundation
Giving Locations: MA
Grant Types: General Support, Multiyear/Continuing Support, Project.

Financial Summary

Total Giving: $817,115 (2004); $897,750 (2002)
Giving Analysis: Giving for 2002 includes: foundation grants to United Way ($3,000)
Assets: $2,528,510 (2004); $1,056,475 (2002)
Gifts Received: $1,974,000 (2004); $763,814 (2002); $425,130 (2000). Note: In 2002, contributions were received from Berkshire Hathaway ($5,814), David Strassler ($203,000), Abbie Strassler ($50,000), Alan Strassler ($30,000), and Robert Strassler ($475,000). In 2000, contributions were received from Berkshire Hathaway ($6,930), David Strassler ($388,200), Abbie Strassler ($20,000), and Kathleen Ward ($10,000). In 1999, contributions were received from Berkshire Hathaway. In 1998,

contributions were received from David H. Strassler. In 1994, contributions were received from Alan Strassler ($20,000), Karen Strassler ($20,000), Matthew Strassler ($30,000), Abbie Strassler ($20,000), Gary and Monica Strassler ($6,000), and Berkshire Hathaway ($15,719).

Typical Recipients

Arts & Humanities: Arts Associations & Councils, Arts Funds, Dance, Arts & Humanities-General, Historic Preservation, History & Archaeology, Libraries, Museums/Galleries, Music, Theater
Civic & Public Affairs: Community Foundations, Civic & Public Affairs-General, Hispanic Affairs, Public Policy, Urban & Community Affairs, Women's Affairs
Education: Arts/Humanities Education, Colleges & Universities, Continuing Education, Education-General, International Studies, Private Education (Precollege), Science/Mathematics Education, Student Aid
Environment: Environment-General, Resource Conservation, Wildlife Protection
Health: AIDS/HIV, Cancer, Children's Health/Hospitals, Clinics/Medical Centers, Emergency/Ambulance Services, Hospices, Hospitals, Long-Term Care, Mental Health, Single-Disease Health Associations
International: Foreign Educational Institutions, Human Rights, International Affairs, International Development, Missionary/Religious Activities
Religion: Jewish Causes, Religious Organizations
Social Services: Community Service Organizations, Crime Prevention, Family Planning, Family Services, Food/Clothing Distribution, People with Disabilities, United Funds/United Ways

Application Procedures

Application Requirements: No specific application deadlines.
Deadlines: None.

Foundation Officials

David H. Strassler: president
Robert B. Strassler: secretary, treasurer

Grants Analysis

Disclosure Period: calendar year ending 2004
Total Grants: $817,115
Number of Grants: 112
Average Grant: $5,519*
Highest Grant: $90,500
Lowest Grant: $500
Typical Range: $1,000 to $10,000
*****Note:** Average grant excludes three highest grants ($215,500).

Recent Grants

Note: Grants derived from 2001 Form 990.

General

75,000	Princeton University, Princeton, NJ
65,800	Recording for the Blind, Lenox, MA
65,000	Medici Archive Project, New York, NY
54,000	Aston Magna Foundation for Music, Danbury, CT
51,000	Simons Rock College of Bard, Great Barrington, MA
45,000	Ackerman Institute for Family Therapy, New York, NY
33,000	Anti-Defamation League of B'nai B'rith, New York, NY
26,000	Clark University, Worcester, MA
25,000	ACCION International, Boston, MA
25,000	American Academy in Rome, New York, NY

GERALDINE AND R. A. BARROWS FOUNDATION

Giving Contact

Stephen J. Campbell, Trust Officer
c/o UMB Bank
1010 Grand
Kansas City, MO 64106
Phone: (816)860-7711

Description

Founded: 1979
EIN: 431184875
Organization Type: Private Foundation
Giving Locations: MO: Kansas City
Grant Types: Endowment, General Support, Research.

Donor Information

Founder: the late G. M. Barrows

Financial Summary

Total Giving: $365,636 (2001)
Assets: $8,024,702 (2001)
Gifts Received: In 1991, contributions were received from a trust under the will of G.M. Barrows for benefit of Helen Bueker.

Typical Recipients

Arts & Humanities: Arts Institutes, Ballet, Libraries, Museums/Galleries, Music, Opera, Performing Arts, Public Broadcasting, Theater
Civic & Public Affairs: Botanical Gardens/Parks, Community Foundations, Economic Policy, Civic & Public Affairs-General, Housing, Rural Affairs, Women's Affairs, Zoos/Aquariums
Education: Colleges & Universities, Education-General, Private Education (Precollege)
Health: Cancer, Children's Health/Hospitals, Clinics/Medical Centers, Health Organizations, Hospices, Hospitals, Medical Rehabilitation, Medical Research, Single-Disease Health Associations
Religion: Churches, Religious Welfare, Seminaries
Social Services: At-Risk Youth, Child Welfare, Day Care, Domestic Violence, People with Disabilities, Recreation & Athletics, Scouts, YMCA/YWCA/YMHA/YWHA, Youth Organizations

Application Procedures

Initial Contact: The foundation requests applications be made in writing.
Deadlines: None.

Restrictions

Limited to underprivileged children and cancer research in the Kansas City, MO area.

Additional Information

Trust(s): UMB Bank

Grants Analysis

Disclosure Period: calendar year ending 2001
Total Grants: $365,636
Number of Grants: 20
Average Grant: $12,665*
Highest Grant: $125,000
Lowest Grant: $1,000
Typical Range: $5,000 to $30,000
*****Note:** Average grant figure excludes highest grant.

Recent Grants

Note: Grants derived from 2002 Form 990.
Library-Related

5,000	Harry S. Truman Library Institute, Independence, MO

General

125,000	Agricultural Future of America, Kansas City, MO
50,000	Barstow School, Kansas City, MO

50,000	Kansas City Rose Society, Kansas City, KS
50,000	KCPT Public Television 19, Kansas City, MO
50,000	Teel Institute, Kansas City, MO
25,000	Boy Scouts of America
25,000	Kansas City Symphony, Kansas City, MO -- for operating expenses
17,500	Camp Fire Heartland Council, Columbia, MO
10,000	Central United Methodist Church, Kansas City, MO
10,000	Heart of America Family Services, Kansas City, MO

BARSTOW FOUNDATION

Giving Contact

Bruce M. Groom, Senior Vice President & Senior Trust Officer
c/o Chemical Bank and Trust Co.
235 E. Main St.
Midland, MI 48640
Phone: (989)839-5305

Description

Founded: 1967
EIN: 386151026
Organization Type: Private Foundation
Giving Locations: MI: Midland County
Grant Types: General Support, Operating Expenses, Project.

Donor Information

Founder: the late Florence K. Barstow

Financial Summary

Total Giving: $297,500 (2004); $517,100 (2001)
Assets: $8,070,610 (2004); $6,557,896 (2001)
Gifts Received: $469,188 (2001); $16,000 (2000); $100,057 (1993). Note: In 2001, contributions were received from Ruth Dixon. In 2000, contributions were received from Sedona Community Food Bank, Seconda, AZ. In 1993, contributions were received from the final distribution of the F. K. Barstow Charitable Annuity Trust.

Typical Recipients

Arts & Humanities: Arts Centers, Dance, Ethnic & Folk Arts, Arts & Humanities-General, History & Archaeology, Libraries, Museums/Galleries, Music, Theater
Civic & Public Affairs: Community Foundations, Civic & Public Affairs-General, Housing, Municipalities/Towns, Urban & Community Affairs
Education: Afterschool/Enrichment Programs, Arts/Humanities Education, Colleges & Universities, Elementary Education (Private), Environmental Education, Faculty Development, Education-General, Literacy, Minority Education, Science/Mathematics Education, Student Aid
Environment: Air/Water Quality, Forestry, Environment-General, Protection, Resource Conservation, Watershed
Health: AIDS/HIV, Cancer, Mental Health, Prenatal Health Issues, Single-Disease Health Associations
International: Health Care/Hospitals, International Relief Efforts
Religion: Churches, Religious Welfare
Science: Science Museums, Scientific Centers & Institutes
Social Services: Animal Protection, Camps, Community Centers, Community Service Organizations, Domestic Violence, Emergency Relief, Family Services, Food/Clothing Distribution, Homes, Recreation & Athletics, Shelters/Homelessness, Social Services-General, Youth Organizations

Application Procedures

Initial Contact: Send cover letter and full proposal. Include organization's pamphlet or brochure, if available.
Deadlines: July 31.

Restrictions

Does not support individuals or research programs, or provide loans, scholarships, or fellowships.

Foundation Officials

David O. Barstow: trustee
John C. Barstow: trustee
Richard G. Barstow: co-chairman, trustee
Robert G. Barstow: trustee
Dr. Robert O. Barstow: trustee
Ruth B. Dixon: co-chairman, trustee
William R. Dixon: trustee
Bruce M. Groom: secretary, trustee

Grants Analysis

Disclosure Period: calendar year ending 2004
Total Grants: $297,500
Number of Grants: 11
Average Grant: $8,250*
Highest Grant: $215,000
Lowest Grant: $1,000
Typical Range: $5,000 to $25,000
*Note: Average grant figure excludes highest grant.

Recent Grants

Note: Grants derived from 2004 Form 990.
General

215,000	City of Midland, Midland, TX -- for recreation
25,000	Cooperative for Assistance and Relief Everywhere, Atlanta, GA -- for 2004 world hunger campaign
25,000	United States Fund for UNICEF, New York, NY -- towards HIV/AIDS in twelve Sub-Saharan nations
10,000	Helpmate Inc., Asheville, NC
8,000	Friends of the Blue Ridge Parkway, Roanoke, VA
5,000	American Red Cross, Washington, DC -- for disaster relief
5,000	Brevard Music Center, Brevard, NC -- towards scholarship
1,500	Presbyterian Home for Children, Austin, TX
1,000	Leukemia and Lymphoma Society, Pittsfield, MA
1,000	Park Day School, Oakland, CA

THE THEODORE H. BARTH FOUNDATION, INC.

Giving Contact

Ellen S. Berelson, President
Theodore H. Barth Foundation, Inc.
45 Rockefeller Plaza, Suite 2037
New York, NY 10111
Phone: (212)332-3466

Description

Founded: 1953
EIN: 136103401
Organization Type: General Purpose Foundation
Giving Locations: MA; NY
Grant Types: General Support, Scholarship.

Donor Information

Founder: Incorporated in 1953 by the late Theodore H. Barth.

Financial Summary

Total Giving: $1,337,563 (2001)
Assets: $28,963,033 (2001)

Typical Recipients

Arts & Humanities: Ballet, Dance, History & Archaeology, Libraries, Literary Arts, Museums/Galleries, Music, Opera, Performing Arts, Public Broadcasting, Theater, Visual Arts
Civic & Public Affairs: Botanical Gardens/Parks, Clubs, Community Foundations, Economic Development, Legal Aid, Urban & Community Affairs, Zoos/Aquariums
Education: Arts/Humanities Education, Colleges & Universities, Education Reform, Education-General, Legal Education, Literacy, Private Education (Precollege), Science/Mathematics Education, Special Education
Environment: Air/Water Quality, Environment-General, Resource Conservation, Wildlife Protection
Health: Children's Health/Hospitals, Clinics/Medical Centers, Health Funds, Health Organizations, Hospices, Hospitals, Kidney, Medical Research, Mental Health, Nursing Services, Public Health, Research/Studies Institutes, Single-Disease Health Associations, Speech & Hearing, Transplant Networks/Donor Banks
International: Foreign Arts Organizations
Religion: Churches, Jewish Causes, Religious Welfare
Science: Science Museums
Social Services: At-Risk Youth, Big Brothers/Big Sisters, Child Welfare, Community Centers, Community Service Organizations, Counseling, Day Care, Family Planning, Family Services, Food/Clothing Distribution, People with Disabilities, Recreation & Athletics, Scouts, Shelters/Homelessness, United Funds/United Ways, Youth Organizations

Application Procedures

Initial Contact: The foundation requests a general letter of interest.
Deadlines: None.

Restrictions

Grants are not made to individuals.

Foundation Officials

Ellen S. Berelson: vice president, director
Thelma D. Berelson: secretary, director

Grants Analysis

Disclosure Period: calendar year ending 2001
Total Grants: $1,337,563*
Number of Grants: 107
Average Grant: $8,775*
Highest Grant: $225,000
Lowest Grant: $750
Typical Range: $1,000 to $20,000
*Note: Giving includes scholarships. Average grant figure excludes three highest grants totaling $425,000.

Recent Grants

Note: Grants derived from 2001 Form 990.
Library-Related

20,000	New York Public Library, New York, NY

General

225,000	League for the Hard of Hearing, New York, NY
100,000	Metropolitan Opera Association, Inc., New York, NY
100,000	Southcoast Health Systems, Inc., New Bedford, MA
30,000	National Book Foundation, New York, NY
25,000	Metropolitan Museum of Art, New York, NY
25,000	New York City Opera, Inc., New York, NY
25,000	New York Law School, New York, NY
25,000	New York Philharmonic Symphony Society, New York, NY

20,000   City Harvest, New York, NY
20,000   Citymeals on Wheels, New York, NY

BARTLETT & CO.

Company Headquarters
4800 Main Street, Suite 600
Kansas City, MO 64112
Web: http://www.bartlettandco.com

Company Description
Employees: 525
SIC(s): 0211 Beef Cattle Feedlots, 2041 Flour &
Other Grain Mill Products, 5153 Grain & Field Beans.
Parent Company: Legg Mason Inc., PO Box 1476,
Baltimore, MD, United States

Bartlett & Co. Grain Charitable Foundation

Giving Contact
Arnold Wheeler, Chief Financial Officer
4800 Main Street, Suite 600
Kansas City, MO 64112-2510
Phone: (816)753-6300
Fax: (816)753-0062

Description
Founded: 1986
EIN: 436323269
Organization Type: Corporate Foundation
Giving Locations: MO
Grant Types: General Support.

Financial Summary
Total Giving: $78,350 (fiscal year ending April 30,
2004); $96,500 (fiscal 2001)
Assets: $1,736,566 (fiscal 2004); $1,990,016 (fiscal
2001)

Typical Recipients
Arts & Humanities: Arts & Humanities-General, History & Archaeology, Libraries, Museums/Galleries,
Music, Opera, Public Broadcasting, Theater
Civic & Public Affairs: Botanical Gardens/Parks,
Business/Free Enterprise, Community Foundations,
Civic & Public Affairs-General, Law & Justice, Legal
Aid, Professional & Trade Associations, Public Policy, Rural Affairs, Urban & Community Affairs
Education: Agricultural Education, Business Education, Colleges & Universities, Education Funds, Faculty Development, Education-General, Private Education (Precollege), Public Education (Precollege)
Environment: Resource Conservation
Health: AIDS/HIV, Children's Health/Hospitals, Clinics/Medical Centers, Health-General, Preventive
Medicine/Wellness Organizations, Public Health, Single-Disease Health Associations, Trauma Treatment
International: International-General
Religion: Religion-General, Jewish Causes, Ministries, Religious Welfare
Science: Science-General, Science Museums, Scientific Centers & Institutes
Social Services: At-Risk Youth, Child Welfare, Community Service Organizations, Crime Prevention,
People with Disabilities, Recreation & Athletics,
Scouts, Social Services-General

Application Procedures
Initial Contact: Send a brief letter of inquiry.
Application Requirements: Include a description of
organization, amount requested, and purpose of
funds sought.
Deadlines: None.

Restrictions
Does not support individuals, religious organizations
for sectarian purposes, or organizations outside operating areas.

Corporate Officials
Paul Dana Bartlett, Jr.: chairman, director B Kansas
City, MO September 16, 1919. ED Yale University BA
(1941). PRIM CORP EMPL chairman, director: Bartlett & Co. CORP AFFIL director: United Missouri
Bancshares; director: United Missouri Bank Financial
Corp.
James B. Hebenstreit: president PRIM CORP
EMPL president: Bartlett & Co.
Arnold Wheeler: chief financial officer PRIM CORP
EMPL chief financial officer: Bartlett & Co.

Foundation Officials
Paul Dana Bartlett, Jr.: trustee (see above)
James B. Hebenstreit: trustee (see above)

Grants Analysis
Disclosure Period: fiscal year ending April 30, 2004
Total Grants: $78,350
Number of Grants: 48
Average Grant: $1,241*
Highest Grant: $20,000
Lowest Grant: $100
Typical Range: $500 to $2,500
***Note:** Average grant figure excludes highest grant.

Recent Grants
Note: Grants derived from fiscal 2004 Form 990.
Library-Related
6,000   Linda Hall Library, Kansas City, MO
5,000   Harry S. Truman Library Institute, Independence, MO
General
20,000   Lyric Opera, Kansas City, MO
5,000   Kansas City Free Health Clinic, Kansas City, MO
5,000   Kemper Museum of Contemporary Art and Design, Kansas City, MO
3,600   UMKC Conservatory of Music, Kansas City, MO
3,000   Nelson Gallery Foundation, Kansas City, MO
2,500   Agriculture Future of America, Kansas City, MO
2,500   Lyric Opera, Kansas City, MO
2,500   Missouri Repertory Theatre, Kansas City, MO

BAT HANADIV FOUNDATION NO. 3

Giving Contact
Jerome Caufield, Attorney
Care of Carter Leoyard & Milburn
2 Wall Street, 13th Floor
New York, NY 10005
Phone: (212)732-3200
Fax: (212)732-3232

Description
Founded: 1981
EIN: 133091620
Organization Type: Specialized/Single Purpose
Foundation
Giving Locations: Israel
Grant Types: Fellowship, General Support, Operating Expenses, Project.

Donor Information
Founder: Established in 1981. All support received
since its inception has come from non-U.S. organizations, including Bat Hanadiv Foundation and Bat
Hanadiv Foundation No. 2.

Financial Summary
Total Giving: $5,943,848 (2003); $6,000,000 (2001)
Assets: $473,719,176 (2003); $224,696,237 (2001)

Typical Recipients
Arts & Humanities: Film & Video, Arts & Humanities-General, Museums/Galleries, Music
Civic & Public Affairs: Botanical Gardens/Parks,
Business/Free Enterprise, Community Foundations,
Employment/Job Training, Gay/Lesbian Issues, Civic
& Public Affairs-General, Law & Justice
Education: Colleges & Universities, Continuing Education, Economic Education, Education Associations,
Education Reform, Education-General, Private Education (Precollege), Religious Education, Science/
Mathematics Education
Environment: Environment-General, Resource
Conservation
Health: Hospices, Hospitals
International: Foreign Arts Organizations, Foreign
Educational Institutions, International-General,
Health Care/Hospitals, International Development,
International Environmental Issues, International Organizations, Missionary/Religious Activities
Religion: Jewish Causes
Science: Science-General, Scientific Centers & Institutes, Scientific Organizations
Social Services: Child Welfare, Substance Abuse

Application Procedures
Initial Contact: The foundation has no formal grant
application procedure or application form.
Deadlines: None.

Additional Information
The foundation lists the Doder Trust, Ltd., Hamilton,
Bermuda, as a corporate trustee.
The foundation reports that it is a foreign foundation
and that the majority of funds go to international organizations.

Grants Analysis
Disclosure Period: calendar year ending 2003
Total Grants: $5,943,848*
Typical Range: $5,000 to $100,000
***Note:** No grants list available for 2003

Recent Grants
Note: Grants derived from 2001 Form 990.
General
946,060   OUI -- new campus at Ra'Anana
600,000   CET - Center for Educational Technology, Tel Aviv Israel -- research & developments
550,000   OUI Fully Integrated Learning Environments
550,000   Water Research Institute, Haifa Israel
371,171   Ramat Hanadiv Israel -- construction visitors' center
347,934   C E T, Washington, DC -- English on-line
218,477   Ramat Hanadiv, Zichron Yaakov Israel -- for Nature Reserve-Spni 2001
192,698   Tel Aviv University -- study of Mediterranean Civilizations
169,195   Weizman Institute, Rehovot Israel -- for Scientific Archaeology Center
153,416   Victor Rothschild Memorial Symposia, Jerusalem Israel

BATTS FOUNDATION

Giving Contact
3855 Sparks Drive SE, Suite 222
Grand Rapids, MI 49546
Phone: (616)956-3053

Description

EIN: 382782168
Organization Type: Private Foundation
Giving Locations: MI: Grand Rapids, Holland
Grant Types: General Support.

Financial Summary

Total Giving: $109,500 (2004); $224,350 (2001)
Assets: $2,378,983 (2004); $2,555,399 (2001)
Gifts Received: $250,000 (1994); $250,000 (1992).
Note: In 1994, contributions were received from the Batts Group, Ltd.

Typical Recipients

Arts & Humanities: Arts Associations & Councils, Arts Centers, Arts Festivals, Film & Video, Arts & Humanities-General, History & Archaeology, Libraries, Museums/Galleries, Music, Opera, Performing Arts, Public Broadcasting
Civic & Public Affairs: Botanical Gardens/Parks, Chambers of Commerce, Clubs, Community Foundations, Economic Development, Employment/Job Training, Civic & Public Affairs-General, Housing, Municipalities/Towns, Nonprofit Management, Parades/Festivals, Philanthropic Organizations, Urban & Community Affairs, Women's Affairs, Zoos/Aquariums
Education: Business Education, Colleges & Universities, Community & Junior Colleges, Education Funds, Elementary Education (Private), Education-General, Private Education (Precollege), Public Education (Precollege), Science/Mathematics Education, Student Aid
Environment: Environment-General, Resource Conservation
Health: Cancer, Children's Health/Hospitals, Emergency/Ambulance Services, Health Funds, Health Organizations, Hospices, Hospitals, Long-Term Care, Medical Rehabilitation, Multiple Sclerosis, Public Health, Research/Studies Institutes, Trauma Treatment
International: Health Care/Hospitals, International Relief Efforts
Religion: Churches, Religious Organizations, Religious Welfare
Social Services: Community Service Organizations, Family Planning, Family Services, Food/Clothing Distribution, Homes, Scouts, Senior Services, Social Services-General, Substance Abuse, United Funds/United Ways, Youth Organizations

Application Procedures

Initial Contact: The foundation has no formal grant application procedure or application form.
Deadlines: None.

Foundation Officials

James L. Batts: director
John H. Batts: president, director
John T. Batts: director
Michael A. Batts: director
Robert H. Batts: director

Grants Analysis

Disclosure Period: calendar year ending 2004
Total Grants: $109,500
Number of Grants: 21
Average Grant: $3,658*
Highest Grant: $20,000
Lowest Grant: $500
Typical Range: $1,000 to $5,000
*Note: Average grant figure excludes two highest grants ($40,000).

Recent Grants

Note: Grants derived from 2004 Form 990.
Library-Related
20,000   Howard Miller Library, Holland, MI
General
20,000   Forest Hills Fine Arts Center, Grand Rapids, MI

20,000   Hope College, Holland, MI
10,000   DeVos Children's Hospital, Grand Rapids, MI
10,000   Porter Hills Foundation, Grand Rapids, MI
5,000   Davenport University, Grand Rapids, MI -- for Davenport foundation
5,000   Lost Tree Charitable Foundation, North Palm Beach, FL
5,000   Multiple Sclerosis Society, Grand Rapids, MI
2,500   Hospice of Holland, Holland, MI
1,500   Waterfront Festival, Saugatuck, MI -- for film festival

BAUER FAMILY FOUNDATION

Giving Contact

Paul D. Bauer, Trustee
60 Waterfront Cir.
Buffalo, NY 14202
Phone: (716)856-7020

Description

Founded: 1991
EIN: 161390793
Organization Type: Private Foundation
Grant Types: General Support.

Financial Summary

Total Giving: $119,041 (2003); $86,650 (2001)
Giving Analysis: Giving for 2003 includes: foundation scholarships ($1,000); 2001: foundation scholarships ($21,000)
Assets: $949,542 (2003); $1,092,458 (2001)
Gifts Received: $42,000 (2000); $33,000 (1993). Note: In 1993 and 2000, contributions were received from Paul D. Bauer.

Typical Recipients

Arts & Humanities: Libraries
Civic & Public Affairs: Civic & Public Affairs-General, Women's Affairs
Education: Colleges & Universities, Private Education (Precollege), Special Education, Student Aid
Health: AIDS/HIV, Cancer, Children's Health/Hospitals, Hospices, Hospitals
International: Foreign Educational Institutions, International Organizations, Missionary/Religious Activities
Religion: Churches, Dioceses, Religion-General, Ministries, Religious Organizations, Religious Welfare, Seminaries
Social Services: At-Risk Youth, Child Welfare, Community Service Organizations, Emergency Relief, Family Services, Food/Clothing Distribution, People with Disabilities, Shelters/Homelessness, Substance Abuse

Application Procedures

Initial Contact: Send a one-page brief letter.
Application Requirements: Include a a description of organization, amount requested, and proof of tax-exempt status.
Deadlines: None.

Foundation Officials

David P. Bauer: trustee
Lisa M. Bauer: trustee
Mary Grace Bauer: trustee
Paul D. Bauer: trustee

Grants Analysis

Disclosure Period: calendar year ending 2003
Total Grants: $118,041*
Number of Grants: 21

Average Grant: $4,752*
Highest Grant: $23,000
Lowest Grant: $500
Typical Range: $1,000 to $5,000
*Note: Giving excludes scholarships. Average grant figure excludes highest grant.

Recent Grants

Note: Grants derived from 2003 Form 990.
General
23,000   D'Youville College, Buffalo, NY
9,000   Catholic Charities, Buffalo, NY
9,000   St. Louis Church, Buffalo, NY
8,500   Catholic Health System, Buffalo, NY
6,000   Dominican Nuns, Buffalo, NY
5,000   Niagara University, Niagara Falls, NY
5,000   St. Joseph's Orphanage, Madras, TN India
3,000   Children's Hospital of Buffalo, Buffalo, NY
2,000   Canisius High School, Buffalo, NY
2,000   St. Adalbert's Parish, Buffalo, NY -- donation for food for needy

CHARLES M. BAUERVIC FOUNDATION

Giving Contact

Executive Director
10260 East Hilltop Road
Suttons Bay, MI 49682
Phone: (248)643-4545

Description

Founded: 1967
EIN: 386146352
Organization Type: Private Foundation
Giving Locations: MI
Grant Types: General Support, Operating Expenses, Project.

Donor Information

Founder: the late Charles M. Bauervic

Financial Summary

Total Giving: $109,000 (2003)
Assets: $3,938,214 (2003)

Typical Recipients

Arts & Humanities: Arts Centers, Arts Outreach, History & Archaeology, Libraries, Museums/Galleries, Music, Opera, Performing Arts
Civic & Public Affairs: Civil Rights, Employment/Job Training, Civic & Public Affairs-General, Housing, Legal Aid, Public Policy, Safety, Urban & Community Affairs
Education: Arts/Humanities Education, Colleges & Universities, Continuing Education, Elementary Education (Private), Education-General, Leadership Training, Medical Education, Minority Education, Private Education (Precollege), Religious Education, Science/Mathematics Education, Secondary Education (Private), Student Aid
Health: Alzheimer's Disease, Clinics/Medical Centers, Emergency/Ambulance Services, Health-General, Health Organizations, Hospices, Long-Term Care, Medical Research, Public Health
International: Foreign Educational Institutions, Health Care/Hospitals
Religion: Dioceses, Religious Organizations, Religious Welfare, Social/Policy Issues
Science: Science Exhibits & Fairs
Social Services: At-Risk Youth, Camps, People with Disabilities, Social Services-General, Special Olympics, Youth Organizations

Application Procedures

Initial Contact: Return completed application form. Include title and description of project, itemized bud-

get, proof of tax-exempt status, any material that will supplement the project proposal, two copies of the past five year's financial reports, and a report of all funds received to date.
Deadlines: April 30.

Restrictions

Grants are awarded primarily for educational purposes.

Additional Information

Publications: Application Form

Foundation Officials

Kathryn Leonard: director
Patricia A. Leonard: president, secretary
Theodore J. Leonard: treasurer
Timothy J. Leonard: director

Grants Analysis

Disclosure Period: calendar year ending 2003
Total Grants: $109,000
Number of Grants: 26
Average Grant: $4,192
Highest Grant: $10,000
Lowest Grant: $1,000
Typical Range: $1,000 to $10,000

Recent Grants

Note: Grants derived from 2001 Form 990.
General

15,000	Institute in Basic life Principles, Oak Brook, IL -- for character first program
10,000	Educational Center for Life, Troy, MI -- for educational materials for radio and internet publicity
10,000	Everest Academy, Clarkston, MI -- for library books and the music program
10,000	Franciscan University of Steubenville, Steubenville, OH -- for computer lab equipment update
10,000	Hillsdale College, Hillsdale, MI -- for the Center for Teacher Training
10,000	Madonna University, Livonia, MI -- for dietetics equipment to access therapeutic nutrition
10,000	Seton Home Study School, Front Royal, VA -- for printing of new 5th grade books
10,000	Southwest College of Naturopathic Medicine, Tempe, AZ -- for three document cameras and for visiting instructors education and promotion costs
10,000	Walsh College, Troy, MI -- for Online Learning Program
8,000	Right to Life of Michigan, Grand Rapids, MI -- for Direct Connect Program

BAUERVIC-PAISLEY FOUNDATION

Giving Contact

Beverly Paisley, President & Director
501 E. Mullet Lake Rd.
Indian River, MI 49749
Phone: (231)238-7817

Description

Founded: 1984
EIN: 382494390
Organization Type: Private Foundation
Giving Locations: MI
Grant Types: Capital, General Support, Operating Expenses.

Financial Summary

Total Giving: $10,000 (2004); $73,500 (2001)
Assets: $1,199,467 (2004); $1,725,357 (2001)

Typical Recipients

Arts & Humanities: Arts Associations & Councils, Libraries, Museums/Galleries, Music, Opera
Civic & Public Affairs: Clubs, Community Foundations, Civic & Public Affairs-General, Municipalities/Towns, Urban & Community Affairs
Education: Afterschool/Enrichment Programs, Business-School Partnerships, Colleges & Universities, Education Funds, Elementary Education (Private), Education-General, International Exchange, Private Education (Precollege), Public Education (Precollege), Science/Mathematics Education, Secondary Education (Private), Student Aid
Health: Alzheimer's Disease, Children's Health/Hospitals, Heart, Hospices, Hospitals, Long-Term Care, Mental Health, Prenatal Health Issues, Public Health
Religion: Religious Organizations, Religious Welfare
Science: Scientific Centers & Institutes, Scientific Labs
Social Services: At-Risk Youth, Camps, Community Centers, Community Service Organizations, Delinquency & Criminal Rehabilitation, Family Services, People with Disabilities, Recreation & Athletics, Social Services-General, Substance Abuse, Volunteer Services, Youth Organizations

Application Procedures

Initial Contact: Contact the foundation to obtain an application form.
Application Requirements: Include title and description of project, itemized budget, approval from the institution where the project will be done, year-end financial statement, proof of tax-exempt status, and the way in which project completion will be visually confirmed.
Deadlines: October 1.

Restrictions

No grants are awarded to individuals.

Foundation Officials

Beverly Paisley: president, director
Bonnie Paisley: director
Charles Paisley: director
Martha Paisley: vice president, director
Peter Paisley, Jr.: director
Peter W. Paisley: director

Grants Analysis

Disclosure Period: calendar year ending 2004
Total Grants: $10,000
Number of Grants: 6
Highest Grant: $5,000
Lowest Grant: $1,000
Typical Range: $1,000 to $5,000

Recent Grants

Note: Grants derived from 2001 Form 990.
Library-Related

2,500	St. Mary Catholic Central High -- for Alumni Program

General

10,000	Hospice of the Straits -- for building addition
10,000	Skidmore College, Saratoga Springs, NY -- for Athletic Program
5,000	Academy of Sacred Heart, New Orleans, LA -- for After School Learning Center
5,000	Cheboygan Youth Center, Cheboygan, MI -- enhancement of children's programming
5,000	Friends of the Broadway, Mt. Pleasant, MI -- to organize Broadway Children's Group
5,000	Henry Ford Museum and Greenfield Village, Dearborn, MI -- School Partnership and Scholarship Program
5,000	Hospice of Little Traverse Bay, Petoskey, MI -- counselor for Bereavement Program

5,000	Tuscarora Township, Indian River, MI -- for Project Playland
3,500	Wellspring, Fairfax, VA -- for Academic and Job Development Program
3,400	Novi Community That Cares, Novi, MI -- for building addition

BAUGHMAN FOUNDATION

Giving Contact

Eugene W. Slaymaker, President
PO Box 1356
Liberal, KS 67905-1356
Phone: (620)624-1371
Fax: (620)624-4177
E-mail: baughman@swko.net

Description

Founded: 1958
EIN: 486108797
Organization Type: General Purpose Foundation
Giving Locations: KS: Liberal
Grant Types: Capital, Endowment, Operating Expenses, Project, Scholarship.

Donor Information

Founder: Incorporated in 1958 by the late Robert W. Baughman and John W. Baughman Farms Co.

Financial Summary

Total Giving: $1,290,771 (2001)
Giving Analysis: Giving for 2001 includes: foundation grants to United Way ($2,000)

Typical Recipients

Arts & Humanities: Arts Associations & Councils, Arts Funds, Arts Outreach, Ethnic & Folk Arts, Historic Preservation, History & Archaeology, Libraries, Museums/Galleries, Music, Public Broadcasting
Civic & Public Affairs: Botanical Gardens/Parks, Chambers of Commerce, Community Foundations, Economic Development, Employment/Job Training, Civic & Public Affairs-General, Housing, Law & Justice, Municipalities/Towns, Parades/Festivals, Philanthropic Organizations, Public Policy, Safety, Urban & Community Affairs, Women's Affairs
Education: Agricultural Education, Colleges & Universities, Community & Junior Colleges, Economic Education, Education Funds, Faculty Development, Education-General, Leadership Training, Legal Education, Medical Education, Preschool Education, Private Education (Precollege), Public Education (Precollege), Religious Education, Science/Mathematics Education, Student Aid, Vocational & Technical Education
Environment: Environment-General
Health: Alzheimer's Disease, Children's Health/Hospitals, Clinics/Medical Centers, Diabetes, Emergency/Ambulance Services, Health Organizations, Hospitals, Mental Health, Single-Disease Health Associations
Religion: Ministries, Missionary Activities (Domestic), Religious Organizations, Religious Welfare
Science: Science Museums
Social Services: Animal Protection, Big Brothers/Big Sisters, Child Welfare, Community Centers, Community Service Organizations, Counseling, Crime Prevention, Day Care, Domestic Violence, Emergency Relief, Family Services, Homes, People with Disabilities, Recreation & Athletics, Scouts, Senior Services, Sexual Abuse, Shelters/Homelessness, Social Services-General, Substance Abuse, United Funds/United Ways, Youth Organizations

Application Procedures

Initial Contact: The foundation requests applications be made in writing.
Application Requirements: Applicants should sub-

mit proposal stating need, availability of other funding, and amount requested.

Deadlines: None. Applicants must submit proposals prior to 10 a.m. Central Time on the second Wednesday of each month to be reviewed at that month's meeting.

Review Process: The foundation reviews proposals on a monthly basis.

Restrictions

Grants are made only to organizations with tax-exempt status under IRS section 501(c)(3) and which are not private foundations. No grants are given to individuals.

Foundation Officials

Carol Feather-Francis: vice president, trustee
Eugene W. Slaymaker: president, trustee
James R. Yoxall: secretary, treasurer, trustee PRIM CORP EMPL treasurer: Hitch Land & Cattle Co. Inc. CORP AFFIL secretary: Keating Tractor & Equipment.

Grants Analysis

Disclosure Period: calendar year ending 2001
Total Grants: $1,288,771*
Number of Grants: 93
Average Grant: $13,858
Highest Grant: $160,000
Lowest Grant: $500
Typical Range: $1,000 to $20,000
***Note:** Giving includes United Way.

Recent Grants

Note: Grants derived from 2002 Form 990.
Library-Related

10,000	Liberal Memorial Library, Liberal, KS -- towards book fund
6,275	Kismet Public Library, Kismet, KS -- towards upgrades and furniture for computers

General

217,500	SCCC Development Foundation, Liberal, KS -- for scholarship funds, student liability and dorms
105,000	USD 480, Liberal, KS -- for sound system and books for schools
70,000	Southwest Kansas Technical School, Liberal, KS -- for scholarships
40,000	Baker Arts Center, Liberal, KS -- operations & new parking lot
39,633	Washington Elementary and Middle Schools, Liberal, KS -- towards student achievement program
35,000	Original Town of Liberal Revitalization Inc, Liberal, KS -- to purchase renovate and sell two properties
35,000	Seward County Historical Museum, Liberal, KS -- for staff development and termite extermination
34,600	City of Liberal Police Dept., Liberal, KS -- for equipment
32,000	City of Liberal Parks and Recreation Dept., Liberal, KS -- for recreation and summer programs
25,700	City of Liberal Parks and Recreation Dept., Liberal, KS -- for bleachers cover and pave parking lot

BAUSCH & LOMB INC.

Company Headquarters

Rochester, NY
Web: http://www.bausch.com

Company Description

Founded: 1853
Ticker: BOL

Exchange: NYSE
Revenue: US$1.816 billion (2002)
Employees: 11600 (2003)
SIC(s): 3479 Metal Coating & Allied Services, 3634 Electric Housewares & Fans, 3827 Optical Instruments & Lenses, 3851 Ophthalmic Goods.

Operating Locations

Bausch & Lomb Inc. (CA--Yorba Linda; CT--Lebanon, Storrs; FL--Miami, Sarasota, Summerland Key; GA--Atlanta, Colbert, Tucker; IL--Roanoke; ME--Windham; MA--Norwood, Southbridge, West Brookfield, Wilmington; MI--Portage; MN--Golden Valley; MO--O'Fallon; NE--Omaha; NH--Pittsfield; NJ--Newfield; NY--Stone Ridge; NC--Williamston; PA--Reinholds, Williamsport; SC--Greenville; TX--Houston, San Antonio; VA--Lynchburg)
Note: Operates in Canada, the Caribbean, Latin America, Europe, Australia, and Asia.

Nonmonetary Support

Type: In-kind Services

Bausch & Lomb Foundation, Inc.

Giving Contact

Barbara M. Kelley, Vice President
One Bausch & Lomb Place
Rochester, NY 14604-2701
Phone: (585)338-6000
Fax: (585)338-6007

Description

EIN: 166039442
Organization Type: Corporate Foundation
Giving Locations: NY: Rochester
Grant Types: General Support.

Financial Summary

Total Giving: $473,700 (fiscal year ending December 29, 2003); $1,075,784 (fiscal 2001). Note: Contributes through corporate direct giving program and foundation.
Assets: $1,308,249 (fiscal 2003); $1,987,200 (fiscal 2001)
Gifts Received: $386,736 (fiscal 2000); $789,103 (fiscal 1999); $815,000 (fiscal 1998). Note: Contributions were received from Bausch & Lomb Inc.

Typical Recipients

Arts & Humanities: Dance, History & Archaeology, Libraries, Museums/Galleries, Music, Performing Arts, Public Broadcasting, Theater
Civic & Public Affairs: Botanical Gardens/Parks, Business/Free Enterprise, Community Foundations, Economic Development, Employment/Job Training, Civic & Public Affairs-General, Housing, Public Policy, Urban & Community Affairs, Women's Affairs, Zoos/Aquariums
Education: Arts/Humanities Education, Business Education, Colleges & Universities, Community & Junior Colleges, Education-General, Minority Education, Private Education (Precollege), Science/Mathematics Education
Environment: Environment-General
Health: Clinics/Medical Centers, Geriatric Health, Medical Rehabilitation, Nursing Services
Science: Science Museums, Scientific Centers & Institutes
Social Services: Child Welfare, Community Centers, Community Service Organizations, Emergency Relief, Homes, People with Disabilities, Recreation & Athletics, Special Olympics, United Funds/United Ways, Veterans, Youth Organizations

Application Procedures

Initial Contact: Send a written letter proposal.
Application Requirements: Include a full proposal,

a brief description, a budget showing revenue and expenses, a list of the organization's board of directors, and proof of tax-exempt status.
Deadlines: None.
Evaluative Criteria: Preference is given to Rochester, NY based projects and organizations.

Additional Information

Company is currently reviewing its policy on international giving.

Corporate Officials

Alan H. Resnick: vice president, treasurer B Boston, MA 1943. ED Tufts University BS (1965); Columbia University MBA (1967). PRIM CORP EMPL vice president, treasurer: Bausch & Lomb Inc. NONPR AFFIL treasurer: Visiting Nurse Foundation Inc.
William H. Waltrip: chairman, director B 1937. PRIM CORP EMPL chairman, director: Bausch & Lomb Inc. CORP AFFIL chairman: Technology Solutions Co.; director: Thomas & Betts Corp.

Foundation Officials

Jean F. Geisel: secretary
Barbara M. Kelley: vice president, director PRIM CORP EMPL vice president corporate communications: Bausch & Lomb Inc.
Stephen C. McCluski: president, director
Alan H. Resnick: treasurer, director (see above)
Robert Stiles: director

Grants Analysis

Disclosure Period: fiscal year ending December 29, 2003
Total Grants: $473,700
Number of Grants: 11
Average Grant: $17,370*
Highest Grant: $300,000
Lowest Grant: $1,500
Typical Range: $5,000 to $40,000
***Note:** Average grant figure excludes highest grant.

Recent Grants

Note: Grants derived from 2003 Form 990.
General

300,000	University of Rochester, Rochester, NY -- towards the B & L Science Award Program
77,500	UNCGR Foundation, Rochester, NY
50,000	Seneca Park Zoological Society, Rochester, NY
11,500	Rochester Museum and Science Center, Rochester, NY
11,000	Neighborhood Housing Services, Rochester, NY
11,000	Rochester Bus Education Alliance, Rochester, NY
5,000	St. Ann's Community Center, Rochester, NY
3,700	George Eastman House, Rochester, NY
2,500	Partners for Livable Communities, Washington, DC
1,500	Monroe County Special Olympics, Pittsford, NY

BAY FOUNDATION

Giving Contact

Frederick Bay, Executive Director
17 W. 94th St.
New York, NY 10025
Phone: (212)663-1115
Fax: (212)932-0316
E-mail: info@bayandpaulfoundations.org
Web: http://www.bayandpaulfoundations.org/

Description

Founded: 1950
EIN: 135646283
Organization Type: General Purpose Foundation
Giving Locations: nationally, with some preference for the East Coast.
Grant Types: General Support, Project, Research.

Donor Information

Founder: The foundation was established in 1950 by Charles Ulrick Bay and Josephine Bay. Mr. Bay was an industrialist and former U.S. ambassador to Norway. His enterprises included surgical bandages, petroleum, shipping, and finance. He died in 1955.

Financial Summary

Total Giving: $703,389 (2003); $775,878 (2002); $826,221 (2001)
Giving Analysis: Giving for 2003 includes: foundation grants to United Way ($1,000); foundation gifts to individuals ($100,000); 2001: foundation gifts to individuals ($150,000)
Assets: $17,375,055 (2003); $15,812,591 (2002); $20,252,858 (2001)

Typical Recipients

Arts & Humanities: Arts Associations & Councils, Arts Centers, Arts Institutes, Arts Outreach, Dance, Film & Video, Arts & Humanities-General, Historic Preservation, History & Archaeology, Libraries, Literary Arts, Museums/Galleries, Music, Opera, Public Broadcasting, Theater
Civic & Public Affairs: Botanical Gardens/Parks, Employment/Job Training, Civic & Public Affairs-General, Hispanic Affairs, Municipalities/Towns, Native American Affairs, Zoos/Aquariums
Education: Arts/Humanities Education, Colleges & Universities, Education Reform, Elementary Education (Public), Engineering/Technological Education, Environmental Education, Education-General, Medical Education, Private Education (Precollege), Public Education (Precollege), Science/Mathematics Education, Special Education
Environment: Air/Water Quality, Environment-General, Protection, Resource Conservation, Wildlife Protection
Health: Medical Rehabilitation, Research/Studies Institutes, Single-Disease Health Associations
International: Foreign Arts Organizations, Foreign Educational Institutions, International Environmental Issues, International Peace & Security Issues, International Relief Efforts
Religion: Religious Organizations, Religious Welfare
Science: Science Museums, Scientific Centers & Institutes, Scientific Labs, Scientific Research
Social Services: At-Risk Youth, Child Welfare, Community Centers, Community Service Organizations, Family Services, Social Services-General, Youth Organizations

Application Procedures

Initial Contact: Send a brief letter and proposal. Include proof of tax-exempt status.
Deadlines: March1, September 1, and December 1.

Restrictions

Grants restricted to conservation sciences, early education, and the care of cultural collections. Funding is not available for individuals, building campaigns, or non-publicly supported charities.

Additional Information

The foundation reports that first time grants generally fall within the $2,000 to $6,000 range.
Publications: Annual Report

Foundation Officials

Robert W. Ashton: chairman B Memphis, TN 1937. ED University of Michigan BA (1960); Vanderbilt University LLB (1964). OCCUPATION pvt practice. NONPR AFFIL director: Saint Lukes Orchestra; board directors: Saint Matthews & Saint Timothys Neighborhood Center; member: New York City Bar Association; member: New York State Bar Association; member: Century Association; director: Millay Colony Arts; member: American Bar Association. CLUB AFFIL Estate Lawyers Club.
Frederick Bay: executive director
Hans A. Ege: vice president
Synnova Bay Hayes: president, treasurer
Corrine Steel: secretary

Grants Analysis

Disclosure Period: calendar year ending 2003
Total Grants: $602,389*
Number of Grants: 144
Average Grant: $4,183
Highest Grant: $35,000
Lowest Grant: $150
Typical Range: $1,000 to $10,000
*Note: Giving excludes United Way; gifts to individuals.

Recent Grants

Note: Grants derived from 2001 Form 990.
General

125,000	Center for Marine Conservation, Washington, DC
35,000	Heritage Preservation, Inc., Washington, DC
30,000	First Nations Development Institute, Fredericksburg, VA
20,000	Greenwich Village Youth Council, New York, NY
20,000	Mary McDowell Center for Learning, Brooklyn, NY
20,000	Native American Rights Fund, Boulder, CO
18,000	Alliance for Arts, New York, NY
15,000	Environmental Defense Fund
15,000	Goddard Riverside Community Center, New York, NY
15,000	International Biodiversity Observation Year

BAY STATE BANCORP INC.

Company Headquarters

1299 Beacon St.
Brookline, MA 02446
Web: http://www.baystatefederal.com

Company Description

Founded: 1997
Ticker: BYS
Exchange: AMEX
Assets: US$491.9 million (2001)
Employees: 109 (2001)
SIC(s): 6035 Federal Savings Institutions, 6712 Bank Holding Companies.

Bay State Federal Savings Charitable Foundation

Giving Contact

Jill W. Power, Corporate Secretary
Bay State Federal Savings Charitable Foundation
55 Cambridge Pkwy.
Cambridge, MA 02142
Phone: (617)225-6945

Description

Founded: 1999
EIN: 043415547
Organization Type: Corporate Foundation

Giving Locations: Bank's market area, or subject to approval.

Financial Summary

Total Giving: $388,070 (fiscal year ending March 31, 2003); $474,566 (fiscal 2002); $211,523 (fiscal 2001)
Giving Analysis: Giving for fiscal 2003 includes: foundation grants to United Way ($250)
Assets: $11,315,958 (fiscal 2003); $6,746,634 (fiscal 2002); $4,638,726 (fiscal 2001)

Typical Recipients

Arts & Humanities: Arts Centers, History & Archaeology, Libraries, Music, Public Broadcasting, Theater
Civic & Public Affairs: Botanical Gardens/Parks, Business/Free Enterprise, Chambers of Commerce, Clubs, Community Foundations, Economic Development, Civic & Public Affairs-General, Municipalities/Towns, Parades/Festivals, Public Policy
Education: Elementary Education (Private), Elementary Education (Public), Private Education (Precollege), Public Education (Precollege), Secondary Education (Public), Student Aid
Environment: Watershed
Health: AIDS/HIV, Cancer, Children's Health/Hospitals, Clinics/Medical Centers, Emergency/Ambulance Services, Geriatric Health, Health Funds, Health Organizations, Heart, Hospitals, Medical Research, Prenatal Health Issues, Respiratory, Single-Disease Health Associations
Religion: Churches, Jewish Causes, Religious Organizations, Religious Welfare
Social Services: Child Welfare, Community Centers, Community Service Organizations, Day Care, Emergency Relief, Food/Clothing Distribution, Homes, People with Disabilities, Recreation & Athletics, Senior Services, Substance Abuse, United Funds/United Ways, Veterans, YMCA/YWCA/YMHA/YWHA, Youth Organizations

Application Procedures

Initial Contact: Send a grant application package or a written letter.
Application Requirements: Include proof of tax-exempt status.
Deadlines: None.

Foundation Officials

Anthony Caruso: director
Michael O. Gilles: senior vice president, treasurer
John E. Murphy: chairman, president, chief executive officer
Phyllis Penta: director
Jill W. Power: corporate secretary
Denise M. Renaghan: executive vice president, director

Grants Analysis

Disclosure Period: fiscal year ending March 31, 2003
Total Grants: $387,820*
Number of Grants: 187
Average Grant: $1,706*
Highest Grant: $70,500
Lowest Grant: $100
Typical Range: $500 to $5,000
*Note: Giving excludes United Way. Average grant figure excludes highest grants.

Recent Grants

Note: Grants derived from 2004 Form 990.
Library-Related

2,500	Brookline Library Foundation, Brookline, MA

General

50,000	Brookline Senior Center, Brookline, MA
30,000	Brookline 21st Century Fund, Brookline, MA
12,000	Brookline Access Television, Brookline, MA
10,000	Coolidge Corner Theater, Brookline, MA

10,000	Westwood Elementary School Coalition, Westwood, MA
6,500	Lown Cardiovascular Foundation, Washington, DC
5,000	Brookline Community Fund, Brookline, MA
5,000	C. Brendan Noonan, Cambridge, MA
5,000	Fiddlehead Theatre, Norwood, MA
3,500	Friends of Walpole Council on Aging, Walpole, MA

BCR FOUNDATION

Giving Contact
Nancy Rainwater, President
1900 Leyden St.
Denver, CO 80220
Phone: (303)759-3720

Description
Founded: 1986
EIN: 592728836
Organization Type: Private Foundation
Giving Locations: FL
Grant Types: General Support.

Financial Summary
Total Giving: $4,875,000 (fiscal year ending August 31, 2004)
Giving Analysis: Giving for fiscal 2004 includes: foundation grants to United Way ($50,000)
Assets: $103,511 (fiscal 2004)
Gifts Received: $1,798,824 (fiscal 1998). Note: Contributions were received from the Crawford Rainwater Estate.

Typical Recipients
Arts & Humanities: Arts Associations & Councils, Community Arts, Dance, History & Archaeology, Libraries, Music, Theater
Civic & Public Affairs: Civic & Public Affairs-General, Housing, Urban & Community Affairs
Education: Business Education, Colleges & Universities, Community & Junior Colleges, Education-General, Journalism/Media Education, Literacy, Private Education (Precollege)
Environment: Environment-General, Resource Conservation, Wildlife Protection
Health: AIDS/HIV, Emergency/Ambulance Services, Geriatric Health, Health Organizations, Medical Rehabilitation, Medical Research, Public Health, Single-Disease Health Associations
International: Health Care/Hospitals, International Environmental Issues
Religion: Churches, Ministries, Religious Welfare
Science: Scientific Centers & Institutes
Social Services: Big Brothers/Big Sisters, Child Welfare, Community Service Organizations, Crime Prevention, Day Care, Family Planning, Food/Clothing Distribution, People with Disabilities, Scouts, Senior Services, Sexual Abuse, Social Services-General, United Funds/United Ways, Youth Organizations

Application Procedures
Initial Contact: The foundation has no formal grant application procedure or application form.
Deadlines: None.

Restrictions
Does not support individuals.

Grants Analysis
Disclosure Period: fiscal year ending August 31, 2004
Total Grants: $4,825,000*
Number of Grants: 20
Average Grant: $26,563*
Highest Grant: $4,000,000

Lowest Grant: $5,000
Typical Range: $10,000 to $50,000
*Note: Giving excludes United Way. Average grant figure excludes four highest grants ($4,400,000).

Recent Grants
Note: Grants derived from 2001 Form 990.
Library-Related

4,000	Friends of the Pensacola Library, Pensacola, FL -- operations

General

925,036	Endowment Trust of Christ Church -- operations
10,200	Learn to Read, Pensacola, FL -- operations
10,000	Charles Darwin Foundation, Pensacola, FL -- operations
10,000	Council On Aging, Pensacola, FL -- operations
6,000	Favor House, Pensacola, FL -- operations
5,000	Habitat for Humanity, Westminster, CA -- operations
4,000	Crime Stoppers, Pensacola, FL -- operations
4,000	United Ministries, Pensacola, FL -- operations
3,000	Children's Service Center, Pensacola, FL -- operations
3,000	Junior Achievement, Pensacola, FL -- operations

BEAL FOUNDATION

Giving Contact
Spencer E. Beal, Trustee
104 S. Pecos
Midland, TX 79701
Phone: (432)682-3753

Alternate Contact
Bryan Limmer, Trustee
c/o American State Bank
PO Box 1401
Lubbock, TX 79401
Phone: (806)767-7196

Description
Founded: 1962
EIN: 756034480
Organization Type: Private Foundation
Giving Locations: TX: Midland
Grant Types: General Support.

Donor Information
Founder: Carlton Beal, W. R. Davis

Financial Summary
Total Giving: $918,000 (2003). Note: 1996 Giving includes United Way ($140,000).
Giving Analysis: Giving for 2003 includes: foundation grants to United Way ($40,000)
Assets: $8,456,034 (2003)

Typical Recipients
Arts & Humanities: Arts Associations & Councils, Ballet, History & Archaeology, Libraries, Museums/Galleries, Music
Civic & Public Affairs: Chambers of Commerce, Civic & Public Affairs-General, Hispanic Affairs, Housing, Public Policy, Safety, Urban & Community Affairs
Education: Business Education, Colleges & Universities, Community & Junior Colleges, Continuing Education, Education-General, Private Education (Precollege), Special Education, Student Aid
Health: Cancer, Children's Health/Hospitals, Hospices, Hospitals, Medical Rehabilitation, Medical Research, Public Health, Single-Disease Health Associations
International: Health Care/Hospitals
Religion: Ministries, Religious Organizations, Religious Welfare
Social Services: At-Risk Youth, Big Brothers/Big Sisters, Child Welfare, Community Service Organizations, Crime Prevention, Day Care, Domestic Violence, Family Planning, Family Services, Food/Clothing Distribution, People with Disabilities, Scouts, Sexual Abuse, Social Services-General, Substance Abuse, United Funds/United Ways, YMCA/YWCA/YMHA/YWHA, Youth Organizations

Application Procedures
Initial Contact: Request application and guidelines.
Deadlines: Two weeks before board meetings. Board meets on April 1 and November 1.

Additional Information
Publications: Application; Guidelines

Foundation Officials
Barry A. Beal: trustee
Carlton E. Beal, Jr.: chairman
Keleen H. Beal: trustee
Kelly S. Beal: trustee
Spencer E. Beal: trustee
Larry Bell: trustee
Robert J. Cowen: trustee
Karlene Beal Garber: trustee
Bill J. Hill: secretary, treasurer
Jane B. Ramsland: trustee

Grants Analysis
Disclosure Period: calendar year ending 2003
Total Grants: $878,000*
Number of Grants: 62
Average Grant: $10,310*
Highest Grant: $100,000
Lowest Grant: $1,000
Typical Range: $5,000 to $20,000
*Note: Giving excludes United Way. Average grant figure excludes four highest grants ($280,000).

Recent Grants
Note: Grants derived from 2003 Form 990.
General

100,000	YMCA of Midland, Midland, TX
65,000	Trinity School of Midland, Midland, TX
65,000	Trinity School of Midland, Midland, TX
50,000	Trinity School of Midland, Midland, TX
40,000	United Way of Midland, Midland, TX
35,000	Midland Chamber of Commerce Foundation Inc., Midland, TX
25,000	Palmer Drug Abuse, Midland, TX
25,000	Saint John's Health Center, Santa Monica, CA
20,000	Breaking Bread Kitchen, Midland, TX
20,000	Hillcrest School, Midland, TX

NORWIN S. AND ELIZABETH N. BEAN FOUNDATION

Giving Contact
PO Box 326
Manchester, NH 03105-0326
Phone: (603)625-6464
Fax: (603)225-1700
E-mail: ns@nsa.org

Description
Founded: 1957
EIN: 026013381
Organization Type: Private Foundation

Giving Locations: NH: Amherst, Manchester
Grant Types: Conference/Seminar, Emergency, General Support, Loan, Project, Scholarship, Seed Money.

Donor Information
Founder: the late Norwin S. Bean, the late Elizabeth N. Bean

Financial Summary
Total Giving: $489,600 (2003)
Assets: $13,331,010 (2003)

Typical Recipients
Arts & Humanities: Arts Associations & Councils, Arts Centers, Arts Festivals, Arts Institutes, Arts Outreach, Community Arts, Historic Preservation, History & Archaeology, Libraries, Museums/Galleries, Music, Performing Arts, Theater
Civic & Public Affairs: Chambers of Commerce, Community Foundations, Employment/Job Training, Civic & Public Affairs-General, Hispanic Affairs, Housing, Municipalities/Towns, Native American Affairs, Nonprofit Management, Parades/Festivals, Philanthropic Organizations, Safety, Urban & Community Affairs, Women's Affairs
Education: Afterschool/Enrichment Programs, Arts/Humanities Education, Colleges & Universities, Education Reform, Environmental Education, Faculty Development, Education-General, Literacy, Preschool Education, Private Education (Precollege), Public Education (Precollege), School Volunteerism, Science/Mathematics Education, Secondary Education (Private), Secondary Education (Public)
Environment: Forestry, Environment-General, Resource Conservation, Watershed
Health: AIDS/HIV, Alzheimer's Disease, Cancer, Children's Health/Hospitals, Clinics/Medical Centers, Emergency/Ambulance Services, Health Organizations, Heart, Mental Health, Nursing Services, Prenatal Health Issues, Respiratory
Religion: Churches, Ministries, Religious Welfare
Social Services: At-Risk Youth, Big Brothers/Big Sisters, Child Welfare, Community Service Organizations, Counseling, Delinquency & Criminal Rehabilitation, Family Services, Food/Clothing Distribution, People with Disabilities, Recreation & Athletics, Scouts, Senior Services, Shelters/Homelessness, Substance Abuse, United Funds/United Ways, YMCA/YWCA/YMHA/YWHA, Youth Organizations

Application Procedures
Initial Contact: Send a cover sheet and a proposal with appropriate enclosures.
Application Requirements: Explain the purpose of the project and describe how that purpose will be accomplished.
Deadlines: December 1, April 1, and September 1 for meetings in February, June, and November.

Restrictions
Does not support individuals or provide funds for scholarships.

Additional Information
Publications: Annual Report; Informational Brochure (including Application Guidelines)

Foundation Officials
Thomas J. Donovan: senior trustee
William G. Steele, Jr.: senior trustee

Grants Analysis
Disclosure Period: calendar year ending 2003
Total Grants: $489,600
Number of Grants: 41
Average Grant: $10,990*
Highest Grant: $50,000
Lowest Grant: $500
Typical Range: $5,000 to $20,000
*Note: Average grant figure excludes highest grant.

Recent Grants
Note: Grants derived from 2003 Form 990.
General

50,000	City of Manchester Department of Health, Manchester, NH -- for third year of the adolescent pregnancy prevention program that has reduced adolescent birth rates
36,000	New Hampshire Charitable Foundation, Concord, NH -- for professional and administrative services to the non-profit sector
25,000	Families in Transition, Manchester, NH -- for development of historic mill as mixed use affordable housing
25,000	Families in Transition, Manchester, NH -- for core operating support and assistance for the development function
25,000	Manchester Neighborhood Housing Services, Manchester, NH -- for core operating support and program costs
25,000	New Horizons for New Hampshire, Manchester, NH -- for improved services at the emergency shelter and at Angie's place
20,000	Peabody Mill Environmental Center, Amherst, NH -- for structural renovations to the education building
15,000	Child Health Services, Manchester, NH -- to support the media smart program to bring parent education and awareness programs to the community
15,000	Girls Incorporated of New Hampshire, Manchester, NH -- for capital campaign to acquire and renovate their own building
14,400	Child and Family Services of New Hampshire, Manchester, NH -- to complete renovations for the teen outreach resource center for runaway and street youth

LUCY AND EMILY BEASLEY CHARITABLE TRUST

Giving Contact
Thomas D. Barsody, Trust Officer
c/o Bank One Akron NA
50 S. Main St.
Akron, OH 44308
Phone: (330)972-1732

Description
Founded: 1981
EIN: 341350747
Organization Type: Private Foundation
Giving Locations: OH

Donor Information
Founder: Robert P. Beasley Trust

Financial Summary
Total Giving: $250,000 (fiscal year ending September 30, 2004)
Assets: $7,504,484 (fiscal 2004)
Gifts Received: $224 (fiscal 1999); $35,251 (fiscal 1998); $227,211 (fiscal 1997). Note: In 1999, contributions were received from Robert P. Beasley Trust. In fiscal 1996, contributions were received from the Robert P. Beasley Trust ($1,888) and the estate of Robert P. Beasley ($31,052).

Typical Recipients
Arts & Humanities: Libraries
Civic & Public Affairs: Clubs, Employment/Job Training, Civic & Public Affairs-General, Zoos/Aquariums
Education: Colleges & Universities, Education-

General, Private Education (Precollege), Public Education (Precollege)
Environment: Environment-General
Health: Health Organizations
Religion: Churches, Ministries, Religious Welfare
Social Services: Animal Protection, Community Service Organizations, Domestic Violence, Family Services, People with Disabilities, Scouts

Application Procedures
Initial Contact: Send a brief letter of inquiry.
Application Requirements: Include a description of organization and purpose of funds sought.
Deadlines: None.

Additional Information
Trust(s): Bank One Akron NA

Foundation Officials
Howard W. Cable, Jr.: trustee

Grants Analysis
Disclosure Period: fiscal year ending September 30, 2004
Total Grants: $250,000
Number of Grants: 18
Average Grant: $9,375*
Highest Grant: $50,000
Lowest Grant: $2,000
Typical Range: $2,000 to $20,000
*Note: Average grant figure excludes two highest grants ($100,000).

Recent Grants
Note: Grants derived from fiscal 2001 Form 990.
General

100,000	Akron Zoological Park, Akron, OH
75,000	H.M. Life Opportunity Services, Akron, OH
75,000	Interval Brotherhood Home, Akron, OH
50,000	Access, Akron, OH
25,000	Project Learn to Summit County, Akron, OH
20,000	University of Akron Foundation, Akron, OH
10,000	Cumberland College, Williamsburg, KY
5,000	Gennesaret, Akron, OH
5,000	Goodwill Industries, Akron, OH
5,000	Great Trail Council, Akron, OH

CORDELIA LEE BEATTIE FOUNDATION

Giving Contact
Debra M. Jacobs, Administrator
1800 2nd St., Suite 750
Sarasota, FL 34236
Phone: (941)957-0442
Fax: (941)957-3135
E-mail: djacobs@selbyfdn.org
Web: http://www.selbyfdn.org/cordeliaLee.html

Description
Founded: 1975
EIN: 596540711
Organization Type: Private Foundation
Giving Locations: FL: Sarasota County
Grant Types: General Support.

Donor Information
Founder: the late Cordelia Lee Beattie

Financial Summary
Total Giving: $104,550 (fiscal year ending October 31, 2002); $150,792 (fiscal 2001)
Assets: $2,168,005 (fiscal 2002); $2,487,788 (fiscal 2001)

Typical Recipients

Arts & Humanities: Arts Associations & Councils, Arts Centers, Arts Festivals, Ballet, Community Arts, Dance, Film & Video, Libraries, Literary Arts, Museums/Galleries, Music, Opera, Performing Arts, Theater, Visual Arts
Civic & Public Affairs: Botanical Gardens/Parks
Education: Arts/Humanities Education, Private Education (Precollege)
Environment: Environment-General
Health: Children's Health/Hospitals
Social Services: Animal Protection

Application Procedures

Initial Contact: Contact the foundation or visit the foundation's web site to obtain guidelines and application format.
Deadlines: November 15.
Notes: The Selby Foundation manages the Cordelia Lee Beattie Foundation's grantmaking.

Restrictions

Does not support endowments, deficit financing, debt reduction, or ordinary operating expenses; conferences, seminars, workshops, travel, surveys, advertising, fundraising costs, or research; annual giving campaigns; projects that have already been completed; or individuals.

Additional Information

Publications: Application Guidelines

Foundation Officials

Debra M. Jacobs: administration agent NONPR AFFIL vice president: Ringling School Art & Design.
Dr. Robert E. Perkins: admin agent

Grants Analysis

Disclosure Period: fiscal year ending October 31, 2002
Total Grants: $104,550
Number of Grants: 9
Average Grant: $11,617*
Highest Grant: $30,000
Lowest Grant: $4,800
Typical Range: $2,500 to $15,000
*Note: Average grant excludes highest grant.

Recent Grants

Note: Grants derived from 2002 Form 990.
General

30,000	Florida West Coast Symphony, Sarasota, FL -- Youth Orchestra Program
20,000	Asolo Performing Arts Center, Sarasota, FL -- for Kaleidoscope Touring Company
13,000	Marie Selby Botanical Gardens, Sarasota, FL -- for Sunday Garden Music series
10,750	Florida Studio Theater, Sarasota, FL -- for VIP Program
10,000	Sarasota Ballet, Sarasota, FL -- for the Nutcracker children's costumes
6,000	Gloria Musicae, Sarasota, FL -- for Venice High School Project
5,000	Theater Works, Sarasota, FL -- for mainstage season
4,800	Pines of Sarasota Inc., Sarasota, FL -- for Continuation of Arts Program

CORDELIA LUNCEFORD BEATTY TRUST

Giving Contact

James R. Rodgers, Trustee
105 North Main
PO Box 514
Blackwell, OK 74631-0514
Phone: (580)363-3684

Description

Founded: 1943
EIN: 736094952
Organization Type: Private Foundation
Giving Locations: OK: Blackwell
Grant Types: General Support, Scholarship.

Financial Summary

Total Giving: $109,150 (2003)
Giving Analysis: Giving for 2003 includes: foundation scholarships ($42,421)
Assets: $2,809,844 (2003)

Typical Recipients

Arts & Humanities: Libraries, Music
Civic & Public Affairs: Clubs, Civic & Public Affairs-General, Municipalities/Towns, Safety
Education: Afterschool/Enrichment Programs, Agricultural Education, Colleges & Universities, Literacy, Private Education (Precollege), Public Education (Precollege), Religious Education, School Volunteerism, Secondary Education (Public), Special Education, Student Aid
Health: Emergency/Ambulance Services
Religion: Churches, Religious Welfare
Social Services: Community Service Organizations, Food/Clothing Distribution, People with Disabilities, Recreation & Athletics, Scouts, Substance Abuse, United Funds/United Ways, YMCA/YWCA/YMHA/YWHA, Youth Organizations

Application Procedures

Initial Contact: The foundation has no formal grant application procedure or application form.
Deadlines: None.

Foundation Officials

James R. Rodgers: trustee
William W. Rodgers: trustee

Grants Analysis

Disclosure Period: calendar year ending 2003
Total Grants: $66,729*
Number of Grants: 50
Average Grant: $1,158*
Highest Grant: $10,000
Lowest Grant: $94
Typical Range: $100 to $3,000
*Note: Giving excludes scholarships. Average grant figure excludes highest grant.

Recent Grants

Note: Grants derived from 2001 Form 990.

Library-Related

1,000	Blackwell Public Library, Blackwell, OK -- children's books

General

25,000	City of Blackwell, Blackwell, OK -- tennis courts
7,500	Northern Oklahoma Youth Services, Ponca City, OK -- capital improvement fund
6,500	Blackwell Youth Center, Blackwell, OK
2,000	Associated Charities of Blackwell, Blackwell, OK
2,000	Pee Wee Football, Blackwell, OK
1,996	Rotary Club, Blackwell, OK -- Christmas Party for Kids
1,600	Blackwell High School, Blackwell, OK -- pitching machine
1,514	Wal-Mart, Blackwell, OK -- school supplies
1,500	Blackwell High School, Blackwell, OK -- incidental student expense fund
1,500	Blackwell Public Schools, Blackwell, OK -- accelerated Reader Program

BEAUCOURT FOUNDATION

Giving Contact

Peter A. Wilson, President, Treasurer, & Director
c/o Testa, Hurwitz & Thibeault
125 High St.
Boston, MA 02110
Phone: (617)248-7426
Fax: (617)248-7100

Description

Founded: 1988
EIN: 042979426
Organization Type: Private Foundation
Giving Locations: MA: Boston; NY
Grant Types: General Support.

Financial Summary

Total Giving: $200,000 (2003); $235,000 (2001)
Assets: $3,155,311 (2003); $3,934,666 (2001)

Typical Recipients

Arts & Humanities: Libraries
Education: Business Education, Colleges & Universities, Education-General, International Studies
International: Foreign Educational Institutions

Application Procedures

Initial Contact: The foundation has no formal grant application procedure or application form.
Deadlines: None.

Restrictions

Must be an IRS approved charity.

Foundation Officials

Henry W. Comstock, Jr.: secretary, director

Grants Analysis

Disclosure Period: calendar year ending 2003
Total Grants: $200,000
Number of Grants: 2
Highest Grant: $120,000
Lowest Grant: $80,000

Recent Grants

Note: Grants derived from 2001 Form 990.
Library-Related

85,000	French Library and Cultural Center, Boston, MA
70,000	French Library and Cultural Center, Boston, MA

General

80,000	Insead Management Education Foundation, New York, NY

BEAZLEY FOUNDATION

Giving Contact

Richard S. Bray, Jr., President
3720 Brighton Street
Portsmouth, VA 23707
Phone: (757)393-1605
Fax: (757)393-4708
E-mail: info@beazleyfoundation.org
Web: http://www.beazleyfoundation.org

Description

Founded: 1948
EIN: 540550100
Organization Type: General Purpose Foundation
Giving Locations: VA: Portsmouth Hampton Roads, VA area.
Grant Types: Capital, General Support, Operating Expenses, Project, Scholarship, Seed Money.

Donor Information

Founder: Established in December 1948 with funds provided by the late Fred W. Beazley, his wife Marie C. Beazley, and son Fred W. Beazley Jr., all of Portsmouth, VA. A sister foundation, Foundation Boys Academy was founded by Mr. Beazley in 1956. In 1986, the charter of Foundation Boys Academy was amended, the name changed to Frederick Foundation and its purpose changed to fund charitable and religious, in addition to educational endeavors. However, in 1993, the Frederick Foundation merged into the Beazley Foundation and now follows its program interests.

The main goal of the chief benefactor of the foundations, Mr. Beazley, was to provide what was not otherwise available to the citizens of Portsmouth, primarily to the youth. He was interested in a quality secondary education for deserving youngsters, as well as recreational facilities for the children of the city. He established the City Dental Clinic in cooperation with the city of Portsmouth to provide dental care to those who could not afford it. Affordable rental housing was also one of his most satisfying accomplishments.

Financial Summary

Total Giving: $1,800,000 (2003 approx); $2,700,179 (2002); $2,947,056 (2001)
Giving Analysis: Giving for 2002 includes: foundation grants to United Way ($300,000)
Assets: $45,000,000 (2003 approx); $54,956,444 (2002)

Typical Recipients

Arts & Humanities: Arts Centers, Historic Preservation, History & Archaeology, Libraries, Museums/Galleries, Music
Civic & Public Affairs: African American Affairs, Botanical Gardens/Parks, Business/Free Enterprise, Community Foundations, Economic Development, Employment/Job Training, Civic & Public Affairs-General, Housing, Municipalities/Towns, Nonprofit Management, Parades/Festivals, Philanthropic Organizations, Professional & Trade Associations, Safety, Urban & Community Affairs, Zoos/Aquariums
Education: Afterschool/Enrichment Programs, Agricultural Education, Arts/Humanities Education, Business Education, Colleges & Universities, Community & Junior Colleges, Education Funds, Elementary Education (Private), Elementary Education (Public), Engineering/Technological Education, Environmental Education, Faculty Development, Education-General, Gifted & Talented Programs, Leadership Training, Legal Education, Literacy, Medical Education, Minority Education, Preschool Education, Private Education (Precollege), Public Education (Precollege), School Volunteerism, Science/Mathematics Education, Secondary Education (Private), Student Aid
Environment: Forestry, Resource Conservation, Wildlife Protection
Health: AIDS/HIV, Cancer, Children's Health/Hospitals, Clinics/Medical Centers, Emergency/Ambulance Services, Health-General, Geriatric Health, Health Organizations, Hospitals, Hospitals (University Affiliated), Medical Rehabilitation, Public Health, Single-Disease Health Associations
International: Foreign Arts Organizations, International Organizations
Religion: Churches, Ministries, Religious Organizations, Religious Welfare, Seminaries
Science: Observatories & Planetariums, Science Museums
Social Services: At-Risk Youth, Camps, Child Abuse, Child Welfare, Community Centers, Community Service Organizations, Crime Prevention, Day Care, Delinquency & Criminal Rehabilitation, Domestic Violence, Emergency Relief, Family Services, Food/Clothing Distribution, Homes, People with Disabilities, Recreation & Athletics, Scouts, Senior Services, Shelters/Homelessness, Social Services-General, Substance Abuse, United Funds/United Ways, Volunteer Services, YMCA/YWCA/YMHA/YWHA, Youth Organizations

Application Procedures

Initial Contact: Applicants are encouraged to call the foundation to request grant application guidelines.
Deadlines: March 1, June 1, September 1, and December 1.

Restrictions

The foundation does not fund individuals, conferences, symposia, publications or media projects, international or national programs and institutions, and environmental protection projects. Generally, limited grants are given to the arts and only to programs providing art education directly to elementary and secondary school students.

Additional Information

Publications: Application Guidelines; Foundation Policy; Annual Report

Foundation Officials

Jeannette C. Bridgeman: treasurer, assistant secretary
Leroy T. Canoles, Jr.: trustee B 1925. ED University of Virginia Law School (1951). PRIM CORP EMPL president, director: Kaufman and Canoles PC.
Diane P. Griffin: trustee
Lawrence W. I'Anson, Jr.: president, executive director
W. Ashton Lewis: secretary, trustee
P. Ward Robinett, Jr.: trustee PRIM CORP EMPL president: Branch Banking Trust Co. of Virginia.

Grants Analysis

Disclosure Period: calendar year ending 2002
Total Grants: $2,670,179*
Number of Grants: 75
Average Grant: $30,678*
Highest Grant: $400,000
Lowest Grant: $70
Typical Range: $10,000 to $50,000
*Note: Giving excludes United Way. Average grant figure excludes highest grant.

Recent Grants

Note: Grants derived from 2002 Form 990.

General

200,000	Portsmouth Community Health Center, Portsmouth, VA -- to assist in the Beazley Dental Center
100,000	Portsmouth Self Sufficiency Project, Portsmouth, VA
100,000	Virginia Sports Hall of Fame & Museum, Portsmouth, VA
90,000	Portsmouth Public Schools, Portsmouth, VA -- for Beazley Scholarships
90,000	Virginia Foundation for Independent Colleges, Richmond, VA -- for Beazley Scholarship Program
80,000	Tidewater Scholarship Foundation, Norfolk, VA -- ACCESS endowment
75,000	Portsmouth Public Schools, Portsmouth, VA -- to assist in the ACCESS Program
59,227	United Cerebral Palsy of Southeastern & Central Virginia, Virginia Beach, VA -- for the new building
50,000	Battleship Wisconsin Foundation, Norfolk, VA
50,000	Chesapeake Bay Academy, Virginia Beach, VA

HILDEGARDE D. BECHER FOUNDATION

Giving Contact

Lawrence Dix, Treasurer
PO Box 11
Hartsdale, NY 10530-0011
Phone: (914)997-9888

Description

Founded: 1995
EIN: 133744010
Organization Type: Private Foundation
Grant Types: General Support, Scholarship.

Financial Summary

Total Giving: $215,100 (2003); $272,300 (2001)
Giving Analysis: Giving for 2003 includes: foundation scholarships ($20,000) 2001: foundation scholarships ($19,800)
Assets: $4,400,573 (2003); $4,928,876 (2001)

Typical Recipients

Arts & Humanities: Libraries, Museums/Galleries, Music, Opera
Education: Arts/Humanities Education, Colleges & Universities, Medical Education, Student Aid
Health: Cancer, Clinics/Medical Centers, Diabetes, Hospices, Hospitals, Hospitals (University Affiliated), Medical Research, Preventive Medicine/Wellness Organizations, Respiratory
International: Foreign Arts Organizations
Social Services: Animal Protection, Camps, Child Welfare, Substance Abuse, YMCA/YWCA/YMHA/YWHA

Application Procedures

Initial Contact: Send a brief letter of inquiry.
Deadlines: None.

Foundation Officials

Alan Berg: vice president
Lawrence Dix: treasurer
Jack Geoghegan: secretary
Herbert Kroner: president

Grants Analysis

Disclosure Period: calendar year ending 2003
Total Grants: $195,100*
Number of Grants: 25
Average Grant: $6,046*
Highest Grant: $50,000
Lowest Grant: $1,000
Typical Range: $2,500 to $10,000
*Note: Giving excludes scholarship. Average grant figure excludes highest grant.

Recent Grants

Note: Grants derived from 2004 Form 990.
General

50,000	Leukemia and Lymphoma Society, New York, NY -- for medical research
25,000	Happiness is Camping Inc., Bronx, NY
25,000	New York University Medical Center, New York, NY -- for medical research
20,000	Mannes College of Music, New York, NY -- for scholarship
10,000	American Lung Association, New York, NY
10,000	Leukemia and Lymphoma Society, White Plains, NY
7,500	Juvenile Diabetes Research Foundation, New York, NY -- for medical research
7,500	Samaritan Village, Briarwood, NY
5,500	Calvary Hospital, Bronx, NY
5,000	Sound Shore Medical Center, New Rochelle, NY

HAROLD R. BECHTEL CHARITABLE REMAINDER UNI-TRUST

Giving Contact
R. Richard Bittner, Trustee
201 W. 2nd St., Suite 1000
Davenport, IA 52801
Phone: (563)328-3333
Fax: (563)328-3352

Description
Founded: 1987
EIN: 426288501
Organization Type: Private Foundation
Giving Locations: IA: Scott County
Grant Types: Capital, General Support, Scholarship.

Financial Summary
Total Giving: $1,194,510 (fiscal year ending April 30, 2002); $1,226,439 (fiscal 2001)
Assets: $24,134,888 (fiscal 2002); $22,922,281 (fiscal 2001)

Typical Recipients
Arts & Humanities: Arts Institutes, Museums/Galleries, Music, Theater
Civic & Public Affairs: Economic Development, Civic & Public Affairs-General, Municipalities/Towns, Urban & Community Affairs
Education: Business Education, Colleges & Universities, Education-General, Medical Education, Private Education (Precollege), Public Education (Precollege), School Volunteerism, Science/Mathematics Education, Secondary Education (Private)
Environment: Environment-General
Health: Alzheimer's Disease
Religion: Churches, Religious Welfare
Science: Science Museums
Social Services: At-Risk Youth, Big Brothers/Big Sisters, Child Welfare, Community Centers, Community Service Organizations, Counseling, Family Services, Food/Clothing Distribution, Recreation & Athletics, Shelters/Homelessness, Social Services-General, Substance Abuse, United Funds/United Ways, YMCA/YWCA/YMHA/YWHA, Youth Organizations

Application Procedures
Initial Contact: Send letter requesting application form.
Deadlines: None.

Foundation Officials
R. Richard Bittner: trustee

Grants Analysis
Disclosure Period: fiscal year ending April 30, 2002
Total Grants: $1,194,510
Number of Grants: 30
Average Grant: $39,817
Highest Grant: $150,000
Lowest Grant: $2,000
Typical Range: $20,000 to $100,000

Recent Grants
Note: Grants derived from fiscal 2002 Form 990.
General

152,000	Scott County Family YMCA, Davenport, IA -- funding for Camp Abe Lincoln
150,000	City of Davenport, Davenport, IA -- funds to lessen the burdens of government
150,000	Palmer Chiropractic University Foundation, Davenport, IA -- research program
150,000	St. Ambrose University, Davenport, IL -- capital funding for construction
100,000	Museum of Art Foundation, Davenport, IA -- capital funding for construction
100,000	Putnam Museum of History and Natural Science, Davenport, IA -- capital funding for construction
100,000	River Mont Collegiate, Bettendorf, IA -- capital funding for construction of new facility
50,000	Davenport One Foundation, Davenport, IA
50,000	Family Resources, Inc., Davenport, IA -- capital fund drive to build residential treatment cottage
50,000	Friends of Brady Street Stadium, Davenport, IA -- capital funding for renovation

MARIE H. BECHTEL CHARITABLE REMAINDER UNI-TRUST

Giving Contact
R. Richard Bittner, Trustee
201 West 2nd Street, Ste. 1000
Davenport, IA 52801
Phone: (563)328-3333
Fax: (563)328-3352

Description
Founded: 1978
EIN: 426288500
Organization Type: General Purpose Foundation
Giving Locations: IA: Scott County
Grant Types: Capital, Challenge, Emergency, Endowment, General Support, Matching, Operating Expenses, Scholarship.
Note: A limited number of emergency grants, endowments, operating grants are given.

Donor Information
Founder: The Marie H. Bechtel Charitable Remainder Uni-Trust, established in 1978, is the largest of four trusts and a corporate foundation which were created either by Harold R. Bechtel or by Marie H. Bechtel during their lifetimes. The other charitable organizations are the following: the Bechtel Foundation, the H. Reimers Bechtel Uni-Trust, the H. R. Bechtel Testamentary Charitable Trust, and the Harold R. Bechtel Charitable Remainder Uni-Trust.
The Bechtels were lifetime residents of Scott County, IA. Harold R. Bechtel was one of Iowa's foremost bankers until his death in 1987. Marie H. Bechtel was highly regarded for her cultural activities and interests in Scott County, as well as her devotion to the health care needs of the community.
Both Harold and Marie were born in Davenport, IA. Harold served in both World War I and World War II, rising to the rank of lieutenant colonel. He became engaged in the banking industry in 1935 when the Bechtel Trust Company received its state banking charter.

Financial Summary
Total Giving: $1,454,670 (2003); $1,504,544 (2002); $1,008,100 (2001)
Assets: $35,632,645 (2003); $28,732,455 (2002); $30,861,450 (2001)

Typical Recipients
Arts & Humanities: Arts Associations & Councils, Arts Institutes, Community Arts, Libraries, Museums/Galleries, Music
Civic & Public Affairs: Community Foundations, Economic Development, Employment/Job Training, Civic & Public Affairs-General, Housing, Inner-City Development, Legal Aid, Municipalities/Towns, Philanthropic Organizations
Education: Afterschool/Enrichment Programs, Business Education, Colleges & Universities, Community & Junior Colleges, Education Funds, Education-General, Medical Education, Private Education (Precollege), Science/Mathematics Education, Secondary Education (Private)
Environment: Environment-General
Health: Cancer, Public Health, Single-Disease Health Associations
Religion: Churches, Religion-General, Religious Organizations, Religious Welfare
Science: Science Museums
Social Services: At-Risk Youth, Big Brothers/Big Sisters, Child Welfare, Community Centers, Community Service Organizations, Delinquency & Criminal Rehabilitation, Food/Clothing Distribution, Recreation & Athletics, Senior Services, Shelters/Homelessness, Social Services-General, Substance Abuse, YMCA/YWCA/YMHA/YWHA

Application Procedures
Initial Contact: Contact the trust to request a copy of the grant application. Such contact should be written and should provide a brief description of the requested use for funds.
Application Requirements: Grant applications will require the following: a brief a description of organization, including its legal name, history, activities, purpose, and governing body; a clear description of the purpose for which the grant is requested and the goals to be achieved; the amount requested and a list of other current and potential sources of financial support; a copy of the organization's most recent audited financial statement; a copy of the IRS tax-exempt determination letter; and a copy of the organization's last 990-income tax return.
Deadlines: None.
Review Process: The trust will send a written notice to applicants within a reasonable time, whether the request for a grant has been approved or declined.

Restrictions
The foundation generally does not support endowment funds; past operating deficits or debt retirement; general and continuing operating support; or basic scholarly research within established academic disciplines.
Grants are currently confined to nonprofit, public tax-exempt organizations to be used for their charitable purposes. Grants may be made to individuals in the future, but are not currently available.
Grants are generally made to Scott County, IA, with the noted exceptions.

Additional Information
Publications: Guidelines; Application Form; Brochure Explaining Uni-Trust's Philosophy

Foundation Officials
R. Richard Bittner: trustee, director

Grants Analysis
Disclosure Period: calendar year ending 2003
Total Grants: $1,454,670
Number of Grants: 24
Average Grant: $45,667*
Highest Grant: $250,000
Typical Range: $20,000 to $100,000
*Note: Average grant figure excludes two highest grants ($450,000).

Recent Grants
Note: Grants derived from 2002 Form 990.
General

226,000	Scott County Family Y, Davenport, IA -- towards new facility at North High School, aquatic swim program, Downtown Davenport initiative and timing system
220,000	St. Ambrose University, Davenport, IA -- towards construction of a new student center and renovation of McMullen Hall
180,000	Palmer Chiropractic University, Davenport, IA -- towards construction of a new

	Fountainhead Research Center and expansion of various campus facilities
150,000	City of Davenport, Davenport, IA -- fund for public parking garage
100,000	Museum of Art Foundation, Davenport, IA -- towards construction of new art museum
100,000	Putnam Museum of History and Natural Science, Davenport, IA -- towards construction of I-MAX theater
100,000	RiverMont Collegiate, Bettendorf, IA -- towards construction of a new facility for students
50,000	DavenportOne Foundation, Davenport, IA
50,000	Friends of Brady Street Stadium, Davenport, IA -- towards renovation of Brady Street stadium
50,000	Gilda Club Quad Cities, Davenport, IA -- fund for expansion of the carriage house

BECHTEL GROUP INC.

Company Headquarters

San Francisco, CA
Web: http://www.bechtel.com

Company Description

Operating Revenue: US$11.6 billion (2002)
Employees: 44000 (2003)
SIC(s): 1522 Residential Construction Nec, 1541 Industrial Buildings & Warehouses, 1542 Nonresidential Construction Nec, 1611 Highway & Street Construction.

Operating Locations

Bechtel Group, Inc. (CA--Concord, Englewood, Los Angeles; DC--Washington; NV--North Las Vegas; NJ--Florence, Hainesport; NC--Charlotte; PA--Pittsburgh; SC--Cayce; TN--Kingsport)

Nonmonetary Support

Type: In-kind Services
Note: Co. provides limited nonmonetary support.

Bechtel Foundation

Giving Contact

LeeAnne M. Lang, Assistant Secretary
Bechtel Foundation
50 Beale Street
San Francisco, CA 94105
Phone: (415)768-7158
Fax: (415)768-0263
E-mail: foundtn@bechtel.com
Web: http://www.bechtel.com/foundation.htm

Alternate Contact

Susan Grisso
Bechtel Foundation
50 Beale Street
San Francisco, CA 94105
Phone: (415)768-5444

Description

EIN: 946078120
Organization Type: Corporate Foundation
Giving Locations: internationally, in major operating locations.
Grant Types: Employee Matching Gifts, General Support.
Note: Foundation matches employee gifts to colleges and universities in the United States.

Financial Summary

Total Giving: $2,548,935 (2003); $2,634,453 (2002); $3,120,277 (2001). Note: Contributes through foundation only.

Giving Analysis: Giving for 2002 includes: foundation grants to United Way ($165,500); 2001: foundation scholarships ($69,611); foundation grants to United Way ($220,500); foundation ($2,830,166)
Assets: $12,678,130 (2003); $14,438,993 (2002); $15,653,616 (2001)
Gifts Received: $75,000 (2003); $3,000,000 (2002). Note: Contributions were received from Bechtel Corp.

Typical Recipients

Arts & Humanities: Arts Centers, Arts Outreach, Community Arts, Ethnic & Folk Arts, Historic Preservation, Libraries, Museums/Galleries, Performing Arts
Civic & Public Affairs: African American Affairs, Botanical Gardens/Parks, Business/Free Enterprise, Chambers of Commerce, Clubs, Community Foundations, Economic Development, Economic Policy, Ethnic Organizations, Civic & Public Affairs-General, Hispanic Affairs, Housing, Legal Aid, Minority Business, Municipalities/Towns, Native American Affairs, Nonprofit Management, Philanthropic Organizations, Professional & Trade Associations, Public Policy, Urban & Community Affairs, Zoos/Aquariums
Education: Business Education, Business-School Partnerships, Colleges & Universities, Education Funds, Education Reform, Elementary Education (Public), Engineering/Technological Education, Environmental Education, Education-General, International Exchange, International Studies, Legal Education, Literacy, Medical Education, Minority Education, Private Education (Precollege), Public Education (Precollege), Science/Mathematics Education, Secondary Education (Public), Social Sciences Education, Student Aid, Vocational & Technical Education
Environment: Air/Water Quality, Environment-General, Resource Conservation
Health: Adolescent Health Issues, AIDS/HIV, Cancer, Children's Health/Hospitals, Emergency/Ambulance Services, Hospitals, Prenatal Health Issues, Research/Studies Institutes
International: Foreign Arts Organizations, Foreign Educational Institutions, Health Care/Hospitals, International Affairs, International Development, International Environmental Issues, International Organizations, International Peace & Security Issues, International Relations, Missionary/Religious Activities
Religion: Jewish Causes, Religious Welfare
Science: Science Exhibits & Fairs, Science Museums, Scientific Centers & Institutes, Scientific Organizations, Scientific Research
Social Services: Child Welfare, Community Service Organizations, Emergency Relief, Food/Clothing Distribution, Recreation & Athletics, Scouts, Social Services-General, Special Olympics, Substance Abuse, United Funds/United Ways, YMCA/YWCA/YMHA/YWHA, Youth Organizations

Application Procedures

Initial Contact: Send a one- or two-page letter of request.
Application Requirements: Include a description of organization; amount requested; purpose of funds sought; recently audited financial statement; proof of tax-exempt status; and a few pages of backup material.
Deadlines: None.
Notes: Most grants are under $5,000.

Restrictions

The foundation does not support individuals; fraternal, social, or religious organizations; entertainment; limited interest organizations; fellowships, internships, or residencies; endowed or named chairs at educational or research institutions; catalogs and publications; conferences and events.

Corporate Officials

Riley Peart Bechtel: chairman, chief executive officer, director B 1952. ED University of California,

Davis BA (1975); Stanford University MBA (1980); Stanford University JD (1980). CORP AFFIL director: Sequoia Ventures Inc.; member: Trilateral Commission; member: National Petroleum Council; chairman, director: Overseas Bechtel Inc.; director: Indian School Business Governing Board; director: JP Morgan Chase & Co.; director: Fremont Group LLC; director: Fremont Investors Inc. NONPR AFFIL member deans advisory council: Stanford University Law School; trustee: Thacher School; member: JP Morgan International Advisory Council; member advisory council: Stanford University Graduate School Business; member policy committee: Business Roundtable; member: California Business Roundtable; member: American Bar Association; member: Business Council.
Donald J. Gunther: director B 1938. ED University of Missouri BScE (1960). PRIM CORP EMPL director: Bechtel Group, Inc. CORP AFFIL president: Bechtel Americas; executive vice president: Bechtel Corp.
Adrian Zaccaria: vice chairman, president, director B 1944. ED United States Merchant Marine Academy BS (1966). PRIM CORP EMPL vice chairman, president, director: Bechtel Group, Inc. CORP AFFIL officer: Bechtel Systems Infrastructure; administration: International Bechtel S De RL; president: Bechtel Overseas Corp.; president: Bechtel Leasing Services Inc.; president: Bechtel North America Power Corp.; executive vice president, director: Bechtel Corp.; president: Bechtel International Inc.; president: America Bechtel Inc.; vice chairman: Bechtel Construction Operations Inc.

Foundation Officials

Riley Peart Bechtel: chairman, director (see above)
R. M. Burt: senior vice president, director
T. A. Carlson: assistant treasurer
M. S. Knox: vice president, treasurer
LeeAnne M. Lang: assistant secretary
J. P. Laspa: president, director
Adrian Zaccaria: director (see above)

Grants Analysis

Disclosure Period: calendar year ending 2003
Total Grants: $2,400,435*
Number of Grants: 518
Average Grant: $2,961*
Highest Grant: $869,625
Lowest Grant: $25
Typical Range: $1,000 to $5,000
*Note: Giving excludes United Way. Average grant figure excludes highest grant.

Recent Grants

Note: Grants derived from 2003 Form 990.

General

869,625	Institute for International Studies, Stanford, CA
125,000	Nevada Test Site Historical Foundation, Las Vegas, NV
110,000	United Way of the Bay Area, San Francisco, CA
90,000	Charities Aid Foundation, Alexandria, VA
60,000	National Action Council for Minorities in Engineering, White Plains, NY
50,000	American School in London Foundation, London United Kingdom
50,000	Citizens' Scholarship Foundation of America, Minneapolis, MN
31,550	Stanford University, Stanford, CA
30,000	Eisenhower Exchange Fellowship, Philadelphia, PA
30,000	Houston Golf Association, Humble, TX

ARNOLD AND MABEL BECKMAN FOUNDATION

Giving Contact

Jacqueline Dorrance, Executive Director
100 Academy Drive
Irvine, CA 92617
Phone: (949)721-2222
Fax: (949)721-2225
E-mail: k.williams@beckman-foundation.com
Web: http://www.beckman-foundation.com

Description

Founded: 1977
EIN: 953169713
Organization Type: Specialized/Single Purpose Foundation
Giving Locations: nationally.
Grant Types: Award, General Support, Research.

Donor Information

Founder: Established in 1977 by Arnold Orville Beckman and his wife, the late Mabel Meinzer Beckman (d. 1989). In 1934, while a professor of chemistry at the California Institute of Technology, Dr. Beckman invented the glass electrode pH meter. In 1941, he invented the quartz spectrophotometer. He went on to found Beckman Instruments, a company which develops and manufactures analytical and electronic instruments, precision components, and chemical products for medical, industrial, environmental, and scientific applications.

Financial Summary

Total Giving: $17,457,722 (fiscal year ending August 31, 2003); $20,719,938 (fiscal 2002); $20,000,000 (fiscal 2001 approx)
Giving Analysis: Giving for fiscal 2003 includes: foundation matching gifts ($106,850); foundation scholarships ($1,137,425); fiscal 2002: foundation scholarships ($907,725)
Assets: $350,492,105 (fiscal 2003); $334,260,791 (fiscal 2002)
Gifts Received: $95 (fiscal 2002); $55,150 (fiscal 1999); $19,908,399 (fiscal 1997). Note: In fiscal 1999, contributions were received from Dr. Arnold Beckman.

Typical Recipients

Civic & Public Affairs: Civic & Public Affairs-General, Professional & Trade Associations, Urban & Community Affairs, Zoos/Aquariums
Education: Colleges & Universities, Engineering/Technological Education, Education-General, Science/Mathematics Education, Student Aid, Vocational & Technical Education
Health: Cancer, Clinics/Medical Centers, Eyes/Blindness, Hospitals, Medical Research, Research/Studies Institutes, Speech & Hearing
Science: Science-General, Science Museums, Scientific Centers & Institutes, Scientific Organizations, Scientific Research
Social Services: Community Service Organizations

Application Procedures

Initial Contact: The foundation encourages all applicants to go to website for guidelines and application.
Application Requirements: The proposal should consist of a brief four-page description of proposed work, including the rationale for the work, its potential importance, methods of implementation, progress to date, and any significant outcomes; curriculum vitae for the principal investigator; three letters of reference; the completed two-page application. References, diagrams, and drawings should be incorporated with the four page limitations. One copy of all of the proposal materials must be submitted.
Deadlines: October 1 for consideration in the following fiscal year.
Review Process: Recommendations of the founda-

tion's Grants Advisory Council are forwarded to the foundation's board, whose decisions on awards are final. Notifications of awards are made in the spring. Approved grants will normally be paid quarterly over three years.
Notes: Projects will be supported for periods of one to four years. While the foundation has no fixed limits on the size of grants, grants will normally be about $240,000 over the term of the project.

Restrictions

Funding will not be considered for the following: general institutional expenses; general fundraising campaign expenses, such as dinners and mass mailings; unified funds or organizations that grant funds to other organizations; and social science, religious, political, or other research that does not fall within the foundation's areas of interest.

Additional Information

Funding is limited to principal investigators who have completed no more than three years of their initial appointment as independent researcher (tenure-track assistant professor or equivalent) by the application deadline.
Publications: Statement of Research Grant Policy and Procedures

Corporate Officials

Gavin Shearer Herbert, Jr.: co-founder, chairman emeritus B Los Angeles, CA 1932. ED University of Southern California BS (1954). PRIM CORP EMPL co-founder, chairman emeritus: Allergan. CORP AFFIL director:; director: Cytel Corp. NONPR AFFIL member: Research Prevent Blindness; trustee: University Southern California; member: Pharmaceutical Manufacturer Association; director: Estelle Doheny Eye Foundation; director: Richard Nixon Presidential Foundation; member: Beta Theta Pi. CLUB AFFIL Pacific Club; Big Canyon Country Club; Newport Harbor Yacht Club; Balboa Bay Yacht Club.

Foundation Officials

George L. Argyros: chairman, director B Detroit, MI 1937. ED Michigan State University; Chapman College BS (1959). PRIM CORP EMPL chairman, chief executive officer: Arnel & Affiliates. CORP AFFIL director: Verteq Inc.; director: Newhall Land and Farming Co.; director: Tecstar Inc.; director: Harper Leather Goods Inc.; director: DST Systems Inc.; director: First America Corp.; director: Doskocil Manufacturing Co. NONPR AFFIL chairman: Nixon Center; chairman: Richard Nixon Library & Birthplace Foundation; chairman board trustee: Chapman University; director: Independent Colleges of Southern California; director: Beckman Foundation; trustee: California Institute of Technology.
Arnold W. Beckman: director
G. Patricia Beckman: director NONPR AFFIL trustee: California Institute of Technology.
Theodore Lawrence Brown: director B Green Bay, WI 1928. ED Illinois Institute of Technology BS (1950); Michigan State University PhD (1956). NONPR AFFIL member: Sigma Xi; emeritus professor: University Illinois; member: American Chemical Society; member: American Academy of Arts & Sciences; fellow: American Association Advancement Science; member: Alpha Chi Sigma.
Jackie Dorrance: executive director
Gerald E. Gallwas: director ED San Diego State University BS.
Harry Barkus Gray: director B Woodburn, KY November 14, 1935. ED Western Kentucky University BS (1957); Northwestern University PhD (1960). NONPR AFFIL vis professor: University Witwatersrand; visitors professor: University Yeshiva; visitors professor: University Copenhagen; visitors professor: University Iowa; member: Royal Danish Academy Science & Letters; visitors professor: University Canterbury; visitors professor: Rockefeller University; visitors professor: Pennsylvania State University; member: Phi Lambda Upsilon; professor chem: California

Institute Technology; visitors professor: Harvard University; fellow: American Association Advancement Science; member: American Chemical Society; member: Alpha Chi Sigma.
Gavin Herbert, Sr.: director
Gary H. Hunt: director B 1948. ED Long Island University BA (1970). NONPR AFFIL director: Irvine Health Foundation.
William H. May: director
Gary T. Wescombe: treasurer, chief financial officer

Grants Analysis

Disclosure Period: fiscal year ending August 31, 2003
Total Grants: $16,213,447*
Number of Grants: 13
Average Grant: $1,004,727*
Highest Grant: $4,156,723
Lowest Grant: $75,052
Typical Range: $100,000 to $1,500,000
*Note: Giving excludes scholarships; matching gifts. Average grant figure excludes highest grant.

Recent Grants

Note: Grants derived from 2003 Form 990.
General

4,156,723	Beckman Young Investigator, CA
2,052,450	California Institute of Technology, Pasadena, CA
2,052,450	University of Illinois, Urbana, IL
1,667,000	Doheny Eye Institute, Los Angeles, CA
1,608,300	Stanford University, Stanford, CA
1,500,000	San Diego Zoological Society, San Diego, CA
1,386,225	City of Hope, Duarte, CA
1,137,425	Beckman Scholars Program, Irvine, CA
811,700	Beckman and Science, Santa Ana, CA
584,000	Beckman Laser Institute, Irvine, CA

J. L. BEDSOLE FOUNDATION

Giving Contact

Mabel B. Ward, Executive Director
PO Box 1137
Mobile, AL 36633
Phone: (251)432-3369
Fax: (251)432-1134
E-mail: bedsole2@bellsouth.net

Alternate Contact

Ken Niemeyer, Vice President and Trust Officer
AmSouth Bank, N.A.
Drawer 1628
Mobile, AL 36633
Phone: (334)438-8260

Description

Founded: 1949
EIN: 237225708
Organization Type: General Purpose Foundation
Giving Locations: AL: Southwest part of the state, Mobile
Grant Types: Award, Capital, Conference/Seminar, Endowment, General Support, Operating Expenses, Professorship, Scholarship.

Donor Information

Founder: Established in 1949 by a small donation from J. L. Bedsole to help young people achieve a college education, the foundation was fully funded in 1988 after Mr. Bedsole's death in 1975.
Joseph Linyer Bedsole was born August 7, 1881 in Clarke County, AL. In 1919, he moved to Mobile where he organized the Bedsole-Colvin Drug Company. He was a director of the First National Bank of Mobile for over fifty years and also served as a director of the Alabama Power Company for twenty years.

Mr. Bedsole was active in many charitable enterprises. In 1947, as chairman of the Mobile Infirmary Campaign, he organized the fundraising campaign to build the new hospital, which was dedicated in 1952. In 1951, he was named "Mobilian of the Year" and was selected "Man of the Year" by Howard College (now Samford University), where he served on the board of trustees from 1939-62. Mr. Bedsole also received the first honorary degree awarded by the University of Mobile, where he served as chairman of the board of trustees from 1962-67.

He was married in 1910 to Phala Bradford. Their only child, Lt. Joseph Linyer Bedsole, Jr., a B-17 Bomber pilot with the U.S. Army Air Corps and holder of the Distinguished Flying Cross, was killed in a bomber raid over Germany in April 1944.

Financial Summary

Total Giving: $3,219,220 (2002)
Giving Analysis: Giving for 2002 includes: foundation gifts to individuals ($28,500); foundation scholarships ($551,900)
Assets: $70,100,596 (2002)

Typical Recipients

Arts & Humanities: Arts Associations & Councils, Arts Centers, Arts Festivals, Ballet, Arts & Humanities-General, Historic Preservation, History & Archaeology, Libraries, Museums/Galleries, Music, Opera, Performing Arts, Public Broadcasting, Theater, Visual Arts

Civic & Public Affairs: Botanical Gardens/Parks, Business/Free Enterprise, Chambers of Commerce, Clubs, Community Foundations, Economic Development, Civic & Public Affairs-General, Housing, Municipalities/Towns, Parades/Festivals, Philanthropic Organizations, Public Policy, Rural Affairs, Safety, Urban & Community Affairs

Education: Business Education, Colleges & Universities, Community & Junior Colleges, Economic Education, Education Associations, Education Funds, Elementary Education (Private), Elementary Education (Public), Engineering/Technological Education, Education-General, International Exchange, Leadership Training, Legal Education, Literacy, Medical Education, Private Education (Precollege), Public Education (Precollege), Science/Mathematics Education, Secondary Education (Public), Social Sciences Education, Special Education, Student Aid, Vocational & Technical Education

Environment: Forestry, Environment-General, Research

Health: Children's Health/Hospitals, Clinics/Medical Centers, Eyes/Blindness, Health-General, Health Funds, Health Organizations, Hospitals, Mental Health, Outpatient Health Care, Public Health, Single-Disease Health Associations

International: Foreign Arts Organizations, International Relief Efforts

Religion: Churches, Religion-General, Religious Organizations, Religious Welfare

Science: Observatories & Planetariums, Science Museums, Scientific Centers & Institutes, Scientific Research

Social Services: Animal Protection, Big Brothers/Big Sisters, Camps, Child Welfare, Community Centers, Community Service Organizations, Day Care, Emergency Relief, Family Services, Food/Clothing Distribution, People with Disabilities, Recreation & Athletics, Scouts, Shelters/Homelessness, Social Services-General, Substance Abuse, United Funds/United Ways, Veterans, Volunteer Services, YMCA/YWCA/YMHA/YWHA, Youth Organizations

Application Procedures

Initial Contact: Applicants should submit a written request to the foundation. Application forms and descriptive brochures for the Bedsole Scholarship Program are sent to high school counselors in southwest Alabama. Application forms are also sent to individuals upon request.
Application Requirements: The preliminary letter

should be short and include the organization name, proof of tax-exempt status, a brief description of the project and the name, address, and telephone number of the contact person.
Deadlines: None for grant requests. Application forms for the Bedsole Scholars Program are due November 30.
Review Process: The board meets every other month. If the foundation has an interest in the proposal then the applicant will be requested to furnish additional information about the project and the organization.

Restrictions

Grants are limited to Southwest Alabama. Bedsole Scholarships are awarded only to graduates of southwest Alabama high schools who achieve a minimum high school GPA of 2.50. Preference is given to high school seniors attending public or private schools in Mobile, Baldwin, Clarke, Monroe, or Washington Counties and Sweet Water High School in Marengo County.

Additional Information

Publications: Application Form
Trust(s): AmSouth Bank, NA

Foundation Officials

M. Palmer Bedsole: member distribution committee B 1928. PRIM CORP EMPL president, chief executive officer, director: Bedsole Medical Companies Inc.
T. Massey Bedsole: chairman distribution committee, trustee ADD CORP EMPL member: Hand Arendall LLC. CORP AFFIL vice president: Mobile Fixture & Equipment Co.
Travis M. Bedsole, Jr.: member distribution committee
Ken Niemeyer: trustee PRIM CORP EMPL trustee officer: AmSouth Bank.
Mabel B. Ward: executive director
T. Bestor Ward, III: mem distribution comm
Robert Williams: member distribution committee

Grants Analysis

Disclosure Period: calendar year ending 2002
Total Grants: $2,638,820*
Number of Grants: 51
Average Grant: $35,184*
Highest Grant: $500,000
Lowest Grant: $1,000
Typical Range: $10,000 to $50,000
*Note: Giving excludes gifts to individuals and scholarships. Average grant figure excludes three highest grants ($950,000).

Recent Grants

Note: Grants derived from 2002 Form 990.
Library-Related
150,000	Mobile Public Library, Mobile, AL
10,000	Grove Hill Public Library, Grove Hill, AL
10,000	Monroe County Public Library, Monroe County, IN

General
551,900	J. L. Bedsole Scholars Program, Mobile, AL
500,000	Center for the Living Arts, Mississauga, ON Canada
250,000	Spring Hill College, Mobile, AL
200,000	Mobile Area Chamber of Commerce Foundation Inc., Mobile, AL
175,000	University of Mobile, Mobile, AL
111,250	Gulf Coast Exploreum Museum of Science, Mobile, AL
100,000	Mobile Historic Development Commission, Mobile, AL
100,000	Mobile Museum of Art, Mobile, AL
80,000	University of South Alabama - J. L. Bedsole International Scholars, Mobile, AL
75,000	Dumas Wesley Community Center, Mobile, AL

FLORENCE SIMON BEECHER FOUNDATION

Giving Contact

c/o Sky Trust, Trust Dept.
PO Box 479
Youngstown, OH 44501-0479
Phone: (330)742-7035

Description

Founded: 1969
EIN: 346613413
Organization Type: Private Foundation
Giving Locations: OH: Youngstown
Grant Types: Capital, General Support, Scholarship.

Donor Information

Founder: Florence Simon Beecher

Financial Summary

Total Giving: $292,000 (2003); $475,233 (2002); $186,766 (2001)
Giving Analysis: Giving for 2003 includes: foundation scholarships ($10,000); foundation grants to United Way ($12,500); 2002: foundation scholarships ($10,000); foundation grants to United Way ($37,500)
Assets: $8,609,018 (2003); $8,123,933 (2002); $9,028,198 (2001)
Gifts Received: $2,150,729 (1992). Note: In 1992, contributions were received from the Florence Simon Beecher Trust.

Typical Recipients

Arts & Humanities: Arts Centers, Arts Institutes, Historic Preservation, History & Archaeology, Libraries, Music, Performing Arts, Theater
Civic & Public Affairs: Botanical Gardens/Parks, Business/Free Enterprise, Urban & Community Affairs
Education: Colleges & Universities, Education-General, Private Education (Precollege), Student Aid
Health: Health Organizations, Hospitals, Long-Term Care, Nursing Services, Public Health, Speech & Hearing
Religion: Churches, Religion-General, Religious Welfare
Social Services: Camps, Community Service Organizations, Domestic Violence, Family Planning, Homes, People with Disabilities, Senior Services, United Funds/United Ways, YMCA/YWCA/YMHA/YWHA, Youth Organizations

Application Procedures

Initial Contact: Send a brief letter of inquiry.
Application Requirements: Include a description of organization, amount requested, purpose of funds sought, recently audited financial statement, and proof of tax-exempt status.
Deadlines: None.

Restrictions

Does not support individuals, religious organizations for sectarian purposes, political or lobbying groups, or organizations outside operating areas.

Additional Information

Trust(s): Sky Trust.

Foundation Officials

Eleanor Beecher Flad: chairman
Erle L. Flad: director
Ward Beecher Flad: director
Gregory L. Ridler: director
Patrick A. Sebastiano: director

Grants Analysis

Disclosure Period: calendar year ending 2003
Total Grants: $269,500*
Number of Grants: 19
Average Grant: $7,029*

Highest Grant: $100,000
Lowest Grant: $1,500
Typical Range: $5,000 to $10,000
*Note: Giving excludes United Way; scholarships. Average grant figure excludes two highest grants ($150,000).

Recent Grants

Note: Grants derived from 2001 Form 990.
General

25,000	Friends of Fellows Gardens, Youngstown, OH -- for Sheridan Memorial Gardens
18,920	Shrine of Our Lady Comforter, Youngstown, OH -- for painting and repair of windows
18,700	Shrine of Our Lady Comforter, Youngstown, OH -- for roof repair
13,000	Butler Institute of American Art, Youngstown, OH -- for installation of Viola Exhibit
12,500	St. Patrick's Church, Youngstown, OH -- for restoration of stained glass windows
11,000	Youngstown and Mahoning Valley United Way, Youngstown, OH -- for leadership
10,000	Mahoning Valley Historical Society, Youngstown, OH -- endowment fund
10,000	Park Vista Retirement Community, Youngstown, OH -- for Life Care Fund
10,000	St. Elizabeth Development Foundation, Youngstown, OH -- for mobile clinic
10,000	Youngstown Playhouse, Youngstown, OH -- for playhouse presentations

BELK STORES SERVICES INC.

Company Headquarters

Charlotte, NC
Web: http://www.belk.com

Company Description

Employees: 2,300
SIC(s): 7389 Business Services Nec, 8721 Accounting, Auditing & Bookkeeping.

Operating Locations

Belk Stores Services Inc. (AL; AR; FL; GA; MD; MS; NC; SC; TX; VA; WV)

Nonmonetary Support

Note: In 1998, 10,681 shares of North Carolina Railroad (NCRR) were contributed to 12 different charities at fair market value.

✳ Belk Foundation

Giving Contact

Paul B. Wyche, Jr., Trustee
2801 West Tyvola Road
Charlotte, NC 28217-4500
Phone: (704)357-1000
Fax: (704)357-1883
Web: http://belk.com/main/
about_philanthropic.jsp?bmUID=1029805668286

Alternate Contact

Susan Blount, Administrative Assistant
E-mail: susan_blount@belk.com

Description

Founded: 1988
EIN: 566046450
Organization Type: Corporate Foundation
Giving Locations: GA; NC; SC
Grant Types: Capital, General Support, Multiyear/Continuing Support, Project.

Financial Summary

Total Giving: $2,592,461 (fiscal year ending May 31, 2003); $2,915,731 (fiscal 2002); $2,900,000 (fiscal 2001 approx)
Giving Analysis: Giving for fiscal 2003 includes: foundation scholarships ($110,000); foundation grants to United Way ($304,250); fiscal 2001: foundation grants to United Way ($87,725); foundation ($2,730,679)
Assets: $47,929,032 (fiscal 2003); $50,253,778 (fiscal 2002)
Gifts Received: $941,104 (fiscal 2003); $511,170 (fiscal 2002); $595,651 (fiscal 2000). Note: In fiscal 2002 and 2003, contributions were received from Belk Inc. In 1994, contributions were received from Belk stores throughout Georgia and North and South Carolina.

Typical Recipients

Arts & Humanities: Arts Associations & Councils, Ethnic & Folk Arts, History & Archaeology, Libraries, Museums/Galleries, Music, Opera, Public Broadcasting
Civic & Public Affairs: African American Affairs, Botanical Gardens/Parks, Business/Free Enterprise, Clubs, Community Foundations, Employment/Job Training, Civic & Public Affairs-General, Housing, Parades/Festivals, Urban & Community Affairs, Women's Affairs
Education: Afterschool/Enrichment Programs, Arts/Humanities Education, Business Education, Business-School Partnerships, Colleges & Universities, Community & Junior Colleges, Economic Education, Education Associations, Education Funds, Education Reform, Elementary Education (Private), Elementary Education (Public), Literacy, Medical Education, Minority Education, Preschool Education, Private Education (Precollege), Public Education (Precollege), Religious Education, Science/Mathematics Education, Secondary Education (Private), Student Aid, Vocational & Technical Education
Environment: Environment-General, Resource Conservation
Health: Arthritis, Cancer, Children's Health/Hospitals, Emergency/Ambulance Services, Health Funds, Health Organizations, Heart, Hospitals, Hospitals (University Affiliated), Medical Rehabilitation
Religion: Churches, Ministries, Religious Organizations, Religious Welfare, Seminaries
Social Services: Child Welfare, Community Service Organizations, Emergency Relief, Family Planning, Family Services, Homes, Recreation & Athletics, Scouts, Senior Services, Shelters/Homelessness, Social Services-General, Substance Abuse, United Funds/United Ways, YMCA/YWCA/YMHA/YWHA, Youth Organizations

Application Procedures

Initial Contact: Send a request for grant summary form. Unsolicited grant proposals are not accepted.
Application Requirements: Include with completed form: a description of organization; amount requested; purpose of funds sought; recently audited financial statement; proof of tax-exempt status; and whether single-year or multi-year grant is requested.
Deadlines: None.
Decision Notification: Foundation will review grant request and contact organization if interested in funding proposal.

Additional Information

Each of the Belk stores operates as an individual corp., but contributes through the foundation, including the Belk-Tyler Foundation in Rocky Mountain, NC and Belk-Simpson Foundation in Greenville, SC.
Publications: Grant Summary Form

Corporate Officials

John Montgomery Belk: chairman, chief executive officer B Charlotte, NC 1920. ED Davidson College (1943). PRIM CORP EMPL chairman, chief executive officer: Belk Inc. ADD CORP EMPL chief executive officer, chairman: Belk Stores Services Inc. CORP AFFIL director: Texas Industries Inc.; director: Coca-Cola Bottling Co. Consolidated; director: Brothers Investment Co.; director: Chaparral Steel Co.; chairman: Belk-Hudson Inc. Spartanburg SC. NONPR AFFIL member: National Retail Federation.

Foundation Officials

Claudia W. Belk: member board advisors
John Montgomery Belk: chairman, member board advisors (see above)
James K. Glenn, Jr.: member board advisors
B. Frank Matthews, II: member board advisors B 1928. PRIM CORP EMPL executive vice president, director: Matthews-Belk Co. CORP AFFIL officer: Public Service Co. NC.
Katherine B. Morris: member board advisors
Leroy Robinson: member board advisors CORP AFFIL director: Belk-Gallant, La Grange Georgia; director: Charlotte Belk Inc.; director: Belk Department Store, Rock Hill.

Grants Analysis

Disclosure Period: fiscal year ending May 31, 2003
Total Grants: $2,178,211*
Number of Grants: 56
Average Grant: $30,513*
Highest Grant: $500,000
Lowest Grant: $1,000
Typical Range: $5,000 to $100,000
*Note: Giving excludes scholarship and United Way. Average grant figure excludes highest grant.

Recent Grants

Note: Grants derived from 2003 Form 990.
General

1,500,000	Belk College of Business UNCC, Charlotte, NC -- fund for int'l business program at UNCC
1,000,000	Charlotte Country Day School, Charlotte, NC -- for Believe and Achieve campaign
700,000	Union Theological Seminary, New York, NY -- fund for Satellite Program at Queens College
500,000	Central Piedmont Community College, Charlotte, NC -- to assist in Criminal Justice Program
500,000	Converse College, Spartanburg, SC -- fund to remodel Belk Dormitory
500,000	UNCC - Belk College of Business, Charlotte, NC -- to assist in pledge payment
375,000	High Point University, High Point, NC -- fund for the renovation of the restoration of the MIB residence hall
250,000	Charlotte Latin, Charlotte, NC -- to assist in Legacy of Excellence campaign
250,000	Crossnore School, Crossnore, NC -- fund in honor of Mrs. Mary I. Belk
250,000	Gaston Day School, Gastonia, NC -- to support new athletic complex

S. LEWIS AND LUCIA B. BELL FOUNDATION

Giving Contact

Joseph M. McElwee
PO Box 832
Chester, SC 29706-0832
Phone: (803)581-9198

Description

Founded: 1991
EIN: 570932788
Organization Type: Private Foundation
Giving Locations: gives nationally.
Grant Types: General Support.

Financial Summary

Total Giving: $80,110 (2003); $74,235 (2001)
Giving Analysis: Giving for 2003 includes: foundation grants to United Way ($1,000)
Assets: $1,646,241 (2003); $1,541,531 (2001)
Gifts Received: $130,000 (2004); $130,000 (2001); $130,000 (2000). Note: In 1994, contributions were received from the Lucia Beason Bell Trust.

Typical Recipients

Arts & Humanities: Art History
Civic & Public Affairs: Municipalities/Towns, Urban & Community Affairs
Education: Afterschool/Enrichment Programs, Colleges & Universities, Education Funds, Education-General, Public Education (Precollege), Vocational & Technical Education
Health: Emergency/Ambulance Services, Health-General, Hospices
Religion: Churches, Religious Welfare
Social Services: Community Service Organizations, Emergency Relief, People with Disabilities, Scouts, Social Services-General, United Funds/United Ways, YMCA/YWCA/YMHA/YWHA, Youth Organizations

Application Procedures

Initial Contact: Send a brief letter of inquiry.
Application Requirements: a description of organization and purpose of funds sought.
Deadlines: None.

Restrictions

Restricted to Chester County, SC.

Foundation Officials

Ladson F. Stringfellow: trustee
D. C. Wylie, Jr.: trustee

Grants Analysis

Disclosure Period: calendar year ending 2003
Total Grants: $79,110*
Number of Grants: 11
Average Grant: $3,123*
Highest Grant: $31,000
Lowest Grant: $500
Typical Range: $1,000 to $5,000
*Note: Giving excludes United Way. Average grant figure excludes two highest grants ($51,000).

Recent Grants

Note: Grants derived from 2003 Form 990.
General

31,000	York Tech College Foundation, York, SC
20,000	Chester County School District, Chester, SC
10,000	Erskine College, Due West, SC
3,500	Salvation Army, Chester, SC
2,110	Chester County 4-H, Chester, SC
2,000	Chester County Department of Social Services, Chester, SC
2,000	Chester Hospice, Chester, SC
2,000	Chester Rescue Squad, Chester, SC
2,000	Great Falls Home Town Association, Great Falls, SC
2,000	Great Falls Rescue Squad, Great Falls, SC

DALE J. BELLAMAH FOUNDATION

Giving Contact

Frank A. Potenziani, Vice President & Director
PO Box 676370
Rancho Santa Fe, CA 92067
Phone: (858)756-1154
Fax: (858)756-3856
E-mail: dwilson@mnttrust.com

Web: http://www.mnttrust.com

Description

Founded: 1972
EIN: 237177691
Organization Type: Family Foundation
Former Name: Dale J. Bellamah Foundation (2002).
Giving Locations: NM
Grant Types: Capital, Endowment, Fellowship, General Support, Research, Scholarship.

Donor Information

Founder: Established in 1972 by the late Dale J. Bellamah.

Financial Summary

Total Giving: $1,156,000 (2002)
Assets: $31,043,901 (2002)
Gifts Received: $340,665 (1993)

Typical Recipients

Arts & Humanities: Theater
Civic & Public Affairs: Civic & Public Affairs-General, Public Policy
Education: Agricultural Education, Business Education, Colleges & Universities, Education Funds, Engineering/Technological Education, Education-General, Legal Education, Medical Education, Private Education (Precollege), Public Education (Precollege), Science/Mathematics Education, Student Aid
Health: Arthritis, Cancer, Diabetes, Hospitals, Single-Disease Health Associations
International: Foreign Educational Institutions, International Development, International Organizations, International Relief Efforts
Religion: Churches, Religion-General, Religious Welfare
Social Services: Big Brothers/Big Sisters, Community Service Organizations, People with Disabilities, Recreation & Athletics, Youth Organizations

Application Procedures

Initial Contact: Send a brief letter of inquiry describing program or project.
Deadlines: None.

Restrictions

Grants are not made to individuals.

Foundation Officials

Kathleen Guggimio: director
A. F. Potenziani: president, director, manager
Frank A. Potenziani: vice president, director
Martha M. Potenziani: director
William Potenziani: director

Grants Analysis

Disclosure Period: calendar year ending 2002
Total Grants: $1,156,000*
Number of Grants: 15
Average Grant: $77,067
Highest Grant: $468,000
Lowest Grant: $1,000
Typical Range: $10,000 to $100,000 and $5,000 to $45,000
*Note: Giving includes scholarships and fellowships.

Recent Grants

Note: Grants derived from 2002 Form 990.
General

468,000	University of Notre Dame, Notre Dame, IN -- scholarships, Student International Business Council
105,000	Big Brothers and Big Sisters, Philadelphia, PA
100,000	American Diabetes Association, Kansas City, MO -- research projects
100,000	Gilmour Academy, Gates Mills, OH
100,000	Marion Military Academy, Aurora, IL -- campus fund
100,000	University of San Diego High School, San Diego, CA -- academic/athletic scholarships
50,000	American Diabetes Association, Albuquerque, NM -- Youth Program
45,000	University of San Diego, San Diego, CA -- Student International Business Council
30,000	Musical Theater Southwest, Albuquerque, NM
25,000	Benedictine College, Atchison, KS -- Student International Business Council

BELLSOUTH CORP.

Company Headquarters

1155 Peachtree Street NE
Atlanta, GA 30309-3610
Phone: (404)249-2000
Fax: (404)249-5599
Web: http://www.bellsouthcorp.com

Company Description

Ticker: BLS
Exchange: NYSE
Revenue: US$22.729 billion (2004)
Profit: US$4.758 billion (2004)
Employees: 75743 (2003)
Fortune Rank: 87, per FORTUNE Magazine's list of 500 Largest U.S. Corporations (2004).
SIC(s): 4813 Telephone Communications Except Radiotelephone, 6719 Holding Companies Nec.

Nonmonetary Support

Type: Loaned Executives
Note: Co. also offers corporate leadership and management training conferences.

BellSouth Foundation

Giving Contact

Greg Norton, Grants Administrator
1155 Peachtree Street, NE, Room 7H08
Atlanta, GA 30309-3610
Phone: (404)249-2396
Fax: (404)249-5696
E-mail: grants.manager@bellsouth.com
Web: http://www.bellsouthfoundation.org

Alternate Contact

401 S. Tryon Street, 4th Floor
Charlotte, NC 28288-1159

Description

Founded: 1986
EIN: 581708046
Organization Type: Corporate Foundation
Giving Locations: principally near operating locations and to national organizations.
Grant Types: Capital, Conference/Seminar, Emergency, Employee Matching Gifts, Endowment, Fellowship, General Support, Matching, Multiyear/Continuing Support.
Note: Employee matching gift ratio: 2 to 1 for education gifts; 1 to 1 for cultural gifts. Corporate contributions fund operating expenses, employee matching gifts, and conference/seminar gifts. Foundation funds policy studies.

Financial Summary

Total Giving: $1,968,078 (2003); $2,619,737 (2002); $3,006,850 (2001). Note: Contributes through corporate direct giving program and foundation.
Assets: $57,623,848 (2003); $46,792,285 (2002); $55,726,884 (2001)
Gifts Received: $14,000,000 (1996). Note: In 1996, contributions were received from BellSouth Corp.

Typical Recipients

Arts & Humanities: Libraries, Museums/Galleries, Visual Arts

Civic & Public Affairs: Business/Free Enterprise, Chambers of Commerce, Employment/Job Training, Civic & Public Affairs-General, Public Policy, Urban & Community Affairs

Education: Arts/Humanities Education, Business Education, Business-School Partnerships, Colleges & Universities, Community & Junior Colleges, Education Associations, Education Funds, Education Reform, Elementary Education (Private), Elementary Education (Public), Engineering/Technological Education, Faculty Development, Education-General, Health & Physical Education, International Exchange, Leadership Training, Legal Education, Literacy, Medical Education, Minority Education, Preschool Education, Private Education (Precollege), Public Education (Precollege), School Volunteerism, Science/Mathematics Education, Secondary Education (Public), Special Education, Vocational & Technical Education

Environment: Resource Conservation

Health: Health-General

International: International-General, Human Rights, International Organizations

Science: Science Museums, Scientific Centers & Institutes

Social Services: Child Abuse, Child Welfare, Day Care, Family Services, People with Disabilities, Recreation & Athletics, Social Services-General, Youth Organizations

Application Procedures

Initial Contact: Visit website for information on requests for proposals and to apply for an opportunity grant. All applications must be submitted through the website.

Application Requirements: Opportunity grant requests must be submitted as a two-page concept paper using the template available on the website.

Deadlines: Late winter or early spring for foundation Opportunity Grants; the corporation reviews requests on a continuous basis.

Evaluative Criteria: Opportunity Grants will be awarded to programs or projects that: mesh tightly with one of the foundation's strategies; appear to be interesting and valuable endeavors; offer a complementary strategy for the foundation's other work; offer a new and innovative approach to a priority issue; provide a supportive policy-level effort to supplement a foundation priority; or serve as a collaborative practice for a foundation initiative. learned and in replication of successful practices; and are most likely to produce measurable results. learned and in replication of successful practices; and are most likely to produce measurable results. learned and in replication of successful practices; and are most likely to produce measurable results.

Decision Notification: Applicants will receive an email response to an online request. Foundation will invite suitable applicants to submit a full proposal. Board meets in late spring to make final decisions.

Restrictions

The foundation does not support capital or building campaigns; endowments; general operating expenses; education product development; individuals; individual study, research, or travel grants; for-profit entities or start-up businesses; fundraising events or dinners; scholarships; single K-12 schools that are not part of a larger district reform effort; single discipline curricula unrelated to comprehensive school reform; equipment acquisition; programs that are primarily recreational or community-based and not connected to the educational system; any organization that discriminates on the basis of race, creed, ethnicity, gender, sexual orientation, national origin, or disability; programs outside of operating locations, except when invited; or non-tax-exempt organizations.

Additional Information

Publications: Bellsouth Foundation Grant Guidelines 1996-2000; New Strategies for the Bellsouth Foundation; Annual Report on Grantmaking Activity of the Bellsouth Foundation

Corporate Officials

F. Duane Ackerman: chief executive officer, chairman, president, director B Plant City, FL 1942. ED Massachusetts Institute of Technology MS; Rollins College BS (1964); Rollins College MS (1970). PRIM CORP EMPL president, chief executive officer: BellSouth Corp. CORP AFFIL director: Allstate Corp. NONPR AFFIL chairman: National Security Telecommunications Advisory Committee; trustee: Rollins College; member: Homeland Security Advisory Council; chairman: Council on Competitiveness.

Keith O. Cowan: vice president corporate development B Hartford, CT 1956. ED University of North Carolina BS (1978); University of Virginia School of Law JD (1982). PRIM CORP EMPL vice president corporate development: BellSouth Corp. CORP AFFIL director: Medirisk Inc.

Foundation Officials

Alicia Adams: secretary
Valencia Adams: trustee
Bonnie Bush: assistant trustee
Ralph De La Vega: trustee
Suzanne H. Detlefs: trustee, vice president PRIM CORP EMPL president: BellSouth Advertising & Publishing Corp.
Fran Dramis: trustee
Mark E. Droege: trustee
Margaret H Green: trustee, chairman PRIM CORP EMPL group president: Bell South Telecommunications Inc.
Isaiah Harris: trustee
Tom Harvey: assistant treasurer
Nan Johnson: assistant trustee
Donna Lee: trustee
Donna Malone: assistant trustee
Eva Mayhew: assistant trustee
Linda McCann: assistant trustee
John McCullouch: trustee
Charlotte Mitchell: assistant trustee
Kim Mulkey: director, Technology program
Roderick Odom: trustee
William C. Pate: chairman PRIM CORP EMPL vice president advertising and Public Relations: BellSouth Corp.
Ramon L. Rodriguez: associate director grantmaking
Fred Shaftman: trustee
Jacquelyn Tatum: assistant trustee
Krista Tillman: trustee
Michael Watson: trustee

Grants Analysis

Disclosure Period: calendar year ending 2003
Total Grants: $1,818,961*
Number of Grants: 77
Average Grant: $23,623
Highest Grant: $100,000
Lowest Grant: $1,000
Typical Range: $15,000 to $60,000
*Note: Giving excludes gifts to individuals.

Recent Grants

Note: Grants derived from 2003 Form 990.

General

100,000	Center for Leadership in School Reform, Louisville, KY
100,000	Center for Leadership in School Reform, Louisville, KY
100,000	Fifth Third Bank of Kentucky, KY
86,000	Mississippi Department of Education, Jackson, MS
55,000	Fundacion Mario Santo Domingo
55,000	Fundacion Mario Santo Domingo
55,000	North Carolina State Treasurer, Raleigh, NC
50,000	Association Concien
50,000	Association Conciencia
50,000	Mississippi State University, MS

BELO CORP.

Company Headquarters

400 S. Record Street
Dallas, TX 75202
Phone: (214)977-6606
Fax: (214)977-7655
Web: http://www.belo.com

Company Description

Founded: 1842
Ticker: BLC
Exchange: NYSE
Former Name: A.H. Belo Corp. (2000).
Revenue: US$1.427 billion (2002)
Employees: 7900 (2003)
SIC(s): 2711 Newspapers, 4833 Television Broadcasting Stations.

Operating Locations

A.H. Belo Corp. (CA--Sacramento; LA--Gretna, New Orleans; OK--Tulsa; TX--Cedar Hill, Dallas, Houston, Plano; VA--Hampton, Norfolk; WA--Seattle)

Belo Foundation

Giving Contact

Judith Garrett Segura, President, Executive Director
The Belo Foundation
PO Box 655237
Dallas, TX 75265-5237
Phone: (214)977-6661
Fax: (214)977-6620
Web: http://www.belo.com/aboutbelo/philanthropy.html

Description

Founded: 1952
EIN: 752564365
Organization Type: Corporate Foundation
Former Name: Dallas Morning News-WFAA Foundation.
Former Name: A. H. Belo Corp. FND (2001).
Giving Locations: CA: Claremont, Oakland, Pasadena; DC: Washington; GA: Atlanta; ID: Boise; IL: Charleston; KY: Louisville; NY: New York; TX: Austin, Dallas, Ft. Worth, Irving; VA: Arlington, Reston
Grant Types: Capital, Endowment, General Support.

Financial Summary

Total Giving: $1,977,875 (2002); $3,191,428 (2001).
Note: Contributes through corporate direct giving program and foundation.
Assets: $34,480,889 (2002); $45,491,589 (2001)
Gifts Received: $4,050,000 (2001); $250,000 (1993). Note: Contributions are received from Belo Corp.

Typical Recipients

Arts & Humanities: Arts Associations & Councils, Arts Centers, Arts Institutes, Ethnic & Folk Arts, Arts & Humanities-General, Historic Preservation, History & Archaeology, Libraries, Museums/Galleries, Music, Public Broadcasting, Theater, Visual Arts

Civic & Public Affairs: African American Affairs, Botanical Gardens/Parks, Community Foundations, Economic Development, Employment/Job Training, First Amendment Issues, Civic & Public Affairs-General, Hispanic Affairs, Law & Justice, Municipalities/Towns, Nonprofit Management, Parades/

Festivals, Professional & Trade Associations, Public Policy, Safety, Urban & Community Affairs
Education: Afterschool/Enrichment Programs, Arts/Humanities Education, Colleges & Universities, Economic Education, Education Funds, Education-General, Journalism/Media Education, Legal Education, Literacy, Secondary Education (Private)
Health: AIDS/HIV, Diabetes, Health Organizations, Hospitals
International: International-General, Human Rights
Religion: Dioceses
Social Services: Child Welfare, Community Service Organizations, Family Planning, Shelters/Homelessness, Social Services-General, United Funds/United Ways, Youth Organizations

Application Procedures

Initial Contact: Send a brief letter of inquiry. Phone calls in advance of the application are encouraged.
Application Requirements: Include a minimum of background material, a list of officers and directors, and proof of tax-exempt status.
Deadlines: None.
Review Process: The foundation is governed by a board of trustees; smaller requests are reviewed year-round for community service support; however, capital and endowment grants in the foundation's focus areas are considered three times a year.
Notes: The foundation encourages calls and letters of inquiry before the submission of a full proposal.

Additional Information

A.H. Belo Corp.'s companion philanthropic foundation was established in 1952, named in honor of G.P. Dealey, founder of *The Dallas Morning News* and majority owner of Belo from 1926 until his death in 1946. Its name changed to the Dallas Morning News-WFAA Foundation in 1983, and in 1995, it was renamed the A.H. Belo Corp. Foundation. In 2000, the foundation was one again renamed the Belo Foundation. The above profile reflects contributions by Belo Corp., *The Dallas Morning News,* and WFAA-TV. Wholly-owned operating companies handle local requests for support and public service announcements independently. Contact the appropriate company directly.

Corporate Officials

Robert William Decherd: chairman, president, chief executive officer, director B Dallas, TX 1951. ED Harvard University BA (1973). PRIM CORP EMPL chairman, president, chief executive officer, director: A.H. Belo Corp. CORP AFFIL chairman: Owensboro Messenger Inquirer; chairman: Henderson Gleaner; director: Kimberly-Clark Corp.; chairman, chief executive officer: Audubon Printers Ink Ltd. NONPR AFFIL member: Newspaper Association America; trustee: Tomas Rivera Policy Institute.
Ward L. Huey, Jr.: president broadcast division, vice chairman, director B Dallas, TX 1938. ED Southern Methodist University BA (1960). PRIM CORP EMPL president broadcast division, vice chairman, director: A.H. Belo Corp. CORP AFFIL president: WWL TV Inc.; vice chairman: Maxium Service Television; president: 3rd Avenue Television Inc. NONPR AFFIL member executive committee: State Fair Texas; member: TV Bureau Advertising; trustee: Southern Methodist University; member executive committee: Southern Methodist University Meadows School Arts; director: Dallas Foundation; member: Maxium Service TV Association; Member: Dallas Advertising League; member: Association Broadcast Executives Texas. CLUB AFFIL Salesmanship Club Dallas; Dallas Country Club.
Burl Osborne: president publishing division, director B Jenkins, KY 1937. ED University of Kentucky (1955-1957); Marshall University BA (1960); Harvard University Graduate School of Business Administration AMP (1984); Long Island University MBA (1984). PRIM CORP EMPL president publishing division, director: A.H. Belo Corp. CORP AFFIL director, publisher, editor: Dallas Morning News. NONPR AFFIL member: Organization Professional Journalists;

member: Southern Newspaper Publishers Association; director: Newspaper Association America; board member: Nieman Foundation; board member: Harvard University; member journalism advisory committee: Knight Foundation; member: American Society Newspaper Editors.

Foundation Officials

Robert William Decherd: trustee (see above)
Judith M. Garrett: president, executive director
Ward L. Huey, Jr.: vice president, trustee (see above)
Amy Mettlen Meadows: executive director
James McQueen Moroney, Jr.: trustee B Dallas, TX 1921. ED University of Texas BBA (1943). CORP AFFIL director: A.H. Belo Corp. NONPR AFFIL chairman: University Dallas.
Becky W. Odlozil: executive director
Burl Osborne: chairman, trustee (see above)

Grants Analysis

Disclosure Period: calendar year ending 2002
Total Grants: $1,717,875*
Number of Grants: 22
Average Grant: $10,375*
Highest Grant: $1,500,000
Lowest Grant: $2,000
Typical Range: $2,000 to $25,000
*Note: Giving excludes United Way. Average grant figure excludes highest grant.

Recent Grants

Note: Grants derived from 2003 Form 990.
General

1,500,000	Southern Methodist University, Dallas, TX
260,000	United Way of Metropolitan Dallas Inc., Dallas, TX
30,000	City of Dallas, Dallas, TX
25,000	Boys and Girls Clubs, Dallas, TX
25,000	Southern Methodist University, Dallas, TX
20,000	Dallas City Plan Inc., Dallas, TX
20,000	Museum of Television and Radio New York, New York, NY
15,000	American Press Institute Inc., Reston, VA
15,000	Tomas Rivera Center Claremont California, Claremont, CA
10,000	American Society of Newspaper Editors Foundation, Reston, VA

BEMIS COMPANY INC.

Company Headquarters

222 S. Ninth Street
Suite 2300
Minneapolis, MN 55402-4099
Phone: (612)376-3000
Web: http://www.bemis.com

Company Description

Founded: 1858
Ticker: BMS
Exchange: NYSE
Revenue: US$2.369 billion (2002)
Employees: 11500 (2003)
SIC(s): 2672 Coated & Laminated Paper Nec, 3565 Packaging Machinery.

Operating Locations

Bemis Co., Inc. (CO--Highlands Ranch; FL--Altamonte Springs; IL--Peoria; KS--Shawnee Mission; MI--De Witt; NE--Omaha; NJ--Flemington; NY--Huntington; OH--Cuyahoga Falls; PA--Doylestown, Hazleton; TX--Magnolia, Richardson; WI--Middleton, Neenah)

Bemis Co. Foundation

Giving Contact

Gene H. Seashore, Trustee
Bemis Co. Foundation
222 South 9th Street, Suite 2300
Minneapolis, MN 55402-4099
Phone: (612)376-3008
E-mail: contactbemis@bemis.com
Web: http://www.bemis.com/corp_citizenship/grant_procedure.html

Description

Founded: 1959
EIN: 416038616
Organization Type: Corporate Foundation
Giving Locations: MN: Minneapolis principally near operating locations and to national organizations.
Grant Types: Capital, Employee Matching Gifts, General Support, Matching, Scholarship.
Note: Employee matching gift ratio: 2 to 1 for education and Food Shelves. Annual budget is committed to multi-year grants and no more than 20% of annual budget is committed to capital programs.

Financial Summary

Total Giving: $2,271,764 (2003); $2,036,417 (2002); $2,558,438 (2001). Note: Contributes through corporate direct giving program and foundation.
Giving Analysis: Giving for 2002 includes: foundation matching gifts ($53,543); foundation grants to United Way ($352,061); foundation scholarships ($520,085); 2001: foundation matching gifts ($288,222); foundation grants to United Way ($310,553); foundation scholarships ($442,046); foundation ($1,517,617)
Assets: $995,028 (2003); $957,700 (2002); $958,191 (2001)
Gifts Received: $2,365,000 (2003); $2,035,000 (2002); $2,615,000 (2001). Note: In 2002 and 2003, contributions were received from Bemis Company, Inc.

Typical Recipients

Arts & Humanities: Arts Appreciation, Arts Associations & Councils, Arts Centers, Arts Institutes, Arts Outreach, History & Archaeology, Libraries, Museums/Galleries, Music, Opera, Performing Arts, Public Broadcasting, Theater, Visual Arts
Civic & Public Affairs: African American Affairs, Botanical Gardens/Parks, Business/Free Enterprise, Community Foundations, Economic Development, Employment/Job Training, Civic & Public Affairs-General, Housing, Public Policy, Safety, Urban & Community Affairs, Women's Affairs, Zoos/Aquariums
Education: Business Education, Colleges & Universities, Community & Junior Colleges, Education Associations, Education Funds, Education Reform, Elementary Education (Private), Engineering/Technological Education, Education-General, Health & Physical Education, International Studies, Legal Education, Medical Education, Minority Education, Preschool Education, Private Education (Precollege), Public Education (Precollege), Religious Education, Science/Mathematics Education, Student Aid, Vocational & Technical Education
Environment: Environment-General
Health: Clinics/Medical Centers, Diabetes, Emergency/Ambulance Services, Health-General, Health Policy/Cost Containment, Health Funds, Health Organizations, Heart, Hospices, Hospitals, Mental Health, Nursing Services, Prenatal Health Issues, Public Health, Single-Disease Health Associations, Speech & Hearing
International: International Environmental Issues, International Peace & Security Issues
Religion: Bible Study/Translation, Ministries, Religious Welfare
Science: Science Museums
Social Services: Child Abuse, Child Welfare, Com-

munity Centers, Community Service Organizations, Counseling, Day Care, Domestic Violence, Emergency Relief, Family Planning, Family Services, Food/Clothing Distribution, Homes, People with Disabilities, Recreation & Athletics, Scouts, Senior Services, Shelters/Homelessness, Social Services-General, Substance Abuse, United Funds/United Ways, Volunteer Services, YMCA/YWCA/YMHA/YWHA, Youth Organizations

Application Procedures

Initial Contact: Send a brief letter or proposal by mail.

Application Requirements: Include organization's name and certificate; outline of proposed project; proposed budget; brief description of objectives and how they are to be attained; list of officers and board members; and proof of tax-exempt status.

Deadlines: None.

Evaluative Criteria: Project is within giving categories and proposal displays an innovative approach to effectively serving people. Preference is given to institutions that are supported by Bemis employees through contributions of time or money.

Restrictions

Grants do not support non tax-exempt organizations, individuals, organizations for religious or political purposes, or lobbying efforts or campaigns. Company prefers not to give to educational capital funds, endowments, or trips or tours.

Grants will not exceed 5% of total requirements of any organization or campaign. No grants are approved for more than three years.

Additional Information

The basis for charitable contributions is 2% of company's domestic pretax profits.

Publications: Annual Community Relations Report

Corporate Officials

Benjamin R. Field, III: senior vice president, chief financial officer, treasurer B Hartford, CT 1938. ED Williams College BA (1961); Harvard University Graduate School of Business Administration MBA (1963). PRIM CORP EMPL senior vice president, chief financial officer, treasurer: Bemis Co., Inc.

Foundation Officials

Gene C. Wulf: trustee B 1950. PRIM CORP EMPL vice president, chief financial officer, treasurer: Bemis Co. Inc. CORP AFFIL vice president: Curwood Inc.; treasurer: Perfecseal Inc.

Grants Analysis

Disclosure Period: calendar year ending 2003
Total Grants: $930,171*
Number of Grants: 972
Average Grant: $700*
Highest Grant: $250,000
Lowest Grant: $50
Typical Range: $100 to $2,500
*Note: Giving includes matching gifts; scholarship; United Way. Average grant figure excludes highest grant.

Recent Grants

Note: Grants derived from 2003 Form 990.
Library-Related
23,000	Drake Free Public Library, Centerville, IA

General
555,460	Scholarship America Inc., St. Peter, MN
250,000	Science Museum of Minnesota, St. Paul, MN
100,000	Youth Futures, Appleton, WI
75,000	United Way of Minneapolis Area, Minneapolis, MN
55,000	United Way of Wabash Valley, Terre Haute, IN
50,000	Vigo County Education Foundation, Terre Haute, IN

26,510	Gateway United Way of Clinton, Clinton, IA
25,000	Guthrie Theater, Minneapolis, MN
25,000	Kids First, Minneapolis, MN
25,000	Mental Health Association in Vigo County, Terre Haute, IN

BEMIS MANUFACTURING CO.

Company Headquarters

300 Mill Street
PO Box 901
Sheboygan Falls, WI 53085
Phone: 800-558-7651
Fax: (920)467-8573
E-mail: corp@BemisMfg.com
Web: http://www.bemismfg.com

Company Description

Employees: 1200 (2003)
SIC(s): 2499 Wood Products Nec, 2511 Wood Household Furniture, 3084 Plastics Pipe, 3089 Plastics Products Nec, 3944 Games, Toys & Children's Vehicles, 3991 Brooms & Brushes.

F.K. Bemis Family Foundation

Giving Contact

Richard A. Bemis, President
PO Box 901
Sheboygan Falls, WI 53085-0901
Phone: (920)467-4621
Fax: (920)467-8573
E-mail: corp@BemisMfg.com

Description

Founded: 1953
EIN: 396067930
Organization Type: Corporate Foundation
Giving Locations: MA; WI: Sheboygan County
Grant Types: Capital, General Support, Scholarship.

Donor Information

Founder: Bemis Manufacturing

Financial Summary

Total Giving: $223,200 (2003); $307,700 (2002); $409,100 (2001). Note: Contributes through foundation only.

Giving Analysis: Giving for 2001 includes: foundation ($2,000); foundation scholarships ($9,000); foundation ($398,100)

Assets: $105,205 (2003); $17 (2002); $17 (2001)

Gifts Received: $132,160 (2003); $307,700 (2002); $409,100 (2001). Note: Contributions were received from Bemis Manufacturing Co.

Typical Recipients

Arts & Humanities: Arts Associations & Councils, Arts Centers, Arts Festivals, Arts Institutes, Ballet, Historic Preservation, History & Archaeology, Libraries, Museums/Galleries, Music, Performing Arts, Public Broadcasting, Theater

Civic & Public Affairs: Botanical Gardens/Parks, Business/Free Enterprise, Clubs, Employment/Job Training, Civic & Public Affairs-General, Professional & Trade Associations, Urban & Community Affairs

Education: Afterschool/Enrichment Programs, Business Education, Colleges & Universities, Education Funds, Engineering/Technological Education, Education-General, Private Education (Precollege), Public Education (Precollege), Student Aid, Vocational & Technical Education

Environment: Environment-General

Health: Cancer, Children's Health/Hospitals, Clinics/Medical Centers, Emergency/Ambulance Services, Hospitals, Medical Research

International: Foreign Educational Institutions

Religion: Churches, Religious Welfare

Social Services: Camps, Child Welfare, Community Service Organizations, Day Care, Family Services, People with Disabilities, Recreation & Athletics, Scouts, Social Services-General, Special Olympics, United Funds/United Ways, YMCA/YWCA/YMHA/YWHA

Application Procedures

Initial Contact: Send a brief letter of inquiry.
Application Requirements: Include purpose of funds sought and proof of tax-exempt status.
Deadlines: None.

Corporate Officials

Richard A. Bemis: president, chief executive officer, director B 1941. ED Denison College BA (1963). PRIM CORP EMPL president, chief executive officer, director: Bemis Manufacturing Co. CORP AFFIL director: WPS Resources Corp.

Peter Lukaszewicz: treasurer, director PRIM CORP EMPL treasurer, director: Bemis Manufacturing Co.

Foundation Officials

Peter F. Bemis: vice president B 1947. ED Carroll College BS (1969). PRIM CORP EMPL vice president, secretary: Bemis Manufacturing Co. NONPR AFFIL chairman: Lakeland College.

Richard A. Bemis: president (see above)

Karen E. Hoefler: secretary

Grants Analysis

Disclosure Period: calendar year ending 2003
Total Grants: $221,200*
Number of Grants: 31
Average Grant: $3,834*
Highest Grant: $60,000
Lowest Grant: $250
Typical Range: $1,000 to $5,000
*Note: Giving excludes United Way. Average grant figure excludes two highest grants ($110,000).

Recent Grants

Note: Grants derived from 2003 Form 990.
General
50,000	Lakeland College, Sheboygan, WI
50,000	St Norbert College, De Pere, WI
30,000	Society of Plastics Industry, Washington, DC
25,000	Quit Quit Oc, Plymouth, WI
10,000	Sheboygan Falls, Sheboygan Falls, WI
7,500	John Michael Kohler Arts Center, Sheboygan, WI
7,500	Sheboygan County Historical Museum, Sheboygan, WI
5,000	YMCA, Sheboygan, WI -- towards family memberships/debt retirement campaign
4,000	Sheboygan Falls High School, Madison, WI -- for scholarship
2,000	Bay-Lakes Council, Menasha, WI

BEN & JERRY'S HOMEMADE INC.

Company Headquarters

Waterbury, VT
Web: http://www.benjerry.com

Company Description

Employees: 751 (1999)
SIC(s): 2024 Ice Cream & Frozen Desserts, 5143 Dairy Products Except Dried or Canned, 5812 Eating Places.

Operating Locations

Ben & Jerry's Homemade Inc. (AZ--Scottsdale, Tempe, Tucson; CA--Agoura Hills, Glendale, Los Angeles, Malibu, Manhattan Beach, Roseville, Sacramento, San Diego, San Francisco, San Ramon, Santa Monica, Sherman Oaks, Torrance; CO--Boulder, Denver; CT--Groton, Norwalk; DC--Washington; FL--Key West, Palm Harbor, Sarasota; IL--Vernon Hills, Villa Park; IN--Bloomington, Nashville, West Lafayette; KY--Saratoga Springs; MA--Arlington, Hingham, North Eastham, Pittsfield, Provincetown; NY--Spring Valley; RI--Cranston, Narragansett, Newport, Providence; VT--Rutland; VA--Alexandria, Norfolk, Virginia Beach, Williamsburg)

Nonmonetary Support

Type: Cause-related Marketing & Promotion; Donated Products
Contact: Laura Cunningham-Firkey, Donations Coordinator
Note: Company provides nonmonetary support.

Ben & Jerry's Foundation

Giving Contact

Lisa Pendolino, Executive Director
Ben & Jerry's Foundation
30 Community Drive
South Burlington, VT 05403-6828
Phone: (802)651-9600
Fax: (802)846-1610
Web: http://www.benjerry.com/foundation

Alternate Contact

Debbie Kessler
Phone: (802)846-1500
Note: Phone extension is 7567.

Description

Founded: 1977
EIN: 030300865
Organization Type: Corporate Foundation
Giving Locations: VT: focusing on Community Action Teams U.S.-based organizations.
Grant Types: Award, General Support, Project.

Donor Information

Founder: Ben & Jerry's Homemade

Financial Summary

Total Giving: $1,904,072 (2003); $2,262,475 (2002); $1,824,994 (2001). Note: Contributes through corporate direct giving program and foundation.
Assets: $4,994,526 (2003); $5,772,927 (2002); $5,864,790 (2001)
Gifts Received: $1,148,262 (2003); $2,159,262 (2002); $1,429,857 (2001). Note: Contributions were received from Ben & Jerry's, Inc., Ben Cohen, and Jerry Greenfield.

Typical Recipients

Arts & Humanities: Arts Associations & Councils, Arts Outreach, Ethnic & Folk Arts, Film & Video, Arts & Humanities-General, Historic Preservation, Libraries, Music, Public Broadcasting
Civic & Public Affairs: African American Affairs, Asian American Affairs, Business/Free Enterprise, Civil Rights, Clubs, Community Foundations, Economic Development, Economic Policy, Employment/Job Training, Ethnic Organizations, Gay/Lesbian Issues, Civic & Public Affairs-General, Hispanic Affairs, Housing, Inner-City Development, Law & Justice, Municipalities/Towns, Native American Affairs, Philanthropic Organizations, Professional & Trade Associations, Public Policy, Rural Affairs, Safety, Urban & Community Affairs, Women's Affairs
Education: Colleges & Universities, Education Associations, Elementary Education (Private), Elementary Education (Public), Faculty Development, Education-General, Leadership Training, Literacy, Private Education (Precollege), Secondary Education (Private), Secondary Education (Public), Social Sciences Education
Environment: Air/Water Quality, Forestry, Environment-General, Protection, Resource Conservation, Watershed, Wildlife Protection
Health: AIDS/HIV, Cancer, Health Funds, Medical Rehabilitation, Mental Health
International: Human Rights, International Development, International Environmental Issues, International Peace & Security Issues, International Relief Efforts
Religion: Churches, Religion-General, Religious Welfare, Social/Policy Issues
Science: Scientific Organizations
Social Services: Animal Protection, Camps, Child Welfare, Community Centers, Community Service Organizations, Counseling, Crime Prevention, Emergency Relief, Family Services, Food/Clothing Distribution, People with Disabilities, Recreation & Athletics, Refugee Assistance, Senior Services, Shelters/Homelessness, Social Services-General, YMCA/YWCA/YMHA/YWHA, Youth Organizations

Application Procedures

Initial Contact: Call, write, or see website for guidelines, then send two copies of a one-page initial letter of interest attached to foundation cover page.
Application Requirements: Include: a description of organization and indication of competence in the area of proposal; outline of the project, including who will benefit, design of project, and outcomes expected; brief overview of budget, income sources, and expenses for the project.
Deadlines: None for initial inquiries; applications should be submitted by the first of March, July, or November for invited full proposals.
Review Process: Foundation reviews initial requests within eight weeks of receipt, and then invites full proposals for large grants (using the National Network of Grantmakers Common Grant Application); full proposals and small requests (less than $1,000) are reviewed 3 times a year.
Evaluative Criteria: Funds projects that will: lead to societal, institutional, and/or environmental change; address the root causes of social or environmental problems; lead to new ways of thinking and acting. Projects must: help ameliorate an unjust or destructive situation by empowering constituents; facilitate leadership development and strengthen the self-empowerment efforts of those who have traditionally been disenfranchised in our society; support movement building and social action. Applicants should: develop a plan for long-tern viability; articulate a clear analysis of the underlying causes of the problem; outline specific goals and strategies of their organizing campaign or program.
Decision Notification: Initial letters are reviewed within six weeks of receipt; final decisions are announced within ten weeks after review meetings.
Notes: Express delivery of packages is strongly discouraged; faxed proposals and inquiries are not accepted. Letters of interest must be readable (with at least a 10-point font, and one-inch margins). The Foundation encourages the use of recycled paper and double-sided copying; avoid using plastic covers, sheet protectors, and glossy photos. Do not send additional backup materials, videos, or cassettes.

Restrictions

Grants are not made to support basic or direct service programs.

Foundation does not fund: discretionary or emergency requests, colleges or universities, individuals, scholarship programs, research projects, capital campaigns, state agencies, religious programs, international or foreign-based programs, or social services programs.

Additional Information

The Foundation generally supports organizations with budgets under $250,000.

Ben and Jerry's Foundation was established in 1985 through a donation of stock in Ben and Jerry's Homemade, Inc.

Approximately 7.5% of pre-tax profits is set aside annually for philanthropy; the foundation, the Community Action Team, and corporate philanthropy each receive a portion of this total.

In April 2000, an agreement was made to sell Ben & Jerry's Homemade, Inc. to Unilever. As part of the terms of agreement, Ben & Jerry's will operate separately from Unilever's existing U.S. ice cream business. In addition, Ben & Jerry's will have an independent board of directors which will concentrate on maintaining Ben & Jerry's social mission and brand integrity.

Publications: Application Packet; Annual Report

Corporate Officials

Jerry Greenfield: co-founder, vice chairman B New York, NY 1950. ED Oberlin College BA (1973). PRIM CORP EMPL co-founder, vice chairman: Ben & Jerry's Homemade Inc.

Foundation Officials

Elizabeth Bankowski: secretary B Boston, MA 1947. ED Boston College (1970). PRIM CORP EMPL director: Ben & Jerry's Homemade, Inc.
Jeffrey Furman: treasurer PRIM CORP EMPL director: Ben & Jerry's Homemade Inc.
Jerry Greenfield: president (see above)

Grants Analysis

Disclosure Period: calendar year ending 2003
Total Grants: $1,878,201*
Number of Grants: 350 (approx)
Average Grant: $5,366
Highest Grant: $150,000
Lowest Grant: $10
Typical Range: $1,000 to $10,000
*Note: Giving excludes matching gifts.

Recent Grants

Note: Grants derived from 2003 Form 990.
General

15,000	Eyak Preservation Council, Cordova, AK
15,000	Kentucky Environmental Foundation, Berea, KY
15,000	Kingsport Citizens for a Clean Environment, Kingsport, TN
15,000	Louisiana Bucket Brigade, New Orleans, LA
15,000	Padres Unidos
15,000	Samara Foundation of Vermont, Burlington, VT
15,000	Seattle Young People's Project, Seattle, WA
15,000	Southeast Regional Economic Justice Network, Durham, NC
15,000	Working Films, Wilmington, NC
10,000	Brecht Forum, New York, NY

LEGLER BENBOUGH FOUNDATION

Giving Contact

Peter K. Ellsworth, President & Director
2550 5th Ave., Suite 132
San Diego, CA 92103
Phone: (619)235-8099

Description

Founded: 1985
EIN: 330105049
Organization Type: Private Foundation

Giving Locations: CA: San Diego
Grant Types: General Support, Research.

Donor Information
Founder: Legler Benbough

Financial Summary
Total Giving: $1,814,833 (2003); $1,661,900 (2001)
Giving Analysis: Giving for 2003 includes: foundation grants to United Way ($17,500)
Assets: $40,546,444 (2003); $40,595,501 (2001)
Gifts Received: $2,247,335 (2001); $9,412,674 (2000); $23,013,030 (1999). Note: In 2001, contributions were received from Legler Benbough Trust. In 2000, contributions were received from Legler Benbough Trust ($5,144,551) and La Jolla Camino Trust ($4,262,123). In 1998 and 1999, contributions were received from the Legler Benbough Trust.

Typical Recipients
Arts & Humanities: Arts Associations & Councils, Community Arts, Ethnic & Folk Arts, Historic Preservation, History & Archaeology, Libraries, Museums/Galleries, Music, Performing Arts, Theater, Visual Arts
Civic & Public Affairs: African American Affairs, Botanical Gardens/Parks, Community Foundations, Civic & Public Affairs-General, Housing, Public Policy, Safety, Urban & Community Affairs, Zoos/Aquariums
Education: Colleges & Universities, Education Funds, Literacy, Private Education (Precollege), Science/Mathematics Education, Secondary Education (Public)
Health: Alzheimer's Disease, Arthritis, Cancer, Children's Health/Hospitals, Clinics/Medical Centers, Eyes/Blindness, Health Funds, Health Organizations, Hospices, Medical Research, Prenatal Health Issues, Public Health, Research/Studies Institutes, Single-Disease Health Associations
International: Health Care/Hospitals
Religion: Churches, Religious Organizations, Religious Welfare, Social/Policy Issues
Science: Science Museums, Scientific Centers & Institutes
Social Services: Animal Protection, Big Brothers/Big Sisters, Camps, Child Welfare, Community Service Organizations, Crime Prevention, Domestic Violence, Emergency Relief, Family Services, Food/Clothing Distribution, People with Disabilities, Recreation & Athletics, Scouts, Senior Services, Social Services-General, Special Olympics, Volunteer Services, Youth Organizations

Application Procedures
Initial Contact: Send a brief letter of inquiry.
Application Requirements: Include pertinent information.
Deadlines: March 15 for April 15 grants and September 15 for October 15 grants.

Foundation Officials
Thomas E. Cisco: vice president, secretary, treasurer, director
Peter Kennedy Ellsworth: president, director B Los Angeles, CA 1931. ED Stanford University BA (1953); Stanford University JD (1956). PRIM CORP EMPL president, chief executive officer: Sharp Healthcare. NONPR AFFIL member: California Bar Association; member: Rotary; fellow: American Bar Association.

Grants Analysis
Disclosure Period: calendar year ending 2003
Total Grants: $1,797,333*
Number of Grants: 46
Average Grant: $24,937*
Highest Grant: $300,000
Lowest Grant: $2,500
Typical Range: $10,000 to $50,000
*Note: Giving excludes United Way. Average grant figure excludes four highest grants ($750,000).

Recent Grants
Note: Grants derived from 2003 Form 990.
General

300,000	Zoological Society of San Diego, San Diego, CA	
250,000	San Diego Natural History Museum, San Diego, CA	
100,000	San Diego Foundation, San Diego, CA -- for wildfire relief	
100,000	USS San Diego CL53 Memorial Association Inc., Coronado, CA	
75,000	Old Globe Theatre, San Diego, CA	
75,000	Salk Institute for Biological Studies, San Diego, CA	
75,000	Sydney Kimmel Cancer Center, San Diego, CA	
50,000	American Red Cross, San Diego, CA -- for San Diego & Imperial counties	
50,000	Balboa Park Cultural Partnership, San Diego, CA	
50,000	San Diego Food Bank, San Diego, CA	

BENDER FOUNDATION

Giving Contact
Julie Bender-Silver, President
1120 Connecticut Ave. NW, Suite 1200
Washington, DC 20036
Phone: (202)828-9000
Fax: (202)785-9347

Description
Founded: 1958
EIN: 526054193
Organization Type: Private Foundation
Giving Locations: DC: Washington
Grant Types: General Support.

Donor Information
Founder: the late Jack I. Bender

Financial Summary
Total Giving: $1,008,033 (2003)
Assets: $13,396,872 (2003)
Gifts Received: $522,629 (2003); $1,563,688 (2000); $890,000 (1999). Note: In 2003, contributions were received from Howard M. Bender. In 1999, contributions were received from the Estate of D.G. Bender, and Howard M. Bender.

Typical Recipients
Arts & Humanities: Arts Centers, Arts Festivals, Arts Institutes, Ballet, Dance, Historic Preservation, History & Archaeology, Libraries, Museums/Galleries, Music, Performing Arts, Theater
Civic & Public Affairs: Botanical Gardens/Parks, Civic & Public Affairs-General, Urban & Community Affairs
Education: Colleges & Universities, Education Funds, Elementary Education (Public), Education-General, International Exchange, International Studies, Private Education (Precollege), School Volunteerism, Secondary Education (Private), Secondary Education (Public), Special Education, Student Aid
Health: Cancer, Children's Health/Hospitals, Clinics/Medical Centers, Health-General, Heart, Hospitals, Medical Rehabilitation, Multiple Sclerosis, Prenatal Health Issues, Public Health, Respiratory, Single-Disease Health Associations
International: Foreign Arts Organizations, Foreign Educational Institutions, Health Care/Hospitals, International Organizations, International Peace & Security Issues, International Relief Efforts, Missionary/Religious Activities
Religion: Jewish Causes, Religious Organizations, Religious Welfare
Science: Science Museums

Social Services: Child Welfare, Community Centers, Community Service Organizations, Day Care, Delinquency & Criminal Rehabilitation, Domestic Violence, Family Planning, Family Services, Food/Clothing Distribution, People with Disabilities, Recreation & Athletics, Senior Services, Substance Abuse, United Funds/United Ways, YMCA/YWCA/YMHA/YWHA, Youth Organizations

Application Procedures
Initial Contact: Send a brief letter of inquiry.
Application Requirements: Include brochures describing the program or project, amount requested, proof of charitable status, and purpose of funds sought.
Deadlines: November 30.

Restrictions
Does not support individuals, or political or lobbying groups.

Foundation Officials
Julie Bender Belinkie: president
Barbara A. Bender: vice president
David S. Bender: vice president
Howard Marvin Bender: executive vice president B Paterson, NJ 1930. ED University of Maryland (1948-1950). PRIM CORP EMPL chairman, director: Blake Construction Co. CORP AFFIL president: Best Mechanical. NONPR AFFIL director: Jewish Community Center Greater Washington; member: Tau Epsilon Phi.
Sondra D. Bender: chairman
Stanley Seymour Bender: secretary B Paterson, NJ 1929. ED University of Maryland. PRIM CORP EMPL executive vice president, director: Blake Construction Co. NONPR AFFIL member: Washington Board Realtors.
Eileen Bender Greenberg: vice president

Grants Analysis
Disclosure Period: calendar year ending 2003
Total Grants: $1,008,033
Number of Grants: 83
Average Grant: $10,130*
Highest Grant: $100,000
Lowest Grant: $250
Typical Range: $1,000 to $20,000
*Note: Average grant figure excludes two highest grants ($187,500).

Recent Grants
Note: Grants derived from 2001 Form 990.

Library-Related

50,000	Genesis Foundation, New York, NY -- library dedication	
20,000	Genesis Foundation, New York, NY	

General

87,500	Jewish Community Center of Greater Washington, Washington, DC -- Fitness Center	
50,000	Discovery Creek Children's Museum, Washington, DC	
50,000	UJA Federation of Greater Washington, Rockville, MD	
25,000	Anti-Defamation League, Washington, DC -- concert against hate	
25,000	Suburban Hospital, Bethesda, MD -- emergency department expansion	
20,000	Bullis School, Potomac, MD	
20,000	Colorado Academy, Denver, CO	
20,000	Greater Washington Jewish Community Foundation, Rockville, MD	
20,000	Greater Washington Jewish Community Foundation, Rockville, MD	
15,000	National Symphony Orchestra Association, Washington, DC -- annual fund	

LEO H. BENDIT CHARITABLE FOUNDATION

Giving Contact
Dr. Kurt J. Bloch, Trustee
81 Arlington Rd.
Chestnut Hill, MA 02467
Phone: (617)734-3284

Description
Founded: 1963
EIN: 136143764
Organization Type: Private Foundation
Grant Types: General Support.

Financial Summary
Total Giving: $144,166 (2002); $158,503 (2001)
Giving Analysis: Giving for 2002 includes: foundation grants to United Way ($5,000)
Assets: $2,667,438 (2002); $3,003,839 (2001)
Gifts Received: $42,490 (2002); $48,032 (2001); $83,550 (2000). Note: In 1999, 2000, 2001, and 2002, contributions were received from Margot Bloch. In 1998, contributions were received from Kurt J. Bloch.

Typical Recipients
Arts & Humanities: Historic Preservation, Libraries, Museums/Galleries, Music, Public Broadcasting
Civic & Public Affairs: Civic & Public Affairs-General, Urban & Community Affairs
Education: Colleges & Universities, Education-General, Medical Education, Private Education (Precollege), Secondary Education (Private), Special Education, Student Aid
Environment: Environment-General, Wildlife Protection
Health: AIDS/HIV, Arthritis, Cancer, Emergency/Ambulance Services, Health-General, Health Organizations, Heart, Hospitals, Long-Term Care, Nursing Services, Respiratory, Single-Disease Health Associations
International: Human Rights, International Affairs, International Peace & Security Issues
Religion: Jewish Causes, Religious Welfare
Social Services: Community Service Organizations, Emergency Relief, Family Planning, Food/Clothing Distribution, People with Disabilities, Shelters/Homelessness, United Funds/United Ways

Application Procedures
Initial Contact: Send a brief letter of inquiry.
Deadlines: None.

Restrictions
Grants are not made to individuals.

Foundation Officials
Donald B. Bloch: trustee
Kenneth D. Bloch: trustee
Dr. Kurt Julius Bloch: trustee B Germany 1929. ED City College of New York BS (1951); New York University MD (1955). PRIM CORP EMPL physician, chief clinical immunology: Massachusetts General Hospital. CORP AFFIL professor: Harvard Medical School. NONPR AFFIL member: American Society Clinical Investigation; diplomate: Diagnostic Laboratory Immunology; diplomate: American Board Internal Medicine; member: American Association Physicians; diplomate: American Board Allergy & Immunology.

Grants Analysis
Disclosure Period: calendar year ending 2002
Total Grants: $139,166*
Number of Grants: 49
Average Grant: $2,066*
Highest Grant: $40,000

Lowest Grant: $100
Typical Range: $1,000 to $5,000
*****Note:** Giving excludes United Way. Average grant figure excludes highest grant.

Recent Grants
Note: Grants derived from 2001 Form 990.
General

40,000	Massachusetts General Hospital, Boston, MA
23,203	United Jewish Communities, New York, NY
10,000	American Red Cross of Massachusetts Bay, Boston, MA
10,000	Beth Israel Hospital, Boston, MA
10,000	New York Foundation for Nursing Homes, Jamaica, NY
10,000	Planned Parenthood League of Massachusetts, Cambridge, MA
10,000	Self Help Community Services, New York, NY
5,000	Jewish Family and Children's Service, Boston, MA
5,000	United Way of Massachusetts, Boston, MA
4,000	Pine Street Inn, Boston, MA

BENEFICIA FOUNDATION

Giving Contact
Feodor U. Pitcairn, Executive Secretary, Director
1 Pitcairn Place, Suite 3000
Jenkintown, PA 19046-3593
Phone: (215)887-6700
Fax: (215)881-6092
E-mail: ak3371@pitcairn.com

Description
Founded: 1953
EIN: 246015630
Organization Type: Family Foundation
Giving Locations: no restrictions.
Grant Types: General Support, Project.

Donor Information
Founder: Established in 1953 by members of the Theodore Pitcairn family.

Financial Summary
Total Giving: $1,002,000 (fiscal year ending April 30, 2003); $1,600,000 (fiscal 2002 approx); $1,625,000 (fiscal 2001). Note: The foundation did not give grants in fiscal 1996.
Assets: $12,119,188 (fiscal 2003); $15,993,427 (fiscal 2001)

Typical Recipients
Arts & Humanities: Arts Centers, Arts Institutes, Arts Outreach, Historic Preservation, Libraries, Museums/Galleries, Music, Opera, Performing Arts, Public Broadcasting, Theater
Civic & Public Affairs: Botanical Gardens/Parks, Civil Rights, Clubs, Economic Development, Civic & Public Affairs-General, Law & Justice, Legal Aid, Public Policy, Urban & Community Affairs, Women's Affairs, Zoos/Aquariums
Education: Arts/Humanities Education, Colleges & Universities, Education Funds, Education Reform, Education-General, Journalism/Media Education, Medical Education, Private Education (Precollege), Science/Mathematics Education, Special Education, Student Aid
Environment: Air/Water Quality, Forestry, Environment-General, Protection, Research, Resource Conservation, Watershed, Wildlife Protection
Health: Cancer, Children's Health/Hospitals, Health-General, Nursing Services, Nutrition
International: International Environmental Issues

Religion: Churches, Religious Organizations, Religious Welfare
Science: Scientific Centers & Institutes, Scientific Organizations, Scientific Research
Social Services: Child Welfare, Community Centers, Community Service Organizations, Crime Prevention, People with Disabilities, United Funds/United Ways, Youth Organizations

Application Procedures
Initial Contact: All applications should be made in writing and addressed to either the Environmental Committee or Arts Committee.
Application Requirements: Applications should include the organization's name and address, proof of U.S. tax-exempt status or affiliation with U.S. based nonprofit, annual report, and a one page project summary. A brief proposal, 10 pages or less, which includes project objectives, project description, expected outcomes, a timetable, a complete budget, and the qualifications of key personnel involved should also be included.
Deadlines: January 31.
Review Process: Committee chairs select proposals for preliminary review at committee meetings in February or March. The full board of directors meets in May to conduct final proposal reviews and make recommendations for funding. Applicants whose proposals are approved will be notified by May 31.
Notes: A final report is required from all grant recipients at the end of the grant year.

Additional Information
Foundation favors programs which are innovative, catalytic, address unmet needs, and strive toward self-sustainability.
Publications: Brochure; Grant List

Foundation Officials
Deana Duncan: director
John Daniel Mitchell: vice president, director B New York, NY 1957. NONPR AFFIL fellow: Linnean Society London; honorary curator: New York Botanical Garden; member: International Association Plant Taxonomists; vice chairman: BAT Conservation International; member: Ecological Society America; member: American Association Advancement Science. CLUB AFFIL Philadelphia Botanical Club; Organization for Flora Neotropica; Explorers Club; New England Botanical Club.
Miriam Pitcairn Mitchell: director
Eshowe P. Pennink: director
Mark J. Pennink: treasurer, director B 1957. PRIM CORP EMPL partner: Pitcairn Group LP. CORP AFFIL president: Pennink & Arrimour; partner: Pitcairn Finance Management Corp.
Feodor Urban Pitcairn: executive secretary, director B Bergen, Netherlands 1934. ED University of Pennsylvania AB (1959). PRIM CORP EMPL chairman: Pitcairn Financial Management Group. CORP AFFIL director: Infotron System. NONPR AFFIL vice chairman, member: Montgomery County Planning Committee; president: Pennypack Watershed Association; member: Bryn Athyn Planning Committee; director: Center Marine Conservation; trustee: Academy Natural Science; member: Bryn Athyn Borough Authority. CLUB AFFIL Racquet Club.
Kirstin Odhner Pitcairn: director
Laren Pitcairn: president, director PRIM CORP EMPL president: Chief Logan Associates Ltd. CORP AFFIL director: Old York Road Bancorp; director: Pitcairn Co.; director: Bank & Trust Old York Road.
Mary Eleanor Pitcairn: director
Sharon R. Pitcairn: director
Heather C. Reynolds: director

Grants Analysis
Disclosure Period: fiscal year ending April 30, 2003
Total Grants: $1,002,000
Number of Grants: 45
Average Grant: $22,267
Highest Grant: $50,000

Lowest Grant: $10,000
Typical Range: $10,000 to $50,000

Recent Grants

Note: Grants derived from fiscal 2003 Form 990.
General

50,000	Philadelphia Society of the Lord's New Church, Bryn Athyn, PA
45,000	Opera Company of Philadelphia, Philadelphia, PA
38,000	Ocean Conservancy, Washington, DC -- towards preserving Alaska's ocean wilderness
37,000	Academy of the New Church, Bryn Athyn, PA -- for performing art center
35,000	Clean Air Council of Philadelphia, Philadelphia, PA -- towards PA wind, low emissions vehicle and children's environment
35,000	Nature Conservancy of New Jersey, NJ -- for Andros National Park, impact of invasive plant
34,000	Academy of Vocal Arts, Philadelphia, PA
30,000	Center for Coastal Studies, Provincetown, MA -- towards Humpback Whale studies program
28,000	Missouri Botanical Garden, St. Louis, MO
26,000	New York Botanical Garden, Bronx, NY -- towards Neotropical plant research; support of rain forest

FRANCES AND BENJAMIN BENENSON FOUNDATION

Giving Contact

Charles B. Benenson, President
708 3rd Avenue, 28th Floor
New York, NY 10017
Phone: (212)867-0990
Fax: (212)983-1952

Description

Founded: 1983
EIN: 133267113
Organization Type: Family Foundation
Giving Locations: NY: New York
Grant Types: General Support, Scholarship.

Donor Information

Founder: Established in 1983 by Charles B. Benenson.

Financial Summary

Total Giving: $1,800,000 (fiscal year ending November 30, 2003 approx); $2,146,488 (fiscal 2002); $1,900,000 (fiscal 2001)
Giving Analysis: Giving for fiscal 2002 includes: foundation grants to United Way ($5,425)
Assets: $30,000,000 (fiscal 2003 approx); $35,195,874 (fiscal 2002)
Gifts Received: $1,500,000 (fiscal 2002); $2,050,000 (fiscal 2000); $1,400,000 (fiscal 1998).
Note: In fiscal 2002, contributions were received from CBB Management Corp. ($1,000,000), Dollar Land Syndicate ($250,000) and Dollar Land 2 ($250,000). In fiscal 2000, contributions were received from Marx Realty and Improvement Co., Inc. ($250,000) and Charles B. Benenson ($1,800,000). In fiscal 1998, contributions were received from Benenson Capital Company and Marx Realty and Improvement Co., Inc. In fiscal 1996, contributions were received from Benenson Capital Co. ($1,075,000) and Marx Realty & Improvement Co., Inc. ($187,500).

Typical Recipients

Arts & Humanities: Arts Associations & Councils, Arts Centers, Arts Institutes, Ethnic & Folk Arts, Film & Video, Arts & Humanities-General, Libraries, Museums/Galleries, Music, Opera, Performing Arts, Public Broadcasting, Theater
Civic & Public Affairs: Botanical Gardens/Parks, Civil Rights, Clubs, Economic Development, Ethnic Organizations, Civic & Public Affairs-General, Housing, Law & Justice, Municipalities/Towns, Philanthropic Organizations, Professional & Trade Associations, Urban & Community Affairs
Education: Afterschool/Enrichment Programs, Arts/Humanities Education, Business Education, Colleges & Universities, Community & Junior Colleges, Education Funds, Education Reform, Elementary Education (Private), Elementary Education (Public), Education-General, Gifted & Talented Programs, International Studies, Literacy, Minority Education, Private Education (Precollege), Secondary Education (Public), Social Sciences Education, Student Aid
Environment: Air/Water Quality, Environment-General, Resource Conservation, Wildlife Protection
Health: AIDS/HIV, Cancer, Children's Health/Hospitals, Clinics/Medical Centers, Diabetes, Emergency/Ambulance Services, Health Organizations, Hospitals, Research/Studies Institutes, Single-Disease Health Associations, Trauma Treatment
International: Foreign Arts Organizations, Foreign Educational Institutions, Human Rights, International Relations, International Relief Efforts, Missionary/Religious Activities
Religion: Jewish Causes, Religious Organizations, Religious Welfare, Synagogues/Temples
Science: Scientific Organizations
Social Services: Animal Protection, Camps, Child Welfare, Community Centers, Community Service Organizations, Crime Prevention, Family Planning, Family Services, People with Disabilities, Recreation & Athletics, Shelters/Homelessness, Social Services-General, Substance Abuse, United Funds/United Ways, Youth Organizations

Application Procedures

Initial Contact: The foundation requests applications be made in writing.
Application Requirements: Include a description of organization and amount requested.
Deadlines: None.
Notes: The foundation considers all proposals.

Restrictions

Grants are not made to individuals.

Foundation Officials

Bruce W. Benenson: vice president
Charles B. Benenson: president
Richard Kessler: secretary
Lloyd Starner: treasurer

Grants Analysis

Disclosure Period: fiscal year ending November 30, 2002
Total Grants: $2,141,063*
Number of Grants: 186
Average Grant: $6,438*
Highest Grant: $950,000
Lowest Grant: $100
Typical Range: $1,000 to $10,000
*Note: Giving excludes United Way. Average grant excludes highest grant.

Recent Grants

Note: Grants derived from fiscal 2002 Form 990.
Library-Related

4,458,500	New York Public Library, New York, NY

General

95,000,000	Yale University Art Gallery, New Haven, CT
14,925,000	Inner-City Scholarship, New York, NY
10,000,000	UJA Federation of New York, New York, NY
5,000,000	Chess-In-The-Schools, New York, NY
5,000,000	Purchase College Foundation, Purchase, NY
3,400,000	UJA Federation of New York, New York, NY
2,604,027	New York Junior Tennis League, Long Island City, NY
2,500,000	American Assoc Ben-Gurion University, Be'er Sheva Israel
2,500,000	American Assoc Ben-Gurion University, Be'er Sheva Israel
2,500,000	Duke University, Durham, NC

BENETTON U.S.A. CORP.

Company Headquarters

New York, NY
Web: http://www.benetton.com

Company Description

Employees: 20
SIC(s): 2300 Apparel & Other Textile Products.
Parent Company: Bennetton Group S.p.A., Via Villa Minelli 1, Ponzano, Treviso, Italy

Operating Locations

Benetton U.S.A. Corp. (NC--New York)

Nonmonetary Support

Type: Donated Products

Giving Contact

Mark Major, Communications Director
597 5th Avenue, 11th Floor
New York, NY 10017-1020
Phone: (212)593-0290
Fax: (212)371-1438

Description

Organization Type: Corporate Giving Program
Giving Locations: no restrictions.
Grant Types: General Support.

Typical Recipients

Arts & Humanities: Dance, Historic Preservation, Libraries, Museums/Galleries, Performing Arts
Education: Colleges & Universities, Private Education (Precollege), Public Education (Precollege)
Health: Hospitals, Medical Research, Single-Disease Health Associations
Science: Scientific Organizations
Social Services: Community Service Organizations, Domestic Violence, People with Disabilities, Refugee Assistance, Substance Abuse, United Funds/United Ways, Youth Organizations

Application Procedures

Initial Contact: Send a brief letter.
Application Requirements: Applications should include a description of organization, amount requested, and purpose of funds sought.
Deadlines: Setember.

Restrictions

Benetton does not support political or lobbying groups.

Corporate Officials

Luciano Benetton: chairman, president, chief executive officer, director B Treviso, Italy 1935. PRIM CORP EMPL chairman, president, chief executive officer; director: Benetton Corp. ADD CORP EMPL cofdr: Colors Publications; chairman: Fratelli Benetton. CORP AFFIL director: Eliodona Publs.
Carlo Tunioli: vice president, general manager PRIM CORP EMPL vice president, general manager: Benetton U.S.A. Corp.

Grants Analysis

Typical Range: $10,000 to $25,000

CLAUDE BENNETT FAMILY FOUNDATION

Giving Contact

Harold I. Apolinsky, Trustee
2311 Highland Avenue South
Birmingham, AL 35205
Phone: (205)945-4687

Description

Founded: 1993
EIN: 582052917
Organization Type: Private Foundation
Grant Types: General Support.

Financial Summary

Total Giving: $48,120 (2003); $86,450 (2001)
Giving Analysis: Giving for 2001 includes: foundation grants to United Way ($2,500)
Assets: $1,613,897 (2003); $1,712,454 (2001)

Typical Recipients

Arts & Humanities: Arts & Humanities-General, Libraries, Museums/Galleries, Music, Opera
Civic & Public Affairs: Botanical Gardens/Parks, Clubs, Civic & Public Affairs-General, Urban & Community Affairs, Zoos/Aquariums
Education: Colleges & Universities, Elementary Education (Private), Education-General, Medical Education, Private Education (Precollege), Student Aid
Health: AIDS/HIV, Alzheimer's Disease, Clinics/Medical Centers, Health-General, Health Organizations, Heart, Hospices, Medical Rehabilitation, Medical Research, Prenatal Health Issues, Public Health, Trauma Treatment
International: Health Care/Hospitals
Religion: Churches, Religion-General, Ministries
Science: Science Museums
Social Services: At-Risk Youth, Camps, Child Welfare, Community Centers, Community Service Organizations, Family Planning, Family Services, Food/Clothing Distribution, Senior Services, Shelters/Homelessness, United Funds/United Ways

Application Procedures

Initial Contact: Applications should be submitted in writing.
Application Requirements: Identify the organization, give the organization's tax exempt number and proof of tax-exempt status, state the purpose of funds sought, state the prior experience of the applicant in carrying out such purpose, provide the applicant's plan for carrying out the purpose, list the personnel to be involved in the project, and attach financial statements for the current and the two preceding years.
Deadlines: None.

Foundation Officials

Harold I. Apolinsky: trustee
Clark Bennett: trustee
Katherine Bennett O'Leary: trustee
J. Miller Piggott: trustee

Grants Analysis

Disclosure Period: calendar year ending 2003
Total Grants: $48,120
Number of Grants: 31
Average Grant: $1,552
Highest Grant: $8,500
Lowest Grant: $90
Typical Range: $200 to $3,000

Recent Grants

Note: Grants derived from 2001 Form 990.
General

15,000	Birmingham Episcopal Camp, Birmingham, AL
14,200	St. Luke's Episcopal Church
10,650	Alzheimer's of Central Alabama, AL
10,000	Samford University, Birmingham, AL
5,000	Alabama Symphony Orchestra, Birmingham, AL
4,750	South Highland Presbyterian Church, Birmingham, AL
3,000	Food Bank of Larimar County
2,500	United Way, Dubuque, IA
2,000	Botanical Gardens
2,000	Crossroads Safe House, Ft. Collins, CO

BENWOOD FOUNDATION

Giving Contact

Corinne A. Allen, Executive Director
Benwood Foundation, Inc.
1600 Suntrust Bank Building
Chattanooga, TN 37402
Phone: (423)267-4311
Fax: (615)267-9049
E-mail: benwoodfnd@benwood.org

Description

Founded: 1944
EIN: 620476283
Organization Type: General Purpose Foundation
Giving Locations: TN: Chattanooga
Grant Types: Challenge, General Support, Matching, Project.

Donor Information

Founder: Established in 1944 by George T. Hunter, who was chairman of the board of the Coca-Cola Bottling Company (Thomas, Inc.) at the time of his death in 1950. Mr. Hunter's uncle, Benjamin F. Thomas, was one of the founders of the Coca-Cola bottling industry. Most of Mr. Hunter's holdings in the bottling company were bequeathed to the foundation.

Financial Summary

Total Giving: $4,295,077 (2003); $4,209,591 (2002)
Giving Analysis: Giving for 2003 includes: foundation grants to United Way ($100,000); 2002: foundation grants to United Way ($100,000)
Assets: $102,969,700 (2003); $93,924,813 (2002)

Typical Recipients

Arts & Humanities: Arts Associations & Councils, Arts Funds, Arts Institutes, Ballet, Arts & Humanities-General, Historic Preservation, History & Archaeology, Libraries, Museums/Galleries, Music, Opera, Performing Arts, Public Broadcasting, Theater
Civic & Public Affairs: African American Affairs, Botanical Gardens/Parks, Business/Free Enterprise, Chambers of Commerce, Clubs, Community Foundations, Economic Development, Civic & Public Affairs-General, Housing, Legal Aid, Municipalities/Towns, Parades/Festivals, Professional & Trade Associations, Public Policy, Safety, Urban & Community Affairs, Zoos/Aquariums
Education: Arts/Humanities Education, Business Education, Colleges & Universities, Continuing Education, Education Associations, Education Funds, Education Reform, Elementary Education (Private), Elementary Education (Public), Education-General, Legal Education, Literacy, Medical Education, Minority Education, Private Education (Precollege), Public Education (Precollege), Religious Education, School Volunteerism, Secondary Education (Private), Secondary Education (Public)
Environment: Air/Water Quality, Environment-General, Protection, Resource Conservation, Wildlife Protection
Health: AIDS/HIV, Alzheimer's Disease, Children's Health/Hospitals, Clinics/Medical Centers, Emergency/Ambulance Services, Health Funds, Health Organizations, Hospitals, Medical Research, Mental Health, Preventive Medicine/Wellness Organizations, Public Health, Research/Studies Institutes
International: Health Care/Hospitals, International Organizations
Religion: Bible Study/Translation, Churches, Jewish Causes, Ministries, Religious Organizations, Religious Welfare, Social/Policy Issues
Social Services: Big Brothers/Big Sisters, Camps, Child Welfare, Community Centers, Community Service Organizations, Emergency Relief, Family Services, Food/Clothing Distribution, Homes, People with Disabilities, Recreation & Athletics, Scouts, Senior Services, Shelters/Homelessness, Social Services-General, Substance Abuse, United Funds/United Ways, YMCA/YWCA/YMHA/YWHA, Youth Organizations

Application Procedures

Initial Contact: A two-page letter of inquiry should be sent to the foundation.
Application Requirements: The letter should include the need that will be met by the proposed project, how the need will be met, and who will be served; why the applicant is qualified to implement the project and what staff will carry out the project; other sources of possible support; how the project will be measured, how the project will be supported after the requested grant expires, and the timetable for the project; and the amount requested by the foundation to fund the project. In addition to the application letter, a brief background of the organization, a list of officers and board members, a copy of the most recent audited financial statement, a copy of the organization's current operating budget, and an IRS letter of determination indicating tax-exempt status should also be submitted. Applicants should submit six copies of the application.
Deadlines: The board of trustees meets annually in January to consider applications.
Review Process: The board looks favorably on proposals for projects dealing with education, health, the humanities, religion, and social welfare, particularly in and around Chattanooga. The trustees reserve the right to delay final decision on grant requests for a two-month period.

Restrictions

The foundation does not award grants for general operating expenses, endowments, financing deficits, political organizations, fund raising, multi-year grants, agencies outside the United States, or requests that are submitted by an organization that has received funding within the same year. Further, the foundation does not give funds for scholarship, fellowships, or grants directly to individuals.

Additional Information

Publications: Application Form; Guidelines

Foundation Officials

Corinne A. Allen: executive director
Sebert Brewer, Jr.: president
Paul K. Brock, Jr.: trustee
E. Y. Chapin, III: vice president CORP AFFIL director: SunTrust Bank Chattanooga NA.
William Chapin: trustee
Susan R. Randolph: chairman
Martha T. Robinson: trustee

Grants Analysis

Disclosure Period: calendar year ending 2003
Total Grants: $4,195,077*
Number of Grants: 106
Average Grant: $30,429*
Highest Grant: $1,000,000
Lowest Grant: $300
Typical Range: $5,000 to $50,000
***Note:** Giving excludes United Way. Average grant excludes highest grant.

Recent Grants

Note: Grants derived from 2003 Form 990.

Library-Related

21,000	Chattanooga Indigenous Resources Center and Library, Chattanooga, TN

General

1,000,000	Public Education Foundation, Chattanooga, TN
751,900	Children's Home, Mt. Holly, NJ
400,000	Ronald McDonald House Charities, Oak Brook, IL
251,000	Chattanooga Chamber Foundation, Chattanooga, TN
250,000	21st Century Waterfront Trust, Chattanooga, TN
210,000	Allied Arts, Oklahoma City, OK
100,000	Southern Environmental Law Center
100,000	United Way of Greater Chattanooga, Chattanooga, TN
65,000	Southeast Tennessee Legal Services, Chattanooga, TN
50,000	Baylor School, Chattanooga, TN

DORIS L. BENZ TRUST

Giving Contact

Judith Burrows
N.H. Charitable Foundation
37 Pleasant Street
Concord, NH 03301
Phone: (603)225-6641

Description

Founded: 1984
EIN: 046504871
Organization Type: Private Foundation
Giving Locations: MA; NH
Grant Types: General Support, Scholarship.

Donor Information

Founder: the late Doris L. Benz

Financial Summary

Total Giving: $270,304 (fiscal year ending June 30, 2004); $397,677 (fiscal 2001)
Giving Analysis: Giving for fiscal 2004 includes: foundation scholarships ($176,404)
Assets: $9,064,130 (fiscal 2004); $9,786,155 (fiscal 2001)

Typical Recipients

Arts & Humanities: Community Arts, History & Archaeology, Libraries, Music, Public Broadcasting, Theater
Civic & Public Affairs: Community Foundations, Economic Development, Civic & Public Affairs-General, Philanthropic Organizations, Safety, Urban & Community Affairs, Zoos/Aquariums
Education: Arts/Humanities Education, Business Education, Colleges & Universities, Community & Junior Colleges, Education Funds, Private Education (Precollege), Public Education (Precollege), Secondary Education (Public), Student Aid
Environment: Environment-General
Health: AIDS/HIV, Cancer, Children's Health/Hospitals, Clinics/Medical Centers, Heart, Home-Care Services, Hospices, Hospitals, Mental Health, Nursing Services, Single-Disease Health Associations
Social Services: Child Welfare, Community Centers, Community Service Organizations, Day Care, Food/Clothing Distribution, People with Disabilities, Recreation & Athletics, Senior Services, Special Olympics, United Funds/United Ways, YMCA/YWCA/YMHA/YWHA, Youth Organizations

Application Procedures

Initial Contact: Return completed application form along with most recent high school or college tran-

scripts, applicant appraisal, and application fee.
Deadlines: None.

Restrictions

No support for religious purposes.

Additional Information

Provides scholarships to residents of Sandwich or Carroll County, NH, who have graduated from high schools in these areas.

Foundation Officials

Wendell P. Weyland: trustee

Grants Analysis

Disclosure Period: fiscal year ending June 30, 2004
Total Grants: $93,900
Number of Grants: 15
Average Grant: $4,921*
Highest Grant: $25,000
Lowest Grant: $200
Typical Range: $1,000 to $10,000
***Note:** Average grant figure excludes highest grant.

Recent Grants

Note: Grants derived from fiscal 2001 Form 990.
Library-Related

25,000	Gilmanton Year Round Library, Gilmanton, NH
10,000	Cook Memorial Library, Tamworth, NH

General

217,477	N.H. Charitable Fund, Concord, NH
40,000	Community School, South Tamworth, NH
15,000	Lynn YMCA, Lynn, MA
14,000	Poore Family Foundation, The, Colebrook, NH
12,500	Endicott College, Beverly, MA
10,000	Helen Fava Scholarship Fund, The, Boxford, MA
10,000	North Shore Association for Retarded Citizens, Salem, MA
10,000	North Shore Medical Center, Lynn, MA
5,000	Bear Camp Valley School, Tamworth, NH
5,000	Boys and Girls Club of Lynn, Lynn, MA

BERE FOUNDATION

Giving Contact

Barbara Van Dellen-Bere, President & Director
641 S. Elm Street
Hinsdale, IL 60521-4623
Phone: (312)322-8511

Description

Founded: 1983
EIN: 363272779
Organization Type: Private Foundation
Giving Locations: IL
Grant Types: General Support.

Donor Information

Founder: James F. Bere

Financial Summary

Total Giving: $682,500 (2003); $819,750 (2001)
Giving Analysis: Giving for 2003 includes: foundation grants to United Way ($500); 2001: foundation grants to United Way ($500)
Assets: $7,144,872 (2003); $8,335,833 (2001)
Gifts Received: $200,000 (2003). Note: In 2003, contributions were received from Barbara V. Bere. In 1991, contributions were received from James F. and Barbara L. Bere.

Typical Recipients

Arts & Humanities: Arts Institutes, History & Archaeology, Libraries, Museums/Galleries, Music, Opera, Performing Arts, Public Broadcasting

Civic & Public Affairs: African American Affairs, Botanical Gardens/Parks, Economic Development, Employment/Job Training, Civic & Public Affairs-General, Urban & Community Affairs, Zoos/Aquariums
Education: Business Education, Colleges & Universities, Education Reform, Education-General, Legal Education, Private Education (Precollege), Public Education (Precollege), Religious Education, Secondary Education (Private), Student Aid
Health: Children's Health/Hospitals, Health Organizations, Hospitals, Kidney, Medical Rehabilitation, Preventive Medicine/Wellness Organizations, Public Health
International: International Organizations, International Relief Efforts, Missionary/Religious Activities
Religion: Bible Study/Translation, Churches, Religion-General, Ministries, Missionary Activities (Domestic), Religious Organizations, Religious Welfare, Seminaries
Science: Science Museums
Social Services: Child Welfare, Community Service Organizations, Day Care, Family Services, Recreation & Athletics, Social Services-General, United Funds/United Ways, YMCA/YWCA/YMHA/YWHA, Youth Organizations

Application Procedures

Initial Contact: The foundation has no formal grant application procedure or application form.
Deadlines: None.

Foundation Officials

Barbara Van Dellen Bere: president, director
David L. Bere: secretary, treasurer, director
James Frederick Bere, Jr.: vice president, director B Chicago, IL 1922. ED Northwestern University (1946); Northwestern University (1950). CORP AFFIL director: Temple-Inland Tribune Co.; director: York International Corp.; director: K-Mart Corp.; director: Abbott Laboratories; director: Ameritech Corp.
Robert P. Bere: vice president, director
Becky B. Sigfusson: vice president, director
Lynn B. Stine: vice president, director

Grants Analysis

Disclosure Period: calendar year ending 2003
Total Grants: $682,000*
Number of Grants: 45
Average Grant: $6,558*
Highest Grant: $200,000
Lowest Grant: $200
Typical Range: $1,000 to $10,000
***Note:** Giving excludes United Way. Average grant figure excludes two highest grants ($400,000).

Recent Grants

Note: Grants derived from 2003 Form 990.

General

200,000	Fuller Seminary
200,000	Millenium Park Inc., Chicago, IL
100,300	World Vision
53,000	Christ Church of Oak Brook, Oak Brook, IL
25,000	Fox Cities Performing Arts Center, Appleton, WI
12,000	Lawndale Community Church, Chicago, IL
10,000	Marian College, Indianapolis, IN
7,000	Art Institute of Chicago, Chicago, IL
5,000	Chicago Symphony Orchestra, Chicago, IL
5,000	Lyric Opera of Chicago, Chicago, IL

FRANK AND LYDIA BERGEN FOUNDATION

Giving Contact
Thomas Chiolo
Wachovia Bank
401 S. Tyron Street, 4th Floor
Charlotte, NC 28288-1159
Phone: (704)383-5589

Alternate Contact
Wachovia Bank
190 Riverpond
Summit, NJ 07901
Note: Address for application submissions.

Description
Founded: 1983
EIN: 226359304
Organization Type: Private Foundation
Giving Locations: NJ: Young American Conductor Projects run throughout the US.
Grant Types: Conference/Seminar, General Support, Multiyear/Continuing Support, Project, Scholarship.

Donor Information
Founder: the late Charlotte V. Bergen

Financial Summary
Total Giving: $667,960 (2004); $597,195 (2001)
Giving Analysis: Giving for 2001 includes: foundation scholarships ($130,850)
Assets: $10,448,545 (2004); $9,870,592 (2001)

Typical Recipients
Arts & Humanities: Arts Associations & Councils, Arts Centers, Arts Festivals, Arts Funds, Arts Institutes, Arts Outreach, Ballet, Dance, Libraries, Music, Opera, Performing Arts, Public Broadcasting
Civic & Public Affairs: Native American Affairs
Education: Arts/Humanities Education, Colleges & Universities, Faculty Development, Private Education (Precollege), Student Aid
Religion: Jewish Causes, Religious Welfare
Social Services: Youth Organizations

Application Procedures
Initial Contact: Send cover letter and a full proposal.
Application Requirements: Include a description of organization, amount requested, purpose of funds sought, recently audited financial statement, and proof of tax-exempt status.
Deadlines: March 15 through September 15.

Restrictions
Grants not made to individuals, endowments, political or lobbying groups, loans, fundraising events, or operating expenses.

Additional Information
Publications: Annual Report; Informational Brochure (including Application Guidelines)
Trust(s): Wachovia Bank

Grants Analysis
Disclosure Period: calendar year ending 2004
Total Grants: $667,960*
Typical Range: $5,000 to $10,000
*Note: No grants list available for 2004.

Recent Grants
Note: Grants derived from 2001 Form 990.
General

45,000	New Jersey Symphony Orchestra, Newark, NJ
31,500	Community School of the Arts
25,000	Montclair State University, Upper Montclair, NJ
24,000	New Jersey Chamber Music Society, Montclair, NJ
21,000	Colonial Symphony, Basking Ridge, NJ
19,600	Community Center on the Palisades Music Development, Pacific Palisades, CA
18,000	Bay Atlantic Symphony, Bridgeton, NJ
17,500	Westfield Symphony Orchestra, Westfield, CT
15,000	Mason Gross School of the Arts, New Brunswick, NJ
12,500	New Jersey City University Foundation, New Jersey City, NJ

LOUIS AND SANDRA BERKMAN FOUNDATION

Giving Contact
Linda L. Pinkle, Secretary
PO Box 576
Steubenville, OH 43952
Phone: (740)283-3722
Fax: (740)283-1224

Description
Founded: 1952
EIN: 346526694
Organization Type: Private Foundation
Giving Locations: MA; OH; PA
Grant Types: General Support.

Donor Information
Founder: Established in 1952 by the late Louis Berkman Sr., Mrs. Louis Berkman, the Louis Berkman Co., Follansbee Steel Corp., and others.

Financial Summary
Total Giving: $328,928 (2001)
Assets: $14,004,765 (2001)
Gifts Received: $100,000 (2000); $240,773 (1996); $100 (1995). Note: In 1996 and 2000, contributions were received from the Louis Berkman Co.

Typical Recipients
Arts & Humanities: Arts Festivals, Historic Preservation, History & Archaeology, Music
Civic & Public Affairs: Clubs, Community Foundations, Ethnic Organizations, Civic & Public Affairs-General, Housing, Municipalities/Towns, Parades/Festivals, Safety, Urban & Community Affairs, Zoos/Aquariums
Education: Arts/Humanities Education, Colleges & Universities, Community & Junior Colleges, Education Funds, Elementary Education (Private), Minority Education, Private Education (Precollege), Religious Education, Secondary Education (Private), Secondary Education (Public), Special Education, Student Aid
Health: Cancer, Children's Health/Hospitals, Clinics/Medical Centers, Emergency/Ambulance Services, Eyes/Blindness, Health Organizations, Heart, Hospices, Hospitals, Medical Research, Prenatal Health Issues, Public Health, Single-Disease Health Associations, Transplant Networks/Donor Banks
Religion: Churches, Religion-General, Jewish Causes, Ministries, Missionary Activities (Domestic), Religious Organizations, Religious Welfare, Synagogues/Temples
Science: Scientific Centers & Institutes
Social Services: Community Service Organizations, Crime Prevention, Day Care, Emergency Relief, Family Planning, Food/Clothing Distribution, Recreation & Athletics, Scouts, Social Services-General, United Funds/United Ways, Veterans, Youth Organizations

Application Procedures
Initial Contact: Send a brief letter of inquiry with a complete explanation of purpose of funds sought and a full description of the applicant.
Deadlines: July 1.

Foundation Officials
Louis Berkman: president, trustee B Canton, OH 1909. PRIM CORP EMPL chairman, president, chief executive officer, treasurer, director: Louis Berkman Co. CORP AFFIL president: Scott Lumber; president: Swenson Spreader; president: Meyer Products; president: Orrville Products; president, director: Follansbee Steel Corp.; president: IDL Supplies; chairman: Ampco-Pittsburgh Corp.; president: Dover Parkersburg.
John Koren: secretary, trustee
Linda Pirkle: assistant secretary

Grants Analysis
Disclosure Period: calendar year ending 2001
Total Grants: $328,928*
Number of Grants: 43
Average Grant: $2,754*
Highest Grant: $100,000
Lowest Grant: $25
Typical Range: $1,000 to $5,000
*Note: Giving excludes scholarships. Average grant figure excludes three highest grants ($210,498).

Recent Grants
Note: Grants derived from 2002 Form 990.
General

100,000	Cornell University, Ithaca, NY
50,000	Franciscan University of Steubenville, Steubenville, OH
50,000	West Liberty State College, West Liberty, WV
30,000	Franciscan University of Steubenville, Steubenville, OH
20,000	Rodef Shalom Congregation, Pittsburgh, PA
10,000	Brooke-Hancock Veterans Group
10,000	Rodef Shalom Congregation, Pittsburgh, PA
10,000	Steubenville Kiwanis Youth Society, Steubenville, OH
10,000	Temple Beth Israel, Austin, TX
5,000	American Friends of the Progressive Jews

ARNOLD BERNHARD FOUNDATION

Giving Contact
Jean B. Buttner, President
220 East 42nd Street, 6th Floor
New York, NY 10017-5806
Phone: (212)907-1620
Fax: (212)226-3935

Description
Founded: 1976
EIN: 136100457
Organization Type: Private Foundation
Giving Locations: CT; NY: nationally.
Grant Types: General Support, Scholarship.

Donor Information
Founder: The foundation was founded by the Arnold Bernhard Charitable Annuity Trust I and the Arnold Bernhard Charitable Annuity Trust II.

Financial Summary
Total Giving: $499,500 (2003); $461,470 (2001)
Giving Analysis: Giving for 2001 includes: foundation gifts to individuals ($10,000)

Assets: $7,112,824 (2003); $8,437,378 (2001)
Gifts Received: $75,000 (2001); $86,124 (2000); $447,739 (1999). Note: In 2001, contributions were received from Stanford Business School. In 2000, contributions were received from Janet K. Bernhard Charitable Annuity Trusts I and II. In 1999, contributions were received from Arnold Bernhard Charitable Annuity Trust II.

Typical Recipients

Arts & Humanities: Libraries, Opera, Public Broadcasting
Civic & Public Affairs: Economic Development, Employment/Job Training, Civic & Public Affairs-General, Safety
Education: Business Education, Colleges & Universities, Medical Education, Private Education (Precollege), Secondary Education (Private), Student Aid
Environment: Air/Water Quality, Environment-General
Health: Clinics/Medical Centers, Emergency/Ambulance Services, Hospitals, Hospitals (University Affiliated), Medical Research, Single-Disease Health Associations
Religion: Churches, Religious Welfare
Social Services: Domestic Violence, Food/Clothing Distribution, Recreation & Athletics, Veterans, Youth Organizations

Application Procedures

Initial Contact: Send a brief letter of inquiry.
Deadlines: None.

Foundation Officials

Howard A. Brecher: vice president, director
Jean Bernhard Buttner: president, director B New Rochelle, NY 1934. ED Vassar College BA (1957); Harvard University (1958). PRIM CORP EMPL chairman, chief executive officer, president, director: Value Line. CORP AFFIL chairman, president, chief executive officer, chief operating officer, director: Arnold Bernhard & Co.; chairman, director: Value Line Fund. NONPR AFFIL member visitation committee: Harvard University Business School; trustee: Williams College.

Grants Analysis

Disclosure Period: calendar year ending 2003
Total Grants: $499,500
Number of Grants: 11
Average Grant: $16,611*
Highest Grant: $250,000
Lowest Grant: $500
Typical Range: $10,000 to $20,000
*Note: Average grant figure excludes two highest grants ($350,000).

Recent Grants

Note: Grants derived from 2003 Form 990.
General

250,000	McLean Hospital, Belmont, MA -- for psychiatric research
100,000	Harvard Business School, Boston, MA -- for women's initiative fund
50,000	Choate Rosemary Hall School, Wallingford, CT
50,000	Vassar College, Poughkeepsie, NY
20,000	Skidmore College, Saratoga Springs, NY
15,000	Jerusalem Foundation Inc., New York, NY -- towards Arnold Bernhard library, Israel
10,000	Emma Willard School, Troy, NY
2,000	Columbia University College of Physicians and Surgeons, New York, NY -- for psychiatric inpatient care
1,000	Disabled American Veterans, Cincinnati, OH
1,000	Paralyzed Veterans of America, Washington, DC

GRACE AND FRANKLIN BERNSEN FOUNDATION

Giving Contact

Sandra L. Griffin, Administrator
15 West 6th St., Suite 1308
Tulsa, OK 74119-5407
Phone: (918)584-4711
Fax: (918)584-4713
E-mail: info@bernsen.org
Web: http://www.bernsen.org

Alternate Contact

E-mail: Gfbernsen@aol.com

Description

Founded: 1985
EIN: 237009414
Organization Type: Family Foundation
Giving Locations: OK: Tulsa
Grant Types: Capital, Emergency, Matching, Multiyear/Continuing Support, Operating Expenses, Project, Seed Money.

Donor Information

Founder: Established in 1968 by the late Grace Bernsen and the late Franklin Bernsen.

Financial Summary

Total Giving: $1,517,604 (fiscal year ending 0, 2001)
Assets: $30,863,180 (fiscal 2001)

Typical Recipients

Arts & Humanities: Arts Associations & Councils, Arts Centers, Arts Funds, Ballet, Community Arts, Dance, Historic Preservation, History & Archaeology, Literary Arts, Museums/Galleries, Music, Opera, Performing Arts, Theater
Civic & Public Affairs: Botanical Gardens/Parks, Business/Free Enterprise, Clubs, Community Foundations, Economic Development, Civic & Public Affairs-General, Nonprofit Management, Philanthropic Organizations, Professional & Trade Associations, Public Policy, Urban & Community Affairs, Women's Affairs, Zoos/Aquariums
Education: Business Education, Colleges & Universities, Community & Junior Colleges, Economic Education, Education Funds, Education-General, International Studies, Leadership Training, Literacy, Medical Education, Preschool Education, Private Education (Precollege), Public Education (Precollege), Science/Mathematics Education, Special Education
Environment: Energy, Resource Conservation
Health: Alzheimer's Disease, Cancer, Children's Health/Hospitals, Clinics/Medical Centers, Emergency/Ambulance Services, Eyes/Blindness, Health Funds, Health Organizations, Heart, Hospices, Hospitals, Medical Rehabilitation, Medical Research, Mental Health, Multiple Sclerosis, Nursing Services, Prenatal Health Issues, Public Health, Respiratory, Single-Disease Health Associations, Speech & Hearing
International: International Affairs, International Relations
Religion: Churches, Ministries, Religious Organizations, Religious Welfare, Seminaries, Social/Policy Issues
Science: Scientific Research
Social Services: Animal Protection, At-Risk Youth, Big Brothers/Big Sisters, Camps, Child Abuse, Child Welfare, Community Service Organizations, Crime Prevention, Day Care, Delinquency & Criminal Rehabilitation, Domestic Violence, Family Services, Food/Clothing Distribution, People with Disabilities, Scouts, Senior Services, Sexual Abuse, Shelters/Homelessness, Social Services-General, Special Olympics, Substance Abuse, United Funds/United Ways, Volunteer Services, YMCA/YWCA/YMHA/YWHA, Youth Organizations

Application Procedures

Initial Contact: Submit a brief letter of inquiry.
Application Requirements: Applications should be submitted in writing by the chief executive officer of the applicant organization. In a summary letter, provide a brief description of the program in need of funding, including an explanation of its importance and clear statement of its goal. Cite the financial need, including the other sources of funds, if any. Attachments should include a list of current officers and board of trustees, documentation of tax-exempt status, most recent audited financial statement, current year-to-date financial statements and budget, project budget and plans to support the project after grant period.
Deadlines: None.
Review Process: Applications are considered at monthly or bi-monthly board meetings. Site visits are often scheduled by the board; proposals are typically processed within two months.
Decision Notification: Decisions on applications are reported in writing or by personal visit.
Notes: There are no set deadlines, but the foundation does request that applications be received by the 12th of each month before the next scheduled board meeting.

Restrictions

The foundation's trustees generally consider funding requests from Tulsa area charitable organizations for projects that will provide a defined benefit, such as capital projects, building programs, or specific program needs of the organizations. The trustees generally only make gifts that will be meaningful in amount and benefit to the recipient. The foundation discourages applications for general support, debt, or continuing support for the same program, although a single grant may extend over a period of several years. No grants are made to elementary or secondary schools, unless the programs are for at-risk, handicapped, or learning disabled children, or if they are innovative and apply to all schools in the system; to individuals; or for the benefit of specific individuals.

Additional Information

Publications: Annual Report; An Introduction to the Grace and Franklin Bernsen Foundation (Brochure); Guidelines

Foundation Officials

Sandra L. Griffin: admin
J. Warren Jackman: trustee
Donald F. Marlar: trustee PRIM CORP EMPL president: Jackman, Pray, Walker.
Donald E. Pray: trustee B Tulsa, OK 1932. ED University of Tulsa BS (1955); University of Oklahoma LLB (1963). PRIM CORP EMPL counsel: Jackman, Pray, Walker. NONPR AFFIL member: American Bar Association; fellow: American Bar Foundation. CLUB AFFIL president: Summit Club.
John D. Strong, Jr.: trustee
W. Bland Williamson: secretary, trustee PRIM CORP EMPL secretary, director: Lasmo America Ltd.

Grants Analysis

Total Grants: $1,517,604
Number of Grants: 42
Average Grant: $30,917*
Highest Grant: $250,000
Typical Range: $5,000 to $50,000
*Note: Average grant figure excludes highest grant.

Recent Grants

Note: Grants derived from fiscal 2002 Form 990.
General

202,500	University of Tulsa, Tulsa, OK
200,000	Camp Loughridge, Tulsa, OK -- for providing funds for capital campaign
100,000	Family and Children's Services, Tulsa, OK -- for providing funds for a capital campaign

100,000	Oklahoma Centennial Commemoration Fund, Oklahoma City, OK
50,000	Junior Achievement of Tulsa, Tulsa, OK -- for providing funds for an education program
50,000	Phillips Theological Seminary, Tulsa, OK -- for providing funds for a capital campaign
41,667	Mental Health Association of Tulsa, Tulsa, OK -- for providing funds for programs and capital needs
40,000	Child Abuse Network, Tulsa, OK -- for providing funds to relocate
37,500	Junior League of Tulsa, Tulsa, OK -- for providing funds for programs
25,000	Little Light House, Tulsa, OK -- for providing funds for an education program

LOREN M. BERRY FOUNDATION

Giving Contact

William T. Lincoln, Treasurer & Trustee
3055 Kettering Boulevard, Suite 418
Dayton, OH 45439
Phone: (937)293-0398

Description

Founded: 1960
EIN: 316026144
Organization Type: Family Foundation
Giving Locations: OH: Dayton
Grant Types: General Support.

Donor Information

Founder: Established in 1960 by the late Loren M. Berry, who developed a predecessor to today's telephone yellow pages. Berry, who was one of the largest telephone directory publishers in the country, died in 1980.

Financial Summary

Total Giving: $900,000 (2002 approx); $848,100 (2001)
Giving Analysis: Giving for 2001 includes: foundation scholarships ($25,000)
Assets: $16,163,977 (2001)

Typical Recipients

Arts & Humanities: Arts Associations & Councils, Arts Centers, Arts Institutes, Ballet, Community Arts, History & Archaeology, Libraries, Museums/Galleries, Music, Public Broadcasting, Theater
Civic & Public Affairs: Botanical Gardens/Parks, Business/Free Enterprise, Ethnic Organizations, Civic & Public Affairs-General, Inner-City Development, Philanthropic Organizations, Public Policy, Urban & Community Affairs, Women's Affairs
Education: Business Education, Colleges & Universities, Community & Junior Colleges, Economic Education, Education Funds, Elementary Education (Private), Environmental Education, Education-General, Literacy, Private Education (Precollege), Public Education (Precollege), Secondary Education (Private), Social Sciences Education, Special Education, Student Aid
Environment: Air/Water Quality, Environment-General, Wildlife Protection
Health: Alzheimer's Disease, Cancer, Children's Health/Hospitals, Clinics/Medical Centers, Emergency/Ambulance Services, Eyes/Blindness, Geriatric Health, Health Organizations, Heart, Hospices, Hospitals, Medical Rehabilitation, Single-Disease Health Associations, Transplant Networks/Donor Banks
International: Human Rights, International Affairs
Religion: Churches, Religious Welfare, Seminaries
Science: Science Museums, Scientific Organizations

Social Services: Animal Protection, At-Risk Youth, Big Brothers/Big Sisters, Camps, Child Welfare, Community Centers, Community Service Organizations, Crime Prevention, Domestic Violence, Family Planning, Family Services, Food/Clothing Distribution, Homes, People with Disabilities, Recreation & Athletics, Scouts, Social Services-General, United Funds/United Ways, YMCA/YWCA/YMHA/YWHA, Youth Organizations

Application Procedures

Initial Contact: Applicants should send a proposal in letter form.
Application Requirements: The letter should include the organization's charitable activities, its history, needs, and goals.
Deadlines: None. Requests may be submitted at any time.
Review Process: Letters are reviewed by the board of trustees.

Restrictions

The foundation does not support individuals.

Foundation Officials

Charles D. Berry: trustee
David L. Berry: trustee B 1927. PRIM CORP EMPL president: Berry & Berry Inc. CORP AFFIL president: Madera Valley Inn Inc.; president: Westgate Building Materials; president: Berry Construction; president: Best Western.
George W. Berry: trustee
John William Berry, Jr.: president, trustee B 1947. PRIM CORP EMPL president, chief executive officer, director: L.M. Berry & Co. CORP AFFIL chief executive officer: Berry Investments Inc.; chairman, director: AcuSport Corp.; chairman: Berry Braiding Inc. NONPR AFFIL director: Air Force Museum Foundation.
Martha B. Fraim: trustee
William L. Fraim: trustee B Santa Monica, CA 1951. ED Occidental College (1974). PRIM CORP EMPL president, director: AcuSport Corp. CORP AFFIL member: National Association Sporting Goods Wholesalers; president, director: Go Sportsmens Supply Inc.; president, director: Midwest Warehouse. NONPR AFFIL member: Benevolent Protectorate Elks.
Elizabeth B. Gray: trustee
Leland W. Henry: trustee
William T. Lincoln: treasurer, trustee B 1943. PRIM CORP EMPL president, director: Berry Investments Inc. ADD CORP EMPL secretary, director: AcuSport Corp.; treasurer: Berry Braiding Inc.; director: Go Sportsmens Supply Inc.
James O. Payne: trustee B 1937. ED University of Dayton; Xavier University MBA. PRIM CORP EMPL executive vice president financial & administration: L.M. Berry & Co. CORP AFFIL treasurer, director: Microwave Sensors Inc.; secretary: Berry Investments Inc. NONPR AFFIL director: Design Forum Inc.

Grants Analysis

Disclosure Period: calendar year ending 2001
Total Grants: $823,100*
Number of Grants: 69
Average Grant: $11,929
Highest Grant: $60,000
Lowest Grant: $150
Typical Range: $5,000 to $20,000
*Note: Giving excludes scholarships.

Recent Grants

Note: Grants derived from 2002 Form 990.
General

50,000	Second & Main Ltd., Dayton, OH
50,000	United Rehabilitation, Dayton, OH
40,000	Cedarville College, Cedarville, OH
40,000	Dayton Public TV, Dayton, OH
30,000	Sinclair Community, Dayton, OH
25,000	2003 Committee
25,000	Aullwood Audubon, Dayton, OH

25,000	Camping and Education
25,000	Catholic Social Services, Cincinnati, OH
25,000	Catholic Social Services, Cincinnati, OH

BERTHA FOUNDATION

Giving Contact

PO Box 1110
Graham, TX 76450
Phone: (940)549-1400

Description

Founded: 1967
EIN: 756050023
Organization Type: Private Foundation
Giving Locations: TX: Young County
Grant Types: General Support, Operating Expenses, Scholarship.

Donor Information

Founder: E. Bruce Street, M. Boyd Street Foundation

Financial Summary

Total Giving: $59,060 (2003)
Giving Analysis: Giving for 2003 includes: foundation scholarships ($5,983)
Assets: $8,648,030 (2003)
Gifts Received: $8,855 (1999); $41,600 (1998); $1,787,085 (1996). Note: In 1998, contributions were received from E. Bruce Street Charitable Trust ($20,800) and M. Boyd Street Charitable Trust ($20,800). In 1996, contributions were received from E. Bruce Street ($814,305), M. Boyd Street ($931,100), E. Bruce Street Charitable Trust ($20,800), and M. Boyd Street Charitable Trust ($20,800).

Typical Recipients

Arts & Humanities: Arts Associations & Councils, Arts Festivals, Libraries, Literary Arts, Museums/Galleries, Music
Civic & Public Affairs: Botanical Gardens/Parks, Chambers of Commerce, Clubs, Civic & Public Affairs-General, Inner-City Development, Municipalities/Towns, Rural Affairs, Safety
Education: Business-School Partnerships, Colleges & Universities, Education Funds, Faculty Development, Literacy, Medical Education, Public Education (Precollege), Science/Mathematics Education, Student Aid
Health: Clinics/Medical Centers, Health Organizations, Hospices, Hospitals, Mental Health, Preventive Medicine/Wellness Organizations, Public Health
Religion: Jewish Causes, Religious Organizations
Science: Science Exhibits & Fairs
Social Services: Community Service Organizations, Counseling, Family Services, Scouts, Senior Services, Social Services-General, Substance Abuse, Youth Organizations

Application Procedures

Initial Contact: Send a brief letter of inquiry.
Application Requirements: Include name, address, telephone number, and purpose of funds sought.
Deadlines: None.

Foundation Officials

Sandra Street Estess: director
J. R. Montgomery: secretary, treasurer
Alice Ann Street: president, director
E. Bruce Street: director
Malcolm Boyd Street, Jr.: director

Grants Analysis

Disclosure Period: calendar year ending 2003
Total Grants: $53,077*
Number of Grants: 16

Average Grant: $2,456*
Highest Grant: $16,236
Lowest Grant: $25
Typical Range: $1,000 to $5,000
*Note: Giving excludes scholarships. Average grant figure excludes highest grant.

Recent Grants

Note: Grants derived from 2003 Form 990.
General

16,236	Graham Senior Citizens Center, Graham, TX -- for construction and furnishing new facility
7,200	Graham Independent School District, Graham, TX -- for teacher training
6,853	City of Graham, Graham, TX -- for maintenance and landscaping at the library
6,381	Graham Independent School District, Graham, TX -- for teacher mini grants
5,983	Rotary Club of Graham, Graham, TX -- for scholarship funding
5,000	City of Graham, Graham, TX -- for memorial auditorium renovations
3,500	Graham Regional Medical Center, Graham, TX -- to sponsor health fair
1,952	City of Graham, Graham, TX -- to replace compressor in children's department for library
1,650	Graham Area Crisis Center, Graham, TX -- to tint all glass on front of the building
1,000	Graham Chamber of Commerce, Graham, TX -- for art splash on the square program

BERWIND GROUP

Company Headquarters

3000 Centre Square West
1500 Market Street
Philadelphia, PA 19102
Phone: (215)563-2800
Fax: (215)563-8347
Web: http://www.berwind.com

Company Description

Founded: 1874
Employees: 4,800 (1998)
SIC(s): 2834 Pharmaceutical Preparations, 2865 Cyclic Crudes & Intermediates, 3441 Fabricated Structural Metal, 6519 Real Property Lessors Nec.

Operating Locations

Berwind Corp. (KY--Kimper, Pikeville; MA--Ashland, Sharon; MI--Port Huron; NJ--Neptune; NY--Amherst; OR--Portland; PA--King of Prussia, Philadelphia, Warminster, West Point; TN--LaVergne; WV--Charleston)

Nonmonetary Support

Type: Donated Equipment

Giving Contact

Mary LaRue, Chairperson, Contributions Committee
3000 Centre Square West
1500 Market Street
Philadelphia, PA 19102
Phone: (215)563-2800
Fax: (215)563-1493
E-mail: mlarue@berwind.com
Web: http://www.berwind.com

Alternate Contact

Jennifer Green, Executive Assistant

Description

Organization Type: Corporate Giving Program
Giving Locations: headquarters area only.
Grant Types: Emergency, Employee Matching Gifts,
General Support, Matching, Project.
Note: Employee matching gift ratio: 1 to 1 up to $1,000, for education only. $5,000 maximum per employee per year.

Financial Summary

Total Giving: $500,000 (2003 approx); $500,000 (2002); $1,000,000 (2001). Note: Contributes through corporate direct giving program only.

Typical Recipients

Arts & Humanities: Arts Institutes, Arts & Humanities-General, Libraries, Museums/Galleries, Music, Performing Arts, Public Broadcasting, Theater
Civic & Public Affairs: Civic & Public Affairs-General, Women's Affairs, Zoos/Aquariums
Education: Business Education, Colleges & Universities, Education-General, Legal Education, Minority Education
Environment: Environment-General
Health: Health-General, Hospitals
Science: Scientific Centers & Institutes
Social Services: Child Welfare, Community Centers, Delinquency & Criminal Rehabilitation, Family Planning, Food/Clothing Distribution, Senior Services, United Funds/United Ways

Application Procedures

Initial Contact: Send a letter of inquiry.
Application Requirements: Include a description of organization, amount requested, purpose of funds sought, list of organizations which support the work done by your organization, list of board of directors, and IRS 501(c)(3) tax-determination letter.
Deadlines: By November for proceeding year.

Restrictions

Does not support political or lobbying groups.

Grants Analysis

Typical Range: $1,000 to $2,500

BESSER FOUNDATION

Giving Contact

J. Richard Wilson, President
123 N. 2nd Ave.
Alpena, MI 49707-2801
Phone: (989)354-4722
Fax: (989)354-8099
E-mail: bessfdtn@freeway.net

Description

Founded: 1944
EIN: 386071938
Organization Type: Private Foundation
Giving Locations: MI: Alpena
Grant Types: Challenge, General Support, Multi-year/Continuing Support, Operating Expenses.

Donor Information

Founder: the late J. H. Besser, Besser Co.

Financial Summary

Total Giving: $874,908 (2004); $819,649 (2001)
Giving Analysis: Giving for 2004 includes: foundation grants to United Way ($45,000); 2001: foundation grants to United Way ($42,000)
Assets: $17,289,894 (2004); $16,883,920 (2001)

Typical Recipients

Arts & Humanities: Arts Associations & Councils, Arts Institutes, Libraries, Museums/Galleries, Theater
Civic & Public Affairs: Community Foundations, Civic & Public Affairs-General, Housing, Legal Aid, Nonprofit Management, Philanthropic Organizations, Professional & Trade Associations, Safety
Education: Business Education, Colleges & Universities, Community & Junior Colleges, Engineering/Technological Education, Education-General, Public Education (Precollege), School Volunteerism, Science/Mathematics Education, Secondary Education (Public), Student Aid, Vocational & Technical Education
Environment: Environment-General
Health: Clinics/Medical Centers, Health-General, Health Organizations, Hospices, Hospitals, Medical Rehabilitation, Mental Health
International: Health Care/Hospitals, International Relief Efforts, Missionary/Religious Activities
Religion: Churches, Religious Organizations, Religious Welfare
Science: Scientific Centers & Institutes
Social Services: At-Risk Youth, Big Brothers/Big Sisters, Camps, Child Welfare, Community Service Organizations, Domestic Violence, Family Services, Food/Clothing Distribution, Recreation & Athletics, Shelters/Homelessness, Substance Abuse, United Funds/United Ways, Volunteer Services, Youth Organizations

Application Procedures

Initial Contact: Submit a written request.
Application Requirements: Provide a detailed prospectus of the project, including the project name, purpose and historical background of the problem to be addressed; proposal objective, plan of development, expected results, and method of evaluation; how and by whom the expected results will be used, and how results might lead to new methods, changes in practice, service, etc.; detailed information concerning personnel involved with the project; complete financial budget; projected calendar, including stages and the points and which partial results and progress reports will be available; whether similar projects have been undertaken previously; whether support has been or is being requested of other foundations; and the name of the organization sponsoring or proposing the project and a copy of its letter of tax-exempt status.
Deadlines: The end of the first month of each calendar quarter.

Restrictions

Does not support individuals, endowment funds, meeting or conference expenses, or travel expenses. The foundation does not generally consider grant requests from organizations located outside of Alpena, MI.

Additional Information

Publications: Annual Report (including Application Guidelines)

Foundation Officials

Gary Dawley: trustee
Patricia Gardner: trustee
James Charles Park: vice president, secretary B Alpena, MI 1937. ED University of Michigan (1959); University of Michigan (1961). PRIM CORP EMPL chairman, president, chief executive officer, director: Besser Co. CORP AFFIL chairman: Lithibar Corp.; chairman: Proneq Industries Montreal; chairman: Besser Canada Ltd.; director: Besser Appco. CLUB AFFIL Rotary Club.
Carl F. Reitz: treasurer
Harold A. Ruemenapp: trustee
J. Richard Wilson: president

Grants Analysis

Disclosure Period: calendar year ending 2004
Total Grants: $829,908*
Number of Grants: 45
Average Grant: $9,533*
Highest Grant: $220,000
Lowest Grant: $600
Typical Range: $1,000 to $15,000
*Note: Giving excludes United Way. Average grant excludes two highest grants ($420,000).

Recent Grants

Note: Grants derived from 2001 Form 990.
General

220,000	Jesse Besser Museum, Alpena, MI -- for operating expenses
100,000	Alpena Community College, Alpena, MI -- World Center for Concrete Technology
50,000	Jesse Besser Museum, Alpena, MI -- operating support
42,000	United Way of Alpena County, Alpena, MI -- for administrative expenses
40,000	Child and Family Services, Alpena, MI -- operating expenses
35,000	Sunrise Mission, Alpena, MI -- shelter renovation
26,500	Africare, Washington, DC -- Baroueli School Project
25,000	Boys and Girls Club of Alpena, Alpena, MI -- operating expenses
25,000	Salvation Army, Alpena, MI -- relocation of thrift store
25,000	Thunder Bay Soccer Association, Alpena, MI -- new soccer fields

BEST BUY CO.

Company Headquarters

7075 Flying Cloud Drive
Eden Prairie, MN 55344
Web: http://www.bestbuy.com

Company Description

Ticker: BBY
Exchange: OTC
Acquired: Musicland (2001).
Revenue: US$24.901 billion (2004)
Profit: US$705 million (2004)
Employees: 24,500
Fortune Rank: 77, per FORTUNE Magazine's list of 500 Largest U.S. Corporations (2004).
SIC(s): 5722 Household Appliance Stores, 5734 Computer & Software Stores, 5946 Camera & Photographic Supply Stores, 5999 Miscellaneous Retail Stores Nec.

Best Buy Children's Foundation

Giving Contact

Richard M. Schulze, Chairman, Director
Best Buy Children's Foundation
c/o Community Relations Department
PO Box 9312
Minneapolis, MN 55440-9312
Phone: (952)947-2000
Web: http://www.bestbuy.com/About/CommunityRelations/ChildrensFoundation.asp

Description

Founded: 1995
EIN: 411784382
Organization Type: Corporate Foundation

Financial Summary

Total Giving: $10,059,510 (fiscal year ending February 28, 2004); $11,564,699 (fiscal 2003); $4,449,912 (fiscal 2002)
Giving Analysis: Giving for fiscal 2001 includes: foundation grants to United Way ($24,000); foundation ($1,877,105)
Assets: $6,324,815 (fiscal 2004); $17,072,761 (fiscal 2003); $20,837,143 (fiscal 2002)
Gifts Received: $101,587 (fiscal 2004); $2,079,047 (fiscal 2003); $16,065,002 (fiscal 2002). Note: In fiscal 2004, contributions were received from Inscape,

Inc. ($5,000), John Tyler Enterprises ($5,000), Weisman Enterprises ($5,000), and OPUS ($50,000). In fiscal 2003, contributions were received from Best Buy Co. ($2,000,000), RHR International Co. ($5,000), American Color Graphics ($5,000), PGA Minnesota ($5,000), Robustelli Travel ($5,000), and Discover Card ($20,000). In fiscal 2000 and 2001, substantial contributions were received from Richard M. Schulze.

Typical Recipients

Arts & Humanities: Arts Centers, Arts Institutes, Film & Video, Arts & Humanities-General, Libraries, Museums/Galleries, Music, Performing Arts, Public Broadcasting, Theater
Civic & Public Affairs: Botanical Gardens/Parks, Community Foundations, Ethnic Organizations, Civic & Public Affairs-General, Law & Justice, Native American Affairs, Public Policy, Urban & Community Affairs
Education: Afterschool/Enrichment Programs, Business Education, Colleges & Universities, Community & Junior Colleges, Education Funds, Education Reform, Education-General, Private Education (Precollege), Public Education (Precollege), Student Aid
Health: Cancer, Children's Health/Hospitals
Religion: Religious Welfare
Science: Science Museums
Social Services: Big Brothers/Big Sisters, Camps, Child Abuse, Child Welfare, Community Centers, Community Service Organizations, Crime Prevention, Domestic Violence, Family Services, People with Disabilities, Scouts, Sexual Abuse, Social Services-General, United Funds/United Ways, YMCA/YWCA/YMHA/YWHA, Youth Organizations

Application Procedures

Application Requirements: Proposals must include the following information: complete Best Buy Children's Foundation application form; description of the proposed program and the evaluation criteria that will be used to measure specific outcomes along with the purpose of program, need being addressed, describe specific activities, time table, specific neightborhood or geographic area served; organization's current operating budget, project or program income and expense budget, including top five donors and amounts; list of past successful programs; most recent IRS 501(c)(3) nonprofit determination letter; list of organization's officers and directors and their affiliations; latest annual report; financial statemtns from the most recently completed fiscal year; current completed 990 tax form; and a list of Best Buy employees who volunteer with the organization and a list of volunteer opportunities.

Additional Information

In 2002, the foundation reported that it was refocusing its giving guidelines. Until the foundation's new guidelines are released, the foundation will only be funding continuation grants for its established nonprofit partners. The foundation's web site will provide updates as the new guidelines become available.

Corporate Officials

Bradbury H. Anderson: vice chairman, chief executive officer PRIM CORP EMPL vice chairman, chief executive officer: Best Buy Co. Inc. NONPR AFFIL director: Retail Industry Leaders Association; trustee: Waldorf College; director: Minnesota Public Radio; director: American Film Institute; director: Junior Achievement.
Susan S. Hoff: senior vice president public affairs PRIM CORP EMPL senior vice president public affairs: Best Buy Co. Inc.
Joseph M. Joyce: senior vice president, general counsel, assistant secretary ED University of Minnesota BA; William Mitchell College of Law JD. PRIM CORP EMPL senior vice president, general counsel, assistant secretary: Best Buy Co. Inc.
Allen U. Lenzmeier: president, chief operating officer ED Mankato State University (1965). PRIM

CORP EMPL president, chief operating officer: Best Buy Co. Inc. NONPR AFFIL national trustee: Boys & Girls Clubs of America; director: Catholic Community Foundation.
Richard M. Schulze: founder, chairman B 1941. PRIM CORP EMPL founder, chairman: Best Buy Co. Inc. NONPR AFFIL trustee: University of St. Thomas; chairman: University of St. Thomas Business School.

Foundation Officials

Bradbury H. Anderson: director (see above)
Ruby Anik: director
Susan S. Hoff: president (see above)
Allen U. Lenzmeier: director (see above)
Tim McGeehan: director
Ryan Robinson: treasurer, director
Richard M. Schulze: chairman, director (see above)
John R. Thompson: director
Barbara VanLoenen: director, treasurer
Judy Weigel: treasurer, director ED Marquette University BA.
Nancy Wigchers: secretary, director

Grants Analysis

Disclosure Period: fiscal year ending February 28, 2004
Total Grants: $8,146,026*
Number of Grants: 1612
Average Grant: $4,866*
Highest Grant: $307,500
Lowest Grant: $50
Typical Range: $1,000 to $10,000
*Note: Giving excludes United Way. Average grant figure excludes highest grant.

Recent Grants

Note: Grants derived from fiscal 2004 Form 990.
Library-Related

250,000	Friends of the Minneapolis Public Library, Minneapolis, MN

General

968,000	Ball State University, Muncie, IN
892,785	United Way of America, Alexandria, VA
500,000	Children's Theatre Co., Minneapolis, MN
500,000	Southlake Women's Club Foundation, Southlake, TX
338,493	United Way of America, Alexandria, VA
307,500	YWCA of the USA, Washington, DC
253,000	March of Dimes, White Plains, NY
250,000	American Film Institute, Los Angeles, CA
250,000	Marine Toys for Tots, Quantico, VA
250,000	Plymouth Christian Youth Center, Minneapolis, MN

BURTON G. BETTINGEN CORP.

Giving Contact

Patricia A. Brown, Executive Director
The Burton G. Bettingen Corporation
9777 Wilshire Boulevard Suite 615
Beverly Hills, CA 90212
Phone: (310)276-4115
Fax: (310)276-4693
E-mail: burtonbet@aol.com

Description

Founded: 1984
EIN: 953942826
Organization Type: General Purpose Foundation
Giving Locations: CA: Los Angeles nationally
Grant Types: Capital, Endowment, General Support, Project, Research.

Donor Information

Founder: Established in 1984 by the late Burton G. Bettingen.

Financial Summary

Total Giving: $1,873,285 (fiscal year ending September 30, 2002); $1,867,620 (fiscal 2001)
Giving Analysis: Giving for fiscal 2002 includes: foundation scholarships ($120,000)
Assets: $15,718,032 (fiscal 2002); $15,718,032 (fiscal 2001)
Gifts Received: $1,482,145 (fiscal 2002); $1,482,145 (fiscal 1999); $1,482,144 (fiscal 1998). Note: In Fiscal 1998, contributions were received from the Burton G. Bettingen Charitable Lead Annuity Trust.

Typical Recipients

Arts & Humanities: Ethnic & Folk Arts, Libraries, Museums/Galleries, Music, Public Broadcasting
Civic & Public Affairs: Botanical Gardens/Parks, Business/Free Enterprise, Community Foundations, Economic Policy, Civic & Public Affairs-General, Hispanic Affairs, Law & Justice, Legal Aid, Native American Affairs, Nonprofit Management, Philanthropic Organizations, Public Policy, Urban & Community Affairs
Education: Afterschool/Enrichment Programs, Arts/Humanities Education, Colleges & Universities, Community & Junior Colleges, Environmental Education, Faculty Development, Education-General, Medical Education, Minority Education, Private Education (Precollege), Public Education (Precollege), Religious Education, Science/Mathematics Education, Secondary Education (Private), Secondary Education (Public), Special Education, Student Aid
Environment: Environment-General, Resource Conservation
Health: AIDS/HIV, Alzheimer's Disease, Cancer, Children's Health/Hospitals, Emergency/Ambulance Services, Health Policy/Cost Containment, Health Organizations, Home-Care Services, Hospitals, Hospitals (University Affiliated), Long-Term Care, Medical Research, Mental Health, Preventive Medicine/Wellness Organizations, Research/Studies Institutes, Respiratory, Single-Disease Health Associations
International: Health Care/Hospitals, International Environmental Issues, International Relief Efforts
Religion: Dioceses, Religious Organizations, Religious Welfare
Social Services: At-Risk Youth, Camps, Child Abuse, Child Welfare, Community Service Organizations, Counseling, Crime Prevention, Day Care, Family Planning, Family Services, Homes, People with Disabilities, Sexual Abuse, Shelters/Homelessness, Substance Abuse, YMCA/YWCA/YMHA/YWHA, Youth Organizations

Application Procedures

Initial Contact: Letters of inquiry stating the applicant's background, goals, and objectives and its specific need for funding are welcome; however, the corporation does not generally award unsolicited grant requests.
Application Requirements: Applications must include the applicant's most recent audited financial statements, Form 990, brief budgetary information related to the request (including other funding sources), a copy of the applicant's IRS determination of not-for-profit tax-exempt status, and a list of the applicant's governing board.
Deadlines: Proposals must be received by December 31 for consideration in April of the following year.
Evaluative Criteria: The Corporation primarily provides operating, capital, research, and endowment support to organizations providing educational, health, and welfare services to child prostitutes, runaways, and abandoned children.
Notes: Consult the corporation's Grant Policy and Application Guidelines for further information.

Restrictions

The corporation does not award grants to individuals, or to organizations that are themselves grantmaking bodies. In addition, the corporation does not support general fundraising events, dinners, or mass mailings.

Additional Information

Publications: Application Guidelines

Foundation Officials

Patricia A. Brown: secretary, treasurer, executive director, director PRIM CORP EMPL administration director, director: Burton G. Bettingen Corp.
Regina Covitt: assistant treasurer
Sandra G. Nowicki: president, director PRIM CORP EMPL president, director: Burton G. Bettingen Corp.
Stuart B. Tobisman: vice president, director, counsel B Detroit, MI 1942. ED University of California, Los Angeles BA (1966); University of California, Los Angeles JD (1969). PRIM CORP EMPL partner: O'Melveny & Myers. CORP AFFIL director: Burton G. Bettingen Corp. NONPR AFFIL Order Coif; member: Phi Beta Kappa; fellow: American College Trust & Estate Counsel.
Jane Van Zyl: director

Grants Analysis

Disclosure Period: fiscal year ending September 30, 2002
Total Grants: $1,753,285*
Number of Grants: 36
Average Grant: $5,415*
Highest Grant: $700,000
Lowest Grant: $75
Typical Range: $10,000 to $100,000
*Note: Giving excludes scholarships. Average grant figure excludes four highest grantss ($1,700,000).

Recent Grants

Note: Grants derived from fiscal 2002 Form 990.
General

700,000	Children's Hospital of Los Angeles, Los Angeles, CA
250,000	Hamburger Home (AVIVA), Los Angeles, CA
200,000	Children's Defense Fund, Oakland, CA
200,000	St. John's Hospital and Health Care Center, Santa Monica, CA
100,000	Public Counsel Center, Los Angeles, CA
100,000	Public Television for Southern and Central California (KCET), Los Angeles, CA
85,000	Alliance for Children's Rights, Los Angeles, CA
80,000	Rape Treatment Center, Santa Monica, CA
50,000	Phoenix House, New York, NY
35,000	Center for Neighborhood Enterprises, Washington, DC

BETTS INDUSTRIES

Company Headquarters

1800 Pennsylvania Ave. W.
Warren, PA 16365

Company Description

Employees: 220
SIC(s): 3300 Primary Metal Industries, 3400 Fabricated Metal Products, 3600 Electronic & Other Electrical Equipment, 3700 Transportation Equipment.

Betts Foundation

Giving Contact

Richard T. Betts, Trustee
Betts Foundation
1800 Pennsylvania Avenue W.
Box 88
Warren, PA 16365

Phone: (814)723-1250

Description

EIN: 256035169
Organization Type: Corporate Foundation
Giving Locations: PA: Warren County
Grant Types: General Support, Scholarship.

Financial Summary

Total Giving: $169,517 (2003); $181,281 (2001). Note: 1996 Giving includes scholarship (21,800).
Giving Analysis: Giving for 2003 includes: foundation grants to United Way ($16,000); foundation scholarships ($25,500); 2001: foundation scholarships ($30,738)
Assets: $2,931,891 (2003); $3,120,062 (2001)
Gifts Received: $25,000 (2003); $25,000 (2001); $75,000 (2000). Note: Contributions were received from Betts Industries.

Typical Recipients

Arts & Humanities: Arts Associations & Councils, Arts Institutes, Historic Preservation, Libraries, Music, Performing Arts, Theater
Civic & Public Affairs: Botanical Gardens/Parks, Business/Free Enterprise, Civil Rights, Economic Development, Economic Policy, Civic & Public Affairs-General, Inner-City Development, Municipalities/Towns, Parades/Festivals, Public Policy, Safety, Urban & Community Affairs, Women's Affairs
Education: Business Education, Colleges & Universities, Community & Junior Colleges, Economic Education, Education Associations, Education Funds, Engineering/Technological Education, Education-General, Public Education (Precollege), Secondary Education (Private), Secondary Education (Public), Student Aid, Vocational & Technical Education
Health: Emergency/Ambulance Services, Health Organizations, Hospices, Hospitals
Religion: Churches, Religious Welfare
Social Services: Animal Protection, Camps, Child Welfare, Community Service Organizations, Day Care, Delinquency & Criminal Rehabilitation, Family Services, Homes, Recreation & Athletics, Scouts, Senior Services, Social Services-General, Substance Abuse, United Funds/United Ways, Veterans, Volunteer Services, YMCA/YWCA/YMHA/YWHA, Youth Organizations

Application Procedures

Initial Contact: Telephone the foundation or send a brief letter describing program.
Deadlines: None.

Restrictions

Preference is given to educational studies for residents of Warren County, Pennsylvania.

Additional Information

Provides scholarships for higher education.

Corporate Officials

Richard T. Betts: chairman, president, director PRIM CORP EMPL chairman, president, director: Betts Industries.

Foundation Officials

C. R. Betts: trustee
R. E. Betts: trustee
Richard T. Betts: trustee (see above)
M. D. Hedges: trustee

Grants Analysis

Disclosure Period: calendar year ending 2003
Total Grants: $139,479*
Number of Grants: 26
Average Grant: $4,579*
Highest Grant: $25,000
Lowest Grant: $150
Typical Range: $1,000 to $10,000
*Note: Giving excludes scholarships. Average grant figure excludes highest grant.

Recent Grants
Note: Grants derived from 2003 Form 990.
Library-Related

15,000	Warren Public Library, Warren, PA
5,000	Youngsville Public Library, Youngsville, PA

General

25,000	Warren General Hospital, Warren, PA
23,250	Salvation Army, Warren, PA
16,000	United Fund of Warren County, Warren, PA
15,200	Struthers Library Theatre, Warren, PA
15,000	Penn Lakes Girl Scout Council, Edinboro, PA
5,000	City of Warren, Warren, PA
5,000	Family Services of Warren County, North Warren, PA
3,000	Jamestown Community College, Jamestown, NY
2,727	Betts Foundation Drug Education Program, Warren, PA
2,500	North Warren Volunteer Fire Department, North Warren, PA

FRANK STANLEY BEVERIDGE FOUNDATION, INC.

Giving Contact
Philip Caswell, President
301 Northeast 51st Street, Suite 1130
Boca Raton, FL 33431-4929
Phone: (561)241-8388
Fax: (561)241-8332
E-mail: administrator@beveridge.org
Web: http://www.beveridge.org

Description
Founded: 1947
EIN: 046032164
Organization Type: Family Foundation
Giving Locations: CA: Orange County; FL: Boca Raton; HI: Kauai County; MA: Hampden County, Hampshire County; NH; RI
Grant Types: Award, Capital, Emergency, General Support, Project, Research, Seed Money.

Donor Information
Founder: Established in 1947 in Massachusetts by the late Frank Stanley Beveridge, who was born in Canada on April 17, 1879. In March 1900, having traveled from Pembrooke Shores, near Yarmouth, Nova Scotia, he arrived at Mount Hermon School in Northfield, MA, with only a quarter. Following Mount Hermon School, Frank moved to upstate New York, married, and he and his wife, Theresa, had two daughters -- Evelyn and Ruth. Later, Mr. Beveridge joined the Fuller Brush Company in Hartford, CT, where he became director of sales.

In 1933, Beveridge founded Stanley Home Products, Inc. in Westfield, MA (Stanhome, Inc.), which was renamed Enesco Group Inc. in 1998. Enesco boasts annual sales of nearly $250 million.

In 1947, he founded the Frank Stanley Beveridge Foundation. In 1949, he founded the Stanley Park of Westfield, Inc. Today, Stanley Park consists of over 200 acres of formal gardens, a carillon tower, trails, sports fields, and a substantial nature area. The park is the principal recipient of funds from the foundation.

Financial Summary
Total Giving: $1,290,811 (2003); $1,587,641 (2002); $1,833,809 (2001)
Assets: $34,700,502 (2002); $38,879,821 (2001)

Typical Recipients
Arts & Humanities: Arts Associations & Councils, Arts Centers, Arts Funds, Dance, Historic Preservation, Libraries, Literary Arts, Museums/Galleries, Music, Performing Arts, Public Broadcasting, Theater, Visual Arts
Civic & Public Affairs: African American Affairs, Botanical Gardens/Parks, Business/Free Enterprise, Community Foundations, Economic Development, Civic & Public Affairs-General, Housing, Nonprofit Management, Philanthropic Organizations, Professional & Trade Associations, Rural Affairs, Urban & Community Affairs, Women's Affairs, Zoos/Aquariums
Education: Arts/Humanities Education, Colleges & Universities, Community & Junior Colleges, Education Associations, Education Funds, Education Reform, Faculty Development, Education-General, Journalism/Media Education, Medical Education, Preschool Education, Private Education (Precollege), Science/Mathematics Education, Secondary Education (Private), Secondary Education (Public), Special Education
Environment: Forestry, Environment-General, Resource Conservation, Watershed, Wildlife Protection
Health: Cancer, Clinics/Medical Centers, Diabetes, Emergency/Ambulance Services, Eyes/Blindness, Geriatric Health, Health Funds, Health Organizations, Heart, Hospices, Hospitals, Mental Health, Nursing Services, Prenatal Health Issues, Public Health, Research/Studies Institutes, Single-Disease Health Associations
Religion: Churches, Dioceses, Ministries, Religious Organizations, Religious Welfare, Seminaries
Science: Science Museums
Social Services: Animal Protection, At-Risk Youth, Camps, Child Welfare, Community Centers, Community Service Organizations, Day Care, Domestic Violence, Emergency Relief, Family Services, Food/Clothing Distribution, People with Disabilities, Recreation & Athletics, Scouts, Senior Services, United Funds/United Ways, Volunteer Services, YMCA/YWCA/YMHA/YWHA, Youth Organizations

Application Procedures
Initial Contact: According to foundation, applications must be made through web site only.
Deadlines: February 1 and August 1. Applications must be submitted no later than 5:00 p.m. on the first day of the month, two months prior to the next regularly scheduled meeting.
Review Process: Board of directors meets each April and October. Applicants are notified in writing of the action taken by the board relative to grant proposals usually within one month after board meetings.

Restrictions
The foundation usually does not support international affairs programs or foreign organizations or expenditures; member benefit organizations; collection management and preservation; endowments; organizations outside the approved geographic area; individuals, scholarships, professorships, and fellowships; employee matching gifts; operating expenses, except for research or start-up programs; faculty or staff development; budget deficits; program-related investment loans; income and management development; conferences and seminars; units of government; private educational institutions not attended by members of the Beveridge family; other private foundations excluding private operating foundations; federated drives and their foundations, including Catholic Charities, United Jewish Appeal, and United Way; chiefly tax-supported institutions and their foundations; or organizations that receive more than 50% of their operating revenues from taxes.

Any requests outside Hampden or Hampshire County, MA, require the support of one or more directors. Applicants should not solicit such support. The foundation will contact these applicants if interested, after initial proposals are received.

Additional Information
Publications: Annual Report; Guidelines; Application Form

Foundation Officials
Christa Palmer Bigue: director
Philip Caswell: president, director
Ward S. Caswell: director, clerk
Latimer B. Eddy: director
Alfred L. Griggs: director, assistant clerk B 1940. PRIM CORP EMPL chief executive officer: A.L. Griggs Industries Inc. CORP AFFIL chief executive officer: Classic Foods Coffee Service; chief executive officer: Classic Foods Spring Water; chief executive officer: Classic Foods.
Carol A. Leary, PhD: director
Carole S. Lenhart: vice president, treasurer
Ian Campbell Palmer: director
Joseph Beveridge Palmer: director
Frederick William Stecher: director
Patsy Palmer Stecher: director

Grants Analysis
Disclosure Period: calendar year ending 2003
Total Grants: $1,290,811
Number of Grants: 89
Average Grant: $11,114*
Highest Grant: $231,759
Lowest Grant: $276
Typical Range: $5,000 to $25,000
*Note: Average grant figure excludes highest grant.

Recent Grants
Note: Grants derived from 2002 Form 990.
Library-Related

25,000	Friends of the Chicopee Public Library, Chicopee, MA

General

110,000	Stanley Park of Westfield Inc., Westfield, MA -- grant to recreation
65,000	Dunn School, Los Olivos, CA
61,241	Beveridge Family Foundation Inc., Boca Raton, FL
60,000	Bay Path College, Longmeadow, MA
50,000	Domus Incorporated
50,000	Hospice by the Sea Inc., Boca Raton, FL
50,000	Laura's House, San Juan Capistrano, CA
50,000	Naismith Memorial Basketball Hall of Fame Inc., Springfield, MA
50,000	Northfield Mount Hermon School, Northfield, MA
50,000	Safe Passage Inc., Johnson City, TN -- to support the non-profit management services

KATHRYNE BEYNON FOUNDATION

Giving Contact
Robert D. Bannon, Trustee
199 S. Los Robles Ave., Suite 711
Pasadena, CA 91101
Phone: (626)584-8800
Fax: (626)584-8807

Description
Founded: 1967
EIN: 956197328
Organization Type: Private Foundation
Giving Locations: CA
Grant Types: Capital, Endowment, General Support.

Donor Information
Founder: the late Kathryne Beynon

Financial Summary

Total Giving: $332,210 (fiscal year ending October 31, 2001)
Giving Analysis: Giving for fiscal 2001 includes: foundation scholarships ($30,000)
Assets: $9,184,681 (fiscal 2001)

Typical Recipients

Arts & Humanities: Arts Associations & Councils, Arts Centers, Ethnic & Folk Arts, Historic Preservation, History & Archaeology, Libraries
Civic & Public Affairs: Clubs, Employment/Job Training, Civic & Public Affairs-General, Hispanic Affairs, Philanthropic Organizations, Public Policy, Safety
Education: Colleges & Universities, Legal Education, Preschool Education, Private Education (Precollege), Secondary Education (Private), Secondary Education (Public), Student Aid
Health: AIDS/HIV, Cancer, Children's Health/Hospitals, Clinics/Medical Centers, Home-Care Services, Hospitals, Medical Rehabilitation, Prenatal Health Issues, Respiratory
Religion: Churches, Religious Welfare
Social Services: At-Risk Youth, Child Welfare, Community Service Organizations, Day Care, Family Planning, Family Services, Homes, People with Disabilities, Scouts, Social Services-General, Substance Abuse, Youth Organizations

Application Procedures

Initial Contact: Send a brief letter of inquiry.
Application Requirements: Include amount requested, purpose of funds sought, financial statements, and proof of tax-exempt status.
Deadlines: None.

Restrictions

Limited to publicly supported charities in child welfare, education, hospital respiratory units, and alcohol treatment in Southern CA.

Foundation Officials

Mel B. Bannon: trustee
Robert D. Bannon: trustee
Alexandra Laboutin Bannon: trustee
Mary Ellen Lubow: trustee

Grants Analysis

Disclosure Period: fiscal year ending October 31, 2001
Total Grants: $302,210*
Number of Grants: 22
Average Grant: $11,534*
Highest Grant: $60,000
Lowest Grant: $2,500
Typical Range: $5,000 to $20,000
***Note:** Giving excludes scholarships. Average grant excludes highest grant.

Recent Grants

Note: Grants derived from 2002 Form 990.
General

50,000	Huntington Memorial Hospital, Pasadena, CA -- asthma project
34,000	Hillside Home for Children, Pasadena, CA -- for permanent endowment
27,500	St. Anne's Maternity Home, Los Angeles, CA -- transition housing fund
22,000	Assistance League of Southern California, Los Angeles, CA -- for day nursery and children club
20,000	Boys and Girls Club of Pasadena, Pasadena, CA -- scholarships
19,500	Boys and Girls Club of Hollywood, Hollywood, CA
18,000	Boys and Girls Club of Santa Clarita Valley, Santa Clarita, CA -- athletic equipment
18,000	Orthopedic Hospital Foundation, Los Angeles, CA
16,500	Westmont College, Santa Barbara, CA -- scholarship
16,500	Young and Healthy, Pasadena, CA

BICKNELL FUND

Giving Contact

Robert G. Acklin, Secretary & Treasurer
c/o Advisory Services Inc.
1422 Euclid Ave., Rm. 1010
Cleveland, OH 44115-2078
Phone: (216)363-6482
Web: http://fdncenter.org/grantmaker/bicknellfund/

Description

Founded: 1949
EIN: 346513799
Organization Type: Private Foundation
Giving Locations: OH: Cleveland
Grant Types: Capital, General Support, Project, Seed Money.

Donor Information

Founder: Kate H. Bicknell, the late Warren Bicknell, Jr., Warren Bicknell III, Kate B. Kirkham

Financial Summary

Total Giving: $341,867 (2004); $384,765 (2002); $750,000 (2001). Note: 1997 Giving includes United Way ($35,000).
Giving Analysis: Giving for 2003 includes: foundation grants to United Way ($30,000); 2002: foundation grants to United Way ($40,000)
Assets: $8,093,418 (2004); $6,354,388 (2002); $8,853,247 (2001)
Gifts Received: $913,436 (1995); $10,683 (1994); $183,600 (1993). Note: In 1995, contributions were received from Kate H. Bicknell.

Typical Recipients

Arts & Humanities: Arts Associations & Councils, Museums/Galleries, Music, Performing Arts, Theater
Civic & Public Affairs: Botanical Gardens/Parks, Economic Development, Employment/Job Training, Civic & Public Affairs-General, Housing, Urban & Community Affairs, Women's Affairs, Zoos/Aquariums
Education: Colleges & Universities, Community & Junior Colleges, Education-General, Medical Education, Private Education (Precollege), Public Education (Precollege), Special Education, Student Aid
Environment: Protection
Health: Children's Health/Hospitals, Clinics/Medical Centers, Emergency/Ambulance Services, Eyes/Blindness, Health-General, Health Funds, Medical Rehabilitation, Medical Research, Mental Health, Nursing Services, Public Health, Single-Disease Health Associations
Religion: Ministries, Religious Welfare
Social Services: Animal Protection, At-Risk Youth, Camps, Child Abuse, Child Welfare, Community Service Organizations, Counseling, Domestic Violence, Family Planning, Family Services, Food/Clothing Distribution, People with Disabilities, Scouts, Senior Services, Shelters/Homelessness, Substance Abuse, United Funds/United Ways, YMCA/YWCA/YMHA/YWHA, Youth Organizations

Application Procedures

Initial Contact: Send cover letter and full proposal.
Application Requirements: Include current income and expense statement of operation, projected budget showing how the requested funds will be utilized, a description of organization, amount requested, and proof of tax-exempt status.
Deadlines: May 1 and October 1.

Restrictions

Does not support individuals or provide loans.

Additional Information

Majority of grants are for community, medical, and educational purposes.
Publications: Application Guidelines

Foundation Officials

Robert G. Acklin: secretary, treasurer
Warren Bicknell, III: vice president, trustee
Wendy H. Bicknell: trustee
Samantha K. Crowley: trustee
Kate B. Luzius: president, trustee
Henry L. Meyer, III: trustee B Cleveland, OH 1949. ED Colgate University BA (1972); Harvard University MBA (1978). PRIM CORP EMPL chairman, president, chief operating officer: KeyBank of Cleveland. CORP AFFIL director: Society Mortgage Co.; director: National Finance Services Corp.; director: Society Investor Services Corp. NONPR AFFIL trustee: Cleveland Museum Natural History; trustee: Federation for Neighborhood Progress; trustee: American Cancer Society Cuyahoga County Unit; trustee: A. M. McGregor Home. CLUB AFFIL Kirtland Country Club; Union Club.
Alexander S. Taylor, II: trustee PRIM CORP EMPL senior vice president: McDonald & Co.

Grants Analysis

Disclosure Period: calendar year ending 2004
Total Grants: $311,867*
Number of Grants: 45
Average Grant: $5,952*
Highest Grant: $50,000
Lowest Grant: $367
Typical Range: $1,000 to $10,000
***Note:** Giving excludes United Way. Average grant figure excludes highest grant.

Recent Grants

Note: Grants derived from 2001 Form 990.
General

150,000	South Kent School, South Kent, CT -- for capital campaign
77,000	Salvation Army of Greater Cleveland, Cleveland, OH -- for program funding and operational support
50,000	Cleveland Botanical Garden, Cleveland, OH -- for program funding
38,000	United Way Services, Cleveland, OH -- for operational support
35,000	American Red Cross, Cleveland, OH -- for operational support
25,000	Cleveland Museum of Natural History, Cleveland, OH -- capital campaign
20,000	Hattie Larlham Foundation, Mantua, OH -- for research institute
20,000	Hiram House, Chagrin Falls, OH -- for capital campaign
12,000	Preterm, Cleveland, OH -- for operational support
10,000	Achievement Center for Children, Cleveland, OH -- for operational support

MARY DUKE BIDDLE FOUNDATION

Giving Contact

Dr. James H. Semans, Chairman
1044 West Forest Hills Boulevard
Durham, NC 27707
Phone: (919)493-5591
Fax: (919)489-0118

Alternate Contact

Douglas C. Zinn, Executive Director

Description
Founded: 1956
EIN: 136068883
Organization Type: General Purpose Foundation
Giving Locations: NY; NC
Grant Types: Award, Project, Seed Money.

Donor Information
Founder: Established by a trust agreement signed by Mary Lillian Duke Biddle on September 14, 1956. The first board of trustees included her children, Nicholas Duke Biddle and Mary Duke Biddle Trent Semans, and her son-in-law, Dr. James H. Semans. Mary Lillian Duke Biddle, the daughter of Sarah Pearson Angier and Benjamin Newton Duke, was born on November 16, 1887, in Durham, NC. In 1907, she graduated from Trinity College (later Duke University) with an English degree. Mrs. Biddle was an accomplished singer and musician. She was active in the civic and cultural life of Durham until she married and moved to New York in 1915. Mrs. Biddle and her husband, A.J. Drexel Biddle, Jr., lived in Irvington-on-Hudson and New York City. They had two children, Mary and Nicholas.

Mrs. Biddle was a niece of James Buchanan Duke, the electric power and tobacco magnate who was a founder of Duke University, and the daughter of Benjamin N. Duke, also one of the University's founders. The personal and business interests of the Duke family have always been centered in North Carolina and New York, the two areas of concern to the Biddle Foundation.

Until her death in 1960, Mrs. Biddle supported the arts, civic organizations, education, religion, and social concerns. She emphasized support of Duke University and other efforts that would "strengthen communities, educate minds, heal bodies, and further the sustaining enrichment of the arts."

The Mary Duke Biddle Foundation is one of three foundations established by members of the Duke family. The others are the Duke Endowment and the Doris Duke Foundation. When Mrs. Biddle died, her will provided for the bulk of her $40 million estate to go to the foundation, which had been established four years earlier. The will also stipulated that half of the annual income of the foundation should go to Duke University for various programs and activities.

Financial Summary
Total Giving: $1,151,724 (2001)
Assets: $28,094,557 (2001)

Typical Recipients
Arts & Humanities: Arts Associations & Councils, Arts Centers, Arts Festivals, Arts Funds, Arts Institutes, Arts Outreach, Ballet, Dance, Ethnic & Folk Arts, Film & Video, Historic Preservation, History & Archaeology, Literary Arts, Museums/Galleries, Music, Opera, Performing Arts, Public Broadcasting, Theater
Civic & Public Affairs: Botanical Gardens/Parks, Community Foundations, Economic Development, Civic & Public Affairs-General, Nonprofit Management, Public Policy
Education: Agricultural Education, Arts/Humanities Education, Business Education, Colleges & Universities, Community & Junior Colleges, Education Funds, Environmental Education, Faculty Development, Education-General, International Exchange, International Studies, Legal Education, Medical Education, Minority Education, Public Education (Precollege), Science/Mathematics Education, Social Sciences Education, Student Aid
Environment: Environment-General
Health: AIDS/HIV, Cancer, Clinics/Medical Centers, Health-General, Geriatric Health, Health Organizations, Hospices, Hospitals (University Affiliated), Medical Rehabilitation, Mental Health
International: Foreign Arts Organizations, International Relations
Religion: Churches, Ministries, Religious Welfare

Social Services: At-Risk Youth, Community Centers, Community Service Organizations, Emergency Relief, People with Disabilities, Senior Services

Application Procedures
Initial Contact: The foundation suggests that applicants call for application guidelines and procedures.
Application Requirements: Letters should include a description of the organization, project description, amount needed, estimated project budget, list of board of directors and staff, and other sources of support. A copy of the applying organization's 501(c)(3) form should also be submitted.
Deadlines: For specific deadlines, please call the foundation.
Review Process: Applicants are notified of the board's decision, usually within one month after the board meeting. A detailed description of the project may be requested at that time. Grant decisions are made at board meetings which are generally held in March, June, September, and December.

Restrictions
Support is not given to individuals or for general operating support, public education, bricks-and-mortar projects, or endowments. Giving is restricted to New York and North Carolina.

Additional Information
Thompson, Siegel & Walmsley of Richmond, VA, gives the foundation investment advice.
Publications: Annual Report

Foundation Officials
Mary Duke Trent Jones: second vice chairman, assistant secretary, assistant treasurer, trustee
John G. Mebane, Jr.: trustee, mem investments comm
James Duke Biddle Trent Semans: trustee
James H. Semans: chairman, trustee, secretary grants comm
Mary Duke Biddle Trent Semans: vice chairman, chairman grants comm, donor daughter B New York, NY February 21, 1920. NONPR AFFIL member: League Women Voters; director: North Carolina School Arts; director: Goodwill Industries Research Triangle Area; chairman: Angier B. Duke Memorial; director: Executive Mansion Fine Arts Committee; member: Business Professional Womens Club. CLUB AFFIL Rotary Club; Altrusa Club; Half Century Club.
Douglas C. Zinn: executive director

Grants Analysis
Disclosure Period: calendar year ending 2000
Total Grants: $1,060,560*
Number of Grants: 236
Average Grant: $4,494
Highest Grant: $37,576
Typical Range: $1,000 to $10,000
*Note: Giving excludes scholarships and fellowships.

Recent Grants
Note: Grants derived from 2002 Form 990.
General

63,336	Duke University, Music Department, Durham, NC -- for Robert Ward's American music theater project
51,693	Duke University, Durham, NC -- Dance Program, for Tyler Walters's ballet instruction
44,616	Duke University, Music Department, Durham, NC -- for Mary Duke Biddle graduate fellowship in composition
36,950	Duke University, Museum of Art, Durham, NC -- for education/outreach coordinator
27,339	Duke University, Durham, NC -- Dance Program, for salary support for musician John Hanks
27,000	Duke University, Institute of the Arts, Durham, NC -- for institute presentations and campus sponsorships
25,016	Duke University, Durham, NC -- Dance Program - for salary support for instructor-Ava Vinesett
25,000	Duke University, Durham, NC -- Focus Program - student travel-field trips
25,000	North Carolina School of the Arts, Salem, NC -- toward support of scholarships
25,000	North Carolina School of the Arts, Salem, NC -- toward support of scholarships

F. R. BIGELOW FOUNDATION

Giving Contact
Carleen K. Rhodes, Secretary
55 5th Street E, Suite 600
St. Paul, MN 55101-1797
Phone: (651)224-5463
Fax: (651)224-8123
E-mail: inbox@frbigelow.org
Web: http://www.frbigelow.org/

Description
Founded: 1934
EIN: 510232651
Organization Type: General Purpose Foundation
Giving Locations: MN: St. Paul
Grant Types: Capital, Endowment, General Support, Matching, Multiyear/Continuing Support, Operating Expenses, Project, Research, Seed Money.

Donor Information
Founder: Established in 1934 by the late Frederic Russell Bigelow, who served for many years as president and chairman of the board of directors of the St. Paul Fire and Marine Insurance Company, a subsidiary of the St. Paul Companies.

Financial Summary
Total Giving: $4,523,458 (2003); $5,470,965 (2002)
Giving Analysis: Giving for 2003 includes: foundation grants to United Way ($389,364); 2002: foundation grants to United Way ($444,667)
Assets: $131,801,077 (2003); $107,213,943 (2002)
Gifts Received: $14,035 (2003); $205,094 (2002); $270,034 (2000). Note: In 2002 and 2003, contributions were received from Bigelow Foundation and SIT Investments. In 2000, contributions were received from Estate of V.J. & I.C. Knutson ($242,966) and Estate of Ida C. Knutson ($4,068).

Typical Recipients
Arts & Humanities: Arts Associations & Councils, Ballet, Community Arts, Historic Preservation, History & Archaeology, Libraries, Literary Arts, Museums/Galleries, Music, Opera, Performing Arts, Public Broadcasting, Theater
Civic & Public Affairs: African American Affairs, Asian American Affairs, Botanical Gardens/Parks, Community Foundations, Economic Development, Economic Policy, Employment/Job Training, Ethnic Organizations, Civic & Public Affairs-General, Hispanic Affairs, Housing, Inner-City Development, Law & Justice, Legal Aid, Minority Business, Municipalities/Towns, Native American Affairs, Nonprofit Management, Parades/Festivals, Philanthropic Organizations, Rural Affairs, Urban & Community Affairs, Women's Affairs, Zoos/Aquariums
Education: Business Education, Colleges & Universities, Continuing Education, Economic Education, Education Associations, Education Funds, Education Reform, Faculty Development, Education-General, Literacy, Minority Education, Private Education (Precollege), Public Education (Precollege), School Volunteerism, Science/Mathematics Education, Secondary Education (Private), Special Education, Student Aid, Vocational & Technical Education

Environment: Environment-General, Resource Conservation, Watershed

Health: Alzheimer's Disease, Cancer, Children's Health/Hospitals, Emergency/Ambulance Services, Health-General, Health Funds, Health Organizations, Hospices, Hospitals, Medical Rehabilitation, Mental Health, Preventive Medicine/Wellness Organizations, Public Health, Research/Studies Institutes, Single-Disease Health Associations

International: Human Rights, International Environmental Issues

Religion: Churches, Religion-General, Jewish Causes, Religious Welfare, Seminaries, Social/Policy Issues

Science: Science Museums

Social Services: At-Risk Youth, Camps, Child Welfare, Community Centers, Community Service Organizations, Counseling, Domestic Violence, Emergency Relief, Family Planning, Family Services, Food/Clothing Distribution, Homes, People with Disabilities, Recreation & Athletics, Scouts, Senior Services, Shelters/Homelessness, Social Services-General, Substance Abuse, United Funds/United Ways, Volunteer Services, YMCA/YWCA/YMHA/YWHA, Youth Organizations

Application Procedures

Initial Contact: The foundation has a set of application requirements available upon request. The applicant may wish to submit a preliminary proposal to ascertain whether the project falls within foundation interests and guidelines. Full proposals may be submitted without preliminary reports.

Application Requirements: Preliminary summary proposals must address the questions in the application concisely, in no more than two or three pages. In the past, the foundation has stipulated that full proposals must include the applicant's name and address; a description of organization's general purpose and objectives; indication of the scope of its operations; copy of the IRS determination letter of tax-exempt status; amount requested; statement of project purpose and objectives; significance of project to society; and an estimate of the number of Minnesota citizens that will benefit from the project. Applicants should also include a project evaluation plan; the applicant's relationship to the organization; detailed budget; indication of other sources of support; statement of need; verification that donated funds will be used solely for the purposes requested and that the applicant will submit progress reports to the foundation; proposed length of time for support (including schedule of support commencement and termination); names and affiliations of board members; qualifications of principal staff members for project implementation; staff availability throughout duration of the project and replaceability should they not be available; recent balance sheet and audited income sheet; acknowledgement that payment of funds will be at the convenience of the foundation and that modifications of original payment agreements may occur; and indication that application has been received and endorsed by the governing body of applicant organization. If possible, a formal board resolution confirming this should be included. Two copies of the proposal must be submitted.

Deadlines: None. The board of trustees meets three times a year, usually in April, August, and November. Generally, full proposals must be received approximately three and a half months prior to a meeting date.

Review Process: Applicants must allow time for ample review prior to formal trustee consideration. Applications that are not adequately reviewed in time for one Trustee meeting are carried forward to the next one. The foundation encourages interviews with applicants when possible. Grant decisions are relayed three to six months after applications are received.

Restrictions

Normally, the foundation will not act as the only source of financial support for a project; make annual or annual operating grants; support sectarian religious groups; make grants to individuals; fund medical research; or make ongoing, open-ended grants.

Additional Information

Publications: Annual Report; List of Application Requirements

Foundation Officials

James H. Bradshaw: trustee
Carolyn J. Brusseau: vice chairman, trustee
John G. Couchman: assistant secretary
Judi Dutcher: president Minnesota community
Joan L. Gardner: trustee CORP AFFIL director: Lifecore Biomedical Inc.
Louise G. Jones: trustee
Elizabeth M. Kiernat: treasurer, trustee NONPR AFFIL director: Amherst H. Wilder Foundation.
Constance B. Kunin: trustee
Bert J. McKasy: trustee
Douglas D. McMillan: trustee
Galen T. Pate: trustee PRIM CORP EMPL chairman, chief executive officer, director: Park Financial Corp. ADD CORP EMPL president, director: United Community Bancshares. CORP AFFIL director: Park National Bank; chairman, director: Signal Bank Inc.; director: Goodhue County National Bank; director: Park Financial Bank.
Sally D. Peterson: trustee
Jack H. Pohl: assistant treasurer
Carleen K. Rhodes: secretary
John M. Scanlan: trustee
Jon A. Theobald: chairman, trustee B Saint Paul, MN 1945. ED Saint John's University (1967); Saint John's University (1970). PRIM CORP EMPL executive vice president: Resource Trust Co.

Grants Analysis

Disclosure Period: calendar year ending 2003
Total Grants: $4,134,094*
Number of Grants: 86
Average Grant: $45,107*
Highest Grant: $300,000
Lowest Grant: $5,000
Typical Range: $10,000 to $75,000
***Note:** Giving excludes United Way. Average grant figure excludes highest grant.

Recent Grants

Note: Grants derived from 2003 Form 990.
General

350,000	Neighborhood House, St. Paul, MN	
250,000	Saint Paul Foundation, St. Paul, MN	
200,000	Amherst H. Wilder Foundation, St. Paul, MN	
200,000	Saint Paul Riverfront Corporation, St. Paul, MN	
150,000	Grand Excursion, St. Paul, MN	
150,000	People Incorporated, St. Paul, MN	
113,048	Children's Home Society & Family Services, St. Paul, MN	
100,000	Cathedral of Saint Paul, St. Paul, MN	
100,000	Catholic Charities of the Archdiocese of St. Paul and Minnesota, Minneapolis, MN	
100,000	Como Zoo and Conservatory Society, St. Paul, MN	

WILLIAM BINGHAM FOUNDATION

Giving Contact

Laura H. Gilbertson, Director
20325 Center Ridge Rd., Suite 629
Rocky River, OH 44116-3554

Phone: (440)331-6350
E-mail: www.info@wbinghamfoundation.org
Web: http://www.fdncenter.org/grantmaker/bingham/

Description

Founded: 1955
EIN: 346513791
Organization Type: Family Foundation
Giving Locations: CA; DC; NY; OH; RI: United States only.
Grant Types: Award, Capital, Conference/Seminar, Endowment, General Support, Matching, Operating Expenses, Project.

Donor Information

Founder: Incorporated in 1955 by Elizabeth Bingham Blossom in memory of her brother, William Bingham, II.

Initially, the foundation contributed to a wide variety of organizations in education, the arts, health, and human services in the Cleveland area. After the death of Mrs. Blossom in 1970, the foundation continued under the leadership of her daughter, Mary Blossom Lee (d. 1976) and her daughter-in-law, Emily E. Blossom. Over the years, many of the current trustees, all descendants of the founder, have relocated to regions away from Cleveland, and as a result the foundation's objectives have broadened to reflect the needs of the communities in which the Trustees reside.

Financial Summary

Total Giving: $200,000 (2003 approx); $693,175 (2001)
Assets: $20,000,000 (2003 approx); $20,830,856 (2001)
Gifts Received: $667,693 (1994); $1,000 (1993); $1,000 (1992). Note: In 1994, contributions were received from Society National Bank, trustee for Elizabeth B. Blossom Pension Fund Trust.

Typical Recipients

Arts & Humanities: Arts Appreciation, Arts Associations & Councils, Arts Centers, Arts Funds, Arts Outreach, Ballet, Dance, Film & Video, Historic Preservation, Libraries, Literary Arts, Museums/Galleries, Music, Performing Arts, Public Broadcasting, Theater, Visual Arts

Civic & Public Affairs: Botanical Gardens/Parks, Economic Development, Employment/Job Training, Civic & Public Affairs-General, Housing, Legal Aid, Nonprofit Management, Professional & Trade Associations, Women's Affairs, Zoos/Aquariums

Education: Afterschool/Enrichment Programs, Arts/Humanities Education, Business Education, Colleges & Universities, Community & Junior Colleges, Continuing Education, Economic Education, Education Associations, Education Funds, Elementary Education (Public), Engineering/Technological Education, Environmental Education, Faculty Development, Education-General, Gifted & Talented Programs, International Exchange, International Studies, Legal Education, Preschool Education, Private Education (Precollege), Public Education (Precollege), Science/Mathematics Education, Secondary Education (Private), Special Education, Student Aid

Environment: Air/Water Quality, Environment-General, Protection, Resource Conservation, Sanitary Systems, Watershed, Wildlife Protection

Health: Cancer, Clinics/Medical Centers, Diabetes, Hospices, Hospitals, Medical Rehabilitation, Multiple Sclerosis, Nursing Services, Public Health

International: International Environmental Issues, International Relief Efforts, Missionary/Religious Activities

Religion: Religion-General, Ministries

Science: Science Museums, Scientific Centers & Institutes, Scientific Labs, Scientific Organizations

Social Services: Animal Protection, Camps, Child Welfare, Community Service Organizations, Domestic Violence, People with Disabilities, Recreation &

Athletics, Scouts, Senior Services, Sexual Abuse, Shelters/Homelessness, Substance Abuse, YMCA/YWCA/YMHA/YWHA, Youth Organizations

Application Procedures
Initial Contact: Submit a one- to two-page letter; no other attachments or documentation should be included.
Application Requirements: Include the nature of the project, budget requirements, and the amount requested.
Deadlines: None.
Review Process: If the project corresponds with the foundation's interests, the executive director or a trustee may request a meeting or a full proposal. If the foundation requests a full grant proposal, the proposal must be submitted two months before the next meeting of the board of trustees. The trustees act on full grant applications, when requested, at their semi-annual meetings, which occur in the spring and fall.
Notes: The foundation encourages applicants to seek additional funding sources and asks applicants to inform the foundation of other grants received. The foundation expects a grantee to report at least annually on the progress of its program, and to account for funds at the completion of the grant period.

Restrictions
The foundation does not make grants to individuals or to organizations outside the United States.

Additional Information
Publications: Guidelines

Foundation Officials
Thomas F. Allen: secretary
C. Bingham Blossom: trustee, president, chairman investment committee
C. Perry Blossom: trustee, treasurer
Laurel Blossom: trustee, chairman grant eval committee
Robin Dunn Blossom: trustee, chairman education committee
Laura H. Gilbertson: director
Elizabeth Blossom Heffernan: vice president, trustee, chairman public information committee

Grants Analysis
Disclosure Period: calendar year ending 2001
Total Grants: $693,175
Number of Grants: 22
Average Grant: $31,508
Highest Grant: $99,000
Lowest Grant: $5,000
Typical Range: $5,000 to $50,000

Recent Grants
Note: Grants derived from 2002 Form 990.
General

50,000	Cleveland Botanical Garden, Cleveland, OH -- toward the Environmental Education Center and the Eleanor Armstrong Smith Glasshouse
40,000	Ocean Institute, Dana Point, CA -- toward Ocean Institute's High School Certification Program
40,000	Radcliffe Institute for Advanced Study, Cambridge, MA -- toward a permanent endowment
35,000	National Association of College & University Attorneys, Washington, DC -- funds for planning
30,000	Girl Scouts of Rhode Island Inc., Providence, RI -- funds for camp renovation
20,000	Natural Resources Defense Council Inc., New York, NY -- funds for operating expenses
20,000	Vocational Guidance Services, Cleveland, OH -- funds for building construction

18,000	Shaker Lakes Regional Nature Center, Cleveland, OH -- funds for environmental education
9,000	City College 21st Century Foundation, New York, NY -- toward the Poetry Outreach Center
3,000	Foundation Center, New York, NY -- funds for the Cleveland Field Office

WILLIAM BINGHAM SECOND BETTERMENT FUND

Giving Contact
114 W. 47th St.
New York, NY 10036
Phone: (212)852-1000

Description
Founded: 1955
EIN: 136072625
Organization Type: General Purpose Foundation
Giving Locations: ME: Western Mountain region.
Grant Types: Capital, Endowment, General Support, Scholarship.

Financial Summary
Total Giving: $2,081,510 (2003)
Giving Analysis: Giving for 2003 includes: foundation scholarships ($40,000)
Assets: $38,285,500 (2003)

Typical Recipients
Arts & Humanities: Arts Associations & Councils, Arts Festivals, Film & Video, Arts & Humanities-General, History & Archaeology, Libraries, Museums/Galleries, Music, Public Broadcasting
Civic & Public Affairs: Chambers of Commerce, Civil Rights, Community Foundations, Economic Development, Economic Policy, Employment/Job Training, Gay/Lesbian Issues, Civic & Public Affairs-General, Housing, Law & Justice, Municipalities/Towns, Nonprofit Management, Philanthropic Organizations, Public Policy, Rural Affairs, Urban & Community Affairs, Women's Affairs
Education: Agricultural Education, Arts/Humanities Education, Colleges & Universities, Education Funds, Education Reform, Environmental Education, Faculty Development, Education-General, Health & Physical Education, International Studies, Leadership Training, Literacy, Medical Education, Private Education (Precollege), Public Education (Precollege), Science/Mathematics Education, Student Aid, Vocational & Technical Education
Environment: Air/Water Quality, Forestry, Environment-General, Resource Conservation, Wildlife Protection
Health: Cancer, Children's Health/Hospitals, Clinics/Medical Centers, Diabetes, Health Funds, Health Organizations, Home-Care Services, Hospitals, Long-Term Care, Medical Research, Nursing Services, Preventive Medicine/Wellness Organizations, Public Health, Respiratory
Religion: Ministries
Science: Science-General, Scientific Labs
Social Services: Camps, Child Welfare, Community Centers, Community Service Organizations, Counseling, Crime Prevention, Family Planning, Family Services, Food/Clothing Distribution, Homes, Recreation & Athletics, Substance Abuse, YMCA/YWCA/YMHA/YWHA, Youth Organizations

Application Procedures
Initial Contact: Applicants should submit, in duplicate, a grant application cover sheet with an accompanying letter. The cover sheet is available from the

foundation.
Application Requirements: A more detailed letter may accompany the application form, but applicants are urged to be succinct. After studying the proposal the trustees will request any additional information needed.
Deadlines: Proposals should be submitted by the last day of January, April, July, and October.
Review Process: The fund tries to answer each inquiry it receives, except general mailings and applicants that lie outside the geographical area or fields of interest of the fund. The trustees normally meet in March, June, September and December.
Notes: Each organization receiving a grant is expected to submit an evaluation of the project within six months after the payment of the grant.

Restrictions
The foundation does not make grants or loans to individuals, or for the support of religious activities or programs.

Additional Information
The United States Trust Company of New York is the fund's corporate trustee.
The fund uses the following criteria for grant selection: whether the program is innovative; evidence of substantial support from constituency; ability to demonstrate sufficient fiscal responsibility and management skills; whether organization can demonstrate a realistic plan for the continuance of program or organization after the grant is completed; and collaborative proposals which involve several organizations or groups in the community are given priority.
Publications: Annual Report; Guidelines; Application Form

Foundation Officials
William P. Clough, III: trustee
Carol Berg Geist: trustee
Andrew L. Tansey: trustee
William M. Throop, Jr.: trustee PRIM CORP EMPL partner, chief executive officer: Davidson, Dawson & Clark.
William B. Winship: trustee
Carolyn S. Wollen: trustee NONPR AFFIL vice president, director: Gould Academy.

Grants Analysis
Disclosure Period: calendar year ending 2003
Total Grants: $2,041,510*
Number of Grants: 75
Average Grant: $27,220
Highest Grant: $113,600
Lowest Grant: $100
Typical Range: $10,000 to $50,000
*Note: Giving excludes scholarships.

Recent Grants
Note: Grants derived from 2001 Form 990.
Library-Related

50,000	Maine Community Foundation, Ellsworth, ME
25,000	Brown Memorial Library, East Baldwin, ME
25,000	Ludden Memorial Library, Dixfield, ME
25,000	Maine Community Foundation, Ellsworth, ME
25,000	Norway Medical Library, Norway, ME
25,000	Norway Memorial Library, Norway, ME

General

150,000	Gould Academy, Bethel, ME
100,000	Gould Academy, Bethel, ME
100,000	Maine Public Broadcasting Corporation, Portland, ME
100,000	University of New England, Biddeford, ME
75,000	Appalachian Trail Conference, Harpers Ferry, WV
50,000	Maine Humanities Council, Portland, ME
50,000	New England Forestry Foundation, Cambridge, MA

50,000	New England Medical Center, Boston, MA
50,000	Portland Museum of Art, Portland, ME
35,000	Eastern Maine Technical College, Bangor, ME

BINNEY & SMITH INC.

Company Headquarters
1100 Church Lane
Easton, PA 18042
Phone: (610)559-6610
Fax: (610)559-6691
Web: http://www.crayola.com

Company Description
Employees: 1,600
SIC(s): 2891 Adhesives & Sealants, 3944 Games, Toys & Children's Vehicles, 3952 Lead Pencils & Art Goods.
Parent Company: Hallmark Cards Inc., 2501 McGee Street, Kansas City, MO, United States

Nonmonetary Support
Type: Donated Products
Note: Company provides nonmonetary support.
Volunteer Programs: The company provides volunteers for special events.
Contact: Margaret Heckman, Philanthropy Administrator

Giving Contact
Mary Ellyn Volden, Director, Global Corporate affairs
PO Box 431
1100 Church Ln.
Easton, PA 18044-0431
Phone: (610)559-6607
Fax: (610)559-6691
E-mail: mvoden@binney-smith.com

Alternate Contact
Cindy McCase, Executive assistant
Note: Cindy McCase extension is 6628

Description
Organization Type: Corporate Giving Program
Giving Locations: PA: Easton
Grant Types: Capital, Employee Matching Gifts.

Financial Summary
Total Giving: Contributes through corporate direct giving program only.

Typical Recipients
Arts & Humanities: Arts Appreciation, Arts Associations & Councils, Arts Centers, Arts Festivals, Arts Funds, Arts Institutes, Community Arts, Dance, Film & Video, Historic Preservation, Libraries, Literary Arts, Museums/Galleries, Music, Opera, Performing Arts, Public Broadcasting, Theater, Visual Arts
Civic & Public Affairs: Business/Free Enterprise, Civil Rights, Community Foundations, Economic Development, Economic Policy, First Amendment Issues, Civic & Public Affairs-General, Hispanic Affairs, Philanthropic Organizations
Education: Afterschool/Enrichment Programs, Arts/Humanities Education, Business Education, Colleges & Universities, Community & Junior Colleges, Continuing Education, Economic Education, Education Associations, Education Funds, Elementary Education (Private), Education-General, Literacy, Preschool Education, Private Education (Precollege), Public Education (Precollege), Secondary Education (Private), Secondary Education (Public), Social Sciences Education, Special Education, Student Aid
Environment: Environment-General, Wildlife Protection
Health: Children's Health/Hospitals, Emergency/

Ambulance Services, Health-General, Speech & Hearing
International: International Relations
Social Services: At-Risk Youth, Child Welfare, Community Centers, Domestic Violence, Family Services, Sexual Abuse, Shelters/Homelessness, Social Services-General, United Funds/United Ways, Volunteer Services, Youth Organizations

Application Procedures
Initial Contact: Submit a letter of request on organization letterhead.
Application Requirements: Include purpose and background information of the organization, amount requested, purpose of funds sought, recently audited financial statements, copy of IRS 501 (c)(3) tax determination letter, population served, time frame in which contribution is needed, planned use of contributions, and follow-up evaluation of contributions impact.
Deadlines: September 1 prior to the year for which funding is sought.
Review Process: Major contributions are reviewed annually by corporate contributions committee.

Restrictions
The company does not support individuals, individual schools, religious organizations for sectarian purposes, athletic groups, fraternal organizations, national or international organizations, individual child care centers, nursing and convalescent homes, prisoners, conventions, hospitals, endowment funds, labor groups, social clubs, or veteran's organizations. Generally, funding is not given for past operating deficits, travel, conferences, events, non-product goodwill advertising, or undefined operational support. Gives to local organizations only. Does not have out of state beneficiaries.

Additional Information
Publications: Informational Brochure (including Guidelines)

Corporate Officials
Mary Ellen Volden: director global philanthropy

Grants Analysis
Total Grants: $0
Average Grant: $0
Typical Range: $1,000 to $2,500

BINSWANGER COS.

Company Headquarters
Philadelphia, PA
Web: http://www.cbbi.com

Company Description
Employees: 150
SIC(s): 6531 Real Estate Agents & Managers, 6799 Investors Nec.

Binswanger Foundation

Giving Contact
John K. Binswanger, President
2 Logan Square, 4th Floor
Philadelphia, PA 19103
Phone: (215)448-6000
Fax: (215)448-6238
E-mail: info@cbbi.com

Description
EIN: 236296506
Organization Type: Corporate Foundation
Giving Locations: PA
Grant Types: General Support.

Donor Information
Founder: Binswanger Corp.

Financial Summary
Total Giving: $205,431 (2003); $341,213 (2002); $418,592 (2001). Note: Contributes through foundation only.
Giving Analysis: Giving for 2001 includes: foundation grants to United Way ($29,000); foundation ($389,592)
Assets: $19,984 (2003); $195,018 (2002); $635,716 (2001)
Gifts Received: $25,000 (2003); $175,000 (2000); $25,000 (1998). Note: In 2003, contributions were received from John K. Binswanger. In 2000, contributions were received from John K Binswanger ($25,000) and the Estate of Elizabeth Binswanger ($150,000). In 1998, contributions were received from John K. Binswanger.

Typical Recipients
Arts & Humanities: Arts Associations & Councils, Arts Centers, Arts Festivals, Ballet, Community Arts, Arts & Humanities-General, Historic Preservation, History & Archaeology, Libraries, Museums/Galleries, Music, Performing Arts, Public Broadcasting, Theater
Civic & Public Affairs: African American Affairs, Botanical Gardens/Parks, Business/Free Enterprise, Chambers of Commerce, Clubs, Economic Development, Employment/Job Training, Ethnic Organizations, Civic & Public Affairs-General, Housing, Law & Justice, Municipalities/Towns, Professional & Trade Associations, Public Policy, Urban & Community Affairs, Zoos/Aquariums
Education: Arts/Humanities Education, Business Education, Business-School Partnerships, Colleges & Universities, Education-General, Minority Education, Private Education (Precollege), Public Education (Precollege)
Health: Cancer, Children's Health/Hospitals, Emergency/Ambulance Services, Eyes/Blindness, Health Funds, Health Organizations, Hospitals, Hospitals (University Affiliated), Medical Rehabilitation, Medical Research, Mental Health, Multiple Sclerosis, Public Health, Single-Disease Health Associations
International: Foreign Educational Institutions, International Affairs, International Organizations, International Relations, Missionary/Religious Activities
Religion: Jewish Causes, Religious Organizations, Religious Welfare, Social/Policy Issues
Science: Science Museums, Scientific Centers & Institutes
Social Services: Child Welfare, Community Service Organizations, Crime Prevention, Day Care, Delinquency & Criminal Rehabilitation, Family Planning, Family Services, People with Disabilities, Recreation & Athletics, Scouts, Shelters/Homelessness, Substance Abuse, United Funds/United Ways, YMCA/YWCA/YMHA/YWHA, Youth Organizations

Application Procedures
Initial Contact: Send a brief letter of inquiry.
Application Requirements: Include all information pertinent to a decision.
Deadlines: None.
Notes: The foundation has no formal grant application procedure or application form.

Additional Information
Foundation reports their grant making is suspended, but they are still in operation.

Corporate Officials
David R. Binswanger: president, chief executive officer B Abington, PA 1956. ED Bowdoin College (1978); Harvard University MBA (1982). PRIM CORP EMPL president, chief executive officer: Binswanger Companies. CORP AFFIL president: Binswanger International; president: Binswanger Management Corp.

Frank G. Binswanger, Jr.: co-chairman, director B Philadelphia, PA 1928. ED Wesleyan University (1950). PRIM CORP EMPL co-chairman, director: Binswanger Companies. CORP AFFIL cochairman: Binswanger International; chairman: Binswanger Management Corp.

John K. Binswanger: co-chairman, director B Philadelphia, PA 1932. ED Wesleyan University (1954). PRIM CORP EMPL co-chairman, director: Binswanger Companies. CORP AFFIL chairman: Binswanger Management Corp.; co-chairman: Chesterton Blumenauer Binswanger.

Michael J. Brennan: chief financial officer, executive vice president B Philadelphia, PA 1958. ED LaSalle University (1979); Villanova University (1989). PRIM CORP EMPL chief financial officer, executive vice president: Binswanger Companies. CORP AFFIL executive vice president, chief financial officer: Binswanger Management Corp.

Foundation Officials

David R. Binswanger: treasurer (see above)
Frank G. Binswanger, III: secretary CORP AFFIL chief executive officer: Binswanger International; president: Binswanger Management Corp.
John K. Binswanger: president (see above)
Robert B. Binswanger: vice chairman

Grants Analysis

Disclosure Period: calendar year ending 2003
Total Grants: $185,431*
Number of Grants: 35
Average Grant: $5,298
Highest Grant: $62,500
Lowest Grant: $100
Typical Range: $250 to $10,000
***Note:** Giving excludes United Way.

Recent Grants

Note: Grants derived from 2003 Form 990.
Library-Related

1,000	Free Library of Philadelphia, Philadelphia, PA

General

62,500	Wesleyan University, Middletown, CT
40,000	Jewish Federation of Greater Philadelphia, Philadelphia, PA
20,000	United Way of SEPA, Philadelphia, PA
16,750	Children's Hospital of Philadelphia, Philadelphia, PA
12,000	Anti-Defamation League, New York, NY
10,000	Police Athletic League of Philadelphia, Philadelphia, PA
8,700	Franklin Institute, Philadelphia, PA
7,898	Fairmount Park Commission, Philadelphia, PA
5,000	Fox Chase Cancer Center, Philadelphia, PA
3,583	National Constitution Center, Philadelphia, PA

BIRDS EYE FOODS INC.

Company Headquarters

90 Linden Oaks
Rochester, NY 14602-0670
Web: http://www.birdseyefoods.com

Company Description

Former Name: (Parent) Agway, Inc.; Agrilink Foods (2002).
Revenue: US$1 billion (2001)
Employees: 3200 (2003)
SIC(s): 2032 Canned Specialties, 2033 Canned Fruits & Vegetables, 2037 Frozen Fruits & Vegetables, 2038 Frozen Specialties Nec.
Parent Company: Pro-Fac Cooperative Inc., 90 Linden Oaks, Rochester, NY, United States

Operating Locations

Agrilink Foods, Inc. (GA--Montezuma; IL--Collinsville, Ridgeway; IA--Wall Lake; MI--Benton Harbor, Coloma, Fennville, Sodus; NJ--Vineland; NY--Alton, Barker, Bergen, Gorham, LeRoy, Leicester, Lyons, Red Creek, Shortsville, Waterport; OH--Lodi; PA--Berlin; TX--Alamo; WA--Tacoma)

Nonmonetary Support

Range: $500 - $1,000
Type: Donated Products; Workplace Solicitation
Contact: Bea Slizewski, vice president, corporate communications
Note: Nonmonetary support requests are handled individually by each division.

Birds Eye Foods Foundation

Giving Contact

Susan C. Riker, Secretary
PO Box 20670
Rochester, NY 14602-0670
Phone: (585)264-3155
Fax: (585)383-1606
Web: http://www.birdseyefoods.com/corp/about/foundation.asp

Description

EIN: 166071142
Organization Type: Corporate Foundation
Former Name: Agrilink Foods/Pro-Fac Foundation (2003).
Giving Locations: headquarters and operating communities.
Grant Types: Capital, Emergency, Endowment, General Support, Matching, Operating Expenses, Scholarship.

Financial Summary

Total Giving: $120,916 (fiscal year ending June 31, 2004); $283,357 (fiscal 2003); $298,000 (fiscal 2002 approx). Note: Contributes through foundation only.
Giving Analysis: Giving for fiscal 2003 includes: foundation scholarships ($19,150); foundation grants to United Way ($78,337); fiscal 2002: foundation ($17,600); corporate direct giving ($280,000); fiscal 2001: foundation scholarships ($17,700); corporate direct giving ($23,850); foundation grants to United Way ($85,225); foundation ($188,950)
Assets: $111,536 (fiscal 2004); $132,017 (fiscal 2003); $146,000 (fiscal 2002 approx)
Gifts Received: $100,100 (fiscal 2004); $300,000 (fiscal 2003); $300,000 (fiscal 2002). Note: In fiscal 2003, contributions were received from Birds Eye Foods Inc. In 2001 and 2002, contributions were received from Pro-Fac. Contributions were received from Curtice-Burns Foods Inc.

Typical Recipients

Arts & Humanities: Arts Associations & Councils, Arts Centers, Community Arts, History & Archaeology, Libraries, Museums/Galleries, Music, Performing Arts, Public Broadcasting, Theater
Civic & Public Affairs: African American Affairs, Botanical Gardens/Parks, Business/Free Enterprise, Chambers of Commerce, Civil Rights, Clubs, Community Foundations, Economic Development, Employment/Job Training, Civic & Public Affairs-General, Housing, Inner-City Development, Nonprofit Management, Professional & Trade Associations, Rural Affairs, Safety, Urban & Community Affairs, Women's Affairs
Education: Afterschool/Enrichment Programs, Agricultural Education, Business Education, Colleges & Universities, Community & Junior Colleges, Education Funds, Education-General, Legal Education, Literacy, Minority Education, Preschool Education, Private Education (Precollege), Special Education,

Student Aid, Vocational & Technical Education
Environment: Environment-General, Resource Conservation
Health: Cancer, Children's Health/Hospitals, Clinics/Medical Centers, Emergency/Ambulance Services, Eyes/Blindness, Geriatric Health, Health Organizations, Heart, Hospices, Hospitals, Medical Rehabilitation, Mental Health, Multiple Sclerosis, Nursing Services, Public Health, Single-Disease Health Associations
Religion: Religious Welfare
Science: Science Museums, Scientific Research
Social Services: Animal Protection, Big Brothers/Big Sisters, Child Welfare, Community Centers, Community Service Organizations, Counseling, Day Care, Delinquency & Criminal Rehabilitation, Domestic Violence, Emergency Relief, Family Planning, Family Services, Food/Clothing Distribution, Homes, People with Disabilities, Recreation & Athletics, Scouts, Senior Services, Shelters/Homelessness, Social Services-General, Substance Abuse, United Funds/United Ways, Veterans, Volunteer Services, YMCA/YWCA/YMHA/YWHA, Youth Organizations

Application Procedures

Initial Contact: Brief letter or proposal.
Application Requirements: a description of organization, amount requested, purpose of funds sought, recently audited financial statement, and copy of IRS 501(c)(3) letter
Deadlines: None.

Restrictions

Contributions are not made to individuals, political groups, dinners or special events, international projects, fraternal organizations, goodwill advertising, or religious activities for sectarian purposes. No awards given outside the United States.

Corporate Officials

Dennis M. Mullen: president, chief executive officer, director B Newark, NJ December 09, 1953. ED Saint Leo College BA. PRIM CORP EMPL president, executive officer, director: Agrilink Foods, Inc.
Beatrice B. Slizewski: vice president corporate communications B Rochester, NY 1943. ED State University of New York (1986). PRIM CORP EMPL vice president corporate communications: Agrilink Foods, Inc.

Foundation Officials

Thomas Facer: trustee
Virginia Ford: trustee CORP AFFIL director: Agrilink Foods, Inc.
Dennis M. Mullen: trustee (see above)
William D. Rice: trustee B Saint Paul, MN 1934. ED Harvard University AB (1956); Harvard University Graduate School of Business Administration MBA (1961). CORP AFFIL regional director: Chase Lincoln First Bank NA; senior vice president strategic development, secretary: Agrilink Foods, Inc. NONPR AFFIL trustee: National Food Processors Association.
Susan Riker: secretary, trustee
Paul Roe: chairman, trustee

Grants Analysis

Disclosure Period: fiscal year ending June 31, 2004
Total Grants: $56,950*
Number of Grants: 29
Average Grant: $1,964
Highest Grant: $10,000
Lowest Grant: $100
Typical Range: $100 to $3,000
***Note:** Giving excludes scholarship; United Way

Recent Grants

Note: Grants derived from 2003 Form 990.
General

10,000	Rochester Children's Theatre, Rochester, NY
10,000	Rochester Philharmonic, Rochester, NY

10,000	St. Bonaventure University, St. Bonaventure, NY
7,000	United Way of Pierce County, Tacoma, WA
5,500	WXXI, Rochester, NY
3,000	Boys and Girls Clubs of Geneva, Geneva, NY
3,000	Wilson Commencement Park, Rochester, NY
2,250	Rebuilding Together Greater Green Bay, Green Bay, WI
2,000	Lakeshore Habitat for Humanity, Holland, MI
1,500	Memorial Art Gallery, Rochester, NY

A. G. BISHOP CHARITABLE TRUST

Giving Contact

Margo M. Chicosky, Assistant Vice President
c/o Bank One
111 E. Court Street, Suite 100
Flint, MI 48502
Phone: (810)237-3765
Fax: (810)237-3809
Note: Application address.

Alternate Contact

c/o Bank One Trust Co.
PO Box 1308
Milwaukee, WI 53201
Phone: (414)765-2769

Description

Founded: 1944
EIN: 386040693
Organization Type: Private Foundation
Giving Locations: MI: Flint-Genesee County
Grant Types: Capital, Emergency, Multiyear/Continuing Support, Operating Expenses.

Donor Information

Founder: the late Arthur Giles Bishop

Financial Summary

Total Giving: $531,133 (2003); $671,016 (2001)
Giving Analysis: Giving for 2003 includes: foundation grants to United Way ($107,500); 2001: foundation grants to United Way ($100,000)
Assets: $11,609,979 (2003); $12,794,893 (2001)

Typical Recipients

Arts & Humanities: Arts Associations & Councils, Arts Centers, Arts Institutes, Community Arts, Dance, Ethnic & Folk Arts, Historic Preservation, History & Archaeology, Libraries, Museums/Galleries, Music, Public Broadcasting, Theater, Visual Arts
Civic & Public Affairs: Botanical Gardens/Parks, Community Foundations, Economic Development, Civic & Public Affairs-General, Hispanic Affairs, Housing, Law & Justice, Urban & Community Affairs
Education: Arts/Humanities Education, Business Education, Colleges & Universities, Community & Junior Colleges, Engineering/Technological Education, Education-General, Private Education (Precollege), Public Education (Precollege)
Environment: Environment-General
Health: Children's Health/Hospitals, Clinics/Medical Centers, Emergency/Ambulance Services, Eyes/Blindness, Geriatric Health, Health Organizations, Medical Research, Public Health, Single-Disease Health Associations
International: International Organizations
Religion: Churches, Ministries, Religious Welfare
Science: Science Museums
Social Services: Animal Protection, Big Brothers/Big Sisters, Child Abuse, Child Welfare, Community Service Organizations, Crime Prevention, Domestic Violence, Family Planning, People with Disabilities, Recreation & Athletics, Scouts, Shelters/Homelessness, Special Olympics, Substance Abuse, United Funds/United Ways, Volunteer Services, YMCA/YWCA/YMHA/YWHA, Youth Organizations

Application Procedures

Initial Contact: The foundation requests applications be made in writing.
Deadlines: None.

Restrictions

Grants are restricted to qualified tax-exempt organizations.

Additional Information

Trust(s): Bank One

Foundation Officials

Robert J. Bellairs: co-trustee
Elizabeth B. Wentworth: co-trustee

Grants Analysis

Disclosure Period: calendar year ending 2003
Total Grants: $423,633*
Number of Grants: 44
Average Grant: $8,689*
Highest Grant: $50,000
Lowest Grant: $1,000
Typical Range: $1,000 to $20,000
*Note: Giving excludes United Way. Average grant figure excludes highest grant.

Recent Grants

Note: Grants derived from 2003 Form 990.
General

50,000	Flint Cultural Center, Flint, MI
33,300	University of Minnesota Public Television, Minneapolis, MN
25,000	Flint Institute of Art, Flint, MI
25,000	Flint Institute of Music, Flint, MI
25,000	Genesee County Historical Society, Flint, MI
20,000	YMCA
20,000	YWCA of Greater Flint, Flint, MI
11,000	Flint Institute of Music, Flint, MI
10,000	Fair Winds Girl Scout Council, Flint, MI
10,000	Flint Genesee Economic Growth Alliance, Flint, MI

E. K. AND LILLIAN F. BISHOP FOUNDATION

Giving Contact

Tom J. Nevers, Grants Manager
Care of Bank of America, Trustee
701 5th Avenue, Floor 47
Seattle, WA 98104
Phone: (520)749-2004
Fax: (520)749-2990
E-mail: thomas.nevers@azbar.org

Description

Founded: 1971
EIN: 916116724
Organization Type: General Purpose Foundation
Giving Locations: WA, Grays Harbor County
Grant Types: Award, Capital, General Support, Matching, Project, Seed Money.

Donor Information

Founder: Established in 1971 by the late E. K. Bishop and the late Lillian F. Bishop.

Financial Summary

Total Giving: $2,089,302 (fiscal year ending April 30, 2004); $2,098,737 (fiscal 2003)
Assets: $16,175,014 (fiscal 2004); $17,064,339 (fiscal 2003)

Typical Recipients

Arts & Humanities: Arts Associations & Councils, Arts Centers, Ballet, Community Arts, Dance, History & Archaeology, Libraries, Museums/Galleries, Music, Opera, Performing Arts, Theater
Civic & Public Affairs: Asian American Affairs, Botanical Gardens/Parks, Business/Free Enterprise, Clubs, Community Foundations, Economic Development, Employment/Job Training, Civic & Public Affairs-General, Housing, Inner-City Development, Municipalities/Towns, Native American Affairs, Parades/Festivals, Philanthropic Organizations, Rural Affairs, Safety, Urban & Community Affairs, Women's Affairs, Zoos/Aquariums
Education: Afterschool/Enrichment Programs, Agricultural Education, Arts/Humanities Education, Business Education, Colleges & Universities, Community & Junior Colleges, Education Associations, Education Funds, Elementary Education (Private), Elementary Education (Public), Education-General, Leadership Training, Private Education (Precollege), Public Education (Precollege), Science/Mathematics Education, Secondary Education (Private), Secondary Education (Public), Special Education, Student Aid
Health: Children's Health/Hospitals, Clinics/Medical Centers, Diabetes, Emergency/Ambulance Services, Eyes/Blindness, Health Funds, Heart, Hospitals, Kidney, Medical Research, Nursing Services, Research/Studies Institutes, Single-Disease Health Associations, Trauma Treatment
International: Health Care/Hospitals, Human Rights
Religion: Churches, Dioceses, Missionary Activities (Domestic), Religious Welfare
Science: Science-General, Science Museums, Scientific Centers & Institutes
Social Services: At-Risk Youth, Big Brothers/Big Sisters, Camps, Child Abuse, Child Welfare, Community Centers, Community Service Organizations, Domestic Violence, Family Planning, Family Services, Food/Clothing Distribution, Recreation & Athletics, Scouts, Shelters/Homelessness, Special Olympics, Substance Abuse, United Funds/United Ways, Volunteer Services, YMCA/YWCA/YMHA/YWHA, Youth Organizations

Application Procedures

Initial Contact: Applicants seeking grants should write to the foundation for a brochure and an application form.
Application Requirements: An original and four copies of the application should be submitted with the following: certificate of tax-exemption from the IRS; list of the applicant's senior officers and directors; most recent financial statements (preferably audited); and proposed budget for use of requested funds.
Deadlines: Applications must be received by the first business day of January, April, July, or October.
Review Process: The awards committee meets quarterly.
Notes: Foundation requests no videotapes be sent. Trustees may request an interview with the applicant or conduct a visit at the applicant's organization.

Restrictions

Grants only made to non-profits for programs that benefit youth (0-23) in the State of Washington.

Additional Information

Priority is accorded to grants that encourage community involvement and are joined with matching funds, public, private, or both. Seafirst Bank is the foundation's corporate trustee.
Publications: Application Guidelines; Application Form

Foundation Officials

Isabelle Smith Lamb: director B Quebec, QC Canada 1922. ED Carleton University (1947). PRIM CORP EMPL president, treasurer, director: Enterprises International Inc. ADD CORP EMPL treasurer, director: EII Ltd./Limitee; vice president, director: Lamb-Grays Harbor Co.; vice president, director: Meridian Machine Works Inc.; treasurer, director: Ovalstrapping Inc. NONPR AFFIL director: Independent College Washington.

James C. Mason: director B 1955. CORP AFFIL president: Mason Timber Inc.

Thomas J. Nevers: grant mgr

Kate Webster: director

Grants Analysis

Disclosure Period: fiscal year ending April 30, 2004
Total Grants: $2,089,302
Number of Grants: 122
Average Grant: $9,912*
Highest Grant: $500,000
Lowest Grant: $1,450
Typical Range: $1,000 to $20,000
*Note: Average grant figure excludes two highest grants ($900,000).

Recent Grants

Note: Grants derived from fiscal 2004 Form 990.
General

500,000	Grays Harbor Community Foundation, Hoquiam, WA
400,000	GH Pacific Counties Food Bank
64,500	City of Aberdeen Parks, Aberdeen, WA
59,784	City of Ocean Shores, Ocean Shores, WA -- tennis court project
59,540	Quinault Lake Schools, Amanda Park, WA
50,000	7th Street Theatre Association, Hoquiam, WA
50,000	Children's Hospital Foundation, Calgary, AB Canada
50,000	Children's Hospital Foundation, Calgary, AB Canada -- telemedicine program
50,000	City of Westport, Westport, WA
50,000	Grays Harbor Young Life, Hoquiam, WA

VERNON AND DORIS BISHOP FOUNDATION

Giving Contact

Vernon Bishop, Trustee
1616 Fieldcrest Road
Lebanon, PA 17042-6413
Phone: (717)273-1462

Description

Founded: 1957
EIN: 236255835
Organization Type: Private Foundation
Giving Locations: PA
Grant Types: General Support.

Financial Summary

Total Giving: $352,300 (2003); $359,840 (2001)
Giving Analysis: Giving for 2003 includes: foundation grants to United Way ($35,000); 2001: foundation grants to United Way ($36,140)
Assets: $4,177,944 (2003); $4,420,648 (2001)
Gifts Received: $351 (1998); $200,000 (1996); $100,000 (1995). Note: In 1996, contributions were received from the Lebanon Chemical Corp.

Typical Recipients

Arts & Humanities: Arts Associations & Councils, Historic Preservation, History & Archaeology, Libraries, Museums/Galleries, Music, Public Broadcasting, Theater
Civic & Public Affairs: Clubs, Employment/Job Training, Civic & Public Affairs-General, Philanthropic Organizations, Professional & Trade Associations, Public Policy

Education: Business Education, Colleges & Universities, Education Funds, Engineering/Technological Education, Education-General, Private Education (Precollege), Religious Education, Secondary Education (Private)
Health: Clinics/Medical Centers, Emergency/Ambulance Services, Health Funds, Health Organizations, Hospitals, Medical Research, Mental Health, Prenatal Health Issues, Public Health
International: Missionary/Religious Activities
Religion: Churches, Ministries, Religious Organizations, Religious Welfare
Science: Scientific Centers & Institutes
Social Services: At-Risk Youth, Camps, Community Service Organizations, People with Disabilities, Scouts, United Funds/United Ways, YMCA/YWCA/YMHA/YWHA, Youth Organizations

Application Procedures

Initial Contact: The foundation requests applications be made in writing.
Deadlines: None.

Foundation Officials

Vernon Bishop: trustee

Grants Analysis

Disclosure Period: calendar year ending 2003
Total Grants: $317,300*
Number of Grants: 38
Average Grant: $3,170*
Highest Grant: $200,000
Lowest Grant: $100
Typical Range: $1,000 to $5,000
*Note: Giving excludes United Way. Average grant figure excludes highest grant.

Recent Grants

Note: Grants derived from 2003 Form 990.
General

200,000	Good Samaritan Health Services Foundation, Lebanon, PA
35,000	United Way of Lebanon County, Lebanon, PA
20,000	Lebanon Catholic High School, Lebanon, PA
20,000	Lebanon Valley Christian Ministries, Lebanon, PA
10,000	Chemical Heritage Foundation, Philadelphia, PA
10,000	Lebanon Valley College, Annville, PA
10,000	Luthercare, Lititz, PA
10,000	Phi Gamma Delta Educational Foundation, Lexington, PA
6,500	Pennsylvania Dutch Council Boy Scouts of America, Lancaster, PA
5,000	St. Andrews Presbyterian Church, Lebanon, PA

MONA BISMARCK CHARITABLE TRUST

Giving Contact

Russell M. Porter, Trustee
1133 Avenue of the Americas
New York, NY 10036-6710
Phone: (212)336-2960

Description

Founded: 1986
EIN: 133244269
Organization Type: Private Foundation
Grant Types: General Support.

Donor Information

Founder: Russell M. Porter

Financial Summary

Total Giving: $923,000 (2003)
Assets: $16,506,165 (2003)
Gifts Received: $1,697,843 (2003)

Typical Recipients

Arts & Humanities: History & Archaeology, Libraries
Education: Colleges & Universities
Health: Research/Studies Institutes
International: Foreign Arts Organizations, Foreign Educational Institutions, International-General, International Organizations, International Peace & Security Issues, International Relations, International Relief Efforts

Application Procedures

Initial Contact: Send a brief letter of inquiry describing program or project.
Deadlines: None.

Restrictions

Does not support individuals.

Foundation Officials

Russell M. Porter: trustee

Grants Analysis

Disclosure Period: calendar year ending 2003
Total Grants: $923,000
Number of Grants: 3
Highest Grant: $900,000
Lowest Grant: $3,000

Recent Grants

Note: Grants derived from 2001 Form 990.
Library-Related

3,000	American Library of Paris, New York, NY -- purchase books

General

700,000	Mona Bismaeck Foundation, Inc., Paris France -- meet expense on cultural events
20,000	Lafayette Escadrille Memorial Day Association, New York, NY -- upkeep of monument

BLANDIN FOUNDATION

Giving Contact

Linda Gibeau, Grants Manager
100 North Pokegama Avenue
Grand Rapids, MN 55744
Phone: (218)326-0523
Fax: (218)327-1949
E-mail: bfinfo@blandinfoundation.org
Web: http://www.blandinfoundation.org

Description

Founded: 1941
EIN: 416038619
Organization Type: General Purpose Foundation
Giving Locations: MN
Grant Types: General Support, Multiyear/Continuing Support, Project, Scholarship, Seed Money.

Donor Information

Founder: Established in 1941 by the late Charles K. Blandin. As owner of a paper mill, Mr. Blandin began his career with the *St. Paul Pioneer Press and Dispatch*, and by the late 1920s, rose to the position of owner and publisher. Eventually he sold the newspaper but retained ownership of the Blandin Paper Company and various other companies. After his death, most of Mr. Blandin's estate was placed in trust for the foundation. Although the trustees sold the trust's stock in Blandin Paper Company in 1977, the foundation remains committed to serving the community where its income was earned. Most of the foundation's income is derived from the Blandin Residuary Trust.

Mr. Blandin set no specific funding restrictions on the foundation's areas of interest.

Financial Summary

Total Giving: $8,929,673 (2003); $9,949,739 (2002); $15,418,132 (2001)

Giving Analysis: Giving for 2003 includes: foundation grants to United Way ($10,000); foundation matching gifts ($32,070); foundation scholarships ($632,518); 2002: foundation grants to United Way ($10,000); foundation scholarships ($770,734)

Assets: $386,458,834 (2003); $333,701,300 (2002); $389,600,831 (2001)

Gifts Received: $15,486,707 (2003); $14,914,140 (2002); $18,097,047 (2001). Note: Contributions were received from C.K. Blandin Residuary Trust.

Typical Recipients

Arts & Humanities: Arts Appreciation, Arts Associations & Councils, Arts Centers, Arts Institutes, Arts Outreach, Historic Preservation, History & Archaeology, Libraries, Literary Arts, Museums/Galleries, Music, Opera, Performing Arts, Public Broadcasting, Theater

Civic & Public Affairs: Botanical Gardens/Parks, Business/Free Enterprise, Chambers of Commerce, Clubs, Community Foundations, Economic Development, Employment/Job Training, Ethnic Organizations, Civic & Public Affairs-General, Housing, Inner-City Development, Legal Aid, Municipalities/Towns, Native American Affairs, Nonprofit Management, Philanthropic Organizations, Professional & Trade Associations, Public Policy, Rural Affairs, Safety, Urban & Community Affairs

Education: Agricultural Education, Arts/Humanities Education, Colleges & Universities, Community & Junior Colleges, Education Associations, Education Reform, Elementary Education (Public), Engineering/Technological Education, Environmental Education, Faculty Development, Education-General, Leadership Training, Medical Education, Minority Education, Preschool Education, Public Education (Precollege), Science/Mathematics Education, Secondary Education (Public), Social Sciences Education, Special Education, Student Aid

Environment: Air/Water Quality, Forestry, Environment-General, Resource Conservation

Health: Children's Health/Hospitals, Clinics/Medical Centers, Emergency/Ambulance Services, Health Policy/Cost Containment, Health Funds, Health Organizations, Hospices, Long-Term Care, Medical Research, Mental Health, Nursing Services, Outpatient Health Care, Prenatal Health Issues, Public Health

Religion: Religious Organizations, Religious Welfare

Science: Scientific Research

Social Services: Animal Protection, At-Risk Youth, Camps, Child Welfare, Community Centers, Community Service Organizations, Crime Prevention, Domestic Violence, Emergency Relief, Family Services, Food/Clothing Distribution, People with Disabilities, Recreation & Athletics, Substance Abuse, United Funds/United Ways, Volunteer Services, YMCA/YWCA/YMHA/YWHA, Youth Organizations

Application Procedures

Initial Contact: Submit a short preliminary letter of inquiry, by conventional mail or through the foundation's online inquiry form on the foundation's web site, concerning the nature of request.

Deadlines: The board meets three times a year; January 2, for the April meeting; May 1 for the August meeting; and September 1, for the January meeting.

Review Process: Each proposal is assigned to a member of the program staff when it is received. The staff member presents the proposal, along with the results of any related investigation, and the program staff's composite recommendation to the Board of Trustees. The board commits all grant funds.

Notes: Guidelines differ for organizations located in the foundation's home community of Grand Rapids

and Itasca County, MN. Applicants from Grand Rapids/Itasca County should contact the foundation to obtain local grantmaking guidelines and a local grant application form.

The foundation will also accept the Minnesota Common Grant Form.

Restrictions

The foundation does not funds organizations outside the state of Minnesota; capital campaigns for construction, renovation, or purchase of equipment or endowments outside of the greater Grand Rapids/Itasca County area; religious activities; medical research; publications; films or videos; travel grants for individuals or groups; camping programs; ordinary governments services; grants to individuals, except the Blandin Educational Awards Program; grants intended to influence legislation; or general operating funds outside of the greater Grand Rapids/Itasca County area.

Additional Information

In addition to making grants, the foundation provides services for conferences and community leadership training for rural Minnesota.

Publications: Annual Report; Application Guidelines; Program Policy Statement

Foundation Officials

Marian Barcus: trustee
Dr. M. James Bensen: trustee
Tim Bonner, MD: trustee
Karen Diver: trustee
James Hamilton: trustee
Peter A. Heegaard: trustee PRIM CORP EMPL executive vice president: Norwest Bank Minnesota.
James Hoolihan: president, trustee B 1952. ED University of Minnesota (1973-1977); William Mitchell College of Law JD (1979). PRIM CORP EMPL president, director: Industrial Lubricant Co.
Mike Johnson: trustee
Helen Klassen: trustee
Sandy Layman: secretary, trustee
Kenneth Lundgren: trustee, chairman
Marcie Mclaughlin: trustee
Gene Radecki: trustee
Bruce W. Stender: trustee B 1942. ED Florida State University PhD (1969). PRIM CORP EMPL president, chief operating officer, director: Lyric Block Development Corp. ADD CORP EMPL president, chief operating officer: Holiday Inn; president, chief operating officer: Labovitz Enterprises Inc. CORP AFFIL director: Minnesota Power Inc.; director: Minnesota Power & Light Co.
George Thompson: trustee

Grants Analysis

Disclosure Period: calendar year ending 2003
Total Grants: $7,622,567*
Number of Grants: 113
Average Grant: $54,978*
Highest Grant: $800,000
Lowest Grant: $975
Typical Range: $25,000 to $100,000
*Note: Giving excludes United Way; matching gifts; scholarship. Average grant figure excludes three highest grants ($1,575,000).

Recent Grants

Note: Grants derived from 2003 Form 990.
General

800,000	Greater Minnesota Housing Fund, St. Paul, MN -- towards affordable housing to residence
632,518	Blandin Educational Awards Program, Grand Rapids, MN -- towards scholarship program
450,000	Grand Rapids Area Community Foundation, Grand Rapids, MN -- towards capital support for Bigfork Fine Arts Center
375,000	City of Cambridge, Cambridge, MN -- to redevelop the Regional Treatment Center
375,000	Minnesota Public Radio, St. Paul, MN -- to provided main street radio throughout rural Minnesota
279,000	Grand Rapids Area Community Foundation, Grand Rapids, MN
260,000	Itasca Community College, Grand Rapids, MN -- towards financial assistance for Itasca County students
259,694	City of Fairmont, Fairmont, MN -- for the development of a kingship mentoring program and youth council
255,000	Itasca Community College, Grand Rapids, MN -- towards financial aid for Itasca County Students
240,000	Minnesota Diversified Industries, St. Paul, MN -- towards rotary die cutter to increase efficiency and productivity

RENE BLOCH FOUNDATION

Giving Contact

Care of U.S. Bank Trust Group
PO Box 3168
Portland, OR 97208-3168
Phone: (503)275-4327

Description

Founded: 1997
EIN: 916448421
Organization Type: Private Foundation
Giving Locations: nationally.
Grant Types: General Support.

Financial Summary

Total Giving: $60,000 (2001)
Giving Analysis: Giving for 2001 includes: foundation scholarships ($1,000)
Assets: $1,058,698 (2001)
Gifts Received: $13,842 (1998); $1,036,518 (1997). Note: In 1998, contributions were received from Rene Bloch estate.

Typical Recipients

Arts & Humanities: Libraries, Opera, Theater
Civic & Public Affairs: Civic & Public Affairs-General, Hispanic Affairs
Education: Colleges & Universities, Education-General, Health & Physical Education
Health: Geriatric Health, Health Organizations, Hospitals, Multiple Sclerosis, Public Health
Religion: Jewish Causes, Ministries
Social Services: Community Service Organizations, People with Disabilities, Youth Organizations

Application Procedures

Deadlines: September 30.

Additional Information

Trusts: US Bank NA OR.
Trust(s): US Bank NA OR

Grants Analysis

Disclosure Period: calendar year ending 2001
Total Grants: $59,000*
Number of Grants: 28
Average Grant: $2,107
Highest Grant: $6,000
Lowest Grant: $1,000
Typical Range: $1,000 to $5,000
*Note: Giving excludes scholarships.

Recent Grants

Note: Grants derived from 2001 Form 990.
Library-Related

3,000	Library Foundation, Los Angeles, CA
2,500	Gunn Memorial Library, Washington, CT

General

6,000	Seeds of Peace, New York, NY
4,000	New Milford Hospital, New Milford, MA
3,000	Greater Washington Coalition for Jewish Life, Washington, CT
3,000	National Multiple Sclerosis Society, Portland, OR
3,000	Oregon Health Sciences Foundation, Portland, OR
3,000	Scripps College, Claremont, CA
2,500	Lewis & Clark College, Portland, OR
2,500	Oregon Council for Hispanic Advancement, Portland, OR
2,000	Brookdale Center on Aging, Brookdale, NY
2,000	Music Theater Works, New York, NY

WALTER A. BLOEDORN FOUNDATION

Giving Contact

F. Elwood Davis, Chairman
888 17th St. NW, Suite 1075
Washington, DC 20006
Phone: (202)452-8553
Fax: (202)293-8973

Description

Founded: 1966
EIN: 520846147
Organization Type: Private Foundation
Giving Locations: DC: Washington metropolitan area
Grant Types: Capital, General Support, Professorship, Scholarship.

Donor Information

Founder: the late Walter A. Bloedorn

Financial Summary

Total Giving: $255,000 (2004); $185,000 (2002); $292,000 (2001). Note: Contributes through foundation only.
Giving Analysis: Giving for 2003 includes: foundation scholarships ($15,000); 2002: foundation scholarships ($6,000)
Assets: $7,843,108 (2004); $6,715,349 (2002); $8,060,156 (2001)

Typical Recipients

Arts & Humanities: Dance, Historic Preservation, History & Archaeology, Libraries, Museums/Galleries, Music, Public Broadcasting
Civic & Public Affairs: Business/Free Enterprise, Employment/Job Training, Municipalities/Towns, Philanthropic Organizations, Urban & Community Affairs
Education: Colleges & Universities, Legal Education, Medical Education, Private Education (Precollege), Religious Education, Secondary Education (Private), Social Sciences Education, Special Education, Student Aid
Health: AIDS/HIV, Alzheimer's Disease, Children's Health/Hospitals, Emergency/Ambulance Services, Heart, Home-Care Services, Hospices, Hospitals, Hospitals (University Affiliated), Long-Term Care, Outpatient Health Care, Public Health
International: International Relief Efforts
Religion: Churches, Missionary Activities (Domestic), Religious Welfare
Science: Scientific Centers & Institutes, Scientific Organizations
Social Services: Child Welfare, Community Service Organizations, Counseling, Family Services, Food/Clothing Distribution, Homes, People with Disabilities, Recreation & Athletics, Senior Services, Social Services-General, United Funds/United Ways, Youth Organizations

Application Procedures

Initial Contact: Send letter describing program or project.
Application Requirements: Include proof of tax-exempt status.
Deadlines: December 31.
Review Process: Board meets in April.

Foundation Officials

F. Elwood Davis: chairman, director
Robert Edwin Davis: president, treasurer, director B Madison, IL 1931. ED University of Missouri BS (1953); Washington University (1953). PRIM CORP EMPL managing director: Axcess Corp. CORP AFFIL director: USF&G Corp.; director: HIMONT; director: Rheometric Science; director: H&R Block. NONPR AFFIL member: American Management Association. CLUB AFFIL Saint Andrews Club; Marriott Seaview Club.
Jack Kleh: assistant secretary, director
John A. Sargent: director
Anne D. Spratt: secretary, director
John Winkel: director

Grants Analysis

Disclosure Period: calendar year ending 2004
Total Grants: $240,000*
Number of Grants: 26
Average Grant: $9,231
Highest Grant: $30,000
Lowest Grant: $1,000
Typical Range: $1,000 to $15,000
*Note: Giving excludes scholarships.

Recent Grants

Note: Grants derived from 2001 Form 990.
General

30,000	George Washington University, Washington, DC -- for WAB Multimedia Center in the Medical School Library
30,000	National Geographic Society Education Foundation, Washington, DC -- for endowment fund for State of Maryland
30,000	Salvation Army, Washington, DC -- for Turning Point Program
25,000	Boys and Girls Club of Greater Washington, Silver Spring, MD
15,000	Easter Seal Society for Disabled Children and Adults, Washington, DC
15,000	Ingleside Presbyterian Retirement Community, Washington, DC
15,000	Ivymount School, Rockville, MD -- for School to Work Program
10,000	Boys and Girls Club of America, Atlanta, GA
10,000	Decatur House, Washington, DC
10,000	Heights School, Potomac, MD -- for scholarships

BLOOD-HORSE CHARITABLE FOUNDATION

Giving Contact

Mr. Stacy V. Bearse, Treasurer
PO Box 4038
Lexington, KY 40544
Phone: (859)278-2361

Description

Founded: 1989
EIN: 611142154
Organization Type: Private Foundation
Grant Types: General Support.

Financial Summary

Total Giving: $78,416 (fiscal year ending May 31, 2004); $63,031 (fiscal 2001)
Giving Analysis: Giving for fiscal 2004 includes: foundation grants to United Way ($1,500)
Assets: $122,619 (fiscal 2004); $112,932 (fiscal 2001)
Gifts Received: $55,000 (fiscal 2004); $53,900 (fiscal 2001); $42,000 (fiscal 1999). Note: In fiscal 2004, contributions were received from Blood-Horse. In fiscal 1995 and 1999, contributions were received from Morven Stud, Ltd. ($6,000) and Blood-Horse ($36,000).

Typical Recipients

Arts & Humanities: Libraries, Museums/Galleries, Public Broadcasting
Civic & Public Affairs: Philanthropic Organizations
Education: Arts/Humanities Education, Business Education, Colleges & Universities, Medical Education, Science/Mathematics Education, Student Aid
Health: Cancer, Children's Health/Hospitals, Health Organizations, Medical Research
Religion: Ministries
Social Services: Animal Protection, Community Service Organizations, People with Disabilities, Recreation & Athletics, Social Services-General, YMCA/YWCA/YMHA/YWHA

Application Procedures

Initial Contact: Requests should be made in writing.
Application Requirements: Include the purpose of the organization, amount requested, purpose of funds sought, proof of tax-exempt status, and any other pertinent information.
Deadlines: April1.

Foundation Officials

Stacy V. Bearse: treasurer
G. Watts Humphrey, Jr.: president PRIM CORP EMPL chairman, chief executive officer, chief operating officer: Conair Group.
Raymond S. Paulick: secretary

Grants Analysis

Disclosure Period: fiscal year ending May 31, 2004
Total Grants: $76,916*
Number of Grants: 31
Average Grant: $756*
Highest Grant: $30,000*
Lowest Grant: $10
Typical Range: $100 to $1,500
*Note: Giving excludes United Way. Average grant figure excludes two highest grants ($55,000).

Recent Grants

Note: Grants derived from 2001 Form 990.
Library-Related

1,000	Stonington Free Library, Stonington, CT -- contribution to support organization

General

30,000	University of Kentucky Equine Research Foundation, Lexington, KY -- to support research into the Fetal Loss Syndrome
5,000	Cornell University, Ithaca, NY -- to sponsor the "Cornell at Saratoga Symposium on Equine Health Care"
5,000	High Hope Steeplechase, Lexington, KY -- sponsorship of the Blood Horse Sportsman's Challenge
3,560	University of Illinois Foundation, Urbana, IL -- to sponsor student participation in AAEP national conference
2,500	United States Equestrian Team, Foxboro, MA -- contribution to support organization
1,546	Thoroughbred Retirement Foundation, Shrewsbury, NJ -- contribution to support organization
1,400	WUKY, Lexington, KY -- to sponsor luncheon at Keeneland and to support organization

1,147   American Association of Equine Practitioners, Lexington, KY -- to fund purchase of item for annual fundraising auction

1,000   American Academy of Equine Art, Lexington, KY -- contribution to support organization

1,000   American Cancer Society, Florence, KY -- contribution to support organization

MILDRED WEEDON BLOUNT EDUCATIONAL AND CHARITABLE FOUNDATION

Giving Contact
Arnold B. Dopson, Chairman
Mildred Weedon Blount Educational and Charitable Foundation
PO Box 706
Tallassee, AL 36078
Phone: (334)283-6581
Fax: (334)283-2310

Description
Founded: 1981
EIN: 630817472
Organization Type: Private Foundation
Giving Locations: AL: Elmore County
Grant Types: General Support, Scholarship.

Donor Information
Founder: the late Mildred W. Blount

Financial Summary
Total Giving: $150,100 (fiscal year ending June 30, 2004); $196,000 (fiscal 2001)
Giving Analysis: Giving for fiscal 2003 includes: foundation scholarships ($54,000); fiscal 2001: foundation scholarships ($51,500)
Assets: $3,601,003 (fiscal 2004); $3,667,748 (fiscal 2001)

Typical Recipients
Arts & Humanities: Arts Associations & Councils, Arts Centers, Community Arts, Libraries, Museums/Galleries, Music, Theater
Civic & Public Affairs: Civic & Public Affairs-General, Municipalities/Towns, Urban & Community Affairs, Women's Affairs
Education: Business Education, Colleges & Universities, Medical Education, Public Education (Precollege), Secondary Education (Public)
Health: Emergency/Ambulance Services, Hospitals
Religion: Churches
Social Services: Community Service Organizations, Scouts, Substance Abuse, United Funds/United Ways, Youth Organizations

Application Procedures
Initial Contact: For grants, send a brief letter of inquiry. Students should submit general information to scholarship committees of Elmore County high schools.
Deadlines: Early May.

Additional Information
Provides scholarships for higher education to students from Elmore County, AL.
Publications: Application Procedures

Foundation Officials
John I. Cottle, III: secretary
Arnold B. Dopson: chairman
Lloyd F. Emfinger, Jr.: trustee
Charles B. Funderburk: trustee

Teddy O. Taylor: trustee
Daniel P. Wilbanks: vchairman

Grants Analysis
Disclosure Period: fiscal year ending June 30, 2003
Total Grants: $96,100*
Number of Grants: 21
Average Grant: $4,576
Highest Grant: $10,000
Lowest Grant: $600
Typical Range: $1,000 to $10,000
*Note: Giving excludes scholarships.

Recent Grants
Note: Grants derived from fiscal 2001 Form 990.
Library-Related
10,000   Community Library
General
15,000   Tallassee High School, Tallassee, AL -- support Women's Show Choir
10,000   Community Hospital Foundation, Grand Junction, CO
10,000   Elmore County High School
10,000   Reeltown High School, Tallassee, AL -- support athletic department
10,000   Reeltown High School, Tallassee, AL
10,000   St. Vincent de Paul Catholic Church
10,000   Tallassee Historical Preservation Society, Tallassee, AL
10,000   Tallassee Mt. Vernon Theatre, Inc., Tallassee, AL
7,500   Tallassee City Schools, Tallassee, AL -- basketball
5,000   ACTS

BLOWITZ-RIDGEWAY FOUNDATION

Giving Contact
Tina M. Erickson, Administrator
One Northfield Plaza, Suite 528
570 Frontage Road
Northfield, IL 60093-1213
Phone: (847)446-1010
E-mail: brf_mcw@sbcglobal.net
Web: http://fdncenter.org/grantmaker/blowitz/

Description
Founded: 1984
EIN: 362488355
Organization Type: General Purpose Foundation
Giving Locations: IL
Grant Types: Capital, General Support, Operating Expenses, Project, Research.
Note: Foundation also makes program-related investments through the Illinois Facilities Fund.

Donor Information
Founder: The Blowitz-Ridgeway Foundation was founded in 1984 using the proceeds of the sale of Chicago's Ridgeway Hospital, a non-profit, psychiatric facility focusing on low-income adolescents.

Financial Summary
Total Giving: $1,295,678 (fiscal year ending September 30, 2001)
Assets: $23,616,527 (fiscal 2001)

Typical Recipients
Arts & Humanities: Arts Funds, Arts Institutes, Arts Outreach, Libraries, Public Broadcasting, Theater
Civic & Public Affairs: Economic Development, Employment/Job Training, Ethnic Organizations, Civic & Public Affairs-General, Housing, Legal Aid, Municipalities/Towns, Nonprofit Management
Education: Afterschool/Enrichment Programs, Business Education, Colleges & Universities, Faculty De-

velopment, Education-General, Literacy, Minority Education, Preschool Education, Private Education (Precollege), Science/Mathematics Education, Secondary Education (Private), Special Education, Student Aid
Environment: Resource Conservation
Health: AIDS/HIV, Alzheimer's Disease, Arthritis, Cancer, Children's Health/Hospitals, Clinics/Medical Centers, Emergency/Ambulance Services, Eyes/Blindness, Health-General, Health Organizations, Home-Care Services, Hospices, Hospitals, Hospitals (University Affiliated), Long-Term Care, Medical Rehabilitation, Medical Research, Mental Health, Nursing Services, Outpatient Health Care, Prenatal Health Issues, Public Health, Respiratory, Single-Disease Health Associations, Speech & Hearing
Religion: Religion-General, Ministries, Religious Organizations, Religious Welfare
Social Services: At-Risk Youth, Big Brothers/Big Sisters, Child Abuse, Child Welfare, Community Centers, Community Service Organizations, Counseling, Crime Prevention, Domestic Violence, Emergency Relief, Family Planning, Family Services, Food/Clothing Distribution, Homes, People with Disabilities, Scouts, Senior Services, Sexual Abuse, Shelters/Homelessness, Social Services-General, Special Olympics, Youth Organizations

Application Procedures
Initial Contact: Write the foundation for a formal application form.
Deadlines: None.
Review Process: The board meets monthly.
Evaluative Criteria: Foundation prefers to fund organizations whose programs or services benefit persons who have not yet reached their majority and/or are for the care of individuals who lack sufficient resources to provide for themselves.
Decision Notification: Applications are reviewed in the order they are received. Committee may decline, recommend board approval, request additional information, schedule a site visit, or invite applicant for an interview by the board.
Notes: The foundation reports that the only funding done outside of the state of Illinois is for medical research, unless an out-of-state applicant has been specifically invited to apply.

Restrictions
The foundation does not support government agencies or organizations which subsist mainly on third party funding. Grants are not made to individuals. Grants will not be made for religious or political purposes, nor for the production of audio-visual materials. Fundraising and administrative costs must be within reasonable limits; grants are only made to the organization providing the service to the end user or is conducting the program for which funding is sought. Applicants must be equal opportunity employers and provide equal access to programs or services.

Additional Information
Applicants, if declined, may not reapply for at least one year from the date of the application. Although the foundation does support operating budgets, applicants should not consider the foundation a source of continuing annual funding.
Publications: Annual Report; Guidelines; Application Form

Foundation Officials
Arthur R. Collision: trustee
Anthony M. Dean: treasurer, trustee
Rev. James W. Jackson: secretary, trustee
Daniel L. Kline: vice president, trustee
Pierre R. LeBreton, PhD: trustee
Patricia A. MacAlister: trustee
Max Pastin: president, trustee
Marvin J. Pitluk, PhD: trustee
Samuel G. Winston: trustee

Grants Analysis

Disclosure Period: fiscal year ending September 30, 2001
Total Grants: $1,333,160*
Number of Grants: 106
Average Grant: $11,976*
Highest Grant: $63,700
Typical Range: $1,000 to $50,000
***Note:** Average grant figure excludes highest grant.

Recent Grants

Note: Grants derived from fiscal 2002 Form 990.
General

50,000	New England Medical Center /Tufts University School of Medicine, Boston, MA -- fund for "Evaluation of constitutively active dopamine receptors as a potential therapeutic strategy for Parkinson's Disease"
50,000	Southern Illinois University School of Medicine, Carbondale, IL -- fund for its brain research project
50,000	University of Chicago, Chicago, IL -- fund for research project titled "Regulation of Airway Epithelial Aptoptosis by Beta-Adrenergic Agonists"
50,000	University of Connecticut, Farmington, CT -- in support of the project titled "The Effects of HBV Infection on HCV Replication on a Non-Primate Animal Model of HCV Infection"
40,000	University of Chicago-HIV Program, Chicago, IL -- fund for social workers / case managers for its Pediatric and Adolescent HIV Program
36,121	University of Chicago-Doula Project, Chicago, IL -- fund for Doula Project to bring awareness in mothers about upbringing of children
35,000	Hug-A-Book, Chicago, IL -- fund for expansion of program to set up lending libraries and classroom libraries at Head Start and day care sites serving children ages two to five
35,000	Literacy Chicago Reach Out & Read, Chicago, IL -- in support of Reach Out and Read program, which provides early literacy support and books to underserved families
30,000	Cradle, Evanston, IL -- fund for Nursery & Special Needs Program, a 24 hour, on-site nursery for infants awaiting adoption
30,000	Will Grundy Medical Clinic, Joliet, IL -- fund to provide nursing services at its free medical and dental clinic

BLUE BELL INC.

Company Headquarters

Greensboro, NC
Web: http://www.bluebell.com

Company Description

SIC(s): 2253 Knit Outerwear Mills, 2311 Men's/Boys' Suits & Coats, 2321 Men's/Boys' Shirts, 2325 Men's/Boys' Trousers & Slacks.
Parent Company: VF Corp., Greensboro, NC, United States

Operating Locations

Blue Bell, Inc. (AL--Birmingham, Mobile, Montgomery, Mooresville; FL--Panama City; KS--Kansas City; LA--Baton Rouge, Ruston; MS--Jackson; OK--Broken Arrow, Oklahoma City; TX--Alvin, Beaumont, Big Spring, Fort Worth, Harlingen, Humble, Lancaster, Lewisville, Longview, New Braunfels, San Antonio, Waco)

Blue Bell Foundation

Giving Contact

Charles Conkin, Vice President Human Resources & Foundation Contact
Blue Bell Foundation
PO Box 21488
Greensboro, NC 27420
Phone: (910)373-3412

Description

EIN: 566041057
Organization Type: Corporate Foundation
Giving Locations: principally near operating locations and to national organizations.
Grant Types: Employee Matching Gifts, General Support.

Financial Summary

Total Giving: $225,730 (2003); $279,804 (2002); $198,587 (2001). Note: Contributes through corporate direct giving program and foundation.
Giving Analysis: Giving for 2002 includes: foundation scholarships ($21,590); foundation matching gifts ($37,225)
Assets: $5,874,723 (2003); $5,393,698 (2002); $6,274,401 (2001)

Typical Recipients

Arts & Humanities: Arts Associations & Councils, Arts Centers, Arts Festivals, Arts Funds, Community Arts, Historic Preservation, Libraries, Museums/Galleries, Music, Theater
Civic & Public Affairs: Botanical Gardens/Parks, Chambers of Commerce, Clubs, Community Foundations, Economic Development, Employment/Job Training, Civic & Public Affairs-General, Housing, Law & Justice, Legal Aid, Municipalities/Towns, Professional & Trade Associations, Public Policy, Safety, Urban & Community Affairs, Women's Affairs, Zoos/Aquariums
Education: Afterschool/Enrichment Programs, Agricultural Education, Arts/Humanities Education, Business Education, Colleges & Universities, Community & Junior Colleges, Economic Education, Education Associations, Education Funds, Elementary Education (Public), Engineering/Technological Education, Education-General, Literacy, Minority Education, Private Education (Precollege), Public Education (Precollege), Science/Mathematics Education, Secondary Education (Private), Secondary Education (Public), Special Education, Student Aid, Vocational & Technical Education
Environment: Environment-General, Resource Conservation, Wildlife Protection
Health: Cancer, Children's Health/Hospitals, Clinics/Medical Centers, Diabetes, Emergency/Ambulance Services, Health Organizations, Heart, Hospices, Hospitals, Medical Rehabilitation, Medical Research, Multiple Sclerosis, Prenatal Health Issues, Preventive Medicine/Wellness Organizations, Public Health, Respiratory, Single-Disease Health Associations
International: Foreign Arts Organizations, Health Care/Hospitals, International Development
Religion: Churches, Jewish Causes, Ministries, Religious Organizations, Religious Welfare, Social/Policy Issues
Science: Science Museums, Scientific Centers & Institutes
Social Services: Animal Protection, At-Risk Youth, Camps, Child Abuse, Child Welfare, Community Centers, Community Service Organizations, Counseling, Day Care, Domestic Violence, Emergency Relief, Family Services, Food/Clothing Distribution, Homes, People with Disabilities, Recreation & Athletics, Scouts, Senior Services, Social Services-General, Special Olympics, Substance Abuse, United Funds/United Ways, YMCA/YWCA/YMHA/YWHA, Youth Organizations

Application Procedures

Initial Contact: Send a letter of request.
Application Requirements: Include a description of organization; IRS tax determination letter; and amount requested.
Deadlines: None.
Decision Notification: Board meets two times per year.

Restrictions

Foundation does not support individuals; grants are made to organizations that directly benefit company's employees.

Additional Information

Trust(s): Wachovia Bank NA

Corporate Officials

John P. Schamberger: president, chairman jeanswear coalition B 1948. ED Saint John's University BS (1969); Saint John's University MBA (1974). PRIM CORP EMPL president, chairman jeanswear coalition: VF Corp.

Foundation Officials

Donald P. Laws: member advisory committee PRIM CORP EMPL president, Wrangler Westernwear: VF Jeanswear Inc. CORP AFFIL president: VF Corp.
Robert Matthews: member advisory committee
T. L. Weatherford: member advisory committee

Grants Analysis

Disclosure Period: calendar year ending 2003
Total Grants: $73,020*
Number of Grants: 96
Average Grant: $761
Highest Grant: $25,000
Lowest Grant: $25
Typical Range: $500 to $2,000
***Note:** Giving excludes United Way; scholarship.

Recent Grants

Note: Grants derived from 2003 Form 990.
Library-Related

500	Friends of Greensboro Public Library, Greensboro, NC

General

50,000	United Way of Greater Greensboro, Greensboro, NC
21,730	Citizens Scholarship Foundation, Bedford, MA
10,000	East Market Street Development Corporation, Greensboro, NC
10,000	Greensboro Symphony, Greensboro, NC
7,500	Town of Shenandoah, Shenandoah, VA
5,000	American Diabetes Association, Alexandria, VA
5,000	American Diabetes Association, Alexandria, VA
5,000	American Heart Association, Dallas, TX
5,000	Brook Wood Baptist Church, Birmingham, AL
5,000	Children's Home Society, Greensboro, NC

BLUM-KOVLER FOUNDATION

Giving Contact

Jonathan Kovler, President
Blum-Kovler Foundation
919 North Michigan Avenue, Suite 2800
Chicago, IL 60611
Phone: (312)664-5050
Fax: (312)664-8983

Description
Founded: 1957
EIN: 362476143
Organization Type: General Purpose Foundation
Giving Locations: DC: Washington; IL: Chicago metropolitan area; NY: New York
Grant Types: General Support.

Donor Information
Founder: Established in 1953 by the late Harry Blum and Everette Kovler, both of whom served as chairman of the James B. Distilling Company, a subsidiary of American Brands, Inc. The Blum-Kovler Foundation is administered primarily by family members. Maribel Blum, widow of Harry Blum, served as the foundation's chairperson until her death in 1985.

Financial Summary
Total Giving: $3,726,449 (2002); $4,207,199 (2001)
Assets: $84,103,656 (2002); $82,188,153 (2001)

Typical Recipients
Arts & Humanities: Arts Associations & Councils, Arts Centers, Arts Festivals, Arts Funds, Arts Institutes, Dance, Ethnic & Folk Arts, Film & Video, Arts & Humanities-General, Historic Preservation, History & Archaeology, Libraries, Museums/Galleries, Music, Opera, Performing Arts, Public Broadcasting, Theater
Civic & Public Affairs: African American Affairs, Asian American Affairs, Botanical Gardens/Parks, Business/Free Enterprise, Civil Rights, Community Foundations, Ethnic Organizations, Civic & Public Affairs-General, Housing, Law & Justice, Legal Aid, Philanthropic Organizations, Public Policy, Urban & Community Affairs, Women's Affairs, Zoos/Aquariums
Education: Arts/Humanities Education, Business Education, Business-School Partnerships, Colleges & Universities, Economic Education, Education Associations, Education Funds, Education Reform, Education-General, International Studies, Leadership Training, Legal Education, Medical Education, Minority Education, Preschool Education, Private Education (Precollege), Public Education (Precollege), Science/Mathematics Education, Secondary Education (Private), Social Sciences Education, Student Aid, Vocational & Technical Education
Environment: Environment-General, Protection
Health: Cancer, Children's Health/Hospitals, Clinics/Medical Centers, Diabetes, Health Funds, Health Organizations, Hospices, Hospitals, Hospitals (University Affiliated), Medical Rehabilitation, Medical Research, Mental Health, Public Health, Research/Studies Institutes, Single-Disease Health Associations, Transplant Networks/Donor Banks
International: Foreign Educational Institutions, International-General, Health Care/Hospitals, International Affairs, International Peace & Security Issues, International Relations, International Relief Efforts, Missionary/Religious Activities
Religion: Churches, Jewish Causes, Religious Organizations, Synagogues/Temples
Science: Science-General, Science Museums
Social Services: Animal Protection, Child Welfare, Community Centers, Community Service Organizations, Family Services, Food/Clothing Distribution, Homes, People with Disabilities, Recreation & Athletics, Refugee Assistance, Shelters/Homelessness, Substance Abuse, United Funds/United Ways, YMCA/YWCA/YMHA/YWHA, Youth Organizations

Application Procedures
Initial Contact: Interested parties may submit proposals, as well as proof of tax exemption under IRS Code 501(c)(3), to the foundation office.
Deadlines: None.

Grants Analysis
Disclosure Period: calendar year ending 2003
Total Grants: $3,726,449

Number of Grants: 241
Average Grant: $13,425*
Highest Grant: $504,350
Lowest Grant: $250
Typical Range: $5,000 to $50,000 and $100,000 to $200,000
*Note: Average grant figure excludes highest grant.

Recent Grants
Note: Grants derived from 2002 Form 990.
General

550,000	Jewish United Fund, Chicago, IL
500,000	Lincoln Park Zoological Society, Chicago, IL
305,000	Center for National Policy, Washington, DC
265,400	Museum of Contemporary Art, Chicago, IL
250,000	Community Foundation for National Capital Region, Washington, DC
250,000	Northwestern Memorial Hospital, Chicago, IL
150,000	Children's Diabetes Foundation, Denver, CO
125,000	Chicago Institute of Neurosurgery and Neuroresearch (CINN), Chicago, IL
104,500	Sidwell Friends School, Washington, DC
102,000	Dartmouth College, Hanover, NH

BLUMENTHAL FOUNDATION

Giving Contact
Philip Blumenthal, Director
PO Box 34689
Charlotte, NC 28234-4689
Phone: (704)377-6555
Fax: (704)377-9237
Web: http://www.blumenthalfoundation.org
Note: Mr. Blumenthal's phone extention is 2477.

Alternate Contact
Peggy Gartner, Administrator
Radiator Specialty Co.
1900 Wilkinson Boulevard
Charlotte, NC 28208
E-mail: foundation@gunk.com
Note: Foundation office location.

Description
Founded: 1953
EIN: 560793667
Organization Type: Family Foundation
Former Name: Blumenthal Foundation for Charity, Religion and Education.
Giving Locations: NC: Charlote headquarters.
Grant Types: Capital, Challenge, Endowment, General Support, Operating Expenses, Professorship, Project, Research, Scholarship.

Donor Information
Founder: Established in 1953 by members of the Blumenthal family including the late I. D. Blumenthal. Two trustees of the foundation sit on the board of the Radiator Specialty Company. Herman Blumenthal and Alan Blumenthal serve as the chairman and president, respectively.

Financial Summary
Total Giving: $790,000 (fiscal year ending April 30, 2003 approx); $898,000 (fiscal 2002 approx); $1,771,607 (fiscal 2001)
Giving Analysis: Giving for fiscal 2001 includes: foundation grants to United Way ($13,206)
Assets: $20,746,923 (fiscal 2001)
Gifts Received: $1,722,230 (fiscal 1999); $65,000 (fiscal 1995); $75,600 (fiscal 1994). Note: Contributions were received from various contributors.

Typical Recipients
Arts & Humanities: Arts Associations & Councils, Arts Centers, Arts Festivals, Arts Institutes, Dance, Libraries, Museums/Galleries, Music, Opera, Performing Arts, Public Broadcasting, Theater
Civic & Public Affairs: Civil Rights, Economic Policy, Ethnic Organizations, Civic & Public Affairs-General, Nonprofit Management, Philanthropic Organizations, Zoos/Aquariums
Education: Arts/Humanities Education, Business Education, Colleges & Universities, Community & Junior Colleges, Education Funds, Education Reform, Education-General, Preschool Education, Private Education (Precollege), Religious Education, Science/Mathematics Education
Environment: Environment-General, Resource Conservation, Wildlife Protection
Health: Adolescent Health Issues, AIDS/HIV, Clinics/Medical Centers, Health Organizations, Hospitals, Mental Health, Single-Disease Health Associations
International: Foreign Arts Organizations, International Affairs, Missionary/Religious Activities
Religion: Churches, Jewish Causes, Ministries, Religious Organizations, Religious Welfare, Synagogues/Temples
Science: Science Museums
Social Services: Child Welfare, Community Centers, Community Service Organizations, Family Planning, Family Services, Food/Clothing Distribution, Scouts, Senior Services, Social Services-General, Substance Abuse, United Funds/United Ways, YMCA/YWCA/YMHA/YWHA, Youth Organizations

Application Procedures
Initial Contact: Applicants should send one copy of a brief letter proposal.
Application Requirements: The proposal should be signed by an authorized official of the petitioning organization and the first paragraph should contain the amount and purpose of the request. The proposal should also include the following: a concise description of the project; what the project hopes to accomplish; total project cost and its duration; funds currently committed or pledged to the project and from what sources; other prospective funding sources; an evaluation plan and, if needed, how future funding will be obtained. Also include a phone number where a contact person for the project may be reached during normal business hours and the name to whom the check is to be made payable. In addition, materials should be attached to the proposal including the following: a line-item budget for the proposed project, if applicable, and a budget for the organization's total operations including expected income and expenditure; a list of the governing board of the petitioning organization; and a copy of the IRS tax-exempt determination letter, except in the cases of governmental agencies and churches.
Deadlines: None.
Review Process: The foundation's board of trustees meets quarterly to consider grant applications.

Restrictions
No grants are made to individuals for any purpose; does not provide scholarships, fellowships, or loans.

Additional Information
The Blumenthal Foundation addresses additional community needs through the Foundation for the Carolinas, including: The Neighborhood Grants Program, to offer support to low-income neighborhoods through leadership development initiatives; Underwriting for the Peirce Report, an in-depth analysis of the Charlotte region offering recommendations on how to deal with growth and development issues; Underwriting for Central Carolina Choices, to develop a regional network of citizens to solve problems by building consensus; The Summer Freedom School, a Children's Defense Fund Program directed at getting "at-risk" children off the street and into summer enrichment programs. enrichment programs.

Publications: Procedures; Requirements for Submitting Grant Proposals; American Jewish Times Outlook (monthly)

Foundation Officials

Alan Blumenthal: trustee B 1947. ED University of North Carolina (1969). PRIM CORP EMPL president: Radiator Specialty Co.

Anita Blumenthal: trustee

Philip Blumenthal: trustee B 1950. ED University of North Carolina (1972). NONPR AFFIL president, director: Wildacres Retreat.

Samuel Blumenthal, PhD: trustee

Peggy Gartner: admin

Grants Analysis

Disclosure Period: fiscal year ending April 30, 2001
Total Grants: $1,753,401*
Number of Grants: 191
Average Grant: $9,180*
Highest Grant: $100,000
Typical Range: $1,000 to $15,000
*Note: Giving excludes United Way. Average grant figure excludes two highest grants ($200,000).

Recent Grants

Note: Grants derived from fiscal 2002 Form 990.
General

500,000	Foundation of Shalom Park Inc., Charlotte, NC -- for expansion of Shalom Park and addition of a camp facility, classroom, gymnasium, and refurbishing of existing building
100,000	Arts & Science Council, Charlotte, NC -- towards Mint museum of Craft and Design establishment and locating Tryon Arts Center in uptown Charlotte
100,000	Arts & Science Council, Charlotte, NC -- towards Mint museum of Craft and Design establishment and locating Tryon Arts Center in uptown Charlotte
100,000	Jewish Community Center, Charlotte, NC -- towards a multi-year grant for the endowment of center
74,088	Wildacres Retreat, Little Switzerland, NC -- towards help to underwrite support of the retreat
50,000	Jewish Federation of Greater Charlotte, Charlotte, NC -- for support of the 2002 Annual Campaign
50,000	Jewish Federation of Greater Charlotte, Charlotte, NC -- for support of the 2002 Annual Campaign
50,000	Jewish Federation of Greater Charlotte, Charlotte, NC -- for support of the 2002 Annual Campaign
50,000	Jewish Federation of Greater Charlotte, Charlotte, NC -- for support of the 2002 Annual Campaign
50,000	Jewish Federation of Greater Charlotte, Charlotte, NC -- for support of the 2002 Annual Campaign
50,000	Jewish Federation of Greater Charlotte, Charlotte, NC -- for support of the 2002 Annual Campaign

BODMAN FOUNDATION

Giving Contact

Joseph S. Dolan, Secretary & Executive Director
767 Third Avenue, 4th Floor
New York, NY 10017
Phone: (212)644-0322
Fax: (212)759-6510
E-mail: main@archelis-bodman-fnds.org
Web: http://fdncenter.org/grantmaker/achelis-bodman/

Description

Founded: 1945
EIN: 136022016

Organization Type: General Purpose Foundation
Giving Locations: NJ: Northern New Jersey; NY: New York metropolitan area
Grant Types: Capital, Conference/Seminar, Emergency, Employee Matching Gifts, General Support, Matching.

Donor Information

Founder: Established in 1945 by the late George M. Bodman (d. 1950), a senior partner in the New York City brokerage firm of Cyrus J. Lawrence and Sons. Both Mr. Bodman and his wife, the late Louise C. Bodman (d. 1955), were active in civic and charitable causes in New York City and Monmouth County, NJ, during their lifetimes.

Financial Summary

Total Giving: $5,030,000 (2003); $2,779,525 (2002); $3,505,000 (2001)
Giving Analysis: Giving for 2001 includes: foundation scholarships ($100,000)
Assets: $55,500,000 (2003 approx); $53,570,560 (2002); $65,762,884 (2001)

Typical Recipients

Arts & Humanities: Arts Funds, Ballet, Dance, Historic Preservation, History & Archaeology, Libraries, Museums/Galleries, Music, Opera, Performing Arts, Public Broadcasting, Theater

Civic & Public Affairs: African American Affairs, Asian American Affairs, Botanical Gardens/Parks, Business/Free Enterprise, Civil Rights, Economic Development, Employment/Job Training, Civic & Public Affairs-General, Hispanic Affairs, Housing, Law & Justice, Legal Aid, Nonprofit Management, Philanthropic Organizations, Public Policy, Urban & Community Affairs, Zoos/Aquariums

Education: Afterschool/Enrichment Programs, Arts/Humanities Education, Business Education, Business-School Partnerships, Colleges & Universities, Economic Education, Education Associations, Education Funds, Education Reform, Elementary Education (Private), Elementary Education (Public), Education-General, Leadership Training, Legal Education, Literacy, Medical Education, Minority Education, Preschool Education, Private Education (Precollege), Public Education (Precollege), School Volunteerism, Science/Mathematics Education, Social Sciences Education, Special Education, Student Aid, Vocational & Technical Education

Environment: Air/Water Quality, Environment-General, Protection, Resource Conservation, Wildlife Protection

Health: AIDS/HIV, Alzheimer's Disease, Cancer, Children's Health/Hospitals, Clinics/Medical Centers, Emergency/Ambulance Services, Eyes/Blindness, Health Policy/Cost Containment, Health Funds, Health Organizations, Hospices, Hospitals, Medical Rehabilitation, Medical Research, Outpatient Health Care, Public Health, Single-Disease Health Associations, Speech & Hearing, Transplant Networks/Donor Banks, Trauma Treatment

International: Human Rights, International Affairs, International Development, Missionary/Religious Activities

Religion: Churches, Dioceses, Religion-General, Jewish Causes, Religious Organizations, Religious Welfare, Seminaries

Science: Science Museums, Scientific Centers & Institutes, Scientific Labs, Scientific Organizations, Scientific Research

Social Services: Animal Protection, At-Risk Youth, Big Brothers/Big Sisters, Child Abuse, Child Welfare, Community Centers, Community Service Organizations, Counseling, Delinquency & Criminal Rehabilitation, Domestic Violence, Family Services, Food/Clothing Distribution, Homes, People with Disabilities, Recreation & Athletics, Scouts, Senior Services, Shelters/Homelessness, Social Services-General, Substance Abuse, Veterans, Volunteer Services, YMCA/YWCA/YMHA/YWHA, Youth Organizations

Application Procedures

Initial Contact: The foundation has no standard application form. One short, but comprehensive proposal should be made in writing and sent to the foundation. Introductory letters should be no longer than two pages.

Application Requirements: All requests should briefly include the history, purpose, and financial statement of the applying organization, as well as descriptions of current activities and programs. In addition, grant requests should contain names of board members, personnel involved in the project, a vita of author or researcher, purpose of the request, amount needed, research basis, expected client or participant outcomes and measurable program results, and financial data or IRS information supporting the organization's tax-exempt status. Proposals should not exceed five pages.

Deadlines: None.

Review Process: The foundation's trustees meet in May, September, and December to decide on grant requests. When the board makes final decisions on grants, it takes into account the recommendations of its professional staff. Applicants typically receive a written response within six weeks. Personal interviews and site visits are arranged when necessary.

Evaluative Criteria: Special consideration given to self-help, leadership and character development, parental involvement, consumer choice, economic empowerment, independent research, prevention and early intervention, advancing the state of the art, faith-based program, strengthening the two-percent intact family, and client/participant outcomes and measurable program results.

Restrictions

No grants are made to individuals. Foundation does not make loans. Generally, grant requests for conferences, travel, films, housing, and publications are discouraged. The foundation generally will not fund national health and mental health organizations, small performing arts groups, annual appeals, dinner functions, fund raising events, international projects, deficits, endowments, annual capital campaigns, housing, or government-affiliated organizations and agencies. The Foundation funds primarily in New York City, occasionally in New Jersey.

Additional Information

Publications: Biennial Report; Guidelines

Foundation Officials

Horace I. Crary, Jr.: treasurer, trustee

Walter Joseph Patrick Curley, Jr.: trustee B Pittsburgh, PA 1922. ED Yale University BA (1944); Harvard University MBA (1948); University of Oslo (1948). PRIM CORP EMPL president: Curley Land Co. OCCUPATION diplomat, investment banker. CORP AFFIL director: Sotheby Holdings Inc.; director: France Growth Fund. NONPR AFFIL honorary chairman: French-American Foundation; trustee: Frick Collection; member: Counsel Foreign Relations. CLUB AFFIL Yale Club; Saint Stephen's Green Club; Travelers Club; New York Racquet & Tennis Club; Rolling Rock Club; Knickerbocker Club; The Links Club; Golf Morfontaine Club; Kildare Street Club; Bedford Golf Club.

Joseph S. Dolan: executive director, secretary

Anthony Drexel Duke, Sr.: trustee B New York, NY July 28, 1918. ED Princeton University (1941). NONPR AFFIL chairman, president, founder: Boys Harbor.

Peter Frelinghuysen: vice president, trustee ED Princeton University (1963); Yale University (1968). PRIM CORP EMPL attorney: Morris & McVeigh. CORP AFFIL secretary: K O A Holdings Inc.

John N. Irwin, III: chairman, chief executive officer, treasurer, trustee B 1954. ED Princeton University (1976). PRIM CORP EMPL vice president, managing director: Hillside Industries Inc. CORP AFFIL vice president, managing director, director: Hillside Capital Inc. De Corp.

Leslie Lenkowsky, PhD: trustee PRIM NONPR EMPL president, chief executive officer: Hudson Institute Inc. CORP AFFIL director: ITT Educational Services Inc.

Russell Parsons Pennoyer: president, trustee B New York, NY 1951. ED Harvard University BA (1974); Columbia University School of Law JD (1982). PRIM CORP EMPL partner: Benedetto, Gartland & Company Inc.

Mary Stone Phipps: vice president, trustee NONPR AFFIL member-at-large, director: Girl Scout Council Greater New York. CLUB AFFIL Somerset Club; Pilgrims Club; Piping Rock Club; The Links Club; Meadow Brook Club; Colony Club.

Guy G. Rutherfurd: chairman emeritus, trustee B New York, NY 1913. ED Princeton University BA (1938); University of Virginia LLB (1942). PRIM CORP EMPL partner: Morris & McVeigh.

Grants Analysis

Disclosure Period: calendar year ending 2003
Total Grants: $5,030,000
Number of Grants: 127
Average Grant: $39,606
Highest Grant: $150,000
Lowest Grant: $10,000
Typical Range: $25,000 to $75,000

Recent Grants

Note: Grants derived from 2002 Form 990.
General

150,000	Explore Charter School, Brooklyn, NY
100,000	Civic Builders Inc., New York, NY
100,000	Institute for American Values, New York, NY
100,000	John A. Reisenbach Charter School, New York, NY
100,000	New York Eye and Ear Infirmary, New York, NY
75,000	Boys and Girls Clubs of Newark Inc., Newark, NJ
75,000	Inner-City Scholarship Fund, NY
75,000	Public/Private Ventures, Philadelphia, PA
50,000	American Council on Science and Health, New York, NY
50,000	American Council of Trustees and Alumni, Washington, DC

BOE BROTHERS FOUNDATION

Giving Contact

Allen D. Faechner, Co-Trustee
PO Box 1396
Great Falls, MT 59403-1396
Phone: (406)727-4200

Description

Founded: 1997
EIN: 841378691
Organization Type: Private Foundation
Giving Locations: MT: North Central portion of MT known as the Golden Triangle Area
Grant Types: General Support.

Financial Summary

Total Giving: $251,658 (2003); $479,288 (2001)
Assets: $5,355,210 (2003); $5,093,611 (2001)

Typical Recipients

Arts & Humanities: Libraries, Museums/Galleries
Civic & Public Affairs: Clubs, Economic Development, Civic & Public Affairs-General, Municipalities/Towns
Education: Agricultural Education, Colleges & Universities, Public Education (Precollege), Special Education, Student Aid
Health: Health Organizations, Hospitals
Religion: Churches

Application Procedures

Initial Contact: Send a brief letter of inquiry.
Deadlines: None.

Restrictions

The trust generally supports organizations located in the north central portion of Montana.

Foundation Officials

Allen D. Faechner: trustee

Grants Analysis

Disclosure Period: calendar year ending 2003
Total Grants: $251,658*
Typical Range: $1,000 to $10,000
***Note:** No grants list available for 2003.

Recent Grants

Note: Grants derived from 2000 Form 990.
General

20,000	Concordia College, Moorhead, MN
20,000	Fairfield High School, Fairfield, MT
20,000	Saint Paul Lutheran Church, Fairfield, MT
10,000	Montana State University Foundation, Bozeman, MT -- for scholarship
5,000	Fairfield High Special Education, Fairfield, MT
5,000	Montana State University Foundation, Bozeman, MT -- for scholarship
4,000	Greenfield School District 75 -- for scholarships
4,000	Power High School -- for scholarships
4,000	Teton Medical Center Foundation, Choteau, MT
3,000	Choteau High School, Choteau, MT -- for scholarships

BOETTCHER FOUNDATION

Giving Contact

Timothy W. Schultz, President & Executive Director
600 Seventeenth Street, Suite 2210 South
Denver, CO 80202
Phone: (303)534-1937
E-mail: grants@boettcherfoundation.org
Web: http://www.boettcherfoundation.org

Description

Founded: 1937
EIN: 840404274
Organization Type: General Purpose Foundation
Giving Locations: CO: Denver
Grant Types: Capital, Challenge, General Support, Scholarship.

Donor Information

Founder: Established in 1937 in Colorado by the Boettcher family, with substantial gifts from Charles and Fanny Augusta Boettcher, their son Claude K. Boettcher, his wife Edna Boettcher, and other family members. Charles Boettcher (1852-1948), a German immigrant, helped organize the Great Western Sugar Company and the Ideal Cement Company.

Financial Summary

Total Giving: $8,876,619 (2003); $8,702,323 (2002 approx)
Giving Analysis: Giving for 2003 includes: foundation grants to United Way ($125,000); foundation scholarships ($1,851,400)
Assets: $223,593,214 (2003); $195,018,192 (2002 approx)

Typical Recipients

Arts & Humanities: Arts Associations & Councils, Arts Centers, Ballet, Dance, Historic Preservation, History & Archaeology, Libraries, Museums/Galleries, Music, Opera, Performing Arts, Public Broadcasting, Theater
Civic & Public Affairs: African American Affairs, Botanical Gardens/Parks, Business/Free Enterprise, Clubs, Community Foundations, Economic Development, Employment/Job Training, Civic & Public Affairs-General, Hispanic Affairs, Housing, Legal Aid, Municipalities/Towns, Parades/Festivals, Public Policy, Rural Affairs, Urban & Community Affairs, Women's Affairs, Zoos/Aquariums
Education: Afterschool/Enrichment Programs, Arts/Humanities Education, Business Education, Colleges & Universities, Community & Junior Colleges, Economic Education, Education Funds, Education Reform, Elementary Education (Private), Elementary Education (Public), Engineering/Technological Education, Education-General, International Studies, Leadership Training, Literacy, Medical Education, Preschool Education, Private Education (Precollege), Public Education (Precollege), Religious Education, Science/Mathematics Education, Secondary Education (Public), Student Aid
Environment: Forestry, Environment-General, Resource Conservation
Health: AIDS/HIV, Alzheimer's Disease, Children's Health/Hospitals, Clinics/Medical Centers, Emergency/Ambulance Services, Eyes/Blindness, Health-General, Health Policy/Cost Containment, Health Funds, Hospices, Hospitals, Long-Term Care, Medical Rehabilitation, Medical Research, Mental Health, Multiple Sclerosis, Preventive Medicine/Wellness Organizations, Public Health, Research/Studies Institutes, Single-Disease Health Associations
Religion: Churches, Jewish Causes, Ministries, Religious Welfare
Science: Science Museums, Scientific Centers & Institutes
Social Services: At-Risk Youth, Child Welfare, Community Centers, Community Service Organizations, Day Care, Domestic Violence, Emergency Relief, Family Planning, Family Services, Food/Clothing Distribution, Homes, People with Disabilities, Recreation & Athletics, Scouts, Senior Services, Sexual Abuse, Shelters/Homelessness, Social Services-General, Substance Abuse, United Funds/United Ways, Volunteer Services, YMCA/YWCA/YMHA/YWHA, Youth Organizations

Application Procedures

Initial Contact: A preliminary letter should be sent, signed by the head of organization and describing the project for which funding is requested. The letter should include a statement related to the priority of the project within the organization. The Foundation will ask the organization to submit a full proposal if interested.
Application Requirements: Send a full proposal with a copy of recent IRS statement of tax-exempt status; list of officers and directors, including occupations and places of employment; a brief description of organization, including historical background, services provided, population served and measurements of success; a recent audited financial statement; a current operating budget; description of project for which funding is being requested, including amount requested; budget for project showing expenses and anticipated sources of revenue; and statement of the funds currently committed to the project and other requests pending.
Deadlines: None.
Review Process: A preliminary response is made as soon as possible. Applicants should allow two or three months before a final decision.

Restrictions

No new grants are awarded for endowments, scholarships, operations, purchase of tables or tickets for events, out of state projects, conferences, seminars, workshops, travel, media presentations, or to individuals.

Additional Information

Grantees are required to submit reports on the use of grants and project results.

The foundation also makes program-related investments. Applicants should already have between 50% and 75% of the funding goal committed before foundation will consider proposal.

Publications: Annual Report; Biennial Scholarship Report

Foundation Officials

Marcia Z. Ashton: trustee
Pamela D. Beardsley: trustee
Paul H. Chan: trustee
James P. Craig: trustee
Claudia Boettcher Merthan: chairman, trustee
M. Ann Penny: trustee
Harris D. Sherman: trustee
J. William Sorensen: trustee
Edward D. White, III: trustee
Thomas Williams: trustee

Grants Analysis

Disclosure Period: calendar year ending 2003
Total Grants: $6,900,219*
Number of Grants: 138
Average Grant: $50,002
Highest Grant: $400,000
Typical Range: $25,000 to $100,000
*Note: Giving excludes scholarships; United Way.

Recent Grants

Note: Grants derived from 2003 Form 990.
General

717,083	Colorado College, Colorado Springs, CO -- 2003 Boettcher scholarships
641,455	University of Denver, Denver, CO -- 2003 Boettcher scholarships
492,862	University of Colorado, Boulder, CO -- 2003 Boettcher scholarships
400,000	Eleanor Roosevelt Institute, Denver, CO -- recoverable grant
375,000	Denver Museum of Nature and Science, Denver, CO -- toward capital expansion campaign
300,000	Denver Art Museum, Denver, CO -- toward capital expansion project
250,000	Educare Colorado, Denver, CO -- in support of program implementation in 3 Colorado countries over a period of 3 years
175,000	saint Joseph Hospital, Denver, CO -- toward the E Atwill Center of Maternal and Child Health
175,000	Western Colorado Community Foundation, Grand Junction, CO -- toward community foundation in western Colorado
166,667	University of Colorado, Boulder, CO -- in honor of J Quigg Newton Endowed Leadership Chair

BOISE CASCADE CORP.

Company Headquarters

Boise, ID
Web: http://www.bc.com

Company Description

Founded: 1957
Ticker: BCC
Exchange: NYSE
Revenue: US$8.245 billion (2003)
Profit: US$8.3 million (2003)
Employees: 55618 (2003)
SIC(s): 2421 Sawmills & Planing Mills--General,

2436 Softwood Veneer & Plywood, 2439 Structural Wood Members Nec, 2493 Reconstituted Wood Products.

Operating Locations

Boise Cascade Corp. (AL--Jackson; AZ--Phoenix; CA--City of Commerce; CO--Denver; ID--Burley, Emmett, Idaho Falls, Nampa; LA--Florien, Oakdale; MN--International Falls; MT--Billings; OR--Medford, Monmouth, Portland, St. Helens; UT--Lake City; WA--Kettle Falls, Spokane, Wallula, Yakima)

Nonmonetary Support

Range: $50,000 - $400,000
Type: Donated Equipment; Donated Products

Giving Contact

Linda Alden, Corporate Communications
1111 West Jefferson Street
PO Box 50
Boise, ID 83728-0001
Phone: (208)384-6161
Fax: (208)384-7224

Description

Organization Type: Corporate Giving Program
Giving Locations: headquarters and operating communities.
Grant Types: Capital, Employee Matching Gifts, Project.
Note: Matching gifts for education only.

Financial Summary

Total Giving: Contributes through corporate direct giving program only.

Typical Recipients

Arts & Humanities: Community Arts, Dance, Libraries, Museums/Galleries, Music, Opera, Performing Arts, Theater
Civic & Public Affairs: Business/Free Enterprise, Civil Rights, Economic Development, Economic Policy, Public Policy, Women's Affairs, Zoos/Aquariums
Education: Business Education, Colleges & Universities, Community & Junior Colleges, Economic Education, Engineering/Technological Education, Literacy, Minority Education, Special Education
Environment: Environment-General
Health: Emergency/Ambulance Services, Hospitals
Social Services: Community Centers, Homes, Recreation & Athletics, Senior Services, Substance Abuse, United Funds/United Ways, Youth Organizations

Application Procedures

Initial Contact: Write to nearest Boise Cascade facility.
Application Requirements: Include a description of the organization and its purpose; proof of tax-exempt status; list of officers a directors; current operating budget and sources of funding; recently audited financial statement or most recent Form 990; purpose of grant; project budget and estimated fund-raising costs; and sources of funding, both committed and proposed.
Deadlines: None.
Decision Notification: Proposals are reviewed on an ongoing basis.

Restrictions

Company does not support organizations located in areas where the company has few or no operations; individuals; private foundations; international organizations; fraternal, social, labor, or veterans' organizations; requests of a political nature and organizations or programs that are sensitive, controversial, harmful, or which pose a potential conflict of interest for the company; operating expenses of United Way member agencies; school trips or tours; athletic teams; scholarships, or sport vehicles; courtesy advertising; testimonial dinners; loans or investments; or churches or religious organizations.

Company generally will not arrange loans, or support memorials, grants to cover operating deficits, or projects that are primarily fund-raising events; organizations that channel funds to donee agencies, except for United Way; or endowments at educational institutions or funds or associations whose sole purpose is to raise funds for educational institutions or other organizations.

Additional Information

Priority is given to organizations and programs in communities where the company operates and to those in which company employees are involved. Operating locations manage and distribute their own funds. Grant seekers should contact the location nearest them.
Publications: Guidelines

Grants Analysis

Typical Range: $1,000 to $10,000

BONFILS-STANTON FOUNDATION

Giving Contact

Dorothy Harrell, Executive Director
1601 Arapahoe St., Suite 500
Denver, CO 80202
Phone: (303)825-3774
Fax: (303)825-0802
Web: http://www.bonfils-stantonfoundation.org

Description

Founded: 1962
EIN: 846029014
Organization Type: Private Foundation
Giving Locations: CO
Grant Types: Capital, General Support, Research.

Donor Information

Founder: the late Charles E. Stanton

Financial Summary

Total Giving: $2,549,225 (fiscal year ending June 30, 2004); $3,872,749 (fiscal 2001)
Giving Analysis: Giving for fiscal 2004 includes: foundation scholarships ($27,000); foundation gifts to individuals ($75,000); fiscal 2001: foundation matching gifts ($21,500); foundation scholarships ($25,310); foundation gifts to individuals ($50,000)
Assets: $72,276,689 (fiscal 2004); $71,286,373 (fiscal 2001)
Gifts Received: $640,787 (fiscal 2001); $403,466 (fiscal 2000); $1,875,045 (fiscal 1997). Note: In fiscal 1996, substantial contributions were received from the estate of Charles Stanton.

Typical Recipients

Arts & Humanities: Arts Associations & Councils, Arts Centers, Ballet, Dance, Historic Preservation, History & Archaeology, Libraries, Museums/Galleries, Music, Opera, Public Broadcasting, Theater
Civic & Public Affairs: Asian American Affairs, Botanical Gardens/Parks, Economic Development, Employment/Job Training, Civic & Public Affairs-General, Public Policy, Urban & Community Affairs, Women's Affairs, Zoos/Aquariums
Education: Arts/Humanities Education, Colleges & Universities, Community & Junior Colleges, Continuing Education, Elementary Education (Private), Education-General, Literacy, Minority Education, Private Education (Precollege), Science/Mathematics Education
Environment: Environment-General, Resource Conservation
Health: Cancer, Children's Health/Hospitals, Clinics/

Medical Centers, Emergency/Ambulance Services, Eyes/Blindness, Home-Care Services, Hospices, Hospitals, Long-Term Care, Medical Rehabilitation, Medical Research, Single-Disease Health Associations
Religion: Jewish Causes, Seminaries
Science: Science Museums, Scientific Centers & Institutes
Social Services: At-Risk Youth, Child Abuse, Child Welfare, Community Centers, Community Service Organizations, Domestic Violence, Family Planning, Family Services, Food/Clothing Distribution, Homes, People with Disabilities, Senior Services, Substance Abuse, YMCA/YWCA/YMHA/YWHA, Youth Organizations

Application Procedures

Initial Contact: Send a brief letter of inquiry, signed by president or chairman, requesting guidelines.
Deadlines: January 1, April 1, July 1, October 1.

Restrictions

Foundation generally does not support individuals, religious organizations for sectarian purposes, political or lobbying groups, or organizations outside operating areas of Colorado.

Additional Information

Publications: Annual Report (including Application Guidelines)

Foundation Officials

Louis J. Duman, MD: trustee
W. Eileen Greenawalt: secretary, trustee
Dorothy Harrell: executive director
Flaminia Odescalchi Kelly: trustee
Johnston R. Livingston: chairman emeritus, trustee B Foochow, People's Republic of China 1923. ED Yale University BS (1947); Harvard University MBA (1949). CORP AFFIL director: Construction Tech. NONPR AFFIL member: Sigma Xi; member: Tau Beta Ti; director: Rocky Mountain World Trade Association; director: National Repertory Orchestra; chairman: Rocky Mountain Regional Institute International Education; trustee: Bonfils Stanton Foundation; director: National Home Improvement Council. CLUB AFFIL Denver Country Club.
J. Landis Martin: chairman, trustee
John E. Repine, MD: trustee

Grants Analysis

Disclosure Period: fiscal year ending June 30, 2004
Total Grants: $2,447,225*
Number of Grants: 89
Average Grant: $19,508*
Highest Grant: $500,000
Lowest Grant: $129
Typical Range: $5,000 to $50,000
*Note: Giving excludes scholarships and gifts to individuals. Average grant figure excludes two highest grants ($750,000).

Recent Grants

Note: Grants derived from fiscal 2004 Form 990.
General
500,000	Denver Art Museum, Denver, CO -- for $3.5 million pledge for the naming of the modern and contemporary galleries in the museum expansion
250,000	Colorado Symphony Association, Denver, CO -- to strengthen fund development capacity in such areas as corporate solicitation, planned giving, endowment gifts and prospect identification
150,000	Colorado Seminary/University of Denver, Denver, CO -- for the capital campaign for the graduate school of social work, namely the completion of Craig Hall
125,000	Colorado Seminary/University of Denver, Denver, CO -- for the capital campaign for the graduate school of social work

100,000	Colorado Symphony Association, Denver, CO -- to support the guest conductor and guest artist fund of the orchestra
100,000	Denver Zoological Foundation Inc., Denver, CO -- to help with the creation of the Colorado trail exhibit
85,000	Women's Bean Project, Denver, CO -- to strengthen organizational capacity through market research, technology, staff and board development, and fundraising expertise
75,000	Central City Opera House Association, Denver, CO -- to provide underwriting for the 2003 summer opera festivals "Gabriel's daughter: The story of Clara Brown"
50,000	Denver Museum of Nature and Science, Denver, CO -- to support the development and implementation of 'Space Odyssey'
40,000	Opera Colorado, Denver, CO -- for the production of La Boheme

BOOTH FERRIS FOUNDATION

Giving Contact

Hildy Simmons, Co-Trustee
Care of J.P. Morgan Chase Bank
345 Park Avenue, 4th Fl.
New York, NY 10154
Phone: (212)464-2487

Description

Founded: 1957
EIN: 136170340
Organization Type: General Purpose Foundation
Giving Locations: NY: New York metropolitan area nationally.
Grant Types: Capital, Challenge, General Support, Matching, Multiyear/Continuing Support, Operating Expenses, Project, Seed Money.

Donor Information

Founder: Founded in 1957 through trusts established by Mrs. Chancie Ferris Booth (d. 1957) and from the estate of Willis H. Booth (d. 1958). The combined trusts created the Booth Ferris Foundation in 1964. For many years, Willis Booth served as vice president of Guaranty Trust Company (now Morgan Guaranty Trust Company), and acted as trustee for many different corporations.

Financial Summary

Total Giving: $9,467,000 (2003); $10,069,000 (2002)
Giving Analysis: Giving for 2003 includes: foundation grants to United Way ($100,000)
Assets: $226,897,391 (2003); $201,670,170 (2002)
Gifts Received: $64,831 (1998)

Typical Recipients

Arts & Humanities: Arts Associations & Councils, Arts Centers, Arts Festivals, Arts Funds, Arts Institutes, Arts Outreach, Ballet, Community Arts, Dance, Ethnic & Folk Arts, Film & Video, Arts & Humanities-General, Historic Preservation, History & Archaeology, Libraries, Literary Arts, Museums/Galleries, Music, Opera, Performing Arts, Public Broadcasting, Theater
Civic & Public Affairs: African American Affairs, Asian American Affairs, Botanical Gardens/Parks, Business/Free Enterprise, Community Foundations, Economic Development, Employment/Job Training, Civic & Public Affairs-General, Hispanic Affairs, Housing, Law & Justice, Legal Aid, Municipalities/Towns, Nonprofit Management, Philanthropic Organizations, Professional & Trade Associations, Public

Policy, Urban & Community Affairs, Women's Affairs
Education: Afterschool/Enrichment Programs, Arts/Humanities Education, Business Education, Colleges & Universities, Education Funds, Education Reform, Engineering/Technological Education, Faculty Development, Education-General, International Studies, Literacy, Minority Education, Private Education (Precollege), Public Education (Precollege), Science/Mathematics Education, Social Sciences Education, Vocational & Technical Education
Environment: Air/Water Quality, Environment-General, Protection, Wildlife Protection
Health: Children's Health/Hospitals, Emergency/Ambulance Services, Eyes/Blindness, Health Funds, Health Organizations, Hospitals, Nutrition, Research/Studies Institutes
International: Foreign Arts Organizations, International Peace & Security Issues
Religion: Churches, Jewish Causes, Ministries, Religious Organizations, Religious Welfare, Seminaries, Synagogues/Temples
Science: Science Museums, Scientific Labs
Social Services: At-Risk Youth, Child Welfare, Community Centers, Community Service Organizations, Day Care, Emergency Relief, Family Planning, Family Services, Food/Clothing Distribution, People with Disabilities, Recreation & Athletics, Senior Services, Shelters/Homelessness, Social Services-General, Substance Abuse, United Funds/United Ways, YMCA/YWCA/YMHA/YWHA, Youth Organizations

Application Procedures

Initial Contact: Send a formal proposal.
Application Requirements: Include annual report and financial data, including current budget and latest audited financial report.
Deadlines: None.

Restrictions

The foundation does not give support to organizations operating outside the United States, to individuals, for federated campaigns, to educational institutions for scholarships and fellowships, for restricted endowments, to social service and cultural programs outside the New York City metropolitan area, for specific diseases and disabilities, or for individual research.

Additional Information

Morgan Guaranty Trust Company of New York serves as corporate trustee for the foundation.
Publications: Annual Report
Trust(s): J.P. Morgan Chase Bank

Grants Analysis

Disclosure Period: calendar year ending 2003
Total Grants: $9,367,000*
Number of Grants: 110
Average Grant: $85,155
Highest Grant: $200,000
Lowest Grant: $7,000
*Note: Giving excludes United Way.

Recent Grants

Note: Grants derived from 2003 Form 990.
Library-Related
200,000	Queens Library Foundation, Jamaica, NY -- towards final planning and design phase of the children's discovery center
150,000	New York Public Library, New York, NY -- towards technology enhancement
125,000	Pierpont Morgan Library, New York, NY -- towards the expansion and renovation program

General
200,000	Gallaudet University, Washington, DC -- towards student academic center
200,000	New York Botanical Garden, Bronx, NY -- towards electronic ticketing and audience tracking system
200,000	New York Foundling Hospital, New York, NY

150,000	Bowdoin College, Brunswick, ME
150,000	College of Mount Saint Vincent, Riverdale, NY
150,000	Gettysburg College, Gettysburg, PA -- towards curriculum enhancement
150,000	Mannes College of Music, New York, NY
150,000	New York Shakespeare Festival, New York, NY -- towards technology enhancement
150,000	Union College, Schenectady, NY
125,000	Furman University, Greenville, SC -- towards education curriculum center

CHARLES H. AND BERTHA L. BOOTHROYD FOUNDATION

Giving Contact
Donald C. Gancer, President
120 W. Madison Street, Suite 14-L
Chicago, IL 60602
Phone: (312)346-8333

Description
Founded: 1958
EIN: 366047045
Organization Type: Private Foundation
Giving Locations: IL
Grant Types: Research, Scholarship.

Donor Information
Founder: the late Mary T. Palzkill, Agnes K. McAvoy Trust

Financial Summary
Total Giving: $268,500 (fiscal year ending June 30, 2002); $294,000 (fiscal 2001)
Giving Analysis: Giving for fiscal 2002 includes: foundation scholarships ($35,000)
Assets: $5,792,306 (fiscal 2002); $6,213,814 (fiscal 2001)
Gifts Received: $67,166 (fiscal 2002); $260,000 (fiscal 2001); $3 (fiscal 1992). Note: In fiscal 2001 and 2002, contributions were received from Gudrun Alcock Trust. In 1992, contributions were received from Agness K. McAvoy.

Typical Recipients
Arts & Humanities: Arts Institutes, Libraries, Music, Opera, Theater
Civic & Public Affairs: Economic Development, Civic & Public Affairs-General, Law & Justice, Legal Aid, Municipalities/Towns, Women's Affairs
Education: Arts/Humanities Education, Colleges & Universities, Medical Education, Private Education (Precollege), Student Aid
Environment: Resource Conservation
Health: Alzheimer's Disease, Clinics/Medical Centers, Health Funds, Health Organizations, Hospitals, Medical Research, Mental Health, Nursing Services, Single-Disease Health Associations
Religion: Religious Welfare
Social Services: Community Service Organizations, Senior Services

Application Procedures
Initial Contact: Send brief letter.
Application Requirements: Individual and organizational applicants must submit a brief resume of academic qualifications, purpose of funds sought, and proof of tax-exempt status. Research grants must include an outline of the proposed investigation and proposed budget.
Deadlines: None.

Foundation Officials
Gudrun Alcock: vice president
Bruce E. Brown: vice president
Donald Charles Gancer: president B Chicago, IL 1933. ED Marquette University LLB (1957). PRIM CORP EMPL principal: Querrey & Harrow Ltd. NONPR AFFIL member: Illinois State Bar Association; member: WI Bar Association; member: Chicago Bar Association; member: Chicago Council Lawyers; member: American Bar Association. CLUB AFFIL Union League Club; Oak Park Tennis Club.
Thomas C. Kaufmann: vice president
Lorraine Marcus: secretary
Dennis A. Marks: vice president

Grants Analysis
Disclosure Period: fiscal year ending June 30, 2002
Total Grants: $268,500
Number of Grants: 17
Average Grant: $19,029
Highest Grant: $35,000
Lowest Grant: $2,500
Typical Range: $8,500 to $20,000

Recent Grants
Note: Grants derived from fiscal 2002 Form 990.
Library-Related

2,500	Newberry Library, Chicago, IL

General

35,000	N. W. University Arts & Sciences, Evanston, IL
26,000	University of Chicago Department of Psychiatry, Chicago, IL
20,000	Bethel New Life, Chicago, IL
20,000	Evans Scholars Foundation, Golf, IL
20,000	H.O.M.E., Chicago, IL
20,000	St. Ignatius College Prep, Chicago, IL
15,000	Alzheimer's Association, Skokie, IL
15,000	Chicago Volunteer Legal Services, Chicago, IL
15,000	Daniel Murphy Scholarship Fund, Chicago, IL
15,000	Golden Apple, Chicago, IL

ALBERT AND ELAINE BORCHARD FOUNDATION

Giving Contact
Willard A. Beling, Chairman & Director
22055 Clarendon St., Suite 210
Woodland Hills, CA 91367
Phone: (818)888-2871

Description
Founded: 1978
EIN: 953294377
Organization Type: Private Foundation
Grant Types: General Support, Scholarship.

Financial Summary
Total Giving: $609,290 (fiscal year ending July 31, 2001)
Giving Analysis: Giving for fiscal 2001 includes: foundation matching gifts ($5,000); foundation fellowships ($25,000)
Assets: $14,952,424 (fiscal 2001)
Gifts Received: $5,000 (fiscal 2001); $25,027 (fiscal 2000). Note: In fiscal 2001, contributions were received from Alzheimer's Association. In fiscal 2000, contributions were received from B. Lawrence Brennan ($5,027), Richard E. Kipper ($5,000), O.W. Moyle III ($5,000), Robert K. Johnson ($5,000), and the Alzheimer's Association ($5,000).

Typical Recipients
Arts & Humanities: History & Archaeology, Libraries, Museums/Galleries, Public Broadcasting,

Theater
Civic & Public Affairs: Clubs, Employment/Job Training, Housing, Law & Justice, Legal Aid
Education: Afterschool/Enrichment Programs, Arts/Humanities Education, Colleges & Universities, Economic Education, Education Associations, Education Funds, Education Reform, International Exchange, International Studies, Legal Education, Medical Education, Science/Mathematics Education, Social Sciences Education, Special Education
Environment: Protection
Health: Adolescent Health Issues, Alzheimer's Disease, Cancer, Children's Health/Hospitals, Emergency/Ambulance Services, Geriatric Health, Health Policy/Cost Containment, Health Organizations, Medical Research, Prenatal Health Issues, Single-Disease Health Associations
International: Foreign Arts Organizations, Health Care/Hospitals
Religion: Religious Welfare
Social Services: Child Abuse, Child Welfare, Community Centers, Community Service Organizations, Crime Prevention, Delinquency & Criminal Rehabilitation, Family Planning, Family Services, People with Disabilities, Senior Services, United Funds/United Ways, Youth Organizations

Application Procedures
Initial Contact: Submit a written grant request, in triplicate.
Application Requirements: Include full proposal and proof of tax-exempt status.
Deadlines: None.

Restrictions
Does not support individuals.

Foundation Officials
Betty Beling: assoc director
Willard A. Beling: chairman, director B Great Bend, ND 1919. ED University of California, Los Angeles BA (1943); Princeton University PhD (1947). NONPR AFFIL professor: University Southern California.
Carol Spurgeon: assoc director
Edward Dutcher Spurgeon: president, director B Newton, NJ 1939. ED Princeton University AB (1961); Stanford University LLB (1964); New York University LLM (1968). NONPR AFFIL president, director: Sibert & Elaine Borchard Foundation; professor, dean sch law: University GA; member: American Bar Association; member: American Bar Foundation.

Grants Analysis
Disclosure Period: fiscal year ending July 31, 2001
Total Grants: $579,290*
Number of Grants: 62
Average Grant: $9,343
Highest Grant: $33,333
Lowest Grant: $250
Typical Range: $1,000 to $20,000
***Note:** Giving excludes fellowships and matching gifts.

Recent Grants
Note: Grants derived from 2002 Form 990.
General

33,334	University of Southern California School of Medicine, Los Angeles, CA -- for new IGM genomics lab space
30,435	University of Georgia Foundation, Athens, GA -- for fellowship
30,000	University of Southern California, Los Angeles, CA -- for two studies
25,000	Regents of the University of California, La Jolla, CA -- for conference
25,000	Regents of the University of California, La Jolla, CA -- for UCLA's Paris Program
25,000	Regents of the University of California, La Jolla, CA -- for Lyon Opera Ballet's performance of Cinderella

25,000	San Diego State University, San Diego, CA -- for conference on Cross Cultural Issues in Women's Health
25,000	University of Southern California, Los Angeles, CA -- for two Borchard Museum Studies
25,000	University of Southern California, Los Angeles, CA -- for Urban Sprawl in France
20,000	University of Southern California, Los Angeles, CA -- for Borchard Overseas Dissertation Research Fellowship

BORKEE-HAGLEY FOUNDATION

Giving Contact
Henry H. Silliman, Jr., President
PO Box 4590
Greenville, DE 19807
Phone: (302)652-8616

Description
Founded: 1955
EIN: 516011644
Organization Type: Private Foundation
Giving Locations: DE
Grant Types: Capital, General Support.

Financial Summary
Total Giving: $427,500 (2003)
Assets: $8,806,714 (2003)

Typical Recipients
Arts & Humanities: History & Archaeology, Libraries, Museums/Galleries
Civic & Public Affairs: Clubs, Employment/Job Training, Civic & Public Affairs-General, Housing, Professional & Trade Associations, Public Policy, Urban & Community Affairs, Women's Affairs
Education: Arts/Humanities Education, Business Education, Colleges & Universities, Environmental Education, Education-General, Private Education (Precollege), Public Education (Precollege), Vocational & Technical Education
Environment: Environment-General, Resource Conservation
Health: Emergency/Ambulance Services, Geriatric Health, Health Organizations, Hospices, Hospitals, Long-Term Care, Preventive Medicine/Wellness Organizations, Public Health
Religion: Jewish Causes, Ministries, Religious Organizations, Religious Welfare
Social Services: Big Brothers/Big Sisters, Child Welfare, Community Centers, Community Service Organizations, Day Care, Family Planning, Family Services, Food/Clothing Distribution, Homes, People with Disabilities, Recreation & Athletics, Senior Services, Social Services-General, Special Olympics, YMCA/YWCA/YMHA/YWHA, Youth Organizations

Application Procedures
Initial Contact: Send a brief letter of inquiry on organization's stationery.
Application Requirements: Includes organization's purpose, proof of tax-exempt status, and details about the area of need for funds requested.
Deadlines: November 1.

Restrictions
Preference is given to organizations engaged in activities benefiting the elderly.

Foundation Officials
Thomas F. Husbands: assistant secretary
Eleanor Silliman Maroney: secretary
Henry Harper Silliman, Jr.: president, treasurer
NONPR AFFIL trustee emeritus: St. Andrews School.

John E. Silliman: vice president B Scarsdale, NY 1934. ED Yale University BA (1956); Columbia University LLB (1959). PRIM CORP EMPL partner: Murtha, Cullina, Richter & Pinney.
Robert M. Silliman: director ED Yale University.
Doris Silliman Stockly: director

Grants Analysis
Disclosure Period: calendar year ending 2003
Total Grants: $427,500
Number of Grants: 54
Average Grant: $7,917
Highest Grant: $25,000
Lowest Grant: $1,000
Typical Range: $1,000 to $10,000

Recent Grants
Note: Grants derived from 2001 Form 990.
General

25,000	Delaware Nature Society, Hockessin, DE -- capital
25,000	St. Anne's Episcopal School, Middletown, DE -- capital
25,000	Tower Hill School, Wilmington, DE -- capital
25,000	Wilmington Youth Rowing Association, Wilmington, DE -- capital
20,000	Christiana Care Foundation, Wilmington, DE -- capital
20,000	Delaware Elwyn, Inc., Wilmington, DE -- capital
20,000	Habitat for Humanity, Wilmington, DE -- capital
20,000	Pilot School, Wilmington, DE -- capital
20,000	Wellness Community, Wilmington, DE -- capital
16,000	Sanford School, Hockessin, DE -- capital

THE BOSTON GLOBE

Company Headquarters
Boston, MA
Web: http://www.boston.com

Company Description
Revenue: US$201 million (2002)
Employees: 2175 (2002)
SIC(s): 2711 Newspapers.
Parent Company: New York Times Co., 229 W. 43rd Street, New York, NY, United States

Operating Locations
The Boston Globe (MA--Billerica, Waltham)

Nonmonetary Support
Type: Cause-related Marketing & Promotion; In-kind Services
Note: Co. provides nonmonetary support. Supports the Globe Santa Program, which raises funds from readers to provide Christmas donations to needy families.

Boston Globe Foundation

Giving Contact
Mrs. Bailey
135 Morrissey Boulevard, 2nd Floor
Boston, MA 02107
Phone: (617)929-3467
Fax: (617)929-2041
E-mail: foundation@globe.com
Web: http://bostonglobe.com/community/index.stm

Description
EIN: 222821421
Organization Type: Corporate Foundation
Giving Locations: MA: Boston, Cambridge, Chelsea, Somerville
Grant Types: Capital, Employee Matching Gifts, General Support, Multiyear/Continuing Support.
Note: Employee matching gift ratio: 1 to 1 to education.

Financial Summary
Total Giving: $345,566 (2001). Note: Contributes through foundation only. In 2000, the foundation changed from a fiscal year to a calendar year; giving figure for 2000 includes contributions made from July 31, 1999 to December 31, 2000.
Assets: $108,774 (2001)
Gifts Received: $1,241,638 (2001); $1,573,249 (2000); $1,999,315 (1999). Note: Contributions received from Globe Newspaper Company.

Typical Recipients
Arts & Humanities: Arts Associations & Councils, Arts Festivals, Arts Funds, Arts Outreach, Ballet, Dance, Ethnic & Folk Arts, Arts & Humanities-General, Libraries, Museums/Galleries, Music, Performing Arts, Public Broadcasting, Theater, Visual Arts
Civic & Public Affairs: Botanical Gardens/Parks, Business/Free Enterprise, Economic Development, Employment/Job Training, Hispanic Affairs, Housing, Nonprofit Management, Philanthropic Organizations, Professional & Trade Associations, Safety, Urban & Community Affairs, Women's Affairs, Zoos/Aquariums
Education: Afterschool/Enrichment Programs, Business-School Partnerships, Colleges & Universities, Education Reform, Elementary Education (Private), Environmental Education, Faculty Development, Education-General, Journalism/Media Education, Literacy, Medical Education, Minority Education, Preschool Education, Private Education (Precollege), Public Education (Precollege), Science/Mathematics Education, Special Education, Student Aid
Environment: Environment-General, Protection
Health: AIDS/HIV, Children's Health/Hospitals, Clinics/Medical Centers, Health Organizations, Hospitals, Medical Research, Mental Health, Nutrition
International: Foreign Arts Organizations, Human Rights
Religion: Religious Welfare
Science: Science Museums
Social Services: Camps, Child Welfare, Community Centers, Community Service Organizations, Counseling, Crime Prevention, Day Care, Domestic Violence, Family Services, Food/Clothing Distribution, Homes, People with Disabilities, Recreation & Athletics, Shelters/Homelessness, Substance Abuse, United Funds/United Ways, Youth Organizations

Application Procedures
Initial Contact: Apply using the Associated Grantmakers of Massachusetts (AGM) Common Proposal Format and a Boston Globe Foundation Addendum. Contact the AGM and Boston Globe Foundation for forms.
Application Requirements: Completed proposal following the AGM Common Proposal Format and answers to all questions asked on the Boston Globe Foundation's Addendum.
Deadlines: None.
Review Process: Proposals reviewed by foundation staff, agencies investigated, budgetary requirements evaluated, and recommendation made to foundation board which meets February, June and in the fall.
Evaluative Criteria: The foundation's primary funding criteria is to support programs and operations of well-managed, financially viable charitable organizations based in Boston, Cambridge, Somerville and Chelsea, MA that serve youth ages 0-22 who live primarily in low-income neighborhoods. Secondary

funding criteria include a preference for programs that foster inclusion of youth not participating fully in society; build bridges for youth across divides (neighborhood borders, varied backgrounds); link youth programs with other neighborhood initiatives, as participants in an integrated community effort; and demonstrate effective and consistent constituency involvement in creation and implementation of programs. The foundation also evaluates whether an agency values inclusion and diversity among staff, clientele and decision-makers; has active governing bodies knowledgeable about the organization's mission and constituents; addresses systemic causes of a problem, or educates the public on important issues.

Decision Notification: Allow four to six months for processing.

Notes: Foundation sponsors meetings on how to shape proposals. Call the foundation for more information regarding community information meetings.

Restrictions

The foundation does not make grants to individuals or for the purchase of tables, tickets, or advertising. The foundation does not make more than one grant per fiscal year to any one organization.

Additional Information

The Globe Santa Fund solicits through advertising and publicity contributions to purchase Christmas gifts for needy children. The company also administers several scholarship programs, including the L.L. Winship Scholarship Fund (for children of full-time company employees), the I. Arthur Seigel Scholarship Fund (athletic), the Marjorie L. Adams Scholarship Fund (for children of employees), and the Louis Shriber Scholarship Fund (for Globe newsboys). The company also sponsors scholastic art awards and the Globe Interscholastic Festival.

The foundation holds bi-weekly informational meetings for grantsseekers to help shape proposals. Staff explains funding priorities and application procedures. The contact for these meetings is Sylvia Payton, at (617)929-2895.

The New York Times Company acquired the Globe Newspaper Co.'s parent corporation, Affiliated Publications, in 1993.

Publications: Application; Guidelines; Report to the Community

Foundation Officials

Richard H. Gilman: director
Leslie Griffin: director
Richard Gula: president, director
Al Larkin: president
Suzanne W. Maas: executive director
Mary Marty: assistant treasurer B 1942. ED Marycrest College (1964). PRIM CORP EMPL treasurer: Affiliated Publications Inc. ADD CORP EMPL treasurer: Globe SPLty Products Inc.
Loretta McLaughlin: director
Mary Jane Patrone: director, clerk
Sylvia Payton: program officer
Mariella Puerto: project director
Randall K. Short: assistant treasurer
Benjamin B. Taylor: director B 1947. ED Harvard University. PRIM CORP EMPL president, publisher chairman: Globe Newspaper Co. NONPR AFFIL trustee: Park School; trustee: Radcliffe College.

Grants Analysis

Disclosure Period: calendar year ending 2001
Total Grants: $345,566
Number of Grants: 28 (approx)
Average Grant: $10,129*
Highest Grant: $72,090 (approx)
Lowest Grant: $2,500 (approx)
Typical Range: $10,000 to $50,000
*Note: Average grant figure excludes highest grant.

Recent Grants

Note: Grants derived from 1996 Form 990.

General

70,000	University of Massachusetts Boston, Boston, MA -- support 1996 Taylor Scholars Program
50,000	Boston Globe Foundation, Boston, MA -- for Lead Action Plan
39,000	Project Bread, Boston, MA -- for Emergency Feeding Network
20,000	New England Aquarium, Boston, MA -- program support, capital campaign
15,000	Black Church Capacity Building Project -- support of Black Church Capacity Building Project
15,000	Boston Children's Services, Boston, MA -- for Project Excel
15,000	HSPC Diversity Initiative -- support arts and humanities organizations
15,000	Roca, Inc., Chelsea, MA -- renovations
15,000	WGBH Educational Foundation, Springfield, MA -- for National Center for Accessible Media
13,400	Associated Grantmakers of Massachusetts, Boston, MA -- support services

THE BOTHIN FOUNDATION

Giving Contact

Lyman H. Casey, Executive Director & Treasurer
Presidio Blvd., Suite 1016
PO Box 29906
San Francisco, CA 94129-0906
Phone: (415)561-6540
Fax: (415)561-6477
Web: http://www.pacificfoundationservices.com

Description

Founded: 1926
EIN: 941196182
Organization Type: General Purpose Foundation
Giving Locations: CA: San Francisco metropolitan area
Grant Types: Capital.

Donor Information

Founder: Established as a private foundation in the State of California on September 28, 1917 by Henry E. Bothin, his wife, Ellen Chabot Bothin, and his daughter, Genevieve Bothin de Limur. The foundation is administered by a board of directors, several of whom are members of the Bothin family and was formerly known as the Bothin Helping Fund.

Financial Summary

Total Giving: $1,500,000 (2002 approx); $1,557,117 (2001)
Assets: $38,027,684 (2001)

Typical Recipients

Arts & Humanities: Arts Associations & Councils, Arts Centers, Arts Festivals, Arts Outreach, Ethnic & Folk Arts, Film & Video, Arts & Humanities-General, Libraries, Museums/Galleries, Music, Public Broadcasting, Theater
Civic & Public Affairs: Asian American Affairs, Botanical Gardens/Parks, Business/Free Enterprise, Community Foundations, Economic Development, Employment/Job Training, Civic & Public Affairs-General, Hispanic Affairs, Housing, Legal Aid, Urban & Community Affairs, Women's Affairs, Zoos/Aquariums
Education: Afterschool/Enrichment Programs, Business Education, Colleges & Universities, Education Funds, Elementary Education (Private), Environmental Education, Education-General, Gifted & Talented Programs, Leadership Training, Preschool Education, Private Education (Precollege), School Volun-

teerism, Science/Mathematics Education, Secondary Education (Private), Secondary Education (Public), Special Education, Student Aid
Environment: Environment-General, Protection, Resource Conservation, Wildlife Protection
Health: AIDS/HIV, Cancer, Clinics/Medical Centers, Emergency/Ambulance Services, Eyes/Blindness, Health Funds, Health Organizations, Home-Care Services, Hospices, Hospitals, Hospitals (University Affiliated), Kidney, Medical Rehabilitation, Medical Research, Mental Health, Prenatal Health Issues, Preventive Medicine/Wellness Organizations, Speech & Hearing, Transplant Networks/Donor Banks
International: Human Rights, International Environmental Issues, International Relations
Religion: Churches, Ministries, Religious Welfare
Science: Scientific Centers & Institutes, Scientific Research
Social Services: Animal Protection, At-Risk Youth, Camps, Child Abuse, Child Welfare, Community Centers, Community Service Organizations, Counseling, Day Care, Domestic Violence, Family Planning, Family Services, Food/Clothing Distribution, People with Disabilities, Recreation & Athletics, Senior Services, Sexual Abuse, Shelters/Homelessness, Social Services-General, Substance Abuse, Volunteer Services, YMCA/YWCA/YMHA/YWHA, Youth Organizations

Application Procedures

Initial Contact: Applicants should submit a brief preliminary letter of request.
Application Requirements: Requests for support should include a description of the goals and objectives of the proposed project; purpose and history of the applying organization; names and qualifications of the project's staff; total operating budget, estimated or proposed budget for the project; amount requested; other sources of income; and proof of tax exemption. If additional information is needed, the foundation will contact the applicant.
Deadlines: Applications should be submitted 12 weeks prior to board meetings.
Review Process: All requests satisfying the guidelines are submitted to the advisory committee for preliminary review before being presented to the board of directors. The board meets three times per year, in February, May, and October. Applicants should expect a waiting period of up to three months before funding decisions are made. All requests are answered with a written response within a reasonable period of time.

Restrictions

Grants are not made to individuals, for endowment drives, general operating expenses, films or other media presentations, religious groups for sectarian purposes, medical research, conferences, program support, or educational institutions other than those directly serving the developmentally or learning disabled. Grants are not made for events, annual appeals, or scholarships.

Additional Information

The foundation prefers that a full three years elapse between grants.
Publications: Biennial Report

Foundation Officials

A. Michael Casey: vice president, treasurer ED University of California at Berkeley (1964); University of California Hastings School Law JD (1967).
Lyman H. Casey: executive director
Genevieve Bothin Lyman di San Faustino: president, director, donor granddaughter
Stephanie MacColl: director NONPR AFFIL director: San Francisco Foundation.
Edmona Lyman Mansell: vice president, director
Gordon E. Miller: director
Rhoda Schultz: director

Grants Analysis

Disclosure Period: calendar year ending 2001
Total Grants: $1,557,117
Number of Grants: 95
Average Grant: $16,390
Highest Grant: $185,000
Lowest Grant: $1,000
Typical Range: $5,000 to $30,000

Recent Grants

Note: Grants derived from 2002 Form 990.
General

415,000	Families on Track, CA -- towards support of the academic programs and social services for at risk students and families at Parkway Heights Middle
25,000	Bay Area Discover Museum, Sausalito, CA -- for the capital campaign of My Place By the Bay and towards expansion and renovation of campus buildings and outdoor sites
25,000	Commonweal, Bolinas, CA -- towards renovation of office space and creation of a chapel in the existing building
25,000	Episcopal Community Services of San Diego, San Diego, CA -- for the capital campaign to build a supportive housing facility for homeless
25,000	Family House Inc., San Francisco, CA -- for buying 60 beds and 3 entertainment centers as temporary housing for families of cancer patients undergoing treatment at UCSF medical center
25,000	Project Open Hand, San Francisco, CA -- for the purchase of kitchen equipment for agency providing meals for clients with HIV and homebound seniors
25,000	San Francisco General Hospital Foundation, San Francisco, CA -- towards purchasing of a bone densitometer
25,000	Trips for Kids Marin, San Rafael, CA -- support renovation of building and purchase of a van for program providing bicycle trips for inner city youth
22,000	Sonoma County People for Economic Opportunity, Santa Rosa, CA -- towards instillation of security equipment at the South Park Center
21,000	Youth and Family Assistance, Redwood City, CA -- for renovating the health clinic and transitional housing facilities for runaway and homeless youth in San Mateo County

BOURNS INC.

Company Headquarters

1200 Columbia Avenue
Riverside, CA 92507
Phone: (909)781-5500
Fax: (909)781-5006
Web: http://www.bourns.com

Company Description

Revenue: US$9 million (2001)
Employees: 150 (2001)
SIC(s): 3676 Electronic Resistors, 3679 Electronic Components Nec, 3699 Electrical Equipment & Supplies Nec.

Operating Locations

Recon-Optical, Inc. (CA--Riverside)

Nonmonetary Support

Type: Donated Equipment

Bourns Foundation

Giving Contact

Gordon L. Bourns, President
1200 Columbia Ave.
Riverside, CA 92507
Phone: (909)781-5084
Fax: (909)781-5203

Description

EIN: 956044472
Organization Type: Corporate Foundation
Giving Locations: CA: focusing on Inland Empire area of Southern California; UT
Grant Types: Capital, Endowment, General Support, Multiyear/Continuing Support, Scholarship.

Financial Summary

Total Giving: $133,000 (fiscal year ending November 30, 2003); $16,450 (fiscal 2002); $31,000 (fiscal 2001). Note: Contributes through foundation only.
Giving Analysis: Giving for fiscal 2002 includes: foundation scholarships ($5,500)
Assets: $321,804 (fiscal 2003); $447,078 (fiscal 2002); $449,648 (fiscal 2001)
Gifts Received: $1,188,234 (fiscal 2000); $1,328,313 (fiscal 1999); $1,800,000 (fiscal 1998). Note: Contributions were received from Bourns, Inc.

Typical Recipients

Arts & Humanities: Arts & Humanities-General, Museums/Galleries
Civic & Public Affairs: Clubs, Economic Development, Civic & Public Affairs-General
Education: Arts/Humanities Education, Business Education, Colleges & Universities, Education Funds, Engineering/Technological Education, Education-General, Private Education (Precollege), Public Education (Precollege), Religious Education, Science/Mathematics Education, Student Aid
Health: Cancer, Children's Health/Hospitals, Diabetes, Health-General, Hospices, Hospitals, Mental Health
Religion: Religious Welfare
Social Services: Community Service Organizations, Recreation & Athletics, Scouts, Shelters/Homelessness, Social Services-General, United Funds/United Ways, YMCA/YWCA/YMHA/YWHA, Youth Organizations

Application Procedures

Initial Contact: Send a brief letter of inquiry.
Application Requirements: Include description of program, including benefits, and purpose of funds sought.
Deadlines: None.

Corporate Officials

Gordon L. Bourns: chairman finance, chief financial officer, treasurer B 1949. ED University of California, Los Angeles BSEE (1971); University of California, Los Angeles MBA (1973). PRIM CORP EMPL chairman: Bourns, Inc.
William P. McKenna: vice president finance, chief financial officer, treasurer B 1947. ED College of the Holy Cross MA (1968); University of Southern California MBA (1976). PRIM CORP EMPL vice president finance, chief financial officer, treasurer: Bourns, Inc.

Foundation Officials

Gordon L. Bourns: president, director (see above)
Linda A. Hill: vice president, director
Anita I. MacBeth: director CORP AFFIL director: Bourns Inc.
Denise L. Moyles: director
Karen J. Smarr: secretary, treasurer, director
Gerald T. Young: director

Grants Analysis

Disclosure Period: fiscal year ending November 30, 2003

Total Grants: $130,000*
Number of Grants: 4
Highest Grant: $100,000
Lowest Grant: $2,000
*****Note:** Giving excludes scholarships.

Recent Grants

Note: Grants derived from fiscal 2003 Form 990.
General

100,000	UC Riverside Foundation, Riverside, CA -- fund for engineering program
25,000	Utah State University, Logan, UT -- donation for engineering college building fund
3,000	UC Riverside Foundation, Riverside, CA
3,000	UC Riverside Foundation, Riverside, CA -- fund for engineering scholarships
2,000	UC Riverside Foundation, Riverside, CA -- fund for alumni & visitor center

BOUTELL MEMORIAL FUND

Giving Contact

Helen James, Trust Officer
c/o CB Wealth Management
101 N. Washington
Saginaw, MI 48607
Phone: (989)776-7368

Description

Founded: 1961
EIN: 386040492
Organization Type: Private Foundation
Giving Locations: MI: Saginaw County
Grant Types: General Support.

Donor Information

Founder: the late Arnold and Gertrude Boutell

Financial Summary

Total Giving: $474,067 (fiscal year ending March 31, 2004); $470,236 (fiscal 2002); $344,697 (fiscal 2001)
Giving Analysis: Giving for fiscal 2001 includes: foundation grants to United Way ($23,000)
Assets: $11,489,299 (fiscal 2004); $11,829,470 (fiscal 2002); $12,169,683 (fiscal 2001)

Typical Recipients

Arts & Humanities: Arts Festivals, Community Arts, Dance, Libraries, Music, Public Broadcasting
Civic & Public Affairs: Botanical Gardens/Parks, Community Foundations, Economic Development, Employment/Job Training, Civic & Public Affairs-General, Housing, Municipalities/Towns, Parades/Festivals, Rural Affairs, Safety, Urban & Community Affairs, Zoos/Aquariums
Education: Business-School Partnerships, Colleges & Universities, Public Education (Precollege)
Health: Emergency/Ambulance Services, Health Funds, Hospitals, Prenatal Health Issues
Religion: Religious Welfare
Social Services: At-Risk Youth, Child Abuse, Child Welfare, Community Service Organizations, Crime Prevention, Domestic Violence, Family Services, Recreation & Athletics, Shelters/Homelessness, United Funds/United Ways, YMCA/YWCA/YMHA/YWHA, Youth Organizations

Application Procedures

Initial Contact: Send letter requesting application guidelines. There are no deadlines.

Restrictions

Does not support individuals.

Additional Information

Trust(s): CB Wealth Management
Publications: Application Guidelines

Grants Analysis

Disclosure Period: fiscal year ending March 31, 2004
Total Grants: $474,067
Number of Grants: 25
Average Grant: $16,628*
Highest Grant: $75,000
Lowest Grant: $3,000
Typical Range: $5,000 to $25,000
*Note: Average grant excludes highest grant.

Recent Grants

Note: Grants derived from 2000 Form 990.
General

100,000	Saginaw County Parks and Recreation Commission, Saginaw, MI
95,100	City of Saginaw School District, Saginaw, MI
75,000	Boys & Girls Club, Saginaw, MI
50,000	City Rescue Mission, Saginaw, MI
50,000	Saginaw Community Foundation, Saginaw, MI
40,000	Opportunities Industrialization, Saginaw, MI
30,000	Healthy Delivery Inc., Saginaw, MI
25,000	Neighborhood Renewal Services, Saginaw, MI
25,000	Neighborhood Renewal Services of Saginaw, Saginaw, MI
25,000	Saginaw Valley State University, University Center, MI

MERVIN BOVAIRD FOUNDATION

Giving Contact

R. Casey Cooper, President & Trustee
401 S. Boston, Suite 3300
Tulsa, OK 74103-4070
Phone: (918)592-3300

Description

Founded: 1955
EIN: 736102163
Organization Type: General Purpose Foundation
Giving Locations: OK: Tulsa metropolitan area
Grant Types: Capital, Challenge, Conference/Seminar, General Support, Matching, Multiyear/Continuing Support, Operating Expenses, Project, Research, Scholarship.

Donor Information

Founder: Established in 1955 by the late Mabel W. Bovaird (1893-1979) to honor her deceased husband, Mervin Bovaird (1890-1949). The Bovairds were long-time residents of Tulsa, OK.

Financial Summary

Total Giving: $903,550 (2002); $1,787,776 (2001). Note: 1996 Giving includes scholarship ($402,000) and pledges ($915,000).
Giving Analysis: Giving for 2002 includes: foundation scholarships ($183,000); 2001: foundation grants to United Way ($15,000)
Assets: $37,755,733 (2002); $42,664,096 (2001)

Typical Recipients

Arts & Humanities: Art History, Arts Associations & Councils, Arts Institutes, Ballet, Dance, Libraries, Literary Arts, Museums/Galleries, Music, Opera, Public Broadcasting, Theater
Civic & Public Affairs: African American Affairs, Botanical Gardens/Parks, Community Foundations, Civic & Public Affairs-General, Legal Aid, Municipalities/Towns, Safety, Urban & Community Affairs, Women's Affairs, Zoos/Aquariums
Education: Business-School Partnerships, Colleges

& Universities, Community & Junior Colleges, Education Associations, Education Funds, Education Reform, Elementary Education (Private), Elementary Education (Public), Engineering/Technological Education, Education-General, Gifted & Talented Programs, Legal Education, Medical Education, Preschool Education, Private Education (Precollege), Social Sciences Education, Special Education, Student Aid
Environment: Environment-General, Resource Conservation
Health: Adolescent Health Issues, Alzheimer's Disease, Arthritis, Cancer, Children's Health/Hospitals, Clinics/Medical Centers, Diabetes, Emergency/Ambulance Services, Health Policy/Cost Containment, Health Organizations, Heart, Hospices, Hospitals, Kidney, Long-Term Care, Medical Rehabilitation, Medical Research, Mental Health, Multiple Sclerosis, Prenatal Health Issues, Preventive Medicine/Wellness Organizations, Single-Disease Health Associations, Speech & Hearing
Religion: Churches, Religion-General, Religious Welfare
Social Services: At-Risk Youth, Big Brothers/Big Sisters, Camps, Child Welfare, Community Service Organizations, Day Care, Domestic Violence, Emergency Relief, Family Planning, Family Services, Food/Clothing Distribution, Homes, People with Disabilities, Scouts, Senior Services, Sexual Abuse, Shelters/Homelessness, Social Services-General, Substance Abuse, United Funds/United Ways, Volunteer Services, YMCA/YWCA/YMHA/YWHA, Youth Organizations

Application Procedures

Initial Contact: General grant applicants should send a brief letter to the foundation.
Application Requirements: General grant proposals should include legal name and address of organization; name, title, address, and phone number of primary contact; a description of organization, including summary of its background and qualifications in funding area sought; description of project, its expected achievements, and its importance; descriptions of people, organizations, or groups expected to benefit from project and ways they would benefit; detailed expenditure budget for project, indicating how major elements of expense were estimated, how requested funds are to be spent, and during what periods; description of other possible sources of support, including funds received or pledged; and grant amount sought.
In an appendix, also include photocopies of most recent IRS Section 501(c)(3) and 509(a) rulings; statement signed by CEO that organization's purpose, character, or operations have not changed since IRS's determination; most recently audited completed fiscal year, or most recent IRS Form 990; interim financial statement for current fiscal period; and list of names and primary professional affiliations of governing body, and names and titles of officers.
Deadlines: The general application deadline is November 15, and the scholarship application deadline is in May.
Review Process: Scholarship recipients are chosen by the schools, based on need and ability. The foundation is governed by trustees, presently five, who meet periodically to consider requests for gifts. The bulk of applications will be acted on by the trustees on or about December 1 each year. When an application has been acted on by the trustees, it will be accepted or rejected in writing with a determination being sent to the applicant's mailing address.

Restrictions

Grants are restricted to the metropolitan Tulsa, OK, area. The foundation does not make loans. The foundation makes grants only to nonprofit, tax-exempt organizations in existence at least three years, and occasionally to local government. As a general rule, the foundation does not contribute to any organization

whose administrative expense, including fund-raising expense, exceeds 25% of its annual budget.
Scholarship support for Tulsa, OK, high school and Tulsa Community College graduates attending University of Tulsa is based on a student's ability to maintain proper scholastic standing. Scholarships are for undergraduate study only and are limited to $6,000 each per academic year.

Additional Information

Publications: Policies and Procedures

Foundation Officials

Wanda W. Brown: secretary
Richard Casey Cooper: president, trustee B Tulsa, OK 1942. ED University of Tulsa BSBA (1965); University of Tulsa JD (1967). PRIM CORP EMPL managing partner: Boesche McDermott & Eskridge. NONPR AFFIL member: Tulsa County Bar Association; trustee: Tulsa Philharmonic Orchestra; trustee: Philbrook Art Museum; member: American Bar Association; member: Oklahoma Bar Association. CLUB AFFIL Southern Hills Country Club.
T. Hillis Eskridge: trustee, assistant to president
David B. McKinney: vice president, treasurer, trustee B Tulsa, OK 1951. ED Rice University BA (1974); Columbia University JD (1975). PRIM CORP EMPL partner: Boesche McDermott & Eskridge. NONPR AFFIL member, founder: Tulsa Health Care Attorneys; member: Tulsa Pension Attorneys; member: National Health Lawyers Association; trustee: Metropolitan Christian Academy; member: National Association College & University Attorneys.
Lance Stockwell: trustee
Thomas H. Trower: trustee

Grants Analysis

Disclosure Period: calendar year ending 2002
Total Grants: $720,550*
Number of Grants: 48
Average Grant: $14,001*
Highest Grant: $62,500
Lowest Grant: $500
Typical Range: $5,000 to $30,000
*Note: Giving excludes scholarships. Average grant figure excludes highest grant.

Recent Grants

Note: Grants derived from 2002 Form 990.
General

62,500	Town & Country School, Tulsa, OK -- towards property acquisition
56,900	Bacone College, Muskogee, OK
55,000	Tulsa Opera Inc., Tulsa, OK
50,000	American Lung Association, Tulsa, OK
50,000	Center for Physically Limited, Tulsa, OK
50,000	Family & Children's Services, Tulsa, OK
50,000	Tulsa Philharmonic Society, Tulsa, OK -- towards public concert
50,000	Tulsa Ronald McDonald House, Tulsa, OK
25,000	Barthelmes Conservatory, Tulsa, OK
24,600	Salvation Army, Tulsa, OK -- towards benefit dinner

BOWATER INC.

Company Headquarters

55 East Camperdown Way
Greenville, SC 29601
Phone: (864)271-7733
Fax: (864)282-9482
Web: http://www.bowater.com

Company Description

Ticker: BOW
Exchange: NYSE
Revenue: US$2.449 billion (2001)

Employees: 8200 (2003)
SIC(s): 2421 Sawmills & Planing Mills--General, 2611 Pulp Mills, 2621 Paper Mills, 2672 Coated & Laminated Paper Nec.

Operating Locations
Bowater Inc. (AL--Albertville; IL--Moline; ME--Millinocket; SC--Catawba; TN--Calhoun)
Note: Also operates in Halifax, Nova Scotia, Canada.

Nonmonetary Support
Type: Donated Products

Giving Contact
Gordon Manuel, Director, Government Affairs
55 East Camperdown Way
Greenville, SC 29601-3597
Phone: (864)271-7733
Fax: (864)282-9594

Description
Organization Type: Corporate Giving Program
Giving Locations: headquarters and operating communities.
Grant Types: Capital, Employee Matching Gifts, General Support.
Note: Employee matching gift ratio: 1 to 1.

Financial Summary
Total Giving: $1,000,000 (2005 approx); $1,000,000 (2004); $1,000,000 (2003 approx). Note: Contributes through corporate direct giving program only.
Assets: $5,000,000,000 (2002)

Typical Recipients
Arts & Humanities: Arts Associations & Councils, Arts Centers, Community Arts, Libraries, Music, Performing Arts, Public Broadcasting
Civic & Public Affairs: Economic Development, Urban & Community Affairs
Education: Business Education, Colleges & Universities, Community & Junior Colleges, Continuing Education, Economic Education, Engineering/Technological Education, Minority Education
Environment: Environment-General
Health: Health Organizations, Hospitals
Social Services: United Funds/United Ways, Youth Organizations

Application Procedures
Initial Contact: letter of inquiry
Application Requirements: a description of organization, amount requested, purpose of funds sought, recently audited financial statement, and IRS tax-determination letter
Deadlines: for small grants, None; for larger grants, July 31.
Evaluative Criteria: requires that the organization requesting funds truly needs the money; that the donation ultimately benefits the company, a significant number of employees, or the operating community; that the contribution must meet the standards of the community and be an appropriate amount; and, whenever possible, donations should be backed by appropriate community participation

Restrictions
Does not support individuals, religious organizations for sectarian purposes, or political or lobbying groups. If the organization requesting a donation is supported by a united fund or if an agency which the contributions committee believes should be a member of a united fund, company will not make a donation.

Additional Information
Each company division has its own contributions budget, with varying application procedures.
Publications: Bowater Incorporated Criteria for Corporate Giving

Corporate Officials
David G. Maffucci: executive vice president, chief financial officero B Stamford, CT 1950. ED Sacred Heart University BA (1972). PRIM CORP EMPL executive vice president, chief financial officer: Bowater Inc. NONPR AFFIL member: Financial Executives Institute; member: National Association Accountants; member: American Institute CPAs.
Arnold M. Nemirow: chairman, president, chief executive officer B March 25, 1943. ED Harvard University AB (1966); University of Michigan JD (1969). PRIM CORP EMPL chairman, president, chief executive officer: Bowater Inc.

Giving Program Officials
Deborah L. Humphrey: director PRIM CORP EMPL director corporate relations: Bowater Inc.

Grants Analysis
Typical Range: $250 to $1,000

ETHEL N. BOWEN FOUNDATION

Giving Contact
R. W. Wilkinson, President
c/o First Century Bank
500 Federal St.
Bluefield, WV 24701
Phone: (304)325-8181

Description
Founded: 1968
EIN: 237010740
Organization Type: Private Foundation
Giving Locations: VA: Southwestern Virginia; WV: Southern West Virginia
Grant Types: General Support, Scholarship.

Donor Information
Founder: the late Ethel N. Bowen

Financial Summary
Total Giving: $475,076 (2003)
Giving Analysis: Giving for 2003 includes: foundation grants to United Way ($2,500); foundation scholarships ($250,553).
Assets: $10,648,597 (2003)
Gifts Received: $20,000 (2000)

Typical Recipients
Arts & Humanities: Arts Associations & Councils, Arts Centers, Film & Video, Historic Preservation, History & Archaeology, Libraries, Music
Civic & Public Affairs: Business/Free Enterprise, Clubs, Community Foundations, Economic Policy, Civic & Public Affairs-General, Law & Justice, Municipalities/Towns, Parades/Festivals, Public Policy, Urban & Community Affairs
Education: Business Education, Colleges & Universities, Community & Junior Colleges, Education Funds, Elementary Education (Private), Elementary Education (Public), Education-General, International Studies, Legal Education, Literacy, Medical Education, Private Education (Precollege), Public Education (Precollege), Religious Education, Science/Mathematics Education, Secondary Education (Private), Secondary Education (Public), Social Sciences Education, Student Aid
Health: Cancer, Children's Health/Hospitals, Emergency/Ambulance Services, Home-Care Services, Prenatal Health Issues, Public Health
Religion: Bible Study/Translation, Churches, Religious Organizations, Religious Welfare
Science: Science-General, Scientific Centers & Institutes
Social Services: Animal Protection, Camps, Child

Welfare, Community Centers, Counseling, Crime Prevention, Homes, Recreation & Athletics, Scouts, Shelters/Homelessness, Social Services-General, United Funds/United Ways, YMCA/YWCA/YMHA/YWHA, Youth Organizations

Application Procedures
Initial Contact: The foundation has no formal grant application procedure or application form. Students must submit transcripts.
Deadlines: prior to beginning of academic year.

Additional Information
Provides scholarships for higher education to residents of southern WV and southwestern VA.
Trust(s): First Century Bank

Foundation Officials
Henry Bowen: director
Basil L. Jackson, Jr.: vice president B Portsmouth, VA 1924. ED Virginia Polytechnic Institute & State University (1950); University of Wisconsin (1961). PRIM CORP EMPL chairman: First National Bank of Bluefield. CORP AFFIL director: Flat Top Insurance Agency; chairman: Pocahontas Bankshares Corp.; director: Bluefield Area Development Corp.
Byron K. Satterfield: treasurer PRIM CORP EMPL executive vice president, trust officer, director: First Century Bank NA.
Frank W. Wilkinson: secretary
Richard W. Wilkinson: president B Welch, WV 1932. ED University of Virginia (1955-1962); University of Virginia JD (1962). PRIM CORP EMPL president, chief executive officer, director: First Century Bank NA. CORP AFFIL president, director: Pocahontas Bankshares.

Grants Analysis
Disclosure Period: calendar year ending 2003
Total Grants: $122,023*
Number of Grants: 67
Average Grant: $1,470*
Highest Grant: $25,000
Lowest Grant: $100
Typical Range: $500 to $3,000
*Note: Giving excludes United Way; scholarship. Average grant figure excludes highest grant.

Recent Grants
Note: Grants derived from 2003 Form 990.
General

25,000	Virginia Athletic Foundation Inc.
10,000	City of Bluefield, Bluefield, WV
10,000	Science Center of West Virginia, Bluefield, WV
10,000	Virginia Athletic Foundation
5,000	Elizabeth Bowen Jones Memorial United Methodist Church
5,000	Mercer County Board of Education, Princeton, WV
5,000	University of Virginia Law School Foundation, Charlottesville, VA
3,800	Bluefield High School, Bluefield, WV
3,000	Bluefield State College Foundation, Bluefield, WV
3,000	East River Soccer Association

WAYNE AND IDA BOWMAN FOUNDATION

Giving Contact
Donald W. Bowman, President & Director
PO Box 24540
St. Simons Island, GA 31522
Phone: (912)638-8670

Description

Founded: 1995
EIN: 621600157
Organization Type: Private Foundation
Grant Types: General Support, Scholarship.

Financial Summary

Total Giving: $115,450 (fiscal year ending September 30, 2004); $146,518 (fiscal 2001)
Giving Analysis: Giving for fiscal 2004 includes: foundation scholarships ($46,000) fiscal 2001: foundation scholarships ($74,000)
Assets: $520,562 (fiscal 2004); $902,827 (fiscal 2001)
Gifts Received: $1,014,391 (fiscal 1996). Note: In fiscal 1996, contributions were received from the Wayne L. Bowman Residuary Trust ($534,634) and the estate of Ida S. Bowman ($479,757).

Typical Recipients

Arts & Humanities: Arts Associations & Councils, Libraries
Civic & Public Affairs: Civic & Public Affairs-General
Education: Arts/Humanities Education, Colleges & Universities, Student Aid
Health: AIDS/HIV
International: Missionary/Religious Activities
Religion: Bible Study/Translation, Churches, Religion-General, Religious Welfare
Social Services: Animal Protection

Application Procedures

Initial Contact: Contact foundation for application instructions.
Deadlines: None.

Foundation Officials

David S. Bowman: director
Donald W. Bowman: president, director
Mayne J. Bowman: vice president
William H. Bowman: secretary, director

Grants Analysis

Disclosure Period: fiscal year ending September 30, 2004
Total Grants: $69,450*
Number of Grants: 10
Average Grant: $5,494*
Highest Grant: $20,000
Lowest Grant: $1,000
Typical Range: $2,000 to $10,000
***Note:** Giving excludes scholarships. Average grant figure excludes highest grant.

Recent Grants

Note: Grants derived from fiscal 2004 Form 990.
General

20,450	Georgia, Florida, Oregon & Oklahoma Department of Corrections -- for libraries
20,000	Montgomery AIDS Outreach Inc., Montgomery, AL
16,000	University of North Carolina at Chapel Hill, Chapel Hill, NC -- for scholarships
13,000	Berea College, Berea, KY -- for scholarships
10,000	Ankerberg Theological Research Institute, Chattanooga, TN
6,000	Brushy Fork Institution, Berea, KY -- for scholarship
5,000	All Saints Episcopal Church, Montgomery, AL
5,000	Bryan College, Dayton, TN -- for scholarships
5,000	Lindsey Wilson College, Berea, KY -- for educational program
3,000	Elmore County Humane Society, Montgomery, AL

J. BOWMAN PROPER CHARITABLE TRUST

Giving Contact

Stephen P. Kosak, Consultant
PO Box 374
Oil City, PA 16301
Phone: (814)677-5085

Description

Founded: 1993
EIN: 251670828
Organization Type: Private Foundation
Giving Locations: PA
Grant Types: General Support, Scholarship.

Financial Summary

Total Giving: $108,995 (fiscal year ending September 30, 2004); $141,523 (fiscal 2001)
Giving Analysis: Giving for fiscal 2001 includes: foundation scholarships ($15,000)
Assets: $2,274,309 (fiscal 2004); $2,347,471 (fiscal 2001)

Typical Recipients

Arts & Humanities: Historic Preservation, History & Archaeology, Libraries
Civic & Public Affairs: Community Foundations, Civic & Public Affairs-General, Municipalities/Towns, Safety, Urban & Community Affairs
Education: Agricultural Education, Public Education (Precollege), Student Aid
Health: Emergency/Ambulance Services, Hospitals, Public Health
Religion: Churches, Ministries, Religious Welfare
Social Services: Child Welfare, Community Centers, Community Service Organizations, Family Services, Recreation & Athletics, Substance Abuse, Veterans, YMCA/YWCA/YMHA/YWHA, Youth Organizations

Application Procedures

Initial Contact: Request application guidelines with a letter explaining purpose of funds sought, amount requested, and when the funds are needed.
Deadlines: April 30.

Additional Information

Publications: Application Guidelines
Trust(s): National City Bank PA

Foundation Officials

Stephen P. Kosak: consultant

Grants Analysis

Disclosure Period: fiscal year ending September 30, 2004
Total Grants: $108,995
Number of Grants: 16
Average Grant: $5,166*
Highest Grant: $31,508
Lowest Grant: $450
Typical Range: $1,000 to $10,000
***Note:** Average grant figure excludes highest grant.

Recent Grants

Note: Grants derived from fiscal 2004 Form 990.
General

31,508	Tionesta Fire Department, Tionesta, PA
13,700	Venango Area Community Foundation, Oil City, PA
13,000	Focus on Forest's Future, Tionesta, PA
10,000	Tionesta Borough, Tionesta, PA -- funds for computer software
7,790	Tionesta Borough, Tionesta, PA -- for vine street water project
6,500	Titusville Area Hospital, Titusville, PA
5,000	Jefferson DeFrees Family Center, Warren, PA
4,438	Forest County Historical Society, Tionesta, PA
3,852	Tionesta Borough, Tionesta, PA -- funds for may river streets water project
3,000	West Forest Area Youth Sports Association, Tionesta, PA

ROBERT BOWNE FOUNDATION

Giving Contact

Lena Townsend, Executive Director
345 Hudson St.
New York, NY 10014
Phone: (212)924-5500
Fax: (212)229-3400
E-mail: ltownsend@robertbownefoundation.org
Web: http://www.robertbownefoundation.org/index.phpl

Description

Founded: 1968
EIN: 132620393
Organization Type: Private Foundation
Giving Locations: NY: Manhattan Boroughs outside of Manhattan, New York
Grant Types: General Support, Multiyear/Continuing Support, Operating Expenses, Project, Seed Money.

Donor Information

Founder: Edmund A. Stanley, Jr., members of the Stanley family

Financial Summary

Total Giving: $1,311,475 (2003); $1,300,850 (2001)
Assets: $16,771,431 (2003); $18,608,408 (2001)
Gifts Received: $100,000 (2003); $100,000 (2001); $100,000 (2000). Note: Contributions were received from Thomas O. Stanley and Bowne of New York City, Inc.

Typical Recipients

Arts & Humanities: Art History, Arts Centers, Arts & Humanities-General, History & Archaeology, Libraries, Museums/Galleries
Civic & Public Affairs: Economic Development, Employment/Job Training, Civic & Public Affairs-General, Hispanic Affairs, Housing, Nonprofit Management, Urban & Community Affairs, Women's Affairs
Education: Afterschool/Enrichment Programs, Arts/Humanities Education, Education Reform, Leadership Training, Literacy, Science/Mathematics Education, Special Education, Vocational & Technical Education
Health: Clinics/Medical Centers
Religion: Churches, Religious Welfare
Social Services: At-Risk Youth, Child Welfare, Community Centers, Community Service Organizations, Family Services, Recreation & Athletics, Refugee Assistance, Shelters/Homelessness, YMCA/YWCA/YMHA/YWHA, Youth Organizations

Application Procedures

Initial Contact: Initial request should be a letter outlining the project.
Deadlines: None.
Decision Notification: The foundation usually responds to requests within four weeks.

Restrictions

Focus is specifically on innovation in both new and existing youth programs that are willing to take risks and that aspire to make literacy education an integral part of their work. Does not support religious organizations, primary or secondary schools, colleges or universities, except when some aspect of their work is an integral part of a program supported by the foundation. Also does not support individuals, capital campaigns, or endowments.

Additional Information

Publications: Informational Brochure

Foundation Officials

Suzanne C. Carothers: vice president

Dianne Kangisser: trustee

Edmund Allport Stanley, Jr.: trustee B New York, NY 1924. ED Princeton University AB (1949). PRIM CORP EMPL chairman executive committee: Bowne & Co. Inc. CLUB AFFIL Bond New York Club; Pilgrims Club.

Jennifer Stanley: chairman, president, trustee

Franz von Ziegesar: trustee B Sao Paulo, SP Brazil 1924. ED Yale University BA (1948). PRIM CORP EMPL chairman, chief executive officer, director: Bowne & Co. Inc. CORP AFFIL director: Southeastern Industries; director: Zarn Inc.

Grants Analysis

Disclosure Period: calendar year ending 2003

Total Grants: $1,311,475

Number of Grants: 55

Average Grant: $23,845

Highest Grant: $50,000

Lowest Grant: $5,000

Typical Range: $10,000 to $50,000

Recent Grants

Note: Grants derived from 2001 Form 990.

General

70,000	Innovation Network, Inc, Washington, DC
70,000	St. Nicholas Neighborhood Preservation Corporation, Brooklyn, NY
50,000	Interfaith Neighbors, New York, NY
35,000	Concourse House Housing Development Fund Company, Inc., Bronx, NY
35,000	Jamaica Center For Art's & Learning, Inc., Jamaica, NY
34,000	Hartley House, New York, NY
33,500	Mary Mitchell Family and Youth Center, Bronx, NY
30,000	Brooklyn Bureau of Community Service, Brooklyn, NY
30,000	Catholic Charities
30,000	Crenulated Company, LTD, Bronx, NY

BOWSHER-BOOHER FOUNDATION

Giving Contact

Tom Lower, Trust Officer
c/o Wells Fargo Bank of Indiana NA
112 W. Jefferson Blvd.
South Bend, IN 46601
Phone: (219)237-3340
Fax: (219)237-3317

Description

Founded: 1980

EIN: 310979401

Organization Type: Private Foundation

Giving Locations: IN: St. Joseph County, South Bend

Grant Types: General Support.

Financial Summary

Total Giving: $95,000 (fiscal year ending May 31, 2004); $70,600 (fiscal 2002); $87,900 (fiscal 2001)

Assets: $1,958,686 (fiscal 2004); $2,043,627 (fiscal 2002); $2,332,061 (fiscal 2001)

Typical Recipients

Arts & Humanities: Dance, Historic Preservation, History & Archaeology, Libraries

Civic & Public Affairs: African American Affairs, Chambers of Commerce, Clubs, Community Foundations, Civic & Public Affairs-General, Hispanic Affairs,

Housing, Legal Aid, Minority Business, Urban & Community Affairs, Women's Affairs

Education: Afterschool/Enrichment Programs, Colleges & Universities, Education Funds, Literacy, Preschool Education, Science/Mathematics Education, Student Aid

Environment: Environment-General

Health: AIDS/HIV, Health Organizations, Prenatal Health Issues

Religion: Ministries, Religious Organizations, Religious Welfare

Social Services: Big Brothers/Big Sisters, Camps, Child Welfare, Community Centers, Community Service Organizations, Family Services, People with Disabilities, Scouts, Shelters/Homelessness, United Funds/United Ways, YMCA/YWCA/YMHA/YWHA, Youth Organizations

Application Procedures

Initial Contact: The foundation requests applications be made in writing.

Application Requirements: Include a description of organization, amount requested, purpose of funds sought, recently audited financial statement, and proof of tax-exempt status.

Deadlines: April 1 and October 1.

Additional Information

Trust(s): Wells Fargo Bank IN NA

Grants Analysis

Disclosure Period: fiscal year ending May 31, 2004

Total Grants: $95,000

Number of Grants: 2

Highest Grant: $65,000

Lowest Grant: $30,000

Recent Grants

Note: Grants derived from 2004 Form 990.

General

65,000	Open Door Preschool, Augusta, GA
30,000	Community Foundation of St. Joseph County, South Bend, IN

DONALD C. BRACE FOUNDATION

Giving Contact

Robert A. Beer, Trustee
c/o Cummings & Lockwood
PO Box 120
Stamford, CT 06904-0120
Phone: (203)351-4294

Description

Founded: 1987

EIN: 133442680

Organization Type: Private Foundation

Giving Locations: Northeast region of US.

Grant Types: General Support.

Donor Information

Founder: Donna Brace Ogilvie

Financial Summary

Total Giving: $717,450 (2004); $542,500 (2002); $728,500 (2001)

Assets: $6,882,834 (2004); $6,451,278 (2002); $8,938,347 (2001)

Gifts Received: $218,997 (2000); $512,000 (1993).

Note: In 1993 and 2000, contributions were received from Donna Brace Ogilvie.

Typical Recipients

Arts & Humanities: Arts Associations & Councils, Arts Centers, Arts Institutes, History & Archaeology, Libraries, Literary Arts, Museums/Galleries, Music,

Theater

Civic & Public Affairs: Employment/Job Training, Civic & Public Affairs-General

Education: Arts/Humanities Education, Colleges & Universities, Literacy, Private Education (Precollege)

Environment: Environment-General, Protection

Health: Geriatric Health, Health Organizations, Hospices, Hospitals, Medical Research, Multiple Sclerosis

Social Services: Community Centers, Community Service Organizations, Food/Clothing Distribution, People with Disabilities, Senior Services, YMCA/YWCA/YMHA/YWHA, Youth Organizations

Application Procedures

Initial Contact: Send brief letter describing program.

Deadlines: None.

Foundation Officials

Robert A. Beer: trustee

Katharine Butler: trustee B Chicago Heights, IL 1925. ED Western Michigan University BA (1950); Western Michigan University MA (1953); Western Michigan University EdS (1961); Michigan State University PhD (1967). PRIM CORP EMPL professor research, director speech & hearing center: San Jose State University PRIM NONPR EMPL professor research, director: Western Michigan University. CORP AFFIL consult: Virginia Hosp. NONPR AFFIL member: New York Saint Speech Language Hearing Association; researchprofessor, director: Syracuse University Center Language Research; member, treasurer: International Association Applied Psycholinguistics; member: International Association Logopedics & Phonetics; member: Higher Education Consortium Special Education; fellow: International Academy Research Learning Disabilities; director: HEW Office Education; member: California Speech & Hearing Association; member: Council Exceptional Children; director: Bur Education Handicapped; member: California Association Prof Special Education; member: American Psychological Association; fellow, trustee: American Speech Language Hearing Association.

John Brace Latham: trustee

Donna Brace Ogilvie: trustee

Karen Scheid: trustee

Grants Analysis

Disclosure Period: calendar year ending 2004

Total Grants: $717,450

Number of Grants: 12

Average Grant: $10,929*

Highest Grant: $150,000

Lowest Grant: $5,000

Typical Range: $5,000 to $20,000

*Note: Average grant figure excludes five highest grants ($640,950).

Recent Grants

Note: Grants derived from 2001 Form 990.

General

150,000	Girls, Inc., Bloomington, IN -- endowment
150,000	Phillips Academy, Andover, MA -- Richard L. Gelb Science Center
150,000	Phillips Academy, Andover, MA -- Richard L. Gelb Science Center
150,000	Stamford Health Foundation, Inc, Stamford, CT -- Brace Community Conference Center
75,000	Stamford Health Foundation, Inc, Stamford, CT -- Brace Community Conference Center
25,000	Friends of the Teton River -- projects to improve the condition of Teton River
15,000	Westhampton Cultural Consortium, Inc., Westhampton Beach, NY -- concerts on the Village Green in Westhampton Beach
10,000	Stamford Land Conservation Trust, Stamford, CT -- purchase of "Treetops"

2,500   Stamford Center for the Arts, Stamford, CT -- Reach Out and Arts in Education Program

1,000   Meals on Wheels, Stamford, CT -- meals for the homebound

HELEN BRACH FOUNDATION

Giving Contact

John Hagnell
55 W. Wacker Dr., Suite 701
Chicago, IL 60601
Phone: (312)372-4417
Fax: (312)372-0290
Note: Foundation accepts faxed requests.

Description

Founded: 1974
EIN: 237376427
Organization Type: General Purpose Foundation
Giving Locations: IL: nationally.
Grant Types: Conference/Seminar, Department, General Support, Operating Expenses, Project, Scholarship.

Donor Information

Founder: Incorporated in 1974 in Chicago, IL. Helen V. Brach was the wife of Frank Brach, owner of the E.J. Brach and Sons Candy Company in Chicago. Frank Brach's father founded the company, which in 1966 was sold upon Frank's retirement. After his death in 1970, Helen Brach became heir to the family fortune.

In February 1977, Helen Brach disappeared without a trace. Seven years later, she was declared legally dead, with her death presumed to have occurred in 1977. As the foundation was the primary beneficiary under her will, it received a significant bequest from her estate when she was declared deceased. Charles M. Vorhees (Helen Brach's brother) was an original member and director of the foundation, and remains on the board of directors.

Financial Summary

Total Giving: $4,114,545 (fiscal year ending March 31, 2004); $5,461,000 (fiscal 2002)
Giving Analysis: Giving for fiscal 2004 includes: foundation grants to United Way ($15,000)
Assets: $105,239,605 (fiscal 2004)
Gifts Received: $95,636 (fiscal 1999). Note: In fiscal 1999, contributions were received from the estate of Helen V. Brach.

Typical Recipients

Arts & Humanities: Arts Centers, Arts Institutes, Community Arts, Dance, Arts & Humanities-General, Historic Preservation, Libraries, Museums/Galleries, Music, Performing Arts, Theater

Civic & Public Affairs: Community Foundations, Economic Development, Employment/Job Training, Civic & Public Affairs-General, Hispanic Affairs, Housing, Inner-City Development, Philanthropic Organizations, Public Policy, Urban & Community Affairs, Women's Affairs, Zoos/Aquariums

Education: Afterschool/Enrichment Programs, Arts/Humanities Education, Business Education, Colleges & Universities, Community & Junior Colleges, Continuing Education, Education Associations, Education Funds, Elementary Education (Private), Education-General, Legal Education, Minority Education, Preschool Education, Private Education (Precollege), Public Education (Precollege), Religious Education, Science/Mathematics Education, Secondary Education (Private), Special Education, Student Aid, Vocational & Technical Education

Environment: Environment-General, Protection, Research, Wildlife Protection

Health: AIDS/HIV, Children's Health/Hospitals, Clinics/Medical Centers, Diabetes, Health-General, Geriatric Health, Health Funds, Health Organizations, Hospices, Hospitals, Long-Term Care, Medical Rehabilitation, Medical Research, Mental Health, Nursing Services, Nutrition, Preventive Medicine/Wellness Organizations, Public Health, Trauma Treatment

International: International Environmental Issues, Missionary/Religious Activities, Trade

Religion: Churches, Dioceses, Ministries, Missionary Activities (Domestic), Religious Organizations, Religious Welfare

Science: Science Museums, Scientific Research

Social Services: Animal Protection, At-Risk Youth, Child Welfare, Community Centers, Community Service Organizations, Counseling, Family Services, Food/Clothing Distribution, People with Disabilities, Recreation & Athletics, Senior Services, Shelters/Homelessness, Volunteer Services, Youth Organizations

Application Procedures

Initial Contact: Applicants should contact the foundation by letter for application form and a report on the foundation.
Application Requirements: The foundation requires seven copies of the completed application form, together with one copy of the following: a cover letter containing a brief summary of the background and purposes of the prospective grantee and the particular project or activity for which funds are requested; a list of the members of the governing board of the requesting organization; evidence of the approval for the submission of the request from the chief executive officer or other authorized individual; a copy of the organization's most recent audited financial statement; and IRS determination of tax exempt status under 501(c)(3) of the Internal Revenue Code.
Deadlines: December 31 for consideration by March 31. To receive optimum consideration, proposals should be received by the foundation in completed form several months before the end of the year and precede a December board meeting.
Review Process: The board follows a schedule of regular quarterly meetings to consider grant applications and to review the progress of currently funded projects. Final consideration is given to all applications received in any year at the board's first meeting the following year, which is usually in March. At the foundation's discretion, a site visit or interview may be scheduled as part of the review process. All eligible requests will be acknowledged.

Restrictions

Except for well-established organizations which the foundation has supported in the past, the board prefers to consider relatively smaller grants and to distribute them among a number of applicants.

The foundation does not make grants to individuals, political campaigns or lobbying groups, or governmental bodies or tax-supported institutions. Grants are not made in excess of 10% of a group's operating budget.

The foundation usually does not make multiyear grants or commitments. Except where the foundation has made an express commitment for successive years' funding, a grant made in one year in no way implies the recipient will receive priority for funding in future years. The foundation does not give internationally.

Additional Information

Publications: Biennial Report; Guidelines; Application Form

Foundation Officials

James John O'Connor: director B Chicago, IL 1937. ED College of the Holy Cross BS (1958); Harvard University MBA (1960); Georgetown University JD (1963). PRIM CORP EMPL chairman, chief executive officer, director: Unicom Corp. CORP AFFIL director: Tribune Co.; director: UAL Corp.; director: Smurfit-Stone Container Corp.; director: Corning Inc.; director: First National Bank Chicago; director: America National Canada Co.; chairman: Advanced Reactor Corp. NONPR AFFIL trustee: Museum Science & Industry; trustee: Northwestern University; director: Lyric Opera Chicago; member: Illinois Bar Association; member: Illinois Business Roundtable; member: Hundred Club Cook County; director: Chicago Urban League; member: Chicagoland Chamber of Commerce; member: Chicago Symphony Orchestra; director: Chicago Board Trade; member: Chicago Convention & Tourism Bureau; member: Chicago Bar Association; member executive board: Boy Scouts America Chicago Area Council; member: Business Council; trustee: Adler Planetarium. CLUB AFFIL member: Hundred Cook County Club.
Toni Perille: associate director
John J. Sheridan: director
R. Matthew Simon: vice chairman, director
Raymond F. Simon: president, director
Charles A. Vorhees: director

Grants Analysis

Disclosure Period: fiscal year ending March 31, 2004
Total Grants: $4,101,545*
Number of Grants: 465 (approx)
Average Grant: $8,821
Highest Grant: $100,000
Lowest Grant: $100
Typical Range: $1,000 to $10,000
***Note:** Giving excludes United Way.

Recent Grants

Note: Grants derived from 2003 Form 990.
General

150,000   Loyola University of Chicago, Chicago, IL -- to help underwrite the cost of constructing a new life science education & research building

100,000   Big Shoulders Fund, Chicago, IL -- operating funds for inner-city schools to adapt buildings for computers, buy books, enhance programs & improve facilities

100,000   Misericordia , Chicago, IL -- to help fund a 125 bed skilled nursing facility to serve the medically fragile children and adults

78,000   Wild Animal Orphanage, San Antonio, TX -- to educate people about the plight of surplus animals

75,000   Big Shoulders, Chicago, IL

50,000   Catholic Charities of Chicago, Chicago, IL -- funding to support medical needs of residents of the maternity and adoption department

50,000   Catholic Extension Society, Chicago, IL -- helping to provide mobile hospital for poor people of Chicago area

50,000   Council of Medical Specialty Societies, Lake Bluff, IL -- funding to find the stress level of doctors

50,000   Food Animal Concerns Trust, Chicago, IL -- funding to support for farming research

50,000   Friends of Animals, Inc., Darien, CT -- research grant to support of continuing field study of Alaskan wolves

GEORGE W. BRACKENRIDGE FOUNDATION

Giving Contact

Gilbert M. Denman, Jr., Trustee
711 Navarro Street, Suite 535
San Antonio, TX 78205

Phone: (210)224-1011
Fax: (210)223-3657

Description
Founded: 1920
EIN: 746034977
Organization Type: General Purpose Foundation
Giving Locations: TX
Grant Types: Endowment, General Support, Project, Research, Scholarship.

Donor Information
Founder: Established in 1920 by the late George W. Brackenridge.

Financial Summary
Total Giving: $1,244,250 (2003); $1,184,882 (2001)
Giving Analysis: Giving for 2003 includes: foundation scholarships ($899,750); 2001: foundation grants to United Way ($154,000)
Assets: $24,532,840 (2003); $27,603,708 (2001)

Typical Recipients
Arts & Humanities: Arts Associations & Councils, Arts Institutes, Arts Outreach, Ballet, Ethnic & Folk Arts, Libraries, Museums/Galleries, Music, Performing Arts, Public Broadcasting
Civic & Public Affairs: Community Foundations, Nonprofit Management, Parades/Festivals, Philanthropic Organizations, Zoos/Aquariums
Education: Afterschool/Enrichment Programs, Arts/Humanities Education, Colleges & Universities, Education Funds, Elementary Education (Private), Engineering/Technological Education, Faculty Development, Education-General, Gifted & Talented Programs, Health & Physical Education, Leadership Training, Medical Education, Minority Education, Private Education (Precollege), Public Education (Precollege), Science/Mathematics Education, Social Sciences Education, Student Aid
Health: Clinics/Medical Centers, Hospitals (University Affiliated), Medical Training
Science: Scientific Research
Social Services: YMCA/YWCA/YMHA/YWHA, Youth Organizations

Application Procedures
Initial Contact: The foundation requests that the application be made in writing on the organization's letterhead and signed by a member of its board of directors or an officer of the organization.
Application Requirements: The application should contain specific information related to the desired use of the grant, a copy of the organization's charter and by-laws, and a copy of the organization's exemption letter from the IRS, including the most recent financial statement.
Deadlines: None.
Review Process: The board meets in March, June, September, and December.

Restrictions
The organization must be located in Texas and must be an accredited education organization, or the grant must support one or more accredited educational organizations. The foundation does not support individuals; provide general support, continuing support, seed money, or matching gifts; or fund emergency funds, operating budgets, annual campaigns, deficit financing, or land acquisition.

Foundation Officials
Leroy G. Denman, Jr.: trustee B San Antonio, TX 1918. ED University of Texas BA (1939); University of Texas LLB (1939). PRIM CORP EMPL attorney: Denman, Franklin & Denman. CORP AFFIL vice president, director: King Ranch Saddle Shop Inc.; vice president, director: Running W Saddle Shop; director: King Ranch Holdings Inc.
Emily D. Thuss: trustee

Grants Analysis
Disclosure Period: calendar year ending 2003
Total Grants: $344,500*
Number of Grants: 23
Average Grant: $20,265
Highest Grant: $30,000
Lowest Grant: $5,000
Typical Range: $10,000 to $30,000
***Note:** Giving excludes scholarships.

Recent Grants
Note: Grants derived from 2002 Form 990.
Library-Related

20,000	San Antonio Public Library, San Antonio, TX -- towards born to read program
10,000	Keystone School, San Antonio, TX -- towards library support program
10,000	St. Mary's Hall, San Antonio, TX -- towards library support program
10,000	San Antonio Academy, San Antonio, TX -- towards library support program

General

765,000	University of Texas, San Antonio, TX -- towards educational program - visiting professor program
130,000	Trinity University, San Antonio, TX -- towards scholarship and educational program
36,000	St. Mary's University, San Antonio, TX -- towards scholarship program
30,000	Arts San Antonio, San Antonio, TX -- towards educational program
30,000	San Antonio Independent School District, San Antonio, TX -- for educational program - field trips purpose
25,000	University of Texas Health Science Center, San Antonio, TX -- towards educational program - nursing program
20,000	KLRU - TV, Austin, TX -- towards educational program
20,000	San Antonio Museum of Art, San Antonio, TX -- towards educational program - Arts, field trips
17,500	San Antonio Zoological Society, San Antonio, TX -- towards educational program
15,000	Southwest School of Arts and Crafts, San Antonio, TX -- charitable purpose for educational program

GEORGE AND RUTH BRADFORD FOUNDATION

Giving Contact
Myrna Oglesby, Director
PO Box 720
Ukiah, CA 95482
Phone: (707)462-6694

Description
Founded: 1985
EIN: 943015722
Organization Type: Private Foundation
Giving Locations: CA: San Francisco Peninsula
Grant Types: General Support, Scholarship.

Donor Information
Founder: Ruth Bradford

Financial Summary
Total Giving: $112,500 (fiscal year ending June 30, 2004); $169,600 (fiscal 2001)
Assets: $2,573,733 (fiscal 2004); $2,515,972 (fiscal 2001)
Gifts Received: $500 (fiscal 2001); $250 (fiscal 2000); $250 (fiscal 1999)

Typical Recipients
Arts & Humanities: Libraries, Museums/Galleries, Music, Performing Arts, Public Broadcasting, Theater
Civic & Public Affairs: Botanical Gardens/Parks, Business/Free Enterprise, Community Foundations, Employment/Job Training, Civic & Public Affairs-General, Rural Affairs, Zoos/Aquariums
Education: Afterschool/Enrichment Programs, Agricultural Education, Business Education, Colleges & Universities, Education Associations, Education Reform, Elementary Education (Public), Engineering/Technological Education, Environmental Education, Education-General, Literacy, Religious Education, Secondary Education (Private), Secondary Education (Public), Special Education
Environment: Environment-General, Resource Conservation, Wildlife Protection
Health: Cancer, Children's Health/Hospitals, Clinics/Medical Centers, Diabetes, Hospices, Hospitals, Long-Term Care, Mental Health, Public Health
Religion: Religious Welfare
Science: Observatories & Planetariums, Science Museums, Scientific Centers & Institutes
Social Services: Big Brothers/Big Sisters, Child Welfare, Community Centers, Community Service Organizations, Counseling, Family Services, Food/Clothing Distribution, People with Disabilities, Scouts, Senior Services, Shelters/Homelessness, Social Services-General, Volunteer Services, YMCA/YWCA/YMHA/YWHA, Youth Organizations

Application Procedures
Initial Contact: Send a brief letter of inquiry.
Deadlines: None.

Restrictions
Does not support individuals.

Foundation Officials
Robert Bradford: director

Grants Analysis
Disclosure Period: fiscal year ending June 30, 2004
Total Grants: $112,500
Number of Grants: 35
Average Grant: $3,015*
Highest Grant: $10,000
Lowest Grant: $1,000
Typical Range: $1,000 to $5,000
***Note:** Average grant figure excludes highest grant.

Recent Grants
Note: Grants derived from fiscal 2004 Form 990.

General

10,000	Anderson Valley Unified School District, Boonville, CA -- towards arts and music
10,000	Castilleja School, Palo Alto, CA -- towards the school for the blind
6,000	Hospice of Ukiah, Ukiah, CA
5,000	Hidden Villa, Los Altos Hills, CA -- for leadership circle
5,000	Plowshares, Ukiah, CA -- for homeless shelter
5,000	Point Reyes Bird Observatory, Stinson Beach, CA -- for Farallones projects
5,000	Santa Rosa High School, Santa Rosa, CA -- for music program
5,000	Ukiah Valley Christmas Effort, Ukiah, CA -- for Christmas donations
5,000	University of California Davis College of Engineering, Davis, CA -- for R. Krone chair
4,000	Community Foundation of Mendocino County, Ukiah, CA -- towards aid for the needy

LYNDE AND HARRY BRADLEY FOUNDATION

Giving Contact
Michael W. Grebe, President, Chief Executive Officer & Director
Lynde and Harry Bradley Foundation
1241 N. Franklin Pl.
PO Box 510860
Milwaukee, WI 53202-2901
Phone: (414)291-9915
Fax: (414)291-9991
Web: http://www.bradleyfdn.org

Description
Founded: 1942
EIN: 396037928
Organization Type: General Purpose Foundation
Giving Locations: WI: nationally.
Grant Types: Capital, Conference/Seminar, Fellowship, General Support, Matching, Operating Expenses, Project, Research, Scholarship.

Donor Information
Founder: Incorporated as the Allen-Bradley Foundation in Wisconsin in 1942 and funded by contributions from Harry L. Bradley, Caroline D. Bradley, Margaret B. Bradley, the Margaret Loock Trust, and the Allen-Bradley Company. The Allen-Bradley Company, an electronics manufacturing firm, was sold to Rockwell International in 1985, after which the foundation acquired proceeds from that sale. The foundation adopted its present name in April 1985.

Financial Summary
Total Giving: $26,000,000 (2003 approx); $25,146,793 (2002); $35,304,281 (2001)
Assets: $532,048,536 (2002); $579,739,000 (2001)

Typical Recipients
Arts & Humanities: Arts Associations & Councils, Ballet, Dance, Film & Video, Historic Preservation, History & Archaeology, Museums/Galleries, Music, Opera, Performing Arts, Public Broadcasting, Theater, Visual Arts
Civic & Public Affairs: African American Affairs, Botanical Gardens/Parks, Business/Free Enterprise, Civil Rights, Community Foundations, Economic Development, Economic Policy, Employment/Job Training, Ethnic Organizations, Civic & Public Affairs-General, Hispanic Affairs, Law & Justice, Legal Aid, Nonprofit Management, Parades/Festivals, Philanthropic Organizations, Professional & Trade Associations, Public Policy, Safety
Education: Afterschool/Enrichment Programs, Arts/Humanities Education, Colleges & Universities, Continuing Education, Economic Education, Education Associations, Education Funds, Education Reform, Engineering/Technological Education, Faculty Development, Education-General, Gifted & Talented Programs, International Exchange, International Studies, Journalism/Media Education, Public Education (Precollege), School Volunteerism, Science/Mathematics Education, Secondary Education (Private), Secondary Education (Public), Social Sciences Education, Student Aid, Vocational & Technical Education
Environment: Environment-General
Health: Children's Health/Hospitals, Clinics/Medical Centers, Health Policy/Cost Containment, Hospitals, Transplant Networks/Donor Banks
International: Foreign Educational Institutions, Human Rights, International Affairs, International Development, International Peace & Security Issues, International Relations
Religion: Churches, Jewish Causes, Missionary Activities (Domestic), Religious Organizations, Religious Welfare, Social/Policy Issues
Science: Scientific Centers & Institutes
Social Services: Community Centers, Community Service Organizations, Crime Prevention, Family Services, People with Disabilities, Recreation & Athletics, Substance Abuse, Veterans, YMCA/YWCA/YMHA/YWHA, Youth Organizations

Application Procedures
Initial Contact: Applicants should write a brief letter of inquiry to the foundation describing the applicant's organization and intended project. If the foundation determines the project to be within its current program interests, the applicant will be invited to submit a formal proposal.
Application Requirements: The proposal should include a letter presenting a concise description of the project, its objectives and significance, and the qualifications of the organizations and individuals involved. Included with the letter should be a project budget, amount requested, other sources of support, a copy of the IRS determination letter 501(c)(3), and a completed Grantee Tax Exempt Status Information form included with the program guidelines.
Deadlines: Deadlines for full proposals are December 1, March 1, June 1, and September 1.
Review Process: The board meets in February, May or June, September, and November. If the foundation is interested in funding the project, the applicant will receive information regarding the foundation and its guidelines for proposals. Final notification arrives within three to five months.

Restrictions
No grants are made to individuals, organizations that do not have 501(c)(3) tax-exempt status, or strictly denominational organizations. Foundation favors projects not normally financed by public tax funds. Capital requests are considered, but foundation limits grants to a fraction of the total project cost.

Additional Information
The foundation conducts an annual evaluation of grants, and recipients are requested to provide periodic reports on the progress of their work.
Publications: Annual Report; Application Guidelines; Proposal Checklist

Foundation Officials
Reed Coleman: vice chairman, director CORP AFFIL director: PUENTE Learning Systems; chairman, chief executive officer: Madison-Kipp Corporate. NONPR AFFIL chairman: Sand County Foundation Inc.; director: Ten Chimneys Foundation; vice chairman: NCPCR; director: Institute for Education Advancement.
Terry Considine: director
Pierre S. DuPont, IV: director
Terri L. Famer: assistant secretary
Cynthia K. Friauf: vice president finance, treasurer, assistant secretary
Michael W. Grebe: president, chief executive officer, director B Peoria, IL 1940. ED United States Military Academy BS (1962); University of Michigan JD (1970). PRIM CORP EMPL partner: Foley & Lardner. CORP AFFIL director: Milwaukee Brewers Baseball Club; director: Oshkosh Truck Corporate; director: Church Mutual Insurance Co. NONPR AFFIL member: Philanthropy Roundtable; member: State Bar Wisconsin; member: Milwaukee Bar Association; Order Coif.
R. Michael Lempke: vice president inventor
Thomas L. Rhodes: chairman, director CORP AFFIL vice chairman: American Land Lease Inc.; president, director: National Review; director: AIMCO.
Daniel P. Schmidt: vice president program
Thomas L. Smallwood: secretary, director NONPR AFFIL trustee: Evan and Marion Helfaer Foundation; chairman council: Milwaukee Symphony Orchestra.
Brother Bob Smith: director NONPR AFFIL president: Messmer High School.
David V. Uihlein, Jr.: director PRIM CORP EMPL president: Uihlein Archts. CORP AFFIL president: Uihlein-Wilson Architects. NONPR AFFIL regent: Milwaukee School of Engineering.

Grants Analysis
Disclosure Period: calendar year ending 2002
Total Grants: $25,146,793
Number of Grants: 400 (approx)
Average Grant: $62,867
Highest Grant: $3,500,000
Typical Range: $20,000 to $200,000

Recent Grants
Note: Grants derived from 2002 Form 990.
General

2,000,000	Milwaukee School of Engineering, Milwaukee, WI -- to support the Rader School of Business
1,000,000	Milwaukee Art Museum Inc., Milwaukee, WI
500,000	Milwaukee Rescue Mission, Milwaukee, WI
297,800	American Enterprise Institute for Public Policy Research, Washington, DC -- to support the Charles Murray Fellowship, the Bradley Lecture Series, the Foreign and Defense policy studies program, and the new Atlantic initiative
250,000	WisconsinEye Public Affairs Network Inc., Madison, WI -- to support efforts to provide citizens with access to their government via technology
200,000	Wisconsin Policy Research Institute Inc., Mequon, WI
195,243	Princeton University, Princeton, NJ -- to support the James Madison Center
185,000	Brewers Charities, Milwaukee, WI -- to support the 2002 Student Achiever' program
182,500	Milwaukee Symphony Orchestra Inc., Milwaukee, WI
176,058	Milwaukee Symphony Orchestra Inc., Milwaukee, WI

BRADY FOUNDATION

Giving Contact
James C. Brady, President, Treasurer & Trustee
Brady Foundation
PO Box 351
Gladstone, NJ 07934
Phone: (908)439-9941

Description
Founded: 1953
EIN: 136167209
Organization Type: Private Foundation
Giving Locations: NJ
Grant Types: General Support.

Donor Information
Founder: the late Helen M. Cutting, Nicholas Brady

Financial Summary
Total Giving: $255,977 (2003)
Giving Analysis: Giving for 2003 includes: foundation grants to United Way ($2,000)
Assets: $7,393,539 (2003)
Gifts Received: $700 (2000); $500 (1999); $300 (1995)

Typical Recipients
Arts & Humanities: Arts Associations & Councils, Arts Funds, Arts Outreach, Ballet, Dance, Historic Preservation, Libraries, Literary Arts, Museums/Galleries, Music, Public Broadcasting
Civic & Public Affairs: Community Foundations, Civic & Public Affairs-General, Municipalities/Towns, Philanthropic Organizations, Safety, Urban & Community Affairs
Education: Arts/Humanities Education, Education-General, Gifted & Talented Programs, Medical Edu-

cation, Private Education (Precollege)

Environment: Air/Water Quality, Environment-General, Resource Conservation, Watershed, Wildlife Protection

Health: Alzheimer's Disease, Cancer, Children's Health/Hospitals, Clinics/Medical Centers, Emergency/Ambulance Services, Health Funds, Health Organizations, Hospitals, Medical Research, Mental Health, Prenatal Health Issues, Public Health, Research/Studies Institutes, Single-Disease Health Associations

Religion: Churches, Religion-General

Science: Scientific Centers & Institutes

Social Services: Big Brothers/Big Sisters, Camps, Child Welfare, Community Service Organizations, People with Disabilities, Recreation & Athletics, Scouts, United Funds/United Ways, YMCA/YWCA/YMHA/YWHA, Youth Organizations

Application Procedures

Initial Contact: The foundation requests applications be made in writing. and should include a description of organization and amount requested.
Deadlines: None.

Restrictions

The foundation does not fund individuals or political or lobbying groups.

Foundation Officials

James C. Brady, Jr.: president, treasurer, trustee
Nicholas Frederick Brady: trustee B New York, NY 1930. ED Yale University BA (1952); Harvard University MBA (1954). CORP AFFIL director: Amerada Hess Corp. NONPR AFFIL trustee: Boys Club Newark. CLUB AFFIL Lunch Club; Bond New York Club; The Links Club.
Karen Wisnosky: secretary, assistant treasurer

Grants Analysis

Disclosure Period: calendar year ending 2003
Total Grants: $253,977*
Number of Grants: 33
Average Grant: $4,967*
Highest Grant: $50,000
Lowest Grant: $100
Typical Range: $500 to $10,000
*Note: Giving excludes United Way. Average grant figure excludes two highest grants ($100,000).

Recent Grants

Note: Grants derived from 2001 Form 990.
General

110,000	New Jersey Performing Arts Center, Newark, NJ
100,000	Church of Our Lady of Perpetual Help, Bernardsville, NJ
33,900	Boys and Girls Club of Newark, Newark, NJ
20,000	Metropolitan Museum of Art, New York, NY
15,000	Morristown Memorial Health Foundation, Morristown, NJ
10,000	Nature Conservancy of New Jersey, Inc., Arlington, VA
10,000	New Jersey SEEDS, Newark, NJ
9,883	Morristown Beard School, Morristown, NJ
5,000	Alzheimer's Disease and Related Disorders, St. Louis, MO
5,000	Business Partnership of Somerset County, Newark, NJ

BRAEMAR CHARITABLE TRUST

Giving Contact

Martha B. Cox, Trustee
c/o Trust Management Services

PO Box 1990
Waldport, OR 97394
Phone: (541)563-7279

Description

Founded: 1994
EIN: 936272124
Organization Type: Private Foundation
Giving Locations: OR
Grant Types: General Support.

Donor Information

Founder: Established in 1994 by Hobart and Marian A. Bird.

Financial Summary

Total Giving: $710,589 (fiscal year ending September 30, 2004); $860,444 (fiscal 2001)
Assets: $26,262,324 (fiscal 2004); $15,462,143 (fiscal 2001)
Gifts Received: $1,276,728 (fiscal 2001); $1,500,000 (fiscal 1998); $1,500,000 (fiscal 1996). Note: Contributions were received from Hobart M. and Marian A. Bird.

Typical Recipients

Arts & Humanities: Arts Associations & Councils, Ballet, History & Archaeology, Libraries, Museums/Galleries, Opera, Public Broadcasting

Civic & Public Affairs: Economic Development, Employment/Job Training, Housing, Legal Aid, Nonprofit Management, Women's Affairs

Education: Afterschool/Enrichment Programs, Agricultural Education, Community & Junior Colleges, Education Funds, Literacy, Private Education (Precollege), Public Education (Precollege), Science/Mathematics Education, Vocational & Technical Education

Environment: Environment-General, Resource Conservation

Health: Children's Health/Hospitals, Geriatric Health, Heart, Home-Care Services, Nursing Services, Nutrition

Religion: Religious Welfare

Science: Science Museums

Social Services: At-Risk Youth, Child Abuse, Child Welfare, Community Service Organizations, Counseling, Crime Prevention, Domestic Violence, Family Services, Food/Clothing Distribution, People with Disabilities, Scouts, Senior Services, Shelters/Homelessness, Substance Abuse, Volunteer Services, Youth Organizations

Application Procedures

Initial Contact: The foundation requests applications be made in writing.
Application Requirements: Include proof of tax-exempt status, a copy of by-laws and constitution, recently audited financial statement, statement of specific endeavor, record of prior results of similar efforts, and any other pertinent information.
Deadlines: Vary by region in Oregon; contact foundation.

Restrictions

Grants are not made to individuals.

Additional Information

Grants are limited to tax-exempt organizations within Oregon. Maximum grant is $8,000.

Foundation Officials

Hobart M. Bird: trustee
Marian A. Bird: trustee
Martha B. Cox: trustee
Molly Sue Snyder: trustee

Grants Analysis

Disclosure Period: fiscal year ending September 30, 2004
Total Grants: $710,589
Number of Grants: 103

Average Grant: $6,899
Highest Grant: $8,000
Lowest Grant: $778
Typical Range: $3,000 to $8,000

Recent Grants

Note: Grants derived from fiscal 2004 Form 990.
General

8,000	A. C. Gilbert's Discovery Village, Salem, OR -- for two new exhibits
8,000	Albany Boys and Girls Club Foundation, Albany, OR -- for 'make and take' computer project
8,000	Alsea Community Effort, Alsea, OR -- towards afterschool & summer programs
8,000	Arc of Lane County, Eugene, OR -- to enhance & expand current recreation programs
8,000	Bandon Historical Society, Bandon, OR -- to transfer newspapers to CD & photos
8,000	Benton County Committee for the Prevention of Child Abuse, Corvallis, OR -- to support the parent enhancement program
8,000	Blanchet Catholic School, Salem, OR -- to enhance the music library
8,000	Boys and Girls Clubs of Western Lane, Florence, OR -- for Amicore volunteer and materials for RAPP
8,000	Chemeketa Community College Foundation, Salem, OR -- for lift truck for the viticulture program
8,000	Court Appointed Special Advocates of Lane County Foundation, Springfield, OR -- to support community volunteers

R. B. O. BRAGG CHARITABLE TRUST

Giving Contact

Care of Bank of America
PO Box 831041
Dallas, TX 75283-1041
Phone: (214)508-2005

Description

Founded: 1999
EIN: 756521856
Organization Type: Private Foundation
Grant Types: General Support.

Financial Summary

Total Giving: $53,000 (fiscal year ending February 28, 2001)
Assets: $1,419,600 (fiscal 2001)
Gifts Received: $1,078,114 (fiscal 1998). Note: In fiscal 1998, contributions were received from Dorothy Watson Bragg.

Typical Recipients

Arts & Humanities: Libraries
Education: Colleges & Universities
Health: Children's Health/Hospitals, Health Organizations

Additional Information

Trust(s): Bank of America NA TX

Grants Analysis

Disclosure Period: fiscal year ending February 28, 2001
Total Grants: $53,000
Number of Grants: 4
Highest Grant: $17,666
Lowest Grant: $5,889

Recent Grants

Note: Grants derived from fiscal 2001 Form 990.

Library-Related

5,889   Fairfield Library Association, Fairfield, TX -- for charitable purposes

General

17,666   Shriners Hospital for Children, Galveston, TX -- for charitable purpose

14,723   East Texas Medical Center Foundation, Fairfield, TX -- for equipment, real estate, construction or purchase of hospital facilities

14,722   College of the Ozarks, Pt. Lookout, MO -- for charitable purposes

BRAITMAYER FOUNDATION

Giving Contact

Robert L. Kirkpatrick, Jr., Advisory
Middlesex Corp. Center
49 Main St.
Middletown, CT 06457
Phone: (860)638-4688
Fax: (860)638-4667
Web: http://www.braitmayerfoundation.org

Description

Founded: 1964
EIN: 046112131
Organization Type: Private Foundation
Giving Locations: nationally.
Grant Types: Challenge, General Support, Matching, Seed Money.

Donor Information

Founder: The Braitmayer Foundation, located in Marion, Massachusetts, was established in 1964 through a gift from Marian S. Braitmayer.

Financial Summary

Total Giving: $161,975 (2004); $170,720 (2002); $227,700 (2001)
Assets: $4,598,949 (2004); $4,181,191 (2002); $4,970,454 (2001)

Typical Recipients

Arts & Humanities: Libraries, Museums/Galleries, Music, Public Broadcasting, Theater
Civic & Public Affairs: Botanical Gardens/Parks, Community Foundations, Civic & Public Affairs-General, Housing, Municipalities/Towns, Urban & Community Affairs
Education: Colleges & Universities, Elementary Education (Public), Faculty Development, Education-General, Leadership Training, Private Education (Precollege), Public Education (Precollege), Religious Education, Science/Mathematics Education, Secondary Education (Private), Secondary Education (Public), Special Education, Student Aid
Environment: Environment-General, Resource Conservation
Religion: Churches
Science: Scientific Centers & Institutes
Social Services: Child Welfare, Community Service Organizations, Day Care, Family Services, People with Disabilities, Recreation & Athletics, YMCA/YWCA/YMHA/YWHA, Youth Organizations

Application Procedures

Initial Contact: Contact the foundation for their detailed Objectives and Guidelines sheet.
Application Requirements: For grants up to $10,000, applicants should submit an original and seven copies of the following documents: a three page proposal describing the project, including timeframe (appendices should be limited); proposed budget; and proof of 501 (c)(3) status or other tax-exempt ruling letter. For grants up to $35,000, applicants

should submit an original and seven copies of the following documents: a two page letter of inquiry describing the proposed project, including timeframe (appendices should be limited); proposed budget; and proof of 501 (c)(3) status or other tax-exempt ruling letter.
Deadlines: June 30th for grants up to $35,000. By September 1st, the trustees will invite selected organizations to submit full proposals due November 15th. June 30th or November 15th for grants up to $10,000.
Decision Notification: Decisions will be announced by March 15th for grants up to $35,000. Successful organizations must wait two years before reapplication. For grants up to $10,000, decisions will be announced by September 1st and March 15th. Successful organizations must wait two years before reapplication for a grant up to $10,000 or before beginning application for a grant up to $35,000.

Restrictions

The foundation does not make grants to individuals, multi-year grants, nor grants for endowment purposes or building programs. Unless a small percentage of the total amount requested, normally the foundation does not make grants for childcare, prekindergarten, or after school programs nor for equipment including hardware, software, and books.

Foundation Officials

Eric A. Braitmayer: trustee
John W. Braitmayer: trustee
Karen L. Braitmayer: trustee
Nancy W. Corkery: trustee
Kristina B. Hewey: trustee
Anne B. Webb: trustee
R. Davis Webb, Jr.: trustee

Grants Analysis

Disclosure Period: calendar year ending 2004
Total Grants: $161,975
Number of Grants: 20
Average Grant: $8,099
Highest Grant: $35,000
Lowest Grant: $150
Typical Range: $1,000 to $10,000

Recent Grants

Note: Grants derived from 2004 Form 990.

General

35,000   Heritage College, Toppenish, WA -- to support the life sciences learning center

35,000   Snow Hill Primary School, Snow Hill, NC -- to support the instructional coaching initiative

33,000   Cesar Chavez Public Charter, Washington, DC -- to support the teacher center initiative

10,000   Cumberland County School -- to support the reading is fundamental program and for the performing arts

10,000   Oneida Special School District, Oneida, TN -- to support the professional development network for Boston - area teacher initiative

10,000   Saint Mary's College, Notre Dame, IN -- to support and strengthen the IBO accreditation initiative

8,775   Rocky Mountain Deaf School, Lakewood, CO -- to support and strengthen TE program

1,000   Mattapoisett Congregational Church, Mattapoisett, MA

1,000   New Bedford Whaling Museum, New Bedford, MA

1,000   Salisbury School, Salisbury, CT

OTTO BREMER FOUNDATION

Giving Contact

John Kostishack, Executive Director
445 Minnesota Street, Suite 2250
St. Paul, MN 55101-2107
Phone: (651)227-8036
Fax: (651)312-3665
E-mail: obf@bremer.com
Web: http://fdncenter.org/grantmaker/bremer/
Note: Proposals may be submitted through local Bremer First American Bank affiliates. Toll Free: (888)291-1123

Description

Founded: 1944
EIN: 416019050
Organization Type: General Purpose Foundation
Giving Locations: MN; MT; ND; WI
Grant Types: Capital, Challenge, General Support, Loan, Matching, Multiyear/Continuing Support, Operating Expenses, Project, Seed Money.

Donor Information

Founder: Otto Bremer, a German immigrant of humble origins, has become an established symbol of philanthropy in the Minnesota, North Dakota, and Wisconsin regions. He began his career as a bookkeeper in the National German American Bank in St. Paul, initiating what proved to be an enduring attachment to that area. Mr. Bremer was an active participant in a wide variety of community affairs throughout his lifetime. In 1921, he became chairman of the American National Bank, and in 1939, he assumed the presidency of the Schmidt Brewing Company.

In addition to these corporate activities, Mr. Bremer was treasurer of the City of St. Paul, aided in the formation of the Minnesota Democratic Farmer-Labor Party, counseled Presidents Woodrow Wilson and Franklin D. Roosevelt, and administered the Federal Home Owners' Loan Corporation in Minnesota. Yet, it was his participation in banking that was most important to Otto Bremer. His holdings were vast, yet his association with "countryside banks" proved to be most satisfying. One of his creeds was that "banks should be home banks, independently operated by people of their communities."

In a biography of Otto Bremer, he is described as firmly believing that individuals do not live or grow in isolation; they fulfill themselves only by helping one another. It was his commitment to this belief that led Mr. Bremer to act with concern for the rural communities in his area that were threatened by poverty. During the Depression, Mr. Bremer liquidated personal assets and placed them in banks serving these rural communities. His support sustained these struggling banks and communities. Later, Mr. Bremer became concerned with maintaining support to these communities after his death. In 1943, he established the Bremer Financial Corporation which received assets from the banks of which Mr. Bremer was principal shareholder. The assets from the Bremer Financial Corporation were then transferred to the Otto Bremer Foundation, which was formed in 1944 due to his deep concern for his holdings in Minnesota, North Dakota, and Wisconsin. Through the foundation, he sought to insure the perpetuation of the Bremer banks and the ultimate return of his wealth to the trade territories of the banks and the city of St. Paul. Money placed in Otto Bremer's banks was funneled into the corporation, and finally to the foundation, which dispensed it to needy causes in the community. In this way, Mr. Bremer formulated an enduring system which would continue to use his wealth to "serve the community in which it was invested first, last and always."

Financial Summary

Total Giving: $19,329,403 (2003); $20,000,000 (2002 approx); $16,080,448 (2001)
Giving Analysis: Giving for 2003 includes: foundation grants to United Way ($17,250); foundation program-related investments ($3,679,104)
Assets: $455,434,351 (2003); $393,777,842 (2001)

Typical Recipients

Arts & Humanities: Ethnic & Folk Arts, Libraries, Music, Public Broadcasting
Civic & Public Affairs: African American Affairs, Asian American Affairs, Botanical Gardens/Parks, Civil Rights, Community Foundations, Economic Development, Employment/Job Training, Civic & Public Affairs-General, Hispanic Affairs, Housing, Legal Aid, Municipalities/Towns, Native American Affairs, Nonprofit Management, Philanthropic Organizations, Public Policy, Rural Affairs, Urban & Community Affairs, Women's Affairs
Education: Agricultural Education, Colleges & Universities, Community & Junior Colleges, Continuing Education, Education Funds, Environmental Education, Faculty Development, Education-General, Gifted & Talented Programs, International Exchange, Leadership Training, Legal Education, Literacy, Medical Education, Minority Education, Preschool Education, Private Education (Precollege), Public Education (Precollege), Religious Education, Science/Mathematics Education, Social Sciences Education, Vocational & Technical Education
Environment: Environment-General, Resource Conservation
Health: AIDS/HIV, Clinics/Medical Centers, Diabetes, Emergency/Ambulance Services, Health-General, Geriatric Health, Health Organizations, Hospices, Hospitals, Long-Term Care, Mental Health, Nursing Services, Outpatient Health Care, Public Health
International: Human Rights, International Development
Religion: Churches, Jewish Causes, Religious Welfare
Science: Scientific Centers & Institutes
Social Services: At-Risk Youth, Camps, Child Welfare, Community Centers, Community Service Organizations, Counseling, Crime Prevention, Day Care, Domestic Violence, Emergency Relief, Family Services, Food/Clothing Distribution, Homes, People with Disabilities, Recreation & Athletics, Refugee Assistance, Senior Services, Sexual Abuse, Shelters/Homelessness, Social Services-General, Substance Abuse, United Funds/United Ways, YMCA/YWCA/YMHA/YWHA, Youth Organizations

Application Procedures

Initial Contact: Applicants should write or call the foundation for an application and for assistance in the development of a proposal. A video on how to apply for a grant is available through the foundation and through First National Bank affiliates.
Application Requirements: A proposal includes the following: legal name, address, and phone number of organization, and name and phone number of contact person; brief a description of organization, including goals, purposes, and short history, if appropriate; description of project for which funds are being sought, what it is designed to achieve, how this will be accomplished; the specific amount requested; documentation of organization's nonprofit and tax-exempt status; names and qualifications of individuals responsible for implementing project; evidence that request is endorsed by board of directors of applicant organization an d list of members; complete budget for project, with projected revenues and expenses; audited financial statement, if available, for organization's previous fiscal year, current operational budget, and copy of most recent IRS Form 990; indication of other funding sources to be used to support project; description of project's future funding plans, where appropriate; description of procedure for reporting expenditures of grant funds and progress of project.
Deadlines: The board of trustees meets monthly; however, proposals should be submitted for review three months prior to the date the funding decision is required. Most applicants are reviewed in a two-step process over two consecutive monthly meetings, about 6-8 weeks on average timetable.
Review Process: All complete proposals will be reviewed first by the staff and then submitted to the trustees, with whom final responsibility for grant approval resides. Applicants receive written notification of board action within a week of the board meeting.
Notes: Grant guidelines are available on the internet.

Restrictions

Grants are given only to projects within the service areas of Bremer-affiliated organizations in Wisconsin, North Dakota, Minnesota, Montana, and within the city of St. Paul. Grants are rarely made to organizations in other communities unless they affect these specified geographic areas. Grants are not made to individuals, K-12 education, sporting activities, or to endowment funds, or to organizations which are not tax exempt as defined under section 501 (c)(3) of the Internal Revenue Service code. Requests for annual fund drives, benefit events, camps, economic development, or medical research are discouraged. The Foundation does not support theatrical productions, books, motion pictures, or other media projects.

Additional Information

Grants are evaluated at the conclusion of the first year of funding. Grants made for more than one year may be reconsidered at the end of each year.
Publications: Annual Report; Guidelines; And Video

Foundation Officials

Charlotte S. Johnson: trustee PRIM CORP EMPL vice president: Bremer Financial Corp.
John Kostishack: executive director B 1941. ED University of Notre Dame; University of Wisconsin.
Mark Lindberg: senior program officer
William H. Lipschultz: trustee B Saint Paul, MN 1930. ED University of Minnesota (1956). PRIM CORP EMPL vice president, treasurer, director, chairman: Bremer Financial Corp. CORP AFFIL chairman, director: Bremer Financial Corporate; vice president: Stone Container Corp. Halper Box Division.
Lynda Marrone: grants mgr
Elsa Vega Perez: senior program officer NONPR AFFIL advisory board: COMPAS.
Daniel C. Reardon: trustee NONPR AFFIL chairman: Center for Rural Policy and Development.
Karen Starr: senior program officer

Grants Analysis

Disclosure Period: calendar year ending 2003
Total Grants: $15,633,049*
Number of Grants: 718
Average Grant: $21,773
Highest Grant: $250,000
Lowest Grant: $1,000
Typical Range: $5,000 to $50,000
***Note:** Giving excludes United Way. Giving excludes program related investments, which are eventually repaid to the foundation.

Recent Grants

Note: Grants derived from 2003 Form 990.
General

250,000	Hispanics in Philanthropy, San Francisco, CA -- towards organizational effectiveness work with Latino communities in Minnesota, Montana, North Dakota and Wisconsin
250,000	YWCA of Fargo Moorhead, Fargo, ND -- towards purchasing land and constructing an emergency shelter
200,000	Tri College University, Fargo, ND -- towards establishing the Red River basin institute
194,025	Northwest Minnesota Foundation, Bemidji, MN -- towards a technical assistance program for nonprofit organizations
160,000	Higher Education Consortium for Urban Affairs Inc., St. Paul, MN -- towards partners internship program
150,000	Minneapolis American Indian Center, Minneapolis, MN -- towards renovation and expansion of the center
140,000	North Dakota Human Rights Coalition, Fargo, ND -- towards establishing the human rights coalition
134,400	Northwest Medical Center, Thief River Falls, MN -- towards implementing a regional health care telecommunications network
130,000	Beyond Shelter Inc., Fargo, ND -- towards the Graver inn project that provides affordable housing
125,000	East Side Neighborhood Development Company Inc., St. Paul, MN -- towards the opportunity housing initiative that will develop affordable housing

BRETZLAFF FOUNDATION

Giving Contact

Michael J. Malarkey, Secretary
Bretzlaff Foundation, Inc.
Weigand Center
165 Liberty Street
Reno, NV 89501
Phone: (775)333-0330

Description

Founded: 1989
EIN: 880241424
Organization Type: Private Foundation
Giving Locations: DC; HI; MI; NV: Northern part of state
Grant Types: Research.

Donor Information

Founder: Established in 1989 by Hazel C. Van Allen.

Financial Summary

Total Giving: $853,827 (fiscal year ending June 30, 2004); $1,210,500 (fiscal 2001)
Giving Analysis: Giving for fiscal 2004 includes: foundation scholarships ($29,000); fiscal 2001: foundation scholarships ($20,000)
Assets: $17,682,030 (fiscal 2004); $19,084,601 (fiscal 2001)
Gifts Received: $1,833 (fiscal 2004); $322,121 (fiscal 2001); $1,848,262 (fiscal 2000). Note: In 2001, contributions were received from the estate of Hazel Van Allen ($156,095), Ruthmary S. Cobb ($7,729), Beverly K. McClendon ($76,222), and Stephen C. Baker ($76,222). Contributions were received from the estate of Hazel C. Van Allen.

Typical Recipients

Arts & Humanities: Arts Associations & Councils, Arts Centers, Ethnic & Folk Arts, Historic Preservation, History & Archaeology, Libraries, Museums/Galleries, Music, Public Broadcasting, Theater
Civic & Public Affairs: Employment/Job Training, Civic & Public Affairs-General, Law & Justice, Legal Aid, Public Policy
Education: Arts/Humanities Education, Colleges & Universities, Legal Education, Science/Mathematics Education, Student Aid
Environment: Research, Resource Conservation
Health: Health Funds, Health Organizations, Hospices, Hospitals, Medical Rehabilitation, Medical Research, Public Health, Research/Studies Institutes
Religion: Religious Welfare
Social Services: At-Risk Youth, Big Brothers/Big

Sisters, Child Welfare, Community Service Organizations, Delinquency & Criminal Rehabilitation, Family Services, Recreation & Athletics, Youth Organizations

Application Procedures

Initial Contact: Send a brief letter of inquiry.
Application Requirements: Include type of organization, its purpose and nature, and purpose of funds sought.
Deadlines: December 31.

Restrictions

Does not support individuals, religious organizations for sectarian purposes, political or lobbying groups, or organizations outside operating areas.

Foundation Officials

Richard Gilbert: president
William G. Van Allen: treasurer

Grants Analysis

Disclosure Period: fiscal year ending June 30, 2004
Total Grants: $824,827*
Number of Grants: 40
Average Grant: $16,021*
Highest Grant: $200,000
Lowest Grant: $2,000
Typical Range: $5,000 to $30,000
***Note:** Giving excludes scholarships. Average grant figure excludes highest grant.

Recent Grants

Note: Grants derived from fiscal 2004 Form 990.
Library-Related

10,000	Washoe County Library Foundation, Reno, NV -- towards enhancements in-line village library

General

200,000	Hawaii Justice Foundation, Honolulu, HI
57,627	University of Nevada Reno Foundation, Reno, NV -- towards scholarship endowments
55,000	Boys and Girls Club of the Truckee Meadows, Reno, NV -- for youth programs
20,000	Honolulu Theater for Youth, Honolulu, HI
20,000	KNPB, Reno, NV -- for programming endowment
20,000	Reno Chamber Orchestra, Reno, NV -- towards concerto competition
20,000	Reno Philharmonic Association, Reno, NV
10,000	Washoe County Sheriff, Reno, NV -- towards summer program
10,000	Washoe Medical Foundation, Reno, NV -- towards Washoe cancer center

BRIDGESTONE AMERICAS HOLDING INC.

Company Headquarters

50 Century Blvd.
Nashville, TN 37214
Web: http://www.bridgestone-firestone.com

Company Description

Founded: 1990
Also Known As: Bridgestone/Firestone.
Revenue: US$389 million (2002)
Employees: 45000 (2002)
SIC(s): 2296 Tire Cord & Fabrics, 3011 Tires & Inner Tubes, 3069 Fabricated Rubber Products Nec, 5014 Tires & Tubes.
Parent Company: Bridgestone Corp., 10-1 Kyobashi 1-chome, Chuo-ku, Tokyo, Japan

Operating Locations ✓

Bridgestone/Firestone Credit Services Co. (OH--Brook Park); Bridgestone/Firestone, Inc. (AR--Russellville; CA--Irvine; FL--Mary Esther, West Palm Beach; GA--Marietta, Norcross, Tucker; IL--Bloomington, Decatur, Rolling Meadows; IN--Indianapolis; IA--Des Moines; MA--Quincy; MI--Southfield; MN--Minneapolis; NY--Clifton Park; NC--Wilson; OH--Akron; OK--Oklahoma City; TN--LaVergne; TX--Corpus Christi, Grand Prairie, Houston); Bridgestone/Firestone Information Services Co. (OH--Akron); Bridgestone/Firestone Off-Road Tire Co. (TN--Nashville); Bridgestone/Firestone Original Equipment Tire Sales Co. (MI--Southfield); Bridgestone/Firestone Research Laboratories (OH--Akron); Bridgestone/Firestone Retail Operations (IL--Rolling Meadows); Bridgestone/Firestone Technology Co. (OH--Akron); Bridgestone/Firestone Tire Manufacturing Operations (TN--Nashville); Bridgestone/Firestone Tire Sales Co. (TN--Nashville); Dayton Tire (OK--Oklahoma City); Firestone Agricultural Tire Co. (IA--Des Moines); Firestone Building Products Co. (IN--Carmel); Firestone Fibers & Textiles Co. (NC--Kings Mountain); Firestone Industrial Products Co. (IN--Carmel); Firestone Synthetic Rubber & Latex Co. (OH--Akron); Firestone Tube Co. (AR--Russellville)
Note: Also operate in Canada, Mexico, Europe, South and Central America, Liberia, and Singapore.

The Bridgestone/ Firestone Trust Fund

Giving Contact

Bernice Csaszar, Administrator
The Bridgestone/Firestone Trust Fund
535 Marriott Dr., 11th Fl.
Nashville, TN 37214
Phone: (615)872-1415
Fax: (615)872-1414
E-mail: bfstrustfund@bfsusa.com

Description

Founded: 1952
EIN: 346505181
Organization Type: Corporate Foundation
Former Name: Bridgestone/Firestone, Inc. (2003).
Giving Locations: headquarters and operating communities.
Grant Types: Capital, Challenge, Employee Matching Gifts, General Support, Operating Expenses, Project, Scholarship, Seed Money.

Donor Information

Founder: Bridgestone/Firestone, Inc.

Financial Summary

Total Giving: $4,115,349 (2003); $4,593,895 (2002); $6,131,633 (2001). Note: Contributes through foundation only.
Giving Analysis: Giving for 2002 includes: foundation grants to United Way ($546,332)
Assets: $23,703,149 (2003); $18,854,646 (2002); $38,681,621 (2001)

Typical Recipients

Arts & Humanities: Arts Associations & Councils, Arts Institutes, Arts Outreach, Ballet, Community Arts, Dance, Arts & Humanities-General, Historic Preservation, Libraries, Museums/Galleries, Music, Opera, Public Broadcasting, Theater
Civic & Public Affairs: African American Affairs, Business/Free Enterprise, Chambers of Commerce, Civil Rights, Clubs, Community Foundations, Economic Development, Employment/Job Training, Civic & Public Affairs-General, Housing, Law & Justice, Municipalities/Towns, Professional & Trade Associations, Public Policy, Rural Affairs, Urban & Community Affairs, Zoos/Aquariums

Education: Afterschool/Enrichment Programs, Agricultural Education, Arts/Humanities Education, Business Education, Colleges & Universities, Community & Junior Colleges, Economic Education, Education Funds, Engineering/Technological Education, Education-General, International Studies, Medical Education, Minority Education, Public Education (Precollege), Religious Education, Science/Mathematics Education, Special Education, Student Aid, Vocational & Technical Education
Environment: Air/Water Quality, Forestry, Environment-General, Resource Conservation, Watershed, Wildlife Protection
Health: AIDS/HIV, Children's Health/Hospitals, Clinics/Medical Centers, Emergency/Ambulance Services, Eyes/Blindness, Health Policy/Cost Containment, Health Funds, Health Organizations, Hospices, Hospitals, Medical Research, Nursing Services, Single-Disease Health Associations
Religion: Ministries, Religious Organizations
Science: Science Museums, Scientific Centers & Institutes, Scientific Organizations
Social Services: At-Risk Youth, Camps, Child Welfare, Community Centers, Community Service Organizations, Emergency Relief, Family Planning, Family Services, People with Disabilities, Recreation & Athletics, Scouts, Senior Services, Social Services-General, Substance Abuse, United Funds/United Ways, Volunteer Services, YMCA/YWCA/YMHA/YWHA, Youth Organizations

Application Procedures

Initial Contact: Send a brief letter or proposal; organizations in communities where Bridgestone/Firestone operates should write to local major facility.
Application Requirements: Include a description of organization, amount requested, purpose of funds sought, recently audited financial statement, proof of tax-exempt status, 501(C)(3) Federation IRS Form 990 or letter, board of directors, current operating budget, and list of major donors, including each of their contributions.
Deadlines: None.
Review Process: Proposals are reviewed upon receipt; those proposals meeting basic criteria are held for review by the committee that meets several times a year; applicants are notified of committee's decision.

Restrictions

Recipients must have 501(c)(3) status and must operate in accordance with the principle of equal opportunity.
Grants do not support groups that discriminate, partisan political organizations, or groups limited to a single religious organization.

Additional Information

In 1992, the company relocated its corporate headquarters from Akron, OH, to Nashville, TN.
In 1989, Bridgestone U.S.A., Inc., merged with Firestone Tire & Rubber Co. to become Bridgestone/Firestone, Inc., a wholly-owned subsidiary of Bridgestone Corp. of Japan.
Publications: Guidelines

Corporate Officials

Masatoshi Ono: chairman, chief executive officer B 1937. ED Kumamoto University (Japan) BS (1959). PRIM CORP EMPL chairman, chief executive officer: Bridgestone/Firestone, Inc.

Foundation Officials

Bernice Csaszar: administrator
Christine Karbowiak: chairman
Gene Stephens: member
Ronald Tepner: member

Grants Analysis

Disclosure Period: calendar year ending 2003
Total Grants: $3,407,849*
Number of Grants: 900 (approx)

Average Grant: $3,786
Highest Grant: $462,000
Lowest Grant: $50
Typical Range: $1,000 to $5,000
*Note: Giving excludes United Way; scholarship.

Recent Grants
Note: Grants derived from 2003 Form 990.
General

207,500	National Merit Scholarship Corporation, Evanston, IL
75,000	United Way of Decatur/Macon County, Decatur, IL
65,000	United Way of Summit County, Akron, OH
50,000	Championship Auto Racing Auxiliary, Miamisburg, OH
50,000	Middle Tennessee State University Foundation, Murfreesboro, TN
50,000	Tennessee Economic Partnership, Maryville, TN
48,000	Public Forum, Roseburg, OR
40,000	United Way of Wilson County Inc., Wilson, NC
35,000	United Way of Metro Nashville, Nashville, TX
29,000	YMCA, Nashville, TN

BRIGHT FAMILY FOUNDATION

Giving Contact
Calvin E. Bright, President
1620 N. Carpenter Rd., Bldg. B
Modesto, CA 95351
Phone: (209)526-8242
Fax: (209)526-8886
Web: http://www.bright-homes.com

Description
Founded: 1986
EIN: 770126942
Organization Type: Private Foundation
Giving Locations: CA
Grant Types: General Support, Operating Expenses.

Donor Information
Founder: Calvin Bright, Marjorie Bright

Financial Summary
Total Giving: $377,500 (2003)
Assets: $7,895,314 (2003)
Gifts Received: $700,000 (1999); $700,000 (1998); $700,000 (1996). Note: In 1998 and 1999, contributions were received from Calvin and Marjorie Bright.

Typical Recipients
Arts & Humanities: Arts & Humanities-General, Libraries, Museums/Galleries, Music, Performing Arts, Public Broadcasting, Theater
Civic & Public Affairs: Clubs, Economic Development, Civic & Public Affairs-General, Housing, Native American Affairs, Philanthropic Organizations, Safety, Women's Affairs
Education: Arts/Humanities Education, Colleges & Universities, Community & Junior Colleges, Medical Education, Private Education (Precollege), Public Education (Precollege), Secondary Education (Public), Student Aid
Health: Cancer, Clinics/Medical Centers, Health Organizations, Hospices, Hospitals, Research/Studies Institutes, Single-Disease Health Associations
International: Health Care/Hospitals, International Environmental Issues, International Organizations
Religion: Churches, Jewish Causes, Missionary Activities (Domestic), Religious Organizations, Religious Welfare
Science: Science Museums
Social Services: Child Welfare, Community Service Organizations, Crime Prevention, Domestic Violence, People with Disabilities, Recreation & Athletics, Scouts, Shelters/Homelessness, United Funds/United Ways, Youth Organizations

Application Procedures
Initial Contact: Send a brief letter of inquiry.
Application Requirements: Include a statement of charitable purpose on organization letterhead, including tax I.D. number, or submit information on Bright Family foundations grant application form.
Deadlines: December 1.

Additional Information
Publications: Application Form

Foundation Officials
Calvin E. Bright: president
Lyn Bright: director
Marjorie H. Bright: director

Grants Analysis
Disclosure Period: calendar year ending 2003
Total Grants: $377,500
Number of Grants: 40
Average Grant: $7,756*
Highest Grant: $75,000
Lowest Grant: $500
Typical Range: $1,000 to $10,000
*Note: Average grant figure excludes highest grant.

Recent Grants
Note: Grants derived from 2001 Form 990.
General

50,000	Central Valley Performing Arts Committee, Modesto, CA
40,000	Children's Crisis Center, Modesto, CA
30,000	California State University Stanislaus, Turlock, CA
30,000	Campus Crusade for Christ, Orlando, FL
30,000	Modesto Gospel Mission, Modesto, CA
30,000	University of California San Francisco School of Medicine, San Francisco, CA
26,000	Modesto Junior College Foundation, Modesto, CA
25,000	Community Hospice, Modesto, CA
25,000	Modesto Junior College Foundation, Modesto, CA
20,000	Shelter Cove Community Church, Modesto, CA

BRILLION IRON WORKS

Company Headquarters
200 Park Avenue
Brillion, WI 54110
Web: http://www.brillionironworks.com

Company Description
Founded: 1934
Revenue: US$126 million (2002)
Employees: 800 (2002)
SIC(s): 3321 Gray & Ductile Iron Foundries, 3523 Farm Machinery & Equipment, 3624 Carbon & Graphite Products.
Parent Company: Transportation Technologies Industries Inc., 980 N. Michigan Ave., Chicago, IL, United States

Brillion Foundation

Giving Contact
Harold J. Wolf, Secretary & Treasurer
Brillion Foundation
200 Park Ave., Box 127
Brillion, WI 54110-0127
Phone: (920)756-2121

Description
EIN: 396043916
Organization Type: Corporate Foundation
Giving Locations: WI: Brillion
Grant Types: Capital, Challenge, General Support, Operating Expenses, Scholarship.

Financial Summary
Total Giving: $50,065 (fiscal year ending June 30, 2004); $61,810 (fiscal 2001). Note: Fiscal 1997 Giving includes scholarship ($7,350).
Giving Analysis: Giving for fiscal 2004 includes: foundation scholarships ($6,500); fiscal 2001: foundation scholarships ($5,700)
Assets: $300,066 (fiscal 2004); $327,692 (fiscal 2001)
Gifts Received: $50,000 (fiscal 2001); $50,000 (fiscal 1999); $50,000 (fiscal 1997). Note: In fiscal 1999 and fiscal 2001, contributions were received from Brillion Iron Works Inc.

Typical Recipients
Arts & Humanities: Historic Preservation, History & Archaeology, Libraries, Music, Public Broadcasting
Civic & Public Affairs: Botanical Gardens/Parks, Clubs, Civic & Public Affairs-General, Municipalities/Towns, Urban & Community Affairs
Education: Agricultural Education, Business Education, Colleges & Universities, Economic Education, Education-General, Journalism/Media Education, Public Education (Precollege)
Environment: Environment-General
Health: Cancer, Children's Health/Hospitals, Health Organizations, Public Health, Single-Disease Health Associations
International: International Peace & Security Issues
Religion: Churches, Religion-General, Religious Organizations, Religious Welfare
Science: Observatories & Planetariums
Social Services: Animal Protection, Community Service Organizations, Food/Clothing Distribution, People with Disabilities, Recreation & Athletics, Scouts, Special Olympics, Substance Abuse, Youth Organizations

Application Procedures
Initial Contact: Send brief letter.
Deadlines: None.

Additional Information
Include a description of organization, amount requested, purpose of funds sought, audited financial statement, and proof of tax-exempt status. Provides support for churches, public broadcasting, community services, and restricted scholarships.

Corporate Officials
Dennis L. Graven: chief financial officer, vice president finance PRIM CORP EMPL chief financial officer, vice president finance: Brillion Iron Works.
John David McClain: president, chief executive officer B Camp Lajune, NC 1944. ED North Carolina State University (1967). PRIM CORP EMPL president, chief executive officer: Brillion Iron Works.

Foundation Officials
Carl Miller: director
Lowell O. Reese: vice president, director
Lin Wittmann: director
Harold J. Wolf: treasurer, director

Grants Analysis
Disclosure Period: fiscal year ending June 30, 2004
Total Grants: $43,565*
Number of Grants: 16
Average Grant: $2,723
Highest Grant: $8,815
Lowest Grant: $250

Typical Range: $500 to $5,000
*Note: Giving excludes scholarships.

Recent Grants

Note: Grants derived from fiscal 2004 Form 990.
General
8,815	Brillion Athletic Association, Brillion, WI
5,000	Faith United Methodist Church
5,000	Holy Family Parish, Arcadia, WI
5,000	Peace United Church of Christ
5,000	St. Bartholomew Lutheran Church
5,000	Trinity Evangelical Lutheran Church, Waukesha, WI
3,850	Brillion City Community Drive, Brillion, WI
2,500	Brillion Community Church, Brillion, WI
700	St. Vincent DePaul Food Pantry
600	Brillion Cub Scouts

BRISTOL-MYERS SQUIBB CO.

Company Headquarters

345 Park Ave.
New York, NY 10154-0037
Web: http://www.bms.com

Company Description

Ticker: BMY
Exchange: NYSE
Revenue: US$21.886 billion (2004)
Profit: US$2.388 billion (2004)
Employees: 44000 (2003)
Fortune Rank: 93, per FORTUNE Magazine's list of 500 Largest U.S. Corporations (2004).

Nonmonetary Support

Value: $35,000,000 (2000 approx)
Type: Donated Products
Note: Contact local operating facilities for local nonmonetary giving. Contact Frank Cifuni at the Edition, NJ, facility for international product requests.

Bristol-Myers Squibb Foundation Inc.

Giving Contact

John L. Damonti, Foundation Coordinator
Bristol-Myers Squibb Foundation Inc.
345 Park Avenue
New York, NY 10154
Phone: (212)546-4000
Web: http://www.bms.com/aboutbms/founda/data/index.html

Alternate Contact

David Fritzsche
Bristol-Myers Squibb Company-Wallingford
PO Box 5100
Wallingford, CT 06492-5100
Note: Contact for nonprofit organizations in the Wallingford, Connecticut community

Description

Founded: 1990
EIN: 133127947
Organization Type: Corporate Foundation
Giving Locations: headquarters and operating communities; internationally; nationally.
Grant Types: Employee Matching Gifts, General Support, Project, Research.
Note: Employee matching gift ratio: 1 to 1.

Donor Information

Founder: Bristol-Myers Squibb Co., divisions, and subsidiaries

Financial Summary

Total Giving: $18,561,106 (2003); $19,820,876 (2002); $21,716,953 (2001). Note: Contributes through corporate direct giving program and foundation. Giving includes corporate direct giving, foundation, domestic subsidiaries, international subsidiaries, nonmonetary support.
Assets: $16,604,318 (2003); $29,014,663 (2002); $40,005,806 (2001)
Gifts Received: $7,750,000 (2003); $6,500,000 (2002); $32,500,000 (2001). Note: Contributions were received from Bristol-Myers Squibb Co.

Typical Recipients

Arts & Humanities: Arts Associations & Councils, Arts Centers, Arts Funds, Arts Institutes, Arts Outreach, Historic Preservation, Libraries, Museums/Galleries, Music, Opera, Performing Arts, Public Broadcasting, Theater
Civic & Public Affairs: African American Affairs, Botanical Gardens/Parks, Business/Free Enterprise, Community Foundations, Economic Development, Employment/Job Training, Civic & Public Affairs-General, Housing, Law & Justice, Municipalities/Towns, Professional & Trade Associations, Public Policy, Rural Affairs, Safety, Urban & Community Affairs, Women's Affairs, Zoos/Aquariums
Education: Arts/Humanities Education, Business Education, Colleges & Universities, Education Funds, Education Reform, Education-General, Leadership Training, Legal Education, Medical Education, Minority Education, Private Education (Precollege), Religious Education, Social Sciences Education, Special Education, Student Aid
Environment: Air/Water Quality, Environment-General, Resource Conservation
Health: AIDS/HIV, Cancer, Children's Health/Hospitals, Clinics/Medical Centers, Diabetes, Emergency/Ambulance Services, Health-General, Geriatric Health, Health Funds, Health Organizations, Heart, Hospitals, Medical Rehabilitation, Medical Research, Medical Training, Mental Health, Nutrition, Public Health, Research/Studies Institutes, Transplant Networks/Donor Banks
International: Foreign Educational Institutions, International-General, Health Care/Hospitals, International Affairs, International Organizations, International Relations, International Relief Efforts, Missionary/Religious Activities
Religion: Religion-General, Jewish Causes, Missionary Activities (Domestic), Religious Welfare
Science: Science-General, Science Museums, Scientific Centers & Institutes, Scientific Organizations, Scientific Research
Social Services: Community Service Organizations, Crime Prevention, Emergency Relief, Family Services, Food/Clothing Distribution, People with Disabilities, Recreation & Athletics, Shelters/Homelessness, Substance Abuse, United Funds/United Ways, Volunteer Services, Youth Organizations

Application Procedures

Initial Contact: Send a brief letter or proposal no more than five pages.
Application Requirements: Include brief statement of history, goals, and accomplishments to date; amount requested; purpose of funds sought; list of current funding sources; recently audited financial statement; current year's operating budget; current annual report; list of board members; proof of tax-exempt status; most recent IRS Form 990.
Deadlines: October 1; organizations should not submit more than one grant application in a 12-month period.

Restrictions

The foundation does not support organizations receiving support through the United Way or other federated campaigns; conferences, special events, or videos; political, fraternal, social, or veterans organi-

zations; religious or sectarian activities, unless they benefit entire community; endowments; courtesy advertising; or individuals

Additional Information

Organizations located in communities where the company maintains facilities may apply directly to the local office.
Publications: Report of Charitable Contributions

Corporate Officials

Harrison MacKellar Bains, Jr.: vice president vice president, human resources B Pasadena, CA 1943. ED University of Redlands BA (1964); University of California MBA (1966); Harvard University Graduate School of Business Administration (1983). PRIM CORP EMPL vice president, treasurer: Bristol-Myers Squibb Co. ADD CORP EMPL treasurer: Boclaro Inc.; treasurer: Bristol Caribbean Inc.; treasurer: Bristol-Myers Squibb Laboratories; treasurer: Squibb Manufacturing Inc. CORP AFFIL director: PriVest Bank. NONPR AFFIL member: National Association of Corporate Treasurers; trustee: Overlook Hospital Foundation; treasurer: Food Safety Council; member: Financial Executives Institute.
Stephen E. Bear: senior vice president, human resources B 1952.
Peter R. Dolan: chairman, chief executive officer B 1956. ED Dartmouth University MBA; Tufts University BA. PRIM CORP EMPL president, chief executive officer, director: Bristol-Myers Squibb Co. CORP AFFIL chairman elect: PhRMA; director: American Express Co. NONPR AFFIL director: National Center on Addiction & Substance Abuse; trustee: Tufts University; member: Business Roundtable; member: Business Council.
Sandra Leung: vice president, secretary B 1961.
John L. Skule, III: senior vice president environment affairs B 1944. PRIM CORP EMPL senior vice president public affairs: Bristol-Myers Squibb Co.

Foundation Officials

Harrison MacKellar Bains, Jr.: treasurer (see above)
Stephen E. Bear: director (see above)
John L. Damonti: director
Peter R. Dolan: chairman (see above)
Jeffrey Galik: assistant treasurer
Sandra Leung: secretary (see above)
John L. McGoldrick: director B 1941. CORP AFFIL director: Zimmer Holdings Inc..
John L. Skule, III: director (see above)
Laurie Smaldone, MD: director
Richard L. Thompson: director ED Catholic University JD; SUNY BA; Syracuse University MBA.
Sonia Vora: assistant secretary

Grants Analysis

Disclosure Period: calendar year ending 2003
Total Grants: $18,561,106*
Number of Grants: 281
Average Grant: $58,968*
Highest Grant: $2,050,000
Lowest Grant: $700
Typical Range: $10,000 to $100,000
*Note: Giving includes matching gifts, scholarship, United Way. Average grant figure excludes highest grant.

Recent Grants

Note: Grants derived from 2003 Form 990.
General
2,050,000	United Way of Tristate, New York, NY
650,000	Robert Wood Johnson University Hospital Foundation, New Brunswick, NJ
500,000	Children's Health Fund, New York, NY
500,000	Hamilton College, Clinton, NY
400,000	Catholic Medical Mission Board, New York, NY
395,724	National Merit Scholarship, Evanston, IL
338,844	Yale School of Medicine, New Haven, CT
311,526	United Way, Evansville, IN

290,000   Hungarian Hospice Foundation, Budapest Hungary
217,847   EUFAMI, Kessel-Lo Belgium

BRITTON FUND

Giving Contact

Nick Valentino, Treasurer
1422 Euclid Avenue, Suite 1010
Cleveland, OH 44115-2078
Phone: (216)363-6489

Description

Founded: 1952
EIN: 346513616
Organization Type: Private Foundation
Giving Locations: OH: Greater Cleveland including Cayahoga, Geauga, and lake counties
Grant Types: Capital, Department, Endowment, General Support, Multiyear/Continuing Support, Scholarship.

Donor Information

Founder: Established in 1952 by Gertrude H. Britton, Charles S. Britton, and Brigham Britton.

Financial Summary

Total Giving: $1,598,516 (2002); $1,818,600 (2001)
Giving Analysis: Giving for 2002 includes: foundation grants to United Way ($10,000)
Assets: $20,383,532 (2002); $25,610,926 (2001)
Gifts Received: $75 (1998); $1,250 (1997); $419,697 (1995). Note: In 1995, contributions were received from the estate of Gertrude H. Britton.

Typical Recipients

Arts & Humanities: Arts Centers, Arts Festivals, Arts Funds, Historic Preservation, History & Archaeology, Libraries, Museums/Galleries, Music, Performing Arts, Public Broadcasting, Theater
Civic & Public Affairs: Botanical Gardens/Parks, Economic Development, Employment/Job Training, Civic & Public Affairs-General, Housing, Philanthropic Organizations, Urban & Community Affairs, Women's Affairs
Education: Arts/Humanities Education, Colleges & Universities, Continuing Education, Education Associations, Education Funds, Elementary Education (Private), Education-General, Medical Education, Minority Education, Private Education (Precollege), Secondary Education (Private), Special Education, Student Aid
Environment: Environment-General, Protection, Research
Health: Alzheimer's Disease, Cancer, Children's Health/Hospitals, Clinics/Medical Centers, Emergency/Ambulance Services, Eyes/Blindness, Geriatric Health, Health Organizations, Hospitals (University Affiliated), Long-Term Care, Medical Rehabilitation, Medical Research, Mental Health, Multiple Sclerosis, Nursing Services, Prenatal Health Issues, Preventive Medicine/Wellness Organizations, Single-Disease Health Associations, Speech & Hearing
Religion: Religious Welfare
Science: Science Museums
Social Services: Animal Protection, Camps, Child Welfare, Community Centers, Community Service Organizations, Counseling, Day Care, Domestic Violence, Emergency Relief, Family Planning, Family Services, Food/Clothing Distribution, Homes, People with Disabilities, Senior Services, Sexual Abuse, Shelters/Homelessness, United Funds/United Ways, YMCA/YWCA/YMHA/YWHA, Youth Organizations

Application Procedures

Initial Contact: Send a brief letter of inquiry and a full proposal.

Application Requirements: Include a description of organization, amount requested, purpose of funds sought, and proof of tax-exempt status.
Deadlines: April 30 and Oct. 31.

Restrictions

Does not support individuals.

Additional Information

Publications: Annual Report

Foundation Officials

Lynda R. Britton: president, trustee
Terence B. Britton: vice president, trustee
Timothy C. Britton: vice president, trustee
Gloria Kirkwood: secretary
Nick Valentino: treasurer

Grants Analysis

Disclosure Period: calendar year ending 2002
Total Grants: $1,588,516*
Number of Grants: 38
Average Grant: $28,425*
Highest Grant: $300,000
Lowest Grant: $2,000
Typical Range: $10,000 to $50,000
*Note: Giving excludes scholarships. Average grant figure excludes two highest grants ($565,200).

Recent Grants

Note: Grants derived from 2002 Form 990.
General

300,000	Cleveland Museum of Natural History, Cleveland, OH -- grant to support pledge payment
265,200	Institute of Pathology, Cleveland, OH -- grant to Alzheimer research
200,000	Hathaway Brown School, Shaker Heights, OH
100,000	Cleveland Center for Contemporary Art, Cleveland, OH -- for exhibit support
100,000	Marine Environmental Research Institute, Blue Hill, ME -- grant to laboratory improvements and construction
55,000	North Coast Community Homes, Cleveland, OH -- for installation of sprinkling system
50,000	Cleveland Center for Contemporary Art, Cleveland, OH -- for general operating support
50,000	Hiram House, Chagrin Falls, OH -- grant to pledge payments
40,000	Salvation Army, Alexandria, VA -- for general operating support
30,000	Ohio Foundation of Independent Colleges, Columbus, OH

BROADHURST FOUNDATION

Giving Contact

Ann S. Cassidy, Chairman
Broadhurst Foundation
8116 E. 63rd St.
Tulsa, OK 74133
Phone: (918)294-9789

Description

Founded: 1951
EIN: 736061115
Organization Type: Private Foundation
Giving Locations: OK: Midwest region of US.
Grant Types: Capital, Fellowship, Loan, Multiyear/Continuing Support, Research, Scholarship, Seed Money.

Donor Information

Founder: William Broadhurst

Financial Summary

Total Giving: $194,735 (2003); $273,737 (2001)
Giving Analysis: Giving for 2001 includes: foundation scholarships ($131,000)
Assets: $7,366,636 (2003); $7,380,696 (2001)

Typical Recipients

Arts & Humanities: Arts Centers, Ballet, Libraries, Museums/Galleries, Music, Opera
Civic & Public Affairs: Civic & Public Affairs-General, Urban & Community Affairs, Zoos/Aquariums
Education: Colleges & Universities, Education-General, Legal Education, Literacy, Medical Education, Minority Education, Preschool Education, Private Education (Precollege), Religious Education, Student Aid
Health: Cancer, Children's Health/Hospitals, Diabetes, Emergency/Ambulance Services, Eyes/Blindness, Health Organizations, Heart, Medical Research, Mental Health, Multiple Sclerosis, Respiratory, Single-Disease Health Associations
Religion: Churches, Jewish Causes, Religious Organizations, Religious Welfare, Seminaries
Social Services: Animal Protection, Child Welfare, Community Service Organizations, Crime Prevention, Food/Clothing Distribution, People with Disabilities, Scouts, Senior Services, Shelters/Homelessness, United Funds/United Ways, Youth Organizations

Application Procedures

Initial Contact: Send a brief letter of inquiry outlining needs.
Application Requirements: Include a description of organization.
Deadlines: None.

Restrictions

Generally limited to educational, religious, and medical research institutions in the Midwest.

Additional Information

Publications: Annual Report

Foundation Officials

Ann S. Cassidy: chairman
John Cassidy, Jr.: trustee
Clint V. Cox: trustee
Ernestine Broadhurst Howard: vchairman
Wishard Lemons: trustee

Grants Analysis

Disclosure Period: calendar year ending 2003
Total Grants: $194,735*
Number of Grants: 24
Average Grant: $7,525*
Highest Grant: $21,666
Lowest Grant: $50
Typical Range: $1,000 to $10,000
*Note: Average grant figure excludes highest grant.

Recent Grants

Note: Grants derived from 2003 Form 990.
General

21,666	Indian Nations Council, Boy Scouts of America, Tulsa, OK
18,000	Asbury Theological Seminary, Wilmore, KY
10,000	Center for the Physically Limited, Tulsa, OK
10,000	John Brown University, Siloam Springs, AR
10,000	Mental Health Association, Tulsa, OK
10,000	National Jewish Center, Denver, CO
10,000	Oklahoma City University, Oklahoma City, OK
8,637	First United Methodist Church, Tulsa, OK
7,500	South Nazarene University, Bethany, OK
7,000	DePauw University, Greencastle, IN

BRODBECK ENTERPRISES

Company Headquarters
1035 E US Hwy. 151
Platteville, WI 53818

Company Description
Employees: 900
SIC(s): 5400 Food Stores.

Brodbeck Foundation

Giving Contact
Barry J. Brodbeck, President & Chief Executive Officer
1891 Country Rd. B
Platteville, WI 53818
Phone: (608)348-2343

Description
Founded: 1987
EIN: 391605932
Organization Type: Corporate Foundation
Giving Locations: WI: Southwestern part of the state
Grant Types: General Support.

Donor Information
Founder: Brodbeck Enterprises

Financial Summary
Total Giving: $11,622 (fiscal year ending August 31, 2004); $53,380 (fiscal 2001)
Giving Analysis: Giving for fiscal 2001 includes: foundation grants to United Way ($4,500)
Assets: $198,230 (fiscal 2004); $240,374 (fiscal 2001)
Gifts Received: $88,516 (fiscal 2001); $118,909 (fiscal 2000); $98,965 (fiscal 1998). Note: In fiscal 1994, 2000, and 2001 contributions were received from Brodbeck Enterprises.

Typical Recipients
Arts & Humanities: Arts Centers, History & Archaeology, Libraries, Museums/Galleries, Performing Arts, Theater
Civic & Public Affairs: Chambers of Commerce, Civic & Public Affairs-General, Public Policy, Urban & Community Affairs
Education: Colleges & Universities, Education Funds, Education-General, Student Aid
Health: Geriatric Health, Health Organizations, Hospitals, Nutrition, Prenatal Health Issues
Science: Science-General
Social Services: Camps, Community Centers, Community Service Organizations, Food/Clothing Distribution, Recreation & Athletics, Scouts, Senior Services, United Funds/United Ways, YMCA/YWCA/YMHA/YWHA

Application Procedures
Initial Contact: Send a brief letter of inquiry.
Application Requirements: Include background information.
Deadlines: None.

Corporate Officials
Robert J. Brodbeck: president, chief executive officer, director PRIM CORP EMPL president, chief executive officer, director: Brodbeck Enterprises.
Richard Taggart: vice president financial, chief financial officer B 1949. ED Adrian College BA (1971); University of Detroit MBA (1976). PRIM CORP EMPL vice president financial, chief financial officer: Brodbeck Enterprises ADD CORP EMPL east secretary: Brodbeck Realty Corp.

Foundation Officials
Barry J. Brodbeck: president, treasurer PRIM CORP EMPL vice president human resources, director: Brodbeck Enterprises.
Helen S. Brodbeck: director
Robert J. Brodbeck: vice president, secretary (see above)

Grants Analysis
Disclosure Period: fiscal year ending August 31, 2004
Total Grants: $11,622
Number of Grants: 3
Highest Grant: $5,000
Lowest Grant: $2,500

Recent Grants
Note: Grants derived from 2004 Form 990.
General
5,000	Rollo Jamison Association, Platteville, WI -- for self-guided tour equipment
4,122	Platteville Youth Baseball League Inc., Platteville, WI -- for public address system
2,500	University Wisconsin - Platteville Foundation, Platteville, WI -- towards signs for pioneer farm

BRODERBUND L.L.C.

Company Headquarters
500 Redwood Blvd.
Novato, CA 94947
Web: http://www.broderbund.com

Company Description
Former Name: Broderbund Corp.
Revenue: US$68 million (2001)
Employees: 1,129
SIC(s): 3944 Games, Toys & Children's Vehicles, 7372 Prepackaged Software.
Parent Company: Riverdeep Group PLC, Styne House, 3rd Fl., Upper Hatch St., Dublin, Ireland

Operating Locations
Broderbund Software, Inc. (OH--Avon Lake; TX--Dallas)

Carlston Family Foundation

Giving Contact
Nancy Klussman
PO Box 10162
San Rafael, CA 94912
Phone: (415)388-4763
Fax: (415)382-4500

Description
Founded: 1988
EIN: 680154752
Organization Type: Corporate Foundation
Giving Locations: CA: San Francisco Bay area
Grant Types: General Support.

Donor Information
Founder: Broderbund Corp.

Financial Summary
Total Giving: $111,896 (2003). Note: Contributes through foundation only.
Assets: $3,956,291 (2003)
Gifts Received: $15,062 (1999); $220,216 (1997); $918,000 (1996). Note: Contributions were received from Alice Carlston.

Typical Recipients
Arts & Humanities: Ethnic & Folk Arts, History & Archaeology, Libraries, Literary Arts, Museums/Galleries, Music, Theater
Civic & Public Affairs: Business/Free Enterprise, Employment/Job Training, Civic & Public Affairs-General, Hispanic Affairs, Housing, Native American Affairs, Parades/Festivals, Rural Affairs, Zoos/Aquariums
Education: Afterschool/Enrichment Programs, Agricultural Education, Arts/Humanities Education, Colleges & Universities, Leadership Training, Literacy, Medical Education, Minority Education, Preschool Education, Public Education (Precollege), Religious Education, Science/Mathematics Education, Secondary Education (Private), Secondary Education (Public), Student Aid
Environment: Forestry, Environment-General, Resource Conservation, Wildlife Protection
Health: AIDS/HIV, Alzheimer's Disease, Cancer, Children's Health/Hospitals, Emergency/Ambulance Services, Heart, Hospices, Hospitals, Mental Health, Nursing Services, Preventive Medicine/Wellness Organizations, Public Health, Respiratory, Single-Disease Health Associations
International: Health Care/Hospitals, International Environmental Issues, International Peace & Security Issues
Religion: Religion-General, Ministries, Religious Welfare
Science: Science Museums, Scientific Centers & Institutes
Social Services: Animal Protection, At-Risk Youth, Big Brothers/Big Sisters, Child Abuse, Child Welfare, Community Service Organizations, Counseling, Day Care, Domestic Violence, Family Services, Food/Clothing Distribution, People with Disabilities, Scouts, Senior Services, Sexual Abuse, Shelters/Homelessness, Special Olympics, Substance Abuse, United Funds/United Ways, Volunteer Services, Youth Organizations

Application Procedures
Initial Contact: Send a brief letter of inquiry.
Application Requirements: Include the organization's statement of purpose, amount requested, proposed use of grant and proof of tax-exempt status.
Deadlines: None.
Evaluative Criteria: Employee involvement is a consideration. Preference is given to health, educational social welfare, and environmental organizations in the San Francisco Bay area.

Corporate Officials
Douglas G. Carlston: chairman, chief operating officer PRIM CORP EMPL chairman: Broderbund Software Inc.
Joseph P. Durrett: chief executive officer B 1945. ED Duke University BA; University of Pennsylvania MBA. PRIM CORP EMPL chief executive officer: Broderbund Software Inc.
William M. McDonagh: president, chief operating officer PRIM CORP EMPL president, chief operating officer: Broderbund Software Inc.

Foundation Officials
Douglas G. Carlston: president, director (see above)
Erin G. Carlston: director
William M. McDonagh: director (see above)

Grants Analysis
Disclosure Period: calendar year ending 2003
Total Grants: $111,896
Number of Grants: 13
Average Grant: $8,607
Highest Grant: $15,000
Lowest Grant: $532

Recent Grants
Note: Grants derived from 2003 Form 990.

General

5,000	Azusa High School, Azusa, CA -- for school donation for teacher
5,000	Edison High School, Fresno, CA -- for school donation for teacher
5,000	Gladstone High School, Covina, CA -- for school donation for teacher
5,000	Independence High School, San Jose, CA -- for school donation for teacher
5,000	San Bernardino High School, San Bernardino, CA -- for school donation for teacher

GUY I. BROMLEY RESIDUARY TRUST

Giving Contact
David P. Ross, Senior Vice President & Trust Officer
Bank of America, NA
1200 Main St., 14th Fl.
PO Box 419119
Kansas City, MO 64141-6119
Phone: (816)979-7481

Description
Founded: 1964
EIN: 436157236
Organization Type: Private Foundation
Giving Locations: KS; MO: Kansas City
Grant Types: General Support, Project.

Donor Information
Founder: Guy I. Bromley

Financial Summary
Total Giving: $708,474 (2003); $254,747 (2001)
Giving Analysis: Giving for 2003 includes: foundation grants to United Way ($500); 2001: foundation grants to United Way ($500)
Assets: $5,302,697 (2003); $6,984,073 (2001)

Typical Recipients
Arts & Humanities: Arts Associations & Councils, Arts Centers, Arts Festivals, Arts Outreach, Ballet, History & Archaeology, Museums/Galleries, Music, Opera, Theater, Visual Arts
Civic & Public Affairs: Civil Rights, Community Foundations, Economic Development, Employment/Job Training, Civic & Public Affairs-General, Housing, Nonprofit Management, Urban & Community Affairs, Zoos/Aquariums
Education: Agricultural Education, Colleges & Universities, Continuing Education, Education-General, Private Education (Precollege), Public Education (Precollege), Religious Education, Science/Mathematics Education, Secondary Education (Private), Student Aid
Environment: Environment-General, Resource Conservation
Health: Emergency/Ambulance Services, Medical Rehabilitation, Mental Health
Religion: Churches, Dioceses, Religion-General, Religious Organizations, Religious Welfare
Social Services: Child Welfare, Community Centers, Community Service Organizations, Counseling, Crime Prevention, Emergency Relief, Family Services, United Funds/United Ways, YMCA/YWCA/YMHA/YWHA, Youth Organizations

Application Procedures
Initial Contact: Send brief letter of no more than three pages with appropriate attachments.
Deadlines: None.

Additional Information
Trust(s): Bank of America NA MO

Grants Analysis
Disclosure Period: calendar year ending 2003
Total Grants: $707,974*
Number of Grants: 25
Average Grant: $21,166*
Highest Grant: $200,000
Lowest Grant: $100
Typical Range: $5,000 to $50,000
*****Note:** Giving excludes United Way. Average grant figure excludes highest grant.

Recent Grants
Note: Grants derived from 2001 Form 990.
General

52,947	Catholic Charities Archdiocese of Kansas City, Kansas City, KS
30,000	St. Lawrence Catholic Campus Center, Lawrence, KS -- technology improvements
30,000	Visitation Church, Kansas City, MO -- computer science lab
25,000	Baker University, Baldwin City, KS -- library capital campaign
25,000	Kansas City Church Community Organization, Kansas City, MO -- challenge
25,000	RLDS for Community of Christ, Independence, MO -- 2001 Peace Prize
17,000	Surplus Exchange, Kansas City, MO
12,000	Foundation for Inclusive Religious Education (FIRE), Kansas City, MO -- operating budget
10,000	Bishop Seabury Academy, Lawrence, KS
10,000	Junction City Family YMCA, Junction City, KS -- Water Safety Program

BROOK FAMILY FOUNDATION

Giving Contact
Paul Brook, Secretary/Treasurer
9 Korhonen Road
Norway, ME 04268
Phone: (207)743-5690

Description
Founded: 1997
EIN: 010499178
Organization Type: Private Foundation
Giving Locations: ME; RI; VT
Grant Types: General Support.

Financial Summary
Total Giving: $170,801 (fiscal year ending March 31, 2004); $180,795 (fiscal 2001)
Assets: $2,354,259 (fiscal 2004); $2,860,645 (fiscal 2001)

Typical Recipients
Arts & Humanities: Libraries, Museums/Galleries
Civic & Public Affairs: Civic & Public Affairs-General
Education: Arts/Humanities Education, Environmental Education, Private Education (Precollege), Public Education (Precollege), Secondary Education (Public), Student Aid, Vocational & Technical Education
Health: Emergency/Ambulance Services, Health-General, Hospices
Social Services: Community Service Organizations, Crime Prevention, Recreation & Athletics

Foundation Officials
Jacqueline C. Brook: director
Paul F. Brook: secretary, treasurer
Robert L. Brook: director
Shirley W. Brook: director

Grants Analysis
Disclosure Period: fiscal year ending March 31, 2004
Total Grants: $170,801
Number of Grants: 19
Average Grant: $7,267*
Highest Grant: $40,000
Lowest Grant: $110
Typical Range: $1,000 to $10,000
*****Note:** Average grant figure excludes highest grant.

Recent Grants
Note: Grants derived from 2001 Form 990.
Library-Related

30,000	Oakland Public Library, Oakland, ME -- educational

General

48,000	Uxbridge Public Schools, Uxbridge, MA -- educational
15,000	Brattleboro Union High School, Brattleboro, VT -- educational
10,000	American Red Cross, Auburn, ME -- for disaster relief
10,000	HOPE, South Paris, ME -- for social tolerance
10,000	Inside Out Playground, Waterville, ME -- for youth programs
10,000	Whitingham School, Wilmington, VT -- educational
8,355	Western Maine Health, Norway, ME -- medical
7,000	Rockingham Arts and Museum, Bellow Falls, VT -- for Arts Programs
5,000	Cranston Public Schools, Cranston, RI -- educational
5,000	Grammar School, Putney, VT -- educational

BROOKDALE FOUNDATION

Giving Contact
Stephen L. Schwartz, President
950 Third Ave., 19th Fl.
New York, NY 10022
Phone: (212)644-0774
Fax: (212)750-0132
Web: http://www.brookdalefoundation.org

Description
Founded: 1950
EIN: 136076863
Organization Type: Private Foundation
Giving Locations: nationally.
Grant Types: Fellowship, Project, Research, Seed Money.

Donor Information
Founder: the late Henry L. Schwartz and his brothers

Financial Summary
Assets: $7,503,299 (fiscal year ending June 30, 2004)

Typical Recipients
Arts & Humanities: Libraries, Visual Arts
Civic & Public Affairs: Civic & Public Affairs-General, Legal Aid, Municipalities/Towns, Public Policy, Urban & Community Affairs
Education: Colleges & Universities, Education-General, Health & Physical Education, Legal Education, Medical Education
Environment: Environment-General
Health: Alzheimer's Disease, Cancer, Clinics/Medical Centers, Geriatric Health, Hospitals, Hospitals (University Affiliated), Long-Term Care, Nursing Services, Research/Studies Institutes
Religion: Dioceses, Jewish Causes, Religious Organizations, Religious Welfare

Social Services: Child Welfare, Community Centers, Community Service Organizations, Family Services, Recreation & Athletics, Scouts, Senior Services, Sexual Abuse, YMCA/YWCA/YMHA/YWHA, Youth Organizations

Application Procedures

Initial Contact: Send a brief letter of inquiry.
Application Requirements: Include a description of organization, amount requested, purpose of funds sought, and proof of tax-exempt status.

Restrictions

The foundation does not support individuals.

Additional Information

Publications: Program Policy Statement; Descriptions of Initiatives

Foundation Officials

Victor Biggs: assistant vice president
Arthur Norman Field: director B New York, NY 1935. ED City College of New York BBA (1955); Harvard University LLB (1958). PRIM CORP EMPL partner: Shearman & Sterling. CORP AFFIL director: Sunset Realty Corp. NONPR AFFIL member: New York State Bar Association; fellow: New York State Bar Foundation; member: Association Bar New York City; member: New York County Lawyers Association; fellow: American Bar Foundation; member: American Law Institute; member: American Bar Association.
Stephen L. Schwartz: president, director
Mary Ann Van Clief: vice president, director PRIM CORP EMPL vice president: Brookdale Management Co.

Grants Analysis

Disclosure Period: fiscal year ending June 30, 2004
Note: No grants were awarded in 2004.

Recent Grants

Note: Grants derived from fiscal 1999 Form 990.
General

75,000	Research Foundation of the City of New York, New York, NY
70,000	National Institute on Aging, Bethesda, MD
67,500	Fishberg Research Center for Neurobiology, New York, NY
67,500	Regents of the University of California, La Jolla, CA
61,568	Johns Hopkins University, Baltimore, MD
60,000	Baylor College of Medicine, Houston, TX
60,000	Johns Hopkins University School of Medicine, Baltimore, MD
60,000	Trustees of University of PA, Philadelphia, PA
59,814	Trustees of Tufts College, Boston, MA
59,151	Boston University, Boston, MA

GLADYS BROOKS FOUNDATION

Giving Contact

Jessica L. Rutledge, Administrative Assistant
Gladys Brooks Thayer Foundation
PO Box 7689
Garden City, NY 11530
Phone: (516)746-6103
Fax: (516)877-1758
Web: http://www.gladysbrooksfoundation.org

Alternate Contact

90 Broad Street
New York, NY 10005

Description

Founded: 1981
EIN: 132955337
Organization Type: General Purpose Foundation
Giving Locations: CT; DE; ME; MD; MA; NH; NJ; NY; NC; OH; PA; RI; SC; VT; VA; WA; WV
Grant Types: Capital, Endowment, Scholarship.

Donor Information

Founder: Established in 1981 by the late Gladys Brooks Thayer.

Financial Summary

Total Giving: $1,570,293 (2002); $1,285,000 (2001)
Assets: $32,042,157 (2002); $36,000,000 (2001)

Typical Recipients

Arts & Humanities: Arts & Humanities-General, Historic Preservation, History & Archaeology, Libraries, Museums/Galleries
Civic & Public Affairs: Civic & Public Affairs-General, Urban & Community Affairs
Education: Arts/Humanities Education, Business Education, Colleges & Universities, Education-General, Medical Education, Preschool Education, Private Education (Precollege), Public Education (Precollege), Secondary Education (Private), Special Education, Student Aid
Health: Cancer, Children's Health/Hospitals, Clinics/Medical Centers, Emergency/Ambulance Services, Hospices, Hospitals, Medical Research, Nursing Services, Research/Studies Institutes, Single-Disease Health Associations
International: Foreign Educational Institutions, Missionary/Religious Activities
Religion: Churches, Religious Organizations, Religious Welfare
Science: Observatories & Planetariums, Scientific Labs
Social Services: Child Welfare, Day Care, Family Services, People with Disabilities, Social Services-General, Youth Organizations

Application Procedures

Initial Contact: The foundation requests applicants obtain a formal application form from the foundation. A form is available for download from the foundation Web site.
Application Requirements: When submitting application form. the Foundation also requests: a specific budget for the grant, financial statements for the latest fiscal year; an annual report or a brief description of organization; and a specific budget for the project. Applications must be submitted in duplicate.
Deadlines: Within 45 days from the date of the letter from the foundation furnishing the application to the applicant or from the date of download.
Notes: It is the policy of the Foundation not to acknowledge receipt of grant application or indicate reason for non-approval of the same.

Restrictions

As a matter of policy, the foundation will make grants only to private, publicly supported, nonprofit, tax-exempt organizations. Grant applications will only be considered if outside funding (including governmental) is not available; or, if the project will be largely funded by the grant and will not be part of a larger project; or, if the funds will be used for capital projects, including equipment or endowments. In addition, grant applications will only be considered for major expenditures, generally between $50,000 and $100,000. The board follows the practice of determining, at the beginning of each calendar year, a limited scope of activities for which it will consider grant applications for that year. The foundation does not make grants to individuals or to support research projects.

Additional Information

Publications: Program Policy Statement; Annual Report (including Application Guidelines)
Trust(s): US Trust Company of NY

Foundation Officials

James J. Daly: member board governors
Thomas Q. Morris, MD: member board governors B Yonkers, NY 1933. ED University of Notre Dame BS (1954); Columbia University MD (1958). PRIM NONPR EMPL senior associate vice president health sciences: Columbia University College Physicians Surgeons. NONPR AFFIL vice dean faculty medicine: Columbia University College Physicians & Surgeons; senior advisor: New York Academy Medicine. CLUB AFFIL Century Club; Harvey Society.
Jessica L. Rutledge: administrative assistant

Grants Analysis

Disclosure Period: calendar year ending 2002
Total Grants: $1,570,293
Number of Grants: 26
Average Grant: $60,396
Highest Grant: $200,000
Lowest Grant: $5,000
Typical Range: $50,000 to $100,000 and $5,000 to $15,000

Recent Grants

Note: Grants derived from 2002 Form 990.
Library-Related

10,000	Friends of the Shelter Island Public Library Society, Shelter Island, NY

General

100,000	National Center for Disability Services, Albertson, NY
96,900	Cameron M. Neely Foundation for Cancer Care, Inc., Boston, MA
50,000	Colleges of the Seneca Hobart and William Smith Colleges, St. Geneva, NY
50,000	St. Mary's Hospital for Children, Bayside, NY
20,000	Helen Keller Service for the Blind, Brooklyn, NY
15,000	University of Notre Dame, Notre Dame, IN
10,000	East End Hospice, West Hampton Beach, NY
5,000	Five Towns Child Care Center, Inwood, NY
5,000	Friends of Rock Hall, Inc., Lawrence, NY
5,000	New Hampshire Historical Society, Concord, NH

BROOMFIELD CHARITABLE FOUNDATION

Giving Contact

William S. Broomfield, President
9910 E. Bexhill Dr.
Kensington, MD 20895
Phone: (301)942-4882

Description

Founded: 1993
EIN: 383083449
Organization Type: Private Foundation
Grant Types: General Support.

Financial Summary

Total Giving: $33,850 (fiscal year ending November 30, 2001)
Assets: $859,754 (fiscal 2001)
Gifts Received: $517,688 (fiscal 1993). Note: In fis-

cal 1993, contributions were received from the Broomfield Campaign Committee.

Typical Recipients

Arts & Humanities: History & Archaeology, Libraries, Museums/Galleries
Civic & Public Affairs: Clubs, Community Foundations, Civic & Public Affairs-General, Municipalities/Towns
Education: Education Funds, Elementary Education (Public), Private Education (Precollege), Secondary Education (Private), Student Aid
Health: Alzheimer's Disease, Arthritis, Cancer, Children's Health/Hospitals, Clinics/Medical Centers, Hospitals, Medical Research, Mental Health, Multiple Sclerosis, Single-Disease Health Associations
Religion: Religious Welfare
Science: Scientific Centers & Institutes
Social Services: Camps, Child Welfare, Community Service Organizations, Delinquency & Criminal Rehabilitation, Domestic Violence, Family Services, People with Disabilities, Scouts, Substance Abuse, Youth Organizations

Application Procedures

Initial Contact: Applications should include an outline of the proposed project and its objectives, a proposed budget, and proof of tax-exempt status.
Deadlines: None.

Restrictions

Foundation does not support individuals or political or lobbying groups.

Additional Information

Trust(s): Bank One

Foundation Officials

Jane Broomfield: vice president, secretary, treasurer
William S. Broomfield: president
Nancy Broomfield Aiken: director
Barbara Broomfield Shaffer: director

Grants Analysis

Disclosure Period: fiscal year ending November 30, 2001
Total Grants: $33,850
Number of Grants: 21
Average Grant: $1,612*
Highest Grant: $5,000
Lowest Grant: $100
Typical Range: $500 to $2,500
*Note: Average grant figure excludes highest grant.

Recent Grants

Note: Grants derived from fiscal 2002 Form 990.
Library-Related
500	Orion Township Public Library, Lake Orion, MI

General
7,500	Connelly School of the Holy Child, Potomac, MD
7,500	GRACF - Rochester Hills Museum, Rochester, MI
5,000	Dondero High School Scholarship Fund, Royal Oak, MI
3,000	Suburban Hospital Foundation, Bethesda, MD
2,500	Children's Hospital of Michigan, Detroit, MI
2,500	WJHS Booster Club, Bethesda, MD
2,000	St. Joseph Mercy Hospital, Pontiac, MI
1,000	St. Jude's Children's Research Hospital, Memphis, TN
1,000	Salvation Army, Royal Oak, MI
750	Alzheimer's Foundation, Alexandria, VA

WILLIAM AND JEMIMA BROSSMAN CHARITABLE FOUNDATION

Giving Contact

Carl Brubaker, Trust Officer
William and Jemima Brossman Charitable Foundation
c/o Ephrata National Bank
31 E. Main St., PO Box 457
Ephrata, PA 17522
Phone: (717)733-6576

Description

Founded: 1986
EIN: 236087844
Organization Type: Private Foundation
Giving Locations: PA: South Central area of state
Grant Types: General Support.

Donor Information

Founder: the late Bertha Brossman Blair

Financial Summary

Total Giving: $1,096,100 (fiscal year ending October 31, 2004); $1,048,820 (fiscal 2001)
Giving Analysis: Giving for fiscal 2004 includes: foundation grants to United Way ($33,500); foundation scholarships ($355,500); fiscal 2001: foundation grants to United Way ($11,000); foundation scholarships ($408,000)
Assets: $9,732,028 (fiscal 2004); $20,852,111 (fiscal 2001)
Gifts Received: $36,083 (fiscal 2004); $1,346 (fiscal 1993). Note: In fiscal 2004, contributions were received from Anne B. Sweigart Irrevocable Trust. In fiscal 1993, contributions were received from the estate of Bertha B. Blair.

Typical Recipients

Arts & Humanities: Arts Associations & Councils, Arts Centers, Arts & Humanities-General, Historic Preservation, History & Archaeology, Libraries, Museums/Galleries, Music, Opera, Performing Arts, Public Broadcasting, Theater, Visual Arts
Civic & Public Affairs: Civic & Public Affairs-General, Housing, Zoos/Aquariums
Education: Arts/Humanities Education, Business Education, Colleges & Universities, Community & Junior Colleges, Education Funds, Engineering/Technological Education, Leadership Training, Private Education (Precollege), Science/Mathematics Education, Student Aid
Health: Alzheimer's Disease, Cancer, Emergency/Ambulance Services, Eyes/Blindness, Geriatric Health, Health Organizations, Heart, Hospices, Hospitals, Preventive Medicine/Wellness Organizations, Public Health
International: Foreign Educational Institutions, Missionary/Religious Activities
Religion: Churches, Jewish Causes, Ministries, Religious Welfare, Seminaries
Science: Scientific Centers & Institutes
Social Services: Big Brothers/Big Sisters, Community Service Organizations, Emergency Relief, Family Planning, Recreation & Athletics, Scouts, United Funds/United Ways, YMCA/YWCA/YMHA/YWHA

Application Procedures

Initial Contact: The foundation has no formal grant application procedure or application form. Send a full proposal.
Application Requirements: Include a description of organization, amount requested, purpose of funds sought, and proof of tax-exempt status.
Deadlines: None.

Restrictions

The foundation does not support individuals or political or lobbying groups. Recipients must be 501(c)(3) organizations.

Additional Information

Trust(s): Ephrata Natl Bank

Grants Analysis

Disclosure Period: fiscal year ending October 31, 2004
Total Grants: $707,100*
Number of Grants: 112
Average Grant: $6,313*
Highest Grant: $50,000
Lowest Grant: $25
Typical Range: $1,000 to $10,000
*Note: Giving excludes scholarships; United Way.

Recent Grants

Note: Grants derived from 2004 Form 990.
General
325,000	Brossman Family Charitable Trust for Scholarships, Ephrata, PA
50,000	Lancaster Health Alliance, Lancaster, PA -- for women and babies hospital
50,000	Lebanon Valley College, Annville, PA -- towards great expectations campaign
50,000	Rider University, Lawrenceville, NJ
41,400	American Red Cross, Lancaster, PA -- for fire hurts media campaign
40,000	Boy Scouts of America, Lancaster, PA -- for Pennsylvania Dutch council
40,000	Harrisburg Area Community College, Harrisburg, PA -- for library and learning center
40,000	LutherCare, Lititz, PA -- for wellness center
40,000	Millersville University, Millersville, PA -- for Roddy science building
30,000	Thaddeus Stevens Foundation, Lancaster, PA

BROWN FOUNDATION

Giving Contact

Nancy Pittman, Executive Director
PO Box 130646
Houston, TX 77219-0646
Phone: (713)523-6867
Fax: (713)523-2917
E-mail: bfi@brownfoundation.org
Web: http://www.brownfoundation.org

Description

Founded: 1951
EIN: 746036466
Organization Type: General Purpose Foundation
Giving Locations: TX: particularly Houston
Grant Types: Capital, Challenge, Employee Matching Gifts, Endowment, Fellowship, General Support, Matching, Operating Expenses, Project.

Donor Information

Founder: Established in July 1951 by Margrett Root Brown, Herman Brown, Alice Pratt Brown, and George R. Brown. Herman and George were founders of Brown & Root, Inc., a construction company whose subsidiaries included oil and gas companies, hotels, real estate companies, paper mills, and mines. Until 1958, all funding was restricted to organizations in Texas. The charter was amended to allow a small amount of funding to be distributed elsewhere in the United States. All of the original donors are now deceased.

Financial Summary

Total Giving: $36,177,237 (fiscal year ending June 30, 2003); $69,463,862 (fiscal 2002); $62,456,909 (fiscal 2001)

Giving Analysis: Giving for fiscal 2003 includes: foundation grants to United Way ($125,000); foundation scholarships ($226,000); fiscal 2001: foundation scholarships ($100,000); foundation grants to United Way ($125,000)

Assets: $1,555,287,602 (fiscal 2003); $1,040,221,987 (fiscal 2002); $1,323,011,734 (fiscal 2001)

Gifts Received: $1,096 (fiscal 1996)

Typical Recipients

Arts & Humanities: Arts Associations & Councils, Arts Centers, Arts Funds, Arts Institutes, Arts Outreach, Ballet, Dance, Ethnic & Folk Arts, Arts & Humanities-General, Historic Preservation, History & Archaeology, Libraries, Literary Arts, Museums/Galleries, Music, Opera, Performing Arts, Public Broadcasting, Theater, Visual Arts

Civic & Public Affairs: African American Affairs, Botanical Gardens/Parks, Community Foundations, Economic Development, Civic & Public Affairs-General, Hispanic Affairs, Housing, Inner-City Development, Public Policy, Rural Affairs, Urban & Community Affairs, Women's Affairs, Zoos/Aquariums

Education: Arts/Humanities Education, Business Education, Colleges & Universities, Education Associations, Education Funds, Education Reform, Elementary Education (Private), Elementary Education (Public), Engineering/Technological Education, Environmental Education, Faculty Development, Education-General, International Exchange, International Studies, Leadership Training, Literacy, Medical Education, Preschool Education, Private Education (Precollege), Public Education (Precollege), Religious Education, Science/Mathematics Education, Secondary Education (Private), Social Sciences Education, Special Education, Student Aid, Vocational & Technical Education

Environment: Environment-General, Resource Conservation, Wildlife Protection

Health: Adolescent Health Issues, Alzheimer's Disease, Cancer, Children's Health/Hospitals, Clinics/Medical Centers, Emergency/Ambulance Services, Health Funds, Health Organizations, Heart, Hospices, Hospitals, Medical Research, Mental Health, Research/Studies Institutes, Single-Disease Health Associations

International: Foreign Arts Organizations, Foreign Educational Institutions, International Environmental Issues, International Organizations, International Relief Efforts

Religion: Churches, Religious Welfare

Science: Science Museums, Scientific Centers & Institutes

Social Services: Animal Protection, At-Risk Youth, Camps, Child Abuse, Child Welfare, Community Centers, Community Service Organizations, Counseling, Crime Prevention, Day Care, Delinquency & Criminal Rehabilitation, Domestic Violence, Family Planning, Family Services, People with Disabilities, Recreation & Athletics, Scouts, Shelters/Homelessness, United Funds/United Ways, YMCA/YWCA/YMHA/YWHA, Youth Organizations

Application Procedures

Initial Contact: Applicants should submit a written proposal. Contact the foundation or visit the foundation's web site to obtain guidelines and a Proposal Summary Form.

Application Requirements: Completed Proposal Summary Forms must be accompanied by the following supporting information: list of board members/officers/advisory board, including the percentage of directors who have contributed financially to the endeavor and the total amount of their contributions; the organization's current operating budget and a budget for the specific program to be funded; a list of other sources of funding for the project, including amounts committed and pending; recently audited financial statement; financial statement of income and expenses from time of last audit to present; and proof of tax-exempt status. The foundation requests that applications be signed by both the chief administrator/executive officer and by the board president or chair, if applicable.

Deadlines: Proposals should be submitted at least four months before funding will be needed but are accepted at any time.

Review Process: Applicants should not inquire about proposal status. Applicants will be informed, in writing, that their proposal has been received at the foundation's office and of the decision of the trustees after the grant review process, usually within 90 days.

Evaluative Criteria: The foundation prefers to fund projects which address root causes of a concern rather than treating symptoms; serve as a catalyst for collaborative efforts by several sectors of the community; result in a growing, long-term impact on the situation beyond the value of the grant itself; and reflect and encourage sound financial planning and management practices in project administration.

Notes: If the foundation requests additional information, failure to submit such within 30 days will result in removal of the proposal from the review process. Video and audio tapes are not accepted.

Restrictions

The foundation does not support individuals; religious organizations for sectarian purposes; testimonial dinners, fundraising events, or marketing efforts; political candidates or causes; private foundations; or grants to cover past operating deficits or debt retirements.

Additional Information

Only one grant request from an organization will be considered in a twelve month period. No proposal from an organization previously funded by the foundation will be reviewed until a full report of the expenditure of the previous grant has been submitted.

Publications: Application Guidelines; Application Form; Annual Report; Proposal Summary Form

Foundation Officials

John F. Fort, III: secretary, trustee CORP AFFIL director: Roper Industries Inc.; advisory director: Tyco International Ltd..

Isabel S. Lummis: trustee

Travis A. Mathis: trustee NONPR AFFIL trustee: Bat Conservation International.

Nancy B. Negley: trustee, first vice president

W. Walter Negley: trustee NONPR AFFIL trustee: The Kinkaid School.

George R. O'Connor: trustee

Maconda Brown O'Connor: chairman, trustee B 1930. PRIM CORP EMPL partner: George R. Brown Partnership. NONPR AFFIL honorary trustee: The Brookings Institution; member: Greater Houston Collaborative for Children.

Nancy Pittman: executive director

Ann Prescott: treasurer

Christopher B. Sarofim: trustee CORP AFFIL vice president: Fayez Sarofim & Co. NONPR AFFIL board of directors development: University of Texas Health Science Center.

Louisa Stude Sarofim: president, trustee ED Smith College. PRIM CORP EMPL partner: George R. Brown Partnership. NONPR AFFIL trustee: Houston Ballet Foundation.

Herman L. Stude: assistant secretary

Mike S. Stude: vice president, trustee B 1939. PRIM CORP EMPL partner: George R. Brown Partnership. NONPR AFFIL board of directors: Houston Parks Board Inc..

Isabel Brown Wilson: vice president, trustee PRIM CORP EMPL partner: George R. Brown Partnership. NONPR AFFIL advisory board: Nature Discovery Center.

Grants Analysis

Disclosure Period: fiscal year ending June 30, 2003

Total Grants: $35,826,237*

Number of Grants: 511

Average Grant: $65,587*

Highest Grant: $1,258,725

Lowest Grant: $1,000

Typical Range: $10,000 to $100,000

*Note: Giving excludes scholarships and United Way. Average grant excludes two highest grants ($2,442,225).

Recent Grants

Note: Grants derived from fiscal 2003 Form 990.

General

1,285,725	University of Texas Health, Houston, TX
1,156,500	University of Texas Health, Houston, TX
973,720	Houston Zoo Inc., Houston, TX
951,500	Pine Manor College, Chestnut Hill, MA
840,000	University of Arkansas Foundation, Fayetteville, AR
820,400	University of Texas Health, Houston, TX
728,000	Child-Centered Schools Initiative, Houston, TX
605,500	University of Arkansas Foundation, Fayetteville, AR
602,630	William Marsh Rice University, Houston, TX
600,000	Texas Southern University Foundation, Houston, TX

JAMES GRAHAM BROWN FOUNDATION, INC.

Giving Contact

Dodie McKenzie, Program Officer
4350 Brownsboro Road
Suite 200
Louisville, KY 40207
Phone: (502)896-2440
Fax: (502)896-1774
E-mail: mason@jgbf.org
Web: http://www.jgbf.org

Description

Founded: 1943

EIN: 610724060

Organization Type: General Purpose Foundation

Giving Locations: KY

Grant Types: Capital, Challenge, Endowment, General Support, Scholarship.

Donor Information

Founder: Established in 1943 and funded by the late James Graham Brown and his sister, the late Agnes B. Duggan. Mr. Brown's business pursuits included timberland, lumber, mineral holdings, and hotels. His philanthropic interests included the Louisville Zoo and a new Red Cross Blood Bank in Louisville. Each organization received $1.5 million in grants. When Mr. Brown died in March 1969, his will specified twelve bequests to religious and educational institutions totaling $3.05 million. The remainder of his estate, one of the largest ever probated in Kentucky, was left to the foundation.

Financial Summary

Total Giving: $16,998,909 (2003); $19,935,253 (2002); $21,843,310 (2001)

Giving Analysis: Giving for 2003 includes: foundation grants to United Way ($875,000)

Assets: $407,351,088 (2003); $377,430,797 (2002); $426,367,510 (2001)

Typical Recipients

Arts & Humanities: Arts Centers, Arts Institutes, Ballet, Ethnic & Folk Arts, Historic Preservation, History

& Archaeology, Libraries, Museums/Galleries, Music, Opera, Public Broadcasting, Visual Arts

Civic & Public Affairs: African American Affairs, Botanical Gardens/Parks, Business/Free Enterprise, Chambers of Commerce, Clubs, Community Foundations, Economic Development, Employment/Job Training, Ethnic Organizations, Civic & Public Affairs-General, Housing, Inner-City Development, Law & Justice, Municipalities/Towns, Nonprofit Management, Parades/Festivals, Public Policy, Urban & Community Affairs, Women's Affairs, Zoos/Aquariums

Education: Afterschool/Enrichment Programs, Arts/Humanities Education, Business Education, Colleges & Universities, Economic Education, Education Funds, Education Reform, Education-General, Literacy, Preschool Education, Private Education (Precollege), Public Education (Precollege), Secondary Education (Private), Special Education

Environment: Environment-General, Protection, Resource Conservation

Health: Arthritis, Cancer, Children's Health/Hospitals, Clinics/Medical Centers, Emergency/Ambulance Services, Eyes/Blindness, Geriatric Health, Health Policy/Cost Containment, Health Organizations, Hospices, Hospitals, Medical Rehabilitation, Mental Health, Multiple Sclerosis, Prenatal Health Issues, Respiratory, Single-Disease Health Associations

Religion: Jewish Causes, Ministries, Religious Organizations, Religious Welfare, Social/Policy Issues

Science: Science Museums, Scientific Centers & Institutes

Social Services: Animal Protection, Camps, Child Abuse, Child Welfare, Community Centers, Community Service Organizations, Counseling, Crime Prevention, Emergency Relief, Family Planning, Family Services, Food/Clothing Distribution, Homes, People with Disabilities, Recreation & Athletics, Scouts, Senior Services, Shelters/Homelessness, Special Olympics, Substance Abuse, United Funds/United Ways, Veterans, Volunteer Services, YMCA/YWCA/YMHA/YWHA, Youth Organizations

Application Procedures

Initial Contact: Contact the foundation or visit the foundation web site to obtain a pre-grant application form.

Application Requirements: The Pre-Grant Application must include the name and phone number of contact person; name of the organization's board chair and president or CEO; percentage of board members contributing to the project or campaign; a description of organization; project description; total project cost; amount requested; evidence of community support; board of directors list; and project budget.

Deadlines: October 1. Funds are dispersed annually at the end of each calendar year; applications received after October 1 will be considered in the following calendar year.

Review Process: The board reviews inquiries and applications monthly. Applicants will receive written notification of the next step, if any, in the application process.

Restrictions

The foundation does not fund grant requests related either directly or indirectly to the performing arts, requests from individuals, primary or secondary schools, national organizations, political entities, religious organizations for religious purposes, annual operating support, or debt reduction.

Additional Information

Publications: Grant application

Foundation Officials

Stanley S. Dickson: trustee
Joan R. Dudley: treasurer
Frank B. Hower, Jr.: trustee
Stanley Hugenberg, Jr.: trustee PRIM CORP EMPL

president: Jack Antom Sales Co. CORP AFFIL director: Churchill Downs Inc. NONPR AFFIL director: Kentucky Derby Museum Corp.

Sylvia Watson Jaeger: trustee
Graham B. Loper: vice president, trustee
Dorma J. McKenzie: program officer
W. Barrett Nichols: trustee B 1950. PRIM CORP EMPL secretary: Micropak Inc.
Alex Rankin: trustee
Joe M. Rodes: president, trustee CORP AFFIL director: PNC Bank.
Robert Rounsavall, III: trustee B 1943. PRIM CORP EMPL chief executive officer: Dixie Warehouse Cartage Inc. CORP AFFIL director: PNC Bank Kentucky; chairman: Prolift Industrial Equipment Co.
Robert Lewis Royer: trustee B Louisville, KY 1928. ED Rose-Hulman Institute Technology BS (1949). PRIM CORP EMPL chairman emeritus: Louisville Gas & Electric Co. NONPR AFFIL member: Louisville Chamber of Commerce; member, board managers: Rose-Hulman Institute Technology; member: Executives Club Louisville; member: Institute Electrical & Electronics Engineers. CLUB AFFIL Pendennis Club; Rotary Club; Hurstbourne Country Club.
Mason B. Rummel: executive director, secretary

Grants Analysis

Disclosure Period: calendar year ending 2003
Total Grants: $16,123,909*
Number of Grants: 47
Average Grant: $166,296*
Highest Grant: $5,000,000
Lowest Grant: $500
Typical Range: $50,000 to $300,000
*Note: Giving excludes United Way. Average grant figure excludes five highest grants ($9,139,488).

Recent Grants

Note: Grants derived from 2003 Form 990.
General

5,000,000	University of Louisville, Louisville, KY
1,500,000	Louisville Zoological Foundation, Louisville, KY
902,300	Kentucky Wesleyan College, Owensboro, KY
893,788	Centre College, Danville, KY
875,000	Metro United Way, Louisville, KY
843,400	Thomas More College, Crestview Hills, KY
760,000	Bellarmine University, Louisville, KY
700,000	Alice Lloyd College, Pippa Passes, KY
526,100	Georgetown College, Georgetown, KY
500,000	Community Foundation of Louisville Inc., Louisville, KY

M. K. BROWN FOUNDATION

Giving Contact

Leland W. Waters, Secretary & Treasurer
PO Box 581
Pampa, TX 79066-0581
Phone: (806)669-6890

Description

Founded: 1960
EIN: 756034058
Organization Type: Private Foundation
Giving Locations: TX: Gray County, Pampa County, Panhandle area of Texas
Grant Types: General Support.

Donor Information

Founder: the late M. K. Brown

Financial Summary

Total Giving: $200,413 (2004)
Giving Analysis: Giving for 2004 includes: founda-

tion grants to United Way ($15,000)
Assets: $3,897,546 (2004)

Typical Recipients

Arts & Humanities: Arts Associations & Councils, Ballet, Dance, Arts & Humanities-General, Historic Preservation, History & Archaeology, Libraries, Museums/Galleries, Music

Civic & Public Affairs: Economic Development, Civic & Public Affairs-General, Municipalities/Towns, Safety, Urban & Community Affairs

Education: Colleges & Universities, Engineering/Technological Education, Medical Education, Public Education (Precollege)

Environment: Environment-General

Health: Alzheimer's Disease, Cancer, Hospices, Prenatal Health Issues, Single-Disease Health Associations, Transplant Networks/Donor Banks

Religion: Churches, Religious Welfare

Science: Scientific Centers & Institutes

Social Services: At-Risk Youth, Camps, Child Welfare, Community Service Organizations, Day Care, Family Planning, Food/Clothing Distribution, People with Disabilities, Recreation & Athletics, Scouts, Senior Services, Substance Abuse, United Funds/United Ways, Veterans, Youth Organizations

Application Procedures

Initial Contact: The foundation requests applications be made in writing.

Application Requirements: Include a description of organization, purpose of funds sought, affiliation with any other organization, and proof of tax-exempt status.

Deadlines: July 1 and December 1.

Grants Analysis

Disclosure Period: calendar year ending 2004
Total Grants: $185,413*
Number of Grants: 19
Average Grant: $8,579*
Highest Grant: $31,000
Lowest Grant: $1,913
Typical Range: $5,000 to $10,000
*Note: Giving excludes United Way. Average grant figure excludes highest grant.

Recent Grants

Note: Grants derived from 2001 Form 990.
General

16,310	Gray County, Texas, Pampa, TX
15,000	Texas Plains Girl Scouts, Lubbock, TX -- for operations
10,000	Body of Christ Church, Pampa, TX -- for operations
10,000	Good Samaritan Christian Service, Pampa, TX -- for operations
7,500	White Deer Land Museum, Pampa, TX -- for building project
5,000	KANZA Society, Garden City, KS -- for operations
5,000	Texas Plains Girl Scouts, Lubbock, TX -- for operations
3,500	Coffee Memorial Blood Center, Amarillo, TX -- for operations
1,000	Pampa Fine Arts Association, Pampa, TX
250	Macedonia Baptist Church, Pampa, TX -- for operations

W. L. LYONS BROWN FOUNDATION

Giving Contact

Ina Hamilton-Bond, President
850 Dixie Hwy.
Louisville, KY 40210
Phone: (502)895-6363
E-mail: Brown-Forman@b-f.com

Web: http://www.brown-forman.com

Description
Founded: 1962
EIN: 610598511
Organization Type: Private Foundation
Giving Locations: KY: Louisville
Grant Types: Capital, General Support.

Donor Information
Founder: the late W. L. Lyons Brown

Financial Summary
Total Giving: $935,891 (2001). Note: 1997 Giving includes United Way ($23,000).
Giving Analysis: Giving for 2001 includes: foundation grants to United Way ($28,000)
Assets: $20,424,812 (2001)

Typical Recipients
Arts & Humanities: Arts Festivals, Arts Funds, Ballet, Community Arts, Ethnic & Folk Arts, Arts & Humanities-General, Historic Preservation, History & Archaeology, Libraries, Museums/Galleries, Music, Public Broadcasting, Theater
Civic & Public Affairs: Botanical Gardens/Parks, Clubs, Community Foundations, Economic Development, Civic & Public Affairs-General, Housing, Philanthropic Organizations, Public Policy, Urban & Community Affairs, Zoos/Aquariums
Education: Business Education, Colleges & Universities, Education Reform, Environmental Education, Faculty Development, Legal Education, Private Education (Precollege), Public Education (Precollege), Science/Mathematics Education, Secondary Education (Private)
Environment: Air/Water Quality, Forestry, Environment-General, Resource Conservation, Wildlife Protection
Health: Cancer, Clinics/Medical Centers, Hospitals, Nursing Services, Prenatal Health Issues
International: International Environmental Issues
Religion: Churches, Dioceses, Religious Welfare
Science: Science Museums, Scientific Centers & Institutes
Social Services: Community Service Organizations, Counseling, Family Planning, Family Services, Homes, People with Disabilities, United Funds/United Ways

Application Procedures
Initial Contact: The foundation requests applications be made in writing.
Application Requirements: Include pertinent information that will enable the board to determine if the request satisfies foundation's guidelines.
Deadlines: None.

Restrictions
Priority is given to organizations that seek to improve the quality of life in Louisville, KY, such as zoos, museums, parks, educational institutions, and organizations that support the arts. Support will not be given to organizations operating in fields where there is substantial governmental financial assistance.

Foundation Officials
Ina B. Hamilton Bond: president, trustee
Martin S. Brown: trustee PRIM CORP EMPL chairman, chief executive officer: Jack Daniels Distillery. CORP AFFIL director: Blue Grass Cooperage Co.; director: Brown-Forman Corp.
Owsley Brown, II: treasurer, trustee B Louisville, KY September 10, 1942. ED Yale University BA (1964); Stanford University MBA (1966). PRIM CORP EMPL president, chief executive officer: Brown-Forman Corp. NONPR AFFIL treasurer, trustee: W L Lyons Brown Foundation; director: Greater Louisville Fund Arts. CLUB AFFIL Wynn Stay Club; Louisville Country Club; Pendennis Club; Filson Club.
Mrs. W. L. Lyons Brown: secretary, trustee
William Lee Lyons Brown, Jr.: trustee B Louisville,

KY 1936. ED University of Virginia BA (1958); American Graduate School of International Management BS (1960). PRIM CORP EMPL chairman: Brown-Forman Corp. CORP AFFIL director: Stone & Webster; director: National City Corp. Cleveland; director: Standex International Corp.; director: Carter Hawley Hale Stores Inc.; director: National City Corp.; director: Bank Boston Corp.; director: Bradley Real Estate Trust. NONPR AFFIL member: Presidents Advisory Committee Trade Policy & Negotiations; member: University Virginia Alumni Association; member business committee: Metropolitan Museum Art; chairman: American Business Conference. CLUB AFFIL Travelers Club; University Club; Pendennis Club; River Valley Club; Fishers Club; Louisville Country Club.
Benjamin H. Morris: trustee

Grants Analysis
Disclosure Period: calendar year ending 2001
Total Grants: $907,891*
Number of Grants: 22
Average Grant: $30,395*
Highest Grant: $200,000
Lowest Grant: $4,000
Typical Range: $10,000 to $50,000
*Note: Giving excludes United Way. Average grant figure excludes two highest grants ($300,000).

Recent Grants
Note: Grants derived from 2002 Form 990.
General

500,000	Woods Hole Research Center, Woods Hole, MA -- global warming grant
150,000	River Fields, Inc., Louisville, KY -- land conservation grant for environmental impact
100,000	Brown Theatre, Columbia, SC -- art grant for building renovation
100,000	Community Foundation of Louisville, Louisville, KY -- philanthropy
100,000	Healing Place, Louisville, KY -- child abuse treatment agency
50,000	Bernheim Arboretum and Research Forest, Clermont, KY -- to create critically need infrastructure
50,000	Harrods Creek Baptist Church -- capital campaign - construction of community center
50,000	Louisville Ballet, Louisville, KY -- arts grant operations
50,000	Muhammad Ali Center, Louisville, KY -- grant to promote peace and non-violence
50,000	Transylvania University, Lexington, NY -- educational grant for excellence in teaching

BROWN & WILLIAMSON TOBACCO CORP.

Company Headquarters
401 South 4th Avenue, Suite 200
PO Box 35090
Louisville, KY 40232-5090
Phone: (502)568-7000
Fax: (502)568-7494
Web: http://www.bw.com

Company Description
Employees: 6,600
SIC(s): 2111 Cigarettes, 2131 Chewing & Smoking Tobacco.
Parent Company: R.J. Reynolds Tobacco, 401 N. Main Street, Winston-Salem, NC, United States

Operating Locations
Brown & Williamson Tobacco Corp. (NC--Wilson, Winston-Salem)

Nonmonetary Support
Type: Donated Equipment; Workplace Solicitation

Giving Contact
Gail Strange, Senior Manager, Corp. and Community Relations
Brown & Williamson Tower 200
401 S. Fourth St.
PO Box 35090
Louisville, KY 40202
Phone: (502)568-7000
Fax: (502)568-8262

Alternate Contact
Brennan Dawson, Vice President

Description
Organization Type: Corporate Giving Program
Giving Locations: headquarters and operating communities.
Grant Types: Award, Capital, Employee Matching Gifts, General Support, Operating Expenses, Research, Scholarship.

Financial Summary
Total Giving: $1,800,000 (2003 approx); $1,800,000 (2002); $3,000,000 (2001 approx). Note: Contributes through corporate direct giving program only.

Typical Recipients
Arts & Humanities: Arts Associations & Councils, Dance, Ethnic & Folk Arts, Historic Preservation, Libraries, Museums/Galleries, Public Broadcasting
Civic & Public Affairs: Business/Free Enterprise, Economic Development, Employment/Job Training, Law & Justice, Public Policy, Urban & Community Affairs, Women's Affairs, Zoos/Aquariums
Education: Colleges & Universities, Education Associations, Minority Education, Science/Mathematics Education
Environment: Environment-General
Science: Scientific Organizations
Social Services: Child Welfare, Community Centers, Community Service Organizations, Family Services, Senior Services, Substance Abuse, United Funds/United Ways

Application Procedures
Initial Contact: letter requesting formal application form
Application Requirements: description of the organization, amount requested, purpose of funds sought, recently audited financial statement, and proof of tax-exempt status
Deadlines: August.

Restrictions
The company does not support individuals, dinners or special events, fraternal organizations, goodwill advertising, member agencies of united funds, political or lobbying groups, or religious organizations for sectarian purposes.

Corporate Officials
Brennan Dawson: vice president external affairs PRIM CORP EMPL vice president external affairs: Brown & Williamson Tobacco Co.
Susan Ivey: president, chief executive officer PRIM CORP EMPL president, chief executive officer: Brown & Williamson Tobacco Corp.
Michael J. McGraw: senior vice president law & human resources PRIM CORP EMPL senior vice president law & human resources: Brown & Williamson Tobacco Corp.

Grants Analysis
Typical Range: $2,500 to $5,000

BROYHILL FAMILY FOUNDATION

Giving Contact
Paul H. Broyhill, Chairman & Manager
PO Box 500
Golfview Park
Lenoir, NC 28645
Phone: (828)758-6100

Description
Founded: 1945
EIN: 566054119
Organization Type: Family Foundation
Giving Locations: NC: preference to Cardwell County and surrounding areas
Grant Types: General Support, Scholarship.

Donor Information
Founder: Established in 1945. Broyhill Furniture Industries and the Broyhill family members are donors.

Financial Summary
Total Giving: $1,845,545 (2002); $1,920,508 (2001)
Giving Analysis: Giving for 2002 includes: foundation grants to United Way ($12,000); foundation scholarships ($29,400); 2001: foundation grants to United Way ($24,000)
Assets: $37,625,356 (2002); $41,848,607 (2001)

Typical Recipients
Arts & Humanities: Arts Associations & Councils, Arts Centers, Community Arts, Arts & Humanities-General, History & Archaeology, Libraries, Museums/Galleries, Music
Civic & Public Affairs: Botanical Gardens/Parks, Business/Free Enterprise, Chambers of Commerce, Community Foundations, Economic Development, Economic Policy, Employment/Job Training, Civic & Public Affairs-General, Philanthropic Organizations, Professional & Trade Associations, Public Policy, Safety
Education: Arts/Humanities Education, Business Education, Colleges & Universities, Community & Junior Colleges, Continuing Education, Education Funds, Education Reform, Education-General, International Studies, Leadership Training, Medical Education, Minority Education, Private Education (Precollege), Public Education (Precollege), Religious Education, School Volunteerism, Science/Mathematics Education, Student Aid
Health: Children's Health/Hospitals, Clinics/Medical Centers, Emergency/Ambulance Services, Eyes/Blindness, Health-General, Health Funds, Health Organizations, Hospices, Hospitals, Medical Research, Mental Health, Preventive Medicine/Wellness Organizations, Public Health, Research/Studies Institutes, Single-Disease Health Associations
Religion: Bible Study/Translation, Churches, Ministries, Missionary Activities (Domestic), Religious Organizations, Religious Welfare, Seminaries
Social Services: At-Risk Youth, Camps, Child Welfare, Community Centers, Community Service Organizations, Counseling, Homes, People with Disabilities, Recreation & Athletics, Scouts, Senior Services, Special Olympics, Substance Abuse, United Funds/United Ways, Volunteer Services, YMCA/YWCA/YMHA/YWHA, Youth Organizations

Application Procedures
Initial Contact: Potential applicants should submit a brief letter to the foundation.
Deadlines: None.
Review Process: The foundation's board meets quarterly to review proposals.

Restrictions
The foundation does not give loans or scholarships directly to students.

Foundation Officials
Clarence E. Beach: director
E. D. Beach: secretary, treasurer, director PRIM CORP EMPL secretary, treasurer, director: Broyhill Investments Inc.
Faye A. Broyhill: director
M. Hunt Broyhill: president, director B 1964. ED Wake Forest University (1984). PRIM CORP EMPL president, director: Broyhill Investments Inc.
Paul Hunt Broyhill: chairman, director B Lincolnton, NC 1924. ED University of North Carolina (1948). PRIM CORP EMPL chairman, chief operating officer: Broyhill Investments Inc. CORP AFFIL chairman: Broyhill Realty. NONPR AFFIL chairman: BMC Fund, Inc.
Lee E. Pritchard: assistant secretary, assistant treasurer

Grants Analysis
Disclosure Period: calendar year ending 2002
Total Grants: $1,804,145*
Number of Grants: 219
Average Grant: $6,732*
Highest Grant: $150,000
Lowest Grant: $50
Typical Range: $1,000 to $10,000
*Note: Giving excludes United Way; scholarships. Average grant figure excludes three highest grants ($350,000).

Recent Grants
Note: Grants derived from 2002 Form 990.
General

150,000	Ridge
135,000	T.H. Broyhill Park Authority, Lenoir, NC
100,000	Broyhill Memorial Park, Lenoir, NC
100,000	Paul H. Broyhill Foundation
100,000	Tomorrow's America Foundation
66,666	Converse College, Spartanburg, SC
60,000	Baptist Children's Homes of North Carolina, Thomasville, NC -- toward cost of book publication
50,000	Appalachian State University Foundation, Washington, DC -- funds for Appalachian House
50,000	Baptist Children's Homes of North Carolina, Thomasville, NC -- toward the Light Their Way Campaign
50,000	Eckerd Youth Alternatives North Carolina Camps, Candor, NC

EVA L. AND JOSEPH M. BRUENING FOUNDATION

Giving Contact
Janet E. Narten, Executive Director
1422 Euclid Avenue, Suite 627
Cleveland, OH 44115-1901
Phone: (216)621-2632
Fax: (216)621-8198
Web: http://www.fmscleveland.com/bruening

Description
Founded: 1988
EIN: 341584378
Organization Type: General Purpose Foundation
Giving Locations: OH: Cuyahoga County
Grant Types: Capital, General Support, Multiyear/Continuing Support, Project, Seed Money.

Donor Information
Founder: Established in 1988 from the estate of the late Eva L. Bruening (d. 1987) and the late Joseph M. Bruening (d. 1987). Although natives of Cincinnati, OH, the Bruenings were residents of Cleveland, OH, for more than 65 years. Mr. Bruening owned the Ohio Ball Bearing Company, which later became Bearings, Inc.

Mr. Bruening was a founding member of Bluecoats, Inc., the organization that helps families of police officers and firefighters killed in the line of duty. Mr. Bruening served many nonprofit organizations during his lifetime including the Cleveland Rotary Club, American Cancer Society, Notre Dame College of Ohio, Society for Crippled Children, Cleveland Zoological Society, and St. Vincent Charity Hospital.

Financial Summary
Total Giving: $4,418,246 (2004); $1,148,300 (2003); $3,944,766 (2002)
Assets: $61,416,516 (2003); $66,694,994 (2001)
Gifts Received: $8,695 (1994); $45 (1993); $1,350 (1992)

Typical Recipients
Arts & Humanities: Ballet, Dance, Historic Preservation, Libraries, Museums/Galleries, Music, Performing Arts, Public Broadcasting, Theater
Civic & Public Affairs: Botanical Gardens/Parks, Business/Free Enterprise, Clubs, Community Foundations, Economic Development, Employment/Job Training, Civic & Public Affairs-General, Hispanic Affairs, Housing, Municipalities/Towns, Nonprofit Management, Parades/Festivals, Urban & Community Affairs, Women's Affairs, Zoos/Aquariums
Education: Afterschool/Enrichment Programs, Arts/Humanities Education, Business Education, Colleges & Universities, Community & Junior Colleges, Education Funds, Education Reform, Elementary Education (Private), Faculty Development, Education-General, International Studies, Literacy, Minority Education, Private Education (Precollege), Public Education (Precollege), Religious Education, Science/Mathematics Education, Secondary Education (Private), Secondary Education (Public), Special Education, Student Aid
Health: Adolescent Health Issues, AIDS/HIV, Alzheimer's Disease, Cancer, Children's Health/Hospitals, Clinics/Medical Centers, Emergency/Ambulance Services, Eyes/Blindness, Geriatric Health, Health Organizations, Hospices, Hospitals, Long-Term Care, Medical Rehabilitation, Mental Health, Nursing Services, Prenatal Health Issues, Preventive Medicine/Wellness Organizations, Public Health, Research/Studies Institutes, Single-Disease Health Associations, Speech & Hearing
Religion: Churches, Dioceses, Jewish Causes, Ministries, Religious Organizations, Religious Welfare, Seminaries
Science: Science Museums, Scientific Centers & Institutes
Social Services: At-Risk Youth, Big Brothers/Big Sisters, Child Welfare, Community Centers, Community Service Organizations, Counseling, Day Care, Domestic Violence, Family Planning, Family Services, Food/Clothing Distribution, People with Disabilities, Recreation & Athletics, Senior Services, Sexual Abuse, Shelters/Homelessness, Social Services-General, Substance Abuse, United Funds/United Ways, Volunteer Services, YMCA/YWCA/YMHA/YWHA, Youth Organizations

Application Procedures
Initial Contact: Applicants are encouraged to contact the foundation for further clarification of its grant-making policies before submitting a proposal.
Application Requirements: Applications must include two copies of the following: a one-page summary signed by the organization's chief operating officer and chief volunteer officer; a proposal including a description of organization's mission and programs, the problem or issue to be addressed, the clients to be served, the program objectives and methods, the project budget, and an evaluation plan; list of the board of trustees; and a copy of the organization's current operating budget. In addition, applicants should submit organization's IRS letter designating its nonprofit status and a copy of the most recent au-

dited financial statement and/or annual report.

Deadlines: March 1, July 1, and October 1.

Review Process: The distribution committee reviews grant requests three times a year in May, August, and December. Qualifying applicants will receive written notification of the foundation's decision within several weeks of each meeting.

Notes: Proposal pages should be attached with a paper clip and the use of binders or notebooks is discouraged.

Restrictions

The foundation will not make a permanent commitment of support to any type of project. In most cases, the foundation will not consider requests for endowments, general operations, research, publications, symposiums, or seminars. No grants will be awarded to individuals, or in response to mass mailings or annual campaign appeals. Grants are limited to the Greater Cleveland area.

Additional Information

Publications: Annual Report

Trust(s): KeyBank NA

Foundation Officials

Douglas Bannerman: member distribution committee

Kim Cowan: program officer

Marilyn A. Cunin: chairman distribution committee

John A. Favret: member distribution committee

CORP AFFIL director: Gorman-Lavelle Corp.

Janet E. Narten: executive director

Karen R. Nestor: member distribution committee

Cristin Slesh: program officer

Anne B. Springer: member distribution committee

Cathy A. Starkey: administration assistant

Margaret S. Wheeler: senior program officer

Grants Analysis

Disclosure Period: calendar year ending 2004

Total Grants: $4,418,246

Number of Grants: 121

Average Grant: $33,485*

Highest Grant: $400,000

Lowest Grant: $400

Typical Range: $10,000 to $50,000

*Note: Average grant figure excludes highest grant.

Recent Grants

Note: Grants derived from 2003 Form 990.

General

100,000	Achievement Centers for Children, Cleveland, OH -- for the capital campaign for a new facility
100,000	Center for Families and Children, Cleveland, OH -- for mental health advocacy coalition
100,000	Cuyahoga County Commissioners, Cleveland, OH -- for the early childhood initiative
75,000	Mental Health Services Inc., Cleveland, OH
60,000	Alzheimer's Disease and Related Disorders, Cleveland, OH -- to implement a centralized information system for programs and services
50,000	Cuyahoga Community College Foundation, Cleveland, OH
50,000	Eliza Bryant Village, Cleveland, OH -- to hire a clinical nurse specialist to serve as coordinator of the skilled care unit
50,000	Jennings Center, Garfield Heights, OH
50,000	Providence House Inc., Cleveland, OH
50,000	West Side Catholic Center, Cleveland, OH

CHARLES E. AND EDNA T. BRUNDAGE CHARITABLE, SCIENTIFIC, AND WILDLIFE CONSERVATION FOUNDATION

Giving Contact

Francis X. O'Brien, Secretary & Trustee

c/o Carpenter, Bennett & Morrissey

3 Gateway Ctr.

100 Mulberry St.

Newark, NJ 07102-4079

Phone: (973)622-7711

Description

Founded: 1955

EIN: 226050185

Organization Type: Private Foundation

Giving Locations: NJ

Grant Types: General Support.

Donor Information

Founder: Edna T. Brundage

Financial Summary

Total Giving: $195,000 (2004); $200,500 (2002); $167,500 (2001)

Assets: $4,060,799 (2004); $3,471,866 (2002); $4,170,392 (2001)

Gifts Received: $5,481 (1999); $510,000 (1996); $25,000 (1994). Note: In 1999, contributions were received from William B. Cater, Jr. In 1996, contributions were received from the estate of Edna T. Brundage.

Typical Recipients

Arts & Humanities: Arts Associations & Councils, Community Arts, History & Archaeology, Libraries, Museums/Galleries, Music, Opera, Performing Arts, Public Broadcasting, Theater

Civic & Public Affairs: African American Affairs, Clubs, Community Foundations, Civic & Public Affairs-General, Safety, Urban & Community Affairs

Education: Arts/Humanities Education, Business Education, Colleges & Universities, Education Funds, Education-General, Leadership Training, Literacy, Preschool Education, Private Education (Precollege), Science/Mathematics Education, Student Aid

Environment: Environment-General, Resource Conservation, Wildlife Protection

Health: Children's Health/Hospitals, Clinics/Medical Centers, Emergency/Ambulance Services, Health Funds, Health Organizations, Home-Care Services, Hospices, Prenatal Health Issues, Research/Studies Institutes

International: Health Care/Hospitals, International Organizations

Religion: Churches, Religious Welfare

Science: Science Museums, Scientific Centers & Institutes

Social Services: Camps, Community Centers, Community Service Organizations, Crime Prevention, Delinquency & Criminal Rehabilitation, Family Planning, Family Services, Food/Clothing Distribution, Recreation & Athletics, United Funds/United Ways

Application Procedures

Initial Contact: Send a brief letter of inquiry.

Deadlines: None.

Foundation Officials

Charles B. Cater: vice president, treasurer, trustee

June B. Cater: vice president, trustee

Kerry Cater: vice president, trustee

William B. Cater: vice president, trustee

William B. Cater, Jr.: president, trustee

James A. Jukosky: vice president, trustee

Susan Jukosky: vice president, trustee

Thomas L. Morrissey: vice president, trustee

Francis X. O'Brien: vice president, trustee

Laurence Reich: assistant vice president

Grants Analysis

Disclosure Period: calendar year ending 2004

Total Grants: $195,000

Number of Grants: 51

Average Grant: $3,824

Highest Grant: $27,000

Lowest Grant: $500

Typical Range: $1,000 to $5,000

Recent Grants

Note: Grants derived from 2001 Form 990.

General

12,000	New Jersey Symphony Orchestra, Newark, NJ -- operating fund
10,000	Dartmouth College, Hanover, NH
10,000	Newark Museum, Newark, NJ -- Science Center
10,000	Newark Museum, Newark, NJ -- operating fund
8,000	Electronic Information and Education Service, South Orange, NJ -- operating fund
6,000	Vermont Studio Center, Johnson, VT
5,500	Kiwanis Foundation of New Jersey, Clinton, NJ
5,000	Greater Newark Christmas Fund, Newark, NJ
5,000	Lebanon Opera House, Lebanon, NH -- capital campaign
5,000	WNYC Radio Foundation, New York, NY

JOSEPH S. BRUNO CHARITABLE FOUNDATION

Giving Contact

Jera Stribling, Executive Director

PO Box 530727

Birmingham, AL 35253

Phone: (205)879-0799

Description

Founded: 1985

EIN: 630936234

Organization Type: Private Foundation

Giving Locations: AL

Grant Types: General Support, Research.

Donor Information

Founder: Joseph S. Bruno

Financial Summary

Total Giving: $368,897 (fiscal year ending November 30, 2003); $441,000 (fiscal 2001)

Assets: $10,234,443 (fiscal 2003); $9,980,597 (fiscal 2001)

Gifts Received: $1,722,282 (fiscal 1996); $108,063 (fiscal 1994); $545,313 (fiscal 1993). Note: In fiscal 1996, contributions were received from the estate of Joseph S. Bruno.

Typical Recipients

Arts & Humanities: Arts Festivals, Ballet, Dance, Arts & Humanities-General, Libraries, Museums/Galleries, Music, Performing Arts

Civic & Public Affairs: Civic & Public Affairs-General, Zoos/Aquariums

Education: Arts/Humanities Education, Business Education, Colleges & Universities, Education Funds,

Education Reform, Education-General, Medical Education, Preschool Education, Private Education (Pre-college), Secondary Education (Private), Student Aid
Environment: Environment-General
Health: Cancer, Children's Health/Hospitals, Health-General, Heart, Hospitals, Medical Research, Mental Health, Single-Disease Health Associations
Religion: Churches, Dioceses, Jewish Causes, Religious Organizations, Religious Welfare
Social Services: Camps, Child Welfare, Community Service Organizations, People with Disabilities, Scouts, Social Services-General, United Funds/United Ways, Youth Organizations

Application Procedures

Initial Contact: Contact the executive director for application and deadline information.

Restrictions

Does not support idd.

Foundation Officials

Richard Cohn: director
Anne LaRussa: director
Benny M. LaRussa, Jr.: vice president, treasurer
Robert H. Sprain, Jr.: vice president, secretary
Theresa Sprain: director
Jera G. Stribling: executive director

Grants Analysis

Disclosure Period: fiscal year ending November 30, 2003
Total Grants: $368,897
Number of Grants: 29
Average Grant: $11,389*
Highest Grant: $50,000
Lowest Grant: $1,000
Typical Range: $5,000 to $20,000
***Note:** Average grant figure excludes highest grant.

Recent Grants

Note: Grants derived from fiscal 2003 Form 990.
General

50,000	Birmingham Zoo, Birmingham, AL
30,000	John Carroll Catholic High School Education Foundation, Birmingham, AL
25,000	Birmingham Southern College, Birmingham, AL
25,000	First Look, Birmingham, AL
25,000	Lakeshore Foundation, Birmingham, AL
20,000	St. Francis Xavier Church, Birmingham, AL
20,000	United Cerebral Palsy, Birmingham, AL
12,800	First Look, Birmingham, AL
11,870	Capstone College of Nursing, Tuscaloosa, AL
10,000	Alabama Symphony Orchestra, Birmingham, AL

BRUNSWICK CORP.

Company Headquarters

1 North Field Court
Lake Forest, IL 60045
Phone: (847)735-4469
Fax: (847)735-4481
Web: http://www.brunswickcorp.com

Company Description

Founded: 1845
Ticker: BC
Exchange: NYSE
Revenue: US$5.229 billion (2004)
Profit: US$269.8 million (2004)
Employees: 23225 (2003)
Fortune Rank: 377, per FORTUNE Magazine's list of 500 Largest U.S. Corporations (2004).
SIC(s): 3519 Internal Combustion Engines Nec, 3732 Boat Building & Repairing, 3949 Sporting & Athletic Goods Nec.

Operating Locations

Brunswick Corp. (CA--Orange; GA--Norcross; IL--Glendale Heights, Lombard; PA--Philadelphia)

Brunswick Foundation

Giving Contact

B. Russell Lockridge, President
One North Field Court
Lake Forest, IL 60045
Phone: (847)735-4667

Description

EIN: 366033576
Organization Type: Corporate Foundation
Giving Locations: principally near operating locations and to national organizations.
Grant Types: Fellowship, General Support, Project, Research, Scholarship.

Financial Summary

Total Giving: $503,896 (2003); $675,850 (2001). Note: Contributes through foundation only.
Assets: $5,844,890 (2003); $6,921,257 (2001)
Gifts Received: $100,000 (1998); $3,895,243 (1996); $1,984,000 (1995). Note: In 1998, contributions were received from Brunswick Corp.

Typical Recipients

Arts & Humanities: Arts Festivals, Arts Funds, Arts Institutes, Community Arts, Dance, Historic Preservation, Libraries, Museums/Galleries, Music, Performing Arts, Theater
Civic & Public Affairs: Asian American Affairs, Botanical Gardens/Parks, Civil Rights, Clubs, Community Foundations, Economic Development, Ethnic Organizations, Civic & Public Affairs-General, Legal Aid, Professional & Trade Associations, Public Policy, Rural Affairs, Urban & Community Affairs, Women's Affairs, Zoos/Aquariums
Education: Afterschool/Enrichment Programs, Business Education, Colleges & Universities, Community & Junior Colleges, Economic Education, Education Associations, Education Funds, Engineering/Technological Education, Environmental Education, Education-General, Gifted & Talented Programs, International Exchange, International Studies, Leadership Training, Literacy, Minority Education, Private Education (Precollege), Public Education (Precollege), Science/Mathematics Education, Secondary Education (Private), Special Education, Student Aid, Vocational & Technical Education
Environment: Environment-General, Wildlife Protection
Health: Cancer, Children's Health/Hospitals, Clinics/Medical Centers, Diabetes, Emergency/Ambulance Services, Health Organizations, Heart, Hospices, Hospitals, Mental Health, Nursing Services, Prenatal Health Issues, Research/Studies Institutes, Single-Disease Health Associations
International: International Affairs, International Relations
Religion: Ministries, Religious Welfare
Social Services: At-Risk Youth, Big Brothers/Big Sisters, Child Welfare, Community Centers, Community Service Organizations, Day Care, Delinquency & Criminal Rehabilitation, Emergency Relief, Family Planning, Family Services, Food/Clothing Distribution, People with Disabilities, Recreation & Athletics, Scouts, Senior Services, Shelters/Homelessness, Social Services-General, Special Olympics, Substance Abuse, United Funds/United Ways, Volunteer Services, YMCA/YWCA/YMHA/YWHA, Youth Organizations

Application Procedures

Initial Contact: Send a brief letter requesting application form.
Application Requirements: Completed applications will include objectives and purpose for which grant is sought; plans for implementation and evaluation of project; benefits expected; evidence of need for project; budget; list of board of directors, IRS 501(c)(3) verification; and most recently audited financial statement.
Deadlines: None.
Decision Notification: Committee meets as needed.
Notes: Foundation does not accept telephone solicitations.

Restrictions

Foundation does not make grants to individuals or provide loans. Does not support organizations that are not tax-exempt; religious or political organizations, veterans' groups, fraternal orders or labor groups; preschool, or trips, tours, tickets, dinners, special events or advertising. Does not donate company equipment or products.

Additional Information

Foundation is in the process of reorganization.
Publications: Annual Report; Application Forms

Corporate Officials

Peter N. Larson: chairman, chief executive officer, director B Los Angeles, CA 1939. ED Oregon State University BS (1960); Seton Hall University JD (1972). PRIM CORP EMPL chairman, chief executive officer, director: Brunswick Corp. CORP AFFIL director: Coty Corp.; Kimberly-Clark Corp.; director: CIGNA Corp.; director: Compaq Computer Corp.

Foundation Officials

George W. Buckley: director
Kathryn J. Chieger: vice president
B. Russell Lockridge: president, director
William L. Metzger: vice president, treasurer
Victoria J. Reich: director
Marschall I. Smith: vice president, secretary, director

Grants Analysis

Disclosure Period: calendar year ending 2003
Total Grants: $92,396*
Number of Grants: 80
Average Grant: $1,043*
Highest Grant: $10,000
Lowest Grant: $150
Typical Range: $500 to $2,000
***Note:** Giving excludes scholarship. Average grant figure excludes highest grant.

Recent Grants

Note: Grants derived from 2003 Form 990.

General

10,000	Craven County YMCA Inc., New Bern, NC
5,000	Brain Research Foundation, Chicago, IL
5,000	Breck School, Minneapolis, MN
5,000	Chicago Symphony Orchestra, Chicago, IL
5,000	Hadley School for the Blind, Winnetka, IL
5,000	Johns Hopkins University, Baltimore, MD
5,000	Junior Achievement of Chicago, Chicago, IL
5,000	Regents of the University of Michigan, Ann Arbor, MI
5,000	Trustees of Westminster School Inc., Simsbury, CT
5,000	University of Florida Foundation Inc., Gainesville, FL

BRUSH FOUNDATION

Giving Contact
3135 Euclid Avenue, Suite 102
Cleveland, OH 44115
Phone: (216)881-5121
Fax: (216)881-1834

Description
Founded: 1928
EIN: 346000445
Organization Type: Private Foundation
Giving Locations: Third World countries, nationally, and locally.
Grant Types: Conference/Seminar, Emergency, General Support, Multiyear/Continuing Support, Operating Expenses, Project, Research, Seed Money.

Donor Information
Founder: the late Charles F. Brush, Maurice Perkins

Financial Summary
Total Giving: $235,300 (2003)
Assets: $6,345,092 (2003)

Typical Recipients
Arts & Humanities: History & Archaeology, Libraries
Civic & Public Affairs: Botanical Gardens/Parks, Civil Rights, Civic & Public Affairs-General, Legal Aid, Nonprofit Management, Public Policy, Women's Affairs
Education: Business Education, Colleges & Universities, Education-General, Legal Education, Medical Education, Public Education (Precollege), Student Aid
Health: Clinics/Medical Centers, Health-General, Health Organizations, Prenatal Health Issues, Public Health
International: Health Care/Hospitals, International Environmental Issues, International Organizations, International Peace & Security Issues
Religion: Ministries, Religious Organizations, Social/Policy Issues
Social Services: Big Brothers/Big Sisters, Child Welfare, Family Planning, Family Services, Food/Clothing Distribution, Scouts, Youth Organizations

Application Procedures
Initial Contact: Send a brief letter of inquiry. Include grant request and purpose of funds sought.
Application Requirements: Include a description of organization, grant request and purpose of funds sought.
Deadlines: None.
Decision Notification: Decisions are made by the Managers at their November and May board meetings.

Restrictions
Grants will be awarded to finance efforts contributing toward betterment of the human stock through research in the field of eugenics and toward regulation of the population. Does not support individuals or provide loans.

Additional Information
Trust(s): Key Trust Co OH NA

Foundation Officials
Barbara Brush Wright: president
Cindie Carroll-Pankhurst: secretary
Virginia P. Carter: treasurer
Meacham Hitchcock: vice president

Grants Analysis
Disclosure Period: calendar year ending 2003
Total Grants: $235,300
Number of Grants: 17
Average Grant: $13,841
Highest Grant: $25,000
Typical Range: $5,000 to $25,000

Recent Grants
Note: Grants derived from 2001 Form 990.
General
50,000	Planned Parenthood Federation of America, New York, NY
25,000	Amazonian Peoples Resources Initiative/APRI, Lawrence, KS
25,000	Pathfinder, Watertown, MA
10,765	State University of New York, New York, NY
5,300	Center for Reproduction Law & Policy, New York, NY

BRYAN FOODS

Company Headquarters
PO Box 1177
West Point, MS 39773
Web: http://www.bryanfoods.com

Company Description
Employees: 2,200
SIC(s): 2000 Food & Kindred Products, 2011 Meat Packing Plants.
Parent Company: Sara Lee Corp., Chicago, IL, United States

Nonmonetary Support
Type: Donated Products
Volunteer Programs: Company is a partner in education with local public schools.

Giving Contact
Jadas Blissard, Human Resources Assistant
PO Box 1177
West Point, MS 39773
Phone: (662)495-4000
Fax: (662)495-4439
E-mail: hakola@bryanfoods.com

Description
Organization Type: Corporate Giving Program
Giving Locations: headquarters and operating communities.

Typical Recipients
Arts & Humanities: Arts Festivals, Arts Outreach, Community Arts, Arts & Humanities-General, Libraries, Performing Arts
Civic & Public Affairs: African American Affairs, Civil Rights, Community Foundations, Economic Development, Civic & Public Affairs-General
Education: Afterschool/Enrichment Programs, Arts/Humanities Education, Business Education, Business-School Partnerships, Elementary Education (Public), Faculty Development, Education-General, Minority Education, Preschool Education, Public Education (Precollege), Special Education
Environment: Resource Conservation, Wildlife Protection
Health: Cancer, Diabetes, Multiple Sclerosis
Social Services: At-Risk Youth, Child Welfare, Domestic Violence, Food/Clothing Distribution, People with Disabilities, Shelters/Homelessness, United Funds/United Ways, Volunteer Services, Youth Organizations

Application Procedures
Initial Contact: Send a brief letter of inquiry and a full proposal.
Application Requirements: Include a description of organization, amount requested, recently audited financial statement, proof of tax-exempt status, and purpose of funds sought.

Restrictions
Does not support individuals, religious organizations for sectarian purposes, political or lobbying groups, or

organizations outside operating areas. Most contributions are made to preselected organizations.

Corporate Officials
John Bryan, III: chairman, president, chief executive officer PRIM CORP EMPL chairman, president, chief executive officer: Bryan Foods.
Brad Egbert: chief financial officer PRIM CORP EMPL chief financial officer: Bryan Foods.

Grants Analysis
Typical Range: $10 to $1,000
Note: A more recent grants list was unavailable.

Recent Grants
Note: Grants derived from 1996 grants list.
GeneralClay County Public Schools, Pheba, MSGardner Simmons Home for Girls, Tupelo, MSKidtown Committee, West Point, MSMississippi Troopers, Jackson, MSSafe Haven, Columbus, MSSally Kate Winters Home for Children, West Point, MSSheriff's Boys and Girls Club, Columbus, MSSpecial Olympics, Jackson, MSWest Point Public Schools, West Point, MSNAACP, West Point, MS

THE BRYANT FOUNDATION

Giving Contact
Arthur H. Bryant, II, President & Treasurer
PO Box 1239
Stephens City, VA 22655-1239
Phone: (540)868-2183

Description
Founded: 1949
EIN: 546032840
Organization Type: Family Foundation
Giving Locations: VA
Grant Types: General Support.

Donor Information
Founder: Established in 1949 by the late J. C. Herbert Bryant.

Financial Summary
Total Giving: $1,159,255 (2003); $2,321,332 (2002)
Assets: $10,163,719 (2003); $10,088,966 (2002)

Typical Recipients
Arts & Humanities: Art History, Arts Associations & Councils, Arts Centers, Historic Preservation, History & Archaeology, Libraries, Museums/Galleries, Theater
Civic & Public Affairs: Clubs, Community Foundations, Civic & Public Affairs-General, Housing, Municipalities/Towns, Nonprofit Management, Philanthropic Organizations, Safety, Urban & Community Affairs, Women's Affairs, Zoos/Aquariums
Education: Colleges & Universities, Community & Junior Colleges, Education Associations, Education Funds, Elementary Education (Private), Education-General, Legal Education, Preschool Education, Private Education (Precollege), Public Education (Precollege), Religious Education, Science/Mathematics Education, Secondary Education (Private), Social Sciences Education, Student Aid
Environment: Forestry, Environment-General, Resource Conservation, Wildlife Protection
Health: Cancer, Clinics/Medical Centers, Emergency/Ambulance Services, Health-General, Health Funds, Health Organizations, Hospitals, Long-Term Care, Medical Rehabilitation, Medical Research, Prenatal Health Issues, Public Health, Respiratory, Single-Disease Health Associations
International: International Peace & Security Issues

Religion: Churches, Religious Organizations, Religious Welfare, Seminaries
Science: Science Museums, Scientific Centers & Institutes
Social Services: Animal Protection, At-Risk Youth, Child Welfare, Community Centers, Community Service Organizations, Day Care, Emergency Relief, Food/Clothing Distribution, Homes, Recreation & Athletics, Social Services-General, Volunteer Services, Youth Organizations

Application Procedures

Initial Contact: The foundation has no formal grant application procedure or application form.
Deadlines: None.

Restrictions

The foundation reports that grants are made only to nonprofit, charitable organizations. Grants are not made to individuals.

Foundation Officials

Arthur H. Bryant, Jr.: secretary
Arthur Herbert Bryant, II: president, treasurer B Washington, DC 1942. ED University of Miami (1963). PRIM CORP EMPL chairman, chief executive officer: O'Sullivan Corp. CORP AFFIL chairman: O'Sullivan Plastics Corp.; chairman: Regalite Plastics Corp. CLUB AFFIL treasurer: Birdwood Golf Course.
Alexander W. Neal, Jr.: trustee

Grants Analysis

Disclosure Period: calendar year ending 2003
Total Grants: $1,159,255
Number of Grants: 64
Average Grant: $11,440*
Highest Grant: $250,000
Lowest Grant: $1000
Typical Range: $1,000 to $20,000
***Note:** Average grant figure excludes two highest grants ($450,000).

Recent Grants

Note: Grants derived from 2003 Form 990.
Library-Related
2,000	Alexandria Library, Alexandria, VA

General
250,000	Episcopal High School, Alexandria, VA
200,000	Hill School, Middleburg, VA
100,000	Our Health, Winchester, VA
100,000	Shenandoah University, Winchester, VA
100,000	Virginia Institute of Marine Science, Gloucester Point, VA
100,000	Virginia Institute of Marine Science, Gloucester Point, VA
75,000	Robert E. Lee Memorial Association, Stratford, VA
55,000	Chesapeake Academy, Irvington, VA
14,500	Virginia Institute of Marine Science, Gloucester Point, VA
11,000	Virginia Institute of Marine Science, Gloucester Point, VA

BLANCHE BRYDEN FOUNDATION

Giving Contact

Judy K. Wilson, Manager
800 SW Jackson St., Suite 910
Topeka, KS 66612-1216
Phone: (785)357-1316

Description

Founded: 1992
EIN: 481117045
Organization Type: Private Foundation
Giving Locations: KS: Topeka
Grant Types: General Support.

Donor Information

Founder: the late Blanche Bryden

Financial Summary

Total Giving: $90,050 (fiscal year ending June 30, 2004); $117,671 (fiscal 2001)
Giving Analysis: Giving for fiscal 2004 includes: foundation scholarships ($31,860); fiscal 2001: foundation scholarships ($48,800).
Assets: $2,376,704 (fiscal 2004); $2,898,130 (fiscal 2001)

Typical Recipients

Arts & Humanities: Libraries, Music, Public Broadcasting
Civic & Public Affairs: Employment/Job Training, Safety
Education: Afterschool/Enrichment Programs, Colleges & Universities, Health & Physical Education, International Studies, Medical Education, Public Education (Precollege), Student Aid, Vocational & Technical Education
Health: Arthritis, Clinics/Medical Centers, Hospices, Mental Health
Religion: Religious Welfare, Synagogues/Temples
Social Services: Animal Protection, Child Welfare, Scouts, Senior Services, Substance Abuse, YMCA/YWCA/YMHA/YWHA, Youth Organizations

Application Procedures

Initial Contact: Send a full proposal.
Application Requirements: Include a description of organization, amount requested, purpose of funds sought, recently audited financial statement, and proof of tax-exempt status. Send a brief letter of inquiry.
Deadlines: None.
Evaluative Criteria: Include purpose of funds sought and proof of tax-exempt status.

Restrictions

Grants are not made to individuals.

Additional Information

Trust(s): Mercantile Bank

Foundation Officials

Katherine G. Kent: trustee

Grants Analysis

Disclosure Period: fiscal year ending June 30, 2004
Total Grants: $58,190*
Number of Grants: 18
Average Grant: $3,233
Highest Grant: $11,000
Lowest Grant: $440
Typical Range: $1,000 to $5,000
***Note:** Giving excludes scholarships.

Recent Grants

Note: Grants derived from fiscal 2001 Form 990.
Library-Related
500	Topeka and Shawnee County Public Library, Topeka, KS

General
26,800	Washburn Endowment Association, Topeka, KS -- scholarship fund
12,000	Villages, Topeka, KS -- summer education and recreation programs
10,000	Marian Clinic, Topeka, KS -- nurses' salaries
10,000	Stormont-Vail Foundation, Topeka, KS -- for nurses' scholarships
10,000	Topeka High School Stars Program, Topeka, KS
8,500	Washburn University, Topeka, KS -- for Blanche Bryden Sunflower Music Festival Institute
5,000	Stormont-Vail Foundation, Topeka, KS -- for Allied Health Professional scholarships
5,000	Topeka Youth Project, Topeka, KS
5,000	Washburn Endowment Association, Topeka, KS -- for KTWU Channel 11
5,000	Washburn Endowment Association, Topeka, KS -- for Women's Alliance Scholarship Fund

BRYN MAWR BANK CORP.

Company Headquarters

801 Lancaster Avenue
Bryn Mawr, PA 19010-3396
Web: http://www.bmtc.com

Company Description

Founded: 1986
Ticker: BMTC
Exchange: NASDAQ
Assets: US$577.4 million (2002)
Employees: 242 (2002)
SIC(s): 6000 Depository Institutions.

Operating Locations

Bryn Mawr Trust Co. (PA--Havertown, Poole, Wayne)

Nonmonetary Support

Note: Meeting Rooms

Giving Contact

Joe Smith, Vice President
801 Lancaster Ave.
Bryn Mawr, PA 19010
Phone: (610)525-1700
Fax: (610)520-7278
E-mail: joesmith@bmtc.com

Description

Organization Type: Corporate Giving Program
Giving Locations: headquarters area only.
Grant Types: Operating Expenses, Scholarship.

Typical Recipients

Arts & Humanities: Arts Associations & Councils, Arts Centers, Arts Festivals, Arts Funds, Arts Institutes, Community Arts, Arts & Humanities-General, Historic Preservation, Libraries, Museums/Galleries, Music, Opera, Performing Arts, Theater
Civic & Public Affairs: African American Affairs, Botanical Gardens/Parks, Business/Free Enterprise, Chambers of Commerce, Civil Rights, Community Foundations, Economic Development, Civic & Public Affairs-General, Housing, Inner-City Development, Municipalities/Towns, Parades/Festivals, Professional & Trade Associations, Zoos/Aquariums
Education: Arts/Humanities Education, Colleges & Universities, Education-General
Environment: Air/Water Quality, Environment-General, Resource Conservation
Health: Arthritis, Cancer, Children's Health/Hospitals, Clinics/Medical Centers, Emergency/Ambulance Services, Health-General, Geriatric Health, Heart, Home-Care Services, Hospices, Hospitals, Long-Term Care, Nursing Services, Prenatal Health Issues, Preventive Medicine/Wellness Organizations
Social Services: Community Centers, Community Service Organizations, Counseling, Day Care, Food/Clothing Distribution, Recreation & Athletics, Senior Services, Shelters/Homelessness, Social Services-General, United Funds/United Ways, Volunteer Services, YMCA/YWCA/YMHA/YWHA

Application Procedures

Initial Contact: Send a brief letter of inquiry.
Application Requirements: Include a description of organization, amount requested, purpose of funds sought, recently audited financial statement, and

proof of tax-exempt status.
Deadlines: None.

Restrictions

Does not support individuals, religious organizations for sectarian purposes, political or lobbying groups, or organizations outside operating areas.

Corporate Officials

Joseph W. Rebl: senior vice president financeeo PRIM CORP EMPL senior vice president finance: Bryn Mawr Trust Co.
Robert L. Stevens: chairman, president, chief executive officer B 1937. PRIM CORP EMPL chairman, president, chief executive officer: Bryn Mawr Trust Co. ADD CORP EMPL president: Bryn Mawr Bank Corp.

Grants Analysis

Typical Range: $100 to $1,000

CAROL FRANC BUCK FOUNDATION

Giving Contact

Marya A. Beam, Administrative Assistant
PO Box 6085
Incline Village, NV 89450
Phone: (775)831-6366
Fax: (775)831-8655

Description

Founded: 1979
EIN: 880163505
Organization Type: Private Foundation
Giving Locations: Western US.
Grant Types: Endowment, General Support, Multiyear/Continuing Support, Project.

Donor Information

Founder: Carol S. Sells, John E. Sells

Financial Summary

Total Giving: $550,600 (fiscal year ending November 30, 2003); $805,700 (fiscal 2001)
Assets: $14,103,183 (fiscal 2003); $15,230,142 (fiscal 2001)
Gifts Received: $1,016,287 (fiscal 1994). Note: In fiscal 1994, contributions were received from Carol Plummer.

Typical Recipients

Arts & Humanities: Arts Associations & Councils, Arts Centers, Arts Festivals, Arts Funds, Arts Institutes, Arts Outreach, Ballet, Dance, Arts & Humanities-General, History & Archaeology, Museums/Galleries, Music, Opera, Performing Arts, Public Broadcasting, Theater, Visual Arts
Civic & Public Affairs: Civic & Public Affairs-General, Urban & Community Affairs
Education: Arts/Humanities Education, Colleges & Universities, Public Education (Precollege), Secondary Education (Public)

Application Procedures

Initial Contact: Telephone foundation or send brief letter of inquiry.
Deadlines: June 1 and December 1.
Review Process: Board meets in January, April, July, and October. Decisions are made within three months.
Evaluative Criteria: Prefer applications from visual and performing arts organizations or for education in the arts.

Restrictions

Does not support individuals or provide funds for deficit financing, land acquisition, renovations, scholarships, fellowships, or loans.

Foundation Officials

Carol F. Buck: trustee
Christian P. Erdman: trustee
Helen J. O'Hanlon: trustee

Grants Analysis

Disclosure Period: fiscal year ending November 30, 2003
Total Grants: $550,600
Number of Grants: 12
Average Grant: $12,575*
Highest Grant: $250,000
Lowest Grant: $2,500
Typical Range: $5,000 to $25,000
***Note:** Average grant figure excludes four highest grants ($450,000).

Recent Grants

Note: Grants derived from fiscal 2003 Form 990.
General

250,100	San Francisco Opera, San Francisco, CA -- underwrite Kata Kabanova
100,000	Houston Grand Opera, Houston, TX -- underwrite: La Traviata
50,000	San Francisco Lyric Opera, San Francisco, CA -- for production underwriting support
50,000	Santa Fe Opera, Santa Fe, NM -- to support its 2003 production of La Belle Helene
30,000	Long Beach Opera, Long Beach, CA -- underwrite: 'Jenufa' and 'Arianna in Creta'
25,000	Uptown Downtown C/R Town, Reno, NV -- for Artown summer festival
11,000	Juneau Symphony, Juneau, AK -- Juneau student symphony educational travel program
10,000	KUNR - FM, Reno, NV -- underwrite Saturday morning opera broadcasts
10,000	Reno Chamber Orchestra, Reno, NV -- for defray production costs 2003/2004 season
7,000	Central California Youth Symphony, Fresno, CA -- student costs for 2004 cultural exchange tour to Spain

FRANK H. AND EVA B. BUCK FOUNDATION

Giving Contact

Kathy Hazen, Executive Director
PO Box 5610
Vacaville, CA 95696-5610
Phone: (760)446-7700

Description

Founded: 1989
EIN: 770233870
Organization Type: Private Foundation
Giving Locations: CA: Sacramento County, San Joaquin County, Solano County, Solano County, Yolo County, Yolo County
Grant Types: Scholarship.

Donor Information

Founder: Robert B. Buck

Financial Summary

Total Giving: $3,122,984 (fiscal year ending March 31, 2003)
Giving Analysis: Giving for fiscal 2001 includes: foundation grants to United Way ($50); foundation scholarships ($2,817,029)
Assets: $49,689,136 (fiscal 2003)
Gifts Received: $12,432 (fiscal 1996); $3,616,157 (fiscal 1995); $2,095,900 (fiscal 1994)

Typical Recipients

Arts & Humanities: Arts & Humanities-General, Libraries, Museums/Galleries
Civic & Public Affairs: Chambers of Commerce, Clubs, Civic & Public Affairs-General, Parades/Festivals
Education: Colleges & Universities, Elementary Education (Public), Education-General, Literacy, Public Education (Precollege), Secondary Education (Public)
Health: Health Organizations
Social Services: Child Welfare, Community Service Organizations, Social Services-General, Special Olympics, United Funds/United Ways

Application Procedures

Initial Contact: Submit application, teacher's assessment, and parental authorization for release of school records.
Deadlines: December 15.

Restrictions

Additional Information

Provides scholarships to students in the third congressional district of CA.
Publications: Application Form

Foundation Officials

Carol Buck: president
Paul Buck: director
Walter Buck: secretary
Christian P. Erdman: treasurer
Kathy Hazen: executive director
Stacey Morris: director

Grants Analysis

Disclosure Period: fiscal year ending March 31, 2000
Total Grants: $305,405*
Number of Grants: 26*
Average Grant: $2,236*
Highest Grant: $250,000
Lowest Grant: $20
Typical Range: $500 to $25,000
***Note:** Giving excludes largest grants. Total number of grants excludes scholarships.

Recent Grants

Note: Grants derived from 2003 Form 990.
Library-Related

250,000	Solano County Library Foundation, Fairfield, CA

General

25,000	Tools of Learning for Children, Fairfield, CA
20,000	Solano Community Foundation, Vacaville, CA
1,500	Festival of Trees, Vacaville, CA
1,150	Advocates for the Arts, Suisun, CA
1,000	Partners in Achieving Literacy, Vacaville, CA
1,000	Vacaville High School, Vacaville, CA -- Grad Nite
1,000	Vanden Sober Grad Nite, Fairfield, CA
1,000	Will C. Wood Grad Nite, Vacaville, CA
530	Markham Elementary School, Vacaville, CA
500	Christmas Wish, Vacaville, CA

TEMPLE HOYNE BUELL FOUNDATION

Giving Contact

Susan J. Steele, Executive Director
Temple Hoyne Buell Foundation
1666 South University Boulevard, Suite B
Denver, CO 80210
Phone: (303)744-1688
Fax: (303)744-1601
E-mail: info@buellfoundation.org
Web: http://www.buellfoundation.org

Description

Founded: 1962
EIN: 846037604
Organization Type: Family Foundation
Giving Locations: CO
Grant Types: Capital, General Support, Operating Expenses, Project.
Note: The foundation provides technical assistance.

Donor Information

Founder: Incorporated in 1962 by the late Temple Hoyne Buell.

Financial Summary

Total Giving: $4,674,720 (fiscal year ending June 30, 2004); $4,500,000 (fiscal 2003 approx); $4,793,350 (fiscal 2002)
Giving Analysis: Giving for fiscal 2004 includes: foundation matching gifts ($5,455); foundation scholarships ($65,000); fiscal 2002: foundation matching gifts ($10,750); foundation scholarships ($111,750).
Assets: $138,547,018 (fiscal 2004); $118,589,966 (fiscal 2003); $111,471,094 (fiscal 2002)
Gifts Received: $358,000 (fiscal 1996); $1,478 (fiscal 1995); $94,505 (fiscal 1994)

Typical Recipients

Arts & Humanities: Arts Centers, Arts Funds, Arts Outreach, Historic Preservation, Libraries, Museums/Galleries, Music, Performing Arts, Theater
Civic & Public Affairs: African American Affairs, Botanical Gardens/Parks, Business/Free Enterprise, Chambers of Commerce, Clubs, Community Foundations, Economic Development, Civic & Public Affairs-General, Hispanic Affairs, Housing, Municipalities/Towns, Native American Affairs, Nonprofit Management, Urban & Community Affairs, Women's Affairs, Zoos/Aquariums
Education: Afterschool/Enrichment Programs, Arts/Humanities Education, Business Education, Colleges & Universities, Community & Junior Colleges, Education Funds, Elementary Education (Public), Engineering/Technological Education, Education-General, Gifted & Talented Programs, Leadership Training, Literacy, Minority Education, Preschool Education, Private Education (Precollege), Public Education (Precollege), Science/Mathematics Education, Special Education, Student Aid
Health: Cancer, Children's Health/Hospitals, Diabetes, Health Organizations, Heart, Hospitals, Kidney, Mental Health, Prenatal Health Issues, Preventive Medicine/Wellness Organizations, Public Health, Research/Studies Institutes, Single-Disease Health Associations, Speech & Hearing
International: Foreign Educational Institutions
Religion: Churches, Ministries, Religious Organizations, Religious Welfare
Social Services: At-Risk Youth, Camps, Child Welfare, Community Centers, Community Service Organizations, Counseling, Crime Prevention, Day Care, Domestic Violence, Family Planning, Family Services, Food/Clothing Distribution, People with Disabilities, Shelters/Homelessness, Social Services-General, United Funds/United Ways, Veterans, YMCA/YWCA/YMHA/YWHA, Youth Organizations

Application Procedures

Initial Contact: The Foundation request that applicants call the office to receive the appropriate forms. The Foundation uses the Common Grant Application form and asks the applicants to make sure the "Purpose of Grant" fits the foundation's guidelines and that the applicants indicate their "focus area".
Application Requirements: For requests of $5,000 and under, include: a limited version of the Common Grant Application; a letter of intent describing the organization and purpose of request; Summary of Applicant Organization (attached form); balance sheet and income and expense statement for previous fiscal year; program budget or organization's budget (if requesting general support); 501(c)(3) determination letter; anti-discrimination statement; and list of board of directors.
For request over $5,000 submit a Full Common Grant Application with described attachments.
Deadlines: The first business day of January, May and September by 5:00 p.m.
Decision Notification: Final grant decisions are made and monies released approximately four months after each deadline.
Notes: Do not use bulky notebooks, binders, or include videotapes.

Restrictions

Grants are not made to or for the following: individuals; to cover past operating expenses; the retirement of debt; testimonial dinners; events, annual campaigns, membership drives or conferences; loans; litigation; sectarian programs promoting religion; legislative lobbying or support of political candidates; international organizations; medical programs; multi-year awards; or endowments. No grant request will be considered from an organization unless that organization is determined to be tax-exempt under 501(c)(3) of the Internal Revenue Code and "not a private foundation" under section 509(a) of the Code.

Additional Information

Publications: Application Form; Guidelines; Annual Report

Foundation Officials

Arthur H. Bosworth, II: trustee
Merle Catherine Chambers: vice president, trustee B Chicago, IL 1946. ED University of California at Berkeley BA (1968); University of California, San Francisco JD (1977); University of Denver LLM (1984). PRIM CORP EMPL president, chief executive officer: Axem Resources Inc. CORP AFFIL chairman executive committee: Clipper Express Co. NONPR AFFIL member: Colorado Women's Bar Association; director: Women Foundations; member: California Bar Association; member: Colorado Bar Association; director: 1066 Foundation; member: American Bar Association.
Thomas J. Curnes: treasurer, trustee
Marilie Hart: grants manager, program officer
Deedee Gale Mayer: trustee
Daniel Lee Ritchie: president, trustee B Springfield, IL 1931. ED Harvard University BA (1954); Harvard University MBA (1956). PRIM NONPR EMPL chancellor: University of Denver. CORP AFFIL owner: Rancho Cielo; owner: Grand River Ranch. NONPR AFFIL chancellor: Colorado Seminary.
Justice Luis Dario Rovira: trustee, secretary B San Juan, PR 1923. ED University of Colorado BA (1948); University of Colorado LLB (1950). NONPR AFFIL trustee: Denver Foundation; member: Phi Alpha Delta; member: Denver Bar Association; member: Colorado Association Retarded Children; member: Colorado Bar Association; member: American Bar Association; director: Childrens Hospital; member: Alpha Tau Omega. CLUB AFFIL Athletic Club; Denver Country Club.
Marguerite Salazar: trustee
Susan J. Steele: executive director

Grants Analysis

Disclosure Period: fiscal year ending June 30, 2004
Total Grants: $4,604,265*
Number of Grants: 157
Average Grant: $27,912*
Highest Grant: $250,000
Lowest Grant: $100
Typical Range: $10,000 to $50,000
*Note: Giving excludes scholarships and matching gifts. Average grant excludes highest grant.

Recent Grants

Note: Grants derived from fiscal 2003 Form 990.
Library-Related

29,000	Denver Public Library Friends Foundation, Denver, CO -- operating support of read aloud and design ongoing evaluation programs

General

250,000	Kidstart Inc., Denver, CO -- fund for Mesa county quality improvement initiative
131,050	Durango 4-C Council Inc., Durango, CO -- fund for early childhood professional development project
100,000	First Visitor, Colorado Springs, CO
89,270	Clayton Foundation, Denver, CO -- fund for early childhood enhanced professional development program
85,000	Colorado Children's Campaign, Denver, CO
85,000	Trinidad State Junior College, Creede, CO -- fund for San Luis Valley professional development project
80,000	Boys & Girls Club of Pueblo County Inc., Pueblo, CO
75,000	Children's Museum of Denver, Denver, CO -- fund for outreach program to serve low-income children
70,000	Child Care Connections, Colorado Springs, CO
67,000	University of Denver, Denver, CO

BUHL FOUNDATION (PA)

Giving Contact

Doreen E. Boyce, President
650 Smithfield St., Suite 2300
Pittsburgh, PA 15222
Phone: (412)566-2711
Fax: (412)566-2714
E-mail: buhl@buhlfoundation.org

Description

Founded: 1927
EIN: 250378910
Organization Type: General Purpose Foundation
Giving Locations: PA: Pittsburgh metropolitan area
Grant Types: Award, General Support, Seed Money.

Donor Information

Founder: The Buhls, a German merchant family for nine generations, immigrated to Zelienople, PA, around 1800. The Buhls established a legacy of concerned citizenship in Pennsylvania, as evidenced by their last heir, Henry Buhl Jr. Trained as a merchant, he and his friend, Russell H. Boggs, established a profitable dry goods store in 1869. As he neared the end of his life, Mr. Buhl considered the future of his fortune. Because he had no children or other direct heirs, he established the Buhl Foundation as a memorial to his wife, Louise C. Buhl, and dedicated it to "charitable, educational, and public uses and purposes," to benefit "the citizens of the City of Pittsburgh and the County of Allegheny, Pennsylvania" first and foremost where he lived and "engaged in business activities and formed friendships." Henry Buhl, Jr., died in 1927.

Financial Summary

Total Giving: $3,032,509 (fiscal year ending June 30, 2004); $2,598,107 (fiscal 2002); $4,396,118 (fiscal 2001)

Giving Analysis: Giving for fiscal 2002 includes: foundation matching gifts ($25,498); fiscal 2001: foundation matching gifts ($23,336)

Assets: $79,593,881 (fiscal 2004); $72,319,732 (fiscal 2002); $80,664,699 (fiscal 2001)

Typical Recipients

Arts & Humanities: Arts Associations & Councils, Arts Funds, Arts Institutes, Arts Outreach, Ballet, Dance, Film & Video, Arts & Humanities-General, Historic Preservation, History & Archaeology, Libraries, Literary Arts, Museums/Galleries, Music, Opera, Performing Arts, Public Broadcasting, Theater

Civic & Public Affairs: African American Affairs, Botanical Gardens/Parks, Business/Free Enterprise, Community Foundations, Economic Development, Economic Policy, Employment/Job Training, Civic & Public Affairs-General, Housing, Inner-City Development, Legal Aid, Minority Business, Nonprofit Management, Philanthropic Organizations, Professional & Trade Associations, Public Policy, Urban & Community Affairs, Women's Affairs

Education: Afterschool/Enrichment Programs, Arts/Humanities Education, Business Education, Colleges & Universities, Community & Junior Colleges, Education Associations, Education Funds, Education Reform, Elementary Education (Private), Environmental Education, Faculty Development, Education-General, Gifted & Talented Programs, Leadership Training, Literacy, Minority Education, Preschool Education, Private Education (Precollege), Public Education (Precollege), School Volunteerism, Science/Mathematics Education, Secondary Education (Private), Secondary Education (Public), Social Sciences Education, Special Education, Vocational & Technical Education

Environment: Environment-General, Resource Conservation, Wildlife Protection

Health: Cancer, Children's Health/Hospitals, Emergency/Ambulance Services, Health Organizations, Heart, Hospitals, Mental Health, Nursing Services, Respiratory

Religion: Ministries, Religious Organizations, Religious Welfare

Science: Observatories & Planetariums, Scientific Centers & Institutes

Social Services: At-Risk Youth, Child Abuse, Child Welfare, Community Service Organizations, Crime Prevention, Day Care, Delinquency & Criminal Rehabilitation, Emergency Relief, Family Services, Food/Clothing Distribution, People with Disabilities, Recreation & Athletics, Scouts, Sexual Abuse, Shelters/Homelessness, Social Services-General, Substance Abuse, YMCA/YWCA/YMHA/YWHA, Youth Organizations

Application Procedures

Initial Contact: Send a letter of inquiry to the president. A formal proposal will be requested if the foundation is interested.

Application Requirements: Statement of objectives for the project and the means by which they will be achieved, including staff qualifications and a timetable; proof of need for the project, its uniqueness in comparison to other work being done in a similar area, and the result anticipated; documentation of procedures for evaluation of anticipated results; itemized budget indicating resources required for the project, other possible funding sources, and the amount requested of them; general information about the applying agency including its name, address, telephone number, contact person, executive director, members of the board, brief history, mission, tax-exempt status, and ability to initiate and sustain the project; and a statement that the proposal has been approved for submission to the foundation by the executive director of the applying organization.

Deadlines: None. Organizations should submit proposals at least two months before consideration may be given by the board.

Review Process: If the foundation is interested in the proposed project, an interview will be scheduled. Grant decisions are made at monthly board meetings.

Restrictions

Grants generally are not made for building funds, overhead costs, accumulated deficits, ordinary operating budgets, fundraising campaigns, loans, scholarships, fellowships, nationally funded organized groups, conferences, seminars (unless grant-related), propaganda, sectarian religious activities, or lobbying. Grants are not made to other foundations or to individuals.

Additional Information

Grant recipients will be expected to confer with the foundation on schedules of grant payments, progress reports on program achievements, and an evaluation upon completion of the program.

Publications: Annual Report; Program Guidelines

Foundation Officials

Dr. Doreen Elizabeth Boyce: president B Antofagasta, Chile 1934. ED Oxford University BA (1956); Oxford University MA (1960); University of Pittsburgh PhD (1983); Westminster College B Humane Lit (1986); Washington & Jefferson College DHL (1993). PRIM NONPR EMPL president: Buhl Foundation. CORP AFFIL director: Orbeco Analytical Services, Inc.; director: Duquesne Light Co.; director: Microbac Laboratories Inc.; director: Dollar Bank, FSB; director: DQE Inc. NONPR AFFIL director: Research for Better School; member appeals committee: Somerville College (Oxford, England); member: Grantmakers of Western Pennsylvania; member: International Womens Forum; director: Council Independent Colleges; trustee: Franklin & Marshall College; member: American Economic Association; trustee: Carnegie Science Center; member: American Association Higher Education. CLUB AFFIL member: Duquesne Club.

Helen S. Faison: trustee, director

Peter F. Mathieson: trustee, director

Francis B. Nimick, Jr.: trustee, director ED Princeton University (1939); Harvard University (1941). NONPR AFFIL chairman: Allegheny General Hospital; vice president, director: W Pennsylvania School Deaf.

Jean A. Robinson: trustee, director

Albert Clarence Van Dusen: trustee, director B Tampa, FL August 30, 1915. ED University of Florida BS (1937); University of Florida AM (1938); Northwestern University PhD (1942). CORP AFFIL director: Dollar Bank, FSB. NONPR AFFIL member: W Pennsylvania Council Economic Education; director: YMCA Pittsburgh; member: Sigma Xi; vice chancellor emeritus: University Pittsburgh; member: Pittsburgh Psychological Association; member: Professional School World Affairs Comm; vice chairman board trustees: Pittsburgh History & Landmarks Foundation; member: Pennsylvania Public Television Network Committee; member: Phi Beta Kappa; vice chancellor emeritus, professor emeritus: Northwestern University; fellow: Pennsylvania Psychological Association; fellow: International Foundation Social Economic Development; member: Midwest Psychological Association; member: International Association School Institute Administration; member: Friends Art Pittsburgh Schools; member: International Association Applied Psychology; member: Beta Theta Pi; member: Eastern Psychological Association; member: Association Deans Dir Summer Sessions; member: Beta Gamma Sigma; fellow: American Psychological Society; member: American Personal Guidance Association; fellow: American Psychological Association; member: American College Public Relations Association; director: American Japan Society Pittsburgh. CLUB AFFIL University Pittsburgh Club; Duquesne Club.

Marsha Zahumensky: secretary, treasurer

Grants Analysis

Disclosure Period: fiscal year ending June 30, 2004

Total Grants: $3,032,509

Number of Grants: 82

Average Grant: $25,406*

Highest Grant: $500,000

Lowest Grant: $500

Typical Range: $10,000 to $50,000

*Note: Average grant figure excludes two highest grants ($1,000,000).

Recent Grants

Note: Grants derived from fiscal 2003 Form 990.

General

500,000	Carnegie Science Center, Pittsburgh, PA
500,000	Pittsburgh Children's Museum, Pittsburgh, PA
100,000	Board of Education of the School District, Pittsburgh, PA
100,000	Center for Creative Play, Pittsburgh, PA
100,000	Robert Morris University, Pittsburgh, PA
75,000	Family Resources, Pittsburgh, PA
75,000	Manchester Bidwell Corporation, Pittsburgh, PA
70,000	Allegheny Conference on Community Development, Pittsburgh, PA
55,000	Watson Institute, Sewickley, PA
50,000	Carnegie Science Center, Pittsburgh, PA

BUILDING 19 FOUNDATION

Giving Contact

Les MacDonald, Director
319 Lincoln St.
Hingham, MA 02043-1600
Phone: (781)749-6900

Description

Founded: 1990
EIN: 043064072
Organization Type: Private Foundation
Grant Types: Capital, General Support, Scholarship.

Donor Information

Founder: Established in 1990 by Building 19, Inc.; S & S Domestic, Inc.; IFC, Inc.; and Paperworks 19, Inc.

Financial Summary

Total Giving: $93,205 (2003); $121,118 (2001)
Assets: $930,174 (2003); $1,027,944 (2001)
Gifts Received: $170,182 (1994); $187,000 (1993); $213,800 (1992). Note: In 1994, contributions were received from Building 19 Inc. ($83,182), International Floorcrafts ($26,400), Paperworks 19 Inc. ($19,200), and Furniture 19 ($10,800); seven other donors made contributions of $8,400 or less each.

Typical Recipients

Arts & Humanities: Arts Centers, Libraries, Museums/Galleries, Opera

Civic & Public Affairs: Clubs, Economic Development, Civic & Public Affairs-General, Urban & Community Affairs, Zoos/Aquariums

Education: Colleges & Universities, Public Education (Precollege), Secondary Education (Public), Student Aid

Environment: Wildlife Protection

Health: AIDS/HIV, Cancer, Clinics/Medical Centers, Health Organizations, Hospices, Hospitals, Medical Rehabilitation, Mental Health, Multiple Sclerosis, Outpatient Health Care, Single-Disease Health Associations, Trauma Treatment

International: Foreign Educational Institutions, Missionary/Religious Activities
Religion: Churches, Jewish Causes
Science: Science Museums
Social Services: Animal Protection, At-Risk Youth, Community Centers, Community Service Organizations, Domestic Violence, Emergency Relief, Food/Clothing Distribution, Homes, People with Disabilities, Recreation & Athletics, Senior Services, Shelters/Homelessness, Special Olympics

Application Procedures

Initial Contact: Send a brief letter of inquiry.
Deadlines: None.

Foundation Officials

Brian Callum: director
Phyllis Devaney: director
Debra Elovitz: director
Elaine Elovitz: director
Gerald Elovitz: director

Grants Analysis

Disclosure Period: calendar year ending 2003
Total Grants: $93,205
Number of Grants: 263
Average Grant: $318*
Highest Grant: $10,000
Lowest Grant: $25
Typical Range: $100 to $500
*Note: Average grant figure excludes highest grant.

Recent Grants

Note: Grants derived from 2000 Form 990.
Library-Related
1,000	Hingham Public Library, Hingham, MA

General
26,827	Weymouth United Methodist
5,000	Dana Farber Cancer Institute, Boston, MA
2,500	Germaine Lawrence, Arlington, MA
2,000	Project Bread, Boston, MA
1,500	Anti-Defamation League
1,000	American Association Ben Gurion University
1,000	Friends of Beth Israel Deaconess Medical Center
1,000	Hebrew Rehabilitation Center, MA
1,000	Hingham High Baseball, Hingham, MA
1,000	Interbarth

BULLITT FOUNDATION

Giving Contact

Marilyn Fike, Administrator
1212 Minor Avenue
Seattle, WA 98101-2825
Phone: (206)343-0807
Fax: (206)343-0822
E-mail: info@bullitt.org
Web: http://www.bullitt.org

Description

Founded: 1952
EIN: 916027795
Organization Type: Specialized/Single Purpose Foundation
Giving Locations: AK: Coastal Rainforests; ID; MT: Western part of state; OR; WA; Canada : BC
Grant Types: Award, Challenge, Emergency, Employee Matching Gifts, General Support, Operating Expenses, Project.
Note: Emergency grant requests for $10,000 or less are possible, but not encouraged, and are designed to deal with unpredictable emergencies that require immediate and critical action. They are not intended as interim funding or as a replacement for meeting established funding deadlines. Emergency requests face a more challenging review.

Donor Information

Founder: Established in 1952 by the founder of King Broadcasting Company, Dorothy Stimson Bullitt, who passed away in 1989 at the age of 97. Her three children, Priscilla B. Collins, Charles Stimson Bullitt, and Harriet S. Bullitt, serve as officers and trustees of the foundation. Priscilla Collins and Harriet Bullitt have recently sold the Seattle-based King Broadcasting Company. Bullitt began her business career without a college education when she was left alone to manage the family's real estate business. In the span of three years in the 1930s, Dorothy Bullitt lost her father, Charles D. Stimson, her husband, Alexander Scott Bullitt, and her brother, Thomas Stimson. Bullitt's pioneering business accomplishments paralleled her civic commitments and charitable contributions. She served on Washington's Unemployment Relief Commission during the Great Depression, which led to the construction of the Grand Coulee Dam. In 1958, she served on the University of Washington's board of regents. Some of her other favorite projects were A Contemporary Theatre, Seattle Public Library, and Children's Hospital. The foundation created the Dorothy Stimson Bullitt Memorial Fund to "award special, one-time gifts to organizations to which she was particularly attached."

Financial Summary

Total Giving: $4,332,625 (2003); $6,802,772 (2002); $5,050,645 (2001)
Assets: $84,399,287 (2002); $102,977,986 (2001)
Gifts Received: $25,000 (1997 approx); $258,035 (1996 approx); $25,000 (1995 approx). Note: In fiscal 1993, the foundation received $5,000 from Stimson Bullitt and $250 from Douglass Raff.

Typical Recipients

Arts & Humanities: Libraries, Public Broadcasting
Civic & Public Affairs: Botanical Gardens/Parks, Civil Rights, Civic & Public Affairs-General, Hispanic Affairs, Native American Affairs, Nonprofit Management, Public Policy, Rural Affairs, Urban & Community Affairs
Education: Agricultural Education, Colleges & Universities, Education Funds, Education Reform, Environmental Education, Faculty Development, Private Education (Precollege)
Environment: Air/Water Quality, Energy, Forestry, Environment-General, Protection, Research, Resource Conservation, Watershed, Wildlife Protection
Health: Preventive Medicine/Wellness Organizations
International: International Environmental Issues
Social Services: Recreation & Athletics, Social Services-General, YMCA/YWCA/YMHA/YWHA

Application Procedures

Initial Contact: Applicants should send an Application Cover Sheet (available from the foundation) and a letter of five pages or less. Examples of how to fill out the cover sheet are available at the foundation's website: www.bullitt.org/sample.htm.
Application Requirements: Letter of Inquiry pre-screening process is not used by the foundation. Include a brief description of the project, its significance, intended accomplishments, and prospects for success; work plan, with timetable, describing what tangible results are expected within the period of the grant and how those results can be discerned; specific funding request and how it will be applied; project budget, funding plan, history of the organization, qualifications of project personnel, and list of board members; copy of the IRS letter verifying tax-exempt status; an audited financial statement for the prior year (or the IRS 990 report); and a cover page with summary information including name and address of the organization, contact person, telephone number, size of the grant request, and a one-paragraph synopsis of the program or project. Other attachments may be included if they are essential for the foundation to understand the proposal, but unnecessary attachments are discouraged.
Deadlines: May 1 and November 1. The foundation prefers to avoid faxed proposals, express mail, and personal deliveries.
Review Process: Board decisions require roughly five months. For the May 1 deadline, a decision is available in early October; for the November 1 deadline, expect an early April decision.
Evaluative Criteria: The foundation uses the following questions to evaluate an application: If the project is successful, what impact will it have? How likely is the project to succeed? What is the track record of the organization submitting the proposal? Is a gifted leader or a talented team associated with the effort? Is the infrastructure in place to support the effort? Is the project timely? Is the proposed strategy well thought out and creative? Who are prospective supporters and opponents, and what resources do they command? Is the proposal scientifically sound? If successful, can the project be replicated?
The foundation favors projects that focus on high priority needs, produce tangible results, leverage resources, have multiplier effects, and use diverse funding sources. Bullitt Foundation Grant Application Guidelines and Final Report Procedures
Decision Notification: Applicants will be notified of the foundation's decision by letter.

Restrictions

Foundation is no longer accepting applications for environmental education projects. The majority of awarded grants will be for projects requesting $15,000 to $30,000. The foundation prefers to give no more than one grant per year to an organization. All requests from the same organization should be consolidated into a single submission.
The foundation does not support political elections or lobbying, individuals, university overhead costs, or capital projects.

Additional Information

The foundation reports that it convenes conferences. In 1995, the foundation changed its fiscal year end date from February 28 to December 31.
Publications: Application Guidelines; Annual Report

Foundation Officials

Harriett Stimson Bullitt: trustee B 1925. ED University of Washington. CORP AFFIL vice president, director: Classic Radio Inc.
Katharine M. Bullitt: vice president, trustee
Anne Fennessy: trustee
Marilyn Fike: director of admin
Denis Allen Hayes: president B Wisconsin Rapids, WI. ED Clark College AA (1964); Stanford University BA (1969); Stanford University JD (1985). NONPR AFFIL member, director: Federation American Scientists; chairman, chief executive officer: Green Seal; member: American Solar Energy Society; member, director: California Environmental Trust.
B. Gerald Johnson: trustee
Estella Leopold: trustee
Hubert Gaylord Locke: trustee B Detroit, MI 1934. ED Wayne State University AB (1955); University of Chicago BD (1959); University of Michigan AM (1961). NONPR AFFIL fellow: Society Values Higher Education; professor: University Washington Graduate School Public Affairs; trustee, fellow: National Academy Public Administration; board governors: Institute European Studies; associate editor: Journal Holocaust Genocide Studies; fellow: William O Douglas Institute.
Tomoko Moriguchi-Matsuno: trustee
Maggie Walker: trustee
Steven C. Whitney: program officer
James Youngren: trustee B 1940. PRIM CORP EMPL president: Great Northwest Store Inc. CORP AFFIL president: Chicken & Egg Productions Inc.; president: El Puerco Lloron Inc.

Grants Analysis

Disclosure Period: calendar year ending 2003
Total Grants: $4,332,625
Number of Grants: 155
Average Grant: $27,952
Highest Grant: $100,000
Lowest Grant: $5,000
Typical Range: $10,000 to $50,000

Recent Grants

Note: Grants derived from 2002 Form 990.

Library-Related

250,000	Seattle Public Library Foundation, Seattle, WA

General

1,300,000	Seattle Parks Foundation, Seattle, WA
175,000	National Audubon Society, New York, NY
140,000	Tides Center, San Francisco, CA
135,000	Long Live the Kings, Seattle, WA
128,000	People for Puget Sound, Seattle, WA
125,000	Earth Island Institute, San Francisco, CA
110,000	Natural Resources Defense Council, New York, NY
105,000	Oregon Environmental Council, Portland, OR
105,000	Sierra Club of British Columbia Foundation, Victoria, BC Canada
100,000	Skagitonians to Preserve Farmland, Mt. Vernon, WA

BUNBURY CO., INC.

Giving Contact

Samuel W. Lambert III, Treasurer
2 Railroad Place
Hopewell, NJ 08525
Phone: (609)333-8800
Fax: (609)333-8900
E-mail: BunburyCo@aol.com
Web: http://www.bunburycompany.org

Description

Founded: 1952
EIN: 136066172
Organization Type: General Purpose Foundation
Giving Locations: , Burlington County, NJ , Camden County , Hunterdon County , Middlesex County , Monmouth County , Ocean County , Somerset County, Mercer County
Grant Types: Capital, Challenge, Endowment, General Support, Matching, Project, Seed Money.
Note: Also funds special initiatives.

Donor Information

Founder: Incorporated in New York in 1952 by the late Dean Mathey.

Financial Summary

Total Giving: $1,084,167 (2001)
Giving Analysis: Giving for 2001 includes: foundation grants to United Way ($1,000)
Assets: $24,045,158 (2001)

Typical Recipients

Arts & Humanities: Arts Associations & Councils, Arts Centers, Arts Outreach, Ballet, Dance, Historic Preservation, History & Archaeology, Libraries, Museums/Galleries, Music, Performing Arts, Public Broadcasting, Theater
Civic & Public Affairs: Botanical Gardens/Parks, Clubs, Community Foundations, Economic Development, Civic & Public Affairs-General, Hispanic Affairs, Housing, Law & Justice, Municipalities/Towns, Nonprofit Management, Philanthropic Organizations, Professional & Trade Associations, Public Policy, Rural Affairs, Safety, Urban & Community Affairs, Women's Affairs, Zoos/Aquariums
Education: Afterschool/Enrichment Programs, Arts/ Humanities Education, Colleges & Universities, Education Funds, Education Reform, Elementary Education (Public), Environmental Education, Faculty Development, Education-General, Health & Physical Education, International Exchange, Literacy, Minority Education, Preschool Education, Private Education (Precollege), Secondary Education (Private), Secondary Education (Public), Special Education, Student Aid, Vocational & Technical Education
Environment: Air/Water Quality, Forestry, Environment-General, Resource Conservation, Watershed
Health: Adolescent Health Issues, AIDS/HIV, Cancer, Children's Health/Hospitals, Clinics/Medical Centers, Emergency/Ambulance Services, Hospitals, Medical Research, Mental Health, Nursing Services, Public Health
International: Foreign Educational Institutions, Health Care/Hospitals
Religion: Churches, Ministries, Religious Organizations, Religious Welfare
Science: Observatories & Planetariums, Science Museums, Scientific Centers & Institutes
Social Services: Animal Protection, At-Risk Youth, Child Welfare, Community Centers, Community Service Organizations, Domestic Violence, Family Planning, Family Services, Food/Clothing Distribution, Homes, People with Disabilities, Recreation & Athletics, Senior Services, Shelters/Homelessness, Substance Abuse, United Funds/United Ways, YMCA/YWCA/YMHA/YWHA, Youth Organizations

Application Procedures

Initial Contact: Request guidelines from the foundation via a letter of inquiry or from the foundation's web site.
Application Requirements: Application packages must include seven copies of the following information in this order: complete standard Bunbury application form; cover letter signed by the applicant organization's executive director or project director; a one-page executive summary of the project (separate from the body of the proposal), including purpose of funds sought, goal, collaborative partners, total project cost, and amount requested; proposal narrative (three pages or less) that includes a brief history of the organization and its range of programs and activities, project description, goals, objectives, and timeline, collaborative partners and community support for the project, methods of measuring outcomes, and a plan to complete or sustain project funding, if applicable; profiles or resumes of project staff; lists of board of directors and institutional funding sources over $1,000; IRS 501(c)(3) determination letter or proof of public supported 509(a) status; and financial information including organization budget for current year, year-end figures for previous year, most recent audit, and detailed project budget for its complete duration.
Deadlines: Exact dates vary, but fall within the months of April, June, September, and December. Contact the foundation for this year's deadlines.
Review Process: Grants are reviewed by a joint committee of Bunbury and its sister foundation, the Windham Foundation.
Evaluative Criteria: Although several New Jersey counties are eligible to apply for grants, preference is given to applicants in Mercer County. The foundation reports that it is, "...particularly interested in innovative ideas that can be sustained over time or that can be replicated elsewhere. Collaborative efforts, demonstrating broad community support and the ability to impact positively the quality of life within the community, are highly encouraged."
"In making decisions, the Foundation will look to the accomplishments of the applicant organization, the stability of its financial base, the strength of its leadership, and the long-term viability of the program in question."
The Foundation uses the following four criteria to evaluate applications:
"Ability to impact positively the target area and audience; Significance and depth of project; Feasibility - ability to complete the project successfully, within a realistic time frame, and according to budgeted goals; Ability to measure and evaluate proposed outcomes."
Decision Notification: Applicants are notified of the foundation's decision by mail within 8-10 weeks of the submission deadline.

Restrictions

The foundation does not make grants to individuals, out-of-state organizations, or for building funds, fellowships, or loans.

Additional Information

The foundation is affiliated with the Windham Foundation in Grafton, VT.
Publications: Annual Report; Application Guidelines

Foundation Officials

Charles B. Atwater: director
James Richard Cogan: treasurer, director B Jersey City, NJ 1928. ED Yale University BA (1950); Columbia University LLB (1953). PRIM CORP EMPL partner: Walter Conston Alexander & Green PC. CORP AFFIL chairman board: Grafton Village Cheese Co. NONPR AFFIL trustee: Charlotte Palmer Phillips Foundation; chairman board trustees: Windham Foundation; member: New York County Lawyers Association; member: Association Bar New York City; director: Corporate Relief Widows & Children Clergymen; director: American Friends Plantin-Moretus Museum; member: American Bar Association; member: American College Trust & Estate Counsel. CLUB AFFIL Salmagundi Artists Club; Yale Club.
Samuel Waldron Lambert, III: president, trustee B New York, NY 1938. ED Yale University BA (1960); Harvard University LLB (1963). PRIM CORP EMPL partner: Drinker, Biddle & Reath. NONPR AFFIL member: New Jersey Bar Association; member: Princeton Bar Association; member: American Bar Association.
William McGuigan: assistant treasurer
Stephan A. Morse: director B 1947. PRIM CORP EMPL president, director: Old Tavern at Grafton Inc. ADD CORP EMPL president, administration, director: Grafton Village Cheese Co. CORP AFFIL director: United Bank; director: Vermont Finance Services.
Robert M. Olmsted: director
Barbara L. Ruppert: assistant secretary
Edward Joseph Toohey: president, director B Jersey City, NJ 1930. ED Yale University BA (1953). CORP AFFIL vice president: Old Tavern Grafton Inc. NONPR AFFIL director emeritus: New York City Ballet; vice chairman: Peddie School. CLUB AFFIL Yale Club; Sky Club; University Club; Canoe Brook Country Club; Georgetown Club.
Charles C. Townsend, Jr.: secretary, director PRIM CORP EMPL secretary: The Bunbury Co. CORP AFFIL director: HTI Voice Solutions Inc.; director: Project Orbis International; director: Cary Institutional PRPTS Inc.
William Bigelow Wright: director B Rutland, VT 1924. ED Princeton University AB (1950). NONPR AFFIL president: Princeton Alumni Association Vermont; member, vice president executive committee Class '47: Princeton University Alumni Council; trustee: Calvin Coolidge Memorial Foundation. CLUB AFFIL Ivy Club; Princeton Club.
Edward R. Zuccaro: director B New York, NY 1943. PRIM CORP EMPL partner: Zuccaro, Willis & Bent. CORP AFFIL clerk, director: Phelps Enterprises; clerk, director: Phelps Real Estate; clerk, director: Music Shop; vice president, secretary, director: Old Tavern Grafton Inc.; treasurer: Grafton Village Cheese Co.; clerk, director: Movie World; clerk, director: Dana Jewelry.

Grants Analysis

Disclosure Period: calendar year ending 2001
Total Grants: $1,084,167*
Number of Grants: 124
Average Grant: $8,743
Highest Grant: $60,000

Lowest Grant: $500
Typical Range: $1,000 to $5,000
*Note: Giving excludes United Way.

Recent Grants
Note: Grants derived from 2002 Form 990.
Library-Related

33,333	Princeton Public Library Foundation, Princeton, NJ
15,000	Grafton Public Library, Grafton, IA

General

50,000	Council of New Jersey Grantmakers, Trenton, NJ
40,000	Windham Foundation Inc., Grafton, VT
30,000	Isles Inc., Trenton, NJ
30,000	Princeton Academy of the Sacred Heart, Princeton, NJ
20,000	HiTops, Princeton, NJ
20,000	Invention Factory Science Center, Trenton, NJ
20,000	Marlboro College, Marlboro, VT
20,000	Putney School, Putney, VT
20,000	Stuart Country Day School, Princeton, NJ
15,000	Children's Home Society of New Jersey, Trenton, NJ

CHARLES E. BURCHFIELD FOUNDATION

Giving Contact
John P. Dee, Attorney
Blair & Roach LLP
2645 Sheridan Dr.
Tonawanda, NY 14150
Phone: (716)834-9181

Description
Founded: 1966
EIN: 166073522
Organization Type: Private Foundation
Giving Locations: CA; DE; NY
Grant Types: Capital, General Support, Multiyear/Continuing Support, Operating Expenses, Scholarship.

Donor Information
Founder: the late Charles E. Burchfield

Financial Summary
Total Giving: $50,755 (2004); $540,600 (2001)
Assets: $2,216,825 (2004); $2,498,042 (2001)
Gifts Received: $235,000 (1993). Note: In 1993, contributions were received in the form of paintings.

Typical Recipients
Arts & Humanities: Arts Centers, Arts Institutes, Arts & Humanities-General, History & Archaeology, Libraries, Museums/Galleries
Civic & Public Affairs: Civic & Public Affairs-General, Municipalities/Towns
Education: Arts/Humanities Education

Application Procedures
Initial Contact: Send a brief letter of inquiry; full proposal.
Application Requirements: Include a description of organization.
Deadlines: None.

Additional Information
Publications: Annual Report

Foundation Officials
C. Arthur Burchfield: president, director
Violet P. Burchfield: vice president, director

Grants Analysis
Disclosure Period: calendar year ending 2004
Total Grants: $50,755
Number of Grants: 8
Highest Grant: $40,000
Lowest Grant: $353

Recent Grants
Note: Grants derived from 2001 Form 990.
General

51,000	Town of West Seneca, West Seneca, NY -- exhibition, recreation and education
20,000	Burchfield Homestead Society, Salem, OH -- exhibition
17,500	Burchfield Penney Art Center, Buffalo, NY -- for endowment, exhibition and restoration
1,100	Friends of Art Valparaiso University, Valparaiso, IN -- for memorial
1,000	Taconic Resources for Independence, Poughkeepsie, NY -- for exhibition

✳BURLINGTON INDUSTRIES INC.

Company Headquarters
Greensboro, NC
Web: http://www.burlington.com

Company Description
Founded: 1923
Ticker: BRLG
Exchange: OTC
Revenue: US$933.3 million (2002)
Employees: 7600 (2002)
SIC(s): 2211 Broadwoven Fabric Mills--Cotton, 2221 Broadwoven Fabric Mills--Manmade, 2231 Broadwoven Fabric Mills--Wool, 2273 Carpets & Rugs.

Operating Locations
Burlington Industries, Inc. (CA--San Francisco; DC--Washington; GA--Calhoun, Dahlonega; IL--Chicago; KS--Overland Park; NY--New York; NC--Belmont, Burlington, Denton, Forest City, Gastonia, Mooresville, Mount Olive, Oxford, Rocky Mount, Smithfield, St. Pauls; SC--Bishopville, Greenville; TN--Johnson City; VA--Halifax, Hillsville; WA--Seattle)
Note: Operates in 10 states and 42 communities and maintains plants in Mexico.

Nonmonetary Support
Type: Donated Products; Loaned Executives
Volunteer Programs: Company does not have a formal employee volunteer program, but it provides meeting space on the premises or time off to individual employees who volunteer for Junior Achievement. Company also sponsors two Red Cross Blood Drives annually.
Note: Co. provides nonmonetary support

Burlington Industries Foundation

Giving Contact
Dolores C. Sides, Executive Director
PO Box 21207
Greensboro, NC 27420-1207
Phone: (336)379-2303
Fax: (336)379-4504

Description
EIN: 566043142
Organization Type: Corporate Foundation
Giving Locations: NC; SC; VA: principally near operating locations and to national organizations.
Grant Types: Award, Capital, Conference/Seminar, Employee Matching Gifts, General Support.
Note: Employee matching gift ratio: 1 to 1 up to $5,000 for current employees; up to $1,000 for retired employees.

Financial Summary
Total Giving: $367,347 (fiscal year ending September 30, 2003); $489,809 (fiscal 2002); $691,212 (fiscal 2001). Note: Contributes from foundation only.
Giving Analysis: Giving for fiscal 2002 includes: foundation gifts to individuals ($5,950); foundation matching gifts ($91,393); foundation grants to United Way ($96,550).
Assets: $2,130,707 (fiscal 2003); $2,186,211 (fiscal 2002); $2,810,901 (fiscal 2001)
Gifts Received: $400,005 (fiscal 2000); $1,000,000 (fiscal 1999); $100 (fiscal 1998)

Typical Recipients
Arts & Humanities: Arts Associations & Councils, Arts Funds, Historic Preservation, Libraries, Museums/Galleries, Music
Civic & Public Affairs: Botanical Gardens/Parks, Business/Free Enterprise, Clubs, Community Foundations, Employment/Job Training, Civic & Public Affairs-General, Housing, Law & Justice, Minority Business, Municipalities/Towns, Nonprofit Management, Philanthropic Organizations, Public Policy, Safety, Urban & Community Affairs
Education: Afterschool/Enrichment Programs, Agricultural Education, Business Education, Colleges & Universities, Community & Junior Colleges, Continuing Education, Economic Education, Education Associations, Education Funds, Education Reform, Elementary Education (Public), Engineering/Technological Education, Faculty Development, Education-General, Literacy, Minority Education, Private Education (Precollege), Public Education (Precollege), Science/Mathematics Education, Secondary Education (Private), Student Aid, Vocational & Technical Education
Environment: Environment-General, Protection, Resource Conservation
Health: AIDS/HIV, Cancer, Children's Health/Hospitals, Clinics/Medical Centers, Emergency/Ambulance Services, Health Organizations, Hospices, Hospitals, Multiple Sclerosis, Outpatient Health Care, Preventive Medicine/Wellness Organizations, Respiratory, Single-Disease Health Associations
International: International Affairs, International Organizations, International Relations
Religion: Jewish Causes, Ministries, Religious Welfare
Science: Science Museums, Scientific Centers & Institutes
Social Services: Child Welfare, Community Centers, Community Service Organizations, Delinquency & Criminal Rehabilitation, Family Services, People with Disabilities, Recreation & Athletics, Scouts, Shelters/Homelessness, Special Olympics, Substance Abuse, United Funds/United Ways, Volunteer Services, YMCA/YWCA/YMHA/YWHA, Youth Organizations

Application Procedures
Initial Contact: Send a brief letter or proposal.
Application Requirements: Include a description of organization, including its aims and purpose; need and justification for program; evidence that organization and its programs are developed and have direction; information on organization's reputation, efficiency, management ability, financial status, and other income sources; proof that organization is tax-exempt and is not a private foundation.
Deadlines: None.
Notes: Foundation may request additional information.

Restrictions

Contributions generally are not made to national organizations; organizations that are not tax-exempt; fraternal, labor, or veterans' organizations; churches; endowment funds; organizations supported through federated campaigns; private secondary schools; historic preservation projects; outdoor dramas; individuals; workshops, conferences, or seminars; production of films, documentaries, or other similar projects; operating expenses; political organizations, parties, or candidates; or medical research.

Corporate Officials

James M. Guin: vice president human resources & public relations B 1943. ED North Carolina State University BS (1966). PRIM CORP EMPL vice president human resources & public relations: Burlington Industries, Inc.

George W. Henderson, III: chief executive officer, chairman B Roanoke, VA 1948. ED University of North Carolina BA (1970); Emory University MBA (1974). PRIM CORP EMPL president, chief executive officer, director: Burlington Industries, Inc. CORP AFFIL director: Wachovia Bank NA; director: Wachovia Corp.; director: Jefferson Pilot Corp.; director: Jefferson Pilot Life Insurance Co.

Foundation Officials

Park R. Davidson: trustee B Keosauqua, IA 1934. ED University of Iowa (1955); University of Iowa Law School (1957).

George W. Henderson, III: trustee (see above)

Charles A. McLendon: trustee ED University of North Carolina (1946).

Dolores C. Sides: executive director

Grants Analysis

Disclosure Period: fiscal year ending September 30, 2003

Total Grants: $161,379*

Number of Grants: 33

Average Grant: $4,890

Highest Grant: $15,000

Lowest Grant: $100

Typical Range: $1,000 to $10,000

***Note:** Giving excludes United Way; matching gifts; and gifts to individuals.

Recent Grants

Note: Grants derived from fiscal 2003 Form 990.

General

40,500	United Way of Greater Greensboro Inc., Greensboro, NC
25,000	Community Foundation of Greater Greensboro, Greensboro, NC
15,000	Independent College Fund of North Carolina (ICFNC), Raleigh, NC
14,350	Greensboro Day School, Greensboro, NC
12,500	Bishop McGuinness Catholic High School, Oklahoma City, OK
12,000	North Carolina Textile Foundation (NCTF Inc.), Raleigh, NC
10,000	Greensboro Urban Ministry, Greensboro, NC
7,675	Duke University, Durham, NC
7,591	University of North Carolina at Chapel Hill, NC
7,500	Cleveland Institute of Music, Cleveland, OH

BURLINGTON NORTHERN SANTA FE CORP.

Company Headquarters

2650 Lou Menk Drive, 2nd Floor
PO Box 961057
Fort Worth, TX 76161-0057
Phone: (817)333-2000
Web: http://www.bnsf.com

Company Description

Founded: 1995
Ticker: BNI
Exchange: NYSE
Revenue: US$10.946 billion (2004)
Profit: US$791 million (2004)
Employees: 36500 (2003)
Fortune Rank: 200, per FORTUNE Magazine's list of 500 Largest U.S. Corporations (2004).
SIC(s): 4011 Railroads--Line-Haul Operating, 4613 Refined Petroleum Pipelines.

Nonmonetary Support

Type: Donated Equipment
Note: Company provides nonmonetary support.

Burlington Northern Santa Fe Foundation

Giving Contact

Richard A. Russack, President
5601 West 26th Street
Cicero, IL 60804
Phone: (708)924-5615
E-mail: sharon.heft@bnsf.com

Alternate Contact

2500 Lou Menk Drive
Ft. Worth, TX 76161
Phone: (817)352-3425

Description

EIN: 366051896
Organization Type: Corporate Foundation
Giving Locations: principally near operating locations and to national organizations.
Grant Types: Capital, Emergency, Employee Matching Gifts, General Support, Matching, Multiyear/Continuing Support, Project, Scholarship.

Financial Summary

Total Giving: $3,235,146 (2002); $3,378,438 (2001). Note: Contributes through corporate direct giving program and foundation.
Giving Analysis: Giving for 2001 includes: foundation matching gifts ($248,777); foundation scholarships ($315,934); foundation grants to United Way ($763,688).
Assets: $1,888,257 (2002); $1,901,074 (2001)
Gifts Received: $3,186,000 (2002); $4,675,000 (2001); $3,502,000 (2000). Note: Contributions received from Burlington Northern Santa Fe Corp.

Typical Recipients

Arts & Humanities: Arts Associations & Councils, Arts Centers, Ballet, Dance, Historic Preservation, History & Archaeology, Libraries, Museums/Galleries, Music, Opera, Performing Arts
Civic & Public Affairs: Botanical Gardens/Parks, Chambers of Commerce, Civic & Public Affairs-General, Zoos/Aquariums
Education: Agricultural Education, Colleges & Universities, Education Funds, Education-General, Literacy, Minority Education, Private Education (Precollege), Science/Mathematics Education, Student Aid
Health: Children's Health/Hospitals, Multiple Sclerosis

Science: Science Museums
Social Services: Child Welfare, Emergency Relief, United Funds/United Ways, YMCA/YWCA/YMHA/YWHA, Youth Organizations

Application Procedures

Initial Contact: Send a brief letter requesting application form; application packet will be sent pending determination of eligibility.

Application Requirements: Include with completed application: description of the organization, amount requested, copy of IRS tax-exempt ruling, current budget, principal sources and amounts of ongoing annual support, copy of most recently filed Form 990, information on the purpose, need for and relevance of the project, the approach to implementing the project, description of local support and coordination; method of project evaluation; how grant funds will be used; the competence of the organization and its personnel, and outside contractors in a direct or indirect supervisory position over the project; outline of future funding of on-going projects, list of other sources of support.

Deadlines: None.

Review Process: Consideration is given to each proposal to determine eligibility; declined organizations receive notification by mail; approved organizations receive funds shortly after approval.

Evaluative Criteria: Relevance to community needs, management capability, ability to achieve program's objectives, impact on community, level of volunteer participation, current and future sources of financial support

Decision Notification: As long as six months after application.

Restrictions

In general, the foundation does not support individuals; political, religious, fraternal, or veterans organizations; national health organizations or their local chapters; goodwill advertising; tours, conferences, dinners, seminars, workshops, or testimonials; endowment funds; tax-supported educational institutions or governmental agencies; pre-school, primary and secondary educational institutions; organizations already receiving United Way support; community and other foundations that also provide grants; or programs beyond stated geographic areas of interest.

Additional Information

Burlington Northern Santa Fe Corporation was formed by the merger of Burlington Northern Inc. and Santa Fe Pacific Corporation

Corporate Officials

Thomas N. Hund: executive vice president, chief financial officer ED Loyola University Chicago BBA; University of Chicago MBA. PRIM CORP EMPL executive vice president, chief financial officer: Burlington Northern Santa Fe Corp.

Carl R. Ice: executive vice president, chief operating officer PRIM CORP EMPL executive vice president, chief operating officer: Burlington Northern Santa Fe Corp.

Matthew K. Rose: president, chief executive officer, director B April 1959. ED University of Missouri BS (1980). PRIM CORP EMPL president, chief executive officer, director: Burlington Northern Santa Fe Corp.

Foundation Officials

Thomas N. Hund: director (see above)
Carl R. Ice: director (see above)
Jeffrey Moreland: director
Matthew K. Rose: director (see above)
Richard A. Russack: president, director ED Union College BS (1959); New York University BA (1960). PRIM CORP EMPL vice president corporate relations: Burlington Northern Santa Fe Corp.

Grants Analysis

Disclosure Period: calendar year ending 2002
Total Grants: $1,876,934*

Number of Grants: 382
Average Grant: $4,913
Highest Grant: $100,000
Lowest Grant: $100
Typical Range: $250 to $25,000
*Note: Giving excludes matching gifts; scholarship; United Way.

Recent Grants

Note: Grants derived from 2003 Form 990.
General

290,000	Scholarship Program Administrators Inc., Nashville, TN
150,000	United Way of Metropolitan Tarrant, Ft. Worth, TX
100,000	Museum Of Science And Industry, Chicago, IL
100,000	Performing Arts Fort Worth, Ft. Worth, TX
70,000	Boys And Girls Clubs of America, Richardson, TX
60,000	Fort Worth Museum of Science And History, Ft. Worth, TX
53,060	National Merit Scholarship Corporation, Evanston, IL
50,000	Amon Carter Museum, Ft. Worth, TX
50,000	Fort Worth Symphony Association, Ft. Worth, TX
50,000	Fort Worth Zoo, Ft. Worth, TX

BURLINGTON RESOURCES INC.

Company Headquarters

5051 Westheimer, Ste. 1400
Houston, TX 77056
Web: http://www.br-inc.com

Company Description

Ticker: BR
Exchange: NYSE
Revenue: US$5.618 billion (2004)
Profit: US$1.527 billion (2004)
Employees: 2111 (2003)
Fortune Rank: 353, per FORTUNE Magazine's list of 500 Largest U.S. Corporations (2004).

Burlington Resources Foundation

Giving Contact

Gavin H. Smith, President
5051 Westheimer, Suite 1400
Houston, TX 77056-5604
Phone: (817)347-2000

Description

EIN: 760453686
Organization Type: Corporate Foundation
Giving Locations: nationally.
Grant Types: Capital, Employee Matching Gifts, General Support.
Note: Employee matching gift ratio: 2 to 1.

Financial Summary

Total Giving: $4,410,533 (2002); $4,553,336 (2001). Note: Contributes through corporate direct giving program and foundation.
Giving Analysis: Giving for 2001 includes: foundation grants to United Way ($168,900); foundation matching gifts ($306,896); foundation ($4,077,540).
Assets: $21,899,256 (2002); $22,272,848 (2001)
Gifts Received: $3,137,367 (2002); $14,726,291 (2001); $6,280,087 (2000). Note: In 2000, 2001 and 2002, contributions were received from Burlington

Resources Inc. In 1993 and 1994, contributions were received from Meridian Oil Inc.

Typical Recipients

Arts & Humanities: Arts Associations & Councils, Arts Festivals, Arts Funds, Community Arts, Dance, Libraries, Museums/Galleries, Music, Opera, Public Broadcasting, Theater
Civic & Public Affairs: Clubs, Economic Policy, Hispanic Affairs, Housing, Native American Affairs, Philanthropic Organizations, Urban & Community Affairs, Zoos/Aquariums
Education: Afterschool/Enrichment Programs, Arts/Humanities Education, Business Education, Colleges & Universities, Education Associations, Education Funds, Education Reform, Elementary Education (Public), Engineering/Technological Education, Faculty Development, Education-General, International Studies, Literacy, Medical Education, Minority Education, Private Education (Precollege), Public Education (Precollege), Science/Mathematics Education, Student Aid
Environment: Environment-General, Protection, Resource Conservation, Wildlife Protection
Health: Alzheimer's Disease, Cancer, Children's Health/Hospitals, Clinics/Medical Centers, Emergency/Ambulance Services, Heart, Hospices, Medical Research, Nursing Services, Prenatal Health Issues, Preventive Medicine/Wellness Organizations, Public Health, Single-Disease Health Associations
International: International Organizations
Religion: Religious Welfare, Seminaries
Science: Science Museums
Social Services: At-Risk Youth, Child Abuse, Child Welfare, Family Services, Food/Clothing Distribution, Homes, People with Disabilities, Recreation & Athletics, Scouts, Senior Services, United Funds/United Ways, Volunteer Services, YMCA/YWCA/YMHA/YWHA, Youth Organizations

Application Procedures

Initial Contact: Request application form.
Application Requirements: Include the completed application form; financial information, including your total current budget and the principal sources and amounts of ongoing annual support; proof of tax-exempt status; and copy of the organization's most recent Form 990.
Deadlines: None.
Decision Notification: Allow four months for a decision.
Notes: Foundation discourages telephone calls or personal visits. Copies of application forms are not accepted. Forms should not be placed in binders or other types of covers.

Restrictions

Does not support religious organizations for religious purposes; veteran or fraternal organizations; general endowment funds; national health organizations or programs; individuals; fund-raising events; corporate memberships, chambers of commerce, taxpayer associations, and other bodies whose activities are not expected to directly benefit the company; political organizations, campaigns, or candidates; and computers or related computer related projects.

Additional Information

Burlington Resources was separated from Burlington Northern Inc. in 1988. It operates its own foundation out of Ft. Worth, TX.
Burlington Resources Foundation gives on behalf of El Paso Natural Gas Co., El Paso, TX; Glacier Park Co., Seattle, WA; Meridian Oil Inc., Houston, TX; and Meridian Minerals Co., Englewood, CO.

Corporate Officials

Jeffery P. Monte: secretary

Foundation Officials

Ernesto Gomez: tax officer
L. David Hanower: senior vice president B New

York, NY 1959. ED Harvard University (1981); University of Chicago Law School (1985). PRIM CORP EMPL senior vice president law: Burlington Resources Inc.
Daniel D. Hawk: vice president, treasurer
Joseph P. McCoy: vice president, controller
Jeffery P. Monte: secretary (see above)
Frederick J. Plaeger, II: senior vice president, assistant secretary, general counsel
Steven J. Shapiro: senior vice president, chief financial officer
Gavin H. Smith: president, director
Anne V. Vaughan: assistant secretary

Grants Analysis

Disclosure Period: calendar year ending 2002
Total Grants: $3,831,392*
Number of Grants: 310
Average Grant: $8,795*
Highest Grant: $300,000
Lowest Grant: $100
Typical Range: $500 to $25,000
*Note: Giving excludes matching gifts and United Way. Average grant figure excludes four highest grants ($1,140,000).

Recent Grants

Note: Grants derived from 2003 Form 990.
General

300,000	Baylor College of Medicine, Houston, TX
300,000	Texas Children's Hospital, Houston, TX
300,000	University of Texas MD Anderson Cancer Center, Houston, TX
240,000	Habitat for Humanity International, Americus, GA
100,000	Texas Heart Institute, Houston, TX
74,667	Mai Tec
69,669	United Way of Calgary and Area, Calgary, AB Canada
68,273	University of Kansas Center for Research Inc., Lawrence, KS
60,000	YMCA of the Greater Houston Area, Houston, TX
55,740	United Way of the Texas Gulf Coast, Houston, TX

ALPHONSE A. BURNAND MEDICAL AND EDUCATIONAL FOUNDATION

Giving Contact

Audrey S. Burnand, President
PO Box 59
Borrego Springs, CA 92004
Phone: (760)767-5314
Fax: (760)767-5912

Description

Founded: 1957
EIN: 956083677
Organization Type: Private Foundation
Giving Locations: CA: San Diego County, Borrego Springs
Grant Types: General Support.

Financial Summary

Total Giving: $421,000 (2003)
Assets: $4,205,887 (2003)

Typical Recipients

Arts & Humanities: Libraries, Music, Performing Arts, Public Broadcasting
Civic & Public Affairs: Botanical Gardens/Parks, Chambers of Commerce, Clubs, Civic & Public Affairs-General, Legal Aid, Safety, Urban & Community

Affairs, Women's Affairs, Zoos/Aquariums
Education: Colleges & Universities, Education Funds, Education-General, Public Education (Precollege), Special Education, Student Aid
Environment: Resource Conservation
Health: Cancer, Children's Health/Hospitals, Emergency/Ambulance Services, Health Organizations, Hospitals, Medical Research, Public Health, Single-Disease Health Associations, Transplant Networks/Donor Banks
International: Health Care/Hospitals, International Organizations
Religion: Churches
Social Services: Animal Protection, Camps, Child Welfare, Community Centers, Community Service Organizations, Day Care, Domestic Violence, People with Disabilities, Recreation & Athletics, Scouts, United Funds/United Ways, YMCA/YWCA/YMHA/YWHA, Youth Organizations

Application Procedures
Initial Contact: Send a brief letter of inquiry.
Application Requirements: Include a full explanation of request and proof of tax-exempt status.
Deadlines: None.

Restrictions
Does not support individuals.

Foundation Officials
Audrey Steele Burnand: president
Alice G. Hansen: secretary

Grants Analysis
Disclosure Period: calendar year ending 2003
Total Grants: $421,000
Number of Grants: 25
Average Grant: $10,045*
Highest Grant: $100,000
Lowest Grant: $1,000
Typical Range: $1,000 to $20,000
*Note: Average grant figure excludes three highest grants ($200,000).

Recent Grants
Note: Grants derived from 2001 Form 990.
Library-Related

5,000	San Diego County Library, San Diego, CA -- charitable	

General

50,000	Borrego Community Health Foundation, Borrego Springs, CA -- charitable
50,000	Boys and Girls Club of Borrego Springs, Ramona, CA -- charitable
25,000	Borrego Springs Fire Protection District, Borrego Springs, CA -- charitable
15,000	Borrego Springs Little League, Borrego Springs, CA -- charitable
15,000	Borrego Springs Performing Arts Center, Borrego Springs, CA -- charitable
10,000	Borrego Springs Educational Foundation, Borrego Springs, CA -- charitable
10,000	Borrego Springs Youth Center, Borrego Springs, CA -- charitable
10,000	Christmas Circle Community Park, Borrego Springs, CA -- charitable
5,500	Braille Institute, Los Angeles, CA -- charitable
5,000	Borrego Springs Children's Center, Borrego Springs, CA -- charitable

LEO BURNETT CO.

Company Headquarters
Chicago, IL
Web: http://www.leoburnett.com

Company Description
Employees: 9,029
SIC(s): 7311 Advertising Agencies.

Operating Locations
Leo Burnett Co. (CA--Los Angeles; FL--Coral Gables; NY--New York)

Nonmonetary Support
Type: Cause-related Marketing & Promotion
Volunteer Programs: Company sponsors "Give Back Day," a day when about 500 employees volunteer in local schools.

Leo Burnett Co. Charitable Foundation

Giving Contact
Kristin Anderson, Vice President
35 West Wacker Drive
Chicago, IL 60601
Phone: (312)220-5959
Fax: (312)220-6523

Description
EIN: 363379336
Organization Type: Corporate Foundation
Giving Locations: IL: Chicago
Grant Types: Employee Matching Gifts, General Support, Operating Expenses, Project.

Financial Summary
Total Giving: $439,731 (2002); $1,149,773 (2001). Note: Contributes through corporate direct giving program and foundation.
Giving Analysis: Giving for 2002 includes: foundation matching gifts ($307,492)
Assets: $759,257 (2002); $1,016,301 (2001)
Gifts Received: $185,000 (2002); $250,000 (2001); $149,231 (1998). Note: Contributions were received from the Leo Burnett Co.

Typical Recipients
Arts & Humanities: Arts Centers, Arts Funds, Arts Institutes, Ballet, Film & Video, Arts & Humanities-General, Historic Preservation, History & Archaeology, Libraries, Museums/Galleries, Music, Opera, Performing Arts, Public Broadcasting, Theater
Civic & Public Affairs: African American Affairs, Business/Free Enterprise, Chambers of Commerce, Civil Rights, Economic Development, Civic & Public Affairs-General, Hispanic Affairs, Housing, Law & Justice, Municipalities/Towns, Professional & Trade Associations, Public Policy, Rural Affairs, Urban & Community Affairs, Women's Affairs, Zoos/Aquariums
Education: Afterschool/Enrichment Programs, Agricultural Education, Arts/Humanities Education, Business Education, Colleges & Universities, Community & Junior Colleges, Education Funds, Education Reform, Elementary Education (Private), Engineering/Technological Education, Education-General, International Studies, Leadership Training, Medical Education, Minority Education, Preschool Education, Private Education (Precollege), Public Education (Precollege), Science/Mathematics Education, Secondary Education (Private), Student Aid
Environment: Environment-General, Resource Conservation, Wildlife Protection
Health: AIDS/HIV, Arthritis, Cancer, Children's Health/Hospitals, Clinics/Medical Centers, Emergency/Ambulance Services, Health Organizations, Heart, Hospices, Hospitals, Medical Research, Mental Health, Multiple Sclerosis, Single-Disease Health Associations
International: Foreign Arts Organizations, Health Care/Hospitals, Human Rights, International Affairs, International Environmental Issues, International Organizations, International Peace & Security Issues, International Relations, International Relief Efforts, Missionary/Religious Activities
Religion: Jewish Causes, Religious Organizations, Religious Welfare
Science: Science-General, Observatories & Planetariums, Science Museums, Scientific Centers & Institutes
Social Services: Animal Protection, At-Risk Youth, Big Brothers/Big Sisters, Child Welfare, Community Centers, Community Service Organizations, Emergency Relief, Family Planning, Family Services, Food/Clothing Distribution, People with Disabilities, Recreation & Athletics, Scouts, Senior Services, Shelters/Homelessness, United Funds/United Ways, YMCA/YWCA/YMHA/YWHA, Youth Organizations

Application Procedures
Initial Contact: Send a brief letter of inquiry.
Application Requirements: Include a description of organization, financial statement, listing of board of directors and IRS statement.
Deadlines: None.
Evaluative Criteria: Supports disadvantaged groups in the Chicago area; supports social and economic structure of Chicago; supports education in the creative fields.
Decision Notification: After bi-annual meetings.

Restrictions
The foundation does not provide grants to individuals or religious groups.

Corporate Officials
Kristin Anderson: vice president, director community affairs PRIM CORP EMPL vice president, director community affairs: Leo Burnett Co.
Richard B. Fizdale: chairman, chief executive officer, director B 1938. PRIM CORP EMPL chairman, chief executive officer, director: Leo Burnett Co. Inc. CORP AFFIL chairman: Leo Burnett Worldwide Inc.

Foundation Officials
Cheryl Berman: vice president
Robert Brennan: president
Michele Casey: treasurer
Flinn Dallis: fund mgr.
Jonathan Davis: fund mgr.
Ken Gilberg: fund mgr.
Eric Martinez: director
Carla Michelotti: secretary
Linda Wolf: director

Grants Analysis
Disclosure Period: calendar year ending 2002
Total Grants: $132,239*
Number of Grants: 66
Average Grant: $2,004
Highest Grant: $25,000
Lowest Grant: $25
Typical Range: $1,000 to $5,000
*Note: Giving excludes matching gifts.

Recent Grants
Note: Grants derived from 2003 Form 990.

General

25,000	Advertising Council Inc., New York, NY
10,400	Peak
10,000	FT Hays State University, Hays, KS
10,000	Virginia Commonwealth University, Richmond, VA
9,212	American Cancer Society
8,750	Avon Breast Cancer 3 Day
5,880	Aids Cycle Inc., Federal Way, WA
5,750	Francis W. Parker School, Chicago, IL
5,711	Off the Street Club, Chicago, IL
5,625	University of Illinois, Chicago, IL

THE BURNETT FOUNDATION

Giving Contact
Thomas F. Beech, Executive Vice President
801 Cherry Street
Unit 16
Ft. Worth, TX 76102-6881
Phone: (817)877-3344
Fax: (817)338-0448

Description
Founded: 1978
EIN: 751638517
Organization Type: General Purpose Foundation
Giving Locations: NM: Santa Fe; TX: Ft. Worth occasionally grants are provided nationally, at the trustee's discretion.
Grant Types: Capital, Challenge, Endowment, General Support, Matching, Operating Expenses.

Donor Information
Founder: Established in 1978 by Anne Burnett Tandy in memory of her husband, Charles D. Tandy (d. 1978). Mr. Tandy bought Radio Shack in 1963 and built it from a debt-ridden chain of nine electronics stores to a national chain with over 7,000 outlets.

Financial Summary
Total Giving: $19,005,818 (2003); $11,625,000 (2002 approx); $13,880,745 (2001)
Giving Analysis: Giving for 2003 includes: foundation grants to United Way ($50,000)
Assets: $214,810,610 (2003); $205,000,000 (2002 approx); $268,115,338 (2001)

Typical Recipients
Arts & Humanities: Arts Associations & Councils, Arts Centers, Arts Festivals, Arts Institutes, Arts Outreach, Ballet, Dance, Historic Preservation, Libraries, Museums/Galleries, Music, Opera, Performing Arts, Public Broadcasting, Theater, Visual Arts
Civic & Public Affairs: African American Affairs, Botanical Gardens/Parks, Community Foundations, Economic Development, Employment/Job Training, Civic & Public Affairs-General, Hispanic Affairs, Housing, Municipalities/Towns, Nonprofit Management, Parades/Festivals, Public Policy, Rural Affairs, Urban & Community Affairs, Women's Affairs, Zoos/Aquariums
Education: Afterschool/Enrichment Programs, Arts/Humanities Education, Colleges & Universities, Education Funds, Education Reform, Elementary Education (Private), Engineering/Technological Education, Environmental Education, Faculty Development, Education-General, Leadership Training, Legal Education, Medical Education, Minority Education, Preschool Education, Private Education (Precollege), Public Education (Precollege), Secondary Education (Public), Special Education, Student Aid
Environment: Research
Health: AIDS/HIV, Alzheimer's Disease, Cancer, Children's Health/Hospitals, Clinics/Medical Centers, Emergency/Ambulance Services, Health Policy/Cost Containment, Hospitals, Medical Research, Mental Health, Prenatal Health Issues, Research/Studies Institutes, Single-Disease Health Associations
International: Health Care/Hospitals, International Affairs, International Development
Religion: Ministries, Religious Organizations, Religious Welfare, Social/Policy Issues
Science: Science Museums
Social Services: At-Risk Youth, Big Brothers/Big Sisters, Child Abuse, Child Welfare, Community Centers, Community Service Organizations, Counseling, Crime Prevention, Day Care, Domestic Violence, Emergency Relief, Family Planning, Family Services, Food/Clothing Distribution, People with Disabilities, Recreation & Athletics, Scouts, Senior Services, Sexual Abuse, Shelters/Homelessness, Social Services-

General, Substance Abuse, United Funds/United Ways, YMCA/YWCA/YMHA/YWHA, Youth Organizations

Application Procedures
Initial Contact: Applicants are encouraged to write a letter of inquiry.
Application Requirements: Include a description of organization, the specific program to be considered, the amount requested, and a budget summary.
Deadlines: None.
Review Process: If the program fits within the foundation's guidelines and priorities, a more detailed application will be requested. Formal grant review meetings are held three times a year, usually in March, June, and November.

Restrictions
Funding is limited to organizations with 501(c)(3) status. The foundation will not fund individuals.

Additional Information
Publications: Annual Report; Guidelines

Foundation Officials
Thomas Foster Beech: executive vice president B Saint Paul, MN 1939. ED Carleton College BA (1961).
Benjamin J. Fortson: trustee
Anne Windfohr Grimes: trustee
Edward R. Hudson, Jr.: vice president, trustee, secretary, treasurer
Anne W. Marion: president, trustee B 1939. ED Briarcliffe Junior College; University of Geneva; University of Texas. NONPR AFFIL trustee: Modern Art Museum Fort Worth; honorary trustee: Texas Technology University; member: Memorial Sloan-Kettering Cancer Center; member executive committee: Fort Worth Stock Show; director: Fort Worth Zoological Association.
John Louis Marion: trustee B New York, NY 1933. ED Fordham University BS (1956); Columbia University (1960-1961). PRIM CORP EMPL honorary chairman: Sotheby's Inc. CORP AFFIL director: Sotheby Holdings Inc. NONPR AFFIL member: Appraisers Association America; director: International Foundation Art Research; chairman financee arts committee: American Cancer Society New York City. CLUB AFFIL Shady Oaks Country Club; Vintage Club; Eldorado Country Club; Lotos Club.

Grants Analysis
Disclosure Period: calendar year ending 2003
Total Grants: $18,955,818*
Number of Grants: 60
Average Grant: $74,923*
Highest Grant: $4,137,503
Lowest Grant: $2,500
Typical Range: $10,000 to $150,000
*Note: Giving excludes United Way. Average grant figure excludes six highest grants ($14,910,003).

Recent Grants
Note: Grants derived from 2001 Form 990.
General

2,300,000	Georgia O'Keeffe Museum, Santa Fe, NM
1,650,000	Georgia O'Keeffe Museum, Santa Fe, NM
1,600,000	FPA Foundation, Ft. Worth, TX
1,000,000	Fort Worth Museum of Science and History, Ft. Worth, TX
1,000,000	Fort Worth Symphony Orchestra, Ft. Worth, TX
1,000,000	Georgia O'Keeffe Museum, Santa Fe, NM
1,000,000	PAFW, Ft. Worth, TX
914,725	Fort Worth Modern Art Museum, Ft. Worth, TX
650,000	SIFL Santa Fe, Santa Fe, NM
300,000	National Cowgirl Museum and Hall of Fame, Ft. Worth, TX

MARGARET E. BURNHAM CHARITABLE TRUST

Giving Contact
Thomas M. Pierce, Trustee
Care of H.M. Payson & Co.
PO Box 31
Portland, ME 04112-0031
Phone: (207)772-3761
Fax: (207)871-7508
Web: http://www.megrants.org/Burnham.htm

Description
Founded: 1995
EIN: 010496879
Organization Type: Private Foundation
Giving Locations: ME
Grant Types: General Support.

Typical Recipients
Arts & Humanities: Ethnic & Folk Arts, Historic Preservation, History & Archaeology, Libraries, Museums/Galleries, Music
Civic & Public Affairs: Civic & Public Affairs-General, Safety, Urban & Community Affairs, Zoos/Aquariums
Education: Arts/Humanities Education, Colleges & Universities, Education Funds, Education-General, Leadership Training, Public Education (Precollege), Student Aid, Vocational & Technical Education
Environment: Environment-General, Resource Conservation
Health: AIDS/HIV, Clinics/Medical Centers, Emergency/Ambulance Services, Health Organizations, Home-Care Services, Hospitals, Single-Disease Health Associations
Religion: Religious Welfare
Social Services: Camps, Child Welfare, Community Centers, Community Service Organizations, Counseling, Domestic Violence, Emergency Relief, Scouts, Social Services-General, Substance Abuse, United Funds/United Ways, Volunteer Services, YMCA/YWCA/YMHA/YWHA, Youth Organizations

Application Procedures
Initial Contact: Send completed application form supplied by the foundation.
Application Requirements: Include proof of tax-exempt status, recently audited financial statement, and a list of officers or directors.
Deadlines: October 15.

Foundation Officials
Thomas M. Pierce: trustee
Clifford H. Sinnett: trustee

Grants Analysis
Disclosure Period: calendar year ending 2000
Total Grants: $341,200*
Number of Grants: 86
Average Grant: $3,967
Highest Grant: $15,000
Typical Range: $1,000 to $5,000
*Note: Giving excludes United Way.

Recent Grants
Note: Grants derived from 2001 Form 990.
Library-Related

5,000	Brown Memorial Library, East Baldwin, ME
5,000	Falmouth Memorial Library, Falmouth, ME

General

20,000	United Way of Greater Portland, Portland, ME
10,000	Falmouth Education Foundation, Falmouth, MA
10,000	Maine Medical Center, Portland, ME
10,000	Portland Museum of Art, Portland, ME
10,000	Rippleffect, Portland, OR

7,500	Catholic Charities, ME
7,500	Gulf of Maine Aquarium, Portland, ME
7,500	Miles Memorial Hospital, Damariscotta, ME
7,500	St. Lawrence Arts and Community Center, Portland, ME
7,500	University of New England, Biddeford, ME

BURNS & MCDONNELL

Company Headquarters
9400 Ward Parkway
Kansas City, MO 64114
Web: http://www.burnsmcd.com

Company Description
Former Name: Burns & McDonnell Engineering Co.
Operating Revenue: US$186 million (2002)
Employees: 1500 (2002)
SIC(s): 8700 Engineering & Management Services, 8711 Engineering Services, 8712 Architectural Services, 8748 Business Consulting Services Nec.

Burns & McDonnell Foundation

Giving Contact
Gregory M. Graves, Chairman, President, & Director
Burns & McDonnell Foundation
PO Box 419173
Kansas City, MO 64141-6173
Phone: (816)333-9400
Fax: (816)333-3690

Description
Founded: 1988
EIN: 431448871
Organization Type: Corporate Foundation
Giving Locations: MO: Kansas City metropolitan area
Grant Types: General Support.

Donor Information
Founder: the Burns & McDonnell Corporation

Financial Summary
Total Giving: $216,269 (2003); $155,598 (2001)
Giving Analysis: Giving for 2003 includes: foundation grants to United Way ($63,400); 2001: foundation ($58,000)
Assets: $3,952,564 (2003); $4,097,914 (2001)
Gifts Received: $18,000 (1993); $36,000 (1992). Note: In 1993, contributions were received from Burns & McDonnell Engineering Co.

Typical Recipients
Arts & Humanities: Arts Funds, Ballet, Arts & Humanities-General, Historic Preservation, History & Archaeology, Libraries, Museums/Galleries, Music, Opera, Public Broadcasting, Theater
Civic & Public Affairs: Economic Development, Civic & Public Affairs-General, Housing, Professional & Trade Associations, Public Policy, Urban & Community Affairs, Women's Affairs, Zoos/Aquariums
Education: Colleges & Universities, Education Funds, Engineering/Technological Education, Education-General, International Exchange, Minority Education, Science/Mathematics Education, Vocational & Technical Education
Environment: Environment-General
Health: Cancer, Clinics/Medical Centers, Diabetes, Health Funds, Heart, Medical Research, Multiple Sclerosis, Single-Disease Health Associations
Science: Scientific Organizations
Social Services: Child Welfare, Community Service

Organizations, Crime Prevention, Domestic Violence, Recreation & Athletics, Scouts, United Funds/United Ways, Youth Organizations

Application Procedures
Initial Contact: The foundation has no formal grant application procedure or application form.
Deadlines: None.

Restrictions
The foundation does not make contributions to political or religious causes.

Additional Information
Company reports 60% of contributions support education; 30% civic and public affairs; and 5% each to arts and health/human services programs.

Corporate Officials
Gerard T. Bukowski, Jr.: vice president, counsel PRIM CORP EMPL vice president, counsel: Burns & McDonnell.
Darrell M. Hosler: executive vice president, secretary, director B Beloit, KS 1936. ED Kansas State University (1959). PRIM CORP EMPL executive vice president, secretary, director: Burns & McDonnell. CORP AFFIL president, managing director: Burns & McDonnell International; director: Nofsinger Co.
Dave G. Ruf, Jr.: chairman, president, chief executive officer, director B Kansas City, MO 1938. ED Kansas City Junior College (1958); University of Kansas (1960). PRIM CORP EMPL chairman, president, chief executive officer, director: Burns & McDonnell.
Mark H. Taylor: vice president PRIM CORP EMPL vice president: Burns & McDonnell ADD CORP EMPL vice president: Burns McDonnell Engineering Co.

Foundation Officials
Gerard T. Bukowski, Jr.: secretary (see above)
Joel A. Cerwick: director
Barbara L. Graham: assistant secretary
Gregory M. Graves: chairman, president, director
Donald F. Greenwood: director
Paul A. Hustad: director
James Schorgl: assistant treasurer
Mark H. Taylor: treasurer, director (see above)

Grants Analysis
Disclosure Period: calendar year ending 2003
Total Grants: $152,869*
Number of Grants: 66
Average Grant: $2,316*
Highest Grant: $24,000
Lowest Grant: $25
Typical Range: $500 to $5,000
*Note: Giving excludes United Way.

Recent Grants
Note: Grants derived from 2003 Form 990.
General

63,400	United Way
24,000	Kansas City Public Television, Kansas City, MO
24,000	KCPTV
6,500	University of Missouri, Columbia, MO
6,500	University of Missouri, Columbia, MO
6,400	Iowa State University, Ames, IA
6,400	Iowa State University, Ames, IA
6,300	University of Nebraska, Lincoln, NE
6,300	University of Nebraska, Lincoln, ME
6,200	University of Kansas, Lawrence, KS

J.W. BURRESS INC.

Company Headquarters
Roanoke, VA
Web: http://www.jwburress.com

Company Description
Employees: 130

Operating Locations
J.W. Burress (NC--Winston-Salem)

J.W. Burress Foundation

Giving Contact
John W. Burress, III, President & Treasurer
J.W. Burress Foundation
380 Knollwood Street, Suite 610
Winston-Salem, NC 27103
Phone: (336)725-7992
E-mail: jwburress@jwburress.com

Description
Founded: 1986
EIN: 561554131
Organization Type: Corporate Foundation
Giving Locations: NC; VA
Grant Types: General Support.

Financial Summary
Total Giving: $65,000 (2003); $430,000 (2002); $147,000 (2001)
Giving Analysis: Giving for 2002 includes: foundation grants to United Way ($100,000)
Assets: $381,011 (2003); $330,394 (2002); $1,066,445 (2001)
Gifts Received: $1,357,773 (1997); $300,000 (1996); $20,000 (1993). Note: In 1996, contributions were received from J.W. Burress Inc.

Typical Recipients
Arts & Humanities: Arts Associations & Councils, Arts Centers, Arts Institutes, Ballet, Arts & Humanities-General, History & Archaeology, Libraries, Museums/Galleries, Music, Public Broadcasting, Theater
Civic & Public Affairs: Asian American Affairs, Botanical Gardens/Parks, Civil Rights, Clubs, Community Foundations, Ethnic Organizations, Civic & Public Affairs-General, Housing, Philanthropic Organizations
Education: Arts/Humanities Education, Business Education, Colleges & Universities, Education Associations, Education Funds, Education-General, International Studies, Minority Education, Private Education (Precollege), Public Education (Precollege), Religious Education, Secondary Education (Private), Special Education, Student Aid
Environment: Environment-General, Protection, Resource Conservation
Health: Adolescent Health Issues, Cancer, Children's Health/Hospitals, Clinics/Medical Centers, Eyes/Blindness, Hospices, Hospitals (University Affiliated), Mental Health, Preventive Medicine/Wellness Organizations, Single-Disease Health Associations, Transplant Networks/Donor Banks
Religion: Churches, Religion-General, Ministries, Religious Organizations, Religious Welfare
Social Services: Big Brothers/Big Sisters, Child Abuse, Child Welfare, Community Centers, Counseling, Family Services, Food/Clothing Distribution, Homes, People with Disabilities, Senior Services, United Funds/United Ways, YMCA/YWCA/YMHA/YWHA, Youth Organizations

Application Procedures
Initial Contact: The foundation has no formal grant application procedure or application form.
Deadlines: None.

Corporate Officials
John W. Burress, III: chairman, president, chief executive officer B 1935. ED University of North Carolina. PRIM CORP EMPL chairman, president, chief executive officer: J.W. Burress Inc.

Foundation Officials

John W. Burress, III: president, treasurer (see above)
Sue Burress Wall: secretary
R. C. Vaughn: assistant secretary

Grants Analysis

Disclosure Period: calendar year ending 2003
Total Grants: $65,000
Number of Grants: 13
Average Grant: $3,636*
Highest Grant: $15,000
Lowest Grant: $1,000
Typical Range: $1,000 to $5,000
*Note: Average grant figure excludes two highest grants ($25,000).

Recent Grants

Note: Grants derived from 2003 Form 990.
General

15,000	Episcopal High School, Alexandria, VA
10,000	North Carolina Botanical Garden, Chapel Hill, NC
5,500	Senior Services, Winston-Salem, NC
5,000	Bethlehem Center Inc., Winston-Salem, NC
5,000	Carolina Ballet, Raleigh, NC
5,000	NAMI-Mental Health Alliance, Richmond, VA
5,000	Wake Forest University Baptist Medical Center, Winston-Salem, NC
4,000	Nature Conservancy, Durham, NC
4,000	Southeastern Center for Contemporary Art (SECCA), Winston-Salem, NC
2,500	UNC Institute for Arts & Humanities, Chapel Hill, NC

ROBERT HAROLD BURTON PRIVATE FOUNDATION

Giving Contact

Richard G. Horne, executive Director
c/o Wells Fargo Bank
PO Box 58477
Salt Lake City, UT 84158
Phone: (801)715-7140

Description

Founded: 1985
EIN: 742425567
Organization Type: Private Foundation
Giving Locations: UT: Salt Lake County
Grant Types: General Support.

Donor Information

Founder: the late Robert H. Burton

Financial Summary

Total Giving: $1,371,405 (2003)
Assets: $33,851,928 (2003)
Gifts Received: $5,996 (1995); $2,613 (1993)

Typical Recipients

Arts & Humanities: Arts Centers, Dance, Ethnic & Folk Arts, Libraries, Literary Arts, Museums/Galleries, Music, Opera, Performing Arts, Public Broadcasting, Theater
Civic & Public Affairs: Botanical Gardens/Parks, Civic & Public Affairs-General, Law & Justice, Legal Aid, Public Policy, Safety, Urban & Community Affairs
Education: Arts/Humanities Education, Colleges & Universities, Elementary Education (Public), Engineering/Technological Education, Faculty Development, Education-General, Legal Education, Literacy, Medical Education, Preschool Education, Private Ed-

ucation (Precollege), Public Education (Precollege), Secondary Education (Private), Student Aid, Vocational & Technical Education
Environment: Resource Conservation, Wildlife Protection
Health: Children's Health/Hospitals, Emergency/Ambulance Services, Health-General, Health Organizations, Long-Term Care, Nursing Services
Religion: Churches, Religious Welfare, Social/Policy Issues
Science: Science Museums
Social Services: Child Welfare, Community Centers, Community Service Organizations, Crime Prevention, Family Services, Social Services-General, Substance Abuse, United Funds/United Ways, YMCA/YWCA/YMHA/YWHA, Youth Organizations

Application Procedures

Initial Contact: The foundation has no formal grant application procedure or application form.
Deadlines: None.

Additional Information

Trust(s): Wells Fargo Bank NA

Foundation Officials

Richard R. Burton: member
Fred A. Moreton, Jr.: vice chairman
Judith Burton Moyle: chairman

Grants Analysis

Disclosure Period: calendar year ending 2003
Total Grants: $1,371,405
Number of Grants: 57
Average Grant: $13,873*
Highest Grant: $200,000
Lowest Grant: $1,000
Typical Range: $5,000 to $20,000
*Note: Average grant figure excludes five highest grants ($650,000).

Recent Grants

Note: Grants derived from 2001 Form 990.
General

414,776	University of Utah, Salt Lake City, UT
264,000	Red Butt Gardens and Arboretum, Salt Lake City, UT
200,000	Western Folklife, Elko, NV
150,000	Life Care, Salt Lake City, UT
100,000	And Justice For All, Salt Lake City, UT
100,000	Westminster College, Salt Lake City, UT
77,068	KUED, Salt Lake City, UT
50,000	Guadalupe Schools, Salt Lake City, UT
50,000	National Conference For Community and Justice, Salt Lake City, UT
50,000	Ronald McDonald House Charities, Salt Lake City, UT

EDYTH BUSH CHARITABLE FOUNDATION, INC.

Giving Contact

David A. Odahowski, President, Chief Executive Officer
199 East Welbourne Avenue
PO Box 1967
Winter Park, FL 32790-1967
Phone: 888-647-4322
Fax: (407)647-7716
E-mail: dhessler@edythbush.org
Web: http://www.edythbush.org

Description

Founded: 1966
EIN: 237318041

Organization Type: General Purpose Foundation
Giving Locations: FL: Lake County, Orange County, Osceola County, Seminole County
Grant Types: Award, Capital, Challenge, General Support, Matching, Multiyear/Continuing Support, Project.

Donor Information

Founder: Incorporated in 1966 in Minnesota by the late Edyth Bush and reincorporated in 1973 in Florida.

Financial Summary

Total Giving: $567,654 (fiscal year ending August 31, 2004); $2,644,634 (fiscal 2003); $2,093,342 (fiscal 2002)
Giving Analysis: Giving for fiscal 2001 includes: foundation matching gifts ($98,764)
Assets: $64,797,956 (fiscal 2002); $75,176,198 (fiscal 2001)

Typical Recipients

Arts & Humanities: Arts Appreciation, Arts Festivals, Arts Outreach, Arts & Humanities-General, Museums/Galleries, Music, Public Broadcasting, Theater
Civic & Public Affairs: Business/Free Enterprise, Community Foundations, Civic & Public Affairs-General, Housing, Municipalities/Towns, Nonprofit Management, Philanthropic Organizations, Professional & Trade Associations, Urban & Community Affairs, Zoos/Aquariums
Education: Business Education, Colleges & Universities, Education-General, Literacy, Public Education (Precollege), Science/Mathematics Education, Student Aid
Health: Alzheimer's Disease, Cancer, Clinics/Medical Centers, Eyes/Blindness, Health Funds, Health Organizations, Hospitals, Mental Health, Nursing Services, Respiratory, Single-Disease Health Associations
Religion: Churches, Dioceses, Ministries, Religious Organizations, Religious Welfare
Science: Scientific Centers & Institutes
Social Services: Animal Protection, At-Risk Youth, Big Brothers/Big Sisters, Child Welfare, Community Centers, Community Service Organizations, Counseling, Delinquency & Criminal Rehabilitation, Emergency Relief, Family Services, Food/Clothing Distribution, People with Disabilities, Senior Services, Shelters/Homelessness, Social Services-General, Volunteer Services, YMCA/YWCA/YMHA/YWHA, Youth Organizations

Application Procedures

Initial Contact: Applicants are encouraged to contact the foundation first by telephone. The foundation requests applications be made in writing.
Application Requirements: The foundation specifies that it needs two sets of a proposal. Requests for support should include contact information, amount requested with statement of why the grant is needed, position or relationship to the applicant organization of the individual signing the grant request, list of contributions received during each of the preceding three years and current year, and a list of potential funding sources. Applications should include a description of goals the grant is expected to accomplish, the method of financing the project after funds from the foundation are expended, and the criteria judging the effectiveness of the grant. Also required are a detailed project budget, statement that applicant will furnish a report detailing fund expenditures, timetable for project, and the names, occupations, and business affiliations of each of the board members, trustees, and key personnel. Applicants also must furnish copies of most recent 501(c)(3) letter of exemption and 509(a) status letter; statement that 501(c)(3) and 509(a) status has not been revoked or modified; latest annual balance sheet and detailed income statement; and the most recent quarterly or monthly management financial state-

ment, if the annual statement is more than three months old.

Applicants submitting construction or renovation requests should provide a current contractor's estimate of costs broken down by subcontracts. Requests for loans require a list of collateral to be tendered and a schedule of principal and interest payments. The foundation suggests talking with its officers before filing a loan request.

Deadlines: None.

Review Process: The foundation conducts a site visit after a complete grant request has been received. A representative of the foundation will meet with both the organization's staff and board members or trustees, and review the organization's operations. After the site visit, completed requests are presented to the grants committee and then to the board of directors. The board generally meets in February, May, August, and November.

Restrictions

The foundation ordinarily will not fund tax-supported institutions, individual scholarships or individual research; alcohol or drug abuse programs; foreign organizations or foreign use of funds; travel projects; fellowships; organizations for sacramental, denominational, or interdenominational purposes; advocacy organizations; cultural or arts organizations, unless their work is of a demonstrated, nationally recognized quality, or for the demonstrated educational value of children, K-12th grade; or organizations having revenues from memberships or contributions of less than $25,000 in the previous year. The foundation discourages requests for routine operating expenses, to pay off deficits, or for endowment funds. The foundation will not accept proposals by facsimile.

Additional Information

Approximately 50% of foundation grants are made on a challenge or match basis. Large grants are typically paid in installments over two or three years. The foundation also provides program-related investment loans to nonprofit organizations

Publications: Outline of Grant Request Requirements; Grants Policies and Procedures; Guidelines

Foundation Officials

Frederick Belloff: director
Mary Gretchen Belloff: vice chairman, director
Michael R. Cross: vice president finance, treasurer
Deborah Hessler: secretary
Gerald F. Hilbrich: director
H. Clifford Lee: chairman, director
John S. Lord: director
David A. Odahowski: president, director
Robert E. Waggoner: director

Grants Analysis

Disclosure Period: fiscal year ending August 31, 2004
Total Grants: $567,654
Number of Grants: 8
Average Grant: $53,236*
Highest Grant: $195,000
Lowest Grant: $10,000
Typical Range: $20,000 to $100,000
*Note: Average grant figure excludes highest grant.

Recent Grants

Note: Grants derived from 2002 Form 990.
General

223,233	CITE the Lighthouse for Central Florida, Orlando, FL -- provides Leesburg center
191,000	Boys & Girls Club of Central Florida Inc., Orlando, FL -- offers planned giving program
156,004	Rollins College, Winter Park, FL -- for philanthropy and nonprofit leadership center
143,904	Birth, Education, Training, Acceptance Inc., Orlando, FL -- for capital campaign
132,052	Florida Nonprofit Resource Center, Winter Park, FL -- for raising more money

117,525	Canine Companions for Independence Inc., Orlando, FL -- for a structural fundraising challenge grant
107,400	Mustard Seed of Central Florida Inc., Longwood, FL -- offers funding for facility space, racking and equipment
100,000	Florida Philanthropic Network, Winter Park, FL -- provides Florida foundation services initiative
98,800	PACE Center for Girls Inc., Jacksonville, FL -- for preserving and expanding intervention options
96,747	Frontline Outreach Inc., Orlando, FL -- provides a fundraising department and strategy

BUSH FOUNDATION

Giving Contact

Anita M. Pampusch, President
332 Minnesota Street, E-900
St. Paul, MN 55101
Phone: (651)227-0891
Fax: (651)297-6485
E-mail: info@bushfoundation.org
Web: http://www.bushfoundation.org

Description

Founded: 1953
EIN: 416017815
Organization Type: General Purpose Foundation
Giving Locations: MN; ND; SD: nationally.
Grant Types: Capital, Fellowship, General Support, Multiyear/Continuing Support, Project.

Donor Information

Founder: Established in 1953 by Archibald Granville Bush and his wife, Edyth Bassler Bush. Mr. Bush was born in 1887 on his family farm near Granite Falls, MN, the third of five children. He grew up on the farm, attended the Granite Falls public schools, and intended to be a farmer. However, hay fever allergy in 1908 forced him to seek a more pollen-free climate. He moved to Duluth, MN, enrolled in the six-month business course at Duluth Business University, and in 1909 went to work for the 3M Company as assistant bookkeeper. His 57-year career at 3M was mainly in sales and general management. He was chairman of the corporation's executive committee at his death in 1966. Bush also was active in St. Paul civic affairs, and was a trustee of Hamline University.

In 1919, Bush married Edyth Bassler of Chicago, a professional actress and dancer. Although Mrs. Bush ceased her stage career, she maintained a strong interest in theater and the arts. In St. Paul, she founded the Edyth Bush Theatre and served there as playwright, producer, and occasional actress. She was chairman of the board of The Bush Foundation from 1966 until her death in 1972. Ill health, however, prevented her active participation in that role for most of those years.

Financial Summary

Total Giving: $32,882,895 (fiscal year ending November 30, 2003); $36,360,000 (fiscal 2002 approx); $37,181,023 (fiscal 2001)
Giving Analysis: Giving for fiscal 2003 includes: foundation fellowships ($2,800,000); fiscal 2001: foundation grants to United Way ($500,000); foundation fellowships ($2,664,414)
Assets: $650,594,179 (fiscal 2003); $608,650,000 (fiscal 2002 approx); $726,484,372 (fiscal 2001)
Gifts Received: $463,900 (fiscal 2003); $900,000 (fiscal 2001). Note: In fiscal 2001 and 2003, contributions were received from the Hewlett Foundation.

Typical Recipients

Arts & Humanities: Arts Associations & Councils, Arts Centers, Arts Outreach, Ethnic & Folk Arts, Arts & Humanities-General, Historic Preservation, History & Archaeology, Libraries, Museums/Galleries, Music, Opera, Performing Arts, Public Broadcasting, Theater, Visual Arts

Civic & Public Affairs: Asian American Affairs, Civil Rights, Community Foundations, Economic Development, Employment/Job Training, Civic & Public Affairs-General, Housing, Legal Aid, Native American Affairs, Nonprofit Management, Public Policy, Rural Affairs, Urban & Community Affairs, Women's Affairs, Zoos/Aquariums

Education: Arts/Humanities Education, Business Education, Colleges & Universities, Community & Junior Colleges, Education Associations, Education Funds, Engineering/Technological Education, Environmental Education, Faculty Development, Education-General, International Exchange, Leadership Training, Legal Education, Literacy, Medical Education, Minority Education, Private Education (Precollege), Public Education (Precollege), School Volunteerism, Science/Mathematics Education, Secondary Education (Private), Social Sciences Education, Special Education, Vocational & Technical Education

Environment: Air/Water Quality, Energy, Environment-General, Resource Conservation, Wildlife Protection

Health: AIDS/HIV, Children's Health/Hospitals, Clinics/Medical Centers, Health-General, Geriatric Health, Health Organizations, Medical Rehabilitation, Medical Training, Mental Health, Nursing Services, Public Health, Research/Studies Institutes

Religion: Churches, Religion-General, Jewish Causes, Religious Organizations, Religious Welfare, Seminaries

Science: Science Museums

Social Services: At-Risk Youth, Big Brothers/Big Sisters, Child Welfare, Community Centers, Community Service Organizations, Day Care, Domestic Violence, Emergency Relief, Family Planning, Family Services, Food/Clothing Distribution, Homes, People with Disabilities, Recreation & Athletics, Refugee Assistance, Senior Services, Sexual Abuse, Shelters/Homelessness, Social Services-General, Substance Abuse, United Funds/United Ways, Youth Organizations

Application Procedures

Initial Contact: The foundation encourages potential applicants to submit a brief letter of inquiry.

Application Requirements: Letters of inquiry should include a project description, amount requested, and the length of time for the expenditure of grant funds. A full proposal should be submitted in duplicate and should include a cover sheet form (available from the foundation); proof of tax-exempt status and the organization's IRS status as a private foundation, private operating foundation, or not a private foundation; the names and primary professional affiliations of the organization's directors and trustees; a description of organization, including its background, purpose, and experience in the area for which funds are requested (limit to one page); the organization's financial information, including operating income and expense projections in a multi-year format for the organization's immediate past year, current year, and for one or more future fiscal years (include line items for major expense categories and sources of support and the main assumptions upon which the projections are based such as inflation rates and program growth); a copy of the organization's latest complete audit; a proposal narrative, and a proposal budget.

Deadlines: Effective June 1, 2004, Ecological Health Letter of Inquiry Deadlines Change to April 15, August 15 and December 15. March 1, for consideration at the July board meeting; July 1, for consideration at the November meeting; and November 1, for consideration at the March meeting.

Review Process: Foundation staff reviews letters of

inquiry to help applicants gauge the likelihood of Foundation support for a particular proposal. Replies generally range from "possible" to "unlikely." Applicants may then take this assessment into account when determining whether or not to submit a full proposal.

The board meets to consider proposals in March, July, and November. Ordinarily, one member of the program staff is assigned to work on a specific proposal. As necessary, this individual will contact the applicant, seek outside opinions, obtain consultant review assistance, and undertake background research. The results will be presented to the grants committee and the board. The grants committee reviews proposals and makes recommendations to the board. All commitments of grant funds are made by the board. Written notice of grant decisions is usually sent within ten days of a board meeting.

Restrictions

The foundation only contributes to nonprofit, tax-exempt organizations. The foundation does not make grants to individuals except through its fellowship programs. The foundation is unlikely to approve grants for general and continuing operating support; past operating deficits, cash reserve funds, or debt reduction; endowment of health and human service agencies, and of public colleges and universities; small remodeling projects or the purchase of office furnishings, computers, vehicles, and other equipment that are not part of a comprehensive capital campaign; individual concerts or concert series, individual exhibitions, festivals, conferences, performances, or one-time cultural events; media projects such as manuscripts, films, television shows, documentaries, or video projects; capital projects to preserve individual, historic structures; capital or program grants for county historical societies; building purchase, construction, or remodeling projects for charter schools, church sanctuaries, community centers, nursing homes, day care centers for children or adults, municipal and other government agencies, nature centers, public colleges, and universities; research in the biomedical and health sciences and in established academic disciplines; projects outside the United States; efforts to increase public awareness of a social problem without suggesting an approach to prevent, solve, or reduce it; general grants to individual day care centers for children or adults, nature centers, nursing homes, senior citizen centers, and youth recreation and camping programs; newly established arts and humanities organizations; arts organizations that do not pay artistic personnel; or government agencies.

Additional Information

The foundation requires progress reports from grant recipients. The reports should include a list of expenditures. Uncommitted funds must be returned at the end of the grant period.

Fellowship grants limited to Minnesota, North Dakota, South Dakota, and western Wisconsin.

Publications: Annual Report; Application Form; Guidelines

Foundation Officials

Esperanza Guerro Anderson: 1st vice chairman, director

Lee-Hoon Benson: program officer

Ivy S. Bernhardson: 2nd vice chairman, director B Fargo, ND 1951. ED Gustavus Adolphus College (1973); University of Minnesota (1978). PRIM CORP EMPL vice president, associate general counsel, corporate secretary: General Mills, Inc. CORP AFFIL partner: Leonard, Street and Deinard. NONPR AFFIL member: Hennepin County Bar Association; member: Minneapolis Bar Association; director: Fairview Hospital & Healthcare Services; director: Fairview Southdale Hospital; member: American Bar Association; member: American Society Corporate Secretary.

Shirley M. Clark: director PRIM CORP EMPL vice

chancellor academic affairs: Oregon State System Higher Education. NONPR AFFIL administrative board of directors: Oregon State System of Higher Education; adj professor education policy & management: University Oregon.

Dudley Cocke: secretary, director

Roxanne Givens Copeland: director CORP AFFIL chief executive officer: Ethnic Homes. NONPR AFFIL honorary member: Givens Foundation for African American Literature.

Steve Goldstein: director

Jose Gonzalez: program officer health

Dwight Gourneau: director

Robert J. Jones: director

Diana E. Murphy: director B Faribault, MN 1934. ED University of Minnesota BA (1954); Johannes Gutenberg University (1954-1955); University of Minnesota (1955-1958); University of Minnesota JD (1974). PRIM NONPR EMPL judge: U.S. Court Appeals. NONPR AFFIL treasurer: University Minnesota Foundation; trustee: University Saint Thomas; member: University Minnesota Alumni Association; chairman: U.S. Sentencing Commission; director: United Way Minneapolis; member: Phi Beta Kappa; board overseers school theology: Saint Johns University; member: Order Coif; member: National Association Governing Boards Universitys Colleges; treasurer: National Association Women Judges; director: Minnesota Opera; member: Minnesota Women Lawyers; member: Minnesota Bar Association; member: Federal Judicial Center; member: Hennepin County Bar Association; member: American Judicature Society; member: American Law Institute; member: American Bar Association; fellow: American Bar Foundation.

Anita Marie Pampusch, PhD: president B Saint Paul, MN 1938. ED College of Saint Catherine BA (1962); University of Notre Dame MA (1970); University of Notre Dame PhD (1972). NONPR AFFIL chairman, trustee: William Mitchell Colorado Law; member executive committee: Women's College Coalition; member: Saint Paul Chamber of Commerce; member: Phi Beta Kappa; district chairman: Rhodes Scholarship Selection Committee; member advisory committee: Columbia University Institutional Leadership Project; member, chairman: Council Independent Colleges; member: American Philosophical Association. CLUB AFFIL Minneapolis Club; Saint Paul Athletic Club.

William Peter Pierskalla: chairman, director B Saint Cloud, MN 1934. ED Harvard University AB Economics (1956); Harvard University MBA (1958); University of Pittsburgh MS Math (1962); Stanford University PhD (1965); University of Pennsylvania MA (1978). PRIM NONPR EMPL dean, professor: John E. Anderson Graduate School of Management, UCLA. CORP AFFIL director: North Trust Corp. California. NONPR AFFIL member: Operations Research Society America; consult: Project Hope; member: Omega Rho; member: Institute for Management Sciences; member: International Federation Operational Research Society.

Catherine V. Piersol: director

Kathryn H. Tunheim: treasurer, director CORP AFFIL president: Tunheim Partners.

Ann Wynia: director B Fort Worth, TX 1943. ED University of Texas BA (1965); University of Wisconsin MA (1968). NONPR AFFIL commissioner: Minnesota Department Human Services; instructor: North Hennepin Community College.

Grants Analysis

Disclosure Period: fiscal year ending November 30, 2003

Total Grants: $23,620,000*

Number of Grants: 165

Average Grant: $143,152

Highest Grant: $3,000,000

Typical Range: $25,000 to $300,000

*Note: Giving excludes fellowships.

Recent Grants

Note: Grants derived from fiscal 2003 Form 990.

General

1,000,000	Benedict College, Columbia, SC
900,000	Florida Memorial College, Miami, FL
780,000	Youth and Family Services Inc., Rapid City, SD
710,000	Concordia University, St. Paul, MN
700,000	Philander Smith College, Little Rock, AR
650,000	West Side Community Health Services Inc., St. Paul, MN
500,000	College of Saint Catherine, St. Paul, MN
500,000	Minnesota Landscape Arboretum Foundation, Chanhassen, MN
500,000	Rochester Art Center, Rochester, MN
500,000	St. Olaf College, Northfield, MN

PATRICK AND AIMEE BUTLER FAMILY FOUNDATION

Giving Contact

Kerrie Blevins, Foundation Director
Patrick and Aimee Butler Family Foundation
332 Minnesota Street, Suite E-1420
St. Paul, MN 55101-1369
Phone: (651)222-2565
E-mail: kerrieb@butlerfamilyfoundation.org
Web: http://www.butlerfamilyfoundation.org

Description

Founded: 1951
EIN: 416009902
Organization Type: Private Foundation
Giving Locations: MN: Minneapolis, St. Paul
Grant Types: General Support, Multiyear/Continuing Support, Project.

Donor Information

Founder: the late Patrick Butler and family

Financial Summary

Total Giving: $2,014,400 (2004); $1,398,442 (2003); $3,558,470 (2001)

Giving Analysis: Giving for 2004 includes: foundation grants to United Way ($30,000); 2001: foundation scholarships ($10,000); foundation grants to United Way ($40,000)

Assets: $55,596,316 (2003); $53,238,857 (2001)

Gifts Received: $378,767 (2003); $350,000 (2001); $424,048 (2000). Note: In 2003, 2001, 2000, and 1999, contributions were received from Aimee Mott Butler Irrevocable Trust. In 1996, contributions were received from the estate of Aimee Mott Butler ($834,630), the Aimee Mott Butler Irrevocable Trust ($350,000), and Sandra K. Butler ($4,032).

Typical Recipients

Arts & Humanities: Arts Centers, Arts Institutes, Community Arts, Historic Preservation, Libraries, Literary Arts, Museums/Galleries, Public Broadcasting, Theater

Civic & Public Affairs: Botanical Gardens/Parks, Community Foundations, Economic Development, Employment/Job Training, Civic & Public Affairs-General, Housing, Native American Affairs, Rural Affairs, Urban & Community Affairs, Women's Affairs, Zoos/Aquariums

Education: Arts/Humanities Education, Education-General, Leadership Training, Literacy, Minority Education

Environment: Air/Water Quality, Environment-General, Resource Conservation

Religion: Jewish Causes, Religious Welfare

Science: Science Museums

Social Services: Child Welfare, Community Centers,

Community Service Organizations, Counseling, Domestic Violence, Family Services, Senior Services, Sexual Abuse, Shelters/Homelessness, Social Services-General, Substance Abuse, United Funds/United Ways, Youth Organizations

Application Procedures

Initial Contact: Contact foundation for application form, then send a full proposal.
Application Requirements: Include a description of organization, amount requested, purpose of funds sought, recently audited financial statement, proof of tax-exempt status, and Butler Family Foundation application form.
Deadlines: Call for deadlines.

Restrictions

Does not support criminal justice, economic education, employment and vocational programs, films, health, hospitals, loans, or grants to individuals, medicine research secondary and elementary education, music, or dance.

Additional Information

Faxed applications not accepted.
Publications: Financial Statement; Annual Report; Informational Brochure (including Application Guidelines)

Foundation Officials

Kerrie Blevins: foundation director
Brigid M. Butler: trustee
Cecelia M. Butler: trustee
John K. Butler: treasurer, trustee
Patricia M. Butler: trustee
Patrick Butler, Jr.: vice president, trustee
Peter M. Butler: president, trustee

Grants Analysis

Disclosure Period: calendar year ending 2004
Total Grants: $1,984,400*
Number of Grants: 118
Average Grant: $14,647*
Highest Grant: $100,000
Lowest Grant: $2,000
Typical Range: $1,000 to $20,000
***Note:** Giving excludes United Way. Average grant figure excludes three highest grants ($100,000).

Recent Grants

Note: Grants derived from 2003 Form 990.

General

42,000	Greater Twin Cities United Way, Minneapolis, MN
40,442	Iron Range Resources and Rehabilitation Agency, Chisholm, MN -- support for archival materials processing project
30,000	Catholic Community Foundation, St. Paul, MN -- support for the catholic community foundation builders administrative endowment
30,000	Coalition Against Trafficking in Women, North Amherst, MA
30,000	Minnesota Children's Museum, St. Paul, MN -- towards endowment support
30,000	Project for Pride in Living Inc., Minneapolis, MN
30,000	Twin Cities Habitat for Humanity, Minneapolis, MN
25,000	Cathedral of Saint Paul, St. Paul, MN -- support for historic preservation
25,000	Conservation Fund, Arlington, VA -- support for the green infrastructure, twin cities collar countries project
25,000	Headwaters Fund, Minneapolis, MN -- support for the social change grants pool

BYDALE FOUNDATION

Giving Contact

Milton D. Solomon, Vice President, Secretary & Trustee
445 Hamilton Ave.
White Plains, NY 10601
Phone: (845)928-0804

Description

Founded: 1965
EIN: 136195286
Organization Type: Private Foundation
Giving Locations: NY: New York
Grant Types: Conference/Seminar, General Support, Multiyear/Continuing Support, Operating Expenses, Project, Research, Seed Money.

Donor Information

Founder: the late James P. Warburg

Financial Summary

Total Giving: $713,250 (2004); $748,250 (2001)
Assets: $13,268,639 (2004); $13,591,815 (2001)

Typical Recipients

Arts & Humanities: Arts Centers, Arts Outreach, Film & Video, Libraries, Literary Arts, Music, Opera, Performing Arts, Public Broadcasting
Civic & Public Affairs: Botanical Gardens/Parks, Civil Rights, Economic Policy, Civic & Public Affairs-General, Nonprofit Management, Parades/Festivals, Professional & Trade Associations, Public Policy, Rural Affairs, Urban & Community Affairs, Women's Affairs
Education: Arts/Humanities Education, Colleges & Universities, Engineering/Technological Education, Education-General, International Studies, Literacy, Private Education (Precollege), Vocational & Technical Education
Environment: Air/Water Quality, Environment-General
International: Foreign Arts Organizations, Human Rights, International Affairs, International Environmental Issues, International Peace & Security Issues, International Relations, Missionary/Religious Activities
Religion: Jewish Causes, Religious Organizations, Religious Welfare, Synagogues/Temples
Social Services: Community Service Organizations, Day Care, Family Planning, Family Services, Food/Clothing Distribution, Social Services-General, YMCA/YWCA/YMHA/YWHA

Application Procedures

Initial Contact: Send a brief letter of inquiry describing program or project.
Deadlines: November 1.

Restrictions

Does not support individuals or provide funds for loans, deficit financing, demonstration projects, capital funds, scholarships, or fellowships.

Foundation Officials

Sarah W. Bliumis: trustee
Frank J. Kick: treasurer
Milton D. Solomon: vice president, secretary, trustee
James P. Warburg, Jr.: trustee
Jennifer J. Warburg: trustee
Joan M. Warburg: president, trustee
Philip N. Warburg: trustee

Grants Analysis

Disclosure Period: calendar year ending 2004
Total Grants: $713,250
Number of Grants: 69
Average Grant: $10,337
Highest Grant: $50,000

Lowest Grant: $1,000
Typical Range: $5,000 to $20,000

Recent Grants

Note: Grants derived from 2001 Form 990.
General

90,000	American for Peace Now, Washington, DC
50,000	Foundation on Economic Trends, Washington, DC
50,000	Grassroots Policy Project, Washington, DC
30,000	New Israel Fund, Washington, DC
25,000	Poets House, New York, NY
25,000	WNYC Radio Foundation, New York, NY
20,000	Equality Now, New York, NY
20,000	Public Media, Inc., New York, NY
15,000	Channel 13, New York, NY
15,000	Feminist Majority Foundation

BYRNE FOUNDATION

Giving Contact

Dorothy M. Byrne, President
3 Laramie Road, Box 599
Etna, NH 03750
Phone: (603)643-4555

Description

Founded: 1993
EIN: 020462931
Organization Type: Private Foundation
Giving Locations: NH: Upper Valley Region; VT: Upper Valley Region
Grant Types: General Support.

Donor Information

Founder: Established in 1993 by John J. Byrne.

Financial Summary

Total Giving: $5,048,135 (2003); $4,488,625 (2002)
Giving Analysis: Giving for 2003 includes: foundation grants to United Way ($17,000)
Assets: $25,505,755 (2003); $19,492,495 (2002)
Gifts Received: $6,733,000 (2003); $1,206 (2000); $2,436 (1998). Note: In 1996, contributions were received from John J. Byrne. In 1996, contributions were received from John J. Byrne ($13,000) and Berkshire Hathaway ($14,400).

Typical Recipients

Arts & Humanities: Arts Funds, Community Arts, History & Archaeology, Libraries, Museums/Galleries, Music, Opera, Performing Arts, Public Broadcasting
Civic & Public Affairs: Business/Free Enterprise, Civil Rights, Clubs, Community Foundations, Economic Development, Economic Policy, Gay/Lesbian Issues, Civic & Public Affairs-General, Housing, Law & Justice, Parades/Festivals, Philanthropic Organizations, Public Policy, Safety, Urban & Community Affairs
Education: Business Education, Colleges & Universities, Education Funds, Elementary Education (Private), Environmental Education, Faculty Development, Education-General, Literacy, Minority Education, Private Education (Precollege), Public Education (Precollege), Science/Mathematics Education, Secondary Education (Private), Student Aid
Environment: Air/Water Quality, Environment-General, Protection, Resource Conservation
Health: Cancer, Children's Health/Hospitals, Clinics/Medical Centers, Emergency/Ambulance Services, Health-General, Health Funds, Health Organizations, Hospices, Hospitals, Medical Rehabilitation, Medical Research, Mental Health, Multiple Sclerosis, Nursing Services, Preventive Medicine/Wellness Organizations, Public Health, Respiratory

International: Foreign Educational Institutions, International-General, Human Rights, International Organizations, International Relations, International Relief Efforts, Missionary/Religious Activities

Religion: Churches, Dioceses, Religion-General, Jewish Causes, Ministries, Religious Welfare

Science: Scientific Centers & Institutes, Scientific Research

Social Services: At-Risk Youth, Child Abuse, Child Welfare, Community Centers, Community Service Organizations, Emergency Relief, Family Services, Food/Clothing Distribution, People with Disabilities, Recreation & Athletics, Senior Services, Shelters/Homelessness, Special Olympics, Substance Abuse, United Funds/United Ways, Youth Organizations

Application Procedures

Initial Contact: Send a brief letter of inquiry.
Deadlines: None.

Restrictions

Primary interests are cancer research, Dartmouth Community College, and general philanthropy.

Foundation Officials

Dorothy M. Byrne: president
John J. Byrne, III: director
Mark J. Byrne: director
Patrick M. Byrne: director
Robert E. Snyder: secretary, treasurer

Grants Analysis

Disclosure Period: calendar year ending 2003
Total Grants: $5,031,135*
Number of Grants: 265
Average Grant: $13,426*
Highest Grant: $800,000
Lowest Grant: $100
Typical Range: $1,000 to $20,000
***Note:** Giving excludes United Way. Average grant excludes two highest grants ($1,500,000).

Recent Grants

Note: Grants derived from 2003 Form 990.
Library-Related
25,000	Howe Public Library, Hanover, NH

General
800,000	Dartmouth College, Hanover, NH
700,000	Dartmouth Hitchcock Palliative, Lebanon, NH
121,332	Bermuda Biological Station for Research Inc., New York, NY
100,000	Visiting Nurse Alliance, White River Junction, VT
96,000	NEED Inc., Phoenix, AZ
90,000	Council on Foreign Relations, New York, NY
80,000	Coachella Valley Boys & Girls Club, Palm Desert, CA
80,000	Martha's Village and Kitchen, Indio, CA
75,000	Upper Valley Land Trust, Norwich, VT
74,000	Saint Denis Catholic Church, Hanover, NH

C. E. And S. Foundation

Giving Contact

Bruce A. Maza, Executive Director
1650 National City Tower
Louisville, KY 40202
Phone: (502)583-0546
Fax: (502)583-7648
E-mail: bruce@cesfoundation.com
Web: http://www.cesfoundation.com/

Description

Founded: 1984
EIN: 592466943
Organization Type: Private Foundation
Giving Locations: KY: Louisville Louisville, KY
Grant Types: Capital, Endowment, General Support, Scholarship.

Donor Information

Founder: David A. Jones

Financial Summary

Total Giving: $2,301,578 (2003); $2,418,776 (2002); $2,904,055 (2001)
Giving Analysis: Giving for 2003 includes: foundation scholarships ($36,000); 2002: foundation scholarships ($120,500); foundation matching gifts ($167,900); foundation grants to United Way ($200,000); 2001: foundation matching gifts ($48,550); foundation grants to United Way ($200,000).
Assets: $42,396,206 (2003); $40,000,000 (2002 approx); $37,033,833 (2001)
Gifts Received: $616 (2001); $1,000,000 (2000); $1,945,575 (1999). Note: In 2001, contributions were received from David. A. Jones. In 2000, contributions were received from W. T. Young Foundation. In 1999, contributions were received from David A. Jones ($1,807,272) and J.G. Funding ($138,303). In 1996 and 1998, contributions were received from David A. Jones.

Typical Recipients

Arts & Humanities: Arts Centers, Community Arts, History & Archaeology, Libraries, Music, Performing Arts, Public Broadcasting

Civic & Public Affairs: African American Affairs, Botanical Gardens/Parks, Community Foundations, Housing

Education: Afterschool/Enrichment Programs, Arts/Humanities Education, Business Education, Colleges & Universities, Faculty Development, Education-General, International Studies, Legal Education, Literacy, Private Education (Precollege), Religious Education, Science/Mathematics Education, Social Sciences Education, Student Aid, Vocational & Technical Education

Environment: Resource Conservation

International: Foreign Educational Institutions, Health Care/Hospitals, International Development, International Relations, International Relief Efforts, Missionary/Religious Activities

Religion: Churches, Ministries, Religious Welfare, Seminaries

Social Services: Community Centers, Community Service Organizations, Food/Clothing Distribution, Homes, People with Disabilities, United Funds/United Ways, Youth Organizations

Application Procedures

Initial Contact: Request executive director to request an application form.
Deadlines: None.

Foundation Officials

Bruce A. Maza: executive director

Grants Analysis

Disclosure Period: calendar year ending 2003
Total Grants: $2,265,578*
Number of Grants: 142
Average Grant: $14,141*
Highest Grant: $200,000
Lowest Grant: $250
Typical Range: $5,000 to $25,000
***Note:** Giving excludes scholarships. Average grant figure excludes two highest grants ($300,000).

Recent Grants

Note: Grants derived from 2001 Form 990.

General
1,000,000	Transylvania University, Lexington, KY -- Clive M. Beck Athletic Recreation Center
478,500	University of Louisville Foundation, Louisville, KY -- higher education initiative
200,000	Metro United Way, Inc., Louisville, KY -- participate in business challenge
100,000	Yale China Association, New Haven, CT -- centennial campaign
85,000	Louisville Presbyterian Theological Seminary, Louisville, KY -- support of foreign and domestic seminary students
81,440	Bellarmine College, Louisville, KY -- support teacher formation
75,000	Yale University, New Haven, CT -- Yale Law School China Institute
69,500	Cathedral Heritage Foundation, Louisville, KY -- community dining room
57,535	Yale University, New Haven, CT -- Global Constitutionalism Symposium of Yale Law School
50,000	Bellarmine College, Louisville, KY -- to fund international student travel, internships and foreign language, faculty development

C. Louis And Mary C. Cabe Foundation

Giving Contact

Anita Cabe, Secretary & Treasurer
108 Front St.
Gurdon, AR 71743
Phone: (870)353-2063

Description

Founded: 1990
EIN: 710685612
Organization Type: Private Foundation
Giving Locations: AR; TX
Grant Types: Capital, General Support.

Donor Information

Founder: Established in 1990 by Mary C. Cabe and C. Louis Cabe.

Financial Summary

Total Giving: $104,623 (2003); $84,306 (2001)
Giving Analysis: Giving for 2001 includes: foundation grants to United Way ($1,000)
Assets: $2,225,822 (2003); $2,321,758 (2001)
Gifts Received: $750,000 (1996). Note: In 1989, contributions were received from from C. Louis Cabe ($250,000) and Mary C. Cabe ($250,000).

Typical Recipients

Arts & Humanities: Libraries, Museums/Galleries
Civic & Public Affairs: African American Affairs, Civic & Public Affairs-General, Municipalities/Towns
Education: Arts/Humanities Education, Colleges & Universities, Education Funds, Literacy, Public Education (Precollege), Secondary Education (Public), Student Aid
Environment: Environment-General
Health: Children's Health/Hospitals, Hospitals, Preventive Medicine/Wellness Organizations
Religion: Churches, Religious Welfare
Social Services: Camps, Child Welfare, Recreation & Athletics, Senior Services, Social Services-General, Youth Organizations

Application Procedures

Initial Contact: Applicants should contact the foundation for an application form.
Deadlines: None.

Restrictions

Grants are usually restricted to charitable and educational organizations operating in AR and TX.

Foundation Officials

Anita B. Cabe: secretary, treasurer, director
Charles L. Cabe, Jr.: president, director
Marianne Cabe Long: vice president, director

Grants Analysis

Disclosure Period: calendar year ending 2003
Total Grants: $104,623
Number of Grants: 65
Average Grant: $1,610
Highest Grant: $5,000
Lowest Grant: $40
Typical Range: $500 to $3,000

Recent Grants

Note: Grants derived from 2001 Form 990.
General

5,000	Arkansas Sheriff Boys and Girls Ranches, Batesville, AR
5,000	Children's Village, New York, NY
5,000	Fishing Hall of Fame Inc.
5,000	Gurdon Schools, Gurdon, AR -- football
4,500	Arkansas Children's Hospital, Little Rock, AR
3,000	Clark County T.E.A Coalition
3,000	Gurdon Schools, Gurdon, AR -- scholarships
3,000	Gurdon Schools, Gurdon, AR -- auditorium fund
3,000	Gurdon Schools, Gurdon, AR -- football
3,000	Hot Springs Documentary Film Institute, Hot Springs, AR

ROBERT G. CABELL III AND MAUDE MORGAN CABELL FOUNDATION

Giving Contact

John B. Werner, Executive Director
PO Box 85678
Richmond, VA 23285-5678
Phone: (804)780-2000
Fax: (804)697-2989

Description

Founded: 1957
EIN: 546039157
Organization Type: Family Foundation
Giving Locations: VA: Richmond
Grant Types: Capital, General Support, Matching.

Donor Information

Founder: Incorporated in 1957 by the late Robert G. Cabell II and the late Maude Morgan Cabell.

Financial Summary

Total Giving: $4,486,500 (2003); $4,071,000 (2002); $4,400,000 (2001)
Assets: $86,854,851 (2003); $76,485,426 (2002)
Gifts Received: $38,502,636 (1997). Note: In 1997, contributions were received from Morgan A. Reynolds.

Typical Recipients

Arts & Humanities: Arts Associations & Councils, Arts Centers, Arts Funds, Arts Institutes, Arts & Humanities-General, Historic Preservation, History & Archaeology, Libraries, Museums/Galleries, Music, Opera, Performing Arts, Public Broadcasting, Theater

Civic & Public Affairs: Botanical Gardens/Parks, Clubs, Community Foundations, Economic Development, Employment/Job Training, Civic & Public Affairs-General, Housing, Municipalities/Towns, Philanthropic Organizations, Urban & Community Affairs, Women's Affairs, Zoos/Aquariums
Education: Agricultural Education, Arts/Humanities Education, Colleges & Universities, Education Associations, Education Funds, Faculty Development, Education-General, Gifted & Talented Programs, Legal Education, Literacy, Religious Education, Science/Mathematics Education, Social Sciences Education
Environment: Air/Water Quality, Forestry, Environment-General, Protection, Resource Conservation
Health: Alzheimer's Disease, Arthritis, Children's Health/Hospitals, Clinics/Medical Centers, Diabetes, Emergency/Ambulance Services, Eyes/Blindness, Health-General, Geriatric Health, Health Funds, Health Organizations, Heart, Hospitals, Multiple Sclerosis, Public Health, Research/Studies Institutes, Single-Disease Health Associations, Transplant Networks/Donor Banks
Religion: Churches, Religion-General, Ministries, Religious Organizations, Religious Welfare, Seminaries
Science: Science Museums
Social Services: Animal Protection, Child Abuse, Child Welfare, Community Centers, Community Service Organizations, Domestic Violence, Family Planning, Family Services, Food/Clothing Distribution, Homes, People with Disabilities, Recreation & Athletics, Scouts, Senior Services, Shelters/Homelessness, United Funds/United Ways, YMCA/YWCA/YMHA/YWHA, Youth Organizations

Application Procedures

Initial Contact: The foundation has no formal grant procedure or grant application form. Submit proposals in writing.
Application Requirements: Include a brief description of the mission; how the specific project supports the mission; planned budget; additional sources of support; current operating budget and recent financial statement; a list of officer's and Board of Directors; support for non-exempt status; a cover letter from the CEO, stating support for proposal.
Deadlines: April 1 and October 1.

Restrictions

Grants are restricted to the state of Virginia. The foundation does not support individuals, endowment funds, operating budgets, special interest groups, or research programs.

Additional Information

Publications: Application Guidelines

Foundation Officials

Joseph L. Antrim, III: director PRIM CORP EMPL executive vice president, director: Davenport & Co. LLC.
J. Read Branch, Jr.: director
J. Read Branch: president, treasurer
Patteson Branch, Jr.: director
Charles L. Cabell: secretary PRIM CORP EMPL attorney: Williams Mullen Christian & Dobbins. CORP AFFIL director: Pleasants Hardware Inc.; director: CF Sauer Co. Inc.; director: High's Ice Cream Corp.; director: Metrolina Plastics Inc.; director: C & T Refinery Quincy Inc.; director: Dean Foods Co.; director: C & T Quincy Inc.
John Branch Cabell: director
Elizabeth Cabell Jennings: director
Edmund A. Rennolds, Jr.: vice president
John B. Werner: executive director B Saint Marys, PA 1931. ED Randolph-Macon College BA (1953); University of Virginia postgrad (1953-1955); Rutgers University postgrad (1965). PRIM CORP EMPL senior executive vice president: Sovran Fin Corp. NONPR AFFIL member: Robert Morris Associates; member: Virginia Chamber of Commerce; trustee, member finance committee: Randolph-Macon College; member: Comptroller Currencys National Advisory Comm; member: Poplar Forest Foundation.

CLUB AFFIL Commonwealth Club.
Mary Z. Zeugner: director

Grants Analysis

Disclosure Period: calendar year ending 2003
Total Grants: $4,486,500
Number of Grants: 40
Average Grant: $112,163
Highest Grant: $350,000
Lowest Grant: $5,000
Typical Range: $50,000 to $200,000

Recent Grants

Note: Grants derived from 2003 Form 990.
Library-Related

50,000	Madison County Library Inc., Madison, VA

General

350,000	Virginia Historical Society, Richmond, VA
300,000	College of William and Mary in Virginia, Williamsburg, VA
300,000	Hampden-Sydney College, Hampden-Sydney, VA
300,000	Randolph-Macon College, Ashland, VA
300,000	Virginia Military Institute, Lexington, VA
250,000	Hampden-Sydney College, Hampden-Sydney, VA
250,000	United Networks for Organ Sharing, Richmond, VA
210,000	American Heart Association, Richmond, VA
200,000	Bolling Haxall House Foundation, Richmond, VA
200,000	Colonial Williamsburg Foundation, Williamsburg, VA

CABOT CORP.

Company Headquarters

Boston, MA
Web: http://www.cabot-corp.com

Company Description

Founded: 1882
Ticker: CBT
Exchange: NYSE
Revenue: US$1.557 billion (2002)
Employees: 4400 (2003)
SIC(s): 2819 Industrial Inorganic Chemicals Nec, 2821 Plastics Materials & Resins, 2895 Carbon Black, 3061 Mechanical Rubber Goods.

Operating Locations

Cabot Corp. (MA--Billerica)

Nonmonetary Support

Type: Donated Equipment; Donated Products; In-kind Services; Loaned Employees; Loaned Executives
Note: Nonmonetary support is provided by the co. and the foundation. For information on nonmonetary support, contact local Cabot facilities manager.

Cabot Corp. Foundation

Giving Contact

Peter S. Gregory, Managing Director
Two Seaport Ln., Ste. 1300
Boston, MA 02210-2019
Phone: (617)342-6105
Fax: (617)342-6320
E-mail: peter_gregory@cabot-corp.com

Description

EIN: 046035227
Organization Type: Corporate Foundation

Giving Locations: international operating locations; principally near operating locations and to national organizations.

Grant Types: Challenge, Employee Matching Gifts, Fellowship, General Support, Multiyear/Continuing Support, Professorship, Project, Research, Scholarship, Seed Money.

Note: Employee matching gift ratio: 1 to 1 for schools and united funds only.

Financial Summary

Total Giving: $729,482 (fiscal year ending September 30, 2003); $728,715 (fiscal 2002); $1,035,082 (fiscal 2001). Note: Contributes through corporate direct giving program and foundation. Giving includes foundation.

Assets: $1,716,357 (fiscal 2003); $1,360,964 (fiscal 2002); $1,627,896 (fiscal 2001)

Gifts Received: $325,000 (fiscal 2002); $500,000 (fiscal 2001); $1,571,760 (fiscal 1999). Note: Contributions were received from Cabot Corp.

Typical Recipients

Arts & Humanities: Arts Appreciation, Arts Associations & Councils, Arts Centers, Arts Funds, Arts Institutes, Arts Outreach, Community Arts, Dance, Ethnic & Folk Arts, Arts & Humanities-General, Historic Preservation, Libraries, Literary Arts, Museums/Galleries, Music, Opera, Performing Arts, Public Broadcasting, Theater

Civic & Public Affairs: African American Affairs, Botanical Gardens/Parks, Business/Free Enterprise, Community Foundations, Economic Development, Economic Policy, Employment/Job Training, Civic & Public Affairs-General, Housing, Law & Justice, Legal Aid, Municipalities/Towns, Philanthropic Organizations, Public Policy, Safety, Urban & Community Affairs, Women's Affairs, Zoos/Aquariums

Education: Afterschool/Enrichment Programs, Business Education, Colleges & Universities, Community & Junior Colleges, Economic Education, Education Funds, Education Reform, Elementary Education (Private), Elementary Education (Public), Engineering/Technological Education, Faculty Development, Education-General, Health & Physical Education, International Exchange, International Studies, Literacy, Medical Education, Minority Education, Preschool Education, Private Education (Precollege), Public Education (Precollege), Science/Mathematics Education, Social Sciences Education, Special Education, Student Aid, Vocational & Technical Education

Environment: Air/Water Quality, Environment-General, Resource Conservation, Wildlife Protection

Health: Cancer, Children's Health/Hospitals, Clinics/Medical Centers, Diabetes, Health-General, Health Organizations, Heart, Hospitals, Prenatal Health Issues, Public Health

International: Foreign Arts Organizations, Foreign Educational Institutions, International-General, Health Care/Hospitals, International Development, International Environmental Issues, International Organizations, International Relations, International Relief Efforts

Religion: Ministries

Science: Science Exhibits & Fairs, Science Museums, Scientific Organizations

Social Services: At-Risk Youth, Camps, Child Abuse, Child Welfare, Community Centers, Community Service Organizations, Counseling, Day Care, Domestic Violence, Emergency Relief, Food/Clothing Distribution, Homes, People with Disabilities, Recreation & Athletics, Scouts, Senior Services, Shelters/Homelessness, Social Services-General, Special Olympics, Substance Abuse, United Funds/United Ways, Volunteer Services, YMCA/YWCA/YMHA/YWHA, Youth Organizations

Application Procedures

Initial Contact: Send a written proposal. Organizations should contact local Cabot facilities for application information.

Application Requirements: Include statement of proposed project (no more than two pages), including its purpose, long-term goals and specific short-term objectives; an explanation of how project is consistent with Cabot business interests; potential for lasting community impact; potential for significant and measurable outcomes; brief background information on organization, board of directors, and those leading proposed effort; proof of tax-exempt status; total project cost, present and potential funding sources, and amount requested of Cabot; include latest audited financial statement if organization's budget exceeds $100,000.

Deadlines: Proposals must be received at least one month before quarterly board meetings.

Review Process: Grant requests for/from communities where Cabot has operations are reviewed at the local level by community relations teams; if appropriate for foundation funding, they are forwarded to the executive director; further information and site visits may be necessary; approval is made by the directors of the foundation.

Evaluative Criteria: Year-end reports, audits, community relations team recommendation, employee involvement.

Decision Notification: Quarterly in January, April, July and October.

Notes: All proposals should be submitted electronically via e-mail.

Restrictions

Cabot Corporation Foundation does not make contributions to individuals, political, fraternal, athletic, or veterans organizations; religious institutions; advertising; tickets or dinner-table sponsorship; capital and endowment campaigns; and sponsorship of local groups or individuals to participate in competitions, conferences, or events.

Additional Information

Cabot strongly encourages requests from projects under way in plant locations. The contributions program has expanded its involvement in plant communities, tying contributions more closely to the nature of business, encouraging greater employee participation in community volunteer activities, and addressing significant societal concerns. Foundation particularly considers recommendations from teams formed by local employees, which initiate community projects and consider local requests for support.

Company prefers to support specific projects or programs rather than general operating expenses.

Strong consideration is given to projects that combine financial support with company manpower, technical assistance, or in-kind support to achieve objectives. Company often conducts "needs assessments" surveys to determine if projects will have a long-term effect on the community they serve.

Cabot is especially interested in projects involved with science and technology.

Organizations receiving grants are expected to provide periodic progress reports.

Publications: Guidelines

Corporate Officials

Kennett F. Burnes: chairman, chief executive officer, president PRIM CORP EMPL chairman, chief executive officer, president: Cabot Corp.

Foundation Officials

Jane A. Bell: clerk
Christina Bramante: director
Kennett F. Burnes: president, director (see above)
Charles Agustus Gray: director B Washington, DC 1938. ED Cornell University BSChE (1961); Massachusetts Institute of Technology PhD (1965). PRIM CORP EMPL vice president Information Systems, director: Cosi, Inc..
Peter S. Gregory: managing director, director
Ho-il Kim: director
John J. Lawler: director, treasurer
Karen M. Morressey: vice president, director

Robbie D. Sisco: director
Scott E. Squillace: director

Grants Analysis

Disclosure Period: fiscal year ending September 30, 2003
Total Grants: $727,482*
Number of Grants: 57
Average Grant: $9,443
Highest Grant: $25,000
Lowest Grant: $500
Typical Range: $1,000 to $20,000
*Note: Giving excludes matching gifts; scholarship; United Way.

Recent Grants

Note: Grants derived from fiscal 2003 Form 990.
Library-Related

7,500	St. Mary Parish Library System, Franklin, LA

General

70,000	United Way of Boyertown, Boyertown, PA
66,000	Citizens Scholarship Foundation of America, Minneapolis, MN
65,000	Boston Private School Science Collaboration Project, Boston, MA
50,000	Massachusetts General Hospital, Boston, MA
38,000	Billercia Council on Aging, Billerica, MA
30,000	Courageous Sailing Center, Boston, MA
25,000	Caritas St. Josef's Workshop, Frankfurt Germany
25,000	Massachusetts State Sciences Fair Inc., Boston, MA
22,600	Boston University School of Education, Cilegon Indonesia
22,252	United Way of South Louisiana, Franklin, LA

CABOT FAMILY CHARITABLE TRUST

Giving Contact

Ruth C. Scheer, Executive Director
70 Federal St.
Boston, MA 02110
Phone: (617)451-1744

Description

Founded: 1942
EIN: 046036446
Organization Type: Private Foundation
Giving Locations: CA; MA
Grant Types: Capital, Endowment, General Support, Multiyear/Continuing Support, Project.

Donor Information

Founder: Established in 1942 by the late Godfrey L. Cabot.

Financial Summary

Total Giving: $1,785,500 (2002); $3,034,500 (2001)
Giving Analysis: Giving for 2001 includes: foundation grants to United Way ($25,000)
Assets: $42,133,389 (2002); $53,100,042 (2001)
Gifts Received: $750,000 (1996). Note: In 1996, contributions were received from the estate of Thomas D. Cabot.

Typical Recipients

Arts & Humanities: Arts Associations & Councils, Arts Funds, Arts Institutes, Arts Outreach, Ballet, Dance, Film & Video, Arts & Humanities-General, Historic Preservation, History & Archaeology, Libraries, Literary Arts, Museums/Galleries, Music, Opera, Public Broadcasting, Theater

Civic & Public Affairs: Business/Free Enterprise,

Civil Rights, Clubs, Community Foundations, Economic Development, Employment/Job Training, Civic & Public Affairs-General, Housing, Municipalities/ Towns, Native American Affairs, Philanthropic Organizations, Public Policy, Urban & Community Affairs, Women's Affairs, Zoos/Aquariums

Education: Afterschool/Enrichment Programs, Colleges & Universities, Education Associations, Education-General, Health & Physical Education, International Studies, Journalism/Media Education, Leadership Training, Legal Education, Medical Education, Private Education (Precollege), Public Education (Precollege), Science/Mathematics Education, Secondary Education (Private), Secondary Education (Public)

Environment: Forestry, Environment-General, Protection, Resource Conservation

Health: Cancer, Children's Health/Hospitals, Clinics/ Medical Centers, Health Organizations, Hospitals, Mental Health, Public Health

International: Foreign Educational Institutions, Health Care/Hospitals, Human Rights, International Development, International Environmental Issues, International Peace & Security Issues, International Relief Efforts

Religion: Churches, Jewish Causes, Social/Policy Issues

Science: Science Museums, Scientific Centers & Institutes, Scientific Labs, Scientific Organizations, Scientific Research

Social Services: At-Risk Youth, Camps, Child Welfare, Community Centers, Community Service Organizations, Counseling, Day Care, Family Planning, Family Services, Food/Clothing Distribution, People with Disabilities, Recreation & Athletics, Refugee Assistance, Shelters/Homelessness, United Funds/ United Ways, YMCA/YWCA/YMHA/YWHA, Youth Organizations

Application Procedures

Initial Contact: Send a brief letter of inquiry.
Deadlines: April 1 and October 1.

Restrictions

Limited to organizations that deal with population control, environmental quality, and educational awards.

Additional Information

Publications: Annual Report

Foundation Officials

Jane C. Bradley: trustee
John Godfrey Lowell Cabot: trustee B Rio de Janeiro, RJ Brazil 1934. ED Harvard University AB (1956); Harvard University MBA (1960). PRIM CORP EMPL vice chairman, director: Cabot Corp. CORP AFFIL director: Eaton Vance Corp.; director: Hollingsworth & Vose Co.; director: Distrigas Massachusetts Corp.; director: America Oil & Gas Corp.; director: Cabot Oil & Gas Corp. NONPR AFFIL trustee: Tufts University; overseer: WGBH Education Foundation; overseer, government: New England Medical Center; member corporate: Massachusetts General Hospital; chairman, director: New England Legal Foundation.
Louis Wellington Cabot: trustee B Boston, MA 1921. ED Harvard University AB (1943); Harvard University MBA (1948). CORP AFFIL director: Kendall Sq Research. NONPR AFFIL member: Sigma Xi; member: U.S. Chamber of Commerce; member: Phi Beta Kappa; trustee: National Humanities Center; trustee: Northeastern University; member: National Council US-China Trade; member corporate: Massachusetts Institute Technology; trustee: Museum Science Boston; member: Massachusetts Business Roundtable; member: Conference Board; member: Council Foreign Relations; trustee: Brookings Institution; member: Business Council; fellow: American Academy of Arts & Sciences. CLUB AFFIL Wianno Club; Somerset Club; New York Yacht Club; River Club; Metropolitan Club; Commercial Club; Harvard

Club.
Ruth C. Scheer: executive director

Grants Analysis

Disclosure Period: calendar year ending 2002
Total Grants: $1,785,500*
Typical Range: $10,000 to $50,000
***Note:** Incomplete grant list for 2002.

Recent Grants

Note: Grants derived from 2002 Form 990.
General

100,000	Brookings Institution, Washington, DC
50,000	Agassiz Neighborhood Council, Cambridge, MA
50,000	Children's Hospital, Boston, MA
50,000	Dana Farber, Boston, MA
50,000	Phillips Academy, Andover, MA
50,000	SEA Education Association, Woods Hole, MA
35,000	City School, Dorchester, MA
30,000	Island Institute, Rockland, ME
25,000	Appalachian Mountain Club, Boston, MA
25,000	Boston Chinatown Neighborhood Center, Boston, MA

CHARLES AND MARIE CAESTECKER FOUNDATION

Giving Contact

Thomas E. Caestecker, Trustee
Charles and Marie Caestecker Foundation
20 S. Clark, Suite 2310
Chicago, IL 60603-1802
Phone: (312)726-2468
Fax: (312)726-2741

Alternate Contact

Guidance Counselor
Green Lake Public High School
Green Lake, WI 54941
Note: Alternate address is for scholarship applications.

Description

Founded: 1967
EIN: 363154453
Organization Type: Private Foundation
Giving Locations: AZ; WI
Grant Types: Operating Expenses, Scholarship.

Donor Information

Founder: the late Charles E. Caestecker

Financial Summary

Total Giving: $110,583 (fiscal year ending April 30, 2002); $164,707 (fiscal 2001)
Giving Analysis: Giving for fiscal 2002 includes: foundation scholarships ($39,583); fiscal 2001: foundation scholarships ($37,707)
Assets: $1,715,124 (fiscal 2002); $1,906,838 (fiscal 2001)
Gifts Received: $3,000 (fiscal 2002)

Typical Recipients

Arts & Humanities: Historic Preservation, History & Archaeology, Libraries
Education: Colleges & Universities, Engineering/ Technological Education, Religious Education, Science/Mathematics Education, Student Aid
Health: Clinics/Medical Centers, Hospitals
Religion: Churches, Religious Welfare
Social Services: Community Service Organizations

Application Procedures

Initial Contact: Request application form for scholarships.
Deadlines: February 1 of graduation year.

Additional Information

Provides scholarships to graduates of Green Lake, WI, public high schools for attendance at a four-year college or university.

Foundation Officials

Thomas E. Caestecker: trustee
Frank Andrew Karaba: trustee B Chicago, IL 1927. ED Northwestern University BS (1949); Northwestern University JD (1951). PRIM CORP EMPL senior counsel: Crowley, Barrett & Karaba. CORP AFFIL director: A&R Printers; director: Lyrick Corp. NONPR AFFIL member: Illinois Bar Association; member: Order Coif; member: American Bar Association; assistant counselor: Emergency Commission Crime. CLUB AFFIL Law Club; Legal Club.

Grants Analysis

Disclosure Period: fiscal year ending April 30, 2002
Total Grants: $71,000*
Number of Grants: 5
Average Grant: $14,200
Highest Grant: $25,000
Lowest Grant: $1,000
Typical Range: $10,000 to $25,000
***Note:** Giving excludes scholarships.

Recent Grants

Note: Grants derived from fiscal 2002 Form 990.
Library-Related

25,000	Caestecker Public Library Foundation, Green Lake, WI

General

25,000	Ripon College, Ripon, WI
14,583	University of Wisconsin Eau Claire, Eau Claire, WI
12,500	Arizona State University, Tempe, AZ
12,500	Lawrence University, Appleton, WI -- scholarship
10,000	Berlin Memorial Hospital, Berlin, WI
10,000	Ripon Medical Center Foundation, Ripon, WI
1,000	Ripon College, Ripon, WI -- Education Foundation

MORRIS AND GWENDOLYN CAFRITZ FOUNDATION

Giving Contact

Kathleen Zeifang, Acting Executive Director
1825 K Street Northwest, Suite 1400
Washington, DC 20006
Phone: (202)223-3100
Fax: (202)296-7567
E-mail: info@cafritzfoundation.org
Web: http://www.cafritzfoundation.org

Description

Founded: 1948
EIN: 526036989
Organization Type: General Purpose Foundation
Giving Locations: DC: Washington including metropolitan area
Grant Types: Award, Challenge, General Support, Matching, Operating Expenses, Project, Scholarship, Seed Money.

Donor Information

Founder: Established in 1948 by the late Morris Cafritz (d. 1964), a major real estate developer and prominent philanthropist in the Washington, DC, area, and his wife, the late Gwendolyn Cafritz (d. 1988).

Financial Summary

Total Giving: $16,203,989 (fiscal year ending April 30, 2003); $16,706,820 (fiscal 2002); $16,648,176 (fiscal 2001)
Assets: $353,323,712 (fiscal 2003); $346,922,783 (fiscal 2002); $336,242,000 (fiscal 2001)
Gifts Received: $7,188,739 (fiscal 1999); $1,575,477 (fiscal 1997); $19,041,036 (fiscal 1995). Note: In fiscal 1999, contributions were received from the Gwendolyn D. Cafritz Estate.

Typical Recipients

Arts & Humanities: Arts Associations & Councils, Arts Centers, Arts Festivals, Arts Institutes, Arts Outreach, Ballet, Community Arts, Dance, Historic Preservation, History & Archaeology, Libraries, Literary Arts, Museums/Galleries, Music, Opera, Performing Arts, Public Broadcasting, Theater
Civic & Public Affairs: Botanical Gardens/Parks, Business/Free Enterprise, Civil Rights, Community Foundations, Economic Development, Employment/ Job Training, Hispanic Affairs, Housing, Legal Aid, Nonprofit Management, Philanthropic Organizations, Professional & Trade Associations, Urban & Community Affairs
Education: Afterschool/Enrichment Programs, Arts/ Humanities Education, Business Education, Colleges & Universities, Education Associations, Education Funds, Education Reform, Environmental Education, Faculty Development, Education-General, International Studies, Medical Education, Minority Education, Preschool Education, Private Education (Precollege), Public Education (Precollege), Science/ Mathematics Education, Secondary Education (Private), Secondary Education (Public), Special Education, Student Aid, Vocational & Technical Education
Environment: Air/Water Quality, Environment-General, Protection, Resource Conservation, Watershed
Health: Adolescent Health Issues, AIDS/HIV, Children's Health/Hospitals, Diabetes, Emergency/ Ambulance Services, Geriatric Health, Health Organizations, Hospices, Hospitals, Long-Term Care, Medical Rehabilitation, Mental Health, Nursing Services, Prenatal Health Issues, Single-Disease Health Associations
Religion: Jewish Causes, Religious Welfare
Science: Scientific Centers & Institutes, Scientific Organizations, Scientific Research
Social Services: At-Risk Youth, Child Welfare, Community Centers, Community Service Organizations, Counseling, Crime Prevention, Day Care, Delinquency & Criminal Rehabilitation, Domestic Violence, Emergency Relief, Family Planning, Family Services, Food/Clothing Distribution, People with Disabilities, Recreation & Athletics, Refugee Assistance, Scouts, Senior Services, Shelters/Homelessness, Social Services-General, Substance Abuse, United Funds/ United Ways, Volunteer Services, Youth Organizations

Application Procedures

Initial Contact: The foundation requests that all grantseekers use the Washington Regional Association of Grantmakers Common Grant Application Format. Send one unbound copy of the properly formatted proposal.
Application Requirements: The application should include a maximum two page cover letter; a ten-page maximum narrative, including organization information, purpose of grant and evaluation; financial information, including project budget, previous and current operating budget, most recent annual financial statement, other sources of funding, and agency affiliation with federation funds or public agencies. Include the following attachments: a copy of IRS determination letter, list of Board of Directors, letters of

support, annual report and relevant articles or reviews about organizations pro grams.
Deadlines: Submit proposals by March 1, July 1, and November 1 by 4:00 p.m. Applications received between deadlines will be held until the next deadline.
Review Process: Applicants are notified as soon as possible after proposals are reviewed by the foundation's advisory board or board of directors. It takes six-to-nine months from the deadline date to process a proposal before submitting it to the board of directors.

Restrictions

Grants generally are made on a project basis. Support is not given to individuals, or for capital purposes, special events or endowments. It is not a general policy to commit funds for a project for more than one year at a time. Grants are only awarded to organizations that are tax-exempt under the IRS code.

Additional Information

Publications: Annual Report; Application Procedures; Grant Guidelines

Foundation Officials

John H. C. Barron, Jr.: secretary
Calvin Cafritz: chairman, president, chief executive officer B Washington, DC 1931. PRIM CORP EMPL founder, president: Calvin Cafritz Enterprises. CORP AFFIL director: Cafritz Co.
Daniel J. Callahan, III: director, vice chairman, treasurer PRIM CORP EMPL chairman, chief executive officer, director: USLICO Corp.
Terence C. Golden: director B Honesdale, PA 1944. ED University of Notre Dame BS (1966); Massachusetts Institute of Technology MS (1967); Harvard University MBA (1970). PRIM CORP EMPL chairman: Bailey Management Corp. ADD CORP EMPL director: Host Mariott Corp. CORP AFFIL president, chief executive officer: Host Marriott Corp.; director: Prime Retail; director: D.R. Horton; chairman: Bailey Realty Corp.; director: Cousins Properties Inc.
Guy T. Steuart, II: director B 1934. PRIM CORP EMPL president, director: Steuart Investment Co. CORP AFFIL director: Steuart Kret Development Co.; director: Steuart Petroleum; chairman: Half Moon Bay Ltd.; vice president: Steuart Holding Co.
Kathleen H. Zeifang: acting executive director

Grants Analysis

Disclosure Period: fiscal year ending April 30, 2003
Total Grants: $16,203,989
Number of Grants: 561
Average Grant: $28,884
Highest Grant: $250,000
Lowest Grant: $100
Typical Range: $5,000 to $50,000

Recent Grants

Note: Grants derived from fiscal 2003 Form 990.
General

250,000	Bell Multicultural High School, Washington, DC -- for educational programs
237,500	Round House Theatre, Bethesda, MD -- for expansion transition into three new sites, for education and outreach programs
200,000	Field School, Washington, DC -- scholarship assistance to minority and other disadvantaged students
200,000	Washington Ballet, Washington, DC -- for a new Nutcracker ballet
166,667	Saint Coletta School, Washington, DC -- For a state of the art building to house people with mental retardation, autism and secondary disabilities
162,500	Shakespeare Theatre, Washington, DC -- for academy for classical training
150,000	Bethesda Academy of Performing Arts, Kern County, CA
133,333	Washington Regional Association of Grant Makers, Washington, DC -- for general support for the Washington AIDS partnership
133,333	Washington Regional Association of Grant Makers, Washington, DC -- for general support for the Washington AIDS partnership
125,000	Cultural Development Corporation, Washington, DC -- For development of the live/work space for artists at the Mother building

GORDON AND MARY CAIN FOUNDATION

Giving Contact

James D. Weaver, President
8 Greenway Plaza, Suite 702
Houston, TX 77046
Phone: (713)960-9283
Fax: (713)877-8107

Description

Founded: 1988
EIN: 760251558
Organization Type: Family Foundation
Giving Locations: FL: Lake Wales; NC: Linville Houston, TX.
Grant Types: Capital, General Support, Multiyear/ Continuing Support, Operating Expenses, Project, Research.

Donor Information

Founder: Established in 1988 by Gordon A. Cain and Mary H. Cain.

Financial Summary

Total Giving: $4,300,750 (2003); $5,620,316 (2002)
Giving Analysis: Giving for 2003 includes: foundation matching gifts ($5,000); foundation scholarships ($748,000)
Assets: $117,565,805 (2003); $101,619,856 (2002)
Gifts Received: $3,418,789 (2003); $54,197,348 (2000); $6,087,500 (1998). Note: In 2003, contributions were received from Gordon A. Cain. In 1998 and 2000, contributions were received from Gordon and Mary Cain.

Typical Recipients

Arts & Humanities: Arts Associations & Councils, Arts Centers, Arts Outreach, Ballet, Dance, History & Archaeology, Libraries, Literary Arts, Museums/ Galleries, Music, Opera, Public Broadcasting, Theater
Civic & Public Affairs: African American Affairs, Botanical Gardens/Parks, Business/Free Enterprise, Clubs, Community Foundations, Economic Development, Economic Policy, Civic & Public Affairs-General, Housing, Law & Justice, Legal Aid, Parades/Festivals, Philanthropic Organizations, Professional & Trade Associations, Public Policy, Urban & Community Affairs, Women's Affairs, Zoos/ Aquariums
Education: Arts/Humanities Education, Business Education, Business-School Partnerships, Colleges & Universities, Community & Junior Colleges, Economic Education, Education Associations, Education Funds, Education Reform, Engineering/ Technological Education, Environmental Education, Faculty Development, Education-General, Literacy, Medical Education, Minority Education, Private Education (Precollege), Religious Education, Science/ Mathematics Education, Secondary Education (Private), Special Education, Student Aid
Environment: Environment-General, Protection, Research, Resource Conservation, Wildlife Protection

Health: AIDS/HIV, Cancer, Children's Health/Hospitals, Clinics/Medical Centers, Diabetes, Emergency/Ambulance Services, Eyes/Blindness, Health Policy/Cost Containment, Health Funds, Heart, Hospices, Hospitals, Medical Rehabilitation, Medical Research, Public Health, Single-Disease Health Associations

International: International-General, Health Care/Hospitals, International Organizations

Religion: Churches, Jewish Causes, Religious Welfare

Science: Science Museums, Scientific Centers & Institutes

Social Services: At-Risk Youth, Camps, Child Abuse, Child Welfare, Community Centers, Community Service Organizations, Day Care, Domestic Violence, Family Planning, Family Services, Homes, People with Disabilities, Recreation & Athletics, Scouts, Shelters/Homelessness, Social Services-General, Substance Abuse, United Funds/United Ways, YMCA/YWCA/YMHA/YWHA, Youth Organizations

Application Procedures

Initial Contact: The foundation has no application form. Written requests should be mailed directly to the foundation.

Application Requirements: Written proposals should include a statement of purpose of the organization; project description, including objectives and community need; brief history of the organization and those whom it serves; most recent audited financial statement, budget with balance sheet, fund balance, and number of employees; current and itemized annual budget and project budget if applicable; amount of grant being requested; list of major sources of support, staff description, breakdown of proposed expenses, and list of Board of Trustees; the latest copy of the organization's IRS 501(c)(3) tax-exempt status letter; a description of an evaluation plan; and specifics of why organization will make a difference and how program will be stable enough to survive.

Deadlines: Proposals should be received on the last day of the month prior to a board meeting, generally April 30, August 31, and November 30.

Review Process: The board meets three times a year, usually in May, September, and December. Applicants should contact the foundation to determine the date of the next board meeting.

Restrictions

Grants are not made to individuals.

Additional Information

Publications: Guidelines

Foundation Officials

Gordon R. Cain: trustee
Mary H. Cain: vice president
William A. McMinn: vice president B 1931. PRIM CORP EMPL director, chairman: Texas Petrochemical Holdings ADD CORP EMPL chairman: Texas Petrochemicals Corp. CORP AFFIL director: Sterling Chemicals; director: Purina Mills Inc.; director: Lexicon Genetics Inc.; director: P M Holdings Corp. NONPR AFFIL trustee: Vanderbilt University.
Margaret W. Oehmig: vice president
William C. Oehmig: secretary, treasurer PRIM CORP EMPL principal: Sterling Group. CORP AFFIL director: PM Holdings Corp.; director: Purina Mills Inc.
John M. Sullivan: assistant secretary, assistant treasurer
James D. Weaver: president B 1918. PRIM CORP EMPL chairman board, director: Weaver Trucking Inc.
Sharyn A. Weaver: vice president

Grants Analysis

Disclosure Period: calendar year ending 2003
Total Grants: $3,547,750*
Number of Grants: 77
Average Grant: $33,290*

Highest Grant: $551,000
Lowest Grant: $3,000
Typical Range: $10,000 to $50,000
***Note:** Giving excludes matching gifts, scholarships. Average grant figure excludes two highest grants ($1,051,000).

Recent Grants

Note: Grants derived from 2003 Form 990.
General

551,250	Rice University, Houston, TX
500,000	Texas Children's Hospital, Houston, TX
390,000	University of Houston-Downtown (UHD), Houston, TX
300,000	Rice University, Houston, TX
250,000	Cannon Sloop Health Care Foundation, Linville, NC
250,000	University of Texas Health Science Center at Houston, Houston, TX
150,000	Linville Foundation Scholarship Fund, Linville, NC
125,000	Houston Museum of Natural Science, Houston, TX
100,000	Appalachian State University, Boone, NC
100,000	Education Foundation Inc., Chapel Hill, NC

LOUIS CALDER FOUNDATION

Giving Contact

Alison Sargent, Senior Program Manager
175 Elm Street
P.O. Box 636
New Canaan, CT 06840
Phone: (203)966-8925

Description

Founded: 1951
EIN: 136015562
Organization Type: General Purpose Foundation
Giving Locations: New York City.
Grant Types: Capital, Endowment, General Support, Multiyear/Continuing Support, Project, Scholarship.

Donor Information

Founder: Established in 1951 by the late Louis Calder (d. 1963), who was chairman of the board of Perkins-Goodwin Co. The foundation was funded by gifts from Mr. Calder during his lifetime and later by a residuary bequest in his will.

Financial Summary

Total Giving: $5,640,831 (fiscal year ending October 31, 2003); $6,058,120 (fiscal 2002)
Assets: $140,490,659 (fiscal 2003); $129,594,089 (fiscal 2002)

Typical Recipients

Arts & Humanities: Arts Centers, Arts Institutes, Arts Outreach, Ballet, Libraries, Museums/Galleries, Music, Opera, Public Broadcasting, Theater, Visual Arts
Civic & Public Affairs: Botanical Gardens/Parks, Business/Free Enterprise, Community Foundations, Economic Development, Employment/Job Training, Civic & Public Affairs-General, Housing, Legal Aid, Nonprofit Management, Urban & Community Affairs
Education: Afterschool/Enrichment Programs, Arts/Humanities Education, Business-School Partnerships, Colleges & Universities, Education Funds, Elementary Education (Private), Faculty Development, Education-General, Health & Physical Education, Leadership Training, Literacy, Medical Education, Minority Education, Private Education (Precollege), Public Education (Precollege), Religious Education, School Volunteerism, Science/Mathematics Educa-

tion, Secondary Education (Private), Special Education, Student Aid
Health: Adolescent Health Issues, AIDS/HIV, Cancer, Children's Health/Hospitals, Health Organizations, Heart, Hospitals, Research/Studies Institutes
Religion: Churches, Religious Organizations, Religious Welfare
Science: Science Museums, Scientific Centers & Institutes
Social Services: At-Risk Youth, Big Brothers/Big Sisters, Child Welfare, Community Centers, Community Service Organizations, Crime Prevention, Day Care, Family Services, People with Disabilities, Recreation & Athletics, Scouts, Social Services-General, United Funds/United Ways, YMCA/YWCA/YMHA/YWHA, Youth Organizations

Application Procedures

Initial Contact: The foundation has no formal application form, but requests organizations use the New York Regional Association of Grantmakers Common Application Form. The foundation does not accept unsolicited formal proposals from organizations unfamiliar to the foundation, but such organizations may submit a letter of inquiry. If the request falls within the parameters of the foundation's current grantmaking interests, the foundation will request a full proposal.

Application Requirements: Proposals should consist of a one- to three-page letter with a concise statement of the purpose of the grant and the amount. The letter should be accompanied by a copy of IRS 501(c)(3) determination letter; brief a description of organization's history and activities; current list of organization members, trustees, directors, and officers; latest audited financial report; detailed project or organization budget; and an accounting of other foundation support.

Deadlines: None.

Review Process: The trustees have no set schedule of meetings.

Decision Notification: Decisions are base upon the nature of the proposal, availability of funding, and the applicant's fiscal year. It is contemplated that all decisions upon pending proposals will be determined by September 30.

Restrictions

Grants are not made to individuals, private foundations, government organizations, or publicly operated educational and medical institutions. Grants for endowments, building funds, capital development, and grants payable over several years are made occasionally. Grants to performing arts institutions or to private colleges and universities are made only at the invitation of the Foundation.

Additional Information

Chase Manhattan Bank is listed as a trustee of the foundation.
Publications: Annual Report; Guidelines

Foundation Officials

Paul R. Brenner: trustee B Yonkers, NY 1942. ED Fordham University AB (1964); Fordham University JD (1967); New York University LLM (1968). PRIM CORP EMPL partner, attorney: Kelley, Drye & Warren.
Peter D. Calder: executive director, trustee ED University of Rhode Island BA (1974); University of Rhode Island MA (1977).
Alison Sargent: senior program manager

Grants Analysis

Disclosure Period: fiscal year ending October 31, 2003
Total Grants: $5,640,831
Number of Grants: 153
Average Grant: $36,868
Highest Grant: $200,000
Lowest Grant: $1,000
Typical Range: $10,000 to $50,000

Recent Grants

Note: Grants derived from 2003 Form 990.

Library-Related

50,000	Brooklyn Public Library, Brooklyn, NY -- renewed support for children's educational programs
50,000	New York Public Library, New York, NY -- match for city funding and purchase of books

General

200,000	American Museum of Natural History, New York, NY -- continued development of the educational website
200,000	American Museum of Natural History, New York, NY -- continued development of the education website, with the addition of new content increased accessibility and functionality and broader dissemination
175,000	Brooklyn Children's Museum, Brooklyn, NY -- technology project
130,000	Educational Broadcasting Corporation, New York, NY -- renewed after school exchange
125,000	YMCA of Greater New York, New York, NY -- capital campaign for kids
110,654	College of Saint Rose, Albany, NY -- develop, design, implement and evaluate model programs of education
100,000	Boys' Club of New York, New York, NY -- New Horizons
100,000	Boys and Girls Club of Northern Westchester, Mt. Kisco, NY -- to support program expansion at the Tarrytown clubhouse
100,000	Goddard Riverside Community Center, New York, NY -- OPTIONS college access center replication project
100,000	Little Sisters of the Assumption, New York, NY -- request for grant to construct new building at east street

KENNETH L. CALHOUN CHARITABLE TRUST

Giving Contact

Karen Krino, Trust Administrator
c/o Key Trust Co. of Ohio NA
157 S. Main St.
Akron, OH 44308
Phone: (330)379-1647

Description

Founded: 1982
EIN: 341370330
Organization Type: Private Foundation
Giving Locations: OH: Akron including surrounding area
Grant Types: General Support.

Donor Information

Founder: the late Kenneth Calhoun

Financial Summary

Total Giving: $135,000 (fiscal year ending July 31, 2004); $481,033 (fiscal 2001)
Giving Analysis: Giving for fiscal 2001 includes: foundation fellowships ($4,000)
Assets: $4,907,797 (fiscal 2004); $6,355,413 (fiscal 2001)

Typical Recipients

Arts & Humanities: Arts Associations & Councils, Ballet, Film & Video, Historic Preservation, History & Archaeology, Libraries, Museums/Galleries, Music, Performing Arts, Public Broadcasting, Theater
Civic & Public Affairs: Botanical Gardens/Parks, Community Foundations, Economic Development, Civic & Public Affairs-General, Law & Justice, Parades/Festivals, Urban & Community Affairs, Zoos/Aquariums
Education: Arts/Humanities Education, Colleges & Universities, Education Funds, Education Reform, Education-General, Medical Education, Minority Education, Private Education (Precollege), Public Education (Precollege), Secondary Education (Private), Special Education
Health: Children's Health/Hospitals, Emergency/Ambulance Services, Health Organizations, Heart, Hospices, Hospitals, Medical Research, Mental Health, Nursing Services, Public Health
International: International Environmental Issues
Religion: Churches, Ministries, Religious Organizations, Religious Welfare
Science: Science Museums, Scientific Centers & Institutes
Social Services: Big Brothers/Big Sisters, Child Welfare, Community Service Organizations, Crime Prevention, Delinquency & Criminal Rehabilitation, Domestic Violence, Family Services, Food/Clothing Distribution, People with Disabilities, Scouts, Senior Services, Shelters/Homelessness, United Funds/United Ways, Volunteer Services, YMCA/YWCA/YMHA/YWHA, Youth Organizations

Application Procedures

Initial Contact: Send a brief letter of inquiry describing program or project.
Application Requirements: Include a description of organization, date and amount requested, purpose of funds sought, and proof of tax-exempt status.
Deadlines: June 30.

Additional Information

Trust(s): Key Bank Co OH NA.
Trust(s): Key Trust Co OH NA

Grants Analysis

Disclosure Period: fiscal year ending July 31, 2004
Total Grants: $135,000
Number of Grants: 17
Average Grant: $4,833*
Highest Grant: $37,500
Lowest Grant: $2,000
Typical Range: $2,000 to $7,000
*Note: Average grant figure excludes two highest grants ($62,500).

Recent Grants

Note: Grants derived from 2001 Form 990.

General

25,000	Akron General Development Foundation, Akron, OH
15,000	University of Akron Foundation, Akron, OH
13,000	Ohio Chamber Ballet, Akron, OH
10,000	Daybreak Productions, Aurora, OH
10,000	Hanna Perkins School, Akron, OH
10,000	In His Steps Foundation
10,000	Kevin Coleman Foundation, Kent, OH
10,000	University of Akron Foundation, Akron, OH
10,000	YMCA, Akron, OH
8,000	American Heart Association, Akron, OH

CALIFORNIA BANK & TRUST

Company Headquarters

San Francisco, CA
Web: http://www.calbanktrust.com

Company Description

Acquired: Sumitomo Bank of California (1998).
Employees: 1,500
SIC(s): 6082 Foreign Trade & International Banks.
Parent Company: Zions Bancorp, Salt Lake City, UT, United States

Operating Locations

California Bank & Trust (CA--Albany, Alhambra, Anaheim, Brea, Claremont, Costa Mesa, Cupertino, Fresno, Gardena, Hacienda Heights, Hayward Millbrae, La Palma, Long Beach, Los Angeles, Monterey, Mountain View, Oxnard, Pleasant Hill, Pomona, Sacramento, San Francisco, San Jose, San Mateo, Santa Monica, Stockton, Torrance, Watsonville, West Hollywood); Sumitomo Bank of California (CA--San Francisco); Sumitomo Bank Capital Markets (NY--New York); Sumitomo Bank Financial Services (NY--New York); Sumitomo Bank Investment Management (NY--New York); Sumitomo Bank Leasing & Finance (NY--New York); Sumitomo Bank, Ltd.-Atlanta Agency (GA--Atlanta); Sumitomo Bank, Ltd., Chicago Branch (IL--Chicago); Sumitomo Bank, Ltd.-Houston Agency (TX--Houston); Sumitomo Bank, Ltd., Los Angeles Branch (CA--Los Angeles); Sumitomo Bank, Ltd., New York Branch (NY--New York); Sumitomo Bank, Ltd., San Francisco Branch (CA--San Francisco); Sumitomo Bank, Ltd.-Seattle Representative Office (WA--Seattle); Sumitomo Bank of New York Trust Co. (NY--New York); Sumitomo Bank Securities (NY--New York)

Nonmonetary Support

Type: Donated Equipment; In-kind Services; Loaned Employees
Volunteer Programs: Employees are encouraged to become involved in their communities through participation in local civic and government groups and whose primary focus is to improve economic development in the community.
Contact: Steve Nelson

Giving Contact

Lynda Buckner, Vice President and Manager
Community Development Department
11622 El Camino Real, Suite 200
San Diego, CA 92130
Phone: (858)793-7470
Fax: (858)793-7438
Web: http://www.calbanktrust.com/contactus

Description

Organization Type: Corporate Giving Program
Giving Locations: CA: Supports organizations within the state of California with priority given to those with whom we have a banking relationship headquarters area only.
Grant Types: General Support, Loan, Operating Expenses.
Note: Employee matching gift ratio: 1 to 1.

Financial Summary

Total Giving: $1,000,000 (2005 approx); $1,000,000 (2004); $750,000 (2001 approx)
Assets: $9,500,000,000 (2004 approx); $9,500,000,000 (2003)

Typical Recipients

Arts & Humanities: Community Arts, Libraries, Museums/Galleries, Music
Civic & Public Affairs: Economic Development, Employment/Job Training, Housing, Urban & Community Affairs
Education: Colleges & Universities, Public Education (Precollege)
Health: Health Organizations
Social Services: Community Service Organizations, Family Services, People with Disabilities, United Funds/United Ways, Youth Organizations

Application Procedures

Initial Contact: Send a written proposal.
Application Requirements: Send a a description of organization and name of contact person, a statement of purpose, a request for a specific amount of

funding, an explanation of why funds are needed and how they will be used, a list of contributors, list of board of directors and their business affiliations, a recently audited financial statement including income and expenses, proof of tax-exempt status.

Deadlines: None.

Notes: Individual branches administer small budgets; large grants are referred to the Community Development Department or the Regional Headquarters in San Francisco, Los Angeles, or San Diego.

Restrictions

Does not support individuals, religious organizations for sectarian purposes, or organizations outside operating areas.

Additional Information

In March 1997, Sumitomo Bank announced its 1997 Community Outreach Plan, which contains the bank's CRA (Community Reinvestment Act) goals. The bank has doubled a commitment made in 1993 and will target $1 billion in CRA loans by the year 2003. In addition, the company expanded its Community Advisory Board from five to ten members, and expects to aim for greater diversity in its use of vendors and in its philanthropic support of community organizations. In 1997, the company's goal was to donate 2% of net income, with a greater emphasis given to educational, business, and job development needs in the communities it serves.

Publications: Guidelines Sheet; Annual Report

Grants Analysis

Disclosure Period: calendar year ending 1999
Total Grants: $827,500*
Number of Grants: 293
Average Grant: $2,800
Highest Grant: $40,000
Typical Range: $2,500 to $5,000
*Note: Grants analysis provided by company.

CALLAWAY FOUNDATION, INC.

Giving Contact

H. Speer Burdette, III, President
209 Broome Street, PO Box 790
PO Box 790
LaGrange, GA 30241
Phone: (706)884-7348
Fax: (706)884-0201

Description

Founded: 1943
EIN: 580566147
Organization Type: General Purpose Foundation
Giving Locations: GA: LaGrange including Troup County
Grant Types: Capital, Challenge, General Support, Matching.

Financial Summary

Total Giving: $7,511,398 (fiscal year ending September 30, 2003); $10,768,709 (fiscal 2002); $10,414,462 (fiscal 2001)
Giving Analysis: Giving for fiscal 2003 includes: foundation grants to United Way ($48,243); fiscal 2002: foundation grants to United Way ($45,875)
Assets: $187,791,860 (fiscal 2003); $179,572,264 (fiscal 2002); $196,549,371 (fiscal 2001)

Typical Recipients

Arts & Humanities: Arts Associations & Councils, Arts Centers, Ballet, Community Arts, Historic Preservation, History & Archaeology, Libraries, Museums/ Galleries, Music, Performing Arts, Theater
Civic & Public Affairs: African American Affairs, Bo-

tanical Gardens/Parks, Business/Free Enterprise, Clubs, Community Foundations, Economic Development, Employment/Job Training, Civic & Public Affairs-General, Housing, Municipalities/Towns, Philanthropic Organizations, Urban & Community Affairs, Women's Affairs, Zoos/Aquariums
Education: Arts/Humanities Education, Business Education, Colleges & Universities, Economic Education, Education Associations, Education Funds, Education Reform, Elementary Education (Private), Engineering/Technological Education, Education-General, International Exchange, Literacy, Medical Education, Preschool Education, Private Education (Precollege), Public Education (Precollege), Special Education, Student Aid, Vocational & Technical Education
Environment: Air/Water Quality, Environment-General, Protection, Resource Conservation
Health: AIDS/HIV, Alzheimer's Disease, Cancer, Clinics/Medical Centers, Emergency/Ambulance Services, Eyes/Blindness, Health Policy/Cost Containment, Health Organizations, Heart, Hospitals, Long-Term Care, Medical Rehabilitation, Public Health, Single-Disease Health Associations, Transplant Networks/Donor Banks
International: Foreign Educational Institutions
Religion: Churches, Jewish Causes, Ministries, Religious Organizations, Religious Welfare, Synagogues/Temples
Science: Science Museums, Scientific Centers & Institutes, Scientific Labs
Social Services: Animal Protection, Camps, Community Centers, Community Service Organizations, Emergency Relief, Family Planning, People with Disabilities, Recreation & Athletics, Scouts, Social Services-General, Special Olympics, Substance Abuse, United Funds/United Ways, Youth Organizations

Application Procedures

Initial Contact: Applicants should send a letter containing pertinent information about the organization to the foundation office.
Application Requirements: Initial letters should contain an outline of the purpose of the request, a proposed budget, amount raised, the needs of the applicant, other material information substantiating the validity of the project, and proof of tax-exempt status. Notification will be given if additional information or interviews are considered necessary.
Deadlines: None. The board of trustees meets in January, April, July, and October; optimum time for application is four to six weeks before the quarterly meetings.

Restrictions

Grants are not made for endowment, debt retirement, loans, or repetitive year-to-year funds for a program. No grants are made to individuals.

Additional Information

The foundation prefers to support organizations on a one-time basis rather than on a long-term basis.
Publications: Annual Report

Foundation Officials

H. Speer Burdette, III: president, general manager
Mark Clayton Callaway: trustee B 1956. ED LaGrange College BA (1981); New York University (1981-1982). CLUB AFFIL Piedmont Driving Club; Rotary Club; Highland Country Club.
Jane Alice Craig: trustee
James Thomas Gresham: president, general manager, treasurer B Griffin, GA 1937. ED Georgia Technology University BS (1960). PRIM CORP EMPL director: Atlantic Realty Co. NONPR AFFIL member: Sigma Chi; honorary member: Tau Beta Pi; honorary member: Phi Kappa Phi; trustee: Georgia Technology Research Corp.; trustee: Medical Park Foundation; trustee: Georgia Heart Clinic Inc.; trustee: Georgia Technology Foundation; deacon: First Baptist Church, LaGrange; president, trustee: Enoch Callaway Cancer Clinic. CLUB AFFIL member: Highland

Country Club.
Ellen H. Harris: trustee
Charles D. Hudson, Jr.: trustee
D. Ray McKenzie, Jr.: vice president
C. L. Pitts: secretary
Esther S. Rainey: treasurer
Ida H. Russell: trustee

Grants Analysis

Disclosure Period: fiscal year ending September 30, 2003
Total Grants: $7,463,155*
Number of Grants: 75
Average Grant: $50,865*
Highest Grant: $2,000,000
Lowest Grant: $500
Typical Range: $10,000 to $100,000
*Note: Giving excludes United Way. Average grant figure excludes two highest grants ($3,750,000).

Recent Grants

Note: Grants derived from fiscal 2003 Form 990.
General

2,000,000	Troup County, Lagrange, GA -- to assist recreational endowment fund
1,750,000	Lagrange College, Lagrange, GA -- to support Callaway Campus endowment fund
600,000	D.A.S.H. for Lagrange Inc., Lagrange, GA -- for rehabilitation fund
330,000	Trinity United Methodist Church, Lagrange, GA -- for permanent improvements
300,000	D.A.S.H. for Lagrange Inc., Lagrange, GA -- to support land acquisition fund
285,000	Lagrange Performing Arts Center Inc., Lagrange, GA -- fund for relocation of radio tower
250,000	Lagrange Performing Arts Center Inc., Lagrange, GA -- to support Lagrange theatre building project
200,000	Troup County, Lagrange, GA -- fund for recreation additions and improvements
157,500	D.A.S.H. for Lagrange Inc., Lagrange, GA -- to support in the operations of Housing Center
155,000	Lafayette Society for Performing Arts Inc., Lagrange, GA

APOLLOS CAMP AND BENNET HUMISTON TRUST

Giving Contact

Neil C. Bach, Chairman
300 W. Washington St.
Pontiac, IL 61764
Phone: (815)844-6155
Fax: (815)842-2977

Description

Founded: 1925
EIN: 370701044
Organization Type: Private Foundation
Giving Locations: IL: Pontiac
Grant Types: Capital, General Support, Operating Expenses.

Financial Summary

Total Giving: $329,898 (fiscal year ending April 30, 2004); $334,226 (fiscal 2002); $312,470 (fiscal 2001)
Assets: $7,924,840 (fiscal 2004); $7,895,757 (fiscal 2002); $7,844,591 (fiscal 2001)
Gifts Received: $50 (fiscal 1997); $5,451 (fiscal 1996). Note: In fiscal 1996, contributions were received from Humiston Haven.

Typical Recipients

Arts & Humanities: Historic Preservation, Libraries, Music, Performing Arts

Civic & Public Affairs: Botanical Gardens/Parks, Chambers of Commerce, Clubs, Economic Development, Civic & Public Affairs-General, Housing, Municipalities/Towns, Parades/Festivals, Safety, Urban & Community Affairs, Zoos/Aquariums

Education: Arts/Humanities Education, Education-General, Public Education (Precollege), Secondary Education (Public)

Environment: Environment-General

Health: Clinics/Medical Centers, Health-General, Long-Term Care, Public Health

Religion: Religious Welfare

Social Services: Child Welfare, Community Service Organizations, Family Services, People with Disabilities, Recreation & Athletics, Social Services-General, Substance Abuse, Youth Organizations

Application Procedures

Initial Contact: The foundation requests applications be made in writing. Include amount requested and purpose of funds sought.

Deadlines: None.

Foundation Officials

Neil C. Bach: chairman, trustee
David R. Harding: trustee
William C. Harris: trustee
Louis Lyons: trustee

Grants Analysis

Disclosure Period: fiscal year ending April 30, 2004
Total Grants: $329,898
Number of Grants: 14
Average Grant: $15,940*
Highest Grant: $73,695
Lowest Grant: $750
Typical Range: $5,000 to $25,000
***Note:** Average grant figure excludes two highest grants ($138,615).

Recent Grants

Note: Grants derived from fiscal 2004 Form 990.
General

73,695	Boys and Girls Club of Livingston County, Pontiac, IL -- for asset purchase
64,920	Humiston Woods Nature Center, Pontiac, IL
50,000	Futures Unlimited, Pontiac, IL -- for capital improvement
30,000	Pontiac School District 429, Pontiac, IL -- for asset purchase
21,000	Livingston County Public Health, Pontiac, IL
20,000	Livingston Family Care Center, Pontiac, IL
18,835	Washington Grade School, Pontiac, IL -- for playground equipment
11,000	Kiwanis Club of Pontiac, Pontiac, IL -- for equipment/renovate
10,000	Pontiac Needy Kids Fund, Pontiac, IL -- for Christmas expense
10,000	Pontiac Township High School, Pontiac, IL -- for asset purchase

CAMP YOUNTS FOUNDATION

Giving Contact

Bobby B. Worrell, Executive Director
SunTrust Bank
PO Box 4655
Atlanta, GA 30302
Phone: (404)230-5541

Description

Founded: 1955
EIN: 586026001
Organization Type: Family Foundation
Giving Locations: VA: southeastern states.
Grant Types: General Support.

Donor Information

Founder: Established in 1955 by the late Charles Younts and the late Willie Camp Younts.

Financial Summary

Total Giving: $1,951,832 (2003); $2,465,607 (2002); $2,817,157 (2001)
Giving Analysis: Giving for 2003 includes: foundation grants to United Way ($2,480); 2002: foundation grants to United Way ($8,000)
Assets: $41,003,200 (2003); $36,273,616 (2002); $46,276,243 (2001)
Gifts Received: $97,384 (1993)

Typical Recipients

Arts & Humanities: Arts Centers, Arts Funds, Community Arts, Historic Preservation, History & Archaeology, Libraries, Museums/Galleries, Music, Performing Arts, Public Broadcasting, Theater

Civic & Public Affairs: Botanical Gardens/Parks, Community Foundations, Civic & Public Affairs-General, Inner-City Development, Municipalities/Towns, Philanthropic Organizations, Public Policy, Urban & Community Affairs

Education: Agricultural Education, Business Education, Colleges & Universities, Community & Junior Colleges, Education Associations, Education Funds, Education Reform, Engineering/Technological Education, Environmental Education, Education-General, Journalism/Media Education, Medical Education, Private Education (Precollege), Public Education (Precollege), Science/Mathematics Education, Special Education, Student Aid, Vocational & Technical Education

Environment: Environment-General, Wildlife Protection

Health: Cancer, Geriatric Health, Hospitals, Mental Health, Nursing Services, Single-Disease Health Associations

International: International Organizations

Religion: Churches, Ministries, Religious Organizations, Religious Welfare

Science: Science Museums, Scientific Research

Social Services: Animal Protection, Child Welfare, Community Centers, Community Service Organizations, Food/Clothing Distribution, Homes, People with Disabilities, Recreation & Athletics, Senior Services, Shelters/Homelessness, United Funds/United Ways, YMCA/YWCA/YMHA/YWHA, Youth Organizations

Application Procedures

Initial Contact: Applications must be made in writing.
Application Requirements: Application must include an IRS tax-exempt letter.
Deadlines: None.

Restrictions

Grants are not made to individuals.

Foundation Officials

Harold S. Atkinson, Jr.: trustee
John M. Camp, Jr.: trustee
Paul C. Marks: trustee
Harry Webster Walker, II: trustee B Bridgeport, CT 1921. PRIM CORP EMPL president, chief executive officer, director: Sunsweet Fruit Inc. CORP AFFIL president: Indian River Elite Citrus Inc.; director: Walker Group Inc.; director: Carpenter Technology Corp. NONPR AFFIL director: Vero Beach YMCA; devel board: Yale University; member: United States Yacht Racing Union; chairman: Piedmont College; member: Rotary Club; chairman: Olympic International Star Class Yacht Racing Association; director: Blue Ridge Assemblies, Inc.; member: National Boating Safety; member: Association Yale University Alumni.

Grants Analysis

Disclosure Period: calendar year ending 2003
Total Grants: $1,949,352*
Number of Grants: 388
Average Grant: $4,594*
Highest Grant: $91,500
Lowest Grant: $500
Typical Range: $1,000 to $10,000
***Note:** Giving excludes United Way. Average grant figure excludes two highest grants ($176,032).

Recent Grants

Note: Grants derived from 2003 Form 990.
General

91,500	Southhampton Academy, Courtland, VA
84,532	Elms Foundation, Tauranga New Zealand
30,000	Boys and Girls Club of South, Tacoma, WA
30,000	Southhampton County, Courtland, VA
30,000	Yale University, New Haven, CT
30,000	Yale University, New Haven, CT
25,000	Blue Ridge Assembly Inc. YMCA
25,000	Franklin Baptist Church, Murfreesboro, TN
25,000	Jamestown-Yorktown Foundation, Williamsburg, VA
25,000	North Carolina Agricultural Foundation, NC

BUSHROD H. CAMPBELL AND ADAH E. HALL CHARITY FUND

Giving Contact

Brenda K. Taylor, Foundation Administrator
c/o Palmer & Dodge
111 Huntington Ave., 18th Fl.
Boston, MA 02199
Phone: (617)239-0100

Description

Founded: 1956
EIN: 046013598
Organization Type: Private Foundation
Giving Locations: MA: Boston including metropolitan area
Grant Types: Capital, Conference/Seminar, Fellowship, General Support, Multiyear/Continuing Support, Operating Expenses, Project, Seed Money.

Donor Information

Founder: the late Bushrod H. Campbell, the late Adah F. Hall

Financial Summary

Total Giving: $837,350 (fiscal year ending May 31, 2004); $1,074,085 (fiscal 2001)
Assets: $19,120,443 (fiscal 2004); $22,184,381 (fiscal 2001)

Typical Recipients

Arts & Humanities: Historic Preservation, Libraries, Opera, Public Broadcasting

Civic & Public Affairs: Asian American Affairs, Civil Rights, Economic Development, Employment/Job Training, Civic & Public Affairs-General, Hispanic Affairs, Housing, Urban & Community Affairs, Women's Affairs

Education: Afterschool/Enrichment Programs, Colleges & Universities, Engineering/Technological Education, Education-General, Literacy, Medical Education, Minority Education, School Volunteerism,

Special Education

Health: AIDS/HIV, Alzheimer's Disease, Clinics/ Medical Centers, Geriatric Health, Health Funds, Health Organizations, Home-Care Services, Hospices, Hospitals, Long-Term Care, Medical Research, Nursing Services, Public Health

International: Health Care/Hospitals

Religion: Churches, Religious Organizations, Social/ Policy Issues

Social Services: Community Service Organizations, Day Care, Domestic Violence, Family Planning, Family Services, Food/Clothing Distribution, People with Disabilities, Senior Services, Shelters/ Homelessness, Social Services-General, United Funds/United Ways, YMCA/YWCA/YMHA/YWHA, Youth Organizations

Application Procedures

Initial Contact: Send cover letter and formal proposal.

Application Requirements: Include a description of organization, amount requested, purpose of funds sought, recently audited financial statement, and proof of tax-exempt status.

Deadlines: January 1, April 1, August 1, and October 1.

Restrictions

Preference is given to teaching hospitals, organizations providing services to the elderly, and population control efforts.

Additional Information

Publications: Application Guidelines

Foundation Officials

Casimir de Rham, Jr.: trustee B New York, NY 1924. ED Yale University (1943-1944); Harvard University AB (1946); Harvard University JD (1949). PRIM CORP EMPL officer counsel: Palmer & Dodge. NONPR AFFIL treasurer, trustee: Mt Auburn Hospital; director: Womens Education & Industry Union; member: Massachusetts Bar Association; trustee: Mt Auburn Foundation; treasurer: Little Harbor Chapel; member: Masons; honorary trustee: Sterling & Francine Clark Art Institute; trustee: Commonwealth School; member: Cambridge-Arlington-Belmont Bar Association; honorary trustee: Center Blood Research Boston; member: Boston Bar Association; sr advisory board: Boys & Girls Clubs Boston; member: American Bar Foundation; member: American Legion; member: American Bar Association. CLUB AFFIL Saint Botolph Club.

Arthur B. Page: trustee

Curtis Prout, MD: trustee B Swampscott, MA October 13, 1915. ED Harvard University AB (1937); Harvard University MD (1941). OCCUPATION physician. NONPR AFFIL director, treasurer: Medical Foundation; director: National Comm Correctional Health Care; fellow: Massachusetts Medicine Society; fellow: American College Physicians; member: American Medical Association; member: American Clinical & Climatological Association.

Grants Analysis

Disclosure Period: fiscal year ending May 31, 2004

Total Grants: $837,350

Number of Grants: 106

Average Grant: $7,403*

Highest Grant: $60,000

Lowest Grant: $2,000

Typical Range: $5,000 to $10,000

*Note: Average grant figure excludes highest grant.

Recent Grants

Note: Grants derived from 2004 Form 990.

General

60,000	Medical Foundation, Boston, MA -- for postdoctoral research fellowship program
18,750	Medical Foundation, Boston, MA -- for research fellowship
12,500	Boston Partners in Education, Boston, MA -- for voluntary recruitment initiative
12,500	Roca Inc., Chelsea, MA -- for youth STAR health promotion project
12,000	Clarke School for the Deaf, Northampton, MA
12,000	Crittenton Hastings House, Boston, MA -- for renovation project
10,000	Boston Aging Concerns-Young and Old United, Boston, MA -- for intergenerational housing
10,000	Carroll Center for the Blind, Newton, MA
10,000	Pathfinder International, Watertown, MA
10,000	Women's Educational and Industrial Union, Boston, MA -- for home health care services

J. BULOW CAMPBELL FOUNDATION

Giving Contact

Betsy Hamilton, Associate Director
50 Hurt Plaza, Suite 850
Atlanta, GA 30303-2917
Phone: (404)658-9066
Fax: (404)659-4802

Description

Founded: 1940

EIN: 580566149

Organization Type: General Purpose Foundation

Giving Locations: AL; FL; GA: Atlanta including surrounding area; NC; SC; TN

Grant Types: Capital, Challenge.

Donor Information

Founder: Established in 1940 in accordance with the will of J. Bulow Campbell (1870-1946), who was chairman of the Campbell Coal Company. He was also chairman of the Berry Schools and Rabun Gap-Nacoochee School, chairman of the executive committee of Columbia Theological Seminary, and a trustee of Agnes Scott College and the YMCA. Mr. Campbell's philanthropic interests were strongly influenced by his Christian faith and close ties to the Southern Presbyterian Church.

Financial Summary

Total Giving: $30,074,098 (2003); $32,000,000 (2002 approx); $35,983,616 (2001)

Assets: $643,669,441 (2003); $600,000,000 (2002 approx); $641,312,031 (2001)

Gifts Received: $60,000 (2000); $145,970,246 (1999); $2,587,459 (1998). Note: In 1999 and 2000, contributions were received from The estate of Virginia C. Courts. In 1998, contributions were received from the J. Bulow Campbell Trust.

Typical Recipients

Arts & Humanities: Arts Centers, Arts Festivals, History & Archaeology, Libraries, Museums/Galleries, Music

Civic & Public Affairs: Botanical Gardens/Parks, Chambers of Commerce, Community Foundations, Civic & Public Affairs-General, Hispanic Affairs, Housing, Inner-City Development, Law & Justice, Legal Aid, Municipalities/Towns, Nonprofit Management, Philanthropic Organizations, Urban & Community Affairs, Zoos/Aquariums

Education: Arts/Humanities Education, Business Education, Colleges & Universities, Economic Education, Education Reform, Education-General, Health & Physical Education, International Studies, Literacy, Medical Education, Private Education (Precollege), Religious Education, Science/Mathematics Education, Special Education, Student Aid

Environment: Environment-General, Resource Conservation

Health: Cancer, Children's Health/Hospitals, Clinics/ Medical Centers, Emergency/Ambulance Services, Health Organizations, Hospices, Hospitals, Long-Term Care, Medical Research, Mental Health, Nursing Services, Single-Disease Health Associations

International: Missionary/Religious Activities

Religion: Bible Study/Translation, Churches, Religion-General, Jewish Causes, Ministries, Religious Organizations, Religious Welfare, Seminaries

Science: Science Museums

Social Services: Animal Protection, At-Risk Youth, Big Brothers/Big Sisters, Camps, Child Abuse, Child Welfare, Community Service Organizations, Counseling, Emergency Relief, Family Services, Homes, People with Disabilities, Recreation & Athletics, Scouts, Senior Services, Shelters/Homelessness, Social Services-General, Substance Abuse, United Funds/United Ways, YMCA/YWCA/YMHA/YWHA, Youth Organizations

Application Procedures

Initial Contact: The foundation does not provide an application form. Initial contact should be made through a letter of request.

Application Requirements: The letter of request must be limited to one page. It should include the full legal name and a concise description of organization, its purpose, and its program; specific amount requested; brief description of the purpose for which the grant would be used; definite plan and timetable for successful completion of the project; and the signature of the principal officer of the governing board and the chief administrative officer of the institution. A copy of the organization's IRS determination letter of tax-exempt status should be enclosed.

Deadlines: Applications submitted by January 1, April 1, July 1, and October 1 will be given preliminary consideration at the board meeting held in each of those months. However, organizations are encouraged to submit applications well in advance of the deadlines.

Review Process: All grants must be approved by the seven-member board of trustees. During preliminary consideration, the board will decide whether or not to consider an application. The applicant will be notified in writing either that the board has declined the proposal or that it has decided to pursue the matter. If further consideration is undertaken, foundation staff will conduct a more detailed study of the proposal. The staff will usually conduct at least one site visit at this stage and submit a report to the board for consideration at the next quarterly board meeting. executive director are often helpful, as are consultations with him prior to submitting a formal letter of application. executive director are often helpful, as are consultations with him prior to submitting a formal letter of application.

Restrictions

The foundation makes no grants or loans of any kind to individuals. It discourages requests from local church congregations. Grants are generally limited exclusively to Georgia, but will occasionally consider grants in South Carolina, North Carolina, Tennessee, Alabama, and Florida.

Additional Information

The Trust Company of Georgia serves as corporate trustee for the foundation.

Applicants are asked to wait at least one year from the date of any previous application before submitting another request.

Publications: General Information Pamphlet; Application Guidelines

Trust(s): SunTrust Bank, Atlanta

Foundation Officials

David E. Boyd: member NONPR AFFIL trustee: Emory University; trustee: Lagrange Colorado.

Peter M. Candler: member

Bickerton W. Cardwell, Jr.: member

R. W. Courts, II: chairman
Betsy Hamilton: grants director
Larry L. Prince: vice chairman, trustee B Dyersburg, TN 1937. PRIM CORP EMPL chairman, chief executive officer, director: Genuine Parts Co. CORP AFFIL director: John H. Harland Co.; director: SunTrust Banks Inc.; director: Crawford & Co.; director: Equifax Inc.
Joseph T. Spence: member
John W. Stephenson: executive director ED Emory University (1970).
Barry L. Teague: member

Grants Analysis

Disclosure Period: calendar year ending 2003
Total Grants: $30,074,098
Number of Grants: 48
Average Grant: $512,758*
Highest Grant: $3,000,000
Lowest Grant: $8,275
Typical Range: $100,000 to $1,000,000
*****Note:** Average grant figure three excludes highest grants ($7,000,000).

Recent Grants

Note: Grants derived from 2003 Form 990.
General

8,000,000	High Museum of Art, Atlanta, GA
2,000,000	Atlanta Union Mission, Atlanta, GA
2,000,000	Piedmont Hospital, Atlanta, GA
2,000,000	Presbyterian Homes of Georgia, Quitman, GA
1,500,000	Girl Scout Council of Northwest, Atlanta, GA
1,250,000	Pace Academy, Atlanta, GA
1,000,000	Atlanta International School, Atlanta, GA
1,000,000	Community Foundation for Greater Atlanta, Atlanta, GA
1,000,000	Galloway School, Atlanta, GA
965,531	Clark Atlanta University, Atlanta, GA

CAMPBELL FOUNDATION (MD)

Giving Contact

William B. Campbell, President
100 W. Pennsylvania Avenue
Baltimore, MD 21204
Phone: (410)825-0545

Description

EIN: 520794348
Organization Type: Private Foundation
Giving Locations: MD: Baltimore including metropolitan area
Grant Types: Capital, Endowment, General Support, Operating Expenses, Project.

Donor Information

Founder: R. McLean Campbell

Financial Summary

Total Giving: $155,000 (2003)
Assets: $2,892,216 (2003)
Gifts Received: $10,000 (1996). Note: In 1996, contributions were received from the estate of Bruce S. Campbell, Jr.

Typical Recipients

Arts & Humanities: Arts Centers, Arts Institutes, Arts Outreach, Community Arts, Arts & Humanities-General, Historic Preservation, History & Archaeology, Libraries, Museums/Galleries, Music, Opera, Performing Arts, Theater
Civic & Public Affairs: Botanical Gardens/Parks, Clubs, Economic Development, Employment/Job Training, Civic & Public Affairs-General, Housing, Parades/Festivals, Professional & Trade Associations, Urban & Community Affairs, Zoos/Aquariums
Education: Arts/Humanities Education, Colleges & Universities, Education Funds, Environmental Education, Education-General, Literacy, Medical Education, Minority Education, Private Education (Precollege), Science/Mathematics Education, Special Education, Student Aid
Environment: Environment-General, Resource Conservation
Health: AIDS/HIV, Children's Health/Hospitals, Clinics/Medical Centers, Eyes/Blindness, Hospices, Hospitals, Research/Studies Institutes
Science: Scientific Centers & Institutes
Social Services: Animal Protection, Camps, Child Welfare, Community Service Organizations, Counseling, Crime Prevention, Family Planning, Food/Clothing Distribution, People with Disabilities, Recreation & Athletics, Shelters/Homelessness, Special Olympics, Substance Abuse, United Funds/United Ways, YMCA/YWCA/YMHA/YWHA, Youth Organizations

Application Procedures

Initial Contact: Send a full proposal.
Application Requirements: Include a description of organization, amount requested, purpose of funds sought, recently audited financial statement, and proof of tax-exempt status, and description of project.
Deadlines: October 15.

Restrictions

Grants are primarily in support of education, civic, cultural, and health programs. Does not support individuals.

Foundation Officials

Carolyn C. Beall: secretary
Bruce S. Campbell, III: treasurer
J. Tyler Campbell: director
Mary Jo Campbell: director
William B. Campbell: president

Grants Analysis

Disclosure Period: calendar year ending 2003
Total Grants: $155,000
Number of Grants: 78
Average Grant: $1,987
Highest Grant: $8,000
Lowest Grant: $500
Typical Range: $500 to $5,000

Recent Grants

Note: Grants derived from 2001 Form 990.
Library-Related

5,000	Baltimore County Public Library, Towson, MD -- capital campaign

General

15,000	Roland Park Country School, Baltimore, MD -- capital campaign
15,000	St. Paul's School for Girls, Brooklandville, MD -- capital campaign
10,000	Odyssey School, Baltimore, MD -- capital campaign
10,000	Walters Art Gallery, Baltimore, MD -- for capital campaign
5,000	Independent College Fund of Maryland, Baltimore, MD
5,000	Jubilee Baltimore, Inc., Baltimore, MD -- capital campaign
5,000	St. James Academy, Baltimore, MD -- capital campaign
3,000	Baltimore Educational Scholarship Trust, Baltimore, MD
2,500	Women's Industrial Exchange, Baltimore, MD -- capital campaign
2,000	Center for Poverty Solutions, Baltimore, MD -- capital campaign

RUTH AND HENRY CAMPBELL FOUNDATION

Giving Contact

Donald D. Koonce, Trust Officer
c/o Bank of America
PO Box 26903
Richmond, VA 23261
Phone: (804)788-2573

Description

Founded: 1957
EIN: 546031023
Organization Type: Private Foundation
Giving Locations: VA
Grant Types: General Support.

Financial Summary

Total Giving: $541,660 (2003)
Assets: $13,364,408 (2003)
Gifts Received: $30,500 (2000); $4,000 (1999); $35,500 (1998)

Typical Recipients

Arts & Humanities: Arts Associations & Councils, Arts Funds, Ballet, Ethnic & Folk Arts, Historic Preservation, History & Archaeology, Libraries, Museums/Galleries, Opera, Theater
Civic & Public Affairs: Clubs, Community Foundations, Civic & Public Affairs-General, Inner-City Development, Municipalities/Towns, Parades/Festivals, Philanthropic Organizations, Public Policy, Safety, Urban & Community Affairs
Education: Agricultural Education, Arts/Humanities Education, Business Education, Colleges & Universities, Community & Junior Colleges, Education Funds, Faculty Development, Minority Education, Private Education (Precollege), Public Education (Precollege), Religious Education, Student Aid
Environment: Environment-General, Resource Conservation, Wildlife Protection
Health: Children's Health/Hospitals, Clinics/Medical Centers, Health Organizations, Heart, Home-Care Services, Hospices, Hospitals, Nursing Services
Religion: Churches, Dioceses, Religious Welfare, Seminaries
Science: Science Museums, Scientific Centers & Institutes
Social Services: Child Welfare, Community Centers, Community Service Organizations, Emergency Relief, Family Services, Homes, People with Disabilities, Recreation & Athletics, Scouts, United Funds/United Ways, Volunteer Services, YMCA/YWCA/YMHA/YWHA, Youth Organizations

Application Procedures

Initial Contact: The foundation requests applications be made in writing.
Application Requirements: Include information about individual or organization.
Deadlines: None.

Additional Information

Trust(s): Bank of America

Foundation Officials

John M. Camp, Jr.: director
Paul D. Camp, III: director
Paul Camp Marks: director
Harry W. Walker, III: director

Grants Analysis

Disclosure Period: calendar year ending 2003
Total Grants: $541,660
Number of Grants: 46
Average Grant: $6,451*
Highest Grant: $132,810
Lowest Grant: $500
Typical Range: $1,000 to $10,000

*Note: Average grant figure excludes two highest grants ($257,810).

Recent Grants

Note: Grants derived from 2001 Form 990.

Library-Related

39,000	City of Franklin, Franklin, VA
15,000	Ruth Camp Campbell Memorial Library, Franklin, VA

General

56,415	Elms Foundation, Franklin, VA
50,000	Paul D. Camp Community College, Franklin, VA
33,500	Jamestown-Yorktown Foundation, Inc., Williamsburg, VA
30,000	James L Camp Jr. YMCA, Franklin, WV
24,000	Chowan College, Murfreesboro, NC
22,300	Children's Hospital of the Kings Daughter, Norfolk, VA
21,000	Children's Center the Texle Camp Marks, Boston, MA
20,000	Carolina Ballet Theatre, Inc., Raleigh, NC
15,000	Good Shepherd Ministries, Wilmington, NC
15,000	Murfreesboro Historical Society, Murfreesboro, NC

CAMPBELL SOUP CO.

Company Headquarters

Camden, NJ
Web: http://www.campbellsoup.com

Company Description

Founded: 1922
Ticker: CPB
Exchange: NYSE
Revenue: US$7.109 billion (2004)
Profit: US$647 million (2004)
Employees: 25000 (2003)
Fortune Rank: 297, per FORTUNE Magazine's list of 500 Largest U.S. Corporations (2004).
SIC(s): 2032 Canned Specialties, 2037 Frozen Fruits & Vegetables, 2051 Bread, Cake & Related Products, 2052 Cookies & Crackers.

Operating Locations

Campbell Soup Co. (CA--Dixon, Modesto, Sacramento, Stockton; CT--Norwalk; GA--Douglas; IL--Downers Grove, West Chicago; IN--Brighton; MI--Bridgeport, Glenn, Memphis, West Bloomfield; NE--Omaha, Tecumseh; NY--New York; NC--Maxton; OH--Jackson, Napoleon, Wauseon; PA--Denver, Downingtown, Evansville, Reading; TX--Paris); Campbell Soup Co. (WI); Campbell Soup Co. (WI--Paris)
Note: Operates in Europe and South America.

Nonmonetary Support

Range: $1,000,000 - $4,000,000
Type: Donated Equipment; Donated Products; In-kind Services; Workplace Solicitation
Volunteer Programs: Foundation operates a Dollars for Doers fund to support and reward company employees who volunteer in their communities; also supports a program in which employees tutor disadvantaged youth. Giving to the United Way is determined by employee involvement.
Contact: Joan Berger, Grant Administrator

Campbell Soup Foundation

Giving Contact

Jerry S. Buckley, Chairman
Campbell Place
Camden, NJ 08103-1799
Phone: (856)342-4800
Web: http://www.campbellsoupcompany.com/community_center.asp

Description

EIN: 216019196
Organization Type: Corporate Foundation
Giving Locations: headquarters and operating communities.
Grant Types: Challenge, Employee Matching Gifts, General Support, Project.
Note: Employee matching gift ratio: 1 to 1 for education and the United Way.

Financial Summary

Total Giving: $1,457,437 (fiscal year ending June 31, 2004); $1,925,114 (fiscal 2002); $1,930,413 (fiscal 2001). Note: Contributes through corporate direct giving program and foundation.
Giving Analysis: Giving for fiscal 2002 includes: foundation matching gifts ($101,887); foundation program-related investments ($423,308); foundation grants to United Way ($485,000); fiscal 2001: foundation matching gifts ($228,287); foundation program-related investments ($398,595); foundation grants to United Way ($647,125); foundation ($656,406)
Assets: $19,799,887 (fiscal 2004); $19,842,767 (fiscal 2002); $23,747,296 (fiscal 2001)
Gifts Received: $1,000,000 (fiscal 1995); $2,000,000 (fiscal 1994). Note: Contributions were received from the Campbell Soup Company.

Typical Recipients

Arts & Humanities: Arts Centers, Community Arts, Arts & Humanities-General, Historic Preservation, Libraries, Museums/Galleries, Music, Performing Arts, Public Broadcasting, Theater, Visual Arts
Civic & Public Affairs: African American Affairs, Asian American Affairs, Botanical Gardens/Parks, Business/Free Enterprise, Chambers of Commerce, Community Foundations, Economic Development, Economic Policy, Employment/Job Training, Civic & Public Affairs-General, Hispanic Affairs, Housing, Inner-City Development, Law & Justice, Minority Business, Professional & Trade Associations, Urban & Community Affairs, Zoos/Aquariums
Education: Afterschool/Enrichment Programs, Business Education, Colleges & Universities, Community & Junior Colleges, Education Associations, Education Funds, Education Reform, Elementary Education (Public), Faculty Development, Education-General, Gifted & Talented Programs, Legal Education, Literacy, Medical Education, Minority Education, Private Education (Precollege), Public Education (Precollege), Science/Mathematics Education, Student Aid, Vocational & Technical Education
Health: AIDS/HIV, Cancer, Children's Health/Hospitals, Clinics/Medical Centers, Diabetes, Emergency/Ambulance Services, Eyes/Blindness, Health-General, Health Organizations, Heart, Hospitals, Kidney, Medical Research, Nutrition, Preventive Medicine/Wellness Organizations, Research/Studies Institutes, Single-Disease Health Associations
International: International Development, International Relief Efforts
Religion: Churches, Ministries, Religious Organizations, Religious Welfare, Synagogues/Temples
Science: Science Museums
Social Services: Animal Protection, Big Brothers/Big Sisters, Camps, Child Welfare, Community Centers, Community Service Organizations, Counseling, Crime Prevention, Day Care, Domestic Violence, Emergency Relief, Family Services, Food/Clothing Distribution, Recreation & Athletics, Scouts, Shelters/Homelessness, Social Services-General, Special Olympics, United Funds/United Ways, YMCA/YWCA/YMHA/YWHA, Youth Organizations

Application Procedures

Initial Contact: Submit a succinct proposal in letter form.
Application Requirements: Summary grant proposal and full narrative proposal, including: description of the organization, including name, address, and telephone number of contact; project objective; target population; major activities planned; timetable; project staff; means of measuring goals; historical sketch of agency and statement of current goals; statement of primary interest; project budget; other sources of funding; and proof of tax-exempt status.
Deadlines: None.
Review Process: An initial review is conducted by foundation staff; qualifying proposals are forwarded to board of trustees for a final decision. The review process may take up to three months.
Evaluative Criteria: Proposal must apply to one of the foundation's giving areas; organization must demonstrate it has a positive history and strong leadership; proposal must be clear and compelling as well as produce measurable results; project must be visible enough to solicit additional support from other funding sources.
Decision Notification: Applicant will be notified of any delays. Decision is received in writing.

Restrictions

The foundation does not make multiyear grants.
The foundation only accepts proposals submitted in writing. An organization can only submit similar proposals once in a 12-month period. Grants do not exceed $100,000.
The foundation does not support individuals; organizations outside the United States; discriminatory organizations; organizations not defined as tax-exempt under Section 501(c)(3) of the Internal Revenue Code; fraternal, political, or lobbying organizations; or goodwill advertising, dinners, or special events. tax-exempt under Section 501(c)(3) of the Internal Revenue Code; fraternal, political, or lobbying organizations; or goodwill advertising, dinners, or special events.

Additional Information

The foundation is increasing emphasis on reinforcing employee charitable activities. Because of this increased emphasis, the foundation is no longer funding initiatives in the area of diet and health.
Publications: Foundation Annual Report

Corporate Officials

Jerry S. Buckley: senior vice president public affairs B 1954. PRIM CORP EMPL vice president public affairs: Campbell Soup Co.
Ellen O. Kaden: senior vice president B New York, NY 1951. ED Cornell University BA (1972); Chicago State University MA (1973); Columbia University JD (1977). PRIM CORP EMPL senior vice president Law & government: Campbell Soup Co. NONPR AFFIL trustee: Institute Judicial Administration; member: National Legal Aid & Defender Association; trustee: Columbia University; member: Committee Civil Rights.

Foundation Officials

Jerry S. Buckley: chairman, trustee (see above)
Carlos del Sol: vice chairman, trustee
A. Fred George: trustee PRIM CORP EMPL branch manager: Campbell Soup Co.
Steve M. Jander: trustee
J. Gonzalez Joseph: program director
K. Lewis: trustee
M. Linder: trustee
G. S. Lord: controller
W. Milanese: secretary
W. J. O'Shea: treasurer

Grants Analysis

Disclosure Period: fiscal year ending June 31, 2004
Total Grants: $995,170*
Number of Grants: 74
Average Grant: $12,057*
Highest Grant: $115,000
Lowest Grant: $2,000
Typical Range: $1,000 to $20,000
***Note:** Giving excludes matching gifts; United Way; and program-related investments. Average grant figure excludes highest grant.

Recent Grants

Note: Grants derived from 2003 Form 990.
General

40,989	United Way of Henry County & Martinsville, Martinsville, VA
36,102	United Way of Lancaster County, Lancaster, PA
35,550	United Way of Lamar County, Paris, TX
29,702	United Way of Norwalk & Wilton, Norwalk, CT
25,000	Boys & Girls Clubs of America, Atlanta, GA
25,000	Neighborhood Center Inc.
25,000	Rowan - CHAMP Summer Camp, Camden, NJ
25,000	Walt Whitman Cultural Arts Center, Camden, NJ
21,000	Perkins Center for the Arts, Moorestown, NJ
21,000	Philadelphia Youth Tennis Inc., Manayunk, PA

FRANK A. CAMPINI FOUNDATION

Giving Contact

Paul J. Ruby, Director
220 Sansome St., Suite 700
San Francisco, CA 94104
Phone: (415)421-4171
Fax: (415)391-9997

Description

Founded: 1960
EIN: 946107956
Organization Type: Private Foundation
Giving Locations: CA: San Francisco Bay Area
Grant Types: General Support.

Donor Information

Founder: the late Frank A. Campini

Financial Summary

Total Giving: $1,040,000 (2003); $1,156,000 (2001)
Giving Analysis: Giving for 2003 includes: foundation scholarships ($11,000); 2001: foundation scholarships ($34,000)
Assets: $22,736,050 (2003); $23,176,214 (2001)

Typical Recipients

Arts & Humanities: Libraries, Museums/Galleries, Music, Opera, Public Broadcasting, Theater
Civic & Public Affairs: Botanical Gardens/Parks, Civic & Public Affairs-General, Urban & Community Affairs, Zoos/Aquariums
Education: Colleges & Universities, Economic Education, Environmental Education, Health & Physical Education, International Studies, Private Education (Precollege), Secondary Education (Public), Student Aid
Environment: Forestry, Environment-General, Resource Conservation
Health: AIDS/HIV, Cancer, Children's Health/Hospitals, Clinics/Medical Centers, Hospices, Medical Research, Preventive Medicine/Wellness Organi-

zations, Single-Disease Health Associations
International: Foreign Educational Institutions, Missionary/Religious Activities
Religion: Jewish Causes, Religious Welfare
Science: Scientific Centers & Institutes
Social Services: Child Welfare, Community Service Organizations, Crime Prevention, Domestic Violence, Family Services, Food/Clothing Distribution, Homes, Youth Organizations

Application Procedures

Initial Contact: Send a brief letter of inquiry.
Application Requirements: Include a description of organization, proof of tax-exempt status, amount requested, recently audited financial statement, and purpose of funds sought.
Deadlines: October 1.

Restrictions

Does not support individuals, religious organizations for sectarian purposes, political or lobbying groups, or organizations outside operating areas.

Foundation Officials

Hendrika C. Neys: director
Patricia Neys: secretary, treasurer
Paul J. Ruby: director

Grants Analysis

Disclosure Period: calendar year ending 2003
Total Grants: $1,029,000*
Number of Grants: 60
Average Grant: $15,746*
Highest Grant: $100,000
Lowest Grant: $1,000
Typical Range: $5,000 to $25,000
***Note:** Giving excludes scholarships. Average grant figure excludes highest grant.

Recent Grants

Note: Grants derived from 2001 Form 990.
General

104,000	Boys and Girls Club of San Francisco, San Francisco, CA
60,000	Audubon Canyon Ranch, Stinson Beach, CA
50,000	Alan Neys Memorial Fund
50,000	Family House, San Francisco, CA -- capital campaign
50,000	Fine Arts Museums of San Francisco, San Francisco, CA -- Rebuild de Young Fund
50,000	Friends of Recreation and Parks, San Francisco, CA -- Windmill Project
50,000	Jewish Federation of the Greater East Bay, San Francisco, CA
47,000	University of California San Francisco, San Francisco, CA -- Scientist Fellow Program
35,000	University of California San Francisco, San Francisco, CA -- Pediatric Oncology Clinical Research
25,000	California Academy of Sciences, San Francisco, CA

CANDLESTICKS INC.

Company Headquarters

New York, NY

Company Description

Employees: 5
SIC(s): 2300 Apparel & Other Textile Products, 5100 Wholesale Trade--Nondurable Goods.

Lawrence Foundation

Giving Contact

Leonard Bernstein, Trustee
Lawrence Foundation
112 West 34th Street
New York, NY 10120-0101
Phone: (212)947-8900
Fax: (212)643-9653

Description

EIN: 132880731
Organization Type: Corporate Foundation
Grant Types: General Support.

Financial Summary

Total Giving: $64,500 (fiscal year ending September 30, 2004); $62,300 (fiscal 2001)
Giving Analysis: Giving for fiscal 2004 includes: foundation scholarships ($4,000); fiscal 2001: foundation scholarships ($4,000)
Assets: $1,199,682 (fiscal 2004); $1,284,378 (fiscal 2001)
Gifts Received: $5,000 (fiscal 2004); $5,000 (fiscal 2001); $43,000 (fiscal 2000). Note: Contributions were received from Candlesticks, Inc. and Lancaster Industries.

Typical Recipients

Arts & Humanities: History & Archaeology, Libraries, Literary Arts, Public Broadcasting
Civic & Public Affairs: African American Affairs, Civil Rights, Economic Development, Gay/Lesbian Issues, Civic & Public Affairs-General, Law & Justice, Safety, Urban & Community Affairs
Education: Elementary Education (Private), School Volunteerism
Environment: Air/Water Quality
Health: AIDS/HIV, Cancer, Hospitals
International: Human Rights, International Peace & Security Issues, International Relations
Religion: Churches, Jewish Causes, Religious Organizations, Religious Welfare
Social Services: Animal Protection, Camps, Community Centers, Community Service Organizations, Crime Prevention, Delinquency & Criminal Rehabilitation, Domestic Violence, Food/Clothing Distribution, Senior Services, Shelters/Homelessness, Substance Abuse

Application Procedures

Initial Contact: Send a brief letter of inquiry.
Application Requirements: Include a description of organization, purpose of funds sought, and proof of tax-exempt status.
Deadlines: None.

Restrictions

Foundation does not support individuals or religious organizations.

Additional Information

Provides scholarships to students of Donegal High School, Mount Joy, PA.

Corporate Officials

Leonard S. Bernstein: chairman, president, chief executive officer B 1931. PRIM CORP EMPL chairman, president, chief executive officer: Candlesticks ADD CORP EMPL president: Donegal Industries Inc.; president: Lawrence Childrens Underwear Co.

Foundation Officials

Jay S. Bernstein: trustee B 1934. PRIM CORP EMPL vice president: Candlesticks Inc. ADD CORP EMPL vice president: Donnegal Industries Inc.; secretary: Lawrence Children's Underwear Co.
Lawrence Bernstein: trustee PRIM CORP EMPL vice president: Candlesticks Inc.
Leonard S. Bernstein: trustee (see above)

Grants Analysis

Disclosure Period: fiscal year ending September 30, 2004
Total Grants: $60,500*
Number of Grants: 19
Average Grant: $3,184
Highest Grant: $7,000
Lowest Grant: $500
Typical Range: $1,000 to $5,000
*Note:** Giving excludes scholarship.

Recent Grants

Note: Grants derived from fiscal 2004 Form 990.
General

7,000	American Civil Liberties Union Foundation, New York, NY
7,000	Center to Prevent Handgun Violence, Washington, DC
7,000	Coalition for the Homeless, Albany, NY
7,000	Fresh Air Fund, New York, NY
5,000	Phoenix House, New York, NY
5,000	Variety Child Learning Center, Syosset, NY
3,000	Coalition Against Domestic Violence, Denver, CO
3,000	Gay Men's Health Crisis, New York, NY
3,000	God's Love We Deliver, New York, NY
3,000	Memorial Sloan-Kettering Cancer Center, New York, NY

THE CANNON FOUNDATION, INC.

Giving Contact

Frank Davis, Executive Director
57 Union Street South
PO Box 548
Concord, NC 28026-0548
Phone: (704)786-8216
Fax: (704)785-2052
E-mail: fdavis@cannonfoundationinc.org
Web: http://www.thecannonfoundationinc.org

Description

Founded: 1943
EIN: 566042532
Organization Type: General Purpose Foundation
Giving Locations: NC
Grant Types: Capital, Challenge, General Support, Project.

Donor Information

Founder: Established in 1943 by the late Charles A. Cannon, who was president and chairman of Cannon Mills for more than 50 years.

Financial Summary

Total Giving: $9,016,318 (fiscal year ending September 30, 2003); $9,800,000 (fiscal 2002 approx); $9,822,749 (fiscal 2001)
Assets: $167,292,016 (fiscal 2003); $156,823,687 (fiscal 2002 approx); $182,160,484 (fiscal 2001)

Typical Recipients

Arts & Humanities: Arts Centers, Historic Preservation, History & Archaeology, Libraries, Museums/Galleries, Music, Performing Arts, Theater
Civic & Public Affairs: Clubs, Employment/Job Training, Civic & Public Affairs-General, Housing, Inner-City Development, Legal Aid, Nonprofit Management, Philanthropic Organizations, Public Policy, Rural Affairs, Safety, Urban & Community Affairs, Women's Affairs, Zoos/Aquariums
Education: Agricultural Education, Arts/Humanities Education, Business-School Partnerships, Colleges & Universities, Community & Junior Colleges, Education Associations, Education Funds, Environmental Education, Faculty Development, Education-General, Health & Physical Education, Literacy, Minority Education, Private Education (Precollege), Public Education (Precollege), Religious Education, Science/Mathematics Education, Social Sciences Education
Environment: Air/Water Quality, Energy, Forestry, Resource Conservation
Health: Adolescent Health Issues, AIDS/HIV, Cancer, Children's Health/Hospitals, Clinics/Medical Centers, Emergency/Ambulance Services, Health-General, Geriatric Health, Health Organizations, Home-Care Services, Hospices, Hospitals, Hospitals (University Affiliated), Nutrition, Prenatal Health Issues, Preventive Medicine/Wellness Organizations, Public Health, Research/Studies Institutes, Transplant Networks/Donor Banks
Religion: Bible Study/Translation, Churches, Ministries, Religious Organizations, Religious Welfare, Seminaries
Science: Science Museums, Scientific Centers & Institutes
Social Services: Camps, Child Welfare, Community Centers, Community Service Organizations, Domestic Violence, Emergency Relief, Family Planning, Family Services, Food/Clothing Distribution, Homes, People with Disabilities, Recreation & Athletics, Scouts, Senior Services, Social Services-General, Special Olympics, Substance Abuse, YMCA/YWCA/YMHA/YWHA, Youth Organizations

Application Procedures

Initial Contact: Applicants should send a proposal of no more than five pages to the foundation. The foundation provides an application form.
Application Requirements: Proposals should include an explanation of the need for the project; objectives and purposes, and how they will be met; description of applying organization; qualifications of persons responsible for project or program; form 990; location and duration of program; evaluative criteria; most recent audit report and one-page line item budget; list of the organization's governing board; and proof of tax-exempt status.
Deadlines: The foundation receives and considers applications on a quarterly basis. Applications are due by January 15, April 15, July 15, or October 15.

Restrictions

The foundation does not make loans or grants to individuals or for endowments. Scholarship grants and recurring grants are not funded.

Additional Information

Applicants must show evidence that the project can be sustained on a continuing basis.
Publications: Guidelines; Application Form

Foundation Officials

William C. Cannon, Jr.: director, president
William M. Connolly: director, member
William S. Fisher: vice president, director, member
Thomas M. Grady: member, director
Dan L. Gray: secretary, treasurer, director, member
Mariam C. Hayes: director, member B 1918. PRIM CORP EMPL president: Central Distributing Co.
Robert C. Hayes: director, member
George W. Liles, Jr.: director, member
Elizabeth L. Quick: director, member B Izmir, Turkey 1948. ED Duke University AB (1970); University of North Carolina JD (1974). PRIM CORP EMPL attorney: Womble Carlyle Sandridge & Rice. NONPR AFFIL member: Forsyth County Bar Association; member: North Carolina Bar Association; member: American Bar Association; member: Fellow American College Trust & Estate Counsel.

Grants Analysis

Disclosure Period: fiscal year ending September 30, 2003
Total Grants: $9,016,318
Number of Grants: 121
Average Grant: $54,759*
Highest Grant: $2,000,000
Lowest Grant: $1,400
Typical Range: $25,000 to $100,000
*Note:** Average grant figure excludes highest two grants ($2,500,000).

Recent Grants

Note: Grants derived from fiscal 2003 Form 990.
General

2,000,000	Cabarrus Memorial Hospital, Concord, NC -- towards interventional radiology services and pediatric renovations
500,000	Hospice of Cabarrus County Inc., Concord, NC
430,000	Cabarrus Memorial Hospital, Concord, NC -- towards professional educational program
350,000	Cabarrus County Schools, Concord, NC -- towards dance learning centers
250,000	Cabarrus Cooperative Christian Ministry Inc., Concord, NC
250,000	Cabarrus County, Concord, NC
250,000	Central North Carolina Council Boy Scouts of America Inc., Albemarle, NC -- for camp Barnhardt aquatics facility
250,000	Charles A. Cannon Jr. Memorial Hospital Inc., Linville, NC
250,000	Community Free Clinic, Concord, NC -- for facility acquisition
250,000	NorthEast Medical Center Foundation Inc., Concord, NC

CANON U.S.A. INC.

Company Headquarters

1 Canon Plaza
Great Neck, NY 11024-1198
Web: http://www.usa.canon.com

Company Description

Employees: 8,700
SIC(s): 3577 Computer Peripheral Equipment Nec.
Parent Company: Canon Inc., 30-2, Shimomaruko 3-chome, Ohta-ku, Tokyo, Japan

Operating Locations

Ambassador Office Equipment (IL--Schaumburg); Astro Business Solutions (CA--Gardena); Canon Computer Systems (CA--Costa Mesa); Canon Financial Services (NJ--Burlington); Canon Latin America (FL--Miami); Canon U.S.A. (NY--Lake Success); Dupli-fax (NJ--Burlington); MCS Business Solutions (NY--New York)

Nonmonetary Support

Type: Donated Equipment; Donated Products

Giving Contact

John Lese, Asst. Dir. Corp. Programs
One Canon Plz.
Lake Success, NY 11042
Phone: (516)328-4928
Fax: (516)328-5149

Description

Organization Type: Corporate Giving Program

Typical Recipients

Arts & Humanities: Arts Centers, Historic Preservation, Libraries, Museums/Galleries, Performing Arts, Public Broadcasting
Civic & Public Affairs: Municipalities/Towns, Urban & Community Affairs, Women's Affairs
Education: Colleges & Universities, Elementary Education (Private)
Environment: Resource Conservation
Health: Health Organizations, Medical Research

Religion: Religious Organizations
Social Services: Community Service Organizations, People with Disabilities, United Funds/United Ways, Youth Organizations

Application Procedures
Initial Contact: Send a brief introductory letter on organizational letterhead.

Additional Information
Canon U.S.A. sponsors a "Clean Earth Campaign" in conjunction with the National Wildlife Federation and the Nature Conservancy. The program has several purposes: it helps to keep the environment clean by encouraging customers to return used toner cartridges to the company, free of charge, instead of disposing of them in the trash; it conserves industrial resources by utilizing the recyclable portion of the cartridge to create new ones; and it helps to protect wildlife and the environment because the National Wildlife Federation and the Nature Conservancy share equally a $1-per-cartridge contribution from Canon. For more information, contact Canon U.S.A., Inc., at 1-800-962-2708. Canon also has manufacturing subsidiaries operating in California and Virginia and research and development operations in California.

Corporate Officials
Seymour Liebman: executive vice president finance, chief financial officer PRIM CORP EMPL executive vice president finance, chief financial officer: Canon U.S.A.
Haruo Murase: chairman, president, chief executive officer PRIM CORP EMPL chairman, president, chief executive officer: Canon U.S.A.

CAPE BRANCH FOUNDATION

Giving Contact
Scarlet S. Johnson, Trustee
PO Box 86
Oldwick, NJ 08858
Phone: (908)439-2357
Fax: (609)452-1025

Description
Founded: 1964
EIN: 226054886
Organization Type: Private Foundation
Giving Locations: NJ
Grant Types: Capital, General Support, Research.

Financial Summary
Total Giving: $1,532,165 (2003); $1,536,060 (2001)
Assets: $23,171,271 (2003); $23,068,840 (2001)

Typical Recipients
Arts & Humanities: Arts Associations & Councils, Arts Centers, Arts Outreach, Dance, Arts & Humanities-General, Libraries, Museums/Galleries, Music, Performing Arts
Civic & Public Affairs: Civic & Public Affairs-General, Law & Justice, Municipalities/Towns, Urban & Community Affairs, Women's Affairs
Education: Arts/Humanities Education, Colleges & Universities, Education Funds, Education-General, Literacy, Medical Education, Private Education (Precollege), Public Education (Precollege), Secondary Education (Private), Student Aid
Environment: Air/Water Quality, Environment-General, Protection, Resource Conservation, Watershed
Health: AIDS/HIV, Health-General, Hospitals, Medical Rehabilitation, Medical Research, Research/Studies Institutes, Single-Disease Health Associa-

tions
International: Health Care/Hospitals
Religion: Churches, Jewish Causes, Religious Welfare
Science: Scientific Research
Social Services: Camps, Community Service Organizations, Day Care, Family Planning, Family Services, People with Disabilities, Recreation & Athletics, Youth Organizations

Application Procedures
Initial Contact: Send a brief letter of inquiry.
Application Requirements: Outline purpose of funds sought and include amount requested.
Deadlines: None.

Restrictions
The foundation does not support individuals, religious organizations for sectarian purposes, or political or lobbying groups.

Foundation Officials
Gordon O. Danser: trustee
Frank Joseph Hoenemeyer: trustee CORP AFFIL director: American International Group.
Gretchen W. Johnson: trustee, director
James Lawrence Johnson: director B Vernon, TX 1927. ED Texas Technology University BBA (1949). PRIM CORP EMPL chairman emeritus: GTE Corp. CORP AFFIL director: Walter Industries Inc.; director: First Federal Savings & Loan Association; director: Mutual Life Insurance Co.; director: CellStar Corp.; director: BC Telecommunications Co.; director: Bloomington Unlimited. NONPR AFFIL member: Wesleyan Associates; member: Wesleyan University; member: National Association Accountants; director: McLean County Association Commerce Industries; trustee, member advisory council: Mennonite Hospital; member advisory council: Illinois State University College Business; director: Illinois Telephone Association; member: Financial Executives Institute. CLUB AFFIL Rotary Club; Woodway Country Club; Bloomington Country Club; Crestwicke Country Club.

Grants Analysis
Disclosure Period: calendar year ending 2003
Total Grants: $1,532,165
Number of Grants: 11
Average Grant: $51,508*
Highest Grant: $733,593
Lowest Grant: $5,000
Typical Range: $20,000 to $100,000
*Note: Average grant figure excludes two highest grants ($1,068,593).

Recent Grants
Note: Grants derived from 2001 Form 990.

General

500,000	Willow School, Gladstone, NJ
201,889	Edison Wetlands Association, Edison, NJ
150,000	Matheny School and Hospital, Peapack, NJ -- arts auditorium campaign
125,000	Institute for Democracy Studies, New York, NY
100,000	Town of Jupiter Island, Hobe Sound, FL -- for land conservation
100,000	United States Equestrian Team, Gladstone, NJ
75,000	Artistic Realization Technologies, Inc., Belle Mead, NJ
52,171	Blairsden Association, New York, NY
50,000	Center for Law and Reproductive Policy, New York, NY
50,000	Girls, Inc., New York, NY

CAPE COD FIVE CENTS SAVINGS BANK

Company Headquarters
PO Box 10
Orleans, MA 02653
Web: http://www.capecodfive.com

Cape Cod Five Cents Savings Bank Charitable Trust

Giving Contact
Ronald E. Reed, Treasurer
Cape Cod Five Cents Savings Bank Charitable Trust
PO Box 10
Orleans, MA 02653-0010
Phone: (508)240-0555

Description
Founded: 1998
EIN: 043423249
Organization Type: Corporate Foundation
Giving Locations: primarily Massachusetts.
Grant Types: Capital, General Support, Matching, Scholarship.

Financial Summary
Total Giving: $273,367 (2003); $251,103 (2002); $206,282 (2001)
Giving Analysis: Giving for 2001 includes: foundation grants to United Way ($2,000)
Assets: $10,452,172 (2003); $6,011,236 (2002); $4,281,145 (2001)
Gifts Received: $3,834,931 (2003); $1,740,000 (2002); $1,427,350 (2001). Note: Contributions received from Cape Cod Five Cents Savings Bank.

Typical Recipients
Arts & Humanities: Arts Associations & Councils, History & Archaeology, Libraries, Museums/Galleries, Music, Performing Arts, Public Broadcasting, Theater
Civic & Public Affairs: Botanical Gardens/Parks, Business/Free Enterprise, Housing
Education: Community & Junior Colleges, Education-General, Student Aid
Environment: Air/Water Quality, Energy, Environment-General, Protection, Resource Conservation
Health: AIDS/HIV, Clinics/Medical Centers, Health-General, Health Funds, Health Organizations, Hospices, Medical Rehabilitation, Nursing Services
Social Services: Big Brothers/Big Sisters, Child Welfare, Community Centers, Community Service Organizations, People with Disabilities, Recreation & Athletics, Senior Services, Shelters/Homelessness

Application Procedures
Initial Contact: The foundation has no specific application procedure. Submit a brief letter of inquiry.
Application Requirements: Include a description of organization, amount requested, purpose of funds sought, recently audited financial statement, and proof of tax-exempt status.
Deadlines: None.

Restrictions
Requests must be for more than $250 and must be for a publicly support entity.

Foundation Officials
Elliot Carr: chairman
Ronald Reed: treasurer
David Williard: secretary

Grants Analysis

Disclosure Period: calendar year ending 2003
Total Grants: $273,367
Number of Grants: 161
Average Grant: $1,698*
Highest Grant: $19,104
Lowest Grant: $200
Typical Range: $500 to $3,000
*Note: Average grant figure excludes highest grant.

Recent Grants

Note: Grants derived from 2001 Form 990.
General

10,000	Cape Cod Concert Opera Inc., North Chatham, MA -- new technology building
10,000	Healthcare Foundation of Cape Cod, Inc., Cape Cod, MA -- Long Pond Medical Center
7,500	National Marine Life Center, Buzzards Bay, MA
5,000	Compact of Cape Cod Conservation Trusts, Barnstable, MA -- development of Chase Park
5,000	Dennis Conservation Trust, East Dennis, MA -- land purchase
5,000	Friends of Pleasant Bay Inc., South Orleans, MA
5,000	Healthcare Foundation of Cape Cod, Inc., Cape Cod, MA -- purchase blanket warmer
5,000	O'Neill Health Center Inc, Hyannis, MA -- Nauset Regional High School
5,000	Orenda Wildlife Trust, West Barnstable, MA -- land purchase
3,700	Berkshire Area Health Education Center, Pittsfield, MA -- Ellen Jones Dental Center

CARGILL INC.

Company Headquarters

Minneapolis, MN
Web: http://www.cargill.com

Company Description

Revenue: US$50.826 billion (2002)
Employees: 98000 (2003)
SIC(s): 2041 Flour & Other Grain Mill Products, 4424 Deep Sea Domestic Transportation of Freight, 5153 Grain & Field Beans, 6221 Commodity Contracts Brokers & Dealers.

Operating Locations

Cargill Inc. (CA--Newark; FL--Riverview; ID--Idaho Falls; IL--Chicago; MA--Beverly; MN--Minnetonka, Monticello, Wayzata; TN--Cordova; WI--Jefferson, Sheboygan).

Nonmonetary Support

Type: Donated Equipment; Donated Products; Loaned Executives
Contact: Mark Murphy
Note: Co. provides nonmonetary support.

Cargill Foundation

Giving Contact

Toni Green, Senior Program Officer
Cargill Foundation
PO Box 5650
Minneapolis, MN 55440-5632
Phone: (952)742-6290
E-mail: toni_green@cargill.com
Web: http://www.cargill.com/commun/found.htm

Alternate Contact

Stacey Smida, Grants Administrator
Cargill Foundation
Phone: (952)742-4311
E-mail: stacey_smida@cargill.com

Description

EIN: 416020221
Organization Type: Corporate Foundation
Giving Locations: MN: Minneapolis including western and northern suburbs headquarters and operating locations; internationally; nationally.
Grant Types: Capital, Emergency, Employee Matching Gifts, General Support, Multiyear/Continuing Support, Project.

Financial Summary

Total Giving: $5,600,000 (2003); $5,402,465 (2002); $6,122,457 (2001). Note: Contributes through corporate direct giving program and foundation.
Giving Analysis: Giving for 2001 includes: foundation grants to United Way ($1,109,268); foundation ($5,013,189).
Assets: $69,221,492 (2003); $50,409,647 (2002); $66,814,267 (2001)
Gifts Received: $12,000,000 (2003); $250,000 (2001); $2,600,000 (1999). Note: Contributions were received from Cargill, Inc., Cargill Financial Services Corp., and North Star Steel Co.

Typical Recipients

Arts & Humanities: Arts Associations & Councils, Arts Centers, Arts Institutes, Arts Outreach, Ethnic & Folk Arts, Arts & Humanities-General, Historic Preservation, History & Archaeology, Libraries, Museums/Galleries, Music, Opera, Public Broadcasting, Theater
Civic & Public Affairs: African American Affairs, Botanical Gardens/Parks, Chambers of Commerce, Community Foundations, Economic Development, Employment/Job Training, Ethnic Organizations, Civic & Public Affairs-General, Housing, Law & Justice, Legal Aid, Minority Business, Native American Affairs, Nonprofit Management, Professional & Trade Associations, Public Policy, Rural Affairs, Safety, Urban & Community Affairs, Women's Affairs, Zoos/Aquariums
Education: Afterschool/Enrichment Programs, Agricultural Education, Arts/Humanities Education, Business Education, Colleges & Universities, Community & Junior Colleges, Economic Education, Education Funds, Education Reform, Elementary Education (Private), Engineering/Technological Education, Faculty Development, Education-General, Leadership Training, Literacy, Medical Education, Minority Education, Preschool Education, Private Education (Precollege), Public Education (Precollege), Religious Education, Science/Mathematics Education, Social Sciences Education, Special Education, Student Aid, Vocational & Technical Education
Environment: Environment-General, Resource Conservation
Health: AIDS/HIV, Cancer, Children's Health/Hospitals, Clinics/Medical Centers, Emergency/Ambulance Services, Eyes/Blindness, Health Organizations, Hospitals
International: International Environmental Issues, International Relief Efforts
Religion: Churches, Religious Welfare
Science: Science Museums, Scientific Centers & Institutes
Social Services: At-Risk Youth, Big Brothers/Big Sisters, Child Welfare, Community Centers, Community Service Organizations, Crime Prevention, Day Care, Domestic Violence, Family Planning, Family Services, Food/Clothing Distribution, People with Disabilities, Recreation & Athletics, Scouts, Senior Services, Sexual Abuse, Shelters/Homelessness, Substance Abuse, United Funds/United Ways, YMCA/YWCA/YMHA/YWHA, Youth Organizations

Application Procedures

Initial Contact: Contact the foundation or visit the foundation's web site to obtain guidelines and an application cover sheet.
Application Requirements: Initial applications should be no more than two typed pages plus a completed application cover sheet. All applications should include proof of tax-exempt status; a description of organization, its mission, and a brief organization history; and a statement of what type of funding is being requested (General Operating, Project, Program, Innovation, or Capital). The foundation requests that all applications (except Capital Grant requests) address the following questions in this order: (1) How does your organization, project, program or concept "Prepare the next generation for success in school, work and life?" (2) How does your organization and/or program demonstrate leadership and effectiveness? (3) Describe the project, program or proposed concept for which you are requesting funds, and explain the need. If a project or program, is it existing or new? If existing, how old is it? (4) Which Cargill Foundation priority or priorities does your organization, project, program, or proposed concept serve? (6) Is there a specific gender or ethnic group that your organization, project, program, or proposed concept serves? For a Capital Grant, the following questions should be answered: Why is capital support needed? Are you currently in a capital campaign? If so, how much have you raised to date? How will capital dollars strengthen your organization?
Deadlines: None.
Review Process: The initial application is reviewed by foundation staff to ensure that the applicant's activities and programs coincide with the foundation's mission. If the foundation approves of the initial application, the applicant will be asked to schedule a site visit. The site visit will allow the foundation staff to observe the organization and its programs, and discuss the applicant's proposal. Upon a successful site visit, the foundation will send a letter confirming its interest in the applicant's proposal, and will request additional information to generate a formal proposal. Formal proposals are considered by foundation staff prior to being presented to the foundation's board of directors.
Evaluative Criteria: The foundation prefers to fund organizations with a well-articulated mission; a clear strategic plan; programs that are considered models in their field; a strong executive director and motivated staff; solid financial reporting and performance; a board the governs responsibly; an entrepreneurial approach; carefully-determined program goals and objectives with documented results; and a demonstrated willingness and ability to take calculated risks.
Decision Notification: Initial applications are responded to by mail within four weeks.
Notes: The Cargill Citizenship Committee addresses regional and national organizations seeking support for community service initiatives or projects in the company's operating communities outside the Twin Cities area. The Committee's corporate grantmaking guidelines were under review at press time. The company reported that revised guidelines should be available on Cargill's web site in late 2003.

Restrictions

The foundation does not support individuals; athletic scholarships; religious organizations for sectarian purposes; membership in civic organizations or trade associations; benefit fundraising events or tickets; endowments or endowment campaigns; recognition or testimonial events; fundraising campaigns for disease-specific organizations or for medical research; fraternal, veterans', or professional associations; public service or political campaigns/lobbying; conferences; or travel expenses.

Due to funding limitations, no funding is provided for youth facing physical or mental challenges; programs that primarily serve adults; summer programs; juvenile offender programs; faith-based organizations;

programs that serve children whose parents are incarcerated or have serious medical problems; homes or shelters for children; or organizations that serve the medical or dental needs of children.

Additional Information
Cargill is taking steps toward achieving a target of two percent of domestic pre-tax earnings for its U.S.-based contributions.
Publications: Guidelines Sheet

Corporate Officials
Robbin S. Johnson: corporate vice president public affairs PRIM CORP EMPL senior vice president, corporate affairs: Cargill Inc.
James D. Moe: corporate vice president, general counsel, secretary ED Stanford University AB (1962); University of Minnesota LLB (1965). PRIM CORP EMPL corporate vice president, general counsel, secretary: Cargill Inc.
Nancy P. Siska: corp. vice president human resources PRIM CORP EMPL corp. vice president human resources: Cargill Inc..
Warren R. Staley: chairman, chief executive officer B May 14, 1942. ED Kansas State University BA (1965); Cornell University MBA (1967). PRIM CORP EMPL chairman, chief executive officer: Cargill Inc.
Tyrone K. Thayer: corp. vice president PRIM CORP EMPL corp. vice president: Cargill Inc. CORP AFFIL director: North Star Steel Co.

Giving Program Officials
James D. Moe: member contributions committee (see above)
Nancy P. Siska: member contributions committee (see above)
Warren R. Staley: member contributions committee (see above)
Tyrone K. Thayer: member contributions committee (see above)

Foundation Officials
Robbin S. Johnson: vice president (see above)
Katherine Kersten: director, treasurer PRIM NONPR EMPL chairman: Center for the American Experiment.
Thomas O. Moe: secretary B Des Moines, IA 1938. ED University of Minnesota BA (1960); University of Minnesota LLB (1963). PRIM CORP EMPL chairman: Dorsey & Whitney. NONPR AFFIL member: Order Coif.
Frank L. Sims: director, vice president
Warren R. Staley: president (see above)

Grants Analysis
Disclosure Period: calendar year ending 2003
Total Grants: $4,800,000*
Number of Grants: 71
Average Grant: $45,797*
Highest Grant: $1,000,000
Lowest Grant: $1,000
Typical Range: $10,000 to $100,000
*Note: Giving excludes United Way. Average grant figure excludes two highest grants ($1,640,000).

Recent Grants
Note: Grants derived from 2003 Form 990.
General
1,000,000	University of Minnesota Foundation, Minneapolis, MN
800,000	Greater Twin Cities United Way, Minneapolis, MN
640,000	Neighborhood Involvement Program Inc., Minneapolis, MN
179,825	Minnesota Humanities Commission, St. Paul, MN
128,874	Neighborhood Involvement Program Inc., Minneapolis, MN
125,000	Learning Disabilities Association Inc., Minneapolis, MN
116,400	Stages Theatre Company, Hopkins, MN
100,000	Achieve! Minneapolis, Minneapolis, MN
100,000	Neighborhood Involvement Program Inc., Minneapolis, MN
80,000	Gilder Lehrman Institute of American History, New York, NY

CARILLON IMPORTERS LTD.

Company Headquarters
Teaneck, NJ

Company Description
Employees: 54
SIC(s): 2084 Wines, Brandy & Brandy Spirits, 2085 Distilled & Blended Liquors.
Parent Company: Diageo PLC, 8 Henrietta Place, London, United Kingdom

Grand Marnier Foundation

Giving Contact
Serge Bellanger
717 Fifth Ave., 22nd Fl.
New York, NY 10022

Description
EIN: 133258414
Organization Type: Corporate Foundation
Giving Locations: CA; MD; NY: nationally.
Grant Types: General Support.

Financial Summary
Total Giving: $849,087 (2003); $485,900 (2001).
Note: Contributes through foundation only.
Assets: $4,235,143 (2003); $5,665,145 (2001)

Typical Recipients
Arts & Humanities: Arts Associations & Councils, Arts Centers, Arts Funds, Arts Institutes, Arts Outreach, Ballet, Dance, Ethnic & Folk Arts, Film & Video, Arts & Humanities-General, History & Archaeology, Libraries, Museums/Galleries, Music, Opera, Performing Arts, Public Broadcasting, Theater, Visual Arts
Civic & Public Affairs: Botanical Gardens/Parks, Clubs, Employment/Job Training, Ethnic Organizations, Civic & Public Affairs-General, Hispanic Affairs, Housing, Native American Affairs, Parades/Festivals, Philanthropic Organizations, Professional & Trade Associations, Women's Affairs
Education: Arts/Humanities Education, Business Education, Colleges & Universities, Continuing Education, Engineering/Technological Education, Education-General, International Exchange, International Studies, Leadership Training, Literacy, Medical Education, Minority Education, Private Education (Precollege), Public Education (Precollege), Science/ Mathematics Education, Social Sciences Education, Student Aid, Vocational & Technical Education
Environment: Air/Water Quality
Health: AIDS/HIV, Alzheimer's Disease, Cancer, Children's Health/Hospitals, Clinics/Medical Centers, Emergency/Ambulance Services, Health Organizations, Heart, Hospitals, Medical Research, Nutrition, Single-Disease Health Associations
International: Foreign Arts Organizations, Foreign Educational Institutions, International Development, International Organizations, International Peace & Security Issues, International Relations, International Relief Efforts, Missionary/Religious Activities
Religion: Churches, Jewish Causes, Religious Welfare, Synagogues/Temples
Science: Scientific Research
Social Services: Child Abuse, Child Welfare, Com-munity Service Organizations, Crime Prevention, Emergency Relief, Family Services, Food/Clothing Distribution, People with Disabilities, Recreation & Athletics, Shelters/Homelessness, Social Services-General, Youth Organizations

Application Procedures
Initial Contact: Submit a brief letter.
Application Requirements: Include a description of organization, amount requested, purpose of funds sought, recently audited financial statement, and proof of tax-exempt status.
Deadlines: None.

Corporate Officials
Michel Roux: president, chief executive officer, director B 1941. PRIM CORP EMPL president, chief executive officer, director: Carillon Importers, Ltd.

Foundation Officials
Jerry Ciraulo: treasurer, director PRIM CORP EMPL chief executive officer: Carillon Importers Ltd.
Maxime Coury: director B Alexandria, Egypt 1925.
Michel Roux: president, director (see above)

Grants Analysis
Disclosure Period: calendar year ending 2003
Total Grants: $849,087
Number of Grants: 124
Average Grant: $5,032*
Highest Grant: $80,000
Lowest Grant: $200
Typical Range: $1,000 to $10,000
*Note: Average grant figure excludes four highest grants ($245,250).

Recent Grants
Note: Grants derived from 2003 Form 990.
Library-Related
12,500	New York Public Library, New York, NY

General
80,000	Flagler College, St. Augustine, FL
64,000	City Meals-on-Wheels, New York, NY
55,000	Pascal Rioult Dance Theatre Inc., New York, NY
46,250	Friends of the Israel Defense Forces (FIDF), New York, NY
37,000	French Institute Alliance Francaise (FIAF), New York, NY
20,000	Atlantic Center for the Arts, Smyrna Beach, FL
20,000	Brooklyn Academy of Music, Brooklyn, NY
20,000	John F. Kennedy Center for the Performing Arts, Washington, DC
20,000	Midori Foundation Inc., New York, NY
18,237	Columbia University in the City of New York, New York, NY

CARLS FOUNDATION

Giving Contact
Elizabeth A. Stieg, Executive Director
333 W. Fort Street, Suite 1940
Detroit, MI 48226
Phone: (313)965-0990
Fax: (313)965-0547
Web: http://www.carlsfdn.org/

Description
Founded: 1961
EIN: 386099935
Organization Type: Private Foundation
Giving Locations: MI: Huron Valley
Grant Types: General Support, Scholarship.

Donor Information
Founder: William Carls

Financial Summary

Total Giving: $4,324,873 (2003); $6,245,242 (2001)
Assets: $108,182,115 (2003); $109,738,312 (2001)
Gifts Received: $36,446,672 (1998); $6,915,833 (1996); $110,000 (1995). Note: In 1998, contributions were received from William Carls Estate Trust.

Typical Recipients

Arts & Humanities: Libraries, Music
Civic & Public Affairs: Community Foundations, Employment/Job Training, Civic & Public Affairs-General
Education: Colleges & Universities, Engineering/Technological Education, Environmental Education, Education-General, Minority Education, Private Education (Precollege), Public Education (Precollege), Special Education, Student Aid, Vocational & Technical Education
Environment: Resource Conservation
Health: Alzheimer's Disease, Cancer, Children's Health/Hospitals, Clinics/Medical Centers, Diabetes, Eyes/Blindness, Geriatric Health, Health Organizations, Home-Care Services, Hospitals, Mental Health, Prenatal Health Issues, Public Health, Speech & Hearing, Transplant Networks/Donor Banks
International: Health Care/Hospitals, International Relief Efforts
Religion: Ministries, Religious Welfare
Science: Scientific Centers & Institutes
Social Services: Big Brothers/Big Sisters, Camps, Child Welfare, Community Service Organizations, Day Care, Family Services, Homes, People with Disabilities, Senior Services, Substance Abuse, YMCA/YWCA/YMHA/YWHA, Youth Organizations

Application Procedures

Initial Contact: The foundation has no formal grant application procedure or application form. Send a brief letter of inquiry.
Deadlines: November 1, March 1, and July 1. Board meets in January, May, and September.

Restrictions

Grants are awarded for the purpose of providing for children's welfare, with special emphasis on the prevention and treatment of hearing impairment and recreational, educational, and welfare programs, especially for children who are disadvantaged for economic and/or health reasons. Grants also awarded for preservation of natural areas, open space and historic buildings and areas having special beauty or significance in maintaining America's heritage and historic ideals, through assistance to land trusts and conservancies and directly related to environmental educational programs.

Additional Information

Provides scholarships to students of the Huron Valley public school system.

Foundation Officials

Arthur B. Derisley: trustee
Henry Fleischer: trustee
Theresa R. Krieger: trustee
Elizabeth A. Stieg: executive director
Harold E. Stieg: trustee

Grants Analysis

Disclosure Period: calendar year ending 2003
Total Grants: $4,324,873
Number of Grants: 37
Average Grant: $35,602*
Highest Grant: $1,500,000
Lowest Grant: $3,000
Typical Range: $10,000 to $50,000
***Note:** Average grant figure excludes four highest grant ($3,150,000).

Recent Grants

Note: Grants derived from 2001 Form 990.

General

750,000	Detroit Institute for Children, Detroit, MI -- for the renovation of the facility
500,000	Central Michigan University, Mt. Pleasant, MI -- capital support for clinical wing
500,000	Community Foundation for Southeast Michigan, Detroit, MI -- for GreenWays Initiative
500,000	Detroit 300, Inc., Detroit, MI -- for conservancy endowment
500,000	Detroit Science Center, Detroit, MI -- for Science Stage Air Show, Power of Air, and the Williams Carls Exhibit
500,000	North Oakland Medical Center, Pontiac, MI -- support renovation of Neonatal Intensive Care Unit
375,000	Grand Traverse Regional Land Conservancy, Traverse City, MI -- for Lasting Landscapes Project
300,000	Lion's Visually Impaired Youth Camp, Lake Orion, MI -- for construction of Main Lodge for a camp for children with physical disabilities
250,000	Alternatives for Girls, Detroit, MI -- for capital funds
250,000	Mel Trotter Ministries, Grand Rapids, MI -- for the purchase of a new camp serving the homeless inner city youth

CARLSON COMPANIES INC.

Company Headquarters

1405 Xenium Lane N.
Plymouth, MN 55441
Web: http://www.carlson.com

Company Description

Founded: 1938
Revenue: US$6.5 billion (2002)
Employees: 180,000 (2002)
SIC(s): 4729 Passenger Transportation Arrangement Nec, 5812 Eating Places, 5961 Catalog & Mail-Order Houses, 7359 Equipment Rental & Leasing Nec.

Curtis L. Carlson Family Foundation

Giving Contact

Donna Snyder, Secretary
301 Carlson Parkway, Suite 102
Minnetonka, MN 55305
Phone: (952)404-5600
Fax: (952)404-5601

Description

Founded: 1959
EIN: 416028973
Organization Type: Corporate Foundation
Giving Locations: MN
Grant Types: General Support.

Donor Information

Founder: Curtis L. Carlson, Arleen M. Carlson, Glen D. Nelson, Marylyn C. Nelson

Financial Summary

Total Giving: $2,106,315 (2003); $2,518,248 (2001). Note: Contributes through corporate direct giving program and foundation.
Assets: $67,150,544 (2003); $54,571,233 (2001)
Gifts Received: $5,371,752 (2003); $7,432,483 (2001); $7,488,060 (2000). Note: In 2003, contributions were received from Arleen M. Carlson Charitable Annuity Trust. In 2000 and 2001, contributions were received from Arleen M. Carlson. In 1997, contributions were received from Edwin C. Gage and Barbara C. Gage.

Typical Recipients

Arts & Humanities: Arts Centers, Arts Festivals, Arts Funds, Arts Institutes, Community Arts, Libraries, Museums/Galleries, Music, Opera, Public Broadcasting, Theater
Civic & Public Affairs: Business/Free Enterprise, Chambers of Commerce, Clubs, Community Foundations, Ethnic Organizations, Civic & Public Affairs-General, Housing, Philanthropic Organizations, Professional & Trade Associations, Public Policy, Urban & Community Affairs, Women's Affairs, Zoos/Aquariums
Education: Afterschool/Enrichment Programs, Business Education, Colleges & Universities, Education Funds, Education-General, Gifted & Talented Programs, International Studies, Leadership Training, Minority Education, Private Education (Precollege), Public Education (Precollege), Student Aid
Environment: Forestry, Wildlife Protection
Health: AIDS/HIV, Cancer, Children's Health/Hospitals, Clinics/Medical Centers, Diabetes, Emergency/Ambulance Services, Eyes/Blindness, Health Organizations, Heart, Hospitals, Medical Research, Multiple Sclerosis, Public Health, Research/Studies Institutes, Single-Disease Health Associations, Transplant Networks/Donor Banks
International: Health Care/Hospitals, International Organizations, International Relations
Religion: Churches, Jewish Causes, Ministries, Religious Organizations, Religious Welfare, Seminaries
Science: Science Museums, Scientific Centers & Institutes
Social Services: Animal Protection, Big Brothers/Big Sisters, Camps, Child Abuse, Child Welfare, Community Service Organizations, Family Services, Food/Clothing Distribution, People with Disabilities, Recreation & Athletics, Scouts, Senior Services, Shelters/Homelessness, Substance Abuse, United Funds/United Ways, Volunteer Services, YMCA/YWCA/YMHA/YWHA, Youth Organizations

Application Procedures

Initial Contact: Write to request application guidelines, then send a written proposal.
Application Requirements: Include name of organization, address, and contact information; history and general purpose of the organization; three-year budget history and projected budget of organization; copy of IRS tax-exempt ruling; copy of most recent Form 990; list of board of directors and their affiliations; purpose of request; amount requested; program budget; evidence of cooperation with other similar agencies; evidence of evaluation system for program; and description of how program will be funded on an ongoing basis.
Deadlines: September 1 for organizations seeking grants before the end of the calendar year.
Review Process: Contributions committee reviews requests.
Evaluative Criteria: Purpose of grant, other sources of support, practicality of proposed plan, plans for future support. Supported programs meet one or more of the following guidelines: self-sufficiency, self-sustaining, performance, potential benefit, and cooperation and coordination.
Decision Notification: Quarterly.

Restrictions

Foundation generally does not fund dinners, benefits, or conferences; travel costs; individuals; political activities or causes; athletic events; endowments; and organizations that are not tax-exempt.

Additional Information

Company has operating locations in nearly all 50 states.
Publications: Guidelines and Policy

Corporate Officials

Barbara C. Gage: director vice president, chief financial officer PRIM CORP EMPL director: Carlson Companies Inc. ADD CORP EMPL director: Carlson Holdings Inc. CORP AFFIL director: Gage Marketing Group LLC.

Marilyn Carlson Nelson: chairman, chief executive officer B Minneapolis, MN August 19, 1939. ED Smith College BA (1961). PRIM CORP EMPL chairman, chief executive officer: Carlson Companies Inc. CORP AFFIL director: ExxonMobil Corp.; director: US West Inc.; chairman, director: Citizens State Bank Waterville; director, president: Carlson Holdings Inc.; chairman: Citizens State Bank Montgomery; president: Adams Martin & Nelson Inc.

Martyn R. Redgrave: executive vice president, chief financial officer B 1952. ED New York University MBA; Princeton University BA. PRIM CORP EMPL executive vice president, chief financial officer: Carlson Companies Inc. CORP AFFIL chief financial officer: Carlson Holdings Inc.

Foundation Officials

Barbara C. Gage: president (see above)
Kelly K. Gage: trustee
Richard C. Gage: trustee
Scott C. Gage: trustee
Diana L. Nelson: trustee
Marilyn Carlson Nelson: trustee (see above)
Marjorie A. Nelson: trustee
Wendy M. Nelson: trustee
Donna D. Snyder: secretary

Grants Analysis

Disclosure Period: calendar year ending 2003
Total Grants: $1,765,707*
Number of Grants: 117
Average Grant: $12,851*
Highest Grant: $275,000
Lowest Grant: $50
Typical Range: $1,000 to $20,000
***Note:** Giving excludes United Way, scholarship, and matching gifts. Average grant figure excludes highest grant.

Recent Grants

Note: Grants derived from 2003 Form 990.
General

275,000	Mayo Foundation for Medical Education and Research, Rochester, MN -- fund for transplantation & medical research
190,000	Greater Twin Cities United Way, Minneapolis, MN
166,666	Children's Theatre Company, Minneapolis, MN
125,000	Mayo Foundation for Medical Education and Research, Rochester, MN
100,000	Walker Art Center, Minneapolis, MN
75,000	Bakken, Minneapolis, MN -- fund for Science education program
75,000	Johnson & Wales University, Providence, RI
70,000	American Hotel & Lodging Educational Foundation, Washington, DC -- fund for new century campaign
70,000	SchoolStart, St. Paul, MN
50,000	Blake School, Hopkins, MN

CARNAHAN-JACKSON FOUNDATION

Giving Contact

Carnahan-Jackson Foundation
c/o Fleet Trust Co.
PO Box 3326
Jamestown, NY 14702
Phone: (716)726-8050

Description

Founded: 1972
EIN: 166151608
Organization Type: Private Foundation
Giving Locations: NY: Jamestown
Grant Types: Capital, General Support, Project, Scholarship, Seed Money.

Donor Information

Founder: the late Katharine J. Carnahan

Financial Summary

Total Giving: $483,487 (fiscal year ending July 31, 2004); $564,700 (fiscal 2001). Note: Fiscal 1997 Giving includes United Way ($10,000).
Giving Analysis: Giving for fiscal 2004 includes: foundation grants to United Way ($10,000); fiscal 2001: foundation grants to United Way ($10,000)
Assets: $11,378,768 (fiscal 2004); $13,469,505 (fiscal 2001)

Typical Recipients

Arts & Humanities: Ballet, Dance, Arts & Humanities-General, History & Archaeology, Libraries, Music, Performing Arts, Public Broadcasting
Civic & Public Affairs: Clubs, Economic Development, Municipalities/Towns
Education: Business Education, Colleges & Universities, Education Funds, Medical Education, Minority Education, Preschool Education, Public Education (Precollege), Student Aid
Environment: Environment-General, Resource Conservation, Wildlife Protection
Health: Hospitals
International: International Organizations
Religion: Churches, Religious Welfare
Social Services: Animal Protection, Child Welfare, Community Centers, Community Service Organizations, Crime Prevention, Day Care, People with Disabilities, Recreation & Athletics, Scouts, Substance Abuse, United Funds/United Ways, YMCA/YWCA/YMHA/YWHA, Youth Organizations

Application Procedures

Initial Contact: Send a brief letter of inquiry.
Application Requirements: Include purpose of funds sought and proof of tax-exempt status.
Deadlines: Applications are considered in June and September.

Restrictions

Preference is given to educational institutions and charitable organizations in the Jamestown, NY, area.

Additional Information

Trust(s): Fleet Trust Co

Grants Analysis

Disclosure Period: fiscal year ending July 31, 2004
Total Grants: $473,487*
Number of Grants: 27
Average Grant: $10,939*
Highest Grant: $100,000
Lowest Grant: $2,500
Typical Range: $5,000 to $20,000
***Note:** Giving excludes United Way. Average grant figure excludes two highest grants ($200,000).

Recent Grants

Note: Grants derived from 1999 Form 990.
Library-Related

100,000	James Prendergast Library, Jamestown, NY
25,000	Patterson Library, Westfield, NY
25,000	Sinclairville Free Library, Sinclairville, NY
5,000	Cuba Circulating Library, Cuba, NY

General

237,300	Chautauqua Institution, Jamestown, NY
65,000	Denison University, Granville, OH
50,000	YMCA Camp Onyahsa
25,000	WNEO Public Broadcasting Association, Youngstown, OH
15,000	Chautauqua Regional Youth Ballet, Jamestown, NY
15,000	Davis & Elkins College, Elkins, WV
15,000	Nature Conservancy
13,900	Jamestown Audubon Society, Jamestown, NY
13,000	Junior Achievement, Providence, RI
10,000	Independent College Fund

CARNEGIE CORP. OF NEW YORK

Giving Contact

Adam Liebling, Grants Associate
437 Madison Avenue
New York, NY 10022
Phone: (212)371-3200
Fax: (212)754-4073
Web: http://www.carnegie.org

Description

Founded: 1938
EIN: 131628151
Organization Type: General Purpose Foundation
Giving Locations: internationally, especially to countries that are or have been members of the British commonwealth.
Grant Types: General Support, Project, Research, Seed Money.

Donor Information

Founder: Andrew Carnegie was born in Scotland in 1835. He moved to the United States 13 years later, beginning work as a bobbin boy in the cotton mill. After holding various jobs with Western Union and the Pennsylvania Railroad, Carnegie resigned in 1865 to establish his own business enterprises and eventually organized the Carnegie Steel Company. At the turn of the century, he sold his major Pittsburgh steel company to J.P. Morgan for $400 million. Carnegie was one of the first wealthy Americans to believe that the well-to-do had a moral responsibility to assist the less fortunate. Carnegie's personal philanthropy began in his thirties with a large gift to his hometown of Dunfermline, Scotland. One of his earliest interests was the establishment of free public libraries throughout the United States, a cause to which he donated over $56 million. Other interests included adult education and education in the fine arts. Over the years, Carnegie established seven philanthropic and educational organizations in the United States, and several more in Europe to carry out theses and other programs. In the United States, he established the Carnegie Foundation for the Advancement of Teaching, the Carnegie Institute (Pittsburgh), the Carnegie Mellon University (formed by the 7 merger of the Mellon Institute and the Carnegie Institute of Technology), the Carnegie Endowment for International Peace, and the Carnegie Institution of Washington. Overseas, Mr. Carnegie established the Carnegie Trust for the Universities of Scotland to assist students and fund expansion and research, and the Carnegie Dunfermline and United Kingdom Trusts to improve social conditions in his native town, and the well-being of the people of Great Britain and Ireland through aid to community service, arts and crafts, and leadership training. Mr. Carnegie also established hero funds in the United States, the United Kingdom, and Europe to recognize heroic acts performed in peaceful nations. In all, Mr. Carnegie's gifts and bequests totaled over $350 million.

Financial Summary

Total Giving: $74,542,133 (fiscal year ending September 30, 2003); $76,301,020 (fiscal 2002);

$84,353,909 (fiscal 2001)

Assets: $1,824,314,932 (fiscal 2003); $1,627,733,524 (fiscal 2002); $1,711,510,640 (fiscal 2001)

Gifts Received: $4,636,000 (fiscal 2003); $50,015 (fiscal 1999). Note: In fiscal 2003, contributions were received from an anonymous contributor. In fiscal 1999, contributions were received from the estate of Peter Economos.

Typical Recipients

Arts & Humanities: Libraries, Public Broadcasting
Civic & Public Affairs: African American Affairs, Asian American Affairs, Civil Rights, Community Foundations, Economic Development, Economic Policy, Civic & Public Affairs-General, Hispanic Affairs, Law & Justice, Legal Aid, Native American Affairs, Nonprofit Management, Philanthropic Organizations, Professional & Trade Associations, Public Policy, Urban & Community Affairs, Women's Affairs
Education: Afterschool/Enrichment Programs, Arts/Humanities Education, Colleges & Universities, Education Associations, Education Funds, Education Reform, Elementary Education (Public), Engineering/Technological Education, Faculty Development, Education-General, Health & Physical Education, International Exchange, International Studies, Journalism/Media Education, Leadership Training, Legal Education, Literacy, Medical Education, Minority Education, Preschool Education, Public Education (Precollege), Science/Mathematics Education, Secondary Education (Public), Social Sciences Education, Special Education, Student Aid, Vocational & Technical Education
Health: Adolescent Health Issues, Children's Health/Hospitals, Clinics/Medical Centers, Health Policy/Cost Containment, Health Funds, Health Organizations, Medical Research, Mental Health, Prenatal Health Issues, Public Health
International: Foreign Arts Organizations, Foreign Educational Institutions, International-General, Health Care/Hospitals, Human Rights, International Affairs, International Development, International Organizations, International Peace & Security Issues, International Relations, Missionary/Religious Activities, Trade
Science: Scientific Centers & Institutes, Scientific Organizations
Social Services: At-Risk Youth, Child Abuse, Child Welfare, Community Service Organizations, Crime Prevention, Day Care, Family Planning, Family Services, Refugee Assistance, Substance Abuse, Volunteer Services, Youth Organizations

Application Procedures

Initial Contact: The corporation does not have application forms. Initial contact should be by letter.
Application Requirements: The initial proposal should be a brief written statement describing the project's aims, duration, methods, personnel, and the amount of financial support required.

The following points may be helpful in preparing a proposal or preproposal. Although the questions need not be answered individually, they indicate the types of concerns program staff members have in mind when reviewing requests: What problem does your project address? Why is this issue significant? What is the relationship of the problem/issue to the corporation's program? How will your project or activity deal with the stated problem? What do you intend to demonstrate or prove? What means will you use, and what methodology will you apply? If the project is already under way, what have you accomplished so far? What outcomes do you expect for the project, both immediate and long term? How will you assess the success or effectiveness of your work? What strengths and skills do the organization and personnel bring to this project? In short, what makes this organization the right one to conduct this project? If the organization has not received a grant from the corporation before, please include background information such as an annual report, audited financial statement,

or mission statement. Finally, what is the overall cost of the project? How much are you requesting and over how long a period? What other sources of support are you pursuing for this project?

Corporation officers will request supplementary information or a personal discussion when necessary. The endorsement of the administrative head of the requesting institution need not be sent with the initial proposal, but it will be required before a favorable recommendation is made to the corporation's trustees.
Deadlines: None.
Review Process: Corporation officers consider each project. If they decide to evaluate a project for funding, a more developed project proposal will be requested. Specific criteria will be given in the descriptions of each program area. The corporation's board meets in October, February, April, and June.
Notes: The corporation does not, as a matter of policy, provide to prospective grantseekers copies of successful proposals.

Restrictions

The corporation does not operate scholarship, fellowship, or travel grant programs; it does not make grants for basic operating expenses, endowments, or facilities of educational or human services institutions; nor does it make program-related investments. The corporation does not generally make grants to individuals. On occasion, it will make a grant to a highly qualified individual for a project that is central to its stated program interests.

Additional Information

The corporation also does not fund individual schools, or curriculum projects within individual schools.
Publications: Annual Report; General Information Pamphlet; Carnegie Quarterly; Carnegie Special Report; Carnegie Meeting Papers

Foundation Officials

Thomas R. Pickering: trustee ED Bowdoin College BA (1953); Tufts University MA (1954); University of Melbourne MA (1956). CORP AFFIL senior vice president international relations: The Boeing Co. NONPR AFFIL member: Council on Foreign Relations; member: International Institute of Strategic Studies.

Richard W. Riley: trustee

Janet L. Robinson: trustee

Patricia L. Rosenfield: chairman Carnegie Scholars program ED Bryn Mawr College AB; Johns Hopkins University PhD. NONPR AFFIL board of directors: Harry Frank Guggenheim Foundation; member: Johns Hopkins University Council for the School of Engineering; secretary: Global Fund for Children; member: Council on Foreign Relations; board of directors: Future Generations.

Robert J. Seman: finance director ED Mercy College BS.

Edward M. Sermier: vice president, chief administrative officer, corp. secretary ED Columbia University MBA; Manhattan College BS. NONPR AFFIL trustee: Services for the Underserved.

D. Ellen Shuman: vice president, chief investment officer ED Bowdoin College BA; Yale University School of Management MBA. NONPR AFFIL inventor advisory: Independent Sector; director: The Investment Fund for Foundations; vice chairman, trustee: Bowdoin College; inventor advisory: Edna McConnell Clark Foundation.

Raymond W. Smith: trustee B Pittsburgh, PA 1937. ED Carnegie Mellon University BS (1959); University of Pittsburgh MBA (1967). CORP AFFIL chairman: Verizon Ventures; chairman: Rothschild Inc.; director: USAirways Group Inc.; director: Banneker Technologies Inc.; director: Five Arrows Investments. NONPR AFFIL trustee: Carnegie-Mellon University; member national advisory board: Private Sector Councils; member board advisors: Arden Theatre Co.

David C. Speedie, III: director Islam Project ED University of St. Andrews MA; University of St. Andrews MLitt.

Grants Analysis
Disclosure Period: fiscal year ending September 30, 2003
Total Grants: $74,542,133
Number of Grants: 547
Average Grant: $106,658*
Highest Grant: $2,521,575
Lowest Grant: $975
Typical Range: $25,000 to $250,000
*Note: Average grant figure excludes ten highest grants ($17,266,646).

Recent Grants
Note: Grants derived from fiscal 2003 Form 990.

General
2,521,575 Academy for Educational Development Inc., Washington, DC -- towards reforming and improving the education of teachers
2,508,333 Woodrow Wilson International Center for Scholars, Washington, DC -- for creation of centers for advanced study and education in Russia
2,093,000 Chattanooga Hamilton County Public Education Fund, Chattanooga, TN -- for district-wide reform in secondary school education
1,894,000 Rhode Island Children's Crusade for Higher Education, Providence, RI -- for district-wide reform in secondary school education
1,868,000 Linking Education and Economic Development in Sacramento, Rancho Cordova, CA -- for district-wide reform in secondary school education
1,600,000 Clark University, Worcester, MA -- for district-wide reform in secondary school education

1,475,000 Obafemi Awolowo University, Lle Lfe Nigeria -- for institutional strengthening and gender equity projects
1,449,700 New Visions for Public Schools Inc., New York, NY -- for the New Century High Schools Consortium for New York City
1,408,000 Child Centered Schools Initiative of Houston, Houston, TX -- for district-wide reform in secondary school education
1,322,038 Carnegie Corporation of New York, New York, NY

CARNIVAL CORP.

Company Headquarters
3655 Northwest 87th Avenue
Miami, FL 33178-2428
Phone: (305)599-2600
Fax: (305)406-4758
Web: http://www.carnivalcorp.com

Company Description
Founded: 1974
Ticker: CCL
Exchange: NYSE
Revenue: US$4.535 billion (2001)
Employees: 66000 (2003)
SIC(s): 7999 Amusement & Recreation Nec.

Operating Locations
Carnival Cruise Lines Inc. (FL--Miami); Gray Line (AK--Anchorage, Fairbanks, Healy); Holland America Line (WA--Seattle)

Ted Arison Family Foundation USA, Inc.

Giving Contact
Madelon Rosenberg, Assistant to the President
3655 NW 87th Avenue
Miami, FL 33178-2428
Phone: (305)599-2600

Description
Founded: 1981
EIN: 592128429
Organization Type: Corporate Foundation
Former Name: Arison Foundation.
Giving Locations: FL: Miami including surrounding area
Grant Types: General Support.

Financial Summary
Total Giving: $11,321,554 (2003); $3,297,350 (2002); $10,151,522 (2001). Note: Contributes through corporate direct giving program and foundation.
Giving Analysis: Giving for 2001 includes: foundation grants to United Way ($1,400,000); foundation ($8,751,522)
Assets: $276,400,419 (2003); $219,543,763 (2002); $250,771,018 (2001).
Gifts Received: $1,500 (2003); $750,000 (2002); $630,000 (2001). Note: In 2002, contributions were received from Marilyn Arison. In 2001, contributions were received from the Ted Arison Charitable Trust. In 1999, contributions were received from Shari Arison.

Typical Recipients
Arts & Humanities: Arts Associations & Councils, Arts Festivals, Arts Funds, Dance, Film & Video, Arts & Humanities-General, History & Archaeology, Museums/Galleries, Music, Performing Arts, Theater, Visual Arts
Civic & Public Affairs: Civil Rights, Clubs, Commu-

nity Foundations, Economic Policy, Ethnic Organizations, Civic & Public Affairs-General, Municipalities/Towns, Philanthropic Organizations, Public Policy, Urban & Community Affairs
Education: Arts/Humanities Education, Business Education, Colleges & Universities, Education Associations, Education Funds, Engineering/Technological Education, Education-General, International Studies, Medical Education, Minority Education, Public Education (Precollege), Religious Education, Science/Mathematics Education, Special Education, Student Aid
Health: Cancer, Children's Health/Hospitals, Clinics/Medical Centers, Eyes/Blindness, Health-General, Geriatric Health, Health Funds, Health Organizations, Hospices, Hospitals, Medical Research, Public Health, Single-Disease Health Associations
International: Foreign Arts Organizations, Foreign Educational Institutions, International-General, Health Care/Hospitals, International Environmental Issues, International Organizations, International Peace & Security Issues, International Relations, International Relief Efforts, Missionary/Religious Activities
Religion: Religion-General, Jewish Causes, Religious Welfare, Social/Policy Issues, Synagogues/Temples
Science: Science-General
Social Services: At-Risk Youth, Child Welfare, Community Service Organizations, People with Disabilities, Recreation & Athletics, Shelters/Homelessness, Social Services-General, United Funds/United Ways, Youth Organizations

Application Procedures
Initial Contact: Send brief letter or proposal.
Application Requirements: Include a description of organization, amount requested, purpose of funds sought, recently audited financial statement, and proof of tax-exempt status.
Deadlines: None.

Additional Information
Foundation's giving is very limited in scope and frequently committed well in advance.

Corporate Officials
M. Micky Arison: chairman, chief executive officer, director secretary B Tel Aviv, Israel 1949. ED University of Miami. PRIM CORP EMPL chairman, chief executive officer, director: Carnival Corp. CORP AFFIL director: CHC International Inc.; managing general partner: Miami Heat; chairman, chief executive officer, managing partner: Carnival Cruise Lines; chairman: Air Holding Co.; chairman: Carnival plc.
Shari Arison Glazer: director PRIM CORP EMPL director: Carnival Corp.
Arnaldo Perez: vice president, general counsel, secretary B 1960. ED Miami University BBA (1982); Columbia University JD (1985). PRIM CORP EMPL vice president, general counsel, secretary: Carnival Corp. Carnival plc CORP AFFIL vice president, general counsel, secretary:.

Foundation Officials
David Arison: trustee
Jason Arison: trustee
M. Micky Arison: trustee (see above)
Madeleine Arison: trustee
Marilyn Arison: trustee ED Skidmore College BA (1976).
Shari Arison Glazer: president (see above)
Arnaldo Perez: vice president (see above)

Grants Analysis
Disclosure Period: calendar year ending 2003
Total Grants: $11,118,548*
Number of Grants: 94
Average Grant: $76,544*
Highest Grant: $4,000,000
Lowest Grant: $79
Typical Range: $5,000 to $50,000 and $100,000 to

$1,000,000

*Note: Giving excludes scholarships and United Way. Average grant figure excludes highest grant.

Recent Grants

Note: Grants derived from 2002 Form 990.
General

993,000	Matan - Your Way to give to Israel, Tel Aviv Israel
503,000	Greater Miami Jewish Federation, Miami, FL
250,000	Association of Friends of Tel Aviv Sourasky Medical Center, New York, NY
200,000	Kav Lachyim, New York, NY
200,000	United Way International, Alexandria, VA
100,000	PEF Israel Endowment Funds Inc., New York, NY -- society of friends of Sieff hospital
100,000	University of Miami Middle East Studies Institute, Coral Gables, FL
80,000	Interdisciplinary Herzilla, Herzaliya Israel -- construction of the Arison school of Business
60,000	American Friends of the Soroka Medical Center of the Negev, New York, NY -- for lung functioning machine
59,000	Israel America Foundation, New York, NY

CARPENTER FOUNDATION

Giving Contact

Jane Carpenter, President, Trustee
711 E. Main St., Suite 10
Medford, OR 97504
Phone: (541)772-5851

Description

Founded: 1957
EIN: 930491360
Organization Type: Private Foundation
Giving Locations: OR: Jackson and Josephine counties
Grant Types: General Support, Operating Expenses, Seed Money.

Donor Information

Founder: the late Helen Bundy Carpenter, the late Alfred S.V. Carpenter, Harlow Carpenter

Financial Summary

Total Giving: $534,440 (fiscal year ending June 30, 2004); $935,725 (fiscal 2001). Note: Fiscal 1997 Giving includes United Way ($16,500).
Giving Analysis: Giving for fiscal 2004 includes: foundation grants to United Way ($35,000); foundation scholarships ($97,130); fiscal 2001: foundation grants to United Way ($35,000); foundation scholarships ($127,130)
Assets: $17,388,401 (fiscal 2004); $18,538,935 (fiscal 2001)
Gifts Received: $212,266 (fiscal 2001); $1,000 (fiscal 1997); $1,000 (fiscal 1996)

Typical Recipients

Arts & Humanities: Arts Associations & Councils, Arts Festivals, Arts Outreach, Arts & Humanities-General, History & Archaeology, Libraries, Literary Arts, Museums/Galleries, Music, Opera, Performing Arts, Public Broadcasting, Theater, Visual Arts
Civic & Public Affairs: Economic Development, Employment/Job Training, Civic & Public Affairs-General, Hispanic Affairs, Housing, Legal Aid, Municipalities/Towns, Native American Affairs, Parades/Festivals
Education: Afterschool/Enrichment Programs, Colleges & Universities, Community & Junior Colleges, Education Funds, Elementary Education (Public),

Faculty Development, International Studies, Preschool Education, Public Education (Precollege), Secondary Education (Public), Student Aid
Environment: Air/Water Quality, Forestry, Environment-General, Resource Conservation
Health: Children's Health/Hospitals, Clinics/Medical Centers, Long-Term Care, Mental Health, Nursing Services, Public Health
Social Services: At-Risk Youth, Child Abuse, Child Welfare, Community Centers, Community Service Organizations, Counseling, Crime Prevention, Day Care, Delinquency & Criminal Rehabilitation, Domestic Violence, Emergency Relief, Family Services, Food/Clothing Distribution, People with Disabilities, Recreation & Athletics, Scouts, Senior Services, Shelters/Homelessness, Substance Abuse, United Funds/United Ways, YMCA/YWCA/YMHA/YWHA, Youth Organizations

Application Procedures

Initial Contact: Send a brief letter of inquiry.
Application Requirements: Include a description of organization, proof of tax-exempt status, purpose of funds sought, organization budget, project budget, plan employed to accomplish the project, evidence of other financial support for the project, and a list of the board of directors.
Deadlines: None.

Restrictions

Grants are not made outside Jackson or Josephine counties, or to individuals. Grants are not made to individuals.

Additional Information

Publications: Application Guidelines; Annual Report

Foundation Officials

Karen C. Allan: secretary, trustee
Dunbar Carpenter: treasurer, trustee
Jane H. Carpenter: president, trustee
William R. Moffat: trustee
Brian Mostue: trustee
Emily C. Mostue: vice president, trustee

Grants Analysis

Disclosure Period: fiscal year ending June 30, 2004
Total Grants: $402,310*
Number of Grants: 77
Average Grant: $5,225
Highest Grant: $25,000
Lowest Grant: $1,000
Typical Range: $1,000 to $10,000
*Note: Giving excludes United Way and scholarship.

Recent Grants

Note: Grants derived from fiscal 2004 Form 990.
General

25,000	La Clinica del Valle, Medford, OR -- funds for west Medford clinic expansion
25,000	Rogue Community College, Medford, OR -- for Jackson and Josephine county student scholarship 2004-2005
25,000	Southern Oregon University, Ashland, OR -- in support of faculty development opportunities, which improve teaching
25,000	United Way of Jackson County, Medford, OR -- in support of human service programs
20,000	Britt Festivals, Medford, OR -- support for 2004 classical music season
20,000	Oregon Shakespeare Festival, Ashland, OR -- special matinee program for student and seniors
20,000	Rogue Valley Family YMCA, Medford, OR -- progress program for youth
19,800	North Medford High School, Medford, OR -- towards scholarship
19,800	South Medford High School, Medford, OR -- towards scholarship
14,630	Central Point High School, Central Point, OR -- towards scholarship

E. RHODES AND LEONA B. CARPENTER FOUNDATION

Giving Contact

Joseph A. O'Connor, Jr., Executive Director
PO Box 58880
Philadelphia, PA 19102-8880
Phone: (215)963-5212

Description

Founded: 1975
EIN: 510155772
Organization Type: General Purpose Foundation
Giving Locations: VA: east of the Mississippi River.
Grant Types: Capital, Challenge, Emergency, General Support, Project, Scholarship.

Donor Information

Founder: Established in 1975 by the late E. Rhodes Carpenter and Leona B. Carpenter.

Financial Summary

Total Giving: $10,188,874 (2002); $11,277,058 (2001)
Assets: $165,363,628 (2002); $208,212,715 (2001)
Gifts Received: $7,158 (1996); $2,492,586 (1995); $2,000,000 (1993). Note: In 1995, the foundation received a gift of $2,492,586 form the estate of Leona B. Carpenter.

Typical Recipients

Arts & Humanities: Arts Associations & Councils, Arts Centers, Arts Funds, Arts Institutes, Arts Outreach, Ballet, Community Arts, Dance, Ethnic & Folk Arts, Film & Video, Historic Preservation, History & Archaeology, Libraries, Museums/Galleries, Music, Opera, Performing Arts, Public Broadcasting, Theater
Civic & Public Affairs: Asian American Affairs, Botanical Gardens/Parks, Community Foundations, Economic Development, Civic & Public Affairs-General, Housing, Municipalities/Towns, Philanthropic Organizations, Women's Affairs
Education: Arts/Humanities Education, Colleges & Universities, Education Funds, Elementary Education (Private), Elementary Education (Public), Education-General, Health & Physical Education, International Studies, Medical Education, Public Education (Precollege), Religious Education, Science/Mathematics Education, Secondary Education (Public), Student Aid
Environment: Environment-General
Health: AIDS/HIV, Cancer, Children's Health/Hospitals, Clinics/Medical Centers, Emergency/Ambulance Services, Health Policy/Cost Containment, Health Organizations, Home-Care Services, Hospices, Hospitals, Medical Rehabilitation, Mental Health, Nursing Services, Public Health, Research/Studies Institutes, Single-Disease Health Associations
International: Foreign Arts Organizations, International Environmental Issues, International Peace & Security Issues, International Relations, Missionary/Religious Activities
Religion: Churches, Jewish Causes, Ministries, Religious Organizations, Religious Welfare, Seminaries
Science: Science Museums, Scientific Centers & Institutes
Social Services: Child Welfare, Community Centers, Community Service Organizations, Counseling, Day Care, Delinquency & Criminal Rehabilitation, Domestic Violence, Emergency Relief, Family Planning, Family Services, Food/Clothing Distribution, Homes, People with Disabilities, Recreation & Athletics, Senior Services, Sexual Abuse, Shelters/Homelessness, Substance Abuse, Youth Organizations

Application Procedures

Initial Contact: Informal letter applications are sufficient.

Application Requirements: The letter application should include a brief history of the purpose of the organization, the dollar amount requested, a description of the specific project or program for which the amount is being requested, and a copy of the organization's ruling that it is a 509(a)(1) or (2) institution.

Deadlines: Applications should be postmarked or fax dated on or before March 15 to be considered at the spring meeting and on or before September 15 for the autumn meeting.

Restrictions

Generally, the foundation will not consider grant requests to support private secondary education, nor will it as a general rule consider grant requests from large public charities such as the Red Cross, American Cancer Society, or United Fund. Also the foundation generally will not transfer funds from its endowment to the endowment of another organization. Grants are made for specific projects or programs. The foundation does not support individuals.

Additional Information

Publications: Application Guidelines

Foundation Officials

Ann B. Day: president, director

Paul B. Day, Jr.: vice president, secretary, treasurer, director

M. H. Reinhart: director PRIM CORP EMPL president: E.R. Carpenter Co.

Grants Analysis

Disclosure Period: calendar year ending 2002
Total Grants: $10,188,874
Number of Grants: 220
Average Grant: $39,525*
Highest Grant: $400,000
Lowest Grant: $2,000
Typical Range: $10,000 to $50,000
*Note: Average grant figure excludes five highest grants ($1,690,959).

Recent Grants

Note: Grants derived from 2002 Form 990.

General

400,000	Science Museum of Virginia, Richmond, VA -- fund towards 'new and continuing initiatives' program
390,959	Richmond Symphony, Richmond, VA
300,000	Mary Baldwin College, Staunton, VA -- to support the new graduate-level program in Shakespeare and Renaissance
300,000	Mary Baldwin College, Staunton, VA -- to support the new graduate-level program in Shakespeare and Renaissance
300,000	Walters Art Museum, Baltimore, MD -- fund towards renovation, conservation and installation of two galleries
200,000	Center for Prevention of Sexual and Domestic Violence, Seattle, WA -- to help the continuation of its seminary project
200,000	Cultural Activities Center, Temple, TX -- to support in construction of an all purpose community room
200,000	National Hospice Foundation, Alexandria, VA -- to cover costs of producing a TV public service announcement
160,000	Lewisburg Elementary School, Lewisburg, KY -- fund towards purchase of computers and related equipment
150,000	Virginia Opera, Richmond, VA -- to support the second premiere series 2002-2003 season

CARROLL CHARITABLE FOUNDATION

Giving Contact

Francis R. Carroll, President
554 Main Street
PO Box 15104
Worcester, MA 01615-0014
Phone: (508)756-3513
Fax: (508)770-0528
E-mail: fcarroll@sbsb.com

Description

EIN: 222546670
Organization Type: Private Foundation
Former Name: Small Business Service Bureau Charitable Foundation (2001).
Giving Locations: MA; NY
Grant Types: General Support.

Financial Summary

Total Giving: $37,727 (fiscal year ending June 30, 2003)
Assets: $378,783 (fiscal 2003)
Gifts Received: $50,458 (fiscal 2003); $50,285 (fiscal 1998); $56,203 (fiscal 1997). Note: In fiscal 2003, contributions were received from Carroll Enterprises, Inc. ($50,000) and miscellaneous sources ($458).

Typical Recipients

Arts & Humanities: Historic Preservation, Libraries, Music, Performing Arts, Public Broadcasting
Civic & Public Affairs: Clubs, Civic & Public Affairs-General, Public Policy
Education: Colleges & Universities, Education-General, Medical Education, Private Education (Precollege), Special Education, Student Aid, Vocational & Technical Education
Health: Arthritis, Cancer, Children's Health/Hospitals, Clinics/Medical Centers, Diabetes, Heart, Hospices, Single-Disease Health Associations
International: Foreign Educational Institutions, Health Care/Hospitals
Religion: Churches, Jewish Causes, Religious Organizations, Religious Welfare
Social Services: Child Welfare, Community Service Organizations, Crime Prevention, Senior Services, Shelters/Homelessness, Special Olympics, United Funds/United Ways, Youth Organizations

Application Procedures

Initial Contact: Send a brief letter of inquiry.
Application Requirements: Include a description of organization.
Deadlines: None.

Restrictions

Scholarships are restricted to the study of small businesses.

Corporate Officials

Francis R. Carroll: president, director PRIM CORP EMPL president, director: Small Bus Service Bur.

Foundation Officials

Francis R. Carroll: trustee (see above)
Mary M. Carroll: trustee
Patricia A. Greenlaw: trustee

Grants Analysis

Disclosure Period: fiscal year ending June 30, 2003
Total Grants: $37,727
Number of Grants: 8
Average Grant: $3,961*
Highest Grant: $10,000
Lowest Grant: $1,000
Typical Range: $1,000 to $5,000
*Note: Average grant figure excludes highest grant.

Recent Grants

Note: Grants derived from fiscal 2003 Form 990.
General

10,000	Church of Worcester, Worcester, MA
9,161	UMass Memorial Children's Medical Center, Worcester, MA
5,000	American Heart Association, Dallas, TX
5,000	National Legal Center for Public Interest, Washington, DC
4,000	Emerald Club Inc., Worcester, MA
2,000	Arthritis Foundation, Atlanta, GA
1,566	Telegram and Gazette, Worcester, MA
1,000	AIND / Giant Steps, Fairfield, CT

CARTER FAMILY FOUNDATION

Giving Contact

Debbie Lester
Carter Family Foundation
c/o United National Bank, Trust Department
129 Main Street
Beckley, WV 25801
Phone: (304)256-7262

Description

Founded: 1981
EIN: 550606479
Organization Type: Private Foundation
Giving Locations: WV: Raleigh County
Grant Types: General Support, Project, Scholarship.

Donor Information

Founder: Bernard E. Carter, the late Georgia Carter

Financial Summary

Total Giving: $552,668 (fiscal year ending June 30, 2004); $74,400 (fiscal 2001). Note: Fiscal 1997 Giving includes scholarships ($10,000); United Way ($2,000).
Giving Analysis: Giving for fiscal 2004 includes: foundation grants to United Way ($3,000)
Assets: $15,364,576 (fiscal 2004); $13,316,260 (fiscal 2001)
Gifts Received: $258,009 (fiscal 1998); $1,500 (fiscal 1995); $50,000 (fiscal 1994). Note: In 1998, contributions were received from Bernard E. Carter. In fiscal 1994, contributions were received from the estate of Bernard E. and Georgia Carter.

Typical Recipients

Arts & Humanities: Libraries, Museums/Galleries, Public Broadcasting, Theater
Civic & Public Affairs: Community Foundations, Employment/Job Training, Housing, Women's Affairs
Education: Colleges & Universities, Engineering/Technological Education, Medical Education, Minority Education, Private Education (Precollege), Religious Education, Secondary Education (Public), Student Aid, Vocational & Technical Education
Environment: Protection
Health: Alzheimer's Disease, Arthritis, Cancer, Children's Health/Hospitals, Emergency/Ambulance Services, Eyes/Blindness, Health Organizations, Heart, Hospices, Hospitals, Kidney, Medical Research, Multiple Sclerosis, Prenatal Health Issues, Single-Disease Health Associations
International: Health Care/Hospitals, International Peace & Security Issues, International Relief Efforts, Missionary/Religious Activities
Religion: Bible Study/Translation, Churches, Religious Organizations, Religious Welfare, Synagogues/Temples
Social Services: Animal Protection, Camps, Child Welfare, Community Service Organizations, Homes, Scouts, Shelters/Homelessness, United Funds/

United Ways, YMCA/YWCA/YMHA/YWHA, Youth Organizations

Application Procedures

Initial Contact: Send letter and resume.
Deadlines: None.
Notes: The foundation provides scholarships and student loans to individuals willing to continue their education and teaching profession within the state of West Virginia.

Additional Information

Trust(s): United National Bank

Grants Analysis

Disclosure Period: fiscal year ending June 30, 2004
Total Grants: $549,668*
Number of Grants: 70
Average Grant: $5,551*
Highest Grant: $166,667
Lowest Grant: $4,400
Typical Range: $1,000 to $10,000
*Note: Giving excludes United Way. Average grant figure excludes highest grant.

Recent Grants

Note: Grants derived from fiscal 2001 Form 990.
Library-Related
10,000	Friends of Shady Spring Library

General
50,000	YMCA Youth Soccer Complex
10,000	Theater West Virginia, Beckley, WV
4,400	Ohio West Virginia YMCA Youth Opportunity Camp

AMON G. CARTER FOUNDATION

Giving Contact

John H. Robinson, Grant Administrator-Executive Vice President
PO Box 1036
Ft. Worth, TX 76101-1036
Phone: (817)332-2783
Fax: (817)332-2787
E-mail: terry@agcf.org
Web: http://www.agcf.org

Description

Founded: 1945
EIN: 756000331
Organization Type: General Purpose Foundation
Giving Locations: TX: Fort Worth including Tarrant County
Grant Types: Capital, Challenge, Endowment, General Support, Matching, Operating Expenses, Project, Scholarship, Seed Money.

Donor Information

Founder: Established in 1945 by Amon G. Carter, publisher of the *Fort Worth Star Telegram* and founder of Carter Publications. Ruth Carter Stevenson, the donor's daughter and the only living member of the Carter family, is president of the foundation. The Carter family's interests in art are reflected in the Amon Carter Museum, which specializes in western and early American art.

Financial Summary

Total Giving: $15,800,755 (2003); $14,640,000 (2002 approx)
Giving Analysis: Giving for 2003 includes: foundation scholarships ($57,900); foundation grants to United Way ($100,000).
Assets: $363,369,813 (2003); $284,000,000 (2002 approx)

Typical Recipients

Arts & Humanities: Arts Associations & Councils, Arts Centers, Arts Festivals, Ballet, Community Arts, Ethnic & Folk Arts, Film & Video, Arts & Humanities-General, Historic Preservation, History & Archaeology, Libraries, Museums/Galleries, Music, Opera, Performing Arts, Public Broadcasting, Theater
Civic & Public Affairs: Botanical Gardens/Parks, Chambers of Commerce, Community Foundations, Economic Development, Employment/Job Training, Civic & Public Affairs-General, Housing, Law & Justice, Municipalities/Towns, Philanthropic Organizations, Public Policy, Safety, Urban & Community Affairs, Women's Affairs, Zoos/Aquariums
Education: Afterschool/Enrichment Programs, Arts/Humanities Education, Colleges & Universities, Community & Junior Colleges, Economic Education, Education Associations, Education Funds, Education Reform, Elementary Education (Private), Engineering/Technological Education, Faculty Development, Education-General, Medical Education, Minority Education, Private Education (Precollege), Public Education (Precollege), Religious Education, School Volunteerism, Science/Mathematics Education, Secondary Education (Private), Secondary Education (Public), Special Education, Student Aid
Environment: Air/Water Quality, Environment-General, Wildlife Protection
Health: AIDS/HIV, Alzheimer's Disease, Cancer, Children's Health/Hospitals, Clinics/Medical Centers, Diabetes, Emergency/Ambulance Services, Eyes/Blindness, Health Policy/Cost Containment, Health Funds, Health Organizations, Hospices, Hospitals, Hospitals (University Affiliated), Medical Rehabilitation, Medical Research, Mental Health, Nursing Services, Prenatal Health Issues, Public Health, Research/Studies Institutes, Respiratory, Single-Disease Health Associations, Transplant Networks/Donor Banks
International: International Affairs, International Relief Efforts
Religion: Churches, Dioceses, Religious Organizations, Religious Welfare
Science: Science Exhibits & Fairs, Science Museums, Scientific Research
Social Services: At-Risk Youth, Big Brothers/Big Sisters, Camps, Child Abuse, Child Welfare, Community Centers, Community Service Organizations, Counseling, Crime Prevention, Day Care, Delinquency & Criminal Rehabilitation, Domestic Violence, Emergency Relief, Family Planning, Family Services, Food/Clothing Distribution, Homes, People with Disabilities, Recreation & Athletics, Scouts, Senior Services, Shelters/Homelessness, Social Services-General, Substance Abuse, United Funds/United Ways, Volunteer Services, YMCA/YWCA/YMHA/YWHA, Youth Organizations

Application Procedures

Initial Contact: Applicants should contact the foundation by letter.
Application Requirements: Letters of request should include proof of the organization's tax-exempt status and the purpose of the requested grant. The foundation may require additional information at a later date.
Deadlines: None.
Review Process: All grants must be approved by the five-member board of directors, which meets three times a year.

Restrictions

No grants are made to individuals or for loans. Applying organizations usually must qualify for exemption under Section 501(c)(3) of the Internal Revenue Code. Special consideration is required if an applying organization is not exempt as a private foundation under Section 509(a) of the Code. Grants outside the Fort Worth area are initiated only by the staff and board of directors.

Additional Information

Publications: Annual Report; Policy and Guidelines Statement

Foundation Officials

Robert William Brown, MD: vice president, director B Seattle, WA 1924. ED Tulane University MD (1950). PRIM CORP EMPL president: American Baseball League.
W. Patrick Harris: executive vice president investments ED Louisiana State University. NONPR AFFIL treasurer: Amon Carter Museum Western Art.
Kate L. Johnson: director
Mark L. Johnson: treasurer, director
Sheila B. Johnson: secretary, director
John H. Robinson: executive vice president
Ruth Carter Stevenson: president, director, donor daughter B Fort Worth, TX 1925. ED Sarah Lawrence College BA (1945). NONPR AFFIL president: Amon Carter Museum Western Art.

Grants Analysis

Disclosure Period: calendar year ending 2003
Total Grants: $15,642,855*
Number of Grants: 171
Average Grant: $21,152*
Highest Grant: $7,618,750
Typical Range: $10,000 to $100,000
*Note: Giving excludes United Way; scholarships. Average grant excludes two highest grants ($12,068,191).

Recent Grants

Note: Grants derived from 2002 Form 990.
General
7,000,000	Amon Carter Museum, Ft. Worth, TX
500,000	All Saints Health Foundation, Ft. Worth, TX
500,000	Trinity Valley School, Ft. Worth, TX
400,000	WARM Place, Ft. Worth, TX
375,000	Community Enrichment Center, North Richland Hills, TX
250,000	Cancer Care Services Inc., Ft. Worth, TX
250,000	Tarrant County Youth Collaboration, Ft. Worth, TX
250,000	Texas Christian University, Ft. Worth, TX
225,000	Fort Worth Country Day School, Ft. Worth, TX
200,000	Casa Manana Musicals Inc., Ft. Worth, TX

BEIRNE CARTER FOUNDATION

Giving Contact

Lucille A. Lindamood, Grant Administrator
1802 Bayberry Ct., Suite 401
Richmond, VA 23226
Phone: (804)521-0272
Fax: (804)521-0274
E-mail: bcarterfn@aol.com
Web: http://www.bcarterfdn.org

Alternate Contact

Phone: (804)788-2288

Description

Founded: 1986
EIN: 541397827
Organization Type: General Purpose Foundation
Giving Locations: VA
Grant Types: Capital, Conference/Seminar, General Support, Project, Research, Scholarship, Seed Money.

Donor Information

Founder: Established in 1986 by the late Beirne B. Carter.

Financial Summary

Total Giving: $1,122,663 (2003); $1,293,000 (2001)
Assets: $27,803,845 (2003); $28,373,630 (2001)
Gifts Received: $3,243 (1995). Note: In 1995, contributions were received from the refund of 1994 990-PF excise tax.

Typical Recipients

Arts & Humanities: Arts Associations & Councils, Arts Centers, Arts Festivals, Arts Funds, Ballet, Ethnic & Folk Arts, Film & Video, Arts & Humanities-General, Historic Preservation, History & Archaeology, Libraries, Museums/Galleries, Music, Opera, Performing Arts, Public Broadcasting, Theater
Civic & Public Affairs: Botanical Gardens/Parks, Clubs, Community Foundations, Economic Development, Civic & Public Affairs-General, Hispanic Affairs, Housing, Legal Aid, Nonprofit Management, Philanthropic Organizations, Professional & Trade Associations, Public Policy, Urban & Community Affairs, Women's Affairs, Zoos/Aquariums
Education: Afterschool/Enrichment Programs, Agricultural Education, Arts/Humanities Education, Business Education, Colleges & Universities, Community & Junior Colleges, Education Funds, Engineering/Technological Education, Environmental Education, Education-General, Medical Education, Private Education (Precollege), Public Education (Precollege), Science/Mathematics Education, Social Sciences Education, Special Education, Student Aid
Environment: Air/Water Quality, Forestry, Environment-General, Protection, Resource Conservation, Watershed, Wildlife Protection
Health: AIDS/HIV, Arthritis, Cancer, Children's Health/Hospitals, Clinics/Medical Centers, Emergency/Ambulance Services, Hospices, Hospitals, Hospitals (University Affiliated), Medical Research, Mental Health, Nursing Services, Preventive Medicine/Wellness Organizations, Public Health, Research/Studies Institutes, Respiratory, Single-Disease Health Associations, Transplant Networks/Donor Banks
International: Human Rights
Religion: Churches, Ministries, Religious Welfare, Seminaries
Science: Science Museums
Social Services: Animal Protection, At-Risk Youth, Big Brothers/Big Sisters, Camps, Child Abuse, Child Welfare, Community Centers, Community Service Organizations, Day Care, Domestic Violence, Emergency Relief, Family Planning, Family Services, Food/Clothing Distribution, Homes, People with Disabilities, Recreation & Athletics, Scouts, Senior Services, Shelters/Homelessness, Social Services-General, YMCA/YWCA/YMHA/YWHA, Youth Organizations

Application Procedures

Initial Contact: The foundation requests applications be made in writing and be submitted in quadruplicate. Applications should be accompanied by an Application Summary Form, which can be obtained from the foundation's web site or directly from the foundation.
Application Requirements: Brief description of the organization, its history, and its purpose; a concise description of the project or activity proposed, including the specific purpose for which the grant is requested, the benefits to be provided, and the needs to be met; a detailed financial plan that includes the total cost, amount requested, amount raised to date, plans for procuring the remainder, other funding sources, and provision for contingencies and ongoing support; brief biographical information on the person who will conduct or supervise the proposed project; plans for evaluating the project's results and for sustaining the project after grant funds expire; the names and affiliations of the organization's trustees, directors, administrators, and principal staff; and a cover letter from an official of the organization stating that the organization has formally approved the proposed project. One copy of the following attachments should be included with a proposal: proof of tax-exempt status and financial statements for the current and two prior years. A new organization should submit prospective pro forma financial statements to assure statements covering at least two years are provided.
Deadlines: February 1 and August 1.
Review Process: The board meets in the spring and fall to review applications.

Restrictions

The foundation does not make grants to individuals. In general, grants are not made to endowment funds, for ongoing general operating expenses, existing deficits, debt reduction, organizations supported primarily by government funds, or to churches and related organizations.

Additional Information

Funding requests that are not of a recurring nature are given preference.
Publications: Informational Brochure (including Application Guidelines)

Foundation Officials

Mary Ross Carter Hutcheson: president
Talfourd H. Kemper: secretary, treasurer PRIM CORP EMPL principal: Woods Rogers & Hazlegrove PLC.
Kenneth C. Laughon: vice president, director

Grants Analysis

Disclosure Period: calendar year ending 2003
Total Grants: $1,122,663
Number of Grants: 40
Average Grant: $8,273*
Highest Grant: $800,000
Lowest Grant: $500
Typical Range: $1,000 to $20,000
*Note: Average grant excludes highest grant.

Recent Grants

Note: Grants derived from 2002 Form 990.
Library-Related

2,500	Charlotte County Library, Charlotte Court House, VA -- fund towards renovation and expansion

General

425,000	Beirne B Carter Center for Immunology Research, Charlottesville, VA
50,000	American Frontier Culture Foundation, Staunton, VA -- to acquire and relocate an 18th century fortified homestead (Bowman House)
50,000	Beirne B Carter Center for Immunology Research, Charlottesville, VA -- fund towards development director's salary
50,000	MCV - Massey Cancer Center, Richmond, VA -- fund towards construction of research facility
50,000	Virginia Genealogical Society, Richmond, VA -- fund towards research and publication of genealogical information
50,000	YMCA of Greater Richmond, Roanoke, VA -- fund to construct a new facility in Goochland County, Virginia
35,000	Habitat for Humanity International, Richmond, VA -- fund to purchase building supplies for new houses to be built in Southwest Virginia
30,000	Virginia Foundation for Independent Colleges, Richmond, VA -- fund towards handicapped accessibility improvements
25,000	Academy of Music, Lynchburg, VA -- fund towards the restoration of theater and construction of a performing arts complex
25,000	Achievement Center, Roanoke, VA -- to construct a new school facility

EVELYN C. CARTER TRUST

Giving Contact

Care of Bank One Trust Co.
PO Box 1308
Milwaukee, WI 53201
Phone: (414)765-2017

Description

Founded: 1997
EIN: 556129783
Organization Type: Private Foundation
Giving Locations: WV: Bridgeport
Grant Types: General Support.

Financial Summary

Total Giving: $82,508 (2003); $72,800 (2001)
Giving Analysis: Giving for 2003 includes: foundation scholarships ($20,627); 2001: foundation scholarships ($18,203)
Assets: $1,724,795 (2003); $1,793,617 (2001)

Typical Recipients

Arts & Humanities: Libraries
Civic & Public Affairs: Safety
Religion: Churches

Application Procedures

Initial Contact: No specific format is required.
Deadlines: April 30.

Restrictions

Scholarships are restricted to graduates of Bridgeport High School who are attending West Virginia University and demonstrate financial need.

Additional Information

Trust(s): Bank One Trust Company

Grants Analysis

Disclosure Period: calendar year ending 2003
Total Grants: $61,881*
Number of Grants: 3
Highest Grant: $20,627
Lowest Grant: $20,627
*Note: Giving excludes scholarships.

Recent Grants

Note: Grants derived from 2001 Form 990.
Library-Related

18,199	Bridgeport Public Library, Bridgeport, WV

General

18,199	Bridgeport United Methodist Church, Bridgeport, WV
18,199	Bridgeport Volunteer Fire Department, Bridgeport, WV

THOMAS AND AGNES CARVEL FOUNDATION

Giving Contact

Ann McHugh, Vice President, Treasurer
35 East Grassy Sprain Road
Yonkers, NY 10710
Phone: (914)793-7300
Fax: (914)793-7381

Description

Founded: 1976
EIN: 132879673
Organization Type: General Purpose Foundation
Giving Locations: NY: Westchester County
Grant Types: Capital, General Support.

Donor Information

Founder: Established in 1976 by the late Agnes Carvel and the late Thomas Carvel. The foundation is also affiliated with the International Institute of Health Foods, Inc.

Financial Summary

Total Giving: $1,986,900 (fiscal year ending November 30, 2003); $2,520,800 (fiscal 2002 approx)
Assets: $35,208,516 (fiscal 2003); $30,726,890 (fiscal 2002 approx)
Gifts Received: $6,075,650 (fiscal 2003); $214,500 (fiscal 2002); $22,304,500 (fiscal 1999). Note: In fiscal 2003, contributions were received from The Agnes Carvel 1991 Trust ($4,650) and Estate of Thomas and Agnes Carvel ($6,071,000). In 2002, contributions were received from the Agnes Carvel 1991 Trust.

Typical Recipients

Arts & Humanities: Arts Centers, Ballet, Arts & Humanities-General, History & Archaeology, Libraries, Museums/Galleries, Music, Performing Arts, Public Broadcasting, Theater
Civic & Public Affairs: Civil Rights, Community Foundations, Economic Development, Civic & Public Affairs-General, Women's Affairs
Education: Arts/Humanities Education, Colleges & Universities, Education Funds, Elementary Education (Private), Elementary Education (Public), Education-General, Private Education (Precollege), Secondary Education (Private), Social Sciences Education, Special Education, Student Aid
Environment: Environment-General, Resource Conservation, Wildlife Protection
Health: AIDS/HIV, Cancer, Children's Health/Hospitals, Clinics/Medical Centers, Emergency/Ambulance Services, Health-General, Health Organizations, Home-Care Services, Hospices, Hospitals, Medical Rehabilitation, Medical Research, Nursing Services, Nutrition, Outpatient Health Care, Prenatal Health Issues, Research/Studies Institutes, Single-Disease Health Associations, Transplant Networks/Donor Banks
International: International Organizations
Religion: Churches, Dioceses, Religion-General, Religious Organizations, Religious Welfare, Seminaries
Social Services: At-Risk Youth, Camps, Child Welfare, Community Centers, Community Service Organizations, Day Care, Domestic Violence, People with Disabilities, Recreation & Athletics, Senior Services, Shelters/Homelessness, Social Services-General, Substance Abuse, United Funds/United Ways, Volunteer Services, Youth Organizations

Application Procedures

Initial Contact: Applications must be made in writing.
Application Requirements: Applications must be supported by a budget and any additional information that may seem necessary.
Deadlines: October 1.

Foundation Officials

Robert H. Abplanalp: director
Brendan Byrne: director
William E. Griffin: president, director B 1932. PRIM CORP EMPL president: Griffin Coogan & Venaruso PC. CORP AFFIL chairman, director: Hudson Valley Bank; chairman, director: Hudson Valley Holding Corp.; secretary: Adirondack Fisheries Inc.
Ann McHugh: vice president, treasurer, director
Salvador Molella: vice president, director

Grants Analysis

Disclosure Period: fiscal year ending November 30, 2003
Total Grants: $1,986,900
Number of Grants: 54
Average Grant: $23,738*
Highest Grant: $200,000

Lowest Grant: $2,000
Typical Range: $10,000 to $50,000
*Note: Average grant figure excludes four highest grants ($800,000).

Recent Grants

Note: Grants derived from fiscal 2002 Form 990.
General

400,000	Children's Hospital Foundation
400,000	Helping Hands, Medfield, MA
200,000	New York Foundling Hospital, New York, NY
200,000	St. Joseph Medical Center, Towson, MD
165,000	Blythedale Children's Hospital, Valhalla, NY
150,000	Richmond Children Center, Yonkers, NY
100,000	Garden State Cancer Center, Belleville, NJ
100,000	Music Conservatory of Westchester, White Plains, NY
50,000	All Hallows High School, Bronx, NY
50,000	Fordham Preparatory School, Bronx, NY

ROY J. CARVER CHARITABLE TRUST

Giving Contact

Troy K. Ross, Executive Administrator
202 Iowa Avenue
Muscatine, IA 52761-3733
Phone: (563)263-4010
Fax: (563)263-1547
E-mail: info@carvertrust.org
Web: http://www.carvertrust.org

Description

Founded: 1982
EIN: 421186589
Organization Type: General Purpose Foundation
Giving Locations: IA: organizations with which the founder had significant involvement.
Grant Types: Award, Capital, Challenge, General Support, Project, Research, Scholarship, Seed Money.

Donor Information

Founder: Established in 1982 under the will of Roy J. Carver, an Iowa industrialist and philanthropist whose interests and activities were worldwide. Mr. Carver founded Bandag, Inc., the Carver Pump Company, and Carver Foundry Products, and remained active in the management of each firm until his death in 1981.

Financial Summary

Total Giving: $12,711,715 (fiscal year ending April 30, 2004); $11,103,580 (fiscal 2003); $14,473,871 (fiscal 2001)
Assets: $275,013,648 (fiscal 2004); $273,351,348 (fiscal 2001)

Typical Recipients

Arts & Humanities: Arts Outreach, Community Arts, Ethnic & Folk Arts, History & Archaeology, Libraries, Museums/Galleries, Music, Public Broadcasting, Visual Arts
Civic & Public Affairs: Asian American Affairs, Community Foundations, Employment/Job Training, Civic & Public Affairs-General, Hispanic Affairs, Municipalities/Towns, Philanthropic Organizations, Urban & Community Affairs, Zoos/Aquariums
Education: Arts/Humanities Education, Colleges & Universities, Community & Junior Colleges, Education Funds, Education Reform, Elementary Education (Private), Engineering/Technological Education, Education-General, Leadership Training, Legal Education, Literacy, Medical Education, Private Education

(Precollege), Public Education (Precollege), School Volunteerism, Science/Mathematics Education, Secondary Education (Private), Student Aid, Vocational & Technical Education
Environment: Environment-General, Research, Resource Conservation, Wildlife Protection
Health: AIDS/HIV, Alzheimer's Disease, Cancer, Children's Health/Hospitals, Emergency/Ambulance Services, Eyes/Blindness, Hospitals (University Affiliated), Medical Research, Nursing Services
Religion: Religious Welfare
Science: Observatories & Planetariums, Science Museums, Scientific Centers & Institutes, Scientific Research
Social Services: At-Risk Youth, Child Abuse, Child Welfare, Community Service Organizations, Day Care, Domestic Violence, Emergency Relief, Family Services, People with Disabilities, Recreation & Athletics, Scouts, Senior Services, Special Olympics, YMCA/YWCA/YMHA/YWHA, Youth Organizations

Application Procedures

Initial Contact: The Trust encourages initial telephone or written inquires.
Application Requirements: The proposal should contain a complete standardized application cover sheet, which is provided by the foundation; a description of organization, including its purpose, activities, and governing board; clear description of the desired purpose and goals; amount of the request and potential sources of funding; a statement of why support from the trust is vital to the success of the project; a plan for evaluating the project; and information on possible sources of funding after the grant period. Applicants should also include a copy of the IRS determination letter indicating 501(c)(3) tax-exempt status, copy of the organization's most recent audited financial statement, name of the contact person, and telephone number. contact person, and telephone number.
Deadlines: None.
Review Process: The board of trustees meets in January, April, July, and October and makes decisions on the third Friday of each of these months. Staff will consider meeting with applicants after reading their proposals. All grants are acted upon by the board of trustees after thorough screening and evaluation by the staff. The trust will send written notices to applicants within a reasonable time period.

Restrictions

The trust does not provide annual operating support or award endowments except under unusual circumstances, direct grants to individuals, or fund religious activities. It does not support political parties, offices, or candidates; fund-raising benefits; program advertising, or organizations without 501(c)(3) status.

Additional Information

Once a grant is approved, the grantee must accept the terms and conditions of an Agreement of Donee, which includes financial reporting and summary results. This practice enables the trust to review and evaluate grant performance periodically.
Publications: Biennial Report; Guidelines for Youth Recreation and Iowa Public Library; Application Form

Foundation Officials

John A. Carver: trustee
Roy James Carver, Jr.: chairman, trustee B Davenport, IA 1943. ED University of Iowa MA (1968); University of California at Berkeley (1970). PRIM CORP EMPL chairman, chief executive officer: Carver Pump Co. CORP AFFIL director: Met-Coil System Corp.; chief executive officer, director: RM Acquisitions Inc.; director: Iowa First Bancshares Inc.; director: GlobalKey; chief executive officer, chairman: Harrington Signal Inc.; president: Downtown Drug & Hardware; president: Carver Hotel Enterprises Inc.; director: Catalyst International Inc.; president: Carver Hardware Inc.; director: Bandag Inc.; president: Carver Aero Inc.

William F. Cory: secretary, trustee
J. Larry Griffith: vice chairman, trustee B 1937. PRIM CORP EMPL president, director: Mosebach Griffith.
D. Scott Ingstad: trustee
David M. Utley: trustee

Grants Analysis

Disclosure Period: fiscal year ending April 30, 2003
Total Grants: $11,103,580
Number of Grants: 85
Average Grant: $77,720*
Highest Grant: $3,600,000
Lowest Grant: $2,995
Typical Range: $25,000 to $200,000
*Note: Average grant excludes two highest grants ($4,652,811). Grants list incomplete for 2004.

Recent Grants

Note: Grants derived from fiscal 2003 Form 990.
Library-Related
82,042 Musser Public Library, Muscatine, IA -- toward upgrading technology and establishing digital image archive
60,000 Brown Memorial Library, Dumont, IA -- funding to construct new addition
60,000 Cedar Falls Public Library, Cedar Falls, IA -- funding to purchase security and self-checkout system
60,000 Community Public Library Foundation, West Point, IA -- funding for constructing a new library facility
60,000 Ely Public Library, Ely, IA -- toward library remodeling project
60,000 Iowa City Public Library Foundation, Iowa City, IA -- funding for renovation and expansion of the library
60,000 Missouri Valley Public Library, Missouri Valley, IA -- funding for library expansion
60,000 Mount Pleasant Library & Community Center, Mt. Pleasant, IA -- toward library renovation
60,000 Panora Public Library Foundation, Panora, IA -- funding for purchase of technology for the new library
60,000 Polk City Public Library Foundation, Polk City, IA -- toward construction of new library and purchase of furnishings
General
3,600,000 University of Iowa Foundation, Iowa City, IA -- toward endowment and capital projects in the College of Medicine

MARY FLAGLER CARY CHARITABLE TRUST

Giving Contact

Edward A. Ames, Trustee
122 E 42nd St., Rm. 3505
New York, NY 10168
Phone: (212)953-7700
Fax: (212)953-7720
E-mail: info@carytrust.org
Web: http://www.carytrust.org

Description

Founded: 1968
EIN: 136266964
Organization Type: General Purpose Foundation
Giving Locations: NY: New York City including metropolitan area; for music and urban environment grants eastern coastal states for conservation grants.
Grant Types: General Support, Matching, Operating Expenses, Project.

Donor Information

Founder: Established in 1968 under the will of the late Mary Flagler Cary, the daughter of Harry Hark-

ness and Anne Lamont Flagler and the wife of Melbert B. Cary, Jr., a graphic design expert. Her family was involved in the original Standard Oil Company. Mrs. Cary was interested in music, particularly the problems of young musicians trying to develop professional careers. She was also interested in the beauty of the countryside and natural landscape. Mrs. Cary owned over 1,800 acres of farmland near Millbrook, NY. Other interests are evident in the Carys' collections of fine prints, music manuscripts, and playing cards.

Financial Summary

Total Giving: $7,401,159 (fiscal year ending June 30, 2004); $6,705,918 (fiscal 2003); $8,140,089 (fiscal 2002)
Assets: $106,011,328 (fiscal 2004); $103,859,190 (fiscal 2003); $100,000,000 (fiscal 2002)

Typical Recipients

Arts & Humanities: Arts Associations & Councils, Arts Centers, Arts Funds, Arts Institutes, Arts Outreach, Community Arts, Dance, Arts & Humanities-General, Historic Preservation, Libraries, Museums/Galleries, Music, Opera, Performing Arts, Theater
Civic & Public Affairs: Asian American Affairs, Botanical Gardens/Parks, Economic Development, Employment/Job Training, Civic & Public Affairs-General, Hispanic Affairs, Inner-City Development, Law & Justice, Nonprofit Management, Philanthropic Organizations, Urban & Community Affairs
Education: Arts/Humanities Education, Colleges & Universities, Engineering/Technological Education, Environmental Education
Environment: Air/Water Quality, Environment-General, Protection, Research, Resource Conservation, Watershed, Wildlife Protection
International: International Environmental Issues
Science: Scientific Research
Social Services: Child Welfare, Community Service Organizations

Application Procedures

Initial Contact: The trust does not use an application form; send a written request.
Application Requirements: After studying a letter of request, if the trustees decide that there is a possibility of support, additional information will be requested. Trustees will want to see complete tax information, including a concise statement of the program or project; amount requested and how it fits within the applicant's overall budget; a description of organization; proof of tax-exempt status; a copy of the applicant's most recent audited financial statement; its legal name; an official letter of request on the organization's letterhead, signed by its chief executive officer on behalf of its governing body; and current list of officers, directors or trustees.
Deadlines: None. Guidelines, including application deadlines, are available for music commissioning and recording grants.
Review Process: The trustees meet at least once every month.

Restrictions

Grants are not made to individuals, international organizations, or primary or secondary schools. With certain exceptions, grants are not made to colleges, universities, or private foundations, or for building or endowment funds. Grants under the trust's music and urban environment programs are restricted to New York City.

Additional Information

Publications: Annual Report; Program Guidelines; General Information Pamphlet

Foundation Officials

Edward A. Ames: trustee
Paul Bernard Guenther: trustee B New York, NY 1940. ED Fordham University BS (1962); Columbia University MBA (1964). CORP AFFIL director: Con-

solidated Freightways; member advisory committee: Walden Capital Partners LP. NONPR AFFIL chairman: Philharmonic Symphony Society New York; trustee governing committee: Scholastic Achievement, Mary Flagler Cary Charitable Trust; chairman: Frost Valley YMCA; member: Institute Chartered Financial Analysts; member board overseers: Columbia University; trustee: Fordham University.
Phyllis J. Mills: trustee NONPR AFFIL vice chairman, director: Philharmonic Symphony Society New York.
Gayle Morgan: program director music
Lois M. Regan: consultant

Grants Analysis

Disclosure Period: fiscal year ending June 30, 2004
Total Grants: $7,401,159*
Number of Grants: 115
Average Grant: $25,796*
Highest Grant: $3,486,159
Lowest Grant: $5,000
Typical Range: $10,000 to $50,000
*Note: Average grant figure excludes two highest grants ($4,486,159).

Recent Grants

Note: Grants derived from fiscal 2002 Form 990.
General
3,671,159 Institute of Ecosystem Studies Inc., Millbrook, NY
1,450,000 Nature Conservancy, Inc., Arlington, VA -- support for the Broadwater Project of the Virginia Coast Reserve
340,000 American Music Center, Inc., New York, NY -- support for 2002 Live Music for Dance program
286,000 Citizens Committee for New York City, Inc., New York, NY
179,870 Concert Artists Guild, Inc., New York, NY -- support for commissioning a program
150,000 Chesapeake Bay Foundation, Inc., Annapolis, MD -- support for the conservation of natural resources on the Eastern shore of Maryland and Virginia
131,000 Trust for Public Land, New York, NY -- support for the neighborhood Open Space Management Program
75,000 Rockefeller University, New York, NY -- support for the Field research Scholars Program at the University's Field Research Center for Ecology and Ethology
55,000 South Carolina Coastal Conservation League Inc., Charleston, SC -- general support towards efforts to protect coastal resources in South Carolina
50,000 Natural Resources Defense Council Inc., New York, NY -- for NRDC's work to restore freshwataer flows to Everglades National Park & Florida Bay

EUGENE B. CASEY FOUNDATION

Giving Contact

Betty Brown-Casey, Chairman, President & Treasurer
800 South Frederick Avenue
Suite 100
Gaithersburg, MD 20877
Phone: (301)948-4595
Fax: (301)948-9159

Description

Founded: 1981
EIN: 526220316
Organization Type: General Purpose Foundation
Giving Locations: DC: Washington including metro-

politan area

Grant Types: Capital, General Support.

Donor Information

Founder: The foundation was established in 1981 by Eugene B. Casey.

Financial Summary

Total Giving: $12,540,500 (fiscal year ending August 31, 2003); $52,470,000 (fiscal 2002 approx)

Giving Analysis: Giving for fiscal 2002 includes: foundation scholarships ($5,000) foundation (approx $185,000)

Assets: $171,300,260 (fiscal 2003); $171,703,050 (fiscal 2002 approx)

Gifts Received: $4,500,000 (fiscal 2003); $4,900 (fiscal 1999); $68,000 (fiscal 1997). Note: In fiscal 2003, contributions were received from Betty Brown Casey. In fiscal 1999, contributions were received from Heartland Development. In fiscal 1997, contributions were received from Blandford Casey, Rockville Development, and Nancy Corp.

Typical Recipients

Arts & Humanities: Arts Associations & Councils, Arts Institutes, Ballet, Historic Preservation, History & Archaeology, Libraries, Museums/Galleries, Opera, Performing Arts, Public Broadcasting, Theater, Visual Arts

Civic & Public Affairs: Business/Free Enterprise, Civil Rights, Clubs, Community Foundations, Economic Development, Economic Policy, Employment/ Job Training, Civic & Public Affairs-General, Housing, Law & Justice, Native American Affairs, Parades/ Festivals, Philanthropic Organizations, Public Policy, Rural Affairs, Women's Affairs

Education: Arts/Humanities Education, Colleges & Universities, Education Reform, Environmental Education, Faculty Development, Education-General, Journalism/Media Education, Literacy, Medical Education, Minority Education, Private Education (Precollege), Secondary Education (Private), Social Sciences Education, Special Education, Student Aid

Environment: Environment-General, Protection

Health: Cancer, Children's Health/Hospitals, Clinics/ Medical Centers, Emergency/Ambulance Services, Eyes/Blindness, Health Funds, Health Organizations, Heart, Hospices, Hospitals, Hospitals (University Affiliated), Medical Research, Mental Health, Nutrition, Single-Disease Health Associations, Speech & Hearing

Religion: Churches, Religion-General, Religious Organizations, Religious Welfare, Social/Policy Issues

Science: Scientific Centers & Institutes

Social Services: Camps, Child Abuse, Child Welfare, Community Centers, Community Service Organizations, Domestic Violence, Family Planning, Food/ Clothing Distribution, People with Disabilities, Recreation & Athletics, Senior Services, Shelters/ Homelessness, Substance Abuse, Veterans, YMCA/ YWCA/YMHA/YWHA, Youth Organizations

Application Procedures

Initial Contact: The foundation has no formal grant application procedure or grant application form.

Application Requirements: Applicants should submit written proposals that include an annual report, the purpose for which the funds are requested, form of project control, and the amount and proportions of funds requested compared with the total sought from other organizations.

Deadlines: None.

Foundation Officials

Betty Brown Casey: chairman, president, treasurer, trustee B 1928. ED Washington College. PRIM CORP EMPL president: Casey Engineering.

William James Price, IV: trustee B Baltimore, MD 1924. ED Yale University BS (1949). NONPR AFFIL trustee: Saint Pauls School; trustee: Washington College; member: National Association Securities Deal-

ers.

John S. Saia: trustee

Grants Analysis

Disclosure Period: fiscal year ending August 31, 2003

Total Grants: $12,540,500*

Number of Grants: 22

Average Grant: $51,444*

Highest Grant: $6,514,500

Lowest Grant: $5,000

Typical Range: $10,000 to $100,000

*Note: Average grant figure excludes four highest grants ($11,614,500)

Recent Grants

Note: Grants derived from 2003 Form 990.

General

6,814,500	Washington Opera, Washington, DC
3,100,000	Suburban Hospital, Bethesda, MD
1,000,000	Massachusetts Ear and Eye Infirmary, Boston, MA -- for Voice Restoration program
1,000,000	Shugar Foundation, Bethesda, MD
135,000	Montgomery Hospice Foundation, Rockville, MD -- for Eugene B. Casey endowment fund at Casey House
100,000	Duke Ellington School for Arts, Washington, DC -- for Dennis Graves endowment fund
100,000	Georgetown University Medical Center, Washington, DC
100,000	Georgetown Visitation School, Washington, DC
20,000	Boys and Girls Clubs of Central Maryland, Baltimore, MD
20,000	Clean and Sober Streets, Washington, DC

O. W. CASPERSEN FOUNDATION FOR AID TO HEALTH AND EDUCATION

Giving Contact

Lucille Keegan, Secretary
PO Box 617
Gladstone, NJ 07934-0617
Phone: (908)719-6592

Description

Founded: 1964

EIN: 510101350

Organization Type: Private Foundation

Giving Locations: East coast.

Grant Types: Capital, Emergency, General Support, Multiyear/Continuing Support, Operating Expenses, Research.

Donor Information

Founder: the late O. W. Caspersen

Financial Summary

Total Giving: $1,656,000 (2003)

Assets: $13,953,027 (2003)

Gifts Received: $482,381 (2003); $743,028 (2000); $961,358 (1999). Note: In 1998, 1999, and 2003, contributions were received from the Freda R. Caspersen Charitable Lead Unitrust.

Typical Recipients

Arts & Humanities: Arts Associations & Councils, Arts Funds, Historic Preservation, Libraries

Civic & Public Affairs: Civic & Public Affairs-General

Education: Colleges & Universities, Education-

General, Legal Education, Private Education (Precollege), Science/Mathematics Education

Environment: Environment-General, Resource Conservation, Watershed, Wildlife Protection

Health: Emergency/Ambulance Services, Geriatric Health, Health Funds, Health Organizations, Hospitals, Single-Disease Health Associations

Religion: Churches

Social Services: Child Welfare, Recreation & Athletics, Scouts, Social Services-General, YMCA/YWCA/ YMHA/YWHA

Application Procedures

Initial Contact: The foundation has no formal grant application procedure or application form.

Deadlines: None.

Restrictions

Support is given for health and education grants only.

Foundation Officials

Barbara M. Caspersen: vice president, treasurer

Erik Michael Westby Caspersen: vice president, director

Finn M. W. Caspersen, Jr.: vice president, director

Finn M. W. Caspersen, Sr.: president B New York, NY 1941. ED Brown University BA (1963); Harvard University LLB (1966). CORP AFFIL vice president: Westby Corp.; director: Beneficial Bank PLC; member executive committee, director: Beneficial National Bank. NONPR AFFIL director: Shelter Harbor Fire District; chairman: U.S. Equestrian Team; chairman: Prosperity New Jersey; member: Partnership for New Jersey; trustee, chairman: Peddie School; member: New York State Bar Association; chairman dean advisory board: Harvard University Law School; advisory board: Institute for Law & Economic; member: Harvard Resources Comm; member: Florida Bar Association; chairman: Gladstone Equestrian Association Inc.; director: Drumthwacket Foundation; chairman: Coalition Better Transportation; chairman: Coalition Service Industry; emeritus trustee: Brown University; member: American Finance Services Association; trustee: BGCN Life Camp Inc. CLUB AFFIL Wilmington Country Club; Knickerbocker Club; University Club; Harvard Club.

Samuel Michael Westby Caspersen: vice president, director

Grants Analysis

Disclosure Period: calendar year ending 2003

Total Grants: $1,656,000

Number of Grants: 17

Average Grant: $15,000*

Highest Grant: $891,000

Lowest Grant: $1,000

Typical Range: $5,000 to $25,000

*Note: Average grant figure excludes two highest grants ($1,431,000).

Recent Grants

Note: Grants derived from 2001 Form 990.

General

225,000	Princeton International Regatta Association, Gladstone, NJ
200,000	Gladstone Equestrian Association, Gladstone, NJ
143,489	Save Ellis Island Foundation, Gladstone, NJ
26,000	Shipley School, Bryn Mawr, PA
25,000	Drew University, Madison, NJ
25,000	French and Pickering Creeks Conservation Trust, Pottstown, PA
25,000	Hospital for Special Surgery Fund, New York, NY
25,000	Kimberton Waldorf School, Kimberton, PA
21,000	Cardigan Mountain School, Canaan, NH
20,000	Brown University, Providence, RI

LOUIS N. CASSETT FOUNDATION

Giving Contact
Malcolm B. Jacobson, Trustee
1 Penn Center, Suite 1220
Philadelphia, PA 19103
Phone: (215)563-8886

Description
Founded: 1946
EIN: 236274038
Organization Type: Private Foundation
Giving Locations: Northeast.
Grant Types: Capital, General Support.

Donor Information
Founder: the late Louis N. Cassett

Financial Summary
Total Giving: $410,400 (2003). Note: 1996 Giving includes United Way ($15,000).
Giving Analysis: Giving for 2003 includes: foundation grants to United Way ($18,000)
Assets: $9,240,025 (2003)

Typical Recipients
Arts & Humanities: Arts Centers, Arts Institutes, Arts Outreach, Ballet, Community Arts, Arts & Humanities-General, Historic Preservation, Libraries, Museums/Galleries, Music, Performing Arts, Public Broadcasting, Theater
Civic & Public Affairs: Civil Rights, Civic & Public Affairs-General, Law & Justice, Public Policy, Zoos/Aquariums
Education: Arts/Humanities Education, Colleges & Universities, Education-General, Legal Education, Minority Education, Special Education
Environment: Environment-General, Resource Conservation
Health: Alzheimer's Disease, Cancer, Children's Health/Hospitals, Clinics/Medical Centers, Diabetes, Emergency/Ambulance Services, Geriatric Health, Hospitals, Medical Research, Nursing Services, Nutrition, Public Health, Single-Disease Health Associations
International: International Relief Efforts, Missionary/Religious Activities
Religion: Churches, Jewish Causes, Religious Organizations, Religious Welfare
Social Services: Big Brothers/Big Sisters, Child Welfare, Community Service Organizations, Day Care, Family Planning, People with Disabilities, Recreation & Athletics, Senior Services, Substance Abuse, United Funds/United Ways, Volunteer Services

Application Procedures
Initial Contact: Send a brief letter of inquiry.
Application Requirements: Include a description of organization, amount requested, purpose of funds sought, recently audited financial statement, and proof of tax-exempt status.
Deadlines: None.

Restrictions
Does not support individuals.

Foundation Officials
Carol Gerstley: trustee
Malcolm B. Jacobson: trustee

Grants Analysis
Disclosure Period: calendar year ending 2003
Total Grants: $392,400*
Number of Grants: 155
Average Grant: $2,532
Highest Grant: $15,000
Lowest Grant: $500
Typical Range: $1,000 to $5,000
*Note: Giving excludes United Way.

Recent Grants
Note: Grants derived from 2001 Form 990.
General

30,000	United Cerebral Palsy, New York, NY
27,500	Philadelphia Geriatric Center, Philadelphia, PA
17,500	Tiferet Bet Israel Synagogue, Blue Bell, PA
15,000	Federation Allied Jewish Appeal, Philadelphia, PA
15,000	Philadelphia Orchestra, Philadelphia, PA
15,000	United Way, Philadelphia, PA
10,000	American Red Cross of Palm Beach County, West Palm Beach, FL
10,000	Children's Hospital Trust, West Palm Beach, FL
10,000	Fairfield University, Fairfield, CT
10,000	Friends of the Unitarian Universalist Union, Boston, MA

HAROLD K. L. CASTLE FOUNDATION

Giving Contact
Christine B. Plunkett, Grants Program Manager
146 Hekili Street, Suite 203A
Kailua, HI 96734
Phone: (808)262-9413
Fax: (808)261-6918
E-mail: bradenkf@aloha.com
Web: http://www.castlefoundation.org

Description
Founded: 1962
EIN: 996005445
Organization Type: General Purpose Foundation
Giving Locations: HI: focusing on Windward Oahu
Grant Types: Capital, Challenge, General Support, Matching, Multiyear/Continuing Support, Seed Money.
Note: Grants are awarded for program start-up or expansion through matching, challenge, and multiyear grants. Capital grants are awarded up to five years and project/program grants up to three years.

Donor Information
Founder: The foundation was established in 1962, with the late Harold K. L. Castle and his wife, the late Alice Hedemann Castle, as donors. Mr. Castle, a prominent landowner and community leader, owned the Kaneohe Ranch. The ranch company was dissolved upon Mr. Castle's death; some of the land and commercial properties from the original ranch provide the base for the foundation's assets. The foundation is the largest private foundation based in Hawaii.

Financial Summary
Total Giving: $6,183,231 (2004); $8,645,114 (2003); $5,507,800 (2002)
Assets: $180,000,000 (2003 approx); $180,000,000 (2002)

Typical Recipients
Arts & Humanities: Arts Associations & Councils, Arts Centers, Community Arts, Dance, Ethnic & Folk Arts, Arts & Humanities-General, Historic Preservation, History & Archaeology, Libraries, Museums/Galleries, Music, Opera, Performing Arts, Public Broadcasting, Theater, Visual Arts
Civic & Public Affairs: Botanical Gardens/Parks, Business/Free Enterprise, Community Foundations, Economic Development, Employment/Job Training, Civic & Public Affairs-General, Housing, Legal Aid, Philanthropic Organizations, Public Policy, Urban & Community Affairs, Zoos/Aquariums
Education: Afterschool/Enrichment Programs, Arts/Humanities Education, Colleges & Universities, Community & Junior Colleges, Economic Education, Education Associations, Education Funds, Elementary Education (Private), Elementary Education (Public), Environmental Education, Education-General, Gifted & Talented Programs, International Studies, Literacy, Preschool Education, Private Education (Precollege), Public Education (Precollege), Science/Mathematics Education, Secondary Education (Private), Secondary Education (Public), Student Aid
Environment: Air/Water Quality, Environment-General, Resource Conservation, Wildlife Protection
Health: AIDS/HIV, Cancer, Children's Health/Hospitals, Clinics/Medical Centers, Emergency/Ambulance Services, Health Funds, Health Organizations, Heart, Hospices, Hospitals, Medical Rehabilitation, Mental Health, Prenatal Health Issues, Single-Disease Health Associations
International: International Affairs, International Development, International Environmental Issues
Religion: Churches, Dioceses, Ministries, Religious Organizations, Religious Welfare
Science: Science-General, Science Museums, Scientific Centers & Institutes
Social Services: Animal Protection, At-Risk Youth, Big Brothers/Big Sisters, Camps, Child Abuse, Community Centers, Community Service Organizations, Day Care, Delinquency & Criminal Rehabilitation, Domestic Violence, Emergency Relief, Family Planning, Family Services, Food/Clothing Distribution, People with Disabilities, Scouts, Senior Services, Sexual Abuse, Shelters/Homelessness, Substance Abuse, United Funds/United Ways, YMCA/YWCA/YMHA/YWHA, Youth Organizations

Application Procedures
Initial Contact: Applicants should mail, fax or e-mail a letter no longer than 2 pages.
Application Requirements: Within one month of receipt of your inquiry, the foundation will write either to invite you to submit a full proposal or to inform you that the Foundation will be unable to consider your request due to a mismatch with current Foundation priorities.
Deadlines: None. Submit proposals by the first of the month prior to the month of the meeting date (i.e., January 1, March 1, May 1, etc.). The board generally meets every other month.
Review Process: The foundation directors will generally notify recipients within one week of the meeting. Larger grants (more than $100,000) are usually paid in December.

Restrictions
Eligible grantees include nonprofit organizations in Hawaii with IRS code Section 501(c)(3) "public" charity status, and government in areas not primarily tax-supported. The foundation does not give grants to individuals. Presentations cannot be made at a meeting of the foundation's directors.

Additional Information
All funded organizations are required to sign a written grant agreement detailing the use of the grant funds, reporting requirements, and other specifics of the grant.
The foundation approves about 30-35% of all proposals it receives.
Organizations should not resubmit a proposal until the next fiscal year.
As stated in the guidelines, applicants are welcome to contact staff prior to submittal to discuss proposals.
Publications: Annual Report; Guidelines

Foundation Officials
Carlton K. C. Au: chief financial officer, treasurer
William E. Aull: director B 1922. PRIM NONPR EMPL treasurer, director: Mid Pacific Institute. CORP AFFIL director: Victoria Ward Ltd. NONPR AFFIL director: Hawaii Pacific University; treasurer: Mid-Pacific Institute.
Henry Mitchell D'Olier: president, chief executive officer, director B Chicago, IL 1946. ED University of

Iowa BA (1968); University of Iowa JD (1972). PRIM CORP EMPL partner tax & health management committee: Goodsil, Anderson, Quinn & Stifel. CORP AFFIL president: Victoria Ward Ltd.; director: Reyns Mens Wear. NONPR AFFIL vice president: Central Union Church.

Randolph G. Moore: director B Honolulu, HI 1939. ED Swarthmore College (1961); Stanford University (1963). PRIM CORP EMPL chief executive officer: Kaneohe Ranch. CORP AFFIL director: Hawaii Stevedores; director: Maui Land & Pineapple Co.; director: Grove Farm Co. Ltd.

Grants Analysis

Disclosure Period: calendar year ending 2004
Total Grants: $6,183,231
Number of Grants: 54
Average Grant: $78,929*
Highest Grant: $2,000,000
Lowest Grant: $2,500
Typical Range: $25,000 to $100,000
*Note: Average grant figure excludes highest grant.

Recent Grants

Note: Grants derived from 2002 Form 990.
General

900,000	Iolani School, Honolulu, HI -- to upgrade and expand facilities campus-wide
750,000	Maui Community Arts & Cultural Center, Maui, HI
600,000	Honolulu Academy of Arts, Honolulu, HI
500,000	Le Jardin D'Enfants Inc., Kailua, HI
400,000	Chaminade University of Honolulu, Honolulu, HI -- toward the multi-phase renovation of the laboratories for the natural sciences and mathematics division
400,000	Hawaii Pacific University, Honolulu, HI -- towards improvements and expansion of the Hawaii Loa campus
400,000	Mid-Pacific Institute, Honolulu, HI -- towards the capital campaign for a new mathematics and science technology complex
400,000	University of Oregon, Eugene, OR
350,000	Hanahauoli School, Honolulu, HI -- to enable the school to implement a model multiage curriculum
333,333	University of Hawaii Foundation, Honolulu, HI -- towards renovation, expansion and staffing of the reproductive and developmental biology laboratory

SAMUEL N. AND MARY CASTLE FOUNDATION

Giving Contact

Alfred L. Castle, Executive Director, Treasurer
The Pacific Garden Center, Makai Tower
733 Bishop Street, Suite 1275
Honolulu, HI 96813
Phone: (808)522-1101
Fax: (808)522-1103
E-mail: acastle@aloha.net
Web: http://fdncenter.org/grantmaker/castle/

Description

Founded: 1925
EIN: 996003321
Organization Type: General Purpose Foundation
Giving Locations: HI
Grant Types: Award, Capital, Challenge, General Support, Multiyear/Continuing Support, Project, Seed Money.

Donor Information

Founder: In 1898, Mary Tenney Castle (d. 1907), the widow of Samuel Northrop Castle (1809-1894), set aside one quarter of her estate to establish the Mary Castle Fund. Her husband had been a congregational missionary and a businessman who co-founded Castle & Cooke, one of Hawaii's largest corporations. In 1925, the Samuel N. and Mary Castle Foundation was incorporated with the transfer of assets from the Mary Castle Fund.

Financial Summary

Total Giving: $1,834,058 (2004); $2,010,570 (2003); $2,299,407 (2002)
Assets: $39,725,321 (2002); $50,200,263 (2001)
Gifts Received: $1,350 (2001)

Typical Recipients

Arts & Humanities: Arts Centers, Arts Festivals, Arts Outreach, Arts & Humanities-General, History & Archaeology, Libraries, Literary Arts, Museums/Galleries, Music, Opera, Public Broadcasting, Theater, Visual Arts

Civic & Public Affairs: Asian American Affairs, Botanical Gardens/Parks, Community Foundations, Economic Development, Employment/Job Training, Civic & Public Affairs-General, Nonprofit Management, Parades/Festivals, Public Policy, Urban & Community Affairs, Women's Affairs

Education: Afterschool/Enrichment Programs, Arts/Humanities Education, Business Education, Colleges & Universities, Education Associations, Education Funds, Education Reform, Elementary Education (Private), Elementary Education (Public), Environmental Education, Faculty Development, Education-General, Gifted & Talented Programs, International Studies, Literacy, Minority Education, Preschool Education, Private Education (Precollege), Public Education (Precollege), Religious Education, Science/Mathematics Education, Secondary Education (Private), Secondary Education (Public), Special Education, Student Aid, Vocational & Technical Education

Environment: Environment-General, Research, Resource Conservation

Health: AIDS/HIV, Cancer, Children's Health/Hospitals, Clinics/Medical Centers, Emergency/Ambulance Services, Health Funds, Health Organizations, Hospices, Hospitals, Mental Health, Prenatal Health Issues, Respiratory, Speech & Hearing

International: Foreign Educational Institutions, International Affairs, International Organizations, International Relations

Religion: Churches, Religion-General, Ministries, Missionary Activities (Domestic), Religious Organizations, Religious Welfare

Science: Scientific Centers & Institutes

Social Services: Animal Protection, At-Risk Youth, Camps, Child Welfare, Community Centers, Community Service Organizations, Day Care, Emergency Relief, Family Services, Food/Clothing Distribution, People with Disabilities, Recreation & Athletics, Scouts, Special Olympics, Substance Abuse, United Funds/United Ways, YMCA/YWCA/YMHA/YWHA, Youth Organizations

Application Procedures

Initial Contact: Applicants should write or call the foundation for priorities and grantmaking policies. Grant seekers are encouraged to call, visit, or e-mail the foundation to determine the appropriateness of an application before submitting a complete proposal.

Application Requirements: Written proposals must contain a brief summary describing the organization, with history, mission, goals and major achievements; population to be served and any relevant characteristics; community opportunity or need which proposal addresses; program or project objectives, a summary of activities to be funded, and any other programmatic details that help clarify the request; amount requested, the duration of time over which foundation funds will be needed, and anticipated sources of support when foundation funding ceases; proposed methods of program/project evaluation; and information about the applicant organization's staff, including those responsible for the program/project.

One copy of each of the following attachments should be included with a proposal: IRS determination letter; the organization's charter and bylaws; most recently completed financial statements for the organization's operation for a full year, preferably audited, showing the year's income and expenses, fund balances at year's end and an explanation for anything unusual in the statements; a copy of the organization's current operating budget; a cover letter signed by the presiding officer of the board and the executive director of the organization, indicating that both the board and the chief staff person have approved the proposal; and the name and phone number of the contact person.

Proposals should also be accompanied by two copies of the following: a one or two-page executive summary; an expense budget for the proposed activity and the revenue plan for the budget with two categories of sources and amounts; and a list of the board of directors, with occupations or positions and a statement of board involvement and functions within the organization.

Deadlines: February 1 for the April meeting, June 1 for the August meeting, and October 1 for the December meeting. Organizations seeking $25,000 or more for major capital must submit proposals by October 1, for review at the December meeting.

Restrictions

Grants are not made to organizations that cannot confirm their 501(c)(3) status. The foundation does not generally award grants to organizations located outside of the state of Hawaii; for programs or projects for which funds are based solely on an organizational need rather than in response to a documented community need; where foundation support would exceed 50% of the program or project budget; to endowment funds; or to third party regranting organizations. Program and project support does not generally exceed three years, and all funding must be applied for on a yearly basis.

Additional Information

Organizations requesting funds from the Henry and Dorothy Castle Memorial Fund should submit requests directly to the Samuel N. and Mary Castle Foundation.

Organizations receiving support from the foundation must submit a brief report summarizing the outcome of the project and a financial accounting of the grant expenditures.

Publications: Annual Report; Requests for Proposals for the Henry and Dorothy Castle Memorial Fund
Trust(s): Bank of Hawaii

Foundation Officials

John C. Baldwin: vice president, trustee B 1937. PRIM CORP EMPL treasurer: HNJ2 Inc. CORP AFFIL officer: Walker Industries Ltd.

Alfred L. Castle: executive director, treasurer, trustee B Washington, DC 1948. ED University of New Mexico; Colorado State University BA (1971); Colorado State University MA (1972); Columbia University (1980). PRIM NONPR EMPL vice president development: Hawaii Pacific University. NONPR AFFIL member: San Diego Council Grantmakers; trustee: Trimble Charitable Trust; trustee: Robert Black Memorial Trust; trustee: Hawaiian Historical Society; executive director: NMMI Federation; trustee: Hawaii School Girls; member: Governors Council Children Youth; trustee: Hawaii Food Bank; member: Council Foundations; member: Association Grantmakers Hawaii; trustee: Henry & Dorothy Castle Fund; trustee: Academy Pacific.

James C. McIntosh: vice president, trustee
Rod McPhee: president, trustee
Cynthia Quisenberry: secretary, trustee

Grants Analysis

Disclosure Period: calendar year ending 2004
Total Grants: $1,834,058
Number of Grants: 70
Average Grant: $26,201
Highest Grant: $150,000
Lowest Grant: $1,628
Typical Range: $10,000 to $50,000

Recent Grants

Note: Grants derived from 2002 Form 990.
Library-Related

10,000	Hoover Presidential Library Association, West Branch, IA -- fund towards W.R. Castle, Jr. Fellowship program

General

300,000	Seabury Hall, Makawao, HI -- fund towards expansion and upgrade of educational facilities
250,000	YMCA of Honolulu, Honolulu, HI -- fund towards 'reaching for tomorrow' capital campaign
100,000	American Red Cross, Honolulu, HI -- fund towards renovation of the Diamond Head facility
100,000	Castle Medical Center, Kailua, HI -- fund towards planning and design of phase II of capital improvement
100,000	Iolani School, Honolulu, HI -- fund towards renovation and construction of facilities
100,000	Le Jardin Windward Oahu Academy, Kailua, HI -- fund towards construction of a new facility
80,000	Chaminade University of Honolulu, Honolulu, HI -- fund towards Castle colleagues program
55,000	Hawaii Pacific University, Honolulu, HI -- fund towards improvements to the Hawaii Loa campus
50,000	City of Refuge Christian Church, Waipahu, HI -- fund towards renovation of the preschool/daycare building
50,000	Doris Todd Memorial Christian School, Paia, HI -- fund towards the construction of classrooms

CASTLE ROCK FOUNDATION

Giving Contact

Sally W. Rippey, Executive Director
4100 East Mississippi Avenue, Suite 1850
Denver, CO 80246
Phone: (303)388-1683
Fax: (303)388-1684
E-mail: generalinfo@castlerockfdn.org
Web: http://www.castlerockfoundation.org

Alternate Contact

John W. Jackson, National Program Advisor

Description

Founded: 1993
EIN: 841243301
Organization Type: Private Foundation
Giving Locations: nationally.
Grant Types: General Support, Project, Scholarship.

Financial Summary

Total Giving: $2,145,850 (fiscal year ending November 30, 2003); $2,630,800 (fiscal 2002); $3,397,000 (fiscal 2001)
Assets: $47,100,918 (fiscal 2003); $40,978,334 (fiscal 2002); $50,862,306 (fiscal 2001)
Gifts Received: $36,596,253 (fiscal 1994). Note:

Contributions were received from Adolph Coors Foundation.

Typical Recipients

Arts & Humanities: Ethnic & Folk Arts, Historic Preservation, History & Archaeology, Libraries, Museums/Galleries, Public Broadcasting
Civic & Public Affairs: African American Affairs, Botanical Gardens/Parks, Business/Free Enterprise, Civil Rights, Community Foundations, Economic Development, Economic Policy, Civic & Public Affairs-General, Law & Justice, Legal Aid, Native American Affairs, Philanthropic Organizations, Professional & Trade Associations, Public Policy, Urban & Community Affairs, Women's Affairs
Education: Arts/Humanities Education, Colleges & Universities, Economic Education, Education Associations, Education Funds, Education Reform, Faculty Development, Education-General, Journalism/Media Education, Leadership Training, Legal Education, Minority Education, Private Education (Precollege), Social Sciences Education, Student Aid
Environment: Environment-General, Research
Health: Cancer, Children's Health/Hospitals, Clinics/Medical Centers, Health Policy/Cost Containment, Hospices, Medical Research, Preventive Medicine/Wellness Organizations
International: Health Care/Hospitals
Religion: Dioceses, Ministries, Religious Organizations, Religious Welfare, Social/Policy Issues
Social Services: Community Centers, Family Services, Scouts, Youth Organizations

Application Procedures

Initial Contact: One copy of a proposal.
Application Requirements: Legal name and address of organization; most recent copy of IRS letter of exemption; date of establishment, brief history and mission statement; purpose and amount of grant, as well as a description of the project and a project budget; current and/or proposed income and expense budget for the organization; anticipated results; financial statements for most recent fiscal year (preferably copy of audit); funding sources and amounts; names and occupations of board of directors and officers; names and addresses of those who have benefited from the organization's work.
Deadlines: April 30.
Review Process: The board of trustees meets once a year in the late fall to consider requests. An on-site visit may be conducted.

Restrictions

The foundation will generally not consider support of the following: human service agencies; museums or museum projects; organizations primarily supported by tax-derived funding; individuals; endowments; scientific or medical research projects; publications or production of films or other media-related projects; churches or church projects; funding of deficits or retirement of debt; special events; out of country projects; or purchase of computer equipment.

Additional Information

Publications: Annual Report

Foundation Officials

Holland H. Coors: trustee
Jeffrey H. Coors: treasurer B Denver, CO 1944. ED Cornell University BSChE (1967); Cornell University MSChE (1968). PRIM CORP EMPL co-president, chief executive officer: ACX Technologies Inc. CORP AFFIL officer: Golden Photon Inc.; president, chief executive officer: Graphic Packaging Corp.; officer: Golden Genesis Co. Inc.
Peter Coors: trustee
William K. Coors: trustee B Golden, CO August 11, 1916. ED Princeton University BSChE (1938); Princeton University MSChE (1939). PRIM CORP EMPL chairman, president, chief executive officer, director: Adolph Coors Co.
Rev. Robert G. Windsor: trustee

Grants Analysis

Disclosure Period: fiscal year ending November 30, 2003
Total Grants: $2,145,850
Number of Grants: 43
Average Grant: $41,362*
Highest Grant: $250,000
Lowest Grant: $5,000
Typical Range: $20,000 to $75,000
***Note:** Average grant figure excludes two highest grants ($450,000).

Recent Grants

Note: Grants derived from fiscal 2003 Form 990.
Library-Related

100,000	Laura Bush Foundation for America's Libraries, Washington, DC

General

250,000	Episcopal Diocese of Massachusetts, Boston, MA -- capital support for camp and conference center
200,000	Heritage Foundation, Washington, DC
138,850	Hillsdale College, Hillsdale, MI -- towards managed endowment fund
75,000	Institute for Justice, Washington, DC
75,000	Leadership Institute, Arlington, VA
75,000	Mountain States Legal Foundation, Lakewood, CO
55,000	Landmark Legal Foundation, Herndon, VA
50,000	American Enterprise Institute for Public Policy Research, Washington, DC
50,000	American Legislative Exchange Council, Washington, DC
50,000	Becket Fund for Religious Liberty, Washington, DC

CATERPILLAR INC.

Company Headquarters

100 NE Adams St.
Peoria, IL 61629
Web: http://www.cat.com

Company Description

Founded: 1925
Ticker: CAT
Exchange: NYSE
Revenue: US$30.251 billion (2004)
Profit: US$2.035 billion (2004)
Employees: 69169 (2003)
Fortune Rank: 57, per FORTUNE Magazine's list of 500 Largest U.S. Corporations (2004).
SIC(s): 3272 Concrete Products Nec, 3511 Turbines & Turbine Generator Sets, 3519 Internal Combustion Engines Nec, 3531 Construction Machinery.

Operating Locations

Caterpillar Inc. (AL--Opelika; AZ--Green Valley; CO--Denver; DC--Washington; FL--Jacksonville; GA--Atlanta; IL--Aurora, Decatur, Joliet, Lisle, Morton Grove, Mossville, Pontiac, Springfield; IN--Indianapolis, Lafayette; MS--Corinth; NC--Clayton; PA--Camp Hill, York; TX--Houston, Irving; WA--Spokane; WI--Edgerton)

Nonmonetary Support

Value: $700,000 (1999)
Type: Donated Equipment; In-kind Services; Loaned Executives
Contact: Henry Holling

Caterpillar Foundation

Giving Contact

Henry Holling, Vice President
Caterpillar Foundation

100 NE Adams Street
Peoria, IL 61629-1480
Phone: (309)675-4464
Fax: (309)675-5815
Web: http://www.cat.com/foundation

Description
Founded: 1952
EIN: 376022314
Organization Type: Corporate Foundation
Giving Locations: operating locations; educational matching gifts program is international.
Grant Types: Capital, Employee Matching Gifts, General Support, Scholarship.
Note: Employee matching gift ratio: 1 to 1 for higher education only.

Donor Information
Founder: Caterpillar

Financial Summary
Total Giving: $11,880,006 (2003); $11,297,890 (2002); $11,753,614 (2001)
Giving Analysis: Giving for 2001 includes: foundation grants to United Way ($1,053,750); foundation ($10,699,864)
Assets: $53,137,342 (2003); $53,806,089 (2002); $54,805,299 (2001)
Gifts Received: $11,209,816 (2003); $10,452,000 (2002); $14,100,000 (2001). Note: Contributions are received from Caterpillar, Inc.

Typical Recipients
Arts & Humanities: Arts Centers, Arts Funds, Community Arts, Arts & Humanities-General, Historic Preservation, History & Archaeology, Museums/Galleries, Music, Opera, Performing Arts, Public Broadcasting, Theater
Civic & Public Affairs: African American Affairs, Botanical Gardens/Parks, Business/Free Enterprise, Civil Rights, Community Foundations, Economic Development, Economic Policy, Employment/Job Training, Ethnic Organizations, Civic & Public Affairs-General, Hispanic Affairs, Housing, Law & Justice, Municipalities/Towns, Nonprofit Management, Professional & Trade Associations, Public Policy, Safety, Urban & Community Affairs
Education: Afterschool/Enrichment Programs, Business Education, Colleges & Universities, Community & Junior Colleges, Economic Education, Education Funds, Education Reform, Engineering/Technological Education, Faculty Development, Education-General, International Studies, Medical Education, Minority Education, Private Education (Precollege), Public Education (Precollege), Science/Mathematics Education, Student Aid, Vocational & Technical Education
Environment: Forestry, Environment-General, Resource Conservation
Health: Cancer, Children's Health/Hospitals, Emergency/Ambulance Services, Health Organizations, Hospices, Hospitals, Medical Rehabilitation, Mental Health, Public Health, Single-Disease Health Associations
International: International Environmental Issues, International Peace & Security Issues, Trade
Religion: Religion-General, Ministries, Missionary Activities (Domestic), Religious Organizations, Religious Welfare
Science: Science Museums
Social Services: Camps, Child Welfare, Community Centers, Community Service Organizations, Domestic Violence, Emergency Relief, Family Services, Homes, People with Disabilities, Scouts, Senior Services, Sexual Abuse, Social Services-General, Special Olympics, Substance Abuse, United Funds/United Ways, YMCA/YWCA/YMHA/YWHA, Youth Organizations

Application Procedures
Initial Contact: Submit a brief proposal to the nearest Caterpillar facility.

Application Requirements: Include the date; organization's name, address, phone and fax; name, address, phone and position of contact person; a description of organization; proof of tax-exempt status; purpose of the project or campaign, total goal, portion of the total already on hand, and if the funds will be used for operating or capital items; reason that Caterpillar should contribute to the cause, and the benefit to Caterpillar; list of other organizations providing similar support and how they provide it; amount requested and why; number of Caterpillar employees or family members are members of the applicant organization; number of Caterpillar employees or family members that might benefit from this project and how; whether the proposal is for an annual request for funds; whether funds are also being sought or obtained from others such as governmental bodies, United Way, etc., and to what degree; and, where appropriate, information on the details of the proposal, copy of current budget, copy of the most recent audited financial report, list of major donors/pledges, and list of board members and their affiliations.
Deadlines: None.
Decision Notification: Notice of approval or rejection is usually sent within one month of proposal receipt.

Restrictions
In general, company does not support individuals, fraternal organizations, religious organizations whose services are limited to any one sectarian group, political activity, tickets or advertising for fund-raising benefits, or general operations or ongoing programs of agencies funded by the United Way.

Foundation Officials
R. D. Beran: treasurer
J. B. Buda: secretary
T. L. Elder: director, vice president
Henry W. Holling: vice president ED Bradley University BA (1965). NONPR AFFIL director: Associated Colleges of Illinois.
R. P. Lavin: vice president
T. L. May: vice president
Ted McDougal: director, vice president
J. W. Owens: director, vice president
J. M. Rooney: assistant secretary

Grants Analysis
Disclosure Period: calendar year ending 2003
Total Grants: $8,775,105*
Number of Grants: 310
Average Grant: $23,601*
Highest Grant: $753,000
Lowest Grant: $100
Typical Range: $1,000 to $25,000
***Note:** Giving excludes matching gifts, scholarship, and United Way. Average grant figure excludes two highest grants ($1,506,000).

Recent Grants
Note: Grants derived from 2003 Form 990.

General

950,000	United Way HOIUW Excellence Fund, Alexandria, VA
673,500	Bradley University, Peoria, IL
550,000	Illinois State University, Normal, IL
400,000	Abraham Lincoln Presidential Library and Museum Foundation, Springfield, IL
343,865	Salvation Army, New York, NY
325,000	Eureka College, Eureka, IL
306,070	Illinois Central College Foundation, East Peoria, IL
300,000	Monmouth College, Monmouth, IL
256,765	YMCA
200,000	American Battle Monuments Commission, Arlington, VA

JOHN AND MILDRED CAUTHORN CHARITABLE TRUST

Giving Contact
Jessie Kerbow, Secretary
PO Box 678
Sonora, TX 76950
Phone: (325)387-3529

Description
Founded: 1985
EIN: 751977779
Organization Type: Private Foundation
Giving Locations: TX: including the Sutton County area
Grant Types: General Support, Operating Expenses, Scholarship.

Financial Summary
Total Giving: $726,679 (2003); $725,117 (2001)
Giving Analysis: Giving for 2003 includes: foundation scholarships ($67,800); 2001: foundation scholarships ($61,000)
Assets: $7,854,432 (2003); $5,779,105 (2001)

Typical Recipients
Arts & Humanities: Historic Preservation, History & Archaeology, Libraries, Music
Civic & Public Affairs: Clubs, Community Foundations, Housing, Municipalities/Towns, Urban & Community Affairs
Education: Agricultural Education, Education Reform, Education-General, Leadership Training, Public Education (Precollege), Special Education, Student Aid
Health: Cancer, Emergency/Ambulance Services, Health Funds, Hospitals
Religion: Churches, Religious Organizations, Religious Welfare
Social Services: Child Welfare, Community Service Organizations, Homes, Scouts, Senior Services, Youth Organizations

Application Procedures
Initial Contact: The foundation has no formal grant application procedure or application form.
Deadlines: None.

Restrictions
Giving is restricted to entities and individuals in Sutton County, Texas.

Foundation Officials
Michael V. Hale: trustee
JoAnn Jones: trustee
Nelda Mayfield: trustee

Grants Analysis
Disclosure Period: calendar year ending 2003
Total Grants: $657,379*
Number of Grants: 13
Average Grant: $2,456*
Highest Grant: $271,346
Lowest Grant: $500
Typical Range: $500 to $5,000
***Note:** Giving excludes scholarships. Average grant figure excludes four highest grants ($635,279).

Recent Grants
Note: Grants derived from 2001 Form 990.
General

293,890	Presbyterian Children Services, Austin, TX -- operating funds
195,927	Church of the Good Shepherd, Sonora, TX -- operating funds
140,000	Sutton County, Sonora, TX -- building repair

61,000	Sonora Independent School District, Sonora, TX -- scholarship
16,400	Bronco Booster Club, Sonora, TX -- school athletic
9,500	Sonora Ministerial Alliance, Sonora, TX -- operating funds
3,000	Community Action Team, Sonora, TX -- Project Graduation
1,500	American Cancer Society, Sonora, TX -- operating fund
1,000	Helping Hand Fund, Sonora, TX -- operating funds
1,000	Sutton County Child Protection, Sonora, TX -- operating funds

CAYUGA FOUNDATION

Giving Contact
Edwin Diener, Trust Officer
c/o Key Trust Co. of Ohio
PO Box 10099
Toledo, OH 43699-0099
Phone: (419)259-8372

Description
Founded: 1960
EIN: 346504822
Organization Type: Private Foundation
Giving Locations: NY; OH, Toledo
Grant Types: Capital, General Support, Scholarship.

Financial Summary
Total Giving: $144,000 (2003); $200,000 (2001)
Giving Analysis: Giving for 2001 includes: foundation grants to United Way ($4,000)
Assets: $3,157,091 (2003); $3,290,939 (2001)

Typical Recipients
Arts & Humanities: Community Arts, Libraries, Museums/Galleries, Public Broadcasting
Civic & Public Affairs: Botanical Gardens/Parks, Economic Development, Civic & Public Affairs-General, Housing, Municipalities/Towns, Public Policy, Safety, Urban & Community Affairs
Education: Colleges & Universities, Elementary Education (Public), Environmental Education, International Exchange, Leadership Training, Minority Education, Preschool Education, Private Education (Precollege), Public Education (Precollege)
Environment: Environment-General, Research, Resource Conservation, Wildlife Protection
Health: Cancer, Clinics/Medical Centers, Health-General, Health Organizations, Hospices, Hospitals, Long-Term Care, Medical Rehabilitation, Single-Disease Health Associations
International: Foreign Educational Institutions, Human Rights, International Environmental Issues, International Organizations, International Relations
Religion: Churches, Ministries, Religious Organizations, Religious Welfare
Social Services: Child Welfare, Community Service Organizations, Family Planning, Family Services, Recreation & Athletics, Scouts, United Funds/United Ways, Volunteer Services, Youth Organizations

Application Procedures
Initial Contact: Send brief letter and a full proposal. Include a description of organization, recently audited financial statement, proof of tax-exempt status, and purpose of funds sought.
Deadlines: None.

Restrictions
The foundation does not support individuals, religious organizations for sectarian purposes, political or lobbying groups, or organizations outside operating areas.

Additional Information
Trust(s): Key Trust Co OH NA

Foundation Officials
Sandra Fritch: adv
Donald J. Keune: adv
Elizabeth M. Pfenninger: adv

Grants Analysis
Disclosure Period: calendar year ending 2003
Total Grants: $144,000
Number of Grants: 35
Average Grant: $4,114
Highest Grant: $9,000
Lowest Grant: $1,500
Typical Range: $2,000 to $7,500

Recent Grants
Note: Grants derived from 2001 Form 990.
Library-Related

6,000	Aurora Free Library Association, Aurora, NY

General

32,000	New York City Outward Bound, New York, NY
12,000	Comfortcare of Cayuga County, Inc, Auburn, NY -- for operations
12,000	United Ministry, Aurora, NY -- for operations
12,000	Village of Cayuga, Cayuga, NY -- for operations
10,000	Peachtown Elementary School, Aurora, NY -- educational
10,000	Wells College, Aurora, NY -- for operations
8,000	Cayuga County Habitat for Humanity, Inc, Auburn, NY -- for operations
8,000	Faatz Crofut Home for the Elderly, Auburn, NY -- for operations
8,000	Ocean Reef Volunteer Fire Department, Inc, Key Largo, FL -- for operations
8,000	Sloan-Kettering Institute for Cancer Research, New York, NY -- for operations and medical research

CBS CORP.

Company Headquarters
51 West 52nd Street
New York, NY 10019
Phone: (212)975-4321
Fax: (212)975-4516
Web: http://www.cbs.com

Company Description
Employees: 28,900 (1999)
Parent Company: Viacom Inc., 1515 Broadway, New York, NY, United States

Nonmonetary Support
Type: In-kind Services

Viacom Foundation

Giving Contact
Karen Zatorski, Foundation Contact
Viacom, Inc.
1515 Broadway
New York, NY 10036
Phone: (212)258-6000

Description
EIN: 136099759
Organization Type: Corporate Foundation
Giving Locations: markets where CBS has major ownership presence.

Grant Types: General Support, Multiyear/Continuing Support, Operating Expenses, Project.

Financial Summary
Total Giving: $230,770 (2003); $1,958,253 (2002); $1,203,158 (2001)
Giving Analysis: Giving for 2002 includes: foundation grants to United Way ($273,000); foundation ($1,685,253)
Assets: $402,545 (2003); $98,134 (2002); $2,066,970 (2001)
Gifts Received: $553,000 (2003); $802,555 (2000).
Note: In 2003, contributions were received from Viacom Inc. In 2000, contributions were received from Westinghouse Foundation.

Typical Recipients
Arts & Humanities: Arts Associations & Councils, Arts Centers, Dance, Film & Video, Arts & Humanities-General, Libraries, Literary Arts, Museums/Galleries, Music, Performing Arts, Public Broadcasting, Theater
Civic & Public Affairs: African American Affairs, Botanical Gardens/Parks, Business/Free Enterprise, Chambers of Commerce, Civil Rights, Clubs, Community Foundations, Employment/Job Training, Ethnic Organizations, Civic & Public Affairs-General, Hispanic Affairs, Law & Justice, Municipalities/Towns, Nonprofit Management, Professional & Trade Associations, Public Policy, Urban & Community Affairs, Women's Affairs
Education: Afterschool/Enrichment Programs, Arts/Humanities Education, Business-School Partnerships, Colleges & Universities, Education Funds, Education Reform, Education-General, Journalism/Media Education, Leadership Training, Minority Education, Science/Mathematics Education, Secondary Education (Public), Social Sciences Education, Special Education, Student Aid
Environment: Air/Water Quality, Environment-General
Health: AIDS/HIV, Cancer, Health-General, Geriatric Health, Health Funds, Health Organizations, Hospitals, Medical Research, Single-Disease Health Associations
International: International-General
Religion: Religious Welfare
Science: Scientific Centers & Institutes
Social Services: Child Abuse, Child Welfare, Community Service Organizations, Emergency Relief, Family Planning, People with Disabilities, Social Services-General, United Funds/United Ways, Volunteer Services, YMCA/YWCA/YMHA/YWHA, Youth Organizations

Application Procedures
Initial Contact: Submit a full proposal.
Application Requirements: Include an outline of project and expected benefits; a copy of 501(c)(3) determination letter; financial plan; list of board of directors and officers; and a copy of organization's latest audited financial statements.
Deadlines: None.

Restrictions
Company only supports charitable organizations with IRS 501(c)(3) tax-exempt status.
Does not support projects that are directly associated with the internal operations of divisions of CBS; organizations via advertisements in journals; endowment or capital costs, including construction, renovation, and/or equipment; internal programs and institutions; or individuals.

Additional Information
In December 1997, the corporation changed its name from Westinghouse Electric Corp. to CBS Corp., recognizing it was nearing completion of its transformation to a pure media company.

Corporate Officials

Preston Robert Tisch: co-chairman, co-chief executive officer, director B Brooklyn, NY 1926. ED Bucknell University (1943-1944); University of Michigan BA (1948). PRIM CORP EMPL co-chairman, director: Loews Corp. ADD CORP EMPL owner, chief executive officer, chairman: New York Football Giants Inc. CORP AFFIL director: Transcontinental Insurance Co. New York; director: Hasbro Inc.; director: Rite Aid Corp.; director: CNA Financial Corp.; director: Bulova Corp. NONPR AFFIL trustee: New York University; member: Sigma Alpha Mu; chairman emeritus: New York Convention & Visitor Bureau; president: Citymeals Wheels; member: Governments Business Advisory Council New York. CLUB AFFIL Rye Racquet Club; Century Country Club.

Foundation Officials

Carl Folta: president
Martin Franks: vice president
W. Keyes Hill-Edgar: general counsel, secretary
Karen O. Zatorski: vice president, treasurer

Grants Analysis

Disclosure Period: calendar year ending 2003
Total Grants: $187,770
Number of Grants: 12
Average Grant: $7,979*
Highest Grant: $100,000
Lowest Grant: $270
Typical Range: $5,000 to $10,000
***Note:** Average grant figure excludes highest grant.

Recent Grants

Note: Grants derived from 2003 Form 990.
General

100,000	Fulfillment Fund, Los Angeles, CA
33,000	Kennedy Center, Washington, DC
20,000	Diddy Runs the City, New York, NY
15,000	Radio Hall of Fame, London United Kingdom
12,500	Motion Picture Pioneers, Toluca Lake, CA
10,000	AMFAR, New York, NY
10,000	Boston University, Boston, MA
10,000	Broadcasting & Cable, North Hollywood, CA
10,000	Committee to Protect Journalists, New York, NY
5,000	American Cinematheque, Hollywood, CA

CCB FINANCIAL CORP.

Company Headquarters

Durham, NC
Web: http://www.ccbonline.com

Company Description

Employees: 2,891
SIC(s): 6022 State Commercial Banks, 6712 Bank Holding Companies.

Operating Locations

CCB Financial Corp. (SC--Durham)

CCB Foundation

Giving Contact

David Kimball, Board Membership
CCB Foundation
PO Box 931
Durham, NC 27702-0931
Phone: (919)683-7251
Fax: (919)682-3870

Description

Founded: 1985
EIN: 581611223
Organization Type: Corporate Foundation
Giving Locations: headquarters area only.
Grant Types: General Support, Matching.

Financial Summary

Total Giving: $1,609,745 (2003); $1,321,303 (2001)
Giving Analysis: Giving for 2001 includes: foundation scholarships ($26,000); foundation matching gifts ($62,637); foundation grants to United Way ($322,114)
Assets: $2,597,418 (2003); $1,719,608 (2001)
Gifts Received: $1,825,000 (2003); $1,585,833 (2001); $1,661,125 (2000). Note: In 2000 and 2003, contributions were received from Central Carolina Bank ($1,660,000); Durham Crime Stoppers, Inc. ($1,000); and North Carolina State University ($125). In 1998, contributions were received from Central Carolina Bank.

Typical Recipients

Arts & Humanities: Arts Associations & Councils, Arts Funds, Dance, Arts & Humanities-General, History & Archaeology, Libraries, Museums/Galleries, Music, Performing Arts, Public Broadcasting, Theater
Civic & Public Affairs: Botanical Gardens/Parks, Business/Free Enterprise, Chambers of Commerce, Economic Development, Civic & Public Affairs-General, Housing, Parades/Festivals, Urban & Community Affairs
Education: Arts/Humanities Education, Business Education, Colleges & Universities, Community & Junior Colleges, Education Funds, Education Reform, Faculty Development, Education-General, Health & Physical Education, Public Education (Precollege), Religious Education, Student Aid
Environment: Resource Conservation
Health: Cancer, Children's Health/Hospitals, Emergency/Ambulance Services, Health-General, Health Funds, Health Organizations, Hospices, Hospitals
Religion: Religious Welfare
Science: Science Museums
Social Services: Child Welfare, Community Service Organizations, Crime Prevention, Emergency Relief, Family Services, Food/Clothing Distribution, Recreation & Athletics, Senior Services, Shelters/Homelessness, Social Services-General, Substance Abuse, United Funds/United Ways, YMCA/YWCA/YMHA/YWHA

Application Procedures

Initial Contact: Send a full proposal.
Application Requirements: Include a description of organization, amount requested, purpose of funds sought, and proof of tax-exempt status.
Deadlines: None.
Review Process: Requests are considered on a monthly basis.

Restrictions

Does not support individuals, religious organizations for sectarian purposes, political or lobbying groups, or organizations outside operating areas.

Foundation Officials

William L. Burns, Jr.: board membership
Scott Edwards: secretary, treasurer
Richard Furr: board membership
David Kimball: board membership
John D. Ramsey: president

Grants Analysis

Disclosure Period: calendar year ending 2003
Total Grants: $1,217,664*
Number of Grants: 191
Average Grant: $4,674*
Highest Grant: $234,363
Lowest Grant: $500
Typical Range: $1,000 to $10,000

***Note:** Giving excludes matching gifts; United Way. Average grant figure excludes two highest grants ($334,363).

Recent Grants

Note: Grants derived from 2003 Form 990.
General

234,363	Durham Central Park, Durham, NC
140,000	Triangle United Way, Morrisville, NC
100,000	North Carolina State Engineering Foundation Inc., Raleigh, NC
32,334	United Way of Greenville County, Greenville, SC
25,000	Hurricane Isabel Relief Fund, Goldsboro, NC
25,000	UNC Hospitals Family House, NC -- medical funds
20,000	Campbell University, Buies Creek, NC
20,000	North Carolina Museum of Art, Raleigh, NC
18,000	Carolina Theatre, Durham, NC
15,000	Duke Community Hospice Services, Hillsborough, NC

CEMALA FOUNDATION

Giving Contact

Priscilla P. Taylor, Executive Director
Cemala Foundation
330 S. Greene Street, Suite 101
Greensboro, NC 27401-2842
Phone: (336)274-3541
E-mail: Cemala@cemala.org
Web: http://www.cemala.org

Description

Founded: 1986
EIN: 561528982
Organization Type: Private Foundation
Giving Locations: NC: Guilford County
Grant Types: Capital, General Support.

Donor Information

Founder: the late Martha A. Cone, the late Ceasar Cone II

Financial Summary

Total Giving: $2,143,897 (2003); $2,889,540 (2002); $1,512,210 (2001)
Giving Analysis: Giving for 2003 includes: foundation grants to United Way ($67,250); 2002: foundation grants to United Way ($181,000)
Assets: $42,865,605 (2003); $38,486,684 (2002); $43,476,576 (2001)
Gifts Received: $12,409,058 (1998); $420,000 (1997); $412,277 (1996). Note: Contributions were received from the Martha A. Cone Trust.

Typical Recipients

Arts & Humanities: Historic Preservation, History & Archaeology, Libraries, Museums/Galleries, Music, Public Broadcasting, Visual Arts
Civic & Public Affairs: Community Foundations, Economic Development, Civic & Public Affairs-General, Law & Justice, Nonprofit Management, Public Policy, Rural Affairs, Urban & Community Affairs, Women's Affairs
Education: Business Education, Colleges & Universities, Elementary Education (Private), Private Education (Precollege), Public Education (Precollege)
Environment: Environment-General
Health: AIDS/HIV, Cancer, Clinics/Medical Centers, Emergency/Ambulance Services, Health Organizations, Hospices
Religion: Religion-General, Ministries, Religious Welfare
Science: Science Museums, Scientific Centers & Institutes

Social Services: Child Welfare, Community Centers, Community Service Organizations, Emergency Relief, Family Planning, Family Services, People with Disabilities, Scouts, Shelters/Homelessness, Social Services-General, United Funds/United Ways, YMCA/YWCA/YMHA/YWHA

Application Procedures

Initial Contact: Submit a completed application form signed and dated by the chief executive officer or chairman of the organization. A proposal of not more than two pages should also be sent, and should include (in this order): a short introductory paragraph with a concise statement of the purpose of funds sought and amount requested; a detailed project description covering the issue being addressed, what will be different and why it is important, the outcomes to be achieved, plans for accomplishing the outcomes and project timetable, capacity of the organization to carry out the plan; if this is a collaborative effort, the role of each partner, and how the success and effectiveness of the program will be evaluated; a description of organization, its history, mission, and activities; project budget; organization operating budget; list of board members and their affiliations; recently audited financial statement; and proof of tax-exempt status.
Deadlines: March 1 and September 1.

Restrictions

Does not provide endowment or operating funds.

Additional Information

Publications: Application Form; Guidelines

Foundation Officials

Carole W. Bruce: director
Ceasar Cone, III: vice chairman, director
Janet G. Cone: director
Walter C. Cone: treasurer
Betty T. Day: assistant secretary, assistant treasurer
John Richmond: treasurer
Katherine K. Richmond: director
Merritt Richmond: secretary
William R. Rogers: director
Priscilla P. Taylor: executive director
Martha C. Wright: chairman, director

Grants Analysis

Disclosure Period: calendar year ending 2003
Total Grants: $2,076,647*
Number of Grants: 49
Average Grant: $24,295*
Highest Grant: $910,497
Lowest Grant: $2,500
Typical Range: $10,000 to $50,000
*Note:** Giving excludes United Way. Average grant figure excludes highest grant.

Recent Grants

Note: Grants derived from 2001 Form 990.
Library-Related
25,000	Conservation Trust for North Carolina, Raleigh, NC -- for operations

General
150,000	Greensboro Urban Ministry, Greensboro, NC -- for operations
125,000	Hospice at Greensboro, Inc., Greensboro, NC -- for operations
100,000	Triad Stage, Greensboro, NC -- for operations
70,000	Community Foundation of Greater Greensboro, Greensboro, NC -- for operations
60,000	United Way of Greater High Point, Inc., High Point, NC -- for operations
50,000	North Carolina Institute of Government Foundation, Chapel Hill, NC -- for operations
50,000	September 11th Fund, New York, NY -- for operations
50,000	Women's Resource Center, Greensboro, NC -- for operations
44,000	United Way of Greater Greensboro, Greensboro, NC -- for operations
40,000	Junior Achievement of Central North Carolina, Greensboro, NC -- for operations

CENTERPOINT ENERGY INC.

Company Headquarters

1111 Louisiana St.
Houston, TX 77002
Web: http://www.centerpointenergy.com

Company Description

Founded: 1976
Ticker: CNP
Exchange: NYSE
Former Name: Houston Industries, Inc. (1999); Reliant Energy, Inc. (2002).
Revenue: US$10.61 billion (2004)
Profit: (US$904.7 million) (2004)
Employees: 11046 (2003)
Fortune Rank: 209, per FORTUNE Magazine's list of 500 Largest U.S. Corporations (2004).
SIC(s): 4841 Cable & Other Pay Television Services, 4911 Electric Services, 5063 Electrical Apparatus & Equipment, 6719 Holding Companies Nec.

Operating Locations

Reliant Energy HL&P (TX--Houston); Reliant Energy Minnegasco (MN--Minneapolis); Reliant Enrergy Arkla (AR--Little Rock); Reliant Entex (TX--Houston)

Nonmonetary Support

Type: Donated Equipment; In-kind Services; Loaned Employees; Loaned Executives

Reliant Resources Foundation

Giving Contact

Cyndy Garza-Roberts, President
PO Box 148
Houston, TX 77002
Phone: (713)207-5155
Fax: (713)207-0207
E-mail: corporateoutreach@reliant.com
Web: http://www.reliantenergy.com/corporate/
1,1003,CID319452,00.html?1id=227037&2id=227287

Description

Founded: 1997
EIN: 760537222
Organization Type: Corporate Foundation
Former Name: Houston Industries, Inc. (1999).
Former Name: Reliant Energy Foundation.
Giving Locations: headquarters and operating communities, mainly TX.
Grant Types: Capital, General Support, Research, Seed Money.

Financial Summary

Total Giving: $2,135,077 (2003); $3,133,837 (2002); $5,818,098 (2001). Note: Contributes through corporate direct giving program and foundation. Company does not disclose contributions figures.
Assets: $10,012,358 (2003); $11,321,336 (2002); $14,960,363 (2001)
Gifts Received: $363,736 (2000). Note: In 2000, contributions were received from Reliant Energy Ventures.

Typical Recipients

Arts & Humanities: Arts Associations & Councils, Arts Centers, Arts Funds, Community Arts, Dance, Ethnic & Folk Arts, Historic Preservation, Libraries, Museums/Galleries, Music, Performing Arts, Public Broadcasting, Theater
Civic & Public Affairs: African American Affairs, Botanical Gardens/Parks, Business/Free Enterprise, Community Foundations, Economic Development, Employment/Job Training, Civic & Public Affairs-General, Housing, Inner-City Development, Law & Justice, Minority Business, Municipalities/Towns, Parades/Festivals, Philanthropic Organizations, Professional & Trade Associations, Public Policy, Rural Affairs, Safety, Urban & Community Affairs, Women's Affairs, Zoos/Aquariums
Education: Afterschool/Enrichment Programs, Business Education, Business-School Partnerships, Colleges & Universities, Community & Junior Colleges, Economic Education, Education Associations, Education Funds, Engineering/Technological Education, Environmental Education, Education-General, Legal Education, Literacy, Medical Education, Minority Education, Private Education (Precollege), Public Education (Precollege), Science/Mathematics Education, Student Aid, Vocational & Technical Education
Environment: Environment-General, Protection, Resource Conservation, Watershed, Wildlife Protection
Health: Cancer, Children's Health/Hospitals, Diabetes, Emergency/Ambulance Services, Health Funds, Health Organizations, Heart, Hospitals, Hospitals (University Affiliated), Medical Research, Mental Health, Single-Disease Health Associations
Religion: Religious Welfare
Science: Science Museums, Scientific Centers & Institutes, Scientific Organizations
Social Services: Animal Protection, Camps, Child Welfare, Community Centers, Community Service Organizations, Delinquency & Criminal Rehabilitation, Family Services, Food/Clothing Distribution, People with Disabilities, Recreation & Athletics, Refugee Assistance, Scouts, Senior Services, Shelters/Homelessness, Social Services-General, Substance Abuse, United Funds/United Ways, Volunteer Services, YMCA/YWCA/YMHA/YWHA, Youth Organizations

Application Procedures

Initial Contact: The foundation requests applications be made in writing.
Application Requirements: Include name of organization, contact person, address, phone and fax numbers setting out specifically the amount and purpose of the request. A copy of the IRS tax status letter, Form 990, financial statements and list of board of directors should accompany the request.
Deadlines: None.

Restrictions

Does not support dinners or special events, fraternal organizations, individuals, political or lobbying groups, or religious organizations for sectarian purposes.

Corporate Officials

Robert W. Harvey: vice chairman, executive vice president, chief financial officer PRIM CORP EMPL vice chairman: Reliant Energy Inc.
Lee W. Hogan: vice chairman, executive vice president PRIM CORP EMPL vice chairman, executive vice president: Reliant Energy Inc.
R. Steve Letbetter: chairman, president, chief executive officer PRIM CORP EMPL chairman, president, chief executive officer: Reliant Energy Inc.
Stephen W. Naeve: vice chairman, executive vice president, chief financial officer PRIM CORP EMPL vice chairman, executive vice president, chief financial officer: Reliant Energy Inc.

Foundation Officials

Cyndy Garza-Roberts: president
Catherine B. Guy: vice president
Michael L. Jines: secretary
Joel V. Staff: chairman
William S. Waller, Jr.: treasurer
Andrew P. Weaver: assistant treasurer
Wendi S. Zerwas: assistant secretary

Grants Analysis

Disclosure Period: calendar year ending 2003
Total Grants: $1,627,255*
Number of Grants: 66
Average Grant: $21,189*
Highest Grant: $250,000
Lowest Grant: $500
Typical Range: $5,000 to $50,000
*Note: Giving excludes United Way. Average grant figure excludes highest grant.

Recent Grants

Note: Grants derived from 2003 Form 990.
General

447,412	United Way of the Texas Gulf Coast, Houston, TX
250,000	Texas Southern University, Houston, TX
200,000	Houston Civic Improvement, Houston, TX
186,667	University of Texas at Austin, Houston, TX
167,000	Rice University, Houston, TX
125,000	Hobby Center for the Performing Arts, Houston, TX
66,000	Baylor College of Medicine, Houston, TX
65,000	Community Family Centers, Houston, TX
50,000	Barbara Bush Foundation for Family Literacy, Houston, TX
35,000	Tides Center, San Francisco, CA

CENTRAL HUDSON GAS & ELECTRIC CORP.

Company Headquarters

Poughkeepsie, NY
Web: http://www.cenhud.com

Company Description

Employees: 1,260
SIC(s): 4900 Electric, Gas & Sanitary Services.

Nonmonetary Support

Type: Donated Equipment; Loaned Employees; Loaned Executives

Giving Contact

Joseph J. DeVirgilio, Jr., Vice President, Human Resources & Administration
284 South Ave.
Poughkeepsie, NY 12601
Phone: (845)452-2000
Fax: (845)486-5894
E-mail: jdvirgilio@cenhud.com

Description

Organization Type: Corporate Giving Program
Giving Locations: corporate operating locations.
Grant Types: Capital, Matching.

Typical Recipients

Arts & Humanities: Arts Associations & Councils, Arts Funds, Historic Preservation, Libraries, Performing Arts
Civic & Public Affairs: Economic Development, Housing, Philanthropic Organizations, Professional & Trade Associations
Education: Colleges & Universities, Science/Mathematics Education
Health: Hospices, Hospitals, Mental Health

Science: Science Exhibits & Fairs
Social Services: Child Welfare, Community Centers, Community Service Organizations, Domestic Violence, Food/Clothing Distribution, Homes, Senior Services, Shelters/Homelessness, United Funds/United Ways, Volunteer Services, Youth Organizations

Application Procedures

Initial Contact: Send brief letter of inquiry.
Application Requirements: Include a description of organization, amount requested, purpose of funds sought, recently audited financial statments, and proof of tax-exempt status.
Deadlines: None.

Restrictions

Does not support individuals, religious organizations for sectarian purposes, organizations outside the company's service territory, or political or lobbying groups.

Corporate Officials

Paul J. Ganci: president, chief operating officer B New York, NY 1938. ED Rensselaer Polytechnic Institute (1960); Union College (1969). PRIM CORP EMPL president, chief operating officer: Central Hudson Gas & Electric Corp. CORP AFFIL director: Fleet Bank Southeast New York; director: Mid Hudson Pattern Progress. NONPR AFFIL trustee: Mt Saint Marys College; vice chairman: Vassar Brothers Hospital.
Steven V. Lant: chief financial officer B Albany, NY 1957. ED State University of New York Albany (1979); State University of New York Albany (1984). PRIM CORP EMPL chief financial officer: Central Hudson Gas & Electric Corp.
John E. Mack, III: chairman, chief executive officer B Poughkeepsie, NY 1934. ED Siena College BS (1956); Siena College MBA (1966); Mount Saint Mary's College LHD (1994). PRIM CORP EMPL chairman, chief executive officer: Central Hudson Gas & Electric Corp. CORP AFFIL president: Empire State Electric Energy Research Corp.; director: New York Business Development Corp. NONPR AFFIL chairman executive committee: New York Power Pool; chairman: New York Saint Energy Association; director: Mid Hudson Medical Center; director: Edison Electric Institute; director: Marist College; director: Astor Home for Children; president: Boy Scouts America Hudson Valley Council; member: American Gas Association.

CENTRAL MAINE POWER CO.

Company Headquarters

83 Edison Dr.
Augusta, ME 04336
Web: http://www.cmpco.com

Company Description

Employees: 1,607 (1999)
SIC(s): 4931 Electric & Other Services Combined.
Parent Company: Energy East Corp., PO Box 12904, Albany, NY, United States

Operating Locations

Central Maine Power Co. (ME--West Buxton); Yankee Atomic Electric Co. (ME--West Buxton)
Note: Operates 14 district offices throughout Maine.

Nonmonetary Support

Range: $25,000 - $50,000
Type: Donated Equipment; Donated Products; In-kind Services
Note: Provides mentoring-engineering help with science program. Portland employees employees donate time in elementary schools.

Giving Contact

John H. Carroll, Community Relations Specialist
83 Edison Dr.
Augusta, ME 04336
Phone: (207)623-3521
Fax: (207)623-5908
E-mail: john.carrol@cmpco.com
Note: Mr. Carroll's extension is 2493.

Description

Organization Type: Corporate Giving Program
Giving Locations: ME: primarily central and southern Maine
Grant Types: Award, Capital, Challenge, Conference/Seminar, Emergency, Employee Matching Gifts, General Support, Matching, Multiyear/Continuing Support, Project, Research, Scholarship, Seed Money.
Note: Employee matching gift ratio: 1 to 1.

Financial Summary

Total Giving: $125,000 (2005 approx); $125,000 (2004); $100,000 (2002 approx). Note: Contributes through corporate direct giving program only.

Typical Recipients

Arts & Humanities: Arts Associations & Councils, Arts Festivals, Arts Institutes, Community Arts, Dance, Ethnic & Folk Arts, Arts & Humanities-General, Historic Preservation, Libraries, Literary Arts, Museums/Galleries, Music, Performing Arts, Public Broadcasting, Theater, Visual Arts
Civic & Public Affairs: Civil Rights, Economic Development, Economic Policy, Employment/Job Training, Housing, Professional & Trade Associations, Public Policy, Rural Affairs, Safety, Urban & Community Affairs, Women's Affairs
Education: Arts/Humanities Education, Business Education, Colleges & Universities, Community & Junior Colleges, Continuing Education, Economic Education, Education Associations, Education Funds, Elementary Education (Private), Engineering/Technological Education, Faculty Development, Literacy, Minority Education, Preschool Education, Public Education (Precollege), Science/Mathematics Education, Social Sciences Education, Student Aid
Environment: Environment-General
Health: Emergency/Ambulance Services, Health-General, Geriatric Health, Health Organizations, Hospices, Hospitals, Medical Rehabilitation, Mental Health, Nutrition, Public Health, Single-Disease Health Associations
Science: Science Exhibits & Fairs, Scientific Centers & Institutes
Social Services: Child Welfare, Community Centers, Community Service Organizations, Counseling, Day Care, Delinquency & Criminal Rehabilitation, Domestic Violence, Emergency Relief, Family Planning, Family Services, Food/Clothing Distribution, People with Disabilities, Recreation & Athletics, Senior Services, Shelters/Homelessness, Social Services-General, Substance Abuse, United Funds/United Ways, Volunteer Services, Youth Organizations

Application Procedures

Initial Contact: Send a brief letter of inquiry.
Application Requirements: Include a description of organization, amount requested, purpose of funds sought, recently audited financial statement, and proof of tax-exempt status.
Deadlines: None.
Decision Notification: Proposals are reviewed monthly.

Restrictions

Company does not support individuals, religious organizations for sectarian purposes, political or lobbying groups, or organizations outside operating areas.

Additional Information

In December 1999, the company's future merge with Energy East was approved.

Corporate Officials

Sara J. Burns: president, director PRIM CORP EMPL president, director: Central Maine Power Co. **Curtis Call:** treasurer

Grants Analysis

Disclosure Period: calendar year ending 2000
Total Grants: $100,000 (approx)
Typical Range: $250 to $5,000

CENTRAL NATIONAL BANK

Company Headquarters

8th & Washington
Junction City, KS 66441

Company Description

Employees: 150
SIC(s): 6000 Depository Institutions.

Central Charities Foundation

Giving Contact

Edward C. Rolfs, Chairman, President & Chief Executive Officer
PO Box 700
Junction City, KS 66441-0700
Phone: (785)238-4114
Fax: (785)238-6299

Description

EIN: 486143983
Organization Type: Corporate Foundation
Giving Locations: KS: including surrounding areas
Grant Types: General Support.

Financial Summary

Total Giving: $110,270 (2003); $108,500 (2001). Note: 1996 Giving includes United Way ($7,512).
Giving Analysis: Giving for 2003 includes: foundation grants to United Way ($18,644); 2001: foundation grants to United Way ($15,957)
Assets: $1,525,096 (2003); $1,576,239 (2001)
Gifts Received: $32,968 (2003); $21,170 (2001); $66,293 (2000). Note: In 1998, contributions were received from Genevieve M. Beerhalter Trust ($58,966), and miscellaneous donations of less than $5,000 each ($12,207).

Typical Recipients

Arts & Humanities: Arts Associations & Councils, Historic Preservation, Libraries, Literary Arts, Museums/Galleries, Opera, Theater
Civic & Public Affairs: Business/Free Enterprise, Economic Policy, Civic & Public Affairs-General, Safety
Education: Agricultural Education, Colleges & Universities, Economic Education, Private Education (Precollege), Secondary Education (Public)
Environment: Wildlife Protection
Health: Cancer, Children's Health/Hospitals, Clinics/Medical Centers, Emergency/Ambulance Services, Health-General, Geriatric Health, Hospices, Hospitals
Religion: Churches, Religious Welfare
Social Services: At-Risk Youth, Community Centers, Community Service Organizations, Crime Prevention, Emergency Relief, Recreation & Athletics,

Scouts, United Funds/United Ways, YMCA/YWCA/YMHA/YWHA

Additional Information

Publications: Application Form

Corporate Officials

Edward C. Rolfs: chairman, president, chief executive officer, director PRIM CORP EMPL chairman, president, chief executive officer, director: Central National Bank.

Foundation Officials

Edward J. Rolfs: mem PRIM CORP EMPL chairman: Central National Bank.

Grants Analysis

Disclosure Period: calendar year ending 2003
Total Grants: $91,626*
Number of Grants: 29
Average Grant: $3,196
Highest Grant: $12,155
Lowest Grant: $15
Typical Range: $1,000 to $5,000
*Note: Giving excludes United Way.

Recent Grants

Note: Grants derived from 2001 Form 990.
Library-Related
1,752	Frank Carlson Library

General
11,000	Junction City Family YMCA, Junction City, KS
10,250	Coronado Area Council, BSA, Salina, KS
10,000	Geary County Extension, Junction City, KS
10,000	Geary County Red Cross, ARC, Junction City, KS
10,000	Geary County Salvation Army, Junction City, KS
10,000	Junction City Good Samaritan Center, Junction City, KS
10,000	Kaw Valley Girl Scout, Topeka, KS
9,611	United Way Junction City/ Geary County, Junction City, KS
5,000	Art of the Ages
3,094	United Way of Greater Topeka, Topeka, KS

CENTRAL VERMONT PUBLIC SERVICE CORP.

Company Headquarters

Rutland, VT
Web: http://www.cvps.com

Company Description

Founded: 1929
Ticker: CV
Exchange: NYSE
Assets: US$521.7 million (2001)
Employees: 535 (2003)
SIC(s): 4911 Electric Services.

Operating Locations

Central Vermont Public Service Corp. (VT--Middleburg, Montpelier, Randolph, St. Albans, St. Johnsbury, Woodstock); Vermont Yankee Nuclear Power Corp. (VT--Woodstock)

Giving Contact

Andrea Bove, Exec. Asst.
77 Grove Street
Rutland, VT 05701
Phone: (802)747-5672
Fax: (802)747-2188
E-mail: above@cvps.com

Alternate Contact

Dale Rocheleau, Senior Vice President Public Affairs

Description

Organization Type: Corporate Giving Program
Giving Locations: VT
Grant Types: Emergency, Endowment, General Support, Multiyear/Continuing Support.

Financial Summary

Total Giving: $145,000 (2005 approx); $145,000 (2004); $145,000 (2003)

Typical Recipients

Arts & Humanities: Community Arts, Libraries, Museums/Galleries, Music, Public Broadcasting
Civic & Public Affairs: Economic Development, Nonprofit Management
Education: Colleges & Universities
Environment: Environment-General
Health: Mental Health
Science: Science Exhibits & Fairs
Social Services: Community Service Organizations

Application Procedures

Initial Contact: Send brief letter of inquiry, including a description of organization, amount requested, and purpose of funds sought. Deadline for January 1 Fiscal year is August 15th.

Restrictions

Does not support individuals, religious organizations for sectarian purposes, political or lobbying groups, or organizations outside operating areas.

Corporate Officials

Frederic Howard Bertrand: chairman, chief executive officer B Montpelier, VT 1936. ED Norwich University BScE (1958); Georgetown University Law Center (1961-1963); College of William & Mary JD (1967); Carnegie Mellon University (1967-1968). PRIM CORP EMPL chairman: Central Vermont Public Service Corp. CORP AFFIL director: Union Mutual Fire Insurance Co.; director: New England Guaranty Insurance Co.; director: Chittenden Trust Co.; chairman, chief executive officer: National Life Insurance Co.; director: Central Vermont Public Services Corp. NONPR AFFIL director: Vermont Business Roundtable; member: Washington County Bar Association; member: Vermont Bar Association; member: Epsilon Tau Sigma; member: Theta Chi; director: Central Vermont Economic Development Corp.; member: American Council Life Insurance.
F. Ray Keyser, Jr.: chairman, director B Chelsea, VT 1927. ED Boston University Law School LLB (1952); Tufts University LLD (1961); Norwich University LLD (1962). PRIM CORP EMPL chairman, director: Central Vermont Public Service Corp. CORP AFFIL director: Vermont Yankee Nuclear Power Co.; director: Vermont Electric Power Corp.; director: Lakey Hitchcock Clinic; director: Union Mutual Fire Insurance Co.; director: Keystone Custodian Funds; director: ICI Mutual Insurance Co.; of counsel: Keyser Crowley Meub Zayden Kulig & Sullivan PC; director: Grand Trunk Corp. NONPR AFFIL member: Masons; member: Vermont Bar Association; member: American Legion; member: American Bar Association.
Robert Harris Young: president, chief executive officer B New York, NY 1947. ED Beloit College (1970); Stanford University (1975). PRIM CORP EMPL president, chief executive officer: Central Vermont Public Service Corp. CORP AFFIL president, chief executive officer, director: SmartEnergy Services; president, chief executive officer, director: Summersville Hydro Corp.; director: Rutland Regional Medical Center; president, chief executive officer, director: Gauley River Management Corp.; director: Green Mountain Bank; president, chief executive officer, director: East Barnet Hydroelectric; president, chief executive officer, director: Equinox Vermont Corp.; president, chief executive officer, director: CV Energy Resources;

president, chief executive officer, director: CV Realty; president, chief executive officer, director: Catamount Williams Lake Ltd.; president, chief executive officer, director: Connecticut Valley Electric Co.; president, chief executive officer, director: Catamount Thetford Corp.; president, chief executive officer, director: Catamount Rumford; president, chief executive officer, director: Catamount Rupert Corp.; president, chief executive officer, director: Catamount Energy Corp.; president, chief executive officer, director: Catamount Glenns Ferry Corp.; president, chief executive officer, director: Appomattox Vermont Corp.; director: Associated Industries Vermont.

Grants Analysis
Typical Range: $1,000 to $2,500

CESSNA AIRCRAFT CO.

Company Headquarters
5211 E. Pawnee St.
Wichita, KS 67218
Web: http://www.cessna.com

Company Description
Employees: 6,900
SIC(s): 3721 Aircraft, 3728 Aircraft Parts & Equipment Nec.

Operating Locations
Cessna Aircraft Co. (OH--Vandalia)

Cessna Foundation, Inc.

Giving Contact
Marilyn Richwine, Secretary & Treasurer
Cessna Foundation
PO Box 7706
Wichita, KS 67277-7706
Phone: (316)517-7810
Fax: (316)517-7812

Description
Founded: 1952
EIN: 486108801
Organization Type: Corporate Foundation
Giving Locations: KS: Wichita including surrounding area principally near operating locations and to national organizations.
Grant Types: Capital, Emergency, Employee Matching Gifts, General Support, Multiyear/Continuing Support.
Note: Employee matching gift ratio: 2 to 1.

Donor Information
Founder: Cessna Aircraft Co.

Financial Summary
Total Giving: $1,524,513 (2003); $1,744,180 (2001)
Assets: $16,476,094 (2003); $15,561,756 (2001)
Gifts Received: $900,000 (2003); $1,500,000 (2001); $2,250,000 (2000). Note: Contributions were received from Cessna Aircraft Co.

Typical Recipients
Arts & Humanities: Arts Associations & Councils, Arts Centers, Arts Institutes, Arts Outreach, Libraries, Museums/Galleries, Music, Performing Arts, Theater
Civic & Public Affairs: African American Affairs, Clubs, Community Foundations, Employment/Job Training, Civic & Public Affairs-General, Housing, Professional & Trade Associations, Safety, Urban & Community Affairs, Women's Affairs, Zoos/Aquariums
Education: Afterschool/Enrichment Programs, Agricultural Education, Business Education, Colleges &

Universities, Community & Junior Colleges, Economic Education, Education Associations, Education Funds, Education Reform, Engineering/Technological Education, Medical Education, Private Education (Precollege), Public Education (Precollege), Science/Mathematics Education, Special Education, Student Aid, Vocational & Technical Education
Health: AIDS/HIV, Cancer, Children's Health/Hospitals, Clinics/Medical Centers, Emergency/Ambulance Services, Health Funds, Health Organizations, Heart, Hospices, Hospitals, Multiple Sclerosis, Preventive Medicine/Wellness Organizations, Single-Disease Health Associations
International: Missionary/Religious Activities
Religion: Churches, Ministries, Missionary Activities (Domestic), Religious Organizations, Religious Welfare, Social/Policy Issues
Science: Science Museums, Scientific Centers & Institutes
Social Services: Animal Protection, Big Brothers/Big Sisters, Child Welfare, Community Centers, Community Service Organizations, Emergency Relief, Family Services, Food/Clothing Distribution, People with Disabilities, Recreation & Athletics, Scouts, Special Olympics, Substance Abuse, United Funds/United Ways, Volunteer Services, YMCA/YWCA/YMHA/YWHA, Youth Organizations

Application Procedures
Initial Contact: Send a brief letter or proposal.
Application Requirements: Include a description of organization, amount requested, purpose of funds sought, recently audited financial statement, and proof of tax-exempt status.
Deadlines: None for grants; board meets quarterly. Scholarship applications are due May 15.

Corporate Officials
Charles B. Johnson: president vice president human resources B 1949. ED Simpson College. PRIM CORP EMPL executive vice president operation: Cessna Aircraft Co.
John E. Moore: executive vice president human resources B Charleston, WV 1943. ED Washington & Lee University BS (1965); University of Kentucky JD (1968). PRIM CORP EMPL executive vice president human resources: Cessna Aircraft Co.

Foundation Officials
Jordan L. Haines: trustee CORP AFFIL director: KN Energy Inc.; director: Q'west Communication International Inc.
Russell William Meyer, Jr.: president B Davenport, IA 1932. ED Yale University BA (1954); Harvard University LLB (1961). CORP AFFIL director: Western Resources Inc.; director: Public Broadcasting System; director: Cessna Finance Corp.; director: NationsBank Corp. NONPR AFFIL trustee: Wesley Hospital Endowment Association; chairman, director: Wichita Chamber of Commerce; trustee: Wake Forest University; board governors: United Way America; director: United Way Wichita & Sedgwick County; member: Ohio Bar Association; member: Kansas Bar Association; member: Latrobe Chamber of Commerce; member: General Aviation Manufacturers Association; president appointee: Aviation Safety Commission; member: Cleveland Bar Association; member: American Bar Association. CLUB AFFIL Wichita Country Club; Pine Valley Club; Wichita Club; Flint Hills National Club; Cypress Hunt Club; Double Eagle Chamber of Commerce.
Jack Pelton: vice president
Marilyn Richwine: secretary, treasurer, trustee
Kenneth J. Wagnon: trustee
Jim Walters: trustee

Grants Analysis
Disclosure Period: calendar year ending 2003
Total Grants: $785,733*
Number of Grants: 50
Average Grant: $12,634*

Highest Grant: $166,666
Lowest Grant: $250
Typical Range: $1,000 to $20,000
***Note:** Giving excludes matching gifts and United Way. Average grant figure excludes highest grant.

Recent Grants
Note: Grants derived from 2003 Form 990.
General

208,250	United Way of the Plains, Wichita, KS
100,000	United Way of the Plains, Wichita, KS
100,000	United Way of the Plains, Wichita, KS
100,000	United Way of the Plains, Wichita, KS
83,333	Kansas Food Bank, Wichita, KS
83,333	Kansas Food Bank, Wichita, KS
50,000	Big Brothers Big Sisters, Philadelphia, PA
50,000	Kansas State University, Manhattan, KS
50,000	Kansas University Endowment Association, Lawrence, KS
50,000	Wichita State University College of Engineering, Wichita, KS

CH FOUNDATION

Giving Contact
Kay Sanford, President
PO Box 94038
Lubbock, TX 79493
Phone: (806)792-0448

Description
Founded: 1976
EIN: 751534816
Organization Type: Private Foundation
Giving Locations: TX: South Plains including surrounding area
Grant Types: Capital, General Support, Matching, Research, Scholarship.

Donor Information
Founder: the late Christine DeVitt

Financial Summary
Total Giving: $3,879,212 (2003)
Giving Analysis: Giving for 2003 includes: foundation grants to United Way ($104,635)
Assets: $93,776,935 (2003)

Typical Recipients
Arts & Humanities: Arts Centers, Ballet, Ethnic & Folk Arts, Arts & Humanities-General, Historic Preservation, History & Archaeology, Libraries, Literary Arts, Museums/Galleries, Music, Public Broadcasting, Theater
Civic & Public Affairs: Community Foundations, Civic & Public Affairs-General, Hispanic Affairs, Urban & Community Affairs
Education: Agricultural Education, Arts/Humanities Education, Colleges & Universities, Education Reform, Elementary Education (Private), Elementary Education (Public), Engineering/Technological Education, Faculty Development, Literacy, Medical Education, Preschool Education, Private Education (Precollege), Public Education (Precollege), Science/Mathematics Education, Secondary Education (Public), Student Aid
Environment: Environment-General
Health: Alzheimer's Disease, Cancer, Children's Health/Hospitals, Eyes/Blindness, Health-General, Health Organizations, Hospices, Hospitals, Medical Research
Science: Science Museums, Scientific Centers & Institutes, Scientific Organizations
Social Services: At-Risk Youth, Child Welfare, Community Centers, Family Services, Food/Clothing Distribution, People with Disabilities, Scouts, Senior Services, United Funds/United Ways, Volunteer

Services, YMCA/YWCA/YMHA/YWHA, Youth Organizations

Application Procedures

Initial Contact: Send a brief letter of inquiry and a full proposal.
Application Requirements: Include background of the organization, a description of the project and its objectives and goals, purpose of funds sought, a detailed budget, other sources of funding, a specific amount requested, proof of tax-exempt status, recently audited financial statement, a statement of approval of the request signed by the chief administrator and the chairman of the board and the name of the primary contact person, and the plan for sustaining the project after grant funds expire.
Deadlines: May 1.

Foundation Officials

Don Graf: executive director, secretary
Kevin G. McMahon: treasurer
Kay Sanford: president
Nelda Thompson: trustee
Louise Wilson Arnold: vice president

Grants Analysis

Disclosure Period: calendar year ending 2003
Total Grants: $3,774,577*
Number of Grants: 89
Average Grant: $31,892*
Highest Grant: $500,000
Lowest Grant: $3,000
Typical Range: $10,000 to $50,000
*****Note:** Giving excludes United Way. Average grant figure excludes two highest grants ($1,000,000).

Recent Grants

Note: Grants derived from 2001 Form 990.
General

1,250,000	Texas Tech University Museum, Lubbock, TX -- for Helen Jones Auditorium
600,000	Museum Association, Lubbock, TX -- grant
600,000	National Ranching Heritage Association, Lubbock, TX -- grant
178,000	Lubbock Area Foundation, Texas Aviation, Lubbock, TX -- endowment
150,000	Vatican Exhibit Fund, Lubbock, TX -- grant
129,287	Covenant Health System Foundation, Lubbock, TX -- grant
103,294	International Cultural Center, Lubbock, TX -- grant
100,000	South Plains College, Levelland, TX -- grant
75,000	Texas Tech University, Lubbock, TX -- for Fine Arts Library
75,000	Texas Tech University, College of Human Sciences, Lubbock, TX -- grant

DOROTHY JORDAN CHADWICK FUND

Giving Contact

c/o US Trust Co. of NY
114 West 47th Street
New York, NY 10036
Phone: (212)852-1000

Description

Founded: 1957
EIN: 136069950
Organization Type: Private Foundation
Giving Locations: DC: Washington; NY: New York
Grant Types: General Support.

Donor Information

Founder: the late Dorothy J. Chadwick, Dorothy R. Kidder

Financial Summary

Total Giving: $1,540,200 (fiscal year ending May 31, 2004); $1,443,600 (fiscal 2001)
Assets: $19,788,556 (fiscal 2004); $27,077,858 (fiscal 2001)
Gifts Received: $3,046,464 (fiscal 1996)

Typical Recipients

Arts & Humanities: Arts Associations & Councils, Arts Centers, Arts Outreach, Arts & Humanities-General, Libraries, Literary Arts, Museums/Galleries, Music, Performing Arts, Public Broadcasting, Theater
Civic & Public Affairs: Botanical Gardens/Parks, Community Foundations, Civic & Public Affairs-General, Municipalities/Towns, Urban & Community Affairs, Zoos/Aquariums
Education: Arts/Humanities Education, Colleges & Universities, Education Reform, Environmental Education, Education-General, Private Education (Precollege), Science/Mathematics Education, Student Aid
Environment: Environment-General, Resource Conservation, Wildlife Protection
Health: Alzheimer's Disease, Clinics/Medical Centers
International: International Environmental Issues, International Peace & Security Issues
Religion: Churches, Religion-General
Social Services: At-Risk Youth, Camps, Child Welfare, Food/Clothing Distribution, Senior Services, Youth Organizations

Application Procedures

Initial Contact: Send a brief letter of inquiry.
Application Requirements: Describe program or project.
Deadlines: None.

Additional Information

Trust(s): US Trust Co NY

Foundation Officials

Berkley D. Johnson, Jr.: trustee

Grants Analysis

Disclosure Period: fiscal year ending May 31, 2004
Total Grants: $1,540,200
Number of Grants: 32
Average Grant: $40,503*
Highest Grant: $125,600
Lowest Grant: $1,500
Typical Range: $25,000 to $50,000
*****Note:** Average grant figure excludes three highest grants ($365,600).

Recent Grants

Note: Grants derived from 2000 Form 990.
General

125,600	Proctor Academy, Andover, NH -- operational
99,521	Friends of the Natural Arboretum -- operational
90,000	Warner Christian Academy -- religious
80,000	African Wildlife Foundation, Washington, DC -- operational
70,000	African Wildlife Foundation, Washington, DC -- operational
50,000	Unity Health Care, Washington, DC -- operational
41,079	Camp Dudley YMCA, Westport, NY -- operational
40,000	Washington College, Chestertown, MD -- educational
38,600	Proctor Academy, Andover, NH -- operational
38,600	Voyage of The Spray, Inc, Salem, MA -- operational

CHAMBERLAIN FOUNDATION

Giving Contact

Calvin M. Chamberlain, President, Director
1680 Crooks Rd.
Troy, MI 48084
Phone: (248)273-4306

Description

Founded: 1989
EIN: 382837915
Organization Type: Private Foundation
Grant Types: Department, General Support.

Financial Summary

Total Giving: $7,450 (fiscal year ending May 31, 2004); $18,975 (fiscal 2001)
Assets: $65,627 (fiscal 2004); $155,878 (fiscal 2001)
Gifts Received: $1,500 (fiscal 1996). Note: In fiscal 1996, contributions were received from Calvin M. Chamberlain.

Typical Recipients

Arts & Humanities: Arts Outreach, Libraries
Civic & Public Affairs: Civic & Public Affairs-General, Hispanic Affairs, Housing, Municipalities/Towns, Public Policy, Safety, Urban & Community Affairs
Education: Colleges & Universities, Education Funds, International Exchange, Medical Education, Private Education (Precollege), Secondary Education (Private), Student Aid
Environment: Resource Conservation
Health: Alzheimer's Disease, Cancer, Children's Health/Hospitals, Clinics/Medical Centers, Diabetes, Hospices, Medical Research, Multiple Sclerosis, Prenatal Health Issues, Public Health, Single-Disease Health Associations
International: Health Care/Hospitals, International Relief Efforts
Religion: Churches, Religious Welfare
Social Services: At-Risk Youth, Child Welfare, Community Service Organizations, People with Disabilities, Recreation & Athletics, Special Olympics, Substance Abuse, United Funds/United Ways, Youth Organizations

Application Procedures

Initial Contact: Send a brief letter of inquiry.
Application Requirements: Include a description of organization and purpose of funds sought.
Deadlines: None.

Foundation Officials

Calvin M. Chamberlain: president, director

Grants Analysis

Disclosure Period: fiscal year ending May 31, 2004
Total Grants: $7,450
Number of Grants: 12
Average Grant: $621
Highest Grant: $3,400
Lowest Grant: $100
Typical Range: $200 to $1,600

Recent Grants

Note: Grants derived from 2004 Form 990.
General

3,400	First Presbyterian Church, Royal Oak, MI
1,600	Michigan State University, East Lansing, MI
750	Salvation Army, Pontiac, MI
300	Alzheimer's Disease Research, Chicago, IL
300	Common Ground, Bloomfield Hills, MI
300	Michigan Special Olympics, Mt. Pleasant, MI
200	MADD, Des Moines, IA
200	March of Dimes, Detroit, MI

100	Jimmy Fund, Brookline, MA
100	Matthaei Foundation, Birmingham, MI

CHAMIZA FOUNDATION

Giving Contact
Sandra Edelman, Executive Director
1301 Luisa St., Suite G
Santa Fe, NM 87505
Phone: (505)986-5044

Description
Founded: 1989
EIN: 850373197
Organization Type: Private Foundation
Giving Locations: NM
Grant Types: Project.

Donor Information
Founder: Established in 1989 by Gifford Phillips.

Financial Summary
Total Giving: $157,635 (2003)
Assets: $3,693,414 (2003)
Gifts Received: $1,043,843 (2003); $100 (2000); $55,000 (1999). Note: In 2003, contributions were received from Gifford and Joann Phillips. In 1999, contributions were received from Gifford Phillips.

Typical Recipients
Arts & Humanities: Arts Associations & Councils, Arts Centers, Community Arts, Ethnic & Folk Arts, Arts & Humanities-General, Historic Preservation, History & Archaeology, Libraries, Museums/Galleries, Music
Civic & Public Affairs: Community Foundations, Civic & Public Affairs-General, Housing, Native American Affairs, Women's Affairs
Education: Arts/Humanities Education, Education-General, Literacy, Minority Education, Private Education (Precollege), Public Education (Precollege), Social Sciences Education
Environment: Environment-General, Resource Conservation
Health: Preventive Medicine/Wellness Organizations
Social Services: Child Welfare, Family Services

Application Procedures
Initial Contact: Submit applications in letter format.
Application Requirements: Include description of the project, amount requested, personnel to implement the project, expected impact on the Pueblo Indian community.
Deadlines: January 20, April 15, August 15.

Restrictions
Grants are made only for cultural preservation and education projects among the Pueblo Indian population of NM.

Foundation Officials
Jonathan Batkin: director
Agnes M. Dill: director
Sandra A. Edelman: executive director
Mrs. Paul C. Frank: president, director
Julia Herrera: director
Robert Montoya: treasurer, director
Gifford Phillips: director
James L. Phillips: chairman
Joann K. Phillips: secretary, assistant treasurer, director
Diane Reyna: vice president, director
Joe Sando: director

Grants Analysis
Disclosure Period: calendar year ending 2003
Total Grants: $157,635
Number of Grants: 26

Average Grant: $5,081*
Highest Grant: $30,605
Lowest Grant: $500
Typical Range: $1,000 to $10,000
***Note:** Average grant figure excludes highest grant.

Recent Grants
Note: Grants derived from 2003 Form 990.
General

30,605	Lina, Acoma Pueblo, NM -- for Keres Training Institute
11,950	New Mexico Culture Net, Santa Fe, NM -- for Pueblo artist video portrait
10,500	Oo-Oonah Art Center, Taos, NM -- to support Taos day school program
9,000	Cornerstones, Santa Fe, NM -- for traditional building programs
8,000	Santa Clara Pueblo, Santa Clara Pueblo, NM -- for library programs
7,000	Santo Domingo Pueblo, Santo Domingo Pueblo, NM -- for summer art program
6,900	Pueblo of Cochiti Housing Authority, Cochiti Pueblo, NM -- for Santa Fe institute native Hispanic cultures
6,630	Pueblo of Zia, Zia Pueblo, NM -- for language program
6,435	Pueblo of Picuris, Picuris Pueblo, NM
5,000	Pueblo of Iselta, Iselta Pueblo, NM -- for language/arts program

CHAMPLIN FOUNDATION

Giving Contact
Keith Lang, Executive Director
300 Centerville Road, Suite 300S
Warwick, RI 02886-0226
Phone: (401)736-0370
Fax: (401)736-7248
E-mail: champlinfdns@worldnet.att.net
Web: http://fdncenter.org/grantmaker/champlin/

Description
Founded: 1932
EIN: 516010168
Organization Type: General Purpose Foundation
Giving Locations: RI: Providence
Grant Types: Capital.
Note: Capital grants generally take the form of direct grants for the purchase of equipment or real property, the reduction of mortgages, and construction or renovation.

Donor Information
Founder: The Champlin Foundation Trust was established in 1932 in Delaware by George S. Champlin (d. 1980), Hope C. Neaves (d. 1987), and Florence C. Hamilton (d. 1970). They founded the Second Champlin Foundation Trust in 1947. In 1975, George S. Champlin founded the Third Champlin Foundation.

Financial Summary
Total Giving: $4,416,451 (2003); $18,700,000 (2002 approx); $20,742,979 (2001)
Assets: $102,343,141 (2003); $400,000,000 (2002 approx); $432,332,498 (2001)

Typical Recipients
Arts & Humanities: Arts Centers, Historic Preservation, History & Archaeology, Libraries, Museums/Galleries, Music, Opera, Performing Arts, Theater
Civic & Public Affairs: African American Affairs, Botanical Gardens/Parks, Economic Development, Employment/Job Training, Civic & Public Affairs-General, Hispanic Affairs, Inner-City Development, Legal Aid, Municipalities/Towns, Nonprofit Management, Philanthropic Organizations, Professional & Trade Associations, Rural Affairs, Safety, Urban & Community Affairs, Women's Affairs, Zoos/Aquariums
Education: Afterschool/Enrichment Programs, Agricultural Education, Arts/Humanities Education, Business Education, Colleges & Universities, Community & Junior Colleges, Education Associations, Engineering/Technological Education, Education-General, International Studies, Private Education (Precollege), Public Education (Precollege), Science/Mathematics Education, Secondary Education (Private), Secondary Education (Public), Special Education, Vocational & Technical Education
Environment: Environment-General, Protection, Resource Conservation, Watershed, Wildlife Protection
Health: AIDS/HIV, Clinics/Medical Centers, Diabetes, Emergency/Ambulance Services, Health-General, Geriatric Health, Health Funds, Health Organizations, Heart, Hospices, Hospitals, Long-Term Care, Medical Rehabilitation, Nursing Services, Prenatal Health Issues, Public Health, Transplant Networks/Donor Banks
Religion: Churches, Dioceses, Religion-General, Jewish Causes, Religious Welfare
Science: Science Museums
Social Services: Animal Protection, Camps, Child Welfare, Community Centers, Community Service Organizations, Crime Prevention, Domestic Violence, Emergency Relief, Family Planning, Family Services, Food/Clothing Distribution, Homes, People with Disabilities, Recreation & Athletics, Refugee Assistance, Scouts, Senior Services, Shelters/Homelessness, Social Services-General, Substance Abuse, United Funds/United Ways, Volunteer Services, YMCA/YWCA/YMHA/YWHA, Youth Organizations

Application Procedures
Initial Contact: Applicants should send a one-page letter.
Application Requirements: The letter should include a description of the project and its intended purpose, costs, amount requested, an accounting of other fund-raising efforts, and a listing of other sources of available funds. An applicant should also submit copies of its IRS 501(c)(3) exemption and 509(a) letters.
Deadlines: Requests should be submitted between March 1 and June 30. The distribution committees meet annually in November to accept or reject grant recommendations. Funds are distributed in December. The foundations report that funds are seldom available for applications filed at the last minute.
Review Process: After acknowledging a request, the foundations may request additional information concerning fund-raising efforts. The foundations like to see fund-raising plans with some favorable results. If fund-raising is not totally successful, the foundations are interested in what parts of the project will proceed and the costs. Mortgage status and evidence of ability to pay for increased operating costs may also be requested.
Site visits by members of the investigating committee are scheduled between May 1 and September 30. Committee members prefer to meet with the chief of operations, selected staff members, and the treasurer in a very informal manner. Prepared speeches and slide shows should be omitted.

Restrictions
Grants are not awarded on a continuing basis, but applicants may qualify annually. Grants are not made for program or operating expenses. No grants are awarded to individuals. Public school requests are considered only if they are solicited by the foundation.

Additional Information
Publications: Annual Report; Guidelines
Trust(s): PNC Bank-Delaware

Foundation Officials
John Gorham: chairman distribution comm, mem investigating comm
Louis R. Hampton: mem distribution comm B Hartford, CT 1920. ED University of Rhode Island BSME

(1942). PRIM CORP EMPL chairman executive committee, director: Providence Energy Corp.

Earl W. Harrington, Jr.: mem distribution comm ED Brown University (1941).

Robert W. Kenyon: mem distribution comm NONPR AFFIL president: Greater Providence Chamber of Commerce.

David A. King: member distribution committee

Norma B. LaFreniere: member distribution comm

Keith H. Lang: executive director ED American University BA (1976).

Grants Analysis

Disclosure Period: calendar year ending 2003
Total Grants: $4,416,451
Number of Grants: 58
Average Grant: $76,146
Highest Grant: $400,000
Lowest Grant: $861
Typical Range: $25,000 to $200,000

Recent Grants

Note: Grants derived from 2003 Form 990.
General

617,000	YMCA of Greater Providence, Providence, RI -- for handicapped accessibility at Newman boat house
400,000	Rhode Island Hospital, Providence, RI -- for emergency department expansion
225,000	McAuley Corporation, Providence, RI -- towards the shortfall regarding construction project
225,000	Self Help, East Providence, RI -- to replace the sloped mansard roof and upper flat roof
200,000	Newport Art Museum, Newport, RI -- towards foundation site work on the Griswold house
200,000	Women & Infants Hospital, Providence, RI -- towards the purchase of a computer aided detection system and a digital mammography machine
166,398	Rhode Island College, Providence, RI -- for the school of management and technology and for department of nursing
155,000	Tides Family Services, West Warwick, RI -- towards building renovations
108,000	Orlando R. Smith Trust, Westerly, RI -- for a new period roof gutters leaders and repointing of chimney bricks at Babcock Smith House
105,050	NE Institute of Technology, Warwick, RI -- for a turning center and for prototyping equipment

CHAPIN FOUNDATION OF MYRTLE BEACH, SOUTH CAROLINA

Giving Contact

Harold D. Clardy, Chairman Emeritus
PO Box 2568
Myrtle Beach, SC 29577
Phone: (803)255-7411

Description

Founded: 1943
EIN: 566039453
Organization Type: Private Foundation
Grant Types: General Support, Operating Expenses.

Donor Information

Founder: S. B. Chapin

Financial Summary

Total Giving: $995,304 (fiscal year ending July 31, 2004); $492,400 (fiscal 2001)
Assets: $25,150,531 (fiscal 2004); $26,414,566 (fiscal 2001)

Typical Recipients

Arts & Humanities: Libraries
Civic & Public Affairs: Civic & Public Affairs-General
Education: Elementary Education (Public), Private Education (Precollege)
Religion: Churches, Dioceses, Jewish Causes, Ministries, Religious Organizations, Religious Welfare, Synagogues/Temples
Social Services: Animal Protection, Community Service Organizations, YMCA/YWCA/YMHA/YWHA, Youth Organizations

Application Procedures

Initial Contact: Send a brief letter of inquiry.
Application Requirements: Include proof of tax-exempt status and statement of purpose.
Deadlines: None.

Restrictions

Generally grants are restricted to Myrtle Beach, SC, area.

Foundation Officials

Harold D. Clardy: chairman emeritus
Claude M. Epps, Jr.: chairman
Ruth T. Gore: vice chairman
Harold Hartshorne, Jr.: director

Grants Analysis

Disclosure Period: fiscal year ending July 31, 2004
Total Grants: $995,304
Number of Grants: 16
Average Grant: $21,955*
Highest Grant: $296,700
Lowest Grant: $7,000
Typical Range: $10,000 to $50,000
***Note:** Average grant figure excludes four highest grants ($731,850).

Recent Grants

Note: Grants derived from 2004 Form 990.

Library-Related

204,750	Chapin Memorial Library, Myrtle Beach, SC

General

296,700	First Presbyterian Church, Myrtle Beach, SC
124,500	Ocean View Baptist Church, Myrtle Beach, SC
105,000	First United Methodist Church, Myrtle Beach, SC
60,000	Grand Strand Humane Society, Myrtle Beach, SC
35,000	Trinity Episcopal Church, Myrtle Beach, SC
25,000	Chabad of Myrtle Beach, Myrtle Beach, SC
25,000	St. John Greek Orthodox Church, Myrtle Beach, SC
24,500	Corner Stone Church of God, Myrtle Beach, SC
20,000	Cathedral Baptist Ministries, Myrtle Beach, SC

HOWARD AND BESS CHAPMAN CHARITABLE CORP.

Giving Contact

Peter M. Dunn, Secretary & General Counsel
Care of Alliance Bank, Trust Dept.
160 Main Street
Oneida, NY 13421-1675
Phone: (315)363-1409

Description

Founded: 1991
EIN: 161373396
Organization Type: Private Foundation
Giving Locations: NY: Oneida including surrounding area
Grant Types: Capital, General Support.

Donor Information

Founder: Established in 1991 from the estate of Howard Chapman.

Financial Summary

Total Giving: $80,500 (fiscal year ending October 31, 2003); $187,552 (fiscal 2001)
Giving Analysis: Giving for fiscal 2004 includes: foundation grants to United Way ($2,000) fiscal 2001: foundation grants to United Way ($2,000)
Assets: $2,887,716 (fiscal 2003); $3,419,453 (fiscal 2001)
Gifts Received: In fiscal 1991, contributions were received from the estate of Howard Chapman.

Typical Recipients

Arts & Humanities: Arts Associations & Councils, Arts Centers, Arts & Humanities-General, Historic Preservation, History & Archaeology, Libraries, Music
Civic & Public Affairs: Clubs, Civic & Public Affairs-General, Philanthropic Organizations, Urban & Community Affairs
Education: Colleges & Universities, Education Funds, Education-General, Literacy, School Volunteerism, Student Aid
Health: Emergency/Ambulance Services, Health Organizations, Hospitals
Religion: Churches, Religious Welfare
Social Services: Camps, Child Welfare, Community Centers, Community Service Organizations, Day Care, Food/Clothing Distribution, People with Disabilities, Recreation & Athletics, Senior Services, Social Services-General, United Funds/United Ways, YMCA/YWCA/YMHA/YWHA, Youth Organizations

Application Procedures

Initial Contact: Send a brief letter of inquiry and a full proposal.
Application Requirements: Include a description of organization, amount requested, purpose of funds sought, recently audited financial statement, and proof of tax-exempt status.
Deadlines: None.

Restrictions

Does not support individuals, religious organizations for sectarian purposes, political or lobbying groups, or organizations outside operating areas.

Foundation Officials

Peter M. Dunn, Esq.: secretary, general counsel
Robert H. Fearon, Jr.: vice president
John G. Haskell: president
Dr. Steven Schneeweiss: treasurer
Rowland Stevens: trustee

Grants Analysis

Disclosure Period: fiscal year ending October 31, 2003
Total Grants: $78,500*

Number of Grants: 9
Average Grant: $3,563*
Highest Grant: $50,000
Lowest Grant: $1,000
Typical Range: $1,000 to $5,000
*Note: Giving excludes United Way. Average grant figure excludes highest grant.

Recent Grants

Note: Grants derived from 2003 Form 990.
General

50,000	Tri-Valley YMCA, Oneida, NY
5,000	Oneida Area Daycare, Oneida, NY
5,000	Oneida Healthcare Facility, Oneida, NY
5,000	Syracuse Symphony, Syracuse, NY
4,500	Sherrill-Kenwood Comchest, Sherrill, NY
2,500	Madison County Historical Society, Oneida, NY
2,500	Oneida Community Mansion, Oneida, NY
2,000	Heritage Farm Inc., Bouckville, NY
2,000	United Way of Greater Oneida, Oneida, NY
2,000	VVS Dollars for Scholars, Sherrill, NY

H. A. AND MARY K. CHAPMAN CHARITABLE TRUST

Giving Contact

Donne Pitman, Trustee
One Warren Place, Suite 1816
6100 South Yale Avenue
Tulsa, OK 74136
Phone: (918)496-7882
Fax: (918)496-7887

Alternate Contact

J. Jerry Dickman, Trustee

Description

Founded: 1976
EIN: 736177739
Organization Type: General Purpose Foundation
Giving Locations: OK: Tulsa
Grant Types: Award, Capital, Conference/Seminar, Emergency, General Support, Matching, Multiyear/Continuing Support.

Donor Information

Founder: The H. A. and Mary K. Chapman Charitable Trust was established in 1976 by the late H. A. Chapman.

Financial Summary

Total Giving: $3,230,950 (2003); $3,508,250 (2002); $3,880,000 (2001 approx)
Giving Analysis: Giving for 2002 includes: foundation grants to United Way ($90,000)
Assets: $66,725,114 (2003); $61,035,771 (2002); $75,000,000 (2001 approx)

Typical Recipients

Arts & Humanities: Arts Associations & Councils, Arts Centers, Arts Institutes, Ballet, Dance, History & Archaeology, Libraries, Literary Arts, Museums/Galleries, Music, Opera, Performing Arts
Civic & Public Affairs: Botanical Gardens/Parks, Business/Free Enterprise, Clubs, Ethnic Organizations, Civic & Public Affairs-General, Law & Justice, Municipalities/Towns, Nonprofit Management, Philanthropic Organizations, Urban & Community Affairs, Zoos/Aquariums
Education: Afterschool/Enrichment Programs, Business Education, Colleges & Universities, Continuing Education, Education Associations, Education Funds, Education Reform, Education-General, Inter-

national Studies, Legal Education, Literacy, Medical Education, Preschool Education, Private Education (Precollege), Public Education (Precollege), Religious Education, Science/Mathematics Education, Secondary Education (Private), Special Education, Student Aid
Environment: Environment-General, Research, Resource Conservation, Wildlife Protection
Health: Cancer, Children's Health/Hospitals, Clinics/Medical Centers, Health-General, Geriatric Health, Health Organizations, Hospices, Hospitals, Medical Research, Mental Health, Nursing Services, Prenatal Health Issues, Preventive Medicine/Wellness Organizations, Public Health, Research/Studies Institutes, Respiratory, Single-Disease Health Associations, Speech & Hearing, Transplant Networks/Donor Banks
Religion: Churches, Religion-General, Ministries, Religious Organizations, Religious Welfare, Seminaries
Science: Science Museums
Social Services: Animal Protection, At-Risk Youth, Camps, Child Abuse, Child Welfare, Community Service Organizations, Day Care, Domestic Violence, Emergency Relief, Family Services, Food/Clothing Distribution, Homes, People with Disabilities, Scouts, Senior Services, Shelters/Homelessness, Social Services-General, Special Olympics, Substance Abuse, United Funds/United Ways, Volunteer Services, YMCA/YWCA/YMHA/YWHA, Youth Organizations

Application Procedures

Initial Contact: Applications will be mailed upon request.
Application Requirements: Organizations must submit proof of IRS 501(c)(3) status, and public charity classification. Applications and required information are to be presented in triplicate and hole-punched for insertion into a 3-ring binder.
Deadlines: February 20, May 20, August 20, and November 20.

Foundation Officials

J. Jerry Dickman: trustee
Donne W. Pitman: trustee B 1940. PRIM CORP EMPL president, director: Chapman Exploration Inc. CORP AFFIL director: F & M Bank Trust Co.

Grants Analysis

Disclosure Period: calendar year ending 2003
Total Grants: $3,230,950
Number of Grants: 129
Average Grant: $25,046
Highest Grant: $250,000
Lowest Grant: $500
Typical Range: $10,000 to $50,000

Recent Grants

Note: Grants derived from 2003 Form 990.

General

250,000	University of Tulsa, Tulsa, OK
140,000	Oklahoma Medical Research Foundation, Oklahoma City, OK
140,000	Saint John Medical Center, Tulsa, OK
125,000	M.D. Anderson Cancer Center, Houston, TX -- funding for medical research
125,000	M.D. Anderson Cancer Center, Houston, TX -- toward medical research
125,000	Salk Institute for Biological Studies, La Jolla, CA -- funding for medical research
100,000	El Pomar Foundation, Colorado Springs, CO -- toward nature and wildlife
100,000	Philbrook Museum of Art, Tulsa, OK
90,000	Tulsa Area United Way, Tulsa, OK -- toward social services
75,000	Oklahoma Baptist University, Shawnee, OK

CHARITABLE VENTURE FOUNDATION

Giving Contact

William D. Dessingue, Executive Director
747 Pierce Road
Clifton Park, NY 12065
Phone: (518)877-8454
Fax: (518)877-6260

Alternate Contact

c/o Conway, Lavelle & Finn
450 New Karner Road
Albany, NY 12205

Description

Founded: 1992
EIN: 141751211
Organization Type: Private Foundation
Giving Locations: NY
Grant Types: General Support, Loan, Multiyear/Continuing Support, Scholarship.

Donor Information

Founder: Established in 1992 by Herbert K. Liebich and Isabel C. Liebich.

Financial Summary

Total Giving: $490,915 (2004); $1,320,244 (2001)
Giving Analysis: Giving for 2001 includes: foundation scholarships ($111,000)
Assets: $4,264,551 (2004); $6,223,011 (2001)
Gifts Received: $117,605 (1999); $14,494 (1996); $5,018,750 (1992). Note: In 1999, contributions were received from New York State. In 1996, contributions were received from Herbert K. Leibich.

Typical Recipients

Arts & Humanities: Arts & Humanities-General
Civic & Public Affairs: African American Affairs, Botanical Gardens/Parks, Community Foundations, Employment/Job Training, Civic & Public Affairs-General, Hispanic Affairs, Housing, Urban & Community Affairs
Education: Business Education, Colleges & Universities, Education Reform, Engineering/Technological Education, Faculty Development, Education-General, Literacy, Medical Education, Public Education (Precollege), Science/Mathematics Education, Secondary Education (Public), Student Aid, Vocational & Technical Education
Environment: Resource Conservation
Health: Alzheimer's Disease, Hospitals, Medical Rehabilitation
Religion: Religious Welfare
Social Services: At-Risk Youth, Community Service Organizations, Crime Prevention, Family Services, People with Disabilities, Recreation & Athletics, Social Services-General, Youth Organizations

Application Procedures

Initial Contact: Send a brief letter of inquiry (maximum of 2 pages).
Application Requirements: Include a description of organization, amount requested, and purpose of funds sought.
Deadlines: None.

Restrictions

The foundation does not award grants to arts organizations. Applicants should have limited resources.

Foundation Officials

Arthur Bates: trustee
Jennifer Cornell: secretary
William Dessingue: executive director
Richard C. Liebich: trustee

Grants Analysis

Disclosure Period: calendar year ending 2004
Total Grants: $490,915
Number of Grants: 14
Average Grant: $21,743*
Highest Grant: $130,000
Lowest Grant: $5,000
Typical Range: $10,000 to $50,000
*Note: Average grant figure excludes two highest grants ($230,000).

Recent Grants

Note: Grants derived from 2001 Form 990.
General

350,000	Project Lead The Way Inc. -- PLTW Programs
176,000	Foundation for Excellent Schools, Cornwall, VT -- Adirondack Excellent Schools Program
114,723	Council of Community Services, Albany, NY -- Community Voice Mail Program
111,000	College of Saint Rose, Albany, NY -- future applied technology educators scholarship fund
105,000	University of Albany Foundation, Albany, NY -- science research
53,709	Junior Achievement Capital District New York, Schenectady, NY -- Rural Outreach Program
40,540	Career Links, Albany, NY -- Opportunities that Last Program
38,023	Interfaith Partnership for the Homeless, Albany, NY -- Homeless Intervention Program
35,000	Parsons Child and Family Center, Albany, NY -- work appreciation for youth
34,544	Merrimack Valley CSD, Penacook, NH -- school equipment

CHARITY RANDALL FOUNDATION

Giving Contact

Robert P. Randall, President
71 Progress Avenue
Cranberry Township, PA 16066-3511
Phone: (724)776-7000

Description

EIN: 251329778
Organization Type: Private Foundation
Giving Locations: headquarters and operating communities.
Grant Types: General Support, Scholarship.

Donor Information

Founder: Earl R. Randall

Financial Summary

Total Giving: $190,000 (fiscal year ending June 30, 2004); $220,040 (fiscal 2002); $205,750 (fiscal 2001)
Giving Analysis: Giving for fiscal 2002 includes: foundation scholarships ($20,000)
Assets: $4,512,817 (fiscal 2004); $4,163,963 (fiscal 2002); $4,643,698 (fiscal 2001)
Gifts Received: $50,000 (fiscal 2002); $201,100 (fiscal 2001); $200,025 (fiscal 1999). Note: In fiscal 1998, 2000, and 2002, contributions were received from Three Rivers Aluminum Co.; and miscellaneous contributions of $50 also was received. In fiscal 1999 contributions were received from Three Rivers Aluminum Co. ($200,000) and miscellaneous contributions of $25 also was received.

Typical Recipients

Arts & Humanities: Arts Associations & Councils, Arts Centers, Ballet, Dance, History & Archaeology, Libraries, Literary Arts, Museums/Galleries, Music, Opera, Performing Arts, Public Broadcasting, Theater
Civic & Public Affairs: Botanical Gardens/Parks, Employment/Job Training, Civic & Public Affairs-General, Inner-City Development, Public Policy, Zoos/Aquariums
Education: Arts/Humanities Education, Colleges & Universities, Economic Education, Education Funds, Private Education (Precollege), Student Aid
Environment: Environment-General, Protection, Resource Conservation, Wildlife Protection
Health: Cancer, Children's Health/Hospitals, Hospitals
International: Foreign Arts Organizations, International Environmental Issues
Science: Scientific Centers & Institutes
Social Services: Animal Protection, Big Brothers/Big Sisters, Community Service Organizations, Youth Organizations

Application Procedures

Initial Contact: Send a brief letter of inquiry.
Application Requirements: Individuals should include a brief resume of academics. Research grants should include outline of proposed investigation and proposed budget. Organizations should request the Foundation's grant application.
Deadlines: None.
Decision Notification: Applicants are usually notified within one month of application.

Restrictions

Does not support individuals, religious organizations for sectarian purposes, political or lobbying groups, or organizations outside operating areas.

Additional Information

Grants to individuals are limited to people attending educational institutions beyond the secondary level. Recipients are selected on the basis of need, prior scholastic achievements, and area of study, with preference given to literary and environmental conservation endeavors.
Publications: Application Form

Foundation Officials

Robert G. Panagulias: assistant treasurer
Brett R. Randall: treasurer
Robert P. Randall: president
Robin S. Randall: secretary

Grants Analysis

Disclosure Period: fiscal year ending June 30, 2004
Total Grants: $190,000
Number of Grants: 18
Average Grant: $3,824*
Highest Grant: $125,000
Lowest Grant: $1,000
Typical Range: $1,000 to $5,000
*Note: Average grant figure excludes highest grant.

Recent Grants

Note: Grants derived from fiscal 2004 Form 990.
General

125,000	University of Pittsburgh, Pittsburgh, PA
30,000	Pittsburgh Zoo, Pittsburgh, PA
7,000	International Poetry Forum, Pittsburgh, PA
5,000	Extra Mile Education Foundation, Pittsburgh, PA
5,000	Pittsburgh Civic Light Opera, Pittsburgh, PA
2,500	Pittsburgh Cultural Trust, Pittsburgh, PA
2,500	Pittsburgh Public Theater, Pittsburgh, PA
2,000	Gateway to the Arts, Pittsburgh, PA
2,000	Pittsburgh Musical Theatre, Pittsburgh, PA
1,000	Animal Friends, Pittsburgh, PA

CHARTWELL FOUNDATION

Giving Contact

Margaret Perenchio, President
1999 Avenue of the Stars, Suite 3050
Los Angeles, CA 90067
Phone: (310)556-7600
Fax: (310)556-3568

Description

Founded: 1986
EIN: 954080111
Organization Type: Private Foundation
Giving Locations: CA
Grant Types: General Support.

Donor Information

Founder: A. Jerrold Perenchio

Financial Summary

Total Giving: $0 (fiscal year ending November 30, 2003)
Assets: $8,013 (fiscal 2003)
Gifts Received: $634,509 (fiscal 1999); $11,090,763 (fiscal 1996); $1,199,629 (fiscal 1995). Note: In fiscal 1996 and 1999, contributions were received from A. Jerrold Perenchio.

Typical Recipients

Arts & Humanities: Arts Centers, Arts Funds, Arts Institutes, Film & Video, Historic Preservation, History & Archaeology, Libraries, Museums/Galleries, Music, Opera, Performing Arts, Public Broadcasting
Civic & Public Affairs: African American Affairs, Civic & Public Affairs-General, Hispanic Affairs, Public Policy, Women's Affairs
Education: Arts/Humanities Education, Business Education, Colleges & Universities, Continuing Education, Education Reform, Engineering/Technological Education, Literacy, Medical Education, Private Education (Precollege), Public Education (Precollege), Religious Education, Student Aid
Environment: Air/Water Quality, Environment-General, Resource Conservation
Health: AIDS/HIV, Alzheimer's Disease, Cancer, Children's Health/Hospitals, Clinics/Medical Centers, Diabetes, Emergency/Ambulance Services, Eyes/Blindness, Hospitals, Medical Research, Mental Health, Multiple Sclerosis, Prenatal Health Issues, Research/Studies Institutes, Single-Disease Health Associations, Transplant Networks/Donor Banks
International: Foreign Arts Organizations, Foreign Educational Institutions, Human Rights, International Organizations, International Relief Efforts, Missionary/Religious Activities
Religion: Jewish Causes, Missionary Activities (Domestic), Religious Welfare, Social/Policy Issues
Social Services: Child Welfare, Community Centers, Community Service Organizations, Domestic Violence, Family Planning, Family Services, Food/Clothing Distribution, People with Disabilities, Recreation & Athletics, Scouts, Senior Services, Sexual Abuse, Shelters/Homelessness, Substance Abuse, Veterans, Volunteer Services, Youth Organizations

Application Procedures

Initial Contact: The foundation requests applications be made in writing.
Application Requirements: Includes proof of tax-exempt status.
Deadlines: None.

Restrictions

Does not support individuals.

Foundation Officials

Robert V. Cahill: vice president
Andrew Jerrold Perenchio: executive vice president, chairman B Fresno, CA 1930. ED University of

California, Los Angeles BS (1954). PRIM CORP EMPL president: Chartwell Partnerships Group. CLUB AFFIL Friars Club; Westchester Country Club; Bel-Air Country Club.

Grants Analysis
Disclosure Period: fiscal year ending November 30, 2003
Total Grants: $0*
*Note: No grants were awarded in 2003.

Recent Grants
Note: Grants derived from fiscal 1999 Form 990.
General

400,000	American Jazz Philharmonic, Los Angeles, CA
400,000	Children's Scholarship Fund, New York, NY
400,000	Geffen Playhouse, Los Angeles, CA
334,000	Los Angeles County Museum of Art, Los Angeles, CA
250,000	Motion Picture and Television Fund Foundation, Woodland Hills, CA
250,000	Muhammad Ali Center, Louisville, KY
150,000	Metropolitan Opera Association, New York, NY
100,000	American Red Cross - Los Angeles Chapter, Los Angeles, CA
81,600	American Friends of the National Gallery London, New York, NY
50,000	AMFAR, New York, NY

ALFRED E. CHASE CHARITY FOUNDATION

Giving Contact
Kerry Herlihy-Sullivan, Directory, Fleet Foundation and Philanthropic Service
PO Box 1802
Providence, RI 02901
Phone: (401)276-7316

Description
Founded: 1956
EIN: 046026314
Organization Type: Private Foundation
Giving Locations: MA
Grant Types: Capital, General Support, Operating Expenses, Project.

Donor Information
Founder: the late Alfred E. Chase

Financial Summary
Total Giving: $362,500 (fiscal year ending October 31, 2004); $363,000 (fiscal 2001)
Assets: $8,226,600 (fiscal 2004); $8,336,654 (fiscal 2001)
Gifts Received: $3 (fiscal 1992)

Typical Recipients
Arts & Humanities: Arts Festivals, Ballet, Ethnic & Folk Arts, Libraries, Music, Performing Arts, Public Broadcasting
Civic & Public Affairs: Asian American Affairs, Economic Development, Employment/Job Training, Ethnic Organizations, Civic & Public Affairs-General, Hispanic Affairs, Housing, Philanthropic Organizations, Urban & Community Affairs
Education: Colleges & Universities, Education Reform, Education-General, Preschool Education, Private Education (Precollege), Public Education (Precollege)
Environment: Environment-General
Health: Cancer, Clinics/Medical Centers, Health Funds, Hospices, Hospitals, Mental Health, Prenatal Health Issues, Single-Disease Health Associations

International: International Peace & Security Issues
Religion: Religion-General, Religious Organizations
Science: Science Museums
Social Services: Animal Protection, Child Abuse, Child Welfare, Community Centers, Community Service Organizations, Day Care, Delinquency & Criminal Rehabilitation, Domestic Violence, Family Services, Food/Clothing Distribution, Homes, People with Disabilities, Shelters/Homelessness, United Funds/United Ways, YMCA/YWCA/YMHA/YWHA, Youth Organizations

Application Procedures
Initial Contact: Send a brief letter of inquiry requesting guidelines.
Deadlines: February 15.

Restrictions
Videotapes are not accepted. Grants not made to individuals.

Additional Information
Preference is given to minority education, preventative health care, and family Service.
Publications: Application Guidelines; Application Form
Trust(s): Fleet National Bank MA NA

Foundation Officials
Kerry H. Sullivan: director grant making PRIM CORP EMPL vice president: Fleet Investment Services.

Grants Analysis
Disclosure Period: fiscal year ending October 31, 2004
Total Grants: $362,500
Number of Grants: 30
Average Grant: $12,083
Highest Grant: $40,000
Lowest Grant: $1,000
Typical Range: $5,000 to $25,000

Recent Grants
Note: Grants derived from 2000 Form 990.
General

50,000	St. Mary's Women and Infants Center, Boston, MA
25,000	Boston Renaissance Charter School, Boston, MA
25,000	Colonel Daniel Marr, Dorchester, MA
25,000	Colonel Marr Boys and Girls, Dorchester, MA
20,000	Germaine Lawrence Inc., Arlington, MA
15,000	Boys and Girls Club of Lynn, Lynn, MA
10,000	Community Minority Center, Lynn, MA
10,000	Help for Abused Women, Salem, MA
10,000	Steppingstone Foundation, Boston, MA
5,000	Boston Chinatown Neighborhood Center, Boston, MA

ALICE P. CHASE TRUST

Giving Contact
c/o Mellon Trust of New England
PO Box 185
Pittsburgh, PA 15230
Phone: (617)722-3891

Description
Founded: 1956
EIN: 046093897
Organization Type: Private Foundation
Giving Locations: MA: Boston including the North Shore area, Lynn
Grant Types: Capital, General Support, Project.

Donor Information
Founder: the late Alice P. and Alfred E. Chase

Financial Summary
Total Giving: $310,000 (fiscal year ending August 31, 2004)
Assets: $6,199,787 (fiscal 2004)

Typical Recipients
Arts & Humanities: Arts Associations & Councils, Arts Centers, Arts Institutes, Ballet, Community Arts, Dance, Ethnic & Folk Arts, History & Archaeology, Libraries, Museums/Galleries, Music
Civic & Public Affairs: Botanical Gardens/Parks, Clubs, Community Foundations, Economic Development, Civic & Public Affairs-General, Hispanic Affairs, Housing, Municipalities/Towns, Native American Affairs, Philanthropic Organizations, Urban & Community Affairs
Education: Arts/Humanities Education, Colleges & Universities, Education-General, Leadership Training, Medical Education, Private Education (Precollege), Public Education (Precollege), Vocational & Technical Education
Environment: Environment-General
Health: AIDS/HIV, Cancer, Children's Health/Hospitals, Clinics/Medical Centers, Diabetes, Health Organizations, Hospitals, Medical Research, Public Health
International: Health Care/Hospitals
Religion: Churches, Religious Welfare
Science: Science Museums
Social Services: Camps, Child Welfare, Community Centers, Community Service Organizations, Crime Prevention, Family Services, Food/Clothing Distribution, Recreation & Athletics, Shelters/Homelessness, United Funds/United Ways, Veterans, YMCA/YWCA/YMHA/YWHA, Youth Organizations

Application Procedures
Initial Contact: Send a brief letter of inquiry.
Application Requirements: a concise statement of the purpose of funds sought, the current year's operating budget, recently audited financial statement, a list of board members, resumes of all key staff people, and proof of tax-exempt status.
Deadlines: in February, May, August, and November.

Restrictions
Does not support individuals or provide funds for matching gifts.

Additional Information
Publications: Application Guidelines
Trust(s): Mellon Bank

Grants Analysis
Disclosure Period: fiscal year ending August 31, 2004
Total Grants: $310,000
Number of Grants: 10
Average Grant: $31,000
Highest Grant: $40,000
Lowest Grant: $10,000
Typical Range: $10,000 to $40,000

Recent Grants
Note: Grants derived from 2004 Form 990.
General

40,000	Boston Cares, Boston, MA
40,000	Families First Parenting Program, Cambridge, MA
40,000	Horizons for Homeless Children, Dorchester, MA
40,000	Museum of Afro-American History, Boston, MA
30,000	Bay Cove Human Services, Boston, MA
30,000	Boston Center for the Arts, Boston, MA
30,000	Cambridge Public Health Department, Medford, MA

30,000   YMCA of Greater Boston/Training, Boston, MA

20,000   Boston Parks & Recreation, Boston, MA

10,000   Everyone Wins Metro Boston, Cambridge, MA

CHATLOS FOUNDATION

Giving Contact
William J. Chatlos, President, Chief Executive Officer, & Chief Investment Officer
PO Box 915048
Longwood, FL 32791-5048
Phone: (407)862-5077
E-mail: cj@chatlos.org
Web: http://www.chatlos.org

Description
Founded: 1953
EIN: 136161425
Organization Type: Family Foundation
Giving Locations: nationally.
Grant Types: General Support, Matching, Operating Expenses, Project.

Donor Information
Founder: William Frederick Chatlos, the foundation's donor, was born in Bridgeport, CT, in 1889. In his youth, he began working for a builder and lumberman while studying the drafting of housing plans in night school at the YMCA. At the age of 17, Mr. Chatlos built his first house. He continued to construct buildings in Connecticut, New York, New Jersey, and Florida until his death in 1977. Mr. Chatlos established the foundation in 1953.

Financial Summary
Total Giving: $4,011,590 (2003); $4,000,000 (2002 approx); $5,403,717 (2001)
Assets: $87,264,404 (2003); $100,000,000 (2002 approx); $90,840,657 (2001)
Gifts Received: $221,442 (2003); $50,000 (1999); $50,000 (1998)

Typical Recipients
Arts & Humanities: Historic Preservation, Libraries
Civic & Public Affairs: Civic & Public Affairs-General, Housing, Legal Aid, Professional & Trade Associations, Safety, Women's Affairs
Education: Afterschool/Enrichment Programs, Colleges & Universities, Education Funds, Faculty Development, Leadership Training, Medical Education, Minority Education, Religious Education, Science/Mathematics Education, Special Education, Student Aid
Environment: Protection
Health: AIDS/HIV, Arthritis, Cancer, Children's Health/Hospitals, Clinics/Medical Centers, Emergency/Ambulance Services, Eyes/Blindness, Health Funds, Health Organizations, Heart, Hospitals, Hospitals (University Affiliated), Long-Term Care, Medical Research, Nursing Services, Public Health, Trauma Treatment
International: Foreign Educational Institutions, International-General, Health Care/Hospitals, International Development, International Environmental Issues, International Peace & Security Issues, International Relief Efforts, Missionary/Religious Activities
Religion: Bible Study/Translation, Churches, Ministries, Missionary Activities (Domestic), Religious Organizations, Religious Welfare, Seminaries, Social/Policy Issues
Social Services: Child Welfare, Community Centers, Community Service Organizations, Emergency Relief, Food/Clothing Distribution, People with Disabilities, Recreation & Athletics, Senior Services, Shelters/Homelessness, Substance Abuse, Youth Organizations

Application Procedures
Initial Contact: The foundation requests that all inquiries be submitted in writing.
Application Requirements: All requests must include a cover letter with the amount requested and plans for the monies; most recent budget; a one- to two-page proposal summary; and evidence of IRS tax exempt status. Include a completed application form, which may be obtained by writing the foundation or from the foundation's web site. If a proposal is to be brought before the full board, additional information will be requested to make the file complete, including: a full proposal, not to exceed ten pages; notarized affidavit certifying current tax exempt status and adherence to IRS criteria; copies of the organization's audited financial statement and Form 990's as submitted to the IRS; project budget; a listing of actual commitments toward the projected budget of the project, and any other information which may be necessary in consideration of your request; and a listing of all current officers and directors.
Deadlines: None. Although there are no deadlines, proposals may be forwarded for consideration at a subsequent meeting.
Review Process: The full board meets in February, May, August and November. A preliminary review committee considers all proposals at its monthly meetings. If significant interest is evidenced, a proposal is considered by the full board. Applicants are notified if their proposal is to be considered by the full board and will be asked to provide additional information. Meetings with the foundation are by appointment only, and are not granted initially.
Decision Notification: Requests are responded to in writing. The review process takes approximately 120 days.

Restrictions
The foundation does not support medical research, individual church congregations, individuals, the arts, state universities, primary or secondary schools, or organizations in existence for less than two years. It also does not provide seed money, loans, deficit financing, or endowment funds. Grants requests for bricks and mortar, conference and administrative expenses, multi-year support, and computer implementation are given very low priority. Do not bind proposals.

Additional Information
Organizations are allowed to submit a proposal every six months. However, no more than one project will be funded in a twelve month period.
The Foundation does not make scholarship grants directly to individuals but rather to educational institutions which in turn select recipients.
For first time applicants, the foundation tends to fund requests for amounts less than $10,000.
For first time applicants, the foundation tends to fund requests for amounts less than $10,000.
Publications: Application Guidelines; Application Form

Foundation Officials
Carol J. Chatlos: vice chairman, secretary, trustee
William J. Chatlos: president, chief executive officer, chief investment officer, trustee CORP AFFIL president: Sun Ray Homes Inc.
Charles O. Morgan, Jr.: trustee
Kathryn A. Randle: chairman, executive vice president, trustee
Cindee Random: trustee
Michele C. Roach: vice president, treasurer, trustee

Grants Analysis
Disclosure Period: calendar year ending 2003
Total Grants: $4,011,590
Number of Grants: 279
Average Grant: $14,378
Highest Grant: $400,000
Lowest Grant: $100
Typical Range: $5,000 to $25,000

Recent Grants
Note: Grants derived from 2003 Form 990.
General

400,000   Foundation Fighting Blindness Inc., Owings Mills, MD -- to support retinal degenerative disease health and education programs

100,000   Asbury Theological Seminary, Wilmore, KY -- to support defray expenses until enrollment reaches the leave to support recent faculty additions and facility expansion

100,000   Moody Bible Institute, Chicago, IL -- fund towards the Beyond the Horizons campaign

100,000   Sun System Development Corporation, Orlando, FL -- fund towards a new community After Hours Medical Clinic for the uninsured and working uninsured

62,500   Baptist Bible College of Pennsylvania, Clarks Summit, PA -- fund towards the construction and renovation of the Phelps student center

60,000   Dallas Theological Seminary, Dallas, TX -- fund towards the 2002-2004 student emergency fund

60,000   Davis College, Bible School Park, NY -- fund towards library and classroom upgrades to enable the college to move toward MSA accreditation

50,000   Campus Crusade for Christ International, Orlando, FL -- fund towards expenses at Here's Life Inner City - NY

50,000   Florida College, Temple Terrace, FL -- fund towards the completion of William F. Chatlos library

50,000   Mercy Medical Airlift, Virginia Beach, VA -- fund to further develop charitable air transportation system for rare disease patients

CHAZEN FOUNDATION

Giving Contact
Jerome A. Chazen, Trustee
Chazen Foundation
767 5th Avenue, 26th Floor
New York, NY 10153
Phone: (212)269-4141

Description
Founded: 1985
EIN: 133229474
Organization Type: Private Foundation
Giving Locations: NY: New York
Grant Types: Capital.

Donor Information
Founder: Jerome A. Chazen

Financial Summary
Total Giving: $968,102 (2003); $2,194,715 (2001)
Giving Analysis: Giving for 2003 includes: foundation grants to United Way ($5,000); foundation scholarships ($128,000)
Assets: $32,606,029 (2003); $37,127,964 (2001)
Gifts Received: $2,145,313 (2000); $1,527,003 (1999); $3,175,000 (1998). Note: In 1999, contributions were received from Jerome Chazen ($1,507,500) and Sean Sovak ($19,503). In 1994 and 1998, contributions were received from Jerome and Simona Chazen.

Typical Recipients

Arts & Humanities: Arts Associations & Councils, Arts Centers, Arts Funds, Arts Institutes, Community Arts, Dance, Ethnic & Folk Arts, Libraries, Museums/Galleries, Music, Opera, Performing Arts, Public Broadcasting, Theater, Visual Arts

Civic & Public Affairs: Civil Rights, Economic Development, Gay/Lesbian Issues, Civic & Public Affairs-General, Hispanic Affairs, Nonprofit Management, Parades/Festivals, Public Policy, Urban & Community Affairs, Women's Affairs

Education: Arts/Humanities Education, Business Education, Colleges & Universities, Education-General, Medical Education, Private Education (Precollege), Secondary Education (Public), Social Sciences Education, Student Aid

Environment: Air/Water Quality, Forestry

Health: AIDS/HIV, Arthritis, Cancer, Emergency/Ambulance Services, Eyes/Blindness, Health Organizations, Heart, Hospitals, Medical Research, Prenatal Health Issues, Single-Disease Health Associations

International: Foreign Arts Organizations, Foreign Educational Institutions, International Relations, Missionary/Religious Activities

Religion: Religion-General, Jewish Causes, Religious Organizations, Religious Welfare, Social/Policy Issues, Synagogues/Temples

Science: Science Museums

Social Services: Animal Protection, Camps, Child Welfare, Community Centers, Community Service Organizations, Counseling, Emergency Relief, Family Planning, Family Services, People with Disabilities, Recreation & Athletics, Scouts, Shelters/Homelessness, United Funds/United Ways, Volunteer Services, YMCA/YWCA/YMHA/YWHA, Youth Organizations

Application Procedures

Initial Contact: Send a letter stating the purpose of funds sought.
Deadlines: None.

Foundation Officials

Simona A. Chazen: trustee

Grants Analysis

Disclosure Period: calendar year ending 2003
Total Grants: $835,102*
Number of Grants: 88
Average Grant: $7,265*
Highest Grant: $203,080
Lowest Grant: $300
Typical Range: $1,000 to $10,000
*Note: Giving excludes scholarships; United Way. Average grant figure excludes highest grant.

Recent Grants

Note: Grants derived from 2001 Form 990.

General

89,930	Playing to Win, New York, NY
60,000	American Craft Museum, New York, NY
39,620	Volunteer Counseling Service, Rockland, NY
33,480	Jazz Aspen, Aspen, CO
31,000	National Jewish Center for Immunological and Respiratory Medicine, Denver, CO
25,000	92nd Street Y, New York, NY
23,000	Helen Hayes Performing Arts Center
18,600	United Jewish Appeal Federation, New York, NY
15,500	NOW Legal Defense and Education Fund, New York, NY
14,900	Temple Beth Torah, New York, NY

CHC FOUNDATION

Giving Contact

Ralph Isom, President
PO Box 1644
Idaho Falls, ID 83403
Phone: (208)522-2368

Description

Founded: 1984
EIN: 820211282
Organization Type: Private Foundation
Giving Locations: ID: especially eastern ID
Grant Types: Capital, General Support, Matching.

Financial Summary

Total Giving: $789,666 (2003); $1,019,736 (2001)
Giving Analysis: Giving for 2001 includes: foundation grants to United Way ($10,000)
Assets: $12,772,347 (2003); $14,364,307 (2001)
Gifts Received: $3,878,561 (2000)

Typical Recipients

Arts & Humanities: Arts Associations & Councils, History & Archaeology, Libraries, Museums/Galleries, Music, Performing Arts, Public Broadcasting, Theater

Civic & Public Affairs: Botanical Gardens/Parks, Chambers of Commerce, Clubs, Economic Development, Employment/Job Training, Civic & Public Affairs-General, Housing, Municipalities/Towns, Safety, Urban & Community Affairs, Zoos/Aquariums

Education: Agricultural Education, Arts/Humanities Education, Colleges & Universities, Education Funds, Elementary Education (Public), Education-General, Gifted & Talented Programs, Public Education (Precollege), Secondary Education (Public), Vocational & Technical Education

Environment: Environment-General, Resource Conservation, Wildlife Protection

Health: Emergency/Ambulance Services, Health Organizations, Hospices, Hospitals, Prenatal Health Issues

Religion: Ministries

Science: Science Museums, Scientific Centers & Institutes

Social Services: Animal Protection, At-Risk Youth, Child Welfare, Community Service Organizations, Counseling, Crime Prevention, Domestic Violence, Emergency Relief, Family Planning, Family Services, Homes, People with Disabilities, Recreation & Athletics, Scouts, Senior Services, Social Services-General, Substance Abuse, Volunteer Services, YMCA/YWCA/YMHA/YWHA

Application Procedures

Initial Contact: Send 13 copies of a written proposal detailing the project and budget.
Application Requirements: Include a description of organization, amount requested, purpose of funds sought, recently audited financial statement, and proof of tax-exempt status.
Deadlines: Proposals are due in spring and fall; March 15, and September 1.

Restrictions

Foundation supports only tax-exempt nonprofit organizations. Foundation does not support individuals; religious groups or churches; political or legislative action groups; athletic teams, bands, trips or tours; contests and competitions; scholarships; general operating expenses of organizations; annual fund drives; advertising for benefit purposes; general activities not clearly linked to specific charitable objectives; general planning or work in which achievements cannot be measured; projects that involve the basic delivery of educational services, except for unique or innovative special programs that serve students or enhance teaching skills or otherwise add a desirable educational dimension not provided by or appropriately printed by regular school operating budgets; national or regional organizations except as may be a specific project or activity within the foundation's region. Foundation prefers short-term projects.

Additional Information

The CHC Foundation, an independent philanthropic foundation, was created in 1985. Its immediate antecedent was Community Hospital of Idaho Falls, which owned the hospital until 1984.

Foundation Officials

Milton F. Adam: director
Donald R. Bjornson, MD: vice president
Ralph Isom: director
Forde Johnson: president
Janice C. Matthews: director
Charles M. Rice: treasurer
John I. Sackett: director
Peggy Sharp: secretary
Anne S. Voilleque: director

Grants Analysis

Disclosure Period: calendar year ending 2003
Total Grants: $789,666
Number of Grants: 52
Average Grant: $12,282*
Highest Grant: $163,293
Lowest Grant: $152
Typical Range: $5,000 to $30,000
*Note: Average grant figure excludes highest grant.

Recent Grants

Note: Grants derived from 2001 Form 990.

General

242,338	City of Idaho Falls Tautphaus Park Zoo, Idaho Falls, ID -- charitable
80,000	Eagle Rock Art Guild, Idaho Falls, ID -- charitable
56,000	Lemhi County Crisis Intervention Center, Salmon, ID -- charitable
39,780	Idaho Falls Symphony, Idaho Falls, ID -- charitable
39,780	Idaho Falls Symphony, Idaho Falls, ID -- charitable
36,000	Family Care Center, Carondelet, MO -- charitable
35,000	Shepeherds Inn, Idaho Falls, ID -- charitable
29,648	Teton Valley Museum, Idaho Falls, ID -- charitable
27,000	Ashton Memorial Hospital, Ashton, ID -- charitable
25,000	American Red Cross, Idaho Falls, ID -- charitable

OWEN CHEATHAM FOUNDATION

Giving Contact

Celeste W. Cheatham, President & Director
530 Park Ave., Suite 18J
New York, NY 10021
Phone: (212)753-4733

Description

Founded: 1957
EIN: 136097798
Organization Type: Private Foundation
Giving Locations: NY
Grant Types: General Support, Operating Expenses, Project, Scholarship.

Donor Information

Founder: the late Gwen Robertson Cheatham, the late Celeste W. Cheatham

Financial Summary

Total Giving: $339,310 (2003); $404,830 (2001)
Assets: $6,045,846 (2003); $6,942,145 (2001)

Typical Recipients

Arts & Humanities: Arts Associations & Councils, Arts Funds, Arts Institutes, Ballet, Community Arts, Dance, Historic Preservation, Libraries, Museums/Galleries, Music, Opera, Performing Arts, Public Broadcasting, Theater
Civic & Public Affairs: Civic & Public Affairs-General, Philanthropic Organizations, Public Policy
Education: Colleges & Universities, Legal Education, Minority Education, Private Education (Precollege)
Environment: Environment-General
Health: Alzheimer's Disease, Cancer, Clinics/Medical Centers, Emergency/Ambulance Services, Eyes/Blindness, Heart, Hospices, Hospitals, Hospitals (University Affiliated), Kidney, Medical Research, Mental Health, Single-Disease Health Associations
International: Foreign Arts Organizations, Foreign Educational Institutions, Human Rights, International Development, International Organizations
Religion: Churches, Jewish Causes, Religious Organizations, Religious Welfare, Synagogues/Temples
Social Services: Animal Protection, At-Risk Youth, Child Welfare, Community Service Organizations, Family Services, People with Disabilities, Recreation & Athletics, Shelters/Homelessness, Social Services-General, Substance Abuse, United Funds/United Ways, Youth Organizations

Application Procedures

Initial Contact: Send a request on organization's stationery giving complete details of the purpose of funds sought.
Deadlines: None.

Foundation Officials

MacDonald Budd: secretary, director
Celeste Wickliffe Cheatham: president, director
Kenneth Kennerly: director
Edward Arthur Reilly: vice president, treasurer B New York, NY 1943. ED Princeton University AB (1965); Duke University JD (1968). PRIM CORP EMPL partner: Morris & McVeigh. NONPR AFFIL member: Florida Bar Association; member: New York State Bar Association; fellow: American College Trust & Estate Counsel; member: Connecticut Bar Association.

Grants Analysis

Disclosure Period: calendar year ending 2003
Total Grants: $339,310
Number of Grants: 46
Average Grant: $6,429*
Highest Grant: $50,000
Lowest Grant: $100
Typical Range: $1,000 to $10,000
*Note: Average grant figure excludes highest grant.

Recent Grants

Note: Grants derived from 2001 Form 990.

General

50,000	Fore Augusta Foundation, Augusta, GA
39,300	Lenox Hill Hospital, New York, NY
29,000	Choate Rosemary Hall, Wallingford, CT
26,000	Miami City Ballet, Miami, FL
26,000	Spence School, New York, NY
15,200	Hospice of Wake County, Raleigh, NC
15,000	Flushing Town Hall
15,000	New Concord Presbyterian Church, New Concord, OH
10,000	Freedom Institute, New York, NY
10,000	Metropolitan Opera Association, New York, NY

TRUST FOR THE CHEEK FAMILY FOUNDATION

Giving Contact

Ronald Lelen, Vice President & Trust Officer
c/o JP Morgan Chase Bank
345 Park Avenue
New York, NY 10154
Phone: (212)789-4076

Description

Founded: 1990
EIN: 136930808
Organization Type: Private Foundation
Grant Types: General Support.

Financial Summary

Total Giving: $89,250 (fiscal year ending 8, 2004); $88,880 (fiscal 2001)
Giving Analysis: Giving for fiscal 2003 includes: foundation grants to United Way ($12,000)
Assets: $1,524,831 (fiscal 2004); $1,823,524 (fiscal 2001)

Typical Recipients

Arts & Humanities: Ballet, History & Archaeology, Libraries, Music, Opera
Civic & Public Affairs: Civic & Public Affairs-General, Housing, Urban & Community Affairs
Education: Colleges & Universities, Student Aid
Health: Cancer
Religion: Churches, Religious Organizations
Social Services: Animal Protection, Child Welfare, United Funds/United Ways, YMCA/YWCA/YMHA/YWHA

Application Procedures

Initial Contact: Send a brief letter of inquiry.
Deadlines: None.

Additional Information

Trust(s): J.P. Morgan Chase Bank

Grants Analysis

Total Grants: $77,250*
Number of Grants: 40
Average Grant: $1,931
Highest Grant: $10,000
Lowest Grant: $250
Typical Range: $500 to $5,000
*Note: Giving excludes United Way.

Recent Grants

Note: Grants derived from fiscal 2001 Form 990.

Library-Related

5,000	Thomas Jefferson Memorial Foundation, Charlottesville, VA

General

10,000	United Way Services, Richmond, VA
10,000	University of Richmond, Richmond, VA
5,000	Better Housing Coalition, Richmond, VA
5,000	Gore Place Society, Waltham, MA
5,000	Richmond Ballet, Richmond, VA
5,000	Trustees of Reservations
5,000	YWCA
3,000	Richmond Ballet, Richmond, VA
2,500	Richmond Society for Prevention of Cruelty to Animals, Richmond, VA
2,500	Virginia Union University, Richmond, VA

MRS. CHEEVER PORTER FOUNDATION

Giving Contact

Clifford E. Starkins, Director
c/o Adams and Becker CPA's

22 Oakwood Road
Huntington, NY 11743
Phone: (631)423-6634

Description

Founded: 1962
EIN: 136093181
Organization Type: Private Foundation
Giving Locations: NH; NJ; NY
Grant Types: General Support.

Financial Summary

Total Giving: $298,500 (fiscal year ending June 30, 2001)
Assets: $3,398,278 (fiscal 2001)

Typical Recipients

Arts & Humanities: Arts Associations & Councils, Arts Centers, Ballet, Libraries, Literary Arts, Museums/Galleries, Music, Opera, Public Broadcasting, Theater
Civic & Public Affairs: Botanical Gardens/Parks, Chambers of Commerce, Civic & Public Affairs-General, Municipalities/Towns, Public Policy, Safety, Urban & Community Affairs, Zoos/Aquariums
Education: Colleges & Universities, Medical Education, Private Education (Precollege)
Environment: Air/Water Quality, Environment-General, Resource Conservation, Wildlife Protection
Health: Cancer, Children's Health/Hospitals, Clinics/Medical Centers, Health-General, Geriatric Health, Hospitals, Hospitals (University Affiliated), Medical Research, Prenatal Health Issues
International: Foreign Arts Organizations, Foreign Educational Institutions
Religion: Churches, Religious Welfare
Science: Scientific Centers & Institutes
Social Services: Animal Protection, Community Service Organizations, Day Care, Family Planning, Homes, People with Disabilities, Scouts, Social Services-General, Youth Organizations

Application Procedures

Initial Contact: Send brief letter describing program.
Deadlines: None.

Foundation Officials

Alton Emil Peters: director B Albany, NY 1935. ED Harvard University AB (1955); Harvard University LLB (1958). PRIM CORP EMPL partner: Kelley, Drye & Warren. NONPR AFFIL fellow: Pierpont Morgan Library; honorary trustee: Signet Associates; member: New York State Bar Association; chairman executive committee, managing director: Metropolitan Opera Association; president: Metropolitan Opera Guild; director: Lincoln Center Performing Arts; fellow: Frick Collection; chairman, director: Goodwill Industries Greater New York; director: English Speaking Union U.S. New York Branch; trustee: Cathedral Saint John Divine; member: Century Association; member: Association Bar New York City; chairman, director: British American Arts Association; member council: American Museum Britain; vice president, director: American Friends Covent Garden & Royal Balet; member: American Judicature Society; member: American College Probate Counsel; treasurer, trustee: Academy American Poets; member: American Bar Association. CLUB AFFIL Pilgrims Club; Church Club; Harvard Club.
Edgar Scott, Jr.: director
Clifford E. Starkins: director

Grants Analysis

Disclosure Period: fiscal year ending June 30, 2001
Total Grants: $298,500
Number of Grants: 61
Average Grant: $4,893
Highest Grant: $30,000
Lowest Grant: $1,000
Typical Range: $1,000 to $15,000

Recent Grants

Note: Grants derived from fiscal 2001 Form 990.
General

30,000	Huntington Townwide Fund, Yorktown Heights, NY
25,000	Nassau Suffolk Autism Society
15,000	AOH
10,000	Pederson-Krag Center, Huntington Station, NY
10,000	Philips Exeter Academy, Exeter, NH
10,000	St. Paul's Center, NY
8,000	Cooley's Anemia Foundation
6,000	Metropolitan Museum of Art, New York, NY
5,000	Babylon Child Care Center, Inc., West Babylon, NY
5,000	Bridgehampton Child Care, Bridgehampton, NY

BEN B. CHENEY FOUNDATION

Giving Contact

Bradbury F. Cheney, Executive Director, President, Director
3110 Ruston Way, Suite A
Tacoma, WA 98402
Phone: (253)572-2442
Fax: (253)572-2902
E-mail: info@benbcheneyfoundation.org
Web: http://www.benbcheneyfoundation.org

Description

Founded: 1955
EIN: 916053760
Organization Type: General Purpose Foundation
Giving Locations: CA: Del Norte, Humboldt, Lassen, Shasta, Siskiyou, and Trinity Counties in northern CA, especially northern CA; OR: especially southwestern OR; WA: especially southwestern WA, Tacoma-Pierce County
Grant Types: Capital, Emergency, General Support, Project, Seed Money.

Donor Information

Founder: The foundation was established in 1955 by the late Ben B. Cheney, who died in 1971, and Marian Cheney Olrogg, who died in 1975. Mr. Cheney founded the Cheney Lumber Company in 1936, and remained in the industry until his death. In 1975, the foundation began active grant making and offices were established in Tacoma, WA.

Financial Summary

Total Giving: $3,298,450 (2002); $4,039,700 (2001)
Giving Analysis: Giving for 2002 includes: foundation scholarships ($280,000)
Assets: $63,608,385 (2002); $78,702,955 (2001)

Typical Recipients

Arts & Humanities: Arts Associations & Councils, Arts Centers, Arts Outreach, Ballet, Community Arts, Dance, Arts & Humanities-General, Historic Preservation, History & Archaeology, Libraries, Museums/Galleries, Music, Opera, Performing Arts, Public Broadcasting, Theater, Visual Arts
Civic & Public Affairs: African American Affairs, Botanical Gardens/Parks, Community Foundations, Economic Development, Employment/Job Training, Civic & Public Affairs-General, Housing, Inner-City Development, Municipalities/Towns, Nonprofit Management, Parades/Festivals, Philanthropic Organizations, Safety, Urban & Community Affairs, Women's Affairs, Zoos/Aquariums
Education: Afterschool/Enrichment Programs, Arts/Humanities Education, Business Education, Colleges & Universities, Community & Junior Colleges, Educa-

tion Associations, Education Funds, Education Reform, Faculty Development, Education-General, Literacy, Private Education (Precollege), Science/Mathematics Education, Secondary Education (Private), Special Education, Student Aid
Environment: Forestry, Environment-General, Resource Conservation, Wildlife Protection
Health: AIDS/HIV, Cancer, Children's Health/Hospitals, Clinics/Medical Centers, Emergency/Ambulance Services, Eyes/Blindness, Health Funds, Health Organizations, Heart, Hospitals, Long-Term Care, Medical Training, Mental Health, Single-Disease Health Associations, Speech & Hearing
Religion: Ministries, Missionary Activities (Domestic), Religious Organizations, Religious Welfare
Science: Science Exhibits & Fairs, Science Museums, Scientific Centers & Institutes
Social Services: Animal Protection, Big Brothers/Big Sisters, Camps, Child Welfare, Community Centers, Community Service Organizations, Counseling, Day Care, Domestic Violence, Emergency Relief, Family Services, Food/Clothing Distribution, Homes, People with Disabilities, Recreation & Athletics, Scouts, Senior Services, Shelters/Homelessness, Social Services-General, Special Olympics, Substance Abuse, United Funds/United Ways, Volunteer Services, YMCA/YWCA/YMHA/YWHA, Youth Organizations

Application Procedures

Initial Contact: Applicants should mail a one- to two-page query letter to the executive director.
Application Requirements: Query letters should provide a short history and mission of the applicant, the scope of operations, and summarize the proposal to be considered. This summary should include the nature of the need(s) to be addressed, the goal of the project, and the amount and purpose of funds requested of the foundation, the total project budget, and a plan for how other monies will be raised.
Deadlines: None.
Review Process: Agenda items for board meetings are set six to eight weeks in advance of meetings. Board meetings are held in April, June, September, and December.
The foundation considers requests on the basis of priorities and funds available. Queries go to a review committee, and if the committee deems a proposal to be of interest to the foundation, a staff contact and application form will follow. The foundation responds to all serious inquiries.

Restrictions

The foundation does not contribute to programs where government funding is available; for operating budgets, research, loans, or endowments; religious organizations for sectarian purposes; the preparation or publication of books, videos, or films; for seminars; to individuals; or for groups raising money for school-related tours.

Additional Information

The foundation awards grants primarily in southwestern Washington, Tacoma-Pierce County, southern Oregon (particularly around Medford), and the seven northernmost counties of California where the Cheney Lumber Company was active.
CF Investments of Tacoma, WA, provides accounting and investment services.
Publications: Application Guidelines; Application Form; Annual Report

Foundation Officials

Bradbury B. Cheney: president, executive director, director
Carolyn Cheney: director
Piper Cheney: treasurer, director
R. Gene Grant: director
John F. Hansler: secretary, director
Elgin E. Olrogg: vice president, director
Kenneth I. Ristine: senior program officer

Grants Analysis

Disclosure Period: calendar year ending 2002
Total Grants: $3,018,450*
Number of Grants: 134
Average Grant: $22,526
Highest Grant: $100,000
Lowest Grant: $1,250
Typical Range: $5,000 to $50,000
*Note: Giving excludes scholarships.

Recent Grants

Note: Grants derived from 2002 Form 990.
Library-Related

30,000	Friends of Jacksonville Library, Jacksonville, OR -- to provide enhancements for children's programs at the new library

General

100,000	Franciscan Foundation, Tacoma, WA -- fund to support the 'circle of care' campaign
100,000	University of Washington, Tacoma, WA -- to assist the creation of a technology center
70,000	University of Puget Sound, Tacoma, WA -- fund to upgrade the softball field to meet NCAA standards
65,000	Ben B Cheney Scholarship Program, Tacoma, WA -- to provide college scholarships to Pierce County high school students
50,000	Ashland Family YMCA, Ashland, OR -- fund towards the expansion of the YMCA
50,000	Columbia Memorial Hospital Foundation, Astoria, OR -- fund to equip a surgical suite in the birthing unit
50,000	Gig Harbor Peninsula Historical Society, Gig Harbor, WA -- fund to build the Gig Harbor heritage center
50,000	Habitat for Humanity, Tacoma, WA -- fund towards infrastructure improvements for a multi-home site
50,000	Listen and Talk, Bothell, WA -- to establish a public relations and fund raising program
50,000	Mercy Foundation North, Redding, CA -- fund to build a regional cancer center in Mount Shasta

ELIZABETH F. CHENEY FOUNDATION

Giving Contact

Elizabeth Geraghty, III, Administrative Director
120 S. LaSalle St., Suite 1740
Chicago, IL 60603
Phone: (312)782-1234
E-mail: egeraghty@cheneyfoundation.org
Web: http://www.cheneyfoundation.org/

Description

Founded: 1985
EIN: 363375377
Organization Type: Private Foundation
Giving Locations: IL: Chicago
Grant Types: General Support.
Note: project.

Donor Information

Founder: Elizabeth F. Cheney Trust

Financial Summary

Total Giving: $784,497 (fiscal year ending May 31, 2004); $862,095 (fiscal 2001)
Assets: $13,548,827 (fiscal 2004); $15,298,388 (fiscal 2001)

Typical Recipients

Arts & Humanities: Arts Associations & Councils, Arts Centers, Arts Festivals, Arts Institutes, Ballet, Community Arts, Dance, Historic Preservation, History & Archaeology, Libraries, Museums/Galleries, Music, Opera, Performing Arts, Public Broadcasting, Theater
Civic & Public Affairs: Employment/Job Training, Civic & Public Affairs-General, Parades/Festivals
Education: Colleges & Universities

Application Procedures

Initial Contact: Application forms available from foundation administration director. ICI a brief letter of inquiry.
Application Requirements: purpose of funds sought, proof of tax-exempt status.
Deadlines: 30 days prior to quarterly meetings of directors.

Restrictions

Most grants awarded to artistic and cultural organizations.

Additional Information

Publications: Application Form

Foundation Officials

Lawrence L. Belles: president, director
Allan I. Drebin: treasurer, director
Howard McDowell McCue, III: secretary, director B Sumter, SC 1946. ED Princeton University AB (1968); Harvard University JD (1971). PRIM CORP EMPL partner: Mayer, Brown & Platt. NONPR AFFIL director: Lawrence Hall Youth Services; director, chairman board governors: Northwestern University Library Council; member: Illinois Bar Association; director: International Academy Estate & Trust Law; adj professor: Chicago Kent College Law; director: Harvard Law Society Illinois; director, member: Chicago Bar Foundation; director: Art Institute of Chicago; member federal tax committee: Chicago Bar Association; member: American College Trust & Estate Counsel; member: American Bar Association; member: American College Tax Counsel. CLUB AFFIL Chicago Club.

Grants Analysis

Disclosure Period: fiscal year ending May 31, 2004
Total Grants: $784,497
Number of Grants: 117
Average Grant: $5,566*
Highest Grant: $50,000
Lowest Grant: $500
Typical Range: $1,000 to $10,000
*Note: Average grant figure excludes three highest grants ($150,000).

Recent Grants

Note: Grants derived from 2004 Form 990.
General

50,000	Chicago Symphony Orchestra, Chicago, IL -- for civic orchestra program
50,000	Lyric Opera of Chicago, Chicago, IL -- lyric at grant park and rising stars concert
50,000	Ravinia Festival, Highland Park, IL -- for Emerson string quartet and postludes
33,000	Northwestern University, Evanston, IL -- for winter chamber music festival
29,000	Windows to the World, Chicago, IL
25,000	Art Institute of Chicago, Chicago, IL -- for Seurat - digital color analysis
25,000	Hubbard Street Dance, Chicago, IL -- for the performance with Chicago symphony
25,000	Joffrey Ballet, Chicago, IL -- for live music for 2003-2004 season
20,000	Chicago Opera Theatre, Chicago, IL -- for Britten's midsummer night's dream
20,000	Goodman Theatre, Chicago, IL -- for concert readings of seven new plays and musicals

CHESAPEAKE CORP.

Company Headquarters

Richmond, VA
Web: http://www.cskcorp.com

Company Description

Founded: 1918
Ticker: CSK
Exchange: NYSE
Revenue: US$822.2 million (2002)
Employees: 5875 (2003)
SIC(s): 2435 Hardwood Veneer & Plywood, 2621 Paper Mills, 2631 Paperboard Mills, 2653 Corrugated & Solid Fiber Boxes.

Operating Locations

Chesapeake Corp. (IA--West Des Moines; KY--Louisville; MD--Pocomoke City, Princess Anne; NJ--Pennsauken; NY--Binghamton, Buffalo, North Tonawanda, Scotia; NC--Elizabeth City, Greensboro, Winston-Salem; OH--Madison, Sandusky; VA--Keysville, Milford, Norfolk, West Point, Williamsburg; WI--Appleton, Menasha)

Nonmonetary Support

Contact: Molly Remes, Director, Corporate Communications
Note: Co. provides nonmonetary support to nonprofits.

Chesapeake Corp. Foundation

Giving Contact

PO Box 2350
Richmond, VA 23218-2350
Phone: (804)697-1132
Fax: (804)697-1199

Alternate Contact

Fran Boroughs, Assistant Secretary

Description

EIN: 540605823
Organization Type: Corporate Foundation
Giving Locations: operating locations.
Grant Types: Award, Capital, Employee Matching Gifts, General Support, Multiyear/Continuing Support, Operating Expenses, Scholarship.

Financial Summary

Total Giving: $134,780 (2003); $235,171 (2001). Note: Contributes through corporate direct giving program and foundation.
Giving Analysis: Giving for 2001 includes: foundation matching gifts ($54,530); foundation scholarships ($71,371)
Assets: $1,499,567 (2003); $1,526,044 (2002); $1,617,138 (2001)
Gifts Received: $605,580 (1999); $540,000 (1998); $512,500 (1996). Note: Contributions were received from the Chesapeake Corporation.

Typical Recipients

Arts & Humanities: Arts Associations & Councils, Arts Centers, Arts Funds, Community Arts, Historic Preservation, History & Archaeology, Libraries, Museums/Galleries, Music, Theater
Civic & Public Affairs: African American Affairs, Asian American Affairs, Botanical Gardens/Parks, Community Foundations, Economic Development, Employment/Job Training, Civic & Public Affairs-General, Housing, Municipalities/Towns, Nonprofit Management, Philanthropic Organizations, Professional & Trade Associations, Public Policy, Safety, Urban & Community Affairs, Women's Affairs
Education: Agricultural Education, Arts/Humanities Education, Business Education, Colleges & Universities, Community & Junior Colleges, Continuing Education, Education Associations, Education Funds, Engineering/Technological Education, Environmental Education, Education-General, Literacy, Minority Education, Private Education (Precollege), Public Education (Precollege), School Volunteerism, Science/Mathematics Education, Secondary Education (Private), Special Education, Student Aid, Vocational & Technical Education
Environment: Air/Water Quality, Forestry, Environment-General, Resource Conservation, Watershed, Wildlife Protection
Health: Cancer, Children's Health/Hospitals, Clinics/Medical Centers, Diabetes, Emergency/Ambulance Services, Health Organizations, Hospitals, Medical Rehabilitation, Mental Health, Multiple Sclerosis, Research/Studies Institutes
International: Health Care/Hospitals, International Relief Efforts
Religion: Religious Welfare
Science: Observatories & Planetariums, Science Museums, Scientific Centers & Institutes
Social Services: Child Welfare, Community Centers, Community Service Organizations, Domestic Violence, Family Services, Homes, People with Disabilities, Recreation & Athletics, Scouts, Social Services-General, United Funds/United Ways, YMCA/YWCA/YMHA/YWHA, Youth Organizations

Application Procedures

Initial Contact: Send a letter of inquiry with a brief statement of the applicant's need for funds; foundation will respond to all preliminary inquiries.
Application Requirements: If the foundation requests a full proposal, it should include specific purpose of request and results sought; budget for project including the month in which it is requested that the grant be paid; recently audited financial statement; identity and qualifications of personnel involved in project; members of governing body; a list of other primary funding sources, particularly the United Way; evidence of tax-exempt status; statement that application has been reviewed and approved by organization's governing body.
Deadlines: December 1 for full grant applications; foundation trustees meet in January.
Decision Notification: Decisions are made at trustee meetings; secretary attempts to promptly notify organizations that do not fall within the foundation's scope.
Notes: Applications for operating grants should be for amounts not less than $1,000. Applications for capital grants should be for amounts not less than $5,000 and should not be payable over more than five years.

Restrictions

Foundation does not support individuals, organizations which are not tax-exempt under IRS standards, school athletic programs or athletic scholarships, religious or fraternal groups unless activities support the general community, political or lobbying groups organizations or candidates, or activities outside the company's geographical operating areas.

Additional Information

After the organization has received a grant, the Foundation requires an accounting of the distribution of funds and recent financial statements.
The Foundation reviews all specific requests for funds but does not respond to routine fund-raising appeals.
A budget for the year is finalized in January and includes grants to education, health, community service, and cultural organizations to which the foundation regularly contributes.
Company gives directly through marketing or public affairs departments within each operating group.

Corporate Officials

Christopher R. Burgess: assistant vice president PRIM CORP EMPL assistant vice president: Chesapeake Corp.

John Paul Causey, Jr.: senior vice president, secretary, general counsel B Takoma Park, MD 1943. ED Davidson College AB (1965); University of Richmond TC Williams School of Law JD (1968). PRIM CORP EMPL senior vice president, secretary, general counsel: Chesapeake Corp. NONPR AFFIL member: American Corporate Counsel Association; member: American Society of Corporate Secretaries.

Joseph Carter Fox: chairman, president, chief executive officer B Petersburg, VA 1939. ED Washington & Lee University BS (1961); University of Virginia MBA (1963). PRIM CORP EMPL chairman, president, chief executive officer: Chesapeake Corp. CORP AFFIL director: Crestar Financial Corp. NONPR AFFIL director: American Forest & Paper Association.

Louis K. Matherne: treasurer B Brownsville, TN 1951. ED University of Virginia (1973); University of Pennsylvania (1978). PRIM CORP EMPL treasurer: Chesapeake Corp.

Foundation Officials

John Paul Causey, Jr.: president, trustee, secretary (see above)

Joseph Carter Fox: vice president, trustee (see above)

Joel K. Mostrom: treasurer

Bruce M. Pinover: trustee PRIM CORP EMPL vice president: Chesapeake Display & Packaging Co.

Brenda L. Skidmore: trustee

E. Massey Valentine, Sr.: trustee ED University of Virginia (1956).

Grants Analysis

Disclosure Period: calendar year ending 2003
Total Grants: $42,513*
Number of Grants: 17
Average Grant: $2,501
Highest Grant: $10,000
Lowest Grant: $1,000
Typical Range: $1,000 to $5,000
*Note: Giving excludes matching gifts; scholarship; United Way.

Recent Grants

Note: Grants derived from 2003 Form 990.
General

54,600	Employee Children's Scholarship, Chapel Hill, NC
10,000	Lexington County Memorial Hospital
10,000	Robinson/Sture Olsson Auditorium & Fine Art Center, West Point, VA
5,000	Davidson's vision, Milwaukee, WI
3,000	Virginia College Fund, Richmond, VA
2,500	Seamark Ranch, Jacksonville, FL
2,500	United Way of Greater Richmond, Richmond, VA
1,000	Arts Council, Richmond, VA
1,000	Chesapeake Bay Foundation, Richmond, VA
1,000	Hand Workshop Art Center, Richmond, VA

CHEVRONTEXACO CORP.

Company Headquarters

6001 Bollinger Canyon Rd.
San Ramon, CA 94583
Web: http://www.chevrontexaco.com

Company Description

Founded: 1926
Ticker: CVX
Exchange: NYSE
Acquired: Texaco (2001);
Former Name: Chevron Corp. (2001).
Revenue: US$147.967 billion (2004)
Profit: US$13.328 billion (2004)
Employees: 50582 (2003)
Fortune Rank: 6, per FORTUNE Magazine's list of 500 Largest U.S. Corporations (2004).
SIC(s): 1311 Crude Petroleum & Natural Gas, 1382 Oil & Gas Exploration Services, 2911 Petroleum Refining, 2992 Lubricating Oils & Greases.

Operating Locations

Chevron Corp. (AK--Delta Junction, Glennallen; CA--Anaheim, Concord, El Segundo, La Habra, Oxnard, Richmond, San Francisco, San Ramon, Ventura; CO--Denver, Englewood, Rangely; FL--Hollywood; GA--Athens, Atlanta; HI--Hilo, Kahului; IN--Elkhart; LA--Winnsboro; MD--Baltimore; MS--Pascagoula; NM--Santa Fe; OR--Portland, St. Helens; PA--Mercer; TX--Bryan, El Paso, Fredericksburg, Houston, Port Arthur, San Antonio, Segno, Silsbee; UT--Park City, Salt Lake City; WA--Spokane; WY--Evanston); ChevronCorp. (WA--Seattle)

Nonmonetary Support

Type: Donated Equipment
Note: Equipment is book value. Chevron has also donated land. Contact Chevron operating locations for local nonmonetary support.

Giving Contact

Manager, Corporate Contributions
ChevronTexaco Corp. Area Gifts & Grants
Worldwide Headquarters
6001 Bollinger Canyon Rd.
San Ramon, CA 94583
Phone: (925)842-1000
Fax: (415)894-3583
E-mail: comment@chevrontexaco.com
Web: http://www.chevrontexaco.com/social_responsibility/community

Alternate Contact

Phone: (925)842-2684

Description

Organization Type: Corporate Giving Program
Giving Locations: corporate operating locations nationally and internationally.
Grant Types: Award, Employee Matching Gifts, General Support.
Note: Employee/director/retiree matching programs are available for educational institutions and arts and cultural organisation. Gifts to higher educational institutions will be matched up to $5,000 for employees, and up to $1,000 for retirees. Arts-related cultural gifts and gifts to precollege educational institutions will be matched up to $500 per individual annually.

Financial Summary

Total Giving: $61,000,000 (2003 approx); $48,518,964 (2002). Note: Contributes through corporate direct giving program only. Total giving for 1998 and 1999 reflects Chevron's corporate giving. Total giving for 2000 reflects the combined totals of Chevron corporate contributions program and Texaco Foundation giving.

Typical Recipients

Arts & Humanities: Arts Associations & Councils, Arts Centers, Arts Festivals, Arts Funds, Ballet, Community Arts, Dance, Film & Video, Historic Preservation, Libraries, Museums/Galleries, Music, Opera, Performing Arts, Public Broadcasting, Theater

Civic & Public Affairs: African American Affairs, Business/Free Enterprise, Economic Development, Economic Policy, Employment/Job Training, Civic & Public Affairs-General, Hispanic Affairs, Housing, Law & Justice, Legal Aid, Municipalities/Towns, Nonprofit Management, Professional & Trade Associations, Public Policy, Rural Affairs, Safety, Urban & Community Affairs, Women's Affairs, Zoos/Aquariums

Education: Agricultural Education, Arts/Humanities Education, Business Education, Colleges & Universities, Economic Education, Education Associations, Education Funds, Education Reform, Elementary Education, Engineering/Technological Education, Faculty Development, Education-General, International Studies, Journalism/Media Education, Literacy, Minority Education, Public Education (Precollege), Science/Mathematics Education, Student Aid

Environment: Environment-General, Resource Conservation, Wildlife Protection

Health: AIDS/HIV, Clinics/Medical Centers, Emergency/Ambulance Services, Health Policy/Cost Containment, Health Funds, Health Organizations, Hospices, Hospitals, Medical Rehabilitation, Mental Health, Public Health, Single-Disease Health Associations

International: Foreign Educational Institutions, International-General, Health Care/Hospitals, International Affairs, International Development, International Environmental Issues, International Peace & Security Issues, International Relations, International Relief Efforts

Science: Observatories & Planetariums, Science Exhibits & Fairs, Scientific Centers & Institutes, Scientific Organizations

Social Services: Child Welfare, Community Centers, Community Service Organizations, Crime Prevention, Day Care, Delinquency & Criminal Rehabilitation, Domestic Violence, Emergency Relief, Family Services, Food/Clothing Distribution, Homes, People with Disabilities, Refugee Assistance, Senior Services, Shelters/Homelessness, Substance Abuse, United Funds/United Ways, Volunteer Services, Youth Organizations

Application Procedures

Initial Contact: ChevronTexaco is currently undergoing a review of its grant programs and guidelines. As of press time, the company was not accepting grant proposals. Once new guidelines become available, they will be posted on the company's web site.

Additional Information

In October 2001, Chevron and Texaco merged to become ChevronTexaco. The company is honoring all existing commitments to community partnership programs and grants made by Chevron, Texaco, and Caltex. At press time for this edition, the company was developing grant guidelines that will reflect the new company's program focus. not been deleted from this entry. When new information is available, the entry will be re-written.

When grants are approved, Chevron requires recipients to sign grant agreements which state that financial and progress reports will be submitted to Chevron to help it monitor the effectiveness of its program. Chevron also requires completion of a substantiation form for grants totaling $250 or more.

Please do not send video or audio tapes. Submitted materials use as a guide for proposals.

If funding is sought for the environment or education, and it is broad in scope, requests for a Chevron Investment Grant application form should be made. Unsolicited proposals outside these two areas of emphasis are not encouraged by this grant program.

Publications: Philanthropy Report

Corporate Officials

Lydia I. Beebe: corporate secretaryo, director B McPherson, KS 1952. ED University of Kansas BA (1974); University of Kansas BA (1974); University of Kansas JD (1977); University of Kansas JD (1977); Golden Gate University MBA (1980). PRIM CORP EMPL corporate secretary: Chevron Corp. NONPR AFFIL trustee: Presidio Trust; trustee: Seneca Network; trustee: Golden Gate University; trustee: American Society of Corporate Secretaries; member: California Bar Association; member: American Bar Association.

David J. O'Reilly: chairman, chief executive officer, director B Dublin, Ireland January 1947. ED University College of Dublin BS (1968). PRIM CORP EMPL chairman, chief executive officer, director: Chevron-Texaco Corp. NONPR AFFIL member: National Petroleum Council; member: Western Studies Petroleum Association; director: Institute for International Economics; member: JP Morgan International Council; member: Business Council; member: Business Roundtable; chairman: American Petroleum Institute; member: Bay Area Council.

Giving Program Officials
Skip Rhodes: manager corporate contributions ED University of California Berkeley BA. NONPR AFFIL member: Commonwealth Club of California.

Foundation Officials
David J. O'Reilly: chairman, chief executive (see above)

Grants Analysis
Disclosure Period: calendar year ending 2000
Total Grants: $34,520,367*
Typical Range: $2,000 to $10,000 and $25,000 to $100,000
*Note: Grants analysis includes Chevron corporate contributions and Texaco Foundation grants made in 2000.

Recent Grants
Note: Grants derived from 1998 Form 990.
General

980,000	Unrestricted Fund, San Francisco, CA
671,077	Stanford University, Stanford, CA
550,000	Contra Costa County Department of Health Services, Martinez, CA
272,376	Ugborodo Town Relocation Project, Ugborodo Nigeria
270,005	University of California, Berkeley, Berkeley, CA
258,039	TB Moblie Clinic Kazakhstan
248,294	Nigerian Conservation Foundation, Lagos Nigeria
232,015	Dolisie Project, Dolisie Republic of the Congo
219,205	Chevron Scholarship Progam for Employees' Children
217,500	Yayasan Sosial Chevron dan Texaco Indonesia, Jakarta Indonesia

CHICAGO BOARD OF TRADE

Company Headquarters
Chicago, IL
Web: http://www.cbot.com

Company Description
Revenue: US$2.027 billion (2001)
Employees: 700 (2001)
SIC(s): 6231 Security & Commodity Exchanges.

Chicago Board of Trade Foundation

Giving Contact
Ellen Paparelli, Administrator
141 W. Jackson Blvd.
Chicago, IL 60604
Phone: (312)435-3500

Description
Founded: 1984
EIN: 363348469

Organization Type: Corporate Foundation
Giving Locations: IL
Grant Types: General Support.

Donor Information
Founder: Chicago Board of Trade

Financial Summary
Total Giving: $203,750 (fiscal year ending June 30, 2004); $190,280 (fiscal 2001)
Assets: $3,955,009 (fiscal 2004); $3,924,656 (fiscal 2001)
Gifts Received: $509,802 (fiscal 2004); $764 (fiscal 2001); $203,010 (fiscal 1994). Note: In fiscal 2004, contributions were received from Trader's Foundation Endowment Fund.

Typical Recipients
Arts & Humanities: Arts Festivals, Arts Institutes, Ballet, Community Arts, History & Archaeology, Libraries, Museums/Galleries, Music, Opera, Public Broadcasting, Theater
Civic & Public Affairs: Employment/Job Training, Civic & Public Affairs-General, Law & Justice, Legal Aid, Parades/Festivals, Philanthropic Organizations, Urban & Community Affairs, Zoos/Aquariums
Education: Business-School Partnerships, Education Associations, Literacy, Private Education (Precollege), Secondary Education (Private), Social Sciences Education, Special Education, Student Aid
Environment: Resource Conservation
Health: Cancer, Children's Health/Hospitals, Clinics/Medical Centers, Diabetes, Medical Rehabilitation, Medical Research, Multiple Sclerosis, Preventive Medicine/Wellness Organizations, Public Health, Single-Disease Health Associations, Speech & Hearing
Religion: Jewish Causes, Ministries, Religious Organizations, Religious Welfare
Science: Observatories & Planetariums, Science Museums, Scientific Centers & Institutes
Social Services: At-Risk Youth, Child Welfare, Community Service Organizations, Domestic Violence, Emergency Relief, Food/Clothing Distribution, Homes, People with Disabilities, Recreation & Athletics, Scouts, Shelters/Homelessness, Substance Abuse, United Funds/United Ways, Youth Organizations

Application Procedures
Initial Contact: Send brief letter describing program.
Deadlines: None.

Restrictions
Does not support: individuals, religious organizations for sectarian purposes, political or lobbying groups, or hospitals.

Corporate Officials
Patrick H. Arbor: chairman, chief executive officer PRIM CORP EMPL chairman: Chicago Board of Trade.
Thomas Roy Donovan: president, chief executive officer B Chicago, IL 1937. ED Illinois Institute of Technology BA (1972); Illinois Institute of Technology MPA (1975). PRIM CORP EMPL president, chief executive officer: Chicago Board of Trade. CORP AFFIL director: MidAm. NONPR AFFIL director, member: National Futures Association; council: Northwestern University Associates; director: Illinois Leadership Council Agricultural Education; director, member: De La Salle Institute; council: Grad School Business University; director, member executive committee: Chicago Association Commerce Industry; member: Chicago Central Area Comm. CLUB AFFIL Communal Chicago Club; Executive Club Chicago.

Foundation Officials
Charles P. Carey: chairman
Robert Corvino: vice chairman
Thomas P. Cunningham: director
Michael Daley: director
Jill A. Harley: treasurer

Nickalas Neubauer: director
Ellen Paparelli: administrator

Grants Analysis
Disclosure Period: fiscal year ending June 30, 2004
Total Grants: $203,750
Number of Grants: 36
Average Grant: $5,660
Highest Grant: $20,000
Lowest Grant: $2,500
Typical Range: $2,500 to $10,000

Recent Grants
Note: Grants derived from fiscal 2004 Form 990.
General

20,000	INFANT Inc., Winnetka, IL
12,500	Children's Memorial, Chicago, IL
10,000	Brookfield Zoo, Brookfield, IL
10,000	J. Kyle Braid Foundation, Villa Grove, CO
10,000	Providence St. Mel's, Chicago, IL
10,000	SOS Children's, Chicago, IL
10,000	Sunshine Gospel Ministries, Chicago, IL
10,000	Visitation Scholarship Fund, Chicago, IL
5,000	Canavan Research, Rolling Meadows, IL
5,000	Center for Disability and Elder Law, Chicago, IL

CHICAGO RAWHIDE CO.

Company Headquarters
735 Tollgate Road
Elgin, IL 60123-9332
Web: http://www.chicago-rawhide.com

Company Description
Former Name: CR Industries.
Employees: 1,800
SIC(s): 3053 Gaskets, Packing & Sealing Devices, 3714 Motor Vehicle Parts & Accessories.
Parent Company: SKF U.S.A. Inc., Northtown, PA, United States
Parent Revenue: US$5,096,900,000 (2001)

Operating Locations
Chicago Rawhide Manufacturing Co. (IL--Elgin); Chicago Rawhide Manufacturing Co. (IN; KS; MO; OK; SD)

Nonmonetary Support
Type: Donated Equipment; Loaned Executives

Giving Contact
Wally Borduer, Development Manager
900 N. State
Elgin, IL 60123
Phone: (847)742-7840
Fax: (847)742-0970

Description
Organization Type: Corporate Giving Program
Giving Locations: headquarters and operating communities.
Grant Types: Capital, Challenge, Endowment, General Support, Project, Research, Seed Money.

Typical Recipients
Arts & Humanities: Arts Associations & Councils, Arts Centers, Historic Preservation, Libraries, Museums/Galleries, Music, Performing Arts
Civic & Public Affairs: Business/Free Enterprise, Economic Development, Law & Justice, Professional & Trade Associations, Public Policy, Urban & Community Affairs, Zoos/Aquariums
Education: Business Education, Colleges & Universities, Economic Education, Engineering/Technological Education
Health: Hospitals
Social Services: Community Service Organizations,

People with Disabilities, Substance Abuse, United Funds/United Ways

Application Procedures
Initial Contact: Submit a brief letter or proposal, including proof of tax-exempt status, a description of organization, and the purpose of funds sought. Applications are accepted any time.

Restrictions
The following are not considered for charitable contributions: fraternal organizations, goodwill advertising, or religious organizations for fraternal purposes.

Corporate Officials
Kent Alcott: chief financial officer, chief executive officer PRIM CORP EMPL chief financial officer: Chicago Rawhide Manufacturing Co.
Gary Butcher: president, chief executive officer PRIM CORP EMPL president, chief executive officer: Chicago Rawhide Manufacturing Co.

Grants Analysis
Typical Range: $1,000 to $2,500

CHICAGO TITLE CORP.

Company Headquarters
171 N. Clark Street
Chicago, IL 60601
Phone: (312)630-2000
Fax: (312)223-5955
Web: http://www.ctt.com

Company Description
Employees: 10,550 (1998)
Parent Company: Fidelity National Financial Inc., 3916 State St., Suite 300, Santa Barbara, CA, United States

Chicago Title and Trust Co. Foundation

Giving Contact
Eileen Hughes, Treasurer
410 N. Michigan Avenue, Suite 590
Chicago, IL 60611
Phone: (312)644-6720

Description
Founded: 1951
EIN: 366036809
Organization Type: Corporate Foundation
Giving Locations: IL: Chicago
Grant Types: Award, Employee Matching Gifts, General Support, Matching.

Donor Information
Founder: Chicago Title and Trust Co.

Financial Summary
Total Giving: $458,677 (2002); $285,577 (2001). Note: Contributes through corporate direct giving program and foundation.
Assets: $1,818,932 (2002); $2,399,779 (2001)
Gifts Received: $650,000 (2000); $360,000 (1998); $180,000 (1997). Note: In 1998, contributions were received from Chicago Title and Trust Co.

Typical Recipients
Arts & Humanities: Arts Appreciation, Arts Centers, Arts Festivals, Arts Institutes, Community Arts, Arts & Humanities-General, Libraries, Museums/Galleries, Music, Opera, Performing Arts, Public Broadcasting, Theater
Civic & Public Affairs: African American Affairs,

Asian American Affairs, Botanical Gardens/Parks, Business/Free Enterprise, Chambers of Commerce, Clubs, Community Foundations, Economic Development, Employment/Job Training, Ethnic Organizations, Civic & Public Affairs-General, Housing, Law & Justice, Legal Aid, Nonprofit Management, Philanthropic Organizations, Public Policy, Urban & Community Affairs, Women's Affairs, Zoos/Aquariums
Education: Business Education, Colleges & Universities, Economic Education, Education Funds, Education-General, Journalism/Media Education, Education Literacy, Medical Education, Minority Education, Private Education (Precollege), Public Education (Precollege), School Volunteerism, Secondary Education (Private), Social Sciences Education, Student Aid
Health: Cancer, Children's Health/Hospitals, Clinics/Medical Centers, Diabetes, Emergency/Ambulance Services, Eyes/Blindness, Health Funds, Health Organizations, Hospitals, Long-Term Care, Multiple Sclerosis, Respiratory, Single-Disease Health Associations, Trauma Treatment
Religion: Jewish Causes, Religious Welfare
Social Services: At-Risk Youth, Big Brothers/Big Sisters, Child Abuse, Child Welfare, Community Service Organizations, Crime Prevention, Delinquency & Criminal Rehabilitation, Family Planning, Food/Clothing Distribution, People with Disabilities, Scouts, Senior Services, Shelters/Homelessness, United Funds/United Ways, Volunteer Services, YMCA/YWCA/YMHA/YWHA, Youth Organizations

Application Procedures
Initial Contact: Send a written proposal.
Application Requirements: Include a description of organization, its purpose, history, programs, and achievements; statement describing the specific purpose of grant request; a plan for evaluating program; current operating budget and budget for proposed project; audited financial statement; copy of certificate of tax exemption; list of officers and board members; and sources of income.
Deadlines: March 1 and September 1.
Evaluative Criteria: Applicant organization contributes to improving the quality of community life, with an emphasis on the urban community; organization is tax-exempt; organization does not show evidence of discrimination; and program qualifies under established priorities of foundation.
Decision Notification: The board meets in April and October.
Notes: Proposals should generally not exceed 10 pages in length. Elaborate, costly proposals are discouraged.

Restrictions
Foundation does not support religious or political activities, funds for reducing or eliminating a budget deficit, or individuals.

Additional Information
Although multi-year grants may be made, grants are not automatically renewed. Requests must be submitted annually, along with a financial statement and an account of accomplishments with the expenditure of funds.
Publications: Application Guidelines

Corporate Officials
Stuart Douglas Bilton: president, chief executive officerhuman resources B Croydon, United Kingdom 1946. ED London School of Economics (1967); University of Wisconsin (1970). PRIM CORP EMPL president, chief executive officer: Chicago Trust Co. CORP AFFIL executive vice president: Chicago Title & Trust Co.; director: Security Trust Co.; president: Alleghany Asset Management Inc.; director: Baldwin & Lyons Inc.
Richard L. Pollay: vice chairman emeritus, director B 1932. ED University of Chicago BS (1952); University of Chicago JD (1955). PRIM CORP EMPL vice chairman emeritus, director: Chicago Title and Trust

Co.
Richard Paul Toft: chairman B Saint Louis County, MO 1936. ED University of Missouri (1958). PRIM CORP EMPL chairman: Chicago Title and Trust Co. CORP AFFIL director: Cologne Life Reinsurance Co.; director: Peoples Energy Corp.; chairman, chief executive officer: Alleghany Asset Management Inc.; chairman: Chicago Title Insurance Co.
S. LaNette Zimmerman: senior vice president human resources B Newark, AR 1944. ED University of Wisconsin (1969); University of Wisconsin (1975). PRIM CORP EMPL executive vice president, chief human resources officer: Chicago Title and Trust Co.

Foundation Officials
Stuart Douglas Bilton: trustee (see above)
Norman Robins: trustee
Edson Burton: trustee
William Foley: vice chairman
Thomas Hodges: secretary
Eileen Hughes: treasurer
Nancy Labik: foundation coord
Marguerite Leanne Lachman: trustee B Vancouver, BC Canada 1943. ED University of Southern California BA (1964); Claremont Graduate School MA (1966). PRIM CORP EMPL managing director: Schroder Real Estate Associates. CORP AFFIL managing director: Schroder Mortgage Associates; director: Liberty Property Trust; director: Lincoln National Corp.; director: Chicago Title Corp. NONPR AFFIL trustee, vice president: Urban Land Foundation; trustee, vice president: Urban Land Institute; member: New York Womens Forum. CLUB AFFIL Commercial Club Chicago.
Peter Leemputte: trustee
Margaret (Pontius) "Mardie" Mac Kimm: trustee B Chicago, IL 1933. ED College of William & Mary BA (1955). PRIM CORP EMPL senior vice president corporate communications: Kraft Foods, Inc. CORP AFFIL director: FW Woolworth Co.; director: E.I. du Pont de Nemours & Co.; director: Venator Group Inc.; director: Chicago Title Insurance Co.; director: Chicago Title & Trust Co. NONPR AFFIL executive committee: Chicago Community Trust. CLUB AFFIL Womens Athletic Club.
Richard L. Pollay: trustee (see above)
John E. Rau: trustee B Milwaukee, WI 1948. ED Boston College BS (1970); Harvard University Graduate School of Business Administration MBA (1972). ADD CORP EMPL president: Chicago Title & Trust Co.; president: Chicago Title Insurance Co. MO; president: Security Union Title Insurance Co.; president, chief executive officer: Ticor Title Insurance Co. CORP AFFIL director: LaSalle National Bank; director: Nicor Inc.; director: Borg-Warner Automotive Inc.; director: First Industrial Realty Corp.
Robert Stuker: trustee
Richard Paul Toft: trustee (see above)
Richard Williamson: trustee
S. LaNette Zimmerman: trustee (see above)

Grants Analysis
Disclosure Period: calendar year ending 2002
Total Grants: $438,677*
Number of Grants: 60
Average Grant: $7,311
Highest Grant: $40,000
Lowest Grant: $500
Typical Range: $1,000 to $10,000
*Note: Giving excludes United Way.

Recent Grants
Note: Grants derived from 2003 Form 990.
General

40,000	Chicago Symphony Lyric Opera, Chicago, IL
30,000	Chicago Shakespeare Theater, Chicago, IL
30,000	Commercial Club Foundation, Chicago, IL
20,000	Neighborhood Housing Services, Chicago, IL

20,000	United Way of Metropolitan Chicago, Chicago, IL
12,000	Signal Hill Inc., Kansas City, MO
12,000	Signal Hill Inc., Kansas City, MO
12,000	Signal Hill Inc., Kansas City, MO
12,000	Signal Hill Inc., Kansas City, MO
10,000	Chicago Humanities Festival, Chicago, IL

CHICAGO TRIBUNE DIRECT MARKETING

Company Headquarters
505 NW Ave.
Northlake, IL 60164
Web: http://www.tribune.com

Company Description
Employees: 10,700
SIC(s): 2711 Newspapers, 7331 Direct Mail Advertising Services, 8742 Management Consulting Services.
Parent Company: Tribune Co., 435 N. Michigan Avenue, Chicago, IL, United States

Operating Locations
Chicago Tribune Co. (FL--Hollywood; GA--Atlanta; IL--Countryside, Freeport, Homewood, Rosemont, Schaumburg, Vernon Hills, Warrenville; NY--New York; TX--Dallas)

Nonmonetary Support
Type: Cause-related Marketing & Promotion
Volunteer Programs: The company's TribUnity program directs volunteer efforts toward reading and hunger issues.
Note: Nonmonetary support is no longer offered.

Chicago Tribune Foundation

Giving Contact
Frank Gihan, President
Chicago Tribune Foundation
435 N. Michigan Ave., Suite 200
Chicago, IL 60611-4041
Phone: (312)222-4300
Fax: (312)222-3751
E-mail: ctcommunityrelations@tribune.com
Web: http://about.chicagotribune.com/community/foundation.htm

Description
EIN: 366050792
Organization Type: Corporate Foundation
Giving Locations: IL: Chicago including metropolitan area
Grant Types: Employee Matching Gifts, General Support, Project.
Note: Employee matching gift ratio: 2 to 1.

Financial Summary
Total Giving: $720,762 (2003); $863,029 (2002); $685,614 (2001). Note: Contributes through corporate direct giving program and foundation.
Assets: $6,131,103 (2003); $6,253,937 (2002); $6,001,961 (2001).
Gifts Received: $100,000 (2002); $408,893 (1999); $867,446 (1998). Note: Contributions were received from the Chicago Tribune Company.

Typical Recipients
Arts & Humanities: Arts Associations & Councils, Arts Centers, Arts Funds, Arts Institutes, Arts Outreach, Community Arts, Dance, Ethnic & Folk Arts, Arts & Humanities-General, History & Archaeology,

Libraries, Literary Arts, Museums/Galleries, Music, Opera, Performing Arts, Public Broadcasting, Theater, Visual Arts
Civic & Public Affairs: African American Affairs, Asian American Affairs, Chambers of Commerce, Civil Rights, Clubs, Economic Development, Employment/Job Training, Civic & Public Affairs-General, Hispanic Affairs, Housing, Law & Justice, Minority Business, Municipalities/Towns, Native American Affairs, Nonprofit Management, Philanthropic Organizations, Professional & Trade Associations, Public Policy, Urban & Community Affairs, Women's Affairs, Zoos/Aquariums
Education: Arts/Humanities Education, Business Education, Colleges & Universities, Economic Education, Education Funds, Engineering/Technological Education, Education-General, Journalism/Media Education, Legal Education, Literacy, Minority Education, Private Education (Precollege), Public Education (Precollege), Religious Education, Secondary Education (Public), Student Aid, Vocational & Technical Education
Environment: Environment-General
Health: AIDS/HIV, Cancer, Children's Health/Hospitals, Emergency/Ambulance Services, Health Organizations, Prenatal Health Issues, Transplant Networks/Donor Banks
International: Human Rights
Religion: Churches, Jewish Causes, Ministries, Religious Organizations, Religious Welfare
Science: Science Museums
Social Services: Child Abuse, Child Welfare, Community Service Organizations, Crime Prevention, Delinquency & Criminal Rehabilitation, Domestic Violence, Family Services, Food/Clothing Distribution, People with Disabilities, Scouts, Senior Services, Shelters/Homelessness, Social Services-General, Substance Abuse, United Funds/United Ways, Volunteer Services, Youth Organizations

Application Procedures
Initial Contact: Send cover letter and grant proposal, preferably using the Chicago Area Grant Application Form. For application forms and information, call (312) 222-4300.
Application Requirements: The application should be accompanied by a one-sided, one-page list of board of directors; copy of the most recent IRS tax-exempt status form; audited financial statements or Form 990 from the most recent fiscal year; organization budget for year in which funding is being sought; sources of support, listing which funds have been committed; annual report or other literature on the organization's programmatic, financial, and managerial accomplishments.
Deadlines: February 1 for culture proposals, June 1 for journalism proposals. Civic proposals are considered by invitation only.
Decision Notification: Board meeting for culture proposals is held in late May and for journalism proposals in late September. All requests for support will be acknowledged.

Restrictions
Grants are generally not made to capital campaigns, endowments, or individuals. Because grants are a more cost-effective mode of support, the company does not generally purchase tables at fund-raising events benefiting nonprofit organizations. The company does not fund international projects.

Additional Information
The Chicago Tribune Company works in partnership with the Robert R. McCormick Tribune Foundation to assist local philanthropy. Company assists foundation in raising monies for two of its funds: Chicago Tribune Charities and the Chicago Tribune Holiday Fund. The Chicago Tribune uses articles, columns, and other aspects of the newspaper to solicit donations from its readers to finance the Chicago Tribune Holiday Fund, which addresses the needs of children, the homeless, hunger and developmental disability in

metropolitan Chicago. These funds are matched by the McCormick Tribune Foundation and used to disburse gifts of toys and books to children during the holiday season. Support also goes to organizations that combat child abuse and developmental delay. Other areas of support include programs or organizations that provide immediate shelter needs for the homeless, and hunger programs that subsidize food banks or alleviate hunger. Chicago Tribune Charities receives funds from the sponsorship endeavors of the Chicago Tribune Company. These monies are used to combat illiteracy and unemployment in the Chicago area. Eligible programs include job preparation and training as well as adult education programs, GED preparation and English as a Second Language programs. The Robert R. McCormick Tribune Foundation also supports programs that enhance the independence of persons with debilitating mental and physical disabilities. All money donated by the public or raised through sponsorship by the Chicago Tribune is matched by the Robert R. McCormick Tribune Foundation. Requests for support in these areas require a completed application form to be sent to the foundation in care of the Chicago Tribune Charities or the Chicago Tribune Holiday Fund at 435 North Michigan Avenue, Chicago, Illinois, 60611. Fund at 435 North Michigan Avenue, Chicago, Illinois, 60611. Fund at 435 North Michigan Avenue, Chicago, Illinois, 60611. Fund at 435 North Michigan Avenue, Chicago, Illinois, 60611. Fund at 435 North Michigan Avenue, Chicago, Illinois, 60611.
Publications: Annual Report; Grantmaking Guidelines

Corporate Officials
Denise Palmer: vice president, strategy & finance B 1957. ED Northwestern University Kellogg Graduate School of Business Administration; University of Dayton BS. PRIM CORP EMPL vice president, strategy & finance: Chicago Tribune Co.

Foundation Officials
Sheila C. Davidson: director
Paulette Dodson: secretary
Philip B. Doherty: treasurer
Frank Gilhan: president, director
Scott C. Smith: chairman, director
Don Wycliff: director
Owen Youngman: director

Grants Analysis
Disclosure Period: calendar year ending 2003
Total Grants: $584,720*
Number of Grants: 52
Average Grant: $11,245
Highest Grant: $35,000
Lowest Grant: $920
Typical Range: $5,000 to $20,000
*Note: Giving excludes matching gifts.

Recent Grants
Note: Grants derived from 2003 Form 990.
General

35,000	Art Institute of Chicago, Chicago, IL -- educational and audience development programs and educational outreach
29,500	Literary Awards, Chicago, IL -- Nelson Algen, Heartland and Young authors awards presented by the Chicago Tribune
25,000	American Society of Newspaper Editors Foundation, Reston, VA -- diversity programs in journalism
25,000	Investigative Reporters and Editors Inc., Columbia, MO -- investigative reporting training, minority fellowships and support of the IRE
25,000	Spanish Coalition for Jobs Inc., Chicago, IL -- support of job training and placement
25,000	United Negro College Fund Inc., Fairfax, VA -- support of college education at African-American colleges

24,000   Chicago Tribune Illinois High School Academic team, Chicago, IL -- college scholarships for outstanding high school students

20,000   Foundation for American Communications, Pasadena, CA -- educational programs for journalists

20,000   Roosevelt University, Chicago, IL -- a multi-media computer lab for journalism students

20,000   Youth Communication/Chicago Center, Chicago, IL -- a monthly teen newspaper

CHILDREN'S FOUNDATION OF ERIE COUNTY

Giving Contact
Ann M. Denman, Treasurer
P.O. Box 560
Kenmore, NY 14217
Phone: (716)877-0418

Description
Founded: 1836
EIN: 166000171
Organization Type: Private Foundation
Giving Locations: NY: Erie County
Grant Types: General Support.

Donor Information
Founder: Founded by the late Ida Z. Welt.

Financial Summary
Total Giving: $195,500 (2003); $262,400 (2001)
Assets: $4,538,232 (2003); $4,818,865 (2001)
Gifts Received: $25 (1996); $1,540 (1995); $395 (1994). Note: In 1994, contributions were received from the estate of Ida Z. Welt.

Typical Recipients
Arts & Humanities: Arts Outreach, Arts & Humanities-General, Libraries, Music, Theater
Civic & Public Affairs: Civic & Public Affairs-General, Urban & Community Affairs
Education: Arts/Humanities Education, Education Reform, Education-General, Leadership Training, Preschool Education, Private Education (Precollege), Special Education
Environment: Air/Water Quality, Environment-General
Health: Children's Health/Hospitals, Diabetes, Heart, Hospices, Single-Disease Health Associations
International: International Affairs
Religion: Churches, Ministries, Religious Welfare
Social Services: At-Risk Youth, Camps, Child Welfare, Community Centers, Community Service Organizations, Day Care, Family Planning, Family Services, People with Disabilities, Recreation & Athletics, Scouts, Social Services-General, United Funds/United Ways, YMCA/YWCA/YMHA/YWHA, Youth Organizations

Application Procedures
Initial Contact: Send a brief letter of inquiry requesting application guidelines.
Application Requirements: Include a description of program for which funds are requested, amount requested, purpose of funds sought, recently audited financial statement, proof of tax-exempt status, and how the program will benefit at-risk minors.
Deadlines: January 15.

Restrictions
Limited to organizations serving needy children in Erie County, NY.

Foundation Officials
Hilary P. Bradford: trustee
Winthrop Lawrence Buck: trustee
David Edmunds: trustee
Rosa Gonzelez: trustee
Charles J. Hahn: secretary
Calvin J. Haller: trustee B Buffalo, NY 1925. ED University of Buffalo BS (1949). NONPR AFFIL chairman board trustee: YMCA Greater Buffalo; trustee: YMCA Metropolitan Buffalo & Erie County; member: University Buffalo Alumni Association; director: Niagara Lutheran Nursing Home; director: Savings Banks Association New York State; member: New York Society Security Analysts; member: Newcomen Society North America; member: National Association Mutual Savings Banks; member: Masons; member: National Association Business Economists; director: Cerebral Palsy Association; director: Children's Foundation; director: Buffalo Federation Neighborhood Center; member: Beta Gamma Sigma; member: Buffalo Area Chamber of Commerce; member: American Institute Banking. CLUB AFFIL Equality Club; Buffalo Country Club; Bond Club; Buffalo Club.
Lewis F. Hazel: trustee emeritus
Betsy Mitchell: president, trustee
Susan Warren Russ: vice president
Edward F. Walsh, Jr.: trustee

Grants Analysis
Disclosure Period: calendar year ending 2003
Total Grants: $195,500
Number of Grants: 62
Average Grant: $3,153
Highest Grant: $10,000
Lowest Grant: $1,500
Typical Range: $1,000 to $5,000

Recent Grants
Note: Grants derived from 2000 Form 990.
Library-Related
20,000   The Library Foundation of Buffalo
General
30,000   Success by 6
10,000   Planned Parenthood
9,000   Gateway-Longview Day Care Center
7,800   Buffalo Audubon Society
7,000   Child & Family Services
7,000   The Salvation Army
5,000   Buffalo Federation of Neighborhood Centers
5,000   Camp Fire Boys & Girls of Buffalo
5,000   Parents Anonymous of Buffalo
5,000   St. Augustine's Center Inc.

ROBERTA M. CHILDS CHARITABLE FOUNDATION

Giving Contact
John R.D. McClintock, Trustee
PO Box 639
North Andover, MA 01845-0639
Phone: (978)685-4113

Description
Founded: 1978
EIN: 042660275
Organization Type: Private Foundation
Giving Locations: MA
Grant Types: General Support, Operating Expenses.

Donor Information
Founder: the late Roberta M. Childs

Financial Summary
Total Giving: $270,000 (fiscal year ending March 31, 2004); $641,500 (fiscal 2002)
Assets: $6,548,153 (fiscal 2004); $6,837,285 (fiscal 2002)

Typical Recipients
Arts & Humanities: Ethnic & Folk Arts, Historic Preservation, Libraries, Public Broadcasting
Civic & Public Affairs: Economic Development, Civic & Public Affairs-General, Housing, Law & Justice, Philanthropic Organizations, Urban & Community Affairs
Education: Colleges & Universities, Education-General, Legal Education, Medical Education, Minority Education, Private Education (Precollege), Public Education (Precollege), Special Education, Student Aid
Environment: Environment-General, Resource Conservation, Wildlife Protection
Health: Children's Health/Hospitals, Clinics/Medical Centers, Home-Care Services, Hospitals, Medical Rehabilitation, Medical Research, Single-Disease Health Associations, Trauma Treatment
Religion: Ministries, Religious Organizations, Religious Welfare
Social Services: Animal Protection, At-Risk Youth, Child Welfare, Community Service Organizations, Counseling, Delinquency & Criminal Rehabilitation, Emergency Relief, Family Services, Homes, People with Disabilities, Refugee Assistance, Senior Services, Shelters/Homelessness, Substance Abuse, YMCA/YWCA/YMHA/YWHA, Youth Organizations

Application Procedures
Initial Contact: The foundation has no formal grant application procedure or application form.
Deadlines: None.

Foundation Officials
John R. D. McClintock: trustee

Grants Analysis
Disclosure Period: fiscal year ending March 31, 2004
Total Grants: $270,000*
Typical Range: $3,000 to $10,000
*Note: Grant list incomplete for 2004.

Recent Grants
Note: Grants derived from 2004 Form 990.
General
5,000   Adolescent Consultation Services Inc., Cambridge, MA
5,000   Alice Lloyd College, Pippa Passes, KY
5,000   Center for Captive Chimpanzee Care, Ft. Pierce, FL
5,000   Family Service Inc., Lawrence, MA
5,000   Freedom from Chemical Dependency Educational Services Inc., Newton, MA
5,000   Gifford Youth Activity Center, Vero Beach, FL
5,000   Nantucket Boys' & Girls' Club, Nantucket, MA
5,000   Nantucket Cottage Hospital, Nantucket, MA
5,000   National Education for Assistance Dog Services, West Boylston, MA
5,000   Pine Street Inn, Boston, MA

CHILES FOUNDATION

Giving Contact
Earle M. Chiles, President & Trustee
111 Southwest Fifth Avenue, Suite 4050
Portland, OR 97204

Phone: (503)222-2143
Fax: (503)228-7079
E-mail: cf@qwest.net

Description

Founded: 1941
EIN: 936031125
Organization Type: Family Foundation
Giving Locations: primarily Pacific Northwest.
Grant Types: General Support, Project, Research, Scholarship.

Donor Information

Founder: Incorporated in 1949 in Oregon by the late Eva Chiles Meyer, the late Earle A. Chiles, and Virginia H. Chiles.

Financial Summary

Total Giving: $1,607,804 (2003); $1,989,100 (2002); $1,784,150 (2001)
Giving Analysis: Giving for 2001 includes: foundation ($2,021,100).
Assets: $15,245,050 (2003); $13,543,249 (2002); $19,325,175 (2001)

Typical Recipients

Arts & Humanities: Arts Festivals, Dance, Film & Video, Arts & Humanities-General, Historic Preservation, History & Archaeology, Libraries, Museums/Galleries, Music, Opera, Performing Arts, Public Broadcasting, Theater
Civic & Public Affairs: African American Affairs, Botanical Gardens/Parks, Community Foundations, Ethnic Organizations, Civic & Public Affairs-General, Municipalities/Towns, Public Policy, Rural Affairs, Safety, Urban & Community Affairs, Women's Affairs, Zoos/Aquariums
Education: Afterschool/Enrichment Programs, Agricultural Education, Arts/Humanities Education, Business Education, Colleges & Universities, Education Funds, Education-General, International Studies, Leadership Training, Legal Education, Minority Education, Private Education (Precollege), Public Education (Precollege), Religious Education, Science/Mathematics Education, Secondary Education (Private), Secondary Education (Public), Student Aid
Environment: Environment-General, Resource Conservation
Health: Cancer, Clinics/Medical Centers, Emergency/Ambulance Services, Eyes/Blindness, Health Funds, Health Organizations, Heart, Hospitals, Medical Research, Multiple Sclerosis, Nursing Services, Prenatal Health Issues, Public Health, Single-Disease Health Associations
International: Foreign Educational Institutions, International-General, Health Care/Hospitals, International Affairs, International Organizations, International Peace & Security Issues, International Relations, Missionary/Religious Activities
Religion: Churches, Dioceses, Religion-General, Jewish Causes, Religious Organizations, Religious Welfare
Science: Science Museums
Social Services: Child Welfare, Community Service Organizations, Homes, Recreation & Athletics, Scouts, Youth Organizations

Application Procedures

Initial Contact: Applicants should contact a foundation officer by phone to obtain an application form before submitting a complete proposal.
Deadlines: Proposals are accepted from January 1 to February 15 of each year.
Review Process: The trustees meet periodically to consider proposals.

Restrictions

Grants are not made to individuals. No grants are made for deficit financing, mortgage reduction, litigation projects, loans, or conferences already in progress.

Additional Information

Publications: Informational Brochure

Foundation Officials

Michael E. Arthur: secretary, trustee
Earle M. Chiles: president, trustee
Pedro Garcia: trustee
Sharron D. Mathews: assistant secretary

Grants Analysis

Disclosure Period: calendar year ending 2003
Total Grants: $1,607,804
Number of Grants: 38
Average Grant: $16,891*
Highest Grant: $349,000
Lowest Grant: $1,000
Typical Range: $1,000 to $30,000
*Note: Average grant figure excludes four highest grants ($1,033,504).

Recent Grants

Note: Grants derived from 2002 Form 990.
General

546,200	Boston University, Boston, MA
310,000	University of Portland, Portland, OR
185,000	Ludwig-Maximilians University, Munich Germany
150,000	St. Vincent Medical Foundation, Dallas, TX
147,000	Stanford University, Stanford, CA
106,100	Providence Portland Medical Foundation, Portland, OR
85,000	Boston Symphony Association, Boston, MA
83,100	High Desert Museum, Bend, OR
67,500	Menlo College, Atherton, CA
44,000	Oregon State University Foundation, Corvallis, OR

M. A. CHISHOLM FOUNDATION

Giving Contact

c/o US Trust Co. of New York
114 W. 47th St.
New York, NY 10036-1510
Phone: (212)852-1000

Description

Founded: 1995
EIN: 136984354
Organization Type: Private Foundation
Giving Locations: nationally.
Grant Types: General Support.

Donor Information

Founder: Established in 1995 by the late Margaret A. Chisholm.

Financial Summary

Total Giving: $797,500 (fiscal year ending November 30, 2001)
Assets: $13,802,086 (fiscal 2001)
Gifts Received: $28,624 (fiscal 1996); $486,998 (fiscal 1994). Note: In fiscal 1994, contributions were received from the estate of Margaret A. Chisholm.

Typical Recipients

Arts & Humanities: Arts Outreach, Historic Preservation, History & Archaeology, Libraries, Museums/Galleries, Music, Opera, Performing Arts, Theater
Civic & Public Affairs: Asian American Affairs, Botanical Gardens/Parks, Community Foundations, Employment/Job Training, Civic & Public Affairs-General, Municipalities/Towns, Women's Affairs
Education: Arts/Humanities Education, Colleges & Universities, Community & Junior Colleges, Faculty

Development, International Studies, Leadership Training, Private Education (Precollege), Religious Education, Student Aid
Environment: Resource Conservation, Wildlife Protection
Health: Health-General, Health Policy/Cost Containment, Transplant Networks/Donor Banks
Religion: Churches, Religion-General, Seminaries
Social Services: Child Welfare, Social Services-General, Youth Organizations

Application Procedures

Initial Contact: Send a brief letter of inquiry.
Application Requirements: Include purpose of funds sought.
Deadlines: None.

Additional Information

Trust(s): US Trust Co NY

Foundation Officials

Cynthia C. Saint-Amand: trustee

Grants Analysis

Disclosure Period: fiscal year ending November 30, 2001
Total Grants: $797,500
Number of Grants: 59
Average Grant: $13,517
Highest Grant: $50,000
Lowest Grant: $100
Typical Range: $5,000 to $30,000

Recent Grants

Note: Grants derived from fiscal 2001 Form 990.
Library-Related

25,000	Morgan Library, New York, NY
10,000	Morgan Library, New York, NY

General

50,000	Greenwich Country Day School, Greenwich, CT
50,000	Juilliard School, New York, NY
50,000	Mississippi Center for Non-Profit, MS
50,000	Mount Vernon Association, Mt. Vernon, VA
50,000	St. John's Episcopal Church, Newark, NJ
50,000	Washington State University, Pullman, WA
25,000	Grace Children's Foundation, New York, NY
25,000	Grameen USA Poverty Alleviation Collaborative, Washington, DC
25,000	Lauren Rogers Museum of Art, Laurel, MS
25,000	Metropolitan Opera Guild, New York, NY

L. C. CHRISTENSEN CHARITABLE AND RELIGIOUS FOUNDATION

Giving Contact

Stephen J. Smith, Secretary
L. C. Christensen Charitable and Religious Foundation
c/o Hostak, Henzl and Bichler
PO Box 516
Racine, WI 53401-0516
Phone: (414)632-7541

Alternate Contact

Harold K. Christensen, Jr.
403 Spruce St.
Abbotsford, WI 54405
Phone: (715)223-6345

Description
Founded: 1966
EIN: 396096022
Organization Type: Private Foundation
Giving Locations: WI: Abbotsford, Racine nationally.
Grant Types: General Support.

Donor Information
Founder: the late Harold K. Christensen, Sr.

Financial Summary
Total Giving: $151,690 (2003); $149,150 (2001)
Assets: $2,909,400 (2003); $3,413,827 (2001)

Typical Recipients
Arts & Humanities: Arts Associations & Councils, Arts Funds, Arts Outreach, Community Arts, Historic Preservation, Libraries, Museums/Galleries, Music, Performing Arts, Theater
Civic & Public Affairs: Botanical Gardens/Parks, Housing, Municipalities/Towns, Safety, Urban & Community Affairs, Women's Affairs, Zoos/Aquariums
Education: Colleges & Universities, Education Funds, Leadership Training, Literacy, Minority Education, Private Education (Precollege), Public Education (Precollege), Science/Mathematics Education, Secondary Education (Private), Secondary Education (Public), Student Aid
Environment: Environment-General
Health: Children's Health/Hospitals, Geriatric Health, Health Organizations, Medical Research
Religion: Churches, Religious Welfare
Social Services: Camps, Child Welfare, Community Service Organizations, Family Services, Homes, People with Disabilities, Recreation & Athletics, Scouts, Senior Services, Social Services-General, Substance Abuse, YMCA/YWCA/YMHA/YWHA, Youth Organizations

Application Procedures
Initial Contact: The foundation requests applications be made in writing. Send cover letter and six copies of proposal.
Application Requirements: Include a description of organization, amount requested, purpose of funds sought, and proof of tax-exempt status.
Deadlines: None.

Restrictions
Primarily supports preselected organizations.

Foundation Officials
Carol Christensen: director
Harold K. Christensen, Jr.: president
John E. Erskine, Jr.: director
Russel L. Kortendick, Sr.: vice president
Dennis C. Schelling: treasurer
Stephen J. Smith: secretary

Grants Analysis
Disclosure Period: calendar year ending 2003
Total Grants: $151,690
Number of Grants: 46
Average Grant: $3,298*
Highest Grant: $30,000
Lowest Grant: $350
Typical Range: $1,000 to $5,000
*Note: Average grant figure excludes highest grant.

Recent Grants
Note: Grants derived from 2001 Form 990.
Library-Related

5,000	Abbotsford Library, Abbotsford, WI -- for 10 books on CD format and encyclopedias

General

30,000	Wastum Museum Art Association, Racine, WI -- capital campaign
24,000	Racine Theatre Guild, Inc., Racine, WI -- for final payment on grant
12,000	Racine YMCA, Racine, WI -- for youth programs and capital campaign
8,500	Christ Lutheran Church, Abbotsford, WI -- for church and parking lot
8,500	St. Monica's Senior Citizens Home, Racine, WI -- towards replacing water pipes and computers
6,000	Marshfield Medical Research Foundation, Marshfield, WI -- for Man to Man Prostate Cancer Education and Support Group
6,000	Racine Habitat for Humanity, Racine, WI -- to assist in a building new house
5,500	St. Paul's Lutheran Church, Curtiss, WI -- toward paying for church
5,000	Luther College, Deborah, IA -- towards theater and dance design club
4,800	City of Abbotsford-Abby Athletic Youth Association and Baseball Team, Abbotsford, WI -- for new bases and field screens

CHRISTIAN DIOR PERFUMES INC.

Company Headquarters
9 W. 57th Street, Suite 39
New York, NY 10019
Web: http://www.dior.com

Company Description
Employees: 50
SIC(s): 6700 Holding & Other Investment Offices.
Parent Company: Christian Dior S.A., 30, Avenue Montaigne, Paris, France

Operating Locations
Christian Dior New York (NY--New York)

Nonmonetary Support
Type: Donated Products

Giving Contact
Amy Raiter, Events Planner
712 5th Ave., 37th Fl.
New York, NY 10019
Phone: (212)582-0500
Fax: (212)581-0788
E-mail: araiter@christiandior.fr

Alternate Contact
Danielle McGarr, Special Events

Description
Organization Type: Corporate Giving Program
Giving Locations: NY: New York nationally.

Financial Summary
Total Giving: Company does not disclose contributions figures.

Typical Recipients
Arts & Humanities: Art History, Arts Appreciation, Arts Associations & Councils, Arts Centers, Arts Festivals, Arts Funds, Arts Institutes, Arts Outreach, Ballet, Community Arts, Dance, Ethnic & Folk Arts, Film & Video, Arts & Humanities-General, Historic Preservation, History & Archaeology, Libraries, Literary Arts, Museums/Galleries, Music, Opera, Performing Arts, Public Broadcasting, Theater, Visual Arts
Education: Colleges & Universities, Education Associations, Education-General, International Studies
Health: AIDS/HIV, Cancer, Health-General, Single-Disease Health Associations, Speech & Hearing
Social Services: People with Disabilities, Social Services-General, Youth Organizations

Application Procedures
Initial Contact: Send a brief letter or proposal, including a description of the organization and purpose of funds sought.

Corporate Officials
Jillian Hirsch: chief financial officer, chief executive officer PRIM CORP EMPL chief financial officer: Christian Dior New York.
Thierry Letrillart: president, chief executive officer PRIM CORP EMPL president, chief executive officer: Christian Dior New York.

CHRISTY-HOUSTON FOUNDATION

Giving Contact
Robert B. Mifflin, Executive Director
1296 Dow Street
Murfreesboro, TN 37130
Phone: (615)898-1140
Fax: (615)895-9524
E-mail: christy-houston@mindspring.com

Description
Founded: 1987
EIN: 621280998
Organization Type: General Purpose Foundation
Giving Locations: TN: Rutherford County
Grant Types: Capital, General Support, Operating Expenses.

Donor Information
Founder: The foundation was established in 1987 with funding from the sale of a hospital.

Financial Summary
Total Giving: $3,929,451 (2002); $4,641,636 (2001)
Giving Analysis: Giving for 2002 includes: foundation scholarships ($7,500)
Assets: $71,367,397 (2002); $80,075,099 (2001)

Typical Recipients
Arts & Humanities: Historic Preservation, History & Archaeology, Libraries, Museums/Galleries, Music
Civic & Public Affairs: Civic & Public Affairs-General, Rural Affairs
Education: Colleges & Universities, Medical Education, Private Education (Precollege), Student Aid, Vocational & Technical Education
Health: Cancer, Children's Health/Hospitals, Clinics/Medical Centers, Emergency/Ambulance Services, Health Funds, Health Organizations, Heart, Hospices, Hospitals, Kidney, Public Health
Religion: Religious Welfare
Social Services: Animal Protection, Community Service Organizations, Domestic Violence, Food/Clothing Distribution, People with Disabilities, Scouts, YMCA/YWCA/YMHA/YWHA, Youth Organizations

Application Procedures
Initial Contact: Interested organizations should contact the foundation for application information and forms.
Application Requirements: All applicants will be requested to provide the following information: the name and address of the applicant; specific geographic target area; affiliations with any other organization; list of any other organizations doing the same or similar work in that geographic area; and a statement explaining how future funding for the project will be handled. The applicant will also be requested to submit a program description which includes the objectives and purposes of the project, a planned method for evaluation, and the amount of funding requested with an explanation of why funding from the Christy-Houston Foundation is needed. Along with

the application, organizations will be required to attach a copy of their most recent determination letter from the IRS, a copy of their most recent Form 990, a list of governing board members and their affiliations, a list of any officers or paid staff, identity of other sources of funding currently solicited, and a copy of their most recent financial statement together with a line-item operating budget incidental to the proposed project.

Deadlines: 28–February to be considered for a grant in March.

Review Process: All applications are evaluated on individual merit, and final approval is determined by the board of directors which meets monthly.

Restrictions

The foundation does not support organizations that do not have tax-exempt status, legislative or lobbying efforts, religious organizations or endeavors, veterans organizations, any program supported with tax funds, or payment to physicians or surgeons except for radical or extraordinary treatment. Public charities located in Rutherford County have priority and in most instances, those charities exhaust the funds.

Additional Information

Publications: Application Form

Foundation Officials

James A. Arnhart: director emeritus
Granville S. R. Bouldin: director
Henry King Butler, MD: director
Ed Delbridge: chairman, president, director
Ed Elam: director
Larry N. Haynes: director
Tom Hord: director
William H. Huddleston, III: director B 1929. ED Yale University (1950). PRIM CORP EMPL president: Huddleston Steel Engineering.
Ed C. Loughry, Jr.: secretary, treasurer, director
Roger C. Maples: director
Hubert L. McCullough, Jr.: director
Robert B. Mifflan: executive director
Edward E. Miller, Jr.: director emeritus
Matt B. Murfree, III: director
Myers B. Parsons: director emeritus

Grants Analysis

Disclosure Period: calendar year ending 2002
Total Grants: $3,921,951*
Number of Grants: 15
Average Grant: $104,669*
Highest Grant: $1,048,401
Lowest Grant: $3,172
Typical Range: $25,000 to $500,000
*Note: Giving excludes scholarships. Average grant excludes two highest grants ($2,561,260).

Recent Grants

Note: Grants derived from 2002 Form 990.
Library-Related

122,500	Lavergne Public Library, Lavergne, TN -- furnishing for new library building

General

1,512,859	Middle Tennessee Medical Center, Murfreesboro, TN -- to purchase land for new hospital
1,048,401	Domestic Violence Program Inc., Murfreesboro, TN -- construction of shelter building for domestic violence victims
560,914	Primary Care and Hope Clinic, Murfreesboro, TN -- to purchase clinic building
153,600	American Heart Association, Nashville, TN -- 48 defibrillators for all schools in this county
100,000	Jesse C Beesley Animal Humane Foundation Inc., Murfreesboro, TN -- for land and building for new spay-neuter clinic
100,000	Vanderbilt Children's Hospital, Nashville, TN -- purchase of pediatric ambulance

75,000	Sam Davis Memorial Association, Smyrna, TN -- construction of visitor center for historical site
65,000	Community Helpers, Murfreesboro, TN -- prescriptions for needy
60,000	Boys & Girls Club of Rutherford County, Murfreesboro, TN -- for buses, signs and lighting
50,000	American Cancer Society, Nashville, TN -- construction of hope lodge

CHURCH & DWIGHT COMPANY INC.

Company Headquarters

469 N. Harriston St.
Princeton, NJ 08540
Web: http://www.churchdwight.com

Company Description

Founded: 1846
Ticker: CHD
Exchange: NYSE
Revenue: US$1.047 billion (2002)
Employees: 2099 (2002)
SIC(s): 2812 Alkalies & Chlorine, 2819 Industrial Inorganic Chemicals Nec, 2841 Soap & Other Detergents, 2842 Polishes & Sanitation Goods.

Operating Locations

Church & Dwight Co., Inc. (CA--Irvine, Petaluma; CO--Evergreen; FL--Altamonte Springs; GA--Norcross; MA--Wakefield; MN--Apple Valley; MO--Nixa; OH--Old Fort; SC--Taylors; TX--Dallas; WA--Federal Way)

Nonmonetary Support

Type: Donated Equipment; Donated Products; In-kind Services; Loaned Employees; Loaned Executives

Giving Contact

Steven Cugini, Vice President, Human Resources
Church & Dwight Co., Inc.
469 North Harrison Street
Princeton, NJ 08543-5297
Phone: (609)683-5900
Fax: (609)497-7177
Web: http://www.churchdwight.com

Description

Organization Type: Corporate Giving Program
Giving Locations: NJ
Grant Types: Employee Matching Gifts, Research.

Financial Summary

Total Giving: $100,000 (2001). Note: Contributes through corporate direct giving program only. Giving includes corporate direct giving; domestic subsidiaries.

Typical Recipients

Arts & Humanities: Community Arts, Historic Preservation, Libraries, Museums/Galleries, Music, Public Broadcasting
Civic & Public Affairs: Urban & Community Affairs
Education: Agricultural Education, Arts/Humanities Education, Business Education, Colleges & Universities
Environment: Environment-General
Health: Emergency/Ambulance Services, Health Funds, Health Organizations, Hospitals, Medical Research, Mental Health
Science: Scientific Organizations
Social Services: Animal Protection, Community Service Organizations, Emergency Relief, Food/Clothing Distribution, United Funds/United Ways, Youth Organizations

Application Procedures

Initial Contact: letter of inquiry
Application Requirements: a description of organization, amount requested, purpose of funds sought, recently audited financial statements, and proof of tax-exempt status
Deadlines: None.

Restrictions

Does not support individuals, religious organizations for sectarian purposes, or political or lobbying groups.

Corporate Officials

Dwight Church Minton: chairman, director B North Hills, NY 1934. ED Yale University BA (1959); Stanford University Graduate School of Business Administration MBA (1961). PRIM CORP EMPL chairman, director: Church & Dwight Co., Inc. CORP AFFIL director: Medusa Corp.; director: Medusa Cement Corp.; director: Crane Co.; director: First Brands Corp. NONPR AFFIL trustee: Morehouse College; trustee: National Environmental Education & Training Foundation; chairman: Greater Yellowstone Coalition; member: Grocery Manufacturer America; member: Chemical Manufacturers Association. CLUB AFFIL Yale Club; Racquet & Tennis Club; Seawanhaka Corinthian Yacht Club; Lotos Club.

CIBC WORLD MARKETS

Company Headquarters

200 Liberty St.
New York, NY 10281
Web: http://www.cibcwm.com

Company Description

Former Name: Canadian Imperial Bank of Commerce; CIBC Wood Gundy Securities Corp.
Employees: 185
SIC(s): 6211 Security Brokers & Dealers, 6221 Commodity Contracts Brokers & Dealers.
Parent Company: Canadian Imperial Bank of Commerce, Commerce Ct., Toronto, ON, Canada

Operating Locations

Canadian Imperial Holding Co. (DE--Wilmington; NY--New York); Canadian Imperial Service Co. (NY--New York); CIBC (GA--Atlanta; NY--New York); CIBC Aviation (NY--New York); CIBC Oppenheimer (CA--Los Angeles, San Francisco; GA--Atlanta; IL--Chicago; NY--New York; TX--Houston); CIBC Wood Gundy Securities Corp. (NY--New York); Oppenheimer Capital (NY--New York)

Nonmonetary Support

Type: Cause-related Marketing & Promotion; Donated Equipment

Giving Contact

Ashley Johansen, Charitable Contributions Coordinator
300 Madison Avenue
New York, NY 10017
Phone: (212)856-4000
Fax: (212)856-3996
E-mail: a.johansen@us.cibc.com
Web: http://www.cibcwm.com

Description

Organization Type: Corporate Giving Program
Giving Locations: CA: Los Angeles, Menlo Park, San Francisco; DC; FL: Boca Raton, Fort Lauderdale, Miami; GA: Atlanta; IL: Chicago; MA: Boston; MO: Saint Louis; NY: New York City; TX: Dallas, Houston; WA: Seattle headquarters and operating communities.
Grant Types: General Support, Loan, Operating Expenses, Project, Seed Money.

Financial Summary

Total Giving: Contributes through corporate direct giving program only.

Typical Recipients

Arts & Humanities: Libraries
Civic & Public Affairs: Chambers of Commerce, Economic Development, Employment/Job Training, Housing, Inner-City Development, Legal Aid, Municipalities/Towns, Urban & Community Affairs
Education: Business Education
Social Services: United Funds/United Ways, YMCA/YWCA/YMHA/YWHA

Restrictions

Does not support individuals, religious organizations for sectarian purposes, political or lobbying groups, or organizations outside operating areas.

Additional Information

The company is restructuring its giving program.

Corporate Officials

Al Flood: chairman, chief executive officer, director B Monkton, ON Canada 1935. ED Harvard University. PRIM CORP EMPL chairman, chief executive officer: Canadian Imperial Bank of Commerce. CORP AFFIL chairman, chief executive officer: CIBC Subs. NONPR AFFIL director: Council for Canadian Unity; trustee: Hospital for Sick Children; chairman: Business Council National Issues.
John Hunkin: president B Toronto, ON Canada 1945. ED University of Manitoba BS (1967); York University MBA (1969). PRIM CORP EMPL president: CIBC Oppenheimer.
Matt Singleton: vice president, chief executive officer, director PRIM CORP EMPL vice president, chief executive officer, director: CIBC Oppenheimer.

Grants Analysis

Typical Range: $1,000 to $2,500

CIGNA CORP.

Company Headquarters

Philadelphia, PA
Web: http://www.cigna.com

Company Description

Founded: 1982
Ticker: CI
Exchange: NYSE
Revenue: US$18.176 billion (2004)
Profit: US$1.438 billion (2004)
Employees: 41200 (2003)
Fortune Rank: 122, per FORTUNE Magazine's list of 500 Largest U.S. Corporations (2004).
SIC(s): 6282 Investment Advice, 6311 Life Insurance, 6331 Fire, Marine & Casualty Insurance, 6719 Holding Companies Nec.

Operating Locations

CIGNA Corp. (CT--Hartford)

Nonmonetary Support

Value: $6,900,000 (2000 approx); $47,250 (1998)
Type: Cause-related Marketing & Promotion; Donated Equipment
Volunteer Programs: Foundation sponsors three "Employee Recognition Awards," which acknowledge employee volunteer efforts. Through the "Grants for Givers" program, employees and retirees who volunteer a significant amount of their time to qualifying nonprofits can request foundation grants of $100 for their organizations. If three or more employees volunteer for the same project, the organization could receive up to $5,000 through the CIGNA Team Award. The Volunteer of the Month award recognizes superi-

or employee volunteer efforts with a $500 grant to the organization benefiting from the employee's volunteerism.
Contact: Deborah Veney Robinson, Technical Consultant

CIGNA Foundation

Giving Contact

Deborah Veney-Robinson, Director, Civic Affairs
CIGNA Contributions and Civic Affairs
Tax Department
1601 Chestnut Street, TL06A
Philadelphia, PA 19192
Phone: (215)761-1000
Fax: (215)761-5632
E-mail: deborah.veney-robinson@cigna.com
Web: http://www.cigna.com/general/about/community/index.html

Alternate Contact

Arnold W. Wright, Jr., Director of Civic Affairs
900 Cottage Grove Road, W-A
Hartford, CT 06152-5001
Phone: (215)761-1000
Note: Alternate contact is for the Hartford area only.

Description

EIN: 236261726
Organization Type: Corporate Foundation
Giving Locations: CT: Hartford including metropolitan area; PA: Philadelphia including metropolitan area
Grant Types: Conference/Seminar, Department, Employee Matching Gifts, General Support, Operating Expenses, Project.
Note: Employee matching gift ratio: 1 to 1 for culture and art organisation.

Financial Summary

Total Giving: $6,732,601 (2002); $9,265,851 (2001). Note: Contributes through corporate direct giving program and foundation.
Giving Analysis: Giving for 2002 includes: foundation matching gifts ($718,970); foundation grants to United Way ($1,510,785)
Assets: $1,020,379 (2002); $1,209,158 (2001)
Gifts Received: $8,271,916 (2002); $8,724,515 (2001); $6,445,287 (2000)

Typical Recipients

Arts & Humanities: Arts Associations & Councils, Arts Festivals, Ballet, Ethnic & Folk Arts, Arts & Humanities-General, History & Archaeology, Libraries, Literary Arts, Museums/Galleries, Music, Opera, Performing Arts, Public Broadcasting, Theater
Civic & Public Affairs: African American Affairs, Business/Free Enterprise, Chambers of Commerce, Community Foundations, Economic Development, Economic Policy, Employment/Job Training, Civic & Public Affairs-General, Hispanic Affairs, Law & Justice, Municipalities/Towns, Nonprofit Management, Philanthropic Organizations, Professional & Trade Associations, Public Policy, Safety, Urban & Community Affairs, Women's Affairs, Zoos/Aquariums
Education: Arts/Humanities Education, Business Education, Business-School Partnerships, Colleges & Universities, Education Associations, Education Funds, Education Reform, Elementary Education (Private), Faculty Development, Education-General, Health & Physical Education, International Exchange, Legal Education, Literacy, Medical Education, Private Education (Precollege), Public Education (Precollege), Secondary Education (Public), Special Education, Student Aid
Environment: Energy, Resource Conservation
Health: Adolescent Health Issues, Cancer, Children's Health/Hospitals, Clinics/Medical Centers, Health-General, Health Organizations, Hospitals, Prenatal Health Issues, Public Health

International: Human Rights
Religion: Religious Welfare
Science: Science Museums, Scientific Centers & Institutes
Social Services: Big Brothers/Big Sisters, Child Abuse, Child Welfare, Community Service Organizations, Crime Prevention, Family Services, Food/Clothing Distribution, People with Disabilities, Social Services-General, Special Olympics, United Funds/United Ways, Volunteer Services

Application Procedures

Initial Contact: Send one- or two-page letter of inquiry.
Application Requirements: Include a description of organization (including name, history, activities, purpose, and board members); description of program for which grant is requested; objectives and evaluative criteria; most recently audited financial statement; copy of IRS 501(c)(3) letter; copy of the most recent Form 990.
Deadlines: None; however, the foundation recommends that proposals be submitted by September 1 for funding in the next year.
Decision Notification: Ongoing; allow six weeks for initial review.

Restrictions

CIGNA Foundation generally will not provide funds to the following categories: individuals, political organizations, religious activities or organizations that are denominational or sectarian, organizations receiving substantial support through United Way or other CIGNA-supported federated funding agencies, endowment drives or capital campaigns, or hospital capital improvements or expansions.

Additional Information

Publications: Annual Report; Contributions Report

Corporate Officials

H. Edward Hanway: chairman, chief executive officer B West Chester, PA 1952. ED Loyola College BA (1974); Widener University MBA (1984). PRIM CORP EMPL president, chief executive officer: CIGNA Corp. NONPR AFFIL member: PICPA; member: World Affairs Council Philadelphia; member: American Institute CPAs.
Judith Soltz: executive vice president PRIM CORP EMPL chief counsel: CIGNA Corp.

Foundation Officials

H. Edward Hanway: director (see above)
Lee R. Hoffman: assistant secretary
Donald M. Levinson: director B 1946. ED Columbia University (1967); Columbia University (1968). NONPR AFFIL member: American Psychological Society.
Judith Soltz: chairman, director (see above)
Carol J. Ward: secretary B 1957. ED Yale University (1978); Emory University School of Law (1983). ADD CORP EMPL secretary: CIGNA Eagle Lodge Properties. NONPR AFFIL member: American Corporate Counsel Association; member: American Society of Corporate Secretaries; member: American Bar Association.
Arnold W. Wright, Jr.: vice president, executive director

Grants Analysis

Disclosure Period: calendar year ending 2002
Total Grants: $4,502,846*
Number of Grants: 141 (approx)*
Average Grant: $23,235*
Highest Grant: $1,250,000
Typical Range: $5,000 to $50,000
*Note: Giving excludes United Way and matching gifts. Number of grants also excludes grants of less than $5,000 each not listed. Average grant amount requested excludes highest grants.

Recent Grants

Note: Grants derived from 2003 Form 990.
General

1,250,000	American Enterprise Institute, Washington, DC
501,896	United Way Field Agencies, Alexandria, VA
407,500	March of Dimes Birth Defects Foundation, White Plains, NY
405,000	United Way of Southeastern Pennsylvania, Philadelphia, PA
401,100	United Way of the Capital Area Connecticut, Hartford, CT
268,480	Susan G Komen Breast Cancer Foundation, Dallas, TX
251,000	March of Dimes Birth Defects Foundation, East Hartford, CT
202,789	United Way of New York City, New York, NY
125,000	National Black Women's Health, Washington, DC
125,000	News for Students Foundation

JAMES AND BARBARA CIMINO FOUNDATION

Giving Contact

Christine Bender, Secretary, Treasurer & Director
James and Barbara Cimino Foundation
PO Box 448
Sun Valley, ID 83353-0448
Phone: (208)622-4556

Description

Founded: 1995
EIN: 820474867
Organization Type: Private Foundation

Financial Summary

Total Giving: $81,200 (fiscal year ending June 30, 2001)
Assets: $1,138,565 (fiscal 2001)
Gifts Received: $60,000 (fiscal 2001); $954,308 (fiscal 1996). Note: In fiscal 2001, contributions were received from J & B Cimino. In fiscal 1996, contributions were received from James Cimino ($182,929), Barbara Cimino ($71,379), James and Barbara Cimino ($450,000), and Robert Cimino ($250,000).

Typical Recipients

Arts & Humanities: Arts Associations & Councils, Libraries, Public Broadcasting
Civic & Public Affairs: Civic & Public Affairs-General, Hispanic Affairs
Education: Colleges & Universities, Community & Junior Colleges, Education Funds, Elementary Education (Private), Elementary Education (Public), Student Aid
Environment: Environment-General, Resource Conservation, Wildlife Protection
Health: Hospices
International: Foreign Educational Institutions, Health Care/Hospitals
Religion: Churches
Social Services: At-Risk Youth

Application Procedures

Initial Contact: Send a brief letter of inquiry.
Application Requirements: Include a specific explanation of the program for which funds are sought and proof of tax-exempt status.
Deadlines: None.

Additional Information

Trust(s): Bank AM IL

Foundation Officials

Christine Bender: secretary, treasurer, director
Barbara Cimino: vice president, director
David Cimino: director
James A. Cimino: director
James N. Cimino: president, director
Robert Cimino: director

Grants Analysis

Disclosure Period: fiscal year ending June 30, 2001
Total Grants: $81,200
Number of Grants: 21
Average Grant: $2,810*
Highest Grant: $25,000
Typical Range: $1,000 to $5,000
*Note: Average grant figure excludes highest grant.

Recent Grants

Note: Grants derived from fiscal 2001 Form 990.
Library-Related

5,000	Community Library Association, Ketchum, ID

General

25,000	DePaul University, Chicago, IL
5,000	Idaho Public Television, Boise, ID
5,000	Nature Conservancy of Idaho, Sun Valley, ID
5,000	Peregrine Fund, Boise, ID
5,000	Rinaldi Foundation
4,000	Boise State University, Boise, ID
2,500	Mills College Alumnae Foundation, Oakland, CA
2,500	National Foundation for Advancement in the Arts, Miami, FL
2,500	University of Waitako, Hamilton New Zealand
2,000	Hospice of Wood River Valley, Ketchum, ID

CINERGY CORP.

Company Headquarters

139 E. 4th St.
Cincinnati, OH 45202
Web: http://www.cinergy.com

Company Description

Founded: 1994
Ticker: CIN
Exchange: NYSE
Revenue: US$4.688 billion (2004)
Profit: US$400.9 million (2004)
Employees: 7693 (2003)
Fortune Rank: 412, per FORTUNE Magazine's list of 500 Largest U.S. Corporations (2004).

Nonmonetary Support

Value: $30,000 (1998 approx)
Type: Cause-related Marketing & Promotion; Donated Equipment; Donated Products; In-kind Services; Loaned Employees; Loaned Executives; Workplace Solicitation
Contact: Karol King, Cinergy Foundation

Cinergy Foundation

Giving Contact

J. Joseph Hale, Jr., President
1000 E. Main St.
Plainfield, IN 46168
Phone: (513)287-2410
Fax: (513)651-9196
Web: http://www.cinergy.com/Community/default.asp

Description

Founded: 1992
EIN: 351755088
Organization Type: Corporate Foundation
Former Name: PSI Energy Foundation.
Giving Locations: IN: company service area; KY: Northern Kentucky (company service area); OH: company service area
Grant Types: Award, Employee Matching Gifts, Matching, Multiyear/Continuing Support, Project, Research, Scholarship.

Financial Summary

Total Giving: $3,457,018 (2003); $3,279,825 (2002); $3,816,667 (2001)
Assets: $73,787 (2003); $18,305 (2002)
Gifts Received: $3,512,500 (2003); $3,352,662 (2002); $3,780,000 (2001)

Typical Recipients

Arts & Humanities: Arts Associations & Councils, Arts Centers, Arts Festivals, Arts Funds, Ballet, Community Arts, Arts & Humanities-General, Historic Preservation, History & Archaeology, Libraries, Museums/Galleries, Music, Opera, Performing Arts, Public Broadcasting, Theater
Civic & Public Affairs: African American Affairs, Botanical Gardens/Parks, Chambers of Commerce, Community Foundations, Economic Development, Civic & Public Affairs-General, Municipalities/Towns, Nonprofit Management, Public Policy, Urban & Community Affairs, Zoos/Aquariums
Education: Afterschool/Enrichment Programs, Arts/Humanities Education, Business Education, Business-School Partnerships, Colleges & Universities, Community & Junior Colleges, Education Associations, Education Funds, Education Reform, Elementary Education (Private), Elementary Education (Public), Engineering/Technological Education, Faculty Development, Education-General, Journalism/Media Education, Leadership Training, Literacy, Medical Education, Private Education (Precollege), Public Education (Precollege), Religious Education, Student Aid
Environment: Environment-General, Resource Conservation
Health: Cancer, Children's Health/Hospitals, Emergency/Ambulance Services, Health-General, Health Funds, Health Organizations, Hospices, Hospitals, Mental Health, Prenatal Health Issues, Single-Disease Health Associations
International: Health Care/Hospitals
Religion: Religious Welfare
Social Services: Child Welfare, People with Disabilities, Recreation & Athletics, Scouts, Social Services-General, Special Olympics, Substance Abuse, United Funds/United Ways, YMCA/YWCA/YMHA/YWHA, Youth Organizations

Application Procedures

Initial Contact: Telephone to request application guidelines and grant application form, then send full proposal.
Application Requirements: Grant application form requests the following information: organization name, address, phone number, and federal tax identification number; name and title of contact person; a brief a description of organization's mission, goals, and objectives; and project information, including name and dates of project, total project cost, dollar amount requested, number of people project benefits, county within which project is located, additional counties benefiting from project, plan for recognizing contributors, project description, a list of Cinergy employees involved in the project and a description of their roles. Attachments requested include a copy of 501(c)(3) tax exemption letter; a copy of organization's current budget and the project budget, showing all project revenues and expenses; timetable for becoming self-sufficient; plan for project evaluation; the names and addresses of the organization's board of

directors; clear, measurable project objectives; and other supplementary material that describes the organization.

Deadlines: The 15th of March, June, and September.

Review Process: Grant requests are reviewed on a quarterly basis; applicants are encouraged to submit grant applications as far in advance of the project dates above as possible.

Evaluative Criteria: How project benefits citizens and communities, especially within company's service area.

Decision Notification: organizations receive notification of grant approximately six weeks after submission deadline. Applications received after the deadline will automatically be considered at the next grant application deadline.

Notes: Applicants are encouraged to call the foundation to discuss their proposals prior to submission. Applicants are requested to submit their grant application to the district office closest to them for review and endorsement by the district manager. Managers and employees are involved in the decision-making process, and the foundation reports it is important for the Cinergy district manager in applicant's service area to be well informed about project.

Restrictions

The foundation does not fund capital campaigns; advertising; membership dues; non-tax exempt organizations; post-prom or post-graduation activities; programs posing a conflict of interest; recognition or academic awards programs (unless part of a staff or workforce development program); technology and audiovisual equipment; travel expenses; uniforms; post-event funding; organizations benefiting an individual or a few persons; capital or endowment campaigns; construction projects; auctions, textbooks purchases, for schools or fundraising events; or veterans, labor, religious, political, or fraternal groups. Generally, gifts for competitions, golf events, and athletic programs and facilities are beyond the scope of foundation's program.

Additional Information

Company is looking for partnerships between the company and organizations that enhance the future of Indiana communities. Grants are for specific projects or designated programs. Grants are made on a one-year basis. Re-application is necessary for consideration of a grant renewal. Special consideration is given to programs with a statewide scope that benefit citizens in company's service area. Some organizations receiving grants from the Cinergy Foundation will be offered the added benefit of an energy audit of their facilities at Cinergy's expense. The audit provides the organization with recommendations to save on energy costs.

Publications: Guidelines; Annual Report

Corporate Officials

William J. Grealis: vice president, president, chief executive officer, director B Olmsted Falls, OH 1945. ED Ohio University (1967); University of Akron (1972). PRIM CORP EMPL vice president: Cinergy Corp. ADD CORP EMPL president, director: Cinergy Investments; president, director: Cinergy Communication Inc.; president: Lawrenceburg Gas Co. CORP AFFIL president corp. development, chief strategic officer: Cincinnati Gas & Electric Co. Inc.

James E. Rogers, Jr.: vice chairman, president, chief executive officer, director B Birmingham, AL 1947. ED University of Kentucky BBA (1970); University of Kentucky JD (1974). PRIM CORP EMPL vice chairman, president, chief executive officer, director: Cinergy Corp. ADD CORP EMPL president: Cinergy Service Inc.; vice chairman: Lawrenceburg Gas Co.; chief executive officer: PSI Energy Inc.; chairman: Power Equipment Supply Co.; vice chairman: Union Light Heat & Power Co. Inc. CORP AFFIL vice president: Roger Petroleum Service Inc.; director: Duke

Realty Investments Inc.; director: Fifth Third Bancorp. NONPR AFFIL director: Edison Electric Institute.

Foundation Officials

Wendy Aumiller: treasurer

Phillip R. Cox: director B 1946. ED Xavier University (1967-1969). PRIM CORP EMPL president: Cox Financial Corp. ADD CORP EMPL secretary: Crown Mortgage Services Inc. CORP AFFIL director: Cincinnati Bell Inc.; director: Cinergy Corp.

Michael J. Cyrus: director

Gregory C. Ficke: director

J. Joseph Hale, Jr.: president, director PRIM CORP EMPL vice president corporate communications: Cinergy Corp.

Julia S. Janson: secretary

George C. Juilfs: director B 1939. PRIM CORP EMPL president, chief executive officer: SENCORP. CORP AFFIL director: Cinergy Corp.; chairman: SENCO Products Inc.

Marc E. Manly: director

Frederick J. Newton, III: director

Kay E. Pashos: director

James E. Rogers, Jr.: chairman, director (see above)

Mary Schapiro: director

Philip R. Sharp: director

James L. Turner: director

Grants Analysis

Disclosure Period: calendar year ending 2003

Total Grants: $3,457,018

Number of Grants: 750 (approx)

Average Grant: $4,609

Highest Grant: $300,000

Lowest Grant: $25

Typical Range: $500 to $5,000

Recent Grants

Note: Grants derived from 2003 Form 990.

General

300,000	Children's Museum at Cincinnati Museum Center, Cincinnati, OH
120,000	Fine Arts Fund, Cincinnati, OH
75,000	Wellness Community Central Indiana Inc., Indianapolis, IN
50,000	Indiana State Museum Foundation, Indianapolis, IN
35,000	National Speaking of Women's Health Foundation, Cincinnati, OH
33,333	Cincinnati Zoo and Botanical Garden, Cincinnati, OH
29,469	United Way of Central Indiana, Indianapolis, IN
25,000	Greater Cincinnati Television Educational Foundation Inc, Cincinnati, OH
25,000	Greenwood Community Schools, Greenwood, IN
25,000	Hebrew Union College, New York, NY

CISCO SYSTEMS INC.

Company Headquarters

San Jose, CA

Web: http://www.cisco.com

Company Description

Founded: 1984

Ticker: CSCO

Exchange: NASDAQ

Revenue: US$22.045 billion (2004)

Profit: US$4.401 billion (2004)

Employees: 34501 (2003)

Fortune Rank: 91, per FORTUNE Magazine's list of 500 Largest U.S. Corporations (2004).

SIC(s): 3577 Computer Peripheral Equipment Nec.

Cisco Systems Foundation

Giving Contact

Lynne Elliott
170 West Tasman Drive
San Jose, CA 95134
Phone: (408)526-3040
Web: http://www.cisco.com/go/philanthropy

Description

EIN: 770443347

Organization Type: Corporate Foundation

Giving Locations: CA: San Jose area; MA; NY; NC

Grant Types: General Support.

Financial Summary

Total Giving: $8,469,865 (fiscal year ending July 31, 2004); $11,386,465 (fiscal 2002); $7,187,424 (fiscal 2001)

Giving Analysis: Giving for fiscal 2002 includes: foundation grants to United Way ($81,904); foundation matching gifts ($2,835,239); fiscal 2001: foundation matching gifts ($2,494,266); foundation matching ($4,693,158)

Assets: $102,456,013 (fiscal 2004); $99,225,019 (fiscal 2002); $125,001,798 (fiscal 2001)

Gifts Received: $199,559 (fiscal 2001); $91,024,874 (fiscal 2000). Note: In 2001, contributions were received from United Airlines ($184,359) and various contributors donating less than $5,000. In 2000, contributions were received from Cisco Systems Corp.

Typical Recipients

Arts & Humanities: Arts Centers, Arts & Humanities-General, Museums/Galleries, Music, Public Broadcasting

Civic & Public Affairs: Botanical Gardens/Parks, Civil Rights, Clubs, Economic Development, Employment/Job Training, Civic & Public Affairs-General, Hispanic Affairs, Housing, Legal Aid, Municipalities/Towns, Nonprofit Management, Philanthropic Organizations, Professional & Trade Associations, Public Policy, Safety, Urban & Community Affairs, Women's Affairs

Education: Business Education, Education Funds, Education Reform, Elementary Education (Public), Faculty Development, Education-General, Literacy, Private Education (Precollege), Public Education (Precollege), Vocational & Technical Education

Health: AIDS/HIV, Cancer, Children's Health/Hospitals, Clinics/Medical Centers, Health Organizations, Hospices, Mental Health, Single-Disease Health Associations

International: International-General, International Organizations

Religion: Churches, Religion-General, Ministries, Missionary Activities (Domestic), Religious Organizations, Religious Welfare

Science: Science Museums

Social Services: Big Brothers/Big Sisters, Child Abuse, Child Welfare, Community Centers, Community Service Organizations, Crime Prevention, Domestic Violence, Emergency Relief, Family Services, Food/Clothing Distribution, People with Disabilities, Refugee Assistance, Scouts, Shelters/Homelessness, Social Services-General, Substance Abuse, United Funds/United Ways, Volunteer Services, YMCA/YWCA/YMHA/YWHA, Youth Organizations

Application Procedures

Initial Contact: Call or see website for application guidelines, then send a written request.

Application Requirements: Include proof of tax-exempt status.

Deadlines: April and November.

Review Process: Foundation makes funding decisions twice each year, for funding in August and March.

Evaluative Criteria: Organizations must be nonprofits under Section 501(c)(3) and public charities, and must operate within 50 miles of Cisco's San Jose headquarters. Programs must leverage existing resources within the larger organization and community; serve the community at large; and have overhead expenses that do not exceed 25% of total operating budget.

Restrictions

Does not fund athletic events, competitions, or tournaments; capital building funds; conferences/seminars; fundraising events or sponsorships; general operating expenses; individuals; multi-year grants; religious, political, or sectarian organizations; research programs; scholarships or stipends; schools, school systems, or school foundations; start-up programs; or grantmaking organizations.

Additional Information

In May of 2003, Cisco donated $2.6 million in networking equipment and services to China's Ministry of Health in order to fight the spread of Severe Acute Respiratory Syndrome (SARS).

Foundation Officials

Sylvia Allen: trustee
Larry R. Carter: chief financial officer, secretary CORP AFFIL director: QLogic Corp..
John T. Chambers: president, trustee CORP AFFIL director: Washington Banking Co..
Duncan Mitchell: trustee
John P. Morgridge: chairman, trustee
Tae Yoo: trustee NONPR AFFIL director: City Year; director: Smithsonian National Museum of American History; director: Catholic Charities of San Jose.
Mike Yutrzenka: executive director

Grants Analysis

Disclosure Period: fiscal year ending July 31, 2004
Total Grants: $7,107,730*
Number of Grants: 159
Average Grant: $22,098*
Highest Grant: $1,908,784
Lowest Grant: $302
Typical Range: $10,000 to $50,000
*Note: Giving excludes matching gifts. Average grant figure excludes four highest grants ($3,682,542).

Recent Grants

Note: Grants derived from 2003 Form 990.
General
1,623,368	Network for Good, Vienna, VA
763,337	Habitat for Humanity, Americus, CA -- for More than House project
500,319	Urban Institute, Washington, DC -- for center on nonprofits and philanthropy
384,000	City Year National, Boston, MA
350,000	Southern Poverty Law, Montgomery, AL
333,333	Red Cross, Alexandria, VA
300,000	Education Broadcasting Corp, New York, NY
282,411	National Center for Learning Disabilities, New York, NY -- for Get Ready to Read project
250,000	Digital Opportunity Trust, Ottawa Canada
250,000	Philanthropix Partners Inc., San Francisco, CA -- for early development phase of the philanthropix online nonprofit information exchange service

CIT GROUP INC.

Company Headquarters

1 CIT Dr.
Livingston, NJ 07039
Web: http://www.cit.com

Company Description

Founded: 1908
Ticker: CIT
Exchange: NYSE
Revenue: US$4.676 billion (2004)
Profit: US$753.6 million (2004)
Employees: 580 (2003)
Fortune Rank: 413, per FORTUNE Magazine's list of 500 Largest U.S. Corporations (2004).
SIC(s): 6141 Personal Credit Institutions, 6153 Short-Term Business Credit, 6159 Miscellaneous Business Credit Institutions, 6719 Holding Companies Nec.
Parent Company: Dai-Ichi Kangyo Bank Ltd., 1-1-5 Uchi-Saiwaicho, Chiyoda-ku, Tokyo, Japan

Operating Locations

CIT Group/Business Credit (NY--New York); CIT Group/Capital Finance (NY--New York); CIT Group/Commercial Services (NY--New York); CIT Group/Credit Finance (NY--New York); CIT Group/Equipment Financing (NJ--Livingston); CIT Group/Equity Investments (NJ--Livingston); CIT Group Holdings (NY--New York); The CIT Group, Inc. (NJ--Livingston; NY--New York); CIT Group/Industrial Financing (NJ--Livingston); CIT Group/Sales Financing (NJ--Livingston); Dai-Ichi Kangyo Bank of California (CA--San Jose, Torrance); Dai-Ichi Kangyo Bank of California-Los Angeles (CA--Los Angeles); Dai-Ichi Kangyo Bank, Ltd.-Atlanta (GA--Atlanta); Dai-Ichi Kangyo Bank, Ltd.-Chicago (IL--Chicago); Dai-Ichi Kangyo Bank, Ltd.-Houston (TX--Houston); Dai-Ichi Kangyo Bank, Ltd.-Los Angeles (CA--Los Angeles); Dai-Ichi Kangyo Bank, Ltd.-New York (NY--New York); Dai-Ichi Kangyo Bank, Ltd.-San Francisco (CA--San Francisco); Dai-Ichi Kangyo Trust Co. of New York (NY--New York); DKB Data Services (U.S.A.) (NJ--Jersey City); DKB Financial Futures Corp. (IL--Chicago); DKB Financial Products (NY--New York); DKB Securities Corp. (NY--New York)

CIT Group Foundation

Giving Contact

Kelley Gibson, Vice President
CIT Group Foundation
1211 Avenue of the Americas
New York, NY 10036
Phone: (973)740-5000
Fax: (973)740-5264
E-mail: citcorporategiving@cit.com
Web: http://www.cit.com/main/AboutCIT/corpgiving.htm

Description

EIN: 136083856
Organization Type: Corporate Foundation
Giving Locations: nationally, with an emphasis on headquarters area only.
Grant Types: General Support, Scholarship.

Financial Summary

Total Giving: $341,879 (2003); $2,485,864 (2001). Note: Contributes through corporate direct giving program and foundation.
Giving Analysis: Giving for 2001 includes: foundation scholarships ($6,000); foundation grants to United Way ($500,349); foundation ($1,979,515).
Assets: $4,319 (2003); $190,447 (2001)
Gifts Received: $2,500 (2003); $2,663,354 (2001); $2,150,000 (2000). Note: Contributions were received from CIT Group.

Typical Recipients

Arts & Humanities: Arts Funds, Arts Institutes, Community Arts, History & Archaeology, Libraries, Museums/Galleries, Music, Performing Arts, Public Broadcasting, Theater
Civic & Public Affairs: African American Affairs, Business/Free Enterprise, Community Foundations, Economic Development, Economic Policy, Ethnic Organizations, Civic & Public Affairs-General, Housing, Municipalities/Towns, Philanthropic Organizations, Professional & Trade Associations, Public Policy, Urban & Community Affairs, Women's Affairs
Education: Arts/Humanities Education, Business Education, Colleges & Universities, Continuing Education, Education Funds, Education Reform, Engineering/Technological Education, Education-General, Journalism/Media Education, Legal Education, Minority Education, Private Education (Precollege), Public Education (Precollege), Secondary Education (Private), Secondary Education (Public), Special Education, Student Aid, Vocational & Technical Education
Health: AIDS/HIV, Arthritis, Cancer, Children's Health/Hospitals, Clinics/Medical Centers, Diabetes, Emergency/Ambulance Services, Health Funds, Health Organizations, Heart, Hospitals, Medical Research, Mental Health, Nursing Services, Single-Disease Health Associations, Transplant Networks/Donor Banks, Trauma Treatment
International: Foreign Educational Institutions, Health Care/Hospitals, International Peace & Security Issues, International Relations, Missionary/Religious Activities
Religion: Dioceses, Religion-General, Jewish Causes, Religious Organizations, Religious Welfare
Science: Scientific Centers & Institutes
Social Services: At-Risk Youth, Child Welfare, Community Centers, Community Service Organizations, Counseling, Food/Clothing Distribution, Homes, People with Disabilities, Recreation & Athletics, Scouts, Shelters/Homelessness, Social Services-General, Substance Abuse, United Funds/United Ways, Veterans, Volunteer Services, YMCA/YWCA/YMHA/YWHA, Youth Organizations

Application Procedures

Initial Contact: Send a written proposal in letter form.
Application Requirements: Include a description of organization, amount requested, purpose of funds sought, audited financial statement, annual report, and proof of tax-exempt status.
Deadlines: None.

Restrictions

Does not support political or lobbying groups, or grants to individuals.

Corporate Officials

Albert R. Gamper, Jr.: president, chief executive officer, chairman B 1942. ED Harvard University PMD; Rutgers University BA. PRIM CORP EMPL president, chief executive officer, chairman: The CIT Group, Inc.
Joseph M. Leone: executive vice president

Foundation Officials

Albert R. Gamper, Jr.: president, chief executive officer, director (see above)
Kelley Gibson: vice president
Robert J. Ingato: vice president
Joseph M. Leone: vice president, treasurer, controller (see above)
Eric S. Mandelbaum: vice president, secretary
Susan Mitchell: vice president, director
Glenn A. Votek: assistant secretary

Grants Analysis

Disclosure Period: calendar year ending 2003
Total Grants: $220,534*
Number of Grants: 55
Average Grant: $3,223*
Highest Grant: $46,500
Lowest Grant: $100
Typical Range: $1,000 to $5,000
*Note: Giving excludes matching gifts; United Way. Average grant figure excludes highest grant.

Recent Grants

Note: Grants derived from 2003 Form 990.

General

100,000	United Way of Tri State, New York, NY
48,500	Newark Museum, Newark, OH
48,500	NJN Foundation, Trenton, NJ
25,000	Security, New York, NY
12,500	Center, New York, NY
7,600	Maryhaven Center of Hope, Port Jefferson, NY
6,000	Longwood University, Farmville, VA
5,500	Catholic Community Services, Seattle, WA
5,000	Arts, Detroit, MI
4,500	Hospital, New York, NY

CITIGROUP GLOBAL MARKETS HOLDINGS INC.

Company Headquarters

388 Greenwich St.
New York, NY 10013

Company Description

Ticker: ASB
Exchange: AMEX
Formed by Merger of: Salomon Brothers and Smith Barney (1997).
Operating Revenue: US$27.374 billion (2001)
Employees: 39000 (2003)
SIC(s): 2911 Petroleum Refining, 6211 Security Brokers & Dealers, 6221 Commodity Contracts Brokers & Dealers, 6719 Holding Companies Nec.
Parent Company: Citigroup Inc., 399 Park Ave., New York, NY, United States

Operating Locations

Salomon Smith Barney (CA--Los Angeles, San Francisco; CT--Westport; GA--Atlanta; MA--Boston; TX--Dallas)

Giving Contact

Alan Okada, Chief Executive Officer for Citigroup Foundation
850 3rd Avenue, 13th Floor
New York, NY 10022
Phone: (212)559-9842
Fax: (212)793-5944
E-mail: citigroupfoundation@citi.com

Alternate Contact

Patricia Byrne
Phone: (212)793-8885

Description

EIN: 133781879
Organization Type: Corporate Giving Program
Former Name: Salomon Foundation.
Former Name: Traveler's Group Foundation.
Former Name: Traveler's Foundation.
Giving Locations: headquarters and operating communities; nationally.
Grant Types: Employee Matching Gifts, General Support, Scholarship.
Note: Employee matching gift ratio: 1 to 1.

Financial Summary

Total Giving: Contributes through corporate direct giving program only.
Gifts Received: $4,500,000 (1997); $638,445 (1995); $17,332,588 (1994). Note: Contributions are received from Salomon Brothers, Inc., and Salomon Brothers Holding Corp.

Typical Recipients

Arts & Humanities: Ballet, Historic Preservation, Libraries, Museums/Galleries, Music, Opera, Performing Arts, Public Broadcasting, Theater, Visual Arts
Civic & Public Affairs: Economic Development, Em-

ployment/Job Training, Law & Justice, Legal Aid, Women's Affairs, Zoos/Aquariums
Education: Arts/Humanities Education, Business Education, Economic Education, Elementary Education (Private), Literacy, Minority Education, Public Education (Precollege)
Health: Hospitals, Medical Research, Single-Disease Health Associations
Science: Scientific Centers & Institutes
Social Services: Delinquency & Criminal Rehabilitation, Emergency Relief, Family Planning, Food/Clothing Distribution, Recreation & Athletics, Substance Abuse, Youth Organizations

Application Procedures

Initial Contact: Contact the company for specific guidelines.
Deadlines: None.

Restrictions

Fraternal organizations, political or lobbying groups, or religious groups for sectarian purposes are not considered for contributions.

Additional Information

Travelers Foundation and Citicorp Foundation merged to form Citigroup Foundation in 1999. Salomon Smith Barney now gives directly through its Community Investment Program.

Giving Program Officials

Jane E. Heffner: vice president PRIM CORP EMPL vice president corporate contributions: Salomon Brothers Inc.

Grants Analysis

Disclosure Period: calendar year ending 1997
Total Grants: $942,917
Number of Grants: 9
Average Grant: $32,153*
Highest Grant: $250,000
Typical Range: $10,000 to $50,000
*Note: Average grant excludes three highest grants totaling $750,000.

CITIGROUP INC.

Company Headquarters

399 Park Ave.
New York, NY 10043
Phone: (212)559-1000
Fax: (212)793-3946
Web: http://www.citigroup.com

Company Description

Founded: 1998
Ticker: C
Exchange: NYSE
Revenue: US$108.276 billion (2004)
Profit: US$17.046 billion (2004)
Employees: 255000 (2003)
Fortune Rank: 8, per FORTUNE Magazine's list of 500 Largest U.S. Corporations (2004).

Nonmonetary Support

Type: Donated Equipment
Volunteer Programs: The corporation's volunteer incentive program provides up to $500 for organizations to which employees volunteer.

Citigroup Foundation

Giving Contact

Charles V. Raymond, President
Citigroup Foundation
850 Third Avenue, 13th Floor
New York, NY 10043

Phone: (212)559-9163
Fax: (212)793-5944
E-mail: citigroupfoundation@citigroup.com
Web: http://www.citigroup.com

Description

EIN: 133781879
Organization Type: Corporate Foundation
Giving Locations: NY: New York headquarters and operating communities.
Grant Types: Employee Matching Gifts, Fellowship, General Support, Multiyear/Continuing Support, Project.
Note: Employee matching gift ratio: 1 to 1.

Financial Summary

Total Giving: $57,324,707 (2003); $56,788,899 (2002); $67,644,961 (2001). Note: Contributes through corporate direct giving program and foundation.
Giving Analysis: Giving for 2003 includes: foundation matching gifts ($890,247); corporate direct giving ($1,722,500); foundation ($55,395,460); 2001: foundation matching gifts ($1,169,217); corporate direct giving ($3,556,500); domestic and international subsidiaries ($13,355,182); foundation ($49,564,061)
Assets: $131,761,174 (2003); $140,404,667 (2002)
Gifts Received: $51,529,728 (2003); $2,381,908 (2002); $108,991,700 (2000). Note: Foundation receives contributions from Citicorp and Citibank.

Typical Recipients

Arts & Humanities: Arts Appreciation, Arts Associations & Councils, Arts Centers, Arts Festivals, Arts Funds, Arts Institutes, Dance, Ethnic & Folk Arts, Historic Preservation, Libraries, Literary Arts, Museums/Galleries, Music, Opera, Performing Arts, Public Broadcasting, Theater
Civic & Public Affairs: Asian American Affairs, Business/Free Enterprise, Civil Rights, Community Foundations, Economic Development, Economic Policy, Employment/Job Training, Civic & Public Affairs-General, Housing, Native American Affairs, Nonprofit Management, Philanthropic Organizations, Public Policy, Urban & Community Affairs, Women's Affairs, Zoos/Aquariums
Education: Arts/Humanities Education, Business Education, Colleges & Universities, Community & Junior Colleges, Continuing Education, Economic Education, Education Associations, Education Funds, Education Reform, Elementary Education (Private), Faculty Development, Education-General, International Exchange, International Studies, Literacy, Minority Education, Private Education (Precollege), Public Education (Precollege), Science/Mathematics Education, Special Education, Student Aid
Environment: Environment-General
Health: Children's Health/Hospitals, Emergency/Ambulance Services, Health Policy/Cost Containment, Health Organizations, Hospices, Hospitals, Hospitals (University Affiliated), Medical Research, Single-Disease Health Associations, Transplant Networks/Donor Banks
International: Foreign Educational Institutions, International-General, Health Care/Hospitals, International Development, International Peace & Security Issues, International Relations, International Relief Efforts
Religion: Missionary Activities (Domestic)
Science: Science Museums
Social Services: Child Welfare, Community Centers, Community Service Organizations, Day Care, Emergency Relief, Family Services, Food/Clothing Distribution, Homes, People with Disabilities, Shelters/Homelessness, Substance Abuse, United Funds/United Ways, Volunteer Services, YMCA/YWCA/YMHA/YWHA, Youth Organizations

Application Procedures

Initial Contact: Call for guidelines.
Application Requirements: Proposals should include amount requested; proposal objective; itemized

budget; brief statement of organization's history, goals, and accomplishments to date; current annual report; proof of tax-exempt status; current year's budget showing anticipated expenses and income; list of current corporate and foundation funding sources, public and private, with amounts received within the most recent 12 months or last fiscal year (for both the organization and the specific programs for which funds are requested); recently audited financial statement; board of directors list; and list of accrediting agencies, if applicable. Cultural organizations should submit their most recent 12-month audience statistics.

Deadlines: None.

Review Process: Initial review by contributions staff and committee members, who may deny a request or make a recommendation to the full committee or policy committee.

Evaluative Criteria: Provide evidence of clearly delineated goals and effective, innovative programs that conform to bank's giving priorities; have stable management, and sound financial status; strong leadership to strengthen communities in which bank operates and serve as a model for other nonprofits; and opportunities for employee volunteer involvement.

Decision Notification: Ongoing; contributions committee meets as required; in most cases, applicants learn of a decision in writing within sixty to ninety days.

Notes: Many contributions committees use a proposal application form, available from local contact person.

Restrictions

The company does not support individuals; political causes or candidates; religious, veteran, or fraternal organizations, unless project significantly benefits entire community; fundraising dinners, benefits, or events; or courtesy advertising.

Additional Information

Citicorp Foundation and Travelers Foundation merged to form the Citigroup Foundation in 1999. Company and foundation prefer to initiate grants, but will consider unsolicited proposals.

The company generally prefers to support specific, one-year programs in areas of charitable interest. Potential for combination with volunteers, in-kind services, or other direct Citibank involvement is frequently a deciding factor in grant decisions. Citibank also makes housing, small business, and student loans; is involved with programs to hire minority youth and to pay summer interns at community nonprofit organizations; provides technical assistance; and encourages employees to participate in the matching gifts program.

Publications: Public Responsibility at Citibank; Guidelines

Corporate Officials

William Reginald Rhodes: senior vice chairmano, director B New York, NY 1935. ED Brown University BA History (1957). PRIM CORP EMPL senior vice chairman: Citigroup. CORP AFFIL vice chairman, director: Citicorp; director: ConocoPhillips Co. NONPR AFFIL founding member: United States National Council International Management Center Budapest; member executive committee: United States-Russia Business Council; member: United States-Egyptian President Council; chairman: Northfield Mt Hermon School; director: Private Export Funding Corp.; government: New York Presbyterian Hospital; director: New York City Chamber of Commerce; director: New York City Partnership; vice chairman: Metropolitan Museum Business Committee; vice chairman: Institute International Finance Inc.; member: Lincoln Center Corporate Leadership Committee; director: Institute East-West Studies; member: Council Foreign Relations; director: Foreign Policy Association; trustee: Council Americas; member executive committee: Bretton Woods Committee; trustee: Brown University; member: Bankers Roundtable; director: Americas

Society; member: Bankers Association Foreign Trade; director: African-American Institute.

Sanford I. Weill: chairman B New York, NY 1933. ED Cornell University BA (1955); Cornell University Graduate School Business & Public Administration (1954-1955). PRIM CORP EMPL chairman: Citigroup. CORP AFFIL director: United Technologies Inc. NONPR AFFIL member business committee: Museum Modern Art; member: New York Society Security Analysts; trustee: Federal Reserve Bank of New York; chairman, board of overseers: Joan & Sanford I. Weill Medical College; vice chairman advisory council: Cornell University Johnson Graduate School Management; chairman, board overseers: Cornell University Medicine College; chairman: Carnegie Hall Society Inc.; founder: Academy Financial; director: Baltimore Symphony Orchestra. CLUB AFFIL Cornell Club; Harmonie Club; Century Country Club.

Robert B. Willumstad: president, chief operating officer, director ED Adelphi University BA. PRIM CORP EMPL president, chief operating officer, director: Citigroup Inc. CORP AFFIL chief executive officer, president: Citibank NA; director: MasterCard International. NONPR AFFIL board of directors: Financial Services Roundtable; board member: Habitat for Humanity; trustee: American Scandinavian Foundation.

Foundation Officials

Patricia Byrne: vice president
Alan Okada: vice president, treasurer CORP AFFIL vice president health programs: Citibank NA. NONPR AFFIL treasurer, director: AAPIP; member: Soh Daiko.
Charles V. Raymond: president ED Syracuse University BA. NONPR AFFIL director: Dance On Inc.; director: Stamford Center for the Arts; director: Bowery Residents' Committee; director: After-School Corp.; advisory board: Alliance for Downtown New York City.
Daria Sheehan: secretary

Grants Analysis

Disclosure Period: calendar year ending 2003
Total Grants: $48,595,113*
Number of Grants: 2,792 (approx)
Average Grant: $17,405 (approx)
Highest Grant: $1,150,000
Lowest Grant: $500
Typical Range: $5,000 to $50,000
*Note: Giving excludes matching gifts, scholarship, and United Way.

Recent Grants

Note: Grants derived from 2003 Form 990.

General

1,150,000	National Academy Foundation, New York, NY -- towards general operating support
1,000,000	Habitat for Humanity, Americus, GA -- towards Citigroup builds communities US initiative
1,000,000	Raza Development Fund, Phoenix, AR -- towards Citigroup NCLR partnership
800,000	Asia Society New York, New York, NY -- towards program endowment
600,000	Grameen Foundation USA, Washington, DC -- towards Micro Credit in China
550,000	Enterprise Foundation, Columbia, MD -- towards risk capital fund housing and child care initiatives
500,000	Alvin Ailey American Dance Theater, New York, NY -- towards campaign for Ailey
500,000	National Community Reinvestment Coalition, Washington, DC -- towards Citigroup Financial Literacy Leadership initiative
470,000	Microfinance Opportunities, Washington, DC -- towards Financial education for microborrowers
400,000	Women's World Banking, New York, NY -- towards integrated service offerings

CITIZENS FINANCIAL GROUP INC.

Company Headquarters
1 Citizens Plaza
Providence, RI 02903
Web: http://www.citizensbank.com

Company Description
Employees: 2,167
SIC(s): 6022 State Commercial Banks.
Parent Company: Royal Bank of Scotland PLC, 30 St. Andrew Sq., Edinburgh, United Kingdom

Operating Locations
Citizens Bank of Connecticut (CT--New London); Citizens Bank of Massachusetts (MA--Fairhaven); Citizens Financial Group (RI--Providence); Citizens Financial Services Corp. (RI--Providence); Citizens Leasing Corp. (RI--Providence); Citizens Mortgage Corp. (GA--Atlanta); Citizens Savings Bank (RI--Providence); Citizens Trust Co. (RI--Providence); Gulf State Mortgage (GA--Atlanta); Royal Bank of Scotland Plc (CA--San Francisco; NY--New York)

Nonmonetary Support
Type: Cause-related Marketing & Promotion; Donated Equipment; Loaned Employees

Citizens Charitable Foundation

Giving Contact
Pat Zeller
Citizens Charitable Foundation
1 Citizens Plaza
Providence, RI 02903-1339
Phone: (401)456-7689
Fax: (401)456-7644

Description
EIN: 056022653
Organization Type: Corporate Foundation
Giving Locations: headquarters and operating communities.
Grant Types: General Support.

Financial Summary
Total Giving: $6,790,315 (2003); $3,635,968 (2002); $2,749,785 (2001). Note: Contributes through foundation only.
Giving Analysis: Giving for 2001 includes: foundation scholarships ($40,000); foundation grants to United Way ($476,365); foundation ($2,233,420)
Assets: $12,223,063 (2003); $12,561,651 (2002); $10,650,030 (2001)
Gifts Received: $5,250,885 (2003); $6,326,266 (2002); $526,139 (2001). Note: Contributions were received from Citizens Bank of Rhode Island, Citizens Bank of Connecticut, Citizens Bank of New Hampshire and Citizens Bank of Massachusetts.

Typical Recipients
Arts & Humanities: Arts Associations & Councils, Arts Centers, Arts Funds, Arts Institutes, Arts & Humanities-General, History & Archaeology, Libraries, Literary Arts, Museums/Galleries, Music, Performing Arts, Theater
Civic & Public Affairs: African American Affairs, Botanical Gardens/Parks, Business/Free Enterprise, Community Foundations, Economic Development, Employment/Job Training, Civic & Public Affairs-General, Hispanic Affairs, Housing, Inner-City Development, Law & Justice, Municipalities/Towns, Parades/Festivals, Philanthropic Organizations, Public Policy, Urban & Community Affairs, Women's Affairs, Zoos/Aquariums

Education: Afterschool/Enrichment Programs, Arts/ Humanities Education, Business Education, Colleges & Universities, Community & Junior Colleges, Economic Education, Education Associations, Education Funds, Education-General, Literacy, Medical Education, Private Education (Precollege), Secondary Education (Public), Student Aid
Environment: Environment-General, Protection, Watershed
Health: AIDS/HIV, Children's Health/Hospitals, Clinics/Medical Centers, Emergency/Ambulance Services, Geriatric Health, Health Organizations, Hospices, Hospitals, Medical Rehabilitation, Medical Research, Mental Health, Nursing Services, Prenatal Health Issues, Public Health, Research/Studies Institutes, Single-Disease Health Associations
International: Foreign Arts Organizations, Health Care/Hospitals
Religion: Churches, Dioceses, Jewish Causes, Ministries, Missionary Activities (Domestic), Religious Organizations, Religious Welfare
Science: Science Museums, Scientific Centers & Institutes
Social Services: Camps, Child Welfare, Community Centers, Community Service Organizations, Day Care, Emergency Relief, Family Services, Food/ Clothing Distribution, Homes, People with Disabilities, Recreation & Athletics, Scouts, Senior Services, Sexual Abuse, Shelters/Homelessness, Social Services-General, Substance Abuse, United Funds/ United Ways, Volunteer Services, YMCA/YWCA/ YMHA/YWHA, Youth Organizations

Application Procedures

Initial Contact: Send a letter of proposal.
Application Requirements: Include a description of agency, its purpose, history, and programs; summary of need, amount requested, and description of agencies providing similar services; financial data on organization, such as independent audit, budget with sources of income, breakdown of expenditures by program, administration, and personnel; brief explanation why Citizens Charitable Foundation would be an appropriate donor; list of board of directors; copy of IRS tax-determination letter; and copy of affirmative action/equal opportunity policy.
Deadlines: None.
Decision Notification: Board meets quarterly; allow 60 to 90 days for a reply.

Restrictions

The foundation does not award grants to the following: member agencies of federated organizations, including United Way agencies, except for major capital campaigns; sectarian programs, including capital campaigns for church buildings; public and quasi-governmental agencies and organizations; operating budget deficits of any agencies; annual campaigns; local affiliates of national organizations; endowments and funds for general operating support; individuals; agencies and organizations outside of the geographical area served by Citizens bank; labor and fraternal organizations or programs and projects of a political nature; or advertising and fund-raising activities. or advertising and fund-raising activities.

Additional Information

All organizations requesting funding must agree to evaluation procedures including on-site visits and community interviews. The foundation may request periodic reports from organizations receiving funding. The foundation will not contribute in excess of 1% of the total goal to capital fund campaigns. Generally, payments are made within a three- to five-year period in order to eliminate an accumulation of substantial pledges in future years.
Publications: Annual Report (including Application Guidelines)
Trust(s): Citizens Bank

Corporate Officials

Lawrence K. Fish: chairman, chief executive officer, president B Chicago, IL 1944. ED Drake University (1966); Harvard University Graduate School of Business Administration MBA (1968). PRIM CORP EMPL chairman, chief executive officer, president: Citizens Financial Group Inc. CORP AFFIL director: Master-Card Inc.; director: Textron Inc.; chairman: Citizens Bank Massachusetts; director: John Hancock Mutual Life Insurance Co.; chairman, chief executive officer: Bank New England. NONPR AFFIL president: Institute Contemporary Art Boston; overseer: New England Conservatory Music. CLUB AFFIL Longwood Club.
Mark J. Formica: vice president, director B 1948. PRIM CORP EMPL president: Citizens Bank Rhode Island.

Foundation Officials

Lawrence K. Fish: trustee (see above)

Grants Analysis

Disclosure Period: calendar year ending 2003
Total Grants: $6,154,284*
Number of Grants: 500 (approx)
Average Grant: $12,309
Highest Grant: $100,000
Lowest Grant: $500
Typical Range: $1,000 to $25,000
*Note: Giving excludes scholarship and United Way.

Recent Grants

Note: Grants derived from 2003 Form 990.

Library-Related
25,000	Library and Archives of New Hampshire's Political Tradition, Concord, NH

General
185,000	Rhode Island State Council of Churches, RI
130,000	Housing Partnership, St. Paul, MN
125,000	Women's Institute
100,000	Easter Seals, Chicago, IL
75,000	Concilio Hispano De Cambridge, Cambridge, MA
65,000	Northeastern University, Boston, MA
60,000	United Way
50,000	Boston Center for the Arts, Boston, MA
50,000	Chittenden Emergency Food shelf, Burlington, VT
50,000	City of Nashua, Nashua, NH

CITIZENS FIRST NATIONAL BANK

Company Headquarters
606 S. Main Street
Princeton, IL 61356
Web: http://www.citizens1st.com

Company Description
Assets: US$420 million (2001)
Employees: 200 (2001)
SIC(s): 6000 Depository Institutions.
Parent Company: First National Corp., 950 John C. Calhoun Dr., SE, Orangeburg, SC, United States

Operating Locations
Citizens First National Bank (IA--Storm Lake)

Citizens First National Bank Foundation

Giving Contact
George H. Schaller, Trustee
Drawer 1227
Storm Lake, IA 50588-1227
Phone: (712)732-5440

Description
EIN: 426073539
Organization Type: Corporate Foundation
Giving Locations: IA: Early, Storm Lake
Grant Types: Capital, General Support.

Financial Summary
Total Giving: $20,560 (2004)
Assets: $439,218 (2004)
Gifts Received: $2,935 (2000)

Typical Recipients
Arts & Humanities: Arts Associations & Councils, Historic Preservation, History & Archaeology, Libraries, Museums/Galleries
Civic & Public Affairs: Botanical Gardens/Parks, Business/Free Enterprise, Clubs, Community Foundations, Economic Development, Employment/Job Training, Civic & Public Affairs-General, Housing, Municipalities/Towns, Safety
Education: Colleges & Universities, Education-General, Private Education (Precollege), Public Education (Precollege), Secondary Education (Public), Student Aid
Health: Emergency/Ambulance Services, Health Organizations, Hospitals
Religion: Bible Study/Translation, Churches, Religion-General, Religious Organizations, Religious Welfare
Social Services: Community Service Organizations, Crime Prevention, Delinquency & Criminal Rehabilitation, Domestic Violence, Food/Clothing Distribution, Recreation & Athletics, Shelters/Homelessness, United Funds/United Ways

Application Procedures
Initial Contact: Send brief letter describing program. Include any information relevant to the request.
Deadlines: November 1.

Corporate Officials
George H. Schaller: president, chief executive officer PRIM CORP EMPL president, chief executive officer: Citizens First National Bank.
Harry P. Schaller: chairman B Storm Lake, IA 1905. ED Columbia University (1926). PRIM CORP EMPL chairman: Citizens First National Bank. CORP AFFIL chairman, director: First National Co.; president, director: Schaller Co.; chairman: Citizens Credit Corp.; chairman: First Leasing Co.

Foundation Officials
Gaylord A. Sadusky: trustee
George H. Schaller: trustee (see above)
Harry P. Schaller: trustee (see above)

Grants Analysis
Disclosure Period: calendar year ending 2004
Total Grants: $20,560
Number of Grants: 54
Average Grant: $381
Highest Grant: $5,000
Lowest Grant: $50
Typical Range: $100 to $500

Recent Grants
Note: Grants derived from 2001 Form 990.
General
3,030	Early Community Foundation, Early, IA
3,000	Buena Vista University, Storm Lake, IA
3,000	Gingerbread House, Storm Lake, IA

3,000	Methodist Manor, Storm Lake, IA
1,500	Concordia Lutheran School, Storm Lake, IA
1,000	Church of Christ, Storm Lake, IA
1,000	First Baptist Church, Storm Lake, IA
1,000	Friends of St. Mary's, Storm Lake, IA
900	Lakeside Presbyterian Church, Storm Lake, IA
500	Genesis Development Center, Storm Lake, IA

CITIZENS UNION BANK

Company Headquarters
200 N. East St.
Greensboro, GA 30642

Company Description
Employees: 43
SIC(s): 6000 Depository Institutions.

Citizens Union Bank Foundation

Giving Contact
Bobby Voyles, Chairman
PO Box 89
Greensboro, GA 30642
Phone: (706)453-2236
Fax: (706)453-9172

Alternate Contact
Dean B. Rizner, Secretary & Treasurer

Description
EIN: 581541701
Organization Type: Corporate Foundation
Giving Locations: GA: Greene County
Grant Types: General Support, Scholarship.

Financial Summary
Total Giving: $13,100 (2003); $15,345 (2001)
Giving Analysis: Giving for 2003 includes: foundation scholarships ($10,100); 2001: foundation scholarships ($11,000)
Assets: $471,425 (2003); $478,978 (2001)
Gifts Received: $50,000 (2000); $150,895 (1998). Note: In 2000, contributions were received from Citizens Union Bank. In 1998, contributions were received from Citizens Union Bank ($150,000) and the Rotary Club of Greene County ($895).

Typical Recipients
Arts & Humanities: Libraries
Education: Continuing Education, Education-General, Secondary Education (Public), Student Aid, Vocational & Technical Education
Health: Hospitals
Religion: Churches
Social Services: Animal Protection

Application Procedures
Initial Contact: Recipients are nominated by students and faculty. All information is submitted by the local high school.
Deadlines: None.

Restrictions
Does not support individuals, religious organizations for sectarian purposes, political or lobbying groups, or organizations outside operating areas.

Additional Information
Provides scholarships for higher education to residents of Greene County, GA.

Corporate Officials
Harold Reynolds: chairman, chief executive officer PRIM CORP EMPL chairman, chief executive officer: Citizens Union Bank.
Bobby L. Voyles: president PRIM CORP EMPL president: Citizens Union Bank.

Foundation Officials
Neal Dolvin: director
Dean B. Rizner: secretary, treasurer
Frances Strickland: director
Bobby L. Voyles: chairman, director (see above)

Grants Analysis
Disclosure Period: calendar year ending 2003
Total Grants: $3,000*
Number of Grants: 2
Highest Grant: $2,000
Lowest Grant: $1,000
*Note: Giving excludes scholarships.

Recent Grants
Note: Grants derived from 2003 Form 990.
General

5,000	Nathaniel Greene Academy, Siloam, GA -- towards scholarship
2,000	Greensboro Georgia Dreamers, Greensboro, GA
1,000	Greene County High School, Greensboro, GA -- for educational exhibit
100	New Springfield Baptist Church Scholarship Fund, Siloam, GA

CITY NATIONAL BANK & TRUST CO.

Company Headquarters
PO Box 873
Gloversville, NY 12078
Web: http://www.citynatlbank.com

Company Description
Employees: 74
SIC(s): 6021 National Commercial Banks.
Parent Company: CNB Bancorp Inc., 10-24 N. Main St., Gloversville, NY, United States

City National Bank Foundation

Giving Contact
William N. Smith, President
14 N. Main St.
Gloversville, NY 12078
Phone: (518)773-7911
Fax: (518)773-8867

Description
EIN: 222816974
Organization Type: Corporate Foundation
Giving Locations: NY: Gloversville
Grant Types: General Support.

Financial Summary
Total Giving: $55,000 (2003); $60,173 (2001)
Giving Analysis: Giving for 2003 includes: foundation grants to United Way ($16,000); 2001: foundation grants to United Way ($16,000)
Assets: $114,380 (2003); $76,311 (2001)
Gifts Received: $70,000 (2003); $50,000 (2001); $70,000 (2000). Note: Contributions were received from City National Bank and Trust Company.

Typical Recipients
Arts & Humanities: History & Archaeology, Libraries, Museums/Galleries, Opera, Performing Arts, Theater
Civic & Public Affairs: Chambers of Commerce, Clubs, Civic & Public Affairs-General, Housing, Municipalities/Towns, Safety, Urban & Community Affairs
Education: Agricultural Education, Community & Junior Colleges, Literacy, School Volunteerism, Science/Mathematics Education, Student Aid
Health: Cancer, Children's Health/Hospitals, Emergency/Ambulance Services, Heart, Hospices, Hospitals, Long-Term Care, Medical Research, Respiratory, Single-Disease Health Associations
Religion: Churches, Jewish Causes, Religious Welfare
Social Services: Animal Protection, Child Welfare, Community Centers, Community Service Organizations, Family Services, Food/Clothing Distribution, Homes, Recreation & Athletics, Senior Services, United Funds/United Ways, YMCA/YWCA/YMHA/YWHA

Application Procedures
Initial Contact: Send a brief letter of inquiry.
Application Requirements: Include amount requested and purpose of funds sought.
Deadlines: None.

Restrictions
Grants limited to local organizations and government subdivisions.

Additional Information
Trust(s): City National Bank

Corporate Officials
Michael J. Frank: committee partner, vice president PRIM CORP EMPL committee partner, vice president: City National Bank and Trust Co.
George A. Morgan: executive vice president PRIM CORP EMPL executive vice president: City National Bank and Trust Co.
Bill Smith: chief executive officer PRIM CORP EMPL chief executive officer: City National Bank and Trust Co.
William N. Smith: president, chief executive officer, director PRIM CORP EMPL president, chief executive officer, director: City National Bank and Trust Co.

Foundation Officials
George A. Morgan: trustee (see above)
William N. Smith: president, trustee (see above)

Grants Analysis
Disclosure Period: calendar year ending 2003
Total Grants: $49,000*
Number of Grants: 17
Average Grant: $1,813*
Highest Grant: $20,000
Lowest Grant: $500
Typical Range: $500 to $2,500
*Note: Giving excludes United Way. Average grant figure excludes highest grant.

Recent Grants
Note: Grants derived from 2001 Form 990.
General

20,000	Nathan Littauer Hospital, Gloversville, NY -- for public support
16,000	United Way of Fulton County, Gloversville, NY -- for public support
10,000	Senior Citizens Center, Gloversville, NY -- for public support
5,000	City of Gloversville, Gloversville, NY -- for public support
3,973	Victims and Families Related, Baltimore, MD -- for public support
1,000	Habitat for Humanity, Johnstown, NY -- for public support

1,000	Jewish Community Center, Gloversville, NY -- for public support
1,000	St. Jude's Children Research, Memphis, TN -- for public support
500	Fulton County YMCA, Gloversville, NY -- for public support
500	James Brennan Humane Society, Gloversville, NY -- for public support

LIZ CLAIBORNE AND ART ORTENBERG FOUNDATION

Giving Contact
James Murtaugh, Program Director
650 5th Avenue, 15th Floor
New York, NY 10019
Phone: (212)333-2536
Fax: (212)956-3531
E-mail: lcaof@fcc.net
Web: http://www.lcaof.org

Description
Founded: 1984
EIN: 133200329
Organization Type: General Purpose Foundation
Giving Locations: internationally especially undeveloped countries; Northern Rockies area and nationally.
Grant Types: General Support, Multiyear/Continuing Support, Project.

Donor Information
Founder: The foundation was established in 1984 by Arthur Ortenberg and Elisabeth Claiborne, who founded Liz Claiborne, Inc., the largest seller of women's sportswear in department stores.
The couple started the clothing company in 1976 with an initial investment of $250,000. They contributed $50,000 themselves and borrowed $200,000 from family and friends. Mr. Ortenberg and Ms. Claiborne are no longer on the board of directors of Liz Claiborne, Inc. They no longer hold Liz Claiborne, Inc., stock.
Ms. Claiborne was born in Brussels in 1929 while her father, a banker from New Orleans, was posted overseas. She attended the Art School in Brussels in 1947 and the Academie des Beaux Arts in Paris in 1948, where she studied painting. She decided to remain in the United States when she won a Harper's Bazaar design contest while she was vacationing in New Orleans in 1949. She is a direct descendant of William C. C. Claiborne, Louisiana's governor during the War of 1812.
Ms. Claiborne made a name for herself as a designer in New York at Jonathan Logan, where she spent 16 years designing moderately priced junior dresses. Elisabeth Claiborne and Arthur Ortenberg were married in 1957. They both had children by a previous marriage. He has two children and she has one, Alexander G. Schultz.

Financial Summary
Total Giving: $1,800,000 (fiscal year ending January 31, 2003 approx); $2,778,258 (fiscal 2002); $1,837,149 (fiscal 2001)
Assets: $42,000,000 (fiscal 2003 approx); $44,515,016 (fiscal 2002); $42,315,477 (fiscal 2001)
Gifts Received: $800,000 (fiscal 2002); $75,000 (fiscal 1999); $75,000 (fiscal 1998). Note: Contributions were received from Arthur and Elisabeth C. Ortenberg.

Typical Recipients
Arts & Humanities: Arts Centers, Arts Funds, Historic Preservation, History & Archaeology, Libraries, Museums/Galleries, Music, Public Broadcasting
Civic & Public Affairs: African American Affairs, Botanical Gardens/Parks, Community Foundations, Economic Development, Economic Policy, Ethnic Organizations, Civic & Public Affairs-General, Municipalities/Towns, Native American Affairs, Philanthropic Organizations, Public Policy, Urban & Community Affairs, Women's Affairs
Education: Arts/Humanities Education, Colleges & Universities, Elementary Education (Private), Elementary Education (Public), Environmental Education, Private Education (Precollege), Public Education (Precollege), Science/Mathematics Education
Environment: Air/Water Quality, Forestry, Environment-General, Protection, Research, Resource Conservation, Watershed, Wildlife Protection
Health: AIDS/HIV, Emergency/Ambulance Services, Health Organizations, Hospitals, Single-Disease Health Associations
International: Health Care/Hospitals, Human Rights, International Environmental Issues, International Peace & Security Issues
Religion: Religious Organizations
Science: Science Museums, Scientific Labs
Social Services: Animal Protection, At-Risk Youth, Counseling, Crime Prevention, Delinquency & Criminal Rehabilitation, Family Planning, People with Disabilities, Recreation & Athletics, United Funds/United Ways, YMCA/YWCA/YMHA/YWHA, Youth Organizations

Application Procedures
Initial Contact: Send a brief letter of inquiry. All requests must be in writing.
Application Requirements: Applicants should include a brief description of the project, the amount requested, and the contact person in charge of the project.
Deadlines: None.

Foundation Officials
Robert Dewar: director
James Murtaugh: program director CORP AFFIL director: Hypres Inc.
Arthur Ortenberg: don, trustee, director B 1926.
Elisabeth Claiborne Ortenberg: donor, director, trustee B Brussels, Belgium 1929. ED Art School Brussels (1948-1949); Academie Nice (France) (1950). NONPR AFFIL director: Fire Island Lighthouse Restoration Comm; guest lecturer: Parsons School Design; guest lecturer: Fashion Institute Technology; director: Council American Fashion Designers; member: Fashion Group.
Mary Corliss Pearl: director B New York, NY 1950. ED Yale University BA (1972); Yale University MPh (1976); Yale University PhD (1982). NONPR AFFIL board governors: Society Conservation Biology; assistant director: Wildlife Conservation Society; member: International Union Conservation Nature; trustee: Gomez Foundation; member: International Primatology Society; member: American Society Primatologists; founder: Council Higher Education Group Rainforest Alliance; member: American Association Advancement Science. CLUB AFFIL Explorers Club.
David Quammen: director
Dr. David Western: director

Grants Analysis
Disclosure Period: fiscal year ending January 31, 2002
Total Grants: $2,778,258
Number of Grants: 104
Average Grant: $23,076*
Highest Grant: $401,464
Lowest Grant: $300
Typical Range: $5,000 to $50,000
***Note:** Average grant figure excludes highest grant.

Recent Grants
Note: Grants derived from 2002 Form 990.
Library-Related
| 15,000 | Library of Congress-James Madison Council, Washington, DC |

General
401,464	Montana Historical Society, Helena, MT -- fund for Montana heritage project and 2002-2003 grants
155,250	Wildlife Conservation Society, Bronx, NY
131,900	Wildlife Conservation Society, Bronx, NY -- fund for Russian Far East (Homocker)
120,000	Wildlife Conservation Society, Bronx, NY -- fund for jaguar conservation program
106,000	Wildlife Conservation Society, Bronx, NY -- fund for Congo-Nouable-Ndoki national park
101,850	Wildlife Conservation Society, Bronx, NY
101,400	Wildlife Conservation Society, Bronx, NY -- toward Argentina-Patagonia program
100,000	Nature Conservancy Montana, Helena, MT -- for rocky mountain front programs
93,150	Wildlife Conservation Society, Bronx, NY -- fund for Sumatra conservation action network program
85,000	Montana Audubon, Helena, MT -- for chapter development programs

LIZ CLAIBORNE INC.

Company Headquarters
New York, NY
Web: http://www.lizclaiborne.com

Company Description
Founded: 1976
Ticker: LIZ
Exchange: NYSE
Revenue: US$4.632 billion (2004)
Profit: US$313.6 million (2004)
Employees: 13000 (2003)
Fortune Rank: 418, per FORTUNE Magazine's list of 500 Largest U.S. Corporations (2004).
SIC(s): 2331 Women's/Misses' Blouses & Shirts, 2335 Women's/Misses' Dresses, 2337 Women's/Misses' Suits & Coats, 2339 Women's/Misses' Outerwear Nec.

Operating Locations
Liz Claiborne, Inc. (CA--Los Angeles; GA--Atlanta; NJ--Carlstadt, North Bergen; TX--Dallas)

Nonmonetary Support
Type: Donated Products
Note: Support is very limited, and products are only donated in support of significant employee volunteer involvement.

Liz Claiborne Foundation

Giving Contact
Melanie Lyons, Director
1441 Broadway Avenue
New York, NY 10018
Phone: (212)626-5767
Fax: (212)626-8060
Web: http://www.lizclaiborne.com/lizinc/foundation

Description
Founded: 1981
EIN: 133060673
Organization Type: Corporate Foundation
Giving Locations: AL: Montgomery; NJ: Hudson County; NY: New York; PA: Mount Pocono
Grant Types: Challenge, Employee Matching Gifts, General Support, Multiyear/Continuing Support, Project.
Note: Cash gifts of $25 or more will be matched, up to a total of $10,000 per associate in each calendar year. The maximum amount of match to a single insti-

tution for any associate is $2,000 per year. Groups not eligible for matching gifts include fraternal organizations, clubs, professional associations, programs, or teams, and any organization not designated by the U.S. Department of the Treasury as a qualified charity.

Financial Summary

Total Giving: $1,317,136 (2003); $1,861,673 (2002); $1,742,182 (2001). Note: Contributes through foundation only.
Giving Analysis: Giving for 2002 includes: foundation grants to United Way ($42,185)
Assets: $25,973,562 (2003); $21,699,703 (2002); $26,140,954 (2001)
Gifts Received: $915,483 (1996); $1,171,218 (1995); $1,006,303 (1994). Note: In 1996, contributions were received from Liz Claiborne Inc.

Typical Recipients

Arts & Humanities: Arts Associations & Councils, Arts Centers, Arts Festivals, Ballet, Community Arts, Ethnic & Folk Arts, Arts & Humanities-General, History & Archaeology, Libraries, Museums/Galleries, Music, Opera, Performing Arts, Public Broadcasting, Theater
Civic & Public Affairs: Asian American Affairs, Botanical Gardens/Parks, Clubs, Community Foundations, Economic Development, Employment/Job Training, Gay/Lesbian Issues, Civic & Public Affairs-General, Housing, Inner-City Development, Law & Justice, Nonprofit Management, Philanthropic Organizations, Urban & Community Affairs, Women's Affairs, Zoos/Aquariums
Education: Arts/Humanities Education, Colleges & Universities, Education Funds, Education Reform, Elementary Education (Public), Faculty Development, Education-General, Literacy, Medical Education, Minority Education, Preschool Education, Private Education (Precollege), Public Education (Precollege), Science/Mathematics Education, Secondary Education (Private), Student Aid
Environment: Air/Water Quality, Environment-General
Health: AIDS/HIV, Cancer, Children's Health/Hospitals, Clinics/Medical Centers, Eyes/Blindness, Health Organizations, Hospitals, Long-Term Care, Multiple Sclerosis, Prenatal Health Issues, Public Health, Single-Disease Health Associations
International: Human Rights
Religion: Jewish Causes, Religious Welfare
Science: Science Museums, Scientific Centers & Institutes
Social Services: Big Brothers/Big Sisters, Camps, Child Abuse, Child Welfare, Community Centers, Community Service Organizations, Crime Prevention, Day Care, Delinquency & Criminal Rehabilitation, Domestic Violence, Emergency Relief, Family Services, Food/Clothing Distribution, People with Disabilities, Recreation & Athletics, Senior Services, Shelters/Homelessness, Social Services-General, United Funds/United Ways, Volunteer Services, YMCA/YWCA/YMHA/YWHA, Youth Organizations

Application Procedures

Initial Contact: Call or write for guidelines, then full written proposal.
Application Requirements: Include a statement of goals, history, and accomplishments; statement of purpose or objective; description of how the program or project is to be implemented and the qualifications of the staff involved; the number of clients to be served; plans to evaluate project's success; amount requested; current organization budget and proposed project budget, showing expenses and income, and following year's budgets if the proposal is submitted within three months of new fiscal year; most recent audited financial statements; list of funding sources and amounts contributed in current and previous year; funding pending approval for current year; amount of funding for project supplied by the organization's general budget; number of professional and support staff, with titles; list of board members, with affiliations; and proof of tax-exempt status.
Deadlines: None.
Review Process: Initial staff review, final review, and funding decision by grant-making committee.
Evaluative Criteria: Preference given to direct services; relevance to foundation's priorities and geographic focus; strength of project or program; managerial, planning, and financial capability of organization; other funding sources; employee involvement.
Decision Notification: Board meets in April, July, October, and December.
Notes: The foundation does not accept unsolicited proposals for the arts or the environment.

Restrictions

Contributions are not made to programs and projects based and/or operating outside the United States; religious, fraternal, or veterans' organizations; individuals; research; professional meetings, conferences, or symposia; building funds or equipment; endowments; hospital-based programs or single-disease organizations; film, video, television, or radio projects; courtesy advertising or fundraising events; or for sponsorship of events, performances, or exhibits.

Corporate Officials

Robert Bernard: senior vice president international sales PRIM CORP EMPL senior vice president international sales: Liz Claiborne, Inc.
Harvey L. Falk: president, vice chairman B 1934. ED New York University (1955). PRIM CORP EMPL president, vice chairman: Liz Claiborne, Inc. CORP AFFIL vice chairman: Liz Claiborne Cosmetics Inc.; vice chairman: Liz Claiborne Foreign Holdings Inc.

Foundation Officials

Paul Charron: trustee
Robert McKean: trustee
Michael Scarpa: trustee
Robert Vill: trustee

Grants Analysis

Disclosure Period: calendar year ending 2003
Total Grants: $1,316,361*
Number of Grants: 173
Average Grant: $7,609*
Highest Grant: $75,000
Lowest Grant: $500
Typical Range: $1,000 to $10,000
*Note: Giving excludes United Way. Giving includes matching gifts.

Recent Grants

Note: Grants derived from 2003 Form 990.

Library-Related
15,310	New York Public Library, New York, NY

General
75,000	Tides Foundation, San Francisco, CA
65,000	Break the Cycle, Huntington, WV
51,700	Educational Broadcasting Corporation, New York, NY
50,000	Seedco, New York, NY
50,000	Women's Housing and Economic Development, Bronx, NY
43,100	University at Albany Foundation, Albany, NY
40,000	Figure Skating in Harlem, New York, NY
40,000	Research Foundation of City University of New York, New York, NY
35,000	Lower Eastside Girls Club, New York, NY
32,630	Citizen's Scholarship Foundation of America, Minneapolis, MN

CLANEIL FOUNDATION

Giving Contact

Cathy M. Weiss, Executive Director
Claneil Foundation, Inc.
630 West Germantown Pike, Suite 400
Plymouth Meeting, PA 19462-1074
Phone: (610)828-6331
Fax: (610)828-6405

Description

Founded: 1968
EIN: 236445450
Organization Type: Private Foundation
Giving Locations: MA; PA, Philadelphia metro area
Grant Types: Capital, Conference/Seminar, General Support, Loan, Professorship, Project, Research, Seed Money.

Donor Information

Founder: Established in 1968 the late Henry S. McNeil and Langhorne B. Smith.

Financial Summary

Total Giving: $2,693,645 (2002); $2,948,246 (2001)
Giving Analysis: Giving for 2002 includes: foundation grants to United Way ($10,000); foundation scholarships ($48,700); 2001: foundation scholarships ($35,700) foundation grants to United Way ($59,700)
Assets: $51,103,617 (2002); $51,265,949 (2001)
Gifts Received: $11,402,563 (2002); $13,078,940 (2001); $10,096,939 (2000). Note: In 2001 and 2002, contributions were received from Claneil Enterprises, Inc.

Typical Recipients

Arts & Humanities: Arts Associations & Councils, Arts Institutes, Arts Outreach, Arts & Humanities-General, Historic Preservation, History & Archaeology, Museums/Galleries, Performing Arts, Public Broadcasting, Theater
Civic & Public Affairs: Civil Rights, Community Foundations, Economic Development, Employment/Job Training, Civic & Public Affairs-General, Hispanic Affairs, Housing, Law & Justice, Native American Affairs, Nonprofit Management, Public Policy, Rural Affairs, Safety, Urban & Community Affairs, Women's Affairs, Zoos/Aquariums
Education: Afterschool/Enrichment Programs, Arts/Humanities Education, Colleges & Universities, Community & Junior Colleges, Education Funds, Elementary Education (Private), Environmental Education, Faculty Development, Education-General, Literacy, Medical Education, Minority Education, Preschool Education, Private Education (Precollege), Public Education (Precollege), Special Education, Student Aid, Vocational & Technical Education
Environment: Air/Water Quality, Forestry, Environment-General, Protection, Resource Conservation, Watershed, Wildlife Protection
Health: AIDS/HIV, Alzheimer's Disease, Cancer, Children's Health/Hospitals, Clinics/Medical Centers, Emergency/Ambulance Services, Health-General, Geriatric Health, Health Funds, Health Organizations, Home-Care Services, Hospitals, Long-Term Care, Medical Research, Mental Health, Prenatal Health Issues, Preventive Medicine/Wellness Organizations, Single-Disease Health Associations, Trauma Treatment
International: Foreign Educational Institutions, Health Care/Hospitals, International Organizations, International Relief Efforts
Religion: Churches, Dioceses, Religious Welfare
Science: Science Museums
Social Services: At-Risk Youth, Big Brothers/Big Sisters, Child Abuse, Child Welfare, Community Centers, Community Service Organizations, Domestic Violence, Family Planning, Family Services, Food/Clothing Distribution, Homes, Scouts, Senior Ser-

vices, Shelters/Homelessness, Substance Abuse, United Funds/United Ways, YMCA/YWCA/YMHA/YWHA, Youth Organizations

Application Procedures

Initial Contact: Organizations that have never applied to the Claneil Foundation, those which have applied within the last three years but have not received a grant, and those who are applying for a grant larger than $10,000 must submit a letter of intent prior to submitting a full proposal. All others may submit a full proposal; guidelines may be requested from the foundation.

Application Requirements: Letters of intent should briefly describe the organization and the purpose for which funding is requested.

Deadlines: Letters of intent must be submitted prior to December 15 for the spring cycle and June 30 for the fall cycle. Proposals are accepted from January 1 to March 1 for the spring cycle and from July 1 to August 15 for the fall cycle.

Decision Notification: After reviewing the letters of intent, the Claniel Foundation will notify applicants whether or not a full proposal is invited. Grants resulting from full proposals are awarded in June for the spring cycle and in November for the fall cycle.

Notes: The foundation reports that it is in a transitional period and therefore may change its guidelines from time to time over the short term. It is recommended that potential applicants contact the foundation to obtain updated guidelines.

Restrictions

Does not support individuals. Grants for more than $10,000, or those made outside Southeast Pennsylvania are by invitation only.

Foundation Officials

Joanne S. Bailey: assistant secretary
Marjorie M. Findlay: vice chairman, vice president, director
Geoffrey T. Freeman: director
Barbara M. Jordan: secretary, director
Gretchen M. Jordan: director
Henry A. Jordan: president, chairman, , director
Duncan McFarland: director
Jennifer C. McNeil: secretary, director
Robert D. McNeil: director
Langhorne B. Smith: treasurer, director
Cathy M. Weiss: executive director

Grants Analysis

Disclosure Period: calendar year ending 2002
Total Grants: $2,634,945*
Number of Grants: 219
Average Grant: $11,221*
Highest Grant: $200,000
Lowest Grant: $3,000
Typical Range: $5,000 to $20,000
*Note: Giving excludes scholarships and United Way. Average grant figure excludes highest grant.

Recent Grants

Note: Grants derived from 2002 Form 990.
General

200,000	King's College, London United Kingdom -- towards medical research program
125,000	Glynwood Center, Cold Spring, PA -- towards strategic alliance for mid-size farmers
100,000	Chester County Community Foundation Inc., West Chester, PA -- to assist low-income communities in Chester County
100,000	Sanford School Inc., Hockessin, DE -- towards building fund
100,000	Westtown School, Westtown, PA -- towards building fund
70,000	National Trust for Historic Preservation, Washington, DC -- towards rural heritage program and constructing historical park building
50,000	Food Trust, Philadelphia, PA -- towards school market program
50,000	Support Center for Child Advocates, Philadelphia, PA -- towards facility renovation
50,000	Trustees of Reservations, Beverly, MA -- for bioreserve project in Southeastern Massachusetts
50,000	Wagner Free Institute of Science, PA -- towards facility renovation

GEORGE H. AND ANNE L. CLAPP CHARITABLE AND EDUCATIONAL TRUST

Giving Contact

Annette Calgaro, Assistant Vice President
George H. and Anne L. Clapp Charitable and Educational Trust
c/o Mellon Bank
PO Box 185
Pittsburgh, PA 15230
Phone: (412)234-1634

Description

EIN: 256018976
Organization Type: Private Foundation
Giving Locations: PA: Pittsburgh including metropolitan area
Grant Types: General Support.

Donor Information

Founder: the late George H. Clapp

Financial Summary

Total Giving: $765,000 (fiscal year ending September 30, 2004); $1,025,500 (fiscal 2001)
Assets: $17,838,791 (fiscal 2004); $20,036,379 (fiscal 2001)

Typical Recipients

Arts & Humanities: Historic Preservation, History & Archaeology, Libraries, Museums/Galleries, Music, Opera, Public Broadcasting
Civic & Public Affairs: Economic Development, Employment/Job Training, Civic & Public Affairs-General, Housing, Public Policy, Safety, Women's Affairs, Zoos/Aquariums
Education: Business Education, Colleges & Universities, Education Funds, Education Reform, Engineering/Technological Education, Education-General, Legal Education, Minority Education, Private Education (Precollege), Public Education (Precollege), Science/Mathematics Education, Special Education, Student Aid
Environment: Environment-General, Resource Conservation
Health: Cancer, Children's Health/Hospitals, Clinics/Medical Centers, Emergency/Ambulance Services, Eyes/Blindness, Health Organizations, Hospices, Hospitals, Long-Term Care, Medical Rehabilitation, Medical Research, Mental Health, Multiple Sclerosis, Nursing Services, Nutrition, Prenatal Health Issues, Single-Disease Health Associations
International: International Environmental Issues
Religion: Religious Organizations, Religious Welfare
Science: Science Museums, Scientific Centers & Institutes
Social Services: Child Welfare, Community Centers, Community Service Organizations, Family Planning, Family Services, Food/Clothing Distribution, People with Disabilities, Sexual Abuse, Shelters/Homelessness, United Funds/United Ways, YMCA/YWCA/YMHA/YWHA, Youth Organizations

Application Procedures

Initial Contact: Phone for application requirements.
Application Requirements: Completed applications will include a description of organization, purpose of funds sought, and proof of tax-exempt status.
Deadlines: Proposals are accepted from January 31 through May 31.

Restrictions

Foundation does not support individuals, religious organizations for sectarian purposes, political or lobbying groups, or organizations outside operating areas.

Additional Information

Trust(s): Mellon Bank NA

Grants Analysis

Disclosure Period: fiscal year ending September 30, 2004
Total Grants: $765,000
Number of Grants: 95
Average Grant: $7,713*
Highest Grant: $40,000
Lowest Grant: $1,000
Typical Range: $1,000 to $10,000
*Note: Average grant figure excludes highest grant.

Recent Grants

Note: Grants derived from fiscal 2000 Form 990.
General

50,000	Carnegie, The, Pittsburgh, PA -- arts and music grant
27,500	Morris Museum of Arts and Sciences, Augusta, GA
25,000	Carnegie Institute, Pittsburgh, PA
25,000	Sewickley YMCA, Sewickley, PA
20,000	Children's Hospital of Pittsburgh, Pittsburgh, PA
20,000	Hotchkiss School, Lakeville, CT
20,000	Laughlin Children's Center, Sawickley, PA
20,000	Sewickley Public Library, Sewickley, PA
20,000	Sewickley Valley Hospital, Sewickley, PA
20,000	University of Pittsburgh, Pittsburgh, PA -- for scholarship fund

CLARCOR INC.

Company Headquarters

Rockford, IL
Web: http://www.clarcor.com

Company Description

Founded: 1904
Ticker: CLC
Exchange: NYSE
Revenue: US$715.6 million (2002)
Employees: 4832 (2003)
SIC(s): 3411 Metal Cans, 3564 Blowers & Fans, 3569 General Industrial Machinery Nec, 3714 Motor Vehicle Parts & Accessories.

Operating Locations

CLARCOR Inc. (AL--Birmingham; CA--Corona; GA--Atlanta; IL--Downers Grove; IN--New Albany; KY--Louisville; NE--Kearney; OH--Cincinnati; TN--Nashville; TX--Dallas, Garland)

Nonmonetary Support

Type: Loaned Executives
Note: Nonmonetary support is for United Way only, and is approximately $20,000 annually.

CLARCOR Foundation

Giving Contact
Pete Nangle, Chairman
2323 6th Street
PO Box 7007
Rockford, IL 61125-7007
Phone: (815)962-8867
Fax: (815)962-0417

Alternate Contact
Susan Berg, Foundation Secretary

Description
EIN: 366032573
Organization Type: Corporate Foundation
Giving Locations: operating locations only.
Grant Types: Capital, Employee Matching Gifts, General Support, Multiyear/Continuing Support.
Note: Employee matching gift ratio: 1 to 1 to educational institutions.

Financial Summary
Total Giving: $372,907 (2003); $425,142 (2002); $512,068 (2001). Note: Contributes through corporate direct giving program and foundation.
Assets: $7,886,424 (2003); $7,063,529 (2002); $8,753,503 (2001)

Typical Recipients
Arts & Humanities: Arts Associations & Councils, Dance, Ethnic & Folk Arts, Arts & Humanities-General, History & Archaeology, Libraries, Museums/Galleries, Music, Opera, Public Broadcasting, Theater
Civic & Public Affairs: African American Affairs, Botanical Gardens/Parks, Community Foundations, Economic Development, Employment/Job Training, Civic & Public Affairs-General, Hispanic Affairs, Housing, Inner-City Development, Minority Business, Municipalities/Towns, Parades/Festivals, Philanthropic Organizations, Safety, Urban & Community Affairs, Women's Affairs
Education: Afterschool/Enrichment Programs, Business Education, Colleges & Universities, Economic Education, Education Funds, Faculty Development, Education-General, Legal Education, Literacy, Minority Education, Private Education (Precollege), Public Education (Precollege)
Health: Alzheimer's Disease, Cancer, Children's Health/Hospitals, Clinics/Medical Centers, Emergency/Ambulance Services, Health Funds, Health Organizations, Hospices, Hospitals, Long-Term Care, Mental Health, Multiple Sclerosis, Nursing Services, Public Health, Respiratory, Single-Disease Health Associations
Religion: Churches, Religion-General, Jewish Causes, Ministries, Religious Organizations, Religious Welfare
Science: Science-General, Science Museums
Social Services: At-Risk Youth, Big Brothers/Big Sisters, Child Welfare, Community Centers, Community Service Organizations, Crime Prevention, Day Care, Emergency Relief, Family Services, Food/Clothing Distribution, Homes, People with Disabilities, Recreation & Athletics, Scouts, Shelters/Homelessness, Social Services-General, Special Olympics, Substance Abuse, United Funds/United Ways, Veterans, YMCA/YWCA/YMHA/YWHA, Youth Organizations

Application Procedures
Initial Contact: Request grant application form.
Application Requirements: Proposals should include completed application form, amount requested, purpose for which funds are sought, a description of organization, recently audited financial statement, and proof of tax-exempt status.
Deadlines: None.
Decision Notification: Quarterly.

Additional Information
In 1988, J.L. Clark Manufacturing Co. was reincorporated as CLARCOR Inc. The foundation name was changed from the Clark Foundation to the CLARCOR Foundation.
Publications: Foundation Guidelines

Corporate Officials
Bruce A. Klein: chief financial officer, vice president B Louisville, KY 1947. ED University of Louisville BA (1973); University of Chicago MBA (1976). PRIM CORP EMPL chief financial officer, vice president: CLARCOR Inc. ADD CORP EMPL treasurer: J.L. Clark Inc. Delaware. CORP AFFIL director: Peoples Insurance Agency; director: Suntec Industries Inc.
William F. Knese: vice president, treasurer B 1948. PRIM CORP EMPL vice president, treasurer: CLARCOR Inc.
David J. Lindsay: vice president B 1955. ED University of Illinois BS (1977). PRIM CORP EMPL vice president: CLARCOR Inc.

Foundation Officials
Susan M. Berg: secretary
Marcia Blaylock: trustee
Norman E. Johnson: trustee B Lake Mills, IA 1948. ED University of Iowa (1970); Drake University (1972). PRIM CORP EMPL president, chief executive officer: Clarcor Inc. CORP AFFIL president: Baldwin Filters Inc.; chairman: JL Clark Inc.
Bruce Klein: trustee
Bruce A. Klein: trustee (see above)
David J. Lindsay: trustee (see above)

Grants Analysis
Disclosure Period: calendar year ending 2003
Total Grants: $222,580*
Number of Grants: 49
Average Grant: $4,542
Highest Grant: $30,000
Lowest Grant: $500
Typical Range: $1,000 to $10,000
*Note: Giving excludes United Way and miscellaneous grants of less than $500 each.

Recent Grants
Note: Grants derived from 2003 Form 990.
General

46,525	United Way of RR Valley, Rockford, IL
33,545	United Way of Kearney, Kearney, NE
30,000	Rockford Pro AM, Rockford, IL
25,000	Lifescape Community Kitchen, Rockford, IL
25,000	YMCA, Rockford, IL
16,917	United Way of Lancaster City, Lancaster, PA
15,452	United Way of Greensboro, Greensboro, NC
13,000	American Red Cross, Rockford, IL
12,500	Rockford Symphony Orchestra, Rockford, IL
11,162	United Way of Yankton, Yankton, SD

CLARK FOUNDATION (NY)

Giving Contact
Charles Hamilton, Executive Director
One Rockefeller Plaza, 31st Floor
New York, NY 10020-2102
Phone: (212)977-6900
Fax: (212)977-3424

Description
Founded: 1931
EIN: 135616528
Organization Type: General Purpose Foundation
Giving Locations: NY: Cooperstown, New York nationally.
Grant Types: Capital, General Support, Scholarship.

Donor Information
Founder: The Clark Foundation was established in 1931 in New York by members of the Clark family, including Edwin Severin Clark, Stephen Carlton Clark, and Frederick Ambrose Clark. The donors were heirs to the Clark family fortune, which originated in the 1800s with Edward Clark, a Cooperstown lawyer who was one of the founders of the Singer Company. The foundation has made major contributions to the residents of Cooperstown through gifts of a museum, a hospital affiliated with Columbia University, a community recreation center, and a college scholarship program for local students. In 1973, the foundation merged with the Scriven Foundation, another Clark endowment. The foundation is governed by a thirteen-member board of directors, including two members of the Clark family.

Financial Summary
Total Giving: $19,380,088 (fiscal year ending June 30, 2003); $17,939,478 (fiscal 2002); $18,533,634 (fiscal 2001)
Giving Analysis: Giving for fiscal 2003 includes: foundation scholarships ($2,860,191); fiscal 2002: foundation fellowships ($156,050); foundation grants to United Way ($1,055,000); foundation scholarships ($2,678,530); fiscal 2001: foundation fellowships ($143,429); foundation grants to United Way ($420,000); foundation scholarships ($2,660,775)
Assets: $444,150,252 (fiscal 2003); $469,042,395 (fiscal 2002); $495,890,546 (fiscal 2001)
Gifts Received: $400 (fiscal 2003); $400 (fiscal 2002); $1,214,221 (fiscal 2001). Note: In fiscal 2001, contributions were received from Trust for Dorothy Dewart. In fiscal 1995, contributions were received from Trust for Frieda Shipley.

Typical Recipients
Arts & Humanities: Ballet, Arts & Humanities-General, History & Archaeology, Libraries, Museums/Galleries, Music, Opera, Performing Arts, Public Broadcasting, Theater
Civic & Public Affairs: Business/Free Enterprise, Civil Rights, Community Foundations, Economic Development, Employment/Job Training, Civic & Public Affairs-General, Housing, Legal Aid, Nonprofit Management, Professional & Trade Associations, Public Policy, Safety, Urban & Community Affairs, Women's Affairs, Zoos/Aquariums
Education: Afterschool/Enrichment Programs, Arts/Humanities Education, Business Education, Colleges & Universities, Education Associations, Education Funds, Education Reform, Elementary Education (Private), Elementary Education (Public), Faculty Development, Education-General, Leadership Training, Literacy, Medical Education, Minority Education, Private Education (Precollege), Public Education (Precollege), School Volunteerism, Social Sciences Education, Special Education, Student Aid, Vocational & Technical Education
Environment: Air/Water Quality, Environment-General, Protection, Resource Conservation, Wildlife Protection
Health: AIDS/HIV, Cancer, Clinics/Medical Centers, Emergency/Ambulance Services, Health Funds, Health Organizations, Hospitals, Hospitals (University Affiliated), Kidney, Long-Term Care, Medical Training, Mental Health, Nursing Services, Outpatient Health Care
International: International Development
Religion: Churches, Religious Organizations, Religious Welfare
Science: Science Museums, Scientific Centers & Institutes
Social Services: At-Risk Youth, Big Brothers/Big Sisters, Child Welfare, Community Centers, Community Service Organizations, Crime Prevention, Day Care, Delinquency & Criminal Rehabilitation, Family Planning, Family Services, Food/Clothing Distribu-

tion, Homes, People with Disabilities, Recreation & Athletics, Senior Services, Shelters/Homelessness, Social Services-General, Substance Abuse, United Funds/United Ways, Veterans, Volunteer Services, YMCA/YWCA/YMHA/YWHA, Youth Organizations

Application Procedures

Initial Contact: Applicants should send a preliminary letter to the foundation.

Application Requirements: The letter should include a description of the project, amount requested, audited financial report, budget, and proof of tax-exempt status. If the foundation is interested in the project, further information will be requested.

Deadlines: None. The foundation's board of directors meets in October and May and at other times during the year. The grants committee, however, meets more frequently.

Review Process: The grants committee has the authority to approve some grants, but its general function is to make recommendations to the board of directors concerning grant requests. Decisions usually are made by the entire board.

Restrictions

The foundation does not fund deficit financing, matching gifts, gifts to individuals, or loans. Grants are not made outside New York.

Additional Information

Publications: Program Policy Statement; Application Guidelines

Foundation Officials

Kent L. Barwick: director B 1941. NONPR AFFIL president: Municipal Art Society of New York.

Felicia H. Blum: director

Jane Forbes Clark: president, donor daughter, director B New York, NY 1955. ED Bennett College AA (1975); Marymount Manhattan College MS (1979). PRIM CORP EMPL chairman: Clark Estates Inc. CORP AFFIL vice president: Otesaga Hotel; vice president: Cooper Inn; vice president: Leatherstocking Corp. NONPR AFFIL vice chairman: National Baseball Hall Fame & Museum; senior vice president, director: U.S. Equestrian Team. CLUB AFFIL vice president: Leatherstocking Golf Course.

William Maxwell Evarts, Jr.: director B New York, NY 1925. ED Harvard University AB (1949); Harvard University LLB (1952). PRIM CORP EMPL partner: Winthrop, Stimson, Putnam & Roberts. NONPR AFFIL director: Trust Public Land; director: Union Hospital Fund New York; director: Scenic Hudson; member: Association Bar New York City; member distr committee: New York Community Trust; member: American Bar Association.

Charles H. Hamilton: secretary

Gates Helms Hawn: director PRIM CORP EMPL chief operating officer: Donaldson, Lufkin & Jenrette Inc. CORP AFFIL chief operating officer: Pershing Trust Co. Division.

Archie F. MacAllaster: director

Joan B. S. McMenamin: director B New York, NY 1925. ED Smith College BA (1946). NONPR AFFIL trustee: Robert College Istanbul Turkey; trustee: WICAT Foundations; member: New York State Association Independent Schools; special advisor: Parents League; trustee: Laurenceville School; member: National Association Principal's Girls School. CLUB AFFIL Bridgehampton Club; Cosmopolitan Club.

Kevin S. Moore: treasurer, director PRIM CORP EMPL chief financial officer, senior vice president, director: Clark Estates Inc. CORP AFFIL director: Leatherstocking Corp.; director: Ducommun Inc. NONPR AFFIL treasurer: National Baseball Hall Fame & Museum.

Thomas Q. Morris: director

Anne Labouisse Peretz: director B 1939. PRIM CORP EMPL co-owner: New Report Inc. NONPR AFFIL president: Family Center Inc.

Edward William Stack: director B Rockville Centre, NY 1935. ED Pace University BBA (1956). PRIM

CORP EMPL president, director: Clark Estates Inc. CORP AFFIL secretary, treasurer, director: New Republic Inc.; director: Otesaga Hotel; director: Cooper Inn; director: Leatherstocking Corp.; regional advisory board: Chase Banking Corporate. NONPR AFFIL secretary, trustee: New York Saint Historical Association; advisory council: Salvation Army Nassau County; trustee: Hartwick College; chairman: National Baseball Hall Fame & Museum; member: Downtown Association; vice chairman, director: Farmers Museum; vice president, trustee: Mary Imogene Bassett Hospital. CLUB AFFIL Mohican Club; director: Leatherstocking Golf Course.

John Hoyt Stookey: director B New York, NY 1930. ED Amherst College BA (1952); Columbia University BS (1955). CORP AFFIL director: US Trust Co.; trustee: US Trust Co. New York; chairman: Per Scholas Inc.; chairman, director: Suburban Propane Partners; director: Chesapeake Corp.; director: Cyprus Amax Minerals Co.; director: ACX Technologies Inc.

Alexander F. Treadwell: vice president, director

Richard C. Vanison: assistant treasurer PRIM CORP EMPL treasurer: Clark Estates Inc. CORP AFFIL treasurer: Leatherstocking Corp.

Clifton R. Wharton, Jr.: director

Grants Analysis

Disclosure Period: fiscal year ending June 30, 2003
Total Grants: $15,343,491*
Number of Grants: 146
Average Grant: $98,921*
Highest Grant: $1,000,000
Lowest Grant: $1,200
Typical Range: $50,000 to $200,000
*Note: Giving excludes scholarships, fellowship, and United Way. Average grant figure excludes highest grant.

Recent Grants

Note: Grants derived from fiscal 2003 Form 990.
General

2,860,191	Clark Foundation Scholarship Program, Cooperstown, NY
1,025,000	United Way of New York City, New York, NY
1,000,000	National Baseball Hall of Fame and Museum, Cooperstown, NY
400,000	Hudson Guild, New York, NY
400,000	St. Christopher Ottilie, Glen Cove, NY
400,000	United Neighborhood Houses of New York, New York, NY
350,000	Doe Fund, New York, NY
325,000	Family Center Inc., Somerville, MA
300,000	Good Shepherd Services, New York, NY
300,000	Public/Private Ventures, New York, NY

ROBERT STERLING CLARK FOUNDATION

Giving Contact

Margaret C. Ayers, Executive Director
135 East 64th Street
New York, NY 10021
Phone: (212)288-8900
Fax: (212)288-1033
Web: http://fdncenter.org/grantmaker/rsclark/

Description

Founded: 1952
EIN: 131957792
Organization Type: General Purpose Foundation
Giving Locations: NY: New York nationally.
Grant Types: General Support, Multiyear/Continuing Support, Project, Research, Scholarship.

Donor Information

Founder: The Robert Sterling Clark Foundation was incorporated in 1952, with funds donated by Robert

Sterling Clark, grandson of one of the original partners in the Singer Sewing Machine Company.

Financial Summary

Total Giving: $4,152,225 (fiscal year ending October 31, 2003); $5,727,208 (fiscal 2002)
Giving Analysis: Giving for fiscal 2003 includes: foundation matching gifts ($8,795); fiscal 2002: foundation grants to United Way ($30,000)
Assets: $93,849,277 (fiscal 2003); $86,385,254 (fiscal 2002)
Gifts Received: $32 (fiscal 1999); $37,872 (fiscal 1998); $300,000 (fiscal 1997). Note: In fiscal 1998, contributions were received from the Robert S. Clark Trust. In 1997, contributions were received from the estate of Constance Guille.

Typical Recipients

Arts & Humanities: Arts Associations & Councils, Arts Centers, Arts Funds, Arts Institutes, Ballet, Dance, Ethnic & Folk Arts, Film & Video, Historic Preservation, Literary Arts, Museums/Galleries, Music, Opera, Performing Arts, Public Broadcasting, Theater, Visual Arts

Civic & Public Affairs: Botanical Gardens/Parks, Civil Rights, Community Foundations, Economic Development, Economic Policy, Employment/Job Training, First Amendment Issues, Civic & Public Affairs-General, Housing, Inner-City Development, Law & Justice, Legal Aid, Nonprofit Management, Philanthropic Organizations, Professional & Trade Associations, Public Policy, Safety, Urban & Community Affairs, Women's Affairs

Education: Afterschool/Enrichment Programs, Arts/Humanities Education, Colleges & Universities, Education Funds, Environmental Education, Education-General, Legal Education, Public Education (Precollege), Secondary Education (Public), Student Aid

Environment: Air/Water Quality, Environment-General, Protection, Resource Conservation

Health: Adolescent Health Issues, Children's Health/Hospitals, Health-General, Health Policy/Cost Containment, Health Organizations, Long-Term Care, Mental Health, Public Health, Research/Studies Institutes

International: Health Care/Hospitals, Human Rights, International Relations

Religion: Jewish Causes, Social/Policy Issues

Science: Scientific Centers & Institutes

Social Services: Child Abuse, Child Welfare, Community Service Organizations, Crime Prevention, Day Care, Domestic Violence, Family Planning, Family Services, Food/Clothing Distribution, Shelters/Homelessness, United Funds/United Ways, Youth Organizations

Application Procedures

Initial Contact: There are no formal application forms. Applicants should send a proposal (the main body of which should not exceed fifteen pages), with a one page summary of the request.

Application Requirements: All proposals must include a one-page summary; past year, current, and projected budgets; most recently audited financial statement; IRS determination letter; names and occupations of board members; major sources of current financial support; resumes of key personnel; and examples of past accomplishments. If an applicant is requesting support for a particular project, the proposal also should include a description of the project, project budget, expected results, detailed work plan, plans for evaluation, plans for future support, other sources of support, and names of other organizations to which the proposal has been submitted.

Deadlines: None.

Review Process: The board of directors meets in January, April, July, and October.

Restrictions

The foundation does not award grants to individuals or for building or endowment funds.

Additional Information
Publications: Annual Report; Guidelines

Foundation Officials
Margaret C. Ayers: executive director
Miner D. Crary, Jr.: secretary B Warren, PA September 08, 1920. ED Amherst College BA (1942); Harvard University MA (1943). NONPR AFFIL president, director: Society Saint Johnland; trustee: Sterling Francine Clark Art Institute; member: New York State Bar Association; member: Association Bar New York City; trustee: Heckscher Art Museum; member: American Bar Association; trustee: American University Cairo. CLUB AFFIL Union League Club; Century Association; Huntington County Country Club.
Winthrop R. Munyan: president
Virginia Hayes Sibbison: director
James Allen Smith: director
John Hoyt Stookey: director B New York, NY 1930. ED Amherst College BA (1952); Columbia University BS (1955). CORP AFFIL director: US Trust Co.; trustee: US Trust Co. New York; chairman: Per Scholas Inc.; chairman, director: Suburban Propane Partners; director: Chesapeake Corp.; director: Cyprus Amax Minerals Co.; director: ACX Technologies Inc.
Joanna Dehaven Underwood: director B New York, NY 1940. ED Bryn Mawr College BA (1962); Sorbonne University (1965). PRIM CORP EMPL president, founder: Inform Inc. NONPR AFFIL director: Rocky Mountain Institute; member: United States Club of Rome; director: Planned Parenthood New York City; director: Keystone Center; director: New York Saint Energy R&D Authority; member: Fellowship Scientists' Institute for Public Information; director: Hampshire Research Institute; member: Aspen Institute Energy Advisory Committee; director: Clean Sites.

Grants Analysis
Disclosure Period: fiscal year ending October 31, 2003
Total Grants: $4,143,430*
Number of Grants: 109
Average Grant: $38,013
Highest Grant: $150,000
Lowest Grant: $1,000
Typical Range: $10,000 to $75,000
*Note: Giving excludes matching gifts.

Recent Grants
Note: Grants derived from 2002 Form 990.

General
325,000	New York Foundation for the Arts, New York, NY
150,000	Center for Reproductive Law and Policy, New York, NY
150,000	National Abortion and Reproductive Rights Action League Foundation, Washington, DC
150,000	Planned Parenthood Federation of America, Albany, NY
125,000	Pre-Choice Public Education Project, New York, NY
100,000	Children's Rights Inc., New York, NY
100,000	Feminist Majority Foundation, Arlington, VA
100,000	Free Expression Policy Project, New York, NY
100,000	National Abortion Federation, Washington, DC
100,000	National Family Planning and Reproductive Health Association, Washington, DC

LYNN AND HELEN CLARK FUND

Giving Contact
Steve Melvin, Trust Officer
c/o First Mainstreet Bank
PO Box 1159
Longmont, CO 80501
Phone: (303)776-5800
Fax: (303)776-8475

Description
Founded: 1993
EIN: 846270492
Organization Type: Private Foundation
Giving Locations: CO: Longmont limited to the St. Vrain School District, including the city of Longmont, CO
Grant Types: General Support.

Financial Summary
Total Giving: $153,073 (fiscal year ending September 30, 2004); $175,192 (fiscal 2001)
Giving Analysis: Giving for fiscal 2001 includes: foundation scholarships ($15,000)
Assets: $2,829,038 (fiscal 2004); $3,036,166 (fiscal 2001)

Typical Recipients
Arts & Humanities: Arts Associations & Councils, Arts Centers, Arts & Humanities-General, Historic Preservation, History & Archaeology, Museums/Galleries, Music
Civic & Public Affairs: Botanical Gardens/Parks, Community Foundations, Civic & Public Affairs-General, Urban & Community Affairs, Women's Affairs
Education: Education Funds, Faculty Development, Education-General, Minority Education, Preschool Education, Public Education (Precollege), Special Education, Student Aid
Health: Emergency/Ambulance Services, Hospices, Hospitals, Medical Rehabilitation, Public Health
Religion: Churches, Religion-General
Social Services: Animal Protection, Child Welfare, Community Centers, Community Service Organizations, Counseling, Domestic Violence, Family Planning, Family Services, Food/Clothing Distribution, Homes, Senior Services, Social Services-General, Substance Abuse, YMCA/YWCA/YMHA/YWHA, Youth Organizations

Application Procedures
Initial Contact: There is no formal application form or guidelines.
Deadlines: May 1.

Restrictions
Grants are limited to St. Vrain Valley School District inhabitants.

Additional Information
The fund is set aside for charitable, religious, literacy, and educational purposes.
Trust(s): First Mainstreet Bank

Grants Analysis
Disclosure Period: fiscal year ending September 30, 2004
Total Grants: $153,073
Number of Grants: 28
Average Grant: $5,467
Highest Grant: $12,000
Lowest Grant: $1,000
Typical Range: $1,500 to $10,000

Recent Grants
Note: Grants derived from fiscal 2004 Form 990.

General
12,000	Safe Shelter of St. Vrain Valley, Longmont, CO
11,223	Tiny Tim Center, Longmont, CO
11,000	YMCA, Longmont, CO
10,000	St. Vrain Historical Society Inc., Longmont, CO
7,500	Addiction Treatment Center of Longmont, Longmont, CO
7,500	Friends First Inc., Longmont, CO -- for Quinceanera mentoring program
7,500	Outreach United Resource Center, Longmont, CO -- for child care center
7,500	Outreach United Resource Center, Longmont, CO -- for basic needs
7,000	First Congregational United Church of Christ, Longmont, CO
5,000	Loomiller Neighborhood Trojan Cafe, Longmont, CO

CLARK-WINCHCOLE FOUNDATION

Giving Contact
Vincent C. Burke, III, President & Trustee
3 Bethesda Metro Center, Suite 550
Bethesda, MD 20814
Phone: (301)654-3607

Description
Founded: 1964
EIN: 526058340
Organization Type: General Purpose Foundation
Giving Locations: DC: Washington including metropolitan area
Grant Types: General Support, Operating Expenses, Scholarship.

Donor Information
Founder: The foundation was established in 1964, with the late Dorothy C. Winchcole and the late Elizabeth G. Clark as donors. The foundation continues to receive contributions from the estate of Dorothy Clark Winchcole.

Financial Summary
Total Giving: $3,549,725 (2003); $3,596,900 (2002). Note: The figure for 1995 includes $45,000 in scholarships.
Giving Analysis: Giving for 2003 includes: foundation scholarships ($423,000)
Assets: $102,442,764 (2003); $83,628,181 (2002)
Gifts Received: The estate of Dorothy Clark Winchcole distributed $737,305 to the foundation in 1987.

Typical Recipients
Arts & Humanities: Arts Associations & Councils, Arts Funds, Arts Institutes, Ballet, Dance, Historic Preservation, History & Archaeology, Libraries, Museums/Galleries, Music, Opera, Performing Arts, Public Broadcasting, Theater
Civic & Public Affairs: Botanical Gardens/Parks, Clubs, Community Foundations, Civic & Public Affairs-General, Hispanic Affairs, Housing, Inner-City Development, Law & Justice, Parades/Festivals, Philanthropic Organizations, Women's Affairs, Zoos/Aquariums
Education: Afterschool/Enrichment Programs, Arts/Humanities Education, Business Education, Colleges & Universities, Education Funds, Education Reform, Elementary Education (Private), Elementary Education (Public), Environmental Education, Faculty Development, Education-General, Literacy, Preschool Education, Private Education (Precollege), Public Education (Precollege), Secondary Education (Private), Special Education, Student Aid
Health: Cancer, Children's Health/Hospitals, Clinics/

Medical Centers, Emergency/Ambulance Services, Health Funds, Health Organizations, Hospices, Hospitals, Long-Term Care, Medical Rehabilitation, Mental Health, Nursing Services, Public Health, Research/Studies Institutes, Single-Disease Health Associations, Speech & Hearing
International: International Peace & Security Issues
Religion: Churches, Dioceses, Ministries, Religious Organizations, Religious Welfare, Seminaries
Social Services: Animal Protection, At-Risk Youth, Child Abuse, Child Welfare, Community Service Organizations, Day Care, Emergency Relief, Family Services, Food/Clothing Distribution, Homes, People with Disabilities, Recreation & Athletics, Scouts, Senior Services, Shelters/Homelessness, Substance Abuse, United Funds/United Ways, Volunteer Services, Youth Organizations

Application Procedures

Initial Contact: Letters of application should be addressed to the foundation's president.
Application Requirements: Letters should explain the charitable purpose of the applicant and the need for the grant. Also send relevant financial material, including a copy of the organization's IRS determination letter of tax-exempt status.
Deadlines: None. Grant proposals should be sent in the first six months of the year.

Restrictions

Grants are made only to publicly supported organizations that are not private foundations.

Additional Information

Publications: Guidelines

Foundation Officials

Vincent C. Burke, III: president, trustee
Vincent C. Burke, Jr.: trustee B 1922. PRIM CORP EMPL attorney: Reasoner Davis & Fox.
Gregory Oyler: secretary, trustee
Grover B. Russell: vice president, trustee
Thomas C. Thompson, Jr.: vice president, trustee
W. Craig Thompson: treasurer, trustee

Grants Analysis

Disclosure Period: calendar year ending 2003
Total Grants: $3,126,725*
Number of Grants: 161
Average Grant: $19,421
Highest Grant: $180,000
Lowest Grant: $1,000
Typical Range: $5,000 to $30,000
*Note: Giving excludes scholarships.

Recent Grants

Note: Grants derived from 2003 Form 990.
Library-Related

40,000	Fairfax County Public Library Foundation, Fairfax, VA -- toward endowment for early literacy program

General

180,000	Wolf Trap Foundation for the Performing Arts, Vienna, VA -- funding for capital campaign and other programs
125,000	Supreme Court Historical Society, Washington, DC -- toward renovation of gift shop
100,000	Georgetown Visitation Preparatory School, Washington, DC -- support for scholarship fund
90,000	Gonzaga College High School, Washington, DC -- toward financial aid for needy students
75,000	Archbishop Carroll High School, Washington, DC -- toward tuition assistance program
70,000	Wesley Theological Seminary of the Methodist Church, Washington, DC -- funding for Urban and Hispanic Lay Ministry Programs
50,000	Archdiocese of Washington, Washington, DC -- funding for renovations to school
50,000	Boys and Girls Clubs of Greater Washington, Silver Spring, MD
50,000	Catholic Charities of the Archdiocese of Washington Inc., Washington, DC -- toward family services centers
50,000	Christmas Pageant of Peace Inc., Washington, DC

JOHN CLARKE TRUST

Giving Contact

PO Box 1802
Providence, RI 02901
Phone: (617)434-4644

Description

EIN: 056006062
Organization Type: Private Foundation
Giving Locations: RI
Grant Types: General Support.

Financial Summary

Total Giving: $232,597 (2004)
Assets: $4,749,761 (2004)

Typical Recipients

Arts & Humanities: Arts Associations & Councils, Libraries, Music, Theater
Civic & Public Affairs: African American Affairs, Chambers of Commerce, Civic & Public Affairs-General, Legal Aid, Municipalities/Towns, Urban & Community Affairs, Women's Affairs
Education: Afterschool/Enrichment Programs, Arts/Humanities Education, Colleges & Universities, Education Funds, Engineering/Technological Education, Education-General, Medical Education, Private Education (Precollege), Public Education (Precollege), Religious Education, Secondary Education (Private), Secondary Education (Public), Student Aid
Environment: Wildlife Protection
Health: Eyes/Blindness, Health Organizations, Home-Care Services, Hospitals, Medical Research, Mental Health, Nursing Services
International: International Affairs
Religion: Churches, Ministries, Religious Organizations, Religious Welfare
Science: Science Museums
Social Services: At-Risk Youth, Big Brothers/Big Sisters, Camps, Child Welfare, Community Centers, Community Service Organizations, Day Care, Domestic Violence, Family Services, Scouts, Shelters/Homelessness, Substance Abuse, United Funds/United Ways, Volunteer Services, YMCA/YWCA, YMHA/YWHA, Youth Organizations

Application Procedures

Initial Contact: The foundation has no formal grant application procedure or application form.
Deadlines: None.

Restrictions

Grants provided for the relief of the poor and education of children.

Additional Information

Trust(s): Fleet National Bank

Foundation Officials

William W. Corcoran, Esq.: co-trustee

Grants Analysis

Disclosure Period: calendar year ending 2004
Total Grants: $232,597
Number of Grants: 49
Average Grant: $4,747
Highest Grant: $10,000
Lowest Grant: $1,000
Typical Range: $1,000 to $10,000

Recent Grants

Note: Grants derived from 2000 Form 990.
Library-Related

5,000	Providence Public Library, Providence, RI

General

10,000	Newport Hospital Foundation, Newport, RI
10,000	Rogers High School, Newport, RI -- scholarships
10,000	University of Rhode Island, Providence, RI
7,200	Community Preparatory School, Providence, RI
5,000	East Providence Community Center, Providence, RI
5,000	Middletown High School, Middletown, RI
5,000	New Visions for Newport County, Newport, RI
5,000	Newman Bird Sanctuary, Middletown, RI
5,000	Portsmouth High School, Portsmouth, RI -- scholarships
5,000	Providence In-Town Churches, Providence, RI

EUGENE M. CLARY FOUNDATION, INC.

Giving Contact

Eugene M. Clary, Chairman & Treasurer
4701 Post Oak Tritt Rd.
Marietta, GA 30062
Phone: (770)993-3562

Description

Founded: 1997
EIN: 582310406
Organization Type: Private Foundation
Grant Types: General Support.

Financial Summary

Total Giving: $94,772 (2003); $104,730 (2001)
Assets: $1,159,707 (2003); $1,351,181 (2001)
Gifts Received: $50,000 (2000); $10,000 (1999); $1,131,523 (1997). Note: In 1997, 1999 and 2000, contributions were received from Eugene M. Clary.

Typical Recipients

Arts & Humanities: Libraries
Civic & Public Affairs: Civic & Public Affairs-General, Urban & Community Affairs
Education: Education Funds, Education-General, Secondary Education (Public), Special Education
Environment: Wildlife Protection
Health: Alzheimer's Disease, Cancer, Children's Health/Hospitals, Diabetes, Emergency/Ambulance Services, Eyes/Blindness, Health-General, Medical Research, Prenatal Health Issues
Religion: Churches, Ministries
Social Services: At-Risk Youth, People with Disabilities, Youth Organizations

Foundation Officials

Eugene M. Clary: chairman, treasurer

Grants Analysis

Disclosure Period: calendar year ending 2003
Total Grants: $94,772
Number of Grants: 26
Average Grant: $616*
Highest Grant: $50,000
Lowest Grant: $45
Typical Range: $100 to $1,000
*Note: Average grant figure excludes two highest grant ($80,000).

Recent Grants

Note: Grants derived from 2003 Form 990.

General

50,000	Georgia Tech Foundation, Atlanta, GA
30,000	Alexander Tharpe Fund, Atlanta, GA
5,000	Jacob's Ladder Learning, Roswell, GA
1,320	Crystal Cathedral Ministry, Garden Grove, CA
1,000	Alpha Tau Omega Foundation, Indianapolis, IN
1,000	Amer Printing House for Blind, Louisville, KY
1,000	Bobby Dodd Institute, Atlanta, GA
1,000	Harlem Methodist Church, Harlem, GA
500	First Baptist Church, Atlanta, GA
480	Campbell High School, Smyrna, GA

CLAY FOUNDATION

Giving Contact

Charles M. Avampato, President
1426 Kanawha Boulevard, East
Charleston, WV 25301
Phone: (304)344-8656
Fax: (304)344-3805
E-mail: cfiwv@aol.com

Description

Founded: 1987
EIN: 550670193
Organization Type: General Purpose Foundation
Giving Locations: WV: Charleston
Grant Types: Award, Challenge, Endowment, General Support, Matching, Research, Seed Money.

Donor Information

Founder: The foundation was established in 1987 by Lyell B. Clay, the chairman of the foundation, and Buckner Clay, also chairman of the foundation. Lyell B. Clay is the chairman of the board of Clay Communications, Inc.

Financial Summary

Total Giving: $1,000,000 (fiscal year ending October 31, 2003 approx); $1,364,338 (fiscal 2002 approx); $1,710,141 (fiscal 2001)
Giving Analysis: Giving for fiscal 2001 includes: foundation scholarships ($25,000); foundation grants to United Way ($65,000).
Assets: $63,000,000 (fiscal 2003 approx); $54,962,179 (fiscal 2002 approx)
Gifts Received: $660,489 (fiscal 1992). Note: Contributions were received from Lyell B. and Buckner W. Clay.

Typical Recipients

Arts & Humanities: Arts Centers, Arts Funds, Historic Preservation, History & Archaeology, Libraries, Museums/Galleries, Music, Opera, Public Broadcasting, Theater
Civic & Public Affairs: Botanical Gardens/Parks, Chambers of Commerce, Community Foundations, Economic Development, Civic & Public Affairs-General, Housing, Law & Justice, Legal Aid, Municipalities/Towns, Nonprofit Management, Philanthropic Organizations, Professional & Trade Associations, Public Policy, Urban & Community Affairs
Education: Afterschool/Enrichment Programs, Arts/Humanities Education, Business-School Partnerships, Colleges & Universities, Continuing Education, Education-General, Health & Physical Education, Legal Education, Literacy, Medical Education, Private Education (Precollege), Public Education (Precollege), Science/Mathematics Education, Social Sciences Education, Student Aid
Health: Children's Health/Hospitals, Clinics/Medical Centers, Health Policy/Cost Containment, Health Organizations, Hospices, Hospitals, Mental Health, Nursing Services, Preventive Medicine/Wellness Organizations, Speech & Hearing
International: International Organizations
Religion: Churches, Religious Organizations, Religious Welfare
Science: Science Museums
Social Services: Animal Protection, At-Risk Youth, Camps, Child Welfare, Community Service Organizations, Counseling, Family Services, Food/Clothing Distribution, Homes, People with Disabilities, Recreation & Athletics, Scouts, Shelters/Homelessness, United Funds/United Ways, Volunteer Services, YMCA/YWCA/YMHA/YWHA, Youth Organizations

Application Procedures

Initial Contact: The foundation reports that applicants should submit, in triplicate, a letter of inquiry (two to three pages) that briefly describes the proposed project.
Application Requirements: Letters should include the name, address, and phone number of the organization; contact's name; descriptive title of project; amount of funds requested; timetable for use of funds; outline of objectives, specific goals, and target population; methods which will be used to accomplish these goals; other sources of funding for the project; and plans for evaluation of the project (if applicable). Attachments should include information about the sponsoring organization, names and brief statements of qualification for individuals who will be involved in the project, most recently audited financial statement, and tax-exempt identification.
Deadlines: None.
Review Process: All grant requests are first reviewed to determine if the request falls within the current program interest of the foundation. Only those requests that clearly fall outside the foundation's priorities are declined on the first review.

In reviewing grant applications, the foundation gives careful consideration to: the potential impact of the request and the number of people who will benefit; the degree to which t he applicant works with, or complements, the services of other community organizations; the organization's fiscal responsibility and management qualifications; the possibility of the use of its grants as seed money for matching funds from other sources; the ability of the program to obtain necessary additional funding to implement the project; the commitment of the organization's board of directors; the imaginative and experimental quality of the proposed project; the extent of local volunteer involvement and support for the project; and the ability of the organization to provide ongoing funding after the term of the grant.

The foundation may request additional information and, in some cases, may arrange for the applicant to meet with the staff for further discussion. A project site visit may be scheduled, and the advice of outside consultants may be sought.

Final approval of each major grant is the responsibility of the board of directors. Certain other grants that require a smaller amount of support may be authorized by the president of the foundation. All grants are subject to the same review and monitoring criteria.

Applicants should allow the foundation 60 working days to review a request. If the foundation's priorities and resources permit consideration of the request, a detailed proposal may be requested. The board of directors meets four times a year, generally in January, April, July, and October.

Restrictions

In general, the foundation does not fund ongoing normal operations, debt retirement or operational deficits, national fundraising campaigns, endowment or scholarship funds, religious organizations for religious purposes, or conduit organizations. The foundation may not award grants to individuals, designate funds for legislation, or support activities that seek to influence the legislative process.

Foundation Officials

Charles M. Avampato: president
James Knight Brown: secretary B Rainelle, WV 1929. ED West Virginia University BS (1951). PRIM CORP EMPL member: Jackson & Kelly. CORP AFFIL director: One Valley Bancorp West Virginia, Inc. NONPR AFFIL member: Phi Beta Kappa; member: West Virginia State Bar; member: Order Coif; member: American Bar Association.
Buckner W. Clay: chairman
Hamilton G. Clay: vice president
Lyell Buffington Clay: chairman B Baltimore, MD 1923. ED Williams College BA (1944); University of Virginia LLB (1948); Marshall University MA (1956); Harvard University (1967); West Virginia University MBA (1975). NONPR AFFIL member: West Virginia Press Association; member: West Virginia State Bar; member: Charleston Area Chamber of Commerce; member: American Newspaper Publishers Association. CLUB AFFIL Charleston Rotary Club.
Whitney Clay Diller: treasurer
Louis Sweetland Southworth, II: assistant secretary-treasurer B Huntington, WV 1943. ED Marshall University AB (1965); West Virginia University JD (1968); New York University LLM (1970). PRIM CORP EMPL attorney: Jackson & Kelly. NONPR AFFIL trustee: Kanawha Valley Foundation; trustee: University Charleston; director: CAMC Foundation; fellow: American College Tax Counsel. CLUB AFFIL Rotary Club; Edgewood Country Club.

Grants Analysis

Disclosure Period: fiscal year ending October 31, 2002
Total Grants: $1,364,338*
Number of Grants: 22
Average Grant: $62,015*
Highest Grant: $596,450
Lowest Grant: $5,000
Typical Range: $7,500 to $50,000 and $5,000 to $150,000
*Note: Giving excludes United Way and scholarships. Average grant figure excludes highest grant.

Recent Grants

Note: Grants derived from 2002 Form 990.

Library-Related

7,500	Kanawha County Public Library, Charleston, WV -- for new library project

General

596,450	University of Charleston, Charleston, WV -- information & science center
150,000	Community Council of Kanawha Valley, Charleston, WV -- for Family Enrichment Center
80,000	BIDCO Foundation, Charleston, WV -- for Economic Development Programs
75,000	Covenant House, Charleston, WV -- for new building
67,750	West Virginia Symphony, Charleston, WV -- for new administrative staff
65,000	United Way Kanawha Valley, Charleston, WV -- annual campaign
60,000	Fund for Arts, Charleston, WV -- annual campaign
50,000	Mount Habitat for Humanity, South Charleston, WV -- for low income housing
40,000	Thomas Memorial Hospital Foundation, South Charleston, WV -- for new emergency room
31,300	Charleston Area Medical Center Foundation, Charleston, WV -- for Adaptive Driving Program

SILAS AND RUTH CLAYPOOL FOUNDATION

Giving Contact
Jimmy Rogers
1719 W. Main St.
PO Box 217
Robinson, IL 62454
Phone: (618)544-2960

Description
Founded: 1991
EIN: 376288069
Organization Type: Private Foundation
Giving Locations: IL: Crawford County
Grant Types: General Support.

Financial Summary
Total Giving: $44,950 (2004); $37,493 (2001)
Assets: $786,662 (2004); $810,515 (2001)
Gifts Received: In 1991, contributions were received from the Ruth Claypool Living Trust.

Typical Recipients
Arts & Humanities: Arts Associations & Councils, Arts Centers, Historic Preservation, History & Archaeology, Libraries, Music, Theater
Civic & Public Affairs: Community Foundations, Civic & Public Affairs-General, Housing, Municipalities/Towns, Safety, Urban & Community Affairs
Education: Afterschool/Enrichment Programs, Agricultural Education, Education-General, Literacy, Preschool Education, Public Education (Precollege), Secondary Education (Public)
Health: Emergency/Ambulance Services
International: International-General, International Affairs
Religion: Churches
Social Services: Animal Protection, Community Service Organizations, Domestic Violence, Food/Clothing Distribution, Recreation & Athletics, Social Services-General, Veterans

Application Procedures
Initial Contact: Send a brief letter of inquiry.
Application Requirements: Include name and address of organization, amount requested, description of project, and the name of the contact person.
Deadlines: May 1 and November 1.

Restrictions
Limited to organizations in Crawford County, IL.

Foundation Officials
Tom Eden: trustee
Allen R. Price: trustee

Grants Analysis
Disclosure Period: calendar year ending 2004
Total Grants: $44,950
Number of Grants: 12
Average Grant: $2,359*
Highest Grant: $19,000
Lowest Grant: $1,000
Typical Range: $1,000 to $4,000
***Note:** Average grant figure excludes highest grant.

Recent Grants
Note: Grants derived from 2004 Form 990.
Library-Related
2,000	Robinson Public Library District, Robinson, IL
1,970	Palestine Public Library, Palestine, IL

General
19,000	Robinson High School, Robinson, IL
6,000	Oblong High School, Oblong, IL
4,380	Clothing Center Workshop, Robinson, IL
2,000	ACE After School Program, Robinson, IL
2,000	Hutsonville Grade School, Hutsonville, IL
2,000	Oblong Grade School, Oblong, IL
1,600	Crawford County Arts, Robinson, IL
1,500	Embarras River Basin Agency, Robinson, IL

CLAYTON FUND

Giving Contact
William Askey
Chase Bank of Texas
600 Travis, 7th Fl.
Houston, TX 77002
Phone: (713)216-1453

Alternate Contact
Anne Bryant

Description
Founded: 1989
EIN: 760285764
Organization Type: General Purpose Foundation
Giving Locations: nationally.
Grant Types: Fellowship, General Support, Professorship.

Donor Information
Founder: Established in Texas as a trust in 1952 through donations by the late William L. Clayton and his late wife, Susan V. Clayton. William L. Clayton, founder of the insurance and food processing company, Anderson, Clayton and Company, was also active in the federal government, including his service as Assistant Secretary of State. He was also vice president of the Export-Import Bank, and wrote extensively on international trade, economics, and foreign affairs. The William L. Clayton Center for International Economic Affairs at the Fletcher School of Law and Diplomacy of Tufts University is named after him.

Financial Summary
Total Giving: $2,020,000 (fiscal year ending December 01, 2003); $2,353,350 (fiscal 2001)
Assets: $41,911,128 (fiscal 2003); $48,832,420 (fiscal 2001)
Gifts Received: $2,501,206 (fiscal 1996); $365,395 (fiscal 1995)

Typical Recipients
Arts & Humanities: Arts Associations & Councils, Historic Preservation, Libraries, Museums/Galleries, Music, Opera, Theater
Civic & Public Affairs: African American Affairs, Botanical Gardens/Parks, Clubs, Community Foundations, Economic Development, Employment/Job Training, Civic & Public Affairs-General, Hispanic Affairs, Housing, Nonprofit Management, Public Policy, Rural Affairs, Urban & Community Affairs
Education: Afterschool/Enrichment Programs, Agricultural Education, Arts/Humanities Education, Business Education, Colleges & Universities, Education Funds, Education Reform, Elementary Education (Private), Engineering/Technological Education, Education-General, Leadership Training, Literacy, Medical Education, Minority Education, Private Education (Precollege), Public Education (Precollege), Religious Education, Secondary Education (Private), Special Education, Student Aid
Environment: Environment-General, Protection, Resource Conservation, Wildlife Protection
Health: Cancer, Children's Health/Hospitals, Clinics/Medical Centers, Emergency/Ambulance Services, Health Organizations, Heart, Hospices, Hospitals, Hospitals (University Affiliated), Medical Rehabilitation, Mental Health, Prenatal Health Issues, Public Health, Single-Disease Health Associations, Speech & Hearing, Transplant Networks/Donor Banks
International: Health Care/Hospitals, International Peace & Security Issues, International Relations, International Relief Efforts, Missionary/Religious Activities
Religion: Churches, Ministries, Religious Welfare
Social Services: At-Risk Youth, Camps, Child Welfare, Community Centers, Community Service Organizations, Domestic Violence, Emergency Relief, Family Planning, Family Services, Food/Clothing Distribution, People with Disabilities, Recreation & Athletics, Scouts, Shelters/Homelessness, Social Services-General, YMCA/YWCA/YMHA/YWHA, Youth Organizations

Application Procedures
Initial Contact: Four copies of a brief proposal
Application Requirements: a summary concerning the applicant, details of the project, amount requested, total amount required for the project, income and expense budget for project, including other sources of funding, a copy of the determination letter issued to the applicant by the I.R.S., and a narrative of three to five pages.
Deadlines: February 1, May 1, August 1, and November 1.
Review Process: Attempts are made to provide applicants with a response within eight weeks of receiving the application.

Restrictions
The foundation generally does not make grants to building or endowment funds. No grants are made to individuals.

Foundation Officials
William Hartman Askey: treasurer, secretary B Williamsburg, PA June 21, 1919. ED Bucknell University BA (1941); University of Pittsburgh JD (1951). PRIM NONPR EMPL magistrate: U.S. District Court. NONPR AFFIL member: Lycoming Law Association; member: Pennsylvania Bar Association; honorary member: Federation Bar Association; member: Federation Magistrate Judges Association; member: American Bar Association. CLUB AFFIL Ross Club; Masons Club.
William C. Baker: trustee
William L. Garwood, Jr.: vice president
Burdine C. Johnson: president

Grants Analysis
Disclosure Period: fiscal year ending December 01, 2003
Total Grants: $2,020,000
Number of Grants: 79
Average Grant: $19,267*
Highest Grant: $250,000
Lowest Grant: $5,000
Typical Range: $10,000 to $40,000
***Note:** Average grant figure excludes four highest grants ($575,000).

Recent Grants
Note: Grants derived from 2001 Form 990.

General
180,000	Planned Parenthood of Houston, Houston, TX
140,000	Bryn Mawr, Baltimore, MD
100,000	Planned Parenthood Federation, New York, NY
90,000	American Red Cross, Houston, TX
75,000	Institute for Rehabilitation & Research Foundation, Houston, TX
50,000	Children's Scholarship Fund, Houston, TX
50,000	Houston CEO Foundation, Houston, TX
50,000	Houston Grand Opera, Houston, TX
50,000	San Migel - Casa Inc., Austin, TX
50,000	Texas Tech University, Lubbock, TX

CLEARY FOUNDATION

Giving Contact
Gail K. Cleary, President
301 Sky Harbour Dr.
La Crosse, WI 54603
Phone: (608)783-7500

Description
Founded: 1982
EIN: 391426785
Organization Type: Private Foundation
Giving Locations: WI
Grant Types: Endowment, General Support.

Donor Information
Founder: Russell G. Cleary, Gail K. Cleary

Financial Summary
Total Giving: $445,008 (fiscal year ending November 30, 2003); $345,805 (fiscal 2001)
Giving Analysis: Giving for fiscal 2003 includes: foundation grants to United Way ($30,000); fiscal 2001: foundation grants to United Way ($30,800)
Assets: $10,767,606 (fiscal 2003); $8,667,682 (fiscal 2001)
Gifts Received: $604,139 (fiscal 2000); $50,439 (fiscal 1998); $15,062 (fiscal 1996). Note: In fiscal 2000, contributions were received from Estate of Lillian Hope Kumm. In fiscal 1996, contributions were received from Russell G. and Gail K. Cleary.

Typical Recipients
Arts & Humanities: Arts Associations & Councils, Arts Funds, Community Arts, Ethnic & Folk Arts, Historic Preservation, History & Archaeology, Libraries, Museums/Galleries, Music, Performing Arts, Public Broadcasting, Theater
Civic & Public Affairs: Clubs, Economic Development, Civic & Public Affairs-General, Housing, Parades/Festivals, Public Policy, Urban & Community Affairs
Education: Business Education, Colleges & Universities, Education Funds, Legal Education, Minority Education, Public Education (Precollege), Student Aid, Vocational & Technical Education
Environment: Resource Conservation, Wildlife Protection
Health: Emergency/Ambulance Services, Health-General, Geriatric Health, Health Funds, Hospitals, Long-Term Care, Medical Research, Single-Disease Health Associations
International: International Organizations
Religion: Churches, Religious Welfare
Social Services: Animal Protection, Community Centers, Community Service Organizations, Counseling, Crime Prevention, Domestic Violence, Family Services, Food/Clothing Distribution, People with Disabilities, Recreation & Athletics, Scouts, Substance Abuse, United Funds/United Ways, YMCA/YWCA/YMHA/YWHA, Youth Organizations

Application Procedures
Initial Contact: Send a brief letter of inquiry describing program.
Application Requirements: Include proof of tax-exempt status, amount requested, and abbreviated amount of supporting detail.
Deadlines: None.

Restrictions
Does not make contributions to individuals.

Foundation Officials
Gail K. Cleary: president, director
Kristine H. Cleary: vice president, secretary, director
Sandra G. Cleary: vice president, treasurer, director

Grants Analysis
Disclosure Period: fiscal year ending November 30, 2003

Total Grants: $415,008*
Number of Grants: 91
Average Grant: $3,168*
Highest Grant: $129,850
Lowest Grant: $25
Typical Range: $500 to $5,000
***Note:** Giving excludes United Way. Average grant figure excludes highest grant.

Recent Grants
Note: Grants derived from fiscal 2003 Form 990.
General

129,850	Girl Scouts of Riverland Council, La Crosse, WI -- for youth education and training
80,200	Family & Children's Center, La Crosse, WI -- towards counseling program for problem students
65,135	Boy's & Girl's Club of La Crosse, La Crosse, WI -- for youth education and rehabilitation
30,000	La Crosse Area United Way, La Crosse, WI -- for community agencies support
20,840	University of Wisconsin - La Crosse Foundation, La Crosse, WI -- for alumni center fund
20,000	La Crosse Historical Society, La Crosse, WI -- for historical preservation efforts
14,100	Western Wisconsin Technical College Foundation, La Crosse, WI -- for educational scholarship and building fund
11,900	Oktoberfest Gemutlichkeit Foundation, La Crosse, WI -- for community and ethnic activities
7,525	La Crosse Symphony Orchestra, La Crosse, WI -- for musical training and appreciation
7,200	Boy Scouts of America, La Crosse, WI -- for youth education

CLEMENS MARKETS

Company Headquarters
1555 Bustard Road
Kulpsville, PA 19443
Web: http://www.clemensmarkets.com

Company Description
Employees: 2,000
SIC(s): 5400 Food Stores.

Clemens Foundation

Giving Contact
Jack Clemons, Jr., Treasurer
P.O. Box 1555
Kulpsville, PA 19443
Phone: (215)361-9000
Web: http://www.clemensmarkets.com/pages/Community_Involvement.htm

Description
EIN: 231675035
Organization Type: Corporate Foundation
Giving Locations: PA
Grant Types: Capital, General Support, Scholarship.

Financial Summary
Total Giving: $126,220 (fiscal year ending September 30, 2003). Note: Fiscal 1997 Giving includes United Way ($13,400); scholarships ($3,000).
Giving Analysis: Giving for fiscal 2003 includes: foundation grants to United Way ($17,540)
Assets: $1,148,324 (fiscal 2003)
Gifts Received: $403,401 (fiscal 2003); $108,411 (fiscal 2000); $80,000 (fiscal 1999). Note: In fiscal

1997 and 1999, contributions were received from Clemens Markets Corp., James S. Clemens Markets, Inc., and Abraham and Lillian Clemens.

Typical Recipients
Arts & Humanities: Historic Preservation, Libraries
Civic & Public Affairs: Civic & Public Affairs-General, Housing, Safety, Urban & Community Affairs
Education: Colleges & Universities, Private Education (Precollege), Religious Education, Secondary Education (Private), Student Aid
Health: Cancer, Children's Health/Hospitals, Emergency/Ambulance Services, Geriatric Health, Hospitals, Medical Rehabilitation, Medical Research, Mental Health
International: Missionary/Religious Activities
Religion: Bible Study/Translation, Churches, Religion-General, Jewish Causes, Ministries, Missionary Activities (Domestic), Religious Organizations, Religious Welfare, Seminaries
Social Services: Camps, Community Service Organizations, Family Services, Food/Clothing Distribution, Homes, United Funds/United Ways, YMCA/YWCA/YMHA/YWHA, Youth Organizations

Application Procedures
Initial Contact: Return completed application form.
Application Requirements: Include recently audited financial statement, list of sources of revenue, actual cost of raising funds, and the compensation of officers, directors, trustees, and officials in charge of overall direction of management.
Deadlines: November 1.

Corporate Officials
James S. Clemens, Jr.: chairman, president, chief executive officer, director PRIM CORP EMPL chairman, president, chief executive officer, director: Clemens Markets.
G. Christian Limbert, Jr.: chief financial officer, treasurer PRIM CORP EMPL chief financial officer, treasurer: Clemens Markets.

Foundation Officials
Suzanne C. Harris: assistant treasurer
Jules Pearlstine: member
Janice C. Tyson: assistant secretary

Grants Analysis
Disclosure Period: fiscal year ending September 30, 2003
Total Grants: $108,500*
Number of Grants: 118
Average Grant: $919
Highest Grant: $5,000
Lowest Grant: $100
Typical Range: $100 to $2,000
***Note:** Giving excludes United Way.

Recent Grants
Note: Grants derived from fiscal 2001 Form 990.
General

8,000	United Way
5,000	Gideon International, Nashville, TN
5,000	Philadelphia Geriatric Center, Philadelphia, PA
5,000	St. Joseph's University, Philadelphia, PA
3,800	Eastern College, St. Davids, PA
3,440	United Way
3,000	Calvary Baptist Church School, Lansdale, PA -- for building fund
3,000	North Penn Valley Boys and Girls Club, Lansdale, PA
2,500	Elizabethtown College, Elizabethtown, PA
2,500	Juniata College, Huntingdon, PA

CLEMENTS FOUNDATION

Giving Contact
Shirley Warren
1901 N. Akard St.
Dallas, TX 75201
Phone: (214)720-0377

Description
Founded: 1968
EIN: 756065076
Organization Type: Private Foundation
Giving Locations: TX: Dallas including metropolitan area
Grant Types: General Support, Scholarship.

Financial Summary
Total Giving: $611,710 (2003). Note: Giving includes United Way ($10,000).
Giving Analysis: Giving for 2003 includes: foundation grants to United Way ($10,500)
Assets: $10,972,225 (2003)
Gifts Received: $350,000 (2003); $255,000 (1993). Note: In 1993 and 2003, contributions were received from William P. Clements, Jr.

Typical Recipients
Arts & Humanities: Arts Outreach, Historic Preservation, History & Archaeology, Libraries, Museums/Galleries
Civic & Public Affairs: Botanical Gardens/Parks, Clubs, Community Foundations, Civic & Public Affairs-General, Parades/Festivals, Philanthropic Organizations, Safety, Urban & Community Affairs, Zoos/Aquariums
Education: Arts/Humanities Education, Colleges & Universities, Education Funds, Engineering/Technological Education, Faculty Development, Education-General, Medical Education, Private Education (Precollege), Public Education (Precollege), Secondary Education (Private), Secondary Education (Public)
Environment: Wildlife Protection
Health: Arthritis, Cancer, Clinics/Medical Centers, Health Organizations, Hospitals, Hospitals (University Affiliated), Nutrition, Public Health
International: Health Care/Hospitals, International Affairs
Religion: Churches, Dioceses, Religious Welfare
Science: Science Museums
Social Services: Child Welfare, Community Service Organizations, Crime Prevention, Family Services, People with Disabilities, Recreation & Athletics, Scouts, Substance Abuse, United Funds/United Ways, YMCA/YWCA/YMHA/YWHA, Youth Organizations

Application Procedures
Initial Contact: Send a detailed, written statement outlining the course of study the applicant wishes to pursue, prior publications (if any), grade reports and/or aptitude scores, and financial need.
Deadlines: None.

Additional Information
Provides scholarships to students pursuing a course of study involving the history of the state of TX, the Greater Southwest, or related matters of historical value.
Publications: Application Guidelines

Foundation Officials
B. Gill Clements: vice president
William P. Clements, Jr.: president B Dallas, TX April 13, 1917. ED Southern Methodist University DHL (1974). CORP AFFIL chairman: SEDCO; director: General Motors Corp.; director: Interfirst Corp. NONPR AFFIL member: Southern Methodist University; member: Southwest Medicine School; member national executive board: Boy Scouts America; member: International Association Drilling Contractors; member: American Association Oil Well Drilling Contractors.

Grants Analysis
Disclosure Period: calendar year ending 2003
Total Grants: $601,210*
Number of Grants: 83
Average Grant: $1,140*
Highest Grant: $360,000
Lowest Grant: $100
Typical Range: $500 to $2,000
*Note: Giving excludes United Way. Average grant figure excludes three highest grants ($510,000).

Recent Grants
Note: Grants derived from 2003 Form 990.
General

360,000	Episcopal Diocese of Dallas, Dallas, TX
100,000	University of Texas Southwestern, Dallas, TX
50,000	Southern Methodist University in Taos, Dallas, TX
11,000	Meadows Museum-Southern Methodist University, Dallas, TX
10,200	Highland Park Independent School District Education Foundation, Dallas, TX
10,000	Friends of Dale Lipshy University Hospital, Dallas, TX
10,000	United Way of Metropolitan Dallas, Dallas, TX
5,200	Old City Park, Dallas, TX
5,000	Boys and Girls Harbor Inc., Houston, TX
5,000	Documents of the Coronado Expedition, Las Vegas, NV

CLEVELAND-CLIFFS INC.

Company Headquarters
1100 Superior Ave., Fl. 18
Cleveland, OH 44114
Web: http://www.cleveland-cliffs.com

Company Description
Founded: 1847
Ticker: CLF
Exchange: NYSE
Revenue: US$330.4 million (2001)
Employees: 3956 (2003)
SIC(s): 1011 Iron Ores.

Operating Locations
Cleveland-Cliffs, Inc. (MI--Ishpeming; TX--Houston)

Nonmonetary Support
Type: Loaned Executives; Workplace Solicitation

The Cleveland-Cliffs Foundation

Giving Contact
Dana W. Byrne, Vice President, Assistant Treasurer
1100 Superior Avenue East, Suite 1500
Cleveland, OH 44114-2589
Phone: (216)694-5700
Fax: (216)694-6741
Web: http://www.cleveland-cliffs.com/general/community/foundation.asp

Description
EIN: 346525124
Organization Type: Corporate Foundation
Giving Locations: DC: Washington; MI; OH; nationally; Canada: nationally.
Grant Types: Capital, Employee Matching Gifts, General Support, Matching, Multiyear/Continuing Support.

Financial Summary
Total Giving: $305,505 (2003); $293,998 (2002); $461,006 (2001). Note: Contributes through foundation only.
Giving Analysis: Giving for 2001 includes: foundation grants to United Way ($57,562); foundation matching gifts ($58,914)
Assets: $163,809 (2003); $468,960 (2002); $638,000 (2001)
Gifts Received: $120,000 (2002); $200,000 (2000); $200,000 (1999). Note: Contributions were received from Cleveland-Cliffs, Inc.

Typical Recipients
Arts & Humanities: Arts Associations & Councils, Arts Centers, Arts Festivals, Ballet, Arts & Humanities-General, Historic Preservation, History & Archaeology, Libraries, Museums/Galleries, Music, Opera, Performing Arts, Public Broadcasting, Theater
Civic & Public Affairs: Botanical Gardens/Parks, Business/Free Enterprise, Chambers of Commerce, Clubs, Community Foundations, Economic Development, Employment/Job Training, Civic & Public Affairs-General, Housing, Law & Justice, Legal Aid, Municipalities/Towns, Parades/Festivals, Philanthropic Organizations, Public Policy, Rural Affairs, Urban & Community Affairs, Zoos/Aquariums
Education: Afterschool/Enrichment Programs, Arts/Humanities Education, Business Education, Business-School Partnerships, Colleges & Universities, Community & Junior Colleges, Continuing Education, Economic Education, Education Associations, Education Funds, Education Reform, Engineering/Technological Education, Environmental Education, Education-General, Literacy, Minority Education, Private Education (Precollege), Public Education (Precollege), Science/Mathematics Education, Secondary Education (Private), Secondary Education (Public), Student Aid, Vocational & Technical Education
Environment: Environment-General, Resource Conservation, Wildlife Protection
Health: Cancer, Children's Health/Hospitals, Clinics/Medical Centers, Emergency/Ambulance Services, Health Organizations, Heart, Hospitals, Mental Health, Nursing Services, Preventive Medicine/Wellness Organizations, Public Health
International: Health Care/Hospitals, International Affairs
Religion: Religious Welfare, Seminaries
Science: Science Museums, Scientific Centers & Institutes
Social Services: At-Risk Youth, Camps, Child Welfare, Community Service Organizations, Counseling, Crime Prevention, Delinquency & Criminal Rehabilitation, Emergency Relief, Family Services, Food/Clothing Distribution, People with Disabilities, Recreation & Athletics, Scouts, Senior Services, Shelters/Homelessness, United Funds/United Ways, Volunteer Services, YMCA/YWCA/YMHA/YWHA, Youth Organizations

Application Procedures
Initial Contact: Submit a brief letter of inquiry.
Application Requirements: Include a description of organization, amount requested, purpose of funds sought, recently audited financial statements, and proof of tax-exempt status.
Deadlines: None.
Review Process: Vice president evaluates requests and submits them to distribution committee for their approval; a letter is sent regarding final decision.

Restrictions
Foundation does not support individuals or political or lobbying groups.

Additional Information
Publications: Guidelines Sheet

Corporate Officials

Cynthia B. Bezik: senior vice president finance B Youngstown, OH 1953. ED Youngstown State University (1970); Case Western Reserve University (1980). PRIM CORP EMPL senior vice president finance: Cleveland-Cliffs, Inc. CORP AFFIL chief financial officer: Cliffs Resources Inc.; manager financial analysis: Pickands Mather; member: Cleveland Cliffs Iron Co. NONPR AFFIL member: National Association Accountants; member: Planning Forum; member: Financial Executives Institute; member: American Iron & Steel Institute; member: American Society Women Accountants. CLUB AFFIL Womens City Club.

John S. Brinzo: president, chief executive officer B Cleveland, OH 1942. ED Kent State University BSBA (1964); Case Western Reserve University MBA (1968). PRIM CORP EMPL chairman, chief executive officer: Cleveland-Cliffs, Inc. NONPR AFFIL member: American Iron & Steel Institute; director: National Mining Association.

William Rushton Calfee: executive vice president, commercial B Cleveland, OH 1946. ED Williams College BA (1968); Harvard University Advanced Management Program (1984). ADD CORP EMPL executive vice president: Ceveland-Cliffs Iron Co.

Edward C. Dowling: senior vice president, operations PRIM CORP EMPL senior vice president, operations: Cleveland-Cliffs, Inc.

Robert Emmet: vice president financial planning, treasurer B 1945. ED Yale University BA (1967); Harvard University MBA (1973). PRIM CORP EMPL vice president financial planning, treasurer: Cleveland-Cliffs, Inc. ADD CORP EMPL vice president: Clevelabd-Cliffs Iron Co.

Donald J. Gallagher: vice president, sales PRIM CORP EMPL vice president, sales: Cleveland-Cliffs, Inc.

John E. Lenhard: secretary, associate general counsel PRIM CORP EMPL secretary, associate general counsel: Cleveland-Cliffs, Inc.

Robert J. Leroux: vice president, controller PRIM CORP EMPL vice president, controller: Cleveland-Cliffs, Inc.

Richard F. Novak: vice president human resources PRIM CORP EMPL vice president human resources: Cleveland-Cliffs, Inc.

Thomas J. O'Neil: president, chief operating officer PRIM CORP EMPL president, chief operating officer: Cleveland-Cliffs, Inc.

John W. Sanders: senior vice president, international development PRIM CORP EMPL senior vice president, international development: Cleveland-Cliffs, Inc.

James A. Trethewey: senior vice president, operations services PRIM CORP EMPL senior vice president, operations services: Cleveland-Cliffs, Inc.

A. Stanley West: senior vice president, sales & commercial planning PRIM CORP EMPL senior vice president, sales & commercial planning: Cleveland-Cliffs, Inc.

Foundation Officials

John S. Brinzo: president, trustee (see above)
Dana W. Byrne: vice president, assistant treasurer
William Rushton Calfee: trustee (see above)
Edward C. Dowling: trustee (see above)
Donald J. Gallagher: vice president, treasurer, trustee (see above)
John E. Lenhard: secretary (see above)

Grants Analysis

Disclosure Period: calendar year ending 2003
Total Grants: $197,500*
Number of Grants: 41
Average Grant: $3,688*
Highest Grant: $50,000
Lowest Grant: $100
Typical Range: $1,000 to $5,000
*Note: Giving excludes matching gifts; United Way. Average grant figure excludes highest grant.

Recent Grants

Note: Grants derived from 2003 Form 990.
General

50,000	SUNTRAC, Ishpeming, MI
40,999	United Way Services, Cleveland, OH
25,000	Iron Industry Museum, Lansing, MI
20,000	Michigan Technological University, Houghton, MI
10,000	William G. Mather Museum, Cleveland, OH
5,000	Bay Cliff Health Camp, Marquette, MI
5,000	Boys and Girls Clubs, Cleveland, OH
5,000	Cleveland Clinic, Cleveland, OH
5,000	Cleveland Health Museum, Cleveland, OH
5,000	Cleveland Institute of Music, Cleveland, OH

CLOROX CO.

Company Headquarters

1221 Broadway
Oakland, CA 94612-1888
Phone: (510)271-7000
Fax: (510)832-1463
Web: http://www.clorox.com

Company Description

Founded: 1913
Ticker: CLX
Exchange: NYSE
Acquired: First Brands Corp. (1999).
Revenue: US$4.324 billion (2004)
Profit: US$549 million (2004)
Employees: 8900 (2003)
Fortune Rank: 445, per FORTUNE Magazine's list of 500 Largest U.S. Corporations (2004).
SIC(s): 2033 Canned Fruits & Vegetables, 2034 Dehydrated Fruits, Vegetables & Soups, 2035 Pickles, Sauces & Salad Dressings, 2842 Polishes & Sanitation Goods.

Operating Locations

Clorox Co. (AL--Birmingham; CA--Laguna Hills, Los Angeles; GA--Forest Park; IL--Chicago, Naperville; MD--Aberdeen; MN--Bloomington; MS--Pearl; MO--Kansas City; NH--Nashua; OH--Cleveland; TX--Farmers Branch, Houston)
Note: Operates over 30 plants in the USA and internationally.

Nonmonetary Support

Type: Donated Equipment; Donated Products; In-kind Services; Workplace Solicitation
Volunteer Programs: The company reports that more than one-third of employees in its General Offices and its Technical Center volunteer time at more than 375 agencies. The Clorox Employee Volunteer Program identifies volunteer opportunities, disseminates information about community agencies and programs to employees, and helps match volunteers with organizations. Company awards $200 grants to organizations where employees volunteer.
Note: Support is given to Second Harvest Food Bank and for disaster relief.

Clorox Co. Foundation

Giving Contact

Clorox Co. Foundation
c/o East Bay Community Foundation
De Domenico Building
200 Frank Ogawa Plaza
Oakland, CA 94612
Phone: (510)836-3223
E-mail: cloroxfndt@eastbaycf.org

Web:
http://www.thecloroxcompany.com/community/
Note: Application address for organizations located in the Oakland, CA, area. Applicants are encouraged to submit applications via the e-mail address above.

Alternate Contact

Clorox Co. Foundation
PO Box 24305
Oakland, CA 94623-9981
Phone: (510)271-2965

Description

Founded: 1980
EIN: 942674980
Organization Type: Corporate Foundation
Giving Locations: CA: Oakland, San Francisco including metropolitan area operating locations.
Grant Types: Capital, Employee Matching Gifts, Endowment, General Support, Operating Expenses, Project, Scholarship.
Note: Employee matching gift ratio: 1 to 1 for educational institutions and the United Way.

Donor Information

Founder: Clorox Co.

Financial Summary

Total Giving: $4,162,435 (fiscal year ending June 31, 2004); $2,592,179 (fiscal 2003); $2,612,538 (fiscal 2002)
Giving Analysis: Giving for fiscal 2003 includes: foundation grants to United Way ($73,560); foundation scholarships ($134,045); foundation matching gifts ($1,214,334); fiscal 2001: foundation grants to United Way ($69,630); foundation program-related investments ($85,000); foundation scholarships ($137,842); foundation ($947,206); foundation matching gifts ($1,164,034)
Assets: $8,817,441 (fiscal 2004); $5,165,516 (fiscal 2003); $7,866,712 (fiscal 2002)
Gifts Received: $8,147,151 (fiscal 2004); $72,804 (fiscal 2003); $7,143,086 (fiscal 2002). Note: Contributions were received from the Clorox Co.

Typical Recipients

Arts & Humanities: Arts Appreciation, Arts Associations & Councils, Arts Centers, Arts Festivals, Arts Funds, Arts Outreach, Ballet, Community Arts, Dance, Ethnic & Folk Arts, Film & Video, Arts & Humanities-General, Historic Preservation, Libraries, Literary Arts, Museums/Galleries, Music, Opera, Performing Arts, Public Broadcasting, Theater, Visual Arts

Civic & Public Affairs: African American Affairs, Asian American Affairs, Botanical Gardens/Parks, Chambers of Commerce, Civil Rights, Clubs, Community Foundations, Economic Development, Employment/Job Training, Civic & Public Affairs-General, Hispanic Affairs, Law & Justice, Legal Aid, Municipalities/Towns, Nonprofit Management, Philanthropic Organizations, Professional & Trade Associations, Public Policy, Safety, Urban & Community Affairs, Women's Affairs, Zoos/Aquariums

Education: Afterschool/Enrichment Programs, Arts/Humanities Education, Business Education, Business-School Partnerships, Colleges & Universities, Community & Junior Colleges, Continuing Education, Economic Education, Education Associations, Education Funds, Education Reform, Elementary Education (Private), Elementary Education (Public), Environmental Education, Faculty Development, Education-General, Journalism/Media Education, Leadership Training, Literacy, Minority Education, Preschool Education, Private Education (Precollege), Public Education (Precollege), Religious Education, School Volunteerism, Science/Mathematics Education, Secondary Education (Public), Special Education, Student Aid

Environment: Environment-General, Resource Conservation, Wildlife Protection

Health: Cancer, Children's Health/Hospitals, Clinics/ Medical Centers, Emergency/Ambulance Services, Geriatric Health, Health Funds, Health Organizations, Hospices, Hospitals, Mental Health, Prenatal Health Issues, Public Health, Research/Studies Institutes, Single-Disease Health Associations

International: International Affairs, International Development

Religion: Religion-General, Jewish Causes, Ministries, Religious Organizations, Religious Welfare

Science: Science Exhibits & Fairs, Science Museums, Scientific Centers & Institutes

Social Services: Animal Protection, At-Risk Youth, Big Brothers/Big Sisters, Child Welfare, Community Centers, Community Service Organizations, Counseling, Day Care, Delinquency & Criminal Rehabilitation, Domestic Violence, Emergency Relief, Family Planning, Family Services, Food/Clothing Distribution, People with Disabilities, Recreation & Athletics, Scouts, Senior Services, Shelters/Homelessness, Special Olympics, Substance Abuse, United Funds/ United Ways, Volunteer Services, YMCA/YWCA/ YMHA/YWHA, Youth Organizations

Application Procedures

Initial Contact: Send a brief letter of inquiry or phone call to request application guidelines and proposal cover sheet form. Guidelines and cover sheet form may also be obtained from the company's web site.

Application Requirements: Include the cover sheet and a typewritten, single-spaced proposal of not more than three pages. The proposal should consist of the following questions answered in the order provided (typing the number and question followed by the answer): 1. What are some of your recent accomplishments? Emphasize achievements of the past year, both quantitative and qualitative. 2. Briefly describe the population that you serve with the funds requested, including the number of individuals, geographic location, age, socio-economic status, race, ethnicity, language, gender, etc. For cultural organizations, include this information for your audience and/or participants. Include a breakdown of the population served by racial/ethnic group and gender using percentages. 3. What are the expected outcomes of the project for which you are requesting funds? Describe the program/activities that will lead to these outcomes. Include the methods that will be used to evaluate the project. 4. Do you collaborate with other agencies? If so, which ones?

Attachments should include a copy of the organization's most recent IRS letter indicating tax status; list of current officers and directors, including professional affiliations; staff list including position titles and indication of full or part-time and number of volunteers, as well as a breakdown of current staff by racial/ethnic group and gender percentages; project budget; agency budget; financial statement; budget narrative explaining any significant changes in revenues or expenses between years, the nature and purpose of any cash reserves or endowment, and a list of in-kind or other non-cash contributions; a list of organization's funders and amounts received during previous fiscal year from all sources; a list of funding sources being solicited for this project indicated committed and pending funds; and a confirmation latter from your fiscal agent (if appropriate).

Deadlines: Applications for foundation grants are accepted August 1 to June 1 of each fiscal year ending June 30; deadlines are July 1, October 1, January 1, and April 1; requests for special events sponsorship should be submitted in writing at least sixty days prior to the event.

Review Process: For grants in excess of $2,500, applications are reviewed by contributions committee, which advises the board of trustees; grants in excess of $10,000 must be reviewed by the board.

Evaluative Criteria: Foundation favors applicants whose programs focus on direct delivery of services; launch programs or services in an innovative manner; promote volunteer participation and citizen involvement; encourage self-reliance and personal growth

among individuals served; have a broad base of financial support and a reasonable fund development plan; and include Clorox employee involvement. Other criteria for selection include: clarity of purpose, outcomes related to performance, strategies that will achieve the stated outcomes, sound evaluation procedures, sound fiscal and management practices, involvement of board members, demonstrated collaborative relationships, fundraising capacity, nondiscrimination policies and practices, and diversity of board, staff, clients, etc.

Decision Notification: Contributions committee meets quarterly.

Notes: Endowment/capital campaign requests include building funds, purchase of major equipment, or general operating reserve funds. However, the foundation discourages contributions to endowments. The company's operating facilities each have their own particular funding priorities and independent review processes. A complete list of contributions programs at Clorox locations is contained within the guidelines.

Restrictions

The foundation will not provide grants to political parties, organizations, candidates, or issues; exclusive membership organizations; religious-based activities for the purpose of furthering religious doctrine; individuals; benefit or raffle tickets; conferences, conventions or meetings; media productions; athletic leagues or events; national projects; advertising or promotional sponsorships; association or membership dues; fundraising events; deficits or retroactive funding; field trips, tours, or travel expenses; or organizations which receive more than 15% of funding from United Way or government sources.

Only one grant request per organization will be considered within a fiscal year time period (July 1 through June 30). Applicants must possess an IRS ruling confirming their classification as a 501(c)(3) organization or be sponsored by a qualified fiscal agent.

Additional Information

First-time grants generally range from $1,000 to $5,000 for general operating support and special projects. The foundation considers itself to be a supplemental funding source, seeking points of intervention where modest grants can be leveraged for greater change.

In addition to cash contributions by the company and foundation, Clorox has invested more than $60 million in low-income housing projects nationwide. Such investments are expected to increase to approximately $100 million.

The Clorox Co. is a U.S. affiliate of Henkel KGAA, which has a 28% investment in Clorox. Other U.S. affiliates are Loctite Corp. (29%) and Ecolab (25%).

The Clorox Co. Foundation recently formed a partnership with the East Bay Community Foundation in the administration of its grants.

Publications: Guidelines; Application Form; Foundation Annual Report

Corporate Officials

Peter D. Bewley: senior vice president, general counsel, secretary B Atlantic City, NJ 1946. ED Princeton University BA (1968); Stanford University JD (1971). PRIM CORP EMPL senior vice president, general counsel, secretary: The Clorox Co. CORP AFFIL secretary: Atlantic Health Group Inc.; senior vice president, secretary, general secretary: Nova Care Inc.

Gerald E. Johnston: president, chief executive officer B 1947. ED California State University, Fullerton BS. PRIM CORP EMPL president, chief executive officer: Clorox Co.

Karen M. Rose: group vice president, chief financial officer B Chicago, IL 1949. ED University of Pennsylvania MBA (1978). PRIM CORP EMPL group vice president, chief financial officer: Clorox Co. ADD CORP EMPL treasurer: Brita Products Co.; treasurer: Clorox International Co. Inc.; treasurer: Clorox Prod-

ucts Manufacturing Co.

G. Craig Sullivan: chairman B 1940. ED Boston College BS (1964). PRIM CORP EMPL chairman: Clorox Co.

Giving Program Officials

Karen M. Rose: member contributions committee (see above)

Foundation Officials

Peter D. Bewley: vice president, secretary (see above)

James A. Hasler: trustee

Daniel Heinrich: vice president, treasurer

Gerald E. Johnston: chairman (see above)

Patricia Martin: trustee

Steven Silberblatt: president

Soraya Wright: trustee

Grants Analysis

Disclosure Period: fiscal year ending June 31, 2004

Total Grants: $1,144,649*

Number of Grants: 80

Average Grant: $10,628*

Highest Grant: $105,000

Lowest Grant: $50

Typical Range: $2,000 to $20,000

*Note: Giving excludes matching gifts, scholarships, United Way. Average grant figure excludes three highest grants ($305,000).

Recent Grants

Note: Grants derived from 2003 Form 990.

General

107,500	East Bay Community Foundation, Oakland, CA
105,500	East Bay Community Foundation, Oakland, CA
105,000	East Bay Community Foundation, Oakland, CA
100,000	Chabot Space and Science Center, Oakland, CA -- for educational programs
100,000	Oakland Zoo, Oakland, CA -- towards children's zoo
97,045	Citizens' Scholarship Foundation of America, Minneapolis, MN -- scholarships for children of Clorox employees
62,500	East Bay Community Foundation, Oakland, CA
60,000	East Bay Community Foundation, Oakland, CA
60,000	Special Olympics Northern California, CA
50,000	F.C. United Soccer Association Inc.

CLOWES FUND

Giving Contact

Elizabeth A. Casselman, Exec. Dir.
320 N. Meridian, Suite 316
Indianapolis, IN 46204-1722
Phone: (317)833-0144
Fax: (317)833-0145
E-mail: staff@clowesfund.org
Web: http://www.clowesfund.org

Description

Founded: 1952
EIN: 351079679
Organization Type: General Purpose Foundation
Giving Locations: IN: Indianapolis; MA
Grant Types: Capital, Endowment, General Support, Matching, Operating Expenses, Professorship, Project, Research, Scholarship, Seed Money.

Donor Information

Founder: The Clowes Fund was established in 1952 by the late Edith W. Clowes, George H. A. Clowes, and Allen W. Clowes.

Financial Summary

Total Giving: $5,587,500 (2004); $2,836,161 (2003); $2,990,452 (2002)

Giving Analysis: Giving for 2003 includes: foundation scholarships ($110,000)

Assets: $71,567,390 (2003); $60,363,210 (2002); $75,947,500 (2001)

Typical Recipients

Arts & Humanities: Arts Associations & Councils, Arts Centers, Arts Institutes, Arts Outreach, Ballet, Community Arts, Dance, Ethnic & Folk Arts, Film & Video, Arts & Humanities-General, Historic Preservation, History & Archaeology, Libraries, Museums/Galleries, Music, Opera, Performing Arts, Public Broadcasting, Theater, Visual Arts

Civic & Public Affairs: African American Affairs, Botanical Gardens/Parks, Community Foundations, Employment/Job Training, Civic & Public Affairs-General, Housing, Law & Justice, Nonprofit Management, Philanthropic Organizations, Public Policy, Urban & Community Affairs, Women's Affairs, Zoos/Aquariums

Education: Afterschool/Enrichment Programs, Arts/Humanities Education, Business-School Partnerships, Colleges & Universities, Education Associations, Education Funds, Elementary Education (Public), Faculty Development, Education-General, Gifted & Talented Programs, Leadership Training, Literacy, Medical Education, Minority Education, Preschool Education, Private Education (Precollege), Public Education (Precollege), Religious Education, Science/Mathematics Education, Secondary Education (Private), Student Aid, Vocational & Technical Education

Environment: Environment-General, Resource Conservation, Wildlife Protection

Health: Adolescent Health Issues, Alzheimer's Disease, Children's Health/Hospitals, Clinics/Medical Centers, Diabetes, Health Funds, Health Organizations, Hospices, Hospitals, Hospitals (University Affiliated), Medical Research, Nursing Services, Outpatient Health Care, Preventive Medicine/Wellness Organizations, Respiratory

International: Foreign Arts Organizations, Foreign Educational Institutions, International Development, International Relief Efforts

Religion: Churches, Ministries, Missionary Activities (Domestic), Religious Organizations, Religious Welfare, Seminaries

Science: Scientific Centers & Institutes, Scientific Labs, Scientific Organizations, Scientific Research

Social Services: At-Risk Youth, Big Brothers/Big Sisters, Camps, Child Abuse, Child Welfare, Community Centers, Community Service Organizations, Day Care, Domestic Violence, Family Planning, Family Services, Food/Clothing Distribution, Homes, People with Disabilities, Recreation & Athletics, Scouts, Senior Services, Shelters/Homelessness, Substance Abuse, United Funds/United Ways, YMCA/YWCA/YMHA/YWHA, Youth Organizations

Application Procedures

Initial Contact: Applicants should submit a letter or proposal to the fund.

Application Requirements: Proposals should include a description of organization, purpose for which the grant is sought, specific amount requested, budget for the proposal, financial statement, and copy of the IRS ruling of tax-exempt status. Two copies of this information is required. If any of the listed criteria is not included in the proposal, it will be considered unacceptable with no written notice given.

Deadlines: January 31.

Review Process: The fund's board meets once a year between April 1 and June 1 to consider proposals.

Restrictions

The fund does not make grants to individuals, or for publications, conferences, seminars, or religious evangelical doctrine.

Additional Information

The fund does not acknowledge receipt of grant proposals. The fund does not make available any kind of printed material for distribution and does not have a printed application.

Foundation Officials

Ben W. Blanton: director
Margaret C. Bowles: secretary
Elizabeth A. Casselman: executive director
Alexander W. Clowes: president B 1946. ED Harvard University AB (1968); Harvard University MD (1972). PRIM NONPR EMPL department vice chairman vascular surgery: University of Washington. NONPR AFFIL member: Society Vascular Surgery; chief division vascular surgery: University Washington; trustee: Seattle Symphony; member: Sigma Xi; trustee: Marine Biology Laboratory (Woods Hole MA); member: Seattle Surgical Society; member: International Society Applied Cardiovascular Biology; member: American Society Cell Biology; member: American Surgical Association; member: American Heart Association; member: American Association Pathologists. CLUB AFFIL Quisset Yacht Club; Cruising Club America Club.
Edith W. Clowes: director
Jonathan J. Clowes: director
Margaret J. Clowes: vice president ED Bryn Mawr College (1937).
Thomas J. Clowes: director
William H. Marshall: treasurer
Donna L. Wiley: director

Grants Analysis

Disclosure Period: calendar year ending 2004
Total Grants: $5,587,500
Number of Grants: 115
Average Grant: $31,469*
Highest Grant: $2,000,000
Lowest Grant: $5,000
Typical Range: $10,000 to $50,000
*Note: Average grant figure excludes highest grant.

Recent Grants

Note: Grants derived from 2003 Form 990.

General

200,000	Case Western Reserve University, Cleveland, OH -- for innovations in medical education
150,000	Oberlin College, Oberlin, OH
125,000	Indiana University Foundation, Bloomington, IN -- to support Thomas M. Lofton scholarship fund
120,000	Indianapolis Museum of Art, Indianapolis, IN -- grant for Clowes Pavilion maintenance
120,000	Seattle Symphony, Seattle, WA
100,000	Herron School of Art, Bloomington, IN
100,000	James Whitcomb Riley Memorial Association, Indianapolis, IN
100,000	Seattle Center Foundation, Seattle, WA
60,000	Planned Parenthood of Central and Southern Indiana Inc., Indianapolis, IN
50,000	Evergreen School, Shoreline, WA

CNA FINANCIAL CORP.

Company Headquarters

CNA Plaza
Chicago, IL 60685
Web: http://www.cna.com

Company Description

Ticker: CNA
Exchange: OTC
Acquired: Buckeye Union Insurance Co..
Assets: US$65.968 billion (2001)
Employees: 12100 (2003)

SIC(s): 6311 Life Insurance, 6321 Accident & Health Insurance, 6331 Fire, Marine & Casualty Insurance.

Operating Locations

CNA (FL--Orlando; PA--Reading; TN--Nashville)

Nonmonetary Support

Type: Donated Equipment; In-kind Services
Note: Co. provides nonmonetary support.

CNA Foundation

Giving Contact

Sarah Pang, Executive Director
CNA Plaza
Chicago, IL 60685
Phone: (312)822-5194

Description

Founded: 1995
EIN: 364029026
Organization Type: Corporate Foundation
Giving Locations: in communities where co. has a presence.
Grant Types: Employee Matching Gifts, General Support, Multiyear/Continuing Support, Operating Expenses, Scholarship.
Note: Employee matching gift ratio: 1 to 1.

Financial Summary

Total Giving: $3,108,362 (2003); $2,286,319 (2001). Note: Contributes through corporate direct giving program and foundation.
Assets: $15,135,270 (2003); $22,309,578 (2001)
Gifts Received: $1,000,000 (1998); $481,000 (1997); $284,694 (1995). Note: Contributions were received from CNA.

Typical Recipients

Arts & Humanities: Arts Associations & Councils, Arts Festivals, Arts Institutes, Arts Outreach, Dance, Historic Preservation, History & Archaeology, Libraries, Literary Arts, Museums/Galleries, Music, Opera, Performing Arts, Theater

Civic & Public Affairs: African American Affairs, Asian American Affairs, Botanical Gardens/Parks, Business/Free Enterprise, Chambers of Commerce, Civil Rights, Clubs, Community Foundations, Employment/Job Training, Civic & Public Affairs-General, Hispanic Affairs, Housing, Law & Justice, Nonprofit Management, Philanthropic Organizations, Professional & Trade Associations, Public Policy, Safety, Urban & Community Affairs, Women's Affairs, Zoos/Aquariums

Education: Afterschool/Enrichment Programs, Arts/Humanities Education, Business Education, Colleges & Universities, Continuing Education, Economic Education, Education Associations, Education Funds, Elementary Education (Private), Faculty Development, Education-General, Literacy, Minority Education, Preschool Education, Private Education (Precollege), Public Education (Precollege), Science/Mathematics Education, Student Aid

Health: AIDS/HIV, Cancer, Children's Health/Hospitals, Diabetes, Emergency/Ambulance Services, Health-General, Health Organizations, Heart, Hospitals, Medical Rehabilitation, Medical Research, Mental Health, Single-Disease Health Associations

International: International Organizations, Missionary/Religious Activities

Religion: Jewish Causes, Religious Organizations, Religious Welfare

Social Services: Child Abuse, Child Welfare, Community Service Organizations, Counseling, Delinquency & Criminal Rehabilitation, Family Services, Food/Clothing Distribution, Homes, People with Disabilities, Recreation & Athletics, Scouts, Shelters/Homelessness, Social Services-General, United Funds/United Ways, YMCA/YWCA/YMHA/YWHA, Youth Organizations

Application Procedures

Initial Contact: Request guidelines; then submit proposal.

Application Requirements: Include a description of the organization with its mission and project to be supported, a needs statement and objectives (no more than one page); amount requested and rationale; latest audited financial statement; proof of tax-exempt status; and names and amounts of other contributors; description of benefits to be realized and population to be served; plans for evaluating and reporting results; a current budget; and the names and affiliations of trustees or board of directors.

Deadlines: None.

Restrictions

Does not support individuals; religious organizations for sectarian purposes; capital campaigns; political or lobbying groups; veterans, labor, alumni, military, or fraternal organizations; social clubs; professional associations; organizations that discriminate by race, color, creed, gender, national origin or disability; endowed chairs or professorships; general endowments; United Way affiliated agencies; ad books, goodwill advertising, raffles, etc.; tickets for testimonials or benefits; documentaries, films, videos, or media projects; national groups whose local chapters receive CNA support; foundations that make grants; trips or travel by student groups; or organizations, programs or projects that pose a conflict of interest. The foundation does not make grants to organizations that are not classified as 501(c)(3) tax-exempt.

Additional Information

Company publishes a corporate contribution guidelines sheet.

CNA Insurance Companies is affiliated with CNA Financial Corporation, Continental Casualty Company, and Continental Assurance Company. Company. Company. Company.

Corporate Officials

Antoinette Cook Bush: partnerchr, co-chief executive officer, director PRIM CORP EMPL partner: Skadden, Arps, Slate, Meagher & Flom. CORP AFFIL director: CNA Financial Corp.

Peter E. Jokiel: senior vice president, chief financial officer B 1947. ED Northern Illinois University (1972). PRIM CORP EMPL senior vice president, chief financial officer: CNA Financial Corp. CORP AFFIL chief financial officer: Transportation Insurance Co.; vice president: Valley Forge Life Insurance Co.; chief financial officer: Transcontinental Insurance Co. New York; chief financial officer: Continental Loss Adjusting Services; vice president: Firemens Insurance Newark New Jersey; vice president: Continental Insurance Co. New Jersey; chief financial officer: Continental Casualty Co.; vice president: Continental Corp.; senior vice president: Continental Assurance Co.; chief financial officer: CNA Casualty California; chief financial officer: Columbia Casualty Corp.; senior vice president: American Casualty Reading Pennsylvania.

Preston Robert Tisch: co-chairman, co-chief executive officer, director B Brooklyn, NY 1926. ED Bucknell University (1943-1944); University of Michigan BA (1948). PRIM CORP EMPL co-chairman, director: Loews Corp. ADD CORP EMPL owner, chief executive officer, chairman: New York Football Giants Inc. CORP AFFIL director: Transcontinental Insurance Co. New York; director: Hasbro Inc.; director: Rite Aid Corp.; director: CNA Financial Corp.; director: Bulova Corp. NONPR AFFIL trustee: New York University; member: Sigma Alpha Mu; chairman emeritus: New York Convention & Visitor Bureau; president: Citymeals Wheels; member: Governments Business Advisory Council New York. CLUB AFFIL Rye Racquet Club; Century Country Club.

Foundation Officials

Joyce Donaly: treasurer
Dennis Hemme: vice president
Lori Komstadius: director
Jim Lewis: director
Steve Lilienthal: chairman, director
Sarah Pang: executive director
Tom Pontarelli: president, director
Sandy Wagman: vice president, secretary
Steve Westman: vice president
Peter Wilson: director

Grants Analysis

Disclosure Period: calendar year ending 2003
Total Grants: $2,226,660*
Number of Grants: 61
Average Grant: $22,815*
Highest Grant: $500,000
Lowest Grant: $250
Typical Range: $5,000 to $50,000
*Note: Giving excludes scholarship; matching gifts. Average grant figure excludes two highest grants ($880,600).

Recent Grants

Note: Grants derived from 2003 Form 990.
Library-Related
50,000	PLUS, Chicago, IL

General
500,000	Mathcounts, Alexandria, VA
380,600	Community Involvement Grant Awards, Chicago, IL
280,000	Kaboomi, Chicago, IL
247,000	USO of Illinois, Chicago, IL
200,000	Boys and Girls Club, Chicago, IL
171,830	National Merit Scholarship, Evanston, IL
80,000	University Scholarships, Chicago, IL
60,000	Junior Achievement, Colorado Springs, CO
50,000	Young Chicago Authors, Chicago, IL
34,000	Starlight Children's Foundation, London United Kingdom

COBB FAMILY FOUNDATION

Giving Contact

Charles E. Cobb, Jr., President
255 Aragon Avenue, Suite 333
Coral Gables, FL 33134
Phone: (305)441-1700
Fax: (305)445-5674

Description

Founded: 1984
EIN: 592477459
Organization Type: Private Foundation
Giving Locations: FL: Dade County
Grant Types: Capital, General Support.

Donor Information

Founder: Charles E. Cobb, Jr.

Financial Summary

Total Giving: $528,345 (fiscal year ending September 30, 2001)

Giving Analysis: Giving for fiscal 2001 includes: foundation scholarships ($2,000); foundation grants to United Way ($35,000).

Assets: $9,194,561 (fiscal 2001)

Gifts Received: $144,688 (fiscal 2001); $216,875 (fiscal 2000); $490,250 (fiscal 1997). Note: In fiscal 1994, 2000, and 2001, contributions were received from Charles E. Cobb, Jr.

Typical Recipients

Arts & Humanities: Arts Centers, Arts Funds, Film & Video, Libraries, Music, Public Broadcasting

Civic & Public Affairs: Clubs, Ethnic Organizations, Civic & Public Affairs-General, Municipalities/Towns, Philanthropic Organizations, Urban & Community Affairs, Zoos/Aquariums

Education: Business Education, Colleges & Universities, Economic Education, Elementary Education (Public), Education-General, International Exchange, Leadership Training, Legal Education, Medical Education, Private Education (Precollege), Science/Mathematics Education, Student Aid

Environment: Environment-General, Resource Conservation

Health: Cancer, Emergency/Ambulance Services, Medical Research, Prenatal Health Issues, Single-Disease Health Associations, Trauma Treatment

International: International Affairs, International Organizations, International Peace & Security Issues, International Relief Efforts, Trade

Religion: Churches, Jewish Causes, Religious Welfare, Social/Policy Issues

Social Services: At-Risk Youth, Camps, Child Welfare, Emergency Relief, Family Services, People with Disabilities, Recreation & Athletics, Shelters/Homelessness, Social Services-General, United Funds/United Ways, Youth Organizations

Application Procedures

Initial Contact: Send a brief letter of inquiry.

Application Requirements: Include a description of organization, list of members of the board of directors and senior executives, current annual budget, percent of management/administration costs to dollars distributed, purpose of funds sought, amount requested, and proof of tax-exempt status.

Deadlines: None.

Restrictions

Contributions are made to institutions of higher education and selected charities that promote the quality of life in communities where the Cobb family has an established interest.

Foundation Officials

Charles E. Cobb, Jr.: president B Fresno, CA 1936. ED Stanford University BA (1958); Stanford University MBA (1962). PRIM CORP EMPL senior partner: Cobb Partners. CORP AFFIL chairman, chief executive officer: Pan America Corp. NONPR AFFIL chairman board trustees: University Miami.

Christian M. Cobb: vice president
Sue M. Cobb: vice president
Tobin T. Cobb: vice president

Grants Analysis

Disclosure Period: fiscal year ending September 30, 2001
Total Grants: $491,345*
Number of Grants: 109
Average Grant: $3,392*
Highest Grant: $125,000
Lowest Grant: $500
Typical Range: $1,000 to $5,000
*Note: Giving excludes scholarships and United Way. Average grant figure excludes highest grant.

Recent Grants

Note: Grants derived from fiscal 2002 Form 990.
General
100,000	Stanford University, Stanford, CA -- for press box for track
75,000	University of Miami, Miami, FL -- for Cobb Stadium endowment
50,000	University of Miami, Miami, FL -- for Cobb Stadium
25,000	Plymouth Church, Coconut Grove, FL -- pledge
25,000	Stanford University, Stanford, CA -- for Cobb track and Angell field

25,000	United Way of Dade County, Miami, FL
25,000	University of Miami, Miami, FL -- for President's Fund
21,000	United Way Jamaica, Kingston Jamaica
20,000	University of Miami, Miami, FL -- for Miller endowed chair
12,500	University of Miami, Miami, FL -- for Hurricane Club

COCA-COLA CO.

Company Headquarters
1 Coca-Cola Plaza
Atlanta, GA 30313
Web: http://www.cocacola.com

Company Description
Founded: 1886
Ticker: KO
Exchange: NYSE
Revenue: US$21.962 billion (2004)
Profit: US$4.847 billion (2004)
Employees: 49000 (2003)
Fortune Rank: 92, per FORTUNE Magazine's list of 500 Largest U.S. Corporations (2004).
SIC(s): 2037 Frozen Fruits & Vegetables, 2086 Bottled & Canned Soft Drinks, 2087 Flavoring Extracts & Syrups Nec, 2099 Food Preparations Nec.

Operating Locations
Coca-Cola Co. (FL--Maitland; IL--Downers Grove; OH--Cincinnati; PA--Blandon)

Nonmonetary Support
Type: Donated Equipment; Donated Products
Note: NOT NOT Company donates computers recently removed from service.
Volunteer Programs: Company sponsors an employee volunteer reaching-out program.
Contact: Kirk Glaze

Coca-Cola Foundation

Giving Contact
Ingrid Saunders-Jones, Chairman
Coca-Cola Foundation
One Coca-Cola Plaza NW
Atlanta, GA 30313
Phone: (404)676-3525
Fax: (404)676-8804
Web: http://www2.coca-cola.com/citizenship/foundation.html

Alternate Contact
Phone: (404)676-6480

Description
Founded: 1984
EIN: 581574705
Organization Type: Corporate Foundation
Giving Locations: internationally; nationally.
Grant Types: Capital, Challenge, Employee Matching Gifts, Endowment, Fellowship, General Support, Multiyear/Continuing Support, Project, Scholarship.
Note: Employee matching gift ratio: 2 to 1.

Financial Summary
Total Giving: $18,537,628 (2003); $15,873,978 (2002); $12,141,774 (2001). Note: Contributes through corporate direct giving program and foundation.
Assets: $27,113,908 (2003); $40,840,716 (2002); $59,075,032 (2001)
Gifts Received: $51,302,278 (2000); $200,001 (1998); $4,928,297 (1996). Note: In 1998 and 1999, contributions were received from the Coca-Cola Company.

Typical Recipients
Arts & Humanities: Arts Festivals, Ballet, Arts & Humanities-General, Historic Preservation, History & Archaeology, Libraries, Museums/Galleries, Music, Opera, Performing Arts, Theater
Civic & Public Affairs: African American Affairs, Botanical Gardens/Parks, Business/Free Enterprise, Civil Rights, Community Foundations, Civic & Public Affairs-General, Hispanic Affairs, Native American Affairs, Public Policy, Urban & Community Affairs
Education: Afterschool/Enrichment Programs, Arts/Humanities Education, Business Education, Colleges & Universities, Continuing Education, Education Associations, Education Funds, Education Reform, Elementary Education (Private), Engineering/Technological Education, Environmental Education, Faculty Development, Education-General, Health & Physical Education, International Exchange, International Studies, Leadership Training, Legal Education, Literacy, Medical Education, Minority Education, Private Education (Precollege), Public Education (Precollege), Science/Mathematics Education, Social Sciences Education, Student Aid, Vocational & Technical Education
Health: Adolescent Health Issues, Children's Health/Hospitals, Mental Health
International: Foreign Arts Organizations, Foreign Educational Institutions, International-General, Health Care/Hospitals, International Affairs, International Development, International Environmental Issues, International Organizations, International Relief Efforts
Science: Science Museums, Scientific Centers & Institutes
Social Services: Community Service Organizations, Emergency Relief, Recreation & Athletics, YMCA/YWCA/YMHA/YWHA, Youth Organizations

Application Procedures
Initial Contact: Call or check the company's web site to obtain an application form.
Application Requirements: Completed application with program summary of no more than five pages. Information should include organization's mission; general program description, an explanation of why it is appropriate for Coca-Cola Foundation to help fund the project; financial statement; board of directors; proof of tax-exempt status; a statement on letterhead indicating that there is no change in purpose of organization since the issuance of the IRS letters; total project cost and amount requested; and a plan for measuring the success of the project.
Deadlines: None.
Decision Notification: Applications are accepted and reviewed continuously; notification is made within 60 days.
Notes: If proposal is being considered for funding, further communication may be required.

Restrictions
Foundation does not make grants to individuals; religious organizations or endeavors; political, legislative, lobbying or fraternal organizations; veterans organizations; fundraising events; advertising, magazines, or articles in professional journals; or organizations that do not have tax-exempt status under IRS Code Section 501(c)(3).

Additional Information
Foundation prefers to support direct service projects and programs rather than making contributions to intermediary funding agencies.
Preference is given to proposals that identify clearly defined need, describe an innovative way to meet that need, demonstrate the applicant's ability to implement the process, and show how the program will benefit the general community.
Special consideration is given to organizations that effectively engage volunteers in reaching their goals.

Corporate Officials
Carlton L. Curtis: vice president, executive vice president ED University of Georgia BA. NONPR AFFIL director: National 4-H Council; trustee: University of Georgia Foundation; board government: Children's Miracle Network; board governors: Howard School of Atlanta.
Gary P. Fayard: chief financial officer, executive vice president ED University of Alabama BA. CORP AFFIL director: Coca-Cola Panamco; director: Coca-Cola SABCO. NONPR AFFIL director: Atlanta Area Council of Boy Scouts; director: Finance Executive Institute; member: American Institute of CPAs.
Ingrid Saunders Jones: senior vice president B Detroit, MI 1945. ED Michigan State University BA (1968); Eastern Michigan University MA (1972). PRIM CORP EMPL senior vice president: The Coca-Cola Co. NONPR AFFIL board of directors: Coca-Cola Scholars Foundation.

Foundation Officials
John H. Downs, Jr.: secretary, director NONPR AFFIL director: Georgia Chamber of Commerce; director: National PTA.
Gary P. Fayard: treasurer, director (see above)
Ingrid Saunders Jones: chairman, director (see above)
Helen Smith Price: director ED Atlanta University MBA; Spelman College BS. NONPR AFFIL trustee: Atlanta Metro College Foundation; advisory committee: Morehouse College Leadership Institute; director: Atlanta Girls' School; director: Alliance Theatre; member: American Institute of CPAs.

Grants Analysis
Disclosure Period: calendar year ending 2003
Total Grants: $17,835,628*
Number of Grants: 124
Average Grant: $128,745*
Highest Grant: $2,000,000
Lowest Grant: $5,000
Typical Range: $10,000 to $200,000
*Note: Giving excludes scholarship. Average grant figure excludes highest grant.

Recent Grants
Note: Grants derived from 2003 Form 990.

General

2,000,000	American Red Cross, Washington, DC -- for national disaster relief fund
1,250,000	Foundation for Community Development Mozambique -- for flood relief
1,000,000	China Youth Development Foundation, Beijing People's Republic of China -- for first generation scholarships
1,000,000	Coca-Cola Africa Foundation, Swaziland Republic of South Africa -- HIV/AIDS educational programs
1,000,000	Coca-Cola Africa Foundation, Swaziland Republic of South Africa -- towards HIV/AIDS awareness programs
600,000	Morehouse College, Atlanta, GA -- towards campaign for a new century
500,000	East Lake Community Foundation, Atlanta, GA -- towards educational village
450,000	Atlanta International School Inc., Atlanta, GA
350,000	Emory University, Atlanta, GA -- towards Donna and Marvin Schwartz center for performing arts
350,000	Hianganani Help Center, Swaziland Republic of South Africa -- towards HIV/AIDS awareness program

COCKRELL FOUNDATION

Giving Contact

M. Nancy Williams, Executive Vice President
1600 Smith, Suite 3250
Houston, TX 77002-7348
Phone: (713)209-7500
Fax: (713)209-7599
E-mail: foundation@cockrell.com
Web: http://www.cockrell.com/foundation/default.asp

Description

Founded: 1966
EIN: 746076993
Organization Type: Family Foundation
Giving Locations: TX: Houston
Grant Types: Capital, Endowment, General Support, Matching, Multiyear/Continuing Support, Operating Expenses, Scholarship.

Donor Information

Founder: Established in 1957 by Mrs. Dula Cockrell and Ernest Cockrell Jr.. Incorporated in 1966, the foundation's assets increased substantially, with almost $4 million bequeathed by Mr. Cockrell's estate. Members of the Cockrell family are among the six-member board of directors.

Financial Summary

Total Giving: $5,910,017 (2003); $8,249,001 (2002); $7,690,000 (2001)
Giving Analysis: Giving for 2003 includes: foundation grants to United Way ($10,000); foundation scholarships ($1,500,000)
Assets: $122,720,966 (2003)

Typical Recipients

Arts & Humanities: Arts Outreach, Arts & Humanities-General, Historic Preservation, Libraries, Museums/Galleries, Music, Theater
Civic & Public Affairs: Botanical Gardens/Parks, Business/Free Enterprise, Clubs, Economic Development, Economic Policy, Civic & Public Affairs-General, Hispanic Affairs, Housing, Law & Justice, Municipalities/Towns, Safety, Urban & Community Affairs, Women's Affairs, Zoos/Aquariums
Education: Business Education, Colleges & Universities, Economic Education, Education Associations, Engineering/Technological Education, Faculty Development, Education-General, Legal Education, Literacy, Medical Education, Public Education (Precollege), Special Education, Student Aid
Environment: Environment-General, Resource Conservation
Health: Adolescent Health Issues, Alzheimer's Disease, Cancer, Children's Health/Hospitals, Clinics/Medical Centers, Diabetes, Emergency/Ambulance Services, Eyes/Blindness, Health Organizations, Heart, Hospices, Hospitals, Medical Research, Mental Health, Prenatal Health Issues, Single-Disease Health Associations, Speech & Hearing
International: International Relief Efforts
Religion: Churches, Jewish Causes, Ministries, Religious Organizations, Religious Welfare
Science: Science Museums
Social Services: At-Risk Youth, Camps, Child Abuse, Child Welfare, Community Centers, Community Service Organizations, Day Care, Family Planning, Family Services, Food/Clothing Distribution, Homes, People with Disabilities, Recreation & Athletics, Scouts, Senior Services, Shelters/Homelessness, Social Services-General, United Funds/United Ways, YMCA/YWCA/YMHA/YWHA, Youth Organizations

Application Procedures

Initial Contact: The foundation has no standard application form. Organizations should send a detailed letter of inquiry outlining their grant proposal.

Application Requirements: Applicants should include in the letter: a brief statement of need; statement of goals; a project budget including the total cost; amount raised to date, including other sources of funding (i.e. private, government, individuals, board members, etc.); plans for raising any uncovered balance; statement of project status; amount requested; description of plans for putting project on self-sustaining basis, plus an estimate of cost; and a list of officers and directors of the organization. Also include a copy of the IRS letter of 501(c)(3) tax exemption, a copy of current annual budget and latest Form 990, and latest audited financial statement.
Deadlines: None.
Review Process: The foundation board meets in Spring and Fall. Generally, decisions are made within six weeks of the meetings.

Restrictions

The foundation does not give to individuals or fund political or lobbying groups.

Additional Information

Publications: Annual Report; Guidelines

Foundation Officials

Douglas E. Bryant: secretary, treasurer
Ernest Harris Cockrell: president, director B Houston, TX 1945. ED University of Texas, Austin BS (1967); University of Texas MBA (1970). PRIM CORP EMPL president, chief executive officer, director: Cockrell Oil Corp. CORP AFFIL director: Pennzoil Co.
Janet S. Cockrell: director
Carol Cockrell Curran: director CORP AFFIL officer: Cockrell Oil Corp.; officer: Cockrell Resources Inc.
Richard B. Curran: director CORP AFFIL director: Intellicall Inc.
Milton T. Graves: vice president, director B Okmulgee, OK 1936. ED Sam Houston State University BBA (1958). PRIM CORP EMPL executive vice president, chief financial officer, director: Cockrell Oil Corp. CORP AFFIL vice president, director: Cockrell Resources Inc.; president, director: Texas Production Co.; president, director: Cockrell Interests Inc.
J. Webb Jennings, III: director
Laura Jennings Turner: director
M. Nancy Williams: executive vice president PRIM CORP EMPL secretary, treasurer: Sprint Press.

Grants Analysis

Disclosure Period: calendar year ending 2003
Total Grants: $4,400,017*
Number of Grants: 43
Average Grant: $25,108*
Highest Grant: $3,345,500
Lowest Grant: $1,000
Typical Range: $5,000 to $50,000
*Note: Giving excludes scholarships and United Way. Average grant figure excludes highest grant.

Recent Grants

Note: Grants derived from 2002 Form 990.
General

3,333,000	Boy Scouts of America, Houston, TX -- constructing Cockrell Memorial Scout Training and Service Center
1,423,320	Baylor College of Medicine, Houston, TX -- funding researchers for clinical research initiative
750,000	Texas Heart Institute, Houston, TX -- capital campaign
550,000	University of Texas Engineering, Austin, TX -- scholarship fund
400,000	TIRR Foundation, Houston, TX -- endowment campaign
300,000	American Red Cross, Houston, TX -- capital campaign "Keeping the Promise"
250,000	Houston CEO Foundation, Houston, TX -- Scholarship program
250,000	University of Texas Health Science Center, Houston, TX -- TexGen Project
200,000	Greater Houston Collaborative for Children, Houston, TX -- program costs and collaborative support
200,000	Houston Museum of Natural Science, Houston, TX -- Technology Improvement Program

GEORGE W. CODRINGTON CHARITABLE FOUNDATION

Giving Contact

Raymond T. Sawyer
c/o Key Trust Co. of OH, N.A.
127 Public Square, 39th Floor
Cleveland, OH 44114
Phone: (216)828-9770

Description

Founded: 1955
EIN: 346507457
Organization Type: Private Foundation
Giving Locations: OH: Cuyahoga County including surrounding area
Grant Types: General Support.

Donor Information

Founder: the late George W. Codrington

Financial Summary

Total Giving: $1,165,820 (2003)
Giving Analysis: Giving for 2003 includes: foundation grants to United Way ($15,000); foundation scholarships ($95,000)
Assets: $17,818,623 (2003)
Gifts Received: $556,880 (1992). Note: In 1992, contributions were received from William S. McKinstry.

Typical Recipients

Arts & Humanities: Arts Centers, Arts Institutes, Arts Outreach, Ballet, Community Arts, Dance, Historic Preservation, History & Archaeology, Libraries, Museums/Galleries, Music, Opera, Performing Arts, Public Broadcasting, Theater
Civic & Public Affairs: Botanical Gardens/Parks, Business/Free Enterprise, Community Foundations, Employment/Job Training, Civic & Public Affairs-General, Legal Aid, Parades/Festivals, Public Policy, Safety, Urban & Community Affairs
Education: Business Education, Colleges & Universities, Community & Junior Colleges, Economic Education, Education Funds, Education Reform, Faculty Development, Education-General, Minority Education, Private Education (Precollege), Public Education (Precollege), Science/Mathematics Education, Social Sciences Education, Student Aid
Environment: Environment-General
Health: AIDS/HIV, Cancer, Children's Health/Hospitals, Clinics/Medical Centers, Diabetes, Emergency/Ambulance Services, Eyes/Blindness, Health-General, Hospitals, Hospitals (University Affiliated), Medical Research, Nursing Services, Prenatal Health Issues, Public Health, Speech & Hearing
International: Foreign Arts Organizations, International Affairs
Religion: Ministries, Religious Organizations, Religious Welfare
Science: Science Museums, Scientific Centers & Institutes
Social Services: Camps, Child Welfare, Community Centers, Community Service Organizations, Domestic Violence, Family Planning, Family Services, Food/Clothing Distribution, People with Disabilities, Recre-

ation & Athletics, Scouts, Senior Services, Social Services-General, Substance Abuse, United Funds/ United Ways, Volunteer Services, YMCA/YWCA/ YMHA/YWHA, Youth Organizations

Application Procedures

Initial Contact: Send a brief letter of inquiry.
Application Requirements: Include amount requested, purpose of funds sought, a brief history of the organization, the area served by the applicant, a description of the applicant's contributions to the area, and a listing of the applicant's officers and trustees.
Review Process: Supervisory board meets in March, June, September, November, and December to review applications.

Restrictions

Provides only annual grants. Does not support individuals or provide loans.

Additional Information

Publications: Annual Report (including Application Guidelines)
Trust(s): Key Bank OH NA

Foundation Officials

John J. Dwyer: mem supervisory board
William E. McDonald: mem supervisory board B Murphy, NC 1942. ED Western Carolina University (1967); East Tennessee State University (1979). PRIM CORP EMPL president, chief operating officer: United Telephone System Southeast. CORP AFFIL president: Sprint Mid-Atlantic Telecom.
Raymond Terry Sawyer: chairman B Cleveland, OH 1943. ED Yale University BA (1965); Harvard University LLB (1968). PRIM CORP EMPL partner: Thompson, Hine & Flory. NONPR AFFIL director: Premix; member: Yale University Alumni Association; secretary, member executive committee: Metro Health System; member: Ohio State Bar Association; member: Cleveland Bar Association; trustee: Cleveland Orchestra; member: American Bar Association; trustee: Cleveland Ballet.
William Robert Seelbach: mem supervisory board B Lakewood, OH 1948. ED Yale University BS (1970); Stanford University MBA (1972). PRIM CORP EMPL chairman: Inverness Partners. CORP AFFIL director: Lumitex Inc. NONPR AFFIL trustee: Playhouse Square Foundation; trustee: University School; trustee: Nebraska Ohio Council; trustee: Enterprise Development Council.

Grants Analysis

Disclosure Period: calendar year ending 2003
Total Grants: $1,055,820*
Number of Grants: 123
Average Grant: $8,584
Highest Grant: $100,000
Typical Range: $1,000 to $10,000
*Note: Giving excludes United Way and scholarships.

Recent Grants

Note: Grants derived from 2001 Form 990.
General
125,000	Enterprise Development, Inc.
100,000	Case Western Reserve University, Cleveland, OH
80,000	United Way Services
75,000	George W. Codorington Charitable Foundation, Cleveland, OH
59,041	Early Stage Partners
40,000	Cleveland Orchestra, Cleveland, OH
35,000	Educational Television Association of Metropolitan Cleveland, Cleveland, OH
30,000	Baldwin-Wallace College, Berea, OH
25,000	Salvation Army, Cleveland, OH
20,000	Children's Aid Society, New York, NY

CHARLES S. AND MARY COEN FAMILY FOUNDATION

Giving Contact

Mona L. Thompson, Trustee
PO Box 34
Washington, PA 15301
Phone: (724)223-5503

Description

Founded: 1959
EIN: 256033877
Organization Type: Private Foundation
Giving Locations: PA: Washington; WV: St. Mary's
Grant Types: General Support.

Donor Information

Founder: the late C. S. Coen, the late Mary Coen, Charles R. Coen, C. S. Coen Land Co.

Financial Summary

Total Giving: $705,010 (fiscal year ending February 28, 2002); $598,090 (fiscal 2001)
Giving Analysis: Giving for fiscal 2002 includes: foundation grants to United Way ($6,000); fiscal 2001: foundation grants to United Way ($4,500)
Assets: $9,050,468 (fiscal 2002); $7,889,299 (fiscal 2001)
Gifts Received: $227,680 (fiscal 2002); $76,000 (fiscal 2001); $50,000 (fiscal 2000). Note: In fiscal 1999, 2000, 2001, and 2002 contributions were received from the estate of C. S. Coen.

Typical Recipients

Arts & Humanities: Historic Preservation, History & Archaeology, Libraries, Museums/Galleries, Music
Civic & Public Affairs: Botanical Gardens/Parks, Clubs, Civic & Public Affairs-General, Housing, Safety
Education: Business Education, Colleges & Universities, Education Funds, Literacy, Minority Education, Private Education (Precollege), Public Education (Precollege)
Environment: Resource Conservation
Health: Children's Health/Hospitals, Clinics/Medical Centers, Health-General, Hospices, Hospitals, Long-Term Care, Medical Research, Single-Disease Health Associations
International: Health Care/Hospitals
Religion: Churches, Religious Welfare
Social Services: Big Brothers/Big Sisters, Camps, Child Welfare, Community Centers, Community Service Organizations, Homes, People with Disabilities, Recreation & Athletics, Scouts, Senior Services, Substance Abuse, United Funds/United Ways, YMCA/YWCA/YMHA/YWHA, Youth Organizations

Application Procedures

Initial Contact: Send a brief letter of inquiry.
Deadlines: None.

Restrictions

Does not support individuals.

Foundation Officials

Charles R. Coen: trustee
Mona Thompson: trustee
Lawrence A. Withum, Jr.: trustee

Grants Analysis

Disclosure Period: fiscal year ending February 28, 2002
Total Grants: $699,010*
Number of Grants: 105
Average Grant: $5,808*
Highest Grant: $95,000
Lowest Grant: $100
Typical Range: $1,000 to $10,000

*Note: Giving excludes United Way. Average grant excludes highest grant.

Recent Grants

Note: Grants derived from fiscal 2002 Form 990.
General
95,000	Presbyterian Senior Care, Washington, PA
70,000	Washington and Jefferson College, Washington, DC
65,000	Wilson College, Chambersburg, PA
56,000	Church of the Covenant, Washington, PA
40,000	Washington Hospital Foundation, Washington, PA
35,000	Central Presbyterian Church, Massillon, OH
26,000	United Cerebral Palsy, Washington, PA
25,000	Colonial Williamsburg Foundation, Williamsburg, VA
25,000	Fourth Presbyterian Church, Washington, PA
25,000	Washington County Health Partners, Inc., Washington, PA

COGSWELL BENEVOLENT TRUST

Giving Contact

David P. Goodwin, Trustee
1001 Elm St.
Manchester, NH 03101
Phone: (603)622-4013

Description

Founded: 1929
EIN: 020235690
Organization Type: Private Foundation
Giving Locations: NH
Grant Types: Endowment, General Support, Operating Expenses.

Donor Information

Founder: the late Leander A. Cogswell

Financial Summary

Total Giving: $1,037,868 (2003); $1,151,296 (2002); $917,749 (2001)
Giving Analysis: Giving for 2003 includes: foundation grants to United Way ($40,000); 2002: foundation grants to United Way ($55,000)
Assets: $25,303,880 (2003); $20,518,169 (2002); $25,230,873 (2001)

Typical Recipients

Arts & Humanities: Arts Associations & Councils, Arts Centers, Community Arts, Arts & Humanities-General, Historic Preservation, History & Archaeology, Libraries, Museums/Galleries, Music, Performing Arts, Public Broadcasting, Theater
Civic & Public Affairs: Botanical Gardens/Parks, Chambers of Commerce, Ethnic Organizations, Civic & Public Affairs-General, Housing, Municipalities/Towns, Urban & Community Affairs
Education: Arts/Humanities Education, Colleges & Universities, Faculty Development, Health & Physical Education, Minority Education, Preschool Education, Private Education (Precollege), Science/Mathematics Education, Secondary Education (Private), Special Education, Student Aid
Environment: Forestry, Environment-General, Resource Conservation, Watershed
Health: AIDS/HIV, Children's Health/Hospitals, Clinics/Medical Centers, Emergency/Ambulance Services, Eyes/Blindness, Geriatric Health, Health Policy/Cost Containment, Hospices, Hospitals, Long-Term Care, Medical Rehabilitation, Mental Health, Prenatal Health Issues, Research/Studies Institutes,

Respiratory
Religion: Churches, Religious Welfare
Science: Scientific Centers & Institutes
Social Services: Animal Protection, At-Risk Youth, Camps, Child Welfare, Community Centers, Community Service Organizations, Day Care, Family Services, Food/Clothing Distribution, Homes, People with Disabilities, Recreation & Athletics, Scouts, Senior Services, Shelters/Homelessness, Social Services-General, Special Olympics, United Funds/United Ways, YMCA/YWCA/YMHA/YWHA, Youth Organizations

Application Procedures

Initial Contact: Send a brief letter of inquiry describing program or project.
Application Requirements: Include amount requested, purpose of funds sought, and name, address, and telephone number of contact person.
Deadlines: None.

Restrictions

The trust is restricted by will to donate 90 percent of funds within NH.

Foundation Officials

David P. Goodwin: trustee
Mark Northridge: trustee
Theodore Wadleigh: trustee

Grants Analysis

Disclosure Period: calendar year ending 2003
Total Grants: $997,868*
Number of Grants: 82
Average Grant: $11,393*
Highest Grant: $75,000
Lowest Grant: $450
Typical Range: $5,000 to $25,000
*Note: Giving excludes United Way. Average grant figure excludes highest grants.

Recent Grants

Note: Grants derived from 2001 Form 990.
General

60,000	Child Health Services, Manchester, NH -- for emergency operating expenses
50,000	Girls Incorporated, NH -- for Norwell Home Program support
50,000	Salvation Army of Manchester, Manchester, NH -- for Camp Expansion Program
50,000	United Way of Greater Manchester, Manchester, NH -- annual campaign
40,000	Weeks Medical Center, Lancaster, NH -- for purchase of mobile health care van
30,000	Cedarcrest Foundation, Keene, NH -- for building expansion project
25,000	Girls Incorporated, NH -- for emergency funding to meet immediate needs of children
25,000	Habitat for Humanity of Mount Washington Valley
25,000	New Horizons of New Hampshire, Manchester, NH -- for 8th annual Thanksgiving breakfast
25,000	Odyssey House, Manchester, NH -- for Youthbuild Odyssey Program

NAOMI AND NEHEMIAH COHEN FOUNDATION

Giving Contact

Alison McWilliams, Associate Director
PO Box 73708
Washington, DC 20056
Phone: (202)234-5454
Fax: (202)234-8797
E-mail: nncf@starpower.net

Description

Founded: 1959
EIN: 526054166
Organization Type: Family Foundation
Giving Locations: DC: Washington; Israel
Grant Types: Capital, General Support, Operating Expenses, Project.

Donor Information

Founder: Established in 1959 by the late Israel Cohen and the late Naomi Cohen. Mr. Cohen left the majority of his estimated $101 million estate to the foundation, boosting the foundation's assets to about $75 million.

Financial Summary

Total Giving: $4,082,500 (2002); $3,379,200 (2001)
Assets: $80,337,648 (2002); $87,419,263 (2001)
Gifts Received: $1,578,583 (2002); $10,208,399 (2001); $35,010,090 (1998). Note: In 2002, contributions were received from Daniel Solomon ($10,000), Diane and Stuart Brown ($10,000), the Estate of Israel Cohen ($8,414) and the estate of Lillian Cohen Solomon ($1,550,169).

Typical Recipients

Arts & Humanities: Arts Centers, Arts & Humanities-General, Libraries, Museums/Galleries, Music, Opera, Performing Arts, Public Broadcasting, Theater
Civic & Public Affairs: Civil Rights, Community Foundations, Economic Development, Economic Policy, Employment/Job Training, Ethnic Organizations, Civic & Public Affairs-General, Housing, Law & Justice, Philanthropic Organizations, Professional & Trade Associations, Public Policy, Safety, Urban & Community Affairs, Women's Affairs
Education: Agricultural Education, Colleges & Universities, Community & Junior Colleges, Education Funds, Environmental Education, Education-General, Legal Education, Medical Education, Minority Education, Preschool Education, Private Education (Precollege), Religious Education, Science/Mathematics Education, Secondary Education (Private), Special Education, Student Aid, Vocational & Technical Education
Environment: Air/Water Quality, Energy, Environment-General, Protection, Research, Resource Conservation, Watershed, Wildlife Protection
Health: Arthritis, Cancer, Children's Health/Hospitals, Clinics/Medical Centers, Diabetes, Emergency/Ambulance Services, Eyes/Blindness, Health-General, Health Organizations, Heart, Hospices, Hospitals, Hospitals (University Affiliated), Long-Term Care, Mental Health, Prenatal Health Issues, Single-Disease Health Associations
International: Foreign Arts Organizations, Foreign Educational Institutions, Health Care/Hospitals, International Organizations, International Peace & Security Issues, Missionary/Religious Activities
Religion: Churches, Religion-General, Jewish Causes, Ministries, Religious Organizations, Religious Welfare, Social/Policy Issues, Synagogues/Temples
Science: Observatories & Planetariums, Scientific Centers & Institutes, Scientific Research
Social Services: At-Risk Youth, Child Welfare, Community Centers, Community Service Organizations, Crime Prevention, Delinquency & Criminal Rehabilitation, Emergency Relief, Family Planning, Food/Clothing Distribution, Homes, People with Disabilities, Recreation & Athletics, Senior Services, Shelters/Homelessness, Social Services-General, Substance Abuse, United Funds/United Ways, Youth Organizations

Application Procedures

Initial Contact: The foundation has no formal grant procedure or grant application form. Send a brief letter of inquiry accompanied by a current operating budget, a list of institutional funders and the amounts

of their grants, and a copy of your organization's IRS determination letter of 501(c)(3) tax-exempt status. Please do not send letters of inquiry by fax, Federal Express, or messenger.
Deadlines: None.

Restrictions

Grants are not made to individuals.

Foundation Officials

Dr. Diane Solomon Brown: secretary
Stuart Brown: treasurer
Daniel Solomon: president
David Solomon: director

Grants Analysis

Disclosure Period: calendar year ending 2002
Total Grants: $4,082,500
Number of Grants: 129
Average Grant: $30,332*
Highest Grant: $200,000
Lowest Grant: $2,000
Typical Range: $10,000 to $50,000
*Note: Average grant figure excludes highest grant.

Recent Grants

Note: Grants derived from 2002 Form 990.
General

250,000	Hadassah Medical Organization, Jerusalem Israel
235,000	PEF Israel Endowment Fund, New York, NY
200,000	Georgetown University Hospital, Washington, DC
140,000	New Israel Fund, Washington, DC
100,000	American Committee for the Weizmann Institute of Science, Washington, DC
100,000	American Friends of the Israel Crisis Center, New York, NY
100,000	Americans for Peace Now, Washington, DC
100,000	Givat Haviva Educational Foundation, New York, NY
90,000	American Friends of Neve Shalom, Sherman Oaks, CA
75,000	Planned Parenthood of Metropolitan Washington, Washington, DC

COLBURN FUND

Giving Contact

Richard D. Colburn, Director
1120 La Collina Road
Beverly Hills, CA 90210
Phone: (310)273-3607
Fax: (310)273-7904

Description

Founded: 1985
EIN: 954018318
Organization Type: Private Foundation
Giving Locations: CA
Grant Types: General Support.

Donor Information

Founder: Richard D. Colburn, Consolidated Electrical Distributors, U.S. Rentals

Financial Summary

Total Giving: $495,132 (2003); $450,011 (2001)
Assets: $427,637 (2003); $185,395 (2001)
Gifts Received: $800,000 (2003); $400,000 (2001); $375,000 (2000). Note: Contributions were received from Consolidated Electrical Distributors, Inc.

Typical Recipients

Arts & Humanities: Arts Associations & Councils, Arts Centers, Arts Funds, Arts Institutes, Community

Arts, Film & Video, Arts & Humanities-General, History & Archaeology, Libraries, Museums/Galleries, Music, Opera, Performing Arts, Public Broadcasting, Theater

Civic & Public Affairs: Community Foundations, Civic & Public Affairs-General, Municipalities/Towns, Parades/Festivals, Philanthropic Organizations, Public Policy, Women's Affairs

Education: Arts/Humanities Education, Colleges & Universities, Continuing Education, Education-General, International Studies, Private Education (Precollege), Social Sciences Education

Environment: Environment-General, Resource Conservation, Wildlife Protection

Health: AIDS/HIV, Cancer, Diabetes, Emergency/ Ambulance Services, Heart, Hospitals, Medical Research, Mental Health

International: Foreign Arts Organizations, International Development, International Environmental Issues, International Organizations, International Relations, Missionary/Religious Activities

Religion: Religion-General, Religious Organizations

Social Services: Community Service Organizations, Family Services, Recreation & Athletics

Application Procedures

Initial Contact: The foundation has no formal grant application procedure or application form.
Deadlines: None.

Additional Information

Emphasis is on music, music related endeavors, fine arts, and performing arts, including their sponsoring organizations, such as orchestral and opera societies, galleries, theatre groups, and civic and other charitable organizations with similar purposes. The fund may also support any other tax exempt organization that is operated exclusively for the charitable, scientific, literary, or educational purposes.

Foundation Officials

Richard Dunton Colburn: director B Carpentersville, IL 1911. ED Antioch College (1933). PRIM CORP EMPL chairman: Decco/Edmundson Electric. CORP AFFIL director: Rolled Alloys Inc.; chairman: U South Rentals Inc.; director: Hajoca Corp.; director: Consolidated Electrical Distributors; director: Edmundson International.
Bernard E. Lyons: director

Grants Analysis

Disclosure Period: calendar year ending 2003
Total Grants: $495,132
Number of Grants: 37
Average Grant: $10,581*
Highest Grant: $114,200
Lowest Grant: $75
Typical Range: $1,000 to $15,000
*Note: Average grant figure excludes highest grant.

Recent Grants

Note: Grants derived from 2001 Form 990.
General

56,200	Colburn School for Performing Arts, CA
50,000	Antioch College, Yellow Springs, OH
33,200	International Festival Society, Los Angeles, CA
31,500	Fraternity of Friends, Los Angeles, CA
25,589	Los Angeles Opera, Los Angeles, CA
25,000	American Friends of the Bayreuth Festival, Los Angeles, CA
25,000	American Friends of the Israel Philharmonic Orchestra, New York, NY
25,000	American Youth Symphony, Los Angeles, CA
25,000	Community Partners FBO Opus Chamber Orchestra
15,000	American Symphony Orchestra, New York, NY

OLIVE B. COLE FOUNDATION

Giving Contact

Maclyn T. Parker, President
6207 Constitution Drive
Ft. Wayne, IN 46804
Phone: (260)436-2182
Fax: (260)432-3146

Description

Founded: 1954
EIN: 356040491
Organization Type: General Purpose Foundation
Giving Locations: IN: North Eastern Indiana, Noble, La Grange, De Kalb, and Steuben counties
Grant Types: Capital, General Support, Loan, Operating Expenses, Project, Scholarship.

Donor Information

Founder: The Olive B. Cole Foundation was established in Indiana in 1954 with funds donated by the late Richard R. Cole and Olive B. Cole. Mr. Cole set up the foundation in honor of his mother. The money for the foundation came from stock in Flint and Walling, a water pump and conditioner manufacturer.

Financial Summary

Total Giving: $1,314,088 (fiscal year ending March 31, 2003); $1,385,846 (fiscal 2002); $1,202,122 (fiscal 2001). Note: Fiscal 1997 Giving includes scholarship ($167,669); 1996 scholarship ($176,217).
Giving Analysis: Giving for fiscal 2001 includes: foundation scholarships ($260,423)
Assets: $24,769,628 (fiscal 2003); $29,533,987 (fiscal 2002); $29,748,768 (fiscal 2001)

Typical Recipients

Arts & Humanities: Arts Appreciation, Arts Institutes, Arts Outreach, Dance, Historic Preservation, Libraries, Literary Arts, Museums/Galleries, Music, Opera, Public Broadcasting, Theater

Civic & Public Affairs: Botanical Gardens/Parks, Business/Free Enterprise, Chambers of Commerce, Community Foundations, Economic Development, Employment/Job Training, Civic & Public Affairs-General, Municipalities/Towns, Parades/Festivals, Philanthropic Organizations, Safety, Urban & Community Affairs, Zoos/Aquariums

Education: Arts/Humanities Education, Business Education, Colleges & Universities, Education Associations, Education Funds, Engineering/ Technological Education, Environmental Education, Education-General, International Studies, Literacy, Private Education (Precollege), Public Education (Precollege), Science/Mathematics Education, Secondary Education (Public), Special Education, Student Aid

Environment: Air/Water Quality, Environment-General, Resource Conservation

Health: AIDS/HIV, Alzheimer's Disease, Cancer, Children's Health/Hospitals, Clinics/Medical Centers, Emergency/Ambulance Services, Health Organizations, Home-Care Services, Hospices, Trauma Treatment

Religion: Churches, Religious Welfare

Science: Science Exhibits & Fairs, Science Museums

Social Services: At-Risk Youth, Big Brothers/Big Sisters, Child Welfare, Community Centers, Community Service Organizations, Crime Prevention, Day Care, Domestic Violence, Emergency Relief, Family Services, Food/Clothing Distribution, People with Disabilities, Recreation & Athletics, Scouts, Senior Services, Shelters/Homelessness, United Funds/ United Ways, Volunteer Services, YMCA/YWCA/ YMHA/YWHA, Youth Organizations

Application Procedures

Initial Contact: A letter of inquiry is the preferred method of initial contact.
Application Requirements: Applicants must complete an application form that is supplied upon request.
Deadlines: None.
Review Process: The board meets in February, May, August, and November. Applicants will be notified of the board's decision after four months.

Restrictions

Scholarship eligibility is limited to residents or graduates of secondary schools in North Eastern Indiana, Noble, La Grange, DeKalb, and Steuben counties in Indiana. Grants are not given to individuals, to religious organizations, or for funds for redistribution.

Additional Information

Scholarship applications also are available at high school offices throughout Noble County, IN.
Publications: Application Form; Statement of Program Policy

Foundation Officials

John E. Hogan: executive vice president, treasurer
Maclyn T. Parker, Esq.: president, director B 1929. ED DePauw University AB (1951); University of Michigan JD (1954). PRIM CORP EMPL member: Baker & Daniels.
Emily E. Pichon: secretary
John N. Pichon, Jr.: chairman
Paul Schirmeyer: director
Gwendlyn I. Tipton: scholarship admin, director

Grants Analysis

Disclosure Period: fiscal year ending March 31, 2001
Total Grants: $936,699*
Number of Grants: 33
Average Grant: $19,897*
Highest Grant: $300,000
Lowest Grant: $660
Typical Range: $10,000 to $40,000
*Note: Giving excludes scholarships. Average grant excludes highest grant.

Recent Grants

Note: Grants derived from 2002 Form 990.
General

300,000	Cole Center Family YMCA, Kendallville, IN -- provides recreational opportunities for all ages
200,000	Kendallville Park and Recreation Department, Kendallville, IN -- for development of Kendallville park system in Noble County
120,000	ELOC, Inc., Ft. Wayne, IN -- provides affordable education to all at all levels and is committed to technological innovation
100,000	Northeast Center for Entrepreneurial Excellence, Ft. Wayne, IN -- serves as a knowledge center for the promotion of entrepreneurial activity and success, regional economic growth, and outreach services
100,000	WFWA PBS-39, Ft. Wayne, IN -- provides high quality telecommunications services to improve the quality of life in the communities through educational programs
70,000	ELOC, Inc, Ft. Wayne, IN -- provides affordable education to all at all levels and is committed to technological innovation
50,000	Fort Wayne Children's Zoo, Ft. Wayne, IN -- provides educational programs and materials for teachers, home schoolers, group leaders, and other educators
25,000	Dean V. Kruse Foundation, Inc., Auburn, IN -- not-for-profit educational institution
20,000	Indiana Technology Partnership, Ft. Wayne, IN -- statewide organization

working to boost technology and create fertile ground for high-tech growth in Indiana

20,000   Shelter Ministries, Auburn, IN -- provides compassionate service to homeless & needy by providing temporary housing

QUINCY COLE TRUST

Giving Contact

Rita Smith, Trust Officer
c/o Bank of America
PO Box 26688
PO Box 26688
Richmond, VA 23261
Phone: (804)788-2143

Description

EIN: 546086247
Organization Type: Private Foundation
Giving Locations: VA: Richmond including metropolitan area
Grant Types: General Support.

Donor Information

Founder: the late Quincy Cole

Financial Summary

Total Giving: $603,570 (fiscal year ending June 30, 2002)
Assets: $8,776,682 (fiscal 2002)

Typical Recipients

Arts & Humanities: Arts Associations & Councils, Arts Centers, Ballet, Community Arts, Dance, Historic Preservation, History & Archaeology, Libraries, Museums/Galleries, Music, Opera, Theater
Civic & Public Affairs: Botanical Gardens/Parks, Clubs, Civic & Public Affairs-General, Municipalities/Towns, Public Policy
Education: Afterschool/Enrichment Programs, Arts/Humanities Education, Colleges & Universities, Private Education (Precollege), Public Education (Precollege), Science/Mathematics Education
Environment: Environment-General
Health: Clinics/Medical Centers, Research/Studies Institutes, Single-Disease Health Associations
International: Foreign Arts Organizations
Religion: Churches, Religious Organizations, Religious Welfare, Seminaries
Science: Science Museums
Social Services: Animal Protection, Child Welfare, Community Service Organizations, Family Services, Food/Clothing Distribution, Homes, People with Disabilities, Recreation & Athletics, Scouts, Shelters/Homelessness, YMCA/YWCA/YMHA/YWHA, Youth Organizations

Application Procedures

Initial Contact: Send a brief letter of inquiry.
Application Requirements: Include a description of organization and purpose of funds sought.
Deadlines: April 20.

Additional Information

Trust(s): Bank of America NA

Grants Analysis

Disclosure Period: fiscal year ending June 30, 2001
Total Grants: $603,570
Number of Grants: 24
Average Grant: $25,148*
Highest Grant: $88,570
Lowest Grant: $5,000
Typical Range: $10,000 to $50,000
*Note: Average grant excludes highest grant.

Recent Grants

Note: Grants derived from fiscal 2002 Form 990.
Library-Related
15,000   Richmond Public Library Foundation, Richmond, VA -- Renovation Project
10,000   Braille Circulating Library, Richmond, VA -- Renovation Project
General
88,570   Windsor Foundation, Richmond, VA -- upkeep and maintenance of house
50,000   Council for Americas First Freedom, Richmond, VA
50,000   Virginia Museum of Fine Arts Foundation, Richmond, VA -- Indian Arts Exhibit
50,000   VMI Foundation, Lexington, VA -- Metro Richmond Student Scholarship
40,000   St. Andrews School, Richmond, VA -- grant for Gothic Building revival
40,000   Science Museum of Virginia Foundation, Richmond, VA
30,000   Richmond Society for the Prevention of Cruelty to Animals, Richmond, VA -- new center development
25,000   Lewis Ginter Botanical Garden, Inc., Richmond, VA -- children's garden
25,000   Little Sisters of the Poor, Richmond, VA -- building renovation
25,000   Virginia Historical Society, Richmond, VA -- grant for exhibition

COLEMAN FOUNDATION (IL)

Giving Contact

Michael W. Hennessy, President & Chief Executive Officer
575 West Madison Street, Suite 4605
Chicago, IL 60661-2549
Phone: (312)902-7120
Fax: (312)902-7124
E-mail: info@colemanfoundation.org
Web: http://www.colemanfoundation.org

Description

Founded: 1953
EIN: 363025967
Organization Type: General Purpose Foundation
Giving Locations: IL: Chicago nationally; especially the Midwest.
Grant Types: Capital, Challenge, Conference/Seminar, General Support, Matching, Multiyear/Continuing Support, Project, Research.

Donor Information

Founder: The Foundation was established in 1953 by the late J. D. Stetson Coleman and the late Dorothy W. Coleman. The Colemans owned Fannie May Candies from 1936 through 1977.

Financial Summary

Total Giving: $5,104,097 (2003); $7,948,017 (2002)
Assets: $151,649,432 (2003); $132,674,460 (2002)

Typical Recipients

Arts & Humanities: Arts Centers, Arts & Humanities-General, History & Archaeology, Libraries, Museums/Galleries, Music, Theater
Civic & Public Affairs: Asian American Affairs, Botanical Gardens/Parks, Business/Free Enterprise, Clubs, Community Foundations, Economic Development, Employment/Job Training, Civic & Public Affairs-General, Hispanic Affairs, Housing, Municipalities/Towns, Nonprofit Management, Philanthropic Organizations, Professional & Trade Associations, Public Policy, Safety, Urban & Community Affairs, Women's Affairs
Education: Business Education, Colleges & Univer-

sities, Education Associations, Education Funds, Elementary Education (Public), Engineering/Technological Education, Education-General, International Studies, Legal Education, Medical Education, Minority Education, Preschool Education, Private Education (Precollege), Public Education (Precollege), Religious Education, Secondary Education (Private), Secondary Education (Public), Student Aid
Health: AIDS/HIV, Cancer, Clinics/Medical Centers, Eyes/Blindness, Health Organizations, Hospices, Hospitals, Hospitals (University Affiliated), Medical Rehabilitation, Medical Research, Preventive Medicine/Wellness Organizations, Public Health, Research/Studies Institutes, Single-Disease Health Associations
Religion: Churches, Dioceses, Jewish Causes, Missionary Activities (Domestic), Religious Welfare
Science: Science-General, Scientific Research
Social Services: Child Welfare, Community Centers, Community Service Organizations, Emergency Relief, Food/Clothing Distribution, People with Disabilities, Sexual Abuse, Shelters/Homelessness, Social Services-General, YMCA/YWCA/YMHA/YWHA, Youth Organizations

Application Procedures

Initial Contact: Submit a brief letter of inquiry (2 pages maximum).
Application Requirements: Include history of the organization, explanation of need, explanation of goals and objectives, amount requested, complete proposal along with project budget, names of other donors with amounts, and alternative sources of funding. All grant applicants must qualify under current IRS Laws and Code Sections 509(a)(1), (2), or (3) or 501(c)(3) and/or other applicable sections of the Internal Revenue Code.
Deadlines: None.
Review Process: The board generally meets in February, May, August, and November. Applicants will be notified of a decision about three months after receipt of proposal.

Restrictions

The foundation does not respond to unsolicited grant proposals, form letters, telephone solicitations, mass mailings, or requests for ticket purchases. The foundation does not make grants to individuals, for deficit financing, for loans, or for programs outside the United States. Applicants should not expect ongoing support. Grant agreements are required before funds are disbursed.

Additional Information

Publications: Financial Statement; Guidelines; Application Procedures and History

Foundation Officials

C. Hugh Albers: director
Trevor C. Davies: chief financial officer treasurer, assistant secretary, director
R. Michael Furlong: director
Michael W. Hennessy: president, chief executive officer, director B 1951. ED University of Colorado (1973). PRIM CORP EMPL chairman, president, chief executive officer, director: Lovejoy Inc.
John Edwin Hughes: chairman, director B Beloit, WI 1927. ED Northwestern University; University of Illinois. PRIM CORP EMPL chairman, president, chief executive officer: J.E. Hughes Enterprises. NONPR AFFIL chairman: Council Entrepreneurship Awareness & Education; member: Institute of Management Accountants; member: American Accounting Association; member: American Institute of Certified Public Accountants.
James H. Jones: secretary, assistant treasurer, director PRIM CORP EMPL treasurer, secretary: Archibald Candy Corp.

Grants Analysis

Disclosure Period: calendar year ending 2003
Total Grants: $5,104,097
Number of Grants: 182
Average Grant: $28,044
Highest Grant: $250,000
Lowest Grant: $500
Typical Range: $5,000 to $50,000

Recent Grants

Note: Grants derived from 2003 Form 990.
Library-Related

59,800	Gilman Area District Library, Gilman, IL -- capital support for arts and culture

General

450,000	Feinburg School of Medicine, Chicago, IL -- program support for scientific research
375,000	United States Association for Small Business and Entrepreneurship, Madison, WI -- program support for education
303,000	Beloit College, Beloit, WI -- program support for education
290,000	Beloit College, Beloit, WI -- capital support for education
280,000	Providence Saint Mel School, Chicago, IL -- program support for education
250,000	Cristo Rey Jesuit High School, Chicago, IL -- capital support for education
250,000	Feinburg School of Medicine, Chicago, IL -- program support for health and rehabilitation
250,000	Providence Saint Mel School, Chicago, IL -- capital support for education
200,000	Feinburg School of Medicine, Chicago, IL -- program support for scientific research
198,000	Saint Louis University, St. Louis, MO -- program support for education

COLLINS FOUNDATION

Giving Contact

Dr. Jerry E. Hudson, Executive Vice President
1618 Southwest 1st Avenue, Suite 505
Portland, OR 97201-5706
Phone: (503)227-7171
Fax: (503)295-3794
E-mail: information@collinsfoundation.org
Web: http://www.collinsfoundation.org

Description

Founded: 1947
EIN: 936021893
Organization Type: Family Foundation
Giving Locations: OR
Grant Types: Award, Capital, Challenge, General Support, Project.

Donor Information

Founder: The Collins Foundation was established in Oregon in 1947 by members of the Collins family. The Collins family is involved in the lumber and wood products industry. Family members serve on the board of directors of the Collins Pine Company.

Financial Summary

Total Giving: $6,573,280 (2003); $7,579,300 (2002); $7,986,550 (2001)
Giving Analysis: Giving for 2003 includes: foundation grants to United Way ($1,000); 2002: foundation grants to United Way ($1,000)
Assets: $166,080,289 (2003); $135,462,593 (2002); $166,235,818 (2001)

Typical Recipients

Arts & Humanities: Arts Associations & Councils, Arts Centers, Arts Festivals, Arts Institutes, Arts Outreach, Ballet, Dance, Ethnic & Folk Arts, Arts & Humanities-General, Historic Preservation, History & Ar-

chaeology, Libraries, Museums/Galleries, Music, Opera, Performing Arts, Public Broadcasting, Theater
Civic & Public Affairs: Botanical Gardens/Parks, Community Foundations, Economic Development, Employment/Job Training, Civic & Public Affairs-General, Housing, Urban & Community Affairs, Zoos/Aquariums
Education: Afterschool/Enrichment Programs, Arts/Humanities Education, Colleges & Universities, Education Funds, Environmental Education, Education-General, Health & Physical Education, Leadership Training, Legal Education, Literacy, Minority Education, Preschool Education, Private Education (Precollege), Religious Education, Science/Mathematics Education, Secondary Education (Private), Special Education, Student Aid
Environment: Air/Water Quality, Forestry, Environment-General, Protection, Resource Conservation
Health: Alzheimer's Disease, Cancer, Children's Health/Hospitals, Clinics/Medical Centers, Emergency/Ambulance Services, Health Policy/Cost Containment, Health Funds, Health Organizations, Heart, Hospices, Hospitals, Hospitals (University Affiliated), Medical Research, Mental Health, Prenatal Health Issues, Preventive Medicine/Wellness Organizations, Public Health, Research/Studies Institutes, Trauma Treatment
International: Health Care/Hospitals, International Environmental Issues
Religion: Churches, Ministries, Religious Organizations, Religious Welfare, Seminaries
Science: Science Museums
Social Services: Animal Protection, Child Welfare, Community Centers, Community Service Organizations, Day Care, Family Planning, Family Services, Food/Clothing Distribution, Homes, People with Disabilities, Recreation & Athletics, Scouts, Senior Services, Shelters/Homelessness, Substance Abuse, United Funds/United Ways, Volunteer Services, YMCA/YWCA/YMHA/YWHA, Youth Organizations

Application Procedures

Initial Contact: Interested organizations should submit a written application to the foundation.
Application Requirements: Applications must include the name of the charitable organization; date the grant is needed; budget; copy of IRS determination letter of tax-exempt status; description of project; list of the board of directors; estimated total funds required and amount needed from the foundation; anticipated sources of remaining funds; list of other contributors; and other sources being approached for funding.
Deadlines: None.
Review Process: Processing of applications requires four to eight weeks.

Restrictions

The foundation does not give grants to individuals.

Additional Information

Publications: Annual Report; Guidelines

Foundation Officials

Timothy R. Bishop: treasurer B 1951. ED University of Oregon BS (1974). PRIM CORP EMPL vice president, treasurer: Collins Pine Co. CORP AFFIL treasurer: Collins Resources Int Ltd.; vice president, treasurer: Ostrander Resources Co.
Ralph Bolliger: vice president, trustee
Maribeth Wilson Collins: president, trustee B Portland, OR October 27, 1918. ED University of Oregon BA (1940). CORP AFFIL director: Ostrander Resources Co.; director: CP Specialties Division; director: Kane Hardwood Division; director: Collins Holding Co.; director: Collins Pine Co.; director: Chester Division; director: Builders Supply Division. NONPR AFFIL member: Gamma Phi Beta; member executive committee, secretary board trustees: Willamette University. CLUB AFFIL University Club.
Truman W. Collins, Jr.: vice president, trustee

Jerry E. Hudson: executive vice president B Chattanooga, TN 1938. ED David Lipscomb College BA (1959); Tulane University MA (1961); Tulane University PhD (1965). CORP AFFIL director: Portland General Electric Co. NONPR AFFIL director: National Association Independent Colleges & Universities; member: Phi Alpha Theta; director: EIIA.
Cherida C. Smith: vice president, trustee CORP AFFIL director: CP Specialties Division; director: Kane Hardwood Division; director: Collins Pine Co.; director: Builders Supply Division; director: Chester Division.

Grants Analysis

Disclosure Period: calendar year ending 2003
Total Grants: $6,572,280*
Number of Grants: 237
Average Grant: $29,839*
Highest Grant: $680,000
Lowest Grant: $500
Typical Range: $5,000 to $50,000
***Note:** Giving excludes United Way. Average grant figure excludes three highest grants ($1,930,000).

Recent Grants

Note: Grants derived from 2001 Form 990.
Library-Related

100,000	Eugene Public Library Foundation, Eugene, OR -- provides construction of library

General

400,000	YMCA of Columbia-Willamette, Portland, OR -- provides renovation and expansion
200,000	Ecumenical Ministries of Oregon, Portland, OR -- provides support of programs and operations
200,000	Lewis & Clark College, Portland, OR -- provides renovation and expansion
200,000	Linfield College, McMinnville, OR -- provides construction of a new library
175,000	Oregon Children's Foundation, Portland, OR -- offers statewide expansion
150,000	Nature Conservancy, Portland, OR -- provides support for the heart of Oregon campaign
150,000	Oregon Graduate Institute of Science and Technology, Beaverton, OR -- offers purchase of chromatography instrumentation
125,000	University of Portland, Portland, OR
125,000	Willamette University, Salem, OR -- provides construction of a new student recreation
100,000	Loaves & Fishes Centers, Portland, OR -- provides purchase and renovation

GEORGE AND JENNIE COLLINS FOUNDATION

Giving Contact

Roger B. Collins, Chairman
2627 E. 21st St., Suite 200
Tulsa, OK 74114-1710
Phone: (918)744-5607

Description

Founded: 1943
EIN: 736093053
Organization Type: Private Foundation
Giving Locations: OK
Grant Types: Capital, General Support, Scholarship.

Donor Information

Founder: George F. Collins, Jr., Liberty Glass Co., and others

Financial Summary

Total Giving: $294,611 (2003); $329,399 (2002); $351,870 (2001)
Assets: $4,775,881 (2003); $5,151,084 (2002); $5,273,647 (2001)
Gifts Received: $100 (1999); $100 (1996); $500 (1995)

Typical Recipients

Arts & Humanities: Community Arts, Arts & Humanities-General, History & Archaeology, Libraries, Museums/Galleries, Music
Civic & Public Affairs: Civic & Public Affairs-General, Housing
Education: Business Education, Colleges & Universities, Education Funds, Faculty Development, Private Education (Precollege)
Health: Alzheimer's Disease, Health Organizations, Hospices, Hospitals
Religion: Churches, Missionary Activities (Domestic), Religious Organizations, Religious Welfare
Social Services: Child Welfare, Community Service Organizations, Recreation & Athletics, Sexual Abuse, Shelters/Homelessness, Social Services-General, United Funds/United Ways, YMCA/YWCA/YMHA/YWHA

Application Procedures

Initial Contact: Send a brief letter of inquiry.
Application Requirements: Include a description of organization amount requested, purpose of funds sought, proof of tax-exempt status.
Deadlines: None.

Restrictions

Does not support individuals, religious organizations for sectarian purposes, political or lobbying groups, organizations outside operating areas

Foundation Officials

Frances R. Collins: trustee
Fulton Collins: trustee B 1943. ED Stanford University BA; Stanford University MS; Stanford University MBA. PRIM CORP EMPL chairman, director: Summit Acceptance Corp.
Roger B. Collins: chairman

Grants Analysis

Disclosure Period: calendar year ending 2003
Total Grants: $294,611
Number of Grants: 12
Average Grant: $9,461*
Highest Grant: $100,000
Lowest Grant: $150
Typical Range: $5,000 to $20,000
***Note:** Average grant figure excludes two highest grants ($200,000).

Recent Grants

Note: Grants derived from 2001 Form 990.
General

150,000	First Presbyterian Church, Tulsa, OK -- for operations
118,000	Holland Hall, Tulsa, OK -- for operations
40,000	Baker University, Baldwin City, KS -- for operations
20,370	Salvation Army, Tulsa, OK -- for operations
10,000	University of Tulsa, Tulsa, OK -- for operations
5,000	Habitat for Humanity, Tulsa, OK -- for operations
3,000	Tulsa Philharmonic, Tulsa, OK -- for operations
1,500	12 and 12, Inc., Tulsa, OK -- for operations
1,500	University of Tulsa, Tulsa, OK -- for operations
1,200	Junior Achievement of Tulsa, Tulsa, OK -- for operations

GEORGE FULTON COLLINS, JR. FOUNDATION

Giving Contact

Fulton Collins, Chairman
1924 S. Utica, Suite 800
Tulsa, OK 74104
Phone: (918)748-9860

Description

Founded: 1968
EIN: 237008179
Organization Type: Private Foundation
Giving Locations: OK
Grant Types: Capital, Scholarship.

Financial Summary

Total Giving: $5,000 (2003); $215,000 (2001)
Assets: $3,164,245 (2003); $3,846,918 (2001)
Gifts Received: $500 (2000); $500 (1996). Note: In 1996, contributions were received from G. Fulton Collins III.

Typical Recipients

Arts & Humanities: Community Arts, Libraries, Museums/Galleries
Civic & Public Affairs: Women's Affairs, Zoos/Aquariums
Education: Colleges & Universities, Literacy, Private Education (Precollege), Public Education (Precollege), Secondary Education (Private)
Health: Emergency/Ambulance Services, Health Funds, Health Organizations
Religion: Churches, Religious Organizations, Religious Welfare
Social Services: Child Welfare, Community Service Organizations, Counseling, Food/Clothing Distribution, Recreation & Athletics, Sexual Abuse, Shelters/Homelessness, YMCA/YWCA/YMHA/YWHA

Application Procedures

Initial Contact: Send a brief letter of inquiry.
Application Requirements: Include purpose of funds sought, amount requested, and how funds will be utilized.
Deadlines: None.

Foundation Officials

Fulton Collins: chairman B 1943. ED Stanford University BA; Stanford University MS; Stanford University MBA. PRIM CORP EMPL chairman, director: Summit Acceptance Corp.
Roger B. Collins: treasurer
Suzanne M. Collins: secretary

Grants Analysis

Disclosure Period: calendar year ending 2003
Total Grants: $5,000
Number of Grants: 1

Recent Grants

Note: Grants derived from 2001 Form 990.
General

215,000	University of Tulsa, Tulsa, OK

COLLINS MEDICAL TRUST

Giving Contact

Nancy L. Helseth, Administrator
1618 SW 1st Avenue, Suite 500
Portland, OR 97201-5706
Phone: (503)227-1219

Description

Founded: 1956
EIN: 936021895
Organization Type: Private Foundation
Giving Locations: OR: OR
Grant Types: General Support, Research, Scholarship.

Donor Information

Founder: the late Truman W. Collins

Financial Summary

Total Giving: $352,154 (fiscal year ending September 30, 2004); $325,600 (fiscal 2001). Note: In fiscal 1997, Giving includes scholarship ($25,000).
Giving Analysis: Giving for fiscal 2005 includes: foundation scholarships ($50,000); fiscal 2001: foundation scholarships ($60,000)
Assets: $7,270,326 (fiscal 2004); $6,559,797 (fiscal 2001)

Typical Recipients

Arts & Humanities: Libraries, Museums/Galleries
Civic & Public Affairs: Civic & Public Affairs-General
Education: Colleges & Universities, Education Funds, Engineering/Technological Education, Health & Physical Education, Medical Education, Science/Mathematics Education, Student Aid
Health: Alzheimer's Disease, Clinics/Medical Centers, Eyes/Blindness, Health-General, Health Policy/Cost Containment, Health Funds, Health Organizations, Heart, Hospices, Hospitals, Medical Research, Medical Training, Nursing Services, Public Health, Single-Disease Health Associations, Speech & Hearing
Science: Scientific Research
Social Services: Child Welfare, Community Service Organizations, Family Services, Veterans

Application Procedures

Initial Contact: Send a brief letter of inquiry.
Application Requirements: Include a description of organization of project, amount requested, and proof of tax-exempt status.
Deadlines: None.

Restrictions

Grants restricted to research, education, and work in the medical research field.

Foundation Officials

Timothy R. Bishop: treasurer B 1951. ED University of Oregon BS (1974). PRIM CORP EMPL vice president, treasurer: Collins Pine Co. CORP AFFIL treasurer: Collins Resources Int Ltd.; vice president, treasurer: Ostrander Resources Co.
Maribeth Wilson Collins: trustee B Portland, OR October 27, 1918. ED University of Oregon BA (1940). CORP AFFIL director: Ostrander Resources Co.; director: CP Specialties Division; director: Kane Hardwood Division; director: Collins Holding Co.; director: Collins Pine Co.; director: Chester Division; director: Builders Supply Division. NONPR AFFIL member: Gamma Phi Beta; member executive committee, secretary board trustees: Willamette University. CLUB AFFIL University Club.
Nancy L. Helseth: admin
James Randolph Patterson: trustee B Lancaster, PA 1942. ED University of Pennsylvania AB (1964); Columbia University MD (1968). CORP AFFIL pulmonary & critical care specialist: Oregon Clinic. NONPR AFFIL member: Pacific Interurban Clinic; member: Pacific Society Internal Medicine; member: Oregon Society Critical Care Medicine; member: Oregon Lung Association; member: Oregon Medicine Association; clinical professor medicine: Oregon Health Sciences University; member: Multnomah County Medicine Society; member: North Pacific Society Internal Medicine; member: American Thoracic Society;

member: American Board Internal Medicine; member: American College Chest Physicians.

Grants Analysis

Disclosure Period: fiscal year ending September 30, 2004
Total Grants: $302,154*
Number of Grants: 11
Average Grant: $26,743*
Highest Grant: $34,811
Lowest Grant: $5,000
Typical Range: $10,000 to $30,000
*Note: Giving excludes scholarships. Average grant figure excludes highest grant.

Recent Grants

Note: Grants derived from fiscal 2004 Form 990.
General

50,000	Linfield College - School of Nursing, Portland, OR -- for paquet nursing scholarships
34,811	Oregon Health Science Foundation, Portland, OR -- for spatial genomics
31,732	Oregon Health Science Foundation, Portland, OR -- for measuring blood flow to the fetal heart muscle resonance imaging
30,000	Providence St. Vincent Medical Foundation, Portland, OR
29,977	Oregon Health Science Foundation, Portland, OR -- enhancing knowledge and building sustainable regional networks between pastoral care and long term care across Oregon
29,268	Oregon Health Science Foundation, Portland, OR -- for research programs to eliminate health disparities in undeserved populations in Oregon
28,416	Geneforum.org, Lake Oswego, OR
27,450	Oregon Health Science Foundation, Portland, OR -- for mechanisms of toxoplasmic retinochoroiditis
27,000	Oregon Health Science Foundation, Portland, OR -- in vivo microscopy studies of herpes simplex keratitis
25,000	Oregon Health Science Foundation, Portland, OR -- for studies on genetics

COLLIS FOUNDATION

Giving Contact

Astrid C. Womble, President & Director
24 Calhoun Dr.
Greenwich, CT 06831
Phone: (203)618-9555

Description

Founded: 1997
EIN: 061472006
Organization Type: Private Foundation
Giving Locations: New England area.
Grant Types: General Support.

Financial Summary

Total Giving: $296,800 (fiscal year ending 8, 2004); $494,500 (fiscal 2002); $388,525 (fiscal 2001)
Giving Analysis: Giving for fiscal 2004 includes: foundation scholarships ($105,800); fiscal 2001: foundation scholarships ($18,000)
Assets: $8,533,251 (fiscal 2004); $9,073,941 (fiscal 2002); $10,304,135 (fiscal 2001)
Gifts Received: $5,000,153 (fiscal 1997). Note: In fiscal 1997, contributions were received from Charles A. Collis.

Typical Recipients

Arts & Humanities: History & Archaeology, Libraries, Museums/Galleries, Music
Civic & Public Affairs: Civic & Public Affairs-

General, Women's Affairs
Education: Education-General, Private Education (Precollege)
Religion: Religious Welfare
Social Services: Community Service Organizations, Food/Clothing Distribution, YMCA/YWCA/YMHA/YWHA, Youth Organizations

Application Procedures

Initial Contact: Submit a two- to three-page letter of inquiry.
Application Requirements: Include a brief statement of the organization's purpose and goals; a description of the project, the need it addresses, and the target population (if applicable); the capability of the leadership to implement the proposed project; anticipated short- and long-term outcomes; method for evaluating success; amount requested; recently audited financial statement; a statement about the total agency budget and project budget, if different; committed and anticipated funding sources for the agency and/or project; proof of tax-exempt status; and a copy of the organization's budget.
Deadlines: None.
Notes: If the proposal is for $1,000 or less, the foundation may be able to evaluate the request based on the letter of inquiry.
Current grantees should contact the executive director before submitting a new proposal.

Restrictions

The foundation funds only charitable organizations located in New England.

Foundation Officials

Charles A. Collis: director
Elfried A. Collis: director
Astrid C. Womble: president, director

Grants Analysis

Total Grants: $191,000*
Number of Grants: 20
Average Grant: $9,550
Highest Grant: $37,000
Lowest Grant: $2,500
Typical Range: $5,000 to $20,000
*Note: Giving excludes scholarships.

Recent Grants

Note: Grants derived from fiscal 2001 Form 990.

Library-Related

10,000	Providence Public Library, Providence, RI -- program for young readers

General

105,025	Community Preparatory School, Providence, RI -- endowment
62,500	Gordon School, Providence, RI -- for capital campaign
40,000	San Miguel Education Center, San Diego, CA -- support of center
25,000	Rhode Island Philharmonic, Providence, RI -- for capital
15,000	Dorcas Place Literacy Center, Providence, RI -- support of center
15,000	Moses Brown School, Providence, RI -- for Access Program
15,000	Moses Brown School, Providence, RI -- for scholarship
15,000	Rhode Island Community Food Bank, Warwick, RI -- for operating budget
10,000	Amos House, Providence, RI -- for operating budget
10,000	Children's Museum of Rhode Island, Providence, RI -- for museum support

COLONIAL GROUP INC.

Company Headquarters

101 N. Lathrop Ave.
Savannah, GA 31415-1054

Company Description

Founded: 1921
Employees: 75
SIC(s): 2911 Petroleum Refining, 5171 Petroleum Bulk Stations & Terminals, 5541 Gasoline Service Stations.
Parent Company: First Colonial Group Inc., 76 S. Main Street, Nazareth, PA, United States

Colonial Foundation

Giving Contact

Francis A. Brown, Vice President, Finance & Chief Financial Officer
PO Box 576
Savannah, GA 31402
Phone: (912)236-1331

Description

Founded: 1986
EIN: 581693323
Organization Type: Corporate Foundation
Giving Locations: GA
Grant Types: General Support.

Donor Information

Founder: Colonial Oil Corp.

Financial Summary

Total Giving: $535,090 (2003); $391,080 (2002); $380,495 (2001)
Giving Analysis: Giving for 2002 includes: foundation grants to United Way ($48,500); 2001: foundation matching gifts ($2,484); foundation grants to United Way ($48,000); foundation ($330,011)
Assets: $4,842,936 (2003); $4,111,189 (2002); $5,012,079 (2001)
Gifts Received: $500,130 (2003); $500,235 (2002); $300,000 (2001). Note: Contributions were received from Colonial Group.

Typical Recipients

Arts & Humanities: Arts Festivals, Arts & Humanities-General, Historic Preservation, History & Archaeology, Libraries, Museums/Galleries, Music, Performing Arts, Public Broadcasting, Theater
Civic & Public Affairs: Business/Free Enterprise, Chambers of Commerce, Civil Rights, Clubs, Community Foundations, Civic & Public Affairs-General, Housing, Law & Justice, Legal Aid, Parades/Festivals, Safety, Urban & Community Affairs
Education: Business Education, Colleges & Universities, Economic Education, Education Associations, Education Funds, Education Reform, Elementary Education, Engineering/Technological Education, Education-General, Literacy, Minority Education, Preschool Education, Private Education (Precollege), Public Education (Precollege), Secondary Education (Private), Secondary Education (Public), Special Education, Student Aid
Environment: Protection, Resource Conservation
Health: Alzheimer's Disease, Arthritis, Cancer, Children's Health/Hospitals, Diabetes, Emergency/Ambulance Services, Health-General, Health Funds, Health Organizations, Hospices, Long-Term Care, Prenatal Health Issues, Respiratory, Single-Disease Health Associations, Transplant Networks/Donor Banks
Religion: Churches, Missionary Activities (Domestic), Religious Organizations, Religious Welfare
Science: Science Museums, Scientific Organizations
Social Services: Animal Protection, At-Risk Youth, Child Welfare, Community Service Organizations,

Counseling, Emergency Relief, Family Services, Food/Clothing Distribution, Homes, People with Disabilities, Recreation & Athletics, Scouts, Sexual Abuse, Shelters/Homelessness, United Funds/United Ways, Volunteer Services, YMCA/YWCA/YMHA/YWHA, Youth Organizations

Application Procedures
Initial Contact: Send a brief letter of inquiry.
Application Requirements: Include proof of tax-exempt status.
Deadlines: None.

Corporate Officials
Francis A. Brown: chief financial officer, director B 1952. PRIM CORP EMPL vice president finance, treasurer, director: Colonial Oil Industries ADD CORP EMPL treasurer: Georgia Kaolin Terminals Inc.; vice president: Chatham Towing Co. Inc.; vice president: Colonial Energy Inc.; vice president: Colonial Group Inc.; vice president: Colonial Marine Industries; treasurer: Colonial Terminals Inc.
Robert H. Demere, Jr.: president, chief executive officer PRIM CORP EMPL president, chief executive officer: Colonial Oil Industries.
Robert H. Demere: chairman B Savannah, GA 1924. ED Yale University (1945). PRIM CORP EMPL chairman: Colonial Oil Industries. CORP AFFIL director: First Union Corp. Georgia; chairman: Interstate Stations; director: First Union Bank Savannah; chairman: Eagle Carriers; chairman: Enmark Stations; chairman: Colonial Marine Industries; chairman: Colonial Terminals; chairman: Chatham Towing Co.; chairman: Colonial Interstate.

Foundation Officials
W. A. Baker, Jr.: vice president
Francis A. Brown: vice president, treasurer (see above)
Robert H. Demere, Jr.: vice president, secretary (see above)
Robert H. Demere: president (see above)

Grants Analysis
Disclosure Period: calendar year ending 2003
Total Grants: $478,040*
Number of Grants: 106
Average Grant: $3,635*
Highest Grant: $50,000
Lowest Grant: $100
Typical Range: $1,000 to $5,000
*Note: Giving excludes United Way; matching gifts; scholarship. Average grant figure excludes two highest grants ($100,000).

Recent Grants
Note: Grants derived from 2003 Form 990.

General

51,000	United Way, Savannah, GA
50,000	Bethesda Home for Boys, Savannah, GA
50,000	Savanna Country Day School, Savannah, GA
50,000	Telfair Academy of Arts and Science, Savannah, GA
50,000	YMCA, Savannah, GA
30,000	Saint Andrew's School, Middletown, DE
20,000	Americas Second Harvest Food Bank, Chicago, IL
20,000	Benedictine Military School, Savannah, GA
20,000	Hospice Savannah's Spirit of Living Campaign, Savannah, GA
20,000	Mercy Housing Southeast, Atlanta, GA

COLONIAL LIFE & ACCIDENT INSURANCE CO.

Company Headquarters
1200 Colonial Life Blvd., W.
Columbia, SC 29210
Web: http://www.coloniallife.com

Company Description
Founded: 1939
Parent Company: UnumProvident, 1 Fountain Sq., Chattanooga, TN, United States

Nonmonetary Support
Type: Donated Equipment; In-kind Services; Loaned Employees; Loaned Executives

Giving Contact
Donna Northam, Assistant Vice President Corporate & External Communication
PO Box 1365
Columbia, SC 29202
Phone: (803)213-5634
Fax: (803)213-7461
E-mail: dcnortham@unum.com

Description
Organization Type: Corporate Giving Program
Giving Locations: SC
Grant Types: General Support.

Financial Summary
Total Giving: Contributes through corporate direct giving program only.

Typical Recipients
Arts & Humanities: Arts Appreciation, Arts Associations & Councils, Arts Centers, Arts Festivals, Arts Institutes, Community Arts, Dance, Ethnic & Folk Arts, Historic Preservation, Libraries, Museums/Galleries, Music, Opera, Performing Arts, Theater, Visual Arts
Civic & Public Affairs: Business/Free Enterprise, Economic Development, Economic Policy, Employment/Job Training, Housing, Law & Justice, Legal Aid, Nonprofit Management, Philanthropic Organizations, Professional & Trade Associations, Safety, Zoos/Aquariums
Education: Agricultural Education, Arts/Humanities Education, Business Education, Colleges & Universities, Community & Junior Colleges, Economic Education, International Exchange, International Studies, Private Education (Precollege), Public Education (Precollege), Student Aid
Environment: Environment-General
Health: Emergency/Ambulance Services, Geriatric Health, Health Policy/Cost Containment, Hospices, Hospitals, Medical Research, Medical Training, Mental Health, Nursing Services, Public Health, Single-Disease Health Associations
Social Services: Animal Protection, Child Welfare, Community Centers, Community Service Organizations, Counseling, Day Care, Delinquency & Criminal Rehabilitation, Domestic Violence, Emergency Relief, Family Planning, Family Services, Food/Clothing Distribution, Homes, People with Disabilities, Recreation & Athletics, Refugee Assistance, Senior Services, Substance Abuse, United Funds/United Ways, Volunteer Services, Youth Organizations

Application Procedures
Initial Contact: Send a brief letter of inquiry.
Application Requirements: Include a description of organization, amount requested, purpose of funds sought, recently audited financial statements, and proof of tax-exempt status.
Deadlines: September 1 for the following year.

Restrictions
The company does not support beauty contests, fashion shows, adversarial groups, individuals, religious organizations for sectarian purposes, or political or lobbying groups.

Giving Program Officials
Edwina Carms: PRIM CORP EMPL community service administration: Colonial Life & Accident Insurance Co.

Grants Analysis
Typical Range: $1,000 to $2,500

COLONIAL OAKS FOUNDATION

Giving Contact
Kristin E. McGlinn, Executive Director
PO Box 5936
Wyomissing, PA 19610
Phone: (610)988-2400

Description
Founded: 1992
EIN: 232705277
Organization Type: Private Foundation
Giving Locations: PA: Berks County
Grant Types: General Support.

Donor Information
Founder: Established in 1992 by Terrence J. McGlinn.

Financial Summary
Total Giving: $841,045 (fiscal year ending September 30, 2003)
Giving Analysis: Giving for fiscal 2003 includes: foundation grants to United Way ($37,500)
Assets: $16,404,740 (fiscal 2003)
Gifts Received: $1,627,000 (fiscal 1998); $6,588,450 (fiscal 1997); $4,000 (fiscal 1996). Note: In 1998, contributions were received from James A. Walker ($5,000) and Terrence J. McGlinn ($1,622,000). In fiscal 1995, contributions were received from Terrence J. McGlinn.

Typical Recipients
Arts & Humanities: Arts Institutes, History & Archaeology, Libraries, Museums/Galleries, Music
Civic & Public Affairs: Clubs, Community Foundations, Civic & Public Affairs-General, Housing, Philanthropic Organizations
Education: Arts/Humanities Education, Business Education, Colleges & Universities, Community & Junior Colleges, Education Funds, Education-General, Literacy, Private Education (Precollege), Public Education (Precollege), Secondary Education (Private), Special Education, Student Aid
Environment: Resource Conservation
Health: AIDS/HIV, Arthritis, Cancer, Children's Health/Hospitals, Clinics/Medical Centers, Emergency/Ambulance Services, Hospices, Hospitals, Long-Term Care, Medical Research, Prenatal Health Issues, Single-Disease Health Associations
Religion: Churches, Jewish Causes, Ministries, Religious Organizations, Religious Welfare
Social Services: At-Risk Youth, Child Welfare, Community Service Organizations, Domestic Violence, Emergency Relief, Food/Clothing Distribution, Recreation & Athletics, Scouts, Shelters/Homelessness, Substance Abuse, United Funds/United Ways, Youth Organizations

Application Procedures
Initial Contact: Send a brief letter of inquiry.
Deadlines: None.

Foundation Officials
Barbara T. McGlinn: assistant secretary
John F. McGlinn, II: assistant treasurer
Terrence J. McGlinn, Jr.: trustee
Terrence J. McGlinn: president
Christine R. McGlinn Auman: secretary
Margaret M. Shields: treasurer

Grants Analysis
Disclosure Period: fiscal year ending September 30, 2003
Total Grants: $803,545*
Number of Grants: 68
Average Grant: $8,463*
Highest Grant: $135,000
Lowest Grant: $250
Typical Range: $5,000 to $10,000
*Note: Giving excludes United Way. Average grant excludes two highest grants ($245,000).

Recent Grants
Note: Grants derived from fiscal 2003 Form 990.
General

135,000	Reading Hospital and Medical Center, Reading, PA -- to support construction of new cancer center
110,000	Holy Name High School, Reading, PA -- for extravaganza annual fundraiser and capital campaign to expand and improve the school
40,000	John Paul II Center for Special Learning, Shillington, PA -- capital campaign to build new school, operating support and scholarships for education of special needs children
38,260	Caron Foundation, Wernersville, PA -- capital campaign to expand facility for treatment of substance abuse and youth prevention program
37,500	United Way of Berks County Inc., Reading, PA -- community campaign for various charitable organizations
28,700	Berks County Community Foundation, Reading, PA -- to provide AED's to community and youth endowment
25,000	Children's Home of Reading, Reading, PA -- shelter and support for troubled and homeless children and capital campaign for building
25,000	Police Athletic League, Reading, PA -- as program support for at-risk kids
20,000	Wood-to-Wonderful, Reading, PA -- to support toy making and reading project for children in need
18,300	American Red Cross, Reading, PA -- for disaster aid and relief

JAMES J. COLT FOUNDATION

Giving Contact
Thomas H. Heard, President & Director
PO Box 9130
Lyndhurst, NJ 07071
Phone: (201)804-8322

Description
Founded: 1952
EIN: 136112997
Organization Type: Private Foundation
Giving Locations: CA; FL: Miami including surrounding area; NY
Grant Types: General Support, Scholarship.

Donor Information
Founder: the late James J. Colt

Financial Summary
Total Giving: $30,500 (2003); $88,450 (2001)
Assets: $106,790 (2003); $266,755 (2001)
Gifts Received: $89,740 (1994). Note: In 1994, contributions were received from the estate of Anita Heard.

Typical Recipients
Arts & Humanities: Historic Preservation, History & Archaeology, Libraries, Literary Arts, Museums/Galleries, Public Broadcasting
Civic & Public Affairs: Clubs, Civic & Public Affairs-General, Municipalities/Towns, Parades/Festivals, Safety, Urban & Community Affairs
Education: Colleges & Universities, Education-General, Medical Education, Preschool Education, Private Education (Precollege), Public Education (Precollege), School Volunteerism
Environment: Environment-General, Resource Conservation
Health: AIDS/HIV, Cancer, Children's Health/Hospitals, Clinics/Medical Centers, Diabetes, Emergency/Ambulance Services, Eyes/Blindness, Health Organizations, Heart, Hospitals, Medical Rehabilitation, Medical Research, Prenatal Health Issues, Single-Disease Health Associations
International: Missionary/Religious Activities
Religion: Churches, Jewish Causes, Ministries, Religious Welfare, Synagogues/Temples
Social Services: Animal Protection, At-Risk Youth, Child Welfare, Community Service Organizations, Crime Prevention, Emergency Relief, Homes, People with Disabilities, Recreation & Athletics, Senior Services, YMCA/YWCA/YMHA/YWHA, Youth Organizations

Application Procedures
Initial Contact: Send a brief letter of inquiry on organization's letterhead.
Application Requirements: Describe program and charitable purpose; include proof of tax-exempt status.
Deadlines: None.

Foundation Officials
Vaughn Durbin: secretary
Jane Heard: director
Karen Heard: director
Thomas H. Heard: vice president, director
Donald Oresman: treasurer B New York, NY 1925. ED Oberlin College BA (1946); Columbia University School of Law LLB (1957). CORP AFFIL officer: Movado Group Inc.; managing partner: Wellspring Associatess.

Grants Analysis
Disclosure Period: calendar year ending 2003
Total Grants: $30,500
Number of Grants: 7
Highest Grant: $12,500
Lowest Grant: $100
Typical Range: $500 to $5,000

Recent Grants
Note: Grants derived from 2001 Form 990.
Library-Related

10,000	Morgan Library, New York, NY

General

20,000	Project Newborn, Miami, FL
20,000	Women's Cancer League and Partners, Miami Beach, FL
10,000	Florida Derby Gala, Gainesville, FL
10,000	Grolier Club, New York, NY
5,000	Jackson Memorial Foundation, Miami, FL
5,000	Thoroughbred Retirement Foundation, Shrewsbury, NJ
2,500	Grace Presbyterian Church, Dalton, GA
2,500	Miami Heart Research Institute, Miami, FL
1,000	American Red Cross Disaster Relief Fund, New York, NY
1,000	Bascom Palmer Eye Institute, Miami, FL

COLUMBIA FOUNDATION

Giving Contact
Susan R. Clark, Executive Director
1016 Lincoln Blvd., Suite 205
San Francisco, CA 94129
Phone: (415)561-6880
Fax: (415)561-6883
E-mail: info@columbia.org
Web: http://www.columbia.org

Description
Founded: 1940
EIN: 941196186
Organization Type: General Purpose Foundation
Giving Locations: CA: especially northern California, San Francisco including metropolitan area; England : London
Grant Types: Capital, General Support, Project, Seed Money.

Donor Information
Founder: The Columbia Foundation was established in 1940 by Madeline Haas Russell, donor and president of the foundation. Mrs. Russell is a member of the Haas family, which owns Levi-Strauss and Company, the nation's largest manufacturer of apparel. Mrs. Russell has been active in Democratic politics, and served on the boards at the San Francisco Museum of Art and the Asia Foundation, located in San Francisco. She has also been active in public broadcasting, health care, and education.
Christine H. Russell, the foundation's treasurer, is also a donor to the foundation.

Financial Summary
Total Giving: $3,211,328 (fiscal year ending May 31, 2003); $3,859,428 (fiscal 2002 approx); $3,398,521 (fiscal 2001)
Giving Analysis: Giving for fiscal 2002 includes: foundation grants to United Way ($30,000)
Assets: $69,216,257 (fiscal 2003); $69,871,970 (fiscal 2002 approx); $80,355,102 (fiscal 2001)
Gifts Received: $33,757 (fiscal 2003); $42,080 (fiscal 2001); $39,274 (fiscal 1999). Note: In fiscal 2003, contributions were received from Madeleine H. Russell 1982 Charitable Lead Trust ($22,067) and SIT Investment ($11,689). In fiscal 2001, contributions were received from Madeleine H. Russell 1982 Charitable Lead Trust ($32,660) and SIT Investment ($9,420). In fiscal 2000, contributions were received from $38,624 from Madeleine H. Russell 1982 Charitable Lead Trust.

Typical Recipients
Arts & Humanities: Arts Associations & Councils, Arts Centers, Arts Funds, Arts Institutes, Ballet, Community Arts, Dance, Ethnic & Folk Arts, Film & Video, Arts & Humanities-General, Historic Preservation, History & Archaeology, Libraries, Literary Arts, Museums/Galleries, Music, Opera, Performing Arts, Public Broadcasting, Theater, Visual Arts
Civic & Public Affairs: Asian American Affairs, Botanical Gardens/Parks, Civil Rights, Clubs, Community Foundations, Economic Development, Economic Policy, Employment/Job Training, First Amendment Issues, Gay/Lesbian Issues, Civic & Public Affairs-General, Hispanic Affairs, Housing, Law & Justice, Legal Aid, Municipalities/Towns, Native American Affairs, Nonprofit Management, Philanthropic Organizations, Professional & Trade Associations, Public Policy, Rural Affairs, Urban & Community Affairs, Women's Affairs
Education: Afterschool/Enrichment Programs, Agricultural Education, Arts/Humanities Education, Business Education, Colleges & Universities, Education

Funds, Environmental Education, Education-General, International Studies, Private Education (Precollege), Public Education (Precollege), Science/Mathematics Education, Vocational & Technical Education

Environment: Air/Water Quality, Forestry, Environment-General, Protection, Research, Resource Conservation, Wildlife Protection

Health: AIDS/HIV, Cancer, Emergency/Ambulance Services, Geriatric Health, Health Policy/Cost Containment, Health Funds, Hospices, Long-Term Care, Medical Research, Nutrition, Preventive Medicine/Wellness Organizations, Public Health

International: Foreign Arts Organizations, Foreign Educational Institutions, International-General, Health Care/Hospitals, Human Rights, International Development, International Environmental Issues, International Organizations, International Peace & Security Issues, International Relations, Missionary/Religious Activities

Religion: Jewish Causes, Ministries, Religious Organizations, Religious Welfare, Synagogues/Temples

Science: Science Museums, Scientific Centers & Institutes, Scientific Research

Social Services: At-Risk Youth, Community Centers, Community Service Organizations, Crime Prevention, Delinquency & Criminal Rehabilitation, Domestic Violence, Food/Clothing Distribution, Homes, Recreation & Athletics, Refugee Assistance, Shelters/Homelessness, Social Services-General, Volunteer Services, Youth Organizations

Application Procedures

Initial Contact: Send a letter of inquiry with an application cover sheet (available from the foundation or from the website). A full proposal will be requested if the foundation selects the application for further consideration.

Application Requirements: The letter of inquiry should be no longer than four pages and include: a description of organization; the purpose for which funds are being requested; amount requested; project budget and other sources of support; plan of action including cooperating agencies, intended results, and measurable objective if applicable. Submission of the cover sheet and letter of inquiry is sufficient for meeting the application deadline.

If the foundation requests a full proposal, it should include: a proposal narrative describing the need for the program or the problem to be addressed; plan of action including a theoretical base or rationale for this approach; the impact and significance of project, including its potential relevance; qualifications of organization and staff to implement project; relationship of program to other similar programs or agencies; how program will be evaluated; and plans for the future of program; including dissemination of results. Financial information should include the following: a line-item budget for fiscal year; statement of actual expenses and revenue for the last two years for the organization and for the project (include an audited statement if available); a list of other contributions and sources of support for project including those currently being considered. Organizational information should include: a history of organization including a description of current activities and an annual report; list of board of directors, including affiliations and occupations; a copy of IRS tax-exempt letter; and copies of articles or other publicity about organization or project.

Deadlines: Deadlines are September 1 for Human Rights; December 15 for Sustainable Communities and Economies; and June 1 for Arts and Culture. February 1. All materials should be postmarked by the application deadline, or the following business day if the deadline falls on a weekend or holiday.

Review Process: A screening process to select applications to be considered further is completed within approximately 10 weeks after the deadline, after which all applicants are notified. At this time, those to be considered are asked to submit a full proposal. After proposals are reviewed, the staff makes recommendations to the board of directors, which makes a final decision at a meeting held in late spring or late fall. The foundation reports that it only grants funds to about thirty new applicants each year.

Notes: The foundation does not accept faxed proposals. Applicants should submit proposals on two-sided recycled paper. The duration of the project may be up to five years on a single application.

Restrictions

The foundation does not customarily provide support for operating budgets of established agencies, for recurring expenses for direct services or ongoing administrative costs, for individual fellowships or scholarships, or for agencies wholly supported by federated campaigns or heavily subsidized by government funds. Primarily supports preselected organizations.

Additional Information

The foundation considers proposals only from organizations certified by the IRS as public charities.

The foundation does not assume an obligation for ongoing support for any activity. It awards a few large multi-year grants of $300,000 to $1,000,000 paid over three to five years, designed to allow an organization to make a major contribution to its field. Grants of $25,000 to $100,000 may be awarded as a single grant or as a multi-year pledge. The foundation focuses its grant making on major arts organizations in San Francisco and London, as well as the Creative Work Fund which, in turn, awards grants to individual artists.

Publications: Application Guidelines; Program Policy Statement; Annual Report; Grants list; Five-year report

Foundation Officials

Susan R. Clark: executive director
Charles P. Russell: president, director
Christine Haas Russell: treasurer, director, donor PRIM CORP EMPL chief financial officer: Persistence Software Inc.
Alice Russell-Shapiro: secretary, director

Grants Analysis

Disclosure Period: fiscal year ending May 31, 2003
Total Grants: $3,211,328
Number of Grants: 94
Average Grant: $32,380*
Highest Grant: $200,000
Lowest Grant: $724
Typical Range: $5,000 to $50,000
*Note: Average grant figure excludes highest grant.

Recent Grants

Note: Grants derived from 2003 Form 990.
General

200,000	Roots of Change Fund, San Francisco, CA -- towards soliciting private and public funding towards agriculture and food systems fellowships and food literacy education
125,000	Proteus Fund, Amherst, MA -- towards the civil marriage collaborative program
100,000	Jewish Home, San Francisco, CA -- towards the end of life care program
100,000	Royal Opera House Foundation, London United Kingdom -- towards commissioning a new opera The Tempest by Thomas Ades
100,000	San Francisco Opera, San Francisco, CA -- towards special contribution for the San Francisco operas program
100,000	San Francisco Opera, San Francisco, CA -- towards general support of the organization
68,000	California Academy of Sciences, San Francisco, CA -- to check viability of giving food service with locally grown organic food & a food center with education programs relating to sustainable food systems
60,000	San Francisco Food Systems Council, San Francisco, CA -- towards organizational development with focusing on increasing access of low income San Franciscans to local produce
55,000	Creative Work Fund, San Francisco, CA -- towards final grant for the coming year to provide funds for individual artists for the creation of a new art works
50,000	Almeida Theatre Company, London United Kingdom -- towards the theatreworks directed by Michael Attenborough and Harrison Birtwistle

COLUMBUS DISPATCH PRINTING CO.

Company Headquarters
Columbus, OH

Company Description
Employees: 1,900
SIC(s): 6200 Security & Commodity Brokers.

Operating Locations
Columbus Dispatch Printing Co. (OH--Columbus)

Nonmonetary Support
Type: In-kind Services

Wolfe Associates, Inc.

Giving Contact
Rita Wolfe, Vice President & Trustee
Wolfe Associates, Inc.
770 Twin Rivers Drive
Columbus, OH 43215
Phone: (614)460-3782
E-mail: comrel@dispatch.com
Web: http://www.dispatch.com

Description
Founded: 1973
EIN: 237303111
Organization Type: Corporate Foundation
Giving Locations: OH: Central Ohio and other areas in which the corporate donors have a substantial presence
Grant Types: Capital, Conference/Seminar, Endowment, General Support, Project, Scholarship.

Financial Summary
Total Giving: $1,591,226 (fiscal year ending June 31, 2002); $3,329,866 (fiscal 2001). Note: Contributes through foundation only.
Giving Analysis: Giving for fiscal 2002 includes: foundation grants to United Way ($521,447); fiscal 2001: foundation grants to United Way ($869,219); foundation ($2,460,647)
Assets: $6,913,829 (fiscal 2002); $8,582,601 (fiscal 2001)
Gifts Received: $989,640 (fiscal 2002); $1,989,860 (fiscal 2001); $734,313 (fiscal 2000). Note: In fiscal 2001, contributions were received from Dispatch. In fiscal 2000, contributions were received from Dispatch ($421,363); WTHR ($191,500); WBNS ($107,000); and DCS ($14,450). In fiscal 1997 contributions were received from Dispatch Printing Co., WBNS-TV, Inc., The Ohio Co., and WTHR.

Typical Recipients
Arts & Humanities: Arts Associations & Councils, Arts Centers, Arts Funds, Arts Institutes, Ballet, Dance, Historic Preservation, History & Archaeology, Libraries, Literary Arts, Museums/Galleries, Music, Opera, Performing Arts, Public Broadcasting, The-

ater

Civic & Public Affairs: African American Affairs, Botanical Gardens/Parks, Business/Free Enterprise, Chambers of Commerce, Clubs, Community Foundations, Economic Development, Economic Policy, Employment/Job Training, Ethnic Organizations, Civic & Public Affairs-General, Housing, Law & Justice, Legal Aid, Municipalities/Towns, Parades/Festivals, Philanthropic Organizations, Public Policy, Safety, Urban & Community Affairs, Zoos/Aquariums

Education: Afterschool/Enrichment Programs, Arts/Humanities Education, Business Education, Colleges & Universities, Economic Education, Education Associations, Education Funds, Education Reform, Education-General, International Studies, Journalism/Media Education, Leadership Training, Legal Education, Literacy, Minority Education, Preschool Education, Private Education (Precollege), Public Education (Precollege), Religious Education, Secondary Education (Private), Social Sciences Education, Student Aid

Environment: Resource Conservation

Health: Cancer, Children's Health/Hospitals, Clinics/Medical Centers, Diabetes, Emergency/Ambulance Services, Health-General, Health Funds, Heart, Hospices, Hospitals, Long-Term Care, Medical Rehabilitation, Medical Research, Single-Disease Health Associations

International: Health Care/Hospitals, International Relations, Trade

Religion: Churches, Dioceses, Jewish Causes, Ministries, Missionary Activities (Domestic), Religious Organizations, Religious Welfare

Science: Scientific Centers & Institutes, Scientific Research

Social Services: Animal Protection, Child Welfare, Community Centers, Community Service Organizations, Crime Prevention, Family Planning, Family Services, Food/Clothing Distribution, People with Disabilities, Recreation & Athletics, Senior Services, Shelters/Homelessness, Social Services-General, United Funds/United Ways, YMCA/YWCA/YMHA/YWHA, Youth Organizations

Application Procedures

Initial Contact: Submit a written request.
Application Requirements: Include a cover letter with a brief summary of purpose of funds sought, amount requested, proof of tax-exempt status, financial statements, and a copy of the organization's most recent Form 990.
Deadlines: None.

Restrictions

Foundation does not support individuals, public school systems, research and demonstration projects, publications, or conferences.

Additional Information

Corporate donors to the foundation are the Dispatch Printing Company, the Ohio Company, WBNS TV Inc., and RadiOhio Inc.

Grants are not automatically renewable and current recipients must reapply annually for continued support.

Foundation may require annual progress reports and notice of any material modification to project during the funding year.

The Columbus Dispatch also provides support directly through their community relations department. They work to develop programs that range from supporting the arts and nurturing Ohio's children, to providing music and excitement for the community through concerts and special events. For more information, contact Community Relations: (614)461-5225.

Corporate Officials

A. Kenneth Pierce, Jr.: vice president, chief financial officer, director B 1930. PRIM CORP EMPL vice president, chief financial officer, director: Dispatch Printing Co. CORP AFFIL vice president, secretary, director: Ohio Magazine Inc.

Foundation Officials

Michael Curtin: vice president, trustee
James H. Gilmour: vice president, treasurer, trustee
Nancy Wolfe Lane: vice president B 1939. ED Bryn Mawr College (1961). PRIM CORP EMPL vice president: Wolfe Associates, Inc.
Sherry L. Lewis: secretary, trustee
Sara Wolfe Perrini: vice president, trustee
John F. Wolfe: chairman, president, trustee
Rita Wolfe: vice president, trustee

Grants Analysis

Disclosure Period: fiscal year ending June 31, 2002
Total Grants: $1,069,779*
Number of Grants: 164
Average Grant: $4,134*
Highest Grant: $200,000
Lowest Grant: $250
Typical Range: $1,000 to $10,000
*Note: Giving excludes United Way. Average grant figure excludes two highest grants ($400,000).

Recent Grants

Note: Grants derived from 2003 Form 990.
General

200,000	Diocese of Columbus, Columbus, OH
107,886	United Way of Franklin County, Columbus, OH
105,298	United Way of Central Ohio, Columbus, OH
51,600	Columbus Symphony Orchestra, Columbus, OH
50,000	Columbus Academy, Columbus, OH
50,000	Columbus Museum of Art, Columbus, OH
32,000	Ohio Foundation of Independent Colleges, Inc, Columbus, OH
30,000	Goodwill Columbus, Columbus, OH
25,000	Franklin Park Conservatory, Columbus, OH
25,000	Wexner Center Foundation, Columbus, OH

COMER FOUNDATION (AL)

Giving Contact

Eleanor F. Wright, Executive Director
31 Inverness Center Parkway, Suite 50
Birmingham, AL 35242
Phone: (256)408-9118

Description

Founded: 1945
EIN: 636004424
Organization Type: Private Foundation
Giving Locations: AL: Birmingham
Grant Types: Capital, General Support, Operating Expenses, Research, Scholarship.

Donor Information

Founder: Avondale Mills, Comer-Avondale Mills, Inc., Cowikee Mills

Financial Summary

Total Giving: $724,600 (2003)
Giving Analysis: Giving for 2003 includes: foundation scholarships ($295,000).
Assets: $13,250,923 (2003)

Typical Recipients

Arts & Humanities: Arts Associations & Councils, Arts Centers, Ballet, Libraries, Museums/Galleries, Music, Theater
Civic & Public Affairs: Botanical Gardens/Parks, Civic & Public Affairs-General, Housing, Municipalities/Towns, Urban & Community Affairs

Education: Afterschool/Enrichment Programs, Colleges & Universities, Economic Education, Education Funds, Education Reform, Engineering/Technological Education, Education-General, Literacy, Medical Education, Public Education (Precollege), Science/Mathematics Education, Special Education, Student Aid, Vocational & Technical Education

Environment: Environment-General

Health: Children's Health/Hospitals, Clinics/Medical Centers, Hospices, Medical Rehabilitation, Medical Research, Medical Training, Nursing Services, Respiratory

Religion: Religious Welfare

Science: Science Exhibits & Fairs, Science Museums

Social Services: Animal Protection, Camps, Child Welfare, Community Service Organizations, Family Services, People with Disabilities, Recreation & Athletics, Scouts, Substance Abuse, United Funds/United Ways, YMCA/YWCA/YMHA/YWHA, Youth Organizations

Application Procedures

Initial Contact: Send a brief letter of inquiry describing program or project.
Deadlines: None.

Foundation Officials

Richard J. Comer, Jr.: trustee
Francis H. Crockard: trustee
Gillian C. Goodrich: chairman
Dr. Hugh C. Nabers, Jr.: trustee
Jane B. Selfe: trustee

Grants Analysis

Disclosure Period: calendar year ending 2003
Total Grants: $429,600*
Number of Grants: 14
Average Grant: $25,354*
Highest Grant: $100,000
Lowest Grant: $100
Typical Range: $5,000 to $40,000
*Note: Giving excludes scholarships. Average grant figure excludes highest grant.

Recent Grants

Note: Grants derived from 2003 Form 990.

Library-Related

50,000	Mountain Brook Library Foundation, Mountain Brook, AL -- for support of plant expansion

General

100,000	Children's Health System, Birmingham, AL -- for the establishment of research and innovation center
70,000	Better Basics, Birmingham, AL -- for support of programs
65,000	Alabama Symphony Orchestra, Birmingham, AL -- for support of programs and endowment fund
56,000	Auburn University, Auburn, AL -- for scholarships
48,000	University of Alabama at Birmingham School of Medicine, Birmingham, AL -- for scholarships
37,500	Sylacauga Parks and Recreation Board, Sylacauga, AL
37,500	University of Alabama, Tuscaloosa, AL -- for scholarships
37,500	University of Alabama at Birmingham School of Nursing, Birmingham, AL -- for scholarships
30,000	Comer Museum and Arts Center, Sylacauga, AL -- for scholarships

COMERICA INC.

Company Headquarters

Comerica Tower
500 Woodward Avenue
Detroit, MI 48226
Phone: (313)222-7356
Fax: (313)222-3240
Web: http://www.comerica.com

Company Description

Founded: 1982
Ticker: CMA
Exchange: NYSE
Revenue: US$2.399 billion (2003)
Profit: US$661 million (2003)
Employees: 11854 (2003)
SIC(s): 6022 State Commercial Banks, 6712 Bank Holding Companies.

Operating Locations

Comerica Inc. (CA--San Jose; FL--Boca Raton; IL--Franklin Park; MI--Battle Creek, Comstock Park, Grand Rapids, Marne; OH--Toledo); Comerica Inc. (TX--Dallas)

Nonmonetary Support

Type: In-kind Services
Volunteer Programs: Company offers Comerica Cares program in which employees participate in volunteer activities of community organizations.
Contact: Charlene Cole, Education/Volunteer Program Manager

Comerica Charitable Foundation

Giving Contact

Caroline Chambers, Vice President, Assistant Secretary, & Director
500 Woodward Avenue
Detroit, MI 48226-3352
Phone: (313)222-3571
Fax: (313)222-8720
E-mail: caroline_chambers@comerica.com
Web: http://www.comerica.com/cma/cda/main/0,1555,4_A_1472,00.html

Description

Founded: 1997
EIN: 383373052
Organization Type: Corporate Foundation
Former Name: Comerica Foundation (2000).
Giving Locations: CA; MI: especially southeastern MI; TX
Grant Types: Capital, Employee Matching Gifts, General Support, Multiyear/Continuing Support, Operating Expenses, Scholarship.
Note: Employee matching gift ratio: 1 to 1 for gifts to colleges and universities, up to $2,000 per employee annually. Company sponsors a special one-time holiday match program.

Financial Summary

Total Giving: $8,319,070 (2003); $7,875,119 (2002); $6,101,689 (2001). Note: Contributes through foundation and corporate direct giving.
Assets: $5,249,021 (2003); $5,754,712 (2002); $12,281,827 (2001)
Gifts Received: $7,987,500 (2003); $2,000,000 (2002); $5,000,000 (2001). Note: Contributions were received from Comerica, Inc. and subsidiaries.

Typical Recipients

Arts & Humanities: Arts Centers, Arts Festivals, Arts Institutes, History & Archaeology, Libraries, Museums/Galleries, Music, Opera, Public Broadcasting
Civic & Public Affairs: Asian American Affairs, Business/Free Enterprise, Chambers of Commerce, Civil Rights, Clubs, Community Foundations, Economic Development, Employment/Job Training, Ethnic Organizations, Civic & Public Affairs-General, Housing, Minority Business, Municipalities/Towns, Nonprofit Management, Parades/Festivals, Public Policy, Rural Affairs, Urban & Community Affairs, Zoos/Aquariums
Education: Afterschool/Enrichment Programs, Arts/Humanities Education, Business Education, Colleges & Universities, Education Funds, Education-General, Legal Education, Minority Education, Private Education (Precollege), Public Education (Precollege), Student Aid
Health: Cancer, Children's Health/Hospitals, Emergency/Ambulance Services, Health Organizations, Hospices, Hospitals, Medical Rehabilitation, Mental Health, Single-Disease Health Associations
Religion: Jewish Causes, Ministries, Religious Welfare
Science: Science Museums, Scientific Centers & Institutes
Social Services: At-Risk Youth, Child Welfare, Community Service Organizations, Food/Clothing Distribution, People with Disabilities, Recreation & Athletics, Scouts, Senior Services, Shelters/Homelessness, Social Services-General, United Funds/United Ways, Volunteer Services, YMCA/YWCA/YMHA/YWHA, Youth Organizations

Application Procedures

Initial Contact: Send a written proposal.
Application Requirements: Include concise statements about project or agency describing programs, need, budget, management, goals, and accomplishments; amount requested; itemized projection of program costs; organizational operating budgets for past two years (preferably audited statements); list of existing funding sources; current board of directors; documentation on the method in which the contribution will be used in the program; and proof of tax-exempt status.
Deadlines: None.
Review Process: After initial staff review, proposals go to corporate contributions committee which determines specific amounts or terms of contributions; organizations will receive written notification of funding decision within 60 days of receipt of request.
Notes: Organizations in Southeastern Michigan may apply to above address; other organizations should contact nearest bank branch. Comerica Foundation board ratifies final decisions concerning contributions allocations.

Restrictions

The company does not support individuals; religious, fraternal, or political organizations; charitable golf events, recreational and athletic programs; multiyear pledges; endowment funds; non-tax-exempt organizations; or organizations supported by united funds. The company avoids controversial organizations and causes.

Additional Information

The company gives primarily to private and public 501(c)(3) organizations, and prefers innovative organizations which demonstrate the ability to solve problems and provide direct services relating to economic development. Approximately 30% of Comerica's contributions are made through headquarters direct giving and 70% of contributions are made through the Comerica Foundation.

The company reports that three permanent funds have been established with the Community Foundation of Southeastern Michigan to address specific needs of the community in the areas of the arts, youth activities, and economic development. Contact the Community Foundation of Southeastern Michigan at (313) 961-6675, or submit a proposal to Vice President of Programs, 333 W. Fort Street, Suite 2010, Detroit, MI 48226.

Publications: Comerica Contributions Policy

Corporate Officials

Elizabeth S. Acton: executive vice president, chief financial officer ED University of Minnesota BA (1973); Indiana University MBA (1976). PRIM CORP EMPL vice president, treasurer: Ford Motor Co.
John D. Lewis: vice chairman B 1950. ED University of Dayton BS; University of Detroit MBA. PRIM CORP EMPL vice chairman: Comerica Inc. ADD CORP EMPL vice chairman: Comerica Bank; director: Comerica Bank California. CORP AFFIL chairman: Oakwood Healthcare Inc. NONPR AFFIL chairman: Bank Administration Institute; trustee: Detroit Institute of Arts Founders Society.

Foundation Officials

Elizabeth S. Acton: director ED University of Minnesota BA (1973); Indiana University MBA (1976).
Paul Burdiss: treasurer
Megan Burkhart: director
Caroline Solomon Chambers: vice president, assistant secretary, director
Frank DeAramas: director
Linda D. Forte: director ED Bowling Green State University BS; University of Michigan MBA. NONPR AFFIL director: National Office Products Association; director: Neighborhood Development Corp.; director: Economic Development Corp.; director: Michigan Women's Foundation.
Mike Fulton: director
Jim Garavaglia: director
John Haggerty: director NONPR AFFIL director: Detroit Neighborhood Housing Services Inc.; vice chairman, michigan region: National Conference for Community & Justice.
John D. Lewis: chairman, director (see above)
Ron Marcinelli: director
Sharon McMurray: director
Albert P. Taylor: director NONPR AFFIL member: Michigan Government Finance Officers Association; director: Starfish Family Services.
Mark Yonkman: vice president, secretary, director
Gregory Yovan: assistant treasurer

Grants Analysis

Disclosure Period: calendar year ending 2003
Total Grants: $7,049,870*
Number of Grants: 650 (approx)
Average Grant: $10,846
Highest Grant: $200,000
Lowest Grant: $50
Typical Range: $1,000 to $25,000
*Note: Giving excludes scholarship and United Way.

Recent Grants

Note: Grants derived from 2003 Form 990.

General

200,000	Detroit Institute of Arts Founders Society, Detroit, MI
187,500	LISC (Local Initiatives Support Corporation), Detroit, MI
167,000	Charles H Wright Museum of African-American History, Detroit, MI
150,000	Detroit Regional Chamber, Detroit, MI
150,000	Detroit Symphony Orchestra Hall, Detroit, MI
115,000	Detroit Public Television - Channel WTVS, Detroit, MI
100,000	ACCESS (Arab American Heritage Campaign), Dearborn, MI
100,000	American Arab Chamber of Commerce, Dearborn, MI
100,000	City Year Inc., Boston, MA
100,000	Cranbrook Institute of Science, Bloomfield Hills, MI

COMMERCE BANCSHARES INC.

Company Headquarters
Kansas City, MO
Web: http://www.commercebank.com

Company Description
Founded: 1966
Ticker: CBSH
Exchange: NASDAQ
Assets: US$13.308 billion (2002)
Employees: 5100 (2003)
SIC(s): 6021 National Commercial Banks, 6712 Bank Holding Companies.

Operating Locations
Commerce Bancshares, Inc. (MO--Springfield); Commerce Bancshares, Inc. (MO--St. Joseph, St. Louis); Commerce Bancshares, Inc. (NE)

Nonmonetary Support
Volunteer Programs: The company actively encourages employee volunteerism. Employees and executives also are active in United Way, Habitat for Humanity, and numerous community organizations.

Commerce Bancshares Foundation

Giving Contact
Michael D. Fields, President
922 Walnut St., 2nd Fl.
Kansas City, MO 64106
Phone: (816)234-2728

Alternate Contact
Sheila Rice
Phone: (816)234-8670

Description
Founded: 1952
EIN: 446012453
Organization Type: Corporate Foundation
Giving Locations: IL: West Central; KS; MO
Grant Types: General Support.

Donor Information
Founder: Commerce Bank of Kansas City, NA, Commerce Bank of Kansas City, NA, Commerce Bank of Springfield, NA

Financial Summary
Total Giving: $1,234,426 (2003); $1,159,337 (2002); $1,265,561 (2001). Note: Contributes through corporate direct giving program and foundation.
Assets: $3,494,575 (2003); $4,689,909 (2002); $2,086,555 (2001)
Gifts Received: $409,653 (2002); $997,639 (1996); $16,453 (1993). Note: In 1996, contributions were received from from Commerce Bancshares Inc.

Typical Recipients
Arts & Humanities: Arts Associations & Councils, Arts Centers, Arts Institutes, Community Arts, Historic Preservation, History & Archaeology, Libraries, Museums/Galleries, Music, Opera, Public Broadcasting, Theater
Civic & Public Affairs: African American Affairs, Botanical Gardens/Parks, Business/Free Enterprise, Community Foundations, Economic Development, Civic & Public Affairs-General, Housing, Inner-City Development, Legal Aid, Municipalities/Towns, Nonprofit Management, Parades/Festivals, Urban & Community Affairs, Zoos/Aquariums
Education: Afterschool/Enrichment Programs, Agricultural Education, Arts/Humanities Education, Busi-

ness Education, Business-School Partnerships, Colleges & Universities, Education Funds, Education-General, Literacy, Private Education (Precollege), Public Education (Precollege), Secondary Education (Private), Secondary Education (Public)
Environment: Environment-General, Protection, Resource Conservation, Wildlife Protection
Health: Cancer, Children's Health/Hospitals, Clinics/Medical Centers, Emergency/Ambulance Services, Health-General, Health Organizations, Hospitals, Public Health, Single-Disease Health Associations
International: International Affairs
Religion: Dioceses, Missionary Activities (Domestic), Religious Organizations, Religious Welfare
Science: Science Exhibits & Fairs, Science Museums, Scientific Centers & Institutes
Social Services: Big Brothers/Big Sisters, Child Welfare, Community Centers, Community Service Organizations, Counseling, Domestic Violence, Emergency Relief, Family Planning, Family Services, Food/Clothing Distribution, Scouts, Shelters/Homelessness, Substance Abuse, United Funds/United Ways, YMCA/YWCA/YMHA/YWHA, Youth Organizations

Application Procedures
Initial Contact: Address letter of inquiry to local branch president.
Application Requirements: Include a description of organization and its purpose, amount requested, time frame, proof of tax-exempt status, a list of the board of directors, an audited financial statement, specific program budget, a list of other donors, and proof of 501(c)(3) status.
Deadlines: None.
Review Process: All requests for support originate from the communities served; local bank presidents forward requests to the foundation; if additional information is required, the foundation requests it.
Evaluative Criteria: Ability to help target constituency.
Decision Notification: Review process is ongoing; organization should set aside at least six months for a specific request.

Restrictions
The foundation does not support private foundations.

Corporate Officials
David Woods Kemper: chairman, president, chief executive officer, director B Kansas City, MO 1950. ED Harvard University AB (1972); Oxford University Worcester College MA (1974); Stanford University Graduate School of Business Administration MBA (1976). PRIM CORP EMPL chairman, president, chief executive officer, director: Commerce Bancshares, Inc. CORP AFFIL director: SLH Corp.; director: Wave Technologies International Inc.; director: Seafield Capital Corp.; director: Lab Holdings Inc.; director: Ralcorp Holdings Inc.; chairman: City National Bank Pittsburgh; director: Commerce Bank Saint Louis; director: Business Mens Assurance Co. NONPR AFFIL trustee: Saint Louis Symphony Orchestra; trustee: Washington University; trustee: Missouri Botanical Gardens; member: American Academy of Arts & Sciences; member: Bankers Roundtable. CLUB AFFIL Saint Louis Country Club; University Club; River Club; Saint Louis Club; Racquet Club; Kansas City Country Club; Old Warson Country Club.

Foundation Officials
Michael D. Fields: president, director
David W. Kemper: director
Jonathan M. Kemper: vice president, assistant secretary, director
Edward J. Reardon, II: vice president, treasurer, director PRIM CORP EMPL director: Commerce Bank, NA.
J. Daniel Stinnett: secretary B Great Falls, MT 1945. ED Vanderbilt University (1967); University of Missouri, Kansas City (1972). PRIM CORP EMPL vice

president, general counsel, secretary: Commerce Bancshares, Inc. CORP AFFIL secretary: Commerce Bank NA.

Grants Analysis
Disclosure Period: calendar year ending 2003
Total Grants: $1,234,426*
Number of Grants: 850 (approx)
Average Grant: $1,452
Highest Grant: $100,000
Lowest Grant: $50
Typical Range: $100 to $3,000
*Note: Giving includes United Way.

Recent Grants
Note: Grants derived from 2003 Form 990.
Library-Related

4,000	Columbus Public Library, Columbus, KS
3,000	St. Louis Public Library, St. Louis, MO

General

52,000	United Way of the Plains, Wichita, KS
47,242	United Way of Greater St. Louis Inc., St. Louis, MO
47,242	United Way of Greater St. Louis Inc., St. Louis, MO
47,242	United Way of Greater St. Louis Inc., St. Louis, MO
47,242	United Way of Greater St. Louis Inc., St. Louis, MO
29,175	Heart of America United Way Inc., Kansas City, MO
29,175	Heart of America United Way Inc., Kansas City, MO
29,175	Heart of America United Way Inc., Kansas City, MO
21,000	Heart of Illinois United Way Inc., Peoria, IL
16,500	United Way of Mclean County, Bloomington, IL

THE COMMONWEALTH FUND

Giving Contact
Andrea C. Landes, Director, Grants Management
1 East 75th Street
New York, NY 10021-2692
Phone: (212)606-3800
Fax: (212)606-3500
E-mail: cmwf@cmwf.org
Web: http://www.cmwf.org

Description
Founded: 1918
EIN: 131635260
Organization Type: General Purpose Foundation
Giving Locations: nationally; some emphasis on New York City.
Grant Types: Fellowship, General Support, Project, Research.

Donor Information
Founder: The Commonwealth Fund was established in 1918 with a gift of about $10 million from Anna M. Harkness. Her husband, Stephen (d. 1888), was a founding investor in Standard Oil Company. Her son, Edward S. Harkness, was the fund's president until his death in 1940 and developed the fund's basic programs. In 1986, the fund was given the assets of the James Picker Foundation.

Financial Summary
Total Giving: $17,621,678 (fiscal year ending June 30, 2003); $17,680,353 (fiscal 2002); $15,349,829 (fiscal 2001)
Giving Analysis: Giving for fiscal 2003 includes: foundation matching gifts ($503,260); foundation fel-

lowships ($1,322,434); fiscal 2002: foundation matching gifts ($574,898); foundation fellowships ($1,245,675); fiscal 2001: foundation matching gifts ($575,858) foundation fellowships ($1,026,175)

Assets: $524,251,893 (fiscal 2003); $533,376,830 (fiscal 2002); $550,680,215 (fiscal 2001)

Gifts Received: $10,000 (fiscal 2003); $3,001,124 (fiscal 2002); $50,000 (fiscal 1999). Note: In 2003, contributions were received from Korrin M. Koran, MD. In 2002, contributions were received from the estate of Professor Frances Cooke Macgregor. In 1999, contributions were received from Professor Frances Cooke Macgregor.

Typical Recipients

Arts & Humanities: Arts Funds, History & Archaeology, Libraries, Public Broadcasting

Civic & Public Affairs: Botanical Gardens/Parks, Business/Free Enterprise, Employment/Job Training, Civic & Public Affairs-General, Housing, Law & Justice, Municipalities/Towns, Nonprofit Management, Philanthropic Organizations, Professional & Trade Associations, Public Policy, Safety, Urban & Community Affairs, Women's Affairs

Education: Business Education, Colleges & Universities, Education Funds, Education Reform, Faculty Development, Education-General, Health & Physical Education, Leadership Training, Legal Education, Medical Education, Public Education (Precollege), Science/Mathematics Education, Social Sciences Education, Special Education, Student Aid, Vocational & Technical Education

Environment: Energy, Environment-General, Resource Conservation, Wildlife Protection

Health: Adolescent Health Issues, Cancer, Children's Health/Hospitals, Clinics/Medical Centers, Diabetes, Health-General, Geriatric Health, Health Policy/Cost Containment, Health Funds, Health Organizations, Heart, Home-Care Services, Hospitals, Hospitals (University Affiliated), Long-Term Care, Medical Research, Medical Training, Mental Health, Nursing Services, Prenatal Health Issues, Preventive Medicine/Wellness Organizations, Public Health, Research/Studies Institutes

International: International-General, Health Care/Hospitals, Human Rights, International Organizations

Science: Scientific Centers & Institutes

Social Services: At-Risk Youth, Child Welfare, Community Service Organizations, Day Care, Domestic Violence, Emergency Relief, Family Planning, Family Services, Homes, Recreation & Athletics, Senior Services, Substance Abuse, Youth Organizations

Application Procedures

Initial Contact: Applicants should submit a letter of inquiry via regular or electronic mail. Letters should be brief and no more than three pages.

Application Requirements: The letter of inquiry should include contact name, legal name of grantee organization, complete mailing address, phone numbers, e-mail address, purpose of grants, description of the project's targeted audience, estimated total project cost, total dollar amount requested from the Fund, project design, including schedule and workplan, description of the project's expected outcomes, and organization staffing and financial resources.

Deadlines: None. Applicants may send requests any time.

Review Process: Applications are reviewed by the staff to judge merit. Applicants will be notified within two months of initial review. Those viewed favorably are reviewed and voted upon by the board of directors, which meets three times a year.

Restrictions

Grants are not provided for general planning, ongoing activities, or work for which achievements cannot be measured. The fund does not make grants to individuals or make contributions used for general support, endowments, buildings, renovations of facilities, or major equipment. The funds does not typically support major media projects or documentaries. Grants rarely provide support for longer than three years.

Additional Information

Preference is given to proposals to clarify the scope of serious and neglected problems, especially those affecting vulnerable groups of Americans; to analyze the impact of policies and trends on well-defined issues; or to develop and test practical solutions.

Publications: Annual Report; Recent Grants Release

Foundation Officials

William R. Brody, MD: director

Benjamin K. Chu, MD: director

Karen Padgett Davis: president, director B Blackwell, OK 1942. ED Rice University BA (1965); Rice University PhD (1969). CORP AFFIL director: Somatix Therapy Corp.

Samuel C. Fleming: director PRIM CORP EMPL chairman, chief executive officer: Decision Resources Inc.

Jane E. Henney, MD: director

Lawrence S. Huntington: director

Lawrence Smith Huntington: chairman finance committee, director B New York, NY 1935. ED Harvard University BA (1957); New York University LLB (1964). PRIM CORP EMPL chairman, chief executive officer, chairman executive committee, director: Fiduciary Trust Co. International. CORP AFFIL director: Princeton Packet Inc. NONPR AFFIL director: Woods Hole Research Center; director: World Wildlife Fund; vice chairman, treasurer, trustee: South Street Seaport Museum; director: Trinity Church; trustee: Saint Lukes Roosevelt Hospital Center; trustee: Santa Fe Institute; member advisory board: New York State Common Retirement Fund; trustee: Opsail; member advisory board: NASD International Markets; chairman: New York Law School; director: Business Executives National Security; trustee: Citizens Budget Committee. CLUB AFFIL trust: New York Yacht Club; American Alpine Club; Century Association.

Helene L. Kaplan: director, vice chairman B New York, NY 1933. ED Barnard College AB (1953); New York University JD (1967). PRIM CORP EMPL of counsel: Skadden, Arps, Slate, Meagher & Flom. CORP AFFIL director: Verizon Communications Inc.; director: May Department Stores Co.; director: Metro Life Insurance Co.; director: JP Morgan Chase; director: ExxonMobil Corp. NONPR AFFIL trustee: Olive Free Library; member: Women's Forum; member: New York State Bar Association; vice chairman, trustee: Mount Sinai Medical Center; vice chairman, trustee: Mount Sinai School of Medicine; trustee: J. Paul Getty Trust; trustee: The Commonwealth Fund; trustee: Institute Advanced Studies; member: Century Association; trustee: Barnard College; member: Carnegie Commission on Science, Technology and Government; fellow: American Philosophical Society; member: Association Bar New York City; trustee, vice chairman: American Museum Natural History; member: American Academy of Arts & Sciences; member: American Bar Association. CLUB AFFIL Cosmopolitan Club.

Dr. Walter Eugene Massey: director B Hattiesburg, MS April 05, 1938. ED Morehouse College BS (1958); Washington University PhD (1966); Washington University MA (1966); Washington University PHD (1966). PRIM NONPR EMPL president: Morehouse College. CORP AFFIL director: McDonalds Corp.; director: Motorola Inc.; director: Conoco Corp.; director: BankAmerica Corp.; director: BP Amoco Corp. NONPR AFFIL member: Sigma Xi; member: United Way of Chicago; trustee: Rand Corp.; president: Morehouse College; member: National Science Foundation; president: American Association Advancement Science.

Robert C. Pozen: director

Cristine Russell: vice chairman, director

James J. Tallon, Jr.: director PRIM CORP EMPL chairman: Educational Resources Systems. NONPR AFFIL director: New York Academy Medicine.

Samuel O. Thier, MD: chairman, director

William Y. Yun: director

Grants Analysis

Disclosure Period: fiscal year ending June 30, 2003

Total Grants: $15,795,984*

Number of Grants: 297

Average Grant: $53,185

Highest Grant: $500,000

Lowest Grant: $1,000

Typical Range: $25,000 to $100,000

*Note: Giving excludes fellowship and matching gifts.

Recent Grants

Note: Grants derived from fiscal 2003 Form 990.

General

792,000	President and Fellows of Harvard College, Cambridge, MA -- towards minority health policy
709,695	Commonwealth Fund, New York, NY -- towards health care policy
414,261	President and Fellows of Harvard College, Cambridge, MA -- towards minority health policy
343,170	Atlantic Health System, Florham Park, NJ -- towards hospital patient safety
339,735	Harvard University John F Kennedy School of Government, Cambridge, MA -- towards commonwealth fund
327,634	Johns Hopkins University Bloomberg School of Public Health, Baltimore, MD -- towards Healthy Steps for young children
302,000	Harris Interactive Inc., New York, NY -- towards national survey of US physicians
270,240	Massachusetts General Hospital, Boston, MA -- towards commonwealth fund quality improvement
240,000	Johns Hopkins University Bloomberg School of Public Health, Baltimore, MD -- towards follow up of Healthy Steps effects
224,994	ICF Incorporated, Baltimore, MD -- towards Healthy Steps for young children

COMMUNITY ENTERPRISES

Giving Contact

William H. Hightower, Jr., President
PO Box 1089
Thomaston, GA 30286
Phone: (706)647-7684
Fax: (706)646-5094

Description

Founded: 1944

EIN: 586043415

Organization Type: Private Foundation

Giving Locations: GA: Thomaston including area within approximately 100 miles of Thomaston

Grant Types: General Support, Multiyear/Continuing Support, Scholarship.

Donor Information

Founder: Julian T. Hightower, Thomaston Cotton Mills

Financial Summary

Total Giving: $446,648 (fiscal year ending June 30, 2004); $568,306 (fiscal 2001). Note: Giving includes United Way ($13,500); scholarship ($364,669).

Giving Analysis: Giving for fiscal 2004 includes: foundation grants to United Way ($10,000); fiscal 2001: foundation grants to United Way ($10,000)

Assets: $10,545,722 (fiscal 2004); $11,002,025 (fiscal 2001)

Typical Recipients

Arts & Humanities: Arts Associations & Councils, Historic Preservation, Libraries

Civic & Public Affairs: Civic & Public Affairs-General, Housing, Municipalities/Towns, Urban & Community Affairs

Education: Business Education, Colleges & Universities, Education Funds, Engineering/Technological Education, Education-General, Private Education (Precollege), Public Education (Precollege), Science/Mathematics Education, Student Aid, Vocational & Technical Education

Environment: Wildlife Protection

Health: Cancer, Heart, Hospitals

Religion: Churches, Missionary Activities (Domestic), Religious Organizations, Religious Welfare

Science: Science Museums

Social Services: Community Service Organizations, Recreation & Athletics, Scouts, Shelters/Homelessness, United Funds/United Ways, Youth Organizations

Application Procedures

Initial Contact: Send a brief letter of inquiry.

Application Requirements: Include a description of organization, amount requested, purpose of funds sought, recently audited financial statement, and proof of tax-exempt status.

Deadlines: December 31.

Additional Information

The foundation is affiliated with Thomaston Mills. See separate entry for financial data on this company.

Foundation Officials

George H. Hightower, Jr.: vice president, trustee PRIM CORP EMPL executive vice president, director: Thomaston Mills.

Neil Hamilton Hightower: trustee B Atlanta, GA 1940. ED Georgia Institute of Technology BS (1963); Harvard University (1974). PRIM CORP EMPL chairman, president, chief executive officer, director: Thomaston Mills. CORP AFFIL director: NationsBank; director: GA NationsBank. NONPR AFFIL director, member: Textile Education Foundation; member: Textile Traffic Association; member: Southern Industry Relations Conf; member: Georgia Textile Manufacturer Association; director, member: National Cotton Council America; member: Georgia Chamber of Commerce; president, member: American Textile Manufacturer Institute; member: American Yarn Spinners Association. CLUB AFFIL Kiwanis Club.

Grants Analysis

Disclosure Period: fiscal year ending June 30, 2004

Total Grants: $436,648*

Number of Grants: 29

Average Grant: $8,452*

Highest Grant: $200,000

Lowest Grant: $1,000

Typical Range: $5,000 to $10,000

*Note: Giving excludes United Way. Average grant figure excludes highest grant.

Recent Grants

Note: Grants derived from fiscal 2004 Form 990.

General

200,000	First United Methodist Church, Marietta, GA
30,000	Georgia Tech Foundation, Atlanta, GA
25,000	Emory University, Atlanta, GA
25,000	Upson County Schools, Thomaston, GA
20,000	Alexander-Tharpe Fund, Atlanta, GA
15,750	Georgia Institute of Technology, Atlanta, GA
10,000	Flint River Technical College Foundation, Thomaston, GA
10,000	Flint River Technical College Foundation, Thomaston, GA
10,000	Gordon College Foundation, Barnesville, GA

10,000	Westwood School, Camilla, GA

COMMUNITY TRUST BANCORP INC.

Company Headquarters

PO Box 2947
Pikeville, KY 41501
Web: http://www.ctbi.com

Company Description

Founded: 1980

Ticker: CTBI

Exchange: NASDAQ

Former Name: Commercial Bank.

Assets: US$2.487 billion (2002)

Employees: 883 (2002)

SIC(s): 6000 Depository Institutions.

Parent Company: Commercial Bank of Grayson, 208 E. Main St., Grayson, KY, United States

Operating Locations

Community Trust Bank (KY--Lexington)

Commercial Bank Foundation

Giving Contact

Jack W. Strother, Trustee
208 E. Main St.
Grayson, KY 41143
Phone: (606)474-7811

Description

EIN: 611087988

Organization Type: Corporate Foundation

Giving Locations: KY: Carter County

Grant Types: Scholarship.

Financial Summary

Total Giving: $24,500 (2003); $33,540 (2001)

Giving Analysis: Giving for 2003 includes: foundation scholarships ($12,000)

Assets: $571,038 (2003); $563,434 (2001)

Gifts Received: $25,000 (2003); $25,000 (2001); $25,000 (2000). Note: Contributions were received from The Commercial Bank.

Typical Recipients

Arts & Humanities: Libraries

Civic & Public Affairs: Civic & Public Affairs-General

Education: Business Education, Colleges & Universities, Private Education (Precollege), Public Education (Precollege), Secondary Education (Public), Student Aid

Religion: Ministries, Religious Welfare

Social Services: Substance Abuse

Application Procedures

Initial Contact: Application form required for scholarships. Other applications should be made in writing. Deadline for graduating seniors is April 15.

Additional Information

Provides higher education scholarships to graduates of Carter County, KY, high schools only.

Publications: Application Form

Corporate Officials

Burlin Coleman: chairman, president, chief executive officer PRIM CORP EMPL chairman, president, chief executive officer: Community Trust Bank.

Richard Levy: chief financial officer PRIM CORP EMPL chief financial officer: Community Trust Bank.

Foundation Officials

Jack W. Strother, Jr.: co-trustee

Grants Analysis

Disclosure Period: calendar year ending 2003

Total Grants: $12,500*

Number of Grants: 3

Highest Grant: $5,000

Lowest Grant: $2,500

*Note: Giving excludes scholarships.

Recent Grants

Note: Grants derived from 2001 Form 990.

General

5,000	Community Hospice, Ashland, KY -- Capital Campaign
5,000	Kentucky Christian College, Grayson, KY
5,000	Kentucky Christian College, Grayson, KY
4,540	Morehead State University, Morehead, KY -- Learning Lab Grant

COMPASS BANK

Company Headquarters

505 20th St. N, Ste. 100
Birmingham, AL 35203
Phone: (205)558-5000
Web: http://www.compassweb.com

Company Description

Former Name: Central Bank of the South.

Employees: 4,300

SIC(s): 6022 State Commercial Banks.

Parent Company: Compass Bancshares Inc., 15 20th Street, Birmingham, AL, United States

Operating Locations

Compass Bank (AL--Decatur; TX--Dallas, Houston)

Note: Maintains 83 locations throughout Alabama.

Compass Bank Foundation

Giving Contact

Jerry W. Powell, Jr.
PO Box 10566
15 S. 20th Street
Birmingham, AL 35233
Phone: (205)933-3960
Fax: (205)933-3336

Description

Founded: 1981

EIN: 630823545

Organization Type: Corporate Foundation

Giving Locations: AL; AZ; FL; TX

Grant Types: Capital, General Support, Scholarship.

Donor Information

Founder: Central Bank of the South

Financial Summary

Total Giving: $1,967,005 (2003); $1,741,952 (2002); $1,645,477 (2001). Note: Contributes through foundation only.

Giving Analysis: Giving for 2002 includes: foundation scholarships ($18,290); foundation grants to United Way ($628,751); foundation ($1,094,912); 2001: foundation scholarships ($20,675); foundation grants to United Way ($515,135); foundation ($1,109,667)

Assets: $7,599,276 (2003); $6,680,746 (2002); $5,925,794 (2001)

Gifts Received: $2,817,000 (2003); $2,359,724 (2002); $4,107,949 (2001). Note: Contributions were received from Compass Bank.

Typical Recipients

Arts & Humanities: Arts Associations & Councils, Arts Festivals, Arts Outreach, Libraries, Museums/ Galleries, Music, Opera, Performing Arts, Public Broadcasting, Theater

Civic & Public Affairs: Botanical Gardens/Parks, Business/Free Enterprise, Chambers of Commerce, Civil Rights, Clubs, Community Foundations, Economic Development, Civic & Public Affairs-General, Hispanic Affairs, Housing, Legal Aid, Minority Business, Municipalities/Towns, Nonprofit Management, Professional & Trade Associations, Public Policy, Rural Affairs, Safety, Urban & Community Affairs, Zoos/Aquariums

Education: Arts/Humanities Education, Business Education, Colleges & Universities, Community & Junior Colleges, Education Funds, Elementary Education (Public), Faculty Development, Education-General, Legal Education, Literacy, Minority Education, Private Education (Precollege), Public Education (Precollege), Religious Education, Science/Mathematics Education, Social Sciences Education, Special Education, Student Aid, Vocational & Technical Education

Environment: Resource Conservation

Health: Cancer, Children's Health/Hospitals, Clinics/ Medical Centers, Diabetes, Emergency/Ambulance Services, Eyes/Blindness, Health Funds, Health Organizations, Heart, Hospices, Hospitals, Kidney, Mental Health, Multiple Sclerosis, Speech & Hearing, Transplant Networks/Donor Banks

International: Health Care/Hospitals, International Organizations

Religion: Ministries, Religious Organizations, Religious Welfare

Science: Science Museums

Social Services: Animal Protection, Child Abuse, Child Welfare, Community Centers, Community Service Organizations, Emergency Relief, Family Services, Food/Clothing Distribution, Homes, People with Disabilities, Recreation & Athletics, Scouts, Shelters/Homelessness, Social Services-General, Special Olympics, United Funds/United Ways, Veterans, YMCA/YWCA/YMHA/YWHA, Youth Organizations

Application Procedures

Initial Contact: Send a brief proposal.

Application Requirements: Include a list of the board of directors, a description of organization, amount requested, purpose of funds sought, recently audited financial statement, and proof of tax-exempt status.

Deadlines: None.

Restrictions

Does not support religious organizations for sectarian purposes, individuals, or political or lobbying groups. Grants are limited to 501(c)(3) organizations.

Corporate Officials

E. Lee Harris, Jr.: executive vice president human resources

Garrett R. Hegel: chief financial officer B Waukegan, IL 1950. ED University of Wisconsin (1973). PRIM CORP EMPL chief financial officer: Compass Bancshares Inc. ADD CORP EMPL chief financial officer: Compass Bank. NONPR AFFIL member: American Society CPAs; member: Federation Executive Institute; member: American Institute CPAs.

D. Paul Jones, Jr.: chairman, chief executive officer B Birmingham, AL 1942. ED University of Alabama BS (1964); University of Alabama JD (1967); New York University LLM (1968). PRIM CORP EMPL chairman, chief executive officer: Compass Bancshares Inc. CORP AFFIL director: Russell Lands Co.; director: Golden Enterprises Inc.; director: Compass Bank; director: Federal Reserve Bank Atlanta. NONPR AFFIL fellow: Society International Business Fellows; board: University Alabama; member: Service Corp. Ret Executives; member: International Fi-

nancial Conference; member: Region 2020 Inc.; partner: Economic Development Partnership Alabama; director: Business Council Alabama. CLUB AFFIL Rotary Club.

Jerry W. Powell: chief financial officer B Montgomery, AL 1950. ED Birmingham-Southern College BA (1972); University of Alabama JD (1975). PRIM CORP EMPL secretary, general counsel: Compass Bancshares Inc. ADD CORP EMPL secretary, general counsel: Compass Bank. CORP AFFIL secretary: Compass Brokerage Inc. NONPR AFFIL member: American Bar Association; member: American Corporate Counsel Association.

Foundation Officials

Garrett R. Hegel: president (see above)
D. Paul Jones, Jr.: trustee (see above)
Jerry W. Powell: trustee (see above)

Grants Analysis

Disclosure Period: calendar year ending 2003
Total Grants: $1,239,213*
Number of Grants: 350 (approx)
Average Grant: $3,541
Highest Grant: $50,000
Lowest Grant: $400
Typical Range: $1,000 to $5,000
*Note: Giving excludes scholarship and United Way.

Recent Grants

Note: Grants derived from 2003 Form 990.
General

80,000	United Way of Dallas County, Dallas, TX
73,000	United Way of Central Alabama, Birmingham, AL
70,000	United way of Central Alabama, Birmingham, AL
50,000	Juvenile Diabetes Research Foundation, New York, NY
40,000	Foundation Communities, Austin, TX
37,500	United way of Northeast Florida Inc., Jacksonville, FL
36,000	United way of Central Alabama, Birmingham, AL
25,000	National Multiple Sclerosis Society, New York, NY
25,000	United Way Capital Area, Hartford, CT
25,000	University of North Florida Inc., Jacksonville, FL

COMSAT INTERNATIONAL

Company Headquarters

6560 Rock Spring Drive
Bethesda, MD 20817
Web: http://www.comsat.com

Company Description

Former Name: Communications Satellite Corp.
Employees: 1,644
SIC(s): 4800 Communications.

Operating Locations

COMSAT Corp. (VA--Sterling); COMSAT Video Enterprises (DC; MD); Lockheed Martin Aeronautics Co. (TX--Fort Worth)

Giving Contact

Charles Manner, V.P. Communications
6560 Rock Springs Dr.
Bethesda, MD 20817
Phone: (301)214-3000
Fax: (301)214-7100

Description

Organization Type: Corporate Giving Program
Giving Locations: nationally.
Grant Types: Employee Matching Gifts.

Financial Summary

Total Giving: Company does not disclose contributions figures.

Typical Recipients

Arts & Humanities: Arts Centers, Community Arts, Arts & Humanities-General, Libraries, Museums/ Galleries, Music, Public Broadcasting, Theater

Education: Colleges & Universities, Community & Junior Colleges, Education Funds, Education-General, Vocational & Technical Education

Restrictions

Does not support individuals, religious organizations for sectarian purposes, or political or lobbying groups.

Corporate Officials

Betty L. Alewine: president, chief executive officer PRIM CORP EMPL president, chief executive officer: COMSAT Corp. ADD CORP EMPL president: Comcast International Communication.

Edwin I. Colodny: chairman PRIM CORP EMPL chairman: COMSAT Corp.

Allen E. Flower: chief financial officer, vice president PRIM CORP EMPL chief financial officer, vice president: COMSAT Corp.

Grants Analysis

Typical Range: $10 to $1,000

CONE-BLANCHARD CORP.

Company Headquarters

7 Everett Lane
Windsor, VT 05089

Company Description

Revenue: US$10.8 million (2001)
Employees: 60 (2001)
SIC(s): 3500 Industrial Machinery & Equipment, 7300 Business Services.

Cone Automatic Machine Co. Charitable Foundation

Giving Contact

W. Red McCullough, Treasurer
PO Box 65
Claremont, NH 03743
Phone: (603)542-6103

Description

EIN: 036004866
Organization Type: Corporate Foundation
Giving Locations: VT: Windsor including surrounding area
Grant Types: General Support, Scholarship.

Financial Summary

Total Giving: $52,000 (fiscal year ending October 31, 2004); $58,500 (fiscal 2001)
Assets: $908,715 (fiscal 2004); $922,818 (fiscal 2001)

Typical Recipients

Arts & Humanities: Arts & Humanities-General, History & Archaeology, Libraries, Museums/Galleries, Public Broadcasting

Civic & Public Affairs: Civic & Public Affairs-General, Urban & Community Affairs

Education: Colleges & Universities, Engineering/ Technological Education, Faculty Development, Education-General, Science/Mathematics Education,

Student Aid, Vocational & Technical Education

Health: Arthritis, Clinics/Medical Centers, Emergency/Ambulance Services, Health-General, Health Organizations, Home-Care Services, Hospitals, Nursing Services, Public Health

Religion: Religious Welfare

Social Services: Community Service Organizations, Homes, People with Disabilities, Scouts, Senior Services, Social Services-General, Volunteer Services, Youth Organizations

Application Procedures

Initial Contact: Send brief letter of inquiry, including a description of organization, amount requested, purpose of funds sought, and proof of tax-exempt status.
Deadlines: August 31.

Restrictions

Does not support individuals (except for scholarships for children or grandchildren of employees), religious organizations for sectarian purposes, or political or lobbying groups.

Corporate Officials

Hunter Banbury: president, chief executive officer, treasurer PRIM CORP EMPL president, chief executive officer, treasurer: Cone-Blanchard Corp.
Jack Keibaum: general manager PRIM CORP EMPL general manager: Cone-Blanchard Corp.

Foundation Officials

Alden P. Dana: trustee
W. R. McCullough: trustee
Wayne E. Pfenning: trustee

Grants Analysis

Disclosure Period: fiscal year ending October 31, 2004
Total Grants: $52,000
Number of Grants: 29
Average Grant: $1,286*
Highest Grant: $16,000
Lowest Grant: $150
Typical Range: $250 to $2,500
*Note: Average grant figure excludes highest grant.

Recent Grants

Note: Grants derived from 2004 Form 990.
General

16,000	Mt. Ascutney Hospital, Windsor, VT
4,500	Mount Holyoke College, South Hadley, MA
3,500	University of Vermont, Burlington, VT
3,000	New Hampshire Community Technical College, Concord, NH
2,500	Champlain College, Burlington, VT
2,500	Hesser College, Concord, NH
2,500	Pace University
2,000	Southern New Hampshire University, Manchester, NH
1,500	American Precision Museum, Windsor, VT
1,500	Wheels Around Windsor

MICHAEL J. CONNELL FOUNDATION

Giving Contact

Michael J. Connell, President & Director
225 S. Lake Avenue, Suite 271
Pasadena, CA 91101
Phone: (323)681-8085

Description

Founded: 1931
EIN: 956000904
Organization Type: Private Foundation

Giving Locations: CA: Los Angeles including metropolitan area
Grant Types: Fellowship, Project.

Donor Information

Founder: the late Michael J. Connell

Financial Summary

Total Giving: $780,615 (fiscal year ending June 30, 2001)
Giving Analysis: Giving for fiscal 2001 includes: foundation grants to United Way ($10,000)
Assets: $14,018,791 (fiscal 2001)

Typical Recipients

Arts & Humanities: Arts Centers, Arts Outreach, Community Arts, Libraries, Museums/Galleries, Music, Public Broadcasting, Theater

Civic & Public Affairs: African American Affairs, Botanical Gardens/Parks, Civic & Public Affairs-General, Nonprofit Management, Safety, Urban & Community Affairs, Zoos/Aquariums

Education: Arts/Humanities Education, Colleges & Universities, Elementary Education (Public), Education-General, Gifted & Talented Programs, Minority Education, Private Education (Precollege), Science/Mathematics Education, Vocational & Technical Education

Environment: Environment-General, Resource Conservation, Wildlife Protection

Health: Children's Health/Hospitals, Emergency/Ambulance Services, Eyes/Blindness, Respiratory

Religion: Religion-General, Religious Welfare

Social Services: Child Welfare, Community Service Organizations, Family Services, Homes, United Funds/United Ways

Application Procedures

Initial Contact: Include a cover letter and a full proposal.
Application Requirements: The cover letter should include the name of the applicant organization; appropriate contact person; an outline of the proposed project and its objectives; total project cost and amount requested; and anticipated date of completion. The proposal must include a description of organization, including the organization's history, current programs, key leadership, and major funding sources; a complete project description, including need, target populations, project strategy, staff requirements and qualifications, and implementation timetable; and an evaluation plan explaining methods of project evaluation and a clear statement of project objetives and an outline of evaluation activities. Financial information must be attached, including management letters and notes for the last two fiscal years; the organization's operating budget and organizational budget for the current fiscal year, with actuals to date (if applicant organization has no audited statements, in-house statements verified and signed by two of the organization's officers are acceptable). Required attachments include copes of both the organization's original and federal tax exemption letter under section 501(c)(3) and the subsequent final determination letter on private foundation status; a letter signed by an officer of the board of directors stating that the proposal is submitted with the board's knowledge and endorsement; and a roster of the organization's board of directors, including each member's full name, address, profession, and notation of office held on board (if applicable).
Deadlines: February 15, May 15, August 15, and November 15.
Review Process: Proposals are initially reviewed to determine whether it fits within the foundation's current areas of interest. Proposals that are aligned with the foundation's interest will be reviewed at the upcoming board meeting.
Decision Notification: The foundation notifies applicants of the receipt of their proposals as soon as possible.
Notes: The Connell Foundation generally discour-

ages unsolicited grant requests because it generally initiates and pursues its own programs in the social, cultural, educational, and medical fields. Application guidelines are supplied for those organizations who desire to apply after taking this into consideration.

Restrictions

Does not support individuals.

Foundation Officials

Mary C. Bayless: director
Michael J. Connell: president, director
Ruth E. Dodd: secretary
Richard A. Grant: vice president, director
Richard A. Wilson: treasurer, director

Grants Analysis

Disclosure Period: fiscal year ending June 30, 2001
Total Grants: $770,615*
Number of Grants: 16
Average Grant: $28,258*
Highest Grant: $250,000
Lowest Grant: $1,826
Typical Range: $10,000 to $50,000
*Note: Giving excludes United Way. Average grant figure excludes two highest grants ($375,000).

Recent Grants

Note: Grants derived from fiscal 2002 Form 990.
General

250,000	Los Angeles Philharmonic Association, Los Angeles, CA
125,000	Archbishop of Los Angeles, Los Angeles, CA
100,000	University of Southern California, Los Angeles, CA
35,000	Concern Resource and Environment, Ojai, CA
34,000	Armory Center for the Arts, Pasadena, CA
33,000	Pasadena Conservatory of Music, Pasadena, CA
25,000	Ganna Walska Lotusland Foundation, Santa Barbara, CA
25,000	Greater Los Angeles Zoo, Los Angeles, CA
15,000	Value Schools, Burbank, CA
10,000	American Youth Symphony, Los Angeles, CA

CONNELLY FOUNDATION

Giving Contact

E. Ann Wilcox, Assistant Vice President
One Tower Bridge, Suite 1450
West Conshohocken, PA 19428
Phone: (610)834-3222
Fax: (610)834-0866
E-mail: info@connellyfdn.org
Web: http://www.connellyfdn.org

Description

Founded: 1955
EIN: 236296825
Organization Type: Family Foundation
Giving Locations: PA: Philadelphia Greater Delaware Valley Region.
Grant Types: Capital, General Support, Operating Expenses, Project, Scholarship.

Donor Information

Founder: John F. Connelly and his wife, Josephine Connelly, established the Connelly Foundation in Pennsylvania in 1955. The foundation's assets consist largely of stock in Crown Cork & Seal Company, of which John Connelly was chairman from 1956 until his death in 1990.

Financial Summary

Total Giving: $9,457,413 (2003); $11,005,804 (2002); $12,033,760 (2001)
Giving Analysis: Giving for 2002 includes: foundation scholarships ($500,000); 2001: foundation grants to United Way ($15,000)
Assets: $200,297,745 (2002); $235,024,454 (2001)

Typical Recipients

Arts & Humanities: Arts Centers, Arts Institutes, Arts Outreach, Historic Preservation, History & Archaeology, Libraries, Museums/Galleries, Music, Opera, Performing Arts, Theater
Civic & Public Affairs: Economic Development, Employment/Job Training, Civic & Public Affairs-General, Hispanic Affairs, Housing, Public Policy, Urban & Community Affairs, Zoos/Aquariums
Education: Afterschool/Enrichment Programs, Arts/Humanities Education, Colleges & Universities, Community & Junior Colleges, Education Associations, Education Funds, Elementary Education (Private), Engineering/Technological Education, Faculty Development, Education-General, Leadership Training, Literacy, Medical Education, Minority Education, Preschool Education, Private Education (Precollege), Public Education (Precollege), Religious Education, School Volunteerism, Science/Mathematics Education, Secondary Education (Private), Secondary Education (Public), Special Education, Student Aid, Vocational & Technical Education
Environment: Environment-General
Health: AIDS/HIV, Alzheimer's Disease, Cancer, Children's Health/Hospitals, Clinics/Medical Centers, Emergency/Ambulance Services, Health-General, Geriatric Health, Health Funds, Health Organizations, Heart, Home-Care Services, Hospices, Hospitals, Hospitals (University Affiliated), Long-Term Care, Medical Rehabilitation, Medical Research, Nursing Services, Outpatient Health Care, Prenatal Health Issues, Preventive Medicine/Wellness Organizations, Public Health, Research/Studies Institutes, Transplant Networks/Donor Banks
International: Foreign Arts Organizations, Foreign Educational Institutions, Health Care/Hospitals, International Relief Efforts, Missionary/Religious Activities
Religion: Churches, Dioceses, Jewish Causes, Ministries, Religious Organizations, Religious Welfare, Seminaries, Social/Policy Issues
Science: Science Museums, Scientific Centers & Institutes, Scientific Organizations
Social Services: Child Abuse, Child Welfare, Community Centers, Community Service Organizations, Crime Prevention, Day Care, Domestic Violence, Family Planning, Family Services, Food/Clothing Distribution, Homes, People with Disabilities, Recreation & Athletics, Senior Services, Shelters/Homelessness, Social Services-General, Substance Abuse, United Funds/United Ways, YMCA/YWCA/YMHA/YWHA, Youth Organizations

Application Procedures

Initial Contact: The foundation provides application guidelines. Initial contact should be in writing.
Application Requirements: Proposals should include the following: an executive summary of the project, its goals, and financial requirements and status (a specific grant amount must be requested); brief history of the organization, an annual report, financial statements from the two most recent years, and the names and occupations of all directors and trustees; detailed proposal including project objectives, budget, revenue plan, timetable and target population (capital expenses must be documented); prospective and committed funding sources to date; evaluation plan and prospects for continued support of the project; resume of project officer and a list of key staff; and a copy of the IRS determination letter granting tax-exempt status.
Deadlines: None.
Review Process: The board of directors meets five times a year with the annual meeting at the foundation's office on the last Monday in January. Proposals are acknowledged upon receipt. The foundation does not grant interviews. Final notification takes three to six months.
Notes: The foundation also accepts the Delaware Valley Grantmakers Application Form.

Restrictions

The foundation does not make grants to individuals, political organizations, or other foundations, nor does it generally respond to annual appeals or letters of solicitation.

Additional Information

Publications: Biennial Report; Guidelines

Foundation Officials

William Joseph Avery: trustee B Chicago, IL 1940. ED University of Chicago (1965). PRIM CORP EMPL chairman: Crown Cork & Seal Co. Inc. CORP AFFIL director: Rohm and Haas Co. NONPR AFFIL chairman: YMCA Philadelphia.
Dr. Lewis William Bluemle, Jr.: senior vice president, trustee B Williamsport, PA 1921. ED Johns Hopkins University AB (1943); Johns Hopkins University MD (1946). CORP AFFIL consult: National Institute Health; director: Teleflex Inc.; director: Greater Philadelphia First Corp.; director, member executive committee: Mellon Bank East. NONPR AFFIL fellow: Royal College Physicians Edinburgh; president: Thomas Jefferson University; member advisory board Philadelphia chapter: Physicians Social Responsibility; member: Phi Beta Kappa; member: Philadelphia Association Clinic Trails; member: Association Academy Health Centers; fellow: College Physicians Philadelphia; member: American Society Artificial Internal Organs; member: American Society Nephrology; member: American Clinical & Climatological Association; fellow: American College Physicians; member: Alpha Omega Alpha. CLUB AFFIL Philadelphia Club; Union League Club.
Andrew J. Bozzelli: trustee
Ira Brind: trustee B Philadelphia, PA 1941. ED University of Pennsylvania AB (1963); University of Pennsylvania JD (1967). PRIM CORP EMPL managing director: Brind Lindsay & Co. Inc. CORP AFFIL director: Today's Man Inc.; director: Trala; director: Shooting Star; director: Thomas Jefferson University Hospital; director: Philadelphia School; director: Delta Paper; director: Nationalease System; director: J. E. Berkowitz LP; director: Blue Ribbon; officer: Aydin Corp. NONPR AFFIL officer: University Arts; director: Wistar Institute of Anatomy & Biology; member: Truck Rental Leasing Association; director: Philadelphia College Arts; member: Philadelphoa Bar Association; member: American Bar Association; member: Pennsylvania Bar Association. CLUB AFFIL Locust Club.
Christine C. Connelly: trustee
Daniele M. Connelly: trustee
Thomas S. Connelly: trustee, donor son B 1945. PRIM CORP EMPL Connelly Containers ADD CORP EMPL manager: Georgia Pacific Corp.
Caroline M. Crowley: trustee
Eleanor L. Davis: trustee
Thomas F. Donovan: trustee B 1934. CORP AFFIL chairman, chief executive officer: Mellon Bank East.
Victoria K. Flaville: vice president
Scott M. Jenkins: trustee
Josephine C. Mandeville: chairman, chief executive officer, president, donor daughter CORP AFFIL director: Crown Cork & Seal Co. Inc.
Lawrence T. Mangan: vice president
Barbara W. Riley: trustee
Emily C. Riley: executive vice president, trustee B 1946. CORP AFFIL director: Connelly Containers. NONPR AFFIL trustee: Villanova University.
Thomas A. Riley: trustee

Grants Analysis

Disclosure Period: calendar year ending 2002
Total Grants: $10,505,804*
Number of Grants: 465

Average Grant: $17,444*
Highest Grant: $581,387
Lowest Grant: $100
Typical Range: $1,000 to $25,000
*Note: Giving excludes scholarships. Average grant figure excludes five highest grants ($2,481,387).

Recent Grants

Note: Grants derived from 2002 Form 990.
General

638,375	Archdiocese of Philadelphia Josephine C Connelly Achievement Awards, Philadelphia, PA -- as tuition scholarship assistance
581,387	Archdiocese of Philadelphia Neumann Scholars Program, Philadelphia, PA -- for assistance for students of Philadelphia and the suburbs to attend catholic high schools
500,000	Country Day School of the Sacred Heart, Bryn Mawr, PA -- for construction of the digital research library to replace the present one
500,000	Gwynedd Mercy Academy, Spring House, PA -- towards support of stage 2 of schools renovation and construction project and renovations to gymnasium
500,000	Merion Mercy Academy, Merion Station, PA -- towards capital support for building a 27000 sq foot addition to the academy and renovate existing space
500,000	Rosemont College, Rosemont, PA -- towards scholarship pledge
400,000	Sacred Heart Hospital, Allentown, PA -- towards renovation and expansion of the department of emergency medicine
300,000	Covenant House Pennsylvania, Philadelphia, PA -- towards support of living the covenant campaign and providing for site renovation of a transitional living program
250,000	MBF Center, Norristown, PA -- for renovation of new facility in East Marshall St Norristown purchased recently
250,000	Project HOME, PA -- for construction of the Honickman Roberts learning center for technology in central north Philadelphia

CONNEMARA FUND

Giving Contact

Polly J. Friess, Trustee
PO Box 11655
Jackson, WY 83002

Description

Founded: 1968
EIN: 566096063
Organization Type: Private Foundation
Giving Locations: New England.
Grant Types: General Support, Multiyear/Continuing Support.

Donor Information

Founder: the late Mary R. Jackson

Financial Summary

Total Giving: $378,005 (fiscal year ending June 30, 2004); $517,000 (fiscal 2001)
Assets: $7,655,706 (fiscal 2004); $8,789,366 (fiscal 2001)

Typical Recipients

Arts & Humanities: Arts Associations & Councils, Arts Centers, Arts & Humanities-General, Libraries, Museums/Galleries, Music, Public Broadcasting
Civic & Public Affairs: Civil Rights, Civic & Public Affairs-General, Legal Aid, Native American Affairs,

Philanthropic Organizations, Professional & Trade Associations, Public Policy, Zoos/Aquariums

Education: Arts/Humanities Education, Colleges & Universities, Elementary Education (Private), Education-General, Leadership Training, Preschool Education, Private Education (Precollege), Religious Education

Environment: Environment-General, Protection, Resource Conservation

Health: Cancer, Children's Health/Hospitals, Emergency/Ambulance Services, Health-General, Hospitals, Medical Research, Mental Health, Prenatal Health Issues, Preventive Medicine/Wellness Organizations, Single-Disease Health Associations

International: International-General, International Affairs, International Development, International Peace & Security Issues, International Relief Efforts, Missionary/Religious Activities

Religion: Churches, Religion-General, Ministries, Missionary Activities (Domestic), Religious Organizations, Religious Welfare, Social/Policy Issues, Synagogues/Temples

Social Services: Child Welfare, People with Disabilities, Shelters/Homelessness, United Funds/United Ways, Youth Organizations

Application Procedures

Initial Contact: Send a brief letter of inquiry.
Application Requirements: Include proof of tax-exempt status.
Deadlines: None.

Restrictions

Does not support individuals.

Foundation Officials

Polly J. Friess: trustee
Herrick Jackson: trustee
Alison Jackson Van Dyk: trustee

Grants Analysis

Disclosure Period: fiscal year ending June 30, 2004
Total Grants: $378,005
Number of Grants: 49
Average Grant: $5,702*
Highest Grant: $60,000
Lowest Grant: $1,000
Typical Range: $1,000 to $10,000
*Note: Average grant figure excludes two highest grants ($110,000).

Recent Grants

Note: Grants derived from fiscal 2004 Form 990.
General

60,000	Temple of Understanding, New York, NY
50,000	Westminster School Inc., Simsbury, CT
15,000	Children's Hospital Trust, Boston, MA
15,000	Grumman Hill Montessori Association, Wilton, CT
10,000	Community of St. John Baptist, Mendham, NJ
10,000	Connecticut Association for Children with Learning Disabilities, East Norwalk, CT
10,000	Connecticut Fund for the Environment, New Haven, CT
10,000	CURE International, Lemoyne, PA
10,000	Ethics and Public Policy Center, Washington, DC
10,000	Harvey School, Katonah, NY

CONSECO INC.

Company Headquarters

11825 N. Pennsylvania St.
Carmel, IN 46032
Web: http://www.conseco.com

Company Description

Founded: 1979
Ticker: CNO
Exchange: NYSE
Former Name: American Life
Chap. 11 Reorg. Bankruptcy (2002);
Acquired: Colonial Penn Life Insurance Co. (1997).
Revenue: US$4.33 billion (2004)
Profit: US$294.8 million (2004)
Employees: 10,400 (2002)
Fortune Rank: 443, per FORTUNE Magazine's list of 500 Largest U.S. Corporations (2004).
SIC(s): 6000 Depository Institutions, 6100 Nondepository Institutions, 6300 Insurance Carriers, 6700 Holding & Other Investment Offices.

Operating Locations

Conseco (IN--Carmel)

Nonmonetary Support

Type: Donated Equipment; In-kind Services
Note: Conseco will consider requests for in-kind contributions. Determinations will be based on need and the availability of resources to provide requested items.

Giving Contact

Sheila Taylor, Supervisor
Conseco Services, LLC
11815 N. Pennsylvania Street
PO Box 1911
Carmel, IN 46082-1911
Phone: 800-888-4918
Fax: (317)817-6721

Description

Organization Type: Corporate Giving Program
Giving Locations: IN: Indianapolis metropolitan area, including Marion County and nine surrounding counties
Grant Types: Capital, Operating Expenses, Research, Seed Money.

Typical Recipients

Arts & Humanities: Art History, Arts Appreciation, Arts Institutes, Ballet, Libraries, Museums/Galleries, Performing Arts, Public Broadcasting, Theater

Civic & Public Affairs: African American Affairs, Botanical Gardens/Parks, Chambers of Commerce, Community Foundations, Economic Development, Inner-City Development, Parades/Festivals, Philanthropic Organizations, Safety, Urban & Community Affairs, Women's Affairs, Zoos/Aquariums

Education: Afterschool/Enrichment Programs, Arts/Humanities Education, Business Education, Colleges & Universities, Continuing Education, Economic Education, Education Reform, Elementary Education (Private), Leadership Training, Literacy, Minority Education, Preschool Education, Private Education (Precollege), Public Education (Precollege), Secondary Education (Private), Secondary Education (Public), Special Education

Environment: Environment-General, Wildlife Protection

Health: Adolescent Health Issues, AIDS/HIV, Alzheimer's Disease, Arthritis, Cancer, Children's Health/Hospitals, Diabetes, Health Organizations, Heart, Hospitals, Hospitals (University Affiliated), Long-Term Care, Medical Research, Medical Training, Mental Health, Multiple Sclerosis, Nursing Services, Single-Disease Health Associations

Social Services: At-Risk Youth, Big Brothers/Big Sisters, Camps, Child Abuse, Child Welfare, Community Centers, Community Service Organizations, Crime Prevention, Domestic Violence, Family Planning, Food/Clothing Distribution, Homes, People with Disabilities, Recreation & Athletics, Scouts, Senior Services, Shelters/Homelessness, Social Services-General, Special Olympics, United Funds/United Ways, Volunteer Services, Youth Organizations

Application Procedures

Deadlines: January 1, April 1, July 1, and October 1. Applicants are encouraged to submit their requests well in advance of the deadline, allowing community relations adequate time for additional research, if necessary. Proposals postmarked on the deadline but not received at Conseco until after the deadline will not be considered until the following quarter. Proposals may not be submitted by fax machine. Applications for Pacers/Colts Charity Program grants are accepted year-round; however, please note that applications for both programs must be received by the July 1 deadline to be considered for the upcoming season.

Restrictions

Requests are not considered from organizations without 501(c)(3) tax-exempt status; veterans groups, service clubs, or fraternal organizations; conferences, workshops, or seminars; religiously-affiliated causes; multiple-year gifts; endowments; projects or groups benefiting an individual or just a few people; re-granting organizations (other than the United Way); political or lobbying groups; or post-event funding.

Additional Information

A proposal asking Conseco to consider providing a portion of the support for a project will generally receive greater preference than one seeking Conseco as the exclusive funding source.

The Community Action Committee requires that proposals offer three sponsorship/donation levels.

For organizations and projects new to the company, it is preferred to start funding at a more modest level and work toward building a relationship.

Conseco's grant-making policy places more emphasis on specific project proposals than on general operating fund or capital campaign proposals.

If renewed funding is desired, an organization must submit a formal request. The Community Action Committee supports new and opportune projects each year. Therefore, a grant given in any one year does not ensure future funding.

The Community Action Committee will consider only one grant request per project in each calendar year. Multiple projects may be submitted during the same funding cycle; a separate application must be filled out for each project.

Organizations that receive a grant will be required to send in a completed Conseco Post-Grant Evaluation form within one month after the completion of the project or program. Future grants will not be awarded to organizations that have a Post Grant Evaluation form outstanding after the deadline.

Grant recipients must use the funds, as agreed upon, within six months of the event or of receiving the funds.

The company sponsors several special programs, including the Pacers/Colts Charity Programs. Each season, Conseco selects 18 community organizations to participate in the Indiana Pacers/Conseco Three-Point Charity Program. Each organization receives 20 admission tickets to two Indiana Pacers home games, as well as a financial contribution at the end of the season. Conseco contributes $50 to a fund for every three-point shot the Pacers make throughout the season. The overall total is divided equally among the participating organizations. One community organization is selected each year to participate in the Indianapolis Colts/Conseco First Down Charity Program. For every first down the Colts make in the RCA Dome, Conseco contributes $75 to the recipient organization. A check presentation is made at the end of the season.

Corporate Officials

Rollin M. Dick: executive vice president, chief financial officers, chief executive officer PRIM CORP EMPL executive vice president, chief financial officer: Conseco.

Stephen C. Hilbert: founder, chairman, president, chief executive officer B 1946. PRIM CORP EMPL founder, chairman, president, chief executive officer: Conseco. CORP AFFIL director: CCP Insurance; chief executive officer: Colonial Penn Life Insurance Co.; director: Bankers Life Holding Corp.

Grants Analysis
Typical Range: $1,500 to $10,000

CONSTELLATION ENERGY GROUP INC.

Company Headquarters
39 W. Lexington Street
Baltimore, MD 21201
Phone: (410)234-5678
Fax: (410)234-5220
Web: http://www.constellationenergy.com

Company Description
Founded: 1995
Ticker: CEG
Exchange: NYSE
Former Name: Baltimore Gas & Electric (1999).
Revenue: US$12.549 billion (2004)
Profit: US$539.7 million (2004)
Employees: 8650 (2003)
Fortune Rank: 167, per FORTUNE Magazine's list of 500 Largest U.S. Corporations (2004).
SIC(s): 4931 Electric & Other Services Combined, 4932 Gas & Other Services Combined, 5722 Household Appliance Stores.

Operating Locations
Baltimore Gas & Electric Co. (MD--Baltimore, Lusby); Baltimore Gas & Electric Home Products & Services Inc. (MD--Columbia, Elkridge, Glen Burnie); Church Street Stateion Inc. (FL--Orlando); Constellation Energy Source (TX--Houston); Safe Harbor Water Power Corp. (PA--Conestoga)

Nonmonetary Support
Value: $50,000 (2003 approx); $43,250 (2002); $59,260 (2001)
Type: Donated Equipment; Donated Products; In-kind Services
Note: NOT Nonmonetary support is provided by the company.
Volunteer Programs: The company sponsors an employee volunteer program aimed at increasing pride, motivation, and participation by allowing volunteers to direct their own program.

Giving Contact
Malinda B. Small, Director, National-State Affairs & Corporate Contributions
Constellation Energy Group
PO Box 1475
Baltimore, MD 21203-1475
Phone: (410)783-3273
Fax: (410)783-3279
E-mail: Malinda.B.Small@constellation.com

Description
Organization Type: Corporate Giving Program
Giving Locations: headquarters and operating communities.
Grant Types: Capital, Employee Matching Gifts, General Support, Multiyear/Continuing Support, Operating Expenses, Project, Scholarship.
Note: Employee matching gift ratio: 1 to 1 between $25 and $2,000 annually per employee.

Donor Information
Founder: Baltimore Gas and Electric Co.

Financial Summary
Total Giving: $6,000,000 (2005 approx); $6,000,000 (2004); $4,000,000 (2003 approx). Note: Contributes through corporate direct giving program and foundation.
Assets: $17,300,000,000 (2005 approx); $17,300,000,000 (2004); $288,895 (2001)
Gifts Received: $1,713,000 (2001); $575,000 (2000); $2,024,500 (1999). Note: In 2001, contributions were received from Constellation Energy Group, Inc. and Baltimore Gas and Electric Company. Contributions prior to 2001 were received from Baltimore Gas and Electric Company.

Typical Recipients
Arts & Humanities: Arts Festivals, Dance, Historic Preservation, History & Archaeology, Libraries, Museums/Galleries, Music, Performing Arts, Theater
Civic & Public Affairs: Business/Free Enterprise, Economic Development, Civic & Public Affairs-General, Housing, Law & Justice, Professional & Trade Associations, Urban & Community Affairs, Zoos/Aquariums
Education: Arts/Humanities Education, Business-School Partnerships, Colleges & Universities, Continuing Education, Education Funds, Faculty Development, Education-General, Health & Physical Education, Literacy, Medical Education, Minority Education, Preschool Education, Religious Education, Science/Mathematics Education, Social Sciences Education, Special Education, Student Aid
Environment: Air/Water Quality, Environment-General, Resource Conservation
Health: Clinics/Medical Centers, Health Organizations, Hospices, Hospitals, Public Health
Religion: Dioceses, Jewish Causes, Ministries, Religious Welfare, Seminaries
Science: Science Museums, Scientific Centers & Institutes, Scientific Research
Social Services: At-Risk Youth, Child Abuse, Child Welfare, Community Service Organizations, Family Services, People with Disabilities, Scouts, Senior Services, Special Olympics, United Funds/United Ways, Veterans, Volunteer Services, YMCA/YWCA/YMHA/YWHA, Youth Organizations

Application Procedures
Initial Contact: Obtain the appropriate guidelines and application forms from the company's web site. Submit two copies of grant requests, or a single copy of sponsorship or in-kind requests.
Deadlines: None for requests of less than $10,000; May 1 and September 1 for requests of $10,000 or more.
Evaluative Criteria: Preference will be given to organizations for which company employees and board members serve as volunteers; organizations whose purposes are aligned with the company's philanthropic focus areas; and organizations that demonstrate a broad base of community support.
Decision Notification: All applicants will receive a response in writing after a funding decision has been made. Allow six to eight weeks for processing grant requests of less than $10,000, sponsorships, and in-kind requests. Grant requests of more than $10,000 are considered at Corporate Contributions Committee meetings in June and October.

Restrictions
Does not normally fund member agencies of the United Way. Company does not support individuals, churches for religious causes, organizations in conflict with company goals, start-up funding, or hospitals' capital campaigns. The company will only consider one contribution request per organization per year.
Applicants must be 501(c)(3) tax-exempt nonprofit organizations located in an area where the company has significant business interests.

Additional Information
Publications: Guidelines

Corporate Officials
Mayo A. Shattuck, III: president, chief executive officer, chairman
Malinda B. Small: director national-state affairs & corporate contributions

Foundation Officials
Christian Herndon Poindexter: chairman, president B Evansville, IN 1938. ED United States Naval Academy BS (1960); Loyola College MBA (1976). ADD CORP EMPL director, president, chairman, chief executive officer: Constellation Energy Group, Inc. CORP AFFIL director: Mercantile Bankshares Corp.; director: Dome Corp.; director: KMS Group Inc.; chairman, chief executive officer: Constellation Investments Inc.; chairman, chief executive officer: Constellation Properties Inc.; chairman, chief executive officer: Constellation Biogas Inc. NONPR AFFIL trustee: Villa Julie College; secretary, director: YMCA Anne Arundel County; trustee: Morgan State University; president, director: Scholarships Scholars Inc.; trustee: Johns Hopkins University; trustee: Maryland Academy Science; member: Engineering Society Baltimore; member: Institute Electrical & Electronics Engineers; member executive board: Boy Scouts America Baltimore Area Council.
Thomas E. Ruszin, Jr.: treasurer ADD CORP EMPL treasurer, assistant secretary: Constellation Energy Group Inc.
Malinda B. Small: assistant secretary, assistant treasurer (see above)

Grants Analysis
Disclosure Period: calendar year ending 2002
Total Grants: $4,000,000*
Number of Grants: 878
Average Grant: $4,120
Highest Grant: $100,000
Lowest Grant: $25
Typical Range: $25,000 to $100,000
*Note: Grants analysis provided by foundation.

Recent Grants
Note: Grants derived from 2001 Form 990.

Library-Related
20,000	Kennedy Krieger Institute, Baltimore, MD -- capital campaign

General
725,000	United Way of Central Maryland, Baltimore, MD -- 2000 corporate campaign
200,000	Johns Hopkins University, Baltimore, MD -- School of Continuing Studies
200,000	United States Naval Academy Foundation, Annapolis, MD -- pledge to capital campaign
125,000	Baltimore Center for Performing Arts, Baltimore, MD -- Hippodrome Performing Arts Center
125,000	Baltimore Children's Museum, Baltimore, MD -- capital campaign
125,000	University of Maryland Foundation, Adelphi, MD -- pledge to BGE Teaching Fund
100,000	Archdiocese of Baltimore, Baltimore, MD -- Partners in Excellence Program
100,000	Baltimore Symphony Orchestra, Baltimore, MD -- sustaining greatness campaign
100,000	University of Maryland College Park, College Park, MD -- "Bright Future" campaign
70,000	Maryland Historical Society, Baltimore, MD -- establishment of new education and Public Programs Center

CONSUMERS ENERGY CO.

Company Headquarters
212 W. Michigan Ave.
Jackson, MI 49201
Web: http://www.consumersenergy.com

Company Description
Revenue: US$4.104 billion (2001)
Employees: 1,475 (2001)
Parent Company: CMS Energy Co., 330 Town Center Dr., Ste. 100, Dearborn, MI, United States

Nonmonetary Support
Type: In-kind Services

Consumers Energy Foundation

Giving Contact
Carolyn A. Bloodworth, Secretary/Treasurer
Consumers Energy Foundation
One Energy Plaza, EP8-228
Jackson, MI 49201
Phone: (517)788-0432
Fax: (517)788-2281
E-mail: foundation@consumersenergy.com
Web: http://www.consumersenergy.com/welcome.htm

Alternate Contact
Phone: 877-501-4952

Description
EIN: 382935534
Organization Type: Corporate Foundation
Giving Locations: MI: nationally.
Grant Types: Capital, Employee Matching Gifts, General Support, Operating Expenses, Project.
Note: Employee matching gift ratio: 1 to 1 for donations to colleges, universities, and Michigan food banks and community foundations, up to $5,000 per employee or retiree annually.

Financial Summary
Total Giving: $600,000 (2004 approx); $963,647 (2003); $1,500,000 (2002)
Assets: $1,000,000 (2004 approx); $2,026,946 (2003); $3,400,000 (2002)
Gifts Received: $110,000 (2003); $7,000,000 (2001); $2,000,000 (2000). Note: Contributions were received from Consumers Energy Company.

Typical Recipients
Arts & Humanities: Arts Associations & Councils, Arts Funds, Arts Institutes, Community Arts, Arts & Humanities-General, Historic Preservation, History & Archaeology, Libraries, Museums/Galleries, Music, Opera, Performing Arts, Public Broadcasting, Theater
Civic & Public Affairs: African American Affairs, Botanical Gardens/Parks, Chambers of Commerce, Civil Rights, Clubs, Community Foundations, Economic Development, Employment/Job Training, Civic & Public Affairs-General, Housing, Municipalities/Towns, Nonprofit Management, Parades/Festivals, Philanthropic Organizations, Professional & Trade Associations, Public Policy, Urban & Community Affairs, Zoos/Aquariums
Education: Agricultural Education, Arts/Humanities Education, Business Education, Business-School Partnerships, Colleges & Universities, Community & Junior Colleges, Economic Education, Education Funds, Engineering/Technological Education, Legal Education, Minority Education, Public Education (Precollege), Science/Mathematics Education, Secondary Education (Public)
Environment: Energy, Environment-General, Resource Conservation, Watershed, Wildlife Protection
Health: Alzheimer's Disease, Cancer, Children's Health/Hospitals, Emergency/Ambulance Services, Hospitals
International: International Relations
Religion: Religious Welfare
Science: Scientific Centers & Institutes
Social Services: Camps, Community Centers, Community Service Organizations, Family Services, Food/Clothing Distribution, People with Disabilities, Recreation & Athletics, Scouts, Senior Services, Shelters/Homelessness, Substance Abuse, United Funds/United Ways, Volunteer Services, YMCA/YWCA/YMHA/YWHA, Youth Organizations

Application Procedures
Initial Contact: Request or see foundation website for application guidelines, then send a cover letter and the Council of Michigan Foundation's Common Grant Application.
Application Requirements: Cover letter should include a description of a program that is supported by the general public, businesses, and other foundations and governments; and should make a strategic link between proposal and foundation's interests. Attachments to completed application should include plans for evaluating the program, current realistic budget including other sources of funding, most recent audited financial statement, list of board of directors, and proof of tax-exempt status.
Deadlines: None; requests reviewed quarterly.
Review Process: Applications are reviewed locally and at company headquarters, then sent to foundation board for consideration; after preliminary review, applicant may be asked to provide additional information. Small grants of less than $5,000 can be approved at any time; larger grants need prior board approval.
Evaluative Criteria: Indications of effective governing board, realistic budget, clearly defined program that is supported by the public, business, and other foundations (if appropriate); and record of accomplishment.
Decision Notification: The foundation tries to respond within six to eight weeks.
Notes: The foundation will not respond to telephone requests. Facsimile requests are discouraged. Funds primarily given to organizations located in the state of Michigan.

Restrictions
Funds only groups to which donations are tax-deductible.
Does not support individuals, political or lobbying groups, endowments, organizations whose operating status is supported by the United Way, religious organizations for sectarian purposes, or labor, veterans, fraternal and social clubs.
Also does not contribute to organizations which discriminate on the basis of sex, age, height, weight, marital status, race, religion, creed, color, nationality or origin, ancestry, disability, handicap, or veteran status. The Foundation does not buy tickets or make payments to events or celebrations to raise funds or charitable purposes, or sponsor advertising to support these efforts.

Additional Information
Consumers Energy Foundation looks for grant recipients that provide solutions to problems faced by individuals and families who are unable to address their own needs without help; protect and enhance the natural environment; improve the availability and quality of education while stressing cost effectiveness; back the improvement and effectiveness of the public's health care systems, with special emphasis on reducing patient costs; participate in community and civic activities for the betterment of the citizenry and their governments; and increase an awareness of the values of artistic and cultural achievements and encourage their growth.

The foundation considers requests from qualified organizations to support operating budgets and capital fund programs for construction, refurbishment or purchase of buildings, structures, equipment or other physical enhancements.
A contribution from Consumers Energy Foundation is more likely to be approved when grant seekers' programs are focused on high priority needs which they are capable of addressing successfully.

Corporate Officials
Paul A. Elbert: president, chief executive officer natural gas B 1950. ED Ohio State University BA; University of Illinois MA. PRIM CORP EMPL president, chief executive officer natural gas: Consumers Energy Co. CORP AFFIL chairman: Michigan Gas Storage Co.; director: Sugar Monitor Co.
David W. Joos: president, chief executive officer electric, executive vice president B Fargo, ND 1953. ED Iowa State University of Science & Technology (1975); Iowa State University of Science & Technology (1976). PRIM CORP EMPL president, chief executive officer electric, executive vice president: Consumers Energy Co. NONPR AFFIL member: American Society Mechanical Engineers; member: Registered Professional Engineers; member: American Nuclear Society.
William Thomas McCormick, Jr.: chairman, chief executive officer, director B Washington, DC 1944. ED Cornell University BS (1966); Massachusetts Institute of Technology PhD (1969). PRIM CORP EMPL chairman, chief executive officer, director: CMS Energy Corp. ADD CORP EMPL chairman: Consumers Energy Co.; chairman: Consumers Power Co. CORP AFFIL director: First Chicago NBD Corp.; director: Rockwell International Corp.; director: Bank One Corp.; chairman, chief executive officer: CMS Enterprises Co. NONPR AFFIL director, member: Greater Detroit Chamber of Commerce; director: Schumberger; director: American Gas Association; director: Edison Electric Institute.

Giving Program Officials
Carolyn A. Bloodworth: secretary-trs PRIM CORP EMPL director community relations: CMS Energy Corp.

Foundation Officials
Carolyn A. Bloodworth: secretary, treasurer (see above)
David W. Joos: director (see above)
David G. Mengebier: president
John G. Russell: director
S. Kinnie Smith, Jr.: director
Thomas J. Webb: director
Kenneth Whipple: chairman

Grants Analysis
Disclosure Period: calendar year ending 2003
Total Grants: $513,500*
Number of Grants: 58
Average Grant: $7,384*
Highest Grant: $50,000
Lowest Grant: $1,000
Typical Range: $1,000 to $10,000
*Note: Giving excludes matching gifts; United Way. Average grant figure excludes two highest grants ($100,000).

Recent Grants
Note: Grants derived from 2003 Form 990.
Library-Related

5,000	Bay County Library System, Bay City, MI

General

99,500	United Way of Jackson County, Jackson, MI
50,000	Detroit Institute of Arts, Detroit, MI
50,000	Detroit Institute of Arts, Detroit, MI
45,000	United Way Community Services, Detroit, MI
30,000	Capital Area United Way, East Lansing, MI

25,000	Detroit Zoological Society, Royal Oak, MI
25,000	Detroit Zoological Society, Royal Oak, MI
25,000	Friends of the Moroccan American Commission Foundation, Washington, DC
22,000	United Way of Bay County, Bay City, MI
20,000	Focus HOPE, Detroit, MI

CONTEMPO COMMUNICATIONS

Company Headquarters
Sherman, CT

Contempo Communications Foundation for the Arts, Inc.

Giving Contact
Joan F. Marshall, Vice President & Director
Contempo Communications Foundation for the Arts, Inc.
17623 Island Inlet
Ft. Myers, FL 33908
Phone: (941)466-7262

Description
EIN: 136209719
Organization Type: Corporate Foundation
Giving Locations: NY: New York including metropolitan area
Grant Types: General Support.

Financial Summary
Total Giving: $7,418 (fiscal year ending March 31, 2004); $9,079 (fiscal 2001)
Giving Analysis: Giving for fiscal 2001 includes: foundation ($9,079)
Assets: $154,066 (fiscal 2004); $179,045 (fiscal 2001)

Typical Recipients
Arts & Humanities: Arts Centers, Dance, Arts & Humanities-General, Libraries, Museums/Galleries, Music, Performing Arts, Public Broadcasting, Theater, Visual Arts
Civic & Public Affairs: Botanical Gardens/Parks, Clubs, Civic & Public Affairs-General, Legal Aid, Municipalities/Towns, Parades/Festivals, Public Policy, Safety, Urban & Community Affairs, Women's Affairs
Education: Arts/Humanities Education, Colleges & Universities, Education-General, Minority Education
Environment: Environment-General, Resource Conservation, Wildlife Protection
Health: Cancer, Emergency/Ambulance Services, Health-General, Hospices, Hospitals, Mental Health, Single-Disease Health Associations
International: Health Care/Hospitals, International Relief Efforts, Missionary/Religious Activities
Religion: Churches, Religion-General, Jewish Causes, Religious Organizations, Synagogues/Temples
Science: Science Museums, Scientific Organizations
Social Services: Child Welfare, Community Service Organizations, Family Planning, Food/Clothing Distribution, United Funds/United Ways, YMCA/YWCA/YMHA/YWHA, Youth Organizations

Application Procedures
Initial Contact: The foundation has no formal grant application procedure or application form. Send a brief letter of inquiry.
Application Requirements: Include all relevant information, including amount requested and purpose of funds sought.
Deadlines: None.

Corporate Officials
Joan F. Marshall: president PRIM CORP EMPL president: Contempo Communications.

Foundation Officials
David B. Marshall: president, director
David L. Marshall: secretary, treasurer, director B Madison, NJ 1939. ED Princeton University (1961); Pennsylvania State University (1962). CORP AFFIL chairman: Brinks.
Joan F. Marshall: vice president, director (see above)

Grants Analysis
Disclosure Period: fiscal year ending March 31, 2004
Total Grants: $7,418
Number of Grants: 28
Average Grant: $53*
Highest Grant: $6,000
Lowest Grant: $25
Typical Range: $25 to $250
*Note: Average grant figure excludes highest grant.

Recent Grants
Note: Grants derived from 2001 Form 990.
General

4,850	University of Michigan, Ann Arbor, MI
1,650	Temple Beth Am, New York, NY
300	United Jewish Appeal Federation, New York, NY
126	American Parkinson's Disease Association, Staten Island, NY
125	City of Sanibel, Sanibel, FL
100	Doctors Without Borders, New York, NY
100	Hillel Foundation, Washington, DC
100	Muscular Dystrophy Association, Denver, CO
100	YWCA
75	Ding Darling Wildlife Society, Sanibel, FL

CONTIGROUP COMPANIES INC.

Company Headquarters
277 Park Ave.
New York, NY 10172
Web: http://www.contigroup.com

Company Description
Former Name: Continental Grain Co. (2001).
Revenue: US$3.3 billion (2001)
Employees: 14500 (2001)
SIC(s): 0211 Beef Cattle Feedlots, 0213 Hogs, 0251 Broiler, Fryer & Roaster Chickens, 2041 Flour & Other Grain Mill Products, 2048 Prepared Feeds Nec, 6159 Miscellaneous Business Credit Institutions.

Operating Locations
Continental Grain Co. (NY--New York)

ContiGroup Companies Foundation

Giving Contact
Susan McIntyre, Assistant Secretary
277 Park Avenue
New York, NY 10172-0003
Phone: (212)207-5879
Fax: (212)207-5163

Description
EIN: 136160912
Organization Type: Corporate Foundation
Giving Locations: NY: Midwest.
Grant Types: General Support, Scholarship.

Financial Summary
Total Giving: $335,922 (fiscal year ending January 31, 2003); $371,970 (fiscal 2002); $274,620 (fiscal 2001)
Giving Analysis: Giving for fiscal 2003 includes: foundation scholarships ($15,406); fiscal 2002: foundation scholarships ($17,330); foundation ($354,640); fiscal 2001: foundation ($274,620)
Assets: $307 (fiscal 2003); $332 (fiscal 2002); $142 (fiscal 2001)
Gifts Received: $335,922 (fiscal 2003); $372,185 (fiscal 2002); $283,230 (fiscal 2001). Note: Contributions were received from ContiGroup Companies.

Typical Recipients
Arts & Humanities: Arts Centers, Arts Outreach, Dance, Arts & Humanities-General, Historic Preservation, Libraries, Museums/Galleries, Music, Opera, Performing Arts, Theater
Civic & Public Affairs: African American Affairs, Asian American Affairs, Botanical Gardens/Parks, Business/Free Enterprise, Chambers of Commerce, Community Foundations, Civic & Public Affairs-General, Law & Justice, Legal Aid, Professional & Trade Associations, Public Policy, Rural Affairs, Urban & Community Affairs, Women's Affairs
Education: Agricultural Education, Arts/Humanities Education, Business Education, Colleges & Universities, Community & Junior Colleges, Education Associations, Education Funds, Education Reform, Elementary Education (Public), Education-General, International Studies, Leadership Training, Legal Education, Literacy, Minority Education, Private Education (Precollege), Public Education (Precollege), Religious Education, Science/Mathematics Education, Secondary Education (Private), Student Aid
Environment: Environment-General, Resource Conservation, Wildlife Protection
Health: Alzheimer's Disease, Cancer, Children's Health/Hospitals, Clinics/Medical Centers, Diabetes, Emergency/Ambulance Services, Health-General, Health Organizations, Hospitals, Multiple Sclerosis, Nursing Services, Single-Disease Health Associations, Trauma Treatment
International: Health Care/Hospitals, Human Rights, International Development, International Organizations, International Peace & Security Issues, International Relations, International Relief Efforts
Religion: Churches, Religion-General, Jewish Causes, Religious Organizations, Religious Welfare, Seminaries
Science: Science Museums, Scientific Research
Social Services: Animal Protection, At-Risk Youth, Child Welfare, Community Service Organizations, Family Services, People with Disabilities, Recreation & Athletics, Scouts, Social Services-General, Substance Abuse, United Funds/United Ways, Volunteer Services, YMCA/YWCA/YMHA/YWHA, Youth Organizations

Application Procedures
Initial Contact: Send a brief letter of inquiry detailing purpose for which grant is requested.
Deadlines: None.

Corporate Officials
James John Bigham: executive vice president, chief financial officer, director B Waterbury, CT 1937. ED Fairfield University BS (1959); Columbia University MBA (1961); Harvard University Graduate School of Business Administration (1970). PRIM CORP EMPL executive vice president, chief financial officer, director: Continental Grain Co.
Dwight C. Coffin: vice president human resources PRIM CORP EMPL vice president human resources:

Continental Grain Co.

Paul J. Fribourg: chairman, president, chief executive officer ED Amherst College BA; Harvard University MA. PRIM CORP EMPL chairman, president, chief executive officer: ContiGroup Companies Inc.

Donald L. Staheli: chairman, director B Hurricane, UT 1931. ED University of Illinois MS; University of Illinois PhD; Utah State University BS. PRIM CORP EMPL chairman, director: Continental Grain Co.

Foundation Officials

Paul J. Fribourg: vice president (see above)

Grants Analysis

Disclosure Period: fiscal year ending January 31, 2003
Total Grants: $320,516*
Number of Grants: 58
Average Grant: $5,526
Highest Grant: $25,000
Lowest Grant: $35
Typical Range: $1,000 to $10,000
*Note: Giving excludes scholarships.

Recent Grants

Note: Grants derived from 2004 Form 990.
Library-Related
20,000	Library of Congress, Washington, DC

General
25,000	Appeal of Conscience Foundation, New York, NY
25,000	Brooklyn Bridge Park Coalition, Brooklyn, NY
25,000	Endeavor, New York, NY
25,000	Jewish Theological Seminary of America, New York, NY
25,000	Lawyers Committee for Human Rights, New York, NY
25,000	Virtual Y, New York, NY
15,000	Museum of Modern Art, New York, NY
15,000	Safed Foundation, New York, NY
11,180	National Merit Scholarship Corporation, Evanston, IL
10,000	Carnegie Hall Society, New York, NY

CONTRAN CORP.

Company Headquarters

5430 Lyndon B. Johnson Freeway, Ste. 1700
Dallas, TX 75240

Company Description

Revenue: US$1.1 billion (2002)
Employees: 7,300 (2002)
SIC(s): 1311 Crude Petroleum & Natural Gas, 2063 Beet Sugar, 2421 Sawmills & Planing Mills--General, 5812 Eating Places.

Harold Simmons Foundation, Inc.

Giving Contact

Lisa Simmons Epstein, President
Harold Simmons Foundation
5430 LBJ Freeway, Suite 1700
Dallas, TX 75240-2697
Phone: (972)233-2134
Fax: (972)448-1456

Alternate Contact

Keith A. Johnson, Controller
Harold Simmons Foundation
Phone: (972)233-1700

Description

Founded: 1988
EIN: 752222091
Organization Type: Corporate Foundation
Giving Locations: TX: Dallas including metropolitan area
Grant Types: Capital, Challenge, General Support, Matching, Multiyear/Continuing Support, Operating Expenses, Research, Scholarship.

Donor Information

Founder: NL Industries and subsidiaries and Contran Corp.

Financial Summary

Total Giving: $1,638,280 (2002); $2,497,353 (2001). Note: Contributes through foundation only.
Assets: $13,511,588 (2002); $7,813,555 (2001)
Gifts Received: $20,655,000 (2002); $450,000 (2001); $1,750,000 (2000). Note: Contributions are received from Contran Corp.

Typical Recipients

Arts & Humanities: Arts Centers, Arts Festivals, Arts Outreach, Dance, Historic Preservation, Libraries, Museums/Galleries, Music, Performing Arts, Public Broadcasting, Theater
Civic & Public Affairs: Botanical Gardens/Parks, Clubs, Community Foundations, Economic Development, Employment/Job Training, Civic & Public Affairs-General, Housing, Nonprofit Management, Parades/Festivals, Philanthropic Organizations, Professional & Trade Associations, Public Policy, Urban & Community Affairs, Women's Affairs, Zoos/Aquariums
Education: Afterschool/Enrichment Programs, Arts/Humanities Education, Business Education, Colleges & Universities, Community & Junior Colleges, Education Associations, Education Funds, Education Reform, Faculty Development, Education-General, Leadership Training, Legal Education, Literacy, Medical Education, Preschool Education, Private Education (Precollege), Public Education (Precollege), Religious Education, Science/Mathematics Education, Secondary Education (Public)
Environment: Environment-General
Health: AIDS/HIV, Cancer, Children's Health/Hospitals, Clinics/Medical Centers, Health Organizations, Hospitals, Hospitals (University Affiliated), Kidney, Medical Research, Mental Health, Multiple Sclerosis, Nursing Services, Prenatal Health Issues, Public Health, Single-Disease Health Associations, Transplant Networks/Donor Banks
International: Health Care/Hospitals, International Development, International Relief Efforts
Religion: Churches, Religion-General, Jewish Causes, Ministries, Missionary Activities (Domestic), Religious Welfare, Social/Policy Issues
Science: Science-General, Science Museums
Social Services: At-Risk Youth, Camps, Child Welfare, Community Centers, Community Service Organizations, Counseling, Crime Prevention, Domestic Violence, Emergency Relief, Family Planning, Family Services, Food/Clothing Distribution, Homes, People with Disabilities, Recreation & Athletics, Scouts, Shelters/Homelessness, Substance Abuse, United Funds/United Ways, Volunteer Services, YMCA/YWCA/YMHA/YWHA, Youth Organizations

Application Procedures

Initial Contact: Send a written proposal. An application form is not required.
Application Requirements: Include a brief history of organization and its purpose; explanation of proposed project, and amount of funds requested; plans for evaluation of project; list of foundation's directors, including professional affiliations; description of staff; description of use of volunteers; list of major donors; copy of organization's tax determination letter from IRS; financial information; most recent audited statement or Form 990; current year's budget for organization and project; fundraising costs and total fundraising goal.
Deadlines: None.
Review Process: If initial criteria are met, further information may be requested.
Decision Notification: Two to three months after receipt of proposal.

Restrictions

Foundation does not support individuals, endowments, deficit financing, or organizations that discriminate on the basis of race, religion, or sex. Multiyear grants are limited in number. Applicants must be classified as a 501(c)(3) organization.

Corporate Officials

Eugene Karl Anderson: vice president, director B Omaha, NE 1935. ED Wayne State University (1958); University of Nebraska (1962). PRIM CORP EMPL vice president, assistant treasurer: Contran Corp. ADD CORP EMPL vice president: NAT City Lines Inc.; vice president: Valcor Inc.; vice president, assistant treasurer: Valhi Inc.

Glenn Reuben Simmons: vice chairman B Golden, TX 1928. ED Texas Christian University; East Texas State University BS (1950). PRIM CORP EMPL vice chairman: Contran Corp. CORP AFFIL director: Valhi Group Inc.; vice chairman: Valhi Inc.; vice chairman: Valcor Inc.; director: NL Industries Inc.; chairman: Sherman Wire Caldwell Inc.; chairman, chief executive officer, director: Keystone Consolidated Industries; vice chairman: National City Lines Inc.; chief executive officer: Fox Valley Steel Wire Co.; chairman: DeSoto Inc.; president: Flight Proficiency Service Inc.

Steven L. Watson: president, director PRIM CORP EMPL president, director: Contran Corp. CORP AFFIL secretary: Flight Proficiency Service Inc.; secretary: National City Lines Inc.; secretary: Dallas Compressor Co.

Foundation Officials

Eugene Karl Anderson: treasurer (see above)
Lisa K. Simmons Epstein: president, director
John Mark Hollingsworth: assistant secretary B Dallas, TX 1951. ED Rhodes College BA (1973); Southern Methodist University JD (1977). PRIM CORP EMPL general corporate counsel: Valhi Inc.
Keith A. Johnson: controller
Harold Clark Simmons: chairman, director B Alba, TX 1931. ED University of Texas BA (1951); University of Texas MA (1952). PRIM CORP EMPL chairman, chief executive officer: Valhi Inc. ADD CORP EMPL chairman, chief executive officer: Contran Corp. CORP AFFIL chairman: Valcor Inc.; director: Kronos Inc.; chairman: NL Industries Inc. NONPR AFFIL member: Phi Beta Kappa.
Steven L. Watson: vice president, secretary, director (see above)

Grants Analysis

Disclosure Period: calendar year ending 2002
Total Grants: $1,521,280*
Number of Grants: 169
Average Grant: $7,357*
Highest Grant: $100,000
Lowest Grant: $500
Typical Range: $1,000 to $25,000
*Note: Giving excludes matching gifts; scholarship; United Way. Average grant figure excludes three highest grants ($300,000).

Recent Grants

Note: Grants derived from 2003 Form 990.
General
100,000	Cooper Institute for Aerobics Research, Dallas, TX
100,000	Crystal Charity Ball, Dallas, TX
100,000	University of Texas at Austin, Austin, TX
50,000	Fellowship of Christian Athletes, Greater Dallas Chapter, Dallas, TX
50,000	March of Dimes, Dallas, TX

50,000	United Way of Metropolitan Dallas Inc., Dallas, TX
40,000	Westmont College, Santa Barbara, CA
25,000	Amyotrophic Lateral Sclerosis Association, Calabasas Hills, CA
25,000	Central Dallas Ministries, Dallas, TX
25,000	Crystal Cathedral Ministries, Garden Grove, CA

CARLE C. CONWAY SCHOLARSHIP FOUNDATION

Giving Contact

Scholarship and Recognition Program
PO Box 6731
Princeton, NJ 08541

Description

Founded: 1950
EIN: 136088936
Organization Type: Private Foundation
Giving Locations: nationally.
Grant Types: Scholarship.

Donor Information

Founder: Continental Can Co., Inc.

Financial Summary

Total Giving: $676,124 (fiscal year ending June 30, 2001). Note: Fiscal 1998 Giving includes scholarship ($265,330).
Giving Analysis: Giving for fiscal 2001 includes: foundation scholarships ($676,124)
Assets: $7,605,445 (fiscal 2001)
Gifts Received: $5,656,069 (fiscal 1994)

Typical Recipients

Arts & Humanities: Libraries
Education: Arts/Humanities Education, Colleges & Universities, Community & Junior Colleges, Engineering/Technological Education, Faculty Development, Education-General, Medical Education, Science/Mathematics Education, Social Sciences Education, Student Aid, Vocational & Technical Education
Social Services: Family Services

Application Procedures

Initial Contact: Send a written application consisting of student and employee information.
Deadlines: November 30.

Restrictions

Maximum grant does not exceed $8,500 a year for four years. Scholarships awarded only to children of employees who have at least six months continuous service up to the Vice President level.

Foundation Officials

R. E. Adams: vice president
Stephen Bermas: president B New York, NY 1925. ED Cornell University BS (1949); Cornell University JD (1950); New York University LLM (1957). PRIM CORP EMPL vice president, general counsel: Continental Plastic Containers. NONPR AFFIL member: American Bar Association.
M. Colten: vice president, secretary, treasurer
J. Hereford: vice president

Grants Analysis

Disclosure Period: fiscal year ending June 30, 2000
Note: Giving excludes scholarship.

Recent Grants

Note: Grants derived from fiscal 2002 Form 990.

General

25,000	Norwalk Community College, Norwalk, CT
20,000	DePaul University, Chicago, IL
20,000	Marquette University, Milwaukee, WI
20,000	Northern Illinois University, De Kalb, IL
20,000	Penn State University, Monaca, PA
20,000	University of Illinois at Urbana-Champaign, Urbana, IL
18,253	Sam Houston State University, Huntsville, TX
10,000	Baldwin Wallace College, Berea, OH
10,000	Brigham Young University, Laie, HI
10,000	California State University, San Marcos, CA

LOUELLA COOK FOUNDATION

Giving Contact

James Bittel, Vice President & Trust Officer
c/o US Trust Company of New York
114 W. 47th Street
New York, NY 10036
Phone: (212)852-1000

Description

Founded: 1976
EIN: 911098016
Organization Type: Private Foundation
Giving Locations: WA: Seattle
Grant Types: Operating Expenses.

Financial Summary

Total Giving: $197,700 (fiscal year ending July 31, 2003)
Giving Analysis: Giving for fiscal 2003 includes: foundation grants to United Way ($2,000)
Assets: $4,488,620 (fiscal 2003)
Gifts Received: $125,002 (fiscal 1998); $200,023 (fiscal 1997). Note: In 1998 contributions were received from Shelley B. Jansing.

Typical Recipients

Arts & Humanities: Libraries
Civic & Public Affairs: Botanical Gardens/Parks, Clubs, Civic & Public Affairs-General, Philanthropic Organizations
Education: Colleges & Universities, Education Funds, Literacy, Private Education (Precollege), Student Aid
Environment: Resource Conservation
Health: Cancer, Children's Health/Hospitals, Clinics/Medical Centers, Emergency/Ambulance Services, Health Funds, Medical Research, Preventive Medicine/Wellness Organizations, Trauma Treatment
International: Human Rights, International Environmental Issues
Religion: Churches, Religion-General, Missionary Activities (Domestic), Religious Organizations, Religious Welfare
Social Services: Child Welfare, Community Centers, Community Service Organizations, Crime Prevention, Day Care, Emergency Relief, Food/Clothing Distribution, Homes, Shelters/Homelessness, United Funds/United Ways, YMCA/YWCA/YMHA/YWHA, Youth Organizations

Application Procedures

Initial Contact: Send a brief letter of inquiry.
Application Requirements: Include purpose of funds sought.
Deadlines: None.

Additional Information

Trust(s): US Trust Co.

Foundation Officials

Caroline C. Jansing: trustee
Christopher C. Jansing: trustee
John Cook Jansing: trustee

Grants Analysis

Disclosure Period: fiscal year ending July 31, 2003
Total Grants: $195,700*
Number of Grants: 41
Average Grant: $4,773
Highest Grant: $25,000
Lowest Grant: $200
Typical Range: $1,000 to $10,000
*Note: Giving excludes United Way.

Recent Grants

Note: Grants derived from 2003 Form 990.
Library-Related

10,000	George Bush Presidential Library Foundation, College Station, TX

General

25,000	Seattle University, Seattle, WA
25,000	Trustees of Dartmouth College, Hanover, NH
23,000	Jupiter Medical Center Foundation Inc., Jupiter, FL
10,000	Hobe Sound Child Care Center Inc., Hobe Sound, FL
10,000	Jupiter Medical Center Foundation Inc., Jupiter, FL
10,000	Mary Institute and Saint Louis Country Day School, St. Louis, MO
10,000	Union Gospel Mission Association of Seattle, Seattle, WA
5,000	American Red Cross, Seattle, WA
5,000	Bread of Life Mission Association Inc., Seattle, WA

KELLY GENE COOK, SR. CHARITABLE FOUNDATION

Giving Contact

Peggy C. Pool, President
278 Waterford Way
Montgomery, TX 77356
Phone: (936)449-6272
E-mail: pegpool@aol.com

Description

Founded: 1986
EIN: 760201807
Organization Type: Specialized/Single Purpose Foundation
Giving Locations: MS: internationally; nationally.
Grant Types: Challenge, Endowment, General Support, Scholarship.

Donor Information

Founder: Established in 1986 by the late Kelly G. Cook and Peggy J. Cook.

Financial Summary

Total Giving: $1,360,626 (2003); $1,622,776 (2001)
Giving Analysis: Giving for 2003 includes: foundation scholarships ($717,717); 2001: foundation scholarships ($540,922)
Assets: $30,800,772 (2003); $33,329,720 (2001)
Gifts Received: $27,977 (1993); $890,296 (1992). Note: Contributions were received from the estate of Kelly Gene Cook.

Typical Recipients

Arts & Humanities: Libraries
Civic & Public Affairs: Civic & Public Affairs-General, Municipalities/Towns, Parades/Festivals,

Philanthropic Organizations

Education: Business Education, Colleges & Universities, Community & Junior Colleges, Education Funds, Education Reform, Elementary Education (Private), Elementary Education (Public), Engineering/Technological Education, Faculty Development, Education-General, Journalism/Media Education, Legal Education, Medical Education, Preschool Education, Private Education (Precollege), Public Education (Precollege), Religious Education, Secondary Education (Public), Special Education, Student Aid

Health: Medical Training, Mental Health

Religion: Religious Organizations, Seminaries

Social Services: Community Service Organizations, Day Care, Domestic Violence, Family Services, People with Disabilities, Shelters/Homelessness, Substance Abuse, Youth Organizations

Application Procedures

Application Requirements: Prospective applicants for scholarships should contact the director of financial aid at Millsaps College, the University of Mississippi, or Mississippi State University. Other scholarship programs are administered at the foundation's initiation.

Deadlines: April 15.

Review Process: Applications are reviewed by the institutions and forwarded to the foundation. The foundation then selects those to be interviewed and notifies the applicant. Individual interviews are administered by the foundation. Recipients are chosen based on financial need, potential, and motivation.

Restrictions

To be eligible, an applicant must: be a full-time student with a minimum of 15 academic hours per semester; maintain a satisfactory grade point average as determined by the foundation; not be a physical education major; not be married or have a child; and demonstrate need.

Additional Information

Scholarship recipients who maintain an overall GPA of 3.0 or above in their undergraduate studies are eligible to receive $4,000 ($2,000 per semester) for the first year of graduate studies.

For more information from a specific institution contact:

Mr. Jack L. Woodward, Director of Financial Aid, Millsaps College, Jackson, MS 39210;

Mr. Thomas G. Hood, Director of Student Financial Aid, Division of Student Personnel, University of Mississippi, University, MS 38677; or

Ms. Teresa Bost, Assistant Director of Scholarships, Mississippi State University, PO Box AB, Mississippi State, MS 39762.

Foundation Officials

Corbin Barnes: treasurer
Robert B. Kneppler, Jr.: director
Jo Ann Mikell: secretary
Peggy Cook Pool: president
Deborah Rochelle: vice president

Grants Analysis

Disclosure Period: calendar year ending 2003
Total Grants: $658,909*
Number of Grants: 40
Average Grant: $11,813*
Highest Grant: $110,000
Lowest Grant: $403
Typical Range: $5,000 to $20,000
*Note: Giving excludes scholarships. Average grant figure excludes two highest grants ($210,000).

Recent Grants

Note: Grants derived from 2002 Form 990.
General

200,000	Mississippi State University, Mississippi State, MS -- for civil engineering department
110,000	Boys and Girls Country, Hockley, TX -- towards campaign for new admin and admission building
100,000	Magnolia Speech School, Jackson, MS
100,000	University of Southern Mississippi, Hattiesburg, MS -- towards school for children with language disorders "DuBard School"
55,406	Millsaps College, Jackson, MS -- towards spring scholarship
50,000	Boys and Girls Country, Hockley, TX -- towards general support
50,000	Briarwood School, Houston, TX -- towards teacher intensive program and endowment
50,000	Holy Child Jesus Catholic School, Canton, MS -- towards teacher intensive program
46,533	Millsaps College, Jackson, MS -- towards spring scholarship
42,802	Mississippi State University, Mississippi State, MS -- spring scholarships for the year 2003

COOKE FOUNDATION

Giving Contact

Lisa Schiff, Grants Administrator
1164 Bishop Street, 8th Floor
Honolulu, HI 96813
Phone: (808)537-6333
Fax: (808)521-6286
E-mail: info@hcf-hawaii.org
Web: http://www.hcf-hawaii.org

Description

Founded: 1920
EIN: 237120804
Organization Type: General Purpose Foundation
Giving Locations: HI: especially Oahu
Grant Types: Capital, Multiyear/Continuing Support, Project.

Donor Information

Founder: The Cooke Foundation was established in 1920 as the Charles M. Cooke and Anna C. Cooke Trust, with funds bequeathed by their estates. The Cooke family was one of the early pioneers in the development of Hawaii. The family was instrumental in the growth of the Honolulu Academy of Arts, and, to this day, in honor of Anna C. Cooke, the first grant authorized by the foundation's trustees each fiscal year goes to the academy. Through the Cooke Foundation, the Cooke family continues to support the interests and needs of Hawaii.

Financial Summary

Total Giving: $1,478,950 (fiscal year ending June 30, 2002); $1,537,970 (fiscal 2001)
Assets: $24,604,882 (fiscal 2002); $29,390,021 (fiscal 2001)
Gifts Received: $500 (fiscal 1999)

Typical Recipients

Arts & Humanities: Arts Associations & Councils, Arts Centers, Arts Festivals, Arts Funds, Ethnic & Folk Arts, Film & Video, Arts & Humanities-General, Historic Preservation, History & Archaeology, Libraries, Literary Arts, Museums/Galleries, Music, Opera, Performing Arts, Public Broadcasting, Theater, Visual Arts

Civic & Public Affairs: Asian American Affairs, Botanical Gardens/Parks, Business/Free Enterprise, Clubs, Community Foundations, Economic Development, Employment/Job Training, Civic & Public Affairs-General, Hispanic Affairs, Housing, Legal Aid, Nonprofit Management, Parades/Festivals, Philanthropic Organizations, Public Policy, Urban & Community Affairs, Zoos/Aquariums

Education: Afterschool/Enrichment Programs, Arts/Humanities Education, Colleges & Universities, Economic Education, Education Funds, Elementary Education (Public), Environmental Education, International Exchange, International Studies, Preschool Education, Private Education (Precollege), Public Education (Precollege), Science/Mathematics Education, Secondary Education (Private), Secondary Education (Public), Social Sciences Education, Special Education, Student Aid

Environment: Air/Water Quality, Environment-General, Resource Conservation, Wildlife Protection

Health: AIDS/HIV, Alzheimer's Disease, Cancer, Children's Health/Hospitals, Clinics/Medical Centers, Emergency/Ambulance Services, Health-General, Health Policy/Cost Containment, Health Organizations, Heart, Hospices, Hospitals, Medical Research, Mental Health, Prenatal Health Issues, Public Health, Single-Disease Health Associations

International: International Environmental Issues, International Organizations

Religion: Churches, Dioceses, Religion-General, Ministries, Missionary Activities (Domestic), Religious Organizations, Religious Welfare, Seminaries

Science: Science-General, Science Museums, Scientific Centers & Institutes, Scientific Research

Social Services: Animal Protection, At-Risk Youth, Big Brothers/Big Sisters, Child Welfare, Community Centers, Community Service Organizations, Counseling, Crime Prevention, Domestic Violence, Emergency Relief, Family Planning, Family Services, Food/Clothing Distribution, People with Disabilities, Recreation & Athletics, Scouts, Senior Services, Shelters/Homelessness, Social Services-General, Substance Abuse, United Funds/United Ways, Volunteer Services, YMCA/YWCA/YMHA/YWHA, Youth Organizations

Application Procedures

Initial Contact: Funding requests must be made in writing and must include foundation request cover sheet. Contact foundation for application guidelines.

Application Requirements: The following information should be included: one copy of a proposal, including a brief summary of organization, its history, mission, goals, and major achievements; population served by project and any relevant characteristics; community need, problem, or opportunity addressed by project; program objectives, and summary of activities to be funded; amount requested, duration of time funds will be needed, anticipated sources of future support; method to determine effectiveness of project; and information on key staff. Attachments will include one copy of the IRS determination letter, organization charter and bylaws, most recent financial statement, organization's current operating budget, signatures indicating that both the board and executive director have approved submission of proposal, and name and phone number of contact person. Include a one- totwo page executive summary of proposal; an expense budget for the proposed activity; and list of the board of directors, including occupations, statement of board involvement, and functions within the organization.

Deadlines: Proposals must be postmarked by July 1 for review at the September meeting; November 1 for the January meeting; and March 1 for the May meeting.

Review Process: Requests for major projects (requests of more than $25,000) are considered at the last meeting of the fiscal year, held in May.

Notes: Organizations receiving grants must submit a brief report summarizing the outcome of the project and an expenditure report at the completion of the project or accounting period.

Restrictions

Grants are not made to individuals; to churches not affiliated with foundation trustees or Cooke family forebears; for scholarships; for re-granting or discretionary funds; or for loans to individuals or institutions.

Only one grant will be awarded to an organization in any one year.

Additional Information

The Hawaii Community Foundation is the grants administrator for the Cooke Foundation, Ltd.
Publications: Annual Report; Application Procedures

Foundation Officials

Dale Bachman: trustee
Anna Derby Blackwell: trustee B Honolulu, HI 1932. ED Vassar College (1950-1952); University of Hawaii (1952-1953); University of Canterbury (New Zealand) (1985); Hawaii Pacific University BA (1991). PRIM CORP EMPL consultant: ANNAgram. NONPR AFFIL member: Women in Communications Inc.; founder: Women's Fund Hawaii; assistant manager: Cathedral Associates Saint Marks; member: Public Relations Society America.
Richard A. Cooke, Jr.: trustee
Samuel A. Cooke: president, trustee PRIM NONPR EMPL chairman: Honolulu Academy Arts.
Betty P. Dunford: vice president, trustee NONPR AFFIL director: Family Support Services West Hawaii.
Lynne Johnson: secretary
Charles C. Spalding: vice president, trustee

Grants Analysis

Disclosure Period: fiscal year ending June 30, 2002
Total Grants: $1,478,950
Number of Grants: 97
Average Grant: $14,364*
Highest Grant: $100,000
Lowest Grant: $2,000
Typical Range: $5,000 to $25,000
*Note: Average grant figure excludes highest grant.

Recent Grants

Note: Grants derived from fiscal 2002 Form 990.
General
121,000	St. Andrew's Priory School, Honolulu, HI -- landscaping for playground at Queen Emma Preschool
100,000	Honolulu Academy of Arts, Honolulu, HI -- for annual grant
50,000	Daughters of Hawaii, Honolulu, HI -- for Queen Emma Summer Palace
50,000	Hanahauoli School, Honolulu, HI -- capital campaign
50,000	La Pietra, Honolulu, HI -- capital campaign
50,000	Volcano Art Center, Hawaii National Park, HI -- for construction of administration and arts education facilities
30,000	Missionary Church, Inc., Mililani, HI -- for Punawai Ola Center Programs
25,000	Academy of the Pacific, Honolulu, HI -- for technology upgrade project
25,000	Assets School, Honolulu, HI -- for library expansion
25,000	Boy Scouts of America Aloha Council, Honolulu, HI -- for capital campaign

V. V. COOKE FOUNDATION CORP.

Giving Contact

Theodore L. Merhoff, Jr., Executive Director
V. V. Cooke Foundation Corp.
PO Box 202
Pewee Valley, KY 40056-0202
Phone: (502)241-0303

Description

Founded: 1947
EIN: 616033714
Organization Type: Private Foundation
Giving Locations: KY
Grant Types: General Support.

Donor Information

Founder: the late V. V. Cooke, Cooke Chevrolet Co., Cooke Pontiac Co.

Financial Summary

Total Giving: $274,500 (fiscal year ending August 31, 2004); $299,510 (fiscal 2001)
Giving Analysis: Giving for fiscal 2004 includes: foundation grants to United Way ($7,000); fiscal 2001: foundation grants to United Way ($9,000)
Assets: $5,554,226 (fiscal 2004); $6,143,748 (fiscal 2001)
Gifts Received: $2,556 (fiscal 1998); $193,390 (fiscal 1997)

Typical Recipients

Arts & Humanities: Arts Centers, Arts Funds, Libraries, Music
Civic & Public Affairs: Botanical Gardens/Parks, Clubs, Civic & Public Affairs-General, Housing, Women's Affairs, Zoos/Aquariums
Education: Business Education, Colleges & Universities, Economic Education, Education Funds, Legal Education, Private Education (Precollege), Public Education (Precollege), Special Education
Environment: Forestry
Health: AIDS/HIV, Alzheimer's Disease, Cancer, Children's Health/Hospitals, Emergency/Ambulance Services, Hospices, Medical Research, Research/Studies Institutes, Single-Disease Health Associations
Religion: Churches, Ministries, Religious Organizations, Religious Welfare, Seminaries
Social Services: At-Risk Youth, Child Welfare, Community Service Organizations, Day Care, Family Services, People with Disabilities, Scouts, Senior Services, United Funds/United Ways, Volunteer Services, YMCA/YWCA/YMHA/YWHA, Youth Organizations

Application Procedures

Initial Contact: Applications may be in letter format.
Application Requirements: Letter should outline the applicant's goals and purposes, the intended use, and the amount of the grant requested. Include proof of tax-exempt status.
Deadlines: Middle of the following months: January, April, July, and October.

Restrictions

Grants are limited to organizations located in the Louisville, KY area. Grant purposes must be religious, educational, civic or humanitarian.

Foundation Officials

V. V. Cooke, Jr.: director
Jane C. Cross: director
Joe D. Cross, Jr.: vice president
Frank P. Hilliard: secretary, treasurer
June C. Hook: director
Robert L. Hook, Jr.: president

Grants Analysis

Disclosure Period: fiscal year ending August 31, 2004
Total Grants: $267,500*
Number of Grants: 76
Average Grant: $2,900*
Highest Grant: $50,000
Lowest Grant: $100
Typical Range: $1,000 to $5,000
*Note: Giving excludes United Way. Average grant figure excludes highest grant.

Recent Grants

Note: Grants derived from 2001 Form 990.
Library-Related
5,000	Prescott Public Library, Prescott, AZ

General
54,000	Walnut Street Baptist Church, Louisville, KY
32,120	Broadway Baptist Church, Louisville, KY
27,750	Baptist Theological Seminary, Richmond, VA
7,000	Metro United Way, Louisville, KY
7,000	St. Paul's Episcopal Church, Alexandria, VA
6,800	St. Francis in the Fields Episcopal Church
6,000	Cabbage Patch Settlement House, Louisville, KY
6,000	University of Virginia, Charlottesville, VA -- for Jefferson Scholars Program
5,000	First Baptist Church of Boynton Beach, Boynton Beach, FL
5,000	Habitat for Humanity - Prescott

COOPER FOUNDATION

Giving Contact

E. Arthur Thompson, President
211 N. 12th St., Suite 304
Lincoln, NE 68508
Phone: (402)476-7571
Fax: (402)476-2356
E-mail: info@cooperfoundation.org
Web: http://www.cooperfoundation.org

Description

Founded: 1934
EIN: 470401230
Organization Type: Private Foundation
Giving Locations: NE: Lincoln including Lancaster County
Grant Types: Emergency, General Support, Research, Scholarship, Seed Money.

Donor Information

Founder: the late Joseph H. Cooper

Financial Summary

Total Giving: $532,208 (2004); $471,215 (2003); $584,612 (2002)
Giving Analysis: Giving for 2004 includes: foundation grants to United Way ($12,383); 2001: foundation scholarships ($15,000); foundation grants to United Way ($24,541)
Assets: $18,461,338 (2003); $14,958,173 (2002); $18,230,822 (2001)
Gifts Received: $250 (2003); $51,689 (2001); $459,376 (1999). Note: In 1999 and 2001, contributions were received from E.N. Thompson.

Typical Recipients

Arts & Humanities: Arts Associations & Councils, Arts Centers, Arts Festivals, Arts Funds, Ballet, Community Arts, Film & Video, Arts & Humanities-General, Historic Preservation, History & Archaeology, Libraries, Literary Arts, Museums/Galleries, Music, Opera, Performing Arts, Public Broadcasting, Theater
Civic & Public Affairs: Asian American Affairs, Botanical Gardens/Parks, Business/Free Enterprise, Community Foundations, Economic Policy, Employment/Job Training, Civic & Public Affairs-General, Hispanic Affairs, Housing, Municipalities/Towns, Native American Affairs, Philanthropic Organizations, Public Policy, Zoos/Aquariums
Education: Afterschool/Enrichment Programs, Arts/Humanities Education, Business Education, Colleges & Universities, Community & Junior Colleges, Economic Education, Education Associations, Education Funds, Elementary Education (Private), Faculty De-

velopment, Education-General, International Studies, Legal Education, Literacy, Medical Education, Minority Education, Preschool Education, Private Education (Precollege), Public Education (Precollege), Religious Education, Science/Mathematics Education, Secondary Education (Private), Secondary Education (Public), Student Aid

Environment: Environment-General, Resource Conservation, Wildlife Protection

Health: Cancer, Children's Health/Hospitals, Emergency/Ambulance Services, Hospitals, Kidney, Mental Health, Prenatal Health Issues, Public Health

International: International Organizations

Religion: Churches, Ministries, Missionary Activities (Domestic), Religious Organizations, Religious Welfare

Social Services: Animal Protection, At-Risk Youth, Big Brothers/Big Sisters, Child Welfare, Community Centers, Community Service Organizations, Crime Prevention, Delinquency & Criminal Rehabilitation, Domestic Violence, Family Services, Food/Clothing Distribution, Homes, People with Disabilities, Recreation & Athletics, Scouts, Shelters/Homelessness, Social Services-General, Substance Abuse, United Funds/United Ways, Volunteer Services, YMCA/YWCA/YMHA/YWHA, Youth Organizations

Application Procedures

Initial Contact: Application form required.
Deadlines: None. Applications are reviewed monthly at board meetings.

Restrictions

Supports programs that benefit children and youth in Lincoln and Lancaster counties, or Nebraska statewide.

Additional Information

Publications: Biennial Report (including Application Guidelines); Informational Brochure

Foundation Officials

Jack D. Campbell: trustee
Kathryn Druliner: trustee
Jane Renner Hood: trustee
Brad Korell: trustee
Robert Nefsky: trustee
Susan K. Renken: trustee
E. Arthur Thompson: president, trustee
Richard J. Vierk: trustee
Norton E. Warner: trustee
John W. White, Jr.: trustee

Grants Analysis

Disclosure Period: calendar year ending 2004
Total Grants: $519,825*
Number of Grants: 50
Average Grant: $10,397
Highest Grant: $30,000
Lowest Grant: $1,200
Typical Range: $5,000 to $20,000
*Note: Giving excludes United Way.

Recent Grants

Note: Grants derived from 2002 Form 990.
General

125,000	YMCA, Lincoln, NE -- for Building Strong Kids campaign
96,189	University of Nebraska Lincoln, Mary Riepma Ross Film Theater, Lincoln, NE -- for New Mary Riepma Ross Media Center - gift from Joseph W Cooper Trust
40,000	University of Nebraska Lincoln, E.N.Thompson Forum on World Issues, Lincoln, NE -- fund for campaign
29,200	First-Plymouth Preschool and Discovery Days, Lincoln, NE -- to support the national curriculum for visual/spatial skills
25,000	Audubon Nebraska, Lincoln, NE -- fund for new education/naturalist position at Rowe Sanctuary
25,000	Nebraska Wesleyan University, Lincoln, NE -- for the development of new Baccalaureate-Plus Program
20,000	Family Service Association -- for second-year funding for CF Star
15,772	Nebraska Association of Teachers of Science, Lincoln, NE -- to support Nebraska teachers in Building a Presence for Science network
15,150	Nebraska Art Association, Lincoln, NE -- fund for exhibition and acquisition of work by Anne Truitt
15,000	Nature Conservancy, Arlington, VA -- for Saline wetlands Coordinator

COOPER INDUSTRIES LTD.

Company Headquarters

600 Travis St., Ste. 5800
Houston, TX 77002-1001
Web: http://www.cooperindustries.com

Company Description

Founded: 1833
Ticker: CBE
Exchange: NYSE
Revenue: US$3.96 billion (2002)
Employees: 27188 (2003)

Nonmonetary Support

Type: Donated Equipment; Donated Products; In-kind Services

Volunteer Programs: The company sponsors a volunteer Spirit Awards program at all of its international locations. In 1996, Cooper recognized 31 volunteers in nine countries, enabling them to direct cash contributions totaling $46,500 to the nonprofit organizations of their choice.

Note: Nonmonetary support is handled through local contacts.

Cooper Industries Foundation

Giving Contact

Beth Dombrowa, Director, Community Affairs
Cooper Industries Foundation
600 Travis, Suite 5800
Houston, TX 77002
Phone: (713)209-8400
Fax: (713)209-8982
Web: http://www.cooperindustries.com/common/aboutCooper/corporateGiving.cfm
Note: Subsidiaries have separate contact persons; call the foundation office for information.

Description

EIN: 316060698
Organization Type: Corporate Foundation
Giving Locations: operating locations.
Grant Types: Capital, Challenge, Emergency, Employee Matching Gifts, General Support, Matching, Multiyear/Continuing Support.
Note: Employee matching gift ratio: 1 to 1; 2 to 1 for volunteer services.

Financial Summary

Total Giving: $2,382,865 (2003); $2,378,525 (2002); $3,032,117 (2001). Note: Contributes through corporate direct giving program and foundation.

Giving Analysis: Giving for 2001 includes: foundation matching gifts ($401,217); foundation grants to United Way ($941,104); foundation ($1,606,751)

Assets: $12,232,767 (2003); $567,932 (2002); $221,782 (2001)

Gifts Received: $14,000,000 (2003); $3,200,000

(2002); $1,500,000 (2001). Note: In 2001 and 2003, contributions were received from Cooper Industries.

Typical Recipients

Arts & Humanities: Arts Associations & Councils, Arts Funds, Ballet, Dance, Historic Preservation, Libraries, Museums/Galleries, Music, Opera, Performing Arts, Public Broadcasting, Theater

Civic & Public Affairs: African American Affairs, Botanical Gardens/Parks, Business/Free Enterprise, Civil Rights, Clubs, Economic Development, Economic Policy, Employment/Job Training, Civic & Public Affairs-General, Hispanic Affairs, Housing, Law & Justice, Municipalities/Towns, Philanthropic Organizations, Professional & Trade Associations, Public Policy, Safety, Urban & Community Affairs, Women's Affairs, Zoos/Aquariums

Education: Afterschool/Enrichment Programs, Arts/Humanities Education, Business Education, Colleges & Universities, Community & Junior Colleges, Economic Education, Education Associations, Education Funds, Engineering/Technological Education, Education-General, Literacy, Medical Education, Minority Education, Private Education (Precollege), Public Education (Precollege), Science/Mathematics Education, Secondary Education (Public), Student Aid, Vocational & Technical Education

Environment: Environment-General

Health: Cancer, Children's Health/Hospitals, Emergency/Ambulance Services, Health Funds, Health Organizations, Heart, Hospices, Hospitals, Mental Health, Single-Disease Health Associations

International: Health Care/Hospitals, International Affairs

Religion: Religious Welfare

Science: Science Museums, Scientific Centers & Institutes, Scientific Organizations

Social Services: Animal Protection, Child Welfare, Community Centers, Community Service Organizations, Emergency Relief, Food/Clothing Distribution, People with Disabilities, Recreation & Athletics, Senior Services, Shelters/Homelessness, Special Olympics, Substance Abuse, United Funds/United Ways, YMCA/YWCA/YMHA/YWHA, Youth Organizations

Application Procedures

Initial Contact: Send a brief letter or proposal.
Application Requirements: Include concise a description of organization and its mission, purpose of funds sought including fundraising goals, amount requested, budget information and funding sources, list of board members, and proof of tax-exempt status.
Deadlines: None; budget is set in the fall for the following year.
Review Process: Review team evaluates requests on an ongoing basis; response within four to six weeks of receipt.
Evaluative Criteria: Programs must benefit a community where Cooper is a significant employer, must be endorsed by local management (where applicable), must not duplicate efforts of company-created programs, must have objectives that coincide with those of the company, and must fulfill an important community need.
Notes: Organizations in communities where Cooper has a plant facility should direct their requests to local facilities.

Restrictions

The following types of organizations normally are not eligible for grants: religious organizations, national health and welfare organizations (except through a local united fund or community chest, or through and for the use and benefit of local chapters), fraternal or veterans' organizations (except for special philanthropic projects that benefit a wide spectrum of community life), endowment funds, political candidates or organizations, labor organizations, or lobbying organizations. The company does not support individuals.

Corporate Officials

D. Bradley McWilliams: chief financial officer, senior vice president financerc B 1941. ED New York University; University of Texas BBA (1966); University of Texas JD (1971). PRIM CORP EMPL chief financial officer, senior vice president finance: Cooper Industries, Inc. CORP AFFIL director: Kronos Data Systems Inc.; director: Kronos Inc.

H. John Riley, Jr.: chairman, president, chief executive officer, director B Syracuse, NY 1940. ED Syracuse University BS (1961); Harvard University (1985). PRIM CORP EMPL chairman, president, chief executive officer, director: Cooper Industries, Inc. CORP AFFIL director: Wyman-Gordon Co.; director: Baker Hughes Inc.; director: Central Houston Inc. NONPR AFFIL trustee: Manufacturers Alliance Productivity & Innovation.

Foundation Officials

Victoria B. Guennewig: president, trustee
Terry Klebe: treasurer, trustee
H. John Riley, Jr.: chairman, trustee (see above)
Diane K. Schumacher: trustee

Grants Analysis

Disclosure Period: calendar year ending 2003
Total Grants: $1,332,733*
Number of Grants: 226
Average Grant: $5,897
Highest Grant: $100,000
Lowest Grant: $100
Typical Range: $1,000 to $10,000
***Note:** Giving excludes matching gifts and United Way.

Recent Grants

Note: Grants derived from 2003 Form 990.
General

100,000	Lowe's Home Safety Council, Wilkesboro, NC
94,513	United Way of Waukesha County, Waukesha, WI
72,534	United Way of Central New York, Syracuse, NY
70,000	Alley Theatre, Houston, TX
68,899	United Way of Texas Gulf Coast, Houston, TX
50,000	Houston Music Hall Foundation, Houston, TX
40,000	Star of Hope Mission, Houston, TX
40,000	YMCA of Greater Houston Area, Houston, TX
35,968	United Way of Greater Saint Louis Inc., St. Louis, MO
35,000	Electrical Safety Foundation International Inc., Rosslyn, VA

COOPER TIRE & RUBBER CO.

Company Headquarters

701 Lima Ave.
Findlay, OH 45840
Web: http://www.coopertire.com

Company Description

Founded: 1914
Ticker: CTB
Exchange: NYSE
Revenue: US$3.933 billion (2004)
Profit: US$201.4 million (2004)
Employees: 22899 (2003)
Fortune Rank: 470, per FORTUNE Magazine's list of 500 Largest U.S. Corporations (2004).

Nonmonetary Support

Type: Donated Equipment; Donated Products

Cooper Tire & Rubber Foundation

Giving Contact

Philip G. Weaver, Trustee
701 Lima Ave.
Findlay, OH 45840
Phone: (419)423-1321
Fax: (419)424-4212

Description

EIN: 237025013
Organization Type: Corporate Foundation
Giving Locations: OH: operating locations.
Grant Types: Employee Matching Gifts, General Support.

Financial Summary

Total Giving: $817,378 (2003); $901,480 (2002); $944,743 (2001). Note: Contributes through corporate direct giving program and foundation.
Giving Analysis: Giving for 2002 includes: foundation grants to United Way ($236,387); 2001: foundation scholarships ($2,200); foundation grants to United Way ($252,978); foundation ($689,569)
Assets: $28,084 (2003); $772,806 (2002); $149,608 (2001)
Gifts Received: $50,569 (2003); $1,696,111 (2002); $38,919 (2001)

Typical Recipients

Arts & Humanities: Arts Associations & Councils, Arts Institutes, Arts & Humanities-General, Libraries, Museums/Galleries, Opera, Public Broadcasting
Civic & Public Affairs: Botanical Gardens/Parks, Chambers of Commerce, Clubs, Community Foundations, Employment/Job Training, Civic & Public Affairs-General
Education: Arts/Humanities Education, Business Education, Colleges & Universities, Community & Junior Colleges, Economic Education, Education Funds, Engineering/Technological Education, Faculty Development, Education-General, Literacy, Private Education (Precollege), Religious Education, Science/Mathematics Education, Secondary Education (Private), Student Aid, Vocational & Technical Education
Health: Cancer, Clinics/Medical Centers, Emergency/Ambulance Services, Health-General, Hospitals, Medical Rehabilitation, Public Health
Religion: Religious Organizations, Religious Welfare, Seminaries
Science: Science Museums, Scientific Centers & Institutes
Social Services: Animal Protection, Community Centers, People with Disabilities, Scouts, Senior Services, Shelters/Homelessness, Social Services-General, United Funds/United Ways, YMCA/YWCA/YMHA/YWHA, Youth Organizations

Application Procedures

Initial Contact: Send a brief letter.
Application Requirements: Include a description of organization, amount requested, purpose of funds sought, recently audited financial statement, and proof of tax-exempt status.
Deadlines: None.

Restrictions

Company does not award grants to individuals.

Corporate Officials

Philip G. Weaver: executive vice president, chief financial officer, trustee PRIM CORP EMPL vice president, chief financial officer, trustee: Cooper Tire & Rubber Co.

Foundation Officials

Philip G. Weaver: trustee (see above)
Eileen B. White: trustee

Grants Analysis

Disclosure Period: calendar year ending 2003
Total Grants: $566,674*
Number of Grants: 262
Average Grant: $2,163
Highest Grant: $33,333
Lowest Grant: $25
Typical Range: $1,000 to $5,000
***Note:** Giving excludes United Way; scholarships.

Recent Grants

Note: Grants derived from 2003 Form 990.
General

97,000	United Way of Hancock County, Findlay, OH
70,000	Findlay Family YMCA, Findlay, OH
33,350	Ferris State University, Big Rapids, MI
30,950	University of Findlay, Findlay, OH
30,000	Tri-State University, Angola, IN
25,000	Ohio Foundation of Independent Colleges, Columbus, OH
20,000	Kettering University, Flint, MI
20,000	United Way, Detroit, MI
19,000	United Way of Greater Texarkana, Texarkana, TX
15,000	United Way of Lee County, Ft. Myers, FL

ADOLPH COORS FOUNDATION

Giving Contact

Salley W. Rippey, Executive Director
4100 East Mississippi Avenue, Suite 1850
Denver, CO 80246
Phone: (303)388-1636
Fax: (303)388-1684
E-mail: generalinfo@acoorsfdn.org
Web: http://www.adolphcoors.org

Description

Founded: 1975
EIN: 510172279
Organization Type: Family Foundation
Giving Locations: CO
Grant Types: Capital, Endowment, General Support, Operating Expenses, Project, Scholarship.

Donor Information

Founder: Adolph Coors, Sr., a native German, came to the United States to escape his country's political and economic oppression. In 1873, he founded the Coors brewery in Golden, CO.
In 1912, Adolph Coors, Jr., became brewery superintendent and continued the profitable operation of the family's brewery and porcelain company. Later, during the prohibition years, he established what has become one of the largest malted milk operations in the country. Adolph Coors Jr., died in 1970. In October 1975, the Adolph Coors Foundation was established with funds from his trust.

Financial Summary

Total Giving: $5,005,530 (fiscal year ending November 30, 2003); $7,248,520 (fiscal 2002); $8,745,315 (fiscal 2001)
Assets: $128,261,386 (fiscal 2003); $113,356,453 (fiscal 2002); $140,247,354 (fiscal 2001)
Gifts Received: $160,795,564 (fiscal 1996); $9,456,288 (fiscal 1995). Note: In fiscal 1995, contributions were received from the Janet H. Coors Estate.

Typical Recipients

Arts & Humanities: Arts Associations & Councils, Arts Centers, Ethnic & Folk Arts, Film & Video, Historic Preservation, History & Archaeology, Libraries, Museums/Galleries, Music, Performing Arts, Public

Broadcasting, Theater

Civic & Public Affairs: Botanical Gardens/Parks, Business/Free Enterprise, Chambers of Commerce, Clubs, Community Foundations, Economic Development, Economic Policy, Employment/Job Training, Ethnic Organizations, First Amendment Issues, Civic & Public Affairs-General, Hispanic Affairs, Housing, Law & Justice, Legal Aid, Municipalities/Towns, Native American Affairs, Nonprofit Management, Parades/Festivals, Professional & Trade Associations, Public Policy, Rural Affairs, Safety, Urban & Community Affairs, Women's Affairs, Zoos/Aquariums

Education: Afterschool/Enrichment Programs, Arts/Humanities Education, Business Education, Colleges & Universities, Continuing Education, Economic Education, Education Associations, Education Funds, Education Reform, Engineering/Technological Education, Education-General, Gifted & Talented Programs, Health & Physical Education, Journalism/Media Education, Leadership Training, Literacy, Minority Education, Private Education (Precollege), Public Education (Precollege), Religious Education, Science/Mathematics Education, Secondary Education (Public), Student Aid

Environment: Environment-General, Protection

Health: AIDS/HIV, Children's Health/Hospitals, Clinics/Medical Centers, Emergency/Ambulance Services, Eyes/Blindness, Health Organizations, Hospitals, Medical Rehabilitation, Medical Research, Mental Health, Nursing Services, Preventive Medicine/Wellness Organizations, Public Health, Single-Disease Health Associations

International: International Development, International Peace & Security Issues

Religion: Churches, Dioceses, Jewish Causes, Ministries, Religious Organizations, Religious Welfare

Science: Science Museums, Scientific Organizations

Social Services: At-Risk Youth, Big Brothers/Big Sisters, Camps, Child Welfare, Community Centers, Community Service Organizations, Day Care, Delinquency & Criminal Rehabilitation, Domestic Violence, Emergency Relief, Family Planning, Family Services, Food/Clothing Distribution, Homes, People with Disabilities, Recreation & Athletics, Scouts, Senior Services, Sexual Abuse, Shelters/Homelessness, Social Services-General, Substance Abuse, United Funds/United Ways, Volunteer Services, YMCA/YWCA/YMHA/YWHA, Youth Organizations

Application Procedures

Initial Contact: A preliminary letter with a general description of the proposed project is suggested and should be sent to the executive director.

Application Requirements: After the initial letter is sent, the applying organization should send one copy of a complete proposal, including the organization's legal name and address; contact person and phone number; proof of tax exemption; history, description, and goals of the organization; factors which set the proposed project apart from similar programs; amount needed and how it will be spent; project budget, proof of need, and expected goals of project; other sources of funding and amounts; list of board members (indicate occupations); financial statement of most recent year (foundation prefers a copy of audit); and current and/or proposed income and expense budget.

Deadlines: Applications must be received at least eight weeks prior to the meeting at which consideration is desired.

Review Process: The board of trustees generally meets in March, July, and October to select grant recipients.

Restrictions

The foundation does not make grants to individuals, or for endowment funds, research, film production or other media projects, churches, preschools, day-care centers, nursing homes, extended care centers, conduit funding, deficit financing or retirement of debt, special benefit programs, purchase of membership,

or purchase of blocks of tickets. Funding is primarily restricted to Colorado programs.

Additional Information

Presentations by applicants are to be made to staff rather than to board members. If possible, an on-site visit will be conducted as a part of the application review process. If a proposal is approved, a grant agreement is required.

Publications: Annual Report

Corporate Officials

Peter Hanson Coors: president, chief executive officer, director B Denver, CO 1946. ED Cornell University BS (1969); University of Denver MBA (1970). CORP AFFIL officer: United States Bancorp; director: Coors Distribution Co.; director: Energy Corp. America; vice chairman, chief executive officer: Coors Brewing Co. NONPR AFFIL director: Wildlife Legislative Fund; member: Young Presidents' Organization; director: Up with People; honorary director: Special Olympics Colorado; trustee: University Northern Colorado; trustee: Presidents Leadership Committee, University Colorado; trustee: Seeds of Hope Foundation; member: Opportunities Centers America; trustee: Outward Bound Colorado; chairman devel committee, trustee: National Commission Future Regis College; member: National Individuals Advancement Council; member executive committee: Ducks Unlimited Inc. CLUB AFFIL Metro Denver Executives Club.

Foundation Officials

Hon. Holland H. Coors: trustee NONPR AFFIL trustee: Heritage Foundation, Washington DC.

Peter Hanson Coors: vice president, trustee (see above)

William K. Coors: president B Golden, CO August 11, 1916. ED Princeton University BSChE (1938); Princeton University MSChE (1939). PRIM CORP EMPL chairman, president, chief executive officer, director: Adolph Coors Co.

Salley W. Rippey: executive director

Grants Analysis

Disclosure Period: fiscal year ending November 30, 2003

Total Grants: $5,005,530

Number of Grants: 109

Average Grant: $28,354*

Highest Grant: $800,000

Lowest Grant: $1,150

Typical Range: $10,000 to $50,000

*Note: Average grant figure excludes three highest grant ($2,000,000).

Recent Grants

Note: Grants derived from fiscal 2003 Form 990.

Library-Related

35,000	Friends of the Pine River Public Library, Bayfield, CO -- towards construction of community room
30,000	Rampart Regional Library District, Woodland Park, CO

General

800,000	Regis University, Denver, CO -- towards renovation of science building
800,000	University of Colorado Foundation President's Leadership Fund, Boulder, CO
400,000	Children's Hospital Foundation, Denver, CO -- towards new children hospital at Fitzsimmons
150,000	Bayaud Industries, Denver, CO -- to purchase current rented building
142,300	Colorado School of Mines Foundation, Golden, CO -- towards Herman Coors endowed chair
100,000	Colorado Leadership Alliance, Denver, CO
100,000	Denver Foundation, Denver, CO -- towards educational options for children
100,000	Inner Place Inc., Denver, CO -- towards building renovation
100,000	Jewish Family Service of Colorado, Denver, CO -- towards capital campaign for new facility
90,000	Mi Casa Resource Center for Women Inc., Denver, CO -- towards renovation of new building

COPIC MEDICAL FOUNDATION

Giving Contact

Kathy Brown, Vice President Marketing & COIs
c/o Copic Insurance Co.
7351 Lowry Blvd.
Denver, CO 80230
Phone: (720)858-6066
Web: http://callcopic.com/cmf/index.htm

Description

Founded: 1992
EIN: 841197083
Organization Type: Private Foundation
Giving Locations: CO
Grant Types: General Support, Operating Expenses.

Donor Information

Founder: Established in 1992 by the Copic Insurance Co.

Financial Summary

Total Giving: $228,938 (2002); $323,662 (2001)
Assets: $3,516,105 (2002); $5,283,954 (2001)
Gifts Received: $250,000 (2001); $250,000 (2000); $500,200 (1999). Note: In 2000 and 2001, contributions were received from In 1999, contributions were received from the COPIC Trust ($500,000) and Valerie Farnham ($200).

Typical Recipients

Arts & Humanities: Libraries
Civic & Public Affairs: Urban & Community Affairs
Education: Education-General, Literacy, Medical Education, Science/Mathematics Education
Health: Alzheimer's Disease, Clinics/Medical Centers, Emergency/Ambulance Services, Health-General, Health Policy/Cost Containment, Health Organizations, Hospitals, Medical Research, Multiple Sclerosis, Nursing Services, Preventive Medicine/Wellness Organizations, Public Health, Research/Studies Institutes, Respiratory, Transplant Networks/Donor Banks
Religion: Religious Welfare
Science: Science Museums
Social Services: Child Welfare, Domestic Violence, Emergency Relief, Family Services, Shelters/Homelessness, Social Services-General, Substance Abuse

Application Procedures

Initial Contact: Send a brief letter of inquiry requesting application form or download application and guidelines from the foundation's web site.

Application Requirements: Proposals should include a completed application, copy of 501(c)(3) letter, total project cost and amount requested, recently audited financial statement, and most recent audit report.

Deadlines: None.

Restrictions

Restricted to purposes related to medicine, medical education, medical research, and other medical charitable purposes. Grants are not made to individuals.

Foundation Officials

A. Lee Anneberg, MD: director
Georgia L. Buford: secretary

George D. Dikeou, Esq.: director
Stuart L. Greisman, D.O.: director
Erroll C. Hossack: treasurer
K. Mason Howard, MD: president, director
Alethia Morgan, MD: director
Ronald C. Ochsner, MD: director
Merlin G. Otteman, MD: director
Barbara Reed, MD: director
Bruce C. Richards, MD: director
Amilu S. Rothhammer, MD: director
Steve Rubin: treasurer
Steven J. Thorson, MD: director
Larry W. Thrower: vice president, director
David M. West, MD: director
Harold Williamson: director

Grants Analysis

Disclosure Period: calendar year ending 2002
Total Grants: $228,938
Number of Grants: 57
Average Grant: $4,016
Highest Grant: $45,000
Lowest Grant: $250
Typical Range: $250 to $10,000

Recent Grants

Note: Grants derived from 2002 Form 990.
General
45,000	Colorado Academy of Family Physicians, Denver, CO -- for program support
30,000	Colorado Medical Society Foundation, Denver, CO -- for program support
25,000	Colorado Prevention Center, Denver, CO -- for program support
15,000	Inner City Health Center, Denver, CO -- for program support
12,000	University of Colorado Health Sciences Center, Denver, CO -- for program support
10,500	Doctors Care, Littleton, CO -- for program support
10,000	Family Pathways of Colorado, Wheat Ridge, CO -- for program support
10,000	Rocky Mountain Multiple Sclerosis Center, Englewood, CO -- for program support
10,000	St. Francis Center, Denver, CO -- for program support
8,250	American Lung Association of Colorado, Denver, CO -- for Champ Camp Scholarship

COPLEY PRESS INC.

Company Headquarters

7776 Ivanhoe Ave.
La Jolla, CA 92037
Web: http://www.copleynews.com

Company Description

Revenue: US$534 million (2001)
Employees: 3500 (2001)
SIC(s): 2711 Newspapers.

Operating Locations

Copley Press, Inc. (CA--San Diego, San Pedro, Santa Monica; IL--Aurora, Elgin, Joliet, Lincoln Park, Springfield, Waukegan)

James S. Copley Foundation

Giving Contact

Terry Gilbert, Secretary
PO Box 1530
La Jolla, CA 92038-1530

Phone: (858)454-0411

Description

EIN: 956051770
Organization Type: Corporate Foundation
Giving Locations: in immediate circulation areas only.
Grant Types: Capital, Employee Matching Gifts, Endowment, General Support, Multiyear/Continuing Support, Scholarship.
Note: Employee matching gift ratio: 1 to 1 for gifts to education institutions, up to $1,000 annually.

Financial Summary

Total Giving: $2,008,972 (2002); $2,600,000 (2001). Note: Contributes through corporate direct giving program and foundation.
Giving Analysis: Giving for 2002 includes: foundation grants to United Way ($405,850); foundation (approx $2,000,000); 2001: foundation (approx $2,600,000)
Assets: $21,317,082 (2002); $25,576,325 (2001)
Gifts Received: $17,262 (2002); $30,531 (2001); $17,160 (2000). Note: Contributions were received from San Diego Union Shoe Fund.

Typical Recipients

Arts & Humanities: Arts Centers, Arts Festivals, Dance, Ethnic & Folk Arts, Arts & Humanities-General, History & Archaeology, Libraries, Literary Arts, Museums/Galleries, Music, Opera, Performing Arts, Public Broadcasting, Theater, Visual Arts
Civic & Public Affairs: Botanical Gardens/Parks, Community Foundations, Civic & Public Affairs-General, Housing, Law & Justice, Professional & Trade Associations, Public Policy, Urban & Community Affairs, Zoos/Aquariums
Education: Afterschool/Enrichment Programs, Arts/Humanities Education, Colleges & Universities, Education Funds, Education-General, Leadership Training, Literacy, Medical Education, Minority Education, Private Education (Precollege), Public Education (Precollege), Secondary Education (Private), Student Aid
Environment: Resource Conservation
Health: AIDS/HIV, Alzheimer's Disease, Children's Health/Hospitals, Clinics/Medical Centers, Health-General, Health Funds, Hospices, Hospitals, Medical Rehabilitation, Mental Health, Preventive Medicine/Wellness Organizations, Public Health, Research/Studies Institutes, Single-Disease Health Associations, Transplant Networks/Donor Banks
International: Foreign Arts Organizations, Foreign Educational Institutions, International Organizations
Religion: Dioceses, Religious Welfare
Science: Science Museums, Scientific Centers & Institutes, Scientific Organizations
Social Services: Animal Protection, Child Abuse, Child Welfare, Community Centers, Community Service Organizations, Food/Clothing Distribution, Homes, People with Disabilities, Recreation & Athletics, Scouts, Senior Services, Shelters/Homelessness, Social Services-General, Substance Abuse, United Funds/United Ways, YMCA/YWCA/YMHA/YWHA, Youth Organizations

Application Procedures

Initial Contact: Submit letter. Average grant figure excludes highest grant.
Application Requirements: Include an outline of the specific need with a copy of tax exempt certificate, a list of board/trustee members, and financial budgetary information.
Deadlines: January 2 yearly for annual meeting held in February; otherwise accepted throughout the year.
Review Process: The board meets sometime in the spring to review requests; usually responds within 30 days.
Notes: The foundation does not accept faxed applications or videotapes.

Restrictions

Foundation does not make grants to individuals, fundraising events, goodwill advertising, or political or lobbying groups. Grants generally are not made for unrestricted purposes, budgetary support, operating expenses, or seed money.
Grants generally are not made to organizations receiving support from United Way; loans; general fund drives or annual appeals; debt retirement or operational deficits; state universities and colleges; grant-making organizations; national organizations; public elementary and secondary schools; organizations whose activities are mainly international; research projects; government and public agencies; religious, fraternal, or athletic organizations; conferences or seminars; organizations for distribution to beneficiaries of their own choosing; or for production costs of films, videos, television programs, or books.
Scholarship funds are only contributed to colleges and universities for distribution, not to individuals. Grants are limited primarily to the immediate circulation areas of Copley Newspapers located in California, Illinois, and Ohio.

Additional Information

Foundation does not grant interviews.
Contributions are made for one year and imply no commitment to repeat donations.
Publications: Giving Guidelines

Corporate Officials

David C. Copley: president, chief executive officer, director, senior management board B 1952. ED Menlo College BSBA. PRIM CORP EMPL president, chief executive officer, director, senior management board: Copley Press, Inc. ADD CORP EMPL publisher: Borrego Sun; president: Copley Northwest Inc.; president: Copley News Service; president: Puller Paper Co. CORP AFFIL member editorial Bd: San Diego Union-Tribune; officer: Peoria Journal Star Inc.; chairman, chief executive officer: Fox Valley Press Inc. NONPR AFFIL president: University San Diego President Club; member president associates: Zoological Society San Diego; member: U.S. Humane Society; director: San Diego Museum Art; member president council: Scripps Clinic & Research Foundation; member president council: San Diego Kind Corp.; member: San Diego Hall Science; member: San Diego Historical Society; trustee: San Diego Crew Classic Foundation; member: San Diego Aerospace Museum; member advisory board: San Diego Automotive Museum; member: National Newspaper Association; director: Saint Vincent de Paul Society; trustee emeritus: Museum Photographic Arts; member: FOCAS; trustee emeritus: La Jolla Playhouse; trustee: Canterbury School; trustee emeritus: American Craft Council. CLUB AFFIL Bachelor San Diego Club.

Dean P. Dwyer: vice president finance, treasurer, senior management board PRIM CORP EMPL vice president finance, treasurer, senior management board: Copley Press, Inc. CORP AFFIL treasurer, director: Fox Valley Press Inc.; assistant secretary: Peoria Journal Star Inc.

Charles F. Patrick: executive vice president, chief operating officer, senior management board PRIM CORP EMPL executive vice president, chief operating officer, senior management board: Copley Press, Inc.

Foundation Officials

David C. Copley: president, trustee (see above)
Helen K. Copley: chairman B Cedar Rapids, IA 1922. ED Hunter College (1945). ADD CORP EMPL publisher: San Diego Union-Tribune. CORP AFFIL chairman, editorial board: Union Tribune Publishing Co.; officer: Peoria Journal Star Inc.; director: Fox Valley Press Inc. NONPR AFFIL honorary chairman: Washington Crossing Foundation; member: YWCA; life member: Scripps Memorial Hospital Auxiliary; life member: Star of India Auxiliary; member: San Diego

Symphony Association; life member: San Diego Zoological Society; member: San Diego Society Natural History; life member: San Diego Hall Science; life member: San Diego Opera Association; honorary chairman: San Diego Council Literacy; life patroness: Makua Auxiliary; member: Newspaper Association America; member: La Jolla Town Council; member: Inter-American Press Association; life member: La Jolla Museum Contemporary Art; life member: Friends of International Center; member: California Press Association; member: California Press Institute; member: California Newspaper Publishers Association; member: American Press Institute. CLUB AFFIL San Francisco Press Club; LA Press Club.

Robert F. Crouch: vice president, trustee CORP AFFIL officer: Fox Valley Press Inc.

Terry Gilbert: secretary

Charles F. Patrick: treasurer, trustee (see above)

Karl ZoBell: vice president, trustee B La Jolla, CA 1932. ED Utah State University (1949-1951); Columbia University (1951-1952); Columbia University AB (1953); Stanford University JD (1958). PRIM CORP EMPL partner: Gray, Cary, Ames & Frye. CORP AFFIL director, founder: La Jolla Bank & Trust Co.; vice president, director: Geisel-Seuss Enterprises Inc. NONPR AFFIL trustee: Dr. Seuss Foundation; member: Lambda Alpha; director: James C. Copley Charitable Foundation; fellow: American College Trust & Estate Counsel; member: California Bar Association; member: American Bar Association. CLUB AFFIL La Jolla Beach & Tennis Club.

Grants Analysis

Disclosure Period: calendar year ending 2002
Total Grants: $1,603,122*
Number of Grants: 246
Average Grant: $4,503*
Highest Grant: $500,000
Lowest Grant: $25
Typical Range: $100 to $10,000
***Note:** Giving excludes United Way.

Recent Grants

Note: Grants derived from 2003 Form 990.
General

500,000	La Jolla Playhouse, La Jolla, CA
250,000	Old Globe Theatre, San Diego, CA -- Corp contribution
200,000	Museum of Photographic Arts, San Diego, CA
200,000	San Diego Natural History Museum, San Diego, CA
100,000	Minger International Museum of Folk Art, San Diego, CA
100,000	Museum of Contemporary Art San Diego, San Diego, CA
56,250	United Way of San Diego County, San Diego, CA
56,250	United Way of San Diego County, San Diego, CA
56,250	United Way of San Diego County, San Diego, CA
56,250	United Way of San Diego County, San Diego, CA

CORBETT FOUNDATION

Giving Contact

Karen P. McKim, Executive Director
127 West 9th Street, Suite 3
Cincinnati, OH 45202
Phone: (513)241-3320
Fax: (513)723-4422

Description

Founded: 1958
EIN: 316050360
Organization Type: General Purpose Foundation

Giving Locations: OH: Cincinnati
Grant Types: Capital, Matching, Project.

Donor Information

Founder: Established in 1958 by the late J. Ralph Corbett and Patricia Corbett.

Financial Summary

Total Giving: $1,924,104 (fiscal year ending April 30, 2002); $1,279,936 (fiscal 2001)
Assets: $19,586,459 (fiscal 2002); $24,103,851 (fiscal 2001)
Gifts Received: $250 (fiscal 1999); $1,500,025 (fiscal 1992). Note: Contributions were received from Patricia A. Corbett.

Typical Recipients

Arts & Humanities: Arts Associations & Councils, Arts Centers, Arts Festivals, Arts Institutes, Arts Outreach, Ballet, Dance, Ethnic & Folk Arts, Film & Video, Arts & Humanities-General, Historic Preservation, History & Archaeology, Libraries, Museums/Galleries, Music, Opera, Performing Arts, Public Broadcasting, Theater
Civic & Public Affairs: Chambers of Commerce, Civic & Public Affairs-General, Urban & Community Affairs, Women's Affairs
Education: Afterschool/Enrichment Programs, Arts/Humanities Education, Colleges & Universities, Private Education (Precollege), Public Education (Precollege), Religious Education, Secondary Education (Public), Special Education, Student Aid
Environment: Environment-General
Health: Alzheimer's Disease, Nutrition, Preventive Medicine/Wellness Organizations
International: Foreign Arts Organizations
Religion: Ministries, Religious Welfare
Science: Science Museums
Social Services: Child Welfare, Community Service Organizations, Senior Services, Substance Abuse, United Funds/United Ways

Application Procedures

Initial Contact: The foundation requests applications be made in writing.
Application Requirements: Applicants should describe the program and need, budget and include a copy of the exempted organization's IRS letter regarding its classification under section 501(c)(3).
Deadlines: None. Proposals are accepted throughout the year.
Review Process: Applicants are usually notified within two months whether the application has been approved, rejected, or if more information is necessary before a decision can be made.

Restrictions

Grants are not made to individuals. The foundation supports projects in the greater Cincinnati area only.

Foundation Officials

Patricia A. Corbett: chairman, president
Thomas R. Corbett: trustee B 1936. ED Williams College (1956). PRIM CORP EMPL president, treasurer: Corbett Lighting Inc. CORP AFFIL president, treasurer: CLI Holdings Inc.
Karen P. McKim: secretary, executive director
Jean S. Reis: vice president, treasurer, trustee
Nancy Walker: trustee

Grants Analysis

Disclosure Period: fiscal year ending April 30, 2001
Total Grants: $1,924,104
Number of Grants: 28
Average Grant: $21,575*
Highest Grant: $600,000
Typical Range: $5,000 to $30,000
***Note:** Average grant figure excludes three highest grants ($1,320,000).

Recent Grants

Note: Grants derived from fiscal 2002 Form 990.

General

600,000	Soc Pres Music Hall
520,000	AAAE -- assist in funding programs
200,000	WCET, Cincinnati, OH
115,000	May Festival
100,000	Cincinnati Art School, Cincinnati, OH
65,000	Cincinnati Opera, Cincinnati, OH
50,000	Cincinnati Institute of Fine Arts, Cincinnati, OH
38,000	WGUC Radio Station, Cincinnati, OH
30,000	School of Creative and Performing Arts, Cincinnati, OH
26,000	American Classical Music Hall of Fame

E. L. CORD FOUNDATION

Giving Contact

William O. Bradley, Trustee
1 East 1st Street, Number 901
Reno, NV 89501
Phone: (775)323-0373
Fax: (775)325-8523

Description

Founded: 1962
EIN: 366072793
Organization Type: General Purpose Foundation
Giving Locations: NV: northern and rural counties
Grant Types: Capital, General Support, Operating Expenses, Project, Scholarship.

Donor Information

Founder: Established in 1962 by the late E. L. Cord, who owned business ventures in automobile manufacturing, airplane and boat engine manufacturing, the airline industry, shipbuilding, electrical appliance manufacturing, real estate, and investments. When Mr. Cord died in 1974, his will provided that the major portion of his estate be given to the foundation after bequests to his family members were paid.

Financial Summary

Total Giving: $4,534,900 (2003)
Assets: $97,522,303 (2003)

Typical Recipients

Arts & Humanities: Arts Associations & Councils, Arts Centers, Arts Festivals, Ballet, Dance, Film & Video, Arts & Humanities-General, Historic Preservation, History & Archaeology, Libraries, Literary Arts, Museums/Galleries, Music, Opera, Performing Arts, Public Broadcasting, Theater
Civic & Public Affairs: Botanical Gardens/Parks, Chambers of Commerce, Clubs, Community Foundations, Employment/Job Training, Civic & Public Affairs-General, Hispanic Affairs, Housing, Law & Justice, Legal Aid, Parades/Festivals, Safety, Women's Affairs, Zoos/Aquariums
Education: Afterschool/Enrichment Programs, Arts/Humanities Education, Business Education, Colleges & Universities, Community & Junior Colleges, Education Funds, Elementary Education (Private), Elementary Education (Public), Engineering/Technological Education, Faculty Development, Education-General, Legal Education, Medical Education, Minority Education, Private Education (Precollege), Public Education (Precollege), Science/Mathematics Education, Secondary Education (Private), Secondary Education (Public), Student Aid
Environment: Research
Health: Cancer, Children's Health/Hospitals, Clinics/Medical Centers, Diabetes, Emergency/Ambulance Services, Health-General, Health Funds, Health Organizations, Hospices, Hospitals, Medical Research, Single-Disease Health Associations
Religion: Churches, Religious Organizations, Religious Welfare
Science: Scientific Centers & Institutes, Scientific

Labs, Scientific Research

Social Services: Camps, Child Abuse, Child Welfare, Community Service Organizations, Counseling, Delinquency & Criminal Rehabilitation, Domestic Violence, Emergency Relief, Family Services, Food/Clothing Distribution, Homes, People with Disabilities, Recreation & Athletics, Scouts, Senior Services, Shelters/Homelessness, Substance Abuse, United Funds/United Ways, Veterans, YMCA/YWCA/YMHA/YWHA, Youth Organizations

Application Procedures

Initial Contact: Applicants should write the foundation for application procedures before submitting a formal application.

Application Requirements: All applications must include a concise statement of the project; a statement of the organization's background and its purpose and objectives (the most recent annual report containing such information will suffice); financial information, including a copy of the audited financial statement for the prior fiscal year, a copy of the organizational budget for the current year, the most recent unaudited operating and other available financial statements, and a statement of the major sources of financial support; a statement of how the applicant and the foundation will be able to determine the results of the project upon its completion; evidence of tax-exempt status copy of the determination letter from the IRS stating that the organization is exempt from taxation as defined under Section 501(c)(3) of the Internal Revenue Code and further that the organization is not a private foundation as defined in Section 509 (a); and a list of names of the board members, showing their business, professional, or community affiliations. Any trustee of the foundation, serving as a member, director, trustee, officer, or employee of an organization requesting a grant, will abstain from voting on any matter pertaining to the organization with which the common relationship exists.

Deadlines: October 15.

Review Process: After an organization submits a formal application, the foundation may request an interview, a site visit to the project, or have a telephone discussion with the applicant before the formal proposal is submitted to the board.

Restrictions

Funding will not be considered for organizations that do not have a tax-exempt status or do not comply with other terms or provisions of the foundation's application procedures; general fund-raising events, campaigns, memorial campaigns, deficit funding, conferences or seminars, dinners, or mass mailings; direct aid to individuals; grants to organizations who use funds to support other organizations; grants to religious organizations for sectarian purposes; or any request that will require permanent or continuing support by the foundation.

Additional Information

Characteristics that the foundation looks for in submitted proposals include: institutions and organizations with a history of achievement and good management; institutions that demonstrate a current stable financial condition; programs and projects that become self-sufficient, rather than continuing dependence on the foundation; and projects with a measurable impact.

Publications: Guidelines

Foundation Officials

Bill Bradley: trustee
Joseph S. Bradley: trustee
William O. Bradley: trustee
Robert L. Sims: trustee

Grants Analysis

Disclosure Period: calendar year ending 2003
Total Grants: $4,534,900
Number of Grants: 156
Average Grant: $29,070

Highest Grant: $200,000
Lowest Grant: $1,000
Typical Range: $10,000 to $50,000

Recent Grants

Note: Grants derived from 2003 Form 990.
General

200,000	Saint Mary's Foundation, Reno, NV -- risk modification clinic for Saint Mary's health network
166,000	Nevada Museum of Art, Reno, NV -- construction of building
150,000	Channel 5 Public Broadcasting KNPB, Reno, NV -- end of fiscal year project expenses
150,000	University of Nevada Reno Foundation, Reno, NV -- creation of new computer laboratory
100,000	Boys & Girls Club of Mason Valley, Yenngton, NV -- to establish a commercial kitchen
100,000	Boys & Girls Club of Truckee Meadows, Reno, NV -- expansion of facilities
100,000	Reno Philharmonic Association, Reno, NV -- programs and operations for youth orchestra
100,000	University of Nevada Reno Foundation, Reno, NV -- operating expenses
75,000	Food Bank of Northern Nevada, Sparks, NV -- operating expenses
75,000	Reno Cancer Foundation, Reno, NV -- operating expenses

PETER C. CORNELL TRUST

Giving Contact

John A. Mitchell, Trustee
c/o Fiduciary Services, Inc.
4050 Harlem Road
Snyder, NY 14226-2783
Phone: (716)839-3005

Description

Founded: 1949
EIN: 951660344
Organization Type: Private Foundation
Giving Locations: NY: Buffalo including Erie County
Grant Types: Capital, Emergency, General Support, Multiyear/Continuing Support, Operating Expenses, Seed Money.

Donor Information

Founder: the late Peter C. Cornell, M.D.

Financial Summary

Total Giving: $258,662 (fiscal year ending September 30, 2003); $523,746 (fiscal 2001)
Assets: $5,576,426 (fiscal 2003); $7,144,694 (fiscal 2001)

Typical Recipients

Arts & Humanities: Arts Institutes, Arts Outreach, Arts & Humanities-General, Historic Preservation, History & Archaeology, Libraries, Music, Opera, Public Broadcasting, Theater

Civic & Public Affairs: African American Affairs, Economic Development, Civic & Public Affairs-General, Housing, Municipalities/Towns, Safety, Urban & Community Affairs, Women's Affairs, Zoos/Aquariums

Education: Arts/Humanities Education, Business-School Partnerships, Colleges & Universities, Continuing Education, Education Funds, Education Reform, Faculty Development, Legal Education, Literacy, Medical Education, Minority Education, Preschool Education, Private Education (Precollege), Public Ed-

ucation (Precollege), Science/Mathematics Education, Special Education, Student Aid

Environment: Wildlife Protection

Health: AIDS/HIV, Alzheimer's Disease, Cancer, Children's Health/Hospitals, Clinics/Medical Centers, Emergency/Ambulance Services, Health Organizations, Hospices, Hospitals, Long-Term Care, Nursing Services, Research/Studies Institutes, Single-Disease Health Associations, Speech & Hearing

International: International-General, International Development, International Organizations

Religion: Churches, Dioceses, Ministries, Religious Organizations, Religious Welfare, Seminaries

Science: Science Museums, Scientific Centers & Institutes, Scientific Organizations

Social Services: Camps, Child Welfare, Community Service Organizations, Counseling, Family Planning, Family Services, Food/Clothing Distribution, People with Disabilities, Scouts, Senior Services, Social Services-General, Substance Abuse, United Funds/United Ways, YMCA/YWCA/YMHA/YWHA, Youth Organizations

Application Procedures

Initial Contact: Request application form and guidelines.

Deadlines: September 15.

Restrictions

Does not provide loans or support individuals, demonstration projects, publications, or conferences.

Additional Information

Publications: Application Form; Guidelines

Foundation Officials

John A. Mitchell: trustee
Susan Cornell Wilkes: trustee

Grants Analysis

Disclosure Period: fiscal year ending September 30, 2003
Total Grants: $258,662
Number of Grants: 21
Average Grant: $8,351*
Highest Grant: $50,000
Lowest Grant: $56
Typical Range: $5,000 to $10,000
*****Note:** Average grant figure excludes two highest grants ($100,000).

Recent Grants

Note: Grants derived from fiscal 2003 Form 990.
General

50,000	Hauptman - Woodward Research Facility, Buffalo, NY
50,000	Roswell Park Cancer Institute, Buffalo, NY
25,000	Buffalo Prep, Buffalo, NY
20,000	Martin House Restoration Campaign, Buffalo, NY
13,386	Nichols School Scholarship, Buffalo, NY
10,000	Results Education Microcredit Summit Conference
10,000	Shakespeare in Delaware Park, Buffalo, NY
10,000	Westminster Early Childhood Programs, Buffalo, NY
7,000	Consumer Credit Counseling of Buffalo, Buffalo, NY
5,000	Pride Africa, Nairobi Kenya

CORNING INC.

Company Headquarters

1 Riverfront Plaza
Corning, NY 14831-0001
Web: http://www.corning.com

Company Description

Founded: 1936
Ticker: GLW
Exchange: NYSE
Acquired: Oak Industries, Inc. (1999).
Revenue: US$3.854 billion (2004)
Profit: (US$2.165 billion) (2004)
Employees: 20600 (2003)
Fortune Rank: 480, per FORTUNE Magazine's list of 500 Largest U.S. Corporations (2004).
SIC(s): 3229 Pressed & Blown Glass Nec, 3661 Telephone & Telegraph Apparatus, 3821 Laboratory Apparatus & Furniture, 3826 Analytical Instruments.

Operating Locations

Corning Inc. (ME--Kennebunk, Scarborough; MA--Acton; NY--Oneonta)

Nonmonetary Support

Type: Loaned Executives
Note: Co. provides nonmonetary support.

Corning Inc. Foundation

Giving Contact

Karen C. Martin, Associate Director
MP-LB-02
Corning, NY 14831
Phone: (607)974-8719
Fax: (607)974-4756
E-mail: martinkc@corning.com
Web: http://www.corning.com/inside_corning/foundation.asp

Description

EIN: 166051394
Organization Type: Corporate Foundation
Giving Locations: headquarters and operating communities and nationally; internationally to U.S.-based organizations.
Grant Types: Employee Matching Gifts, Fellowship, General Support, Project.
Note: Employee matching gift ratio: 1 to 1 up to $5,000 per employee annually; institutions may receive up to $20,000 in matched payments per calendar year.

Financial Summary

Total Giving: $4,349,686 (2002); $4,718,947 (2001). Note: Contributes through corporate direct giving program and foundation.
Giving Analysis: Giving for 2001 includes: foundation scholarships ($50,000); foundation matching gifts ($617,686); foundation grants to United Way ($629,570); foundation grants to United Way ($667,075); foundation ($3,421,691); foundation ($5,180,391)
Assets: $18,294,961 (2002); $22,686,811 (2001)
Gifts Received: $312,965 (2002); $405,058 (2001); $9,350,177 (1999). Note: Contributions were received from Corning, Inc.

Typical Recipients

Arts & Humanities: Arts Associations & Councils, Arts Centers, Arts Outreach, Community Arts, Arts & Humanities-General, Historic Preservation, Libraries, Museums/Galleries, Music, Opera, Performing Arts, Public Broadcasting, Theater, Visual Arts
Civic & Public Affairs: Community Foundations, Economic Development, Employment/Job Training, Civic & Public Affairs-General, Municipalities/Towns, Nonprofit Management, Professional & Trade Associations, Public Policy, Urban & Community Affairs, Women's Affairs, Zoos/Aquariums
Education: Afterschool/Enrichment Programs, Arts/Humanities Education, Business Education, Business-School Partnerships, Colleges & Universities, Community & Junior Colleges, Education Associations, Education Funds, Education Reform, Engineering/Technological Education, Environmental Educa-

tion, Faculty Development, Education-General, International Studies, Minority Education, Public Education (Precollege), Science/Mathematics Education, Student Aid, Vocational & Technical Education
Environment: Environment-General, Resource Conservation
Health: Clinics/Medical Centers, Emergency/Ambulance Services, Health Funds, Hospices, Hospitals (University Affiliated), Medical Rehabilitation
International: Foreign Educational Institutions
Religion: Jewish Causes
Science: Science Museums, Scientific Centers & Institutes, Scientific Organizations
Social Services: At-Risk Youth, Big Brothers/Big Sisters, Community Centers, Community Service Organizations, Family Planning, Recreation & Athletics, Scouts, Senior Services, Substance Abuse, United Funds/United Ways, YMCA/YWCA/YMHA/YWHA, Youth Organizations

Application Procedures

Initial Contact: Send a two- to three-page letter of inquiry signed by the senior administrative officer of the organization.
Application Requirements: When submitting a full proposal, provide a project description, including project's purpose, details on how its objectives are to be attained and evaluated, demonstration of how project promotes cooperation among other organizations in the same field, project timetable, amount requested and when funds are needed, itemized project budget, other potential and secured sources of support, and how the project fits Corning Foundation interests. In addition, a proposal must include a description of organization, list of officers and board members, proof of tax-exempt status, and organization's budget and copy of the organization's latest audited financial statement. Organizations requesting renewed operating support must also include a long-range plan for generating other funding and attaining self-sufficiency.
Deadlines: None.
Decision Notification: Written responses usually follow within four weeks of receipt of inquiries; if interested, foundation will ask for a full proposal. Board meets in March, June, September, and November.
Notes: Eligible organizations located near Corning operations should submit requests for funding directly to local Corning management.

Restrictions

Grants are not made to individuals; political parties, campaigns, or causes; labor or veterans' organizations; religious groups; fraternal orders; for fundraising events; athletic activities; to volunteer emergency squads; or for goodwill advertising.

Additional Information

Publications: Guidelines; Foundation Annual Report

Corporate Officials

James B. Flaws: executive vice president, chief financial officer, director B 1948. ED Tufts University BS (1971); Dartmouth College MBA (1973). PRIM CORP EMPL executive vice president, chief financial officer, director: Corning Inc.
James Richardson Houghton: chairman emeritus B Corning, NY April 06, 1936. ED Harvard University AB (1958); Harvard University MBA (1962). PRIM CORP EMPL chairman emeritus: Corning Inc. CORP AFFIL director: JP Morgan Chase & Co.; director: Harvard Corp.; director: Metropolitan Life Insurance Co.; director: ExxonMobil Corp. NONPR AFFIL member business council: Trilateral Commission. CLUB AFFIL University Club; Tarratine Club; River Club; Rolling Rock Club; Harvard Club; Laurel Valley Golf Club; Brookline Country Club; Corning Country Club; Augusta National Golf Club.
E. Marie McKee: senior vice president B Columbus, IN 1951. ED Simmons College MBA; Purdue University BA (1973); Purdue University MA (1976). PRIM CORP EMPL senior vice president: Corning Inc. ADD

CORP EMPL president: Corning Museum Glass; chairman: Steuben Glass. CORP AFFIL director: Carolina Power Co.
Peter F. Volanakis: president Corning technologies ED Dartmouth College BA; Dartmouth College MA. PRIM CORP EMPL president Corning technologies: Corning Inc.
Wendell P. Weeks: president, chief operating officer, director ED Harvard University MBA; Lehigh University BA. PRIM CORP EMPL president, chief operating officer, director: Corning Inc.

Foundation Officials

Katherine A. Asbeck: trustee
Thomas S. Buechner: trustee B New York, NY 1926. ED Princeton University (1945); Arts Students League New York City (1946); Ecole des Beaux Arts (1946); Institut voor Pictologie (1947); University of Paris (1947). PRIM CORP EMPL counsel: Corning Glass Works. NONPR AFFIL trustee: Pilchuck School; trustee: Rockwell Museum; member: National Collection Fine Arts; member: Century Association; trustee: Corning Museum Glass; member: Brooklyn Institute Arts & Science; director: Brooklyn Museum; trustee: Arnot Art Museum Arts Southern Finger Lakes; member faculty art school: Bild-Werk Fravenau Germany.
William D. Eggers: trustee
James B. Flaws: trustee (see above)
Kirk P. Gregg: trustee
Denise A. Hauselt: secretary
James Richardson Houghton: trustee (see above)
Karen C. Martin: associate director
E. Marie McKee: chairman, trustee (see above)
Joseph A. Miller, Jr.: trustee
Mark S. Rogus: treasurer
Pamela C. Schneider: trustee
Kristin A. Swain: president
Peter F. Volanakis: trustee (see above)
Wendell P. Weeks: trustee (see above)

Grants Analysis

Disclosure Period: calendar year ending 2002
Total Grants: $2,104,313*
Number of Grants: 153
Average Grant: $12,463*
Highest Grant: $210,000
Lowest Grant: $250
Typical Range: $5,000 to $25,000
*Note: Giving excludes matching gifts, fellowship, and United Way. Average grant figure excludes highest grant.

Recent Grants

Note: Grants derived from 2003 Form 990.
General

210,000	Regional Science and Discovery Center Inc., Corning, NY -- towards metals outreach programs
175,000	United Way of the Southern Tier Inc., Corning, NY
175,000	United Way of the Southern Tier Inc., Corning, NY
125,000	Chemung Valley Arts Council, Corning, NY -- towards general program support
115,000	Corning City School District, Painted Post, NY -- towards curriculum staff development
100,000	Economic Opportunity Program Inc. of Chemung County, Elmira, NY -- towards Erass Darss campus project
80,000	Boy Scouts of America, Elmira, NY -- towards capital campaign
60,000	Bucknell University, Lewisburg, PA -- towards curriculum enhancement
60,000	Hospital for Special Surgery Fund Inc., New York, NY -- towards rehabilitation program
50,000	Clarkson University, Potsdam, NY -- towards learning center

COUNTRY CURTAINS INC.

Company Headquarters
705 Pleasant St.
Lee, MA 01238

Company Description
Employees: 137
SIC(s): 2299 Textile Goods Nec.

Operating Locations
Country Curtains, Inc. (CT--Avon, Westport; DE--Greenville; MD--Annapolis; MA--Beverly, Stockbridge, Sturbridge, Sudbury; NJ--Far Hills, Ridgewood, Shrewsbury; NY--Fishkill, Rochester; RI--Cranston; VA--Arlington)

High Meadow Foundation

Giving Contact
John H. Fitzpatrick, President
High Meadow Foundation
PO Box 955
Stockbridge, MA 01262
Phone: (413)298-5565
Fax: (413)243-1067

Description
EIN: 222527419
Organization Type: Corporate Foundation
Giving Locations: MA: Berkshire County
Grant Types: Capital, General Support.

Financial Summary
Total Giving: $1,195,264 (fiscal year ending September 30, 2004); $1,185,811 (fiscal 2003); $1,161,590 (fiscal 2002). Note: Contributes through foundation only.
Assets: $1,572,984 (fiscal 2004); $1,504,999 (fiscal 2003); $1,191,737 (fiscal 2002)
Gifts Received: $1,475,220 (fiscal 2004); $1,236,049 (fiscal 2003); $907,417 (fiscal 2002). Note: Contributions were received from Fitzpatrick Companies, Red Lion Inn, Country Curtains Retail, Country Curtains Mail Order, Housatonic Curtain, More Window Ways, Blantyre, John H. and Jane P. Fitzpatrick, JoAnn Brown, Nancy J. Fitzpatrick, and employee donations through the Zoa Fund.

Typical Recipients
Arts & Humanities: Arts Appreciation, Arts Associations & Councils, Arts Centers, Arts Festivals, Arts Institutes, Dance, Film & Video, Arts & Humanities-General, Historic Preservation, History & Archaeology, Libraries, Museums/Galleries, Music, Opera, Performing Arts, Public Broadcasting, Theater
Civic & Public Affairs: Botanical Gardens/Parks, Business/Free Enterprise, Community Foundations, Economic Development, Civic & Public Affairs-General, Housing, Native American Affairs, Parades/Festivals, Professional & Trade Associations, Public Policy, Safety, Urban & Community Affairs, Women's Affairs, Zoos/Aquariums
Education: Afterschool/Enrichment Programs, Agricultural Education, Arts/Humanities Education, Business Education, Colleges & Universities, Community & Junior Colleges, Economic Education, Education Associations, Education Funds, Education-General, International Studies, Legal Education, Minority Education, Private Education (Precollege), Public Education (Precollege), Secondary Education (Private), Student Aid
Environment: Protection, Resource Conservation
Health: AIDS/HIV, Children's Health/Hospitals, Clinics/Medical Centers, Emergency/Ambulance Services, Hospices, Hospitals, Mental Health, Nursing Services, Public Health

International: Foreign Arts Organizations, Human Rights, Missionary/Religious Activities
Religion: Churches, Religious Welfare
Science: Science Museums
Social Services: Animal Protection, Child Abuse, Child Welfare, Community Centers, Community Service Organizations, Counseling, Family Planning, Family Services, People with Disabilities, Recreation & Athletics, Scouts, Shelters/Homelessness, Substance Abuse, United Funds/United Ways, Youth Organizations

Application Procedures
Initial Contact: Send a brief letter.
Application Requirements: Information includes a description of program, brief history, and amount sought.
Deadlines: None.

Restrictions
The foundation limits the majority of gifts to charitable organizations in Berkshire County, MA.

Corporate Officials
Jane P. Fitzpatrick: chairman, chief executive officer, treasurer B 1925. PRIM CORP EMPL chairman, chief executive officer, treasurer: Country Curtains, Inc. CORP AFFIL treasurer: Housatonic Curtain Co. Inc.; treasurer: Red Lion Inc.; chairman: Country Curtains Mail Order Inc.; chairman: Fitzpatrick Companies Inc.
Robert B. Trask: president, chief operating officer, director B Springfield, MA 1946. ED Western New England College (1971). PRIM CORP EMPL president, chief operating officer, director: The Fitzpatrick Companies Inc. ADD CORP EMPL vice president, clearing houserk, director: Red Lion Inc. CORP AFFIL vice president: Lee Community Development Corp.; director: More Window Ways Inc.; director: Housatonic Curtain Co. Inc.; clerk, director: Country Curtains Retail Inc.; director: Fitzpatrick Retail & Realty Co. Inc.; trustee: City Savings Bank; president, chief operating officer, director: Country Curtains Mail Order Inc.; director: Berkshire Gas Co., Inc.; corporator: Berkshire Health Systems. NONPR AFFIL member: New England Mail Order Association; corporator: North Adams State College Foundation; member: Knights of Columbus; secretary, treasurer: High Meadow Foundation Inc.; member: Institute of Management Accountants; trustee: Berkshire Theatre Festival; member: Direct Marketing Association; member: American Institute CPAs; trustee: Berkshire Community College.

Foundation Officials
JoAnn Fitzpatrick Brown: director
Jane P. Fitzpatrick: treasurer (see above)
John H. Fitzpatrick: president B 1925. PRIM CORP EMPL president, director: Housatonic Curtain Co. Inc. CORP AFFIL vice chairman: Country Curtains Retail Inc.; director: Fitzpatrick Retail & Realty Co. Inc.
Nancy J. Fitzpatrick: director B 1946. ADD CORP EMPL treasurer: Berkshire Collections Inc.; vice president, director: Country Curtains Mail Order Inc.; president: Country Curtains Retail Inc.; executive vice president: Fitzpatrick Companies Inc.; treasurer, director: Fitzpatrick Retail & Realty Co. Inc.; vice president,director: Housatonic Curtain Co. Inc.; president,director: Red Lion Inc.
Tamara T. Stevens: director
Robert B. Trask: clerk (see above)

Grants Analysis
Disclosure Period: fiscal year ending September 30, 2004
Total Grants: $1,127,755*
Number of Grants: 241
Average Grant: $4,282*
Highest Grant: $100,000
Lowest Grant: $100
Typical Range: $1,000 to $10,000

*Note: Giving excludes scholarship; United Way. Average grant figure excludes highest grant.

Recent Grants
Note: Grants derived from fiscal 2004 Form 990.
Library-Related
25,000	Lenox Library Association, Lenox, MA
10,000	Lenox Library Association, Lenox, MA
5,000	Lenox Library, Lenox, MA
5,000	Stockbridge Library Association, Stockbridge, MA

General
100,000	Colonial Theatre Association, Pittsfield, MA
85,000	Berkshire Theatre Festival, Stockbridge, MA
55,000	Boston Symphony Orchestra, Boston, MA
50,000	Austin Riggs Center, Stockbridge, MA
50,000	Norman Rockwell Museum, Stockbridge, MA
40,000	Berkshire Theatre Festival, Stockbridge, MA
40,000	Berkshire United Way, Berkshire, MA
30,000	First Congregational Church, Stockbridge, MA
25,000	Berkshire Country Day School, Lenox, MA
25,000	Buckley School, Camden, SC

COVE CHARITABLE TRUST

Giving Contact
Sandra Brown-McMullen, Trust Officer
c/o Mellon Trust of New England
1 Boston Pl.
Boston, MA 02108
Phone: (617)722-3891

Description
Founded: 1964
EIN: 046118955
Organization Type: Private Foundation
Giving Locations: MA
Grant Types: Capital, General Support, Multiyear/Continuing Support, Operating Expenses, Project, Seed Money.

Donor Information
Founder: the late Aileen Kelly Pratt, the late Edwin H. B. Pratt

Financial Summary
Total Giving: $157,000 (2003); $283,500 (2001)
Assets: $4,566,206 (2003); $4,896,375 (2001)

Typical Recipients
Arts & Humanities: Historic Preservation, History & Archaeology, Libraries, Music, Public Broadcasting
Civic & Public Affairs: Civil Rights, Community Foundations, Civic & Public Affairs-General, Housing, Native American Affairs, Urban & Community Affairs, Women's Affairs
Education: Business Education, Colleges & Universities, Education-General, Health & Physical Education, Leadership Training, Literacy, Student Aid
Environment: Environment-General, Resource Conservation
Health: Emergency/Ambulance Services, Health Funds, Health Organizations, Hospices, Hospitals, Prenatal Health Issues, Preventive Medicine/Wellness Organizations, Public Health
International: International Development
Religion: Churches, Religion-General, Ministries, Religious Organizations, Religious Welfare
Social Services: Animal Protection, Child Welfare,

Community Service Organizations, Domestic Violence, Emergency Relief, Family Services, Food/Clothing Distribution, People with Disabilities, Recreation & Athletics, Social Services-General, YMCA/YWCA/YMHA/YWHA, Youth Organizations

Application Procedures
Initial Contact: Call Ms. Brown-McMullen for application information.
Deadlines: None.

Additional Information
Trust(s): Mellon Trust of New England

Grants Analysis
Disclosure Period: calendar year ending 2003
Total Grants: $157,000
Number of Grants: 17
Average Grant: $9,235
Highest Grant: $26,500
Lowest Grant: $500
Typical Range: $1,000 to $20,000

Recent Grants
Note: Grants derived from 2001 Form 990.
General

55,000	Emmanuel Gospel Center, Boston, MA -- for operations
55,000	Social Action Ministries
33,500	Coalition of Buzzards Bay -- assist in Watershed Campaign
20,000	Bowling Green State University Foundation, Bowling Green, OH -- support for Ned E. Baker Lecture Series
12,500	Sippican Lands Trust, Marion, MA -- for operations
10,000	American Red Cross -- for disaster relief
10,000	Hartford Foundation for Public Giving, Hartford, CT -- support the Boyd and Wendy Hinds Scholarship Fund
10,000	Old Colony Hospice, Inc., Stoughton, MA -- support for the Hospice Housing Project
8,000	New York City Radio, New York, NY -- support to help replace the destroyed tower
7,500	National Association of County and City Health Officials, Washington, DC -- support for Public Health Partners Coalition

LOUETTA M. COWDEN FOUNDATION

Giving Contact
David P. Ross, Senior Vice President & Trust Officer
c/o Bank of America, N.A.
1200 Main Street, 14th Floor
Kansas City, MO 64105
Phone: (816)979-7481
Fax: (816)979-7916

Description
Founded: 1964
EIN: 436052617
Organization Type: Private Foundation
Giving Locations: MO
Grant Types: Capital, Emergency, General Support, Project, Seed Money.

Donor Information
Founder: the late Louetta M. Cowden

Financial Summary
Total Giving: $609,629 (2003)
Assets: $13,369,081 (2003)

Typical Recipients
Arts & Humanities: Ballet, Historic Preservation, Libraries, Literary Arts, Museums/Galleries, Opera, Theater
Civic & Public Affairs: Business/Free Enterprise, Employment/Job Training, Zoos/Aquariums
Education: Colleges & Universities, Education-General, Literacy, Private Education (Precollege), Science/Mathematics Education, Special Education, Student Aid
Environment: Resource Conservation
Health: Children's Health/Hospitals, Hospitals, Mental Health, Nursing Services, Research/Studies Institutes
Religion: Jewish Causes, Ministries, Religious Organizations, Religious Welfare
Science: Science Museums
Social Services: Child Welfare, Community Centers, Community Service Organizations, Counseling, Domestic Violence, Family Services, Food/Clothing Distribution, Recreation & Athletics, Scouts, Senior Services, United Funds/United Ways, YMCA/YWCA/YMHA/YWHA, Youth Organizations

Application Procedures
Initial Contact: Send a brief letter (no more than three pages) with appropriate attachments. Deadlines vary.

Restrictions
Does not support individuals. Grants are limited to organizations in the state of Missouri.

Additional Information
Publications: Application Guidelines
Trust(s): Bank of America, N.A.

Foundation Officials
Arthur H. Bowen, Jr.: trustee

Grants Analysis
Disclosure Period: calendar year ending 2003
Total Grants: $609,629
Number of Grants: 15
Average Grant: $31,510*
Highest Grant: $100,000
Lowest Grant: $10,000
Typical Range: $10,000 to $50,000
***Note:** Average grant figure excludes two highest grants ($200,000).

Recent Grants
Note: Grants derived from 2001 Form 990.

General

86,000	Friends of the Zoo, Kansas City, MO -- support not for profit conservation groups
76,000	Community Linc, Kansas City, MO -- capital campaign
70,000	Genesis School, Kansas City, MO -- compute and software upgrade
60,000	Don Bosco Centers, Kansas City, MO -- Famcare
50,000	Rainbow Center, Blue Springs, MO -- air conditioner and roof repair
50,000	Rose Brooks Center, Kansas City, MO -- capital campaign
50,000	St. Theresa's Academy, Kansas City, MO -- capital campaign
37,500	Learning Exchange, Kansas City, MO -- capital campaign
33,000	Mattie Rhodes Center, Kansas City, MO -- capital campaign
26,000	Heart of America United Way, Kansas City, MO -- Met Alliance for Adult Learning

S. H. COWELL FOUNDATION

Giving Contact
Susan T. Vandiver, Vice President Grants Programs
120 Montgomery St., Suite 2570
San Francisco, CA 94104
Phone: (415)397-0285
Fax: (415)986-6786
Web: http://www.shcowell.org

Description
Founded: 1955
EIN: 941392803
Organization Type: General Purpose Foundation
Giving Locations: CA
Grant Types: Capital, Challenge, General Support, Matching, Project.

Donor Information
Founder: The S. H. Cowell Foundation was established in 1955 through the will of Samuel Henry Cowell. S. H. Cowell's father, Henry, was a noted businessman who made his fortune during the famous California Gold Rush of the 1850s. By 1888, Henry Cowell owned the thriving Henry Cowell Lime and Cement Company, various warehouses and storage companies, prime San Francisco financial district properties, and 82,491 acres of land stretching from Texas Island, Canada, to San Louis Obispo, CA. Henry Cowell's net worth was estimated at $3,000,000. S. H. Cowell, although one of four surviving heirs, eventually inherited this estate in its totality. When S. H. Cowell died in 1955, his will provided for the creation of a foundation that would continue his family's philanthropy. The original assets bequeathed to the foundation exceeded $12,560,363.

Financial Summary
Total Giving: $6,573,163 (2002)
Giving Analysis: Giving for 2002 includes: foundation matching gifts ($93,033)
Assets: $135,621,271 (2002)

Typical Recipients
Arts & Humanities: Arts Institutes, Ballet, Ethnic & Folk Arts, Arts & Humanities-General, History & Archaeology, Libraries, Literary Arts, Museums/Galleries, Opera, Performing Arts, Public Broadcasting, Theater, Visual Arts
Civic & Public Affairs: Asian American Affairs, Botanical Gardens/Parks, Clubs, Community Foundations, Economic Development, Employment/Job Training, Civic & Public Affairs-General, Hispanic Affairs, Housing, Law & Justice, Parades/Festivals, Public Policy, Urban & Community Affairs, Women's Affairs, Zoos/Aquariums
Education: Afterschool/Enrichment Programs, Colleges & Universities, Education Associations, Education Funds, Education Reform, Elementary Education (Private), Elementary Education (Public), Faculty Development, Education-General, Health & Physical Education, Journalism/Media Education, Leadership Training, Literacy, Minority Education, Preschool Education, Private Education (Precollege), Public Education (Precollege), Religious Education, School Volunteerism, Secondary Education (Private), Secondary Education (Public), Special Education, Student Aid
Environment: Environment-General, Protection, Resource Conservation
Health: AIDS/HIV, Cancer, Children's Health/Hospitals, Clinics/Medical Centers, Health Organizations, Medical Research, Nutrition, Public Health, Trauma Treatment
International: Foreign Educational Institutions, Health Care/Hospitals, International Affairs, International Development, International Environmental Issues, International Organizations, International Peace & Security Issues, International Relief Efforts

Religion: Religion-General, Jewish Causes, Religious Organizations, Religious Welfare
Science: Scientific Centers & Institutes
Social Services: Animal Protection, At-Risk Youth, Child Abuse, Child Welfare, Community Centers, Community Service Organizations, Counseling, Day Care, Delinquency & Criminal Rehabilitation, Domestic Violence, Family Planning, Family Services, Food/Clothing Distribution, Homes, People with Disabilities, Recreation & Athletics, Shelters/Homelessness, Social Services-General, Special Olympics, Substance Abuse, United Funds/United Ways, Volunteer Services, YMCA/YWCA/YMHA/YWHA, Youth Organizations

Application Procedures

Initial Contact: Contact the foundation by telephone to discuss the likelihood of support for a project. Applicants may then be asked to submit a brief letter of inquiry.
Application Requirements: The letter should be two or three pages in length and should include a summary of history, purpose, and goals of the applying agency; scope, budget, and timetable for the project; specific amount requested from the foundation and an explanation of the particular uses to which these funds would be applied; list of other funding sources and amount solicited or received; and a copy of the most recent IRS determination letter of tax-exempt status.
Deadlines: None.
Review Process: The foundation board generally meets monthly to consider requests. The foundation will request further information as needed, and in most cases a site visit is arranged. Generally, three to six months are required for review from the time of initial inquiry and action by the board.

Restrictions

The foundation normally does not make grants outside northern California or to support individuals. It generally does not fund start-ups of new organizations not included within its affirmative interests; academic or other research unless significantly related to policies or activities of an organization within its affirmative interest fields; general support, routine program administration, and operating expenses; endowments and repayment of indebtedness, except in unusual cases; annual fund-raising and development campaigns; government or governmental agencies; churches or sectarian religious programs; hospitals or programs and projects under hospital sponsorship; medical research or treatment; conferences, seminars, workshops, symposia, or related activities; media projects, including publications and communications projects; or political lobbying.

Additional Information

Grants to organizations outside northern California are made strictly on the Foundation's initiative.
The foundation "prefers to make grants for unusual capital needs or specific projects, rather than for general support, operating expenses, or repayment of indebtedness." Priority is given to applicants who have not received previous grants from the foundation. The foundation is continually increasing its number of matching and challenge grants to provide agencies with leverage in fund raising and to amplify the effect of its support.
A 1997 education guidelines statement from the foundation stated: "The Foundation is in the process of re-evaluating priorities for education grantmaking. In the meantime... limited funds are available to improve student learning; to increase attendance, graduation rates, parent and neighborhood involvement; and to support winning teachers. Qualified applicants must be established public school programs with a solid track record of successful results. We are also interested in funding private schools for outreach/cooperative programs and scholarships serving public school students. The Foundation has been working in several northern California neighborhoods to

develop family resource centers. We are interested in linking those community-based efforts with local public schools to meet shared goals for the neighborhood, children, and families."
In 1995, the foundation began to phase out its support for food and clothing programs and for disabled assistance.
Publications: Annual Report

Foundation Officials

Ann Alpers: director
Jack W. Chu: treasurer, director ED Golden Gate University MA; University of California at Berkeley BS. PRIM CORP EMPL certified public accountant, founder, managing partner: Chu and Waters LLP. CORP AFFIL director: Community Bank of the Bay; member: American Institute Certified Public Accountants; member: California Society Certified Public Accountants. NONPR AFFIL director: East Bay Asian Local Development Corp.
Ken Doane: program officer
Lise Einfeld Maisano: senior program officer
Mary Seawell Metz: president, director B Rockhill, SC 1937. ED Furman University BA (1958); Institute Phonetique (1962-1963); Sorbonne University (1962-1963); Louisiana State University PhD (1966). CORP AFFIL director: Union Bank; director: SBC Communications Inc.; director: Union Bancal Corp.; director: PacTel PacBell; director: PG&E Corp.; director: Longs Drug Stores Corp.; director: Pacific Telesis Group. NONPR AFFIL member: Women's Forum W; member: World Affairs Council Northern California; member: Women's College Coalition; advisory council: Stanford University Graduate School Business; member: Western College Association; member: Phi Kappa Phi; member: Southern Conference Language Teaching; member: Phi Beta Kappa; associate: Gannett Center Media Studies; member: National Association Independent Colleges & Universities; member: Association Independent Colleges & Universities; member: Business Higher Education Forum.
Fredric C. Nelson: secretary, director
Donald D. Roberts: director
Cora M. Tellez: vice president, director B Manila, Philippines 1949. ED Mills College BA (1972); California State University MA (1979). PRIM NONPR EMPL vice president, regional manager: Kaiser Foundation Health Plan. CORP AFFIL board member: Golden State Bank Board; board member: California Association Health Plans. NONPR AFFIL board member: Institute for the Future; board member: Institute Medical Quality; board member: Holy Names College; board member: Asian Community Mental Health Services.
Susan T. Vandiver: vice president grant programs
Greg Wendt: director ED Harvard University MBA; University of Chicago BS. PRIM CORP EMPL senior vice president: Capital Research Co. NONPR AFFIL director: Larkin Street Youth Services; board member: Teach for America; board member: American Conservatory Theatre San Francisco.
Mary Lee Widener: director PRIM CORP EMPL co-founder, president, chief executive officer: Neighborhood Housing Services America ADD CORP EMPL chairman: Federal Home Loan Bank San Francisco.

Grants Analysis

Disclosure Period: calendar year ending 2002
Total Grants: $6,480,220*
Number of Grants: 83
Average Grant: $78,075
Highest Grant: $300,000
Lowest Grant: $500
Typical Range: $30,000 to $150,000
*Note: Giving excludes matching gifts.

Recent Grants

Note: Grants derived from 2002 Form 990.
General
300,000   Boys & Girls Club of North Lake Tahoe, Kings Beach, CA

250,000	Boys & Girls Clubs of Greater Sacramento Inc., Sacramento, CA
250,000	Boys & Girls Clubs of San Francisco, San Francisco, CA
185,000	Chicken's Network Solano County, CA
175,000	East Bay Agency for Children, Oakland, CA -- for Fremont Family Resource Center
170,000	Yolo Family Resource Center, Woodland, CA
135,000	Community Partnership for Families of San Joaquin, Stockton, CA
130,000	Youth for Change, Paradise, CA
125,000	Milpitas Unified School District, Milpitas, CA -- fund for Milpitas High School
124,000	Safe Passage Family Resource Center, Ft. Bragg, CA

COWLES CHARITABLE TRUST

Giving Contact

Mary Croft, Secretary & Treasurer
PO Box 219
Rumson, NJ 07760
Phone: (732)936-9826

Description

Founded: 1948
EIN: 136090295
Organization Type: Family Foundation
Giving Locations: FL; NY: New York City nationally.
Grant Types: Capital, Emergency, Endowment, General Support, Operating Expenses, Project, Scholarship.

Donor Information

Founder: Established in 1948 by Gardner Cowles Jr. Mr. Cowles, along with his father, Gardner Cowles, Sr., and brother, John Cowles, built a media empire which included the *Des Moines Register*, the *Evening Tribune*, the *Minneapolis Star*, *Look Magazine*, and radio and television stations. In 1985, the Des Moines Register and Tribune Company, owned primarily by the Cowles, sold its newspapers to Gannett Company for $260 million. Cowles Media of Minneapolis, MN, a private corporation, is owned almost entirely by descendants of John Cowles, Sr.

Financial Summary

Total Giving: $950,500 (2001)
Assets: $22,137,911 (2001)

Typical Recipients

Arts & Humanities: Arts Appreciation, Arts Associations & Councils, Arts Centers, Arts Festivals, Arts Funds, Arts Institutes, Ballet, Community Arts, Dance, Arts & Humanities-General, Historic Preservation, History & Archaeology, Libraries, Museums/Galleries, Music, Opera, Performing Arts, Public Broadcasting, Theater, Visual Arts
Civic & Public Affairs: African American Affairs, Botanical Gardens/Parks, Civil Rights, Clubs, Employment/Job Training, Civic & Public Affairs-General, Housing, Legal Aid, Municipalities/Towns, Urban & Community Affairs, Women's Affairs, Zoos/Aquariums
Education: Arts/Humanities Education, Colleges & Universities, Education Funds, Faculty Development, Education-General, International Studies, Literacy, Medical Education, Minority Education, Private Education (Precollege), Public Education (Precollege), Secondary Education (Private), Social Sciences Education, Special Education
Environment: Environment-General, Wildlife Protection
Health: AIDS/HIV, Cancer, Children's Health/

Hospitals, Clinics/Medical Centers, Emergency/Ambulance Services, Health Organizations, Hospitals, Hospitals (University Affiliated), Medical Rehabilitation, Medical Research, Mental Health, Single-Disease Health Associations
International: Foreign Arts Organizations, Foreign Educational Institutions, International Relief Efforts
Religion: Churches, Religious Organizations, Religious Welfare
Science: Scientific Centers & Institutes
Social Services: Animal Protection, At-Risk Youth, Child Welfare, Community Centers, Community Service Organizations, Counseling, Crime Prevention, Delinquency & Criminal Rehabilitation, Domestic Violence, Emergency Relief, Family Planning, Family Services, Food/Clothing Distribution, People with Disabilities, Senior Services, Shelters/Homelessness, Social Services-General, Substance Abuse, United Funds/United Ways, Volunteer Services, Youth Organizations

Application Procedures

Initial Contact: Send a brief letter requesting a foundation application form.
Application Requirements: The application should include a brief a description of organization and scope of current activities; need for project or activity; objectives of project; description of activities to be included and timetable for their accomplishment; and overall cost of project, amount requested from Cowles Charitable Trust, and amounts, sources, and statuses (committed or pending) of additional support. The application packet should also include Cowles Charitable Trust proposal cover sheet, including signature of CEO; project budget, including projected re venue and expenses; organization's current annual operating budget, including revenues and expenses; governing body and officers, showing business, professional, and community affiliations; and single copies of letter from IRS determining organization's tax-exempt status under sections 501(c)(3) and 509(a), most recent audited financial statement, and other supporting documents.
Deadlines: Any eligible request that arrives too late for one meeting will be placed on the agenda of the following meeting. Proposals must be received at the trust office by 5 p.m. on the following dates to be included on the agendas noted: December 1 for January agenda, March 1 for April agenda; June 1 for July agenda; and September 1 for October agenda. If any of the above dates fall on a weekend or holiday, the deadline is 5 p.m. on the first working day following the published deadline.
Review Process: The board meets in January, April, July, and October to review proposals. The trust will notify, in writing, all grant applicants generally within two weeks of a board meeting.
Notes: Only written applications can be considered. The trust does not accept proposals by fax. Videos and other supplementary material cannot be returned to applicants. Material should not be bound, inserted in protective sleeves, or prepared in other notebook form.

Restrictions

Grants are not made to individuals. The trust will also not consider more than one application from any one organization within a 12 month period. The trust does not consider applications from any nonprofit receiving a multiyear grant until payment of that grant is completed.

Additional Information

Publications: Annual Report; Guidelines; Application Form

Foundation Officials

Charles Cowles: trustee B Santa Monica, CA 1941. ED Stanford University (1963). PRIM CORP EMPL president, director: Charles Cowles Gallery. NONPR AFFIL trustee: New York Studio School; trustee: Wolfsonian; member: Art Dealers Association America;

trustee: Lanmeier Sculpture Park.
Gardner Cowles, III: president, trustee B 1936. PRIM CORP EMPL president: Northern Suffolk Publishing Corp.
Jan S. Cowles: trustee B Berkeley, CA 1918.
Mary Croft: secretary, treasurer
Lois Cowles Harrison: trustee B 1934. ED Wellesley College BA (1956). NONPR AFFIL member: Wellesley College Alumnae Association.
Lois Eleanor Harrison: trustee
Kate Cowles Nichols: trustee
Virginia Cowles Schroth: trustee

Grants Analysis

Disclosure Period: calendar year ending 2001
Total Grants: $948,000*
Number of Grants: 144
Average Grant: $6,583
Highest Grant: $37,500
Lowest Grant: $1,000
Typical Range: $1,000 to $10,000
*Note: Giving excludes United Way.

Recent Grants

Note: Grants derived from 2002 Form 990.
General

35,000	Museum of Modern Art, New York, NY
35,000	Stony Brook Health Sciences Center, Stony Brook, NY
30,000	Beth Israel Medical Center North, New York, NY
30,000	Planned Parenthood of Southwest and Central Florida, Sarasota, FL
30,000	Polk Museum of Art, Lakeland, FL
30,000	St. George's School, Middletown, RI
27,500	Allen-Stevenson School, New York, NY
27,500	Artists Space, New York, NY
27,500	Miami Art Museum, Miami, FL
27,500	Parrish Art Museum, Southampton, NY

A. G. Cox Charitable Trust

Giving Contact

Sandra M. Wallick
Bank One Trust Co.
70 W. Madison
Chicago, IL 60670
Phone: (312)732-7785

Description

Founded: 1924
EIN: 366011498
Organization Type: Private Foundation
Giving Locations: CA; IL; WA
Grant Types: General Support.

Financial Summary

Total Giving: $664,646 (2003); $602,333 (2001)
Assets: $13,925,572 (2003); $13,650,810 (2001)

Typical Recipients

Arts & Humanities: History & Archaeology, Libraries
Civic & Public Affairs: Urban & Community Affairs
Education: Colleges & Universities, Education Funds, Education-General, Health & Physical Education, Medical Education, Preschool Education, Special Education, Student Aid
Environment: Environment-General, Resource Conservation
Health: Arthritis, Cancer, Children's Health/Hospitals, Diabetes, Emergency/Ambulance Services, Health Organizations, Heart, Hospitals, Kidney, Medical Rehabilitation, Medical Research, Nursing Services, Prenatal Health Issues, Respiratory, Single-Disease Health Associations
International: Human Rights

Religion: Churches, Religious Organizations, Religious Welfare
Science: Science Museums
Social Services: At-Risk Youth, Child Welfare, Community Service Organizations, Day Care, Domestic Violence, Emergency Relief, People with Disabilities, Scouts, United Funds/United Ways, Veterans, YMCA/YWCA/YMHA/YWHA, Youth Organizations

Application Procedures

Initial Contact: Send a brief letter of inquiry.
Deadlines: None.

Additional Information

Trust(s): Bank One Trust Co.

Grants Analysis

Disclosure Period: calendar year ending 2003
Total Grants: $664,646
Number of Grants: 29
Average Grant: $14,025*
Highest Grant: $100,000
Lowest Grant: $2,000
Typical Range: $5,000 to $30,000
*Note: Average grant figure excludes three highest grants ($300,000).

Recent Grants

Note: Grants derived from 2001 Form 990.
General

100,000	American Red Cross, Chicago, IL
100,000	University of Southern California, Los Angeles, CA
90,000	American Cancer Society, Chicago, IL
61,333	Salvation Army of Chicago, Chicago, IL
35,000	Shriners Hospitals for Children, Chicago, IL
30,000	Rehabilitation Institute of Chicago, Chicago, IL
25,000	Mayo Foundation Cancer Research Center, Scottsdale, AZ
15,000	Virginia Mason Foundation, Seattle, WA
12,000	Amyotropic Lateral Sclerosis Association, Chicago, IL
10,000	American Diabetes Association, Chicago, IL

Jessie B. Cox Charitable Trust

Giving Contact

Susan M. Fish, Grants Administrator
Select Client Services
Hemenway & Barnes
60 State Street
Boston, MA 02109-1899
Phone: (617)227-7940
Fax: (617)227-0781
E-mail: scs@hembar.com
Web: http://www.hembar.com//selectsrv/jbcox/cox.html

Description

Founded: 1982
EIN: 046478024
Organization Type: Family Foundation
Giving Locations: New England.
Grant Types: Challenge, General Support, Multiyear/Continuing Support, Project, Seed Money.

Donor Information

Founder: The trust was established in 1982 by funds from the estate of Jessie B. Cox. Jessie B. Cox (d. 1982) was a granddaughter of Clarence Barron, who launched the Dow Jones media empire. Her husband, William C. Cox (d. 1970), was a senior director of Dow Jones & Company.

Financial Summary

Total Giving: $2,883,230 (2004); $3,590,230 (2003 approx); $3,590,230 (2002 approx)
Assets: The annual range for assets is between $52,000,000 and $60,000,000.

Typical Recipients

Arts & Humanities: Arts Associations & Councils, Arts Outreach, History & Archaeology, Libraries, Museums/Galleries, Music, Performing Arts, Public Broadcasting
Civic & Public Affairs: African American Affairs, Botanical Gardens/Parks, Community Foundations, Employment/Job Training, Civic & Public Affairs-General, Housing, Law & Justice, Nonprofit Management, Philanthropic Organizations, Public Policy, Women's Affairs, Zoos/Aquariums
Education: Arts/Humanities Education, Colleges & Universities, Education Associations, Education Reform, Elementary Education (Private), Environmental Education, Faculty Development, Education-General, Leadership Training, Literacy, Medical Education, Minority Education, Private Education (Precollege), Public Education (Precollege), School Volunteerism, Science/Mathematics Education, Special Education
Environment: Air/Water Quality, Energy, Forestry, Environment-General, Protection, Research, Resource Conservation, Watershed, Wildlife Protection
Health: Adolescent Health Issues, AIDS/HIV, Children's Health/Hospitals, Diabetes, Health-General, Health Policy/Cost Containment, Health Organizations, Home-Care Services, Hospitals, Hospitals (University Affiliated), Medical Research, Mental Health, Nursing Services, Nutrition, Prenatal Health Issues, Preventive Medicine/Wellness Organizations, Public Health, Respiratory
International: International Environmental Issues
Science: Science Museums, Scientific Centers & Institutes, Scientific Labs, Scientific Research
Social Services: Child Welfare, Community Service Organizations, Family Planning, Family Services, Food/Clothing Distribution, People with Disabilities, Senior Services, Substance Abuse

Application Procedures

Initial Contact: The trust recommends that prospective applicants call to discuss the appropriateness of their request. The trust has a two-step application process. All applicants are asked to first submit a three to four page concept paper signed by the Executive Director or Board President.
Application Requirements: A concept paper should describe the background and purpose of the organization, the project, amount desired, and how the project will enable the applicant organization to reach its goals. A budget and evidence of 501(c)(3) status must accompany the concept paper.
Deadlines: Concept papers may be submitted at any time but must be received by January 15 for the March trustees' meeting, April 15 for the June meeting, July 15 for the September meeting, and October 15 for the December meeting.
Review Process: Concept papers are reviewed by the staff and trustees, following which the trustees will invite full proposals from a limited number. Letters requesting a full proposal are mailed within two weeks of meeting. Trustees tend to favor organizations which have not received prior trust support and which suggest new approaches toward problems. Preference is given to organizations located in New England.
Notes: The trust does not accept facsimile submissions.

Restrictions

The trust will consider multiple-year grants where necessary to accomplish the project.
The trust generally will not support capital projects for buildings, equipment or land purchase; endowments, scholarship funds or fundraising activities; loans; defi-

cits or normal operating budgets or where the trust may become the organization's predominant source of support; programs or projects usually supported by the public sector; any attempt to influence legislation; requests from individuals; sectarian religious activity; organizations or activities outside of New England; or recent grantees, or extension of multiple-year awards.

Additional Information

Publications: Annual Report; Guidelines

Foundation Officials

William Coburn Cox, Jr.: trustee B 1931.
Roy A. Hammer: trustee B New York, NY 1934. ED Yale University BA (1956); Columbia University MA (1957). PRIM CORP EMPL partner: Hemenway & Barnes. CORP AFFIL director: Dow Jones & Co. Inc.
Jane Cox MacElree: trustee B 1929. ED University of Pennsylvania (1949). CORP AFFIL director: Dow Jones & Co. Inc.
Katherine S. McHugh: director
Rachel L. Pohl: program officer
George T. Shaw: trustee ED Trinity College (1962); Harvard University (1965). PRIM CORP EMPL partner: Hemenway & Barnes.
Ann Fowler Wallace: program officer

Grants Analysis

Disclosure Period: calendar year ending 2004
Total Grants: $2,883,230
Number of Grants: 89
Average Grant: $32,396
Highest Grant: $70,000
Lowest Grant: $1,000
Typical Range: $10,000 to $50,000
Note: A more recent grants list was unavailable.

Recent Grants

Note: Grants derived from 2001 Form 990.
General

75,000	Center for Public Interest Research, Boston, MA -- New England Climate Action Project
75,000	Essex County Community Foundation, Topsfield, MA -- challenge grant
75,000	University of Pennsylvania, Philadelphia, PA -- The Children's Education Endowment
70,000	Harvard School of Public Health, Boston, MA -- Healthy Public Housing Initiative
65,000	American Cancer Society New England Division, Inc., Framingham, MA -- regional health campaign
60,000	Health Care Without Harm Campaign, Jamaica Plain, MA -- continued support of Boston-New England Organizing Project
55,000	Audubon Society of New Hampshire, Concord, NH -- The New England Science Center
50,000	Alliance for Community Supports, Inc., Concord, NH -- Building Blocks Training Initiative
50,000	American Lung Association of Maine, Augusta, ME -- collaborative of Association and eastern Canada for the International Centre for Action on Air Quality and Human Health
50,000	Cobscook Bay Resource Center, Eastport, ME -- support and strengthen community-based marine conservation and management organizations

COX ENTERPRISES INC.

Company Headquarters

1400 Lake Hearn Dr., NE
Atlanta, GA 30319

Web: http://www.coxenterprises.com

Company Description

Revenue: US$8.805 billion (2002)
Employees: 77000 (2003)
SIC(s): 2711 Newspapers, 4832 Radio Broadcasting Stations, 4833 Television Broadcasting Stations, 4841 Cable & Other Pay Television Services.

Operating Locations

Cox Enterprises Inc. (AZ--Mesa, Phoenix, Yuma; CA--Anaheim, City of Commerce, Eureka, Fresno, Goleta, Los Angeles, Oakland, Riverside, San Diego; CT--Manchester; FL--Gainesville, Lakeland, Ocala, Ocoee, Orlando, Pensacola, St. Petersburg; GA--Atlanta, Macon, Red Oak; IL--Fairview Heights, Moline; IA--Cedar Rapids; LA--Harahan, New Orleans; MA--Woburn, MI--Saginaw, Southfield; MO--Kansas City; NE--Omaha; NY--Great Neck, New York; NC--Charlotte; OH--Dayton; OK--Oklahoma City; PA--Bala-Cynwyd, Gibsonia, Pittsburgh; RI--Cranston; SC--Myrtle Beach; TX--Austin, Lufkin, Waco; VA--Fredericksburg, Roanoke; WA--Spokane; WI--Caledonia)

Nonmonetary Support

Type: Cause-related Marketing & Promotion; Donated Equipment; In-kind Services
Note: Each company operating location can be contacted for nonmonetary support.

James M. Cox Foundation

Giving Contact

Leigh Ann Launius, Assistant Secretary
PO Box 105357
Atlanta, GA 30348
Phone: (678)645-0000
Fax: (404)843-5599
E-mail: LeighAnn.Launius@cox.com

Alternate Contact

PO Box 105720
Atlanta, GA 30348
Phone: (404)843-5300

Description

EIN: 586032469
Organization Type: Corporate Foundation
Giving Locations: GA: Atlanta headquarters and operating communities.
Grant Types: Capital, General Support, Operating Expenses, Project, Scholarship.

Financial Summary

Total Giving: $3,407,200 (2002); $3,242,500 (2001).
Note: Contributes through corporate direct giving program and foundation.
Assets: $5,227,748 (2002); $5,717,486 (2001)
Gifts Received: $3,000,000 (2002); $3,000,000 (2001); $3,000,000 (2000). Note: Contributions received from Cox Enterprises.

Typical Recipients

Arts & Humanities: Arts Associations & Councils, Arts Centers, Arts Festivals, Arts Institutes, Historic Preservation, History & Archaeology, Libraries, Museums/Galleries, Music, Opera, Performing Arts, Public Broadcasting, Theater
Civic & Public Affairs: African American Affairs, Botanical Gardens/Parks, Business/Free Enterprise, Civil Rights, Community Foundations, Economic Development, Employment/Job Training, Ethnic Organizations, Civic & Public Affairs-General, Hispanic Affairs, Housing, Professional & Trade Associations, Public Policy, Urban & Community Affairs, Women's Affairs, Zoos/Aquariums
Education: Arts/Humanities Education, Colleges &

Universities, Community & Junior Colleges, Education Associations, Education Funds, Education Reform, Engineering/Technological Education, Education-General, International Studies, Journalism/Media Education, Leadership Training, Literacy, Medical Education, Private Education (Precollege), Public Education (Precollege), School Volunteerism, Secondary Education (Public), Special Education, Student Aid

Environment: Air/Water Quality, Energy, Environment-General, Protection, Resource Conservation, Wildlife Protection

Health: Arthritis, Cancer, Children's Health/Hospitals, Clinics/Medical Centers, Emergency/Ambulance Services, Health-General, Health Policy/Cost Containment, Heart, Hospices, Hospitals, Hospitals (University Affiliated), Medical Rehabilitation, Mental Health, Multiple Sclerosis, Preventive Medicine/Wellness Organizations, Public Health, Single-Disease Health Associations, Speech & Hearing, Transplant Networks/Donor Banks

International: Health Care/Hospitals, International Relations

Religion: Jewish Causes, Religious Organizations, Religious Welfare

Science: Science Museums, Scientific Centers & Institutes

Social Services: Animal Protection, At-Risk Youth, Big Brothers/Big Sisters, Camps, Child Abuse, Child Welfare, Community Service Organizations, Counseling, Domestic Violence, Emergency Relief, Family Services, Food/Clothing Distribution, Homes, People with Disabilities, Recreation & Athletics, Scouts, Senior Services, Shelters/Homelessness, Social Services-General, Substance Abuse, United Funds/United Ways, Volunteer Services, YMCA/YWCA/YMHA/YWHA, Youth Organizations

Application Procedures

Initial Contact: Send three copies of written request. **Application Requirements:** Outline of needs and goals; copy of IRS tax-exemption letter; list of recent donors, including dollar amounts; annual report and other financial information, including audited financial statements (or most recent Form 990); history of organization; list of board members and officers with salaries; copy of current or project budget.

Deadlines: Established one month before quarterly board meetings.

Review Process: Local management recommends grants; foundation trustees make grant decisions.

Decision Notification: The foundation makes its decision at semi-annual meetings.

Restrictions

All potential recipients must be tax-exempt under IRS standards and have support of local management. Grants are generally restricted to operating areas. No grants are made to individuals.

Additional Information

The foundation does not accept personal interviews.

Corporate Officials

David E. Easterly: president, chief operating officer affairs, secretary B Denison, TX 1942. ED University of Texas; Austin College BA (1965). PRIM CORP EMPL president, chief operating officer: Cox Enterprises Inc. CORP AFFIL director: Cox Communications Inc.; vice president: Grand Junction Newspapers. NONPR AFFIL member: Newspaper Association America; member, director: Southern Newspaper Publishers Association; member: Associated Press.

Timothy W. Hughes: senior vice president B 1943. ED Bellarmine College AB (1965); Cleveland State University JD (1973). PRIM CORP EMPL senior vice president: Cox Enterprises Inc.

Richard J. Jacobson: vice president, treasurer B 1956. ED Georgia State University (1980). PRIM CORP EMPL vice president, treasurer: Cox Enterprises Inc.

James Cox Kennedy: chairman, chief executive officer, director B 1947. ED University of Denver BBA (1970). PRIM CORP EMPL chairman, chief executive officer, director: Cox Enterprises Inc. ADD CORP EMPL chairman, president: National Auto Dealers Exchange. CORP AFFIL director: Manheim Auctions Inc.; director: National Service Industries Inc.; Flagler System Inc.; chairman, director: Cox Communications Inc.; director: Cox Radio Inc.; advisory director: Chase Bank Texas.

Andrew Austin Merdek: vice president legal affairs, secretary B Portland, ME 1950. ED Middlebury College AB (1972); University of Virginia JD (1978). PRIM CORP EMPL vice president legal affairs, secretary: Cox Enterprises Inc. ADD CORP EMPL secretary: Cox Texas Pubs Inc.; secretary: Cox Broadcasting Inc.; secretary: Cox Communications Inc.; secretary: Cox Interactive Media Inc.; secretary: Cox NC Pubs Inc.; secretary: Cox Newspapers Inc.; secretary, director: Dayton Newspapers Inc.; secretary: Eagle Research Group Inc.; secretary, director: GA Television Co.; secretary: Hospitality Network Inc.; secretary, director: Manheim Auction Government Service; secretary: Manheim Auctions Inc.; secretary, director: Manheim Metro Detroit Auto Auction; secretary,director: Palm Beach Newspapers Inc.; secretary: WFTV Inc. NONPR AFFIL member: Order Coif; member: Phi Beta Kappa; chairman: Newspaper Association America Legal Affairs Committee; member: American Corporate Counsel Association; member: American Society of Corporate Secretaries; member: American Bar Association.

Foundation Officials

Barbara Cox Anthony: president, trustee B Honolulu, HI 1923. PRIM CORP EMPL chairman: Dayton Newspapers Inc. CORP AFFIL director: Cox Enterprises Inc.

John G. Boyette: treasurer B 1944. ED Augusta College BBA (1968). PRIM CORP EMPL senior vice president finance & administration: Cox Broadcasting Inc. ADD CORP EMPL vice president: Cox Enterprises Inc.

Anne Cox Chambers: chairman, trustee B Dayton, OH 1919. ED Finch Junior College. PRIM CORP EMPL chairman: Atlanta Journal-Constitution. CORP AFFIL director: Cox Enterprises Inc. NONPR AFFIL director: New York Botanical Garden; member national committee: Whitney Museum American Art; director: Metropolitan Museum Art; trustee: Museum Modern Art; member: LaCoste School Arts; director: MacDowell Colony; director: High Museum Art; director: Emory Museum Art & Archaeology; director: Forward Arts Foundation; director: Cities & Schools; member: Council Foreign Relations; director: American Ambassadors Chmns Council; director: Atlanta Arts Alliance.

Timothy W. Hughes: vice president, trustee (see above)

Leigh Ann (Korns) Launius: assistant secretary PRIM CORP EMPL administration assistant: Cox Enterprises Inc.

Andrew Austin Merdek: secretary (see above)

Grants Analysis

Disclosure Period: calendar year ending 2002
Total Grants: $3,407,200
Number of Grants: 56
Average Grant: $60,396
Highest Grant: $250,000
Lowest Grant: $3,750
Typical Range: $10,000 to $100,000

Recent Grants

Note: Grants derived from 2003 Form 990.

Library-Related

50,000	Jimmy Carter Library and Museum, Atlanta, GA -- for the purpose of special projects

General

250,000	High Museum of Art, Atlanta, GA -- towards capital campaign
250,000	National Cable Television Center & Museum, Denver, CO -- towards endowment
200,000	Carter Center, Atlanta, GA -- towards endowment
200,000	Kennesaw State University Cox Family Enterprise Center, Kennesaw, GA -- for general operating expenses
200,000	Nature Conservancy, Arlington, VA -- towards special projects
200,000	PATH Foundation, Atlanta, GA -- towards capital campaign
150,000	Southern Newspaper Publishers Association Traveling Campus Endowment, Atlanta, GA -- for endowment
100,000	American Cancer Society -- towards general operations
100,000	Animal Medical Center Colorado State University, Pueblo, CO -- for its capital campaign
100,000	Camp Sunshine, Casco, ME -- for its capital campaign

DAVE COY FOUNDATION

Giving Contact

Greg Muenster, Vice President
c/o Bank of America
PO Box 121, Trust Dept.
San Antonio, TX 78291-0121
Phone: (210)270-5371

Description

Founded: 1992
EIN: 746394909
Organization Type: Private Foundation
Giving Locations: TX: Bexar County
Grant Types: General Support.

Financial Summary

Total Giving: $292,000 (fiscal year ending July 31, 2004); $648,456 (fiscal 2001)
Giving Analysis: Giving for fiscal 2001 includes: foundation scholarships ($15,000)
Assets: $1,856,452 (fiscal 2004); $3,416,101 (fiscal 2001)

Typical Recipients

Arts & Humanities: Arts Outreach, Libraries, Museums/Galleries, Music, Public Broadcasting

Civic & Public Affairs: Clubs, Economic Development, Employment/Job Training, Civic & Public Affairs-General, Hispanic Affairs, Housing, Nonprofit Management, Urban & Community Affairs, Women's Affairs

Education: Afterschool/Enrichment Programs, Education Funds, Education-General, Literacy, Private Education (Precollege), Science/Mathematics Education, Secondary Education (Private), Student Aid

Health: AIDS/HIV, Cancer, Children's Health/Hospitals, Clinics/Medical Centers, Emergency/Ambulance Services, Health-General, Health Organizations, Hospitals, Mental Health, Nursing Services, Prenatal Health Issues, Public Health, Single-Disease Health Associations

Religion: Jewish Causes, Ministries, Religious Welfare, Social/Policy Issues

Social Services: At-Risk Youth, Child Welfare, Community Centers, Community Service Organizations, Counseling, Day Care, Domestic Violence, Family Services, Food/Clothing Distribution, People with Disabilities, Scouts, Shelters/Homelessness, YMCA/YWCA/YMHA/YWHA, Youth Organizations

Application Procedures

Initial Contact: Send a full proposal.
Application Requirements: Include description of organization, purpose of funds sought, amount re-

quested, and proof of tax-exempt status.
Deadlines: June 1.

Restrictions

Awards grants to benefit the poor and needy of Bexar County, TX.

Additional Information

Trust(s): Bank of America

Grants Analysis

Disclosure Period: fiscal year ending July 31, 2004
Total Grants: $292,000
Number of Grants: 7
Average Grant: $25,000*
Highest Grant: $142,000
Lowest Grant: $10,000
Typical Range: $10,000 to $40,000
***Note:** Average grant figure excludes highest grant.

Recent Grants

Note: Grants derived from 2004 Form 990.
General

142,000	Baptist Children's Ministries, San Antonio, TX -- towards south Texas campus project
42,000	Carver Academy, San Antonio, TX -- capital campaign-Dave Coy courtyard
28,000	San Antonio Metropolitan Ministry, San Antonio, TX -- towards furniture for a cause project
25,000	Children's Shelter of San Antonio, San Antonio, TX -- to establish permanent children's home
25,000	Salvation Army, San Antonio, TX
20,000	Respite Care of San Antonio, San Antonio, TX -- for emergency funding for operations
10,000	Family Service Association, San Antonio, TX -- for work on 720 Pedro boulevard

CRAIL-JOHNSON FOUNDATION

Giving Contact

Carolyn E. Johnson, President
222 W. 6th St., Suite 1010
San Pedro, CA 90731
Phone: (310)519-7413
Fax: (310)519-7221
E-mail: pat-christopher@crail-johnson.org
Web: http://www.crail-johnson.org/

Description

Founded: 1987
EIN: 330247161
Organization Type: Private Foundation
Giving Locations: CA: Los Angeles
Grant Types: General Support, Project.

Donor Information

Founder: the late Robert Johnson

Financial Summary

Total Giving: $1,765,766 (2003)
Assets: $15,553,538 (2003)
Gifts Received: $1,750,000 (2003); $2,425,000 (2000); $2,150,000 (1999). Note: In 2003, contributions were received from Robert Johnson Charitable Lead Trust. In 1999, contributions were received from Eric C. Johnson, Craig C. Johnson, Alan C. Johnson, and L. Johnson ($100,000 each), and the Robert Johnson Charitable Lead Trust ($1,750,000). In 1996, contributions were received from the Robert Johnson Charitable Lead Trust ($1,750,000), Eric C. Johnson ($103,000), Craig C. Johnson, Alan C. Johnson, and Ann L. Johnson ($100,000 each), and the Jessie L.Crail Trust ($100,000).

Typical Recipients

Arts & Humanities: Ballet, Arts & Humanities-General, Performing Arts
Civic & Public Affairs: African American Affairs, Clubs, Civic & Public Affairs-General, Legal Aid, Non-profit Management, Public Policy, Urban & Community Affairs, Women's Affairs, Zoos/Aquariums
Education: Business Education, Education Reform, Elementary Education (Public), Education-General, Literacy, Minority Education, Preschool Education, Private Education (Precollege), Public Education (Precollege), School Volunteerism, Science/Mathematics Education, Secondary Education (Public), Special Education
Environment: Environment-General
Health: AIDS/HIV, Cancer, Children's Health/Hospitals, Clinics/Medical Centers, Emergency/Ambulance Services, Eyes/Blindness, Health Funds, Heart, Hospices, Hospitals, Prenatal Health Issues, Public Health
Religion: Churches, Religious Welfare
Science: Scientific Centers & Institutes
Social Services: Animal Protection, At-Risk Youth, Big Brothers/Big Sisters, Camps, Child Welfare, Community Centers, Community Service Organizations, Counseling, Crime Prevention, Day Care, Domestic Violence, Emergency Relief, Family Planning, Family Services, Food/Clothing Distribution, Homes, People with Disabilities, Recreation & Athletics, Shelters/Homelessness, Social Services-General, Special Olympics, Substance Abuse, YMCA/YWCA/YMHA/YWHA, Youth Organizations

Application Procedures

Initial Contact: Send letter of inquiry describing applicant organization.
Application Requirements: Include a description of organization, purpose of funds sought, amount requested, proof of tax-exempt status, methods to be employed, the results expected, a preliminary budget, purpose of project and need it meets and duration.
Deadlines: None.
Decision Notification: Applicants will be notified within one month of receipt of request.

Restrictions

Does not support individuals, religious organizations for sectarian purposes, political or lobbying groups, organizations outside operating areas, University level education, or research.

Additional Information

The foundation provides financial support primarily through grants to public non-profit organizations which are exempt under Section 501(c)(3) of the Internal Revenue Service and are not a private foundation under Section 509(a).
Publications: Brochure; Grant application form.

Foundation Officials

John J. Berwald: director
S. L. Hutchison: chief financial officer, director
Alan C. Johnson: director
Ann L. Johnson: director
Carolyn E. Johnson: president, director
Craig C. Johnson: director
Eric C. Johnson: chairman, director
John S. Peterson: general counsel, director

Grants Analysis

Disclosure Period: calendar year ending 2003
Total Grants: $1,765,766
Number of Grants: 113
Average Grant: $14,106*
Highest Grant: $100,000
Lowest Grant: $100
Typical Range: $5,000 to $30,000
***Note:** Average grant figure excludes two highest grants ($200,000).

Recent Grants

Note: Grants derived from 2003 Form 990.
General

103,000	Boys and Girls Club of SO Bay
100,000	Boys and Girls Club of San Pedro, San Pedro, CA
80,000	Accelerated School
75,000	Boys and Girls Club of Wilmington, Wilmington, DE
75,000	San Pedro Penn Hospital Foundation, San Pedro, CA
50,000	House of Hope Foundation, San Pedro, CA
50,000	Tobeerman Settlement House, San Pedro, CA
43,760	Dramatic Results, Long Beach, CA
38,160	SCAP
25,000	Youth Alive, Oakland, CA

CRALLE FOUNDATION

Giving Contact

James T. Crain, Jr., Executive Director
614 W. Main St., Suite 2500
Louisville, KY 40202
Phone: (502)581-1148

Description

Founded: 1990
EIN: 611179672
Organization Type: Private Foundation
Giving Locations: KY
Grant Types: General Support, Scholarship.

Financial Summary

Total Giving: $543,144 (2003); $1,142,508 (2001)
Giving Analysis: Giving for 2003 includes: foundation scholarships ($33,500)
Assets: $11,243,124 (2003); $6,444 (2001)
Gifts Received: $8,066 (2001); $14,650 (2000); $88,573 (1998). Note: In 2001, contributions were received from Joan Day. In 1998, contributions were received from Joan Day and the estate of Lee E. Cralle.

Typical Recipients

Arts & Humanities: Ballet, Dance, Ethnic & Folk Arts, History & Archaeology, Libraries, Museums/Galleries, Public Broadcasting
Civic & Public Affairs: Botanical Gardens/Parks, Community Foundations, Civic & Public Affairs-General, Housing, Philanthropic Organizations, Urban & Community Affairs, Women's Affairs, Zoos/Aquariums
Education: Afterschool/Enrichment Programs, Business Education, Colleges & Universities, Economic Education, Education-General, Medical Education, Preschool Education, Private Education (Precollege), Secondary Education (Private), Special Education
Environment: Environment-General
Health: Emergency/Ambulance Services, Geriatric Health, Preventive Medicine/Wellness Organizations, Single-Disease Health Associations
Religion: Ministries, Religious Organizations, Religious Welfare
Science: Scientific Centers & Institutes
Social Services: At-Risk Youth, Big Brothers/Big Sisters, Camps, Child Welfare, Community Centers, Community Service Organizations, Day Care, Family Planning, Family Services, Food/Clothing Distribution, Homes, People with Disabilities, Scouts, Shelters/Homelessness, Social Services-General, Substance Abuse, YMCA/YWCA/YMHA/YWHA, Youth Organizations

Application Procedures

Initial Contact: Request application form.
Deadlines: None.

Additional Information
Publications: Application Form

Foundation Officials
James T. Crain, Jr.: executive director
James S. Welch: director

Grants Analysis
Disclosure Period: calendar year ending 2003
Total Grants: $509,644*
Number of Grants: 46
Average Grant: $9,103*
Highest Grant: $100,000
Lowest Grant: $150
Typical Range: $1,000 to $10,000
*Note: Giving excludes scholarships. Average grant figure excludes highest grant.

Recent Grants
Note: Grants derived from 2001 Form 990.
General

125,000	Home of the Innocents, Louisville, KY -- capital campaign
75,000	Centre College, Danville, KY -- endowment
57,500	Spina Bifida Association of Kentucky, Louisville, KY -- Cycle for Life Project
50,000	Spalding University, Louisville, KY -- Cralle Scholars
35,000	Louisville Diversified Services, Louisville, KY -- Schlachter House
30,840	Saint Catherine College, St. Catherine, KY -- computers and workstations
25,000	Cathedral Heritage Foundation, Louisville, KY -- festival
25,000	David School, David, KY -- operating costs
25,000	Spava, Louisville, KY -- scholarships
24,483	YMCA, Louisville, KY -- Camp Piomingo

ARTHUR CRAMES FAMILY FOUNDATION

Giving Contact
Arthur Crames, Director
19 Briarcliff Road
Upper Saddle River, NJ 07458
Phone: (212)372-1520

Description
Founded: 1991
EIN: 133544875
Organization Type: Private Foundation
Giving Locations: NJ; NY
Grant Types: General Support.

Financial Summary
Total Giving: $50,750 (2001)
Assets: $63,067 (2001)
Gifts Received: $81,975 (2001); $37,063 (2000); $39,777 (1999). Note: In 2000 and 2001, contributions were received from Arthur Crames. In 1999, contributions were received from Arthur Crames. In 1996, contributions were received from Arthur Crames ($47,000) and the Monterey Fund ($3,874).

Typical Recipients
Arts & Humanities: History & Archaeology, Libraries
Civic & Public Affairs: Clubs, Community Foundations, Civic & Public Affairs-General, Housing, Municipalities/Towns, Safety, Urban & Community Affairs
Education: Colleges & Universities, Private Education (Precollege), Public Education (Precollege), Student Aid
Environment: Environment-General
Health: Cancer, Clinics/Medical Centers, Emergency/Ambulance Services, Eyes/Blindness, Heart, Hospitals, Single-Disease Health Associations
Religion: Religion-General, Jewish Causes, Religious Organizations, Religious Welfare
Social Services: Child Welfare, Community Service Organizations, Crime Prevention, Delinquency & Criminal Rehabilitation, Recreation & Athletics, Social Services-General, Veterans, Volunteer Services, YMCA/YWCA/YMHA/YWHA

Application Procedures
Initial Contact: The foundation has no formal grant application procedure or application form.
Deadlines: None.

Foundation Officials
Arthur Crames: director
Dale Crames: director
Gail T. Winawer: director

Grants Analysis
Disclosure Period: calendar year ending 2001
Total Grants: $50,750
Number of Grants: 19
Average Grant: $2,671
Highest Grant: $14,000
Lowest Grant: $100
Typical Range: $500 to $5,000

Recent Grants
Note: Grants derived from 2002 Form 990.
General

10,000	St. Charles Borromeo School, New York, NY
5,000	DWC Scholarship Foundation Fund, New YorK, NY
5,000	Paramus Ceremonial Honor Guard, Paramus, NJ
3,000	United Jewish Appeal Federation, New York, NY
2,500	Boca Raton Community Hospital, Boca Raton, FL
2,500	Iona College, New Rochelle, NY
1,000	Muscular Dystrophy Association, Tucson, AZ
1,000	Police Pipes and Drums, Upper Saddle River, NJ
1,000	St. Joseph's Indian School, Chamberlain, SD
1,000	Salesian Sisters, Haledon, NJ

CRAMPTON TRUST

Giving Contact
R. B. Doyle, III, Trust Officer
c/o Regions Bank
PO Box 2527
Mobile, AL 36622-0001
Phone: (251)690-1411
Fax: (251)690-1591

Description
Founded: 1994
EIN: 636181261
Organization Type: Private Foundation
Giving Locations: AL
Grant Types: General Support.

Donor Information
Founder: Established in 1994 by the late Katherine C. Cochrane.

Financial Summary
Total Giving: $952,199 (2003)
Assets: $19,589,020 (2003)
Gifts Received: $1,000 (1993). Note: In 1993, contributions were received from the estate of Katherine C. Cochrane.

Typical Recipients
Arts & Humanities: Arts Centers, Ballet, Libraries, Museums/Galleries
Civic & Public Affairs: Civic & Public Affairs-General, Hispanic Affairs, Municipalities/Towns, Safety
Education: Business Education, Colleges & Universities, Elementary Education (Public), Education-General, Medical Education, Private Education (Precollege), Public Education (Precollege), Science/Mathematics Education, Secondary Education (Public), Student Aid
Environment: Environment-General
Health: Cancer, Children's Health/Hospitals, Clinics/Medical Centers, Emergency/Ambulance Services, Health-General, Geriatric Health, Heart, Hospitals, Mental Health, Nutrition, Single-Disease Health Associations
Religion: Churches, Religion-General, Religious Organizations, Religious Welfare
Science: Science Museums
Social Services: At-Risk Youth, Child Welfare, Emergency Relief, Food/Clothing Distribution, Homes, People with Disabilities, Senior Services, United Funds/United Ways, YMCA/YWCA/YMHA/YWHA, Youth Organizations

Application Procedures
Initial Contact: Request guidelines.
Deadlines: None.

Additional Information
Trust(s): Regions Bank

Foundation Officials
John C. Johnson: member
Mabel B. Ward: member

Grants Analysis
Disclosure Period: calendar year ending 2003
Total Grants: $952,199
Number of Grants: 34
Average Grant: $16,797*
Highest Grant: $189,507
Lowest Grant: $4,000
Typical Range: $5,000 to $30,000
*Note: Average grant figure excludes three highest grants ($431,507).

Recent Grants
Note: Grants derived from 2003 Form 990.

General

189,507	Center for the Living Arts, Mobile, AL -- theater preservation and expansion
150,000	UMS-Wright Preparatory School, Mobile, AL
92,000	Mobile Museum of Art, Mobile, AL -- capital campaign
50,000	Franklin Primary Health Care Center, Mobile, AL -- new facility equipment and furnishings
50,000	University of South Alabama, Mobile, AL -- cancer research institute equipment purchase
40,000	University of South Alabama, Mobile, AL -- for medical scholarship
35,000	University of Mobile, Mobile, AL -- for computer system
33,192	University of South Alabama, Mobile, AL -- medical college professorship
30,000	Mercy Medical, Daphne, AL -- capital campaign
27,000	Dearborn YMCA, Mobile, AL -- after school education enhancement

J. FORD CRANDALL MEMORIAL FOUNDATION

Giving Contact
Robert J. Christian, Secretary
26 Market Street, Suite 904
Youngstown, OH 44503
Phone: (330)744-2125

Description
Founded: 1975
EIN: 346513634
Organization Type: Private Foundation
Giving Locations: OH: Mahoning County
Grant Types: Capital, Endowment, General Support, Scholarship.

Donor Information
Founder: the late J. Ford Crandall

Financial Summary
Total Giving: $269,536 (2003); $257,199 (2001)
Assets: $5,229,711 (2003); $5,686,376 (2001)

Typical Recipients
Arts & Humanities: Arts Associations & Councils, Community Arts, Historic Preservation, Libraries, Music, Public Broadcasting
Civic & Public Affairs: Botanical Gardens/Parks, Economic Development, Civic & Public Affairs-General, Legal Aid, Urban & Community Affairs
Education: Colleges & Universities, Education-General, Preschool Education, Private Education (Precollege), Student Aid
Health: Alzheimer's Disease, Children's Health/Hospitals, Clinics/Medical Centers, Emergency/Ambulance Services, Hospices, Hospitals, Research/Studies Institutes
Religion: Churches, Jewish Causes, Missionary Activities (Domestic), Religious Organizations, Religious Welfare
Social Services: Camps, Child Welfare, Community Centers, Community Service Organizations, Counseling, Domestic Violence, Family Services, Food/Clothing Distribution, People with Disabilities, Recreation & Athletics, Senior Services, Shelters/Homelessness, Substance Abuse, United Funds/United Ways, Veterans, Volunteer Services, YMCA/YWCA/YMHA/YWHA, Youth Organizations

Application Procedures
Initial Contact: The foundation has no formal grant application procedure or application form.
Deadlines: December 1.

Foundation Officials
Andrew G. Bresko: trustee

Grants Analysis
Disclosure Period: calendar year ending 2003
Total Grants: $269,536
Number of Grants: 9
Average Grant: $21,192*
Highest Grant: $100,000
Lowest Grant: $4,836
Typical Range: $10,000 to $35,000
***Note:** Average grant figure excludes highest grant.

Recent Grants
Note: Grants derived from 2001 Form 990.
General
62,500	Fellows Riverside Gardens, Youngstown, OH -- for capital improvements
62,500	YMCA, Youngstown, OH -- for capital improvements
35,000	Mill Creek Park Foundation, Canfield, OH -- for operations
25,000	HELP Hotline Crisis Center, Youngstown, OH -- for operations

20,000	Hillsville Charitable Foundation, Lowellville, OH -- for operations
18,570	D & E Counseling Camp Challenge, Youngstown, OH -- for operations
16,580	Volunteer Services Agency, Youngstown, OH -- for operations
15,000	Park Vista Senior Independence, Youngstown, OH -- for operations
1,049	Youngstown Area Arts Council, Youngstown, OH -- for operations
1,000	Rescue Mission, Youngstown, OH -- for operations

CRANSTON PRINT WORKS CO.

Company Headquarters
1381 Cranston St.
Cranston, RI 02920
Web: http://www.cpw.com

Company Description
Employees: 1,175
SIC(s): 2261 Finishing Plants--Cotton, 3552 Textile Machinery, 3554 Paper Industries Machinery.

Operating Locations
Cranston Print Works Co. (LA--Denham Springs; MA--Webster; NY--New York; NC--Fletcher; RI--East Providence, Pawtucket, Providence)

Cranston Foundation

Giving Contact
Carolyn Lake, Administrator
1381 Cranston St.
Cranston, RI 02920
Phone: (401)943-4800
Fax: (401)943-3971
E-mail: cpw@cpw.com

Description
EIN: 056015348
Organization Type: Corporate Foundation
Giving Locations: ME; MA; RI
Grant Types: Employee Matching Gifts, General Support, Scholarship.

Financial Summary
Total Giving: $254,569 (fiscal year ending June 30, 2003); $204,177 (fiscal 2002); $220,283 (fiscal 2001). Note: Contributes through foundation only.
Giving Analysis: Giving for fiscal 2001 includes: foundation scholarships ($154,935)
Assets: $6,874 (fiscal 2003); $17,517 (fiscal 2002); $13,726 (fiscal 2001)
Gifts Received: $244,032 (fiscal 2003); $208,244 (fiscal 2002); $230,307 (fiscal 2001). Note: Contributions received from Cranston Print Works Co.

Typical Recipients
Arts & Humanities: Arts Institutes, Ethnic & Folk Arts, Historic Preservation, History & Archaeology, Libraries, Museums/Galleries
Civic & Public Affairs: Civic & Public Affairs-General, Safety
Education: Arts/Humanities Education, Business Education, Colleges & Universities, Community & Junior Colleges, Engineering/Technological Education, Journalism/Media Education, Medical Education, Minority Education, Religious Education, Science/Mathematics Education, Social Sciences Education, Student Aid, Vocational & Technical Education
Environment: Environment-General, Resource Conservation
Health: AIDS/HIV, Emergency/Ambulance Services,

Health Funds, Hospitals, Kidney, Prenatal Health Issues
Religion: Jewish Causes, Religious Welfare
Social Services: Big Brothers/Big Sisters, Community Service Organizations, Scouts, United Funds/United Ways, YMCA/YWCA/YMHA/YWHA, Youth Organizations

Application Procedures
Initial Contact: Send a written request.
Application Requirements: Include details of project; funding requirements; budget information; organization's management structure, purpose, operation, and goals; copy of IRS classification letter; and recent financial statements.
Deadlines: Before May 15 for funding during that fiscal year.
Decision Notification: Trustees normally meet once per quarter.

Restrictions
The foundation only makes contributions to domestic organizations which have been ruled by the IRS as tax exempt under Section 501(c)(3) of the Internal Revenue Code.

Additional Information
Publications: Guidelines

Corporate Officials
Bryan Adriance: vice president, finance & administration PRIM CORP EMPL vice president finance & administration: Cranston Print Works Co.
George Whitcomb Shuster: president, chief executive officer, director B Trenton, NJ 1946. ED Yale University (1967); Yale University Law School (1973). PRIM CORP EMPL president, chief executive officer, director: Cranston Print Works Co. CORP AFFIL director: Ashwright Inc. NONPR AFFIL director: Kent County Memorial Hospital.

Foundation Officials
Bryan Adriance: trustee (see above)
George Whitcomb Shuster: trustee (see above)
Shelley Wollseiffen: trustee

Grants Analysis
Disclosure Period: fiscal year ending June 30, 2003
Total Grants: $124,450*
Number of Grants: 34
Average Grant: $3,660
Highest Grant: $10,000
Lowest Grant: $200
Typical Range: $250 to $10,000
***Note:** Giving excludes matching gifts, scholarship, United Way.

Recent Grants
Note: Grants derived from fiscal 2004 Form 990.

General
10,000	Bryant College, Smithfield, RI
10,000	Hubbard Regional Hospital, Webster, MA
10,000	Hubbard Regional Hospital, Webster, MA
10,000	Rhode Island School of Design, Providence, RI
10,000	United Way of Rhode Island, Providence, RI
10,000	United Way of Webster, Webster, MA
10,000	YMCA, Providence, RI
5,000	Kent Hospital Foundation, Warwick, RI
5,000	Paper Technology Foundation, Kalamazoo, MI
4,000	Elmira College, Elmira, NY -- scholarship to dependent college of employee

BRUCE L. CRARY FOUNDATION

Giving Contact
Euphemia V. Hall, President
PO Box 396
Elizabethtown, NY 12932
Phone: (518)873-6496

Description
Founded: 1973
EIN: 237366844
Organization Type: Private Foundation
Giving Locations: NY: Essex County
Grant Types: General Support, Scholarship.

Donor Information
Founder: Crary Public Trust, the late Bruce L. Crary

Financial Summary
Total Giving: $366,187 (fiscal year ending June 30, 2004); $397,329 (fiscal 2001). Note: Fiscal 1997 Giving includes scholarship ($292,630).
Giving Analysis: Giving for fiscal 2004 includes: foundation scholarships ($341,145); fiscal 2001: foundation scholarships ($370,785)
Assets: $8,572,682 (fiscal 2004); $9,907,950 (fiscal 2001)
Gifts Received: $5,800 (fiscal 2004); $5,225 (fiscal 2001). Note: In fiscal 2004, contributions were received from The Walbridge Fund Ltd.

Typical Recipients
Arts & Humanities: Arts Centers, Historic Preservation, History & Archaeology, Libraries, Museums/Galleries, Theater
Civic & Public Affairs: Municipalities/Towns, Nonprofit Management, Urban & Community Affairs
Education: Community & Junior Colleges, Literacy, Preschool Education, Secondary Education (Private), Student Aid
Environment: Air/Water Quality, Environment-General
Health: Clinics/Medical Centers, Emergency/Ambulance Services, Hospices, Hospitals, Mental Health
Social Services: Animal Protection, Child Welfare, Community Service Organizations, Domestic Violence, Family Planning

Application Procedures
Initial Contact: Student aid applications are available at guidance offices in area high schools. For charitable grants, there are no formal requirements.
Deadlines: March 31 for student aid.

Additional Information
Provides scholarships to individuals for higher education.

Foundation Officials
Janet Decker: gov
Euphemia V. Hall: president, trustee
Meredith M. Prime: gov
Gail Rogers-Rice: gov
Arthur V. Savage, Esq.: vice president, trustee

Grants Analysis
Disclosure Period: fiscal year ending June 30, 2004
Total Grants: $25,042*
Number of Grants: 11
Average Grant: $595*
Highest Grant: $19,092
Lowest Grant: $100
Typical Range: $100 to $1,000
*Note: Giving excludes scholarships. Average grant excludes highest grant.

Recent Grants
Note: Grants derived from fiscal 2004 Form 990.

Library-Related

450	Wadhams Free Library, Wadhams, NY

General

1,000	Lake Placid Center for the Arts, Lake Placid, NY
1,000	Northern Adirondack Planned Parenthood, Plattsburgh, NY
1,000	Planned Parenthood of Mohawk Hudson, Schenectady, NY
750	Little Peaks Preschool Program, Keene, NY
450	Depot Theater, Westport, NY
450	Essex County Historical Society, Elizabethtown, NY
350	Foundation Center, New York, NY
300	North Country Society for the Prevention of Cruelty to Animals, Westport, NY
100	Adirondack Medical Center, Saranac Lake, NY

E. R. CRAWFORD ESTATE TRUST FUND A

Giving Contact
George F. Young, Jr., Trustee
PO Box 487
McKeesport, PA 15134
Phone: (412)751-2770

Description
Founded: 1936
EIN: 256031554
Organization Type: Private Foundation
Giving Locations: PA
Grant Types: General Support, Operating Expenses, Scholarship.

Donor Information
Founder: E. R. Crawford

Financial Summary
Total Giving: $342,560 (2003)
Giving Analysis: Giving for 2003 includes: foundation gifts to individuals ($1,560)
Assets: $7,089,242 (2003)

Typical Recipients
Arts & Humanities: Arts & Humanities-General, Historic Preservation, History & Archaeology, Libraries, Literary Arts, Music, Theater
Civic & Public Affairs: Chambers of Commerce, Clubs, Civic & Public Affairs-General, Municipalities/Towns, Philanthropic Organizations, Professional & Trade Associations, Women's Affairs
Education: Business Education, Colleges & Universities, Community & Junior Colleges, Education-General, Gifted & Talented Programs, Literacy, Preschool Education, Student Aid
Health: Cancer, Children's Health/Hospitals, Diabetes, Emergency/Ambulance Services, Health Organizations, Hospitals, Medical Research, Multiple Sclerosis, Single-Disease Health Associations
Religion: Churches, Religious Organizations, Religious Welfare, Synagogues/Temples
Social Services: Animal Protection, Child Welfare, Community Service Organizations, Food/Clothing Distribution, Homes, Recreation & Athletics, Senior Services, YMCA/YWCA/YMHA/YWHA, Youth Organizations

Application Procedures
Initial Contact: Individuals should request an application form.
Application Requirements: Public charities should submit a proposal stating general background information, the purposes and nature of the organization, and purpose of funds sought.
Deadlines: None.

Foundation Officials
George F. Young, Jr.: trustee

Grants Analysis
Disclosure Period: calendar year ending 2003
Total Grants: $341,000*
Number of Grants: 105
Average Grant: $3,248
Highest Grant: $30,000
Lowest Grant: $500
Typical Range: $1,000 to $5,000
*Note: Giving excludes gifts to individuals.

Recent Grants
Note: Grants derived from 2001 Form 990.

Library-Related

30,000	Carnegie Free Library of McKeesport, McKeesport, PA

General

45,000	McKeesport Heritage Center, McKeesport, PA
40,000	YMCA of McKeesport, McKeesport, PA
25,000	South Hills Health System Foundation, Jefferson Boro, PA
20,000	McKeesport Area Meals on Wheels, McKeesport, PA
20,000	McKeesport Hospital Foundation, McKeesport, PA
20,000	Salvation Army, McKeesport, PA
15,000	YMCA of McKeesport, McKeesport, PA
10,000	Community Food Bank, McKeesport, PA
10,000	Kane Foundation, McKeesport, PA
10,000	Pauline Auberle Foundation, McKeesport, PA

EVAH C. CRAY RESIDUARY CHARITABLE TRUST

Giving Contact
Gay L. Wright, Trust Officer
UMB Bank
626 Commercial
Atchison, KS 66002
Phone: (913)367-3412
Fax: (913)367-7125

Description
Founded: 1995
EIN: 486320070
Organization Type: Private Foundation
Giving Locations: KS: Atchison County
Grant Types: General Support, Matching.

Financial Summary
Total Giving: $241,580 (fiscal year ending June 30, 2004); $393,417 (fiscal 2001)
Giving Analysis: Giving for fiscal 2004 includes: foundation grants to United Way ($5,000)
Assets: $6,554,060 (fiscal 2004); $4,854,205 (fiscal 2001)

Typical Recipients
Arts & Humanities: Arts Associations & Councils, History & Archaeology, Libraries, Museums/Galleries, Theater
Civic & Public Affairs: Business/Free Enterprise, Chambers of Commerce, Civic & Public Affairs-General, Housing, Municipalities/Towns
Education: Colleges & Universities, Community & Junior Colleges, Education Funds, Elementary Education (Private), Education-General, Private Education (Precollege), Student Aid
Environment: Resource Conservation
Health: Emergency/Ambulance Services, Home-Care Services

International: Health Care/Hospitals
Religion: Churches
Social Services: At-Risk Youth, Community Centers, Community Service Organizations, Counseling, Domestic Violence, Family Services, Scouts, United Funds/United Ways, YMCA/YWCA/YMHA/YWHA

Application Procedures

Initial Contact: The foundation has no formal grant application procedure or application form. Send a brief letter of inquiry.
Application Requirements: Include a description of organization, amount requested, purpose of funds sought, proof of tax-exempt status, proof of matched funds.
Deadlines: None.

Restrictions

Does not support organizations outside operating areas. Grants are generally restricted to charitable organizations within Atchison County, KS.

Additional Information

All requests for funds must be matched.
Trust(s): UMB Bank

Foundation Officials

Cloud L. Cray: co-trustee B Detroit, MI 1922. ED Case Institute of Technology BS (1943). PRIM CORP EMPL president, director: Midwest Solvents Co. of Illinois. CORP AFFIL chairman: Midwest Grain Products Inc. NONPR AFFIL president: Cray Medicine Research Foundation; director: Riverbend Regional Health Systems; chairman: Atchison Hospital Foundation.
Jeri Kurth: co-trustee
June Lynn: co-trustee
Gay Wright: trust officer, trustee

Grants Analysis

Disclosure Period: fiscal year ending June 30, 2004
Total Grants: $236,580*
Number of Grants: 17
Average Grant: $4,500*
Highest Grant: $88,580
Lowest Grant: $500
Typical Range: $1,000 to $10,000
*Note: Giving excludes United Way. Average grant figure excludes three highest grants ($173,580).

Recent Grants

Note: Grants derived from fiscal 2004 Form 990.
General

88,580	Evah C. Cray Home Museum, Atchison, KS
50,000	City of Atchison, Atchison, KS
35,000	Atchison Area Chamber of Commerce Educational Foundation, Atchison, KS
10,000	Happy Hearts Inc., Atchison, KS
7,500	Theatre Atchison, Atchison, KS
5,000	All Faith Counseling Center, Atchison, KS
5,000	Atchison Family YMCA, Atchison, KS
5,000	Bittersweet Homestead, Holton, KS
5,000	Domestic Violence Emergency Services Inc., Atchison, KS
5,000	First Presbyterian Church, Atchison, KS

CREDIT SUISSE FIRST BOSTON CORP.

Company Headquarters

11 Madison Ave.
New York, NY 10010-3629
Web: http://www.csfb.com

Company Description

Former Name: First Boston.
Revenue: US$1.366 billion (2001)

Employees: 28,415 (2001)
SIC(s): 6211 Security Brokers & Dealers.
Parent Company: Credit Suisse Group, Paradeplatz 8, PO Box 1, Zurich, Switzerland

Operating Locations

Credit Suisse First Boston (NY--New York; PR--Hato Rey); Swiss American Securities (NY--New York)
Note: Operates throughout the USA.

Nonmonetary Support

Volunteer Programs: The company encourages employee volunteerism in programs such as Publicolor, Habitat for Humanity, Everybody Wins, and Big Brothers/Big Sisters.

Credit Suisse First Boston Foundation Trust

Giving Contact

Ms. Casey Karel, Vice President
Credit Suisse First Boston Foundation Trust
11 Madison Ave.
New York, NY 10010
Phone: (212)325-2389
Fax: (212)538-4633
E-mail: casey.karel@csfb.com
Web: http://www.csfb.com/about_csfb/company_information/foundation/index.shtml

Description

Founded: 1959
EIN: 046059692
Organization Type: Corporate Foundation
Giving Locations: NY: New York headquarters and operating communities; nationally.
Grant Types: General Support, Project.
Note: The foundation also awards mini-grants to employees.

Donor Information

Founder: The First Boston Corp.

Financial Summary

Total Giving: $5,000,000 (2004 approx); $5,000,000 (2003 approx); $5,985,053 (2002). Note: Contributes through corporate direct giving program and foundation.
Giving Analysis: Giving for 2002 includes: foundation (approx $5,000,000); 2001: foundation (approx $4,422,023); corporate direct giving (approx $10,830,000)
Assets: $24,000,000 (2003 approx); $26,073,853 (2002); $24,677,227 (2001)
Gifts Received: $8,263,172 (2002); $31,675,934 (2001); $4,708,373 (2000). Note: Contributions were received from Credit Suisse First Boston Corporation.

Typical Recipients

Arts & Humanities: Arts Associations & Councils, Arts Centers, Arts Funds, Arts Institutes, Ballet, Dance, Arts & Humanities-General, Libraries, Museums/Galleries, Music, Opera, Performing Arts, Public Broadcasting, Theater
Civic & Public Affairs: African American Affairs, Botanical Gardens/Parks, Business/Free Enterprise, Civil Rights, Clubs, Community Foundations, Economic Development, Economic Policy, Employment/Job Training, Gay/Lesbian Issues, Civic & Public Affairs-General, Housing, Law & Justice, Municipalities/Towns, Philanthropic Organizations, Professional & Trade Associations, Public Policy, Urban & Community Affairs, Women's Affairs
Education: Afterschool/Enrichment Programs, Arts/Humanities Education, Business Education, Colleges & Universities, Continuing Education, Economic Education, Education Funds, Education Reform, Engineering/Technological Education, Faculty Develop-

ment, Education-General, Leadership Training, Literacy, Minority Education, Preschool Education, Private Education (Precollege), Public Education (Precollege), School Volunteerism, Science/Mathematics Education, Special Education, Student Aid, Vocational & Technical Education
Environment: Air/Water Quality, Resource Conservation
Health: Cancer, Children's Health/Hospitals, Clinics/Medical Centers, Emergency/Ambulance Services, Hospitals, Long-Term Care, Medical Research, Mental Health, Prenatal Health Issues, Single-Disease Health Associations, Transplant Networks/Donor Banks
International: Health Care/Hospitals, International Relations
Religion: Religious Welfare
Science: Science Museums
Social Services: At-Risk Youth, Big Brothers/Big Sisters, Camps, Child Welfare, Community Centers, Community Service Organizations, Emergency Relief, Family Services, Food/Clothing Distribution, People with Disabilities, Recreation & Athletics, Scouts, Shelters/Homelessness, Social Services-General, Special Olympics, United Funds/United Ways, Volunteer Services, YMCA/YWCA/YMHA/YWHA, Youth Organizations

Application Procedures

Initial Contact: See website for application guidelines, then submit a letter of inquiry.
Application Requirements: Letters of inquiry should not exceed two pages and must include contact information; a description of organization; purpose of funds sought; population served; estimated overall project budget; and time period for which funds are requested.
Deadlines: None for letters of inquiry. February 15 and August 15 for proposals.
Review Process: If the foundation determines that an inquiry fits the foundation's guidelines and current focus, the applicant will be contacted and invited to submit a full proposal. The foundation's board of trustees holds three grant making meetings from April through September of each year.
Evaluative Criteria: Proposals should be clear and concise. The foundation prefers programs that are consistent with the foundation's mission; provide volunteer opportunities for CSFB employees; for which the foundation's grant money can make a difference; and will be likely to attract the support of other funders in subsequent years. The foundation also strongly prefers organizations with stable financials.
Decision Notification: Letters of inquiry generally receive a response within 90 working days. Review of full proposals may take three to four months.
Notes: Do not send videotapes unless specifically requested.

Restrictions

Foundation does not support capital campaigns; dinners or events; endowments; individuals or scholarship programs; matching gifts; medical research; public or private schools; religious programs; sponsorships; or veteran, fraternal and political programs.

Additional Information

In 1994, the company reported that it changed its name. The company was formerly known as First Boston Inc., but is now known as Credit Suisse First Boston Corp. Additionally, the company's trust has changed its name from First Boston Foundation Trust to Credit Suisse First Boston Foundation Trust.
Publications: Guidelines

Corporate Officials

John J. Mack: chief executive officer
Stephen R. Volk: chairman
Barbara Yastine: chief financial officer

Foundation Officials
Liza Bailey: trustee
Gates Hawn: trustee
Grace Koo: trustee
Christopher Lawrence: trustee
Elisabeth Millard: trustee
Thomas Nides: trustee
Robert C. O'Brien: trustee
David C. O'Leary: deputy chairman, trustee NONPR AFFIL director: Good Shepherd Services.
Douglas L. Paul: trustee
G. T. Sweeney: chairman, trustee

Grants Analysis
Disclosure Period: calendar year ending 2002
Total Grants: $5,940,053*
Number of Grants: 281
Average Grant: $15,600*
Highest Grant: $650,000
Lowest Grant: $500
Typical Range: $1,000 to $30,000
*Note:** Giving excludes United Way. Average grant figure excludes five highest grants ($1,650,000).

Recent Grants
Note: Grants derived from 2003 Form 990.
General
600,000	Robin Hood Foundation, New York, NY
250,000	Gordon A. Rich Memorial Foundation, New York, NY
125,000	Children's Storefront
125,000	Madison Square Park Conservancy, New York, NY
100,000	CityKids Foundation, New York, NY
100,000	Cooperative for Assistance and Relief Everywhere, Atlanta, GA
100,000	Good Shepherd Services, New York, NY
100,000	Habitat for Humanity, Americus, GA
100,000	Henry Street Settlement, New York, NY
100,000	Prep for Prep, New York, NY

CREMER FOUNDATION

Giving Contact
James A. Berkenstadt, Administrator
PO Box 1
Madison, WI 53701
Phone: (608)837-5166
E-mail: mlpp@globaldialog.com
Note: Mr. Berkenstadt may be reached at extension 330.

Description
Founded: 1965
EIN: 396086822
Organization Type: Private Foundation
Giving Locations: WI: Madison and surrounding metropolitan area
Grant Types: General Support, Seed Money.

Financial Summary
Total Giving: $231,650 (2003); $240,680 (2001)
Assets: $3,192,029 (2003); $3,549,126 (2001)
Gifts Received: $70,000 (1996). Note: In 1996, contributions were received from Helen and Garvin Cremer.

Typical Recipients
Arts & Humanities: Arts & Humanities-General, Libraries
Civic & Public Affairs: Community Foundations, Employment/Job Training, Hispanic Affairs, Housing
Education: Education Funds, Literacy, Medical Education, Public Education (Precollege), Special Education, Student Aid
Health: Eyes/Blindness, Health-General, Geriatric Health, Health Funds, Medical Research, Mental Health, Nursing Services
Religion: Churches, Religious Welfare
Social Services: At-Risk Youth, Child Welfare, Community Centers, Community Service Organizations, Domestic Violence, Family Planning, Family Services, Food/Clothing Distribution, Homes, People with Disabilities, Scouts, Senior Services, Shelters/Homelessness, Social Services-General, United Funds/United Ways, YMCA/YWCA/YMHA/YWHA, Youth Organizations

Application Procedures
Initial Contact: The foundation requests applications be made in writing. Send a full proposal.
Application Requirements: Include a description of organization, amount requested, purpose of funds sought, recently audited financial statement, and proof of tax-exempt status; also list sources of other contributionss received.
Deadlines: None.

Restrictions
The foundation does not support individuals, religious organizations for sectarian purposes, political or lobbying groups, or organizations outside operating areas.

Additional Information
Publications: Application Guidelines

Foundation Officials
James A. Berkenstadt: director
Frances H. Cremer: president
Holly L. Cremer: treasurer
Helen A. George: secretary
Robert R. Stroud: vice president
James T. Sykes: director

Grants Analysis
Disclosure Period: calendar year ending 2003
Total Grants: $231,650
Number of Grants: 25
Average Grant: $6,527*
Highest Grant: $75,000
Lowest Grant: $500
Typical Range: $1,000 to $15,000
*Note:** Average grant figure excludes highest grant.

Recent Grants
Note: Grants derived from 2003 Form 990.
General
75,000	Wisconsin Partnership for Housing Development, Madison, WI
34,500	Salvation Army of Dane County, Madison, WI
25,000	Meriter Foundation, Madison, WI
20,000	University of Wisconsin Foundation, Madison, WI
7,000	Sun Prairie YMCA, Madison, WI
6,000	East Madison Community Center, Madison, WI
6,000	Very Special Arts Wisconsin, Madison, WI
5,000	Madison Literary Council, Madison, WI
5,000	Sun Prairie Community Foundation, Sun Prairie, WI
5,000	Youth Services of Southern Wisconsin, Madison, WI

CRESTLEA FOUNDATION

Giving Contact
Stephen A. Martinenza, Secretary & Treasurer
100 W. 10th Street, Suite 1109
Wilmington, DE 19801
Phone: (302)654-2477
Fax: (302)654-2323

Description
Founded: 1955
EIN: 516015638
Organization Type: General Purpose Foundation
Giving Locations: DE: Wilmington including surrounding area
Grant Types: Capital, Seed Money.

Donor Information
Founder: Incorporated in 1955 by the late Henry B. duPont.

Financial Summary
Total Giving: $823,285 (2001)
Giving Analysis: Giving for 2001 includes: foundation grants to United Way ($40,000)
Assets: $35,528,984 (2001)
Gifts Received: $541,101 (2001); $714,442 (2000); $665,062 (1998). Note: In 1998 and 2000, contributions were received from the Wilmington Trust Co.

Typical Recipients
Arts & Humanities: Art History, Arts Centers, Arts Funds, Arts Institutes, Ballet, Arts & Humanities-General, Historic Preservation, History & Archaeology, Libraries, Museums/Galleries, Music, Opera, Performing Arts, Theater, Visual Arts
Civic & Public Affairs: Business/Free Enterprise, Clubs, Community Foundations, Economic Development, Employment/Job Training, Civic & Public Affairs-General, Housing, Law & Justice, Native American Affairs, Nonprofit Management, Professional & Trade Associations, Public Policy, Urban & Community Affairs, Women's Affairs, Zoos/Aquariums
Education: Arts/Humanities Education, Colleges & Universities, Community & Junior Colleges, Education Associations, Education-General, Health & Physical Education, Leadership Training, Literacy, Medical Education, Preschool Education, Private Education (Precollege), Science/Mathematics Education, Secondary Education (Private), Secondary Education (Public), Special Education, Student Aid, Vocational & Technical Education
Environment: Air/Water Quality, Environment-General, Resource Conservation
Health: AIDS/HIV, Alzheimer's Disease, Arthritis, Cancer, Children's Health/Hospitals, Clinics/Medical Centers, Geriatric Health, Health Organizations, Hospices, Hospitals, Long-Term Care, Preventive Medicine/Wellness Organizations, Public Health, Single-Disease Health Associations
Religion: Churches, Ministries, Religious Organizations, Religious Welfare
Science: Science-General, Science Museums, Scientific Centers & Institutes
Social Services: Animal Protection, Camps, Child Welfare, Community Centers, Community Service Organizations, Counseling, Day Care, Family Planning, Family Services, Food/Clothing Distribution, Homes, People with Disabilities, Recreation & Athletics, Scouts, Senior Services, Sexual Abuse, Social Services-General, Special Olympics, United Funds/United Ways, Veterans, YMCA/YWCA/YMHA/YWHA, Youth Organizations

Application Procedures
Initial Contact: The foundation requests applications be made in writing.
Application Requirements: Applicants should include the reason for the grant, any pertinent financial statements, and a copy of the IRS exemption approval letter.
Deadlines: Applications must be received by 3–November 1.

Restrictions
Some grants are made at the discretion of the Board of Trustees regardless of geographic location. Solicitation for grantss are only considered from organizations DE and nearby Southern Chester County, PA. Grants are not made to individuals.

Foundation Officials

Otto C. Fad: vice president
Stephen A. Martinenza: treasurer

Grants Analysis

Disclosure Period: calendar year ending 2001
Total Grants: $783,285*
Number of Grants: 67
Average Grant: $11,691*
Highest Grant: $82,785
Typical Range: $5,000 to $20,000
*Note: Giving excludes United Way. Average grant figure excludes highest grant.

Recent Grants

Note: Grants derived from 2002 Form 990.

Library-Related

15,000	Northeast Harbor Library, Northeast Harbor, ME -- toward operating support
5,000	Library Company of Philadelphia, Philadelphia, PA -- toward operating support

General

1,082,785	Pomfret School, Pomfret, CT -- funding for capital improvements
82,500	Philadelphia Museum of Art, Philadelphia, PA -- toward operating support
50,000	St. Michael's Day Nursery Inc., Wilmington, DE -- toward building acquisition/renovation
40,000	United Way of Delaware, Wilmington, DE -- assistance for annual appeal
25,000	Archmere Academy, Claymont, DE -- toward capital campaign for renovations
25,000	Delaware Museum of Natural History, Wilmington, DE -- toward capital campaign for renovations
25,000	Wilmington Friends School, Wilmington, DE -- funding for facility renovation
20,000	Mystic Seaport Museum Inc., Mystic, CT -- toward operating support
20,000	St. Mary's Church, Northeast Harbor, ME -- toward operating support
20,000	SODAT Counseling & Eval Center, Wilmington, DE -- toward program support

MARY A. CROCKER TRUST

Giving Contact

Charles Crocker, Trustee
233 Post Street, 2nd Floor
San Francisco, CA 94108
Phone: (415)982-0138
Fax: (415)982-0141
E-mail: mact@best.com
Web: http://www.mactrust.org

Description

Founded: 1889
EIN: 946051917
Organization Type: Private Foundation
Giving Locations: CA: San Francisco including metropolitan area
Grant Types: Capital, Emergency, General Support, Project, Seed Money.

Donor Information

Founder: Established by the late Mary A. Crocker.

Financial Summary

Total Giving: $495,000 (2003); $520,000 (2001)
Assets: $13,336,347 (2003); $12,264,570 (2001)

Typical Recipients

Arts & Humanities: Community Arts, Film & Video, Libraries, Museums/Galleries, Public Broadcasting
Civic & Public Affairs: Botanical Gardens/Parks, Business/Free Enterprise, Community Foundations, Employment/Job Training, Ethnic Organizations, Civic & Public Affairs-General, Hispanic Affairs, Housing, Municipalities/Towns, Nonprofit Management, Philanthropic Organizations, Professional & Trade Associations, Public Policy, Rural Affairs, Urban & Community Affairs, Women's Affairs
Education: Colleges & Universities, Education Funds, Education Reform, Environmental Education, Faculty Development, Education-General, Leadership Training, Literacy, Minority Education, Preschool Education, Private Education (Precollege), Public Education (Precollege), School Volunteerism, Science/Mathematics Education, Secondary Education (Private), Secondary Education (Public), Special Education, Student Aid
Environment: Air/Water Quality, Forestry, Environment-General, Research, Resource Conservation, Watershed, Wildlife Protection
Health: Clinics/Medical Centers, Hospitals, Medical Research, Prenatal Health Issues, Research/Studies Institutes
International: Health Care/Hospitals, International Development
Religion: Churches, Religious Welfare
Science: Science Museums, Scientific Centers & Institutes, Scientific Organizations, Scientific Research
Social Services: At-Risk Youth, Child Welfare, Community Centers, Community Service Organizations, Emergency Relief, Family Planning, Family Services, Food/Clothing Distribution, People with Disabilities, Recreation & Athletics, Volunteer Services, Youth Organizations

Application Procedures

Initial Contact: Submit a brief letter of inquiry.
Application Requirements: If the foundation requests a full proposal, it should include amount requested; statement of necessity; description of the project plan, intended outcome, and any innovative features of the proposal; budget and organization budget; information on aid from others; and persons to contact for further information.
Deadlines: None.

Restrictions

Does not support individuals, annual campaigns, continuing support, deficit financing, or sectarian purposes. Building funds, operating budgets, scholarships, and equipment purchases are a low priority. Grants are made primarily to charitable organizations in the San Francisco Bay area.

Additional Information

Publications: Application Guidelines

Foundation Officials

Elizabeth Atcheson: trustee
Charles Crocker: trustee
Tania W. Stepanian: chairperson
Fredrick W. Whitridge: trustee

Grants Analysis

Disclosure Period: calendar year ending 2003
Total Grants: $495,000
Number of Grants: 44
Average Grant: $11,250
Highest Grant: $25,000
Lowest Grant: $1,000
Typical Range: $1,000 to $20,000

Recent Grants

Note: Grants derived from 2001 Form 990.

Library-Related

15,000	San Francisco Public Library, San Francisco, CA -- Wallace Stegner Environmental Center

General

35,000	Kids Turn, San Francisco, CA -- workshops
30,000	Greenbelt Alliance, San Francisco, CA -- protect open space and curb urban sprawl
25,000	Bay Nature, Berekely, CA -- local Bay area magazine launching
25,000	Exploratorium, San Francisco, CA -- training for beginning math and sciences teachers
25,000	First Resort, Oakland, CA -- course teaching consequences of early sexual activity
25,000	Gateway High School, San Francisco, CA -- start up expenses
25,000	Hamilton School, San Francisco, CA -- capital campaign
25,000	Omega Boys Club, San Francisco, CA -- Academic Programs
25,000	Park Day School, Oakland, CA -- Community Outreach Program
25,000	Project HELP, Sunnyvale, CA -- Model Academy safety net

CROSSWICKS FOUNDATION

Giving Contact

Crosswicks Foundation
924 West End Ave., Suite 95
New York, NY 10025
Phone: (860)496-8119

Description

Founded: 1972
EIN: 132732197
Organization Type: Private Foundation
Grant Types: General Support, Multiyear/Continuing Support, Scholarship.

Financial Summary

Total Giving: $193,000 (fiscal year ending November 30, 2004); $182,000 (fiscal 2001)
Assets: $3,700,874 (fiscal 2004); $3,635,375 (fiscal 2001)

Typical Recipients

Arts & Humanities: Arts Associations & Councils, Ballet, Arts & Humanities-General, Libraries, Literary Arts, Music, Opera, Theater
Civic & Public Affairs: Ethnic Organizations, Civic & Public Affairs-General
Education: Arts/Humanities Education, Colleges & Universities, Private Education (Precollege), Religious Education, Secondary Education (Public)
Environment: Forestry, Resource Conservation, Wildlife Protection
Health: Cancer, Eyes/Blindness, Hospices, Hospitals, Long-Term Care
International: Foreign Educational Institutions, Health Care/Hospitals
Religion: Churches, Religion-General, Religious Organizations, Religious Welfare
Social Services: At-Risk Youth, Counseling, Homes, Scouts, Social Services-General, Youth Organizations

Application Procedures

Initial Contact: Send a written request.
Application Requirements: Include a description of organization, amount requested, purpose of funds sought, recently audited financial statement, and proof of tax-exempt status.
Deadlines: November 1.

Restrictions

Grants are not made to individuals.

Foundation Officials

Edward A. Jones: director
Josephine Jones: executive vice president
Madeleine L'Engle Franklin: president B New York, NY 1918. ED Smith College AB (1941); New School for Social Research (1941-1942); Columbia University (1960-1961). CORP AFFIL teacher: Saint Hildas & Saint Hughes Sch; writer-in-residence: Wheaton Coll; writer-in-residence: Cathedral Saint John Divine. NONPR AFFIL member: Colonial Dames; member: Writers Guild America; president, member council & membership committee: Authors Guild; member council: Authors League.
Morton L. Price: secretary
Maria R. Rooney: vice president
Madeleine J. Roy: treasurer

Grants Analysis

Disclosure Period: fiscal year ending November 30, 2004
Total Grants: $193,000
Number of Grants: 34
Average Grant: $5,676
Highest Grant: $10,000
Lowest Grant: $500
Typical Range: $1,000 to $10,000

Recent Grants

Note: Grants derived from fiscal 2004 Form 990.
General

10,000	Action Without Borders, New York, NY
10,000	Cathedral of St. John the Divine, New York, NY
10,000	Cathedral of St. John the Divine, New York, NY
10,000	Charlotte Hungerford Hospital, Torrington, CT
10,000	Community of the Holy Spirit, New York, NY
10,000	Connecticut Junior Republic, Litchfield, CT
10,000	Greenwoods Counseling Center, Litchfield, CT
10,000	Lower Manhattan Cultural Council, New York, NY
10,000	New York City Public Schools, New York, NY
10,000	Wheaton College, Wheaton, IL

HENRY P. AND SUSAN C. CROWELL TRUST

Giving Contact

Paul E. Nelson, Executive Director
1880 Office Club Pointe, Suite 2200
Colorado Springs, CO 80920
Phone: (719)272-8300
Fax: (719)272-8305
E-mail: crowellhp@aol.com

Description

Founded: 1927
EIN: 366038028
Organization Type: Specialized/Single Purpose Foundation
Giving Locations: nationally.
Grant Types: Challenge, General Support, Project.

Donor Information

Founder: The trust was established in 1927 and funded by the late Henry P. Crowell, an early leader of the Quaker Oats Company.

Financial Summary

Total Giving: $2,185,000 (2003); $4,205,000 (2002); $3,947,000 (2001)
Assets: $98,303,575 (2003); $82,862,396 (2002);

$99,932,026 (2001)
Gifts Received: $1,758,348 (2001). Note: In 2001, contributions were received from Henry P. Crowell for Irene Goodson.

Typical Recipients

Arts & Humanities: Libraries, Public Broadcasting
Civic & Public Affairs: Clubs, Economic Development, Civic & Public Affairs-General, Hispanic Affairs, Public Policy, Urban & Community Affairs
Education: Colleges & Universities, Education-General, International Exchange, International Studies, Private Education (Precollege), Religious Education, Science/Mathematics Education, Secondary Education (Private), Student Aid, Vocational & Technical Education
Health: Clinics/Medical Centers, Hospitals
International: Foreign Arts Organizations, Foreign Educational Institutions, International-General, Health Care/Hospitals, International Affairs, International Development, International Environmental Issues, International Organizations, International Relations, International Relief Efforts, Missionary/Religious Activities
Religion: Bible Study/Translation, Churches, Religion-General, Jewish Causes, Ministries, Missionary Activities (Domestic), Religious Organizations, Religious Welfare, Seminaries, Social/Policy Issues
Social Services: Camps, Community Service Organizations, Family Services, Homes, Refugee Assistance, Shelters/Homelessness, Social Services-General

Application Procedures

Initial Contact: Requests should be addressed to the executive director.
Application Requirements: Proposals should clearly set forth the need, purpose, and amount of request. A list of the organization's governing board; history of organization and its mission; problem that project addresses; latest audited financial statement; current year's organizational budget; project budget; and a copy of the organization's IRS letter of tax-exempt and non-private foundation status should be included.
Deadlines: The trust's board meets in May and November. Grant applicants will be advised of meeting date during which the proposal will be considered.

Foundation Officials

John T. Bass: vice chairman, treasurer
Edwin L. Frizen, Jr.: chairman, trustee B Chicago, IL 1925. PRIM NONPR EMPL executive director: Interdenominational Foreign Mission Association ADD NONPR EMPL member missions committee: World Evang Fellowship; treasurer editorial com: Evang Missions Information Service.
Lowell L. Kline: co-trustee, treasurer
Jane Overstreet: co-trustee, secretary
John F. Robinson: co-trustee

Grants Analysis

Disclosure Period: calendar year ending 2003
Total Grants: $2,185,000
Number of Grants: 78
Average Grant: $20,800*
Highest Grant: $750,000
Lowest Grant: $5,000
Typical Range: $10,000 to $30,000
*Note: Average grant figure excludes three highest grants ($625,000).

Recent Grants

Note: Grants derived from 2003 Form 990.
General

200,000	Moody Bible Institute -- towards broadcasting stewardship
200,000	Moody Bible Institute, Chicago, IL
125,000	Pioneers, Orlando, FL -- towards doctors services
90,000	Mission Training International Inc., Palmer Lake, CO
75,000	Mission Aviation Fellowship, Redlands, CA -- for the global ministry
50,000	Columbia International University, Columbia, SC -- for tuitions
50,000	Development Associates International, Colorado Springs, CO
50,000	Overseas Council, Indianapolis, IN -- for the excellence in Christian leadership development
50,000	Partners International, Spokane, WA -- for leadership transition
40,000	Bangui Evangelical School of Theology, Bangui Central African Republic -- scholarship funding

ARIE AND IDA CROWN MEMORIAL

Giving Contact

Susan Crown, President
222 North LaSalle Street, Suite 2000
Chicago, IL 60601
Phone: (312)236-6300
Fax: (312)984-1499
E-mail: aicm@crown-chicago.com

Description

Founded: 1947
EIN: 366076088
Organization Type: General Purpose Foundation
Giving Locations: IL: Chicago including Cook County
Grant Types: Capital, Emergency, Employee Matching Gifts, Endowment, General Support, Multiyear/Continuing Support, Operating Expenses, Project.

Donor Information

Founder: The foundation was established in honor of Arie and Ida Crown by their children in 1947. The Crown family was headed by noted industrialist Henry Crown. Henry and his brother Sol started a building supply company that became the largest in the Chicago area, and the basis for the Crown family fortune.
John J. Crown, Lester Crown and Joanne Crown have all donated more than 2% of the total contributions received by the foundation.

Financial Summary

Total Giving: $9,888,998 (2003); $9,616,115 (2002)
Assets: $224,631,697 (2003); $167,706,021 (2002)
Gifts Received: $13,253,734 (2003); $42,641 (2000); $23,949,096 (1997). Note: In 2003, contributions were received from Rebecca Crown ($66,391), David Crown ($34,686), Judith Crown ($25,594), Lester Crown ($33,932), Arie S. Crown ($695,599), James Crown ($64,252), Patricia Crown ($70,517), Daniel Crown ($26,434), Susan Crown ($33,082), Sara Star ($36,548), Janet Crown ($24,524), Debra Harriman ($30,943), Nancy Crown ($40,950), Elizabeth Crown ($16,350), William Crown ($32,089), Richard Goodman ($22,004), Barbara Manilow ($24,601), Leonard Goodman ($21,086), and the Edward Crown Charitable Fund ($12,572,082). In 2000, contributions were received from Lester Crown.

Typical Recipients

Arts & Humanities: Arts Associations & Councils, Arts Centers, Arts Festivals, Arts Institutes, Community Arts, Dance, History & Archaeology, Libraries, Literary Arts, Museums/Galleries, Music, Opera, Performing Arts, Public Broadcasting, Theater
Civic & Public Affairs: Asian American Affairs, Botanical Gardens/Parks, Civil Rights, Community Foundations, Employment/Job Training, Ethnic Organizations, Civic & Public Affairs-General, Hispanic Affairs, Law & Justice, Municipalities/Towns, Profes-

sional & Trade Associations, Public Policy, Urban & Community Affairs, Women's Affairs, Zoos/Aquariums

Education: Arts/Humanities Education, Business Education, Colleges & Universities, Education Funds, Education Reform, Elementary Education (Private), Engineering/Technological Education, Education-General, Health & Physical Education, Leadership Training, Legal Education, Literacy, Preschool Education, Private Education (Precollege), Public Education (Precollege), Religious Education, Secondary Education (Private), Vocational & Technical Education

Environment: Air/Water Quality, Resource Conservation, Wildlife Protection

Health: Alzheimer's Disease, Children's Health/Hospitals, Clinics/Medical Centers, Diabetes, Eyes/Blindness, Health-General, Health Funds, Health Organizations, Hospitals, Hospitals (University Affiliated), Medical Rehabilitation, Medical Research, Mental Health, Public Health, Single-Disease Health Associations

International: Foreign Educational Institutions, International Affairs, International Peace & Security Issues, International Relations, Missionary/Religious Activities

Religion: Jewish Causes, Seminaries, Synagogues/Temples

Science: Observatories & Planetariums, Science Museums

Social Services: At-Risk Youth, Big Brothers/Big Sisters, Child Welfare, Community Centers, Community Service Organizations, Delinquency & Criminal Rehabilitation, Domestic Violence, Emergency Relief, Family Planning, Family Services, Food/Clothing Distribution, Homes, People with Disabilities, Refugee Assistance, Scouts, Senior Services, Shelters/Homelessness, Substance Abuse, United Funds/United Ways, YMCA/YWCA/YMHA/YWHA, Youth Organizations

Application Procedures

Initial Contact: Prospective applicants should submit a letter of inquiry before submitting a proposal. A full proposal and grant application will be requested by the foundation.

Application Requirements: The letter of intent should not be longer than two pages and include the nature of the organization's work, budget size, proposed project, project budget, amount requested, and an attached copy of IRS determination letter.

Deadlines: None.

Review Process: The board meets twice annually, in the spring and fall.

Restrictions

The foundation does not support government sponsored programs, individuals, special events, conferences, or film projects.

Foundation Officials

Arie Steven Crown: vice president, director B Chicago, IL 1952. ED Claremont McKenna College (1974); University of California, Los Angeles MBA (1977). PRIM CORP EMPL general partner: Henry Crown & Co. CORP AFFIL director: Hilton Hotels Corp.; president: Ojai Resort Management Inc.; director: Aspen Ski Co.; director: Farmers Investment Co.

James Schine Crown: vice president, director B Chicago, IL 1953. ED Hampshire College BA (1976); Stanford University JD (1980). PRIM CORP EMPL general partner: Henry Crown & Co. CORP AFFIL director: Sara Lee Corp.; vice president: Woodard Inc.; principal: Pec Israel Economic Corp.; board directors: General Dynamics Corp.; ltd. partner: New York Yankees Partnership; vice president, director: Exchange Building Corp.; vice president, director: CC Industries Inc.; director: Citation Oil & Gas Corp.; director: Bank One Corp. NONPR AFFIL trustee: Orchestral Association; trustee: University Chicago; trustee: Museum Science & Industry.

Lester Crown: treasurer, director B Chicago, IL

1925. ED Northwestern University BScE (1946); Harvard University MBA (1949). PRIM CORP EMPL chairman, director: Material Service Corp. CORP AFFIL ltd. partner: New York Yankees Partnership; director: Santa Cruz Valley Pecan Co.; director: Maytag Appliances; director: Maytag Corp.; director: Marblehead Lime Co.; chairman: Material Service Resources Co.; chairman executive committee, director: General Dynamics Corp.; director: Green Valley Pecan; general partner: Henry Crown Co.; director: Farmers Investment Co.; chairman, director: CC Industries Inc.; director: Country Estates Pecan; director: 360 Communication Co. NONPR AFFIL trustee: Michael Reese Foundation; member: Tau Beta Pi; member: Phi Eta Sigma; member: Pi Mu Epsilon; director: Lyric Opera Corp.; trustee: Northwestern University; director: Childrens Memorial Medical Center; member: Jewish Theological Seminary; trustee: Aspen Institute Humanistic Studies; member, board advisors: Chicago Zoological Society. CLUB AFFIL Standard Club; Mid-America Club; Northmoor Country Club; Lake Shore Country Club; Marco Polo Club; Economic Club; John Evans Club Northwestern University; Chicago Club; Commercial Club.

Rebecca Crown: vice president, director

Susan Crown: president, director PRIM CORP EMPL vice president: Henry Crown & Co. CORP AFFIL director: Baxter International Inc.; director: Illinois Tool Works Inc.

William Crown: director, vice president

Sara Crown Star: director, vice president

Erica Eisner: program officer

Charles Goodman: vice president, director PRIM CORP EMPL vice president: Henry Crown & Co. CORP AFFIL director: General Dynamics Corp.; vice president, director: Monticello Realty Corp.; vice president, director: Exchange Building Corp.; vice president, director: CC Industries Inc.; director: Citation Oil & Gas Corp.

Jennifer Jacoby: vice president, secretary, director

Barbara Goodman Manilow: vice president, director NONPR AFFIL secretary, director: Chicago Children's Museum.

Maria Emma Smith: executive assistant

Arnold R. Weber: director, vice president

Grants Analysis

Disclosure Period: calendar year ending 2003
Total Grants: $9,888,998
Number of Grants: 690
Average Grant: $9,732*
Highest Grant: $945,690
Lowest Grant: $100
Typical Range: $1,000 to $25,000
*Note: Average grant figure excludes six highest grants ($3,232,173).

Recent Grants

Note: Grants derived from 2002 Form 990.

General

557,967	JPF Foundation, Chicago, IL	
539,350	JPF Foundation, Chicago, IL	
500,000	Syracuse University, Syracuse, NY	
491,650	Jewish United Fund of Metropolitan Chicago, Chicago, IL	
400,000	Window to the World Communications Inc., Chicago, IL	
312,500	Children's Hospital, Boston, MA	
290,000	Duke University, Durham, NC	
250,000	Lincoln Park Zoo, Chicago, IL	
195,232	JPF Foundation, Chicago, IL	
150,000	Claremont Mckenna College, Claremont, CA	

ROY E. CRUMMER FOUNDATION

Giving Contact

Roy E. Crummer, III, President & Trustee
130 Newport Center Dr., No. 140-B
Newport Beach, CA 92660-6923
Phone: (949)644-4702
Fax: (949)252-8959

Description

Founded: 1964
EIN: 886004422
Organization Type: Private Foundation
Giving Locations: CA
Grant Types: General Support.

Financial Summary

Total Giving: $310,000 (2003)
Assets: $6,603,273 (2003)

Typical Recipients

Arts & Humanities: Arts Associations & Councils, Film & Video, Historic Preservation, History & Archaeology, Libraries, Museums/Galleries, Public Broadcasting, Theater

Civic & Public Affairs: Clubs, Civic & Public Affairs-General, Hispanic Affairs, Housing, Parades/Festivals

Education: Colleges & Universities, Education-General, Legal Education, Minority Education, Private Education (Precollege), Religious Education

Environment: Air/Water Quality, Environment-General, Resource Conservation, Wildlife Protection

Health: AIDS/HIV, Cancer, Children's Health/Hospitals, Clinics/Medical Centers, Heart, Hospitals, Medical Research, Single-Disease Health Associations

International: International Environmental Issues, International Relief Efforts, Missionary/Religious Activities

Religion: Churches, Religious Welfare, Social/Policy Issues

Social Services: Animal Protection, At-Risk Youth, Camps, Child Welfare, Community Centers, Community Service Organizations, Day Care, Domestic Violence, Family Planning, Food/Clothing Distribution, Shelters/Homelessness, United Funds/United Ways, YMCA/YWCA/YMHA/YWHA, Youth Organizations

Application Procedures

Initial Contact: Send a brief letter of inquiry.
Application Requirements: Submit a description of the organization, purpose of funds sought, and IRS exemption number.
Deadlines: October 31.

Foundation Officials

Margarite Brown: secretary, treasurer, trustee
Ian F. Gow: trustee
Lee D. Strom: trustee

Grants Analysis

Disclosure Period: calendar year ending 2003
Total Grants: $310,000
Number of Grants: 101
Average Grant: $3,069
Highest Grant: $12,500
Lowest Grant: $500
Typical Range: $1,000 to $5,000

Recent Grants

Note: Grants derived from 2001 Form 990.
General

25,000	Palm Springs Desert Museum, Palm Springs, CA	
20,000	Cate, Carpinteria, CA	
15,000	Living Desert, Oakland, CA	
10,000	Church of Conscious Harmony, Austin, TX	

10,000	PATH
10,000	Pepperdine University, Malibu, CA
10,000	Santa Ynez Valley Hospital, Santa Ynez, CA
10,000	Venice Family Clinic, Venice, CA
7,000	Para Los Ninos, Los Angeles, CA
7,000	San Rogue School, San Rogue, CA

CRYSTAL TRUST

Giving Contact

Stephen C. Doberstein, Director
PO Box 39
Montchanin, DE 19710
Phone: (302)651-0533

Description

Founded: 1947
EIN: 516015063
Organization Type: Family Foundation
Giving Locations: nationally.
Grant Types: Capital, Emergency, General Support, Seed Money.

Donor Information

Founder: The donor of the trust, the late Irenee du Pont, established the trust in 1947. Under the terms of Mr. du Pont's will, the trust received an additional endowment in 1964, and has since operated under its present name. Mr. du Pont served as president of E. I. du Pont de Nemours & Co., a Wilmington-based manufacturing and chemical firm. Currently, the board of advisory trustees includes three descendants of the donor.

Financial Summary

Total Giving: $4,225,200 (2003); $6,057,375 (2002)
Assets: $132,967,262 (2003); $109,756,708 (2002)
Gifts Received: $66,669 (2003); $33,616,222 (2002). Note: Contributions were received from Stephen C. Doberstein, Director.

Typical Recipients

Arts & Humanities: Arts Centers, Arts Funds, Arts Institutes, Arts & Humanities-General, Historic Preservation, History & Archaeology, Libraries, Museums/Galleries, Music, Opera, Public Broadcasting, Theater
Civic & Public Affairs: Clubs, Economic Development, Employment/Job Training, Civic & Public Affairs-General, Hispanic Affairs, Housing, Nonprofit Management, Public Policy, Urban & Community Affairs, Zoos/Aquariums
Education: Arts/Humanities Education, Business Education, Colleges & Universities, Continuing Education, Economic Education, Education Associations, Elementary Education (Private), Elementary Education (Public), Engineering/Technological Education, Education-General, Gifted & Talented Programs, Medical Education, Preschool Education, Private Education (Precollege), Religious Education, Science/Mathematics Education, Secondary Education (Private), Special Education, Student Aid, Vocational & Technical Education
Environment: Environment-General, Protection, Research, Resource Conservation, Watershed, Wildlife Protection
Health: Cancer, Clinics/Medical Centers, Health-General, Geriatric Health, Health Funds, Health Organizations, Hospices, Hospitals, Long-Term Care, Medical Research, Mental Health, Preventive Medicine/Wellness Organizations, Public Health, Single-Disease Health Associations
Religion: Churches, Ministries, Religious Welfare
Science: Observatories & Planetariums, Science Museums, Scientific Centers & Institutes, Scientific Labs, Scientific Organizations, Scientific Research
Social Services: Child Abuse, Child Welfare, Community Centers, Community Service Organizations, Counseling, Day Care, Domestic Violence, Emergency Relief, Family Planning, Family Services, Food/Clothing Distribution, Homes, People with Disabilities, Recreation & Athletics, Scouts, Senior Services, Shelters/Homelessness, Social Services-General, Special Olympics, United Funds/United Ways, Veterans, YMCA/YWCA/YMHA/YWHA, Youth Organizations

Application Procedures

Initial Contact: The trust does not use standard application forms. Detailed letters of request should be submitted.
Application Requirements: Letters should include a history of the applicant organization, organizational purposes and activities, details about the proposal and its priority within the applicant organization, certification of tax-exempt status, and information on the governing group, staff and finances of the organization.
Deadlines: Requests should be submitted by September 30 of each year. Early application is recommended.
Review Process: Grant decisions are made toward the end of the year. Exceptions are considered only when there is a crucial factor of timing.

Restrictions

The trust does not support individuals, endowment funds, research, scholarships, fellowships, matching programs, loans, or continuing expenses of operations or deficits.

Additional Information

In unique cases, requests can be considered at times other than those specified by the trust. One-time support is preferred, usually for capital or for the needs of a program in its early stages.
Requests should be submitted by an appropriate volunteer officer or board member of the organization, or by a member of its executive staff to whom the responsibility is specifically delegated by its governing body.

Foundation Officials

Stephen C. Doberstein: director
Irenee du Pont, Jr.: trustee B 1920. ED Dartmouth College; Massachusetts Institute of Technology. PRIM CORP EMPL vice president: Longwood Gardens.
Eleanor Silliman Maroney: adv trustee
Ernest N. May, Jr.: adv trustee

Grants Analysis

Disclosure Period: calendar year ending 2003
Total Grants: $4,225,200
Number of Grants: 72
Average Grant: $53,217*
Highest Grant: $250,000
Lowest Grant: $5,000
Typical Range: $10,000 to $100,000
*Note: Average grant figure excludes two highest grants ($500,000).

Recent Grants

Note: Grants derived from 2003 Form 990.
Library-Related

150,000	Laurel Public Library, Laurel, DE -- renovations and expansion
50,000	Woodlawn Library, Wilmington, DE -- capital campaign

General

250,000	Independence School, Newark, DE -- capital campaign
250,000	Patrick Center for Environmental Research, Philadelphia, PA -- environment
200,000	Easter Seals, New Castle, DE -- capital campaign
200,000	Goldey Beacom College, Wilmington, DE -- capital needs
200,000	Sanford School, Hockessin, DE -- capital campaign
200,000	Tatnall School, Wilmington, DE -- capital campaign
150,000	Boy Scouts of America, Wilmington, DE -- scouting program
150,000	Saint Francis Foundation, Wilmington, DE -- capital development
120,000	Mount Cuba Astronomical Observatory, Greenville, DE -- equipment needs
100,000	Carnegie Institution of Washington, Washington, DC -- capital campaign

CTW FOUNDATION, INC.

Giving Contact

Robert A. Tucker, President
PO Box 911
Wilmington, DE 19899-0911
Phone: (302)429-9425

Description

Founded: 1954
EIN: 516011637
Organization Type: Private Foundation
Giving Locations: nationally.
Grant Types: Capital, General Support, Scholarship.

Financial Summary

Total Giving: $725,718 (2002); $741,266 (2001)
Giving Analysis: Giving for 2002 includes: foundation scholarships ($50,718)
Assets: $12,679,212 (2002); $15,273,811 (2001)
Gifts Received: $51,156 (2000); $2,628,750 (1998); $800,000 (1997). Note: In 2000, contributions were received from Charles W. Bower. Foundation receives contributions from Beneficial Tax Masters, Inc.

Typical Recipients

Arts & Humanities: Arts Associations & Councils, Arts Festivals, Arts Funds, Libraries, Museums/Galleries, Opera, Theater
Civic & Public Affairs: Botanical Gardens/Parks
Education: Arts/Humanities Education, Colleges & Universities, Economic Education, Education Funds, Engineering/Technological Education, International Studies, Legal Education, Medical Education, Minority Education, Private Education (Precollege), Religious Education, Student Aid
Environment: Environment-General, Resource Conservation
Health: Cancer, Children's Health/Hospitals, Clinics/Medical Centers, Health Funds, Health Organizations, Hospices, Hospitals, Medical Rehabilitation, Medical Research, Medical Training, Preventive Medicine/Wellness Organizations, Public Health
Religion: Churches, Religious Welfare, Seminaries
Social Services: Domestic Violence, Emergency Relief, Homes, People with Disabilities, Scouts, Youth Organizations

Application Procedures

Initial Contact: Send proposal in letter form.
Application Requirements: A description of organization; amount requested; purpose of funds sought; recently audited financial statement; proof of tax-exempt status.
Deadlines: October 1. April 15 for scholarships.
Notes: Application forms are available for scholarships.

Additional Information

Household International acquired Beneficial Corp. in second quarter of 1998. Following the merger, Beneficial Foundation changed its name to CTW Foundation. The foundation is no longer affiliated with either company.

Foundation Officials

Charles W. Bower: treasurer, director
Finn M. W. Caspersen, Jr.: director
Finn M. W. Caspersen, Sr.: vice president, director B New York, NY 1941. ED Brown University BA (1963); Harvard University LLB (1966). CORP AFFIL vice president: Westby Corp.; director: Beneficial Bank PLC; member executive committee, director: Beneficial National Bank. NONPR AFFIL director: Shelter Harbor Fire District; chairman: U.S. Equestrian Team; chairman: Prosperty New Jersey; member: Partnership for New Jersey; trustee, chairman: Peddie School; member: New York State Bar Association; chairman dean advisory board: Harvard University Law School; advisory board: Institute for Law & Economic; member: Harvard Resources Comm; member: Florida Bar Association; chairman: Gladstone Equestrian Association Inc.; director: Drumthwacket Foundation; chairman: Coalition Better Transportation; chairman: Coalition Service Industry; emeritus trustee: Brown University; member: American Finance Services Association; trustee: BGCN Life Camp Inc. CLUB AFFIL Wilmington Country Club; Knickerbocker Club; University Club; Harvard Club.
Eileen D. Dickey: secretary
Theresa A. Reilly: assistant secretary
Robert A. Tucker: president, director B Brooklyn, NY 1926. ED Wesleyan University (1948); Brown University (1951). CORP AFFIL director: Beneficial Corp.
John O. Williams: director

Grants Analysis

Disclosure Period: calendar year ending 2002
Total Grants: $675,000*
Number of Grants: 15
Average Grant: $17,308*
Highest Grant: $250,000
Lowest Grant: $5,000
Typical Range: $5,000 to $25,000
*Note: Giving excludes scholarships. Average grant figure excludes two highest grants ($450,000).

Recent Grants

Note: Grants derived from 2002 Form 990.
Library-Related

250,000	John Carter Brown Library, Providence, RI

General

200,000	Seeing Eye, Morristown, NJ
50,000	Drew University, Madison, NJ
50,000	Peddie School, Hightstown, NJ
25,000	New Jersey Museum of Agriculture, North Brunswick, NJ
20,000	Nature Conservancy, Chester, NJ
15,000	Shakespeare Theater of New Jersey, Madison, NJ
15,000	Wesleyan University, Middletown, CT
10,000	The College Fund, Fairfax, VA
10,000	Harness Racing Museum & Hall of Fame, Goshen, NY
10,000	Widener University of Law

PATRICK AND ANNA M. CUDAHY FUND

Giving Contact

Judith Borchers, Executive Director
1007 Church St., Suite 414
Evanston, IL 60201
Phone: (847)866-0760
Fax: (847)475-0679
E-mail: secretary@cudahyfund.org
Web: http://www.cudahyfund.org

Description

Founded: 1934
EIN: 390991972
Organization Type: Family Foundation
Giving Locations: IL: Chicago; WI internationally; nationally.
Grant Types: General Support, Multiyear/Continuing Support, Operating Expenses, Project.

Donor Information

Founder: Michael F. Cudahy established the Patrick and Anna M. Cudahy Fund in 1934 in honor of his parents, and incorporated it in Wisconsin in 1949. Patrick Cudahy (1849-1919) was a partner in Armour and Company and organized the Cudahy Brothers Packing Company. Michael Cudahy served as president of the fund and was succeeded by his son, Richard D. Cudahy. The current president is Janet S. Cudahy, M.D., wife of Richard D. Cudahy.

Financial Summary

Total Giving: $2,569,278 (2003); $1,936,930 (2002 approx); $2,420,433 (2001)
Assets: $20,358,468 (2003); $23,552,805 (2001)

Typical Recipients

Arts & Humanities: Arts Funds, Arts Institutes, Dance, Historic Preservation, Libraries, Museums/Galleries, Performing Arts, Public Broadcasting
Civic & Public Affairs: African American Affairs, Asian American Affairs, Civil Rights, Economic Development, Employment/Job Training, Ethnic Organizations, Civic & Public Affairs-General, Hispanic Affairs, Housing, Law & Justice, Municipalities/Towns, Nonprofit Management, Professional & Trade Associations, Public Policy, Rural Affairs, Urban & Community Affairs, Women's Affairs
Education: Afterschool/Enrichment Programs, Business Education, Colleges & Universities, Education Funds, Education Reform, Elementary Education (Public), Environmental Education, Education-General, Legal Education, Literacy, Minority Education, Preschool Education, Private Education (Precollege), Public Education (Precollege), Religious Education, Science/Mathematics Education, Secondary Education (Private), Secondary Education (Public), Student Aid, Vocational & Technical Education
Environment: Environment-General
Health: Children's Health/Hospitals, Clinics/Medical Centers, Eyes/Blindness, Geriatric Health, Health Organizations, Long-Term Care, Medical Rehabilitation, Mental Health, Preventive Medicine/Wellness Organizations, Public Health
International: Foreign Educational Institutions, Health Care/Hospitals, Human Rights, International Development, International Environmental Issues, International Organizations, International Relations, Missionary/Religious Activities
Religion: Churches, Dioceses, Religion-General, Ministries, Missionary Activities (Domestic), Religious Organizations, Religious Welfare
Science: Scientific Research
Social Services: At-Risk Youth, Camps, Child Welfare, Community Centers, Community Service Organizations, Day Care, Domestic Violence, Emergency Relief, Family Planning, Family Services, Food/Clothing Distribution, Homes, People with Disabilities, Recreation & Athletics, Scouts, Senior Services, Shelters/Homelessness, Social Services-General, Special Olympics, Substance Abuse, Volunteer Services, YMCA/YWCA/YMHA/YWHA, Youth Organizations

Application Procedures

Initial Contact: Prospective recipients should call or write the fund for guidelines and proposal cover sheet.
Application Requirements: Completed one page Cudahy form entitled "Summary and Request for Funding"; a brief description of the organization and an outline of the proposed project, which should not exceed five pages in length; a projected income and expense breakdown for the organization and the project; a list of the major institutional donors to the organization during the past five years (maximum of ten names with amounts); a complete, current list of the board of directors of the organization; a copy of the Internal Revenue Service ruling that the organization has 501(c)(3) status; a complete copy of the most recent audited financial statement. If the organization is not required to be audited, a detailed balance sheet of actual income and expenses, assets and liabilities for the past fiscal year.
Deadlines: Applicants should submit the proposals eight weeks before a meeting.
Review Process: The board meets quarterly, on January 5, April 5, July 5, and October 5. Notification of decisions will be two weeks after meetings.

Restrictions

No grants are given to individuals or for endowments, and no loans are made. The fund also does not support organizations outside of U.S. who are not represented by a U.S.-based 501(c)(3) organization.

Additional Information

Publications: Guidelines; Application Form; Annual Grants List

Foundation Officials

James D. Bailey: director
Judith Borchers: executive director
Janet S. Cudahy, MD: president, director, donor daughter-in-law
Michaela Cudahy: director
Molly Cudahy: director
Richard D. Cudahy: chairman, director, donor son B Milwaukee, WI 1926. ED United States Military Academy BS (1948); Yale University JD (1955). PRIM NONPR EMPL federal judge: U.S. Court Appeals. NONPR AFFIL judge: U.S. Court Appeals 7th Federal Circuit; member: Wisconsin Bar Association; member: Milwaukee Bar Association; member board directors: Federal Judges Association; member: Law Club Chicago; trustee: Catholic Theological Union; member: Chicago Bar Association; member: American Law Institute; member: American Bar Association; board selectors: American Institute Public Service.
Annette Stoddard Freeman: director
Dudley J. Godfrey, Jr.: secretary, treasurer, director B 1926. ED University of Wisconsin BBA (1949); University of Michigan LLB (1952). PRIM CORP EMPL senior partner: Godfrey & Kahn SC. CORP AFFIL director: Manpower Inc.; director: Powers Holding Inc.
Jean Holtz: director
Wesley L. Scott: director

Grants Analysis

Disclosure Period: calendar year ending 2003
Total Grants: $2,569,278
Number of Grants: 165
Average Grant: $15,571
Highest Grant: $50,000
Lowest Grant: $500
Typical Range: $5,000 to $25,000

Recent Grants

Note: Grants derived from 2003 Form 990.
General

50,000	Maryknoll Sisters, Maryknoll, NY -- for Emusoi Center construction
20,000	Northwestern University School of Law, Chicago, IL
18,000	Milwaukee Habitat for Humanity Inc., Milwaukee, WI -- to sponsor one habitat home
17,939	Maryknoll Sisters, Maryknoll, NY -- to support Good Samaritan Hostel for Women in Taiwan
15,000	Depaul University College of Law, Chicago, IL -- fund for Chiapas Project

15,000	Oxfam America, Boston, MA -- to support the Domestic Program
15,000	Salvatorian Mission Warehouse, New Holstein, WI -- to assist in shipping costs
15,000	Special Olympics, Madison, WI -- to support the Athlete Recognition Awards
12,500	Hunger Task Force of Milwaukee Inc., Milwaukee, WI -- to assist in Emergency Food Program
12,500	Second Harvest of Wisconsin, Milwaukee, WI -- fund for food

THE CULLEN FOUNDATION

Giving Contact
Alan M. Stewart, Executive Director
601 Jefferson, Suite 4000
Houston, TX 77002
Phone: (713)651-8835
Fax: (713)651-2374
Web: http://www.cullenfdn.org

Description
Founded: 1947
EIN: 746048769
Organization Type: Family Foundation
Giving Locations: TX: Houston including surrounding area
Grant Types: Capital, Endowment, Fellowship, General Support, Matching, Multiyear/Continuing Support, Operating Expenses, Professorship, Project, Research, Scholarship.

Donor Information
Founder: The Cullen foundation was established in 1947 by Hugh Roy Cullen, a Houston oilman. The original grant funding the foundation was in the form of oil properties. The donor's daughter and grandsons serve on the board of trustees.

Financial Summary
Total Giving: $10,450 (2003 approx); $12,485,000 (2002); $14,001,667 (2001)
Assets: $180,000,000 (2002)

Typical Recipients
Arts & Humanities: Arts Associations & Councils, Ballet, Dance, Film & Video, Historic Preservation, History & Archaeology, Libraries, Museums/Galleries, Music, Opera, Public Broadcasting, Theater, Visual Arts
Civic & Public Affairs: African American Affairs, Botanical Gardens/Parks, Employment/Job Training, Civic & Public Affairs-General, Hispanic Affairs, Housing, Legal Aid, Municipalities/Towns, Philanthropic Organizations, Safety, Zoos/Aquariums
Education: Afterschool/Enrichment Programs, Arts/Humanities Education, Colleges & Universities, Education Reform, Education-General, Legal Education, Literacy, Medical Education, Private Education (Precollege), Public Education (Precollege), Science/Mathematics Education, Secondary Education (Private), Special Education, Student Aid
Environment: Environment-General
Health: AIDS/HIV, Alzheimer's Disease, Cancer, Children's Health/Hospitals, Clinics/Medical Centers, Emergency/Ambulance Services, Heart, Hospices, Hospitals, Medical Rehabilitation, Medical Research, Speech & Hearing
Religion: Churches, Religious Welfare, Social/Policy Issues
Science: Science Museums, Scientific Centers & Institutes
Social Services: Animal Protection, At-Risk Youth, Camps, Child Abuse, Family Planning, Food/Clothing Distribution, Scouts, Shelters/Homelessness, Substance Abuse, United Funds/United Ways, YMCA/YWCA/YMHA/YWHA, Youth Organizations

Application Procedures
Initial Contact: Send a letter of application on the organization's letterhead signed by the chief executive officer (e.g. president, executive) and including a statement that the chief executive officer has seen and approved the request, and endorses the request as a priority.
Application Requirements: Provide the name, title, and telephone number of the contact person; evidence from the IRS that the applicant organization is a public charity and not a private foundation, and that the donee organization is exempt from federal income taxes under section 501(c)(3) or 170(c) of the Internal Revenue Code. Als include a brief statement of the grant request, including amount requested, total funds needed for the project, and timing of the grant, including installation payments if required; purpose of funds sought and statement of need; other sources of funds received or anticipated for the project, as well as the existence of a challenge grant, including the name of the grantor; sources of funds available for project apart from grants; how project will be funded after the Foundation's funding ends; and proposed method for evaluating the project. In addition, provide, a description of organization that describes where the organization has previously or is currently operating under a name other than the name on the IRS determination letter; purpose, scope of operations, history, and affiliations (if any); a list of the trustees or directors, officers, and managers; a list of principal contributors during past years and currently, including dollar amounts of major grants; the most recent year's income and expense statement or audited financial report; a complete copy of the organization's most recent IRS Form 990; and balance sheet and budget for the coming year. If the request is for building construction, renovation, or purchase of real property, also attach an architectural rendering or drawing of the facilities to be built or renovated or a photograph of property to be acquired; a description of the property including such items as type of construction, square footage, and special features; and a cost estimate.
Deadlines: None. However, if funding is needed by a specific date, the foundation suggests that applications be submitted four to six months in advance.
Review Process: The review process may take several months.
Decision Notification: Funding decisions are communicated in writing.

Restrictions
Grants and rewards are restricted to Texas-based organizations, primarily in Houston. The foundation makes grants only to 501(c)(3) or 170(c)(1) organizations, and does not make grants to businesses, individuals, or for loans. The foundation prefers not to fund galas, testimonials, and other fundraising events; organizations that in turn provide grants to others; activities whose sole purpose is the promotion or support of a specific religion, denomination or church; purchase of uniforms, equipment, or trips for school-related organizations or amateur sports teams. Generally, the foundation will not consider applications from an organization more than once every 12 months or an organization that has received a multi-year grant from the foundation until all payments of that grant have been made.

Additional Information
Publications: Guidelines

Foundation Officials
Isaac Arnold, Jr.: vice president, trustee B 1932. CORP AFFIL director: Nuevo Energy Co.; chairman, president, director: Quintana Petroleum Corp.
Bert Louis Campbell: trustee B Tyler, TX 1939. ED University of Texas BA (1961); University of Texas JD (1970). PRIM CORP EMPL partner: Vinson & Elkins.

CORP AFFIL secretary: Quintana Minerals Corp. NONPR AFFIL member: Houston Bar Association; member: Texas Bar Association; member: American Health Lawyers Association; member: American Arbitration Association; member: American Bar Association.
Roy Henry Cullen: president, trustee B 1929. CORP AFFIL director: Quintana Petroleum Corp.
William H. Drushel, Jr.: trustee B 1938. ED University of Texas Law School (1960). PRIM CORP EMPL partner: Vinson & Elkins. CORP AFFIL secretary: Quintana Petroleum Corp.
Wilhelmina Cullen Robertson Morian: secretary-treasurer, trustee B 1923. ED Sweet Briar College. CORP AFFIL director: Quintana Petroleum Corp.
Alan M. Stewart: executive director

Grants Analysis
Disclosure Period: calendar year ending 2000
Total Grants: $14,387,749*
Number of Grants: 61
Average Grant: $148,065*
Highest Grant: $3,000,000
Lowest Grant: $17,500
Typical Range: $50,000 to $400,000
*Note: Giving excludes United Way. Average grant figure excludes three highest grants ($5,800,000).

Recent Grants
Note: Grants derived from 2000 Form 990.
General

3,000,000	Baylor College of Medicine, Houston, TX -- The Cullen Endowment
1,800,000	University of Houston System, Houston, TX -- restoration of Robertson Stadium
1,000,000	University of Houston System, Houston, TX -- for expansion and renovations
600,000	Museum of Fine Arts of Houston, Houston, TX -- for new museum building and renovation of existing one
500,000	Neighborhood Center, Houston, TX -- for capital campaign
500,000	Texas Heart Institute, Houston, TX -- for "Raising the Standard: The Texas Heart Institute Campaign"
400,000	Houston Music Hall Foundation, Houston, TX -- toward construction of new Hobby Center for the Performing Arts
400,000	Memorial Hermann Healthcare System, Houston, TX -- the capital campaign
333,333	Episcopal High School, Bellaire, TX -- for construction of a new Field House
333,333	Houston Christian High School, Houston, TX -- construction of the new high school

DAPHNE SEYBOLT CULPEPER MEMORIAL FOUNDATION

Giving Contact
Nicholas J. Nardi, Secretary & Treasurer
PO Box 206
Norwalk, CT 06852-0206
Phone: (203)762-3984

Description
Founded: 1983
EIN: 222478755
Organization Type: Private Foundation
Giving Locations: CT; FL
Grant Types: General Support, Multiyear/Continuing Support.

Donor Information
Founder: the late Daphne Seybolt Culpeper

Financial Summary

Total Giving: $964,350 (2002)
Giving Analysis: Giving for 2002 includes: foundation grants to United Way ($10,500)
Assets: $15,537,552 (2002)

Typical Recipients

Arts & Humanities: Arts Centers, Historic Preservation, History & Archaeology, Libraries, Museums/Galleries, Music, Opera, Theater
Civic & Public Affairs: Botanical Gardens/Parks, Civil Rights, Housing, Zoos/Aquariums
Education: Arts/Humanities Education, Colleges & Universities, Community & Junior Colleges, Education-General, International Education, Legal Education, Medical Education, Minority Education, Private Education (Precollege), School Volunteerism, Science/Mathematics Education, Secondary Education (Private), Special Education, Student Aid, Vocational & Technical Education
Environment: Environment-General
Health: AIDS/HIV, Cancer, Clinics/Medical Centers, Emergency/Ambulance Services, Health Organizations, Heart, Hospices, Hospitals, Medical Research, Prenatal Health Issues, Single-Disease Health Associations
International: International Relief Efforts
Religion: Churches, Religious Organizations, Religious Welfare
Science: Scientific Centers & Institutes
Social Services: Child Welfare, Community Service Organizations, Counseling, Crime Prevention, Day Care, Domestic Violence, Family Services, Food/Clothing Distribution, People with Disabilities, Recreation & Athletics, Scouts, Senior Services, Shelters/Homelessness, United Funds/United Ways, YMCA/YWCA/YMHA/YWHA, Youth Organizations

Application Procedures

Initial Contact: Send a brief letter of inquiry.
Application Requirements: Provide a description of the proposed program; proof of tax-exempt status; recently audited financial statement; detailed budget, with starting and completing dates; list of names, residences, and business addresses of governing board; and sources of other support.
Deadlines: None.

Restrictions

Does not provide fund individuals; endowments, conferences, forums, seminars, gratuities, honorariums, travel, meals and lodging; or loans.

Additional Information

Publications: Application Guidelines

Foundation Officials

Rodney S. Eielson: president
Nicholas J. Nardi: secretary, treasurer

Grants Analysis

Disclosure Period: calendar year ending 2002
Total Grants: $953,850*
Number of Grants: 283
Average Grant: $3,370
Highest Grant: $75,000
Typical Range: $1,000 to $10,000
***Note:** Giving excludes United Way.

Recent Grants

Note: Grants derived from 2002 Form 990.
General

75,000	Bethesda Hospital Foundation Inc., Boynton Beach, FL -- for Critical Care services and Emergency Services Center
65,000	Advent Lutheran Church, Boca Raton, FL -- for Mosaic and additional lighting
50,000	Florida Atlantic University, Boca Raton, FL -- for multiple myeloma cancer research
50,000	Norwalk Hospital Foundation, Norwalk, CT -- for departments of medicine and emergency medicine
35,000	AIDS Project New Haven, Inc., New Haven, CT
25,000	All Saints Catholic School, Madison Lake, MN -- for Technology Program
25,000	Bethany Covenant Church, Berlin, CT -- for Construction Program
25,000	Boca Raton Museum of Art, Boca Raton, FL -- for Educational and Visual Arts Program
25,000	Habitat for South Palm Beach, Boca Raton, FL
25,000	Norwalk Community College Foundation, Norwalk, CT -- for computer security laboratory equipment

THE FRANCES L. AND EDWIN L. CUMMINGS MEMORIAL FUND

Giving Contact

J. Andrew Lark, Co-Trustee
501 Fifth Ave., Suite 708
New York, NY 10017-6103
Phone: (212)286-1778
Fax: (212)682-9458
Note: Faxed proposals are not accepted.

Description

Founded: 1982
EIN: 136814491
Organization Type: General Purpose Foundation
Giving Locations: NY: New York including surrounding area
Grant Types: Challenge, Endowment, General Support, Professorship, Project, Seed Money.
Note: The fund also reports that it gives grants for program expansion, staff additions, and technical assistance.

Donor Information

Founder: "The fund was established by Frances L. Cummings and Edwin L. Cummings in 1982. Fran and Ed Cummings were a couple with simple tastes and generally frugal tendencies. They did not "strike it rich" through speculative ventures nor did they amass a fortune through personal business successes. It was not until 1958 that the Cummings received a sizable block of IBM stock from a wealthy, childless aunt. Despite their new-found wealth, the Cummings refrained from significantly enhancing their "middle class" ways. Indeed, like many Americans who had endured the hard times of the great Depression in the 1930s, they retained a fiscally conservative lifestyle. By their later years, the Cummings, who had no children, saw their IBM stock increase considerably in value, and decided that the bulk of their estates should be distributed for charitable purposes." The Frances L. & Edwin Cummings Memorial Fund Biennial Report 2001-2002

Financial Summary

Total Giving: $1,876,000 (fiscal year ending July 31, 2002); $2,365,700 (fiscal 2001). Note: Fiscal 2001 giving includes board designated grants ($8,000).
Assets: $34,493,934 (fiscal 2002); $41,741,286 (fiscal 2001)

Typical Recipients

Arts & Humanities: Libraries
Civic & Public Affairs: African American Affairs, Asian American Affairs, Business/Free Enterprise, Clubs, Community Foundations, Economic Development, Employment/Job Training, Gay/Lesbian Issues, Civic & Public Affairs-General, Hispanic Affairs, Housing, Law & Justice, Legal Aid, Municipalities/Towns, Nonprofit Management, Philanthropic Organizations, Public Policy, Safety, Urban & Community Affairs, Women's Affairs
Education: Afterschool/Enrichment Programs, Colleges & Universities, Education Associations, Education Reform, Elementary Education (Public), Environmental Education, Education-General, Journalism/Media Education, Literacy, Minority Education, Preschool Education, Private Education (Precollege), Public Education (Precollege), Religious Education, Secondary Education (Private), Secondary Education (Public), Social Sciences Education, Special Education, Student Aid
Environment: Environment-General
Health: AIDS/HIV, Cancer, Children's Health/Hospitals, Clinics/Medical Centers, Eyes/Blindness, Health Organizations, Home-Care Services, Hospitals, Medical Rehabilitation, Medical Research, Medical Training, Mental Health, Outpatient Health Care, Public Health
Religion: Churches, Religion-General, Ministries, Religious Organizations, Religious Welfare, Synagogues/Temples
Social Services: At-Risk Youth, Big Brothers/Big Sisters, Child Abuse, Child Welfare, Community Centers, Community Service Organizations, Counseling, Crime Prevention, Day Care, Delinquency & Criminal Rehabilitation, Domestic Violence, Emergency Relief, Family Planning, Family Services, People with Disabilities, Senior Services, Shelters/Homelessness, Social Services-General, Substance Abuse, Volunteer Services, YMCA/YWCA/YMHA/YWHA, Youth Organizations

Application Procedures

Initial Contact: The organization should submit one original and three copies of a concise statement, no longer than seven pages in length, which describes the project. Contact foundation for detailed guidelines.
Application Requirements: Attached to the letter should be a specific amount of the request and an itemized project budget including the portion(s) of the budget being requested from the Fund; population to be served, how they are selected, the number involved, and how they will benefit; specific and measurable goals of the project which the organization hopes to meet at the conclusion of the grant period and how the results will be measured; and an indication of the relevance of this program to both present objectives of the application organization and to future plans. An indication of plans to secure future funding for the program should also be included.
All applicants collate the following attachments with the original and copies of the proposal: audited financial statements; organization's operating budget; names of other foundations, corporations, and/or individuals to whom same grant request is being submitted and the respective amounts solicited; and names of other foundations, corporations, and/or individuals who have already significantly contributed to the project, and their respective amounts. Additionally, an organization must submit one copy of its IRS tax-exempt letter. Proposals should be clipped or stapled together, not permanently bound.
Deadlines: April 1 for review in June and October 1 for review in December. Early submissions are encouraged. Groups submitting early will have a greater chance of having a site visit.
Review Process: The Co-Trustees and Board of Advisors meet twice a year to consider grant requests. Once a full proposal has been received, the Co-Trustees will review the request to determine whether it will be submitted to the Board of Advisors for their consideration. If the Co-Trustees should decide to deny funding for any request without submitting it to the Board of Advisors, organizations will be notified prior to the Board meeting. The Co-Trustees have final responsibility for all grant proposal approvals and rejections.

Site visits are given high priority by the Co-Trustees of the Cummings Fund. They are, however, arranged only at the request of the Co-Trustees. The Co-Trustees will not meet with any organization until a complete grant request together with all supporting documentation has been submitted to the Fund.
Notes: The Cummings Fund will agree to consider up to two different grant requests at any given time from any one organization.

Restrictions

The Cummings Fund is legally restricted from contributing, in any manner, to the cultural arts. Further, as a matter of practice, the Fund does not approve grant requests within the following categories: general operating expenses; building, equipment, and other capital expenses; capital campaigns; legal aid programs; support to private individuals; activities which function primarily outside of the New York metropolitan area; organizations which are not tax-exempt under section 501(c)(3) of the Internal Revenue Code; organizations without audited financial statements; alcoholism and drug addiction treatment programs; camping programs; conferences; day care programs; environmental programs; moving expenses; public opinion polls, surveys, and research studies; public policy and/or advocacy groups; programs for senior citizens; soup kitchens and/or food banks; and well-endowed institutions. Also not funded are documentaries, films, and videos; private elementary and secondary schools; and scholarship programs. The Co-Trustees generally give higher priority to programs which have not received prior support from the fund.

Additional Information

The trust discourages elaborate, expensively prepared proposals. The value of the proposal lies in the quality of its ideas. Grant requests which lack sophistication will never be discarded on that basis alone. The Board of Advisors may direct $1,000 per member to charities of their choosing annually.
To enable the trust's small professional staff to actively work with grantees, the fund generally prefers to support worthwhile nonprofit groups operating in its region. The fund usually makes one-year grants, and considers up to two requests per organization at any given time.
Publications: Biennial Report; Application Guidelines
Trust(s): Bank of New York

Foundation Officials

Elizabeth Costas: administration director
J. Andrew Lark: co-trustee
Dottye Riley-Chen: secretary

Grants Analysis

Disclosure Period: fiscal year ending July 31, 2002
Total Grants: $1,876,000
Number of Grants: 58
Average Grant: $32,345
Highest Grant: $100,000
Lowest Grant: $500
Typical Range: $10,000 to $50,000

Recent Grants

Note: Grants derived from 2002 Form 990.
General

100,000	Boys & Girls Clubs of America, Atlanta, GA
100,000	Center for Educational Innovation - Public Education Association, New York, NY
100,000	Rutgers, The State University of New Jersey, Newark, NJ
100,000	Teach for America Inc., New York, NY
75,000	Bronx Preparatory Charter School, Bronx, NY
75,000	Learning Project, New York, NY
60,000	Lawyers Alliance for New York, New York, NY
50,000	American Foundation for AIDS Research, New York, NY
50,000	Children's Village Inc., New York, NY
50,000	Court Appointed Special Advocates of New Jersey Inc., Green Village, NJ

CUMMINS INC.

Company Headquarters

PO Box 3005
Columbus, IN 47202
Web: http://www.cummins.com

Company Description

Founded: 1919
Ticker: CUM
Exchange: NYSE
Former Name: Cummins Engine Co..
Revenue: US$8.438 billion (2004)
Profit: US$350 million (2004)
Employees: 24200 (2003)
Fortune Rank: 257, per FORTUNE Magazine's list of 500 Largest U.S. Corporations (2004).
SIC(s): 3519 Internal Combustion Engines Nec, 3714 Motor Vehicle Parts & Accessories, 7549 Automotive Services Nec.

Operating Locations

Cummins Engine Co. (AL--Huntsville; IN--Columbus, Seymour; IA--Lake Mills; MN--Fridley; NY--Jamestown; NC--Rocky Mount; OH--Findlay; SC--Charleston; TN--Cookeville, Memphis; TX--El Paso)

Nonmonetary Support

Type: Donated Equipment; Donated Products; Loaned Executives

Cummins Foundation

Giving Contact

Gayle Dudley Nay
Cummins Foundation
500 Jackson St.
Columbus, IN 47201
Phone: (812)377-3114
Fax: (812)377-7897
Web: http://www.cummins.com/na/pages/en/whoweare/foundation.cfm

Alternate Contact

Sheri W. Bishop
Cummins Foundation
500 Jackson Street
Columbus, IN 47201
Phone: (812)377-5000
Fax: (812)377-3334

Description

EIN: 356042373
Organization Type: Corporate Foundation
Former Name: Cummins Engine Foundation.
Giving Locations: operating locations.
Grant Types: General Support, Multiyear/Continuing Support.

Financial Summary

Total Giving: $1,369,672 (2003); $1,368,878 (2002); $3,010,805 (2001). Note: Contributes through corporate direct giving program and foundation.
Giving Analysis: Giving for 2002 includes: corporate direct giving ($143,022); 2001: corporate direct giving ($337,319); foundation ($2,665,214)
Assets: $1,740,466 (2003); $166,566 (2002); $1,724,498 (2001)
Gifts Received: $2,130,073 (2003); $729,549 (2002); $353,600 (2001). Note: Contributions were received from Cummins, Inc. In 1999, contributions were received from Fleetguard, Inc.

Typical Recipients

Arts & Humanities: Arts Appreciation, Arts Associations & Councils, Arts Festivals, Arts Funds, Arts Outreach, Community Arts, Dance, Historic Preservation, History & Archaeology, Libraries, Museums/Galleries, Music, Performing Arts, Public Broadcasting, Theater
Civic & Public Affairs: African American Affairs, Botanical Gardens/Parks, Business/Free Enterprise, Chambers of Commerce, Civil Rights, Community Foundations, Economic Development, Economic Policy, Employment/Job Training, Civic & Public Affairs-General, Hispanic Affairs, Housing, Legal Aid, Municipalities/Towns, Nonprofit Management, Philanthropic Organizations, Public Policy, Rural Affairs, Safety, Urban & Community Affairs, Women's Affairs, Zoos/Aquariums
Education: Afterschool/Enrichment Programs, Arts/Humanities Education, Business Education, Business-School Partnerships, Colleges & Universities, Community & Junior Colleges, Education Associations, Education Funds, Education Reform, Elementary Education (Private), Elementary Education (Public), Engineering/Technological Education, Education-General, International Exchange, Minority Education, Private Education (Precollege), Public Education (Precollege), Science/Mathematics Education, Student Aid
Environment: Environment-General, Resource Conservation, Wildlife Protection
Health: Children's Health/Hospitals, Eyes/Blindness, Heart, Hospices, Hospitals, Mental Health, Preventive Medicine/Wellness Organizations, Public Health, Research/Studies Institutes
International: Foreign Arts Organizations, Foreign Educational Institutions, Human Rights, International Organizations, International Peace & Security Issues, International Relations
Religion: Religious Welfare, Seminaries
Social Services: Child Welfare, Community Centers, Community Service Organizations, Counseling, Day Care, Domestic Violence, Emergency Relief, Family Planning, Family Services, Food/Clothing Distribution, Recreation & Athletics, Scouts, Senior Services, Shelters/Homelessness, Substance Abuse, United Funds/United Ways, Volunteer Services, YMCA/YWCA/YMHA/YWHA, Youth Organizations

Application Procedures

Initial Contact: Submit a preliminary proposal. Local projects outside Indiana should be sent to local plant manager; proposals from Indiana communities should be directed to the foundation.
Application Requirements: Inquiries should include a brief description of problem being addressed, what the programs aims to achieve, operating plan and cost, description of key leadership, criteria for evaluating program success, and documentation of tax-exempt status.
Deadlines: None.
Review Process: Foundation staff will respond regarding the possibility of funding.
Decision Notification: Directors meet three to four times a year; small grants are made from a discretionary budget between meetings.

Restrictions

Does not support political causes or candidates, sectarian religious activities, or individuals.

Additional Information

Cummins contributes 5% of its domestic pretax profits and 1% of its international profits for charitable activities.

Corporate Officials

Jean Blackwell: vice president, human resources
Jack Kenneth Edwards: executive president, group president power generation B Erie, PA 1944. ED

Claremont McKenna College BA (1966); Vanderbilt University MA (1972). PRIM CORP EMPL president: Cummins Engine Co. Inc.

Mark R. Gerstle: vice president, cummins business services

Thomas Linebarger: vice president, chief financial officer ED Stanford University MBA (1994); Stanford University MS (1994). PRIM CORP EMPL vice president, chief financial officer: Cummins Engine Co.

Frank J. McDonald: vice president, quality

Rick J. Mills: president, fleetguard

Theodore Matthew Solso: chairman, chief executive officer, director B Spokane, WA 1947. ED De-Pauw University (1969); Harvard University MBA (1971). PRIM CORP EMPL chairman, chief executive officer, director: Cummins Engine Co. Inc. CORP AFFIL director: Cyprus Amax Minerals Co.; director: Irwin Financial Corp.; director: BP Amoco Corp.; president: Cummins Americas Inc.

Christina M. Vujovich: vice president environmental policy

John C. Wall: vice president, chief technical office

Foundation Officials

Jean Blackwell: secretary, treasurer (see above)
Steve Chapman: director
Thomas Linebarger: director (see above)
F. Joseph Loughrey: director
Will Miller: director
Rick J. Mills: director (see above)
Tim Solso: chairman
Tracy H. Souza: president
John C. Wall: director (see above)

Grants Analysis

Disclosure Period: calendar year ending 2003
Total Grants: $1,369,672*
Typical Range: $1,000 to $15,000
***Note:** Grants list unavailable for 2003.

Recent Grants

Note: Grants derived from 2002 Form 990.
General

427,500	United Way of Bartholomew County, Columbus, IN
100,000	Columbus Child Care Center, Columbus, IN
68,751	United Way of Minneapolis, Minneapolis, MN
50,000	Heritage Fund of Bartholomew County, Columbus, IN -- toward capital endowment campaign
50,000	National Civil Rights Museum, Nashville, TN
40,000	Association Filantropica
38,189	Senior Center, Columbus, IN
28,009	United Way of Jackson County, Jackson, MI
25,000	ABC School, Columbus, IN
25,000	Wilberforce University, Wilberforce, OH -- toward the Ted Marston Scholarship Fund

CUNA MUTUAL GROUP

Company Headquarters

Madison, WI
Web: http://www.cunamutual.com

Company Description

Assets: US$3.921 billion (2001)
Employees: 6000 (2003)
SIC(s): 6311 Life Insurance, 6321 Accident & Health Insurance, 6399 Insurance Carriers Nec.

Operating Locations

CUNA Mutual Group (CA--Pomona; GA--Duluth; IA--Waverly; MI--Bingham Farms; NY--Albany; PA--Harrisburg; TX--Dallas; WA--Federal Way)

Nonmonetary Support

Type: Donated Equipment
Volunteer Programs: The company's Dollars for Doers program provides cash grants to qualifying nonprofit organizations for which employees and company board members volunteer.
Note: Nonmonetary support budget is approximately $5,000 annually.

CUNA Mutual Group Foundation, Inc.

Giving Contact

Steven Goldberg, Executive Director
CUNA Mutual Group Foundation
5910 Mineral Point Rd.
Madison, WI 53705
Phone: (608)231-7755
Fax: (608)236-7908
Web:
http://www.cunamutual.com/cmg/freeFormDetail/0,1248,888,00.html
Note: Toll free: (800)937-2644. Foundation is the point of contact for contributions in Madison or field locations.

Alternate Contact

Corporate Contributions
CUNA Mutual Life Insurance Co.
200 Heritage Way
Waverly, IA 50677
Phone: (319)483-2333
Fax: (319)352-1272
Note: Contact for requests in Waverly.

Description

EIN: 396105418
Organization Type: Corporate Foundation
Former Name: CUNA Mutual Foundation, Inc.
Giving Locations: CA: Rancho Cucamonga primary location; GA: Duluth secondary location; IA: Waverly primary location; MI: Southfield secondary location; MN: Bloomington secondary location; NY: Albany secondary location; TX: Dallas secondary location; WI: Madison primary location generally in communities where CUNA Mutual is located.
Grant Types: Capital, Emergency, Employee Matching Gifts, Matching, Multiyear/Continuing Support.
Note: The company matches employee and retiree gifts to institutions of higher learning, the Filene Research Institute, and the Credit Union Foundation.

Financial Summary

Total Giving: $771,223 (2003); $542,845 (2002); $751,691 (2001). Note: Contributes through corporate direct giving program and foundation.
Assets: $408,785 (2003); $469,326 (2002); $497,182 (2001)
Gifts Received: $662,055 (2003); $552,899 (2002); $660,000 (2001). Note: Contributions were received from CUNA Mutual Group and its companies.

Typical Recipients

Arts & Humanities: Arts Associations & Councils, Arts Centers, Arts Festivals, Arts Funds, Community Arts, Dance, Arts & Humanities-General, Historic Preservation, History & Archaeology, Libraries, Museums/Galleries, Music, Opera, Performing Arts, Public Broadcasting, Theater
Civic & Public Affairs: African American Affairs, Botanical Gardens/Parks, Business/Free Enterprise, Community Foundations, Economic Development, Employment/Job Training, Civic & Public Affairs-General, Housing, Law & Justice, Minority Business, Municipalities/Towns, Nonprofit Management, Parades/Festivals, Philanthropic Organizations, Public Policy, Safety, Urban & Community Affairs, Zoos/Aquariums
Education: Business Education, Business-School Partnerships, Colleges & Universities, Economic Education, Education Associations, Education Funds, Elementary Education (Private), Elementary Education (Public), Engineering/Technological Education, Education-General, Gifted & Talented Programs, Legal Education, Minority Education, Private Education (Precollege), Public Education (Precollege), Religious Education, Science/Mathematics Education, Secondary Education (Public), Student Aid, Vocational & Technical Education
Environment: Energy, Environment-General, Resource Conservation
Health: AIDS/HIV, Cancer, Children's Health/Hospitals, Clinics/Medical Centers, Diabetes, Emergency/Ambulance Services, Health-General, Geriatric Health, Health Policy/Cost Containment, Health Funds, Health Organizations, Hospitals, Medical Rehabilitation, Medical Research, Mental Health, Multiple Sclerosis, Nursing Services, Prenatal Health Issues, Public Health, Single-Disease Health Associations
International: International Organizations
Religion: Churches, Ministries, Religious Welfare
Social Services: At-Risk Youth, Big Brothers/Big Sisters, Camps, Child Welfare, Community Centers, Community Service Organizations, Crime Prevention, Day Care, Emergency Relief, Family Services, Food/Clothing Distribution, Homes, People with Disabilities, Recreation & Athletics, Scouts, Senior Services, Shelters/Homelessness, Social Services-General, Special Olympics, United Funds/United Ways, Veterans, YMCA/YWCA/YMHA/YWHA, Youth Organizations

Application Procedures

Initial Contact: Call to request guidelines and application.
Application Requirements: Include completed application form, list of current board of directors, most recent audited financial statement, current operating budget (and project budget, if applicable), copy of annual report, copy of IRS tax exemption letter, and any supporting material.
Deadlines: None, for funding under $5,000; requests over $5,000 must be received six weeks before the board meets to be considered for funding at the meeting; contact the foundation executive director for exact dates.
Evaluative Criteria: Program serves communities where company employees live and work or where employees are active volunteers; involves training, management assistance, and involvement by employees and not just monetary assistance; leverages funds through challenge grants, matching funds or cooperative funding from other sources; reduces duplication and provides cost-effective services; proposal benefits a large section of the community at a low per-capita cost; provides direct services rather than general operations; and demonstrates significant, measurable outcomes.
Decision Notification: Board reviews proposals three times annually, in February, May, and October.

Restrictions

The foundation will not provide grants for organizations without IRS 501(c)(3) nonprofit status; individuals; political parties, candidates, or partisan political campaigns; professional associations; religious purposes; endowment funds; the purchase of tickets or items for fundraising events; or for organizations that conflict with the company's goals, products, or policy-owners.

The foundation will generally not consider grants for travel funds, benefit tickets, or courtesy advertising; athletic activities; regional or national programs; organizations that receive a major portion of their funding from government sources; grantmaking bodies; service clubs; general operating support; capital campaigns, unless approved by the Capital Fund Raising Committee in Madison, Wisconsin; or programs that receive United Way funding. Community Cornerstone Funding is not available for secondary locations.

Additional Information

Madison, WI; Pomona, CA; and Waverly, IA are considered "primary locations" for grant consideration. The foundation has four corporate giving and volunteer strategies: Community Cornerstone Grants supporting community organizations; Focused Grants supporting a specific community challenge (the current target population is families of working poor and individuals transitioning from welfare to work); Employee Involvement Grants, which has two major programs, including Dollars for Doers providing cash grants and The Matching Gift Program; and Credit Union Movement Grants supporting charitable causes related to credit unions.
Publications: Application Guidelines; Application Form

Corporate Officials

Loretta M. Burd: chairman
Terri Fiez: manager community relations
Michael B. Kitchen: president, chief executive officer, director B Toronto, ON Canada 1945. ED Ryerson Polytechnic Institute (1968). PRIM CORP EMPL president, chief executive officer, director: CUNA Mutual Insurance Group ADD CORP EMPL president: Members Life Insurance Co.; president: CUNA Mutual Insurance Society; president: CUNA Mutual Insurance Agency; president: CUNA Mutual Investment Corp.; president: CUNA Mutual Life Insurance Co. CORP AFFIL director: CUMIS General Insurance Co.; director: CUMIS Life Insurance Co.; director: Canadian Northern Shield Insurance Co.

Foundation Officials

Larry H. Blanchard: assistant secretary, assistant treasurer
Loretta M. Burd: president, director (see above)
Janice C. Doyle: assistant secretary
Steven A. Goldberg: executive director
Michael B. Kitchen: secretary, treasurer, director (see above)
Tracy K. Lien: assistant secretary
Geoffrey McCloskey: assistant treasurer
Brian McDonnell: vice president, director
Faye A. Patzner: assistant secretary

Grants Analysis

Disclosure Period: calendar year ending 2003
Total Grants: $487,223*
Number of Grants: 179
Average Grant: $2,722
Highest Grant: $30,000
Lowest Grant: $25
Typical Range: $1,000 to $5,000
*Note: Giving excludes United Way.

Recent Grants

Note: Grants derived from 2003 Form 990.

General

271,000	United Way of Dane County, Madison, WI
112,500	Worldwide Foundation for CU
30,000	Bartels Lutheran Home, Waverly, IA
25,000	Waverly Childcare and Preschool, Waverly, IA
21,000	YMCA of Madison Inc., Madison, WI
20,000	Family Centers Inc.
18,000	American Red Cross, Washington, DC
15,150	Edgewood College, Madison, WI
15,000	Bremwood Lutheran Children's Home, Waverly, IA
15,000	CommonWealth Development

LAURA MOORE CUNNINGHAM FOUNDATION

Giving Contact

Harry L. Bettis, President
PO Box 1157
Boise, ID 83701
Phone: (208)365-2512

Description

Founded: 1964
EIN: 826008294
Organization Type: General Purpose Foundation
Giving Locations: ID
Grant Types: Capital, Endowment, General Support, Scholarship.

Donor Information

Founder: The foundation was established in 1964 by the late Laura Moore Cunningham.

Financial Summary

Total Giving: $3,283,666 (fiscal year ending August 31, 2003); $3,333,850 (fiscal 2002); $3,023,000 (fiscal 2001)
Giving Analysis: Giving for fiscal 2003 includes: foundation scholarships ($1,533,000); fiscal 2002: foundation scholarships ($1,453,000); fiscal 2001: foundation scholarships ($1,603,000)
Assets: $76,617,642 (fiscal 2003); $70,000,000 (fiscal 2002); $79,812,443 (fiscal 2001)
Gifts Received: $421,800 (fiscal 2003); $370,000 (fiscal 2002); $240,000 (fiscal 2001). Note: Contributions were received from Harry L. Bettis.

Typical Recipients

Arts & Humanities: Arts Centers, Ballet, Community Arts, Historic Preservation, Libraries, Museums/Galleries, Music, Opera, Public Broadcasting, Theater
Civic & Public Affairs: Botanical Gardens/Parks, Economic Development, Economic Policy, Civic & Public Affairs-General, Hispanic Affairs, Municipalities/Towns, Safety, Zoos/Aquariums
Education: Afterschool/Enrichment Programs, Agricultural Education, Arts/Humanities Education, Colleges & Universities, Community & Junior Colleges, Education Associations, Education Funds, Elementary Education (Private), Engineering/Technological Education, Faculty Development, Education-General, Legal Education, Literacy, Medical Education, Private Education (Precollege), Public Education (Precollege), Secondary Education (Private), Special Education, Student Aid
Environment: Environment-General, Research, Wildlife Protection
Health: Children's Health/Hospitals, Clinics/Medical Centers, Emergency/Ambulance Services, Health-General, Health Organizations, Heart, Hospices, Hospitals, Hospitals (University Affiliated), Long-Term Care, Nursing Services, Prenatal Health Issues, Preventive Medicine/Wellness Organizations, Single-Disease Health Associations
International: International Relief Efforts
Religion: Bible Study/Translation, Religious Organizations, Religious Welfare
Social Services: Animal Protection, At-Risk Youth, Child Abuse, Child Welfare, Community Centers, Community Service Organizations, Delinquency & Criminal Rehabilitation, Emergency Relief, Family Planning, Family Services, Food/Clothing Distribution, Homes, People with Disabilities, Senior Services, Shelters/Homelessness, Social Services-General, Youth Organizations

Application Procedures

Initial Contact: Contact the foundation to receive an application form.

Deadlines: February 28.
Review Process: The board considers requests at its annual meeting in the spring.

Restrictions

The foundation does not support individuals. Grants and scholarships will only be made to institutions, business students, or hospitals located in Idaho.

Additional Information

Publications: Application Form

Foundation Officials

Harry Little Bettis: president, director
Laura Bettis: secretary, treasurer
Janelle Bettis Wise: vice president

Grants Analysis

Disclosure Period: fiscal year ending August 31, 2003
Total Grants: $1,750,666*
Number of Grants: 21
Average Grant: $47,540*
Highest Grant: $799,866
Lowest Grant: $5,000
Typical Range: $20,000 to $100,000
*Note: Giving excludes scholarships. Average grant figure excludes highest grant.

Recent Grants

Note: Grants derived from 2003 Form 990.
Library-Related

25,000	Lewiston City Library, Lewiston, ID -- capital improvements
18,200	Fruitland Community Library, Fruitland, ID -- maintenance and improvement
15,000	Priest Lake Public Library, Coolin, ID -- capital improvements

General

799,866	University of Idaho, Moscow, ID -- capital campaign
280,000	Albertson College of Idaho, Caldwell, ID -- scholarships
280,000	Northwest Nazarene University, Nampa, ID -- scholarships
250,000	Idaho Public Television, Boise, ID -- local production underwriting
210,000	Boise State University, Boise, ID -- scholarships
180,000	University of Idaho, Moscow, ID -- scholarships
165,000	Idaho State University Foundation, Boise, ID -- scholarships
100,000	Peregrine Fund Inc., Boise, ID -- educational programs
100,000	Wildlife Conservation Society, Bellevue, ID -- educational programs
60,000	Brigham Young University, Rexburg, ID -- scholarships

D&B

Company Headquarters

1 Diamond Hill Rd.
Murray Hill, NJ 07974-1218
Web: http://www.dnb.com

Company Description

Founded: 1841
Ticker: DNB
Exchange: NYSE
Former Name: Dun & Bradstreet Corp. (2001).
Operating Revenue: US$1.275 billion (2002)
Employees: 6100 (2003)
SIC(s): 2731 Book Publishing, 2741 Miscellaneous Publishing, 7319 Advertising Nec, 7323 Credit Reporting Services.

Operating Locations

Dun & Bradstreet Corp. (CA--Campbell, San Diego, San Jose; CO--Aurora; FL--Cape Coral, Hollywood; IL--Carbondale; LA--New Orleans; MD--Rockville; MS--Jackson; NJ--Berkeley Heights, Florham Park, New Providence; NY--Amherst, New York; NC--Greensboro; OR--Eugene; PA--Pittsburgh; TN--Oak Ridge; UT--Salt Lake City; VA--Falls Church, Richmond)

Dun & Bradstreet Corp. Foundation, Inc.

Giving Contact

Rosanne Miller
Dun & Bradstreet Corp. Foundation
1 Diamond Hill Road
Murray Hill, NJ 07974
Phone: (908)665-8052
Fax: (908)665-5022

Alternate Contact

512 Seventh Avenue
11th Floor
New York, NY 10018
Phone: (908)665-5000

Description

EIN: 136148188
Organization Type: Corporate Foundation
Giving Locations: nationally.
Grant Types: Employee Matching Gifts, General Support.

Financial Summary

Total Giving: $946,251 (2001). Note: Contributes through foundation only.
Assets: $576,771 (2001)
Gifts Received: $550,000 (2001); $2,250,000 (2000); $1,200,000 (1999)

Typical Recipients

Arts & Humanities: Arts Associations & Councils, Arts Centers, Dance, Arts & Humanities-General, Historic Preservation, Libraries, Museums/Galleries, Performing Arts, Public Broadcasting, Theater
Civic & Public Affairs: African American Affairs, Business/Free Enterprise, Civil Rights, Clubs, Economic Development, Economic Policy, Law & Justice, Municipalities/Towns, Professional & Trade Associations, Public Policy, Urban & Community Affairs
Education: Business Education, Colleges & Universities, Community & Junior Colleges, Education Associations, Education Funds, Education-General, International Studies, Literacy, Minority Education, Student Aid
Health: AIDS/HIV, Cancer, Emergency/Ambulance Services, Health Organizations, Hospitals, Mental Health, Single-Disease Health Associations, Speech & Hearing
Religion: Religious Welfare
Science: Scientific Centers & Institutes
Social Services: At-Risk Youth, Child Welfare, Community Centers, Community Service Organizations, Family Services, Food/Clothing Distribution, People with Disabilities, Recreation & Athletics, Special Olympics, Substance Abuse, United Funds/United Ways, YMCA/YWCA/YMHA/YWHA, Youth Organizations

Application Procedures

Initial Contact: Send brief letter or proposal.
Application Requirements: Include a description of organization, amount requested, purpose of funds sought, recently audited financial statement, and copy of IRS Code Section 501(c)(3) tax-exempt status.
Deadlines: None.

Restrictions

Foundation does not make grants for dinners or special events, fraternal organizations, political or lobbying groups, religious organizations for sectarian purposes, goodwill advertising, or individuals.
Foundation will not consider organizations without an IRS 501(c)(3) tax exempt status.

Additional Information

In 1997 the foundation restructured its giving guidelines and priorities.

Corporate Officials

Allan Z. Loren: chairman, chief executive officer, director B May 03, 1938. ED Queens College BS (1960). PRIM CORP EMPL chairman, chief executive officer, director: Dun & Bradstreet Corp.

Foundation Officials

Edwin A. Bescherer, Jr.: trustee B Brooklyn, NY 1933. ED Purdue University BS (1955). NONPR AFFIL member: Financial Executives Institute.
Dennis N. Pidherny: assistant treasurer PRIM CORP EMPL assistant treasurer: Dun & Bradstreet Corp.

Grants Analysis

Disclosure Period: calendar year ending 2001
Total Grants: $604,519*
Number of Grants: 175 (approx)
Average Grant: $3,454 (approx)*
Typical Range: $500 to $5,000
*Note: Giving excludes matching gifts. Number of grants and average grant figures are approximate. A more recent grants list was unavailable.

Recent Grants

Note: Grants derived from 1996 Form 990.

General

250,000	United Way Tri-State Area, New York, NY
200,000	University of Connecticut, Stamford, CT
60,558	National Merit Scholarship Fund, Evanston, IL
60,000	Wilton Family Y, Wilton, CT
55,000	United Way, New York, NY
50,000	Norwalk Community College, Norwalk, CT
41,567	National Merit Scholarship Fund, Evanston, IL
36,000	Jackie Robinson Foundation, New York, NY
30,000	Fairfield County Commission, Norwalk, CT
30,000	Wilton Family Y, Wilton, CT

DAILY NEWS L.P.

Company Headquarters

450 W. 33rd St.
New York, NY 10001
Web: http://www.nydailynews.com

Company Description

Founded: 1919
Employees: 1,600
SIC(s): 2711 Newspapers.

Operating Locations

Daily News (CA--Woodland Hills)

Tribune New York Foundation

Giving Contact

John Campi, Vice President, Promotions
220 E. 42nd Street, 10th Floor
New York, NY 10017
Phone: (212)210-2686

Description

Founded: 1958
EIN: 136161525
Organization Type: Corporate Foundation
Former Name: Daily News Foundation.
Giving Locations: CT; NJ; NY: New York
Grant Types: General Support.
Note: Employee matching gift ratio: 2 to 1. $25 is the minimum for individual matching grants. A specified fund or particular area of support may by indicated.

Donor Information

Founder: New York News

Financial Summary

Total Giving: $396,510 (2003); $341,260 (2001)
Assets: $6,024,380 (2003); $6,413,707 (2001)

Typical Recipients

Arts & Humanities: Arts Associations & Councils, Arts Centers, Arts Funds, Arts Institutes, Arts Outreach, Ballet, Community Arts, Dance, Ethnic & Folk Arts, Film & Video, Arts & Humanities-General, Historic Preservation, Libraries, Museums/Galleries, Music, Performing Arts, Public Broadcasting, Theater, Visual Arts
Civic & Public Affairs: African American Affairs, Asian American Affairs, Botanical Gardens/Parks, Clubs, Economic Development, Employment/Job Training, Ethnic Organizations, Gay/Lesbian Issues, Civic & Public Affairs-General, Hispanic Affairs, Housing, Law & Justice, Municipalities/Towns, Public Policy, Women's Affairs, Zoos/Aquariums
Education: Afterschool/Enrichment Programs, Arts/Humanities Education, Colleges & Universities, Education Funds, Education Reform, Journalism/Media Education, Legal Education, Minority Education, Private Education (Precollege), Religious Education, School Volunteerism, Special Education, Student Aid
Environment: Resource Conservation, Wildlife Protection
Health: Cancer, Hospitals, Long-Term Care, Medical Research, Preventive Medicine/Wellness Organizations, Single-Disease Health Associations
International: Foreign Arts Organizations, Foreign Educational Institutions
Religion: Churches, Dioceses, Religion-General, Jewish Causes, Religious Organizations, Religious Welfare
Science: Science Museums, Scientific Centers & Institutes
Social Services: At-Risk Youth, Child Welfare, Community Service Organizations, Crime Prevention, Family Planning, Family Services, Food/Clothing Distribution, People with Disabilities, Recreation & Athletics, Scouts, Senior Services, Substance Abuse, United Funds/United Ways, Volunteer Services, Youth Organizations

Application Procedures

Initial Contact: Contact the foundation for an application form and guidelines.
Application Requirements: Return the application, in the exact form specified by the guidelines, accompanied by a certificate of tax-exempt status signed by an officer of the organization; the organization's most recent tax-exempt determination letter; recently audited financial statement or IRS Form 990; line-item budget for the organization for the year of the request; a line-item program budget, if applicable; a list of board members, with principal business or profes-

sional affiliations; a list of the five largest grants received from corporations and/or foundations during the same fiscal year of the audit or Form 990 included with the application, including dollar amounts; and an annual report, if available. If the proposal is for salary support, include a job description and, if available, the resume of the person who will fill the position.
Deadlines: None.
Notes: Handwritten applications are not accepted. Application materials should not be bound, nor should they be submitted on colored paper.

Restrictions
For matching grants, non-eligible parties include, university athletic associations or booster clubs, memberships, subscriptions, fees or tuition, or payment for services.

Corporate Officials
Fred Drasner: co-founder, president, chief executive officer, co-publisher, director PRIM CORP EMPL co-founder, president, chief executive officer, co-publisher, director: U.S. News & World Report.
Les Goodstein: president

Foundation Officials
Carlos Austin: secretary, director
Betty Ellen Berlamino: president, director
Catherine Davis: treasurer, assistant secretary, director
Timothy Knight: director
Steve Mulderrig: director
Bill Shaw: director

Grants Analysis
Disclosure Period: calendar year ending 2003
Total Grants: $390,000*
Number of Grants: 58
Average Grant: $6,724
Highest Grant: $15,000
Lowest Grant: $2,500
Typical Range: $2,500 to $10,000
*Note: Giving excludes matching gifts.

Recent Grants
Note: Grants derived from 2003 Form 990.
Library-Related
5,000	Brooklyn Public Library, Brooklyn, NY

General
15,000	Emma Bowen Foundation, New York, NY
15,000	International Radio and Television Society Foundation, New York, NY
15,000	Jersey City Museum, Jersey City, NJ
12,500	Steve Jacobson Fund, Wingdale, NY
10,000	City Meals on Wheels, New York, NY
10,000	Diversity Foundation, New York, NY
10,000	Futures in Education, Brooklyn, NY
10,000	John A. Reisenbach Foundation, New York, NY
10,000	Long Island Coalition of Fair Broadcasting, Garden City, NY
10,000	Museum of Television and Radio, New York, NY

DAIMLERCHRYSLER AG

Company Headquarters
Epplestrasese 225
D-70546 Stuttgart, Germany
Fax: GER 711 17-94022
Web: http://www.daimlerchrysler.com/

Company Description
Founded: 1998
Ticker: DCX
Exchange: NYSE
Formed by Merger of: Daimler-Benz AG; Chrysler Corp.

Revenue: US$156.838 billion (2002)
Employees: 362063 (2003)
SIC(s): 3700 Transportation Equipment, 6100 Non-depository Institutions, 6500 Real Estate, 6700 Holding & Other Investment Offices.

Nonmonetary Support
Type: Donated Equipment; Donated Products
Note: Nonmonetary support is principally in the form of vehicles donated to educational institutions for use in training mechanics.

DaimlerChrysler Corp. Fund

Giving Contact
Brian G. Glowiak, Vice President & Secretary
DaimlerChrysler Corp. Fund
1000 Chrysler Dr., CIMS 485-12-30
Auburn Hills, MI 48326-2766
Phone: (248)512-2500
Fax: (248)512-2503

Description
Founded: 1953
EIN: 386087371
Organization Type: Corporate Foundation
Giving Locations: headquarters and operating communities and nationally.
Grant Types: Emergency, Employee Matching Gifts, General Support, Project.
Note: Employee matching gift ratio: 2 to 1 up to $5,000 per employee annually.

Donor Information
Founder: Chrysler Corp.

Financial Summary
Total Giving: $22,115,853 (2003); $36,003,334 (2002); $21,832,877 (2001). Note: Contributes through corporate direct giving program and foundation.
Assets: $13,756,308 (2003); $31,835,812 (2002); $46,799,509 (2001)
Gifts Received: $25,000,000 (2003); $10,324,553 (2002); $255,928 (2001). Note: Contributions were received from DaimlerChrysler Corp., formerly Chrysler Corp.

Typical Recipients
Arts & Humanities: Arts Associations & Councils, Arts Centers, Arts Festivals, Arts Funds, Arts Institutes, Community Arts, Ethnic & Folk Arts, Arts & Humanities-General, Historic Preservation, History & Archaeology, Libraries, Museums/Galleries, Music, Opera, Performing Arts, Public Broadcasting, Theater
Civic & Public Affairs: African American Affairs, Business/Free Enterprise, Chambers of Commerce, Community Foundations, Economic Development, Economic Policy, Employment/Job Training, Ethnic Organizations, Civic & Public Affairs-General, Hispanic Affairs, Housing, Law & Justice, Minority Business, Municipalities/Towns, Nonprofit Management, Parades/Festivals, Professional & Trade Associations, Public Policy, Rural Affairs, Safety, Urban & Community Affairs, Women's Affairs, Zoos/Aquariums
Education: Afterschool/Enrichment Programs, Agricultural Education, Arts/Humanities Education, Business Education, Colleges & Universities, Community & Junior Colleges, Continuing Education, Economic Education, Education Associations, Education Funds, Education Reform, Engineering/Technological Education, Faculty Development, Education-General, Health & Physical Education, International Studies, Literacy, Minority Education, Private Education (Precollege), Public Education (Precollege), Science/Mathematics Education, Student Aid,

Vocational & Technical Education
Environment: Environment-General
Health: Cancer, Diabetes, Emergency/Ambulance Services, Eyes/Blindness, Health Organizations, Hospices, Hospitals, Mental Health, Speech & Hearing
International: Foreign Educational Institutions, International-General, International Development, International Relief Efforts
Religion: Jewish Causes, Religious Welfare
Science: Scientific Centers & Institutes
Social Services: Animal Protection, Child Welfare, Community Centers, Community Service Organizations, Emergency Relief, Food/Clothing Distribution, People with Disabilities, Recreation & Athletics, Scouts, Senior Services, Substance Abuse, United Funds/United Ways, Volunteer Services, YMCA/YWCA/YMHA/YWHA, Youth Organizations

Application Procedures
Initial Contact: Requests from organizations that are located in Southeastern Michigan or that are national or international in scope must be submitted using the company's on-line application tool (available at http://www.daimlerchrysler.com/company/dccfund/dccfund_e.htm). Local requests (from organizations outside of Michigan) should be submitted in writing to your local DaimlerChrysler facility.
Application Requirements: National, international, or Southeastern Michigan applicants should have the following items available prior to beginning the on-line application process: the organization's IRS determination letter, most recent annual report and a summary description or synopsis outlining the proposal. The synopsis should provide, as briefly as possible, information on the following topics: a. What issue or problem does your program or project address? b. How does this issue relate to DaimlerChrysler Corporation Fund's goals, areas of focus and criteria? c. What are the credentials or special capabilities of your organization to address this issue? d. What is the scope of your program? e. Who are the clients, audience or people served by this program? f. What is the goal or expected outcome of the program for which you seek support? g. What specifically are you requesting of DaimlerChrysler Corporation Fund? h. What is the rationale for this request and the amount requested of the Fund? i. What are the key program or deadline dates? j. How will you measure results or success of this program? k. How will you sustain this program after DaimlerChrysler Corporation Fund support ends? l. What will your organization expect of the Fund in the future?
Local requests should follow the same guidelines, but should be submitted in writing to the local DaimlerChrysler facility.
Deadlines: None.
Evaluative Criteria: Supported programs demonstrate: leadership, innovation, a model of effective change, organizational self-sufficiency, empowered people, involved employees, teamwork, continuous improvement, and results; grants are increasingly made on the initiative of the company or through competitive grants.
Notes: The fund asks that organizations review guidelines prior to submitting a formal letter. Applications are accepted online.

Restrictions
The fund does not support organizations without 501(c)(3) status; individuals; discriminatory organizations; endowment funds; conferences, seminars, trips, tours or similar events; religious organizations for religious purposes; fraternal, athletic, or social clubs; veterans or labor organizations, or similar associations; political organizations or campaigns; requests for loans or debt retirement programs; programs or projects involving the delivery of direct health care; disease-specific organizations; multi-year requests; capital campaigns; operating expenses of United Way local agencies (except through the company's support of annual United Way cam-

paigns in operating communities); fund-raising activities related to individual sponsorship; or the purchase of courtesy advertising.

No support is given to organizations that might in any way pose a conflict with Chrysler's mission, goals, programs, products or employees. Projects and organizations without connection to a major DaimlerChrysler Corp. plant community will not be considered. Neither the DaimlerChrysler Corp. Fund nor DaimlerChrysler Corp. donates vehicles for on-road use.

Additional Information

In May of 1998, Daimler-Benz of Stuttgart, Germany, and Chrysler Corp. of Auburn Hills, MI, merged to create DaimlerChrysler.
Publications: Community Involvement Guidelines

Corporate Officials

Dr. Manfred Bischoff: aerospace and industrial businesses PRIM CORP EMPL aerospace and industrial businesses: DaimlerChrysler Corp. CORP AFFIL chairman, director: EADS.

W. Frank Fountain, Jr.: senior vice president government affairs B Brewton, AL 1944. ED Hampton University BA (1966); University of Pennsylvania MBA (1973). PRIM CORP EMPL vice president government affairs: DaimlerChrysler Corp. NONPR AFFIL vice chairman: New Detroit; director: WTVS Public Television; director: Museum of African American History; director: Music Hall; vice chairman: Joint Center for Political & Economic Studies; director: Michigan Manufacturers Association; director: Hudson-Webber Foundation; vice chairman: Detroit Regional Chamber of Commerce; chairman of trustee: Hampton University; director: Dennis W. Archer Foundation; chairman: Detroit Public Schools Board of Education; member: Business Council of Alabama; director: Community Foundation of SE Michigan; director: Africare.

Arthur C. Liebler: vice president communications B Pittsburgh, PA 1942. ED Wayne State University; Marquette University AB (1964). PRIM CORP EMPL vice president communications: DaimlerChrysler Corp. NONPR AFFIL board of directors: Detroit Symphony Orchestra; director: Public Relations Society America; director: American Advertising Federation. CLUB AFFIL member: Detroit Adcraft Club; member: Detroit Golf Club.

Jurgen E. Schrempp: chairman B Stuttgart, Germany 1944. PRIM CORP EMPL chairman of management board: DaimlerChrysler. CORP AFFIL director: Sasol Ltd.; director: Vodafone Group Plc; director: Richemont SA.

Gary C. Valade: executive vice president, chief financial officer B Detroit, MI 1942. ED Michigan State University BS (1966); Michigan State University MBA (1968). PRIM CORP EMPL executive vice president finance, chief financial officer: Chrysler Corp. ADD CORP EMPL global procurement: DaimlerChrysler Corp. NONPR AFFIL chairman: Michigan Colleges Foundation; member, director: Michigan State University Eli Broad College Business Alumni Association; trustee: Adrian College; vice chairman: Interlochen Center Arts.

Foundation Officials

Doug J. Brown: assistant treasurer
Timothy P. Dykstra: vice president, treasurer
Joachim W. Eberhardt: trustee
Frank J. Ewasyshyn: trustee
W. Frank Fountain, Jr.: president (see above)
Brian G. Glowiak: vice president, secretary
Marilyn F. Graham: assistant vice president, assistant secretary
E. S. Harris: controller
Robert G. Liberatore: trustee
Nancy A. Rae: trustee
Eric R. Ridenour: trustee
Gary C. Valade: trustee (see above)

Grants Analysis

Disclosure Period: calendar year ending 2003
Total Grants: $19,829,803*
Number of Grants: 735 (approx)
Average Grant: $23,486*
Highest Grant: $1,518,332
Lowest Grant: $96
Typical Range: $1,000 to $50,000
*****Note:** Giving excludes United Way. Average grant figure excludes two highest grants ($2,614,632).

Recent Grants

Note: Grants derived from 2003 Form 990.
General

2,286,050	United Way Community Services, Detroit, MI
1,518,332	Detroit Institute of Arts, Detroit, MI
1,096,300	Detroit Renaissance Foundation, Detroit, MI
717,600	Scholarship America, St. Peter, MN
500,000	Focus: HOPE, Detroit, MI
460,000	New Detroit Inc., Detroit, MI
400,000	Automotive Youth Educational Systems, Troy, MI
400,000	Detroit Zoological Society, Royal Oak, MI
350,000	Detroit Symphony Civic Orchestra, Detroit, MI
312,000	Tom Joyner Foundation, Dallas, TX

HARRY L. DALTON FOUNDATION

Giving Contact

Elizabeth D. Brand, President, Treasurer & Director
736 Wachovia Center
Charlotte, NC 28285
Phone: (704)332-5380
Fax: (704)332-5380

Description

Founded: 1979
EIN: 566061267
Organization Type: Private Foundation
Grant Types: General Support.

Financial Summary

Total Giving: $302,217 (fiscal year ending July 31, 2004); $373,058 (fiscal 2001). Note: 1997 Giving includes United Way ($4,000).
Giving Analysis: Giving for fiscal 2004 includes: foundation grants to United Way ($6,500); fiscal 2001: foundation grants to United Way ($10,000)
Assets: $6,200,521 (fiscal 2004); $5,645,734 (fiscal 2001)
Gifts Received: $595,366 (fiscal 2004)

Typical Recipients

Arts & Humanities: Arts Associations & Councils, Community Arts, Historic Preservation, Libraries, Museums/Galleries, Music, Opera, Performing Arts, Theater
Civic & Public Affairs: Clubs, Community Foundations, Civic & Public Affairs-General, Minority Business, Zoos/Aquariums
Education: Colleges & Universities, Education-General, Private Education (Precollege)
Environment: Environment-General
Health: Cancer, Health Organizations, Hospitals
International: International Affairs, International Relief Efforts
Religion: Churches, Ministries, Religious Welfare
Social Services: Child Abuse, Child Welfare, Community Service Organizations, Day Care, Recreation & Athletics, Shelters/Homelessness, Special Olympics, Substance Abuse, United Funds/United Ways, YMCA/YWCA/YMHA/YWHA, Youth Organizations

Application Procedures

Initial Contact: Send brief letter describing program.
Deadlines: None.

Foundation Officials

Elizabeth D. Brand: president, treasurer, director
R. Alfred Brand, III: vice president, director
Deeda Coffey: secretary, director

Grants Analysis

Disclosure Period: fiscal year ending July 31, 2004
Total Grants: $295,717*
Number of Grants: 26
Average Grant: $4,915*
Highest Grant: $107,750
Lowest Grant: $500
Typical Range: $1,000 to $5,000
*****Note:** Giving excludes United Way. Average excludes two highest grants ($177,750).

Recent Grants

Note: Grants derived from 2004 Form 990.
General

107,750	Charlotte Country Day School, Charlotte, NC
70,000	Mint Museum of Art, Charlotte, NC
41,667	Agnes Scott College, Decatur, GA
33,700	Family Center, Charlotte, NC
13,000	Henry T. Herald Center for Education, Orlando, FL
6,500	United Way of Central Carolinas, Charlotte, NC
5,000	Lifespan, Charlotte, NC
5,000	North Carolina Blumenthal Performing Arts, Charlotte, NC
3,000	Lynnwood Foundation, Charlotte, NC
2,500	Opera Carolina, Charlotte, NC

ELEANOR NAYLOR DANA CHARITABLE TRUST

Giving Contact

c/o Trustees
375 Park Avenue, Suite 3807
New York, NY 10152
Phone: (212)754-2890
Fax: (212)754-2892
Note: All correspondence should be addressed to the trustees. A contact person is not listed.

Description

Founded: 1979
EIN: 132992855
Organization Type: General Purpose Foundation
Giving Locations: NY: New York including the East Coast.
Grant Types: General Support, Project, Research.

Donor Information

Founder: Established in 1979 by the late Eleanor Naylor Dana, the wife of Charles A. Dana (also deceased), an attorney and New York State legislator who founded Dana Corporation. The Danas established the Charles A. Dana Foundation in 1950.

Financial Summary

Total Giving: $3,091,088 (fiscal year ending May 31, 2003); $3,072,518 (fiscal 2002)
Assets: $9,837,509 (fiscal 2003); $9,060,633 (fiscal 2002)
Gifts Received: $4,197,096 (fiscal 2003); $4,197,096 (fiscal 2002); $4,197,096 (fiscal 2000). Note: Contributions were received from a trust established by Eleanor N. Dana.

Typical Recipients

Arts & Humanities: Arts Associations & Councils, Arts Centers, Arts Festivals, Arts Funds, Arts Institutes, Ballet, Dance, Ethnic & Folk Arts, Arts & Humanities-General, History & Archaeology, Libraries, Music, Opera, Performing Arts, Public Broadcasting, Theater

Civic & Public Affairs: Botanical Gardens/Parks, Community Foundations, Municipalities/Towns, Philanthropic Organizations

Education: Arts/Humanities Education, Business Education, Colleges & Universities, Education Associations, Elementary Education (Private), Legal Education, Medical Education, Private Education (Precollege), Public Education (Precollege), Secondary Education (Private)

Environment: Wildlife Protection

Health: AIDS/HIV, Cancer, Children's Health/Hospitals, Clinics/Medical Centers, Diabetes, Emergency/Ambulance Services, Eyes/Blindness, Health Funds, Heart, Hospitals, Hospitals (University Affiliated), Medical Research, Mental Health, Public Health, Research/Studies Institutes, Transplant Networks/Donor Banks, Trauma Treatment

International: Health Care/Hospitals, International Affairs, International Development

Religion: Churches, Jewish Causes, Religious Welfare

Science: Scientific Research

Social Services: Family Planning, People with Disabilities, Senior Services, Youth Organizations

Application Procedures

Initial Contact: Initial inquiries should be submitted as a brief letter of intent, not to exceed one thousand words. Selected applicants will be invited to submit detailed proposals.

Deadlines: February 1, May 1, September 1 and November 1.

Additional Information

In general, biomedical research grants are limited to no more than three years and must not exceed $100,000. Performing arts grants must not exceed $100,000 and must show: anticipated benefit and long-range potential as a result of grant; stature of organization; need for the grant; and financial viability.

Publications: Informational Brochure

Foundation Officials

Robert Alan Good, MD: trustee B Crosby, MN 1922. ED University of Minnesota BA (1944); University of Minnesota MB (1946); University of Minnesota PhD (1947); University of Minnesota MD (1947). NONPR AFFIL professor department pediatrics: University South Florida; member: Western Association Immunologists; member: Transplantion Society; member: Society Experimental Biology & Medicine; member: Society Pediatric Research; member: Sigma Xi; member: Reticuloendothelial Society; fellow: Royal Society Medicine; member: Practitioners Society; honorary fellow: Philippine Pediatric Society; member: Pioneer; member: Phi Beta Kappa; fellow: New York Academy Science; member: Northwest Pediatric Society; member: National Academy Sciences Institute Medicine; member: Minnesota State Medicine Association; member: National Academy Sciences; member: Minneapolis Pediatric Society; member: International Society Nephrology; member: International Society for Transplantation Biology; member: International Society Immunopharmacology; member: International Society Blood Transfusion; member: International Society Experimental Hematology; member advisory committee: International Bone Marrow Transplant Registry; member: Infectious Diseases Society America; member: International Academy Pathology; member: Harvey Society; member: Central Society Clinical Research; member: Detroit Surgical Association; member: Association American Physicians; member: American Society Microbiology; honorary member: American Society Transplant Sur-

geons; member: American Rheumatism Association; member: American Federation Clinical Research; member: American Pediatric Society; fellow: American College Allergy & Immunology; member: American Association Pathologists; member: American Clinical & Climatological Association; member: American Association Immunologists; member: American Association Anatomists; member: American Association History Medicine; fellow: American Association Advancement Science; fellow: American Academy of Arts & Sciences; fellow: American Academy Pediatrics; member: Alpha Omega Alpha; fellow: Academy Multidisciplinary Research; physician-in-chief: All Childrens Hospital; foreign advisor: Academy Medical Science.

Valerie Harper: admin
Carlos Moseley: trustee
A. J. Signorile: trustee
Stephen A. Signorile: trustee
Robert Edward Wise, MD: trustee B Pittsburgh, PA May 21, 1918. ED University of Pittsburgh BS (1941); University of Maryland MD (1943). PRIM NONPR EMPL chief executive officer, chairman board governors, radiologist: Lahey Clinic Foundation. CORP AFFIL director: Bay Saint Skills Corp. NONPR AFFIL member: Radiological Society North America; chairman: Robert E. Wise Medicine Research Education Institute; member: New England Roentgen Ray Society; member: North Suburban Chamber of Commerce; member: Massachusetts Radiological Society; corporator: New England Deaconess Hospital; member: Massachusetts Medicine Society; chairman: Lahey Clinic Foundation; trustee: Lahey Clinic Hospital; board governor: Historical Society Palm Beach County; adj staff: Cleveland Clinic Foundation; member: Eastern Radiological Society; clinical professor radiology: Boston University Medicine School; director: Boston Opera Association; director: Boston Public Library Foundation; member: American Medical Association; trustee: Boston Ballet Co.; member: American College Radiology. CLUB AFFIL Webhannet Golf Club; Kennebunk River Club; La Coquille Club; Braeburn Country Club; Atlantis Golf Club; Beach Club; Algonquin Club.

Grants Analysis

Disclosure Period: fiscal year ending May 31, 2003
Total Grants: $3,091,088
Number of Grants: 162
Average Grant: $19,081
Highest Grant: $200,000
Lowest Grant: $1,000
Typical Range: $5,000 to $50,000

Recent Grants

Note: Grants derived from 2003 Form 990.

General

200,000	Lahey Clinic Foundation, Burlington, MA -- fund for digital mammography program
100,000	Cleveland Clinic, Ft. Lauderdale, FL
100,000	David Mahoney Institute of Brain Initiatives, Palm Beach, FL
100,000	Jewish Communal Fund, New York, NY
100,000	Metropolitan Opera Association, New York, NY
100,000	New York City Opera, New York, NY
100,000	Vanguard Charitable, Southeastern, PA
80,000	University of South Florida, St. Petersburg, FL -- for study of non-nyekiabkative bone marrow stem cell transplantation in BXSB lupus mice model
77,500	University of South Florida, St. Petersburg, FL -- study on hematopoetic stem cells in tissues other than bone marrow to treat autoimmune diseases
74,000	University of South Florida, St. Petersburg, FL -- fund for non-myeloblative transplants for experimental lupus erythematosus

DANA CORP.

Company Headquarters
4500 Dorr St.
Toledo, OH 43615
Web: http://www.dana.com

Company Description
Founded: 1904
Ticker: DCN
Exchange: NYSE
Revenue: US$10.939 billion (2004)
Profit: US$82 million (2004)
Employees: 45000 (2003)
Fortune Rank: 201, per FORTUNE Magazine's list of 500 Largest U.S. Corporations (2004).

Nonmonetary Support
Type: Donated Equipment; In-kind Services; Loaned Employees; Loaned Executives
Note: Nonmonetary support is provided by the foundation and the company.

Dana Corp. Foundation

Giving Contact
Ed McNeal, Administrator
Dana Corp. Foundation
PO Box 1000
Toledo, OH 43697
Phone: (419)535-4500
Fax: (419)535-4896

Description
EIN: 346544909
Organization Type: Corporate Foundation
Giving Locations: principally near operating locations and to national organizations.
Grant Types: Award, Capital, Challenge, Emergency, General Support, Matching, Multiyear/Continuing Support.

Financial Summary
Total Giving: $2,513,661 (fiscal year ending March 31, 2004); $2,854,459 (fiscal 2003); $2,879,492 (fiscal 2001). Note: Contributes through corporate direct giving program and foundation.
Giving Analysis: Giving for fiscal 2003 includes: foundation scholarships ($14,000); foundation matching gifts ($403,677); foundation grants to United Way ($792,995); fiscal 2001: foundation scholarships ($20,000); foundation matching gifts ($409,172); foundation grants to United Way ($808,050); foundation ($1,642,270)
Assets: $4,762,609 (fiscal 2004); $6,884,701 (fiscal 2003); $10,760,175 (fiscal 2001)
Gifts Received: $50,000 (fiscal 2004); $470,000 (fiscal 2003); $3,000,000 (fiscal 2000). Note: In fiscal 2004, contributions were received from UBS. In fiscal 2003, contributions were received from Dana Corp.

Typical Recipients
Arts & Humanities: Arts Associations & Councils, Arts Centers, Arts Institutes, Ballet, Historic Preservation, Libraries, Museums/Galleries, Music, Opera, Public Broadcasting, Theater
Civic & Public Affairs: Botanical Gardens/Parks, Business/Free Enterprise, Chambers of Commerce, Civil Rights, Community Foundations, Economic Development, Civic & Public Affairs-General, Housing, Inner-City Development, Municipalities/Towns, Professional & Trade Associations, Public Policy, Urban & Community Affairs, Women's Affairs, Zoos/Aquariums
Education: Afterschool/Enrichment Programs, Agricultural Education, Business Education, Colleges & Universities, Community & Junior Colleges, Economic Education, Education Funds, Elementary Education (Private), Elementary Education (Public), Engi-

neering/Technological Education, Education-General, Health & Physical Education, Literacy, Medical Education, Minority Education, Private Education (Precollege), Public Education (Precollege), Science/Mathematics Education, Secondary Education (Public), Special Education, Student Aid, Vocational & Technical Education

Environment: Air/Water Quality, Environment-General

Health: AIDS/HIV, Alzheimer's Disease, Cancer, Clinics/Medical Centers, Emergency/Ambulance Services, Eyes/Blindness, Health Organizations, Hospices, Hospitals, Mental Health, Preventive Medicine/Wellness Organizations, Single-Disease Health Associations

Religion: Ministries, Religious Organizations, Religious Welfare

Science: Science Museums, Scientific Centers & Institutes

Social Services: Big Brothers/Big Sisters, Camps, Child Welfare, Community Centers, Community Service Organizations, Delinquency & Criminal Rehabilitation, Emergency Relief, Family Planning, Family Services, Food/Clothing Distribution, Homes, People with Disabilities, Recreation & Athletics, Scouts, Senior Services, Shelters/Homelessness, Social Services-General, Substance Abuse, United Funds/United Ways, Volunteer Services, YMCA/YWCA/YMHA/YWHA, Youth Organizations

Application Procedures

Initial Contact: Send a letter or proposal; requests from local organizations should be sent to headquarters of the nearest Dana Corp. facility.

Application Requirements: Include the overall objectives of the organization, purpose of project, an organizational chart, the most recent financial statement and tax return, and any supplemental information which would be beneficial.

Deadlines: None.

Review Process: Seven regional screening committees review requests.

Evaluative Criteria: Clear articulation of objectives and plans; incorporation of active volunteer boards, respected leadership, competent administrations and a broad base of support; demonstration of a measurable and potentially lasting impact through the projects/services provided; 501(c)3 status under the Internal Revenue Code.

Decision Notification: Board meets quarterly.

Restrictions

Foundation does not make grants to individuals, organizations that practice discrimination, religious organizations for programs exclusively denominational or sectarian in purpose, political organizations or campaigns, or United Way affiliated organizations that are applying for operating expense support.

Additional Information

In July 1998, Echlin Inc. merged with Dana Corp.

Corporate Officials

Don M. Decker: vice president corporate services PRIM CORP EMPL vice president corporate services: Dana Corp.

Bob Fesenmyer: general manager, vice president PRIM CORP EMPL general manager, vice president: Dana Corp., Spicer Driveshaft Division.

Joseph M. Magliochetti: president, chief executive officer, director B 1942. ED University of Illinois. PRIM CORP EMPL president, chief executive officer, director: Dana Corp. CORP AFFIL director: Danaven; director: Spicer SA; director: AMP Inc. NONPR AFFIL member: Equipment Manufacturers Institute; director: Motor Equipment Manufacturers Association; member: Automotive Original Equipment Manufacturers Association; member: Automotive Service Indiana Association.

John Shaner: vice president corporate relations PRIM CORP EMPL vice president corporate relations: Dana Corp.

Foundation Officials

Kathy Chang: treasurer, director
Bob Fesenmyer: director (see above)
Cheryl Kline: director
Mike Laisure: president, director
Ann Marie Riley: director
Tony Shelbourn: vice president, director
Joe Stancaxi: secretary, director

Grants Analysis

Disclosure Period: fiscal year ending March 31, 2004
Total Grants: $1,873,432*
Number of Grants: 375 (approx)
Average Grant: $4,996
Highest Grant: $50,000
Typical Range: $1,000 to $10,000
*Note: Giving excludes matching gifts, scholarships, and United Way.

Recent Grants

Note: Grants derived from 2003 Form 990.
General

55,000	United Way of Gaston County, Gastonia, NC
50,000	Central Cities Ministries, Toledo, OH
50,000	Toledo Museum of Arts, Toledo, OH
44,000	United Way of Muskegon, Muskegon, MI
35,000	Public Broadcasting of Northwest Ohio, Toledo, OH
30,000	Junior Achievement of Northwestern Ohio, Toledo, OH
27,000	United Way of McHenry County, McHenry, WI
26,500	United Way of Greater Kalamazoo, Kalamazoo, MI
25,000	Crawford County Foundation, Cuba, MO
25,000	Maumee Valley Girl Scouts, Toledo, OH

CHARLES A. DANA FOUNDATION

Giving Contact

William Safire, Chairman & Chief Executive Officer
745 Fifth Avenue, Suite 900
New York, NY 10151
Phone: (212)223-4040
Fax: (212)317-8721
E-mail: danainfo@dana.org
Web: http://www.dana.org

Description

Founded: 1950
EIN: 066036761
Organization Type: General Purpose Foundation
Giving Locations: nationally.
Grant Types: Award, Challenge, Conference/Seminar, General Support, Project, Research.

Donor Information

Founder: Established in 1950 by Charles A. Dana.

Financial Summary

Total Giving: $14,014,984 (2003); $13,023,389 (2002); $12,184,332 (2001)
Assets: $299,243,979 (2003); $270,941,414 (2002); $324,635,937 (2001)

Typical Recipients

Arts & Humanities: Arts Associations & Councils, Arts Festivals, Film & Video, History & Archaeology, Libraries, Literary Arts, Museums/Galleries, Music, Opera, Performing Arts, Public Broadcasting, Theater

Civic & Public Affairs: Municipalities/Towns, Professional & Trade Associations, Public Policy, Zoos/Aquariums

Education: Arts/Humanities Education, Colleges & Universities, Economic Education, Education Associations, Education Funds, Education Reform, Elementary Education (Private), Engineering/Technological Education, Faculty Development, Education-General, Legal Education, Literacy, Medical Education, Minority Education, Private Education (Precollege), Public Education (Precollege), School Volunteerism, Science/Mathematics Education, Social Sciences Education, Special Education, Student Aid

Environment: Environment-General, Wildlife Protection

Health: AIDS/HIV, Cancer, Children's Health/Hospitals, Clinics/Medical Centers, Emergency/Ambulance Services, Health-General, Geriatric Health, Health Policy/Cost Containment, Health Funds, Health Organizations, Heart, Hospitals, Hospitals (University Affiliated), Medical Research, Medical Training, Mental Health, Multiple Sclerosis, Public Health, Research/Studies Institutes, Single-Disease Health Associations, Speech & Hearing

International: Foreign Educational Institutions, Health Care/Hospitals

Religion: Religious Welfare

Science: Scientific Centers & Institutes, Scientific Labs, Scientific Research

Social Services: Day Care, Emergency Relief, People with Disabilities, Recreation & Athletics, Substance Abuse, Volunteer Services

Application Procedures

Initial Contact: Science and health grants are generally provided through a Request for Proposals (RFP) process and invitational programs for research grants. Requests for Proposals are generally sent to the deans of U.S. Schools of Medicine and Public Health and other invited institutions. Additional information on these programs can be found on the foundation's web site.

The foundation's Arts Education program is not currently accepting inquiries or proposals. Updates on this program and its guidelines can be obtained from the foundation's web site. The foundation's grant support of innovations in K-12 education is provided through the Dana Center for Educational Innovation (www.utdanacenter.org). All other foundation support of educational projects is generally by invitation only. Charles A. Dana Awards are by nomination only.

Deadlines: The board of directors meets in April, June, and October to consider grant proposals.

Review Process: The foundation acknowledges receipt of proposals and grants interviews with applicants after a proposal letter has passed review. Supporting materials should not be submitted until requested and should include proof of the organization's tax-exempt status.

Notes: Faxed proposals will not be accepted; however, letters of inquiry may be submitted by e-mail at the above address.

Restrictions

Requests from organizations outside the United States or organizations that conduct activities outside the United States are not considered for grants. Aside from the Dana Awards, grants are not made directly to individuals. The foundation generally declines requests to support operating funds of professional organizations. Requests for endowment and support for facilities generally are not accepted, although they are not excluded. The grantees are generally expected to share the cost of the project or raise matching funds. No grants are made for deficit reduction, capital campaigns, or individuals sabbaticals.

Additional Information

The Charles A. Dana Awards for Pioneering Achievements in Health and Education Program is suspended.

Publications: Annual Report; Quarterly Newsletter; Guidelines

Foundation Officials

Barbara D. Best: director, member relations
Edward Bleier: director
Wallace L. Cook: director
Charles A. Dana, III: director
Josephine C. Donahue: director administration
Barbara E. Gill: vice president public affairs CLUB AFFIL Union Club.
Dr. LaSalle D. Leffall, Jr.: director
Hildegarde E. Mahoney: director
Donald Baird Marron: director B Goshen, NY 1934. ED City University of New York Bernard M. Baruch College (1957). ADD CORP EMPL chairman, chief executive officer: Paine Webber Inc. CORP AFFIL co-founder: Data Resources. NONPR AFFIL director: New York City Partnership; member: President Committee Arts & Humanities; member board overseers: Memorial Sloan-Kettering Cancer Center; vice chairman board trustee: Museum Modern Art; member: Council Foreign Relations; member: Governor School & Business Alliance Task Force; director: Business Committee Arts.
Ann McLaughlin Korologos: director
Burton M. Mirsky: vice president finance
Jane Nevins: vice president, Dana Press editor
L. Guy Palmer, II: director B New York, NY.
Edward F. Rover: president, director B New York, NY 1938. ED Fordham University AB (1961); Harvard University JD (1964). PRIM CORP EMPL partner: White & Case. CORP AFFIL director: Cranshaw Corp. NONPR AFFIL director: Rumsey-Carter Foundation; director: Waterford School; member: New York State Bar Association; director: Norton Simon Art Museum; director: Harvard-Mahoney Neuroscience Institute; member: New York County Bar Association; director: EN Dana Institute; secretary: Guggenheim Museum; director: Brearley School; member: Century Association; member: American Bar Association; member: Association Bar New York City. CLUB AFFIL Scarsdale Golf Club; Harvard Club.
William L. Safire: chairman, director B New York, NY 1929. ED Syracuse University (1947-1949). PRIM CORP EMPL columnist: New York Times Co. NONPR AFFIL member: Pulitzer Prize Board; trustee: Syracuse University.
Herbert Jay Siegel: director B Philadelphia, PA 1928. ED Lehigh University BA (1950). PRIM CORP EMPL chairman, president: Chris-Craft Industries Inc. CORP AFFIL chairman: United Television.
Clark M. Whittemore, Jr.: director
Clark M. Whittemore, Jr.: director ED Harvard University AB; University of Virginia LLB. PRIM CORP EMPL attorney: Whitman & Ransom.

Grants Analysis

Disclosure Period: calendar year ending 2003
Total Grants: $14,014,984
Number of Grants: 155
Average Grant: $60,141*
Highest Grant: $3,313,366
Lowest Grant: $1,500
Typical Range: $25,000 to $100,000
*Note: Average grant figure excludes two highest grants ($4,813,366).

Recent Grants

Note: Grants derived from 2002 Form 990.

General
3,077,503	Dana Alliance for Brain Initiatives Inc., New York, NY -- for public education campaign on neuroscience research
1,500,000	Dana-Farber Cancer Institute, Boston, MA -- fund for David Mahoney Center for Neuro-oncology Immuno-defense
922,211	Yale University School of Medicine, New Haven, CT
750,000	Science Museum United Kingdom -- fund for establishing the Dana Center
500,000	Brown University, Providence, RI -- for fellowships and research in brain sciences
433,000	Cold Spring Harbor Laboratory, Cold Spring Harbor, NY -- to train doctoral scholars in biological sciences
350,000	University of Texas at Austin, Austin, TX -- grant for Dana Center for Educational Innovation
300,000	Weill Medical College of Cornell University, New York, NY -- grant for Neuroimmunology
266,667	Weill Medical College of Cornell University, New York, NY -- for fellowships in neuroscience
250,000	Arizona State University, Tempe, AZ -- fund for Immuno-defense

DANIEL FOUNDATION OF ALABAMA

Giving Contact

S. Garry Smith, Executive Director
820 Shades Creek Parkway, Suite 1200
Birmingham, AL 35209
Phone: (205)879-0902
Fax: (205)879-0906

Description

Founded: 1977
EIN: 630736444
Organization Type: General Purpose Foundation
Giving Locations: AL: southeastern states.
Grant Types: General Support.

Donor Information

Founder: The Daniel Foundation of Alabama was founded in 1977, with assets transferred from the Daniel Foundation of South Carolina. The latter was established posthumously in 1947 by Charles E. Daniel and R. Hugh Daniel. Charles E. Daniel (1895-1964) organized, and was chairman of, Daniel Construction Company. He also was a trustee of Clemson University.

Financial Summary

Total Giving: $4,344,200 (2003); $3,711,500 (2002); $3,409,000 (2001)
Giving Analysis: Giving for 2003 includes: foundation grants to United Way ($25,000); 2002: foundation grants to United Way ($25,000); 2001: foundation grants to United Way ($25,000)
Assets: $99,688,202 (2003); $82,541,745 (2002); $81,804,260 (2001)

Typical Recipients

Arts & Humanities: Arts Associations & Councils, Arts Festivals, Arts Funds, Arts Institutes, Ballet, Dance, History & Archaeology, Libraries, Museums/Galleries, Music, Opera, Theater
Civic & Public Affairs: Botanical Gardens/Parks, Business/Free Enterprise, Clubs, Community Foundations, Economic Development, Economic Policy, Civic & Public Affairs-General, Housing, Municipalities/Towns, Nonprofit Management, Safety, Urban & Community Affairs, Zoos/Aquariums
Education: Afterschool/Enrichment Programs, Arts/Humanities Education, Business Education, Colleges & Universities, Community & Junior Colleges, Economic Education, Education Associations, Education Funds, Education Reform, Elementary Education (Public), Engineering/Technological Education, Education-General, Leadership Training, Legal Education, Literacy, Medical Education, Private Education (Precollege), Public Education (Precollege), Religious Education, Science/Mathematics Education, Secondary Education (Private), Special Education, Student Aid
Environment: Environment-General, Protection, Resource Conservation, Wildlife Protection
Health: AIDS/HIV, Cancer, Children's Health/Hospitals, Clinics/Medical Centers, Eyes/Blindness, Health Funds, Health Organizations, Hospices, Hospitals, Long-Term Care, Medical Rehabilitation, Medical Research, Mental Health, Multiple Sclerosis, Preventive Medicine/Wellness Organizations, Public Health, Research/Studies Institutes, Single-Disease Health Associations
International: Health Care/Hospitals
Religion: Churches, Jewish Causes, Ministries, Religious Welfare
Science: Science Museums, Scientific Centers & Institutes
Social Services: Animal Protection, At-Risk Youth, Camps, Child Abuse, Child Welfare, Community Service Organizations, Counseling, Delinquency & Criminal Rehabilitation, Family Services, People with Disabilities, Recreation & Athletics, Scouts, Senior Services, Social Services-General, Substance Abuse, United Funds/United Ways, YMCA/YWCA/YMHA/YWHA, Youth Organizations

Application Procedures

Initial Contact: Preliminary contact should be made in writing.
Application Requirements: The letter should include a description of the proposed program, its purpose, and a breakdown of how the grant will be used. Any applicable brochures regarding the organization, as well.
Deadlines: None. Applications should be received in time for board meetings in April and October.

Restrictions

Limited to organizations located in the southeast region of U.S.

Foundation Officials

Charles W. Daniel: president CORP AFFIL director: Compass Bancshares; director: Compass Bank.
Martha Cobb Daniel: chairman
Marion Daniel Head: vice president
James F. Hughey, Jr.: director
S. Garry Smith: executive director

Grants Analysis

Disclosure Period: calendar year ending 2003
Total Grants: $4,319,200*
Number of Grants: 93
Average Grant: $41,513*
Highest Grant: $500,000
Lowest Grant: $2,000
Typical Range: $10,000 to $75,000
*Note: Giving excludes United Way. Average grant figure excludes highest grant.

Recent Grants

Note: Grants derived from 2003 Form 990.
Library-Related
50,000	Parnell Memorial Library Foundation Inc., Montevallo, AL
10,000	Daleville Public Library, Daleville, AL

General
500,000	Citadel, Charleston, SC
300,000	Children's Hospital of Alabama, Birmingham, AL
250,000	Alabama Institute for the Deaf and Blind, Birmingham, AL
250,000	Birmingham Southern College, Birmingham, AL
250,000	Birmingham Zoo Inc., Birmingham, AL
200,000	Tuskegee University, Tuskegee, AL
100,000	Alabama Ballet, Birmingham, AL
100,000	Alabama Symphonic Association, Birmingham, AL
100,000	Discovery 2000 Inc. McWane Center, Birmingham, AL
100,000	Marion Military Institute, Marion, AL

FRED HARRIS DANIELS FOUNDATION

Giving Contact
Fred Daniels, President
Fred Harris Daniels Foundation
Care of Fleet National Bank
Attn: Brian Hite
100 Front St., 19th Fl.
Worcester, MA 01608-1438
Phone: (617)434-1670

Description
Founded: 1949
EIN: 046014333
Organization Type: Private Foundation
Giving Locations: MA: Worcester
Grant Types: Capital, Emergency, Endowment, Fellowship, General Support, Multiyear/Continuing Support, Operating Expenses, Professorship, Project.

Donor Information
Founder: the late Fred H. Daniels, Riley Stoker Co.

Financial Summary
Total Giving: $522,000 (fiscal year ending October 31, 2004); $555,000 (fiscal 2001)
Giving Analysis: Giving for fiscal 2004 includes: foundation grants to United Way ($35,000); fiscal 2001: foundation grants to United Way ($5,000)
Assets: $17,707,587 (fiscal 2004); $16,555,562 (fiscal 2001)
Gifts Received: $1,725 (fiscal 1995); $2,928 (fiscal 1994)

Typical Recipients
Arts & Humanities: Ethnic & Folk Arts, Historic Preservation, History & Archaeology, Libraries, Museums/Galleries, Music, Public Broadcasting, Theater
Civic & Public Affairs: Botanical Gardens/Parks, Community Foundations, Civic & Public Affairs-General, Safety, Urban & Community Affairs
Education: Colleges & Universities, Community & Junior Colleges, Education-General, Literacy, Preschool Education, Private Education (Precollege), Public Education (Precollege), Secondary Education (Public), Student Aid, Vocational & Technical Education
Environment: Environment-General
Health: Cancer, Clinics/Medical Centers, Health Funds, Health Organizations, Hospitals, Medical Research, Nursing Services, Public Health
Science: Scientific Centers & Institutes, Scientific Labs
Social Services: Big Brothers/Big Sisters, Child Welfare, Community Service Organizations, Emergency Relief, Family Planning, Family Services, Social Services-General, United Funds/United Ways, YMCA/YWCA/YMHA/YWHA, Youth Organizations

Application Procedures
Initial Contact: Send a brief letter of inquiry.
Application Requirements: Include a description of organization, proof of tax-exempt status, amount requested and purpose of funds sought.
Deadlines: None.
Review Process: Meetings are held in March, June, September, and December to review applications.

Restrictions
Does not support individuals or provide funds for seed money or deficit financing.

Foundation Officials
Jonathan D. Blake: director
Eleanor D. Bronson-Hodge: director
Fred H. Daniels, II: director
Janet B. Daniels: director
Amy Bronson Key: director
Sarah D. Morse: director
David A. Nicholson: director
William S. Nicholson: director
William O. Pettit, Jr.: director
Meridith D. Wesby: director

Grants Analysis
Disclosure Period: fiscal year ending October 31, 2004
Total Grants: $487,000*
Number of Grants: 59
Average Grant: $8,254
Highest Grant: $40,000
Lowest Grant: $1,000
Typical Range: $5,000 to $20,000
***Note:** Giving excludes United Way.

Recent Grants
Note: Grants derived from 2004 Form 990.
Library-Related
30,000	American Antiquarian Society, Worcester, MA

General
50,000	Nichols College - Daniels Hall
40,000	Worcester Polytechnic Institute, Worcester, MA
35,000	United Way of Central Massachusetts, Worcester, MA
25,000	Bancroft School, Worcester, MA
25,000	Worcester Academy, Worcester, MA
25,000	Worcester Historical Museum, Worcester, MA
15,000	American Red Cross, Worcester, MA
15,000	VNA Care Network Inc., Worcester, MA
15,000	Worcester Vocational High School, Worcester, MA

DARBY FOUNDATION

Giving Contact
Katherine Brady, Trustee
PO Box 1410
Easton, MD 21601
Phone: (410)820-4300

Description
Founded: 1966
EIN: 136212178
Organization Type: Private Foundation
Giving Locations: northeastern United States.
Grant Types: General Support.

Donor Information
Founder: Nicholas F. Brady

Financial Summary
Total Giving: $178,500 (2003); $191,000 (2001)
Giving Analysis: Giving for 2001 includes: foundation grants to United Way ($5,000)
Assets: $2,279,583 (2003); $2,244,789 (2001)

Typical Recipients
Arts & Humanities: Arts Associations & Councils, Historic Preservation, History & Archaeology, Libraries, Museums/Galleries, Opera, Performing Arts, Theater
Civic & Public Affairs: Botanical Gardens/Parks, Clubs, Civic & Public Affairs-General, Public Policy, Safety, Zoos/Aquariums
Education: Business Education, Colleges & Universities, Education-General, Medical Education, Private Education (Precollege), Student Aid
Environment: Environment-General, Resource Conservation
Health: Clinics/Medical Centers, Diabetes, Emergency/Ambulance Services, Eyes/Blindness, Hospices, Hospitals, Medical Research, Research/Studies Institutes, Single-Disease Health Associations
International: Foreign Educational Institutions, Health Care/Hospitals, Human Rights, International Development, Missionary/Religious Activities
Religion: Churches
Social Services: Big Brothers/Big Sisters, Child Abuse, Child Welfare, Community Service Organizations, Day Care, Delinquency & Criminal Rehabilitation, Domestic Violence, Food/Clothing Distribution, Recreation & Athletics, Scouts, Senior Services, Shelters/Homelessness, Social Services-General, United Funds/United Ways, YMCA/YWCA/YMHA/YWHA, Youth Organizations

Application Procedures
Initial Contact: Send a brief letter of inquiry.
Deadlines: None.

Restrictions
Primarily supports preselected organizations.

Foundation Officials
Katherine D. Brady: trustee

Grants Analysis
Disclosure Period: calendar year ending 2003
Total Grants: $178,500
Number of Grants: 20
Average Grant: $8,925
Highest Grant: $25,000
Lowest Grant: $2,500
Typical Range: $5,000 to $10,000

Recent Grants
Note: Grants derived from 2001 Form 990.
General
25,000	Skillman Association
25,000	Vice President's House
15,000	Lyford Cay Foundation, Nassau Bahamas
10,000	C.S.W.I.
10,000	Friends of the Island Academy, NY
10,000	Iona Senior Services, Washington, DC
10,000	National Gallery of Art, Washington, DC
10,000	National Museum of Racing, Saratoga Springs, NY
10,000	National Museum of Women in the Arts, Washington, DC
10,000	Talbot Hospice Foundation, Easton, MD

HUGH AND HAZEL DARLING FOUNDATION

Giving Contact
Richard L. Stack, Trustee
520 S. Grand Ave. 7th Floor
Los Angeles, CA 90071-2645
Phone: (213)683-5200
Fax: (213)627-7795
E-mail: rstack@dhrlaw.com

Description
Founded: 1988
EIN: 956874901
Organization Type: General Purpose Foundation
Giving Locations: CA
Grant Types: Capital, Endowment, General Support, Multiyear/Continuing Support, Scholarship.

Donor Information
Founder: The foundation was established in 1988 from the estate of Hugh Darling and Hazel Darling after Mr. Darling passed away in 1986 and Mrs. Darling passed away in 1987.
Mr. Darling was a prominent lawyer in Southern California for more than 50 years. As an undergraduate, he attended the University of California at Berkeley, and he received his LL.B degree from the University of Southern California School of Law in 1927. He

opened a law office with a partner in 1928 that today is known as the law firm of Darling, Hall & Rae in Los Angeles, CA. Mr. Darling developed an expertise in aviation law and served on the board of directors for Western Airlines.

He also belonged to many civic associations, and served as the mayor of Beverly Hills in 1960-61. A former president of the Los Angeles County Bar Association, he visited law schools as a speaker and used his influence to further the support of legal education in California.

Financial Summary

Total Giving: $1,800,000 (2002); $2,003,500 (2001)
Giving Analysis: Giving for 2002 includes: foundation scholarships ($40,000); 2001: foundation scholarships ($130,000)
Assets: $28,188,565 (2002); $32,209,866 (2001)
Gifts Received: $27,000,000 (1996); $135,664 (1995); $102,000 (1994). Note: The foundation received a one time gift from the will of Thomas C. Case.

Typical Recipients

Arts & Humanities: Libraries, Public Broadcasting
Civic & Public Affairs: Civic & Public Affairs-General, Law & Justice, Legal Aid, Public Policy
Education: Afterschool/Enrichment Programs, Business Education, Colleges & Universities, Education Funds, Elementary Education (Private), Education-General, Legal Education, Private Education (Precollege), Religious Education, Science/Mathematics Education, Secondary Education (Private), Special Education, Student Aid
Health: Eyes/Blindness, Speech & Hearing
International: Foreign Educational Institutions
Religion: Religious Welfare, Seminaries
Science: Science Museums
Social Services: At-Risk Youth, Community Centers, Crime Prevention, People with Disabilities, Recreation & Athletics, Scouts, Social Services-General, YMCA/YWCA/YMHA/YWHA, Youth Organizations

Application Procedures

Initial Contact: Applicants should submit a detailed one- or two-page letter of proposal.
Application Requirements: Letters should include appropriate contact and mailing information, a description of the project, and the amount requested.
Deadlines: None.

Restrictions

Grants are limited to California educational institutions with a primary emphasis on legal education. The foundation does not make grants to individuals.

Foundation Officials

Richard L. Stack: trustee B Los Angeles, CA 1947. ED University of California, Los Angeles BA (1969); Loyola University JD (1973). PRIM CORP EMPL attorney: Darling Hall & Rae. NONPR AFFIL member: Saint Thomas More Society.

Grants Analysis

Disclosure Period: calendar year ending 2002
Total Grants: $1,760,000*
Number of Grants: 21
Average Grant: $83,810
Highest Grant: $250,000
Lowest Grant: $5,000
Typical Range: $25,000 to $200,000
***Note:** Giving excludes scholarships.

Recent Grants

Note: Grants derived from 2002 Form 990.
General

250,000	Azusa Pacific University, Azusa, CA -- funding for construction for education complex
250,000	Chapman University School of Law, Orange, CA -- toward books and publications for library
250,000	Loyola Law School, Los Angeles, CA -- toward renovation of library
200,000	Hope International University, Fullerton, CA -- assistance for construction of facilities
200,000	University of San Francisco-School of Law, San Francisco, CA -- toward renovation of facilities
200,000	University of Southern California-Law School, Los Angeles, CA -- toward library renovation
100,000	California Lutheran University, Thousand Oaks, CA -- toward construction of facilities
50,000	Optimist Youth Public Foundation, Los Angeles, CA -- funding for library construction
50,000	Pacific Research Institute, San Francisco, CA -- toward public education
35,000	Phi Alpha Delta Legal Fraternity, Los Angeles, CA -- for California award endowment

CHARLES H. DATER FOUNDATION

Giving Contact

Bruce A. Krone, Secretary & Trustee
602 Main Street, Suite 302
Cincinnati, OH 45202
Phone: (513)241-2658
Fax: (513)241-2731
E-mail: info@DaterFoundation.org
Web: http://www.daterfoundation.org

Description

Founded: 1985
EIN: 311150951
Organization Type: Private Foundation
Giving Locations: OH: Cincinnati including the greater metropolitan area
Grant Types: Capital, General Support, Multiyear/Continuing Support, Project, Scholarship, Seed Money.

Financial Summary

Total Giving: $1,724,665 (fiscal year ending August 31, 2003); $2,633,500 (fiscal 2001)
Giving Analysis: Giving for fiscal 2003 includes: foundation scholarships ($65,000); fiscal 2001: foundation scholarships ($60,000)
Assets: $41,384,146 (fiscal 2003); $51,474,475 (fiscal 2001)
Gifts Received: $17,502,704 (fiscal 1995); $3,646,578 (fiscal 1994); $78,285 (fiscal 1992). Note: In fiscal 1995, contributions were received from the Charles H. Dater Trust.

Typical Recipients

Arts & Humanities: Arts Associations & Councils, Arts Outreach, Arts & Humanities-General, Historic Preservation, History & Archaeology, Libraries, Museums/Galleries, Music, Opera, Performing Arts, Public Broadcasting, Theater
Civic & Public Affairs: Clubs, Community Foundations, Women's Affairs, Zoos/Aquariums
Education: Arts/Humanities Education, Business Education, Colleges & Universities, Education Funds, Education-General, International Studies, Literacy, Private Education (Precollege), Public Education (Precollege), Secondary Education (Public), Special Education, Student Aid
Environment: Environment-General
Health: Cancer, Children's Health/Hospitals, Hospitals, Multiple Sclerosis, Prenatal Health Issues, Public Health, Single-Disease Health Associations, Speech & Hearing

International: International Peace & Security Issues
Religion: Churches, Dioceses, Ministries, Religious Organizations, Religious Welfare, Social/Policy Issues
Science: Science Museums
Social Services: Child Abuse, Child Welfare, Community Centers, Community Service Organizations, Day Care, Delinquency & Criminal Rehabilitation, Domestic Violence, Family Services, Food/Clothing Distribution, Homes, People with Disabilities, Recreation & Athletics, Shelters/Homelessness, United Funds/United Ways, YMCA/YWCA/YMHA/YWHA, Youth Organizations

Application Procedures

Initial Contact: Return completed application form. along with proof of tax-exempt status.
Deadlines: None.

Restrictions

Focus is on the children in the greater Cincinnati, OH, area. Also does not fund individuals, capital funds, or scholarships directly to individuals.

Additional Information

Publications: Application Form

Foundation Officials

Stanley J. Frank, Jr.: treasurer, director
Bruce A. Krone: secretary, director
Dorothy G. Krone: director emeritus
John Donald Silvati: vice president, director B Cincinnati, OH 1937. ED Xavier University BSBA (1959). PRIM CORP EMPL president, manager: Merrill Lynch. NONPR AFFIL member: Institute Certified Financial Planners; member: International Association Financial Planners. CLUB AFFIL member: Kenwood Country Club.

Grants Analysis

Disclosure Period: fiscal year ending August 31, 2003
Total Grants: $1,659,665*
Number of Grants: 86
Average Grant: $16,622*
Highest Grant: $100,000
Lowest Grant: $2,892
Typical Range: $5,000 to $30,000
***Note:** Giving excludes scholarships. Average grant figure excludes three highest grants ($280,000).

Recent Grants

Note: Grants derived from 2003 Form 990.
Library-Related

80,000	Public Library of Cincinnati and Hamilton County, Cincinnati, OH -- for Westwood branch library expansion

General

100,000	Taft Museum, Cincinnati, OH -- for education room expansion/renovation
100,000	YMCA - Clippard Family Branch -- towards the campaign for the children's activity pool
65,000	Cincinnati Scholarship Foundation, Cincinnati, OH -- contribution to the new horizons scholarship fund
60,000	Emanuel Community Center Inc., Cincinnati, OH -- for outdoor playground and related security fences contiguous to center
50,000	Catholic Inner-City Schools Education Fund, Cincinnati, OH -- for accelerated math and accelerated reading programs
50,000	Children's Theatre, Cincinnati, OH -- for season sponsorship
50,000	Cincinnati Opera, Cincinnati, OH -- for education and outreach program
50,000	Greater Cincinnati Foundation Learning Links, Cincinnati, OH -- for learning links program
50,000	Starfire Council of Greater Cincinnati Inc., Cincinnati, OH -- for community service

outings for teens/young adults with disabilities

DAVENPORT-HATCH FOUNDATION

Giving Contact
Bill McKee, Contact
Care of Fleet Trust Co.
1 East Ave.
Rochester, NY 14604
Phone: (716)238-3300

Description
Founded: 1952
EIN: 166027105
Organization Type: General Purpose Foundation
Giving Locations: NY: Rochester including surrounding metropolitan area
Grant Types: Capital, Multiyear/Continuing Support, Project, Scholarship, Seed Money.

Donor Information
Founder: Established in 1952 by the late Augustus Hatch.

Financial Summary
Total Giving: $1,858,620 (fiscal year ending May 31, 2002); $2,105,376 (fiscal 2001)
Assets: $37,645,592 (fiscal 2002); $42,178,183 (fiscal 2001)
Gifts Received: $4,569 (fiscal 1992)

Typical Recipients
Arts & Humanities: Arts Festivals, Arts Outreach, Dance, Film & Video, Historic Preservation, History & Archaeology, Libraries, Museums/Galleries, Music, Opera, Performing Arts, Public Broadcasting, Theater
Civic & Public Affairs: African American Affairs, Business/Free Enterprise, Clubs, Economic Development, Employment/Job Training, Civic & Public Affairs-General, Housing, Urban & Community Affairs, Women's Affairs, Zoos/Aquariums
Education: Arts/Humanities Education, Business Education, Colleges & Universities, Community & Junior Colleges, Elementary Education (Private), Engineering/Technological Education, Education-General, Literacy, Medical Education, Private Education (Precollege), Public Education (Precollege), Science/Mathematics Education, Secondary Education (Private), Student Aid
Health: AIDS/HIV, Alzheimer's Disease, Cancer, Clinics/Medical Centers, Emergency/Ambulance Services, Health-General, Geriatric Health, Health Organizations, Heart, Home-Care Services, Hospices, Hospitals, Kidney, Long-Term Care, Medical Rehabilitation, Medical Research, Medical Training, Mental Health, Multiple Sclerosis, Nursing Services, Prenatal Health Issues, Public Health, Single-Disease Health Associations, Speech & Hearing, Trauma Treatment
International: Foreign Arts Organizations, International Peace & Security Issues
Religion: Churches, Religion-General, Jewish Causes, Religious Organizations, Religious Welfare, Synagogues/Temples
Science: Science Museums, Scientific Centers & Institutes, Scientific Research
Social Services: Camps, Child Welfare, Community Centers, Community Service Organizations, Crime Prevention, Day Care, Domestic Violence, Emergency Relief, Family Planning, Family Services, Homes, People with Disabilities, Recreation & Athletics, Scouts, Senior Services, Shelters/Homelessness, Social Services-General, Substance Abuse, United Funds/United Ways, Veterans, Volunteer Services, YMCA/YWCA/YMHA/YWHA, Youth Organizations

Application Procedures
Initial Contact: The foundation has no formal grant procedure or grant application form.
Deadlines: None.

Restrictions
The foundation does not make grants to individuals.

Foundation Officials
Robert J. Brinkman: director B 1944. ED University of Denver BA (1967). PRIM CORP EMPL president: Albert Gates Inc.
William L. Ely: director B 1940. ED Syracuse University BS (1962). PRIM CORP EMPL president, treasurer, secretary: Samuel Sloan & Co. Inc. ADD CORP EMPL president: Heyer Metro Distributors Inc.; president: Metro Associates. CORP AFFIL officer: Saint Augustine Road Corp.
Helen H. Heller: secretary, treasurer, director
A. Thomas Hildebrandt: director
Austin E. Hildebrandt: president, director
Mary Hildebrandt: director
Lindsey Knoble: director
John Ross: director
David H. Taylor: vice president, director B 1944. PRIM CORP EMPL president, treasurer, director: Hart Taylor Lincoln Mercury.
Douglas F. Taylor: director PRIM CORP EMPL vice president, secretary, director: Hart Taylor Lincoln Mercury.
Shirley Warren: director

Grants Analysis
Disclosure Period: fiscal year ending May 31, 2002
Total Grants: $1,803,620*
Number of Grants: 50
Average Grant: $36,072
Highest Grant: $200,000
Lowest Grant: $1,000
Typical Range: $10,000 to $75,000
*Note: Giving excludes United Way.

Recent Grants
Note: Grants derived from 2002 Form 990.
General

200,000	Eastman School of Music, Rochester, NY -- for capital
125,000	Hillside Children's Center, Rochester, NY -- for capital
100,000	Al Sigl Center, Rochester, NY -- for the Respite Home Campaign
100,000	American Red Cross, New York, NY -- for New York City Relief Fund
100,000	Lakeside Health System, Brockport, NY -- building for next generation
100,000	Nazareth College, Rochester, NY -- for capital
100,000	RIT -- for new field house and activities center
100,000	University of Rochester, Rochester, NY -- for Resource Center
75,000	Otetiana Council -- for Camp Pioneer facilities
70,000	Geva Theater, Rochester, NY -- to refurbish main stage area

DAVENPORT TRUST FUND

Giving Contact
Richard E. Jackson, Trustee
65 Front St.
Bath, ME 04530
Phone: (207)443-3431

Description
Founded: 1927
EIN: 016009246
Organization Type: Private Foundation

Giving Locations: ME: Bath
Grant Types: General Support, Loan, Scholarship.

Donor Information
Founder: the late George P. Davenport

Financial Summary
Total Giving: $328,133 (2003); $319,060 (2001). Note: Giving includes scholarships ($125,000).
Giving Analysis: Giving for 2003 includes: foundation scholarships ($170,000); 2001: foundation scholarships ($140,000)
Assets: $6,595,495 (2003); $6,721,170 (2001)
Gifts Received: $2,515 (2003); $126,185 (2001); $500 (2000). Note: In 2001, contributions were received from Ruby G. Beggs Charitable Remainder Unitrust. In 1993, contributions were received from the Maine Woman's Christian Temperance Union ($3,000).

Typical Recipients
Arts & Humanities: Libraries, Public Broadcasting
Civic & Public Affairs: Clubs, Civic & Public Affairs-General, Municipalities/Towns, Urban & Community Affairs, Women's Affairs
Education: Arts/Humanities Education, Colleges & Universities, Engineering/Technological Education, Education-General, Literacy, Medical Education, Public Education (Precollege), Special Education, Student Aid, Vocational & Technical Education
Health: Clinics/Medical Centers, Health Organizations, Hospitals, Medical Rehabilitation, Mental Health, Public Health
Religion: Churches, Religion-General, Religious Organizations, Religious Welfare
Social Services: Animal Protection, At-Risk Youth, Big Brothers/Big Sisters, Child Welfare, Emergency Relief, Food/Clothing Distribution, People with Disabilities, YMCA/YWCA/YMHA/YWHA, Youth Organizations

Application Procedures
Initial Contact: Application form required for scholarships. For non-scholarship grants send a brief letter of inquiry.
Application Requirements: Include amount requested, purpose of funds sought, and a budget and financial statements.
Deadlines: None.

Additional Information
Provides undergraduate scholarships to local students.
Publications: Application Form

Foundation Officials
J. Franklin Howe: trustee
Richard E. Jackson: trustee
Barry M. Sturgeon: trustee

Grants Analysis
Disclosure Period: calendar year ending 2003
Total Grants: $158,133*
Number of Grants: 34
Average Grant: $4,651
Highest Grant: $27,000
Lowest Grant: $250
Typical Range: $1,000 to $10,000
*Note: Giving excludes scholarships.

Recent Grants
Note: Grants derived from 2001 Form 990.
General

25,000	Merrymeeting Center for Child Development
24,000	Elmhurst, Inc., Bath, ME
18,090	City Bath, Bath, ME
15,000	Small Point Baptist Church, Small Point, ME
10,100	Bath Area Family YMCA, Bath, ME
10,000	American Red Cross
10,000	Midcoast Hospital, Inc., Brunswick, ME

9,000	University of Southern Maine, Portland, ME
7,000	Catholic Charities of Maine, Portland, ME
6,000	Colby-Sawyer College, New London, NY

EDWARD H. DAVIES BENEVOLENT FUND

Giving Contact
John D. Duncan, Trustee
c/o Verrill and Dana
1 Portland Sq.
PO Box 586
Portland, ME 04112-0586
Phone: (207)774-4000

Description
Founded: 1992
EIN: 010473137
Organization Type: Private Foundation
Giving Locations: ME: Portland
Grant Types: General Support.

Financial Summary
Total Giving: $88,500 (2003); $145,410 (2001)
Giving Analysis: Giving for 2003 includes: foundation grants to United Way ($30,000) 2001: foundation grants to United Way ($58,000)
Assets: $2,048,345 (2003); $2,270,042 (2001)

Typical Recipients
Arts & Humanities: Ballet, Arts & Humanities-General, Historic Preservation, History & Archaeology, Libraries, Museums/Galleries, Music, Performing Arts, Theater
Civic & Public Affairs: African American Affairs, Civic & Public Affairs-General, Housing, Urban & Community Affairs, Women's Affairs, Zoos/Aquariums
Education: Arts/Humanities Education, Business Education, Colleges & Universities, Leadership Training, Student Aid
Environment: Environment-General, Resource Conservation
Health: AIDS/HIV, Cancer, Clinics/Medical Centers, Emergency/Ambulance Services, Hospices
Religion: Churches, Religious Welfare
Social Services: Camps, Child Welfare, Community Centers, Community Service Organizations, Counseling, Emergency Relief, Family Services, Food/Clothing Distribution, People with Disabilities, Substance Abuse, United Funds/United Ways, YMCA/YWCA/YMHA/YWHA, Youth Organizations

Application Procedures
Initial Contact: Send a written proposal.
Application Requirements: Include general information about the program or project, financial information, and proof of tax-exempt status.
Decision Notification: Decisions are made in early December.

Restrictions
Contributionss are awarded to IRS approved tax-exempt organizations engaged in charitable activities, in the Portland, ME area.

Foundation Officials
John D. Duncan, Esq.: trustee
Alden Sawyer, Jr.: trustee
Frederic Thompson: trustee

Grants Analysis
Disclosure Period: calendar year ending 2003
Total Grants: $58,500*
Number of Grants: 28
Average Grant: $2,089
Highest Grant: $4,500
Lowest Grant: $1,000
Typical Range: $1,000 to $3,000
*Note: Giving excludes United Way.

Recent Grants
Note: Grants derived from 2003 Form 990.
General

30,000	United Way of Greater Portland, Portland, ME
4,500	American Red Cross
3,000	Children's Museum of Maine, Portland, ME
3,000	English as 2nd Language Scholarship Fund
3,000	Greater Portland Landmarks, Portland, ME
3,000	Oxford House Fellowship of Maine, Portland, ME
2,500	Cumberland County YMCA, Portland, ME
2,500	Portland Museum of Art, Portland, ME
2,500	Portland Trails, Portland, ME
2,000	AIDS Lodging House, Portland, ME

EDWIN W. AND CATHERINE M. DAVIS FOUNDATION

Giving Contact
Bette D. Moorman, President & Director
30 E. 7th St., Suite 2000
St. Paul, MN 55101
Phone: (651)228-0935

Description
Founded: 1956
EIN: 416012064
Organization Type: Family Foundation
Giving Locations: nationally.
Grant Types: Fellowship, General Support, Operating Expenses, Project, Research, Scholarship.

Donor Information
Founder: Edwin Weyerhaeuser Davis, members of the Davis family

Financial Summary
Total Giving: $799,950 (2003)
Giving Analysis: Giving for 2003 includes: foundation grants to United Way ($10,000); foundation scholarships ($152,000)
Assets: $18,788,558 (2003)
Gifts Received: $191,348 (2000); $67,944 (1999); $84,733 (1998). Note: In 2000, contributions were received from 1993 Irrevocable Trust of M. E. Davis ($81,348) and the Estate Trust of Anne O'C Davis ($110,000). In 1998 and 1999, contributions were received from 1993 Irrevocable Trust of M. E. Davis.

Typical Recipients
Arts & Humanities: Arts Associations & Councils, Arts Centers, Arts Outreach, Historic Preservation, History & Archaeology, Libraries, Museums/Galleries, Music, Opera, Public Broadcasting, Theater
Civic & Public Affairs: Asian American Affairs, Botanical Gardens/Parks, Business/Free Enterprise, Civil Rights, Community Foundations, Civic & Public Affairs-General, Housing, Nonprofit Management, Philanthropic Organizations, Public Policy, Safety, Zoos/Aquariums
Education: Colleges & Universities, Education Reform, Elementary Education (Public), Education-General, International Studies, Medical Education, Minority Education, Private Education (Precollege), Religious Education, Social Sciences Education, Student Aid
Environment: Environment-General, Resource Conservation, Wildlife Protection
Health: AIDS/HIV, Cancer, Children's Health/Hospitals, Clinics/Medical Centers, Emergency/Ambulance Services, Eyes/Blindness, Health-General, Health Policy/Cost Containment, Health Funds, Health Organizations, Hospitals, Medical Rehabilitation, Medical Research, Mental Health, Nursing Services, Research/Studies Institutes, Single-Disease Health Associations
International: Health Care/Hospitals, Human Rights, International Environmental Issues, International Peace & Security Issues, International Relations, International Relief Efforts
Religion: Churches
Science: Science Museums
Social Services: Animal Protection, Camps, Child Welfare, Community Service Organizations, Day Care, Emergency Relief, Family Planning, Family Services, Recreation & Athletics, Refugee Assistance, Social Services-General, United Funds/United Ways, YMCA/YWCA/YMHA/YWHA, Youth Organizations

Application Procedures
Initial Contact: Send a brief letter of inquiry.
Application Requirements: Include proof of tax-exempt status.
Deadlines: None.

Restrictions
The foundation does not make grants to individuals, although it may support scholarships, fellowships, and research programs of established organizations. The foundation generally does not make grants for capital purposes, building and equipment, endowment, or loans. The foundation also prefers not to make long-term commitments in order to preserve flexibility for changing social conditions.

Additional Information
The Davis family is related to the Weyerhaeuser family, who founded the Weyerhaeuser Company.
Publications: Report on Programs; Policies and Procedures

Foundation Officials
Frederick W. Davis, II: secretary, director
Mary E. Davis: vice president, director
Richard T. Holm: assistant treasurer
Bette D. Moorman: president, director CORP AFFIL director: NCR Corp.

Grants Analysis
Disclosure Period: calendar year ending 2003
Total Grants: $637,950*
Number of Grants: 50
Average Grant: $9,673*
Highest Grant: $163,650
Lowest Grant: $1,000
Typical Range: $1,000 to $20,000
*Note: Giving excludes scholarships; United Way. Average grant figure excludes highest grant.

Recent Grants
Note: Grants derived from 2001 Form 990.
Library-Related

50,000	Friends of the St. Paul Public Library, St. Paul, MN -- for Albert J. Moorman Fund

General

108,000	University of California Los Angeles Foundation, Los Angeles, CA -- for nursing program
76,362	Fulfillment Fund, Los Angeles, CA -- children's program
75,000	National Tropical Botanical Garden, Lawai, HI -- for capital campaign
30,000	National Medical Fellowships, New York, NY -- for scholarships
25,000	Population Action International, Washington, DC -- for operating support

25,000	Teach for America, Oakland, CA -- for operating support
25,000	Yale University, New Haven, CT -- for the School of Forestry and Environmental Studies
23,000	International Rescue Committee, New York, NY -- for operating support and relief work in Afghanistan
20,000	Children's Health Council, Palo Alto, CA -- scholarship
20,000	Doctors Without Borders, New York, NY -- for operating support

EVELYN Y. DAVIS FOUNDATION

Giving Contact
Evelyn Y. Davis, Trustee
Watergate Office Building
2600 Virginia Ave., NW, Suite 215
Washington, DC 20037-1905
Phone: (202)737-7755

Description
Founded: 1989
EIN: 521632305
Organization Type: Private Foundation
Grant Types: General Support.

Financial Summary
Total Giving: $105,000 (2003); $137,002 (2001)
Assets: $2,246,964 (2003); $1,772,040 (2001)
Gifts Received: $300,000 (2003); $300,000 (2001); $300,000 (2000). Note: In 2000, 2001, and 2003, contributions were received from Evelyn Y. Davis. In 1993, contributions were received from Evelyn Y. Davis.

Typical Recipients
Arts & Humanities: Arts Associations & Councils, Arts Centers, Arts Institutes, Libraries, Museums/Galleries, Music, Performing Arts
Civic & Public Affairs: Botanical Gardens/Parks, Civic & Public Affairs-General
Education: Colleges & Universities, Journalism/Media Education, Student Aid
Health: Cancer, Hospitals
Social Services: Community Service Organizations, People with Disabilities, Senior Services

Application Procedures
Initial Contact: Application should be in writing describing the organization requesting funds and the purpose of funds sought. The application should be signed by the executive director or president of the organization.
Deadlines: November 15.

Restrictions
Special emphasis is placed on activities in journalism and business.

Foundation Officials
Evelyn Y. Davis: trustee

Grants Analysis
Disclosure Period: calendar year ending 2003
Total Grants: $105,000
Number of Grants: 4
Highest Grant: $48,000
Lowest Grant: $2,000

Recent Grants
Note: Grants derived from 2003 Form 990.
General

50,000	University of Miami, Coral Gables, FL
48,000	Northwestern Memorial Hospital, Chicago, IL
5,000	Carnegie Hall, New York, NY
2,000	American Democracy Foundation, Washington, DC

IRENE E. AND GEORGE A. DAVIS FOUNDATION

Giving Contact
Mary E. Walachy, Executive Director
One Monarch Place, Suite 1450
Springfield, MA 01144
Phone: (413)734-8336
Fax: (413)734-7845
E-mail: info@davisfdn.org
Web: http://www.davisfdn.org

Description
Founded: 1970
EIN: 237102734
Organization Type: General Purpose Foundation
Giving Locations: MA
Grant Types: Award, Challenge, General Support, Matching, Multiyear/Continuing Support, Scholarship.

Donor Information
Founder: Established in 1970 by the late Irene E. Davis and George A. Davis, and was incorporated under the laws of the Commonwealth of Massachusetts in 1972.

Financial Summary
Total Giving: $4,840,840 (2003); $4,689,902 (2002)
Assets: $68,692,395 (2003); $63,529,950 (2002)
Gifts Received: $58,619 (2003); $2,002,720 (2000); $4,006,314 (1998). Note: In 2003, contributions were received from Mary E. Davis Charitable Lead Unitrust. In 1998 and 2000, contributions were received from American Saw and Manufacturing Co.

Typical Recipients
Arts & Humanities: Arts Associations & Councils, Arts Festivals, Arts Funds, Historic Preservation, History & Archaeology, Libraries, Museums/Galleries, Performing Arts, Public Broadcasting
Civic & Public Affairs: African American Affairs, Asian American Affairs, Business/Free Enterprise, Clubs, Community Foundations, Economic Development, Employment/Job Training, Civic & Public Affairs-General, Housing, Native American Affairs, Nonprofit Management, Public Policy, Urban & Community Affairs, Women's Affairs, Zoos/Aquariums
Education: Arts/Humanities Education, Business Education, Colleges & Universities, Education Associations, Education Funds, Education Reform, Elementary Education (Public), Education-General, International Exchange, International Studies, Minority Education, Private Education (Precollege), Public Education (Precollege), School Volunteerism, Science/Mathematics Education, Secondary Education (Private), Secondary Education (Public), Special Education, Student Aid, Vocational & Technical Education
Environment: Environment-General, Wildlife Protection
Health: AIDS/HIV, Children's Health/Hospitals, Clinics/Medical Centers, Emergency/Ambulance Services, Geriatric Health, Health Organizations, Hospitals, Mental Health, Nursing Services, Prenatal Health Issues, Public Health, Research/Studies Institutes, Single-Disease Health Associations
International: Foreign Arts Organizations, Foreign Educational Institutions, Health Care/Hospitals, International Affairs
Religion: Churches, Dioceses, Religion-General, Jewish Causes, Missionary Activities (Domestic), Religious Welfare
Social Services: Animal Protection, At-Risk Youth, Big Brothers/Big Sisters, Child Welfare, Community Centers, Community Service Organizations, Domestic Violence, Family Services, Food/Clothing Distribution, People with Disabilities, Recreation & Athletics, Scouts, Social Services-General, United Funds/United Ways, Volunteer Services, YMCA/YWCA/YMHA/YWHA, Youth Organizations

Application Procedures
Initial Contact: Send letter of intent or call to request an application.
Application Requirements: Initial letter should outline the purpose, scope, estimated cost, and method of evaluation of specific goals. The organization will be notified if the foundation would like to review a full proposal. If requested, the original proposal (and two copies) should be submitted, unbound, and must include a complete application form; a copy of the most recent letter of exemption under Section 501(c)(3) of the IRS Code; a copy of a form or letter classifying the applicant under Section 509(a) of the IRS Code; an affirmation letter on separate letterhead of the organization, signed by a responsible officer, director, trustee, or chief executive officer, that the IRS determination has not been revoked and that the present operation and sources of support are not inconsistent with the organization's continuing classification as set forth in the determination letter; one copy of the latest audited statement; the project budget; a list of sources of funding; three bids if the funding is for a construction project; a statement that the grant request is executed by a person authorized to submit on behalf of the organization; the names and affiliation of board members responsible for project management; and the name and qualifications of the proposed grant administrator. All proposals should include a description of the measurable program objectives to be achieved.
Deadlines: Complete proposals must be received no later than February 1, May 1, August 1, or November 1 for review at the next regularly scheduled meeting. Scholarship application deadline is March 31.
Review Process: The trustees meet quarterly (March, June, September, December) to review proposals. Applicants will be notified in writing of the action taken by the foundation, usually within two weeks of the board meeting.

Restrictions
The foundation's guidelines usually preclude support for individuals, endowments, scholarships, internships, continuing support of current programs, debt reduction, multiple proposals per year from the same organization, other private foundations, and program-related loans. Limited to the Hamden County, Massachusetts area.

Additional Information
The foundation encourages collaborative proposals involving multiple providers.

Foundation Officials
John H. Davis: trustee B 1949. ED Nichols College (1972). PRIM CORP EMPL president, treasurer, director: America Saw & Manufacturing Co.
Stephen A. Davis: trustee B 1957. PRIM CORP EMPL president: America Saw & Manufacturing Co.
Mary E. Walacky: executive director

Grants Analysis
Disclosure Period: calendar year ending 2003
Total Grants: $4,840,840
Number of Grants: 213
Average Grant: $22,727
Highest Grant: $250,000
Lowest Grant: $75
Typical Range: $5,000 to $50,000

Recent Grants
Note: Grants derived from 2002 Form 990.

General

250,000	YMCA Of Greater Springfield, Inc., Springfield, MA
250,000	YWCA of Western Massachusetts, Springfield, MA
200,000	Bay Path College, Longmeadow, MA
200,000	Roman Catholic Diocese of Springfield, Springfield, MA
100,000	Baystate Health Systems (Baystate Health Foundation Inc.), Springfield, MA
100,000	Boston College, Chestnut Hill, MA
100,000	Holyoke Hospital (Valley Health Systems, Inc), Holyoke, MA
100,000	Springfield College, Springfield, MA
90,000	Community United Way of Pioneer Valley, Springfield, MA
80,000	Spirit Of Springfield, Springfield, MA

JAMES A. AND JULIET L. DAVIS FOUNDATION

Giving Contact

Merl F. Sellers, President
1 Compound Drive
Hutchinson, KS 67502
Phone: (620)662-8331

Description

Founded: 1954
EIN: 486105748
Organization Type: Private Foundation
Giving Locations: KS: Hutchinson including metropolitan area
Grant Types: General Support, Scholarship.

Financial Summary

Total Giving: $188,854 (2003); $244,965 (2001)
Giving Analysis: Giving for 2003 includes: foundation gifts to individuals ($16,000); foundation scholarships ($73,339); 2001: foundation gifts to individuals ($16,000); foundation scholarships ($71,100)
Assets: $4,437,446 (2003); $4,676,348 (2001)

Typical Recipients

Arts & Humanities: Arts Associations & Councils, Community Arts, History & Archaeology, Libraries, Museums/Galleries, Music, Public Broadcasting, Theater
Civic & Public Affairs: Clubs, Community Foundations, Employment/Job Training, Civic & Public Affairs-General, Housing, Zoos/Aquariums
Education: Afterschool/Enrichment Programs, Colleges & Universities, Community & Junior Colleges, Education Funds, Literacy, Preschool Education, Private Education (Precollege), Public Education (Precollege), Science/Mathematics Education, Student Aid
Environment: Energy, Environment-General
Health: Clinics/Medical Centers, Emergency/ Ambulance Services, Health-General, Hospices, Mental Health, Single-Disease Health Associations
Religion: Churches, Dioceses, Ministries, Religious Organizations, Religious Welfare
Social Services: Big Brothers/Big Sisters, Child Welfare, Community Service Organizations, Day Care, Emergency Relief, Family Planning, Food/Clothing Distribution, People with Disabilities, Scouts, Shelters/Homelessness, United Funds/United Ways, YMCA/YWCA/YMHA/YWHA, Youth Organizations

Application Procedures

Initial Contact: The foundation has no formal grant application procedure or application form.
Deadlines: March 15.

Additional Information

Provides scholarships to students graduating from Hutchinson High School.

Foundation Officials

William Y. Chalfant: secretary, treasurer
Ray E. Dillon, III: trustee
R. A. Edwards: trustee
Allen K. Fee: trustee
Kent Longenecker: vice president
Merl F. Sellers: president
V. Carol Winkley: assistant secretary, assistant treasurer

Grants Analysis

Disclosure Period: calendar year ending 2003
Total Grants: $99,515*
Number of Grants: 37
Average Grant: $1,875*
Highest Grant: $32,000
Lowest Grant: $150
Typical Range: $500 to $5,000
***Note:** Giving excludes gifts to individuals; scholarships. Average grant figure excludes highest grant.

Recent Grants

Note: Grants derived from 2001 Form 990.
General

50,000	Reno County Historical Society, Hutchinson, KS -- for Salt Museum and supplies for children's place
25,000	New Beginnings Homeless Shelter, Hutchinson, KS -- for operations and public building fund
25,000	Salvation Army, Hutchinson, KS -- for public building fund
8,000	Boys and Girls Club of Hutchinson, Hutchinson, KS
8,000	Hutchinson Community College, Hutchinson, KS -- for scholarships
5,500	Training and Evaluation Center of Hutchinson, Inc., Hutchinson, KS -- for public unrestricted
3,000	Hutchinson Community Foundation, Hutchinson, KS -- living land foundation
2,500	Interfaith Housing Services, Hutchinson, KS
2,000	New Beginnings Homeless Shelter, Hutchinson, KS -- for operations and public building fund
2,000	Reno County Historical Society, Hutchinson, KS -- for Salt Museum and supplies for children's place

JOE C. DAVIS FOUNDATION

Giving Contact

William R. Deloache, Trustee
28 White Bridge Road, Suite 210
Nashville, TN 37205
Phone: (615)352-2080
Fax: (615)463-2763

Alternate Contact

Shannon Barton, Program Officer
4343 Sneed Road
Nashville, TN 37215
Phone: (615)292-1249
E-mail: bartonshan@home.com

Description

Founded: 1976
EIN: 626125481
Organization Type: General Purpose Foundation
Giving Locations: TN: Nashville including metropolitan area
Grant Types: Capital, Challenge, Loan, Matching, Project, Research, Scholarship, Seed Money.

Donor Information

Founder: The foundation was established in 1976 by the late Joe C. Davis.

Financial Summary

Total Giving: $4,189,150 (fiscal year ending September 30, 2003); $4,042,770 (fiscal 2002)
Giving Analysis: Giving for fiscal 2003 includes: foundation scholarships ($558,000); fiscal 2002: foundation scholarships ($298,000)
Assets: $87,169,734 (fiscal 2003); $76,992,110 (fiscal 2002)
Gifts Received: $34,999 (fiscal 2003); $69,999 (fiscal 2002); $70,038 (fiscal 1999). Note: In 2003, contributions were received from the JCD Lead Trust fbo MPD. In fiscal 2002, contributions were received from the JCD Lead Trust fbo JCD ($26,250) and the JCD Lead Trust fbo MPD ($43,749).

Typical Recipients

Arts & Humanities: Libraries, Performing Arts
Civic & Public Affairs: Botanical Gardens/Parks, Clubs, Community Foundations, Economic Development, Civic & Public Affairs-General, Housing, Legal Aid, Municipalities/Towns, Nonprofit Management, Philanthropic Organizations, Public Policy, Urban & Community Affairs
Education: Afterschool/Enrichment Programs, Arts/ Humanities Education, Business Education, Colleges & Universities, Continuing Education, Education Funds, Education Reform, Education-General, Legal Education, Medical Education, Preschool Education, Private Education (Precollege), Public Education (Precollege), Student Aid
Health: Alzheimer's Disease, Cancer, Children's Health/Hospitals, Clinics/Medical Centers, Diabetes, Eyes/Blindness, Health Policy/Cost Containment, Health Organizations, Hospices, Hospitals, Hospitals (University Affiliated), Medical Research, Public Health, Speech & Hearing
Religion: Churches, Ministries, Religious Organizations, Religious Welfare
Social Services: At-Risk Youth, Big Brothers/Big Sisters, Camps, Child Welfare, Community Centers, Community Service Organizations, Counseling, Crime Prevention, Day Care, Family Services, Food/ Clothing Distribution, Homes, Recreation & Athletics, Scouts, Senior Services, Sexual Abuse, Shelters/ Homelessness, Social Services-General, Substance Abuse, United Funds/United Ways, YMCA/YWCA/ YMHA/YWHA, Youth Organizations

Application Procedures

Initial Contact: Send a two page letter proposal.
Application Requirements: Describe purpose, need, and budget.
Deadlines: July 1.

Restrictions

The foundation seeks to help people help themselves, encouraging individual initiative and responsibility. The foundation prefers one-time grants, rather than funding operating costs on a multi-year basis. The foundation only supports 501(c)(3) organizations.

Additional Information

Publications: Guidelines

Foundation Officials

Shannon Barton: program officer
Bond D. DeLoache: co-trustee
William R. DeLoache, Jr.: co-trustee
Dr. William R. DeLoache: co-trustee B Camden, SC March 27, 1920. ED Furman University (1937-1938); Vanderbilt University BA (1941); Vanderbilt University MD (1943). NONPR AFFIL member: Southern Society Pediatric Research; member advisory board: Vanderbilt University Medical Center; member: Southern Perinatal Association; senior associate: Greenville Memorial Hospital; member: South Caroli-

na Medical Association; member: Greenville County Medical Society; member: American Medical Association; member: Greenville Chamber of Commerce; member: American Academy Pediatrics. CLUB AFFIL Poinsett Club; Rotary Club; Greenville Country Club.

Grants Analysis

Disclosure Period: fiscal year ending September 30, 2003
Total Grants: $3,631,150*
Number of Grants: 29
Average Grant: $54,684*
Highest Grant: $2,100,000
Lowest Grant: $1,000
Typical Range: $10,000 to $100,000
*Note: Giving excludes scholarships. Average grant figure excludes highest grant.

Recent Grants

Note: Grants derived from fiscal 2003 Form 990.
General

2,100,000	Community Foundation of Middle Tennessee, Nashville, TN -- donor advised fund
500,000	Belmont University, Nashville, TN -- nursing scholarships
340,000	Vanderbilt Medical Center/Dept. of Urology, Nashville, TN -- for research projects
300,000	Vanderbilt University Bill Wilkerson Center, Nashville, TN -- national center
255,000	Harpeth Hall School, Nashville, TN -- for middle school building
200,000	Girl Scout Council of Cumberland Valley, Nashville, TN -- for camp renovation
100,000	Matthew Walker Comprehensive Health Center, Nashville, TN -- for new facility
50,000	Jason Foundation, Hendersonville, TN
50,000	Montgomery Bell Academy, Nashville, TN -- for teacher award program
50,000	Project Reflect, Nashville, TN

ARTHUR VINING DAVIS FOUNDATIONS

Giving Contact

Dr. Jonathan T. Howe, Executive Director
225 Water St., Ste. 1510
Jacksonville, FL 32202-5185
Phone: (904)359-0670
Fax: (904)359-0675
E-mail: arthurvining@bellsouth.net
Web: http://www.jvm.com/davis

Description

Founded: 1952
EIN: 256018909
Organization Type: General Purpose Foundation
Giving Locations: nationally.
Grant Types: Capital, Challenge, Department, Endowment, Fellowship, General Support, Operating Expenses, Professorship, Project, Research, Scholarship.

Financial Summary

Total Giving: $8,378,068 (2003); $361,643 (2001)
Assets: $227,318,646 (2002); $7,377,420 (2001)

Typical Recipients

Arts & Humanities: Arts Centers, Film & Video, History & Archaeology, Libraries, Museums/Galleries, Music, Public Broadcasting, Theater
Civic & Public Affairs: Civic & Public Affairs-General, Nonprofit Management
Education: Arts/Humanities Education, Colleges & Universities, Continuing Education, Engineering/Technological Education, Environmental Education, Faculty Development, Education-General, International Studies, Leadership Training, Literacy, Medical Education, Minority Education, Private Education (Precollege), Public Education (Precollege), Religious Education, Science/Mathematics Education, Social Sciences Education, Student Aid
Environment: Resource Conservation
Health: Cancer, Children's Health/Hospitals, Clinics/Medical Centers, Health-General, Health Policy/Cost Containment, Health Organizations, Hospices, Hospitals, Hospitals (University Affiliated), Medical Research, Mental Health, Research/Studies Institutes
International: Foreign Educational Institutions, International Peace & Security Issues, Missionary/Religious Activities
Religion: Religious Organizations, Religious Welfare, Seminaries
Science: Scientific Centers & Institutes, Scientific Labs, Scientific Research
Social Services: Community Service Organizations, United Funds/United Ways

Application Procedures

Initial Contact: Applicants should submit a simple statement describing the proposed project. A budget outline should also be appended.
Application Requirements: All proposals must emanate from the president or other primary executive of an institution.
Deadlines: None.
Review Process: After evaluation of the initial proposal, further detailed information may be requested. Copies of audited financial statements for the past three years are normally requested.
Notes: Additional information is available from the Annual Report, guidelines, and the foundations Website: www.jvm.com/davis/.

Restrictions

The foundations do not support organizations outside of the U.S. and its possessions; individuals, except participants chosen by the grantee institution under an organized scholarship program; voter registration drives; voter education; efforts to influence elections or legislation; expenditures for non-charitable purposes; institutions primarily supported by governmental funds (except in healthcare and secondary education programs); projects incurring obligations extending over several years; private foundations within Sec. 509(A) of the 1969 Tax Reform Act.

Additional Information

The three foundations' assets are invested by corporate trustees and administered as separate legal entities. For the purposes of grantmaking, however, the three foundations function as a single philanthropic organization. The foundations also share a single administrative office in Jacksonville, FL.
Grants generally are made out of annual income, with minimal future commitments. Grantees are expected to prepare a brief written progress report one year after receipt of a grant, or sooner if the project is completed. A more detailed final report also will be required.
The foundations state that a decision not to fund a project is more often the result of funding limitations rather than a judgment of the quality of an applicant or its program. A decision not to fund does not preclude the future submission of a new proposal.
Mellon Bank, N.A., of Pittsburgh, PA, serves as corporate trustee for Foundations No. 1 and No. 2. SunTrust/North Florida, N.A., of Jacksonville, FL, serves as corporate trustee for Foundation No. 3.
Publications: Annual Report; Guidelines

Foundation Officials

Caleb N. Davis: trustee
Holbrook R. Davis: trustee ED Harvard University (1943).
J. H. Dow Davis: chairman
Joel P. Davis: trustee PRIM CORP EMPL senior vice president corporate planning & development: Gillette Co.
Nathanael V. Davis: chairman emeritus
Jane M. Estes: chief financial officer
Doreen A. Flippin: vice president administrator
Rev. Davis Given: trustee
Dr. Jonathan T. Howe: executive director B San Diego, CA 1935. ED United States Naval Academy BS (1957); Tufts University MA (1968); Tufts University PhD (1969).
William C. Keator: program director
Dorothy Davis Kee: trustee
Mrs. John L. Kee, Jr.: trustee
Margaret Davis Maiden: trustee
Dr. Max King Morris: trustee B Springfield, MO 1924. ED United States Naval Academy BS (1947); Tufts University MA Law (1960); Tufts University MA Economics (1961); Tufts University PhD (1967). PRIM CORP EMPL: Thalassa Res Co. CORP AFFIL director: Jacksonville Electric Authority. NONPR AFFIL member: Middle East Institute; member: U.S. Naval Institute; member: Institute International Strategic Studies; member: Council Foreign Relations. CLUB AFFIL New York Yacht Club; Ponte Vedra Club; Belfry Club; Florida Yacht Club.
William R. Wright: trustee emeritus

Grants Analysis

Disclosure Period: calendar year ending 2003
Total Grants: $8,378,068
Number of Grants: 79
Average Grant: $106,051
Highest Grant: $400,000
Typical Range: $50,000 to $200,000

Recent Grants

Note: Grants derived from 2000 Form 990.
General

50,000	Hamilton College, Clinton, NY
50,000	University of Notre Dame, Notre Dame, IN
29,930	Institute for Educational Inquiry, Seattle, WA
25,000	DePauw University, Greencastle, IN
25,000	KCET Hollywood Bowl, Los Angeles, CA -- Woodrow Wilson Series
25,000	Pacific School of Religion, Berkeley, CA
25,000	University of Georgia, Athens, GA
25,000	Wofford College, Spartanburg, SC
24,506	University of Virginia School of Medicine, Charlottesville, VA
20,000	WETA, Washington, DC -- A Force More Powerful

WILLAMETTA K. DAY FOUNDATION

Giving Contact

Jonathan D. Jaffrey, Vice President, Secretary
865 S. Figueroa St., Suite 700
Los Angeles, CA 90017
Phone: (213)891-6300
Fax: (213)891-6300

Description

Founded: 1954
EIN: 956092476
Organization Type: Private Foundation
Giving Locations: CA
Grant Types: General Support.

Donor Information

Founder: the late Willametta K. Day

Financial Summary

Total Giving: $2,319,275 (2003)
Giving Analysis: Giving for 2003 includes: foundation grants to United Way ($10,000)
Assets: $56,307,538 (2003)

Typical Recipients

Arts & Humanities: Arts Institutes, Community Arts, Film & Video, Arts & Humanities-General, Historic Preservation, History & Archaeology, Libraries, Museums/Galleries, Music, Opera

Civic & Public Affairs: Clubs, Community Foundations, Civic & Public Affairs-General, Hispanic Affairs, Housing, Legal Aid, Municipalities/Towns, Public Policy, Urban & Community Affairs

Education: Agricultural Education, Arts/Humanities Education, Business Education, Colleges & Universities, Community & Junior Colleges, Education Reform, Elementary Education (Public), Education-General, Legal Education, Medical Education, Private Education (Precollege), Public Education (Precollege), Secondary Education (Public)

Environment: Environment-General

Health: AIDS/HIV, Cancer, Children's Health/Hospitals, Clinics/Medical Centers, Diabetes, Health Organizations, Hospices, Hospitals

International: Foreign Educational Institutions, International Affairs, International Organizations, International Relations, International Relief Efforts

Religion: Dioceses, Religious Organizations, Religious Welfare

Science: Science Museums, Scientific Centers & Institutes

Social Services: At-Risk Youth, Child Welfare, Community Service Organizations, Delinquency & Criminal Rehabilitation, Food/Clothing Distribution, Recreation & Athletics, United Funds/United Ways, YMCA/YWCA/YMHA/YWHA, Youth Organizations

Application Procedures

Initial Contact: The foundation has no formal grant application procedure or application form.

Restrictions

Does not support individuals.

Foundation Officials

Dorothy W. Day: trustee
Howard M. Day: president, trustee PRIM CORP EMPL general partner: Crescent Investment Co.
Robert A. Day, Jr.: chairman, trustee B 1945. ED Claremont McKenna College (1965). PRIM CORP EMPL founder, chairman, chief executive officer: TCW Asset Management Co. CORP AFFIL chairman, chief executive officer, director: Trust Co. West; director: Fisher Scientific International Inc. NONPR AFFIL chairman investments committee, trustee: Claremont McKenna College.
Tammis M. Day: vice president, trustee PRIM CORP EMPL general partner: Crescent Investment Co.
Theodore J. Day: vice president, trustee PRIM CORP EMPL general partner: Crescent Investment Co. CORP AFFIL senior partner: Hale Day Gallagher; director: Sierra Pacific Resources.
Thomas Joseph Deegan-Day: trustee
Lucinda Fournier: trustee NONPR AFFIL board of governors: Boys & Girls Club of Central Oregon.
Jonathan D. Jaffrey: vice president, secretary NONPR AFFIL chairman: USC Hillel Foundation.

Grants Analysis

Disclosure Period: calendar year ending 2003
Total Grants: $2,309,275*
Number of Grants: 136
Average Grant: $8,772*
Highest Grant: $1,125,000
Lowest Grant: $300
Typical Range: $1,000 to $20,000
*Note: Giving excludes UNW. Average grant figure excludes highest grant.

Recent Grants

Note: Grants derived from 2001 Form 990.
General
333,333	Oldfield School, Oldfield, MD
225,000	Lynfield College, Auckland New Zealand
200,000	York School, Monterey, CA
200,000	York School, Monterey, CA
150,000	Robert Louis Stevenson School, Carmel, CA
100,000	Stevenson School, Pebble Beach, CA
90,000	Saint Mary's Foundation, Evansville, IN
75,000	Cathedral of Our Lady for the Angels, Los Angeles, CA
75,000	Los Angeles County Museum of Art, Los Angeles, CA
75,000	University of Nevada Reno Foundation, Reno, NV

DAYTON POWER AND LIGHT CO.

Company Headquarters

1900 Dryden Rd.
Dayton, OH 45439
Web: http://www.waytogo.com/

Company Description

Employees: 2,908
SIC(s): 4911 Electric Services, 4924 Natural Gas Distribution, 4961 Steam & Air-Conditioning Supply.
Parent Company: DPL Inc., 1065 Woodman Dr., Dayton, OH, United States

Nonmonetary Support

Range: $30,000 - $50,000
Type: Donated Equipment; In-kind Services
Note: Funds goodwill advertising, and dinner/benefit tickets. Requests for nonmonetary support are handled directly by area managers.

Dayton Power and Light Co. Foundation

Giving Contact

Virginia Strausburg, Executive Director
Dayton Power and Light Co. Foundation
1065 Woodman Dr.
Dayton, OH 45432
Phone: (937)259-7925
Fax: (937)259-7923
Web: http://www.waytogo.com/cc/cc.phtm

Description

EIN: 311138883
Organization Type: Corporate Foundation
Giving Locations: headquarters and operating communities.
Grant Types: Capital, General Support, Multiyear/Continuing Support, Project, Scholarship.

Financial Summary

Total Giving: $1,533,700 (2003); $1,111,953 (2002); $1,695,807 (2001). Note: Contributes through corporate direct giving program and foundation.
Giving Analysis: Giving for 2002 includes: foundation grants to United Way ($210,000)
Assets: $29,969,663 (2003); $30,492,307 (2002); $33,287,502 (2001)
Gifts Received: $12,504,041 (2000)

Typical Recipients

Arts & Humanities: Arts Associations & Councils, Arts Centers, Arts Funds, Arts Institutes, Arts Outreach, Ballet, Dance, Ethnic & Folk Arts, Arts & Humanities-General, Historic Preservation, History & Archaeology, Libraries, Museums/Galleries, Music, Opera, Performing Arts, Public Broadcasting, Theater, Visual Arts

Civic & Public Affairs: African American Affairs, Botanical Gardens/Parks, Clubs, Community Foundations, Economic Development, Economic Policy, Employment/Job Training, Civic & Public Affairs-General, Housing, Law & Justice, Municipalities/Towns, Nonprofit Management, Parades/Festivals, Philanthropic Organizations, Public Policy, Urban & Community Affairs, Women's Affairs

Education: Arts/Humanities Education, Business Education, Colleges & Universities, Community & Junior Colleges, Education Funds, Education Reform, Engineering/Technological Education, Environmental Education, Faculty Development, Education-General, Literacy, Minority Education, Private Education (Precollege), Public Education (Precollege), Science/Mathematics Education, Secondary Education (Public), Student Aid

Environment: Energy, Environment-General, Resource Conservation

Health: Alzheimer's Disease, Cancer, Children's Health/Hospitals, Health Funds, Heart, Hospices, Transplant Networks/Donor Banks

Religion: Churches, Religious Welfare, Social/Policy Issues

Science: Science-General, Science Exhibits & Fairs, Science Museums

Social Services: Big Brothers/Big Sisters, Child Welfare, Community Service Organizations, Crime Prevention, Domestic Violence, Emergency Relief, Family Services, Food/Clothing Distribution, People with Disabilities, Recreation & Athletics, Scouts, Senior Services, Substance Abuse, United Funds/United Ways, Veterans, YMCA/YWCA/YMHA/YWHA, Youth Organizations

Application Procedures

Initial Contact: Send a proposal letter with financial attachments.
Application Requirements: Include description of the history, structure, purpose and program of the organization; amount requested, and purpose of funds sought; a specific description of the support needed; status and results of any programs previously supported by DP&L Foundation; and a list of donors and level of support received, committed, or requested. Proposals must be accompanied by detailed organizational financial data, including an independent financial audit, budget, sources of income, and expenditures by programs, administration and fundraising; proof of tax-exempt status; and a copy of the organization's most recent Form 990.
Deadlines: None.
Decision Notification: Distribution committee normally meets quarterly.

Restrictions

Does not support individuals; individual members of federated campaigns; fraternal, labor, or veterans organizations; political or lobbying groups; religious organizations; conduit organizations; college fundraising associations; capital campaigns; endowment or development funds; hospital operating budgets; sports leagues; telephone or mass-mail solicitations; or national organizations outside the DP&L service territory. The foundation rarely makes contributions to tax supported institutions.

Corporate Officials

Allen M. Hill: president, chief executive officer, chief financial officer B Dayton, OH 1945. ED University of Dayton BS (1967); University of Dayton MBA (1972). PRIM CORP EMPL president, chief executive officer: Dayton Power & Light Co. NONPR AFFIL president, chief executive officer, director: DPL Inc.
Caroline E. Muhlenkamp: group vice president, chief financial officer

Foundation Officials

Peter Hans Forster: director B Berlin, Germany 1942. ED University of Wisconsin BS (1964); Brooklyn Law School JD (1972). CORP AFFIL director: Comair Inc.; chairman, chief executive officer, president, director: DPL Inc.; director: Comair Holdings Inc.; director: Amcast Industries Corp.; director: Bank One Dayton NA. NONPR AFFIL trustee: Medical

American Health Systems; member: Ohio Bar Association; director: Dayton Business Committee; member: American Bar Association; member: Dayton Bar Association.

Jane Haley: director

Allen M. Hill: director (see above)

Stephen F. Koziar, Jr.: president, director B Webster, MA 1944. ED University of Dayton BSIE (1967); Salmon P. Chase College of Law JD (1971). PRIM CORP EMPL president, chief executive officer: Dayton Power & Light Co. CORP AFFIL president: Miami Valley Development Co.; president: Miami Valley Resources Inc.; secretary: DPL Inc.

Caroline E. Muhlenkamp: treasurer, trustee (see above)

Virginia M. Strausburg: executive director

Judy Wyatt: secretary, trustee

Grants Analysis

Disclosure Period: calendar year ending 2003
Total Grants: $1,521,700*
Number of Grants: 61
Average Grant: $15,622*
Highest Grant: $350,000
Lowest Grant: $1,000
Typical Range: $5,000 to $25,000
*Note: Giving excludes United Way. Average grant figure excludes two highest grants ($600,000).

Recent Grants

Note: Grants derived from 2003 Form 990.
General

350,000	Inventing Flight, Dayton, OH
250,000	Montgomery County Historical Society, Dayton, OH
70,000	Dayton Urban League, Dayton, OH
49,000	University of Dayton, Dayton, OH
25,000	Miami Valley Council BSA, Dayton, OH
25,000	Wilmington College
20,500	Central State University, Wilberforce, OH
20,000	Dayton Art Institute, Dayton, OH
20,000	Fort Recovery Local Schools, Ft. Recovery, OH
20,000	Victoria Theatre Association, Dayton, OH

DAYWOOD FOUNDATION

Giving Contact

William W. Booker, Secretary & Treasurer
PO Box 2031
1600 Bank One Center
Charleston, WV 25301
Phone: (304)345-8900

Description

Founded: 1958
EIN: 556018107
Organization Type: Private Foundation
Giving Locations: WV: Barbour County, Charleston County, Greenbrier County, Kanawha County, Lewisburg County
Grant Types: Capital, Emergency, General Support, Seed Money.

Donor Information

Founder: the late Ruth Woods Dayton

Financial Summary

Total Giving: $891,542 (2003)
Giving Analysis: Giving for 2003 includes: foundation grants to United Way ($65,000); foundation scholarships ($82,500)
Assets: $23,193,072 (2003)

Typical Recipients

Arts & Humanities: Arts Centers, Arts Funds, Community Arts, Film & Video, Arts & Humanities-General, History & Archaeology, Libraries, Museums/ Galleries, Music, Opera, Theater
Civic & Public Affairs: Economic Development, Civic & Public Affairs-General
Education: Colleges & Universities, Education Funds, Faculty Development, Education-General, Minority Education, Student Aid
Health: Health-General, Health Organizations, Hospices, Mental Health
Social Services: At-Risk Youth, Camps, Child Welfare, Community Service Organizations, Counseling, Domestic Violence, Emergency Relief, Family Services, Food/Clothing Distribution, Recreation & Athletics, Scouts, Senior Services, Shelters/ Homelessness, Social Services-General, United Funds/United Ways, YMCA/YWCA/YMHA/YWHA, Youth Organizations

Application Procedures

Initial Contact: Submit a brief letter of inquiry.
Application Requirements: Include a description of organization, amount requested, purpose of funds sought, proof of tax-exempt status, and a recently audited financial statement.
Deadlines: September 15.

Restrictions

The foundation does not make grants to individuals, political or lobbying groups, organizations outside operating areas.

Foundation Officials

William W. Booker: secretary, treasurer

Richard Edmond Ford: vice president B Ronceverte, WV 1927. ED University of North Carolina (1950); West Virginia University BS (1951); West Virginia University LLB (1954). PRIM CORP EMPL partner: Hayne Ford & Rowe. CORP AFFIL director: WV Power Co.; director: First National Bank Ronceverte; director: Greenbrier Cable Corp. NONPR AFFIL member: WV University Alumni Association; director: WV University Foundation; member: WV Bar Association; member: WV Law School Association; member: Phi Delta Phi; member: Sigma Chi; member: Phi Beta Kappa; member: National Conference Commrs Uniform Saint Laws; member: Order of Vandalia; member: Greenbrier County Bar Association; director: Faculty Merit Foundation; member advisory board: Greenbrier Community College Center; vice president, director: Daywood Foundation; fellow: American Judicature Society; member executive board: Boy Scouts America; member: American College Real Estate Lawyers; member: American Bar Association; fellow: American Bar Foundation. CLUB AFFIL Shriners Club; Lewisburg Elks Club; Masons Club; Kentucky Club.

John Oscar Kizer: secretary, treasurer B Wheeling, WV March 06, 1913. ED West Virginia University AB (1934); West Virginia University LLB (1936). PRIM CORP EMPL partner: Kay, Casto, Chaney, Love & Wise. NONPR AFFIL member: WV Bar Association; member: WV State Bar; member: Delta Tau Delta; member: American Bar Association; director, past president: Childrens Museum Charleston. CLUB AFFIL Berry Hills Country Club.

L. Newton Thomas, Jr.: president

Grants Analysis

Disclosure Period: calendar year ending 2003
Total Grants: $744,042*
Number of Grants: 47
Average Grant: $8,756*
Highest Grant: $250,000
Lowest Grant: $1,500
Typical Range: $5,000 to $10,000
*Note: Giving excludes United Way and scholarship. Average grant figure excludes two highest grants ($350,000).

Recent Grants

Note: Grants derived from 2003 Form 990.

Library-Related

50,000	Greenbrier County Library, Lewisburg, WV -- for capital campaign

General

250,000	Clay Center for the Arts and Sciences, Charleston, WV -- for capital campaign
100,000	West Virginia University Foundation College of Law Chair, Morgantown, WV
50,000	United Way of Kanawha Valley, Charleston, WV
36,000	Carnegie Hall Inc., Lewisburg, WV -- for education director position
32,500	Davis and Elkins College, Elkins, WV -- for scholarships program
30,000	West Virginia Wesleyan College, Buckhannon, WV -- for scholarships
25,000	Sunrise Foundation Inc., Charleston, WV -- for art education curriculum
20,000	University of Charleston, Charleston, WV -- for nursing scholarships
15,000	United Way of Greenbrier County, Lewisburg, WV

DBH FOUNDATION FOR LAW, LAND, AND THE FELICITOUS ENVIRONMENT

Giving Contact

Dr. Suzanne Keller, Chairman
Princeton University
Department of Sociology
Princeton, NJ 08540
Phone: (201)684-4100

Description

Founded: 1992
EIN: 222953497
Organization Type: Private Foundation
Giving Locations: NY
Grant Types: General Support.

Financial Summary

Gifts Received: $19,477 (1998); $3,000 (1992). Note: In 1998, contributions were received from Charles M. Haar.

Typical Recipients

Arts & Humanities: Arts Associations & Councils, Dance, Libraries, Museums/Galleries, Theater
Civic & Public Affairs: Clubs, Civic & Public Affairs-General, Law & Justice, Legal Aid, Urban & Community Affairs
Education: Colleges & Universities, Legal Education, Private Education (Precollege), Social Sciences Education
Environment: Environment-General
Health: Heart
International: Foreign Educational Institutions, International Organizations
Religion: Jewish Causes, Seminaries, Synagogues/ Temples
Social Services: Social Services-General

Application Procedures

Initial Contact: Request guidelines. Send a brief letter of inquiry and a full proposal.
Deadlines: None.

Restrictions

Does not support religious organizations for sectarian purposes, or political or lobbying groups.

Additional Information

Publications: Guidelines

Foundation Officials
Charles M. Haar: director
Susan E. Haar: director
Steven G. Horowitz: director
Jerold Kayden: director
Dr. Suzanne Keller: chairman

Grants Analysis
Disclosure Period: calendar year ending 2000
Total Grants: $28,100
Number of Grants: 24
Average Grant: $1,171
Highest Grant: $5,000
Lowest Grant: $100
Typical Range: $100 to $5,000

Recent Grants
Note: Grants derived from 2000 Form 990.
General
5,000	Carlo Mongardini Amalfi Foundation
3,000	World Society of Ekistics, Athens Greece
2,500	Princeton University Department of Sociology, Princeton, NJ
1,800	Stern College for Women, New York, NY
1,000	American Academy of the Arts and Sciences, Cambridge, MA
1,000	Citizens Union Foundation, New York, NY
1,000	Contemporary Dance Theater, New York, NY
1,000	Fogg Art Museum
1,000	Harvard Hillel
1,000	Lawyers Alliance, New York, NY

SARAH K. DE COIZART PERPETUAL CHARITABLE TRUST

Giving Contact
Philip DiMaulo, Vice President
c/o Chase Manhattan Bank
1211 Avenue of the Americas, 34th Floor
New York, NY 10036
Phone: (212)789-4159

Description
Founded: 1995
EIN: 137046581
Organization Type: Private Foundation
Giving Locations: nationally.
Grant Types: General Support.

Donor Information
Founder: Established in 1995 by the late Sarah de Coizart and with funds from the Andre de Coizart Interim Trust.

Financial Summary
Total Giving: $1,150,925 (fiscal year ending January 31, 2001)
Giving Analysis: Giving for fiscal 2001 includes: foundation grants to United Way ($25,000)
Assets: $39,276,619 (fiscal 2001)
Gifts Received: $10,000 (fiscal 2001); $3,109,301 (fiscal 2000); $10,268,407 (fiscal 1997). Note: In fiscal 1996, contributions were received from the estate of Sarah de Coizart ($3,500,000) and the Andre de Coizart Interim Trust ($10,649,355).

Typical Recipients
Arts & Humanities: Community Arts, Libraries, Museums/Galleries
Civic & Public Affairs: Civic & Public Affairs-General, Philanthropic Organizations, Urban & Community Affairs
Education: Colleges & Universities

Environment: Protection, Resource Conservation
Health: Arthritis, Cancer, Eyes/Blindness, Health-General, Hospitals, Nursing Services, Public Health
Religion: Religious Welfare
Science: Science Museums
Social Services: At-Risk Youth, Child Welfare, Community Centers, Community Service Organizations, Family Services, People with Disabilities, Recreation & Athletics, United Funds/United Ways, YMCA/YWCA/YMHA/YWHA

Application Procedures
Initial Contact: The foundation has no formal grant application procedure or application form.
Deadlines: None.

Additional Information
Trust(s): Chase Manhattan Bank

Foundation Officials
Carl S. Forsythe, III: trustee

Grants Analysis
Disclosure Period: fiscal year ending January 31, 2001
Total Grants: $1,125,925*
Number of Grants: 83
Average Grant: $13,567
Highest Grant: $40,000
Typical Range: $5,000 to $50,000
***Note:** Giving excludes United Way.

Recent Grants
Note: Grants derived from 2001 Form 990.
Library-Related
25,000	Desert Foothills Library, Carefree, AZ
20,000	Museum of Modern Art, New York, NY

General
40,000	VNA of Hudson Valley
35,000	Arthritis Foundation, Reno, NV
35,000	Family Centers, Inc, Greenwich, CT
30,000	Bruce Museum, Greenwich, CT
30,000	Greenwich Land Trust, Greenwich, CT
30,000	Interplast, Inc., Mountain View, CA
25,000	Interfaith Neighbors, Inc., Asbury Park, NJ
25,000	Manchester Health Services, Manchester Center, VT
25,000	Northshire Civic Center, Manchester Center, VT
25,000	Posse Foundation, The, New York, NY

DE QUEEN REGIONAL MEDICAL CENTER

Giving Contact
Charles Long
c/o Cossatot Technical College
De Queen, AR 71832
Phone: (870)584-4471
Fax: (870)584-4100

Description
Founded: 1984
EIN: 710405256
Organization Type: Private Foundation
Grant Types: General Support, Scholarship.

Typical Recipients
Arts & Humanities: Libraries, Museums/Galleries
Civic & Public Affairs: Urban & Community Affairs
Education: Colleges & Universities, Student Aid, Vocational & Technical Education
Health: Emergency/Ambulance Services, Health-General, Hospitals
Social Services: People with Disabilities, Youth Organizations

Application Procedures
Initial Contact: Applications available at Cossatot Technical College.
Deadlines: None.

Additional Information
Provides scholarships to individuals studying for a medical profession.

Foundation Officials
Donn Allison: secretary
Frank Daniel, MD: director
C. E. Hendrix, Jr.: president
Jonathon Hoyt, MD: director
Charles N. Jones, MD: vice president
Ray Kimball: director
Jim Pearce: treasurer
Randell Wright: director

Grants Analysis
Disclosure Period: calendar year ending 1999
Total Grants: $2,058,000*
Number of Grants: 4
Highest Grant: $2,000,000
Typical Range: $100 to $25,000
***Note:** Giving excludes scholarships.

Recent Grants
Note: Grants derived from 2002 Form 990.
General
114,576	De Queen General Hospital, De Queen, AR -- for payroll expenses

IRA W. DECAMP FOUNDATION

Giving Contact
Herbert Faber, Trustee
Care of J.P. Morgan Chase Bank
1211 Sixth Ave., 34th Fl.
New York, NY 10036
Phone: (212)789-4073
Web: http://fdncenter.org/grantmaker/decamp/

Description
Founded: 1975
EIN: 510138577
Organization Type: Specialized/Single Purpose Foundation
Giving Locations: NY: New York including the metropolitan area
Grant Types: Capital, General Support, Multiyear/Continuing Support, Research, Scholarship.

Donor Information
Founder: Established in New York in 1975 with funds from the estate of the late Elizabeth DeCamp McInerny.

Financial Summary
Total Giving: $4,005,000 (fiscal year ending October 31, 2003); $4,350,000 (fiscal 2002); $4,915,000 (fiscal 2001 approx)
Assets: $76,579,255 (fiscal 2003); $72,767,931 (fiscal 2002); $87,725,298 (fiscal 2001)
Gifts Received: $89 (fiscal 1992)

Typical Recipients
Arts & Humanities: Historic Preservation, Libraries, Public Broadcasting
Civic & Public Affairs: Community Foundations, Economic Development, Employment/Job Training, Civic & Public Affairs-General, Hispanic Affairs, Housing, Inner-City Development, Legal Aid, Municipalities/Towns, Nonprofit Management, Philanthropic Organizations, Professional & Trade Associations, Urban & Community Affairs, Women's Affairs

Education: Arts/Humanities Education, Business Education, Colleges & Universities, Education Funds, Education Reform, Engineering/Technological Education, Education-General, Health & Physical Education, International Studies, Journalism/Media Education, Legal Education, Medical Education, Preschool Education, Private Education (Precollege), Religious Education, Science/Mathematics Education, Special Education, Student Aid, Vocational & Technical Education

Environment: Environment-General

Health: AIDS/HIV, Alzheimer's Disease, Cancer, Children's Health/Hospitals, Clinics/Medical Centers, Emergency/Ambulance Services, Eyes/Blindness, Health-General, Geriatric Health, Health Funds, Health Organizations, Heart, Hospices, Hospitals, Hospitals (University Affiliated), Kidney, Long-Term Care, Medical Rehabilitation, Medical Research, Medical Training, Mental Health, Nursing Services, Outpatient Health Care, Public Health, Research/Studies Institutes, Single-Disease Health Associations, Speech & Hearing, Transplant Networks/Donor Banks

International: Health Care/Hospitals, International Environmental Issues, International Organizations

Religion: Churches, Religion-General, Religious Organizations, Religious Welfare, Seminaries

Science: Scientific Labs, Scientific Organizations, Scientific Research

Social Services: Big Brothers/Big Sisters, Child Abuse, Child Welfare, Community Centers, Community Service Organizations, Counseling, Delinquency & Criminal Rehabilitation, Family Services, Food/Clothing Distribution, Homes, People with Disabilities, Recreation & Athletics, Scouts, Senior Services, Shelters/Homelessness, Social Services-General, Substance Abuse, United Funds/United Ways, Volunteer Services, Youth Organizations

Application Procedures

Initial Contact: Applicants should contact foundation for funding guidelines and application requirements.
Application Requirements: Full proposals will include primary goals of organization, need or problem addressed, and population served; most recent annual report; brief history of the organization; list of directors or trustees with affiliations; brief biography of executive director and key project staff; most recent financial audit; current operating budget; list of foundation and corporate support with amounts for the most recently completed fiscal year; proof of tax-exempt status and Form 990; description of project, including statement of primary purpose and need addressed, population served and how they will benefit, anticipated duration, current budget, and list of funding sources.
Deadlines: March 15 and July 15.
Review Process: Grants are reviewed in the spring and fall. Applicants generally will be notified of the foundation's final decision on their proposal within six weeks of the trustees' meeting.

Restrictions

No grants are made to individuals, private foundations, endowments, scholarships, fellowships, or for matching gifts or loans.

Additional Information

J.P. Morgan Chase Bank serves as a corporate trustee for the foundation.

Foundation Officials

Herbert Faber: trustee

Grants Analysis

Disclosure Period: fiscal year ending October 31, 2003
Total Grants: $4,005,000
Number of Grants: 56
Average Grant: $71,518
Highest Grant: $245,000
Typical Range: $25,000 to $150,000

Recent Grants

Note: Grants derived from 2003 Form 990.
General

245,000	Community Health Care Association of New York, New York, NY -- towards grant for community health care association of New York State
170,000	Medical and Health Research Association of New York, New York, NY -- as grant towards the association
165,000	Inner City Scholarship Fund Inc., New York, NY -- towards grant payment for the preschool support initiative
150,000	Charles B. Wang Community, New York, NY -- towards technology upgrades
150,000	Duke University Medical Center, Durham, NC -- towards grant for the medical center
150,000	New York Presbyterian, New York, NY -- towards renovations of the Allen pavilion emergency department
150,000	United Hospital Fund, New York, NY -- grant towards the united hospital fund of New York
140,000	Advocates for Children, New York, NY -- towards project achieve grant for the current year
140,000	Structured Employment, New York, NY -- towards grant for structured employment and economic development corporation
125,000	Graham Windham, New York, NY -- as grant towards the organization

DECHERD FOUNDATION

Giving Contact

Vickie King
400 S. Record St., 2nd Fl.
Dallas, TX 75202-4819
Phone: (214)977-8293

Description

Founded: 1993
EIN: 752507229
Organization Type: Private Foundation
Giving Locations: TX: nationally and internationally.
Grant Types: General Support.

Donor Information

Founder: Established in 1993 by Mr. and Mrs. Robert Decherd.

Financial Summary

Total Giving: $289,500 (2003)
Giving Analysis: Giving for 2003 includes: foundation grants to United Way ($23,500)
Assets: $4,460,380 (2003)
Gifts Received: $305,215 (2003); $5,313,781 (1998); $1,171,443 (1996). Note: In 1998 and 2003, contributions were received from Mr. and Mrs. Robert Decherd.

Typical Recipients

Arts & Humanities: Libraries
Civic & Public Affairs: Business/Free Enterprise
Education: Colleges & Universities, Education Funds, Education-General, Minority Education, Private Education (Precollege), Student Aid
Health: Eyes/Blindness, Health Funds, Mental Health
Religion: Churches, Religious Welfare
Social Services: Community Centers, Community Service Organizations, Substance Abuse, United Funds/United Ways, Volunteer Services, YMCA/YWCA/YMHA/YWHA, Youth Organizations

Application Procedures

Initial Contact: Send a brief letter of inquiry.
Application Requirements: Include proof of tax-exempt status, recently audited financial statement, and list of board of directors.
Deadlines: None.

Foundation Officials

William Bennett Cullum: secretary, treasurer
Maureen H. Decherd: president
Robert William Decherd: chairman B Dallas, TX 1951. ED Harvard University BA (1973). PRIM CORP EMPL chairman, president, chief executive officer, director: A.H. Belo Corp. CORP AFFIL chairman: Owensboro Messenger Inquirer; chairman: Henderson Gleaner; director: Kimberly-Clark Corp.; chairman, chief executive officer: Audubon Printers Ink Ltd. NONPR AFFIL member: Newspaper Association America; trustee: Tomas Rivera Policy Institute.

Grants Analysis

Disclosure Period: calendar year ending 2003
Total Grants: $266,000*
Number of Grants: 9
Average Grant: $4,929*
Highest Grant: $131,500
Lowest Grant: $500
Typical Range: $500 to $10,000
*Note: Giving excludes United Way. Average grant figure excludes two highest grants ($231,500).

Recent Grants

Note: Grants derived from 2003 Form 990.
Library-Related

1,000	Friends of the Dallas Public Library, Dallas, TX

General

131,500	St. Mark's School of Texas, Dallas, TX -- for the campaign of St. Mark's
100,000	Gladney Center, Ft. Worth, TX -- for capital campaign outreach education fund
23,500	United Way of Metropolitan Dallas, Dallas, TX
22,000	Saint Michael and All Angels Episcopal Church, Dallas, TX -- for annual stewardship campaign
5,000	Hockaday School, Dallas, TX -- funds for Decherd family endowment
5,000	St. Mark's School of Texas, Dallas, TX -- for long-term funds
500	Junior League of Dallas, Dallas, TX -- for annual sustainers campaign
500	Retina Foundation of the Southwest, Dallas, TX -- towards research fund
500	St. Phillip's School and Community Center, Dallas, TX

ARTHUR J. DECIO FOUNDATION

Giving Contact

Ronald F. Kloska, Trustee
c/o Skyline Corp.
2520 By-Pass Rd.
Elkhart, IN 46515
Phone: (574)294-6521
Fax: (574)293-7574

Description

Founded: 1970
EIN: 237083597
Organization Type: Private Foundation
Giving Locations: IN
Grant Types: General Support.

Donor Information

Founder: Arthur J. Decio

Financial Summary

Total Giving: $262,200 (fiscal year ending September 30, 2004); $85,500 (fiscal 2001)

Assets: $3,350,121 (fiscal 2004); $2,317,725 (fiscal 2001)

Gifts Received: $210,000 (fiscal 2004). Note: In fiscal 2004, contributions were received from Arthur J. Decio.

Typical Recipients

Arts & Humanities: Arts Festivals, Arts Outreach, Arts & Humanities-General, History & Archaeology, Libraries, Music, Performing Arts, Public Broadcasting

Civic & Public Affairs: Community Foundations, Employment/Job Training, Ethnic Organizations, Civic & Public Affairs-General, Parades/Festivals, Women's Affairs

Education: Business Education, Colleges & Universities, Education Funds, Education-General, Private Education (Precollege), Student Aid

Health: Cancer, Emergency/Ambulance Services, Heart, Hospices, Hospitals, Medical Research, Mental Health, Single-Disease Health Associations

Religion: Religious Organizations, Religious Welfare, Seminaries

Social Services: Community Service Organizations, Domestic Violence, Family Planning, People with Disabilities, Substance Abuse, Youth Organizations

Application Procedures

Initial Contact: Send a brief letter of inquiry.
Deadlines: None.

Foundation Officials

Arthur J. Decio: trustee B Elkhart, IN 1930. ED DePaul University (1949-1950); University of Notre Dame LLD (1975); Indiana State University LLD (1978). PRIM CORP EMPL chairman, chief executive officer, director: Skyline Corp. CORP AFFIL director: Schwarz Paper Co.; director: NIPSCO Industries Inc.; director: Quality Housing. NONPR AFFIL fellow, trustee: University Notre Dame; member: World Business Council; director: Special Olympics International; member: Mobile Home Manufacturer Association; life member, vice chairman advisory board: National Salvation Army; life member, trust: Marmion Military Acad; member: Knights Malta; member: Manufactured Housing Institute; trustee: Holy Cross College; president: Elkhart General Hospital Foundation; member advisory board: Goshen College; member: Chief Executives Organization; counc adv: Center Homeless; member: Chicago Presidents Association. CLUB AFFIL Tavern Club; Ocean Florida Club; Signal Point Country Club; Delray Beach Yacht Club; Chicago Club; Country Club Florida.

Patricia C. Decio: trustee
Terrence M. Decio: trustee
Ronald Frank Kloska: trustee B Grand Rapids, MI 1933. ED University of Montreal MBA (1955); University of Michigan PhB (1957). PRIM CORP EMPL vice chairman, deputy chief executive officer, chief administrative officer, director: Skyline Corp. CORP AFFIL director: NBD Bank. NONPR AFFIL member: Indiana Certified Public Accountant Society; member: Michigan Society CPA's; member: American Institute of CPA's. CLUB AFFIL SouthBend Country Club.

Richard M. Treckelo: trustee B Elkhart, IN 1926. ED University of Michigan AB (1951); University of Michigan JD (1953). PRIM NONPR EMPL partner: Barnes & Thornburg. NONPR AFFIL director: Elkhart Park Foundation; member: Indiana Bar Association; director: Elkhart General Hospital Foundation; cochairman: Elkhart Constitutional Bicentennial Comm; member: Elkhart County Bar Association; member: American Bar Association; member: Elkhart City Bar Association. CLUB AFFIL Rotary Club; Christiana Country Club; Presidents University Michigan Club.

Grants Analysis

Disclosure Period: fiscal year ending September 30, 2004
Total Grants: $262,200
Number of Grants: 45
Average Grant: $5,107*

Highest Grant: $37,500
Lowest Grant: $250
Typical Range: $1,000 to $10,000
*Note: Average grant figure excludes highest grant.

Recent Grants

Note: Grants derived from fiscal 2004 Form 990.
General

37,500	WNIT Public Television, Elkhart, IN
30,000	Indiana University Foundation, Bloomington, IN
25,000	United Way of Elkhart County, Elkhart, IN
21,000	Salvation Army, Indianapolis, IN
20,000	Ara Parseghian Medical Research Foundation, Tucson, AZ
20,000	St. Thomas the Apostle Church, West Hempstead, NY
10,000	Hillsdale College, Hillsdale, MI
10,000	Mayo Foundation, Rochester, MN
10,000	Saint Joe
10,000	St. Mary's College, Notre Dame, IN

DR. G. CLIFFORD AND FLORENCE B. DECKER FOUNDATION

Giving Contact

Gerald E. Putman, Executive Director
8 Riverside Dr.
Binghamton, NY 13901
Phone: (607)722-0211

Description

Founded: 1979
EIN: 161131704
Organization Type: Private Foundation
Giving Locations: NY
Grant Types: General Support, Scholarship.

Donor Information

Founder: the late G. Clifford Decker

Financial Summary

Total Giving: $1,238,417 (2004); $2,814,034 (2001)
Giving Analysis: Giving for 2004 includes: foundation grants to United Way ($61,000); foundation scholarships ($100,000); 2001: foundation grants to United Way ($55,000); foundation scholarships ($200,000)
Assets: $35,296,162 (2004); $41,084,733 (2001)
Gifts Received: $179,854 (1999). Note: In 1999, contributions were received from the Mrs. Korn Trust.

Typical Recipients

Arts & Humanities: Arts Associations & Councils, Arts Outreach, Arts & Humanities-General, History & Archaeology, Libraries, Museums/Galleries, Music, Opera, Performing Arts, Public Broadcasting

Civic & Public Affairs: Economic Development, Civic & Public Affairs-General, Legal Aid, Nonprofit Management, Professional & Trade Associations, Public Policy, Urban & Community Affairs

Education: Arts/Humanities Education, Colleges & Universities, Community & Junior Colleges, Education-General, Health & Physical Education, Literacy, Medical Education, Preschool Education, Science/Mathematics Education, Student Aid

Health: Clinics/Medical Centers, Emergency/Ambulance Services, Health Organizations, Home-Care Services, Hospitals, Mental Health, Public Health

Religion: Churches, Religious Welfare
Science: Science Museums, Scientific Centers & Institutes
Social Services: Child Welfare, Community Service Organizations, Counseling, Day Care, Family Services, Food/Clothing Distribution, People with Disabilities, Recreation & Athletics, United Funds/United Ways, YMCA/YWCA/YMHA/YWHA, Youth Organizations

Application Procedures

Initial Contact: Request application form.
Application Requirements: Include proof of tax-exempt status along with complete summary form, history, and development of organization, needs to be met by project, purpose of program, name, position and qualification of people in charge of project. Include funding list of actual and potential funding sources and how project will be funded in the future and current board members. See application form. for full requirements.
Deadlines: None.

Additional Information

Publications: Grant application form.

Foundation Officials

Ferris G. Akel: chairman PRIM CORP EMPL director: Bsb Bancorp Inc. ADD CORP EMPL director: Bsb Bank & Trust Co.

James A. Carrigg: trustee B Johnson City, NY 1933. ED Broome Community College AAS; University of Michigan Graduate School of Business Administration; Union College (1951-1953). PRIM CORP EMPL chairman, president, chief executive officer: New York State Electric & Gas Co. CORP AFFIL director: Utilities Mutual Insurance Co.; director: Security Mutual Life Insurance Co.; chairman: UN MedManagement Inc.; director: Security Equity Life Insurance Co.; director: M&T Bank-Endicott Trust Division; director: Partnership 2000; director: First Empire State Corp.; director: Home Mutual Insurance Co.; director: Empire State Electric Energy Research Corp. NONPR AFFIL director: United Health Services Hospitals Inc.; director: United Health Services Inc.; trustee: Public Policy Institute; trustee: Independent College Fund; director: New York Business Development Corp.; director: Broome County Community Charities; director: Foundation SUNY; trustee: Broome Community College. CLUB AFFIL Broome Country Club.

Mary Lou Faust: secretary
Douglas Johnson: treasurer
Gerald Putman: executive director
Alice Wales: vchairman

Grants Analysis

Disclosure Period: calendar year ending 2004
Total Grants: $1,077,417*
Number of Grants: 14
Average Grant: $20,985*
Highest Grant: $295,400
Lowest Grant: $500
Typical Range: $5,000 to $65,000
*Note: Giving excludes United Way and scholarships. Average grant figure excludes four highest grants ($867,566).

Recent Grants

Note: Grants derived from 2001 Form 990.
General

650,000	Roberson Memorial, Inc. -- capital campaign
500,000	Lourdes Hospital Foundation, Binghamton, NY -- 2001 renew campaign
500,000	Phelps Mansion Foundation, Binghamton, NY -- replicate mansard roof
250,000	Discovery Center of Southern Tier, Inc. -- capital project
200,000	Broome Community College Foundation, Binghamton, NY -- endowment for scholarships
150,000	Broome County Council of Churches, Binghamton, NY -- expansion and renovation and relocation

150,000	Imaginarium for Health, Healing and The Arts, Inc. -- development and implementation of After-School Program
125,000	Tri-Cities Opera, Binghamton, NY -- expanding and upgrading
100,000	Foundation of the State University of New York, Binghamton, NY -- equipment for Doctoral Program
55,000	United Way of Broome County, Binghamton, NY -- annual campaign

DEDALUS FOUNDATION

Giving Contact

Richard Rubin, Chairman
555 W. 57th St., Suite 1222
New York, NY 10019
Phone: (212)220-4220

Description

Founded: 1981
EIN: 133091704
Organization Type: Private Foundation
Grant Types: General Support.

Donor Information

Founder: the late Robert Motherwell

Financial Summary

Total Giving: $740,679 (2003)
Giving Analysis: Giving for 2003 includes: foundation gifts to individuals ($114,000)
Assets: $48,106,632 (2003)
Gifts Received: $9,915,470 (1996); $19,442,993 (1993). Note: In 1993, contributions were received from the estate of Robert Motherwell.

Typical Recipients

Arts & Humanities: Arts Centers, Arts Funds, Arts Institutes, Arts Outreach, Arts & Humanities-General, Libraries, Literary Arts, Museums/Galleries, Visual Arts
Education: Arts/Humanities Education, Colleges & Universities
Health: Children's Health/Hospitals
International: Foreign Arts Organizations
Religion: Jewish Causes

Application Procedures

Initial Contact: Send a brief letter of inquiry followed by a full proposal.
Application Requirements: Include a description of organization, amount requested, purpose of funds sought, and proof of tax-exempt status.
Deadlines: October 1.

Restrictions

Primarily supports preselected organizations.

Additional Information

Although the foundation gives grants to preselected organizations and does not accept unsolicited requests for funds, it does have three separate grant programs offered to individuals. They are: Senior Fellowship Program, which is open to art historians, critics, and curators pursuing projects related to the study of modern art and modernism. The applicant does not have to be affiliated with an educational institution or a museum and cannot be a candidate for a degree. Applicants must be a U.S. citizen. Awards will be made for a period of up to one year, with a maximum of $20,000 annually. The application must be submitted by December 1st. Decisions made by the following April; the PhD Dissertation Fellowship, provides support for a graduate student studying any aspect of the modernist tradition. Departments of art history at colleges and universities in the United States are invited to nominate one student each for

consideration. Nominees must have completed all course requirements and examinations and must have advanced to candidacy for the PhD. The foundation mails the program information and application to the chairperson of graduate departments a few months in advance of the deadline. The amount of award is $20,000 for award year July 1 to June 30. Nominations and all accompanying materials must be received at the foundation no later than December 1st. Decisions made the following April; and the MFA Fellowship, provides support for graduate students of painting and sculpture who are about to enter their last year of candidacy for the MFA degree at an American college, university, or art school. Graduate departments of art are invited to nominate one student each for consideration. The foundation mails the program information and application to the chairperson of graduate departments a few months in advance of the deadline. Nomination and all accompanying materials must be received at the foundation no later than July 1st. Decisions made in December.

Foundation Officials

Dore Ashton: director B Newark, DE 1925. ED University of Wisconsin BA (1949); Harvard University MA (1950). PRIM CORP EMPL professor: Cooper Union. NONPR AFFIL member advisory board: John Simon Guggenheim Foundation; member: Phi Beta Kappa.
Joan Banach: secretary
John Elderfield: director
Jack Flam: president, treasurer
Lynn Kearney: director
David Rosand: director B Brooklyn, NY 1938. ED Columbia College AB (1959); Columbia University MA (1962); Columbia University PhD (1965). PRIM CORP EMPL professor art history: Meyer Schapiro. NONPR AFFIL member executive board: Renaissance Society America; member general committee: Save Venice; member: Ateneo Veneto; member: College Art Association America.
Richard Rubin: chairman

Grants Analysis

Disclosure Period: calendar year ending 2003
Total Grants: $626,679*
Number of Grants: 20
Average Grant: $16,076*
Highest Grant: $257,500
Lowest Grant: $1,000
Typical Range: $10,000 to $25,000
***Note:** Giving excludes individuals. Average grant figure excludes two highest grants ($337,311).

Recent Grants

Note: Grants derived from 2003 Form 990.
General

257,500	Judith Rothschild Foundation, New York, NY -- to educate the public about the art of Robert Motherwell and modernism
79,811	Walker Art Center, Minneapolis, MN -- support for printing of the new Robert Motherwell prints catalogue raisonne
45,000	Everson Museum of Art, Syracuse, NY -- to educate the public about the art of Robert Motherwell and modernism
40,000	Center Georges Pompidou, Paris France -- to educate the public about the art of Robert Motherwell and modernism
33,333	Maria Fereri Children's Hospital at Westchester, Valhalla, NY -- support for a three-year art and art studio program
25,000	International Foundation for Art Research, New York, NY -- support for the catalogue raisonne initiative program
25,000	Modern Art Museum of Fort Worth, Ft. Worth, TX -- support for the Anselm Kiefer retrospective exhibition
25,000	Young Audiences New York, New York, NY -- support for the breaking the rules project

| 15,000 | Harlem School of Arts Inc., New York, NY -- support for the 2003-2004 opportunities for learning program |
| 15,000 | New York University, New York, NY -- support for the 2003-2004 Dedalus foundation fellow in conservation (Corey D'Augustine) at the institute of Fine |

LAWRENCE T. AND JANET T. DEE FOUNDATION

Giving Contact

David Buchman, Trust Officer
c/o Wells Fargo Bank, NA
PO Box 30007
Salt Lake City, UT 84130
Phone: (801)246-5363

Description

Founded: 1971
EIN: 876150803
Organization Type: Private Foundation
Giving Locations: UT
Grant Types: Capital, Emergency, General Support, Research, Scholarship.

Donor Information

Founder: the late L. T. Dee, the late Janet T. Dee

Financial Summary

Total Giving: $584,000 (2003)
Assets: $12,947,249 (2003)
Gifts Received: $100,000 (1996); $404,802 (1995); $350,000 (1994)

Typical Recipients

Arts & Humanities: Arts Centers, Ballet, Community Arts, Dance, Arts & Humanities-General, Historic Preservation, History & Archaeology, Libraries, Museums/Galleries, Music, Opera, Performing Arts, Public Broadcasting, Theater
Civic & Public Affairs: Botanical Gardens/Parks, Civic & Public Affairs-General, Legal Aid, Native American Affairs, Urban & Community Affairs, Women's Affairs
Education: Arts/Humanities Education, Colleges & Universities, Education-General, Literacy, Medical Education, Private Education (Precollege), Public Education (Precollege)
Environment: Environment-General, Resource Conservation
Health: Alzheimer's Disease, Arthritis, Cancer, Children's Health/Hospitals, Emergency/Ambulance Services, Eyes/Blindness, Health Organizations, Hospitals, Prenatal Health Issues, Respiratory, Single-Disease Health Associations
Religion: Churches, Religious Welfare
Science: Science Museums, Scientific Research
Social Services: Camps, Child Welfare, Community Centers, Community Service Organizations, Family Planning, People with Disabilities, Senior Services, YMCA/YWCA/YMHA/YWHA, Youth Organizations

Application Procedures

Initial Contact: Send a brief letter of inquiry.
Deadlines: September 30.

Additional Information

Trust(s): Wells Fargo Bank NA

Grants Analysis

Disclosure Period: calendar year ending 2003
Total Grants: $584,000*
Number of Grants: 82
Average Grant: $6,284*
Highest Grant: $75,000
Lowest Grant: $1,000

Typical Range: $1,000 to $10,000
*Note: Average grant figure excludes highest grant.

Recent Grants

Note: Grants derived from 2001 Form 990.
General

75,000	Nature Conservancy of Utah, Salt Lake City, UT
60,000	Weber State University, Ogden, UT -- College of Health Professions
57,500	University of Utah, Salt Lake City, UT -- Department of Educational Psychology
50,000	University of Utah, Salt Lake City, UT -- J. Willard Marriott Library
40,000	Ogden Nature Center, Ogden, UT
30,000	Westminster College, Salt Lake City, UT
25,000	Utah Open Lands, Salt Lake City, UT
25,000	Utah State University College of Humanities, Logan, UT
20,000	Utah Symphony, Salt Lake City, UT
15,000	Kolob Foundation, Salt Lake City, UT

DEERE & CO.

Company Headquarters

Moline, IL
Web: http://www.johndeere.com

Company Description

Founded: 1837
Ticker: DE
Exchange: NYSE
Revenue: US$19.986 billion (2004)
Profit: US$1.406 billion (2004)
Employees: 43221 (2003)
Fortune Rank: 106, per FORTUNE Magazine's list of 500 Largest U.S. Corporations (2004).
SIC(s): 3519 Internal Combustion Engines Nec, 3523 Farm Machinery & Equipment, 3524 Lawn & Garden Equipment, 3531 Construction Machinery.

Operating Locations

Deere & Co. (GA--Conyers; IA--Ankeny, Davenport, Dubuque; KS--St. Marys; MN--Bloomington; MO--Kansas City; NY--Syracuse; OR--Portland; SC--Clover; TX--Dallas)

Nonmonetary Support

Type: Donated Products; Loaned Executives
Note: Nonmonetary support is provided by the company.

John Deere Foundation

Giving Contact

Jim H. Collins, President
One John Deere Pl.
Moline, IL 61265
Phone: (309)748-7951
Fax: (309)765-9855
E-mail: collinsjamesh@johndeere.com
Web: http://www.deere.com/en_US/compinfo/ johndeere_foundations/contacts.html

Description

EIN: 366051024
Organization Type: Corporate Foundation
Giving Locations: principally near operating locations and to national organizations.
Grant Types: Award, Capital, Department, Emergency, Fellowship, General Support, Multiyear/ Continuing Support, Project, Scholarship.

Financial Summary

Total Giving: $5,969,656 (fiscal year ending October 31, 2003); $5,883,725 (fiscal 2001). Note: Contrib-

utes through corporate direct giving program and foundation.
Giving Analysis: Giving for fiscal 2001 includes: corporate direct giving ($1,700,000); foundation ($5,800,000)
Assets: $33,132,092 (fiscal 2003)
Gifts Received: $7,051,587 (fiscal 2003); $1,495,000 (fiscal 2000); $5,987,805 (fiscal 1999). Note: In fiscal 2003, contributions were received from Deere & Co. Contributions were received from Deere & Co., John Deere Insurance Company, Deere & Company - Kansas City Branch, Heritage National Healthplan Services, Inc.

Typical Recipients

Arts & Humanities: Arts Associations & Councils, Arts Centers, Community Arts, Arts & Humanities-General, Historic Preservation, History & Archaeology, Libraries, Museums/Galleries, Music, Opera, Public Broadcasting, Theater, Visual Arts
Civic & Public Affairs: Botanical Gardens/Parks, Business/Free Enterprise, Chambers of Commerce, Community Foundations, Economic Development, Civic & Public Affairs-General, Municipalities/Towns, Parades/Festivals, Professional & Trade Associations, Public Policy, Rural Affairs, Urban & Community Affairs, Zoos/Aquariums
Education: Afterschool/Enrichment Programs, Agricultural Education, Arts/Humanities Education, Business Education, Colleges & Universities, Community & Junior Colleges, Economic Education, Education Funds, Engineering/Technological Education, Environmental Education, Education-General, Minority Education, Private Education (Precollege), Public Education (Precollege), Science/Mathematics Education, Secondary Education (Private), Vocational & Technical Education
Environment: Environment-General, Research, Resource Conservation
Health: Emergency/Ambulance Services, Health-General, Health Policy/Cost Containment, Health Organizations, Hospices, Outpatient Health Care, Public Health, Transplant Networks/Donor Banks
International: Foreign Educational Institutions, International-General, International Relief Efforts
Religion: Missionary Activities (Domestic), Religious Welfare
Science: Science Museums
Social Services: Child Welfare, Community Centers, Community Service Organizations, Day Care, Domestic Violence, Emergency Relief, Family Services, Homes, People with Disabilities, Recreation & Athletics, Scouts, Senior Services, Social Services-General, Substance Abuse, United Funds/United Ways, YMCA/YWCA/YMHA/YWHA, Youth Organizations

Application Procedures

Initial Contact: Request guidelines, then send written proposal. Organizations in the Moline, IL area and organizations of a national scope should send applications to the foundation. OrganizationS serving other operating communities should direct inquiries to the general manager of the local unit.
Application Requirements: Applications should include a description of organization and statement of objectives and goals; recent audited financial statement; annual report; program budget if the request is for a specific project; proof of tax-exempt status; complete explanation of the activity; goals of program and deadlines for results; description of benefits; geographic area to be served.
Deadlines: None.
Review Process: Requests are reviewed in order of receipt; board meets as needed; initial response can be expected in four to six weeks.
Evaluative Criteria: "The John Deere Foundation considers requests only from tax-exempt, nonprofit organizations, located in the U.S. or its possessions.... Supports programs that address specific community needs, solve problems, and develop activities that create opportunities for individuals to gain

skills and knowledge that will assist them in accomplishing positive social goals. The Contributions Committee at Deere & Company, a second grant-making group, evaluates requests on their business merits. Priority funding centers upon programs in this order: health and human services; education, including K-12, university, and college efforts that are important to our employee recruiting, research, and training; community revitalization efforts; and cultural organizations." *Deere & Company Corporate Contributions Program 2000 Report of Contributions*
Notes: Organizations located in Moline, IL area or which are national in scope should direct requests to the foundation; other organizations should send requests to the manager of operating unit in community.

Restrictions

John Deere Foundation will not provide support for individuals; dinners or special events; fraternal organizations; goodwill advertising; or political or lobbying groups.

Additional Information

Publications: Annual Contributions Report

Corporate Officials

John K. Lawson: senior vice president B Moline, IL 1940. ED Iowa State University BA (1962). PRIM CORP EMPL senior vice president: John Deere & Co. ADD CORP EMPL vice president: John Deere Commercial Products. CORP AFFIL director: Deere Marketing Services Inc. NONPR AFFIL director: Iowa State University Foundation; director: Research Board; governor: Iowa College Foundation; director: Arrowhead Ranch.

Giving Program Officials

Donald R. Margenthaler: president, director PRIM CORP EMPL director community relations: Deere Co.

Foundation Officials

Samuel R. Allen: director
James H. Becht: secretary
James H. Collins: president, director
James R. Jenkins: director
Nathan J. Jones: director
Robert W. Lane: vice president, director
Dennis R. Schwartz: assistant treasurer
Lisa A. Whitaker: assistant treasurer

Grants Analysis

Disclosure Period: fiscal year ending October 31, 2003
Total Grants: $5,233,256*
Number of Grants: 520 (approx)
Average Grant: $10,064
Highest Grant: $500,000
Lowest Grant: $500
Typical Range: $1,000 to $20,000
*Note: Giving excludes United Way.

Recent Grants

Note: Grants derived from 2003 Form 990.
General

824,350	United Way of the Quad Cities Area, Davenport, IA
500,000	Lincoln Park Zoo, Chicago, IL
320,000	Cedar Valley United Way, Waterloo, IA
250,000	Museum of Art Foundation, Davenport, IA -- towards cultural centers
200,000	Dubuque County Historical Society, Dubuque, IA -- towards community development
145,000	Skip-A-Long Day Care Center, Moline, IL -- for youth agencies
125,000	Northwestern University, Evanston, IL
125,000	Putnam Museum, Davenport, IA
108,000	United Way Service Inc., Dubuque, IA
105,000	United Way of Central Iowa, Des Moines, IA

MIGNON SHERWOOD DELANO FOUNDATION

Giving Contact
Dorothy L. Sullivan, Senior Vice President & Senior Trust Officer
c/o NCB
PO Box 50246
Kalamazoo, MI 49005
Phone: (616)771-8576

Description
Founded: 1985
EIN: 382557743
Organization Type: Private Foundation
Giving Locations: MI: Allegan
Grant Types: General Support.

Donor Information
Founder: the late Mignon Sherwood Delano

Financial Summary
Total Giving: $192,235 (2003)
Assets: $4,163,841 (2003)

Typical Recipients
Arts & Humanities: Arts Associations & Councils, Arts Festivals, Arts Funds, Community Arts, Historic Preservation, History & Archaeology, Libraries, Theater
Civic & Public Affairs: Botanical Gardens/Parks, Civic & Public Affairs-General, Housing, Municipalities/Towns, Urban & Community Affairs, Women's Affairs
Education: Agricultural Education, Arts/Humanities Education, Colleges & Universities, Elementary Education (Public), Education-General, Literacy, Preschool Education, Public Education (Precollege), School Volunteerism
Environment: Energy
Health: Cancer, Clinics/Medical Centers, Emergency/Ambulance Services, Eyes/Blindness, Health Organizations, Hospices, Hospitals, Mental Health, Preventive Medicine/Wellness Organizations
Religion: Religion-General, Religious Welfare
Social Services: Camps, Child Abuse, Child Welfare, Community Centers, Community Service Organizations, Domestic Violence, Family Planning, Family Services, Food/Clothing Distribution, People with Disabilities, Recreation & Athletics, Social Services-General, Special Olympics, Substance Abuse, United Funds/United Ways, Volunteer Services, Youth Organizations

Application Procedures
Initial Contact: Application form required.
Deadlines: September 15.

Additional Information
Publications: Application Form
Trust(s): National City Bank MI NA

Foundation Officials
Ellen Altamore: vice president
Rebecca Burnett: director
G. Phillip Dietrich: secretary
Bernard Riker: president

Grants Analysis
Disclosure Period: calendar year ending 2003
Total Grants: $192,235
Number of Grants: 22
Average Grant: $8,738
Highest Grant: $22,525
Lowest Grant: $1,500
Typical Range: $2,000 to $10,000

Recent Grants
Note: Grants derived from 2003 Form 990.

General
22,525	Allegan Area Community Center, Allegan, MI -- funds for equipments
15,528	Allegan County Prevention of Child Abuse and Neglect Council, Allegan, MI -- funds for programming
15,000	Allegan County Crisis Response Services Inc., Allegan, MI -- funds for programming
15,000	Wings of Hope Hospice, Allegan, MI -- funds for programming
13,000	City of Allegan, Allegan, MI
11,765	Allegan County Medical Care Facility, Allegan, MI -- for equipment
11,600	Allegan Wellness and Sports Complex, Allegan, MI -- funds for equipment
10,000	Allegan County Parks and Recreation Commission, Allegan, MI -- for equipment
10,000	Allegan Ministerium Central Food Pantry, Allegan, MI
8,000	Center for Women in Transition, Allegan, MI

HAZEL DELL FOUNDATION

Giving Contact
Joy Dunlop, Hazel Dell Foundation
103 Foulk Road, Suite 202
Wilmington, DE 19803
Phone: (704)383-2885

Description
Founded: 1956
EIN: 136161744
Organization Type: Private Foundation
Giving Locations: CT; MA; NJ
Grant Types: General Support.

Donor Information
Founder: the late Harry C. McClarity

Financial Summary
Total Giving: $33,700 (2003)
Assets: $1,984,922 (2003)
Gifts Received: $526,019 (1996). Note: In 1996, contributions were received from the June McClarity Powers Trust.

Typical Recipients
Arts & Humanities: Arts Festivals, Ballet, Libraries, Music, Theater
Civic & Public Affairs: Civic & Public Affairs-General, Housing, Municipalities/Towns, Native American Affairs, Parades/Festivals, Safety
Education: Arts/Humanities Education, Colleges & Universities, Engineering/Technological Education, Medical Education, Minority Education, Private Education (Precollege), Public Education (Precollege), Secondary Education (Public)
Environment: Wildlife Protection
Health: Children's Health/Hospitals, Clinics/Medical Centers, Emergency/Ambulance Services, Health Organizations, Hospitals, Medical Rehabilitation, Medical Research
International: Health Care/Hospitals, International Environmental Issues, International Relief Efforts, Missionary/Religious Activities
Religion: Churches, Religion-General, Religious Welfare
Social Services: Animal Protection, Child Welfare, Community Service Organizations, Counseling, Crime Prevention, Family Services, Recreation & Athletics, United Funds/United Ways, Youth Organizations

Application Procedures
Initial Contact: The foundation has no formal grant application procedure or application form.
Deadlines: None.

Restrictions
No support for individuals.

Foundation Officials
Joy S. Dunlop: president, director
William J. Sullivan: treasurer, director PRIM CORP EMPL director advisor: Rolex Watch U.S.A. Inc.

Grants Analysis
Disclosure Period: calendar year ending 2003
Total Grants: $33,700
Number of Grants: 26
Average Grant: $788*
Highest Grant: $14,000
Lowest Grant: $300
Typical Range: $300 to $2,000
***Note:** Average grant figure excludes highest grant.

Recent Grants
Note: Grants derived from 2001 Form 990.
General
24,000	United States Rugby Football Foundation, Boston, MA
2,500	Fairfield Fire Department, Fairfield, CT
2,500	New England Ballet Company, Orange, CT
2,000	Hospital for Special Surgery, New York, NY
2,000	Montana Wildlife Federation, Helena, MT
2,000	Mount Ida College, Newton Center, MA
2,000	New England College, Henniker, NH
2,000	Rocky Mountain Elk Foundation, Missoula, MT
2,000	St. Luke's Catholic Church, Westport, CT
2,000	Sisters of New Skete, Cambridge, NY

GLADYS KRIEBLE DELMAS FOUNDATION

Giving Contact
Joseph C. Mitchell, Trustee
521 5th Avenue, Suite 1612
New York, NY 10175-1699
Phone: (212)687-0011
Fax: (212)687-8877
E-mail: info@delmas.org
Web: http://www.delmas.org

Description
Founded: 1976
EIN: 510193884
Organization Type: Private Foundation
Giving Locations: nationally and internationally.
Grant Types: General Support, Research.

Donor Information
Founder: the late Gladys Krieble Delmas, the late Jean Delmas

Financial Summary
Total Giving: $2,362,439 (2003). Note: 1996 Giving includes scholarships.
Giving Analysis: Giving for 2003 includes: foundation scholarships ($25,000); foundation matching gifts ($25,000); foundation fellowships ($112,000); foundation gifts to individuals ($112,912).
Assets: $53,620,463 (2003)
Gifts Received: $701,899 (1995); $818,586 (1993); $30,229,874 (1992). Note: In 1995, contributions were received from the estate of Gladys K. Delmas.

Typical Recipients

Arts & Humanities: Arts Associations & Councils, Arts Festivals, Arts Outreach, Ballet, Dance, Arts & Humanities-General, Historic Preservation, History & Archaeology, Libraries, Literary Arts, Museums/ Galleries, Music, Opera, Performing Arts, Theater
Civic & Public Affairs: Civic & Public Affairs-General, Nonprofit Management, Parades/Festivals, Professional & Trade Associations, Public Policy
Education: Arts/Humanities Education, Colleges & Universities, Continuing Education, Education Associations, Education-General, International Studies, Legal Education, Private Education (Precollege), Social Sciences Education, Student Aid
Environment: Environment-General
Health: Hospitals, Research/Studies Institutes
International: Foreign Arts Organizations, Foreign Educational Institutions, International Organizations, International Relations, Missionary/Religious Activities
Science: Scientific Centers & Institutes
Social Services: Community Service Organizations, Social Services-General

Application Procedures

Initial Contact: Application to the humanities, library, and performing arts programs are by invitation only. For other programs and deadline information, contact foundation.

Foundation Officials

Joseph C. Mitchell: trustee
David Harry Stam: trustee B Paterson, NJ 1935. ED Wheaton College BA (1955); University of Edinburgh New College (1955-1956); Rutgers University MLS (1962); City University of New York (1963-1964); Northwestern University PhD (1978). PRIM CORP EMPL senior scholar: Syracuse University. NONPR AFFIL member: American Antiquarian Society; member: American Historical Association. CLUB AFFIL Princeton New York Club; Caxton Club; Grolier Club.

Grants Analysis

Disclosure Period: calendar year ending 2003
Total Grants: $2,087,527*
Number of Grants: 126
Average Grant: $13,808*
Highest Grant: $102,900
Lowest Grant: $400
Typical Range: $5,000 to $20,000
*Note: Giving excludes fellowships; matching gifts; scholarships; gifts to individuals. Average grant figure excludes four highest grants ($402,900).

Recent Grants

Note: Grants derived from 2001 Form 990.
Library-Related
50,000	Library Company of Philadelphia, Philadelphia, PA -- dissertation fellowship
40,000	Frick Collection, New York, NY -- historic archives

General
141,000	Woodrow Wilson National Fellowship Foundation, Princeton, NJ -- Millicent C. McIntosh Fellowships Program
100,000	New York City Ballet, New York, NY -- Archive Project
100,000	New York City Opera, Inc., New York, NY -- support for seasons
100,000	Woodrow Wilson National Fellowship Foundation, Princeton, NJ -- Woodrow Wilson Postdoctoral Fellowships
70,000	People and Stories, Trenton, NJ -- operating support
50,000	Bennington College Corporation, Bennington, VT -- Masters Program
50,000	Brooklyn Academy of Music, Brooklyn, NY -- theater programs
50,000	Brooklyn Academy of Music, Brooklyn, NY -- opera
50,000	University of Toronto, Toronto, ON Canada
50,000	Yale University, New Haven, CT

N. DEMOS FOUNDATION

Giving Contact

Diane Day, Secretary
c/o The Northern Trust Co.
50 S. LaSalle St.
Chicago, IL 60675
Phone: (312)630-6000
Fax: (312)444-4122
E-mail: ddm@ntrs.com

Description

Founded: 1964
EIN: 366165689
Organization Type: Private Foundation
Giving Locations: Greece
Grant Types: General Support, Scholarship.

Donor Information

Founder: the late Nicholas Demos

Financial Summary

Total Giving: $303,500 (fiscal year ending June 30, 2004); $419,000 (fiscal 2001)
Assets: $4,526,673 (fiscal 2004); $5,178,252 (fiscal 2001)

Typical Recipients

Arts & Humanities: Arts Centers, Libraries
Civic & Public Affairs: Civic & Public Affairs-General
Education: Agricultural Education, Arts/Humanities Education, Colleges & Universities, Education-General, Private Education (Precollege)
Health: Children's Health/Hospitals, Clinics/Medical Centers, Medical Research, Mental Health
International: Foreign Educational Institutions, International-General, Health Care/Hospitals, International Organizations, International Peace & Security Issues, International Relief Efforts, Missionary/ Religious Activities
Religion: Religious Organizations, Religious Welfare
Social Services: Child Welfare, Community Service Organizations, Family Services, People with Disabilities, Social Services-General, Veterans, Youth Organizations

Application Procedures

Initial Contact: Send a brief letter of inquiry, then a full proposal.
Application Requirements: Include a description of organization, amount requested, purpose of funds sought, recently audited financial statement, and proof of tax-exempt status.
Deadlines: Applications are due by annual meeting.

Restrictions

Limited to charities in Greece involved in various social work activities.

Additional Information

Publications: Application Guidelines

Foundation Officials

Mrs. Desi Bakalis: director
Elizabeth R. Gebhard: director
Charles M. Gray: president
Metropolitan Iakovos: director
Judge Paul C. Lillios: director
Robert F. Reusche: chairman B New Rochelle, NY 1927. ED Ohio State University BS (1949); University of Chicago MBA (1955). PRIM CORP EMPL vice chairman, director: Northern Trust Co. CORP AFFIL chairman, director: Northern Trust FloridaCorp.; director: Banque Scandinave Suisse; director: Griffin Group. NONPR AFFIL director: JR Bowman Health Center; trustee: Ravinia Festival Association; member: Financial Analysts Federation; trustee: Chicago Home Incurables; member: Corp. Fiduciary Association; member: American Bankers Association; member advisory board: Catholic Charities.

Grants Analysis

Disclosure Period: fiscal year ending June 30, 2004
Total Grants: $303,500
Number of Grants: 26
Average Grant: $8,896*
Highest Grant: $50,000
Lowest Grant: $5,000
Typical Range: $5,000 to $10,000
*Note: Average grant figure excludes two highest grants ($90,000).

Recent Grants

Note: Grants derived from fiscal 2004 Form 990.
General
40,000	Cerebral Palsy Greece Greece
38,000	Social Work Foundation, Attika Greece
25,000	Anatolia College Greece
15,000	American Farm School, New York, NY
15,000	Friends of the Deaf Greece
15,000	Patriarchal Institute for Patristic Studies Greece
12,500	American School of Classical Studies
10,000	American College of Greece, Aghia Paraskevi Greece
10,000	Association of Autistic Persons
10,000	Center D'estudes D'asie Meneure

DEMOULAS SUPERMARKETS INC.

Company Headquarters

875 E. St.
Tewksbury, MA 01876

Company Description

Founded: 1954
Revenue: US$1.9 billion (2001)
Employees: 7,000
SIC(s): 5411 Grocery Stores, 6512 Nonresidential Building Operators.

Operating Locations

Demoulas Supermarkets Inc. (MA--Andover, Bellingham, Burlington, Chelmsford, Chelsea, Danvers, Haverhill, Lawrence, Leominster, Lowell, Middleton, Newburyport, North Andover, North Billerica, Raynham, Rowley, Westford, Wilmington, Woburn; NH--Concord, Hudson, Londonderry, Milford, Plaistow, Portsmouth, Rindge, Rochester, Seabrook, Somersworth, Stratham)

Demoulas Foundation

Giving Contact

Arthur T. Demoulas, Trustee
Demoulas Foundation
286 Chelmsford Street
Chelmsford, MA 01824
Phone: (978)224-1024
Fax: (978)640-8392

Description

Founded: 1964
EIN: 042723441
Organization Type: Corporate Foundation
Giving Locations: primarily New England.
Grant Types: Endowment, General Support.

Donor Information

Founder: Demoulas Supermarkets, Inc., and members of the Demoulas family

Financial Summary

Total Giving: $1,897,205 (2003); $2,029,300 (2002); $1,276,100 (2001). Note: Contributes through foundation only.
Assets: $35,513,383 (2003); $36,293,556 (2002); $36,142,070 (2001)

Typical Recipients

Arts & Humanities: Arts Associations & Councils, Arts Centers, Arts Festivals, Ballet, Dance, Arts & Humanities-General, Historic Preservation, History & Archaeology, Libraries, Literary Arts, Museums/Galleries, Music, Opera, Performing Arts, Public Broadcasting
Civic & Public Affairs: Botanical Gardens/Parks, Clubs, Civic & Public Affairs-General, Housing, Inner-City Development, Municipalities/Towns, Parades/Festivals, Philanthropic Organizations, Safety, Urban & Community Affairs, Women's Affairs
Education: Arts/Humanities Education, Business Education, Colleges & Universities, Education Funds, Education-General, International Studies, Leadership Training, Medical Education, Minority Education, Private Education (Precollege), Religious Education, Secondary Education (Private), Special Education, Student Aid
Environment: Environment-General
Health: Cancer, Children's Health/Hospitals, Diabetes, Geriatric Health, Health Funds, Health Organizations, Hospices, Hospitals, Hospitals (University Affiliated), Long-Term Care, Medical Rehabilitation, Medical Research, Nursing Services, Respiratory, Single-Disease Health Associations, Trauma Treatment
Religion: Churches, Dioceses, Religion-General, Religious Organizations, Religious Welfare
Science: Science Museums
Social Services: Camps, Community Centers, Community Service Organizations, Food/Clothing Distribution, Homes, People with Disabilities, Recreation & Athletics, Scouts, Senior Services, Social Services-General, Substance Abuse, Veterans, YMCA/YWCA/YMHA/YWHA, Youth Organizations

Application Procedures

Initial Contact: Send a brief letter of inquiry.
Application Requirements: Include a brief history of organization and description of need.
Deadlines: None.

Corporate Officials

Julien Lacourse: executive vice president

Foundation Officials

Arthur T. Demoulas: trustee B 1955. ED Bentley College (1976). ADD CORP EMPL president, chief executive officer, treasurer: Market Basket Inc.
D. Harold Sullivan: fiscal officer B 1923.

Grants Analysis

Disclosure Period: calendar year ending 2003
Total Grants: $1,897,205
Number of Grants: 181
Average Grant: $4,984*
Highest Grant: $1,000,000
Lowest Grant: $500
Typical Range: $1,000 to $10,000
*Note: Average grant figure excludes highest grant.

Recent Grants

Note: Grants derived from 2003 Form 990.
General
1,000,000	Boston College, Chestnut Hill, MA
30,000	Central Catholic High School, Pittsburgh, PA
25,000	Catholic Schools Foundation Inc., Boston, MA
25,000	Clinical Scholar Fund
21,555	Metropolitan Opera, New York, NY
15,000	Boys and Girls Club of Lawrence, Lawrence, KS
15,000	Hellenic College Inc. School of Theology
15,000	Lowell Community Broadcast, Lowell, MA
14,500	Celebrity Series, Boston, MA
11,000	Lowell Festival Foundation, Lowell, MA

DENDROICA FOUNDATION

Giving Contact

Leonard Richards, Vice President
Mellon Bank, NA
One Mellon Bank Center, Suite 3725
Pittsburgh, PA 15258
Phone: (412)234-5892

Description

Founded: 1997
EIN: 237912826
Organization Type: Private Foundation
Giving Locations: Northeastern United States.
Grant Types: General Support, Project.

Financial Summary

Total Giving: $14,831,031 (2003)
Assets: $11,018,962 (2003)
Gifts Received: $241,337 (2003); $7,096,000 (2000); $61,659 (1997). Note: In 2003, contributions were received from Peter Blanchard.

Typical Recipients

Arts & Humanities: Libraries, Museums/Galleries
Civic & Public Affairs: Botanical Gardens/Parks, Civic & Public Affairs-General, Zoos/Aquariums
Education: Environmental Education, Student Aid
Environment: Environment-General, Resource Conservation, Wildlife Protection

Application Procedures

Initial Contact: Contact the foundation for application procedures.
Notes: Most grantees are pre-selected by the distribution committee.

Restrictions

Grants are almost exclusively in the areas of nature conservation, preservation of biological diversity, and environmental education and research.

Additional Information

Trust(s): Mellon Bank NA

Grants Analysis

Disclosure Period: calendar year ending 2003
Total Grants: $14,831,031
Number of Grants: 1

Recent Grants

Note: Grants derived from 2001 Form 990.
Library-Related
10,000	New York Botanical Gardens, Bronx, NY

General
50,000	Maine Coast Heritage Trust, Brunswick, ME
50,000	Nature Conservancy Maine Chapter, New York, NY
50,000	RARE Center for Tropical Conservation, Philadelphia, PA
30,000	Nature Conservancy Maine Chapter, New York, NY
25,000	American Farmland Trust, Saratoga Springs, NY
20,000	Natural Resources Council of Maine, Augusta, ME
10,000	American Museum of Natural History, New York, NY
10,000	Mosby Heritage Area, Middleburg, VA
10,000	Wildlife Conservation Society, New York, NY
10,000	Yale University School of Forestry and Environmental Studies, New Haven, CT

HELEN PUMPHREY DENIT TRUST FOR CHARITABLE AND EDUCATIONAL PURPOSES

Giving Contact

Richard Adams, Trust Officer
c/o Bank of America
100 South Charles Street, MD4-325-09-03
Baltimore, MD 21201
Phone: (410)547-4333
Fax: (410)837-3096
E-mail: richard.adams@am.bankofamerica.com
Web: http://www.bankofamerica.com

Alternate Contact

Phone: 800-527-5394

Description

Founded: 1989
EIN: 526401248
Organization Type: Private Foundation
Giving Locations: DC
Grant Types: General Support.

Donor Information

Founder: the late Helen P. Denit

Financial Summary

Total Giving: $900,000 (fiscal year ending June 30, 2002 approx); $1,030,000 (fiscal 2001)
Assets: $6,500,000 (fiscal 2002 approx); $10,227,077 (fiscal 2001)

Typical Recipients

Arts & Humanities: Arts Festivals, History & Archaeology, Libraries, Museums/Galleries, Theater
Civic & Public Affairs: Botanical Gardens/Parks, Community Foundations, Civic & Public Affairs-General, Zoos/Aquariums
Education: Arts/Humanities Education, Colleges & Universities, Private Education (Precollege), Religious Education, Student Aid
Health: Cancer, Health-General, Heart, Hospitals
Religion: Jewish Causes, Seminaries
Social Services: Child Abuse, Child Welfare, Food/Clothing Distribution, Recreation & Athletics

Application Procedures

Initial Contact: Send a brief letter of inquiry.
Application Requirements: Include amount requested and purpose of funds sought.
Deadlines: None.

Additional Information

Foundation/Giving Program still in operation, but grant making has been suspended. We have preferred charities indicated by Mrs. Denits will, and several multiyear commitments that will effectively limit consideration of additional grants for at least the next five years.
Trust(s): Bank of America

Grants Analysis

Disclosure Period: fiscal year ending June 30, 2001
Total Grants: $1,030,000
Number of Grants: 18
Average Grant: $51,176*
Highest Grant: $160,000
Typical Range: $5,000 to $60,000

*Note: Average grant figure excludes highest grant. Grant analysis provided by foundation.

Recent Grants

Note: Grants derived from fiscal 2002 Form 990.
General

100,000	American Heart Association - Mid Council, Baltimore, MD
100,000	George Washington University, Washington, DC
100,000	Life Bridge Health, Baltimore, MD
100,000	Montgomery General Hospital Health Foundation, Inc., Olney, MD
100,000	University of Baltimore Educational Foundation, Baltimore, MD
100,000	University of Maryland Medical System Foundation, Baltimore, MD
100,000	Wesley Theological Seminary, Washington, DC
100,000	Western Maryland College, Westminster, MD
10,000	Babe Ruth Birthplace Foundation, Baltimore, MD
10,000	Baltimore and Ohio Railroad Museum, Baltimore, MD

DENTSPLY INTERNATIONAL INC.

Company Headquarters

PO Box 872
York, PA 17405-0872
Web: http://www.dentsply.com

Company Description

Founded: 1899
Ticker: XRAY
Exchange: NASDAQ
Revenue: US$1.513 billion (2002)
Employees: 7800 (2002)
SIC(s): 3800 Instruments & Related Products.

Operating Locations

Dentsply International Inc. (DE--Milford; OH--Cincinnati, Maumee)
Note: Includes division locations

Nonmonetary Support

Type: Donated Equipment; Donated Products

Dentsply International Foundation

Giving Contact

Dentsply International Foundation
Tax Dept.
570 W. College Ave.
York, PA 17404
Phone: (717)845-7511

Description

EIN: 236297307
Organization Type: Corporate Foundation
Giving Locations: nationally.
Grant Types: Award, Capital, General Support, Multiyear/Continuing Support, Research.

Financial Summary

Total Giving: $196,050 (2003); $120,710 (2001)
Giving Analysis: Giving for 2003 includes: foundation grants to United Way ($41,000); 2001: foundation grants to United Way ($48,000); foundation ($72,710)
Assets: $62,273 (2003); $75,616 (2001)
Gifts Received: $211,000 (2003); $160,000 (2001);

$125,000 (2000). Note: Contributions were received from Dentsply International.

Typical Recipients

Arts & Humanities: Arts Funds, Arts & Humanities-General, Historic Preservation, History & Archaeology, Libraries, Museums/Galleries, Music, Performing Arts, Theater
Civic & Public Affairs: Botanical Gardens/Parks, Chambers of Commerce, Clubs, Community Foundations, Civic & Public Affairs-General, Hispanic Affairs, Housing, Philanthropic Organizations, Professional & Trade Associations, Public Policy, Safety, Urban & Community Affairs
Education: Arts/Humanities Education, Business Education, Colleges & Universities, Continuing Education, Education-General, Health & Physical Education, Medical Education, Minority Education, Public Education (Precollege), Student Aid
Environment: Resource Conservation
Health: AIDS/HIV, Cancer, Children's Health/Hospitals, Clinics/Medical Centers, Diabetes, Health-General, Geriatric Health, Health Organizations, Heart, Hospices, Hospitals, Medical Research, Nursing Services, Public Health, Single-Disease Health Associations, Transplant Networks/Donor Banks
Religion: Churches, Religion-General, Religious Organizations, Religious Welfare
Social Services: Animal Protection, At-Risk Youth, Big Brothers/Big Sisters, Child Abuse, Child Welfare, Community Service Organizations, Day Care, Family Services, Food/Clothing Distribution, People with Disabilities, Recreation & Athletics, Senior Services, Shelters/Homelessness, United Funds/United Ways, YMCA/YWCA/YMHA/YWHA, Youth Organizations

Application Procedures

Initial Contact: The foundation has no formal grant application procedure or application form.
Deadlines: None.

Restrictions

Does not support individuals, religious organizations for sectarian purposes, political or lobbying groups, or organizations outside operating areas.

Additional Information

Provides grants for dental health and higher education.

Corporate Officials

Leslie A. Jones: chairman vice president, chief financial officer PRIM CORP EMPL chairman: Dentsply International.
Gary K. Kunkle: president, chief operating officer PRIM CORP EMPL president, chief operating officer: Dentsply International.
John C. Miles, II: president, chief executive officer, director B Portland, ME 1942. ED Lehigh University (1964); New York University (1971). PRIM CORP EMPL president, chief executive officer, director: Dentsply International. CORP AFFIL director: Dental Manufacturers America.
Edward D. Yates: senior vice president, chief financial officer PRIM CORP EMPL senior vice president, chief financial officer: Dentsply International.

Foundation Officials

Brian M. Addison: secretary, trustee
Gary K. Kunkle: chairman, trustee (see above)

Grants Analysis

Disclosure Period: calendar year ending 2003
Total Grants: $155,050*
Number of Grants: 44
Average Grant: $1,617*
Highest Grant: $85,500
Lowest Grant: $275
Typical Range: $500 to $3,500
*Note: Giving excludes United Way. Average grant figure excludes highest grant.

Recent Grants

Note: Grants derived from 2001 Form 990.
Library-Related

500	Intercollegiate Studies Institute, Inc., Wilmington, DE -- community service

General

40,500	United Way of York County, York, PA -- community service
10,000	New York Fire Fighters Fund, New York, NY -- community service
7,000	United Way of Delaware, Wilmington, DE -- community service
2,500	Junior Achievement of Delaware, Wilmington, DE -- community service
1,000	American Heart Association, Georgetown, DE -- community service
1,000	Community Programs Council, Inc., York, PA -- community service
1,000	Friends of the Capitol Theater, Dover, DE -- community service
1,000	Manito, Inc., PA -- community service
1,000	Noah's Place, York, PA -- community service
1,000	Tressler Lutheran Services -- community service

DEROY TESTAMENTARY FOUNDATION

Giving Contact

Julie Rodecker Holly, Vice President
26999 Central Park Boulevard, Suite 160
Southfield, MI 48076
Phone: (248)827-0920
Fax: (248)827-0922
E-mail: DeRoyFdtn@aol.com

Description

Founded: 1979
EIN: 382208833
Organization Type: General Purpose Foundation
Giving Locations: MI: Metropolitan Detroit
Grant Types: Award, General Support, Multiyear/Continuing Support, Professorship, Project, Scholarship.

Donor Information

Founder: Established in 1979 by the late Helen L. DeRoy.

Financial Summary

Total Giving: $2,057,483 (2003); $2,061,695 (2002); $1,920,612 (2001)
Giving Analysis: Giving for 2003 includes: foundation grants to United Way ($9,000); 2001: foundation grants to United Way ($34,000)
Assets: $50,436,917 (2003); $43,621,392 (2002); $46,724,275 (2001)

Typical Recipients

Arts & Humanities: Arts Associations & Councils, Arts Centers, Arts Funds, Arts Institutes, Arts Outreach, Arts & Humanities-General, Historic Preservation, History & Archaeology, Libraries, Literary Arts, Museums/Galleries, Music, Opera, Performing Arts, Public Broadcasting, Theater
Civic & Public Affairs: Clubs, Ethnic Organizations, Civic & Public Affairs-General, Housing, Municipalities/Towns, Parades/Festivals, Public Policy, Urban & Community Affairs, Women's Affairs, Zoos/Aquariums
Education: Agricultural Education, Arts/Humanities Education, Business Education, Colleges & Universities, Community & Junior Colleges, Education Funds, Engineering/Technological Education, Faculty Development, Education-General, International Exchange, Leadership Training, Legal Education, Medical Edu-

cation, Minority Education, Preschool Education, Private Education (Precollege), Public Education (Precollege), Religious Education, Science/Mathematics Education, Secondary Education (Private), Special Education, Student Aid
Environment: Air/Water Quality, Environment-General
Health: Cancer, Children's Health/Hospitals, Clinics/Medical Centers, Emergency/Ambulance Services, Eyes/Blindness, Health Funds, Health Organizations, Hospices, Hospitals, Long-Term Care, Medical Rehabilitation, Medical Research, Mental Health, Nursing Services, Prenatal Health Issues, Preventive Medicine/Wellness Organizations, Public Health, Research/Studies Institutes, Trauma Treatment
Religion: Churches, Jewish Causes, Religious Organizations, Religious Welfare, Synagogues/Temples
Science: Scientific Centers & Institutes
Social Services: Animal Protection, At-Risk Youth, Camps, Child Abuse, Child Welfare, Community Centers, Community Service Organizations, Counseling, Day Care, Domestic Violence, Family Planning, Family Services, Food/Clothing Distribution, Homes, People with Disabilities, Recreation & Athletics, Senior Services, United Funds/United Ways, Youth Organizations

Application Procedures

Initial Contact: The foundation reports that applications may vary depending upon the nature of the request.
Deadlines: None.

Restrictions

The foundation reports that it principally makes grants to institutions of established excellence in Michigan. Grants are not made to individuals.

Foundation Officials

Arthur Rodecker: president, trustee B 1926. PRIM CORP EMPL president: Rodecker & Co. Investment Brokers.

Grants Analysis

Disclosure Period: calendar year ending 2003
Total Grants: $2,048,483*
Number of Grants: 163
Average Grant: $12,567
Highest Grant: $100,000
Lowest Grant: $200
Typical Range: $5,000 to $25,000
*Note: Giving excludes United Way.

Recent Grants

Note: Grants derived from 2002 Form 990.

Library-Related
| 8,000 | Friends of the Detroit Public Library, Detroit, MI |

General
250,000	Detroit Symphony Orchestra Hall Inc., Detroit, MI
100,000	Detroit Science Center, Detroit, MI
97,000	Oakland Family Services, Pontiac, MI
75,000	Detroit Institute of Arts, Detroit, MI
75,000	Providence Health Foundation, Southfield, MI
60,000	Hospice of Michigan, Detroit, MI
50,000	Interlochen Center for the Arts, Interlochen, MI
50,000	Jewish Federation of Metropolitan Detroit, Bloomfield Hills, MI
50,000	Michigan State University, East Lansing, MI
50,000	Society of St. Vincent de Paul, Detroit, MI

GEORGE H. DEUBLE FOUNDATION

Giving Contact

Andrew H. Deuble, Secretary & Trustee
c/o DCC Corp.
5757 Mayfair Rd.
PO Box 2288
North Canton, OH 44720-1546
Phone: (330)828-9770

Description

Founded: 1947
EIN: 341806245
Organization Type: Private Foundation
Giving Locations: OH
Grant Types: Capital, Fellowship, Operating Expenses, Scholarship.

Donor Information

Founder: Established in 1947 by the late George H. Deuble.

Financial Summary

Total Giving: $1,364,438 (2002 approx)
Giving Analysis: Giving for 2002 includes: foundation scholarships ($1,000); foundation scholarships ($38,333); foundation grants to United Way ($86,125)
Assets: $24,628,535 (2002 approx)

Typical Recipients

Arts & Humanities: Arts Centers, Arts Festivals, Historic Preservation, Libraries, Museums/Galleries, Music
Civic & Public Affairs: African American Affairs, Community Foundations, Economic Development, Civic & Public Affairs-General, Housing, Minority Business, Urban & Community Affairs
Education: Business Education, Colleges & Universities, Education Funds, Education Reform, Education-General, Private Education (Precollege), Public Education (Precollege), Science/Mathematics Education, Student Aid
Health: Health Funds, Health Organizations, Heart, Hospitals, Medical Research
Religion: Churches, Religious Welfare
Social Services: Child Welfare, Community Service Organizations, Day Care, Emergency Relief, Family Services, Recreation & Athletics, Scouts, Social Services-General, United Funds/United Ways, YMCA/YWCA/YMHA/YWHA, Youth Organizations

Application Procedures

Initial Contact: Send a brief letter of inquiry.
Application Requirements: purpose of funds sought and amount requested.
Deadlines: None.

Foundation Officials

Andrew H. Deuble: secretary, trustee
Steven G. Deuble: president, trustee B Canton, OH 1947. ED Ohio Wesleyan University (1969). PRIM CORP EMPL chief executive officer, director: DCC Corp. CORP AFFIL president, director: Massillon Plaque Co.
Walter C. Deuble: trustee B 1921. PRIM CORP EMPL chairman board, director: DCC Corp.
Walter J. Deuble: trustee

Grants Analysis

Disclosure Period: calendar year ending 2002
Total Grants: $1,238,980*
Number of Grants: 123
Average Grant: $10,073*
Highest Grant: $125,000
Lowest Grant: $75
Typical Range: $1,000 to $10,000
*Note: Giving excludes United Way; scholarships and fellowship

Recent Grants

Note: Grants derived from 2002 Form 990.
Library-Related
| 50,000 | National First Ladies Library, Canton, OH |
General
125,000	Walsh University, Canton, OH
115,000	Canton Ex-Newsboys Association, Canton, OH
100,000	North Canton Medical Foundation, Canton, OH
56,833	Hartville Area Community Charitable Trust, Canton, OH
55,125	United Way Central Stark County, Canton, OH
50,000	First Tee of Canton, Canton, OH
39,125	Canton Negro Oldtimers, Canton, OH
35,000	Blue Coats Drum and Bugle Corp., North Canton, OH
33,333	Stark State College of Technology, Canton, OH
30,000	Ohio Foundation of Independent Colleges, Columbus, OH

DEVORE FOUNDATION

Giving Contact

Richard A. DeVore, President & Secretary
PO Box 782615
Wichita, KS 67278-2615
Phone: (316)634-1275

Description

Founded: 1953
EIN: 486109754
Organization Type: Private Foundation
Giving Locations: KS: Wichita
Grant Types: Capital, Endowment, General Support, Multiyear/Continuing Support, Operating Expenses, Project.

Donor Information

Founder: the late Floyd DeVore, Richard A. DeVore, William O. DeVore

Financial Summary

Total Giving: $237,850 (fiscal year ending November 30, 2001)
Giving Analysis: Giving for fiscal 2001 includes: foundation grants to United Way ($5,000)
Assets: $7,584,791 (fiscal 2001)
Gifts Received: $5,000 (fiscal 2000); $5,000 (fiscal 1997); $142,000 (fiscal 1996). Note: In fiscal 1997 and 2000, contributions were received from Devore and Sons. In fiscal 1996, contributions were received from R.A. Devore and William Devore.

Typical Recipients

Arts & Humanities: Arts Associations & Councils, Arts Centers, Arts & Humanities-General, History & Archaeology, Libraries, Museums/Galleries, Music, Performing Arts
Civic & Public Affairs: Business/Free Enterprise, Clubs, Community Foundations, Employment/Job Training, Civic & Public Affairs-General, Municipalities/Towns, Native American Affairs, Public Policy, Urban & Community Affairs, Zoos/Aquariums
Education: Colleges & Universities, Education Funds, Education-General, Literacy, Private Education (Precollege), Student Aid
Environment: Air/Water Quality, Environment-General
Health: AIDS/HIV, Cancer, Children's Health/Hospitals, Geriatric Health, Hospices, Hospitals, Medical Research, Public Health, Single-Disease Health Associations
Religion: Churches, Ministries, Religious Welfare
Social Services: At-Risk Youth, Big Brothers/Big Sisters, Child Welfare, Community Service Organiza-

tions, Crime Prevention, Family Services, Homes, People with Disabilities, Scouts, Senior Services, Social Services-General, Special Olympics, Substance Abuse, United Funds/United Ways, YMCA/YWCA/YMHA/YWHA, Youth Organizations

Application Procedures

Initial Contact: Send a brief letter of inquiry.
Application Requirements: Include a description of organization, amount requested, purpose of funds sought, recently audited financial statement, and proof of tax-exempt status.
Deadlines: None.
Decision Notification: Contributions are planned in advance and donations requiring a rapid decision are rarely made.

Restrictions

The foundation makes contributions to operating and educational organizations only.

Additional Information

Publications: Application Guidelines; Annual Report

Foundation Officials

Richard A. DeVore: president, secretary
William O. DeVore: vice president, treasurer

Grants Analysis

Disclosure Period: fiscal year ending November 30, 2001
Total Grants: $232,850*
Number of Grants: 101
Average Grant: $1,140*
Highest Grant: $90,000
Lowest Grant: $100
Typical Range: $100 to $5,000
*Note: Giving excludes United Way. Average grant figure excludes two highest grants ($120,000).

Recent Grants

Note: Grants derived from fiscal 2002 Form 990.
General

100,000	Wichita Art Museum, Wichita, KS
50,000	Wichita Art Museum, Wichita, KS
50,000	Wichita Community Foundation, Wichita, KS
20,000	Desert Caballeros Western Museum, Wickenburg, AZ
12,000	Wichita Art Museum, Wichita, KS
11,250	First Presbyterian Church, Wichita, KS
11,250	First Presbyterian Church, Wichita, KS
10,000	City of Wichita, Wichita, KS -- Excellence in Public Service
10,000	United Way of the Plains, Wichita, KS
10,000	Wichita State University, Wichita, KS

RICHARD AND HELEN DEVOS FOUNDATION

Giving Contact

Ginny Vander Hart, Foundation Director
126 Ottawa Northwest, Suite 500
Grand Rapids, MI 49503
Phone: (616)454-4114
Fax: (616)454-0970
E-mail: virginiav@rdvcorp.com

Description

Founded: 1969
EIN: 237066873
Organization Type: Family Foundation
Giving Locations: FL: including central Florida; MI: Grand Rapids nationally.
Grant Types: Capital, Challenge, General Support, Matching, Operating Expenses, Project, Seed Money.

Donor Information

Founder: The foundation was established in Michigan in 1969 by Richard M. DeVos, co-founder and president of the Amway Corporation, and his wife, Helen DeVos. Periodic contributions from the DeVos family increase the foundation's asset level. Executive personnel of the Amway Corporation provide management and administrative aid to the foundation.
Mr. Devos purchased the National Basketball Association's Orlando Magic franchise in 1991 for a reported $85 million.

Financial Summary

Total Giving: $31,911,100 (2003); $33,226,280 (2002); $26,574,754 (2001)
Giving Analysis: Giving for 2003 includes: foundation grants to United Way ($50,000); 2002: foundation grants to United Way ($350,000)
Assets: $95,613,488 (2003); $81,564,122 (2002); $97,048,407 (2001)
Gifts Received: $32,208,394 (2003); $5,408,394 (2002); $3,596,869 (2001). Note: In 2003, contributions were received from Richard M. Devos Clat 2 ($7,208,394) and Alticor Inc. ($25,000,000). In 2001 and 2002, contributions were received from Richard M. Devos Clat 2. In 1998, contributions were received from Amway Corp. ($4,000,000) and Richard Devos ($14,416,788).

Typical Recipients

Arts & Humanities: Arts Associations & Councils, Arts Centers, Arts Funds, Libraries, Museums/Galleries, Music, Public Broadcasting
Civic & Public Affairs: Botanical Gardens/Parks, Business/Free Enterprise, Civil Rights, Community Foundations, First Amendment Issues, Civic & Public Affairs-General, Housing, Inner-City Development, Law & Justice, Philanthropic Organizations, Public Policy, Urban & Community Affairs, Zoos/Aquariums
Education: Afterschool/Enrichment Programs, Business Education, Business-School Partnerships, Colleges & Universities, Education Associations, Education Funds, Education Reform, Engineering/Technological Education, Education-General, Journalism/Media Education, Leadership Training, Private Education (Precollege), Religious Education, Secondary Education (Public), Student Aid
Environment: Air/Water Quality, Environment-General
Health: Clinics/Medical Centers, Emergency/Ambulance Services, Health-General, Health Funds, Health Organizations, Hospitals, Long-Term Care, Medical Research, Prenatal Health Issues, Public Health, Single-Disease Health Associations, Transplant Networks/Donor Banks
International: Health Care/Hospitals, International Affairs, International Development, International Organizations, International Relations, International Relief Efforts, Missionary/Religious Activities
Religion: Bible Study/Translation, Churches, Religion-General, Ministries, Missionary Activities (Domestic), Religious Organizations, Religious Welfare, Seminaries, Social/Policy Issues
Social Services: Camps, Child Welfare, Community Centers, Community Service Organizations, Delinquency & Criminal Rehabilitation, Family Planning, Family Services, Food/Clothing Distribution, Homes, People with Disabilities, Recreation & Athletics, Scouts, Senior Services, Social Services-General, United Funds/United Ways, Volunteer Services, YMCA/YWCA/YMHA/YWHA, Youth Organizations

Application Procedures

Initial Contact: Prospective applicants should send a letter of proposal.
Application Requirements: In the preliminary letter, describe the project and organization for which funds are sought. The foundation asks that applicants specify amounts.
Deadlines: None.

Additional Information

Publications: Guidelines

Foundation Officials

William Boer: vice president, assistant secretary
Helen June (Van Wesep) DeVos: president
Robert H. Schierbeek: treasurer
Jerry L. Tubergen: vice president, secretary, chief operating officer CORP AFFIL director: Genmar Holdings Inc. CLUB AFFIL member: Economic Club of Grand Rapids.

Grants Analysis

Disclosure Period: calendar year ending 2003
Total Grants: $31,861,100*
Number of Grants: 167
Average Grant: $77,195*
Highest Grant: $3,600,000
Lowest Grant: $500
Typical Range: $20,000 to $200,000
*Note: Giving excludes United Way. Average grant excludes twelve highest grants ($19,895,925).

Recent Grants

Note: Grants derived from 2002 Form 990.
General

6,470,000	Blodgett Butterworth Health Care Foundation, Grand Rapids, MI
2,044,800	Gospel Communications International, Muskegon, MI
2,015,000	Calvin College, Grand Rapids, MI
2,010,000	National Constitutional Center, Philadelphia, PA
1,400,000	Grand Valley University Foundation, Grand Rapids, MI
1,260,000	Grand Rapids Symphony, Grand Rapids, MI
1,030,000	Holland Home, Grand Rapids, MI
1,028,000	Grand Rapids Christian School Association, Grand Rapids, MI
1,005,000	Ada Christian School, Grand Rapids, MI
1,000,000	Lee University, Cleveland, TN

DEWAR FOUNDATION

Giving Contact

Sidney Levine, President & Director
16 Dietz St.
Oneonta, NY 13820
Phone: (607)432-1811

Description

Founded: 1947
EIN: 166054329
Organization Type: Private Foundation
Giving Locations: NY: including Oneonta and surrounding area
Grant Types: General Support.

Donor Information

Founder: the late Jessie Smith Dewar

Financial Summary

Total Giving: $598,000 (2004)
Giving Analysis: Giving for 2005 includes: foundation grants to United Way ($5,000)
Assets: $12,235,428 (2004)
Gifts Received: $7,995 (1994); $2,221,500 (1993). Note: In 1994, contributions were received from the estate of Wendall F. Couse.

Typical Recipients

Arts & Humanities: Arts Centers, History & Archaeology, Libraries, Museums/Galleries, Music, Opera, Public Broadcasting, Theater
Civic & Public Affairs: Employment/Job Training, Civic & Public Affairs-General, Municipalities/Towns, Rural Affairs, Safety, Urban & Community Affairs

Education: Colleges & Universities, Community & Junior Colleges, Education-General, Legal Education, Minority Education, Private Education (Precollege), Public Education (Precollege), Science/ Mathematics Education, Student Aid
Environment: Environment-General
Health: Cancer, Emergency/Ambulance Services, Heart, Hospices, Hospitals, Medical Research, Single-Disease Health Associations
Religion: Churches, Jewish Causes, Religious Organizations, Religious Welfare, Synagogues/Temples
Social Services: Animal Protection, Child Welfare, Community Service Organizations, Family Planning, Family Services, Homes, People with Disabilities, Recreation & Athletics, Scouts, Senior Services, Social Services-General, United Funds/United Ways, YMCA/YWCA/YMHA/YWHA, Youth Organizations

Application Procedures

Initial Contact: Send a brief letter of inquiry describing program or project.
Application Requirements: Include statement of need and purpose of funds sought.
Deadlines: None.

Foundation Officials

Michael F. Getman: treasurer, secretary
Sidney Levine: president

Grants Analysis

Disclosure Period: calendar year ending 2004
Total Grants: $593,000*
Number of Grants: 78
Average Grant: $6,078*
Highest Grant: $125,000
Lowest Grant: $1,000
Typical Range: $1,000 to $10,000
*Note: Giving excludes United Way. Average grant figure excludes highest grant.

Recent Grants

Note: Grants derived from 2001 Form 990.
General

150,000	State University College Oneonta, Oneonta, NY
125,000	Fox Memorial Hospital, Oneonta, NY
55,000	Temple Beth El, Oneonta, NY
51,000	Saint Mary's School, Oneonta, NY
35,000	Catskill Area Hospice and Palliative Care, Inc., Oneonta, NY
25,000	College Foundation at Delhi, Inc., Delhi, NY
25,000	College of St. Rose, Albany, NY
25,000	Greater Oneonta Historical Society, Oneonta, NY
25,000	Opportunities for Otsego, Inc., Oneonta, NY
25,000	SUNY Cobleskill, Cobleskill, NY

HENRIETTA DEXTER CHARITABLE TRUST

Giving Contact

Thea Katsounakis, Trust Officer
c/o Fleet PCG
Charitable Trusts
PO Box 6767
Providence, RI 02940-6767

Description

Founded: 1946
EIN: 046018698
Organization Type: Private Foundation
Giving Locations: MA, Sringfield including greater metropolitan are
Grant Types: Capital, Conference/Seminar, General Support, Seed Money.

Donor Information

Founder: the late Henrietta F. Dexter

Financial Summary

Total Giving: $448,939 (2004); $740,681 (2001)
Assets: $14,394,578 (2004); $14,427,429 (2001)

Typical Recipients

Arts & Humanities: Arts Associations & Councils, Arts Centers, Arts Festivals, Community Arts, History & Archaeology, Libraries, Literary Arts, Museums/ Galleries, Music, Performing Arts, Theater
Civic & Public Affairs: African American Affairs, Asian American Affairs, Business/Free Enterprise, Community Foundations, Economic Development, Employment/Job Training, Ethnic Organizations, Civic & Public Affairs-General, Hispanic Affairs, Housing, Municipalities/Towns, Philanthropic Organizations, Professional & Trade Associations, Urban & Community Affairs, Zoos/Aquariums
Education: Arts/Humanities Education, Colleges & Universities, Education Reform, Education-General, International Studies, Leadership Training, Literacy, Minority Education, Public Education (Precollege), School Volunteerism, Special Education, Student Aid
Environment: Environment-General
Health: AIDS/HIV, Children's Health/Hospitals, Clinics/Medical Centers, Emergency/Ambulance Services, Health Organizations, Hospitals, Mental Health, Nursing Services, Outpatient Health Care, Prenatal Health Issues, Research/Studies Institutes
International: Foreign Arts Organizations, International Affairs
Religion: Churches, Jewish Causes, Religious Organizations, Religious Welfare
Social Services: At-Risk Youth, Child Welfare, Community Centers, Community Service Organizations, Crime Prevention, Day Care, Family Planning, Family Services, Food/Clothing Distribution, People with Disabilities, Recreation & Athletics, Scouts, Senior Services, Shelters/Homelessness, United Funds/ United Ways, YMCA/YWCA/YMHA/YWHA, Youth Organizations

Application Procedures

Initial Contact: Send a brief letter of inquiry.
Deadlines: None.

Restrictions

Does not support individuals. Gives only to charitable organizations in the city of Springfield, Massachusetts.

Additional Information

Publications: Informational Brochure (including Application Guidelines)
Trust(s): Fleet National Bank NA

Grants Analysis

Disclosure Period: calendar year ending 2004
Total Grants: $448,939
Number of Grants: 46
Average Grant: $9,760
Highest Grant: $36,400
Lowest Grant: $1,700
Typical Range: $2,000 to $20,000

Recent Grants

Note: Grants derived from 2001 Form 990.
General

26,500	Springfield Southwest Community Health Center, Springfield, MA
26,500	Springfield Southwest Community Health Center, Springfield, MA
25,000	Springfield Home for Friendless Women and Children, Inc., Springfield, MA
23,000	Western New England College, Springfield, MA
21,000	Friends of the Homeless, Springfield, MA
20,000	Springfield Library and Museums Association, Springfield, MA
20,000	Trinity United Methodist Church, Springfield, MA
15,164	Community Foundation of Western Massachusetts, Springfield, MA
15,164	Community Foundation of Western Massachusetts, Springfield, MA
15,164	Community Foundation of Western Massachusetts, Springfield, MA

DIBNER FUND

Giving Contact

Marci B. Sternheim, Executive Director
PO Box 7575
Wilton, CT 06897
Phone: (203)761-9904
Fax: (203)761-9989
E-mail: Dibnerfund@worldnet.att.net

Description

Founded: 1957
EIN: 066038482
Organization Type: Family Foundation
Giving Locations: nationally and internationally.
Grant Types: Conference/Seminar, General Support, Scholarship.

Donor Information

Founder: The fund was established in 1957 by David Dibner, the late Bern Dibner, and the late Barbara Dibner. It continues to be supported by the Dibner family.

Financial Summary

Total Giving: $3,982,048 (2003); $3,772,739 (2002)
Giving Analysis: Giving for 2003 includes: foundation grants to United Way ($7,500); 2002: foundation grants to United Way ($7,500)
Assets: $73,102,284 (2003); $73,729,737 (2002)
Gifts Received: $250,314 (2000); $725,546 (1999); $319,200 (1997). Note: In 2000, contributions were received from the Barbara Dibner Trust ($125,449) and the Bern Dibner Trust ($124,865). In 1997, contributions were received from the Bern Dibner Trust ($159,600) and the Barbara Dibner Trust ($159,600).

Typical Recipients

Arts & Humanities: Film & Video, Arts & Humanities-General, Historic Preservation, History & Archaeology, Libraries, Literary Arts, Museums/Galleries, Music, Public Broadcasting
Civic & Public Affairs: Botanical Gardens/Parks, Civil Rights, Ethnic Organizations, Civic & Public Affairs-General, Law & Justice, Municipalities/Towns, Native American Affairs, Nonprofit Management, Philanthropic Organizations, Professional & Trade Associations, Public Policy, Urban & Community Affairs, Zoos/Aquariums
Education: Business Education, Colleges & Universities, Education Funds, Education Reform, Engineering/Technological Education, Education-General, Health & Physical Education, International Studies, Leadership Training, Literacy, Minority Education, Private Education (Precollege), Public Education (Precollege), Science/Mathematics Education, Student Aid, Vocational & Technical Education
Environment: Air/Water Quality, Environment-General, Protection, Research, Resource Conservation, Watershed
Health: Cancer, Children's Health/Hospitals, Diabetes, Emergency/Ambulance Services, Eyes/ Blindness, Health Policy/Cost Containment, Health Funds, Home-Care Services, Hospices, Hospitals, Medical Rehabilitation, Single-Disease Health Associations, Transplant Networks/Donor Banks
International: Foreign Arts Organizations, Foreign Educational Institutions, International-General, Health Care/Hospitals, International Organizations,

International Relief Efforts, Missionary/Religious Activities

Religion: Churches, Jewish Causes

Science: Science Exhibits & Fairs, Science Museums, Scientific Centers & Institutes, Scientific Organizations, Scientific Research

Social Services: Animal Protection, At-Risk Youth, Community Centers, Community Service Organizations, Emergency Relief, Family Services, People with Disabilities, Recreation & Athletics, Refugee Assistance, Shelters/Homelessness, United Funds/United Ways, Youth Organizations

Application Procedures

Initial Contact: No special form is required.
Application Requirements: Customary grant request data should be included in proposal.
Deadlines: None.

Restrictions

The Dibner Fund considers grants on a very focused and limited basis in the areas of history of science and technology and science education, and specifically discourages unsolicited applications removed from its fields of interest. It specifically avoids grants for capital programs, general-purpose support, individuals, and religious institutions.

Additional Information

Publications: Guidelines Mission Statement

Foundation Officials

Dr. Paul Busch: trustee
Michael Cohen: trustee
Brent Dibner: trustee
Daniel Dibner: trustee
David Dibner: president, treasurer, trustee B New York, NY 1927. PRIM CORP EMPL chairman: Bundy Corp.
Frances K. Dibner: vice president, treasurer, trustee
Stewart Greenfield: trustee B 1931. ED Saint John's College (1949-1953). PRIM CORP EMPL partner: Alternative Investment LP. CORP AFFIL partner: Oak Investment Partners II.
Stephen Shapiro: trustee
Warren Shine: trustee
Marci B. Sternheim: executive director
George Michael Szabad: secretary, treasurer, trustee B Nizhni Novgorod, Russia February 21, 1917. ED Columbia University BS (1937); Columbia University LLB (1939). PRIM CORP EMPL attorney: Blum Haimoff Gersen Lipson Slavin & Szabad. NONPR AFFIL member: American Federal Bar Association; member: Association Bar New York City; member: American Arbitration Association.

Grants Analysis

Disclosure Period: calendar year ending 2003
Total Grants: $3,974,548*
Number of Grants: 99
Average Grant: $23,048*
Highest Grant: $1,715,858
Lowest Grant: $1,000
Typical Range: $5,000 to $50,000
*Note: Giving excludes United Way. Average grant figure excludes highest grants.

Recent Grants

Note: Grants derived from 2002 Form 990.
Library-Related

147,557	Burndy Library, Cambridge, MA
57,600	Smithsonian Institution Libraries, Washington, DC
25,000	American Society for Technion Israel Institute of Technology Dibner Library, New York, NY
15,000	National Yiddish Book Center, Amherst, MA

General

873,444	Dibner Institute for the History of Science & Technology, Cambridge, MA
500,000	Dibner Institute for the History of Science & Technology, Cambridge, MA
200,000	PolyTechnic University, Brooklyn, NY
185,000	PolyTechnic University, Brooklyn, NY
150,000	Teach for America, New York, NY
112,700	Columbia University Earth Engineering Center, New York, NY
110,000	American Associates Ben Gurion University of the Negev, New York, NY
75,000	Doctors Without Borders USA Inc., New York, NY
75,000	Handicap International, Lyon France
75,000	Interplast Inc., Dobbs Ferry, NY

VOLNEY E. DIBRELL CHARITABLE TRUST

Giving Contact

William Clyborne, Vice President & Trust Officer
c/o Frost National Bank
PO Box 2950
San Antonio, TX 78299-2950
Phone: (210)220-4449

Description

Founded: 1993
EIN: 746396825
Organization Type: Private Foundation
Giving Locations: TX
Grant Types: General Support.

Financial Summary

Total Giving: $36,638 (fiscal year ending March 31, 2004); $21,205 (fiscal 2001)
Giving Analysis: Giving for fiscal 2004 includes: foundation grants to United Way ($8,943)
Assets: $851,287 (fiscal 2004); $968,027 (fiscal 2001)
Gifts Received: $692,152 (fiscal 1993)

Typical Recipients

Education: Public Education (Precollege)
Health: Children's Health/Hospitals, Health Organizations, Medical Research
Social Services: Community Service Organizations, Family Planning, Recreation & Athletics

Application Procedures

Initial Contact: Written application should include charter and by-laws, financial statement, and proof of tax-exempt status.
Deadlines: None.

Restrictions

Limited to TX.

Additional Information

Trust(s): Frost National Bank

Grants Analysis

Disclosure Period: fiscal year ending March 31, 2004
Total Grants: $27,695*
Number of Grants: 3
Highest Grant: $10,000
Lowest Grant: $7,695
*Note: Giving excludes United Way.

Recent Grants

Note: Grants derived from 2001 Form 990.
General

6,000	Children's Inn, Boerne, TX
6,000	Little League Baseball, Inc.-Alamo Heights, San Antonio, TX
6,000	National Kidney Foundation of Southeast Texas, Houston, TX
5,205	Planned Parenthood of San Antonio, San Antonio, TX

HARRIET FORD DICKENSON FOUNDATION

Giving Contact

James Largey, Vice President
Care of Morgan Guaranty Trust Trustee
3450 Park Avenue
New York, NY 10154
Phone: (212)464-1937
Fax: (212)464-1919

Description

Founded: 1958
EIN: 136047225
Organization Type: Private Foundation
Giving Locations: NY: Broome County
Grant Types: General Support.

Donor Information

Founder: Harriet Ford Dickenson

Financial Summary

Total Giving: $1,458,000 (2001)
Assets: $43,626,741 (2001)
Gifts Received: $193,617 (1998)

Typical Recipients

Arts & Humanities: Arts Associations & Councils, Ballet, Arts & Humanities-General, Historic Preservation, History & Archaeology, Libraries, Museums/Galleries, Music, Opera, Performing Arts, Public Broadcasting, Theater

Civic & Public Affairs: Botanical Gardens/Parks, Clubs, Community Foundations, Civic & Public Affairs-General, Housing, Inner-City Development, Law & Justice, Legal Aid, Urban & Community Affairs

Education: Arts/Humanities Education, Colleges & Universities, Community & Junior Colleges, Education Funds, Legal Education, Private Education (Precollege), Student Aid

Environment: Air/Water Quality, Environment-General, Protection, Resource Conservation

Health: Health Funds, Hospitals, Single-Disease Health Associations

Religion: Churches, Religious Organizations, Religious Welfare

Science: Science Museums, Scientific Centers & Institutes, Scientific Organizations

Social Services: Camps, Child Welfare, Community Service Organizations, Counseling, Day Care, Family Planning, Family Services, Food/Clothing Distribution, Homes, People with Disabilities, Recreation & Athletics, Scouts, Social Services-General, United Funds/United Ways, Veterans, YMCA/YWCA/YMHA/YWHA

Application Procedures

Initial Contact: Send a brief letter of inquiry.
Application Requirements: Describe program and amount requested.
Deadlines: None.

Additional Information

Trust(s): Morgan Guaranty Trust

Foundation Officials

Gillian Attfield: advisory committee member
Ann Hubbard: advisory committee member
David Hubbard: advisory committee member
Tom Hubbard: advisory committee member
John Keeler: advisory committee member
Shirley Keeler: advisory committee member

Grants Analysis

Disclosure Period: calendar year ending 2000
Total Grants: $20,121,300*
Number of Grants: 85
Average Grant: $236,721
Highest Grant: $2,200,000
Lowest Grant: $1,000

Typical Range: $1,000 to $25,000 and $500,000 to $2,200,000

***Note:** Does not include grants to United Way.

Recent Grants

Note: Grants derived from 2002 Form 990.

Library-Related

30,000	Pierpont Morgan Library, New York, NY
5,000	New York Public Library, New York, NY
3,500	Cornwall Library Association, Cornwall, CT

General

2,330,000	New York City Ballet, New York, NY
2,305,000	New York Botanical Garden, Bronx, NY
2,000,000	Community Foundation for South Central New York, Binghamton, NY
100,000	Metropolitan Opera Association, New York, NY
100,000	Parkinson's Disease Foundation Inc., New York, NY
91,250	Smith College, Northampton, MA
85,000	United Church of Christ, Cornwall, CT
45,000	Binghamton University Foundation, Binghamton, NY
25,000	Adirondack Council, Elizabethtown, NY
25,000	Michael J. Fox Foundation for Parkinson's Research, New York, NY

DICKLER FAMILY FOUNDATION

Giving Contact

Lauren Katzowtiz
130 E. 59th St., 12th Fl.
New York, NY 10022
Phone: (212)836-1577

Description

Founded: 1996
EIN: 133864553
Organization Type: Private Foundation
Former Name: Ruth and Gerald Dickler Foundation (2000).
Giving Locations: NY: also areas where trustees reside
Grant Types: General Support.

Financial Summary

Total Giving: $575,000 (2001)
Assets: $11,591,357 (2001)
Gifts Received: $104,089 (1996)

Typical Recipients

Arts & Humanities: Museums/Galleries, Music
Civic & Public Affairs: Economic Policy, Civic & Public Affairs-General, Women's Affairs
Education: Arts/Humanities Education, Education Reform, Literacy, Special Education
Health: Health-General
Social Services: Child Welfare, Community Service Organizations, Family Planning, Family Services

Application Procedures

Initial Contact: Send a brief letter of inquiry.
Application Requirements: Include description of organization, past and present year's budget, and references.
Deadlines: None.

Restrictions

Emphasis is on international population control and New York City early childhood education.

Foundation Officials

Ruth Dickler: president
Susan Dickler: executive vice president
Fred C. Farkouh: treasurer

Lauren Katzowitz: secretary
Jane Lebow: vice president
Abby Pratt: vice president

Grants Analysis

Disclosure Period: calendar year ending 2001
Total Grants: $575,000*
Number of Grants: 67
Average Grant: $8,582
Highest Grant: $25,000
Lowest Grant: $1,000
Typical Range: $1,000 to $20,000
***Note:** Giving excludes scholarships.

Recent Grants

Note: Grants derived from 2001 Form 990.

General

25,000	American Museum of Natural History, New York, NY -- to establish and maintain the museum and library of natural history
25,000	IPAS, New York, NY -- to increase women's abortion access in South Africa
20,000	Campaign for Fiscal Equality, New York, NY -- to reform the system of funding for public education throughout New York State
20,000	Education Through Music, New York, NY -- teaches music to children in public schools to improve academic skills
20,000	New Visions for Public Schools, New York, NY -- aims to improve the quality of education children received in NYC public schools
20,000	Population Media Center, Shelburne, VT -- to promote the use of effective communication strategies for promoting behavior change to encourage family and reproductive health
20,000	Studio In A School Association, New York, NY -- to work with New York City Public Schools and child care center to make art a part of children's daily life
17,500	United Neighborhood Houses, New York, NY -- to initiate a collaboration to replicate the east side house settlement's early childhood transition program
15,000	Abortion Access Project, Inc., Cambridge, MA -- to implement and expand its advocacy organizing education training and policy work
15,000	Henry Street Settlement, New York, NY -- to provide arts instructions and cultural programs to student and staff at PS 20 in New York City

WILLIAM B. DIETRICH FOUNDATION

Giving Contact

William B. Dietrich, President
PO Box 58177
Philadelphia, PA 19102-8177
Phone: (215)979-1919

Description

Founded: 1936
EIN: 231515616
Organization Type: Private Foundation
Giving Locations: PA
Grant Types: Capital, Operating Expenses, Project, Research.

Donor Information

Founder: Daniel W. Dietrich Foundation, the late Henry D. Dietrich, Dietrich American Foundation

Financial Summary

Total Giving: $988,700 (2001)
Assets: $17,349,999 (2001)
Gifts Received: $189 (1998); $500,000 (1993); $375,000 (1992). Note: In 1993, contributions were received from Dietrich American Foundation.

Typical Recipients

Arts & Humanities: Arts Associations & Councils, Community Arts, Ethnic & Folk Arts, Arts & Humanities-General, Historic Preservation, History & Archaeology, Libraries, Museums/Galleries, Music
Civic & Public Affairs: Botanical Gardens/Parks, Civic & Public Affairs-General, Housing, Municipalities/Towns, Safety, Urban & Community Affairs, Zoos/Aquariums
Education: Arts/Humanities Education, Colleges & Universities, Medical Education, Private Education (Precollege), Religious Education
Environment: Watershed
Health: AIDS/HIV, Cancer, Children's Health/Hospitals, Emergency/Ambulance Services, Geriatric Health, Health Organizations, Hospices, Hospitals, Medical Research, Single-Disease Health Associations
Religion: Churches
Science: Scientific Centers & Institutes
Social Services: Animal Protection, Community Service Organizations, Crime Prevention, Food/Clothing Distribution, People with Disabilities, Recreation & Athletics, Senior Services, YMCA/YWCA/YMHA/YWHA

Application Procedures

Initial Contact: Send a brief letter of inquiry.
Application Requirements: Include a description of organization, purpose of funds sought, and proof of tax-exempt status.
Deadlines: None.

Foundation Officials

Frank G. Cooper, Esq.: secretary, assistant treasurer
William B. Dietrich: president, treasurer

Grants Analysis

Disclosure Period: calendar year ending 2001
Total Grants: $988,700
Number of Grants: 39
Average Grant: $13,965*
Highest Grant: $237,000
Lowest Grant: $500
Typical Range: $5,000 to $25,000
***Note:** Average grant figure excludes two highest grants ($472,000).

Recent Grants

Note: Grants derived from 2002 Form 990.

General

325,000	Philadelphia Museum of Art, Philadelphia, PA -- for restoration of Mount Pleasant Mansion
141,450	Riverton Steamboat Landing Foundation, Riverton, NJ -- for second floor restoration
127,079	Rosenbach Museum and Library, Philadelphia, PA
75,000	Calcutta House, Philadelphia, PA -- for costs of constructing Calcutta House II
30,000	MANNA, Washington, DC -- for expansion of meal provisions services
19,600	Northwestern Human Services Foundation, Inc., Lafayette Hill, PA -- for exterior painting of historic home at Upland Woods
18,040	St. Mary's Episcopal Church, Elverson, PA -- for painting of steeple and belfry
6,000	Options in Aging, Ardmore, PA -- funding for Daily Hot Lunch Program

5,000   Associated Services for Blind, Philadelphia, PA -- for purchase of new Braille embosser and printer

5,000   Church Farm School, Paoli, PA

DILLON FOUNDATION

Giving Contact
Peter W. Dillon, President & Director
PO Box 537
Sterling, IL 61081
Phone: (815)626-9000
Fax: (815)626-4000

Description
Founded: 1953
EIN: 366059349
Organization Type: Family Foundation
Giving Locations: IL: Sterling including metropolitan area
Grant Types: Capital, Emergency, Fellowship, General Support, Matching, Multiyear/Continuing Support, Research, Scholarship, Seed Money.

Donor Information
Founder: Incorporated in 1953 by members of the Dillon family.

Financial Summary
Total Giving: $3,493,758 (fiscal year ending October 31, 2003); $3,746,795 (fiscal 2002); $3,885,286 (fiscal 2001)
Giving Analysis: Giving for fiscal 2003 includes: foundation grants to United Way ($89,850); fiscal 2002: foundation grants to United Way ($112,500)
Assets: $79,487,197 (fiscal 2003); $71,183,935 (fiscal 2002); $75,770,685 (fiscal 2001)

Typical Recipients
Arts & Humanities: Historic Preservation, History & Archaeology, Libraries, Museums/Galleries, Music, Opera, Visual Arts
Civic & Public Affairs: Botanical Gardens/Parks, Community Foundations, Economic Development, Employment/Job Training, Civic & Public Affairs-General, Housing, Inner-City Development, Legal Aid, Municipalities/Towns, Safety, Urban & Community Affairs, Zoos/Aquariums
Education: Colleges & Universities, Community & Junior Colleges, Economic Education, Education Associations, Education Funds, Elementary Education (Public), Education-General, Medical Education, Private Education (Precollege), Public Education (Precollege), Science/Mathematics Education, Secondary Education (Private), Secondary Education (Public)
Environment: Environment-General, Resource Conservation, Wildlife Protection
Health: Cancer, Children's Health/Hospitals, Clinics/Medical Centers, Emergency/Ambulance Services, Health Funds, Health Organizations, Hospices, Hospitals, Medical Rehabilitation, Medical Research, Public Health, Research/Studies Institutes, Single-Disease Health Associations
International: International Organizations
Religion: Churches, Dioceses, Religious Organizations, Religious Welfare
Science: Science Museums
Social Services: At-Risk Youth, Child Welfare, Community Service Organizations, Family Planning, People with Disabilities, Recreation & Athletics, Scouts, Senior Services, Social Services-General, United Funds/United Ways, YMCA/YWCA/YMHA/YWHA, Youth Organizations

Application Procedures
Initial Contact: The foundation requests applications be made in writing.
Application Requirements: Written proposals should describe the details of the program or project for which the applicant is requesting assistance.
Deadlines: None.

Restrictions
No grants are made to individuals. The foundation does not make loans.

Foundation Officials
James M. Boesen: secretary, director
Margo Dillon: assistant treasurer, director
Patrick Dillon: director
Peter W. Dillon: president, director
Douglas Inglee: director
Gale D. Inglee: assistant secretary, director
Tom Lexvold: director

Grants Analysis
Disclosure Period: fiscal year ending October 31, 2003
Total Grants: $3,403,908*
Number of Grants: 111
Average Grant: $12,499*
Highest Grant: $2,029,048
Lowest Grant: $400
Typical Range: $5,000 to $25,000
***Note:** Giving excludes United Way. Average grant figure excludes highest grant.

Recent Grants
Note: Grants derived from 2003 Form 990.
Library-Related
17,500   Sterling Public Library, Sterling, IL
General
2,029,048 Sterling Park District, Sterling, IL
260,584   Community Unit School District, Sterling, IL
129,300   Sterling Schools Foundation, Sterling, IL
129,131   City of Sterling, Sterling, IL
120,000   Greater Sterling Development Corporation, Sterling, IL
89,850   United Way of Sterling Rock Falls Inc., Sterling, IL
66,245   Sauk Valley Community College Foundation, Sterling, IL
38,000   Sterling Park District Museum Association, Sterling, IL
30,000   Grace Episcopal Church, Sterling, IL
29,842   Sterling Township, Sterling, IL

DIME BANK OF NORWICH CONNECTICUT

Company Headquarters
290 Salem Turnpike
Norwich, CT 06360
Web: http://www.dimesavingsbank.com

Dime Savings Bank of Norwich Foundation

Giving Contact
Wilma Sullivan, Secretary
Dime Savings Bank Foundation
290 Salem Turnpike
Norwich, CT 06360-0070
Phone: (860)889-2317

Description
Founded: 1998
EIN: 061507800
Organization Type: Corporate Foundation
Giving Locations: CT
Grant Types: General Support.

Financial Summary
Total Giving: $72,597 (2004); $73,309 (2001)
Assets: $1,479,293 (2004); $1,367,087 (2001)
Gifts Received: $4,490 (2004); $309,978 (2001).
Note: In 2001, contributions were received from Dime Savings Bank of Norwich.

Typical Recipients
Arts & Humanities: Arts & Humanities-General, Libraries
Civic & Public Affairs: Civic & Public Affairs-General, Housing
Education: Business Education, Public Education (Precollege)
Health: Children's Health/Hospitals, Clinics/Medical Centers, Health-General, Hospices, Hospitals, Medical Rehabilitation, Nursing Services
Social Services: Community Centers, Community Service Organizations, Family Services, People with Disabilities

Application Procedures
Initial Contact: Submit a brief letter of inquiry.
Application Requirements: Include a description of organization, amount requested, purpose of funds sought, recently audited financial statement, and proof of tax-exempt status.
Deadlines: September 30.

Restrictions
Applicants must be located within the company's operating area.

Foundation Officials
Michael G. Betten: director
Francis J. Buckley, Jr.: director
James P. Cronin: president
James P. Cronin: director
Roland J. Harris: director
Paul M. Higgins, Jr.: director
James M. Kirker: director
Richard J. Legare: director
Robert A. Staley: director
Wilma J. Sullivan: secretary
Charles O. Treat: vice president

Grants Analysis
Disclosure Period: calendar year ending 2004
Total Grants: $72,597
Number of Grants: 31
Average Grant: $2,342
Highest Grant: $4,000
Lowest Grant: $1,500
Typical Range: $1,500 to $5,000

Recent Grants
Note: Grants derived from 2001 Form 990.
Library-Related
2,800   Otis Library, Los Angeles, CA -- financial assistance for microfilming archived local newspaper
General
10,000   WW Backus Hospital -- radiation therapy building
5,000   AmeriCares, New Canaan, CT -- funding for walk-in clinic in Norwich
5,000   Ledyard Center School PTO -- purchase library equipment
5,000   Norwich Social Services Safety Net Team, Norwich, CT -- funding for fuel, food, children's supplies
5,000   Southeastern Association the Retarded -- recreational and respite services for families with retarded dependents
3,750   High Horses Therapeutic Riding, Etna, NH -- scholarships for special needs student
3,500   East Lyme High School -- student fine arts publication
3,000   Madonna Place, Norwich, CT -- staffing for court ordered supervised visits

3,000	Thames River Community Service, Inc. -- funding support for families in transition from public assistance
2,900	Easter Seals, CT -- purchase of therapeutic devices

DIMEO CONSTRUCTION CO.

Company Headquarters

75 Chapman Street
Providence, RI 02905-5496
Web: http://www.dimeo.com

Company Description

Operating Revenue: US$149 million (2002)
Employees: 200 (2002)
SIC(s): 1500 General Building Contractors, 1700 Special Trade Contractors, 8700 Engineering & Management Services.

Nonmonetary Support

Type: In-kind Services; Loaned Executives; Workplace Solicitation

Giving Contact

Kimberly Hall
75 Chapman St.
Providence, RI 02905
Phone: (401)781-9800
Fax: (401)461-4580

Description

Organization Type: Corporate Giving Program
Giving Locations: RI
Grant Types: General Support.

Typical Recipients

Arts & Humanities: Arts Appreciation, Arts Associations & Councils, Arts Centers, Arts Festivals, Community Arts, Historic Preservation, Libraries, Museums/Galleries, Music, Opera, Performing Arts, Theater
Civic & Public Affairs: Economic Development, Housing, Municipalities/Towns, Safety, Women's Affairs, Zoos/Aquariums
Education: Arts/Humanities Education, Business Education, Colleges & Universities, Community & Junior Colleges, Continuing Education, Economic Education
Health: Health Funds, Health Organizations, Hospitals, Mental Health, Nutrition, Single-Disease Health Associations
International: International Peace & Security Issues
Religion: Churches, Religious Organizations, Synagogues/Temples
Social Services: Animal Protection, Child Welfare, Community Centers, Community Service Organizations, Counseling, Family Planning, Senior Services, Substance Abuse

Application Procedures

Initial Contact: Send a brief letter of inquiry.
Application Requirements: Include a description of organization, amount requested, purpose of funds sought, recently audited financial statement, and proof of tax-exempt status.
Deadlines: None.

Restrictions

Does not support individuals.

Corporate Officials

Bradford S. Dimeo: vice president PRIM CORP EMPL vice president: Dimeo Construction Co.
Thomas P. Dimeo: chairman, president, chief executive officer, director B Providence, RI 1930. ED

Brown University BA (1952). PRIM CORP EMPL chairman, president, chief executive officer, director: Dimeo Enterprises. CORP AFFIL director: Old Stone Bank; director: Providence Mutual Fire Insurance Co.; chairman: Dimeo Construction Co. NONPR AFFIL member corporate: RI Hospital; director: YMCA Greater Providence; trustee: Cathedral Saint John Divine; trustee: Johnson Wales College.

DIMMER FAMILY FOUNDATION

Giving Contact

Diane C. Dimmer, Executive Director
1019 Pacific Avenue, Suite 916
Tacoma, WA 98402
Phone: (253)759-1318

Description

Founded: 1994
EIN: 911622059
Organization Type: Private Foundation
Giving Locations: WA: Pierce County, Tacoma County
Grant Types: General Support.

Donor Information

Founder: Established in 1994 by John C. Dimmer.

Financial Summary

Total Giving: $492,240 (2003)
Assets: $10,868,138 (2003)
Gifts Received: $5,027 (2003); $456,994 (2000); $8,509,628 (1999). Note: In 1998, 1999, 2000, and 2003 contributions were received from John C. Dimmer and Key Bank. In 1994, contributions were received from John C. Dimmer.

Typical Recipients

Arts & Humanities: Arts Associations & Councils, Arts & Humanities-General, History & Archaeology, Libraries, Museums/Galleries, Music, Opera, Performing Arts, Theater
Civic & Public Affairs: Clubs, Employment/Job Training, Civic & Public Affairs-General, Housing, Parades/Festivals, Zoos/Aquariums
Education: Business Education, Colleges & Universities, Community & Junior Colleges, Education Funds, Elementary Education (Public), Environmental Education, Education-General, Legal Education, Literacy, Private Education (Precollege), Science/Mathematics Education, Special Education, Student Aid
Environment: Wildlife Protection
Health: AIDS/HIV, Arthritis, Cancer, Children's Health/Hospitals, Health Funds, Heart, Hospitals, Mental Health, Prenatal Health Issues, Single-Disease Health Associations
Religion: Churches, Ministries, Religious Welfare
Science: Science Museums, Scientific Centers & Institutes
Social Services: Animal Protection, Camps, Child Welfare, Community Service Organizations, Crime Prevention, Day Care, Food/Clothing Distribution, Homes, People with Disabilities, Recreation & Athletics, Scouts, YMCA/YWCA/YMHA/YWHA, Youth Organizations

Application Procedures

Initial Contact: Send a brief letter of inquiry or complete application.
Application Requirements: Include a description of organization, purpose of funds sought, amount requested, and recently audited financial statement.
Deadlines: None.

Restrictions

Restricted to Tacoma-Pierce county, WA organizations which qualify as 501(c)(3).

Foundation Officials

Carolyn J. Dimmer: vice president
Diane C. Dimmer: secretary
John B. Dimmer: treasurer
John C. Dimmer: president
Marilyn J. Dimmer: vice president

Grants Analysis

Disclosure Period: calendar year ending 2003
Total Grants: $492,240
Number of Grants: 128
Average Grant: $3,220*
Highest Grant: $56,000
Lowest Grant: $100
Typical Range: $1,000 to $5,000
***Note:** Average grant figure excludes two highest grants ($86,500).

Recent Grants

Note: Grants derived from 2003 Form 990.
General

56,000	Museum of Glass, Tacoma, WA
30,500	Boys and Girls Club, Tacoma, WA
17,000	Washington Women's Employment and Education, Tacoma, WA
15,191	University of Oregon Foundation, Eugene, OR
15,000	Franciscan Health System, Tacoma, WA
14,500	Zoo Society, Tacoma, WA
13,645	Eugene Symphony, Eugene, OR
12,500	Tacoma Rotary, Tacoma, WA
12,000	Museum of Flight Foundation, Seattle, WA
11,321	Children's Museum of Tacoma, Tacoma, WA

MICHAEL D. DINGMAN FOUNDATION

Giving Contact

Lenore Jennings, Assistant Secretary
1 Liberty Ln.
Hampton, NH 03842
Phone: (603)929-2203

Description

Founded: 1986
EIN: 943080164
Organization Type: Private Foundation
Giving Locations: nationally.
Grant Types: Department, General Support.

Donor Information

Founder: Henley Manufacturing Charitable Fdn.

Financial Summary

Total Giving: $163,921 (2004); $1,185,596 (2001)
Assets: $237,626 (2004); $707,666 (2001)
Gifts Received: $32,000 (2004); $32,000 (2001); $32,000 (2000). Note: Contributions were received from Michael D. Dingman, and Winthrop, Inc.

Typical Recipients

Arts & Humanities: Historic Preservation, History & Archaeology, Libraries, Museums/Galleries, Music, Theater
Civic & Public Affairs: Botanical Gardens/Parks, Business/Free Enterprise, Economic Policy, Employment/Job Training, Civic & Public Affairs-General, Housing, Legal Aid, Public Policy, Safety, Urban & Community Affairs, Zoos/Aquariums
Education: Agricultural Education, Business Education, Colleges & Universities, Education Funds, Edu-

cation-General, Minority Education, Private Education (Precollege), Student Aid

Environment: Environment-General, Resource Conservation, Wildlife Protection

Health: Cancer, Clinics/Medical Centers, Emergency/Ambulance Services, Eyes/Blindness, Health-General, Health Funds, Health Organizations, Hospices, Hospitals, Medical Rehabilitation, Medical Research, Nursing Services, Public Health, Single-Disease Health Associations

International: Foreign Arts Organizations, Foreign Educational Institutions, Health Care/Hospitals, International Development, International Organizations, International Relations, Missionary/Religious Activities

Religion: Churches, Jewish Causes, Ministries, Missionary Activities (Domestic), Religious Organizations, Religious Welfare

Science: Science Museums

Social Services: Animal Protection, Camps, Child Welfare, Community Service Organizations, Crime Prevention, Emergency Relief, People with Disabilities, Recreation & Athletics, Social Services-General, Substance Abuse, United Funds/United Ways, Volunteer Services, Youth Organizations

Application Procedures

Initial Contact: Send a brief letter of inquiry.
Deadlines: None.

Foundation Officials

Edwin H. Danenhauer: assistant secretary
Elizabeth T. Dingman: vice president
Michael David Dingman: president, chief financial officer B New Haven, CT 1931. ED University of Maryland. PRIM CORP EMPL president, chief executive officer: Shipston Group Ltd. CORP AFFIL director: Ford Motor Co.; director: Fisher Scientific International Inc. NONPR AFFIL member: Institute Electrical & Electronics Engineers. CLUB AFFIL San Diego Yacht Club; Union Club; New York Yacht Club; The Links Club; Lyford Cay Club; La Jolla Country Club; Bohemian Club; Cruising Club America Club.
Lenore Jennings: assistant secretary

Grants Analysis

Disclosure Period: calendar year ending 2004
Total Grants: $163,921
Number of Grants: 21
Average Grant: $5,696*
Highest Grant: $50,000
Lowest Grant: $1,000
Typical Range: $1,000 to $10,000
*Note: Average grant figure excludes highest grant.

Recent Grants

Note: Grants derived from 2001 Form 990.

General

400,000	Business & Management Foundation of MD, Inc., College Park, MD
116,440	Lyford Cay School Development Fund, Nassau Bahamas
100,000	Bahamas Mission of Florida, Inc., Nassau Bahamas
55,000	St. George's School, Newport, RI
50,000	Boston College, Chestnut Hill, MA
50,000	Historic Charleston Foundation, Charleston, SC
50,000	Historic Deerfield, Inc, Deerfield, MA
50,000	Hun School of Princeton, Princeton, NJ
50,000	Medical University of South Carolina, Charleston, SC
20,000	Farnsworth Art Museum, Rockland, ME

H. E. AND KATE DISHMAN CHARITABLE FOUNDATION TRUST

Giving Contact

Trust Officer
c/o Hibernia National Bank
PO Box 3928
Beaumont, TX 77704-3928
Phone: (409)880-1415

Description

Founded: 1985
EIN: 766024806
Organization Type: Private Foundation
Giving Locations: TX: Georgetown
Grant Types: Capital, General Support, Project.

Donor Information

Founder: Dishman Foundation, the late H. E. Dishman, Kate Dishman Foundation

Financial Summary

Total Giving: $166,633 (2003); $195,542 (2001)
Assets: $3,224,103 (2003); $3,523,101 (2001)

Typical Recipients

Arts & Humanities: Arts Associations & Councils, Arts Outreach, Libraries, Museums/Galleries, Music, Public Broadcasting, Theater

Civic & Public Affairs: African American Affairs, Community Foundations, Civic & Public Affairs-General, Housing, Nonprofit Management, Philanthropic Organizations

Education: Business Education, Colleges & Universities, Education-General, Public Education (Precollege), Science/Mathematics Education, Secondary Education (Private)

Health: Emergency/Ambulance Services, Hospitals, Medical Research, Nutrition, Single-Disease Health Associations, Transplant Networks/Donor Banks

Religion: Churches, Religious Organizations, Religious Welfare

Science: Science Museums

Social Services: At-Risk Youth, Camps, Child Welfare, Community Service Organizations, Crime Prevention, Family Services, Food/Clothing Distribution, Homes, People with Disabilities, Scouts, Senior Services, Shelters/Homelessness, Social Services-General, Substance Abuse, United Funds/United Ways, Veterans, Volunteer Services

Application Procedures

Initial Contact: Send a brief letter of inquiry and a full proposal.
Application Requirements: Include a description of organization, amount requested, purpose of funds sought, and proof of tax-exempt status.
Deadlines: None.

Restrictions

Does not support individuals, religious organizations for sectarian purposes, political or lobbying groups, or organizations outside operating areas.

Additional Information

Trust(s): Hiberia National Bank

Grants Analysis

Disclosure Period: calendar year ending 2003
Total Grants: $166,633*
Number of Grants: 11
Average Grant: $13,263*
Highest Grant: $35,000
Lowest Grant: $2,500
Typical Range: $5,000 to $25,000
*Note: Average grant figure excludes highest grant.

Recent Grants

Note: Grants derived from 2001 Form 990.
General

32,442	Habitat for Humanity, Beaumont, TX -- for the habitat re-store and house the kids built
30,000	KVLU, Beaumont, TX -- equipment for digital conversion
30,000	Some Other Place, Beaumont, TX -- for new school clothing and funds to supply food
25,000	Beaumont Community Players, Beaumont, TX -- for expenses related to construction of a new theatre
25,000	Garth House, Beaumont, TX -- to purchase the house where the program operates
15,000	Spindletop MHMR Services, Beaumont, TX -- to assist in providing the maximum education
15,000	Trinity Army, Beaumont, TX -- to build a 3-bedroom 1 1/2 bath home
11,100	Family Services of Southeast Texas, Inc., Beaumont, TX -- upgrade of communication and accounting systems
10,000	Fire Museum of Texas, Beaumont, TX -- for memorial plaza construction
2,000	Heartbeats of Hope, Vidor, TX -- for books for children

WALT DISNEY CO.

Company Headquarters

Burbank, CA
Web: http://www.disney.go.com

Company Description

Founded: 1938
Ticker: DIS
Exchange: NYSE
Revenue: US$30.752 billion (2004)
Profit: US$2.345 billion (2004)
Employees: 114000 (2003)
Fortune Rank: 54, per FORTUNE Magazine's list of 500 Largest U.S. Corporations (2004).
SIC(s): 6531 Real Estate Agents & Managers, 7812 Motion Picture & Video Production, 7996 Amusement Parks.

Operating Locations

Walt Disney Co. (CA--Anaheim, Glendale, Hollywood; FL--Lake Buena Vista, Orlando; NJ--Edison; NY--New York)

Walt Disney Co. Foundation

Giving Contact

Tillie J. Baptie, Executive Director
The Walt Disney Co. Foundation
500 South Buena Vista Street
Burbank, CA 91521-0987
Phone: (818)560-1006

Description

EIN: 956037079
Organization Type: Corporate Foundation
Giving Locations: CA: Los Angeles County, Orange County; FL: Orange County, Osceola County headquarters and operating communities.
Grant Types: Capital, Challenge, General Support, Operating Expenses, Project, Research, Scholarship.

Financial Summary

Total Giving: $3,327,946 (fiscal year ending September 30, 2003); $5,538,631 (fiscal 2002); $5,548,269 (fiscal 2001). Note: Contributes through corporate direct giving program and foundation.

Assets: $1,617,522 (fiscal 2003); $718,312 (fiscal 2002); $2,973,312 (fiscal 2001)

Gifts Received: $4,299,039 (fiscal 2003); $3,076,521 (fiscal 2002); $5,479,509 (fiscal 2001). Note: In fiscal 2003, contributions were received from the Walt Disney Co. ($3,500,000) and miscellaneous contributions from the employees of the Walt Disney Co. ($521,039). In fiscal 2002, contributions were received from the Walt Disney Co. ($1,500,000) and miscellaneous contributions from the employees of the Walt Disney Co. ($1,576,521). In fiscal 2001, contributions were received from the Walt Disney Co. ($5,000,000) and miscellaneous contributions from the employees of the Walt Disney Co. ($479,509). Contributions are received from the Walt Disney Company.

Typical Recipients

Arts & Humanities: Arts Associations & Councils, Arts Centers, Arts Festivals, Arts Funds, Arts Institutes, Arts Outreach, Ethnic & Folk Arts, Film & Video, Arts & Humanities-General, History & Archaeology, Libraries, Museums/Galleries, Music, Performing Arts, Public Broadcasting, Theater

Civic & Public Affairs: African American Affairs, Asian American Affairs, Business/Free Enterprise, Community Foundations, Economic Development, Employment/Job Training, Ethnic Organizations, Civic & Public Affairs-General, Hispanic Affairs, Law & Justice, Legal Aid, Native American Affairs, Philanthropic Organizations, Public Policy, Urban & Community Affairs, Zoos/Aquariums

Education: Afterschool/Enrichment Programs, Arts/Humanities Education, Business Education, Business-School Partnerships, Colleges & Universities, Education Funds, Education Reform, Engineering/Technological Education, Education-General, Health & Physical Education, Legal Education, Medical Education, Minority Education, Science/Mathematics Education, Special Education, Student Aid

Environment: Environment-General, Resource Conservation, Wildlife Protection

Health: Cancer, Children's Health/Hospitals, Clinics/Medical Centers, Diabetes, Emergency/Ambulance Services, Eyes/Blindness, Health-General, Health Funds, Health Organizations, Hospitals, Medical Rehabilitation, Mental Health, Public Health, Single-Disease Health Associations

International: International Environmental Issues, International Relations

Religion: Missionary Activities (Domestic), Religious Welfare

Science: Scientific Centers & Institutes, Scientific Labs

Social Services: Animal Protection, Camps, Child Abuse, Child Welfare, Community Centers, Community Service Organizations, Domestic Violence, Emergency Relief, Family Services, Food/Clothing Distribution, People with Disabilities, Recreation & Athletics, Scouts, Senior Services, Shelters/Homelessness, Social Services-General, Substance Abuse, United Funds/United Ways, Volunteer Services, YMCA/YWCA/YMHA/YWHA, Youth Organizations

Application Procedures

Initial Contact: Send brief letter or proposal.

Application Requirements: Include financial statements, preferably audited; list of major contributors and sources of income; list of board members, including their affiliations; history of the organization; and proof of tax exemption.

Deadlines: Proposals should be submitted by December 31 to be evaluated the following summer; scholarship applications due by October 1 to be issued the following summer.

Review Process: Applications reviewed by foundation staff as received, then passed on to the donations committee.

Evaluative Criteria: Recipients must be tax-exempt, must have been in operation for at least three years, and must make significant use of volunteers.

Decision Notification: Donations committee makes its final decision at its annual summer meeting.

Restrictions

Foundation does not support public agencies, educational institutions, or other nonprofit organizations supported predominantly by tax dollars; agencies receiving funds from United Way, Permanent Charities Committee, or other similar consolidated giving programs to which the foundation contributes; sectarian organizations; agency building campaigns; agency start-up campaigns or for seed money purposes; medical research programs; or individuals.

Additional Information

In past years, most grants have gone to repeat recipients.

Scholarship applicant qualifications include: must be a high school senior or academic equivalent with the expectation of graduating within the 12-month period following October 1 of that year; must be in upper one-third of high school graduating class; must be qualified, upon graduation, to enroll at an accredited four-year college or university; must be a child, stepchild or adopted child of a qualified employee (a full time regular employee who has completed at least one year of continuous service and is a resident or citizen of the United States); must file an official application form which must be received no later than October 1 of the year in which the candidate is eligible to apply.

Publications: Guidelines

Corporate Officials

Michael Dammann Eisner: chairman, chief executive officer, director B Mount Kisco, NY 1942. ED Denison University BA (1964). PRIM CORP EMPL chairman, chief executive, director: Walt Disney Co. Inc. ADD CORP EMPL president: Buena Vista International; president: WCO Parent Corp. CORP AFFIL principal: Disneyland International; chairman: Hollywood Records Inc.; chairman: Anaheim Sports Inc.; chairman: Disney Enterprises Inc. NONPR AFFIL trustee: Denison University; director: University California Los Angeles Board Medicine Science; director: Conservative International; director: American Hospital of Paris Foundation; trustee: California Institute Arts.

Sanford M. Litvack: member, director B Brooklyn, NY 1936. ED University of Connecticut BA (1956); Georgetown University LLB (1959). PRIM CORP EMPL Antigenics Inc. CORP AFFIL director: Buena Vista Home Entertainment; director: Disney International.

Foundation Officials

Tilly J. Baptie: executive director

Michael Dammann Eisner: president, trustee (see above)

Robert A. Iger: treasurer, trustee

Marsha L. Reed: secretary

Grants Analysis

Disclosure Period: fiscal year ending September 30, 2003

Total Grants: $2,090,330*

Number of Grants: 46

Average Grant: $35,341*

Highest Grant: $500,000

Lowest Grant: $1,000

Typical Range: $10,000 to $50,000

*Note: Giving excludes scholarships; matching gifts. Average grant figure excludes highest grant.

Recent Grants

Note: Grants derived from fiscal 2003 Form 990.

General

500,000	California Institute of the Arts, Valencia, CA
200,000	St. Joseph Medical Center Foundation, Bryan, TX
100,000	California Science Center, Los Angeles, CA
100,000	Children's Hospital Foundation of Orange County, Orange, CA
100,000	Entertainment Industry Foundation, Studio City, CA
100,000	Hispanic Culture Foundation Inc., Albuquerque, NM
100,000	Orlando Science Center, Orlando, FL
100,000	United Arts of Central Florida, Maitland, FL
69,830	Junior Achievement, Colorado Springs, CO
50,000	American Red Cross, Santa Ana, CA

CLIFTON C. AND HENRYETTA C. DOAK CHARITABLE TRUST

Giving Contact

Kenneth Loke, Trust Officer
c/o Wells Fargo Bank Texas
PO Drawer 913
Bryan, TX 77805-0913
Phone: (979)776-3267

Description

Founded: 1993
EIN: 746402510
Organization Type: Private Foundation
Giving Locations: TX: Brazos County
Grant Types: General Support.

Donor Information

Founder: Established in 1993 by the late Henryetta C. Doak.

Financial Summary

Total Giving: $217,667 (2003); $258,800 (2001)

Giving Analysis: Giving for 2003 includes: foundation grants to United Way ($7,500); 2001: foundation grants to United Way ($10,000)

Assets: $3,835,087 (2003); $4,055,197 (2001)

Gifts Received: $9,840 (2001); $28,454 (2000); $3,094,886 (1993). Note: In 2000 and 2001, contributions were received from Christopher Lew Trust. In 1993, contributions were received from the estate of Henryetta C. Doak.

Typical Recipients

Arts & Humanities: Arts & Humanities-General, Libraries, Museums/Galleries, Music

Civic & Public Affairs: Clubs, Civic & Public Affairs-General, Housing, Municipalities/Towns, Urban & Community Affairs

Education: Colleges & Universities, Elementary Education (Public), Private Education (Precollege), Student Aid

Health: Clinics/Medical Centers, Emergency/Ambulance Services, Health-General, Health Organizations, Hospices, Medical Rehabilitation, Mental Health

Religion: Religious Welfare

Science: Science Museums

Social Services: Food/Clothing Distribution, Homes, Social Services-General, United Funds/United Ways, Veterans, Youth Organizations

Application Procedures

Initial Contact: submit requests on bank trust department's grant application form

Deadlines: March 15.

Additional Information
Trust(s): Wells Fargo Bank Texas

Grants Analysis
Disclosure Period: calendar year ending 2003
Total Grants: $210,167*
Number of Grants: 21
Average Grant: $10,008
Highest Grant: $30,000
Lowest Grant: $300
Typical Range: $5,000 to $15,000
*Note: Giving excludes United Way.

Recent Grants
Note: Grants derived from 2001 Form 990.
Library-Related

12,500	Bryan City Library, Bryan, TX -- for educational purposes	

General

31,000	Hospice Brazos Valley, Bryan, TX -- for charitable purposes
30,000	Brazos Valley Museum, Bryan, TX -- for educational purposes
30,000	Habitat for Humanity, Bryan, TX -- for charitable purposes
20,000	Brazos Valley Rehabilitation Center, Bryan, TX -- for charitable purposes
15,000	Brazos Food Bank, Bryan, TX -- for charitable purposes
15,000	Doak Carter Boys Club, Bryan, TX -- for charitable purposes
15,000	Trinity University, San Antonio, TX -- for educational purposes
14,000	Health for All, Inc., Bryan, TX -- for health care improvements and education
12,500	College Station City Library, College Station, TX -- for educational purposes
10,500	University of North Texas, Denton, TX -- for educational purposes

DR. SEUSS FOUNDATION

Giving Contact
Audrey S. Geisel, President & Assistant Secretary
7301 Encelia Dr.
La Jolla, CA 92037-5279
Phone: (858)454-7384

Description
Founded: 1958
EIN: 956029752
Organization Type: Private Foundation
Giving Locations: CA: national organizations.
Grant Types: General Support.

Donor Information
Founder: the late Theodor S. Geisel

Financial Summary
Total Giving: $227,305 (2004); $207,642 (2001)
Assets: $1,844,482 (2004); $2,192,308 (2001)

Typical Recipients
Arts & Humanities: Arts Funds, Arts Outreach, Ballet, Dance, Ethnic & Folk Arts, Arts & Humanities-General, Libraries, Literary Arts, Museums/Galleries, Music, Opera, Performing Arts, Public Broadcasting, Theater, Visual Arts
Civic & Public Affairs: Botanical Gardens/Parks, Civil Rights, Community Foundations, Civic & Public Affairs-General, Hispanic Affairs, Parades/Festivals, Philanthropic Organizations, Public Policy, Rural Affairs, Safety, Urban & Community Affairs, Women's Affairs, Zoos/Aquariums
Education: Business Education, Colleges & Universities, Education Funds, Education Reform, Education-General, Literacy, Private Education (Precollege), Public Education (Precollege), Secondary

Education (Private), Special Education
Environment: Forestry, Environment-General
Health: AIDS/HIV, Alzheimer's Disease, Cancer, Children's Health/Hospitals, Clinics/Medical Centers, Emergency/Ambulance Services, Hospices, Hospitals (University Affiliated), Medical Research, Mental Health, Prenatal Health Issues, Preventive Medicine/Wellness Organizations, Research/Studies Institutes
International: Foreign Arts Organizations, Health Care/Hospitals, Human Rights, International Affairs, International Organizations, International Relief Efforts
Religion: Churches, Religious Welfare
Science: Science Museums, Scientific Organizations
Social Services: Child Welfare, Family Planning, Food/Clothing Distribution, Homes, People with Disabilities, Recreation & Athletics, Scouts, Senior Services, Social Services-General, Substance Abuse, YMCA/YWCA/YMHA/YWHA, Youth Organizations

Application Procedures
Initial Contact: The foundation has no formal grant application procedure or application form.
Deadlines: None.

Restrictions
Grants are not made to individuals.

Foundation Officials
Audrey S. Geisel: president, assistant secretary
Edward Lathem: director
Claudia Prescott: chief financial officer
Karl ZoBell: secretary B La Jolla, CA 1932. ED Utah State University (1949-1951); Columbia University (1951-1952); Columbia University AB (1953); Stanford University JD (1958). PRIM CORP EMPL partner: Gray, Cary, Ames & Frye. CORP AFFIL director, founder: La Jolla Bank & Trust Co.; vice president, director: Geisel-Seuss Enterprises Inc. NONPR AFFIL trustee: Dr. Seuss Foundation; member: Lambda Alpha; director: James C. Copley Charitable Foundation; fellow: American College Trust & Estate Counsel; member: California Bar Association; member: American Bar Association. CLUB AFFIL La Jolla Beach & Tennis Club.

Grants Analysis
Disclosure Period: calendar year ending 2004
Total Grants: $227,305
Number of Grants: 141
Average Grant: $1,612
Highest Grant: $14,850
Lowest Grant: $150
Typical Range: $500 to $5,000

Recent Grants
Note: Grants derived from 2001 Form 990.

General

10,000	San Diego Opera, San Diego, CA
10,000	University of California San Diego Affairs Development, San Diego, CA
8,900	UC Regents, Los Angeles, CA
7,195	San Diego Museum of Art, San Diego, CA
6,750	Vista Hill Foundation, San Diego, CA
5,100	University of California San Diego Foundation, San Diego, CA
3,900	Salvation Army Women's Auxiliary, Dallas, TX
3,500	Episcopal Community Service
3,500	San Diego Symphony, San Diego, CA
3,000	City Ballet, Knoxville, TN

CLEVELAND H. DODGE FOUNDATION

Giving Contact
Phyllis M. Criscuoli, Executive Director & Treasurer
670 West 247th Street
Riverdale, NY 10471
Phone: (718)543-1220
Fax: (718)543-0737
E-mail: info@chdodgefoundation.org
Web: http://www.chdodgefoundation.org

Description
Founded: 1917
EIN: 136015087
Organization Type: General Purpose Foundation
Giving Locations: AZ; NM; NY: New York including metropolitan area
Grant Types: Capital, Endowment, General Support, Matching, Multiyear/Continuing Support, Operating Expenses, Project.

Donor Information
Founder: The Cleveland H. Dodge Foundation was established in 1917 by Cleveland Hoadley Dodge, whose father headed Phelps Dodge Corporation, a copper company.

Financial Summary
Total Giving: $3,513,668 (2003); $2,139,299 (2002); $2,334,905 (2001). Note: 1996 Giving includes matching gifts ($284,723). 1995 Giving includes matching gifts ($278,304).
Giving Analysis: Giving for 2002 includes: foundation matching gifts ($376,914); 2001: foundation grants to United Way ($250,000); foundation matching gifts ($396,260)
Assets: $39,846,818 (2002); $49,217,356 (2001)

Typical Recipients
Arts & Humanities: Arts Associations & Councils, Arts Outreach, Historic Preservation, History & Archaeology, Libraries, Museums/Galleries, Performing Arts, Public Broadcasting
Civic & Public Affairs: Botanical Gardens/Parks, Civil Rights, Clubs, Community Foundations, Employment/Job Training, Civic & Public Affairs-General, Nonprofit Management, Philanthropic Organizations, Public Policy, Urban & Community Affairs, Zoos/Aquariums
Education: Afterschool/Enrichment Programs, Arts/Humanities Education, Colleges & Universities, Education Reform, Elementary Education (Public), Faculty Development, Education-General, International Exchange, International Studies, Leadership Training, Legal Education, Minority Education, Preschool Education, Private Education (Precollege), Public Education (Precollege), School Volunteerism, Science/Mathematics Education, Secondary Education (Private), Student Aid
Environment: Air/Water Quality, Environment-General, Wildlife Protection
Health: Emergency/Ambulance Services, Health Organizations, Nursing Services, Public Health
International: Foreign Educational Institutions, Health Care/Hospitals, International Affairs, International Environmental Issues, International Organizations, International Peace & Security Issues, International Relations
Religion: Churches, Religious Welfare
Science: Observatories & Planetariums, Science Museums
Social Services: Big Brothers/Big Sisters, Child Abuse, Child Welfare, Community Centers, Community Service Organizations, Counseling, Emergency Relief, Family Planning, Family Services, People with Disabilities, Recreation & Athletics, Scouts, Senior Services, Shelters/Homelessness, United Funds/United Ways, Volunteer Services, YMCA/YWCA/YMHA/YWHA, Youth Organizations

Application Procedures

Initial Contact: To apply for a grant, organizations may send a brief letter to the foundation's executive director and treasurer. There are no application forms.

Application Requirements: Letters of application should describe the proposed project and include a budget. After a preliminary review, a detailed proposal may be requested.

Deadlines: None.

Review Process: At the board meetings, the directors review the activities of recipient organizations to ensure that they are "being maintained at a satisfactory level." The remainder of the yearly income is disbursed in the form of one-time grants for capital campaigns and special projects.

Restrictions

The foundation does not make loans or grants to individuals. Low priority is given to cultural organizations, such as museums, libraries, or exhibitions; and to research institutes, preparatory schools, colleges, and universities. The foundation generally does not fund medical research or health care and training, and it is not interested in managing programs or projects of non-established organizations.

Additional Information

"To encourage the descendants of the Founder to take an interest in philanthropy, the Foundation matches, to a limited extent, their individual grants made to agencies in which they are actively involved."

Publications: Annual Report

Foundation Officials

Alice D. Berkeley: director
Louis E. Black: secretary, director
Phyllis M. Criscuoli: executive director, treasurer
Bayard Dodge: vice president, director
Cleveland Earl Dodge, Jr.: director, member executive committee, member finance committee B New York, NY 1922. ED Princeton University BSME (1943). PRIM CORP EMPL president, treasurer, director: International Dodge Inc.
David S. Dodge: mem executive comm, director NONPR AFFIL chairman, director: Near East Foundation.
Robert Garrett: director
Alfred H. Howell, Jr.: director
Sally Dodge Mole: director
Dodge Olmsted: director
Bayard D. Rea: director
William Dodge Rueckert: president, chairman fin committee, chairman executive committee ED University of New Hampshire (1977).
Jennifer Rea Schmitt: director
Ingrid R. Warren: director

Grants Analysis

Disclosure Period: calendar year ending 2002
Total Grants: $1,761,385*
Number of Grants: 102
Average Grant: $17,142*
Highest Grant: $300,000
Lowest Grant: $200
Typical Range: $5,000 to $20,000
*Note: Giving excludes matching gifts. Average grant figure excludes highest grant.

Recent Grants

Note: Grants derived from 2002 Form 990.
Library-Related
5,000	New York Public Library, New York, NY

General
300,000	children's Aid Society, New York, NY
250,000	New York Botanical Garden, Bronx, NY
100,000	Antique Boat Museum, New York, NY
100,000	Planned Parenthood of New York City Inc., New York, NY
100,000	Springfield College, Springfield, MA
100,000	Teachers College, New York, NY
75,000	Princeton University, Princeton, NJ
50,000	Kingsbridge Heights Community Center, Bronx, NY
50,000	Near East Foundation, New York, NY
25,000	American University of Beirut, New York, NY

GERALDINE R. DODGE FOUNDATION

Giving Contact

David R. Grant, Executive Director
163 Madison Avenue
PO Box 1239
Morristown, NJ 07962-1239
Phone: (973)540-8442
Fax: (973)540-1211
E-mail: info@grdodge.org
Web: http://www.grdodge.org

Description

Founded: 1974
EIN: 237406010
Organization Type: General Purpose Foundation
Giving Locations: NJ: nationally.
Grant Types: Challenge, Conference/Seminar, Department, Emergency, Employee Matching Gifts, General Support, Matching, Operating Expenses, Project, Seed Money.

Donor Information

Founder: Established in 1974 in accordance with the will of the late Geraldine R. Dodge (d. 1973), the daughter of William Rockefeller (a former president of Standard Oil) and the niece of John D. Rockefeller. Her husband, Marcellus Hartley Dodge, was chairman of the Remington Arms Co. Mrs. Dodge was an avid dog breeder and pet lover and she established an animal shelter at the time of her death.

Financial Summary

Total Giving: $17,687,405 (2003); $23,243,333 (2002); $20,689,816 (2001)
Giving Analysis: Giving for 2003 includes: foundation matching gifts ($30,349)
Assets: $291,246,939 (2003); $270,796,051 (2002); $306,376,880 (2001)
Gifts Received: $30,000 (2003); $65,200 (2002); $135,050 (1997). Note: In 2003, contributions were received from Kenneth A. Scott Charitable Trust.

Typical Recipients

Arts & Humanities: Arts Appreciation, Arts Associations & Councils, Arts Centers, Arts Festivals, Arts Outreach, Ballet, Community Arts, Dance, Ethnic & Folk Arts, History & Archaeology, Libraries, Literary Arts, Museums/Galleries, Music, Opera, Performing Arts, Public Broadcasting, Theater, Visual Arts
Civic & Public Affairs: Botanical Gardens/Parks, Business/Free Enterprise, Employment/Job Training, Civic & Public Affairs-General, Nonprofit Management, Public Policy, Rural Affairs, Urban & Community Affairs, Women's Affairs
Education: Afterschool/Enrichment Programs, Arts/Humanities Education, Colleges & Universities, Education Associations, Education Reform, Elementary Education (Private), Elementary Education (Public), Engineering/Technological Education, Environmental Education, Faculty Development, Education-General, Gifted & Talented Programs, International Exchange, International Studies, Leadership Training, Literacy, Medical Education, Minority Education, Private Education (Precollege), Public Education (Precollege), School Volunteerism, Science/Mathematics Education, Secondary Education (Public), Social Sciences Education, Student Aid

Environment: Air/Water Quality, Energy, Forestry, Environment-General, Protection, Resource Conservation, Watershed, Wildlife Protection
Health: Medical Research
International: Health Care/Hospitals, International Affairs, International Development, International Environmental Issues, International Peace & Security Issues
Science: Science Museums, Scientific Centers & Institutes
Social Services: Animal Protection, Domestic Violence, Family Planning, Family Services, Recreation & Athletics, Shelters/Homelessness, Youth Organizations

Application Procedures

Initial Contact: A one-page letter of inquiry is encouraged, to determine if a project falls within the foundation's guidelines.

Application Requirements: The Foundation accepts the New York Area Common Application Form. Grant proposals should begin with a one-page summary of the project, followed by the main body, which should be a fuller description of no more than six pages. The foundation prefers 12-point type or larger for the text. The proposal should describe the project and the need for it; the qualifications and past accomplishments of the sponsoring organization; how the project is to proceed and who is to carry it out; a time frame and budget; the benefits to be gained and for whom; and the plans for evaluating and funding the project in the future. Also included should be a recent financial statement, together with the names and occupations of the trustees of the organization, as well as IRS confirmation of tax-exempt status. The foundation requests that the proposal be presented in an environmentally sensitive manner. Proposals should use two-sided copies without binders or plastic packaging. No faxed proposals are accepted, and the foundation prefers that express mail carriers not be used.

Deadlines: Program deadlines are November 1 for education requests, March 1 for arts grants, May 1 for Morris County, June 1 for environmental requests (formerly critical issues), and January 15 for welfare of animals applications.

Review Process: A team of program staff reviews proposals received and determines which ones fall within current grantmaking strategy. Applicants that are preliminarily determined to be within the foundation's funding strategy will be contacted by a member of the program staff to schedule a site visit or telephone interview.

Restrictions

The foundation does not consider grants for higher education, health, or religion. Grants are not usually made for capital programs, equipment purchases, indirect costs, endowment funds, or deficit operations. Grants typically are not made to individuals, scholarship funds, or grants to conduit organizations. The foundation does not support lobbying efforts.

Additional Information

Grant recipients are asked to make periodic progress reports, and at the termination of a grant, to submit a narrative report and an accounting of all disbursements. It is customary for an organization, whether it is funded or not, to wait one year before submitting another proposal.

Publications: Annual Report; Guidelines

Foundation Officials

Robert Hayes Burns Baldwin: chairman emeritus B East Orange, NJ July 09, 1920. CORP AFFIL director: ORC Worldwide.
Ross Danis: program director, education
Brenda S. Davis: trustee NONPR AFFIL council member: Art Educators of New Jersey.
Barbara Knowles Debs: trustee B Eastham, MA 1931. ED Vassar College BA (1953); Harvard University PhD (1967); New York Law School LLD (1979);

Manhattanville College LHD (1985). NONPR AFFIL member: Renaissance Society America; member: Young Audiences; director: New York Historical Society; member: Phi Beta Kappa; honorary trustee: Manhattanville College; vice chairman: Midori & Friends; board governors: Foreign Policy Association; member advisory board: Greenwich Historical Society; member: College Art Association; member: Council Foreign Relations; member executive board: Bard Center Decorative Arts; trustee: Brooklyn Museum Art; member: American Council Education. CLUB AFFIL Hundred Club Westchester; Century Association; Cosmopolitan Club.

Christopher J. Elliman: president, trustee CORP AFFIL member: Seifert Group; director: Barrett Associates. NONPR AFFIL vice chairman: Environmental Defense Fund.

David Grant: executive director

John Lloyd Huck: trustee emeritus B Brooklyn, NY 1922. ED Pennsylvania State University BS (1946). NONPR AFFIL fellow: John Simon Guggenheim Memorial Foundation. CLUB AFFIL Pipers Landing Country Club; Morris County Golf Club.

Robert LeBuhn: chairman, chief executive officer, trustee B Davenport, IA 1932. ED Northwestern University BS (1954); University of Pennsylvania MBA (1957). PRIM CORP EMPL chairman: Investor International Inc. CORP AFFIL director: Cambrex Corp.; director: Enzon Pharmaceuticals Inc.

Nancy D. Lindsay: trustee emeritus NONPR AFFIL chairman of overseers: AKC Museum of the Dog; trustee: Westminster Kennel Foundation.

Betsy S. Michel: trustee CORP AFFIL director: Tri-Continental Corp.; director: Seligman Income Fund Inc.; director: Seligman Common Stock Fund; director: Seligman Growth Fund Inc.; director: Seligman Cash Management Fund. NONPR AFFIL trustee: World Learning Inc..

Walter J. Neppl: trustee emeritus

Paul J. O'Donnell: trustee emeritus

Robert T. Perry: program director environment B Mexico City, Mexico. ED City University of New York MA; Cornell University BA (1974).

Preston D. Pinkett, III: trustee ED Cornell University BS; University of Pennsylvania MBA. CORP AFFIL senior vice president: PNC Development Bank. NONPR AFFIL board of directors: National Housing Institute; chairman: New Jersey Community Loan Fund; trustee: Montclair State University; board of directors: Central New Jersey Inroads; board of directors: Coopers Ferry Development Corp.

James W. Stevens: treasurer, trustee ED New York University MBA; Williams College BA. CORP AFFIL director: Markem Corp.; director: Maxcor Financial Group.

John Edward Yingling, Jr.: chief administrative and financial officer B Baltimore, MD 1935. ED Yale University BA (1955); Johns Hopkins University MLA (1967); New York University MBA (1977). CLUB AFFIL Yale Central New Jersey Club.

Grants Analysis

Disclosure Period: calendar year ending 2003
Total Grants: $17,657,056*
Number of Grants: 545 (approx)
Average Grant: $32,398
Highest Grant: $300,000
Lowest Grant: $500
Typical Range: $10,000 to $50,000
*Note: Giving excludes matching gifts.

Recent Grants

Note: Grants derived from 2002 Form 990.

General

1,000,000 New Jersey Symphony Orchestra, Newark, NJ

375,000 Geraldine R. Dodge Foundation, New Jersey Animal Assistance Program, Morristown, NJ -- to support the efforts of 33 humane organizations in New Jersey

350,000 New Jersey Teaching and Learning Collaborative, NJ -- to establish a new statewide intermediary education organization

300,000 Woodrow Wilson National Fellowship Foundation, Princeton, NJ -- to continue the expansion of "Teachers as Scholars"

250,000 Network for Family Life Education, New Brunswick, NJ -- to continue implementation of the New Jersey Sexuality Education Staff Development Initiative

200,000 Association of New Jersey Environmental Commission, Mendham, NJ -- to support a "Smart Growth Assistance Program"

200,000 Eastern Environmental Law Center, Newark, NJ -- to support two activities at the Center

200,000 Geraldine R. Dodge Foundation Initiative for Veterinary Students, Morristown, NJ -- to again fund the "Frontiers for Veterinary Medicine" Program

200,000 New Jersey Conservation Foundation, Far Hills, NJ -- to support the Garden State Greenways Initiative

200,000 Newark Lighthouse Initiative, Trenton, NJ -- to develop three models of early care and educational excellence in Newark, New Jersey

DODGE JONES FOUNDATION AND SUBSIDIARY

Giving Contact

Lawrence Gill, Grants Administrator
PO Box 176
Abilene, TX 79604
Phone: (325)673-6429
Fax: (325)673-2028

Description

Founded: 1954
EIN: 756006386
Organization Type: General Purpose Foundation
Giving Locations: TX
Grant Types: Capital, Challenge, General Support, Operating Expenses.

Donor Information

Founder: The foundation was established in 1954 by the late Ruth Leggett Jones.

Financial Summary

Total Giving: $6,283,340 (2002); $7,017,637 (2001)
Giving Analysis: Giving for 2002 includes: foundation scholarships ($52,500); foundation grants to United Way ($55,000)
Assets: $97,995,368 (2002); $106,756,286 (2001)
Gifts Received: $580,500 (2001); $250 (1994); $6,900 (1993). Note: In 2001, contributions were received from Julia Jones Matthews.

Typical Recipients

Arts & Humanities: Art History, Arts Associations & Councils, Ethnic & Folk Arts, Arts & Humanities-General, Historic Preservation, History & Archaeology, Libraries, Literary Arts, Museums/Galleries, Music, Opera, Performing Arts, Public Broadcasting, Theater, Visual Arts

Civic & Public Affairs: African American Affairs, Botanical Gardens/Parks, Business/Free Enterprise, Chambers of Commerce, Civil Rights, Clubs, Community Foundations, Economic Development, Employment/Job Training, Civic & Public Affairs-General, Housing, Inner-City Development, Legal Aid, Municipalities/Towns, Nonprofit Management, Professional & Trade Associations, Public Policy, Rural Affairs, Safety, Urban & Community Affairs, Zoos/Aquariums

Education: Afterschool/Enrichment Programs, Agricultural Education, Business Education, Business-School Partnerships, Colleges & Universities, Education Associations, Education Funds, Elementary Education (Private), Engineering/Technological Education, Faculty Development, Education-General, Health & Physical Education, Legal Education, Literacy, Medical Education, Private Education (Precollege), Public Education (Precollege), Science/Mathematics Education, Secondary Education (Private), Secondary Education (Public), Social Sciences Education, Special Education, Student Aid, Vocational & Technical Education

Environment: Environment-General

Health: Adolescent Health Issues, AIDS/HIV, Alzheimer's Disease, Cancer, Children's Health/Hospitals, Clinics/Medical Centers, Emergency/Ambulance Services, Geriatric Health, Health Policy/Cost Containment, Health Funds, Health Organizations, Heart, Hospices, Hospitals, Medical Rehabilitation, Medical Research, Mental Health, Public Health, Speech & Hearing

International: Foreign Arts Organizations

Religion: Churches, Ministries, Religious Organizations, Religious Welfare

Science: Science Museums, Scientific Organizations

Social Services: At-Risk Youth, Big Brothers/Big Sisters, Camps, Child Welfare, Community Centers, Community Service Organizations, Counseling, Crime Prevention, Day Care, Family Planning, Family Services, Food/Clothing Distribution, People with Disabilities, Recreation & Athletics, Scouts, Senior Services, Shelters/Homelessness, Social Services-General, Substance Abuse, United Funds/United Ways, Volunteer Services, YMCA/YWCA/YMHA/YWHA, Youth Organizations

Application Procedures

Initial Contact: The foundation reports that applicants should submit a letter of request describing the purpose for the proposed funding.
Deadlines: None.

Restrictions

The foundation does not make grants to individuals, or to organizations on behalf of individuals.

Foundation Officials

Thomas R. Allen: vice president, chief financial officer

Linda Buckner: secretary, treasurer

Joseph E. Canon: executive vice president, executive director CORP AFFIL director: First Financial Bankshares.

Lawrence Gill: vice president

Joseph B. Matthews: director

Julia Jones Matthews: president, director

Kade L. Matthews: director

Jill Matthews Wilkinson: director

Grants Analysis

Disclosure Period: calendar year ending 2002
Total Grants: $6,175,840*
Number of Grants: 154
Average Grant: $23,780*
Highest Grant: $1,093,775
Lowest Grant: $500
Typical Range: $5,000 to $50,000
*Note: Giving excludes United Way and scholarships. Average grant excludes four highest grants ($2,608,775).

Recent Grants

Note: Grants derived from 2002 Form 990.
General

1,093,775 Grace Museum, Abilene, TX -- as part of an agency endowment fund grant

515,000 Taylor County Historical Foundation, Taylor, TX -- towards providing funds for the Texas forts trail visitors center

500,000   Ben Richey Boys Ranch, Abilene, TX -- towards completion of the Abilene facility

500,000   Meals on Wheels Plus Inc., Abilene, TX -- towards construction of a new facility

500,000   Salvation Army, Alexandria, VA -- towards capital campaign

250,000   Advanced Placement Strategies, Dallas, TX -- for support of the advanced placement incentive program in the Abilene ISD

250,000   Angelo State University, San Angelo, TX -- towards construction and equipping of a food safety and product lab

200,000   Abilene Goodwill Industries, Abilene, TX -- towards purchase of equipment necessary for expansion

166,666   City of Abilene, Abilene, TX -- for support of the Texas tech university Abilene center for engineering excellence

160,000   Down Home Ranch, Elgin, TX -- towards building and equipping a garden and training center

CARRIE ESTELLE DOHENY FOUNDATION TRUST

Giving Contact

Shirley Bernard, Grants Administrator
707 Wilshire Boulevard, Suite 4960
Los Angeles, CA 90017
Phone: (213)488-1122
Fax: (213)488-1544
E-mail: doheny@dohenyfoundation.org
Web: http://www.dohenyfoundation.org

Description

Founded: 1948
EIN: 952051633
Organization Type: General Purpose Foundation
Giving Locations: nationally.
Grant Types: Award, Capital, Challenge, General Support, Matching, Multiyear/Continuing Support, Research.

Donor Information

Founder: Mrs. Edward Lawrence Doheny established the foundation in 1948, as a result of her lifelong devotion to charitable and public benefactions. Her husband (1856-1935) was chairman of Petroleum Securities Company, and president of Doheny-Stone Drilling Company and Los Nietos Producing and Refining Company. Mrs. Doheny spent years helping the sick, needy, and those suffering from loss and impairment of vision. Her interest in optical problems led her to set up the Estelle Doheny Eye Foundation, which receives annual contributions from the foundation, to support laboratory research and services, and an eye bank. Today, the eye foundation is considered one of the leading opthalmological facilities.

Financial Summary

Total Giving: $6,709,405 (2003); $7,062,099 (2002)
Assets: $166,637,032 (2003); $141,145,166 (2002)

Typical Recipients

Civic & Public Affairs: Employment/Job Training, Civic & Public Affairs-General, Hispanic Affairs, Housing, Nonprofit Management, Urban & Community Affairs, Women's Affairs
Education: Colleges & Universities, Continuing Education, Education Associations, Education Funds, Education-General, Literacy, Preschool Education, Private Education (Precollege), Public Education (Precollege), Religious Education, Secondary Education (Private), Secondary Education (Public), Student Aid, Vocational & Technical Education

Health: Cancer, Children's Health/Hospitals, Clinics/Medical Centers, Emergency/Ambulance Services, Eyes/Blindness, Health Funds, Health Organizations, Heart, Hospitals, Long-Term Care, Medical Research, Medical Training, Nutrition, Prenatal Health Issues, Public Health, Research/Studies Institutes, Single-Disease Health Associations, Speech & Hearing
International: Missionary/Religious Activities
Religion: Churches, Dioceses, Religion-General, Missionary Activities (Domestic), Religious Organizations, Religious Welfare, Seminaries
Social Services: At-Risk Youth, Big Brothers/Big Sisters, Child Welfare, Community Centers, Community Service Organizations, Counseling, Delinquency & Criminal Rehabilitation, Domestic Violence, Emergency Relief, Family Planning, Family Services, Food/Clothing Distribution, Homes, People with Disabilities, Recreation & Athletics, Scouts, Senior Services, Shelters/Homelessness, Social Services-General, United Funds/United Ways, Youth Organizations

Application Procedures

Initial Contact: The foundation currently has no formal grant application procedure or application form; requests should be made in letter form. Beginning in 2001, and application form will be required. The form will be available via mail, fax, or website.
Application Requirements: Requests should be concise and contain a brief description of the project, clearly stating its objectives; preliminary budget; and a description of organization. Copies of an IRS determination letter of tax exemption must be included, along with financial statements.
Deadlines: None.
Review Process: The board of directors meets monthly to review proposals.
Notes: Video tapes cannot be returned.

Restrictions

No grants are made to organizations not certified as nonprofit and tax-exempt by the IRS, individuals, or tax-supported entities; or for scholarships, political purposes, goodwill advertisement, travel funds, radio or television programming, or book publishing.

Additional Information

Publications: Annual Report

Foundation Officials

Robert F. Erburu: director B Ventura, CA 1930. ED University of Southern California BA (1952); Harvard University JD (1955). CORP AFFIL director: Marsh & McLennan Companies Inc. NONPR AFFIL trustee: National Gallery Art; director: Pacific Council on International Policy; life director: Independent Colleges Southern California; member: American Bar Association; chairman board trustee: H.E. Huntington Library Art Gallery.
Austin F. Gavin: director
George Gibbs: director
Joseph Nally: director B 1934. PRIM NONPR EMPL president: Pacific-Western Inc.
Rev. William Piletic: director
Mrs. Terry Seidler: director PRIM CORP EMPL tru: Loyola Marymount University.
Robert A. Smith, III: director

Grants Analysis

Disclosure Period: calendar year ending 2003
Total Grants: $6,709,405
Number of Grants: 246
Average Grant: $20,409*
Highest Grant: $800,000
Lowest Grant: $1,000
Typical Range: $5,000 to $50,000
*Note: Average grant excludes three highest grants ($1,750,000).

Recent Grants

Note: Grants derived from 2003 Form 990.

General

800,000   Doheny Eye Institute, Los Angeles, CA

650,000   Archdiocese of Los Angeles Cathedral, Los Angeles, CA -- construction of our lady of the angels cathedral

300,000   Archdiocese of Los Angeles Inner City Schools, Los Angeles, CA -- maintenance & repair of poor inner-city elementary schools

150,000   University of San Diego, San Diego, CA -- construction of new science building

125,000   Loyola Marymount University, Los Angeles, CA -- support for university hall purchase

120,000   Independent Colleges of Southern California, Los Angeles, CA -- support for the independent colleges

120,000   St. Vincent Medical Center, Los Angeles, CA -- four community outreach programs

100,000   Cathedral High School, Los Angeles, CA -- Doheny scholarship program

100,000   Mount St. Mary's College, Los Angeles, CA -- 2003 repairs and maintenance for the Doheny campus

100,000   St. Joseph Center, Venice, CA

HENRY L. AND GRACE DOHERTY CHARITABLE FOUNDATION

Giving Contact

Walter R. Brown, President
Henry L. and Grace Doherty Charitable Foundation
Care of McGrath, Doyle & Phair
150 Broadway, Suite 1703
New York, NY 10038
Phone: (212)571-2300

Description

Founded: 1947
EIN: 136401292
Organization Type: Private Foundation
Giving Locations: nationally.
Grant Types: General Support, Research.

Donor Information

Founder: the late Mrs. Henry L. Doherty, the late Helen Lee Lassen

Financial Summary

Total Giving: $749,950 (2003); $897,275 (2001)
Giving Analysis: Giving for 2003 includes: foundation grants to United Way ($11,000); 2001: foundation grants to United Way ($10,000)
Assets: $19,298,957 (2003); $19,024,391 (2001)

Typical Recipients

Arts & Humanities: Arts Associations & Councils, Arts Centers, Arts & Humanities-General, History & Archaeology, Libraries, Museums/Galleries, Music, Theater
Civic & Public Affairs: Asian American Affairs, Civic & Public Affairs-General, Parades/Festivals, Urban & Community Affairs
Education: Colleges & Universities, Engineering/Technological Education, Faculty Development, Education-General, Leadership Training, Legal Education, Minority Education, Private Education (Precollege), Public Education (Precollege), Science/Mathematics Education
Environment: Environment-General, Resource Conservation, Wildlife Protection
Health: Alzheimer's Disease, Cancer, Clinics/Medical Centers, Diabetes, Emergency/Ambulance Services, Health Organizations, Hospices, Hospitals, Medical Research, Mental Health, Nursing Services,

Single-Disease Health Associations
International: Foreign Educational Institutions, Health Care/Hospitals, International Organizations, International Relations, International Relief Efforts
Religion: Churches, Religious Organizations, Religious Welfare
Science: Observatories & Planetariums, Scientific Centers & Institutes, Scientific Labs
Social Services: At-Risk Youth, Camps, Child Welfare, Community Service Organizations, Crime Prevention, People with Disabilities, Scouts, Senior Services, United Funds/United Ways, YMCA/YWCA/YMHA/YWHA, Youth Organizations

Application Procedures

Initial Contact: Send a brief letter of inquiry.
Application Requirements: Include a description of organization, its activities, and its purpose; proof of tax-exempt status; a statement regarding if the applicant is controlled by, related to, connected with, or sponsored by another organization; a list of board members; whether the applicant has applied for a grant from this foundation in the past; purpose of funds sought; amount requested; and the name of contact person who will be administering the proposed program.
Deadlines: None.

Restrictions

Preference is given to marine research and oceanography. Does not support individuals.

Foundation Officials

James R. Billegsly: director
Helen Lee Billingsley: director
James Ray Billingsley: vice president, treasurer, director B Rome, GA 1927. ED New York University (1945); North Georgia College (1945); University of Mississippi JD (1950). PRIM CORP EMPL managing partner: Tolten LP. CORP AFFIL senior vice president: AT&T. NONPR AFFIL member: New York State Bar Association; member, board advisors: University Mississippi Center Telecommunications; member: Fed Communications Bar Association; member: American Bar Association.
Kiyoko O. Brown: director
Walter R. Brown: president, director
Jacob C. Hardin, Jr.: director

Grants Analysis

Disclosure Period: calendar year ending 2003
Total Grants: $738,950*
Number of Grants: 39
Average Grant: $3,860*
Highest Grant: $400,000
Lowest Grant: $100
Typical Range: $1,000 to $5,000
*Note: Giving excludes United Way. Average grant figure excludes three highest grants ($600,000).

Recent Grants

Note: Grants derived from 2001 Form 990.
Library-Related

15,000	Rye Free Reading Room, Rye, NY

General

500,000	University of Mississippi Foundation, University, OK
100,000	Florida Institute of Technology, Melbourne, FL
100,000	Marine Biological Laboratories, Woods Hole, MA
50,000	Charles Hollister Foundation, Woods Hole, MA
15,000	Hackley School, Tarrytown, NY
15,000	Huntington Museum of Art, Huntington, WV
10,200	National Maritime Historical Society, Peekskill, NY
10,000	Charlottesville Catholic School, Charlottesville, VA
10,000	Maine Coast Heritage Trust, Topsham, ME
10,000	St. Joseph Catholic Church, Huntington, WV

DOMINIC FOUNDATION

Giving Contact

Richard A. Berlanti, President
777 S. Wadsworth Boulevard
Suite 4-280
Lakewood, CO 80226
Phone: (303)985-0041

Description

Founded: 1995
EIN: 521905243
Organization Type: Private Foundation
Giving Locations: nationally and internationally.
Grant Types: General Support.

Donor Information

Founder: Established in 1995 by Richard A. Berlanti, Todd A. Berlanti and Merryl A. Berlanti.

Financial Summary

Total Giving: $39,000 (2004); $92,500 (2001)
Assets: $2,788,436 (2004); $2,564,947 (2001)
Gifts Received: $1,410,938 (1994). Note: In 1994, contributions were received from Richard A. Berlanti, Todd A. Berlanti, and Merryl A. Berlanti ($470,313) each.

Typical Recipients

Arts & Humanities: Arts Festivals, Ballet, Arts & Humanities-General, History & Archaeology, Libraries, Museums/Galleries
Civic & Public Affairs: Clubs, Civic & Public Affairs-General, Safety
Education: Arts/Humanities Education, Colleges & Universities, Secondary Education (Private), Special Education
Environment: Resource Conservation
Health: Cancer, Children's Health/Hospitals, Hospices
Religion: Churches, Religious Welfare
Science: Science Museums
Social Services: Animal Protection, Child Welfare, Community Service Organizations, Family Services, Food/Clothing Distribution, Homes, People with Disabilities, Recreation & Athletics, Shelters/Homelessness

Application Procedures

Initial Contact: Applicant must submit letter with exemption certificate attached.
Deadlines: None.

Foundation Officials

Merryl A. Berlanti: vice president
Richard A. Berlanti: president
Todd A. Berlanti: secretary, treasurer
John P. Hill, Jr.: administrator

Grants Analysis

Disclosure Period: calendar year ending 2004
Total Grants: $39,000
Number of Grants: 9
Average Grant: $2,875*
Highest Grant: $16,000
Lowest Grant: $500
Typical Range: $1,000 to $5,000
*Note: Average grant figure excludes highest grant.

Recent Grants

Note: Grants derived from 2001 Form 990.
Library-Related

5,000	Mary S. Biesecker Library, Somerset, PA

General

10,000	Northern New Mexico Animal Protection Society, Espanola, NM
9,000	Laurel Arts, Somerset, PA
5,000	Boca Raton Museum of Art, Boca Raton, FL
5,000	Humanitarian Society, Boca Raton, FL
5,000	Meals on Wheels, Somerset, PA
5,000	Norton Museum of Art, West Palm Beach, FL
4,000	James P. Beckwourth Mountain Club, Denver, CO
3,500	Children's Aid Home and Society of Somerset County, Somerset, PA
3,500	Children's Place at Home Safe, Lake Worth, FL
3,000	Borough of Somerset, Somerset, PA

DOMINION

Company Headquarters

120 Tredegar Street
Richmond, VA 23219
Phone: (804)819-2000
E-mail: dominion_resources@domres.com
Web: http://www.dom.com

Company Description

Founded: 1983
Ticker: D
Exchange: NYSE
Revenue: US$13.98 billion (2004)
Profit: US$1.249 billion (2004)
Employees: 16700 (2003)
Fortune Rank: 151, per FORTUNE Magazine's list of 500 Largest U.S. Corporations (2004).

Nonmonetary Support

Type: Donated Equipment; In-kind Services; Loaned Employees; Loaned Executives

Giving Contact

Renee Johnson, Philanthropy Coordinator
PO Box 26532
Richmond, VA 23261
Phone: (804)819-2580
Fax: (804)819-2217
E-mail: reneejohnson@dom.com

Description

Organization Type: Corporate Giving Program
Giving Locations: operating locations.
Grant Types: Capital, Employee Matching Gifts, General Support.
Note: Employee matching gift ratio: 0.5 to 1. The company matches gifts from $25 to $1,000 per employee annually.

Financial Summary

Total Giving: $1,000,000 (2004 approx); $1,000,000 (2003); $2,150,000 (2002 approx). Note: Contributes through corporate direct giving program only.

Typical Recipients

Arts & Humanities: Arts Associations & Councils, Arts Centers, Arts Festivals, Community Arts, Dance, Libraries, Literary Arts, Museums/Galleries, Music, Opera, Performing Arts, Public Broadcasting, Theater, Visual Arts
Civic & Public Affairs: Employment/Job Training, Housing, Safety, Urban & Community Affairs, Women's Affairs
Education: Colleges & Universities, Education Funds, Engineering/Technological Education
Environment: Environment-General
Health: Emergency/Ambulance Services, Health Organizations, Hospices, Hospitals, Mental Health
Social Services: Child Welfare, Food/Clothing Distri-

bution, Homes, People with Disabilities, Senior Services, Shelters/Homelessness, Substance Abuse

Application Procedures

Initial Contact: Submit a letter or proposal.
Application Requirements: Include organization's purpose and goals, most recent financial statement, proof of tax-exempt status, amount of grant requested and total goal for contributions from individuals and corp.s, and a description of intended use of requested funds.
Deadlines: None.
Evaluative Criteria: Priority is given to organizations that address issues critical to the company's objectives; organizations that promote research and coalition-building rather than duplicating efforts; organizations that are tax-exempt; and organizations that operate within the northeastern quadrant of the United States.
Decision Notification: Statewide requests are reviewed quarterly and notices are sent in April, July, October, and December; other organizations receive notice within approximately 45 days.

Restrictions

Support is not given to organizations benefiting an individual or family; religious, political, fraternal, veteran, professional or membership organization; operating grants to organizations supported by the United Way; historic restoration; individual Scout troops, except area scouting councils that are not supported by the United Way; organizations that discriminate on the basis of race, creed, color, sex or national origin; or elementary and secondary schools.

In the area of human and social services the company does not make grants to national health organizations; for medical equipment or research; tax-supported hospitals or hospitals operated for-profit; or campaigns for sponsorship through program advertising.

In the area of education the company does not support private foundations benefiting from tax-supported education institutions; individual research or scholarship; operating support for individual universities; or athletic and extracurricular activities.

In the area of arts and humanities the company does not support film or video projects; endowment programs; or individual high school or college performing arts groups.

In the area of the environment the company does not make grants to groups whose objectives are inconsistent with the company's best interests; political or lobbying groups; or research or issues for which significant information is already available.

Additional Information

In January 2000, Dominion Resources merged with Consolidated Natural Gas Co. Under the terms of the merger agreement, Consolidated Natural Gas Co. became a direct subsidiary of Dominion.

Local community organizations should apply to nearest company offices. Addresses and phone numbers are listed in the Corporate Giving Program brochure, available upon request from the contributions administrator.

Grants for economic development are administered as a separate program by the Economic Development section of the company's Customer Service and Marketing Department.

Organizations that receive a capital grant must wait two years after receiving final payment to apply for another grant.

Publications: Corporate Giving Program Brochure

Giving Program Officials

Eva S. Teig: PRIM CORP EMPL senior vice president: Virginia Electric & Power Co. NONPR AFFIL director: Christian Childrens Fund Inc.

OLIVER S. AND JENNIE R. DONALDSON CHARITABLE TRUST

Giving Contact

Linda Franciscovich, Managing Director
P.O. Box 2004
New York, NY 10109-1910
Phone: (212)852-1000
Fax: (212)852-3377

Description

Founded: 1969
EIN: 046229044
Organization Type: General Purpose Foundation
Giving Locations: northeastern United States.
Grant Types: General Support, Operating Expenses, Project, Research, Seed Money.

Donor Information

Founder: Established in 1969 by the late Oliver S. Donaldson.

Financial Summary

Total Giving: $1,529,500 (2002); $1,753,750 (2001)
Giving Analysis: Giving for 2002 includes: foundation fellowships ($10,000) 2001: foundation scholarships ($66,600)
Assets: $27,046,854 (2002); $28,833,712 (2001)
Gifts Received: $24,397 (1993)

Typical Recipients

Arts & Humanities: Arts Associations & Councils, Arts Festivals, Arts & Humanities-General, Historic Preservation, Libraries, Museums/Galleries, Music, Opera, Public Broadcasting, Theater
Civic & Public Affairs: Botanical Gardens/Parks, Clubs, Community Foundations, Employment/Job Training, Civic & Public Affairs-General, Hispanic Affairs, Housing, Urban & Community Affairs, Zoos/Aquariums
Education: Afterschool/Enrichment Programs, Colleges & Universities, Community & Junior Colleges, Education Associations, Education Funds, Legal Education, Medical Education, Private Education (Precollege), Secondary Education (Private), Secondary Education (Public)
Environment: Forestry, Environment-General, Protection, Resource Conservation, Watershed, Wildlife Protection
Health: Cancer, Children's Health/Hospitals, Clinics/Medical Centers, Emergency/Ambulance Services, Health-General, Health Funds, Health Organizations, Heart, Hospitals, Medical Research, Mental Health, Nursing Services, Preventive Medicine/Wellness Organizations, Research/Studies Institutes, Single-Disease Health Associations
International: Health Care/Hospitals, Human Rights, International Affairs, International Environmental Issues, International Relations
Religion: Churches, Religious Organizations, Religious Welfare, Synagogues/Temples
Science: Scientific Centers & Institutes, Scientific Labs
Social Services: Animal Protection, At-Risk Youth, Big Brothers/Big Sisters, Child Abuse, Child Welfare, Community Centers, Community Service Organizations, Emergency Relief, Family Services, Homes, People with Disabilities, Recreation & Athletics, Senior Services, Social Services-General, United Funds/United Ways, Volunteer Services, YMCA/YWCA/YMHA/YWHA, Youth Organizations

Application Procedures

Initial Contact: The foundation requests applications be made in writing, using a common application form.
Deadlines: Applicants should fax the foundation to request guidelines and application form.

Review Process: Grants are generally made twice a year.

Restrictions

Funds are restricted to the U.S.; no requests from international organizations will be considered. Grants are not made to individuals.

Additional Information

Publications: Application Guidelines; Application Forms

Foundation Officials

Marjorie Atwood: trustee
Carolyn Lark: vice president
Dr. Elizabeth Atwood Lawrence: trustee
William E. Murray: trustee B 1926. PRIM CORP EMPL chairman board, chief executive officer, director: East Bay Company Ltd.
John F. Sisk: trustee

Grants Analysis

Disclosure Period: calendar year ending 2002
Total Grants: $1,519,500*
Number of Grants: 33
Average Grant: $34,500*
Highest Grant: $250,000
Lowest Grant: $4,000
Typical Range: $10,000 to $50,000
*Note: Giving excludes fellowship. Average grant figure excludes two highest grants ($450,000).

Recent Grants

Note: Grants derived from 2002 Form 990.
General

250,000	University of Medical Associates of the Medical University of South Carolina, Charleston, SC
200,000	Spoleto Festival USA, Charleston, SC
115,000	General Hospital Corporation, Boston, MA
100,000	Mayo Foundation, Rochester, MN
100,000	Mayo Foundation, Rochester, MN -- towards clinical trial for the treatment of ovarian cancer
100,000	Newport Hospital Foundation Inc., Newport, RI -- towards Hospital's medical information system's upgradation
100,000	Rappahannock Westminster Canterbury Foundation, Irvington, VA
100,000	University of Medical Associates of the Medical University of South Carolina, Charleston, SC
43,000	Woods Hole, Woods Hole, MA
40,000	Thomas Chew Memorial Boys Club Inc., Fall River, MA -- towards expansion and renovation project

DONALDSON COMPANY INC.

Company Headquarters

Minneapolis, MN
Web: http://www.donaldson.com

Company Description

Founded: 1915
Ticker: DCI
Exchange: NYSE
Revenue: US$1.218 billion (2003)
Employees: 9409 (2003)
SIC(s): 3519 Internal Combustion Engines Nec.

Operating Locations

Donaldson Co., Inc. (CA--Covina, San Ramon, Santa Ana; FL--Plantation; IL--Dixon, Galesburg; IN--Frankfort, Indianapolis, South Bend; IA--Grinnell,

Oelwein; KS--Shawnee Mission; LA--Jefferson; MI--Brighton; MO--Chillicothe; NY--Skaneateles; NC--Morrisville; OH--Cincinnati, Cleveland, Reynoldsburg; OK--Oklahoma City; PA--Pittsburgh; TX--Houston, Richardson; WA--Bellevue; WI--Baldwin, Brookfield, Stevens Point)

Note: Operates plants in all locations.

Donaldson Foundation

Giving Contact
Norman C. Linnell, President & Trustee
PO Box 1299 MS 100
Minneapolis, MN 55440
Phone: (952)703-4999
Fax: (952)887-3005
E-mail: donaldsonfoundation@mail.donaldson.com
Web: http://www.donaldson.com/en/about/community/foundation.html

Description
EIN: 416052950
Organization Type: Corporate Foundation
Giving Locations: headquarters and operating communities.
Grant Types: Award, Capital, General Support, Multiyear/Continuing Support, Scholarship.

Financial Summary
Total Giving: $848,655 (fiscal year ending July 31, 2004); $842,353 (fiscal 2003); $857,536 (fiscal 2002). Note: Contributes through corporate direct giving program and foundation.
Giving Analysis: Giving for fiscal 2001 includes: foundation matching gifts ($14,530); foundation scholarships ($131,860); foundation grants to United Way ($264,052); foundation ($426,275)
Assets: $3,175,374 (fiscal 2004); $3,959,067 (fiscal 2003); $2,251,448 (fiscal 2002)
Gifts Received: $2,500,000 (fiscal 2003); $900,000 (fiscal 2001); $2,310,000 (fiscal 1998). Note: Contributions were received from Donaldson Company.

Typical Recipients
Arts & Humanities: Arts Associations & Councils, Arts Centers, Arts Funds, Arts Institutes, Community Arts, Dance, Historic Preservation, History & Archaeology, Libraries, Museums/Galleries, Music, Opera, Performing Arts, Public Broadcasting, Theater
Civic & Public Affairs: Botanical Gardens/Parks, Business/Free Enterprise, Clubs, Community Foundations, Economic Development, Employment/Job Training, Civic & Public Affairs-General, Hispanic Affairs, Housing, Nonprofit Management, Safety, Women's Affairs, Zoos/Aquariums
Education: Agricultural Education, Business Education, Business-School Partnerships, Colleges & Universities, Community & Junior Colleges, Economic Education, Education Funds, Education Reform, Elementary Education (Private), Elementary Education (Public), Engineering/Technological Education, Faculty Development, Education-General, Health & Physical Education, Legal Education, Literacy, Minority Education, Private Education (Precollege), Public Education (Precollege), Science/Mathematics Education, Secondary Education (Private), Secondary Education (Public), Special Education, Student Aid, Vocational & Technical Education
Environment: Forestry, Environment-General, Resource Conservation, Wildlife Protection
Health: Children's Health/Hospitals, Clinics/Medical Centers, Emergency/Ambulance Services, Health Funds, Health Organizations, Hospices, Hospitals, Medical Rehabilitation, Mental Health, Preventive Medicine/Wellness Organizations, Public Health
Religion: Religious Welfare
Science: Observatories & Planetariums, Science Museums
Social Services: Big Brothers/Big Sisters, Child Welfare, Community Centers, Community Service Organizations, Counseling, Day Care, Delinquency & Criminal Rehabilitation, Domestic Violence, Emergency Relief, Family Planning, Family Services, Food/Clothing Distribution, Homes, People with Disabilities, Recreation & Athletics, Senior Services, Shelters/Homelessness, Substance Abuse, United Funds/United Ways, Volunteer Services, YMCA/YWCA/YMHA/YWHA, Youth Organizations

Application Procedures
Initial Contact: Send a brief letter of inquiry.
Application Requirements: Provide a description of organization, a list of officers and directors, a description of the program or project needing assistance, explanation of current progress toward goal, a budget and list of contributors, IRS tax exemption letter, and IRS letter stating organization is not a private foundation.
Deadlines: None.
Decision Notification: Trustees review grants in September, January, and May; annual budget set at August meeting.

Restrictions
The foundation limits its support to local or regional drives in communities where Donaldson employees live. The foundation does not support individuals, organizations for religious purposes, groups that influence legislation, political campaigns, or national drives. Applicants must qualify for tax exemption under the IRS Code and cannot be a private foundation.

Additional Information
The foundation considers capital grants, but limits them to 30% of annual giving.
Applicants receiving grants are furnished with a Statement of Donee form, which must be returned to the foundation before payments can be made. The statement may be recalled for any future grant payments.
Publications: Application Guidelines; Annual Report

Corporate Officials
Norman C. Linnell: vice president, general counselo, director B 1959. ED University of Minnesota (1981); University of Minnesota (1984). PRIM CORP EMPL vice president, general counsel: Donaldson Co., Inc.
William Grant Van Dyke: chairman, president, chief executive officer, director B Minneapolis, MN 1945. ED University of Minnesota BA (1967); University of Minnesota MBA (1972). PRIM CORP EMPL chairman, president, chief executive officer, director: Donaldson Co., Inc. ADD CORP EMPL president: Advanced Filtration Systems. CORP AFFIL director: Graco Inc. NONPR AFFIL member: Kappa Sigma Alumni Association.

Foundation Officials
Marty Barris: trustee
Jim Burrows: director
Becky Cahn: trustee
H. Young Chung: trustee
Patrick Fischer: trustee
Karen Geronime: trustee
Dennis Grigal: trustee
Sandra Johnson: secretary
Norman C. Linnell: president, trustee (see above)
Jeff May: trustee
Julie Rumsey: director

Grants Analysis
Disclosure Period: fiscal year ending July 31, 2004
Total Grants: $848,655*
Typical Range: $1,000 to $5,000
*Note: No grant list available for 2004.

Recent Grants
Note: Grants derived from 2002 Form 990.

Library-Related
1,500	Sterling Public Library, Sterling, IL -- for library operation

General
187,000	United Way of Minneapolis Area, Minneapolis, MN
122,720	Citizens' Scholarship Foundation, St. Peter, MN -- towards scholarship
70,000	University of Minnesota Foundation, Minneapolis, MN -- for education
50,000	United Way September 11 Fund, New York, NY
48,000	SHAPE -- towards self-sufficiency
45,000	Rebuild Resources, St. Paul, MN -- towards self-sufficiency
40,000	Community Action Council, St. Paul, MN -- towards self-sufficiency
35,000	Women in Transition, Philadelphia, PA -- towards self-sufficiency
31,000	Tree Trust, St. Paul, MN -- towards self-sufficiency
22,964	United Way of Portage County, Ravenna, OH

R.R. Donnelley & Sons Co.

Company Headquarters
Chicago, IL
Web: http://www.rrdonnelley.com

Company Description
Ticker: DNY
Exchange: OTC
Revenue: US$7.79 billion (2004)
Profit: US$178.3 million (2004)
Employees: 30000 (2003)
Fortune Rank: 275, per FORTUNE Magazine's list of 500 Largest U.S. Corporations (2004).
SIC(s): 2732 Book Printing, 2752 Commercial Printing-Lithographic, 2754 Commercial Printing--Gravure, 2759 Commercial Printing Nec.

Operating Locations
R.R. Donnelley & Sons Co. (AR--Fayetteville; CA--Emeryville, Irvine, Los Angeles, San Francisco, Santa Clara, Sherman Oaks, Torrance; CO--Denver; CT--Hartford, Old Saybrook, Stamford; FL--Eatonville, Tampa; GA--Atlanta; IL--Burbank, Dwight, Elgin, Hinsdale, Lisle, Mendota; IN--Crawfordsville, Warsaw; KY--Danville; ME--Portland; MA--Boston, Waltham, Wrentham; MN--Minneapolis; MS--Senatobia; NV--Reno; NC--Charlotte; OH--Willard; OR--Beaverton, Portland; PA--Lancaster, Pittsburgh; SC--Spartanburg; TN--Brentwood, Gallatin; TX--Dallas, Fort Worth, Houston, McAllen; VA--Falls Church, Harrisonburg, Richmond; WA--Bellevue)

Nonmonetary Support
Type: Donated Equipment; Loaned Executives
Volunteer Programs: The company sponsors the Donnelley Dollars for Doers program, which provides grants to organizations for which Donnelley employees or retirees volunteer. Grant amounts are based on the number of hours donated by the employee or retiree, to a maximum of $500 per employee and $5,000 to any one organization.
Note: Company donates only used equipment. Company loans executives to the United Way only.

Giving Contact
Susan M. Levy, Vice President
R.R. Donnelley Foundation
111 South Wacker Drive
Chicago, IL 60606
Phone: (312)326-8102
Fax: (312)326-8262
E-mail: susan.levy@rrd.com

Alternate Contact
Phone: (312)326-8175

Description
Organization Type: Corporate Giving Program
Giving Locations: principally near operating locations and to national organizations.
Grant Types: Capital, Emergency, Employee Matching Gifts, General Support, Multiyear/Continuing Support, Scholarship, Seed Money.
Note: Employee matching gift ratio: 1 to 1 for educational and cultural gifts.

Financial Summary
Total Giving: $2,000,000 (2004 approx); $2,000,000 (2003); $2,406,000 (2002). Note: Contributes through corporate direct giving program and foundation. 2000 giving excludes corporate scholarships of an undisclosed amount; matching gifts includes corporate matching gifts to educational institutions, arts organizations, and to match employee volunteer efforts. 1998 and 1999 giving includes nonmonetary support.

Typical Recipients
Arts & Humanities: Arts Institutes, Historic Preservation, Libraries, Literary Arts, Museums/Galleries, Performing Arts, Theater
Civic & Public Affairs: Employment/Job Training, Public Policy, Urban & Community Affairs, Zoos/Aquariums
Education: Colleges & Universities, Education Associations, Literacy
Health: Hospitals, Mental Health
Social Services: Domestic Violence, Family Services, People with Disabilities, Shelters/Homelessness, United Funds/United Ways, Youth Organizations

Application Procedures
Initial Contact: Submit a short written proposal.
Application Requirements: Include a description of organization, its activities and clients; a clear statement of what is being requested; an explanation of what will be accomplished; proof of tax-exempt status; a list of board members; and an audited financial statement.
Deadlines: Proposals are accepted between January 1 and November 1.
Review Process: Requests are reviewed by the foundation's board of directors, which meets on a quarterly basis.
Notes: Organizations located in operating communities should contact local manufacturing division; requests from the Chicago area should be directed to the foundation's headquarters.

Restrictions
Neither the foundation nor the company contribute printing; award scholarships, except through the company's established programs for children of employees; or make grants for individuals, religious organizations, hospitals, disease specific organizations, clinical care, medical research or equipment, television, radio, film or video.

Additional Information
Part of Donnelley's annual giving is administered by manufacturing divisions, although division grants tend to be smaller than those awarded by the corporate office. In general, manufacturing divisions award grants ranging from $25 to $15,000 each, while the corporate office awards grants ranging from $1,000 to $125,000 each.
Publications: Corporate Contributions Annual Report

Corporate Officials
Haven E. Cockerham: senior vice president human resources PRIM CORP EMPL senior vice president human resources: R.R. Donnelly & Sons Co.
William L. Davis: chairman, president, chief executive officer B 1943. ED Princeton University BA (1965). PRIM CORP EMPL chairman, president, chief executive officer: R.R. Donnelley & Sons Co. CORP AFFIL director: Mallinckrodt Inc.
James R. Donnelley: director B Chicago, IL 1935. ED Dartmouth College BA (1957); University of Chicago MBA (1962). PRIM CORP EMPL vice chairman: R.R. Donnelley & Sons Co. CORP AFFIL director: Sierra Pacific Power Co.; director: Sierra Pacific Resources; director: Pacific Magazines & Printing Ltd.
Cheryl A. Francis: executive vice president, chief financial officer B Toledo, OH 1954. ED Cornell University BS (1976); University of Chicago MBA (1978). PRIM CORP EMPL executive vice president, chief financial officer: R.R. Donnelley & Sons Co. ADD CORP EMPL director investor relations: FMC Corp. NONPR AFFIL member: Financial Executives Institute; member: International Womens Forum.
Susan M. Levy: director community relations PRIM CORP EMPL community relations manager, director: R.R. Donnelley & Sons Co.
Cheryl Malmloff: community relations administrator PRIM CORP EMPL community relations administrator: R.R. Donnelley & Sons Co.

Giving Program Officials
Cheryl A. Francis: member (see above)

Foundation Officials
William L. Davis: chief financial officer, director (see above)
James R. Donnelley: director (see above)
Susan M. Levy: vice president (see above)

Grants Analysis
Typical Range: $1,000 to $10,000

DOROT FOUNDATION

Giving Contact
Prof. Ernest S. Frerichs, President
439 Benefit Street
Providence, RI 02903
Phone: (401)351-8866
Fax: (401)351-4975
E-mail: info@dorot.org
Web: http://www.dorot.org

Description
Founded: 1958
EIN: 136116927
Organization Type: General Purpose Foundation
Giving Locations: U.S.-based affiliates of Israeli organizations; northeast United States.
Grant Types: Fellowship.

Donor Information
Founder: The foundation was established in 1958 by Joy G. Ungerleider-Mayerson, D.S., and the R. H. Gottesman Foundation.

Financial Summary
Total Giving: $3,314,140 (fiscal year ending March 31, 2004); $11,866,252 (fiscal 2002); $2,877,927 (fiscal 2001)
Giving Analysis: Giving for fiscal 2004 includes: foundation fellowships ($534,012); fiscal 2001: foundation fellowships ($703,092).
Assets: $57,829,735 (fiscal 2004); $49,704,771 (fiscal 2002); $49,662,944 (fiscal 2001)
Gifts Received: $2,683,030 (fiscal 2004); $2,683,031 (fiscal 2002); $2,683,031 (fiscal 2001). Note: In fiscal 2004, contributions were received from Yesod Fund. In fiscal 2001, contributions were received from Jeane Ungerleider. In fiscal 1999, contributions were received from the Yesod Fund.

Typical Recipients
Arts & Humanities: Arts Appreciation, Arts Centers, Arts Festivals, Arts Funds, Film & Video, Historic Preservation, History & Archaeology, Libraries, Museums/Galleries, Performing Arts, Public Broadcasting, Theater
Civic & Public Affairs: Civil Rights, Community Foundations, Ethnic Organizations, Civic & Public Affairs-General, Law & Justice, Legal Aid, Public Policy, Safety, Urban & Community Affairs, Women's Affairs
Education: Arts/Humanities Education, Colleges & Universities, Economic Education, Education-General, Gifted & Talented Programs, International Exchange, International Studies, Medical Education, Preschool Education, Private Education (Precollege), Religious Education, Secondary Education (Private), Special Education, Student Aid, Vocational & Technical Education
Environment: Environment-General
Health: AIDS/HIV, Children's Health/Hospitals, Clinics/Medical Centers, Hospices, Medical Research, Medical Training, Mental Health, Public Health, Single-Disease Health Associations
International: Foreign Arts Organizations, Foreign Educational Institutions, International-General, Human Rights, International Environmental Issues, International Organizations, International Peace & Security Issues, Missionary/Religious Activities
Religion: Bible Study/Translation, Churches, Religion-General, Jewish Causes, Religious Organizations, Religious Welfare, Synagogues/Temples
Science: Scientific Centers & Institutes
Social Services: Big Brothers/Big Sisters, Camps, Child Welfare, Community Centers, Community Service Organizations, Emergency Relief, Family Services, Food/Clothing Distribution, People with Disabilities, Recreation & Athletics, Senior Services, Social Services-General, Substance Abuse, YMCA/YWCA/YMHA/YWHA, Youth Organizations

Application Procedures
Initial Contact: Applicants should submit a preliminary letter of proposal. The foundation reports that it does not have any formal proposal guidelines. Fellowship applications and guidelines may be downloaded from the foundation's Web site.

Foundation Officials
Ernest S. Frerichs: president B Staten Island, NY 1925. ED Brown University AB (1948); Harvard University AM (1949); Boston University STB (1952); Boston University PhD (1957); Hebrew Union College DHL (1992). NONPR AFFIL member: Phi Beta Kappa; member: Society Biblical Literature; professor religious studies, director Judaic stud: Brown University; member: American Academy Religion; vice president, trustee: American Schools Oriental Research; trustee: Albright Institute Archeological Research.
Michael Hill: executive vice president

Grants Analysis
Disclosure Period: fiscal year ending March 31, 2004
Total Grants: $2,780,128*
Number of Grants: 46
Average Grant: $43,089*
Highest Grant: $841,111
Lowest Grant: $2,500
Typical Range: $10,000 to $100,000
***Note:** Giving excludes fellowship. Average grant figure excludes highest grant.

Recent Grants
Note: Grants derived from 2003 Form 990.
General
835,000   New Israel Fund-Joint venture
327,912   Public Employees Federation, Albany, NY
200,000   Justice for Athletes, Eugene, OR
150,000   Jewish Women's Archive, Brookline, MA

135,000	Jewish Museum, New York, NY
100,000	American Parkinson Disease Association, Staten Island, NY
100,000	Skirball Cultural Center, Los Angeles, CA
90,000	Alliance for Justice, Washington, DC
75,000	Doernbecher Children's Hospital Foundation, Portland, OR
75,000	National Foundation for Jewish Culture, New York, NY

DORRANCE FAMILY FOUNDATION

Giving Contact

Bennett Dorrance, President
Dorrance Family Foundation
7600 East Doubletree Ranch Road Suite 300
Scottsdale, AZ 85258
Phone: (480)367-7000

Description

Founded: 1991
EIN: 860691863
Organization Type: Private Foundation
Giving Locations: AZ
Grant Types: General Support, Scholarship.

Donor Information

Founder: Established in 1991 by Bennett Dorrance.

Financial Summary

Total Giving: $3,795,436 (2002); $3,172,715 (2001)
Giving Analysis: Giving for 2002 includes: foundation scholarships ($619,465); 2001: foundation grants to United Way ($10,000); foundation scholarships ($621,185)
Assets: $38,724,483 (2002); $51,695,885 (2001)
Gifts Received: $100,000 (2002); $7,553,750 (2001); $19,119,822 (2000). Note: In 2001 and 2002, contributions were received from Bennett Dorrance.

Typical Recipients

Arts & Humanities: Arts Associations & Councils, Arts Centers, Arts Funds, Ballet, Community Arts, Libraries, Museums/Galleries, Music, Performing Arts, Public Broadcasting, Theater
Civic & Public Affairs: Botanical Gardens/Parks, Community Foundations, Housing, Municipalities/Towns, Public Policy, Urban & Community Affairs, Women's Affairs, Zoos/Aquariums
Education: Afterschool/Enrichment Programs, Business Education, Colleges & Universities, Education Funds, Preschool Education, Private Education (Precollege), Secondary Education (Private), Special Education, Student Aid
Environment: Resource Conservation
Health: AIDS/HIV, Arthritis, Cancer, Children's Health/Hospitals, Diabetes, Health-General, Health Funds, Health Organizations, Heart, Hospices, Hospitals, Kidney, Medical Research, Nursing Services, Public Health
Religion: Religion-General, Religious Organizations, Religious Welfare
Science: Science Museums, Scientific Centers & Institutes
Social Services: Animal Protection, Big Brothers/Big Sisters, Child Welfare, Community Centers, Domestic Violence, Family Planning, Family Services, People with Disabilities, Sexual Abuse, Shelters/Homelessness, Substance Abuse, United Funds/United Ways, Volunteer Services, Youth Organizations

Application Procedures

Initial Contact: Application should be in writing by qualified organization under Sec. 501(C)(3).
Application Requirements: Include a statement of request and purpose for the grant.
Deadlines: None.

Foundation Officials

Bennett Dorrance, Jr.: vice president, director
Bennett Dorrance: president, director B 1945. ED University of Arizona. ADD CORP EMPL trustee: DMB Ltd.; ltd. partner: DMB Property Ventures LP. CORP AFFIL director: The Larson Co. NONPR AFFIL committee member: Big Brothers Big Sisters; director: Desert Botanical Garden; director: Arizona Community Foundation; director: American Graduate School International Management.
Jacquelynn W. Dorrance: secretary, treasurer, director

Grants Analysis

Disclosure Period: calendar year ending 2002
Total Grants: $3,175,971*
Number of Grants: 32
Average Grant: $12,808*
Highest Grant: $1,600,000
Lowest Grant: $200
Typical Range: $5,000 to $25,000
*Note: Giving excludes scholarships. Average grant figure excludes four highest grants ($2,817,359).

Recent Grants

Note: Grants derived from 2002 Form 990.
General

1,600,000	New Moon Foundation, Kapaau, HI -- towards capital restoration and rehabilitation of historic site for a new use as a retreat center
608,965	Bourgade Catholic High School, Phoenix, AZ -- for providing quality education to students at an affordable price and capital development study fee
592,359	Arizona Community Foundation, Phoenix, AZ -- towards scholarship programs charitable causes community needs in Arizona and support of the Leave A Legacy program
425,000	Phoenix Country Day School, Phoenix, AZ -- towards the 40th anniversary capital campaign and project excellence
200,000	Mayo Foundation, Scottsdale, AZ -- towards supporting the cellular immunology laboratory at Mayo clinic Scottsdale
50,000	Florence Crittenton Services of Arizona, Phoenix, AZ -- towards the building new beginnings campaign
50,000	Fresh Start Women's Foundation, Phoenix, AZ -- towards funding of the Fresh Start Women's resource center
50,000	Hospice of the Valley, Phoenix, AZ -- towards capital campaign for a new hospice home
50,000	Scottsdale Healthcare Foundation, Scottsdale, AZ -- towards the Virginia G Piper cancer center
40,000	Desert Botanical Gardens, Phoenix, AZ -- towards the capital development campaign

M. S. DOSS FOUNDATION, INC.

Giving Contact

Joe K. McGill, President
PO Box 1677
Seminole, TX 79360-1677
Phone: (432)758-2770
Fax: (432)758-9591

Description

Founded: 1984
EIN: 751945227
Organization Type: General Purpose Foundation
Giving Locations: NM: eastern New Mexico; TX: western Texas
Grant Types: Capital, General Support, Scholarship.

Donor Information

Founder: Established by the late M. S. Doss and the late Meek Lane Doss.

Financial Summary

Total Giving: $2,534,659 (2003); $1,375,243 (2002 approx); $2,388,043 (2001)
Giving Analysis: Giving for 2003 includes: foundation scholarships ($563,516); 2001: foundation scholarships ($3,437)
Assets: $56,676,222 (2003); $53,439,176 (2001)
Gifts Received: $8,100 (1993)

Typical Recipients

Arts & Humanities: Historic Preservation, Libraries, Museums/Galleries, Music, Theater
Civic & Public Affairs: Botanical Gardens/Parks, Community Foundations, Economic Development, Civic & Public Affairs-General, Housing, Inner-City Development, Municipalities/Towns, Nonprofit Management, Parades/Festivals, Philanthropic Organizations, Professional & Trade Associations, Rural Affairs, Urban & Community Affairs
Education: Afterschool/Enrichment Programs, Agricultural Education, Business Education, Colleges & Universities, Engineering/Technological Education, Education-General, Literacy, Medical Education, Private Education (Precollege), Public Education (Precollege), Student Aid
Health: Children's Health/Hospitals, Clinics/Medical Centers, Diabetes, Health Funds, Hospices, Hospitals, Medical Rehabilitation, Single-Disease Health Associations
Religion: Churches, Dioceses, Religion-General, Religious Organizations, Religious Welfare
Science: Scientific Centers & Institutes
Social Services: Animal Protection, At-Risk Youth, Big Brothers/Big Sisters, Camps, Child Abuse, Child Welfare, Community Centers, Community Service Organizations, Counseling, Day Care, Delinquency & Criminal Rehabilitation, Domestic Violence, Family Services, Food/Clothing Distribution, Homes, People with Disabilities, Recreation & Athletics, Scouts, Senior Services, Shelters/Homelessness, Social Services-General, Special Olympics, Substance Abuse, Volunteer Services, YMCA/YWCA/YMHA/YWHA, Youth Organizations

Application Procedures

Initial Contact: The foundation reports that organizations submitting a proposal for the first time should send a brief letter of inquiry. Organizations applying for grants for a second time should send a grant application packet.
Deadlines: None.

Restrictions

Applications for youth organizations are restricted to West Texas and East New Mexico. Scholarship applications are restricted to Gaines County youth homes to which the foundation has made grants.

Additional Information

The foundation also funds scholarships for certain needy students, and supports the Community Chapel, the Doss Museum, and the Scout Center, all in Seminole, TX. The foundation prefers to support charitable youth organizations.

Foundation Officials

Joe K. McGill: president, chairman, trustee
Rebecca S. Narvarte: trustee emeritus
Julia Narvarte Romanow: assistant treasurer, trustee
Stuart Robertson: treasurer, trustee
Richard Spraberry: vice president, trustee

Billie Thompson: secretary, trustee PRIM CORP EMPL vice president: First National Bank Temple.

Grants Analysis

Disclosure Period: calendar year ending 2003
Total Grants: $1,971,143*
Number of Grants: 31
Average Grant: $33,931*
Highest Grant: $325,085
Lowest Grant: $1,750
Typical Range: $10,000 to $50,000
*Note: Giving excludes scholarships. Average grant figure excludes four highest grants ($1,055,010).

Recent Grants

Note: Grants derived from 2003 Form 990.
General

325,085	Seminole Hospital District, Seminole, TX -- towards building construction photographs
300,000	Yoakum County, Plains, TX -- towards expansion renovations and equipment
226,330	UMC Foundation, Lubbock, TX -- towards equipment programs and campership fees
203,625	Ector County Hospital District, Odessa, TX -- towards equipment software and maintenance
100,000	Meals on Wheels Plus Inc., Abilene, TX -- towards equipment
100,000	Tarleton State University, Stephenville, TX -- towards scholarship endowment
100,000	Tarrant County College Foundation, Ft. Worth, TX -- towards scholarship endowment
90,000	Meals on Wheels Inc. of Tarrant County, Ft. Worth, TX -- towards debt retirement
90,000	New Mexico Junior College Foundation, Hobbs, NM -- towards scholarship endowment
90,000	Weatherford College Development Foundation Inc., Weatherford, TX -- towards scholarship endowment

ALFRED AND MARY DOUTY FOUNDATION

Giving Contact

Judith L. Bardes, Executive Director & Trustee
PO Box 540
Plymouth Meeting, PA 19462
Phone: (610)828-8145
Fax: (610)834-8175

Description

Founded: 1968
EIN: 236463709
Organization Type: Private Foundation
Giving Locations: PA: Philadelphia including metropolitan area in Philadelphia and Montgomery counties
Grant Types: General Support, Project, Seed Money.

Donor Information

Founder: the late Alfred Douty, the late Mary M. Douty

Financial Summary

Total Giving: $280,420 (2003); $292,950 (2001)
Assets: $6,122,014 (2003); $6,585,650 (2001)
Gifts Received: $180,158 (1995). Note: In 1995, contributions were received from Alfred and Mary Douty Unitrust.

Typical Recipients

Arts & Humanities: Community Arts, Arts & Humanities-General, Libraries, Performing Arts

Civic & Public Affairs: Asian American Affairs, Botanical Gardens/Parks, Community Foundations, Economic Development, Employment/Job Training, Civic & Public Affairs-General, Hispanic Affairs, Housing, Law & Justice, Philanthropic Organizations, Safety, Urban & Community Affairs, Women's Affairs
Education: Afterschool/Enrichment Programs, Arts/Humanities Education, Colleges & Universities, Community & Junior Colleges, Education Funds, Education Reform, Elementary Education (Public), Education-General, Literacy, Minority Education, Preschool Education, Private Education (Precollege), Public Education (Precollege), School Volunteerism, Science/Mathematics Education
Health: Adolescent Health Issues, Children's Health/Hospitals, Prenatal Health Issues, Public Health
Religion: Ministries
Social Services: At-Risk Youth, Camps, Child Welfare, Community Centers, Community Service Organizations, Crime Prevention, Delinquency & Criminal Rehabilitation, Domestic Violence, Family Planning, Family Services, Homes, Social Services-General, YMCA/YWCA/YMHA/YWHA, Youth Organizations

Application Procedures

Initial Contact: Request application guidelines in a brief letter of inquiry, then send full proposal.
Application Requirements: Include name and a description of organization; purpose of funds sought; special nature of the project; leadership involved in the project; evidence that staff involved in the project are able to work with and understand the needs of the population to be served; amount requested and total funds needed; other funds available or anticipated; recently audited financial statement including most recent audited annual report, annual budget, and balance sheet; information on the organization's leadership, including board of directors/trustees; and proof of tax-exempt status.
Deadlines: February 15, April 15, and October 15.
Evaluative Criteria: The foundation favors educational projects and projects that promote positive social change and benefit disadvantaged people.

Restrictions

Foundation does not support individuals, nor religious or political organizations. The following are low funding priorities for the foundation: capital expenditures; endowments; or agency promotion such as marketing, development, publication of annual reports, or fundraising events.

Additional Information

Publications: Annual Report (including Application Guidelines)
Trust(s): PNC Bank NA

Foundation Officials

Richard G. Alexander: trustee
Judith L. Bardes: executive director, trustee
Lynette E. Campbell: trustee
Norma Elias: trustee
Thomas B. Harvey, Esq.: trustee
Nancy J. Kirby: trustee
Carrolle F. Perry Devonish: trustee

Grants Analysis

Disclosure Period: calendar year ending 2003
Total Grants: $280,420
Number of Grants: 101
Average Grant: $2,776
Highest Grant: $10,000
Lowest Grant: $620
Typical Range: $1,000 to $5,000

Recent Grants

Note: Grants derived from 2001 Form 990.
Library-Related

5,000	Free Library of Philadelphia, Philadelphia, PA -- for cultural and educational programming

General

10,000	Children's Hospital of Philadelphia, Philadelphia, PA -- for Bridging the Gaps Consortium
10,000	Delaware Valley Habitat for Humanity, Philadelphia, PA
6,000	Greater Philadelphia Federation of Settlements, Philadelphia, PA -- for 2001 Summer Career Exploration Program
6,000	Korean Community Development Services Center, Philadelphia, PA -- for 2001 Summer Career Exploration Program
6,000	Respond, Camden, NJ -- for 2001 Summer Career Exploration Program
5,000	Asian Arts Initiative, Philadelphia, PA -- for Youth Arts Workshop
5,000	Assets Montco, Norristown, PA
5,000	CHOICE, Philadelphia, PA -- for Teen Pregnancy Prevention Program
5,000	Community Learning Center, Philadelphia, PA
5,000	Family Care Solutions, Inc., Philadelphia, PA

DOVER FOUNDATION

Giving Contact

Hoyt Q. Bailey, President
PO Box 208
Shelby, NC 28151
Phone: (704)487-8890
Fax: (704)482-6818
E-mail: doverfnd@shelby.net

Description

Founded: 1944
EIN: 560769897
Organization Type: General Purpose Foundation
Giving Locations: NC
Grant Types: Challenge, Endowment, General Support, Operating Expenses, Scholarship.

Donor Information

Founder: The Dover foundation was founded in 1944 by John Randolph Dover Jr. and Charles Irvin Dover for the purpose of assisting religious, charitable, scientific, literary, and educational organizations.

Financial Summary

Total Giving: $1,500,000 (fiscal year ending August 31, 2002); $1,317,675 (fiscal 2001)
Giving Analysis: Giving for fiscal 2001 includes: foundation grants to United Way ($5,000); foundation scholarships ($60,000)
Assets: $23,000,000 (fiscal 2002 approx); $25,823,307 (fiscal 2001)
Gifts Received: In 1991, contributions were received from the estate of Charles I. Dover.

Typical Recipients

Arts & Humanities: Arts Associations & Councils, Arts Funds, Arts Institutes, Dance, Libraries, Museums/Galleries, Theater
Civic & Public Affairs: Botanical Gardens/Parks, Clubs, Community Foundations, Employment/Job Training, Civic & Public Affairs-General, Housing, Law & Justice, Municipalities/Towns, Safety, Urban & Community Affairs
Education: Afterschool/Enrichment Programs, Agricultural Education, Arts/Humanities Education, Colleges & Universities, Community & Junior Colleges, Education-General, Medical Education, Preschool Education, Private Education (Precollege), Public Education (Precollege), Science/Mathematics Education, Secondary Education (Public), Student Aid
Environment: Resource Conservation
Health: Cancer, Clinics/Medical Centers, Emergency/Ambulance Services, Geriatric Health, Health

Funds, Health Organizations, Heart, Hospices, Hospitals, Kidney, Medical Research, Mental Health, Preventive Medicine/Wellness Organizations, Public Health, Research/Studies Institutes, Respiratory
Religion: Churches, Ministries, Religious Organizations, Religious Welfare
Science: Science Museums
Social Services: Animal Protection, At-Risk Youth, Child Abuse, Child Welfare, Community Centers, Community Service Organizations, Crime Prevention, Domestic Violence, Emergency Relief, Family Planning, Family Services, Homes, Recreation & Athletics, Scouts, Senior Services, Shelters/Homelessness, United Funds/United Ways, YMCA/YWCA/YMHA/YWHA, Youth Organizations

Application Procedures

Initial Contact: A formal grant request may be submitted to the foundation by letter.
Application Requirements: The applicant's proposal letter must include the following information: the full legal name of the organization; a brief description of the organization, its purpose, and program; the specific amount of money requested; a brief description of the purpose for which the grant would be used; a definite plan for the successful completion of the project; the signature of the principal officer of the governing board; and the signature of the organization's chief administrative officer. Detailed supporting information about the program or project may be attached to the grant request. The applicant must also attach a copy of the organization's most recent tax exemption letter from the IRS and a list of the organization's board of directors. One copy of the proposal is sufficient.
Deadlines: Deadlines for grant requests to be considered at the next meeting are: December 1, for the January meeting; March 1, for the April meeting; June 1, for the July meeting; and September 1, for the October meeting.
Review Process: The foundation board of directors meets four times a year to consider grant awards. These meetings are in January, April, July, and October.

Restrictions

The foundation does not ordinarily make grants to political entities or for their activities, to individuals or their projects, advertising, newsletters, magazines, books, trips, tours, or to organizations whose principal activities take place outside the United States.

Additional Information
Publications: Application Form; Guidelines

Foundation Officials
Hoyt Q. Bailey: president
W. W. Gainey, Jr.: treasurer
Harvey B. Hamrick: secretary
Kathleen D. Hamrick: vice president

Grants Analysis
Disclosure Period: fiscal year ending August 31, 2001
Total Grants: $1,252,675*
Number of Grants: 156
Average Grant: $6,107*
Highest Grant: $200,000
Lowest Grant: $100
Typical Range: $1,000 to $10,000
*****Note:** Giving excludes scholarships and United Way. Average grant figure excludes highest grant.

Recent Grants
Note: Grants derived from 2002 Form 990.
General
105,500	American Red Cross, Shelby, NC
100,000	Gardner Webb University, Boiling Springs, NC
100,000	Life Enrichment Center of Cleveland County, Shelby, NC
100,000	YMCA, Charlotte, NC
75,000	Cleveland County Council on Aging, Shelby, NC
60,000	Dover Scholarships
50,000	Heineman Medical Research Center, Charlotte, NC
45,000	Kings Mountain Baptist Association, Shelby, NC
30,500	North Carolina State University, Raleigh, NC
30,000	Abuse Prevention Council

DOW CORNING CORP.

Company Headquarters
PO Box 994
Midland, MI 48686-0994
Phone: (517)496-4400
Web: http://www.dowcorning.com

Company Description
Employees: 6,000
SIC(s): 2821 Plastics Materials & Resins, 2869 Industrial Organic Chemicals Nec.
Parent Company: Dow Chemical Co., 2030 Dow Center, Midland, MI, United States

Operating Locations
Dow Corning Corp. (CA--Irvine; DC--Washington; GA--Roswell; IA--Davenport; KY--Carrollton, Elizabethtown; MI--Freeland, Hemlock; NJ--Budd Lake; NC--Greensboro; SC--Fort Mill; WA--Silverdale)

Dow Corning Foundation

Giving Contact
Anne M. DeBoer, Executive Director
CO2210
Midland, MI 48686-0994
Phone: (989)496-6290
Fax: (989)496-4393
E-mail: a.m.deboer@dowcorning.com
Web: http://www.dowcorning.com/content/about/aboutcomm/default.asp

Alternate Contact
2200 W. Salzburg Road
PO Box 994
Midland, MI 48686-0994

Description
EIN: 382376485
Organization Type: Corporate Foundation
Giving Locations: headquarters and operating communities.
Grant Types: Capital, Fellowship, General Support, Matching, Multiyear/Continuing Support, Professorship, Project.

Financial Summary
Total Giving: $1,495,496 (2003); $1,618,121 (2002); $970,900 (2001). Note: Contributions through foundation.
Assets: $15,161,419 (2003); $13,537,200 (2002); $13,578,940 (2001)
Gifts Received: $3,000,000 (2002); $1,262 (1994); $350 (1993). Note: Contributions were received from Dow Corning Corp.

Typical Recipients
Arts & Humanities: Arts Associations & Councils, Arts Centers, Arts Festivals, Arts Institutes, Community Arts, Dance, Arts & Humanities-General, Historic Preservation, Libraries, Museums/Galleries, Music, Performing Arts, Public Broadcasting, Theater, Visual Arts

Civic & Public Affairs: Chambers of Commerce, Clubs, Community Foundations, Economic Development, Employment/Job Training, Civic & Public Affairs-General, Municipalities/Towns, Native American Affairs, Nonprofit Management, Parades/Festivals, Philanthropic Organizations, Professional & Trade Associations, Safety, Urban & Community Affairs, Women's Affairs, Zoos/Aquariums
Education: Afterschool/Enrichment Programs, Arts/Humanities Education, Business-School Partnerships, Colleges & Universities, Community & Junior Colleges, Economic Education, Education Funds, Engineering/Technological Education, Faculty Development, Education-General, International Exchange, International Studies, Minority Education, Public Education (Precollege), Science/Mathematics Education, Student Aid, Vocational & Technical Education
Environment: Environment-General
Health: Medical Research, Public Health
Religion: Religious Welfare
Science: Science Exhibits & Fairs, Scientific Centers & Institutes
Social Services: Camps, Child Abuse, Community Centers, Community Service Organizations, Family Services, Recreation & Athletics, Scouts, Senior Services, Substance Abuse, United Funds/United Ways, Volunteer Services, YMCA/YWCA/YMHA/YWHA, Youth Organizations

Application Procedures
Initial Contact: Contributions can be made by individual Dow Corning sites, through the US Corporate Contributions Committee, or by the Dow Corning Foundation. Individual sites make small contributions that benefit local communities; US Corporate Contributions funds projects that drive change in operating communities, and grants range from $2,000 to $25,000; the Foundation focuses on education and environmental projects, and grants range from $10,000 to $100,000. Contact appropriate giving program via telephone or letter for detailed application guidelines.
Review Process: Foundation executive director reviews applications and makes a recommendation to the foundation board, which meets quarterly.
Evaluative Criteria: Foundation-supported applicants must meet the following criteria: address a clearly defined need, and describe organization's ability and qualifications to meet the need; outline expected improvements, results, beneficiaries, and how they will be impacted by the program; include plan to secure ongoing funding; contain measurable objectives and plan for reporting progress.
Decision Notification: For foundation grants, decisions are communicated within three weeks following a board meeting.
Notes: Foundation requires a final report from grantees.

Restrictions
Does not support individuals; political or veterans organizations; religious organizations for sectarian purposes; intercollegiate athletics; health-related research or services; public advertisements; conferences, travel costs, dinners or fund-raising events; or ongoing operational support. Foundation does not fund scholarships or provide on-going support.

Additional Information
Contributions of Dow Corning products, material, or equipment are not provided; promotional items and samples are distributed when appropriate.
Dow Corning also sponsors a speakers' bureau.
Publications: Guidelines

Corporate Officials
Gary E. Anderson: chairman, president, chief executive officero PRIM CORP EMPL chairman, president, chief executive officer: Dow Corning Corp.
Gifford E. Brown: global vice president, chief finan-

cial officer PRIM CORP EMPL global vice president, chief financial officer: Dow Corning Corp.

Foundation Officials

Mohamed Ahmed: trustee
Anne M. DeBoer: executive director
Marie N. Eckstein: vice president, trustee B New York, NY 1917. ED Pace University BA. PRIM CORP EMPL secretary, treasurer: Fred Heinzelman & Sons, Inc.
Scott Fuson: trustee
Thomas H. Lane: trustee
Feifei Lin: trustee
Paul A. Marcela: secretary, trustee
Jere D. Marciniak: president, trustee
Brad Sauve: treasurer, trustee
James White: trustee

Grants Analysis

Disclosure Period: calendar year ending 2003
Total Grants: $785,263*
Number of Grants: 31
Average Grant: $20,181*
Highest Grant: $100,000
Lowest Grant: $3,000
Typical Range: $10,000 to $40,000
*Note: Giving excludes matching gifts; fellowship; United Way. Average grant figure excludes two highest grants ($200,000).

Recent Grants

Note: Grants derived from 2003 Form 990.
General

233,300	United Way of Midland County, Midland, MI
100,000	Delta College, University Center, MI -- for purchase of digital broadcasting tower and equipment
75,000	Purdue University School of Chemical Engineering, West Lafayette, IN
58,024	United Way of Central Kentucky, Elizabethtown, KY
50,000	North Midland Family Center, Midland, MI -- for construction of new building
50,000	South Dakota School of Mines and Technology, Rapid City, SD
34,000	Connect Michigan Alliance, Lansing, MI -- for promotion of volunteerism
33,000	Midland County Council on Aging, Midland, MI
30,000	Arts Midland of Midland Center for the Arts, Midland, MI
30,000	Saginaw County Vision 2020, Saginaw, MI -- for community programs

HERBERT H. AND GRACE A. DOW FOUNDATION

Giving Contact

Margaret Ann Riecker, President
1018 West Main Street
Midland, MI 48640-4292
Phone: (989)631-3699
Fax: (989)631-0675
E-mail: info@hhdowfoundation.org
Web: http://www.hhdowfdn.org/

Description

Founded: 1936
EIN: 381437485
Organization Type: Family Foundation
Giving Locations: MI: statewide, Midland
Grant Types: Capital, Endowment, General Support, Matching, Multiyear/Continuing Support, Operating Expenses, Project, Seed Money.

Donor Information

Founder: The foundation was established by Mrs. Grace A. Dow in 1936 in memory of her husband, Dr. Herbert H. Dow, founder of the Dow Chemical Company. Dr. Dow maintained two strong interests during his lifetime: horticulture and an obligation to the workers and families at Dow Chemical Company "to share in the growing physical and cultural benefits which an industrially healthy community could provide." Mrs. Dow was a school teacher in Midland, and avidly studied the town's history. The foundation's trustees hope to perpetuate and expand its donors' interests in these areas.

Financial Summary

Total Giving: $19,809,887 (2003); $20,761,460 (2002); $23,722,000 (2001)
Giving Analysis: Giving for 2003 includes: foundation grants to United Way ($190,000); 2001: foundation grants to United Way ($140,000); foundation grants to United Way ($150,000)
Assets: $473,184,000 (2003); $387,861,935 (2002); $446,515,000 (2001)
Gifts Received: $1,889 (2000); $1,855,995 (1998); $56,000 (1997). Note: In 1998, contributions were received from Dorothy D. Arbury. In 1996, donations were received from the Dow Chemical Company, Dept. of Agriculture, Awards Management Division, and other undisclosed sources.

Typical Recipients

Arts & Humanities: Arts Centers, Arts Institutes, Historic Preservation, History & Archaeology, Libraries, Museums/Galleries, Opera, Public Broadcasting, Theater
Civic & Public Affairs: Botanical Gardens/Parks, Business/Free Enterprise, Chambers of Commerce, Community Foundations, Economic Development, Economic Policy, Employment/Job Training, Civic & Public Affairs-General, Inner-City Development, Municipalities/Towns, Native American Affairs, Nonprofit Management, Parades/Festivals, Philanthropic Organizations, Professional & Trade Associations, Public Policy, Safety, Urban & Community Affairs, Zoos/Aquariums
Education: Agricultural Education, Colleges & Universities, Continuing Education, Education Associations, Education Funds, Elementary Education (Public), Faculty Development, Education-General, Journalism/Media Education, Leadership Training, Preschool Education, Private Education (Precollege), Public Education (Precollege), Science/Mathematics Education, Secondary Education (Public), Student Aid
Environment: Environment-General, Protection, Resource Conservation, Watershed, Wildlife Protection
Health: Children's Health/Hospitals, Clinics/Medical Centers, Emergency/Ambulance Services, Geriatric Health, Health Policy/Cost Containment, Hospitals, Medical Rehabilitation, Public Health
Religion: Churches, Ministries, Religious Organizations, Religious Welfare, Synagogues/Temples
Science: Science-General, Science Museums, Scientific Centers & Institutes
Social Services: At-Risk Youth, Community Centers, Community Service Organizations, Crime Prevention, Family Services, Homes, People with Disabilities, Recreation & Athletics, Scouts, Senior Services, Social Services-General, Special Olympics, Substance Abuse, United Funds/United Ways, Youth Organizations

Application Procedures

Initial Contact: The foundation has no formal application form. Applicants should submit a written proposal.
Application Requirements: Proposals should include a letter setting forth the nature and potential results of the program for which funding is sought; total project cost including any endowment for operations; amount requested, and how and over what period of

time the grant may be disbursed; proof of tax-exempt status; a detailed annual budget and audited financial statement for the organization; and the names of the organization's management and trustees/directors.
Deadlines: None.
Review Process: After initial evaluation, proposals are referred to the appropriate program committee for full consideration. Additional information, site visits, or meetings in Midland may be requested. The board meets periodically during the year to make final grant decisions. Grants and installments on grants are usually disbursed late in December.
Evaluative Criteria: The trustees have a preference for funding opportunities where a grant of seed money or a matching grant will stimulate broad public participation in an artistic, recreational or cultural project so that the project can become self-sustaining. Projects that benefit youngsters or senior citizens are of special interest. The foundation also may be interested in a program that needs launching or requires changes. Requests for general support for ongoing programs are unlikely to be funded.

Restrictions

The foundation does not fund individuals, organizations outside of Michigan, or those which are not tax-exempt; political or lobbying groups; organizations that discriminate by race, sex, creed, age, or national origins; and religious organizations for sectarian purposes (except churches in the Midland community).

Additional Information

Publications: Annual Report

Foundation Officials

Julie Carol Arbury: trustee, donor great granddaughter
Herbert Dow Doan: chairman, trustee B Midland, MI 1922. ED Cornell University BS (1949). PRIM CORP EMPL chairman: Doan Resources Group. CORP AFFIL board of directors: Dendritech Inc.; director: Neogen Corp. NONPR AFFIL co-chairman: Michigan Venture Capital Task Force; member: Sigma Xi; member: Commission Physical Sciences Math Applications; board of directors: Michigan Molecular Institute; member: American Chemical Society; member: American Institute Chemical Engineers.
Michael Lloyd Dow: vice president, treasurer, trustee B Saginaw, MI 1935. ED Williams College (1953-1956); Michigan State University BS (1961). PRIM CORP EMPL chairman: Michael L. Dow, Associates. CORP AFFIL director: Chemical Finance Corp. NONPR AFFIL trustee: Little Traverse Conservancy.
Diane D. Hullet: trustee
Andrew N. Liveris: trustee ED University of Queensland BAE. CORP AFFIL board of directors: Dow Corning Corp.; advisory board of directors: Comerica Bank; president, chief executive officer, director: Dow Chemical Co. NONPR AFFIL member: Institute of Chemical Engineers.
Bonnie B. Matheson: trustee ED George Mason University BA.
Terence F. Moore: trustee ED Central Michigan University MBA; Central Michigan University BS; Washington University MS. CORP AFFIL board of directors: Chemical Financial Corp.; president, chief executive officer: MidMichigan Health. NONPR AFFIL board of directors: Michigan Molecular Institute; trustee: Northwood University.
Margaret E. Thompson: trustee
Ruth B. Wheeler: trustee
Helen Dow Whiting: trustee NONPR AFFIL trustee: Macauley and Helen Dow Whiting Foundation.
Macauley Whiting, Jr.: secretary, trustee ED Princeton University BSE. CORP AFFIL president, co-founder: Decker Energy International Inc. NONPR AFFIL trustee: Macauley and Helen Dow Whiting Foundation.

Grants Analysis

Disclosure Period: calendar year ending 2003
Total Grants: $19,619,887*

Number of Grants: 116
Average Grant: $131,449*
Highest Grant: $1,105,000
Lowest Grant: $985
Typical Range: $50,000 to $200,000
***Note:** Giving excludes United Way. Average grant figure excludes five highest grants ($5,029,000).

Recent Grants

Note: Grants derived from 2002 Form 990.
Library-Related

166,667	Bay County Library, MI -- towards operating expenses
100,000	Coleman Area Library, Coleman, MI -- towards operating expenses

General

1,007,005	Central Michigan University, Mt. Pleasant, MI -- towards the health professions building
1,000,000	Interlochen Center for the Arts, Interlochen, MI -- towards operating expenses
1,000,000	Kalamazoo College, Kalamazoo, MI -- towards operating expenses
1,000,000	Midland County Council on Aging, Midland, MI -- towards operating expenses
1,000,000	Midland County Historical Society, Midland, MI -- towards the museum
999,727	Hope College, Holland, MI -- towards operating expenses
999,028	Albion College, Albion, MI -- towards operating expenses
500,000	Alma College, Alma, MI -- towards operating expenses
500,000	Education Training Connection, Midland, MI -- towards operating expenses
500,000	Ferris State University, Big Rapids, MI -- towards operating expenses

DOW JONES & COMPANY INC.

Company Headquarters
New York, NY
Web: http://www.dowjones.com

Company Description
Ticker: DJ
Exchange: OTC
Employees: 8,300
SIC(s): 2711 Newspapers.

Operating Locations
Dow Jones & Co., Inc. (AZ--Phoenix; AR--Little Rock; CA--Fresno, Los Angeles, Palo Alto, San Diego; CO--Englewood; DC--Washington; FL--Coral Gables, Jacksonville, Tampa; GA--Atlanta; IL--Chicago, Highland, Lisle, Niles, Northbrook; IN--Indianapolis; IA--West Des Moines; MD--Baltimore, Silver Spring; MA--Boston; MI--Detroit; MO--St. Louis; NJ--Monmouth, Union; NY--Albany, Buffalo, Liverpool; NC--Charlotte; OH--Bowling Green; OK--Tulsa; PA--Philadelphia, West Middlesex; RI--East Providence; TX--Dallas, Houston, Irving, Lubbock; UT--Holladay; VA--Richmond; WA--Bellevue; WI--Milwaukee)
Note: Operates internationally.

Dow Jones Foundation

Giving Contact
Leonard E. Doherty, Administrative Officer
Dow Jones Foundation
PO Box 300
Princeton, NJ 08543
Phone: (609)520-5143
Fax: (609)520-5180

Description
EIN: 136070158
Organization Type: Corporate Foundation
Giving Locations: principally near operating locations and to national organizations.
Grant Types: General Support.

Financial Summary
Total Giving: $1,218,066 (2002); $1,519,446 (2001). Note: Contributes through corporate direct giving program and foundation.
Giving Analysis: Giving for 2002 includes: foundation scholarships ($274,032); 2001: foundation grants to United Way ($299,700); foundation scholarships ($317,346); foundation ($902,400)
Assets: $1,352,398 (2002); $314,100 (2001)
Gifts Received: $2,261,000 (2002); $1,500,000 (2001); $1,000,000 (1998). Note: In 1998, 2001, and 2002, contributions were received from Dow Jones and Co.

Typical Recipients
Arts & Humanities: Arts Associations & Councils, Arts Festivals, History & Archaeology, Libraries, Museums/Galleries, Music, Theater
Civic & Public Affairs: African American Affairs, Asian American Affairs, Botanical Gardens/Parks, Business/Free Enterprise, Civil Rights, Clubs, Economic Development, Economic Policy, First Amendment Issues, Gay/Lesbian Issues, Civic & Public Affairs-General, Hispanic Affairs, Housing, Native American Affairs, Professional & Trade Associations, Public Policy, Urban & Community Affairs, Women's Affairs
Education: Arts/Humanities Education, Business Education, Colleges & Universities, Education Associations, Education-General, International Exchange, International Studies, Journalism/Media Education, Minority Education, Private Education (Precollege), Special Education, Student Aid
Health: Clinics/Medical Centers, Hospitals
International: Human Rights, International Organizations, International Relations
Social Services: Child Welfare, Community Service Organizations, Family Services, People with Disabilities, Substance Abuse, United Funds/United Ways, Volunteer Services, Youth Organizations

Application Procedures
Initial Contact: Send brief letter or proposal.
Application Requirements: Include outline of proposed purpose of grant and proof of tax-exempt status.
Deadlines: None.
Decision Notification: Annual meeting in November.

Restrictions
Does not currently support medical and scientific research or cultural activities.

Additional Information
Foundation has policy of considering contributions to institutions and causes where there has been a history of active participation and support by company employees.
Foundation reports U.S. Trust Co. of New York as corporate trustee.
The Dow Jones Foundation routinely makes its largest grant to the Dow Jones Newspaper Fund, a program which supports journalism education for minority high school and college students. The fund also provides internships and fellowships. internships and fellowships. internships and fellowships. internships and fellowships.

Corporate Officials
Kenneth L. Burenga: president, chief operating officer, chief executive officer B Somerville, NJ 1944. ED Rider College BS (1970). PRIM CORP EMPL president, chief operating officer, chief executive officer: Dow Jones & Co., Inc. CORP AFFIL general manager: Wall Street Journal; director: Telerate Holdings Inc.; chief executive officer: Dow Jones Telerate Inc.; director: Ottaway Newspapers Inc. NONPR AFFIL chairman: Better Business Bureau New York Inc.
Peter Robert Kann: chairman, chief executive officer, director B New York, NY December 13, 1942. ED Harvard University BA (1964). PRIM CORP EMPL chairman, chief executive officer, director: Dow Jones & Co., Inc. ADD CORP EMPL publisher: Wall Street Journal. NONPR AFFIL trustee: Aspen Institute; trustee: Institute Advanced Study. CLUB AFFIL Spee Club.
James Haller Ottaway, Jr.: senior vice president, director B Binghamton, NY 1938. ED Yale University BA (1960). PRIM CORP EMPL senior vice president, director: Dow Jones & Co., Inc. CORP AFFIL chairman, director, chief executive officer: Ottaway Newspapers Inc.; chairman: Inquirer & Mirror Inc. NONPR AFFIL chairman: World Press Freedom Comm; trustee: World Wildlife Foundation USA; trustee: Storm King Art Center; member: Newspaper Association America; trustee: Phillip Exeter Academy; president: Magazine Group; member: American Society Newspaper Editors; director: Arden Hill Hospital Foundation; trustee: American School Classical Studies Athens; member: American Newspaper Publishers Association.

Grants Analysis
Disclosure Period: calendar year ending 2002
Total Grants: $769,084*
Number of Grants: 65
Average Grant: $11,832
Highest Grant: $25,000
Lowest Grant: $200
Typical Range: $1,000 to $20,000
***Note:** Giving excludes United Way and scholarships.

Recent Grants
Note: Grants derived from 2003 Form 990.
Library-Related

12,500	Friends of the Princeton Public Library Inc., Princeton, NJ
10,000	New York Public Library, New York, NY
10,000	South Brunswick Public Library Foundation Inc., Monmouth Junction, NJ

General

375,000	United Way of West Georgia Inc., La Grange, GA
274,032	Citizens Trust Company
40,400	Mile High United Way, Denver, CO
31,500	United Way of Mercer County, Sharon, PA
25,000	Children's Art Carnival, New York, NY
20,000	Learning Leaders Inc., New York, NY
17,100	Freedom House Inc., Washington, DC
14,800	United Way of Central Iowa, Des Moines, IA
14,800	United Way of Greater Toledo, Toledo, OH
12,500	Jersey City Medical Center, Jersey City, NJ

DOYLE FOUNDATION

Giving Contact
Frederick E. Fisher, Director
The Doyle Foundation
1901 Ulmerton Rd., Suite 750
Clearwater, FL 33762
Phone: (727)942-7003

Description
Founded: 1995
EIN: 593311469

Organization Type: Private Foundation
Grant Types: General Support.

Donor Information
Founder: Established in 1995 by Dan Doyle.

Financial Summary
Total Giving: $165,000 (2003); $106,500 (2001)
Assets: $3,326,890 (2003); $3,021,847 (2001)
Gifts Received: $1,105,390 (1996). Note: In 1996, contributions were received from Dan Doyle.

Typical Recipients
Arts & Humanities: Arts Centers, Arts Funds, Ballet, Libraries, Performing Arts
Civic & Public Affairs: Community Foundations, Civic & Public Affairs-General, Zoos/Aquariums
Education: Colleges & Universities, Economic Education, Private Education (Precollege), Public Education (Precollege)
Health: Clinics/Medical Centers, Health Funds, Public Health
Religion: Churches, Religious Organizations, Religious Welfare
Social Services: Child Abuse, Child Welfare, Community Service Organizations, Food/Clothing Distribution, People with Disabilities, Recreation & Athletics, Shelters/Homelessness, Social Services-General, Youth Organizations

Application Procedures
Initial Contact: Request application form.
Application Requirements: Return completed application form with proof of tax-exempt status, evidence of current accreditation (for educational institutions), recently audited financial statement, and a list of current board members.
Deadlines: Applications are accepted from October 1 to November 30.

Foundation Officials
Daniel M. Doyle, Jr.: director
Daniel M. Doyle: president, director
Rosaleen J. Doyle: vice president, director
Frederick E. Fisher: secretary, director

Grants Analysis
Disclosure Period: calendar year ending 2003
Total Grants: $165,000
Number of Grants: 13
Average Grant: $12,692
Highest Grant: $25,000
Lowest Grant: $5,000
Typical Range: $5,000 to $20,000

Recent Grants
Note: Grants derived from 2003 Form 990.

General

25,000	Community Foundation of Tampa Bay, Tampa, FL
25,000	Enterprise Village Inc., Largo, FL
20,000	Morton Plant Mease Foundation, Clearwater, FL
20,000	PAC Foundation, Clearwater, FL
20,000	Tampa Bay Performing Arts Center, Tampa, FL
10,000	Children's Home Society of Florida, St. Petersburg, FL
10,000	Clearwater Free Clinic, Clearwater, FL
10,000	Religious Community Services, Clearwater, FL
8,500	Clearwater for Youth Inc., Clearwater, FL
6,500	Homeless Emergency Project, Clearwater, FL

DREYFUS CORP.

Company Headquarters
200 Park Avenue, 7th Floor
New York, NY 10166-0039
Web: http://www.dreyfus.com

Company Description
Employees: 1,800
SIC(s): 6200 Security & Commodity Brokers.

Operating Locations
Dreyfus Corp. (NJ--East Orange)

Giving Contact
Patrice M. Kozolowski, Vice President, Corporate Communications
200 Park Ave., 55th Fl.
New York, NY 10166
Phone: (212)922-6000
Fax: (212)922-8620
E-mail: stile.j@dreyfus.com

Description
Organization Type: Corporate Giving Program
Giving Locations: principally near operating locations and to national organizations.
Grant Types: Employee Matching Gifts, General Support, Scholarship.

Financial Summary
Total Giving: Company does not disclose contributions figures.

Typical Recipients
Arts & Humanities: Arts Appreciation, History & Archaeology, Libraries, Museums/Galleries, Opera, Theater
Civic & Public Affairs: Public Policy, Women's Affairs
Education: Afterschool/Enrichment Programs, Business Education, Colleges & Universities, Economic Education, Education Funds, Journalism/Media Education, Literacy
Environment: Protection
Health: Adolescent Health Issues, Children's Health/Hospitals, Clinics/Medical Centers, Diabetes, Health Organizations, Hospitals, Medical Research, Multiple Sclerosis, Prenatal Health Issues, Research/Studies Institutes, Single-Disease Health Associations
International: International Affairs
Religion: Religious Welfare
Science: Science Museums
Social Services: At-Risk Youth, Community Centers, Recreation & Athletics, Volunteer Services, Youth Organizations

Application Procedures
Initial Contact: Send a brief letter of inquiry and a full proposal. Include a description of organization, amount requested, and purpose of funds sought.

Additional Information
Company reports 40% of contributions support education. Approximately 20% each support the arts and humanities, health and human services, and neighborhood/economic development.

Corporate Officials
Christopher M. Condron: president, chief executive officer PRIM CORP EMPL president, chief executive officer: Dreyfus Corp.
William Thomas Sandalls, Jr.: senior vice president, chief financial officer B Newport, RI 1944. ED Yale University (1966); Harvard University Graduate School of Business Administration (1972). PRIM CORP EMPL senior vice president, chief financial officer: Dreyfus Corp. CORP AFFIL chairman, director: Cirrus System; director: MasterCard International Inc. NONPR AFFIL trustee: Taxpayers Foundation; chair-

man finance committee: Town Weston MA; member: Tax Executives Institute; member: Financial Executives Institute; member: Massachusetts Society Certified Public Accountants; director-at-large: Bank Administration Institute; corporateorator: Boston Museum Science; member: American Institute of CPA's.
W. Keith Smith: chairman PRIM CORP EMPL chairman: Dreyfus Corp.

Recent Grants
Note: Grants derived from 1998 Form 990.
Library-Related
New York Public Library, New York, NY
General
American Ireland Fund, New York, NY
American Museum of Natural History, New York, NY
Columbia University Business School, New York, NY
Council on Economic Priorities, New York, NY
Cystic Fibrosis Foundation, New York, NY
Financial Women's Association, New York, NY
Franciscan Sisters of the Poor, New York, NY
March of Dimes, Long Island, NY
Reach Out and Read, New York, NY
Metropolitan Museum of Art, New York, NY

MAX AND VICTORIA DREYFUS FOUNDATION, INC.

Giving Contact
Lucy Gioia, Office Administrator
50 Main Street, Suite 1000
White Plains, NY 10606
Phone: (914)682-2008

Description
Founded: 1965
EIN: 131687573
Organization Type: General Purpose Foundation
Giving Locations: nationally.
Grant Types: General Support, Project, Research.

Donor Information
Founder: The foundation was established in New York in 1965 by the late Victoria Dreyfus. When Mrs. Dreyfus died in 1976, her assets were bequeathed to the foundation. Mrs. Dreyfus was the wife of the late Max Dreyfus, a leading figure in the music publishing business and one of the founding members of ASCAP.

Financial Summary
Total Giving: $3,020,400 (2003); $3,489,400 (2002)
Giving Analysis: Giving for 2003 includes: foundation scholarships ($30,000); 2002: foundation scholarships ($55,000)
Assets: $64,617,163 (2003); $55,039,895 (2002)

Typical Recipients
Arts & Humanities: Arts Appreciation, Arts Associations & Councils, Arts Centers, Arts Festivals, Arts Institutes, Arts Outreach, Ballet, Community Arts, Dance, Ethnic & Folk Arts, Arts & Humanities-General, Historic Preservation, Libraries, Literary Arts, Museums/Galleries, Music, Opera, Performing Arts, Public Broadcasting, Theater, Visual Arts
Civic & Public Affairs: Botanical Gardens/Parks, Community Foundations, Economic Development, Employment/Job Training, Hispanic Affairs, Housing, Law & Justice, Legal Aid, Municipalities/Towns, Native American Affairs, Nonprofit Management, Parades/Festivals, Philanthropic Organizations, Public Policy, Safety, Urban & Community Affairs, Zoos/Aquariums
Education: Afterschool/Enrichment Programs, Agri-

cultural Education, Arts/Humanities Education, Business Education, Colleges & Universities, Education Associations, Education Funds, Engineering/Technological Education, Environmental Education, Education-General, Leadership Training, Legal Education, Medical Education, Minority Education, Private Education (Precollege), Public Education (Precollege), Science/Mathematics Education, Secondary Education (Private), Secondary Education (Public), Special Education, Student Aid, Vocational & Technical Education

Environment: Environment-General, Resource Conservation, Wildlife Protection

Health: AIDS/HIV, Alzheimer's Disease, Cancer, Children's Health/Hospitals, Clinics/Medical Centers, Emergency/Ambulance Services, Eyes/Blindness, Health-General, Health Funds, Health Organizations, Heart, Home-Care Services, Hospices, Hospitals, Hospitals (University Affiliated), Medical Rehabilitation, Medical Research, Mental Health, Nutrition, Preventive Medicine/Wellness Organizations, Single-Disease Health Associations, Speech & Hearing

Religion: Churches, Dioceses, Religion-General, Jewish Causes, Religious Organizations, Religious Welfare

Science: Science Museums, Scientific Research

Social Services: Animal Protection, At-Risk Youth, Child Welfare, Community Centers, Community Service Organizations, Counseling, Crime Prevention, Day Care, Delinquency & Criminal Rehabilitation, Domestic Violence, Emergency Relief, Family Planning, Family Services, Food/Clothing Distribution, People with Disabilities, Recreation & Athletics, Refugee Assistance, Scouts, Senior Services, Sexual Abuse, Shelters/Homelessness, Social Services-General, Substance Abuse, United Funds/United Ways, Volunteer Services, YMCA/YWCA/YMHA/YWHA, Youth Organizations

Application Procedures

Initial Contact: Send a letter of request, not exceeding three pages.

Application Requirements: An outline of the project, a copy of an IRS tax-exempt determination letter, budget sheet for project/program and explanation of purpose of grants.

Deadlines: None.

Decision Notification: The board reviews applications every four months.

Restrictions

The foundation does not support individuals or foreign organizations.

Additional Information

Publications: Guidelines

Foundation Officials

Lucy Gioia: office administrator

Nancy E. Oddo: vice president, director

Norman S. Portenoy: vice president, director B 1919. PRIM CORP EMPL chairman: PSC Systems Inc. CORP AFFIL officer: EMP Industries Inc.; officer: RJ Simpson Ltd.; officer: Business Link Systems Inc.

Winifred Riggs Portenoy: president, director

Mary P. Surrey: secretary, treasurer, director

Sara R. Surrey: vice president, director

Grants Analysis

Disclosure Period: calendar year ending 2003
Total Grants: $2,990,400*
Number of Grants: 389
Average Grant: $7,687
Highest Grant: $50,000
Lowest Grant: $700
Typical Range: $1,000 to $10,000
*Note: Giving excludes scholarships.

Recent Grants

Note: Grants derived from 2003 Form 990.

General

55,000	Thirteen WNET New York/Educational Broadcasting Corporation, New York, NY -- funding for production of Broadway: The American Musical
50,000	New York Weill Cornell Medical Center, New York, NY -- toward fellowship training program
50,000	United States Merchant Marine Academy Foundation Inc., Kings Point, NY -- toward museum program/education curriculum
40,000	St. Andrew's Cripple Children's Clinic Inc., Nogales, AZ -- toward orthotics program and clinic needs
32,000	Studio Theatre Inc., Washington, DC -- funding for performance/education
30,000	Arizona Theatre Company, Tucson, AZ -- toward cultural education programs for youth
30,000	St. Paul the Apostle Church, Clemson, SC -- funding for building program
30,000	Sheltering Arms Children's Service, New York, NY -- toward kitchen renovations at Harlem Center
28,500	Washington Ballet, Washington, DC -- funding for performing arts
20,000	52nd Street Project, New York, NY -- funding for teen program

JEAN AND LOUIS DREYFUS FOUNDATION

Giving Contact

Edmee de Montmollin-Firth, Executive Director
420 Lexington Avenue, Suite 626
New York, NY 10170
Phone: (212)599-1931
Fax: (212)599-2956
E-mail: jldreyfusfdtn@hotmail.com
Web: http://fdncenter.org/grantmaker/dreyfus/

Description

Founded: 1978
EIN: 132947180
Organization Type: Family Foundation
Giving Locations: NY: New York
Grant Types: General Support, Matching.

Donor Information

Founder: Incorporated in 1979 by the late Louis Dreyfus, a music publisher, and his wife, Jean.

Financial Summary

Total Giving: $1,093,000 (2002); $1,352,500 (2001)
Assets: $18,158,693 (2002); $22,000,000 (2001 approx)

Typical Recipients

Arts & Humanities: Arts Associations & Councils, Arts Centers, Arts Festivals, Arts Funds, Arts Institutes, Arts Outreach, Ballet, Dance, Ethnic & Folk Arts, Historic Preservation, Libraries, Literary Arts, Museums/Galleries, Music, Opera, Performing Arts, Theater, Visual Arts

Civic & Public Affairs: Asian American Affairs, Botanical Gardens/Parks, Business/Free Enterprise, Community Foundations, Economic Development, Employment/Job Training, Ethnic Organizations, Gay/Lesbian Issues, Civic & Public Affairs-General, Hispanic Affairs, Housing, Law & Justice, Legal Aid, Municipalities/Towns, Parades/Festivals, Public Policy, Urban & Community Affairs, Women's Affairs

Education: Afterschool/Enrichment Programs, Arts/Humanities Education, Colleges & Universities, Education Reform, Elementary Education (Private), Education-General, Literacy, Medical Education, Minority

Education, Private Education (Precollege), Public Education (Precollege), Secondary Education (Private), Special Education, Student Aid

Environment: Air/Water Quality, Environment-General

Health: Adolescent Health Issues, AIDS/HIV, Alzheimer's Disease, Cancer, Children's Health/Hospitals, Clinics/Medical Centers, Geriatric Health, Health Policy/Cost Containment, Health Funds, Health Organizations, Home-Care Services, Hospitals, Long-Term Care, Medical Training, Mental Health, Nursing Services, Nutrition, Prenatal Health Issues, Public Health

International: Foreign Educational Institutions, Health Care/Hospitals, International Organizations

Religion: Churches, Religion-General, Jewish Causes, Religious Welfare

Social Services: At-Risk Youth, Child Welfare, Community Centers, Community Service Organizations, Crime Prevention, Day Care, Delinquency & Criminal Rehabilitation, Family Planning, Family Services, Food/Clothing Distribution, Scouts, Senior Services, Shelters/Homelessness, Social Services-General, Substance Abuse, Volunteer Services, YMCA/YWCA/YMHA/YWHA, Youth Organizations

Application Procedures

Initial Contact: Submit an initial inquiry consisting of a one- to two-page letter.

Application Requirements: Include a description of organization and an outline of the project.

Deadlines: Letters of inquiry are due February 1 and August 1 for spring and fall board meetings, respectively.

Review Process: All inquiries will be acknowledged in writing indicating whether or not an application is justified. If so, the foundation will provide an application form. result in a request for repayment to the foundation or discontinuance of payment by the foundation. result in a request for repayment to the foundation or discontinuance of payment by the foundation.

Restrictions

The Foundation has no direct charitable activities. Grants are not made to individuals. Grants are made only to tax-exempt organizations.

Foundation Officials

Edmee de Montmollin Firth: executive director
Katherine V. Firth: vice president
Nicholas L. D. Firth: president NONPR AFFIL director: American Society Composers Authors Publishers.
Thomas J. Hubbard: secretary NONPR AFFIL chairman, director: Metropolitan Opera Guild.

Grants Analysis

Disclosure Period: calendar year ending 2002
Total Grants: $1,093,000
Number of Grants: 67
Average Grant: $16,313
Highest Grant: $75,000
Lowest Grant: $5,000
Typical Range: $5,000 to $20,000

Recent Grants

Note: Grants derived from 2002 Form 990.

Library-Related

15,000	Queens Library Foundation, Jamaica, NY

General

75,000	New York City Opera, New York, NY
30,000	Columbia University-Taub Institute, New York, NY
25,000	Brady Center to Prevent Gun Violence, Washington, DC
25,000	Chamber Music Society of Lincoln Center, New York, NY
25,000	Institute for Democracy Studies, New York, NY
25,000	KIPP Academy, Bronx, NY
25,000	New York City Opera, New York, NY

25,000	St Luke's Roosevelt Hospital Center, New York, NY
25,000	Sunnyside Community Services, Sunnyside, NY
20,000	ASPIRA of New York, Inc., New York, NY

DRISCOLL FOUNDATION

Giving Contact
W. John Driscoll, President & Director
332 Minnesota St., Suite 2100
St. Paul, MN 55101-1308
Phone: (651)228-0935

Description
Founded: 1962
EIN: 416012065
Organization Type: Private Foundation
Giving Locations: CA: San Francisco; MN: Minneapolis, Saint Paul
Grant Types: Capital, General Support, Research.

Donor Information
Founder: members of the Driscoll family

Financial Summary
Total Giving: $730,000 (fiscal year ending February 28, 2001). Note: Fiscal 1997 Giving includes United Way ($20,000).
Assets: $14,482,018 (fiscal 2001)
Gifts Received: $421,260 (fiscal 2001); $214,713 (fiscal 2000); $235,988 (fiscal 1998). Note: In fiscal 2001, contributions were received from the Revocable Trust of W. John Driscoll ($410,550) and Berkshire Hathaway ($10,710). In fiscal 2000, contributions were received from the Revocable Trust of W. John Driscoll ($205,209) and Berkshire Hathaway ($9,504).

Typical Recipients
Arts & Humanities: Arts Centers, Arts Festivals, Arts Funds, Arts Institutes, Ballet, Community Arts, History & Archaeology, Libraries, Museums/Galleries, Music, Opera, Performing Arts, Public Broadcasting, Theater
Civic & Public Affairs: Botanical Gardens/Parks, Civic & Public Affairs-General, Public Policy, Women's Affairs
Education: Arts/Humanities Education, Colleges & Universities, International Studies, Literacy, Minority Education, Private Education (Precollege), Religious Education, Special Education
Environment: Environment-General, Resource Conservation, Wildlife Protection
Health: AIDS/HIV, Children's Health/Hospitals, Hospitals, Medical Research, Speech & Hearing
International: Foreign Educational Institutions, International Environmental Issues
Religion: Seminaries
Science: Science Museums, Scientific Centers & Institutes
Social Services: Child Welfare, Community Service Organizations, Emergency Relief, Family Services, Recreation & Athletics, Substance Abuse, United Funds/United Ways, Volunteer Services, Youth Organizations

Application Procedures
Initial Contact: Send cover letter and full proposal.
Application Requirements: Include a description of organization, amount requested, purpose of funds sought, recently audited financial statement, and proof of tax-exempt status.
Deadlines: None.

Restrictions
Does not support individuals or provide funds for conferences, travel, publications, or films.

Additional Information
Publications: Annual Report; Application Guidelines

Foundation Officials
Elizabeth S. Driscoll: director
Rudolph Weyerhaeuser Driscoll: vice president, director B Saint Paul, MN 1933. ED Yale University BA (1955).
Walter John Driscoll: president, director B Saint Paul, MN 1929. ED Yale University BS (1951). CORP AFFIL director: Northern Studies Power Co.; director: Weyerhaeuser Co.
Michael J. Giefer: treasurer
Joseph S. Micallef: secretary B 1933. PRIM CORP EMPL president, chief executive officer, treasurer, director: Fiduciary Counselling Inc. PRIM NONPR EMPL sec-treas: Rock Island Co. CORP AFFIL secretary, treasurer: Rock Island Co.

Grants Analysis
Disclosure Period: fiscal year ending February 28, 2001
Total Grants: $730,000
Number of Grants: 15
Average Grant: $21,167*
Highest Grant: $250,000
Lowest Grant: $1,000
Typical Range: $10,000 to $30,000
*Note: Average grant figure excludes three highest grant ($476,000).

Recent Grants
Note: Grants derived from fiscal 2002 Form 990.
General

250,000	American University in Cairo, New York, NY -- for landscaping fund
125,000	Santa Fe Opera, Santa Fe, NM -- opera underwriting
101,000	Minnesota Historical Society, St. Paul, MN -- for St. Anthony Fall Project and North Star Heritage Fund
101,000	Walker Art Center, Minneapolis, MN -- capital campaign and annual fund
51,000	Vassar College, Warwick, NY -- for reunion fund and annual fund
31,000	Yale University, New Haven, CT -- for Davenport College renovation
15,000	Minneapolis Institute of Arts, Minneapolis, MN -- endowment fund/annual fund
10,000	American Council for Capital Formation Center for Policy Research, Washington, DC -- for operating support
10,000	Marine Corps University Foundation, Quantico, VA -- for operating support
10,000	Minnesota Landscape Arboretum, Chanhassen, MN -- for Slade Perennial Gardens

JOSEPH DROWN FOUNDATION

Giving Contact
Wendy Wachtell, Vice President, Program Director
1999 Avenue of the Stars, Suite 2330
Los Angeles, CA 90067
Phone: (310)277-4488
Fax: (310)277-4573
E-mail: staff@jdrown.org
Web: http://www.jdrown.org

Description
Founded: 1953
EIN: 956093178
Organization Type: General Purpose Foundation
Giving Locations: CA
Grant Types: General Support, Matching, Operating Expenses, Project, Research, Scholarship.

Donor Information
Founder: The foundation was established in 1953 in California by Joseph W. Drown (d. 1982). Mr. Drown was a hotel builder and developer in California. His prize hotel, which he personally developed in 1945, was the Hotel Bel-Air in Los Angeles, CA. The foundation still has the original officers chosen by Mr. Drown.

Financial Summary
Total Giving: $4,500,402 (fiscal year ending March 31, 2003); $4,767,660 (fiscal 2002); $5,290,671 (fiscal 2001)
Giving Analysis: Giving for fiscal 2003 includes: foundation scholarships ($80,000)
Assets: $90,017,572 (fiscal 2003); $90,190,854 (fiscal 2002); $92,370,042 (fiscal 2001)

Typical Recipients
Arts & Humanities: Arts Centers, Film & Video, Arts & Humanities-General, Libraries, Museums/Galleries, Music, Public Broadcasting, Theater
Civic & Public Affairs: African American Affairs, Botanical Gardens/Parks, Business/Free Enterprise, Community Foundations, Economic Development, Civic & Public Affairs-General, Hispanic Affairs, Legal Aid, Native American Affairs, Nonprofit Management, Philanthropic Organizations, Public Policy, Urban & Community Affairs, Women's Affairs
Education: Afterschool/Enrichment Programs, Arts/Humanities Education, Business Education, Colleges & Universities, Education Funds, Education Reform, Elementary Education (Public), Engineering/Technological Education, Faculty Development, Education-General, Gifted & Talented Programs, Health & Physical Education, Leadership Training, Legal Education, Literacy, Medical Education, Minority Education, Preschool Education, Public Education (Precollege), Science/Mathematics Education, Student Aid, Vocational & Technical Education
Environment: Protection
Health: Adolescent Health Issues, AIDS/HIV, Alzheimer's Disease, Arthritis, Cancer, Children's Health/Hospitals, Clinics/Medical Centers, Diabetes, Emergency/Ambulance Services, Eyes/Blindness, Health-General, Geriatric Health, Health Funds, Health Organizations, Heart, Hospitals (University Affiliated), Long-Term Care, Medical Research, Mental Health, Outpatient Health Care, Preventive Medicine/Wellness Organizations, Research/Studies Institutes, Single-Disease Health Associations, Speech & Hearing
International: Foreign Educational Institutions, Health Care/Hospitals, International Relief Efforts, Missionary/Religious Activities
Religion: Churches, Jewish Causes
Science: Scientific Centers & Institutes, Scientific Research
Social Services: Animal Protection, At-Risk Youth, Child Welfare, Community Service Organizations, Crime Prevention, Day Care, Family Planning, Family Services, Food/Clothing Distribution, People with Disabilities, Senior Services, Social Services-General, Substance Abuse, United Funds/United Ways, YMCA/YWCA/YMHA/YWHA, Youth Organizations

Application Procedures
Initial Contact: Prospective applicants should send a proposal and description of their organization.
Application Requirements: Proposals should include: a letter with information about both the organization as a whole and the particular project; an IRS tax-exempt determination letter; the most recent dited financial statement; budget information of the most recent Form 990 filed with th a list of the organization's officers an additional materials, such as a press releases, may also be
Deadlines: Applications mus fore January 15, April 15, July

Review Process: The board meets in the second month following each deadline. All proposals must be received by 5 p.m. on the day of the deadline to be considered.
Notes: Proposals should be addressed to Norman C. Obrow, President of the foundation.

Restrictions

The foundation does not make grants to individuals, endowments, capital campaigns, or building funds. It does not underwrite annual meetings, conferences, or special events. Does not fund religious programs or purchase tickets to events. No unsolicited proposals for medical and scientific research are funded. Funding is limited to California organizations.

Additional Information

Publications: Guidelines

Foundation Officials

Philip S. Magaram: director B 1937. ED University of California, Los Angeles Law School. PRIM CORP EMPL president: Rose Valensi & Plc Magaram.
Elaine Mahoney: director
Thomas C. Marshall: director
Norman C. Obrow: chairman, president, director
Wendy Wachtell: vice president, director, program director B White Plains, NY 1961. ED Wellesley College BA (1983); University of Southern California MA (1987). NONPR AFFIL advisor: Psychological Trauma Center; director: Southern California Association Philanthropy; board directors: Los Angeles Urban Funders; oversight committee: Big Sisters Los Angeles Pathways Project; advisor: Center Talented Youth.

Grants Analysis

Disclosure Period: fiscal year ending March 31, 2003
Total Grants: $4,420,402*
Number of Grants: 129
Average Grant: $34,267
Highest Grant: $250,000
Lowest Grant: $5,000
Typical Range: $10,000 to $50,000
*****Note:** Giving excludes scholarship.

Recent Grants

Note: Grants derived from 2004 Form 990.

General

250,000	Accelerated School, Los Angeles, CA -- fund for capital campaign
175,537	Agua Caliente Band of Cahuilla Indians, Palm Springs, CA
100,000	Baruch College, New York, NY -- fund for faculty awards for excellence in teaching
100,000	Buck Institute for Age Research, Novato, CA -- to support research on novel therapeutics for Alzheimer's disease
100,000	Cornell University School of Hotel Administration, Ithaca, NY -- fund for foundation loan
100,000	Division of Hematology/Oncology University of California, San Francisco, CA -- fund for research on the urokinase-urokinase receptor complex in cancer
100,000	Office of the President California State University, Northridge, CA
75,000	UCLA Graduate School of Education & Information Studies (GSE&IS), Los Angeles, CA
75,000	United Hostesses' Charities, Beverly Hills, CA -- fund for cardiac/stroke emergency care unit
'00	Roosevelt Elementary School, Santa Monica, CA -- fund for instruction reform

DTE ENERGY CO.

Company Headquarters

2000 2nd Ave.
Detroit, MI 48226-1279
Web: http://www.dteenergy.com

Company Description

Founded: 1995
Ticker: DTE
Exchange: NYSE
Former Name: Detroit Edison Co.;
Acquired: Michigan Consolidated Gas Co..
Revenue: US$7.114 billion (2004)
Profit: US$431 million (2004)
Employees: 11099 (2003)
Fortune Rank: 296, per FORTUNE Magazine's list of 500 Largest U.S. Corporations (2004).

Nonmonetary Support

Value: $50,000 (2000)
Type: Donated Equipment; In-kind Services
Note: NOT The company also donates office space.

DTE Energy Foundation

Giving Contact

Karla Hall, Secretary & Director
DTE Energy Foundation
2000 Second Avenue, Rm. 1046 WCB
Detroit, MI 48226-1279
Phone: (313)235-9271
Fax: (313)235-0285
E-mail: hallk@dteenergy.com
Web: http://www.dteenergy.com/community/foundation/index.html
Note: Ms. Hall is also Administrator, Corporate Contributions.

Description

EIN: 382708636
Organization Type: Corporate Foundation
Giving Locations: MI: headquarters and operating communities, Detroit
Grant Types: Capital, Emergency, Employee Matching Gifts, Endowment, General Support, Matching, Multiyear/Continuing Support, Operating Expenses, Project, Seed Money.
Note: Foundation matches employee gifts to all educational and Michigan cultural institutions up to a limit of $5,000 per donor annually. Foundation also sponsors "Holiday Season Matching Gifts" program between November 1 and December 31 annually, through which it matches employee gifts to agencies that provide emergency food and shelter services.

Financial Summary

Total Giving: $6,324,325 (2003); $5,846,649 (2002); $5,192,560 (2001). Note: Contributes through corporate direct giving program and foundation.
Giving Analysis: Giving for 2001 includes: foundation matching gifts ($304,405); foundation grants to United Way ($1,842,714)
Assets: $27,340,988 (2003); $14,250,514 (2002); $21,131,377 (2001)
Gifts Received: $15,000,000 (2003); $3,000,000 (1998); $2,240,000 (1997). Note: Contributions were received from the Detroit Edison Co.

Typical Recipients

Arts & Humanities: Arts Associations & Councils, Arts Centers, Arts Institutes, Arts Outreach, Ethnic & Folk Arts, Arts & Humanities-General, Historic Preservation, History & Archaeology, Libraries, Museums/Galleries, Music, Opera, Performing Arts, Public Broadcasting, Theater
Civic & Public Affairs: African American Affairs, Botanical Gardens/Parks, Business/Free Enterprise, Chambers of Commerce, Civil Rights, Community

Foundations, Economic Development, Economic Policy, Ethnic Organizations, Civic & Public Affairs-General, Housing, Municipalities/Towns, Nonprofit Management, Parades/Festivals, Professional & Trade Associations, Public Policy, Safety, Urban & Community Affairs, Women's Affairs, Zoos/Aquariums
Education: Agricultural Education, Arts/Humanities Education, Business Education, Business-School Partnerships, Colleges & Universities, Community & Junior Colleges, Economic Education, Education Associations, Education Funds, Education Reform, Engineering/Technological Education, Environmental Education, Education-General, Literacy, Medical Education, Minority Education, Private Education (Precollege), Public Education (Precollege), School Volunteerism, Science/Mathematics Education, Student Aid, Vocational & Technical Education
Environment: Environment-General, Protection, Resource Conservation, Wildlife Protection
Health: Children's Health/Hospitals, Emergency/Ambulance Services, Eyes/Blindness, Health Funds, Health Organizations, Hospices, Hospitals, Mental Health, Public Health, Single-Disease Health Associations
Religion: Jewish Causes, Religious Welfare
Science: Scientific Centers & Institutes, Scientific Organizations
Social Services: Child Welfare, Community Centers, Community Service Organizations, Delinquency & Criminal Rehabilitation, Family Services, Food/Clothing Distribution, Recreation & Athletics, Scouts, Substance Abuse, United Funds/United Ways, Youth Organizations

Application Procedures

Initial Contact: Submit a written proposal.
Application Requirements: The foundation uses the Council of Michigan Common Grant Application Procedure. The foundation requests that applicants complete the Common Grant Application Cover Sheet, and include a cover letter signed by the applicant organization's chief executive or senior development officer of the organization or chair of the volunteer board. The foundation has a specific format for applications, which can be referenced on the web at: http://www.dteenergy.com/community/apply.html.
Applications should be typed double-space, and must include a Narrative comprised of the Executive Summary, Purpose of Grant, Evaluation, Budget Narrative/Justification, Organization Information, and Donor Recognition. The Executive Summary should describe why the organization is requesting funds, how the money will be spent, and anticipated outcomes. Purpose of Grant must include a statement of needs to be addressed, description of target population and how they will benefit; project goals, measurable objectives, action plans, and statements as to whether this is a new or ongoing initiative for the organization; a timetable for implementation; a list of any partners in the project and their roles; a description of similar existing projects, how this proposal differs from them, and what effort might be made to work cooperatively; an explanation of the active involvement of constituents in defining the needs/problems to be addressed and in making policy and planning the program; and long-term strategies for funding the project at the end of the grant period. Evaluation should include plans for project evaluation; how evaluation results will be used and/or disseminated; and a description of how constituents will be actively involved in the evaluation process. The Budget Narrative/Justification section should provide a grant budget, an explanation of how each budget item relates to the project and how the budget was calculated; other sources of funding and current funding requests; and an indication of priority items in the budget in the event that the full request cannot be accommodated. Organization Information should include the organization's history and goals; description of current projects, activities, and accomplishments; and an organizational chart, including board, staff and volunteer

involvement. Attachments must include proof of tax-exempt status; list of the board of directors and their affiliations; organization's current annual operating budget, including expenses and revenue; and most recent annual financial statement (and Form 990 if financial statement is unaudited). The Donor Recognition section should list various donor recognition opportunities and provide key publicity-related dates, if available. Optional attachments include letters of support, annual report, and donor recognition opportunities, key publicity-related dates, fundraising plan, a list of other corporate and foundation funders with amounts, description of any cooperative actions with similar organizations to advance mutual goals and prevent duplication, and a description of quantity and types of support given by non-volunteer boards.

Deadlines: April 15, August 15, and December 15.
Review Process: Proposals are reviewed upon receipt and then referred to contributions committee for consideration.
Evaluative Criteria: Evidence of cooperative working arrangements among local organizations addressing same or similar goals.
Decision Notification: Quarterly, usually within 60-90 days after receipt of proposal.
Notes: Faxes and videos are discouraged. Requests must be made in writing.

Restrictions

Support is not provided for individuals (including direct scholarships); political parties, organizations, or activities; religious organizations for sectarian purposes; organizations that cannot demonstrate a commitment to equality and diversity; student group trips; single purpose health organizations; hospitals, for building or equipment needs; national or international organizations, unless providing benefits directly to DTE Energy service-area residents; projects which may result in undue personal benefit to a member of the DTE Energy Foundation board or any DTE Energy director or employee; or conferences unless they are aligned with DTE Energy's business interests.

Additional Information

Prefers to fund specific projects rather than annual operating budgets or multi-purpose capital campaigns.
Publications: Guidelines; Application Form; Annual Report

Corporate Officials

Susan M. Beale: vice president, secretary chief financial officer B Richmond, IN 1948. ED Michigan State University BS (1970); University of Michigan JD (1976). PRIM CORP EMPL vice president, corporate secretary: DTE Energy Co. ADD CORP EMPL vice president, secretary: Detroit Edison Co. CORP AFFIL director: Edison Illuminating Co. Detroit; director: Saint Clair Energy Corp.
Robert J. Buckler: chief operating officer, president B Flint, MI 1949. ED University of Michigan BSME (1971); University of Michigan MSME (1973). PRIM CORP EMPL president, chief operating officer: DTE Energy Distribution Inc.
Anthony Francis Earley, Jr.: chairman, president, chief executive officer, chief operating officer B Jamaica, NY July 29, 1949. ED University of Notre Dame BS (1971); University of Notre Dame MS (1979); University of Notre Dame MS (1979). PRIM CORP EMPL chairman, president, chief executive officer, chief operating officer: DTE Energy Co. CORP AFFIL director: Mutual America. NONPR AFFIL vice chairman: Michigan Chamber of Commerce; member advisory council: University Notre Dame College Engineering; member: American Bar Association.
Karla Hall: administrator corporate contributions
David E. Meador: senior vice president, chief financial officer ED Wayne State University BA; Wayne State University MBA. PRIM CORP EMPL senior vice president, chief financial officer: DTE Energy Co.
Frederick E. Shell: vice president corporate & governmental affairs PRIM CORP EMPL vice president

corporate & governmental affairs: DTE Energy Co.
S. Martin Taylor: senior vice president human resources & corporate affairs ED Western Michigan University BS. PRIM CORP EMPL senior vice president human resources & corporate affairs: DTE Energy Co. ADD CORP EMPL senior vice president human resources: Detroit Edison Co.

Foundation Officials

Susan M. Beale: director (see above)
Robert J. Buckler: director (see above)
James F. Connelly: director
Lynne Ellyn: director
Stephen E. Ewing: director
Karla Hall: secretary, director (see above)
Naif A. Khouri: treasurer, director
Michael C. Porter: director
Frederick E. Shell: president, director (see above)
Larry E. Steward: director
S. Martin Taylor: vice president, director (see above)

Grants Analysis

Disclosure Period: calendar year ending 2003
Total Grants: $5,467,021*
Number of Grants: 377
Average Grant: $14,501
Highest Grant: $275,000
Lowest Grant: $100
Typical Range: $1,000 to $20,000
*Note: Giving excludes matching gifts; United Way.

Recent Grants

Note: Grants derived from 2003 Form 990.
General

497,792	United Way Community Services, Detroit, MI
275,000	Detroit Symphony Orchestra Hall Inc., Detroit, MI
200,000	United Way Community Services, Detroit, MI
100,000	Boys and Girls Clubs of Southeastern Michigan, Farmington Hills, MI
100,000	University of Detroit Mercy, Detroit, MI
88,677	United Way of Monroe County Inc., Monroe, MI
75,000	Mexicantown Community Development Corporation, Detroit, MI
75,000	Youth Connection, Detroit, MI
72,200	Detroit Renaissance Foundation, Detroit, MI
61,841	United Way of St. Clair County, Port Huron, MI

E.I. Du Pont De Nemours & Co.

Company Headquarters

Wilmington, DE
Web: http://www.dupont.com

Company Description

Founded: 1802
Ticker: DD
Exchange: NYSE
Acquired: Pioneer Hi-Bred (1999);
Former Name: E.I. du Pont de Nemours & Co. (2005).
Revenue: US$24.006 billion (2002)
Employees: 93000 (2003)
SIC(s): 1222 Bituminous Coal--Underground, 1311 Crude Petroleum & Natural Gas, 1321 Natural Gas Liquids, 2822 Synthetic Rubber.

Operating Locations

E.I. du Pont de Nemours & Co. (AL--Axis; AR--Hazen, Lonoke; CA--Antioch, Santa Clara; CO--Commerce City, Rangely; CT--Danbury; DE--Edge

Moor, Glasgow, Newark, Newport, Wilmington; FL--Starke; GA--Athens; IL--El Paso; IN--East Chicago, Kokomo; IA--Fort Madison; KS--Kansas City; KY--Wurtland; LA--Darrow, Egan, Grand Chenier, Lake Charles, Westlake; MA--Boston; MI--Mason, Montague, Mount Clemens, Troy; MS--Pass Christian; NJ--Deepwater, Gibbstown, Linden, Pompton Lakes; NM--Bloomfield, Maljamar; NY--Buffalo, Niagara Falls, Rochester; NC--Brevard, Denton, Fayetteville, Kinston, Wilmington; OH--Circleville, Findlay, Stow, Toledo; OK--Ada, Hennessy, Medford, Ponca City, Tuttle; PA--Boothwyn, Philadelphia, Pittsburgh, Towanda; SC--Camden, Florence; TN--Chattanooga, Memphis, New Johnsonville; TX--Beaumont, El Dorado, Hamlin, Houston, La Porte, McKinney, Mertzon, Mont Belvieu, Orla, Pasadena, Round Rock, San Angelo, Victoria; VA--Front Royal, Martinsville, Mavisdale, Waynesboro; WV--Belle, Martinsburg, Moundsville)

Subsidiary Companies

IA: Pioneer Hi-Bred International Inc., Des Moines

Nonmonetary Support

Type: Donated Equipment
Note: Company also donates property. For nonmonetary support contact nearest company site.

Giving Contact

Pat Eggert, Contributions Coordinator
DuPont Public Affairs
Corporate Contributions Office
1007 Market Street
Wilmington, DE 19898
Phone: (302)774-2036
Fax: (302)773-2919
Web: http://www.dupont.com/corp/community.html

Alternate Contact

DuPont Office of Education
Barley Mill Plaza 16/2150
PO Box 80016
Wilmington, DE 19880-0016
Note: Contact for DuPont Education programs.

Description

Organization Type: Corporate Giving Program
Giving Locations: headquarters and operating communities.
Grant Types: Capital, Conference/Seminar, Emergency, Fellowship, General Support, Multiyear/Continuing Support.

Financial Summary

Total Giving: Contributes through corporate direct giving program only.

Typical Recipients

Arts & Humanities: Arts Appreciation, Arts Associations & Councils, Arts Centers, Arts Festivals, Arts Funds, Arts Institutes, Community Arts, Dance, Ethnic & Folk Arts, Historic Preservation, Libraries, Literary Arts, Museums/Galleries, Music, Opera, Performing Arts, Public Broadcasting, Theater, Visual Arts
Civic & Public Affairs: Business/Free Enterprise, Civil Rights, Economic Development, Economic Policy, Employment/Job Training, Housing, Law & Justice, Legal Aid, Municipalities/Towns, Nonprofit Management, Philanthropic Organizations, Professional & Trade Associations, Public Policy, Safety, Urban & Community Affairs, Women's Affairs, Zoos/Aquariums
Education: Agricultural Education, Business Education, Colleges & Universities, Community & Junior Colleges, Economic Education, Education Associations, Education Funds, Engineering/Technological Education, Faculty Development, International Exchange, International Studies, Journalism/Media Education, Legal Education, Literacy, Minority Education, Preschool Education, Private Education (Precollege), Public Education (Precollege), Science/Mathematics Education, Social Sciences Education,

Student Aid
Environment: Environment-General
Health: Emergency/Ambulance Services, Geriatric Health, Health Policy/Cost Containment, Health Organizations, Hospices, Hospitals, Medical Rehabilitation, Medical Research, Medical Training, Mental Health, Single-Disease Health Associations
International: Foreign Educational Institutions, Health Care/Hospitals, International Peace & Security Issues, International Relations
Science: Science Exhibits & Fairs, Scientific Centers & Institutes, Scientific Organizations
Social Services: Animal Protection, Child Welfare, Community Centers, Community Service Organizations, Counseling, Day Care, Delinquency & Criminal Rehabilitation, Domestic Violence, Emergency Relief, Family Services, Food/Clothing Distribution, Homes, People with Disabilities, Recreation & Athletics, Senior Services, Shelters/Homelessness, Substance Abuse, United Funds/United Ways, Volunteer Services, Youth Organizations

Application Procedures

Initial Contact: Submit a written proposal.
Application Requirements: Provide a one-to two-page a description of organization and program to be funded and an explanation of how it relates to the mission, operating philosophy, and areas of support of the DuPont Community Involvement Program.
Requests should be sent to the above address to the attention of the appropriate committee:
The Committee on Contributions and Memberships reviews all requests for non-education financial contributions.
The Committee on Educational Aid reviews requests for financial contributions to educational institutions.
Deadlines: None.
Review Process: The Committee on Contributions and Memberships generally reviews requests in May and September.
Evaluative Criteria: For Community Social Progress and Economic Success requests, DuPont prefers programs that both address a community need and reflect positively on the reputation and image of DuPont; programs that have extensive DuPont employee volunteer involvement; proposals that have well-defined goals and objectives and a method for evaluating results; and programs designed with long-lasting results in mind.
In the area of Environmental Excellence, DuPont has a preference for organizations that can provide evidence of demonstrated, credible environmental performance; proposals that leverage non-cash resources; proposals that involve partnerships and collaboration between industry, governmental, and community-based organizations; programs which involve DuPont employees; and programs that reflect favorably on DuPont's reputation and image.
DuPont focuses its funding in the Education program area on learning readiness, hands-on science, discovery math, work force readiness, and teacher preparation.
Decision Notification: Applicants are notified in writing.

Restrictions

DuPont does not support U.S. nonprofit organizations not eligible for support under the U.S. IRS Code; disease-specific organizations; endowments; fraternal and veterans groups; individuals; political organizations or campaigns; sectarian organizations whose programs are limited to members of one religious group; organizations which discriminate based on age, race, religion, color, sex, disability, national origin, ancestry, marital status, sexual orientation, or veteran status. presence.

Additional Information

The company awards between 5,000 and 6,000 grants annually.
DuPont contributions are focused on three areas of support:

Community Social Progress and Economic Success, particularly those programs that provide access to opportunity to people for whom that access does not currently adequately exist; help children, youth and families; foster understanding and respect between community members; revitalize neighborhoods; and help people achieve self-sufficiency.
Environmental Excellence, through support of initiatives that produce significant, measurable results in four major areas of environmental quality: conservation, public policy, research and education, and environmental management.
Send non-education requests to the DuPont Corporate Contributions Office.
Education, by funding programs that support improvements in pre-school to grade 12 education. At the college/university level, DuPont opens access to leading-edge research and introduces talented students to the company.
Send education-related requests to the DuPont Office of Education.
Publications: Brochure

Corporate Officials

Thomas M. Connelly, Jr.: senior vice president, chief science & technology officer B Toledo, OH. ED University of Cambridge PhD. PRIM CORP EMPL senior vice president, chief science & technology officer: E.I. du Pont de Nemours & Co.
Richard R. Goodmanson: executive vice president, chief operating officer PRIM CORP EMPL executive vice president, chief operating officer: E.I. du Pont de Nemours & Co. CORP AFFIL director: Boise Cascade Corp.
Charles O. Holliday, Jr.: chairman, chief executive officer, director B March 09, 1948. ED University of Tennessee BS. PRIM CORP EMPL chairman, chief executive officer, director: E.I. du Pont de Nemours & Co. CORP AFFIL director: HCA. NONPR AFFIL chairman: Business Council; trustee: Winterthur Museum and Gardens.
Stacey J. Mobley: senior vice president, chief administrative officer, general counsel B Chester, PA. PRIM CORP EMPL senior vice president, chief administrative officer, general counsel: E.I. du Pont de Nemours & Co. CORP AFFIL director: Wilmington Trust Corp.

Grants Analysis

Disclosure Period: calendar year ending 2000
Total Grants: $30,000,000 (approx)
Typical Range: $5,000 to $10,000

DUCHOSSOIS FAMILY FOUNDATION

Giving Contact

Kimberly T. Duchossois, President
Duchossois Family Foundation
845 Larch Ave.
Elmhurst, IL 60126-1196
Phone: (847)381-6278
Fax: (847)381-4102

Description

Founded: 1985
EIN: 363327987
Organization Type: Private Foundation
Former Name: Duchossois Foundation.
Giving Locations: IL: Chicago
Grant Types: General Support, Multiyear/Continuing Support.

Financial Summary

Total Giving: $501,177 (2001). Note: Contributes through foundation only.
Giving Analysis: Giving for 2001 includes: founda-

tion scholarships ($3,500); foundation grants to United Way ($4,000); foundation ($493,677)
Assets: $3,905,550 (2001)
Gifts Received: $3,715,574 (2000); $2,500,000 (1998); $2,000,000 (1997). Note: In 2000, contributions were received from Duchossois Technology Partners, LLC. In 1998 and 1997, contributions were received from Duchossois Industries.

Typical Recipients

Arts & Humanities: Arts Associations & Councils, Arts Festivals, Arts Funds, Arts Institutes, Arts Outreach, Ballet, Community Arts, Dance, Ethnic & Folk Arts, Arts & Humanities-General, Historic Preservation, History & Archaeology, Libraries, Literary Arts, Museums/Galleries, Music, Opera, Performing Arts, Public Broadcasting, Theater, Visual Arts
Civic & Public Affairs: Botanical Gardens/Parks, Business/Free Enterprise, Chambers of Commerce, Clubs, Community Foundations, Economic Development, Ethnic Organizations, Civic & Public Affairs-General, Hispanic Affairs, Housing, Nonprofit Management, Parades/Festivals, Philanthropic Organizations, Public Policy, Safety, Urban & Community Affairs, Women's Affairs, Zoos/Aquariums
Education: Afterschool/Enrichment Programs, Arts/Humanities Education, Business Education, Colleges & Universities, Community & Junior Colleges, Education Funds, Education Reform, Elementary Education (Private), Engineering/Technological Education, Faculty Development, Education-General, Medical Education, Minority Education, Private Education (Precollege), Public Education (Precollege), Secondary Education (Public), Special Education, Student Aid
Environment: Forestry, Environment-General, Resource Conservation, Watershed
Health: AIDS/HIV, Cancer, Children's Health/Hospitals, Clinics/Medical Centers, Diabetes, Health-General, Geriatric Health, Health Funds, Health Organizations, Hospices, Hospitals, Hospitals (University Affiliated), Medical Rehabilitation, Medical Research, Mental Health, Prenatal Health Issues, Preventive Medicine/Wellness Organizations, Research/Studies Institutes, Single-Disease Health Associations, Speech & Hearing
International: International-General, Health Care/Hospitals, International Affairs, International Environmental Issues, Missionary/Religious Activities
Religion: Churches, Jewish Causes, Religious Organizations, Religious Welfare, Seminaries
Science: Science Museums, Scientific Organizations
Social Services: Animal Protection, At-Risk Youth, Child Welfare, Community Centers, Community Service Organizations, Family Services, Homes, People with Disabilities, Recreation & Athletics, Scouts, Shelters/Homelessness, Social Services-General, Substance Abuse, United Funds/United Ways, Volunteer Services, Youth Organizations

Application Procedures

Initial Contact: Send a one-page summary-request letter.
Application Requirements: Include a description of organization; its specific needs and purposes; the amount of support requested; list of board of directors and their business or professional affiliations. Attach proof of tax-exempt status and latest annual report.
Deadlines: None.
Review Process: Foundation will either reject initial inquiry or request a full proposal.
Decision Notification: Board meets semi-annually or as needed; major funding commitments are made at the January meeting.

Restrictions

The foundation does not support individuals, including scholarships or fellowships; lobbying groups; religious organizations for sectarian purposes; or organizations that are not tax-exempt.

Additional Information

Publications: Guidelines

Corporate Officials

Craig J. Duchossois: chief executive officer B 1944. ED Southern Methodist University MBA (1968). PRIM CORP EMPL chief executive officer: Duchossois Industries Inc. CORP AFFIL chairman: Saco Defense Inc.; chairman, chief executive officer, director: Thrall Car Manufacturing Co.; chairman: Chamberlain Group Inc.; director: Hill n Dale Farms Inc.

Richard Louis Duchossois: chairman, chief executive officer, director B Chicago, IL 1921. ED Washington & Lee University. PRIM CORP EMPL chairman, chief executive officer, director: Duchossois Industries Inc. CORP AFFIL chairman: Transportation Corp. Am; vice chairman: Thrall Car Manufacturing Co.; chairman: Duchossois Communication Co.; director: Hill n Dale Farms Inc.; director: Chamberlain Manufacturing Corp.; chairman: Arlington Management Services; director: Chamberlain Group Inc.; chairman: Arlington International Racecourse Ltd. NONPR AFFIL member: Chief Executives Organization. CLUB AFFIL Executive Club; Jockey Club; Economic Club.

Foundation Officials

Craig J. Duchossois: director (see above)
Dayle Paige Duchossois: director
Kimberly Duchossois: president
Richard Louis Duchossois: secretary (see above)

Grants Analysis

Disclosure Period: calendar year ending 2001
Total Grants: $493,677*
Number of Grants: 52
Average Grant: $7,719*
Highest Grant: $100,000
Lowest Grant: $500
Typical Range: $1,000 to $20,000
*Note: Giving excludes United Way and scholarships. Average grant figure excludes highest grant.

Recent Grants

Note: Grants derived from 2002 Form 990.
General

100,000	Northwestern University Medical School, Chicago, IL -- for research
30,000	Chicago Charter School Foundation, Chicago, IL
25,000	American Cancer Society, Chicago, IL -- relay for life
20,000	University of Chicago Hospitals, Chicago, IL -- towards cancer research
15,000	American Cancer Society, Chicago, IL -- relay for life
10,000	Barrington Area Community Foundation, Barrington, IL
10,000	Boy Scouts of America, Mt. Prospect, IL -- for Northwest Suburban Council
10,000	Boys & Girls Clubs of America, Chicago, IL
10,000	Cancer Treatment Research Foundation, Arlington Heights, IL
10,000	Chicago House, Chicago, IL

DUCOMMUN AND GROSS FOUNDATION

Giving Contact

Robert Ducommun, President
1155 Park Avenue
New York, NY 10128

Description

Founded: 1968
EIN: 956210834
Organization Type: Private Foundation
Giving Locations: CA; DC: Washington; MA; NY:

New York
Grant Types: General Support.

Financial Summary

Total Giving: $276,000 (2003); $247,000 (2001)
Assets: $6,267,925 (2003); $5,202,645 (2001)
Gifts Received: $194,641 (2003); $197,087 (2001); $194,640 (2000). **Note:** Contributions were received from Charles E. and Palmer G. Ducommun Charitable Annuity Trust.

Typical Recipients

Arts & Humanities: Historic Preservation, Libraries, Museums/Galleries, Public Broadcasting
Civic & Public Affairs: Clubs, Community Foundations, Civic & Public Affairs-General, Safety, Zoos/Aquariums
Education: Colleges & Universities, Private Education (Precollege), Public Education (Precollege)
Environment: Environment-General, Resource Conservation
Health: Children's Health/Hospitals, Emergency/Ambulance Services, Medical Research
Science: Science Museums, Scientific Centers & Institutes
Social Services: Child Welfare, Day Care, Emergency Relief, Food/Clothing Distribution, Recreation & Athletics, Scouts, Youth Organizations

Application Procedures

Initial Contact: Send a brief letter of inquiry.
Application Requirements: Include a description of organization, amount requested, purpose of funds sought, and proof of tax-exempt status.
Deadlines: None.

Restrictions

Does not support individuals, religious organizations for sectarian purposes, or political or lobbying groups.

Foundation Officials

Robert E. Ducommun: president
Electra Ducommun Depeyster: vice president, treasurer
Courtlandt D. Gross: adv director
Frederick Alexander Richmand: secretary
Anthony C. Ward: adv director

Grants Analysis

Disclosure Period: calendar year ending 2003
Total Grants: $276,000
Number of Grants: 20
Average Grant: $10,053*
Highest Grant: $85,000
Lowest Grant: $2,500
Typical Range: $5,000 to $20,000
*Note: Average grant figure excludes highest grant.

Recent Grants

Note: Grants derived from 2001 Form 990.

Library-Related

2,500	David Hale Library, Larkspur, CA

General

60,000	Stanford University, Stanford, CA
25,000	Saint Georges School, Newport, RI
20,000	National Public Radio, Washington, DC
20,000	Woods Hole Oceanographic Institute, Woods Hole, MA
15,000	Harvard College Fund, Cambridge, MA
15,000	Sarah Lawrence College, Bronxville, NY
11,000	National History Museum, Los Angeles, CA
10,000	American Red Cross, Los Angeles, CA
10,000	City of Hope, Los Angeles, CA
10,000	KQED, San Francisco, CA

DUCOMMUN INC.

Company Headquarters

PO Box 22677
Long Beach, CA 90801-5677
Web: http://www.ducommun.com

Company Description

Founded: 1849
Ticker: DCO
Exchange: NYSE
Revenue: US$212.4 million (2002)
Employees: 1300 (2002)
SIC(s): 3600 Electronic & Other Electrical Equipment, 3700 Transportation Equipment, 5000 Wholesale Trade--Durable Goods.

Operating Locations

Ducommun Inc. (CA--Carson)

Giving Contact

Kenneth R. Pearson, Vice President, Human Resources
111 W. Ocean Bld., Ste. 900
Long Beach, CA 90802
Phone: (562)951-1742
Fax: (562)624-0799

Description

Organization Type: Corporate Giving Program

Typical Recipients

Arts & Humanities: Historic Preservation, Libraries, Museums/Galleries, Public Broadcasting
Civic & Public Affairs: Economic Development, Zoos/Aquariums
Education: Colleges & Universities, Private Education (Precollege), Student Aid
Environment: Environment-General
Health: Emergency/Ambulance Services, Medical Research
International: International Environmental Issues
Science: Science Museums, Scientific Centers & Institutes
Social Services: Youth Organizations

Corporate Officials

Norman A. Barkeley: chairman emeritus B Grand Rapids, MI 1930. ED Michigan State University BS BA (1953). PRIM CORP EMPL chairman emeritus: Ducommun Inc. CORP AFFIL director: Golden Sys Inc.
Joseph C. Berenato: president, chief executive officer B Atlantic City, NJ. ED United States Military Academy (1969); University of Virginia MS (1976); New York University MBA (1979). PRIM CORP EMPL president, chief executive officer: Ducommun.
James S. Heiser: chief financial officer B Evanston, IL 1956. ED University of Virginia (1977); Stanford University (1980). PRIM CORP EMPL chief financial officer: Ducommun. NONPR AFFIL member: American Bar Association.

Grants Analysis

Note: A more recent grants list was unavailable.

Recent Grants

Note: Grants derived from 1997 Form 990.
Library-Related

2,500	David Hale Library, Larkspur, CA

General

30,000	St. George's School, Newport, RI
15,000	National Public Radio, Washington, DC
10,000	American Red Cross, Los Angeles, CA
10,000	Design Industries Foundation, New York, NY
10,000	Harvard College Fund, Cambridge, MA -- for financial aid
10,000	Monterey Bay Aquarium, Monterey, CA
10,000	Stanford University Art Museum for Print, Stanford, CA

10,000 Stanford University School of Education, Stanford, CA
10,000 WGBH, Brighton, MA
10,000 Woods Hole Oceanographic Institute, Woods Hole, MA

DUFFIELD FAMILY FOUNDATION

Giving Contact
Laurie E. Peek, Secretary
2223 Santa Clara Ave., Ste. B
Alameda, CA 94501
Phone: (510)337-8989
Fax: (510)337-8988
E-mail: info@maddiesfund.org
Web: http://www.maddiesfund.org

Description
Founded: 1995
EIN: 680339626
Organization Type: Private Foundation
Giving Locations: CA
Grant Types: General Support.

Donor Information
Founder: Established in 1995 by David A. Duffield.

Financial Summary
Total Giving: $6,028,855 (fiscal year ending August 31, 2003); $8,357,545 (fiscal 2002); $8,267,988 (fiscal 2001)
Assets: $144,462,499 (fiscal 2003); $128,478,755 (fiscal 2002); $181,435,997 (fiscal 2001)
Gifts Received: $10,971,080 (fiscal 2003); $37,499,133 (fiscal 2002); $40,314,200 (fiscal 2001).
Note: Contributions were received from David A. Duffield.

Typical Recipients
Arts & Humanities: Museums/Galleries
Civic & Public Affairs: Professional & Trade Associations, Zoos/Aquariums
Education: Colleges & Universities, Medical Education
Environment: Environment-General, Protection, Wildlife Protection
Health: Cancer, Children's Health/Hospitals
International: Health Care/Hospitals
Social Services: Animal Protection, Child Abuse, Community Service Organizations, People with Disabilities, United Funds/United Ways, Youth Organizations

Application Procedures
Initial Contact: Send a brief letter of inquiry.
Application Requirements: Applications should include a description of organization, purpose of funds sought, and proposed follow-up with the foundation.
Deadlines: None.

Restrictions
Support is limited to programs for domestic animal welfare.

Foundation Officials
Richard Avanzino: president, director
Cheryl D. Duffield: director
David A. Duffield: director
Michael D. Duffield: director
Laurie E. Peek: director
Margaret L. Taylor: treasurer, chief financial officer
Amy D. Zeifang: chairman, director

Grants Analysis
Disclosure Period: fiscal year ending August 31, 2003

Total Grants: $6,028,855
Number of Grants: 32
Average Grant: $101,036*
Highest Grant: $1,238,810
Lowest Grant: $750
Typical Range: $25,000 to $200,000
*Note: Average grant excludes three highest grants ($3,098,814).

Recent Grants
Note: Grants derived from 2003 Form 990.
General

1,238,810 Texas Veterinary Medical Association, Austin, TX -- toward Maddie's Spay/Neuter Project
1,078,950 Best Friends Animal Sanctuary, Kanab, UT -- funding for no more homeless pets
781,054 Best Friends Animal Sanctuary, Kanab, UT -- funding for no more homeless pets
603,309 Alabama Veterinary Medical Association, Montgomery, AL -- toward Maddie's big fix for Alabama
500,000 Tony La Russa's Animal Rescue, Walnut Creek, CA -- funding for Maddie's animal care center
308,231 University of California, Davis Veterinary Medical Teaching Hospital, Davis, CA -- toward Maddie's shelter medicine program
254,151 Western University College of Veterinary Medicine, Pomona, CA -- toward Maddie's shelter medicine program
201,176 Alachua County Humane Society, Gainesville, FL -- toward Maddie's pet rescue project
192,645 Arizona Animal Welfare League, Phoenix, AZ -- funding for Maddie's pet rescue project
183,130 Arizona Animal Welfare League, Phoenix, AZ -- funding for Maddie's pet rescue project

DUKE ENDOWMENT

Giving Contact
David H. Roberson, Director, Communications
100 North Tryon Street, Suite 3500
Charlotte, NC 28202-4012
Phone: (704)376-0291
Fax: (704)376-9336
E-mail: droberson@tde.org
Web: http://www.dukeendowment.org

Description
Founded: 1924
EIN: 560529965
Organization Type: General Purpose Foundation
Giving Locations: NC; SC
Grant Types: Capital, Challenge, Conference, Seminar, Department, Emergency, Endowment, Fellowship, General Support, Loan, Matching, Multiyear/Continuing Support, Operating Expenses, Professorship, Project, Research, Scholarship, Seed Money.

Donor Information
Founder: Established in 1924 by James Buchanan Duke (d. 1925) with a $40 million endowment. The Duke family derived its wealth from tobacco, textiles, and the development of hydroelectric power in North and South Carolina. The family tobacco business began shortly after the Civil War. In 1884, the small firm gambled on an innovation--automation--and the cottage industry grew into the American Tobacco Company with James Duke as president. The company was dissolved in 1911 when the Supreme Court upheld the Sherman Anti-Trust Act; but the Duke family had already turned their attention to hydroelectric power in 1905. This led to the founding of Duke

Power Company in 1907. Mr. Duke also had business investments in textiles and blocks of shares of Aluminum Company of America.
During the family's years of prosperity, they generously contributed to orphanages, hospitals, the Methodist Church, and Trinity College, which became Duke University when the Duke Endowment was founded.
The Duke Endowment is also closely affiliated with Angier B. Duke Memorial, NC, and Nanaline Duke Fund for Duke University, NC. Doris Duke, former trustee and late daughter of the donor, established the Doris Duke Charitable Foundation under her will. Ms. Duke died in April 1993.

Financial Summary
Total Giving: $105,346,441 (2003); $116,554,909 (2002); $105,192,626 (2001)
Giving Analysis: Giving for 2003 includes: foundation scholarships ($6,415,000)
Assets: $2,307,706,953 (2003); $2,100,000,000 (2002 approx); $2,489,158,509 (2001)
Gifts Received: $127,260,880 (1995)

Typical Recipients
Arts & Humanities: Libraries
Civic & Public Affairs: Botanical Gardens/Parks
Education: Arts/Humanities Education, Colleges & Universities, Engineering/Technological Education, Faculty Development, International Studies, Leadership Training, Medical Education, Minority Education, Religious Education, Science/Mathematics Education, Social Sciences Education, Student Aid
Health: Adolescent Health Issues, AIDS/HIV, Alzheimer's Disease, Cancer, Children's Health/Hospitals, Clinics/Medical Centers, Diabetes, Emergency/Ambulance Services, Health-General, Geriatric Health, Health Policy/Cost Containment, Health Organizations, Heart, Home-Care Services, Hospices, Hospitals, Hospitals (University Affiliated), Long-Term Care, Medical Rehabilitation, Medical Research, Medical Training, Nursing Services, Nutrition, Outpatient Health Care, Prenatal Health Issues, Preventive Medicine/Wellness Organizations, Public Health, Respiratory
Religion: Churches, Religious Organizations, Religious Welfare, Seminaries
Social Services: Camps, Child Welfare, Day Care, Family Planning, Family Services, Homes, People with Disabilities, Substance Abuse

Application Procedures
Initial Contact: Applicants should mail a letter of inquiry describing the proposed project. Eligible requests will be referred to the appropriate program officer in education, health care, child care, or the rural Methodist church.
Application Requirements: A program officer may request a full proposal, including project description, budget, funding sources, proof of tax-exempt status, audited financial statements, list of board members, and other pertinent information.
Deadlines: None. The board makes final decisions at its meetings which are held ten times per year.
Review Process: Applications are screened by trustee committees and sent with recommendations to the full board. Letters of inquiry are usually answered within thirty days. If a meeting is desirable, the program officer will arrange it. It may take between two and six months for a final decision on a proposal.

Additional Information
In addition to its grant-making activities, the endowment also sponsors conferences, seminars/workshops, and technical assistance consulting for eligible beneficiaries. The endowment's library is designated a Foundation Center cooperating collection. Their library is open to grantseekers daily, Monday through Friday. Grantsmanship seminars are also held for area nonprofits.
Publications: Annual Report; Guidelines; Brochures; Issues Magazine

Foundation Officials

William George Anlyan, MD: trustee B Alexandria, Egypt 1925. ED Yale University BS (1945); Yale University MD (1949). NONPR AFFIL member: Surgical Biology Club II; member: Allen O. Whipple Surgical Society; member: Southern Medicine Association; member: Southern Surgical Association; member: Society University Surgeons; member: Society Vascular Surgery; member: Society Medical Administrations; member: Sigma Xi; member: Society Clinical Surgery; member: Phi Beta Kappa; member: Research America; member: International Cardiovascular Society; member: National Academy of Sciences Institute Medicine; member: Industrial Research Roundtable - NAS; director: Friends of the National Library of Medicine; member: Halsted Society; member: Council Deans; chancellor emeritus: Duke University; member: Association American Medical Colleges; member: Coordinating Council Medicine Education; member: Association Academy of Health Centers; member: American Medical Association; member: American Surgical Association; member: American Heart Association; member: Alpha Omega Alpha; fellow: American College Surgeons. CLUB AFFIL Rotary Club.

Dennis M. Campbell, PhD: trustee B TX. ED Duke University AB (1967); Yale University Divinity School BD (1970); Duke University PhD (1973); Duke University PhD (1973). PRIM NONPR EMPL headmaster: Woodbury Forest School. NONPR AFFIL advisory board chair: WHTJ Charlottesville Public Television; headmaster: Woodberry Forest School; advisory board: Boys & Girls Club Charlottesville; director: Family Health International.

Hugh McMaster Chapman: vice chairman, trustee B Spartanburg, SC September 11, 1932. ED University of North Carolina BSBA (1955); Rutgers University Stonier Graduate School of Banking (1966). CORP AFFIL director: Williams Co.; director: Scana Resources Inc.; director: West Point Stevens; director: SCANA Corp.; director: SCANA Propane Gas, Inc.; director: PrintPark Inc.; director: Inman Holding Co.; director: Inman Mills. NONPR AFFIL chairman: East Lake Community Foundation; member: South Carolina Business Hall of Fame.

Eugene W. Cochrane, Jr.: president

Constance F. Gray: trustee

Richard Hampton Jenrette: trustee B Raleigh, NC 1929. ED University of North Carolina BA (1951); Harvard University MBA (1957). CORP AFFIL senior advisor: Donaldson Lufkin & Jenrette Inc.; director: Alliance Capital Management. NONPR AFFIL member: Phi Beta Kappa; member, board directors, executive committee: Securities Industry Association; member: Institute Chartered Financial Analysts; member: New York Society Security Analysts; director: Business Roundtable; director: Historic Hudson Valley; director: Business Foundation North Carolina. CLUB AFFIL University Club; Harvard Club; The Links Club; Carolina Yacht Club; Harvard Business School Club; Brook Club.

Mary Duke Trent Jones: trustee

Thomas Stephen Kenan, III: trustee B Durham, NC 1937. ED University of North Carolina BA (1959). CORP AFFIL director: Kenan Transport Co.; director: Flagler System Inc. NONPR AFFIL trustee: National Tropical Botanical Garden; honorary trustee: NC School of the Arts; restoration committee: Liberty Hall; trustee: Council National Trust Historic Preservation. CLUB AFFIL Treyburn Country Club; University Club; Landfall Golf & Tennis Club; Breakers Beach & Golf Club; Hope Valley Country Club.

Charles C. Lucas, III: trustee NONPR AFFIL member steering committee: Close to a Cure; trustee: North Carolina School Arts.

Rhett N. Mabry: director child care division

John Grimes Medlin, Jr.: trustee B Benson, NC 1933. ED University of North Carolina BS (1956). PRIM CORP EMPL chairman emeritus, director: Wachovia Corp. CORP AFFIL chairman emeritus: Wacjpvoa Corp. NONPR AFFIL trustee: Research

Triangle Fund; trustee: Wake Forest University; member: North Carolina Business Hall of Fame; member: Phi Delta Theta; director: Kenan Institute Arts; trustee: National Humanities Center.

Russell M. Robinson, II: chairman, trustee B Charlotte, NC 1932. ED Princeton University (1950-1952); Duke University School of Law LLB (1956). PRIM CORP EMPL partner: Robinson, Bradshaw & Hinson. CORP AFFIL director: Caraustar Indiana Inc.; officer: Robinson, Bradshaw & Hinson PA; director: Cadmus Communications Corp.

Mary Duke Biddle Trent Semans: trustee B New York, NY February 21, 1920. NONPR AFFIL member: League Women Voters; director: North Carolina School Arts; director: Goodwill Industries Research Triangle Area; chairman: Angier B. Duke Memorial; director: Executive Mansion Fine Arts Committee; member: Business Professional Womens Club. CLUB AFFIL Rotary Club; Altrusa Club; Half Century Club.

Minor Mickel Shaw: trustee ED University of North Carolina BA (1969). CORP AFFIL president: Micco Corp.; president: Mickel Investment Group. NONPR AFFIL director: United Way of Greenville County; member: Urban League of the Upstate; director: United Way Association of South Carolina; director: Greenville Hospital System Foundation; director: SC Governor's School for the Arts Foundation; director: Daniel-Mickel Foundation; member: Greater Greenvile Chamber of Commerce.

Jean G. Spaulding, MD: trustee ED Columbia University; Duke University MD. OCCUPATION psychiatrist. NONPR AFFIL director: Cardinal Health Inc.; director: North Carolina Biotechnology Center.

Neil Williams: trustee B Charlotte, NC 1936. ED Duke University AB (1958); Duke University JD (1961). PRIM CORP EMPL partner: Alston & Bird. NONPR AFFIL trustee: Vasser Woolley Foundation; chairman: Woodruff Arts Center; member: Phi Beta Kappa; member: State Bar Georgia; trustee emeritus: Duke university; member: Omicron Delta Kappa; member: Atlanta Chamber of Commerce; trustee: Brevard Music Center; member: American Law Institute; director: American Symphony Orchestra; member: American Bar Association; member: American Bar Foundation. CLUB AFFIL member: Piedmont Driving Club; member: University Club; member: Commerce Club.

Grants Analysis

Disclosure Period: calendar year ending 2003
Total Grants: $98,931,441*
Number of Grants: 750 (approx)
Average Grant: $107,786*
Highest Grant: $6,415,000
Lowest Grant: $200
Typical Range: $20,000 to $200,000
*Note: Average grant figure excludes three highest grants ($18,415,000).

Recent Grants

Note: Grants derived from 2001 Form 990.

General

5,106,623	Duke Endowment, Durham, NC -- to establish the Duke Endowment for Flood Relief
4,000,000	Benjamin N. Duke Leadership Program, Durham, NC
3,500,000	Angier B. Duke Memorial Scholarship Program Endowment, Durham, NC
3,500,000	Benjamin N. Duke Leadership Summer Project, Durham, NC
2,000,000	Davidson College, Davidson, NC
2,000,000	Duke University Divinity School, Durham, NC -- chapel
1,900,000	Furman University, Greenville, SC -- James B. Duke Library
1,693,000	Davidson College, Davidson, NC
1,693,000	Furman University, Greenville, SC -- capital campaign
1,297,000	Johnson C. Smith University, Charlotte, NC

DUKE ENERGY CORP.

Company Headquarters

526 S. Church St.
Charlotte, NC 28202-1803
Web: http://www.duke-energy.com

Company Description

Ticker: DUK
Exchange: OTC
Former Name: Duke Power Co.
Revenue: US$22.779 billion (2004)
Profit: US$1.49 billion (2004)
Employees: 23800 (2003)
Fortune Rank: 86, per FORTUNE Magazine's list of 500 Largest U.S. Corporations (2004).
SIC(s): 4911 Electric Services.

Operating Locations

Duke Energy (DE--Wilmington; NC--Burlington, Chapel Hill, Gastonia, Greensboro, Hendersonville, Hickory, Rutherfordton, Salisbury, Winston-Salem; SC--Anderson, Lancaster, Spartanburg)

Subsidiary Companies

MA: Algonquin Gas Transmission Co., Brighton

Nonmonetary Support

Type: Donated Equipment; In-kind Services
Volunteer Programs: Community Volunteer Grants provide $1,000 for materials for employees and retirees who volunteer time to one-time, hands-on projects, and $1,000 grants to organizations where employees help achieve significant strategic objectives.
Note: Co. provides nonmonetary support.

Duke Energy Foundation

Giving Contact

Hilary Davidson, Vice President
422 S. Church Street
Charlotte, NC 28202
Phone: (704)382-7200
Web: http://www.duke-energy.com/company/community/foundation/

Description

EIN: 581586283
Organization Type: Corporate Foundation
Former Name: Duke Power Co. Foundation.
Giving Locations: NC; SC: headquarters and operating communities.
Grant Types: Award, Capital, Challenge, Conference/Seminar, Employee Matching Gifts, General Support, Multiyear/Continuing Support, Project, Scholarship.
Note: Employee matching gift ratio: 1 to 1 for gifts up to $5,000 per employee annually with a $50 minimum, for gifts to education, culture and the arts, and medical organizations.

Financial Summary

Total Giving: $14,908,663 (2003); $10,046,968 (2002); $17,531,797 (2001). Note: Contributes through corporate direct giving program and foundation.
Giving Analysis: Giving for 2001 includes: foundation grants to United Way ($46,674)
Assets: $42,875,062 (2003); $56,408,909 (2002); $12,457,452 (2001)
Gifts Received: $755,553 (2003); $53,252,617 (2002); $24,113,400 (2001). Note: In 2001 and 2003, contributions were received from Duke Energy Corp. ($23,330,000) and general public ($783,400). In 2000, contributions were received from Duke Energy Corp. ($3,000,000), and general public ($679,890).

Typical Recipients

Arts & Humanities: Arts Associations & Councils, Arts Centers, Arts Festivals, Arts Funds, Ballet, Community Arts, Dance, Ethnic & Folk Arts, Historic Preservation, History & Archaeology, Libraries, Museums/Galleries, Music, Opera, Performing Arts, Theater

Civic & Public Affairs: African American Affairs, Business/Free Enterprise, Chambers of Commerce, Civil Rights, Community Foundations, Economic Development, Civic & Public Affairs-General, Housing, Legal Aid, Municipalities/Towns, Philanthropic Organizations, Professional & Trade Associations, Public Policy, Rural Affairs, Safety, Urban & Community Affairs, Women's Affairs, Zoos/Aquariums

Education: Agricultural Education, Arts/Humanities Education, Business Education, Colleges & Universities, Economic Education, Education Associations, Education Funds, Education Reform, Elementary Education (Private), Engineering/Technological Education, Faculty Development, Education-General, Leadership Training, Literacy, Medical Education, Minority Education, Private Education (Precollege), Public Education (Precollege), Religious Education, Science/Mathematics Education, Social Sciences Education, Student Aid, Vocational & Technical Education

Environment: Environment-General, Resource Conservation

Health: Adolescent Health Issues, Emergency/Ambulance Services, Health-General, Health Policy/Cost Containment, Health Organizations, Hospices, Hospitals, Mental Health, Nutrition, Single-Disease Health Associations

International: International Development, International Peace & Security Issues, International Relations

Religion: Churches, Jewish Causes, Ministries, Religious Welfare

Science: Science Exhibits & Fairs, Science Museums, Scientific Centers & Institutes, Scientific Organizations

Social Services: Animal Protection, Child Abuse, Child Welfare, Community Centers, Community Service Organizations, Counseling, Day Care, Domestic Violence, Emergency Relief, Family Planning, Family Services, Food/Clothing Distribution, People with Disabilities, Recreation & Athletics, Scouts, Senior Services, Substance Abuse, United Funds/United Ways, Volunteer Services, YMCA/YWCA/YMHA/YWHA, Youth Organizations

Application Procedures

Initial Contact: Call or write for application form, then submit written proposal.

Application Requirements: Completed application form; proposal including a description of organization, amount requested, purpose of funds sought; proof of tax-exempt status; list of board members with affiliations; current budget.

Deadlines: None; February 15 for scholarships.

Evaluative Criteria: Broad base of support, affects company service area, annual budget approved by board, board is active and responsible, clear statement of purpose, measurable objectives, nonduplication of services. Each grant must have an internal Duke Energy business "sponsor" and a clear business reason for making the contribution.

Notes: Foundation indicates that most grant money is already dedicated to certain causes or organizations. Almost no funds are available for unsolicited grant applications.

Restrictions

Foundation does not support organizations that discriminate by race, creed, gender, age or national origin; political activities and organizations; individual agencies of the United Way or the Charlotte Arts and Science Council; health or human service agencies, besides the United Way; capital campaigns and endowments, except in extremely rare and specialized situations that relate directly to company's areas of expertise in business; individuals; athletics, including individual sports teams and all-star teams; underwriting of films, video and television productions; reducing the cost of utility service; sectarian or religious activities; conferences, trips, or tours; fraternal, veteran or labor groups serving only their members; advertising; membership fees or association fees. Dinners or tables at fundraisers are rarely considered.

Additional Information

In June of 1997, Duke Power Company and PanEnergy Corporation merged to create Duke Energy Corporation.

Foundation also matches gifts to the Share the Warmth program, a heating bill assistance program, with a maximum corporate contribution of $500,000 annually.

Publications: Application Form

Corporate Officials

Paul M. Anderson: chairman, chief executive officer B 1945. ED University of Vermont BSME (1967); Stanford University Graduate School of Business Administration MBA (1969). PRIM CORP EMPL chairman, chief executive officer: Duke Energy Corp. CORP AFFIL director: MDS Inc.; director: Quantas Airways Ltd.; director: Albany Molecular Research; director: Communications Systems Inc..

Fred J. Fowler: president, chief operating officer ED Oklahoma State University BS (1968). PRIM CORP EMPL president, chief operating officer: Duke Energy Corp. CORP AFFIL director: Duke Energy Field Services.

Richard J. Osborne: group vice president B Gastonia, NC. ED Tufts University BA; University of North Carolina MBA. PRIM CORP EMPL executive vice president: Duke Energy Corp. CORP AFFIL director: Duke Energy Field Services. NONPR AFFIL director: Nuclear Electric Insurance Ltd.; director: United Way of Central Carolinas; trustee: Johnson C. Smith University; director: Museum of the New South; director: Charlotte Symphony; member: Edison Electric Institute.

Ruth G. Shaw: president B February 19, 1948. ED University of Texas PhD. PRIM CORP EMPL group president Duke Power: Duke Energy Corp. CORP AFFIL director: Medcath Corp.; director: Wachovia Corp.

Foundation Officials

Paul M. Anderson: trustee (see above)

Roberta B. Bowman: president ED Tufts University BA. PRIM CORP EMPL senior vice president public affairs, chief communications officer: Duke Energy Corp. NONPR AFFIL trustee: Foundation of the Public Relations Society of America.

Dale Carpenter: treasurer

Micah Cline: assistant secretary

Hilary Davidson: vice president

Bill Easter: trustee

Bobby Evans: trustee

Fred J. Fowler: trustee (see above)

David Hauser: trustee

Jim Mogg: trustee

A. R. Mullinax: trustee

Tom O'Connor: trustee

Richard J. Osborne: chairman, trustee (see above)

Kay Saville: secretary

Ruth G. Shaw: trustee (see above)

Martha Wyrsch: trustee

Grants Analysis

Disclosure Period: calendar year ending 2003
Total Grants: $14,908,663
Number of Grants: 2,000 (approx)
Average Grant: $7,454
Highest Grant: $350,000
Lowest Grant: $100
Typical Range: $1,000 to $20,000

Recent Grants

Note: Grants derived from 2003 Form 990.

General

327,111	Arts & Science Council, Charlotte, NC
299,500	Foundation of the University of North Carolina at Charlotte Inc., Charlotte, NC
290,000	Foundation for the Carolinas Duke Energy Scholars Fund, Charlotte, NC
268,446	North Carolina State University Foundation Inc., Raleigh, NC
110,650	Foundation for the Carolinas, Charlotte, NC
100,000	Clemson University, Clemson, SC
96,500	Houston Symphony Society, Houston, TX
75,000	Georgia Technical Foundation Inc., Atlanta, GA
75,000	National Association for Community Leadership, Indianapolis, IN
70,000	McDowell Technical Community College, Marion, NC

DORIS DUKE FOUNDATION

Giving Contact

Director of Operations and Administration
650 Fifth Avenue, 19th Fl.
New York, NY 10019
Phone: (212)974-7006

Description

Founded: 1934
EIN: 131655241
Organization Type: Private Foundation
Giving Locations: CA; NJ; NY
Grant Types: General Support, Multiyear/Continuing Support.

Donor Information

Founder: the late Doris Duke

Financial Summary

Total Giving: $74,039 (2003)
Assets: $6,516,446 (2003)
Gifts Received: $3 (1994); $10,726,840 (1993); $755,000 (1992)

Typical Recipients

Arts & Humanities: Arts Associations & Councils, Ballet, Dance, Ethnic & Folk Arts, Historic Preservation, History & Archaeology, Libraries, Museums/Galleries

Civic & Public Affairs: Botanical Gardens/Parks, Clubs, Civic & Public Affairs-General, Safety, Women's Affairs, Zoos/Aquariums

Education: Agricultural Education, Arts/Humanities Education, Colleges & Universities, Medical Education, Secondary Education (Private)

Environment: Wildlife Protection

Health: AIDS/HIV, Cancer, Children's Health/Hospitals, Clinics/Medical Centers, Emergency/Ambulance Services, Eyes/Blindness, Hospitals, Medical Research, Single-Disease Health Associations

International: Foreign Arts Organizations, Health Care/Hospitals, Human Rights, International Relief Efforts

Religion: Churches, Dioceses, Religious Organizations, Religious Welfare

Science: Scientific Organizations

Social Services: Animal Protection, At-Risk Youth, Child Welfare, Community Service Organizations, Crime Prevention, Delinquency & Criminal Rehabilitation, People with Disabilities, Recreation & Athletics, Senior Services, Social Services-General, United Funds/United Ways, YMCA/YWCA/YMHA/YWHA, Youth Organizations

Application Procedures

Initial Contact: Submit a proposal in letter form.
Application Requirements: The foundation has no prescribed proposal format.
Deadlines: None.

Grants Analysis

Disclosure Period: calendar year ending 2003
Total Grants: $74,039
Number of Grants: 7
Highest Grant: $20,000
Lowest Grant: $466
Typical Range: $1,000 to $10,000

Recent Grants

Note: Grants derived from 2003 Form 990.
General

20,000	Colonial Williamsburg, Williamsburg, VA
13,584	Robert Hull - Fleming Museum, Burlington, VT -- for artwork
12,500	John N Brown, Providence, RI
10,000	Diocese of Rockville Center, Rockville, NY
10,000	Phillips Collection, Washington, DC
7,489	Los Angeles County Museum of Art, Los Angeles, CA -- for artwork
466	Newark Museum, Newark, NJ

CALEB C. AND JULIA W. DULA EDUCATIONAL AND CHARITABLE FOUNDATION

Giving Contact

James F. Mauze, General Counsel
112 South Hanley Road, 2nd Floor
St. Louis, MO 63105-3418
Phone: (314)726-2800
Fax: (314)863-3821

Description

Founded: 1939
EIN: 431716767
Organization Type: General Purpose Foundation
Giving Locations: MO; NY
Grant Types: Operating Expenses.

Donor Information

Founder: Established in 1939 by the late Julia W. Dula.

Financial Summary

Total Giving: $1,836,000 (2002)
Assets: $35,122,269 (2002)

Typical Recipients

Arts & Humanities: Arts Associations & Councils, Arts Centers, Arts Funds, Arts Outreach, Dance, Film & Video, Historic Preservation, History & Archaeology, Libraries, Museums/Galleries, Music, Opera, Performing Arts, Public Broadcasting, Theater
Civic & Public Affairs: Botanical Gardens/Parks, Business/Free Enterprise, Clubs, First Amendment Issues, Civic & Public Affairs-General, Parades/Festivals, Public Policy, Urban & Community Affairs, Zoos/Aquariums
Education: Afterschool/Enrichment Programs, Agricultural Education, Arts/Humanities Education, Colleges & Universities, Education-General, Health & Physical Education, Medical Education, Private Education (Precollege), Secondary Education (Public), Special Education, Student Aid
Environment: Environment-General, Protection, Resource Conservation, Wildlife Protection
Health: Adolescent Health Issues, Alzheimer's Disease, Cancer, Children's Health/Hospitals, Clinics/Medical Centers, Diabetes, Emergency/Ambulance Services, Health Organizations, Hospitals, Nursing Services, Preventive Medicine/Wellness Organizations, Single-Disease Health Associations
Religion: Churches, Missionary Activities (Domestic), Religious Organizations, Religious Welfare
Science: Science Museums, Scientific Centers & Institutes
Social Services: Animal Protection, At-Risk Youth, Camps, Child Welfare, Community Service Organizations, Crime Prevention, Day Care, Delinquency & Criminal Rehabilitation, Family Planning, Family Services, Food/Clothing Distribution, People with Disabilities, Scouts, Senior Services, Shelters/Homelessness, Social Services-General, United Funds/United Ways, Youth Organizations

Application Procedures

Initial Contact: The foundation has no formal grant application procedure or application form.
Deadlines: Proposals must be sent to the trustees by April 1 for the Spring meeting and by October 1 for the Fall meeting.
Review Process: The trustees generally meet four times a year to consider the distribution of funds.

Restrictions

Grants are made only to tax-exempt organizations. The foundation does not support individuals or make loans.

Foundation Officials

Margaret C. Gunter: trustee
Margaret W. Kobusch: trustee
Orrin S. Wightman, III: trustee

Grants Analysis

Disclosure Period: calendar year ending 2002
Total Grants: $1,836,000
Number of Grants: 96
Average Grant: $19,125
Highest Grant: $105,000
Lowest Grant: $5,000
Typical Range: $5,000 to $35,000

Recent Grants

Note: Grants derived from 2002 Form 990.
General

105,000	World Dance Arts Foundation, Bradenton, FL
100,000	Whitfield School, St. Louis, MO
100,000	Williams College, Hanover, NH
75,000	Center of Contemporary Arts, University City, MO
75,000	Eaglebrook School, Deerfield, MA
75,000	Stages St. Louis, St. Louis, MO
55,000	Film Arts Foundation, San Francisco, CA
55,000	Northern Michigan Hospital Foundation, Petoskey, MI
50,000	Long Meadow Rescue Ranch, St. Louis, MO
50,000	Missouri Botanical Garden, St. Louis, MO

DUNAGAN FOUNDATION

Giving Contact

Kathlyn C. Dunagan, President
PO Box 387
Monahans, TX 79756
Phone: (432)943-2571

Description

Founded: 1976
EIN: 751561848
Organization Type: Private Foundation
Giving Locations: TX

Grant Types: General Support, Professorship, Project, Scholarship.

Donor Information

Founder: J. Conrad Dunagan, Kathlyn C. Dunagan, John C. Dunagan

Financial Summary

Total Giving: $164,700 (2003); $236,775 (2002); $305,429 (2001)
Assets: $4,251,842 (2003); $4,056,284 (2002); $4,344,820 (2001)
Gifts Received: $2,750 (2003); $1,000 (2002); $7,375 (2001). Note: In 1999, 2000, 2001, and 2002, contributions were received from William C. Dunagan. In 1998, contributions were received from Deanna Dunagan ($212,938), John Charles Dunagan ($58,375), William C. Dunagan ($7,882), and Kathleen Dunagan ($115,786). In 1996, contributions were received from Deanna Dunagan ($5,000), John Charles Dunagan ($5,000), Carol Husbands ($500), and Kathleen Dunagan ($500).

Typical Recipients

Arts & Humanities: Arts Centers, Arts & Humanities-General, Historic Preservation, History & Archaeology, Libraries, Literary Arts, Museums/Galleries, Public Broadcasting, Theater
Civic & Public Affairs: Botanical Gardens/Parks, Community Foundations, Employment/Job Training, Civic & Public Affairs-General, Housing
Education: Business Education, Colleges & Universities, Education Funds, Education-General, Legal Education, Medical Education, Private Education (Precollege), Public Education (Precollege), Student Aid
Environment: Air/Water Quality, Environment-General, Resource Conservation, Wildlife Protection
Health: AIDS/HIV, Cancer, Children's Health/Hospitals, Clinics/Medical Centers, Health Funds, Hospices, Hospitals, Hospitals (University Affiliated), Medical Research, Mental Health, Public Health, Research/Studies Institutes, Single-Disease Health Associations
International: Health Care/Hospitals, International Peace & Security Issues
Religion: Churches, Dioceses, Religious Organizations, Religious Welfare
Science: Science Museums, Scientific Centers & Institutes
Social Services: Child Welfare, Community Service Organizations, Counseling, Family Planning, Family Services, Scouts, United Funds/United Ways, Veterans, Youth Organizations

Application Procedures

Initial Contact: Send a brief letter of inquiry.
Application Requirements: Include a description of organization, purpose of funds sought, latest budget information, latest financial statement, and proof of tax-exempt status.
Deadlines: None.

Restrictions

Foundation makes contributions to organizations with exempt certification from the IRS.

Foundation Officials

John C. Dunagan: vice president
Kathleen Dunagan: secretary
Kathlyn C. Dunagan: president
Rena Shelton: assistant secretary

Grants Analysis

Disclosure Period: calendar year ending 2003
Total Grants: $164,700
Number of Grants: 27
Average Grant: $4,988*
Highest Grant: $20,000
Lowest Grant: $250
Typical Range: $1,000 to $10,000

*Note: Average grant figure excludes two highest grants ($40,000).

Recent Grants

Note: Grants derived from 2001 Form 990.
General

60,000	University of Texas of the Permian Basin, Odessa, TX -- to support educational activities
40,000	Lawrenceville School, Lawrenceville, NJ -- support educational activities
35,000	Boys and Girls Club of Monahans, Monahans, TX -- to support charitable activities
21,000	Mary Institute and St. Louis Country Day School, St. Louis, MO -- to support educational activities
20,000	Dana-Farber Cancer Institute, Boston, MA -- to support medical activities
20,000	Green Farms Academy, Farm, CT -- to support educational activities
11,110	Permian Historical Society, Midland, TX -- to support literary activities
11,000	Parks and Wildlife Foundation, Dallas, TX -- to support parks and wildlife activities
10,000	Buffalo Trail Council of Boy Scouts, Midland, TX -- support charitable activities
10,000	KOCV-TV, Odessa, TX -- to support literacy activities

L. H. AND C. W. DUNCAN FOUNDATION

Giving Contact

Karla Siemens
Salient Partners
4265 San Felipe, Suite 900
Houston, TX 77027
Phone: (713)993-4679

Description

Founded: 1964
EIN: 746064215
Organization Type: Private Foundation
Giving Locations: TX
Grant Types: General Support.

Donor Information

Founder: the late C. W. Duncan

Financial Summary

Total Giving: $293,800 (fiscal year ending September 30, 2004); $500,600 (fiscal 2001)
Giving Analysis: Giving for fiscal 2004 includes: foundation grants to United Way ($22,000)
Assets: $6,768,176 (fiscal 2004); $7,041,776 (fiscal 2001)
Gifts Received: $496,006 (fiscal 2000). Note: In 2000, contributions were received from Lillian H. Duncan CRAT.

Typical Recipients

Arts & Humanities: Ballet, Ethnic & Folk Arts, Film & Video, Arts & Humanities-General, Historic Preservation, Libraries, Museums/Galleries, Music, Performing Arts, Theater
Civic & Public Affairs: Botanical Gardens/Parks, Community Foundations, Civic & Public Affairs-General, Hispanic Affairs, Housing, Municipalities/Towns, Public Policy, Urban & Community Affairs, Zoos/Aquariums
Education: Arts/Humanities Education, Business Education, Colleges & Universities, Education Associations, Education Reform, Elementary Education (Private), Medical Education, Preschool Education, Private Education (Precollege), Public Education (Precollege), School Volunteerism, Science/Mathematics Education, Special Education

Environment: Resource Conservation, Wildlife Protection
Health: AIDS/HIV, Cancer, Children's Health/Hospitals, Clinics/Medical Centers, Eyes/Blindness, Health-General, Geriatric Health, Heart, Hospices, Hospitals, Hospitals (University Affiliated), Long-Term Care, Medical Research, Multiple Sclerosis, Prenatal Health Issues, Speech & Hearing
International: International Affairs
Religion: Churches, Dioceses, Jewish Causes, Ministries, Missionary Activities (Domestic), Religious Organizations, Religious Welfare
Science: Science Museums
Social Services: Child Welfare, Community Service Organizations, People with Disabilities, Recreation & Athletics, Substance Abuse, United Funds/United Ways, Volunteer Services, YMCA/YWCA/YMHA/YWHA, Youth Organizations

Application Procedures

Initial Contact: Submit a brief letter of inquiry.
Application Requirements: Include a description of organization, amount requested, purpose of funds sought, proof of tax-exempt status.
Deadlines: None.

Foundation Officials

C. W. Duncan, III: vice president, director
Charles William Duncan, Jr.: chairman, director B Houston, TX 1926. ED Rice University BSChE (1947); University of Texas (1948-1949). CORP AFFIL director: United Technologies Inc.; director: American Express Co.; director: Newfield Exploration Co. NONPR AFFIL member: Sigma Alpha Epsilon; member: Sigma Iota Epsilon; trustee emeritus: Rice University; member: Council Foreign Relations. CLUB AFFIL River Oaks Country Club; Allegro Club; Houston Country Club.
John H. Duncan, Jr.: vice president, director
John H. Duncan, Sr.: president, director B Houston, TX 1928. ED University of Texas BBA (1949). CORP AFFIL director: Texas Commerce Bancshares; director: Mosher Inc.; director: Proler International Corp.; director: Group 1 Automotive; director: King Ranch Inc. NONPR AFFIL member: Sigma Alpha Epsilon. CLUB AFFIL Houston Country Club; River Oaks Country Club.
Robert J. Faust: secretary, treasurer

Grants Analysis

Disclosure Period: fiscal year ending September 30, 2004
Total Grants: $271,800*
Number of Grants: 31
Average Grant: $7,393*
Highest Grant: $50,000
Lowest Grant: $1,000
Typical Range: $5,000 to $10,000
*Note: Giving excludes United Way. Average grant figure excludes highest grant.

Recent Grants

Note: Grants derived from fiscal 2004 Form 990.

General

50,000	Rise School, Houston, TX
25,000	DePelchin, Houston, TX
20,000	Kincaid School, Houston, TX
20,000	Rise School, Houston, TX
20,000	Texas Heart Institute, Houston, TX
20,000	United Way of the Texas Gulf Coast, Houston, TX
10,000	Communities in Schools, Houston, TX
10,000	Communities in Schools, Houston, TX
10,000	Museum of Fine Arts, Houston, TX
10,000	Rise School, Houston, TX

JOHN G. DUNCAN TRUST

Giving Contact

Yvonne Baca, Trust Officer
c/o Wells Fargo Bank
PO Box 5825
Denver, CO 80217
Phone: (303)392-5324

Description

Founded: 1955
EIN: 846016555
Organization Type: Private Foundation
Giving Locations: CO
Grant Types: General Support.

Donor Information

Founder: the late John G. Duncan

Financial Summary

Total Giving: $341,449 (2003); $445,600 (2002); $399,669 (2001)
Giving Analysis: Giving for 2003 includes: foundation grants to United Way ($2,000)
Assets: $6,813,540 (2003); $6,420,041 (2002); $7,261,244 (2001)

Typical Recipients

Arts & Humanities: Arts Centers, Arts Outreach, History & Archaeology, Libraries, Museums/Galleries, Music, Opera, Performing Arts, Public Broadcasting, Theater
Civic & Public Affairs: African American Affairs, Botanical Gardens/Parks, Clubs, Community Foundations, Employment/Job Training, Civic & Public Affairs-General, Hispanic Affairs, Housing, Legal Aid, Native American Affairs, Urban & Community Affairs, Women's Affairs, Zoos/Aquariums
Education: Afterschool/Enrichment Programs, Colleges & Universities, Continuing Education, Elementary Education (Private), Education-General, Minority Education, Preschool Education, Private Education (Precollege), Science/Mathematics Education
Environment: Forestry
Health: Alzheimer's Disease, Cancer, Children's Health/Hospitals, Clinics/Medical Centers, Emergency/Ambulance Services, Geriatric Health, Health Organizations, Heart, Home-Care Services, Hospices, Hospitals, Long-Term Care, Medical Rehabilitation, Medical Research, Public Health, Respiratory, Single-Disease Health Associations, Speech & Hearing, Transplant Networks/Donor Banks
International: Health Care/Hospitals, International Organizations, International Peace & Security Issues, International Relief Efforts
Religion: Jewish Causes, Religious Organizations, Religious Welfare, Synagogues/Temples
Social Services: Animal Protection, At-Risk Youth, Big Brothers/Big Sisters, Child Welfare, Community Centers, Community Service Organizations, Crime Prevention, Domestic Violence, Emergency Relief, Family Services, Food/Clothing Distribution, Homes, People with Disabilities, Recreation & Athletics, Scouts, Senior Services, Shelters/Homelessness, Special Olympics, Substance Abuse, Volunteer Services, Youth Organizations

Application Procedures

Initial Contact: The foundation requests applications be made in writing.
Deadlines: None.

Additional Information

Publications: Application Guidelines
Trust(s): Wells Fargo Bank

Grants Analysis

Disclosure Period: calendar year ending 2003
Total Grants: $339,449*
Number of Grants: 99

Average Grant: $3,429
Highest Grant: $10,000
Lowest Grant: $1,000
Typical Range: $1,000 to $5,000
*Note: Giving excludes United Way.

Recent Grants

Note: Grants derived from 2001 Form 990.
General

24,535	Denver Museum of Nature and Science, Denver, CO
18,000	Youth Biz, Inc., Denver, CO
14,715	Children's Hospital Foundation
10,418	National Center for Children, Families and Communities
10,000	American Red Cross, Atchison, KS
10,000	Boys and Girls Club of Pueblo County, Inc, Pueblo, CO
10,000	Denver Botanical Gardens, Denver, CO
10,000	Denver Summerbridge, Denver, CO
10,000	Kids In Need of Dentistry, Denver, CO
10,000	St. Francis Center, Denver, CO

LOUISE HEAD DUNCAN TRUST

Giving Contact

David Wolfe, Trust Officer
PO Box 248
La Grange, KY 40031
Phone: (606)231-2428
Fax: (606)231-2694

Alternate Contact

Bank One Trust Co.
PO Box 1308
Milwaukee, WI 53201
Phone: (414)765-2017

Description

Founded: 1991
EIN: 616183556
Organization Type: Private Foundation
Giving Locations: KY: Oldham County
Grant Types: General Support.

Donor Information

Founder: Established in 1991 by the late Louise Head Duncan.

Financial Summary

Total Giving: $455,488 (2001)
Assets: $8,465,627 (2001)
Gifts Received: $683,651 (1992). Note: In 1992, contributions were received from the estate of Louise Duncan.

Typical Recipients

Arts & Humanities: History & Archaeology, Libraries, Performing Arts
Civic & Public Affairs: African American Affairs, Botanical Gardens/Parks, Employment/Job Training, Civic & Public Affairs-General, Housing, Law & Justice, Municipalities/Towns, Safety, Urban & Community Affairs, Women's Affairs
Education: Afterschool/Enrichment Programs, Arts/Humanities Education, Business Education, Elementary Education (Public), Education-General, Private Education (Precollege), Public Education (Precollege)
Environment: Environment-General, Wildlife Protection
Health: Emergency/Ambulance Services, Health Organizations
Religion: Churches, Religion-General, Religious Organizations
Social Services: Big Brothers/Big Sisters, Child Welfare, Community Centers, Community Service Organizations, Family Services, People with Disabilities, Recreation & Athletics, Scouts, Shelters/Homelessness, Social Services-General, YMCA/YWCA/YMHA/YWHA, Youth Organizations

Application Procedures

Initial Contact: Send letter to the foundation requesting application form and guidelines.

Restrictions

Grants limited to 501(c)(3) organizations benefiting residents of Oldham County, Kentucky.

Additional Information

Publications: Application Form
Trust(s): Bank One Trust Company NA

Foundation Officials

Thomas W. Gaines, Jr.: adv comm
J. W. Hall, Jr.: adv comm
Rose Ethel Hall: adv comm
John F. Payne: adv comm

Grants Analysis

Disclosure Period: calendar year ending 2001
Total Grants: $455,488
Number of Grants: 22
Average Grant: $12,024*
Highest Grant: $115,000
Lowest Grant: $2,225
Typical Range: $5,000 to $25,000
*Note: Average grant figure excludes two highest grants ($215,000).

Recent Grants

Note: Grants derived from 2001 Form 990.
General

115,000	Oldham County Historical Society, Inc., Prospect, KY
100,000	Oldham County Family YMCA, La-Grange, KY
50,000	Yew Dell, Inc., Crestwood, KY
28,000	Center For Women in Crisis, LaGrange, KY
25,000	City of La Grange, La Grange, GA
25,000	Greenways for Oldham County, Inc., Crestwood, PA
18,000	Applepatch Community, Crestwood, KY
10,000	First Baptist Church of LaGrange, La-Grange, KY
10,000	Oldham Little League, LaGrange, KY
8,100	Ballardsville Fire Protection Dist., Crestwood, KY

DUNKIN' DONUTS INC.

Company Headquarters

Randolph, MA 02368
Web: http://www.dunkindonuts.com

Company Description

Founded: 1950
Acquired: Mister Donut (1990).
Employees: 1345
SIC(s): 2024 Ice Cream & Frozen Desserts, 5812 Eating Places, 6794 Patent Owners & Lessors.

Operating Locations

Dunkin' Ventures Corp. (MA--Randolph); Mister Donut of America (MA--Randolph); Wine Alliance (CA--Healdsburg)

Nonmonetary Support

Type: Donated Equipment; Donated Products; In-kind Services

Giving Contact

Attn: Dunkin Donuts
15 Pacella Dr.
PO Box 317
Randolph, MA 02368
Phone: (781)961-4020
Fax: (781)986-7490

Description

Organization Type: Corporate Giving Program
Grant Types: General Support.

Financial Summary

Total Giving: Company does not disclose contributions figures.

Typical Recipients

Arts & Humanities: Libraries
Education: Education-General
Health: Alzheimer's Disease, Children's Health/Hospitals, Diabetes, Heart
Social Services: At-Risk Youth, Child Welfare, Shelters/Homelessness, Volunteer Services

Application Procedures

Initial Contact: Send a letter of inquiry and brief proposal.

Additional Information

Company reported in June 1998 that Allied Domecq Plc merged three of its U.S. subsidiaries, Baskin-Robbins, Dunkin' Donuts, and Togo's, into one entity, Allied Domecq Retailing U.S.A.

Corporate Officials

Stephen Alexander: chief executive
Tony Hales: chairman
Sir Christopher Anthony Hogg: chairman B London, United Kingdom 1936. ED Oxford University Trinity College BA (1960); Harvard University MBA (1962). PRIM CORP EMPL chairman: Allied Domecq PLC. NONPR AFFIL chairman: Royal National Theatre.
Kim Lopdrup: board member
Jack Shafer: board member
John (Jack) D. Shafer: president PRIM CORP EMPL president: Allied Domecq Retailing U.S.A.

DUNSPAUGH-DALTON FOUNDATION

Giving Contact

William A. Lane, Jr., President
Dunspaugh Dalton Foundation, Inc.
1533 Sunset Drive, Suite 150
Coral Gables, FL 33143
Phone: (305)668-4192
Fax: (305)361-2818

Description

Founded: 1963
EIN: 591055300
Organization Type: General Purpose Foundation
Giving Locations: CA; FL: Dade County; NC nationally.
Grant Types: Capital, Endowment, General Support, Multiyear/Continuing Support, Project, Research.

Donor Information

Founder: The will of Ann V. Dalton created the Dunspaugh-Dalton Foundation in 1963.

Financial Summary

Total Giving: $2,188,867 (2002); $1,741,500 (2001)
Giving Analysis: Giving for 2001 includes: foundation scholarships ($40,000)
Assets: $31,565,609 (2002); $46,473,590 (2001)

Typical Recipients

Arts & Humanities: Arts Associations & Councils, Arts Centers, Arts Festivals, Arts Outreach, Ballet, Community Arts, Dance, Historic Preservation, History & Archaeology, Museums/Galleries, Music, Performing Arts, Public Broadcasting, Theater

Civic & Public Affairs: Botanical Gardens/Parks, Civil Rights, Clubs, Civic & Public Affairs-General, Housing, Law & Justice, Legal Aid, Parades/Festivals, Public Policy, Safety, Urban & Community Affairs, Zoos/Aquariums

Education: Afterschool/Enrichment Programs, Arts/Humanities Education, Colleges & Universities, Education Funds, Elementary Education (Public), Engineering/Technological Education, Faculty Development, Education-General, Health & Physical Education, International Studies, Legal Education, Medical Education, Minority Education, Private Education (Precollege), Public Education (Precollege), Social Sciences Education, Special Education

Environment: Environment-General, Resource Conservation

Health: Alzheimer's Disease, Cancer, Children's Health/Hospitals, Clinics/Medical Centers, Emergency/Ambulance Services, Geriatric Health, Health Funds, Health Organizations, Hospices, Hospitals, Hospitals (University Affiliated), Long-Term Care, Medical Rehabilitation, Medical Research, Mental Health, Nursing Services, Research/Studies Institutes, Single-Disease Health Associations, Speech & Hearing, Transplant Networks/Donor Banks, Trauma Treatment

International: Foreign Educational Institutions

Religion: Churches, Jewish Causes, Ministries, Missionary Activities (Domestic), Religious Organizations, Religious Welfare

Science: Observatories & Planetariums

Social Services: At-Risk Youth, Big Brothers/Big Sisters, Camps, Child Welfare, Community Centers, Community Service Organizations, Counseling, Emergency Relief, Family Planning, Family Services, Food/Clothing Distribution, Homes, People with Disabilities, Recreation & Athletics, Scouts, Senior Services, Sexual Abuse, Shelters/Homelessness, Social Services-General, Special Olympics, Substance Abuse, United Funds/United Ways, YMCA/YWCA/YMHA/YWHA, Youth Organizations

Application Procedures

Initial Contact: The foundation has no formal guidelines for application. Prospective grantees should submit a letter of inquiry.

Application Requirements: Letters of inquiry should provide the organization's name and address, project name, and IRS exemption number.

Deadlines: None.

Restrictions

Grants restricted to United States and its territories, for religious, educational, or scientific purposes.

Additional Information

Publications: Annual Report

Foundation Officials

Sarah H. Bonner: vice president, trustee

William A. Lane, Jr.: president, trustee B 1954. PRIM CORP EMPL president, director: Lane Winpak Inc.

Thomas H. Wakefield: secretary, treasurer, trustee

Grants Analysis

Disclosure Period: calendar year ending 2002

Total Grants: $2,188,867

Number of Grants: 82

Average Grant: $21,736*

Highest Grant: $250,000

Lowest Grant: $238

Typical Range: $5,000 to $50,000

*Note: Average grant figure excludes two highest grants ($450,000).

Recent Grants

Note: Grants derived from 2002 Form 990.

General

500,000	Duke University, Carlsbad, CA -- towards the department of athletics
324,000	Barry University, Miami Shores, FL
200,000	Barry University, Miami Shores, FL -- towards a new commitment in this year for dollars
100,000	Carmel by the Sea Sunset Center for the Arts, Carmel, CA
65,000	Palmar Trinity School, Miami, FL
60,000	Close Up Foundation, Alexandria, VA
55,000	Santa Catalina School, Monterey, CA
45,000	American Red Cross, Washington, DC
35,000	Monterey Bay Aquarium Foundation, Monterey Bay, CA
35,000	Stanford University Medical Center, Stanford, CA

ALFRED I. DUPONT FOUNDATION

Giving Contact

Rosemary C. Wills, Director
4600 Touchton Rd. East, Bldg. 200, Suite 120
Jacksonville, FL 32246
Phone: (904)232-4123

Description

Founded: 1936

EIN: 591297267

Organization Type: General Purpose Foundation

Giving Locations: FL; southeastern United States.

Grant Types: Emergency, General Support.

Donor Information

Founder: The foundation was incorporated in 1936 by the late Jessie Dew Ball duPont.

Financial Summary

Total Giving: $1,376,640 (2001)

Giving Analysis: Giving for 2001 includes: foundation gifts to individuals ($442,524)

Assets: $34,267,614 (2001)

Typical Recipients

Arts & Humanities: Arts Associations & Councils, Historic Preservation, History & Archaeology, Libraries, Museums/Galleries, Music, Theater

Civic & Public Affairs: Economic Policy, Employment/Job Training, Civic & Public Affairs-General, Law & Justice, Philanthropic Organizations, Professional & Trade Associations, Public Policy, Zoos/Aquariums

Education: Afterschool/Enrichment Programs, Agricultural Education, Colleges & Universities, Community & Junior Colleges, Continuing Education, Education Funds, Education-General, Medical Education, Minority Education, Private Education (Precollege), Religious Education, Science/Mathematics Education, Special Education, Student Aid

Environment: Environment-General

Health: Alzheimer's Disease, Arthritis, Children's Health/Hospitals, Clinics/Medical Centers, Emergency/Ambulance Services, Health Organizations, Hospices, Long-Term Care, Medical Rehabilitation, Multiple Sclerosis, Nursing Services, Preventive Medicine/Wellness Organizations, Public Health, Single-Disease Health Associations

International: Foreign Educational Institutions, Health Care/Hospitals

Religion: Churches, Ministries, Religious Organizations, Religious Welfare

Science: Science Museums

Social Services: At-Risk Youth, Camps, Child Abuse, Child Welfare, Community Service Organizations, Emergency Relief, Food/Clothing Distribution, Homes, People with Disabilities, Senior Services, Shelters/Homelessness, Social Services-General, United Funds/United Ways, YMCA/YWCA/YMHA/YWHA, Youth Organizations

Application Procedures

Initial Contact: The foundation reports that requests should be made for a formal application form.

Application Requirements: Grants are given to individuals and charitable organizations. Individual grants are generally limited to elderly individuals residing in the southeastern U.S. who are in distressed economic situations.

Deadlines: None.

Review Process: After receiving request, forms are mailed to the applicant.

Restrictions

The foundation reports that individual grants are generally limited to elderly individuals residing in the southeastern United States who are in distressed economic situations.

Foundation Officials

Edward Carter Brownlie: assistant secretary, assistant treasurer B Birmingham, AL 1937. ED Samford University (1963). PRIM CORP EMPL vice president administration: St Joe Paper Co. CORP AFFIL vice president, director: Saint Joseph Land & Development Co.; director: Saint Joseph Tel & Tel Co.

Lillie S. Land: secretary, director

Robert E. Nedley: president B 1938. PRIM CORP EMPL president, chief operating officer, director: St Joe Paper Co. CORP AFFIL president: Saint Joe Industries Inc.; vice president, director: Saint Joseph Tel & Tel Co.

Rosemary C. Wills: assistant secretary, assistant treasurer

Grants Analysis

Disclosure Period: calendar year ending 2001

Total Grants: $934,115*

Number of Grants: 119

Average Grant: $7,000

Highest Grant: $75,000

Lowest Grant: $250

Typical Range: $1,000 to $10,000

*Note: Giving excludes gifts to individuals.

Recent Grants

Note: Grants derived from 2002 Form 990.

General

75,000	Maclay School, Tallahassee, FL
52,000	North Carolina State University, Raleigh, NC -- for pulp & paper foundation
50,000	Chipola Junior College, Marianna, FL
50,000	Gulf Coast Community College Foundation, Panama City, FL
36,000	Stetson University, Deland, FL
35,000	Flagler College, St. Augustine, FL
25,000	Cumberland College, Williamsburg, KY
20,000	BETA Inc., Santa Barbara, CA
20,000	Florida 4-H Foundation, Gainesville, FL -- for North West/North East County camps
20,000	Southern Scholarship Foundation Inc., Tallahassee, FL

CHICHESTER DUPONT FOUNDATION

Giving Contact

Gregory F. Fields, Secretary
3120 Kennett Pike
Wilmington, DE 19807
Phone: (302)658-5244
Fax: (302)658-5091

Description

Founded: 1946
EIN: 516011641
Organization Type: Family Foundation
Giving Locations: mid-Atlantic United States; northeastern United States.
Grant Types: Capital, Endowment, General Support, Operating Expenses.

Donor Information

Founder: The foundation was incorporated in 1946 by A. Felix duPont Jr., Alice duPont Mills, the late Lydia Chichester duPont, and the late Mary Chichester duPont Clark.

Financial Summary

Total Giving: $2,600,000 (2003); $2,600,000 (2002); $3,000,000 (2001)
Assets: $51,983,186 (2003); $47,245,480 (2002); $53,831,614 (2001)

Typical Recipients

Arts & Humanities: Arts Associations & Councils, Arts Centers, Arts Festivals, Arts Funds, Arts Institutes, Ballet, Community Arts, Historic Preservation, History & Archaeology, Libraries, Museums/Galleries, Music, Opera, Performing Arts, Theater
Civic & Public Affairs: Botanical Gardens/Parks, Civil Rights, Economic Development, Employment/Job Training, Civic & Public Affairs-General, Housing, Inner-City Development, Municipalities/Towns, Rural Affairs, Safety, Urban & Community Affairs, Zoos/Aquariums
Education: Business Education, Colleges & Universities, Community & Junior Colleges, Education Funds, Environmental Education, Education-General, Literacy, Medical Education, Preschool Education, Private Education (Precollege), Public Education (Precollege), Science/Mathematics Education, Secondary Education (Private), Secondary Education (Public), Special Education, Student Aid
Environment: Air/Water Quality, Forestry, Environment-General, Protection, Research, Resource Conservation, Watershed, Wildlife Protection
Health: Arthritis, Cancer, Children's Health/Hospitals, Clinics/Medical Centers, Emergency/Ambulance Services, Health Funds, Health Organizations, Heart, Hospices, Hospitals, Long-Term Care, Medical Rehabilitation, Medical Research, Mental Health, Nursing Services, Prenatal Health Issues, Preventive Medicine/Wellness Organizations, Public Health, Research/Studies Institutes, Single-Disease Health Associations
Religion: Churches, Religion-General, Ministries, Religious Welfare
Science: Science Museums
Social Services: Animal Protection, Camps, Child Abuse, Child Welfare, Community Centers, Community Service Organizations, Counseling, Crime Prevention, Day Care, Family Planning, Food/Clothing Distribution, Homes, People with Disabilities, Recreation & Athletics, Senior Services, Sexual Abuse, Shelters/Homelessness, Social Services-General, Special Olympics, Substance Abuse, United Funds/United Ways, YMCA/YWCA/YMHA/YWHA, Youth Organizations

Application Procedures

Initial Contact: The foundation has no formal grant application procedure or application form. Applicants should provide a complete statement of the grant request.
Deadlines: October 1.

Restrictions

Grants are not made to individuals.

Foundation Officials

Lynne L. Dorsey: trustee
Christopher T. du Pont: treasurer, trustee
Allaire duPont: trustee

Gregory F. Fields: secretary, trustee
Alexis duPont Gahagan: trustee
Katharine G. Gahagan: president, trustee
Sophie Mills: trustee
Caroline J. du Pont Prickett: vice president, trustee B 1942. PRIM CORP EMPL chairman, director: Summit Aviation Inc.
Mary Mills Abel Smith: trustee
Phyllis Mills Wyeth: trustee NONPR AFFIL trustee: National Trust Historic Preservation.

Grants Analysis

Disclosure Period: calendar year ending 2003
Total Grants: $2,600,000
Number of Grants: 49
Average Grant: $45,615*
Highest Grant: $410,500
Lowest Grant: $5,000
Typical Range: $10,000 to $100,000
***Note:** Average grant figure excludes highest grant.

Recent Grants

Note: Grants derived from 2002 Form 990.
General

515,000	children's Beach House, Wilmington, DE -- towards annual operating budget and maintenance repair and replacement fund and for the search of a new executive director
150,000	Community School, Sun Valley, ID -- costs incurred due to construction of the elementary school at the Sagewillow campus
150,000	St. Andrews School, Middletown, DE -- towards the arts center building
100,000	Easter Seals, New Castle, DE -- towards community based early intervention program
100,000	Herring Gut, Port Clyde, ME -- towards building of a new center
90,000	Poplar Forest, Forest, VA -- towards preservation
75,000	Chesapeake Bay Foundation, Annapolis, MD -- towards the initiative of heart of the Chesapeake
75,000	University of Pennsylvania, Philadelphia, PA -- towards conversion of radiology department
65,000	University of Delaware Early Learning Center, Newark, DE -- towards establishing the early learning center
60,000	Meadowood Special Education Art Therapy Express Program, Newark, DE -- towards the art therapy express program

DYNAMET INC.

Company Headquarters

195 Museum Rd.
Washington, PA 15301
Phone: 800-237-9655
Web: http://www.dynamet.com

Company Description

Founded: 1967
Employees: 290
SIC(s): 3356 Nonferrous Rolling & Drawing Nec, 3463 Nonferrous Forgings, 3599 Industrial Machinery Nec.
Parent Company: Carpenter Technology Corp., 1047 North Park Road, Wyomissing, PA, United States

Operating Locations

Dynamet, Inc. (PA--Washington)

Giving Contact

Lisa McGregor, Director of Communications
101 West Burn Street
Reading, PA 19601
Phone: (610)208-2000
Fax: (610)736-6232

Alternate Contact

Phone: (610)208-3479

Description

Organization Type: Corporate Giving Program
Giving Locations: PA: Pittsburgh
Grant Types: General Support.

Financial Summary

Total Giving: Contributes through corporate direct giving program only. Foundation dissolved in 1997.
Gifts Received: $7,304,979 (1997); $1,172,500 (1996); $500,000 (1993). Note: Contributions received from Dynamet, Inc.

Typical Recipients

Arts & Humanities: Arts Centers, Arts Funds, Arts Institutes, Ballet, Film & Video, Historic Preservation, History & Archaeology, Libraries, Museums/Galleries, Music, Opera, Performing Arts, Public Broadcasting, Theater
Civic & Public Affairs: Economic Development, Employment/Job Training, Housing, Parades/Festivals, Philanthropic Organizations, Public Policy, Urban & Community Affairs, Zoos/Aquariums
Education: Colleges & Universities, Economic Education, Education Reform, Engineering/Technological Education, Education-General, Preschool Education, Religious Education, Science/Mathematics Education, Secondary Education (Public), Special Education
Environment: Resource Conservation
Health: Cancer, Children's Health/Hospitals, Clinics/Medical Centers, Diabetes, Emergency/Ambulance Services, Eyes/Blindness, Health Organizations, Hospices, Hospitals, Kidney, Medical Rehabilitation, Medical Research, Mental Health, Single-Disease Health Associations
International: Health Care/Hospitals, International Affairs, International Organizations, International Relations
Religion: Religious Organizations, Religious Welfare, Seminaries
Science: Scientific Centers & Institutes, Scientific Organizations, Scientific Research
Social Services: Camps, Child Welfare, Community Centers, Community Service Organizations, Food/Clothing Distribution, Homes, People with Disabilities, Recreation & Athletics, Scouts, Senior Services, Shelters/Homelessness, Special Olympics, Substance Abuse, United Funds/United Ways, Volunteer Services, YMCA/YWCA/YMHA/YWHA, Youth Organizations

Application Procedures

Initial Contact: Contact co.

Additional Information

Foundation has recently dissolved; contact company for direct giving.

Corporate Officials

Alan Rossin: materials director PRIM CORP EMPL materials director: Dynamet Inc.

Grants Analysis

Disclosure Period: calendar year ending 1998
Total Grants: $775,640*
Number of Grants: 50
Average Grant: $15,513
Highest Grant: $250,000
Typical Range: $1,000 to $50,000
***Note:** Giving excludes United Way.

Recent Grants
Note: Grants derived from 1998 Form 990.
Library-Related

| 10,000 | Carnegie Institute, Pittsburgh, PA -- Scientific research |
| 1,000 | Carnegie Institute, Pittsburgh, PA -- Powdermill Natural Program |

General

250,000	Pittsburgh Theological Seminary, Pittsburgh, PA -- Educational assistance
250,000	Washington and Jefferson College, Washington, PA -- Educational assistance
125,000	Carnegie Mellon University, Pittsburgh, PA -- Educational programs
25,000	South Dakota School of Mines and Technology, Rapid City, SD -- Educational assistance
25,000	Washington Hospital Foundation, Inc., Washington, PA -- Scientific charity
20,000	Coalition for Christian Outreach, Pittsburgh, PA -- Ministry on college campus
10,000	Pittsburgh Trust for Cultural Resources, Pittsburgh, PA -- Recreational cultural organization
10,000	The United Way of Southwest Pennsylvania, Pittsburgh, PA -- United Way
5,000	Childrens Hospital of Pittsburgh, Pittsburgh, PA -- Scientific research
5,000	St. Vincent Archabbey, Latrobe, PA -- Church related renovations

DYSON FOUNDATION

Giving Contact
Diana M. Gurieva, Executive Vice President
25 Halcyon Road
Millbrook, NY 12545-9611
Phone: (845)677-0644
Fax: (845)677-0650
E-mail: info@dyson.org
Web: http://www.dyson.org

Description
Founded: 1957
EIN: 136084888
Organization Type: General Purpose Foundation
Giving Locations: NY: Mid-Hudson Valley nationally.
Grant Types: Capital, Challenge, Conference/Seminar, Fellowship, General Support, Loan, Matching, Multiyear/Continuing Support, Professorship, Project, Research, Scholarship, Seed Money.

Donor Information
Founder: The Dyson Foundation was established in 1957 by Charles H. Dyson and Margaret M. Dyson as a means of formalizing and furthering their family's charitable giving. Their daughter, Anne E. Dyson, MD, serves as the foundation's president, and their son, Robert R. Dyson is on the foundation's board of directors. Margaret M. Dyson passed away in 1990. Charles H. Dyson died in 1997.

Financial Summary
Total Giving: $13,667,121 (fiscal year ending December 30, 2003); $14,400,000 (fiscal 2002); $12,503,211 (fiscal 2001)
Giving Analysis: Giving for fiscal 2003 includes: foundation grants to United Way ($221,000); foundation scholarships ($562,100); fiscal 2001: foundation grants to United Way ($40,000); foundation scholarships ($423,500)
Assets: $287,031,659 (fiscal 2003); $253,919,204 (fiscal 2002); $296,307,874 (fiscal 2001)
Gifts Received: $576,180 (fiscal 2001); $5,523,289 (fiscal 1999); $150,410,144 (fiscal 1998). Note: In 2001, contributions were received from The Dyson

Kissner-Moran Corp. ($500,000) and the estate of Margaret M. Dyson ($76,180).

Typical Recipients
Arts & Humanities: Arts Associations & Councils, Arts Funds, Arts Outreach, Ballet, Dance, Historic Preservation, History & Archaeology, Libraries, Museums/Galleries, Music, Opera, Performing Arts, Public Broadcasting
Civic & Public Affairs: Botanical Gardens/Parks, Business/Free Enterprise, Community Foundations, Economic Development, Civic & Public Affairs-General, Housing, Law & Justice, Legal Aid, Nonprofit Management, Public Policy, Rural Affairs, Women's Affairs, Zoos/Aquariums
Education: Afterschool/Enrichment Programs, Arts/Humanities Education, Business Education, Colleges & Universities, Education Funds, Environmental Education, Faculty Development, Education-General, Legal Education, Literacy, Medical Education, Preschool Education, Private Education (Precollege), Religious Education, Science/Mathematics Education, Secondary Education (Public), Social Sciences Education, Special Education, Student Aid
Environment: Air/Water Quality, Environment-General, Protection, Sanitary Systems, Wildlife Protection
Health: AIDS/HIV, Cancer, Children's Health/Hospitals, Eyes/Blindness, Geriatric Health, Health Funds, Health Organizations, Hospitals, Hospitals (University Affiliated), Medical Rehabilitation, Medical Research, Prenatal Health Issues, Preventive Medicine/Wellness Organizations, Public Health, Trauma Treatment
Religion: Churches, Ministries, Religious Organizations, Religious Welfare
Science: Science Museums
Social Services: Camps, Child Welfare, Community Centers, Community Service Organizations, Counseling, Crime Prevention, Day Care, Family Planning, Family Services, Food/Clothing Distribution, Homes, People with Disabilities, Recreation & Athletics, Scouts, Substance Abuse, United Funds/United Ways, Volunteer Services, YMCA/YWCA/YMHA/YWHA, Youth Organizations

Application Procedures
Initial Contact: The foundation welcomes telephone inquiries concerning its interest in charitable projects. The foundation does not accept unsolicited proposals, but applicants may send brief (two- or three-page) letters of inquiry.
Application Requirements: Submit a two- to three-page letter of inquiry addressing the following guidelines: Include a brief statement of the organizations purpose and goals; a description of the project, the need, and its targeted population; information about the capability of the leadership; expected outcomes; grant amount, total project budget, and other funding sources being approached, detailing committed and projected sources of support. Do not include annual reports, brochures, or additional pages of illustrative materials. Please do not send unsolicited videotapes, curricula, reports, etc.
Deadlines: None.
Review Process: All potential applicants will receive a written response to their letter of inquiry. If interested, the foundation will invite applicants to submit a fully developed proposal. During the review, representatives of the foundation will research the proposal through telephone inquiries, site visits, and meetings with staff, board, volunteers, and clients as necessary. Generally, it can take at least six months from time of inquiry to the accrual award of a grant. Directors of the Dyson Foundation meet quarterly.
Evaluative Criteria: The foundation supports organizations that are tax-exempt under Sec. 501(c)(3) of the IRS Code, and are not classified as foundations under Sec. 509(A) of the Code. Occasionally the foundation will consider grants to eligible organizations acting as fiscal sponsors to other non-qualifying organizations. Generally the foundation does not

fund projects sponsored by governmental bodies (such as public schools) but will evaluate particularly innovative requests on a case-by-case basis.
Notes: The Foundation prefers to fund special projects rather than general operating expenses. It will consider grants for management or technical assistance, demonstration or pilot projects, start-up costs, evaluation, advocacy, limited equipment purchases, and small-scale publications or conferences. The Foundation will also consider multi-year awards, as well as challenge grants.

Restrictions
The foundation will not make grants to individuals (this includes scholarships, which are only provided though grants to academic institutions) or international projects (to organizations operating outside the U.S.). It will not make grants for debt reduction, direct-mail campaigns, and fund-raising events. Exceptions may occasionally be made for an organization that has an established long-term relationship with the Foundation. The foundation will not award grants support to organizations which, in their constitution, bylaws or practices, discriminate against a person or group on the basis of age, race, national origin, ethnicity, gender, disability, sexual orientation, political affiliation or religious belief. (Grantees may target services to a particular population when the targeted groups require specialized programs to meet specific needs not shared by the general population.)

Additional Information
The foundation is affiliated with the Dyson Charitable Fund, also located in New York.
The foundation prefers to fund special projects rather than general operating expenses.
The Foundation's interests are ever-changing. Potential applicants should review the current year's guidelines for areas of interest and not rely on what or whom the Foundation has funded in the past.
Publications: Annual Report; Guidelines

Foundation Officials
Robert R. Dyson: president, director B 1946. ED Cornell University MBA; Marietta College BA. PRIM CORP EMPL chairman, chief executive officer: Dyson-Kissner-Moran Corp. CORP AFFIL chairman, chief executive officer: D K M Ltd.; chairman: Kearney-National Inc.; director: Centre Foundry & Machine Co.; director: Chrisolm Corp.
Marc Feldman: treasurer
John S. FitzSimons: secretary, director B 1948. ED Princeton University BA (1970); New York University JD (1973). PRIM CORP EMPL secretary, general counsel: Dyson-Kissner-Moran Corp. ADD CORP EMPL secretary, general counsel: DKM Properties Corp. CORP AFFIL secretary, director: Kearney-National Inc.
Diana M. Gurieva: executive vice president
Raymond A. Lamontagne: director
Timmian C. Massie: director
Lynn A. McCluskey: assistant secretary, assistant treasurer PRIM CORP EMPL treasurer, secretary: M.S. Chambers & Sons. CORP AFFIL vice president, secretary, director: Patterson Planning & Services.
Michael P. Murphy: director
David G. Nathan, MD: director

Grants Analysis
Disclosure Period: fiscal year ending December 30, 2003
Total Grants: $12,884,021*
Number of Grants: 167
Average Grant: $57,423*
Highest Grant: $3,351,845
Lowest Grant: $1,500
Typical Range: $25,000 to $100,000
*Note: Giving excludes United Way, scholarships. Average grant excludes highest grant.

Recent Grants
Note: Grants derived from 2002 Form 990.

General

1,000,000	Marietta College, Marietta, OH -- towards support for the renovation and expansion of the Ban Johnson field house
777,000	children's Hospital, Boston, MA -- towards creation of a national program office for the Dyson initiative
500,000	High Mowing School, Wilton, NH -- towards capital campaign grant of 2000000 dollars over three years
500,000	Weill Medical College of Cornell University, New York, NY -- towards new innovations for medical campaign
441,845	Bardavon 1869 Opera house, Poughkeepsie, NY -- towards a multi part institutional support grant for programming endowment and capital improvements
400,000	Hudson River Housing Inc., Poughkeepsie, NY -- towards purchase of new facility in order to relocate and expand emergency transitional permanent housing services
363,000	children's Hospital, Boston, MA -- towards Dyson Fellowship in Pediatric advocacy
300,000	Mid Hudson children's Museum, Poughkeepsie, NY -- towards renovation and relocation costs associated with moving to a downtown Poughkeepsie site
251,000	children's Hospital of Philadelphia, Philadelphia, PA -- towards pediatric residency innovation
250,000	Columbia University, New York, NY -- towards pediatric residency training innovation

EARHART FOUNDATION

Giving Contact

David B. Kennedy, President
2200 Green Road, Suite H
Ann Arbor, MI 48105
Phone: (734)761-8592
Fax: (734)761-2722

Description

Founded: 1929
EIN: 386008273
Organization Type: Specialized/Single Purpose Foundation
Grant Types: Fellowship, Research, Scholarship.

Donor Information

Founder: The foundation was organized in 1929 by the late Harry Boyd Earhart, the principal donor. Born in Pennsylvania, Mr. Earhart was the son of a village storekeeper. After completing the eighth grade and a brief commercial business course, he became a cargo broker on the Great Lakes, a designer and salesman of logging machinery, and a manufacturer and distributor of lubricating oils and related petroleum products. Mr. Earhart founded the White Star Refining Company, now a part of Mobil Oil Corporation.

Financial Summary

Total Giving: $4,323,116 (2003); $4,705,024 (2002)
Giving Analysis: Giving for 2003 includes: foundation fellowships ($1,658,012)
Assets: $73,877,282 (2003); $66,670,425 (2002)
Gifts Received: $200,000 (1995)

Typical Recipients

Arts & Humanities: Historic Preservation, History & Archaeology, Libraries, Literary Arts
Civic & Public Affairs: Civil Rights, Community Foundations, Economic Policy, Employment/Job Training, Civic & Public Affairs-General, Law & Justice, Philanthropic Organizations, Public Policy,

Urban & Community Affairs
Education: Arts/Humanities Education, Business Education, Colleges & Universities, Continuing Education, Economic Education, Education Associations, Education Funds, Education Reform, Engineering/Technological Education, Faculty Development, Education-General, International Exchange, International Studies, Journalism/Media Education, Legal Education, Literacy, Religious Education, Science/Mathematics Education, Secondary Education (Public), Social Sciences Education, Student Aid
Environment: Environment-General, Research
International: Foreign Educational Institutions, International-General, International Affairs, International Development, International Environmental Issues, International Organizations, International Peace & Security Issues, International Relations, Missionary/Religious Activities
Religion: Social/Policy Issues
Social Services: Community Centers, People with Disabilities

Application Procedures

Initial Contact: Organizations or individuals may submit a letter of inquiry or may telephone the foundation for complete application guidelines.
Application Requirements: Institutions seeking grants must complete an application including a general a description of organization, status of eligibility for support from private foundations, current audit or financial statement, list of other institutional supporters, statement of the project with amount requested and budget, and an evaluation with follow-up procedures.
Individuals applying for fellowship research grants must include a personal history statement, full description of proposed research, abstract of approximately 250 words or one page, intended use or publication, budget and time schedule, list of references, and a statement of applications pending elsewhere. elsewhere.
Deadlines: None. The foundation will acknowledge receipt of proposals. In the case of individuals seeking fellowship research grants, applications should be submitted at least 120 days before the commencement of the projected work.
Review Process: If an institutional project is of interest, one copy of a completed proposal will be required. Interviews may be requested.

Restrictions

No grants are made for capital, building, or endowment funds; conferences; operating budgets; continuing support; annual campaigns; seed money; emergency funds; deficit financing; matching gifts; or loans.

Additional Information

H. B. Earhart Fellowships are awarded only to individuals who are nominated by designated faculty sponsors. Direct applications from candidates or from non-invited sponsors are not accepted.
A copy of foundation's annual report is available at the foundation's office for inspection during normal office hours.
Publications: Annual Report

Foundation Officials

Dennis L. Bark: chairman, trustee ED Stanford University (1964).
Thomas Joseph Bray: trustee B New York, NY 1941. ED Princeton University AB (1963). PRIM CORP EMPL editorial page editor: Detroit News. NONPR AFFIL member: American Society Newspaper Editors; member: National Conference Editorial Writers. CLUB AFFIL mem: Birmingham Athletic Club; mem: Detroit Athletic Club.
Elayne J. Ellis: assistant secretary, trustee
Cheryl Gorski: assistant treasurer
Ingrid A. Gregg: secretary, trustee
Earl I. Heenan, III: trustee
Ann K. Irish: trustee NONPR AFFIL board member,

director: North Central Michigan College; secretary, director: Northern Michigan Hospital.
David Boyd Kennedy: president, trustee B Ann Arbor, MI 1933. ED McGill University (1951-1952); University of Michigan (1952-1954); Indiana University AB (1958); University of Michigan LLB (1963). NONPR AFFIL director: Philanthropy Roundtable; member: Wyoming Bar Association; member: Mont Pelerin Society; chairman, director: Institute Justice; member: Michigan Bar Association; director: Citizens Research Council Michigan.
Kathleen B. Mason: treasurer
Kimberly B. Mason: trustee
John H. Moore: trustee
Robert L. Queller: trustee
Susan Woodward: vice president, trustee

Grants Analysis

Disclosure Period: calendar year ending 2003
Total Grants: $2,665,104*
Number of Grants: 181
Average Grant: $14,724
Highest Grant: $50,000
Lowest Grant: $500
Typical Range: $5,000 to $20,000
***Note:** Giving excludes fellowship.

Recent Grants

Note: Grants derived from 2003 Form 990.
General

60,000	Jamestown Foundation, Washington, DC
50,000	Citizens Research Council of Michigan, Livonia, MI
50,000	Intercollegiate Studies Institute (ISI), Wilmington, DE
50,000	Social Philosophy and Policy Center, Bowling Green, OH
40,000	Institute of World Politics, Washington, DC
40,000	Princeton University, Princeton, NJ -- towards James Madison Program in American Ideals and Institutions
35,000	American Friends Fund of the Institute of US Studies, Washington, DC -- to provide assistance for a lecture
35,000	Critical Review Foundation, Princeton, NJ
35,000	Manhattan Institute, New York, NY
35,000	Russell Kirk Center for Cultural Renewal, Grand Rapids, MI

EARLY FOUNDATION

Giving Contact

Jeanette B. Early, President
6319 Mimosa Ln.
Dallas, TX 75230
Phone: (214)373-7114

Description

Founded: 1963
EIN: 756011853
Organization Type: Private Foundation
Giving Locations: TX
Grant Types: General Support.

Donor Information

Founder: Jeannette B. Early

Financial Summary

Gifts Received: $30,000 (fiscal year ending May 31, 1996)

Typical Recipients

Arts & Humanities: Arts Centers, Ballet, Dance, History & Archaeology, Libraries, Museums/Galleries, Music, Opera, Performing Arts, Public Broadcasting, Theater

Civic & Public Affairs: Economic Development, Gay/Lesbian Issues, Civic & Public Affairs-General, Hispanic Affairs, Housing, Parades/Festivals, Public Policy, Urban & Community Affairs, Zoos/Aquariums
Education: Arts/Humanities Education, Business Education, Colleges & Universities, Community & Junior Colleges, Education Reform, Engineering/Technological Education, Education-General, Leadership Training, Literacy, Medical Education, Minority Education, Private Education (Precollege), Public Education (Precollege), Religious Education, Special Education, Student Aid
Environment: Environment-General
Health: Alzheimer's Disease, Children's Health/Hospitals, Clinics/Medical Centers, Eyes/Blindness, Health Organizations, Heart, Hospices, Medical Research, Mental Health, Nursing Services, Prenatal Health Issues, Single-Disease Health Associations
International: Foreign Arts Organizations, International Development, International Relations, International Relief Efforts, Missionary/Religious Activities
Religion: Churches, Religion-General, Ministries, Religious Organizations, Religious Welfare, Seminaries
Science: Science Museums
Social Services: Child Welfare, Community Service Organizations, Delinquency & Criminal Rehabilitation, Family Services, Homes, People with Disabilities, Substance Abuse, United Funds/United Ways, Volunteer Services, YMCA/YWCA/YMHA/YWHA, Youth Organizations

Application Procedures

Initial Contact: The foundation has no formal grant application procedure or application form.
Application Requirements: Proof of tax exempt satus is required.
Deadlines: None.

Additional Information

Publications: Annual Report

Foundation Officials

Jeannette B. Early: president

Grants Analysis

Disclosure Period: fiscal year ending May 31, 2000
Total Grants: $247,650
Number of Grants: 34
Average Grant: $7,284
Highest Grant: $25,000
Typical Range: $2,000 to $15,000

Recent Grants

Note: Grants derived from 2002 Form 990.
General

25,000	Dallas Children's Theater, Dallas, TX -- provides drama programs and theater to the children of Dallas
25,000	Grace Presbyterian Village, Dallas, TX -- for retirement home and hospital care for retired citizens
25,000	Total Learning Project, Centennial, CO -- support schools and provides training to those with learning disabilities
20,000	Total Learning Project, Centennial, CO -- support schools and provides training to those with learning disabilities
15,000	Presbyterian Children's Home and Service Agency, Austin, TX -- provides homes and special services to children
15,000	Presbyterian Pan American School, Kingsville, TN -- preparatory school for students to learn English before going to college
15,000	Science Place, Dallas, TX -- provides hands-on physics gallery and science center to 225,000 school children year round
10,000	Agape Medical Clinic, Dallas, TX -- care of persons in need of health care in East Dallas
10,000	Austin Presbyterian Theological Seminary, Austin, TX -- for graduate school to train church professionals for positions in US and abroad
10,000	Austin Presbyterian Theological Seminary, Austin, TX -- for graduate school to train church professionals for positions in US and abroad

ANDREW H. AND ANNE O. EASLEY TRUST

Giving Contact

Andrew H. and Anne O. Easley Trust
PO Box 27602
Richmond, VA 23261
Phone: (804)697-6901

Description

Founded: 1968
EIN: 546074720
Organization Type: Private Foundation
Giving Locations: VA: Lynchburg
Grant Types: General Support.

Donor Information

Founder: the late Andrew H. Easley

Financial Summary

Total Giving: $400,355 (fiscal year ending June 30, 2004); $508,498 (fiscal 2001)
Assets: $9,551,179 (fiscal 2004); $407,887,389 (fiscal 2001)

Typical Recipients

Arts & Humanities: Arts Associations & Councils, Arts Centers, Community Arts, Historic Preservation, Libraries, Museums/Galleries, Music, Performing Arts, Theater
Civic & Public Affairs: Economic Development, Employment/Job Training, Civic & Public Affairs-General, Housing, Legal Aid, Native American Affairs, Urban & Community Affairs, Women's Affairs
Education: Agricultural Education, Arts/Humanities Education, Colleges & Universities, Community & Junior Colleges, Education Associations, Education-General, Private Education (Precollege), Science/Mathematics Education
Environment: Forestry, Environment-General
Health: Public Health, Single-Disease Health Associations
International: Human Rights
Religion: Religious Welfare
Social Services: Animal Protection, Camps, Child Welfare, Community Centers, Community Service Organizations, Day Care, Family Planning, Family Services, Food/Clothing Distribution, Homes, Recreation & Athletics, Shelters/Homelessness, United Funds/United Ways, YMCA/YWCA/YMHA/YWHA, Youth Organizations

Application Procedures

Initial Contact: Request application guidelines.
Deadlines: April 1 and October 1.

Additional Information

Publications: Application Guidelines
Trust(s): Wachovia Bank

Grants Analysis

Disclosure Period: fiscal year ending June 30, 2004
Total Grants: $400,355
Typical Range: $3,000 to $50,000
Note: No grants list available for 2004.

Recent Grants

Note: Grants derived from fiscal 2001 Form 990.

General

50,000	Arc of Central Virginia, Richmond, VA
25,000	Lynchburg Sheltered Industries, Inc., Lynchburg, VA
15,345	Virginia School of the Arts, Lynchburg, VA
15,000	Central Virginia Community College, Lynchburg, VA
15,000	Ferrum College, Ferrum, VA
15,000	Hampden-Sydney College, Hampden-Sydney, VA
15,000	Lynchburg College, Lynchburg, VA
15,000	Randolph-Macon Woman's College, Lynchburg, VA
15,000	Sweet Briar College, Sweet Briar, VA
13,550	Adult Care Center

EAST CAMBRIDGE SAVINGS BANK

Company Headquarters

292 Cambridge St.
Cambridge, MA 02141
Web: http://www.ecsb.com

Company Description

Founded: 1854

East Cambridge Savings Charitable Foundation

Giving Contact

East Cambridge Savings Bank
292 Cambridge Street
East Cambridge, MA 02141-1263
Phone: (617)354-7700

Description

Founded: 1997
EIN: 043399319
Organization Type: Corporate Foundation
Giving Locations: , MA
Grant Types: General Support, Scholarship.

Financial Summary

Total Giving: $108,131 (2003); $110,850 (2001)
Giving Analysis: Giving for 2003 includes: foundation grants to United Way ($5,000); foundation scholarships ($10,500); 2001: foundation grants to United Way ($5,000) foundation scholarships ($6,000)
Assets: $121,910 (2003); $351,951 (2001)

Typical Recipients

Arts & Humanities: Arts Centers, Libraries, Music
Civic & Public Affairs: Community Foundations, Ethnic Organizations, Civic & Public Affairs-General, Housing, Municipalities/Towns, Philanthropic Organizations
Education: Arts/Humanities Education, Colleges & Universities, Faculty Development, Public Education (Precollege)
Health: Nursing Services
Religion: Churches
Social Services: Child Welfare, Community Service Organizations, Counseling, Family Services, Refugee Assistance, United Funds/United Ways, YMCA/YWCA/YMHA/YWHA, Youth Organizations

Application Procedures

Initial Contact: Write the foundation to request an application form.

Foundation Officials

Joseph A. Amoroso, Jr.: director
Charles Aufieror: director

Lee C. Craig: director
Tyler H. Foster: director
Susan LaPierre: vice president community relations
Daniel A. Leone: director
Gisela L. Margotta: treasurer
William F. McGilvreay: president, director
Gilda M. Nogueira: clerk
Albert M. Pacheco: director
Arthur C. Spears: executive vice president
Philip A. Trussell: director
George E. Wilson: director

Grants Analysis

Disclosure Period: calendar year ending 2003
Total Grants: $92,631*
Number of Grants: 86
Average Grant: $1,077
Highest Grant: $10,000
Lowest Grant: $25
Typical Range: $500 to $5,000
*Note: Giving excludes scholarships; United Way.

Recent Grants

Note: Grants derived from 2003 Form 990.
General

10,000	Cambridge Family YMCA, Cambridge, MA
10,000	East End House, Cambridge, MA
8,340	Cambridge Housing Assistance Fund, Cambridge, MA -- for sponsorship
5,000	Cambridge Community Foundation, Cambridge, MA
5,000	United Way of Massachusetts, Boston, MA
4,050	Longy School of Music, Cambridge, MA
3,000	Cambridge Family and Children's Service, Cambridge, MA
3,000	Consumer Credit Counseling Service of Southern New England, Boston, MA
3,000	Just-A-Start Corporation, Cambridge, MA
2,000	Watertown Community Housing Inc., Watertown, MA

EASTERN BANK

Company Headquarters

Salem, MA
Web: http://www.easternbank.com

Company Description

Employees: 731

Operating Locations

Eastern Bank (MA--Beverly, Boston, Braintree, Hingham, Lynnfield, Malden, Medford, Melrose, Quincy, Salem, Saugus, Shrewsbury, Stoughton, Swampscott, Wakefield, Weymouth)

Eastern Bank Charitable Foundation

Giving Contact

Sumner W. Jones, Executive Vice President
605 Broadway, LF41
Saugus, MA 01906
Phone: (781)581-4219
Web: http://www.easternbank.com/ a_charitable_foundation.html

Description

Founded: 1985
EIN: 223317340
Organization Type: Corporate Foundation
Giving Locations: MA: market area
Grant Types: Capital, General Support, Scholarship.

Financial Summary

Total Giving: $1,221,930 (2004); $1,130,517 (2003); $1,163,582 (2001). Note: Contributes through foundation only.
Giving Analysis: Giving for 2001 includes: foundation scholarships ($6,425); foundation grants to United Way ($52,000); foundation matching gifts ($206,475); foundation ($758,887).
Assets: $34,516,194 (2004); $24,108,302 (2003); $17,571,769 (2001)
Gifts Received: $4,628,775 (2003); $202,396 (1995); $105 (1993). Note: Contributions were received from Eastern Bank.

Typical Recipients

Arts & Humanities: Arts Centers, Community Arts, Arts & Humanities-General, Historic Preservation, History & Archaeology, Libraries, Museums/ Galleries, Music, Performing Arts, Public Broadcasting
Civic & Public Affairs: African American Affairs, Asian American Affairs, Business/Free Enterprise, Chambers of Commerce, Civil Rights, Clubs, Community Foundations, Economic Development, Employment/Job Training, Ethnic Organizations, Civic & Public Affairs-General, Hispanic Affairs, Housing, Law & Justice, Native American Affairs, Nonprofit Management, Parades/Festivals, Philanthropic Organizations, Public Policy, Safety, Urban & Community Affairs, Women's Affairs
Education: Afterschool/Enrichment Programs, Arts/ Humanities Education, Business-School Partnerships, Colleges & Universities, Community & Junior Colleges, Education Associations, Education Funds, Education Reform, Education-General, Medical Education, Private Education (Precollege), Science/ Mathematics Education, Secondary Education (Private), Student Aid
Health: AIDS/HIV, Cancer, Children's Health/ Hospitals, Clinics/Medical Centers, Health-General, Health Organizations, Heart, Hospices, Hospitals, Mental Health, Preventive Medicine/Wellness Organizations, Single-Disease Health Associations
International: International Affairs
Religion: Churches, Religion-General, Jewish Causes, Religious Welfare, Synagogues/Temples
Science: Scientific Research
Social Services: At-Risk Youth, Big Brothers/Big Sisters, Camps, Child Welfare, Community Centers, Community Service Organizations, Counseling, Crime Prevention, Day Care, Delinquency & Criminal Rehabilitation, Domestic Violence, Emergency Relief, Family Services, Food/Clothing Distribution, Homes, People with Disabilities, Recreation & Athletics, Scouts, Senior Services, Shelters/ Homelessness, Social Services-General, Substance Abuse, United Funds/United Ways, YMCA/YWCA/ YMHA/YWHA, Youth Organizations

Application Procedures

Initial Contact: Contact foundation for guidelines, then letter or full proposal.
Application Requirements: For grants under $10,000: brief letter describing background of organization, amount requested and purpose of funds sought, and proof of tax-exempt status; grants of $10,000 or more must be requested using Associated Grantmakers of Massachusetts application form and Eastern Bank Donation Request form.
Deadlines: For grants $10,000 to $25,000: the 1st of May or November; for grants of less than $10,000: None.
Decision Notification: Major gifts ($10,000 to $25,000) are considered in June and December.

Restrictions

Recipients of major gifts may not reapply for funding for three years.
Does not support individuals or political or lobbying groups.

Additional Information

Foundation divides its annual giving budget, with half of contributions going to a few major gifts ($10,000 to $25,000), and half distributed broadly with smaller grants.
Publications: Annual Report

Corporate Officials

Sumner Jones: executive vice presidento PRIM CORP EMPL executive vice president: Eastern Bank.
Stanley J. Lukowski: chairman, chief executive officer PRIM CORP EMPL chairman, chief executive officer: Eastern Bank ADD CORP EMPL chairman: Eastern Bank Corp.; chairman: Eastern Bank and Trust Co. Inc.; chairman: Eastern Securities Corp. NONPR AFFIL chairman: Massachusetts Bankers Association.

Foundation Officials

Richard C. Bane: trustee
William F. Collins, Jr.: trustee
Daryl A. Hellman: trustee
Deborah C. Jackson: trustee
Andre C. Jasse, Jr.: trustee ED Georgia Institute of Technology BS (1963); Boston College LLB (1966). PRIM CORP EMPL chairman: Brown Rudnick Freed Gesmer. CORP AFFIL secretary: WNA Carthage Inc.; clerk: WNA Comet East Inc.; director: Waddington North America; vice president: Filemark Corp.; clerk: Pericomp Corp.
Wendell J. Knox: trustee
Stanley J. Lukowski: trustee (see above)
George E. Massaro: trustee
Nills P. Peterson: trustee
Roger D. Scoville: trustee
Michael B. Sherman: trustee

Grants Analysis

Disclosure Period: calendar year ending 2004
Total Grants: $1,014,202*
Number of Grants: 400 (approx)
Average Grant: $2,536
Highest Grant: $75,000
Lowest Grant: $50
Typical Range: $1,000 to $5,000
*Note: Giving excludes matching gifts; United Way.

Recent Grants

Note: Grants derived from 2003 Form 990.

General

100,000	Salem State College Foundation, Salem, MA
75,000	Peabody Essex Museum, Salem, MA
50,000	North Shore Arc, Danvers, MA
25,000	American Red Cross of Massachusetts Bay, Boston, MA
25,000	Easter Seals, Chicago, IL
25,000	Girl Scouts, Patriots' Trail Council Inc., Boston, MA
25,000	Peabody Lynnfield YMCA
25,000	St. Mary's High School, Calgary, AB Canada
25,000	YMCA of the North Shore, Beverly, MA
17,500	United Way of Massachusetts Bay, Boston, MA

EASTERN S.L.A.

Company Headquarters

257 Main St.
Norwich, CT 06360
Phone: (860)889-7381

Eastern Savings and Loan Foundation

Giving Contact

Carol A. Cieslukowski, Secretary
Eastern Savings & Loan Foundation
257 Main Street
PO Box 709
Norwich, CT 06360-5837
Phone: (860)889-7381
Fax: (860)889-4779
Note: Phone ext. 145.

Description

Founded: 1999
EIN: 061539443
Organization Type: Corporate Foundation
Giving Locations: , CT

Financial Summary

Total Giving: $23,000 (fiscal year ending 0, 2004); $21,000 (fiscal 2001)
Assets: $469,566 (fiscal 2004); $394,588 (fiscal 2001)
Gifts Received: $22,000 (fiscal 2004); $10,000 (fiscal 2001). Note: Contributions were received from Eastern Savings and Loan Association.

Typical Recipients

Arts & Humanities: Libraries
Civic & Public Affairs: Community Foundations, Civic & Public Affairs-General, Women's Affairs
Health: Hospices, Hospitals
Social Services: At-Risk Youth, Community Service Organizations, Family Services, Food/Clothing Distribution

Application Procedures

Initial Contact: Contact the foundation to request a grant application form.
Deadlines: March 31.
Decision Notification: The board's funding decisions are communicated by mail in May.
Notes: Grants are distributed in June.

Restrictions

Grants must be used for a specific program, project or scholarships. Grants are not provided for general operating expenses.

Foundation Officials

Linda M. Adelman: director
Carol A. Cieslukowski: secretary
Donald A. Cipriani: president
Joseph A. Fatone: director
John R. FitzGerald: director
Richard A. Friedrich, Sr.: vice president
Anthony G. Madiera: treasurer
Andre J. Messier, Jr.: director
Jerald I. Navick: director
Bernard G. Park: director

Grants Analysis

Total Grants: $23,000
Number of Grants: 16
Average Grant: $1,438
Highest Grant: $2,500
Lowest Grant: $1,000
Typical Range: $1,000 to $2,000

Recent Grants

Note: Grants derived from fiscal 2001 Form 990.
Library-Related
2,000   Slater Library -- purchase series of 86 books "Opposing Viewpoints"
1,000   Voluntown Public Library, Voluntown, CT -- expand and re-do youth biography section of library

General
2,500   Natchaug Hospital, Mansfield Center, CT -- renovation project to provide 42,500sq ft to in-patient, out-patient, and education facilities
2,000   Bethesda Community, Inc. -- assisting in creating computer training center to train women for entering workplace
2,000   Madonna Place, Norwich, CT -- family visitation center program
2,000   Martin House, Trenton, NJ -- contributions match for adult education program
1,000   Griswold Volunteer Fire Department -- purchase thermal imaging camera
1,000   Hospice of Southeastern Connecticut, Uncasville, CT -- support of services and equipment provided to patients
1,000   Norwich Arts Council, Norwich, CT -- provide performance at Winter Festival
1,000   Norwich Social Services Safety Net Team, Norwich, CT -- assist people to become self-sufficient through various programs
1,000   Salvation Army, Norwich, CT -- provide 8 scholarships to children for Camp Connri for one week
1,000   Thames River Family Program -- to staff alumni organization

EASTMAN KODAK CO.

Company Headquarters

Rochester, NY
Web: http://www.kodak.com

Company Description

Founded: 1881
Ticker: EK
Exchange: NYSE
Revenue: US$13.829 billion (2004)
Profit: US$649 million (2004)
Employees: 70000 (2003)
Fortune Rank: 153, per FORTUNE Magazine's list of 500 Largest U.S. Corporations (2004).
SIC(s): 2843 Surface Active Agents, 2865 Cyclic Crudes & Intermediates, 3081 Unsupported Plastics Film & Sheet, 3861 Photographic Equipment & Supplies.

Operating Locations

Eastman Kodak Co. (AL--Huntsville, Mobile; AK--Anchorage; AZ--Scottsdale; AR--Little Rock; CA--Fresno, Irvine, Los Angeles, San Diego, San Francisco, San Jose, Ventura, Woodland Hills; CO--Englewood, Windsor; DC--Washington; FL--Fort Lauderdale, Miami, Orlando, Pensacola, Winter Park; GA--Atlanta, Norcross; HI--Mililani; ID--Boise; IL--Chicago, Hinsdale, Springfield; KS--Overland Park, Wichita; KY--Lexington, Louisville; LA--Lafayette, New Orleans; MD--Columbia, Severna Park; MA--Chelmsford, Wellesley Hills; MI--Bingham Farms, Bloomfield Hills, Grand Rapids, Lansing; MN--Minnetonka; MS--Jackson; MO--St. Louis; NV--Las Vegas; NJ--Princeton; NY--Albany, Amherst, Endwell, Fishkill, Latham, New York, Rome, Scottsville, Uniondale; NC--Charlotte, Greensboro, Morrisville; OH--Cincinnati, Dayton, Dublin, Hudson, Toledo; OR--Portland; PA--Camp Hill, Erie, Horsham; SC--Charleston; TN--Knoxville, Nashville; TX--Fort Worth, Houston, Irving, San Antonio; VA--Arlington, Herndon, Norfolk, Reston, Richmond; WA--Spokane; WI--Madison, Middleton, Waukesha)

Nonmonetary Support

Type: Donated Equipment; Donated Products
Volunteer Programs: Company offers "Dollars for Doers" program through which it makes small donations to nonprofit organizations where company employees serve as volunteers; supports Global Service Day; when all employees are encouraged to volunteer in their communities.
Note: Co. donates property. Nonmonetary support budget is separate from the corporate giving budget.

Eastman Kodak Charitable Trust

Giving Contact

Essie B. Calhoun, Director
343 State Street
Rochester, NY 14650-0552
Phone: (585)724-2434
Fax: (585)724-1376
Web: http://www.kodak.com/US/en/corp/community.shtml

Alternate Contact

Care of JP Morgan Chase Bank
PO Box 31412
Rochester, NY 14603
Phone: (585)258-5322

Description

EIN: 166015274
Organization Type: Corporate Foundation
Giving Locations: nationally, especially in operating locations.
Grant Types: Award, Capital, Department, Emergency, Endowment, Fellowship, General Support, Matching, Multiyear/Continuing Support, Research, Scholarship.

Donor Information

Founder: The Eastman Kodak Co. was founded in 1892 by the late George Eastman (1854-1932).

Financial Summary

Total Giving: $5,998,400 (2003); $6,819,700 (2002); $10,905,115 (2001). Note: Contributes through corporate direct giving program and foundation.
Giving Analysis: Giving for 2002 includes: foundation grants to United Way ($2,314,700)
Assets: $264,703 (2003); $251,228 (2002); $62,916 (2001)
Gifts Received: $6,000,000 (2003); $7,051,603 (2002); $10,866,809 (2001)

Typical Recipients

Arts & Humanities: Arts Associations & Councils, Arts Funds, Dance, Film & Video, Arts & Humanities-General, History & Archaeology, Libraries, Museums/Galleries, Music, Performing Arts, Theater
Civic & Public Affairs: African American Affairs, Botanical Gardens/Parks, Business/Free Enterprise, Chambers of Commerce, Clubs, Community Foundations, Economic Development, Economic Policy, Employment/Job Training, Ethnic Organizations, Civic & Public Affairs-General, Hispanic Affairs, Housing, Law & Justice, Minority Business, Parades/Festivals, Professional & Trade Associations, Public Policy, Safety, Urban & Community Affairs, Women's Affairs, Zoos/Aquariums
Education: Afterschool/Enrichment Programs, Arts/Humanities Education, Business Education, Colleges & Universities, Community & Junior Colleges, Economic Education, Education Funds, Education Reform, Elementary Education (Public), Engineering/Technological Education, Education-General, Health & Physical Education, International Studies, Literacy, Minority Education, Preschool Education, Private Education (Precollege), Public Education (Precollege), Religious Education, School Volunteerism, Science/Mathematics Education, Secondary Education (Private), Secondary Education (Public), Special Education, Student Aid, Vocational & Technical Education
Environment: Environment-General, Resource Conservation, Wildlife Protection

Health: Adolescent Health Issues, AIDS/HIV, Cancer, Clinics/Medical Centers, Emergency/Ambulance Services, Health-General, Health Funds, Health Organizations, Hospitals, Medical Rehabilitation, Mental Health, Nursing Services, Single-Disease Health Associations

International: Foreign Arts Organizations, Foreign Educational Institutions, International-General, Health Care/Hospitals, International Development, International Environmental Issues, International Organizations, International Relations, International Relief Efforts, Missionary/Religious Activities

Religion: Jewish Causes, Religious Welfare

Science: Science Museums, Scientific Centers & Institutes, Scientific Organizations

Social Services: Animal Protection, At-Risk Youth, Child Welfare, Community Centers, Community Service Organizations, Day Care, Emergency Relief, Family Services, Food/Clothing Distribution, Homes, People with Disabilities, Recreation & Athletics, Scouts, United Funds/United Ways, Youth Organizations

Application Procedures

Initial Contact: Send a written proposal.

Application Requirements: Cover letter should include legal name of the organization, mission statement, grant amount requested, and purpose of grant. Proposal (not to exceed five pages) should include proposal summary (one or two pages); mission of the organization; history of the organization; need for the project (in view of related work by others); project description; audience served; goals, objectives, and action plan; expected quantifiable outcomes or results; method of evaluation of proposed outcomes; other sources of support; and, if appropriate, plan for continuing the project beyond company support. Attachments should include most recent organizational financial statement and income and expense budget, list of other current and projected sources of funding, most recent Form 990, proof of tax-exempt status, and list of board members and affiliations.

Deadlines: Applications are accepted between January 1 and April 30.

Review Process: Kodak board of directors approves budget based on recommendation of company's corporate contributions council.

Evaluative Criteria: Funded programs support societal needs in communities where substantial numbers of active and potential employees live and work, and reflect global corporate goals in recruitment, technology strength, market growth, public policy, diversity, and environment.

Decision Notification: Within 45 days of receipt.

Restrictions

Kodak does not support individuals; a commitment beyond three to five years (unless a specific strategic rationale exists and the contribution is reviewed in three years); endowed chairs or university capital campaigns; event sponsorships; operating costs of organizations that receive funds from a Kodak-supported United Way; legislators, political organizations, or campaigns; or sectarian organizations whose programs are limited to members of one religious group.

Additional Information

Charitable trust generally does not solicit funding requests.

Kodak recycles more than a half billion pounds of material a year and supports a World Wildlife Fund program to increase the environmental literacy of students. Copies of Kodak's annual environmental report are available by writing: Principles and Progress, Coordinator of Environmental Communications, Eastman Kodak Company, Rochester, NY 14650-0518.

Publications: Contributions Program Brochure

Corporate Officials

Michael P. Benard: vice president, director communications & public affairs B 1948. ED John Carroll University BA; Temple University MEd. PRIM CORP EMPL vice president, director communications & public affairs: Eastman Kodak Co.

Daniel A. Carp: chairman, chief executive officer, director B 1948. ED Massachusetts Institute of Technology MS; Ohio University MBA; Ohio University BBA. PRIM CORP EMPL chairman, chief executive officer, director: Eastman Kodak Co. CORP AFFIL director: Texas Instruments Inc.

Giving Program Officials

Michael P. Benard: member (see above)

Foundation Officials

Essie L. Calhoun: vice president PRIM CORP EMPL director community relations & contributions: Eastman Kodak Co.

Grants Analysis

Disclosure Period: calendar year ending 2003

Total Grants: $5,278,400*

Number of Grants: 68

Average Grant: $77,624

Highest Grant: $200,000

Lowest Grant: $1,500

Typical Range: $25,000 to $100,000

***Note:** Giving excludes United Way.

Recent Grants

Note: Grants derived from 2003 Form 990.

General

500,000	United Way of Greater Rochester, Rochester, NY
500,000	United Way of Greater Rochester, Rochester, NY
250,000	University of Rochester, Rochester, NY
200,000	Clarkson University, Potsdam, NY
200,000	People for the American Way, Washington, DC
190,000	United Kingdom Committee for UNICEF, London United Kingdom
150,000	Ministry of Health, Beijing People's Republic of China
150,000	Nazareth College, Rochester, NY
140,000	Rensselaer Polytechnic Institute, Troy, NY
125,000	Al Sigl Center, Rochester, NY

EATON CORP.

Company Headquarters

Eaton Center
Cleveland, OH 44114-2584
Phone: (216)523-5000
Fax: (216)523-4787
Web: http://www.eaton.com

Company Description

Founded: 1916
Ticker: ETN
Exchange: NYSE
Acquired: Aeroquip-Vickers (1999).
Revenue: US$9.817 billion (2004)
Profit: US$648 million (2004)
Employees: 51000 (2003)
Fortune Rank: 227, per FORTUNE Magazine's list of 500 Largest U.S. Corporations (2004).
SIC(s): 3452 Bolts, Nuts, Rivets & Washers, 3559 Special Industry Machinery Nec, 3561 Pumps & Pumping Equipment, 3714 Motor Vehicle Parts & Accessories.

Operating Locations

Eaton Corp. (AL--Arab; CA--Costa Mesa, El Segundo, San Diego; CT--Bethel, Danbury; FL--Oldsmar,

Sarasota; IL--Carol Stream, Rochelle; IN--Auburn, Greenfield, Hamilton, Winamac; IA--Belmond, Shenandoah, Spencer; KS--Hutchinson; MD--Elkridge; MA--Beverly; MI--Galesburg, Marshall, Rochester Hills, Saginaw, Three Rivers; MO--Eden Prairie; NE--Hastings; NY--Horseheads; NC--Asheville, Charlotte, Fayetteville, Fletcher, Kings Mountain, Laurinburg, Roxboro, Sanford, Selma; OH--Brunswick, Cleveland, Eastlake, Westerville; OK--Oklahoma City, Shawnee; PA--Beaver, Pittsburgh; SC--Greenville, Pageland, Sumter; TN--Cleveland, Shelbyville; TX--Austin, Brownsville; WA--Everett; WI--Milwaukee, Watertown, Wauwatosa)

Nonmonetary Support

Value: $19,723 (2002); $31,152 (2001)

Type: Donated Products

Volunteer Programs: Volunteer services of all types are encouraged. Volunteers support many causes including teaching reading to the illiterate, coaching little league softball, organizing school aid programs, serving food at hunger centers, building houses for the needy, and chairing United Way campaigns. Company sponsors the James R. Stover Awards to recognize employee volunteers, and makes cash grants to organizations where employees contribute their time and talents.

Eaton Charitable Fund

Giving Contact

James L. Mason, Vice President, Community Initiatives
1111 Superior Avenue
Cleveland, OH 44114-2584
Phone: (216)828-9770
Fax: (216)479-7013
E-mail: jamesmason@eaton.com

Description

Founded: 1953
EIN: 346501856
Organization Type: Corporate Foundation
Giving Locations: corporate operating locations.
Grant Types: Capital, Employee Matching Gifts, General Support, Project.
Note: Employee matching gift ratio: 1 to 1 to arts, and cultural institutions; American Red Cross; Salvation Army; and Habitat for Humanity. Employee matching gift ratio: 2 to 1 to accredited colleges, universities, and secondary schools. Also matches employee gifts to United Way organizations that average at least 50 percent of the employee donations in the prior year.

Financial Summary

Total Giving: $4,308,465 (2003); $1,814,290 (2002); $4,937,778 (2001). Note: Contributes through corporate direct giving program and foundation.

Giving Analysis: Giving for 2001 includes: nonmonetary support ($31,152); corporate direct giving ($113,904); foundation matching gifts ($631,914); foundation grants to United Way ($1,724,855); foundation ($2,435,953)

Assets: $7,812,084 (2003); $12,008,122 (2002); $5,748,748 (2001)

Gifts Received: $12,475 (2000); $10,000,000 (1998); $400,000 (1995). Note: Contributions were received from Eaton Corporation.

Typical Recipients

Arts & Humanities: Arts Associations & Councils, Arts Centers, Arts Festivals, Arts Funds, Ballet, Community Arts, Dance, Historic Preservation, Libraries, Museums/Galleries, Music, Opera, Performing Arts, Public Broadcasting, Theater, Visual Arts

Civic & Public Affairs: African American Affairs, Botanical Gardens/Parks, Business/Free Enterprise, Community Foundations, Economic Development, Economic Policy, Employment/Job Training, Civic & Public Affairs-General, Hispanic Affairs, Housing,

Law & Justice, Legal Aid, Municipalities/Towns, Parades/Festivals, Professional & Trade Associations, Public Policy, Rural Affairs, Safety, Urban & Community Affairs, Zoos/Aquariums

Education: Business Education, Colleges & Universities, Community & Junior Colleges, Economic Education, Education Associations, Education Funds, Education Reform, Engineering/Technological Education, Education-General, Medical Education, Minority Education, Private Education (Precollege), Public Education (Precollege), Religious Education, Science/Mathematics Education, Secondary Education (Public), Student Aid

Environment: Environment-General, Watershed

Health: Cancer, Clinics/Medical Centers, Diabetes, Emergency/Ambulance Services, Health Policy/Cost Containment, Health Funds, Health Organizations, Hospices, Hospitals, Hospitals (University Affiliated), Nursing Services, Preventive Medicine/Wellness Organizations, Public Health, Single-Disease Health Associations

International: Health Care/Hospitals, International Organizations, International Relations

Religion: Ministries, Religious Welfare, Seminaries

Science: Science Museums, Scientific Centers & Institutes

Social Services: Child Welfare, Community Centers, Community Service Organizations, Counseling, Delinquency & Criminal Rehabilitation, Emergency Relief, Family Services, Food/Clothing Distribution, Homes, People with Disabilities, Recreation & Athletics, Scouts, Senior Services, Shelters/Homelessness, Social Services-General, United Funds/United Ways, Volunteer Services, YMCA/YWCA/YMHA/YWHA, Youth Organizations

Application Procedures

Initial Contact: Contact the company for guidelines; then submit an unbound written proposal.

Application Requirements: Proposals should consist of three components: a cover letter, program detail summary, and attachments. A one-page cover letter (on the organization's letterhead) should summarize the project, its purpose, amount requested, primary program activities, and the population that will benefit from the grant. The program detail component should be three pages or less, and must provide a written summary of the program, including specific project goals and how they relate the applicant organization's mission and to Eaton's grant guidelines; specific population that will benefit; description of what will be accomplished during the grant period; project budget; and an explanation of how the effectiveness of the project will be evaluated and communicated to Eaton and the community. The following attachments are required: the organization's history and purpose; identification of other sources of funding for the program and the amounts committed; names of Eaton employees and a description of their involvement, if applicable; recently audited financial statement and current budget; names and affiliations of officers and directors/trustees; and proof of tax-exempt status.

Deadlines: None.

Review Process: Requests should be made through local Eaton plant or human resources manager. Eaton managers submit requests to the Corporate Contributions Committee, which meets regularly to review requests; written notification of decisions is sent.

Evaluative Criteria: The evaluative process takes into account the importance of the project to Eaton Corporation employees and their families; importance to the community with significant Eaton Corporation employment; contributions from other companies similar to Eaton Corporation; participation of Eaton Corporation employees in direction of the institution; and recommendation by an Eaton manager. Projects supported are aimed at prevention rather than reaction, have clearly defined objectives, measurable results and benchmarks to evaluate progress, efficient administration, ethical fundraising

methods, and adequate budgetary controls.

Notes: Grants are typically limited to one year, except in the case of capital grants. Eaton requests that proposals not be submitted in binders or with videotapes, CD-ROMs, and/or in other costly manners.

Restrictions

Grants not awarded to religious, fraternal, or labor organizations; to individuals or individual endeavors; to annual operating budgets of United Way agencies or hospitals; for endowment funds; for fundraising benefits and sponsorships; for medical research; or debt retirement.

Additional Information

Branch facilities may make grants up to $1,000 without headquarters approval.

Eaton limits funding to specific projects or programs which address their priorities or to capital campaigns which meet their criteria. The priorities are education and community improvement.

In April 1999, Eaton Corp. acquired Aeroquip-Vickers, Inc.

Publications: Contributions Guidelines

Corporate Officials

Kristen Bihary: vice president corporate communications

Alexander MacDonald Cutler: chairman, president, chief executive officer B Milwaukee, WI May 28, 1951. ED Yale University BA (1973); Dartmouth College MBA (1975). NONPR AFFIL executive committee visitors committee: Weatherhood Subcommittee Metropolitan; member: Yale University Alumni Association; director: United Way Service Cleveland; class agent alumni fund: Loomis-Chaffee School; board governors: National Electrical Manufacturers Association; member: Amos Tuck School Dartmouth College; trustee: Cleveland Playhouse. CLUB AFFIL Chagrin Valley Hunt Club; Electric Manufacturer Club.

James L. Mason: vice president community initiatives B Joliet, IL 1938. ED John Carroll University (1960); Case Western Reserve University (1967).

Grants Analysis

Disclosure Period: calendar year ending 2003
Total Grants: $2,125,380*
Number of Grants: 250 (approx)
Average Grant: $8,501
Highest Grant: $100,000
Lowest Grant: $500
Typical Range: $1,000 to $20,000
*Note: Giving excludes United Way; matching gifts

Recent Grants

Note: Grants derived from 2003 Form 990.

General

100,000	Case Western Reserve University, Cleveland, OH
100,000	United Way Services, Cleveland, OH
78,000	Cleveland Scholarship Programs, Cleveland, OH
50,000	Carnegie Science Center, Pittsburgh, PA
50,000	Musical Arts Association Cleveland Orchestra, Cleveland, OH
40,000	Belmond Community Hospital, Belmond, IA
30,000	Kearney Public Schools, Kearney, NE
30,000	Kearney Public Schools, Kearney, NE
26,125	United Way of Allegheny County, Pittsburgh, PA
26,125	United Way of Allegheny County, Pittsburgh, PA

CYRUS EATON FOUNDATION

Giving Contact

Henry W. Gulick, Treasurer & Trustee
24200 Chagrin Blvd., Suite 233
Beachwood, OH 44122-5531
Phone: (216)360-9550

Description

Founded: 1955
EIN: 237440277
Organization Type: Private Foundation
Giving Locations: OH: Cleveland
Grant Types: Endowment, General Support, Project, Seed Money.

Financial Summary

Total Giving: $190,000 (2003)
Assets: $3,288,830 (2003)

Typical Recipients

Arts & Humanities: Arts Associations & Councils, Arts Centers, Arts Festivals, Arts Funds, Arts Institutes, Arts Outreach, Community Arts, Dance, Arts & Humanities-General, Historic Preservation, History & Archaeology, Libraries, Museums/Galleries, Music, Opera, Performing Arts, Public Broadcasting, Theater

Civic & Public Affairs: African American Affairs, Botanical Gardens/Parks, Clubs, Economic Development, Economic Policy, First Amendment Issues, Gay/Lesbian Issues, Civic & Public Affairs-General, Municipalities/Towns, Public Policy, Urban & Community Affairs

Education: Arts/Humanities Education, Colleges & Universities, Community & Junior Colleges, Education-General, International Studies, Private Education (Precollege), Student Aid

Environment: Protection, Resource Conservation

Health: AIDS/HIV, Children's Health/Hospitals, Clinics/Medical Centers, Hospices, Medical Research, Multiple Sclerosis, Single-Disease Health Associations

International: Foreign Educational Institutions, Health Care/Hospitals, International Environmental Issues, International Organizations, International Peace & Security Issues

Science: Science-General, Science Museums, Scientific Centers & Institutes

Social Services: Camps, Child Welfare, Community Centers, Community Service Organizations, Domestic Violence, Family Planning, Shelters/Homelessness

Application Procedures

Initial Contact: Send a brief letter of inquiry.
Application Requirements: budget for project, financial statements, and proof of tax-exempt status.
Deadlines: October 31.

Foundation Officials

Barring Coughlin: trustee B Wilkes-Barre, PA December 19, 1913. ED Princeton University BA (1935); Harvard University JD (1938). NONPR AFFIL trustee: Gun Safety Institute; member: Ohio Bar Association; member: American Law Institute; member: American Bar Association. CLUB AFFIL Union Club; Edgewater Yacht Club; Princeton Club; City Club; Adirondack League Club; Chagrin Valley Hunt Club.

Mary Stephens Eaton: vice president, trustee
Alice J. Gulick: trustee, secretary
Henry W. Gulick: treasurer, trustee
Ralph P. Higgins: assistant treasurer, trustee
Raymond Szabo: president, trustee

Grants Analysis

Disclosure Period: calendar year ending 2003
Total Grants: $190,000
Number of Grants: 42

Average Grant: $4,524
Highest Grant: $15,000
Lowest Grant: $1,000
Typical Range: $1,000 to $10,000

Recent Grants

Note: Grants derived from 2003 Form 990.
General

15,000	Cleveland Museum of Natural History, Cleveland, OH
15,000	US Pugwash, Washington, DC
5,000	Free Medical Clinic of Greater Cleveland, Cleveland, OH
5,000	Friends of the Cleveland School of the Arts, Cleveland, OH
5,000	McMaster University, Hamilton, ON Canada
3,000	Cleveland Opera, Cleveland, OH
3,000	Family Transitional Housing, Cleveland, OH
3,000	Great Lakes Theater Festival, Cleveland, OH
3,000	Greater Cleveland Community Shares, Cleveland, OH
3,000	Trust for Public Land, Cleveland, OH

EBERLY FOUNDATION

Giving Contact

Robert E. Eberly, Sr., President
The Eberly Foundation
PO Box 2023
Uniontown, PA 15401-1643
Phone: (724)437-7557

Description

Founded: 1963
EIN: 237070246
Organization Type: Private Foundation
Giving Locations: PA
Grant Types: General Support, Scholarship.

Financial Summary

Total Giving: $2,769,478 (2003); $2,324,916 (2002); $3,494,803 (2001)
Giving Analysis: Giving for 2003 includes: foundation scholarships ($25,000); foundation matching gifts ($314,195); 2002: foundation matching gifts ($92,854).
Assets: $12,250,930 (2003); $14,076,225 (2002); $17,694,731 (2001)
Gifts Received: $51,198 (1995); $16,918,780 (1994); $1,650,000 (1993). Note: In 1995, contributions were received from Greystone Productions.

Typical Recipients

Arts & Humanities: Arts Centers, Arts Outreach, Dance, Ethnic & Folk Arts, Arts & Humanities-General, Historic Preservation, History & Archaeology, Libraries, Museums/Galleries, Music, Opera, Performing Arts, Public Broadcasting, Theater
Civic & Public Affairs: Botanical Gardens/Parks, Chambers of Commerce, Community Foundations, Economic Development, Economic Policy, Civic & Public Affairs-General, Minority Business, Municipalities/Towns, Public Policy, Safety, Urban & Community Affairs
Education: Afterschool/Enrichment Programs, Business Education, Colleges & Universities, Education Reform, Elementary Education (Public), Faculty Development, Medical Education, Public Education (Precollege), Science/Mathematics Education, Student Aid
Environment: Air/Water Quality, Environment-General, Watershed
Health: Cancer, Children's Health/Hospitals, Clinics/Medical Centers, Emergency/Ambulance Services, Heart, Hospitals

International: International Organizations
Religion: Religious Welfare
Science: Scientific Centers & Institutes
Social Services: Camps, Community Centers, Community Service Organizations, Family Services, People with Disabilities, Recreation & Athletics, Scouts, Senior Services, United Funds/United Ways, YMCA/YWCA/YMHA/YWHA, Youth Organizations

Application Procedures

Initial Contact: Send a brief letter of inquiry.
Application Requirements: Include purpose of funds sought, employer identification number, copy of latest Form 990, and proof of tax-exempt status.
Deadlines: August 1.

Restrictions

None.

Foundation Officials

Carolyn E. Blaney: president, director
Ruth Ann Carter: director
Carolyn Jill Drost: director
Paul O. Eberly: director
Robert E. Eberly, Sr.: director B Greensboro, PA July 14, 1918. ED Pennsylvania State University BA (1939). PRIM CORP EMPL chairman: Eberly & Meade. CORP AFFIL chairman: Greystone Resources; director: Integra Financial Corp.; chairman: Chalk Hill Gas; chairman: Gallatin National Bank. NONPR AFFIL director: WQED/WQEX-TV; member: WV Oil Gas Association; member: Western Pennsylvania Conservancy; trustee emeritus: Uniontown Hospital Association; director: Uniontown Industry Fund; member: Pennsylvania Geological Society; member: Pennsylvania Oil Gas Association; director: Penns Southwest Association; member: OK Independent Petroleum Association; member: OK Oil Gas Association; member: Indepdendent Petroleum Association; member: Ohio Oil Gas Association; member: Greater Uniontown Chamber of Commerce; treasurer: Campaign Penn St; director: Fayette Heritage.
Robert E. Eberly, Jr.: director
Patricia Hillman Miller: vice president, secretary, director

Grants Analysis

Disclosure Period: calendar year ending 2003
Total Grants: $2,430,283*
Number of Grants: 7
Average Grant: $171,713*
Highest Grant: $1,400,000
Lowest Grant: $150
Typical Range: $500 to $200,000
*Note: Giving excludes matching gifts; scholarships. Average grants figure excludes highest grant.

Recent Grants

Note: Grants derived from 2003 Form 990.
General

1,400,000	Pennsylvania State University, Philadelphia, PA
250,000	Fay Penn Economic Development Council, Uniontown, PA
88,099	Touchstone Center for Crafts, Farmington, PA
53,185	Touchstone Center for Crafts, Farmington, PA
47,818	Touchstone Center for Crafts, Farmington, PA
43,101	Touchstone Center for Crafts, Farmington, PA
26,605	Touchstone Center for Crafts, Farmington, PA -- for student housing and infrastructure
25,000	Pennsylvania Free Enterprise Week, Erie, PA -- toward scholarships for Fayette County students
21,272	Touchstone Center for Crafts, Farmington, PA
18,000	Greater Uniontown Heritage Consortium, Uniontown, PA

EBSCO INDUSTRIES INC.

Company Headquarters

Birmingham, AL
Web: http://www.ebsco.com

Company Description

Revenue: US$1.375 billion (2002)
Employees: 4500 (2003)
SIC(s): 2542 Partitions & Fixtures Except Wood, 2721 Periodicals, 2752 Commercial Printing--Lithographic, 2759 Commercial Printing Nec.

Operating Locations

Ebsco Industries, Inc. (IL--Belleville; MD--Bowie; MN--Long Lake; NJ--Shrewsbury; PA--Horsham, Pittsburgh; TX--Plano)

Nonmonetary Support

Type: Donated Products; Workplace Solicitation

Giving Contact

Dell Brooke, Corp. Sec.
PO Box 1943
Birmingham, AL 35201
Phone: (205)991-1197
Fax: (205)995-1517
E-mail: wdimon@ebsco.com

Description

Organization Type: Corporate Giving Program
Giving Locations: AL
Grant Types: General Support.

Financial Summary

Total Giving: Contributes through corporate direct giving program only.

Typical Recipients

Arts & Humanities: Arts & Humanities-General, Libraries
Civic & Public Affairs: Civic & Public Affairs-General
Education: Education-General
Health: Health-General
Social Services: Social Services-General

Application Procedures

Initial Contact: Send a breif letter of inquiry. Deadlines: 2/None.
Deadlines: None.
Notes: The company is not currently accepting proposals.

Additional Information

The directors of the giving program report that the office is overwhelmed with requests that they do not have the time to read or the funds to support. Funding to new programs or organizations has ceased.
The company gives approximately 5% of pre-tax earnings.

Corporate Officials

Elton Bryson Stephens: founder, chairman B Clio, AL August 04, 1911. ED Birmingham-Southern College BA (1932); University of Alabama Law School LLB (1936). PRIM CORP EMPL founder, chairman: Ebsco Industries, Inc. CORP AFFIL chairman: Highland Bank; chairman, secretary: Ebsco Investment Services Inc.; chairman, vice president: Franklin Square Agency Overseas Inc.; chairman: CANEBSCO Subscription Services Ltd.; trustee, founder: Ebsco Employee Savings & Profit Sharing Trust; director: RA Brown Agency Ltd.; trustee: AlabamaBancorp Savings & Profit Sharing Trust; chairman: Bennett-Ebsco Subscription Services; chairman, founder: AlabamaBancorp. NONPR AFFIL chairman: TN-Tombigbee Waterway Authority Economic Pension Comm; member, don: United Arts Fund/Metropolitan

Arts Council; member: Phi Alpha Delta; chairman: Birmingham-Southern College Executive Comm; member: Omicron Delta Kappa; trustee: Birmingham Metropolitan YMCA; member: Alpha Tau Omega; director: Birmingham Chamber of Commerce. CLUB AFFIL Shades Valley Rotary Club; Summit Club; Mountain Brook Country Club; Birmingham Press Club; The Club.

James T. Stephens: president, director B 1939. ED Yale University BA (1961); Harvard University MBA (1964). PRIM CORP EMPL president, director: Ebsco Industries, Inc. CORP AFFIL president: Plastic Research & Development Corp.

Giving Program Officials

Elton Bryson Stephens: (see above)

WILLARD L. ECCLES CHARITABLE FOUNDATION

Giving Contact

Clark P. Giles
PO Box 628
Salt Lake City, UT 84110
Phone: (801)532-1500

Description

Founded: 1981
EIN: 942759395
Organization Type: Family Foundation
Giving Locations: UT: primarily Salt Lake City and Ogden
Grant Types: Capital, Challenge, Fellowship, General Support, Multiyear/Continuing Support, Project, Research.

Donor Information

Founder: The Willard L. Eccles Charitable Foundation was established in 1981 in Utah.

Financial Summary

Total Giving: $1,727,500 (fiscal year ending March 31, 2003)
Assets: $32,520,898 (fiscal 2003)
Gifts Received: $1,381 (fiscal 1997); $54,854 (fiscal 1995); $8,006 (fiscal 1992)

Typical Recipients

Arts & Humanities: Arts Centers, Arts Funds, Ballet, Arts & Humanities-General, Historic Preservation, Libraries, Museums/Galleries, Opera, Performing Arts, Public Broadcasting, Theater
Civic & Public Affairs: Clubs, Community Foundations, Municipalities/Towns, Professional & Trade Associations, Safety, Urban & Community Affairs, Zoos/Aquariums
Education: Colleges & Universities, Education Funds, Environmental Education, Education-General, Medical Education, Private Education (Precollege), Public Education (Precollege), School Volunteerism, Science/Mathematics Education, Secondary Education (Public), Special Education
Environment: Environment-General, Protection, Resource Conservation, Wildlife Protection
Health: AIDS/HIV, Alzheimer's Disease, Cancer, Children's Health/Hospitals, Clinics/Medical Centers, Emergency/Ambulance Services, Eyes/Blindness, Health-General, Health Organizations, Hospices, Hospitals, Medical Research, Medical Training, Mental Health, Multiple Sclerosis, Nursing Services, Prenatal Health Issues, Preventive Medicine/Wellness Organizations, Public Health, Respiratory, Single-Disease Health Associations
Religion: Religious Organizations, Religious Welfare
Science: Science Museums, Scientific Research

Social Services: Animal Protection, At-Risk Youth, Big Brothers/Big Sisters, Camps, Child Abuse, Child Welfare, Community Centers, Community Service Organizations, Counseling, Domestic Violence, Family Planning, Family Services, Food/Clothing Distribution, People with Disabilities, Recreation & Athletics, Scouts, Senior Services, Shelters/Homelessness, Social Services-General, United Funds/United Ways, Volunteer Services, YMCA/YWCA/YMHA/YWHA, Youth Organizations

Application Procedures

Initial Contact: Applicants should submit a brief letter or proposal, no specific form is required.
Application Requirements: Requests for grants should specifically describe the purpose of the grant and the proposed use of the funds and the benefits to be derived by the public from the grant. If the requesting organization has not previously submitted a request, background information with respect to the organization and evidence of tax-exempt status should be included. Where practicable, eight copies should be submitted.
Deadlines: Requests may be submitted at any time, but the deadline for consideration at the subsequent meetings of the Advisory Committee are February 1, June 1, and September 1.
Review Process: Proposals are reviewed at the next committee meeting.

Restrictions

The foundation does not support individuals, only exempt charitable organizations; grants for land acquisition, construction or building purposes, or endowments are limited to special circumstances.

Foundation Officials

Barbara E. Coit: committee member
Susan E. Coit: committee member
William E. Coit: committee member
Julie Denkers: committee member
Stephen G. Denkers: committee member
Susan E. Denkers: committee member

Grants Analysis

Disclosure Period: fiscal year ending March 31, 2003
Total Grants: $1,727,500
Number of Grants: 60
Average Grant: $18,009*
Highest Grant: $250,000
Lowest Grant: $2,500
Typical Range: $5,000 to $40,000
*Note: Average grant figure excludes three highest grants ($701,000).

Recent Grants

Note: Grants derived from 2003 Form 990.
General

250,000	McKay Dee Foundation, Ogden, UT -- for the exempt purpose of this organization
250,000	Nature Conservancy of Oregon, Portland, OR -- for the exempt purpose of this organization
201,000	Nature Conservancy of Utah, Salt Lake City, UT -- for the exempt purpose of this organization
150,000	University of Utah - Honors Program, Salt Lake City, UT -- for the exempt purpose of this organization
134,000	Rowland Hall-St. Marks, Salt Lake City, UT -- for the exempt purpose of this organization
54,000	Utah State University, Logan, UT -- for the exempt purpose of this organization
50,000	Christmas Box House, Salt Lake City, UT -- for the exempt purpose of this organization
50,000	University of Utah, Salt Lake City, UT -- for the exempt purpose of this organization
30,000	Planned Parenthood of Utah, Salt Lake City, UT -- for the exempt purpose of this organization
30,000	Riverdale School District 51J, Portland, OR -- for the exempt purpose of this organization

GEORGE S. AND DOLORES DORE ECCLES FOUNDATION

Giving Contact

Lisa Eccles, Executive Director
Deseret Building
79 South Main Street, 12th Floor
Salt Lake City, UT 84111
Phone: (801)246-5351
Fax: (801)350-3510

Description

Founded: 1958
EIN: 876118245
Organization Type: General Purpose Foundation
Giving Locations: UT: preference for Intermountain area of United States.
Grant Types: Challenge, Department, Fellowship, General Support, Multiyear/Continuing Support, Operating Expenses, Project, Scholarship.

Donor Information

Founder: Established in 1958 by George Stoddard Eccles and Dolores Dore 'Lolie' Eccles. George and Dolores Eccles met as undergraduates at Columbia University in New York City, married in 1925, and "became partners in a lifelong adventure -- a spirited trek through banking, international business and civic responsibility."

Throughout his respected business career, George Eccles sat on the boards of many corporations including Texas Gulf Sulfur Co., Amalgamated Sugar, Utah Construction, Union Pacific, and Husky Oil. He was also an original board member for the Salt Lake City-based First Security Corporation. George Eccles died on January 20, 1982, and his estate continues to fund the foundation.

Dolores Dore Eccles is known for her dedication to charities. Besides having served on the boards of several nonprofits including Ballet West and Westminster College, she also founded the Ogden Junior League. Dolores Dore Eccles continues to attend every meeting of the foundation's directors.

In 1981, the foundation absorbed the Lillian Ethel Dufton Charitable Trust.

Financial Summary

Total Giving: $24,577,149 (2003); $9,819,334 (2002); $20,621,709 (2001)
Giving Analysis: Giving for 2003 includes: foundation grants to United Way ($122,000)
Assets: $529,926,232 (2003)
Gifts Received: $50,000,000 (1995 approx); $749,700 (1994). Note: Contributions were received from the estate of George S. Eccles.

Typical Recipients

Arts & Humanities: Arts Associations & Councils, Arts Centers, Arts Festivals, Arts Funds, Arts Outreach, Ballet, Community Arts, Dance, Film & Video, Arts & Humanities-General, Historic Preservation, History & Archaeology, Libraries, Literary Arts, Museums/Galleries, Music, Opera, Performing Arts, Public Broadcasting, Theater
Civic & Public Affairs: Botanical Gardens/Parks, Business/Free Enterprise, Chambers of Commerce, Clubs, Community Foundations, Economic Development, Economic Policy, Civic & Public Affairs-

General, Housing, Law & Justice, Legal Aid, Municipalities/Towns, Parades/Festivals, Urban & Community Affairs, Zoos/Aquariums

Education: Arts/Humanities Education, Business Education, Colleges & Universities, Community & Junior Colleges, Economic Education, Education Associations, Education Funds, Education Reform, Elementary Education (Public), Engineering/Technological Education, Education-General, Health & Physical Education, International Studies, Leadership Training, Legal Education, Medical Education, Minority Education, Preschool Education, Private Education (Precollege), Public Education (Precollege), Science/Mathematics Education, Secondary Education (Public), Student Aid, Vocational & Technical Education

Environment: Air/Water Quality, Environment-General, Protection, Resource Conservation

Health: Arthritis, Clinics/Medical Centers, Eyes/Blindness, Health-General, Health Funds, Health Organizations, Hospices, Hospitals, Medical Research, Mental Health, Nursing Services, Outpatient Health Care, Preventive Medicine/Wellness Organizations, Public Health, Research/Studies Institutes, Single-Disease Health Associations, Speech & Hearing

Religion: Churches, Religious Organizations, Religious Welfare, Synagogues/Temples

Science: Science-General, Science Museums, Scientific Centers & Institutes

Social Services: At-Risk Youth, Camps, Child Welfare, Community Centers, Community Service Organizations, Counseling, Domestic Violence, Family Services, Homes, People with Disabilities, Recreation & Athletics, Scouts, Senior Services, Shelters/Homelessness, Substance Abuse, United Funds/United Ways, YMCA/YWCA/YMHA/YWHA, Youth Organizations

Application Procedures

Initial Contact: Prospective applicants should request an application form from the foundation.

Application Requirements: Organizations should complete the application form and send one additional copy to the foundation; attachments should include proof of tax-exempt status, financial statement and most recent operating budget, list of board of directors, and any additional information.

Deadlines: None. Proposals should reach the foundation four weeks prior to quarterly meetings.

Review Process: The board meets quarterly to set policies, review proposals, and make final decisions on awarding grants.

Notes: The foundation only accepts requests from organizations exempt by 501(c)(3) status under the Internal Revenue Code.

Restrictions

The foundation does not make grants to individuals, or for loans or endowment funds. Also not funded are operating costs, conduit organizations such as united funds, conferences and seminars, or governmental or quasi-governmental entities other than colleges and universities.

The foundation primarily funds organizations in Utah.

Additional Information

In addition to reviewing proposals submitted by qualified organizations and institutions, the foundation will seek out grant opportunities on its own initiative as funds permit and as the purposes of the foundation are seen as being served by such initiatives.

Publications: Application Form

Foundation Officials

Lisa Eccles: executive director
Robert M. Graham: treasurer
Alonzo Wallace Watson, Jr.: secretary, director B Salt Lake City, UT 1922. ED University of Utah AB (1943); Georgetown University BSFS (1947); University of Utah JD (1951). PRIM CORP EMPL chairman, director: Ray, Quinney & Nebeker.

Grants Analysis

Disclosure Period: calendar year ending 2003
Total Grants: $24,455,149*
Number of Grants: 387
Average Grant: $48,312*
Highest Grant: $2,000,000
Lowest Grant: $550
Typical Range: $5,000 to $100,000
*Note: Giving excludes United Way. Average grant excludes five highest grants ($6,000,000).

Recent Grants

Note: Grants derived from 2003 Form 990.
General

2,000,000	Westminster College, Salt Lake City, UT -- to construct health, wellness and athletic center
1,500,000	Utah Athletic Foundation, Salt Lake City, UT -- to support Olympic winter games
1,250,000	University of Utah, Salt Lake City, UT -- to establish the Presidential endowed chair in Pharmaceutics
1,250,000	University of Utah, Salt Lake City, UT -- to establish a Presidential chair in the David Eccles School of Business
1,000,000	Dixie State College, St. George, UT -- to construct fine arts center on their campus
600,000	Utah Symphony & Opera, Salt Lake City, UT -- to support Symphony programs
500,000	Ballet West, Salt Lake City, UT -- to construct new facility
500,000	Children & Youth Services Inc., West Jordan, UT -- to construct Utah girl's town campus
500,000	Foundation of Dixie Regional Medical Center, St. George, UT -- to help construct new medical center
500,000	University of Utah, Salt Lake City, UT -- to fund the new John A. Moran eye center

MARRINER S. ECCLES FOUNDATION

Giving Contact

Shannon K. Toronto, Executive Director
299 S. Main
Salt Lake City, UT 84111
Phone: (801)246-1436

Description

Founded: 1973
EIN: 237185855
Organization Type: General Purpose Foundation
Giving Locations: UT
Grant Types: General Support, Matching, Operating Expenses, Professorship, Project, Research, Scholarship.

Donor Information

Founder: The foundation was established in 1979. Marriner Eccles (1890-1977) was the son of banker David Eccles, a co-founder of Utah Construction, which built railroads, bridges, and the Grand Coulee and Hoover Dams. The company, which became Utah International, also had extensive coal and copper mining interests. Marriner S. Eccles was chairman of the company until 1971. Mr. Eccles was Federal Reserve chairman for fourteen years, and proposed many of the New Deal economic reforms, including the minimum wage and federal bank-deposit insurance. His widow, Sara M. Eccles, was the foundation's chairman.

Financial Summary

Total Giving: $1,506,500 (fiscal year ending March 31, 2004); $2,172,334 (fiscal 2001)
Giving Analysis: Giving for fiscal 2001 includes:

foundation grants to United Way ($37,500)
Assets: $33,527,343 (fiscal 2004); $36,488,522 (fiscal 2001)
Gifts Received: $123,635 (fiscal 2001); $7,843 (fiscal 1997); $78,944 (fiscal 1995). Note: Contributions were received from the estate of Marriner Eccles.

Typical Recipients

Arts & Humanities: Arts Associations & Councils, Arts Centers, Arts Festivals, Ballet, Community Arts, Dance, Libraries, Museums/Galleries, Music, Opera, Performing Arts, Public Broadcasting, Theater

Civic & Public Affairs: Botanical Gardens/Parks, Community Foundations, Economic Development, Employment/Job Training, Civic & Public Affairs-General, Housing, Law & Justice, Legal Aid, Native American Affairs, Nonprofit Management, Rural Affairs, Urban & Community Affairs, Zoos/Aquariums

Education: Afterschool/Enrichment Programs, Arts/Humanities Education, Business Education, Colleges & Universities, Community & Junior Colleges, Engineering/Technological Education, Environmental Education, Education-General, Legal Education, Medical Education, Private Education (Precollege), Vocational & Technical Education

Environment: Environment-General

Health: AIDS/HIV, Arthritis, Cancer, Children's Health/Hospitals, Clinics/Medical Centers, Diabetes, Emergency/Ambulance Services, Eyes/Blindness, Health-General, Geriatric Health, Health Funds, Health Organizations, Hospices, Hospitals, Hospitals (University Affiliated), Mental Health, Nursing Services, Public Health, Respiratory, Single-Disease Health Associations

International: Foreign Arts Organizations

Religion: Churches, Religious Organizations, Religious Welfare

Science: Science Museums

Social Services: Camps, Child Welfare, Community Centers, Community Service Organizations, Counseling, Day Care, Family Planning, Family Services, Food/Clothing Distribution, Homes, People with Disabilities, Recreation & Athletics, Senior Services, Shelters/Homelessness, Social Services-General, Special Olympics, Substance Abuse, YMCA/YWCA/YMHA/YWHA, Youth Organizations

Application Procedures

Initial Contact: Call or write for application form.
Application Requirements: Application must include an IRS form 501 (c)(3), an outline of the Organization, statement of request, and description of project and determination.
Deadlines: April 15.
Review Process: The foundation's board meets approximately four times a year.

Restrictions

Capital grants are made for equipment acquisition but not for bricks-and-mortar projects. Grants are strictly limited to organizations located within the state of Utah. Grants are not made to individuals.

Additional Information

Wells Fargo Bank, N.A. serves as a corporate trustee for the foundation.
Publications: Application Form; Application Guidelines

Foundation Officials

C. Hope Eccles: committee member
Spencer Fox Eccles: committee member B Ogden, UT 1934. ED University of Utah BS (1956); Columbia University MA (1959). PRIM CORP EMPL chairman, chief executive officer, director, president: First Security Corp. CORP AFFIL director: Zions Corp. Mercantile Institute; director: Zions Corp.; director: First Security Insurance Inc.; director: Union Pacific Corp.; director: Anderson Lumber Co. NONPR AFFIL director: Merc Institute; member advisory council: University Utah Business College; member: Bankers Roundtable; member: American Bankers Associa-

tion. CLUB AFFIL mem: Alta Club; mem: Salt Lake Country Club.
James M. Steele: committee member
Shannon K. Toronto: executive director
Elmer D. Tucker: comm mem
Alonzo Wallace Watson, Jr.: committee member B Salt Lake City, UT 1922. ED University of Utah AB (1943); Georgetown University BSFS (1947); University of Utah JD (1951). PRIM CORP EMPL chairman, director: Ray, Quinney & Nebeker.

Grants Analysis
Disclosure Period: fiscal year ending March 31, 2004
Total Grants: $1,506,500
Number of Grants: 123
Average Grant: $12,248
Highest Grant: $95,000
Lowest Grant: $2,000
Typical Range: $5,000 to $25,000

Recent Grants
Note: Grants derived from 2004 Form 990.
General

95,000	Utah Symphony & Opera, Salt Lake City, UT
50,000	Wasatch Homeless Healthcare, Salt Lake City, UT
50,000	Westminster College, Salt Lake City, UT
45,000	University of Utah KUED 7, Salt Lake City, UT
41,000	Guadalupe Schools, Salt Lake City, UT
40,000	Ballet West, Salt Lake City, UT
40,000	University of Utah - Utah Museum of Fine Arts, Salt Lake City, UT
40,000	Utah State University College of Engineering, Logan, UT
35,000	Boys & Girls Club of Greater SL, Salt Lake City, UT
25,000	Arthritis Foundation, Salt Lake City, UT

RALPH M. AND ELLA M. ECCLES FOUNDATION

Giving Contact
Emily Eisenman, Trust Officer
c/o National City Bank of Pennsylvania
20 Stanwix St.
Pittsburgh, PA 15222
Phone: (216)222-3668

Description
Founded: 1972
EIN: 237261807
Organization Type: Private Foundation
Giving Locations: PA: limited to Union School District of Clarion County
Grant Types: Capital, Emergency, General Support, Multiyear/Continuing Support, Operating Expenses.

Financial Summary
Total Giving: $141,620 (2003)
Assets: $3,869,268 (2003)

Typical Recipients
Arts & Humanities: Libraries
Civic & Public Affairs: Economic Development, Municipalities/Towns, Safety
Education: Colleges & Universities, Education Funds, Environmental Education, Public Education (Precollege), School Volunteerism
Health: Clinics/Medical Centers, Hospitals, Prenatal Health Issues
Religion: Churches, Religious Welfare
Social Services: Community Service Organizations, Food/Clothing Distribution, Recreation & Athletics, Youth Organizations

Application Procedures
Initial Contact: Send a brief letter of inquiry.
Application Requirements: Include purpose of funds sought and proof of tax-exempt status.
Deadlines: None.

Restrictions
Foundation contributes to organizations serving Clarion County.

Additional Information
Trust(s): Natl City Bank PA

Grants Analysis
Disclosure Period: calendar year ending 2003
Total Grants: $141,620
Number of Grants: 8
Highest Grant: $62,200
Lowest Grant: $900

Recent Grants
Note: Grants derived from 2001 Form 990.
Library-Related

187,333	Eccles Lesher Memorial Library, Rimersburgh, PA

General

19,369	Rimbersburg Medical Center, Rimersburg, PA
18,000	Rimersburg Little League, Rimersburg, PA
3,500	United Methodist Church, Rimersburg, PA
1,000	United Together Food Bank, Sligo, PA

ECG FOUNDATION

Giving Contact
Amber Carden, Trust Officer
c/o Bank of America
PO Box 908
Austin, TX 78781
Phone: (512)397-2717

Description
Founded: 1986
EIN: 742418070
Organization Type: Private Foundation
Giving Locations: TX: nationally.
Grant Types: General Support.

Donor Information
Founder: Ellen Clayton Garwood

Financial Summary
Total Giving: $105,000 (fiscal year ending April 30, 2004); $185,742 (fiscal 2001)
Giving Analysis: Giving for fiscal 2004 includes: foundation grants to United Way ($3,000) fiscal 2001: foundation grants to United Way ($5,000)
Assets: $2,688,337 (fiscal 2004); $3,557,200 (fiscal 2001)

Typical Recipients
Arts & Humanities: Arts Associations & Councils, Film & Video, Historic Preservation, Libraries, Literary Arts, Museums/Galleries, Music, Performing Arts, Public Broadcasting, Theater
Civic & Public Affairs: Civil Rights, Civic & Public Affairs-General, Hispanic Affairs, Legal Aid, Public Policy, Urban & Community Affairs, Women's Affairs
Education: Colleges & Universities, Education-General, International Studies, Private Education (Precollege), Secondary Education (Public), Social Sciences Education, Vocational & Technical Education
Health: Cancer, Children's Health/Hospitals, Clinics/Medical Centers, Heart, Hospitals
International: International Peace & Security Issues,

International Relations
Religion: Religious Organizations, Religious Welfare
Social Services: Big Brothers/Big Sisters, Camps, Child Welfare, Community Service Organizations, Counseling, Domestic Violence, Family Services, Recreation & Athletics, United Funds/United Ways, Youth Organizations

Application Procedures
Initial Contact: Request application form.
Deadlines: None.

Restrictions
Limited to organizations with section 501(c)(3) IRS code status.

Additional Information
Publications: Application Form
Trust(s): Bank of America

Foundation Officials
Mary Margaret Farabee: secretary
William L. Garwood, Jr.: vice president, director
Lew Little: treasurer
Howard Yancy: president, director

Grants Analysis
Disclosure Period: fiscal year ending April 30, 2004
Total Grants: $102,000*
Number of Grants: 15
Average Grant: $3,615*
Highest Grant: $30,000
Lowest Grant: $1,000
Typical Range: $1,000 to $5,000
*Note: Giving excludes United Way. Average grant figure excludes two highest grants ($55,000).

Recent Grants
Note: Grants derived from fiscal 2004 Form 990.
General

30,000	Caritas, Austin, TX
25,000	St. Andrew's Episcopal School, Austin, TX
10,000	Any Baby Can of Austin, Austin, TX
5,000	Austin Theatre Alliance, Austin, TX
5,000	Big Brothers Big Sisters, Austin, TX
5,000	LifeWorks, Austin, TX
5,000	SafePlace, Austin, TX
3,000	United Way, Austin, TX
2,500	Austin Film Festival, Austin, TX
2,500	Austin High School Debate, Austin, TX

SAMUEL AND RAE ECKMAN CHARITABLE FOUNDATION

Giving Contact
Stephen F. Selig, President & Director
c/o Baer, Marks & Upham
900 3rd Avenue
New York, NY 10022
Phone: (212)895-2000

Description
Founded: 1970
EIN: 237051411
Organization Type: Private Foundation
Giving Locations: NY: primarily New York City
Grant Types: General Support, Research.

Donor Information
Founder: the late Rae Eckman, the late Samuel Eckman

Financial Summary
Total Giving: $246,500 (2003)
Assets: $1,680,217 (2003)

Typical Recipients

Arts & Humanities: Arts Centers, Ballet, Dance, Arts & Humanities-General, Libraries, Museums/Galleries, Music, Opera, Performing Arts, Theater

Civic & Public Affairs: Botanical Gardens/Parks, Economic Policy, Ethnic Organizations, Gay/Lesbian Issues, Civic & Public Affairs-General, Municipalities/Towns, Safety, Urban & Community Affairs

Education: Colleges & Universities, Legal Education

Environment: Air/Water Quality

Health: AIDS/HIV, Cancer, Clinics/Medical Centers, Emergency/Ambulance Services, Health Funds, Hospitals, Medical Research, Public Health, Single-Disease Health Associations

International: Missionary/Religious Activities

Religion: Jewish Causes, Ministries, Religious Organizations, Synagogues/Temples

Social Services: Community Service Organizations, People with Disabilities, Senior Services, YMCA/YWCA/YMHA/YWHA

Application Procedures

Initial Contact: Send a brief letter of inquiry. Include a description of organization, amount requested, purpose of funds sought, recently audited financial statement, and proof of tax-exempt status.

Deadlines: None.

Restrictions

Grants are awarded for medical research, assistance to and support for aged persons, and education of indigent or underprivileged children.

Foundation Officials

Abraham Jacob Briloff: assistant secretary, assistant treasurer B New York, NY July 19, 1917. ED City College of New York BBA (1937); City College of New York MS (1941); New York University PhD (1965). PRIM CORP EMPL partner: AJ & LA Briloff PRIM NONPR EMPL professor emeritus: City University of New York, Baruch College. NONPR AFFIL member: New York Saint Society Certified Public Accountants; member: New York State Society of CPA's; member: American Institute of CPA's.

Arthur Murphy: director

William Benjamin Norden, Esq.: secretary, treasurer, director B Brooklyn, NY 1945. ED Brooklyn College BS (1967); New York University JD (1969). PRIM CORP EMPL partner: Baer Marks & Upham.

Stephen F. Selig, Esq.: president, director

Grants Analysis

Disclosure Period: calendar year ending 2003

Total Grants: $246,500

Number of Grants: 29

Average Grant: $8,500

Highest Grant: $20,000

Lowest Grant: $2,500

Typical Range: $5,000 to $10,000

Recent Grants

Note: Grants derived from 2003 Form 990.

Library-Related

15,000	New York Public Library, New York, NY

General

20,000	American Friends Aids Research
15,000	Brooklyn Museum of Art, Brooklyn, NY
12,500	Jewish Guild for the Blind, New York, NY
12,000	Metropolitan Museum of Art, New York, NY
12,000	United Jewish Appeal-Federation, New York, NY
10,000	American Ballet Theatre, New York, NY
10,000	Calvary Fund, Bronx, NY
10,000	Memorial Sloan-Kettering of New York, New York, NY
10,000	Philharmonic Society of New York, New York, NY

ECOLAB INC.

Company Headquarters

370 N. Wabasha St.
St. Paul, MN 55102
Web: http://www.ecolab.com

Company Description

Founded: 1923
Ticker: ECL
Exchange: NYSE
Revenue: US$4.184 billion (2004)
Profit: US$310.5 million (2004)
Employees: 20800 (2003)
Fortune Rank: 455, per FORTUNE Magazine's list of 500 Largest U.S. Corporations (2004).
SIC(s): 2841 Soap & Other Detergents, 2879 Agricultural Chemicals Nec, 2899 Chemical Preparations Nec, 7342 Disinfecting & Pest Control Services.

Operating Locations

Ecolab (MN--St. Paul); Ecolab Inc. (AL--Birmingham, Mobile; CA--Carlsbad, Roseville, San Jose, Simi Valley, Tulare; CO--Denver; CT--Tolland; DC--Washington; FL--Altamonte Springs, Fort Myers, Tampa; GA--McDonough; HI--Honolulu; IL--Glen Ellyn, Joliet, Lombard, Peoria; IN--Granger, Huntington, Indianapolis; IA--West Des Moines; KS--Lenexa; LA--Shreveport, St. Rose; ME--Brewer; MD--Gaithersburg, Ocean City; MA--Norwood, Wilmington; MI--Farmington Hills, Traverse City; MN--Eagan, Mendota Heights, Minnetonka; MO--Kansas City, Springfield; NE--Omaha; NV--Las Vegas, Reno; NH--Amherst, Lebanon; NM--Albuquerque; NY--East Syracuse, New Hyde Park, New York, Rochester; NC--Burlington, Charlotte, Winston-Salem; OH--Cleveland, Hebron, Pickerington; OK--Oklahoma City, Tulsa; PA--Allentown, Erie, Harrisburg, Lancaster, Plumsteadville; PR--Dorado; SC--Columbia, North Charleston; TN--Brentwood, Knoxville, Memphis, Murfreesboro; TX--Garland, Grand Prairie, Houston; UT--Midvale; VA--Roanoke, Virginia Beach; WA--Gig Harbor, Renton; WI--Janesville, Milwaukee, Sun Prairie)

Nonmonetary Support

Type: In-kind Services
Note: NOT NOT In-kind services are offered in times of disasters.
Volunteer Programs: Employees volunteer as classroom speakers and with Business/Education Partnership. Company also provides technical assistance and coordinates volunteer projects for two weekends of the United Way's Week of Caring, Volunteer Fair, and provides contributions to nonprofit organizations to reward employee volunteers.
Contact: James Dietz, Distribution
Note: Foundation provides nonmonetary support.

Ecolab Foundation

Giving Contact

Kris J. Taylor, Director, Community & Public Relations
Ecolab Inc.
370 North Wabasha Street N.
St. Paul, MN 55102
Phone: (651)293-2259
Fax: (651)225-3123
Web: http://www.ecolab.com/companyprofile/foundation/default.asp

Alternate Contact

Phone: (651)293-2255

Description

EIN: 411372157
Organization Type: Corporate Foundation
Giving Locations: MN: St. Paul areas where compa-

ny has a major presence, and large numbers of employees live and work.
Grant Types: General Support.

Financial Summary

Total Giving: $6,216,771 (2003); $2,916,435 (2002); $3,034,923 (2001). Note: Contributes through corporate direct giving program and foundation.

Assets: $6,167,737 (2003); $5,979,435 (2002); $5,485,860 (2001)

Gifts Received: $3,312,299 (2003); $3,238,050 (2002); $3,402,584 (2001). Note: In 2000, 2001, and 2002, contributions were received from Ecolab Inc. In 1998, contributions were received from the Ida C. Koran Trust.

Typical Recipients

Arts & Humanities: Arts Associations & Councils, Arts Funds, Arts Institutes, Arts Outreach, Arts & Humanities-General, History & Archaeology, Libraries, Museums/Galleries, Music, Opera, Performing Arts, Public Broadcasting, Theater

Civic & Public Affairs: African American Affairs, Business/Free Enterprise, Economic Development, Employment/Job Training, Ethnic Organizations, Civic & Public Affairs-General, Hispanic Affairs, Housing, Law & Justice, Municipalities/Towns, Nonprofit Management, Parades/Festivals, Professional & Trade Associations, Urban & Community Affairs, Women's Affairs, Zoos/Aquariums

Education: Business Education, Business-School Partnerships, Colleges & Universities, Continuing Education, Economic Education, Education Associations, Education Funds, Education Reform, Elementary Education (Public), Environmental Education, Faculty Development, Education-General, International Exchange, Minority Education, Public Education (Precollege), School Volunteerism, Science/Mathematics Education, Secondary Education (Public), Special Education, Student Aid

Environment: Environment-General, Protection, Resource Conservation

Health: AIDS/HIV, Cancer, Children's Health/Hospitals, Clinics/Medical Centers, Diabetes, Emergency/Ambulance Services, Hospitals, Long-Term Care, Medical Rehabilitation, Nutrition, Public Health, Speech & Hearing

International: Foreign Arts Organizations, International Environmental Issues

Religion: Churches, Religion-General, Jewish Causes, Religious Welfare

Science: Science Museums

Social Services: Animal Protection, At-Risk Youth, Big Brothers/Big Sisters, Child Welfare, Community Service Organizations, Day Care, Delinquency & Criminal Rehabilitation, Emergency Relief, Family Planning, Family Services, Food/Clothing Distribution, People with Disabilities, Scouts, Senior Services, Shelters/Homelessness, Social Services-General, Substance Abuse, United Funds/United Ways, Volunteer Services, YMCA/YWCA/YMHA/YWHA, Youth Organizations

Application Procedures

Initial Contact: Submit a one-page letter describing the program and how it fits within the foundation's guidelines.

Application Requirements: Full proposals to the foundation should be made using the Minnesota Common Grant Application Form, and must include proof of tax-exempt status.

Deadlines: August 31.

Review Process: The foundation will respond to initial proposals within 2-4 weeks with a postcard indicating whether or not a complete proposal is requested.

Evaluative Criteria: Priority given to programs in company operating areas that leverage corporate dollars with volunteer time and technical expertise; encourage self-sufficiency among disadvantaged groups in the community; encompass creative programs that are not duplicated through existing community organizations and resources; involve a significant number of employees; and have a direct impact on the end user.

Decision Notification: Most funding decisions are made in late fall for the following year, and grantees are notified after January 15.

Restrictions

Grants are made for general operations and specific projects. The company does not award grants for individuals; fundraisers or advertisements; religious organizations for sectarian or denominational programs; disease-specific organizations; sports or athletic programs; industry, trade, political, professional, or business associations; or loans or investments.

Additional Information

Company sponsors an Employee Volunteer Bonus Program (to provide grants to nonprofits in recognition of significant employee volunteer commitments), a Community Involvement Program (to recognize employees who serve on the boards of nonprofits), and a matching gifts program.

The company allocates 1% of pretax U.S. profits to charitable contributions each year.

Ecolab is a U.S. affiliate of Henkel KGAA, which has a 25% investment in the company. Other U.S. affiliates are Loctite Corp. (29%) and Clorox Co. (28%).

Publications: Annual Giving Report; Application Guidelines

Corporate Officials

Douglas Baker, Jr.: president, chief operating officer
Lawrence T. Bell: vice president law, general counsel B 1947. PRIM CORP EMPL vice president law, general counsel: Ecolab Inc.
Bruno Deschamps: president, chief operating officer PRIM CORP EMPL president, chief operating officer: Ecolab Inc.
John G. Forsythe: vice president tax and public affairs B Chicago, IL 1947. ED Loyola University (1969); Northwestern University (1973). PRIM CORP EMPL vice president tax and public affairs: Ecolab Inc. NONPR AFFIL chairman: Chemical Specialties Manufacturing Association.
Steven L. Fritze: vice president, controller B Saint Paul, MN 1954. ED University of Minnesota (1975); University of Minnesota (1977). PRIM CORP EMPL vice president, chief financial officer: Ecolab Inc. NONPR AFFIL member: Financial Executives Institute.
Kenneth A. Iverson: vice president, corporate secretary B 1945. ED College of Saint Thomas BA (1967); University of Notre Dame JD (1970). PRIM CORP EMPL vice president, corporate secretary: Ecolab Inc.
Diana D. Lewis: vice president human resources PRIM CORP EMPL vice president human resources: Ecolab Inc.
Richard L. Marcantonio: vice president, chairman PRIM CORP EMPL vice president, chairman: Ecolab Inc.
Michael J. Monahan: vice president external affairs PRIM CORP EMPL vice president external affairs: Ecolab Inc.
Maurizio Nisita: senior vice president global operations PRIM CORP EMPL senior vice president global operations: Ecolab Inc.
Allan L. Schuman: chairman, chief executive officer, director B Sheridan, WY May 24, 1934. ED New York University BS (1955). PRIM CORP EMPL president, chief executive officer: Ecolab Inc. CORP AFFIL director: Northern Studies Power Co.; director: Northern Studies Power Co. Minnesota; chairman: Industrial Maintenance Corp.

Giving Program Officials

Lawrence T. Bell: member, corporate contributions committee (see above)
John G. Forsythe: member corporate contributions committee (see above)

Diana D. Lewis: member corporate contributions committee (see above)
William A. Mathison: member corporate contributions committee PRIM CORP EMPL vice president, general manager food & bev North America: Ecolab Inc.
Michael J. Monahan: president corporate contributions committee (see above)

Foundation Officials

Lawrence T. Bell: vice president, director (see above)
Dave F. Duvick: secretary
John G. Forsythe: vice president (see above)
Thomas J. Hill: treasurer
Diana D. Lewis: vice president (see above)
Michael J. Monahan: president, director (see above)
Thomas W. Schnack: vice president
Allan L. Schuman: chairman (see above)
Kris J. Taylor: vice president

Grants Analysis

Disclosure Period: calendar year ending 2003
Total Grants: $5,635,304*
Number of Grants: 1,000 (approx)
Average Grant: $5,635
Highest Grant: $100,000
Lowest Grant: $500
Typical Range: $1,000 to $10,000
*****Note:** Giving excludes scholarship and United Way.

Recent Grants

Note: Grants derived from 2003 Form 990.
General

150,000	Guthrie Theatre, Minneapolis, MN
100,000	Minnesota Public Radio, St. Paul, MN
52,500	Greater Twin Cities United Way, Minneapolis, MN
52,500	Greater Twin Cities United Way, Minneapolis, MN
52,500	Greater Twin Cities United Way, Minneapolis, MN
52,500	Greater Twin Cities United Way, Minneapolis, MN
50,000	Ordway Center for the Performing Arts, St. Paul, MN
50,000	Ordway Center for the Performing Arts, St. Paul, MN
42,000	United Way of Greater Greensboro, Greensboro, NC
35,000	Best Education Foundation

C. K. EDDY FAMILY MEMORIAL FUND

Giving Contact

Helen James, Trust Administrator
c/o Citizens Bank Saginaw
101 N. Washington Ave., MC 332021
Saginaw, MI 48607
Phone: (517)776-7368
Fax: (517)776-7309

Description

Founded: 1925
EIN: 386040506
Organization Type: Private Foundation
Giving Locations: MI: limited to Saginaw County
Grant Types: Project, Scholarship.

Donor Information

Founder: the late Arthur D. Eddy

Financial Summary

Total Giving: $589,927 (fiscal year ending June 30, 2003)
Assets: $15,168,128 (fiscal 2003)

Gifts Received: $247,578 (fiscal 1997); $269,788 (fiscal 1996)

Typical Recipients

Arts & Humanities: Dance, Historic Preservation, History & Archaeology, Libraries, Museums/Galleries, Music, Performing Arts, Theater
Civic & Public Affairs: African American Affairs, Business/Free Enterprise, Community Foundations, Employment/Job Training, Civic & Public Affairs-General, Housing, Municipalities/Towns, Safety, Urban & Community Affairs, Zoos/Aquariums
Education: Business Education, Colleges & Universities, Engineering/Technological Education, Private Education (Precollege), Public Education (Precollege), Student Aid
Health: Children's Health/Hospitals, Clinics/Medical Centers, Emergency/Ambulance Services, Health Funds, Hospitals, Medical Rehabilitation, Nursing Services
Religion: Religion-General, Religious Welfare
Social Services: Big Brothers/Big Sisters, Child Abuse, Child Welfare, Community Centers, Community Service Organizations, Counseling, Crime Prevention, Food/Clothing Distribution, People with Disabilities, Recreation & Athletics, United Funds/United Ways, Volunteer Services, YMCA/YWCA/YMHA/YWHA, Youth Organizations

Application Procedures

Initial Contact: For scholarships, return completed application form along with transcripts and financial information; for grants, send a proposal with a one-page cover letter.
Application Requirements: Include explanation of name of program, purpose of funds sought, amount requested, period of program or project, contact person, a description of organization, statement of expected accomplishments, time schedule for completion of project, program budget, and future activities and funding.
Deadlines: None, for scholarships; May 1 for grants

Restrictions

Limited to organizations and residents of Saginaw County or City, MI.

Additional Information

Provides scholarships to residents of Saginaw County for higher education.
Publications: Application Guidelines
Trust(s): Citizens Bank Saginaw

Grants Analysis

Disclosure Period: fiscal year ending June 30, 2003
Total Grants: $589,927*
Number of Grants: 22
Average Grant: $19,746*
Highest Grant: $100,000
Lowest Grant: $3,000
Typical Range: $15,000 to $100,000 and $10,000 to $50,000
*****Note:** Giving excludes scholarships to individuals totaling $195,000 (two largest grants).

Recent Grants

Note: Grants derived from fiscal 2003 Form 990.
General

100,000	Mid-Michigan Children's Museum, Saginaw, MI
95,000	Saginaw Concert Band, Saginaw, MI
50,000	Saginaw Habitat for Humanity, Saginaw, MI
50,000	Saginaw Valley State University, Saginaw, MI
46,000	Saginaw Valley Rail Trail, Saginaw, MI
33,334	Delta College, University Center, MI
33,333	Delta College, University Center, MI
30,000	Westlund Guidance Clinic, Saginaw, MI
25,000	Saginaw Symphony Association, Saginaw, MI
20,000	United Way, Saginaw, MI

EDEN HALL FOUNDATION

Giving Contact
George C. Greer, Chairman
Eden Hall Foundation
600 Grant, Suite 3232
Pittsburgh, PA 15219
Phone: (412)642-6697
Fax: (412)642-6698

Alternate Contact
Josephine K. Crane, Administrations Manager

Description
Founded: 1984
EIN: 251384468
Organization Type: General Purpose Foundation
Giving Locations: PA: primarily western area
Grant Types: Capital, Endowment, General Support, Project, Research, Scholarship.

Donor Information
Founder: The Eden Hall Foundation was established in 1984 by Eden Hall Farm.

Financial Summary
Total Giving: $21,388,600 (2003); $9,637,466 (2002)
Giving Analysis: Giving for 2003 includes: foundation scholarships ($73,000); foundation grants to United Way ($300,000); 2002: foundation scholarships ($120,000)
Assets: $161,136,807 (2003); $141,245,359 (2002)

Typical Recipients
Arts & Humanities: Arts Associations & Councils, Arts Centers, Arts Institutes, Arts Outreach, Ballet, Arts & Humanities-General, Historic Preservation, History & Archaeology, Libraries, Museums/Galleries, Music, Opera, Public Broadcasting, Theater
Civic & Public Affairs: African American Affairs, Botanical Gardens/Parks, Business/Free Enterprise, Chambers of Commerce, Clubs, Community Foundations, Economic Development, Economic Policy, Employment/Job Training, Civic & Public Affairs-General, Housing, Parades/Festivals, Philanthropic Organizations, Public Policy, Urban & Community Affairs, Women's Affairs, Zoos/Aquariums
Education: Afterschool/Enrichment Programs, Arts/Humanities Education, Business Education, Colleges & Universities, Education Associations, Education Funds, Environmental Education, Education-General, Gifted & Talented Programs, Health & Physical Education, Literacy, Medical Education, Minority Education, Preschool Education, Private Education (Precollege), Religious Education, Science/Mathematics Education, Special Education, Student Aid
Environment: Environment-General, Wildlife Protection
Health: AIDS/HIV, Arthritis, Cancer, Children's Health/Hospitals, Clinics/Medical Centers, Diabetes, Emergency/Ambulance Services, Health Funds, Health Organizations, Hospices, Hospitals, Kidney, Medical Rehabilitation, Mental Health, Multiple Sclerosis, Nursing Services, Prenatal Health Issues, Research/Studies Institutes, Single-Disease Health Associations
International: International Affairs
Religion: Religion-General, Ministries, Religious Organizations, Religious Welfare
Science: Scientific Centers & Institutes
Social Services: Big Brothers/Big Sisters, Camps, Child Welfare, Community Centers, Community Service Organizations, Counseling, Day Care, Delinquency & Criminal Rehabilitation, Domestic Violence, Family Planning, Family Services, Food/Clothing Distribution, Homes, People with Disabilities, Scouts, Senior Services, Shelters/Homelessness, Substance Abuse, United Funds/United Ways, YMCA/YWCA/YMHA/YWHA, Youth Organizations

Application Procedures
Initial Contact: Initial requests should be in letter form.
Application Requirements: Requests should include the purpose of the applying organization, current financial statement including the organization's other sources of funding, specific purposes for which the grant is to be used, and proof of IRS tax-exempt status.
Organizations receiving funds must acknowledge receipt in writing, stating that the grant will be used for the purpose for which it was made. When the organization expends the funds, a written report giving details and verification of the expenditures is required by the foundation.
Deadlines: None.
Review Process: The board of directors usually meets quarterly to consider grant proposals. Applicants will receive notification of the board's decision.

Restrictions
Requests to cover operating expenses, accumulated deficits, and general fund-raising campaigns are discouraged. Grants are not made to individuals or private foundations.

Additional Information
Interviews or site visits may be required for additional information and confirmation.
Publications: Application Guidelines

Foundation Officials
D. S. Foster: secretary
George C. Greer: chairman B Sharon, PA 1932. ED Pennsylvania State University (1954); University of Pennsylvania School of Law (1957). PRIM CORP EMPL vice president organization development & administration: H.J. Heinz Co. CORP AFFIL director: Hartwell-Pacific (HK) Ltd.
John M. Mazur: treasurer
E. H. Shifler: director

Grants Analysis
Disclosure Period: calendar year ending 2003
Total Grants: $21,015,600*
Number of Grants: 87
Average Grant: $232,740*
Highest Grant: $1,000,000
Lowest Grant: $1,000
Typical Range: $50,000 to $500,000
*Note: Giving excludes scholarships; United Way. Average grant figure excludes highest grant.

Recent Grants
Note: Grants derived from 2003 Form 990.
General
1,000,000	Pittsburgh Parks Conservancy, Pittsburgh, PA
500,000	Chatham College, Pittsburgh, PA -- for new athletic facility
500,000	Point Park College, Pittsburgh, PA -- for purchase of two buildings to house four dance studios
500,000	Seton Hill College, Greensburg, PA -- towards construction of a new athletic facility
500,000	Washington & Jefferson College, Washington, PA -- for construction of the Vilar technology center
400,000	Three Rivers Youth, Pittsburgh, PA -- for capital improvements associated with improvements to use service facilities
400,000	War for Empire Regional Enterprise Tower, Pittsburgh, PA
300,000	Manchester Craftsmen's Guild, Pittsburgh, PA -- towards learning and training initiatives in Reizenstein, Frick International Studies Academy, South Hills and Columbus Middle school
300,000	Rankin Christian Center, Rankin, PA
300,000	United Way, Pittsburgh, PA

CHARLES EDISON FUND

Giving Contact
John Keegan, Chairman, President
Charles Edison Fund
One Riverfront Plaza, 4th Floor
Newark, NJ 07102
Phone: (973)648-0500
Fax: (973)648-0400
E-mail: info@charlesedisonfund.org
Web: http://www.charlesedisonfund.org/home2.html

Description
Founded: 1948
EIN: 221514861
Organization Type: General Purpose Foundation
Giving Locations: NJ: primarily metropolitan area; NY: primarily metropolitan area
Grant Types: General Support, Multiyear/Continuing Support, Project, Research, Seed Money.

Donor Information
Founder: The Charles Edison Fund was incorporated in 1948 as the Brook Foundation. Charles Edison, who died in 1969, was the founder and principal donor. The son of inventor Thomas A. Edison, he left the bulk of his estate (between $8 and $12 million) to the Brook Foundation, which later became the Charles Edison Fund.
Charles Edison was born in Llewellyn Park, West Orange, NJ, in 1890 and spent most of his life there. He attended the Hotchkiss School, Lakeville, CT, and received a degree in electrical engineering at Massachusetts Institute of Technology in 1913. He went on to become governor of New Jersey and secretary of the Navy. His personal interests were music and literature.

Financial Summary
Total Giving: $1,509,235 (2003); $2,091,605 (2002)
Assets: $32,854,046 (2003); $30,487,543 (2002)
Gifts Received: $465 (2003); $2,014 (2000); $3,779 (1998)

Typical Recipients
Arts & Humanities: Arts Associations & Councils, Arts Institutes, Film & Video, Arts & Humanities-General, Historic Preservation, History & Archaeology, Libraries, Museums/Galleries, Music, Performing Arts, Public Broadcasting
Civic & Public Affairs: Botanical Gardens/Parks, Community Foundations, Ethnic Organizations, Civic & Public Affairs-General, Municipalities/Towns, Nonprofit Management, Parades/Festivals, Philanthropic Organizations, Professional & Trade Associations, Public Policy, Urban & Community Affairs, Women's Affairs
Education: Arts/Humanities Education, Colleges & Universities, Community & Junior Colleges, Education Associations, Engineering/Technological Education, Education-General, Medical Education, Minority Education, Private Education (Precollege), Public Education (Precollege), Science/Mathematics Education, Secondary Education (Private), Secondary Education (Public), Social Sciences Education, Special Education, Student Aid
Environment: Energy, Wildlife Protection
Health: Arthritis, Cancer, Children's Health/Hospitals, Clinics/Medical Centers, Diabetes, Eyes/Blindness, Heart, Hospices, Hospitals, Hospitals (University Affiliated), Medical Rehabilitation, Medical Research, Medical Training, Mental Health, Prenatal Health Issues, Single-Disease Health Associations, Speech & Hearing, Trauma Treatment
International: Foreign Arts Organizations

Religion: Churches, Religious Organizations, Religious Welfare

Science: Science-General, Scientific Centers & Institutes, Scientific Organizations

Social Services: At-Risk Youth, Camps, Community Service Organizations, People with Disabilities, Recreation & Athletics, Scouts, Senior Services, Veterans, YMCA/YWCA/YMHA/YWHA, Youth Organizations

Application Procedures

Initial Contact: The fund does not have a formal grant application. Applicants may submit a request on organization's letterhead, signed by an official on behalf of the governing board.

Application Requirements: Proposal should detail the applying organization's history, explain the project, and outline its expected costs. A financial report, current budget, and proof of tax exemption also should be included.

Deadlines: None, but requests must be submitted three weeks prior to meeting to be considered at that meeting.

Review Process: The fund meets in February or March, June, and December. Applicants will be notified of the board's decision within three months.

Notes: Progress reports and a final accounting of the use of grant funds are required and determine eligibility for continuing grants.

Restrictions

No grants are made to individuals, or for endowments or building funds. Continuing grants are made only under special circumstances.

Additional Information

In addition to its grant-making function, the fund provides a variety of services to museums, libraries, and educational institutions. Some of the trustees and staff members pay periodic visits to museums and render assistance in special projects. The fund also provides the services of a professional museum coordinator who visits the more than 80 museums at which it has exhibits, and works closely with producers of educational films and documentaries on Thomas A. Edison.

The Charles Edison Fund cooperates with various public television stations throughout the country, providing listings of educational science films and videos, and is associated with the Library of Congress Motion Picture Section and the Smithsonian Institute Department of Science and Invention.

Other services of the fund include: providing Edison science-oriented teaching kits; arranging science exhibits; repairing Edison phonographs at museums throughout the country; promoting experimentation in speech therapy through its phonograph collection at Syracuse University, in conjunction with the Voice Foundation of America; loaning rubber molds for the casting of bronze busts of Thomas A. Edison to museums and historical organizations; and working with various state energy educational departments throughout the nation in conjunction with conservation of energy and ecology.

The fund cooperates with the New Jersey Historical Society, New Jersey Historical Commission, Friends of Edison National Historic Site (West Orange, NJ), Edison Birthplace Museum (Milan, OH), Edison Institute (Dearborn, MI), and Edison Winter Home Museum and Laboratory (Ft. Myers, FL). It also assists the Edison Tower of Light (Menlo Park, NJ) and the Thomas A. Edison Papers Project, a twenty-year program identifying and organizing millions of historic papers, laboratory notes, photographs, related correspondence and inventions of Thomas Edison.

The fund has completed its commitment to the Science of Technology Center in New Jersey, a "hands-on" museum, which will, in part, memorialize Thomas A. Edison and his achievements.

Publications: Brochure (including Guidelines for Application)

Foundation Officials

Edward Lee Allman: trustee B Poplar, MD 1926. ED Georgia Institute of Technology BS (1948). PRIM CORP EMPL chairman: Meggitt-USA Inc. CORP AFFIL director: Canterbury Shaker Village; office: Oneida Tableware Group; director: Amoskeag Industries.

Nancy Miller Arnn: trustee

Alberta Ench: secretary

William M. Henderson: trustee NONPR AFFIL director: Saint Margaret Memorial Hospital Foundation.

James Everett Howe: trustee B New York, NY 1930. ED Williams College BA (1952); Columbia University MBA (1954). NONPR AFFIL member: New York Society Security Analysts; member: Princeton Co.; member: Machinery Analysts New York; member: Environmental Control Analysts New York; member: Jamestown Society; member: Alpha Kappa Psi; member: Association Investment Management & Research. CLUB AFFIL Genesee Valley Club; Short Hills Club.

John Phillip Keegan: president, chairman, trustee B 1927.

Robert E. Murray: vice president, trustee

John N. Schullinger, MD: trustee

J. Thomas Smoot, Jr.: trustee CORP AFFIL president: Smoot Adams Edwards Green Pennsylvania.

Thomas J. Ungerland: trustee

Grants Analysis

Disclosure Period: calendar year ending 2003

Total Grants: $1,509,235

Number of Grants: 23

Average Grant: $8,602

Highest Grant: $1,320,000

Lowest Grant: $100

Typical Range: $1,000 to $20,000

Recent Grants

Note: Grants derived from 2003 Form 990.

General

1,320,000	Edison Preservation Foundation, Newark, NJ -- towards historical preservation
26,307	Columbia University, New York, NY -- towards medical facilities
25,000	Greenwood School, Putney, VT
20,000	Thomas Edison Media Arts -- towards education
19,000	College of Saint Elizabeth, Morristown, NJ
15,040	Seton Hall Preparatory School, West Orange, NJ -- towards education
10,000	Edison Ford Winter Estate Foundation, Ft. Myers, FL -- towards historical preservation
10,000	Georgetown University, Washington, DC
10,000	Rutgers University, New Brunswick, NJ -- towards education
10,000	St. Vincent Academy, Newark, NJ -- towards education

EDISON INTERNATIONAL

Company Headquarters

2244 Walnut Grove Avenue
Rosemead, CA 91770
Phone: (626)302-1212
Fax: (626)302-2517
Web: http://www.edison.com

Company Description

Founded: 1987
Ticker: EIX
Exchange: NYSE
Also Known As: Southern California Edison.
Revenue: US$11.499 billion (2004)
Profit: US$916 million (2004)
Employees: 15407 (2003)

Fortune Rank: 187, per FORTUNE Magazine's list of 500 Largest U.S. Corporations (2004).

SIC(s): 4911 Electric Services.

Operating Locations

Edison International (AZ--Phoenix; CA--Alhambra, Apple Valley, Arcadia, Barstow, Bell, Bell Gardens, Bellflower, Brea, Buena Park, Burbank, Camarillo, Cathedral City, Cerritos, Chino, Claremont, Corona, Costa Mesa, Covina, Cudahy, Cypress, Delano, Downey, Duarte, Fontana, Fountain Valley, Fullerton, Garden Grove, Glendora, Hanford, Hawthorne, Hemet, Highland, Huntington Beach, Huntington Park, Inglewood, La Canada, La Habra, La Mirada, La Puente, Laguna Beach, Lakewood, Lancaster, Lawndale, Long Beach, Los Angeles, Lynwood, Manhattan Beach, Mission Viejo, Monrovia, Montclair, Montebello, Moorpark, Moreno Valley, Newport Beach, Norco, Ontario, Orange, Oxnard, Palm Springs, Palo Verde, Paramount, Pico Rivera, Placentia, Port Hueneme, Porterville, Rancho Cucamonga, Rancho Palos Verdes, Redondo Beach, Rialto, Ridgecrest, Rosemead, San Bruno, San Dimas, San Fernando, San Gabriel, Santa Barbara, Santa Clarita, Santa Monica, Santa Paula, Simi Valley, South Gate, South Pasadena, Stanton, Thousand Oaks, Torrance, Tulare, Tustin, Victorville, Visalia, Walnut, West Covina, Westminster, Whittier, Yorba Linda)

Nonmonetary Support

Type: Donated Equipment; In-kind Services; Loaned Executives

Contact: Marilyn Kalenda, Corp. Contributions Budget Analyst

Giving Contact

Lucia Galindo, Manager, Corporate Contributions
Southern California Edison Co.
Edison International
8631 Rush St., Room 100 G04
PO Box 800
Rosemead, CA 91770
Phone: (626)302-2222
Fax: (626)302-8114
E-mail: Lucia.Galindo@sce.com

Description

Organization Type: Corporate Giving Program

Giving Locations: CA: primarily in company's Southern CA service area; strategic giving outside traditional service territory

Grant Types: Employee Matching Gifts, General Support.

Note: Also awards special initative grants.

Financial Summary

Total Giving: $10,000,000 (2005 approx); $7,000,000 (2004); $2,700,000 (2003 approx). Note: Contributes through corporate direct giving program and foundation.

Typical Recipients

Arts & Humanities: Arts Associations & Councils, Arts Centers, Arts Institutes, Community Arts, Dance, Ethnic & Folk Arts, Historic Preservation, Libraries, Museums/Galleries, Music, Opera, Performing Arts, Public Broadcasting, Theater

Civic & Public Affairs: Business/Free Enterprise, Civil Rights, Economic Development, Economic Policy, Housing, Law & Justice, Professional & Trade Associations, Public Policy, Safety, Urban & Community Affairs, Women's Affairs, Zoos/Aquariums

Education: Business Education, Colleges & Universities, Economic Education, Engineering/Technological Education, Faculty Development, Education-General, Literacy, Minority Education, Private Education (Precollege), Science/Mathematics Education, Special Education

Environment: Environment-General

Health: Geriatric Health, Health Organizations, Hospices, Hospitals, Nursing Services

Science: Science Exhibits & Fairs, Scientific Centers & Institutes, Scientific Organizations

Social Services: Child Welfare, Community Centers, Community Service Organizations, Counseling, Emergency Relief, Family Services, People with Disabilities, Recreation & Athletics, Senior Services, Substance Abuse, United Funds/United Ways, Volunteer Services, Youth Organizations

Application Procedures

Initial Contact: Send a brief letter or proposal.
Application Requirements: Include organization name and contact information; a description of organization, including objectives, accomplishments, and current programs; amount requested and purpose of funds sought, list of officers and board of directors; list of current contributors and partners; recently audited financial statement, and proof of tax-exempt status.
Deadlines: None.

Restrictions

Company does not support fraternal, political, veterans, religious organizations, labor groups, commercial for-profit agencies, or public agencies.

Additional Information

Edison International is the parent company of Southern California Edison and handles all requests for charitable contributions.
Publications: Guidelines

Corporate Officials

Stephen E. Frank: president, chief operating officer, director B 1938. PRIM CORP EMPL president, chief executive officer, director: Southern California Edison Co. CORP AFFIL director: Edison International; director: Arkwright Insurance Co. NONPR AFFIL director: University Virginia.

Grants Analysis

Typical Range: $500 to $10,000

DEAN S. EDMONDS FOUNDATION

Giving Contact

Marjorie Thompson, Vice President
c/o The Bank of New York
1 Wall St., 28th Fl.
New York, NY 10286
Phone: (212)635-1520

Description

Founded: 1959
EIN: 136161381
Organization Type: Private Foundation
Grant Types: General Support.

Financial Summary

Total Giving: $94,000 (2003)
Assets: $2,611,010 (2003)

Typical Recipients

Arts & Humanities: Arts & Humanities-General, Historic Preservation, History & Archaeology, Libraries, Museums/Galleries, Music, Opera, Performing Arts, Public Broadcasting
Civic & Public Affairs: Clubs, Community Foundations, Civic & Public Affairs-General, Philanthropic Organizations, Professional & Trade Associations, Public Policy, Rural Affairs, Safety, Women's Affairs
Education: Arts/Humanities Education, Business Education, Colleges & Universities, Continuing Education, Engineering/Technological Education, Faculty Development, Medical Education, Private Education (Precollege), Science/Mathematics Education, Student Aid

Health: Cancer, Children's Health/Hospitals, Diabetes, Eyes/Blindness, Hospices, Hospitals
International: Foreign Educational Institutions
Religion: Churches
Science: Science-General, Scientific Organizations
Social Services: Community Service Organizations, Emergency Relief, Scouts

Application Procedures

Deadlines: January 31.

Restrictions

Does not fund individuals or political or lobbying groups. Primarily supports preselected organizations.

Additional Information

Trust(s): The Bank New York

Foundation Officials

Dean S. Edmonds, III: trustee

Grants Analysis

Disclosure Period: calendar year ending 2003
Total Grants: $94,000
Number of Grants: 37
Average Grant: $2,541
Highest Grant: $10,000
Lowest Grant: $1,000
Typical Range: $1,000 to $5,000

Recent Grants

Note: Grants derived from 2001 Form 990.
General

78,500	National Gallery of Art, Washington, DC
20,000	Metropolitan Opera Association, New York, NY
10,000	Aero Club of New England, Boston, MA
10,000	Boston University School of Music, Boston, MA
10,000	Connecticut Valley Railroad Museum, Hartford, CT
10,000	Swift Water Girl Scout Council, Manchester, NH
10,000	Taft School, Watertown, CT
6,000	Boston University, Boston, MA
6,000	Naples Player, Naples, FL
6,000	Philharmonic Center for the Arts, Naples, FL

EDUCATIONAL FOUNDATION OF AMERICA

Giving Contact

Diane M. Allison, Executive Director
EducationAL Foundation of America
35 Church Lane
Westport, CT 06880-3515
Phone: (203)226-6498
Fax: (203)227-0424
E-mail: efa@efaw.org
Web: http://www.efaw.org

Description

Founded: 1959
EIN: 133424750
Organization Type: Family Foundation
Giving Locations: nationally.
Grant Types: Project, Seed Money.

Donor Information

Founder: Established in 1959 by Richard Prentice Ettinger, who died in 1971. Although he provided the initial funding, other family members have added capital to the asset base over the years.
Mr. Ettinger began his career as a law professor at New York University, and later helped establish the

Prentice-Hall publishing company. His career remained closely tied to higher education, as his publishing company concentrated on the development of teaching materials. Mr. Ettinger also was one of the first to grant financial aid scholarships to community and junior college graduates to further their education at four-year institutions.
Afflicted by cancer, he also became interested in cancer research and health care. He inaugurated a cancer fellowship program and the idea of minimum-care floors for ambulatory patients in hospitals.

Financial Summary

Total Giving: $10,265,242 (2003); $14,087,616 (2001)
Giving Analysis: Giving for 2003 includes: foundation matching gifts ($26,250)
Assets: $203,806,691 (2003); $221,978,974 (2001)
Gifts Received: $532,917 (2001); $69,214 (2000); $69,214 (1998). Note: In 2001 contributions were received from Virginia P. Andrews Trust and Helen Russo Trust.

Typical Recipients

Arts & Humanities: Arts Institutes, Dance, Libraries, Museums/Galleries, Music, Opera, Performing Arts, Theater
Civic & Public Affairs: Botanical Gardens/Parks, Community Foundations, Economic Policy, Employment/Job Training, Civic & Public Affairs-General, Legal Aid, Native American Affairs, Nonprofit Management, Philanthropic Organizations, Professional & Trade Associations, Public Policy, Rural Affairs, Safety, Women's Affairs
Education: Agricultural Education, Arts/Humanities Education, Business Education, Colleges & Universities, Community & Junior Colleges, Education Associations, Elementary Education (Public), Environmental Education, Faculty Development, Education-General, Leadership Training, Legal Education, Medical Education, Minority Education, Preschool Education, Private Education (Precollege), Public Education (Precollege), Science/Mathematics Education, Social Sciences Education, Special Education, Student Aid
Environment: Air/Water Quality, Energy, Forestry, Environment-General, Protection, Research, Resource Conservation, Watershed, Wildlife Protection
Health: Cancer, Children's Health/Hospitals, Clinics/Medical Centers, Health-General, Geriatric Health, Medical Research, Mental Health, Prenatal Health Issues, Public Health, Research/Studies Institutes
International: International-General, Health Care/Hospitals, Human Rights, International Affairs, International Environmental Issues, International Peace & Security Issues
Religion: Religious Organizations, Social/Policy Issues
Science: Scientific Centers & Institutes, Scientific Labs
Social Services: Animal Protection, At-Risk Youth, Child Welfare, Community Service Organizations, Day Care, Family Planning, Food/Clothing Distribution, Senior Services, Substance Abuse

Application Procedures

Initial Contact: Applicants should submit a letter of inquiry prior to consideration of a proposal. Foundation staff will review the letter and notify applicant if a full proposal is required.
Application Requirements: A letter of inquiry should be no more than two pages printed back to back on one sheet of unbleached recycled paper. The letter should identify the organization, including its mission, date of founding, location, region of focus, past and current projects, name(s) and brief description of the founder(s), and affiliations with other organizations; description of purpose of project, intended results, timeline, amount requested, and funding strategy for project; total amount budgeted for project, total amount budgeted for organization for the

current year and a copy of the IRS determination letter.

Proposal should be submitted only after letter of inquiry has been approved. Send a completed EFA Information Request Form along with two copies of proposal. Proposal should be unbound, printed back to back on unbleached paper, single spaced, in 10 to 12 point font and no more than ten pages. Proposals should include the following: an executive summary; statement of problem being addressed; solution to problem, including organization's mission, goals and objectives, brief history and record of achievements; describe other organizations modeled after, influenced by, or building on your organization's work; description of project for which funding is sought, including specifics such as plan of execution, time frame, intended impact, amount requested and an explanation of project budget; describe any other organizations working on similar projects and how the two projects could cooperate; describe methods to evaluate objective, specific and quantifiable criteria, as well as subjective, general, and qualitative criteria; and explanation of funding sources. Also include the following attachments: a line item budget for project; line item annual budget for organization; most current financial statement; brief biographical information and qualification of key staff; list of board members and related qualifications (one page maximum); and a copy of the most recent IRS tax exempt letter and Form 990. and Form 990. and Form 990.

Deadlines: None.

Review Process: When a full proposal is received it will be reviewed by the staff. If all guidelines have been met and review receives a favorable evaluation, staff will then submit it to the Board of EFA for consideration at the next director's meeting. EFA normally meets quarterly. If the Board is interested in the proposal, a letter of invitation and guidelines will be sent describing how to submit a full proposal.

Evaluative Criteria: Characteristics that the foundation focuses on during review of letters of inquiry and proposals include an organization's record of achievement, intended broad impact, sound financial practices, increasing independence, and correspondence with EFA objectives.

Decision Notification: Staff will notify applicants of a decision usually within two weeks after the meeting at which the proposal was considered.

Notes: A final report is required from all grantees.

Restrictions

Foundation does not provide funds for endowments, endowed faculty chairs, building programs, annual fund-raising campaigns, religious purposes, indirect costs, overhead or general support, or to individuals.

Additional Information

Adjunct directors are related to the founder.
Publications: Annual Report; Guidelines

Foundation Officials

Diane M. Allison: executive director B 1953.
Jerry Babicka: director
Laren Babicka: adjunct director
Lynn P. Babicka: director
James Bohart, Jr.: adjunct director
Barbara P. Ettinger: director
Christian P. Ettinger: adjunct director
Heidi P. Ettinger: director
Leland P. Ettinger: adjunct director
Matthew Ettinger: adjunct director
Wendy W. P. Ettinger: director
Barbara Hapgood: director
Elaine P. Hapgood: president
Rev. Fletcher Harper: director
Sven Huseby: director
Derek McLane: director
John P. Powers: director
Trevor Renner: director
Wendy Wasserstein: director

Grants Analysis

Disclosure Period: calendar year ending 2003
Total Grants: $10,238,992*
Number of Grants: 295
Average Grant: $28,024*
Highest Grant: $2,000,000
Lowest Grant: $200
Typical Range: $10,000 to $50,000
***Note:** Giving excludes matching gifts. Average grant figure excludes highest grant.

Recent Grants

Note: Grants derived from 2002 Form 990.

General

280,000	Colorado Public Interest Research Foundation Inc., Denver, CO -- towards Colorado democracy project
175,000	Oil and Gas Accountability Project (OGAP), Durango, CO -- towards western coalbed methane project
165,000	Colorado Environmental Coalition Inc., Denver, CO -- towards Colorado capacity building program
150,000	children's AID Society, New York, NY -- towards community school initiative PS 50
150,000	Earth Rights International Inc., Washington, DC -- towards legal resource center
150,000	International Center for Technology Assessment, Washington, DC -- towards patent watch project
150,000	United States Public Interest Research Group Education Fund, Washington, DC -- towards campaign to cut polluter pork and environmental defense campaign
125,000	Friends of Action Group on Erosion Technology and Concentration Inc., Winnipeg, MB Canada -- towards biopiracy and intellectual property biotechnology and food security
125,000	Land Institute, Salina, KS -- towards natural systems agriculture
125,000	Planned Parenthood of Connecticut, New Haven, CT -- towards for teens only initiative

EL PASO CORP.

Company Headquarters

1001 Louisana St.
Houston, TX 77002
Web: http://www.epenergy.com

Company Description

Founded: 1928
Ticker: EP
Exchange: NYSE
Former Name: El Paso Natural Gas Co.;
Acquired: Sonat (1999);
Former Name: El Paso Energy Co. (2001);
Acquired: Coastal Corp. (2001).
Revenue: US$6.64 billion (2004)
Profit: (US$1.024 billion) (2004)
Employees: 11855 (2003)
Fortune Rank: 314, per FORTUNE Magazine's list of 500 Largest U.S. Corporations (2004).
SIC(s): 4923 Gas Transmission & Distribution.

Operating Locations

El Paso Energy Co. (TX--Agua Dulce, El Paso, Freeport, Houston)

El Paso Corporate Foundation

Giving Contact

Gloria Moritz, Community Relations Coordinator
1001 Louisiana Street
Houston, TX 77002
Phone: (713)420-5192

Description

Founded: 1992
EIN: 742638185
Organization Type: Corporate Foundation
Former Name: El Paso Energy Foundation.
Giving Locations: AZ; CA; CO; NM; TX: western area nationally.
Grant Types: Award, Challenge, Department, Employee Matching Gifts, General Support, Matching, Multiyear/Continuing Support.

Financial Summary

Total Giving: $5,327,658 (2003); $8,812,462 (2002); $9,670,078 (2001). Note: Contributes through foundation only.
Assets: $18,662,243 (2003); $22,201,315 (2002); $20,852,761 (2001)
Gifts Received: $12,000,000 (2002); $18,000,000 (2001); $4,300,000 (2000). Note: In 2001, contributions were received from El Paso Corp.

Typical Recipients

Arts & Humanities: Arts Associations & Councils, Arts Centers, Ballet, History & Archaeology, Libraries, Museums/Galleries, Music, Opera, Performing Arts, Public Broadcasting, Theater
Civic & Public Affairs: Chambers of Commerce, Civil Rights, Clubs, Community Foundations, Economic Development, Economic Policy, Civic & Public Affairs-General, Hispanic Affairs, Housing, Native American Affairs, Nonprofit Management, Public Policy, Safety, Urban & Community Affairs, Women's Affairs, Zoos/Aquariums
Education: Afterschool/Enrichment Programs, Agricultural Education, Arts/Humanities Education, Business Education, Colleges & Universities, Community & Junior Colleges, Education Funds, Education Reform, Engineering/Technological Education, Education-General, International Studies, Legal Education, Literacy, Medical Education, Minority Education, Private Education (Precollege), Public Education (Precollege), School Volunteerism, Science/Mathematics Education, Student Aid
Environment: Protection, Resource Conservation
Health: Alzheimer's Disease, Cancer, Children's Health/Hospitals, Clinics/Medical Centers, Hospices, Hospitals (University Affiliated), Medical Rehabilitation, Medical Research, Nursing Services, Prenatal Health Issues, Public Health
International: Foreign Arts Organizations, International Development, International Organizations
Religion: Ministries, Religious Welfare
Science: Scientific Centers & Institutes
Social Services: Animal Protection, At-Risk Youth, Child Abuse, Child Welfare, Community Centers, Community Service Organizations, Day Care, Domestic Violence, Emergency Relief, Family Services, Food/Clothing Distribution, People with Disabilities, Recreation & Athletics, Scouts, Senior Services, Substance Abuse, United Funds/United Ways, YMCA/YWCA/YMHA/YWHA, Youth Organizations

Application Procedures

Initial Contact: Send letter requesting an application form.
Application Requirements: When submitting a completed application form, the following attachments are required: a financial statement, preferably audited; proof of tax-exempt status; and a copy of the organization's most recent Form 990. information on the use of outside consultants.

Deadlines: None.
Review Process: The evaluation process takes four months. The foundation requests that no inquiries be made during this process.
Decision Notification: All applicants receive written notification of a funding decision when it has been reached.
Notes: The foundation emphasizes that incomplete applications or applications incorrectly completed will be returned.

Restrictions

Does not support religious organizations for religious purposes; war veterans and fraternal service organizations; endowment funds; national health organizations and programs; grants or loans to individuals; fundraising events, including tickets, dinners, and telethons; corporate memberships or contributions to chambers of commerce, taxpayer associations, and other bodies whose activities are expected to directly benefit the company; political organizations, campaigns, or candidates; computers or computer-related projects; or operating expenses.

The foundation does not generally fund scholarship programs, as the foundation supports its own scholarship program.

Additional Information

Company was formerly known as the El Paso Natural Gas Company.
Publications: application form. and Funding guidelines

Corporate Officials

H. Brent Austin: president, chief operating officer, director B Dallas, TX 1954. ED University of Texas BA (1975); University of Texas MBA (1978). PRIM CORP EMPL executive vice president, chief financial officer, director: El Paso Corp. CORP AFFIL portfolio manager: Private Investment Partnership. NONPR AFFIL board visitors: Southwestern University.

Norma F. Dunn: senior vice president investor & public relations ED University of Texas El Paso BS. PRIM CORP EMPL vice president investor & public relations: El Paso Energy Co. CORP AFFIL senior vice president, corp. communications: Aquila Inc..

Douglas L. Foshee: president, chief executive officer, director ED Southwest Texas State University BA (1982); Rice University MBA (1992). NONPR AFFIL member: Independent Petroleum Association of America; director: Texas Business Hall of Fame Foundation; director: Goodwill Industries; director: Central Houston; director: Children's Museum of Houston.

Peggy A. Heeg: executive vice president, general counsel ED University of Louisville BA (1983); University of Louisville JD (1986). CORP AFFIL partner: Fulbright & Jaworski LLP. NONPR AFFIL member: Kentucky Bar Association; member: Texas Bar Association; director: DePelchin Children's Center; member: Energy Bar Association; member: American Bar Association; member: DC Bar Association.

Ronald L. Kuehn, Jr.: chairman, chief executive officer B Brooklyn, NY 1935. ED Fordham University BS (1957); Fordham University LLB (1964). PRIM CORP EMPL chairman, chief executive officer: El Paso Corp. CORP AFFIL director: Praxair Inc.; director: America South Bancorp; director: Dun & Bradstreet Corp. NONPR AFFIL trustee: Tuskegee University; member president council: University Alabama Birmingham; member: New York Bar Association; member: Newcomen Society; director: Interstate Natural Gas Association America; director: National Petroleum Council; member: Fed Energy Bar Association; director: Gas Research Institute; trustee: Boys Club America; member: Bretton Woods Committee; member: Association Bar New York City; director: Boy Scouts America; member: American Bar Association.

Robert G. Phillips: president, El Paso Field Services ED University of Texas BS (1977); South Texas College of Law JD (1981). CORP AFFIL president, chief executive officer: Enterprise Products Partners LP.

D. Dwight Scott: executive vice president, chief financial officer

John W. Somerhalder, II: president, El Paso Pipeline Group CORP AFFIL director: Interstate Pipeline Co..

Foundation Officials

Robert W. Baker: senior vice president, general counsel, director B 1958. NONPR AFFIL advisory board: Institute for Energy Law.

Jeffrey I. Beason: senior vice president, controller

John J. Hopper: vice president, treasurer CORP AFFIL president, chief executive officer: Falcon Gas Storage Co. Inc..

Kelly J. Jameson: assistant secretary NONPR AFFIL member: Texas Bar Association.

Greg G. Jenkins: director

Ronald L. Kuehn, Jr.: chairman, chief executive officer, director (see above)

Robert G. Phillips: director (see above)

Margaret E. Roark: assistant secretary NONPR AFFIL member: ASCS; member: PACE.

D. Dwight Scott: executive vice president, chief financial officer, director (see above)

David L. Siddall: vice president, associate general counsel, corporate section

Clark C. Smith: director

John W. Somerhalder, II: director (see above)

Judy A. Vandagriff: senior vice president

Gregory W. Watkins: vice president

Basil R. Woller: senior vice president, general auditor NONPR AFFIL director: Institute of Internal auditors.

David E. Zerhusen: senior vice president, director

Grants Analysis

Disclosure Period: calendar year ending 2003
Total Grants: $3,828,484*
Number of Grants: 546
Average Grant: $6,107*
Highest Grant: $500,000
Lowest Grant: $50
Typical Range: $1,000 to $10,000
*Note: Giving excludes United Way. Average grant figure excludes highest grant.

Recent Grants

Note: Grants derived from 2003 Form 990.
General

1,122,486	United Way of the Texas Gulf Coast, Houston, TX
500,000	Rice University, Houston, TX
135,465	United Way of Central Alabama Inc., Birmingham, AL
108,993	National Merit Scholarship Corporation, Evanston, IL
100,000	United Way of the Texas Gulf Coast, Houston, TX
100,000	University of Texas at Austin, Austin, TX
100,000	YMCA of Greater Houston, Houston, TX
85,500	Hobby Center for the Performing Arts, Houston, TX
85,426	Pikes Peak United Way, Colorado Springs, CO
80,500	Hobby Center for the Performing Arts, Houston, TX

EL POMAR FOUNDATION

Giving Contact

William J. Hybl, Chairman & Chief Executive Officer
10 Lake Circle
Colorado Springs, CO 80906
Phone: (719)633-7733
Fax: (719)577-5702
E-mail: grants@elpomar.org
Web: http://www.elpomar.org

Alternate Contact

Phone: 800-554-7711
Note: Toll-free telephone number.

Description

Founded: 1937
EIN: 846002373
Organization Type: General Purpose Foundation
Giving Locations: CO
Grant Types: Capital, General Support, Project.

Donor Information

Founder: The El Pomar Foundation was established in 1937 by the late Spencer Penrose. Upon his death in 1939, the foundation received a portion of his estate. Mrs. Spencer Penrose, who died in 1956, also made gifts to the foundation. Mr. Penrose and his associate, Charles L. Tutt, were involved in the gold and copper mining and real estate businesses. He was founder of the Utah Copper Company, and built the Broadmoor Hotel in Colorado Springs. His private zoo became the Cheyenne Mountain Zoo, which the foundation still supports.

Financial Summary

Total Giving: $12,029,165 (2003); $14,017,720 (2002); $15,755,587 (2001)
Giving Analysis: Giving for 2003 includes: foundation matching gifts ($133,386) 2001: foundation grants to United Way ($176,048)
Assets: $440,860,434 (2003); $398,973,064 (2002); $464,243,436 (2001)
Gifts Received: $161,352 (2003); $202,487 (2002); $29,812 (2000). Note: In 2003, contributions were received from H.A. & Mary K. Chapman Charitable Trust ($100,000) and Urs J. Steck ($30,000). In 2000, contributions were received from Penrose Trust ($29,762) and other donors.

Typical Recipients

Arts & Humanities: Arts Associations & Councils, Arts Centers, Community Arts, Dance, Ethnic & Folk Arts, Historic Preservation, History & Archaeology, Libraries, Museums/Galleries, Music, Opera, Performing Arts, Public Broadcasting, Theater
Civic & Public Affairs: African American Affairs, Botanical Gardens/Parks, Chambers of Commerce, Community Foundations, Economic Development, Civic & Public Affairs-General, Hispanic Affairs, Housing, Legal Aid, Municipalities/Towns, Nonprofit Management, Parades/Festivals, Public Policy, Safety, Urban & Community Affairs, Zoos/Aquariums
Education: Afterschool/Enrichment Programs, Arts/Humanities Education, Business Education, Colleges & Universities, Community & Junior Colleges, Continuing Education, Economic Education, Education Funds, Education Reform, Elementary Education (Private), Education-General, Leadership Training, Minority Education, Preschool Education, Private Education (Precollege), Public Education (Precollege), Student Aid
Environment: Environment-General, Resource Conservation
Health: Alzheimer's Disease, Arthritis, Cancer, Children's Health/Hospitals, Clinics/Medical Centers, Diabetes, Emergency/Ambulance Services, Eyes/Blindness, Health-General, Health Funds, Health Organizations, Hospices, Hospitals, Long-Term Care, Medical Rehabilitation, Medical Research, Mental Health, Nursing Services, Preventive Medicine/Wellness Organizations, Public Health, Transplant Networks/Donor Banks
International: Foreign Educational Institutions
Religion: Churches, Jewish Causes, Religious Welfare, Seminaries
Science: Science Museums, Scientific Centers & Institutes, Scientific Organizations
Social Services: At-Risk Youth, Child Welfare, Community Centers, Community Service Organizations, Day Care, Domestic Violence, Emergency Relief, Family Services, Food/Clothing Distribution, Homes,

People with Disabilities, Recreation & Athletics, Scouts, Senior Services, Shelters/Homelessness, Substance Abuse, United Funds/United Ways, Volunteer Services, YMCA/YWCA/YMHA/YWHA, Youth Organizations

Application Procedures

Initial Contact: There are no set application forms. A detailed and complete application should be sent to: Board of Trustees, El Pomar Foundation, 10 Lake Circle, Colorado Springs, CO 80906.

Application Requirements: One copy of the application should be sent. Include the name and address of the tax exempt organization applying; a description of organization, including its mission, history, programs, and accomplishments; concise statement of purpose of funds sought and amount requested, including anticipated outcomes and methods for measuring the project's success; organization's budget for the current year and project budget, including total amount to be raised, anticipated funding sources, and long-term funding solutions, if applicable; and a statement indicating whether the applicant has sought aid from other foundations during the previous three years, and a list of the granting foundation(s) and amount received from each, if any. In addition, the applicant should furnish the relationship and capacity of the person signing the application; a list of members of the governing body; a statement that notes that the grant purpose has been approved by the applicant's governing body; endorsement from outside authorities, and copies of regulatory agency approvals, if necessary; copy of current IRS determination letter; the organization's three most recent years of audited financial statements, and the organization's latest IRS Form 990. The foundation also requests that applicants furnish up to three pictures (photographs, architectural renderings, etc.) that portray the specific project, issue, or operations of the organization for use in presenting the application to the board of trustees.

Applications for funding of a technology projects must clearly state how the project will benefit the functioning of the nonprofit organization. The foundation considers technology projects under the categories of software applications, computers and peripheral devices, network equipment, and internetworking equipment. Such requests should also include an itemization of equipment and/or software, including a description and purchase price; implementation costs of the technology project, such as installation, consulting or training; and a description of how the project will be implemented including, where applicable, the timeline for installation and training.

Deadlines: None.

Decision Notification: Applications are acted upon within 90 days of receipt.

Restrictions

The foundation does not grant funds for the following: an organization which grants money to recipients of its own selection; discriminatory organizations; deficits, debt elimination, or endowments; making films or other media projects; K-12 education (except for capital requests from non-publicly funded secondary schools); research or studies; organizations which do not have fiscal responsibility for the project; nonprofit organizations that do not have proof of active 501(c)(3) status; travel, conferences, conventions, group meetings, or seminars; camps, camp programs, or other seasonal activities; individuals; religious organizations for support of religious programs; political or lobbying groups; or funding for software development projects. Grant requests of more than $500,000 will rarely be considered. Applicants must be based in Colorado or have a proposed activity that takes place within Colorado. Grantees are precluded from applying for a grant for three years following notification of a grant. Applicants whose proposals are not funded must wait one year before they are eligible to submit another proposal.

Additional Information

The foundation reports that it also sponsors a limited number of seminars, workshops, and conferences. The foundation requires grant recipients to report on expended grant funds and to return any unexpended funds. If a grant is made, grant recipients should not use plaques or memorials relating to El Pomar Foundation without the foundation's approval.

Publications: Annual Report; Guidelines; Program Brochures

Foundation Officials

Judy Bell: trustee

Cortland S. Dietler: trustee B Denver, CO 1921. ED University of Tulsa (1947); Hillsdale College (1996). PRIM CORP EMPL chairman, chief executive officer: Transmontaigne Oil Co. CORP AFFIL director: PanEnergy Corp.; director: Key Production Co. Inc.; director: Grease Monkey Holding Corp.; director: Hallador Petroleum Co. NONPR AFFIL trustee: University Tulsa.

Theophilus Gregory: associate vice president

Robert J. Hilbert: secretary, treasurer, senior vice president admin, trustee PRIM CORP EMPL secretary, treasurer, director: Garden City Co.

William J. Hybl: chairman, chief executive officer, trustee B Des Moines, IA 1942. ED Colorado College BA (1964); University of Colorado JD (1967). PRIM CORP EMPL vice chairman, director: Broadmoor Hotel, Inc. CORP AFFIL director: Manitou & Pikes Peak RY Co.; director: USAA; director: KN Energy Inc.; director: FirstBank Vail; president, director: Garden City Co.; director: FirstBank Holding Co. Colorado.

Kent Oliver Olin: trustee B Chicago, IL 1930. ED Ripon College BS (1955). CORP AFFIL board directors: Bank One Colorado. NONPR AFFIL trustee: Falcon Foundation. CLUB AFFIL Broadmoor Golf Club.

David J. Palenchar: senior vice president operations, trustee

Brenda J. Smith: trustee

Russell Thayer Tutt, Jr.: president, chief investment officer, trustee B 1955. ED Princeton University (1977); Duke University (1979). PRIM CORP EMPL vice president, director: Garden City Co. CORP AFFIL director: Bank One Colorado Springs NA; treasurer, director: Broadmoor Hotel Inc.

William R. Ward: trustee

Grants Analysis

Disclosure Period: calendar year ending 2003

Total Grants: $10,856,587*

Number of Grants: 572

Average Grant: $13,871*

Highest Grant: $1,550,000

Lowest Grant: $175

Typical Range: $5,000 to $25,000

*Note: Giving excludes matching gifts; United Way; gifts in-kind totaling $1,039,192. Average grant figure excludes two highest grants ($2,950,000).

Recent Grants

Note: Grants derived from 2003 Form 990.

Library-Related

50,000	Denver Public Library, Denver, CO -- funding for cataloging mining collection

General

1,550,000	Denver Art Museum, Denver, CO -- funding for new museum building
1,400,000	Partners in Housing Inc., Colorado Springs, CO -- toward construction of transitional housing
804,000	Cheyenne Mountain Zoo, Colorado Springs, CO
333,333	Denver Museum of Natural History, Denver, CO -- funding for El Pomar Space activity center
300,000	Colorado College, Colorado Springs, CO -- funding for hockey program
300,000	Community Health Centers, Colorado Springs, CO -- funding for direct service programs
263,000	University of Colorado Foundation, Boulder, CO -- funding for building Beth El College of Nursing
250,000	Goodwill Industries of Colorado Springs, Colorado Springs, CO -- toward construction of new retail center
177,880	Pikes Peak United Way, Colorado Springs, CO -- funding for administrative expenses
175,000	Urban Peak-Colorado Springs, Colorado Springs, CO -- toward homeless shelter for youth

ELF ATOCHEM NORTH AMERICA INC.

Company Headquarters

Philadelphia, PA

Company Description

Employees: 3,600

SIC(s): 1479 Chemical & Fertilizer Mining Nec, 2812 Alkalies & Chlorine, 2813 Industrial Gases, 2819 Industrial Inorganic Chemicals Nec.

Operating Locations

Accecones Ricci U.S.A. (NY--New York); Ato-Findley (WI--Wauwatosa); Atochem (MI--Wyandotte; MN--Blooming Prairie; OK--Pryor; SC--Andrews); Atochem Services (PA--Valley Forge); Aviation & Performance Chemicals Division (PA--Philadelphia); Decco Division (CA--Monrovia); Elf Aquitaine (NY--New York); Elf Aquitaine Asphalt (MO--St. Louis); Elf Atochem North America, Agrichemicals Division (PA--Philadelphia); Elf Atochem North America Basic Chemicals Division (PA--Philadelphia); Elf Atochem North America, Fluorochemical Division (PA--Philadelphia); Elf Atochem North America, Inc. (AL--Mobile; CA--Los Angeles, Monrovia; GA; KY--Calvert City, Carrollton; MI--Wyandotte; NY--Buffalo, Homer; OH--Delaware; OK--Pryor, Tulsa; PA--Cornwells Heights, King of Prussia, Philadelphia; TX--Beaumont, Seagraves; WA--Tacoma); Elf Atochem Organic Peroxides Plant (NY--Buffalo); Elf Exploration (TX--Houston); Elf Sanofi (NY--New York); Elf Trading (TX--Houston); Genetic Systems Corp. (WA--Seattle); Parfums Van Cleef & Arpels (NY--New York); Pharmasol Corp. (MA--South Easton); Sanofi (IA--Fort Dodge); Sanofi Beaute (NY--New York); Sanofi Diagnostias Pasteur (MN--Chaska); Sanofi Pharmaceuticals (NY--New York); Sanofi Research (NY--New York); Sanofi Research Division (PA--Malvern); Specialty Chemicals (PA--Philadelphia); Stendhal (NY--New York); Turco Products Division (CA--Long Beach, Westminster; OH--Marion)

Atofina Chemicals Foundation

Giving Contact

Diane L. Milici

c/o Atofina Chemicals, Inc.

2000 Market Street

Philadelphia, PA 19103-3222

Phone: (215)419-7000

Fax: (215)419-5494

Description

Founded: 1957

EIN: 236256818

Organization Type: Corporate Foundation

Giving Locations: nationally; operating location

communities.

Grant Types: Capital, Employee Matching Gifts, General Support, Scholarship.

Note: Employee matching gift ratio: 1 to 1 to colleges and universities, public broadcasting and cultural and performing arts organizations.

Donor Information

Founder: Atochem North America

Financial Summary

Total Giving: $490,829 (2002); $562,036 (2001). Note: Contributes through corporate direct giving program and foundation.

Giving Analysis: Giving for 2002 includes: foundation matching gifts ($25,768); 2001: foundation grants to United Way ($54,000)

Assets: $55,753 (2002); $42,753 (2001)

Gifts Received: $511,000 (2002); $600,000 (2001); $600,000 (2000). Note: In 2000, 2001, and 2002, contributions were received from Atofina Chemicals, Inc. In 1998 and 1999, contributions were received from Elf Atochem North American, Inc.

Typical Recipients

Arts & Humanities: Arts Centers, Ballet, Community Arts, Dance, Historic Preservation, History & Archaeology, Libraries, Museums/Galleries, Music, Opera, Performing Arts, Public Broadcasting, Theater

Civic & Public Affairs: Botanical Gardens/Parks, Business/Free Enterprise, Chambers of Commerce, Economic Development, Economic Policy, Employment/Job Training, Civic & Public Affairs-General, Law & Justice, Municipalities/Towns, Philanthropic Organizations, Professional & Trade Associations, Public Policy, Safety, Urban & Community Affairs, Zoos/Aquariums

Education: Arts/Humanities Education, Business Education, Colleges & Universities, Community & Junior Colleges, Economic Education, Education Funds, Education Reform, Elementary Education (Private), Engineering/Technological Education, Environmental Education, Education-General, Minority Education, Private Education (Precollege), Public Education (Precollege), Science/Mathematics Education, Student Aid

Environment: Environment-General

Health: Clinics/Medical Centers, Emergency/Ambulance Services, Health Organizations, Hospitals, Medical Rehabilitation, Medical Research

International: Foreign Educational Institutions

Science: Science Museums, Scientific Centers & Institutes, Scientific Organizations

Social Services: Big Brothers/Big Sisters, Community Service Organizations, People with Disabilities, United Funds/United Ways, Volunteer Services, YMCA/YWCA/YMHA/YWHA, Youth Organizations

Application Procedures

Initial Contact: Send a brief letter or proposal.

Application Requirements: Include a description of organization, amount requested, purpose of funds sought, recently audited financial statement, proof of tax-exempt status.

Deadlines: None.

Restrictions

The foundation generally does not support political or lobbying groups, member agencies of united funds, or international organizations.

Additional Information

In 1991, the company changed its name from Atochem North America to Elf Atochem North America. The company was also formerly known as Pennwalt Corp.

The Foundation gives preference to qualified charitable organizations whose activities enhance Elf Atochem North America, Inc.'s employees' health and welfare (social, cultural or educational) and/or neighborhoods surrounding the company's plants and offices.

Corporate Officials

Bernard Azoulay: president, chief executive officeraffairs B 1940. ED Ecole Polytechnique (1977). PRIM CORP EMPL president, chief executive officer: Atofina Chemical Inc.

Peter John McCarthy: vice president public affairs B Philadelphia, PA 1943. ED Temple University; LaSalle College (1964). PRIM CORP EMPL vice president public affairs: Elf Atochem North America, Inc.

Foundation Officials

F. H. Lauchert: trustee

Peter John McCarthy: trustee (see above)

Grants Analysis

Disclosure Period: calendar year ending 2002

Total Grants: $405,202*

Number of Grants: 22

Average Grant: $6,676*

Highest Grant: $151,677

Lowest Grant: $10

Typical Range: $50 to $5,000

*Note: Giving excludes matching gifts and United Way. Average grant figure excludes two highest grants ($271,677).

Recent Grants

Note: Grants derived from 2003 Form 990.

General

123,233	Atofina Chemicals, Philadelphia, PA -- science teachers grant
120,000	Philadelphia Museum of Art, Philadelphia, PA
25,000	Philadelphia Museum of Art, Philadelphia, PA
18,030	United Way, Mobile, AL
17,672	Atofina Chemicals, Philadelphia, PA
15,015	Calvert Area United Way, Prince Frederick, MD
15,000	Philadelphia Orchestra, Philadelphia, PA
10,000	Academy of Natural Sciences, Philadelphia, PA
10,000	Fairmount Park Conservancy, Philadelphia, PA
10,000	Franklin Institute, Philadelphia, PA

MARGARET AND JAMES A. ELKINS, JR. FOUNDATION

Giving Contact

James A. Elkins, Jr., President
Margaret and James A. Elkins Jr. Foundation
1001 Fannin St., Suite 1166
Houston, TX 77002
Phone: (713)651-9400

Description

Founded: 1956

EIN: 746051746

Organization Type: Private Foundation

Giving Locations: TX: Houston

Grant Types: Endowment, General Support.

Financial Summary

Total Giving: $1,524,256 (fiscal year ending October 31, 2002)

Giving Analysis: Giving for fiscal 2002 includes: foundation grants to United Way ($25,000)

Assets: $22,889,538 (fiscal 2002)

Gifts Received: $10,056,282 (fiscal 1998); $5,815,344 (fiscal 1997); $2,212,568 (fiscal 1995). Note: In fiscal 1998, contributions were received from James A. Elkins, Jr., and Margaret Elkins.

Typical Recipients

Arts & Humanities: Community Arts, Dance, History & Archaeology, Libraries, Literary Arts, Museums/

Galleries, Music, Opera, Performing Arts, Public Broadcasting, Theater

Civic & Public Affairs: Botanical Gardens/Parks, Community Foundations, Economic Development, Housing, Municipalities/Towns, Safety, Urban & Community Affairs, Zoos/Aquariums

Education: Arts/Humanities Education, Colleges & Universities, Engineering/Technological Education, Education-General, International Studies, Literacy, Medical Education, Private Education (Precollege), Public Education (Precollege), Secondary Education (Private)

Environment: Environment-General

Health: Cancer, Children's Health/Hospitals, Emergency/Ambulance Services, Eyes/Blindness, Geriatric Health, Hospices, Hospitals, Prenatal Health Issues

International: Health Care/Hospitals

Religion: Churches, Dioceses, Religious Organizations, Religious Welfare, Social/Policy Issues

Social Services: Animal Protection, Child Welfare, Community Centers, Community Service Organizations, Day Care, Family Planning, Family Services, Food/Clothing Distribution, Homes, Scouts, Shelters/Homelessness, Substance Abuse, United Funds/United Ways, Youth Organizations

Application Procedures

Initial Contact: Send a brief letter of inquiry.

Application Requirements: Include a description of organization, amount requested, purpose of funds sought, recently audited financial statement, and proof of tax-exempt status. Also include a list of donors.

Deadlines: None.

Restrictions

Does not support individuals or political or lobbying groups. Does not make grants for operating support.

Foundation Officials

James Anderson Elkins, Jr.: president B Galveston, TX March 24, 1919. ED Princeton University BA (1941). CORP AFFIL director: Central Houston Inc. NONPR AFFIL member: Christ Cathedral; director: Houston Grand Opera; chairman, trustee: Baylor University College Medicine.

Pete Seale: treasurer

Grants Analysis

Disclosure Period: fiscal year ending October 31, 2002

Total Grants: $1,499,625*

Number of Grants: 14*

Average Grant: $107,116*

Highest Grant: $500,000

Lowest Grant: $5,000

Typical Range: $10,000 to $50,000

*Note: Giving excludes United Way.

Recent Grants

Note: Grants derived from 2002 Form 990.

General

500,000	University of Texas at Austin, Austin, TX -- for campaign fund
250,000	Central Houston Civic Center, Houston, TX -- for campaign fund
250,000	St. John's School, Houston, TX -- for campaign fund
150,000	Rice University, Houston, TX -- for campaign fund
100,000	Episcopal Diocese of Texas, Houston, TX -- for campaign fund
75,000	Hill School, Houston, TX -- for campaign fund
50,000	Gathering Place, Houston, TX -- for campaign fund
50,000	Parish School, Houston, TX -- for new campus
25,000	Stella Link Redevelopment Association, Houston, TX -- for completion of main campus

25,000   United Way of the Texas Gulf Coast, Houston, TX -- for campaign fund

ELLIS FOUNDATION

Giving Contact
Michael Ellis, Director
PO Box 9478
Rancho Santa Fe, CA 92067
Phone: (619)490-5222

Description
Founded: 1997
EIN: 330771069
Organization Type: Private Foundation
Grant Types: General Support.

Financial Summary
Total Giving: $73,980 (2003)
Assets: $94,524 (2003)
Gifts Received: $100,000 (2003). Note: In 2003, contributions were received from Michael J. Ellis II.

Typical Recipients
Arts & Humanities: Libraries
Civic & Public Affairs: Civic & Public Affairs-General, Rural Affairs
Education: Colleges & Universities, Education-General, Public Education (Precollege)
Health: Hospitals
Social Services: Community Service Organizations, Youth Organizations

Foundation Officials
Michael Ellis, II: director
Monica Ellis: director

Grants Analysis
Disclosure Period: calendar year ending 2003
Total Grants: $73,980
Number of Grants: 9
Highest Grant: $25,000
Lowest Grant: $500

Recent Grants
Note: Grants derived from 2001 Form 990.
Library-Related
10,000   San Diego Public Library, San Diego, CA
General
500,000   Campanile Foundation, San Diego, CA
135,000   Community Education Enhancement, San Diego, CA
25,000   St. Jude Hospital, Memphis, TN
22,500   Sweetwater High School, San Diego, CA
20,000   South Bay Community Services, San Diego, CA
5,000   Country Friends, Santa Fe, CA
5,000   Laurels for Leaders, San Diego, CA
2,000   Children's Experimental Trust, Zeeland, MI
1,000   Boys and Girls Club, San Diego, CA

RUTH H. AND WARREN A. ELLSWORTH FOUNDATION

Giving Contact
Sumner B. Tilton, Jr., Trustee
Ruth H. and Warren A. Ellsworth Foundation
370 Main Street, 12th Floor
Worcester, MA 01608

Phone: (508)798-8621
Fax: (508)791-6454
E-mail: stilton@ftwaw.com

Description
Founded: 1964
EIN: 046113491
Organization Type: Private Foundation
Giving Locations: MA: Worcester
Grant Types: Capital, Emergency, General Support, Multiyear/Continuing Support, Operating Expenses.

Donor Information
Founder: the late Ruth H. Ellsworth

Financial Summary
Total Giving: $635,550 (2003); $976,250 (2001)
Giving Analysis: Giving for 2003 includes: foundation grants to United Way ($23,000); foundation matching gifts ($43,211); 2001: foundation grants to United Way ($4,000); foundation matching gifts ($46,250)
Assets: $19,156,812 (2003); $19,465,677 (2001)

Typical Recipients
Arts & Humanities: Community Arts, Historic Preservation, History & Archaeology, Libraries, Museums/Galleries, Music, Theater
Civic & Public Affairs: Clubs, Community Foundations, Housing, Urban & Community Affairs
Education: Colleges & Universities, Education Reform, Engineering/Technological Education, Education-General, Private Education (Precollege), Science/Mathematics Education, Secondary Education (Private), Student Aid
Environment: Environment-General, Resource Conservation
Health: Cancer, Children's Health/Hospitals, Clinics/Medical Centers, Health Funds, Health Organizations, Hospices, Hospitals, Hospitals (University Affiliated), Medical Rehabilitation, Medical Research, Nursing Services, Public Health, Research/Studies Institutes
International: Foreign Arts Organizations
Religion: Churches, Dioceses, Jewish Causes
Science: Scientific Centers & Institutes, Scientific Organizations, Scientific Research
Social Services: At-Risk Youth, Big Brothers/Big Sisters, Child Abuse, Child Welfare, Community Centers, Community Service Organizations, Crime Prevention, Family Planning, Family Services, Senior Services, United Funds/United Ways, YMCA/YWCA/YMHA/YWHA, Youth Organizations

Application Procedures
Initial Contact: Send a brief letter of inquiry.
Application Requirements: Include goals and objectives of the request, plan for accomplishing these goals, proof of tax-exempt status, and project budget.
Deadlines: June 1.

Restrictions
Organizations must be recognized by the IRS in the cumulative listing.

Foundation Officials
David H. Ellsworth: trustee
Joy W. Hall: trustee
Sumner B. Tilton, Jr.: trustee PRIM CORP EMPL clerk: New England Newspaper Supply Co. CORP AFFIL clerk: Whitinsville Water Co.; clerk: Whiteater Inc.; clerk: NDI Inc.; clerk: R H White Co. Inc.; officer: Fletcher, Tilton & Whipple PC. NONPR AFFIL president: Greater Worcester Community Foundation.
Mark R. Wetzel: trustee
Todd H. Wetzel: trustee

Grants Analysis
Disclosure Period: calendar year ending 2003
Total Grants: $569,339*
Number of Grants: 36
Average Grant: $14,553*

Highest Grant: $60,000
Lowest Grant: $1,000
Typical Range: $5,000 to $25,000
*Note: Giving excludes United Way and matching gifts. Average grant figure excludes highest grant.

Recent Grants
Note: Grants derived from 2001 Form 990.
Library-Related
30,000   Friends of the Worcester Public Library, Worcester, MA -- capital project for the expansion and renovation of Salem Square
General
125,000   Bancroft School, Worcester, MA -- for campus programs and needs
100,000   Children's Friend, Inc., Worcester, MA -- for capital campaign Putting Kids First
60,000   New England Science Center, Worcester, MA -- capital campaign support
60,000   New England Science Center, Worcester, MA -- for construction projects
60,000   Worcester Art Museum, Worcester, MA -- centennial campaign
60,000   YOU, Worcester, MA -- for Children's Diagnostic Center
40,000   Massachusetts College of Pharmacy and Health Sciences, Boston, MA -- for the creation of Worcester Campus
30,000   Assumption College, Worcester, MA -- for science building
30,000   Greater Worcester Community Foundation, Worcester, MA -- for December 3rd Fund
30,000   UMASS Memorial Health Care, Worcester, MA -- for Ambulatory Center at Hahnemann Campus

FRED L. EMERSON FOUNDATION, INC.

Giving Contact
Ronald D. West, Executive Director & Secretary
PO Box 276
Auburn, NY 13021
Phone: (315)253-9621
Fax: (315)253-5235

Description
Founded: 1943
EIN: 156017650
Organization Type: Family Foundation
Giving Locations: NY: Cayuga County, Upstate, Auburn
Grant Types: Capital, Challenge, Emergency, Endowment, General Support, Matching, Multiyear/Continuing Support, Project, Research, Scholarship.

Donor Information
Founder: Established in 1932 by the late Fred L. Emerson, president of Dunn and McCarthy, Inc., a manufacturer of women's shoes in Auburn, NY.

Financial Summary
Total Giving: $3,501,954 (2003); $4,001,628 (2002)
Giving Analysis: Giving for 2003 includes: foundation grants to United Way ($134,830); 2002: foundation grants to United Way ($137,370)
Assets: $73,600,787 (2003); $67,691,512 (2002)

Typical Recipients
Arts & Humanities: Arts Associations & Councils, Arts Centers, Arts Festivals, Dance, Historic Preservation, History & Archaeology, Libraries, Museums/Galleries, Music, Opera, Performing Arts, Public Broadcasting, Theater
Civic & Public Affairs: African American Affairs, Bo-

tanical Gardens/Parks, Chambers of Commerce, Community Foundations, Economic Development, Civic & Public Affairs-General, Municipalities/Towns, Nonprofit Management, Parades/Festivals, Philanthropic Organizations, Public Policy, Safety, Urban & Community Affairs

Education: Arts/Humanities Education, Business Education, Colleges & Universities, Community & Junior Colleges, Education Associations, Education Funds, Education Reform, Elementary Education (Public), Environmental Education, Faculty Development, Education-General, Leadership Training, Preschool Education, Private Education (Precollege), Science/Mathematics Education, Student Aid, Vocational & Technical Education

Environment: Air/Water Quality

Health: Cancer, Children's Health/Hospitals, Emergency/Ambulance Services, Eyes/Blindness, Health-General, Health Funds, Health Organizations, Heart, Hospices, Hospitals, Long-Term Care, Medical Rehabilitation, Medical Research, Mental Health, Preventive Medicine/Wellness Organizations, Single-Disease Health Associations

International: Missionary/Religious Activities

Religion: Churches, Ministries, Religious Welfare

Science: Science Museums

Social Services: Animal Protection, Child Welfare, Community Service Organizations, Crime Prevention, Emergency Relief, Family Planning, Homes, People with Disabilities, Recreation & Athletics, Scouts, Senior Services, Shelters/Homelessness, Social Services-General, Substance Abuse, United Funds/United Ways, Veterans, Volunteer Services, YMCA/YWCA/YMHA/YWHA, Youth Organizations

Application Procedures

Initial Contact: Applicants should send a proposal in letter form to the foundation.

Application Requirements: Proposals should detail the project for which support is sought. Attachments should include copies of current financial statements, a list of other sources of support, and a copy of the IRS determination letter of tax-exempt status.

Deadlines: Proposals should be received no later than May 1 and November 1.

Review Process: Most major grants are made in early December. Meetings may be arranged with the foundation's grants officers if the applicant's program falls within the foundation's areas of interest.

Restrictions

The foundation does not make grants to individuals or for deficit financing or loans. The foundation prefers not to fund operating expenses.

Additional Information

Publications: Application Guidelines

Foundation Officials

William Finch Allyn: director B Auburn, NY 1935. ED Dartmouth College BA (1958); Syracuse University (1960). PRIM CORP EMPL president: Welch Allyn Inc. CORP AFFIL director: Perfex Corp.; director: Syracuse Research Corp.; director: Oneida Tableware Group; director: Oneida Silver; director: Oneida Silversmiths Division; director: Oneida Ltd.; director: Niagara Mohawk Holdings Inc.; president, chief executive officer: Niagara Mohawk Power Corp.; director: M T Bank; president, director: Grason-Stadler Inc.; president: GSI; president director: C E L Instruments, Ltd.

Christopher S. Emerson: director

David L. Emerson: president, director

Heather A. Emerson: director

Peter J. Emerson: director PRIM NONPR EMPL executive vice president: Dunn & McCarthy Inc.

W. Gary Emerson: director

Anthony D. Franceschelli: vice president

Dr. J. David Hammond: treasurer

Lori E. Robinson: director

Kristen E. Rubacka: director

Sally E. Wagner: director

Ronald D. West: executive director, secretary

Grants Analysis

Disclosure Period: calendar year ending 2003

Total Grants: $3,367,124*

Number of Grants: 59

Average Grant: $49,433*

Highest Grant: $500,000

Lowest Grant: $250

Typical Range: $10,000 to $100,000

*Note: Giving excludes United Way. Average grant figure excludes highest grant.

Recent Grants

Note: Grants derived from 2003 Form 990.

Library-Related

25,000	Seymour Library Foundation Inc., Auburn, NY

General

500,000	Rochester Institute of Technology, Rochester, NY
333,333	Colgate University, Hamilton, NY
280,500	Auburn Hospital System Foundation, Auburn, NY
251,000	Ithaca College, Ithaca, NY
250,000	Cayuga County Boy Scouts of America, Auburn, NY
250,000	Sage Colleges, Troy, NY
194,500	Cayuga County Community College Foundation, Auburn, NY
171,666	Hamilton College, Clinton, NY
165,500	Foundation Historical Association Inc., Auburn, NY
150,000	Keuka College, Geneva, NY

THOMAS J. EMERY MEMORIAL

Giving Contact

Lee A. Carter, President
2120 US Bank Center
425 Walnut St.
Cincinnati, OH 45202
Phone: (513)621-3124
Fax: (513)651-8403

Description

Founded: 1925

EIN: 310536711

Organization Type: General Purpose Foundation

Giving Locations: OH: Cincinnati

Grant Types: Capital, General Support, Matching, Project, Seed Money.

Donor Information

Founder: Incorporated in 1925 by the late Mary Muhlenberg Emery.

Financial Summary

Total Giving: $1,391,000 (2002); $1,350,633 (2001)

Giving Analysis: Giving for 2002 includes: foundation grants to United Way ($122,500); 2001: foundation grants to United Way ($115,500)

Assets: $25,039,665 (2002); $29,854,500 (2001)

Gifts Received: $26,000 (1996); $133,000 (1995).

Note: In 1996, contributions were received from C. G. & E.

Typical Recipients

Arts & Humanities: Arts Associations & Councils, Arts Centers, Arts Institutes, Arts Outreach, Ballet, Arts & Humanities-General, Historic Preservation, History & Archaeology, Libraries, Museums/Galleries, Music, Opera, Performing Arts, Public Broadcasting, Theater

Civic & Public Affairs: African American Affairs, Bo-

tanical Gardens/Parks, Clubs, Community Foundations, Economic Development, Employment/Job Training, Civic & Public Affairs-General, Housing, Legal Aid, Municipalities/Towns, Nonprofit Management, Parades/Festivals, Public Policy, Urban & Community Affairs, Women's Affairs, Zoos/Aquariums

Education: Arts/Humanities Education, Business Education, Colleges & Universities, Continuing Education, Economic Education, Education Funds, Elementary Education (Private), Education-General, Minority Education, Preschool Education, Private Education (Precollege), Public Education (Precollege), Science/Mathematics Education, Secondary Education (Private), Secondary Education (Public), Special Education, Student Aid, Vocational & Technical Education

Environment: Environment-General

Health: AIDS/HIV, Cancer, Children's Health/Hospitals, Clinics/Medical Centers, Diabetes, Emergency/Ambulance Services, Eyes/Blindness, Health-General, Health Organizations, Hospices, Hospitals, Long-Term Care, Medical Rehabilitation, Mental Health, Multiple Sclerosis, Nursing Services, Prenatal Health Issues, Public Health, Research/Studies Institutes, Single-Disease Health Associations, Speech & Hearing, Transplant Networks/Donor Banks

International: International Development

Religion: Churches, Dioceses, Religion-General, Ministries, Religious Organizations, Religious Welfare, Seminaries

Science: Observatories & Planetariums

Social Services: Child Welfare, Community Centers, Community Service Organizations, Counseling, Day Care, Domestic Violence, Emergency Relief, Family Planning, Family Services, Food/Clothing Distribution, Homes, People with Disabilities, Recreation & Athletics, Scouts, Senior Services, Shelters/Homelessness, Social Services-General, Substance Abuse, United Funds/United Ways, YMCA/YWCA/YMHA/YWHA, Youth Organizations

Application Procedures

Initial Contact: The foundation requests that applicants call for application guidelines.

Application Requirements: Send a brief letter of inquiry.

Deadlines: None.

Review Process: The board meets in April, September, and December.

Additional Information

Publications: Guidelines

Foundation Officials

John F. Barrett: treasurer B 1949. ED University of Cincinnati (1971). PRIM CORP EMPL president, chief executive officer, director: Western & Southern Life Insurance Co. ADD CORP EMPL president: Western Southern Life Assurance Co. CORP AFFIL director: Fifth Third Bank; director: Fifth Third Bancorp; director: Cincinnati Bell Inc.; director: Convergys Corp.; director: Andersons Inc. NONPR AFFIL vice chairmanr: Greater Cincinnati Chamber of Commerce.

Lee A. Carter: president, trustee

John T. Lawrence, Jr.: vice president, trustee

James S. Wachs: secretary, trustee

Thomas L. Williams: trustee

Grants Analysis

Disclosure Period: calendar year ending 2002

Total Grants: $1,268,500*

Number of Grants: 53

Average Grant: $21,510*

Highest Grant: $150,000

Lowest Grant: $400

Typical Range: $10,000 to $50,000

*Note: Giving excludes United Way. Average grant figure excludes highest grant.

Recent Grants

Note: Grants derived from 2002 Form 990.
General

150,000	Cincinnati Development Fund, Cincinnati, OH
122,500	United Way, Cincinnati, OH
115,000	Cincinnati Institute of Fine Arts, Cincinnati, OH
100,000	Cincinnati Country Day School, Cincinnati, OH
100,000	Seven Hills School, Cincinnati, OH
100,000	Taft Museum of Art, Cincinnati, OH
75,000	LISC Gr Cincinnati & Northern KY, Cincinnati, OH
50,000	Contemporary Arts Center, Cincinnati, OH
50,000	National Underground Railroad Freedom Center, Cincinnati, OH
33,000	Cincinnati Art Museum, Cincinnati, OH

EMPLOYERS MUTUAL CASUALTY CO.

Company Headquarters

Des Moines, IA
Web: http://www.emcins.com

Company Description

Employees: 1,795
SIC(s): 6311 Life Insurance, 6321 Accident & Health Insurance, 6331 Fire, Marine & Casualty Insurance.
Parent Company: Employers Mutual Inc., 1000 Riverside Ave., Ste. 400, Jacksonville, FL, United States
Parent Assets: US$758,300,000 (2001)

Operating Locations

Employers Mutual Casualty Co. (AL--Birmingham; IL--Oak Brook; IA--Des Moines; ND--Bismarck)
Note: Operates branch offices in 17 states.

Nonmonetary Support

Type: Donated Equipment; Loaned Executives

Employers Mutual Charitable Foundation

Giving Contact

Joe Smith, Manager, Executive Director
Employers Mutual Charitable Foundation
PO Box 712
Des Moines, IA 50303-0712
Phone: (515)280-2171
Web: http://www.emcins.com/about/communityinvolvement.htm

Description

EIN: 421343474
Organization Type: Corporate Foundation
Giving Locations: IA
Grant Types: Capital, General Support.

Financial Summary

Total Giving: $864,208 (2002); $477,360 (2001). Note: Contributes through foundation only.
Assets: $2,134,644 (2002); $2,753,559 (2001)
Gifts Received: $202,902 (2002); $48,350 (2001); $94,756 (1998). Note: Contributions are received from Employers Mutual Charitable Trust and Employers Mutual Casualty Company.

Typical Recipients

Arts & Humanities: Arts Associations & Councils, Arts Centers, Arts Festivals, Ballet, Arts & Humanities-General, Historic Preservation, History & Archae-ology, Libraries, Literary Arts, Museums/Galleries, Music, Opera, Performing Arts, Public Broadcasting, Theater
Civic & Public Affairs: African American Affairs, Botanical Gardens/Parks, Business/Free Enterprise, Civil Rights, Clubs, Community Foundations, Economic Development, Civic & Public Affairs-General, Housing, Law & Justice, Municipalities/Towns, Parades/Festivals, Public Policy, Safety, Urban & Community Affairs, Women's Affairs, Zoos/Aquariums
Education: Afterschool/Enrichment Programs, Business Education, Colleges & Universities, Education Funds, Education Reform, Elementary Education (Private), Elementary Education (Public), Education-General, International Studies, Minority Education, Preschool Education, Private Education (Precollege), Public Education (Precollege), Secondary Education (Public), Special Education, Student Aid
Environment: Environment-General, Resource Conservation
Health: Cancer, Children's Health/Hospitals, Diabetes, Emergency/Ambulance Services, Eyes/Blindness, Health-General, Health Policy/Cost Containment, Hospices, Hospitals, Multiple Sclerosis
International: International Relations
Religion: Religion-General, Jewish Causes, Religious Welfare
Science: Scientific Centers & Institutes
Social Services: Camps, Child Welfare, Community Centers, Community Service Organizations, Emergency Relief, Family Services, Food/Clothing Distribution, People with Disabilities, Recreation & Athletics, Scouts, Senior Services, Shelters/Homelessness, Social Services-General, Special Olympics, United Funds/United Ways, Volunteer Services, YMCA/YWCA/YMHA/YWHA, Youth Organizations

Application Procedures

Initial Contact: Send a letter of inquiry.
Application Requirements: Include intended use of funds, verification of tax-exempt status, and a list of major donors.
Deadlines: None.

Corporate Officials

Richard W. Hoffmann: general counsel, chief operating officer B Des Moines, IA 1953. ED Dartmouth College (1976); University of Colorado (1979). PRIM CORP EMPL general counsel: Employers Mutual Casualty Co. ADD CORP EMPL general counsel: American Liberty Insurance Co.; general counsel: Illinois EMCASCO Insurance Co.; general counsel: Dakota Fire Insurance Co.; general counsel: EMC Insurance Group Inc.; general counsel: EMC Reinsurance Co.; general counsel: EMCASSCO Insurance Co.; general counsel: Employers Modern Life Co.; general counsel: Farm and City Insurance Co.; general counsel: Union Insurance Co. of Providence ADD NONPR EMPL member legal committee: Alliance of American Insurers. NONPR AFFIL member: American Corp. Counsel Association; member: American Council Life Insurers; member: American Bar Association.
Fredrick A. Schiek: executive vice president, chief operating officer B Readlyn, IA 1934. ED Drake University (1959). PRIM CORP EMPL director: EMC Insurance Group Inc. CORP AFFIL director: Mutual Reinsurance Bureau. NONPR AFFIL director: Employers Mutual; vice chairman: Union Insurance Co. of Providence; director: CCIC; director: Alliance American Insurers.

Foundation Officials

Ronald D. Herman: treasurer
Richard W. Hoffmann: secretary (see above)
Bruce Gunn Kelley: president, chief executive officer B Philadelphia, PA 1954. ED Dartmouth College AB (1976); University of Iowa Law School JD (1979). PRIM CORP EMPL president, chief executive officer, director: Employers Mutual Casualty Co. ADD CORP EMPL president, chief executive officer: EMC Insurance Group Inc.; treasurer: EMC Underwriters Ltd. Inc. CORP AFFIL chairman: Illinois Emcasco Insurance Co.; chief executive officer: Employers Modern Life Co.; chairman: Farm City Insurance Co.; director: Alliance America Insurance Co.; chairman: American Liberty Insurance Co. NONPR AFFIL president: Mid-Iowa Council Boy Scouts America; trustee: National Committee Drunk Drivers; member: Iowa Bar Association; member advisory board: Iowa Public Employees Retirement Systems; director: Des Moines Arts Center; director: Greater Des Moines Sports Authority. CLUB AFFIL Masons Club; Rotary Club; Des Moines Club.
George W. Kochheiser: vice president
Joseph A. Smith: manager, executive director

Grants Analysis

Disclosure Period: calendar year ending 2002
Total Grants: $690,399*
Number of Grants: 68
Average Grant: $2,824*
Highest Grant: $404,000
Lowest Grant: $50
Typical Range: $100 to $8,000
*****Note:** Giving excludes scholarship and United Way. Average grant figure excludes two highest grants ($504,000).

Recent Grants

Note: Grants derived from 2003 Form 990.
General

404,000	Drake University, Des Moines, IA
165,809	United Way, Des Moines, IA
100,000	Salisbury House Foundation, Des Moines, IA
25,000	Iowa Dollars for Scholars, Des Moines, IA
25,000	Living History Farms, Des Moines, IA
20,000	Des Moines Symphony, Des Moines, IA
14,500	Explorer Post, Des Moines, IA
10,000	Civic Center of Greater Des Moines, Des Moines, IA
8,000	Iowa College Foundation, Des Moines, IA
8,000	Junior Achievement, Des Moines, IA

ENERGEN CORP.

Company Headquarters

605 Richard Arrington Jr. Boulevard, N.
Birmingham, AL 35203-2707
Web: http://www.energen.com

Company Description

Founded: 1978
Ticker: EGN
Exchange: NYSE
Revenue: US$677.2 million (2002)
Employees: 1,533 (2002)
SIC(s): 4900 Electric, Gas & Sanitary Services.
Parent Company: Energen Corp., 605 Richard Arrington Jr. Boulevard, N., Birmingham, AL, United States

Nonmonetary Support

Type: Donated Equipment; In-kind Services; Loaned Employees; Loaned Executives; Workplace Solicitation

Giving Contact

R. William Barber, Director, Corporate Contributions & New Business Administration
605 Richard Arrington, Jr. Blvd N.
Birmingham, AL 35203-2707
Phone: (205)326-8198

Description

Organization Type: Corporate Giving Program
Giving Locations: headquarters area only.
Grant Types: Award, Capital, Emergency, Employee Matching Gifts, General Support, Multiyear/

Continuing Support, Operating Expenses, Professorship, Scholarship.

Typical Recipients

Arts & Humanities: Arts Associations & Councils, Arts Festivals, Ballet, Community Arts, Dance, Arts & Humanities-General, Historic Preservation, Libraries, Museums/Galleries, Music, Opera, Performing Arts, Public Broadcasting, Theater
Civic & Public Affairs: Chambers of Commerce, Civil Rights, Community Foundations, Civic & Public Affairs-General, Inner-City Development, Law & Justice, Philanthropic Organizations, Public Policy, Urban & Community Affairs, Zoos/Aquariums
Education: Colleges & Universities, Education Funds, Elementary Education (Public), Faculty Development, Education-General, Literacy, Minority Education, Science/Mathematics Education, Secondary Education (Public)
Health: AIDS/HIV, Arthritis, Cancer, Children's Health/Hospitals, Clinics/Medical Centers, Diabetes, Eyes/Blindness, Health-General, Heart, Hospices, Hospitals, Kidney, Medical Rehabilitation, Mental Health, Multiple Sclerosis, Respiratory, Single-Disease Health Associations
Religion: Religious Welfare
Social Services: At-Risk Youth, Child Welfare, Community Service Organizations, Family Services, People with Disabilities, Recreation & Athletics, Scouts, Senior Services, Shelters/Homelessness, Social Services-General, United Funds/United Ways, Volunteer Services, YMCA/YWCA/YMHA/YWHA

Application Procedures

Initial Contact: Send a brief letter of inquiry and a full proposal. Include a description of organization, amount requested, purpose of funds sought, recently audited financial statement, and proof of tax-exempt status. Also include a listing of salaries and benefits paid to staff members of the organizations requesting a contribution.

Restrictions

Does not support individuals, religious organizations for sectarian purposes, political or lobbying groups, organizations outside operating areas, or fraternal organizations.

Additional Information

Publications: Guidelines

Corporate Officials

Geoff C. Ketcham: executive vice president, treasurer, chief financial officero, director B Birmingham, AL 1951. ED Auburn University. PRIM CORP EMPL executive vice president, treasurer, chief financial officer: Alabama Gas Corp.
William Michael Warren, Jr.: chairman, president, chief executive officer, chief operating officer, director B Bryan, TX 1947. ED Auburn University BA (1968); Duke University JD (1971). PRIM CORP EMPL chairman, president, chief executive officer, chief operating officer, director: Energen Corp. ADD CORP EMPL chief executive officer: Alabama Gas Co.; chief executive officer: Energen Resources Corp. CORP AFFIL director: AmSouth Bank NA.

Recent Grants

Note: Grants derived from 1998 Form 990.
General
Big Oak Ranch, Gadsden, AL
United Negro College Fund, Birmingham, AL
United Way, Birmingham, AL -- operating support
YWCA Capital Camp, Birmingham, AL
Alabama Independent Colleges, Birmingham, AL

MICHAEL S. ENGL FAMILY FOUNDATION

Giving Contact

Michael S. Engl, Director
PO Box 2500
Sun Valley, ID 83353-2500
Phone: (208)726-8151

Description

Founded: 1994
EIN: 820474079
Organization Type: Private Foundation
Grant Types: General Support.

Financial Summary

Total Giving: $128,276 (2003); $150,500 (2001)
Assets: $2,676,247 (2003); $2,825,495 (2001)
Gifts Received: $486,976 (1999); $1,029,910 (1994). Note: In 1994 and 1999, contributions were received from Michael S. Engl.

Typical Recipients

Arts & Humanities: Arts Centers, Museums/Galleries, Performing Arts
Civic & Public Affairs: Civic & Public Affairs-General, Municipalities/Towns
Education: Colleges & Universities, Minority Education, Private Education (Precollege), Public Education (Precollege), Secondary Education (Private), Special Education
Environment: Environment-General, Resource Conservation
Religion: Churches, Religious Organizations

Application Procedures

Initial Contact: The foundation requests applications be made in writing. Include purpose of funds sought and a description of organization.
Deadlines: None.

Foundation Officials

Dana Riley DeGroot: director
Leslie Engl: director
Michael S. Engl: director

Grants Analysis

Disclosure Period: calendar year ending 2003
Total Grants: $128,276
Number of Grants: 13
Average Grant: $9,867
Highest Grant: $32,500
Lowest Grant: $1,500
Typical Range: $5,000 to $15,000

Recent Grants

Note: Grants derived from 2003 Form 990.
General

32,500	Lensic Performing Arts Center, Santa Fe, NM -- for annual gift-board discretion and office renovation
25,000	Georgia O'Keefe Museum, Santa Fe, NM -- towards exhibitions, education and public programs
20,000	College of Southern Idaho, Hailey, ID -- for mountain wellness festival
9,776	Community School, Sun Valley, ID -- towards faculty enrichment and parents' associations
8,000	Santa Fe Preparatory School, Santa Fe, NM -- for headmaster's discretion
7,500	Sun Valley Center for the Art, Sun Valley, ID -- for whole salmon exhibition
5,000	Citizens for Smart Growth, Hailey, ID -- for board discretion
5,000	Santa Catalina School, Monterey, CA -- towards faculty endowment and scholarships
5,000	Sawtooth Valley Chapel, Stanley, ID -- for chapel improvements

5,000	Wood River Land Trust, Hailey, ID -- for open space preservation

ENSIGN-BICKFORD INDUSTRIES

Company Headquarters

Simsbury, CT
Web: http://www.ensign-bickford.com

Company Description

Employees: 153
SIC(s): 2672 Coated & Laminated Paper Nec, 2823 Cellulosic Manmade Fibers.

Nonmonetary Support

Type: Donated Equipment

Ensign-Bickford Foundation

Giving Contact

Janet DeLissio, Secretary, Treasurer, & Director
100 Grist Mill Road
Simsbury, CT 06070
Phone: (860)658-4411
Fax: (860)843-2805
Web: http://www.e-bind.com/community.html

Description

Founded: 1952
EIN: 066041097
Organization Type: Corporate Foundation
Giving Locations: CT: Avon, Simsbury primarily in areas of company operations.
Grant Types: Capital, Conference/Seminar, Employee Matching Gifts, General Support, Multiyear/Continuing Support, Project, Research, Scholarship, Seed Money.

Donor Information

Founder: Ensign-Bickford Industries, Inc.

Financial Summary

Total Giving: $190,854 (2003); $267,775 (2002); $223,190 (2001). Note: Contributes through corporate direct giving program and foundation.
Giving Analysis: Giving for 2002 includes: foundation grants to United Way ($13,656)
Assets: $213,676 (2003); $140,556 (2002); $147,272 (2001)
Gifts Received: $250,000 (2003); $250,000 (2002); $250,000 (2001). Note: Contributions were received from Ensign-Bickford Industries.

Typical Recipients

Arts & Humanities: Arts Associations & Councils, Arts Centers, Dance, Arts & Humanities-General, Historic Preservation, History & Archaeology, Libraries, Museums/Galleries, Music, Opera, Performing Arts, Public Broadcasting, Theater
Civic & Public Affairs: Botanical Gardens/Parks, Chambers of Commerce, Clubs, Economic Development, Employment/Job Training, Civic & Public Affairs-General, Housing, Legal Aid, Municipalities/Towns, Parades/Festivals, Professional & Trade Associations, Public Policy, Safety, Urban & Community Affairs, Women's Affairs
Education: Afterschool/Enrichment Programs, Arts/Humanities Education, Business Education, Colleges & Universities, Education Associations, Education Funds, Elementary Education (Public), Engineering/Technological Education, Education-General, Medical Education, Private Education (Precollege), Public Education (Precollege), Secondary Education (Pub-

lic), Student Aid
Environment: Environment-General, Resource Conservation, Sanitary Systems, Watershed
Health: Cancer, Children's Health/Hospitals, Diabetes, Health-General, Health Funds, Health Organizations, Heart, Hospitals, Medical Research, Multiple Sclerosis, Nursing Services, Respiratory, Single-Disease Health Associations
International: Health Care/Hospitals
Religion: Churches, Religious Organizations, Religious Welfare
Science: Science-General, Science Museums, Scientific Centers & Institutes, Scientific Organizations
Social Services: Big Brothers/Big Sisters, Camps, Child Welfare, Community Centers, Community Service Organizations, Crime Prevention, Emergency Relief, Food/Clothing Distribution, Homes, People with Disabilities, Recreation & Athletics, Scouts, Senior Services, Social Services-General, United Funds/United Ways, Volunteer Services, YMCA/YWCA/YMHA/YWHA, Youth Organizations

Application Procedures

Initial Contact: Send brief letter.
Application Requirements: Include purpose of request, annual budget, other funding, and geographic areas in which proceeds will be distributed.
Deadlines: None.

Restrictions

Grants are generally given to organizations within the local geographic area of the foundation's corporate offices.

Corporate Officials

Linda W. Angelastro: director corporate communications PRIM CORP EMPL director corporate communications: Ensign-Bickford Industries.
Herman J. Fonteyne: president, chief executive officer, director B Ghent, Belgium 1939. ED University of Louvain (1961); University of Ghent (1963). PRIM CORP EMPL president, chief executive officer, director: Ensign-Bickford Industries Inc. CORP AFFIL officer: Ensign-Bickford Haz-Pros Inc.; chairman: Ensign-Bickford Realty Corp.; director: CT Natural Gas Corp.; chairman, chief executive officer, director: Ensign-Bickford Co.
Joseph Ensign Lovejoy: chairman, director B Boston, MA 1940. ED Nichols College (1963). PRIM CORP EMPL chairman, director: Ensign-Bickford Industries Inc. ADD CORP EMPL director: Ensign-Bickford Co.

Foundation Officials

Robert Edward Darling, Jr.: chairman B Oakland, CA 1937. ED San Francisco State University BA (1959); Yale University School of Drama MFA (1963). PRIM CORP EMPL artistic producer: Acorn Theatre. CORP AFFIL manager: MG Taylor Corp.; manager: Darling Associates Garden Design; director: Ensign-Bickford Industries; vice president: Bushnell Horace Memorial Hall Corp. NONPR AFFIL member: United Scenic Artists; member: Washington Daffodil Society; member, panelist: Opera America; panelist: National Institute Music Theater; panelist: National Opera Institute; member: Logan Circle Association; member: Actors Equity - Canada; member: American Guild Musical Artists.
Janet DeLissio: secretary, treasurer, director
Ralph Harnett: director
Michael Thomas Long: director B Hartford, CT 1942. ED University of Notre Dame BA (1964); University of Connecticut JD (1967). PRIM CORP EMPL vice president, general counsel, secretary: Ensign-Bickford Industries Inc. CORP AFFIL director: Windsor Locks; president, director: Ensign-Bickford Haz-Pros Inc.; secretary, director: Ensign-Bickford Realty Corp.; administration, director: Ensign-Bickford Co. NONPR AFFIL member: International Society Explosive Engineers; scholarship chairman: University Notre Dame Alumni Clubs Greater Hartford; member: Hartford County Bar Association; board governors:

Institute Makers Explosives; member: Connecticut Bar Association; member: Greater Hartford Chamber of Commerce; director: American Corporate Counsel Association; chairman: Bradley International Airport Committee; member: American Bar Association. CLUB AFFIL Simsbury Farms Men's Club; Hop Meadow Country Club.
Kevin Shultz: director

Grants Analysis

Disclosure Period: calendar year ending 2003
Total Grants: $181,353*
Number of Grants: 34
Average Grant: $3,980*
Highest Grant: $50,000
Lowest Grant: $100
Typical Range: $1,000 to $5,000
*Note: Giving excludes United Way. Average grant figure excludes highest grant.

Recent Grants

Note: Grants derived from 2003 Form 990.
Library-Related

1,000	Simsbury Public Library, Simsbury, CT

General

50,000	Simsbury Land Trust, Simsbury, CT
25,000	Hartford Hospital, Hartford, CT
20,000	Farmington Valley YMCA, Granby, CT
12,185	United Way Golf Tournament Funds
10,000	Learning Corridor, Hartford, CT
8,772	United Way, Alexandria, VA
7,500	Hartford Hospital, Hartford, CT
7,000	Hartford Hospital, Hartford, CT
6,650	Farmington Valley Arts Center (FVAC), Avon, CT
6,200	McLean Golf Tournament, Simsbury, CT

EQUIFAX INC.

Company Headquarters

Atlanta, GA
Web: http://www.equifax.com

Company Description

Founded: 1899
Ticker: EFX
Exchange: NYSE
Revenue: US$1.139 billion (2001)
Employees: 4600 (2003)
SIC(s): 6411 Insurance Agents, Brokers & Service, 7323 Credit Reporting Services, 7374 Data Processing & Preparation, 7389 Business Services Nec.

Operating Locations

Equifax Inc. (AL--Lillian; AZ--Phoenix; AR--Little Rock; CA--Oroville, San Bruno; DE--New Castle; FL--Fort Lauderdale, Orlando, St. Petersburg; GA--Atlanta, Doraville, Marietta; ID--Boise; IL--Chicago, Downers Grove, Lisle, Westchester; KS--Shawnee Mission; MD--Pikesville; MA--Woburn; MI--Grand Rapids, Southfield; MN--Brooklyn Center; NJ--Eatontown; NM--Albuquerque; NY--Albany, Amherst, Troy, Yonkers; NC--Charlotte; OK--Oklahoma City; OR--Portland; PA--Pittsburgh; SC--North Augusta; TX--Arlington, El Paso, San Antonio, Willis; VA--Glen Allen, Richmond; WA--Federal Way; WI--Wisconsin Rapids)
Note: Operates throughout the USA; locations above include affiliate operations.

Nonmonetary Support

Value: $100,000 (2001 approx)
Type: Donated Equipment; Loaned Employees; Loaned Executives; Workplace Solicitation
Volunteer Programs: The Hearts and Hands program recognizes employees for volunteer efforts in their communitys. Employees who reach milestones in hours of service are rewarded with Hearts and

Hands shirts, event tickets, etc. Volunteers may participate in company-organized activities or may initiate activities on their own.

Equifax Foundation

Giving Contact

Kirby Thompson
Equifax Foundation
1550 Peachtree Street NW, Drop H-46
Atlanta, GA 30309
Phone: (404)885-8000
Fax: (404)885-8215
E-mail: kirby.thompson@equifax.com
Web: http://www.equifax.com

Description

EIN: 581296807
Organization Type: Corporate Foundation
Giving Locations: GA: Atlanta primarily metro area
Grant Types: Capital, Emergency, Employee Matching Gifts, Endowment, General Support, Matching, Multiyear/Continuing Support.

Financial Summary

Total Giving: $522,031 (2003); $1,000,000 (2002 approx); $824,060 (2001). Note: Contributes through corporate direct giving program and foundation.
Giving Analysis: Giving for 2001 includes: non-monetary support ($100,000); foundation ($364,133).
Assets: $1,848,217 (2003); $1,687,898 (2001)
Gifts Received: $400,000 (2003); $300,000 (2001); $475,000 (2000). Note: Contributions were received from Equifax Inc.

Typical Recipients

Arts & Humanities: Arts Associations & Councils, Arts Centers, Arts Festivals, Arts Funds, Ballet, Ethnic & Folk Arts, Historic Preservation, Libraries, Music, Performing Arts, Theater
Civic & Public Affairs: Botanical Gardens/Parks, Business/Free Enterprise, Chambers of Commerce, Civil Rights, Community Foundations, Economic Development, Economic Policy, Employment/Job Training, Ethnic Organizations, Civic & Public Affairs-General, Housing, Legal Aid, Municipalities/Towns, Nonprofit Management, Philanthropic Organizations, Professional & Trade Associations, Urban & Community Affairs, Women's Affairs, Zoos/Aquariums
Education: Afterschool/Enrichment Programs, Agricultural Education, Arts/Humanities Education, Business Education, Business-School Partnerships, Colleges & Universities, Economic Education, Education Associations, Education Funds, Education Reform, Engineering/Technological Education, Education-General, Literacy, Medical Education, Minority Education, Preschool Education, Private Education (Precollege), Special Education
Environment: Environment-General
Health: Adolescent Health Issues, AIDS/HIV, Cancer, Children's Health/Hospitals, Diabetes, Emergency/Ambulance Services, Health-General, Health Organizations, Heart, Hospices, Hospitals, Kidney, Medical Rehabilitation, Multiple Sclerosis, Nursing Services, Prenatal Health Issues, Preventive Medicine/Wellness Organizations, Public Health, Research/Studies Institutes, Single-Disease Health Associations
International: Foreign Arts Organizations, Health Care/Hospitals, International Development, International Organizations, International Peace & Security Issues, International Relations, Missionary/Religious Activities
Religion: Jewish Causes, Religious Welfare
Science: Observatories & Planetariums, Science Museums
Social Services: Big Brothers/Big Sisters, Camps, Child Abuse, Child Welfare, Community Centers, Community Service Organizations, Counseling, Day Care, Delinquency & Criminal Rehabilitation, Domes-

tic Violence, Emergency Relief, Family Services, Food/Clothing Distribution, People with Disabilities, Recreation & Athletics, Senior Services, Shelters/ Homelessness, Social Services-General, Special Olympics, Substance Abuse, United Funds/United Ways, Volunteer Services, YMCA/YWCA/YMHA/ YWHA, Youth Organizations

Application Procedures

Initial Contact: Request application guidelines, then send written proposal.

Application Requirements: Include a description of organization, purpose of funds sought, proof of tax-exempt status, explanation of how funds will be used, annual report, list of officers and directors, and why Equifax would be an appropriate donor.

Review Process: Proposals reviewed by foundation vice president prior to consideration by donations committee, then submitted to foundation committee for approval; committee consists of four executives.

Restrictions

Foundation primarily supports organizations with which it has an established relationship.

Does not support fraternal organizations, goodwill advertising, individuals, political or lobbying groups, member agencies of united funds, or religious organizations for sectarian purposes.

In general, will not give grants for memorials, to cover operating deficits, to projects that are primarily fundraising events, or to local or regional chapters of national organizations. that are primarily fundraising events, or to local or regional chapters of national organizations.

Additional Information

Grants are not renewed automatically. Organizations must re-apply for funding each year unless multi-year campaigns have been approved by the Donations Committee.

The Donations Committee, the panel which directs Equifax's contributions program, is made up of executive officers.

Trust Company Bank, Atlanta, GA, is also listed as the foundation's corporate trustee. corporate trustee. corporate trustee. corporate trustee.

Corporate Officials

John T. Chandler: corporate vice president, chief administrative officer B 1948. PRIM CORP EMPL corporate vice president, chief administrative officer: Equifax Inc. ADD CORP EMPL vice president: Equifax Payment Service Inc.

Karen H. Gaston: chief executive officer PRIM CORP EMPL chief executive officer: Equifax Inc.

David A. Post: corporate vice president, chief financial officer B Canfield, OH 1953. ED Ohio University BBA (1975). PRIM CORP EMPL corporate vice president, chief financial officer: Equifax Inc. ADD CORP EMPL chief financial officer: Equifax Credit Information Service.

Foundation Officials

Thomas F. Chapman: trustee
Karen H. Gaston: trustee (see above)
Philip J. Mazzilli: trustee
Kirby A. Thompson: trustee

Grants Analysis

Disclosure Period: calendar year ending 2003
Total Grants: $219,334*
Number of Grants: 59
Average Grant: $2,704*
Highest Grant: $62,500
Lowest Grant: $500
Typical Range: $1,000 to $5,000
*Note: Giving excludes matching gifts and United Way. Average grant figure excludes highest grant.

Recent Grants

Note: Grants derived from 2003 Form 990.

General

111,000	United Way of Metro Atlanta, Atlanta, GA
62,500	Woodruff Arts Center, Atlanta, GA
33,334	East Lake Community Foundation Inc., Atlanta, GA
18,000	Myeloma Institute for Research, Little Rock, AR
15,000	Literacy Action, Atlanta, GA
12,000	United Negro College Fund, Fairfax, VA
10,000	Greater Atlanta Inner City Games, Atlanta, GA
6,500	Woodruff Arts Center, Atlanta, GA
5,000	Center for Puppetry Arts, Atlanta, GA
5,000	Children's Healthcare of Atlanta, Atlanta, GA

ARMAND G. ERPF FUND

Giving Contact

Sue E. Van de Bovenkamp, President
640 Park Ave.
New York, NY 10021
Phone: (212)535-6678

Description

Founded: 1951
EIN: 136085594
Organization Type: Private Foundation
Giving Locations: NY
Grant Types: General Support.

Donor Information

Founder: the late Armand G. Erpf

Financial Summary

Gifts Received: $287,493 (fiscal year ending November 30, 2000); $251,469 (fiscal 1999); $206,283 (fiscal 1998). Note: In fiscal 1998, 1999 and 2000, contributions were received from from the ERPF Charitable Trust.

Typical Recipients

Arts & Humanities: Arts Associations & Councils, Arts Centers, Arts Institutes, Ballet, Community Arts, Dance, Historic Preservation, Libraries, Museums/ Galleries, Music, Opera, Public Broadcasting, Theater

Civic & Public Affairs: Asian American Affairs, Botanical Gardens/Parks, Economic Development, Ethnic Organizations, Civic & Public Affairs-General, Philanthropic Organizations, Zoos/Aquariums

Education: Arts/Humanities Education, Colleges & Universities, Environmental Education, Education-General, International Studies, Private Education (Precollege)

Environment: Environment-General, Resource Conservation, Wildlife Protection

Health: Hospitals, Single-Disease Health Associations

International: Foreign Educational Institutions, Health Care/Hospitals, International Development, International Environmental Issues, International Organizations, International Peace & Security Issues, International Relations, International Relief Efforts

Religion: Churches, Religious Organizations

Science: Science Museums, Scientific Centers & Institutes, Scientific Labs

Social Services: Child Welfare, Crime Prevention, Youth Organizations

Application Procedures

Initial Contact: The foundation has no formal grant application procedure or application form.
Deadlines: None.

Foundation Officials

Gina Caimi: secretary
Douglas Campbell: vice president

Armand B. Erpf: director
Cornelia A. Erpf: director
Henry B. Hyde: director
Carl L. Kempner: treasurer
Robert B. Oxnam: director NONPR AFFIL president emeritus: Asia Society.
Roger David Stone: director B New York, NY 1934. ED Yale University BA (1955). NONPR AFFIL director: Scenic Hudson; president: Sustainable Development Institute; vice chairman: ECO; member: Century Association; member: Council Foreign Relations; member: Center Inter-American Relations; director: Asian Institute Technology Foundation; director: Caribbean Conservation Corp.; member: Arts International; member: ACCION International; member: Ams Foundation.
Sue Erpf Van de Bovenkamp: president, director

Grants Analysis

Disclosure Period: fiscal year ending November 30, 2000
Total Grants: $517,213
Number of Grants: 126
Average Grant: $4,105
Highest Grant: $50,000
Typical Range: $1,000 to $10,000

Recent Grants

Note: Grants derived from fiscal 2002 Form 990.

Library-Related

10,000	New York Public Library, New York, NY

General

50,000	Amazon Conservation Team, Washington, DC
35,000	Wildlife Conservation Society, New York, NY
30,000	World Wildlife Fund, Washington, DC
25,000	Catskill Center for Conservation and Development, Arkville, NY
25,000	Catskill Center for Conservation and Development, Arkville, NY
25,000	Conservation International, Washington, DC
25,000	Wildlife Conservation Society, New York, NY
20,000	World Wildlife Fund, Washington, DC
20,000	World Wildlife Fund, Washington, DC
15,000	Convent of the Sacred Heart, New York, NY

ERVING INDUSTRIES

Company Headquarters

120 E. Main St.
Erving, MA 01344
Web: http://www.fiberclaycouncil.org/erving

Company Description

Former Name: Erving Paper Mills.
Employees: 500
SIC(s): 2621 Paper Mills, 6719 Holding Companies Nec.

Operating Locations

Erving Industries (MA--Erving)

Housen Foundation

Giving Contact

Denis L. Emmett, Treasurer
Erving Industries, Inc.
97 E. Main Street
Erving, MA 01344-9756
Phone: (413)422-2723
Fax: (978)544-2865

Description

Founded: 1968
EIN: 046183673
Organization Type: Corporate Foundation
Giving Locations: MA
Grant Types: Award, Capital, Emergency, Employee Matching Gifts, Endowment, Fellowship, General Support, Multiyear/Continuing Support, Operating Expenses, Project, Scholarship.

Donor Information

Founder: Erving Paper Mills, Brattleboro Paper Products, Inc.

Financial Summary

Total Giving: $33,502 (2003); $117,757 (2002); $172,252 (2001)
Assets: $13,049 (2003); $46,257 (2002); $164,441 (2001)
Gifts Received: $100,000 (2000); $150,000 (1999); $40,000 (1998). Note: Contributions were received from Erving Paper Mills.

Typical Recipients

Arts & Humanities: Arts Associations & Councils, Arts Funds, Arts & Humanities-General, Libraries, Music, Performing Arts
Civic & Public Affairs: Botanical Gardens/Parks, Clubs, Community Foundations, Ethnic Organizations, Civic & Public Affairs-General, Housing, Law & Justice, Municipalities/Towns, Philanthropic Organizations, Women's Affairs
Education: Afterschool/Enrichment Programs, Business-School Partnerships, Colleges & Universities, Community & Junior Colleges, Education Funds, Elementary Education (Private), Elementary Education (Public), Engineering/Technological Education, Education-General, Health & Physical Education, Literacy, Medical Education, Private Education (Precollege), Public Education (Precollege), Science/Mathematics Education, Secondary Education (Public), Social Sciences Education, Student Aid, Vocational & Technical Education
Health: Cancer, Children's Health/Hospitals, Clinics/Medical Centers, Emergency/Ambulance Services, Health-General, Heart, Home-Care Services, Hospices, Hospitals, Hospitals (University Affiliated), Medical Research, Preventive Medicine/Wellness Organizations
International: International Peace & Security Issues, Missionary/Religious Activities
Religion: Churches, Religion-General, Jewish Causes, Synagogues/Temples
Science: Science Museums
Social Services: At-Risk Youth, Child Abuse, Child Welfare, Crime Prevention, Domestic Violence, Food/Clothing Distribution, Recreation & Athletics, Scouts, Shelters/Homelessness, Social Services-General, United Funds/United Ways, Veterans, YMCA/YWCA/YMHA/YWHA, Youth Organizations

Application Procedures

Initial Contact: Application forms are available upon request from the personnel administrator.
Deadlines: February 28.

Restrictions

Does not support individuals (except employee-related scholarships).

Additional Information

Provides scholarships to children of employees of Erving Industries and its subsidiaries.

Corporate Officials

Denis L. Emmett: chief financial officer, president, chief executive officer, director B 1954. ED University of Massachusetts BA (1976). PRIM CORP EMPL treasurer: Industries Inc. ADD CORP EMPL treasurer: Erving Paper Products Inc.; treasurer: Erving Paper Mills Inc.

Charles B. Housen: chairman, president, chief executive officer, director B 1932. PRIM CORP EMPL chairman, president, chief executive officer, director: Erving Industries Inc. ADD CORP EMPL chairman: Erving Paper Miles Inc.; president: Erving Paper Products Inc.; president: Flamingo Products Inc. CORP AFFIL director: Massachusetts Electric Co.

Foundation Officials

Denis L. Emmett: treasurer, assistant clerk (see above)
Charles B. Housen: president, director (see above)
Marjorie G. Housen: director
Morris Housen: director, vice president, assistant treasurer, clerk PRIM CORP EMPL treasurer: Erving Industries Inc. ADD CORP EMPL assistant treasurer: Erving Paper Products Inc.

Grants Analysis

Disclosure Period: calendar year ending 2003
Total Grants: $31,702*
Number of Grants: 4
Highest Grant: $20,000
Lowest Grant: $1,500
Typical Range: $2,500 to $20,000
*Note: Giving excludes scholarship.

Recent Grants

Note: Grants derived from 2003 Form 990.
General

20,000	Greater Worcester Community Foundation, Worcester, MA
7,702	Erving Elementary School, Erving, MA
2,500	YMCA in Greenfield, Greenfield, MA
1,500	Athol Area YMCA, Athol, MA
1,500	Greenfield Community College, Greenfield, MA
300	Hofstra University, Hempstead, NY

ESSICK FOUNDATION

Giving Contact

Robert Essick, President, Treasurer
1379 La Solana Dr.
Altadena, CA 91001
Phone: (818)449-1120

Description

Founded: 1947
EIN: 956048985
Organization Type: Private Foundation
Giving Locations: CA: primarily in southern area; MA; NY; VA; WA
Grant Types: General Support.

Donor Information

Founder: the late Jeanette Marie Essick, Bryant Essick, Essick Investment Co.

Financial Summary

Total Giving: $143,000 (2004); $136,300 (2001)
Assets: $3,203,328 (2004); $3,024,853 (2001)

Typical Recipients

Arts & Humanities: Arts Institutes, Ethnic & Folk Arts, Libraries, Literary Arts, Museums/Galleries, Public Broadcasting
Civic & Public Affairs: Clubs, Philanthropic Organizations, Zoos/Aquariums
Education: Business Education, Colleges & Universities, Education Funds, Engineering/Technological Education, Science/Mathematics Education, Vocational & Technical Education
Health: Alzheimer's Disease, Children's Health/Hospitals, Clinics/Medical Centers, Emergency/Ambulance Services, Eyes/Blindness, Health Organizations, Hospitals, Medical Research, Prenatal Health Issues, Preventive Medicine/Wellness Organizations, Research/Studies Institutes, Single-Disease Health Associations, Speech & Hearing
International: Foreign Arts Organizations
Religion: Churches, Religious Welfare
Social Services: Child Welfare, Community Service Organizations, Homes, People with Disabilities, Recreation & Athletics, Scouts, Special Olympics, United Funds/United Ways, Volunteer Services, YMCA/YWCA/YMHA/YWHA, Youth Organizations

Application Procedures

Initial Contact: Send a brief letter of inquiry.
Application Requirements: Include purpose of funds sought and proof of tax-exempt status.
Deadlines: None.

Foundation Officials

Robert N. Essick: president, treasurer B Los Angeles, CA 1942. PRIM NONPR EMPL professor: University of California, Riverside. NONPR AFFIL member, board overseers: Huntington Library; member: Modern Language Association.
Jenijoy LaBelle: vice president, secretary
Dr. James Stanger: chief financial officer

Grants Analysis

Disclosure Period: calendar year ending 2004
Total Grants: $143,000
Number of Grants: 5
Highest Grant: $66,000
Lowest Grant: $5,000
Typical Range: $8,000 to $50,000

Recent Grants

Note: Grants derived from 2001 Form 990.
Library-Related

97,300	Huntington Library, San Marino, CA

General

25,000	University of Virginia, Charlottesville, VA
5,000	University of Rochester, Rochester, NY
4,000	California Institute of Technology, Pasadena, CA
3,000	William College Alumni, Williamstown, MA
1,000	Boy Scouts of America, Redlands, CA
1,000	Boy Scouts of America, Tacoma, WA

ETHYL CORP.

Company Headquarters

Richmond, VA
Web: http://www.ethyl.com

Company Description

Founded: 1942
Ticker: EY
Exchange: NYSE
Revenue: US$656.4 million (2002)
Employees: 1100 (2003)
SIC(s): 2869 Industrial Organic Chemicals Nec, 5169 Chemicals & Allied Products Nec.
Parent Company: NewMarket Corporation, 330 South Fourth St., Richmond, VA, United States

Operating Locations

Ethyl Corp. (DC--Washington; MI--Southfield; NY--Clarence Center; TX--Houston)

Nonmonetary Support

Type: Donated Equipment; Loaned Employees

Giving Contact

Diane Hazelwood
Services Coordinator
330 S. 4th St.
Richmond, VA 23219
Phone: (804)788-5522
Fax: (804)788-6084

E-mail: contributions@ethyl.com
Note: Also contact nearest field location.

Alternate Contact

Bruce R. Hazelgrove, III, Vice President Corporate Resources

Description

Organization Type: Corporate Giving Program
Giving Locations: headquarters and operating communities.
Grant Types: Capital, Challenge, Employee Matching Gifts, Endowment, General Support, Professorship, Scholarship.
Note: Employee matching gift ratio: 1 to 1.

Financial Summary

Total Giving: Contributes through corporate direct giving program only.

Typical Recipients

Arts & Humanities: Arts Associations & Councils, Arts Centers, Arts Funds, Community Arts, Historic Preservation, Libraries, Museums/Galleries, Music, Opera, Performing Arts, Public Broadcasting
Civic & Public Affairs: Business/Free Enterprise, Economic Development, Urban & Community Affairs
Education: Colleges & Universities, Economic Education, Science/Mathematics Education
Environment: Environment-General
Health: Emergency/Ambulance Services, Health Organizations, Hospitals
Science: Observatories & Planetariums, Science Exhibits & Fairs, Scientific Centers & Institutes, Scientific Organizations
Social Services: Community Service Organizations, Shelters/Homelessness, United Funds/United Ways, Youth Organizations

Application Procedures

Initial Contact: Send a brief letter of inquiry.
Application Requirements: Include a statement of purpose; brief description of nature and scope of activities; current financial condition (balance sheet); list of board members and staff manager; copy of IRS determination letter; rationale for why company is appropriate donor.
Deadlines: Before September 1.
Review Process: The program is administered from headquarters; community relations committees (plant manager, office manager, department head, deputy) determine involvement on local level, with vice president of external affairs acting as liaison; top management official at each field location responsible for budgeting annual support.
Decision Notification: The annual budget is presented and approved in late fall; contributions on an unbudgeted basis are extremely limited.

Restrictions

Contributions are not made to religious organizations for religious purposes, individuals in support of a personal project for profit, fraternal groups, local organizations in communities where company does not have significant operations, or in response to telephone or mass mail solicitations.
The corporation does not directly support political contributions. However, limited contributions are made through Ethyl Corporation Political Action Committee, which consists of funds contributed by Ethyl employees. Political Action Committee, which consists of funds contributed by Ethyl employees. Foundation primarily funds preselected organizations.

Additional Information

Company annually budgets a limited amount to support charitable organizations with small advertisements in printed programs aimed at raising funds.

Corporate Officials

Thomas E. Gottwald: president, chief executive officer B 1962. ED Virginia Military Institute BS (1983);

Harvard University MBA (1984). PRIM CORP EMPL president, chief executive officer: Ethyl Corp. ADD CORP EMPL president, director: Ethyl Petroleum Additives Inc.; president: Ethyl Additives Corp.

Giving Program Officials

Thomas E. Gottwald: (see above)
Henry C. Page, Jr.: PRIM CORP EMPL vice president human resources & external affairs: Ethyl Corp.

Grants Analysis

Typical Range: $1,000 to $5,000

EDWARD P. EVANS FOUNDATION

Giving Contact

Edward P. Evans, Officer
Edward P. Evans Foundation
PO Box 46, Route 602
Casanova, VA 20139
Phone: (212)765-9500

Description

Founded: 1991
EIN: 256232129
Organization Type: Private Foundation
Grant Types: General Support.

Donor Information

Founder: Established in 1991 by Edward P. Evans.

Financial Summary

Total Giving: $137,720 (fiscal year ending November 30, 2004); $287,514 (fiscal 2001)
Assets: $3,105,466 (fiscal 2004); $4,026,953 (fiscal 2001)
Gifts Received: $2,142,538 (fiscal 1999). Note: In fiscal 1999, contributions were received from The Evans Foundation. In fiscal 1989, contributions were received from Edward P. Evans.

Typical Recipients

Arts & Humanities: Arts Associations & Councils, Ballet, Dance, Historic Preservation, Libraries, Museums/Galleries, Music
Civic & Public Affairs: Botanical Gardens/Parks, Civic & Public Affairs-General, Law & Justice, Zoos/Aquariums
Education: Business Education, Colleges & Universities, Education Reform, Elementary Education (Private), Education-General, Private Education (Precollege), Public Education (Precollege), Social Sciences Education, Student Aid
Environment: Environment-General, Resource Conservation, Wildlife Protection
Health: AIDS/HIV, Cancer, Children's Health/Hospitals, Hospices, Hospitals, Medical Research, Single-Disease Health Associations
International: Foreign Arts Organizations, Foreign Educational Institutions, Human Rights, International Affairs
Religion: Churches
Social Services: Animal Protection, Child Welfare, Community Service Organizations, Recreation & Athletics, United Funds/United Ways

Application Procedures

Initial Contact: The foundation has no formal grant application procedure or application form.
Deadlines: None.

Foundation Officials

Edward Parker Evans: off B Pittsburgh, PA 1942. ED Yale University BA (1964); Harvard University MBA (1967). CORP AFFIL owner: Spring Hill Farm Virginia; director: HBD Industries. NONPR AFFIL

member: Andover Development Board. CLUB AFFIL Round Hill Club; Spouting Rock Beach Association; Rolling Rock Club; Lyford Cay Club; River Club; Harvard Business School Club; Blind Brook Country Club; Duquesne Club.
Dorsey Gardner: trustee
Charles J. Queenan, Jr.: trustee

Grants Analysis

Disclosure Period: fiscal year ending November 30, 2004
Total Grants: $137,720
Number of Grants: 25
Average Grant: $3,663*
Highest Grant: $49,800
Lowest Grant: $95
Typical Range: $1,000 to $5,000
***Note:** Average grant figure excludes highest grant.

Recent Grants

Note: Grants derived from fiscal 2004 Form 990.
General

49,800	Washington Ballet, Washington, DC
15,000	Fauquier County Society for Prevention of Cruelty to Animals, Casanova, VA
15,000	Fauquier County Society for Prevention of Cruelty to Animals, Casanova, VA
15,000	Human Rights First, New York, NY
10,000	Piedmont Environmental Council, Warrenton, VA
8,500	Washington Ballet, Washington, DC
4,750	Society of Memorial Sloan - Kettering Cancer Center
3,000	Piedmont Environmental Council, Warrenton, VA
2,500	2004 Annual Appeal of Memorial Sloan - Kettering Cancer Center
2,400	Thoroughbred Retirement Foundation

THOMAS J. EVANS FOUNDATION

Giving Contact

J. Gilbert Reese, Chairman & Chief Executive Officer
36 N. 2nd Street
Newark, OH 43055-0764
Phone: (740)345-3431

Description

Founded: 1965
EIN: 316055767
Organization Type: General Purpose Foundation
Giving Locations: OH: Licking County
Grant Types: Capital, General Support, Operating Expenses, Scholarship, Seed Money.

Donor Information

Founder: the late Thomas J. Evans

Financial Summary

Total Giving: $678,593 (fiscal year ending October 31, 2004); $395,292 (fiscal 2001)
Assets: $23,229,637 (fiscal 2004); $21,886,153 (fiscal 2001)
Gifts Received: $40,710 (fiscal 2004); $700 (fiscal 2000). Note: In fiscal 2004, contributions were received from Dan & Peggy Evans.

Typical Recipients

Arts & Humanities: Arts Associations & Councils, Arts Centers, Historic Preservation, History & Archaeology, Libraries, Museums/Galleries, Theater, Visual Arts
Civic & Public Affairs: Botanical Gardens/Parks, Clubs, Community Foundations, Economic Development, Civic & Public Affairs-General, Housing, Municipalities/Towns, Urban & Community Affairs

Education: Colleges & Universities, Education Reform, Elementary Education (Public), Public Education (Precollege), Student Aid
Environment: Environment-General, Resource Conservation
Religion: Churches, Ministries, Religious Organizations, Religious Welfare
Social Services: Community Service Organizations, People with Disabilities, Recreation & Athletics, Senior Services, Social Services-General, YMCA/YWCA/YMHA/YWHA, Youth Organizations

Application Procedures

Initial Contact: The foundation has no formal grant application procedure or application form. Send a brief letter of inquiry.
Deadlines: None.

Restrictions

Grants are not made to individuals. Grants are restricted to organizations in Licking County, Ohio.

Foundation Officials

J. Gilbert Reese: chairman, chief executive officer B 1926. PRIM CORP EMPL chairman board, director: First Federal Saving & Loan Association.
Louella H. Reese: vice president, treasurer
Sarah R. Wallace: president, secretary PRIM CORP EMPL chairman: First Federal Saving & Loan Association.

Grants Analysis

Disclosure Period: fiscal year ending October 31, 2004
Total Grants: $678,593
Number of Grants: 12
Average Grant: $843*
Highest Grant: $350,000
Lowest Grant: $60
Typical Range: $100 to $1,000
*Note: Average grant figure excludes three highest grants ($671,000).

Recent Grants

Note: Grants derived from 2004 Form 990.
General

350,000	First Federal Foundation -- for works fund
300,000	First Federal Foundation -- for Midland theatre fund
21,000	City of Newark, Newark, OH -- for Cherry valley
5,335	Carol Strawn Center, Newark, OH -- for roof repair
1,000	Licking Land Trust, Granville, OH
329	Newark Monument, Newark, OH -- for plaque Shakespeare
262	Licking County Recorder, Newark, OH -- for leases
216	St. Luke's Episcopal Church, Niles, OH -- for florals
174	Art and Clay, Lancaster, OH -- towards city chair project
145	FLO Lawn

EVERETT CHARITABLE TRUST

Giving Contact

c/o Fleet National Bank, Trustee
One East Avenue
Rochester, NY 14604
Phone: (716)546-9289

Description

Founded: 1957
EIN: 156018093
Organization Type: Private Foundation

Giving Locations: NY: Auburn and Cayuga counties, NY
Grant Types: General Support.

Donor Information

Founder: the late Fred M. Everett

Financial Summary

Total Giving: 1996 Giving includes United Way ($49,991).
Gifts Received: $1,725 (1992)

Typical Recipients

Arts & Humanities: Arts Associations & Councils, Arts Centers, Historic Preservation, History & Archaeology, Libraries, Museums/Galleries, Music, Performing Arts
Civic & Public Affairs: Civic & Public Affairs-General
Education: Colleges & Universities, Community & Junior Colleges, Student Aid
Health: Emergency/Ambulance Services, Hospitals, Long-Term Care
International: Human Rights
Religion: Churches
Social Services: Animal Protection, Child Welfare, Community Service Organizations, Recreation & Athletics, Scouts, United Funds/United Ways, YMCA/YWCA/YMHA/YWHA, Youth Organizations

Application Procedures

Initial Contact: Send a brief letter of inquiry.
Application Requirements: Include amount requested, and purpose of funds sought.
Deadlines: November 1

Additional Information

Trust(s): Fleet Trust Co

Grants Analysis

Disclosure Period: calendar year ending 2000
Total Grants: $46,525*
Number of Grants: 17
Average Grant: $2,737
Highest Grant: $8,930
Typical Range: $1,000 to $5,000
*Note: Giving excludes United Way.

Recent Grants

Note: Grants derived from 2002 Form 990.
General

48,369	United Way of Cayuga County, Auburn, NY
11,173	Westminster Presbyterian Church, Austin, TX
5,586	Auburn Memorial Hospital, Auburn, NY
5,586	Trinity United Church of Christ, Union Springs, NY
5,586	YMCA of Auburn, Auburn, NY
2,500	United Way of Cayuga County, Auburn, NY
2,500	United Way of Cayuga County, Auburn, NY
2,500	United Way of Cayuga County, Auburn, NY

H. T. EWALD FOUNDATION

Giving Contact

Shelagh Kuprenski, Secretary
15450 E. Jefferson Ave., Suite 180
Grosse Pointe Park, MI 48230
Phone: (313)821-1278

Description

Founded: 1928
EIN: 386007837

Organization Type: Private Foundation
Giving Locations: MI: Detroit including metropolitan area
Grant Types: General Support, Scholarship.

Donor Information

Founder: the late Henry T. Ewald

Financial Summary

Total Giving: $92,400 (2003)
Giving Analysis: Giving for 2003 includes: foundation scholarships ($91,500).
Assets: $2,674,899 (2003)
Gifts Received: $29,723 (2003); $435 (2000); $1,470 (1999). Note: In 2003, contributions were received from James Bashaw ($1,000), Holly Ewald ($1,500), Kristi Ewald ($3,000), Boyd Chapin ($10,000), Carolyn Kratzet ($10,500), and miscellaneous donations of less than $300 each. In 1999, contributions were received from James and Dorothy Bashaw ($1,000) and miscellaneous donations of less than $500 each. In 1994, contributions were received from Mr. and Mrs. Henry Ewald ($100,000), and Charles B. Johnson ($500).

Typical Recipients

Arts & Humanities: Arts Institutes, Film & Video, History & Archaeology, Libraries, Public Broadcasting
Civic & Public Affairs: Clubs, Civic & Public Affairs-General, Housing, Law & Justice, Urban & Community Affairs, Women's Affairs, Zoos/Aquariums
Education: Arts/Humanities Education, Business Education, Colleges & Universities, Engineering/Technological Education, Education-General, Legal Education, Literacy, Minority Education, Private Education (Precollege), Student Aid
Health: Cancer, Hospices
Religion: Religion-General, Ministries, Religious Welfare
Social Services: At-Risk Youth, Camps, Child Welfare, Community Service Organizations, Recreation & Athletics, United Funds/United Ways, Veterans, YMCA/YWCA/YMHA/YWHA, Youth Organizations

Application Procedures

Initial Contact: send complete application
Application Requirements: three letters of recommendation, a photo biography, high school transcripts, and SAT or ACT scores
Deadlines: April 1.

Additional Information

Provides scholarships to residents of the metropolitan Detroit, MI, area all residents must be in their senior year to apply.
Publications: Informational Brochure (including Application Guidelines)

Foundation Officials

Holly Ewald: vice president
John Clifford Ewald: treasurer
Kristi Ewald: president
Carolyn T. Ewald Kratzet: vice president emeritus
Shelagh Kuprenski: secretary
Shirley E. Pfeifer: vice president emeritus

Grants Analysis

Disclosure Period: calendar year ending 2003
Total Grants: $900*
Number of Grants: 2
Highest Grant: $500
Lowest Grant: $400
*Note: Giving excludes scholarships.

Recent Grants

Note: Grants derived from 2001 Form 990.
Library-Related

100	Friends of the Detroit Public Library, Detroit, MI
100	Grosse Pointe Library, Grosse Pte., MI

General

500	Detroit Zoo, Royal Oak, MI
400	Goodfellows
360	Salvation Army, Kenosha, WI
300	Detroit Area Films and Television, Detroit, MI
250	Arbor Hospice, Detroit, MI
200	Junior Achievement
200	St. Vincent de Paul, Baltimore, MD
150	WTVS, Detroit, MI
100	Abigayle Ministries, Port Huron, MI
100	Ann Arbor Film Festival, Ann Arbor, MI

EXCEL CORP.

Company Headquarters

2901 N. Mead St.
Wichita, KS 67219-4242
Web: http://www.excelmeats.com

Company Description

Founded: 1974
Revenue: US$12.5 billion (2002)
Employees: 30,000 (2002)
SIC(s): 2000 Food & Kindred Products.
Parent Company: Cargill Inc., Minneapolis, MN, United States

Operating Locations

Excel Corp. (KS--Wichita; MN--Minneapolis)

Nonmonetary Support

Type: Donated Products

Giving Contact

Gilbert Contreras, Recruiting Manager
151 North Main Street
Wichita, KS 67202
Phone: (316)291-2500
Fax: (316)291-2547
E-mail: contactexcel@cargill.com

Description

Organization Type: Corporate Giving Program
Giving Locations: headquarters and operating communities.
Grant Types: Employee Matching Gifts, Multiyear/Continuing Support, Scholarship.

Financial Summary

Total Giving: Contributes through corporate direct giving program only.

Typical Recipients

Arts & Humanities: Libraries, Literary Arts, Public Broadcasting
Civic & Public Affairs: Chambers of Commerce, Community Foundations, Civic & Public Affairs-General, Zoos/Aquariums
Education: Agricultural Education, Colleges & Universities, Elementary Education (Public), Education-General, Literacy
Health: Health-General, Medical Rehabilitation
Social Services: At-Risk Youth, Emergency Relief, Social Services-General, United Funds/United Ways

Corporate Officials

Bill Buckner: president, chief executive officer
Derek Kennedy: chief financial officer

Grants Analysis

Typical Range: $10 to $1,000

EXCHANGE BANK

Company Headquarters

PO Box 403
Santa Rosa, CA 95402
Web: http://www.exchangebank.com

Company Description

Founded: 1890
Ticker: EXSR
Exchange: OTC
Assets: US$974.2 million (2001)
Employees: 450 (2001)
SIC(s): 6000 Depository Institutions.

Operating Locations

Exchange Bank (CA--Santa Rosa)

Exchange Bank Foundation

Giving Contact

C. William Reinking, Chairman
Exchange Bank
PO Box 403
Santa Rosa, CA 95402
Phone: (707)524-3117

Alternate Contact

Shirley Kielty
Exchange Bank
Note: Contact to request application form.

Description

Founded: 1979
EIN: 942576480
Organization Type: Corporate Foundation
Giving Locations: CA: Sonoma County
Grant Types: Capital, General Support, Scholarship.

Financial Summary

Total Giving: $55,783 (2003); $57,430 (2001)
Giving Analysis: Giving for 2003 includes: foundation scholarships ($4,000); 2001: foundation scholarships ($4,000)
Assets: $71,821 (2003); $63,090 (2001)
Gifts Received: $60,000 (2003); $100,000 (2001); $50,000 (1999). Note: Contributions were received from Exchange Bank.

Typical Recipients

Arts & Humanities: Arts Associations & Councils, Arts Centers, Libraries, Museums/Galleries, Music, Opera, Performing Arts, Theater
Civic & Public Affairs: Economic Development, Employment/Job Training, Civic & Public Affairs-General, Safety
Education: Business Education, Business-School Partnerships, Colleges & Universities, Community & Junior Colleges, Elementary Education (Public), Education-General, Preschool Education, Student Aid
Environment: Resource Conservation
Health: AIDS/HIV, Children's Health/Hospitals, Clinics/Medical Centers, Health Funds, Hospices, Hospitals, Medical Rehabilitation, Research/Studies Institutes, Respiratory
Religion: Religious Welfare
Science: Observatories & Planetariums
Social Services: Animal Protection, At-Risk Youth, Camps, Child Welfare, Community Centers, Community Service Organizations, Counseling, Family Services, People with Disabilities, Recreation & Athletics, Scouts, Senior Conservation, Shelters/Homelessness, Volunteer Services, YMCA/YWCA/YMHA/YWHA, Youth Organizations

Application Procedures

Initial Contact: Call the foundation contact to request an application form.
Application Requirements: Provide a completed application form including description of the benefit to be achieved, number of people that will benefit, names of other contributors and amount requested from each, budget for current fiscal year, copy of most recent annual audit, list of board of directors and their business and/or home addresses, organization's by-laws and articles of incorporation, proof of tax-exempt status, a geographic breakdown of the area served, and organization's membership structure
Deadlines: None.

Restrictions

Preference is given to organizations supporting youth, the disabled, or the indigent. No grants are made for scholarships, seed money, private schools, or for program or operating expenses.

Additional Information

The company's largest shareholder is the Doyle Trust, which recently has contributed more than $3.5 million annually to the Doyle Scholarship Program for students attending Santa Rosa Junior College.
Publications: Application Form; Guidelines

Corporate Officials

Bruce DeCrona: chief financial officer, controller, vice president finance PRIM CORP EMPL chief financial officer, controller, vice president finance: Exchange Bank.
C. William Reinking: president, chief executive officer, director PRIM CORP EMPL president, chief executive officer, director: Exchange Bank.
Andrew J. Shepard: chairman, director B Chicago, IL 1924. ED Stanford University (1949); Pacific Coast Banking School (1954). PRIM CORP EMPL chairman, director: Exchange Bank. NONPR AFFIL chairman: LPGA.

Foundation Officials

Marlene S. Barney: director
Charles R. Bartley, Sr.: vchairman
Jean E. Destruel: director
C. William Reinking: chairman (see above)
James M. Ryan: director
Andrew J. Shepard: director (see above)
Robert G. Stone: director

Grants Analysis

Disclosure Period: calendar year ending 2003
Total Grants: $51,783*
Number of Grants: 16
Average Grant: $3,236
Highest Grant: $5,000
Lowest Grant: $1,500
Typical Range: $2,000 to $5,000
*Note: Giving excludes scholarship.

Recent Grants

Note: Grants derived from 2003 Form 990.
General

6,500	Sonoma State University, Rohnert Park, CA -- for scholarship fund and athletic department
5,000	Boys and Girls Club of Santa Rosa, Santa Rosa, CA -- to assist with cost of building renovation
5,000	Doyle Park School, Santa Rosa, CA -- to purchase computer equipment for their new computer laboratory
5,000	Santa Rosa Junior College, Santa Rosa, CA -- capital campaign
5,000	Sebastopol Community Center, Sebastopol, CA -- to assist with cost of refurbishing the Brook Haven school tennis courts
5,000	Valley of the Moon Children's Foundation, Santa Rosa, CA -- to assist with

	costs of construction and equipping a professional kitchen
3,334	Westminster Woods, Occidental, CA -- towards building campaign
3,000	Northern Sonoma County Healthcare Foundation, Healdsburg, CA -- to purchase a wheelchair desk with laptop and cell phone
2,849	Santa Rosa City School District, Santa Rosa, CA -- to purchase a Vineyard Flamer for the district's vineyard project
2,600	Native Sons of the Golden West, Santa Rosa, CA -- to assist with costs of painting their building, putting in a new front porch and shale for their parking lot

EXELON

Company Headquarters

10 S. Dearborn Street, 37th Floor
Chicago, IL 60690-3005
Phone: (312)394-7398
Web: http://www.exeloncorp.com

Company Description

Founded: 2000
Ticker: EXC
Exchange: NYSE
Acquired: Unicom Corp. (2000);
Former Name: PECO Energy Co. (2000).
Revenue: US$14.515 billion (2004)
Profit: US$1.864 billion (2004)
Employees: 29000 (2003)
Fortune Rank: 145, per FORTUNE Magazine's list of 500 Largest U.S. Corporations (2004).
SIC(s): 4931 Electric & Other Services Combined.

Operating Locations

PECO Energy Co. (NJ--Hancock's Bridge; PA--Bristol, Chester, Eddystone, Limerick Township, New Florence, Peach Bottom, Philadelphia, Shelocta)

Nonmonetary Support

Type: Donated Equipment; In-kind Services; Loaned Employees; Loaned Executives

Giving Contact

Steve Soloman
senior manager of Corporate Citizenship
PO Box 767
Chicago, IL 60690
Phone: (312)394-4361
Fax: (312)394-8693
E-mail: steve.soloman@exeloncorp.com

Description

Organization Type: Corporate Giving Program
Giving Locations: PA: Bucks County, Chester County, Delaware County, Montgomery County, York County
Grant Types: Capital, General Support, Operating Expenses.

Financial Summary

Total Giving: $18,000,000 (2005 approx); $18,000,000 (2004); $2,500,000 (2003). Note: Contributes through corporate direct giving program only.

Typical Recipients

Arts & Humanities: Arts Funds, Dance, Ethnic & Folk Arts, Libraries, Music, Opera
Civic & Public Affairs: Housing, Law & Justice, Urban & Community Affairs
Education: Business Education, Colleges & Universities, Community & Junior Colleges, Education Funds, Education-General, Public Education (Precollege)
Environment: Environment-General

Health: Hospitals
Social Services: Child Welfare, United Funds/United Ways

Application Procedures

Initial Contact: brief letter
Application Requirements: a description of organization and its mission; detailed description of project and amount requested; list of organization's board of directors, trustees, officers, and other key people and their affiliations; copy of current year's organizational budget and/or project budget; and copy of 501(c)(3) letter of determination
Deadlines: None.

Corporate Officials

Corbin Asahel McNeill, Jr.: president, chief executive officer, director, chairman B Santa Fe, NM 1939. ED United States Naval Academy BS (1962); Naval Nuclear Power School (1962-1963); University of California at Berkeley (1975-1976); Syracuse University (1983-1984). PRIM CORP EMPL president, chief executive officer, director, chairman: PECO Energy Co. CORP AFFIL president, chief executive officer, chairman: Philadelphia Electric Co.; president: Adwin Equipment Co.; president, director: Adwin Realty Co. NONPR AFFIL director: Drexel University; director: Nuclear Utility Management Resources Council; director: American Nuclear Energy Council; member: American Nuclear Society; director: American Gas Association.

Foundation Officials

Anne Baker: manager corporate contributions

EXXONMOBIL CORP.

Company Headquarters

5959 Las Colinas Blvd.
Irving, TX 75039-2298
Web: http://www2.exxonmobil.com

Company Description

Founded: 1999
Ticker: XOM
Exchange: NYSE
Revenue: US$270.772 billion (2004)
Profit: US$25.33 billion (2004)
Employees: 92500 (2003)
Fortune Rank: 2, per FORTUNE Magazine's list of 500 Largest U.S. Corporations (2004).

Exxon Mobil Foundation

Giving Contact

Edward F. Ahnert, Manager, Contributions
Exxon Mobil Corp. Contributions
5959 Las Colinas Boulevard
Irving, TX 75039-2298
Phone: (972)444-1104
Fax: (972)444-1405
E-mail: contributions@exxonmobil.com
Web: http://exxonmobil.com/corporate/Citizenship/CCR4/ccr_home.asp

Alternate Contact

Matching Gifts Program
PO Box 7288
Princeton, NJ 08543-7288
Phone: 877-807-0204
E-mail: exxonmobil@easymatch.com

Description

EIN: 136082357
Organization Type: Corporate Foundation

Former Name: Exxon Education Foundation (1999).
Giving Locations: internationally; nationally.
Grant Types: Employee Matching Gifts, General Support, Matching, Multiyear/Continuing Support.
Note: Employee matching gift ratio: 3 to 1 up to $5,000 per employee per year to colleges and universities, and to the United Negro College Fund, the American Indian College Fund, and the Hispanic Association of Colleges & Universities. Educational matching gifts are handled through the foundation. Employee matching gift ratio: 1 to 1 up to $1,000 per employee annually to the arts and humanities. Cultural matching gifts are handled through the corporation. Matching gift contact information should be used by employees, retirees, and surviving.

Financial Summary

Total Giving: $48,745,497 (2003); $47,304,345 (2002); $32,667,911 (2001). Note: Contributes through corporate direct giving program and foundation.
Giving Analysis: Giving for 2001 includes: corporate direct giving ($18,152,241); foundation matching gifts (approx $20,000,000)
Assets: $64,582,649 (2003); $67,890,706 (2002); $70,171,738 (2001)
Gifts Received: $42,792,563 (2003); $46,689,850 (2002); $36,749,080 (2001). Note: In 2003, contributions were received from Exxon Mobil Corp. In 2001, contributions were received from Exxon Mobil Corp. ($35,400,000) and Enjay Inc. ($1,349,080). In 2000, contributions were received from Exxon Corporation ($21,550,000) and ExxonMobil Biomedical Sciences ($5,000,000). In 1999, contributions were received from ExxonMobil Research Engineering Co. ($58,000,000); Exxon Corporation ($19,636,000); ExxonMobil Biomedical Sciences ($15,000,000) and other ExxonMobil companies. In 1998, contributions were received from Exxon Corporation.

Typical Recipients

Arts & Humanities: Arts Associations & Councils, Arts Centers, Arts Festivals, Arts Institutes, Arts Outreach, Community Arts, Dance, Ethnic & Folk Arts, Historic Preservation, Libraries, Museums/Galleries, Music, Opera, Performing Arts, Public Broadcasting, Theater
Civic & Public Affairs: African American Affairs, Botanical Gardens/Parks, Business/Free Enterprise, Community Foundations, Economic Development, Economic Policy, Employment/Job Training, Civic & Public Affairs-General, Hispanic Affairs, Housing, Law & Justice, Minority Business, Municipalities/Towns, Nonprofit Management, Professional & Trade Associations, Public Policy, Safety, Urban & Community Affairs, Women's Affairs, Zoos/Aquariums
Education: Business Education, Business-School Partnerships, Colleges & Universities, Economic Education, Education Associations, Education Funds, Education Reform, Engineering/Technological Education, Environmental Education, Faculty Development, Education-General, Health & Physical Education, International Studies, Leadership Training, Medical Education, Minority Education, Public Education (Precollege), Science/Mathematics Education, Secondary Education (Public), Special Education, Student Aid
Environment: Air/Water Quality, Energy, Forestry, Environment-General, Resource Conservation, Wildlife Protection
Health: Cancer, Clinics/Medical Centers, Emergency/Ambulance Services, Health Organizations, Hospitals, Medical Rehabilitation, Medical Research, Medical Training, Nursing Services, Public Health
International: Health Care/Hospitals, International Affairs, International Environmental Issues, International Peace & Security Issues, International Relations
Science: Science-General, Science Museums, Scientific Centers & Institutes, Scientific Labs, Scientific Research
Social Services: At-Risk Youth, Child Welfare, Com-

munity Service Organizations, Counseling, Day Care, Delinquency & Criminal Rehabilitation, Emergency Relief, Family Services, Scouts, Shelters/ Homelessness, Substance Abuse, United Funds/ United Ways, Volunteer Services, YMCA/YWCA/ YMHA/YWHA, Youth Organizations

Application Procedures

Initial Contact: The foundation has no formal grant application procedure or application form. Submit a brief written request (preferably under five pages).
Application Requirements: Grant requests should include a brief history of the organization, a description of its current work, and an explanation of the significance of that work; the organization's current general operating budget; recently audited financial statement; background information on those responsible for administering and developing the organization's programs; a list of the members of the board of directors; a list of current public and private contributors, including their levels of support; and proof of tax-exempt status. If the request is for a specific project, the request should also include a description of the project and explanation of its significance; background information on the individuals who will be carrying out the project; total project budget; amount requested; and a list of others who are or will be providing project funds.
Deadlines: None.
Decision Notification: Review process is continuous.
Notes: All requests will be considered by both the foundation and the corporation.

Restrictions

Neither the company nor the foundation makes grants to individuals, local organizations or activities (unless they are geographically located in an area where Exxon Mobil has significant facilities or numbers of employees), or for political or religious causes. Generally, support is not provided for endowments or operating support to agencies funded by the United Way. Scholarships are provided only on a preselected basis and are offered by ExxonMobil recruiters to attract selected students to employment with the company.

Additional Information

The Exxon Education Foundation's name was changed to Exxon Mobil Foundation as a result of the merger of Exxon Corp. and Mobil Corp. in 1999. The Exxon Mobil Foundation gives to education only and is separate from the corporate direct giving program and the Mobil Foundation.
The National Fish and Wildlife Foundation and Exxon Corp. established the Save the Tiger Fund in 1995 to help fund tiger conservation projects in Asia and research at universities and zoos. The funds also supports education programs to make the public aware that the tiger is near extinction in the wilderness.

Corporate Officials

Edward F. Ahnert: corporate contribution manager ED Princeton University MA; Rice University BA. PRIM CORP EMPL corporate contribution manager: Exxon Mobil Corp. NONPR AFFIL director: Save the Tiger Fund; director: Van Cliburn Foundation.
Ken P. Cohen: vice president, public affairs
Edward G. Galante: senior vice president B Inwood, NY 1951. ED Northeastern University BS. PRIM CORP EMPL senior vice president: Exxon Mobil Corp. NONPR AFFIL board overseers: Northeastern University; trustee, vice chairman: US Council for International Business; director: Junior Achievement Worldwide; director: Council of the Americas; director: Council for the United States & Italy; member: 25 Year Club of the Petroleum Industry.
Harry J. Longwell: executive vice president, director B Bunkie, LA 1941. ED Louisiana State University BA (1963). PRIM CORP EMPL executive vice president, director: Exxon Mobil Corp. NONPR AFFIL trustee: University of Dallas; board visitors: University of

Texas M.D. Anderson Cancer Center; member: Society of Petroleum Engineers; advisory board: Dallas Area Habitat for Humanity; director: National Action Council for Minorities in Engineering; member: American Petroleum Institute.
Lee R. Raymond, PhD: chairman, chief executive officer B Watertown, SD 1938. ED University of Wisconsin BSChE (1960); University of Minnesota PhD (1963). PRIM CORP EMPL chairman, chief executive officer: Exxon Mobil Corp. ADD CORP EMPL senior vice president, director: Esso International-AM Inc. CORP AFFIL director: JP Morgan Chase & Co. NONPR AFFIL member: University Wisconsin Foundation; trustee: Wisconsin Alumni Research Foundation; director: United Negro College Fund; member: Singapore-U.S. Business Council; member: Trilateral Commission; director: Project Shelter Pro-Am; partner emeritus: New York City Partnership; member: President's Export Council; member: National Petroleum Council; member: Innovations in Medicine Leadership Council; member, director: National Academy Engineering; member: Emergency Committee American Trade; director: Dallas Citizens Council; member: Dallas Committee Foreign Relations; member: Council Foreign Relations; member: Business Council; member: Business Roundtable; member, founder: American Society Royal Botanical Garden; director, member: American Petroleum Institute; member national advisory council: American Society Engineering; trustee, vice chairman: American Enterprise Institute; member: American Council Germany.
F. A. Risch: vice president, treasurer ED Carnegie Mellon University MS; Penn State University BS.
F. B. Sprow: vice president, safety, health & environment ED Massachusetts Institute of Technology BS (1962); Massachusetts Institute of Technology MS (1963); University of California Berkeley PhD (1965).

Foundation Officials

Edward F. Ahnert: president (see above)
F. W. Bass: trustee
C. L. Birdsall: assistant secretary
S. E. Carter: trustee
Ken P. Cohen: chairman, trustee (see above)
W. N. Huplits: assistant controller
Arleen E. Lawson: executive director
B. G. Macklin: trustee ED Manhattan College BS. NONPR AFFIL director: Junior Achievement Houston.
S. B.L. Penrose: treasurer
T. Plemenos: secretary
F. A. Risch: trustee (see above)
D. H. Samson: assistant treasurer
F. B. Sprow: trustee (see above)
P. A. Wetz: trustee

Grants Analysis

Disclosure Period: calendar year ending 2003
Total Grants: $29,866,401*
Number of Grants: 2000 (approx)
Average Grant: $14,933
Highest Grant: $6,000,000
Lowest Grant: $250
Typical Range: $1,000 to $30,000
*Note: Giving excludes matching gifts.

Recent Grants

Note: Grants derived from 2001 Form 990.
General
4,173,500	Volunteer Involvement Fund, Irving, TX -- for program
2,000,000	Educational Alliance Program, Irving, TX
1,315,000	National Science Teachers Association, Arlington, VA
500,000	National Fish and Wildlife Foundation, Washington, DC -- for programs
500,000	National Fish and Wildlife Foundation, Washington, DC -- for Tiger Program
459,000	California Foundation on the Environment and the Economy, San Francisco, CA -- for clean air challenge

448,748	Mobil Retiree Volunteer Program, Irving, TX -- for program
330,000	Harvard University School of Public Health, Boston, MA -- for Harvard Malaria Initiative
300,000	Carnegie Mellon University, Pittsburgh, PA -- for center for the study and improvement of regulations
270,000	National Action Council for Minorities in Engineering, New York, NY

FAB STEEL PRODUCTS CO.

Company Headquarters
Clovis, NM

Fab Steel Products Foundation

Giving Contact
Kevin W. Cooper, Secretary, Treasurer & Director
Fab Steel Products Foundation
4600 Mabry Drive
Clovis, NM 88101
Phone: (505)763-4414

Description
EIN: 850339249
Organization Type: Corporate Foundation
Giving Locations: NM; TX
Grant Types: General Support.

Financial Summary
Total Giving: $10,000 (2003)
Assets: $168,230 (2003)
Gifts Received: $9,634 (2000); $10,000 (1999); $19,000 (1997)

Typical Recipients
Arts & Humanities: Libraries
Education: Student Aid
Religion: Churches, Religious Welfare
Social Services: Camps, Youth Organizations

Application Procedures
Initial Contact: Send a formal written request.
Deadlines: None.

Corporate Officials
Stanley Glenn: president, chief executive officer PRIM CORP EMPL president, chief executive officer: Fab Steel Product Co.

Foundation Officials
M. Virginia Glenn: president, director

Grants Analysis
Disclosure Period: calendar year ending 2003
Total Grants: $10,000
Number of Grants: 5
Highest Grant: $8,000
Lowest Grant: $500

Recent Grants
Note: Grants derived from 2001 Form 990.
General
5,400	New Mexico Girls and Boys Ranch, Albuquerque, NM -- for budget
3,000	New Mexico Girls and Boys Ranch, Albuquerque, NM -- for endowment
1,800	Lighthouse Mission, Clovis, NM -- for budget

FAIR OAKS FOUNDATION

Giving Contact
Rose Hoover, Secretary
Fair Oaks Foundation
600 Grant Street, Suite 4600
Pittsburgh, PA 15219
Phone: (412)456-4418

Description
Founded: 1988
EIN: 251576560
Organization Type: Private Foundation
Giving Locations: NY
Grant Types: General Support, Scholarship.

Donor Information
Founder: Pittsburgh Forgings Foundation, Ampco-Pittsburgh Foundation

Financial Summary
Total Giving: $263,155 (2004)
Giving Analysis: Giving for 2004 includes: foundation grants to United Way ($27,500)
Assets: $5,842,683 (2004)

Typical Recipients
Arts & Humanities: Arts Associations & Councils, Arts Centers, Arts Festivals, Ballet, Community Arts, History & Archaeology, Libraries, Museums/Galleries, Music, Opera, Public Broadcasting, Theater
Civic & Public Affairs: African American Affairs, Asian American Affairs, Botanical Gardens/Parks, Civil Rights, Clubs, Economic Development, Civic & Public Affairs-General, Parades/Festivals, Professional & Trade Associations, Public Policy, Safety, Urban & Community Affairs, Women's Affairs, Zoos/Aquariums
Education: Business Education, Colleges & Universities, Community & Junior Colleges, Education Funds, Legal Education, Medical Education, Minority Education, Private Education (Precollege), Student Aid
Environment: Environment-General
Health: Arthritis, Cancer, Children's Health/Hospitals, Emergency/Ambulance Services, Hospitals, Single-Disease Health Associations
International: International Affairs, International Relief Efforts
Religion: Jewish Causes, Religious Organizations, Religious Welfare, Social/Policy Issues
Social Services: Community Centers, Community Service Organizations, Crime Prevention, Family Planning, Food/Clothing Distribution, People with Disabilities, Recreation & Athletics, Scouts, Substance Abuse, United Funds/United Ways, YMCA/YWCA/YMHA/YWHA, Youth Organizations

Application Procedures
Initial Contact: The foundation has no formal grant application procedure or application form.
Deadlines: October 31.

Additional Information
Provides scholarships to individuals for higher education.

Foundation Officials
Louis Berkman: chairman, trustee B Canton, OH 1909. PRIM CORP EMPL chairman, president, chief executive officer, treasurer, director: Louis Berkman Co. CORP AFFIL president: Scott Lumber; president: Swenson Spreader; president: Meyer Products; president: Orrville Products; president, director: Follansbee Steel Corp.; president: IDL Supplies; chairman: Ampco-Pittsburgh Corp.; president: Dover Parkersburg.
Rose Hoover: vice president, secretary
Robert Arthur Paul: president, trustee B New York,

NY 1937. ED Cornell University AB (1959); Harvard University JD (1962); Harvard University MBA (1964). PRIM CORP EMPL president, chief executive officer, director: Ampco-Pittsburgh Corp. CORP AFFIL partner: Romar Trading Co.; partner: National City Corp.; executive vice president, assistant secretary, director, trustee: Louis Berkman Co. NONPR AFFIL member: Massachusetts Bar Association; trustee: Presbyterian University Hospital; trustee: Cornell University; member: American Bar Association. CLUB AFFIL Pittsburgh Athletic Association; Harvard Club; Concordia Club; Duquesne Club.

Grants Analysis
Disclosure Period: calendar year ending 2004
Total Grants: $235,655*
Number of Grants: 91
Average Grant: $962*
Highest Grant: $100,000
Lowest Grant: $50
Typical Range: $100 to $3,000
*Note: Giving excludes United Way. Average grant figure excludes two highest grants ($150,000).

Recent Grants
Note: Grants derived from 2001 Form 990.
Library-Related
5,000	Lauri Ann West Memorial Library, Pittsburgh, PA -- support programs

General
200,000	Harvard University, Boston, MA -- support programs
100,000	Cornell University, Ithaca, NY -- support program
50,000	United Jewish Federation, Pittsburgh, PA -- support programs
20,000	Hillman Cancer Center, Pittsburgh, PA -- support programs
20,000	United Way of Allegheny County, Pittsburgh, PA -- support programs
5,000	Harvard Business School, Boston, MA -- support programs
3,000	United Way of Central Virginia, Lynchburg, VA -- support programs
2,500	United Way of Tonawandas, Tonawanda, NY -- support programs
2,000	United Way of Porter County, Inc., Valparaiso, IN -- support programs
1,250	Shadyside Hospital Foundation, Pittsburgh, PA -- support programs

FAIR PLAY FOUNDATION

Giving Contact
Blaine T. Phillips, Executive Director
100 W. 10th Street, Suite 1010
Wilmington, DE 19801
Phone: (302)777-4711
Fax: (302)658-1192
E-mail: bthillips@pac.delware.com

Description
Founded: 1983
EIN: 516017779
Organization Type: Private Foundation
Giving Locations: DE
Grant Types: Capital, General Support.

Financial Summary
Total Giving: $622,900 (2003)
Assets: $12,792,011 (2003)

Typical Recipients
Arts & Humanities: Arts Centers, Arts Festivals, Arts Institutes, Arts & Humanities-General, Historic Preservation, History & Archaeology, Libraries, Museums/Galleries, Music, Public Broadcasting, Theater
Civic & Public Affairs: Botanical Gardens/Parks,

Community Foundations, Civic & Public Affairs-General, Philanthropic Organizations, Public Policy, Urban & Community Affairs, Zoos/Aquariums
Education: Agricultural Education, Arts/Humanities Education, Colleges & Universities, Education Funds, Environmental College, Legal Education, Private Education (Precollege)
Environment: Air/Water Quality, Environment-General, Protection, Research, Resource Conservation, Watershed, Wildlife Protection
Health: Arthritis, Hospices, Long-Term Care, Medical Research, Single-Disease Health Associations
International: International Environmental Issues, International Relief Efforts
Religion: Churches
Science: Science Museums, Scientific Centers & Institutes
Social Services: Child Welfare, Community Service Organizations, Day Care, Family Planning, Family Services, Recreation & Athletics, YMCA/YWCA/YMHA/YWHA, Youth Organizations

Application Procedures
Initial Contact: Send a brief letter of inquiry describing program or project.
Deadlines: None.

Foundation Officials
James F. Burnett: vice president, trustee
Thomas H. Fooks, V: trustee
L. E. Grimes: treasurer, trustee
Blaine T. Phillips: president, trustee
D. P. Ross, Jr.: trustee

Grants Analysis
Disclosure Period: calendar year ending 2003
Total Grants: $622,900
Number of Grants: 60
Average Grant: $9,710*
Highest Grant: $50,000
Lowest Grant: $400
Typical Range: $5,000 to $20,000
*Note: Average grant figure excludes highest grant.

Recent Grants
Note: Grants derived from 2001 Form 990.
General
100,000	Chesapeake Bay Foundation, Annapolis, MD -- oyster restoration, crab protection program
50,000	Winterthur Museum, Greenville, DE -- for grounds projects
25,000	Academy of the Arts, Easton, MD -- for changing special exhibits
25,000	African Wildlife Foundation, Washington, DC -- for research
25,000	Brandywine Conservancy, Chadds Ford, PA -- for Kuerner Farm
25,000	Conservation Fund, Arlington, VA -- for protection of open space and wildlife habitat
25,000	Delaware Wild Lands, Odessa, DE -- for habitat project
25,000	Hagley Museum and Library, Wilmington, DE -- for new boiler in Hall of Records
25,000	Nabb Research Center, Salisbury, MD -- for study and research
25,000	Stroud Water Research Center, Avondale, PA -- for stream and pond protections

SHERMAN FAIRCHILD FOUNDATION, INC.

Giving Contact
Bonnie Himmelman, President & Director
5454 Wisconsin Ave. Suite 1205
Chevy Chase, MD 20815

Phone: (301)913-5990
Fax: (301)913-9444

Description

Founded: 1955
EIN: 131951698
Organization Type: General Purpose Foundation
Giving Locations: NY: New York including metropolitan area nationally.
Grant Types: Capital, Endowment, Fellowship, General Support, Project, Research, Scholarship.

Donor Information

Founder: The Sherman Fairchild Foundation was incorporated in 1955 by Sherman M. Fairchild, inventor of the Fairchild aerial camera, chairman of Fairchild Camera Instrument Co. and of Fairchild Hiller Corp., owner of Fairchild Recording Equipment Co., and one of the largest single stockholders of IBM. When Mr. Fairchild died in 1971, he left most of his estate to the foundation.

Financial Summary

Total Giving: $14,649,180 (2002); $18,955,435 (2001)
Giving Analysis: Giving for 2002 includes: foundation scholarships ($5,000,000)
Assets: $382,834,201 (2002); $435,835,204 (2001)
Gifts Received: $4,475 (1998); $4,346 (1996); $2,608 (1995). Note: The foundation receives contributions from the Sherman M. Fairchild Annuity Trust.

Typical Recipients

Arts & Humanities: Arts Centers, Arts Institutes, Arts & Humanities-General, Historic Preservation, Libraries, Museums/Galleries, Music, Performing Arts, Visual Arts
Civic & Public Affairs: Botanical Gardens/Parks, Civic & Public Affairs-General, Housing
Education: Arts/Humanities Education, Colleges & Universities, Education Funds, Engineering/Technological Education, Faculty Development, Education-General, International Studies, Legal Education, Medical Education, Minority Education, Private Education (Precollege), Religious Education, Science/Mathematics Education, Secondary Education (Private), Student Aid, Vocational & Technical Education
Environment: Protection
Health: Cancer, Children's Health/Hospitals, Clinics/Medical Centers, Health Funds, Health Organizations, Hospitals, Medical Research
International: International Peace & Security Issues
Religion: Dioceses, Religion-General, Jewish Causes, Missionary Activities (Domestic), Religious Welfare, Seminaries
Science: Science Museums, Scientific Research
Social Services: Animal Protection, At-Risk Youth, Child Welfare, Community Service Organizations, Family Services, Recreation & Athletics, Shelters/Homelessness, YMCA/YWCA/YMHA/YWHA, Youth Organizations

Application Procedures

Initial Contact: Send a a brief letter of inquiry.
Application Requirements: Include a description of the proposed project and proof of the organization's tax-exempt status.
Deadlines: None.

Restrictions

No grants are made to individuals.

Foundation Officials

Walter Burke: treasurer, director
Walter F. Burke, III: director, chairman
Bruce Dresner: director
Robert P. Henderson: director PRIM CORP EMPL managing partner: Greylock Ltd. Partnership. CORP AFFIL director: Cabot Corp.; director: Allmerica Asset Management; director: Allmerica Financial Corp. NONPR AFFIL chairman: Museum Fine Arts Boston.

Bonnie Himmelman: president, director
Michele Tolela Myers: director B Rabat, Morocco 1941. ED University of Paris (1962); University of Denver MA (1966); University of Denver PhD (1967); Trinity University MA (1977). PRIM CORP EMPL president: Sarah Lawrence College. NONPR AFFIL director, member: American Council Education; director: National Association Independent Colleges & Universities. CLUB AFFIL 100 San Antonio Club.
Charles Pierce: director
Dr. Agnar Pytte: director B Kongsberg, Norway 1932. ED Princeton University AB (1953); Harvard University AM (1954); Harvard University PhD (1958). PRIM CORP EMPL president: Case Western Reserve University. CORP AFFIL director: AO Smith Corp.; director: Goodyear Tire & Rubber Co. NONPR AFFIL director: United Way; trustee: University Research Association; director: Sherman Fairchild Foundation Inc.; member: Sigma Xi; member: Ohio Science Technology Council; member: Phi Beta Kappa; trustee: Ohio Aerospace Institute; member: Ohio Council Research & Economic Development; member: Cleveland Roundtable; member: Cleveland Technology Leadership Council; trustee: Cleveland Institute Music; trustee: Cleveland Orchestra; member: American Physical Society; director: Cleveland Growth Association.
James Wright: director
James Wright: director

Grants Analysis

Disclosure Period: calendar year ending 2002
Total Grants: $9,649,180*
Number of Grants: 48
Average Grant: $112,254*
Highest Grant: $1,710,000
Lowest Grant: $10,000
Typical Range: $50,000 to $200,000
*Note: Giving excludes scholarships. Average grant figure excludes four highest grants ($4,710,000).

Recent Grants

Note: Grants derived from 2002 Form 990.

Library-Related

250,000	Pierpont Morgan Library, New York, NY -- towards general support
30,000	Pierpont Morgan Library, New York, NY -- towards conservation fellows

General

5,000,000	California Institute of Technology, Pasadena, CA -- towards postdoctoral scholars program PMA division
3,000,000	Phillips Collection, Washington, DC -- for the center for studies in modern art
1,710,000	Metropolitan Museum of Art, New York, NY -- towards works on paper and photographs conservation center
1,666,666	Museum of Fine Arts, Boston, MA -- towards construction on conservation wing
1,000,000	Boys and Girls Club of Greater New York, New York, NY -- towards construction of Flushing clubhouse
1,000,000	Case Western Reserve, Cleveland, OH -- towards professorship in Physics program PMA division
1,000,000	Sarah Lawrence College, Bronxville, NY -- towards construction of new visual arts center
500,000	Denison University, Greenville, OH -- towards faculty enhancement fund
500,000	New York University Institute of Fine Arts, New York, NY -- towards endowment
500,000	Salvation Army of Greater New York, New York, NY -- towards general use

FREEMAN E. FAIRCHILD-MEEKER CHARITABLE TRUST

Giving Contact

Judy Dowling, Trust Officer
c/o Wells Fargo Bank
633 17th St.
Denver, CO 80270
Phone: (303)293-5365
Fax: (303)293-5632

Description

Founded: 1969
EIN: 846068906
Organization Type: Private Foundation
Giving Locations: CO: Meeker
Grant Types: General Support, Scholarship.

Donor Information

Founder: the late Freeman E. Fairfield

Financial Summary

Total Giving: $174,790 (fiscal year ending November 30, 2001). Note: Fiscal 1997 Giving includes scholarship ($173,415).
Giving Analysis: Giving for fiscal 2001 includes: foundation scholarships ($63,400)
Assets: $4,801,106 (fiscal 2001)

Typical Recipients

Arts & Humanities: Community Arts, Historic Preservation, History & Archaeology, Libraries, Music
Civic & Public Affairs: Chambers of Commerce, Economic Development, Civic & Public Affairs-General, Municipalities/Towns, Parades/Festivals, Safety, Urban & Community Affairs
Education: Colleges & Universities, Community & Junior Colleges, Education Funds, Engineering/Technological Education, Education-General, Literacy, Medical Education, Private Education (Precollege), Public Education (Precollege), Science/Mathematics Education, Secondary Education (Public), Student Aid
Health: Health-General, Hospitals, Medical Rehabilitation
Religion: Churches, Religious Welfare
Social Services: Community Service Organizations, Family Planning, Family Services, Recreation & Athletics, Scouts, Social Services-General, Veterans, Youth Organizations

Application Procedures

Initial Contact: Send a brief letter of inquiry describing program.
Deadlines: None.

Additional Information

Provides scholarships to graduates of Meeker High School.
Trust(s): Wells Fargo Bank

Foundation Officials

Rev. Paul Brisbane: trustee
Kim Cook: trustee
Dave McGraw: trustee
Larry Shutis: trustee
Glenn Trobster: trustee
Pete Waller: trustee

Grants Analysis

Disclosure Period: fiscal year ending November 30, 2001
Total Grants: $111,390*
Number of Grants: 14
Average Grant: $3,646*
Highest Grant: $37,640
Lowest Grant: $1,000
Typical Range: $1,000 to $5,000

*Note: Giving excludes scholarships. Average grant figure excludes two highest grants ($67,640).

Recent Grants

Note: Grants derived from fiscal 2002 Form 990.
General

110,000	Fairfield Community Center, Meeker, CO
36,300	Meeker School District Re-1, Meeker, CO
11,800	Colorado Northwestern Community College Foundation, Rangely, CO -- scholarship
9,600	Mesa State College, Grand Junction, CO -- scholarship
9,000	Garfield Youth Services, Glenwood Springs, CO
8,639	Meeker Civic Improvement Corporation, Meeker, CO -- charitable
8,000	Colorado State University, Ft. Collins, CO -- scholarship
6,000	University of Colorado at Boulder, Boulder, CO
4,800	Fort Lewis College, Durango, CO -- scholarship
4,000	Freeman E. Fairfield Meeker Charity, Meeker, CO

FAITH FOUNDATION

Giving Contact

Daniel L. Kerr, Secretary & Treasurer
Attn: Grants
2746 Front St. NE
Salem, OR 97303-6554
Phone: (503)364-6777

Description

Founded: 1993
EIN: 931115227
Organization Type: Private Foundation
Giving Locations: OR
Grant Types: Loan.

Donor Information

Founder: Established in 1993 by Richard Faith.

Financial Summary

Total Giving: $86,898 (2003)
Assets: $20,426,580 (2003)
Gifts Received: $1,000,500 (2003); $2,000,000 (2000); $2,201,000 (1999). Note: In 1998, 1999, 2000, and 2003 contributions were received from Richard Faith. In 1996, contributions were received from Richard Faith & Dan Kerr. In 1995, contributions were received from Richard Faith.

Typical Recipients

Arts & Humanities: Libraries
Civic & Public Affairs: Civic & Public Affairs-General, Housing
Education: Private Education (Precollege), Public Education (Precollege)
International: Foreign Educational Institutions, International Environmental Issues, International Organizations, Missionary/Religious Activities
Religion: Churches, Ministries, Missionary Activities (Domestic), Religious Welfare
Social Services: Child Welfare, Delinquency & Criminal Rehabilitation, Recreation & Athletics, Social Services-General, Youth Organizations

Application Procedures

Initial Contact: Send a brief letter of inquiry
Application Requirements: a description of organization, amount requested, purpose of funds sought, proof of tax-exempt status, project description and timeline.
Deadlines: None.

Restrictions

Does not support individuals.

Additional Information

The foundation funds causes through low interest capital improvement loans.

Foundation Officials

Richard G. Faith: president, director
Daniel L. Kerr: secretary, treasurer
Jennifer Rowland: vice president
Jodie Schwanke: vice president

Grants Analysis

Disclosure Period: calendar year ending 2003
Total Grants: $86,898
Number of Grants: 9
Average Grant: $8,362*
Highest Grant: $20,000
Lowest Grant: $2,500
Typical Range: $5,000 to $10,000
*Note: Average grant figure excludes highest grant.

Recent Grants

Note: Grants derived from 2003 Form 990.
General

20,000	Frontier Lodge, St. Hermenegilde, QC Canada -- funds for septic system
16,000	Boys and Girls Club, Salem, OR -- building fund
12,398	Salem Area Habitat for Humanity, Salem, OR -- building fund
10,000	Salem Academy Christian School, Salem, OR
9,000	Northside Fellowship, Keizer, OR
7,000	Salvation Army, Salem, OR -- hi-cube van
5,000	Lourdes School, Scio, OR
5,000	Onesimus Ministries, Salem, OR -- Samaritan's Inn
2,500	Feed the Children, Oklahoma City, OK -- funds for feeding the children

MAURICE FALK FUND

Giving Contact

Sigo Falk, Chairman
3315 Grant Bldg.
Pittsburgh, PA 15219
Phone: (412)261-2485

Description

Founded: 1960
EIN: 251099658
Organization Type: Private Foundation
Former Name: Maurice Falk Medical Fund.
Giving Locations: PA
Grant Types: Conference/Seminar, Endowment, General Support, Multiyear/Continuing Support, Project, Seed Money.

Donor Information

Founder: Maurice and Laura Falk Foundation

Financial Summary

Total Giving: $609,531 (fiscal year ending August 31, 2004); $520,578 (fiscal 2001)
Assets: $17,454,936 (fiscal 2004); $17,559,288 (fiscal 2001)
Gifts Received: $18,268 (fiscal 2004); $37,663 (fiscal 2001); $33,294 (fiscal 2000). Note: In fiscal 2004, contributions were received from Loti G. Gaffney ($7,500) and Jeannette Falk ($10,768). In fiscal 2001, contributions were received from Loti G. Gaffney ($25,389) and Jeannette Falk ($12,274). In fiscal 2000, contributions were received from Loti G. Gaffney ($23,332) and Jeannette Falk ($9,962). In fiscal 1996, contributions were received from Loti G. Gaffney.

Typical Recipients

Arts & Humanities: Arts Centers, Arts Funds, Arts Outreach, Community Arts, Film & Video, Historic Preservation, History & Archaeology, Libraries, Public Broadcasting, Theater, Visual Arts
Civic & Public Affairs: African American Affairs, Civil Rights, Economic Development, Civic & Public Affairs-General, Housing, Legal Aid, Nonprofit Management, Philanthropic Organizations, Public Policy, Urban & Community Affairs, Women's Affairs
Education: Colleges & Universities, Education Funds, Health & Physical Education, International Studies, Medical Education, Minority Education, Private Education (Precollege), Public Education (Precollege), Social Sciences Education
Health: AIDS/HIV, Health Funds, Health Organizations, Hospitals, Mental Health, Public Health, Research/Studies Institutes, Single-Disease Health Associations
International: Foreign Arts Organizations, Health Care/Hospitals, International Organizations, International Peace & Security Issues, International Relations
Religion: Religious Organizations, Religious Welfare
Science: Scientific Research
Social Services: Child Welfare, Community Centers, Counseling, Crime Prevention, Family Planning, Family Services, People with Disabilities, Shelters/Homelessness, Social Services-General, Youth Organizations

Application Procedures

Initial Contact: Send detailed letter of inquiry describing program or project.
Application Requirements: Include history of organization, goals of project, budget, endorsements, and proof of tax-exempt status.
Deadlines: None.

Restrictions

Grants are made primarily to projects in mental health and health related fields. Does not support individuals or provide loans.

Additional Information

Publications: Application Guidelines; Occasional Report

Foundation Officials

Bertram S. Brown, MD: trustee
Estelle Comay: secretary, treasurer
Sigo Falk: chairman B Pittsburgh, PA 1934. ED Harvard University (1957); Carnegie Mellon University (1960). CORP AFFIL trustee: McKee Income Realty Trust; director: National Intergroup; director: DQE Inc.; director: Duquesne Light Co.
Kerry J. O'Donnell: president
Eric W. Springer: trustee B New York, NY 1929. ED Rutgers University AB (1950); New York University LLB (1953). CORP AFFIL director: Duquesne Light Co. NONPR AFFIL fellow: American Public Health Association; member: National Bar Association; member: American Bar Association; honorary fellow: American College Healthcare Executives; member: Allegany County Bar Association; member: American Academy Hospital attorneys. CLUB AFFIL Order of Coif.

Grants Analysis

Disclosure Period: fiscal year ending August 31, 2004
Total Grants: $609,531*
Typical Range: $100 to $7,000
*Note: Grants list for fiscal 2004 incomplete.

Recent Grants

Note: Grants derived from 2004 Form 990.
General

100,000	Public Interest Projects, New York, NY -- for continuation support of the Racial Justice Collaborative

65,765	University of Pittsburgh, Department of Family Medicine, Pittsburgh, PA -- for support of the ad it up using media literacy program
35,501	University of Pittsburgh, Pittsburgh, PA -- for support of an education specialist for the fathers' collaborative project
35,000	National Alliance for the Mentally Ill of Southwestern Pennsylvania, Pittsburgh, PA -- for advocacy and public policy initiative
31,955	Pittsburgh Public Schools, Pittsburgh, PA -- to televise school board meetings
30,000	American Institute for Social Justice, Washington, DC -- for campaign of financial justice
26,910	Pittsburgh Mercy Foundation, Pittsburgh, PA -- for parish nurse program
25,000	Allegheny County Court Appointed Special Advocates, Pittsburgh, PA -- to establish a case manager position to specialize in addressing needs of older minority foster children
25,000	Bridge to Independence, Braddock, PA -- to hire a clinical assessor
15,000	Center for Victims of Violence and Crime, Pittsburgh, PA -- for symposium series on violence in the lives of African-American women

FANNIE MAE

Company Headquarters
Washington, DC
Web: http://www.fanniemae.com

Company Description
Founded: 1938
Ticker: FNM
Exchange: NYSE
Former Name: Federal National Mortgage Association.
Revenue: US$53.766 billion (2003)
Profit: US$7.904 billion (2003)
Employees: 4800 (2003)
SIC(s): 6111 Federal & Federally-Sponsored Credit.

Operating Locations
Fannie Mae (AL--Birmingham; AZ--Phoenix; CA--Pasadena; CT--Hartford; FL--Orlando; GA--Atlanta; IL--Chicago; IA--Des Moines; MA--Boston; MI--Detroit; MN--St. Paul; MS--Jackson; MO--St. Louis; NE--Lincoln; NY--New York; NC--Charlotte; OH--Columbus; OR--Portland; PA--Philadelphia; TX--Houston, San Antonio; WA--Seattle)
Note: Operates nationally, through headquarters and 5 regional offices.

Nonmonetary Support
Type: Loaned Employees

Fannie Mae Foundation

Giving Contact
Grants Management
Fannie Mae Foundation
North Tower, Suite One
4000 Wisconsin Avenue, NW
Washington, DC 20016-2804
Phone: (202)274-8000
Fax: (202)274-8100
E-mail: grants@fanniemaefoundation.org
Web: http://www.fanniemaefoundation.org

Description
Founded: 1979
EIN: 521172718

Organization Type: Corporate Foundation
Giving Locations: DC: Washington national organizations; operating locations.
Grant Types: Award, Capital, Conference/Seminar, Emergency, Employee Matching Gifts, Endowment, General Support, Loan, Matching, Multiyear/Continuing Support.
Note: Employee matching gift ratio: 2 to 1 up to $500 annually. Employee matching gift ratio: 1 to 1 for gifts over $500.

Financial Summary
Total Giving: $46,086,154 (2003); $38,058,078 (2002); $34,874,351 (2001). Note: Contributes through foundation only.
Giving Analysis: Giving for 2001 includes: foundation grants to United Way ($200,041); foundation gifts to individuals ($567,500); foundation matching gifts ($1,790,862); foundation ($32,276,944)
Assets: $333,496,929 (2002); $468,969,010 (2001)
Gifts Received: $50,000,000 (2003); $25,000,000 (2002); $300,000,000 (2001). Note: Contributions were received from Fannie Mae.

Typical Recipients
Arts & Humanities: Arts Outreach, Dance, History & Archaeology, Museums/Galleries, Music, Opera, Performing Arts, Public Broadcasting, Theater
Civic & Public Affairs: African American Affairs, Asian American Affairs, Business/Free Enterprise, Community Foundations, Economic Development, Employment/Job Training, Ethnic Organizations, Civic & Public Affairs-General, Hispanic Affairs, Housing, Municipalities/Towns, Nonprofit Management, Philanthropic Organizations, Professional & Trade Associations, Public Policy, Rural Affairs, Urban & Community Affairs, Women's Affairs
Education: Afterschool/Enrichment Programs, Business Education, Colleges & Universities, Community & Junior Colleges, Education Associations, Education Funds, Education-General, Legal Education, Minority Education, Public Education (Precollege), Religious Education, Student Aid, Vocational & Technical Education
Environment: Environment-General
Health: AIDS/HIV, Nursing Services, Single-Disease Health Associations
International: Health Care/Hospitals, International Relief Efforts
Religion: Jewish Causes, Religious Welfare
Social Services: Camps, Child Abuse, Community Centers, Community Service Organizations, Emergency Relief, Family Services, Homes, Recreation & Athletics, Refugee Assistance, Senior Services, Shelters/Homelessness, United Funds/United Ways, Volunteer Services, Youth Organizations

Application Procedures
Initial Contact: The foundation accepts unsolicited proposals only once per year--and posts deadlines, guidelines, and other grant information at the website by December 31 each year for the subsequent year.
Application Requirements: The foundation awards most of its grants by soliciting proposals from organizations with both the capacity and proven track record to engage in strong partnerships with the Foundation. In order to allow us also to identify potential future partners or respond to unique community needs, the foundation sets aside a limited amount of grant funding each year for which nonprofit organizations may apply through a competitive process. the program's target population; and geographic area (s) to benefit from the request. The narrative should include a description of organization including its history, mission, programs/services offered, and recent accomplishments; a description of the request, including its principal objectives and anticipated outcomes; problems and issues the program or organization will address; qualifications of the organization and its principal personnel to implement the objectives and achieve the expected outcomes; degree to which the program will build on existing services in

the community rather than duplicating them; funding received to date for the program (or for the organization, if the request is for general operating support), as well as other sources from which
Deadlines: Deadlines posted on the website.
Evaluative Criteria: The foundation's national work is organized around the following four interconnected initiatives: Increase the affordable housing supply. The foundation seeks to produce and preserve high quality affordable housing that sustains healthy neighborhoods and offers opportunities to create individual and community wealth. Generally, we seek to enhance the operations of particularly effective and accountable non-profit organizations working on housing production and/or preservation, rather than to direct our grant funds to specific affordable housing development projects. Create wealth through homeownership: The foundation works to increase sustainable homeownership that builds individual and community wealth. This initiative focuses on providing high-quality, comprehensive personal finance and homeownership information and education and strives to help bring mainstream financial services to underserved communities. Bring Wall Street to Main Street: The Foundation strives to attract Wall Street investors-including individuals, corporations, governments, and foundations-to investments in affordable housing and housing-related community development. The foundation also works to improve the capacity of financial intermediaries, including their interconnection with mainstream players in the larger capital markets. Create and Share Knowledge: The Foundation creates and shares relevant and innovative information in order to help advance practice, policy and through in the fields of affordable housing and community development. Primary audiences for this shared knowledge are nonprofit organization staffs, affordable housing practitioners, government officials, academics and private developers. The Foundation's primary vehicle for sharing data is www.knowledgeplex.org, the Foundation's premier portal for housing and community development information.
Decision Notification: The foundation acknowledges receipt of proposal within 15 days.
Notes: The foundation's Innovation, Research, and Technology grant program have a separate set of guidelines. See the foundation's web site.
The foundation frequently makes Requests For Applications; these initiatives may have specific deadlines.

Restrictions
Does not support projects, programs or organizations that do not fit within the foundation's areas of interest or for which the foundation is asked to serve as the sole funder; individuals; organizations without Section 501(c)(3) status; private foundations; organizations that channel funds received to third parties; political campaigns, candidates or lobbying organizations; sectarian purposes; endowment and capital campaigns; in-classroom components of K-12 public or private schools; existing program or organizational deficits; organizations that already have an active grant with the foundation; or local affiliates of larger national organizations, if the foundation has a relationship with the national organization.

Additional Information
Applications should be sent to regional offices; contact information is included in application guidelines.
Publications: Application Form; Foundation Annual Report; Application Guidelines

Corporate Officials
Kenneth J. Bacon: senior vice presidento B Houston, TX 1954. ED Stanford University (1976); Harvard University (1982). PRIM CORP EMPL senior vice president: Fannie Mae. CORP AFFIL director: National Equity Fund; director: Comcast Corp. NONPR AFFIL trustee: Stanford University; member: Urban Land Institute; member: Executive Leadership Council; member: Real Estate Roundtable; national fi-

nance committee chairman: Communities in Schools.
Louis W. Hoyes: vice president ED City University of New York BS; Harvard University MBA.
Robert J. Levin: executive vice president ED University of Chicago MBA; University of North Carolina BA.
William R. Maloni: senior vice president policy & affairs B Pittsburgh, PA 1944. ED Duquesne University (1968). PRIM CORP EMPL senior vice president policy & affairs: Fannie Mae.
Daniel H. Mudd: vice chairman, chief operating officer ED Harvard University MA; University of Virginia BA. CORP AFFIL director: Oriental and General Fund Ltd.; director: Ryder Systems Inc. NONPR AFFIL director: Local Initiatives Support Corp.; director: National Building Museum; director: Center for the Study of the Presidency.
Barry Zigas: senior vice president B New York, NY 1951. ED Grinnell College (1973). PRIM CORP EMPL senior vice president: Federal National Mortgage Association. NONPR AFFIL director: National Housing Trust; director: Yachad Inc.; trustee: Enterprise Foundation.

Foundation Officials

Kenneth J. Bacon: vice chairman (see above)
Peter Beard: senior vice president ED Davidson College AB; Syracuse University JD. NONPR AFFIL director: Partners for Livable Communities; vice chairman: Rural Development & Finance Corp.; director: Neighborhood Funders Group.
James H. Carr: senior vice president ED Columbia University MA; Hampton University BA; University of Pennsylvania MA; University of Pennsylvania MA. NONPR AFFIL trustee: University of California-Berkeley; trustee: University of Pennsylvania; director: American Real Estate Society; trustee: Harvard University.
Rev. Dr. Floyd Harold Flake: director B Los Angeles, CA January 30, 1945. ED Northeastern University; United Theological Seminary DD; Wilberforce University BA (1967); United Theology Seminary D Ministry (1995). PRIM CORP EMPL pastor: Allen AME Church. NONPR AFFIL pastor: Allen African Methodist Episcopal Church; senior fellow: Manhattan Institute Policy Research.
Stephen Goldsmith: director ED University of Michigan JD (1971). CORP AFFIL director: Waterfield Mortgage Co.; director: Net2Phone Inc.; director: Steak n Shake Co.; senior vice president: ACS State & Local Solutions Inc.; director: Finish Line. NONPR AFFIL chairman: Corp. for National and Community Service; director: Oquirrh Institute; chairman: Center of Civic Innovation at Manhattan Institute.
Chuck Greener: director
Colleen Hernandez: director CORP AFFIL director: Douglass National Bank.
Glen S. Howard: secretary, senior vice president, general counsel ED Harvard University BA; University of Chicago JD. NONPR AFFIL past chairman: Greater DC Cares; president: United Arts Organization of Greater Washington; member: Bar Association of District of Columbia; director: Goodwill of Greater Washington.
Louis W. Hoyes: director (see above)
Stewart Kwoh: director NONPR AFFIL president, executive director: Asian Pacific American Legal Center.
Daniel H. Mudd: chairman (see above)
Rebecca Senhauser: director
Stacey Davis Stewart: president, chief executive officer, director ED Georgetown University AB; University of Michigan MBA.
Karen Hastie Williams: director B Washington, DC 1944. ED University of Neuchatel (Switzerland) (1965); Bates College BA (1966); Tufts University MA (1967); Catholic University America JD (1973). PRIM CORP EMPL partner: Crowell & Moring. CORP AFFIL director: SunTrust Bank; director: Washington Gas Holdings Co.; director: Federal National Mortgage Association; director: Gannett Co. Inc.; director: Continental Airlines Inc.; retired partner: Crowell & Moring; director: Chubb Corp. NONPR AFFIL member: National Contract Management Association; member: Women's Forum; member, director legal defense fund: NAACP; member: National Bar Association; member: Black Women Lawyers' Association; chairman, trustee: Greater Washington Research Center; member: American Bar Association.
Barry Zigas: treasurer (see above)

Grants Analysis

Disclosure Period: calendar year ending 2003
Total Grants: $43,614,338*
Number of Grants: 975 (approx)
Average Grant: $44,733
Highest Grant: $1,750,000
Lowest Grant: $500
Typical Range: $20,000 to $100,000
*Note: Giving excludes gifts to individuals; United Way; matching gifts.

Recent Grants

Note: Grants derived from 2003 Form 990.
General

1,750,000	Local Initiatives Support Corporation, New York, NY -- to assist affordable rental housing and homeownership opportunities in low-income communities
600,000	Mercy Housing Inc., Denver, CO -- for an organization that works to advance service-enriched affordable housing development and preservation initiatives
500,000	Homebuilding Community Foundation, Houston, TX -- for small, community-based nonprofit affordable housing organizations
400,000	National Council of La Raza, Washington, DC -- to support the partnerships of hope program
350,000	Washington Area Women's Foundation, Washington, DC -- fund to launch women and families financial independence initiative
300,000	Housing Partnership Network, Boston, MA -- grant to promote regional nonprofit housing partnerships
200,000	H Street Community Development Corporation, Washington, DC -- for building neighborhood assets
200,000	Low Income Investment Fund, Oakland, CA -- fund for nonprofit organizations to alleviate poverty
200,000	National Housing Trust Enterprise Preservation, Washington, DC -- to assist affordable housing and improvement of rental homes
200,000	Washington Regional Association of Grantmakers, Washington, DC -- grants to offer technical assistance to CDCs

MAX AND MARIAN FARASH CHARITABLE FOUNDATION

Giving Contact

Max M. Farash, Trustee
919 Winton Rd. S.
Rochester, NY 14618-1633
Phone: (585)244-1886

Description

Founded: 1989
EIN: 222948675
Organization Type: Private Foundation
Giving Locations: NY: Rochester including metropolitan area; PA
Grant Types: General Support.

Financial Summary

Total Giving: $178,000 (2003); $431,600 (2001)
Assets: $4,544,211 (2003); $4,115,068 (2001)

Typical Recipients

Arts & Humanities: Arts Associations & Councils, Arts & Humanities-General, History & Archaeology, Libraries, Museums/Galleries, Music, Theater
Civic & Public Affairs: Employment/Job Training, Civic & Public Affairs-General, Urban & Community Affairs
Education: Arts/Humanities Education, Business Education, Colleges & Universities, Community & Junior Colleges, Medical Education, Student Aid
Health: Cancer, Clinics/Medical Centers, Health Organizations, Hospitals, Medical Rehabilitation, Medical Research, Single-Disease Health Associations
International: Missionary/Religious Activities
Religion: Jewish Causes, Religious Organizations
Science: Science Museums
Social Services: Child Welfare, Community Centers, Community Service Organizations, Homes, Senior Services, United Funds/United Ways, Volunteer Services, Youth Organizations

Application Procedures

Initial Contact: Send a brief letter of inquiry on organization's letterhead.
Application Requirements: Include statement of purpose, amount requested, and proof of tax-exempt status.
Deadlines: March 1.

Restrictions

Organized charitable organizations qualifying as such under the Internal Revenue code.

Foundation Officials

Max M. Farash: trustee

Grants Analysis

Disclosure Period: calendar year ending 2003
Total Grants: $178,000
Number of Grants: 7
Highest Grant: $100,000
Lowest Grant: $500

Recent Grants

Note: Grants derived from 2001 Form 990.
General

200,000	Catholic Family Services
100,000	University of Pennsylvania - The Wharton School, Philadelphia, PA
50,000	Jewish Community Center
50,000	Jewish Home Foundation, Rochester, NY
29,100	George Eastman House, Rochester, NY
2,500	Suny College at Alfred

WILLIAM STAMPS FARISH FUND

Giving Contact

Caroline P. Rotan, Secretary
The William Stamps Farish Fund
10000 Memorial Drive, Suite 920
Houston, TX 77024
Phone: (713)686-7373

Description

Founded: 1951
EIN: 746043019
Organization Type: General Purpose Foundation
Giving Locations: NY; TX: Houston
Grant Types: Capital, Challenge, Conference/Seminar, General Support, Project, Research, Scholarship.

Donor Information

Founder: Mrs. Libbie Rice Farish, wife of William Stamps Farish, established the William Stamps Farish Fund in 1951 in Texas. Mr. Farish was one of the Humble Oil Company organizers. The fund receives contributions from various family trusts.

Financial Summary

Total Giving: $8,124,500 (fiscal year ending June 30, 2003); $9,923,500 (fiscal 2002)
Assets: $158,247,857 (fiscal 2003); $173,414,769 (fiscal 2002)

Typical Recipients

Arts & Humanities: Arts Associations & Councils, Arts Centers, Arts Outreach, Ballet, Dance, Film & Video, History & Archaeology, Libraries, Museums/Galleries, Music, Opera, Performing Arts, Public Broadcasting, Theater, Visual Arts
Civic & Public Affairs: Botanical Gardens/Parks, Business/Free Enterprise, Urban & Community Affairs, Women's Affairs
Education: Afterschool/Enrichment Programs, Arts/Humanities Education, Business Education, Colleges & Universities, Economic Education, Education Associations, Education Funds, Faculty Development, Education-General, Literacy, Medical Education, Minority Education, Preschool Education, Private Education (Precollege), Public Education (Precollege), Religious Education, Science/Mathematics Education, Secondary Education (Private), Social Sciences Education, Special Education, Student Aid
Environment: Environment-General, Resource Conservation
Health: Cancer, Children's Health/Hospitals, Clinics/Medical Centers, Emergency/Ambulance Services, Eyes/Blindness, Health-General, Health Funds, Health Organizations, Hospices, Hospitals, Hospitals (University Affiliated), Medical Research, Mental Health, Prenatal Health Issues, Public Health, Single-Disease Health Associations, Speech & Hearing, Transplant Networks/Donor Banks
Religion: Churches, Ministries, Religious Organizations, Religious Welfare
Science: Science Museums, Scientific Centers & Institutes, Scientific Labs, Scientific Research
Social Services: Animal Protection, Camps, Child Abuse, Child Welfare, Community Service Organizations, Day Care, Emergency Relief, Family Planning, Family Services, Food/Clothing Distribution, People with Disabilities, Recreation & Athletics, Scouts, Sexual Abuse, Shelters/Homelessness, Substance Abuse, Volunteer Services, Youth Organizations

Application Procedures

Initial Contact: Applicants should send a copy of a full proposal to the fund.
Application Requirements: Applicants must submit proof of exempt status. A complete proposal must include proof of tax-exempt status; brief history of the organization; description of the proposed project and a concise statement of the necessity for such a project; copy of a detailed financial statement; and an explanation of the proposed use of funds, detailed project budget, other potential sources of funding, and specific amount requested.
Deadlines: None.
Review Process: The board meets annually.

Restrictions

Awards are made only to Houston, Texas, charities unless a trustee is directly involved in the charity. The fund does not make contributions for endowments, ongoing operating expenses, or to individuals.

Additional Information

Publications: Application Guidelines

Foundation Officials

Laura Farish Chadwick: trustee
Cornelia Gerry Corbett: trustee
Martha Farish Gerry: president, trustee NONPR AFFIL director: Cold Spring Harbor Laboratory.
Caroline P. Rotan: secretary
Terry W. Ward: vice president, treasurer

Grants Analysis

Disclosure Period: fiscal year ending June 30, 2003
Total Grants: $8,124,500
Number of Grants: 96
Average Grant: $71,537*
Highest Grant: $500,000
Lowest Grant: $5,000
Typical Range: $10,000 to $100,000
*Note: Average grants figure excludes three highest grants ($1,400,000).

Recent Grants

Note: Grants derived from fiscal 2003 Form 990.
General

500,000	Brandywine Conservancy Inc., Chadds Ford, PA -- for capital campaign and program support
500,000	Texas Children's Hospital, Houston, TX -- new patient rooms and establishment of Autistic Disorder program
450,000	Family and Children's Service Association, Mineola, NY -- capital campaign
316,000	Museum of Fine Arts, Houston, TX -- annual giving
250,000	Baylor College of Medicine, Houston, TX -- for teacher salaries
250,000	Brookwood Community Inc., Brookshire, TX -- renovations to infirmary
250,000	National Gallery of Art, Washington, DC -- acquisition of American art
250,000	New York Presbyterian Hospital Inc., New York, NY -- new children's wing
250,000	North Shore Long Island Jewish Health System Inc., Great Neck, NY -- new emergency room
250,000	Purnell School, Pottersville, NJ -- new education center

FARMER FAMILY FOUNDATION

Giving Contact

Amy F. Joseph, Trustee
c/o Summer Hill
PO Box 625737
Cincinnati, OH 45262-5737
Phone: (513)459-1085

Description

Founded: 1988
EIN: 311256614
Organization Type: Private Foundation
Grant Types: General Support.

Donor Information

Founder: Richard T. Farmer

Financial Summary

Total Giving: $2,684,857 (2003)
Giving Analysis: Giving for 2003 includes: foundation grants to United Way ($5,000)
Assets: $75,695,721 (2003)
Gifts Received: $13,093,820 (2003); $7,673,592 (2000); $4,960,299 (1998). Note: In 2003, contributions were received from Richard T. Farmer 2000 Charitable Trust ($10,035,000), Richard T. Farmer ($2,459,000), Brynne F. Coletti ($107,525), Amy F. Joseph ($221,805), and Scott D. Farmer ($270,490). In 2000, contributions were received from Richard T. Farmer 2000 Charitable Trust ($4,371,416), Richard T. Farmer ($3,101,954) and Scott D. Farmer ($200,222). In 1998, contributions were received from Richard T. Farmer ($4,360,380), Brynne F. Coletti ($199,973), Scott D. Farmer ($199,973), and Amy F. Joseph ($199,973). In 1994, contributions were received from Joyce E. Farmer ($1,390,000) and Brynne F. Coletti ($36,000).

Typical Recipients

Arts & Humanities: Arts Associations & Councils, Arts Centers, Libraries, Museums/Galleries, Performing Arts
Civic & Public Affairs: Community Foundations, Civic & Public Affairs-General, Urban & Community Affairs, Zoos/Aquariums
Education: Business Education, Colleges & Universities, Education Reform, Education-General, Journalism/Media Education, Private Education (Precollege), Student Aid
Environment: Protection
Health: Children's Health/Hospitals, Clinics/Medical Centers, Diabetes, Hospices, Hospitals, Single-Disease Health Associations
Religion: Churches
Science: Scientific Organizations
Social Services: At-Risk Youth, Food/Clothing Distribution, People with Disabilities, Scouts, Volunteer Services, YMCA/YWCA/YMHA/YWHA, Youth Organizations

Application Procedures

Initial Contact: Send a brief letter of inquiry.
Application Requirements: purpose of funds sought, description and background of organization, amount requested, charitable status, and list of board members.
Deadlines: None.

Additional Information

The foundation was established to assist children, the handicapped, and programs that aid people in entering the work force.

Foundation Officials

Brynne F. Coletti: trustee
Robert E. Coletti: trustee, secretary
Amy F. Joseph: trustee

Grants Analysis

Disclosure Period: calendar year ending 2003
Total Grants: $2,679,857*
Number of Grants: 63
Average Grant: $10,768*
Highest Grant: $1,000,000
Lowest Grant: $250
Typical Range: $5,000 to $20,000
*Note: Giving excludes United Way. Average grant figure excludes five highest grants ($2,055,333).

Recent Grants

Note: Grants derived from 2003 Form 990.

Library-Related

100,000	George Bush Presidential Library Foundation, Houston, TX

General

1,000,000	University of Texas, Houston, TX
500,000	Intrepid Museum Foundation, New York, NY
355,333	Summit Country Day School, Cincinnati, OH
100,000	Points of Light Foundation, Houston, TX
77,750	Xavier University, Cincinnati, OH
75,000	Citizens for Community Values, Cincinnati, OH
75,000	Hebrew Union College, Cincinnati, OH
40,000	Little Traverse Conservancy Inc., Harbor Springs, MI
35,000	Ocean Reef Foundation, Key Largo, FL

FARMER JACK SUPERMARKETS

Company Headquarters
18718 Borman St.
Detroit, MI 48228
Web: http://www.farmerjack.com

Company Description
Founded: 1928
Former Name: Borman's Inc..
Employees: 8,500
SIC(s): 5411 Grocery Stores, 5912 Drug Stores & Proprietary Stores.
Parent Company: Great Atlantic & Pacific Tea Company Inc., 2 Paragon Drive, Montvale, NJ, United States

Operating Locations
Borman's Inc. (MI--Southfield)
Note: Operates 2 divisions in Detroit, MI.

Borman's Inc. Fund

Giving Contact
Paul Borman, President
Borman's Inc. Fund
32406 Franklin Rd.
PO Box 250520
Franklin, MI 48025
Phone: (248)203-9333

Description
EIN: 386069267
Organization Type: Corporate Foundation
Giving Locations: MI: Southeastern Michigan
Grant Types: Award, General Support, Project.

Donor Information
Founder: Borman's Inc., Paul Borman

Financial Summary
Total Giving: $31,180 (2003); $78,650 (2002). Note: Contributes through corporate direct giving program and foundation.
Giving Analysis: Giving for 2002 includes: foundation grants to United Way ($500)
Assets: $130,678 (2003); $85,036 (2002)
Gifts Received: $990 (2002); $5,210 (2000); $129,960 (1998). Note: In 1995, contributions were received from Great Atlantic & Pacific Tea Company ($300,000), Paul Borman ($5,000), and other sources ($6,984).

Typical Recipients
Arts & Humanities: Art History, Arts Associations & Councils, Arts Centers, Arts Institutes, Community Arts, Dance, Ethnic & Folk Arts, Historic Preservation, Libraries, Literary Arts, Museums/Galleries, Music, Performing Arts, Public Broadcasting, Theater
Civic & Public Affairs: Business/Free Enterprise, Civil Rights, Civic & Public Affairs-General, Housing, Parades/Festivals, Philanthropic Organizations, Public Policy, Urban & Community Affairs, Zoos/Aquariums
Education: Colleges & Universities, Education Funds, Environmental Education, Education-General, International Exchange, Leadership Training, Minority Education, Private Education (Precollege), Religious Education, Science/Mathematics Education, Secondary Education (Public), Student Aid
Environment: Environment-General
Health: AIDS/HIV, Alzheimer's Disease, Cancer, Children's Health/Hospitals, Clinics/Medical Centers, Diabetes, Emergency/Ambulance Services, Eyes/Blindness, Geriatric Health, Health Organizations, Hospices, Hospitals, Long-Term Care, Mental Health, Multiple Sclerosis, Single-Disease Health Associations

International: Foreign Educational Institutions, Health Care/Hospitals, International Affairs, International Organizations, International Relief Efforts, Missionary/Religious Activities
Religion: Churches, Jewish Causes, Religious Organizations, Religious Welfare, Seminaries, Synagogues/Temples
Science: Science-General, Scientific Centers & Institutes, Scientific Organizations
Social Services: Animal Protection, Child Welfare, Community Centers, Community Service Organizations, Day Care, Delinquency & Criminal Rehabilitation, Domestic Violence, Emergency Relief, Family Planning, Family Services, Food/Clothing Distribution, People with Disabilities, Recreation & Athletics, Senior Services, Shelters/Homelessness, Social Services-General, Substance Abuse, United Funds/United Ways, Youth Organizations

Application Procedures
Initial Contact: Send a written request.
Application Requirements: Include amount needed, purpose of the grant, and organizational and financial information.
Deadlines: None.

Restrictions
The company does not support individuals, political or lobbying groups.

Corporate Officials
Paul Borman: chief executive officer B Detroit, MI 1932. ED Michigan State University (1954). PRIM CORP EMPL chairman: Borman's Inc. CORP AFFIL director: First Federal Michigan.

Foundation Officials
Eric Borman: assistant secretary
Gilbert Borman: secretary, treasurer
Marlene Borman: vice president B Grant County, ND 1936. ED Cleveland Institute of Technology; United States Air Force Institute of Technology. NONPR AFFIL member: American Management Association; member: National Society Professional Engineers.
Paul Borman: president (see above)
Stuart Borman: assistant secretary

Grants Analysis
Disclosure Period: calendar year ending 2003
Total Grants: $31,180
Number of Grants: 10
Average Grant: $1,394*
Highest Grant: $18,635
Lowest Grant: $250
Typical Range: $500 to $3,000
*Note: Average grant figure excludes highest grant.

Recent Grants
Note: Grants derived from 2003 Form 990.

General

18,635	American Port, Bloomfield, MI
3,600	Jewish Community Center, West Bloomfield, MI
3,000	Congregation Shaarey Zedek, Southfield, MI
2,500	National Jewish Center for Learning and Leadership, New York, NY
1,000	Henry Ford Health System, Detroit, MI
1,000	Michigan Thanksgiving Parade, Detroit, MI
500	Cystic Fibrosis Foundation, Bethesda, MI
400	Yadegar, Berkley, MI
295	Yeshiva Beth Yehuda, Detroit, MI
250	Siga delta TAU Foundation, Carel, MI

FRANK M. AND ALICE M. FARR TRUST

Giving Contact
James E. Koepke, Trustee
1101 12th St.
Aurora, NE 68818
Phone: (402)694-3136
Fax: (402)694-3136

Description
Founded: 1985
EIN: 476144457
Organization Type: Private Foundation
Giving Locations: DC; IA; NE: Hamilton County
Grant Types: Capital, Emergency, Endowment, General Support, Operating Expenses.

Financial Summary
Total Giving: $184,519 (2004); $278,017 (2001)
Assets: $5,063,268 (2004); $4,862,853 (2001)

Typical Recipients
Arts & Humanities: Historic Preservation, History & Archaeology, Libraries, Music
Civic & Public Affairs: Botanical Gardens/Parks, Chambers of Commerce, Clubs, Community Foundations, Ethnic Organizations, Civic & Public Affairs-General, Housing, Municipalities/Towns, Rural Affairs, Safety, Urban & Community Affairs
Education: Agricultural Education, Colleges & Universities, Education Funds, Education-General, Private Education (Precollege), Student Aid
Health: Alzheimer's Disease, Cancer, Emergency/Ambulance Services, Health Organizations, Heart, Hospitals, Nursing Services, Public Health
Social Services: Animal Protection, Community Centers, Community Service Organizations, Recreation & Athletics, Scouts, Senior Services, Youth Organizations

Application Procedures
Initial Contact: Send request for application form.
Deadlines: March 1.

Restrictions
Limited to governmental subdivisions or charities in Hamilton County, NE.

Additional Information
Trust(s): Heritage Bank

Foundation Officials
James E. Koepke: trustee

Grants Analysis
Disclosure Period: calendar year ending 2004
Total Grants: $184,519
Number of Grants: 17
Average Grant: $7,253*
Highest Grant: $42,871
Lowest Grant: $251
Typical Range: $1,000 to $10,000
*Note: Average grant figure excludes two highest grants ($75,718).

Recent Grants
Note: Grants derived from 2001 Form 990.
General

63,000	Community Center of Hamilton County
50,000	Nebraska Vocational Aging Foundation, NE
26,575	Hamilton County Senior Center, Aurora, NE
25,000	Hamilton County Information Technology
23,988	Hamilton County Foundation Inc., Aurora, NE
19,516	Hamilton County Senior Center, Aurora, NE

17,678	Hamilton Community Foundation, Aurora, NE
15,000	ADC Foundation, Washington, DC
10,000	Edgerton Education Foundation
7,760	Memorial Hospital Foundation

DRUSILLA FARWELL FOUNDATION

Giving Contact
Leslie Wise, Treasurer
725 Barclay Cir., Suite 230
Rochester Hills, MI 48307
Phone: (248)852-9330

Description
Founded: 1937
EIN: 386082430
Organization Type: Private Foundation
Giving Locations: MI
Grant Types: General Support.

Financial Summary
Total Giving: $173,700 (fiscal year ending August 31, 2004); $243,900 (fiscal 2001)
Assets: $3,069,562 (fiscal 2004); $3,695,069 (fiscal 2001)

Typical Recipients
Arts & Humanities: Arts Associations & Councils, Arts Centers, Arts Funds, Arts Institutes, Community Arts, Arts & Humanities-General, History & Archaeology, Libraries, Museums/Galleries, Music, Opera, Performing Arts, Public Broadcasting, Theater
Civic & Public Affairs: Asian American Affairs, Community Foundations, Civic & Public Affairs-General, Legal Aid, Municipalities/Towns, Professional & Trade Associations, Safety, Urban & Community Affairs, Women's Affairs
Education: Business Education, Colleges & Universities, Legal Education, Medical Education, Private Education (Precollege), Public Education (Precollege), Religious Education, Secondary Education (Private), Secondary Education (Public), Special Education
Health: Alzheimer's Disease, Cancer, Children's Health/Hospitals, Clinics/Medical Centers, Diabetes, Emergency/Ambulance Services, Geriatric Health, Health Organizations, Heart, Hospices, Hospitals, Hospitals (University Affiliated), Medical Research, Multiple Sclerosis, Public Health, Single-Disease Health Associations
International: Foreign Arts Organizations, Missionary/Religious Activities
Religion: Churches, Dioceses, Jewish Causes, Religious Organizations, Religious Welfare, Seminaries
Social Services: Child Abuse, Child Welfare, Community Service Organizations, People with Disabilities, Shelters/Homelessness, Substance Abuse, United Funds/United Ways, Youth Organizations

Application Procedures
Initial Contact: Send brief letter describing program.
Deadlines: None.

Foundation Officials
Randolph Fields: president
Helmuth Krave: trustee
Leslie Wise: secretary, treasurer

Grants Analysis
Disclosure Period: fiscal year ending August 31, 2004
Total Grants: $173,700
Number of Grants: 80
Average Grant: $2,171
Highest Grant: $11,400

Lowest Grant: $200
Typical Range: $1,000 to $5,000

Recent Grants
Note: Grants derived from 2004 Form 990.
General

11,400	AFS-USA Inc., New York, NY
7,000	United Arts of Central Florida, Maitland, FL
6,500	N. Donald Diebel Jr. MD Good Samaritan Fund, Winter Park, FL
6,000	Hickory Woods Elementary School, Novi, MI
6,000	Our Lady of Loretto School, Redford, MI
5,100	McLaren Regional Medical Center, Flint, MI
5,000	Central Michigan University, Mt. Pleasant, MI
5,000	Oakland University, Rochester, MI
3,500	Atlantic Center for the Arts, New Smyrna Beach, FL
3,500	Consortium on Child Abuse and Neglect, Flint, MI

FASKEN FOUNDATION

Giving Contact
Andrew C. Elliott, Jr., Director
PO Box 162786
Austin, TX 78716-2786
Phone: (512)708-1003

Description
Founded: 1955
EIN: 756023680
Organization Type: Private Foundation
Giving Locations: TX
Grant Types: General Support, Scholarship.

Donor Information
Founder: the late Andrew A. Fasken, the late Helen Fasken House, the late Vickie Mallison, the late Howard Marshall Johnson, the late Ruth Shelton

Financial Summary
Total Giving: $900,970 (2003)
Giving Analysis: Giving for 2003 includes: foundation scholarships ($94,970)
Assets: $21,374,483 (2003)
Gifts Received: $50 (1994); $25,000 (1993); $125 (1992)

Typical Recipients
Arts & Humanities: Libraries
Civic & Public Affairs: Chambers of Commerce, Civic & Public Affairs-General, Hispanic Affairs, Housing, Rural Affairs, Safety
Education: Business Education, Colleges & Universities, Engineering/Technological Education, Faculty Development, Literacy, Medical Education, Private Education (Precollege), Public Education (Precollege), Special Education, Student Aid
Health: AIDS/HIV, Children's Health/Hospitals, Clinics/Medical Centers, Health Funds, Hospices, Single-Disease Health Associations
Religion: Ministries, Religious Welfare
Social Services: At-Risk Youth, Big Brothers/Big Sisters, Child Abuse, Child Welfare, Community Service Organizations, Domestic Violence, Family Services, People with Disabilities, Scouts, Senior Services, Sexual Abuse, Social Services-General, Substance Abuse, United Funds/United Ways, YMCA/YWCA/YMHA/YWHA, Youth Organizations

Application Procedures
Initial Contact: Send a brief letter of inquiry.
Application Requirements: list of governing board and proof of tax-exempt status. Grants are reviewed

quarterly and awards are generally made in February and September.

Additional Information
Provides scholarships to graduates of Midland County, TX, public schools.
Publications: Application Guidelines

Foundation Officials
Andrew C. Elliott, Jr.: director
F. Andrew Fasken: vice president
Steven P. Fasken: president
William P. Franklin: trustee B Las Vegas, NM 1933. ED Texas A&M University (1955); University of Texas (1958). PRIM CORP EMPL president, chief executive officer: First City TX - Midland.
B. L. Jones: trustee
Thomas E. Kelly: trustee PRIM CORP EMPL chief financial officer: Cadence Design Systems, Inc.
Susan Fasken Martin: trustee

Grants Analysis
Disclosure Period: calendar year ending 2003
Total Grants: $806,000*
Number of Grants: 58
Average Grant: $12,737*
Highest Grant: $80,000
Lowest Grant: $1,000
Typical Range: $5,000 to $20,000
***Note:** Giving excludes scholarships; United Way. Average grant figure excludes highest grant.

Recent Grants
Note: Grants derived from 2003 Form 990.
General

80,000	Midland Children's Rehabilitation Center, Midland, TX
50,000	Manor Park Inc., Midland, TX
48,000	Trinity Christian Academy, Addison, TX
45,000	Midland Memorial Foundation, Midland, TX
45,000	Multicultural Career Intern Program Inc., Washington, DC
40,000	High Sky Children's Ranch, Midland, TX
40,000	YMCA, Midland, TX
37,500	Coleman County Youth Activity Center, Coleman, TX
25,000	Casa de Amigos, Midland, TX
25,000	Seton Fund, Austin, TX

MARIANNE G. FAULKNER TRUST

Giving Contact
Monica Neal, Vice President
c/o JP Morgan Chase Bank
1211 Ave. of the Americas, 34th Floor
New York, NY 10036
Phone: (212)464-2443

Alternate Contact
Phone: (212)789-4159

Description
Founded: 1959
EIN: 136047458
Organization Type: Private Foundation
Giving Locations: VT: Northeast.
Grant Types: General Support, Operating Expenses.

Donor Information
Founder: the late Marianne Gaillard Faulkner

Financial Summary
Total Giving: $371,270 (2003); $551,544 (2001)
Assets: $10,027,662 (2003); $10,266,131 (2001)

Typical Recipients

Arts & Humanities: Arts Associations & Councils, Arts & Humanities-General, History & Archaeology, Libraries, Literary Arts, Public Broadcasting
Civic & Public Affairs: Civic & Public Affairs-General, Municipalities/Towns, Public Policy, Urban & Community Affairs
Education: Colleges & Universities, Education-General
Environment: Air/Water Quality, Environment-General, Resource Conservation
Health: Clinics/Medical Centers, Health Organizations, Home-Care Services, Hospitals
Religion: Churches, Ministries
Social Services: Child Welfare, Community Centers, Community Service Organizations, Food/Clothing Distribution, Homes, People with Disabilities, Recreation & Athletics, Senior Services, United Funds/ United Ways, Youth Organizations

Application Procedures

Initial Contact: Send a letter of application.
Application Requirements: Include description of project, financial data, and proof of tax-exempt status.
Deadlines: None.

Restrictions

Does not support individuals.

Additional Information

Trust(s): JP Morgan Chase Bank

Grants Analysis

Disclosure Period: calendar year ending 2003
Total Grants: $371,270
Number of Grants: 10
Highest Grant: $70,492
Lowest Grant: $4,480
Typical Range: $10,000 to $18,750

Recent Grants

Note: Grants derived from 2001 Form 990.
General

75,536	Homestead, Inc., Woodstock, VT
75,536	Homestead, Inc., Woodstock, VT
75,535	Homestead, Inc., Woodstock, VT
57,502	Homestead, Inc., Woodstock, VT
57,502	Homestead, Inc., Woodstock, VT
25,000	North University
18,033	Homestead, Inc., Woodstock, VT
10,000	Vermont Council, Essex Junction, VT
10,000	Vermont Public Radio, Essex Junction, VT
9,000	Woodstock Associates, Woodstock Community Recreation Center, Woodstock, VT

FEAR NOT FOUNDATION

Giving Contact

Steven Russo, Director
3002 N. Campbell Ave., Suite 100
Tucson, AZ 85719
Phone: (520)529-1515

Description

Founded: 1991
EIN: 860647136
Organization Type: Private Foundation
Giving Locations: AZ: Tucson
Grant Types: General Support.

Financial Summary

Total Giving: $110,500 (2003); $117,500 (2001)
Assets: $1,196,120 (2003); $1,356,469 (2001)
Gifts Received: $50,288 (2003); $62,475 (1994); $220,179 (1992)

Typical Recipients

Arts & Humanities: Libraries, Museums/Galleries
Civic & Public Affairs: Hispanic Affairs
Education: Arts/Humanities Education, Colleges & Universities, Education Funds, Education Reform, Education-General, Public Education (Precollege), Secondary Education (Private)
Environment: Environment-General, Resource Conservation
Health: Clinics/Medical Centers, Hospices
Religion: Religious Organizations
Social Services: Emergency Relief, Food/Clothing Distribution, People with Disabilities, Recreation & Athletics

Application Procedures

Initial Contact: Send a brief letter of inquiry.
Application Requirements: Include name of requestor, amount requested, purpose of funds sought, and why request is made.
Deadlines: None.

Foundation Officials

Ashley M. Dixon: director
Steven Russo: director
Norman A. Willock: director
Scott Willock: director

Grants Analysis

Disclosure Period: calendar year ending 2003
Total Grants: $110,500
Number of Grants: 4
Highest Grant: $75,000
Lowest Grant: $3,000

Recent Grants

Note: Grants derived from 2003 Form 990.
General

75,000	University of Arizona Foundation, Tucson, AZ
20,000	Nature Conservancy, Tucson, AZ
12,500	Tucson Country Day School, Tucson, AZ
3,000	Tucson Children's Museum, Tucson, AZ

FEDERATED MUTUAL INSURANCE CO.

Company Headquarters

121 E. Park Sq.
Owatonna, MN 55060
Web: http://www.federatedinsurance.com

Company Description

Assets: US$3.476 billion (2001)
Employees: 2800 (2003)
SIC(s): 6321 Accident & Health Insurance, 6331 Fire, Marine & Casualty Insurance.

Operating Locations

Federated Mutual Insurance Co. (AZ--Phoenix; GA--Atlanta; MN--Minneapolis, St. Paul)

Federated Mutual Insurance Foundation

Giving Contact

Brian Brose
121 E. Park Sq.
Owatonna, MN 55060
Phone: (507)446-7411

Description

EIN: 237173646
Organization Type: Corporate Foundation

Giving Locations: operating locations, mainly MN.
Grant Types: General Support, Project, Scholarship.

Financial Summary

Total Giving: $282,311 (2003); $264,253 (2002); $541,532 (2001)
Giving Analysis: Giving for 2001 includes: foundation scholarships ($17,100); foundation grants to United Way ($73,000); foundation ($451,432)
Assets: $283,790 (2003); $243,302 (2002); $225,037 (2001)
Gifts Received: $35,355 (2003); $61,031 (2002); $95,385 (2001). Note: Contributions were received from Federated Mutual Insurance Company.

Typical Recipients

Arts & Humanities: Arts Centers, Arts Festivals, Arts Institutes, Community Arts, Arts & Humanities-General, Libraries, Music, Performing Arts, Public Broadcasting, Theater
Civic & Public Affairs: Chambers of Commerce, Clubs, Community Foundations, Economic Development, Civic & Public Affairs-General, Housing, Law & Justice, Municipalities/Towns, Parades/Festivals, Philanthropic Organizations, Professional & Trade Associations, Safety, Urban & Community Affairs, Women's Affairs, Zoos/Aquariums
Education: Afterschool/Enrichment Programs, Business Education, Business-School Partnerships, Colleges & Universities, Economic Education, Education Funds, Education-General, Public Education (Precollege), Science/Mathematics Education, Student Aid
Environment: Environment-General, Watershed, Wildlife Protection
Health: Cancer, Children's Health/Hospitals, Emergency/Ambulance Services, Health-General, Geriatric Health, Health Policy/Cost Containment, Health Funds, Health Organizations, Heart, Home-Care Services, Hospices, Medical Rehabilitation, Medical Research, Multiple Sclerosis, Public Health
Religion: Religious Organizations, Religious Welfare
Social Services: At-Risk Youth, Big Brothers/Big Sisters, Camps, Child Welfare, Community Service Organizations, Emergency Relief, Family Services, Food/Clothing Distribution, People with Disabilities, Recreation & Athletics, Scouts, Senior Services, Shelters/Homelessness, Social Services-General, Special Olympics, Substance Abuse, United Funds/ United Ways, Youth Organizations

Application Procedures

Initial Contact: Send a brief letter of inquiry.
Deadlines: None.
Notes: The foundation has no formal grant application procedure or application form.

Restrictions

Does not support individuals, religious organizations, political or lobbying groups, or organizations outside operating areas.

Corporate Officials

Raymond R. Stawarz: chief financial officer PRIM CORP EMPL chief financial officer: Federated Mutual Insurance Co.

Foundation Officials

A. T. Annexstad: president
A. D. Lewis: secretary
H. J. Moret: vice president
Raymond R. Stawarz: treasurer (see above)
G. J. Stroik: assistant secretary, assistant treasurer

Grants Analysis

Disclosure Period: calendar year ending 2003
Total Grants: $173,071*
Number of Grants: 137
Average Grant: $1,263
Highest Grant: $15,000
Lowest Grant: $100
Typical Range: $500 to $5,000
*Note: Giving excludes scholarship and United Way.

Recent Grants

Note: Grants derived from 2003 Form 990.
Library-Related

5,000	Owatonna Public Library, Owatonna, MN

General

52,500	United Way of Steele County, Owatonna, MN
15,000	Anti-Defamation League
15,000	NFL Alumni Inc., MN
10,000	American Cancer Society, Atlanta, GA
10,000	Grow Minnesota, St. Paul, MN
6,750	United Way of Metropolitan Atlanta Inc., Atlanta, GA
6,000	Big Brothers-Big Sisters of Steele County, Owatonna, MN
5,000	Federated Holiday Classic Basketball & Wrestling Tournament, MN
5,000	Steele County Family to Family, Owatonna, MN
5,000	Valley of the Sun United Way, Phoenix, AZ

FRANK B. AND VIRGINIA V. FEHSENFELD CHARITABLE FOUNDATION

Giving Contact

H. Warren Smith, Vice President
1107 1st Avenue, No. 1404
Seattle, WA 98101
Phone: (206)621-7962

Description

Founded: 1989
EIN: 382775201
Organization Type: Private Foundation
Giving Locations: DC; MI
Grant Types: Emergency, General Support, Multi-year/Continuing Support.

Financial Summary

Total Giving: $96,000 (2004); $119,500 (2001)
Assets: $1,803,016 (2004); $1,789,320 (2001)
Gifts Received: $250,000 (1999) $250,000 (1995); $200,000 (1994). Note: In 1995 and 1999, contributions were received from Frank B. Fehsenfeld.

Typical Recipients

Arts & Humanities: Libraries, Museums/Galleries, Music
Civic & Public Affairs: Botanical Gardens/Parks, Civic & Public Affairs-General, Housing, Urban & Community Affairs
Education: Colleges & Universities, Education-General
Environment: Environment-General, Resource Conservation
Health: Children's Health/Hospitals, Emergency/Ambulance Services, Eyes/Blindness
International: International Environmental Issues
Religion: Religion-General, Ministries, Religious Welfare
Social Services: Camps, Community Centers, Crime Prevention, Emergency Relief, Family Planning, Scouts, United Funds/United Ways, YMCA/YWCA/YMHA/YWHA, Youth Organizations

Application Procedures

Initial Contact: Send a personal letter stating organization's name, address, exempt status, and needs.
Deadlines: None.

Restrictions

Limited to non-private IRC SEC 501 (C)(3) status organizations.

Foundation Officials

Frank B. Fehsenfeld: president, treasurer
John A. Fehsenfeld: trustee
Thomas V. Fehsenfeld: trustee
William S. Fehsenfeld: trustee
Nancy Fehsenfeld Smith: secretary
H. Warren Smith: vice president

Grants Analysis

Disclosure Period: calendar year ending 2004
Total Grants: $96,000
Number of Grants: 40
Average Grant: $2,400
Highest Grant: $10,000
Lowest Grant: $500
Typical Range: $1,000 to $5,000

Recent Grants

Note: Grants derived from 2001 Form 990.
Library-Related

2,000	Ryerson Library Foundation, Grand Rapids, MI -- annual support

General

15,000	Kent County Parks Foundation, Grand Rapids, MI -- annual support
10,000	St. Cecilia Music Society, Grand Rapids, MI -- annual support
6,500	Baxter Community Center, Grand Rapids, MI -- annual support
5,000	Conservation International Foundation, Washington, DC -- annual support
5,000	Eastern Michigan University, Ypsilanti, MI -- annual support
5,000	Grand Rapids Symphony, Grand Rapids, MI -- annual support
5,000	Land Conservancy of West Michigan, Grand Rapids, MI -- annual support
5,000	University of Michigan, Ann Arbor, MI -- annual support
5,000	Wedgwood Christian Youth and Family Services, Grand Rapids, MI -- annual support
4,000	YWCA, Grand Rapids, MI -- annual support

FEINSTEIN FOUNDATION

Giving Contact

Alan S. Feinstein, President
37-41 Alhambra Cir.
Cranston, RI 02905-3416
Phone: (401)467-5155
Web: http://www.feinsteinfoundation.com

Description

Founded: 1991
EIN: 223142312
Organization Type: Private Foundation
Giving Locations: NY; RI
Grant Types: Emergency, General Support, Scholarship.

Donor Information

Founder: Alan S. Feinstein

Financial Summary

Total Giving: $521,770 (2003); $1,875,120 (2001)
Giving Analysis: Giving for 2003 includes: foundation scholarships ($25,475) 2001: foundation grants to United Way ($7,500)
Assets: $38,126,819 (2003); $32,010,979 (2001)
Gifts Received: $135,881 (2003); $135,741 (2000); $226,429 (1998). Note: In 2003, contributions were received from American Rare Coin. In 1998 and 2000, contributions were received from Alan Shaw Feinstein. In 1994, contributions were received from Alan Shawn Feinstein ($147,611).

Typical Recipients

Arts & Humanities: Libraries, Theater
Civic & Public Affairs: Community Foundations, Civic & Public Affairs-General, Municipalities/Towns, Philanthropic Organizations, Public Policy, Urban & Community Affairs
Education: Colleges & Universities, Education Funds, Education-General, Private Education (Pre-college), Public Education (Precollege), Science/Mathematics Education, Secondary Education (Public), Student Aid
International: International Organizations
Religion: Religious Welfare
Social Services: Child Welfare, Community Centers, Community Service Organizations, Counseling, Family Services, Homes, People with Disabilities, Recreation & Athletics, Scouts, United Funds/United Ways, Youth Organizations

Application Procedures

Initial Contact: The foundation has no formal application procedure.
Application Requirements: Submit an application in any format.
Deadlines: None.

Foundation Officials

Alan Shawn Feinstein: president, director B Boston, MA 1931. ED Boston University BS (1952); Boston State College MS (1956); Johnson & Wales University PhD (1994); Providence College PhD (1995). NONPR AFFIL chairman: Cranston Crime Stoppers; founder: Providence College Institute Public Service.
Edward Walton: director

Grants Analysis

Disclosure Period: calendar year ending 2003
Total Grants: $496,295*
Number of Grants: 10
Highest Grant: $162,436
Lowest Grant: $9,328
Typical Range: $7,500 to $50,000
***Note:** Giving excludes scholarships.

Recent Grants

Note: Grants derived from 2001 Form 990.
General

477,471	Johnson and Wales University, Providence, RI
409,000	University of Rhode Island, Kingston, RI
300,000	International Scholar Athletes
250,000	Chamber Education Program
125,068	Klein Foundation
100,000	University of Rhode Island, Kingston, RI -- Hunger Center
50,000	International Institute of Rhode Island, Providence, RI
10,000	United Way
7,500	Boy Scouts, Rochester, NY

SAMUEL S. FELS FUND

Giving Contact

Helen Cunningham, Executive Director & Secretary
1616 Walnut St., Suite 800
Philadelphia, PA 19103
Phone: (215)731-9455
Fax: (215)731-9457
Web: http://www.samfels.org

Description

Founded: 1935
EIN: 231365325
Organization Type: General Purpose Foundation
Giving Locations: PA: Philadelphia
Grant Types: General Support, Matching, Multiyear/Continuing Support, Operating Expenses, Project, Seed Money.

Donor Information

Founder: Samuel S. Fels established the fund in 1935. Mr. Fels, a Philadelphia philanthropist, civic leader, and president of a soap manufacturing company, was born in Yanceyville, NC, in 1860. He died in Philadelphia in 1950.

Financial Summary

Total Giving: $2,298,919 (2003); $2,211,880 (2002); $3,455,874 (2001)

Giving Analysis: Giving for 2003 includes: foundation grants to United Way ($20,000); 2001: foundation grants to United Way ($25,000).

Assets: $39,638,953 (2002); $49,017,145 (2001)

Gifts Received: GIV Civic Affairs, social services, arts, and education.

Typical Recipients

Arts & Humanities: Arts Associations & Councils, Arts Centers, Arts Festivals, Ballet, Community Arts, Dance, Ethnic & Folk Arts, Arts & Humanities-General, Historic Preservation, History & Archaeology, Libraries, Museums/Galleries, Music, Opera, Performing Arts, Public Broadcasting, Theater, Visual Arts

Civic & Public Affairs: African American Affairs, Asian American Affairs, Botanical Gardens/Parks, Business/Free Enterprise, Civil Rights, Clubs, Economic Development, Economic Policy, Employment/Job Training, Ethnic Organizations, Gay/Lesbian Issues, Civic & Public Affairs-General, Hispanic Affairs, Housing, Inner-City Development, Law & Justice, Legal Aid, Nonprofit Management, Philanthropic Organizations, Public Policy, Urban & Community Affairs, Women's Affairs, Zoos/Aquariums

Education: Afterschool/Enrichment Programs, Arts/Humanities Education, Business Education, Colleges & Universities, Community & Junior Colleges, Continuing Education, Education Funds, Education Reform, Faculty Development, Education-General, Literacy, Minority Education, Private Education (Precollege), Public Education (Precollege), School Volunteerism, Social Sciences Education, Student Aid

Environment: Air/Water Quality, Energy, Environment-General

Health: Adolescent Health Issues, AIDS/HIV, Cancer, Children's Health/Hospitals, Clinics/Medical Centers, Diabetes, Emergency/Ambulance Services, Health Organizations, Home-Care Services, Hospitals, Long-Term Care, Medical Research, Nursing Services, Nutrition, Prenatal Health Issues, Public Health

International: Foreign Arts Organizations, International Affairs, International Organizations, International Relations

Religion: Churches, Jewish Causes, Ministries, Religious Organizations, Religious Welfare

Science: Science Museums, Scientific Centers & Institutes

Social Services: At-Risk Youth, Big Brothers/Big Sisters, Child Abuse, Child Welfare, Community Centers, Community Service Organizations, Crime Prevention, Day Care, Delinquency & Criminal Rehabilitation, Domestic Violence, Family Planning, Family Services, Food/Clothing Distribution, Homes, People with Disabilities, Recreation & Athletics, Refugee Assistance, Senior Services, Shelters/Homelessness, Social Services-General, United Funds/United Ways, Veterans, YMCA/YWCA/YMHA/YWHA, Youth Organizations

Application Procedures

Initial Contact: Organizations may call for further clarification as to whether a project falls within the foundation's priorities, and for a copy of the guidelines and proposal cover sheet. A preliminary letter or abbreviated proposal is not recommended; only complete proposals using the Delaware Valley Grantmakers Common Application Form will be accepted.

Application Requirements: Proposals should include the cover sheet, summary of the proposal (one page or less), and the actual proposal (five pages). In addition, a description of organization's purpose, history, goals, activities, and constituency is required. Funding plans and a program evaluation plan should also be included. The resumes of top staff, the addresses and occupations of the board of directors, budget, funding sources, financial statement, annual report, and proof of tax-exempt status are also required.

Deadlines: Deadlines for arts applications are January 15 and May 15. There are no deadlines for other applications.

Review Process: The board meets eight times a year. Proposals can usually be reviewed within two months. Notification is usually within two weeks after a decision.

Restrictions

The fund does not make grants to individuals, or for conferences, scholarships, fellowships or travel. Ordinarily, the fund also avoids making grants for major programs of large institutions, capital and equipment, endowment, and the routine or direct services of social service agencies. Individual day care and after school programs cannot be accommodated, although agencies that serve these fields may apply.

Additional Information

A written report is required on every grant received, to the satisfaction of the board. Organizations which do not fulfill this requirement will not be considered for subsequent grants.

The foundation allows its offices to be used as a meeting place for local nonprofit groups.

Publications: Annual Report; Guidelines; Application Form

Foundation Officials

Iso Briselli: board member OCCUPATION concert violinist. NONPR AFFIL member: Pennsylvania Council Arts.

Daniel W. Burke: board member B Pittsburgh, PA 1926. ED Catholic University America BA (1949); Catholic University America MA (1952); Catholic University America PhD (1957). PRIM CORP EMPL professor: LaSalle University. NONPR AFFIL member: Phi Beta Kappa; trustee emeritus: University Bethlehem; member: Modern Language Association; professor, art mus director: LaSalle University; trustee emeritus: Manhattan College; executive director: Catholic Commission on Cultural & Intellectual Affairs.

Ida K. Chen: board member, treasurer

Helen Cunningham: executive director, secretary

Sandra Featherman, PhD: vice president, director B Philadelphia, PA 1934. ED University of Pennsylvania BA (1955); University of Pennsylvania PhD (1978); University of Pennsylvania MA (1978). PRIM NONPR EMPL director, president: University New England. NONPR AFFIL president: Maine Independent Colleges Association; president: Pennsylvania Federation Chamber of Congress; director: Guild Maine Aquarium; director: Kennebec Girl Scout Council; member: American Political Science Association; member: Greater Portland Alliance Colleges Universitys; member: AAUW; board governors member executive committee: American Association Colleges Osteopathic Medicine.

David C. Melnicoff: board member

Emanuel Ortiz: board member

Mindy M. Posoff: board member

Anthony Santomero: board member

David Herschel Wice: board member, president B Petersburg, VA February 01, 1908. ED Washington & Lee University AB (1927); Washington & Lee University MA (1928); Hebrew Union College DHL (1933); Washington & Lee University DD (1948). OCCUPATION rabbi. NONPR AFFIL director: Jewish Community Relations; director: Union American Hebrew Congregations New Ams; co-chairman: Hebrew Union College; director: Family Services Association America; director: Federation Jewish Agencies; director: Council Jewish Education; member: Council Religion Independent Schools; member: Central Conference American Rabbis; rabbi emeritus: Congregation Rodeph Shalom, Philadelphia.

Grants Analysis

Disclosure Period: calendar year ending 2003

Total Grants: $2,278,919*

Number of Grants: 198

Average Grant: $11,510

Highest Grant: $150,000

Lowest Grant: $1,000

Typical Range: $1,000 to $20,000

*Note:** Giving excludes United Way.

Recent Grants

Note: Grants derived from 2002 Form 990.

Library-Related

15,000	Friends of the Free Library of Philadelphia, Philadelphia, PA -- towards salary of a branch group coordinator

General

200,000	Regional Performing Arts Center Inc., Philadelphia, PA -- towards new Orchestra Concert Hall
166,000	Franklin Institute, Philadelphia, PA -- towards renovation and modernization of the Fels Planetarium
125,000	Fels Institute for Cancer Research and Molecular Biology, Philadelphia, PA -- towards support for new faculty
50,000	Good Schools Pennsylvania, Philadelphia, PA -- to campaign for public school equity
38,400	Asociacion De Musicos Latino Americanos Inc., Philadelphia, PA -- to fund booking agent position
34,404	Philadelphia Health Management Corporation, Philadelphia, PA -- towards evaluational study on breaking the cycle of homelessness and poverty
30,000	Caring People Alliance, Philadelphia, PA -- towards summer career exploration program
30,000	Evangelical Lutheran Church in America, Philadelphia, PA -- towards Southeast Philadelphia community technology collaborative
30,000	Public Interest Law Center of Philadelphia, Philadelphia, PA -- towards public education advocacy
25,000	Alliance Organizing Project for Educational Reform, Philadelphia, PA

FENTON FOUNDATION

Giving Contact

Frank M. Fenton, Treasurer & Director
310 W. 4th St.
Williamstown, WV 26187
Phone: (304)375-6122

Description

Founded: 1955

EIN: 556017260

Organization Type: Private Foundation

Giving Locations: OH: Washington County; WV: Wood County

Grant Types: General Support.

Financial Summary

Total Giving: $93,653 (2003)

Giving Analysis: Giving for 2003 includes: foundation scholarships ($12,013)

Assets: $3,269,946 (2003)

Gifts Received: $11,733 (2003); $62,559 (2000); $190,762 (1999). Note: In 2000 and 2003, contributions were received from Fenton Gift Shops, Inc. In

1999, contributions were received from Fenton Gift Shops ($62,452) and Fenton Art Glass Co. ($128,310). In 1996, contributions were received from Fenton Gift Shops ($23,935) and Fenton Art Glass Co. ($38,530).

Typical Recipients

Arts & Humanities: Arts Associations & Councils, Arts Centers, Film & Video, Arts & Humanities-General, Libraries, Museums/Galleries, Music, Performing Arts

Civic & Public Affairs: Clubs, Community Foundations, Economic Development, Civic & Public Affairs-General, Municipalities/Towns, Safety, Urban & Community Affairs, Women's Affairs

Education: Arts/Humanities Education, Business-School Partnerships, Colleges & Universities, Education Funds, Education Reform, Elementary Education (Public), Education-General, International Exchange, Medical Education, Private Education (Precollege), Public Education (Precollege), School Volunteerism, Science/Mathematics Education, Secondary Education (Public)

Health: Alzheimer's Disease, Children's Health/Hospitals, Clinics/Medical Centers, Emergency/Ambulance Services, Health-General, Health Organizations, Hospices, Hospitals, Public Health, Research/Studies Institutes, Single-Disease Health Associations

International: Foreign Arts Organizations

Religion: Churches, Religious Organizations, Religious Welfare

Social Services: Child Welfare, Community Service Organizations, Homes, People with Disabilities, Recreation & Athletics, Scouts, Senior Services, Substance Abuse, United Funds/United Ways, Volunteer Services, YMCA/YWCA/YMHA/YWHA

Application Procedures

Initial Contact: Send a brief letter of inquiry.
Deadlines: None.

Restrictions

Does not support individuals.

Foundation Officials

Frank M. Fenton: treasurer, director
Thomas K. Fenton: president, director

Grants Analysis

Disclosure Period: calendar year ending 2003
Total Grants: $81,640*
Number of Grants: 59
Average Grant: $1,235*
Highest Grant: $10,000
Lowest Grant: $100
Typical Range: $500 to $3,000
*Note: Giving excludes United Way. Average grant figure excludes highest grant.

Recent Grants

Note: Grants derived from 2001 Form 990.
General

25,000	First United Methodist Church, Williamstown, WV
25,000	Marietta College, Marietta, OH
8,500	Williamstown United Way, Williamstown, WV
7,500	West Virginia Foundation for Independent Colleges, Charleston, WV
5,000	Williamstown High School, Williamstown, WV
4,500	Spring Heights Education Center, Charleston, WV
4,100	City of Williamstown, Williamstown, WV
4,000	Artsbridge, Parkersburg, WV
4,000	Artsbridge, Parkersburg, WV
3,500	Greater Marietta United Way, Marietta, OH

EUGENE AND ESTELLE FERKAUF FOUNDATION

Giving Contact

Barbara Dor, Trustee
67 Allenwood Rd.
Great Neck, NY 11023
Phone: (516)773-3269

Description

Founded: 1967
EIN: 132621094
Organization Type: Private Foundation
Grant Types: General Support, Multiyear/Continuing Support, Research.

Donor Information

Founder: Eugene Ferkauf, Estelle Ferkauf

Financial Summary

Total Giving: $230,400 (2003)
Assets: $5,369,891 (2003)

Typical Recipients

Arts & Humanities: Arts Funds, History & Archaeology, Libraries, Museums/Galleries, Music, Performing Arts, Public Broadcasting, Theater

Civic & Public Affairs: Botanical Gardens/Parks, Civil Rights, Civic & Public Affairs-General

Education: Colleges & Universities, Continuing Education, Private Education (Precollege), Religious Education, Special Education

Health: AIDS/HIV, Cancer, Children's Health/Hospitals, Health Organizations, Heart, Hospitals, Hospitals (University Affiliated), Long-Term Care, Medical Rehabilitation, Medical Research, Mental Health, Research/Studies Institutes, Single-Disease Health Associations

International: Foreign Educational Institutions, Health Care/Hospitals, International Relief Efforts, Missionary/Religious Activities

Religion: Religion-General, Jewish Causes, Religious Organizations, Synagogues/Temples

Social Services: Child Welfare, Community Centers, Community Service Organizations, Family Services, People with Disabilities, Social Services-General, Substance Abuse, YMCA/YWCA/YMHA/YWHA

Application Procedures

Initial Contact: Send a brief letter of inquiry describing program or project.
Deadlines: None.

Additional Information

Publications: Application Guidelines

Foundation Officials

Lenore Bronstein: trustee
Robert Bronstein: trustee
Richard M. Dicke, Esq.: trustee
Barbara Dor: trustee
Benny Dor: trustee
Estelle Ferkauf: trustee
Eugene Ferkauf: trustee
Amy Shapira: trustee
Israel Shapira: trustee

Grants Analysis

Disclosure Period: calendar year ending 2003
Total Grants: $230,400
Number of Grants: 53
Average Grant: $3,662*
Highest Grant: $40,000
Lowest Grant: $100
Typical Range: $1,000 to $5,000
*Note: Average grant figure excludes highest grant.

Recent Grants

Note: Grants derived from 2001 Form 990.

Library-Related

5,000	Standing Tall, Inc., New York, NY

General

40,000	Jewish Federation of Broward County, Inc., Ft. Lauderdale, FL
27,800	United Jewish Appeal Federation, New York, NY
27,750	Gift of Life, Boynton Beach, FL
20,650	Little Neck Jewish Center, Queens, NY
12,000	Chabad of Great Neck, Great Neck, NY
10,000	Project Judaica, Washington, DC
10,000	Sephardic Home for the Aged, Brooklyn, NY
9,000	Hill Crest Jewish Center, Flushing, NY
6,000	Tracy Fleisher Memorial Fund, Queens, NY
5,000	Aleph Society, New York, NY

FERRIDAY FUND CHARITABLE TRUST

Giving Contact

Douglas J. Boyle
c/o Bank of New York
1290 Ave. of the Americas, 5th Floor
New York, NY 10104
Phone: (212)635-1520

Description

Founded: 1991
EIN: 136967609
Organization Type: Private Foundation
Grant Types: General Support.

Donor Information

Founder: Established in 1991 by the late Carolyn Ferriday.

Financial Summary

Total Giving: $522,645 (fiscal year ending July 31, 2004); $741,750 (fiscal 2001)
Assets: $9,846,606 (fiscal 2004); $11,816,927 (fiscal 2001)
Gifts Received: $150,000 (fiscal 2001); $187,596 (fiscal 1994). Note: In 2001, contributions were received from Milena Knoll Unit-Trust.

Typical Recipients

Arts & Humanities: Arts Associations & Councils, Arts & Humanities-General, Historic Preservation, History & Archaeology, Libraries, Public Broadcasting, Theater

Civic & Public Affairs: African American Affairs, Civic & Public Affairs-General, Law & Justice, Native American Affairs, Public Policy

Education: Business Education, Colleges & Universities, Education Funds, Legal Education, Literacy, Medical Education, Private Education (Precollege), Secondary Education (Private)

Environment: Protection, Resource Conservation

Health: Clinics/Medical Centers, Health-General, Hospitals, Hospitals (University Affiliated), Single-Disease Health Associations

International: Health Care/Hospitals, International Relations

Religion: Churches, Jewish Causes, Religious Welfare

Social Services: At-Risk Youth, Child Welfare, People with Disabilities

Application Procedures

Initial Contact: Send a brief letter of inquiry.
Deadlines: None.

Additional Information

Trust(s): Bank of New York

Foundation Officials
Richard J. Carter, Jr.: trustee

Grants Analysis
Disclosure Period: fiscal year ending July 31, 2004
Total Grants: $522,645
Number of Grants: 79
Average Grant: $6,060*
Highest Grant: $50,000
Lowest Grant: $1,000
Typical Range: $1,000 to $10,000
*Note: Average grant figure excludes highest grant.

Recent Grants
Note: Grants derived from 2000 Form 990.
Library-Related

10,000	Westport Library

General

20,000	Antiquarian & Landmarks Society Inc, New York, NY
20,000	University of Notre Dame, Notre Dame, IN
15,000	Antiquarian & Landmarks Society Inc, New York, NY
10,000	Fordham University School of Law, New York, NY
10,000	Fordham University School of Law, New York, NY
10,000	Hope Worldwide
10,000	IGHL Foundation
10,000	Little Sisters of the Assumption, New York, NY
10,000	Student Conservation Association, Washington, DC
10,000	University of Notre Dame, Notre Dame, IN

FIDELITY INVESTMENTS

Company Headquarters
Boston, MA
Web: http://www.fidelity.com

Company Description
Employees: 7,000
SIC(s): 6719 Holding Companies Nec, 6722 Management Investment--Open-End.
Parent Company: FMR Corp., 82 Devonshire Street, Boston, MA, United States

Operating Locations
Fidelity Investments (KY--Covington; MA--Boston; OH--Cincinnati; TX--Dallas)

Fidelity Foundation

Giving Contact
Margaret H. Morton, Vice President, Program
Fidelity Foundation
82 Devonshire Street S3
Boston, MA 02109
Phone: (617)563-6806
Fax: (617)476-4234
Web: http://www.fidelityfoundation.org

Description
EIN: 046131201
Organization Type: Corporate Foundation
Former Name: Fidelity Investments Charitable Gift Fund Foundation, Inc.
Giving Locations: KY: Covington; MA: Boston, Marlborough; NH: Merrimack; NY: New York; RI: Smithfield; TX: Dallas; UT: Salt Lake City; Canada : Toronto, ON
Grant Types: Capital, Employee Matching Gifts, Endowment, Matching, Project, Research.

Note: Employee matching gift ratio: 2 to 1, up to $1,000; 1 to 1 for $1,000 to $3,500.

Donor Information
Founder: FMR Corp.

Financial Summary
Total Giving: $11,946,743 (2003); $16,589,652 (2002); $20,209,004 (2001). Note: Contributes through foundation only.
Assets: $313,159,282 (2003); $258,548,760 (2002); $306,283,121 (2001)
Gifts Received: $275,792 (2002); $1,769,954 (2001); $38,692,968 (2000). Note: In 2002, contributions were received from Fidelity Ventures Ltd. Contributions are received from FMR Corp. and Fidelity Investors L.P.

Typical Recipients
Arts & Humanities: Art History, Arts Associations & Councils, Arts Centers, Arts Festivals, Arts Funds, Arts Institutes, Arts Outreach, Ballet, Arts & Humanities-General, Historic Preservation, History & Archaeology, Libraries, Museums/Galleries, Music, Opera, Performing Arts, Theater
Civic & Public Affairs: African American Affairs, Asian American Affairs, Business/Free Enterprise, Community Foundations, Economic Development, Economic Policy, Employment/Job Training, Gay/Lesbian Issues, Civic & Public Affairs-General, Housing, Legal Aid, Municipalities/Towns, Native American Affairs, Nonprofit Management, Parades/Festivals, Philanthropic Organizations, Public Policy, Urban & Community Affairs, Women's Affairs, Zoos/Aquariums
Education: Afterschool/Enrichment Programs, Arts/Humanities Education, Business Education, Colleges & Universities, Education Funds, Education Reform, Elementary Education (Private), Education-General, Leadership Training, Literacy, Preschool Education, Private Education (Precollege)
Environment: Environment-General, Protection, Resource Conservation
Health: AIDS/HIV, Cancer, Children's Health/Hospitals, Clinics/Medical Centers, Health Funds, Health Organizations, Hospices, Hospitals, Medical Research, Mental Health, Nursing Services
International: Foreign Arts Organizations, Foreign Educational Institutions, International-General, Health Care/Hospitals, International Environmental Issues, International Organizations, International Relations, International Relief Efforts
Religion: Churches, Dioceses, Religion-General, Religious Organizations, Religious Welfare
Science: Science Museums, Scientific Centers & Institutes, Scientific Labs
Social Services: At-Risk Youth, Big Brothers/Big Sisters, Camps, Child Abuse, Child Welfare, Community Service Organizations, Counseling, Family Services, Food/Clothing Distribution, People with Disabilities, Recreation & Athletics, Scouts, Senior Services, Shelters/Homelessness, Social Services-General, United Funds/United Ways, Volunteer Services, YMCA/YWCA/YMHA/YWHA, Youth Organizations

Application Procedures
Initial Contact: Send a letter of request.
Application Requirements: Include foundation's project summary form; itemized project budget; recent audited financial statements; IRS 501(c)(3) determination letter; history of organization, including objectives and programs; list of officers and directors and their affiliations; list of other funders and status of requests; current operating budget; and a description of request and rationale.
Deadlines: March 30 to receive decision by August 1, and September 30 to receive decision by February 1.
Evaluative Criteria: The foundation seeks evidence of institutional commitment to the project on behalf of the organization's board; a realistic project budget; a

thorough implementation plan, including a plan for performance measurement; net value to the organization and the community it serves; significant support from other funders; and other criteria. Also considered are the organization's financial health; the strength of its management team and board; and evidence of an overall strategic plan.
Notes: Contact the foundation to receive a project summary form. Applications should not be sent in folders, binders or packaging. Limit press clippings and background materials to five pages.

Restrictions
Foundation does not make multi-year grants or award grants to an organization in successive years. Foundation does not make grants to individuals, sectarian or civic organizations, start-up organizations, public school systems, disease-specific organizations, for operating support, scholarships, video or film projects, sponsorships, benefit events or for memberships. Grants do not generally support an entire project's cost. Applicants to the Fidelity Foundation cannot submit simultaneous proposals to the Edward C. Johnson Fund or the Fidelity Non-Profit Management Foundation.

Additional Information
Fidelity Investments created the foundation in 1965 in order to represent the company's philanthropic interests in the communities where it does business.

Foundation Officials
Thomas J. Eberhardt: assistant treasurer
Patricia R. Hurley: secretary
Abigail P. Johnson: director
Edward C. Johnson, III: director, president
Jeffrey P. Resnik: treasurer
Ross E. Sherbrooke: director
Melanie S. Sommer: assistant secretary
Anne-Marie Soulliere: director NONPR AFFIL advisory board: Center for Effective Philanthropy; board of directors: New England Conservatory of Music.

Grants Analysis
Disclosure Period: calendar year ending 2003
Total Grants: $9,891,786*
Number of Grants: 144
Average Grant: $42,084*
Highest Grant: $2,500,000
Lowest Grant: $250
Typical Range: $10,000 to $100,000
*Note: Giving excludes matching gifts; United Way; scholarship. Average grant figure excludes four highest grants ($4,000,000).

Recent Grants
Note: Grants derived from 2003 Form 990.
Library-Related

100,000	Concord Free Public Library Corporation, Concord, MA -- funds for renovation

General

500,000	Boston Symphony Orchestra Inc., Boston, MA
500,000	Children's Museum, Boston, MA -- funds for museum exhibitions
500,000	Museum of Fine Arts, Boston, MA -- funds for museum exhibitions
414,212	Society for the Preservation of New England Antiquities, Boston, MA -- funds for museum exhibitions
250,000	Museum of Fine Arts, Boston, MA -- funds for museum exhibitions
250,000	Museum of Fine Arts, Boston, MA -- funds for museum exhibitions
150,000	Children's Museum, Boston, MA -- funds for museum exhibitions
150,000	Westminster College, Salt Lake City, UT
140,000	Boston Baroque Inc., Cambridge, MA -- funds for performances
100,000	Cincinnati Museum Association, Cincinnati, OH -- funds for renovation

FIELD FOUNDATION OF ILLINOIS

Giving Contact

Handy Lindsey, Jr., President
200 South Wacker Dr., Suite 3860
Chicago, IL 60606
Phone: (312)831-0910
Fax: (312)831-0961
E-mail: hlindsey@fieldfoundation.org
Web: http://www.fieldfoundation.org

Description

Founded: 1960
EIN: 366059408
Organization Type: General Purpose Foundation
Giving Locations: IL: Chicago including metropolitan area
Grant Types: Capital, Employee Matching Gifts, General Support, Matching, Operating Expenses, Project.

Donor Information

Founder: The foundation was established in 1960, with the late Marshall Field IV as donor.

Financial Summary

Total Giving: $1,000,000 (fiscal year ending April 30, 2002 approx); $1,900,088 (fiscal 2001)
Assets: $50,924,371 (fiscal 2001)

Typical Recipients

Arts & Humanities: Arts Associations & Councils, Arts Institutes, Dance, Ethnic & Folk Arts, Libraries, Museums/Galleries, Music, Opera, Public Broadcasting, Theater
Civic & Public Affairs: Asian American Affairs, Civil Rights, Clubs, Community Foundations, Economic Development, Employment/Job Training, Ethnic Organizations, Civic & Public Affairs-General, Housing, Law & Justice, Legal Aid, Municipalities/Towns, Nonprofit Management, Parades/Festivals, Philanthropic Organizations, Professional & Trade Associations, Public Policy, Urban & Community Affairs, Women's Affairs, Zoos/Aquariums
Education: Arts/Humanities Education, Colleges & Universities, Education Funds, Elementary Education (Private), Elementary Education (Public), Faculty Development, Education-General, Literacy, Medical Education, Preschool Education, Public Education (Precollege), Science/Mathematics Education, Secondary Education (Public), Social Sciences Education, Student Aid
Environment: Environment-General, Protection, Resource Conservation
Health: AIDS/HIV, Children's Health/Hospitals, Clinics/Medical Centers, Emergency/Ambulance Services, Health Organizations, Heart, Hospitals, Hospitals (University Affiliated), Medical Rehabilitation, Prenatal Health Issues, Public Health
International: Foreign Educational Institutions
Religion: Ministries, Religious Welfare
Science: Science Museums, Scientific Centers & Institutes, Scientific Organizations
Social Services: Big Brothers/Big Sisters, Child Welfare, Community Centers, Community Service Organizations, Crime Prevention, Day Care, Delinquency & Criminal Rehabilitation, Domestic Violence, Family Services, Food/Clothing Distribution, People with Disabilities, Recreation & Athletics, Sexual Abuse, Shelters/Homelessness, Social Services-General, Substance Abuse, United Funds/United Ways, Volunteer Services, YMCA/YWCA/YMHA/YWHA, Youth Organizations

Application Procedures

Initial Contact: Written requests should be addressed to the foundation. The foundation has a prospective grantees checklist that organizations should request, which will aid in writing a proposal and in determining if the organization fits the criteria to apply.
Application Requirements: Proposal should be accompanied by a cover letter briefly describing the project, the proposed budget, and the history and background of the applicant. Applications should be accompanied by a copy of the organization's IRS determination letter of tax-exempt status, and a list of the membership of the board of directors and their affiliations.
Deadlines: January 15, May 15, September 15.
Review Process: The board meets three times per year, in May, September, and January; the grant evaluation process begins approximately four months before each meeting. A response to all inquiries is provided as quickly as possible.
Notes: For the general grant program, operating support generally is restricted from one to three years; continuing operating support is not considered. Applications for grants from hospitals normally will be considered only if the applicant has a broad teaching and research program; conducts a comprehensive clinic service and provides a substantial amount of free care; has sufficient full-time clinicians in various specialties to secure good teaching and investigation; and if the specific project has distinctive importance or the promise of a unique cont ribution to medicine and/or medical education in Chicago.

Restrictions

Grants are not made to United Way of Chicago member agencies, or to member agencies of other United Ways in the metropolitan area for regular operating support; to endowments; to individuals; for medical research or national health agency appeals; for propaganda or to influence legislation; to fund conferences, seminars, or meetings; to cover costs of printed materials or video equipment; for elimination of accumulated operating deficit; for disease-specific voluntary associations; for theater programs other than outreach to disadvantaged students; for fund-raising events or advertising; for religious purposes; to other grantmaking agencies or foundations for ultimate distribution to agencies or programs of its own choosing; or for operating support of neighborhood health centers or clinics, day care centers for children, or small cultural groups. For the Primary and Secondary Education Grants Program, the foundation does not support scholarships, new building construction, centralized parenting training, city-wide advocacy efforts, endowment campaigns, degree-granting programs for teachers, repairs or improvements to public schools, or general operating needs of schools or of local school councils. An entity will be eligible to receive no more than one (1) grant from the Foundation during a fiscal year of the Foundarion.

Additional Information

In addition to its grant-making activities, the foundation also provides technical assistance to charitable organizations.
Publications: Grant Guidelines and Application Procedures; Grant Guidelines and Application Procedures: Primary and Secondary School Education; Annual Report; Self-Certification Checklist for Prospective Grantees

Foundation Officials

Berlean M. Burris: director
Milton Austin Davis: director PRIM CORP EMPL vice president, director: Shorebank Corp. CORP AFFIL partner: Williams Street Building Partnership.
Marshall Field, IV: director B Charlottesville, VA 1941. ED Harvard University BA (1963). PRIM CORP EMPL chairman: Field Corp. CORP AFFIL chairman, chief executive officer, senior director: Cabot Cabot & Forbes Investment Co. NONPR AFFIL chairman: Rush-Presbyterian-Saint Lukes Medical Center; director: World Wildlife Federation; member: Nature Conservancy; vice chairman, trustee: Field Museum Natural History; director: Lincoln Park Zoological Society; trustee: Chicago Public Library Foundation; director: Field Foundation; active: Chicago Orchestral Association; director: Atlantic Salmon Association; member advisory board: Brookfield Zoo; trustee: Art Institute of Chicago. CLUB AFFIL Shoreacres Club; Racquet Club; River Club; Jupiter Island Club; Onwentsia Club; Harvard Club; Chicago Club; Commercial Club.
Philip Wayne Hummer: director B 1931. PRIM CORP EMPL principal: Wayne Hummer Investments LLC.
Gary H. Kline: secretary
Handy L. Lindsey, Jr.: president
George A. Ranney, Jr.: director B Chicago, IL 1940. ED Harvard University BA (1962); University of Chicago JD (1966). PRIM CORP EMPL partner: Mayer, Brown & Platt PRIM NONPR EMPL president, chief executive officer: Chicago Metropolis 2020. NONPR AFFIL chairman: Task Force on the Future of Illinois; trustee: University Chicago; member: Commerce Counsel Network; trustee: Newberry Library; past president: Chicago Metropolis 2020; trustee: Chicago Public Television; member: American Bar Association; member: Chicago Bar Association.
Tina Tchen: director

Grants Analysis

Disclosure Period: fiscal year ending April 30, 2001
Total Grants: $1,900,088
Number of Grants: 253
Average Grant: $7,510
Highest Grant: $50,000
Lowest Grant: $4,000
Typical Range: $5,000 to $10,000

Recent Grants

Note: Grants derived from fiscal 2002 Form 990.
General

50,000	University of Chicago Hospitals, Chicago, IL -- scholarships for Health administration studies
25,000	Muntu Dance Theatre of Chicago, Chicago, IL -- sponsoring for construction of center for performing arts
25,000	Muntu Dance Theatre of Chicago, Chicago, IL -- sponsoring for construction of center for performing arts
25,000	Muntu Dance Theatre of Chicago, Chicago, IL -- sponsoring for construction of center for performing arts
18,750	Chicago Zoological Society, Brookfield, IL -- financial support for electrical infrastructure renovation plan
18,750	Chicago Zoological Society, Brookfield, IL -- financial support for electrical infrastructure renovation plan
18,750	Chicago Zoological Society, Brookfield, IL -- financial support for electrical infrastructure renovation plan
18,750	Chicago Zoological Society, Brookfield, IL -- financial support for electrical infrastructure renovation plan
12,500	Cambodian Association of Illinois, Chicago, IL -- towards Cambodian community center
12,500	Cambodian Association of Illinois, Chicago, IL -- towards Cambodian community center

FIFTH THIRD BANCORP

Company Headquarters

Fifth Third Center
38 Fountain Sq. Plz.
Cincinnati, OH 45263
Web: http://www.53.com

Company Description

Founded: 1900
Ticker: FITB
Exchange: NASDAQ
Acquired: Old Kent Financial Corp..
Revenue: US$6.579 billion (2004)
Profit: US$1.525 billion (2004)
Employees: 20211 (2003)
Fortune Rank: 317, per FORTUNE Magazine's list of 500 Largest U.S. Corporations (2004).
SIC(s): 6022 State Commercial Banks, 6712 Bank Holding Companies.

Operating Locations

Fifth Third Bancorp (AZ--Scottsdale; FL--Naples; IN--Indianapolis; KY--Florence, Louisville; OH--Cincinnati, Cleveland, Columbus, Dublin, Hamilton, Hillsboro, Toledo)

Fifth Third Foundation

Giving Contact

Lawra Baumann, Foundation Officer
38 Fountain Square Plaza
Dept. 00864
Cincinnati, OH 45263
Phone: (513)579-6034
Fax: (513)579-5461

Description

EIN: 316024135
Organization Type: Corporate Foundation
Giving Locations: OH: Cincinnati including metropolitan area
Grant Types: Capital, Conference/Seminar, Employee Matching Gifts, General Support, Project, Scholarship.
Note: Matches gifts to education.

Financial Summary

Total Giving: $9,518,320 (fiscal year ending September 30, 2003); $6,715,761 (fiscal 2001). Note: Contributes through foundation only.
Giving Analysis: Giving for fiscal 2003 includes: foundation scholarships ($325,000); foundation grants to United Way ($1,722,678); fiscal 2001: foundation matching gifts ($138,105); foundation grants to United Way ($1,445,004); foundation ($5,132,652)
Assets: $20,700,163 (fiscal 2003); $43,334,782 (fiscal 2001)
Gifts Received: $1,050,000 (fiscal 1996); $1,800,000 (fiscal 1995); $1,800,000 (fiscal 1994). Note: Contributions were received from Fifth Third Bank.

Typical Recipients

Arts & Humanities: Arts Associations & Councils, Arts Centers, Arts Festivals, Arts Funds, Arts Institutes, Community Arts, Arts & Humanities-General, Historic Preservation, Museums/Galleries, Music, Opera, Performing Arts, Public Broadcasting, Theater
Civic & Public Affairs: African American Affairs, Botanical Gardens/Parks, Business/Free Enterprise, Chambers of Commerce, Civil Rights, Clubs, Community Foundations, Economic Development, Employment/Job Training, Civic & Public Affairs-General, Housing, Inner-City Development, Law & Justice, Minority Business, Municipalities/Towns, Parades/Festivals, Urban & Community Affairs, Women's Affairs, Zoos/Aquariums
Education: Arts/Humanities Education, Business Education, Colleges & Universities, Community & Junior Colleges, Economic Education, Education Funds, Engineering/Technological Education, Education-General, Medical Education, Private Education (Precollege), Public Education (Precollege), Religious Education, Secondary Education (Public), Special Education, Student Aid
Environment: Protection

Health: Children's Health/Hospitals, Emergency/Ambulance Services, Health Funds, Health Organizations, Hospices, Hospitals, Medical Rehabilitation, Single-Disease Health Associations, Speech & Hearing
Religion: Jewish Causes, Ministries, Religious Organizations, Religious Welfare
Science: Science-General, Scientific Centers & Institutes
Social Services: Child Welfare, Community Centers, Community Service Organizations, Counseling, Family Services, Food/Clothing Distribution, People with Disabilities, Recreation & Athletics, Scouts, Senior Services, Shelters/Homelessness, United Funds/United Ways, YMCA/YWCA/YMHA/YWHA, Youth Organizations

Application Procedures

Initial Contact: Send a brief letter.
Application Requirements: Include a description of program.
Deadlines: None.

Additional Information

Trust(s): Fifth Third Bank

Corporate Officials

Paul Michael Brumm: executive vice president, chief financial officer B Cincinnati, OH 1947. ED University of Cincinnati BA (1969); University of Cincinnati MBA (1976). PRIM CORP EMPL executive vice president, chief financial officer: Fifth Third Bancorp. NONPR AFFIL member: Banking & Finance Markets Committee; member: Delta Mu Delta; member: Bankers Roundtable. CLUB AFFIL Coldstream Country Club; University Club; Athletic Club.
Roger W. Dean: controller, chief administrative officer B 1963. PRIM CORP EMPL controller, chief administrative officer: Fifth Third Bancorp.
George A. Schaefer, Jr.: president B Cincinnati, OH 1945. ED United States Military Academy (1967); Xavier University (1974). PRIM CORP EMPL president: Fifth Third Bank. CORP AFFIL director: WellPoint Inc.; director: Ashland Inc.; president, chief executive officer, director: Fifth Third Bancorp. NONPR AFFIL vice chairman: Greater Cincinnati Chamber of Commerce.

Grants Analysis

Disclosure Period: fiscal year ending September 30, 2003
Total Grants: $7,470,642*
Number of Grants: 713
Average Grant: $10,478
Highest Grant: $200,000
Typical Range: $1,000 to $20,000
***Note:** Giving excludes scholarship; United Way.

Recent Grants

Note: Grants derived from fiscal 2003 Form 990.
General

800,000	Lucas County, Toledo, OH
551,464	Cincinnati Development Fund, Cincinnati, OH
551,464	Cincinnati Development Fund, Cincinnati, OH
375,000	University of Cincinnati Foundation, Cincinnati, OH
350,000	United Way of Greater Cincinnati, Cincinnati, OH
350,000	United Way of Greater Cincinnati, Cincinnati, OH
200,000	Greater Cincinnati Chamber of Commerce, Cincinnati, OH
150,000	Methodist Theological School in Ohio, Delaware, OH
140,000	Grand Action Foundation, Grand Rapids, MI
125,000	United Way, Lombard, IL

FIGTREE FOUNDATION

Giving Contact

Mark Pflaum, President
Figtree Foundation
PO Box 130845
Birmingham, AL 35213
Phone: (205)521-6311
Fax: (205)879-6382

Description

Founded: 1986
EIN: 630932247
Organization Type: General Purpose Foundation
Grant Types: General Support, Project.

Donor Information

Founder: The Figtree Foundation was established in 1986 by Jo Ann Morrison Myers.

Financial Summary

Total Giving: $240,800 (fiscal year ending November 30, 2003); $360,492 (fiscal 2001)
Giving Analysis: Giving for fiscal 2001 includes: foundation grants to United Way ($15,000)
Assets: $39,161 (fiscal 2003); $497,046 (fiscal 2001)
Gifts Received: $220,000 (fiscal 2001). Note: In 2002 Jo Ann Morrison contributed.

Typical Recipients

Arts & Humanities: Arts Festivals, Arts Institutes, Community Arts, Dance, Arts & Humanities-General, History & Archaeology, Libraries, Literary Arts, Museums/Galleries, Music, Performing Arts, Public Broadcasting, Theater
Civic & Public Affairs: Civil Rights, Civic & Public Affairs-General, Housing, Legal Aid, Municipalities/Towns, Philanthropic Organizations, Professional & Trade Associations, Public Policy, Safety
Education: Arts/Humanities Education, Colleges & Universities, Faculty Development, Minority Education, Preschool Education, Private Education (Precollege), Religious Education, Student Aid
Health: Cancer, Health-General, Heart, Hospices, Medical Rehabilitation, Medical Research, Single-Disease Health Associations
International: Foreign Arts Organizations, Foreign Educational Institutions, Health Care/Hospitals, Human Rights, International Organizations, Missionary/Religious Activities
Religion: Religion-General, Jewish Causes, Religious Organizations, Social/Policy Issues, Synagogues/Temples
Science: Science Museums
Social Services: Camps, Child Welfare, Community Service Organizations, Crime Prevention, Family Services, People with Disabilities, Shelters/Homelessness, Social Services-General, Substance Abuse, United Funds/United Ways, YMCA/YWCA/YMHA/YWHA, Youth Organizations

Application Procedures

Initial Contact: Individual requests should be addressed to a trustee.
Deadlines: None.

Additional Information

Publications: Annual Report

Foundation Officials

Alan Engel: vice president, secretary B 1955. ED University of Colorado BS (1976-1977); Northwestern University MBA (1977-1978). PRIM CORP EMPL principal: Crowne Partners Inc. CORP AFFIL partner: Engel Associates.
Donald E. Hess: secretary-treasurer B 1948. ED Dartmouth College BS (1970). PRIM CORP EMPL president, chief executive officer: Parisian Inc. CORP AFFIL director: AmSouth Bancorp; director: Saks Inc.
Donald Marc Hess: president, treasurer B Bern,

Switzerland 1936. PRIM CORP EMPL chairman, chief executive officer: Hess Holding PRIM NONPR EMPL chairman: Hess Collection Winery ADD CORP EMPL chairman: Blue Lake Ltd.; chairman: Hess International; chairman: Hess Ltd.; chairman: Valser Mineral Water Ltd. CORP AFFIL director: Kambly Biscuits; director: Trubschachen CH. NONPR AFFIL co-founder: Kunst Heute Foundation; founder: Napa Contemporary Arts Foundation.

Grants Analysis

Disclosure Period: fiscal year ending November 30, 2003
Total Grants: $240,800
Number of Grants: 6
Highest Grant: $160,000
Lowest Grant: $1,000
Typical Range: $10,000 to $50,000

Recent Grants

Note: Grants derived from fiscal 2002 Form 990.
General
224,750	Chabad, Brooklyn, NY
70,000	Birmingham Jewish Federation, Birmingham, AL
30,000	Chai Tots School
25,000	CIRF, Mestre Italy
20,000	Friends of Milah Inc., GA
15,000	Apple Hill Center for Chamber Music Inc.
15,000	Jerusalem Studies School, Jerusalem Israel
15,000	United Way
10,000	Alabama School of Fine Arts, Birmingham, AL
10,000	Bessie Sobol

LELAND FIKES FOUNDATION

Giving Contact

Nancy J. Solana, Vice President & Secretary
500 North Akard, Suite 3050
Dallas, TX 75201-6696
Phone: (214)754-0144

Description

Founded: 1952
EIN: 756035984
Organization Type: General Purpose Foundation
Giving Locations: TX: Dallas
Grant Types: Capital, Department, Endowment, General Support, Matching, Multiyear/Continuing Support, Operating Expenses, Seed Money.

Donor Information

Founder: The Fikes Foundation was established in 1952 by Leland Fikes, a Texas oil producer and philanthropist. Mr. Fikes was also involved in many other business interests, including real estate. Family members are active in the foundation.

Financial Summary

Total Giving: $3,346,365 (2003); $4,581,062 (2002); $3,259,445 (2001)
Assets: $74,130,349 (2003); $70,942,614 (2002)
Gifts Received: $180,000 (2000); $31,000 (1994); $182,000 (1993). Note: In 2000, contributions were received from the estate of Catherine Fikes.

Typical Recipients

Arts & Humanities: Arts Centers, Arts Outreach, Ethnic & Folk Arts, Film & Video, Arts & Humanities-General, Historic Preservation, Libraries, Museums/Galleries, Music, Performing Arts, Public Broadcasting, Theater
Civic & Public Affairs: African American Affairs, Botanical Gardens/Parks, Civil Rights, Community Foundations, Economic Development, Civic & Public Affairs-General, Hispanic Affairs, Housing, Law & Justice, Legal Aid, Nonprofit Management, Public Policy, Rural Affairs, Urban & Community Affairs, Women's Affairs, Zoos/Aquariums
Education: Afterschool/Enrichment Programs, Colleges & Universities, Community & Junior Colleges, Education Associations, Education Funds, Education Reform, Elementary Education (Private), Education-General, Health & Physical Education, Literacy, Medical Education, Preschool Education, Private Education (Precollege), Public Education (Precollege), Science/Mathematics Education, Secondary Education (Private), Student Aid
Environment: Environment-General, Wildlife Protection
Health: AIDS/HIV, Cancer, Children's Health/Hospitals, Clinics/Medical Centers, Diabetes, Eyes/Blindness, Health-General, Health Policy/Cost Containment, Health Funds, Health Organizations, Heart, Hospitals, Hospitals (University Affiliated), Medical Research, Mental Health, Nursing Services, Prenatal Health Issues, Public Health, Research/Studies Institutes, Single-Disease Health Associations, Transplant Networks/Donor Banks, Trauma Treatment
International: Foreign Educational Institutions, Health Care/Hospitals, Human Rights, International Development, International Environmental Issues, International Organizations, International Peace & Security Issues, Missionary/Religious Activities
Religion: Churches, Jewish Causes, Ministries, Religious Organizations, Religious Welfare, Social/Policy Issues
Science: Observatories & Planetariums, Science Exhibits & Fairs, Science Museums, Scientific Organizations, Scientific Research
Social Services: At-Risk Youth, Camps, Child Abuse, Child Welfare, Community Centers, Community Service Organizations, Counseling, Domestic Violence, Family Planning, Family Services, Food/Clothing Distribution, Homes, People with Disabilities, Recreation & Athletics, Scouts, Senior Services, Shelters/Homelessness, Social Services-General, Substance Abuse, United Funds/United Ways, Volunteer Services, YMCA/YWCA/YMHA/YWHA, Youth Organizations

Application Procedures

Initial Contact: Applicants should submit concise and complete written proposals. The foundation does not have an application form.
Application Requirements: Proposals should contain a cover letter on organization letterhead (signed by the chief executive officer) describing the project, amount requested, and the date by which funds are needed; the names and affiliations of the board of directors or trustees; a brief history of the organization's work and purpose; a specific description of the program for which support is asked; a copy of the total budget showing projected income and expenses for the current year and, in the same format, the budget for the year immediately past with actual numbers; budget information pertaining to the program or project; a statement of financial position (balance sheet); information about the principal staff or volunteers who will implement the program; the name and phone number of contact person for additional information; other funding sources that have responded favorably or are currently considering the project for funding; future funding plans of the program, project, or organization; plans for evaluating the effectiveness of the project; and a copy of letter determining tax-exempt status.
Deadlines: None.
Review Process: All grant requests are acknowledged. After the board of trustees has received proposal, it may request a meeting or additional information.

Restrictions

Grants are not made to individuals.

Additional Information

Publications: Application Guidelines

Foundation Officials

Amy L. Fikes: vice president, trustee
Lee Fikes: president, treasurer, trustee, chairman B 1943. PRIM CORP EMPL president: Bonanza Oil Co. CORP AFFIL president: Denton Hines Properties; president: Denton Hines Properties Inc.
Nancy J. Solana: vice president, secretary

Grants Analysis

Disclosure Period: calendar year ending 2003
Total Grants: $3,346,365
Number of Grants: 60
Average Grant: $44,006*
Highest Grant: $750,000
Lowest Grant: $1,000
Typical Range: $20,000 to $100,000
***Note:** Average grant figure excludes highest grant.

Recent Grants

Note: Grants derived from 2003 Form 990.
Library-Related
100,000	Friends of the Dallas Public library, Dallas, TX -- for renovation

General
750,000	University of Texas Southwestern Medical Center, Dallas, TX -- Hui Sheng stem cell research start up
250,000	Dallas Symphony Association Inc., Dallas, TX -- European tour
200,000	Dallas Center for the Performing Arts Foundation Inc., Dallas, TX -- to build the center
200,000	Saint Mark's School of Texas, Dallas, TX
150,000	Planned Parenthood of North Texas Inc., Dallas, TX -- to educate people on PPNT mission
100,000	Dallas Symphony Association Inc., Dallas, TX -- sustaining fund
100,000	East Dallas Community School, Dallas, TX -- to create public charter school and for operating support of private school
100,000	Hackaday School, Dallas, TX -- new century campaign
100,000	Jubilee Park and Community Center Corporation, Dallas, TX -- for master plan and anti crime program
100,000	Old Red Courthouse Inc., Dallas, TX -- to develop museum

DOAK FINCH FOUNDATION

Giving Contact

J. C. Dorety, Contact
10 Welloskie Dr.
Thomasville, NC 27360

Alternate Contact

c/o Bank of America
Bank of America Place NC1-002-11-18
Charlotte, NC 28255
Phone: (704)387-4562

Description

Founded: 1961
EIN: 566042823
Organization Type: Private Foundation
Giving Locations: NC: Thomasville including surrounding area
Grant Types: General Support.

Donor Information

Founder: the late Doak Finch

Financial Summary

Total Giving: $253,000 (fiscal year ending October 31, 2002); $257,100 (fiscal 2001)
Assets: $4,543,740 (fiscal 2002); $4,170,154 (fiscal 2001)

Typical Recipients

Arts & Humanities: Arts Associations & Councils, Arts & Humanities-General, Libraries, Theater
Civic & Public Affairs: Community Foundations, Civic & Public Affairs-General, Housing, Municipalities/Towns, Urban & Community Affairs
Education: Community & Junior Colleges, Education-General, Private Education (Precollege), Public Education (Precollege), Secondary Education (Public)
Health: Emergency/Ambulance Services, Health-General, Health Funds, Hospices, Hospitals
Religion: Churches, Ministries, Religious Organizations, Religious Welfare
Social Services: Child Welfare, Community Service Organizations, Crime Prevention, Food/Clothing Distribution, Homes, People with Disabilities, Recreation & Athletics, Social Services-General, Substance Abuse, United Funds/United Ways, YMCA/YWCA/YMHA/YWHA, Youth Organizations

Application Procedures

Initial Contact: Send brief letter describing program, purpose of funds sought, amount requested, and proof of tax-exempt status.
Deadlines: None.

Additional Information

trustee
Trust(s): Bank of America NA

Grants Analysis

Disclosure Period: fiscal year ending October 31, 2002
Total Grants: $253,000
Number of Grants: 24
Average Grant: $6,500*
Highest Grant: $60,000
Lowest Grant: $2,500
Typical Range: $2,500 to $10,000
***Note:** Average grant excludes two highest grants ($110,000).

Recent Grants

Note: Grants derived from 2002 Form 990.
General

60,000	Tom A Finch YMCA, Thomasville, NC
50,000	Memorial United Methodist Church, Thomasville, NC
15,000	City of Thomasville Finch Field, Thomasville, NC
15,000	Community Schools of Thomasville, Thomasville, NC
10,000	Arts United for Davidson County, Davidson, NC
10,000	City of Thomasville 150th Project, Thomasville, NC
10,000	Community General Hospital Foundation, Thomasville, NC
10,000	Davidson County Community College, Thomasville, NC
5,000	Crimestoppers, Thomasville, NC
5,000	Meals on Wheels, Thomasville, NC

THOMAS AUSTIN FINCH FOUNDATION

Giving Contact

Linda G. Tilley, Administrator
c/o Wachovia Bank of North Carolina NA

100 N. Main St.
Winston-Salem, NC 27150-7131
Phone: (336)732-5372

Description

Founded: 1944
EIN: 566037907
Organization Type: Private Foundation
Giving Locations: NC: Thomasville including surrounding area
Grant Types: Capital, Emergency, General Support, Matching, Multiyear/Continuing Support, Operating Expenses, Scholarship.

Donor Information

Founder: Ernestine L. Finch Mobley, Thomas Austin Finch, Jr.

Financial Summary

Total Giving: $449,990 (2004); $689,539 (2001)
Giving Analysis: Giving for 2001 includes: foundation scholarships ($21,667); foundation matching gifts ($135,626)
Assets: $10,000,400 (2004); $11,153,122 (2001)

Typical Recipients

Arts & Humanities: Arts Associations & Councils, History & Archaeology, Libraries
Civic & Public Affairs: Community Foundations, Civic & Public Affairs-General, Housing, Municipalities/Towns, Urban & Community Affairs
Education: Colleges & Universities, Community & Junior Colleges, Education-General, Private Education (Precollege), Public Education (Precollege), Secondary Education (Public), Student Aid
Health: Hospices, Hospitals
International: Health Care/Hospitals
Religion: Churches, Ministries, Religious Welfare
Social Services: Community Service Organizations, Crime Prevention, Domestic Violence, Family Services, Food/Clothing Distribution, Recreation & Athletics, Senior Services, Substance Abuse, United Funds/United Ways, YMCA/YWCA/YMHA/YWHA, Youth Organizations

Application Procedures

Initial Contact: Application form required.
Deadlines: None.

Restrictions

Limited to Thomasville, NC area.

Additional Information

Publications: Informational Brochure (including Application Guidelines)
Trust(s): Wachovia Bank NC NA

Foundation Officials

Thomas Austin Finch, Jr.: manager
Ernestine L. Mobley: manager

Grants Analysis

Disclosure Period: calendar year ending 2004
Total Grants: $449,990*
Typical Range: $1,500 to $15,000
***Note:** No grants list available for 2004.

Recent Grants

Note: Grants derived from 2001 Form 990.
General

250,000	Memorial United Methodist Church, Thomasville, NC
135,628	Tom A Finch Community YMCA, Thomasville, NC
100,000	Westchester Academy, High Point, NC
25,000	Memorial United Methodist Church, Thomasville, NC
25,000	Memorial United Methodist Church, Thomasville, NC
20,000	Thomasville Communities in School, Thomasville, NC
15,000	Piedmont School, High Point, NC
15,000	Thomasville Community Foundation, Thomasville, NC
13,667	Davidson County Education Foundation, Lexington, NC
10,000	City of Thomasville, Thomasville, NC

FINK FOUNDATION (NY)

Giving Contact

Romie Shapiro, President
501 5th Avenue, Rm. 909
New York, NY 10017-7853
Phone: (212)687-8098

Description

Founded: 1956
EIN: 136135438
Organization Type: Private Foundation
Giving Locations: MD; NY: New York
Grant Types: General Support.

Donor Information

Founder: David Fink, Nathan Fink

Financial Summary

Total Giving: $148,000 (2003); $334,500 (2001)
Assets: $10,000,400 (2004); $1,160,482 (2003); $1,479,658 (2001)
Gifts Received: $4,995 (1996)

Typical Recipients

Arts & Humanities: Film & Video, Libraries, Museums/Galleries, Music
Civic & Public Affairs: Civic & Public Affairs-General, Women's Affairs
Education: Arts/Humanities Education, Colleges & Universities, Community & Junior Colleges, Education Funds, Faculty Development, Education-General, Legal Education, Minority Education, Private Education (Precollege), Public Education (Precollege), Secondary Education (Private), Student Aid
Health: Geriatric Health, Health Organizations, Hospices, Hospitals, Long-Term Care, Research/Studies Institutes, Respiratory
International: Foreign Arts Organizations, Foreign Educational Institutions, International-General, Health Care/Hospitals, International Peace & Security Issues, Missionary/Religious Activities
Religion: Bible Study/Translation, Religion-General, Jewish Causes, Religious Organizations, Religious Welfare, Seminaries, Synagogues/Temples
Social Services: Camps, Community Service Organizations, Family Services, Homes, People with Disabilities, Scouts, Senior Services, YMCA/YWCA/YMHA/YWHA

Application Procedures

Initial Contact: Applicants should submit a brief resume of academic qualifications.
Application Requirements: For research grants, include an outline of the proposed investigation and budget.
Deadlines: None.

Foundation Officials

Stanley Dalneoff: treasurer
Harold Fink: secretary
David Maurice Levitan: vice president B Tver, Lithuania December 25, 1915. ED Northwestern University BS (1936); Northwestern University MA (1937); University of Chicago PhD (1940); Columbia University JD (1948). PRIM CORP EMPL counsel: Hahn & Hessen. NONPR AFFIL member: New York State Bar Association; chairman board zoning appeals: Village Roslyn Harbor; member: American Society International Law; member: New York City Bar Association; member: American Law Institute; member: American Political Science Association; member:

American Bar Association; fellow: American College Trust & Estate Counsel.
Charles Shanok: director
Romie Shapiro: president
Seymour Zises: director

Grants Analysis

Disclosure Period: calendar year ending 2003
Total Grants: $148,000
Number of Grants: 48
Average Grant: $3,083
Highest Grant: $15,000
Lowest Grant: $1,000
Typical Range: $1,000 to $5,000

Recent Grants

Note: Grants derived from 2001 Form 990.
General

40,000	Friends of Bezalel Academy, New York, NY
35,000	Abraham Joshua Herschel School, New York, NY
25,000	American Friends Open University Israel, New York, NY
25,000	Charles E. Smith Jewish Day School, Rockville, MD
25,000	Hebrew High School of New England, Springfield, MA
25,000	Institute for Advancement in Education, Inc.
10,000	American Committee for Shaare Zedek Hospital, New York, NY
10,000	Hadassah The Womens Zionist Organization of America, Inc.
10,000	Hebrew Home for the Aged, Riverdale, NY
10,000	Jewish Theological Seminary, Broadway, NY

FIREMAN'S FUND INSURANCE CO.

Company Headquarters

777 San Marin Dr.
Novato, CA 94998
Web: http://www.firemansfund.com

Company Description

Founded: 1863
Parent Company: Allianz Life Insurance Company of North America, 5701 Golden Hill Dr., Minneapolis, MN, United States

Nonmonetary Support

Type: Donated Equipment; In-kind Services

Fireman's Fund Foundation

Giving Contact

Phyllis Secosky, Secretary
Fireman's Fund Foundation
777 San Marin Drive
Novato, CA 94998-1406
Phone: (415)899-2757
Fax: (415)899-2012
Web: http://www.firemansfund.com/servlet/dcms?c=about&rkey=112

Description

Founded: 1953
EIN: 946078025
Organization Type: Corporate Foundation
Giving Locations: CA: Marin and Sonoma Counties
Grant Types: Employee Matching Gifts, General

Support, Project.
Note: Employee matching gift ratio: 1 to 1.

Donor Information

Founder: Fireman's Fund Insurance Co. & Subsidiaries

Financial Summary

Total Giving: $670,812 (2003); $742,909 (2002); $1,143,577 (2001). Note: Contributes through foundation only.
Giving Analysis: Giving for 2002 includes: foundation grants to United Way ($49,258)
Assets: $124,679 (2003); $191,760 (2002); $136,017 (2001)
Gifts Received: $600,000 (2003); $792,047 (2002); $1,093,004 (2001). Note: In 2002, contributions were received from Firemen's Fund Insurance Co. In 2001, contributions were received from Firemen's Fund Insurance Co. ($1,023,959) and miscellaneous contributions less than $5,000 each ($69,045).

Typical Recipients

Arts & Humanities: Arts Centers, Arts Funds, Arts Institutes, Arts Outreach, Ballet, Community Arts, Dance, Ethnic & Folk Arts, Arts & Humanities-General, Historic Preservation, History & Archaeology, Libraries, Museums/Galleries, Music, Opera, Performing Arts, Public Broadcasting, Theater, Visual Arts
Civic & Public Affairs: Botanical Gardens/Parks, Economic Development, Employment/Job Training, Gay/Lesbian Issues, Civic & Public Affairs-General, Housing, Law & Justice, Legal Aid, Municipalities/Towns, Nonprofit Management, Parades/Festivals, Philanthropic Organizations, Professional & Trade Associations, Safety, Urban & Community Affairs, Women's Affairs, Zoos/Aquariums
Education: Afterschool/Enrichment Programs, Business Education, Colleges & Universities, Community & Junior Colleges, Continuing Education, Education Funds, Environmental Education, Education-General, Literacy, Preschool Education, Private Education (Precollege), Public Education (Precollege), Religious Education, Science/Mathematics Education, Secondary Education (Public), Special Education
Environment: Environment-General, Resource Conservation
Health: AIDS/HIV, Alzheimer's Disease, Health Organizations, Home-Care Services, Hospices, Hospitals, Medical Rehabilitation, Mental Health, Preventive Medicine/Wellness Organizations
International: International Organizations
Religion: Jewish Causes, Ministries, Religious Organizations, Religious Welfare, Social/Policy Issues
Science: Observatories & Planetariums, Science Exhibits & Fairs, Science Museums
Social Services: At-Risk Youth, Big Brothers/Big Sisters, Child Welfare, Community Centers, Community Service Organizations, Counseling, Day Care, Domestic Violence, Emergency Relief, Family Services, Food/Clothing Distribution, Homes, People with Disabilities, Recreation & Athletics, Senior Services, Shelters/Homelessness, Social Services-General, Substance Abuse, United Funds/United Ways, Volunteer Services, YMCA/YWCA/YMHA/YWHA, Youth Organizations

Application Procedures

Initial Contact: Send a brief letter of not more than two pages, plus attachments.
Application Requirements: Include a description of organization; constituency served; statement of mission, objectives and goals; amount requested, and an explanation of how funds will be used to support a specific program or project; program budget showing expenses and income sources; list of current contributors and amounts; recently audited financial statement; proof of tax-exempt status; and list of board members, executive director and other key staff members.

Deadlines: None.
Review Process: Foundation director reviews proposals prior to consideration by distribution committee.
Evaluative Criteria: Broad community support and proven track record; demonstration of how sustainable, positive change will be achieved; project meets community needs and targets a wide audience; projects have demonstrated impact in the community.
Decision Notification: Distribution committee meets four times a year; grants usually made within 90 days.

Restrictions

Grants are not made to individuals; religious, veterans', labor, or fraternal organizations; capital campaigns, endowment funds or operating expenses; fund-raising or sporting events; subscription fees or admission tickets; insurance premiums; medical research and health organizations; political candidates; political or lobbying groups; dinners or special events; trips or tours; advertisements; public sector services; or videos, films, or television productions.

Additional Information

Publications: Guidelines

Corporate Officials

Gary E. Black: president claims division, director actuary B 1945. PRIM CORP EMPL president claims division, director: Fireman's Fund Insurance Co. CORP AFFIL director: American Insurance Co. Inc.; director: Interstate National Corp.
David R. Pollard: officer PRIM CORP EMPL officer: Fireman's Fund Insurance Co. CORP AFFIL executive vice president: Associated Indemnity Corp.; officer: Interstate Fire & Casualty Co.
Jeffery H. Post: executive vice president, chief financial officer, chief actuary PRIM CORP EMPL executive vice president, chief financial officer, chief actuary: Fireman's Fund Insurance Co. ADD CORP EMPL chief financial officer: American Insurance Co. Inc.; vice president: Associated Indemnity Corp.

Foundation Officials

Bruce Friedberg: director
Thomas Geillser: director
Peter Huehne: director
Janet S. Kloenhammer: chairman, director
H. David Lundgren: director
Jeffery H. Post: director (see above)
Phyllis Secosky: secretary
Alastair Shore: president, director
Linda Wright: treasurer

Grants Analysis

Disclosure Period: calendar year ending 2003
Total Grants: $670,812
Number of Grants: 65
Average Grant: $9,785*
Highest Grant: $44,542
Lowest Grant: $2,500
Typical Range: $5,000 to $15,000
***Note:** Average grant figure excludes highest grant.

Recent Grants

Note: Grants derived from 2003 Form 990.
Library-Related

10,000	LITA (American Library Association), Chicago, IL

General

44,542	Volunteer Center of Sonoma County, Santa Rosa, CA
15,359	Center for Volunteer and Nonprofit Leadership of Marin, San Rafael, CA
15,000	Adopt a Family of Marin, San Rafael, CA
15,000	Bay Area Discovery Museum, Sausalito, CA
15,000	Bernard Osher Marin Jewish Community Center, San Rafael, CA
15,000	Community Action Marin, San Rafael, CA
15,000	Community Institute for Psychotherapy, San Rafael, CA

15,000	Dance Palace, Pt. Reyes Station, CA
15,000	Family Law Center for Women & Children, CA
15,000	Luther Burbank Memorial Foundation, Santa Rosa, CA

HARVEY FIRESTONE, JR. FOUNDATION

Giving Contact
Charles D'Arcy, Trust Officer
c/o Bank One Trust Co. NA
600 Superior Ave.
Cleveland, OH 44114
Phone: 800-557-1332

Description
Founded: 1983
EIN: 341388254
Organization Type: Private Foundation
Giving Locations: east of the Mississippi River.
Grant Types: General Support.

Financial Summary
Total Giving: $1,220,000 (2003)
Giving Analysis: Giving for 2003 includes: foundation grants to United Way ($100,000)
Assets: $22,164,716 (2003)
Gifts Received: $8,001 (1995)

Typical Recipients
Arts & Humanities: Arts & Humanities-General, Historic Preservation, History & Archaeology, Libraries, Museums/Galleries, Music, Public Broadcasting, Theater
Civic & Public Affairs: Community Foundations, Employment/Job Training, Civic & Public Affairs-General, Philanthropic Organizations, Rural Affairs, Urban & Community Affairs
Education: Arts/Humanities Education, Colleges & Universities, Faculty Development, Private Education (Precollege), Science/Mathematics Education, Secondary Education (Public), Special Education
Environment: Resource Conservation
Health: Children's Health/Hospitals, Emergency/Ambulance Services, Health Organizations, Hospices, Hospitals, Nursing Services, Public Health
International: Foreign Arts Organizations, Foreign Educational Institutions
Religion: Churches, Dioceses, Religious Organizations, Religious Welfare, Seminaries
Science: Scientific Labs
Social Services: At-Risk Youth, Child Welfare, Community Centers, Community Service Organizations, Counseling, Family Services, People with Disabilities, Recreation & Athletics, Shelters/Homelessness, United Funds/United Ways, Youth Organizations

Application Procedures
Initial Contact: The foundation has no formal grant application procedure or application form.
Deadlines: None.

Foundation Officials
Anne F. Ball: trustee
Martha F. Ford: trustee

Grants Analysis
Disclosure Period: calendar year ending 2003
Total Grants: $1,120,000*
Number of Grants: 81
Average Grant: $6,662*
Highest Grant: $200,000
Lowest Grant: $500
Typical Range: $1,000 to $10,000
***Note:** Giving excludes United Way. Average grant excludes four highest grants ($607,000).

Recent Grants
Note: Grants derived from 2003 Form 990.
General

188,000	Henry Ford Museum and Greenfield Village, Dearborn, MI
94,000	Christ Church, Grosse Pte., MI
80,000	Pontifical North American College, Bridgeport, CT
60,000	Our Lady of the Elms, Akron, OH
52,000	Miss Porter's School Inc., Farmington, CT
50,000	Bon Secours Cottage Health Services, Grosse Pte., MI
40,000	Vassar College, Poughkeepsie, NY
25,000	College for Creative Studies, Detroit, MI
25,000	Greenwich Hospital, Greenwich, CT
15,000	Foxcroft School, Middleburg, VA

FIRST FINANCIAL BANK

Company Headquarters
1045 Clark St.
Stevens Point, WI 54481

Company Description
Employees: 1,283
SIC(s): 6035 Federal Savings Institutions.
Parent Company: First Financial Corp., 1 First Financial Plaza, Terre Haute, IN, United States

Operating Locations
First Financial Bank (WI--Stevens Point)

Associated Banc-Corp Foundation

Giving Contact
Jonathon Drayna
C/O Associated Bank
112 North Adams Street
PO Box 13307
Green Bay, WI 54307-3307
Phone: (715)341-0400

Alternate Contact
PO Box 408
Neenah, WI 54957-0408

Description
Founded: 1977
EIN: 391277461
Organization Type: Corporate Foundation
Former Name: First Financial Foundation (2002).
Giving Locations: IL: areas of business; WI: areas of business
Grant Types: Capital, Employee Matching Gifts, General Support.

Financial Summary
Total Giving: $8,250 (2003); $38,000 (2002); $64,000 (2001)
Assets: $1,301,308 (2003); $661,704 (2002); $763,893 (2001)
Gifts Received: $500,000 (2003); $360,000 (1997); $90,000 (1996). Note: In 2003, contributions were received from Associated Bank Co. In 1996, contributions were received from First Financial Bank.

Typical Recipients
Arts & Humanities: Arts & Humanities-General, Libraries, Museums/Galleries, Music, Opera, Performing Arts, Public Broadcasting, Theater
Civic & Public Affairs: Botanical Gardens/Parks, Chambers of Commerce, Clubs, Community Foundations, Economic Development, Civic & Public Affairs-

General, Housing, Municipalities/Towns, Public Policy, Safety, Urban & Community Affairs, Women's Affairs
Education: Agricultural Education, Colleges & Universities, Economic Education, Education Reform, Literacy, Private Education (Precollege), Social Sciences Education, Student Aid, Vocational & Technical Education
Environment: Environment-General
Health: AIDS/HIV, Cancer, Children's Health/Hospitals, Clinics/Medical Centers, Geriatric Health, Health Funds, Hospitals, Medical Research, Nursing Services, Public Health, Single-Disease Health Associations
Religion: Missionary Activities (Domestic), Religious Organizations, Religious Welfare
Social Services: Child Welfare, Community Centers, Community Service Organizations, Domestic Violence, Family Planning, Food/Clothing Distribution, People with Disabilities, Recreation & Athletics, Scouts, Senior Services, Shelters/Homelessness, United Funds/United Ways, YMCA/YWCA/YMHA/YWHA, Youth Organizations

Application Procedures
Initial Contact: Request a contribution request form.
Deadlines: September 1.

Restrictions
The foundation does not make contributions to individuals, political or lobbying groups, labor organizations, or veterans' organizations. Contributions to religious organizations are limited to those facilities that offer higher education or hospital care to the general public.

Additional Information
Publications: Application Form

Corporate Officials
John C. Seramur: president, chief executive officer, director B 1943. PRIM CORP EMPL president, chief executive officer, director: First Financial Bank.

Foundation Officials
Brian Bodager: president
Joanne P. Radeske: director

Grants Analysis
Disclosure Period: calendar year ending 2003
Total Grants: $8,250
Number of Grants: 3
Highest Grant: $5,000
Lowest Grant: $750

Recent Grants
Note: Grants derived from 2003 Form 990.
General

5,000	Greater Green Bay Habitat for Humanity, Green Bay, WI
2,500	Public Policy Forum for the Project Blueprint
750	Newist Pledge

FIRST HAWAIIAN INC.

Company Headquarters
1111 S. Beretania St.
Honolulu, HI 96814
Web: http://www.fnb.com

Company Description
Employees: 3,384
SIC(s): 6022 State Commercial Banks, 6159 Miscellaneous Business Credit Institutions, 6719 Holding Companies Nec.

Operating Locations
First Hawaiian, Inc. (HI--Honolulu)

Nonmonetary Support
Volunteer Programs: Company supports employee volunteerism through the YesTeam.

First Hawaiian Foundation

Giving Contact
Sharon Brown, President
First Hawaiian Foundation
999 Bishop Street, 29th Floor
Honolulu, HI 96813
Phone: (808)525-7777
Fax: (808)525-7750

Description
EIN: 237437822
Organization Type: Corporate Foundation
Giving Locations: HI
Grant Types: Capital, Employee Matching Gifts, Endowment, General Support, Project.

Financial Summary
Total Giving: $2,004,654 (2002); $1,637,351 (2001)
Assets: $13,583,800 (2002); $18,387,932 (2001)
Gifts Received: $2,004 (2002); $9,997,317 (2001); $2,004 (2000). Note: In 2002, contributions were received from First Hawaiian Leasing, Inc. In 2001, contributions were received from BancWest Corp. and First Hawaiian Bank. Prior to 2001, contributions were received from First Hawaiian Credit Corp., First Hawaiian Bank, and First Hawaiian Leasing.

Typical Recipients
Arts & Humanities: Arts Associations & Councils, Arts Centers, Arts Festivals, Arts Funds, Film & Video, Historic Preservation, History & Archaeology, Libraries, Museums/Galleries, Music, Public Broadcasting, Theater, Visual Arts
Civic & Public Affairs: Asian American Affairs, Business/Free Enterprise, Chambers of Commerce, Community Foundations, Civic & Public Affairs-General, Housing, Law & Justice, Parades/Festivals, Philanthropic Organizations, Urban & Community Affairs
Education: Agricultural Education, Arts/Humanities Education, Business Education, Colleges & Universities, Continuing Education, Economic Education, Education Funds, Elementary Education (Public), Education-General, Gifted & Talented Programs, International Studies, Literacy, Preschool Education, Private Education (Precollege), Public Education (Precollege), Religious Education, Science/Mathematics Education, Secondary Education (Private), Secondary Education (Public), Social Sciences Education, Special Education, Student Aid
Environment: Environment-General, Resource Conservation
Health: Cancer, Children's Health/Hospitals, Clinics/Medical Centers, Emergency/Ambulance Services, Health Funds, Health Organizations, Hospices, Hospitals, Medical Rehabilitation, Research/Studies Institutes, Single-Disease Health Associations
International: Foreign Educational Institutions, Health Care/Hospitals, International Relief Efforts, Missionary/Religious Activities
Religion: Churches, Ministries, Missionary Activities (Domestic), Religious Organizations, Religious Welfare, Synagogues/Temples
Science: Science Museums, Scientific Centers & Institutes, Scientific Research
Social Services: Animal Protection, Big Brothers/Big Sisters, Child Welfare, Community Centers, Community Service Organizations, Day Care, Domestic Violence, Emergency Relief, Family Services, Food/Clothing Distribution, Homes, People with Disabilities, Recreation & Athletics, Scouts, Senior Services, Shelters/Homelessness, Social Services-General, Substance Abuse, United Funds/United Ways, Volunteer Services, YMCA/YWCA/YMHA/YWHA, Youth Organizations

Application Procedures
Initial Contact: Send letter of request.
Application Requirements: Include a description of organization, amount requested, project budget, purpose of funds sought, recently audited financial statement, proof of tax-exempt status, income level of service area, and list of board members and officers.
Deadlines: None.
Review Process: Board meets quarterly.

Restrictions
Company will only fund organizations with tax-exempt status.

Corporate Officials
Lily K. Yao: director PRIM CORP EMPL director: First Hawaiian, Inc. CORP AFFIL secretary: First Hawaiian Bank. NONPR AFFIL chairman board regents: University Hawaii.

Foundation Officials
William E. Atwater: secretary, director
Anthony R. Guerrero, Jr.: director B Honolulu, HI 1945. ED University of Portland (1967). PRIM CORP EMPL executive vice president: First Hawaiian Bank. CORP AFFIL director: Oahu Transit Service Inc.
Gerald J. Keir: director
Robin Midkif: director
Fredrick J. Shine, III: director
Sheila M. Sumida: director
John K. Tsui: vice president, director B 1938. PRIM CORP EMPL president: First Hawaiian Bank. CORP AFFIL president: Bancwest Corp.; chief executive officer: First Hawaiian Leasing Inc.
Albert M. Yamada: director
Lily K. Yao: president, director (see above)

Grants Analysis
Disclosure Period: calendar year ending 2002
Total Grants: $1,472,584*
Number of Grants: 108
Average Grant: $13,635
Highest Grant: $250,000
Lowest Grant: $1,000
Typical Range: $1,000 to $50,000
*Note: Giving excludes United Way.

Recent Grants
Note: Grants derived from 2003 Form 990.
General

460,070	Aloha United Way Oahu, Honolulu, HI -- towards corporate pledge
250,000	University of Hawaii Foundation, Honolulu, HI -- towards creation of endowed chair at college of business
100,000	Enterprise Honolulu, Honolulu, HI -- towards support of business plan
50,000	American Red Cross Guam Chapter Guam -- towards support of relief and recovery efforts by Typhoon Chataan
50,000	Contemporary Museum, Honolulu, HI -- towards corporate membership
50,000	Washington Place Foundation, Honolulu, HI -- for the support of capital campaign for site improvements
40,000	Hawaii Theater Center, Honolulu, HI -- towards completion of the exterior of the theater
40,000	Iolani School, Honolulu, HI -- towards financial aid program
28,000	Hawaii Island United Way, Hilo, HI -- towards corporate pledge
25,000	Community Development Pacific, Honolulu, HI -- towards the Daniel K. Inouye multimedia project

FIRST TENNESSEE NATIONAL CORP.

Company Headquarters
Memphis, TN
Web: http://www.ftb.com

Company Description
Ticker: FTN
Exchange: OTC
Former Name: First Tennessee Bank.
Assets: US$22.81 billion (2002)
Employees: 11494 (2003)
SIC(s): 6021 National Commercial Banks, 6712 Bank Holding Companies.

Operating Locations
First Tennessee National Corp. (TN--Chattanooga, Cookeville, Dandridge, Dyersburg, Gallatin, Greeneville, Jackson, Johnson City, Knoxville, Maryville, Memphis, Morristown, Nashville)

Nonmonetary Support
Range: $5,000 - $15,000
Type: Donated Equipment; Donated Products; In-kind Services; Loaned Employees; Loaned Executives; Workplace Solicitation
Volunteer Programs: Company sponsors Volunteerbank.
Contact: Sue Jacks, Corporate Communications

First Tennessee Foundation

Giving Contact
J. Terrence Lee, Senior Vice President, Corporate Communications
First Tennessee National Corp.
165 Madison, 3rd Fl.
Memphis, TN 38103
Phone: (901)523-4380
E-mail: jtlee@ftb.com

Description
EIN: 621533987
Organization Type: Corporate Foundation
Giving Locations: TN: headquarters and operating communities
Grant Types: Capital, Challenge, Endowment, General Support, Professorship, Project.

Financial Summary
Total Giving: $4,234,049 (2003); $4,081,385 (2002); $1,731,485 (2001). Note: Contributes through corporate direct giving program and foundation.
Giving Analysis: Giving for 2001 includes: foundation grants to United Way ($380,988)
Assets: $68,990,570 (2003); $55,043,550 (2002); $12,609,200 (2001)
Gifts Received: $9,820,000 (2003). Note: Contributions were received from First Tennessee Bank.

Typical Recipients
Arts & Humanities: Arts Associations & Councils, Arts Centers, Arts Festivals, Arts Funds, Arts Institutes, Community Arts, Dance, Ethnic & Folk Arts, Historic Preservation, History & Archaeology, Libraries, Literary Arts, Museums/Galleries, Music, Opera, Performing Arts, Public Broadcasting, Theater, Visual Arts
Civic & Public Affairs: Botanical Gardens/Parks, Business/Free Enterprise, Chambers of Commerce, Civil Rights, Community Foundations, Economic Development, Ethnic Organizations, Civic & Public Affairs-General, Housing, Philanthropic Organizations, Professional & Trade Associations, Public Policy, Urban & Community Affairs, Women's Affairs, Zoos/

Aquariums

Education: Business Education, Colleges & Universities, Economic Education, Education Funds, Education Reform, Elementary Education (Private), Faculty Development, Minority Education, Preschool Education, Private Education (Precollege), Public Education (Precollege)

Environment: Environment-General, Wildlife Protection

Health: Children's Health/Hospitals, Clinics/Medical Centers, Health-General, Hospitals, Transplant Networks/Donor Banks

Religion: Churches, Religion-General, Ministries

Social Services: Big Brothers/Big Sisters, Child Welfare, Community Service Organizations, Emergency Relief, Family Services, Recreation & Athletics, Scouts, Shelters/Homelessness, United Funds/United Ways, Volunteer Services, YMCA/YWCA/YMHA/YWHA, Youth Organizations

Application Procedures

Initial Contact: a brief letter of inquiry to determine interest; proposal will be invited

Application Requirements: (after interest has been shown by First Tennessee Bank) a proposal that includes: name, address, telephone number and contact person of organization; brief a description of organization's history, accomplishments, and goals; objectives of program to be funded; amount sought in relation to total need; expected project outcomes; proposed evaluation method; geographic area and number of people served; current operating budget, expected project costs, and most recently audited financial statement; other funding sources, including government, individuals, foundations, corporations, and united funds; list of officers, board of directors, and other principles of the organization; involvement of volunteers in the organization; and proof of tax-exempt status volunteers in the organization; and proof of tax-exempt status

Deadlines: by the October prior to the year for which funding is requested

Review Process: after initial inquiry, notification within four weeks if written proposal is sought; complete review may take up to two months

Evaluative Criteria: relation to contributions policy objectives; extent to which project will prevent community problems or develop financial resources to respond to such problems; extent to which funding will promote self-sufficiency; community's need for program and lack of duplication of existing services; organization's record of accomplishment; community support; financial condition, management, and administrative costs of organization

Decision Notification: ongoing basis, with review process taking as long as two months; applicants notified in February of status of requests for that year

Notes: The program is decentralized; apply to Memphis office for proposals with a statewide or Memphis area focus; apply to local bank president for proposals of a local or regional focus. Very few unsolicited requests are accepted.

Restrictions

Grants are not made to individuals; charities sponsored solely by a single civic organization; charities that redistribute funds to other organizations, except recognized united funds and arts funds; member agencies of the United Way or united arts funds; bank "clearinghouse" organizations; religious, veterans, social, athletic, or fraternal organizations; political organizations or other groups promoting a specific ideological point of view; trips or tours; operating budget deficits; multiyear commitments of four years or more; endowments; tickets to fund-raising benefits; goodwill advertising; or member agencies of united funds. tickets to fund-raising benefits; goodwill advertising; or member agencies of united funds.

Foundation Officials

Clyde A. Billings, Jr.: secretary
Harry A. Johnson, III: chairman
Gregg I. Lansky: president, treasurer

Grants Analysis

Disclosure Period: calendar year ending 2001
Total Grants: $653,281*
Number of Grants: 263
Average Grant: $1,539*
Highest Grant: $250,000
Lowest Grant: $500
Typical Range: $1,000 to $5,000
***Note:** Giving excludes United Way. Average grant figure excludes highest grant.

Recent Grants

Note: Grants derived from 2003 Form 990.
Library-Related

32,200	Foundation for the Memphis Shelby County Public Library, Memphis, TN

General

250,000	Church Health Center, Memphis, TN
250,000	Rise Foundation Inc
200,000	Memphis Tomorrow, Memphis, TN
131,272	United Way of the Mid-South, Memphis, TN
130,000	Lifeblood Foundation
116,500	United Way of Greater Knoxville, Knoxville, TN
108,937	United Way of the Midsouth, Memphis, TN
100,000	Goals for Memphis, Memphis, TN
100,000	Goals for Memphis, Memphis, TN
100,000	Greater Memphis Arts Council, Memphis, TN

FISCHBACH FOUNDATION

Giving Contact

Nancy Fischbach, President & Treasurer
PO Box 224
Deep River, CT 06417
Phone: (860)767-8745

Description

Founded: 1944
EIN: 237416874
Organization Type: Private Foundation
Giving Locations: NY; Israel
Grant Types: General Support.

Donor Information

Founder: Established by members of the Fischbach family.

Financial Summary

Total Giving: $138,221 (2003); $148,455 (2001)
Assets: $3,117,323 (2003); $3,406,949 (2001)
Gifts Received: $2,210,611 (1998); $1,500 (1996); $1,500 (1995)

Typical Recipients

Arts & Humanities: Dance, Arts & Humanities-General, History & Archaeology, Libraries, Museums/Galleries, Music, Opera, Public Broadcasting
Civic & Public Affairs: Clubs
Education: Arts/Humanities Education, Colleges & Universities, Engineering/Technological Education, Education-General, Minority Education, Private Education (Precollege), Religious Education, Science/Mathematics Education
Health: AIDS/HIV, Cancer, Clinics/Medical Centers, Diabetes, Emergency/Ambulance Services, Eyes/Blindness, Health-General, Hospitals, Long-Term Care, Medical Rehabilitation, Medical Research, Single-Disease Health Associations
International: Foreign Arts Organizations, International-General, Health Care/Hospitals, International Peace & Security Issues, International Relief Efforts, Missionary/Religious Activities
Religion: Religion-General, Jewish Causes, Ministries, Religious Organizations, Religious Welfare, Synagogues/Temples
Social Services: Child Welfare, Community Centers, Community Service Organizations, Counseling, Food/Clothing Distribution, Shelters/Homelessness, United Funds/United Ways, Youth Organizations

Application Procedures

Initial Contact: Send written request.
Deadlines: None.

Restrictions

Grants are not made to individuals or political or lobbying groups.

Foundation Officials

Nancy Fischbach: president
Beatrice Levenson: secretary

Grants Analysis

Disclosure Period: calendar year ending 2003
Total Grants: $138,221
Number of Grants: 36
Average Grant: $3,024*
Highest Grant: $32,375
Lowest Grant: $250
Typical Range: $1,000 to $5,000
***Note:** Average grant figure excludes highest grant.

Recent Grants

Note: Grants derived from 2001 Form 990.
General

35,000	Gilda's Club Westchester, Purchase, NY -- for informational film
11,200	Congregation Beth Shalom, Deep River, CT -- capital fund
10,000	Project ALS, Inc., New York, NY
9,814	Congregation Beth Shalom, Deep River, CT -- capital fund
5,650	UJA Federation, New York, NY
5,250	Gilda's Club Westchester, Purchase, NY
5,000	American Red Cross, Washington, DC -- for El Salvador earthquake
5,000	American Red Cross, Washington, DC
5,000	Rensselaer Polytechnic Institute, Troy, NY -- for travel grant
5,000	Rensselaer Polytechnic Institute, Troy, NY -- scholarship fund

SONJA AND F. CONRAD FISCHER FOUNDATION

Giving Contact

F. Conrad Fischer, Trustee
c/o William Blair & Co.
222 W. Adams
Chicago, IL 60606
Phone: (312)236-1600

Description

Founded: 1991
EIN: 366941059
Organization Type: Private Foundation
Grant Types: General Support.

Financial Summary

Total Giving: $104,300 (2003)
Giving Analysis: Giving for 2003 includes: foundation grants to United Way ($1,000)
Assets: $2,390,939 (2003)
Gifts Received: $59,319 (2003); $207,271 (2000); $130,000 (1999). Note: In 1996, 1999, 2000, and 2003, contributions were received from Sonja and F. Conrad Fischer.

Typical Recipients

Arts & Humanities: Historic Preservation, Libraries, Museums/Galleries, Music, Theater
Civic & Public Affairs: African American Affairs, Botanical Gardens/Parks, Community Foundations, Civic & Public Affairs-General, Zoos/Aquariums
Education: Colleges & Universities, Education Associations, Education Funds, Education-General, Public Education (Precollege), Secondary Education (Private)
Environment: Resource Conservation
Religion: Religious Organizations, Religious Welfare
Science: Science Museums
Social Services: Child Welfare, Community Service Organizations, Day Care, People with Disabilities, Recreation & Athletics, United Funds/United Ways

Application Procedures

Initial Contact: Send grant proposal with statement of purpose.
Deadlines: November 15.

Foundation Officials

F. Conrad Fischer: trustee
Sonja Fischer: trustee

Grants Analysis

Disclosure Period: calendar year ending 2003
Total Grants: $103,300*
Number of Grants: 21
Average Grant: $2,128*
Highest Grant: $25,000
Lowest Grant: $500
Typical Range: $500 to $5,000
*Note: Giving excludes United Way. Average grant excludes three highest grants ($65,000).

Recent Grants

Note: Grants derived from 2003 Form 990.
General

25,000	Westminister School
20,000	Chicago Child Care, Chicago, IL
20,000	University of Chicago, Chicago, IL
6,000	Field Museum, Chicago, IL
5,000	Chicago Botanic Garden, Glencoe, IL
5,000	Child Care Center, Evanston, IL
5,000	Winnetka Historical Society, Winnetka, IL
3,000	Link Unlimited, Chicago, IL
3,000	Wells College, Aurora, NY
2,000	Kalamazoo College Tennis, Kalamazoo, MI

FISERVE

Company Headquarters

West Des Moines, IA

Company Description

Employees: 85

Trust Foundation

Giving Contact

Greg Bentley, Chairman
Trust Foundation
Regency West 7
4400 Westown Parkway
West Des Moines, IA 50266-6751
Phone: (515)224-8013
Fax: (515)224-8186

Description

Founded: 1988
EIN: 421313172
Organization Type: Corporate Foundation
Former Name: Fiserve Foundation.

Giving Locations: IA: Des Moines
Grant Types: General Support.

Donor Information

Founder: Financial Information Trust

Financial Summary

Gifts Received: $13,708 (2000); $14,976 (1999); $10,356 (1998)

Typical Recipients

Arts & Humanities: Arts Associations & Councils, Arts Centers, Historic Preservation, Libraries, Public Broadcasting
Civic & Public Affairs: Clubs, Civic & Public Affairs-General, Parades/Festivals, Public Policy, Urban & Community Affairs
Education: Colleges & Universities, Secondary Education (Public)
Environment: Wildlife Protection
Health: Alzheimer's Disease, Cancer, Children's Health/Hospitals, Diabetes, Emergency/Ambulance Services, Heart, Hospices, Multiple Sclerosis, Respiratory, Single-Disease Health Associations
Religion: Religious Organizations, Religious Welfare
Science: Observatories & Planetariums, Scientific Centers & Institutes
Social Services: Animal Protection, At-Risk Youth, Big Brothers/Big Sisters, Child Welfare, Community Centers, Community Service Organizations, Family Services, Food/Clothing Distribution, People with Disabilities, Shelters/Homelessness, Special Olympics, YMCA/YWCA/YMHA/YWHA

Application Procedures

Initial Contact: Send a brief letter of inquiry.
Application Requirements: history of organization, financial data, and contact person.
Deadlines: None.

Restrictions

Grants are not made to individuals.

Foundation Officials

Peter A. Anderson: treasurer
Greg Bentley: director
Kim Katch: secretary
Steve Willis: director
Edie C. Winkelman: chairman

Grants Analysis

Disclosure Period: calendar year ending 2000
Total Grants: $15,642
Number of Grants: 37
Average Grant: $423
Highest Grant: $1,500
Typical Range: $200 to $700

Recent Grants

Note: Grants derived from 2002 Form 990.

General

1,500	Blank Children's Hospital Foundation, Des Moines, IA
1,480	Make A Wish Foundation, Chicago, IL
1,214	Foodbank of Iowa, IA
1,162	Hospice of Central Iowa, Des Moines, IA
1,000	Civic Center, Des Moines, IA
750	Family Enrichment Center
683	Ronald McDonald House, Missoula, MT
600	Children's Convalescent Home, Des Moines, IA
520	Amanda the Panda, Des Moines, IA
500	Iowa College Foundation, Des Moines, IA

RAY C. FISH FOUNDATION

Giving Contact

Barbara F. Daniel, President
2001 Kirby Dr., Suite 1005
Houston, TX 77019
Phone: (713)522-0741
Fax: (713)529-4033

Description

Founded: 1957
EIN: 746043047
Organization Type: General Purpose Foundation
Giving Locations: TX: Galveston, Houston including metropolitan area, Kerrville
Grant Types: Capital, Challenge, Endowment, General Support, Matching, Multiyear/Continuing Support, Operating Expenses, Project, Research, Scholarship, Seed Money.

Donor Information

Founder: The late Raymond Clinton Fish established the foundation in Texas in 1957, five years before his death. Mr. Fish was board chairman of the Fish Engineering Corporation and president and director of numerous gas pipeline and petrochemical firms. He helped create the Transcontinental Gas Pipeline System (Transco), the Pacific Northwest Pipeline System, and the Texas-Illinois Pipeline Company. His wife, Mirtha Galvez Fish, chaired the foundation prior to her death in 1967. Large portions of their estates went to benefit the foundation.

Financial Summary

Total Giving: $1,400,000 (fiscal year ending June 30, 2003 approx); $1,400,000 (fiscal 2002 approx); $1,470,640 (fiscal 2001)
Assets: $27,000,000 (fiscal 2003 approx); $27,000,000 (fiscal 2002 approx)
Gifts Received: $68,676 (fiscal 1999); $60,643 (fiscal 1995); $43,419 (fiscal 1994). Note: The foundation has received contributions from the Ray C. and Martha G. Fish Trust in Houston, TX.

Typical Recipients

Arts & Humanities: Arts Associations & Councils, Arts Centers, Ballet, Dance, Ethnic & Folk Arts, Film & Video, Arts & Humanities-General, Historic Preservation, History & Archaeology, Libraries, Museums/Galleries, Music, Opera, Performing Arts, Public Broadcasting, Theater
Civic & Public Affairs: Botanical Gardens/Parks, Business/Free Enterprise, Clubs, Economic Development, Economic Policy, Employment/Job Training, Civic & Public Affairs-General, Hispanic Affairs, Housing, Inner-City Development, Parades/Festivals, Philanthropic Organizations, Professional & Trade Associations, Public Policy, Urban & Community Affairs, Zoos/Aquariums
Education: Business Education, Colleges & Universities, Education Reform, Engineering/Technological Education, Environmental Education, Faculty Development, Education-General, Legal Education, Literacy, Medical Education, Minority Education, Preschool Education, Private Education (Precollege), Public Education (Precollege), Science/Mathematics Education, Secondary Education (Private), Social Sciences Education, Special Education, Student Aid
Environment: Energy, Environment-General, Resource Conservation
Health: Alzheimer's Disease, Cancer, Clinics/Medical Centers, Emergency/Ambulance Services, Health Organizations, Heart, Hospices, Hospitals, Hospitals (University Affiliated), Kidney, Medical Rehabilitation, Medical Research, Research/Studies Institutes, Single-Disease Health Associations
International: Health Care/Hospitals, Missionary/Religious Activities
Religion: Churches, Jewish Causes, Ministries, Reli-

gious Organizations, Religious Welfare, Social/Policy Issues
Science: Science Museums
Social Services: At-Risk Youth, Camps, Child Abuse, Child Welfare, Community Centers, Community Service Organizations, Counseling, Emergency Relief, Family Planning, Food/Clothing Distribution, Homes, People with Disabilities, Recreation & Athletics, Scouts, Senior Services, United Funds/United Ways, Volunteer Services, YMCA/YWCA/YMHA/YWHA, Youth Organizations

Application Procedures
Initial Contact: Proposals should be submitted in writing.
Deadlines: None.
Review Process: The foundation will review the proposal and respond as quickly as possible. The board of trustees may request an interview and supplementary information.

Additional Information
Publications: Guidelines

Foundation Officials
Robert J. Cruikshank: vice president, assistant secretary, trustee CORP AFFIL director: Reliant Energy Inc.; director: Texas Biotechnology Corp.; director: MAXXAM Inc.; director: Kaiser Aluminum Corp.; director: KLU; director: Kaiser Aluminum & Chemical Corp.
Barbara Fish Daniel: president, trustee B 1935. PRIM CORP EMPL vice president: M.J. Daniel Co. Inc.
Christopher J. Daniel: vice president, treasurer, trustee
James L. Daniel, Jr.: vice president, trustee
Paula Hooton: executive administrator

Grants Analysis
Disclosure Period: fiscal year ending June 30, 2001
Total Grants: $1,470,640
Number of Grants: 168
Average Grant: $8,013*
Highest Grant: $132,500
Lowest Grant: $1,000
Typical Range: $1,000 to $25,000
*Note: Average grant excludes highest grant.

HARMES C. FISHBACK FOUNDATION TRUST

Giving Contact
Katharine H. Stapleton, Trustee
8 Village Rd.
Englewood, CO 80110-4908
Phone: (303)789-1753

Description
Founded: 1972
EIN: 846094542
Organization Type: Private Foundation
Giving Locations: CO: Denver including metropolitan area
Grant Types: Endowment, General Support, Multiyear/Continuing Support, Scholarship.

Donor Information
Founder: the late Harmes C. Fishback

Financial Summary
Total Giving: $219,509 (2003)
Assets: $4,053,378 (2003)

Typical Recipients
Arts & Humanities: Arts Centers, Community Arts, Ethnic & Folk Arts, Historic Preservation, History &

Archaeology, Libraries, Museums/Galleries, Music, Opera, Performing Arts, Theater
Civic & Public Affairs: Botanical Gardens/Parks, Economic Development, Civic & Public Affairs-General, Legal Aid, Public Policy, Urban & Community Affairs, Zoos/Aquariums
Education: Colleges & Universities, Continuing Education, Education Funds, Education-General, Gifted & Talented Programs, International Studies, Leadership Training, Private Education (Precollege), Secondary Education (Private), Student Aid
Environment: Environment-General
Health: AIDS/HIV, Arthritis, Cancer, Diabetes, Health-General, Health Funds, Health Organizations, Hospices, Hospitals, Hospitals (University Affiliated), Medical Rehabilitation, Medical Research, Mental Health, Respiratory, Transplant Networks/Donor Banks
Religion: Churches, Dioceses, Religious Welfare
Science: Science Museums
Social Services: Child Welfare, Community Service Organizations, Day Care, Family Planning, Family Services, Food/Clothing Distribution, People with Disabilities, Senior Services, Social Services-General, United Funds/United Ways, YMCA/YWCA/YMHA/YWHA, Youth Organizations

Application Procedures
Initial Contact: Send brief letter describing program.
Deadlines: None.

Restrictions
Does not support individuals.

Foundation Officials
Katharine H. Stapleton: trustee

Grants Analysis
Disclosure Period: calendar year ending 2003
Total Grants: $219,509
Number of Grants: 35
Average Grant: $3,409*
Highest Grant: $54,000
Lowest Grant: $500
Typical Range: $1,000 to $5,000
*Note: Average grant figure excludes two highest grants ($107,000).

Recent Grants
Note: Grants derived from 2003 Form 990.
Library-Related
| 5,000 | Denver Public Library, Denver, CO |
General
54,000	Barstow School, Kansas City, MO
53,000	Institute of International Education, Denver, CO
17,544	Colorado Symphony, Denver, CO
10,000	Amon Carter Museum, Ft. Worth, TX
7,765	University of Colorado Foundation, Boulder, CO
7,500	Denver Art Museum, Denver, CO
7,500	Limb Preservation Foundation, Denver, CO
7,500	St Joseph's Hospital, Denver, CO
5,000	Planned Parenthood, Denver, CO

FISHER FOUNDATION

Giving Contact
Hinda N. Fischer, President & Treasurer
36 Brookside Boulevard
West Hartford, CT 06107
Phone: (860)232-2755

Description
Founded: 1959
EIN: 066039415
Organization Type: Private Foundation

Giving Locations: CT: Hartford including surrounding area
Grant Types: General Support.

Donor Information
Founder: Stanley D. Fisher Trust, FIP Corp.

Financial Summary
Total Giving: $448,550 (2003). Note: 1996 Giving includes scholarship (6,000); United Way ($2,000).
Assets: $10,990,003 (2003)
Gifts Received: $494,482 (1998); $460,100 (1997); $405,043 (1996). Note: In 1997 and 1998, contributions were received from the Stanley D. Fisher Trust. In 1995, contributions were received from the Stanley D. Fisher Trust.

Typical Recipients
Arts & Humanities: Arts Associations & Councils, Arts Centers, Ballet, Dance, Historic Preservation, Libraries, Literary Arts, Museums/Galleries, Music, Performing Arts, Public Broadcasting, Theater
Civic & Public Affairs: Botanical Gardens/Parks, Business/Free Enterprise, Community Foundations, Economic Development, Employment/Job Training, Civic & Public Affairs-General, Hispanic Affairs, Housing, Municipalities/Towns, Nonprofit Management, Urban & Community Affairs, Women's Affairs
Education: Arts/Humanities Education, Colleges & Universities, Education Associations, Education Reform, Education-General, Literacy, Medical Education, Minority Education, Public Education (Precollege), Science/Mathematics Education, Special Education, Student Aid
Health: AIDS/HIV, Children's Health/Hospitals, Clinics/Medical Centers, Eyes/Blindness, Health Organizations, Home-Care Services, Hospices, Hospitals, Long-Term Care, Medical Rehabilitation, Mental Health, Multiple Sclerosis, Nursing Services, Public Health, Speech & Hearing
International: Human Rights, International Relief Efforts
Religion: Churches, Jewish Causes, Religious Organizations, Religious Welfare
Science: Scientific Centers & Institutes
Social Services: At-Risk Youth, Camps, Child Welfare, Community Centers, Community Service Organizations, Counseling, Day Care, Domestic Violence, Emergency Relief, Family Planning, Family Services, Food/Clothing Distribution, Homes, People with Disabilities, Recreation & Athletics, Senior Services, Shelters/Homelessness, Substance Abuse, United Funds/United Ways, YMCA/YWCA/YMHA/YWHA, Youth Organizations

Application Procedures
Initial Contact: The foundation has no formal grant application procedure or application form. Send a brief letter of inquiry.
Deadlines: None.

Foundation Officials
Diane Fisher Bell: vice president
Beverly Boyle: executive director
Lois Fisher Dietzel: vice president
Michael Finkelstein: assistant treasurer
Hinda N. Fisher: president, treasurer
Nancy S. Freeman: secretary
Martha Newman: executive director

Grants Analysis
Disclosure Period: calendar year ending 2003
Total Grants: $448,550*
Typical Range: $1,000 to $10,000
*Note: No grant list available for 2003.

Recent Grants
Note: Grants derived from 2000 Form 990.
General
| 20,000 | Action in Education |
| 14,000 | Greater Hartford Interracial Scholarship, Hartford, CT |

10,000	Bell School Reform Network, McLean, VA
10,000	Boundless Playgrounds, Inc
10,000	Camp Courant, Hartford, CT
10,000	Center City Churches, Hartford, CT
10,000	Children in Placement, Hartford, CT
10,000	Co-op Initiatives, Hartford, CT
10,000	Coon College, Coon Rapid, MN
10,000	CPEP

FLAGLER FOUNDATION

Giving Contact
Bradford B. Sauer, Vice President, Treasurer & Director
PO Box 26665
Suntrust Bank Endowments & Foundations
Richmond, VA 23261
Phone: (804)782-5280

Description
Founded: 1963
EIN: 546051282
Organization Type: General Purpose Foundation
Giving Locations: VA: east of the Mississippi River.
Grant Types: General Support.

Donor Information
Founder: the late Jessie Kenan Wise

Financial Summary
Total Giving: $884,932 (2003); $1,507,796 (2002); $1,351,797 (2001)
Assets: $22,533,420 (2003); $20,110,446 (2002); $24,794,282 (2001)

Typical Recipients
Arts & Humanities: Ballet, Dance, Historic Preservation, History & Archaeology, Libraries, Museums/Galleries, Music, Public Broadcasting, Theater
Civic & Public Affairs: Botanical Gardens/Parks, Clubs, Community Foundations, Economic Policy, Employment/Job Training, Civic & Public Affairs-General, Housing, Municipalities/Towns, Philanthropic Organizations, Professional & Trade Associations, Urban & Community Affairs
Education: Afterschool/Enrichment Programs, Colleges & Universities, Education Funds, Faculty Development, Education-General, Minority Education, Private Education (Precollege), Public Education (Precollege), Secondary Education (Private), Secondary Education (Public), Special Education, Student Aid
Environment: Air/Water Quality, Forestry, Environment-General, Resource Conservation, Wildlife Protection
Health: Cancer, Children's Health/Hospitals, Emergency/Ambulance Services, Eyes/Blindness, Health Organizations, Hospices, Hospitals, Long-Term Care, Nursing Services, Public Health, Single-Disease Health Associations
Religion: Churches, Ministries, Religious Organizations, Religious Welfare
Social Services: Animal Protection, Camps, Child Welfare, Community Centers, Community Service Organizations, Counseling, Day Care, Domestic Violence, Family Planning, Family Services, Homes, People with Disabilities, Scouts, Senior Services, Shelters/Homelessness, United Funds/United Ways, YMCA/YWCA/YMHA/YWHA, Youth Organizations

Application Procedures
Initial Contact: Applications should be submitted in letter proposal form.
Deadlines: March 1.

Restrictions
The foundation does not make grants to support capital programs or long-range projects.

Foundation Officials
William Hill Brown, III: director
Louise Lewis Foster: president, director
Catherine Gray Hathaway: director
Janet P. Lewis Sauer: director
Lewis B. Pollard, Jr.: vice president, director
Susan Fleet Roberts: assistant secretary, director
Bradford B. Sauer: vice president, treasurer, director
Julious P. Smith, Jr.: counsel
B. Briscoe White, III: director
Kenan Lewis White: secretary, director

Grants Analysis
Disclosure Period: calendar year ending 2003
Total Grants: $884,932
Number of Grants: 16
Average Grant: $29,995*
Highest Grant: $435,000
Lowest Grant: $5,000
Typical Range: $10,000 to $50,000
*Note: Average grant figure excludes highest grant.

Recent Grants
Note: Grants derived from 2002 Form 990.
General
425,000	Flagler Home, Richmond, VA
250,000	Massey Cancer Center, Richmond, VA
200,000	Flagler College, Augustine, FL
100,000	Goodwill Industries, Richmond, VA
100,000	Richmond Hill, Richmond, VA
61,796	Lewis Ginter Botanical Garden, Richmond, VA
50,000	Steward School, Richmond, VA
50,000	Woodberry Forest School, Orange, VA
37,000	Adult Care Services, Richmond, VA
30,000	Virginia Supportive Housing, Richmond, VA

FLEISHHACKER FOUNDATION

Giving Contact
Christine Elbel, Executive Director
1016 Lincoln Blvd., No. 12
San Francisco, CA 94129
Phone: (415)561-5350
E-mail: info@fleishhackerfoundation.org
Web: http://www.fleishhackerfoundation.org

Description
Founded: 1947
EIN: 946051048
Organization Type: Private Foundation
Giving Locations: CA: San Francisco including Bay area; NY: New York
Grant Types: Capital, General Support, Project, Seed Money.

Donor Information
Founder: the late Mortimer Fleishhacker, Sr., Janet Fleishhacker Bates

Financial Summary
Total Giving: $693,600 (2004); $111,000 (2002 approx); $600,700 (2001)
Giving Analysis: Giving for 2004 includes: foundation grants to United Way ($3,000); foundation gifts to individuals ($99,500); 2001: foundation gifts to individuals ($3,000); foundation grants to United Way ($54,200)
Assets: $15,587,342 (2004); $13,354,633 (2001)

Gifts Received: $55,000 (1992). Note: In fiscal 1992, contributions were received from the Walter and Elise Haas Fund ($50,000) and Grants for the Arts ($5,000).

Typical Recipients
Arts & Humanities: Arts Appreciation, Arts Associations & Councils, Arts Centers, Arts Festivals, Arts Funds, Arts Institutes, Arts Outreach, Ballet, Community Arts, Dance, Ethnic & Folk Arts, Film & Video, Arts & Humanities-General, Historic Preservation, Libraries, Museums/Galleries, Music, Opera, Performing Arts, Theater
Civic & Public Affairs: Civic & Public Affairs-General, Nonprofit Management, Public Policy, Urban & Community Affairs, Zoos/Aquariums
Education: Arts/Humanities Education, Colleges & Universities, Education Reform, Faculty Development, Education-General, Literacy, Minority Education, Private Education (Precollege), Public Education (Precollege), School Volunteerism, Science/Mathematics Education, Secondary Education (Public), Social Sciences Education
Social Services: Family Services, United Funds/United Ways

Application Procedures
Initial Contact: For grants, send a short letter proposal (2-6 pages) outlining the need for funding, how funds will be used, and the impact on the program's beneficiaries, and a summary of the financial parameters of the program.
Deadlines: January 15 and July 15.
Decision Notification: Decisions are made within two to five months.

Restrictions
Foundation supports arts and culture and precollegiate education in the greater Bay area. Does not provide funds for annual campaigns, deficit financing, matching gifts, financial aid, scholarships, or special events. Primarily supports preselected organizations.

Additional Information
Publications: Application Guidelines

Foundation Officials
Delia Fleishhacker Ehrlich: director
Jodi Ehrlich: director
John Stephen Ehrlich, Jr.: vice president
Christine Elbel: executive director
David Fleishhacker: president B San Francisco, CA 1937. ED Princeton University AB (1959); University of California MA (1965). PRIM CORP EMPL president: Fleishhacker Foundation. NONPR AFFIL member: National Association Prin Girls Schools; director: Saint Josephs Hospital Queen Angels; member: Elementary School Heads Association.
Mortimer Fleishhacker, III: treasurer
William Fleishhacker: director
Lois Gordon: director
Sandra Fleishhacker Randall: director
Edie F. Rindal: director
Deborah Sloss: secretary
Hillary Sloss: director
Laura Sloss: director

Grants Analysis
Disclosure Period: calendar year ending 2004
Total Grants: $591,100*
Number of Grants: 106
Average Grant: $5,576
Highest Grant: $30,000
Lowest Grant: $1,000
Typical Range: $1,000 to $10,000
*Note: Giving excludes United Way and gifts to individuals.

Recent Grants
Note: Grants derived from 2001 Form 990.

General

50,000	9th Street Media Consortium, San Francisco, CA -- capital campaign
32,500	Fine Arts Museum of San Francisco, San Francisco, CA -- capital campaign
25,000	Sonoma Valley Museum of Art, Sonoma, CA -- exhibit support
22,500	Intersection for the Arts, San Francisco, CA -- monthly jazz series
15,000	Earth Island Institute, San Francisco, CA -- annual prize for youth
15,000	Reading Tree, San Francisco, CA -- Book Giveaway Program
15,000	San Francisco Zoo, San Francisco, CA -- capital campaign
15,000	San Jose Repertory Theatre, San Jose, CA -- Playwright Festival
12,000	Hamlin School, San Francisco, CA -- capital campaign
11,000	Northern California Grantmakers, San Francisco, CA -- Summer Youth Project

ROBERT FLEMING AND JANE HOWE PATRICK FOUNDATION

Giving Contact

Adam B. Dantzscher, Executive Director
PO Box 234
Charlotte, VT 05445
Phone: (802)660-9447

Description

Founded: 1989
EIN: 030317962
Organization Type: Private Foundation
Giving Locations: VT
Grant Types: General Support.

Financial Summary

Total Giving: $108,000 (fiscal year ending June 30, 2004); $87,830 (fiscal 2001)
Assets: $1,569,096 (fiscal 2004); $1,976,128 (fiscal 2001)

Typical Recipients

Arts & Humanities: Historic Preservation, History & Archaeology, Libraries, Museums/Galleries, Performing Arts, Public Broadcasting
Civic & Public Affairs: Economic Development, Employment/Job Training, Civic & Public Affairs-General, Housing, Safety, Urban & Community Affairs, Women's Affairs
Education: Colleges & Universities, Education-General, Literacy, Social Sciences Education
Health: AIDS/HIV, Clinics/Medical Centers, Health Organizations, Heart, Hospices, Multiple Sclerosis, Single-Disease Health Associations
Religion: Churches
Social Services: Animal Protection, Child Abuse, Community Service Organizations, Domestic Violence, Emergency Relief, Family Planning, Food/Clothing Distribution, Homes, People with Disabilities, Senior Services, Shelters/Homelessness, YMCA/YWCA/YMHA/YWHA, Youth Organizations

Application Procedures

Initial Contact: Send a brief letter of inquiry.
Application Requirements: Include a description of organization and purpose of funds sought.
Deadlines: None.

Restrictions

Giving is limited to Vermont organizations.

Foundation Officials

Richard Cunningham: vice president, director
Adam B. Dantzscher: executive director
C. Dennis Hill: director
Harriet S. Patrick: president, director
Glen A. Wright: director

Grants Analysis

Disclosure Period: fiscal year ending June 30, 2004
Total Grants: $108,000
Number of Grants: 58
Average Grant: $1,862
Highest Grant: $10,000
Lowest Grant: $500
Typical Range: $500 to $3,000

Recent Grants

Note: Grants derived from fiscal 2004 Form 990.
General

10,000	Champlain Maritime Museum, Vergennes, VT
10,000	Elderly Services, Middlebury, VT -- for program assistance
7,500	Fletcher Allen Health Care, Burlington, VT -- for cardiac rehabilitation center
5,000	Center for the Lake, Burlington, VT
5,000	Community Health Center, Burlington, VT -- for dental program
5,000	Landmark Trust, Dummerston, VT -- for projects/education programs
3,000	Committee on Temporary Shelter, Burlington, VT
3,000	Vermont Foodbank, South Barre, VT
3,000	Vermont Museum and Gallery Alliance, Shelburne, VT -- for program assistance
2,500	Vermont Lion Charities, South Strafford, VT -- for veteran's park

FLEMING FOUNDATION

Giving Contact

G. Malcolm Louden, CPA
500 W. 7th St., Suite 1007
Ft. Worth, TX 76102-4732
Phone: (817)335-3741
Fax: (817)338-4844

Description

Founded: 1936
EIN: 756022736
Organization Type: Family Foundation
Giving Locations: TX: Fort Worth including Tarrant County
Grant Types: Capital, General Support, Operating Expenses.

Donor Information

Founder: The late William Fleming, an oilman and philanthropist, established the Fleming Foundation in Texas in 1936. Mr. Fleming was interested in Baptist churches and schools.

Financial Summary

Total Giving: $341,500 (2003); $546,500 (2001)
Assets: $2,586,266 (2003); $2,582,634 (2001)
Gifts Received: $1,000,000 (1997 approx); $1,000,000 (1996 approx); $665,000 (1995 approx)

Typical Recipients

Arts & Humanities: Arts Associations & Councils, Arts Centers, Arts Festivals, Ballet, Community Arts, Dance, History & Archaeology, Libraries, Museums/Galleries, Music, Opera, Performing Arts, Theater
Civic & Public Affairs: Botanical Gardens/Parks, Clubs, Economic Development, Civic & Public Affairs-General, Hispanic Affairs, Parades/Festivals, Philanthropic Organizations, Rural Affairs, Safety, Urban & Community Affairs, Women's Affairs, Zoos/

Aquariums
Education: Colleges & Universities, Education Associations, Education Funds, Education-General, Private Education (Precollege), School Volunteerism, Special Education
Environment: Environment-General, Wildlife Protection
Health: AIDS/HIV, Alzheimer's Disease, Cancer, Children's Health/Hospitals, Clinics/Medical Centers, Eyes/Blindness, Health Organizations, Heart, Hospitals, Medical Rehabilitation, Mental Health, Research/Studies Institutes, Single-Disease Health Associations
International: Foreign Educational Institutions, International Affairs, International Development, International Relief Efforts
Religion: Bible Study/Translation, Churches, Religion-General, Jewish Causes, Religious Welfare
Science: Science Museums
Social Services: Big Brothers/Big Sisters, Child Welfare, Community Centers, Community Service Organizations, Counseling, Crime Prevention, Family Planning, Family Services, Food/Clothing Distribution, Homes, People with Disabilities, Recreation & Athletics, Scouts, Shelters/Homelessness, Social Services-General, Substance Abuse, United Funds/United Ways, YMCA/YWCA/YMHA/YWHA, Youth Organizations

Application Procedures

Initial Contact: Applicants should submit a written proposal outlining intended use of funds.
Deadlines: None.
Review Process: The board of directors meets in January, April, July, and September.

Restrictions

The foundation does not give grants to individuals, or for capital or endowment funds, deficit financing, matching gifts, fellowships, scholarships, land acquisition, exchange programs, conferences, or publications.
Gives only to local organizations.

Additional Information

The foundation reports that it is closely affiliated with the Walsh Foundation, Ft. Worth, TX. The two foundations share many of the same officers and directors.

Foundation Officials

Gary F. Goble: director PRIM CORP EMPL secretary, treasurer, director: Walsh & Watts Inc.
G. Malcolm Louden: assistant treasurer, assistant secretary, director B 1945. ED Texas Christian University BBA (1969). PRIM CORP EMPL vice president, director: Walsh & Watts Inc. CORP AFFIL director: Overton Bank & Trust National Association; executive vice president, director: F Howard Walsh Jr Oper Co.; director: Overton Bancshares Inc.
F. Howard Walsh, Jr.: treasurer, secretary, trustee B 1941. ED Texas Christian University BA (1963). PRIM CORP EMPL president, director: F Howard Walsh Jr Oper Co. ADD CORP EMPL owner: Walsh Oil Co.
Mary D. Fleming Walsh: president, trustee B Whitewright, TX October 29, 1913. ED Southern Methodist University BA (1934). CORP AFFIL partner: Walsh Co. NONPR AFFIL honorary director: Van Cliburn International Piano Competition; life member: YWCA; member: Texas League Composers; member: Texas Boys Club Auxilliary; member: Texas Christian University Fine Arts Foundation Guild; guarantor: Texas Boys Choir; charter member: Lloyd Shaw Foundation; member: Tarrant County Auxiliary Edna Gladney Home; guarantor: Scholar Cantorum; member: Rae Reimers Bible Study; member: Round Table International; member: National Association Cowbelles; member: Opera Guild; member: Jewel Charity Ball; member: Friends Texas Boys Choir; member: Goodwill Industries Auxiliary; guarantor: Fort Worth Theatre; guarantor: Fort Worth Opera Association;

member: Fort Worth Pan Hellenic; member: Fort Worth Childrens Hospital; member: Fort Worth Ballet Association; member: Fort Worth Boys Club; guarantor, member: Fort Worth Art Council; guarantor, member: Fort Worth Ballet; member: Fort Worth Art Association; member: Childrens Hospital Women's Board; member: Colorado Springs Fine Arts Center; member: Child Study Center; member: Chi Omega Carousel; member: Chi Omega Mothers; member: Chi Omega; member: American Guild Organists; member: Big Brothers Tarrant County; member: American Automobile Association; co-founder: American Field Service Fort Worth; member: American Association University Women. CLUB AFFIL Women's Club; Texas Christian University Women's Club; Ridglea Country Club; Shady Oaks Country Club; Garden of Gods Club; Colonial Country Club; Colorado Springs Country Club.

Grants Analysis

Disclosure Period: calendar year ending 2003
Total Grants: $341,500
Number of Grants: 10
Average Grant: $1,438*
Highest Grant: $170,000
Lowest Grant: $500
Typical Range: $500 to $5,000
***Note:** Average grant figure excludes two highest grants ($330,000).

Recent Grants

Note: Grants derived from 2002 Form 990.
General

135,000	Dorothy Shaw Bell Choir, Ft. Worth, TX
90,000	Littlest Wiseman, Ft. Worth, TX
10,000	Fort Worth Dallas Ballet, Ft. Worth, TX
5,000	Trinity Valley School, Ft. Worth, TX
1,500	Fort Worth Zoo, Ft. Worth, TX
1,000	Boy Scouts of America, Wichita Falls, TX
1,000	Interfaith Ministries, Wichita Falls, TX
1,000	North Texas Rehabilitation Center, Wichita Falls, TX
1,000	Salvation Army, Wichita Falls, TX
1,000	Wichita Falls Faith Missionary, Wichita Falls, TX

FLETCHER FOUNDATION

Giving Contact

Warner S. Fletcher, Secretary, Treasurer & Trustee
370 Main St., 12th Fl.
Worcester, MA 01608
Phone: (508)798-8621
Fax: (508)791-1201
E-mail: wfletcher@ftwlaw.com

Description

Founded: 1981
EIN: 046470890
Organization Type: Private Foundation
Giving Locations: MA: Worcester
Grant Types: General Support.

Donor Information

Founder: the late Paris Fletcher

Financial Summary

Total Giving: $1,162,500 (2003)
Giving Analysis: Giving for 2003 includes: foundation grants to United Way ($20,000)
Assets: $26,042,887 (2003)
Gifts Received: $2,059,813 (1999); $176,612 (1995); $93,765 (1994). Note: In 1999, contributions were received from Warner S. Fletcher ($498,094), Patricia A. Fletcher ($1,082,813), and Allen W. Fletcher ($478,906). In 1995, contributions were received from the estate of Marion S. Fletcher.

Typical Recipients

Arts & Humanities: Arts Associations & Councils, Arts Festivals, Community Arts, Ethnic & Folk Arts, Historic Preservation, History & Archaeology, Libraries, Museums/Galleries, Music, Performing Arts, Public Broadcasting, Theater
Civic & Public Affairs: Business/Free Enterprise, Clubs, Community Foundations, Economic Development, Civic & Public Affairs-General, Hispanic Affairs, Housing, Law & Justice, Legal Aid, Municipalities/Towns, Urban & Community Affairs, Women's Affairs
Education: Colleges & Universities, Community & Junior Colleges, Education Associations, Education Funds, Education Reform, Education-General, Literacy, Medical Education, Private Education (Precollege), Science/Mathematics Education
Environment: Environment-General, Resource Conservation, Wildlife Protection
Health: Cancer, Children's Health/Hospitals, Clinics/Medical Centers, Diabetes, Emergency/Ambulance Services, Health Organizations, Medical Research, Nursing Services, Public Health
Science: Science Museums
Social Services: Animal Protection, At-Risk Youth, Child Welfare, Community Centers, Community Service Organizations, Counseling, Crime Prevention, Day Care, Family Planning, Homes, Senior Services, Shelters/Homelessness, Substance Abuse, United Funds/United Ways, YMCA/YWCA/YMHA/YWHA, Youth Organizations

Application Procedures

Initial Contact: Send brief letter describing program.
Application Requirements: Include proof of tax-exempt status.
Deadlines: None.

Restrictions

Must be listed in federal cumulative listings.

Foundation Officials

Allen W. Fletcher: chairman, trustee B 1948. PRIM CORP EMPL chairman, treasurer: Worcester Publishing Inc. CORP AFFIL chairman, treasurer: Worcester Business Journal; chairman, treasurer: Worcester Magazine; chairman, treasurer: Hartford Business Journal.
Mary F. Fletcher: trustee
Patricia A. Fletcher: trustee
Warner S. Fletcher: secretary, treasurer, trustee B Worcester, MA 1945. ED Williams College BA (1967); Boston University JD (1973). PRIM CORP EMPL treasurer: Fletcher, Tilton & Whipple PC. CORP AFFIL director: Wyman-Gordon Co.

Grants Analysis

Disclosure Period: calendar year ending 2003
Total Grants: $1,142,500*
Number of Grants: 41
Average Grant: $19,539*
Highest Grant: $200,000
Lowest Grant: $2,000
Typical Range: $5,000 to $50,000
***Note:** Giving excludes United Way. Average grant excludes three highest grants ($400,000).

Recent Grants

Note: Grants derived from 2001 Form 990.
Library-Related

150,000	Friends of the Worcester Public Library, Worcester, MA -- expansion and renovations to Salem Square Public Library

General

200,000	Worcester Polytechnic Institute, Worcester, MA -- for Worcester Community Project Center
100,000	Worcester Historic Museum, Worcester, MA -- for leadership challenge
80,000	Quinsigamond Community College Foundation, Worcester, MA -- for renovations to Applied Arts Laboratories

75,000	Bancroft School, Worcester, MA -- towards school's initiative
50,000	Bridge of Central Massachusetts, Northboro, MA -- for capital campaign
50,000	Greater Worcester Land Trust, Worcester, MA -- toward purchase of 100 acre parcel adjacent to Broad Meadow
50,000	Martin Luther King Jr. Business Empowerment Center, Worcester, MA -- for renovations
50,000	YMCA of Greater Worcester, Worcester, MA -- for construction
40,000	Joy of Music Program, Worcester, MA -- for renovations
40,000	Massachusetts College of Pharmacy and Allied Health Sciences, Boston, MA -- towards new facility in downtown Worcester

FLORIDA ROCK INDUSTRIES INC.

Company Headquarters

127 Edgewood Ave., S
Jacksonville, FL 32254
Web: http://www.flarock.com

Company Description

Founded: 1945
Ticker: FRK
Exchange: NYSE
Revenue: US$723.7 million (2002)
Employees: 3127 (2003)
SIC(s): 1442 Construction Sand & Gravel, 3271 Concrete Block & Brick, 3273 Ready-Mixed Concrete.

Operating Locations

Florida Rock Industries (FL--Jacksonville)

Florida Rock Industries Foundation

Giving Contact

John D. Milton, Jr., Secretary & Treasurer
PO Box 4667
Jacksonville, FL 32201
Phone: (904)355-1781
Fax: (904)366-1866

Description

EIN: 592143326
Organization Type: Corporate Foundation
Giving Locations: FL
Grant Types: General Support, Scholarship.

Financial Summary

Total Giving: $440,276 (fiscal year ending September 30, 2003); $364,917 (fiscal 2002); $315,251 (fiscal 2001)
Giving Analysis: Giving for fiscal 2002 includes: foundation grants to United Way ($800); fiscal 2001: foundation scholarships ($5,000); foundation grants to United Way ($41,500); foundation ($268,751)
Assets: $2,733,157 (fiscal 2003); $2,663,821 (fiscal 2002); $3,005,089 (fiscal 2001)
Gifts Received: $250,000 (fiscal 2003); $230,000 (fiscal 2002); $500,000 (fiscal 2001). Note: Contributions were received from Florida Rock Industries.

Typical Recipients

Arts & Humanities: Arts Associations & Councils, Arts Funds, Historic Preservation, History & Archaeology, Libraries, Museums/Galleries, Music, Opera, Performing Arts, Public Broadcasting, Theater
Civic & Public Affairs: African American Affairs, Bo-

tanical Gardens/Parks, Community Foundations, Economic Development, Employment/Job Training, Civic & Public Affairs-General, Legal Aid, Philanthropic Organizations, Public Policy, Urban & Community Affairs, Zoos/Aquariums

Education: Afterschool/Enrichment Programs, Business Education, Colleges & Universities, Community & Junior Colleges, Continuing Education, Education Associations, Education Funds, Elementary Education (Public), Engineering/Technological Education, Faculty Development, Education-General, Leadership Training, Minority Education, Private Education (Precollege), Public Education (Precollege), Special Education, Student Aid, Vocational & Technical Education

Environment: Environment-General, Resource Conservation

Health: Alzheimer's Disease, Cancer, Children's Health/Hospitals, Clinics/Medical Centers, Geriatric Health, Health Funds, Health Organizations, Hospices, Hospitals, Medical Research, Multiple Sclerosis, Single-Disease Health Associations

International: Health Care/Hospitals, International Environmental Issues

Religion: Churches, Dioceses, Religion-General, Jewish Causes, Ministries, Religious Organizations, Religious Welfare

Science: Science Museums, Scientific Research

Social Services: Animal Protection, At-Risk Youth, Camps, Child Welfare, Community Centers, Community Service Organizations, Counseling, Crime Prevention, Family Planning, Family Services, Homes, People with Disabilities, Recreation & Athletics, Scouts, Senior Services, Shelters/Homelessness, United Funds/United Ways, YMCA/YWCA/YMHA/YWHA, Youth Organizations

Application Procedures

Initial Contact: Send brief letter describing program.
Application Requirements: Include recently audited financial statement, description of benefits or services provided, list of board members and leading contributors with amounts, whether activities qualify for "Community Contributions Tax Credit" under the Florida Corporation Tax Act, whether contributions will be for capital or operating funds, and proof of tax-exempt status.
Deadlines: None.

Corporate Officials

Edward L. Baker: chairman, director B 1935. PRIM CORP EMPL chairman, director: Florida Rock Industries. CORP AFFIL chairman, director: FRP Properties; director: Virginia Concrete Co. Inc.; director: Flowers Industries; chairman, director: Arundel Corp.; director: Cardinal Concrete Co.

Foundation Officials

Edward L. Baker: president (see above)
John Daniel Baker, II: vice president B Jacksonville, FL 1948. ED Princeton University BA (1970); University of Florida JD (1973). CORP AFFIL director: Hughes Supply Inc.
John D. Milton, Jr.: secretary, treasurer

Grants Analysis

Disclosure Period: fiscal year ending September 30, 2003
Total Grants: $404,776*
Number of Grants: 89
Average Grant: $4,548
Highest Grant: $40,000
Lowest Grant: $100
Typical Range: $1,000 to $5,000
*Note: Giving excludes United Way.

Recent Grants

Note: Grants derived from fiscal 2003 Form 990.
General

80,000	Police Athletic League, North Palm Beach, FL
60,000	WJCT Foundation Inc., Jacksonville, FL

40,000	Seamark Ranch, Jacksonville, FL
40,000	St Vincent's Foundation, Jacksonville, FL
30,000	RMC Research Foundation Inc., Silver Spring, MD
25,000	Jacksonville Symphony Association, Jacksonville, FL
25,000	Jacksonville Symphony Association, Jacksonville, FL
20,000	ARC of Jacksonville, Jacksonville, FL
20,000	First Coast Educational Leadership Center, Jacksonville, FL
20,000	Greenwood School, Putney, VT

FLORIDA ROCK & TANK LINES

Company Headquarters

5714 Buffalo Ave.
Jacksonville, FL 32208
Web: http://www.patriottrans.com

Company Description

Employees: 537
SIC(s): 4200 Trucking & Warehousing.
Parent Company: Patriot Transportation Holding Inc., 1801 Art MuseumDr., Jacksonville, FL, United States

Operating Locations

Florida Rock & Tank Lines (FL--Jacksonville)

Florida Rock & Tank Lines Foundation

Giving Contact

John D. Milton, Jr., Secretary
Florida Rock & Tank Lines Foundation
PO Box 4667
Jacksonville, FL 32201
Phone: (904)355-1781
Fax: (904)366-1866

Description

EIN: 593050577
Organization Type: Corporate Foundation
Giving Locations: FL
Grant Types: General Support.

Financial Summary

Total Giving: $38,565 (fiscal year ending September 30, 2001)
Giving Analysis: Giving for fiscal 2001 includes: foundation grants to United Way ($1,000)
Assets: $645,720 (fiscal 2001)
Gifts Received: $100,000 (fiscal 1998); $100,000 (fiscal 1997); $100,000 (fiscal 1996). Note: Contributions were received from Florida Rock and Tank Lines.

Typical Recipients

Arts & Humanities: Libraries, Music, Performing Arts
Civic & Public Affairs: Civic & Public Affairs-General, Urban & Community Affairs
Education: Business Education, Colleges & Universities, Leadership Training
Environment: Forestry
Health: Health Organizations, Hospices, Single-Disease Health Associations
Religion: Ministries, Religious Organizations, Religious Welfare
Social Services: Community Service Organizations, Family Services, Recreation & Athletics, Scouts, Special Olympics, United Funds/United Ways, YMCA/YWCA/YMHA/YWHA, Youth Organizations

Application Procedures

Initial Contact: Send a brief letter of inquiry.
Application Requirements: Include a recently audited financial statement, description of benefits or services provided, list of board members and leading contributors and amount of such leading contributions/pledges, whether activities qualify for "Community Contributions Tax Credit" under the Florida Corporation Tax Act, whether contribution will be for capital or operating funds, and proof of tax-exempt status.
Deadlines: None.

Corporate Officials

John Anderson: chairman, chief executive officer PRIM CORP EMPL chairman: Florida Rock & Tank Lines. CORP AFFIL president, chief executive officer: FRP Properties.
John R. Mabbett, III: president, chief executive officer PRIM CORP EMPL president, chief executive officer: Florida Rock & Tank Lines.

Foundation Officials

Edward L. Baker: president B 1935. PRIM CORP EMPL chairman, director: Florida Rock Industries. CORP AFFIL chairman, director: FRP Properties; director: Virginia Concrete Co. Inc.; director: Flowers Industries; chairman, director: Arundel Corp.; director: Cardinal Concrete Co.

Grants Analysis

Disclosure Period: fiscal year ending September 30, 2001
Total Grants: $37,565*
Number of Grants: 14
Average Grant: $1,351*
Highest Grant: $20,000
Lowest Grant: $187
Typical Range: $1,000 to $3,000
*Note: Giving excludes United Way. Average grant figure excludes highest grant.

Recent Grants

Note: Grants derived from fiscal 2001 Form 990.
General

20,000	Jacksonville University, Jacksonville, FL
5,500	Junior Achievement, Jacksonville, FL
3,500	Hospice of Baltimore, Baltimore, MD
2,000	Osmond Foundation for the Children, Salt Lake City, UT
1,000	Boy Scouts of America Flint River Council, Griffin, GA
1,000	Bridge of Northeast Florida, Carrollton, FL
1,000	Jacksonville Community Council, Jacksonville, FL
1,000	United Services Organization, Jacksonville, FL -- golf tournament
1,000	United Way Northeast Florida, Jacksonville, FL
780	Pine Castle, Jacksonville, FL

ALBERT W. AND EDITH V. FLOWERS CHARITABLE TRUST

Giving Contact

Ron B. Tynan, Trust Officer
First Merit Bank, NA
121 South Main Street, Suite 200
Akron, OH 44308-1440
Phone: (330)384-7320

Description

Founded: 1968
EIN: 346608643

Organization Type: Private Foundation
Giving Locations: OH: Stark County
Grant Types: Capital, General Support, Operating Expenses, Scholarship.

Donor Information

Founder: the late Albert W. Flowers, the late Edith V. Flowers

Financial Summary

Total Giving: $197,430 (2001)
Giving Analysis: Giving for 2001 includes: foundation scholarships ($5,000)
Assets: $3,096,667 (2001)

Typical Recipients

Arts & Humanities: Arts Centers, Arts Outreach, Ballet, Arts & Humanities-General, Historic Preservation, History & Archaeology, Libraries, Museums/Galleries, Music, Performing Arts, Theater
Civic & Public Affairs: African American Affairs, Botanical Gardens/Parks, Clubs, Community Foundations, Economic Development, Employment/Job Training, Civic & Public Affairs-General, Housing, Minority Business, Municipalities/Towns, Urban & Community Affairs
Education: Colleges & Universities, Private Education (Precollege), Public Education (Precollege), Secondary Education (Private), Special Education, Student Aid
Environment: Environment-General, Resource Conservation
Health: Children's Health/Hospitals, Emergency/Ambulance Services, Prenatal Health Issues
International: Missionary/Religious Activities
Religion: Bible Study/Translation, Churches, Ministries, Religious Welfare
Social Services: Big Brothers/Big Sisters, Camps, Child Welfare, Community Centers, Community Service Organizations, Family Services, Food/Clothing Distribution, Recreation & Athletics, Scouts, Social Services-General, YMCA/YWCA/YMHA/YWHA, Youth Organizations

Application Procedures

Initial Contact: Send a brief letter of inquiry.
Application Requirements: Include amount requested and purpose of funds sought.
Deadlines: None.

Restrictions

Awards generally granted to qualifying organizations in Stark County.

Additional Information

Trust(s): First Merit Bank NA

Foundation Officials

F. E. McCullough: mem distribution comm
Albert Printz: mem distribution comm
Charles Tyburski: member distribution committee
Ronald B. Tynan: chairman

Grants Analysis

Disclosure Period: calendar year ending 2001
Total Grants: $192,430*
Number of Grants: 31
Average Grant: $6,207
Highest Grant: $12,200
Typical Range: $1,000 to $10,000
***Note:** Giving excludes scholarships.

Recent Grants

Note: Grants derived from 2001 Form 990.
General

15,000	Walsh University, North Canton, OH -- for phase II of capital campaign
12,200	Neo Christian Youth Camp, Lisbon, OH -- for Tafco walk-in cooler and freezer
10,000	Friends of Stark Parks, Canton, OH -- for Ohio and Erie Canal Heritage Corridor
10,000	St. John's Villa, Inc., Carrollton, OH -- for Sisters of Charity Foundation challenge
8,700	Lions Club of Massillon, Massillon, OH -- for Lincoln Theatre Restoration
8,300	Stark Christian Academy, Canton, OH -- for educational items
8,000	Great Trail Girl Scout Council, Canton, OH -- for capital campaign
6,500	Shrine Cripple Children Fund, Canton, OH -- for transportation fund
5,000	Bluecoats Drum and Bugle Corp, Canton, OH -- for 2001 horn fund drive
5,000	Canton Negro Oldtimers, Canton, OH -- for activity center construction

FLUOR CORP.

Company Headquarters

1 Enterprise Dr.
Aliso Viejo, CA 92656-2606
Web: http://www.fluor.com

Company Description

Founded: 1924
Ticker: FLR
Exchange: NYSE
Revenue: US$9.38 billion (2004)
Profit: US$186.7 million (2004)
Employees: 29011 (2003)
Fortune Rank: 241, per FORTUNE Magazine's list of 500 Largest U.S. Corporations (2004).
SIC(s): 1221 Bituminous Coal & Lignite--Surface, 1241 Coal Mining Services, 1541 Industrial Buildings & Warehouses, 1629 Heavy Construction Nec.

Operating Locations

Fluor Corp. (AK--Anchorage; CA--Bakersfield, Irvine; CO--Denver; DC; IL--Chicago; KY; MO--Kansas City; NJ--Marlton; OH--Cincinnati, Dayton; OK--Tulsa; SC--Greenville; TN, Nashville; TX--Corpus Christi, Sugar Land; VA--Falls Church, Richmond; WI--Appleton)

Nonmonetary Support

Type: Donated Equipment; In-kind Services
Volunteer Programs: "The Fluor Community Involvement Team," is a corporate volunteer program in which employees, retirees, and their family and friends carry out service projects in local communities. Employees also volunteer for many education programs: Junior Achievement, school partnerships, mentoring, and classroom presentations.

Fluor Foundation

Giving Contact

Suzanne H. Esber, Manager Community Relations
Fluor Foundation
One Enterprise Dr., F4E
Aliso Viejo, CA 92656-2606
Phone: (949)349-6797
E-mail: community.relations@fluordaniel.com
Web: http://www.fluor.com/communities/default.asp

Description

EIN: 510196032
Organization Type: Corporate Foundation
Giving Locations: operating locations.
Grant Types: Capital, Employee Matching Gifts, Endowment, General Support, Matching, Operating Expenses, Project, Scholarship.
Note: Employee matching gift ratio: 1 to 1.

Financial Summary

Total Giving: $3,268,718 (2003); $3,238,169 (2001).
Note: Contributes through corporate direct giving program and foundation.

Giving Analysis: Giving for 2001 includes: foundation matching gifts ($215,070); foundation scholarships ($567,565); foundation grants to United Way ($961,917); foundation ($1,493,617)
Assets: $12,446,834 (2003); $6,134,266 (2001)
Gifts Received: $4,000,000 (2003); $3,245,714 (2001); $60,815 (2000). Note: Contributions were received from Fluor Corp.

Typical Recipients

Arts & Humanities: Arts Associations & Councils, Arts Centers, Arts Funds, Dance, History & Archaeology, Museums/Galleries, Music, Opera, Performing Arts, Public Broadcasting, Theater
Civic & Public Affairs: Botanical Gardens/Parks, Community Foundations, Economic Development, Employment/Job Training, Civic & Public Affairs-General, Hispanic Affairs, Housing, Nonprofit Management, Professional & Trade Associations, Public Policy, Safety, Urban & Community Affairs, Women's Affairs
Education: Afterschool/Enrichment Programs, Business Education, Business-School Partnerships, Colleges & Universities, Education Associations, Education Funds, Education Reform, Engineering/Technological Education, Environmental Education, Education-General, International Studies, Leadership Training, Literacy, Medical Education, Minority Education, Public Education (Precollege), Science/Mathematics Education, Student Aid, Vocational & Technical Education
Environment: Environment-General
Health: AIDS/HIV, Cancer, Children's Health/Hospitals, Clinics/Medical Centers, Diabetes, Emergency/Ambulance Services, Hospitals, Speech & Hearing
International: International Affairs, International Development
Religion: Religious Welfare
Science: Science Exhibits & Fairs, Scientific Centers & Institutes, Scientific Research
Social Services: Child Welfare, Community Service Organizations, Emergency Relief, Family Services, Scouts, Substance Abuse, United Funds/United Ways, Volunteer Services, YMCA/YWCA/YMHA/YWHA, Youth Organizations

Application Procedures

Initial Contact: Send a preliminary letter of request.
Application Requirements: Include a description of organization, amount requested, purpose of funds sought, recently audited financial statement, and proof of tax-exempt status.
Deadlines: None.
Review Process: After initial request is reviewed, additional information may be requested.
Decision Notification: Three to four months after receipt of request.

Restrictions

Does not provide funding directly to elementary or secondary schools, health initiatives or research, individual artists, film production, publishing activities, individuals, sports organizations, sports programs, veterans, fraternal, labor, religious organizations, lobbying organizations, or campaigns. Foundation prefers to limit operation support to two or three consecutive years, and capital support to one grant in a five-year period.

Additional Information

Giving figures for 2000 reflect a change in the foundation's fiscal year, and are for the period November 1, 2000 through December 31, 2000.

Corporate Officials

Alan L. Boeckmann: chairman, chief executive officer chief financial officer B 1948. ED University of Arizona. PRIM CORP EMPL chairman, chief executive officer: Fluor Corp. CORP AFFIL director: Burlington Northern Santa Fe Corp.; director: American Petroleum Institute. NONPR AFFIL director: Orange County

Performing Arts Center.

John Robert Fluor, II: vice president corporate & public affairs B Orange, CA 1945. ED University of Southern California (1967). PRIM CORP EMPL vice president corporate & public affairs: Fluor Corp. NONPR AFFIL member: California Business Roundtable; member: United Way Orange County.

D. Michael Steuert: senior vice president, chief financial officer B Oklahoma City, OK 1948. ED Carnegie Mellon University (1971). PRIM CORP EMPL senior vice president, chief financial officer: Fluor Corp. NONPR AFFIL member: Leadership Akron Alumni Association; member: Private Sector Council; member: Carnegie Mellon Graduate School Council Finance.

Foundation Officials

Alan L. Boeckmann: trustee (see above)
Suzanne Huffmon Esber: manager, community relationss
L. N. Fisher: secretary
John Robert Fluor, II: president, trustee (see above)
H. S. Gilbert: trustee
J. L. Hopkins: trustee
K. A. Karkut: treasurer
R. W. Oakley: trustee
D. Michael Steuert: trustee (see above)
M. A. Stevens: trustee
D. W. Wilson: trustee

Grants Analysis

Disclosure Period: calendar year ending 2003
Total Grants: $1,432,750*
Number of Grants: 210
Average Grant: $6,823
Highest Grant: $75,000
Lowest Grant: $25
Typical Range: $1,000 to $15,000
*Note: Giving excludes matching gifts; scholarship and United Way.

Recent Grants

Note: Grants derived from 2003 Form 990.
General

653,427	Scholarship America, St. Peter, MN
207,902	United Way of Orange County, Irvine, CA
157,759	United Way of Orange County, Irvine, CA
143,644	United Way of Orange County, Irvine, CA
135,319	United Way of Orange County, Irvine, CA
75,000	Points of Light Foundation, Washington, DC
63,252	United Way of Benton and Franklin Counties, Kennewick, WA
55,000	National Engineers Week Foundation, Alexandria, VA
50,757	United Way of Benton and Franklin Counties, Kennewick, WA
50,000	Texas A and M University, College Station, TX

FMC CORP.

Company Headquarters

Philadelphia, PA
Web: http://www.fmc.com

Company Description

Founded: 1928
Ticker: FMC
Exchange: NYSE
Revenue: US$1.852 billion (2002)
Employees: 5300 (2003)
SIC(s): 1041 Gold Ores, 1044 Silver Ores, 1479 Chemical & Fertilizer Mining Nec, 2819 Industrial Inorganic Chemicals Nec.

Operating Locations

FMC Corp. (AL--Anniston; AK--Anchorage; AZ--Yuma; CA--Anaheim, Fresno, Hacienda Heights, Hollister, Madera, Pomona, Richmond, Riverside, Santa Clara, Ventura, Woodland Hills; CO--Denver; DC--Washington; FL--Coral Gables, Jacksonville, Lakeland, Orlando; GA--Atlanta, Sparks; ID--Boise, Pocatello; IL--Champaign, Chicago, Downers Grove, Summit Argo, Wheeling, Wyoming; IA--Sergeant Bluff; KS--Lawrence; LA--New Orleans, Opelousas; MD--Baltimore, Ridgely; MI--Howell, Warren; MN--Madison Lake; MS--Jackson; NE--Omaha; NV--Battle Mountain; NJ--Carteret, Princeton; NM--Hobbs; NY--Albany, Tonawanda; NC--Charlotte, Gastonia; OK--Lawton, Oklahoma City; PA--Bradford, Homer City, Lansdale, Philadelphia; SC--Aiken; SD--Aberdeen; TX--Austin, Corpus Christi, El Paso, Odessa, Pasadena; VA--Arlington, King George; WA--Vancouver, Walla Walla; WV--Institute, Nitro, South Charleston; WI--Columbus, Green Bay, Waukesha; WY--La Barge, Mills, Rock Springs)

Nonmonetary Support

Volunteer Programs: Through the Dollars for Doers program, the company matches up to $500 of employees' volunteer time at qualifying organizations.

FMC Foundation

Giving Contact

Judith Smeltzer
FMC Foundation
1735 Market Street
Philadelphia, PA 19103
Phone: (215)299-6000

Description

EIN: 946063032
Organization Type: Corporate Foundation
Giving Locations: nationally; operating locations.
Grant Types: Capital, Employee Matching Gifts, General Support.
Note: Employee matching gift ratio: 1 to 1 for qualifying educational and cultural institutions, up to $10,000 annually per employee. Company matches employee United Way contributions up to 60 percent on the dollar based on the percent of employee participation at each company site.

Financial Summary

Total Giving: $101,601 (fiscal year ending November 30, 2002); $2,279,780 (fiscal 2001)
Assets: $420,995 (fiscal 2004); $420,995 (fiscal 2003); $420,995 (fiscal 2002)
Gifts Received: $2,400,000 (fiscal 2001); $2,020,000 (fiscal 2000); $1,350,000 (fiscal 1998)

Typical Recipients

Arts & Humanities: Arts Centers, Arts Festivals, Arts Institutes, Community Arts, Libraries, Museums/Galleries, Music, Opera, Theater
Civic & Public Affairs: African American Affairs, Business/Free Enterprise, Clubs, Economic Development, Economic Policy, Employment/Job Training, Civic & Public Affairs-General, Hispanic Affairs, Law & Justice, Philanthropic Organizations, Professional & Trade Associations, Public Policy, Rural Affairs, Urban & Community Affairs, Zoos/Aquariums
Education: Agricultural Education, Business Education, Colleges & Universities, Community & Junior Colleges, Economic Education, Education Funds, Education Reform, Engineering/Technological Education, Education-General, Gifted & Talented Programs, International Exchange, International Studies, Medical Education, Minority Education, Science/Mathematics Education, Student Aid
Environment: Air/Water Quality, Environment-General, Wildlife Protection
Health: Children's Health/Hospitals, Emergency/Ambulance Services, Health Policy/Cost Contain-

ment, Health Funds, Health Organizations, Heart, Hospitals, Medical Rehabilitation, Public Health, Single-Disease Health Associations
International: Foreign Educational Institutions, International-General, International Affairs, International Environmental Issues, International Peace & Security Issues
Religion: Religious Welfare
Science: Science-General, Science Museums, Scientific Centers & Institutes, Scientific Organizations, Scientific Research
Social Services: Child Welfare, Community Service Organizations, Emergency Relief, Family Services, Recreation & Athletics, United Funds/United Ways, Volunteer Services, YMCA/YWCA/YMHA/YWHA, Youth Organizations

Application Procedures

Initial Contact: Send a brief (no more than two pages) typewritten letter.
Application Requirements: Include a description of organization; statement of organization's activities and programs; specific amount of money requested; explanation of how funds will be used; project location; timetable; proof of tax-exempt status; and list of board of directors.
Deadlines: None; budget determined in fall quarter.
Review Process: If organization is local, request is forwarded for local management review and recommendation; if national, preliminary review by foundation committee, then review by foundation board.
Evaluative Criteria: Strong consideration given to organizations which count a number of FMC employees among their active supporters; emphasizes groups that strive to improve communities in which employees live and work and to improve environment in which company does business; organization must have proven effectiveness and a broad base of community support; priority given to organizations and institutions promoting the free enterprise system.
Decision Notification: Foundation board meets at least twice a year.
Notes: Foundation discourages submission of unsolicited and voluminous support materials. Based on application information listed above, if funding appears possible, foundation will request the following: audited financial report for most recently completed year of operation; organizational budget for current operating year, showing expenses and income by sources; copy of organization's IRS tax-exempt status ruling; and a sample donor list showing corporate and foundation contributors to the organization for the past 12 months.

Local contributions are determined by individual manufacturing plants and operating sites, and not through the foundation or corporate office.

Restrictions

Foundation does not support individuals, state or regional associations of independent colleges, elementary or secondary schools, organizations that receive or qualify for United Way support, dinners or special events, fraternal organizations, goodwill advertising, political or lobbying groups, or religious organizations for sectarian purposes.

Foundation also does not support national health agencies or hospitals for operating expenses, or medical research.

Grants are not pledged for a period longer than one year.

The foundation usually only gives in plant communities.

Additional Information

Requests for special programs at hospitals (for example, outpatient alcoholism programs, drug addiction, or prenatal care) are not given high priority, but are considered individually as funds become available.
Publications: Foundation Annual Report

Corporate Officials

William G. Walter: chairman, chief executive officer, director B 1946. ED Loras College BS (1968); Northwestern University MBA (1971). PRIM CORP EMPL president, chief executive officer, director: FMC Corp.

Foundation Officials

Tom Deas: treasurer
Ken Garrett: president, director
Andrea Utecht: vice president, secretary

Grants Analysis

Disclosure Period: fiscal year ending November 30, 2004
Typical Range: $1,000 to $30,000
Note: No grants awarded in fiscal 2004.

Recent Grants

Note: Grants derived from fiscal 2001 Form 990.
Library-Related

15,000	Newberry Library, Chicago, IL

General

204,291	Dollars for Doers, Chicago, IL
100,000	United Way of New York City, New York, NY -- September 11th Fund
60,000	Orchestral Association of Chicago, Chicago, IL
50,951	Dollars for Doers, Chicago, IL
40,000	Lyric Opera of Chicago, Chicago, IL
30,500	National FFA Foundation, Indianapolis, IN
30,000	Commercial Club Foundation, Chicago, IL
30,000	Houston Golf Association, Woodlands, TX
30,000	Orchestral Association of Chicago, Chicago, IL
30,000	Society of Hispanic Professional Engineers, Los Angeles, CA

FOELLINGER FOUNDATION

Giving Contact

Cheryl K. Taylor, President/Chief Executive Officer
520 East Berry Street
Ft. Wayne, IN 46802
Phone: (260)422-2900
Fax: (260)422-9436
E-mail: info@foelinger.org
Web: http://www.foellinger.org/

Description

Founded: 1958
EIN: 356027059
Organization Type: Family Foundation
Giving Locations: IN: Fort Wayne including Allen County
Grant Types: Capital, Challenge, Emergency, General Support, Matching, Operating Expenses, Project.

Donor Information

Founder: The Foellinger Foundation was established in Indiana in 1958 by the late Helene R. Foellinger (1910-1987) and her mother, the late Esther A. Foellinger (1890-1969). Helene Foellinger's father, Oscar G. Foellinger, was a prominent newspaper publisher and president of the *Ft. Wayne News-Sentinel*. After her father's death in 1936, Helene R. Foellinger served as president of the News Publishing Company until her retirement in November 1981. The foundation was also funded by profits from the News Publishing Company until the sale of the *News-Sentinel* in 1980.

Financial Summary

Total Giving: $6,446,439 (fiscal year ending August 31, 2003); $7,480,896 (fiscal 2002); $7,416,280 (fiscal 2001)
Giving Analysis: Giving for fiscal 2003 includes: foundation grants to United Way ($203,000); fiscal 2002: foundation grants to United Way ($331,000); fiscal 2001: foundation grants to United Way ($190,000)
Assets: $158,721,249 (fiscal 2003); $157,675,585 (fiscal 2002); $172,825,992 (fiscal 2001)
Gifts Received: $2,361 (fiscal 1992). Note: Prior to fiscal 1990, the foundation received contributions from the Helene R. Foellinger Trust. The remainder of funds from this trust have now been received.

Typical Recipients

Arts & Humanities: Arts Appreciation, Arts Associations & Councils, Arts Centers, Arts Funds, Dance, Ethnic & Folk Arts, Arts & Humanities-General, Historic Preservation, Libraries, Museums/Galleries, Music, Public Broadcasting, Theater
Civic & Public Affairs: African American Affairs, Botanical Gardens/Parks, Business/Free Enterprise, Clubs, Community Foundations, Economic Development, Civic & Public Affairs-General, Housing, Professional & Trade Associations, Urban & Community Affairs, Zoos/Aquariums
Education: Afterschool/Enrichment Programs, Business Education, Colleges & Universities, Continuing Education, Economic Education, Education Associations, Education Funds, Elementary Education (Public), Engineering/Technological Education, Education-General, Gifted & Talented Programs, Journalism/Media Education, Literacy, Preschool Education, Private Education (Precollege), Public Education (Precollege), Science/Mathematics Education, Student Aid
Environment: Air/Water Quality, Protection, Resource Conservation
Health: AIDS/HIV, Clinics/Medical Centers, Health Organizations, Medical Rehabilitation, Preventive Medicine/Wellness Organizations, Public Health
Religion: Ministries, Religious Welfare
Science: Science Museums, Scientific Centers & Institutes
Social Services: Big Brothers/Big Sisters, Camps, Child Welfare, Community Centers, Community Service Organizations, Crime Prevention, Day Care, Domestic Violence, Emergency Relief, Family Services, Food/Clothing Distribution, Homes, People with Disabilities, Recreation & Athletics, Scouts, Shelters/Homelessness, Substance Abuse, United Funds/United Ways, YMCA/YWCA/YMHA/YWHA, Youth Organizations

Application Procedures

Initial Contact: Potential recipients should send a letter of intent no longer than two pages to the foundation, after which grantseekers will either be encouraged to submit a full grant application package, refine the current proposal, or explore other funding sources.
Application Requirements: The letter should include the following components, presented in order and under the headings listed: Statement of Purpose: Mission of the organization, goals of the proposed program/project, and specific reasons why the funding request is consistent with the foundation's grant guidelines and priority interests. Proposed Use of Funding: An explanation of how the funding will be used (for general operating support, program support, capital support, or support for some other special project). An outline should describe what, how, and when the program/project will be done. Budget: Estimate of organization's expenses or the expenses of the proposed program/project, amount requested, and a list of other potential sources of funding. IRS letter indicating the organization's status.
Deadlines: See the website for current deadline dates. Applications should be sent 90 days ahead of

the committee meetings, held in February, May, and November.
Review Process: The foundation acknowledges the receipt of grant applications by mail and requests for any additional information. If the directors conclude that the application meets their guidelines, an interview or visit to the project site may be arranged.

Restrictions

Grants are not made to individuals, including scholarship or travel assistance; public or private elementary or secondary schools independent of their school systems; sectarian religious groups or causes; churches for their general operations; projects that taxpayers normally support; endowment purposes; annual campaigns or general appeals for support; the support of projects or programs that have begun or have been completed before the foundation receives a funding request; or to purchase advertising, tickets, or for special events or group trips.

Additional Information

The foundation reports that it also sponsors conferences and assists in planning grants and studies.
Publications: Grant Guidelines; Annual Report

Foundation Officials

Mary F. Barksdale: director
David A. Bobilya: director
Barbara A. Burt: chairman, director
Thomas J. Felts: director
Carolyn R. Hughes: vice chairman, secretary, director
Joanne Baldwin Lantz: director B Defiance, OH 1932. ED University of Indianapolis BS (1953); Indiana University MS (1957); Michigan State University PhD (1969). CORP AFFIL director: Fort Wayne National Corp. NONPR AFFIL member: Sigma Xi; member: Southeast Psychological Association; member: Purdue University Alumni Society Fort Wayne; chancellor emeritus: Indiana University/Purdue University; member: Pi Lambda Theta; member: Indiana School Womens Club; member: Delta Kappa Gamma; director: Delta Kappa Gamma Education Foundation; member: American Psychological Association; member: American Association University Women.
Richard B. Pierce: director
Carl D. Rolfsen: treasurer, director B 1956. CORP AFFIL officer: Graphic Finishing Inc.
Cheryl K. Taylor: president, chief executive officer, director

Grants Analysis

Disclosure Period: fiscal year ending August 31, 2003
Total Grants: $6,243,439*
Number of Grants: 69
Average Grant: $71,495*
Highest Grant: $802,500
Lowest Grant: $1,000
Typical Range: $25,000 to $100,000
*Note: Giving excludes United Way. Average grants figure excludes two largest grants ($1,453,237).

Recent Grants

Note: Grants derived from 2003 Form 990.
Library-Related

144,127	Allen County Public Library Foundation, Ft. Wayne, IN -- towards expansion of the foundation collection services
100,000	Allen County Public Library Foundation, Ft. Wayne, IN -- towards young adult summer reading

General

802,500	Taylor University Inc., Upland, IN -- towards support for Allen County institute for organizational effectiveness
650,737	Fort Wayne Community Schools, Ft. Wayne, IN -- towards program support for summer clubhouse sites

608,000	Fort Wayne Community Schools, Ft. Wayne, IN -- to support for summer clubhouse
395,900	Fort Wayne Community Foundation, Ft. Wayne, IN -- towards community grant making fund and support for operating expenses
250,000	East Allen County Schools, New Haven, IN -- to support for capacity building institutionalization of learning perspectives for selected sites
228,000	East Allen County Schools, New Haven, IN -- towards program support for summer center
150,000	Arts United of Greater Fort Wayne Inc., Ft. Wayne, IN -- towards operating support
150,000	United Way of Allen County Inc., Ft. Wayne, IN -- towards operating support
145,000	Allen County Local Education Fund Inc., Ft. Wayne, IN -- to support parent literacy enrichment
129,000	Taylor University Inc., Upland, IN -- to support for Allen County postsecondary education summer consortium

FONDREN FOUNDATION

Giving Contact

Martie S.H. Herrick, Assistant Secretary-Treasurer
PO Box 2558
Houston, TX 77252-8037
Phone: (713)216-4513

Description

Founded: 1948
EIN: 746042565
Organization Type: Family Foundation
Giving Locations: TX: especially Houston
Grant Types: Capital, General Support, Project, Research.

Donor Information

Founder: Walter William Fondren, a Houston oilman, philanthropist, and founder of Humble Oil and Refining Co., established the Fondren Foundation in Texas in 1948.
Mrs. Walter Fondren administered his estate following his death and became the principal contributor to the foundation.

Financial Summary

Total Giving: $7,174,789 (fiscal year ending October 31, 2003); $8,100,000 (fiscal 2002); $8,255,265 (fiscal 2001)
Giving Analysis: Giving for fiscal 2003 includes: foundation scholarships ($42,083); fiscal 2002: foundation scholarships ($175,000); foundation matching gifts ($456,654); fiscal 2001: foundation scholarships ($38,250)
Assets: $173,745,011 (fiscal 2003); $149,652,569 (fiscal 2002); $172,674,279 (fiscal 2001)

Typical Recipients

Arts & Humanities: Art History, Arts Funds, Arts Outreach, Ballet, Dance, Arts & Humanities-General, Historic Preservation, History & Archaeology, Libraries, Museums/Galleries, Music, Opera, Performing Arts, Public Broadcasting, Theater, Visual Arts
Civic & Public Affairs: Botanical Gardens/Parks, Economic Development, Employment/Job Training, Civic & Public Affairs-General, Hispanic Affairs, Housing, Inner-City Development, Philanthropic Organizations, Public Policy, Safety, Urban & Community Affairs, Women's Affairs, Zoos/Aquariums
Education: Arts/Humanities Education, Business Education, Colleges & Universities, Education Associations, Education Funds, Education Reform, Engineering/Technological Education, Faculty Development, Education-General, Leadership Training, Legal Education, Literacy, Medical Education, Minority Education, Private Education (Precollege), Public Education (Precollege), Religious Education, Science/Mathematics Education, Secondary Education (Private), Social Sciences Education, Special Education, Student Aid
Environment: Environment-General, Resource Conservation, Wildlife Protection
Health: AIDS/HIV, Alzheimer's Disease, Cancer, Children's Health/Hospitals, Clinics/Medical Centers, Emergency/Ambulance Services, Geriatric Health, Heart, Hospices, Hospitals, Medical Rehabilitation, Medical Research, Mental Health, Prenatal Health Issues, Public Health, Research/Studies Institutes, Single-Disease Health Associations, Speech & Hearing, Transplant Networks/Donor Banks
International: International Environmental Issues, International Relations
Religion: Churches, Dioceses, Jewish Causes, Ministries, Religious Welfare
Science: Science Museums, Scientific Centers & Institutes
Social Services: Animal Protection, At-Risk Youth, Camps, Child Abuse, Child Welfare, Community Centers, Community Service Organizations, Domestic Violence, Family Planning, Family Services, Food/Clothing Distribution, People with Disabilities, Recreation & Athletics, Scouts, Senior Services, Substance Abuse, Volunteer Services, YMCA/YWCA/YMHA/YWHA, Youth Organizations

Application Procedures

Initial Contact: Applicants should send a letter with a concise proposal and a copy of the IRS exemption letter.
Application Requirements: Proposals should include a brief narrative history of the organization's purpose and work, specific description of the proposed program or project for which funds are requested, amount requested from the foundation as well as total amount needed, date by which funds are needed, proof of tax-exempt status, and a list of trustees or directors and principal staff.
Deadlines: Proposals should be submitted by the first day of the month preceding the month of a meeting, which are generally held in March, June, September, and December. Contact the foundation for the next scheduled meeting.
Review Process: The board of governors meets on a quarterly basis to consider grant proposals.

Restrictions

Grants are not made to individuals. The foundation does not award grants for annual fund drives.

Foundation Officials

Doris Fondren Allday: board of governors
R. Edwin Allday: board of governors
Laura Trammell Baird: board of governors
Ellanor Allday Beard: board of governors
Celia Whitfield Crank: board of governors
Bentley B. Fondren: board of governors
Leland T. Fondren: board of governors
Robert E. Fondren: board of governors B 1962. PRIM CORP EMPL vice president, director: Trend Development. CORP AFFIL off: Lake Colony Four; off: Plantation Development Corp.; off: CNO Development; off: Companeros Development Co.
Walter W. Fondren, IV: board of governors
Walter W. Fondren, III: board of governors B 1935. PRIM NONPR EMPL chairman: Coastal Conservation Association.
Marie Fondren Hall: vice chairman, board of governors
Martie S. H. Herrick: assistant secretary, assistant treasurer, board of governors
Catherine Fondren Underwood Murray: board of governors
Michael W. Springer: board of governors
Carrie Trammell Sturges: board of governors
Ann Gordon Trammell: secretary, treasurer, board of governors
Harper B. Trammell: board of governors
David M. Underwood, Jr.: board of governors
David M. Underwood: board of governors B 1937. ED Yale University (1959). PRIM CORP EMPL president, director: Feliciana Corp.
Duncan K. Underwood: chairman, board of governors
Lynda Knapp Underwood: board of governors B 1937. PRIM CORP EMPL vice president, director: Feliciana Corp.
Sue Trammell Whitfield: board of governors
Susan T. Whitfield: board of governors
W. Trammell Whitfield: board of governors
William F. Whitfield, Jr.: board of governors
William F. Whitfield, Sr.: board of governors
Frances Fondren Wilson: board of governors

Grants Analysis

Disclosure Period: fiscal year ending October 31, 2003
Total Grants: $7,132,706*
Number of Grants: 111
Average Grant: $64,259
Highest Grant: $300,000
Lowest Grant: $2,500
Typical Range: $20,000 to $100,000
*Note: Giving excludes scholarships.

Recent Grants

Note: Grants derived from 2003 Form 990.
Library-Related

50,000	George Bush Presidential Library Foundation, College Station, TX -- fund to campaign educational programs

General

300,000	Kinkaid School, Houston, TX -- in support of capital and endowment campaign
200,000	Alley Theatre, Houston, TX -- to assist in the capital component of the capital and endowment campaign
200,000	Depelchin Children's Center, Houston, TX -- to assist in the construction of new program services building
200,000	Texas Children's Hospital, Houston, TX -- to assist in building children expansion capital improvements campaign
166,664	Coastal Conservation Association, Houston, TX -- for the construction of permanent, purpose-built facility
166,664	Glenwood Cemetery Historic Preservation Foundation, Houston, TX -- for the prevention of erosion and to preserve the cemetery
166,664	River Oaks Baptist School, Houston, TX -- fund for building additions
166,664	University of St. Thomas, Houston, TX -- grant for second major Mall for campus life activities
164,000	St. Francis Episcopal Day School, Houston, TX -- fund for the construction of the Middle School wing
150,000	Annunciation Orthodox School, Houston, TX -- to support million master facilities plan

FORD FAMILY FOUNDATION

Giving Contact

Norman J. Smith, President
1600 Northwest Stewart Parkway
Roseburg, OR 97470
Phone: (541)957-5574
Fax: (541)957-5720
Web: http://www.tfff.org

Description
Founded: 1957
EIN: 936026156
Organization Type: Private Foundation
Giving Locations: CA: Siskiyou County; OR: rural communities only with population of 30,000 or fewer people
Grant Types: Award, Capital, Challenge, Emergency, General Support, Multiyear/Continuing Support, Scholarship.

Donor Information
Founder: The foundation was established in 1957 by Kenneth and Hallie Ford, to give back to the timber communities of Southwest Oregon. (grant guidelines in 1998 Form 990).

Financial Summary
Total Giving: $19,456,535 (fiscal year ending March 31, 2003); $22,658,625 (fiscal 2002); $15,319,855 (fiscal 2001)
Giving Analysis: Giving for fiscal 2003 includes: foundation grants to United Way ($17,800); foundation scholarships ($6,390,862); fiscal 2002: foundation grants to United Way ($18,800); foundation scholarships ($5,255,665); fiscal 2001: foundation grants to United Way ($41,095); foundation scholarships ($10,699,427)
Assets: $342,464,041 (fiscal 2003); $464,969,576 (fiscal 2002); $483,138,339 (fiscal 2001)
Gifts Received: $501,638 (fiscal 2002); $5,251,710 (fiscal 2001); $5,376,000 (fiscal 1998). Note: Contributions were received from the estate of Kenneth Ford.

Typical Recipients
Arts & Humanities: Arts Appreciation, Arts Associations & Councils, Arts Centers, Arts Institutes, Community Arts, Libraries, Museums/Galleries, Music, Performing Arts, Theater
Civic & Public Affairs: Botanical Gardens/Parks, Community Foundations, Economic Development, Employment/Job Training, Civic & Public Affairs-General, Housing, Inner-City Development, Law & Justice, Municipalities/Towns, Parades/Festivals, Public Policy, Safety, Urban & Community Affairs
Education: Afterschool/Enrichment Programs, Arts/Humanities Education, Colleges & Universities, Community & Junior Colleges, Education Associations, Education Funds, Elementary Education (Private), Elementary Education (Public), Education-General, Minority Education, Preschool Education, Private Education (Precollege), Public Education (Precollege), Religious Education, Science/Mathematics Education, Secondary Education (Private), Secondary Education (Public), Student Aid
Environment: Air/Water Quality, Environment-General
Health: Adolescent Health Issues, Cancer, Children's Health/Hospitals, Clinics/Medical Centers, Emergency/Ambulance Services, Health-General, Health Funds, Health Organizations, Hospices, Hospitals, Mental Health, Prenatal Health Issues
International: International Environmental Issues
Religion: Churches, Missionary Activities (Domestic), Religious Welfare
Science: Science-General, Science Museums, Scientific Centers & Institutes
Social Services: Animal Protection, At-Risk Youth, Child Abuse, Child Welfare, Community Centers, Community Service Organizations, Counseling, Crime Prevention, Day Care, Domestic Violence, Emergency Relief, Family Services, Food/Clothing Distribution, Homes, People with Disabilities, Recreation & Athletics, Scouts, Senior Services, Shelters/Homelessness, Social Services-General, Substance Abuse, United Funds/United Ways, Volunteer Services, YMCA/YWCA/YMHA/YWHA, Youth Organizations

Application Procedures
Initial Contact: Send a brief letter of inquiry.
Application Requirements: Applications should include a description of organization, project description, amount requested, purpose of funds sought, proof of tax-exempt status, list of board members, project timeline and budget, source and amount of committed and projected support, and who will benefit.
Deadlines: March 1.
Review Process: The foundation will respond within approximately four weeks to organizations submitting a pre-application letter. Final decisions may take as long as 12 months, but generally will occur within four months.

Restrictions
The Ford Family Foundation only provides funding to charitable organization, except for recipients of scholarships (see below). Funding will not be considered for endowments or reserve funds, general fund drives overhead expenses, debt reduction, Operating expenses, political or lobbying groups, purchase of art, nor environmental preservation which intends to deprive property owners use of their property. Unsolicited requests for funds are not accepted.

Additional Information
The Roseburg Forest Products Co. endowed the Ford Family Foundation.
Projects which have already secured at least 50% of funding needed to complete the project are eligible to apply.
Contact should be in written form; Foundation discourages phone calls.

Foundation Officials
Gerald E. Bruce: director
Karla S. Chambers: director
Allyn C. Ford: director
Joseph P. Kearns: director
Ronald C. Parker: director
Carmen R. Phillips: director
Norman J. Smith: president NONPR AFFIL director: Roseburg Area Chamber of Commerce.
Charles U. Walker: director
Donna P. Wolford: assistant secretary

Grants Analysis
Disclosure Period: fiscal year ending March 31, 2003
Total Grants: $13,047,873*
Number of Grants: 419
Average Grant: $31,141
Highest Grant: $703,310
Lowest Grant: $50
Typical Range: $5,000 to $75,000
***Note:** Giving excludes scholarships and United Way.

Recent Grants
Note: Grants derived from 2003 Form 990.
Library-Related
325,000   Library Foundation of Milton-Freewater, Milton-Freewater, OR -- towards campaign for the new Milton Freewater public library

166,000   Hood River County Library Foundation, Hood River, OR -- towards library renovation project

150,000   Friends of the Independence Public Library, Independence, OR -- towards the new independence library

General
703,310   Winston Dillard Rural Fire Protection District, Winston, OR -- towards fire station and medical clinic

500,000   City and County of Baker, Baker City, OR -- towards conference center enhancements

500,000   Umpqua Community College, Roseburg, OR -- towards community health career lab

447,337   Douglas Education Service District, Roseburg, OR -- towards administration of national board certified teachers program

400,000   Umpqua Community Development Corporation, Roseburg, OR -- towards Coos county agriculture and community center

313,645   Doernbecher Childrens Hospital Foundation, Portland, OR -- towards Kenneth W Ford northwest childrens cancer center expansion

300,000   Gospel Rescue Mission of Grants Pass, Grants Pass, OR -- towards campus and learning center

300,000   Oregon Independent College Foundation Inc., Portland, OR -- towards independent college support

288,145   Oregon Health & Sciences Foundation, Portland, OR -- towards rural health institutes

275,000   Klamath Ice Sports Inc., Klamath Falls, OR -- towards the sports facility

FORD FOUNDATION

Giving Contact
Barron M. Tenny, Executive Vice President, Secretary
320 East 43rd Street
New York, NY 10017
Phone: (212)573-5000
Fax: (212)351-3677
E-mail: office-of-communications@fordfound.org
Web: http://www.fordfound.org

Description
Founded: 1936
EIN: 131684331
Organization Type: Private Foundation
Giving Locations: internationally, especially Asia, Latin America, and Africa; nationally.
Grant Types: Conference/Seminar, Endowment, Fellowship, General Support, Matching, Multiyear/Continuing Support, Project, Research, Seed Money.

Donor Information
Founder: Established in 1936 by Henry Ford, who founded Ford Motor Company in 1903, and his son, Edsel Ford. The late Henry Ford II (d. 1987), chairman of Ford Motor Company and a son of Edsel Ford, served on the foundation's board from 1943 until 1976. Under his tenure, the foundation evolved from a Michigan charity into a worldwide institutional philanthropy. Today, the foundation has no official ties to the Ford family or the Ford Motor Company.

Financial Summary
Total Giving: $431,643,480 (fiscal year ending September 30, 2003); $506,951,000 (fiscal 2002 approx); $827,695,000 (fiscal 2001 approx)
Giving Analysis: Giving for fiscal 2003 includes: foundation program-related investments (approx $19,000,000); fiscal 2001: foundation gifts to individuals (approx $1,907,865); foundation program-related investments (approx $31,289,859)
Assets: $10,015,612,595 (fiscal 2003); $9,300,140,000 (fiscal 2002 approx); $10,548,500,000 (fiscal 2001 approx)

Typical Recipients
Arts & Humanities: Arts Associations & Councils, Arts Centers, Dance, Ethnic & Folk Arts, Film & Video, Arts & Humanities-General, Historic Preservation, Libraries, Music, Performing Arts, Public Broadcasting, Theater

Civic & Public Affairs: African American Affairs, Business/Free Enterprise, Civil Rights, Community Foundations, Economic Development, Economic Policy, Employment/Job Training, First Amendment Issues, Civic & Public Affairs-General, Hispanic Affairs, Housing, Law & Justice, Legal Aid, Municipalities/Towns, Native American Affairs, Nonprofit Management, Philanthropic Organizations, Public Policy, Rural Affairs, Urban & Community Affairs, Women's Affairs

Education: Agricultural Education, Arts/Humanities Education, Business-School Partnerships, Colleges & Universities, Community & Junior Colleges, Continuing Education, Economic Education, Education Associations, Education Funds, Education Reform, Faculty Development, Education-General, Gifted & Talented Programs, International Studies, Leadership Training, Legal Education, Literacy, Minority Education, Public Education (Precollege), Science/Mathematics Education, Social Sciences Education, Student Aid

Environment: Air/Water Quality, Forestry, Environment-General, Resource Conservation

Health: AIDS/HIV, Health-General, Health Organizations, Medical Research, Nutrition, Public Health

International: Foreign Arts Organizations, Foreign Educational Institutions, International-General, Health Care/Hospitals, Human Rights, International Affairs, International Development, International Environmental Issues, International Organizations, International Peace & Security Issues, International Relations, International Relief Efforts, Missionary/Religious Activities, Trade

Religion: Religious Organizations, Religious Welfare, Social/Policy Issues

Science: Science-General, Scientific Centers & Institutes, Scientific Organizations

Social Services: At-Risk Youth, Child Welfare, Community Service Organizations, Day Care, Delinquency & Criminal Rehabilitation, Domestic Violence, Family Planning, Family Services, Refugee Assistance, Substance Abuse, United Funds/United Ways, Volunteer Services, Youth Organizations

Application Procedures

Initial Contact: Before submitting any application, a brief letter of inquiry is recommended to determine whether the foundation's present interests and funds permit consideration of a proposal. Domestic applications and inquiries should be sent to the foundation's secretary. International applicants should direct their proposals to the nearest field office; field offices are listed in the foundation's annual report and on the foundation's Web site.

Application Requirements: The letter should include the purpose of the project for which funds are being requested; problems and issues the proposed project will address; information about the organization conducting the project; estimated project budget; period of time for which funds are requested; and qualifications of those who will be engaged in the project. After receiving the letter, the foundation may ask the applicant to submit a formal proposal. There is no grant application form. Proposals should include the organization's current budget; a description of the proposed work and how it will be conducted; the names and curriculum vitae of those engaged in the project; a detailed project budget; present means of support and status of applications to other funding sources; and legal and tax status.

Deadlines: None.

Review Process: Applications are considered throughout the year. Normally, applicants may expect to receive within six weeks an indication of whether their proposals are within the foundation's interests and budget limitations.

Restrictions

Activities supported by grants and program-related investments must be charitable, educational, or scientific, as defined under the U.S. Internal Revenue Code and Treasury Regulations. The foundation lim-

its its grants to efforts likely to have wide effect. Support is not usually awarded for routine operating costs or for religious activities. Except in rare cases, funding is not available for construction or maintenance of buildings.

The foundation does not award undergraduate scholarships or make grants for purely personal needs. Support for graduate fellowships is generally provided through grants to universities and other organizations, which are responsible for the selection of recipients. Grants to individuals are most often awarded either through publicly announced competitions or on the basis of nominations from universities and other nonprofit institutions.

Although the foundation also makes grants to individuals, they are few in number relative to demand and are limited to research, training, and other activities related to the foundation's interests.

Additional Information

The foundation publishes and distributes a variety of free publications and also disseminates foundation-supported videos and films. Videos may be purchased or rented. A catalog listing these publications and videos, along with video pricing and ordering information, is available free of charge. Requests for the catalog and other publications, or to be placed on the mailing list, should be sent to the Ford Foundation, Office of Communications, Dept. A, 320 E. 43rd St., New York, NY 10017.

Publications: Annual Report; Current Interests of the Ford Foundation; Ford Foundation Report; Videos and Films; Numerous Reports

Foundation Officials

Alison R. Bernstein: vice president knowledge creativity and freedom ED Columbia University MA; Columbia University Ph.D.; Columbia University PhD; Vassar College BA. NONPR AFFIL advisory board of directors: Smithsonian Institution; member: Tribal Colleges and Universities; advisory board of directors: National Museum of American History.

Susan Vail Berresford: president, trustee B New York, NY 1943. ED Vassar College (1961-1963); Radcliffe College BA (1965). NONPR AFFIL member, board of directors: Council on Foundations; member: Trilateral Commission.

Afsaneh M. Beschloss: trustee CORP AFFIL president: Rock Creek Group; director: Temple-Inland Inc..

Anke A. Ehrhardt: trustee ED University of Munich BA (1961); University of Hamburg MA (1964); University of Dusseldorf PhD (1969). NONPR AFFIL director: HIV Center for Clinical & Behavioral Studies.

Nancy P. Feller: assistant secretary, associate general counsel

Kathryn Scott Fuller: chairman, trustee B New York, NY 1946. ED Brown University BA (1968); University of Texas JD (1976); University of Maryland MS (1980-1982). PRIM NONPR EMPL president, chief executive officer: World Wildlife Fund. NONPR AFFIL member: World Bank Advisory Committee on Sustainable Development; honorary member: Zonta International; member: Texas Bar Association; member advisory committee: Trade Policy Negotiations; member: District of Columbia Bar Association; member advisory committee: President Commission Environmental Quality; director: Brown University.

Barry D. Gaberman: senior vice president B Shanghai, People's Republic of China August 09, 1941. ED University of Wisconsin BS (1966); University of Wisconsin MA (1968). NONPR AFFIL chairman: Foundation Center; board of directors: Independent Sector.

Nicholas M. Gabriel: treasurer, director financial services

Juliet V. Garcia: trustee NONPR AFFIL member: Texas Women's Hall of Fame; president: University of Texas at Brownsville.

Wilmot G. James: trustee ED University of Western Cape South Africa BA (1977); University of Wisconsin M.Sc (1978); University of Wisconsin Ph.D. (1982). NONPR AFFIL chairman: Immigration Advi-

sory Board for South Africa.

Yolanda Kakabadse: trustee NONPR AFFIL board of directors: Millennium Ecosystem Assessment; board of directors: World Resources Institute; executive president: Fundacion Futuro Latinoamericano; President: International Union for Conservation of Nature and Natural Resources.

Wilma Pearl Mankiller: trustee B Tahlequah, OK November 18, 1945. ED Skyline College; San Bruno College (1973); San Francisco State College (1973-1975); Union College BA (1977); University of Arkansas (1979). NONPR AFFIL member: National Women's Hall of Fame.

Yolanda T. Moses: trustee B Los Angeles, CA. ED California State College BS (1968); University of California PhD (1976); University of California PhD (1976). PRIM NONPR EMPL president: City University of New York. NONPR AFFIL member: Valley College Alumni Hall of Fame; member: Women's Forum; president, member: American Anthropological Association; president: City College of New York.

Deval Laurdine Patrick: trustee B Chicago, IL 1956. ED Harvard College AB (1978); Harvard College JD (1982). CORP AFFIL executive vice president, secretary, general counsel: Coca-Cola Company; director: Reebok International Ltd. NONPR AFFIL director: Museum of Fine Arts, Boston; trustee: Saint Andrew's School (Delaware); member: Massachusetts Black Lawyers Association; board overseers: Harvard University; member: Massachusetts Bar Association; board overseers: Harvard Alumni Association; director: A Better Chance Inc.; member: Boston Bar Association; member: American Bar Association.

Bradford K. Smith: vice president peace & social justice ED New School for Social Research MA; University of Michigan BA.

Linda B. Strumpf: vice president, chief investment officer ED Penn State University BA (1969); New York University MBA (1972). NONPR AFFIL board of directors: Penn State University Investment Council; board of directors: Penn State University Liberal Arts Dev. Council; board of directors: New York Society of Security Analysts; board of directors: Associate for Investment Management and Research; board of directors: New York City Professional Women Alumni Interest Group.

Ratan Naval Tata: trustee B Bombay, MH India. ED Cornell University; Harvard University Graduate School of Business Administration. PRIM CORP EMPL chairman: Tata Industries Ltd. CORP AFFIL chairman: Tata Industries Ltd..

Barron M. Tenny: executive vice president, secretary, general counsel

Carl B. Weisbrod: trustee B New York, NY 1944. ED Cornell University BS (1965); New York University JD (1968). PRIM CORP EMPL chairman: National Income Realty Trust PRIM NONPR EMPL president: Alliance for Downtown New York. CORP AFFIL director: Tarragon Corp. NONPR AFFIL president: Alliance for Downtown New York Inc.; president: Downtown-Lower Manhattan Assn..

W. Richard West, Jr.: trustee B San Bernardino, CA January 06, 1943. ED University of Redlands BA (1965); Harvard University MA (1968); Stanford University JD (1971); Stanford University (1971). PRIM NONPR EMPL director: Smithsonian Institute National Museum American Indian. NONPR AFFIL honorary counselor: Wings America; member advisory committee: Winslow Foundation; board of directors: Stanford University; board of directors: National Parks and Conservation Assn.; national support committee: Native American Rights Fund; board of directors: American Indian Resources Institute; director: National Museum of the American Indian; vice chairman: American Assocation of Museums/International Council of Museums; member: American Indian Bar Association.

Grants Analysis

Disclosure Period: fiscal year ending September 30, 2003

Total Grants: $412,643,480*

Number of Grants: 2,750 (approx)
Average Grant: $150,052
Highest Grant: $300,000,000
Typical Range: $10,000 to $500,000
*Note: Giving excludes program-related investments and funding for foundation-administered projects. Giving includes gifts to individuals.

Recent Grants

Note: Grants derived from fiscal 2003 Form 990.
General
8,000,000 National Academy of Sciences, Washington, DC -- for minority predoctoral, dissertation and postdoctoral fellowship programs
5,000,000 Trust for Civil Society in Central and Eastern Europe, Warszawa Poland -- for a sinking fund to provide support for long-term sustainable development of civil society
4,643,750 Institute of International Education, New York, NY -- for the Global Travel and Learning Fund
4,500,000 Academy for Educational Development, Washington, DC -- for the New Voices Fellowship Program
3,000,000 Bangladesh Freedom Foundation, Dhaka Bangladesh -- endowment support to ensure institutional sustainability and a financial base
3,000,000 Fund for the City of New York, New York, NY -- for activities to enhance the operations and improve the performance of public agencies
3,000,000 International Center for Transitional Justice, Inc., New York, NY -- to help countries respond to human rights abuse
2,500,000 Institute of International Education, New York, NY -- support for fellowship program to enhance Asian Scholarship and comparative study within the region
2,500,000 Social Science Research Council, New York, NY -- for international programs
2,000,000 Policy Link, Oakland, CA -- to promote community building at the federal, state and local levels

WALTER AND JOSEPHINE FORD FUND

Giving Contact
David M. Hempstead, Secretary & Trustee
100 Renaissance Center, 34th Floor
Detroit, MI 48243
Phone: (313)259-7777
Fax: (313)393-7579

Description
Founded: 1951
EIN: 386066334
Organization Type: Family Foundation
Giving Locations: ME; MI: Detroit including metropolitan area; NY
Grant Types: General Support, Project.

Donor Information
Founder: The fund was established in 1951, with Walter B. Ford II, the fund's president, and his wife, Josephine F. Ford, the fund's vice president, as donors. Josephine Ford is the granddaughter of Ford Motor Company founder, Henry Ford, and the daughter of Eleanor and Edsel Ford. Walter B. Ford II, from an unrelated Detroit banking family, is chief executive of Ford & Earl Design Associates.

Financial Summary
Total Giving: $580,600 (2002)
Assets: $6,278,300 (2002)

Gifts Received: $258,041 (1997); $232,304 (1996); $194,175 (1995). Note: The fund receives gifts from a trust agreement between Josephine F. Ford and Comerica Bank of Detroit.

Typical Recipients
Arts & Humanities: Arts Associations & Councils, Arts Centers, Arts Funds, Arts Institutes, Historic Preservation, History & Archaeology, Libraries, Museums/Galleries, Music, Performing Arts, Public Broadcasting, Theater
Civic & Public Affairs: Botanical Gardens/Parks, Chambers of Commerce, Clubs, Community Foundations, Economic Development, Civic & Public Affairs-General, Housing, Inner-City Development, Municipalities/Towns, Nonprofit Management, Parades/Festivals, Philanthropic Organizations, Public Policy, Rural Affairs, Urban & Community Affairs, Zoos/Aquariums
Education: Arts/Humanities Education, Colleges & Universities, Education Associations, Education-General, Gifted & Talented Programs, Minority Education, Preschool Education, Private Education (Precollege), Public Education (Precollege), Science/Mathematics Education, Secondary Education (Private), Secondary Education (Public), Special Education, Student Aid
Environment: Forestry, Environment-General, Research, Resource Conservation, Wildlife Protection
Health: Alzheimer's Disease, Cancer, Children's Health/Hospitals, Clinics/Medical Centers, Emergency/Ambulance Services, Health Funds, Health Organizations, Hospitals, Medical Research, Mental Health, Nursing Services, Public Health
International: Foreign Arts Organizations, Human Rights, International Organizations
Religion: Churches, Religious Organizations, Religious Welfare
Science: Scientific Centers & Institutes, Scientific Labs, Scientific Research
Social Services: Animal Protection, At-Risk Youth, Camps, Child Welfare, Community Service Organizations, Day Care, Family Planning, Family Services, People with Disabilities, Recreation & Athletics, Scouts, Social Services-General, Substance Abuse, United Funds/United Ways, Veterans, YMCA/YWCA/YMHA/YWHA, Youth Organizations

Application Procedures
Initial Contact: Send a brief letter of inquiry.
Application Requirements: Include copy of financial statement and copy of IRS letter determining tax status, (unless already listed in cumulative list).
Deadlines: None.

Restrictions
The foundation does not support individuals.

Foundation Officials
Richard M. Cundiff: treasurer
Josephine Clay Ford: president, trustee, mem B 1923.
David M. Hempstead: secretary, trustee PRIM CORP EMPL secretary: Detroit Lions Inc. CORP AFFIL secretary: Higbie-Maxon Inc.
George A. Straitor: assistant treasurer

Grants Analysis
Disclosure Period: calendar year ending 2000
Total Grants: $809,553*
Number of Grants: 76
Average Grant: $8,101*
Highest Grant: $202,000
Lowest Grant: $100
Typical Range: $1,000 to $25,000
*Note: Giving excludes United Way. Average grant figure excludes highest grant.

Recent Grants
Note: Grants derived from 2002 Form 990.

Library-Related
1,000 Northeast Harbor Library, Northeast Harbor, ME
1,000 Seal Harbor Library, Seal Harbor, ME
General
200,000 College for Creative Studies, Detroit, MI
80,000 Detroit Zoological Society, Royal Oak, MI
32,000 Detroit Institute of Arts, Detroit, MI
25,000 Maine Coast Heritage Trust, Northeast Harbor, ME
25,000 Maine Maritime Academy, Castine, ME
25,000 Neighborhood House, Northeast Harbor, ME
21,000 Henry Ford Health System, Detroit, MI
16,000 United Way Community Services, Detroit, MI
12,000 Henry Ford Museum & Greenfield Village, Dearborn, MI
10,000 Children's Hospital of Michigan, Detroit, MI

WILLIAM AND MARTHA FORD FUND

Giving Contact
David M. Hempstead, Secretary, Trustee & Member
William and Martha Ford Fund
100 Renaissance Center, 34th Floor
Detroit, MI 48243
Phone: (313)259-7777

Description
Founded: 1953
EIN: 386066335
Organization Type: Private Foundation
Giving Locations: MI; NY; TX
Grant Types: General Support, Scholarship.

Donor Information
Founder: William Clay Ford, Martha Firestone Ford

Financial Summary
Total Giving: $1,002,500 (2002)
Giving Analysis: Giving for 2002 includes: foundation grants to United Way ($101,000)
Assets: $9,852,270 (2002)
Gifts Received: $10,365,625 (1998); $3,940,821 (1996)

Typical Recipients
Arts & Humanities: Arts Centers, Arts Funds, Arts Institutes, Historic Preservation, History & Archaeology, Libraries, Museums/Galleries, Music, Performing Arts, Public Broadcasting
Civic & Public Affairs: Clubs, Community Foundations, Civic & Public Affairs-General, Housing, Municipalities/Towns, Parades/Festivals, Public Policy, Urban & Community Affairs, Women's Affairs, Zoos/Aquariums
Education: Colleges & Universities, Education-General, Minority Education, Private Education (Precollege), Science/Mathematics Education, Special Education, Student Aid
Environment: Environment-General, Resource Conservation
Health: Children's Health/Hospitals, Clinics/Medical Centers, Emergency/Ambulance Services, Health Organizations, Heart, Hospitals, Medical Research, Mental Health, Nursing Services, Public Health
International: Foreign Arts Organizations, Human Rights
Religion: Churches
Science: Scientific Centers & Institutes, Scientific Labs
Social Services: Child Welfare, Community Service Organizations, Delinquency & Criminal Rehabilitation, Family Planning, Homes, Recreation & Athletics,

Scouts, Substance Abuse, United Funds/United Ways, Youth Organizations

Application Procedures
Initial Contact: Send a brief letter of inquiry.
Application Requirements: Include recently audited financial statement and proof of tax-exempt status.
Deadlines: None.

Restrictions
Awards are generally limited to charitable organizations already favorably known to and of interest to the substantial contributors of the foundation. Does not support individuals.

Foundation Officials
Richard M. Cundiff: treasurer
Martha F. Ford: trustee, mem
William Clay Ford, Sr.: president, trustee, mem B Detroit, MI 1925. ED Yale University BS (1949). CORP AFFIL director: Ford Motor Co.; owner, chairman: Detroit Lions Inc. NONPR AFFIL member: Psi Upsilon; associate member: Society Automotive Engineers; member: K. T. Phelps Association; chairman emeritus: Edison Institute; honorary life trustee: Eisenhower Medical Center; member: Automobile Old Timers. CLUB AFFIL Economic Club Detroit; Masons Club.
David M. Hempstead: secretary, trustee, member PRIM CORP EMPL secretary: Detroit Lions Inc. CORP AFFIL secretary: Higbie-Maxon Inc.
George A. Straitor: assistant treasurer

Grants Analysis
Disclosure Period: calendar year ending 2002
Total Grants: $901,500*
Number of Grants: 62
Average Grant: $7,483*
Highest Grant: $352,500
Lowest Grant: $300
Typical Range: $500 to $50,000 and $300 to $30,000
*Note: Giving excludes United Way. Average grant figure excludes two highest grants $452,500.

Recent Grants
Note: Grants derived from 2002 Form 990.
General

352,500	Henry Ford Health System, Detroit, MI
100,000	Henry Ford Museum and Greenfield Village, Dearborn, MI
100,000	United Way Community Services, Detroit, MI
65,000	Freedom Institute, New York, NY
52,000	Detroit Zoological Society, Royal Oak, MI
50,000	Boys and Girls Clubs of America, Atlanta, GA
30,000	St. Luke's Episcopal Hospital, Houston, TX
25,000	East Hampton Healthcare Foundation, East Hampton, NY
25,000	National Council on Alcoholism and Drug Dependence, New York, NY
15,000	Community Foundation for Southeastern Michigan, Detroit, MI

EDSEL B. FORD II FUND

Giving Contact
David M. Hempstead, Secretary
100 Renaissance Center, 34th Fl.
Detroit, MI 48243-1006
Phone: (313)259-7777

Description
Founded: 1994
EIN: 383153050
Organization Type: Private Foundation

Giving Locations: MI: Detroit metro area some giving nationally.
Grant Types: General Support.

Financial Summary
Total Giving: $292,962 (2003); $303,769 (2001)
Assets: $7,502,033 (2003); $6,602,343 (2001)
Gifts Received: $5,713 (2003); $5,051,922 (1998); $1,165,173 (1993). Note: Contributions were received from Edsel B. Ford II.

Typical Recipients
Arts & Humanities: Arts Institutes, Historic Preservation, History & Archaeology, Libraries, Museums/Galleries
Civic & Public Affairs: Botanical Gardens/Parks, Clubs, Housing, Zoos/Aquariums
Education: Arts/Humanities Education, Business Education, Colleges & Universities, Faculty Development, Education-General, Private Education (Precollege), Public Education (Precollege), Secondary Education (Public)
Health: Cancer, Children's Health/Hospitals, Diabetes, Health Organizations
Religion: Churches, Jewish Causes, Religious Welfare
Science: Scientific Centers & Institutes
Social Services: Camps, Child Welfare, Community Service Organizations, Family Planning, People with Disabilities

Application Procedures
Initial Contact: Send a brief letter of inquiry.
Application Requirements: Financial statement and proof of tax-exempt status.
Deadlines: None.

Restrictions
Awards are generally limited to charitable organizations already favorably known to, and of interest to, the substantial contributors of the foundation. Grants are not made to individuals.

Foundation Officials
Edsel B. Ford, II: president, director, member B 1949. ED Babson University BA (1972). PRIM CORP EMPL vice president, director: Ford Motor Co. CORP AFFIL director: Ford Motor Co. NONPR AFFIL director: Henry Ford Health System; vice chairman, national advisory board: Salvation Army; director: Detroit Metropolitan Wayne County Airport Commission; director: Federal Reserve Bank of Chicago; director: CATCH; director: Detroit 300.

Grants Analysis
Disclosure Period: calendar year ending 2003
Total Grants: $292,962
Number of Grants: 39
Average Grant: $7,512
Highest Grant: $35,500
Lowest Grant: $500
Typical Range: $5,000 to $10,000

Recent Grants
Note: Grants derived from 2003 Form 990.
General

35,500	Salvation Army, Southfield, MI
22,500	Detroit Institute for Children, Detroit, MI
21,762	Babson College, Babson Park, MA
19,000	Juvenile Diabetes Research Foundation, Southfield, MI
17,000	Grosse Pointe Memorial Church, Grosse Pte. Farms, MI
15,000	University Liggett School, Grosse Pte. Woods, MI
12,500	Children's Hospital of Michigan, Detroit, MI
12,000	McCarty Cancer Foundation, St. Clair Shores, MI
10,000	Detroit Zoological Society, Royal Oak, MI
10,000	Rollins College, Winter Park, FL

HENRY FORD II FUND

Giving Contact
David M. Hempstead, Secretary & Trustee
100 Renaissance Center, 34th Floor
Detroit, MI 48243
Phone: (313)259-7777
Fax: (313)393-7579

Description
Founded: 1953
EIN: 386066332
Organization Type: General Purpose Foundation
Giving Locations: MI: Detroit
Grant Types: General Support, Research, Scholarship.

Donor Information
Founder: The fund was established in 1953. The donor was the late Henry Ford II (d. 1987), a grandson of Ford Motor Company founder Henry Ford, and a chairman and chief executive of the automobile company.

Financial Summary
Total Giving: $1,260,000 (2002)
Assets: $23,604,780 (2002)
Gifts Received: $285,628 (1998); $262,434 (1997); $234,137 (1996). Note: In 1998, the fund received gifts from trust agreements between Henry Ford II and Comerica Bank.

Typical Recipients
Arts & Humanities: Arts Institutes, Arts & Humanities-General, Historic Preservation, History & Archaeology, Libraries, Museums/Galleries, Music, Performing Arts, Public Broadcasting
Civic & Public Affairs: Civil Rights, Clubs, Community Foundations, Civic & Public Affairs-General, Housing, Legal Aid, Municipalities/Towns, Urban & Community Affairs
Education: Business-School Partnerships, Colleges & Universities, Community & Junior Colleges, Education Associations, Minority Education, Private Education (Precollege), Secondary Education (Private), Secondary Education (Public), Special Education, Student Aid
Environment: Environment-General, Wildlife Protection
Health: Children's Health/Hospitals, Clinics/Medical Centers, Diabetes, Emergency/Ambulance Services, Eyes/Blindness, Health Organizations, Hospitals, Medical Rehabilitation, Medical Research
Religion: Churches, Religious Welfare
Science: Scientific Centers & Institutes
Social Services: Child Welfare, Community Service Organizations, Family Planning, Food/Clothing Distribution, People with Disabilities, Recreation & Athletics, United Funds/United Ways, Veterans, Volunteer Services, Youth Organizations

Application Procedures
Initial Contact: Send a brief letter of inquiry.
Application Requirements: Include recently audited financial statement and proof of tax-exempt status.
Deadlines: None.

Restrictions
Awards are generally limited to charitable organizations already favorably known to and of interest to the substantial contributors of this foundation. The purpose of each grant or contributions is to provide financial support to corporations, trust, community chests, funds or foundations, organized and operated solely for religious, charitable, scientific, literary or educational purposes, or for the prevention of cruelty to children or animals. The fund does not make grants to individuals.

Foundation Officials

Richard M. Cundiff: treasurer,
Edsel B. Ford, II: president, trustee, mem B 1949. ED Babson University BA (1972). PRIM CORP EMPL vice president, director: Ford Motor Co. CORP AFFIL director: Ford Motor Co. NONPR AFFIL director: Henry Ford Health System; vice chairman, national advisory board: Salvation Army; director: Detroit Metropolitan Wayne County Airport Commission; director: Federal Reserve Bank of Chicago; director: CATCH; director: Detroit 300.
David M. Hempstead: secretary, trustee PRIM CORP EMPL secretary: Detroit Lions Inc. CORP AFFIL secretary: Higbie-Maxon Inc.

Grants Analysis

Disclosure Period: calendar year ending 2000
Total Grants: $1,693,500*
Number of Grants: 19
Average Grant: $89,132
Highest Grant: $300,000
Typical Range: $25,000 to $50,000 and $100,000 to $300,000
*Note: Giving excludes United Way.

Recent Grants

Note: Grants derived from 2002 Form 990.
General

500,000	American Diabetes Association, Alexandria, VA
150,000	Henry Ford Community College, Dearborn, MI
100,000	Detroit Zoological Society, Royal Oak, MI
100,000	Focus Hope, Detroit, MI
100,000	The Gunnery, Washington, CT
50,000	Detroit Institute for Children, Detroit, MI
50,000	National Center for Learning Disabilities, Inc, New York, NY
50,000	Planned Parenthood of Southeast Michigan, Detroit, MI
25,000	Catch, Detroit, MI
25,000	Detroit Downtown Foundation, Detroit, MI

FORD METER BOX CO.

Company Headquarters

775 Manchester Avenue
PO Box 443
Wabash, IN 46992-0443
Phone: (219)563-3171
Fax: (219)563-6781
Web: http://www.fordmeterbox.com

Company Description

Employees: 700 (2003)
SIC(s): 3321 Gray & Ductile Iron Foundries, 3494 Valves & Pipe Fittings Nec, 3822 Environmental Controls, 3823 Process Control Instruments.

Operating Locations

Ford Meter Box Co. (IN--Wabash)

Ford Meter Box Foundation

Giving Contact

Marta D. Gidley, Secretary
PO Box 443
775 Manchester Avenue
Wabash, IN 46992
Phone: (260)563-3171

Description

Founded: 1988
EIN: 351253080

Organization Type: Corporate Foundation
Giving Locations: IN: Wabash County and surrounding area
Grant Types: General Support, Project, Scholarship.

Financial Summary

Total Giving: $684,060 (2003); $1,259,318 (2002); $779,835 (2001). Note: Contributes through foundation only.
Giving Analysis: Giving for 2001 includes: foundation scholarships ($1,000); foundation grants to United Way ($32,500) foundation ($746,335)
Assets: $3,400,698 (2003); $3,959,005 (2002); $3,840,149 (2001)
Gifts Received: $1,000,000 (2002); $500,000 (1998); $500,000 (1996). Note: Contributions were received from Ford Meter Box Co.

Typical Recipients

Arts & Humanities: Arts Associations & Councils, Arts Funds, Community Arts, Dance, Film & Video, Historic Preservation, History & Archaeology, Libraries, Museums/Galleries, Music, Opera, Performing Arts, Theater
Civic & Public Affairs: Botanical Gardens/Parks, Business/Free Enterprise, Clubs, Community Foundations, Economic Development, Economic Policy, Employment/Job Training, Civic & Public Affairs-General, Housing, Law & Justice, Municipalities/Towns, Nonprofit Management, Parades/Festivals, Philanthropic Organizations, Professional & Trade Associations, Public Policy, Safety, Urban & Community Affairs, Zoos/Aquariums
Education: Afterschool/Enrichment Programs, Agricultural Education, Arts/Humanities Education, Business Education, Colleges & Universities, Economic Education, Education Associations, Education Funds, Elementary Education (Private), Elementary Education (Public), Education-General, International Studies, Leadership Training, Preschool Education, Private Education (Precollege), Public Education (Precollege), Religious Education, Science/Mathematics Education, Secondary Education (Public), Student Aid, Vocational & Technical Education
Environment: Protection
Health: Cancer, Children's Health/Hospitals, Diabetes, Emergency/Ambulance Services, Eyes/Blindness, Geriatric Health, Health Funds, Health Organizations, Heart, Hospices, Hospitals, Medical Research, Mental Health, Outpatient Health Care, Prenatal Health Issues, Single-Disease Health Associations
International: Foreign Arts Organizations, Health Care/Hospitals, Missionary/Religious Activities
Religion: Churches, Ministries, Religious Organizations, Religious Welfare
Social Services: Animal Protection, At-Risk Youth, Big Brothers/Big Sisters, Child Abuse, Child Welfare, Community Service Organizations, Counseling, Crime Prevention, Domestic Violence, Emergency Relief, Family Services, Food/Clothing Distribution, Homes, Recreation & Athletics, Scouts, Senior Services, Substance Abuse, United Funds/United Ways, YMCA/YWCA/YMHA/YWHA, Youth Organizations

Application Procedures

Initial Contact: Send written request.
Application Requirements: Include amount requested and purpose for which funds will be used.
Deadlines: None.

Corporate Officials

Thomas W. Hodson: president, drcc
Christopher Shanks: vice president, director

Foundation Officials

Daniel H. Ford: vice chairman
Steven R. Ford: treasurer PRIM CORP EMPL secretary, treasurer: Ford Meter Box Co.
Marta D. Gidley: secretary
Thomas G. Vanosdol: chairman

Grants Analysis

Disclosure Period: calendar year ending 2003
Total Grants: $650,810*
Number of Grants: 44
Average Grant: $3,507*
Highest Grant: $500,000
Lowest Grant: $100
Typical Range: $500 to $5,000
*Note: Giving excludes scholarship; United Way. Average grant figure excludes highest grant.

Recent Grants

Note: Grants derived from 2003 Form 990.
General

500,000	Honeywell Foundation, Wabash, IN
50,000	Quality of Life Foundation, Indianapolis, IN -- for computer automated multi-symptom monitoring pilot project
33,000	Wabash County United Fund, Wabash, IN
30,000	Independent Colleges of Indiana, Indianapolis, IN
10,000	Community Foundation of Wabash County, Manchester, IN -- towards Honeywell house renovation fund
6,500	Wabash County Sheriff's Department, Wabash, IN -- for computer equipment
5,000	Stockdale Mill Foundation, Kokomo, IN
5,000	Teague Barn Project, Wabash, IN -- for barn renovation
5,000	Thirteenth Place Inc., Gadsden, AL -- long term group home for children
5,000	Wabash Marketplace Inc., Wabash, IN -- for revitalization of downtown Wabash

FORD MOTOR CO.

Company Headquarters

1 American Rd.
Dearborn, MI 48126-2798
Web: http://www.ford.com

Company Description

Ticker: F
Exchange: NYSE
Revenue: US$172.233 billion (2004)
Profit: US$3.487 billion (2004)
Employees: 350321 (2004)
Fortune Rank: 4, per FORTUNE Magazine's list of 500 Largest U.S. Corporations (2004).

Nonmonetary Support

Type: Donated Equipment; Donated Products
Volunteer Programs: Ford Motor Company offers every Ford salaried employee 16 hours of paid time off per year to volunteer in teams of co-workers at various agencies.
Contact: Ray Byers, Manager, Contributions Programs
Phone: (313)248-4745
Note: Company also donates land.

Ford Motor Co. Fund

Giving Contact

Sandra E. Ulsh, President
Ford Motor Company Fund
One American Road
PO Box 1899
Dearborn, MI 48126
Phone: 888-313-0102
E-mail: fordfund@ford.com
Web: http://www.ford.com/en/goodWorks/fundingAndGrants/fordMotorCompanyFund/default.htm

Description

EIN: 381459376
Organization Type: Corporate Foundation
Giving Locations: nationally; headquarters and operating communities; nationally.
Grant Types: Capital, Conference/Seminar, Department, Employee Matching Gifts, General Support, Multiyear/Continuing Support.
Note: Employee matching gift ratio: 1 to 1.

Financial Summary

Total Giving: $77,450,320 (2003); $83,899,251 (2002); $56,971,262 (2001). Note: Contributes through corporate direct giving program and foundation.
Giving Analysis: Giving for 2001 includes: foundation scholarships ($1,060,075); foundation matching gifts ($3,143,413); foundation grants to United Way ($12,488,806); foundation ($40,278,968)
Assets: $108,006,099 (2003); $103,911,785 (2002); $144,907,832 (2001)
Gifts Received: $85,020,650 (2003); $70,000,000 (2000); $245,008,771 (1999). Note: Contributions were received from Ford Motor Company and Ford Holdings, Inc.

Typical Recipients

Arts & Humanities: Arts Associations & Councils, Arts Centers, Arts Festivals, Arts Institutes, Community Arts, Ethnic & Folk Arts, Arts & Humanities-General, Historic Preservation, History & Archaeology, Libraries, Museums/Galleries, Music, Opera, Performing Arts, Public Broadcasting, Theater
Civic & Public Affairs: African American Affairs, Asian American Affairs, Botanical Gardens/Parks, Business/Free Enterprise, Chambers of Commerce, Civil Rights, Community Foundations, Economic Development, Economic Policy, Employment/Job Training, Civic & Public Affairs-General, Hispanic Affairs, Housing, Law & Justice, Municipalities/Towns, Philanthropic Organizations, Professional & Trade Associations, Public Policy, Safety, Urban & Community Affairs, Women's Affairs, Zoos/Aquariums
Education: Agricultural Education, Arts/Humanities Education, Business Education, Colleges & Universities, Economic Education, Education Associations, Education Funds, Education Reform, Engineering/Technological Education, Faculty Development, Education-General, Gifted & Talented Programs, Health & Physical Education, Journalism/Media Education, Minority Education, Public Education (Precollege), Religious Education, Science/Mathematics Education, Secondary Education (Public), Student Aid, Vocational & Technical Education
Environment: Environment-General, Resource Conservation, Wildlife Protection
Health: Cancer, Emergency/Ambulance Services, Health Policy/Cost Containment, Health Organizations, Hospices, Hospitals, Kidney, Prenatal Health Issues, Public Health
International: Foreign Arts Organizations, International Development, International Environmental Issues, International Organizations, International Peace & Security Issues, International Relations
Religion: Jewish Causes, Ministries
Science: Science Museums, Scientific Centers & Institutes
Social Services: Camps, Child Welfare, Community Service Organizations, Delinquency & Criminal Rehabilitation, People with Disabilities, Recreation & Athletics, Scouts, Substance Abuse, United Funds/United Ways, Volunteer Services, YMCA/YWCA/YMHA/YWHA, Youth Organizations

Application Procedures

Initial Contact: National organizations should submit a brief written proposal; organizations located in communities where Ford operates may submit requests to the fund or to the community relations committee at local plants. All organizations must complete the grant application enclosed in the Ford Fund annual report.
Application Requirements: Within two pages, the proposal should include a description of organization, amount requested, proposed use of the funds, and a brief description of the project or program, including goals and objectives. In addition, the proposal should include other sources of funding, a detailed budget and financial information, status of related projects previously supported by Ford Motor Company Fund, an explanation of how the Fund will be recognized, summary of past performance (if applicable), and proof of tax-exempt status.
Deadlines: None.
Decision Notification: The fund will send a postcard notifying applicant that proposal has been received. No further notification will occur if there is no interest in the proposal. If there is an interest in the request, applicant will receive notification of the disposition within six weeks of receiving initial acknowledgment card.

Restrictions

The Fund generally does not support animal rights organizations, beauty or talent contests, day-to-day business operations, debt reduction, vehicle donations, endowments, fraternal organizations, individual sponsorship related to fund-raising activities, individuals, labor groups, small business or program-related investment loans, general operating support to hospitals and health care institutions, non-U.S.-based charities, organizations without 501(c)(3) status, political or lobbying groups, private schools, profit-making enterprises, religious organizations for sectarian purposes, species specific organizations, or organizations that may pose a conflict with Ford's mission, goals, programs, products, services, or employees.

Additional Information

Publications: Guidelines; Corporate Citizenship Report (annually); Ford Fund Annual Report (annually)

Corporate Officials

W. Wayne Booker: vice chairman, director ED Purdue University BS. PRIM CORP EMPL vice chairman: Ford Motor Co. CORP AFFIL director: AGCO Corp.; director: BSI Group.
William Clay Ford, Jr.: chairman, chief executive officer B Detroit, MI May 03, 1957. ED Princeton University BA (1979); Michigan Institute of Technology MS (1984). PRIM CORP EMPL chairman, chief executive officer: Ford Motor Co. CORP AFFIL vice chairman: Detroit Lions Inc. NONPR AFFIL chairman, trustee: Henry Ford Museum & Greenfield Village; trustee: Princeton University Brookings Institute; director: Greenfield Village; vice chairman: Detroit Renaissance Foundation.
Allan Dana Gilmour: vice chairman B Burke, VT June 17, 1934. ED Harvard University BA (1956); University of Michigan MBA (1959). PRIM CORP EMPL vice chairman, chief financial officer: Ford Motor Co. CORP AFFIL director: DTE Energy Co.; director: Whirlpool Corp. NONPR AFFIL member: Phi Kappa Phi; member vis committee grad sch business administration: University Michigan; advisory cabinet: Council of Michigan Foundations; trustee: Henry Ford Health Systems; member: Beta Gamma Sigma; trustee: Community Foundation Southeastern Michigan.
Sir Nicholas V. Scheele: president, director B Essex, United Kingdom January 03, 1944. PRIM CORP EMPL president, chief operating officer: Ford Motor Co.

Foundation Officials

Patricia A. Charles: assistant treasurer
Susan M. Cischke: trustee
Alfred B. Ford: trustee B 1934.
Allan Dana Gilmour: chairman, trustee (see above)
Sheila F. Hamp: trustee PRIM CORP EMPL trustee: Henry Ford Museum.
Malcolm S. McDonald: trustee, treasurer
Timothy J. O'Brien: trustee

Peter J. Sherry, Jr.: secretary
Sandy E. Ulsh: president ED Gettysburg College BS; Lehigh University MBA.
Martin B. Zimmerman: trustee B New York, NY June 19, 1946. ED Dartmouth College BA; Massachusetts Institute of Technology PhD. NONPR AFFIL director: National Association of Business Economists; member: Phi Beta Kappa; director: Community Foundation of Southeastern Michigan; director: Citizens Research Council of Michigan; trustee: Committee for Economic Development; director: Business for Social Responsibility.

Grants Analysis

Disclosure Period: calendar year ending 2003
Total Grants: $74,109,558*
Number of Grants: 1,500 (approx)
Average Grant: $49,406
Highest Grant: $5,000,000
Typical Range: $1,000 to $100,000
*Note: Giving excludes matching gifts.

Recent Grants

Note: Grants derived from 2003 Form 990.

General

4,300,000	Conservation International Foundation, Washington, DC
2,000,000	Georgia Institute of Technology, Atlanta, GA
2,000,000	Northwestern University, Evanston, IL
2,000,000	United Way Community Services, Detroit, MI
1,880,000	Berry College, Mt. Berry, GA
1,500,000	Atlanta-Fulton County Zoo Inc., Atlanta, GA
1,500,000	Edison Institute
1,200,000	Chicago's Environmental Fund, Chicago, IL
1,000,000	Dearborn Community Fund, Dearborn, MI
1,000,000	Detroit Institute of Arts, Detroit, MI

FOREST CITY ENTERPRISES INC.

Company Headquarters

50 Public Sq.
Cleveland, OH 44113
Web: http://www.fceinc.com

Company Description

Founded: 1920
Ticker: FCEA
Exchange: NYSE
Revenue: US$906.6 million (2001)
Employees: 4425 (2003)
SIC(s): 1521 Single-Family Housing Construction, 1522 Residential Construction Nec, 1531 Operative Builders, 6531 Real Estate Agents & Managers.

Operating Locations

Forest City Enterprises, Inc. (AL--Homewood; CA--Los Angeles, Newport Beach; FL--Tampa; MN--Minneapolis; NH--Nashua; NY--New York; OH--Brook Park; OR--Beaverton, Bend, Portland; PA--Aliquippa)

Nonmonetary Support

Type: Loaned Employees; Loaned Executives

Forest City Enterprises Charitable Foundation, Inc.

Giving Contact

Allan C. Krulak, Vice President
Forest City Enterprises
50 Public Square, Suite 1100
Cleveland, OH 44113-2201
Phone: (216)621-6060
Fax: (216)263-6208

Description

Founded: 1976
EIN: 341218895
Organization Type: Corporate Foundation
Giving Locations: NY: New York including metropolitan area; OH, Cleveland including metropolitan area operating locations.
Grant Types: General Support, Scholarship.

Financial Summary

Total Giving: $2,933,284 (fiscal year ending January 31, 2003); $3,117,317 (fiscal 2002). Note: Contributes through foundation only.
Giving Analysis: Giving for fiscal 2003 includes: foundation grants to United Way ($114,940)
Assets: $222,000 (fiscal 2003); $227,203 (fiscal 2002)
Gifts Received: $2,909,063 (fiscal 2003); $3,062,794 (fiscal 2002); $2,531,000 (fiscal 2000). Note: Contributions are received from Forest City Enterprises Inc.

Typical Recipients

Arts & Humanities: Arts Associations & Councils, Arts Centers, Arts Funds, Arts Institutes, Ballet, Arts & Humanities-General, History & Archaeology, Libraries, Museums/Galleries, Music, Opera, Performing Arts, Theater, Visual Arts
Civic & Public Affairs: African American Affairs, Business/Free Enterprise, Civil Rights, Clubs, Community Foundations, Economic Development, Ethnic Organizations, Civic & Public Affairs-General, Housing, Law & Justice, Municipalities/Towns, Parades/Festivals, Philanthropic Organizations, Public Policy, Safety, Urban & Community Affairs, Women's Affairs, Zoos/Aquariums
Education: Afterschool/Enrichment Programs, Arts/Humanities Education, Colleges & Universities, Community & Junior Colleges, Education Associations, Education Funds, Education Reform, Engineering/Technological Education, Education-General, Leadership Training, Private Education (Precollege), Religious Education, Secondary Education (Private), Student Aid
Environment: Forestry
Health: AIDS/HIV, Alzheimer's Disease, Arthritis, Cancer, Children's Health/Hospitals, Clinics/Medical Centers, Diabetes, Emergency/Ambulance Services, Eyes/Blindness, Health-General, Health Funds, Health Organizations, Hospices, Hospitals, Hospitals (University Affiliated), Medical Research, Multiple Sclerosis, Nursing Services, Prenatal Health Issues, Preventive Medicine/Wellness Organizations, Public Health, Single-Disease Health Associations
International: International Peace & Security Issues, International Relations, International Relief Efforts, Missionary/Religious Activities
Religion: Churches, Dioceses, Religion-General, Jewish Causes, Ministries, Religious Organizations, Religious Welfare, Seminaries, Social/Policy Issues, Synagogues/Temples
Science: Science Museums, Scientific Centers & Institutes
Social Services: Animal Protection, Camps, Child Welfare, Community Service Organizations, Crime Prevention, Delinquency & Criminal Rehabilitation, Domestic Violence, Family Services, Food/Clothing Distribution, People with Disabilities, Recreation & Athletics, Senior Services, Sexual Abuse, Social Services-General, Substance Abuse, United Funds/United Ways, Volunteer Services, YMCA/YWCA/YMHA/YWHA, Youth Organizations

Application Procedures

Initial Contact: Send a brief letter or proposal.
Application Requirements: Include a description of organization, amount requested, purpose of funds sought, and proof of tax-exempt status.
Deadlines: None; grants committee meets as needed.

Restrictions

Grants are not made to individuals.

Corporate Officials

Allan C. Krulak: vice president corporate & public affairs, director PRIM CORP EMPL vice president corporate & public affairs, director: Forest City Enterprises, Inc.

Grants Analysis

Disclosure Period: fiscal year ending January 31, 2003
Total Grants: $2,818,344*
Number of Grants: 207
Average Grant: $8,706*
Highest Grant: $1,025,000
Lowest Grant: $100
Typical Range: $1,000 to $10,000
*Note: Giving excludes United Way. Average grant figure excludes highest grants.

Recent Grants

Note: Grants derived from 2004 Form 990.
Library-Related

25,000	National First Ladies Library, Canton, OH

General

770,000	Jewish Community Federation, Cleveland, OH
277,283	United Way Services, Cleveland, OH
200,000	Brandeis University, Waltham, MA
160,000	Hebrew Academy of Cleveland, Cleveland, OH
125,000	Park Synagogue, Cleveland, OH
102,500	Ratner School, Lyndhurst, OH
95,836	Case Western Reserve University, Cleveland, OH
50,000	Cleveland Clinic Foundation, Cleveland, OH
50,000	Cleveland Clinic Foundation Taussig Cancer Center, Cleveland, OH
50,000	Cleveland Museum of Art, Cleveland, OH

FOREST FOUNDATION

Giving Contact

Frank D. Underwood, Executive Director
820 A Street, Suite 345
Tacoma, WA 98402
Phone: (253)627-1634
Fax: (253)627-6249

Description

Founded: 1962
EIN: 916020514
Organization Type: Family Foundation
Giving Locations: WA: southwestern Washington; especially Pierce County
Grant Types: Capital, General Support, Operating Expenses, Project.

Donor Information

Founder: Incorporated in 1962 by C. Davis Weyerhaeuser and William T. Weyerhaeuser.

Financial Summary

Total Giving: $1,344,435 (fiscal year ending October 31, 2003); $2,305,513 (fiscal 2001)
Giving Analysis: Giving for fiscal 2003 includes: foundation grants to United Way ($50,000)
Assets: $28,581,201 (fiscal 2003); $29,251,996 (fiscal 2001)

Typical Recipients

Arts & Humanities: Arts Associations & Councils, Arts Funds, Arts Outreach, Ballet, Dance, Ethnic & Folk Arts, Arts & Humanities-General, Historic Preservation, History & Archaeology, Libraries, Museums/Galleries, Music, Opera, Performing Arts, Public Broadcasting, Theater
Civic & Public Affairs: African American Affairs, Asian American Affairs, Botanical Gardens/Parks, Business/Free Enterprise, Civil Rights, Clubs, Community Foundations, Economic Policy, Civic & Public Affairs-General, Housing, Municipalities/Towns, Native American Affairs, Parades/Festivals, Philanthropic Organizations, Public Policy, Safety, Urban & Community Affairs, Women's Affairs
Education: Afterschool/Enrichment Programs, Arts/Humanities Education, Colleges & Universities, Community & Junior Colleges, Continuing Education, Economic Education, Education Funds, Elementary Education (Public), Education-General, Health & Physical Education, Leadership Training, Medical Education, Minority Education, Private Education (Precollege), Public Education (Precollege), Religious Education, Secondary Education (Private), Special Education, Student Aid, Vocational & Technical Education
Environment: Air/Water Quality, Forestry, Environment-General, Resource Conservation, Watershed, Wildlife Protection
Health: AIDS/HIV, Cancer, Clinics/Medical Centers, Emergency/Ambulance Services, Health Funds, Health Organizations, Home-Care Services, Hospitals, Medical Research, Mental Health, Public Health, Single-Disease Health Associations, Transplant Networks/Donor Banks
International: International Relief Efforts
Religion: Churches, Religion-General, Ministries, Religious Organizations, Religious Welfare, Seminaries
Science: Science Museums, Scientific Centers & Institutes
Social Services: Animal Protection, Big Brothers/Big Sisters, Camps, Child Abuse, Child Welfare, Community Centers, Community Service Organizations, Counseling, Crime Prevention, Day Care, Domestic Violence, Family Planning, Family Services, Food/Clothing Distribution, Homes, People with Disabilities, Recreation & Athletics, Scouts, Senior Services, Sexual Abuse, Shelters/Homelessness, United Funds/United Ways, YMCA/YWCA/YMHA/YWHA, Youth Organizations

Application Procedures

Initial Contact: Submit five copies of a complete proposal, including cover letter that describes the project and amount of money requested, and a completed grant request summary sheet, which can be obtained from the foundation. Foundation does not accept faxed or emailed proposals. All proposals must clearly address one or more of the forest foundation outcomes provided in the guidelines.
Deadlines: Each of the program areas has specific deadlines. The Community Building and Development program, March 15 and July 15; Culture and the Arts program, May 15 and November 15; the Dependency to Self Sufficiency program, January 15, May 15 and September 15; the Environment program, March 15 and September 15; Children and Youth Development program, January 15, May 15, and September 15, and the Overcoming Adversity program May 15 and November 15. Contact the foundation to confirm the dates.
Review Process: The foundation meets six times a

year. Decisions on complete proposals in each of the program areas are made at least twice annually. Action will be taken on proposals between 60 and 75 days from the deadline.

Restrictions
The foundation makes grants only to tax-exempt charitable organizations and generally does not support endowment funds; annual appeals; private foundations or operating foundations; individuals; production of films, videos or any publications; lobbying to influence elections or legislation; or school-related tours.

Additional Information
Grantmaker Consultants, Tacoma, WA, provides grant management services.
Publications: Program Policy Statement; Guidelines

Foundation Officials
Nicholas C. Spika: secretary
Frank D. Underwood: executive director, director
Annette B. Weyerhaeuser: vice president, director
Gail T. Weyerhaeuser: president, treasurer, director
William T. Weyerhaeuser: director

Grants Analysis
Disclosure Period: fiscal year ending October 31, 2003
Total Grants: $1,294,435*
Number of Grants: 63
Average Grant: $15,892*
Highest Grant: $200,000
Lowest Grant: $1,000
Typical Range: $10,000 to $50,000
*Note: Giving excludes United Way. Average grant figure excludes two highest grants ($325,000).

Recent Grants
Note: Grants derived from 2003 Form 990.
General

200,000	Tacoma Art Museum, Tacoma, WA
125,000	Seattle Center Foundation, Seattle, WA
50,000	Cowlitz County Historical Museum, Kelso, WA
50,000	Franciscan Health System, Tacoma, WA
50,000	Girl Scouts, Tumwater, WA
50,000	Harold E LeMay Museum, Tacoma, WA
50,000	Museum of Flight Foundation, Seattle, WA
50,000	Northwest Sinfonietta, Tacoma, WA
50,000	United Way of Pierce County, Tacoma, WA
45,000	Tacoma Symphony Orchestra, Tacoma, WA

FOREST OIL CORP.

Company Headquarters
1600 Broadway, Suite 2200
Denver, CO
Web: http://www.forestoil.com

Company Description
Founded: 1916
Ticker: FST
Exchange: NYSE
Revenue: US$475.6 million (2002)
Employees: 500 (2002)
SIC(s): 1300 Oil & Gas Extraction.

Operating Locations
Forest Oil Corp. (PA--Bradford); NO SUBSIDIARIES (CO--Denver)
Note: List includes division location

Nonmonetary Support
Type: Donated Equipment; Workplace Solicitation

Glendorn Foundation

Giving Contact
William F. Higie, Secretary & Manager
Glendorn Foundation
78 Main St.
Bradford, PA 16701
Phone: (814)368-7171

Description
Founded: 1953
EIN: 251024349
Organization Type: Corporate Foundation
Giving Locations: nationally.
Grant Types: Capital, Endowment, General Support, Research.

Donor Information
Founder: Forest Oil Corp., Ruth H. Dorn

Financial Summary
Total Giving: $185,000 (2003)
Assets: $3,260,254 (2003)
Gifts Received: $375 (2000); $895 (1999); $5,675 (1998). Note: Contributions were received from Forest Oil Corp.

Typical Recipients
Arts & Humanities: Arts Festivals, Dance, Historic Preservation, Libraries, Museums/Galleries, Music, Opera, Performing Arts, Theater
Civic & Public Affairs: Business/Free Enterprise, Economic Development, Civic & Public Affairs-General, Hispanic Affairs, Philanthropic Organizations, Zoos/Aquariums
Education: Colleges & Universities, Education-General, Literacy, Medical Education, Private Education (Precollege), Special Education, Student Aid
Health: Cancer, Clinics/Medical Centers, Health Funds, Hospices, Hospitals, Hospitals (University Affiliated), Medical Rehabilitation, Medical Research
International: International Development, Missionary/Religious Activities
Religion: Religious Welfare
Science: Science Museums
Social Services: Animal Protection, Child Welfare, Community Centers, Domestic Violence, Food/Clothing Distribution, People with Disabilities, Shelters/Homelessness, Substance Abuse, United Funds/United Ways, YMCA/YWCA/YMHA/YWHA

Application Procedures
Initial Contact: Due to the backlog of proposed gifts, no solicitations from grantees are desired at this time.

Corporate Officials
Bulent A. Berilgen: vice president, chief operating officer, director PRIM CORP EMPL vice president, chief operating officer, director: Forest Oil Corp.
Robert S. Boswell: president, chief executive officer, director B Tulsa, OK 1949. ED Vanderbilt University (1971); University of Texas (1973). PRIM CORP EMPL president, chief executive officer, director: Forest Oil Corp.
William L. Dorn: chairman, chief executive officer, director B San Antonio, TX 1948. ED University of Texas (1971). PRIM CORP EMPL chairman, chief executive officer, director: Forest Oil Corp.
David H. Keyte: vice president, chief financial officer PRIM CORP EMPL vice president, chief financial officer: Forest Oil Corp.

Foundation Officials
Clayton D. Coburn: trustee
David F. Dorn: trustee B 1924. PRIM CORP EMPL co-chairman, chairman executive committee, director: Forest Oil Corp.
John C. Dorn: trustee B 1927. ED Yale University (1950).
Dale B. Grubb: trustee
William F. Higie: secretary, mgr B Bradford, PA

1926. ED Saint Bonaventure University (1949); Dickinson School of Law (1952). PRIM CORP EMPL vice president, secretary, counsel, director: Forest Oil Corp. NONPR AFFIL vice chairman: Bradford Hospital.
Jeffrey W. Miller: trustee
Carolyn D. Warner: trustee
Leslie D. Young: trustee

Grants Analysis
Disclosure Period: calendar year ending 2003
Total Grants: $185,000
Number of Grants: 8
Average Grant: $23,125
Highest Grant: $50,000
Lowest Grant: $10,000
Typical Range: $12,500 to $40,000

Recent Grants
Note: Grants derived from 2003 Form 990.
General

50,000	New York Presbyterian Hospital, New York, NY
40,000	Midland Memorial Foundation, Midland, TX
37,500	University of Colorado Health Sciences Center, Denver, CO
12,500	Denver Academy, Denver, CO
12,500	Memorial Sloan-Kettering Cancer Center, New York, NY
12,500	University of Pittsburgh, Bradford, PA
10,000	Alamogordo Music Theatre, Alamogordo, NM
10,000	Denver Museum of Nature and Science, Denver, CO

FORMOSA PLASTICS CORPORATION, USA

Company Headquarters
9 Peach Tree Hill Rd.
Livingston, NJ 07039-5702
Web: http://www.fpcusa.com

Company Description
Revenue: US$1.9 billion (2001)
Employees: 2,700 (2001)
SIC(s): 2800 Chemicals & Allied Products, 3000 Rubber & Miscellaneous Plastics Products.
Parent Company: Formosa Plastics Corp., 201 Tun Hwa North Rd., Taipei, Taiwan

Giving Contact
William H. Bauer, Jr., Trustee, Executive Advisory Committee
Formosa Plastics Religious Trust
First National Bank
PO Drawer 7
Port Lavaca, TX 77979
Phone: (361)552-6726

Description
Organization Type: Corporate Giving Program
Giving Locations: TX: Calhoun, Jackson, and Victoria counties
Grant Types: General Support.

Financial Summary
Total Giving: $55,005 (2001)
Giving Analysis: Giving for 2001 includes: foundation ($55,005)
Assets: $1,134,333 (2001)

Typical Recipients
Civic & Public Affairs: Civic & Public Affairs-General
Education: Colleges & Universities, Religious Edu-

cation, Secondary Education (Private)
Health: Cancer
Religion: Churches, Religion-General, Ministries, Religious Organizations

Application Procedures

Initial Contact: Send for grant application.
Application Requirements: Include a description of organization and purpose of funds sought, benefits and costs of program, and evidence that the application is a qualified religious organization.
Deadlines: October 1.

Restrictions

Limited to commonly recognized religious organizations in a three-county area of the Formosa Plastics Corp. plant at Point Comfort, Texas (Calhoun, Jackson, and Victoria)

Corporate Officials

Robert P. H. Ho: chief financial officer, president B Taiwan 1949. ED National Taiwan University BA (1972). PRIM CORP EMPL chief financial officer: Formosa Plastics Corp. U.S.A. CORP AFFIL treasurer: Inteplast Corp.; treasurer: Nan Ya Plastics Corp. America; treasurer: Formosa Plastics Corp. America.
C. T. Lee: president PRIM CORP EMPL president: Formosa Plastics Corp. U.S.A.
Susan Wang: executive, president B 1960. PRIM CORP EMPL executive, president: Formosa Plastics Corp. U.S.A. ADD CORP EMPL executive, vice president: Formosa Plastics Corp. Delaware; executive, vice president: Formosa Plastics Corp. Texas.
Yung-ching Wang: chairman B Taiwan 1916. PRIM CORP EMPL chairman: Formosa Plastics Corp. U.S.A. CORP AFFIL chairman, director: Formosa Plastics Corp. USA; owner: Nan Ya Plastics Corp.; chairman, director: Formosa Plastics Corp. Texas; owner: Formosa Chemicals & Fibre Corp.; chairman, director: Formosa Plastics Corp. LA.

Grants Analysis

Disclosure Period: calendar year ending 2001
Total Grants: $55,005
Number of Grants: 12
Average Grant: $4,584
Highest Grant: $7,500
Lowest Grant: $1,000

Recent Grants

Note: Grants derived from 2001 Form 990.
General

7,500	First Christian Church, Victoria, TX -- video projection system
6,950	Calhoun County Ministerial Alliance, Victoria, TX -- outreach program to counsel married couples and strengthen existing marriages
6,825	Shiloh Missionary Baptist, Newark, OH -- after-school youth program
5,730	Texas Buddhist Association, Houston, TX -- lecture series and youth leadership development program
4,500	First English Lutheran Church, Victoria, TX -- conference to strengthen families
4,000	Jackson County Ministerial Alliance Industrial Commission, Vanderbilt, TX -- Speakers on substance abuse, sexual decisions, delinquent behavior, and related issues
4,000	St. Joseph High School, Victoria, TX -- spiritual retreat for seniors
4,000	Victoria College Library, Victoria, TX -- books on religion and theology
3,800	Faith Academy, Victoria, TX -- library tables and chairs
3,500	Seadrift Cemetery, Seadrift, TX -- construction of chapel at cemetery

JAMES W. AND ELLA B. FORSTER CHARITABLE TRUST

Giving Contact

Trust Officer
Frontier Bank
PO Box 549
Rock Rapids, IA 51246
Phone: (712)472-2567
Fax: (712)472-2620

Description

Founded: 1987
EIN: 421305882
Organization Type: Private Foundation
Giving Locations: IA
Grant Types: Department, General Support.

Donor Information

Founder: the late James W. Forster, the late Ella B. Forster

Financial Summary

Total Giving: $157,431 (fiscal year ending June 30, 2004); $151,982 (fiscal 2001)
Assets: $3,521,853 (fiscal 2004); $3,035,822 (fiscal 2001)

Typical Recipients

Arts & Humanities: Historic Preservation, History & Archaeology, Libraries, Music
Civic & Public Affairs: Clubs, Economic Development, Municipalities/Towns, Parades/Festivals, Safety
Education: Education-General, Public Education (Precollege), Student Aid
Health: Clinics/Medical Centers, Emergency/Ambulance Services, Hospitals
Social Services: Community Centers, Day Care, Recreation & Athletics, Substance Abuse, Youth Organizations

Application Procedures

Initial Contact: Request application form.
Deadlines: September 30.

Additional Information

Publications: Application Form
Trust(s): Frontier Bank

Foundation Officials

John Appel: trustee

Grants Analysis

Disclosure Period: fiscal year ending June 30, 2004
Total Grants: $157,431
Number of Grants: 10
Average Grant: $10,270*
Highest Grant: $65,000
Lowest Grant: $850
Typical Range: $5,000 to $20,000
*Note: Average grant figure excludes highest grant.

Recent Grants

Note: Grants derived from fiscal 2004 Form 990.
Library-Related

4,000	Rock Rapids Public Library, Rock Rapids, IA -- serendipity club (latch-key kids)

General

65,000	City of Rock Rapids, Rock Rapids, IA -- debt service on Forster community center
35,000	Central Lyon Community School District, Rock Rapids, IA -- debt services on central Lyon auditorium
14,581	Merrill Pioneer Community Hospital, Rock Rapids, IA -- for capital improvements to hospital
10,000	Central Lyon Community School District, Rock Rapids, IA -- demolition of former high school and construction of new facility
10,000	City of Rock Rapids, Rock Rapids, IA -- for recreation trail
10,000	Rock Rapids Kids Club, Rock Rapids, IA -- for community daycare
5,000	Central Lyon Community School District, Rock Rapids, IA -- project for central Lyon historical plaza
3,000	City of Rock Rapids, Rock Rapids, IA -- Ramp-Forster field multi-purpose
850	Lyon County Historical Society, Rock Rapids, IA -- purchase copier and fireproof file

FORT WORTH STAR-TELEGRAM INC.

Company Headquarters

400 W 7th St.
Fort Worth, TX 76102
Web: http://www.star-telegram.com

Company Description

Founded: 1982
Revenue: US$4.2 million (2001)
Employees: 12 (2003)
SIC(s): 2711 Newspapers.
Parent Company: ABC Inc., 77 W. 66th St., New York, NY, United States

Operating Locations

Fort Worth Star-Telegram Inc. (TX--Fort Worth)

Amon G. Carter Star Telegram Employees Fund

Giving Contact

Nenetta Carter Tatum, President
PO Box 17480
Ft. Worth, TX 76102
Phone: (817)332-3535

Description

Founded: 1945
EIN: 756014850
Organization Type: Corporate Foundation
Giving Locations: TX: Tarrant County
Grant Types: Capital, General Support, Scholarship.

Financial Summary

Total Giving: $1,169,138 (fiscal year ending April 30, 2004); $1,132,247 (fiscal 2003); $1,630,043 (fiscal 2002). Note: Contributes through foundation only.
Giving Analysis: Giving for fiscal 2001 includes: foundation grants to United Way ($25,000); foundation scholarships ($94,000); foundation gifts to individuals ($195,419); foundation ($1,177,500)
Assets: $26,511,402 (fiscal 2004); $23,132,617 (fiscal 2003); $27,184,234 (fiscal 2002)
Gifts Received: $25 (fiscal 2003); $10,000 (fiscal 1997); $12,000 (fiscal 1996)

Typical Recipients

Arts & Humanities: Arts Associations & Councils, Arts Festivals, Arts Outreach, Ballet, Dance, Arts & Humanities-General, Historic Preservation, History & Archaeology, Libraries, Museums/Galleries, Music, Opera, Performing Arts, Theater
Civic & Public Affairs: Business/Free Enterprise, Clubs, Civic & Public Affairs-General, Housing, Law

& Justice, Municipalities/Towns, Nonprofit Management, Parades/Festivals, Philanthropic Organizations, Safety, Urban & Community Affairs, Women's Affairs, Zoos/Aquariums
Education: Afterschool/Enrichment Programs, Colleges & Universities, Education Associations, Education Reform, Elementary Education (Private), Education-General, Minority Education, Private Education (Precollege), Public Education (Precollege), School Volunteerism, Special Education, Student Aid
Environment: Environment-General
Health: Adolescent Health Issues, AIDS/HIV, Cancer, Children's Health/Hospitals, Diabetes, Eyes/Blindness, Health Funds, Health Organizations, Heart, Hospitals, Hospitals (University Affiliated), Medical Research, Mental Health, Nursing Services, Public Health, Research/Studies Institutes, Single-Disease Health Associations, Transplant Networks/Donor Banks
International: Foreign Arts Organizations, Missionary/Religious Activities
Religion: Bible Study/Translation, Jewish Causes, Religious Organizations, Religious Welfare
Science: Science Museums, Scientific Research
Social Services: At-Risk Youth, Big Brothers/Big Sisters, Camps, Child Welfare, Community Service Organizations, Counseling, Crime Prevention, Day Care, Domestic Violence, Family Planning, Family Services, Food/Clothing Distribution, People with Disabilities, Recreation & Athletics, Scouts, Senior Services, Shelters/Homelessness, Social Services-General, Substance Abuse, United Funds/United Ways, Volunteer Services, YMCA/YWCA/YMHA/YWHA, Youth Organizations

Application Procedures

Initial Contact: Send a brief letter of inquiry.
Application Requirements: One copy of proposal.
Deadlines: None.
Notes: The foundation may request additional information after reviewing initial letter.

Restrictions

Foundation limits its giving to Texas. No grants are given to individuals, except for employee-related scholarships and grants.

Additional Information

Giving is primarily for medical or hardship assistance and pension supplements for Carter Publications, Inc. employees. Scholarships are awarded to children of Star Telegram employees.

Corporate Officials

Richard L. Connor: president, publisher B Bangor, ME 1947. ED Hillsdale College BA (1970). PRIM CORP EMPL president, publisher: Fort Worth Star-Telegram Inc. NONPR AFFIL trustee: Tilton School; director: Wilkes-Barre Chamber of Commerce; trustee: Ft. Worth Academy; trustee: Misericordia College; member: American Society Newspaper Editors; director: Capital Cities Community Minorities Intern Program; member: American Newspaper Publishers Association.

Foundation Officials

Mark L. Johnson: vice president
John H. Robinson: secretary, treasurer
Nenetta Carter Tatum: president NONPR AFFIL director: Carter Amon Museum Western Art.

Grants Analysis

Disclosure Period: fiscal year ending April 30, 2004
Total Grants: $761,230*
Number of Grants: 51
Average Grant: $11,225*
Highest Grant: $200,000
Lowest Grant: $1,000
Typical Range: $2,500 to $25,000
*Note: Giving excludes gifts to individuals; scholarship. Average grant figure excludes highest grant.

Recent Grants

Note: Grants derived from fiscal 2003 Form 990.
General

90,000	YMCA of Metropolitan Tarrant County, Ft. Worth, TX
50,000	All Saints Health Foundation, Ft. Worth, TX
50,000	Carter BloodCare, Ft. Worth, TX
25,000	Amon Carter Museum, Ft. Worth, TX
25,000	Casa Manana Musicals Inc., Ft. Worth, TX
25,000	First Texas Council of Camp Fire, Ft. Worth, TX
20,000	Allied Theater Group, Ft. Worth, TX
20,000	Cook Fort Worth Children's Medical Center, Ft. Worth, TX
20,000	Fort Worth Opera, Ft. Worth, TX
20,000	Summerbridge, Ft. Worth, TX

FORTIS HEALTH

Company Headquarters

501 W. Michigan St.
Milwaukee, WI 53203
Web: http://www.fortishealth.com

Company Description

Founded: 1892
Former Name: Time Insurance Co.
Employees: 2,000
SIC(s): 6311 Life Insurance, 6321 Accident & Health Insurance.
Parent Company: Assurant, One Chase Manhattan Plaza, New York, NY, United States
Parent Revenue: US$40,090,000,000 (2001)

Nonmonetary Support

Type: Donated Equipment; In-kind Services; Loaned Employees; Loaned Executives; Workplace Solicitation
Volunteer Programs: The foundation supports employee volunteer activities, with special consideration given to organizations where employees volunteer that fall within the foundation's focus areas. The foundation does consider grants to organizations where employees volunteer but are not within the foundation focus. However, grants of this nature are limited to $100 per organization, with priority given to programs providing education, training, and direct services.

Fortis Insurance Foundation

Giving Contact

Dawn Krautkramer, Secretary
501 West Michigan Street
Milwaukee, WI 53203-3050
Phone: (414)299-8557
Fax: (414)299-6900

Alternate Contact

Pat Cullen
Phone: (414)271-3011
Note: Pat Cullen may be reached at extension 6722.

Description

Founded: 1973
EIN: 237346436
Organization Type: Corporate Foundation
Former Name: Fortis Insurance Foundation.
Giving Locations: WI: Southeastern Wisconsin
Grant Types: Employee Matching Gifts, General Support.
Note: Employee matching gift ratio: 1 to 1 to social services, education, or cultural institutions, up to

$500 annually. Also provides grants for specific organizational programs within the focus of the foundation.

Donor Information

Founder: Time Insurance Co.

Financial Summary

Total Giving: $308,557 (2002); $368,039 (2001). Note: Contributes through foundation only.
Giving Analysis: Giving for 2001 includes: foundation scholarships ($1,000); foundation matching gifts ($96,511); foundation ($270,528)
Assets: $2,499,906 (2002); $1,232,068 (2001)
Gifts Received: $1,575,000 (2002); $480,000 (2001); $376,000 (2000). Note: In 2002, 2001, 2000 and 1998, contributions were received from Fortis Insurance Co. (formerly known as the Times Industry Co.). In 1999, contributions were received from Fortis Insurance Co. ($181,000) and Diversified Pharmaceutical Services ($1,000).

Typical Recipients

Arts & Humanities: Arts Associations & Councils, Arts Funds, Libraries, Museums/Galleries, Music, Performing Arts, Public Broadcasting
Civic & Public Affairs: African American Affairs, Economic Development, Employment/Job Training, Civic & Public Affairs-General, Hispanic Affairs, Housing, Legal Aid, Minority Business, Nonprofit Management, Philanthropic Organizations, Public Policy, Safety, Urban & Community Affairs, Women's Affairs, Zoos/Aquariums
Education: Afterschool/Enrichment Programs, Business Education, Economic Education, Education-General, Health & Physical Education, Literacy, Medical Education, Minority Education, Private Education (Precollege), Public Education (Precollege), Science/Mathematics Education, Secondary Education (Public), Vocational & Technical Education
Environment: Environment-General
Health: AIDS/HIV, Alzheimer's Disease, Children's Health/Hospitals, Clinics/Medical Centers, Geriatric Health, Health Policy/Cost Containment, Health Funds, Health Organizations, Hospitals, Medical Rehabilitation, Medical Research, Mental Health, Nutrition, Public Health, Respiratory, Single-Disease Health Associations
International: Health Care/Hospitals
Religion: Ministries, Religious Welfare
Science: Science Museums, Scientific Centers & Institutes
Social Services: Camps, Child Welfare, Community Centers, Community Service Organizations, Crime Prevention, Day Care, Delinquency & Criminal Rehabilitation, Domestic Violence, Family Planning, Family Services, Food/Clothing Distribution, People with Disabilities, Scouts, Social Services-General, Substance Abuse, United Funds/United Ways, Veterans, Volunteer Services, YMCA/YWCA/YMHA/YWHA, Youth Organizations

Application Procedures

Initial Contact: Send a letter requesting grant application form.
Application Requirements: Application form requests information on organization's background, its mission, size, and history; description of proposed program, its purpose, budget and goals; description of beneficiaries, including the approximate number of people who will be helped; and information on personnel, including qualifications for those personnel who play a key role in carrying out the objectives of the organization. Accompanying materials must include, financial statements for the past fiscal year, including IRS Form 990; a copy of the most recent IRS ruling under section 501(c)(3); list of officers and directors; actual income and expense statement for the past year, including sources of support; and projected income and expense budget for the current fiscal year.
Deadlines: One month prior to bi-monthly meetings.

Review Process: The board of directors will evaluate the proposal on its merits, its consistency with the foundation's policies, and the availability of funds.

Evaluative Criteria: A preference will be given to proposals that improve the quality, accessibility, and efficiency of health-care services.

Decision Notification: The trustees meet bi-monthly to consider grant applications, in February, April, June, August, October, and December; applicants receive written notice regarding the board's decision within 14 days after the meeting.

Notes: Foundation uses the Common Application Form of the Donors Forum of Wisconsin.

Restrictions

Grants are generally not made to organizations that are primarily political, fraternal, municipal, religious, or labor-related.

Generally does not provide grants for fund-raising events or multiyear grants, nor does it provide endowment grants.

Foundation will not individually support operational grant requests from organizations that receive a substantial amount of their funding from United Way or United Performing Arts Fund. Will not provide matching funds for food and clothing drives, sporting teams, payment for school or tuition expenses, alumni or membership dues, fees for services, unpaid pledges, bequests, subscription fees for publications, or insurance premium payments.

Additional Information

The foundation's grant programs include a Discretionary Grant program, a Community Cornerstone Grant program, and an Employee Matching Grant program. The Discretionary grant program awards grant monies to qualifying organizations addressing the priorities of the foundation: health issues, job creation and economic revitalization of its operating community, hunger/homelessness, long-term care, and other services for children, youth, elderly, and the family. Special consideration is given to organizations where company employees actively volunteer their services. Community Cornerstone grants are made for operational support to established community organizations providing equal and low-cost access to a variety of artistic, cultural, and scientific experiences. These grants are also made to support community-based fundraising initiatives such as the United Way and the United Performing Arts Fund. The Employee Matching Grant program provides for matching of personal employee contributions of $20 or more, to qualifying organizations, up to $500 per year per employee.

Publications: Community Annual Report; Application Guidelines; Application Form

Grants Analysis

Disclosure Period: calendar year ending 2002
Total Grants: $265,500*
Number of Grants: 29
Average Grant: $7,696*
Highest Grant: $50,000
Lowest Grant: $500
Typical Range: $2,000 to $12,000
*Note: Giving excludes matching gifts and scholarship. Average grant figure excludes highest grant.

Recent Grants

Note: Grants derived from 2003 Form 990.
General

169,165	Public Forum Institute, Washington, DC
50,000	Medical College of Wisconsin, Milwaukee, WI
50,000	Medical College of Wisconsin, Milwaukee, WI
25,000	ALEC, Washington, DC
25,000	Galen Institute, Alexandria, VA
25,000	United Way of Greater Milwaukee, Milwaukee, WI

20,000	National Center of Policy Analysis, Dallas, TX
10,000	AAHP Foundation, Washington, DC
10,000	Common Good, New York, NY
5,000	AIDS Resource Center of Wisconsin, WI

FORTUNE BRANDS INC.

Company Headquarters
300 Tower Parkway
Lincolnshire, IL 60069-3640
Web: http://www.fortunebrands.com

Company Description
Ticker: FO
Exchange: NYSE
Former Name: American Brands, Inc.
Revenue: US$7.021 billion (2004)
Profit: US$783.8 million (2004)
Employees: 30988 (2003)
Fortune Rank: 301, per FORTUNE Magazine's list of 500 Largest U.S. Corporations (2004).
SIC(s): 2085 Distilled & Blended Liquors, 2111 Cigarettes, 2121 Cigars, 6719 Holding Companies Nec.

Operating Locations
ACCO North America (IL--Deerfield); ACCO U.S.A. Inc. (NY--Long Island City); Acushnet Co. (MA--Fairhaven); Acushnet Rubber Co. (MA--New Bedford); Aristokraft Distribution Center (WA--Kent); Fortune Brands, Inc. (VA--Richmond; WI--Milwaukee); Jim Beam Brands (KY--Clermont; TX--Bedford); Master Lock Co. (WI--Milwaukee); Masterbrand Industries, Inc. (IL--Lincolnshire); Moen Inc. (NC--Sanford); Moen, Inc. (OH--Elyria); NHB Industries, Inc. (AL--Talladega); Schrock Cabinet Co. (IL--Arthur); Torco P/L (WA--Kalannie); Waterloo Industries Inc. (IA--Waterloo)
Note: Also has major operations in Weybridge, Surrey, England.

Nonmonetary Support
Value: $3,864,378 (1998)
Type: Donated Equipment; Donated Products; In-kind Services
Note: The company also reports that it donates the use of their facilities.

Giving Contact
Joan McGrath, Contributions Administrator
Fortune Brands, Inc. Contributions Program
1700 East Putnam Avenue
Old Greenwich, CT 06870
Fax: (203)698-5577

Description
Organization Type: Corporate Giving Program
Giving Locations: headquarters and operating communities.
Grant Types: Employee Matching Gifts, General Support, Multiyear/Continuing Support, Scholarship.
Note: Employee matching gift ratio: 2 to 1.

Financial Summary
Total Giving: Contributes through corporate direct giving program only. Giving includes corporate direct giving; domestic and international subsidiaries; nonmonetary support.

Typical Recipients
Arts & Humanities: Arts Centers, Community Arts, Historic Preservation, Libraries, Museums/Galleries, Music, Opera, Performing Arts, Public Broadcasting, Theater
Civic & Public Affairs: Civil Rights, Economic Development, Employment/Job Training, Legal Aid, Urban & Community Affairs, Women's Affairs, Zoos/Aquariums

Education: Arts/Humanities Education, Business Education, Colleges & Universities, Community & Junior Colleges, Continuing Education, Economic Education, Education Associations, Elementary Education (Private), Literacy, Minority Education, Private Education (Precollege), Public Education (Precollege), Special Education
Environment: Environment-General
Health: Emergency/Ambulance Services, Health Organizations, Hospitals, Medical Research, Public Health, Single-Disease Health Associations
International: Health Care/Hospitals, International Peace & Security Issues, International Relations
Social Services: Child Welfare, Community Centers, Community Service Organizations, Day Care, Food/Clothing Distribution, People with Disabilities, Recreation & Athletics, Shelters/Homelessness, Substance Abuse, United Funds/United Ways, Volunteer Services, Youth Organizations

Application Procedures
Initial Contact: Send a brief letter of inquiry.
Application Requirements: Include organization's purpose, detailed description of project and amount of funding requested; list of other corporate contributors; and proof of tax-exempt status.
Deadlines: None.
Review Process: All requests are screened and approved by the corporate responsibility committee; operating companies administer local contributions programs.
Evaluative Criteria: Preference given to organizations close to company locations.
Decision Notification: Decisions are made as applications are received; final notification within one month.
Notes: The company reports that requests should be sent to the nearest company facility. The company's contributions program is highly decentralized.

Restrictions
Generally does not support individuals, political parties or candidates, fraternal organizations, member agencies of united funds, or religious organizations for sectarian purposes.

Additional Information
In 1997, American Brands, Inc. divided into two companies--Fortune Brands and Gallaher. Gallaher is based in the United Kingdom.

Corporate Officials
Thomas Chandler Hays: chairman, chief executive officer, director B Chicago, IL 1935. ED California Institute of Technology BS (1957); California Institute of Technology MS (1958); Harvard University Graduate School of Business Administration MBA (1963). PRIM CORP EMPL former chairman and chief executive officer; director: Fortune Brands, Inc. CORP AFFIL director: Fortune Brands Inc. NONPR AFFIL member: Conference Board; director: Southwest Area Commerce & Industry Association; director: Community Foundations Fairfield County; member: Ambassador Roundtable; member: Business Roundtable. CLUB AFFIL Economic Club; Tokeneke Club; Darien Country Club; Bel-Air Bay Club; Cincinnati Country Club.
Norman H. Wesley: president, chief operating officer ED University of Utah MBA. PRIM CORP EMPL president, chief executive officer: Fortune Brands, Inc. ADD CORP EMPL chairman: ACCO World Corp. CORP AFFIL director: R.R. Donnelley & Sons.

Giving Program Officials
Joan S. McGrath: contributions administrator

Grants Analysis
Typical Range: $500 to $5,000

FOSTER CHARITABLE TRUST

Giving Contact
Bernard S. Mars, Trustee
681 Andersen Dr., Suite 300
Pittsburgh, PA 15220-2747
Phone: (412)928-8900

Description
Founded: 1962
EIN: 256064791
Organization Type: Private Foundation
Giving Locations: PA
Grant Types: General Support.

Donor Information
Founder: Foster Industries

Financial Summary
Gifts Received: $161,100 (1999); $196,756 (1998); $327,023 (1996). Note: In 1999, contributions were received from Foster Investment Co. In 1998, contributions were received from Foster Industries, Inc. ($47,588) and Foster Investment Co. ($149,168). In 1992, contributions were received from Foster Industries, Inc.

Typical Recipients
Arts & Humanities: Arts Associations & Councils, Arts Festivals, Arts Funds, Ballet, Ethnic & Folk Arts, Arts & Humanities-General, Libraries, Museums/Galleries, Music, Opera, Performing Arts, Public Broadcasting, Theater
Civic & Public Affairs: Botanical Gardens/Parks, Civic & Public Affairs-General, Philanthropic Organizations
Education: Colleges & Universities, Health & Physical Education, Legal Education, Private Education (Precollege), Religious Education
Health: AIDS/HIV, Alzheimer's Disease, Clinics/Medical Centers, Eyes/Blindness, Hospitals, Medical Rehabilitation, Medical Research, Research/Studies Institutes, Single-Disease Health Associations
International: Foreign Educational Institutions, Missionary/Religious Activities
Religion: Jewish Causes, Religious Organizations, Religious Welfare, Synagogues/Temples
Science: Scientific Centers & Institutes
Social Services: Camps, Child Welfare, Community Centers, Community Service Organizations, People with Disabilities, Shelters/Homelessness, Substance Abuse, United Funds/United Ways, Youth Organizations

Application Procedures
Initial Contact: Send brief typed letter of inquiry.
Application Requirements: Include a description of organization and proof of tax-exempt status.
Deadlines: None.

Foundation Officials
J. R. Foster: trustee
Jay L. Foster: trustee
Lee B. Foster: trustee
Bernard S. Mars: trustee
Peter F. Mars: trustee
Kim Petracca: trustee

Grants Analysis
Disclosure Period: calendar year ending 2000
Total Grants: $319,450*
Number of Grants: 72
Average Grant: $4,189*
Highest Grant: $50,000
Typical Range: $1,000 to $10,000
*Note: Giving excludes United Way. Average grant figure excludes two highest grants ($98,240).

Recent Grants
Note: Grants derived from 2001 Form 990.
General
55,000	United Jewish Federation, Pittsburgh, PA
32,000	Temple Jeremiah, Northfield, IL
26,000	United Way of Allegheny County, Pittsburgh, PA
21,000	Society for Contemporary Craft, Pittsburgh, PA
20,000	Trinity College, Port Hope, ON Canada
14,000	Sarasota Manatee Jewish Federation, Sarasota, FL
11,520	Camp Kon-O-Kwee/Spencer, Fombell, PA
10,500	Chicago Botanic Garden, Glencoe, IL
10,000	University of Pennsylvania, Pittsburgh, PA
6,000	Jewish Education Institute, Pittsburgh, PA

FOSTER FOUNDATION

Giving Contact
Jill Goodsell, Administrator
1929 43rd Avenue East, Suite 300
Seattle, WA 98112
Phone: (206)726-1815

Description
Founded: 1984
EIN: 911265474
Organization Type: Family Foundation
Giving Locations: WA: Seattle
Grant Types: Capital, General Support, Matching, Project, Research, Scholarship, Seed Money.

Donor Information
Founder: Established in 1984 by Evelyn W. Foster.

Financial Summary
Total Giving: $2,371,107 (2003); $2,272,050 (2001)
Giving Analysis: Giving for 2003 includes: foundation grants to United Way ($35,000); 2001: foundation grants to United Way ($35,000)
Assets: $79,299,854 (2003); $39,205,096 (2001)
Gifts Received: $34,727,493 (2003). Note: In 2003, contributions were received from the estate of Evelyn Foster.

Typical Recipients
Arts & Humanities: Arts Associations & Councils, Arts Centers, History & Archaeology, Libraries, Museums/Galleries, Music, Opera, Performing Arts, Theater
Civic & Public Affairs: Employment/Job Training, Housing, Municipalities/Towns, Public Policy, Safety, Urban & Community Affairs, Women's Affairs
Education: Arts/Humanities Education, Business Education, Colleges & Universities, Education Reform, Environmental Education, Literacy, Preschool Education, Private Education (Precollege), Public Education (Precollege)
Environment: Environment-General, Resource Conservation
Health: AIDS/HIV, Cancer, Children's Health/Hospitals, Clinics/Medical Centers, Emergency/Ambulance Services, Eyes/Blindness, Geriatric Health, Health Funds, Health Organizations, Heart, Hospices, Hospitals, Medical Research, Nursing Services, Prenatal Health Issues, Preventive Medicine/Wellness Organizations, Public Health, Research/Studies Institutes, Respiratory, Single-Disease Health Associations
International: Health Care/Hospitals
Religion: Churches, Ministries, Missionary Activities (Domestic), Religious Organizations, Religious Welfare
Science: Scientific Centers & Institutes

Social Services: At-Risk Youth, Big Brothers/Big Sisters, Child Abuse, Child Welfare, Community Centers, Community Service Organizations, Day Care, Domestic Violence, Emergency Relief, Family Planning, Family Services, Food/Clothing Distribution, Homes, People with Disabilities, Senior Services, Shelters/Homelessness, Social Services-General, United Funds/United Ways, YMCA/YWCA/YMHA/YWHA, Youth Organizations

Application Procedures
Initial Contact: Inquiries for funding should be described briefly in letter form. If the inquiry is deemed appropriate, a formal application will be requested.
Application Requirements: Inquiries should include a brief description of the project and its intended purpose. Formal applications must contain the name and address of the organization, proof of tax-exempt status, a list of officers and directors, a brief history of the program and its accomplishments, and financial reports including a budget for the current year. The formal application also must include a project plan defining the need and the methods for achieving the objectives and for evaluating the results, and a detailed budget for the project.
Deadlines: None.
Review Process: Applicants should allow three months for the board to make its decision.

Restrictions
Grants will be awarded to organizations for one year only. Grants to individuals will be made as scholarships through a school, college, or university. The foundation does not support endowment funds, fundraising activities, loans, or unrestricted operating funds.

Foundation Officials
Michael G. Foster, Jr.: director
Jill Goodsell: admin, trustee PRIM CORP EMPL treasurer, director: Foster, Paulsell & Baker, Inc.

Grants Analysis
Disclosure Period: calendar year ending 2003
Total Grants: $2,336,107*
Number of Grants: 80
Average Grant: $22,547*
Highest Grant: $200,000
Lowest Grant: $1,000
Typical Range: $10,000 to $40,000
*Note: Giving excludes United Way. Average grant figure excludes three highest grant ($600,000).

Recent Grants
Note: Grants derived from 2002 Form 990.

Library-Related
250,000	Seattle Public Library Foundation, Seattle, WA

General
200,000	Children's Hospital Foundation, Seattle, WA
200,000	McCaw Hall Seattle Center Foundation, Seattle, WA
200,000	Overlake School, Redmond, WA
150,000	YWCA Shelter Angeline's, Seattle, WA
54,400	Northwest Harvest, Seattle, WA
50,000	Planned Parenthood of Western Washington, Seattle, WA
50,000	Seattle Art Museum, Seattle, WA
50,000	Treehouse, Seattle, WA
50,000	YMCA of Greater Seattle, Seattle, WA
42,350	Make a Wish Foundation, Seattle, WA

FOUNDATION FOR CHILD DEVELOPMENT

Giving Contact
Ruby Takanish, President
145 East 32nd Street
14th Floor
New York, NY 10016-6055
Phone: (212)213-8337
Fax: (212)213-5897
E-mail: inforequest@ffcd.org
Web: http://www.ffcd.org

Description
Founded: 1900
EIN: 131623901
Organization Type: Specialized/Single Purpose Foundation
Giving Locations: New York area.
Grant Types: Conference/Seminar, General Support, Multiyear/Continuing Support, Project, Research.

Donor Information
Founder: The foundation was incorporated as a voluntary agency in New York in 1900, and established as the Association for the Aid of Crippled Children in 1908. It was publicly supported by voluntary contributions until 1944 when substantial funds were received from the estate of Milo M. Belding Jr., as a testament to his wife, Annie K. Belding, who had devoted many years of service to the association. Mr. Belding (1865-1931) was president of Belding Brothers and Company, a firm established by his father, which became the largest silk manufacturer in the world. He was also president of Broadway Trust Company.

In its early years, the association was directly involved with the care of crippled children. In the 1950s, the foundation's focus shifted to the prevention of congenital disabilities, and until the 1970s, it primarily supported research into genetically based disorders and abnormalities of fetal development. In recognition of its evolving program and of its status as a grant-making organization, the association changed its name in 1972 to the Foundation for Child Development.

Financial Summary
Total Giving: $3,599,998 (fiscal year ending March 31, 2004); $3,602,172 (fiscal 2001)
Assets: $103,482,660 (fiscal 2004); $101,462,405 (fiscal 2001)
Gifts Received: $3,000 (fiscal 2001); $716 (fiscal 1999); $350 (fiscal 1998). Note: In fiscal 1996, contributions were received from the estate of Kenneth Nussbaum.

Typical Recipients
Arts & Humanities: Arts & Humanities-General, Libraries, Museums/Galleries, Music, Public Broadcasting
Civic & Public Affairs: African American Affairs, Civil Rights, Community Foundations, Economic Development, Economic Policy, Employment/Job Training, Civic & Public Affairs-General, Hispanic Affairs, Law & Justice, Legal Aid, Nonprofit Management, Philanthropic Organizations, Professional & Trade Associations, Public Policy, Urban & Community Affairs, Women's Affairs
Education: Afterschool/Enrichment Programs, Arts/Humanities Education, Colleges & Universities, Education Associations, Education Funds, Education Reform, Engineering/Technological Education, Faculty Development, Education-General, Medical Education, Preschool Education, Public Education (Precollege), School Volunteerism, Social Sciences Education, Student Aid
Environment: Environment-General
Health: Children's Health/Hospitals, Geriatric Health, Health Funds, Hospitals, Medical Rehabilitation,

Medical Research, Mental Health, Nutrition, Public Health, Research/Studies Institutes
International: International Relations
Religion: Religious Welfare
Science: Scientific Centers & Institutes, Scientific Organizations
Social Services: At-Risk Youth, Child Abuse, Child Welfare, Community Centers, Community Service Organizations, Counseling, Day Care, Delinquency & Criminal Rehabilitation, Domestic Violence, Family Planning, Family Services, Food/Clothing Distribution, People with Disabilities, Senior Services, Shelters/Homelessness, United Funds/United Ways, Volunteer Services, Youth Organizations

Application Procedures
Initial Contact: Send a one- or two-page letter of inquiry to the foundation. Contact the foundation for guidelines.
Application Requirements: Query letters should describe the proposed project, its objectives, and approximate level of funding required. If the project falls within the Foundation's scope of interest, a proposal will be invited and details regarding what the proposal should include will be provided.
Deadlines: None.
Review Process: The board of directors meets in June, September, December, and March to review invited proposals. The foundation replies quickly to query letters with an indication of whether a project fits its program interests.

Restrictions
The foundation does not consider requests for scholarships or grants to individuals, capital campaigns, or the purchase, construction, or renovation of buildings. The foundation does not make grants outside the United States.

Additional Information
The foundation indicates that future grant making will focus on the integration of research, policy, and advocacy or research and practice in the areas of availability and access to early childhood education and care programs and health care for children.
Publications: Annual Report; Guidelines

Foundation Officials
Ruth Ann Burns: secretary, director NONPR AFFIL vice president, director: Educational Broadcasting Corp.
P. Lindsay Chase-Lansdale: chairman, director
Michael I. Cohen: vice chairman, director B Brooklyn, NY 1935. ED Columbia University BA (1956); Columbia University MD (1960). PRIM NONPR EMPL professor pediatrics, department chairman: Albert Einstein College of Medicine. NONPR AFFIL member: Society Adolescent Medicine; member: Society Pediatric Research; member: National Academy Sciences Institute Medicine; member: American Pediatric Society; member: American Psychosomatic Society; member: American Federation Clinical Research; member: American Gastrointestinal Association; member: American Academy Pediatrics; member: Alpha Omega Alpha; member: Ambulatory Pediatrics Association.
John L. Furth: treasurer, director B 1931. PRIM CORP EMPL vice chairman, director: EM Warburg, Pincus & Co. Inc. CORP AFFIL vice chairman: Warburg EM Pincus Co. LLC. NONPR AFFIL president, director: Grand Street Settlement Inc.
Karen N. Gerard: director PRIM CORP EMPL vice president business locations division: Moran, Stahl & Boyer.
Julius Benjamin Richmond: director B Chicago, IL September 26, 1916. ED University of Illinois BS (1937); University of Illinois MD (1939); University of Illinois MS (1939). PRIM NONPR EMPL professor emeritus: Harvard University, School of Medicine. NONPR AFFIL member: Sigma Xi; member: Society Pediatric Research; associate member: New England Council Child Psychiatry; member: Phi Eta

Sigma; professor health policy emeritus: Harvard University Medical School; member: National Academy Sciences Institute Medicine; member: American Public Health Association; advisor child health policy: Childrens Hospital Medical Center; fellow: American Psychiatric Association; member: American Psychosomatic Society; fellow: American Orthopsychiatric Association; member: American Pediatric Society; member: American Academy Pediatrics; member: American Medical Association; member: Alpha Omega Alpha.
Barbara Paul Robinson: director B 1941. ED Bryn Mawr College AB (1962); Yale University LLB (1965). PRIM CORP EMPL partner: Debevoise & Plimpton. NONPR AFFIL director: Yale Council; member: Yale Law School Association New York; member: Women's Forum; member advisory board, lecturer: Practicing Law Institute; director: Wave Hill Inc.; fellow: New York State Bar Foundation; director: Garden Conservancy; member: New York State Bar Association; director: Fund Modern Courts; member: Council Foreign Relations; trustee: William Nelson Cromwell Foundation; member: Association Bar New York City Fund; director: Catalyst for Women Inc.; president: Association Bar New York City; fellow: American College Trust & Estate Counsel; director: American Judicature Society; member: American Bar Association; fellow: American Bar Foundation; arbitrator, director: American Arbitration Association. CLUB AFFIL Washington Club; Yale Club.
Fasaha M. Traylor: senior program officer

Grants Analysis
Disclosure Period: fiscal year ending March 31, 2004
Total Grants: $3,599,998
Number of Grants: 39
Average Grant: $80,263*
Highest Grant: $550,000
Lowest Grant: $22,026
Typical Range: $50,000 to $150,000
*Note: Average grant figure excludes highest grant.

Recent Grants
Note: Grants derived from 2003 Form 990.
General

302,655	University of Maryland Foundation, Inc., College Park, MD
275,000	University of North Carolina at Chapel Hill, Chapel Hill, NC
228,790	New York Academy of Medicine, New York, NY
221,898	Education Commission of the States, Washington, DC
209,696	Georgetown University, Washington, DC
209,590	Yale University, New Haven, CT
209,359	Economic Policy Institute, Seattle, WA
200,000	Strategies for Children, Inc., Boston, MA
165,000	Center on Budget and Policy Priorities, Washington, DC
158,000	French American Foundation, New York, NY

FOUNDATION FOR SEACOAST HEALTH

Giving Contact
Susan R. Bunting, President
100 Campus Dr., Suite 1
Portsmouth, NH 03801
Phone: (603)422-8200
Fax: (603)422-8207
E-mail: ffsh@communitycampus.org
Web: http://www.ffsh.org

Description
Founded: 1984
EIN: 020386319

Organization Type: General Purpose Foundation
Giving Locations: ME: Eliot, Kittery, York; NH: Greenland, New Castle, Newington, North Hampton, Portsmouth, Rye
Grant Types: Award, Challenge, General Support, Matching, Multiyear/Continuing Support, Project, Scholarship, Seed Money.

Donor Information

Founder: Incorporated in 1984 with private endowments and the proceeds from the sale of the Portsmouth Hospital franchise to Hospital Corporation of America.

Financial Summary

Total Giving: $1,618,231 (2002); $1,996,419 (2001)
Giving Analysis: Giving for 2002 includes: foundation scholarships ($96,000)
Assets: $60,649,679 (2002); $67,230,754 (2001)
Gifts Received: $10,953 (2002); $39,094 (2000); $200 (1998). Note: In 2002, contributions were received from Council on Foundations. In 2000, contributions were received from Portsmouth Regional Hospital. In 1998, contributions were received from the Wilder Fund.

Typical Recipients

Arts & Humanities: Arts Outreach, Arts & Humanities-General, Museums/Galleries, Music, Public Broadcasting, Theater
Civic & Public Affairs: Community Foundations, Employment/Job Training, Civic & Public Affairs-General, Municipalities/Towns, Nonprofit Management, Philanthropic Organizations, Professional & Trade Associations, Urban & Community Affairs, Women's Affairs
Education: Afterschool/Enrichment Programs, Arts/Humanities Education, Colleges & Universities, Community & Junior Colleges, Education Funds, Faculty Development, Education-General, Leadership Training, Literacy, Preschool Education, Private Education (Precollege), Public Education (Precollege), Religious Education, School Volunteerism, Special Education
Environment: Air/Water Quality, Environment-General, Resource Conservation
Health: Adolescent Health Issues, AIDS/HIV, Cancer, Children's Health/Hospitals, Clinics/Medical Centers, Diabetes, Emergency/Ambulance Services, Health-General, Geriatric Health, Health Policy/Cost Containment, Health Funds, Health Organizations, Home-Care Services, Hospices, Hospitals, Medical Rehabilitation, Mental Health, Nursing Services, Prenatal Health Issues, Preventive Medicine/Wellness Organizations, Public Health, Single-Disease Health Associations, Trauma Treatment
Religion: Churches, Jewish Causes, Religious Organizations, Religious Welfare
Social Services: Child Welfare, Community Centers, Community Service Organizations, Counseling, Crime Prevention, Day Care, Domestic Violence, Emergency Relief, Family Planning, Family Services, Food/Clothing Distribution, Homes, People with Disabilities, Recreation & Athletics, Scouts, Senior Services, Sexual Abuse, Shelters/Homelessness, Social Services-General, Substance Abuse, United Funds/United Ways, Volunteer Services, YMCA/YWCA/YMHA/YWHA, Youth Organizations

Application Procedures

Initial Contact: Applicants should write, e-mail, or call the foundation for a set of "request for proposals" brochures on the foundation's grant programs.
Application Requirements: Applicants should follow proposal instructions as set forth in the "request for proposals" brochures. Proof of tax-exempt status is required.
Deadlines: For the Scholarship Program, applications are due on February 1, and award notification is made in April. For the Infants, Children, and Adolescents Program, proposals are due on March 1 and grant notification is made in May. For discretionary

fund requests, proposals are due on the last day of each month for grant notification the following month. For the Women's Health Initiative, proposals are due on October 1, with notification in November. For the Promoting Health and Preventing Disease Program, proposals are due June 1, with notification in August. For the discretionary fund, proposals are due on the last day of the month, for nonfiction the following month. for nonfiction the following month.
Review Process: Foundation staff, in researching a grant application, may find it necessary to review any and all of the information submitted with advisors of the foundation's choosing before presentation to the board of trustees.

Restrictions

The foundation does not consider requests for ongoing general expenses; elimination of deficits; support of political activities; grants to individuals other than through the Foundation for Seacoast Health's Scholarship Program; grants for travel, lodging and conferences; grants for bricks and mortar; general fundraising campaigns; capital expenditures; or equipment.

Additional Information

Grant recipients are required to submit quarterly narrative progress reports and an accounting of all funds. Demonstration of accountability by keeping the foundation informed is an important factor in future funding consideration.

In general, a one-time grant will be given the strongest consideration. Multiple-year proposals will only be considered for exceptional projects or programs that demonstrate special circumstances and can identify other resources or in-kind contributions to enhance program stability and longevity. and can identify other resources or in-kind contributions to enhance program stability and longevity.
Publications: Annual Report; Newsletter; "Request for Proposals" Brochures for Each Program

Foundation Officials

Don Albertson, MD: trustee
Peter L. Bergeron: trustee ED University of New Hampshire (1974). PRIM CORP EMPL president: Simplex Technologies Inc.
Rodney G. Brock: trustee
Susan R. Bunting, EdD: president
Kenneth L. Chute: chairman, trustee B 1945. ED University of Massachusetts BA (1968); Rutgers University MBA (1969). PRIM CORP EMPL vice president: Sprague Energy Corp.
Nancy L. Cutter: admin assistant
Eileen D. Foley: trustee PRIM NONPR EMPL mayor: City of Portsmouth, New Hampshire.
Catherine R. Goodwin: trustee
William C. Henson: treasurer, trustee
Thomas M. Keane: vice chairman, trustee PRIM CORP EMPL partner: Taylor Keane Blanchard Lyons & Watson. CORP AFFIL secretary: Flooring Resources Inc.; secretary: Global Trade Group Inc.
Wendy A. McLaughlin, MD: trustee
J. Gregg Sanborn: trustee

Grants Analysis

Disclosure Period: calendar year ending 2002
Total Grants: $1,522,231*
Number of Grants: 15
Average Grant: $30,159*
Highest Grant: $600,000
Lowest Grant: $1,400
Typical Range: $5,000 to $50,000
*Note: Giving excludes scholarships. Average grant figure excludes two highest grants ($1,100,000).

Recent Grants

Note: Grants derived from 2002 Form 990.
General

555,200	Seacoast Mental Health Center, Portsmouth, NH -- towards New Heights Program
475,000	Families First of the Greater Seacoast, Portsmouth, NH -- for family support / health services
250,000	Portsmouth School Department, Portsmouth, NH -- towards Clipper Health Center
96,250	Community Child Care Center, Portsmouth, NH -- towards wage solutions
86,250	Lamprey Health Care, Newmarket, NH -- towards medical financial assistance
15,577	Rockingham City Corn Action Program, Portsmouth, NH -- towards Nutrition Program
12,500	York Hospital Fiscal Agent, York, ME -- towards community wellness coalition
11,000	SeaCare Health Services, Exeter, NH -- towards Dental Net program
8,507	Council on Foundations, Washington, DC -- for membership
5,000	Artists in Residence, Dover, NH -- towards LEAP Program for Portsmouth student

JOHN EDWARD FOWLER MEMORIAL FOUNDATION

Giving Contact

Richard H. Lee, President
1725 K St. NW, Suite 1201
Washington, DC 20006
Phone: (202)728-9080
Fax: (202)728-9082
Web: http://fdncenter.org/grantmaker/fowler

Description

Founded: 1964
EIN: 516019469
Organization Type: General Purpose Foundation
Giving Locations: DC: Washington including immediate metropolitan area
Grant Types: Capital, General Support, Matching.

Donor Information

Founder: Created in 1964 by the late Pearl Gunn Fowler in memory of her husband, John Edward Fowler, who was a businessman and banker in Northern Virginia for forty years.

Financial Summary

Total Giving: $1,352,000 (2003); $911,000 (2002); $1,128,500 (2001)
Assets: $23,678,592 (2003); $22,359,497 (2002); $24,264,652 (2001)

Typical Recipients

Arts & Humanities: Arts Institutes, Arts Outreach, Ballet, Dance, Historic Preservation, Libraries, Literary Arts, Music, Performing Arts, Theater
Civic & Public Affairs: African American Affairs, Botanical Gardens/Parks, Business/Free Enterprise, Civil Rights, Economic Development, Employment/Job Training, Civic & Public Affairs-General, Hispanic Affairs, Housing, Legal Aid, Minority Business, Nonprofit Management, Philanthropic Organizations, Urban & Community Affairs, Women's Affairs
Education: Afterschool/Enrichment Programs, Arts/Humanities Education, Business Education, Colleges & Universities, Community & Junior Colleges, Economic Education, Education Funds, Faculty Development, Education-General, Leadership Training, Literacy, Minority Education, Preschool Education, Private Education (Precollege), Religious Education, School Volunteerism, Secondary Education (Private), Secondary Education (Public), Special Education, Student Aid
Environment: Environment-General
Health: AIDS/HIV, Alzheimer's Disease, Cancer,

Children's Health/Hospitals, Clinics/Medical Centers, Emergency/Ambulance Services, Geriatric Health, Hospices, Hospitals, Hospitals (University Affiliated), Long-Term Care, Mental Health, Multiple Sclerosis, Outpatient Health Care, Prenatal Health Issues, Public Health

International: Health Care/Hospitals, International Development, Missionary/Religious Activities

Religion: Churches, Jewish Causes, Ministries, Missionary Activities (Domestic), Religious Organizations, Religious Welfare, Seminaries

Social Services: Animal Protection, At-Risk Youth, Big Brothers/Big Sisters, Child Welfare, Community Centers, Community Service Organizations, Counseling, Day Care, Delinquency & Criminal Rehabilitation, Domestic Violence, Emergency Relief, Family Services, Food/Clothing Distribution, Homes, People with Disabilities, Recreation & Athletics, Refugee Assistance, Scouts, Senior Services, Shelters/Homelessness, Substance Abuse, Volunteer Services, YMCA/YWCA/YMHA/YWHA, Youth Organizations

Application Procedures

Initial Contact: Send written request.

Application Requirements: The foundation accepts, but does not require, Washington Regional Association of Grantmakers' common grant application form. According to the foundation's guidelines, applicants should submit a concise (two-page) letter describing the project for which funding is sought. In addition, applicants should provide a brief statement (three pages) on the history of the organization, its purposes, its current activities, and evidence of its effectiveness. These letters and the foundation's application form should be submitted along with a copy of the organization's IRS determination letter; a budget for the project and the organization's current general operating budget; financial statements (balance sheet, income statements, and latest audit); a list of the organization's board of directors and officers; and resume of key staff. Applicants should also include any additional information which may be useful in evaluating the request.

Deadlines: None.

Review Process: Receipt of proposals will be acknowledged by postcard. Applicants will receive notification of the board's decision shortly after the board meets, but should expect the process to take at least four months. The foundation rarely conducts interviews or makes on-site visits. Applications outside the metropolitan Washington, DC, area are not accepted.

Restrictions

The foundation does not support individuals, medical research or government agencies. It does not make loans.

Additional Information

Initial grants are usually in the $5,000 range. First time applicants are advised not to make requests in excess of $10,000.

Publications: Application Guidelines; Grants Report; Application Form

Foundation Officials

Michael P. Bentzen: secretary, trustee
Jeffery P. Capron: treasurer, trustee
Richard H. Lee: president, trustee

Grants Analysis

Disclosure Period: calendar year ending 2001
Total Grants: $1,313,500
Number of Grants: 76
Average Grant: $14,849
Highest Grant: $75,000
Lowest Grant: $1,000
Typical Range: $10,000 to $25,000
Note: Grants analysis provided by foundation.

Recent Grants

Note: Grants derived from 2002 Form 990.
General

75,000	Boys & Girls Clubs of Greater Washington, Silver Spring, MD -- towards after school & summer programs for about 1,150 youth that focus on education and life skills development
45,000	Junior Achievement of the National Capital Area Inc., Washington, DC -- towards teaching the fundamentals of free market economy to grades K-6
30,000	Fellowship of Christian Athletes, Fairfax, VA -- fund for various events
30,000	Washington Ballet, Washington, DC -- towards Ballet's outreach program
25,000	Faith in the Family International, Springfield, VA -- building and rebuilding of strong individuals through faith in God
25,000	Metropolitan Washington Airports Interfaith Chapels Inc., Washington, DC -- towards counseling families of 9/11 flight 77 airport employees who lost their jobs
25,000	Montgomery College Foundation, Rockville, MD -- towards scholarship for minority students
25,000	Rachael's Women's Center, Washington, DC -- towards day center for homeless women, housing opportunities & support services for mentally ill women
20,000	Barker Foundation, Cabin John, MD -- towards pregnancy counseling services for poor and minority women
20,000	D.C. Central Kitchen, Washington, DC -- towards distribution of food to social service agencies

EMMA R. FOX CHARITABLE TRUST

Giving Contact

Frank Rizzo, Trustee
National City Bank
PO Box 5756
Cleveland, OH 44101
Phone: (216)575-2507

Description

Founded: 1959
EIN: 346511198
Organization Type: Private Foundation
Giving Locations: OH: northeastern region
Grant Types: General Support.

Donor Information

Founder: the late Emma R. Fox

Financial Summary

Total Giving: $343,800 (2001)
Giving Analysis: Giving for 2001 includes: foundation scholarships ($5,000); foundation grants to United Way ($9,000)
Assets: $9,440,966 (2001)

Typical Recipients

Arts & Humanities: Arts Associations & Councils, Arts Centers, Arts Outreach, Community Arts, History & Archaeology, Libraries, Museums/Galleries, Music, Opera, Performing Arts, Public Broadcasting, Theater, Visual Arts

Civic & Public Affairs: Botanical Gardens/Parks, Business/Free Enterprise, Civil Rights, Economic Development, Economic Policy, Employment/Job Training, Civic & Public Affairs-General, Legal Aid, Nonprofit Management, Parades/Festivals, Public Policy, Safety, Urban & Community Affairs, Women's Affairs

Education: Afterschool/Enrichment Programs, Arts/Humanities Education, Colleges & Universities, Community & Junior Colleges, Economic Education, Education Reform, Education-General, Legal Education, Medical Education, Minority Education, Private Education (Precollege), Religious Education, Special Education, Student Aid

Environment: Environment-General

Health: Children's Health/Hospitals, Clinics/Medical Centers, Emergency/Ambulance Services, Eyes/Blindness, Geriatric Health, Health Funds, Health Organizations, Hospices, Hospitals, Long-Term Care, Medical Rehabilitation, Medical Research, Mental Health, Public Health, Research/Studies Institutes, Single-Disease Health Associations, Speech & Hearing

Religion: Churches, Jewish Causes, Ministries, Religious Organizations, Religious Welfare, Social/Policy Issues

Science: Science Museums, Scientific Centers & Institutes, Scientific Organizations

Social Services: Child Abuse, Child Welfare, Community Service Organizations, Crime Prevention, Day Care, Delinquency & Criminal Rehabilitation, Domestic Violence, Family Planning, Family Services, Food/Clothing Distribution, Homes, People with Disabilities, Senior Services, Shelters/Homelessness, Substance Abuse, United Funds/United Ways, Youth Organizations

Application Procedures

Initial Contact: Send a brief letter of inquiry and full proposal.

Application Requirements: Include a description of organization, amount requested, purpose of funds sought, recently audited financial statement, and proof of tax-exempt status.

Deadlines: May 15; November 15.

Restrictions

Support is not awarded to individuals, religious organizations for sectarian purposes, or political or lobbying groups.

Additional Information

Trust(s): National City Bank

Foundation Officials

Harold Edward Friedman: secretary B Cleveland, OH 1934. ED Ohio State University BS (1956); Case Western Reserve University LLB (1959). PRIM CORP EMPL partner: Ulmer & Berne. NONPR AFFIL member: Ohio Bar Association; director: YES; president: Metropolitan Health Foundation; president: National Association Jewish Vocational Services; director: Jewish Family Service Association; president: Jewish Vocational Services Cleveland; vice chairman endowment fund, director: Jewish Community Federation Cleveland; director: Jewish Convalesce & Rehabilitation Center; president: Cleveland Hillel Foundation; president: International Association Jewish Vocational Services; director: Bur Jewish Education; member: Cleveland Bar Association; director: Bellaire/Jewish Childrens Bureau; director: Big Brothers Greater Cleveland; member: American Bar Association. CLUB AFFIL Oakwood Country Club.

Nancy Friedman: trustee
Frank M. Rizzo: trustee PRIM CORP EMPL vice president: National City Bank.
Mrs. Edward Schweid: chairman

Grants Analysis

Disclosure Period: calendar year ending 2001
Total Grants: $329,800*
Number of Grants: 86
Average Grant: $3,835
Highest Grant: $23,000
Lowest Grant: $1,000
Typical Range: $1,000 to $10,000
*Note: Giving excludes United Way.

Recent Grants

Note: Grants derived from 2001 Form 990.

General

23,000	Jewish Community Federation of Cleveland, Cleveland, OH
10,500	American Civil Liberties, Cleveland, OH
10,000	Boys and Girls Club of Cleveland, Cleveland, OH
10,000	Food Rescue of Northeast Ohio, Cleveland, OH
10,000	Free Clinic of Greater Cleveland, Cleveland, OH
10,000	Metro Health Foundation, Cleveland, OH
9,000	United Way Services, Cleveland, OH
8,000	Cuyahoga Community College, Cleveland, OH
7,500	Hopewell Inn, Mesopotamia, OH
6,000	Cleveland Orchestra, Cleveland, OH

FRANCE-MERRICK FOUNDATION

Giving Contact

Robert W. Schaefer, Executive Director
The Exchange, Suite 118
1122 Kenilworth Drive
Towson, MD 21204
Phone: (410)832-5700
Fax: (410)832-5704

Description

Founded: 1962
EIN: 526072964
Organization Type: Family Foundation
Giving Locations: MD: Baltimore within the metropolitan area
Grant Types: Capital, Challenge, Employee Matching Gifts, Endowment, General Support, Matching, Project, Scholarship, Seed Money.

Donor Information

Founder: The Jacob and Anita France Foundation was established in 1959 by Jacob France. The late Mr. France, a prominent Baltimore attorney and banker, founded the Equitable Trust Company, now known as Equitable Bancorp. The Robert G. and Anne M. Merrick Foundation was established in 1962 by Robert G. Merrick and Anne M. Merrick, both deceased. The association of the two foundations resulted from Mr. France's request in his will that Mr. Merrick be designated as president of the France Foundation. The two foundations were legally merged in 1998.

Financial Summary

Total Giving: $9,212,449 (fiscal year ending May 31, 2003); $10,000,000 (fiscal 2002 approx); $10,784,499 (fiscal 2001)
Giving Analysis: Giving for fiscal 2003 includes: foundation grants to United Way ($118,667); fiscal 2001: foundation scholarships ($1,000)
Assets: $213,535,439 (fiscal 2003); $227,841,999 (fiscal 2001)
Gifts Received: $3,545 (fiscal 1997); $15,977 (fiscal 1996); $1,504 (fiscal 1993)

Typical Recipients

Arts & Humanities: Arts Funds, Arts Institutes, Historic Preservation, History & Archaeology, Libraries, Museums/Galleries, Music, Opera, Performing Arts, Theater
Civic & Public Affairs: Community Foundations, Civic & Public Affairs-General, Housing, Philanthropic Organizations, Professional & Trade Associations, Urban & Community Affairs, Women's Affairs, Zoos/Aquariums
Education: Arts/Humanities Education, Business Education, Business-School Partnerships, Colleges & Universities, Community & Junior Colleges, Education Funds, Education Reform, Environmental Education, Faculty Development, Education-General, Health & Physical Education, Legal Education, Literacy, Medical Education, Private Education (Precollege), Public Education (Precollege), Religious Education, Science/Mathematics Education, Secondary Education (Private), Special Education, Student Aid
Environment: Air/Water Quality, Environment-General, Research, Resource Conservation, Watershed
Health: Adolescent Health Issues, Cancer, Children's Health/Hospitals, Clinics/Medical Centers, Eyes/Blindness, Health-General, Health Funds, Health Organizations, Hospices, Hospitals, Hospitals (University Affiliated), Medical Rehabilitation, Public Health
International: International Affairs, International Relief Efforts
Religion: Churches, Dioceses, Jewish Causes, Religious Organizations, Religious Welfare, Seminaries
Science: Science-General, Science Exhibits & Fairs, Science Museums, Scientific Centers & Institutes, Scientific Research
Social Services: At-Risk Youth, Big Brothers/Big Sisters, Community Service Organizations, Day Care, Domestic Violence, Family Services, Food/Clothing Distribution, Homes, People with Disabilities, Recreation & Athletics, Scouts, Senior Services, Shelters/Homelessness, Social Services-General, Substance Abuse, United Funds/United Ways, Volunteer Services, YMCA/YWCA/YMHA/YWHA, Youth Organizations

Application Procedures

Initial Contact: A cover letter addressed to the Executive Director should accompany the request. Only one copy of a proposal is necessary.
Application Requirements: The proposal should include a description of the project for which the organization is seeking funds; a brief a description of organization, including history, function(s), and goals(s); the amount requested and over what period of time; a copy of the budget for the project; the number of employees the organization has on staff and, if possible, a brief description of their professional backgrounds; a list of the board of directors; a brief description of major funding sources for the proposed project; a copy of the latest audit or details about income and expenses and assets and liabilities; a copy or synopsis of any evaluation that has been done on the project or an indication of how its effectiveness will be gauged; a copy of the organization's tax-exempt ruling stating it is described under 501(c)(3) of the Internal Revenue Code and is not a private foundation.
Deadlines: None.
Review Process: Once a proposal has been received, the requesting organization will be sent a letter of acknowledgement from the foundation. The proposal will then be evaluated by the grant review committee and referred to the board of directors for a decision. This decision will be conveyed to the organization by mail shortly after the board meeting. The grant review committee and the board meet periodically throughout the year.

Restrictions

Applications are limited to organizations that are tax-exempt under section 501(c)(3) of the Internal Revenue Code and that are based in Maryland. Grantees must have the financial potential to sustain the project on a continuing basis after funding has ceased.
The foundation asks that an organization wait one fiscal year after final payment before submitting a subsequent proposal.

Additional Information

Endowment is for scholarships only; not scholarships to individuals.
Publications: Application Guidelines

Foundation Officials

Redmond C.S. Finney: director
Freeman Hrabowski: director
Robert G. Merrick, III: vice president, director
Anne M. Pinkard: chairman emeritus
Gregory C. Pinkard: treasurer CORP AFFIL stockholder: Colliers Pinkard; stockholder: WC Pinkard Co. Inc.
Robert M. Pinkard: secretary
Walter D. Pinkard, Jr.: president, director B 1949. ED Yale University (1971); Harvard University MBA (1975). PRIM CORP EMPL president, director: Colliers Pinkard ADD CORP EMPL president: W.C. Pinkard Co. Inc.
Robert Schaefer: executive director
Donna C. Silbersack: assistant secretary, assistant treasurer

Grants Analysis

Disclosure Period: fiscal year ending May 31, 2003
Total Grants: $9,092,782*
Number of Grants: 176
Average Grant: $34,195*
Highest Grant: $1,008,646
Lowest Grant: $500
Typical Range: $10,000 to $50,000
***Note:** Giving excludes United Way. Average grant figure excludes five highest grants ($3,245,490).

Recent Grants

Note: Grants derived from 2003 Form 990.
General

1,002,000	Hippodrome Performing Arts Center, Baltimore, MD
526,208	Odyssey School, Baltimore, MD
500,000	Safe and Sound Campaign, Baltimore, MD
300,000	Johns Hopkins University Recreation Center, Baltimore, MD
300,000	Lovely Lane United Methodist Church, Baltimore, MD
252,000	Maryland Science Center, Baltimore, MD
251,000	Maryland Historic Society, Baltimore, MD
250,700	Johns Hopkins University Homewood Campus, Baltimore, MD
204,000	Baltimore and Ohio Railroad Museum, Baltimore, MD
202,000	University of Maryland Foundation, Baltimore, MD

FRANCIS FAMILIES FOUNDATION

Giving Contact

Lyn A. Knox, Program Officer
Francis Families Foundation
800 West 47th Street, Suite 717
Kansas City, MO 64112
Phone: (816)531-0077
Fax: (816)531-0077
E-mail: webmaster@francisfoundation.org
Web: http://www.francisfoundation.org

Description

Founded: 1989
EIN: 431492132
Organization Type: Specialized/Single Purpose Foundation
Giving Locations: MO: Kansas City grantss within a 60-mile radius of Kansas City; fellowships, nationally and in Canada.
Grant Types: Capital, Fellowship, General Support, Operating Expenses, Project.

Donor Information

Founder: The Francis Families Foundation was formed in 1989 as the result of a merger between the

Parker B. Francis Foundation and the Parker B. Francis III Foundation. The late Parker B. Francis and his wife, Mary B. Francis, established the Parker B. Francis Foundation as a trust in Missouri in 1951. Mr. Francis was a founder of the Puritan-Bennett Corporation, manufacturer and marketer of specialized hospital medical products and equipment for respiratory care.

As a result of the company's success, the research fellowship program was inaugurated in 1975. A major part of the foundation's income supported that program. In the interest of Mr. Francis and the Puritan Bennett Corporation, fellowship awards were made in fields related to pulmonary disease and anesthesiology.

The Parker B. Francis III Foundation was established in 1962. Its interest was in the principal education and cultural institutions in the metropolitan Kansas City area.

Financial Summary
Total Giving: $4,701,536 (2002)
Giving Analysis: Giving for 2002 includes: foundation fellowships ($1,973,000)
Assets: $97,775,475 (2002)

Typical Recipients
Arts & Humanities: Arts Associations & Councils, Arts Institutes, Ballet, Dance, Arts & Humanities-General, Historic Preservation, History & Archaeology, Libraries, Museums/Galleries, Music, Opera, Performing Arts, Public Broadcasting, Theater, Visual Arts
Civic & Public Affairs: Botanical Gardens/Parks, Community Foundations, Civic & Public Affairs-General, Hispanic Affairs, Public Policy, Zoos/Aquariums
Education: Arts/Humanities Education, Colleges & Universities, Community & Junior Colleges, Education Funds, Elementary Education (Private), Environmental Education, Faculty Development, Education-General, Medical Education, Minority Education, Preschool Education, Private Education (Precollege), Public Education (Precollege), Science/Mathematics Education, Social Sciences Education, Special Education, Student Aid
Health: Children's Health/Hospitals, Clinics/Medical Centers, Health Organizations, Hospitals, Hospitals (University Affiliated), Medical Research, Prenatal Health Issues, Public Health, Research/Studies Institutes, Respiratory, Single-Disease Health Associations
International: Foreign Educational Institutions, Health Care/Hospitals
Religion: Religious Welfare
Social Services: At-Risk Youth, Child Welfare, Community Service Organizations, Counseling, Crime Prevention, Day Care, Family Services, Social Services-General, United Funds/United Ways, Youth Organizations

Application Procedures
Initial Contact: Prospective applicants for religious, chapterritable, educational, scientific, or literary funding should telephone or send the request to the foundation by mail or e-mail. Fellowship applications should be requested from Joseph D. Brain, Director, Parker B. Francis Fellowship Program, Physiology Program, Harvard School of Public Health, Room 1411, Bldg. 1, Harvard University, 665 Huntington Avenue, Boston, MA 02115.
Application Requirements: If an educational or cultural program falls within foundation guidelines, a written proposal will be requested. The proposal should include brief project summary; goals and plans; timetable with specific, measurable objectives; method of evaluation; plan to achieve financial stability during and after funding expiration; project budget; description of additional sources of support; recently audited financial statement and IRS determination letter. Additional information may be requested during the review process.

Deadlines: Varies from year to year for fellowships, but is usually in mid-October. Late applications will not be accepted. Education and culture proposals must be submitted by August 1.
Review Process: The board reviews requests in January.

Restrictions
The applying entity must be geographically located within the greater Kansas City area (60-mile radius). Grants are not made to individualss for any purpose.

Additional Information
In 1989, the Parker B. Francis Foundation and the Parker B. Francis III Foundation merged to form the Francis Families Foundation.

The director of any pulmonary training program may apply on behalf of a candidate for fellowship. Only one award will be approved in a department at a time.
Publications: Annual Report; Guidelines; Application Form; Fellowship Brochure

Foundation Officials
Ann F. Barhoum: director, executive committee
David V. Francis: director, executive committee
J. Scott Francis: director, president
Mary Harris Francis: director
B. Spencer Heddens: director
Ramon Murguia: director

Grants Analysis
Disclosure Period: calendar year ending 2002
Total Grants: $2,728,536*
Number of Grants: 129
Average Grant: $36,872*
Highest Grant: $976,002
Lowest Grant: $500
Typical Range: $20,000 to $100,000 and $125,000 to $250,000
*Note: Giving excludes fellowships. Average grant figure excludes 55 fellowships.

Recent Grants
Note: Grants derived from 2002 Form 990.
Library-Related
125,000	Harry S. Truman Library Institute, Independence, MO
100,000	Kansas City Public Library, Kansas City, MO

General
976,002	Francis Child Development Institute, Kansas City, MO
250,000	KCPT/Channel 19, Kansas City, MO
125,000	Kansas City Art Institute, Kansas City, MO
100,000	Catholic Charities of the Archdiocese of Kansas City, Kansas City, KS
100,000	El Centro, Kansas City, MO
66,667	Metropolitan Council on Child Care, Kansas City, MO
50,000	Children's Mercy Hospital, Kansas City, MO
50,000	Genesis School, Kansas City, MO
50,000	KCPT/Channel 19, Kansas City, MO
50,000	Lyric Opera of Kansas City, Kansas City, MO

A. J. FRANK FAMILY FOUNDATION

Giving Contact
Ryan Banning
PO Drawer 79
Mill City, OR 97360
Phone: (503)897-2371

Description
Founded: 1959
EIN: 930523395
Organization Type: Private Foundation
Giving Locations: OR
Grant Types: General Support.

Donor Information
Founder: A. J. Frank, L. D. Frank, Frank Lumber Co., Inc., Frank Timber Products, Inc., members of the Frank family

Financial Summary
Total Giving: $378,400 (fiscal year ending September 30, 2004)
Assets: $7,968,521 (fiscal 2004)
Gifts Received: $259,000 (fiscal 2004); $13,000 (fiscal 2000); $48,000 (fiscal 1998)

Typical Recipients
Arts & Humanities: Libraries, Museums/Galleries, Music
Civic & Public Affairs: Botanical Gardens/Parks, Community Foundations, Housing, Municipalities/Towns, Safety, Urban & Community Affairs
Education: Agricultural Education, Colleges & Universities, Community & Junior Colleges, Economic Education, Education Funds, Elementary Education (Private), Private Education (Precollege), Secondary Education (Private), Secondary Education (Public)
Health: Cancer, Children's Health/Hospitals, Heart, Hospices, Hospitals, Long-Term Care, Medical Research, Multiple Sclerosis, Single-Disease Health Associations
International: International Affairs, International Environmental Issues, International Relations, International Relief Efforts, Missionary/Religious Activities
Religion: Churches, Dioceses, Religion-General, Ministries, Religious Organizations, Religious Welfare, Social/Policy Issues
Social Services: Animal Protection, Child Welfare, Community Service Organizations, Domestic Violence, Family Planning, Food/Clothing Distribution, Homes, People with Disabilities, Recreation & Athletics, Scouts, Social Services-General, Special Olympics, Substance Abuse, United Funds/United Ways, Youth Organizations

Application Procedures
Initial Contact: Send a brief letter of inquiry.
Application Requirements: Include a description of organization, purpose of funds sought, budget of project, and proof of tax-exempt status.
Deadlines: August 15 and December 15.

Restrictions
Grants are not made to individuals.

Foundation Officials
C. M. Carey: director
Dennis D. Frank: director PRIM CORP EMPL president, chief executive officer: Frank Lumber Co.
J. T. Frank: director

Grants Analysis
Disclosure Period: fiscal year ending September 30, 2004
Total Grants: $378,400
Number of Grants: 44
Average Grant: $6,358*
Highest Grant: $105,000
Lowest Grant: $100
Typical Range: $1,000 to $10,000
*Note: Average grant figure excludes highest grant.

Recent Grants
Note: Grants derived from fiscal 2004 Form 990.
General
105,000	Santiam Catholic Schools, Stayton, OR
30,000	Immaculate Conception, St. Louis, MO

25,000	North Santiam School Foundation, Stayton, OR
23,900	Regis High School, New York, NY
23,500	Habitat for Humanity, Americus, GA
17,000	St. Joseph School, Marietta, GA
15,000	St. Vincent de Paul, San Diego, CA
10,000	Mount Angel Abbey, Mt. Angel, OR
10,000	University of Portland, Portland, OR
8,000	Archdiocese of Portland, Portland, OR

JOHN AND MARY FRANKLIN FOUNDATION INC.

Giving Contact

Dr. Marilu McCarty, Executive Secretary
NC1-002-11-18 Bank of America Plaza
Charlotte, NC 28255
Phone: (404)607-5209

Description

Founded: 1955
EIN: 586036131
Organization Type: General Purpose Foundation
Giving Locations: GA: Atlanta including metropolitan area
Grant Types: Award, Endowment, Fellowship, General Support, Professorship, Project, Research, Scholarship.

Donor Information

Founder: The John and Mary Franklin Foundation was established in Georgia in 1955 by John Leonard Franklin and his wife, Mary Owen Franklin. Mr. Franklin developed the Audichron equipment used by telephone companies to provide time-of-day telephone answering service to customers. The pattern of charitable giving established by the Franklins during their lives forms the basis of the foundation's grant program.

Financial Summary

Total Giving: $1,745,190 (2002); $1,943,200 (2001)
Giving Analysis: Giving for 2002 includes: foundation scholarships ($40,000); foundation matching gifts ($76,010); 2001: foundation grants to United Way ($5,000); foundation matching gifts ($46,500); foundation scholarships ($85,500)
Assets: $29,389,939 (2002); $34,711,872 (2001)

Typical Recipients

Arts & Humanities: Arts Centers, Arts Festivals, Ballet, Historic Preservation, History & Archaeology, Libraries, Museums/Galleries, Music, Performing Arts, Theater
Civic & Public Affairs: Botanical Gardens/Parks, Clubs, Community Foundations, Civic & Public Affairs-General, Housing, Public Policy, Urban & Community Affairs, Zoos/Aquariums
Education: Afterschool/Enrichment Programs, Agricultural Education, Business Education, Colleges & Universities, Community & Junior Colleges, Economic Education, Education Funds, Engineering/Technological Education, Environmental Education, Faculty Development, International Studies, Leadership Training, Legal Education, Literacy, Medical Education, Minority Education, Private Education (Precollege), Religious Education, Science/Mathematics Education, Secondary Education (Private), Special Education, Student Aid, Vocational & Technical Education
Environment: Environment-General, Resource Conservation
Health: Cancer, Children's Health/Hospitals, Clinics/Medical Centers, Emergency/Ambulance Services, Eyes/Blindness, Geriatric Health, Health Policy/Cost Containment, Hospices, Hospitals, Long-Term Care, Medical Rehabilitation, Medical Research, Medical Training, Mental Health, Single-Disease Health Associations, Speech & Hearing
International: Foreign Educational Institutions
Religion: Religious Organizations, Religious Welfare
Science: Science Museums
Social Services: At-Risk Youth, Child Welfare, Community Centers, Community Service Organizations, Family Planning, People with Disabilities, Recreation & Athletics, Scouts, Senior Services, Special Olympics, United Funds/United Ways, Volunteer Services, YMCA/YWCA/YMHA/YWHA, Youth Organizations

Application Procedures

Initial Contact: The foundation does not provide application forms. Initial contact should be a letter describing the program. Applications may be directed to the chairman, secretary, or any member of the board of trustees.
Application Requirements: The letter of application should include a description of the institution, its legal status, organization, officers, trustees or directors, and the purpose for which it was organized. Organizations that are not public institutions must also provide evidence of classification as a 501(c)(3) tax-exempt organization.
Deadlines: None.
Review Process: The board of trustees meets in January and July; the majority of funding decisions are made in January. The executive committee considers each application to determine whether it falls within the purposes of the foundation and whether funds are available for that type of project. The committee then forwards recommendations to the full board of trustees.

Restrictions

The foundation does not support religious denominations or political activities.

Additional Information

Bank South, N.A., in Atlanta, GA, provides administrative services for the foundation.
Publications: Annual Report (for trustees only)

Foundation Officials

Richard Winn Courts, II: trustee B Atlanta, GA. PRIM CORP EMPL chairman, director: Atlantic Investment Co. STI Classic Funds CORP AFFIL director: Southern Mills Inc.; director: SunTrust Bank Georgia Inc.; director: NAPA Auto Parts; director: NAPA Distribution Center; director: Cousins Properties Inc.; director: Genuine Parts Co.; director:.
George T. Duncan: trustee ED Army War College; Auburn University; United States Military Academy BS.
John B. Ellis: trustee B Columbus, GA 1924. ED Louisiana State University BS (1948); Indiana University MBA (1949). PRIM CORP EMPL director: Atlantic Investment Co. CORP AFFIL director: Interstate/Johnson Lane Inc.; director: UAP Inc.; director: Hughes Supply Inc.; director: Columbus Mills Inc.; director: Crystal Farms Inc.
Frank M. Malone, Jr.: trustee B 1936. ED University of North Carolina (1958). PRIM CORP EMPL senior vice president human resources: First Financial Management Corp.
Marilu H. McCarty: executive secretary ED Georgia Southern University BS; Georgia State University MA; Georgia State University PhD. NONPR AFFIL assistant dean: Georgia Institute Technology College Management.
L. Edmund Rast: trustee, member executive committee, chairman ED University of Georgia BCS. PRIM CORP EMPL chairman: Audichron Co.
Alexander Wyly Smith, Jr.: trustee, member executive committee B Atlanta, GA 1923. ED College of the Holy Cross (1941-1942); University of Georgia BBA (1947); University of Georgia LLB (1949). PRIM CORP EMPL partner retired: Smith Gambrell & Russell. NONPR AFFIL director: Our Lady Perpetual Help Free Cancer Home; member: Phi Delta Phi; director: Marist School; member: Chi Phi; member: Georgia Bar Association; member: Atlanta Bar Association; director, planning developmental council: Catholic Archdiocese Atlanta. CLUB AFFIL Peachtree Golf Club; Piedmont Driving Club.
William Maurrelle Suttles: trustee B Ben Hill, GA July 25, 1920. ED Georgia State University BCS (1942); Yale University MDiv (1946); Emory University MTh (1947); Emory University MRE (1953); Auburn University EdD (1958). PRIM NONPR EMPL professor: Georgia State University. CORP AFFIL director: Georgia Federal Bank. NONPR AFFIL member: Sigma Tau Delta; trustee: George M Sparks Scholarship Fund; member: Sigma Nu; member, grand chaplain: Sigma Pi Alpha; member: Phi Eta Sigma; member: Phi Kappa Phi; member: Omicron Delta Kappa; member: Phi Delta Kappa; member: Kappa Phi Kappa; member: Mortar Board; director: John Mercer Foundation; member: Kappa Delta Phi; member: Georgia State University Athletic Association; trustee: Georgia State University Foundation; member: Georgia State University Alumni Association; trustee: Georgia Council Moral Civic Concerns; executive vice president, provost, professor: Georgia State University; trustee: Christian Council; trustee: Georgia Baptist Children's Homes & Families Ministries; member: Atlanta Chamber of Commerce; member: Beta Gamma Sigma; member: Alpha Lambda Delta; member: Alpha Kappa Psi. CLUB AFFIL Masons Club; Shriners Club; Commerce Club; Kiwanis Club; Blue Key Club.

Grants Analysis

Disclosure Period: calendar year ending 2002
Total Grants: $1,629,180*
Number of Grants: 137
Average Grant: $11,892*
Highest Grant: $75,000
Lowest Grant: $100
Typical Range: $1,000 to $15,000
*Note: Giving excludes scholarship, matching gifts.

Recent Grants

Note: Grants derived from 2002 Form 990.
General

100,000	Georgia Institute of Technology, Atlanta, GA -- for John McCarty Chair for electrical engineering
64,000	Auburn University, Auburn, AL -- for the Franklin Littleton lecture series
50,000	Georgia State University Foundation, Atlanta, GA -- funding for science building
50,000	Stepping Stones Education Therapy Center, Atlanta, GA -- funding for general purposes
50,000	University of Georgia School of Law Foundation, Athens, GA -- toward general purposes
35,000	Around the Clock Childcare Home, Atlanta, GA -- assistance for general purposes
35,000	Metropolitan Atlanta Boys and Girls Club, Atlanta, GA -- toward general funds
30,000	Carrie Steele Pitts Home, Atlanta, GA -- assistance for building program
30,000	Center for the Visually Impaired, Atlanta, GA -- assistance for general purposes
30,000	Girls Inc., Atlanta, GA -- funding for general purchases

MARY D. AND WALTER F. FREAR ELEEMOSYNARY TRUST

Giving Contact

Paula Boyce, Grants Administration Officer
c/o Pacific Century Trust

PO Box 3170
Honolulu, HI 96802
Phone: (808)538-4945
E-mail: pboyce@boh.com

Description

Founded: 1936
EIN: 996002270
Organization Type: Private Foundation
Giving Locations: HI
Grant Types: Capital, General Support, Multiyear/Continuing Support, Operating Expenses.

Donor Information

Founder: the late Mary D. Frear, Walter F. Frear

Financial Summary

Total Giving: $1,722,761 (2001)
Assets: $18,372,158 (2001)
Gifts Received: In 1991, contributions were received from Mary D. and Walter F. Frear Special Trust "A".

Typical Recipients

Arts & Humanities: Arts Festivals, Arts Funds, Community Arts, Dance, Arts & Humanities-General, Libraries, Museums/Galleries, Music, Opera, Public Broadcasting, Theater
Civic & Public Affairs: Botanical Gardens/Parks, Community Foundations, Civic & Public Affairs-General, Law & Justice, Women's Affairs
Education: Arts/Humanities Education, Business Education, Colleges & Universities, Economic Education, Faculty Development, Education-General, Literacy, Preschool Education, Private Education (Precollege), Secondary Education (Private), Special Education
Environment: Environment-General, Resource Conservation
Health: Alzheimer's Disease, Clinics/Medical Centers, Hospices, Hospitals, Medical Rehabilitation, Mental Health
Religion: Churches, Ministries, Religious Organizations, Religious Welfare
Social Services: At-Risk Youth, Child Welfare, Community Centers, Community Service Organizations, Day Care, Family Planning, Family Services, Food/Clothing Distribution, People with Disabilities, Recreation & Athletics, Scouts, United Funds/United Ways, Veterans, YMCA/YWCA/YMHA/YWHA, Youth Organizations

Application Procedures

Initial Contact: Send full proposal signed by the presiding officer of the Board of Directors.
Application Requirements: board of directors, a description of organization. Include summary of proposed activity stating need, plan for distribution, population to be served, plan for evaluation effectiveness, total cost of project including other funding sources, both present and future, two or three letters of endorsement, amount requested, purpose of funds sought, recently audited financial statement, and proofs of tax-exempt status.
Deadlines: January 15, April 15, July 15, and October 15.

Restrictions

Does not support individuals or endowments.

Additional Information

The foundation reports that contributions are allocated in the following manner: 42% Health & Human Services; 40% Education; 13% Arts & Humanities, 5% Religion and Environment. PU/annual report (including application guidelines)
Trust(s): Pacific Century Trust

Grants Analysis

Disclosure Period: calendar year ending 2000
Total Grants: $545,365*
Number of Grants: 91
Average Grant: $5,993

Highest Grant: $25,000
Typical Range: $1,000 to $10,000
***Note:** Giving excludes scholarships, matching gifts.

Recent Grants

Note: Grants derived from 2001 Form 990.
General

500,000	Honolulu Symphony Society, Honolulu, HI -- for capacity building and stabilization and establishment of trust fund for education programs
175,000	Hawaii Theatre Center, Honolulu, HI -- for restoration of a vertical sign
50,000	St. Francis Health Care Foundation of Hawaii, Honolulu, HI -- to purchase state of the art dual detector gamma camera
44,229	Boys and Girls Club of Hawaii, Honolulu, HI -- install gymnasium flooring for the Hawaii Ewa Beach Clubhouse
31,500	Hawaiian Island Ministries, Honolulu, HI -- for Honolulu 2002 Youth Night Program
25,000	Hawaii Alliance for Arts Education, Honolulu, HI -- for renovations
25,000	Honolulu Academy of Arts, Honolulu, HI -- for Ambassador Outreach Program
21,000	Modah Community Center, Honolulu, HI -- to purchase a 28 child seat school for the childcare program
20,000	Goodwill Industries, Honolulu, HI -- for Island Career Center Build Out on Britannia Street
20,000	Hawaii Nature Center, Honolulu, HI -- supplies for the Pouhala Project

FREAS FOUNDATION

Giving Contact

David M. Trout, Jr., Manager
c/o First Union National Bank
401 S. Tryon St., 4th Fl.
Charlotte, NC 28288-1159
Phone: (704)383-2885

Description

EIN: 221714810
Organization Type: Private Foundation
Giving Locations: CT; MD; PA; UT; WA
Grant Types: General Support.

Financial Summary

Total Giving: $461,048 (2001)
Assets: $8,464,602 (2001)

Typical Recipients

Arts & Humanities: Arts Centers, Ballet, Historic Preservation, History & Archaeology, Libraries, Museums/Galleries, Opera, Performing Arts, Public Broadcasting, Theater
Civic & Public Affairs: Botanical Gardens/Parks, Community Foundations, Employment/Job Training, Civic & Public Affairs-General, Legal Aid, Urban & Community Affairs, Women's Affairs
Education: Arts/Humanities Education, Colleges & Universities, Health & Physical Education, Journalism/Media Education, Literacy, Medical Education, Private Education (Precollege), Public Education (Precollege), Religious Education, Secondary Education (Private), Secondary Education (Public), Student Aid
Health: Cancer, Emergency/Ambulance Services, Health Organizations, Hospices, Hospitals, Medical Rehabilitation, Nursing Services, Public Health
Religion: Churches, Religious Organizations, Religious Welfare, Seminaries
Social Services: Child Welfare, Community Centers, Community Service Organizations, Counseling, Day Care, Delinquency & Criminal Rehabilitation, Domestic Violence, Family Services, Food/Clothing Distribu-

tion, Homes, People with Disabilities, Scouts, Senior Services, Social Services-General, Substance Abuse, Volunteer Services, YMCA/YWCA/YMHA/YWHA, Youth Organizations

Application Procedures

Deadlines: None.

Additional Information

Trust(s): First Union National Bank

Foundation Officials

Arthur K. Freas: mgr
Margery H. Freas: mgr
David M. Trout, Jr.: mgr
Rebecca F. Trout: mgr

Grants Analysis

Disclosure Period: calendar year ending 2001
Total Grants: $461,048
Number of Grants: 83*
Average Grant: $3,555*
Highest Grant: $166,000
Lowest Grant: $100
Typical Range: $1,000 to $10,000
***Note:** Average grant figure excludes highest grant.

Recent Grants

Note: Grants derived from 2001 Form 990.
Library-Related

5,000	Martin Library, York, PA

General

166,000	Bucknell University, Lewisburg, PA
22,200	Children's Center, Salt Lake City, UT
12,615	York County Heritage Trust, York, PA
12,000	York College of Pennsylvania, York, PA
11,000	Access York, Inc., York, PA
10,100	Strand Capitol Performing Arts Center, York, PA
8,500	Capon Bridge Middle School
6,750	Nine Months in York Town
5,998	York Hospital, York, ME
5,305	York Jewish Community Center

AMBROSE AND IDA FREDRICKSON FOUNDATION

Giving Contact

Tamara I. Morales, Trust Associate
c/o First Union Bank, NA
401 S. Tryon Street, 4th Fl.
Charlotte, NC 28288-1159
Phone: (704)383-5588

Alternate Contact

Phone: (908)598-3576

Description

Founded: 1989
EIN: 226422114
Organization Type: Private Foundation
Giving Locations: NJ: Millburn Township including organizations within a one-hundred mile radius; PA; VA
Grant Types: Capital, General Support, Project, Scholarship.

Financial Summary

Total Giving: $165,350 (2001)
Giving Analysis: Giving for 2001 includes: foundation scholarships ($85,500)
Assets: $2,623,506 (2001)

Typical Recipients

Arts & Humanities: Historic Preservation, History & Archaeology, Libraries, Museums/Galleries, Music,

Opera, Performing Arts, Visual Arts
Civic & Public Affairs: Botanical Gardens/Parks, Economic Development, Civic & Public Affairs-General, Hispanic Affairs, Philanthropic Organizations
Education: Colleges & Universities, Elementary Education (Private), Education-General, Minority Education, Private Education (Precollege), Science/Mathematics Education, Secondary Education (Private), Special Education, Student Aid
Environment: Environment-General, Resource Conservation
Health: AIDS/HIV, Alzheimer's Disease, Cancer, Children's Health/Hospitals, Health Organizations, Medical Rehabilitation
Religion: Religious Organizations, Religious Welfare
Social Services: At-Risk Youth, Child Welfare, Community Centers, Community Service Organizations, Family Services, People with Disabilities, Scouts, Youth Organizations

Application Procedures

Initial Contact: request Grant Proposal Format
Deadlines: December 1, March 1, June 1, and September 1.

Restrictions

Does not support political or lobbying groups.

Additional Information

The foundations primary funding concerns are human services, historic preservation and restoration, educational, conservation and restoration of woodland areas, and the arts.
Trust(s): First Union National Bank NA

Foundation Officials

Frederick A. Coombs: trustee
Andrew Davis: assistant vice president
Rosemary M. Karl: trustee
Hugo M. Pfaltz: trustee
Richard G. Ranck: trustee

Grants Analysis

Disclosure Period: calendar year ending 2001
Total Grants: $79,850*
Number of Grants: 22
Average Grant: $3,630
Highest Grant: $10,000
Typical Range: $2,000 to $10,000
*Note: Giving excludes scholarship.

Recent Grants

Note: Grants derived from 2001 Form 990.
General

20,000	Susquehanna University, Selinsgrove, PA
20,000	Susquehanna University, Selinsgrove, PA
20,000	Susquehanna University, Selinsgrove, PA
20,000	Susquehanna University, Selinsgrove, PA
10,000	Colonial Williamsburg Foundation, Williamsburg, VA -- support their efforts in rare breed conservation
10,000	Scholarship Fund for Inner-City Children, Newark, NJ -- for scholarships for needy elementary and secondary students
5,000	American Cancer Society -- for Reach to Recovery Program
5,000	Chad School Foundation, Newark, NJ -- for operating support
5,000	Girl Scout Council -- for renovation and capital campaign for Jockey Hollow Camp
5,000	Interfaith Council for the Homeless, Plainfield, NJ -- for Volunteers Shelter Program

FREED FOUNDATION

Giving Contact

Elizabeth Freed, President
1025 Thomas Jefferson St. NW, Suite 308E
Washington, DC 20007
Phone: (202)337-5487

Description

Founded: 1954
EIN: 526047591
Organization Type: General Purpose Foundation
Giving Locations: DC: Washington including metropolitan area; NJ; NY
Grant Types: General Support, Multiyear/Continuing Support, Operating Expenses, Project.

Donor Information

Founder: The foundation was incorporated in 1954 by the late Frances W. Freed and the late Gerald A. Freed.

Financial Summary

Total Giving: $900,130 (fiscal year ending May 31, 2001)
Assets: $24,215,934 (fiscal 2001)
Gifts Received: $156,261 (fiscal 2001); $186,254 (fiscal 2000); $186,254 (fiscal 1999). Note: Contributions were received from the estate of Gerald Freed.

Typical Recipients

Arts & Humanities: Arts Festivals, Arts Outreach, Film & Video, Historic Preservation, Libraries, Literary Arts, Museums/Galleries, Music, Public Broadcasting, Theater
Civic & Public Affairs: Botanical Gardens/Parks, Business/Free Enterprise, Community Foundations, Employment/Job Training, Civic & Public Affairs-General, Housing, Minority Business, Nonprofit Management, Philanthropic Organizations, Professional & Trade Associations, Public Policy, Safety, Women's Affairs, Zoos/Aquariums
Education: Afterschool/Enrichment Programs, Arts/Humanities Education, Colleges & Universities, Continuing Education, Education Funds, Environmental Education, Education-General, International Studies, Literacy, Medical Education, Minority Education, Preschool Education, Religious Education, Science/Mathematics Education, Student Aid
Environment: Air/Water Quality, Environment-General, Protection, Resource Conservation, Wildlife Protection
Health: AIDS/HIV, Alzheimer's Disease, Cancer, Children's Health/Hospitals, Clinics/Medical Centers, Emergency/Ambulance Services, Eyes/Blindness, Health Policy/Cost Containment, Health Funds, Hospices, Hospitals, Medical Rehabilitation, Mental Health, Nutrition, Public Health, Research/Studies Institutes, Single-Disease Health Associations
Religion: Jewish Causes
Science: Science Museums, Scientific Centers & Institutes
Social Services: Animal Protection, At-Risk Youth, Big Brothers/Big Sisters, Camps, Child Abuse, Child Welfare, Community Service Organizations, Crime Prevention, Day Care, Domestic Violence, Emergency Relief, Family Planning, Family Services, Food/Clothing Distribution, People with Disabilities, Sexual Abuse, Shelters/Homelessness, Substance Abuse, United Funds/United Ways, Youth Organizations

Application Procedures

Initial Contact: Applicants should write to the foundation for an application form.
Application Requirements: Applicants should submit one copy of their proposal, a budget for the proposal, audited financial statements for the organization, and a copy of IRS tax ruling.
Deadlines: Rolling deadlines.

Restrictions

The foundation does not make grants to individuals, foreign organizations, international projects, conferences, or scholarships.

Additional Information

Publications: Annual Report

Foundation Officials

Lorraine Barnhart: director
Lloyd J. Derrickson: secretary, director
Elizabeth Ann Freed: president, director

Grants Analysis

Disclosure Period: fiscal year ending May 31, 2001
Total Grants: $850,130*
Number of Grants: 26
Average Grant: $26,005*
Highest Grant: $200,000
Lowest Grant: $2,000
Typical Range: $10,000 to $50,000
*Note: Giving excludes United Way. Average grant figure excludes highest grant.

Recent Grants

Note: Grants derived from 2002 Form 990.
General

200,000	Florida State University Foundation, Tallahassee, FL -- towards Mental Health Professorship
200,000	Lenox Hill Hospital, New York, NY -- for Emergency Department Fund
50,000	Discovery Creek Children's Museum of Washington, Washington, DC -- general assistance
50,000	Ford's Theater Society, Washington, DC -- towards education programs
50,000	Monmouth Health Care Foundation, Long Branch, NJ -- towards Palliative Care Program
50,000	Wildlife Conservation Society, Bronx, NY -- towards Adirondack Program
40,000	Washington AIDS Partnership, Washington, DC -- general assistance
35,000	Multicultural Career Intern Program, Washington, DC -- towards Columbia Heights Ed Campus
25,000	Ocean Conservancy, Washington, DC -- general assistance
20,000	Clean Water Fund, Washington, DC -- towards Chesapeake Reg. Projects

SAMUEL FREEMAN CHARITABLE TRUST

Giving Contact

Linda Franciscovich, Vice President
c/o U.S. Trust Company of New York
114 West 47th Street
New York, NY 10036-1532
Phone: (212)852-3629
Fax: (212)852-3377

Description

Founded: 1981
EIN: 136803465
Organization Type: General Purpose Foundation
Giving Locations: mid-Atlantic region.
Grant Types: Challenge, Endowment, General Support.

Donor Information

Founder: Established in 1981 by the late Samuel Freeman.

Financial Summary
Total Giving: $984,700 (2003)
Assets: $39,691,077 (2003)

Typical Recipients
Arts & Humanities: Arts Associations & Councils, Arts Festivals, Ballet, Dance, Arts & Humanities-General, History & Archaeology, Libraries, Museums/Galleries, Music, Opera, Performing Arts, Public Broadcasting, Theater
Civic & Public Affairs: Business/Free Enterprise, Clubs, Civic & Public Affairs-General, Municipalities/Towns, Philanthropic Organizations, Public Policy, Safety, Urban & Community Affairs, Zoos/Aquariums
Education: Arts/Humanities Education, Colleges & Universities, Education Associations, Engineering/Technological Education, Education-General, International Exchange, International Studies, Legal Education, Medical Education, Minority Education, Private Education (Precollege), Public Education (Precollege), Science/Mathematics Education, Student Aid
Environment: Environment-General, Resource Conservation
Health: AIDS/HIV, Cancer, Clinics/Medical Centers, Diabetes, Eyes/Blindness, Health-General, Hospitals, Medical Research, Multiple Sclerosis, Single-Disease Health Associations
International: Foreign Arts Organizations, Health Care/Hospitals, Human Rights, International Environmental Issues, International Organizations, International Relations, International Relief Efforts, Missionary/Religious Activities
Religion: Churches, Jewish Causes, Religious Welfare
Science: Scientific Centers & Institutes
Social Services: Big Brothers/Big Sisters, Community Service Organizations, Emergency Relief, Family Planning, People with Disabilities, Recreation & Athletics, Shelters/Homelessness, Social Services-General, Substance Abuse, YMCA/YWCA/YMHA/YWHA, Youth Organizations

Application Procedures
Initial Contact: The trust requests a two-page proposal.
Application Requirements: The proposal should include a budget, the most recent audit report, and an IRS determination letter.
Deadlines: None.

Restrictions
The trust does not make grants to individuals or private entities. Trust does not answer telephone inquiries.

Additional Information
Publications: Guidelines
Trust(s): US Trust Co.

Foundation Officials
Linda R. Franciscovich: vice president
William E. Murray: trustee B 1926. PRIM CORP EMPL chairman board, chief executive officer, director: East Bay Company Ltd.

Grants Analysis
Disclosure Period: calendar year ending 2003
Total Grants: $984,700
Number of Grants: 84
Average Grant: $8,777*
Highest Grant: $150,000
Lowest Grant: $200
Typical Range: $5,000 to $10,000
***Note:** Average grant figure excludes two highest grants ($265,000).

Recent Grants
Note: Grants derived from 2000 Form 990.

Library-Related

20,000	New York Botanical Gardens, New York, NY

General

200,000	East West Institute, Germantown, MD
183,000	Cold Spring Harbor Laboratory, Cold Spring Harbor, NY
150,000	Cold Spring Harbor Laboratory, Cold Spring Harbor, NY
130,000	Marymount Manhattan College, New York, NY
125,000	St. James School
100,000	Cannon Street YMCA, Charleston, SC
100,000	Cannon Street YMCA, Charleston, SC
75,000	Adirondack Railway Preservation Society, Inc., Thendara, NY
75,000	College of Charleston, Charleston, SC
60,000	Saint Marguerite Bourgeoys, Brookfield, CT

FREEPORT BRICK CO.

Company Headquarters
Freeport, PA

Company Description
Employees: 40
SIC(s): 3500 Industrial Machinery & Equipment.
Parent Company: Freeport Refractories, PO Box F, Freeport, PA, United States

Operating Locations
Freeport Brick Co. (PA--Freeport)

Freeport Brick Co. Charitable Trust

Giving Contact
F. H. Laube, III, Secretary
Drawer F
Freeport, PA 16229-0306
Phone: (724)295-2111

Description
EIN: 256074334
Organization Type: Corporate Foundation
Giving Locations: PA: Freeport, Kittanning
Grant Types: General Support.

Typical Recipients
Arts & Humanities: Historic Preservation, Libraries
Civic & Public Affairs: Botanical Gardens/Parks, Law & Justice, Municipalities/Towns, Safety, Urban & Community Affairs, Zoos/Aquariums
Education: Education-General, Student Aid
Health: Children's Health/Hospitals, Emergency/Ambulance Services, Health Organizations, Hospitals, Medical Research, Single-Disease Health Associations
Social Services: Community Service Organizations, Crime Prevention, Food/Clothing Distribution, Recreation & Athletics, Scouts, Senior Services, United Funds/United Ways, Volunteer Services, Youth Organizations

Application Procedures
Initial Contact: The foundation requests applications be made in writing.
Application Requirements: Include a description of organization, amount requested, and purpose of funds sought.
Deadlines: None.

Corporate Officials
Mildred Cook: chief financial officer, treasurer, secretary PRIM CORP EMPL chief financial officer, treasurer, secretary: Freeport Brick Co.
F. H. Laube, III: chairman, chief executive officer, president PRIM CORP EMPL chairman, chief executive officer, president: Freeport Brick Co.

Foundation Officials
F. H. Laube, III: secretary
Harry R. Laube: assistant secretary, assistant treasurer
J. Terry Medovitch: treasurer
J. C. Overholt: vchairman

Grants Analysis
Disclosure Period: calendar year ending 2000
Total Grants: $33,000
Number of Grants: 9
Highest Grant: $27,000
Lowest Grant: $500

Recent Grants
Note: Grants derived from 2001 Form 990.
General

14,000	Freeport Community Park Corp, Freeport, PA -- community recreation
2,000	Freeport Volunteer Fire Department, Freeport, PA
1,500	South Buffalo Volunteer Fire Department, Freeport, PA
1,000	Freeport Area Library Association, Freeport, PA -- endowment fund
1,000	Pennsylvania State Police Camp Cadet, Kittanning, PA -- youth education
500	Boy Scouts of America, Pittsburgh, PA -- for youth education
500	Pittsburgh Youth Golf Foundation, Pittsburgh, PA -- youth education
500	United Way of Armstrong County, Kittanning, PA
200	Make A Wish Foundation, Newburgh, NY

FREEPORT-MCMORAN COPPER & GOLD INC.

Company Headquarters
1615 Poydras St.
New Orleans, LA 70112
Web: http://www.fcx.com

Company Description
Founded: 1912
Ticker: FCX
Exchange: NYSE
Revenue: US$1.91 billion (2002)
Employees: 14803 (2003)
SIC(s): 1094 Uranium, Radium & Vanadium Ores, 1311 Crude Petroleum & Natural Gas, 1475 Phosphate Rock, 1479 Chemical & Fertilizer Mining Nec.

Operating Locations
Freeport-McMoRan Inc. (LA--New Orleans)

Nonmonetary Support
Type: Donated Equipment; Loaned Employees; Other

Freeport-McMoRan Foundation

Giving Contact
Cynthia M. Molyneux, President & Trustee
1615 Poydras St.
New Orleans, LA 70112
Phone: (504)582-4000
Fax: (504)582-4028

Description

EIN: 721316308
Organization Type: Corporate Foundation
Giving Locations: principally near operating locations and to national organizations.
Grant Types: Award, Emergency, Employee Matching Gifts, Endowment, General Support.
Note: Employee matching gift ratio: 2 to 1 up to $500; 1 to 1 after $500 and up to $20,000 per employee annually.

Financial Summary

Total Giving: $2,504,612 (2003); $1,709,599 (2002); $2,464,660 (2001). Note: Contributes through corporate direct giving program and foundation.
Assets: $935,660 (2003); $916,226 (2002); $1,331,878 (2001)
Gifts Received: $2,614,403 (2003); $1,816,641 (2002); $2,347,000 (2001). Note: In 2003, contributions were received from Freeport-McMoRan Copper & Gold Inc. ($2,518,525), McMoRan Oil & Gas LLC ($71,668), and Freeport McMoRan Sulphur LLC ($24,210). In 2002, contributions were received from Freeport-McMoRan Copper & Gold Inc. ($1,640,415), McMoRan Oil & Gas LLC ($140,180), and Freeport McMoRan Sulphur LLC ($36,046). In 2001, contributions were received from Freeport-McMoRan Copper & Gold Inc. ($1,842,973), Freeport-McMoRan Oil & Gas LLC ($504,027). In 2000, contributions were received from Freeport-McMoRan Copper & Gold Inc. ($1,003,557), Freeport-McMoRan Sulphur LLC ($191,719), and McMoRan Oil & Gas LLC ($267,801).

Typical Recipients

Arts & Humanities: Arts Appreciation, Arts Associations & Councils, Arts Centers, Arts Festivals, Arts Funds, Arts Institutes, Ballet, Community Arts, Dance, Ethnic & Folk Arts, Historic Preservation, History & Archaeology, Libraries, Museums/Galleries, Music, Opera, Performing Arts, Public Broadcasting, Theater
Civic & Public Affairs: African American Affairs, Asian American Affairs, Botanical Gardens/Parks, Business/Free Enterprise, Chambers of Commerce, Civil Rights, Clubs, Community Foundations, Economic Development, Employment/Job Training, Civic & Public Affairs-General, Housing, Law & Justice, Legal Aid, Minority Business, Municipalities/Towns, Native American Affairs, Philanthropic Organizations, Professional & Trade Associations, Public Policy, Rural Affairs, Safety, Urban & Community Affairs, Women's Affairs, Zoos/Aquariums
Education: Agricultural Education, Business Education, Colleges & Universities, Community & Junior Colleges, Economic Education, Education Associations, Education Funds, Education Reform, Elementary Education (Private), Elementary Education (Public), Engineering/Technological Education, Education-General, International Studies, Leadership Training, Legal Education, Literacy, Minority Education, Preschool Education, Private Education (Precollege), Public Education (Precollege), Science/Mathematics Education, Secondary Education (Private), Special Education, Student Aid
Environment: Environment-General, Resource Conservation, Wildlife Protection
Health: AIDS/HIV, Cancer, Children's Health/Hospitals, Clinics/Medical Centers, Emergency/Ambulance Services, Eyes/Blindness, Health-General, Health Organizations, Heart, Hospitals, Medical Research, Mental Health, Nutrition, Prenatal Health Issues, Single-Disease Health Associations
International: Foreign Educational Institutions, International Affairs, International Organizations, International Relief Efforts
Religion: Churches, Dioceses, Religious Organizations, Religious Welfare
Science: Science Exhibits & Fairs, Science Museums, Scientific Centers & Institutes, Scientific Organizations

Social Services: Animal Protection, At-Risk Youth, Big Brothers/Big Sisters, Camps, Child Abuse, Child Welfare, Community Service Organizations, Counseling, Crime Prevention, Delinquency & Criminal Rehabilitation, Domestic Violence, Emergency Relief, Family Services, Food/Clothing Distribution, Homes, People with Disabilities, Recreation & Athletics, Scouts, Senior Services, Shelters/Homelessness, Social Services-General, Special Olympics, Substance Abuse, United Funds/United Ways, Volunteer Services, YMCA/YWCA/YMHA/YWHA, Youth Organizations

Application Procedures

Initial Contact: Call or write foundation to ascertain foundation interest and request application form.
Application Requirements: Proposals should include: summary statement, with history, mission, and goals; description of project and organization; amount and specific purpose of request; need for the project in community; detailed report of how money will be spent; detailed annual operating budget; method of evaluation; list of board members; any collaborative efforts; list of other sources of support; financial statements; and proof of tax-exempt status.
Deadlines: November 30.
Review Process: The executive director and president of the foundation make recommendations to the board of trustees.
Evaluative Criteria: Efficiency of management and employee participation through contributions and volunteerism are considered when evaluating requests.
Decision Notification: A preliminary budget is drawn up in October and finalized in December; grants are announced by the end of February.

Restrictions

Does not support individuals; distributing foundations; national disease agencies; or religious, political, fraternal, labor, veterans, or tax-supported organizations (with the exception of public schools, colleges, and universities). The foundation also does not support sporting events, trips or festivals, organizations supported by the United Way, or discriminatory organizations.

Additional Information

Since 1996, the company has operated the Freeport-McMoRan Foundation and the Research, Environmental, and Corporate Fund.
Giving is based on 1% of pre-tax earnings; therefore the contributions budget varies from year to year.
All contributions are suspended for 1999.
Publications: Giving Annual Report; Application Form

Foundation Officials

Nancy L. Adkerson: executive director
Richard C. Adkerson: trustee
Douglas N. Currault, II: secretary
Dean T. Falgoust: vice president, trustee
William H. Hines: assistant secretary
Cynthia M. Molyneux: president, trustee
Kathleen L. Quirk: vice president, treasurer

Grants Analysis

Disclosure Period: calendar year ending 2003
Total Grants: $2,337,759*
Number of Grants: 384
Average Grant: $6,088
Highest Grant: $100,000
Lowest Grant: $50
Typical Range: $1,000 to $10,000
*Note: Giving excludes United Way.

Recent Grants

Note: Grants derived from 2003 Form 990.
General

137,183	United Way of Greater New Orleans, New Orleans, LA
100,000	Center for the Study of Presidency, Washington, DC
75,000	Horatio Alger Association of Distinguished Americans Inc., Alexandria, VA
75,000	International AIDS Trust, Washington, DC
65,328	Louisiana Philharmonic Orchestra, New Orleans, LA
56,250	United States-Indonesia Society, Washington, DC
54,872	University of New Orleans, New Orleans, LA
52,500	New Orleans Museum of Art, New Orleans, LA
50,230	Friends of City Park, New Orleans, LA
50,000	American Geological Institute Foundation, Houston, TX

D.E. FRENCH FOUNDATION

Giving Contact

Walter M. Lowe, Manager & Director
D.E. French Foundation
120 Genesee Street, Suite 503
Auburn, NY 13021-3620
Phone: (315)253-9321

Description

Founded: 1955
EIN: 166052246
Organization Type: Private Foundation
Giving Locations: NY: Cayuga County
Grant Types: Capital, General Support.

Donor Information

Founder: the late Clara M. French, the late D. E. French

Financial Summary

Total Giving: $162,000 (2003)
Giving Analysis: Giving for 2003 includes: foundation grants to United Way ($23,000); foundation scholarships ($25,500)
Assets: $4,599,292 (2003)

Typical Recipients

Arts & Humanities: Arts Associations & Councils, Arts Centers, History & Archaeology, Libraries, Museums/Galleries, Music, Performing Arts, Theater
Civic & Public Affairs: Botanical Gardens/Parks, Chambers of Commerce, Community Foundations, Employment/Job Training, Civic & Public Affairs-General, Housing, Municipalities/Towns, Safety, Urban & Community Affairs
Education: Colleges & Universities, Community & Junior Colleges, Elementary Education (Public), Medical Education, Private Education (Precollege), Secondary Education (Public), Special Education, Student Aid
Health: Emergency/Ambulance Services, Health Organizations, Heart, Hospitals, Long-Term Care, Medical Rehabilitation, Public Health
Religion: Churches, Religious Welfare
Social Services: Animal Protection, Camps, Child Welfare, Community Centers, Community Service Organizations, Day Care, Emergency Relief, People with Disabilities, Recreation & Athletics, Scouts, Senior Services, United Funds/United Ways, YMCA/YWCA/YMHA/YWHA, Youth Organizations

Application Procedures

Initial Contact: The foundation has no formal grant application procedure or application form.
Deadlines: None.

Foundation Officials

Frederick J. Atkins: director
James P. Costello: director
Walter M. Lowe: manager, director
John P. McLane: director
Ronald D. West: president, director

Grants Analysis

Disclosure Period: calendar year ending 2003
Total Grants: $113,500*
Number of Grants: 19
Average Grant: $4,861*
Highest Grant: $26,000
Lowest Grant: $500
Typical Range: $1,000 to $10,000
***Note:** Giving excludes United Way and scholarships. Average grant figure excludes highest grant.

Recent Grants

Note: Grants derived from 2003 Form 990.
General

26,000	Boy Scouts of America, Auburn, NY -- operating funds to help fund-teaching assistant
23,000	United Way of Cayuga County, Auburn, NY -- support annual campaign
20,000	Cayuga County Community College Foundation, Auburn, NY -- funds for scholarship
15,000	Merry-Go-Round Playhouse, Auburn, NY
10,000	Cayuga County Community College Foundation, Auburn, NY -- funds for scholarship
10,000	YMCA-WEIU, Auburn, NY
6,000	First Church of the Nazarene, Auburn, NY
6,000	Syracuse Symphony Orchestra, Syracuse, NY -- funds for concert program in Auburn
5,000	American Red Cross, Auburn, NY -- disaster relief fund
5,000	Calvary Presbyterian Church, Auburn, NY -- funds for food pantry program

FRENCH OIL MILL MACHINERY CO.

Company Headquarters

PO Box 920
Piqua, OH 45356
Web: http://www.frenchoil.com

Company Description

Revenue: US$9 million (2001)
Employees: 55 (2001)
SIC(s): 3500 Industrial Machinery & Equipment, 3554 Paper Industries Machinery, 3556 Food Products Machinery, 3559 Special Industry Machinery Nec.

Operating Locations

French Oil Mill Machinery Co. (OH--Piqua)

French Oil Mill Machinery Co. Charitable Trust

Giving Contact

Daniel P. French, Jr., President & Chief Executive Officer
French Oil Mill Machinery Co.
c/o Fifth Third Bank of Western Ohio
PO Box 630858
Cincinnati, OH 45263
Phone: (513)579-5310

Description

EIN: 316024511
Organization Type: Corporate Foundation
Giving Locations: OH: Dayton, Piqua
Grant Types: General Support, Seed Money.

Financial Summary

Total Giving: $28,420 (fiscal year ending November 30, 2001)
Giving Analysis: Giving for fiscal 2001 includes: foundation grants to United Way ($12,600); foundation ($15,820)
Assets: $662,871 (fiscal 2001)

Typical Recipients

Arts & Humanities: Arts Associations & Councils, Arts Centers, Arts Festivals, Community Arts, Arts & Humanities-General, Libraries, Performing Arts
Civic & Public Affairs: Chambers of Commerce, Clubs, Community Foundations, Economic Development, Economic Policy, Employment/Job Training, Civic & Public Affairs-General, Legal Aid, Public Policy
Education: Afterschool/Enrichment Programs, Arts/Humanities Education, Business-School Partnerships, Colleges & Universities, Community & Junior Colleges, Economic Education, Education Funds, Education-General, Religious Education, Science/Mathematics Education, Secondary Education (Public)
Environment: Environment-General
Health: Cancer, Emergency/Ambulance Services, Health-General, Heart, Hospices, Medical Rehabilitation, Mental Health, Respiratory
Religion: Religious Organizations
Science: Science-General, Scientific Centers & Institutes
Social Services: Child Welfare, Community Service Organizations, Family Planning, Food/Clothing Distribution, People with Disabilities, Recreation & Athletics, Scouts, Senior Services, Social Services-General, United Funds/United Ways, YMCA/YWCA/YMHA/YWHA, Youth Organizations

Application Procedures

Initial Contact: The foundation has no formal grant application procedure or application form. Send a brief letter of inquiry.
Deadlines: None.

Restrictions

Does not support individuals or political or lobbying groups.

Additional Information

Trust(s): Fifth Third Bank Western OH

Corporate Officials

Dennis Bratton: vice president finance, treasurero, director PRIM CORP EMPL vice president finance, treasurer: French Oil Mill Machinery Co.
Daniel P. French: chairman, president, chief executive officer, director PRIM CORP EMPL chairman, president, chief executive officer, director: French Oil Mill Machinery Co.

Grants Analysis

Disclosure Period: fiscal year ending November 30, 2001
Total Grants: $15,820*
Number of Grants: 37
Average Grant: $428
Highest Grant: $1,175
Typical Range: $250 to $500
***Note:** Giving excludes United Way.

Recent Grants

Note: Grants derived from fiscal 2001 Form 990.
General

12,600	Piqua Area United Fund, Piqua, OH
1,500	National Right to Work Legal Defense and Education Foundation, Springfield, VA
1,175	Piqua Community Foundation, Piqua, OH
1,000	American Legion Ambulance Fund, Moosup, CT
1,000	Edison State Community College, Edison, NJ
1,000	YMCA, Piqua, OH
975	Piqua Area Chamber of Commerce, Piqua, OH
800	Piqua Education Foundation, Piqua, OH
550	Planned Parenthood Association, Dayton, OH
500	Hipple Cancer Research Center, Dayton, OH

ARNOLD D. FRESE FOUNDATION

Giving Contact

James S. Smith, President & Treasurer
10 Rockefeller Plz., Suite 916
New York, NY 10020
Phone: (212)373-1960

Description

Founded: 1966
EIN: 136212507
Organization Type: Private Foundation
Giving Locations: , CA CT: Greenwich; DC: Washington; MA: Cambridge; NY, New York
Grant Types: General Support.

Donor Information

Founder: the late Arnold D. Frese

Financial Summary

Total Giving: $829,000 (2001)
Assets: $4,261,193 (2001)

Typical Recipients

Arts & Humanities: Arts Associations & Councils, Arts Festivals, Arts & Humanities-General, History & Archaeology, Libraries, Museums/Galleries, Music, Performing Arts
Civic & Public Affairs: Civic & Public Affairs-General, Women's Affairs
Education: Afterschool/Enrichment Programs, Colleges & Universities, Legal Education, Medical Education, Private Education (Precollege), Public Education (Precollege), School Volunteerism
Environment: Air/Water Quality, Environment-General
Health: Arthritis, Cancer, Clinics/Medical Centers, Diabetes, Emergency/Ambulance Services, Hospitals, Hospitals (University Affiliated), Long-Term Care, Prenatal Health Issues
International: Health Care/Hospitals, Human Rights, International Organizations, International Peace & Security Issues
Religion: Churches, Religious Welfare
Science: Scientific Centers & Institutes
Social Services: At-Risk Youth, Child Welfare, Community Centers, Day Care, Family Planning, Family Services, Food/Clothing Distribution, People with Disabilities, Recreation & Athletics, Shelters/Homelessness, United Funds/United Ways, Youth Organizations

Application Procedures

Initial Contact: Send a brief letter of inquiry.
Application Requirements: Include purpose of funds sought, amount requested, and proof of tax-exempt status.
Deadlines: None.

Foundation Officials

Hector G. Dowd: secretary
Ines Frese: chairman
Henry D. Mercer, Jr.: trustee
Emil Mosbacher, Jr.: trustee B White Plains, NY 1922. ED Dartmouth College BA (1943). CORP AFFIL director: Federal Insurance Co.; director: Vigilant Insurance Co.; director: Chubb Corp.; director: Avon Products Inc.; director: Chemical Bank; director: Amax Gold Inc. NONPR AFFIL member: U.S. Seniors Golf Association; member: U.S. Yacht Racing Association; member: Pilgrims U.S.; member: Independent Petroleum Association America; trustee: Lenox Hill Hospital; member, board overseers: Hoover Institute.
James S. Smith: president, treasurer
Laura Smith: trustee

Grants Analysis

Disclosure Period: calendar year ending 2001
Total Grants: $829,000
Number of Grants: 29
Average Grant: $2,724*
Highest Grant: $550,000
Lowest Grant: $1,000
Typical Range: $1,000 to $5,000
*****Note:** Average grant figure excludes two highest grants ($750,000).

Recent Grants

Note: Grants derived from 2001 Form 990.
General

550,000	Harvard College, Cambridge, MA
200,000	National Gallery of Art, Washington, DC
10,000	Lighthouse International, New York, NY
7,000	Westchester Association for Retarded Citizens, White Plains, NY
5,000	Family Center, Greenwich, CT
5,000	Fresh Air Fund, New York, NY
5,000	Girls, Incorporated, Greenwich, CT
5,000	Meals on Wheels, Pacific Grove, CA
5,000	Merry Go Round, Inc., Auburn, NY
5,000	Nathaniel Witherell Auxiliary

VIRGINIA FRIEDHOFER CHARITABLE TRUST

Giving Contact

Arnold Seidel, Trustee
8730 Wilshire Blvd., No. 530
Beverly Hills, CA 90211
Phone: (310)360-7541

Description

Founded: 1996
EIN: 956995937
Organization Type: Private Foundation
Giving Locations: CA
Grant Types: General Support.

Donor Information

Founder: Established in 1996 by the Virginia Friedhofer Trust.

Financial Summary

Total Giving: $136,000 (2003)
Assets: $3,668,837 (2003)
Gifts Received: $21,914 (1996); $2,675,534 (1995).
Note: In 1996, contributions were received from the estate of Virginia Friedhofer.

Typical Recipients

Arts & Humanities: Libraries, Music, Opera, Performing Arts, Theater
Civic & Public Affairs: Civic & Public Affairs-General, Safety, Zoos/Aquariums
Education: Colleges & Universities, Education Funds, Engineering/Technological Education, Education-General, Medical Education, School Volunteerism
Health: Cancer, Clinics/Medical Centers, Eyes/Blindness, Heart, Multiple Sclerosis, Single-Disease Health Associations
International: Human Rights, Missionary/Religious Activities
Religion: Jewish Causes, Synagogues/Temples
Social Services: Child Welfare, Community Service Organizations, Counseling, Domestic Violence, Family Planning, Food/Clothing Distribution, People with Disabilities, Recreation & Athletics, YMCA/YWCA/YMHA/YWHA, Youth Organizations

Application Procedures

Initial Contact: Send a written request.
Deadlines: None.

Foundation Officials

Arnold Seidel: trustee

Grants Analysis

Disclosure Period: calendar year ending 2003
Total Grants: $136,000
Number of Grants: 32
Average Grant: $3,581*
Highest Grant: $25,000
Lowest Grant: $1,000
Typical Range: $1,000 to $5,000
*****Note:** Average grant figure excludes highest grant.

Recent Grants

Note: Grants derived from 2001 Form 990.
General

11,000	Friends of the Los Angeles Free Clinic, Los Angeles, CA
10,000	Beverly Hills Community Sports Center, Beverly Hills, CA
10,000	Phoenix House
10,000	Planned Parenthood, Santa Ana, CA
10,000	Regents of University of California, Los Angeles, CA
10,000	University of Washington School of Medicine, Seattle, WA
10,000	Zoological Society of San Diego, San Diego, CA
7,500	Beverly Hills Education Foundation, Beverly Hills, CA
6,000	Recording for the Blind and Dyslexic, Los Angeles, CA
5,000	10th District PTA, Los Angeles, CA

FRIEDMAN FAMILY FOUNDATION

Giving Contact

Lisa M. Kawahara, Grants Manager
PMB 719, 204 E. 2nd Ave.
San Mateo, CA 94401
Phone: (650)342-8750
Fax: (650)342-8750
E-mail: fffdn@aol.com
Web: http://www.friedmanfamilyfoundation.org/

Description

Founded: 1964
EIN: 946109692
Organization Type: Private Foundation
Giving Locations: CA: San Francisco focus on Bay area
Grant Types: General Support, Operating Expenses, Project.

Donor Information

Founder: Established in 1964 by Phyllis K. Friedman and Howard Friedman.

Financial Summary

Total Giving: $1,680,000 (fiscal year ending February 28, 2003); $1,345,300 (fiscal 2001)
Assets: $14,735,602 (fiscal 2003); $21,919,550 (fiscal 2001)
Gifts Received: $12,000 (fiscal 1999); $850,000 (fiscal 1996); $804,602 (fiscal 1995). Note: In fiscal 1999, contributions were received from Mr. and Mrs. Ted Geballe. In fiscal 1996, contributions were received from Phyllis K. Friedman.

Typical Recipients

Arts & Humanities: Arts Associations & Councils, Arts Festivals, Community Arts, Film & Video, Libraries, Museums/Galleries, Music, Public Broadcasting, Theater
Civic & Public Affairs: African American Affairs, Asian American Affairs, Business/Free Enterprise, Community Foundations, Economic Development, Economic Policy, Employment/Job Training, Ethnic Organizations, Civic & Public Affairs-General, Hispanic Affairs, Housing, Law & Justice, Legal Aid, Minority Business, Native American Affairs, Nonprofit Management, Parades/Festivals, Philanthropic Organizations, Professional & Trade Associations, Public Policy, Urban & Community Affairs, Women's Affairs
Education: Afterschool/Enrichment Programs, Business-School Partnerships, Colleges & Universities, Continuing Education, Economic Education, Education Funds, Education Reform, Education-General, International Exchange, Preschool Education, Private Education (Precollege), Public Education (Precollege)
Environment: Environment-General
Health: AIDS/HIV, Children's Health/Hospitals, Clinics/Medical Centers, Emergency/Ambulance Services, Health Policy/Cost Containment, Health Organizations, Heart, Hospitals, Medical Research, Mental Health, Public Health, Single-Disease Health Associations
International: Foreign Educational Institutions, Health Care/Hospitals, Human Rights, International Development, International Organizations, International Relations, International Relief Efforts, Missionary/Religious Activities
Religion: Jewish Causes, Ministries, Religious Organizations, Religious Welfare, Synagogues/Temples
Science: Observatories & Planetariums
Social Services: Animal Protection, At-Risk Youth, Camps, Child Abuse, Child Welfare, Community Centers, Community Service Organizations, Counseling, Domestic Violence, Emergency Relief, Family Services, Food/Clothing Distribution, People with Disabilities, Refugee Assistance, Senior Services, Shelters/Homelessness, Social Services-General, United Funds/United Ways, YMCA/YWCA/YMHA/YWHA, Youth Organizations

Application Procedures

Initial Contact: Letter of inquiry or request application procedures.
Application Requirements: In addition to the application, include the following: one or two client profiles; total project and organization budget for the current year; list of funding sources; list of board of directors with affiliations; proof of tax-exempt status; readily available printed materials describing the organization.
Deadlines: None. The deadlines vary each year.
Review Process: The Foundation board meets three times per year. Allow up to three months for the review process.

Restrictions

The foundation does not fund films, videos, conferences, seminars, capital grants, scholarships, research, individuals, or special or fundraising events.

Additional Information

Publications: Annual Report; Guidelines; Application Form

Foundation Officials

David A. Friedman: secretary PRIM CORP EMPL senior vice president: Heller Financial.
Eleanor Friedman: vice president
Phyllis K. Friedman: president B 1936. PRIM CORP EMPL president: Rochester Diet Inc.
Robert E. Friedman: treasurer

Grants Analysis

Disclosure Period: fiscal year ending February 28, 2003
Total Grants: $1,680,000
Number of Grants: 167
Average Grant: $10,060
Highest Grant: $100,000
Lowest Grant: $500
Typical Range: $5,000 to $20,000

Recent Grants

Note: Grants derived from fiscal 2003 Form 990.
General

100,000	Asian Neighborhood Design, San Francisco, CA
25,000	New Israel Fund, San Francisco, CA
20,000	Arkansas Institute for Social Justice, Little Rock, AR
20,000	Arriba Juntos, San Francisco, CA
20,000	Ashoka, Arlington, VA
20,000	Aspen Institute Inc, Queenstown, MD
20,000	Association for Enterprise Opportunity, Arlington, VA
20,000	Bar Association, Chicago, IL
20,000	Bay Area Video Coalition, San Francisco, CA
20,000	Bay Area Women's & Children's Center, San Francisco, CA

FRIENDSHIP FUND

Giving Contact

Eleanor Millan
c/o Mellon Trust Co.
1 Boston Pl., AIM 024-0104
Boston, MA 02108
Phone: (617)722-3533

Description

Founded: 1918
EIN: 136089220
Organization Type: Private Foundation
Grant Types: Capital, General Support, Project, Scholarship.

Donor Information

Founder: the late Charles R. Crane

Financial Summary

Total Giving: $270,000 (fiscal year ending June 30, 2004); $276,670 (fiscal 2001)
Assets: $4,900,390 (fiscal 2004); $5,576,720 (fiscal 2001)

Typical Recipients

Arts & Humanities: Arts Centers, Film & Video, Historic Preservation, History & Archaeology, Libraries, Museums/Galleries, Music, Opera, Performing Arts, Public Broadcasting
Civic & Public Affairs: Civil Rights, Community Foundations, Civic & Public Affairs-General, Housing, Public Policy, Safety, Urban & Community Affairs, Women's Affairs
Education: Colleges & Universities, Education-General, Legal Education, Private Education (Precollege), Public Education (Precollege), Science/

Mathematics Education, Social Sciences Education, Student Aid
Environment: Air/Water Quality, Forestry, Environment-General, Resource Conservation
Health: Clinics/Medical Centers, Diabetes, Emergency/Ambulance Services, Health Organizations, Hospitals, Mental Health, Nursing Services, Prenatal Health Issues
International: Foreign Educational Institutions, Health Care/Hospitals, International Affairs, International Development, International Environmental Issues, International Organizations, International Peace & Security Issues
Religion: Churches, Religious Organizations, Religious Welfare
Science: Scientific Centers & Institutes, Scientific Labs, Scientific Organizations
Social Services: Community Service Organizations, Family Planning, People with Disabilities, Sexual Abuse, Substance Abuse

Application Procedures

Initial Contact: Organizations seeking support may submit requests in writing.
Application Requirements: Include a concise statement of the purpose of funds sought, current year's operating budget, list of board members, recently audited financial statement, resumes of all key staff people, and proof of tax-exempt status. If a grant is for a specific program, the staff and budget of the program must be described.
Deadlines: April 1; for consideration at the annual meeting held during the first week of August.

Foundation Officials

Darby Bradley: trustee
Charles M. Crane: trustee
Diane Crane: trustee
Sylvia E. Crane: trustee
Thomas S. Crane: treasurer
Josephine DeGive: trustee
Elizabeth McLane-Bradley: trustee
Ellen D. B. F. Tully: president

Grants Analysis

Disclosure Period: fiscal year ending June 30, 2004
Total Grants: $270,000
Number of Grants: 1

Recent Grants

Note: Grants derived from fiscal 2004 Form 990.
General

270,000	Rhode Island Foundation, Providence, RI

FRIST FOUNDATION

Giving Contact

Peter F. Bird, Jr., President, Chief Executive Officer
3100 West End Avenue, Suite 1200
Nashville, TN 37203
Phone: (615)292-3868
Fax: (615)292-5843
E-mail: askfrist@fristfoundation.org
Web: http://www.fristfoundation.org

Description

Founded: 1982
EIN: 621134070
Organization Type: General Purpose Foundation
Giving Locations: TN, Nashville
Grant Types: Capital, Emergency, Employee Matching Gifts, General Support, Multiyear/Continuing Support, Operating Expenses, Project, Seed Money.
Note: Award grants are given through foundation initiative programs.

Donor Information

Founder: The HCA Foundation was established in 1982 as a corporate foundation, sponsored by Hospital Corporation of America. The foundation became fully independent of the company in 1994. It adopted The Frist Foundation name in 1997 to honor the philanthropic influence and creative force of two of its founding directors, Dr. Thomas F. Frist, Jr., who continues as chairman, and Dr. Thomas F. Frist, Sr., a gifted cardiologist, businessman, and philanthropist who died in 1998.

Financial Summary

Total Giving: $9,438,870 (2003); $10,400,000 (2002 approx); $13,363,804 (2001)
Giving Analysis: Giving for 2003 includes: foundation grants to United Way ($297,490)
Assets: $177,701,296 (2003); $151,733,000 (2002); $188,667,000 (2001)

Typical Recipients

Arts & Humanities: Arts Appreciation, Arts Associations & Councils, Arts Centers, Arts Festivals, Arts Funds, Arts Institutes, Arts Outreach, Ballet, Dance, Arts & Humanities-General, Historic Preservation, History & Archaeology, Libraries, Literary Arts, Museums/Galleries, Music, Opera, Performing Arts, Public Broadcasting, Theater, Visual Arts
Civic & Public Affairs: Botanical Gardens/Parks, Business/Free Enterprise, Civil Rights, Clubs, Community Foundations, Economic Development, Economic Policy, Employment/Job Training, Civic & Public Affairs-General, Hispanic Affairs, Housing, Inner-City Development, Law & Justice, Nonprofit Management, Parades/Festivals, Public Policy, Rural Affairs, Safety, Urban & Community Affairs, Women's Affairs, Zoos/Aquariums
Education: Afterschool/Enrichment Programs, Arts/Humanities Education, Business Education, Colleges & Universities, Community & Junior Colleges, Continuing Education, Economic Education, Education Associations, Education Funds, Education Reform, Faculty Development, Education-General, Health & Physical Education, Literacy, Medical Education, Minority Education, Preschool Education, Private Education (Precollege), Public Education (Precollege), Religious Education, Science/Mathematics Education, Social Sciences Education, Student Aid
Environment: Forestry, Environment-General
Health: Children's Health/Hospitals, Clinics/Medical Centers, Emergency/Ambulance Services, Health Policy/Cost Containment, Health Funds, Health Organizations, Medical Training, Mental Health, Nursing Services, Public Health, Speech & Hearing
Religion: Churches, Religious Organizations, Religious Welfare
Science: Science Exhibits & Fairs, Science Museums, Scientific Centers & Institutes
Social Services: Animal Protection, Big Brothers/Big Sisters, Child Abuse, Child Welfare, Community Centers, Community Service Organizations, Day Care, Delinquency & Criminal Rehabilitation, Domestic Violence, Emergency Relief, Family Planning, Family Services, Food/Clothing Distribution, Homes, People with Disabilities, Recreation & Athletics, Scouts, Senior Services, Sexual Abuse, Shelters/Homelessness, Social Services-General, Special Olympics, Substance Abuse, United Funds/United Ways, Volunteer Services, YMCA/YWCA/YMHA/YWHA, Youth Organizations

Application Procedures

Initial Contact: Send a letter of inquiry or complete an online grant application, available on the foundation's website.
Application Requirements: The initial inquiry should describe in no more than two pages the organization, its record of accomplishments, objectives of program to be funded and who will benefit, amount sought from foundation in relation to total need, how foundation funds will be used, and proposed method

of evaluating program's success. Also include an annual report, if available, and a copy of IRS determination letter. Foundation may also request copy of Form 990, budget, list of board members and their affiliations, list of current sources of support and amounts contributed, and list of other funding sources being approached for support.

Deadlines: For Internship Program, December 7; for Technology Program, April 1; for Building Cultures Program, August 1.

Review Process: Decisions on proposals are generally made within one month of submission, except for those requesting more than $50,000, which are scheduled for review at quarterly board of directors meetings. All proposals are acknowledged promptly. results of its effort; what plans the organization has for future funding. Foundation staff review proposals and conducts personal interviews or site visits, as necessary. Requests for more than $1,000 require review and approval by the board of directors.

Evaluative Criteria: Among the issues considered during the evaluation are the organization's history of success, including financial statements reflecting an ability to manage funds well; the program objectives and its intended beneficiaries; the proportion of funding sought from foundation to the total need; whether the program treats the causes of the problem or its effects; duplication of effort of other groups; the organization's efforts to collaborate with others; how the organization proposes to measure the results of its effort; what plans the organization has for future funding. Foundation staff review proposals and conducts personal interviews or site visits, as necessary.

Restrictions

With rare exception, grants are limited to organizations based in the greater Nashville area. Recipients must be tax-exempt under Section 501(c)(3) of the Internal Revenue Code. For legal reasons, the foundation does not support individuals or their projects, private foundations, political activities, advertising or sponsorships. As a matter of policy, the foundation does not ordinarily support disease-specific organizations seeking support for national projects and programs; biomedical or clinical research; hospitals; projects, programs, or organizations that serve a limited audience or a relatively small number of people; organizations whose principal impact is outside the United States; endowments; social events, telethons, or similar fundraising activities; organizations during their first three years of operation; or religious organizations for religious purposes.

Additional Information

Publications: Annual Report; Guidelines; Newsletter; Application Form

Foundation Officials

Peter F. Bird, Jr.: president, chief executive officer
Hon. Frank F. Drowota, III: director B Williamsburg, KY 1938. ED Vanderbilt University BA (1960); Vanderbilt University JD (1965). PRIM NONPR EMPL associate justice: Tennessee Supreme Court.
Dr. Thomas Fearn Frist, Jr.: chairman, director B Nashville, TN 1938. ED Vanderbilt University BS (1961); Washington University MD (1966). PRIM CORP EMPL chairman, chief executive officer: Columbia/HCA Healthcare Corp. CORP AFFIL chairman, director: HCA Health Services Florida; chairman, director: HCA Health Services Louisiana. NONPR AFFIL member: Business Roundtable; vice chairman: International Medicine Group Pennsylvania; honorary fellow: American College Healthcare Executives; member: Business Council. CLUB AFFIL Belle Meade Country Club.
Regina F. Nash: administrative assistant
Kenneth Lewis Roberts: president emeritus, director B Dungannon, VA 1932. ED Vanderbilt University BA (1954); Vanderbilt University LLB (1959). NONPR AFFIL member: Tennessee Bar Association; trustee: Vanderbilt University; member: Nashville Chamber of Commerce; trustee: Montgomery Bell Academy;

member: Nashville Bar Association; director: Leadership Nashville; member: American Bar Association. CLUB AFFIL University Club; Ponte Vedra Inn Club; Belle Meade Country Club; Cumberland Club.

Grants Analysis

Disclosure Period: calendar year ending 2003
Total Grants: $9,141,380*
Number of Grants: 365
Average Grant: $10,671*
Highest Grant: $1,300,000
Lowest Grant: $25
Typical Range: $1,000 to $25,000
*Note: Giving excludes United Way. Average grant figure excludes five highest grants ($5,300,000).

Recent Grants

Note: Grants derived from 2003 Form 990.
General

1,300,000	Frist Center for the Visual Arts, Nashville, TN
1,000,000	Frist Center for the Visual Arts, Nashville, TN
800,000	Frist Center for the Visual Arts, Nashville, TN
200,000	United Way of Metropolitan Nashville, Nashville, TN
190,000	Oasis Center, Nashville, TN
140,000	Center for Nonprofit Management, Nashville, TN
125,000	Nashville Symphony Association, Nashville, TN
100,000	Adventure Science Center, Nashville, TN -- toward renovation and facility expansion
80,000	PENCIL Foundation, Nashville, TN
75,000	Nashville Alliance for Public Education, Nashville, TN

PAUL AND MAXINE FROHRING FOUNDATION

Giving Contact

R. A. Bumblis, CPA
Paul and Maxine Frohring Foundation
3200 National City Center
1900 E. 9th Street, Suite 3200
Cleveland, OH 44114-3485
Phone: (216)861-7976

Description

Founded: 1958
EIN: 346513729
Organization Type: Private Foundation
Giving Locations: FL; MD; MT; OH: Cleveland including northern Ohio; PA
Grant Types: Emergency, General Support.

Donor Information

Founder: Paul R. Frohring, the late Maxine A. Frohring

Financial Summary

Total Giving: $1,498,948 (2001)
Assets: $32,130,596 (2001)
Gifts Received: $242,500 (1993). Note: In 1993, contributions were received from Paul R. Frohring.

Typical Recipients

Arts & Humanities: Libraries, Museums/Galleries
Civic & Public Affairs: Botanical Gardens/Parks, Clubs, Employment/Job Training, Housing, Zoos/Aquariums
Education: Colleges & Universities, Engineering/Technological Education, Education-General, Minority Education, Private Education (Precollege)
Environment: Wildlife Protection

Health: Eyes/Blindness, Health-General, Hospices, Hospitals, Nursing Services, Public Health
International: Foreign Educational Institutions
Religion: Religious Welfare
Social Services: Community Service Organizations, Day Care, Family Planning, People with Disabilities, Senior Services, Substance Abuse, YMCA/YWCA/YMHA/YWHA, Youth Organizations

Application Procedures

Initial Contact: Send a written request.
Application Requirements: Include proof of tax-exempt status.
Deadlines: None.

Foundation Officials

William Wendell Falsgraf: secretary, trustee B Cleveland, OH 1933. ED Amherst College AB (1955); Case Western Reserve University JD (1958). PRIM CORP EMPL partner: Baker & Hostetler. NONPR AFFIL member: Ohio Bar Association; member: Ohio Bar Foundation; chairman board trustees: Hiram College; member: Amherst College Alumni Association; member: Cleveland Bar Association; fellow: American Bar Foundation; president: American Bar Insurance Plans Consult; member: American Bar Association. CLUB AFFIL Country Club; Union Club.
Paul Robert Frohring: president, trustee B Cleveland, OH 1904. ED Ohio State University (1921-1922); Case Institute of Technology BS (1926). CORP AFFIL director: Newbury Industries; director: Horsburg & Scott; director: Irvin & Co.; director: Cleveland Machine Controls; director: Alco Standard Corp.; director: America Home Products Corp. NONPR AFFIL member: Ohio Society; member: Planned Parenthood; member: Newcomen Society; member: Ohio Academy Science; member: Navy League; fellow: New York Academy Sciences; trustee: John Cabot University; fellow: Garfield Society; trustee: Hiram College; trustee, honorary chairman: Cleveland Health Education Museum; trustee: Florida Zoological Society; member: American Oil Chemical Society; overseer: Case Western Reserve University; member: American Dairy Science Association; member: American Association Advancement Science; member: American Chemical Society; member: Alpha Chi Sigma. CLUB AFFIL Union Club; Commodore Club; Key Biscayne Yacht Club; Chagrin Valley Hunt Club.
Elmer Jagow: trustee B West Bend, WI 1922. ED Concordia University BS (1944); Northwestern University MBA (1955). CORP AFFIL director: Cleveland Machine Controls. NONPR AFFIL president emeritus: Hiram College; chairman: John Cabot University; member: Garfield Society. CLUB AFFIL Walden Golf & Tennis Club.
James Kushlan: director
Paula Frohring Kushlan: trustee
Jeffrey LaRich: trustee

Grants Analysis

Disclosure Period: calendar year ending 2001
Total Grants: $1,498,948
Number of Grants: 23
Average Grant: $38,947*
Highest Grant: $301,579
Typical Range: $5,000 to $100,000
*Note: Average grant figure excludes two highest grants ($603,158).

Recent Grants

Note: Grants derived from 2001 Form 990.
Library-Related

5,000	Bainbridge Public Library, Chagrin Falls, OH

General

301,579	Cleveland Botanical Garden, Cleveland, OH
301,579	Cleveland Health Museum, Cleveland, OH
260,000	John Cabot University, Rome Italy
250,000	Hiram College, Hiram, OH

150,790	Geauga YMCA at Heather Hill, Chardon, OH
35,000	Arundel Habitat for Humanity, Arnold, MD
35,000	Salvation Army, Annapolis, MD
30,000	McDonogh School, Owings Mills, MD
25,000	Hospice of Chesapeake, Millerville, MD
25,000	Planned Parenthood, Baltimore, MD

SAUL FROMKES FOUNDATION

Giving Contact
Otto Fromkes, Director
122 E. 42nd St., Rm. 4400
New York, NY 10168-0112
Phone: (212)447-8360

Description
Founded: 1993
EIN: 133682406
Organization Type: Private Foundation
Grant Types: General Support.

Financial Summary
Total Giving: $60,000 (2003)
Assets: $1,290,187 (2003)
Gifts Received: $2,860 (1996); $49,953 (1995); $1,230,350 (1994). Note: In 1994, contributions were received from the estate of Saul Fromkes.

Typical Recipients
Arts & Humanities: Arts Associations & Councils, Dance, Libraries, Museums/Galleries
Civic & Public Affairs: Safety
Education: Colleges & Universities
Health: Cancer, Emergency/Ambulance Services
Religion: Jewish Causes, Religious Welfare

Application Procedures
Initial Contact: Send a brief letter of inquiry.
Application Requirements: Include a description of organization and purpose of funds sought.
Deadlines: None.

Foundation Officials
Otto Fromkes: director
Arthur Richenthal: director

Grants Analysis
Disclosure Period: calendar year ending 2003
Total Grants: $60,000
Number of Grants: 3
Highest Grant: $30,000
Lowest Grant: $15,000

Recent Grants
Note: Grants derived from 2003 Form 990.
General

30,000	Young Dance, Minneapolis, MN
15,000	Cultural Association, New York, NY
15,000	North Plainfield Fire Department, North Plainfield, NJ

FROST NATIONAL BANK

Company Headquarters
100 W. Houston St.
San Antonio, TX 78205-1498
Web: http://www.frostbank.com

Company Description
Employees: 1,700
SIC(s): 6021 National Commercial Banks.

Parent Company: Cullen/Frost Bankers Inc., 100 W. Houston St., No. 100, San Antonio, TX, United States

Operating Locations
Frost National Bank (TX--Austin, Corpus Christi, Houston, McAllen)

Nonmonetary Support
Type: Donated Equipment; Donated Products; In-kind Services; Loaned Employees; Loaned Executives

The Charitable Foundation of Frost National Bank of San Antonio

Giving Contact
Melissa Adams
Frost Bank
100 W. Houston St.
San Antonio, TX 78205
Phone: (210)220-4353
Fax: (210)220-5144

Description
Founded: 1981
EIN: 742058155
Organization Type: Corporate Foundation
Giving Locations: TX
Grant Types: Capital, General Support, Matching, Multiyear/Continuing Support, Scholarship.

Financial Summary
Total Giving: $664,066 (2003); $559,418 (2001). Note: Contributes through foundation only.
Giving Analysis: Giving for 2001 includes: foundation scholarships ($36,000); foundation grants to United Way ($176,000).
Assets: $1,028,928 (2003); $738,571 (2001).
Gifts Received: $750,000 (2003); $250,000 (2001). Note: Contributions were received from Frost National Bank.

Typical Recipients
Arts & Humanities: Arts Appreciation, Arts Associations & Councils, Arts Festivals, Arts Funds, Arts Institutes, Arts Outreach, Community Arts, Dance, Ethnic & Folk Arts, Historic Preservation, History & Archaeology, Libraries, Museums/Galleries, Music, Performing Arts, Public Broadcasting, Theater
Civic & Public Affairs: Botanical Gardens/Parks, Business/Free Enterprise, Economic Development, Employment/Job Training, Civic & Public Affairs-General, Housing, Minority Business, Nonprofit Management, Philanthropic Organizations, Professional & Trade Associations, Zoos/Aquariums
Education: Agricultural Education, Arts/Humanities Education, Business Education, Colleges & Universities, Education Associations, Education Funds, Education Reform, Engineering/Technological Education, Faculty Development, Education-General, Health & Physical Education, International Exchange, Literacy, Medical Education, Minority Education, Pre-school Education, Private Education (Precollege), Public Education (Precollege), Science/Mathematics Education, Student Aid
Environment: Environment-General, Resource Conservation
Health: Cancer, Children's Health/Hospitals, Health Organizations, Hospices, Hospitals, Medical Rehabilitation, Medical Research, Mental Health, Public Health, Single-Disease Health Associations
International: International Relations
Religion: Churches, Religion-General, Ministries, Religious Organizations
Science: Scientific Organizations, Scientific Research

Social Services: Child Welfare, Community Centers, Community Service Organizations, Counseling, Crime Prevention, Delinquency & Criminal Rehabilitation, Domestic Violence, Emergency Relief, Family Services, Food/Clothing Distribution, People with Disabilities, Recreation & Athletics, Scouts, Senior Services, Social Services-General, Substance Abuse, United Funds/United Ways, Volunteer Services, YMCA/YWCA/YMHA/YWHA, Youth Organizations

Application Procedures
Initial Contact: Send a brief letter of inquiry.
Application Requirements: Provide a description of organization, amount requested, purpose of funds sought, recently audited financial statements, proof of tax-exempt status, deadline for project approval, and signature of authorization by organization's highest ranking officer. Also include a copy of the organization's charter and by-laws.
Deadlines: At least three weeks before funds are needed.
Decision Notification: Committee meets weekly.

Corporate Officials
Melissa J. Adams: corporate donations officer PRIM CORP EMPL corporate donations officer: Frost National Bank.
Richard W. Evans, Jr.: chairman, chief executive officer B 1946. ED Southwest Texas Junior College (1965-1966); University of Texas BA (1968). PRIM CORP EMPL chairman, chief executive officer: Frost National Bank.

Giving Program Officials
Melissa J. Adams: member (see above)

Grants Analysis
Disclosure Period: calendar year ending 2003
Total Grants: $405,240*
Number of Grants: 88
Average Grant: $4,605
Highest Grant: $27,500
Lowest Grant: $500
Typical Range: $1,000 to $10,000
*Note: Giving excludes scholarship; United Way.

Recent Grants
Note: Grants derived from 2003 Form 990.

Library-Related

5,000	San Antonio Public Library Foundation, San Antonio, TX

General

175,000	United Way of San Antonio and Bexar County, San Antonio, TX
27,500	United Way of Metropolitan Tarrant County, Ft. Worth, TX
25,000	University of Texas, San Antonio, TX -- towards Uteach program
21,000	Neighborhood Housing Services of San Antonio, San Antonio, TX
20,000	Enterprise San Antonio, San Antonio, TX
20,000	San Antonio Education Partnership, San Antonio, TX -- towards program of partnership school
15,000	White Museum, San Antonio, TX -- towards free Tuesday's program of 2003
15,000	White Museum, San Antonio, TX -- towards free Tuesday program
12,500	Cook Children's Medical Center, San Antonio, TX
12,500	Victory Outreach of Texas Inc. D/B/A Victory Yellow, San Antonio, TX -- towards new victory home

CHARLES A. FRUEAUFF FOUNDATION

Giving Contact

Sue M. Frueauff, Trustee
Three Financial Center
900 South Shackleford, Suite 300
Little Rock, AR 72211
Phone: (501)219-1410
Web: http://www.frueauffoundation.com

Description

Founded: 1950
EIN: 135605371
Organization Type: General Purpose Foundation
Giving Locations: east of the Rocky Mountains.
Grant Types: Capital, Endowment, General Support, Matching, Operating Expenses, Project, Scholarship.

Donor Information

Founder: The foundation was established in 1950, with the late Charles A. Frueauff as donor.

Financial Summary

Total Giving: $5,034,630 (2003); $4,597,900 (2002); $4,844,960 (2001)
Giving Analysis: Giving for 2003 includes: foundation grants to United Way ($60,000); foundation scholarships ($905,000).
Assets: $106,567,029 (2003); $97,526,505 (2002); $109,978,435 (2001)

Typical Recipients

Arts & Humanities: History & Archaeology, Libraries, Museums/Galleries, Music, Performing Arts, Public Broadcasting
Civic & Public Affairs: Community Foundations, Economic Development, Economic Policy, Employment/Job Training, Civic & Public Affairs-General, Law & Justice, Legal Aid
Education: Afterschool/Enrichment Programs, Arts/ Humanities Education, Business Education, Colleges & Universities, Education Associations, Education Funds, Engineering/Technological Education, Faculty Development, Education-General, Literacy, Medical Education, Minority Education, Private Education (Precollege), Public Education (Precollege), Science/ Mathematics Education, Special Education, Student Aid
Health: Children's Health/Hospitals, Clinics/Medical Centers, Diabetes, Emergency/Ambulance Services, Health Funds, Health Organizations, Hospices, Hospitals, Nursing Services, Public Health, Transplant Networks/Donor Banks
Religion: Dioceses, Religious Welfare
Social Services: At-Risk Youth, Child Abuse, Child Welfare, Community Centers, Community Service Organizations, Counseling, Family Services, Food/ Clothing Distribution, Homes, People with Disabilities, Recreation & Athletics, Scouts, Senior Services, Shelters/Homelessness, Substance Abuse, United Funds/United Ways, Veterans, YMCA/YWCA/YMHA/ YWHA, Youth Organizations

Application Procedures

Initial Contact: Organizations should request application guidelines. Phone calls to the foundation are encouraged.
Application Requirements: Proposals should be in the letter form, and should include a history of the organization, project description, purpose of funds sought, objectives, time period, projected budget, evaluation plan, additional funding requested or received from other sources, a list of trustees or directors and key staff, most recent audited financial statements, and proof of tax-exempt status.
Deadlines: Submit the proposal for the May meeting by March 15 and submit the proposal for the November meeting by September 15. Any requests received after September 15 are reviewed at the following May

meeting.
Review Process: The foundation notifies all applicants whether or not they receive a grant.
Notes: The foundation does not review incomplete applications. Pre-proposal letters, videos, and other special supplementary material are discouraged. All grant funds are distributed in December.

Restrictions

The foundation does not support individuals, multi-year grants, international projects, state supported colleges and universities, primary and secondary schools, churches, fundraising drives, or special events.

Additional Information

Grants to new agencies are generally limited to $15,000.
Publications: Informational Brochure

Foundation Officials

James P. Fallon: chief financial officer, trustee
Karl P. Fanning: trustee
Anna Kay Frueauff: trustee
David A. Frueauff: president, chief executive officer, trustee
Sue M. Frueauff: chief administrative officer, trustee
Charles T. Klein: vice president, trustee
A. C. McCully, MD: president emeritus, trustee

Grants Analysis

Disclosure Period: calendar year ending 2003
Total Grants: $4,069,630*
Number of Grants: 121
Average Grant: $33,633
Highest Grant: $110,000
Lowest Grant: $10,000
Typical Range: $20,000 to $50,000
*Note: Giving excludes scholarship; United Way.

Recent Grants

Note: Grants derived from 2003 Form 990.
General

110,000	Boys and Girls Clubs of AR River Valley, Russellville, AR -- program support
100,000	Sweet Briar College, Sweet Briar, VA -- scholarship endowments
80,000	P A R K, Little Rock, AR -- endowment
65,000	Craig Hospital, Eaglewood, CO -- nursing program
65,000	Desert Caballeros Western Museum, Wickenburg, AZ -- renovation and expansion
60,000	America's 2nd Harvest of the Big Bend, Tallahassee, FL -- operating support and expansion
60,000	City Harvest, New York, NY -- operating support
60,000	Melmark, Berwyn, PA -- residential houses renovation endowment
60,000	United Way of Big Bend, Tallahassee, FL -- foods bank support
60,000	Westminster College, Salt Lake City, UT -- faculty technology center

FRUEHAUF FOUNDATION

Giving Contact

Dian Stallings
100 Maple Park Blvd., Suite 106
St. Clair Shores, MI 48081
Phone: (810)774-5130
Fax: (810)774-1152

Description

Founded: 1968
EIN: 237015744
Organization Type: Private Foundation

Giving Locations: MI
Grant Types: General Support, Operating Expenses.

Donor Information

Founder: Angela Fruehauf

Financial Summary

Gifts Received: $21,753 (2000); $12,606 (1999); $191,000 (1996). Note: In 1999 and 2000, contributions were received from Barbara F. Bristol. In 1996, contributions were received from Barbara F. Bristol ($160,000) and Harvey C. Fruehauf, Jr. ($31,000).

Typical Recipients

Arts & Humanities: Arts Funds, Arts Institutes, Historic Preservation, History & Archaeology, Libraries, Music, Public Broadcasting
Civic & Public Affairs: Clubs, Economic Policy, Civic & Public Affairs-General, Law & Justice, Philanthropic Organizations, Public Policy, Safety, Urban & Community Affairs
Education: Business Education, Colleges & Universities, Education Funds, Medical Education, Private Education (Precollege), Public Education (Precollege), Religious Education, Student Aid
Environment: Resource Conservation
Health: AIDS/HIV, Cancer, Children's Health/ Hospitals, Clinics/Medical Centers, Emergency/ Ambulance Services, Eyes/Blindness, Health Funds, Health Organizations, Hospices, Hospitals, Long-Term Care, Medical Research, Mental Health, Nursing Services, Research/Studies Institutes, Single-Disease Health Associations
International: Foreign Educational Institutions, Health Care/Hospitals, International Organizations, International Relief Efforts
Religion: Churches, Ministries, Missionary Activities (Domestic), Religious Organizations, Religious Welfare, Seminaries, Social/Policy Issues
Science: Science Museums
Social Services: Animal Protection, Child Welfare, Community Service Organizations, Family Planning, Family Services, Homes, People with Disabilities, Recreation & Athletics, Scouts, Senior Services, Social Services-General, Substance Abuse, United Funds/United Ways, YMCA/YWCA/YMHA/YWHA, Youth Organizations

Application Procedures

Initial Contact: Send a brief letter of inquiry.
Deadlines: None.

Foundation Officials

Barbara F. Bristol: vice president
Harvey C. Fruehauf, Jr.: president B Grosse Pointe Park, MI 1929. ED University of Michigan (1952). PRIM CORP EMPL president, director: HCF Enterprises Inc. CORP AFFIL president, treasurer, director: HCF Realty Inc.; chairman, president: Miami Oil Producers Inc.; director: Georgia-Pacific Corp.
Robert B. Joslyn: trustee
Frederick R. Keydel: trustee
Julie Stranahan: trustee

Grants Analysis

Disclosure Period: calendar year ending 2000
Total Grants: $163,585
Number of Grants: 44
Average Grant: $2,409*
Highest Grant: $60,000
Typical Range: $500 to $5,000
*Note: Average grant figure excludes highest grant.

Recent Grants

Note: Grants derived from 2001 Form 990.
General

25,000	Church of Jesus Christ Disciples, Cameron, MO -- for Running Child Ministries
25,000	St. Lawrence University, Canton, NY -- for Linda's fund

25,000	Trinity Preparatory School, Winter Park, FL -- for operating expenses
20,000	Houston Museum of Natural Science, Houston, TX -- for mineral specimen
16,250	Lost Tree Chapel, North Palm Beach, FL -- for operating expenses
10,000	Hillsdale College, Hillsdale, MI -- for operating expenses
10,000	University of Texas M. D. Anderson Cancer Center, Houston, TX -- for cancer research
7,500	Lost Tree Chapel, North Palm Beach, FL -- for operating expenses
7,500	St. Francis Episcopal Day School, Houston, TX -- for permanent endowment
5,000	Billy Graham Evangelistic Association, Minneapolis, MN -- for operating expenses

LLOYD A. FRY FOUNDATION

Giving Contact

Unmi Song, Executive Director
120 S LaSalle St., Suite 1950
Chicago, IL 60603
Phone: (312)580-0310
Fax: (312)580-0980
E-mail: usong@fryfoundation.org
Web: http://www.fryfoundation.org

Description

Founded: 1983
EIN: 366108775
Organization Type: General Purpose Foundation
Giving Locations: IL: Chicago
Grant Types: Project, Seed Money.

Donor Information

Founder: Born in San Antonio, TX, in 1895, Lloyd A. Fry established a roofing business in Chicago in 1931. The Lloyd A. Fry Roofing Company grew into the world's largest producer of asphalt roofing products until its sale to Owens-Corning Fiberglas Corporation in 1977. Mr. Fry established the foundation in 1959. Upon his death in 1981, the foundation received a significant testamentary bequest which led to an increase in its philanthropic activity.

Financial Summary

Total Giving: $7,788,419 (fiscal year ending June 30, 2004); $6,000,000 (fiscal 2003 approx); $6,000,000 (fiscal 2002 approx)
Assets: $164,174,514 (fiscal 2004); $160,000,000 (fiscal 2003 approx); $160,000,000 (fiscal 2002 approx)
Gifts Received: $1,039,539 (fiscal 2004); $1,248,303 (fiscal 2000); $1,363,355 (fiscal 1999). Note: The foundation is a residual beneficiary of several trusts established by the estate of the founder.

Typical Recipients

Arts & Humanities: Arts Appreciation, Arts Centers, Arts Festivals, Arts Institutes, Dance, Ethnic & Folk Arts, Historic Preservation, Libraries, Museums/Galleries, Music, Opera, Performing Arts, Public Broadcasting, Theater
Civic & Public Affairs: African American Affairs, Clubs, Community Foundations, Economic Development, Economic Policy, Employment/Job Training, Civic & Public Affairs-General, Housing, Law & Justice, Legal Aid, Nonprofit Management, Public Policy, Urban & Community Affairs, Women's Affairs, Zoos/Aquariums
Education: Afterschool/Enrichment Programs, Arts/Humanities Education, Business Education, Colleges & Universities, Continuing Education, Education Associations, Education Funds, Education Reform, Elementary Education (Private), Faculty Development, Education-General, International Exchange, Leadership Training, Literacy, Minority Education, Preschool Education, Private Education (Precollege), Public Education (Precollege), Science/Mathematics Education, Secondary Education (Private), Secondary Education (Public), Special Education, Student Aid
Environment: Environment-General
Health: AIDS/HIV, Children's Health/Hospitals, Clinics/Medical Centers, Health-General, Geriatric Health, Health Policy/Cost Containment, Health Organizations, Heart, Hospitals, Medical Rehabilitation, Mental Health, Nursing Services, Prenatal Health Issues, Public Health, Single-Disease Health Associations
International: Health Care/Hospitals, International Relations, International Relief Efforts
Religion: Churches, Ministries, Religious Organizations, Religious Welfare, Seminaries
Science: Science Museums, Scientific Centers & Institutes, Scientific Labs
Social Services: At-Risk Youth, Child Abuse, Child Welfare, Community Centers, Community Service Organizations, Counseling, Day Care, Delinquency & Criminal Rehabilitation, Domestic Violence, Emergency Relief, Family Services, Food/Clothing Distribution, People with Disabilities, Refugee Assistance, Senior Services, Shelters/Homelessness, Social Services-General, Substance Abuse, United Funds/United Ways, Volunteer Services, YMCA/YWCA/YMHA/YWHA, Youth Organizations

Application Procedures

Initial Contact: Applicants may submit a brief inquiry before a full proposal. Inquiries should include a brief statement of the project and a project budget.
Application Requirements: Full proposals should include a brief history of the organization with functions and goals; brief proposal summary, including need to be addressed, budget, and an evaluation plan; most recent audited financial report and approved operating budget; other sources of support; list of board members and key personnel; and copy of IRS tax-exempt status letter.
Deadlines: December 1; March 1; June 1; and September 1.
Review Process: The board of directors meets in February, May, August, and November. Although the foundation considers requests for operating support and capital campaigns, it prefers to fund projects directed at the solution of specific problems. Priority is given to proposals for new programs rather than for support of ongoing direct service programs.

Restrictions

Grants rarely are made to organizations outside metropolitan Chicago. No grants are made to individuals, non-tax-exempt organizations, government agencies, fund-raising benefits, or tax-supported educational institutions for services that fall within their normal responsibilities.

Additional Information

Publications: Annual Report; Guidelines

Foundation Officials

Lloyd A. Fry, III: vice chairman, director
Stephanie Pace Marshall, PhD: vice president, director PRIM NONPR EMPL president: Illinois Math & Science Academy. CORP AFFIL director: Tellabs Inc.
M. James Termondt: president, treasurer, director

Grants Analysis

Disclosure Period: fiscal year ending June 30, 2004
Total Grants: $7,788,419
Number of Grants: 358
Average Grant: $21,755
Highest Grant: $200,000
Lowest Grant: $500
Typical Range: $5,000 to $50,000

Recent Grants

Note: Grants derived from fiscal 2003 Form 990.
General

200,000	Marie Sklodowska Curie Metro High School, Chicago, IL -- for the implementation of high school programs
200,000	Millennium Park, Inc., Chicago, IL
175,000	C.A. Prosser Career Academy High School, Chicago, IL -- to support program implementation
150,000	Big Shoulders Fund, Chicago, IL -- for scholarships, technology and professional development
150,000	George Henry Corliss High School, Chicago, IL -- support for program implementation for five years for high school
150,000	George Henry Corliss High School, Chicago, IL -- support for program implementation for five years for high school
150,000	Senn Metro Liberal Arts and Technical High School, Chicago, IL -- for the implementation of high school programs
149,000	Richard T. Crane Tech Prep Common School, Chicago, IL -- for the implementation of high school programs
148,000	Senn Metro Lt. Liberal Arts and Technical High School, Chicago, IL -- for the implementation of high school programs
136,000	Richard T. Crane Tech Prep Common School, Chicago, IL -- for the implementation of high school programs

GOTTFRIED AND MARY FUCHS FOUNDATION

Giving Contact

Gayleene Berry, Trust Officer
c/o Union Bank of California NA
1011 Pacific Ave.
Tacoma, WA 98402
Phone: (206)591-2548

Description

Founded: 1960
EIN: 916022284
Organization Type: Private Foundation
Giving Locations: WA: especially Tahoma and Pierce County, and the lower Puget Sound area
Grant Types: Capital, Emergency, General Support, Multiyear/Continuing Support, Operating Expenses, Project, Research, Scholarship.

Donor Information

Founder: the late Gottfried and Mary Fuchs

Financial Summary

Total Giving: $1,216,320 (2003)
Assets: $21,994,563 (2003)
Gifts Received: $69,559 (2003). Note: In 2003, contributions were received from Gottfried Fuchs Trust.

Typical Recipients

Arts & Humanities: Community Arts, Dance, Historic Preservation, History & Archaeology, Libraries, Museums/Galleries, Music, Opera, Theater
Civic & Public Affairs: African American Affairs, Asian American Affairs, Botanical Gardens/Parks, Clubs, Community Foundations, Employment/Job Training, Civic & Public Affairs-General, Housing, Municipalities/Towns, Parades/Festivals, Urban & Community Affairs, Women's Affairs, Zoos/Aquariums
Education: Colleges & Universities, Community & Junior Colleges, International Studies, Minority Education, Private Education (Precollege), Public Education (Precollege), Religious Education, Special Education, Student Aid, Vocational & Technical

Education
Environment: Environment-General, Resource Conservation, Wildlife Protection
Health: Children's Health/Hospitals, Clinics/Medical Centers, Emergency/Ambulance Services, Geriatric Health, Heart, Hospitals, Mental Health, Prenatal Health Issues, Transplant Networks/Donor Banks, Trauma Treatment
Religion: Churches, Ministries, Religious Organizations, Religious Welfare
Science: Scientific Centers & Institutes
Social Services: Animal Protection, Child Abuse, Child Welfare, Community Centers, Community Service Organizations, Crime Prevention, Day Care, Domestic Violence, Emergency Relief, Family Services, Food/Clothing Distribution, Homes, People with Disabilities, Recreation & Athletics, Refugee Assistance, Scouts, Senior Services, Shelters/Homelessness, Social Services-General, United Funds/United Ways, Volunteer Services, YMCA/YWCA/YMHA/YWHA, Youth Organizations

Application Procedures

Initial Contact: Return completed application form.
Application Requirements: Include proof of tax-exempt status, current financial statement, current budget pertinent to the grant request, resume of the director or person in charge of the program, and a list of board members.
Deadlines: None.

Restrictions

Does not support individuals.

Additional Information

Publications: Application Form; Guidelines
Trust(s): Union Bank CA NA

Grants Analysis

Disclosure Period: calendar year ending 2003
Total Grants: $1,216,320
Number of Grants: 157
Average Grant: $7,747
Highest Grant: $45,000
Lowest Grant: $720
Typical Range: $1,000 to $10,000

Recent Grants

Note: Grants derived from 2001 Form 990.
General

75,000	Bellarmine Preparatory School, Tacoma, WA
50,000	Tacoma Art Museum, Tacoma, WA
50,000	Tacoma Art Museum, Tacoma, WA
50,000	Tacoma Art Museum, Tacoma, WA
45,000	Pierce College Foundation, Tacoma, WA -- for scholarship funds
45,000	Tacoma Community College Foundation, Tacoma, WA -- for scholarship funds
40,000	Pacific Lutheran University, Tacoma, WA -- for scholarship funds
40,000	St. Martin's College, Lacey, WA -- for scholarship funds
40,000	University of Puget Sound, Tacoma, WA -- for scholarship funds
40,000	University of Washington, Tacoma, WA -- for scholarship funds

FUJITSU AMERICA

Company Headquarters

3055 Orchard Drive
San Jose, CA 95134
Web: http://www.fujitsu.com

Company Description

Former Name: Fujitsu American, Inc.
Revenue: US$4.33 billion (2002)

Employees: 188000 (2002)
SIC(s): 3571 Electronic Computers, 3661 Telephone & Telegraph Apparatus.
Parent Company: Fujitsu General America Inc., 3900 NW 79th Ave., Ste. 320, Miami, FL, United States
Parent Revenue: US$42,239,100,000 (2002)

Operating Locations

Fujitsu America (CA--San Jose); Fujitsu America - Information Systems Group (CA--San Jose); Fujitsu America - Super Computer Group (CA--San Jose); Fujitsu Business Communication Systems (CA--Anaheim); Fujitsu Business Communication Systems - Sales & Marketing (AZ--Phoenix); Fujitsu Compound Semiconductor (CA--San Jose); Fujitsu Computer Packaging Technologies (CA--San Jose); Fujitsu Computer Products of America (CA--San Jose); Fujitsu Computer Products of America Manufacturing (OR--Hillsboro); Fujitsu Computer Products of America - Research & Development (CO--Longmont); Fujitsu General America Corp. (NJ--Fairfield); Fujitsu Laboratories of America (CA--San Jose); Fujitsu Ltd. (NY--New York); Fujitsu Microelectronics (CA--San Jose); Fujitsu Microelectronics - Manufacturing (OR--Gresham); Fujitsu Network Switching of America (NC--Raleigh); Fujitsu Network Transmission Systems (TX--Richardson); Fujitsu Networks Industries (CT--Stamford); Fujitsu Open Systems Solutions (CA--San Jose); Fujitsu Personal Systems (CA--Santa Clara); Fujitsu Systems of America (CA--La Jolla); Fujitsu Systems Business of America (CA--Santa Clara); Fujitsu Ten Corp. of America (CA--Torrance); HaL Computer Systems (CA--Campbell); ICL (CA--Irvine); Ross Technology (TX--Austin)

Giving Contact

George Tripshaw, Director, Marketing & Communications
3055 Orchard Dr.
San Jose, CA 95134
Phone: (408)432-1300

Description

Organization Type: Corporate Giving Program
Giving Locations: headquarters and operating communities.
Grant Types: General Support.

Typical Recipients

Arts & Humanities: Libraries, Museums/Galleries
Education: Colleges & Universities, Minority Education
Health: Hospitals, Single-Disease Health Associations
Social Services: Community Service Organizations, United Funds/United Ways

Application Procedures

Initial Contact: Submit a letter at any time, including a description of organization, amount and purpose of request, goals and objectives of the organization, and a list of the board of directors.

Restrictions

Value of monetary and nonmonetary support is not available. Nonmonetary support generally is in the form of donated computers and telecommunications equipment.

Corporate Officials

K. Kojima: chairman, chief executive officer chief financial officer PRIM CORP EMPL chairman, chief executive officer: Fujitsu America.
Motoyasu Matsuzaki: executive vice president, chief financial officer PRIM CORP EMPL executive vice president, chief financial officer: Fujitsu America.

Grants Analysis

Typical Range: $1,000 to $2,500

H.B. FULLER CO.

Company Headquarters

St. Paul, MN
Web: http://www.hbfuller.com

Company Description

Founded: 1887
Ticker: FULL
Exchange: NASDAQ
Revenue: US$1.256 billion (2002)
Employees: 4500 (2003)
SIC(s): 2842 Polishes & Sanitation Goods, 2851 Paints & Allied Products, 2891 Adhesives & Sealants.

Operating Locations

H.B. Fuller Co. (CA--La Mirada, Santa Fe Springs, Tulare; FL--Gainesville; GA--Atlanta; IL--Palatine, Tinley Park; IN; KY; MD--Baltimore; MA--Marlboro; MI--Detroit; MN--Minneapolis, St. Paul, Vadnais Heights; NY--Geneva; NC--Greensboro; OH--Blue Ash; OK; OR--Portland; TN--Memphis; TX--Houston, Mesquite; WA--Vancouver)

Nonmonetary Support

Value: $31,200 (2001); $44,960 (2000)
Type: Donated Equipment; Donated Products; In-kind Services; Loaned Employees

H.B. Fuller Co. Foundation

Giving Contact

Karen P. Muller, Director of Community Affairs
H.B. Fuller Co.
PO Box 64683
St. Paul, MN 55164-0683
Phone: (651)236-5207
Web: http://www.hbfuller.com/About_Us/Community/index.shtml

Alternate Contact

Naida Kissner, Community Affairs Assistant

Description

EIN: 363500811
Organization Type: Corporate Foundation
Giving Locations: internationally; headquarters and operating communities; nationally.
Grant Types: Employee Matching Gifts, General Support, Matching, Operating Expenses, Project.
Note: Employee matching gift ratio: 1 to 1 to education, 0.5 to 1 to the United Way. Company also has a matching gift program for employees serving on boards of community agencies.

Financial Summary

Total Giving: $497,944 (fiscal year ending November 30, 2003); $468,786 (fiscal 2002); $750,755 (fiscal 2001). Note: Contributes through corporate direct giving program and foundation.
Giving Analysis: Giving for fiscal 2001 includes: foundation matching gifts ($43,465); foundation grants to United Way ($138,083); corporate direct giving ($194,086); foundation ($375,121).
Assets: $1,257,655 (fiscal 2003); $1,163,806 (fiscal 2002)
Gifts Received: $562,054 (fiscal 2003); $452,914 (fiscal 2002); $631,410 (fiscal 2001). Note: Contributions were received from H.B. Fuller Company.

Typical Recipients

Arts & Humanities: Arts Associations & Councils, Arts Centers, Arts Funds, Arts Outreach, Dance, Libraries, Literary Arts, Museums/Galleries, Music, Opera, Performing Arts, Public Broadcasting, Theater
Civic & Public Affairs: African American Affairs,

Asian American Affairs, Botanical Gardens/Parks, Business/Free Enterprise, Community Foundations, Economic Development, Employment/Job Training, Ethnic Organizations, Civic & Public Affairs-General, Hispanic Affairs, Housing, Legal Aid, Municipalities/ Towns, Nonprofit Management, Philanthropic Organizations, Public Policy, Urban & Community Affairs, Women's Affairs

Education: Afterschool/Enrichment Programs, Arts/ Humanities Education, Colleges & Universities, Economic Education, Education Funds, Education Reform, Elementary Education (Private), Elementary Education (Public), Education-General, Literacy, Minority Education, Preschool Education, Public Education (Precollege), Religious Education, Science/ Mathematics Education, Secondary Education (Public), Social Sciences Education, Special Education

Environment: Air/Water Quality, Forestry, Environment-General

Health: AIDS/HIV, Clinics/Medical Centers, Emergency/Ambulance Services, Health Organizations, Mental Health, Research/Studies Institutes, Speech & Hearing

International: Foreign Educational Institutions, International-General, Health Care/Hospitals, Human Rights, International Environmental Issues, International Organizations, International Relief Efforts

Religion: Churches, Religion-General, Religious Organizations, Religious Welfare

Science: Science Museums

Social Services: At-Risk Youth, Big Brothers/Big Sisters, Camps, Child Abuse, Child Welfare, Community Centers, Community Service Organizations, Domestic Violence, Family Services, People with Disabilities, Recreation & Athletics, Refugee Assistance, Scouts, Sexual Abuse, Shelters/Homelessness, Social Services-General, Special Olympics, Substance Abuse, United Funds/United Ways, Volunteer Services, YMCA/YWCA/YMHA/YWHA, Youth Organizations

Application Procedures

Initial Contact: Call or send a brief letter of inquiry. The Foundation is the central contact point for all new grant applicants.

Application Requirements: Include a description of organization, amount requested, current budget information, and proof of tax-exempt status.

Deadlines: February 14, June 3, and October 15.

Review Process: Decisions are made by local employee committees and by foundation contributions committee.

Evaluative Criteria: Includes organization's intention to address underlying causes of problems, not merely resulting problems; proximity of organization to company facilities; employee involvement with agency; effectiveness and impact of organization; urgency and need for organization, its leverage, and organizational strength; and multi-level approach to issue or problem.

Decision Notification: Local councils meet monthly and review proposals as they are received; foundation reviews applications three times a year.

Notes: Both foundation and company accept the Minnesota Common Grant Application. The H.B. Fuller Company and Foundation support a wide range of organizations and projects worldwide to reach the needs of the company's international communities. However, in Minnesota, the foundation only approves grants for organizations or programs that directly serve family literacy.

Restrictions

Foundation does not make grants to religious, fraternal, or veterans organizations except for programs that are of direct benefit to the community. Does not support individuals, political/lobbying organizations, basic or applied research, or travel. Does not give to disease-specific organizations, courtesy/public service advertising, or capital or endowment drives. Programs which are the responsibility of governments will not be supported unless the program is a commu-

nity-based effort aimed at improving the delivery of government funded services.

Additional Information

Since 1987, H.B. Fuller's focus issue has been youth development. The company is committed to building strong communities which create economic and educational support for children and their families.

The foundation's primary areas of interest are social services organizations and organizations in which company employees are volunteers. Employees are encouraged to convey the needs of such organizations to the community affairs council for their location.

Recipients of grants are required to submit complete financial reports.

H.B. Fuller allocates 3.5% of pre-tax profits to community affairs activities in the U.S.

In addition to company's community affairs budget, Community Affairs Councils operate in 33 communities in the United States, 23 in Latin America, and 11 in Europe. These councils contribute to over 270 local agencies and also provide nonmonetary support. A list of council chairpersons is available from the foundation.

Publications: Community Affairs Annual Report

Corporate Officials

John Feenan: senior vice president, chief financial officeref executive ED Saint Anselm College; University of North Carolina MBA.

Albert P. L. Stroucken: chairman, president, chief executive B July 09, 1947.

Foundation Officials

Charles Brown: director
Ron Feole: president, director
Keralyn Grolf: director
Richard Kastner: treasurer
Jenny Keyser, PhD: vice president, director
Al Longstreet: director
Greg Mueller: director
Karen P. Muller: executive director, secretary
Albert P. L. Stroucken: director (see above)
Ann Wynia: director B Fort Worth, TX 1943. ED University of Texas BA (1965); University of Wisconsin MA (1968). NONPR AFFIL commissioner: Minnesota Department Human Services; instructor: North Hennepin Community College.

Grants Analysis

Disclosure Period: fiscal year ending November 30, 2003

Total Grants: $362,045*
Number of Grants: 93
Average Grant: $4,108
Highest Grant: $50,000
Lowest Grant: $500
Typical Range: $1,000 to $10,000
*Note: Giving excludes matching gifts and United Way.

Recent Grants

Note: Grants derived from fiscal 2003 Form 990.

Library-Related

5,000	Library Foundation of Hennepin County, Minnetonka, MN -- for read to me, daddy-read to me, mommy

General

50,000	University of Minnesota Foundation, Minneapolis, MN -- Elmer L Anderson library endowment for special collections
30,000	Ready 4 K
20,000	Greater Twin Cities United Way, Minneapolis, MN -- for success by 6
20,000	Lifetrack Resources, St. Paul, MN -- families together program
20,000	Minnesota Humanities Commission, MN -- for family literacy initiatives
20,000	Reading Rx

15,000	Lao Family Community of Minnesota Inc., St. Paul, MN -- for English education program
10,250	University of Minnesota Office of Sponsored Projects Administration, Minneapolis, MN -- HB Fuller McEvoy lecture series
10,000	Mounds View Schools's Family Learning Program
8,650	Bethel College, Mishawaka, IN -- towards family literacy program

FULLER FOUNDATION (DE)

Giving Contact

Nannette Barrigan, Executive Director
269 S. Beverly Dr., 469
Beverly Hills, CA 90212
Phone: (561)655-1980
Fax: (561)655-5677

Description

Founded: 1951
EIN: 756015942
Organization Type: Private Foundation
Giving Locations: nationally.
Grant Types: General Support.

Donor Information

Founder: Andrew P. Fuller, William M. Fuller

Financial Summary

Gifts Received: In 1991, contributions were received from Buffalo News/Berkshire Hathaway ($140) and William M. Fuller ($500).

Typical Recipients

Arts & Humanities: Arts Associations & Councils, Arts Funds, Community Arts, Film & Video, Historic Preservation, History & Archaeology, Libraries, Museums/Galleries, Music, Theater, Visual Arts

Civic & Public Affairs: Botanical Gardens/Parks, Employment/Job Training, Gay/Lesbian Issues, Civic & Public Affairs-General, Housing, Urban & Community Affairs, Zoos/Aquariums

Education: Arts/Humanities Education, Colleges & Universities, Education Funds, Education-General, Legal Education, Literacy, Medical Education, Private Education (Precollege), Science/Mathematics Education, Social Sciences Education

Environment: Environment-General, Resource Conservation

Health: AIDS/HIV, Arthritis, Cancer, Clinics/Medical Centers, Emergency/Ambulance Services, Health Organizations, Heart, Hospices, Hospitals, Hospitals (University Affiliated), Medical Rehabilitation, Medical Research, Mental Health, Multiple Sclerosis, Single-Disease Health Associations, Transplant Networks/ Donor Banks

International: Health Care/Hospitals, Human Rights, International Environmental Issues, International Relief Efforts

Religion: Churches, Jewish Causes, Religious Organizations, Religious Welfare

Social Services: Animal Protection, Camps, Child Welfare, Community Centers, Domestic Violence, Family Planning, Food/Clothing Distribution, Recreation & Athletics, Social Services-General, Substance Abuse, YMCA/YWCA/YMHA/YWHA, Youth Organizations

Application Procedures

Initial Contact: Send proposal in any legible form containing all relevant information about organization.

Deadlines: None.

Foundation Officials

Kenneth S. Beall, Esq.: secretary
Fuller French: treasurer
Geraldine Fuller: president
Gillian Fuller: vice president

Grants Analysis

Disclosure Period: calendar year ending 2000
Total Grants: $342,000
Number of Grants: 36
Average Grant: $8,343*
Highest Grant: $50,000
Typical Range: $1,000 to $15,000
*Note: Average grant excludes highest grant.

Recent Grants

Note: Grants derived from 2001 Form 990.
General

50,000	Friendly Hand Foundation, Los Angeles, CA
31,500	MJ Fox Foundation, New York, NY
25,000	Children of Move, Los Angeles, CA
15,000	United World College, Montezuma, NM
10,000	Loyola Law School, Los Angeles, CA
10,000	St. John's Health Center Foundation, Santa Monica, CA
10,000	St. Joseph's Center, Venice, CA
10,000	Shakespearean Hobarts, Los Angeles, CA
10,000	Tuesday's Child, Culver City, CA
10,000	University of Southern California, Los Angeles, CA

GEORGE F. AND SYBIL H. FULLER FOUNDATION

Giving Contact

Mark W. Fuller, Chairman & Treasurer
370 Main St.
Worcester, MA 01608
Phone: (508)755-1684

Description

Founded: 1955
EIN: 046125606
Organization Type: Family Foundation
Giving Locations: MA: Worcester County
Grant Types: Capital, Challenge, General Support, Loan.

Donor Information

Founder: Established in 1955 by the late George Freeman Fuller (d. 1962), who was an influential figure in the Worcester, MA area. Mr. Fuller served for many years as a trustee of Worcester Polytechnic Institute and worked with many charitable organizations. He was president and chairman of the board of the Wyman-Gordon Company, a leading industrial concern in the forging business. His wife, Sybil Harriet Flagg Fuller, died in 1955. The foundation received a considerable bequest from Mr. Fuller's estate at the time of his death.

Financial Summary

Total Giving: $3,193,450 (2003); $3,386,500 (2002); $3,500,000 (2001)
Giving Analysis: Giving for 2003 includes: foundation grants to United Way ($80,000); 2002: foundation grants to United Way ($75,000).
Assets: $65,986,026 (2003); $61,803,956 (2002); $69,000,000 (2001)

Typical Recipients

Arts & Humanities: Arts Centers, Ethnic & Folk Arts, Arts & Humanities-General, Historic Preservation, History & Archaeology, Libraries, Museums/Galleries, Music, Performing Arts, Public Broadcast-

ing, Theater
Civic & Public Affairs: African American Affairs, Botanical Gardens/Parks, Business/Free Enterprise, Clubs, Community Foundations, Civic & Public Affairs-General, Housing, Minority Business, Professional & Trade Associations, Public Policy, Safety, Urban & Community Affairs
Education: Agricultural Education, Arts/Humanities Education, Colleges & Universities, Community & Junior Colleges, Education Reform, Engineering/Technological Education, Education-General, Literacy, Medical Education, Preschool Education, Private Education (Precollege), Public Education (Precollege), Science/Mathematics Education, Secondary Education (Private), Special Education, Student Aid, Vocational & Technical Education
Environment: Forestry, Environment-General, Protection, Resource Conservation
Health: Cancer, Children's Health/Hospitals, Clinics/Medical Centers, Diabetes, Emergency/Ambulance Services, Health-General, Health Organizations, Hospices, Hospitals, Hospitals (University Affiliated), Medical Research, Nursing Services, Public Health, Single-Disease Health Associations
International: Foreign Arts Organizations
Religion: Churches, Jewish Causes, Ministries, Religious Organizations, Religious Welfare, Seminaries
Science: Science-General, Science Museums, Scientific Centers & Institutes, Scientific Research
Social Services: Big Brothers/Big Sisters, Child Welfare, Community Centers, Community Service Organizations, Counseling, Day Care, Emergency Relief, Family Services, Food/Clothing Distribution, People with Disabilities, Recreation & Athletics, Scouts, Senior Services, Substance Abuse, United Funds/United Ways, YMCA/YWCA/YMHA/YWHA, Youth Organizations

Application Procedures

Initial Contact: The foundation has no formal application requirements or procedures. Initial contact should be a letter of inquiry mailed to the foundation.
Application Requirements: Applications should be made in a reasonably brief narrative form with an appropriate budget. The purpose to be achieved, reasons why the organization is fitted to achieve them, and how these purposes integrate with the existing activities of the institution are also of interest. In addition, included evidence of tax exempt status and the most recent annual report, including the audited financial report. Signature of the Chief Executive Officer is required.
Deadlines: None. The six-member board of trustees meets six times a year.
Review Process: If the foundation is interested in the project, one copy of a full proposal will be requested. The foundation occasionally acknowledges receipt of proposals. Applicants may arrange interviews.

Restrictions

No grants are made to individuals for scholarships or fellowships.

Foundation Officials

Jan Fuller: trustee
Joyce I. Fuller: assistant treasurer, trustee PRIM CORP EMPL executive vice president, clerk, director: REFCO Inc.
Lincoln E. Fuller: trustee PRIM CORP EMPL executive vice president, director: REFCO Inc.
Mark W. Fuller: chairman, treasurer, trustee B 1949. ED Pennsylvania State University (1972). PRIM CORP EMPL president, treasurer, chief executive officer, director: REFCO Inc. CORP AFFIL president: Industrial & Tool Suppliers; president: Leen/Refco Co.
Russell E. Fuller: chairman, trustee B 1925. PRIM CORP EMPL chairman, director: REFCO Inc. CORP AFFIL director: Wyman-Gordon Co.
David P. Hallock: trustee
Dianne Robbins: secretary, trustee

Grants Analysis

Disclosure Period: calendar year ending 2003
Total Grants: $3,113,450*
Number of Grants: 94
Average Grant: $33,122
Highest Grant: $259,000
Lowest Grant: $1,000
Typical Range: $5,000 to $50,000
*Note: Giving excludes United Way.

Recent Grants

Note: Grants derived from 2003 Form 990.
General

259,000	Ecotarium, Worcester, MA
210,000	Assumption College, Worcester, MA
210,000	Worcester Polytechnic Institute, Worcester, MA
200,000	Boylston Historical Society, Boylston, MA
200,000	Worcester Art Museum, Worcester, MA
119,500	Barton Center for Diabetes Education, North Oxford, MA
110,000	Anna Maria College, Paxton, MA
110,000	Becker College, Worcester, MA
110,000	Clark University, Worcester, MA
105,000	Joy of Music Program, Worcester, MA

FULLER FOUNDATION (MA)

Giving Contact

John T. Bottomley, Executive Director & Trustee
PO Box 461
Rye Beach, NH 03871
Phone: (603)964-8998

Description

Founded: 1936
EIN: 042241130
Organization Type: Private Foundation
Giving Locations: MA: Boston; NH: seacoast area
Grant Types: Capital, General Support, Operating Expenses, Scholarship.

Donor Information

Founder: the late Alvan T. Fuller, Sr.

Financial Summary

Total Giving: $527,550 (2003); $730,369 (2001)
Giving Analysis: Giving for 2001 includes: foundation grants to United Way ($500); foundation scholarships ($16,000)
Assets: $14,184,942 (2003); $15,833,289 (2001)

Typical Recipients

Arts & Humanities: Arts Associations & Councils, Arts Centers, Arts Festivals, Arts Institutes, Arts Outreach, Arts & Humanities-General, Historic Preservation, Libraries, Music, Performing Arts, Public Broadcasting
Civic & Public Affairs: Community Foundations, Economic Development, Employment/Job Training, Civic & Public Affairs-General, Philanthropic Organizations, Urban & Community Affairs, Zoos/Aquariums
Education: Colleges & Universities, Elementary Education (Public), Engineering/Technological Education, Leadership Training, Private Education (Precollege), Public Education (Precollege)
Environment: Environment-General, Resource Conservation
Health: AIDS/HIV, Cancer, Children's Health/Hospitals, Emergency/Ambulance Services, Health Organizations, Hospitals, Medical Research
International: International Relief Efforts
Religion: Churches, Jewish Causes, Ministries, Religious Organizations, Religious Welfare
Science: Scientific Centers & Institutes

Social Services: Big Brothers/Big Sisters, Child Welfare, Community Service Organizations, Crime Prevention, Day Care, Emergency Relief, Family Services, Food/Clothing Distribution, Recreation & Athletics, Scouts, Shelters/Homelessness, Social Services-General, Substance Abuse, United Funds/United Ways, Youth Organizations

Application Procedures

Initial Contact: Telephone foundation.
Deadlines: None.

Restrictions

Does not support individuals or provide funds for publications or conferences.

Additional Information

Publications: Application Guidelines

Foundation Officials

Mindy Bocko: trustee
Mrs. George T. Bottomley: honorary trustee
John T. Bottomley: executive director, trustee
Peter Fuller, Jr.: trustee
Peter D. Fuller, Sr.: trustee B Boston, MA 1923. ED Harvard University (1946). PRIM CORP EMPL chairman, president: Cadillac Automobile Co. Boston. CORP AFFIL president, director: Fuller Enterprises.
James D. Henderson: trustee
Susanne Fuller MacDonald: trustee
Sandra Scagliotti: program administrator
Mrs. Frederick W. Swasey: honorary trustee
Melinda F. vanden Henvel: trustee

Grants Analysis

Disclosure Period: calendar year ending 2003
Total Grants: $527,550
Number of Grants: 123
Average Grant: $4,289
Highest Grant: $21,000
Lowest Grant: $250
Typical Range: $1,000 to $10,000

Recent Grants

Note: Grants derived from 2001 Form 990.
General

22,810	Fuller Foundation of New Hampshire, Rye Beach, NH
20,000	Fuller Foundation of New Hampshire, Rye Beach, NH
20,000	Fuller Foundation of New Hampshire, Rye Beach, NH
15,000	Fuller Foundation of New Hampshire, Rye Beach, NH
15,000	Fuller Foundation of New Hampshire, Rye Beach, NH
14,000	Fuller Foundation of New Hampshire, Rye Beach, NH
10,000	Fuller Foundation of New Hampshire, Rye Beach, NH
10,000	Fuller Foundation of New Hampshire, Rye Beach, NH
10,000	Fuller Foundation of New Hampshire, Rye Beach, NH
10,000	Fuller Foundation of New Hampshire, Rye Beach, NH

FULLERTON FOUNDATION

Giving Contact

Walter E. Cavell, Executive Director
PO Box 2208
Gaffney, SC 29342-2208
Phone: (864)489-6678
Fax: (864)487-9946
E-mail: cjbonner@fullertonfoundation.org

Description

Founded: 1954
EIN: 570847444
Organization Type: Family Foundation
Giving Locations: NC; SC
Grant Types: General Support, Matching, Project, Scholarship, Seed Money.

Donor Information

Founder: Established in 1954 by the late Alma H. Fullerton.

Financial Summary

Total Giving: $1,838,000 (fiscal year ending November 30, 2003); $2,005,000 (fiscal 2001)
Giving Analysis: Giving for fiscal 2003 includes: foundation scholarships ($243,000); fiscal 2001: foundation scholarships ($283,000)
Assets: $43,360,402 (fiscal 2003); $43,741,795 (fiscal 2001)

Typical Recipients

Arts & Humanities: Libraries, Museums/Galleries
Civic & Public Affairs: African American Affairs, Civic & Public Affairs-General, Housing
Education: Arts/Humanities Education, Colleges & Universities, Education Funds, Medical Education, Public Education (Precollege), Science/Mathematics Education, Student Aid
Health: Cancer, Children's Health/Hospitals, Clinics/Medical Centers, Emergency/Ambulance Services, Health-General, Geriatric Health, Health Policy/Cost Containment, Health Funds, Health Organizations, Hospices, Hospitals, Hospitals (University Affiliated), Long-Term Care, Medical Rehabilitation, Medical Research, Medical Training, Nursing Services, Nutrition, Outpatient Health Care, Prenatal Health Issues, Preventive Medicine/Wellness Organizations, Public Health, Research/Studies Institutes, Transplant Networks/Donor Banks, Trauma Treatment
Religion: Ministries, Religious Organizations, Religious Welfare
Science: Scientific Organizations
Social Services: Child Welfare, Community Centers, Community Service Organizations, Family Planning, Family Services, Homes, People with Disabilities, Recreation & Athletics, Scouts, United Funds/United Ways, Youth Organizations

Application Procedures

Initial Contact: The foundation requests a brief initial letter of application.
Application Requirements: The letter of application should contain the background of the organization requesting the grant, the purpose of the grant, general financial information, and documentation of section 501(c)(3) federal tax-exempt status.
Deadlines: Deadlines for submitting applications are April 1, August 1, and December 1.

Restrictions

The foundation generally makes grants to health care, medicine, and education. Grants are not made to individuals.

Foundation Officials

Helen T. Baden: director
Catherine Hamrick Beattie: director
Charles J. Bonner: associate director
Walter E. Cavell: executive director
Jean Hamrick Haas: director
A. Wardlaw Hamrick: director
Charles F. Hamrick, II: vice chairman, director
Charles F. Hamrick: director B 1956. PRIM CORP EMPL secretary, treasurer, director: Hamrick Mills Inc.
John M. Hamrick: director B Gaffney, SC 1913. ED Duke University (1934). PRIM CORP EMPL chairman: Hamrick Mills Inc.
Lyman W. Hamrick: secretary, director PRIM CORP EMPL president: Hamrick Mills Inc.

W. Carlisle Hamrick: treasurer
Wylie L. Hamrick: chairman, director B 1926. PRIM CORP EMPL chairman: Hamrick Mills Inc. CORP AFFIL president: Southern Loom Reed Co. Inc.
Frances Reaves Ross: director
Volina Cline Valentine: director

Grants Analysis

Disclosure Period: fiscal year ending November 30, 2003
Total Grants: $1,595,000*
Number of Grants: 21
Average Grant: $69,750*
Highest Grant: $200,000
Lowest Grant: $1,000
Typical Range: $25,000 to $200,000
*Note: Giving excludes scholarships. Average grant figure excludes highest grant.

Recent Grants

Note: Grants derived from fiscal 2003 Form 990.
Library-Related

1,000	Cherokee County Public Library, SC

General

243,000	Fullerton Medical Scholarship Program, Gaffney, SC -- towards assistance for medical students in medical school
200,000	Limestone College, Gaffney, SC -- towards support for the current capital campaign
188,755	Duke University Medical Center, Durham, NC -- towards pathways in caring
175,316	School of Medicine University of South Carolina, Columbia, SC -- towards integration of physician training and biomedical research
150,000	Memory Assessment Clinic and Eldercare Resource Center, Asheville, NC -- towards support expansion of services by hiring additional geriatrician
150,000	School of Medicine University of South Carolina, Columbia, SC -- towards development of surgical residency fellowship program in trauma care
129,239	School of Medicine University of South Carolina, Columbia, SC -- to support a pilot program to develop biomarkers to access colon cancer risk
100,000	Gateway House, Greenville, SC -- towards financing construction of colleague training guesthouse
60,000	Mission Saint Joseph's Health System, Asheville, NC -- towards support for the development of the Fullerton center's education initiatives
50,000	Fellowship of Christian Athletes, Gaffney, SC -- towards support for the continued expansion of FCA in South Carolina

FUND FOR NEW JERSEY

Giving Contact

Mark M. Murphy, Executive Director & Secretary
94 Church Street, Suite 303
New Brunswick, NJ 08901
Phone: (732)220-8656
Fax: (732)220-8654
E-mail: info@fundfornj.org
Web: http://www.fundfornj.org
Note: Proposals are not accepted via e-mail.

Description

Founded: 1969
EIN: 221895028
Organization Type: General Purpose Foundation
Giving Locations: NJ
Grant Types: General Support, Matching, Operating Expenses, Project, Research, Seed Money.

Donor Information

Founder: Established in 1969 by the family of the late Mr. and Mrs. Charles F. Wallace of Westfield, NJ, to "maximize contributions to social improvements." Mr. Charles Wallace declined naming any specific purpose for the fund, stating that only individuals living in and currently aware of existing problems in the community could decide the best use of its fund. The original board of trustees was then augmented with well-informed individuals of standing in the community who could contribute meaningfully to board deliberations.

Financial Summary

Total Giving: $3,149,703 (2004); $3,044,703 (2003); $3,086,840 (2002)
Giving Analysis: Giving for 2002 includes: foundation scholarships ($10,000)
Assets: $69,734,657 (2003); $62,134,075 (2002)
Gifts Received: $839,931 (1998); $620,235 (1995); $2,775,259 (1994)

Typical Recipients

Arts & Humanities: Film & Video, Libraries, Public Broadcasting
Civic & Public Affairs: African American Affairs, Botanical Gardens/Parks, Business/Free Enterprise, Civil Rights, Community Foundations, Economic Development, Economic Policy, Employment/Job Training, Civic & Public Affairs-General, Hispanic Affairs, Housing, Law & Justice, Legal Aid, Municipalities/Towns, Nonprofit Management, Philanthropic Organizations, Professional & Trade Associations, Public Policy, Rural Affairs, Urban & Community Affairs, Women's Affairs, Zoos/Aquariums
Education: Agricultural Education, Arts/Humanities Education, Business Education, Colleges & Universities, Education Associations, Education Funds, Education Reform, Elementary Education (Private), Environmental Education, Education-General, Gifted & Talented Programs, Leadership Training, Legal Education, Literacy, Medical Education, Minority Education, Private Education (Precollege), Public Education (Precollege), Science/Mathematics Education, Social Sciences Education, Student Aid
Environment: Air/Water Quality, Environment-General, Protection, Resource Conservation, Watershed, Wildlife Protection
Health: Adolescent Health Issues, AIDS/HIV, Health Organizations, Hospitals, Prenatal Health Issues, Public Health
International: Health Care/Hospitals, Human Rights, International Affairs, International Development, International Environmental Issues
Religion: Religious Welfare
Science: Science Museums, Scientific Centers & Institutes
Social Services: At-Risk Youth, Child Abuse, Child Welfare, Community Service Organizations, Crime Prevention, Domestic Violence, Family Services, Substance Abuse, United Funds/United Ways, YMCA/YWCA/YMHA/YWHA

Application Procedures

Initial Contact: Applicants are required to submit a one-page summary describing their project.
Application Requirements: The one-page cover sheet should include the following: organization and contact person, with address and telephone number; amount requested requested; a one or two sentence description of the problem or need addressed by the proposed project. The fund encourages applicants to submit in the body of their proposal whatever information they feel is important for consideration. All proposals must be accompanied by a copy of the applicant's IRS tax exemption letter, the names and affiliations of the board of directors, and a budget showing projected sources of income and anticipated expenditures. expenditures.
Deadlines: All proposals must be submitted seven weeks prior to board meetings.

Review Process: The board of trustees meets four times a year (March, June, September, and December) to consider proposals that come to it with staff recommendation. The process may involve a considerable lapse of time before a determination is made on a specific proposal.

Restrictions

The fund stresses that it only makes grantss to organizations that have applied for or have been granted tax-exempt status under Section 501(c)(3) of Internal Revenue Code. The fund does not accept applications for support of individuals, nor for capital projects including acquisition, renovation, or equipment. In general, the fund will not support day care centers, drug treatment programs, arts programs, health care delivery, or scholarships.

Additional Information

A few grantss are provided for local activities, direct services, and general operating support; such proposals are usually considered at the fund's invitation.
Publications: Annual Report (includes Application Guidelines); Agenda New Jersey series (titles include Campaign Reform, Fiscal Responsibility, Better Schools, Building Our Cities, Strengthening Families)

Foundation Officials

Candace McKee Ashmun: vice president, trustee
Ernestine Schlant Bradley: trustee
John W. Cornwall: trustee
Joseph C. Cornwall: chairman emeritus
Hon. Dickinson Richards Debevoise: trustee B Orange, NJ 1924. ED Williams College BA (1948); Columbia University LLB (1951). PRIM NONPR EMPL federal judge: U.S. District Court. NONPR AFFIL member: New Jersey Bar Association; judge: U.S. District Court New Jersey; member: Judicature Society; member: Essex County Bar Association; member: Federal Bar Association; member: Association Federation Bar New Jersey; member: Columbia University Law School Association; member: American Law Institute; member: American Bar Association; fellow: American Bar Foundation.
Linda Dennery: trustee
Dr. Susan H. Fuhrman: trustee
Hon. John Joseph Gibbons: trustee B Newark, NJ 1924. ED College of the Holy Cross BS (1947); Harvard University LLB (1950); Holy Cross College LLD (1970); Seton Hall University LLD (1980); Suffolk University LLD (1982). PRIM NONPR EMPL professor constitutional law: Seton Hall University. NONPR AFFIL adj professor: Suffolk University; member vis committee: University Chicago Law School; trustee: Practicing Law Institute; adj professor: Rutgers University; member: New Jersey Bar Association; member: New Jersey Council Against Crime; member: Holy Cross College General Alumni Association; member: Governors Select Committee Civil Disorder; trustee: Holy Cross College; member: Essex County Bar Association; fellow: American Bar Foundation; adj professor: Duke University; member: American Bar Association.
Gustav Heningburg: trustee
Leonard Lieberman: chairman, trustee B Elizabeth, NJ 1929. ED Yale University BA (1950); Columbia University JD (1953); Harvard University Advanced Management Program (1970). CORP AFFIL director: Republic New York Corp.; director: Sonic Industries; director: Outlet Communication; director: Celestial Seasonings; director: La Petite Academy. NONPR AFFIL member counselor New Jersey affairs: Princeton University Council New Jersey Affairs; member: Regional Plan Association; honorary president, trustee: Newark Beth Israel Medical Center; member: Food Marketing Institute; trustee: New Jersey Center Performing Arts; director: Center Hospital Care Strategies.
Lawrence S. Lustberg: trustee
Mark M. Murphy: secretary, executive director
Clement A. Price: trustee
Gary D. Rose: treasurer, trustee

Richard J. Sullivan: trustee B Green Bay, WI 1949. PRIM CORP EMPL executive vice president: Fleishman-Hillard. NONPR AFFIL member: Public Relations Society America. CLUB AFFIL National Press Club.
Jane W. Thorne: trustee emeritus
Richard L. Wright: trustee

Grants Analysis

Disclosure Period: calendar year ending 2004
Total Grants: $3,149,703
Number of Grants: 60
Average Grant: $52,495
Highest Grant: $175,000
Lowest Grant: $16,000
Typical Range: $25,000 to $100,000

Recent Grants

Note: Grants derived from 2003 Form 990.
General

150,000	New Jersey Policy Perspective, Trenton, NJ -- to support advance a progressive agenda through reports and analysis on major issues in the state
125,000	Eastern Environmental Law Center, Newark, NJ -- to provide legal counsel and advocacy for New Jersey's environmental organizations
125,000	Education Law Center, Newark, NJ -- support for the Abbott implementation initiative
125,000	Housing and Community Development Network of New Jersey, Trenton, NJ -- support for capacity building, resource development efforts, statewide advocacy and public policy work
100,000	Cityworks Inc., Trenton, NJ -- start fund for real estate projects in economically distress neighborhoods
100,000	Clean Water Fund, Belmar, NJ
100,000	Local Initiatives Support Corporation, Trenton, NJ
85,000	Lawyer's Committee for Human Rights, New York, NY -- support for the Asylum Program
85,000	Legal Services of New Jersey, Edison, NJ -- support for the poverty research institute and anti poverty network programs
85,000	Public Agenda, New York, NY

FURTHUR FOUNDATION

Giving Contact

Andre Carothers, Director
1405 McGee Ave.
Berkeley, CA 94703
Phone: (510)524-4000

Description

Founded: 1990
EIN: 680177715
Organization Type: Private Foundation
Giving Locations: CA; NM; OR
Grant Types: General Support.

Financial Summary

Total Giving: $32,450 (fiscal year ending January 31, 2004); $40,800 (fiscal 2001)
Assets: $867,312 (fiscal 2004); $832,808 (fiscal 2001)
Gifts Received: $10,046 (fiscal 2004); $200 (fiscal 2001); $500 (fiscal 2000). Note: In fiscal 1995, contributions were received from Robert H. Weir ($100,000); other miscellaneous contributions totaled $3,135.

Typical Recipients

Arts & Humanities: Libraries

Civic & Public Affairs: Employment/Job Training, Civic & Public Affairs-General, Native American Affairs, Rural Affairs, Women's Affairs

Education: Agricultural Education, Education-General, International Studies, Science/Mathematics Education

Environment: Air/Water Quality, Forestry, Environment-General, Protection, Research, Resource Conservation, Wildlife Protection

Health: AIDS/HIV, Mental Health

International: Foreign Educational Institutions, Health Care/Hospitals, Human Rights, International Affairs, International Environmental Issues, International Relief Efforts

Religion: Social/Policy Issues

Social Services: At-Risk Youth, Camps, Community Centers, Community Service Organizations, Counseling, Family Services, Food/Clothing Distribution, Senior Services

Application Procedures

Initial Contact: The foundation requests applications be made in writing.
Deadlines: January 31.

Restrictions

Foundation does not support individuals or political or lobbying groups.

Additional Information

Publications: Application Form

Foundation Officials

Andre Carothers: director
Ram Dass: director
Robert H. Weir: director

Grants Analysis

Disclosure Period: fiscal year ending January 31, 2004
Total Grants: $32,450
Number of Grants: 33
Average Grant: $983
Highest Grant: $1,500
Lowest Grant: $500
Typical Range: $500 to $1,500

Recent Grants

Note: Grants derived from 2001 Form 990.
General

3,300	Vellecitos Mountain Refuge, Taos, NM
2,500	Cascadia Wildlands Project, Eugene, OR
2,500	Central Cascade Alliance, Hood River, OR
2,500	Haight Ashbury Food Program, San Francisco, CA
2,500	Mountain Light Center/AGP, Taos, NM
2,500	Project Avary, San Rafael, CA
2,500	Smith River Preservation, Guerneville, CA
2,500	Trees Foundation, Redway, CA
2,000	As You Sow Foundation, San Francisco, CA
2,000	No Penny Opera, The, San Francisco, CA

G/S/M INDUSTRIAL INC.

Company Headquarters

345 S. Reading Rd.
Ephrata, PA 17522

Company Description

Employees: 100
SIC(s): 3400 Fabricated Metal Products.

Parent Company: Gooding Simpson Mackes Inc., 345 S. Reading Road, Ephrata, PA, United States

Gooding Group Foundation

Giving Contact

John S. Gooding, President
345 South Reading Road
Ephrata, PA 17522
Phone: (717)733-1247

Description

EIN: 232516754
Organization Type: Corporate Foundation
Giving Locations: PA
Grant Types: General Support.

Financial Summary

Gifts Received: $10,150 (2000); $46,500 (1999); $101,880 (1998). Note: In 2000, contributions were received from GSM Industrial Inc. In 1999, contributions were received from G/S/M Industrial ($30,000), Gooding Delaware, Inc. ($16,000), and Millersville Univ. ($500). In 1998, contributions were received from G/S/M Industrial ($60,000); Gooding Delaware, Inc. ($10,000); and Fern Gooding ($31,880). In 1996, contributions were received from G/S/M Industrial.

Typical Recipients

Arts & Humanities: Arts Associations & Councils, Dance, Historic Preservation, History & Archaeology, Libraries, Museums/Galleries, Opera, Performing Arts

Civic & Public Affairs: Employment/Job Training, Civic & Public Affairs-General, Hispanic Affairs, Housing, Professional & Trade Associations, Safety, Urban & Community Affairs

Education: Business Education, Colleges & Universities, Community & Junior Colleges, Education Funds, Public Education (Precollege), Science/Mathematics Education, Secondary Education (Private), Special Education, Student Aid, Vocational & Technical Education

Environment: Environment-General, Resource Conservation

Health: Cancer, Children's Health/Hospitals, Emergency/Ambulance Services, Eyes/Blindness, Heart, Hospices, Hospitals, Nursing Services

Religion: Bible Study/Translation, Churches, Religious Welfare

Science: Science Museums

Social Services: Big Brothers/Big Sisters, Child Abuse, Community Service Organizations, Counseling, Day Care, Emergency Relief, Family Planning, Family Services, People with Disabilities, Recreation & Athletics, Scouts, Special Olympics, United Funds/United Ways, YMCA/YWCA/YMHA/YWHA, Youth Organizations

Application Procedures

Initial Contact: Send a letter including any information with regards to the request.
Deadlines: None.

Corporate Officials

John S. Gooding: chairman, director PRIM CORP EMPL chairman, director: GSM Industrial.

Foundation Officials

Robert E. Burkholder: secretary, treasurer
John S. Gooding: president (see above)
James K. Towers, III: vice president PRIM CORP EMPL president, chief executive officer, director: GSM Industrial.

Grants Analysis

Disclosure Period: calendar year ending 2000
Total Grants: $31,342*

Number of Grants: 81
Average Grant: $387
Highest Grant: $2,000
Typical Range: $100 to $500
*****Note:** Giving excludes United Way.

Recent Grants

Note: Grants derived from 2001 Form 990.
Library-Related

525	Ephrata Public Library, Ephrata, PA

General

2,000	Millersville University, Millersville, PA
1,000	Boy Scouts of America Pennsylvania Dutch Council, Lancaster, PA
1,000	Elizabethtown College, Elizabethtown, PA
1,000	Lancaster Foundation for Educational Enrichment, Lancaster, PA
1,000	Thaddeus Stevens College of Technology, Lancaster, PA
1,000	United Way of Lancaster County, Lancaster, PA
1,000	University of Pittsburgh, Pittsburgh, PA
1,000	West Chester University, West Chester, PA
750	Fulton Opera House, Lancaster, PA
750	Junior Achievement, Lancaster, PA

ALFRED S. GAGE FOUNDATION

Giving Contact

Roxanna Catto-Hayne, Vice President & Secretary
Alfred S. Gage Foundation
110 E. Crockett Street
San Antonio, TX 78205-2694
Phone: (210)222-2161

Description

Founded: 1990
EIN: 742553574
Organization Type: Private Foundation
Giving Locations: TX: Bexar County, Brewstar County, Kendal County
Grant Types: General Support.

Financial Summary

Total Giving: $105,130 (fiscal year ending June 30, 2004); $63,400 (fiscal 2001)
Assets: $2,943,374 (fiscal 2004); $2,729,347 (fiscal 2001)
Gifts Received: $1,879,278 (fiscal 2001)

Typical Recipients

Arts & Humanities: Arts Institutes, Historic Preservation, History & Archaeology, Libraries, Museums/Galleries, Music, Public Broadcasting, Theater

Civic & Public Affairs: Botanical Gardens/Parks, Clubs, Civic & Public Affairs-General, Hispanic Affairs, Law & Justice, Legal Aid, Public Policy

Education: Arts/Humanities Education, Business Education, Colleges & Universities, Environmental Education, Private Education (Precollege)

Environment: Environment-General, Resource Conservation

Health: Cancer, Health-General, Heart, Hospitals

International: International Affairs

Religion: Churches

Social Services: Animal Protection, Recreation & Athletics

Application Procedures

Initial Contact: Submit a brief letter for initial contact.
Deadlines: None.

Foundation Officials

Roxana Catto Hayne: vice president, secretary
Joan N. Kelleher: president, treasurer

Grants Analysis

Disclosure Period: fiscal year ending June 30, 2004
Total Grants: $105,130
Number of Grants: 37
Average Grant: $2,841
Highest Grant: $10,000
Lowest Grant: $600
Typical Range: $1,000 to $5,000

Recent Grants

Note: Grants derived from fiscal 2001 Form 990.
General

10,000	San Antonio Symphony, San Antonio, TX
10,000	San Antonio Symphony, San Antonio, TX
6,000	Youth Orchestra, San Antonio, TX -- String Camp 2001
5,000	Cancer Therapy and Research Center, San Antonio, TX -- Wellness Center
5,000	Davis Mountains Trans-Pecos Heritage Association, Alpine, TX -- legal fund
5,000	Environmental Education Fund of Texas, Midland, TX
5,000	National Resources Foundation, Midland, TX
5,000	Texas Public Radio, San Antonio, TX
2,500	Texas A & M Foundation, Houston, TX -- Bush Chair Endowment
2,000	Holy Family Catholic Church, San Antonio, TX -- Pop Warner football trip

GAIA FUND

Giving Contact

Mark L. Schlesinger, Managing Trustee
235 Montgomery St., Suite 1011
San Francisco, CA 94104
Phone: (415)391-6943
Web: http://www.gaiafundsf.org/

Description

Founded: 1997
EIN: 943215541
Organization Type: Private Foundation
Giving Locations: CA: San Francisco
Grant Types: Endowment, General Support, Loan, Project.

Donor Information

Founder: Established in 1997 by Christine Haas Russell.

Financial Summary

Total Giving: $499,050 (2003); $650,450 (2001)
Assets: $11,885,330 (2003); $10,845,717 (2001)
Gifts Received: $423,883 (2003); $323,883 (2000); $870,161 (1998). Note: In 2003, contributions were received from M.H. Russell Charitable Lead Trust ($323,883) and the estate of Leon Russell ($100,000). In 2001, contributions were received from Christine H. Russell. In 2000, contributions were received from M.H. Russell Charitable Trust. In 1998, contributions were received from Madeleine H. Russell. In 1997, contributions were received from Christine H. Russell ($3,039,646).

Typical Recipients

Arts & Humanities: Arts Centers, Ballet, History & Archaeology, Libraries, Museums/Galleries, Music, Opera, Public Broadcasting, Theater
Civic & Public Affairs: Botanical Gardens/Parks, Civil Rights, Ethnic Organizations, First Amendment Issues, Civic & Public Affairs-General, Parades/Festivals, Rural Affairs, Urban & Community Affairs, Women's Affairs, Zoos/Aquariums
Education: Colleges & Universities, Faculty Development, Education-General, Private Education (Precollege), Public Education (Precollege), Student Aid
Environment: Air/Water Quality, Forestry, Environ-

ment-General, Protection, Resource Conservation, Wildlife Protection
Health: AIDS/HIV, Medical Research
International: Health Care/Hospitals, Human Rights, International Development, International Environmental Issues, International Relations
Religion: Jewish Causes, Synagogues/Temples
Science: Scientific Centers & Institutes
Social Services: Community Service Organizations, Family Services, Food/Clothing Distribution, United Funds/United Ways

Application Procedures

Initial Contact: Send a brief letter of inquiry.
Application Requirements: Include a description of organization, amount requested, purpose of funds sought, recently audited financial statement, and proof of tax-exempt status
Deadlines: January 15 for spring funding cycle; September 15 for winter funding cycle.

Restrictions

Does not support individuals, political or lobbying groups, or Jewish day schools. Annual budget of grantee must be less than $1.5 million.

Additional Information

The fund considers grant requests that fall within two programmatic areas: the environment and Jewish life. Preference is given to requests for projects that have annual operating budgets of under $1.5 million.

Foundation Officials

Christine Haas Russell: chief executive officer, director PRIM CORP EMPL chief financial officer: Persistence Software Inc.
Mark L. Schlesinger: cfo, secretary, director

Grants Analysis

Disclosure Period: calendar year ending 2003
Total Grants: $499,050
Number of Grants: 36
Average Grant: $11,830*
Highest Grant: $85,000
Lowest Grant: $500
Typical Range: $5,000 to $20,000
*Note: Average grant figure excludes highest grant.

Recent Grants

Note: Grants derived from 2004 Form 990.

General

85,000	Natural Resources Defense Council, New York, NY
62,500	California Academy of Sciences, San Francisco, CA
50,000	Congregation Emanu - El, San Francisco, CA -- for building preservation fund
50,000	San Francisco Symphony, San Francisco, CA -- for a Jewish culture - themed music festival
30,000	Jewish Community Federation, San Francisco, CA
25,000	California Sustainable Agriculture Working Group, Santa Cruz, CA -- for the campaign for the equitable farm policy
25,000	Jewish Home, San Francisco, CA -- to help rebuild the home's onsite synagogue
25,000	Occidental Arts and Ecology Center, Occidental, CA
25,000	People for the American Way Foundation, Washington, DC -- for the election protection program
20,000	Jewish Community High School of the Bay, San Francisco, CA -- for the scholarship campaign

ERNEST GALLO FOUNDATION

Giving Contact

Ruby Abel
PO Box 1130
Modesto, CA 95353
Phone: (209)341-3203
Fax: (209)341-3324

Description

Founded: 1955
EIN: 946061537
Organization Type: Private Foundation
Giving Locations: CA
Grant Types: General Support.

Donor Information

Founder: members of the Gallo family, E. and J. Gallo Winery

Financial Summary

Total Giving: $1,048,000 (fiscal year ending October 31, 2001)
Giving Analysis: Giving for fiscal 2001 includes: foundation grants to United Way ($5,000)
Assets: $21,461,045 (fiscal 2001)
Gifts Received: $4,922,500 (fiscal 1998); $350,000 (fiscal 1994); $350,000 (fiscal 1993). Note: Contributions were received from E. and J. Gallo Winery and Ernest Gallo.

Typical Recipients

Arts & Humanities: Arts Associations & Councils, Arts Centers, Community Arts, Ethnic & Folk Arts, History & Archaeology, Libraries, Museums/Galleries, Music, Opera, Performing Arts
Civic & Public Affairs: Ethnic Organizations, Civic & Public Affairs-General, Women's Affairs
Education: Colleges & Universities, Education Funds, Private Education (Precollege), Secondary Education (Private), Secondary Education (Public)
Health: Cancer, Clinics/Medical Centers, Diabetes, Eyes/Blindness, Heart, Hospices, Hospitals, Medical Research, Single-Disease Health Associations
International: International Organizations, International Relief Efforts
Religion: Churches, Jewish Causes, Religious Organizations, Religious Welfare
Social Services: Community Centers, Community Service Organizations, Domestic Violence, Family Services, People with Disabilities, Shelters/Homelessness, Social Services-General, United Funds/United Ways, YMCA/YWCA/YMHA/YWHA

Application Procedures

Initial Contact: Send a brief letter of inquiry.
Application Requirements: Include name of applicant and purpose of funds sought.
Deadlines: None.

Foundation Officials

Richard M. Beal: treasurer
Ernest Gallo: president B Jackson, CA 1909. PRIM CORP EMPL co-founder, chairman: E&J Gallo Winery, Inc. PRIM NONPR EMPL president, secretary: Ernest Gallo Clinic & Research Center.
Joseph E. Gallo: vice president B 1941. PRIM CORP EMPL co-president: E&J Gallo Winery, Inc. ADD CORP EMPL president: Gallo International Service; president: Gallo Sales Co. Inc.; owner: Joseph Gallo Farms. CORP AFFIL president: Pacific Coast Beverage Distribution; secretary: Valley Vinters Inc.; director: Fairbanks Trucking Inc.; partner: Midcal.
Mary I. Gallo: vice president
Daniel T. Murray: secretary

Grants Analysis

Disclosure Period: fiscal year ending October 31, 2001

Total Grants: $1,043,000*
Number of Grants: 7
Highest Grant: $1,000,000
Lowest Grant: $1,000
Typical Range: $2,000 to $35,000
*Note: Giving excludes United Way.

Recent Grants

Note: Grants derived from 2002 Form 990.
General

1,000,000	University of California San Francisco, San Francisco, CA
5,000	Barry Bonds Family Foundation, San Francisco, CA
5,000	Juvenile Diabetes Foundation, Modesto, CA
5,000	St. Anthony's Family Center, Modesto, CA
5,000	St. Paul's Lutheran Church, Modeston, CA
5,000	United Way of Stanislaus County, Modesto, CA
2,000	KVIE, Inc., Sacramento, CA
1,000	St. Stanislaus Catholic Church, Modesto, CA
1,000	Sisters of The Cross of The Sacred Heart, Modesto, CA

ROBERT GALVIN FOUNDATION

Giving Contact

Robert W. Galvin, President
1295 E. Algonquin Rd.
Schaumburg, IL 60196
Phone: (847)576-5300
Fax: (847)538-5255

Description

Founded: 1953
EIN: 366065560
Organization Type: Private Foundation
Giving Locations: IL
Grant Types: General Support.

Donor Information

Founder: Robert W. Galvin

Financial Summary

Total Giving: $1,067,518 (2004)
Giving Analysis: Giving for 2004 includes: foundation grants to United Way ($45,438)
Assets: $18,686,191 (2004)
Gifts Received: $175,000 (2004); $230,874 (1996); $250,000 (1994). Note: In 1996 and 2004, contributions were received from the Robert Galvin Trust.

Typical Recipients

Arts & Humanities: Arts Centers, Arts Institutes, Dance, Libraries, Music, Opera
Civic & Public Affairs: Business/Free Enterprise, Civic & Public Affairs-General, Hispanic Affairs, Municipalities/Towns, Philanthropic Organizations, Public Policy, Zoos/Aquariums
Education: Arts/Humanities Education, Business Education, Colleges & Universities, Education Associations, Education Reform, Engineering/Technological Education, Education-General, Legal Education, Medical Education, Private Education (Precollege), Science/Mathematics Education, Student Aid, Vocational & Technical Education
Environment: Environment-General
Health: Children's Health/Hospitals, Clinics/Medical Centers, Emergency/Ambulance Services, Home-Care Services, Hospitals, Medical Rehabilitation, Research/Studies Institutes
International: International Affairs, International Relief Efforts

Religion: Churches, Religious Organizations, Religious Welfare
Science: Observatories & Planetariums, Scientific Centers & Institutes
Social Services: Child Welfare, Day Care, Youth Organizations

Application Procedures

Initial Contact: The foundation has no formal grant application procedure or application form. Send a brief letter of inquiry.
Deadlines: None.

Additional Information

The foundation reports that its funds are fully committed.

Foundation Officials

Mary G. Galvin: secretary, treasurer
Robert William Galvin: president B Marshfield, WI 1922. ED University of Chicago; University of Notre Dame. PRIM CORP EMPL chairman executive committee, director: Motorola Inc. CORP AFFIL member: Electronic Industries Association; chairman: Semantech Inc. NONPR AFFIL chairman: U.S. Trade Rep Industry Policy Advisory Comm; trustee: University Notre Dame; chairman: Sematech; chairman: President Advisory Council Private Sector Initiatives; member: President Private Sector Survey Cost Control; chairman, trustee: Illinois Institute Technology; director: Junior Achievement.

Grants Analysis

Disclosure Period: calendar year ending 2004
Total Grants: $1,022,080*
Number of Grants: 60
Average Grant: $15,628*
Highest Grant: $100,030
Lowest Grant: $5,166
Typical Range: $5,000 to $30,000
*Note: Giving excludes United Way. Average grant figure excludes highest grant.

Recent Grants

Note: Grants derived from 2001 Form 990.
General

700,000	Illinois Institute of Technology, Chicago, IL
300,000	Illinois Institute of Technology, Chicago, IL

GAMBLE FOUNDATION

Giving Contact

Launce E. Gamble, President
PO Box 2655
San Francisco, CA 94126
Phone: (415)782-8102
Fax: (415)782-8109

Description

Founded: 1968
EIN: 941680503
Organization Type: Private Foundation
Giving Locations: CA
Grant Types: General Support.

Donor Information

Founder: Launce E. Gamble, Mary S. Gamble, George F. Gamble

Financial Summary

Total Giving: $367,500 (2003); $334,500 (2001)
Assets: $10,567,355 (2003); $7,519,828 (2001)
Gifts Received: $129,188 (2001); $107,500 (2000); $649,750 (1999). Note: Contributions were received from Launce E. Gamble, Sydney Gamble, Mark D.

Gamble, George F. Gamble, Joan Gamble, James A. Gamble, Aimee Gamble Price, and Launce L. Gamble; miscellaneous contributions of less than $5,000 each also were received.

Typical Recipients

Arts & Humanities: Arts Centers, Ballet, History & Archaeology, Libraries, Museums/Galleries, Music, Opera
Civic & Public Affairs: Botanical Gardens/Parks, Clubs, Community Foundations, Economic Development, Employment/Job Training, Civic & Public Affairs-General, Hispanic Affairs, Law & Justice, Legal Aid, Philanthropic Organizations, Public Policy, Safety, Urban & Community Affairs
Education: Afterschool/Enrichment Programs, Agricultural Education, Arts/Humanities Education, Colleges & Universities, Education Funds, Education-General, Leadership Training, Medical Education, Private Education (Precollege), Religious Education, Science/Mathematics Education, Secondary Education (Private), Secondary Education (Public), Student Aid
Environment: Environment-General, Protection, Resource Conservation, Wildlife Protection
Health: AIDS/HIV, Arthritis, Cancer, Children's Health/Hospitals, Clinics/Medical Centers, Emergency/Ambulance Services, Eyes/Blindness, Health Funds, Heart, Hospitals, Medical Rehabilitation, Medical Research, Public Health
International: Foreign Arts Organizations, Foreign Educational Institutions, International Environmental Issues, International Organizations
Religion: Churches, Jewish Causes, Ministries, Religious Welfare
Science: Science Museums
Social Services: Camps, Child Welfare, Community Centers, Community Service Organizations, Counseling, Family Planning, Family Services, Food/Clothing Distribution, Homes, People with Disabilities, Recreation & Athletics, Scouts, Sexual Abuse, Shelters/Homelessness, United Funds/United Ways, Youth Organizations

Application Procedures

Initial Contact: Send a brief letter of inquiry.
Deadlines: None.

Foundation Officials

Paul E. Cameron: assistant secretary, assistant treasurer
George F. Gamble: vice president
Launce E. Gamble: president
Mark D. Gamble: vice president, treasurer
Aimee Gamble Price: vice president, secretary

Grants Analysis

Disclosure Period: calendar year ending 2003
Total Grants: $367,500
Number of Grants: 56
Average Grant: $6,563
Highest Grant: $40,000
Lowest Grant: $500
Typical Range: $1,000 to $10,000

Recent Grants

Note: Grants derived from 2003 Form 990.
General

40,000	Queen of the Valley
40,000	Queen of the Valley Foundation, Napa, CA
30,000	Jack L. Davies Napa Valley Agricultural Land Preservation Fund, Napa, CA
20,000	Calistoga Friends of the Family Center
20,000	Napa Valley Unified Education Foundation, Napa, CA
15,000	Gateway High School, San Francisco, CA
15,000	Juvenile Justice Network
15,000	Land Trust of Napa County's Connelly Ranch, Napa, CA

15,000	McCormick Sanctuary Acorn Soupe, St. Helena, CA
15,000	Omega Boy's Club, San Francisco, CA

GANNETT COMPANY INC.

Company Headquarters

Arlington, VA
Web: http://www.gannett.com

Company Description

Founded: 1906
Ticker: GCI
Exchange: NYSE
Acquired: Central Newspapers Inc. (2000).
Revenue: US$7.381 billion (2004)
Profit: US$1.317 billion (2004)
Employees: 53000 (2003)
Fortune Rank: 283, per FORTUNE Magazine's list of 500 Largest U.S. Corporations (2004).
SIC(s): 2711 Newspapers, 4832 Radio Broadcasting Stations, 4833 Television Broadcasting Stations, 5063 Electrical Apparatus & Equipment.

Operating Locations

Gannett Co., Inc. (AL; AZ; AR; CA; CT; DE; DC; FL; HI; ID; IL; IA; KS; KY; LA; MI; MS; MO; MT; NV; NY; NC; OH; OK; PA; SC; SD; TN; VT; VA; WA; WI)
Note: Application guidelines come with a complete listing of operating cities for the states listed above.

Nonmonetary Support

Type: In-kind Services
Note: Co. provides nonmonetary support in the form of public service announcements and in-kind advertising for nonprofits. This support is handled locally; contact local office.

Gannett Foundation

Giving Contact

Irma E. Simpson, Manager
7950 Jones Branch Drive
McLean, VA 22107
Phone: (703)854-6000
Fax: (703)854-2002
E-mail: isimpson@gannett.com
Web: http://www.gannettfoundation.org
Note: Grant requests should be made to the local CEOs in communities where Gannett has newspapers and broadcast stations.

Description

EIN: 541568843
Organization Type: Corporate Foundation
Giving Locations: operating locations.
Grant Types: Capital, Employee Matching Gifts, General Support, Project, Scholarship.
Note: Employee matching gift ratio: 1 to 1.

Financial Summary

Total Giving: $9,390,364 (2003); $11,144,000 (2002); $17,725,828 (2001). Note: Contributes through corporate direct giving program and foundation.
Giving Analysis: Giving for 2001 includes: foundation scholarships ($30,000); foundation matching gifts ($236,586); foundation grants to United Way ($613,860).
Assets: $15,954,375 (2003); $25,500,132 (2002); $36,299,024 (2001)
Gifts Received: $12,311,850 (2001). Note: Contributions were received from Gannett Co. Inc.

Typical Recipients

Arts & Humanities: Arts Associations & Councils, Libraries, Museums/Galleries, Music, Performing Arts, Public Broadcasting, Visual Arts
Civic & Public Affairs: African American Affairs, Asian American Affairs, Community Foundations, Economic Development, Employment/Job Training, Gay/Lesbian Issues, Civic & Public Affairs-General, Hispanic Affairs, Housing, Professional & Trade Associations, Public Policy
Education: Afterschool/Enrichment Programs, Business Education, Colleges & Universities, Education Funds, Education Reform, Education-General, Journalism/Media Education, Leadership Training, Literacy, Science/Mathematics Education, Student Aid
Environment: Environment-General
Health: Hospitals, Mental Health, Nursing Services, Single-Disease Health Associations
International: International-General
Religion: Religious Organizations, Religious Welfare
Social Services: Child Welfare, Community Centers, Community Service Organizations, Counseling, Emergency Relief, People with Disabilities, Recreation & Athletics, Senior Services, Shelters/Homelessness, Social Services-General, Special Olympics, United Funds/United Ways, Veterans, Youth Organizations

Application Procedures

Initial Contact: Write or e-mail foundation manager, or call local CEO learn about the local operation's priorities, restrictions, and deadlines. If unsure about your organization's eligibility, a one-page letter of inquiry is welcome. Do not send a proposal directly to the foundation's offices in McLean, VA unless it addresses needs in the Washington, DC metropolitan area.
Application Requirements: Submit two copies of your proposal to the local Gannett CEO. Proposals should be no more than five pages, not including attachments. Include a completed application form (available from the local CEO or on the foundation's web site), statement of need, proof of tax-exempt status, project objectives, organization's qualifications to carry out the project, an indication of whether the project is new or ongoing, constituency to be served, community and volunteer involvement, method of evaluating the project, plans for future funding (if applicable), one-page project budget, organizational budget, list of other committed and pending funding sources, and any publications pertinent to the proposal.
Deadlines: None.
Review Process: Management Contributions Committee meets four times per year from February through November; local CEOs will notify applicants of decisions and distribute funds.
Decision Notification: Decisions generally take between 60 and 90 days.
Notes: If the organization has not been determined a tax-exempt organization under 501(c)(3), send a copy of the application for exempt status.

Restrictions

Fund will not make grants to individuals; organizations without IRS section 501 (c)(3) tax-exempt status; national or regional organizations, unless programs address specific local community needs; programs for religious purposes; elementary or secondary schools (except to provide special initiatives or programs not provided by regular school budgets); political action or legislative advocacy groups; endowment funds; multiple-year pledge campaigns; medical or other research organizations; organizations located in or benefiting nations other than the United States and its territories; fraternal groups; athletic teams; bands; veterans organizations; volunteer firefighters or similar organizations; or organizations outside operating areas. nations other than the United States and its territories; fraternal groups; athletic teams; bands; veterans' organizations; volunteer firefighters or similar organizations; or organizations outside operating areas.

Additional Information

Publications: Foundation Annual Report

Corporate Officials

Christopher W. Baldwin: assistant treasurer PRIM CORP EMPL vice president taxes: Gannett Co. Inc.
Thomas Leslie Chapple: senior vice president, general counsel, chief administrative officer B Canandaigua, NY 1947. ED Cornell University BA (1970); Albany Law School JD (1973). PRIM CORP EMPL senior vice president, general counsel, secretary: Gannett Co., Inc. CORP AFFIL secretary, director: Times Herald Co. Inc.; secretary, director: Pensacola News-Journal Inc.; secretary, director: KPNX Broadcasting Co.; secretary, director: KVUE-TV Inc.; secretary, general counsel: Gannett Co. Inc. DE; secretary, director: Detroit News Inc.; secretary: Florida Gannett Broadcasting; secretary, director: Des Moines Register & Tribune Co. NONPR AFFIL member: New York State Bar Association; member: Sigma Pi Phi; member: Association of Corporate Counsel; member: American Bar Association.
Mimi A. Feller: senior vice president public affairs & government relations B Omaha, NE. ED Creighton University BA (1970); Georgetown University JD (1981). PRIM CORP EMPL senior vice president public affairs & government relations: Gannett Co., Inc.
Gracia C. Martore: senior vice president, chief financial officer B Somerville, MA 1951. ED George Washington University; Wellesley College BA (1973). PRIM CORP EMPL senior vice president, chief financial officer, investor contact: Gannett Co., Inc.
Douglas H. McCorkindale: chairman, president, chief executive officer B New York, NY June 14, 1939. ED Columbia University BA (1961); Columbia University LLB (1964). PRIM CORP EMPL chief executive officer, president, chairman: Gannett Co., Inc. CORP AFFIL director: Visalia Newspapers Inc.; director: WFMY Television Corp.; director: USA Weekend Inc.; director: United States of America Today Information Network; director: USA Today International Corp.; director: United States of America Today; director: Television 12 Jacksonville Inc.; director: Times Herald Co. Inc.; director: Stockton Newspapers Inc.; director: Sun Co. San Bernardino California; director: Statesman-Journal Co.; director: Southland Publishing Co.; director: Speidel Newspapers Inc.; vice president, director: Shelter Media Communication Inc.; director: Sioux Falls Newspapers Inc.; vice president, director: Shelter Media Arizona Inc.; director: Salem County Sampler Inc.; director: Salinas Newspapers Inc.; director: Reno Newspapers Inc.; director: Saint Cloud Newspapers Inc.; director: Pensacola News-Journal Inc.; director: Pacific Media Inc.; vice president, director: Pacific & Southern Co. Inc.; director: Oklahoma Press Publishing Co.; vice president, director: New York Subways Advertising Co. Inc.; director: News-Press Publishing Co.; trustee: Mutual Insurance Co. Ltd.; director: Lockheed Martin Corp.; president, director: McClure Newspapers Inc.; director: KVUE-TV Inc.; director: Lend-A-Hand Inc.; director: KPNX Broadcasting Co.; director: High Yield Income Fund; director: High Yield Plus Fund Inc.; director: Louis Harris & Assoc Inc.; director: Louis Harris International Inc.; director: Guam Publications Inc.; vice chairman, chief financial officer, chief administration off, director: Gannett TG Subsidiary Inc.; director: Global Government Plus Fund Inc.; director: Gannett Television; director: Gannett Texas Broadcasting Inc.; director: Gannett Telemarketing Inc.; president, director: Gannett Satellite Information Network; director: Gannett Supply Corp.; director: Gannett River Saint Publishing Corp.; vice president, director: Gannett Pacific Corp.; director: Gannett Retail Advertising Group; director: Gannett Outdoor Co. Texas; director: Gannett News Service; director: Gannett Newspaper Division; director: Gannett National Newspaper Sales Inc.; director: Gannett News Media; director: Gannett Media Technologies International; president, director: Gannett Internation-

al Communication Inc.; director: Gannett Massachusetts Broadcasting Inc.; director: Gannett Direct Marketing Services Inc.; director: Gannett International; director: Gannett Broadcasting Division; director: Fort Collins Newspapers Inc.; director: Frontier Corp.; director: Eleven-Fifty Corp.; director: Federal Publishing Inc.; director: El Paso Times; director: Desert Sun Publishing Co. Inc.; director: Detroit News Inc.; director: Daily News Publishing Co. Inc.; director: Des Moines Register & Tribune Co.; director: Courier-Journal & Louisville Times Co.; director: Continental Airlines Inc.; director: Courier Broadway Corp.; president, director: Combined Communications Corp.; director: Combined Communications Corp. Oklahoma Inc.; director: Citizen Publishing Co.; director: Cape Publishing Inc.; director: Children's Edition Inc.; director: California Newspapers Inc. NONPR AFFIL director: Associated Press; member: Newspaper Association America; member: American Bar Association. CLUB AFFIL Pine Valley Golf Club; Oak Hills Country Club; Burning Tree Club; Mid-Ocean Club.

Foundation Officials

Christopher W. Baldwin: assistant treasurer (see above)

Thomas Leslie Chapple: president, director (see above)

Tara J. Connell: executive director

Daniel S. Ehrman: vice president

Michael A. Hart: treasurer

Gracia C. Martore: vice president (see above)

Todd A. Mayman: secretary

Douglas H. McCorkindale: director (see above)

Irma E. Simpson: manager

Grants Analysis

Disclosure Period: calendar year ending 2003

Total Grants: $1,074,456*

Number of Grants: 150

Average Grant: $7,173

Highest Grant: $164,000

Lowest Grant: $250

Typical Range: $1,000 to $10,000

*Note: Giving excludes matching gifts; scholarships, United Way.

Recent Grants

Note: Grants derived from 2003 Form 990.

Library-Related

52,627	Fairfax County Public Library Foundation, Fairfax, VA -- to assist in the motherhood/ fatherhood program

General

164,000	Southern Newspaper Publishers Association Foundation, Atlanta, GA -- to assist the newsroom training program
164,000	Southern Newspaper Publishers Association Foundation, Atlanta, GA -- to support the national newsroom training program
150,000	University of Iowa Foundation, Iowa City, IA -- fund for naming opportunity within the new journalism school building
115,000	American Press Institute, Reston, VA
65,000	Association for Education in Journalism and Mass Communication, Columbia, SC -- fund to train eventual dean or directorships of college journalism programs
45,000	Foundation for American Communications, Los Angeles, CA -- to support 3 state-wide training programs for working journalists
35,000	Florida International University, North Miami, FL -- to assist a program to introduce Hispanic journalism students to job opportunities
30,000	American Red Cross, Hagatna Guam -- to assist disaster relief for December 2002 typhoon
30,000	Investigative Reporters & Editors, Columbia, MO -- fund for the NICAR conference in Charlotte and the convention in DC

25,000	Hospital Research and Educational Trust/American Organization of Nurse Executives, Washington, DC -- to support Nursing the Future program to attract young people into nursing careers

GAP INC.

Company Headquarters

San Francisco, CA

Web: http://www.gap.com

Company Description

Founded: 1969

Ticker: GPS

Exchange: NYSE

Former Name: Gap Foundation.

Revenue: US$16.267 billion (2004)

Profit: US$1.15 billion (2004)

Employees: 153000 (2003)

Fortune Rank: 130, per FORTUNE Magazine's list of 500 Largest U.S. Corporations (2004).

SIC(s): 5651 Family Clothing Stores.

Operating Locations

Gap, Inc. (CA--San Bruno, San Francisco)

Note: Operates throughout the USA.

Nonmonetary Support

Value: $1,240,000 (1999 approx)

Type: Donated Equipment; Donated Products; In-kind Services

Volunteer Programs: The company sponsors an employee volunteer effort, wherein headquarter's employees receive five hours per month of paid leave to volunteer, and field staff participate in on-going special volunteer projects.

Contact: Molly White, Senior Director

Note: Co. awards merchandise, office equipment (computers), and gift certificates.

Gap Foundation

Giving Contact

Gap Foundation

2 Folsom Street, 14th Floor

San Francisco, CA 94105

Phone: (415)427-2000

Web: http://www.gapinc.com/public/ SocialResponsibility/socialres.shtml

Description

Founded: 1969

EIN: 942474426

Organization Type: Corporate Foundation

Giving Locations: CA: Los Angeles, San Francisco; IL: Chicago; NY: New York headquarters and operating locations.

Grant Types: Employee Matching Gifts, General Support.

Note: Employee matching gift ratio: 1 to 1 up to $2,000 per employee annually, including monies raised by employees via pledges collected for official fundraising events carried on by charitable organizations.

Financial Summary

Total Giving: $5,456,964 (fiscal year ending January 31, 2004); $4,721,525 (fiscal 2003); $5,851,892 (fiscal 2002). Note: Contributes through corporate direct giving program only.

Giving Analysis: Giving for fiscal 2003 includes: foundation grants to United Way ($10,000); foundation matching gifts ($1,599,057); fiscal 2002: foundation ($5,851,892); fiscal 2001: foundation grants to United Way ($15,000); foundation matching gifts

($550,486); foundation ($7,073,091)

Assets: $7,798,771 (fiscal 2004); $6,879,477 (fiscal 2003); $10,993,336 (fiscal 2002)

Gifts Received: $5,629,377 (fiscal 2004); $418,228 (fiscal 2003); $2,060,289 (fiscal 2002). Note: Contributions were received from The Gap, Inc.

Typical Recipients

Arts & Humanities: Arts Associations & Councils, Arts Centers, Arts Festivals, Arts Institutes, Arts Outreach, Ballet, Dance, Film & Video, Arts & Humanities-General, Historic Preservation, Libraries, Museums/Galleries, Music, Opera, Performing Arts, Public Broadcasting, Theater, Visual Arts

Civic & Public Affairs: African American Affairs, Asian American Affairs, Botanical Gardens/Parks, Business/Free Enterprise, Civil Rights, Community Foundations, Economic Development, Employment/ Job Training, Gay/Lesbian Issues, Civic & Public Affairs-General, Hispanic Affairs, Housing, Legal Aid, Municipalities/Towns, Nonprofit Management, Philanthropic Organizations, Urban & Community Affairs, Zoos/Aquariums

Education: Afterschool/Enrichment Programs, Arts/ Humanities Education, Business Education, Colleges & Universities, Community & Junior Colleges, Education Associations, Education Funds, Education Reform, Elementary Education (Public), Engineering/ Technological Education, Education-General, Leadership Training, Medical Education, Minority Education, Private Education (Precollege), Public Education (Precollege), Religious Education, School Volunteerism, Science/Mathematics Education, Student Aid

Environment: Air/Water Quality, Forestry, Environment-General, Protection, Resource Conservation, Watershed, Wildlife Protection

Health: AIDS/HIV, Cancer, Clinics/Medical Centers, Emergency/Ambulance Services, Eyes/Blindness, Health-General, Health Funds, Health Organizations, Hospices, Hospitals, Medical Research, Prenatal Health Issues, Preventive Medicine/Wellness Organizations, Public Health, Research/Studies Institutes, Single-Disease Health Associations, Transplant Networks/Donor Banks, Trauma Treatment

International: Foreign Educational Institutions, International-General, International Relief Efforts, Missionary/Religious Activities

Religion: Churches, Dioceses, Religious Organizations, Religious Welfare

Science: Science-General, Science Museums, Scientific Centers & Institutes

Social Services: Camps, Child Abuse, Child Welfare, Community Centers, Community Service Organizations, Day Care, Delinquency & Criminal Rehabilitation, Domestic Violence, Emergency Relief, Family Services, Food/Clothing Distribution, Recreation & Athletics, Senior Services, Shelters/Homelessness, United Funds/United Ways, Volunteer Services, YMCA/YWCA/YMHA/YWHA, Youth Organizations

Application Procedures

Initial Contact: Unsolicited applications for cash grants are not accepted. The Gap Foundation donates a limited number of GiftCards to public schools and nonprofit youth-serving organizations in New York City and the San Francisco Bay area. To request a GiftCard donation, submit a one-page letter on the applicant organization's letterhead.

Application Requirements: Letters of request should include a description of organization; organization's federal tax-exempt number; a description of the project or event for which the GiftCards will be used; amount requested; date by which the donation is needed; and how the contributions will be acknowledged at the event/program.

Deadlines: None.

Decision Notification: Applicants will be notified only if the foundation approves a request. Allow six weeks for request processing.

Notes: San Francisco Bay area requests for Gift-Cards should be submitted to the attention of the Gift-

Card Program at the foundation address listed above. New York City area requests should be submitted to: GiftCard Program, Gap Foundation, 620 Avenue of the Americas, New York, NY 10011.

Restrictions

Does not donate to individuals, political organizations/candidates, religious organizations, or organizations that discriminate.

Additional Information

The company reports that it will continue to donate 1% of its pre-tax earnings to charitable giving.

The Gap's divisions include Banana Republic, Gap Stores, GapKids, BabyGap, Gap Shoes, Gap Warehouses, and Old Navy.

The Gap reports that it donates cash, gift certificates, and limited contributions of merchandise.

Publications: Annual Report; Funding Guidelines

Corporate Officials

Millard S. Drexler: president, chief executive officer, directorresources, legal, administration B New York, NY 1944. ED State University of New York Buffalo BS; Boston University MBA (1968). PRIM CORP EMPL president, chief executive officer, director: Gap, Inc. CORP AFFIL president: Banana Republic Inc.; director: Williams-Sonoma Inc.; president, chief executive officer, director: Ann Taylor Stores.

Anne B. Gust: executive vice president human resources, legal, administration PRIM CORP EMPL executive vice president human resources, legal, administration: Gap Inc.

Foundation Officials

Donald G. Fisher: chairman, director
Doris F. Fisher: director
Anne B. Gust: secretary, treasurer (see above)
Marka Hansen: director
Paul Pressler: president, director

Grants Analysis

Disclosure Period: fiscal year ending January 31, 2004
Total Grants: $3,601,596*
Number of Grants: 231
Average Grant: $14,293*
Highest Grant: $300,000
Lowest Grant: $250
Typical Range: $5,000 to $30,000
*Note: Giving excludes matching gifts; United Way. Average grant figure excludes highest grant.

Recent Grants

Note: Grants derived from 2004 Form 990.

General

500,000	San Francisco Boys Club, San Francisco, CA
300,000	Lorraine Monroe Leadership Institute, New York, NY
250,000	San Francisco Boys Club, San Francisco, CA
250,000	San Francisco Boys Club, San Francisco, CA
53,000	Hands on San Francisco, San Francisco, CA
50,000	Boys and Girls Clubs of San Francisco, San Francisco, CA
50,000	Community Corps, San Francisco, CA
50,000	Door Career Development Program, New York, NY
50,000	Glide Memorial United Methodist Church, San Francisco, CA
50,000	Harlem Children's Zone Incorporated, New York, NY

GAR FOUNDATION

Giving Contact

Robert W. Briggs, Executive Director
50 South Main Street
PO Box 1500
Akron, OH 44309-1500
Phone: (330)643-0201
Fax: (330)252-5584
E-mail: gar@bdblaw.com
Web: http://www.garfdn.org

Description

Founded: 1967
EIN: 346577710
Organization Type: Family Foundation
Giving Locations: OH: Summit County and 5 surrounding counties
Grant Types: Capital, Challenge, Conference/Seminar, Endowment, Fellowship, General Support, Matching, Multiyear/Continuing Support, Operating Expenses, Project, Scholarship, Seed Money.

Donor Information

Founder: The late Galen Roush and his wife, the late Ruth C. Roush, established the GAR Foundation in 1967 in Ohio. Mr. Roush was a lawyer and the principal founder and chief executive of Roadway Express, one of the country's 25 largest transportation companies. Because they were raised in the Akron-northeastern Ohio area, the Roushes preferred to fund philanthropic organizations based in this section of Ohio. Mrs. Roush, an Oberlin College graduate, was interested in music, art, and education. As a result, the foundation gives significant support to arts and educational programs. Mr. Roush graduated from Hiram College and received his law degree from Case Western Reserve University. Both Mr. and Mrs. Roush firmly believed in the free enterprise system in which they had prospered. The foundation is endowed by their respective estates.

Financial Summary

Total Giving: $7,348,461 (2002); $6,821,126 (2001)
Giving Analysis: Giving for 2002 includes: foundation grants to United Way ($749,100); 2001: foundation grants to United Way ($55,000)
Assets: $180,000,000 (2003 approx); $135,999,035 (2002); $167,850,596 (2001)

Typical Recipients

Arts & Humanities: Arts Centers, Arts Festivals, Arts Institutes, Arts Outreach, Ballet, Community Arts, Historic Preservation, History & Archaeology, Libraries, Museums/Galleries, Music, Opera, Performing Arts, Public Broadcasting, Theater
Civic & Public Affairs: Botanical Gardens/Parks, Business/Free Enterprise, Community Foundations, Economic Development, Employment/Job Training, Civic & Public Affairs-General, Housing, Inner-City Development, Municipalities/Towns, Nonprofit Management, Philanthropic Organizations, Public Policy, Urban & Community Affairs, Zoos/Aquariums
Education: Afterschool/Enrichment Programs, Arts/Humanities Education, Business Education, Colleges & Universities, Education Associations, Education Funds, Education Reform, Elementary Education (Private), Environmental Education, Faculty Development, Education-General, Literacy, Medical Education, Minority Education, Private Education (Precollege), Public Education (Precollege), Religious Education, Science/Mathematics Education, Secondary Education (Private), Secondary Education (Public), Social Sciences Education, Special Education, Student Aid, Vocational & Technical Education
Environment: Environment-General, Protection, Resource Conservation, Wildlife Protection
Health: Alzheimer's Disease, Cancer, Children's Health/Hospitals, Clinics/Medical Centers, Emergency/Ambulance Services, Eyes/Blindness, Health-

General, Health Funds, Health Organizations, Hospices, Hospitals, Mental Health, Multiple Sclerosis, Nursing Services, Prenatal Health Issues, Public Health
International: International Environmental Issues
Religion: Churches, Ministries, Religious Organizations, Religious Welfare
Science: Science Exhibits & Fairs, Science Museums
Social Services: At-Risk Youth, Camps, Community Centers, Community Service Organizations, Day Care, Emergency Relief, Family Planning, Family Services, Food/Clothing Distribution, Homes, People with Disabilities, Recreation & Athletics, Scouts, Senior Services, Shelters/Homelessness, Substance Abuse, United Funds/United Ways, YMCA/YWCA/YMHA/YWHA, Youth Organizations

Application Procedures

Initial Contact: Applicants should request and complete the foundation's application form.
Application Requirements: Application information should include verification of tax-exempt status; detailed budget; latest IRS Form 990; description of general purposes and activities; list of members of governing board; other sources of funding; amount requested; and contact person's name.
Deadlines: The application should be submitted by February 1, May 1, August 1, and November 1. The distribution committee meets the second Thursday of February, May, August, and November.
Review Process: The applicants will receive acknowledgement upon receipt and written notification of the decision within several weeks of each meeting.
Notes: Grants are made to endowment funds, particularly to those of educational institutions, including the endowment of chairs and scholarship funds. However, the foundation has strict guidelines on the means of memorializing endowment funds to ensure that the principal of an endowment grant is not used without the written consent of the GAR Foundation. All recipients of grants must inform the foundation of the project's progress and completion, and provide a fiscal and program summary. Funds not used as designated must be returned to the foundation. Endowment recipients must report on an annual basis that grant funds are intact and only income has been expended in accordance with the endowment policy established by the foundation.

Restrictions

Ordinarily, grants are not made for general operating expenses not directly related to the grantee's purpose, to individuals, to other private non-operating foundations, to mass appeal fund-raising drives, to national organizations, or to hospitals or their affiliated foundations except for collaborative efforts which are permitted under the law and are designed to reduce costs and promote efficient delivery of medical services.

Additional Information

No grant is made for more than a calendar year. No grant will be renewed or made for a new project by the same grantee without a formal application being filed. Renewals cannot be guaranteed from year to year.

The foundation lists National City Bank as a co-trustee.

Publications: Application Form; Guidelines

Foundation Officials

Robert Briggs: co-trustee, executive director ED Duke University BA; Ohio State University JD. NONPR AFFIL trustee: Northeast Ohio Council on Higher Education; trustee: Northeast Ohio Technology Coalition; trustee: Musical Arts Association; chairman, trustee: National Inventors Hall of Fame; trustee: Catholic Diocese of Cleveland Foundation; chairman: Fund for Our Economic Future; co-chairman, board of overseers: Blossom Music Center.

Grants Analysis

Disclosure Period: calendar year ending 2002
Total Grants: $6,599,361*
Number of Grants: 99
Average Grant: $53,406*
Highest Grant: $918,000
Lowest Grant: $3,000
Typical Range: $10,000 to $100,000
*Note: Giving excludes United Way. Average grant figure excludes two highest grants ($1,418,000).

Recent Grants

Note: Grants derived from 2002 Form 990.
General

918,000	Akron Art Museum, Akron, OH -- for endowment and operations
700,000	United Way of Summit County, Akron, OH -- fund for annual campaign
500,000	Community Hall Foundation Inc., Akron, OH -- fund for Kresge Foundation challenges
325,000	Archbishop Hoban High School, Akron, OH -- fund for faculty and financial endowment
250,000	American Red Cross Summit County Chapter, Akron, OH -- to support maintenance and operations
250,000	Center for Nonprofit Excellence, Akron, OH
235,000	East Akron Community House Association, Akron, OH -- fund for construction costs
200,000	Great Trail Council Boy Scouts of America Inc., Akron, OH -- to assist in the off-site sewer project
190,000	National Inventors Hall of Fame Inc., Akron, OH -- fund for development, training, and for five Camp Invention camps in Akron
189,848	Summit Education Initiative, Akron, OH -- for educational project

GARDINER SAVINGS INSTITUTION

Company Headquarters

190 Water St.
Gardiner, ME 04345

Company Description

Employees: 100
SIC(s): 6000 Depository Institutions.

Gardiner Savings Institution Charitable Foundation

Giving Contact

Arthur Markos, President & Chief Executive Officer
190 Water St.
PO Box 190
Gardiner, ME 04345-2109
Phone: (207)582-5550
Fax: (207)582-8029

Description

Founded: 1990
EIN: 010446023
Organization Type: Corporate Foundation
Giving Locations: headquarters and operating communities.
Grant Types: General Support, Scholarship.

Financial Summary

Total Giving: $416,685 (2003)
Giving Analysis: Giving for 2003 includes: foundation grants to United Way ($12,500)
Assets: $2,966,789 (2003)
Gifts Received: $300,000 (2000); $325,000 (1999); $250,000 (1998). Note: In 1996, 1999 and 2000, contributions were received from Gardiner Savings Institution.

Typical Recipients

Arts & Humanities: Arts Centers, Historic Preservation, History & Archaeology, Libraries, Music, Opera, Performing Arts, Public Broadcasting, Theater
Civic & Public Affairs: Botanical Gardens/Parks, Clubs, Civic & Public Affairs-General, Municipalities/Towns, Rural Affairs, Safety, Urban & Community Affairs, Women's Affairs
Education: Colleges & Universities, Education Funds, Elementary Education (Private), Education-General, Literacy, Private Education (Precollege), Public Education (Precollege), School Volunteerism, Secondary Education (Private), Secondary Education (Public), Vocational & Technical Education
Environment: Environment-General, Resource Conservation
Health: Alzheimer's Disease, Emergency/Ambulance Services, Health Funds, Health Organizations, Hospices, Hospitals, Mental Health
Religion: Churches, Ministries, Religious Welfare
Science: Science Museums
Social Services: Child Abuse, Child Welfare, Community Centers, Community Service Organizations, Emergency Relief, Family Services, Food/Clothing Distribution, Homes, Recreation & Athletics, Scouts, Senior Services, Social Services-General, Substance Abuse, United Funds/United Ways, YMCA/YWCA/YMHA/YWHA, Youth Organizations

Application Procedures

Initial Contact: The foundation reports no specific application guidelines. Send a brief letter of inquiry.
Application Requirements: Include statement of purpose, amount requested, and proof of tax-exempt status.
Deadlines: None.

Additional Information

Trust(s): Gardiner Savings Inst

Corporate Officials

Douglas C. Cooper: chairman, chief executive officer PRIM CORP EMPL chairman: Gardiner Savings Institution.
Arthur C. Markos: president, chief executive officer PRIM CORP EMPL president, chief executive officer: Gardiner Savings Institution.

Foundation Officials

Everett L. Ayer: mem
Richard L. Goodwin: vice chairman
Al C. Graceffa: member
George W. Heselton: chairman
Robert P. Lacasse: member
Arthur C. Markos: president, director (see above)
Paul F. McClay: mem
Anita M. Nored: treasurer
John G. Rizzo: member

Grants Analysis

Disclosure Period: calendar year ending 2003
Total Grants: $404,185*
Number of Grants: 236
Average Grant: $873*
Highest Grant: $100,000
Lowest Grant: $41
Typical Range: $200 to $2,000
*Note: Giving excludes United Way. Average grant figure excludes two highest grants ($200,000).

Recent Grants

Note: Grants derived from 2003 Form 990.
Library-Related

6,667	Topsham Public Library, Topsham, ME
5,800	Oakland Library, Oakland, CA

General

100,000	Gardiner Boys/Girls Club, Gardiner, ME
100,000	Kennebec Valley YMCA, Augusta, ME
25,000	Opera House at Boothbay Harbor, Boothbay Harbor, ME
10,000	Boys and Girls Club of Greater Gardiner, Gardiner, ME
8,600	United Way of Kennebec Valley, Augusta, ME
7,000	Johnson Hall, Gardiner, ME
5,000	Bath YMCA, Bath, ME
5,000	Children's Center, Portland, ME
5,000	Lincoln Academy, Newcastle, ME
5,000	Maine General Health Alzheimer's Care Center, Gardiner, ME

GARFINKLE-MINARD FOUNDATION, INC.

Giving Contact

Shivaun McDonagh
133 East 62nd Street
New York, NY 10021
Phone: (212)486-0194

Description

Founded: 1989
EIN: 650104540
Organization Type: Private Foundation
Giving Locations: DC: Washington; NY: New York
Grant Types: General Support.

Financial Summary

Total Giving: $83,525 (2003); $183,095 (2001)
Assets: $945 (2003); $137,265 (2001)
Gifts Received: $136,656 (2001). Note: In 2001, contributions were received from Norton Garfinkle and Sally Minard.

Typical Recipients

Arts & Humanities: Arts Institutes, Historic Preservation, Libraries, Museums/Galleries, Public Broadcasting, Theater
Civic & Public Affairs: Clubs, Civic & Public Affairs-General, Public Policy, Urban & Community Affairs, Women's Affairs
Education: Arts/Humanities Education, Colleges & Universities, Private Education (Precollege), School Volunteerism
Environment: Environment-General, Resource Conservation
Health: AIDS/HIV, Cancer, Hospices
International: Foreign Educational Institutions, International Relations, Missionary/Religious Activities
Religion: Jewish Causes, Religious Welfare
Science: Scientific Centers & Institutes
Social Services: Child Welfare, Emergency Relief, Family Services

Application Procedures

Initial Contact: Submit a letter of inquiry on organization's letterhead.
Application Requirements: Include a description of organization, proof of tax-exempt status, and latest annual report.
Deadlines: None.

Foundation Officials

Gillian Garfinkle: director
Nicholas Garfinkle: director
Norton Garfinkle: chairman, director
Sally Minard: president, director

Grants Analysis

Disclosure Period: calendar year ending 2003
Total Grants: $83,525
Number of Grants: 45
Average Grant: $1,444*
Highest Grant: $20,000
Lowest Grant: $50
Typical Range: $100 to $1,000
*Note: Average grant figure excludes highest grant.

Recent Grants

Note: Grants derived from 2003 Form 990.
General

20,000	New School University, New York, NY
10,840	National Partnership for Women, Washington, DC
8,300	American Red Cross, New York, NY
8,000	New York Landmark Conservancy, New York, NY
5,398	New York Women's Agenda, New York, NY
4,662	White House, New York, NY
4,615	Folksbiene Yiddish Theatre, New York, NY
1,850	East Side House Settlement, Bronx, NY
1,350	Metropolitan Museum of Art, New York, NY
1,200	Conservators Program, New York, NY

DAVID B. GARVER CHARITY FUND

Giving Contact

c/o Bellefonte Elks Lodge
120 High St.
Bellefonte, PA 16823
Phone: (717)780-3037

Description

Founded: 1991
EIN: 256212802
Organization Type: Private Foundation
Giving Locations: PA: Bellefonte
Grant Types: General Support.

Financial Summary

Total Giving: $25,007 (fiscal year ending January 31, 2004)
Giving Analysis: Giving for fiscal 2003 includes: foundation grants to United Way ($12,500)
Assets: $948,821 (fiscal 2004)
Gifts Received: $14,338 (fiscal 1999); $2,000 (fiscal 1997)

Typical Recipients

Arts & Humanities: Arts Funds, History & Archaeology, Libraries, Music
Civic & Public Affairs: Clubs, Civic & Public Affairs-General, Municipalities/Towns, Safety, Urban & Community Affairs
Education: Public Education (Precollege), School Volunteerism, Science/Mathematics Education, Secondary Education (Public)
Health: Cancer, Emergency/Ambulance Services, Home-Care Services, Hospitals
Social Services: Community Service Organizations, Family Services, Recreation & Athletics, Scouts, YMCA/YWCA/YMHA/YWHA, Youth Organizations

Application Procedures

Initial Contact: Send a brief letter of inquiry.
Application Requirements: Include a description of organization, amount requested, reason for request, and proof of tax-exempt status.
Deadlines: Quarterly.

Restrictions

Provides grants for the needy and civic projects in Bellefonte and vicinity.

Additional Information

Trust(s): Mellon Bank

Grants Analysis

Disclosure Period: fiscal year ending January 31, 2004
Total Grants: $25,007
Number of Grants: 19
Average Grant: $1,316
Highest Grant: $3,200
Lowest Grant: $200
Typical Range: $500 to $3,000

Recent Grants

Note: Grants derived from 2001 Form 990.
General

5,000	Snow Shoe Borough Council (Fire Company), Snow Shoe, PA
3,500	Centre County Historical Society, Bellefonte, PA
2,500	American Cancer Society, Baltimore, MD
2,500	Bellefonte Youth Football Association, Bellefonte, PA

EDWARD CHASE GARVEY MEMORIAL FOUNDATION

Giving Contact

Cindy Lewis
Commerce Bank
8000 Forsyth Blvd.
Clayton, MO 63105
Phone: (314)746-7332

Description

Founded: 1970
EIN: 436132744
Organization Type: Private Foundation
Giving Locations: MO: St. Louis
Grant Types: General Support.

Donor Information

Founder: the late Edward C. Garvey

Financial Summary

Total Giving: $250,000 (fiscal year ending September 30, 2003); $320,000 (fiscal 2001)
Assets: $5,032,083 (fiscal 2003); $5,749,535 (fiscal 2001)

Typical Recipients

Arts & Humanities: Arts Centers, Arts Outreach, Community Arts, Dance, Arts & Humanities-General, History & Archaeology, Libraries, Literary Arts, Museums/Galleries, Music, Opera, Performing Arts, Theater
Civic & Public Affairs: Botanical Gardens/Parks, Civic & Public Affairs-General, Zoos/Aquariums
Education: Arts/Humanities Education, Colleges & Universities, Private Education (Precollege), Science/Mathematics Education, Secondary Education (Private), Secondary Education (Public), Special Education, Vocational & Technical Education
Environment: Environment-General, Wildlife Protection
Health: Eyes/Blindness
Science: Scientific Centers & Institutes
Social Services: Animal Protection, Child Welfare, Family Planning, People with Disabilities, Social Services-General, Youth Organizations

Application Procedures

Initial Contact: Send a brief letter of inquiry.
Application Requirements: Include proof of tax-exempt status and most recent budget.
Deadlines: None.

Restrictions

Does not support individuals.

Additional Information

Trust(s): Commerce Bank St Louis

Foundation Officials

Bliss Lewis Shands: trustee

Grants Analysis

Disclosure Period: fiscal year ending September 30, 2003
Total Grants: $250,000
Number of Grants: 29
Average Grant: $8,621
Highest Grant: $25,000
Lowest Grant: $2,000
Typical Range: $2,000 to $16,000

Recent Grants

Note: Grants derived from fiscal 2003 Form 990.
General

20,000	Missouri Botanical Garden, St. Louis, MO
20,000	Opera Theater of St. Louis, St. Louis, MO
20,000	Webster University
18,000	St. George's School
16,000	St. Louis Symphony Orchestra, St. Louis, MO
11,000	Stray Rescue of St. Louis, St. Louis, MO
9,000	Central Institute for the Deaf, St. Louis, MO
9,000	Frank Lloyd Wright House, St. Louis, MO
8,000	Open Door Animal Sanctuary, St. Louis, MO
8,000	Ranken Technical College, St. Louis, MO

GARVEY TEXAS FOUNDATION

Giving Contact

Shirley F. Garvey, President
PO Box 9600
Ft. Worth, TX 76147-2600
Phone: (817)335-5881

Description

Founded: 1962
EIN: 756031547
Organization Type: Private Foundation
Giving Locations: CO; KS; NE; OK; TX
Grant Types: Capital, General Support, Research.

Donor Information

Founder: James S. Garvey, Shirley F. Garvey, Garvey Foundation

Financial Summary

Total Giving: $408,660 (2003)
Assets: $8,853,033 (2003)
Gifts Received: $32,374 (1998); $6,300 (1996); $5,500 (1995). Note: In 1998, contributions were received from Fifty Charitable Trust. In 1996, contributions were received from Fifty Charitable Trust ($1,800) and Garvey, Inc. ($4,500).

Typical Recipients

Arts & Humanities: Arts Associations & Councils, Arts Centers, Arts Festivals, Ballet, Dance, Historic Preservation, History & Archaeology, Libraries, Museums/Galleries, Music, Opera, Performing Arts, Public Broadcasting, Theater

Civic & Public Affairs: Clubs, Civic & Public Affairs-General, Hispanic Affairs, Housing, Municipalities/Towns, Parades/Festivals, Philanthropic Organizations, Public Policy, Safety, Urban & Community Affairs, Zoos/Aquariums
Education: Agricultural Education, Arts/Humanities Education, Colleges & Universities, Community & Junior Colleges, Education Funds, Education Reform, Education-General, Minority Education, Private Education (Precollege), Public Education (Precollege), Student Aid
Environment: Environment-General, Research, Resource Conservation
Health: Alzheimer's Disease, Cancer, Children's Health/Hospitals, Emergency/Ambulance Services, Health Policy/Cost Containment, Health Organizations, Hospices, Hospitals, Medical Research, Public Health, Research/Studies Institutes, Respiratory, Single-Disease Health Associations, Speech & Hearing
International: International Relations
Religion: Churches, Religious Organizations, Religious Welfare
Science: Science Museums
Social Services: Big Brothers/Big Sisters, Child Welfare, Community Centers, Community Service Organizations, Counseling, Crime Prevention, Domestic Violence, Family Planning, Family Services, Food/Clothing Distribution, Homes, Recreation & Athletics, Scouts, Senior Services, Substance Abuse, United Funds/United Ways, YMCA/YWCA/YMHA/YWHA, Youth Organizations

Application Procedures

Initial Contact: Send a brief letter of inquiry. Include a description of organization, amount requested, and proof of tax-exempt status.
Deadlines: None.

Restrictions

Does not support individuals.

Foundation Officials

Richard F. Garvey: secretary PRIM CORP EMPL vice president: JaGee Corp. CORP AFFIL sec: Garvey Enterprises; secretary, director: Jim Garvey Ranches; secretary, director: Garvey Elevators.
Shirley F. Garvey: president
Carol G. Sweat: vice president

Grants Analysis

Disclosure Period: calendar year ending 2003
Total Grants: $408,660
Number of Grants: 93
Average Grant: $3,572*
Highest Grant: $80,000
Lowest Grant: $100
Typical Range: $1,000 to $5,000
*Note: Average grant figure excludes highest grant.

Recent Grants

Note: Grants derived from 2001 Form 990.

General

40,000	National Cowgirl Museum and Hall of Fame, Ft. Worth, TX
30,000	Texas Christian University, Ft. Worth, TX
29,500	Fort Worth Country Day School, Ft. Worth, TX
25,000	Colby United Methodist Church
25,000	Fort Worth Symphony Orchestra Association, Ft. Worth, TX
23,100	First United Methodist Church
20,000	Child Study Center Foundation, Ft. Worth, TX
15,860	Amon Carter Museum, Ft. Worth, TX
15,100	Warm Place, Ft. Worth, TX
12,000	Happy Hill Farm, Ft. Worth, TX

GATES FAMILY FOUNDATION

Giving Contact

C. Thomas Kaesemeyer, Executive Director
3575 Cherry Creek North Drive, Suite 100
Denver, CO 80209
Phone: (303)722-1881
Fax: (303)316-3038
E-mail: info@gatesfamilyfoundation.org
Web: http://www.gatesfamilyfoundation.org

Description

Founded: 1946
EIN: 840474837
Organization Type: Family Foundation
Giving Locations: CO
Grant Types: Capital, General Support, Matching, Multiyear/Continuing Support.

Donor Information

Founder: The Gates Foundation was established in Colorado in 1946 by the late Charles C. Gates Sr., and members of the Gates family. Gates Corporation, an aircraft parts, instruments, and mechanical rubber goods company, was founded in 1911 by Mr. Gates. In 1961, he transferred the presidency of the company to his son, Charles C. Gates, Jr. The company is one of the largest privately-owned companies in the country, and Charles Gates, Jr., remains the chairman, president, and chief executive officer.

Financial Summary

Total Giving: $8,018,744 (2003); $8,733,861 (2002); $9,917,669 (2001). Note: Giving for 2000 includes grants from Bernice Gates Hopper and Robert E. Hopper family funds.
Assets: $237,190,970 (2003); $173,119,408 (2002); $182,031,741 (2001)
Gifts Received: $35,753,141 (2002); $1,000,000 (2001); $1,967,985 (1998). Note: In 2002, contributions were received from the estate of June Swaner Gates. In 2001, contributions were received from Bernice Gates Hopper. In 1998, contributions were received from Bernice Gates Hopper ($983,993) and Robert E. Hopper ($983,993).

Typical Recipients

Arts & Humanities: Arts Associations & Councils, Arts Centers, Arts Funds, Arts Outreach, Ballet, Dance, Ethnic & Folk Arts, Arts & Humanities-General, Historic Preservation, History & Archaeology, Libraries, Museums/Galleries, Music, Opera, Performing Arts, Public Broadcasting, Theater, Visual Arts
Civic & Public Affairs: Botanical Gardens/Parks, Business/Free Enterprise, Clubs, Community Foundations, Economic Development, Employment/Job Training, Civic & Public Affairs-General, Housing, Inner-City Development, Municipalities/Towns, Native American Affairs, Parades/Festivals, Professional & Trade Associations, Public Policy, Rural Affairs, Urban & Community Affairs, Women's Affairs, Zoos/Aquariums
Education: Afterschool/Enrichment Programs, Arts/Humanities Education, Business Education, Colleges & Universities, Community & Junior Colleges, Continuing Education, Economic Education, Education Associations, Education Funds, Education Reform, Elementary Education (Private), Engineering/Technological Education, Faculty Development, Education-General, Gifted & Talented Programs, International Studies, Leadership Training, Literacy, Preschool Education, Private Education (Precollege), Public Education (Precollege), Science/Mathematics Education, Secondary Education (Private), Secondary Education (Public), Social Sciences Education, Student Aid
Environment: Environment-General, Protection, Resource Conservation

Health: Children's Health/Hospitals, Clinics/Medical Centers, Health-General, Health Policy/Cost Containment, Medical Rehabilitation
Religion: Bible Study/Translation, Dioceses, Religion-General, Jewish Causes, Ministries, Religious Welfare
Science: Science Museums, Scientific Centers & Institutes, Scientific Organizations, Scientific Research
Social Services: Animal Protection, At-Risk Youth, Camps, Child Abuse, Child Welfare, Community Centers, Community Service Organizations, Crime Prevention, Day Care, Domestic Violence, Family Planning, Family Services, Food/Clothing Distribution, People with Disabilities, Recreation & Athletics, Scouts, Senior Services, Shelters/Homelessness, Social Services-General, Substance Abuse, United Funds/United Ways, YMCA/YWCA/YMHA/YWHA, Youth Organizations

Application Procedures

Initial Contact: Applicants may call a program officer before submitting a proposal. A letter of inquiry may also be submitted, including a brief narrative description of the proposed project. If interested the foundation will request a completed copy of the Common Grant Application.
Deadlines: January 15 for the April 1 meeting; April 1 for the June 15 meeting; July 1 for the October 1 meeting; and October 1 for the December 15 meeting.
Review Process: The foundation's staff acknowledges and reviews all applications, and notifies each applicant in writing regarding funding decisions within two weeks following each quarterly meeting. Highly specialized requests and proposals requiring on-site study or outside consultation may require even more time for review.
Evaluative Criteria: The Foundation attempts wherever possible to invest its funds in organizations that address root problems with substantive solutions; views as important sound management of an applying organization, with an effective board of trustees that has supported the project to the fullest financial extent possible; expects strong support for the project from the community; believes it is appropriate to support new organizations only when it is clear they will not become a financial burden on others.
Notes: Only one copy of proposal is requested. Trustees will initiate any meetings with applicants.

Restrictions

Generally the foundation does not make grants outside Colorado; to individuals or loans to organizations; for projects that have been completed prior to the next trustees' meeting; to conferences, meetings, or studies that are not initiated by trustees; to organizations engaged in grant making; to retire operating debt; for the purchase of vehicles or office equipment; directly to public schools or public school districts; for the construction of medical facilities or for medical research; or tickets for fundraising dinners, parties, benefits, balls or other social fundraising events. The foundation will not consider more than one application per organization per year. Grants are generally confined to campaigns for capital projects.

Additional Information

Occasionally, the foundation will conduct post-grant evaluation of completed projects; written reports must be submitted by all grantees.
Publications: Annual Report; Common Application Form

Foundation Officials

George B. Beardsley: trustee
Charles G. Cannon: president, trustee
Charles Cassius Gates, Jr.: trustee emeritus B Morrison, CO 1921. ED Massachusetts Institute of Technology (1939-1941); Stanford University BS (1943). PRIM CORP EMPL chairman, director: Cody Energy Co. CORP AFFIL chairman: Gates Capital Management LLC. NONPR AFFIL trustee: Denver Museum

Natural History; trustee: Graland Country Day School Foundation; trustee: Denver Art Museum; trustee: California Institute Technology; Member: Conference Board. CLUB AFFIL Wigwam Club; Waialae Country Club; Roundup Riders Rockies Club; Shikar Safari International Club; Old Baldy Club; Outrigger Canoe Club; Ltd. Club; Country Club Colorado; Denver Country Club; Castle Pines Golf Club; Conquistadores del Cielo Club; Augusta National Golf Club; Boone & Crockett Club.

Valerie Gates: vice president, trustee

C. Thomas Kaesemeyer: executive director, secretary ED Lehigh University BA (1965); University of Washington MA (1969).

Karen W. Mather: grants manager, program officer

Thomas C. Stokes: trustee, treasurer

Christina H. Turissini: comptroller

Diane Gates Wallach: trustee PRIM CORP EMPL director: Gates Rubber Co. CORP AFFIL director: The Gates Corp.

Mike Wilfley: trustee B 1944. ED University of Colorado JD; Claremont McKenna College BA (1962-1970). PRIM CORP EMPL president, director: A R Wilfley & Sons Inc.

Grants Analysis

Disclosure Period: calendar year ending 2003
Total Grants: $8,018,744
Number of Grants: 75
Average Grant: $98,902*
Highest Grant: $700,000
Lowest Grant: $1,000
Typical Range: $25,000 to $200,000
*Note: Average grant figure excludes highest grant.

Recent Grants

Note: Grants derived from 2003 Form 990.
Library-Related

100,000	Dolores Public Library, Denver, CO
100,000	Rampart Regional Library District, Woodland Park, CO
67,000	Friends of the Ridgway Public Library, Ridgway, CO

General

957,000	Children's Hospital
500,000	Colorado Public Radio, Centennial, CO
500,000	National trust for Historic Preservation/ Denver Foundation, Denver, CO
275,000	State of Colorado/Executive Residence, Denver, CO
250,000	Two Rivers Community Foundation
225,000	Colorado Symphony Orchestra, Denver, CO
225,000	Strings in the Mountains, Steamboat Springs, CO
175,000	City of Colorado Springs Confluence Park, Colorado Springs, CO
150,000	Rocky Mountain Public Broadcasting, Grand Junction, CO
126,000	YWCA of Boulder Countys, Boulder, CO

BILL AND MELINDA GATES FOUNDATION

Giving Contact

Patricia Stonesifer, President
PO Box 23350
Seattle, WA 98102
Phone: (206)709-3140
Fax: (206)709-3280
E-mail: info@gatesfoundation.org
Web: http://www.gatesfoundation.org

Alternate Contact

Phone: (206)709-3400
Fax: (206)709-3252
E-mail: libraryinfo@gatesfoundation.org
Note: Contact for information about library programs.

Description

Founded: 1999
EIN: 911663695
Organization Type: Private Foundation
Formed by Merger of: William H. Gates Foundation (1999).
Formed by Merger of: Gates Learning Foundation (1999).
Giving Locations: Pacific Northwest; internationally; nationally.

Donor Information

Founder: The Bill & Melinda Gates Foundation was established in 1999 by William H. Gates III and Melinda French Gates to consolidate the efforts of the William H. Gates Foundation and the Gates Learning Foundation.

Bill Gates developed the programming language BASIC while attending Harvard University. He launched Microsoft Corp. in 1975 with partner Paul Allen to develop software to be used on personal computers. Bill Gates serves as chairman of Microsoft and continues to play an active role in both the management of the corporation and the development of its products.

Melinda French Gates attended Duke University, where she earned a bachelor's degree in computer science and economics in 1986 and a master's degree from Duke's Fuqua School of Business in 1987. She played a role in developing many of Microsoft's multimedia and Web-based products, but retired two years after marrying Bill Gates in order to raise their children and contribute more fully to a number of philanthropic endeavors.

Financial Summary

Total Giving: $1,182,826,639 (2003); $976,737,432 (2002); $1,147,045,501 (2001)
Assets: $26,810,518,000 (2003 approx); $24,081,369,193 (2002); $32,751,464,978 (2001)
Gifts Received: $2,107,500,000 (2001). Note: In 2001, contributions were received from William H. Gates III.

Typical Recipients

Arts & Humanities: Libraries, Public Broadcasting
Civic & Public Affairs: Community Foundations, Employment/Job Training, Civic & Public Affairs-General, Legal Aid, Nonprofit Management, Public Policy, Urban & Community Affairs
Education: Colleges & Universities, Education Associations, Education Funds, Education Reform, Faculty Development, Education-General, Leadership Training, Medical Education, Minority Education, Public Education (Precollege), Religious Education, Student Aid
Health: AIDS/HIV, Children's Health/Hospitals, Eyes/Blindness, Health-General, Health Policy/Cost Containment, Health Organizations, Medical Research, Nutrition, Prenatal Health Issues, Preventive Medicine/Wellness Organizations, Public Health, Research/Studies Institutes, Respiratory
International: Foreign Arts Organizations, Foreign Educational Institutions, International-General, Health Care/Hospitals
Religion: Religious Welfare
Social Services: Child Welfare, Community Service Organizations

Application Procedures

Initial Contact: Submit a brief letter of inquiry not exceeding two pages in length.
Application Requirements: Letters of inquiry should include objectives, including the goals and charitable purpose of the project; information on how the organization will achieve the outlined goals and a project timeline; a brief statement of the organization's need for funding for the stated objectives; organizational information, including past projects, previous grants, the qualifications of those involved in the project, a list of board members (when applicable), the address for

any organizational Web site, and a copy of the organization's IRS tax determination letter. Additional materials should not be sent with a letter of inquiry, as the foundation will not review supporting materials at this stage in the process and is unable to return items to the sender.

The foundation will accept letters of inquiry sent by mail or e-mail (info@gatesfoundation.org).
Deadlines: None.
Review Process: The foundation will review letters of inquiry and may invite those organizations whose goals coincide with the scope and mission of available funding to submit a full proposal.
Notes: The foundation does not generally consider unsolicited proposals. However, the foundation does accept letters of inquiry from tax-exempt, charitable organizations for the following program areas: Global Health, Pacific Northwest, and Public Access to Information.

Restrictions

The foundation cannot accept proposals benefiting individuals or that serve religious organizations for sectarian purposes.

Additional Information

Educational Programs: Gates Millennium Scholars Program, The goal of the scholars program is to increase the number of African-Americans, American Indians/Alaska Natives, Asian Pacific Americans, and Hispanic Americans attending and completing college/university programs, with an emphasis on students studying math, science, engineering, education, or library science. The Bill & Melinda Gates Foundation has committed $1 billion over the next two decades to provide 20,000 scholarships through the scholars program.. Application Procedure: Application is made by nomination of a student by a principal, teacher, counselor, or other education professional. Eligibility criteria and nomination instructions are available on the program's Web site: http://www.gmsp.org. EDU. Deadline: Gates Millennium Scholars Program.

Foundation Officials

Melinda French Gates: co-founder B Dallas, TX 1965. ED Duke University BS (1986); Duke University Fuqua School of Business MBA (1987). CORP AFFIL director: drugstore.com; board member: Third Age Media. NONPR AFFIL co-chairman: Governor's Commission on Learning; technology committee member: Sacred Heart Catholic School (Bellevue, Washington); board trustee: Duke University.

William H. Gates, Sr.: co-chairman, chief executive officer B Bremerton, WA 1925. ED University of Washington BS (1949); University of Washington School of Law (1949-1950). ADD CORP EMPL co-founder: Preston, Gates & Ellis LLP. NONPR AFFIL director: United Way; board of regents: University of Washington; director: Seattle Symphony Foundation; founder: Technology Alliance.

William Henry Gates, III: co-founder B Seattle, WA October 28, 1955. ED Harvard University (1975). PRIM CORP EMPL co-founder, chairman, chief software architect: Microsoft Corp. ADD CORP EMPL chairman: Corbis Corp. CORP AFFIL board of directors: Berkshire Hathaway Inc.; director: ICOS.

Dr. Helene Gayle, MPH: director HIV, TB and reprod health program ED Barnard College BA; Johns Hopkins University MPH; University of Pennsylvania MD; University of Pennsylvania MD. NONPR AFFIL co-chairman: Global HIV Prevention Group.

Allan C. Golston, CPA: chief financial officer, chief administrative officer ED Seattle University MBA; University of Colorado BA. NONPR AFFIL director: Philanthropy Northwest; director: Public Library of Science; trustee: Make-a-Wish Foundation; treasurer: New Futures; fellow: British-American Project; alumnus: INROADS Denver; trustee: Artist Trust; fellow: British-American Project.

Richard D. Klausner, MD: executive director, global health ED Duke University MD; Yale University.

NONPR AFFIL member: Institute of Medicine; member: National Academy of Sciences.

Sylvia M. Mathews: chief operating officer, executive director, libraries, pac northwest B Hinton, WV. ED Oxford University BS; Harvard University BS (1987). CORP AFFIL director: Metlife. NONPR AFFIL member: Pacific Council on International Policy; member: University of Washington Medicine Board; member: CFR Task Force on Transatlantic Relations for Council on Foreign Relations; director: The Aspen Strategy Group.

Dr. N. Regina Rabinovich, MPH: director, infectious disease program ED Southern Illinois University MD; University of Iowa BA; University of Iowa BA; University of North Carolina MPH. NONPR AFFIL director: Malaria Vaccine Initiative.

Greg Shaw: director foundation library & pac northwest advocacy ED Northeastern State University BA. NONPR AFFIL co-chairman: Sound Families Initiative Steering Committee; senior fellow: University Washington Center Communications & Civic Engagement; member: Episcopal Relief & Development AIDS Advisory Council.

Patty Stonesifer: co-chairman, president ED Indiana University BA. PRIM CORP EMPL senior vice president Consumer division: Microsoft Corp. CORP AFFIL director: Viacom Inc.; director: Amazon.com. NONPR AFFIL member: UN General Assembly Special Session on AIDS; member: YWCA King County (Washington); board of regents: Smithsonian Institution; director: Seattle Foundation.

Tom Vander Ark: executive director education NONPR AFFIL director: Partnership for Learning; trustee: Western Governors University; director: Foundation for Early Learning; board of directors: James B. Hunt Jr. Institute for Educational Leadership.

Grants Analysis

Disclosure Period: calendar year ending 2002
Total Grants: $976,737,432
Number of Grants: 2,000 (approx)
Average Grant: $488,369
Typical Range: $100,000 to $1,000,000

Recent Grants

Note: Grants derived from 2002 Form 990.
General

150,000,000 Northwest Educational Service District 189, Mt. Vernon, WA -- fund for Teacher Leadership Project

102,931,250 Washington Education Foundation, Issaquah, WA -- towards Washington State Achievers Scholarship program

100,000,000 International AIDS Vaccine Initiative Inc., New York, NY -- fund for AIDS vaccine

70,000,000 University of Washington Foundation, Seattle, WA -- fund for genome sciences project

50,000,000 Global Fund to Fight AIDS, Tuberculosis and Malaria, Geneva Switzerland -- fund for addressing HIV/AIDS, TB and Malaria in heavily affected poor countries

40,000,000 International Bank for Reconstruction and Development, Washington, DC -- fund for global alliance for improved Nutrition towards elimination of vitamin and mineral deficiencies in developing countries

35,000,000 Duke University, Durham, NC -- towards construction of a new multidisciplinary science facility

25,000,000 International Bank for Reconstruction and Development, Washington, DC -- fund for World Bank's efforts towards Polio eradication in developing countries

20,000,000 Children's Hospital Foundation, Seattle, WA -- towards ambulatory care facilities

20,000,000 Knowledge Works Foundation, Cincinnati, OH -- fund for new and redesigned schools in academic crisis

GATX CORP.

Company Headquarters

Chicago, IL
Web: http://www.gatx.com

Company Description

Founded: 1916
Ticker: GMT
Exchange: NYSE
Operating Revenue: US$1.34 billion (2002)
Employees: 2250 (2003)
SIC(s): 4432 Freight Transportation on the Great Lakes, 4613 Refined Petroleum Pipelines, 4741 Rental of Railroad Cars, 6159 Miscellaneous Business Credit Institutions.

Operating Locations

GATX Corp. (CA--Carson, Compton, Richmond, San Francisco, Wilmington; FL--Jacksonville, Taft, Tampa; IL--Argo, Chicago; IN--East Chicago; LA--Good Hope; NY--Buffalo; OH--Youngstown; OR--Portland; PA; TX--Houston, Norco, Pasadena; UT; WA--Vancouver)

Nonmonetary Support

Value: $10,000 (2001); $125,000 (2000 approx); $100,000 (1999 approx)
Type: Donated Equipment; Donated Products; In-kind Services
Volunteer Programs: GATX employees nationwide are recognized for volunteer efforts from tutoring students to building playgrounds. GATX presents its Spirit of Volunteerism Award twice a year to honor those whose best exemplify principles of community service, teamwork, and good corporate citizenship. Unions service projects during work hours with work release time for eligible employees.

Giving Contact

Allison Dean, Supervisor, Community Affairs
500 West Monroe Street
Chicago, IL 60661-3676
Phone: (312)621-6222
Fax: (312)621-6665
E-mail: communityaffairs@gatx.com

Alternate Contact

Phone: (312)621-4274

Description

Organization Type: Corporate Giving Program
Giving Locations: IL: Chicago operating locations.
Grant Types: Award, Employee Matching Gifts, General Support, Multiyear/Continuing Support, Operating Expenses, Project, Seed Money.

Financial Summary

Total Giving: $991,000 (2002); $1,460,000 (2001 approx)
Giving Analysis: Giving for 2001 includes: nonmonetary support ($10,000); corporate direct giving ($1,460,000)

Typical Recipients

Arts & Humanities: Arts Associations & Councils, Arts Institutes, Arts Outreach, Community Arts, Dance, Ethnic & Folk Arts, Historic Preservation, Libraries, Museums/Galleries, Music, Opera, Performing Arts, Public Broadcasting, Theater, Visual Arts
Civic & Public Affairs: Botanical Gardens/Parks, Civil Rights, Economic Development, Employment/Job Training, Housing, Public Policy, Urban & Community Affairs, Women's Affairs, Zoos/Aquariums
Education: Afterschool/Enrichment Programs, Arts/Humanities Education, Colleges & Universities, Education Associations, Education Reform, Elementary Education (Private), Faculty Development, Education-General, Literacy, Minority Education, Preschool Education, Private Education (Precollege), Science/

Mathematics Education, Special Education, Student Aid
Health: AIDS/HIV, Cancer, Clinics/Medical Centers, Geriatric Health, Health Organizations, Hospices, Hospitals, Medical Rehabilitation, Mental Health, Nutrition, Public Health, Single-Disease Health Associations
International: Human Rights
Religion: Religious Welfare
Science: Science Museums
Social Services: At-Risk Youth, Child Abuse, Child Welfare, Community Centers, Community Service Organizations, Counseling, Delinquency & Criminal Rehabilitation, Domestic Violence, Family Services, Food/Clothing Distribution, People with Disabilities, Senior Services, Shelters/Homelessness, Substance Abuse, United Funds/United Ways, Youth Organizations

Application Procedures

Initial Contact: Call or write for Chicago Area Grant Application Form, then submit a written proposal.
Application Requirements: Proposal should include: statement of purpose and history of organization; current program activities and goals, specifics regarding particular project to be funded; itemized budget for the organization, with both projected revenues and expenses for the current fiscal year; current program budget; current sources of revenue; audited financial statement or Form 990 for the most recently completed fiscal year; annual report; list of board members and affiliations; and proof of tax-exempt status.
Deadlines: By the 15th day of January, April, July, or October.
Review Process: The initial review is done by the supervisor; further review and decision is made by the contributions committee on a quarterly basis.
Evaluative Criteria: Evaluation is based on the involvement of company employees in organization; geographical area served; efficiency of structure and management; cost of fund-raising activities; existence or level of government funding; evidence of broad community support; proven effectiveness of organization in meeting community needs; potential of program to become self-sustaining; and the impact on the community.
Decision Notification: Completed applications will be acknowledged in writing; final decisions are made at meetings in March, June, September, and December, and as necessary.

Restrictions

Corporation does not support individuals; political organizations; religious organizations for sectarian purposes; trips, conferences, or tours; organizations which lack status as a 501(c)(3) organization or equivalent; land acquisition; deficit financing; member organizations of united funds for general operating support; organizations or programs which pose a potential conflict of interest; social, fraternal, athletic, labor, or veterans' groups serving a limited constituency.

Additional Information

Recipients must submit progress reports as a condition of funding.
Grant renewals are not automatic.
Publications: Guidelines; Grants List; Application Form

Corporate Officials

David M. Edwards: president, president, chief executive officer, chief operating officer B Berkeley, CA 1951. ED University of California, Davis AB (1973); University of California, Davis MA (1975). PRIM CORP EMPL president: GATX Corp. CORP AFFIL director: General American Transportation Corp.; director: GATX Capital Corp.; director: GATX Terminals Corp. NONPR AFFIL member: Finance Executive Institute.
Ronald H. Zech: chairman, president, chief execu-

tive officer, chief operating officer B Reedsburg, WI 1943. ED Valparaiso University BSEE (1965); University of Wisconsin MBA (1967). PRIM CORP EMPL chairman, president, chief executive officer, chief operating officer: GATX Corp. CORP AFFIL president, chief executive officer: GATX Capital Corp.; director: McGrath Rentcorp.

Grants Analysis

Disclosure Period: calendar year ending 2001
Total Grants: $1,460,000 (approx)*
Number of Grants: 75
Average Grant: $19,466
Highest Grant: $50,000
Lowest Grant: $10,000
Typical Range: $10,000 to $25,000
*Note: Giving excludes nonmonetary support. Grants analysis provided by the corporation. A more recent grants list was unavailable.

Recent Grants

Note: Grants derived from 1996 grants list.
General

50,000	Music and Dance Theater -- capital campaign
50,000	Music and Dance Theater -- capital campaign
45,000	Heartland Alliance for Human Needs and Human Rights, Chicago, IL -- for Neon Street Programs
45,000	Heartland Alliance for Human Needs and Human Rights, Chicago, IL -- for Neon Street Programs
25,000	Chicago Botanic Garden, Chicago, IL -- for Green Chicago Program
23,600	Robert Crown Center for Health Education, Hinsdale, IL -- for Farren School Family Life
20,000	Associated Colleges of Illinois, Chicago, IL -- for North Central College's Inner-City Tutoring Program, Rosary College's Tutoring Program with Farren School
20,000	Rainbow House/Arco Iris, Chicago, IL -- for Adolescent Services
20,000	Teen Living Programs, Chicago, IL -- for Belfort House
17,500	Big Shoulders Fund, Chicago, IL -- counseling services

GAULT-HUSSEY CHARITABLE TRUST

Giving Contact

Rudy Wrenick, Jr., Senior Vice President & Trust Officer
c/o Bank of America
PO Box 88
Topeka, KS 66601
Phone: (785)295-3463
Fax: (785)295-3450

Description

Founded: 1980
EIN: 486237061
Organization Type: Private Foundation
Giving Locations: KS
Grant Types: Capital, Endowment, General Support, Operating Expenses, Project.

Financial Summary

Total Giving: $144,500 (fiscal year ending November 30, 2001). Note: Fiscal 1997 Giving includes scholarship($23,500); United Way ($10,000).
Giving Analysis: Giving for fiscal 2001 includes: foundation grants to United Way ($14,500).
Assets: $2,733,928 (fiscal 2001)

Typical Recipients

Arts & Humanities: Arts Centers, Arts Funds, Historic Preservation, Libraries, Museums/Galleries, Music, Performing Arts, Theater
Civic & Public Affairs: Community Foundations, Employment/Job Training, Civic & Public Affairs-General, Housing, Public Policy
Education: Business Education, Colleges & Universities, Economic Education, Education Funds, Elementary Education (Public), Medical Education, Public Education (Precollege), Student Aid, Vocational & Technical Education
Environment: Resource Conservation
Health: Alzheimer's Disease, Cancer, Children's Health/Hospitals, Clinics/Medical Centers, Diabetes, Emergency/Ambulance Services, Health Organizations, Home-Care Services, Hospices, Hospitals, Medical Research, Mental Health, Prenatal Health Issues, Respiratory, Single-Disease Health Associations, Trauma Treatment
Religion: Religious Welfare
Social Services: Animal Protection, At-Risk Youth, Child Welfare, Community Service Organizations, Day Care, Domestic Violence, Food/Clothing Distribution, People with Disabilities, Scouts, Senior Services, Shelters/Homelessness, United Funds/United Ways, YMCA/YWCA/YMHA/YWHA, Youth Organizations

Application Procedures

Initial Contact: The foundation has no formal grant application procedure or application form. Send a brief letter of inquiry.
Deadlines: January 1 and July 1.

Restrictions

Priority is given to organizations that seek to fill a community need and whose programs would be unlikely to receive adequate support from any other funding source. Does not support individuals.

Additional Information

Publications: Grant Guidelines
Trust(s): Bank of America

Grants Analysis

Disclosure Period: fiscal year ending November 30, 2001
Total Grants: $130,000*
Number of Grants: 18
Average Grant: $7,222
Highest Grant: $20,500
Lowest Grant: $1,000
Typical Range: $1,000 to $10,000
*Note: Giving excludes United Way.

Recent Grants

Note: Grants derived from fiscal 2002 Form 990.
General

20,000	YWCA, Topeka, KS -- for building fund
19,500	Washburn University, Topeka, KS -- nursing scholarships and athletics
18,000	Capper Foundation, Topeka, KS -- for physically disabled services
14,000	Stormont Vail Regional Medical Center, Topeka, KS -- nursing scholarships
12,000	Kansas Independent College Fund, Topeka, KS -- scholarship for disadvantaged
12,000	United Way of Greater Topeka, Topeka, KS -- community services
6,500	YMCA, Topeka, KS -- youth programs
5,000	Baker University, Baldwin City, KS -- unrestricted contribution
4,500	American Red Cross, Washington, DC -- unrestricted contribution
4,500	Topeka Symphony Society, Topeka, KS -- for program support

GAZETTE CO.

Company Headquarters

Cedar Rapids, IA
Web: http://www.gazettecommunications.com

Company Description

Employees: 650
SIC(s): 2700 Printing & Publishing, 4800 Communications.

Operating Locations

Gazette Co. (IA--Cedar Rapids)

Gazette Foundation

Giving Contact

Joseph F. Hladky, III, President
Gazette Foundation
500 3rd Ave. SE
Cedar Rapids, IA 52401
Phone: (319)398-8280

Description

Founded: 1960
EIN: 426075177
Organization Type: Corporate Foundation
Giving Locations: IA: Cedar Rapids
Grant Types: Capital, General Support, Scholarship.

Donor Information

Founder: The Gazette Co.

Financial Summary

Total Giving: $143,200 (2004); $161,700 (2003)
Giving Analysis: Giving for 2004 includes: foundation scholarships ($3,500); foundation grants to United Way ($65,000)
Assets: $884,826 (2004); $889,879 (2003)
Gifts Received: $124,000 (2004); $92,500 (2003); $47,000 (2000). Note: In 2003, contributions were received from Cedar Rapids Television Co. ($24,000) and Gazette Communications Inc. ($68,500). IIn 2000, contributions were received from Cedar Rapids Television Co. ($12,000) and Gazette Communications Inc. ($35,000). In 1999, contributions were received from Cedar Rapids Television Co. ($12,000) and Gazette Communications Inc. ($48,000). Contributions were received from the Cedar Rapids Television Co., the Cedar Rapids Gazette, the Gazette Co., the Iowa Farmer Today, and Publications, Inc.

Typical Recipients

Arts & Humanities: Arts Associations & Councils, Ethnic & Folk Arts, History & Archaeology, Libraries, Literary Arts, Museums/Galleries, Music, Performing Arts, Theater
Civic & Public Affairs: African American Affairs, Botanical Gardens/Parks, Chambers of Commerce, Clubs, Community Foundations, Civic & Public Affairs-General, Housing, Municipalities/Towns, Philanthropic Organizations, Professional & Trade Associations, Public Policy, Safety, Urban & Community Affairs, Women's Affairs, Zoos/Aquariums
Education: Agricultural Education, Business Education, Colleges & Universities, Community & Junior Colleges, Education Funds, Environmental Education, Education-General, Leadership Training, Literacy, Private Education (Precollege), Public Education (Precollege), Secondary Education (Private), Student Aid
Environment: Environment-General
Health: Cancer, Children's Health/Hospitals, Diabetes, Emergency/Ambulance Services, Health Funds, Health Organizations, Hospitals, Kidney, Multiple Sclerosis, Outpatient Health Care
Religion: Religious Welfare
Science: Science-General, Science Museums
Social Services: Animal Protection, Camps, Child

Welfare, Community Centers, Community Service Organizations, Counseling, Delinquency & Criminal Rehabilitation, Domestic Violence, Emergency Relief, Family Services, Food/Clothing Distribution, Scouts, Senior Services, Substance Abuse, United Funds/United Ways, YMCA/YWCA/YMHA/YWHA, Youth Organizations

Application Procedures

Initial Contact: Return completed application.
Application Requirements: Include a description of organization, proof of tax-exempt status, purpose of funds sought, financial information relating to the project, and project personnel.
Deadlines: None.
Review Process: Review process takes approximately three months.

Restrictions

Does not support individuals.

Additional Information

Publications: Guidelines Sheet

Corporate Officials

Joseph F. Hladky, III: president, chief executive officer, publisher, editor B Cedar Rapids, IA 1940. ED University of Iowa BA (1962). PRIM CORP EMPL president, chief executive officer, publisher, editor: Gazette Co. CORP AFFIL director: Banks IA; director: Merchants National Bank. NONPR AFFIL member: National Association Broadcasters; member: Shriners; member: Masons; member: Inland Daily Press Association; member: Iowa Newspaper Association; director: Coe College; member: American Society Newspaper Editors; director, member: Cedar Rapids Chamber of Commerce; director, member: American Newspaper Publishers Association. CLUB AFFIL Cedar Rapids Country Club.
Ken Slaughter: chief financial officer PRIM CORP EMPL chief financial officer: Gazette Co.

Foundation Officials

Elizabeth T. Barry: director PRIM CORP EMPL secretary: Gazette Co. Inc. ADD CORP EMPL secretary: Cedar Rapids Gazette Inc.; assistant secretary: Cedar Rapids Television Co.
Joseph F. Hladky, III: president, director (see above)
Chuck Peters: director
Ken Slaughter: vice president, secretary, treasurer, director (see above)

Grants Analysis

Disclosure Period: calendar year ending 2003
Total Grants: $100,200*
Number of Grants: 19
Average Grant: $3,692*
Highest Grant: $33,750
Lowest Grant: $500
Typical Range: $1,000 to $5,000
***Note:** Giving excludes United Way; scholarship. Average grant figure excludes highest grant.

Recent Grants

Note: Grants derived from 2003 Form 990.
Library-Related
3,000   Iowa City Public Library, Iowa City, IA -- towards capital campaign
General
53,900   United Way of East Central Iowa, Cedar Rapids, IA
33,750   Greater Cedar Rapids Foundation, Cedar Rapids, IA
10,000   Kernels Foundation, Cedar Rapids, IA -- towards capital campaign
10,000   University of Iowa Foundation, Iowa City, IA -- towards capital campaign
5,000   American Red Cross, Cedar Rapids, IA -- towards capital campaign
5,000   Coe College, Cedar Rapids, IA -- towards capital campaign

5,000   Marion Parks and Recreation Foundation Inc., Marion, IA -- towards capital campaign
5,000   St. Luke's Health Care Foundation, Cedar Rapids, IA -- towards capital campaign
5,000   Science Station, Cedar Rapids, IA -- towards capital campaign
5,000   YMCA, Cedar Rapids, IA -- towards capital campaign

GE CAPITAL CORP.

Company Headquarters

260 Long Ridge Rd.
Stamford, CT 06927
Web: http://www.gecapital.com

Company Description

Acquired: Heller Financial Inc. (2001);
Former Name: GE Capital Corp. (2005).
Employees: 1,250
SIC(s): 6141 Personal Credit Institutions, 6153 Short-Term Business Credit.
Parent Company: General Electric Co., 3135 Easton Turnpike, Fairfield, CT, United States

Operating Locations

Fuji Bank Atlanta (GA--Atlanta); Fuji Bank Chicago Branch (IL--Chicago); Fuji Bank Houston (TX--Houston); Fuji Bank International (CA--San Francisco); Fuji Bank Los Angeles (CA--Los Angeles); Fuji Bank New York Branch (NY--New York); Fuji Bank San Francisco (CA--San Francisco); Fuji Bank & Trust Co. (NY--New York); Fuji Capital Holdings (NY--New York); Fuji Capital Markets Corp. (NY--New York); Fuji Securities - Chicago (IL--Chicago); Fuji Securities - New York (NY--New York); Fuji-Wolfensohn International (NY--New York); Fujilease Corp. (NY--New York); FWI Holdings (DE--Wilmington); Heller International Corp. (IL--Chicago); Miami Representative Office (FL--Miami); Seattle Representative Office (WA--Seattle); Washington, D.C. Representative Office (DC--Washington)

Nonmonetary Support

Type: Donated Equipment
Volunteer Programs: The company has a volunteer committee, an incentive program, and has adopted a public school.

Giving Contact

Leslie Krohn, Vice President Communications
500 West Monroe Street
Chicago, IL 60661
Phone: (312)441-6169
Fax: (312)441-7770

Alternate Contact

Deia Campanelli, Communications Manager

Description

Organization Type: Corporate Giving Program
Giving Locations: headquarters and operating communities.
Grant Types: Employee Matching Gifts, General Support.
Note: Matching gifts are for academic purposes only.

Financial Summary

Total Giving: Contributes through corporate direct giving program only. Giving includes corporate direct giving; nonmonetary support.

Typical Recipients

Arts & Humanities: Libraries, Music, Public Broadcasting
Civic & Public Affairs: Business/Free Enterprise,

Professional & Trade Associations, Public Policy
Education: Colleges & Universities, Elementary Education (Private), Literacy, Minority Education, Private Education (Precollege), Public Education (Precollege)
Health: Mental Health
Social Services: United Funds/United Ways, Youth Organizations

Application Procedures

Initial Contact: brief letter of inquiry, then a full proposal
Application Requirements: a description of the organization, amount requested, purpose of funds sought, list of board of trustees or directors, percentage of budget used for administration and overhead, evidence of 501(c)(3) status, outcomes expected, method of evaluation, and list of funding from other organizations or government agencies
Deadlines: None.

Restrictions

Does not support individuals, organizations outside operating areas, political or lobbying groups, United Way-supported organizations, or religious organizations for sectarian purposes.

Additional Information

The majority of Heller Financial, Inc.'s charitable contributions is distributed by the corporate headquarters office in Chicago, IL, but a small percentage of funding is distributed through various regional offices.

Corporate Officials

Richard Almeida: chairman, chief executive officer B New York, NY 1942. ED George Washington University BA (1963); Syracuse University MA (1965). PRIM CORP EMPL chairman, chief executive officer: Heller Financial Inc. ADD CORP EMPL president: Heller Equity Capital Corp.; chief executive officer: Heller Interstate Inc.
Lauralee Martin: chief financial officer B Minneapolis, MN 1950. ED Oregon State University (1972); University of Connecticut (1979). PRIM CORP EMPL chief financial officer: Heller Financial. CORP AFFIL director: Gables Residental Trust.
Rick Wolfert: president, chief operating officer PRIM CORP EMPL president, chief operating officer: Heller Financial.

Giving Program Officials

Judy Korba: PRIM CORP EMPL contributions manager: Heller Financial.

Grants Analysis

Typical Range: $1,000 to $25,000

GEBBIE FOUNDATION

Giving Contact

Thomas M. Cardman, Executive Director
110 W 3rd Street, No. 308
Jamestown, NY 14701
Phone: (716)487-1062
Fax: (716)484-6401

Description

Founded: 1964
EIN: 166050287
Organization Type: General Purpose Foundation
Giving Locations: NY
Grant Types: Capital, Challenge, General Support, Matching, Multiyear/Continuing Support, Project, Research, Scholarship, Seed Money.

Donor Information

Founder: The foundation was established in 1964 and initially funded by the estates of the late Miss

Marion Bertram Gebbie and the late Mrs. Geraldine Gebbie Bellinger in memory of their parents, Frank and Harriet Louise Hubbell Gebbie. Frank Gebbie was one of the developers (with Gail Borden) of condensed milk, and a founder of the Mohawk Condensed Milk Company in St. Johnsville, NY, in the late 1800s.

Geraldine, the older daughter, studied violin privately in Rochester, NY, but did not choose to have a professional career. In 1908, she married Earl J. Bellinger, a St. Johnsville area resident connected with the Mohawk Dairy. The young couple went to the western New York and northern Pennsylvania areas where they purchased farms and set up dairies. Mrs. Bellinger also managed the Mohawk Condensed Milk Company plant in Sherman. As time passed, Mrs. Bellinger became interested in Chautauqua Institution and was particularly close to the institution when it suffered setbacks in the early 1930s. She became a founding member of the Chautauqua Foundation, serving on its board until her death in 1963. She was also an active member of the Jamestown YWCA Board and the First Presbyterian Church.

Marion, the second daughter, graduated from the Wheaton Female Seminary, now Wheaton College, in 1901. Immediately after college, however, she chose to be helpful to her parents by remaining at home. She was one of the first women in New York to operate a motor car and she enjoyed driving for her parents. She also enjoyed traveling with her father on his business trips. After her mother's death in 1912, she remained with her father until his death in 1928. She eventually lived with her sister in Magnolia. Upon joining Mrs. Bellinger in Chautauqua County, she became an active member of the WCA Hospital Board in Jamestown. She passed away in 1949. In 1952, Mrs. Bellinger and her daughter, Mrs. Parker, provided funds for setting up the WCA snack shop as a memorial to Marion.

Financial Summary

Total Giving: $4,310,943 (fiscal year ending September 30, 2003); $4,018,226 (fiscal 2002); $3,756,141 (fiscal 2001)
Giving Analysis: Giving for fiscal 2003 includes: foundation grants to United Way ($458,000); fiscal 2002: foundation grants to United Way ($505,500); fiscal 2001: foundation grants to United Way ($885,500)
Assets: $68,322,693 (fiscal 2003); $64,842,249 (fiscal 2002); $70,252,260 (fiscal 2001)

Typical Recipients

Arts & Humanities: Arts Associations & Councils, Arts Funds, Arts & Humanities-General, Historic Preservation, History & Archaeology, Libraries, Museums/Galleries, Music, Opera, Performing Arts, Public Broadcasting, Theater
Civic & Public Affairs: Botanical Gardens/Parks, Business/Free Enterprise, Community Foundations, Economic Development, Employment/Job Training, Civic & Public Affairs-General, Housing, Inner-City Development, Legal Aid, Municipalities/Towns, Nonprofit Management, Philanthropic Organizations, Professional & Trade Associations, Public Policy, Urban & Community Affairs
Education: Afterschool/Enrichment Programs, Business-School Partnerships, Colleges & Universities, Community & Junior Colleges, Education Associations, Education Funds, Education Reform, Engineering/Technological Education, Environmental Education, Education-General, Literacy, Medical Education, Minority Education, Private Education (Precollege), Public Education (Precollege), Student Aid
Environment: Air/Water Quality, Environment-General, Resource Conservation, Watershed, Wildlife Protection
Health: AIDS/HIV, Alzheimer's Disease, Cancer, Children's Health/Hospitals, Emergency/Ambulance Services, Health-General, Heart, Hospices, Hospitals, Medical Rehabilitation, Medical Research, Mental Health, Nursing Services, Prenatal Health Issues,

Public Health, Research/Studies Institutes, Speech & Hearing
Religion: Churches, Ministries, Religious Welfare
Science: Scientific Centers & Institutes
Social Services: Animal Protection, Camps, Child Welfare, Community Service Organizations, Counseling, Day Care, Domestic Violence, Family Services, Food/Clothing Distribution, Homes, People with Disabilities, Scouts, Senior Services, Social Services-General, Substance Abuse, United Funds/United Ways, Volunteer Services, YMCA/YWCA/YMHA/YWHA, Youth Organizations

Application Procedures

Initial Contact: Send a letter of inquiry addressed to the executive director of the foundation.
Application Requirements: The letter should contain a brief statement of the need for funds and enough factual information to enable the staff to determine whether or not the application falls within the foundation's areas of preferred interest or warrants consideration as a special project.
If the request falls into the foundation's geographical and interest areas, further information will be solicited, including 13 copies of a formal proposal, IRS determination letter, most recent audited financial statements, most recent Form 990, and current and proposed budgets for the and organization and/or program.
Deadlines: Although proposals may be submitted at any time, they must reach the foundation by December 1 for the March meeting, April 1 for the July meeting, and August 1 for the November meeting.
Review Process: All inquiries and proposals are reported to the board, including those declined at the staff or committee level.

Restrictions

Grants are not made to individuals, or to sectarian or religious organizations; however, traditional support is an exception. Special projects may be supported, but funds are not usually available for general support, endowment purposes, or national appeals.

Additional Information

Progress reports on grants, and annual audits of the grant program or agency, are requested. The foundation also suggests that programs seek funding from other sources.
Publications: Annual Report

Foundation Officials

George Campbell: director
Thomas Cardman: executive director
Martin Coyle: director
Charles T. Hall: director
Rhoe B. Henderson, III: president, director
Daniel E. Kathman: secretary, director
John Lloyd: director
Dr. Lillian V. Ney: vice president, director
Bertram B. Parker: director
Linda Swanson: treasurer, director
Kristy Zabrodsky: director

Grants Analysis

Disclosure Period: fiscal year ending September 30, 2003
Total Grants: $3,852,943*
Number of Grants: 33
Average Grant: $75,420*
Highest Grant: $1,439,500
Lowest Grant: $50
Typical Range: $25,000 to $100,000
*Note: Giving excludes United Way. Average grant figure excludes highest grant.

Recent Grants

Note: Grants derived from fiscal 2003 Form 990.
Library-Related
163,860   Chautauqua Cattaraugus Library System, Jamestown, NY

General
1,439,500   Jamestown Center City Development Corp, Jamestown, NY -- for building construction, renovation project
449,000   United Way of Southern Chautauqua County, Jamestown, NY
300,000   YMCA of Jamestown, Jamestown, NY -- to Camp Anyahsa centennial campaign
250,000   Jamestown Community College, Jamestown, NY -- campus expansion
250,000   WCA Hospital, Jamestown, NY
200,000   Chautauqua Region Community Foundation, Jamestown, NY
111,000   Jamestown Community Learning Council, Jamestown, NY -- for community school
110,000   Northern Chautauqua Community Foundation, Dunkirk, NY
102,103   YMCA of Jamestown, Jamestown, NY -- for team program/Chadakoin building capital
101,000   Chautauqua Institution, Chautauqua, NY -- towards Turner School buildings/grounds & Bellinger Award

GEIFMAN FAMILY FOUNDATION

Giving Contact
Stephen L. Geifman, President
57 W. Burton Pl.
Chicago, IL 60610
Phone: (312)732-6519

Description
Founded: 1964
EIN: 366123096
Organization Type: Private Foundation
Giving Locations: IL
Grant Types: Endowment, General Support.

Financial Summary
Total Giving: $455,863 (2003)
Assets: $2,455,922 (2003)

Typical Recipients
Arts & Humanities: Arts Institutes, Ballet, Community Arts, Dance, History & Archaeology, Libraries, Museums/Galleries, Music, Opera, Theater
Civic & Public Affairs: Botanical Gardens/Parks, Civic & Public Affairs-General, Urban & Community Affairs, Zoos/Aquariums
Education: Colleges & Universities, Legal Education, Private Education (Precollege), Student Aid
Health: Alzheimer's Disease, Cancer, Emergency/Ambulance Services, Heart, Hospitals, Prenatal Health Issues, Public Health, Research/Studies Institutes, Respiratory, Single-Disease Health Associations
International: Foreign Educational Institutions, Health Care/Hospitals, Missionary/Religious Activities
Religion: Jewish Causes, Religious Organizations, Religious Welfare, Social/Policy Issues, Synagogues/Temples
Social Services: Community Centers, Community Service Organizations, Homes, People with Disabilities, Substance Abuse, United Funds/United Ways, Youth Organizations

Application Procedures
Initial Contact: Applications have no set format; however, they must be typewritten.
Deadlines: None.

Foundation Officials
Geraldine Geifman: secretary, director
Stephen L. Geifman: president

Terri Geifman: assistant treasurer, director
Cherie Handler: assistant secretary, director

Grants Analysis

Disclosure Period: calendar year ending 2003
Total Grants: $455,863
Number of Grants: 148
Average Grant: $3,080
Highest Grant: $25,000
Lowest Grant: $14
Typical Range: $500 to $5,000
Note: No grants list available for 2000.

Recent Grants

Note: Grants derived from 2001 Form 990.
General

50,000	Bernard Zell Anshe Emet Day School, Chicago, IL
40,000	River North Dance Company, Chicago, IL
30,000	Museum of Art Foundation, Davenport, IA
25,000	Georgetown University Law School, Washington, DC
25,000	New York University School of Law, New York, NY
25,000	New York University School of Law, New York, NY
21,000	Anshe Emet Synagogue, Chicago, IL
20,000	Mesorah Heritage Foundation, New York, NY
20,000	Washington University, St. Louis, MO
17,000	Latin School, Chicago, IL

CARL GELLERT AND CELIA BERTA GELLERT FOUNDATION

Giving Contact

Peter J. Brusati, Secretary & Director
1169 Market St., Suite 808
San Francisco, CA 94103
Phone: (415)255-2829

Description

Founded: 1958
EIN: 946062858
Organization Type: Private Foundation
Giving Locations: CA: San Francisco Alamada, Contra Costa, Marin, Napa, San Mateo, Santa Clara, Solano, and Sonoma counties in CA
Grant Types: Capital, Endowment, General Support, Multiyear/Continuing Support, Operating Expenses, Project, Research, Scholarship.

Donor Information

Founder: the late Carl Gellert, Atlas Realty Co., Pacific Coast Construction Co., the late Gertrude E. Gellert

Financial Summary

Total Giving: $983,000 (2002); $4,209,940 (2001)
Assets: $46,457,205 (2003); $50,164,865 (2001)
Gifts Received: $33,693,318 (2001); $10,840,544 (2000); $315,000 (1998). Note: In fiscal 2001, contributions were received from the Estate of Celia Ann Gellert. In fiscal 2000, contributions were received from Cecilia A. Gellert ($395,000) and Carl Gellert Trust ($10,445,544). In fiscal 1994 and in fiscal 1998, contributions were received from Celia A. Gellert.

Typical Recipients

Arts & Humanities: Community Arts, Historic Preservation, Libraries, Museums/Galleries, Music, Performing Arts
Civic & Public Affairs: Legal Aid, Municipalities/ Towns, Zoos/Aquariums
Education: Afterschool/Enrichment Programs, Arts/ Humanities Education, Colleges & Universities, Engineering/Technological Education, Private Education (Precollege), Religious Education, Science/ Mathematics Education, Secondary Education (Private), Secondary Education (Public), Special Education, Student Aid
Health: Alzheimer's Disease, Arthritis, Cancer, Clinics/Medical Centers, Emergency/Ambulance Services, Eyes/Blindness, Health Organizations, Home-Care Services, Hospitals, Long-Term Care, Medical Rehabilitation, Medical Research, Mental Health, Nursing Services
International: Health Care/Hospitals
Religion: Churches, Dioceses, Religion-General, Ministries, Religious Organizations, Religious Welfare, Seminaries
Social Services: Animal Protection, Big Brothers/Big Sisters, Child Welfare, Community Centers, Community Service Organizations, Family Planning, Family Services, Food/Clothing Distribution, Homes, People with Disabilities, Recreation & Athletics, Senior Services, Substance Abuse, Youth Organizations

Application Procedures

Initial Contact: Send a brief letter of inquiry of not more than five pages.
Application Requirements: Foundation's application, proof of tax-exempt status, documentation that the organization is not a private foundation, brief background information on organization, and a brief outline of program or project to be funded.
Deadlines: August 15.

Restrictions

Grants are not made to individuals. The foundation does not support organizations outside operating areas, loans, donations, multi-year commitments, sponsorships, fund raising events such as dinner, walk-a-thons, tournaments or fashion show.

Additional Information

Publications: Application Guidelines; Grant Request Application; Form 990; Financial Statements

Foundation Officials

Maria C. Bentley: treasurer, director
Peter J. Brusati: president, director
Andrew A. Cresci: vice president, director
Lorraine D'Elia: director
John J. Fitzpatrick: executive director, secretary
Robert J. Grassilli: vice president, director
J. Malcolm Visbal: director

Grants Analysis

Disclosure Period: calendar year ending 2003
Total Grants: $983,000
Typical Range: $1,000 to $10,000
Note: No grants awarded in 2003.

Recent Grants

Note: Grants derived from 2000 Form 990.
General

55,000	Seton Medical Center, Daly City, CA -- patient bed replacement
25,000	College of Notre Dame, Belmont, CA -- financial aid
25,000	Little Sisters of the Poor, San Francisco, CA -- emergency power load additions
20,000	Immaculate Conception Academy, San Francisco, CA -- scholarship fund
20,000	Junipero Serra High School, San Mateo, CA -- financial aid
20,000	Mercy High School, Burlingame, CA -- tuition assistance
20,000	RCH, Inc, San Francisco, CA -- after school and summer day camp
20,000	RCH, Inc., San Francisco, CA -- After School and Summer Day Camp
20,000	Sacred Heart Cathedral Preparatory, San Francisco, CA -- technology classroom upgrade
20,000	Saint Ignatius College Preparatory, San Francisco, CA -- tuition assistance

GENERAL ELECTRIC CO.

Company Headquarters

3135 Easton Turnpike
Fairfield, CT 06828-0001
Web: http://www.ge.com

Company Description

Ticker: GE
Exchange: NYSE
Revenue: US$152.363 billion (2004)
Profit: US$16.593 billion (2004)
Employees: 305000 (2003)
Fortune Rank: 5, per FORTUNE Magazine's list of 500 Largest U.S. Corporations (2004).

Nonmonetary Support

Type: Donated Equipment; Donated Products; Loaned Executives
Note: NOT The company provides nonmonetary support.
Volunteer Programs: GE supports the United Way and United Way-sponsored agencies where GE volunteers perform a variety of services, including agency clean-ups, refurbishing day care centers, and building houses through Habitat for Humanity. GE also supports Elfun, a global organization of GE employees and retirees who work to improve the company and communities through volunteerism, leadership, and camaraderie.
GE volunteer hours approach $500,000 in billable hours.
Note: For nonmonetary support contact nearest company office.

GE Foundation

Giving Contact

Robert Corcoran, President
3135 Easton Turnpike
Fairfield, CT 06828-0001
Phone: (203)373-3216
Fax: (203)373-3029
E-mail: gefoundation@ge.com
Web: http://www.gefoundation.com

Alternate Contact

Kim Ackerman, Secretary

Description

EIN: 222621967
Organization Type: Corporate Foundation
Former Name: GE Foundations.
Former Name: GE Fund (2003).
Giving Locations: headquarters and operating communities; international organizations; national organizations.
Grant Types: Award, Emergency, Employee Matching Gifts, General Support, Multiyear/Continuing Support, Project, Research.
Note: Employee matching gift ratio: 1 to 1 for education and health and human services.

Financial Summary

Total Giving: $52,381,016 (2004); $50,847,173 (2003); $44,618,926 (2002). Note: Contributes through corporate direct giving program and foundation.
Giving Analysis: Giving for 2001 includes: nonmonetary support (approx $700,000); international subsidiaries (approx $1,900,000); domestic subsidiaries (approx $21,200,000); corporate direct giving (approx $23,100,000); foundation (approx

$52,700,000)
Assets: $719,512 (2003); $11,429 (2002); $29,346,467 (2001)
Gifts Received: $55,200,000 (2003); $16,215,379 (2002); $59,800,007 (2001). Note: Contributions were received from General Electric Company.

Typical Recipients

Arts & Humanities: Arts Associations & Councils, Arts Centers, Arts Funds, Dance, Ethnic & Folk Arts, Historic Preservation, Libraries, Museums/Galleries, Music, Opera, Performing Arts, Public Broadcasting, Theater, Visual Arts
Civic & Public Affairs: African American Affairs, Business/Free Enterprise, Civil Rights, Community Foundations, Economic Development, Economic Policy, Employment/Job Training, Civic & Public Affairs-General, Housing, Law & Justice, Minority Business, Nonprofit Management, Professional & Trade Associations, Public Policy, Urban & Community Affairs, Women's Affairs, Zoos/Aquariums
Education: Afterschool/Enrichment Programs, Arts/Humanities Education, Business Education, Colleges & Universities, Continuing Education, Economic Education, Education Associations, Education Funds, Education Reform, Engineering/Technological Education, Faculty Development, Education-General, International Exchange, International Studies, Legal Education, Literacy, Medical Education, Minority Education, Public Education (Precollege), Science/Mathematics Education, Student Aid
Environment: Energy, Environment-General, Resource Conservation, Watershed, Wildlife Protection
Health: Clinics/Medical Centers, Emergency/Ambulance Services, Health Policy/Cost Containment, Health Organizations, Hospitals, Hospitals (University Affiliated), Medical Research
International: Foreign Educational Institutions, Health Care/Hospitals, International Affairs, International Development, International Environmental Issues, International Organizations, International Peace & Security Issues, International Relations, International Relief Efforts, Missionary/Religious Activities, Trade
Religion: Ministries, Religious Welfare
Science: Scientific Centers & Institutes, Scientific Organizations
Social Services: At-Risk Youth, Child Welfare, Community Centers, Community Service Organizations, Emergency Relief, Family Services, Food/Clothing Distribution, People with Disabilities, Senior Services, Shelters/Homelessness, Social Services-General, Substance Abuse, United Funds/United Ways, Volunteer Services, Youth Organizations

Application Procedures

Initial Contact: Send letter requesting application to Joyce Hergenhan, President, GE Fund, 3135 Easton Turnpike, Fairfield, CT 06828, or telephone (203)373-3216.
Deadlines: None.
Notes: Giving priorities are for pre-college and higher education, arts education programs, international education programs and institutions, and public policy organizations where GE has a presence. A community awards program supports local improvement efforts in selected locations overseas.

Restrictions

The Fund does not provide scholarships or other direct support to individuals, nor does it support capital campaigns, endowments, endowed chairs, ongoing operations, or institutional overhead/indirect costs; capital investment, construction or renovation, solely equipment purchases; grants to individuals and/or private elementary and secondary schools; projects that directly benefit the GE company, employees, or customers; projects for political or religious purposes; special events, such as conferences, sports competitions, and art exhibits; activities of organizations serving primarily their own membership; organizations or projects in countries with which the U.S. government

restricts business dealings; recipients of funds through the GE Fund More Gifts...More Givers matching gifts; or United Way agencies.

Additional Information

Company has operating locations in nearly all 50 states.
In 1994, GE combined its two charitable foundations, the GE Foundation, a trust established in 1952 to make grants in the US, and the GE Foundation, Inc., a corporation established in 1985 to make grants both domestically and internationally. The combined entity is known as the GE Fund and serves as the company's primary vehicle for philanthropic support.
Biographical information above covers the chairperson of each foundation committee. Complete list of committee members is available upon request from foundation office.
Publications: Annual Report

Corporate Officials

William J. Conaty: senior vice president, human resources B Johnson City, NY 1945. ED Bryant College BS (1967). PRIM CORP EMPL senior vice president human resources: General Electric Co. NONPR AFFIL director: Labor Policy Association; fellow: National Academy Human Resources; director: Jobs for Americas Grads.
Dennis Dean Dammerman: vice chairman, director B Fairfield, IA 1945. ED University of Dubuque BS (1967). PRIM CORP EMPL vice chairman, director: General Electric Co. ADD CORP EMPL chairman, chief executive officer: Capital Services. CORP AFFIL director: Genworth Financial Inc.; director: General Electric Financial Services; director: General Electric Capital Corp.; chief executive officer, chairman: General Electric Capital Services. NONPR AFFIL member: Officers Conference Group; member: University Dubuque; member: Financial Executives Institute; trustee: Fairfield University; trustee: Financial Accounting Foundation; member: Council Financial Executives.
Benjamin Walter Heineman, Jr.: senior vice president, law and public affairs B Chicago, IL 1944. ED Harvard University BA (1965); Oxford University Balliol College (1967); Yale University JD (1971); Yale University JD (1971). PRIM CORP EMPL senior vice president, general counsel, secretary: General Electric Co. ADD CORP EMPL director: General Electric Capital Corp.; officer: General Electric Capital SVCs. NONPR AFFIL director: Memorial Sloan-Kettering Cancer Center; member: Phi Beta Kappa; director: Center for Strategic and International Studies; member: American Bar Association; member: American Law Institute.
Henry A. Hubschman: president, chief executive officer, GE Aviation Services B Newark, NJ 1947. ED Rutgers University BA (1969); Harvard University MA (1973); Harvard University JD (1973). PRIM CORP EMPL president: GE Capital Aviation Service Inc. CORP AFFIL director: General Electric Fund. NONPR AFFIL director: Jewish Federation of Greenwich.
Jeffrey R. Immelt: chairman, chief executive officer B February 19, 1956. ED Dartmouth College BA; Harvard University MBA. PRIM CORP EMPL chairman, chief executive officer: General Electric Co. CORP AFFIL director: Catalyst. NONPR AFFIL director: Robin Hood.
Steven Kerr: vice president corporate leadership development ED City University of New York PhD. PRIM CORP EMPL vice president corporate leadership development: General Electric Co. CORP AFFIL chief learning officer, managing director: Goldman Sachs.
Keith S. Sherin: senior vice president finance, chief financial officer B 1959. ED University of Notre Dame BA (1981); Columbia University MBA (1991). PRIM CORP EMPL senior vice president finance, chief financial officer: General Electric Corp.
Lloyd G. Trotter: senior vice president, GE Industrial Systems PRIM CORP EMPL president, chief execu-

tive officer: GE Industrial Systems ADD CORP EMPL president: General Electric Co. CORP AFFIL vice president: First Robinson Financial.

Foundation Officials

Kim Ackerman: secretary
Nani Becalli: director
Jean Collier: controller
William J. Conaty: chairman, director (see above)
Robert Corcoran: president, director
Michael J. Cosgrove: treasurer ED Fordham University BS (1970); St. John's University MBA (1973). PRIM CORP EMPL executive vice president: General Electric Investment Corp. ADD CORP EMPL executive vice president: GE Investment Management Inc. CORP AFFIL trustee: General Electric S&S Program; trustee: General Electric S&S Long Term Fund; chairman: General Electric Mutual Funds; trustee: General Electric Pension Trust; director: Elfun Trusts. NONPR AFFIL director: Fordham University.
Pamela Daley: director
Benjamin Walter Heineman, Jr.: director (see above)
Henry A. Hubschman: director (see above)
Roger Nozaki: executive director
Marc Saperstein: director
Keith S. Sherin: director (see above)
Lloyd G. Trotter: director (see above)

Grants Analysis

Disclosure Period: calendar year ending 2004
Total Grants: $24,252,438*
Number of Grants: 287
Average Grant: $79,508*
Highest Grant: $1,513,292
Lowest Grant: $4,000
Typical Range: $15,000 to $100,000
*Note: Giving excludes matching gifts, scholarships, United Way. Average grant figure excludes highest grant.

Recent Grants

Note: Grants derived from 2003 Form 990.
General

4,131,493	United Way of Tri-State
1,000,000	American Red Cross
979,790	Institute of International Education, Washington, DC
750,000	Junior Achievement International, Colorado Springs, CO
575,000	United Way and Community Chest of Greater Cincinnati, Cincinnati, OH
360,000	International Youth Foundation, Baltimore, MD
355,000	Metro United Way Inc., Atlanta, GA
327,782	Institute of International Education, Washington, DC
317,000	National Action Council for Minorities in Engineering, White Plains, NY
310,500	University of Connecticut, Storrs, CT

GENERAL MILLS INC.

Company Headquarters

Minneapolis, MN
Web: http://www.generalmills.com

Company Description

Founded: 1928
Ticker: GIS
Exchange: NYSE
Revenue: US$11.07 billion (2004)
Profit: US$1.055 billion (2004)
Employees: 27300 (2003)
Fortune Rank: 197, per FORTUNE Magazine's list of 500 Largest U.S. Corporations (2004).
SIC(s): 2026 Fluid Milk, 2034 Dehydrated Fruits,

Vegetables & Soups, 2037 Frozen Fruits & Vegetables, 2043 Cereal Breakfast Foods.

Operating Locations

General Mills, Inc. (AK--Anchorage; CA--Lodi, Los Angeles, Orange; CO--Englewood, Henderson; DC--Washington; FL--Orlando; HI--Waipahu; ID--American Falls, Idaho Falls, Newdale, Pocatello; IL--Gurnee, Hoffman Estates, Lisle, Montgomery, West Chicago; IA--Carlisle, Cedar Rapids, Iowa City; KS--Shawnee Mission; MA--Franklin; MN--Bloomington, Minneapolis; MO--Chesterfield, Kansas City; MT--Broadview, Carter, Chester, Choteau, Cut Bank, Denton, Fort Benton, Geraldine, Gilford, Harlowton, Havre, Hingham, Joplin, Plentywood, Stanford, Sweetgrass, Wolf Point; NV, Winnemucca; OH--North Olmsted, Toledo; OR, Lake Oswego; TN--Chattanooga, Germantown; TX--Dallas, Fort Worth)

Nonmonetary Support

Value: $16,000,000 (2000)
Type: Donated Products; Loaned Employees; Loaned Executives
Volunteer Programs: General Mills' Volunteer Connection and Retirement PLUS programs promote employee volunteerism by matching volunteers with projects, and the Volunteer Advisory Board Steers Company involvement in volunteer endeavors.
Contact: David Nasby, Vice President
Phone: (612)540-4351
Note: Co. donates a substantial amount of food products primarily through Second Harvest food banks.

General Mills Foundation

Giving Contact

Chris L. Shea, President and Executive Director
General Mills Foundation
PO Box 1113
Minneapolis, MN 55440
Phone: (612)540-2579
Fax: (612)540-4114
Web: http://www.generalmills.com/corporate/commitment/foundation.aspx

Alternate Contact

Constance L. Schillings
General Mills Foundation
One General Mills Boulevard
Minneapolis, MN 55426
Note: Contact for volunteer questions and requests only.

Description

Founded: 1954
EIN: 416018495
Organization Type: Corporate Foundation
Giving Locations: nationally; operating locations.
Grant Types: Capital, Employee Matching Gifts, General Support, Multiyear/Continuing Support, Operating Expenses.
Note: Employee matching gift ratio: 1 to 1. Foundation makes a limited number of capital grants and only for special purposes that meet specific community needs within the foundation's funding focus.

Financial Summary

Total Giving: $20,200,000 (fiscal year ending May 31, 2004 approx); $15,000,157 (fiscal 2001). Note: Contributes through corporate direct giving program and foundation.
Assets: $27,829,500 (fiscal 2001)
Gifts Received: $8,000,000 (fiscal 2001); $7,500,000 (fiscal 1996); $9,000,000 (fiscal 1995). Note: Contributions were received from General Mills and its subsidiaries.

Typical Recipients

Arts & Humanities: Arts Associations & Councils, Arts Centers, Arts Funds, Arts Institutes, Dance, Film & Video, Arts & Humanities-General, Historic Preservation, History & Archaeology, Libraries, Literary Arts, Museums/Galleries, Music, Opera, Performing Arts, Public Broadcasting, Theater
Civic & Public Affairs: African American Affairs, Asian American Affairs, Business/Free Enterprise, Civil Rights, Community Foundations, Economic Development, Employment/Job Training, Civic & Public Affairs-General, Hispanic Affairs, Housing, Law & Justice, Legal Aid, Municipalities/Towns, Native American Affairs, Professional & Trade Associations, Public Policy, Urban & Community Affairs, Women's Affairs, Zoos/Aquariums
Education: Agricultural Education, Arts/Humanities Education, Business Education, Business-School Partnerships, Colleges & Universities, Community & Junior Colleges, Continuing Education, Economic Education, Education Associations, Education Funds, Education Reform, Elementary Education (Public), Engineering/Technological Education, Faculty Development, Education-General, Gifted & Talented Programs, International Exchange, International Studies, Legal Education, Literacy, Medical Education, Minority Education, Preschool Education, Private Education (Precollege), Public Education (Precollege), Religious Education, Science/Mathematics Education, Secondary Education (Public), Social Sciences Education, Special Education, Student Aid
Environment: Environment-General
Health: Cancer, Children's Health/Hospitals, Clinics/Medical Centers, Emergency/Ambulance Services, Geriatric Health, Health Policy/Cost Containment, Health Organizations, Hospitals, Medical Rehabilitation, Medical Research, Mental Health, Nutrition
Religion: Churches, Religious Welfare, Social/Policy Issues
Science: Science Museums, Scientific Centers & Institutes
Social Services: At-Risk Youth, Big Brothers/Big Sisters, Child Welfare, Community Centers, Community Service Organizations, Counseling, Day Care, Delinquency & Criminal Rehabilitation, Domestic Violence, Emergency Relief, Family Planning, Family Services, Food/Clothing Distribution, Homes, People with Disabilities, Recreation & Athletics, Refugee Assistance, Scouts, Senior Services, Shelters/Homelessness, Social Services-General, Substance Abuse, United Funds/United Ways, Volunteer Services, YMCA/YWCA/YMHA/YWHA, Youth Organizations

Application Procedures

Initial Contact: Request grant application or download application from the foundation's web site.
Application Requirements: Completed application form; a description of organization and mission statement with a list of its officers and board members, including affiliations; proof of tax-exempt status; a recently audited financial statement; objectives for the current fiscal year; the previous year's major accomplishments; and a major donor list.
Deadlines: None; board meets periodically throughout the year.
Review Process: If proposal meets foundation criteria, application is assigned to a program officer for review; officer analyzes proposal and makes recommendation to foundation's Grants Committee; officer will contact organization if additional information is required.
Evaluative Criteria: Priority is given to organizations whose mission is closely related to the foundation's priorities; programs focus on the needs of families, children, and youth; services are direct and of high quality; programs or activities are based in communities with General Mills facilities and employees; programs or activities involve General Mills employees and retirees.

Decision Notification: Four to six weeks after recommendation to Grants Committee.
Notes: Send proposals to the Community Partnership Council in applicant's region; see foundation guidelines for list of councils.

Restrictions

Foundation does not support organizations without 501(c)(3) and 509(a) status; individuals; travel by groups; social, labor, veterans, alumni or fraternal organizations serving a limited constituency; political causes, candidates, or legislative lobbying efforts; recreational, sporting events or athletic associations; religious organizations for religious purposes; or organizations seeking underwriting for advertising or program sponsorship. Generally, the foundation also does not support: conferences, seminars and workshops; underwriting for program sponsorship; campaigns to eliminate or control specific diseases; or publications, films, or television programs. campaigns to eliminate or control specific diseases; or publications, films, or television programs.

Additional Information

Foundation funding takes four forms: grants to nonprofit organizations; gift-matching to education and arts and culture organizations; match of employee and retiree contributions to annual United Way campaign; and scholarships for children of employees. Foundation grant amounts begin at $1,000 and can exceed $100,000 for a single project.
The foundation conducts both pre- and post-grant evaluations and seeks the participation of the nonprofit in this process. The foundation also keeps a confidential record of all grant requests that have been accepted in the past nine years. Records of grants requests that are declined are kept for three years.
Publications: Annual Report; Application Form

Corporate Officials

Stephen R. Demeritt: vice chairman, director ED Dartmouth College BA (1965); Amos Tuck School of Business Administration MBA (1966). PRIM CORP EMPL vice chairman: General Mills Inc. CORP AFFIL director: Eastman Chemical Co. NONPR AFFIL director: Minnesota Orchestra; board governors: Uniform Code Council.
James A. Lawrence: chief financial officer, executive vice president ED Harvard University MBA; Yale University BA. PRIM CORP EMPL chief financial officer, executive vice president: General Mills, Inc. CORP AFFIL director: Avnet Inc. NONPR AFFIL board overseers: Carlson School of Business, University of Minnesota; director: University of Minnesota Foundation.
Siri S. Marshall: senior vice president, general counsel, secretary B 1949. ED Harvard University BA (1970); Yale University JD (1974). PRIM CORP EMPL senior vice president, general counsel: General Mills Inc. NONPR AFFIL director: Jafra Cosmetics International; trustee: Minneapolis Institute Arts; member: Chief Legal Officers Roundtable; director: American Arbitration Association; member: Association of General Counsel.
Michael A. Peel: senior vice president human resources B 1950. ED James Madison University BA (1971); Columbia University MBA (1983). PRIM CORP EMPL senior vice president human resources: General Mills, Inc. CORP AFFIL director: Select Comfort Corp. NONPR AFFIL vice chairman: Labor Policy Association; director: Walker Art Center.
Stephen W. Sanger: chairman, chief executive officer, director B April 10, 1946. ED DePauw University BA (1968); University of Michigan MBA (1970). PRIM CORP EMPL chairman, chief executive officer, director: General Mills, Inc. CORP AFFIL director: Target Corp.; director: Donaldson Co. Inc. NONPR AFFIL chairman: Guthrie Theater Foundation; director: National Campaign to Prevent Teen Pregnancy; director: Conference Board Inc.; chairman: Grocery Manufacturers of America; director: Catalyst.

David Van Benschoten: vice president, treasurer B 1955. ED University of Minnesota; Bethel College (1976). PRIM CORP EMPL vice president investment management: General Mills, Inc.

Raymond G. Viault: vice chairman, director B New York, NY 1944. ED Brown University (1967); Columbia University (1969). PRIM CORP EMPL vice chairman, director: General Mills, Inc. CORP AFFIL director: Safeway Inc.; director: VF Corp.; director: Newell Rubbermaid Inc..

Foundation Officials

Stephen R. Demeritt: trustee (see above)
Michael A. Peel: trustee (see above)
Stephen W. Sanger: chairman, trustee (see above)
Austin Padraic Sullivan, Jr.: secretary B Washington, DC 1940. ED Princeton University AB (1964). PRIM CORP EMPL senior vice president corporate relations: General Mills, Inc. NONPR AFFIL member: Grocery Manufacturers of America; trustee: Minnesota Public Radio; member: Business Roundtable; board advisors: Democrat Leadership Council.
David Van Benschoten: treasurer (see above)
Raymond G. Viault: trustee (see above)

Grants Analysis

Disclosure Period: fiscal year ending May 31, 2004
Total Grants: $14,491,274 (approx)*
Number of Grants: 802
Average Grant: $18,069
Highest Grant: $500,000
Typical Range: $5,000 to $30,000
*Note: Giving excludes scholarship and United Way.

Recent Grants

Note: Grants derived from 2004 Form 990.
General

500,000	Guthrie Theater Foundation, Minneapolis, MN
406,970	Scholarship America Inc., St. Peter, MN
306,695	Scholarship America Inc., St. Peter, MN
300,000	Walker Art Center, Minneapolis, MN
250,000	Minneapolis Society of Fine Arts, Minneapolis, MN -- bring art to life capital campaign
250,000	Minnesota Orchestral Association, Minneapolis, MN
250,000	Minnesota Public Radio Inc., St. Paul, MN
200,000	City of Minneapolis, Minneapolis, MN -- Minneapolis training and employment program
200,000	Hawthorne Area Community Council Inc., Minneapolis, MN -- north side partnership housing
175,000	Minnesota Public Radio Inc., St. Paul, MN

GENERAL MOTORS CORP.

Company Headquarters

Detroit, MI
Web: http://www.gm.com

Company Description

Founded: 1908
Ticker: GM
Exchange: NYSE
Acquired: Hughes Electronics Corp..
Revenue: US$193.517 billion (2004)
Profit: US$2.805 billion (2004)
Employees: 349000 (2003)
Fortune Rank: 3, per FORTUNE Magazine's list of 500 Largest U.S. Corporations (2004).
SIC(s): 3663 Radio & T.V. Communications Equipment, 3711 Motor Vehicles & Car Bodies, 3743 Railroad Equipment, 3769 Space Vehicle Equipment Nec.

Operating Locations

General Motors Corp. (AL--Athens, Decatur; CA--Ontario, San Francisco; CT--Fairfield, Plainville; DE--Wilmington; FL--Fort Myers; GA--Norcross, Rome; IL--La Grange, Maywood, Morrisonville; IN--Bedford, Bloomington, Fort Wayne, Indianapolis, Marion, Mount Vernon; IA--West Burlington; KS--Arkansas City, Kansas City; KY--Bowling Green, Louisville; LA--Monroe, Shreveport; MD--Baltimore, Rockville; MA--Fitchburg, Lynn; MI--Adrian, Bay City, Coopersville, Detroit, Flint, Grand Blanc, Kalamazoo, Lake Orion, Lansing, Livonia, Orion, Pontiac, Saginaw, Three Rivers, Warren, Waterford, Ypsilanti; MS--Clinton; MO--Springfield; NH--Hooksett, Somersworth; NJ--Camden, Linden; NY--Lockport, Schenectady, Selkirk, Syracuse; NC--Hendersonville, Hickory, Mebane; OH--Bucyrus, Cincinnati, Circleville, Cleveland, Coshocton, Ravenna, Warren; OK--Oklahoma City; PA--Erie, Grove City, King of Prussia, Philadelphia; TN--Columbia; TX--Arlington, Richardson, Wichita Falls; VT--North Clarendon, Rutland; VA--Winchester; WV--Martinsburg, Parkersburg, Washington; WI--Janesville)

Nonmonetary Support

Value: $15,200,000 (1999); $15,500,000 (1998)
Type: Donated Equipment; Donated Products; In-kind Services; Loaned Employees
Volunteer Programs: The GM Volunteer PLUS program recognizes and rewards employees for the time they spend volunteering with charities and allows employees to direct a monetary gift from the GM Foundation to local charities for which they regularly volunteer.
Note: Co. also donates real estate. Co. will not donate products for on-highway use.

General Motors Foundation

Giving Contact

Deborah I. Dingell, Vice Chairman
General Motors Foundation
300 Renaissance Center
MC 482-C16-D25
Detroit, MI 48265
Phone: (313)665-4085
Fax: (313)665-0746
Web:
http://www.gm.com/company/gmability/philanthropy/
Note: Address for general (non-local, non-education) applications. Local grants requests should be directed to the local GM Community Relations Committee.

Alternate Contact

General Motors Education Relations
300 Renaissance Center
MC 482-C09-D36
Detroit, MI 48265
Note: Address for education-related applications.

Description

EIN: 382132136
Organization Type: Corporate Foundation
Giving Locations: nationally; operating locations.
Grant Types: General Support, Project.

Financial Summary

Total Giving: $40,129,969 (2003); $30,819,897 (2002 approx); $36,485,097 (2001). Note: Corporate program-related investment indicated for 1999 reflects the company's participation in charity events.
Assets: $268,277,011 (2003); $253,178,845 (2002); $322,837,455 (2001)
Gifts Received: $286,867,500 (2000); $43,300,000 (1999); $23,700,000 (1998). Note: In 1998, contributions were received from General Motors Corp.

Typical Recipients

Arts & Humanities: Arts Associations & Councils, Arts Centers, Arts Festivals, Arts Funds, Arts Institutes, Dance, Historic Preservation, History & Archaeology, Libraries, Museums/Galleries, Music, Opera, Performing Arts, Public Broadcasting, Theater, Visual Arts
Civic & Public Affairs: African American Affairs, Business/Free Enterprise, Chambers of Commerce, Civil Rights, Community Foundations, Economic Development, Economic Policy, Employment/Job Training, Ethnic Organizations, First Amendment Issues, Civic & Public Affairs-General, Hispanic Affairs, Housing, Law & Justice, Minority Business, Municipalities/Towns, Nonprofit Management, Philanthropic Organizations, Professional & Trade Associations, Public Policy, Rural Affairs, Safety, Urban & Community Affairs, Women's Affairs, Zoos/Aquariums
Education: Agricultural Education, Arts/Humanities Education, Business Education, Business-School Partnerships, Colleges & Universities, Community & Junior Colleges, Continuing Education, Economic Education, Education Associations, Education Funds, Education Reform, Elementary Education (Private), Engineering/Technological Education, Faculty Development, Education-General, Health & Physical Education, International Exchange, International Studies, Legal Education, Literacy, Minority Education, Private Education (Precollege), Public Education (Precollege), Science/Mathematics Education, Student Aid
Environment: Environment-General, Protection, Resource Conservation
Health: Alzheimer's Disease, Cancer, Children's Health/Hospitals, Clinics/Medical Centers, Emergency/Ambulance Services, Health Organizations, Hospices, Hospitals, Medical Rehabilitation, Medical Training, Mental Health, Public Health, Single-Disease Health Associations, Transplant Networks/Donor Banks
International: International Affairs, International Environmental Issues, International Peace & Security Issues, International Relations
Religion: Religious Welfare
Science: Science Exhibits & Fairs, Scientific Centers & Institutes, Scientific Organizations
Social Services: Child Welfare, Community Centers, Community Service Organizations, Crime Prevention, Emergency Relief, Family Services, Food/Clothing Distribution, Homes, People with Disabilities, Recreation & Athletics, Scouts, Senior Services, Shelters/Homelessness, Substance Abuse, United Funds/United Ways, Volunteer Services, YMCA/YWCA/YMHA/YWHA, Youth Organizations

Application Procedures

Initial Contact: Send a one-page cover letter and concept summary; only written requests will be given consideration.
Application Requirements: The cover letter should include the organization name; contact person; project purpose; specific funding, service, or in-kind request; time period; possible strategic link with GM; and total length of time GM support would be needed. The concept summary should include the following information, in bullet format and not exceeding two pages, using the following order and numeric identification: (1) date of application; (2) legal name of organization; (3) year founded; (4) current operating budget; (5) contact person, address, phone and fax; (6) project name; (7) purpose of grant (statement of requested support); (8) project time frame; (9) amount requested; (10) total project cost; (11) geographic area; (12) previous support and requests to GM or GM Foundation over the last five years; (13) other organizations to which requests are being submitted; (14) signature of chairperson and executive director; (15) attachment of latest IRS Form 990, including federal identification number and a copy of the IRS correspondence confirming the organization's tax-exempt status. Indicate if organization has submitted

this or other proposals to other GM units (e.g., marketing divisions) or GM subsidiaries (e.g. GMAC, Hughes Electronics Corp.).

Deadlines: GM and the GM Foundation accept and screen proposals for grants on a continuous basis; however, proposals must be received no less than 45 days prior to the month of the quarterly Contributions Planning Board (CPB) meeting in order to be included in the next review.

Review Process: As of 2002, The GM Contributions Planning Board (CPB) has been eliminated and the Chairperson, Vice-Chairperson, and President of the Foundation have collectively assumed the responsibilities of the CPB and serve as the governing body for all contributions and memberships drawing on interactive staff and operating unit input to guide the overall philanthropic process. The CPB has recommended an annual budget and has set policies, guidelines, criteria, and strategic direction, and has approved major contributions. Under the oversight of the CPB, various contributions subcommittees -- centered on the Foundations identified program areas of education, health, public policy, environment and energy, and community relations -- set strategic direction within their scope as well as review and evaluate proposals prior to submitting recommendations to Foundation. The GM Corporate Relations staff refers regional and local proposals for consideration and handling to the appropriate local committee.

Evaluative Criteria: Primary consideration is given to requests that exhibit a clear purpose and defined need in one of GM's areas of focus; recognize innovative approaches in addressing the defined need; demonstrate an efficient organization and detail the organization's ability to follow through on proposal; explain clearly the benefits to GM and plant city communities; and have a strong commitment to diversity.

Decision Notification: Inappropriate applicants are informed on a timely basis; if recommended, application will be reviewed by the CPB, which meets quarterly in March, June, September and December.

Notes: Based on the outcome of the concept evaluation, GM may request submission of a comprehensive proposal for additional evaluation, including: expanded project description, goals, and objectives; description of persons or groups who will benefit; relevant experience of the project's principal staff; history of organization (most recent annual report); detailed work plan, time frame, and action plan for expected outcome; evaluation plan including criteria for measuring effectiveness of the proposed project; all current and projected sources of funding (list amount requested of other corporations, foundations, and funding sources); detailed budget and long-term funding strategy beyond the initial grant period; current financial statements; current Board of Directors with affiliations. The CPB has been eliminated in 2002. The Chairperson, Vice-Chairperson, and the President of the Foundation have collectively assumed the responsibilities of the CPB.

Restrictions

Does not support organizations that discriminate on the basis of race, religion, creed, gender, age, veteran status, physical challenges, or national origin. In addition, contributions are generally not provided to individuals; religious organizations; political parties or candidates; U.S. hospitals and health care institutions (for general operating support); capital campaigns; endowment funds; or conferences, workshops, or seminars not directly related to GM's business interests. GM believes that giving to capital programs and endowment campaigns does not appropriately utilize the corporation's resources. Does not support multi-year grants; usually only the first year of multi-year requests will be considered and subsequent years will be evaluated annually for future support.

Additional Information

General Motors has established a nonprofit organization, the GM Cancer Research Foundation, which

awards substantial prizes for outstanding individual achievement in cancer research. As an extension of the foundation's ongoing commitment in the fight against cancer, the foundation established an international science journalism awards program in 1989. This program recognizes excellence in reporting about biomedical research with application to cancer and cancer research. Three awards, one each for newspaper, magazine and book, and broadcast coverage, carry a $10,000 cash award and a limited-edition work of art.

In 1999, General Motors established the GM Global Aid program to enable the company to quickly direct funds from the GM Foundation to aid victims of natural disasters around the world. As part of this program, General Motors launched the www.WebHands.org web site which allows employees worldwide to identify nonprofit organizations needing assistance in their community and donate to disaster relief funds.

In addition to its philanthropic activities, General Motors provides funding for numerous educational and public interest programs as a corporate sponsor (an example is the Concept:Cure breast cancer research initiative which raises funds through a design collaboration with the Council of Fashion Designers of America, where fashion designers work with GM's design staff and brand teams to create one-of-a-kind GM vehicles).

Company actively works to increase educational opportunities for minorities and women inside the corporation and in the business community.

Publications: Philanthropic Annual Report

Corporate Officials

John M. Devine: vice chairman, chief financial officer responsibility B Pittsburgh, PA May 13, 1944. ED Duquesne University BS (1967); University of Michigan MBA (1972). PRIM CORP EMPL vice chairman, chief financial officer: General Motors Corp. CORP AFFIL member: GM Automotive Strategy Board.

Roderick D. Gillum: vice president, corp. responsibility B Detroit, MI. ED Michigan State University BA (1972); University School of Law-Boston JD (1975); Massachusetts Institute of Technology MS (1985). CORP AFFIL director: Holcim Inc. NONPR AFFIL director: New Detroit; director: Washington DC Martin Luther King Jr. National Membership Project Foundation; director: National Urban League; director: Michigan Colleges Foundation; director: National Council of LaRaza; director: Detroit Economic Growth Corp.; director: Hispanic Association Corp. Responsibility; director: Congressional Black Caucus Foundation; director: Charles H. Wright Museum of African American History.

G. Richard Wagoner, Jr.: chairman, chief executive officer, director B Wilmington, DE February 09, 1953. ED Duke University BA (1975); Harvard University MBA (1977). PRIM CORP EMPL president, chief executive officer, director: General Motors Corp. CORP AFFIL director: General Motors Acceptance Corp. NONPR AFFIL trustee: Duke University; secretary: Energy Advisory Board.

Foundation Officials

Kevin W. Cobb: chief tax officer
Deborah I. Dingell: vice chairman, trustee ED Georgetown University BA; Cornell University MA (1998). NONPR AFFIL regent: Georgetown University; vice president: House of Representatives Child Day Care Center; vice chairman: Barbara Karmanos Center; chairman: Friends of Wayne County Park.
Roderick D. Gillum: chairperson (see above)
Thomas A. Gottschalk: director
Karen A. Merkle: secretary
Margreta D. Mobley: treasurer
B. J. Rodgers: director
Paul W. Schmidt: chief financial officer
Lorna G. Utley: president

Grants Analysis

Disclosure Period: calendar year ending 2003
Total Grants: $40,129,969*
Number of Grants: 1,323
Average Grant: $30,333
Highest Grant: $2,000,000
Lowest Grant: $50
Typical Range: $10,000 to $50,000
*Note: Giving excludes United Way.

Recent Grants

Note: Grants derived from 2003 Form 990.
Library-Related
250,000   Laura Bush Foundation for America's Libraries, Washington, DC

General
2,000,000   National Safe Kids Campaign, CNMC, Washington, DC
2,000,000   National Safe Kids Campaign, CNMC, Washington, DC
1,125,000   Smithsonian Institution, Washington, DC
1,115,000   GM Cancer Research Foundation
1,000,000   Community Foundation for Southeastern Michigan, Detroit, MI
1,000,000   GM Cancer Research Foundation
1,000,000   GM Cancer Research Foundation
1,000,000   Leon H. Sullivan Foundation, Washington, DC
1,000,000   Museum of African American History, Detroit, MI
1,000,000   United Way Community Services, Alexandria, VA

ELIZABETH MORSE GENIUS CHARITABLE TRUST

Giving Contact

Charles Slamar, Jr., Trust Officer
c/o Bank of America
231 S. Lasalle St.
Chicago, IL 60697
Phone: (312)828-5554
Fax: (312)987-0806

Description

Founded: 1992
EIN: 367010559
Organization Type: Private Foundation
Giving Locations: IL: Chicago
Grant Types: General Support.

Financial Summary

Total Giving: $2,236,163 (fiscal year ending November 30, 2003); $2,627,891 (fiscal 2002); $3,322,639 (fiscal 2001)
Assets: $57,023,558 (fiscal 2003); $52,156,642 (fiscal 2002); $60,027,015 (fiscal 2001)
Gifts Received: $22,934,009 (fiscal 1994). Note: In fiscal 1994, contributions were received from the Richard M. Genius, Jr. Trust.

Typical Recipients

Arts & Humanities: Arts Associations & Councils, Arts Festivals, Arts Funds, Arts Institutes, Community Arts, Dance, Film & Video, Arts & Humanities-General, Libraries, Museums/Galleries, Music, Opera, Performing Arts, Public Broadcasting, Theater

Civic & Public Affairs: Asian American Affairs, Botanical Gardens/Parks, Community Foundations, Economic Development, Employment/Job Training, Civic & Public Affairs-General, Hispanic Affairs, Housing, Nonprofit Management, Public Policy, Safety, Urban & Community Affairs, Women's Affairs, Zoos/Aquariums

Education: Afterschool/Enrichment Programs, Arts/Humanities Education, Colleges & Universities, Education Reform, Education-General, International Studies, Preschool Education, Private Education (Precollege), Public Education (Precollege), Special Education, Student Aid

Environment: Environment-General

Health: AIDS/HIV, Arthritis, Cancer, Children's Health/Hospitals, Clinics/Medical Centers, Emergency/Ambulance Services, Eyes/Blindness, Hospitals, Long-Term Care, Mental Health, Public Health

International: Foreign Arts Organizations

Religion: Jewish Causes, Ministries, Religious Welfare

Science: Science Museums, Scientific Centers & Institutes

Social Services: At-Risk Youth, Child Abuse, Child Welfare, Community Service Organizations, Counseling, Delinquency & Criminal Rehabilitation, Domestic Violence, Family Services, Food/Clothing Distribution, People with Disabilities, Recreation & Athletics, Refugee Assistance, Senior Services, Shelters/Homelessness, Social Services-General, Youth Organizations

Application Procedures

Initial Contact: Send a brief letter of inquiry.
Deadlines: None.
Notes: The foundation has no formal grant application procedure or application form.

Additional Information

Trust(s): Bank Am IL

Foundation Officials

James L. Alexander: co-trustee

Grants Analysis

Disclosure Period: fiscal year ending November 30, 2003
Total Grants: $2,236,163
Number of Grants: 32
Average Grant: $30,397*
Highest Grant: $605,877
Lowest Grant: $2,500
Typical Range: $10,000 to $50,000
*Note: Average grant figure excludes three highest grants ($1,354,657).

Recent Grants

Note: Grants derived from fiscal 2003 Form 990.
Library-Related

10,000	Chicago Public Library, Chicago, IL

General

605,877	Music and Dance Theater, Chicago, IL
384,000	Chicago Metropolis 2020, Chicago, IL
364,780	IT Resource Center, Chicago, IL
102,356	Community Counseling Centers of Chicago (C4), Chicago, IL
75,000	Mount Sinai Hospital, Chicago, IL
62,250	Health and Disabilities Advocates, Chicago, IL
60,000	Jobs For Youth, Chicago, IL
50,000	Access Living, Chicago, IL
50,000	Chicago Children's Advocacy Center, Chicago, IL
50,000	Children's Memorial Hospital, Chicago, IL

GEORGE FOUNDATION

Giving Contact

Roland Adamson, Executive Director
Private Mail Box
310 Morton Street - Suite C
Richmond, TX 77469
Phone: (281)342-6109
Fax: (281)341-7635
E-mail: radamson@thegeorgefoundation.org

Web: http://www.thegeorgefoundation.org

Description

Founded: 1945
EIN: 746043368
Organization Type: General Purpose Foundation
Giving Locations: TX: Fort Bend County and surrounding area
Grant Types: General Support, Matching, Multiyear/Continuing Support, Operating Expenses, Project, Scholarship, Seed Money.

Donor Information

Founder: The George Foundation was established in Texas in 1945 with funds donated by A. P. George and Mamie E. George.

Financial Summary

Total Giving: $5,162,641 (2003); $5,556,015 (2002 approx)
Giving Analysis: Giving for 2003 includes: foundation matching gifts ($55,950); foundation scholarships ($361,000); 2002: foundation grants to United Way ($75,000); foundation scholarships ($353,843); foundation matching gifts ($833,334)
Assets: $146,762,064 (2003); $105,150,461 (2002 approx)
Gifts Received: $56,832 (2002); $288,373 (1993); $150,000 (1992)

Typical Recipients

Arts & Humanities: Arts Associations & Councils, Arts Festivals, Arts Funds, Arts Institutes, Community Arts, Historic Preservation, History & Archaeology, Libraries, Museums/Galleries, Performing Arts, Public Broadcasting, Theater

Civic & Public Affairs: African American Affairs, Botanical Gardens/Parks, Community Foundations, Economic Development, Employment/Job Training, Civic & Public Affairs-General, Hispanic Affairs, Housing, Legal Aid, Municipalities/Towns, Nonprofit Management, Public Policy, Safety, Urban & Community Affairs, Women's Affairs, Zoos/Aquariums

Education: Business Education, Colleges & Universities, Community & Junior Colleges, Continuing Education, Education Associations, Education Funds, Education Reform, Elementary Education (Private), Elementary Education (Public), Education-General, Legal Education, Literacy, Medical Education, Preschool Education, Public Education (Precollege), Science/Mathematics Education, Special Education, Student Aid

Environment: Air/Water Quality, Resource Conservation, Wildlife Protection

Health: Adolescent Health Issues, AIDS/HIV, Alzheimer's Disease, Cancer, Children's Health/Hospitals, Clinics/Medical Centers, Diabetes, Emergency/Ambulance Services, Eyes/Blindness, Geriatric Health, Health Funds, Health Organizations, Hospices, Hospitals, Long-Term Care, Medical Research, Mental Health, Multiple Sclerosis, Prenatal Health Issues, Research/Studies Institutes, Single-Disease Health Associations, Speech & Hearing, Transplant Networks/Donor Banks

Religion: Churches, Jewish Causes, Ministries, Religious Organizations, Religious Welfare, Social/Policy Issues

Science: Science-General, Observatories & Planetariums, Science Museums, Scientific Organizations

Social Services: At-Risk Youth, Big Brothers/Big Sisters, Camps, Child Abuse, Child Welfare, Community Centers, Community Service Organizations, Counseling, Day Care, Delinquency & Criminal Rehabilitation, Domestic Violence, Emergency Relief, Family Planning, Family Services, People with Disabilities, Recreation & Athletics, Scouts, Senior Services, Shelters/Homelessness, Special Olympics, Substance Abuse, United Funds/United Ways, YMCA/YWCA/YMHA/YWHA, Youth Organizations

Application Procedures

Initial Contact: Prospective applicants should submit a letter signed by the executive director and board chairman and fully setting forth the purposes and needs for the requested grant.

Application Requirements: The letter should clearly state the proposed objectives of the project and the need for the grant. It should also provide the organization's plan to achieve identified goals; the methods by which the goals will be reached; the methods, criteria, and plan to evaluate the project's effectiveness; an outline of specific, measurable objectives with a timetable for accomplishment; and the organization's plan to achieve self-sufficiency after the grant term. The grant packet should also include the following: a list of board of director and officers; specific amount requested; budget for the proposed project; list of funding sources for current and prior years; list of persons responsible for project; copy of organization's most recent financial statement; copies of the organization's two most recent IRS Form 990s; a list of organizations asked for support of the specific project, including their responses to date and amount committed; and a copy of the organization's qualifying letter from the Internal Revenue Service; and a statement on the organization's letterhead that there has been no change in IRS status since issuance of ruling letter.

Deadlines: Applications must be submitted ninety days prior to a grant request meeting: October 15, for the January meeting; January 15, for the April meeting; April 15, for the July meeting; and July 15, for the October meeting.

Review Process: During the review process, interviews and site visits may be requested to better evaluate the proposal. When the review process is completed, a final decision will be made by the foundation's trustees at the appropriate quarterly grant meeting. Applicants will be notified within two weeks of the trustees' determination of their application.

Notes: Because the focus of the foundation may change as new areas of concern evolve within the community, previous grant commitments should not be taken as precedents for subsequent grants. The foundation will not consider a grant request, whether granted or denied, more than once in a twelve month period. The foundation encourages matching gifts proposals to leverage funds granted.

Restrictions

The foundation accepts projects which benefit Ft. Bend County, TX and its residents only. No grants are made to the following: individuals; loans; fundraising events; organizations that are not tax exempt; organizations that practice discrimination; proposals that commit the foundation to continued support; or political activities of any nature.

Additional Information

Publications: Application Guidelines

Foundation Officials

Roland Adamson: executive director ED Texas A&M University BS (1976).
Charles Herder: trustee
Dean Leaman: trustee
William A. Little: chairman, trustee B Boston, MA 1929. ED Tufts University BA (1951); Trinity College LTCL (1952); Harvard University MA (1953); Harvard University PhD (1961). NONPR AFFIL visiting professor musicology: University Rochester; professor German & music emeritus: University Virginia; member: MLA; member: Organ Historic Society; registrar, archivist: American Guild Organists Central Florida Chapter; member: American Music Society; member: American Association Teachers German; member, national committee professional education: American Guild Organists.
Gene Reed: trustee
Mike Wells: trustee

Grants Analysis

Disclosure Period: calendar year ending 2003
Total Grants: $4,745,691*
Number of Grants: 75
Average Grant: $46,745*
Highest Grant: $666,667
Lowest Grant: $500
Typical Range: $10,000 to $10,000
*Note: Giving excludes scholarships; matching gifts. Average grant figure excludes two highest grants ($1,333,334).

Recent Grants

Note: Grants derived from 2003 Form 990.
General

666,667	Ryon Memorial Hospital, Richmond, TX
666,666	Ryon Memorial Hospital, Richmond, TX
403,000	Delay Foundation for Kids, Houston, TX
300,000	Memorial Hermann Foundation, Houston, TX
276,934	Memorial Hermann Foundation, Houston, TX
254,900	Sr. Tri-County Child Development Council Inc., Stafford, TX
200,000	Memorial Hermann Foundation, Houston, TX
128,262	Fort Bend Museum Association, Richmond, TX
82,500	Fort Bend Museum Association, Richmond, TX
82,500	Fort Bend Museum Association, Richmond, TX

GEORGIA-PACIFIC CORP.

Company Headquarters

Georgia-Pacific Center
133 Peachtree St. NE
Atlanta, GA 30303
Web: http://www.gp.com

Company Description

Founded: 1927
Ticker: GP
Exchange: NYSE
Revenue: US$19.876 billion (2004)
Profit: US$623 million (2004)
Employees: 65000 (2003)
Fortune Rank: 109, per FORTUNE Magazine's list of 500 Largest U.S. Corporations (2004).

Nonmonetary Support

Type: Donated Equipment; Donated Products
Volunteer Programs: Employee volunteers serve such organizations as United Way, American Red Cross, Boy Scouts of America, Girl Scouts, Better Business Bureaus and councils, and Keep America Beautiful.

Georgia-Pacific Foundation

Giving Contact

Curley M. Dossman, Jr., President
133 Peachtree Street Northeast
Atlanta, GA 30303
Phone: (404)652-4000
Fax: (404)584-1470
Web: http://www.gp.com/center/community/index.html

Description

EIN: 936023726
Organization Type: Corporate Foundation
Giving Locations: operating locations.

Grant Types: Capital, Employee Matching Gifts, Endowment, General Support, Scholarship.
Note: Employee matching gift ratio: 2 to 1. Foundation matches employee gifts to approved educational institutions, cultural organizations, hospitals and other medical institutions, and public radio and television stations.

Financial Summary

Total Giving: $4,873,020 (2001). Note: Contributes through corporate direct giving program and foundation.
Assets: $899,640 (2001)
Gifts Received: $3,755,000 (2001); $3,650,000 (2000); $4,650,000 (1999). Note: Contributions are received from the Georgia-Pacific Corporation.

Typical Recipients

Arts & Humanities: Arts Associations & Councils, Arts Centers, Arts Festivals, Dance, Ethnic & Folk Arts, Historic Preservation, History & Archaeology, Libraries, Museums/Galleries, Music, Opera, Public Broadcasting, Theater
Civic & Public Affairs: African American Affairs, Botanical Gardens/Parks, Business/Free Enterprise, Chambers of Commerce, Civil Rights, Community Foundations, Economic Development, Employment/Job Training, Ethnic Organizations, Civic & Public Affairs-General, Housing, Law & Justice, Municipalities/Towns, Public Policy, Safety, Urban & Community Affairs, Zoos/Aquariums
Education: Arts/Humanities Education, Business Education, Colleges & Universities, Economic Education, Education Associations, Education Funds, Education Reform, Elementary Education (Public), Engineering/Technological Education, Environmental Education, Education-General, Leadership Training, Literacy, Medical Education, Minority Education, Private Education (Precollege), Public Education (Precollege), Science/Mathematics Education, Special Education, Student Aid
Environment: Air/Water Quality, Forestry, Environment-General, Protection, Resource Conservation, Wildlife Protection
Health: Children's Health/Hospitals, Emergency/Ambulance Services, Eyes/Blindness, Health-General, Health Funds, Health Organizations, Hospitals, Hospitals (University Affiliated), Medical Rehabilitation, Medical Research, Single-Disease Health Associations
Religion: Churches, Religion-General, Jewish Causes, Religious Welfare
Science: Science Exhibits & Fairs, Science Museums, Scientific Centers & Institutes
Social Services: At-Risk Youth, Big Brothers/Big Sisters, Camps, Child Abuse, Child Welfare, Community Centers, Community Service Organizations, Family Services, Food/Clothing Distribution, Homes, People with Disabilities, Recreation & Athletics, Scouts, Social Services-General, Substance Abuse, United Funds/United Ways, Volunteer Services, YMCA/YWCA/YMHA/YWHA, Youth Organizations

Application Procedures

Initial Contact: Submit a brief letter or proposal.
Application Requirements: Include background information including name of organization and name of project, project's goal and objective, need project seeks to meet, priority area and company area project will affect, anticipated results, project budget, proof of tax-exempt status and list of board members and staff, including description of qualifications.
Deadlines: October 31.
Decision Notification: Written notification within 45 days of receipt of proposal.

Restrictions

Foundation does not support non-tax exempt organizations; organizations that discriminate on the basis of race, color, creed, nationality or gender; individuals; political causes; religious institutions or schools; social, labor, veterans, alumni or fraternal organiza-

tions; goodwill advertising or fundraising; sports; operating support for members of United Way; national groups whose local chapters already receive support; benefit tickets; operating support for colleges and universities; medical and nursing schools; academic chairs; organizations that channel funds; raffles, telethons, walk-a-thons and trips or tours. chairs; organizations that channel funds; raffles, telethons, walk-a-thons and trips or tours.

Foundation Officials

Curley M. Dossman, Jr.: president
Danny W. Huff: chairman
Phillip M. Johnson: treasurer
Kenneth F. Khoury: vice president B New York, NY 1951. ED Rutgers University Stonier Graduate School of Banking BA (1972); Fordham University School of Law JD (1977). PRIM CORP EMPL vice president, secretary, deputy general counsel: Georgia-Pacific Corp.

Grants Analysis

Disclosure Period: calendar year ending 2001
Total Grants: $3,726,237*
Number of Grants: 578
Average Grant: $6,447
Highest Grant: $138,053
Lowest Grant: $15
Typical Range: $200 to $25,000
*Note: Giving excludes scholarship; United Way.

Recent Grants

Note: Grants derived from 2001 Form 990.
General

138,055	Habitat for Humanity, Atlanta, GA
116,667	Atlanta Symphony Orchestra, Atlanta, GA
100,000	American Red Cross, Albany, NY
100,000	National Park Foundation, Washington, DC
86,000	United Way of Brown County, Green Bay, WI
85,241	United Way of Southeast Georgia, Statesboro, GA
54,855	United Way of South Wood, Wisconsin Rapids, WI
50,000	Augusta Foundation, Inc.
50,000	College Fund, Richmond, VA
50,000	Eastlake Community Foundation, Eastlake, OH

GEORGIA POWER CO.

Company Headquarters

Atlanta, GA
Web: http://www.georgiapowerco.com

Company Description

Assets: US$5 million (2001)
Employees: 8855 (2001)
SIC(s): 4911 Electric Services.
Parent Company: Southern Co., Atlanta, GA, United States

Operating Locations

Georgia Power Co. (AL--Valley; GA--Alma, Americus, Arlington, Ashburn, Atlanta, Augusta, Bainbridge, Baxley, Brunswick, Budford, Buena Vista, Butler, Cartersville, Caton, Cedar Springs, Cedartown, Chickamauga, Clarkesville, Claxton, Clayton, Cochran, Columbus, Comer, Cornelia, Cuthbert, Dahlonega, Dalton, Darien, Donalsonville, Douglas, Eastman, Eastonollee, Ellijay, Evans, Folkston, Forest Park, Fort Gaines, Gainesville, Glennville, Gordon, Gray, Greenville, Hahira, Hartwell, Hawkinsville, Hinesville, Homerville, Jasper, Jefferson, Juliette, Kingsland, La Grange, Lakeland, Lavonia, Lincolnton, Lithonia, Louisville, Madison, Manchester, Mc

Rae, Metter, Millen, Montezuma, Moultrie, Nashville, Newnan, Ocilla, Pearson, Pelham, Pine Mountain, Rabun Gap, Reidsville, Richland, Rockmart, Rome, Royston, Soperton, St. Marys, St. Simons Island, Statesboro, Summerville, Swainsboro, Tallapoosa, Thomasville, Thomson, Tifton, Toccoa, Valdosta, Vidalia, Vienna, Villa Rica, Waycross, Waynesboro, West Point, Winder, Zebulon)

Nonmonetary Support

Value: $594,525 (2003); $80,000 (2002)
Type: In-kind Services
Note: NOT NOT Donated equipment, in-kind services, workplace solicitation.
Volunteer Programs: Company sponsors the Citizens of Georgia Power, a group of employees that volunteers with nonprofit groups throughout the state. The Ambassadors is the same type of program for retired employees. OrganizationS supported include Habitat for Humanity, the March of Dimes, and the American Red Cross.
Contact: Susan M. Carter, Executive Director, Georgia Power Foundation
Note: Annual Sponsorship Budget: $34,000 to $138,000.

Georgia Power Foundation

Giving Contact

Judy M. Anderson, Foundation President
Senior Vice President, Georgia Power Co.
Bin 10131
241 Ralph McGill Boulevard NE
BIN 10131
Atlanta, GA 30308-3374
Phone: (404)506-6784
Fax: (404)506-1485

Alternate Contact

Jim Trupiano, Manager of Charitable Contributions
Phone: (404)506-2960

Description

Founded: 1930
EIN: 581709417
Organization Type: Corporate Foundation
Giving Locations: GA: operating locations and service area
Grant Types: Award, Capital, Conference/Seminar, Emergency, Employee Matching Gifts, Endowment, General Support, Matching, Multiyear/Continuing Support, Professorship, Project, Research.

Financial Summary

Total Giving: $5,507,230 (2003); $9,100,000 (2002); $7,636,518 (2001). Note: Contributes through corporate direct giving program and foundation.
Giving Analysis: Giving for 2002 includes: nonmonetary support ($80,000); 2001: corporate direct giving ($2,541,810); foundation ($7,672,448)
Assets: $105,225,989 (2003); $87,000,000 (2002); $103,127,952 (2001)
Gifts Received: $15,000,000 (2001); $7,000,000 (1996); $2,566,083 (1993). Note: Contributions were received from Georgia Power Co.

Typical Recipients

Arts & Humanities: Arts Associations & Councils, Arts Centers, Arts Festivals, Arts Funds, Arts Institutes, Ballet, Community Arts, Dance, Ethnic & Folk Arts, Arts & Humanities-General, Historic Preservation, Libraries, Museums/Galleries, Music, Performing Arts, Theater
Civic & Public Affairs: African American Affairs, Botanical Gardens/Parks, Chambers of Commerce, Civil Rights, Community Foundations, Economic Development, Economic Policy, Employment/Job Training, Ethnic Organizations, Civic & Public Affairs-

General, Housing, Law & Justice, Legal Aid, Municipalities/Towns, Nonprofit Management, Parades/Festivals, Philanthropic Organizations, Professional & Trade Associations, Rural Affairs, Urban & Community Affairs, Women's Affairs, Zoos/Aquariums
Education: Afterschool/Enrichment Programs, Agricultural Education, Arts/Humanities Education, Business Education, Colleges & Universities, Community & Junior Colleges, Economic Education, Education Associations, Education Funds, Education Reform, Elementary Education (Private), Engineering/Technological Education, Faculty Development, Education-General, Health & Physical Education, International Studies, Journalism/Media Education, Leadership Training, Literacy, Medical Education, Minority Education, Private Education (Precollege), Public Education (Precollege), Science/Mathematics Education, Secondary Education (Public), Student Aid, Vocational & Technical Education
Environment: Environment-General, Protection, Resource Conservation, Wildlife Protection
Health: Alzheimer's Disease, Cancer, Children's Health/Hospitals, Clinics/Medical Centers, Emergency/Ambulance Services, Eyes/Blindness, Geriatric Health, Health Organizations, Heart, Hospices, Hospitals, Medical Rehabilitation, Medical Research, Mental Health, Public Health, Single-Disease Health Associations
International: International Affairs, International Relations
Religion: Ministries, Religious Welfare
Science: Science Museums, Scientific Centers & Institutes
Social Services: At-Risk Youth, Big Brothers/Big Sisters, Camps, Child Abuse, Child Welfare, Community Centers, Community Service Organizations, Day Care, Delinquency & Criminal Rehabilitation, Emergency Relief, Family Planning, Family Services, Food/Clothing Distribution, Homes, People with Disabilities, Recreation & Athletics, Scouts, Senior Services, Shelters/Homelessness, Social Services-General, Special Olympics, Substance Abuse, United Funds/United Ways, Volunteer Services, YMCA/YWCA/YMHA/YWHA, Youth Organizations

Application Procedures

Initial Contact: Send a brief letter or proposal.
Application Requirements: Include a brief a description of organization, list of officers and board members, amount requested, purpose for which funds are sought, sources of other support and the amounts assured or anticipated for the proposed project, audited financial statements detailing current position of organization, list (if any) of Georgia Power and Southern Company employees participating in the organization, and proof of tax-exempt status.
Deadlines: None, but grant proposals should arrive at least three weeks before quarterly board meetings held in March, June, September and December.
Review Process: Each request is organized by category (education, health, etc.) and set up in files as well as on the philanthropy system.
Evaluative Criteria: Must fit strategic focus area; past contributions, survey data, tax status, and support of similar or other corporate or foundation support issues.
Decision Notification: Grants are made quarterly.

Restrictions

Does not give to individuals, private elementary or secondary schools, religious organizations, or political campaigns or causes. Do not send videotapes or supplemental materials with initial inquiry.

Additional Information

The Georgia Power Foundation was established in December 1986 with a $10.5 million grant from Georgia Power Co., although the company also continues to give directly.
Southern Co., Georgia Power's parent company, does not administer a contributions program. However, several other subsidiaries administer direct giving

programs: Alabama Power Co.; Gulf Power Company/Gulf Power Foundation, 500 Bayfront Parkway, PO Box 1151, Pensacola, FL 32520, 904-444-6325; and Mississippi Power Company/Mississippi Power Foundation. 32520, 904-444-6325; and Mississippi Power Company/Mississippi Power Foundation (see separate entry for details).
Publications: Brochure

Corporate Officials

Judy M. Anderson: senior vice president charitable givingower B Jay, FL 1948. ED Troy State University (1971); Atlanta Law School (1979). PRIM CORP EMPL senior vice president charitable giving: Georgia Power Co. ADD CORP EMPL secretary: Piedmont-Forrest Corp. NONPR AFFIL member: American Bar Association.
William C. Archer, III: senior vice president external affairs
Ronnie L. Bates: senior vice president, planning, sales, service
Mickey A. Brown: senior vice president distribution
David M. Ratcliffe: director B Tifton, GA 1948. ED Valdosta State College (1970); Woodrow Wilson College (1975). PRIM CORP EMPL chief financial officer, treasurer, director: Georgia Power Co. ADD CORP EMPL senior vice president external affairs: Southern Co. CORP AFFIL director: CSX Corp.; chairman, chief executive officer, president: Southern Co.
Leslie R. Sibert: vice president transmission ED GA Institute of Technology BS. NONPR AFFIL director: Citizens of GA Power. CLUB AFFIL member: Decator Rotary Club.
Chris Womack: senior vice president, fossil & hydro power

Foundation Officials

Judy M. Anderson: president (see above)
William C. Archer, III: director (see above)
Ronnie L. Bates: director (see above)
Mickey A. Brown: director (see above)
Susan M. Carter: secretary, assistant treasurer
O. Ben Harris: director, assistant secretary
Mike Harrold: director
Richard Holmes: director
Roger S. Steffens, Jr.: treasurer CORP AFFIL executive: Southern Co. NONPR AFFIL director: Children's Museum of Atlanta.
Chris Womack: director (see above)

Grants Analysis

Disclosure Period: calendar year ending 2003
Total Grants: $3,855,061*
Number of Grants: 500 (approx)
Average Grant: $7,710
Highest Grant: $250,000
Lowest Grant: $500
Typical Range: $1,000 to $15,000
*Note: Giving excludes scholarships; United Way; and corporate giving.

Recent Grants

Note: Grants derived from 2003 Form 990.
General

1,496,000	United Way of Metropolitan Atlanta Incorporated, Atlanta, GA
250,000	Robert W Woodruff Arts Center Incorporated, Atlanta, GA
250,000	University of Georgia Research Foundation Incorporated, Atlanta, GA
200,000	Nature Conservancy of Georgia, Atlanta, GA
200,000	Robert W Woodruff Arts Center Incorporated, Atlanta, GA
150,000	Georgia Research Alliance, Atlanta, GA
100,000	United Negro College Fund, Atlanta, GA
76,000	United Way of Central Georgia, Macon, GA
50,000	Atlanta Fulton County Zoo Incorporated, Atlanta, GA
50,000	Atlanta Police Foundation, Atlanta, GA

GERBER PRODUCTS CO.

Company Headquarters

445 State St.
Fremont, MI 49412
Web: http://www.gerber.com

Company Description

Employees: 9,200
SIC(s): 2032 Canned Specialties, 2033 Canned Fruits & Vegetables, 2043 Cereal Breakfast Foods, 2341 Women's/Children's Underwear.
Parent Company: Novartis Corp., 608 Fifth Ave., New York, NY, United States
Parent Revenue: US$23,901,900,000 (2002)

Operating Locations

Biocine Co. (CA--Emeryville); Biotrack (CA--Mountain View); Chiron Diagnostics (CA--Emeryville); CIBA Corning Diagnostics Corp. (CA--Irvine); Ciba Corning Diagnostics Corp. (CA--Palo Alto; MA--East Walpole); CIBA Corning Diagnostics Corp. (MA--Medfield); Ciba Corning Diagnostics Corp. (OH--Oberlin); CIBA-GEIGY Formulated Systems Group (WI--Madison Heights); CIBA-GEIGY Pharmaceutical Production (NY--Suffern); CIBA Seeds (NC--Greensboro); CIBA Self-Medication (NJ--Woodbridge); CIBA Vision Corp. (GA--Duluth); EMS-Togo (MI--Taylor); Fredonia Seed Co. (MN--Golden Valley); Genetic Therapy (MD--Gaithersburg); Geneva Pharmaceuticals (CO--Broomfield); Gerber Finance Co. (MI--Fremont); Gerber Life Insurance Co. (NY--White Plains); Gerber Products Co. (AR--Fort Smith; CA--Anaheim, Fremont; CO--Englewood; GA--Norcross; HI--Honolulu; IL--Schaumburg; IN--Indianapolis; MA--Chelmsford; MI--Fremont, Southfield; NJ--Fort Lee; NC--Asheville, Skyland; OH--Akron; PR; WI--Reedsburg); Gerber Products, Div.-Baby Care (WI--Reedsburg); Gerber Products Overseas (MI--Fremont); Hi-Speed Checkweigher Co. (NY--Ithaca); Hilleshog Mono-Hy, Inc. (CO--Longmont); Ingold Electrodes (MA--Wilmington); International Forest Seed Co. (AL--Odenville); Maag Agrochemicals (FL--Vero Beach); McHutchinson Division (NJ--Ridgefield Park); NK Lawn & Garden (MN--Golden Valley); Northrup King Co. (MN--Golden Valley); Novartis Nutrition Corp. (MN--St. Louis Park); Novartis Pharmaceuticals (NJ--East Hanover); Novartis Seeds (IL--Downers Grove); Ohaus Corp. (NJ--Florham Park); Pedigree Seed Co. (MN--Golden Valley); Red Line Health Care Corp. (MN--Golden Valley); Reed Plastics (MI--Albion; TX--Grand Prairie); Repligen Sandoz Research Corp. (MN--St. Louis Park); Rogers Brothers Seed Co. (ID--Boise); Rogers NK Seed Co. (ID--Boise); Sandoz Agro, Inc. (IL--Des Plaines); Sandoz Argo Corp. (TX--Dallas); Sandoz Chemical Corp. (NC--Charlotte); Sandoz Chemical Corp. Purchasing (NJ--Fair Lawn); Sandoz Clinical & Nutrition Division (MN--Minneapolis); Sandoz Consumer Pharmaceutical (MD--Baltimore; TN--Chattanooga); Sandoz Corp. (NY--New York); Sandoz Food Service & Industrial Division (MN--Minneapolis); Sandoz Pharmaceutical Corp. (AZ--Scottsdale; DC--Washington; NJ--East Hanover); Sandoz Research Institute (NJ--East Hanover); Summit Plastic Co. (OH--Tallmadge); SyStemix (CA--Palo Alto)
Note: Operates in Canada and Costa Rica.

Nonmonetary Support

Type: Donated Products
Contact: Van Hinds, Director, Committee Affairs
Note: Company makes product donations to international relief organizations only.

Gerber Foundation

Giving Contact

Cathy A. Obits, Program Manager
Gerber Foundation
4747 W. 48th Street, Suite 153
Fremont, MI 49412-8119
Phone: (231)924-3175
Fax: (231)924-7906
E-mail: tgf@ncresa.org
Web: http://www.gerberfoundation.org

Description

EIN: 386068090
Organization Type: Corporate Foundation
Giving Locations: nationally.
Grant Types: Award, Employee Matching Gifts, General Support, Matching, Research, Scholarship.
Note: Matching gifts program supports educational institutions and health and human services organizations.

Donor Information

Founder: Foundation was established in 1952 as the Gerber Baby Foods Fund by Dan Gerber and the Gerber Products Company.

Financial Summary

Total Giving: $3,494,202 (2003); $2,733,577 (2002); $4,017,746 (2001). Note: Contributes through foundation.
Giving Analysis: Giving for 2001 includes: foundation matching gifts ($164,512); foundation scholarships ($222,806); foundation ($3,630,428)
Assets: $77,861,904 (2003); $67,611,443 (2002); $83,984,750 (2001)
Gifts Received: $1,969 (1997); $40,292 (1996); $43,037 (1995)

Typical Recipients

Arts & Humanities: Arts Centers, Libraries, Museums/Galleries, Public Broadcasting, Theater
Civic & Public Affairs: African American Affairs, Clubs, Community Foundations, Economic Development, Employment/Job Training, Civic & Public Affairs-General, Hispanic Affairs, Housing, Law & Justice, Legal Aid, Municipalities/Towns, Native American Affairs, Nonprofit Management, Parades/Festivals, Philanthropic Organizations, Professional & Trade Associations, Public Policy, Rural Affairs, Safety, Zoos/Aquariums
Education: Afterschool/Enrichment Programs, Agricultural Education, Arts/Humanities Education, Business Education, Colleges & Universities, Community & Junior Colleges, Education Funds, Elementary Education (Private), Engineering/Technological Education, Education-General, Medical Education, Minority Education, Preschool Education, Private Education (Precollege), Public Education (Precollege), Science/Mathematics Education, Secondary Education (Public), Student Aid, Vocational & Technical Education
Environment: Environment-General
Health: AIDS/HIV, Arthritis, Cancer, Children's Health/Hospitals, Clinics/Medical Centers, Diabetes, Eyes/Blindness, Health-General, Health Policy/Cost Containment, Health Funds, Health Organizations, Heart, Hospices, Hospitals, Medical Rehabilitation, Medical Research, Medical Training, Mental Health, Nursing Services, Nutrition, Prenatal Health Issues, Preventive Medicine/Wellness Organizations, Public Health, Speech & Hearing
International: Health Care/Hospitals, International Relief Efforts
Religion: Churches, Religion-General, Ministries, Religious Welfare, Seminaries
Science: Science Museums, Scientific Centers & Institutes, Scientific Organizations, Scientific Research
Social Services: At-Risk Youth, Camps, Child Abuse, Child Welfare, Community Service Organizations, Domestic Violence, Family Services, Food/Clothing Distribution, Homes, People with Disabilities, Recreation & Athletics, Scouts, Social Services-General, Special Olympics, United Funds/United Ways, Volunteer Services, YMCA/YWCA/YMHA/YWHA, Youth Organizations

Application Procedures

Initial Contact: Call or write for guidelines and application, then submit written proposal.
Application Requirements: Cover letter, signed by senior administrative official, which describes the applicant organization and endorses the proposed project; completed application form; proposal narrative, including: description of organization, current programs, services, and population served, description of project, how it fits within organization, primary project audience, project schedule and anticipated outcomes, evaluation measures, description and status of any collaborations with other organizations, expected impact of the project nationally or regionally, potential for replication, plan of project funding, description of current or expected funding from other donors, plans for continuation of project after funding period; line-item project budget; most recent audited financial statement, or Form 990; board roster, including affiliations; proof of tax-exempt status; supporting information, such as: letters of support, news articles, annual report, newsletters, etc.
Deadlines: February 1, May 1 and August 1.
Review Process: Trustees review proposals in May, August, and November.
Evaluative Criteria: Specific projects with measurable national or regional impact.
Decision Notification: Up to three months after receipt.
Notes: Foundation staff is willing to discuss projects with applicants before a full proposal is submitted.

Restrictions

Grants are not made to agencies based outside of the United States.
Does not support dinners or special events, fraternal organizations, individuals, political or lobbying groups, religious organizations for sectarian purposes, or organizations not tax-exempt under the Internal Revenue Code.
Foundation does not generally support capital, endowment, or local projects.

Additional Information

Publications: Application Form; Guidelines

Corporate Officials

Frank Palantoni: chief executive officer PRIM CORP EMPL chief executive officer: Gerber Products Co.

Foundation Officials

Tracy A. Baker: trustee
William L. Bush: trustee
Ted C. Davis: trustee
Michael G. Ebert: secretary, trustee
Fernando Flores-New: trustee, vice president
Barbara J. Ivens: president, trustee
John J. James: trustee
Jane M. Jeannero: trustee
David C. Joslin: trustee
Carolyn R. Morby: trustee
Nancy Nevin-Folino: trustee
Steven W. Poole: trustee
Randy A. Puff: trustee
Stan M. VanderRoest: treasurer, trustee B Kalamazoo, MI 1961. ED Calvin College (1983); University of Pittsburgh (1984). NONPR AFFIL member: American Institute CPAs.
Dr. William B. Weil, Jr.: trustee

Grants Analysis

Disclosure Period: calendar year ending 2003
Total Grants: $2,642,275*
Number of Grants: 132
Average Grant: $9,289*
Highest Grant: $744,661
Lowest Grant: $50

Typical Range: $500 to $15,000 and $50,000 to $170,000
*Note: Giving excludes matching gifts; scholarship; United Way. Average grant figure excludes two highest grants ($1,434,661).

Recent Grants

Note: Grants derived from 2003 Form 990.
General

744,661	Bethany Christian Services, Fremont, MI
176,395	Children's National Medical Center, Washington, DC -- pediatric health
140,840	Baylor College of Medicine, Houston, TX -- pediatric nutrition
139,983	University of Arizona Health Sciences, Tucson, AZ
133,633	Baylor College of Medicine, Houston, TX -- pediatric health
102,020	DeVos Children's Hospital Foundation, Grand Rapids, MI -- pediatric nutrition
70,000	Fremont Area Community Foundation, Fremont, MI
66,240	Michigan State University, East Lansing, MI
49,999	Kennedy Krieger Foundation Incorporated, Baltimore, MD
32,695	Grand Valley State University, Grand Rapids, MI -- for scholarships

GERMAN PROTESTANT ORPHAN ASYLUM ASSOCIATION FOUNDATION

Giving Contact

Lisa M. Kaichan, Foundation Manager
German Protestant Orphan Asylum Association
PO Box 158
Mandeville, LA 70470-0158
Phone: (504)895-2361
Fax: (504)674-0490
E-mail: gpoafoundation@aol.com

Description

Founded: 1979
EIN: 720423621
Organization Type: Private Foundation
Giving Locations: LA
Grant Types: General Support, Operating Expenses.

Financial Summary

Total Giving: $450,000 (fiscal year ending November 30, 2004); $635,846 (fiscal 2001)
Assets: $12,287,104 (fiscal 2004); $13,097,029 (fiscal 2001)
Gifts Received: $130 (fiscal 2004); $16 (fiscal 2001); $170 (fiscal 2000)

Typical Recipients

Arts & Humanities: Libraries, Museums/Galleries, Public Broadcasting
Civic & Public Affairs: African American Affairs, Clubs, Employment/Job Training, Civic & Public Affairs-General, Housing, Philanthropic Organizations, Women's Affairs
Education: Arts/Humanities Education, Business Education, Colleges & Universities, Education Reform, Education-General, Private Education (Precollege), Public Education (Precollege), Science/Mathematics Education, Vocational & Technical Education
Health: Children's Health/Hospitals, Emergency/Ambulance Services, Health Organizations, Hospitals, Medical Rehabilitation, Research/Studies Institutes, Single-Disease Health Associations

Religion: Churches, Religion-General, Jewish Causes, Religious Organizations, Religious Welfare
Science: Scientific Centers & Institutes
Social Services: At-Risk Youth, Big Brothers/Big Sisters, Child Welfare, Community Centers, Community Service Organizations, Counseling, Day Care, Delinquency & Criminal Rehabilitation, Domestic Violence, Family Planning, Family Services, Homes, People with Disabilities, Scouts, Shelters/Homelessness, Social Services-General, Substance Abuse, Volunteer Services, YMCA/YWCA/YMHA/YWHA, Youth Organizations

Application Procedures

Initial Contact: Contact foundation for application guidelines.
Application Requirements: Proposals should be in the form of a letter signed by an authorized official of the agency and must indicate that the agency's governing body officially approved submitting the proposal. The letter should be sufficient to convey the basic elements of the proposal, but should not exceed three pages. Include the project's short title and the amount requested in the first paragraph; a concise description of the project; what the project hopes to accomplish; qualifications of the personnel involved in the project; estimate of the time involved in carrying out the project and a time chart; and financial requirements of the project, other sources of funding, and amounts to be contributed by other sources. Attachments should include a list of members of the governing body, proof of tax-exempt status, recently audited financial statement, and other appropriate material. Submit ten copies of the proposal.
Deadlines: February 1, May 1, August 1, November 1.

Restrictions

Grants are limited to organizations providing social services to children and youth Louisiana.

Additional Information

Publications: Annual Report (including Application Guidelines)

Foundation Officials

Phillip W. Bohne: trustee
Walter C. Flower, III: secretary
J. Gary Haller: president
Robert L. Hattler: treasurer
Paul Haygood: trustee
Charles B. Mayer: vice president
Charles Monsted, III: trustee
Camille Strachan: trustee

Grants Analysis

Disclosure Period: fiscal year ending November 30, 2004
Total Grants: $450,000
Number of Grants: 47
Average Grant: $6,398*
Highest Grant: $155,703
Lowest Grant: $1,800
Typical Range: $2,500 to $15,000
*Note: Average grant figure excludes highest grant.

Recent Grants

Note: Grants derived from fiscal 2000 Form 990.
General

171,000	Greater New Orleans Foundation, New Orleans, LA
25,200	Bossier Caddo Children's Advocacy Center, Shreveport, LA
25,000	CASA Services, Inc., Ponchatoula, LA
24,780	Youth Service Bureau, Covington, LA
22,000	Young Leader's Academy, The, Baton Rouge, LA
19,631	St. John Lutheran Church, New Orleans, LA
17,000	Family Service GNO, New Orleans, LA
16,500	Catholic Charities - GERT, New Orleans, LA
15,000	Boys and Girls Club of Baton Rouge, Baton Rouge, LA
15,000	CADA of Acadiana, Lafayette, LA

ROLLIN M. GERSTACKER FOUNDATION

Giving Contact

Gail E. Allen-Lanphear, President
812 W. Main
Midland, MI 48640
Phone: (989)631-6097
Fax: (989)832-8842
E-mail: lanphear@concentric.net
Web: http://www.mindnet.org/gf.htm

Alternate Contact

E. N. Brandt, Vice President and Assistant Secretary

Description

Founded: 1957
EIN: 386060276
Organization Type: Family Foundation
Giving Locations: MI: Midland; OH: Cleveland
Grant Types: Capital, Challenge, Endowment, General Support, Multiyear/Continuing Support, Operating Expenses, Project, Research, Seed Money.

Donor Information

Founder: The foundation was established by Mrs. Eda U. Gerstacker in 1957 in memory of her husband, Rollin M. Gerstacker. Its primary purpose is to continue financial support of charities of all types supported by Mr. and Mrs. Gerstacker. Mrs. Gerstacker died in 1975. Family members continue to serve as officers and trustees of the foundation, although a majority of the trustees are non-family. Assets consist primarily of Dow Chemical common stock.

Financial Summary

Total Giving: $8,679,595 (2003); $9,474,964 (2002); $9,737,400 (2001)
Giving Analysis: Giving for 2003 includes: foundation grants to United Way ($193,000); 2002: foundation grants to United Way ($166,000); 2001: foundation grants to United Way ($326,000); foundation ($9,411,726)
Assets: $208,500,655 (2003); $166,073,201 (2002); $188,845,151 (2001)
Gifts Received: $35,009,391 (1997); $14,083,000 (1996); $499,055 (1995). Note: Contributions were received from the estate of Carl A. Gerstacker.

Typical Recipients

Arts & Humanities: Arts Centers, Historic Preservation, History & Archaeology, Libraries, Museums/Galleries, Music, Public Broadcasting, Theater
Civic & Public Affairs: Botanical Gardens/Parks, Business/Free Enterprise, Chambers of Commerce, Community Foundations, Economic Development, Economic Policy, Employment/Job Training, Civic & Public Affairs-General, Housing, Inner-City Development, Law & Justice, Legal Aid, Municipalities/Towns, Native American Affairs, Parades/Festivals, Philanthropic Organizations, Professional & Trade Associations, Public Policy, Safety, Urban & Community Affairs, Zoos/Aquariums
Education: Afterschool/Enrichment Programs, Agricultural Education, Colleges & Universities, Community & Junior Colleges, Education Associations, Education Funds, Engineering/Technological Education, Education-General, Literacy, Minority Education, Private Education (Precollege), Public Education (Precollege), Religious Education, Science/Mathematics Education, Secondary Education (Private)
Environment: Environment-General, Protection, Resource Conservation

Health: AIDS/HIV, Alzheimer's Disease, Arthritis, Cancer, Clinics/Medical Centers, Emergency/Ambulance Services, Eyes/Blindness, Geriatric Health, Health Organizations, Hospitals, Medical Rehabilitation, Medical Research, Mental Health, Multiple Sclerosis, Nursing Services, Public Health, Research/Studies Institutes, Single-Disease Health Associations, Transplant Networks/Donor Banks
Religion: Churches, Religious Welfare, Seminaries
Science: Science-General, Scientific Centers & Institutes, Scientific Organizations
Social Services: At-Risk Youth, Camps, Child Welfare, Community Centers, Community Service Organizations, Domestic Violence, Family Services, Food/Clothing Distribution, Homes, People with Disabilities, Recreation & Athletics, Scouts, Senior Services, Substance Abuse, United Funds/United Ways, YMCA/YWCA/YMHA/YWHA, Youth Organizations

Application Procedures

Initial Contact: Applicants should write the foundation for guidelines, or send a brief letter outlining the project for which funding is sought.
Application Requirements: The application letter should provide a brief description of the program in need of funding, including an explanation of its importance and a clear statement of its goals. Include a budget for the proposed program, information about other potential sources of funding, the amount requested from the foundation, and evidence of tax-exempt status.
Deadlines: Applications should reach the foundation prior to June 1 or December 1.
Review Process: The board meets twice a year, in June and December, to review proposals.

Restrictions

The foundation does not provide funding for scholarships, for individuals, or to religious organizations for sectarian purposes.

Additional Information

Publications: Annual Report

Foundation Officials

Alexio R. Baum: trustee
E. N. Brandt: vice president, assistant secretary, trustee
Frank Gerace: trustee
Thomas L. Ludington: trustee
Paul Fausto Oreffice: trustee B Venice, Italy 1927. ED Purdue University BS (1949). CORP AFFIL director: Saratoga Race Track; director: Coca-Cola USA; director: Minute Maid Co.; director: CIGNA Corp.; director: Coca-Cola Co.; director: Aqueduct Race Track; director: Belmont Park. NONPR AFFIL director: New York Racing Association Inc.
Jean U. Popoff: trustee
William S. Stavropoulos: trustee B Bridgehampton, NY 1939. ED Fordham University BA (1961); University of Washington PhD (1966). PRIM CORP EMPL chairman, director, executive committee: Dow Chemical Co. CORP AFFIL director: Marion Merrell Dow Inc.; director: NCR Corp.; director: Dow Corning Corp.; director: Chemical Bank & Trust Co.; director: Chemical Finance Corp.; director: BellSouth Corp.

Grants Analysis

Disclosure Period: calendar year ending 2003
Total Grants: $8,486,595*
Number of Grants: 243
Average Grant: $30,433*
Highest Grant: $1,000,000
Lowest Grant: $250
Typical Range: $5,000 to $50,000
*Note: Giving excludes United Way. Average grant figure excludes three highest grants ($2,400,000).

Recent Grants

Note: Grants derived from 2003 Form 990.
General
1,000,000 University of Michigan, Ann Arbor, MI

1,000,000	University of Michigan, Ann Arbor, MI
400,000	Albion College, Albion, MI
240,000	SVSU, University Center, MI
200,000	Alma College, Alma, MI
200,000	Grand Traverse Regional, Grand Traverse, MI
200,000	Michigan State University, East Lansing, MI
200,000	Midland Area Community Foundation, Midland, MI
200,000	Midland County Historical Society, Midland, MI
156,250	Midland Soccer Club, Midland, MI

CHARLES M. AND NANCY A. GESCHKE FOUNDATION

Giving Contact

Charles M. Geschke, President
220 University Avenue
Los Altos, CA 94022-3518
Phone: (650)961-4400

Description

Founded: 1987
EIN: 943052556
Organization Type: Private Foundation
Giving Locations: CA
Grant Types: General Support, Scholarship.

Donor Information

Founder: Charles W. and Nancy A. Geschke

Financial Summary

Total Giving: $373,196 (fiscal year ending September 30, 2004); $686,548 (fiscal 2001)
Giving Analysis: Giving for fiscal 2001 includes: foundation scholarships ($13,150)
Assets: $11,211,402 (fiscal 2004); $7,404,912 (fiscal 2001)
Gifts Received: $4,080,402 (fiscal 2000); $990,000 (fiscal 1995); $2,300 (fiscal 1993). Note: In fiscal 1995, 1997 and 2000, contributions were received from Charles M. and Nancy A. Geschke.

Typical Recipients

Arts & Humanities: History & Archaeology, Libraries, Literary Arts, Music, Theater
Civic & Public Affairs: Civic & Public Affairs-General, Hispanic Affairs
Education: Arts/Humanities Education, Colleges & Universities, Public Education (Precollege), Secondary Education (Private), Social Sciences Education
Environment: Protection
Health: Emergency/Ambulance Services
Religion: Churches, Religious Organizations, Religious Welfare
Social Services: Emergency Relief, Senior Services, Social Services-General, Youth Organizations

Application Procedures

Initial Contact: The foundation reports no specific application guidelines. Send a brief letter of inquiry, including statement of purpose, amount requested, and proof of tax-exempt status.
Deadlines: None.

Foundation Officials

Charles Matthew Geschke: president B Cleveland, OH 1939. ED Carnegie Mellon University PhD; Xavier University AB (1962); Xavier University MS (1963). PRIM CORP EMPL co-chairman: Adobe Systems. NONPR AFFIL member: Math Association America; member: National Academy Engineers; member: Association Computer Math.

Kathleen A. Geschke: director
Nancy A. Geschke: secretary, treasurer

Grants Analysis

Disclosure Period: fiscal year ending September 30, 2004
Total Grants: $373,196
Number of Grants: 22
Average Grant: $6,081*
Highest Grant: $245,496
Lowest Grant: $200
Typical Range: $1,000 to $10,000
*Note: Average grant figure excludes highest grant.

Recent Grants

Note: Grants derived from fiscal 2004 Form 990.
General

25,000	Nantucket Atheneum, Nantucket, MA
25,000	San Francisco Symphony, San Francisco, CA
20,000	Nantucket Children's Charity Classic, Siasconset, MA
10,000	Town Crier Holiday Fund, San Jose, CA
7,000	American Red Cross, Palo Alto, CA
5,000	Boys and Girls Club of Silicon Valley, Milpitas, CA
5,000	Bus Barn Stage Company, Los Altos, CA
5,000	Committee for Green Foothills, Palo Alto, CA
5,000	Dominican Sisters of Oakland, San Leandro, CA
5,000	Marygrove College, Detroit, MI

J. PAUL GETTY TRUST

Giving Contact

The Getty Grant Program
1200 Getty Center Dr., Suite 800
Los Angeles, CA 90049-1685
Phone: (310)440-7300
Fax: (310)440-7703
E-mail: enovotny@getty.edu
Web: http://www.getty.edu/grants

Description

Founded: 1953
EIN: 951790021
Organization Type: General Purpose Foundation
Giving Locations: internationally; nationally.
Grant Types: Fellowship, General Support, Matching, Project, Research.

Donor Information

Founder: "The Getty Grant Program is part of the J. Paul Getty Trust, a private operation foundation dedicated to the visual arts and the humanities. In addition to the Grant Program, the Trust has seven operating programs. The Trust's origins date to 1953 and the founding of the J. Paul Getty Museum as a California charitable trust. When most of Mr. Getty's personal estate passed to the Trust in 1992, the trustees decided that -- given the size of the endowment and Mr. Getty's purpose, stated in the trust indenture as 'the diffusion of artistic and general knowledge' -- the Trust should make a greater contribution to the visual arts than the museum could alone." Billionaire J. Paul Getty was the son of Oklahoma oilman George Franklin Getty, who founded the Getty Oil Company.

Financial Summary

Total Giving: $19,308,042 (fiscal year ending June 30, 2003); $21,047,815 (fiscal 2002); $19,579,820 (fiscal 2001)
Giving Analysis: Giving for fiscal 2003 includes: foundation matching gifts ($1,692,328); foundation gifts to individuals ($2,344,617); fiscal 2002: foundation gifts to individuals ($2,472,712); fiscal 2001: foundation matching gifts ($1,584,706); foundation

matching gifts ($1,815,362); foundation gifts to individuals ($2,615,474)

Assets: $9,100,188,385 (fiscal 2003); $8,623,795,970 (fiscal 2002); $8,793,485,757 (fiscal 2001)

Gifts Received: $962,801 (fiscal 2003); $1,698,334 (fiscal 2002); $3,071,442 (fiscal 2001). Note: The J. Paul Getty Trust occasionally receives works of art and reference materials from individuals, libraries, and other museums. These gifts are listed in terms of their fair market value. The Getty Grant program is the philanthropic arm of the J. Paul Getty Trust, a private operating foundation. Figures are for the Trust as a whole.

Typical Recipients

Arts & Humanities: Arts Associations & Councils, Arts Centers, Arts Funds, Arts Institutes, Arts Outreach, Ethnic & Folk Arts, Film & Video, Historic Preservation, History & Archaeology, Libraries, Literary Arts, Museums/Galleries, Performing Arts, Visual Arts

Civic & Public Affairs: Botanical Gardens/Parks, Community Foundations, Ethnic Organizations, Civic & Public Affairs-General, Municipalities/Towns, Nonprofit Management, Public Policy

Education: Arts/Humanities Education, Colleges & Universities, Education Associations, Education Funds, Education Reform, Engineering/Technological Education, Environmental Education, Education-General, International Exchange, Minority Education, Private Education (Precollege), Public Education (Precollege), Science/Mathematics Education, Social Sciences Education, Student Aid, Vocational & Technical Education

Environment: Environment-General, Protection, Resource Conservation

Health: Adolescent Health Issues, Health-General

International: Foreign Arts Organizations, Foreign Educational Institutions, International-General, International Development, International Environmental Issues, International Organizations, International Peace & Security Issues, International Relations, Missionary/Religious Activities

Religion: Dioceses, Religious Organizations

Science: Observatories & Planetariums, Science Museums, Scientific Centers & Institutes

Application Procedures

Initial Contact: Potential applicants should request the Getty Grant Program's funding priorities brochure for information about areas of support. The next step, in most cases, is to submit a preliminary letter. Applicants are welcome to contact the grant program office for assistance with applications. Initial inquiries can be faxed, but final applications must be mailed.

Deadlines: Varies according to grant category.

Review Process: All application materials must be received in the Grant Program Office before the review process can begin. Applications are reviewed by specialists in relevant fields. The Grant Program bases its final decisions on the recommendations of outside reviewers and committee members. Final notification is usually within six months of receipt of the complete application.

Restrictions

The Trust generally will not support operating expenses, indirect costs, endowment funds, building maintenance or construction, or production or acquisition of works of art.

Additional Information

The Getty Grant Program reports that most grants range between $3,000 and $300,000. The majority of grants are under $50,000. Grants also range from one to three years, and are not renewable.

Publications: Guidelines; Grant Program Description; Grants Awarded Report; Biennial Report; application form.

Corporate Officials

David I. Fisher: chairman B Bellmore, NY 1939. ED University of California (1961); University of Missouri (1965). PRIM CORP EMPL chairman: Capital Group Companies Inc.

Foundation Officials

John Herron Biggs: chairman, trustee B Saint Louis, MO 1936. ED Harvard University AB (1958); Washington University PhD (1983). PRIM CORP EMPL chairman, chief executive officer, director: Teachers Insurance Annuity Association/College Retirement Equities Fund. CORP AFFIL director: J.P. Morgan Chase & Co. NONPR AFFIL director: United Way New York City; trustee: Washington University; fellow: Society Actuaries; chairman: National Bureau Economic Affairs; member: New York City Partnership; member: Financial Accounting Foundation; emeritus trustee: Missouri Botanical Gardens; member: Association Governing Board Higher Education; member: Business Higher Education Forum; member: American Academy of Actuaries; member: American Academy of Arts & Sciences. CLUB AFFIL Westchester Country Club; Saint Louis Club; Sky Club; Harvard Club; Log Cabin Club.

Louise Henry Bryson: vice chairman, trustee PRIM CORP EMPL chairman: Community Television of Southern California. NONPR AFFIL director: Cable & Telecommunications Assn. for Marketing; director: Children Now.

Ronald W. Burkle: trustee

Ramon C. Cortines: trustee NONPR AFFIL board of directors: Rural School and Community Trust; board of directors: San Francisco Symphony; executive director: Pew Network for Standards Based Reform; trustee: Brown University; board of directors: National Center for Public Policy and Higher Education.

Lloyd E. Cotsen: trustee B Boston, MA 1929. ED Princeton University BA (1950); Harvard University MBA (1957). NONPR AFFIL trustee: American School of Classical Studies at Athens.

Barbara G. Fleischman: trustee NONPR AFFIL chairman: Smithsonian Archives of American Art.

Agnes Gund: trustee B Cleveland, OH 1938. ED Connecticut College BA (1960); Harvard University MA (1980). PRIM NONPR AFFIL president: Music of Modern Art. NONPR AFFIL president emeritus: Museum of Modern Art; board of directors: World Trade Center Memorial Foundation.

Barry Munitz: president, chief executive officer, trustee B 1941. ED Princeton University PhD; Brooklyn College BA (1963); Princeton University MA (1965); Princeton University PhD (1968). PRIM NONPR EMPL chancellor: California State University System. CORP AFFIL board of directors: Sallie Mae; board of directors: KB Home; director: LeapFrog Enterprises Ltd. NONPR AFFIL trustee: Princeton University; member: Young President Organization; member: National Business Higher Education Forum; member: Phi Beta Kappa; director: KCET-TV.

Luis Guerrero Nogales: trustee B Madera, CA 1943. ED San Diego State University BA (1966); Stanford University JD (1969). PRIM NONPR EMPL attorney, president: Nogales Partners. CORP AFFIL managing Partner: Nogales Investors LLC; director: SCE Corp.; director: Kaufman & Broad Home Corp.; director: KB Home; director: Edison International; chairman, chief executive officer: Embarcadero Media Inc.; director: Arbitron Inc..

Steven B. Sample: trustee

Dr. Blenda Jacqueline Wilson: trustee B Woodbridge, NJ 1941. ED Cedar Crest College AB (1962); Seton Hall University AM (1965); Boston College PhD (1979). PRIM NONPR EMPL president, chief executive officer: Nellie Mae Education Foundation. CORP AFFIL director: Medco Health Solutions Inc. NONPR AFFIL member: Women Foundations; member: Women's Economic Club Detroit; member: Women Executives State Government; advisory board: University Southern California District 60 National Alliance; advisory board: Valley Cultural Cen-

ter; director: University Detroit Jesuit High School; director: United Way Southeast Michigan; chairman: University Corporate; American delegate: United States-UK Dialogue About Quality Judgements Higher Education; member: Race Relations Council Metropolitan Detroit; advisory board: Stanford Institute Higher Education Research; director: Nothridge Hospital Medical Center; visitors committee: PEW Forum K-12 Education Reform U.S.; president, chief executive officer: Nellie Mae Education Foundation; member: Michigan Womens Forum; member: National Coalition 100 Black Women; director, vice chairman: Metropolitan Affairs Corp.; director: Metropolitan Center High Technology; member: International Womens Forum; visitors committee: Harvard College Division Continuing Education Faculty Arts Science; director: International Foundation Education & Self-Help; trustee: J. Paul Getty Music; member: Greater Detroit Interfaith Round Table NCCJ; director, trustee emeritus: Foundation Center; deputy chairman: Federal Reserve Bank of Boston; director: Federated Dorchester Neighborhood Houses; member: College Board; trustee: Sammy Davis Junior National Liver Institute; trustee: Clark University; member: Black Women Higher Education; life trustee: Cambridge College; member: Association Black Professionals & Administrations; member advisory council president: Association Government Boards; director: Arab Community Center Economic Social Services; member: American Association University Women; member higher education colloquium: American Council Education; director: Achievement Council; member: American Association State Colleges & Universities. CLUB AFFIL Economic Club; Rotary Club.

Jay S. Wintrob: trustee

Grants Analysis

Disclosure Period: fiscal year ending June 30, 2003
Total Grants: $15,271,097*
Number of Grants: 219
Average Grant: $61,618*
Highest Grant: $1,000,000
Typical Range: $10,000 to $100,000
*Note: Giving excludes matching gifts; gifts to individuals. Average grant figure excludes two highest grants ($1,900,000).

Recent Grants

Note: Grants derived from fiscal 2003 Form 990.

General

1,000,000	Performing Arts Center of Los Angeles County, Los Angeles, CA -- towards special initiatives
900,000	Courtauld Institute of Art, London United Kingdom -- towards support for charitable activities
350,000	Regents of the University of California, Oakland, CA -- towards special initiatives
349,541	National Gallery London, London United Kingdom
313,991	Katholieke Universiteit Leuven, Leuven Belgium -- towards reference works
269,500	Philadelphia Museum of Art, Philadelphia, PA -- towards collaborative research
250,000	Henry E Huntington Library and Art Gallery, San Marino, CA -- towards electronic cataloguing initiative
250,000	Museum Associates, Los Angeles, CA -- towards electronic cataloguing initiative
250,000	University of Southern California, Los Angeles, CA -- towards preserve LA initiative
250,000	University of Southern California, Los Angeles, CA -- towards archival projects

GHEENS FOUNDATION

Giving Contact
James N. Davis, Executive Director
One Riverfront Plaza, Suite 705
Louisville, KY 40202
Phone: (502)584-4650
Fax: (502)584-4652
E-mail: lindahw@aye.net

Description
Founded: 1957
EIN: 616031406
Organization Type: General Purpose Foundation
Giving Locations: KY: Louisville; LA: LaFourche Parish
Grant Types: Capital, Fellowship, General Support, Matching, Multiyear/Continuing Support, Operating Expenses, Project, Research, Scholarship.

Donor Information
Founder: The foundation was established in 1957, by the late C. Edwin Gheens and the late Mary Jo Gheens Hill. Mr. Gheens owned a successful candy manufacturing company in Louisville, KY. His family, which was successful in the wholesale grocery business, also owned a sugar cane plantation in the New Orleans, LA area. Mr. & Mrs. Gheens were leaders in their church and active in other philanthropic endeavors in Louisville, and founded the Gheens Foundation to continue their interests in education, religious programs and human services.

Financial Summary
Total Giving: $3,768,675 (fiscal year ending October 31, 2003); $3,891,124 (fiscal 2002); $4,868,917 (fiscal 2001)
Giving Analysis: Giving for fiscal 2003 includes: foundation grants to United Way ($80,000); fiscal 2002: foundation grants to United Way ($80,000)
Assets: $75,904,336 (fiscal 2003); $70,468,184 (fiscal 2002); $90,570,318 (fiscal 2001)

Typical Recipients
Arts & Humanities: Arts Associations & Councils, Arts Centers, Arts Festivals, Arts Funds, Ballet, Community Arts, Historic Preservation, History & Archaeology, Libraries, Literary Arts, Museums/Galleries, Music, Opera, Public Broadcasting, Theater
Civic & Public Affairs: African American Affairs, Botanical Gardens/Parks, Clubs, Community Foundations, Economic Development, Employment/Job Training, Civic & Public Affairs-General, Hispanic Affairs, Housing, Law & Justice, Legal Aid, Municipalities/Towns, Parades/Festivals, Philanthropic Organizations, Rural Affairs, Safety, Urban & Community Affairs, Women's Affairs, Zoos/Aquariums
Education: Afterschool/Enrichment Programs, Agricultural Education, Business Education, Colleges & Universities, Economic Education, Education Associations, Education Funds, Education Reform, Elementary Education (Private), Engineering/Technological Education, Education-General, Leadership Training, Legal Education, Literacy, Medical Education, Minority Education, Preschool Education, Private Education (Precollege), Public Education (Precollege), Religious Education, School Volunteerism, Science/Mathematics Education, Secondary Education (Private), Social Sciences Education, Special Education, Student Aid
Environment: Air/Water Quality, Environment-General, Resource Conservation, Wildlife Protection
Health: Cancer, Children's Health/Hospitals, Clinics/Medical Centers, Diabetes, Eyes/Blindness, Geriatric Health, Health Funds, Health Organizations, Hospices, Hospitals, Hospitals (University Affiliated), Long-Term Care, Medical Rehabilitation, Medical Research, Mental Health, Preventive Medicine/Wellness Organizations, Public Health, Single-Disease Health Associations

International: Foreign Educational Institutions
Religion: Churches, Dioceses, Religion-General, Jewish Causes, Ministries, Religious Organizations, Religious Welfare, Seminaries
Science: Science Exhibits & Fairs, Science Museums, Scientific Centers & Institutes
Social Services: At-Risk Youth, Child Welfare, Community Centers, Community Service Organizations, Counseling, Day Care, Family Planning, Family Services, Food/Clothing Distribution, Homes, People with Disabilities, Recreation & Athletics, Scouts, Senior Services, Shelters/Homelessness, Social Services-General, Special Olympics, Substance Abuse, United Funds/United Ways, Volunteer Services, YMCA/YWCA/YMHA/YWHA, Youth Organizations

Application Procedures
Initial Contact: The foundation provides an application form; ten copies of the completed application should be sent to the foundation.
Application Requirements: The application form requests the following information: name of organization, contact person and title, address, program summary describing the activities of the organization and the particular activity that the grant would fund; and a financial summary detailing the amount of the request, total annual budget of the organization, and the budget for the project which the grant would support. The foundation also requires copies of IRS letters confirming the organization's tax-exempt status, and that it is not a private foundation.
Deadlines: None.

Restrictions
Grants are not made to individuals.

Additional Information
Publications: Guidelines; Application Form

Foundation Officials
Morton Boyd: trustee B Louisville, KY 1936. ED University of Virginia BA (1958); Rutgers University Stonier Graduate School of Banking (1964). PRIM CORP EMPL chairman, chief executive officer: National City Bank Kentucky. CORP AFFIL executive vice president: National City Corp.; executive vice president, director: First Kentucky Trust Co.; vice chairman: First National Bank Louisville. NONPR AFFIL chairman: Louisville Central Area; member: Louisville Chamber of Commerce; director: Fund Arts; director: Kentucky Derby Museum Corp.; member: Association Reserve City Bankers.
James N. Davis: executive director
Donald W. Doyle: vice president, trustee
William G. Duncan, Jr.: trustee
Michael B. Mountjoy: trustee, secretary, treasurer B 1942. ED University of Kentucky (1963). PRIM CORP EMPL managing director: Carpenter & Mountjoy PSC. CORP AFFIL secretary-treasurer, director: T-Shirts & More Inc.
Joseph E. Stopher: president, trustee B 1914. ED University of Louisville LLB (1938). PRIM CORP EMPL partner: Boehl Stopher & Graves.
Samuel D. Weakley, MD: trustee

Grants Analysis
Disclosure Period: fiscal year ending October 31, 2003
Total Grants: $3,688,675*
Number of Grants: 122
Average Grant: $30,235*
Highest Grant: $500,000
Lowest Grant: $1,000
Typical Range: $10,000 to $50,000
***Note:** Giving excludes United Way. Average grant figure excludes highest grant.

Recent Grants
Note: Grants derived from 2003 Form 990.
General
500,000	University of Louisville Foundation, Louisville, KY
150,000	Dryades YMCA, New Orleans, LA
110,332	Jefferson County Board of Education, Birmingham, AL
102,239	Jefferson County Board of Education Gheens Academy, Birmingham, AL
100,000	Bellarmine College, Louisville, KY
100,000	Greater Louisville Foundation Inc., Louisville, KY
100,000	Home of the Innocents, Louisville, KY
100,000	Owsley Brown Frazier Historical Arms Museum Foundation, Louisville, KY
100,000	Tulane University, New Orleans, LA
83,333	Episcopal Church Home, New York, NY

GHIDOTTI FOUNDATION

Giving Contact
William Toms, Trustee
3961 De Sabla Rd.
Cameron Park, CA 95682
Phone: (530)677-3994

Description
Founded: 1969
EIN: 946181833
Organization Type: Private Foundation
Giving Locations: CA: Nevada County
Grant Types: General Support, Scholarship.

Donor Information
Founder: William Ghidotti, the late Marian Ghidotti

Financial Summary
Total Giving: $590,454 (2004); $625,316 (2001). Note: 1997 Giving includes scholarship.
Giving Analysis: Giving for 2004 includes: foundation scholarships ($480,333); 2001: foundation scholarships ($494,767)
Assets: $11,896,732 (2004); $13,187,034 (2001)
Gifts Received: $184,916 (1994)

Typical Recipients
Arts & Humanities: Arts & Humanities-General, Historic Preservation, Libraries, Literary Arts, Music, Theater
Civic & Public Affairs: Clubs, Civic & Public Affairs-General, Parades/Festivals, Rural Affairs
Education: Agricultural Education, Elementary Education (Private), Education-General, Literacy, Private Education (Precollege), Public Education (Precollege), Science/Mathematics Education, Secondary Education (Public), Special Education, Student Aid
Environment: Energy, Resource Conservation
Health: Alzheimer's Disease, Home-Care Services, Hospices, Hospitals, Prenatal Health Issues
Religion: Religious Welfare
Social Services: At-Risk Youth, Big Brothers/Big Sisters, Child Abuse, Child Welfare, Community Service Organizations, United Funds/United Ways, Volunteer Services, Youth Organizations

Application Procedures
Initial Contact: Send standard application form by February for new scholarships, August for renewals. Also send transcript of grades, student and family income, and personal resume.

Additional Information
Provides scholarships to graduating seniors residing in and attending Nevada County, CA, high schools.
Trust(s): Wells Fargo Bank

Foundation Officials
Mary Bouma: trustee
Erica Erickson: trustee
Frank Francis: trustee
William Toms: trustee
Ruth Halls Unger: trustee

Grants Analysis

Disclosure Period: calendar year ending 2004
Total Grants: $110,121*
Number of Grants: 17
Average Grant: $5,320*
Highest Grant: $25,000
Lowest Grant: $1,000
Typical Range: $1,000 to $10,000
*Note: Giving excludes scholarships. Average grant figure excludes highest grant.

Recent Grants

Note: Grants derived from 2004 Form 990.
Library-Related

12,000	Friends of the Library

General

25,000	Music in the Mountains, Nevada City, CA
18,871	Nevada County Fair, Grass Valley, CA
13,000	Hospices of the Foothills, Grass Valley, CA
8,500	Foothill Theatre Company, Nevada City, CA
8,000	Miners Fdy Culture Preservation
4,500	Sierra Nevada Memorial Hospital, Grass Valley, CA
3,500	Friendship Club, Nevada City, CA
3,000	Child Advocates of Nevada County, Nevada City, CA
3,000	Nevada County Land Trust, Grass Valley, CA

GIANT EAGLE INC.

Company Headquarters

Pittsburgh, PA
Web: http://www.gianteagle.com

Company Description

Revenue: US$5.943 billion (2002)
Employees: 36000 (2003)
SIC(s): 2032 Canned Specialties, 2033 Canned Fruits & Vegetables, 2051 Bread, Cake & Related Products, 5411 Grocery Stores.

Operating Locations

Giant Eagle Inc. (PA--Pittsburgh)

Giant Eagle Foundation

Giving Contact

Jody Clark, Administrator
101 Kappa Drive
Pittsburgh, PA 15238
Phone: (412)963-6200
Fax: (412)963-2540

Alternate Contact

Ray Huber, Scholarship Administrator

Description

EIN: 256033905
Organization Type: Corporate Foundation
Giving Locations: PA: Pittsburgh
Grant Types: General Support, Research.

Financial Summary

Total Giving: $2,972,426 (fiscal year ending August 31, 2003); $3,162,273 (fiscal 2002); $3,162,273 (fiscal 2001). Note: Contributes through corporate direct giving program and foundation.
Assets: $20,899,050 (fiscal 2003); $17,472,774 (fiscal 2002); $17,472,774 (fiscal 2001)
Gifts Received: $4,434,281 (fiscal 2003); $3,423,466 (fiscal 2002); $3,423,466 (fiscal 2001). Note: Contributions are received from Giant Eagle, Inc.

Typical Recipients

Arts & Humanities: Arts Associations & Councils, Arts Centers, Arts Festivals, Arts Institutes, Ballet, Community Arts, Dance, Ethnic & Folk Arts, Arts & Humanities-General, History & Archaeology, Libraries, Museums/Galleries, Music, Opera, Performing Arts, Public Broadcasting, Theater
Civic & Public Affairs: African American Affairs, Botanical Gardens/Parks, Civil Rights, Clubs, Community Foundations, Economic Development, Economic Policy, Ethnic Organizations, Gay/Lesbian Issues, Civic & Public Affairs-General, Law & Justice, Legal Aid, Municipalities/Towns, Nonprofit Management, Parades/Festivals, Philanthropic Organizations, Public Policy, Urban & Community Affairs, Women's Affairs, Zoos/Aquariums
Education: Business Education, Colleges & Universities, Education Funds, Elementary Education (Private), Faculty Development, Education-General, Medical Education, Minority Education, Private Education (Precollege), Public Education (Precollege), Religious Education, Secondary Education (Private), Special Education, Student Aid
Environment: Environment-General, Resource Conservation, Wildlife Protection
Health: AIDS/HIV, Cancer, Children's Health/Hospitals, Diabetes, Emergency/Ambulance Services, Geriatric Health, Health Funds, Health Organizations, Heart, Hospitals, Kidney, Medical Rehabilitation, Medical Research, Mental Health, Prenatal Health Issues, Preventive Medicine/Wellness Organizations, Public Health, Single-Disease Health Associations
International: Health Care/Hospitals, International Organizations, International Relief Efforts, Missionary/Religious Activities
Religion: Dioceses, Religion-General, Jewish Causes, Religious Organizations, Religious Welfare, Social/Policy Issues, Synagogues/Temples
Science: Scientific Centers & Institutes, Scientific Research
Social Services: At-Risk Youth, Big Brothers/Big Sisters, Child Welfare, Community Centers, Community Service Organizations, Counseling, Delinquency & Criminal Rehabilitation, Domestic Violence, Family Services, Food/Clothing Distribution, Homes, People with Disabilities, Recreation & Athletics, Scouts, Senior Services, Sexual Abuse, Shelters/Homelessness, Substance Abuse, United Funds/United Ways, YMCA/YWCA/YMHA/YWHA, Youth Organizations

Application Procedures

Initial Contact: Send a written proposal.
Application Requirements: Include a description of organization, amount requested, purpose of funds sought, recently audited financial statement, and proof of tax-exempt status.
Deadlines: January 31 for grants; November 1 for scholarship applications.

Restrictions

Does not support individuals or non-501(c)(3) organizations.

Corporate Officials

David S. Shapira: chairman, chief executive officer, director B 1942. ED Oberlin College BA (1964); Stanford University MA (1966). PRIM CORP EMPL chairman, chief executive officer, director: Giant Eagle Inc. CORP AFFIL director: Mellon Bank Corp.; director: Mellon Bank NA; director: Equitable Resources Inc.

Foundation Officials

Gerald Chait: trustee CORP AFFIL director: Giant Eagle Inc.; director: Tamarkin Co. Inc.
Edward Moravitz: trustee B 1925. ED University of Pittsburgh (1948). CORP AFFIL director: Tamarkin Co. Inc.
David S. Shapira: trustee (see above)
Norman Weizenbaum: trustee B 1933. ED University of Pennsylvania (1955). CORP AFFIL director: Giant Eagle Inc.; director: Tamarkin Co. Inc.

Grants Analysis

Disclosure Period: fiscal year ending August 31, 2003
Total Grants: $2,890,426*
Number of Grants: 215
Average Grant: $7,814*
Highest Grant: $1,218,131
Lowest Grant: $170
Typical Range: $1,000 to $10,000
*Note: Giving excludes United Way and scholarships. Average grant figure excludes highest grant.

Recent Grants

Note: Grants derived from 2004 Form 990.
Library-Related

15,000	Columbus Metropolitan Library System, Columbus, OH

General

1,336,500	United Jewish Federation, Pittsburgh, PA
162,250	University of Pittsburgh, Pittsburgh, PA
150,000	Carnegie Mellon University, Pittsburgh, PA
50,000	MetroHealth System, Cleveland, OH
40,000	Cleveland Food Bank, Cleveland, OH
40,000	Pittsburgh Symphony, Pittsburgh, PA
36,000	Kollel Jewish Learning Center, Pittsburgh, PA
35,000	Hillel Academy, Pittsburgh, PA
33,000	Palestine Endowment Fund Israel Endowment Funds, New York, NY
30,500	Catholic Diocese of Cleveland Foundation, Cleveland, OH

GIANT FOOD INC.

Company Headquarters

6300 Sheriff Rd.
Landover, MD 20785
Web: http://www.giantfood.com

Company Description

Revenue: US$5.289 billion (2001)
Employees: 35000 (2001)
SIC(s): 5411 Grocery Stores, 5912 Drug Stores & Proprietary Stores.

Operating Locations

Giant Food Inc. (CA--Fresno; DC--Washington; MD--Baltimore, Burtonsville, Gaithersburg, Jessup, Joppa Heights, Landover, Lutherville, Pikesville, Prince Frederick, Rockville, Silver Spring, Upper Marlboro, Westminster; VA--Annandale, Fredericksburg, Herndon, Lakeridge, McLean, Warrenton)

Nonmonetary Support

Range: $75,000 - $400,000
Type: Cause-related Marketing & Promotion; Donated Equipment; Donated Products; In-kind Services
Contact: Barry F. Scher, Vice President, Public Affairs

Giant Food Foundation

Giving Contact

Richard A. Baird, President
6300 Sheriff Road
Landover, MD 20785
Phone: (301)341-4171
Fax: (301)618-4972
Web: http://www.giantfood.com/corporate/company_charitable.htm

Alternate Contact

Barry Scher, Vice President of Public Affairs
PO Box 1804
Washington, DC 20013
Note: Contact for sponsorship, direct giving and non-monetary support.

Description

Founded: 1950
EIN: 526045041
Organization Type: Corporate Foundation
Giving Locations: DE; DC; MD; NJ; VA
Grant Types: General Support.

Financial Summary

Total Giving: $605,122 (fiscal year ending January 31, 2004); $589,961 (fiscal 2003); $503,266 (fiscal 2001). Note: Contributes through corporate direct giving program and foundation.
Giving Analysis: Giving for fiscal 2001 includes: foundation grants to United Way ($207,450); foundation ($295,816)
Assets: $246,644 (fiscal 2004); $741,605 (fiscal 2003); $715,544 (fiscal 2001)
Gifts Received: $100,000 (fiscal 2004); $99,112 (fiscal 2003); $500,000 (fiscal 1999). Note: Contributions were received from Giant Food Inc.

Typical Recipients

Arts & Humanities: Arts Centers, Ballet, Community Arts, Dance, Historic Preservation, History & Archaeology, Libraries, Museums/Galleries, Music, Opera, Performing Arts, Public Broadcasting, Theater
Civic & Public Affairs: African American Affairs, Business/Free Enterprise, Chambers of Commerce, Community Foundations, Economic Development, Employment/Job Training, Ethnic Organizations, Civic & Public Affairs-General, Housing, Law & Justice, Public Policy, Urban & Community Affairs, Women's Affairs, Zoos/Aquariums
Education: Afterschool/Enrichment Programs, Arts/Humanities Education, Colleges & Universities, Community & Junior Colleges, Education Associations, Education Funds, Education-General, Medical Education, Minority Education, Public Education (Precollege), Religious Education, Science/Mathematics Education, Special Education, Student Aid
Health: Alzheimer's Disease, Cancer, Children's Health/Hospitals, Clinics/Medical Centers, Geriatric Health, Health Funds, Health Organizations, Heart, Hospices, Hospitals, Mental Health, Multiple Sclerosis, Prenatal Health Issues, Single-Disease Health Associations
Religion: Dioceses, Jewish Causes, Religious Organizations, Religious Welfare, Social/Policy Issues
Social Services: Animal Protection, Big Brothers/Big Sisters, Child Abuse, Child Welfare, Community Centers, Community Service Organizations, Counseling, Emergency Relief, Family Services, Food/Clothing Distribution, People with Disabilities, Recreation & Athletics, Scouts, Senior Services, Shelters/Homelessness, Social Services-General, Substance Abuse, United Funds/United Ways, Youth Organizations

Application Procedures

Initial Contact: Submit a brief letter or proposal.
Application Requirements: Include a description of organization, amount requested, purpose of funds sought, recently audited financial statement, and proof of Internal Revenue Service Section 170(c) status
Deadlines: None.

Corporate Officials

Richard A. Baird: president B 1942. PRIM CORP EMPL president, chief executive officer: Giant Food Inc. CORP AFFIL senior vice president: Stop & Stop Co. Inc.
Mark H. Berey: senior vice president, chief financial officer, treasurer B 1951. ED Indiana University BA

(1974); Northwestern University MBA (1975). PRIM CORP EMPL senior vice president, chief financial officer, treasurer: Giant Food Inc.
Michael J. Bush: vice president real estate B Phoenix, AZ 1943. ED Stanford University (1965); Harvard University (1968). PRIM CORP EMPL vice president real estate: Giant Food Inc. CORP AFFIL vice president: GFS Realty Inc.; executive vice president, chief operating officer, director: Movado Group Inc.
Russell B. Fair: vice president pharmacy operations B Nashua, NH 1948. ED Northeastern University (1971). PRIM CORP EMPL vice president pharmacy operations: Giant Food Inc. ADD CORP EMPL vice president: Giant Maryland Inc.
M. Davis Herriman, Jr.: vice president, grocery operations B Washington, DC 1938. ED George Washington University (1961). PRIM CORP EMPL vice president, grocery operations: Giant Food Inc. ADD CORP EMPL vice president: Giant of Maryland Inc.
Odonna Mathews: vice president consumer affairs B Washington, DC 1950. ED University of Maryland (1972); University of Maryland (1981). PRIM CORP EMPL vice president consumer affairs: Giant Food Inc. ADD CORP EMPL vice president: Giant Maryland Inc. NONPR AFFIL member consumer affairs committee: Food Marketing Institute; member: Society of Consumer Affairs Professionals.
David W. Rutstein: senior vice president, general counsel, chief administrative officer B New York, NY 1944. ED University of Pennsylvania BA (1966); George Washington University JD (1969). PRIM CORP EMPL senior vice president, general counsel, chief administrative officer: Giant Food Inc. ADD CORP EMPL senior vice president: Giant Maryland Inc.; senior vice president: Giant of Maryland Inc. NONPR AFFIL member: Washington Metropolitan Area Corporate Counsel Association; treasurer, director: Washington Metropolitan Board Trade; trustee: Greater Washington Research Center; member: District of Columbia Bar Association; treasurer, director, member executive committee: Federal City Council.
Barry F. Scher: vice president public affairs B Richmond, VA 1942. ED College of William & Mary (1964); American University (1965). PRIM CORP EMPL vice president public affairs: Giant Food Inc. ADD CORP EMPL vice president: Giant Maryland Inc. NONPR AFFIL member: Public Relations Society America; director: Second Harvest; vice chairman: Maryland Retailers Association; member: Food Marketing Government Affairs & Communications Division; chairman food bank national task force: Food Marketing Institute.
Samuel E. Thurston: senior vice president distribution B New Haven, CT 1943. ED University of New Haven (1966). PRIM CORP EMPL senior vice president distribution: Giant Food Inc. CORP AFFIL senior vice president: Giant Maryland Inc.

Foundation Officials

Richard A. Baird: president (see above)
Dan Currie: member
Bernie Ellis: member
Robert Evans: member
Barry F. Scher: vice president (see above)
Ann Weiser: member

Grants Analysis

Disclosure Period: fiscal year ending January 31, 2004
Total Grants: $605,122
Number of Grants: 33
Average Grant: $3,285*
Highest Grant: $500,000
Lowest Grant: $250
Typical Range: $1,000 to $5,000
*Note: Average grant figure excludes highest grant.

Recent Grants

Note: Grants derived from 2004 Form 990.

General

500,000	Twin Towers Fund, White Plains, MD -- aid in educational and relief funding
30,000	Genesee County Museum, Flint, MI -- aid in educational and relief funding
12,500	Capital Area Food Bank, Washington, DC -- aid in educational and relief funding
10,000	Project Reap, Washington, DC -- aid in educational and relief funding
8,872	American Red Cross, Washington, DC -- aid in educational and relief funding
6,000	Upper Chesapeake Health Foundation, Bel Air, MD -- aid in educational and relief funding
5,000	Multiple Sclerosis Society, Cockeysville, MD -- aid in educational and relief funding
5,000	Northwest Hospital Center, Randallstown, MD -- aid in educational and relief funding
2,500	Corcoran Gallery Art, Washington, DC -- aid in educational and relief funding
2,500	Greater Baltimore Urban League, Baltimore, MD -- aid in educational and relief funding

GIANT FOOD STORES

Company Headquarters

1149 Harrisburg Pike
Carlisle, PA 17013
Web: http://www.giantpa.com

Company Description

Employees: 3,000
SIC(s): 5411 Grocery Stores.
Parent Company: Royal Ahold N.V., Albert Heijnweg 1, Zaandam, Netherlands

Operating Locations

BI-LO (SC--Greenville); Edwards Super Food Stores (PA--Carlisle); Edwards Super Foods Stores Long Island Division (NY--Garden City); FINAST (OH--Maple Heights); Giant Food Stores (MD, Landover; PA--Carlisle; VA; WV); Stop & Shop Cos. (MA--Quincy); Tops Markets (NY--Amherst)

Nonmonetary Support

Type: Donated Equipment; Donated Products

Giving Contact

Debra Stoven, Consumer Affairs
1149 Harrisburg Pike
Carlisle, PA 17013
Phone: (717)249-4000
Fax: (717)960-1920
Web: http://www.giantpa.com

Description

Organization Type: Corporate Giving Program
Giving Locations: headquarters and operating communities.
Grant Types: Capital, General Support, Seed Money.

Typical Recipients

Arts & Humanities: Arts Associations & Councils, Historic Preservation, Libraries, Public Broadcasting
Civic & Public Affairs: Business/Free Enterprise, Civil Rights, Economic Development, Law & Justice, Municipalities/Towns, Safety, Urban & Community Affairs, Women's Affairs
Education: Colleges & Universities, Literacy, Minority Education, Student Aid
Environment: Environment-General
Health: Health Funds, Health Organizations, Hospitals, Medical Research, Mental Health, Single-Disease Health Associations
Religion: Religious Organizations

Social Services: Child Welfare, Community Centers, Community Service Organizations, Domestic Violence, Family Services, People with Disabilities, Senior Services, Substance Abuse, United Funds/United Ways, Youth Organizations

Application Procedures
Initial Contact: Send a brief letter or proposal.
Application Requirements: Include a description of organization, amount requested, and purpose for which funds are sought; a recently audited financial statement and proof of tax-exempt status occasionally are requested.

Additional Information
Does not support political or lobbying groups.
Giant Food Stores makes contributions to United Way agencies in each of the localities in which it does business. It also supports some capital campaigns for participating agencies, but generally does not support United Way member agencies. Giant's local stores are free to support local individual fund-raising activities at the store manager's discretion and as limited by the individual store's budget.

Corporate Officials
Jim Ferraro: chief financial officer, chief executive officer PRIM CORP EMPL chief financial officer: Giant Food Stores.
Anthony Schiano: president, chief executive officer PRIM CORP EMPL president, chief executive officer: Giant Food Stores Inc. ADD CORP EMPL vice president: May fair Super Markets Inc.

GIDDINGS & LEWIS INC.

Company Headquarters
142 Doty St.
Fond du Lac, WI 54936
Web: http://www.giddings.com

Company Description
Founded: 1859
Revenue: US$165 million (2002)
Employees: 439 (2003)
SIC(s): 3541 Machine Tools--Metal Cutting Types, 3625 Relays & Industrial Controls, 3825 Instruments to Measure Electricity.
Parent Company: ThyssenKrupp AG, August Thyssen Strasse 1, Dusseldorf, Germany

Giddings & Lewis Foundation

Giving Contact
Terri Groth, Treasurer
142 Doty Street
Fond du Lac, WI 54935
Phone: (920)921-9400

Alternate Contact
3155 W. Big Beaver Road
Suite 5084
Troy, MI 48007-5084
Phone: (248)643-3514

Description
Founded: 1952
EIN: 396061306
Organization Type: Corporate Foundation
Giving Locations: CA; MI; OH; WI
Grant Types: General Support.

Donor Information
Founder: Giddings & Lewis Machine Tool Co.

Financial Summary
Total Giving: $181,495 (2003); $373,621 (2001)
Assets: $1,929,160 (2003); $1,864,948 (2002); $2,384,643 (2001)
Gifts Received: $76,369 (2003); $297,180 (1999); $250,000 (1993). Note: CRF Giddings & Lewis, LLC.

Typical Recipients
Arts & Humanities: Arts Associations & Councils, Arts Centers, Community Arts, History & Archaeology, Libraries, Museums/Galleries, Music, Performing Arts, Public Broadcasting, Theater
Civic & Public Affairs: Botanical Gardens/Parks, Business/Free Enterprise, Clubs, Community Foundations, Economic Development, Civic & Public Affairs-General, Housing, Municipalities/Towns, Professional & Trade Associations, Safety, Urban & Community Affairs, Women's Affairs
Education: Business Education, Colleges & Universities, Community & Junior Colleges, Education Funds, Engineering/Technological Education, Faculty Development, Education-General, International Studies, Private Education (Precollege), Public Education (Precollege), Secondary Education (Private), Secondary Education (Public), Student Aid, Vocational & Technical Education
Environment: Wildlife Protection
Health: AIDS/HIV, Cancer, Clinics/Medical Centers, Emergency/Ambulance Services, Health Funds, Heart, Hospices, Hospitals, Multiple Sclerosis, Nursing Services, Prenatal Health Issues, Single-Disease Health Associations, Transplant Networks/Donor Banks
Religion: Religious Organizations, Religious Welfare, Seminaries
Science: Science Museums, Scientific Organizations
Social Services: At-Risk Youth, Big Brothers/Big Sisters, Child Welfare, Community Centers, Community Service Organizations, Homes, People with Disabilities, Recreation & Athletics, Scouts, Senior Services, Social Services-General, Substance Abuse, United Funds/United Ways, YMCA/YWCA/YMHA/YWHA, Youth Organizations

Application Procedures
Initial Contact: Send brief letter describing program.
Application Requirements: Include written proof of tax-exempt status.
Deadlines: None.

Additional Information
The majority of the foundation's giving is through a matching gift program.

Corporate Officials
Joseph R. Coppola: chairman, president, chief executive officer, director PRIM CORP EMPL chairman, president, chief executive officer, director: Giddings & Lewis.

Foundation Officials
Terri L. Groth: treasurer
Stephen M. Peterson: president
Douglas B. Vonderhaar: vice president

Grants Analysis
Disclosure Period: calendar year ending 2003
Total Grants: $74,500*
Number of Grants: 3
Highest Grant: $72,000
Lowest Grant: $1,000
*Note: Giving excludes scholarships, matching gifts, and United Way.

Recent Grants
Note: Grants derived from 2003 Form 990.
General

72,000	Fond Du Lac School District -- for new performing arts center
21,177	United Way
6,912	United Way
6,271	United Way
5000	Chatsworth Hills Academy, Chatsworth, CA
2,820	American Cancer Society Relay for Life
2,225	University of Wisconsin Foundation, Madison, WI
2,015	Dayton United Way, Dayton, OH
1,587	United Way
1,500	Windhover Center for the Arts, Fond du Lac, WI

ROSAMOND GIFFORD CHARITABLE CORP.

Giving Contact
Kathryn Goldfarb, Executive Director
126 N. Salina St., 100 Clinton Sq.
Syracuse, NY 13202
Phone: (315)474-2489
Fax: (315)475-4983
E-mail: kgoldfarb@giffordfd.org
Web: http://www.giffordfd.org

Description
Founded: 1954
EIN: 150572881
Organization Type: General Purpose Foundation
Giving Locations: NY: Syracuse and Onondaga County
Grant Types: Award, Capital, Emergency, Endowment, General Support, Loan, Matching, Multiyear/Continuing Support, Project, Seed Money.

Donor Information
Founder: The foundation was incorporated in 1954 by the late Rosamond Gifford.

Financial Summary
Total Giving: $1,025,010 (2002); $1,380,969 (2001). Note: 1997 Giving includes United Way ($267,300).
Giving Analysis: Giving for 2002 includes: foundation grants to United Way ($125,000)
Assets: $24,547,133 (2002); $27,931,970 (2001)

Typical Recipients
Arts & Humanities: Arts Associations & Councils, Historic Preservation, History & Archaeology, Libraries, Museums/Galleries, Music, Performing Arts, Public Broadcasting, Theater
Civic & Public Affairs: African American Affairs, Botanical Gardens/Parks, Clubs, Community Foundations, Economic Development, Employment/Job Training, Ethnic Organizations, Civic & Public Affairs-General, Housing, Legal Aid, Municipalities/Towns, Nonprofit Management, Parades/Festivals, Rural Affairs, Urban & Community Affairs, Women's Affairs, Zoos/Aquariums
Education: Arts/Humanities Education, Business Education, Colleges & Universities, Community & Junior Colleges, Education Funds, Education-General, Leadership Training, Literacy, Private Education (Precollege), Public Education (Precollege), Social Sciences Education, Student Aid
Environment: Environment-General, Protection
Health: Alzheimer's Disease, Clinics/Medical Centers, Emergency/Ambulance Services, Health-General, Health Organizations, Heart, Hospices, Hospitals, Kidney, Long-Term Care, Medical Research, Mental Health, Nursing Services, Prenatal Health Issues, Public Health, Single-Disease Health Associations
International: International Organizations
Religion: Churches, Jewish Causes, Ministries, Religious Organizations, Religious Welfare, Social/Policy Issues
Science: Scientific Centers & Institutes, Scientific Organizations

Social Services: Animal Protection, Big Brothers/Big Sisters, Camps, Child Welfare, Community Centers, Community Service Organizations, Crime Prevention, Family Planning, Family Services, Food/Clothing Distribution, Homes, People with Disabilities, Recreation & Athletics, Scouts, Senior Services, Sexual Abuse, Shelters/Homelessness, Social Services-General, Special Olympics, Substance Abuse, United Funds/United Ways, Volunteer Services, YMCA/YWCA/YMHA/YWHA, Youth Organizations

Application Procedures

Initial Contact: Applicants should call or write to the corporation to request an application form.
Deadlines: February1; May1; August1; November1.

Restrictions

The corporation does not make grants to individuals, or for continuing support, deficit financing, land acquisition, matching gifts, scholarships, fellowships, or loans.

Additional Information

Publications: Application Guidelines; Program Policy Statement; Annual Report

Foundation Officials

Richard G. Case: assistant secretary
Charles A. Chappell, Jr.: trustee B Syracuse, NY 1924. ED Syracuse University BA (1949). PRIM CORP EMPL chairman: C. E. Chappell & Sons Inc.
Patricia T. Civil: treasurer
Bethaida C. Gonzalez: vice president, trustee
Edward S. Green: president, trustee
Amelia Greiner: trustee
Linda M. Hall: trustee
Billy Harper: trustee
Patrick A. Mannion: trustee PRIM CORP EMPL chief executive officer: Unity Mutual Life Insurance Co. CORP AFFIL director: Germantown Life Insurance Co.
Judith Mower: trustee
Mark D. Muhammad: trustee
Sharon C. Northrup: trustee
Joanne Reddick: trustee
Jack H. Webb: trustee

Grants Analysis

Disclosure Period: calendar year ending 2002
Total Grants: $900,010*
Number of Grants: 62
Average Grant: $11,476*
Highest Grant: $200,000
Lowest Grant: $284
Typical Range: $5,000 to $20,000
*Note: Giving excludes United Way. Average grant figure excludes highest grant.

Recent Grants

Note: Grants derived from 2002 Form 990.
General
200,000	Friends of Burnet Park Zoo, Syracuse, NY -- for educational endowment
125,000	United Way of Central New York, Syracuse, NY -- to support various needs in Onondaga county
100,000	Lemoyne College Theater 2001, Syracuse, NY -- to create theater for children to teach life skills
78,500	Interdenominational Ministerial Alliance -- toward administrative support for coalition against
50,000	Syracuse 20/20 -- funding for general operations
39,750	ENOTA Project, Erie County, NY -- for training of police and community on mutual respect
31,045	Citistates -- for 4 day conference/seminar in SYR on
30,000	MOST, Paris France -- to enhance science & technology educational program for students

30,000	YMCA, Eastside Center, Providence, RI -- towards grant for building fund
26,000	RLS Career Center, Syracuse, NY -- for job training program for youths & adults

PAUL AND OSCAR GIGER FOUNDATION

Giving Contact

Frank A. Blazek, President & Secretary
Paul and Oscar Giger Foundation
Care of Fraser Stryker Law Firm
500 Energy Plz.
409 S. 17th Street
Omaha, NE 68102
Phone: (402)341-6000

Description

Founded: 1985
EIN: 470682708
Organization Type: Private Foundation
Giving Locations: NE: Omaha including metropolitan area; OH
Grant Types: General Support.

Donor Information

Founder: the late Ruth Giger

Financial Summary

Total Giving: $107,200 (2003); $119,700 (2001)
Assets: $2,575,247 (2003); $2,691,095 (2001)

Typical Recipients

Arts & Humanities: Arts Associations & Councils, Ballet, Community Arts, Libraries, Museums/Galleries, Music, Opera, Performing Arts, Public Broadcasting, Theater
Civic & Public Affairs: Botanical Gardens/Parks, Civic & Public Affairs-General, Housing, Philanthropic Organizations, Urban & Community Affairs, Zoos/Aquariums
Education: Arts/Humanities Education, Colleges & Universities, Education-General, Health & Physical Education, Private Education (Precollege), Public Education (Precollege), Religious Education
Environment: Environment-General, Wildlife Protection
Health: Cancer, Emergency/Ambulance Services, Eyes/Blindness, Health Organizations, Nursing Services, Preventive Medicine/Wellness Organizations, Single-Disease Health Associations
International: Missionary/Religious Activities
Religion: Bible Study/Translation, Churches, Ministries, Religious Organizations, Religious Welfare
Social Services: Animal Protection, Child Welfare, Community Service Organizations, Emergency Relief, Family Services, Food/Clothing Distribution, Homes, Scouts, Senior Services, Volunteer Services, Youth Organizations

Application Procedures

Initial Contact: Contact foundation for application form.
Deadlines: May 15 and October 1.

Restrictions

Does not support individuals, private for-profit businesses, private nonoperating foundations, or building funds.

Additional Information

Publications: Application Form; Instructions

Foundation Officials

Janet Acker: secretary B 1951. PRIM CORP EMPL vice president: Airfield Plaza Inn Corp.
Frank A. Blazek: president
Beverly Ingram: vice president

Grants Analysis

Disclosure Period: calendar year ending 2003
Total Grants: $107,200
Number of Grants: 25
Average Grant: $4,288
Highest Grant: $27,000
Lowest Grant: $500
Typical Range: $1,000 to $10,000

Recent Grants

Note: Grants derived from 2001 Form 990.
Library-Related
5,000	Omaha Public Library, Omaha, NE
General
20,000	Fontanel Forest Association, Omaha, NE
20,000	Omaha Botanical Gardens, Omaha, NE
12,500	First Central Congregational Church, Omaha, NE
10,000	Omaha Symphony Association, Omaha, NE
10,000	Omaha Zoo Foundation, Omaha, NE
5,000	American Red Cross, Omaha, NE
5,000	Volunteer Intervening for Equity, Omaha, NE
4,500	Tuesday Musical Concert Series, Omaha, NE
4,000	Nebraska Humane Society, Omaha, NE
3,500	Salvation Army, Omaha, NE

GILLETTE CO.

Company Headquarters

Boston, MA
Web: http://www.gillette.com

Company Description

Founded: 1901
Ticker: G
Exchange: NYSE
Revenue: US$10.477 billion (2004)
Profit: US$1.691 billion (2004)
Employees: 29400 (2003)
Fortune Rank: 215, per FORTUNE Magazine's list of 500 Largest U.S. Corporations (2004).
SIC(s): 2844 Toilet Preparations, 3421 Cutlery, 3634 Electric Housewares & Fans, 3951 Pens & Mechanical Pencils.

Operating Locations

Gillette Co. (CA--Mission Viejo, Santa Monica, Thousand Oaks, Westlake Village; GA--Marietta; IL--Itasca, North Chicago, Schaumburg; MA--Boston, Lynnfield, Norwood; MN--St. Paul; OH--Cleveland)

Nonmonetary Support

Value: $10,500,000 (2000)
Type: Cause-related Marketing & Promotion; Donated Equipment; Donated Products; In-kind Services
Note: In-kind product donations are given to in-need recipients in the locations where the company has a major presence. Except in the event of a natural disaster, production donations are generally reviewed using the same priorities and criteria that are used to select grant recipients. Gillette also works with an international organization which serves as the company's agent in providing product donations. Product requests can be directed to Gifts in Kind International (703) 836-2121.
Volunteer Programs: Company employees volunteer with Making Strides for Breast Cancer, Walk for Hunger, and the AIDS Walk. The Gillette Retiree Outreach Program (GROUP) is a retiree managed program that administers a variety of volunteer activities ranging from literacy programs to blood drives.

Gillette Charitable & Educational Foundation

Giving Contact

Kathy Chizauskas, Director, Civic Affairs
Care of The Gillette Company
Prudential Tower Bldg.
Boston, MA 02199
Phone: (617)463-8608
Fax: (617)421-8484
E-mail: royall_mack@gillette.com
Web: http://www.gillette.com/community/corpcontributions.asp

Alternate Contact

Royall Mack, Director, Civic Affairs

Description

EIN: 136047626
Organization Type: Corporate Foundation
Giving Locations: MA: Boston operating locations.
Grant Types: Employee Matching Gifts, General Support, Operating Expenses, Scholarship.
Note: The company matches employee gifts to most 501(c)(3) charities.

Financial Summary

Total Giving: $3,113,652 (2002)
Assets: $2,648,399 (2002)
Gifts Received: $500,000 (1995)

Typical Recipients

Arts & Humanities: Arts Centers, Dance, Libraries, Museums/Galleries, Music, Public Broadcasting
Civic & Public Affairs: Employment/Job Training, Urban & Community Affairs
Education: Business Education, Colleges & Universities
Health: Clinics/Medical Centers, Emergency/Ambulance Services, Hospitals
Religion: Jewish Causes
Social Services: United Funds/United Ways, Youth Organizations

Application Procedures

Initial Contact: After confirming that proposal falls within Gillette's priorities, submit a written request.
Application Requirements: The request must include responses to the following questions: What is the issue your organization is addressing? What is your organization's mission statement and how does it relate to The Gillette Company's areas of focus? What is your experience and capabilities in dealing with this issue? What is the scope of your program, including objectives, timelines and expected outcomes? What communities, audience or people are the beneficiaries of this program? What results do you expect for the program? How will you track and measure the results? How will you communicate those results to The Gillette Company? What is the time frame of the program? How is your program different from like programs that may also be addressing the issue you have identified? How will you sustain this program after Gillette support ends? Is this a single request of The Gillette Company or will you be seeking additional support? If so, please describe. Do you receive support from The United Way? Does the program or your organization have volunteer opportunities for Gillette employees? How will you acknowledge Gillette Company support? The following supporting documents must also be included with the request: annual report or other information about the applicant organization, its leadership, advisory board, current programs, budget, financial statement, and a list of other current or proposed contributions, and proof of tax-exempt status.
Deadlines: December 31, for grants to be awarded in March; March 31, for grants to be awarded in June; June 30, for grants to be awarded in September; and September 30, for grants to be awarded in December.

Decision Notification: Within six to eight weeks.
Notes: Gillette support to an organization or program is limited to three consecutive years; previously funded organizations may reapply after a two-year hiatus.

Restrictions

Gillette does not fund projects or organizations that are not located within a Gillette community; endowments or capital campaigns; fundraising events; golf tournaments or sporting events; multi-year pledges or commitments; contributions for more than three years to a specific organization; organizations that conflict with Gillette's mission, goals, policies, or products; organizations without IRS 501(c)(3) tax exempt status; organizations that limit membership and services in a discriminatory manner; conferences, seminars, trips, tours or similar events; advertising for benefit or courtesy purposes; operating expenses of organizations supported by United Way; loans or debt retirement; religious or sectarian programs for religious purposes; churches, synagogues, or ministries unless for specific social programs that meet all other foundation criteria; and fraternities, sororities, individuals, scholarships, political action committees, or candidates for political office.

Additional Information

Scholarships provided only through the National Merit Scholarship Program.

Corporate Officials

Cathleen Chizauskas: director, ethnic marketing
Charles W. Cramb: senior vice president finance, chief financial officer ED Dartmouth College BA (1968); University of Chicago MBA (1970). PRIM CORP EMPL senior vice president finance, chief financial officer: The Gillette Co. CORP AFFIL director: Idenix Pharmaceuticals Inc.; director: Tenneco Automotive Inc..
Edward F. DeGraan: vice chairman, director ED Suffolk University. PRIM CORP EMPL president, chief operating officer, director: The Gillette Co. CORP AFFIL director: Becton, Dickinson & Co. NONPR AFFIL trustee: National Urban League.
James M. Kilts: chairman, chief executive officer, director B February 10, 1948. ED Knox College BA (1970); University of Chicago MBA (1974). PRIM CORP EMPL chairman, chief executive officer, director: The Gillette Co. CORP AFFIL director: Whirlpool Corp.; director: May Department Stores Co. NONPR AFFIL trustee: Knox College; director: National Association of Manufacturers; director: International Executive Service Corps.; chairman, director: Grocery Manufacturers of America.

Giving Program Officials

Cathleen Chizauskas: director civic affairs (see above)

Grants Analysis

Disclosure Period: calendar year ending 2000
Total Grants: $21,000,000 (approx)
Typical Range: $300,000 to $500,000

Recent Grants

Note: Grants derived from 1998 Form 990.
General
352,348   United Way New England, Providence, RI

HOWARD GILMAN FOUNDATION

Giving Contact

Jennifer Amis, Program Administrator
111 West 50th Street
New York, NY 10020

Phone: (212)307-1073
Fax: (212)262-4108

Description

Founded: 1981
EIN: 133097486
Organization Type: Family Foundation
Giving Locations: NY: New York internationally; nationally.
Grant Types: General Support, Multiyear/Continuing Support, Operating Expenses, Project, Research.

Donor Information

Founder: The foundation was established in 1981 by Howard Gilman, former chairman of the board of the Gilman Paper Co. Three generations of the Gilman family have worked toward building its philanthropic legacy. Founded in 1884 by Howard Gilman's grandfather, the Gilman Paper Co. is the largest privately-owned paper company in the United States. The company has operations in New York, Florida, and Georgia. Howard Gilman died in 1998.

Financial Summary

Total Giving: $7,790,750 (2002)
Assets: $57,230,970 (2002)
Gifts Received: $3,000,000 (2002); $500 (2000); $6,500,000 (1994). Note: In 2002, contributions were received from the estate of Sylvia P. Gilman. In fiscal 1994, contributions were received from Gilman Securities Corporation. In fiscal 1993, gifts were received from Gilman Investment Company.

Typical Recipients

Arts & Humanities: Arts Appreciation, Arts Associations & Councils, Arts Centers, Arts Funds, Arts Institutes, Arts Outreach, Ballet, Dance, Ethnic & Folk Arts, Film & Video, Arts & Humanities-General, Libraries, Literary Arts, Museums/Galleries, Music, Opera, Performing Arts, Public Broadcasting, Theater, Visual Arts
Civic & Public Affairs: African American Affairs, Botanical Gardens/Parks, Civil Rights, Community Foundations, Employment/Job Training, Ethnic Organizations, Gay/Lesbian Issues, Civic & Public Affairs-General, Municipalities/Towns, Nonprofit Management, Philanthropic Organizations, Professional & Trade Associations, Public Policy, Urban & Community Affairs, Women's Affairs, Zoos/Aquariums
Education: Arts/Humanities Education, Colleges & Universities, Education Funds, Environmental Education, Education-General, Literacy, Medical Education, Social Sciences Education, Student Aid
Environment: Environment-General, Protection, Resource Conservation, Wildlife Protection
Health: AIDS/HIV, Children's Health/Hospitals, Clinics/Medical Centers, Health-General, Health Organizations, Heart, Hospitals, Hospitals (University Affiliated), Medical Research, Preventive Medicine/Wellness Organizations, Public Health, Single-Disease Health Associations
International: Foreign Arts Organizations, International-General, Health Care/Hospitals, Human Rights, International Affairs, International Development, International Environmental Issues, International Organizations, International Peace & Security Issues, International Relations, International Relief Efforts, Missionary/Religious Activities
Religion: Jewish Causes, Religious Organizations, Religious Welfare, Synagogues/Temples
Science: Science-General, Science Museums, Scientific Labs
Social Services: Animal Protection, Child Welfare, Community Service Organizations, Crime Prevention, Family Services, Food/Clothing Distribution, Refugee Assistance, Shelters/Homelessness, Social Services-General, YMCA/YWCA/YMHA/YWHA

Application Procedures

Initial Contact: The foundation requests that prospective applicants check the foundation's web site for program guidelines, as updates are posted each program year.

Application Requirements: Applications are accepted in the Partners for Performing Arts and Training & Mentoring Young Talent program areas. Applications are not accepted for the Cardiovascular Research program area, as Foundation support is provided solely to the Howard Gilman Institute for Valvular Heart Diseases at Weill Medical College of Cornell University. The Foundation also operates the White Oak Plantation, which supports wildlife conservation and performing arts programs on-site. Unsolicited requests are not currently being accepted for the use of White Oak Plantation.

Deadlines: Deadlines vary by program area. Refer to the foundation's web site for details.

Restrictions

The foundation supports charitable organizations classified under IRS Code 509(a)(1),(2), or (3) and 501(c)(3) or private operating foundation under section 4942 (j)(3) only. It does not support political or religious activity, nor individuals. It also will not fund deficit operations, construction or renovation of buildings, capital investments, endowments, scholarships, fellowships, or foreign grantees not satisfying the requirements of the Foundation Tax Excise regulations. The animal program focuses on wildlife, not domesticated animals or humane societies. International AIDS programming is policy-oriented. Arts and Medical focused in NYC.

Additional Information

The foundation is particularly interested in trans-Atlantic cooperation.

In 1999, the Gilman Paper Co. was acquired by Group Industrial Durango of Mexico. The Gilman Paper Co. reported that assets from the acquisition would be given to the Howard Gilman Foundation.

Publications: Guidelines; Background Statement

Foundation Officials

Norman E. Alexander: director
Pierre Apraxine: director
Gwendolyn C. Baker: director
Bernard D. Bergreen: director B 1923. ED New York University AB (1943); Columbia University LLB (1948).
Dr. Jeffrey Borer: vice president, director
Donald Bruce: director
J. D. Campbell: director
Stephen W. Cropper: vice president, director
Justin N. Feldman: director
Harvey Lichtenstein: director
William Henry Luers: director B Springfield, IL 1929. ED Columbia University MA; Hamilton College BA (1951); Northwestern University (1951-1952); Columbia University MA (1957). PRIM NONPR EMPL president: Metropolitan Museum of Art. CORP AFFIL director: Wickes Inc.; director: Wickes Lumber Co.; director: Scudder New Europe Fund; director: Story First Corp.; director: Scudder Equities & Security Funds; director: Scudder Global/International Funds; director: Brazil Fund; director: IDEX Corp. NONPR AFFIL advisory council: Trust Mutual Understanding; president, chief executive officer: UN Association of the US; member: Council Foreign Relations; director: Institute East-West Studies; fellow: American Academy of Arts & Sciences; trustee, advisory council: Appeal Conscience Foundation. CLUB AFFIL board directors: Economic Club New York.
John Lukas: director
Raymond J. McGuire: director
Natalie P. Moody: director
Isabella Rossellini: president, director

Grants Analysis

Disclosure Period: calendar year ending 2002
Total Grants: $7,790,750*
Number of Grants: 119
Average Grant: $31,644*
Highest Grant: $1,600,000
Lowest Grant: $1,000

Typical Range: $5,000 to $50,000 and $100,000 to $500,000
*Note: Average grant figure excludes three highest grants ($4,120,000).

Recent Grants

Note: Grants derived from 2002 Form 990.
General

1,600,000	Weill Medical College of Cornell University, New York, NY -- towards heart research
1,500,000	Brooklyn Academy of Music, Brooklyn, NY -- for Gilman opera house
1,020,000	Gilman International Conservation Foundation, Yulee, FL -- for general support
350,000	White Oak Conference and Residency Center Inc., Yulee, FL -- for general support
300,000	Mark Morris Dance Group, Brooklyn, NY -- for general support
250,000	Howard Gilman, Israel Culture Foundation, Tel Aviv Israel -- for general support
225,000	New York University Medical Center, New York, NY -- for research activities
209,300	International Rhino Foundation, Yulee, FL -- for general support
166,750	St. Marys Riverfront Park, St. Marys, GA -- for Gilman memorial park
150,000	Baryshnikov Dance Foundation, New York, NY -- center for dance

IRVING S. GILMORE FOUNDATION

Giving Contact

Frederick W. Freund, Executive Director & Trustee
136 East Michigan Avenue, Suite 900
Kalamazoo, MI 49007
Phone: (269)342-6411
Fax: (269)342-6465
E-mail: fritz@isgilmorefoundation.org
Web: http://www.isgilmorefoundation.org

Description

Founded: 1972
EIN: 237236057
Organization Type: General Purpose Foundation
Giving Locations: MI: Kalamazoo including greater metropolitan area
Grant Types: Capital, Conference/Seminar, Emergency, General Support, Matching, Multiyear/Continuing Support, Operating Expenses, Project, Seed Money.

Donor Information

Founder: The foundation was established in 1972 with an initial donation of $5,000 by the founder, Irving S. Gilmore of Kalamazoo, MI. Mr. Gilmore died in 1986 and through his will distributed assets valued at $67,010,041 to the foundation.

Financial Summary

Total Giving: $8,325,793 (2003); $7,845,952 (2002)
Giving Analysis: Giving for 2003 includes: foundation matching gifts ($21,389)
Assets: $201,162,334 (2003); $235,737,981 (2002)

Typical Recipients

Arts & Humanities: Arts Associations & Councils, Arts Centers, Arts Festivals, Arts Funds, Arts Institutes, Arts Outreach, Ballet, Community Arts, Dance, Ethnic & Folk Arts, Arts & Humanities-General, Historic Preservation, History & Archaeology, Libraries, Museums/Galleries, Music, Performing Arts, Theater
Civic & Public Affairs: Botanical Gardens/Parks, Business/Free Enterprise, Clubs, Community Foundations, Economic Development, Gay/Lesbian Is-

sues, Civic & Public Affairs-General, Hispanic Affairs, Housing, Municipalities/Towns, Native American Affairs, Nonprofit Management, Parades/Festivals, Philanthropic Organizations, Professional & Trade Associations, Public Policy, Urban & Community Affairs, Women's Affairs, Zoos/Aquariums
Education: Afterschool/Enrichment Programs, Arts/Humanities Education, Business Education, Colleges & Universities, Community & Junior Colleges, Economic Education, Education Associations, Education Funds, Education Reform, Engineering/Technological Education, Education-General, Literacy, Medical Education, Public Education (Precollege), Science/Mathematics Education, Special Education, Student Aid
Environment: Environment-General
Health: AIDS/HIV, Clinics/Medical Centers, Emergency/Ambulance Services, Eyes/Blindness, Health Organizations, Nursing Services, Public Health, Single-Disease Health Associations, Speech & Hearing
International: Foreign Arts Organizations
Religion: Churches, Dioceses, Ministries, Religious Organizations, Religious Welfare
Social Services: At-Risk Youth, Big Brothers/Big Sisters, Camps, Child Welfare, Community Centers, Community Service Organizations, Counseling, Day Care, Emergency Relief, Family Planning, Family Services, Food/Clothing Distribution, Homes, People with Disabilities, Recreation & Athletics, Scouts, Senior Services, Substance Abuse, United Funds/United Ways, Volunteer Services, YMCA/YWCA/YMHA/YWHA, Youth Organizations

Application Procedures

Initial Contact: Applicants should mail a proposal to the foundation.
Application Requirements: The proposal should be unbound, not more than 8-10 pages include the following: a brief history of the organization; description of the project; anticipated outcome; need for the program; amount requested; means by which outcome of project can be achieved; means for evaluating outcome and success; list of the board of directors or trustees and affiliations and occupations; the organization's past and present sources of support and a list of sources of support being sought for the present proposal, both prospective and received; a one-page, line-item project budget; latest audited financial statement including a balance sheet and income and expense statement; all interim and final reports from any grants previously received from the Foundation; and a copy of the IRS tax-exempt determination letter. A cover letter must also be sent, signed by the organization's board president and chief executive officer.
Deadlines: May 15 for the July meeting; July 15 for the September meeting; September 15 for the November meeting; November 15 for the January meeting; January 15 for the March meeting; and March 15 for the May meeting.

Restrictions

Grants are not made to individuals. The foundation only gives to organization in the area of Kalamazoo, MI. No grant applications accepted via e-mail or via fax.

Additional Information

Publications: Annual Report; Application Guidelines

Foundation Officials

Julie Batts: secretary
Frederick W. Freund: executive director, trustee
Russell L. Gabier: secretary, trustee NONPR AFFIL director: Gilmore Music Festival.
Richard M. Hughey, Sr.: president, trustee
Richard M. Hughey, Jr.: program officer CORP AFFIL director: Spring Root Scraper Co.
Floyd L. Parks: vice president, treasurer, trustee
Kay Tomas: secretary

Grants Analysis

Disclosure Period: calendar year ending 2003
Total Grants: $8,304,404*
Number of Grants: 128
Average Grant: $37,434*
Highest Grant: $1,000,000
Lowest Grant: $800
Typical Range: $15,000 to $50,000
*Note: Giving excludes matching gifts. Average grant figure excludes five highest grants ($3,700,000).

Recent Grants

Note: Grants derived from 2002 Form 990.
General

3,015,000	Kalamazoo College, Kalamazoo, MI -- for facilities and programming
900,000	Irving S. Gilmore International Keyboard Festival, Kalamazoo, MI -- for operations
620,450	Kalamazoo Regional Educational Service Agency, Kalamazoo, MI -- for operations and programming
396,254	Western Michigan University Foundation, WMUK, Kalamazoo, MI -- for capital campaign and programming
350,000	Southwest Michigan First Corporation, Kalamazoo, MI -- for operations
318,400	Arts Council of Greater Kalamazoo, Kalamazoo, MI -- for operations and programming
314,000	Glowing Embers Girl Scout Council, Kalamazoo, MI -- for capital campaign and programming
275,000	Kalamazoo Institute of Arts, Kalamazoo, MI -- for operations
180,000	Crescendo Academy of Music, Kalamazoo, MI -- for facilities and operations
171,250	Healthy Futures Inc., Kalamazoo, MI -- for capital campaign and operations

WILLIAM G. GILMORE FOUNDATION

Giving Contact

Faye C. Wilson, Executive Director
120 Montgomery St., Suite 1880
San Francisco, CA 94104
Phone: (415)546-1400
Fax: (415)391-8732

Description

Founded: 1953
EIN: 946079493
Organization Type: Private Foundation
Giving Locations: CA: northern CA
Grant Types: General Support.

Donor Information

Founder: the late William G. Gilmore, Mrs. William G. Gilmore

Financial Summary

Total Giving: $1,035,025 (2003)
Giving Analysis: Giving for 2003 includes: foundation grants to United Way ($10,000)
Assets: $25,508,263 (2003)

Typical Recipients

Arts & Humanities: Arts Associations & Councils, Arts Centers, Ethnic & Folk Arts, Arts & Humanities-General, History & Archaeology, Libraries, Museums/Galleries, Music, Opera, Performing Arts, Public Broadcasting
Civic & Public Affairs: Botanical Gardens/Parks, Community Foundations, Civic & Public Affairs-General, Hispanic Affairs, Legal Aid, Zoos/Aquariums
Education: Afterschool/Enrichment Programs, Colleges & Universities, Continuing Education, Education Funds, Education-General, Private Education (Precollege), Public Education (Precollege), Religious Education, Science/Mathematics Education, Secondary Education (Private), Student Aid
Environment: Resource Conservation, Wildlife Protection
Health: Cancer, Children's Health/Hospitals, Clinics/Medical Centers, Emergency/Ambulance Services, Health Organizations, Hospices, Hospitals, Medical Research, Nursing Services, Single-Disease Health Associations, Speech & Hearing, Trauma Treatment
International: Foreign Arts Organizations
Religion: Churches, Dioceses, Religious Organizations, Religious Welfare
Science: Science Museums, Scientific Centers & Institutes
Social Services: Animal Protection, At-Risk Youth, Camps, Community Centers, Community Service Organizations, Family Services, Food/Clothing Distribution, People with Disabilities, Scouts, Shelters/Homelessness, United Funds/United Ways, YMCA/YWCA/YMHA/YWHA, Youth Organizations

Application Procedures

Initial Contact: Send a brief letter of inquiry.
Application Requirements: Include a description of organization.
Deadlines: December 1.
Review Process: Decisions are made within two months.

Foundation Officials

Thomas B. Boklund: trustee
C. Lee Emerson: vice president, treasurer
V. Neil Fulton: assistant secretary
Patrice Gehrke: trustee
Robert C. Harris: president B San Francisco, CA 1916. ED Stanford University (1937); Harvard University (1940). PRIM CORP EMPL counsel: Heller, Ehrman, White & McAuliffe.
William R. Mackey: trustee
Faye C. Wilson: executive director

Grants Analysis

Disclosure Period: calendar year ending 2003
Total Grants: $1,025,025*
Number of Grants: 135
Average Grant: $7,593
Highest Grant: $50,000
Lowest Grant: $500
Typical Range: $1,000 to $15,000
*Note: Giving excludes United Way.

Recent Grants

Note: Grants derived from 2001 Form 990.
General

50,000	Historic Arkansas Riverwalk of Pueblo Foundation, AR
50,000	Queen of the Valley Hospital, Napa, CA
40,000	Alta Bates Summit Foundation
30,000	Project Open Hand, Atlanta, GA
25,000	Boy Scouts of America San Francisco Bay Area Council, San Francisco, CA
25,000	Children's Charity Ball
25,000	Fine Arts Museum of San Francisco, San Francisco, CA
25,000	Oregon Public Broadcasting, Portland, OR -- NOVA sponsorship
25,000	Portland Art Museum, Portland, OR
25,000	Portland State University, Portland, OR

GLASER FOUNDATION

Giving Contact

R. Thomas Olson, Secretary
PO Box 6548
Bellevue, WA 98008-0548
Phone: (425)881-2485

Description

Founded: 1952
EIN: 916028694
Organization Type: Private Foundation
Giving Locations: WA: Puget Sound area
Grant Types: General Support, Project, Seed Money.

Donor Information

Founder: the late Paul F. Glaser

Financial Summary

Total Giving: $641,998 (fiscal year ending November 30, 2001)
Assets: $13,512,884 (fiscal 2001)

Typical Recipients

Arts & Humanities: Arts Associations & Councils, Arts Centers, Arts Outreach, Ballet, Community Arts, Dance, Ethnic & Folk Arts, Arts & Humanities-General, Libraries, Music, Performing Arts, Theater
Civic & Public Affairs: African American Affairs, Business/Free Enterprise, Clubs, Economic Development, Employment/Job Training, Civic & Public Affairs-General, Hispanic Affairs, Housing, Legal Aid, Professional & Trade Associations, Urban & Community Affairs, Women's Affairs, Zoos/Aquariums
Education: Afterschool/Enrichment Programs, Arts/Humanities Education, Colleges & Universities, Community & Junior Colleges, Education Reform, Elementary Education (Private), Engineering/Technological Education, Education-General, Literacy, Preschool Education, Private Education (Precollege), Public Education (Precollege), Science/Mathematics Education, Secondary Education (Public), Social Sciences Education, Special Education, Student Aid
Environment: Wildlife Protection
Health: AIDS/HIV, Cancer, Children's Health/Hospitals, Clinics/Medical Centers, Diabetes, Geriatric Health, Health Funds, Health Organizations, Heart, Hospices, Hospitals, Medical Research, Mental Health, Nursing Services, Nutrition, Prenatal Health Issues, Public Health, Single-Disease Health Associations, Speech & Hearing, Transplant Networks/Donor Banks
International: International-General
Religion: Religion-General, Ministries, Missionary Activities (Domestic), Religious Welfare
Science: Scientific Centers & Institutes
Social Services: Animal Protection, At-Risk Youth, Camps, Child Abuse, Child Welfare, Community Centers, Community Service Organizations, Counseling, Crime Prevention, Day Care, Domestic Violence, Family Planning, Family Services, Food/Clothing Distribution, Homes, People with Disabilities, Recreation & Athletics, Refugee Assistance, Senior Services, Sexual Abuse, Shelters/Homelessness, Substance Abuse, United Funds/United Ways, YMCA/YWCA/YMHA/YWHA, Youth Organizations

Application Procedures

Initial Contact: Application form in duplicate is required. Pacific Northwest Grantmakers Forum common grant application form is accepted. Phone calls are discouraged.
Deadlines: None.

Restrictions

Emphasis is on direct line services, mainly to children and the elderly in King County and immediately adjoining areas. Does not support individuals or provide loans.

Additional Information

Publications: Application Guidelines

Foundation Officials

R. N. Brandenburg: president
R. William Carlstrom: secretary

R. Thomas Olson: mem
Janet L. Politeo: vice president
Walt Smith: treasurer

Grants Analysis

Disclosure Period: fiscal year ending November 30, 2001
Total Grants: $641,998
Number of Grants: 79
Average Grant: $6,949*
Highest Grant: $100,000
Lowest Grant: $100
Typical Range: $1,000 to $10,000
*Note: Average grant figure excludes highest grant.

Recent Grants

Note: Grants derived from fiscal 2002 Form 990.

General

50,000	Health Housing and Human Services, Bainbridge Island, WA -- Community Connections for Youth Program
50,000	YWCA of Seattle, Seattle, WA -- capital campaign
41,500	Gilda's Club, Seattle, WA -- services to cancer patients
25,000	Hope Heart Institute, Seattle, WA -- Youth Education Program
22,500	South Whidbey Schools Foundation, Langley United Kingdom -- philanthropy in the schools
20,000	Multifaith Works, Seattle, WA -- housing services for women with Multiple Sclerosis
20,000	Park Market Medical Clinic, Seattle, WA -- care for low income patients
13,000	YMCA of Greater Seattle, Seattle, WA -- After-School Program
12,760	Pike Market Child Care and Preschool, Seattle, WA -- tuition assistance for low income families
12,500	Cyberschool Foundation, Freeland, PA -- youth in philanthropy

GLAXOSMITHKLINE PLC

Company Headquarters

Berkeley Sq.
Greenford UB6 0NN, United Kingdom
Phone: ENG 20 89668000
Fax: ENG 20 89668330
Web: http://www.gsk.com

Company Description

Ticker: GSK
Exchange: OTC
Formed by Merger of: SmithKline Beecham;
Former Name: Glaxo Wellcome.
SIC(s): 2800 Chemicals & Allied Products, 5100 Wholesale Trade--Nondurable Goods.

Nonmonetary Support

Value: $15,000,000 (1998)
Type: Donated Equipment; Donated Products
Volunteer Programs: The company maintains an employee volunteering support scheme.
Contact: Jean Glenn, Manager, Community Partnership
E-mail: jean.glenn@sb.com
Note: Product donations are provided for humanitarian relief efforts at the request of government agencies and major charities. Such donations are made on a

GlaxoSmithKline Foundation

Giving Contact

Director, Philanthropic Programs
GlaxoSmithKline
One Franklin Plaza
PO Box 7929
Philadelphia, PA 19101-7929
Phone: (215)751-4668
Fax: (215)751-7655
E-mail: community.partnership@gsk.com
Web: http://corp.gsk.com/community/

Description

Founded: 2001
EIN: 232120418
Organization Type: Corporate Foundation
Giving Locations: internationally; nationally.
Grant Types: Award, Employee Matching Gifts, General Support, Project.
Note: Employee matching gift ratio: 1 to 1 to education, health and human services organizations, and the arts.

Donor Information

Founder: GlaxoSmithKline

Financial Summary

Total Giving: $1,789,985 (2003); $2,490,515 (2002); $5,421,423 (2001). Note: In 2002, total giving figure is for GlaxoSmithKline Foundation. Contributes through corporate direct giving program and foundation. Total giving figures represent SmithKline Beecham giving prior to the company's merger with Glaxo Wellcome.
Giving Analysis: Giving for 2002 includes: foundation matching gifts ($1,770,946)
Assets: $3,074,537 (2003); $4,492,882 (2002); $2,533,175 (2001). Note: In 2002, asset figures are for GlaxoSmithKline Foundation. Asset figures are for the SmithKline Beecham Foundation, prior to SmithKline Beecham's merger with Glaxo Wellcome.
Gifts Received: $3,771,537 (2003); $4,485,560 (2002); $6,655,795 (2001). Note: Gifts received represent contributions received by the SmithKline Beecham Foundation prior to the company merger with Glaxo Wellcome. Contributions were received from SmithKline Beecham Corporation.

Typical Recipients

Arts & Humanities: Arts Associations & Councils, Arts Outreach, Ballet, Ethnic & Folk Arts, History & Archaeology, Libraries, Museums/Galleries, Music, Opera, Performing Arts, Public Broadcasting, Theater
Civic & Public Affairs: Economic Policy, Employment/Job Training, Municipalities/Towns, Nonprofit Management, Philanthropic Organizations, Professional & Trade Associations, Public Policy, Urban & Community Affairs, Women's Affairs, Zoos/Aquariums
Education: Arts/Humanities Education, Business Education, Colleges & Universities, Community & Junior Colleges, Education Funds, Elementary Education (Private), Engineering/Technological Education, Faculty Development, Education-General, International Exchange, Literacy, Medical Education, Private Education (Precollege), Religious Education, Science/Mathematics Education, Secondary Education (Private), Social Sciences Education, Student Aid
Environment: Environment-General
Health: AIDS/HIV, Cancer, Children's Health/Hospitals, Clinics/Medical Centers, Diabetes, Emergency/Ambulance Services, Health-General, Health Funds, Health Organizations, Heart, Hospitals, Hospitals (University Affiliated), Long-Term Care, Medical Research, Single-Disease Health Associations
International: Foreign Educational Institutions, Health Care/Hospitals, International Organizations,

International Relations
Religion: Jewish Causes, Religious Welfare, Seminaries
Science: Science Museums, Scientific Centers & Institutes, Scientific Labs, Scientific Organizations
Social Services: Camps, Community Service Organizations, Crime Prevention, People with Disabilities, Substance Abuse, United Funds/United Ways, Volunteer Services, Youth Organizations

Application Procedures

Initial Contact: Send a one- to two-page letter of inquiry by mail or e-mail.
Application Requirements: Include a summary a description of organization of the organization; a summary of the proposed project or program with description of the problem to be addressed; the proposed solution; how it meets GlaxoSmithKline's support criteria; how GlaxoSmithKline volunteers (if appropriate) can be incorporated; the amount requested and the proposed project budget (with all other anticipated sources of income); a plan to measure and evaluate program results; an explanation of how the request and program relate to GlaxoSmithKline's three focus areas of health care, science education, or community betterment; and a contact name, address, phone number, fax number and e-mail address if available.
Deadlines: None.
Evaluative Criteria: Proposals are screened to ensure that the proposed program identifies targets and possible barriers to success; includes a plan for self-sufficiency; measures and evaluates progress; and has the potential to be replicated.
Decision Notification: If the initial inquiry is unsuccessful, the applicant will be informed in writing with 30 days of receipt. A staff person will contact organization for full proposal if one is desired.
Notes: Company rarely supports unsolicited grant proposals, but prefers to initiate partnerships.

Restrictions

No grants are made to the following: deficit financing or debt retirement; capital campaigns, chairs, or endowments; individuals; political, labor, religious, fraternal, athletic or veterans' organizations; fundraising events and associated advertising; conferences and symposia; lobbying groups; or universities or freestanding scientific research centers for research on GlaxoSmithKline projects or products. Ongoing general operating expenses are rarely funded. Commercial sponsorships and corporate hospitality opportunities are not funded. Multiple grants to the same organization are not made within a calendar year. Recipients must be exempt under IRS 501(c)(3) and do not receive substantial federal, state or local government funding.

Additional Information

A merger between SmithKline Beecham and Glaxo Wellcome was finalized in January 2001. The new company is known as GlaxoSmithKline plc. The Global Community Partnerships program was formed after the merger.
Publications: Guidelines Sheet; Annual Report

Corporate Officials

James Hill: senior vice president corporate affairs
PRIM CORP EMPL senior vice president corporate affairs: SmithKline Beecham Corp.

Foundation Officials

Vincent I. Ahonkhar: director
Carol Ashe: secretary, general counsel
John Barber: director
Robert Carr, MD: president, director
Margaret B. Dardess: director
Thomas K. Kaney: director
Judith Lynch: treasurer, secretary
Geoffrey C. Mitchinson: director
John E. Reardon: director
Catherine A. Sohn: director

Steven Stefano: director
David M. Stout: chairman, director
Jeff D. Strum: director

Grants Analysis

Disclosure Period: calendar year ending 2003
Total Grants: $1,789,985*
*Note: Giving includes matching gifts.

Recent Grants

Note: Grants derived from 2001 Form 990.
Library-Related

11,648	Free Library of Philadelphia, Philadelphia, PA

General

37,054	Trustees of the University Of Pennsylvania, Philadelphia, PA
22,649	Wilson College, Chambersburg, PA
17,238	Magee Memorial Hospital for Convalescents, Philadelphia, PA
16,716	St. Charles Borromeo Seminary, Wynnewood, PA
16,700	University of Notre Dame Du Lac, Notre Dame, IN
16,250	St. Mary School, Schwenksville, PA
15,475	Thomas Jefferson University, Philadelphia, PA
15,130	President and Trustees of Bowdoin College, Brunswick, ME
13,590	Thomas Jefferson University, Philadelphia, PA
12,700	Trustees of Columbia University in the City of New York, New York, NY

GLEASON FOUNDATION

Giving Contact

Ralph E. Harper, Secretary, Treasurer
1000 University Avenue
PO Box 22970
Rochester, NY 14692-2970
Phone: (585)241-4030
Fax: (585)241-4099
E-mail: susy.elniski@gleasonfoundation.org

Description

Founded: 1959
EIN: 166023235
Organization Type: General Purpose Foundation
Former Name: Gleason Memorial Fund.
Giving Locations: NY: Rochester
Grant Types: Capital, Challenge, General Support, Loan, Multiyear/Continuing Support, Operating Expenses, Scholarship.

Donor Information

Founder: Formerly known as the Emmet Blakeney Gleason Memorial Fund, the fund was incorporated in 1959 in New York by the late Miriam Blakeney Gleason in memory of her son. In 1961, it was merged with the J. E. and Eleanor Gleason Trust to form the Gleason Memorial Fund.

Financial Summary

Total Giving: $3,768,213 (2002)
Giving Analysis: Giving for 2002 includes: foundation scholarships ($83,532); foundation grants to United Way ($280,000)
Assets: $95,599,703 (2002)

Typical Recipients

Arts & Humanities: Arts Associations & Councils, Arts Funds, Arts Outreach, Dance, Arts & Humanities-General, Historic Preservation, Libraries, Literary Arts, Museums/Galleries, Music, Public Broadcasting, Theater
Civic & Public Affairs: African American Affairs, Botanical Gardens/Parks, Business/Free Enterprise, Civil Rights, Community Foundations, Economic Development, Economic Policy, Employment/Job Training, Ethnic Organizations, Civic & Public Affairs-General, Hispanic Affairs, Housing, Law & Justice, Legal Aid, Professional & Trade Associations, Public Policy, Urban & Community Affairs, Women's Affairs, Zoos/Aquariums
Education: Afterschool/Enrichment Programs, Business Education, Business-School Partnerships, Colleges & Universities, Community & Junior Colleges, Continuing Education, Education Associations, Education Funds, Elementary Education (Private), Elementary Education (Public), Engineering/Technological Education, Education-General, Minority Education, Private Education (Precollege), Religious Education, Science/Mathematics Education, Secondary Education (Private), Special Education, Student Aid, Vocational & Technical Education
Environment: Environment-General
Health: Children's Health/Hospitals, Clinics/Medical Centers, Emergency/Ambulance Services, Hospitals, Medical Rehabilitation, Medical Research, Nursing Services, Nutrition
International: Foreign Arts Organizations, Foreign Educational Institutions, International-General, Health Care/Hospitals, International Affairs, Missionary/Religious Activities
Religion: Churches, Religion-General, Religious Organizations
Science: Science Museums, Scientific Centers & Institutes, Scientific Research
Social Services: At-Risk Youth, Child Abuse, Child Welfare, Community Centers, Community Service Organizations, Crime Prevention, Domestic Violence, Family Planning, Food/Clothing Distribution, People with Disabilities, Recreation & Athletics, Senior Services, Shelters/Homelessness, Social Services-General, United Funds/United Ways, Volunteer Services, Youth Organizations

Application Procedures

Initial Contact: Applicants should contact the foundation for an application form.
Application Requirements: The proposal should include a history and background of the organization; explanation of the project; amount requested; project budget and time schedule; names of board of directors and responsible staff; detailed financial statements for current and two previous years; a list of present funding sources; and a copy of IRS 501(c)(3) or 509(a) and 990 PF.
Deadlines: None.
Review Process: The board meets quarterly. Final notification occurs after board meetings.

Restrictions

Generally no funding is made for United Way-supported agencies. No grants are made to individuals. Grants are limited to greater Rochester or Monroe County, NY.

Additional Information

The foundation changed its name from the Gleason Memorial Fund to the Gleason Foundation.
Publications: Application Form

Foundation Officials

Dr. Edward C. Atwater: director
James S. Gleason: director B 1934. ED Princeton University (1955); University of Rochester MBA (1973). PRIM CORP EMPL president, chief executive officer, chairman: Gleason Works ADD CORP EMPL chairman, president, chief executive officer, director: Gleason Corp.
Janis F. Gleason: director
Tracy R. Gleason: president, director
Ralph E. Harper: secretary, treasurer, director B Batavia, NY 1933. ED University of Rochester (1956); George Washington University JD (1966). PRIM CORP EMPL vice president, secretary, treasurer: Gleason Corp. CORP AFFIL secretary: Gleason Works.

Gary J. Kimmet: director PRIM CORP EMPL vice president engineering: Gleason Works.
Albert W. Moore: director B Norwood, MA 1934. ED Clarkson College of Technology (1959); University of Rochester (1970). CORP AFFIL director: Gleason Corp. NONPR AFFIL president, director: Association Manufacturing Technology.

Grants Analysis

Disclosure Period: calendar year ending 2002
Total Grants: $3,404,681*
Number of Grants: 54
Average Grant: $42,581*
Highest Grant: $910,485
Lowest Grant: $100
Typical Range: $10,000 to $100,000
*Note: Giving excludes scholarships and United Way. Average grant excludes two highest grants ($1,190,485).

Recent Grants

Note: Grants derived from 2002 Form 990.
Library-Related

10,000	Macedon Public Library, Macedon, NY
10,000	Rundel Library Foundation, Rochester, NY

General

910,485	Ohio State University, Columbus, OH
280,000	Alfred State College Development Fund, Alfred, NY
280,000	United Way of Greater Rochester, Rochester, NY
225,000	Rochester Institute of Technology, Rochester, NY
200,000	Monroe Community College, Rochester, NY
150,000	Strong Museum, Rochester, NY
114,360	National Merit Scholarship Corporation, Chicago, IL
100,000	Allendale Columbia School, Rochester, NY
100,000	Harley School, Rochester, NY
100,000	McQuaid Jesuit High School, Rochester, NY

GLENCOE FOUNDATION

Giving Contact

Ellice McDonald, Jr., President & Director
Greenville Center
3801 Kennett Pke., Suite C-300
Greenville, DE 19807-2377
Phone: (302)654-9933
Fax: (302)429-8472

Description

Founded: 1975
EIN: 510164761
Organization Type: Private Foundation
Giving Locations: Scotland: Highland and Island regions of Scotland.
Grant Types: Capital, Emergency, General Support, Multiyear/Continuing Support, Operating Expenses, Scholarship.

Donor Information

Founder: Ellice McDonald, Jr., Rosa H. McDonald

Financial Summary

Total Giving: $1,049,195 (2001)
Giving Analysis: Giving for 2001 includes: foundation scholarships ($19,410)
Assets: $5,864,154 (2001)
Gifts Received: $1,000 (2001); $1,246,013 (2000); $681,975 (1999). Note: In 1997, 1999, 2000, and 2001, contributions were received from Ellice, Jr. & Rosa H. McDonald.

Typical Recipients
Arts & Humanities: Libraries, Museums/Galleries, Music
Education: Private Education (Precollege)
Health: Hospitals, Mental Health
International: Foreign Arts Organizations, Foreign Educational Institutions, International Development, International Environmental Issues, International Organizations, International Peace & Security Issues, International Relief Efforts, Missionary/Religious Activities

Application Procedures
Initial Contact: Send brief letter requesting application form.
Deadlines: None.

Restrictions
Limited to Scottish and American charitable organizations that promote Scottish-American traditions and culture.

Additional Information
Publications: Application Guidelines; Application Form

Foundation Officials
Gregory A. Inskip: director CLUB AFFIL Ocean Forest Golf Club; Wilmington Country Club.
Walter Jones Laird, Jr.: director B Philadelphia, PA 1926. ED Princeton University BS (1948); Massachusetts Institute of Technology MSCE (1950). PRIM CORP EMPL senior vice president: Dean Witter Reynolds Inc. CORP AFFIL director: Wentz Corp.; director: Meridian Asset Management; director: Sinkler Corp. NONPR AFFIL member: Wilmington Club; chairman emeritus, trust: Winterthur Museum & Gardens; member: Financial Analysts Federation; gov: Society Colonial Wars; director: Delaware Trust Co.
Ellice McDonald, Jr.: president, director
Rosa H. McDonald: vice president, director
John C. Milner: secretary, treasurer
John P. Sinclair, Esq.: director

Grants Analysis
Disclosure Period: calendar year ending 2001
Total Grants: $1,029,785*
Number of Grants: 2
Highest Grant: $773,310
Lowest Grant: $256,475
*Note: Giving excludes scholarships.

Recent Grants
Note: Grants derived from 2002 Form 990.
General

318,138	Clan Donald Lands Trust United Kingdom -- operating grants
150,461	Clan Donald Lands Trust United Kingdom -- museum grants
22,721	Lamond School, Helensburgh United Kingdom -- traditional music scholarship
15,066	Scottish Episcopal Church -- "Gathering in the Isles" appeal

EUGENE AND MARILYN GLICK FOUNDATION

Giving Contact
Eugene Glick, President
Eugene and Marilyn Glick Foundation
PO Box 40177
Indianapolis, IN 46240
Phone: (317)469-5836
E-mail: info@glickco.com
Web: http://www.genebglick.com/about_foundation.asp

Description
Founded: 1982
EIN: 351549707
Organization Type: Private Foundation
Giving Locations: IN: Indianapolis
Grant Types: Capital, General Support, Operating Expenses, Project.

Donor Information
Founder: Eugene B. Glick, Marilyn K. Glick

Financial Summary
Total Giving: $2,665,009 (fiscal year ending November 30, 2001)
Giving Analysis: Giving for fiscal 2001 includes: foundation grants to United Way ($25,400)
Assets: $56,066,363 (fiscal 2001)
Gifts Received: $4,147,434 (fiscal 2001); $3,750,250 (fiscal 2000); $4,411,448 (fiscal 1998).
Note: Contributions were received from Eugene B. and Marilyn K. Glick.

Typical Recipients
Arts & Humanities: Arts Associations & Councils, Arts Centers, Community Arts, Arts & Humanities-General, Historic Preservation, Libraries, Museums/Galleries, Music, Opera, Performing Arts, Public Broadcasting, Theater
Civic & Public Affairs: African American Affairs, Botanical Gardens/Parks, Business/Free Enterprise, Civil Rights, Community Foundations, Employment/Job Training, Civic & Public Affairs-General, Nonprofit Management, Parades/Festivals, Philanthropic Organizations, Public Policy, Urban & Community Affairs, Women's Affairs, Zoos/Aquariums
Education: Business Education, Colleges & Universities, Education Funds, Engineering/Technological Education, Minority Education, Private Education (Precollege), Public Education (Precollege), Student Aid
Health: Cancer, Clinics/Medical Centers, Diabetes, Emergency/Ambulance Services, Eyes/Blindness, Health Organizations, Heart, Hospitals, Medical Research, Mental Health, Public Health, Single-Disease Health Associations
International: Foreign Arts Organizations, Health Care/Hospitals
Religion: Jewish Causes, Missionary Activities (Domestic), Religious Organizations, Religious Welfare, Seminaries, Synagogues/Temples
Social Services: Child Welfare, Community Service Organizations, Domestic Violence, Family Planning, Family Services, Recreation & Athletics, Scouts, Senior Services, Social Services-General, United Funds/United Ways, YMCA/YWCA/YMHA/YWHA, Youth Organizations

Application Procedures
Initial Contact: Submit a brief letter of inquiry.
Application Requirements: Include a description of organization, amount requested, and purpose of funds sought.
Deadlines: None.

Foundation Officials
James T. Bisesi: director
Eugene B. Glick: president, trustee
Marilyn K. Glick: trustee, secretary, treasurer
Barbara Gunn: director
Sharon Kibbe: director

Grants Analysis
Disclosure Period: fiscal year ending November 30, 2001
Total Grants: $2,639,609*
Number of Grants: 167
Average Grant: $1,353*
Highest Grant: $2,415,000
Lowest Grant: $50
Typical Range: $1,000 to $5,000

*Note: Giving excludes United Way. Average grant excludes highest grant.

Recent Grants
Note: Grants derived from fiscal 2002 Form 990.
General

2,625,000	Central Indiana Community Foundation, Indianapolis, IN -- contribution to Gene and Marilyn Glick Foundation Fund
50,000	Children's Bureau, Indianapolis, IN -- PRO-100 Program
25,000	Indiana State Museum Foundation, Indianapolis, IN -- "The Birth of the Earth"
17,000	United Way of Central Indiana, Inc., Indianapolis, IN -- annual contribution
9,000	United Way of Central Indiana, Inc., Indianapolis, IN -- in support of the Forever Fund
8,000	Indiana Repertory Theatre, Indianapolis, IN -- programs
5,000	American Heart Association, Indianapolis, IN
5,000	Cyber-Sight Foundation, Inc., Indianapolis, IN -- support program for people with eye disease
5,000	Indianapolis Downtown, Indianapolis, IN -- Marge Tarplee Downtown Beautification Fund
5,000	Indianapolis Hebrew Congregation, Indianapolis, IN

CHARLES B. GODDARD FOUNDATION

Giving Contact
William R. Goddard, Jr., Trustee
PO Box 1485
Ardmore, OK 73402
Phone: (580)226-6040

Description
Founded: 1958
EIN: 756005868
Organization Type: Private Foundation
Giving Locations: OK: southern OK; TX: northern TX
Grant Types: Capital, Emergency, General Support, Multiyear/Continuing Support, Operating Expenses, Research, Seed Money.

Donor Information
Founder: the late Charles B. Goddard

Financial Summary
Total Giving: $463,650 (fiscal year ending June 30, 2004); $605,277 (fiscal 2002); $561,510 (fiscal 2001)
Giving Analysis: Giving for fiscal 2004 includes: foundation grants to United Way ($3,000); fiscal 2002: foundation grants to United Way ($10,000); fiscal 2001: foundation grants to United Way ($10,000)
Assets: $11,908,201 (fiscal 2004); $11,253,226 (fiscal 2002); $12,509,451 (fiscal 2001)

Typical Recipients
Arts & Humanities: Arts Institutes, Historic Preservation, Libraries, Museums/Galleries, Performing Arts, Public Broadcasting, Theater
Civic & Public Affairs: Chambers of Commerce, Economic Development, Civic & Public Affairs-General, Law & Justice, Legal Aid, Parades/Festivals, Public Policy, Safety, Urban & Community Affairs, Zoos/Aquariums
Education: Colleges & Universities, Education Funds, Education Reform, Elementary Education (Private), Faculty Development, Education-General, Literacy, Private Education (Precollege), Public Education (Precollege), Science/Mathematics Education,

Student Aid

Environment: Wildlife Protection

Health: Children's Health/Hospitals, Clinics/Medical Centers, Diabetes, Health Policy/Cost Containment, Health Organizations, Hospices, Hospitals, Medical Rehabilitation, Medical Research, Nursing Services, Public Health, Respiratory, Single-Disease Health Associations

International: International Affairs

Religion: Churches, Religious Welfare

Science: Science Museums, Scientific Centers & Institutes, Scientific Organizations

Social Services: Animal Protection, At-Risk Youth, Camps, Child Welfare, Community Centers, Community Service Organizations, Crime Prevention, Day Care, Domestic Violence, Family Services, Homes, People with Disabilities, Recreation & Athletics, Scouts, Shelters/Homelessness, Substance Abuse, United Funds/United Ways, YMCA/YWCA/YMHA/YWHA, Youth Organizations

Application Procedures

Initial Contact: Send a brief letter of inquiry.
Deadlines: None.

Foundation Officials

Garland Clay: trustee
Ann G. Corrigan: trustee
William R. Goddard, Jr.: trustee
William M. Johns: trustee

Grants Analysis

Disclosure Period: fiscal year ending June 30, 2004
Total Grants: $460,650*
Number of Grants: 28
Average Grant: $8,626*
Highest Grant: $120,000
Lowest Grant: $100
Typical Range: $5,000 to $10,000
*Note: Giving excludes United Way. Average grant excludes three highest grants ($245,000).

Recent Grants

Note: Grants derived from fiscal 2004 Form 990.
General

120,000	Goddard Youth Foundation, Sulphur, OK -- fund for environmental camp and museum
65,000	Children's Medical center, Dallas, TX -- capital expansion of hospital
60,000	Visiting Nurse Association, Dallas, TX -- for capital campaign
30,000	Ardmore Village, Ardmore, OK -- low-income housing assistance
30,000	Community Activities, Ardmore, OK -- improvements at central park
25,000	Payne Education Center, Ardmore, OK -- for literacy programs
20,000	Ardmore City Schools, Ardmore, OK -- tutoring programs
15,000	Family Shelter of Oklahoma, Ardmore, OK
10,000	National Center for Policy Analysis, Dallas, TX
10,000	Oak Hall Episcopal School, Ardmore, OK

GOEL FOUNDATION

Giving Contact

Prabhu Goel, Secretary
98 Ridgeview Dr.
Atherton, CA 94027-6464
Phone: (408)977-7092

Description

Founded: 1990
EIN: 770269072
Organization Type: Private Foundation

Giving Locations: no restrictions.
Grant Types: General Support.

Donor Information

Founder: Established in 1990 by Prabhu Goel and Poonam Goel.

Financial Summary

Total Giving: $225,764 (fiscal year ending March 31, 2004); $390,033 (fiscal 2002); $403,543 (fiscal 2001)
Assets: $7,212,259 (fiscal 2004); $7,617,778 (fiscal 2002)
Gifts Received: $17,500 (fiscal 1998); $372,500 (fiscal 1997)

Typical Recipients

Arts & Humanities: Ethnic & Folk Arts, Libraries
Civic & Public Affairs: Civic & Public Affairs-General, Native American Affairs, Philanthropic Organizations
Education: Colleges & Universities, Private Education (Precollege), Science/Mathematics Education
Health: AIDS/HIV, Public Health
International: Foreign Arts Organizations, Foreign Educational Institutions, International Peace & Security Issues, International Relief Efforts, Missionary/Religious Activities
Religion: Religious Organizations, Synagogues/Temples
Science: Science Museums
Social Services: Community Service Organizations, Domestic Violence

Application Procedures

Initial Contact: Send a brief letter of inquiry.
Deadlines: None.

Foundation Officials

Poonam Goel: president
Prabhu Goel: secretary

Grants Analysis

Disclosure Period: fiscal year ending March 31, 2004
Total Grants: $225,764
Number of Grants: 1

Recent Grants

Note: Grants derived from 2004 Form 990.
General

225,764	Fidelity Investments Charitable Fund, Boston, MA

DAVID B. GOLD FOUNDATION

Giving Contact

Elaine E. Gold, Director
44 Montgomery Street, Suite 3750
San Francisco, CA 94104
Phone: (415)288-9530
Fax: (415)288-9549

Description

Founded: 1993
EIN: 943169439
Organization Type: Private Foundation
Giving Locations: CA: San Francisco; NY: New York
Grant Types: General Support.

Financial Summary

Total Giving: $2,311,845 (fiscal year ending November 30, 2003); $2,300,683 (fiscal 2001)
Assets: $93,225,739 (fiscal 2003); $57,679,538 (fiscal 2001)
Gifts Received: $27,962,538 (fiscal 2003);

$1,564,505 (fiscal 2001); $2,434,044 (fiscal 2000).
Note: In fiscal 1998, 1999, 2000, 2001, and 2003, contributions were received from David B. Gold Trust. In fiscal 1994 and fiscal 1995, contributions were received from the estate of David B. Gold.

Typical Recipients

Arts & Humanities: Arts Outreach, Libraries, Museums/Galleries, Music, Public Broadcasting, Theater
Civic & Public Affairs: African American Affairs, Botanical Gardens/Parks, Civil Rights, Civic & Public Affairs-General, Hispanic Affairs, Legal Aid, Municipalities/Towns, Public Policy, Safety
Education: Private Education (Precollege), Student Aid
Environment: Air/Water Quality, Environment-General, Protection, Resource Conservation
Health: Cancer, Heart, Medical Research, Prenatal Health Issues
International: Health Care/Hospitals
Religion: Jewish Causes, Religious Welfare
Science: Scientific Organizations
Social Services: Big Brothers/Big Sisters, Child Welfare, Community Centers, Community Service Organizations, Day Care, Domestic Violence, Family Planning, Family Services, Food/Clothing Distribution, Recreation & Athletics, Senior Services, Shelters/Homelessness, Youth Organizations

Application Procedures

Initial Contact: The foundation has no formal grant application procedure or application form.
Deadlines: None.

Foundation Officials

Elaine E. Gold: director
Emily Gold: director
Steven A. Gold: treasurer
Diane Gold-Bubier: secretary, director
Barbara Gold-Lurie: president

Grants Analysis

Disclosure Period: fiscal year ending November 30, 2003
Total Grants: $2,311,845
Number of Grants: 139
Average Grant: $14,216*
Highest Grant: $350,000
Lowest Grant: $500
Typical Range: $5,000 to $30,000
*Note: Average grant figure excludes highest grant.

Recent Grants

Note: Grants derived from fiscal 2001 Form 990.
General

500,000	San Francisco Conservatory of Music, San Francisco, CA -- capital campaign
150,000	Jewish Community Center of San Francisco, San Francisco, CA -- capital campaign
75,000	Cardiac Arrhythmia Center, Minneapolis, MN -- women at risk of sudden death
60,000	Earth Justice Legal Defense Fund, San Francisco, CA -- healthy cities, healthy wildlands
50,000	American Civil Liberties Union, San Francisco, CA -- Racial Justice Project
50,000	Bay Area Legal Aid, Oakland, CA
50,000	Union of Concerned Scientists, Cambridge, MA -- Food and Environment Program
40,000	Pesticide Action Network of North America, San Francisco, CA -- Database and Mapping Project
40,000	Planned Parenthood Golden Gate, San Mateo, CA -- specific project
35,000	Homeless Prenatal Program, San Francisco, CA -- Case Management Program

GOLDBERG FAMILY FOUNDATION

Giving Contact

Avram J. Goldberg, Trustee
225 Franklin St., Suite 2700
Boston, MA 02110-2804
Phone: (617)695-1946

Description

Founded: 1961
EIN: 046039556
Organization Type: Private Foundation
Giving Locations: MA; NY; VT
Grant Types: General Support.

Donor Information

Founder: Avram J. and Carol R. Goldberg

Financial Summary

Total Giving: $674,030 (2003); $820,518 (2001)
Giving Analysis: Giving for 2003 includes: foundation grants to United Way ($105,450); 2001: foundation grants to United Way ($1,000,000)
Assets: $15,092,897 (2003); $15,461,386 (2001)
Gifts Received: $501,258 (2003); $25 (2000); $36,290 (1996). Note: In 1995 and, contributions were received from Avram J. and Carol R. Goldberg. In 1996, contributions were received from Carol Goldberg.

Typical Recipients

Arts & Humanities: Arts Centers, Community Arts, History & Archaeology, Libraries, Museums/Galleries, Music, Performing Arts, Public Broadcasting, Theater
Civic & Public Affairs: Clubs, Economic Development, Civic & Public Affairs-General, Philanthropic Organizations, Public Policy
Education: Arts/Humanities Education, Business Education, Colleges & Universities, Education Funds, Elementary Education (Public), Education-General, Legal Education, Minority Education, Private Education (Precollege), Religious Education, Social Sciences Education
Environment: Environment-General
Health: Children's Health/Hospitals, Clinics/Medical Centers, Geriatric Health, Hospitals, Medical Rehabilitation, Medical Research, Public Health, Single-Disease Health Associations
International: Foreign Arts Organizations, International Organizations, International Relations, Missionary/Religious Activities
Religion: Jewish Causes, Religious Organizations, Synagogues/Temples
Science: Science Museums, Scientific Centers & Institutes
Social Services: Community Service Organizations, Family Planning, People with Disabilities, United Funds/United Ways

Application Procedures

Initial Contact: Send a brief letter of inquiry.
Deadlines: None.

Foundation Officials

Avram Jacob Goldberg: trustee B Brookline, MA 1930. ED Harvard University AB (1951); Harvard University JD (1954). PRIM CORP EMPL chairman: AVCAR Group. CORP AFFIL director: Boston Co. Inc.; director: Boston Safe Deposit & Trust Co.
Carol Rabb Goldberg: trustee B Newton, MA 1931. ED Tufts University BA (1955); Harvard University Graduate School of Business Administration (1969). PRIM CORP EMPL president: AVCAR Group. CLUB AFFIL Commercial Merchants Boston Club.
Deborah Beth Goldberg: trustee
Joshua Rabb Goldberg: trustee

Grants Analysis

Disclosure Period: calendar year ending 2003
Total Grants: $568,580*
Number of Grants: 200
Average Grant: $2,606*
Highest Grant: $50,000
Lowest Grant: $2
Typical Range: $500 to $5,000
*Note: Giving excludes United Way. Average grant figure excludes highest grant.

Recent Grants

Note: Grants derived from 2001 Form 990.
General

158,000	Combined Jewish Philanthropies, Boston, MA
50,000	United Way of Massachusetts Bay, Boston, MA
50,000	United Way of Massachusetts Bay, Boston, MA
49,000	Center for Collaborative Education, New York, NY
37,500	Putney School, Putney, VT
37,000	Combined Jewish Philanthropies, Boston, MA
34,000	Congregation Kehilath Israel, New York, NY
32,000	Combined Jewish Philanthropies, Boston, MA
32,000	Combined Jewish Philanthropies, Boston, MA
31,000	Combined Jewish Philanthropies, Boston, MA

HERMAN GOLDMAN FOUNDATION

Giving Contact

Richard K. Baron, Executive Director
61 Broadway, 18th Floor
New York, NY 10006
Phone: (212)797-9090
Fax: (212)797-9162

Description

Founded: 1943
EIN: 136066039
Organization Type: General Purpose Foundation
Giving Locations: NY: New York including metropolitan area
Grant Types: Award, Capital, Conference/Seminar, Department, Endowment, Fellowship, General Support, Operating Expenses, Project, Research, Scholarship.

Donor Information

Founder: The Herman Goldman Foundation was established in 1943 by the late Herman Goldman, a New York City attorney, tax expert, and philanthropist. During his lifetime, Mr. Goldman was active in the affairs of a number of New York charitable undertakings. Included among his philanthropic interests were Beekman-Downtown, Mount Sinai, and North Shore Hospitals; Hebrew Home for the Aged; Fordham University; and Lincoln Center for the Performing Arts. In addition, he was one of the founders of the Albert Einstein College of Medicine.

Financial Summary

Total Giving: $1,510,200 (fiscal year ending February 28, 2002); $2,117,200 (fiscal 2001)
Assets: $31,883,560 (fiscal 2002); $36,520,252 (fiscal 2001)

Typical Recipients

Arts & Humanities: Arts Centers, Arts Festivals, Arts Funds, Arts Outreach, Ballet, Community Arts, Dance, Libraries, Museums/Galleries, Music, Performing Arts, Public Broadcasting, Theater, Visual Arts
Civic & Public Affairs: Botanical Gardens/Parks, Civil Rights, Clubs, Employment/Job Training, Ethnic Organizations, Civic & Public Affairs-General, Law & Justice, Legal Aid, Nonprofit Management, Philanthropic Organizations, Professional & Trade Associations, Public Policy, Urban & Community Affairs, Women's Affairs
Education: Arts/Humanities Education, Colleges & Universities, Education-General, Legal Education, Literacy, Medical Education, Private Education (Precollege), Public Education (Precollege), Religious Education, Special Education, Student Aid
Environment: Protection
Health: AIDS/HIV, Cancer, Clinics/Medical Centers, Geriatric Health, Health Funds, Health Organizations, Heart, Hospitals, Hospitals (University Affiliated), Long-Term Care, Medical Research, Mental Health, Multiple Sclerosis, Prenatal Health Issues, Single-Disease Health Associations
International: Foreign Educational Institutions, International Peace & Security Issues, International Relief Efforts, Missionary/Religious Activities
Religion: Churches, Jewish Causes, Religious Organizations, Religious Welfare, Seminaries, Synagogues/Temples
Science: Scientific Centers & Institutes
Social Services: Animal Protection, Big Brothers/Big Sisters, Child Welfare, Community Service Organizations, Counseling, Crime Prevention, Family Services, Homes, People with Disabilities, Recreation & Athletics, Senior Services, Shelters/Homelessness, Social Services-General, Veterans, YMCA/YWCA/YMHA/YWHA, Youth Organizations

Application Procedures

Initial Contact: Applicants should send a proposal in the form of a letter.
Application Requirements: Proposal should include: amount requested; a description of existing activities, intended activities and their expected impact; other sources if funding committed and anticipated; prospects for project's continuance; plans for future support; a budget, and a copy of a letter from the IRS exempting the applicant from Federal Income Tax.
Deadlines: None.

Restrictions

Grants are not given to individuals.

Additional Information

Publications: Annual Report

Foundation Officials

Jules M. Baron: director
Richard K. Baron: executive director
David A. Brauner: vice president, director B New York, NY 1942. ED Dickinson College AB (1963); Columbia University JD (1966). PRIM CORP EMPL partner: Baron Rosenzweig Klein & Brauner. NONPR AFFIL member: Maritime Law Association United States; member: New York County Lawyers Association; vice president, director: The Bridge Inc.
Robert N. Davies: director CLUB AFFIL Baltusrol Golf Club.
Michael L. Goldstein: director
David R. Kay: treasurer, director
Allan Nisselson: director
Elias Rosenzweig: director
Gail Schneider: director
Christopher C. Schwabacher: director B New York, NY 1941. ED Harvard University BA (1963); Harvard University LLB (1966); New York University LLM (1967).
Norman H. Sparber: director B Brooklyn, NY 1917. ED Saint John's University BBA (1942); Brooklyn Law School JD (1952). PRIM CORP EMPL attorney: Brauner Baron Rosenzweig Kligler Sparber & Bauman.

Roy M. Sparber: director PRIM CORP EMPL partner: Baron Rosenzweig Klein & Brauner.

Grants Analysis

Disclosure Period: fiscal year ending February 28, 2002
Total Grants: $1,510,200
Number of Grants: 103
Average Grant: $14,662
Highest Grant: $80,000
Lowest Grant: $1,000
Typical Range: $5,000 to $30,000

Recent Grants

Note: Grants derived from fiscal 2002 Form 990.
General

100,000	City College of the City University of New York, New York, NY
100,000	UJA/Federation of Jewish Philanthropies of New York Inc., New York, NY
60,000	American Friends of Maccabee Institute Foundation, Monsey, NY
50,000	Federation of Jewish Philanthropies of New York Inc., New York, NY
50,000	New York University Downtown Hospital, New York, NY
40,000	Rockefeller University, New York, NY
36,000	National Conference of Synagogue Youth of the Union of Orthodox Jewish Congregations of America, New York, NY
28,000	American Cancer Society, Tampa, FL
25,000	Nassau Land Trust, East Norwich, NY
25,000	New York Philharmonic, New York, NY

RICHARD AND RHODA GOLDMAN FUND

Giving Contact

Sam Salkin, Executive Director
One Lombard Street, Suite 303
San Francisco, CA 94111
Phone: (415)788-1090
Fax: (415)788-7890
E-mail: info@goldmanfund.org
Web: http://www.goldmanfund.org

Description

Founded: 1951
EIN: 946064502
Organization Type: Family Foundation
Giving Locations: CA: San Francisco including metropolitan area
Grant Types: Capital, General Support, Multiyear/Continuing Support, Project.

Donor Information

Founder: The fund was incorporated in 1951 by Rhoda H. Goldman and Richard N. Goldman.

Financial Summary

Total Giving: $43,362,780 (2003); $31,859,552 (2002); $47,512,937 (2001)
Assets: $371,761,570 (2002); $466,044,479 (2001)
Gifts Received: $25,084,432 (2002); $152,450,731 (1998); $109,096,827 (1992). Note: In 2002, contributions were received from Richard Goldman. In 1998, contributions were received from the Goldman '96 Charitable Remainder Trust.

Typical Recipients

Arts & Humanities: Arts Centers, Arts Festivals, Arts Institutes, Ballet, Dance, Film & Video, Historic Preservation, History & Archaeology, Libraries, Museums/Galleries, Music, Opera, Public Broadcasting, Theater
Civic & Public Affairs: Asian American Affairs, Botanical Gardens/Parks, Business/Free Enterprise, Civil Rights, Community Foundations, Economic Development, Economic Policy, Employment/Job Training, Civic & Public Affairs-General, Law & Justice, Legal Aid, Native American Affairs, Nonprofit Management, Philanthropic Organizations, Public Policy, Urban & Community Affairs, Women's Affairs, Zoos/Aquariums
Education: Afterschool/Enrichment Programs, Arts/Humanities Education, Business Education, Colleges & Universities, Education Funds, Environmental Education, Faculty Development, Education-General, Health & Physical Education, International Studies, Leadership Training, Literacy, Minority Education, Private Education (Precollege), Secondary Education (Private), Special Education, Student Aid
Environment: Air/Water Quality, Forestry, Environment-General, Protection, Research, Resource Conservation, Watershed, Wildlife Protection
Health: AIDS/HIV, Alzheimer's Disease, Cancer, Children's Health/Hospitals, Clinics/Medical Centers, Health-General, Health Policy/Cost Containment, Health Organizations, Heart, Hospices, Long-Term Care, Medical Research, Medical Training, Nursing Services, Public Health
International: International-General, Health Care/Hospitals, Human Rights, International Environmental Issues, International Organizations, International Peace & Security Issues, International Relations, Missionary/Religious Activities, Trade
Religion: Religion-General, Jewish Causes, Religious Welfare, Social/Policy Issues
Science: Science Museums, Scientific Organizations, Scientific Research
Social Services: Child Abuse, Community Service Organizations, Counseling, Crime Prevention, Day Care, Delinquency & Criminal Rehabilitation, Domestic Violence, Family Planning, Family Services, Food/Clothing Distribution, People with Disabilities, Recreation & Athletics, Senior Services, Shelters/Homelessness, Substance Abuse, United Funds/United Ways, YMCA/YWCA/YMHA/YWHA, Youth Organizations

Application Procedures

Initial Contact: The foundation requests applications be made in writing.
Application Requirements: Letters of inquiry, no longer than two pages plus attachments, should include a one-paragraph executive summary describing the project for which funding is being sought, total project budget, amount requested, and short descriptive project title (proposals will not be accepted without the executive summary paragraph). Also include the name of the primary contact person along with his or her title, address, and phone number; description of project, including its necessity, objectives, significance, and plans for implementation; one-page itemized project budget; other sources or potential sources of funding; total annual budget; and a copy of the IRS letter verifying tax exempt status.
Deadlines: None.
Review Process: If the fund is interested in receiving a full proposal, applicant will be contacted and asked to submit additional information.

Restrictions

The fund does not accept unsolicited proposals for the support of arts organizations or institutions of primary, secondary or higher education, and generally does not accept applications for deficit budgets; endowments, or conferences; basic research; documentary films; and grants or scholarships to individuals.

Additional Information

Publications: Annual Report; Application Guidelines

Foundation Officials

Thomas Ehrlich: director
Mathea Falco: director
Douglas E. Goldman: director, vice president CORP AFFIL chairman: Certain Software. NONPR AFFIL founder: Goldman Genealogy Center; chairman: Stern Grove Festival Assn.; president: Lisa and Douglas Goldman Fund; trustee: Goldman Environmental Foundation.
Richard Nathaniel Goldman: president, director, member executive committee B San Francisco, CA April 16, 1920. ED University of California at Berkeley Boalt Hall School of Law; University of California at Berkeley (1941). PRIM CORP EMPL chairman, chief executive officer: Richard N. Goldman & Co. NONPR AFFIL trustee: World Affairs Council.
Donald H. Seiler: director, member executive committee CORP AFFIL director: Greater Bay Bancorp; director: Ross Stores Inc..
Mason Willrich: director

Grants Analysis

Disclosure Period: calendar year ending 2003
Total Grants: $43,362,780
Number of Grants: 750 (approx)
Average Grant: $57,817
Highest Grant: $1,000,000
Lowest Grant: $1,000
Typical Range: $10,000 to $100,000

Recent Grants

Note: Grants derived from 2002 Form 990.
General

1,000,000	Mendocino Land Trust Inc., Mendocino, CA -- to help purchase the Big River property
1,000,000	National Geographic Society, Washington, DC -- to educate the public & develop a strategy for the restoration & conservation of the nation's marine resources
500,000	Bay Area Discovery Museum, Sausalito, CA -- for capital campaign for children's museum
400,000	PAX Inc., New York, NY -- to redefine the debate over gun ownership as a matter of public safety and good parenting
350,000	NARAL Foundation, Washington, DC -- for "Choice for America" initiative
265,000	Board of Trustees of the Leland Stanford Junior University, Stanford, CA -- for center for environmental science & policy, a multidisciplinary research & teaching program
250,000	Boys and Girls Clubs of San Francisco, San Francisco, CA -- to complete a merger by building the infrastructure necessary to sustain the new, larger institution
250,000	Environmental Defense Fund for Alliance for Environmental Innovation, Boston, MA -- for FedEx project, to help Federal Express a cleaner, more fuel-efficient truck fleet
250,000	Family Violence Prevention Fund, San Francisco, CA -- for a new national initiative safe at home, a constituency building campaign
250,000	Global Fund for Women, San Francisco, CA -- to support & promote women's safety & health including reproductive health

MORRIS GOLDSEKER FOUNDATION OF MARYLAND

Giving Contact

Carol Gilbert, Program Officer
1040 Park Avenue, Suite 310
Baltimore, MD 21201
Phone: (410)837-5100
Fax: (410)837-7927
E-mail: cgilbert@goldsekerfoundation.org

Web: http://www.goldsekerfoundation.org

Description
Founded: 1974
EIN: 520983502
Organization Type: General Purpose Foundation
Giving Locations: MD: Baltimore
Grant Types: Award, General Support, Loan, Matching, Multiyear/Continuing Support, Professorship, Project, Seed Money.
Note: Also provides grants for evaluations, program development, and technical assistance.

Donor Information
Founder: The Morris Goldseker Foundation of Maryland was established in 1973 by the will of Morris Goldseker expressly to support programs directly benefiting the people of the Baltimore metropolitan area.

Financial Summary
Total Giving: $3,472,835 (2003); $5,300,000 (2001 approx)
Assets: $91,831,971 (2003); $100,174,901 (2001)
Gifts Received: $40,948 (1994). Note: In 1994, contributions were received from LISC.

Typical Recipients
Arts & Humanities: Arts Associations & Councils, Arts Centers, Historic Preservation, History & Archaeology, Libraries, Literary Arts, Public Broadcasting
Civic & Public Affairs: African American Affairs, Botanical Gardens/Parks, Business/Free Enterprise, Civil Rights, Community Foundations, Economic Development, Employment/Job Training, Ethnic Organizations, Civic & Public Affairs-General, Hispanic Affairs, Housing, Inner-City Development, Law & Justice, Legal Aid, Municipalities/Towns, Nonprofit Management, Parades/Festivals, Philanthropic Organizations, Professional & Trade Associations, Public Policy, Urban & Community Affairs, Women's Affairs
Education: Colleges & Universities, Education Funds, Elementary Education (Public), Education-General, Leadership Training, Literacy, Medical Education, Preschool Education, Private Education (Precollege), Secondary Education (Private), Special Education, Student Aid, Vocational & Technical Education
Environment: Environment-General, Protection, Watershed
Health: Clinics/Medical Centers, Health Organizations, Mental Health, Research/Studies Institutes
International: International Development
Religion: Churches, Jewish Causes, Ministries, Religious Organizations, Religious Welfare
Science: Scientific Centers & Institutes
Social Services: Animal Protection, At-Risk Youth, Big Brothers/Big Sisters, Child Abuse, Child Welfare, Community Centers, Community Service Organizations, Counseling, Crime Prevention, Domestic Violence, Family Planning, Family Services, Food/Clothing Distribution, Homes, People with Disabilities, Recreation & Athletics, Scouts, Senior Services, Shelters/Homelessness, Substance Abuse, Volunteer Services, YMCA/YWCA/YMHA/YWHA, Youth Organizations

Application Procedures
Initial Contact: Applicants should submit a brief preliminary letter to the foundation. Telephone inquiries are also welcome.
Application Requirements: Applicants should include a description of organization, evidence of IRS tax-exempt status under sections 501(c)(3) and 509(a) of the Internal Revenue Code, background information, statement of need and objectives of the proposed project, methods for accomplishing objectives, projected program budget, and amount sought from the foundation. If foundation staff determine the request is within the foundation's interests and poli-

cies, they will send the applicant a proposal development form.
Deadlines: For full proposals: April 1; August 1; and December 1.
Review Process: The foundation's board meets three times a year, in March, June, and October, to consider proposals. Applicants are notified in writing of the outcome of their requests immediately after each meeting.
Because the foundation is not a long-term source of funds, applicants are encouraged to demonstrate how the proposed activity will be sustained. Applicants are expected to demonstrate adequate administrative capacity and financial stability, and to describe evaluation criteria and methods on their requests.

Restrictions
In order to be considered for funding, an organization must carry on its work and activities principally in the Baltimore metropolitan area.
The foundation does not make grants in support of religious programs or purposes, endowments, individuals, building campaigns, deficit financing, annual giving, or publications. The foundation reports it does not support arts and culture, ongoing operating budgets, political action groups, specific diseases or disabilities, or projects normally financed with public funds. In accordance with the donor's instruction, the foundation awards no more than five percent of its net income in any calendar year to any single recipient. Also, the foundation prefers not to award grants for longer than one year, but may consider requests for longer periods.

Additional Information
The foundation lists NationsBank Trust Company of Baltimore as a corporate trustee represented by Howard M. Weiss. The foundation is affiliated with the Baltimore Community Foundation. Also, the foundation is working with Johns Hopkins Health System, Johns Hopkins University, and the Kennedy Krieger Institute to establish a private community development bank in east and southeast Baltimore, to begin the long-term restoration of an inner-city neighborhood.
Publications: Annual Report; Program Guidelines

Foundation Officials
Timothy D. Armbruster: president, chief executive officer PRIM NONPR EMPL president, director: Baltimore Community Foundation.
Ana Goldseker: trustee
Deby Goldseker: trustee
Sharna Goldseker: trustee
Sheldon Goldseker: chairman, trustee B 1940. PRIM CORP EMPL president: Multi-Properties Inc.
Simon Goldseker: vice chairman, trustee B 1939. PRIM CORP EMPL vice president, director: Multi-Properties Inc. CORP AFFIL partner: Maryland Apartments.
Sheila L. Purkey: secretary, treasurer
Semmes Guest Walsh: member investment committee B Annapolis, MD 1926. ED Yale University BE (1946); Harvard University MBA (1950). NONPR AFFIL director: J. L. Kernan Hospital Foundation.
Howard M. Weiss: corporate co-trustee, member investment committee PRIM CORP EMPL partner, attorney: Fletcher, Heald & Hildreth.

Grants Analysis
Disclosure Period: calendar year ending 2003
Total Grants: $3,472,835
Number of Grants: 79
Average Grant: $35,118*
Highest Grant: $213,000
Lowest Grant: $84
Typical Range: $10,000 to $75,000
***Note:** Average grant figure excludes four highest grants ($839,000).

Recent Grants
Note: Grants derived from 2003 Form 990.
General

213,000	Johns Hopkins University, Baltimore, MD
213,000	Morgan State University, Baltimore, MD
213,000	Preserving and Enhancing Jewish Life, Baltimore, MD
200,000	Baltimore Community Foundation, Baltimore, MD
175,000	Greater Homewood, Baltimore, MD
100,000	Citizens Planning and Housing Association, Baltimore, MD
100,000	Maryland Association of Nonprofit Organization, Baltimore, MD
100,000	Patterson Park Community Development Corporation, Baltimore, MD
100,000	Southeast Community Development Corporation, Baltimore, MD
98,500	Chesapeake Bay Fund, Baltimore, MD

GOLUB CORP.

Company Headquarters
Schenectady, NY
Web: http://www.pricechopper.com

Company Description
Revenue: US$2 billion (2001)
Employees: 20000 (2003)
SIC(s): 5411 Grocery Stores.

Operating Locations
Golub Corp. (MA; NY--Albany, Broom, Clinton, Delaware, Essex, Franklin Square, Fulton, Hamilton, Herkimer, Jefferson, Madison, Oneida, Onondaga, Orange, Oswego, Rensselaer, Saratoga Springs, Schenectady, Schoharie, Washington; PA; VT--Bennington)

Golub Foundation

Giving Contact
Melissa Pabis, Foundation Administrator
501 Duanesburg Rd.
Schenectady, NY 12306
Phone: (518)379-1270

Description
Founded: 1981
EIN: 222341421
Organization Type: Corporate Foundation
Giving Locations: headquarters and operating communities.
Grant Types: Employee Matching Gifts, General Support, Scholarship.

Donor Information
Founder: Golub Corp., Jane Golub, Neil M. Golub

Financial Summary
Total Giving: $671,180 (fiscal year ending March 31, 2003); $478,750 (fiscal 2001). Note: Contributes through foundation only.
Giving Analysis: Giving for fiscal 2003 includes: foundation grants to United Way ($55,000); fiscal 2001: foundation matching gifts ($2,895); corporate grants to United Way ($49,980); foundation scholarships ($51,000); foundation ($374,875)
Assets: $12,797 (fiscal 2003); $477,299 (fiscal 2001)
Gifts Received: $962,265 (fiscal 2001); $300,000 (fiscal 1999); $445,000 (fiscal 1997). Note: Contributions were received from the Golub Corporation.

Typical Recipients
Arts & Humanities: Arts Associations & Councils, Arts Centers, Arts Institutes, Arts Outreach, Ethnic &

Folk Arts, Historic Preservation, Libraries, Literary Arts, Museums/Galleries, Music, Opera, Performing Arts, Theater

Civic & Public Affairs: African American Affairs, Ethnic Organizations, Civic & Public Affairs-General, Housing, Professional & Trade Associations, Public Policy, Urban & Community Affairs

Education: Business Education, Colleges & Universities, Community & Junior Colleges, Education Funds, Engineering/Technological Education, Education-General, Literacy, Medical Education, Preschool Education, Public Education (Precollege), Science/Mathematics Education, Student Aid

Health: Arthritis, Cancer, Children's Health/Hospitals, Clinics/Medical Centers, Diabetes, Eyes/Blindness, Health Funds, Health Organizations, Hospices, Hospitals, Medical Rehabilitation, Nursing Services, Prenatal Health Issues, Single-Disease Health Associations

Religion: Dioceses, Jewish Causes, Religious Organizations, Religious Welfare, Synagogues/Temples

Science: Science Museums

Social Services: Community Centers, Community Service Organizations, Counseling, Family Services, Food/Clothing Distribution, People with Disabilities, Recreation & Athletics, Scouts, Senior Services, United Funds/United Ways, YMCA/YWCA/YMHA/YWHA, Youth Organizations

Application Procedures

Initial Contact: Brief letter for general proposals; letter requesting application form for scholarship awards.

Application Requirements: For grant proposals, a description of organization, amount requested, purpose of funds sought, recently audited financial statement, and proof of tax-exempt status. Scholarship application packet must include applicant's educational history, including courses taken, ACT/SAT scores, class ranking, grades received; activity profile, including honors/awards and extracurricular activities; three reference letters; original essay; and completed application form.

Deadlines: for grant requests: None; for scholarship applications: March.

Notes: Scholarship applicants must plan to attend a school in NY, MA, PA, VT, CT, or NH.

Additional Information

Publications: Informational Brochure

Corporate Officials

Lewis Golub: chairman, chief executive officer, director B 1931. ED Michigan State University BS (1953). PRIM CORP EMPL chairman, chief executive officer, director: Golub Corp. CORP AFFIL director: Taylor Made Co.; chairman, chief executive officer: Price Chopper Oper Co. Massachusetts; chairman, chief executive officer: Price Chopper Oper Co. Pennsylvania; director: CIES; chairman, chief executive officer: Golub Service Stations Inc.; chairman: Central Distributors Inc.; member regional advisory board: Chase Bank; chairman: Cengo Construction Corp. NONPR AFFIL director: Saratoga Performing Arts Center; member advisory board: Union College; director: Proctor's Theater; advisor mba program: Russell Sage College; director: Food Marketing Institute; chairman: New York State Business Council; director: Empire State College Foundation.

Foundation Officials

Mark Boucher: trustee
Pamela Cerrone: trustee
David Golub: trustee
Wesley Holloway, Jr.: trustee

Grants Analysis

Disclosure Period: fiscal year ending March 31, 2003
Total Grants: $555,795*
Number of Grants: 539
Average Grant: $1,031

Highest Grant: $43,125
Typical Range: $300 to $3,000
*Note: Giving excludes matching gifts; scholarships; United Way.

Recent Grants

Note: Grants derived from 2003 Form 990.

General

43,125	United Jewish Federation, Latham, NY
43,125	United Jewish Federation, Latham, NY
43,125	United Jewish Federation, Latham, NY
43,125	United Jewish Federation, Latham, NY
32,681	Golub Corporation, Rotterdam, NY
25,000	Saratoga Automobile Museum, Saratoga Springs, NY
25,000	United Jewish Federation, Latham, NY -- towards 'Israel Now' fund
20,000	Albany Medical Center Foundation, Albany, NY
20,000	Daughters of Sarah Nursing Home, Albany, NY
20,000	Ellis Hospital Foundation Inc., Schenectady, NY

GOOD SAMARITAN

Giving Contact

Edmund N. Carpenter, Jr., President
600 Center Mill Rd.
Wilmington, DE 19807
Phone: (302)654-7558
Fax: (302)654-2376

Description

Founded: 1938
EIN: 516000401
Organization Type: Private Foundation
Giving Locations: East Coast.
Grant Types: General Support.

Donor Information

Founder: the late Elias Ahuja

Financial Summary

Total Giving: 1996 Giving includes scholarship ($318,000).

Typical Recipients

Arts & Humanities: Libraries, Museums/Galleries
Civic & Public Affairs: Community Foundations, Civic & Public Affairs-General, Housing, Law & Justice, Legal Aid, Public Policy, Urban & Community Affairs
Education: Colleges & Universities, Community & Junior Colleges, Education Funds, Elementary Education (Public), Engineering/Technological Education, Environmental Education, Faculty Development, Education-General, Minority Education, Private Education (Precollege), Public Education (Precollege), Religious Education, Science/Mathematics Education, Special Education, Student Aid
Environment: Environment-General, Protection, Resource Conservation, Wildlife Protection
Health: Cancer, Hospices, Hospitals, Long-Term Care, Medical Research, Mental Health, Preventive Medicine/Wellness Organizations
International: Foreign Educational Institutions, International-General
Religion: Ministries
Social Services: At-Risk Youth, Child Welfare, Community Service Organizations, Day Care, Delinquency & Criminal Rehabilitation, Family Planning, People with Disabilities, Recreation & Athletics, YMCA/YWCA/YMHA/YWHA, Youth Organizations

Application Procedures

Initial Contact: Send a written narrative report.
Deadlines: Four weeks before first Thursday in June and four weeks before first Thursday in November.

Restrictions

Grants are not provided for building funds, other capital assets, or conferences.

Additional Information

Publications: Application Guidelines

Foundation Officials

Carroll M. Carpenter: vice president
Edmund Nelson Carpenter, II: secretary, treasurer B Philadelphia, PA 1921. ED Princeton University BA (1943). Harvard University LLB (1948). PRIM CORP EMPL director: Barclays Bank. CORP AFFIL director: Bank DE Corp. Wilmington. NONPR AFFIL trustee: Woodrow Wilson Foundation; trustee: Winterthur Museum; trustee: Wilmington Medical Center; member: Delaware Health Care Injury Insurance Study Commission; director: Good Samaritan; member: Delaware Bar Association; member: American Judicature Society; member: American Trial Lawyers Association; fellow: American College Trial Lawyers; member: American Bar Association; fellow: American Bar Foundation.
Elizabeth Lee DuPont: vice president
Lea C. DuPont: vice president
Jeffrey M. Nielsen: secretary, treasurer
Rev. Edmund K. Sherrill, II: director
H. Sinclair Sherrill: director
Rev. Henry W. Sherrill: president

Grants Analysis

Disclosure Period: calendar year ending 2000
Total Grants: $970,260
Number of Grants: 19
Average Grant: $42,792*
Highest Grant: $200,000
Typical Range: $20,000 to $100,000
*Note: Average grant figure excludes highest grant.

Recent Grants

Note: Grants derived from 2002 Form 990.

Library-Related

250,000	Laurel Public Library, Laurel, DE
200,000	Boston Athenaeum, Boston, MA -- support intern program and establish endowment fund

General

250,000	Brigham and Women's Hospital, Boston, MA -- fund the Patient and Family Waiting Area and Education Center Project
150,000	American Judicature Society, Chicago, IL -- National Jury Center
150,000	Angel Fund, Wakefield, MA -- research
150,000	Shernl House, Inc., Boston, MA -- Bishop Henry Knox Sherrill Fund
150,000	Wilmer Institute of Johns Hopkins Hospital, Baltimore, MD -- research in cataracts and glaucoma
100,000	Brooks School, North Andover, MA -- Bishop Sherrill Scholarship Fund
100,000	Lawrenceville School, Lawrenceville, NJ -- Circle House Initiative
100,000	Massachusetts General Hospital, Boston, MA -- Prenatal Psychiatry Program
50,000	Boys and Girls Club of Delaware, Wilmington, DE -- program enhancement
50,000	Conservation Fund, Arlington, VA -- preserve critical wetlands

GOODMAN FAMILY FOUNDATION

Giving Contact
Roy M. Goodman, Trustee
1035 5th Ave.
New York, NY 10028
Phone: (212)298-5524

Description
Founded: 1970
EIN: 136355553
Organization Type: Private Foundation
Giving Locations: NY: New York
Grant Types: General Support.

Donor Information
Founder: the late Israel Matz

Financial Summary
Total Giving: $280,057 (fiscal year ending June 30, 2004); $196,278 (fiscal 2001)
Assets: $4,618,683 (fiscal 2004); $5,018,845 (fiscal 2001)

Typical Recipients
Arts & Humanities: Arts Associations & Councils, Arts Centers, Arts Festivals, Arts Funds, Arts Outreach, Ballet, Community Arts, Dance, Libraries, Literary Arts, Museums/Galleries, Music, Opera, Performing Arts, Public Broadcasting, Theater
Civic & Public Affairs: Botanical Gardens/Parks, Clubs, Community Foundations, Civic & Public Affairs-General, Philanthropic Organizations, Professional & Trade Associations, Public Policy, Urban & Community Affairs, Women's Affairs
Education: Arts/Humanities Education, Business Education, Colleges & Universities, Education Funds, Faculty Development, International Studies, Medical Education, Minority Education, Private Education (Precollege), Science/Mathematics Education, Social Sciences Education, Special Education, Student Aid
Environment: Wildlife Protection
Health: AIDS/HIV, Cancer, Clinics/Medical Centers, Emergency/Ambulance Services, Hospitals, Hospitals (University Affiliated), Long-Term Care, Medical Research, Research/Studies Institutes
International: Health Care/Hospitals, International Affairs, International Relations, Missionary/Religious Activities
Religion: Churches, Dioceses, Jewish Causes, Religious Organizations, Religious Welfare, Synagogues/Temples
Science: Science Museums
Social Services: Camps, Child Welfare, Community Centers, Community Service Organizations, Crime Prevention, Day Care, Family Services, People with Disabilities, Recreation & Athletics, United Funds/United Ways, Youth Organizations

Application Procedures
Initial Contact: Send a brief letter of inquiry describing program.
Application Requirements: Include a written outline describing the special use of all contributions.
Deadlines: None.

Foundation Officials
Barbara F. Goodman: trustee
Roy Matz Goodman: trustee B New York, NY 1930. ED Harvard University BA (1951); Harvard University MBA (1953). PRIM CORP EMPL member: New York State Senate. NONPR AFFIL member: Omicron Delta Epsilon; trustee: Temple Emanu-El; sponsor: New York Philharmonic Society; member: New York Society Security Analysts; patron: Metropolitan Opera; member council advisor: New York Comm Young Audiences; fellow: Metropolitan Museum Art; trustee: Heart Research Foundation; member visitors committee: John F. Kennedy School Government

Harvard University Overseers; member council advisor: Harvard Comm University Resources; member: Council Foreign Relations; member: Financial Analysts Federation; trustee: Carnegie Hall Society; member: Association Harvard Alumni; trustee: Carnegie Hall Corp.; member: Anti-Defamation League; member: American Young President Organization. CLUB AFFIL Senate New York Saint Club; Harvard Club; Fort Orange Club; Harvard Business School Club; Dutch Treat Club; Century Country Club; City Club; Century Association.

Grants Analysis
Disclosure Period: fiscal year ending June 30, 2004
Total Grants: $280,057
Number of Grants: 94
Average Grant: $2,443*
Highest Grant: $52,900
Lowest Grant: $100
Typical Range: $1,000 to $5,000
*****Note:** Average grant excludes highest grant.

Recent Grants
Note: Grants derived from fiscal 2004 Form 990.
General

52,900	John F. Kennedy Center for Performing Arts, Washington, DC
25,000	Teacher's College Columbia University, New York, NY
10,620	Dalton School, New York, NY
10,000	Chamber Music Society of Lincoln Center, New York, NY
10,000	Citizens Union Foundation, New York, NY
10,000	Lenox Hill Hospital, New York, NY
9,700	City Parks Foundation, New York, NY
7,500	Carnegie Hall Society Inc., New York, NY
7,100	Harvard College Fund, New York, NY
6,000	United Nations Association, New York, NY

GOODNOW FUND

Giving Contact
Edward B. Goodnow, Trustee
36 Old Kings Highway South
Darien, CT 06820-4523
Phone: (203)655-6272
Fax: (203)655-7351

Description
Founded: 1994
EIN: 066395384
Organization Type: Private Foundation
Giving Locations: CT; MA; NY
Grant Types: General Support.

Donor Information
Founder: Established in 1994 by Edward B. Goodnow.

Financial Summary
Total Giving: $331,925 (2003); $1,371,755 (2001)
Assets: $16,621,080 (2003); $15,168,348 (2001)
Gifts Received: $1,500,000 (1995); $3,035,000 (1994); $3,000,100 (1993)

Typical Recipients
Arts & Humanities: History & Archaeology, Libraries, Literary Arts, Museums/Galleries
Civic & Public Affairs: Civic & Public Affairs-General, Housing, Philanthropic Organizations, Professional & Trade Associations, Safety, Urban & Community Affairs
Education: Colleges & Universities, Medical Education, Minority Education, Private Education (Precollege), School Volunteerism, Student Aid
Environment: Air/Water Quality, Protection, Re-

source Conservation, Wildlife Protection
Health: Cancer, Emergency/Ambulance Services, Hospitals, Medical Research, Public Health
International: International Relief Efforts
Religion: Churches, Religious Organizations, Religious Welfare
Social Services: Animal Protection, Camps, Child Welfare, Community Centers, Community Service Organizations, Family Services, Food/Clothing Distribution, People with Disabilities, Scouts, Senior Services, Special Olympics, United Funds/United Ways, Volunteer Services, YMCA/YWCA/YMHA/YWHA, Youth Organizations

Application Procedures
Initial Contact: The foundation has no formal grant application procedure or application form. Send a brief letter of inquiry.
Deadlines: None.

Foundation Officials
Edward B. Goodnow: trustee

Grants Analysis
Disclosure Period: calendar year ending 2003
Total Grants: $331,925*
Typical Range: $100 to $1,000
*****Note:** No grants list available for 2003.

Recent Grants
Note: Grants derived from 2000 Form 990.
Library-Related

20,000	Friends of Darien Library, Darien, CT

General

250,000	Princeton University Trustees, Princeton, NJ
30,000	Salvation Army, Norristown, PA
25,000	Fairfield County Foundation, Fairfield, CT
20,000	Darien United Way, Darien, CT
20,000	Fresh Air Fund, New York, NY
20,000	Stamford Health Foundation, Inc, Stamford, CT
15,000	Jericho Project, The, New York, NY
15,000	Norwalk Hospital Foundation, Norwalk, CT
10,000	Catholic Relief Services
10,000	Hospital for Special Surgery, New York, NY

GOODRICH CORP.

Company Headquarters
4 Coliseum Centre
2730 W. Tyvola Rd.
Charlotte, NC 28217-4578
Web: http://www.goodrich.com

Company Description
Founded: 1870
Ticker: GR
Exchange: NYSE
Revenue: US$4.724 billion (2004)
Profit: US$172.2 million (2004)
Employees: 20600 (2003)
Fortune Rank: 408, per FORTUNE Magazine's list of 500 Largest U.S. Corporations (2004).

Nonmonetary Support
Type: Donated Equipment; In-kind Services; Loaned Employees; Loaned Executives; Workplace Solicitation
Volunteer Programs: Foundation sponsors a Bonus Volunteer Match program in addition to its Donors Match program. The foundation will make an extra 1 to 1 match of employee gifts to eligible organizations for which the employee volunteers, to a maximum of $1,000. The company also sponsors a school partnership in Charlotte, NC.

B.F. Goodrich Foundation, Inc.

Giving Contact
Natalie English, Secretary
B.F. Goodrich Foundation, Inc.
Four Coliseum Center
2730 W. Tyvola Road
Charlotte, NC 28217-4578
Phone: (704)423-7069
Fax: (704)423-7069
Web: http://www.goodrich.com/AboutGoodrich

Description
EIN: 341601879
Organization Type: Corporate Foundation
Giving Locations: nationally; operating locations.
Grant Types: Award, Capital, Employee Matching Gifts, General Support, Multiyear/Continuing Support.
Note: Matching gifts are given to nonprofit organizations through its Partners in Giving Plan. Employee matching gift ratio: 1 to 1, from $50 to $2,500.

Donor Information
Founder: The Goodrich Corp. established the foundation with a contribution in 1988.

Financial Summary
Total Giving: $2,232,637 (2003); $2,507,416 (2002); $2,469,797 (2001). Note: Contributes through corporate direct giving program and foundation.
Giving Analysis: Giving for 2002 includes: foundation grants to United Way ($529,004); 2001: domestic and international subsidiaries ($1,250,000); corporate direct giving ($2,400,000)
Assets: $15,032,248 (2003); $14,083,869 (2002); $14,965,814 (2001)
Gifts Received: $2,000,000 (2001); $1,107,180 (1998); $218,680 (1997). Note: In 1997, contributions were received from Goodrich.

Typical Recipients
Arts & Humanities: Arts Associations & Councils, Arts Centers, Ballet, Community Arts, Dance, Historic Preservation, History & Archaeology, Libraries, Museums/Galleries, Music, Opera, Performing Arts, Public Broadcasting, Theater, Visual Arts
Civic & Public Affairs: African American Affairs, Botanical Gardens/Parks, Business/Free Enterprise, Chambers of Commerce, Community Foundations, Economic Development, Economic Policy, Employment/Job Training, Civic & Public Affairs-General, Housing, Law & Justice, Municipalities/Towns, Parades/Festivals, Philanthropic Organizations, Professional & Trade Associations, Public Policy, Safety, Urban & Community Affairs, Women's Affairs
Education: Afterschool/Enrichment Programs, Business Education, Colleges & Universities, Community & Junior Colleges, Economic Education, Education Associations, Education Funds, Education Reform, Elementary Education (Private), Engineering/Technological Education, Education-General, Minority Education, Private Education (Precollege), Public Education (Precollege), Science/Mathematics Education, Student Aid
Health: Cancer, Children's Health/Hospitals, Clinics/Medical Centers, Emergency/Ambulance Services, Health-General, Geriatric Health, Health Organizations, Hospices, Hospitals, Nursing Services, Preventive Medicine/Wellness Organizations
International: International Affairs
Religion: Religious Organizations, Religious Welfare
Science: Science Exhibits & Fairs, Science Museums, Scientific Centers & Institutes, Scientific Organizations
Social Services: Camps, Child Abuse, Child Welfare, Community Centers, Community Service Organizations, Emergency Relief, Family Services, People with Disabilities, Recreation & Athletics, Scouts,

Senior Services, Social Services-General, Substance Abuse, United Funds/United Ways, YMCA/YWCA/YMHA/YWHA, Youth Organizations

Application Procedures
Initial Contact: Request an application form from the foundation or download an application from the foundation's web site: www.goodrich.com/giving.asp.
Application Requirements: Mail the completed application form and any supporting documentation outlining the project and its impact on the community.
Deadlines: None.
Review Process: Calendar budget cycle begins in February of each year.
Decision Notification: Funding decisions are made by the Foundation Contributions Committee.
Notes: Telephone and e-mail requests are not accepted.

Restrictions
Grants are not made for multi-year grants in excess of five years; individuals, private foundations, endowments, churches or religious programs, fraternal, social, labor, or veterans' organizations; groups with unusually high fundraising or administrative expenses; political parties, candidates, or lobbying activities; travel funds for tours, trips, or exhibitions by individuals or special interest groups; organizations that discriminate because of race, color, religion, national origin; local athletic or sports programs or equipment, courtesy advertising benefits, raffle tickets, and other fundraising events involving the purchase of tables, tickets, or advertisements; organizations that receive sizable portions of their support from government entities; individuals United Way agencies that already benefit from Goodrich contributions to the United Way Campaign; or international organizations. Contributions are made only to 501(c)(3) tax-exempt organizations.

Corporate Officials
David L. Burner: chairman, chief executive officer, director B Lodi, OH April 05, 1939. ED Ohio University BS (1962). PRIM CORP EMPL chairman: Goodrich Corp. ADD CORP EMPL officer: Jcair Inc.; chairman: Simmonds Precision Products. CORP AFFIL director: Brush Wellman Inc. NONPR AFFIL director: Salvation Army Greater Cleveland; director: Summit Education Initiative; director: Greater Cleveland Growth Association; board governor: Aerospace Institute America; director: Cleveland Scholarship Program Inc.
Gary L. Habegger: vice president human resources B Decatur, IN 1944. ED Seattle Pacific University (1966); University of Michigan (1978). PRIM CORP EMPL vice president human resources: B.F. Goodrich Co. ADD CORP EMPL vice president: Simmonds Precision Products.
Robert Jewell: vice president communications PRIM CORP EMPL vice president communications: B.F. Goodrich Co.
Scott E. Kuechle: vice president, treasurer PRIM CORP EMPL vice president, treasurer: B.F. Goodrich Co.
Marshall O. Larsen: president, chief executive officer, director ED Purdue University MS. PRIM CORP EMPL president, chief executive officer, director: Goodrich Corp.
Les C. Vinney: senior vice president, chief financial officer B Cleveland, OH 1948. ED Cornell University BA (1970); Cornell University MBA (1972). PRIM CORP EMPL senior vice president, chief financial officer: B.F. Goodrich Co. CORP AFFIL president, director: Tremco Autobody Technologies; president: Tremco Inc.; treasurer: B.F. Performance Freedom Chem Co.

Foundation Officials
Natalie English: secretary
Scott E. Kuechle: treasurer (see above)
Marshall O. Larsen: vice president (see above)

Terrence G. Linnert: president
Rick Schmidt: vice president

Grants Analysis
Disclosure Period: calendar year ending 2003
Total Grants: $1,984,684*
Number of Grants: 575 (approx)
Average Grant: $3,452
Highest Grant: $100,000
Lowest Grant: $50
Typical Range: $1,000 to $5,000
*Note: Giving excludes United Way.

Recent Grants
Note: Grants derived from 2003 Form 990.
General
247,953	United Way, Charlotte, NC
100,000	Advantage Carolina, Charlotte, NC
100,000	Cleveland Orchestra, Cleveland, OH
100,000	North Carolina Dance Theatre, Charlotte, NC
75,000	Forum for Corporate Conscience, Charlotte, NC
70,000	Field of Dreams, West Hartford, CT
60,000	South Bay YMCA, Chula Vista, CA
56,000	Communities in Schools, Charlotte, NC
55,750	Junior Achievement, Charlotte, NC
55,000	Mint Museum of Art, Charlotte, NC

GOODSTEIN FOUNDATION

Giving Contact
Morris Massey, President
PO Box 2773
Casper, WY 82602
Phone: (307)234-0821

Description
Founded: 1952
EIN: 836003815
Organization Type: Private Foundation
Giving Locations: CO; WY
Grant Types: General Support.

Donor Information
Founder: J. M. Goodstein

Financial Summary
Total Giving: $278,650 (fiscal year ending June 30, 2004); $408,390 (fiscal 2001). Note: Fiscal 1997 Giving includes United Way ($2,500).
Giving Analysis: Giving for fiscal 2004 includes: foundation grants to United Way ($2,500); fiscal 2001: foundation grants to United Way ($2,500)
Assets: $5,930,451 (fiscal 2004); $5,982,781 (fiscal 2001)

Typical Recipients
Arts & Humanities: Community Arts, Libraries, Museums/Galleries, Music, Opera, Public Broadcasting, Theater
Civic & Public Affairs: Botanical Gardens/Parks, Economic Development, Civic & Public Affairs-General, Urban & Community Affairs, Women's Affairs, Zoos/Aquariums
Education: Agricultural Education, Arts/Humanities Education, Colleges & Universities, Education Funds, Education-General, Legal Education, Private Education (Precollege), Science/Mathematics Education, Secondary Education (Private)
Environment: Environment-General
Health: Alzheimer's Disease, Arthritis, Cancer, Children's Health/Hospitals, Clinics/Medical Centers, Diabetes, Health Funds, Health Organizations, Heart, Hospices, Hospitals, Medical Research, Nursing Services, Prenatal Health Issues, Respiratory, Speech & Hearing
International: Health Care/Hospitals, Missionary/

Religious Activities
Religion: Churches, Religion-General, Jewish Causes, Religious Organizations, Religious Welfare
Science: Science Museums
Social Services: Animal Protection, Child Welfare, Community Service Organizations, Crime Prevention, Day Care, Emergency Relief, Family Planning, Food/Clothing Distribution, People with Disabilities, Senior Services, United Funds/United Ways, Youth Organizations

Application Procedures

Initial Contact: The foundation requests applications be made in writing. Clearly outline the purpose of funds sought.
Deadlines: None.

Restrictions

Primarily limited to colleges, universities, churches, hospitals, and like educational and health institutions.

Foundation Officials

Lucy M. Goodstein: vice president
Morris Massey: president

Grants Analysis

Disclosure Period: fiscal year ending June 30, 2004
Total Grants: $276,150*
Number of Grants: 55
Average Grant: $4,503*
Highest Grant: $33,000
Lowest Grant: $250
Typical Range: $1,000 to $10,000
*Note: Giving excludes United Way. Average grant figure excludes highest grant.

Recent Grants

Note: Grants derived from fiscal 2004 Form 990.
General

33,000	Casper College Foundation, Casper, WY
25,000	Boys and Girls Clubs
25,000	Casper Area Economic Development Alliance, Casper, WY
25,000	Mercer House, Savannah, GA
15,000	Central Wyoming Hospice, Casper, WY
10,000	Child Development of Wyoming, Cheyenne, WY
10,000	Children's Hospital
10,000	Hadassah, New York, NY
10,000	Meals on Wheels, Syracuse, NY
10,000	Planned Parenthood, Denver, CO

PEGGY AND YALE GORDON CHARITABLE TRUST

Giving Contact

Sidney S. Sherr, Director
3 Church Ln.
Pikesville, MD 21208
Phone: (410)484-6410

Description

Founded: 1980
EIN: 521174287
Organization Type: Private Foundation
Giving Locations: MD, Baltimore
Grant Types: General Support, Multiyear/Continuing Support.

Donor Information

Founder: The late Yale Gordon.

Financial Summary

Total Giving: $161,542 (2004); $54,600 (2001)
Assets: $4,169,798 (2004); $6,097,181 (2001)

Gifts Received: $38 (1998); $100 (1996); $11,088 (1995). Note: In 1996, contributions were received from Raymond and Alice Gordon.

Typical Recipients

Arts & Humanities: Arts Associations & Councils, Arts Funds, Arts Institutes, Arts Outreach, Community Arts, Historic Preservation, Libraries, Museums/Galleries, Music, Opera, Performing Arts, Public Broadcasting, Theater
Education: Arts/Humanities Education, Colleges & Universities, Private Education (Precollege)
International: Missionary/Religious Activities
Religion: Jewish Causes, Ministries, Religious Organizations, Synagogues/Temples

Application Procedures

Initial Contact: The foundation has no formal grant application procedure or application form. Submit a full proposal.
Application Requirements: Provide a description of organization, amount requested, purpose of funds sought, recently audited financial statement, proof of tax-exempt status.
Deadlines: None.

Restrictions

Does not support individuals, religious organizations for sectarian purposes, political or lobbying groups, or organizations outside operating areas.

Foundation Officials

Loraine Bernstein: assistant director
Judith A. Burke: trustee
Phyllis C. Friedman: trustee
Raymond J. Gordon: trustee
Sidney S. Sherr: director
Robert A. Steinberg: trustee

Grants Analysis

Disclosure Period: calendar year ending 2004
Total Grants: $161,542*
Number of Grants: 10
Average Grant: $12,394*
Highest Grant: $50,000
Lowest Grant: $1,500
Typical Range: $5,000 to $25,000
*Note: Average grant figure excludes highest grant.

Recent Grants

Note: Grants derived from 2001 Form 990.
General

50,000	P and Y Gordan Performing Arts Center, Owings Mills, MD -- new construction and music
2,500	Baltimore Choral Arts Society, Baltimore, MD -- music
1,500	Towson State University, Towson, MD -- music
600	GBMC, Baltimore, MD -- music

THE FLORENCE GOULD FOUNDATION

Giving Contact

John R. Young, President
Cahill, Gordon, and Reindel
80 Pine St., Ste. 1736
New York, NY 10005-1702
Phone: (212)701-3400
Fax: (212)269-5420

Description

Founded: 1957
EIN: 136176855
Organization Type: General Purpose Foundation
Giving Locations: NY: nationally; France

Grant Types: Conference/Seminar, Department, Endowment, General Support, Project, Research.

Donor Information

Founder: Established in 1957 by Florence J. Gould.

Financial Summary

Total Giving: $6,024,395 (2003); $6,592,672 (2002)
Giving Analysis: Giving for 2003 includes: foundation scholarships ($122,850); 2002: foundation scholarships ($59,800)
Assets: $91,368,520 (2003); $101,695,466 (2002)
Gifts Received: $6,494 (1992). Note: Contributions were received from trusts under the will of Florence J. Gould.

Typical Recipients

Arts & Humanities: Arts Associations & Councils, Arts Centers, Ballet, Dance, Ethnic & Folk Arts, Arts & Humanities-General, Historic Preservation, History & Archaeology, Libraries, Literary Arts, Museums/Galleries, Music, Opera, Performing Arts, Public Broadcasting, Theater, Visual Arts
Civic & Public Affairs: Botanical Gardens/Parks, Clubs, Civic & Public Affairs-General, Law & Justice, Philanthropic Organizations, Public Policy, Urban & Community Affairs
Education: Arts/Humanities Education, Colleges & Universities, Continuing Education, Engineering/Technological Education, Education-General, International Exchange, International Studies, Legal Education, Medical Education, Public Education (Precollege), Science/Mathematics Education
Environment: Environment-General
Health: AIDS/HIV, Alzheimer's Disease, Children's Health/Hospitals, Clinics/Medical Centers, Geriatric Health
International: Foreign Arts Organizations, Foreign Educational Institutions, International-General, Health Care/Hospitals, International Affairs, International Development, International Organizations, International Peace & Security Issues, International Relations
Religion: Churches, Jewish Causes, Religious Organizations, Religious Welfare
Science: Science-General, Scientific Labs
Social Services: Community Service Organizations, People with Disabilities, Social Services-General

Application Procedures

Initial Contact: No particular form of application is required.
Deadlines: None.

Foundation Officials

Walter Conway Cliff: assistant treasurer, secretary, director B Detroit, MI 1932. ED University of Detroit BS (1955); University of Detroit LLB (1955); New York University LLM (1956). PRIM CORP EMPL president: Walter C. Cliff PC PRIM NONPR EMPL partner: Cahill Gordon & Reindel. CORP AFFIL partner: Cahill Gordon & Reindel. NONPR AFFIL member collections committee: Harvard University Art Museum; member: New York State Bar Association; member: American Bar Association; member: Association Bar New York City. CLUB AFFIL Stockbridge Golf Club; Downtown Club.
Daniel Pomeroy Davison: vice president, treasurer, ast secretary, director B New York, NY 1925. ED Yale University BA (1949); Harvard University JD (1952).
Daniel Leopold Wildenstein: vice president, director B Verrieres-le-Buisson, France September 11, 1917. PRIM CORP EMPL chairman: Wildenstein & Co. Inc.
John R. Young: president B Milwaukee, WI 1934. ED University of Chicago AB (1953); University of Chicago JD (1956). PRIM CORP EMPL Cahill Gordon & Reindel.

Grants Analysis

Disclosure Period: calendar year ending 2003
Total Grants: $5,901,545*

Number of Grants: 168
Average Grant: $35,238
Highest Grant: $250,000
Lowest Grant: $200
Typical Range: $5,000 to $50,000
*Note: Giving excludes scholarships.

Recent Grants

Note: Grants derived from 2001 Form 990.
Library-Related

| 150,000 | Pierpont Morgan Library, New York, NY |
| 75,000 | Wadsworth Athenaeum, Hartford, CT |

General

250,000	Metropolitan Museum of Art, New York, NY
250,000	Metropolitan Museum of Art, New York, NY
225,000	Brooklyn Academy of Music, Brooklyn, NY
200,000	Agence Comptable Central du Tresor
200,000	Foundation for French Museums, New York, NY
200,000	French Institute Alliance Francaise, New York, NY
175,000	Institut de France, Domaine de Chantilly, Chantilly France
150,000	French Institute Alliance Francaise, New York, NY
150,000	Fund for Independent Publishing, New York, NY
150,000	Roundabout Theater Company, New York, NY

GRABLE FOUNDATION

Giving Contact

Susan H. Brownlee, Executive Director
650 Smithfield Street, Suite 240
Pittsburgh, PA 15222
Phone: (412)471-4550
Fax: (412)471-2267
E-mail: grable@grablefdn.org
Web: http://www.grablefdn.org

Description

Founded: 1977
EIN: 251309888
Organization Type: General Purpose Foundation
Giving Locations: PA: southwest region
Grant Types: General Support, Matching, Multiyear/Continuing Support, Operating Expenses, Project, Research, Seed Money.

Donor Information

Founder: Minnie K. Grable founded the Grable Foundation in 1976.

Financial Summary

Total Giving: $9,116,004 (2003); $8,972,080 (2002); $10,984,014 (2001)
Giving Analysis: Giving for 2003 includes: foundation grants to United Way ($200,000)
Assets: $232,127,387 (2003); $200,793,684 (2002); $234,656,940 (2001)
Gifts Received: $35,013,925 (1997); $27,592,274 (1996); $28,128,119 (1995). Note: In 1996 and 1997, contributions were received from the Minnie K. Grable Trust.

Typical Recipients

Arts & Humanities: Arts Centers, Arts Institutes, Community Arts, Arts & Humanities-General, Historic Preservation, History & Archaeology, Libraries, Museums/Galleries, Public Broadcasting
Civic & Public Affairs: African American Affairs, Botanical Gardens/Parks, Business/Free Enterprise, Community Foundations, Economic Development, Economic Policy, Employment/Job Training, Civic & Public Affairs-General, Law & Justice, Professional & Trade Associations, Public Policy, Urban & Community Affairs, Zoos/Aquariums
Education: Afterschool/Enrichment Programs, Arts/Humanities Education, Business Education, Colleges & Universities, Community & Junior Colleges, Economic Education, Education Associations, Education Funds, Education Reform, Elementary Education (Private), Elementary Education (Public), Environmental Education, Faculty Development, Education-General, International Exchange, Leadership Training, Literacy, Minority Education, Private Education (Precollege), Public Education (Precollege), School Volunteerism, Science/Mathematics Education, Secondary Education (Public), Social Sciences Education, Special Education, Student Aid, Vocational & Technical Education
Environment: Forestry, Protection, Resource Conservation
Health: Children's Health/Hospitals, Clinics/Medical Centers, Health-General, Health Organizations, Hospitals, Mental Health, Prenatal Health Issues
Religion: Religious Organizations, Religious Welfare
Science: Scientific Centers & Institutes
Social Services: Big Brothers/Big Sisters, Child Welfare, Community Service Organizations, Counseling, Day Care, Family Planning, Family Services, Recreation & Athletics, Shelters/Homelessness, Substance Abuse, United Funds/United Ways, Volunteer Services, YMCA/YWCA/YMHA/YWHA, Youth Organizations

Application Procedures

Initial Contact: Send a brief letter of inquiry describing program.
Application Requirements: If notified that the program is within foundation guidelines, applications should include a one-page summary of proposal, a description of organization, description of project, statement of need, description of project supervisor and staff, project budget showing committed and anticipated funds, how project will be sustained after funding, organization's operating budget, description of anticipated outcomes of the project, list of board members, and a copy of IRS tax-exempt certification.
Deadlines: None. The board meets three times a year, usually in March, July, and November.
Notes: The Common Grant Application is also accepted.

Restrictions

Foundation does not support endorsement, capital campaigns, fundraisers or individuals.

Additional Information

Publications: Annual Report Guidelines

Foundation Officials

Susan H. Brownlee: executive director
Charles R. Burke, Jr.: chairman, director
Charles R. Burke: chairman emeritus, director
Patricia G. Burke: director
Steven E. Burke: treasurer
Barbara N. McFadyen: director
Jan Nicholson: president
Marion G. Nicholson: director
William B. Nicholson: director
Merrilynn Young: comptroller

Grants Analysis

Disclosure Period: calendar year ending 2003
Total Grants: $8,916,004*
Number of Grants: 279
Average Grant: $31,957
Highest Grant: $200,000
Lowest Grant: $400
Typical Range: $10,000 to $50,000
*Note: Giving excludes United Way.

Recent Grants

Note: Grants derived from 2002 Form 990.

Library-Related

| 50,000 | Carnegie Library of Pittsburgh, Pittsburgh, PA -- for BLAST school outreach program |

General

850,000	Carnegie Institute, Pittsburgh, PA -- for Carnegie science center capital campaign
259,028	NARSAD, Great Neck, NY -- for 2002 investigators
155,940	Mon Valley Education Consortium, McKeesport, PA -- for grants
150,000	Beginning with Books, Pittsburgh, PA -- for project BEACON
150,000	Education Delivery Systems (EDSYS), Pittsburgh, PA -- for city charter high school
150,000	Family Health Council, Pittsburgh, PA -- for center for adolescent pregnancy prevention
150,000	Sports & Exhibition Authority, Pittsburgh, PA -- for North Shore Riverfront park
150,000	Tides Center, Pittsburgh, PA -- for youthplaces
125,000	Zoological Society of Pittsburgh, Pittsburgh, PA -- for aquarium project
105,000	Shady Lane School, Pittsburgh, PA -- for capacity building

GRACO INC.

Company Headquarters

Minneapolis, MN
Web: http://www.graco.com

Company Description

Founded: 1926
Ticker: GGG
Exchange: NYSE
Revenue: US$487 million (2002)
Employees: 1750 (2003)
SIC(s): 3561 Pumps & Pumping Equipment.

Operating Locations

Graco, Inc. (CA--Los Angeles; CO--Arvada, Denver; GA--Atlanta; IL--Franklin Park; MI--Plymouth; MN--Golden Valley; TX--Dallas)

Nonmonetary Support

Type: Donated Equipment
Volunteer Programs: In the past, employees have volunteered time for education associations such as Junior Achievement and the Business Economics Education Foundation. Graco's program also included year-round volunteer assignments (on boards, etc.) with Junior Achievement, the United Way, Metro Paint-a-Thon, and other events of interest to employees. The company has a Volunteer Coordinator.
Note: Nonmonetary support is limited and contact is initiated through foundation.

Graco Foundation

Giving Contact

Robert M. Mattison, President
PO Box 1441
Minneapolis, MN 55440-1441
Phone: (612)623-6684
Fax: (612)623-6944
Web: http://www.graco.com/Internet/T_Corp.nsf/Webpages/Foundation

Alternate Contact

Nancy Skaalrud, Legal Secretary, Foundation Administrator
E-mail: Nancy_a_Skaalrud@Graco.com

Description
EIN: 416023537
Organization Type: Corporate Foundation
Giving Locations: MN; SD: Sioux Falls operating locations.
Grant Types: Capital, General Support, Scholarship.
Note: Employee matching gift ratio: 1 to 1, up to $2,500.

Financial Summary
Total Giving: $1,731,998 (2003); $1,574,640 (2002); $1,629,109 (2001). Note: Contributes through corporate direct giving program and foundation.
Giving Analysis: Giving for 2001 includes: foundation scholarships ($175,500); foundation grants to United Way ($526,597)
Assets: $3,541,343 (2003); $2,882,740 (2002); $2,950,417 (2001)
Gifts Received: $1,700,000 (2003); $2,100,000 (2002); $1,000,000 (2001). Note: Contributions were received from Graco, Inc.

Typical Recipients
Arts & Humanities: Arts Institutes, Dance, Arts & Humanities-General, History & Archaeology, Libraries, Music, Public Broadcasting, Theater, Visual Arts
Civic & Public Affairs: African American Affairs, Asian American Affairs, Botanical Gardens/Parks, Business/Free Enterprise, Chambers of Commerce, Community Foundations, Economic Development, Employment/Job Training, Ethnic Organizations, Civic & Public Affairs-General, Hispanic Affairs, Housing, Minority Business, Municipalities/Towns, Native American Affairs, Nonprofit Management, Philanthropic Organizations, Public Policy, Urban & Community Affairs, Women's Affairs
Education: Afterschool/Enrichment Programs, Business Education, Colleges & Universities, Economic Education, Education Associations, Education Funds, Education Reform, Elementary Education (Private), Elementary Education (Public), Engineering/Technological Education, Education-General, Literacy, Medical Education, Minority Education, Preschool Education, Private Education (Precollege), Public Education (Precollege), Science/Mathematics Education, Secondary Education (Private), Secondary Education (Public), Special Education, Student Aid, Vocational & Technical Education
Environment: Forestry, Environment-General, Wildlife Protection
Health: AIDS/HIV, Alzheimer's Disease, Cancer, Children's Health/Hospitals, Clinics/Medical Centers, Diabetes, Emergency/Ambulance Services, Health Organizations, Hospitals, Medical Rehabilitation, Mental Health, Research/Studies Institutes, Single-Disease Health Associations
International: Foreign Educational Institutions, International Environmental Issues, International Relief Efforts
Religion: Churches, Jewish Causes, Religious Organizations, Religious Welfare
Science: Science Museums
Social Services: At-Risk Youth, Child Abuse, Child Welfare, Community Centers, Community Service Organizations, Crime Prevention, Day Care, Domestic Violence, Emergency Relief, Family Services, Food/Clothing Distribution, People with Disabilities, Recreation & Athletics, Scouts, Senior Services, Shelters/Homelessness, Social Services-General, United Funds/United Ways, Volunteer Services, YMCA/YWCA/YMHA/YWHA, Youth Organizations

Application Procedures
Initial Contact: Send a brief letter.
Application Requirements: Include a brief outline of the program, including agency background, objectives, and their IRS validation as a qualified applicant.
Deadlines: None.
Review Process: Foundation board of directors reviews requests quarterly.

Evaluative Criteria: Grant requests must address the Foundation's focus areas; emphasis will be on capacity building grants.

Restrictions
Grants are not awarded to individuals; political campaigns; fraternal organizations; national or local campaigns for disease research; for fundraising purposes, travel, special events, dinners, or courtesy advertising; or religious organizations for sectarian purposes.
Grants are limited to northeast Minneapolis, Minnesota and Sioux Falls, South Dakota.

Additional Information
The Foundation also sponsors a scholarship program for college age children of Graco employees. Graco makes 5% of its U.S. pretax earnings available each year for distribution to charitable organizations and community development programs.
Graco sponsors a scholarship program for children of employees.
Publications: Graco Foundation Community Report; Guidelines

Corporate Officials
George Aristides: chairman, chief executive officer, director B 1936. PRIM CORP EMPL president, chief executive officer, director: Graco, Inc.
James Graner: vice president, controller PRIM CORP EMPL vice president, controller: Graco Inc.
David M. Lowe: vice president lubrication equip division B 1956. PRIM CORP EMPL vice president lubrication equip division: Graco Inc.
Mark Sheahan: vice president B Minneapolis, MN 1964. ED University of Minnesota (1986); William Mitchell College of Law (1990). PRIM CORP EMPL treasurer: Graco Inc. NONPR AFFIL member: American Bar Association.

Foundation Officials
Laurie O. Englert: director
Janel French: treasurer
Charles R. Hartl: director
Dale D. Johnson: director
Robert Mayer Mattison: president B Minneapolis, MN 1948. ED Saint John's University BA (1970); University of Minnesota JD (1973). NONPR AFFIL member: Minnesota Bar Association; member: Minnesota Corp. Counsel Association; member: Hennepin County Bar Association; member: American Corporate Counsel Association. CLUB AFFIL Golden Valley Country Club.
Patrick J. McHale: director
Charles L. Rescorla: director
Nancy Skaalrud: secretary

Grants Analysis
Disclosure Period: calendar year ending 2003
Total Grants: $1,158,132*
Number of Grants: 48
Average Grant: $19,070*
Highest Grant: $100,000
Lowest Grant: $3,000
Typical Range: $10,000 to $40,000
*Note: Giving excludes matching gifts; scholarship; United Way. Average grant figure excludes three highest grants ($300,000).

Recent Grants
Note: Grants derived from 2003 Form 990.
Library-Related

100,000	Minneapolis Public Library, Minneapolis, MN
20,000	Minneapolis Public Library, Minneapolis, MN

General

458,571	Greater Twin Cities United Way, Minneapolis, MN
100,000	Courage Center, Minneapolis, MN
100,000	Greater Minneapolis Crisis Nursery, Minneapolis, MN
100,000	McCrossan Boys Ranch, Sioux Falls, SD
77,400	Citizens' Scholarship Foundation of America, Minneapolis, MN
75,000	Project for Pride in Living, Minneapolis, MN
57,552	A Chance to Grow, Minneapolis, MN
50,000	Seed Academy/Harvest Preparatory School, Minneapolis, MN
49,980	Yale Mechanical, New Haven, CT
40,000	Minnesota Independent School Forum, St. Paul, MN

GRAHAM ENGINEERING CORP.

Company Headquarters
1203 Eden Rd.
York, PA 17402
Web: http://www.grahammachinerygroup.com

Company Description
Revenue: US$41 million (2001)
Employees: 175 (2001)

Graham Foundation

Giving Contact
William H. Kerlin, Jr., Trustee
PO Box 1104
York, PA 17405
Phone: (717)849-4045

Description
Founded: 1986
EIN: 236805421
Organization Type: Corporate Foundation
Giving Locations: headquarters area only.
Grant Types: General Support.

Donor Information
Founder: Graham Engineering

Financial Summary
Total Giving: $1,872,345 (fiscal year ending June 30, 2004); $2,028,982 (fiscal 2002); $2,102,810 (fiscal 2001)
Assets: $20,401,760 (fiscal 2004); $19,606,115 (fiscal 2003); $20,810,494 (fiscal 2002)
Gifts Received: $277,917 (fiscal 2004); $30,000 (fiscal 2002); $30,000 (fiscal 2001). Note: Contributions were received from Graham Capital Corp. In fiscal 1999, contributions were received from Donald C. Graham. In fiscal 2001, 2002, and 2004, contributions were received from Graham Packaging Co.

Typical Recipients
Arts & Humanities: Arts Associations & Councils, Arts & Humanities-General, Historic Preservation, History & Archaeology, Libraries, Museums/Galleries, Music, Performing Arts, Public Broadcasting, Theater
Civic & Public Affairs: Botanical Gardens/Parks, Business/Free Enterprise, Chambers of Commerce, Community Foundations, Civic & Public Affairs-General, Hispanic Affairs, Housing, Urban & Community Affairs
Education: Afterschool/Enrichment Programs, Business Education, Colleges & Universities, Economic Education, Education Funds, Elementary Education (Private), Engineering/Technological Education, Education-General, Health & Physical Education, Preschool Education, Private Education (Precollege), Public Education (Precollege), Secondary Education (Private), Student Aid
Environment: Environment-General, Resource Conservation

Health: Cancer, Children's Health/Hospitals, Diabetes, Emergency/Ambulance Services, Health-General, Health Funds, Health Organizations, Heart, Home-Care Services, Hospices, Hospitals, Medical Rehabilitation, Medical Research, Mental Health, Nursing Services, Public Health, Single-Disease Health Associations
Religion: Churches, Jewish Causes, Ministries, Religious Welfare
Science: Science Exhibits & Fairs
Social Services: Camps, Child Welfare, Community Centers, Community Service Organizations, Emergency Relief, Family Planning, Homes, People with Disabilities, Recreation & Athletics, Scouts, Senior Services, Social Services-General, United Funds/United Ways, YMCA/YWCA/YMHA/YWHA, Youth Organizations

Application Procedures

Initial Contact: The foundation has no formal grant application procedure or application form.
Deadlines: None.

Restrictions

Grants are not made to individuals.

Corporate Officials

William H. Kerlin, Jr.: chairman PRIM CORP EMPL chairman: Graham Engineering Corp.

Foundation Officials

Donald C. Graham: trustee
Ingrid A. Graham: trustee
William H. Kerlin, Jr.: trustee (see above)

Grants Analysis

Disclosure Period: fiscal year ending June 30, 2004
Total Grants: $1,812,845*
Number of Grants: 59
Average Grant: $14,015*
Highest Grant: $1,000,000
Lowest Grant: $100
Typical Range: $1,000 to $25,000
*Note: Giving excludes United Way. Average grant excludes highest grant.

Recent Grants

Note: Grants derived from fiscal 2004 Form 990.

Library-Related

10,000	Martin Library Building Fund, York, PA -- capital campaign	

General

1,000,000	University of Michigan, Ann Arbor, MI -- Donald C. Graham endowment fund
248,570	Burke Mountain Academy, East Burke, VT
207,625	Burke Mountain Academy, East Burke, VT -- capital campaign
85,000	Squam Lake Association, Holderness, NH -- capital campaign
60,000	Strand-Capitol Performing Arts Center, York, PA -- capital campaign
59,500	United Way of York County, York, PA
50,000	University of Pennsylvania, Philadelphia, PA -- Munger statue memorial
20,000	York Foundation, York, PA -- capital campaign
12,650	Camp Tecumseh, Center Harbor, NH
12,500	Hershey Gardens, Hershey, PA -- capital campaign

GRAHAM FOUNDATION FOR ADVANCED STUDIES IN THE FINE ARTS

Giving Contact

Richard Solomon, Director
4 West Burton Place
Chicago, IL 60610-1416
Phone: (312)787-4071
E-mail: info@grahamfoundation.org
Web: http://www.grahamfoundation.org

Description

Founded: 1956
EIN: 362356089
Organization Type: General Purpose Foundation
Giving Locations: internationally; nationally.
Grant Types: Award, Conference/Seminar, Fellowship, Project, Research.

Donor Information

Founder: The foundation was established in 1956 by a bequest from Ernest R. Graham (1866-1936), a Chicago architect. Under the guidance of Daniel Burnham, Mr. Graham was the principal assistant in overseeing construction of the 1893 World's Columbian Exhibition and later was associated with the D. H. Burnham & Co. architectural firm. After Mr. Burnham's death in 1912, Graham built the company into one of the nation's largest designers of railroad stations, banks, office buildings, museums, department stores, theaters, and post offices. Ernest Graham died during the Depression, leaving his estate severely undervalued. It took 20 years for his associate and executor, the late Charles F. Murphy, to rebuild the estate and begin the foundation.

Financial Summary

Total Giving: $1,345,845 (2001)
Giving Analysis: Giving for 2001 includes: foundation gifts to individuals ($459,185)
Assets: $35,000,000 (2002 approx); $38,186,292 (2001)
Gifts Received: $5,000 (2001); $9,431 (1998); $15,000 (1992). Note: In 1998, contributions were received from Bright New City.

Typical Recipients

Arts & Humanities: Art History, Arts Appreciation, Arts Associations & Councils, Arts Centers, Arts Festivals, Arts Funds, Arts Institutes, Community Arts, Ethnic & Folk Arts, Film & Video, Arts & Humanities-General, Historic Preservation, History & Archaeology, Libraries, Literary Arts, Museums/Galleries, Performing Arts, Public Broadcasting, Visual Arts
Civic & Public Affairs: African American Affairs, Botanical Gardens/Parks, Business/Free Enterprise, Clubs, Economic Development, Civic & Public Affairs-General, Housing, Municipalities/Towns, Philanthropic Organizations, Professional & Trade Associations, Public Policy, Urban & Community Affairs, Women's Affairs
Education: Arts/Humanities Education, Business Education, Colleges & Universities, Continuing Education, Education Funds, Engineering/Technological Education, Education-General, International Exchange, International Studies, Journalism/Media Education, Minority Education, Private Education (Precollege), Religious Education, Social Sciences Education, Student Aid, Vocational & Technical Education
Environment: Environment-General, Protection
Health: Health Organizations
International: Foreign Arts Organizations, Foreign Educational Institutions, International Development, International Environmental Issues, International Organizations
Religion: Jewish Causes

Social Services: Senior Services, Social Services-General

Application Procedures

Initial Contact: A written proposal should be sent to the foundation. There is no formal application form.
Application Requirements: The application should succinctly specify the grant request's objectives and the applicant's qualifications. All applications should have a first-page summary sheet with the following information: project title; name, address, telephone number, and e-mail address of applicant and names of principal project participants; abstract of 150 words or less describing project; specific amount (in U.S. dollars) sought from foundation; anticipated final products of project; names of people from whom letters of support have been requested; and a list of other funding sources being approached and an indication of the status of those applications.
In addition to the summary sheet, applicants should supply the following: proposal succinctly describing purpose, audience, and outcome of project and addressing applicant's relevant background and capacity to accomplish project; career resumes of principal participants and background information on applying institution; work plan and schedule including applicant's plans for dissemination of completed work; budget, including cost components of total project and identifying other potential sources of support (do not include overhead or fringe benefits); letters from three references knowledgeable in area of project (references should assess worthiness of applicant and project and submit letter in confidence directly to foundation); supplemental information, including visual information, when appropriate; and IRS determination letter.
Deadlines: Applications should be postmarked no later than January 15 and July 15. Only reference letters postmarked up to 15 days after application deadline will be accepted. Deadline for the Carter Manny Award is March 15.
Review Process: Applications are considered twice a year. Notification of the decision on the proposal is usually made within 150 days.
Notes: The foundation will not accept applications or letters by fax or e-mail. If possible, use type no smaller than 10 points in application material.

Restrictions

Typically, grants are not made for endowments, operating expenses, construction or other capital expenditures, architectural fees for construction or renovation, or direct scholarships to students in pursuit of a degree. (However, doctoral candidates are eligible for the Carter Manny Award.) Grants are typically reserved for the early stages of a project.

Additional Information

Grants to individuals do not exceed $10,000. If a large sum of money is requested, other sources of funding should be included. In addition to making grants, the foundation conducts lectures and exhibits. The foundation also reports that it makes its Madlener House available to other organizations, at a nominal fee, for activities that relate to the foundation's purposes and do not conflict with its schedule. Applicants seeking permission to use the house should apply in writing well in advance of the date desired and must comply with strict rules governing use of the building.
Publications: Annual Report; Guidelines

Foundation Officials

Irwin J. Askow: vice president, trustee PRIM CORP EMPL secretary, director: Allied World Travel Inc.
Thomas H. Beeby: trustee B 1941. ED Yale University MS (1962-1965). PRIM CORP EMPL partner: Hammond, Beeby Rupert, Ainge.
Miles Lee Berger: director B Chicago, IL 1930. ED Brown University (1952). PRIM CORP EMPL chairman: Berger Financial Services Corp. CORP AFFIL chairman: Midtown Bank Chicago; vice chairman: Heitman Finance Ltd.; director: Innkeepers, Inc.; vice

chairman: Columbia National Bank Chicago; director: Franklin Holding. NONPR AFFIL member: Society Real Estate Appraisers; member: Society Real Estate Counsellors; member: American Institute of Real Estate Appraisers.

Sally A. Kitt Chappell: trustee PRIM NONPR EMPL professor: DePaul University.

Roberta Feldman: trustee PRIM NONPR EMPL assoc vice chancellor academic aff: University of Illinois, Chicago.

Henry Kuehn: trustee

Carter Hugh Manny, Jr.: director emeritus B Michigan City, IN November 16, 1918. ED Harvard University AB (1941); Illinois Institute of Technology BS (1948). NONPR AFFIL member advisory committee architecture: Art Institute of Chicago; member: Phi Beta Kappa; fellow: American Institute Architects. CLUB AFFIL Tavern Club; Michigan City Yacht Club; Pottawattomie Country Club; Arts Club; Cliff Dwellers Club.

James Nagle: trustee B 1933. ED University of Illinois BSME (1956). PRIM CORP EMPL president: Nagle Pumps Inc.

John I. Schlossman: trustee B Chicago, IL 1931. ED University of Minnesota BA (1953); University of Minnesota BArch (1955); Massachusetts Institute of Technology MArch (1956). PRIM CORP EMPL principal: Loebl, Schlossman & Hackl. NONPR AFFIL architectural society of Art Institute Chicago; trustee: Merit Music Program Inc.; fellow: American Institute Architects. CLUB AFFIL Arts Club; Tavern Club.

John James Schornack: trustee B Chicago, IL 1930. ED Loyola University BS (1951); Northwestern University MBA (1956); Harvard University Graduate School of Business Administration (1969). PRIM CORP EMPL chairman: Binks Sames Corp. CORP AFFIL director: Wintrust Finance Corp.; director: North Shore Bancorp Inc.; director: Binks James Corp. NONPR AFFIL chairman, member: Midwest-Japan Association; trustee: Saint Francis Hospital; trustee: Kohl Childrens Museum; member: Illinois Certified Public Accountant Society; member: Japan American Society; trustee: Chicago Symphony Orchestra; trustee: Graham Foundation; trustee: Catholic Theological Union; member: American Institute of Certified Public Accountants; chairman, trustee: Barat College; member: American Accounting Association. CLUB AFFIL Tavern Club; Glen View Golf Club; Ocean Club; Economic Club; 410 Club; Chicago Club.

Patricia Snyder: admin

Richard Solomon: director

Benjamin Horace Weese: president, trustee B Evanston, IL 1929. ED Harvard University BArch (1951); Ecole des Beaux Arts (1956); Harvard University MArch (1957). PRIM CORP EMPL principal: Weese Langley Weese Ltd. NONPR AFFIL co-founder, president: Glessner House; member: National Council Architectural Registration Boards; fellow: American Institute Architects; co-founder, president: Chicago Architects Foundation.

Robert A. Wislow: trustee B 1945. PRIM CORP EMPL chairman: U.S. Equities Realty Inc. CORP AFFIL chairman: Load Link Inc.

Grants Analysis

Disclosure Period: calendar year ending 2001
Total Grants: $886,660*
Number of Grants: 52
Average Grant: $15,425*
Highest Grant: $100,000
Lowest Grant: $2,500
Typical Range: $5,000 to $25,000
*Note: Giving excludes gifts to individuals. Average grant figure excludes highest grant.

Recent Grants

Note: Grants derived from 2002 Form 990.
General

100,000	Chicago Architecture Foundation, Chicago, IL -- for the Chicago architecture center
100,000	WBEZ Radio, Chicago, IL -- for enhanced architectural programming on WBEZ
46,000	National Endowment for the Arts, Washington, DC -- for Graham fellow in federal service
45,000	2002 Carter Manny Award, Chicago, IL
41,154	Graham Foundation Lectures/Exhibits, Chicago, IL
25,000	Metropolitan Plan Council, Chicago, IL -- for neighborhood zoning guidelines
20,000	Architectural League of New York, New York, NY -- for 'urban life an international look at contemporary housing design'
20,000	Princeton Architectural Press, New York, NY -- for new voices in architecture
15,000	Harvard University, Cambridge, MA -- for Harvard design school project on the city
15,000	Harvard University, Cambridge, MA -- for the CASE series

PHILIP L. GRAHAM FUND

Giving Contact

Candice C. Bryant, President
1150 15th Street, Northwest
Washington, DC 20071
Phone: (202)334-6640
Fax: (202)334-4498
E-mail: plgfund@washpost.com

Description

Founded: 1963
EIN: 526051781
Organization Type: General Purpose Foundation
Giving Locations: DC: Washington including metropolitan area
Grant Types: Award, Capital, Emergency, General Support, Project.

Financial Summary

Total Giving: $5,250,000 (2003); $5,112,500 (2002); $5,033,000 (2001)
Assets: $105,303,463 (2003); $106,176,219 (2002); $98,000,000 (2001 approx)

Typical Recipients

Arts & Humanities: Arts Associations & Councils, Arts Centers, Arts Festivals, Arts Funds, Arts Outreach, Ballet, Dance, Ethnic & Folk Arts, Arts & Humanities-General, Historic Preservation, History & Archaeology, Libraries, Museums/Galleries, Music, Opera, Performing Arts, Public Broadcasting, Theater, Visual Arts

Civic & Public Affairs: African American Affairs, Asian American Affairs, Botanical Gardens/Parks, Community Foundations, Economic Development, Economic Policy, Employment/Job Training, First Amendment Issues, Civic & Public Affairs-General, Hispanic Affairs, Housing, Inner-City Development, Municipalities/Towns, Nonprofit Management, Professional & Trade Associations, Public Policy, Urban & Community Affairs, Women's Affairs

Education: Afterschool/Enrichment Programs, Arts/Humanities Education, Business Education, Colleges & Universities, Economic Education, Education Associations, Education Funds, Education Reform, Elementary Education (Public), Environmental Education, Education-General, International Studies, Journalism/Media Education, Leadership Training, Legal Education, Literacy, Minority Education, Preschool Education, Private Education (Precollege), Public Education (Precollege), Science/Mathematics Education, Secondary Education (Private), Special Education, Student Aid, Vocational & Technical Education

Environment: Environment-General, Watershed
Health: Adolescent Health Issues, AIDS/HIV, Cancer, Children's Health/Hospitals, Clinics/Medical Centers, Diabetes, Emergency/Ambulance Services, Geriatric Health, Health Organizations, Heart, Home-Care Services, Hospices, Hospitals, Long-Term Care, Mental Health, Outpatient Health Care, Prenatal Health Issues, Preventive Medicine/Wellness Organizations, Public Health, Transplant Networks/Donor Banks

International: Foreign Arts Organizations, Human Rights, International Affairs, International Development, International Organizations, International Relations

Religion: Churches, Jewish Causes, Ministries, Religious Organizations, Religious Welfare

Science: Science Museums, Scientific Centers & Institutes, Scientific Research

Social Services: Animal Protection, At-Risk Youth, Child Abuse, Child Welfare, Community Centers, Community Service Organizations, Counseling, Day Care, Delinquency & Criminal Rehabilitation, Domestic Violence, Family Planning, Family Services, Food/Clothing Distribution, Homes, People with Disabilities, Recreation & Athletics, Scouts, Senior Services, Shelters/Homelessness, Social Services-General, Substance Abuse, United Funds/United Ways, Volunteer Services, YMCA/YWCA/YMHA/YWHA, Youth Organizations

Application Procedures

Initial Contact: Request recent summary of grants. If applicant's needs falls within the Fund's areas of interest, send an original and two copies of a proposal letter of ten pages or less.

Application Requirements: The letter of proposal should describe the organization, its purpose, and the people it benefits. Applicants should also include a description of the project, benefits, costs, amount requested, other funding sources, the organization's qualifications to accomplish its goals, potential future support (if relevant), and a summary of prior support received from the Fund. Applicants also should submit a recent audited financial statement or IRS Form 990 for the most recent fiscal year, a current budget, project budget (including expected sources of funding), a copy of the organization's IRS letter of tax-exempt status, and a list of the organization's board of directors. Proposals should not be bound. The Fund accepts, but does not require, the WRAG common grant application form.

Deadlines: Proposals must be received by February 1, May 1, August 1, and October 15 for review at the next meeting.

Review Process: The fund's trustees meet four times a year to make funding decisions.

Evaluative Criteria: Preference is given to proposals that address one-time needs of organizations rather than general operating or program support.

Decision Notification: Organizations will be notified of decisions within 120 days of each application deadline.

Restrictions

Grants are not made to individuals; political, religious, or lobbying activities; membership organizations; for advocacy or litigation; research; conferences, workshops, or seminars; travel expense; benefits or fundraising events; courtesy advertising; national or international organizations; medical care; production of films or publications; annual giving campaigns, independent schools; post-secondary education institutions; or event sponsorships. The Fund generally makes grants only to organizations in the Washington, DC metropolitan area, and only to organizations that have been ruled to be tax-exempt under Section 501(c)(3) of the Internal Revenue Code, and that are not private foundations.

Additional Information

The fund accepts but does not require the WRAG common grant application format. The fund prefers proposals that address specific, special, primarily one-time needs. Proposals should not be bound.

Publications: History and Proposal Guidelines; Summary of Grants

Foundation Officials

Mary Bellor: secretary, secretary

Candice Bryant: president

Martin Cohen: trustee, treasurer B New York, NY 1932. ED Brown University AB (1953); University of Pennsylvania Wharton School MBA (1957). PRIM CORP EMPL vice president, director: Washington Post Co. NONPR AFFIL president: Frenchmans Creek Country Club. CLUB AFFIL Woodmont Country Club.

Donald Edward Graham: trustee B Baltimore, MD 1945. ED Harvard University BA (1966). PRIM CORP EMPL chairman, chief executive officer, director, publisher: Washington Post Co. NONPR AFFIL member: American Antiquarian Society.

Theodore M. Lutz: trustee

Daniel Lynch: assistant treasurer

Lionel Neptune: trustee

Grants Analysis

Disclosure Period: calendar year ending 2003

Total Grants: $5,250,000

Number of Grants: 187

Average Grant: $25,676*

Highest Grant: $300,000

Lowest Grant: $2,000

Typical Range: $5,000 to $50,000

*Note: Average grant excludes two highest grants ($500,000).

Recent Grants

Note: Grants derived from 2003 Form 990.

General

300,000	DC College Access Program, Washington, DC -- to encourage DC public high school students to enroll and graduate from college
200,000	Washington Drama Society dba Arena Stage, Washington, DC
175,000	Shakespeare Theater, Washington, DC -- support for The Shakespeare Theater
125,000	Boys & Girls Club of Greater Washington, Silver Spring, MD -- for underwriting a merger with the Metropolitan Police Boys & Girls Clubs
100,000	Center City Consortium, Washington, DC -- towards capital improvement to inner-city Catholic schools
100,000	DC Habitat for Humanity, Washington, DC -- for infrastructure expenses in 53 homes
100,000	Greater Washington Educational Television Association WETA, Arlington, VA
100,000	Junior Achievement, Washington, DC -- for the new technology-driven infrastructure needed to sustain volunteer mentors
100,000	New Leaders for New Schools, Washington, DC -- to support New Leaders' Fellows in DC
100,000	Nieman Foundation for Journalism at Harvard University, Cambridge, MA -- to enlarge Walter Lippman House to provide a larger seminar room

CHARLES M. AND MARY D. GRANT FOUNDATION

Giving Contact

Jacqueline E. Elias, Vice President
c/o JP Morgan Chase Bank
345 Park Ave., 4th Fl.
New York, NY 10154
Phone: (212)464-2487

Description

Founded: 1967

EIN: 136264329

Organization Type: Private Foundation

Giving Locations: Southeastern U.S.A.

Grant Types: Capital, General Support, Operating Expenses, Project, Seed Money.

Donor Information

Founder: the late Mary D. Grant

Financial Summary

Total Giving: $420,000 (2003); $510,000 (2001)

Assets: $9,327,508 (2003); $9,607,265 (2001)

Typical Recipients

Arts & Humanities: Libraries, Public Broadcasting

Civic & Public Affairs: Botanical Gardens/Parks, Civil Rights, Economic Development, Civic & Public Affairs-General, Legal Aid, Nonprofit Management, Philanthropic Organizations, Public Policy, Rural Affairs, Urban & Community Affairs, Women's Affairs

Education: Afterschool/Enrichment Programs, Arts/Humanities Education, Colleges & Universities, Education Funds, Literacy

Environment: Environment-General

Health: Hospices, Long-Term Care, Medical Research, Public Health

Social Services: Child Welfare, Community Centers, Community Service Organizations, Domestic Violence, Food/Clothing Distribution, Homes, Youth Organizations

Application Procedures

Initial Contact: Send a brief letter of inquiry with pertinent financial information.

Application Requirements: Include information on a description of organization, purpose of funds sought, recently audited financial statement, and proof of tax-exempt status.

Deadlines: None.

Restrictions

Grants are given for education, health, and welfare in the U.S. Does not support individuals or provide individual scholarships or loans.

Additional Information

Trust(s): JP Morgan Chase Bank

Grants Analysis

Disclosure Period: calendar year ending 2003

Total Grants: $420,000

Number of Grants: 12

Average Grant: $35,000

Highest Grant: $50,000

Lowest Grant: $25,000

Typical Range: $25,000 to $40,000

Recent Grants

Note: Grants derived from 2003 Form 990.

General

50,000	Hospice Foundation of Arkansas, Little Rock, AR
40,000	Friends-R-Fun Child Development, Summersville, WV
40,000	Greater New Orleans Educational Television, New Orleans, LA
40,000	MDC Inc., Chapel Hill, NC
35,000	Center for Creative Education, West Palm Beach, FL
35,000	Georgia Legal Services, Atlanta, GA
35,000	Quitman County Development, Marks, MS
35,000	United Negro College Fund, New York, NY
30,000	Berry College, Mt. Berry, GA
30,000	Virginia Quality Life, Kilmarnock, VA

GARLAND AND AGNES TAYLOR GRAY FOUNDATION

Giving Contact

Darcy Oman, President
7325 Beaufont Springs Drive, Suite 210
Richmond, VA 23225
Phone: (804)330-7400

Description

EIN: 546071867

Organization Type: Private Foundation

Giving Locations: VA: Waverly including surrounding area

Grant Types: Capital, Endowment, General Support, Multiyear/Continuing Support, Operating Expenses, Scholarship, Seed Money.

Donor Information

Founder: the late Garland Gray

Financial Summary

Total Giving: $1,025,759 (2001)

Giving Analysis: Giving for 2001 includes: foundation grants to United Way ($3,000)

Assets: $20,600,068 (2001)

Gifts Received: $2,478 (1996); $3,577 (1994). Note: In 1996, contributions were received from Thomas C. Gordon, Jr.

Typical Recipients

Arts & Humanities: Arts Appreciation, Arts Centers, Historic Preservation, History & Archaeology, Libraries, Museums/Galleries

Civic & Public Affairs: Clubs, Community Foundations, Economic Development, Employment/Job Training, Civic & Public Affairs-General, Hispanic Affairs, Housing, Municipalities/Towns, Philanthropic Organizations, Urban & Community Affairs

Education: Agricultural Education, Colleges & Universities, Education Funds, Environmental Education, Education-General, Medical Education, Private Education (Precollege), Public Education (Precollege), Science/Mathematics Education, Student Aid

Environment: Environment-General

Health: Cancer, Clinics/Medical Centers, Health Organizations, Hospitals, Medical Research, Multiple Sclerosis, Research/Studies Institutes, Single-Disease Health Associations

International: International Organizations

Religion: Churches, Religious Welfare

Science: Science Museums

Social Services: Animal Protection, At-Risk Youth, Child Welfare, Community Centers, Community Service Organizations, Crime Prevention, Emergency Relief, Family Services, Homes, People with Disabilities, Recreation & Athletics, Scouts, United Funds/United Ways, YMCA/YWCA/YMHA/YWHA, Youth Organizations

Application Procedures

Initial Contact: Send a brief letter of inquiry.

Deadlines: None.

Restrictions

Foundation does not support individuals or "start-up" organizations.

Additional Information

The Garland and Agnes Taylor Gray Foundation has become a supporting organization of the Community Foundation, a public charity.

Foundation Officials

William Birch Douglass, III: secretary B Richmond, VA 1943. ED Hampden-Sydney College BA (1965); University of Richmond LLB (1968); Harvard University LLM (1969). PRIM CORP EMPL partner: Mc-

Guire, Woods, Battle & Boothe. CORP AFFIL director: Flippo Lumber Corp.; director: Ted Lansing Corp.; director: Air Conditioning Suppliers; director: Carpenter Co. NONPR AFFIL trustee: Hampden-Sydney College; associate: University Richmond; fellow: American College Tax Counsel; fellow: American College Trust & Estate Counsel.

Charles F. Duff: vice president, trustee
C. Taylor Everett: trustee
Thomas Christian Gordon, Jr.: assistant secretary, trustee B Richmond, VA July 14, 1915. ED University of Virginia BS (1936); University of Virginia LLB (1938). NONPR AFFIL trustee: Childrens Hospital Richmond; member: Virginia Bar Association; member: American Bar Association; fellow: American Bar Foundation.
Bruce B. Gray: assistant treasurer, trustee
Elmon T. Gray: president, treasurer, trustee
Garland Gray, II: assistant secretary, trustee
Wallace Stettinius: vice president, trustee B New York, NY 1933. ED University of Virginia BA (1955); University of Virginia MBA (1959). PRIM CORP EMPL chairman, chief executive officer, director: Cadmus Communications Corp. CORP AFFIL director: Chesapeake Corp.
Thomas H. Tullidge: vice president, trustee

Grants Analysis

Disclosure Period: calendar year ending 2001
Total Grants: $1,022,759*
Number of Grants: 56
Average Grant: $15,868*
Highest Grant: $150,000
Lowest Grant: $500
Typical Range: $1,000 to $10,000 and $20,000 to $50,000
*Note: Giving excludes United Way. Average grant excludes highest grant.

Recent Grants

Note: Grants derived from 2001 Form 990.
Library-Related

75,000	Friends of the Waverly Public Library, Waverly, VA

General

150,000	Suffolk Center for Cultural Arts, Suffolk, VA
107,259	Community Foundation, Richmond, VA
104,500	Stuart Hall School, Staunton, VA
87,000	Collegiate Schools, Richmond, VA
55,000	YMCA of Greater Richmond, Richmond, VA
50,000	Horizon Health Services, Ivor, VA
50,000	Virginia Home, Richmond, VA
49,500	Randolph-Macon College, Ashland, VA
40,000	Southeast 4-H Educational Center, Wakefield, VA
22,000	University of Richmond, Richmond, VA

GREAT-WEST LIFE AND ANNUITY INSURANCE CO.

Company Headquarters
PO Box 1700
Denver, CO 80201
Web: http://www.gwl.com

Company Description
Assets: US$28.811 billion (2002)
Employees: 8160 (2002)
SIC(s): 6311 Life Insurance, 6321 Accident & Health Insurance.
Parent Company: Great-West Life Assurance Co., 100 Osborne St. N., Winnipeg, MB, Canada

Operating Locations
Great-West Life & Annuity Insurance Co. (CO--Englewood); Great-West Life Assurance Co. (CO--Englewood); Great-West Realty Investments (CO--Englewood); GWL Properties (CO--Englewood)

Nonmonetary Support
Type: Donated Equipment; In-kind Services; Loaned Employees; Loaned Executives

Giving Contact
John Clayton, Vice President, Corporate Services
8515 East Orchard Road
Englewood, CO 80111
Phone: (303)737-3000

Description
Organization Type: Corporate Giving Program
Giving Locations: headquarters and operating locations.
Grant Types: General Support, Research, Scholarship.

Typical Recipients
Arts & Humanities: Arts Associations & Councils, Arts Centers, Community Arts, Dance, Libraries, Museums/Galleries, Music, Performing Arts
Civic & Public Affairs: Women's Affairs
Education: Business Education, Colleges & Universities, Economic Education, Minority Education, Student Aid
Health: Health Policy/Cost Containment, Hospitals, Medical Research, Mental Health
Social Services: Community Service Organizations, Domestic Violence, Family Services, People with Disabilities, Substance Abuse, United Funds/United Ways, Youth Organizations

Application Procedures
Initial Contact: Company does not have a formal application form, but requests must be made in writing.
Application Requirements: Include a brief description of organization and its purpose; amount requested; specific purpose for which funds are being solicited; the total cost of program or project and the amount that will be spent in the Denver area; list of current contributors and amounts; copy of IRS tax-exemption letter of determination; list of officers and directors; copy of organization's most recent financial statement and annual report; and reasons why you believe Great-West Life should support your organization.
Review Process: Request for support are normally processed within 2 to 3 months from the date of receipt.
Decision Notification: All applicants are notified of the company's decision.

Restrictions
Contributions are not made to political organizations, veterans organizations, labor or fraternal organizations, individuals, or religious organizations for purposes of religious advocacy.

Additional Information
Company gives approximately $125,000 in nonmonetary support each year. This amount is not included in the contributions budget or figures above.
Publications: Contributions Policy and Procedures Sheet

Corporate Officials
William T. McCallum: president, chief executive officer chief financial officer PRIM CORP EMPL president, chief executive officer: Great-West Life Assurance Co.
Douglas Wooden: senior vice president, chief financial officer PRIM CORP EMPL senior vice president, chief financial officer: Great-West Life Assurance Co.

Grants Analysis
Typical Range: $500 to $1,000

GRECA REALTY & DEVELOPMENT CORPORATION INC.

Company Headquarters
6478 N. Oracle Rd.
Tucson, AZ 85704

Joseph and Mary Cacioppo Foundation

Giving Contact
Michael-Anne Young, Executive Director
Joseph and Mary Cacioppo Foundation
4769 E. Camp Lowell Dr.
Tucson, AZ 85712
Phone: (520)326-0703

Description
EIN: 860465698
Organization Type: Corporate Foundation
Giving Locations: AZ
Grant Types: General Support.

Financial Summary
Total Giving: $326,456 (fiscal year ending June 30, 2004); $154,524 (fiscal 2001)
Assets: $8,234,561 (fiscal 2004); $2,095,568 (fiscal 2001)
Gifts Received: $860,000 (fiscal 2001); $235,000 (fiscal 2000); $500 (fiscal 1994)

Typical Recipients
Arts & Humanities: Arts & Humanities-General, History & Archaeology, Libraries, Music, Opera, Theater
Civic & Public Affairs: Civic & Public Affairs-General, Hispanic Affairs, Housing, Parades/Festivals, Philanthropic Organizations, Professional & Trade Associations, Public Policy
Education: Arts/Humanities Education, Colleges & Universities, Education Funds, Education-General, Literacy, Private Education (Precollege), Public Education (Precollege), Secondary Education (Private), Special Education, Student Aid
Environment: Forestry, Resource Conservation
Health: Alzheimer's Disease, Children's Health/Hospitals, Health-General, Home-Care Services, Hospitals, Nursing Services, Single-Disease Health Associations, Speech & Hearing
International: International Peace & Security Issues
Religion: Churches, Religion-General, Religious Organizations, Religious Welfare
Social Services: Animal Protection, At-Risk Youth, Camps, Child Welfare, Community Service Organizations, Counseling, Domestic Violence, Family Planning, Family Services, Food/Clothing Distribution, People with Disabilities, Senior Services, Shelters/Homelessness, Social Services-General, Youth Organizations

Application Procedures
Initial Contact: Send a brief letter of inquiry.
Deadlines: August 31 for existing grantees; January 30 for new applicants.

Restrictions
Does not support individuals or political or lobbying groups.

Corporate Officials
Joseph F. Cacioppo, Jr.: chairman, president, chief executive officer PRIM CORP EMPL chairman, president, chief executive officer: Greca Realty.

Foundation Officials
Ann B. Brown: trustee
Elizabeth Day: trustee

Grants Analysis

Disclosure Period: fiscal year ending June 30, 2004
Total Grants: $326,456
Number of Grants: 169
Average Grant: $1,932
Highest Grant: $2,511
Lowest Grant: $1,256

Recent Grants

Note: Grants derived from fiscal 2004 Form 990.
Library-Related

2,511	Mary Baker Eddy Library, Boston, MA -- for the Betterment of Humanity

General

2,511	Administration of Resources and Choices, Tucson, AZ
2,511	Alzheimer's Association, Tucson, AZ
2,511	Asher Student Foundation, Los Angeles, CA
2,511	Aviva Children's Services, Tucson, AZ
2,511	Branch School, Houston, TX
2,511	Broadview Inc., Los Angeles, CA
2,511	Canterbury Crest Inc., Tigard, OR
2,511	Christian Science Committee on Publication for Arizona, Scottsdale, AZ
2,511	Comin Home, Tucson, AZ
2,511	Community Home Repair Project of Arizona, Tucson, AZ

GREDE FOUNDRIES

Company Headquarters

1320 S. 1st St.
Milwaukee, WI 53204
Web: http://www.grede.com

Company Description

Revenue: US$591 million (2001)
Employees: 4500 (2003)
SIC(s): 3321 Gray & Ductile Iron Foundries, 3325 Steel Foundries Nec.

Grede Foundation

Giving Contact

Burleigh E. Jacobs, President
9898 West Bluemound Road
Milwaukee, WI 53226-0499
Phone: (414)257-3600

Description

EIN: 396042977
Organization Type: Corporate Foundation
Giving Locations: WI
Grant Types: General Support, Scholarship.

Financial Summary

Total Giving: $80,100 (2003); $167,000 (2002); $168,445 (2001)
Giving Analysis: Giving for 2001 includes: foundation scholarships ($22,000); foundation grants to United Way ($31,500); foundation ($114,945)
Assets: $146,177 (2003); $214,547 (2002); $205,617 (2001)
Gifts Received: $2,800 (2003); $171,335 (2002); $165,983 (2000). Note: Contributions were received from Grede Foundries.

Typical Recipients

Arts & Humanities: Arts Associations & Councils, Arts Centers, Libraries, Museums/Galleries, Performing Arts
Civic & Public Affairs: Business/Free Enterprise, Chambers of Commerce, Clubs, Community Foundations, Economic Development, Economic Policy, Civic & Public Affairs-General, Hispanic Affairs, Housing, Law & Justice, Legal Aid, Professional & Trade Associations, Public Policy, Urban & Community Affairs
Education: Afterschool/Enrichment Programs, Arts/Humanities Education, Colleges & Universities, Community & Junior Colleges, Economic Education, Education Funds, Elementary Education (Public), Engineering/Technological Education, Education-General, Medical Education, Private Education (Precollege), Public Education (Precollege), Science/Mathematics Education, Secondary Education (Private), Secondary Education (Public), Student Aid, Vocational & Technical Education
Environment: Environment-General
Health: Cancer, Children's Health/Hospitals, Clinics/Medical Centers, Health Funds, Hospitals, Medical Research, Nursing Services, Single-Disease Health Associations, Speech & Hearing, Transplant Networks/Donor Banks
Religion: Religious Welfare
Science: Science Museums, Scientific Centers & Institutes
Social Services: Child Welfare, Community Centers, Community Service Organizations, Family Services, People with Disabilities, Recreation & Athletics, Scouts, Senior Services, United Funds/United Ways, YMCA/YWCA/YMHA/YWHA, Youth Organizations

Application Procedures

Initial Contact: Call or write to request materials. Request scholarship applications from Jan Winberg (414-257-3600).
Deadlines: Scholarship applications are due December 31 of the year prior to expected enrollment.

Restrictions

Scholarships are awarded only to high school seniors with a parent who is a regular employee of Grede Foundries, Inc or its subsidiaries, and has been employed as such for at least two years prior to application. Children and grandchildren of the Grede Foundation, Inc. board of directors are not eligible.

Additional Information

Publications: Application Form

Corporate Officials

Bruce E. Jacobs: president, chief executive officer B Milwaukee, WI 1947. ED University of Wisconsin (1969). PRIM CORP EMPL president, chief executive officer: Grede Foundries. CORP AFFIL owner: Watermark Press; owner: Watermark West Rare Books; owner: Watermark Books.

Foundation Officials

Susan L. Daigneau: director
Betty G. Davis: director
W. Stewart Davis: secretary, treasurer
Bruce E. Jacobs: vice president, director (see above)
Burleigh Edmund Jacobs: president, director B Milwaukee, WI February 03, 1920. ED University of Wisconsin BA (1942). CORP AFFIL director: Marshall & Ilsley Bank; director: Marshall & Ilsley Corp.; director: Benz Oil Inc.
Mary J. York: director

Grants Analysis

Disclosure Period: calendar year ending 2003
Total Grants: $49,100*
Number of Grants: 24
Average Grant: $2,046
Highest Grant: $6,000

Lowest Grant: $500
Typical Range: $1,000 to $5,000
*Note: Giving excludes scholarships and United Way.

Recent Grants

Note: Grants derived from 2003 Form 990.
General

13,300	Center for the Deaf, Brookfield, WI
10,000	United Way, Milwaukee, WI
7,000	YMCA Strong Kids Campaign, Milwaukee, WI
6,000	Foundry Educational Foundation, Meadows, IL
6,000	United Way of Dickinson County, Traverse City, MI
5,000	Henry County YMCA, Stockbridge, GA
5,000	Reedsburg Area United Way, Reedsburg, WI
5,000	West Suburban Branch YMCA, Milwaukee, WI
2,500	Grede Foundries Inc., Milwaukee, WI
2,500	Medical College of Wisconsin, Milwaukee, WI

GREEN BAY PACKAGING

Company Headquarters

1601 N. Quincy St.
Green Bay, WI 54302
Web: http://www.gbp.com

Company Description

Revenue: US$786 million (2002)
Employees: 2750 (2003)
SIC(s): 2631 Paperboard Mills, 2653 Corrugated & Solid Fiber Boxes, 2657 Folding Paperboard Boxes, 2672 Coated & Laminated Paper Nec.

George Kress Foundation

Giving Contact

John F. Kress, Director
Green Bay Packaging
1700 N. Webster Ave.
Green Bay, WI 54301
Phone: (920)433-5113

Alternate Contact

Care of Associated Trust Company
PO Box 408
Neenah, WI 54957-0408

Description

Founded: 1953
EIN: 396050768
Organization Type: Corporate Foundation
Giving Locations: WI: primarily Green Bay occasionally to state aside from Wisconsin.
Grant Types: General Support, Scholarship.

Financial Summary

Total Giving: $2,115,223 (2003); $2,347,702 (2002); $2,109,628 (2001). Note: In 1998, foundation made grants to itself and its members in turn distributed funds to an organization of their choice ($66,215).
Giving Analysis: Giving for 2002 includes: foundation grants to United Way ($84,200)
Assets: $7,159,297 (2003); $4,998,068 (2002); $7,813,966 (2001)
Gifts Received: $3,500,000 (2003); $12,752 (2002); $2,000,000 (2001). Note: Contributions were received from Green Bay Packaging, Inc.

Typical Recipients

Arts & Humanities: Arts Associations & Councils, Arts Centers, Community Arts, Arts & Humanities-General, History & Archaeology, Libraries, Museums/Galleries, Music, Performing Arts, Public Broadcasting, Theater

Civic & Public Affairs: Botanical Gardens/Parks, Community Foundations, Economic Development, Civic & Public Affairs-General, Housing, Inner-City Development, Municipalities/Towns, Philanthropic Organizations, Professional & Trade Associations, Public Policy, Urban & Community Affairs

Education: Afterschool/Enrichment Programs, Colleges & Universities, Education Funds, Environmental Education, Education-General, Medical Education, Private Education (Precollege), Public Education (Precollege), Religious Education, Science/Mathematics Education, Vocational & Technical Education

Environment: Forestry, Environment-General, Resource Conservation, Wildlife Protection

Health: Children's Health/Hospitals, Emergency/Ambulance Services, Health Funds, Health Organizations, Hospitals, Hospitals (University Affiliated), Public Health, Single-Disease Health Associations

Religion: Churches, Dioceses, Ministries, Religious Organizations, Religious Welfare

Science: Science Museums, Scientific Centers & Institutes, Scientific Research

Social Services: Animal Protection, Big Brothers/Big Sisters, Camps, Child Welfare, Community Centers, Community Service Organizations, Counseling, Crime Prevention, Day Care, Family Services, People with Disabilities, Recreation & Athletics, Shelters/Homelessness, Social Services-General, Substance Abuse, United Funds/United Ways, Volunteer Services, YMCA/YWCA/YMHA/YWHA, Youth Organizations

Application Procedures

Initial Contact: Submit a written request.
Deadlines: None.

Restrictions

Grants are limited to local interests. 2001 Form 990

Corporate Officials

Walter J. Dauska: treasurer, director B 1939. PRIM CORP EMPL treasurer: Green Bay Packaging Inc.
James F. Kress: chairman, director B 1929. ED University of Wisconsin (1951). PRIM CORP EMPL chairman, director: Green Bay Packaging. CORP AFFIL director: HC Prange Co.; director: Shade Information System; director: Krueger International Inc.; director: Marshall & Ilsley Corp.
William F. Kress: president, director PRIM CORP EMPL president, director: Green Bay Packaging.

Foundation Officials

Ingrid Kress: director
James F. Kress: director (see above)
John F. Kress: president, director
William F. Kress: director (see above)
Marilyn Swanson: director
Terry Swanson: director

Grants Analysis

Disclosure Period: calendar year ending 2003
Total Grants: $2,096,673*
Number of Grants: 203
Average Grant: $3,486*
Highest Grant: $500,000
Lowest Grant: $70
Typical Range: $500 to $5,000
*Note: Giving excludes United Way; scholarship. Average grant figure excludes six highest grants ($1,410,000).

Recent Grants

Note: Grants derived from 2003 Form 990.

Library-Related
500,000	Brown County Library, Green Bay, WI

General
310,000	American Foundation of Counseling Services Incorporated, Green Bay, WI
200,000	Bellin Foundation, Green Bay, WI
200,000	YWCA of Green Bay, Green Bay, WI
100,000	Boys and Girls of Green Bay, Green Bay, WI
100,000	Family Services of Northeast Wisconsin Incorporated, Green Bay, WI
31,000	American Foundation of Counseling Services Incorporated, Green Bay, WI
30,000	International Corrugated Packaging Foundation, Appleton, WI
30,000	Notre Dame Academy, Green Bay, WI
30,000	University of Wisconsin Foundation, Madison, WI
25,000	Catholic Foundation of the Diocese, Green Bay, WI

ALLEN P. AND JOSEPHINE B. GREEN FOUNDATION

Giving Contact

Walter G. Staley, Jr., Secretary, Treasurer & Director
Allen P. and Josephine B. Green Foundation
PO Box 523
Mexico, MO 65265
Phone: (573)581-5568
E-mail: nrcox@greenfdn.org
Web: http://www.greenfdn.org

Description

Founded: 1941
EIN: 436030135
Organization Type: Private Foundation
Giving Locations: MO: Mexico including surrounding area
Grant Types: Capital, Conference/Seminar, Emergency, Endowment, Fellowship, Project, Scholarship, Seed Money.

Donor Information

Founder: the late Allen P. Green, the late Mrs. Allen P. Green

Financial Summary

Total Giving: $633,800 (2001)
Giving Analysis: Giving for 2001 includes: foundation scholarships ($5,000)
Assets: $12,978,458 (2001)

Typical Recipients

Arts & Humanities: Historic Preservation, History & Archaeology, Libraries, Museums/Galleries, Opera, Performing Arts, Public Broadcasting, Theater

Civic & Public Affairs: Botanical Gardens/Parks, Clubs, Community Foundations, Employment/Job Training, Housing, Safety, Urban & Community Affairs

Education: Agricultural Education, Colleges & Universities, Community & Junior Colleges, Elementary Education (Public), Environmental Education, Faculty Development, Education-General, Literacy, Medical Education, Preschool Education, Private Education (Precollege), Public Education (Precollege), Religious Education, Science/Mathematics Education, Special Education, Student Aid, Vocational & Technical Education

Environment: Environment-General, Resource Conservation

Health: Arthritis, Cancer, Children's Health/Hospitals, Clinics/Medical Centers, Diabetes, Eyes/Blindness, Hospices, Medical Rehabilitation, Mental Health, Preventive Medicine/Wellness Organizations, Public Health, Speech & Hearing

Religion: Bible Study/Translation, Churches, Religious Organizations, Religious Welfare

Science: Scientific Centers & Institutes

Social Services: Animal Protection, At-Risk Youth, Child Abuse, Child Welfare, Community Service Organizations, Day Care, Family Services, Food/Clothing Distribution, People with Disabilities, Recreation & Athletics, Scouts, Senior Services, Social Services-General, Substance Abuse, Veterans, YMCA/YWCA/YMHA/YWHA, Youth Organizations

Application Procedures

Initial Contact: Contact foundation for application guidelines.
Deadlines: Contact foundation for annual deadlines.

Restrictions

Does not support individuals, scholarships, or fellowships.

Additional Information

Publications: Annual Report

Foundation Officials

Arthur D. Bond, III: president, director
Senator Christopher Samuel Bond: director B Saint Louis, MO 1939. ED Princeton University BA (1960); University of Virginia LLB (1963). PRIM CORP EMPL senior ator: MO. NONPR AFFIL chairman: Midwestern Governments Conf; chairman: Rep Governments Association.
Rev. Robert R. Collins: director
Carl D. Fuemmeler: vice president, director
Judge James F. McHenry: director
Robert E. McIntosh: assistant secretary, assistant treasurer, director
Walter G. Staley, Jr.: secretary, treasurer, director
Nancy G. White: director
George C. Willson, III: president, director
Robert A. Wood: director
Elizabeth Wood Knight: director

Grants Analysis

Disclosure Period: calendar year ending 2001
Total Grants: $628,800*
Number of Grants: 69
Average Grant: $9,113
Highest Grant: $27,000
Lowest Grant: $400
Typical Range: $2,000 to $20,000
*Note: Giving excludes scholarship.

Recent Grants

Note: Grants derived from 2001 Form 990.

General
27,000	Moberly Area Community College, Moberly, MO -- for computer network lab
22,000	NBA Gateways, St. Louis, MO -- for sprinkler system
20,000	City Academy, St. Louis, MO -- for third grade classroom
20,000	Fire Fighters Foundation of Missouri, Mexico, MO -- for new memorial statue
20,000	Independence Center, St. Louis, MO -- programs for individuals with mental illness
20,000	Mexico Athletic Booster Club, Mexico, MO -- for portable concession stand
20,000	Partnership for Youth, St. Louis, MO -- for Americorps St. Louis Partners Program
20,000	St. Charles Regional Child Assessment Center, Wentzville, MO -- equipment for abused victims
17,000	Northeast Community Services Agency, Inc., Mexico, MO -- for Alternative Sentencing Program
15,500	Handi-Shop, Mexico, MO -- for 1997 GMC box van

ROBERT AND SUSAN GREEN FOUNDATION

Giving Contact
Robert L. Green, President
2601 Mariposa St., Suite 100
San Francisco, CA 94110
Phone: (415)865-1700
Fax: (415)865-1700

Description
EIN: 943025003
Organization Type: Private Foundation
Giving Locations: CA
Grant Types: General Support.

Financial Summary
Total Giving: $33,820 (2003). Note: In 1998 and 1996 Giving includes United Way ($25,000).
Assets: $280,617 (2003)
Gifts Received: $219,946 (2003); $43,224 (2000); $91,186 (1999). Note: In 2003, contributions were received from Robert and Susan Green. In 2000, contributions were received from John Doerr ($18,224) and Robert Green ($25,000). In 1999, contributions were received from Mr. John Doerr. In 1996, contributions were received from Fidelity.

Typical Recipients
Arts & Humanities: Arts Associations & Councils, Arts Centers, Arts Funds, Arts Institutes, Ethnic & Folk Arts, Arts & Humanities-General, Historic Preservation, Libraries, Museums/Galleries, Music, Opera, Public Broadcasting, Theater
Civic & Public Affairs: Civic & Public Affairs-General, Philanthropic Organizations, Public Policy, Women's Affairs
Education: Afterschool/Enrichment Programs, Business Education, Colleges & Universities, Education Funds, Elementary Education (Public), Education-General, Leadership Training, Medical Education, Private Education (Precollege), Public Education (Precollege), School Volunteerism, Secondary Education (Private), Secondary Education (Public), Student Aid
Environment: Environment-General, Wildlife Protection
Health: Cancer, Children's Health/Hospitals, Clinics/Medical Centers, Eyes/Blindness, Geriatric Health, Hospitals, Long-Term Care, Prenatal Health Issues, Public Health
International: International Affairs, Missionary/Religious Activities
Religion: Churches, Religion-General, Jewish Causes, Religious Welfare
Social Services: Child Abuse, Child Welfare, Community Service Organizations, Food/Clothing Distribution, Recreation & Athletics, Senior Services, United Funds/United Ways, Volunteer Services, Youth Organizations

Application Procedures
Initial Contact: Send a brief letter of inquiry and a full proposal in writing.
Deadlines: None.

Foundation Officials
Robert L. Green: president

Grants Analysis
Disclosure Period: calendar year ending 2003
Total Grants: $33,820
Number of Grants: 14
Average Grant: $1,517*
Highest Grant: $14,100
Lowest Grant: $100
Typical Range: $500 to $3,000
*****Note:** Average grant figure excludes highest grant.

Recent Grants
Note: Grants derived from 2003 Form 990.
General

14,100	San Francisco Museum of Modern Arts, San Francisco, CA -- funds for advancement of sciences, arts, education etc
6,000	White Nights Foundation of America, New York, NY -- funds for advancement of sciences, arts, education etc
5,000	Knowledge is Power Program Foundation, San Francisco, CA -- funds for advancement of sciences, arts, education etc
2,500	Asian Art Museum, San Francisco, CA -- funds for advancement of sciences, arts, education etc
1,750	Fine Arts Museums of San Francisco, San Francisco, CA -- funds for advancement of sciences, arts, education etc
1,500	Jewish Museum of San Francisco, San Francisco, CA -- funds for advancement of sciences, arts, education etc
750	Corporation of the Fine Arts Museum, San Francisco, CA -- funds for advancement of sciences, arts, education etc
500	San Francisco Education Fund, San Francisco, CA -- funds for advancement of sciences, arts, education etc
500	Summer Search, San Francisco, CA -- funds for advancement of sciences, arts, education etc
500	UCSF Foundation, San Francisco, CA -- funds for advancement of sciences, arts, education etc

ALBERT M. GREENFIELD FOUNDATION

Giving Contact
Priscilla Luce, President
PO Box 30267
Philadelphia, PA 19103
Phone: (215)333-8949

Description
Founded: 1953
EIN: 236050816
Organization Type: Private Foundation
Giving Locations: PA: Philadelphia including metropolitan area
Grant Types: General Support.

Donor Information
Founder: the late Albert M. Greenfield, the late Etelka J. Greenfield

Financial Summary
Total Giving: $607,081 (fiscal year ending August 31, 2003); $556,918 (fiscal 2001)
Assets: $8,659,524 (fiscal 2003); $9,924,198 (fiscal 2001)

Typical Recipients
Arts & Humanities: Arts Associations & Councils, Arts Centers, Arts Institutes, Arts Outreach, Ballet, Community Arts, Dance, History & Archaeology, Libraries, Museums/Galleries, Music, Theater
Civic & Public Affairs: Botanical Gardens/Parks, Economic Policy, Employment/Job Training, Legal Aid, Urban & Community Affairs, Zoos/Aquariums
Education: Arts/Humanities Education, Colleges & Universities, Community & Junior Colleges, Environmental Education, Education-General, Literacy, Private Education (Precollege), Public Education (Precollege), Secondary Education (Public), Student Aid
Health: Eyes/Blindness
Religion: Jewish Causes

Science: Science Museums
Social Services: Camps, Child Abuse, Community Service Organizations, Domestic Violence, Family Planning, Recreation & Athletics, Shelters/Homelessness, Social Services-General, United Funds/United Ways, Youth Organizations

Application Procedures
Initial Contact: The foundation has no formal grant application procedure or application form.
Deadlines: None.

Additional Information
All awards reviewed on an individual basis. Awards are generally given to tax-exempt organizations.

Foundation Officials
Debra G. DeLauro: secretary
Albert M. Greenfield, III: trustee
Bruce Harold Greenfield: trustee B Philadelphia, PA March 12, 1917. ED Duke University BA (1938); Yale University JD (1941). NONPR AFFIL member: Phi Beta Kappa; lecturer: Tulane University; trustee: Albert M Greenfield Foundation; lecturer: New York University; director: American Jewish Committee; lecturer: American University Tax Institute. CLUB AFFIL Yale Club.
Bernard M. Guth: trustee
Janet Guth: trustee
Derek G. Howard: trustee
Priscilla Luce: president
Sarah E. Mark: trustee
Julie G. Six: treasurer

Grants Analysis
Disclosure Period: fiscal year ending August 31, 2003
Total Grants: $607,081
Number of Grants: 13
Average Grant: $37,916*
Highest Grant: $100,000
Lowest Grant: $5,000
Typical Range: $25,000 to $50,000
*****Note:** Average grant figure excludes two highest grants ($190,000).

Recent Grants
Note: Grants derived from 2003 Form 990.
Library-Related

50,000	Library Company of Philadelphia, Philadelphia, PA

General

100,000	Academy of Natural Sciences, Philadelphia, PA
90,000	Wills Eye Hospital, Philadelphia, PA
62,500	Philadelphia Zoo, Philadelphia, PA
50,000	Curtis Institute of Music, Philadelphia, PA
50,000	Moore College of Arts, Philadelphia, PA
50,000	Prince Music Theater, Philadelphia, PA
50,000	Support Center for Child Advocates, Philadelphia, PA
26,781	Center for Literacy, Philadelphia, PA
25,000	William Penn Charter School, Philadelphia, PA

GREENTREE FOUNDATION

Giving Contact
Richard Schaffer, President
400 Madison Avenue, Suite 1001
New York, NY 10017
Phone: (212)888-7755
Fax: (212)888-1574
E-mail: rschaffer@greentreefdn.org

Description
Founded: 1982
EIN: 133132117

Organization Type: Family Foundation
Giving Locations: NY: New York including metropolitan area
Grant Types: General Support, Project.

Donor Information

Founder: Established in 1982 by Betsey C. Whitney.

Financial Summary

Total Giving: $1,857,668 (2003); $2,105,939 (2001)
Assets: $260,582,773 (2003); $278,015,722 (2001)
Gifts Received: $157,880,676 (2000); $72,198,379 (1998); $401,936 (1997). Note: In 2000, contributions were received from the estate of Betsey Cushing Whitney ($156,276,260); John Hay Whitney Charitable Trust ($1,387,944); Sara Wilford ($113,160); and Kate Whitney ($103,312). In 1998, contributions were received from the estate of Betsey C. Whitney-Greentree and John Hay Whitney Charitable Trust.

Typical Recipients

Arts & Humanities: Arts Associations & Councils, Arts Centers, Arts Outreach, Ballet, Community Arts, Dance, Ethnic & Folk Arts, Arts & Humanities-General, Historic Preservation, History & Archaeology, Libraries, Museums/Galleries, Music, Performing Arts, Public Broadcasting, Theater
Civic & Public Affairs: African American Affairs, Botanical Gardens/Parks, Clubs, Community Foundations, Economic Development, Employment/Job Training, Civic & Public Affairs-General, Hispanic Affairs, Professional & Trade Associations, Public Policy, Urban & Community Affairs, Women's Affairs
Education: Afterschool/Enrichment Programs, Arts/Humanities Education, Business Education, Colleges & Universities, Community & Junior Colleges, Education Funds, Education Reform, Elementary Education (Private), Elementary Education (Public), Education-General, International Exchange, Literacy, Medical Education, Minority Education, Private Education (Precollege), Public Education (Precollege), School Volunteerism, Science/Mathematics Education, Special Education, Student Aid
Environment: Air/Water Quality, Environment-General, Resource Conservation
Health: Hospitals, Mental Health, Research/Studies Institutes
Religion: Religious Welfare
Science: Scientific Centers & Institutes
Social Services: At-Risk Youth, Big Brothers/Big Sisters, Camps, Child Abuse, Child Welfare, Community Centers, Community Service Organizations, Counseling, Emergency Relief, Family Planning, Family Services, Food/Clothing Distribution, Recreation & Athletics, Scouts, Senior Services, Shelters/Homelessness, Social Services-General, Volunteer Services, YMCA/YWCA/YMHA/YWHA, Youth Organizations

Application Procedures

Initial Contact: Contact the foundation to request a grant application form.
Application Requirements: The form should be completed and submitted with a grant proposal, which should include a proposal summary, a narrative of no more than five pages, and attachments.
The proposal summary should summarize in a short paragraph the purpose of the organization, explaining the purpose for requesting a grant, the proposed outcomes and achievements, and how the grant funds will be spent.
The narrative portion of the proposal should include organizational background, the grant proposal, and an evaluation. Background information should include a brief description of the organization's history and mission; the need or problem to be addressed; current programs and accomplishments; the population served by the organization, including geographic location, socioeconomic status, race, ethnicity, gender, sexual orientation, age, physical ability, and language; the number of paid full-time staff, number of paid part-time staff, and the number of volunteers;

and the organization's relationships--both formal and informal--with other organizations working to meet the same needs or providing similar services, explaining how the organization differs from these other agencies.
The grant proposal should include a statement of the primary purpose and the need or problem that will be addressed; population the grant will serve and how population will benefit from project; strategies to implement project; names and qualifications of the individuals who will direct the project; anticipated length of project; how project contributes to organization's overall mission; and a list of foundations and corporations, and other sources that funds are being solicited from, and the status of each.
The evaluation section of the proposal should explain how the organization will measure the effectiveness of the activities. Further, describe the organization's criteria for a successful program and the expected results.
The supplemental attachments should be labeled and should include both financial information and other supporting materials. The financial documentation should include the most recent financial statement, audited if available, that reflects actual expenditures and funds received during the most recent fiscal year; the operating budgets (aligned side by side on one page) for the current and most recent fiscal year; a list of foundation and corporate supporters (aligned side by side on one page) and other sources of income, with amounts, for the current and most recent fiscal year; and a current budget for the project (list each staff line separately, include percentage of time spent on the project, and indicate the specific uses of the requested grant).
Other supporting materials should include a list of the board of directors and their affiliations; a copy of the most recent IRS letter indicating tax-exempt status; one paragraph resumes of key staff; the most recent annual report, if available; and no more than three examples of recent articles about, or evaluations of, the organization, if available.
Deadlines: None.
Review Process: The trustees meet to consider proposals in March, June, September, and December. The review of and decision on any pending application depends upon the number and nature of other applications and the availability of funds. The review process can take several months.
Notes: If it appears that the project has a reasonable chance for funding, the foundation will arrange a site visit.

Restrictions

Grants are not made to individuals.

Additional Information

Publications: Grant Application Form

Foundation Officials

Laura E. Butzel: assistant secretary
Robert Carswell: treasurer B Brooklyn, NY 1928. ED Harvard University AB (1949); Harvard University LLB (1952). CORP AFFIL director: Georgia-Pacific Corp.; chairman: Private Export Funding Corp. NONPR AFFIL member: Phi Beta Kappa; member: Saint Andrews Society State New York; member: Harvard University Law School Alumni Association New York; member: Law Council Foreign Relations; member: California State Bar Association; chairman: Carnegie Endowment International Peace; member: American Society International Law; member: Association Bar New York City; member: American Bar Association; member: American Law Institute. CLUB AFFIL The Links New York City Club; Metro Club; Century Association.
Richard Schaffer: president
Franklin A. Thomas: trustee
Kate R. Whitney: vice president, trustee
Ronald A. Wilford: trustee
Sara R. Wilford: vice president, trustee

Grants Analysis

Disclosure Period: calendar year ending 2003
Total Grants: $1,857,668
Number of Grants: 84
Average Grant: $18,996*
Highest Grant: $150,000
Lowest Grant: $500
Typical Range: $5,000 to $25,000
*Note: Average grant figure excludes two highest grants ($300,000).

Recent Grants

Note: Grants derived from 2002 Form 990.
General

200,000	Kingsborough Community College, City University of New York, Brooklyn, NY -- for final grant for the tutorial programs in New York City high schools
200,000	Kingsborough Community College, City University of New York, Brooklyn, NY -- for an after school tutorial program for middle school students in Brooklyn
50,000	After School Corporation, New York, NY -- to identify prospective teachers at after school program sites & to develop a plan for financing their academic & licensing requirements
40,000	Manhattan Country School, New York, NY -- towards the public school outreach program & for the Irwin M. Greelernt mentoring program
35,000	Community Funds Inc., C/o Long Island Community Foundation, Jericho, NY -- for continued support for the "erase racism project"
33,500	Brooks School, North Andover, MA -- towards the African exchange program
25,000	East Harlem Tutorial Program, New York, NY -- towards the parental involvement workshops
25,000	Educational Equity Concepts Inc., New York, NY -- for a collaboration with the river project for the after-school science plus/marine biology internship program
25,000	Forest Hills Community House, Forest Hills, NY -- for tutoring & parent workshops in the after school tutoring program
25,000	New Jersey Performing Arts Center, Newark, NJ -- towards the arts academy residencies in theater & dance in 11 Newark schools

GREENVILLE FOUNDATION

Giving Contact

Virginia Hubbell, Program Director
Care of Conrad Business Services
1100 Main Street, Suite C
Sonoma, CA 95476
Phone: (707)938-9377
Web: http://www.greenville-foundation.org

Description

Founded: 1949
EIN: 954396319
Organization Type: Private Foundation
Giving Locations: AZ; CA; DC; MN; NM; ND; OR; TX; Canada : ON
Grant Types: General Support.

Donor Information

Founder: the late William Miles

Financial Summary

Total Giving: $967,750 (2001)
Assets: $18,317,499 (2001)

Gifts Received: $602,942 (1995); $723,927 (1993). Note: In 1995, contributions were received from the William Miles Charitable Trust.

Typical Recipients

Arts & Humanities: Arts Outreach, Film & Video, Libraries, Public Broadcasting

Civic & Public Affairs: Civil Rights, Economic Development, Employment/Job Training, First Amendment Issues, Civic & Public Affairs-General, Hispanic Affairs, Housing, Law & Justice, Native American Affairs, Public Policy, Rural Affairs, Urban & Community Affairs, Women's Affairs

Education: Colleges & Universities, Environmental Education, International Studies, Leadership Training, Minority Education, Preschool Education, Private Education (Precollege), Religious Education, Science/Mathematics Education, Special Education

Environment: Energy, Forestry, Environment-General, Resource Conservation, Watershed

Health: Public Health

International: International-General, Health Care/Hospitals, Human Rights, International Affairs, International Development, International Environmental Issues, International Peace & Security Issues, International Relations, Missionary/Religious Activities, Trade

Religion: Churches, Jewish Causes, Ministries, Religious Organizations, Religious Welfare

Science: Science Museums, Scientific Organizations

Social Services: Child Abuse, Child Welfare, Community Service Organizations, Domestic Violence, Family Services, Food/Clothing Distribution, People with Disabilities, Recreation & Athletics, Shelters/Homelessness, Social Services-General, Youth Organizations

Application Procedures

Initial Contact: Send a brief outline of proposal or project.

Deadlines: April1 and October1.

Restrictions

Does not provide funds for individuals, scholarship, venture capital, capital improvements, endowments, general classroom-based environmental education programs, individuals species preservation, health, food banks, or temporary shelter.

Foundation Officials

Donald W. Crew: treasurer, director
Herb Crew: director, chairman
John Crew: director, treasurer
Richard A. Crew: chairman, director
Brian Fish: director
Susanne Fish-Sadin: director, secretary
Virginia Hubbell: program director
Pat Miles: secretary, director
William Miles: director

Grants Analysis

Disclosure Period: calendar year ending 2001
Total Grants: $967,750
Number of Grants: 65
Average Grant: $14,888
Highest Grant: $25,000
Typical Range: $5,000 to $25,000

Recent Grants

Note: Grants derived from 2001 Form 990.
General

25,000	Arriba Juntos, San Francisco, CA -- to support a 17-week intensive training program
25,000	New Mexico Conference of Churches, Albuquerque, NM -- to support a part-time coordinator for Standing Together as Communities for Human Dignity and Respect
25,000	Rural Advancement Foundation International, Winnipeg, ON Canada -- to support a State of the World Farmers Report
25,000	Seattle University, Seattle, WA -- to support the School of Theology and Ministry Liturgical Institute's Summer Pilot Program
21,750	Project Alchemy FA Western States Center, Inc., Seattle, WA -- to support and build technology capacity civil rights organizations in the Pacific Northwest
21,000	Center for Ecoliteracy, Berkeley, CA -- to support the Food Systems Project
20,000	Arizona Center for Law in the Public Interest, Phoenix, AZ -- to support litigation challenging
20,000	Californians for Justice, Oakland, CA -- to support youth and parent leadership
20,000	Center for Victims of Torture, Minneapolis, MN -- to support traumatized refugees from Sierra Leone
20,000	Correct Help FA Tides Center, West Hollywood, CA -- to support CorrectHelp

GREENWALL FOUNDATION

Giving Contact

William C. Stubing, President
420 Lexington Avenue, Suite 2500
New York, NY 10170
Phone: (212)679-7266
E-mail: admin@greenwall.org
Web: http://www.greenwall.org

Description

Founded: 1949
EIN: 136082277
Organization Type: General Purpose Foundation
Giving Locations: NY
Grant Types: General Support, Project, Research.

Donor Information

Founder: Frank Greenwall and his wife, Anna Alexander Greenwall, established the foundation in 1949. Anna Alexander Greenwall's father owned a company called National Gum and Mica. In 1920, Frank Greenwall joined the company, which became National Starch and Chemical Corporation in 1959. Mr. Greenwall was chairman and chief executive of the adhesives, resins, and specialty chemical business.

The foundation was originally named the Susan Greenwall Foundation in memory of the Greenwall's daughter. Its focus was on bone cancer research, the disease which took Susan's life at age 16. Frank and Anna were joined as donors to the foundation by their daughter, Nancy Greenwall, and their close friends and colleagues, Alfred A. Halden and Elias D. Cohen. In 1981, after the deaths of both Anna and Nancy, the name of the foundation was changed to the Greenwall Foundation to honor the deceased family members. Frank Greenwall, the last surviving founder, died in 1985.

Financial Summary

Total Giving: $3,454,537 (2003); $4,065,678 (2002)
Assets: $77,978,093 (2003); $68,110,561 (2002)
Gifts Received: $2,750 (1998); $5,000 (1997); $3,500 (1996)

Typical Recipients

Arts & Humanities: Arts Associations & Councils, Arts Funds, Arts Outreach, Ballet, Dance, Ethnic & Folk Arts, Arts & Humanities-General, Historic Preservation, History & Archaeology, Libraries, Literary Arts, Museums/Galleries, Music, Opera, Performing Arts, Public Broadcasting, Theater, Visual Arts

Civic & Public Affairs: Botanical Gardens/Parks, Civic & Public Affairs-General, Law & Justice, Legal Aid, Municipalities/Towns, Nonprofit Management, Professional & Trade Associations, Public Policy, Zoos/Aquariums

Education: Arts/Humanities Education, Colleges & Universities, Education Associations, Education Funds, Education Reform, Engineering/Technological Education, Faculty Development, Education-General, Health & Physical Education, International Studies, Journalism/Media Education, Medical Education, Minority Education, Private Education (Precollege), Public Education (Precollege), School Volunteerism, Science/Mathematics Education

Environment: Environment-General

Health: Alzheimer's Disease, Children's Health/Hospitals, Clinics/Medical Centers, Diabetes, Health Policy/Cost Containment, Health Funds, Health Organizations, Heart, Hospitals, Hospitals (University Affiliated), Long-Term Care, Medical Research, Public Health

International: Human Rights

Science: Science Museums, Scientific Centers & Institutes, Scientific Labs, Scientific Organizations, Scientific Research

Social Services: Community Service Organizations, Volunteer Services, Youth Organizations

Application Procedures

Initial Contact: The foundation does not have an application form or a standard outline for proposals. Initial letter should describe the program, objectives, amount requested, and qualifications of organization and project directors.

Application Requirements: If interested, the foundation will request additional information such as financial statements, itemized budget, tax-exempt status letter, and other relevant material.

Deadlines: Applications must be received by February 1 for consideration at the spring board meeting, or by August 1 for the autumn meeting.

Review Process: The foundation gives special attention to proposals demonstrating innovative approaches.

Restrictions

The foundation generally will not fund private foundations, endowment campaigns, or individuals. Arts organizations that have received contributions from the foundation for three consecutive years are not eligible for renewals for at least one year after foundation support has ceased.

Additional Information

Publications: Annual Report

Foundation Officials

Troyen A. Brennan, MD: director

Christine Karen Cassel, MD: director B Minneapolis, MN 1945. ED University of Chicago AB (1967); University of Massachusetts MD (1976). PRIM CORP EMPL chairman geriatric department, professor geriatric medicine: Mount Sinai. NONPR AFFIL president, director: Physicians Social Responsibility; member: Society Health & Human Values; member: NAS Institute Medicine; fellow bioethics: Institute Health Policy Studies; member: Institute Medicine; fellow: American Geriatrics Society; director: American Society Law & Medicine; member: American Board Internal Medicine; fellow: American College Physicians.

John Edwin Craig, Jr.: director B Lancaster, SC 1944. ED Davidson College BA (1966); Princeton University MA (1968). NONPR AFFIL chairman investment committee: Social Science Research Council; member, board: US-Australia-New Zealand Council; member government council: Rockefeller Archives Center; chairman investment committee: Investment Fund Foundations; chairman: Nonprofit Coordinating Committee; member: Foundation Administration Group; member: Foundation Financial Officer Group; member, board visitors: Davidson College. CLUB AFFIL mem: University Club.

Harvey J. Goldschmid: director B New York, NY 1940. ED Columbia University AB (1962); Columbia

University JD (1965). PRIM CORP EMPL general counsel: Securities & Exchange Commission. NONPR AFFIL member: Phi Beta Kappa; board visitors: University Arizona College Law; member: New York City Bar Association; member: Association American Law Schools; director: National Center Philanthropy & Law; member: American Bar Association; fellow: American Bar Foundation; director, secretary, treasurer: American Association International Committee Jurists. CLUB AFFIL member: Century Association; member: Riverdale Yacht Club.

Rosmarie E. Homberger: corporate secretary

Matina Souretis Horner: chairman, director B Boston, MA 1939. ED Bryn Mawr College AB (1961); University of Michigan MS (1963); University of Michigan PhD (1968). CORP AFFIL director: Neiman Marcus Group Inc.; executive vice president: TIAA-CREF New York City; director: BEC Energy; director: Boston Edison Co. NONPR AFFIL member advisory committee: Women's Leadership Conference National Security; member, board directors, chairman research committee: Women's Research Education Institute; trustee: Twentieth Century Fund; member: Phi Kappa Phi; president emerita: Radcliffe College; member: Phi Beta Kappa; member: Phi Delta Kappa; member: National Organization Women; member executive committee: New England Colleges Fund; trustee: Massachusetts General Hospital Institute Health Professions; member: National Institute Social Sciences; member: Council Foreign Relations; president: American Laryngol Voice Research Education Foundation; trustee: Committee for Economic Development.

Fredrica Jarcho: vice president, program

Edith Levett: secretary emeritus

Gayle Pemberton: director

Joseph George Perpich, MD, JD: vice chairman, director B Hibbing, MN 1941. ED University of Minnesota BA (1963); University of Minnesota MD (1966); Georgetown University JD (1974). PRIM NONPR EMPL vice president: Howard Hughes Medical Institute.

Roger Rosenblatt: director B New York, NY 1940. ED Harvard University PhD. CORP AFFIL contributing editor: Time Inc.; contributing editor: New Republic Inc. NONPR AFFIL essayist: PBS NewsHour with Jim Lehrer.

Richard L. Salzer, Jr.: director NONPR AFFIL treasurer, director: Jewish Home & Hospital Aged.

William C. Stubing: president, director

T. Dennis Sullivan: treasurer, director

James A. Tulsky: director

Grants Analysis

Disclosure Period: calendar year ending 2003
Total Grants: $3,454,537
Number of Grants: 113
Average Grant: $30,571
Highest Grant: $268,927
Lowest Grant: $3,750
Typical Range: $10,000 to $50,000

Recent Grants

Note: Grants derived from 2003 Form 990.
General

580,230	Faculty Scholars Program
268,930	Johns Hopkins University (Faden), Baltimore, MD
213,415	University of California, San Francisco, CA
152,020	University of California, San Francisco, CA
146,285	Johns Hopkins University (Faden/Gearhart), Baltimore, MD
133,965	University of Virginia, Charlottesville, VA
116,995	Harvard Pilgrim Health Care, Massachusetts, ME
106,040	Johns Hopkins University (Faden), Baltimore, MD
100,000	University of Pennsylvania (Mcgee), Philadelphia, PA

99,420	Duke University Medical Center (Swartz), Durham, NC

GREGG-GRANITEVILLE FOUNDATION

Giving Contact

Patricia H. Knight, Secretary-Treasurer
PO Box 418
Graniteville, SC 29829
Phone: (803)663-7552
Fax: (803)663-6435

Description

Founded: 1941
EIN: 570314400
Organization Type: General Purpose Foundation
Giving Locations: GA: Richmond County; SC: Aiken County
Grant Types: Award, General Support, Scholarship.

Donor Information

Founder: "The Gregg-Graniteville Foundation was established in 1941 in honor of William Gregg to carry out his philosophy of genuine concern for people, their betterment, and their well-being."

Financial Summary

Total Giving: $295,860 (2003); $850,000 (2002 approx); $779,430 (2001). Note: 1997 Giving includes scholarships ($72,400) and support for the Gregg Park Civic Center ($257,600).
Giving Analysis: Giving for 2003 includes: foundation scholarships ($98,600)
Assets: $18,695,758 (2003); $19,573,674 (2001)
Gifts Received: $710 (1998). Note: In 1998, contributions were received from Triarc, Inc.

Typical Recipients

Arts & Humanities: Arts Associations & Councils, Arts Centers, Ballet, Community Arts, Dance, Libraries, Museums/Galleries, Music, Opera, Performing Arts

Civic & Public Affairs: Botanical Gardens/Parks, Clubs, Economic Development, Economic Policy, Civic & Public Affairs-General, Housing, Public Policy, Rural Affairs, Safety, Urban & Community Affairs, Women's Affairs

Education: Arts/Humanities Education, Business Education, Colleges & Universities, Community & Junior Colleges, Economic Education, Education Funds, Elementary Education (Private), Elementary Education (Public), Education-General, Health & Physical Education, Minority Education, Private Education (Precollege), Public Education (Precollege), Science/Mathematics Education, Secondary Education (Private), Secondary Education (Public), Student Aid, Vocational & Technical Education

Environment: Environment-General

Health: Cancer, Diabetes, Emergency/Ambulance Services, Eyes/Blindness, Geriatric Health, Health Funds, Health Organizations, Hospitals, Hospitals (University Affiliated), Medical Rehabilitation, Mental Health, Research/Studies Institutes, Single-Disease Health Associations

Religion: Churches, Ministries, Religious Organizations, Religious Welfare

Science: Science Museums, Scientific Centers & Institutes, Scientific Organizations

Social Services: Camps, Community Centers, Community Service Organizations, Domestic Violence, Family Services, Food/Clothing Distribution, People with Disabilities, Recreation & Athletics, Senior Services, Special Olympics, Veterans, Youth Organizations

Application Procedures

Initial Contact: Contact the foundation for a grant application.
Application Requirements: A completed application and a full proposal, which includes a brief description of sponsoring organization, need to be addressed, financial resources available, constituency served by the grant, most recent audited financial statement or current operating budget, and a copy of the IRS tax exemption letter.
Deadlines: Grants None; scholarships June 15.
Review Process: Applications are reviewed at the foundation office before presentation to the board of directors. Applicants are notified of the board's decision following regular meetings, held bimonthly.

Restrictions

Other than scholarships, no grants are made to individuals. Grants are restricted to organizations operating in Georgia and South Carolina. The foundation does not provide grants for operating budgets. ScholarshipS are awarded to children of employees of Avondale Milles, formerly known as Graniteville CO or are residents of Graniteville, Warrenville, and Vacluse South Carolina areas or Augusta, Georgia.

Additional Information

Publications: Annual Report; Guidelines; Application Form

Foundation Officials

Robert Morrall Bell: president, director B Graniteville, SC 1936. ED University of South Carolina AB (1958); University of South Carolina LLB (1965). PRIM CORP EMPL senior partner: Bell & Surasky PRIM NONPR EMPL county attorney: Aiken County. NONPR AFFIL member: South Carolina Trial Lawyers Association; member: Tau Kappa Alpha; member: South Carolina Bar Association; member: Phi Delta Phi; member: Shriners; member: American Trial Lawyers Association; member: Kappa Sigma Kappa; member: American Bar Association; member: Aiken County Bar Association. CLUB AFFIL Masons Club.

Ira E. Coward, II: director

John W. Cunningham: vice president, director

Jerry Ray Johnson: director B Savannah, GA 1926. ED University of South Carolina BSME (1950).

Patricia H. Knight: secretary, director, director

William Sammie Napier: director

Joan F. Phibbs: director

James A. Randall: director

J. Paul Reeves: vice president, director

Robert P. Timmerman: director B Warrenville, SC November 09, 1920. ED Clemson University BA (1941). PRIM CORP EMPL director: Graniteville Co. CORP AFFIL director: Textile Hall Corp.; director: McCampbell Co. Ltd. (Tokyo Japan); chairman: C H Patrick & Co.; chairman, chief executive officer: Graniteville International Sales. NONPR AFFIL chairman: Community Services.

Grants Analysis

Disclosure Period: calendar year ending 2003
Total Grants: $197,260*
Number of Grants: 22
Average Grant: $6,346*
Highest Grant: $64,000
Lowest Grant: $1,000
Typical Range: $1,000 to $10,000
*Note: Giving excludes scholarships. Average grant figure excludes highest grant.

Recent Grants

Note: Grants derived from 2002 Form 990.
General

20,000	South Carolina Independent Colleges and Universities Inc., Columbia, SC
15,000	Southeastern Natural Sciences Academy, Augusta, GA

13,000	Midland Valley High School, Athletic Booster Club, Langley, SC
12,000	Aiken Partnership, University of South Carolina, Aiken, SC -- for Greg-Graniteville library
10,000	Calvary Baptist Church, Graniteville, SC
10,000	Golden Harvest Food Bank, Augusta, GA
10,000	St. Joseph Foundation Inc., Augusta, GA
6,500	Byrd Elementary School, Graniteville, SC
5,000	Aiken Partnership, University of South Carolina, Aiken, SC
5,000	Hale Foundation Inc., Augusta, GA

ROSA MAY GRIFFIN FOUNDATION

Giving Contact

Dan Phillips, Secretary & Treasurer
PO Box 1790
Kilgore, TX 75663
Phone: (903)983-2051

Description

Founded: 1960
EIN: 756011866
Organization Type: Private Foundation
Giving Locations: TX
Grant Types: Capital, Emergency, General Support, Multiyear/Continuing Support, Operating Expenses.

Donor Information

Founder: the late Rosa May Griffin

Financial Summary

Total Giving: $356,088 (2001)
Giving Analysis: Giving for 2001 includes: foundation grants to United Way ($500)
Assets: $6,593,156 (2001)

Typical Recipients

Arts & Humanities: Arts & Humanities-General, Historic Preservation, History & Archaeology, Libraries, Museums/Galleries, Theater
Civic & Public Affairs: Botanical Gardens/Parks, Clubs, Civic & Public Affairs-General, Housing, Safety, Urban & Community Affairs
Education: Arts/Humanities Education, Business Education, Colleges & Universities, Education-General, Literacy, Preschool Education, Private Education (Precollege), Public Education (Precollege), School Volunteerism, Science/Mathematics Education, Secondary Education (Private), Student Aid
Health: Children's Health/Hospitals, Diabetes, Emergency/Ambulance Services, Geriatric Health, Heart, Hospitals, Hospitals (University Affiliated), Long-Term Care, Medical Rehabilitation, Medical Research, Public Health, Research/Studies Institutes
Religion: Churches, Ministries, Religious Organizations, Religious Welfare, Seminaries, Synagogues/Temples
Social Services: Camps, Child Welfare, Community Service Organizations, Counseling, Crime Prevention, Family Services, Homes, People with Disabilities, Recreation & Athletics, Scouts, Senior Services, Substance Abuse, United Funds/United Ways, Youth Organizations

Application Procedures

Initial Contact: Send a brief letter of inquiry.
Application Requirements: Include amount requested, purpose of funds sought, and proof of tax-exempt status.
Deadlines: None.

Restrictions

Does not support individuals.

Additional Information

Publications: Program Policy Statement

Foundation Officials

E. B. Mobley: president
Ebb Mobley: vice president
O. N. Pederson: trustee
Dan Phillips: secretary, treasurer

Grants Analysis

Disclosure Period: calendar year ending 2001
Total Grants: $355,588*
Number of Grants: 27
Average Grant: $11,753*
Highest Grant: $50,000
Lowest Grant: $500
Typical Range: $5,000 to $20,000
*Note: Giving excludes United Way. Average grant excludes highest grant.

Recent Grants

Note: Grants derived from 2001 Form 990.
General

50,000	Laird Hospital Foundation, Kilgore, TX
35,000	Texas Shakespeare Festival, TX
25,000	East Texas Treatment Center, Kilgore, TX
24,850	Schreiner College, Kerrville, TX
20,000	All-Star Music Scholarships, Kilgore, TX
20,000	American Heart Association, Longview, TX
20,000	East Texas Council on Alcoholism and Drug Abuse, Longview, TX
18,571	Kilgore Historical Preservation Foundation, Kilgore, TX
16,667	Evergreen Presbyterian Ministries, Bossier City, LA
15,000	KISD-Baseball Booster Program, Kilgore, TX

GRIFFIS FOUNDATION

Giving Contact

Hughes Griffis, President & Director
c/o Waller, Smith & Palmer
52 Eugene O'Neill Drive
New London, CT 06320
Phone: (860)422-0367

Description

Founded: 1943
EIN: 135678764
Organization Type: Private Foundation
Giving Locations: CT; NY
Grant Types: General Support.

Donor Information

Founder: the late Stanton Griffis, Nixon Griffis

Financial Summary

Total Giving: $702,683 (2003)
Assets: $6,092,494 (2003)
Gifts Received: $10,000 (2003)

Typical Recipients

Arts & Humanities: Arts Associations & Councils, Arts Centers, Arts Institutes, Dance, History & Archaeology, Libraries, Museums/Galleries, Music, Theater, Visual Arts
Civic & Public Affairs: Botanical Gardens/Parks, Community Foundations, Civic & Public Affairs-General, Municipalities/Towns, Philanthropic Organizations, Zoos/Aquariums
Education: Arts/Humanities Education, Colleges & Universities, Education-General, Private Education (Precollege), Public Education (Precollege), Secondary Education (Private)
Health: Cancer, Children's Health/Hospitals, Clinics/

Medical Centers, Emergency/Ambulance Services, Hospices, Hospitals, Medical Research, Single-Disease Health Associations
International: Human Rights
Religion: Religious Welfare
Social Services: Animal Protection, Camps, Family Services, Shelters/Homelessness, United Funds/United Ways, Youth Organizations

Application Procedures

Initial Contact: The foundation has no formal grant application procedure or application form.
Deadlines: None.

Additional Information

Publications: Program Policy Statement; Application Guidelines

Foundation Officials

Hughes Griffis: president, director
Elizabeth Nye: vice president, director
Patricia Morel Shippee: director B Brooklyn, NY 1940. ED Fordham University BA (1981). PRIM NONPR EMPL trustee: Griffis Art Center. NONPR AFFIL director: Connecticut Graphic Arts Center; trustee: Mondrian/Holtzman Trust.

Grants Analysis

Disclosure Period: calendar year ending 2003
Total Grants: $702,683
Number of Grants: 106
Average Grant: $5,795*
Highest Grant: $50,000
Lowest Grant: $100
Typical Range: $1,000 to $10,000
*Note: Average grant figure excludes two highest grants ($100,000).

Recent Grants

Note: Grants derived from 2003 Form 990.
General

50,000	Aspen Country Day School, Aspen, CO
50,000	Hoben Animal Shelter
25,000	Griffis Art Center, New London, CT
25,000	Richard B. Nye Foundation
25,000	Richard B. Nye Foundation
24,110	Convent of the Sacred Heart, New York, NY
22,808	St. David's School, New York, NY
20,000	Glenwood Springs Beauty Academy, Glenwood Springs, CO
15,000	Lyubonair Leuchev
13,072	Ferris State University, Big Rapids, MI

W. C. GRIFFITH FOUNDATION

Giving Contact

Curt Farran
Trustee Contact
c/o National City Bank of Indiana
101 W. Washington Street
Indianapolis, IN 46255
Phone: (317)267-7290
Fax: (317)267-3786 -

Description

Founded: 1959
EIN: 356007742
Organization Type: Private Foundation
Giving Locations: IN: Indianapolis
Grant Types: General Support, Operating Expenses.

Donor Information

Founder: the late William C. and Ruth Perry Griffith

Financial Summary

Total Giving: $481,100 (fiscal year ending November 30, 2003); $974,500 (fiscal 2001)
Assets: $11,437,456 (fiscal 2003); $14,274,037 (fiscal 2001)

Typical Recipients

Arts & Humanities: Arts Associations & Councils, Arts Centers, Ballet, Community Arts, Ethnic & Folk Arts, Historic Preservation, History & Archaeology, Libraries, Museums/Galleries, Music, Opera, Performing Arts, Public Broadcasting, Theater
Civic & Public Affairs: Botanical Gardens/Parks, Economic Development, Employment/Job Training, Civic & Public Affairs-General, Housing, Municipalities/Towns, Parades/Festivals, Public Policy, Safety, Urban & Community Affairs, Zoos/Aquariums
Education: Business Education, Colleges & Universities, Education Funds, Education Reform, Faculty Development, Education-General, International Studies, Private Education (Precollege), Public Education (Precollege), Secondary Education (Private), Student Aid
Environment: Environment-General, Resource Conservation
Health: AIDS/HIV, Cancer, Clinics/Medical Centers, Emergency/Ambulance Services, Health Organizations, Hospitals, Medical Rehabilitation, Medical Research, Mental Health, Preventive Medicine/Wellness Organizations, Single-Disease Health Associations
International: International Organizations, International Relief Efforts
Religion: Churches, Ministries, Religious Organizations, Religious Welfare
Social Services: Animal Protection, At-Risk Youth, Big Brothers/Big Sisters, Child Welfare, Community Service Organizations, Counseling, Family Planning, Food/Clothing Distribution, People with Disabilities, Recreation & Athletics, Scouts, Senior Services, Social Services-General, Substance Abuse, United Funds/United Ways, YMCA/YWCA/YMHA/YWHA, Youth Organizations

Application Procedures

Initial Contact: Send a brief letter of inquiry.
Application Requirements: Include a description of organization and purpose of funds sought.
Deadlines: None.

Restrictions

Does not support individuals or organizations outside the United States.

Foundation Officials

Ruthelen Griffith Burns: adv
Charles P. Griffith, Jr.: adv
Walter S. Griffith: adv
William C. Griffith, III: adv
Wendy Griffith Kortepeter: adv

Grants Analysis

Disclosure Period: fiscal year ending November 30, 2003
Total Grants: $481,100
Number of Grants: 93
Average Grant: $5,182*
Highest Grant: $50,000
Lowest Grant: $500
Typical Range: $1,000 to $10,000
***Note:** Average grant figure excludes two highest grants ($95,000).

Recent Grants

Note: Grants derived from fiscal 2003 Form 990.
General

50,000	James Whitcomb Riley Association, Indianapolis, IN
45,000	Camp Tecumseh YMCA Outdoor Center, Brookston, IN
35,000	Brebeuf Jesuit Preparatory School, Indianapolis, IN
25,000	Eiteljorg Museum, Indianapolis, IN
20,000	Indianapolis Art Center, Indianapolis, IN
20,000	Indianapolis Senior Citizens Center Inc., Indianapolis, IN
10,000	Independent Colleges of Indiana Inc., Indianapolis, IN
10,000	Indianapolis Downtown Inc., Indianapolis, IN
10,000	Oaks Academy, Indianapolis, IN
10,000	Wheeler Mission, Indianapolis, IN

MARY LIVINGSTON GRIGGS AND MARY GRIGGS BURKE FOUNDATION

Giving Contact

Marvin J. Pertzik, Secretary & Treasurer
55 East Fifth Street
1400 5th Street
St. Paul, MN 55101-1792
Phone: (651)227-7683
Fax: (651)602-2670

Description

Founded: 1966
EIN: 416052355
Organization Type: General Purpose Foundation
Giving Locations: MN: Minneapolis, St. Paul; NY: New York
Grant Types: Capital, Challenge, Department, Endowment, General Support, Professorship, Project.

Donor Information

Founder: The Mary Livingston Griggs and Mary Griggs Burke Foundation was established in 1966. The donor was Mary Livingston Griggs.

Financial Summary

Total Giving: $1,627,696 (fiscal year ending June 30, 2004); $2,028,740 (fiscal 2002); $2,479,610 (fiscal 2001)
Giving Analysis: Giving for fiscal 2001 includes: foundation grants to United Way ($42,000)
Assets: $24,359,027 (fiscal 2004); $25,803,733 (fiscal 2002); $29,010,630 (fiscal 2001)

Typical Recipients

Arts & Humanities: Arts Associations & Councils, Arts Centers, Arts Funds, Arts Institutes, Arts Outreach, Ballet, Dance, Arts & Humanities-General, Historic Preservation, History & Archaeology, Libraries, Museums/Galleries, Music, Opera, Performing Arts, Public Broadcasting, Theater, Visual Arts
Civic & Public Affairs: African American Affairs, Botanical Gardens/Parks, Business/Free Enterprise, Employment/Job Training, Civic & Public Affairs-General, Municipalities/Towns, Nonprofit Management, Parades/Festivals, Philanthropic Organizations, Urban & Community Affairs, Zoos/Aquariums
Education: Arts/Humanities Education, Colleges & Universities, Environmental Education, Education-General, International Studies, Literacy, Minority Education, Private Education (Precollege), Science/Mathematics Education, Student Aid
Environment: Environment-General, Resource Conservation, Wildlife Protection
Health: AIDS/HIV, Clinics/Medical Centers, Heart, Hospitals, Medical Research
International: International Environmental Issues, International Peace & Security Issues, International Relations
Science: Science Museums, Scientific Organizations
Social Services: Child Welfare, Day Care, Family Planning, Shelters/Homelessness, United Funds/United Ways

Application Procedures

Initial Contact: Applicants should send a proposal that includes four copies of the cover letter.
Application Requirements: Proposals should include a copy of the IRS tax-exempt determination letter. If the letter is more than one-year old, the foundation requests a statement indicating that there has been no change in the applicant's tax-exempt status. The proposal should also describe, clearly and concisely, the purposes of the grant, amount needed, the budget for the project, and whether or not assistance is sought from any other foundation. The proposal should also include the latest audited financial statements.
Deadlines: None.

Restrictions

The foundation does not make contributions to individuals, for dinners or special events, to fraternal organizations, political or lobbying groups, religious organizations for sectarian purposes, or for goodwill advertising.

Foundation Officials

Eleanor Briggs: director
Mary Griggs Burke: honorary president, director B Saint Paul, MN. ED Columbia University MA; New School for Social Research; Sarah Lawrence College BA. NONPR AFFIL William Beene fellow: New York Zoological Society; member visitors committee: Smithsonian Institute Freer Gallery Art; member visitors committee, member ed committee, member aquis: Metropolitan Museum Art; member international council: Museum Modern Art; director: Hobe Sound Nature Center; honorary life trustee: Japan House Gallery; honorary life trustee: Brooklyn Museum Art; honorary life trustee: Friends Asian Art Freer & Sackler Galleries.
Gale Lansing Davis: vice president, director
C. E. Bayliss Griggs: president, director
Marvin J. Pertzik: secretary, treasurer, director B 1929. PRIM CORP EMPL partner: Moore, Costello & Hart.

Grants Analysis

Disclosure Period: fiscal year ending June 30, 2004
Total Grants: $1,627,696
Number of Grants: 64
Average Grant: $22,344*
Highest Grant: $220,000
Lowest Grant: $1,000
Typical Range: $10,000 to $40,000
***Note:** Average grant figure excludes highest grant.

Recent Grants

Note: Grants derived from fiscal 2002 Form 990.
Library-Related

30,000	Friends of the St. Paul Public Library, St. Paul, MN -- system renewal
15,000	New York Public Library, New York, NY -- for specific programs

General

200,000	Asia Society, Inc., New York, NY -- for capital campaign
200,000	International Crane Foundation, Baraboo, WI -- endowment
200,000	Northland College, Ashland, WI -- science building
200,000	Sarah Lawrence College, Washington, DC -- endowment fund
194,469	Mary and Jackson Burke Foundation, St. Paul, MN -- art acquisition
157,531	Mary and Jackson Burke Foundation, St. Paul, MN -- for administration
120,000	Central Park Conservancy, New York, NY -- Shakespeare Garden
55,450	Metropolitan Museum of Art, New York, NY -- for purchase of art

53,000	Central Park Conservancy, New York, NY
50,000	Minneapolis Society of Fine Arts, Minneapolis, MN -- for challenge

8,000	Bethesda Hospital Association, Boynton Beach, FL
7,000	St. Mary's School, Urbana, OH
6,250	Ohio State University, Columbus, OH
3,000	Boy Scouts of America, Springfield, OH
2,500	Miami University, Oxford, OH

115,000	New Hampshire Association for the Blind, Concord, NH
115,000	Schepens Eye Research Institute, Boston, MA
110,000	Brown University, Providence, RI
64,000	Eastern Nazarene College, Quincy, MA
60,000	Dartmouth-Hitchcock Medical Clinic for Continuing Education, Lebanon, NH
55,000	St. Francis Xavier Foreign Mission, Inc., Wayne, NJ
40,000	Freetown Historical Society, Freetown, MA
30,000	Lown Cardiovascular Research Foundation, Brookline, MA

GRIMES FOUNDATION

Giving Contact
Lewis B. Moore, Trustee
166 Tanglewood Dr.
Urbana, OH 43078
Phone: (937)653-4865

Description
Founded: 1951
EIN: 346528288
Organization Type: Private Foundation
Giving Locations: FL; OH
Grant Types: Capital, General Support, Scholarship.

Donor Information
Founder: Warren G. Grimes

Typical Recipients
Arts & Humanities: Arts Associations & Councils, Ethnic & Folk Arts, Libraries, Museums/Galleries, Theater
Civic & Public Affairs: Economic Development, Civic & Public Affairs-General, Municipalities/Towns, Safety, Urban & Community Affairs
Education: Colleges & Universities, Education Reform, Elementary Education (Private), Elementary Education (Public), Engineering/Technological Education, Faculty Development, Private Education (Precollege), Public Education (Precollege), Science/Mathematics Education, Secondary Education (Public)
Environment: Environment-General
Health: Cancer, Emergency/Ambulance Services, Health-General, Health Organizations, Hospitals, Medical Research
Religion: Churches
Social Services: At-Risk Youth, Community Centers, Community Service Organizations, Day Care, Scouts, Senior Services, YMCA/YWCA/YMHA/YWHA, Youth Organizations

Application Procedures
Initial Contact: The foundation has no formal grant application procedure or application form.
Deadlines: None.

Foundation Officials
Clarence J. Brown, Jr.: trustee
James S. Mihori: trustee
Gregory Moore: trustee
Lewis B. Moore: trustee
Robert S. Oelman: trustee
Steven Posley: trustee

Grants Analysis
Disclosure Period: calendar year ending 2000
Total Grants: $276,248
Number of Grants: 37
Average Grant: $5,590*
Highest Grant: $75,000
Typical Range: $1,000 to $10,000
*Note: Average grant figure excludes highest grant.

Recent Grants
Note: Grants derived from 2001 Form 990.
General

75,000	Urbana University, Urbana, OH
50,000	Champaign YMCA, Urbana, OH
25,000	Main Street Urbana, Urbana, OH
25,000	Morikami Museum, Delray Beach, FL
10,300	Grimes Field Municipal Airport, Urbana, OH

GRIMSHAW-GUDEWICZ CHARITABLE FOUNDATION

Giving Contact
Anne Fazendeiro, Trustee
173 Auburn Street
New Bedford, MA 02740
Phone: (508)997-2297

Description
Founded: 1995
EIN: 046778721
Organization Type: Private Foundation
Giving Locations: MA; NH; RI
Grant Types: General Support.

Typical Recipients
Arts & Humanities: Arts Centers, History & Archaeology, Libraries, Museums/Galleries, Music, Opera, Theater
Education: Colleges & Universities, Community & Junior Colleges, Continuing Education, Education-General, Literacy, Public Education (Precollege), Student Aid
Environment: Forestry
Health: Clinics/Medical Centers, Eyes/Blindness, Health Organizations, Heart, Hospitals, Medical Research, Public Health, Single-Disease Health Associations
International: Missionary/Religious Activities
Religion: Religion-General, Jewish Causes, Religious Welfare, Synagogues/Temples
Social Services: Community Service Organizations, Homes, People with Disabilities, Recreation & Athletics, Social Services-General, YMCA/YWCA/YMHA/YWHA

Application Procedures
Initial Contact: Send a letter indicating purpose of funds sought, and including proof of tax-exempt status and a statement that the organization is currently in good standing.
Deadlines: None.

Foundation Officials
Anne Fazendeiro: trustee
Arthur Parker: trustee
Barry Robbins: trustee
Andrew Shabshelowitz: trustee
Harold Shabshelowitz: trustee
Bernard A. G. Taradash: trustee

Grants Analysis
Disclosure Period: calendar year ending 2000
Total Grants: $1,250,000
Number of Grants: 73
Average Grant: $9,191*
Highest Grant: $125,000
Typical Range: $5,000 to $20,000
*Note: Average grant figures excludes five highest grants ($625,000).

Recent Grants
Note: Grants derived from 2002 Form 990.
General

115,000	Franklin Pierce College, Rindge, NH
115,000	Masonic Education and Charity Trust, Inc., Boston, MA

GRINNELL MUTUAL REINSURANCE CO.

Company Headquarters
4215 Hwy. 146
Grinnell, IA 50112

Company Description
Employees: 650
SIC(s): 6331 Fire, Marine & Casualty Insurance.

Grinnell Mutual Group Foundation

Giving Contact
Steph Meggers, Manager
4215 Highway 146
PO Box 790
Grinnell, IA 50112-0790
Phone: (641)236-6121
Fax: (641)236-6121

Description
EIN: 421308146
Organization Type: Corporate Foundation
Former Name: GMG Foundation (2002).
Giving Locations: IA: headquarters area only
Grant Types: Employee Matching Gifts, General Support, Scholarship.

Financial Summary
Total Giving: $78,897 (2001)
Giving Analysis: Giving for 2001 includes: foundation scholarships ($6,000); foundation matching gifts ($11,670); foundation grants to United Way ($23,470)
Assets: $13,072 (2001)
Gifts Received: $75,000 (2001); $70,000 (2000); $100,000 (1999). Note: Contributions were received from Ginnell Mutual Reinsurance Co.

Typical Recipients
Arts & Humanities: Film & Video, Libraries, Literary Arts, Museums/Galleries, Public Broadcasting, Theater
Civic & Public Affairs: Clubs, Community Foundations, Civic & Public Affairs-General, Parades/Festivals, Rural Affairs, Safety
Education: Agricultural Education, Business Education, Colleges & Universities, Community & Junior Colleges, Secondary Education (Public), Student Aid
Environment: Air/Water Quality, Forestry, Environment-General, Protection, Research, Resource Conservation
Health: Cancer, Clinics/Medical Centers, Emergency/Ambulance Services, Heart, Hospices, Hospitals, Multiple Sclerosis
Social Services: Animal Protection, Big Brothers/Big Sisters, Community Service Organizations, Day Care, Domestic Violence, Emergency Relief, Family

Services, Recreation & Athletics, Social Services-General, United Funds/United Ways

Application Procedures

Initial Contact: Send a brief letter of inquiry and a full proposal.
Application Requirements: Include a description of organization, amount requested, purpose of funds sought, recently audited financial statement, and proof of tax-exempt status.
Deadlines: None.

Restrictions

Does not support individuals, religious organizations for sectarian purposes, political or lobbying groups, or organizations outside operating areas.

Corporate Officials

Dan F. Agnew: president, chief executive officer B Grinnell, IA 1944. ED University of Northern Iowa (1967). PRIM CORP EMPL president, chief executive officer: Grinnell Mutual Reinsurance Co. CORP AFFIL president, director: Grinnell Realty Co.; director: Grinnell Select Insurance Co.; director: Greater Grinnell Development; director: Grinnell Infosystems Inc.; chairman: Big M Agency Inc. NONPR AFFIL member: Ancient Free Accepted Masons; member: Lions International.
Michael J. Fordyce: chairman, director PRIM CORP EMPL chairman, director: Grinnell Mutual Reinsurance Co.
Robert C. Latham: second vice chairman, director PRIM CORP EMPL second vice chairman, director: Grinnell Mutual Reinsurance Co.
Clifford L. Strovers: director PRIM CORP EMPL director: Grinnell Mutual Reinsurance Co.
Jerry Dean Woods: vice president financial B Osceola, IA 1948. ED University of Iowa (1971). PRIM CORP EMPL vice president financial: Grinnell Mutual Reinsurance Co. CORP AFFIL director: Grinnell Life Insurance Co.

Foundation Officials

Dan F. Agnew: president, director (see above)
Tom Bachmann: director
Michael J. Fordyce: director (see above)
Stacy Heinen: director
Larry Jansen: director B Marshalltown, IA 1947. ED University of Iowa (1969). PRIM CORP EMPL vice president: Grinnell Mutual Reinsurance Co. CORP AFFIL president, director: Grinnell Select Insurance Canada.
Brent Larsen: director
Shawn McKay: director
Steph Meggers: manager
Wendy Nelson Munyon: secretary PRIM CORP EMPL assistant general counsel: Grinnell Mutual Reinsurance Co.
Ray Spriggs: director
Phyllis Steffen: director
Clifford L. Strovers: vice president, director (see above)
Ralph LaSalle Thompson: treasurer B Hopkinton, IA 1927. PRIM CORP EMPL treasurer: Grinnell Inco Co. CORP AFFIL treasurer: Grinnell Select Insurance Co.; treasurer: Invest Manager Grinnell Mutual Reinsurance Co.; treasurer, manager: Grinnell Realty Co.; treasurer: Grinnell Infosystems Inc.; treasurer secretary: Grinnell Mutual Life Insurance Co.; treasurer: Big M Agency.
Jerry Dean Woods: treasurer (see above)

Grants Analysis

Disclosure Period: calendar year ending 2001
Total Grants: $35,758*
Number of Grants: 18
Average Grant: $926*
Highest Grant: $20,000
Lowest Grant: $200
Typical Range: $250 to $2,000
***Note:** Giving excludes matching gifts, scholarships, United Way. Average grant excludes highest grant.

Recent Grants

Note: Grants derived from 2002 Form 990.
General

20,000	Grinnell Regional Medical Center, Grinnell, IA -- pledge donation
11,187	United Way of Grinnell, Grinnell, IA -- united way employee match
5,000	Iowa College Foundation, Des Moines, IA -- scholarships
3,000	Grinnell Middle School, Grinnell, IA -- for 2002 pledge
2,500	Farm Safety 4 Just Kids, Earlham, IA
2,285	Montezuma Community Fund, Montezuma, IA -- united way employee match
2,200	Iowa 4-H Foundation, Ames, IA -- sponsorship
2,010	Jasper County United Way, Newton, IA -- united way employee match
2,000	Insurance Education Foundation, Indianapolis, IN
2,000	Iowa Valley Community College, Grinnell, IA -- for 2002 pledge

JOHN C. GRISWOLD FOUNDATION

Giving Contact

Jacqueline G. Moore, President
201 E. 5th St.
Cincinnati, OH 45202
Phone: (312)857-7820

Description

Founded: 1978
EIN: 132978937
Organization Type: Private Foundation
Grant Types: General Support.

Donor Information

Founder: the late John C. Griswold

Financial Summary

Total Giving: $725,000 (fiscal year ending November 30, 2004); $757,000 (fiscal 2001)
Assets: $13,009,405 (fiscal 2004); $13,479,208 (fiscal 2001)
Gifts Received: $500,000 (fiscal 2004); $519,491 (fiscal 2001); $368,446 (fiscal 2000). Note: Contributions were received from the John C. Griswold Charitable Lead Trust.

Typical Recipients

Arts & Humanities: Arts Centers, Arts Funds, Ballet, Historic Preservation, Libraries, Museums/Galleries, Music, Opera, Performing Arts, Public Broadcasting, Theater
Civic & Public Affairs: Community Foundations, Civic & Public Affairs-General, Public Policy, Urban & Community Affairs
Education: Colleges & Universities, Education Associations, Education Reform, Education-General, Medical Education, Private Education (Precollege), Public Education (Precollege), School Volunteerism, Special Education
Environment: Environment-General, Research, Wildlife Protection
Health: Cancer, Children's Health/Hospitals, Clinics/Medical Centers, Diabetes, Hospitals, Medical Rehabilitation, Medical Research, Mental Health, Prenatal Health Issues, Preventive Medicine/Wellness Organizations, Single-Disease Health Associations, Trauma Treatment
International: International Relief Efforts
Religion: Churches, Jewish Causes, Religious Organizations
Science: Scientific Centers & Institutes
Social Services: Child Welfare, Community Service

Organizations, Counseling, Domestic Violence, Family Services, People with Disabilities, Recreation & Athletics, Shelters/Homelessness, Social Services-General, Youth Organizations

Application Procedures

Initial Contact: Send brief letter describing program.
Deadlines: None.

Restrictions

Applicants must be personally known by directors.

Foundation Officials

James R. Donnelley: vice president, treasurer B Chicago, IL 1935. ED Dartmouth College BA (1957); University of Chicago MBA (1962). PRIM CORP EMPL vice chairman: R.R. Donnelley & Sons Co. CORP AFFIL director: Sierra Pacific Power Co.; director: Sierra Pacific Resources; director: Pacific Magazines & Printing Ltd.
Jeffrey W. Earls: vice president
Lynda Earls: secretary
D. Ross Griswold, Jr.: vice president
Jacqueline G. Moore: president

Grants Analysis

Disclosure Period: fiscal year ending November 30, 2004
Total Grants: $725,000
Number of Grants: 68
Average Grant: $8,582*
Highest Grant: $150,000
Lowest Grant: $250
Typical Range: $5,000 to $20,000
***Note:** Average grant figure excludes highest grant.

Recent Grants

Note: Grants derived from fiscal 2004 Form 990.
General

150,000	Greater Cincinnati Foundation, Cincinnati, OH
30,000	Prospect House Foundation Inc., Cincinnati, OH
25,000	Cincinnati Ballet Company, Cincinnati, OH
20,000	Cincinnati Opera, Cincinnati, OH
20,000	Cincinnati Symphony Orchestra, Cincinnati, OH
20,000	John L. Magro Foundation, Cincinnati, OH
20,000	University of Southern California, Los Angeles, CA
15,000	Blind Children's Learning Center of Orange County, Santa Ana, CA
15,000	Community School, Sun Valley, ID
15,000	Operation Enduring Freedom Family Fund, Ridgecrest, CA

LILLIAN SHERWOOD GRISWOLD FOUNDATION

Giving Contact

c/o Griswold Management Co.
1701 Placentia
Costa Mesa, CA 92627
Phone: (949)496-1174

Description

Founded: 1995
EIN: 330668667
Organization Type: Private Foundation
Grant Types: General Support.

Financial Summary

Total Giving: $30,917 (2003); $146,097 (2001)
Assets: $1,385,790 (2003); $2,699,300 (2001)
Gifts Received: $15,000 (2003); $300,000 (1999);

$600,000 (1998). Note: In 2003, contributions were received from David E. Griswold. In 1998 and 1999, contributions were received from Griswold Industries.

Typical Recipients
Arts & Humanities: Arts Centers, Libraries
Civic & Public Affairs: Civic & Public Affairs-General
Education: Colleges & Universities, Education-General
Health: Children's Health/Hospitals, Hospitals, Prenatal Health Issues
Religion: Churches, Religion-General, Missionary Activities (Domestic), Religious Welfare
Social Services: Camps, Child Welfare, Homes, Social Services-General, Volunteer Services, Youth Organizations

Application Procedures
Initial Contact: The foundation has no formal grant application procedure or application form.
Deadlines: None.

Foundation Officials
Lois G. Ericson: off
David E. Griswold: off

Grants Analysis
Disclosure Period: calendar year ending 2003
Total Grants: $30,917
Number of Grants: 6
Highest Grant: $10,306
Lowest Grant: $300
Typical Range: $1,000 to $5,000

Recent Grants
Note: Grants derived from 2003 Form 990.
General

10,306	Orange County Performing Arts Center, Costa Mesa, CA
10,000	Twelveacres Inc., Campbell, CA
5,001	Child Help Village Library Fund, Beaumont, CA
3,005	Klamath Falls Gospel Mission, Klamath Falls, OR
2,300	Gideons International, Nashville, TN

GROTTO FOUNDATION

Giving Contact
Sarah Marquardt, Grants Manager
5323 Lakeland Ave. North, Suite 100
Minneapolis, MN 55429
Phone: (763)277-3434
Fax: (763)277-3444
E-mail: info@grottofoundation.org
Web: http://www.grottofoundation.org

Description
Founded: 1964
EIN: 416052604
Organization Type: Private Foundation
Giving Locations: AK; MN
Grant Types: General Support, Project, Research, Scholarship, Seed Money.

Donor Information
Founder: Louis W. Hill, Jr.

Financial Summary
Total Giving: $709,006 (fiscal year ending April 30, 2004); $712,993 (fiscal 2002); $859,879 (fiscal 2001)
Assets: $22,886,508 (fiscal 2004); $23,982,631 (fiscal 2002); $27,319,413 (fiscal 2001)
Gifts Received: $25,000 (fiscal 2004); $5,000 (fiscal 2002); $65,000 (fiscal 2001)

Typical Recipients
Arts & Humanities: Arts Associations & Councils, Arts Outreach, Film & Video, History & Archaeology, Libraries, Literary Arts, Public Broadcasting, Visual Arts
Civic & Public Affairs: African American Affairs, Asian American Affairs, Civil Rights, Economic Development, Gay/Lesbian Issues, Civic & Public Affairs-General, Hispanic Affairs, Housing, Municipalities/Towns, Native American Affairs, Nonprofit Management, Parades/Festivals, Philanthropic Organizations, Public Policy, Urban & Community Affairs, Women's Affairs
Education: Afterschool/Enrichment Programs, Colleges & Universities, Community & Junior Colleges, Continuing Education, Faculty Development, Education-General, Legal Education, Minority Education, Private Education (Precollege), Public Education (Precollege), School Volunteerism, Secondary Education (Public), Special Education, Student Aid
Environment: Environment-General
Health: AIDS/HIV, Clinics/Medical Centers, Emergency/Ambulance Services, Health Organizations, Hospitals, Public Health
International: Foreign Arts Organizations, Human Rights, International Relations
Religion: Religious Organizations, Religious Welfare
Social Services: Community Service Organizations, Domestic Violence, Family Services, Homes, People with Disabilities, Refugee Assistance, Scouts, Senior Services, Substance Abuse, Youth Organizations

Application Procedures
Initial Contact: Application form required.
Application Requirements: Include in the grant application, organizational information, purpose of funds sought, and evaluation information regarding program effectiveness and criteria. Attachments to application form include an IRS SOI(c)(3) letter; current registration receipt from state attorney general's office; officers list; recent audited report; project financials; projected budget; and any additional information.
Deadlines: January15, March15, July15, November15.

Restrictions
The foundation does not support individuals; scholarships; capital fund programs; subsidies for writing or publishing; multiple years; outside Minnesota; for travel; graduate or under graduate research; general operating expense; government agencies.

Additional Information
Publications: Annual Report (including Application Guidelines)

Foundation Officials
Austin J. Baillon: director emeritus
Ellis F. Bullock: secretary, executive director
Louis Shea Hill: director
Michael Johnson: second vice president
Mary Manuel: director
Malcolm W. McDonald: treasurer, director NONPR AFFIL director: Amherst H. Wilder Foundation.
Elizabeth Pegues-Smart: 1st vice president, director
William B. Randall: president emeritus
Nancy Randall-Dana: director

Grants Analysis
Disclosure Period: fiscal year ending April 30, 2004
Total Grants: $709,006
Number of Grants: 54
Average Grant: $11,491*
Highest Grant: $100,000
Lowest Grant: $5,000
Typical Range: $5,000 to $20,000
*Note: Average grant figure excludes highest grant.

Recent Grants
Note: Grants derived from fiscal 2004 Form 990.
General

55,000	Waadookodaading, Hayward, WI -- to support the salary of third-grade teacher, the addition of fourth grade instruction and curriculum development
45,000	Fond du Lac Tribal and Community College, Cloquet, MN -- to continue Ojibwe language skill development during the first year of student teaching
30,000	Na-way-ee Center School, Minneapolis, MN -- for positive language environment program
20,000	Circle Corporation, Minneapolis, MN -- for financial capacity building
10,000	American Indian Family Center, St. Paul, MN -- for community circle of giving
10,000	Grand Excursion 2004, St. Paul, MN -- towards river exploration trunks
10,000	La Escuelita, Minneapolis, MN -- to support youth-led events, enrichment and community activities that improve education of Latino youth
7,500	La Oportunidad Inc., Minneapolis, MN -- towards El Camino and Latino youth programs
7,500	Minnesota African Refugees and Immigrants Initiatives, Crystal, MN -- to provide mentoring to Liberian youth and their families, school-based tutorials and counseling to access community services
7,500	Twin Cities Neighborhood Housing Services Inc., St. Paul, MN -- towards financial literary program

GRUNDY FOUNDATION

Giving Contact
Roland H. Johnson, Executive Director
680 Radcliffe Street
PO Box 701
Bristol, PA 19007
Phone: (215)788-5460
Fax: (215)788-0915

Description
Founded: 1961
EIN: 231609243
Organization Type: General Purpose Foundation
Giving Locations: PA: Bristol and Bucks County
Grant Types: Capital, General Support, Project.

Donor Information
Founder: The foundation was established in 1961 pursuant to the will of the late Joseph Ridgeway Grundy. Mr. Grundy was president of Grundy and Company (a linen manufacturer) and the Farmers National Bank of Bucks County. He was also appointed by the governor of Pennsylvania to an unexpired term in the U.S. Senate (1929-1930).

Financial Summary
Total Giving: $479,132 (2003); $1,226,666 (2002); $1,275,915 (2001)
Giving Analysis: Giving for 2003 includes: foundation grants to United Way ($134,000)
Assets: $53,351,091 (2003); $53,000,000 (2002); $52,473,285 (2001)
Gifts Received: $35,104 (1993). Note: In 1993, contributions were received from the Johnson Fund.

Typical Recipients
Arts & Humanities: Arts Centers, Arts Festivals, Arts Outreach, Ethnic & Folk Arts, Film & Video, Historic Preservation, History & Archaeology, Libraries, Museums/Galleries, Music, Opera, Performing Arts, Theater

Civic & Public Affairs: Botanical Gardens/Parks, Economic Development, Economic Policy, Civic & Public Affairs-General, Hispanic Affairs, Housing, Inner-City Development, Municipalities/Towns, Parades/Festivals, Public Policy, Safety, Urban & Community Affairs, Women's Affairs

Education: Colleges & Universities, Community & Junior Colleges, Education Associations, Education Funds, Education-General, International Exchange, Literacy, Preschool Education, Public Education (Precollege), Science/Mathematics Education, Secondary Education (Public), Student Aid

Environment: Air/Water Quality, Forestry, Environment-General, Resource Conservation, Wildlife Protection

Health: Cancer, Children's Health/Hospitals, Clinics/Medical Centers, Emergency/Ambulance Services, Health-General, Hospitals, Long-Term Care, Mental Health, Public Health, Respiratory

International: International Affairs, International Relations

Social Services: Animal Protection, Big Brothers/Big Sisters, Camps, Child Welfare, Community Centers, Community Service Organizations, Crime Prevention, Day Care, Domestic Violence, Emergency Relief, Family Planning, Family Services, Food/Clothing Distribution, Homes, People with Disabilities, Recreation & Athletics, Scouts, Senior Services, Sexual Abuse, Shelters/Homelessness, Social Services-General, Substance Abuse, United Funds/United Ways, YMCA/YWCA/YMHA/YWHA, Youth Organizations

Application Procedures

Initial Contact: The foundation has no specific application requirements. Submit a brief letter of inquiry.
Application Requirements: Include a description of organization, amount requested, purpose of funds sought, recently audited financial statement, and proof of tax-exempt status. report. of annual report.
Deadlines: None.
Review Process: Grants are reviewed throughout the year at board meetings. The foundation may request more information or make a site visit before reaching a decision. Applicants are notified by letter within a week of the board meeting at which the decision is made.
Notes: Telephone request for clarification of proposal requirements are accepted, but faxed proposals and videotapes are not.

Restrictions

The foundation does not make grants to nonpublic schools, individuals, religious organizations, or for endowments, loans, research or political activities. The foundation can not consider proposals for operating support from United Way member agencies.

Additional Information

The foundation operates a museum and a library.
Publications: Application Guidelines
Trust(s): Wachovia Bank

Foundation Officials

James M. Gassaway: trustee
Roland H. Johnson: executive director
John Knoell: trustee B 1927. PRIM CORP EMPL president: John Knoell & Sons Inc.
Frederick J. M. La Valley: trustee ED Stanford University (1969); University of Pennsylvania (1972).
Leonard N. Snyder: trustee

Grants Analysis

Disclosure Period: calendar year ending 2003
Total Grants: $345,132*
Number of Grants: 53
Average Grant: $3,826*
Highest Grant: $75,000
Lowest Grant: $1,000
Typical Range: $1,000 to $5,000
***Note:** Giving excludes United Way. Average grant figure excludes two highest grants ($150,000).

Recent Grants

Note: Grants derived from 2002 Form 990.
General

235,000	Bristol Riverside Theater Company Inc., Bristol, PA -- for support of the 2002-2007 seasons
100,000	Borough of Bristol, Bristol, PA
60,000	Bristol Riverside Theater Company Inc., Bristol, PA -- to support the 1999-2002 seasons
57,500	United Way of Bucks County, Fairless Hills, PA -- for the 2001-2002 campaign
50,000	Bristol Riverside Theater Company Inc., Bristol, PA -- for support of the endowment fund
50,000	Historic Delaware Canal Improvement Corp, Doylestown, PA -- to support the restoration of the Delaware canal
50,000	Pennsbury Society, Morrisville, PA -- to support the new visitor's center
20,000	Bristol Borough School District, Bristol, PA -- for renewal of the Leonard N. Snyder scholarship fund
20,000	United Way of Bucks County, Fairless Hills, PA -- to support the 2002-2003 annual campaign
15,000	Bucks County Association for Retired and Senior Citizens, Bristol, PA -- for installation of an elevator at the lower Bucks activity center

GUARANTY BANK & TRUST CO.

Company Headquarters
Cedar Rapids, IA
Web: http://www.guaranty-bank.com

Company Description
Employees: 56
SIC(s): 6022 State Commercial Banks.

Guaranty Bank and Trust Co. Charitable Trust

Giving Contact
Robert Becker, President
PO Box 1807
Cedar Rapids, IA 52406-1807
Phone: (319)286-6200
Fax: (319)362-1295
E-mail: becker@guaranty-bank.com

Description
EIN: 510182485
Organization Type: Corporate Foundation
Giving Locations: IA
Grant Types: General Support.

Financial Summary
Gifts Received: $42,000 (2000); $60,000 (1999); $40,000 (1996). Note: Contributions were received from Guaranty Bank and Trust Co.

Typical Recipients
Arts & Humanities: Arts Festivals, Community Arts, Ethnic & Folk Arts, Historic Preservation, History & Archaeology, Libraries, Museums/Galleries, Music, Theater
Civic & Public Affairs: African American Affairs, Botanical Gardens/Parks, Chambers of Commerce, Clubs, Community Foundations, Civic & Public Affairs-General, Housing, Municipalities/Towns, Parades/Festivals, Professional & Trade Associations, Safety, Urban & Community Affairs, Women's Affairs, Zoos/Aquariums
Education: Business Education, Colleges & Universities, Community & Junior Colleges, Education Funds, Private Education (Precollege), Public Education (Precollege), Science/Mathematics Education
Environment: Environment-General
Health: AIDS/HIV, Alzheimer's Disease, Cancer, Children's Health/Hospitals, Diabetes, Emergency/Ambulance Services, Health Organizations, Hospitals, Kidney, Single-Disease Health Associations
Religion: Churches, Jewish Causes, Religious Welfare
Science: Science-General, Scientific Centers & Institutes
Social Services: Animal Protection, Camps, Community Centers, Community Service Organizations, Domestic Violence, Family Planning, Food/Clothing Distribution, People with Disabilities, Recreation & Athletics, Scouts, Senior Services, Social Services-General, Substance Abuse, United Funds/United Ways, YMCA/YWCA/YMHA/YWHA

Application Procedures
Initial Contact: Send brief letter describing program.
Deadlines: None.

Corporate Officials
Harold M. Becker: chairman, chief executive officer PRIM CORP EMPL chairman, chief executive officer: Guaranty Bank & Trust Co.
B. Larry Johnson: president PRIM CORP EMPL president: Guaranty Bank & Trust Co.
John Waters: chief financial officer PRIM CORP EMPL chief financial officer: Guaranty Bank & Trust Co.

Foundation Officials
Harold M. Becker: director (see above)
Robert D. Becker: director
Nancy H. Evans: director

Grants Analysis
Disclosure Period: calendar year ending 2000
Total Grants: $45,725*
Number of Grants: 66
Average Grant: $693*
Highest Grant: $6,000
Typical Range: $100 to $1,000
***Note:** Giving excludes United Way.

Recent Grants
Note: Grants derived from 2001 Form 990.

General

4,000	United Way of East Central Iowa, Cedar Rapids, IA
3,750	Cedar Rapids Museum of Art, Cedar Rapids, IA
3,000	Cedar Rapids Symphony Orchestra, Cedar Rapids, IA
3,000	Linn County Historical Museum, Cedar Rapids, IA
3,000	Science Station, Cedar Rapids, IA
2,500	City Treasurer, City of Cedar Rapids, Cedar Rapids, IA
2,250	YMCA of Cedar Rapids, Cedar Rapids, IA
2,000	American Red Cross, Cedar Rapids, IA
1,650	National Czech and Slovak Museum and Library, Cedar Rapids, IA
1,600	Marion Historical Museum, Marion, IA

GUARDIAN LIFE INSURANCE COMPANY OF AMERICA

Company Headquarters
New York, NY
Web: http://www.theguardian.com

Company Description
Revenue: US$8.892 billion (2004)
Profit: US$309.4 million (2004)
Employees: 5500 (2003)
Fortune Rank: 251, per FORTUNE Magazine's list of 500 Largest U.S. Corporations (2004).
SIC(s): 6036 Savings Institutions Except Federal, 6311 Life Insurance, 6321 Accident & Health Insurance.

Operating Locations
Guardian Life Insurance Co. of America (PA; WA; WI)

Giving Contact
Karen Olvany, Assistant Corporate Secretary
7 Hanover Square
New York, NY 10004-2616
Phone: (212)598-7499
Fax: (212)919-2944
E-mail: karen_olvany@glic.com

Description
Organization Type: Corporate Giving Program
Giving Locations: PA: Bethlehem; WA: Spokane; WI: Appleton headquarters and operating communities.
Grant Types: General Support.

Financial Summary
Total Giving: $1,000,000 (2004 approx); $1,000,000 (2003); $1,000,000 (2002 approx). Note: Contributes through corporate direct giving program only.
Giving Analysis: Giving for 2001 includes: foundation matching gifts ($131,225)

Typical Recipients
Arts & Humanities: Arts Centers, Community Arts, Historic Preservation, Libraries, Museums/Galleries, Music, Opera, Performing Arts, Public Broadcasting, Theater
Civic & Public Affairs: Business/Free Enterprise, Economic Development, Economic Policy, Law & Justice, Safety, Urban & Community Affairs, Zoos/Aquariums
Education: Arts/Humanities Education, Business Education, Colleges & Universities, Community & Junior Colleges, Economic Education, Education Funds, Literacy
Health: Health Policy/Cost Containment, Hospices, Medical Research, Single-Disease Health Associations
Social Services: Food/Clothing Distribution, Substance Abuse, United Funds/United Ways, Youth Organizations

Application Procedures
Initial Contact: Submit a brief letter of inquiry.
Application Requirements: A description of organization, amount requested and purpose of funds sought, recently audited financial statement, and proof of tax-exempt status.
Deadlines: None.

Restrictions
Does not support individuals, religious organizations for sectarian purposes, or political or lobbying groups.

Additional Information
In 1992, the company began a direct giving program. The Guardian Life Charitable Trust was terminated in December 1993.

Corporate Officials
Peter Lounsbery Hutchings: executive vice president, chief financial officerc B New York, NY 1943. ED Yale University BA (1964). PRIM CORP EMPL executive vice president, chief financial officer: Guardian Life Insurance Co. of America ADD CORP EMPL director: Family Service Lifeline Co.; president, director: First International; director: Guardian Insurance & Annuity Co. Inc.; director: Guardian Investors Services Corp.; president, director: Park Avenue Life; president, director: Sentinel American Life Insurance. NONPR AFFIL member: American Academy of Actuaries; fellow: Society Actuaries; member: Actuarial Society Greater New York; director: 14th Street Business Improvement District; director: 14th Street Union Square Local Development Corp.
Joseph Dudley Sargent: president, chief executive officer, director B Philadelphia, PA 1937. ED Fairfield University AB (1959). PRIM CORP EMPL president, chief executive officer, director: Guardian Life Insurance Co. of America ADD CORP EMPL director: Family Service Life Insurance Co.; president, chief executive officer: Guardian Insurance & Annuity Co. Inc. NONPR AFFIL member: National Association Life Underwriters; director: United Way New York City; director: Life Office Management Association; director: Discovery Museum Bridgeport; director: Life Insurance Marketing & Research Institute.

Giving Program Officials
Karen L. Olvany: contact PRIM CORP EMPL assistant corporate secretary: Guardian Life Insurance Co. of America.

Grants Analysis
Disclosure Period: calendar year ending 2001
Total Grants: $966,900*
Number of Grants: 322
Average Grant: $1,000
Highest Grant: $171,400
Lowest Grant: $250
Typical Range: $500 to $5,000
*****Note:** Giving includes matching gifts, United Way. Grants analysis provided by foundation.

HOMER AND MARTHA GUDELSKY FAMILY FOUNDATION

Giving Contact
Medda Gudelsky, Secretary & Director
11900 Tech Road
Silver Spring, MD 20904
Phone: (301)622-0100
Fax: (301)622-3507

Description
Founded: 1968
EIN: 520885969
Organization Type: Family Foundation
Giving Locations: DC: Washington; FL; MD
Grant Types: Capital, Project, Scholarship.

Donor Information
Founder: Established in 1968 by members of the Gudelsky family, Percontee, Inc., and Axcorp, Inc.

Financial Summary
Total Giving: $1,345,000 (2001)
Assets: $26,626,320 (2001)
Gifts Received: $8,888 (1993)

Typical Recipients
Arts & Humanities: Arts Centers, Arts Funds, Dance, History & Archaeology, Libraries, Museums/Galleries, Theater

Civic & Public Affairs: Clubs, Civic & Public Affairs-General, Hispanic Affairs, Parades/Festivals, Public Policy, Safety, Urban & Community Affairs, Women's Affairs, Zoos/Aquariums
Education: Arts/Humanities Education, Colleges & Universities, Education-General, International Studies, Medical Education, Private Education (Precollege), Public Education (Precollege), Student Aid
Environment: Protection, Resource Conservation
Health: Cancer, Clinics/Medical Centers, Emergency/Ambulance Services, Hospices, Hospitals, Long-Term Care, Mental Health, Research/Studies Institutes
Religion: Churches, Jewish Causes, Religious Organizations, Religious Welfare, Synagogues/Temples
Science: Science-General
Social Services: Child Welfare, Community Service Organizations, Family Services, Food/Clothing Distribution, Homes, Shelters/Homelessness, Substance Abuse, Veterans, Volunteer Services, Youth Organizations

Application Procedures
Initial Contact: Submit a written proposal.
Application Requirements: Applications should include a detailed account of why funds are sought.
Deadlines: None.

Foundation Officials
John Gudelsky: secretary, director B 1956. PRIM CORP EMPL president: Gudelsky Materials Inc.
Martha Gudelsky: president, director B 1922.
Medda Gudelsky: secretary, director PRIM CORP EMPL vice president: Homer Properties Inc.
Rita Regino: vice president, director B 1958. PRIM CORP EMPL president: 495 Trucking Inc. CORP AFFIL officer: Homer Properties Inc.
Holly Stone: vice president, director CORP AFFIL director: Homer Properties Inc.
Joseph Yedlin: treasurer, director PRIM CORP EMPL treasurer, assistant secretary, director: Percontee Inc. CORP AFFIL secretary: Homer Properties Inc.

Grants Analysis
Disclosure Period: calendar year ending 2001
Total Grants: $1,345,000
Number of Grants: 25
Average Grant: $35,208*
Highest Grant: $500,000
Lowest Grant: $1,000
Typical Range: $5,000 to $25,000 and $100,000 to $500,000
*****Note:** Average grant figure excludes highest grant.

Recent Grants
Note: Grants derived from 2002 Form 990.
General

500,000	Mori Kami Museum, Delray Beach, FL -- assists with religious, charitable and educational activities of donee
160,000	Baltimore Zoo, Baltimore, MD -- for religious, charitable and educational activities of donee
160,000	Florence Fuller Child Develop, Boca Raton, FL -- offers religious, charitable and educational activities of donee
100,000	Atlantic General Hospital, Berlin, MD -- assists with religious, charitable and educational activities of donee
100,000	Beth Israel Synagogue, Salisbury, MD -- offers religious, charitable and educational activities of donee
100,000	Capitol College, Laurel, MD -- provides religious, charitable and educational activities of donee
100,000	Mobile Medical Care, Rockville, MD -- provides religious, charitable and educational activities of donee
100,000	Oseh Shalom, Laurel, MD -- assists with religious, charitable and educational activities of donee

25,000	Boca Raton Community Hospital, Boca Raton, FL -- offers religious, charitable and educational activities of donee
25,000	Boca's Promise, Boca Raton, FL -- for religious, charitable and educational activities of donee

HARRY FRANK GUGGENHEIM FOUNDATION

Giving Contact

Karen Colvard, Program Officer
527 Madison Avenue, 15th Floor
New York, NY 10022-4304
Phone: (212)644-4909
Fax: (212)644-5110
E-mail: hfgacf@aol.com
Web: http://www.hfg.org

Description

Founded: 1929
EIN: 136043471
Organization Type: General Purpose Foundation
Giving Locations: nationally and internationally.
Grant Types: Employee Matching Gifts, Fellowship, Matching, Project, Research.

Donor Information

Founder: The foundation was established in 1929 by the late Harry Frank Guggenheim.

Financial Summary

Total Giving: $816,158 (2003); $1,026,212 (2002); $1,800,000 (2001 approx)
Giving Analysis: Giving for 2003 includes: foundation grants to United Way ($1,000); foundation matching gifts ($57,943); foundation gifts to individuals ($697,715); 2001: foundation gifts to individuals ($120,000); foundation matching gifts ($628,654)
Assets: $71,612,076 (2003); $77,628,490 (2002 approx); $78,000,000 (2001 approx)

Typical Recipients

Arts & Humanities: Ethnic & Folk Arts, History & Archaeology, Libraries, Literary Arts, Museums/Galleries, Music, Theater
Civic & Public Affairs: Chambers of Commerce, Community Foundations, Ethnic Organizations, Civic & Public Affairs-General, Nonprofit Management, Philanthropic Organizations, Professional & Trade Associations, Public Policy, Safety, Urban & Community Affairs, Women's Affairs
Education: Arts/Humanities Education, Colleges & Universities, Education Reform, Education-General, International Studies, Leadership Training, Medical Education, Public Education (Precollege), Science/Mathematics Education, Social Sciences Education, Student Aid
Environment: Environment-General
Health: Alzheimer's Disease, Children's Health/Hospitals, Eyes/Blindness, Health Funds, Health Organizations, Hospitals, Kidney, Medical Research
International: Foreign Educational Institutions, International-General, Health Care/Hospitals, Human Rights, International Affairs, International Organizations, International Peace & Security Issues
Religion: Churches, Jewish Causes, Religious Organizations, Synagogues/Temples
Science: Scientific Centers & Institutes, Scientific Research
Social Services: Child Abuse, Child Welfare, Crime Prevention, Family Services, People with Disabilities, Substance Abuse, United Funds/United Ways, Youth Organizations

Application Procedures

Initial Contact: Request a title page and abstract form from the foundation. Submit four copies of a typewritten application in English.
Application Requirements: Applications for research grants should include the title page, the abstract including a description of the project in plain English and its relevance to human dominance, aggression, and violence; curricula vitae and lists of relevant publications for the principal investigator and all professional personnel; an IRS tax-exempt determination letter if proposal is submitted by an institution; a budget in U.S. dollars with justification of each item; a research plan discussing the specific aims, background, and significance of the project; a description of other sources of support; a discussion of how subjects used in the research will be protected; and referee's comments. Applications for dissertation fellowships should include the title page, abstract, advisor's letter, applicant's background, research plan, description of how subjects will be protected, and a list of facilities and resources already available for the proposed research.
Deadlines: New applications for research grants must be received by August 1 for consideration at the December board meeting; applications for continuation may be submitted by August 1 for a decision in December or February 1 for a decision at the June board meeting. Applications for dissertation fellowships must be received by February 1 for a decision in June.
Review Process: Applicants will be informed promptly by letter of the board's decision.
Notes: Faxed applications will not be accepted.

Restrictions

The foundation will not fund overhead costs of institutions, professional meetings and conferences, self-education, elaborate fixed equipment, travel costs, or support while completing the requirements for advanced degrees (apart from those indirectly involved in research assistantships or those awarded through the Dissertation Fellowship program).

Additional Information

The foundation generally gives about 30 research grants and 10 dissertation awards. The research grants range from $15,000 to $35,000; the dissertation awards are $15,000 each.
Publications: Biennial Report; Application Guidelines; Application Form

Foundation Officials

William Oliver Baker: director B Chestertown, MD July 15, 1915. ED Washington College BS (1935); Princeton University PhD (1938). PRIM CORP EMPL director: Summit Trust Co. CORP AFFIL director: General America Investors Co. Inc. NONPR AFFIL advisory council: Special Libraries Association; member, vice chairman: Robert A. Welch Foundation; member: Sigma Xi; visiting lectr: Princeton University; chairman emeritus: Rockefeller University; member: Omicron Delta Kappa; member: Phi Lambda Upsilon; visiting lectr: Northwestern University; member: New Jersey Commission Science & Technology; member advisory council: New Jersey Regional Medicine Library; member: National Materials Program; member: National Security Council Organization Federal Telecommunications System; member: National Cancer Plan; member: National Academy Engineering; member: National Academy Sciences; member council: Marconi Fellowships; chairman emeritus: Andrew W. Mellon Foundation; member: Institute Medicine; member: Industrial Research Institute; co-sponsor: Institute Materials Research; visiting lectr: Duke University; fellow: Franklin Institute; member visitors committee science & math: Drew University; member: Council Trends Perspectives; member: Directors Industry Research; member science advisory board: Committee Science Technology; director: Council Library Resources; member:

Carnegie Forum Education Science Technology & Economic; fellow: American Physical Society; trustee: Charles Babbage Institute; fellow: American Institute Chemists; trustee: American Philosophical Society; member: American Chemical Society; fellow: American Academy of Arts & Sciences; co-chairman national council: American Association Advancement Science. CLUB AFFIL Princeton Northwestern New Jersey Club; honorary member: Chemists Club New York; Cosmos Club.
Peyton S. Cochran, Jr.: director B 1916. ED University of Virginia BA (1950). PRIM CORP EMPL senior vice president, director: Rouse Co. of Saint Louis. CORP AFFIL senior vice president: Governors Square Inc.; senior vice president, director: Salem Mall Inc.; senior vice president: Charlottetown Inc.; senior vice president: Franklin Park Mall Inc.
Karen Colvard: senior program officer
Howard Graves: director
Donald Charles Hood: director B North Merrick, NY 1942. ED State University of New York Harper College BA (1965); Brown University MSc (1968); Brown University PhD (1969). PRIM NONPR EMPL professor psychology: Columbia University. NONPR AFFIL trustee, vice chairman: Smith College; member: Society Experimental Psychology; member: Optical Society of America; James F. Bender professor psychology: Columbia University; member: Eastern Psychology Association; fellow: American Psychonomics Society; member: Association Research Vision & Opthalmology; member: American Association Advancement Science; member: American Association University Professors.
Joseph A. Koenigsberger: treasurer
Carol Langstaff: director
Lewis H. Lapham: director
Peter Orman Lawson-Johnston, II: director B New York, NY 1927. ED University of Virginia (1951). PRIM CORP EMPL senior partner: Guggenheim Brothers PRIM NONPR EMPL pres, trust: Lawrenceville School. CORP AFFIL chairman, director: Zemex Corp.; director: National Review; president, director: Elgerbar Corp.; director: Feldspar Corp. NONPR AFFIL president: Lawrenceville School.
Gillian Lindt: director
Theodore Davidge Lockwood: director B Hanover, NH 1924. ED Trinity College BA (1948); Princeton University MA (1950); Princeton University PhD (1952). NONPR AFFIL member: Phi Beta Kappa; member: Pi Gamma Mu; member: Association American Colleges; member: Greater Hartford Chamber of Commerce.
Tania L-J. McCleery: director
Jeremiah Milbank, III: director ED Trinity College BA (1970); Stanford University MBA (1973); University of Virginia JD (1980). PRIM CORP EMPL chairman: Milbank Associate ADD CORP EMPL vice president: Cypress Woods Corp.; vice president: Turkey Hill Plantation; president: Winthrop Milbank & Co.
Lois Dickson Rice: director B Portland, ME 1933. ED Radcliffe College AB (1954); Columbia University (1954-1955). CORP AFFIL director: UNUM Corp.; director: International Multifoods Corp.; director: McGraw-Hill Inc.; director: Hartford Steam Boiler Inspection & Insurance Co.; director: Fleet Financial Group. NONPR AFFIL member: President Foreign Intelligence Advisory Board; director: Reading Is Fundamental; member: Phi Beta Kappa; guest scholar: Brookings Institute Program Economic Studies; trustee: CNA Corp. Public Agenda Foundation. CLUB AFFIL Cosmos Club.
Mary-Alice Yates: secretary

Grants Analysis

Disclosure Period: calendar year ending 2003
Total Grants: $59,500*
Number of Grants: 8
Average Grant: $4,214*
Highest Grant: $30,000
Lowest Grant: $1,000
Typical Range: $1,000 to $10,000
*Note: Giving excludes matching gifts, gifts to individ-

uals, United Way. Average grant figure excludes highest grant.

Recent Grants

Note: Grants derived from 2002 Form 990.
General

30,000	Friends for Long Island's Heritage, Syosset, NY -- for Falaise museum upkeep
10,000	International Peace Academy, New York, NY -- for International Peace Academy policy award
10,000	Solomon R. Guggenheim Foundation, New York, NY
5,000	UJA-Federation, New York, NY
1,500	Foundation Center, New York, NY
1,000	Middleton Place Foundation, Charleston, SC
1,000	Star Foundation Inc., New York, NY
1,000	United Hospital Fund, New York, NY
1,000	United Way of New York City, New York, NY

GULF COAST MEDICAL FOUNDATION

Giving Contact

Mr. Dee McElroy, Executive Vice President & Foundation Manager
135 West Elm, PO Box 30
PO Box 30
Wharton, TX 77488
Phone: (979)532-0904
Web: http://www.gulfcoastmedical.com

Description

Founded: 1983
EIN: 741285242
Organization Type: Private Foundation
Giving Locations: CO: Matagorda County, Wharton County; TX: Brazoria County, Fort Bend County, Fort Bend County
Grant Types: General Support.

Financial Summary

Total Giving: $703,600 (2002)
Assets: $13,912,889 (2002)

Typical Recipients

Arts & Humanities: Arts Festivals, History & Archaeology, Libraries, Museums/Galleries, Music, Theater
Civic & Public Affairs: Botanical Gardens/Parks, Clubs, Civic & Public Affairs-General, Municipalities/Towns, Nonprofit Management, Parades/Festivals, Safety, Urban & Community Affairs
Education: Afterschool/Enrichment Programs, Agricultural Education, Community & Junior Colleges, Education-General, International Exchange, Literacy, Medical Education, Public Education (Precollege), Science/Mathematics Education, Secondary Education (Public), Student Aid, Vocational & Technical Education
Health: Cancer, Children's Health/Hospitals, Clinics/Medical Centers, Diabetes, Emergency/Ambulance Services, Geriatric Health, Health Organizations, Hospices, Long-Term Care, Mental Health, Nursing Services, Nutrition, Preventive Medicine/Wellness Organizations, Public Health, Transplant Networks/Donor Banks
Religion: Churches, Ministries, Religious Welfare
Science: Scientific Centers & Institutes
Social Services: At-Risk Youth, Child Welfare, Community Centers, Community Service Organizations, Crime Prevention, Day Care, Emergency Relief, Food/Clothing Distribution, People with Disabilities, Recreation & Athletics, Senior Services, Shelters/Homelessness, YMCA/YWCA/YMHA/YWHA, Youth Organizations

Application Procedures

Initial Contact: Write a letter to the foundation requesting a grant application.
Deadlines: None.

Restrictions

Grants are made primarily for medically-related projects.

Additional Information

In 1995, foundation changed from a fiscal year ending May 31 to a calendar year.
Publications: Application Form; Guidelines

Foundation Officials

Laurance H. Armour, III: director
Laurance Hearne Armour, Jr.: director B Chicago, IL 1923. ED Princeton University AA (1945); Northwestern University (1947-1948). NONPR AFFIL member national board governors: Institute Living. CLUB AFFIL Shoreacres Club; New York Yacht Club; Onwentsia Club; Chicago Club; Chicago Yacht Club; Casino Club.
R. B. Caraway, MD: director
Charles Davis, Jr.: treasurer
Charles F. Drees: director
Kent Hill: president
Bert Huebner: director
Dee McElroy: executive vice president, foundation manager
Sylvan Miori: director
Irving Moore, Jr.: secretary B Wharton City, TX 1912. ED University of Texas LLB. CORP AFFIL director: Heritage Bank.
Jack Moore: vice president
Max Rotholz: director
Clive Runnells: director
Clive Runnells, III: director
David Stovall: director
Guy F. Stovall, III: director
C. E. Woodson, MD: director

Grants Analysis

Disclosure Period: calendar year ending 2002
Total Grants: $703,600
Number of Grants: 41
Average Grant: $17,161
Highest Grant: $100,000
Lowest Grant: $100
Typical Range: $5,000 to $50,000 and $2,000 to $25,000

Recent Grants

Note: Grants derived from 2002 Form 990.
General

100,000	Wharton County Junior College, Wharton, TX -- for Management Information System Project
65,500	City of Wharton, Wharton, TX -- for ambulance
60,000	Northside Health Center, El Campo, TX -- for technology, equipment and furnishings for Education Center
50,000	Boys and Girls Club of Wharton, Inc., Wharton, TX -- operating support
50,000	East Fort Bend Human Needs Ministry, Inc., Stafford, TX -- capital campaign
50,000	Lifeline Chaplaincy, Houston, TX -- for Compassionate Touch Program
32,500	East Bernard Volunteer Fire Department, East Bernard, TX -- for the purchase of personal protective equipment
25,000	Brookwood Community, Brookshire, TX -- for construction and implementation of continuing care facility
25,000	Matagorda County Women's Crisis, Matagorda, TX -- for remodeling of new facility
20,000	Matagorda County Women's Crisis, Matagorda, TX -- for family violence seminars

GULF POWER CO.

Company Headquarters

1 Energy Pl.
Pensacola, FL 32520
Web: http://www.gulfpower.com

Company Description

Assets: US$807 million (2001)
Employees: 1500 (2001)
SIC(s): 4911 Electric Services.
Parent Company: Southern Co., Atlanta, GA, United States

Nonmonetary Support

Volunteer Programs: Company reports that it supports, "Junior Achievement, (charity) runs and holiday shopping."

Gulf Power Foundation

Giving Contact

Bernard Jacob, Chairman
1 Energy Place
Pensacola, FL 32520-0786
Phone: (850)444-6806

Alternate Contact

500 Bayfront Parkway
Pensacola, FL 32501
Phone: (850)444-6206

Description

Founded: 1987
EIN: 592817740
Organization Type: Corporate Foundation
Giving Locations: Northwest Florida.
Grant Types: Employee Matching Gifts, General Support, Scholarship.

Donor Information

Founder: Gulf Power Company

Financial Summary

Total Giving: $240,001 (2003); $195,743 (2002); $209,548 (2001)
Giving Analysis: Giving for 2001 includes: foundation matching gifts ($4,395); foundation scholarships ($12,000); foundation grants to United Way ($64,353); foundation ($128,800)
Assets: $1,793,134 (2003); $419,170 (2002); $770,295 (2001)
Gifts Received: $1,500,000 (2003); $200 (1997); $1,082,484 (1993). Note: In 2003, contributions were received from Gulf Power Co. In 1997, contributions were received from J. Lewis Davidson.

Typical Recipients

Arts & Humanities: Arts Associations & Councils, Arts & Humanities-General, Historic Preservation, History & Archaeology, Libraries, Museums/Galleries, Music
Civic & Public Affairs: African American Affairs, Botanical Gardens/Parks, Chambers of Commerce, Community Foundations, Civic & Public Affairs-General, Housing, Parades/Festivals, Safety, Urban & Community Affairs, Women's Affairs
Education: Afterschool/Enrichment Programs, Agricultural Education, Business Education, Colleges & Universities, Community & Junior Colleges, Economic Education, Education Associations, Education Funds, Engineering/Technological Education, Education-General, Literacy, Student Aid
Environment: Environment-General, Protection, Resource Conservation, Wildlife Protection
Health: Cancer, Children's Health/Hospitals, Emergency/Ambulance Services, Health Funds, Health Organizations, Hospices, Hospitals, Prenatal Health Issues, Public Health, Single-Disease Health Associ-

ations, Transplant Networks/Donor Banks
Religion: Ministries, Religious Organizations, Religious Welfare, Social/Policy Issues
Science: Science Museums
Social Services: At-Risk Youth, Child Abuse, Child Welfare, Community Centers, Community Service Organizations, Counseling, Domestic Violence, Emergency Relief, Food/Clothing Distribution, Homes, People with Disabilities, Recreation & Athletics, Scouts, Senior Services, Shelters/Homelessness, Social Services-General, Substance Abuse, United Funds/United Ways, Veterans, Volunteer Services, YMCA/YWCA/YMHA/YWHA, Youth Organizations

Application Procedures
Initial Contact: Contact the foundation to obtain a Grant Request Form.
Deadlines: None.

Restrictions
The foundation does not support individuals or organizations outside service area.

Corporate Officials
Travis J. Bowden: chairman, president, chief executive officer, director B Greenville, AL 1938. ED University of Alabama (1960). PRIM CORP EMPL chairman, president, chief executive officer, director: Gulf Power Co.
Arlan Earl Scarbrough: vice president financial B Carnes, MS 1936. ED University of Southern Mississippi (1958); East Carolina University (1962). PRIM CORP EMPL vice president financial: Gulf Power Co. NONPR AFFIL member: American Institute CPAs.

Foundation Officials
Francis M. Fisher, Jr.: trustee
John E. Hodges, Jr.: chairman PRIM CORP EMPL vice president: Gulf Power Co.
P. Bernard Jacob: chairman
Ronnie R. Labrato: trustee B Pensacola, FL 1953. ED University of West Florida (1974). PRIM CORP EMPL controller: Gulf Power Co.
Susan D. Ritenour: secretary, treasurer
Warren E. Tate: treasurer
Gene L. Ussery: trustee

Grants Analysis
Disclosure Period: calendar year ending 2003
Total Grants: $149,200*
Number of Grants: 48
Average Grant: $2,643*
Highest Grant: $25,000
Lowest Grant: $500
Typical Range: $1,000 to $5,000
*Note: Giving excludes matching gifts, scholarship, and United Way. Average grant figure excludes highest grant.

Recent Grants
Note: Grants derived from 2003 Form 990.
Library-Related

2,500	Bay County Library Foundation, Panama City, FL

General

32,661	United Way of Escambia County, Pensacola, FL
25,000	Pensacola Junior College, Pensacola, FL
15,049	United Way of Northwest Florida, Panama City, FL
10,443	United Way of Santa Rosa County, Milton, FL
10,000	Air Force Armament Museum Foundation, Pensacola, FL
10,000	Naval Aviation Museum Foundation, Pensacola, FL
10,000	YMCA of Greater Pensacola, Pensacola, FL
8,468	United Way of Okaloosa, Ft. Walton Beach, FL

7,500	Baptist Health Care Foundation, Pensacola, FL
5,000	Arts Council of Northwest Florida, Pensacola, FL

JOSEPHINE GUMBINER FOUNDATION

Giving Contact
Julie Meenan, Executive Director
401 E. Ocean View Blvd., Suite 503
Long Beach, CA 90802
Phone: (562)437-2882

Description
Founded: 1989
EIN: 330345249
Organization Type: Private Foundation
Giving Locations: CA: Long Beach; FL; TX
Grant Types: General Support.

Donor Information
Founder: Established in 1989 by the late Josephine S. Gumbiner.

Financial Summary
Total Giving: $602,257 (2001)
Assets: $13,917,615 (2001)
Gifts Received: $9,855 (1999); $100,000 (1998); $250,000 (1996). Note: In 1998, contributions were received from the Gumbiner Family Foundation. In 1996, contributions were received from Josephine S. Gumbiner.

Typical Recipients
Arts & Humanities: Arts Appreciation, Arts Outreach, Ballet, Dance, Ethnic & Folk Arts, Libraries, Museums/Galleries, Music, Opera, Performing Arts, Theater
Civic & Public Affairs: Asian American Affairs, Botanical Gardens/Parks, Clubs, Economic Development, Employment/Job Training, Civic & Public Affairs-General, Hispanic Affairs, Housing, Legal Aid, Nonprofit Management, Urban & Community Affairs, Women's Affairs, Zoos/Aquariums
Education: Afterschool/Enrichment Programs, Arts/Humanities Education, Business Education, Colleges & Universities, Community & Junior Colleges, Education Reform, Elementary Education (Public), Faculty Development, Education-General, Literacy, Preschool Education, Social Sciences Education, Special Education, Student Aid
Health: AIDS/HIV, Alzheimer's Disease, Children's Health/Hospitals, Clinics/Medical Centers, Emergency/Ambulance Services, Heart, Hospices, Medical Research, Medical Training, Mental Health, Prenatal Health Issues, Respiratory
Religion: Churches, Jewish Causes, Religious Welfare
Social Services: At-Risk Youth, Big Brothers/Big Sisters, Child Welfare, Community Service Organizations, Counseling, Day Care, Domestic Violence, Emergency Relief, Family Planning, Family Services, Food/Clothing Distribution, People with Disabilities, Recreation & Athletics, Scouts, Sexual Abuse, Shelters/Homelessness, Social Services-General, Substance Abuse, Volunteer Services, YMCA/YWCA/YMHA/YWHA, Youth Organizations

Application Procedures
Initial Contact: Telephone contact person to request application and guidelines.
Application Requirements: In a complete proposal include the grant application; two-page proposal letter, containing history of organization, statement of need, current accomplishments, description of program, project strategies; one-page project budget; fi-

nancial statements; operating budget; revenue; list of anticipated outcomes; one-paragraph resumes of staff; list of Board of Directors; list of volunteers; and a copy of recent IRS (c) (3) letter.
Deadlines: None.
Review Process: Board of Directors meets quarterly to consider new funding.

Restrictions
The foundation does not make grants to individuals, political or lobbying groups, or any organizations that discriminate on the basis of race, creed, sexual orientation, or national origin.

Additional Information
In 1998, the Gumbiner Family Foundation merged with the Josephine S. Gumbiner Foundation. The organization has an interest in women's and children's issues.
Publications: Application Form; Guidelines

Foundation Officials
Beth Campbell: director
Beth Campbell: director
Art Gottlieb: secretary
Alis Gumbiner: cfo, vp
Burke F. Gumbiner: chief financial officer
Lee Gumbiner: vice president
Julie Meenan: executive director
Dennis Rockway: director

Grants Analysis
Disclosure Period: calendar year ending 2001
Total Grants: $602,257*
Number of Grants: 55
Average Grant: $9,586*
Highest Grant: $37,500
Typical Range: $5,000 to $20,000
*Note: Average grant figure excludes two highest grants. ($75,000).

Recent Grants
Note: Grants derived from 2001 Form 990.
Library-Related

11,700	Long Beach Public Library Foundation, Long Beach, CA

General

37,500	Habitat for Humanity, Immokalee, FL
37,500	SCADD
25,000	Long Beach Nonprofit Partnership, Long Beach, CA
20,500	Boys & Girls Club, Pontiac, IL
20,000	Liberty Hill Foundation, Santa Monica, CA
18,750	Lutheran Social Services, Austin, TX
18,500	Robin Hood Foundation, New York, NY
15,000	Children's Clinic, Long Beach, CA
15,000	Harbor Area Halfway Houses
15,000	Jewish Family and Children's Service, Inc., Baltimore, MD

GEOFFREY GUND FOUNDATION

Giving Contact
Geoffrey Gund, Trustee
40 E. 94th St., Apt. 28-E
New York, NY 10128
Phone: (212)689-3075

Alternate Contact
8075 Leesburg Pike
Vienna, VA 22182

Description
Founded: 1991
EIN: 521509128

Organization Type: Private Foundation
Giving Locations: no restrictions.
Grant Types: Research, Scholarship.

Donor Information

Founder: Established in 1991 by Geoffrey and Felicity Gund.

Financial Summary

Gifts Received: $150,000 (fiscal year ending June 30, 1999); $256,521 (fiscal 1998); $1,300,000 (fiscal 1996). Note: In fiscal 1998 and 1999, contributions were received from Geoffrey Gund.

Typical Recipients

Arts & Humanities: Arts Associations & Councils, Ballet, Film & Video, Arts & Humanities-General, Historic Preservation, History & Archaeology, Libraries, Museums/Galleries, Music, Performing Arts
Civic & Public Affairs: Botanical Gardens/Parks, Civic & Public Affairs-General, Philanthropic Organizations, Public Policy, Women's Affairs
Education: Arts/Humanities Education, Colleges & Universities, Education Funds, Education-General, Minority Education, Private Education (Precollege), Science/Mathematics Education, Student Aid
Environment: Environment-General, Resource Conservation, Wildlife Protection
Health: Emergency/Ambulance Services, Eyes/Blindness, Hospitals, Medical Research, Mental Health
International: Foreign Educational Institutions, Health Care/Hospitals
Religion: Churches, Religion-General, Religious Welfare
Social Services: Child Welfare, Community Service Organizations, Day Care, Family Planning, Food/Clothing Distribution, Recreation & Athletics, Senior Services

Application Procedures

Initial Contact: The foundation has no formal grant application procedure or application form. Send a brief letter of inquiry.
Deadlines: None.

Additional Information

Trust(s): Key Trust Co OH NA

Foundation Officials

Geoffrey de Conde Gund: trustee ED Harvard University (1964).
Donald Kozusko: trustee
James O'Hara: trustee

Grants Analysis

Disclosure Period: fiscal year ending June 30, 2000
Total Grants: $874,140*
Number of Grants: 20
Average Grant: $23,563*
Highest Grant: $300,000
Typical Range: $10,000 to $50,000
*Note: Giving excludes scholarships. Average grant figure excludes two highest grants ($450,000).

Recent Grants

Note: Grants derived from fiscal 2001 Form 990.
General

300,000	Groton School, Groton, MA -- for teaching chair
200,000	National Financial Services Corporation Money Market Pool -- for further gifting
150,000	Ethical Culture Fieldston School, New York, NY -- for operating expenses
100,000	Groton School, Groton, MA -- for scholarship fund
25,000	Museum of Modern Art, New York, NY -- for operating expenses
17,500	Riverdale Presbyterian Church, Bronx, NY -- for stewardship fund
15,000	Foundation Fighting Blindness, Princeton, NJ -- for operating expenses
15,000	Wave Hill, Bronx, NY -- for operating expenses
15,000	Wave Hill, Bronx, NY -- for Garden Access Program
10,000	Cleveland Orchestra, Cleveland, OH -- for sustaining fund

GEORGE GUND FOUNDATION

Giving Contact

David T. Abbott, Executive Director
45 Prospect Avenue West
1845 Guildhall Building
Cleveland, OH 44115
Phone: (216)241-3114
Fax: (216)241-6560
E-mail: info@gundfdn.org
Web: http://www.gundfdn.org

Description

Founded: 1952
EIN: 346519769
Organization Type: General Purpose Foundation
Giving Locations: OH: Cleveland including northeastern Ohio region
Grant Types: General Support, Project, Seed Money.

Donor Information

Founder: Established in 1952 by the late George Gund (d. 1966), former chairman of the board of the Cleveland Trust Company. Mr. Gund was involved in banking and real estate in Seattle, military intelligence during World War I, the Kaffee-Hag Corporation in Cleveland, animal husbandry in Iowa, and ranching in Nevada. He was also devoted to the arts, serving as president of the Cleveland Art Institute; and education, serving as a trustee at several institutions of higher education.

Financial Summary

Total Giving: $19,078,471 (2003); $19,556,406 (2002); $20,345,592 (2001)
Assets: $448,453,097 (2003); $397,249,175 (2002); $424,502,237 (2001)

Typical Recipients

Arts & Humanities: Arts Associations & Councils, Arts Centers, Arts Institutes, Community Arts, Dance, Ethnic & Folk Arts, Film & Video, Arts & Humanities-General, Historic Preservation, History & Archaeology, Libraries, Museums/Galleries, Music, Opera, Performing Arts, Public Broadcasting, Theater
Civic & Public Affairs: African American Affairs, Botanical Gardens/Parks, Business/Free Enterprise, Civil Rights, Clubs, Community Foundations, Economic Development, Economic Policy, Employment/Job Training, Civic & Public Affairs-General, Housing, Inner-City Development, Law & Justice, Legal Aid, Municipalities/Towns, Parades/Festivals, Philanthropic Organizations, Public Policy, Urban & Community Affairs, Women's Affairs
Education: Afterschool/Enrichment Programs, Arts/Humanities Education, Colleges & Universities, Community & Junior Colleges, Education Funds, Education Reform, Engineering/Technological Education, Environmental Education, Faculty Development, Education-General, Leadership Training, Minority Education, Preschool Education, Public Education (Precollege), Science/Mathematics Education, Student Aid, Vocational & Technical Education
Environment: Air/Water Quality, Energy, Environment-General, Protection, Resource Conservation
Health: AIDS/HIV, Children's Health/Hospitals, Clinics/Medical Centers, Emergency/Ambulance Services, Eyes/Blindness, Health Policy/Cost Containment, Health Organizations, Hospitals, Single-Disease Health Associations
International: International Environmental Issues
Religion: Dioceses, Jewish Causes, Ministries, Religious Organizations, Religious Welfare
Science: Science Museums, Scientific Centers & Institutes
Social Services: Child Welfare, Community Centers, Community Service Organizations, Counseling, Crime Prevention, Day Care, Family Planning, Family Services, Food/Clothing Distribution, People with Disabilities, Recreation & Athletics, Social Services-General, United Funds/United Ways, Veterans, YMCA/YWCA/YMHA/YWHA, Youth Organizations

Application Procedures

Initial Contact: Organizations should send a proposal addressed to the executive director.
Application Requirements: Applications must include a one-page cover letter describing the project and the amount being requested. The proposal should also include a one page summary of the project, name and telephone number of contact person, organizational background, need for project implementation, project objectives, project budget, anticipated income including information about other sources approached for funding, steps in implementation, time frame, qualifications of key personnel to be involved, and method of project evaluation. Also include list of current board of trustees, current budget, a proposed budget for the project year(s) showing both income and expenses, copy of IRS classification letter, recent audited financial statement, outline of sources of income, letters of support, and readily available printed material about the organization such as annual reports and brochures.
Deadlines: Submit requests by March 30, June 30, September 30, and December 30 for consideration at the next regularly scheduled meeting of the trustees in March, June, September, and December.
Review Process: Proposals are screened and evaluated by the staff before presentation at the trustees' meeting. Organizations submitting proposals outside of the foundation's priorities and guidelines will be notified promptly. Preference is given to pilot projects, innovative programs, and research endeavors which promise significant benefits and broad application. Grantees must be able to demonstrate administrative capabilities for programs funded and provide periodic reports and a financial account of how funds have been utilized.

Restrictions

No support is given to carry on propaganda, influence legislation and elections, or for voter registration drives; for endowments or capital needs, including renovation, equipment and construction; for debt reduction or to fund benefit events; for services to the physically, mentally or developmentally disabled or the elderly; to individuals; or for purposes and activities outside of the United States. Proposals sent electronically or by fax are not accepted.

Additional Information

Publications: Annual Report (including Application Guidelines)

Foundation Officials

David T. Abbott: executive director B Fremont, OH. ED Denison University BA; Columbia University MS (1975); Harvard University Law School JD (1982).
Marjorie M. Carlson: trustee
Marcia Egbert: senior program officer ED Ohio State University JD; Ohio State University BA. NONPR AFFIL founding board member: Health Policy Institute of Ohio; member: Public Policy Committee of Ohio Grantmakers Forum; member: Grantmakers Income Security Task Force; member: Early Childhood Funders Collaborative; member: Funders Network on Reproductive Health and Rights.
Deena M. Epstein: senior program officer ED Ohio University BS. NONPR AFFIL advisory: Community

Partnership for Arts and Culture; member: Northeast Ohio Advisory Committee of Ohio Grantmakers Forum.

Ann Landreth Gund: secretary, trustee NONPR AFFIL chairman: The Skowhegan School of Painting & Sculpture.

Catherine Gund: trustee NONPR AFFIL co-founder: Third Wave Foundation.

Geoffrey de Conde Gund: president, treasurer, trustee ED Harvard University (1964).

George Gund, III: trustee B Cleveland, OH 1937. ED Case Western Reserve University School of Business Administration. PRIM CORP EMPL chairman: Northstar Financial Corp. CORP AFFIL vice president hockey: Sun Valley Ice Skating Inc.; vice chairman: Gund Investment Corp.; chairman: North Stars Metro Center Management Corp.; film producer: Caipirinha Productions; co-owner: Cleveland Cavaliers; director: Ameritrust Cleveland. NONPR AFFIL director: Sundance Institute; director: University Nevada-Reno Foundation; advisory council: Sierra Club Foundation; director: Sun Valley Center Arts & Humanities; chairman: San Francisco International Film Festival; director: San Francisco Museum Art; member sponsors council: Project Population Action; member international council: Museum Modern Art; collectors committee: National Gallery Art; director: Cleveland Health Museum; director: Cleveland International Film Festival; director: Bay Area Education Television Association; director: California Theatre Foundation. CLUB AFFIL University Club; Union Club; Rainier Club; Rowfant Club; Olympic Club; Cleveland Athletic Club; Kirtland Country Club; California Tennis Club.

Llura A. Gund: vice president, trustee CORP AFFIL president: Gund Investment Corp..

Zachary Gund: trustee

Robert B. Jaquay: associate director ED Cleveland State University MBA; Cleveland State University JD; Harvard University MBA; John Carroll University BS. NONPR AFFIL chairman, advisory board: Foundation Center, Cleveland; treasurer: Neighborhood Funders Group.

Jon Mark Jensen: senior program officer B Norristown, PA 1953. ED Albright College BS (1975); Bucknell University MS (1980). PRIM CORP EMPL president, director: Intecon Inc. NONPR AFFIL founding member: Environmental Grantmakers Association; chairman: Funders Network for Smart Growth and Livable Communities.

Robert Davis Storey: trustee B Tuskegee, AL 1936. ED Harvard University AB (1958); Case Western Reserve University JD (1964). PRIM CORP EMPL partner: Thompson Hine LLP. CORP AFFIL director: Verizon Communications Inc.; director: Procter & Gamble Co. NONPR AFFIL member: Society Benchers; trustee: Spelman College; member: Cleveland Bar Association; member: Alpha Phi Alpha Fraternity; trustee: Case Western Reserve University. CLUB AFFIL University Club; Union Club; Ponce de Leon Club; Rowfant Club.

Grants Analysis

Disclosure Period: calendar year ending 2003
Total Grants: $19,078,471
Number of Grants: 434
Average Grant: $39,533*
Highest Grant: $1,000,000
Lowest Grant: $500
Typical Range: $5,000 to $50,000
***Note:** Average grant figure excludes two highest grants ($2,000,000).

Recent Grants

Note: Grants derived from 2003 Form 990.
General

1,000,000	Foundation Fighting Blindness, Owing Mills, MD -- towards retinal degenerative disease research
1,000,000	Foundation Fighting Blindness, Owing Mills, MD -- towards retinal degenerative disease research
750,000	Cleveland Foundation, Cleveland, OH -- towards the fund for our economic future
500,000	Great Lakes Museum of Science, Environment and Technology, Cleveland, OH -- towards leadership grant
250,000	BioEnterprise Corporation, Cleveland, OH
250,000	Case Western Reserve University, Cleveland, OH -- towards president's initiative fund
250,000	Neighborhood Progress Inc., Cleveland, OH
250,000	Neighborhood Progress Inc., Cleveland, OH
250,000	Neighborhood Progress Inc., Cleveland, OH
210,000	Community Partnership for Arts and Culture, Cleveland, OH

STELLA AND CHARLES GUTTMAN FOUNDATION

Giving Contact

Elizabeth Olofson, Executive Director
122 E. 42nd St., Suite 2010
New York, NY 10168
Phone: (212)371-7082
Fax: (212)371-8936
E-mail: info@guttmanfdn.org
Web: http://www.fdncenter.org/grantmaker/guttman/

Description

Founded: 1959
EIN: 136103039
Organization Type: General Purpose Foundation
Giving Locations: NY: New York including metropolitan area; Israel
Grant Types: General Support, Operating Expenses, Project.

Donor Information

Founder: Incorporated in 1959 by the late Charles Guttman and the late Stella Guttman.

Financial Summary

Total Giving: $1,709,570 (2003); $1,872,234 (2002); $2,142,720 (2001)
Giving Analysis: Giving for 2002 includes: foundation scholarships ($5,000); foundation grants to United Way ($40,000); 2001: foundation scholarships ($25,000); foundation grants to United Way ($40,000)
Assets: $42,266,205 (2002); $48,675,149 (2001)

Typical Recipients

Arts & Humanities: Arts Associations & Councils, Dance, Arts & Humanities-General, Libraries, Museums/Galleries, Music, Public Broadcasting
Civic & Public Affairs: African American Affairs, Asian American Affairs, Botanical Gardens/Parks, Community Foundations, Employment/Job Training, Ethnic Organizations, Civic & Public Affairs-General, Hispanic Affairs, Law & Justice, Legal Aid, Public Policy, Safety, Urban & Community Affairs
Education: Afterschool/Enrichment Programs, Arts/Humanities Education, Colleges & Universities, Education Associations, Education Funds, Education Reform, Elementary Education (Public), Environmental Education, Faculty Development, Education-General, Health & Physical Education, International Studies, Legal Education, Literacy, Medical Education, Minority Education, Preschool Education, Public Education (Precollege), Religious Education, Science/Mathematics Education, Social Sciences Education, Special Education, Student Aid
Environment: Air/Water Quality, Environment-General
Health: Adolescent Health Issues, AIDS/HIV, Alzheimer's Disease, Cancer, Children's Health/Hospitals, Diabetes, Emergency/Ambulance Services, Eyes/Blindness, Geriatric Health, Health Policy/Cost Containment, Health Organizations, Heart, Hospitals, Medical Research, Mental Health, Nutrition, Prenatal Health Issues, Public Health, Single-Disease Health Associations
International: Foreign Educational Institutions, Health Care/Hospitals, Human Rights, International Development, International Peace & Security Issues, International Relations, International Relief Efforts, Missionary/Religious Activities
Religion: Churches, Jewish Causes, Religious Organizations, Religious Welfare
Science: Scientific Centers & Institutes, Scientific Research
Social Services: At-Risk Youth, Big Brothers/Big Sisters, Camps, Child Welfare, Community Centers, Community Service Organizations, Counseling, Day Care, Delinquency & Criminal Rehabilitation, Family Planning, Family Services, Homes, People with Disabilities, Recreation & Athletics, Senior Services, Shelters/Homelessness, Social Services-General, Substance Abuse, United Funds/United Ways, Volunteer Services, YMCA/YWCA/YMHA/YWHA, Youth Organizations

Application Procedures

Initial Contact: Applicants should send a request for funding three to five pages in length.
Application Requirements: Request for funding should include; a statement of the need for the project and population served; explanation of program that will meet need; description of intended results; amount requested; detailed project budget; other sources of support;; summary of staff and board qualifications; current financial statement; most recent IRS Form 990; IRS tax exempt letter; and signed statement by CEO or Chairman that proposal is accurate.
Deadlines: None.
Review Process: The Board of Directors meets at least three times a year to review proposals.
Notes: The Foundation also accepts the New York area common application form.

Restrictions

The foundation does not make grants to religious organizations for religious purposes, public interest litigation, anti-vivisectionist causes, individuals, organizations not qualified as charitable, or for foreign travel or study.

Additional Information

Publications: Funding Guidelines; Application Procedures

Foundation Officials

Charles S. Brenner: director
Edgar H. Brenner: vice president, director B New York, NY 1930. ED Carleton College BA (1951); Yale University JD (1954). PRIM NONPR EMPL national director: Behavioral Law Center. NONPR AFFIL codirector: International University Center Legal Studies; vis. res. professor. law: National Law Center; director: Institute Behavior Resources; fellow: College Problems Drug Dependency; senior counsel terrorism studies program: George Washington University; member: American Bar Association; president, chairman board: Americans Medical Progress. CLUB AFFIL member: Explorers Club; member: Yale Club.
Robert S. Gassman: treasurer, director
Peter A. Herbert: president, director
Elizabeth Olofson: executive director
Sonia Rosenberg: director
Ernest Rubenstein: secretary, director NONPR AFFIL director: Covenant House.

Grants Analysis

Disclosure Period: calendar year ending 2002
Total Grants: $1,827,234*
Number of Grants: 106

Average Grant: $16,545*
Highest Grant: $90,000
Lowest Grant: $500
Typical Range: $5,000 to $25,000
*Note: Giving excludes scholarships and United Way. Average grant figure excludes highest grant.

Recent Grants

Note: Grants derived from 2002 Form 990.
General

95,000	New Israel fund, Washington, DC
50,000	United Jewish Appeal - Federation of Jewish Philanthropies of New York Inc., New York, NY
40,000	New Israel fund, Washington, DC
40,000	United Way of New York City, New York, NY -- toward the Child Care and Early Education Fund
40,000	Yedid, Jerusalem Israel -- for support of Yedid's volunteer-based Citizens Rights Centers
30,000	Elders Share the Arts Inc., Brooklyn, NY -- toward a program that uses trained artists to work with the elderly in senior centers
30,000	Grand Street Settlement Inc., New York, NY -- for support of a service program for immigrant seniors
30,000	Lenox Hill Neighborhood House, New York, NY -- toward a caregiver program to improve the care of frail seniors living at home
30,000	Medicare Rights Center, New York, NY -- toward development of an interactive Medicare counseling and assistance system
30,000	Yale University Law School, New Haven, CT -- toward the Middle East Legal Studies Seminar

H. C. S. FOUNDATION

Giving Contact

L. Thomas Hiltz, Trustee
1801 East 9th Street, Suite 1035
Cleveland, OH 44114-3103
Phone: (216)781-3502
Fax: (216)781-3504

Description

Founded: 1959
EIN: 346514235
Organization Type: General Purpose Foundation
Giving Locations: MD; OH: Cincinnati
Grant Types: Capital, Challenge, Conference/Seminar, General Support, Operating Expenses.

Donor Information

Founder: Established in 1959 by the late Harold C. Schott.

Financial Summary

Total Giving: $3,819,050 (2003); $4,059,200 (2002)
Giving Analysis: Giving for 2002 includes: foundation grants to United Way ($567,000)
Assets: $94,518,810 (2003); $77,561,178 (2002)
Gifts Received: $2,800,000 (1997); $15,000 (1992)

Typical Recipients

Arts & Humanities: Arts Associations & Councils, Arts Centers, Arts & Humanities-General, Historic Preservation, History & Archaeology, Libraries, Museums/Galleries, Music, Opera, Public Broadcasting, Theater
Civic & Public Affairs: Botanical Gardens/Parks, Clubs, Economic Development, Employment/Job Training, Civic & Public Affairs-General, Legal Aid, Municipalities/Towns, Parades/Festivals, Public Poli-

cy, Zoos/Aquariums
Education: Colleges & Universities, Community & Junior Colleges, Education Funds, Elementary Education (Private), Education-General, Legal Education, Literacy, Private Education (Precollege), Public Education (Precollege), Religious Education, Science/Mathematics Education, Secondary Education (Private), Special Education, Student Aid
Environment: Resource Conservation, Wildlife Protection
Health: Cancer, Clinics/Medical Centers, Eyes/Blindness, Health Funds, Health Organizations, Heart, Hospitals, Long-Term Care, Medical Rehabilitation, Mental Health, Prenatal Health Issues, Preventive Medicine/Wellness Organizations, Speech & Hearing, Trauma Treatment
International: Foreign Arts Organizations, International Relations, International Relief Efforts
Religion: Churches, Dioceses, Religion-General, Ministries, Religious Organizations, Religious Welfare, Seminaries
Science: Science Exhibits & Fairs, Science Museums, Scientific Centers & Institutes
Social Services: Animal Protection, At-Risk Youth, Child Welfare, Community Centers, Community Service Organizations, Emergency Relief, Family Planning, Family Services, Food/Clothing Distribution, People with Disabilities, Recreation & Athletics, Shelters/Homelessness, Social Services-General, Substance Abuse, United Funds/United Ways, YMCA/YWCA/YMHA/YWHA, Youth Organizations

Application Procedures

Initial Contact: The foundation has no formal grant application procedure or application form.
Application Requirements: Applications should be in writing and include detailed information about the project, the amount requested, and proof of the organization's tax-exempt status.
Deadlines: None.

Restrictions

Grants are not made to individuals.

Foundation Officials

Francie S. Hiltz: trustee
L. Thomas Hiltz: trustee CORP AFFIL director: Applied Industrial Technologies; director: Drees Co.
Betty Jane Mulcahy: trustee
William Dunne Saal: trustee B 1948. ED University of Cincinnati BA (1970). PRIM CORP EMPL principal: William D. Saal Real Estate. CORP AFFIL president, director: Hyde Park Associates Inc.
Milton B. Schott, Jr.: trustee

Grants Analysis

Disclosure Period: calendar year ending 2003
Total Grants: $3,819,050
Number of Grants: 24
Average Grant: $122,567*
Highest Grant: $1,000,000
Lowest Grant: $3,750
Typical Range: $25,000 to $200,000
*Note: Average grant figure excludes highest grant.

Recent Grants

Note: Grants derived from 2003 Form 990.
General

1,000,000	Otto Armleder Memorial Education Center, Cincinnati, OH -- in support of strong academic program for pre kindergarten
500,000	University of Cincinnati, Cincinnati, OH -- in support of capital improvement project for athletic facilities
300,000	YMCA, Lakewood, OH -- toward construction of a new state-of-the-art facility
265,300	National Underground Railroad Freedom Center, Cincinnati, OH -- in support of completion and operations of the center
250,000	Cincinnati Art Museum, Cincinnati, OH -- towards the museum capital campaign.

250,000	Hanna Perkins Center for Child Development, Shaker Heights, OH -- toward relocating to the Malvern school building
250,000	Taft Museum of Art, Cincinnati, OH -- towards renovations for classroom space, exhibition gallery, lecture hall and improved handicapped access
200,000	Cincinnati Museum Center, Cincinnati, OH -- toward permanent indoor and outdoor lighting and rotunda furniture replacement
200,000	Diocese of Columbus, Columbus, OH -- fourth installment of pledge toward the challenge in changing times campaign
150,000	YMCA, OH -- in support of transforming their community campaign for the West end YMCA

H&R BLOCK INC.

Company Headquarters

4400 Main St.
Kansas City, MO 64111
Web: http://www.hrblock.com

Company Description

Founded: 1955
Ticker: HRB
Exchange: NYSE
Revenue: US$4.205 billion (2004)
Profit: US$697.9 million (2004)
Employees: 11200 (2003)
Fortune Rank: 454, per FORTUNE Magazine's list of 500 Largest U.S. Corporations (2004).
SIC(s): 7291 Tax Return Preparation Services, 8721 Accounting, Auditing & Bookkeeping.

Operating Locations

List includes headquarters offices for Personnel Pool of America, an H&R Block operating company.

Nonmonetary Support

Type: Donated Products; Loaned Employees; Loaned Executives
Volunteer Programs: Individual H&R Block associates actively participate in community programs such as Habitat for Humanity and United Way. The foundation provides strategic support, rewards, and recognition for volunteer efforts.
Contact: Marla Sutton, Volunteer & Community Program Coordinator
Note: Nonmonetary support is provided by the company and foundation.

H&R Block Foundation

Giving Contact

David P. Miles, President
4400 Main Street
Kansas City, MO 64111
Phone: 800-869-9220
Fax: (816)753-1585
E-mail: foundation@hrblock.com
Web: http://www.hrblockfoundation.org

Description

Founded: 1974
EIN: 237378232
Organization Type: Corporate Foundation
Giving Locations: MO: Kansas City
Grant Types: Capital, Employee Matching Gifts, General Support, Multiyear/Continuing Support.
Note: Employee matching gift ratio: 1 to 1 for gifts to education institutions and the September 11 Fund.

Financial Summary

Total Giving: $2,378,529 (2003); $2,545,680 (2002); $3,177,017 (2001). Note: Contributes through corporate direct giving program and foundation.

Assets: $49,309,499 (2003); $42,724,026 (2002); $47,017,571 (2001)

Gifts Received: $2,075,000 (2003); $1,916,500 (2002); $1,800,000 (2001). Note: In 2003, contributions were received from H&R Block Inc. ($1,975,000) and Frank & Sarah Salizzoni Foundation ($100,000). In 1999, contributions were received from HRB Management, Inc. In 1996, 1998, and 2001 contributions were received from H&R Block, Inc.

Typical Recipients

Arts & Humanities: Arts Appreciation, Arts Associations & Councils, Arts Centers, Arts Festivals, Arts Funds, Arts Institutes, Arts Outreach, Ballet, Community Arts, Dance, Ethnic & Folk Arts, Arts & Humanities-General, Libraries, Literary Arts, Museums/ Galleries, Music, Opera, Performing Arts, Public Broadcasting, Theater, Visual Arts

Civic & Public Affairs: Botanical Gardens/Parks, Business/Free Enterprise, Civil Rights, Clubs, Community Foundations, Economic Development, Employment/Job Training, Civic & Public Affairs-General, Housing, Inner-City Development, Law & Justice, Legal Aid, Nonprofit Management, Public Policy, Safety, Urban & Community Affairs, Women's Affairs, Zoos/Aquariums

Education: Afterschool/Enrichment Programs, Agricultural Education, Arts/Humanities Education, Business Education, Colleges & Universities, Community & Junior Colleges, Continuing Education, Economic Education, Education Associations, Education Funds, Education Reform, Environmental Education, Education-General, Legal Education, Literacy, Medical Education, Minority Education, Preschool Education, Private Education (Precollege), Public Education (Precollege), Science/Mathematics Education, Secondary Education (Private), Social Sciences Education, Special Education, Student Aid, Vocational & Technical Education

Environment: Environment-General, Watershed

Health: AIDS/HIV, Cancer, Children's Health/ Hospitals, Clinics/Medical Centers, Geriatric Health, Health Funds, Health Organizations, Heart, Home-Care Services, Hospices, Hospitals, Medical Rehabilitation, Mental Health, Multiple Sclerosis, Prenatal Health Issues, Public Health, Research/Studies Institutes, Single-Disease Health Associations

International: International Relations

Religion: Religion-General, Jewish Causes, Ministries, Missionary Activities (Domestic), Religious Organizations, Religious Welfare, Social/Policy Issues

Science: Science Exhibits & Fairs, Science Museums, Scientific Centers & Institutes, Scientific Research

Social Services: At-Risk Youth, Big Brothers/Big Sisters, Camps, Child Abuse, Child Welfare, Community Centers, Community Service Organizations, Counseling, Crime Prevention, Day Care, Delinquency & Criminal Rehabilitation, Domestic Violence, Emergency Relief, Family Planning, Family Services, Food/Clothing Distribution, Homes, People with Disabilities, Recreation & Athletics, Refugee Assistance, Scouts, Senior Services, Shelters/Homelessness, Social Services-General, Special Olympics, Substance Abuse, United Funds/United Ways, Volunteer Services, YMCA/YWCA/YMHA/YWHA, Youth Organizations

Application Procedures

Initial Contact: Request guidelines, then submit a formal proposal.

Application Requirements: Information should include a cover letter detailing amount requested and grant period; project description (including an explanation of why the project is needed, who will be served and what will be accomplished during a specific time period); information on the sustainability of the project and its lasting benefits to the participants, organization and community; a specific plan for evaluating and reporting outcomes; budget and projected sources of funds for the grant period; recently audited financial statement; proof of tax-exempt status; and a description of organization (including staff, board of directors, history and accomplishments).

Deadlines: July 30 and October 15.

Evaluative Criteria: Demonstrated need; relevance to foundation's funding categories; 501(c)(3) status; location within metropolitan areas of Kansas City, MO; stability of organization's management; financial planning; fiscal soundness; long- and short-range goals and objectives; and measurable evaluation.

Decision Notification: The board of directors considers requests at quarterly meetings in September (annual meeting), December, March, and June; written notification of grants awarded follows each meeting.

Notes: Organizations may be asked to submit additional information or to meet with a member of the foundation's board of directors or staff.

Restrictions

Foundation does not support individuals or businesses; publications; projects for which the Foundation must exercise expenditure responsibility; single-disease agencies; travel or conferences; historic preservation; telethons, dinners, advertising, or other fund-raising events.

Additional Information

Foundation favors making proportionately significant grants to relatively few activities, rather than relatively minor grants to a great many activities. Hands-on contributions have a special place within the foundation's priorities. Generally, grants of less than $500 are not made.

Foundation usually makes one-year grants but, in appropriate circumstances, will consider requests for up to five years for special project funding. Recipients may apply for additional funding after original grant has expired.

H&R Block is no longer affiliated with CompuServe.

Publications: Annual Report; Guidelines

Corporate Officials

Frank L. Salizzoni: chairman, director B 1938. ED Pennsylvania State University BS (1960); George Washington University MS (1964). PRIM CORP EMPL chairman, director: H&R Block Inc. CORP AFFIL director: Orbital Sciences Corp.; director: SKF U.S.A. Inc.; president: Block Financial Corp.; president: H & R Block.

Foundation Officials

Henry Wollman Bloch: chairman, treasurer, director B Kansas City, MO 1922. ED University of Michigan BS (1944). NONPR AFFIL general chairman: United Negro College Fund; president trustees: University Kansas City; director: Saint Lukes Hospital; director, trustee: Nelson-Atkins Museum Art; director: Saint Lukes Foundation; vice chairman, director: Midwest Research Institute; director: Menorah Medical Center Foundation; director: Mid-American Coalition Health Care; vice chairman corporate fund: Kennedy Center for Performing Arts; vice president, director: Kansas City Area Health Planning Council; director: Kansas City Symphony; trustee: Junior Achievement Mid-America; director: HRB Management Inc.; director: International Public Relations Council; member: Greater Kansas City Chamber of Commerce; member: Academy Squires; member: Golden Key National Honor Society. CLUB AFFIL River Club; Kansas City Racquet Club; Oakwood Country Club; Kansas City Country Club; Carriage Club; John Gardiners Tennis Ranch.

Robert L. Bloch: secretary, program officer

Charles E. Curran: director

Mark A. Ernst: director

Edward Taylor Matheny, Jr.: director B Chicago, IL 1923. ED University of Missouri BA (1944); Harvard University JD (1949). NONPR AFFIL Phi Beta Kappa; Sigma Chi; member: Missouri Bar Association; member: Kansas City Bar Association; trustee: Jacob L. and Ella C. Loose Foundation; trustee: Eye Foundation Kansas City. CLUB AFFIL River Club; member: Harvard Club Kansas City; Mission Hills Country Club.

David P. Miles: president

Frank L. Salizzoni: vice chairman, director (see above)

Becky S. Shulman: assistant treasurer

Morton Irvin Sosland: director B Kansas City, MO 1925. ED Harvard University (1946). CORP AFFIL director: H & R Block; director: Kansas City Southern Industries. NONPR AFFIL director: Greater Kansas City Community Foundation; life trustee: Midwest Research Institute.

Bret G. Wilson: assistant secretary

Grants Analysis

Disclosure Period: calendar year ending 2003

Total Grants: $2,278,529*

Number of Grants: 403

Average Grant: $5,655

Highest Grant: $100,000

Lowest Grant: $50

Typical Range: $1,000 to $10,000

*Note: Giving excludes scholarships and United Way.

Recent Grants

Note: Grants derived from 2003 Form 990.

General

200,000	Kansa City Community Development Initiative, Kansas City, MO
157,450	Scholarship America, St. Peter, MN
150,000	Harvesters, Kansas City, MO
100,000	Nelson Gallery Foundation, Kansas City, MO
100,000	Nelson Gallery Foundation, Kansas City, MO
100,000	Operation Breakthrough, Kansas City, MO
75,000	Kansas City Area Life Sciences Institute Inc., Kansas City, MO
50,000	Friends of The Zoo, Kansas City, MO
50,000	Midwest Research Institute, Kansas City, MO
47,414	U.M.K.C University of Missouri, Kansas City, MO

MIRIAM AND PETER HAAS FUND

Giving Contact

Cheryl Polk, Executive Director & Secretary
Miriam and Peter Haas Fund
201 Filbert Street, 5th Floor
San Francisco, CA 94133
Phone: (415)296-9249
Fax: (415)296-8842
E-mail: mphf@mphf.org

Description

Founded: 1982
EIN: 946064551
Organization Type: Family Foundation
Giving Locations: CA: San Francisco County
Grant Types: Capital, Endowment, General Support, Matching, Multiyear/Continuing Support, Operating Expenses, Project.

Donor Information

Founder: The fund was incorporated in 1982 in California by funds from Peter E. Haas Sr., his wife, Miriam Haas, and his mother, the late Elise Haas. Peter E. Haas, Sr., is the great-grandnephew of Levi

Strauss, the founder of Levi Strauss & Company, the world's largest manufacturer of clothing. Mr. Haas, although retired, still operates as the company's chairman of its executive committee.

Financial Summary

Total Giving: $9,296,415 (2003); $11,594,068 (2002)
Giving Analysis: Giving for 2003 includes: foundation grants to United Way ($250,000); 2002: foundation grants to United Way ($250,000)
Assets: $218,699,026 (2003); $190,145,600 (2002)
Gifts Received: $142,434 (1995); $12,947,831 (1994); $63,035,667 (1993). Note: In fiscal 1992 and 1994, contributions were received from the estate of Elise S. Haas. In fiscal 1993, contributions were received from the estate of Elise S. Haas ($60,000,000) and from Peter and Miriam Haas ($3,035,667).

Typical Recipients

Arts & Humanities: Arts Centers, Arts Funds, Arts Institutes, Ballet, Community Arts, Dance, Ethnic & Folk Arts, Film & Video, Arts & Humanities-General, Historic Preservation, History & Archaeology, Libraries, Museums/Galleries, Music, Opera, Performing Arts, Public Broadcasting, Theater, Visual Arts
Civic & Public Affairs: African American Affairs, Asian American Affairs, Botanical Gardens/Parks, Business/Free Enterprise, Community Foundations, Economic Development, Employment/Job Training, Civic & Public Affairs-General, Hispanic Affairs, Housing, Legal Aid, Nonprofit Management, Philanthropic Organizations, Professional & Trade Associations, Public Policy, Urban & Community Affairs, Women's Affairs, Zoos/Aquariums
Education: Afterschool/Enrichment Programs, Arts/Humanities Education, Business Education, Colleges & Universities, Continuing Education, Education Funds, Education Reform, Elementary Education (Public), Education-General, Literacy, Preschool Education, Private Education (Precollege), Public Education (Precollege), Religious Education, Secondary Education (Private), Secondary Education (Public), Social Sciences Education, Vocational & Technical Education
Environment: Environment-General
Health: AIDS/HIV, Cancer, Children's Health/Hospitals, Clinics/Medical Centers, Health Funds, Hospitals, Long-Term Care, Medical Rehabilitation, Medical Research, Mental Health, Public Health, Research/Studies Institutes
International: Foreign Educational Institutions, Human Rights, International Organizations, International Peace & Security Issues, International Relations, Missionary/Religious Activities
Religion: Jewish Causes, Religious Organizations, Religious Welfare, Synagogues/Temples
Science: Science Museums, Scientific Centers & Institutes
Social Services: Child Welfare, Community Centers, Community Service Organizations, Counseling, Day Care, Domestic Violence, Emergency Relief, Family Planning, Family Services, Food/Clothing Distribution, People with Disabilities, Recreation & Athletics, Refugee Assistance, Shelters/Homelessness, Substance Abuse, United Funds/United Ways, YMCA/YWCA/YMHA/YWHA, Youth Organizations

Application Procedures

Initial Contact: The foundation has no formal grant application procedure or application form.
Deadlines: None.

Restrictions

The fund does not support individuals.

Additional Information

The majority of grantmaking is staff and trustee initiated, and the fund works with other organizations to solicit proposals.
Publications: Annual Report

Foundation Officials

Miriam Lurie Haas: don, president, trustee
Cheryl Polk: executive director

Grants Analysis

Disclosure Period: calendar year ending 2003
Total Grants: $9,026,415*
Number of Grants: 280
Average Grant: $18,146*
Highest Grant: $2,000,000
Lowest Grant: $50
Typical Range: $1,000 to $35,000
*Note: Giving excludes United Way. Average grant figure excludes three highest grants ($4,000,000).

Recent Grants

Note: Grants derived from 2003 Form 990.
General

2,000,000	Museum of Modern Art, New York, NY
1,000,000	Museum of Modern Art, New York, NY
1,000,000	University of California Berkeley Foundation, Berkeley, CA
200,000	Council on Foreign Relations, New York, NY -- towards national program outreach
200,000	KQED, San Francisco, CA
155,000	Creative Work Fund, San Francisco, CA
150,000	California Pacific Medical Center Foundation, San Francisco, CA
150,000	San Francisco Unified School District, San Francisco, CA -- towards Child development program
125,000	Asian Art Museum of San Francisco, San Francisco, CA
125,000	California Academy of Sciences, San Francisco, CA

WALTER AND ELISE HAAS FUND

Giving Contact

Pamela H. David, Executive Director
1 Lombard Street, Suite 305
San Francisco, CA 94111-1130
Phone: (415)398-4474
Fax: (415)986-4779
E-mail: information@haassr.org
Web: http://www.haassr.org

Description

Founded: 1953
EIN: 946068564
Organization Type: Family Foundation
Giving Locations: CA: Alameda County, Marin County, San Mateo County, San Francisco the Bay area
Grant Types: Capital, Endowment, General Support, Multiyear/Continuing Support, Project.

Donor Information

Founder: The Walter and Elise Haas Fund was established in 1952 by Walter Abraham Haas and Elise Haas "to provide support for charitable and cultural purposes consistent with traditions and values which they held in regard. In creating the fund, Mr. and Mrs. Haas sought to return to the community benefits which they felt fortunate to have enjoyed as part of their active careers."
Walter Abraham Haas was head of Levi Strauss and Company from 1928 to 1955, during which time the company was developed into the world's largest apparel manufacturer. His wife, Elise Haas, was the daughter of Sigmund Stern, a nephew of Levi Strauss. Mrs. Haas was active in San Francisco cultural and civic life for many years and was involved in the establishment of the Museum of Modern Art, the San Francisco Symphony, the Stern Grove Festival, and Mount Zion Hospital. Mr. Haas died in 1979;

Mrs. Haas continued to serve as vice president of the fund until her death in 1990.

Financial Summary

Total Giving: $9,595,223 (2003); $11,540,210 (2002); $10,697,970 (2001)
Giving Analysis: Giving for 2003 includes: foundation grants to United Way ($120,000); 2002: foundation grants to United Way ($100,000)
Assets: $208,934,387 (2003); $179,244,560 (2002); $213,128,308 (2001)
Gifts Received: $200,000 (1998); $200,000 (1997 approx); $500,000 (1996)

Typical Recipients

Arts & Humanities: Arts Associations & Councils, Arts Centers, Arts Festivals, Arts Institutes, Arts Outreach, Ballet, Dance, Ethnic & Folk Arts, Film & Video, Arts & Humanities-General, Historic Preservation, History & Archaeology, Libraries, Literary Arts, Museums/Galleries, Music, Opera, Performing Arts, Public Broadcasting, Theater, Visual Arts
Civic & Public Affairs: Asian American Affairs, Botanical Gardens/Parks, Business/Free Enterprise, Chambers of Commerce, Civil Rights, Community Foundations, Economic Development, Employment/Job Training, Ethnic Organizations, First Amendment Issues, Civic & Public Affairs-General, Hispanic Affairs, Housing, Law & Justice, Legal Aid, Municipalities/Towns, Native American Affairs, Nonprofit Management, Parades/Festivals, Philanthropic Organizations, Professional & Trade Associations, Public Policy, Urban & Community Affairs, Women's Affairs, Zoos/Aquariums
Education: Afterschool/Enrichment Programs, Arts/Humanities Education, Business Education, Colleges & Universities, Education Associations, Education Funds, Education Reform, Environmental Education, Faculty Development, Education-General, International Exchange, Literacy, Minority Education, Private Education (Precollege), Public Education (Precollege), Religious Education, School Volunteerism, Science/Mathematics Education, Secondary Education (Private), Secondary Education (Public), Social Sciences Education, Special Education, Student Aid
Environment: Energy, Environment-General, Resource Conservation, Wildlife Protection
Health: AIDS/HIV, Children's Health/Hospitals, Clinics/Medical Centers, Diabetes, Health-General, Health Funds, Health Organizations, Hospitals, Long-Term Care, Mental Health, Prenatal Health Issues, Public Health
International: Foreign Arts Organizations, Foreign Educational Institutions, International Affairs, International Relations, Missionary/Religious Activities
Religion: Religion-General, Jewish Causes, Religious Welfare
Science: Science Museums, Scientific Organizations
Social Services: At-Risk Youth, Child Welfare, Community Centers, Community Service Organizations, Counseling, Crime Prevention, Domestic Violence, Emergency Relief, Family Planning, Family Services, Food/Clothing Distribution, Homes, People with Disabilities, Recreation & Athletics, Senior Services, Shelters/Homelessness, Substance Abuse, United Funds/United Ways, Volunteer Services, YMCA/YWCA/YMHA/YWHA, Youth Organizations

Application Procedures

Initial Contact: Submit a letter of inquiry. Letters of inquiry are the preferred form of initial contact, and we have provided a format that can be submitted electronically or printed and sent by mail.
Application Requirements: Proposals should include the organization name and description, names and addresses of contact persons, project name, and project summary. The following attachments should be included: total project budget; annual organization budget; list of other sources of financial support, including amounts of current and proposed funding; financial statement for the previous year; list of the organization's board of directors, proof of tax-exempt

status, and a complete project description.
Deadlines: None.
Review Process: The directors meet quarterly.

Restrictions

No grants are made to individuals; for general fundraising benefits; or for video or film production or distribution. Applications for capital grants are considered if the projects are of interest to the fund. Outside of the San Francisco Bay area, only projects of unusual merit are considered; grants in the categories citizenship and Civic Education and Professional Ethics are awarded to national organizations.

Additional Information

The fund also is related through family membership to three other foundations in California: Evelyn and Walter A. Haas, Jr. Fund, Miriam and Peter Haas Fund, and Richard and Rhoda Goldman Fund.
Publications: Periodic Reports; Annual Reports; Guidelines; Application Forms

Foundation Officials

Elizabeth Haas Eisenhardt: trustee ED University of California at Berkeley (1976). PRIM CORP EMPL partner: Oakland Athletics.
John D. Goldman: trustee CORP AFFIL president, director: Richard N Goldman & Co.; president, director: Goldman Insurance.
Peter Edgar Haas, Jr.: president B San Francisco, CA 1947. ED Stanford University AB (1969); Harvard University MBA (1972). CORP AFFIL director: Levi Strauss & Co.
Peter Edgar Haas, Sr.: honorary president B San Francisco, CA December 20, 1918. ED University of California at Berkeley AB (1940); Harvard University MBA (1943). PRIM CORP EMPL chairman executive committee, director: Levi Strauss & Co. ADD CORP EMPL chairman executive committee, director: Levi Strauss Associates Inc. Holding Corp.
Walter J. Haas: trustee
Jennifer Haas-Dehejia: trustee

Grants Analysis

Disclosure Period: calendar year ending 2003
Total Grants: $9,475,223*
Number of Grants: 327
Average Grant: $27,531*
Highest Grant: $500,000
Lowest Grant: $125
Typical Range: $10,000 to $50,000
*Note: Giving excludes United Way. Average grant figure excludes highest grant.

Recent Grants

Note: Grants derived from 2003 Form 990.
Library-Related
75,000   Libraries for the Future, New York, NY -- toward collaborative initiative of school districts and library

General
625,000   Jewish Community Federation of San Francisco, San Francisco, CA
625,000   Jewish Community Federation of San Francisco, San Francisco, CA
500,000   Stern Grove Festival, San Francisco, CA -- funding for capital and endowment campaign
250,000   Stanford University, Stanford, CA -- toward gift in honor of Peter Haas
240,000   San Francisco Unified School District, San Francisco, CA -- funding for office of Teachers Affairs and CARE
187,000   Regents of the University of California, Berkeley, CA -- toward support for beginning teachers at the New Teacher Center
181,000   Regents of the University of California, Berkeley, CA -- toward support for beginning teachers at the New Teacher Center
150,000   Oakland Private Industry Council Inc., San Francisco, CA -- funding for family in-

dependence initiative and financial incentives
125,000   Asian Art Museum, San Francisco, CA -- funding for capital renovation
120,000   Alliance for California Traditional Arts, Fresno, CA -- funding for mentorship program

EVELYN AND WALTER HAAS, JR. FUND

Giving Contact

Clayton Juan, Grants Administrator
One Market Landmark, Suite 400
San Francisco, CA 94105
Phone: (415)856-1400
Fax: (415)856-1500
E-mail: sitemaster@haasjr.org
Web: http://www.haasjr.org

Description

Founded: 1953
EIN: 946068932
Organization Type: Family Foundation
Giving Locations: CA: Alameda County, San Francisco County
Grant Types: Challenge, Employee Matching Gifts, General Support, Multiyear/Continuing Support, Operating Expenses, Seed Money.

Donor Information

Founder: The Evelyn and Walter Haas, Jr. Fund was established in 1953 by Mr. and Mrs. Walter A. Haas Jr.. Walter A. Haas, Jr., who died in 1995, was the son of Walter A. Haas, the head of Levi Strauss & Company from 1928 to 1955. His mother, Elise Haas, was the daughter of Sigmund Stern, a nephew of Levi Strauss. When Walter Haas, Jr., became president, CEO, and board chair of Levi Strauss & Company, he helped develop the business into the world's largest apparel company. He was also honorary chairman and director of Levi Strauss Associates. He was a trustee of the Ford Foundation and was an early president of the Guardsmen, a group of young men involved in social welfare. A philanthropist with a strong commitment to the Bay Area, he was a leader in San Francisco Urban League inner-city activities, and he helped establish a Boys' Club at Hunter's Point. His wife, Evelyn Haas, serves on the board of the San Francisco Museum of Art and Children's Hospital of San Francisco.

Financial Summary

Total Giving: $23,006,984 (2003); $16,379,852 (2002); $21,769,070 (2001)
Giving Analysis: Giving for 2002 includes: foundation grants to United Way ($55,000)
Assets: $442,781,627 (2002); $488,632,860 (2001)
Gifts Received: $14,031,647 (1994); $110,000,000 (1992)

Typical Recipients

Arts & Humanities: Arts Centers, Arts Funds, Arts Institutes, Ballet, Film & Video, Arts & Humanities-General, Libraries, Museums/Galleries, Music, Opera, Performing Arts, Public Broadcasting
Civic & Public Affairs: Asian American Affairs, Botanical Gardens/Parks, Business/Free Enterprise, Civil Rights, Clubs, Community Foundations, Economic Development, Economic Policy, Employment/Job Training, Ethnic Organizations, Gay/Lesbian Issues, Civic & Public Affairs-General, Hispanic Affairs, Housing, Law & Justice, Legal Aid, Municipalities/Towns, Native American Affairs, Nonprofit Management, Philanthropic Organizations, Professional & Trade Associations, Public Policy, Safety, Urban & Community Affairs, Women's Affairs

Education: Afterschool/Enrichment Programs, Business Education, Business-School Partnerships, Colleges & Universities, Education Funds, Education Reform, Education-General, Gifted & Talented Programs, Journalism/Media Education, Legal Education, Literacy, Minority Education, Private Education (Precollege), Public Education (Precollege), Religious Education, School Volunteerism, Science/Mathematics Education, Special Education
Environment: Environment-General, Resource Conservation
Health: Alzheimer's Disease, Clinics/Medical Centers, Geriatric Health, Health Organizations, Home-Care Services, Hospices, Hospitals, Long-Term Care, Mental Health, Nursing Services, Nutrition, Research/Studies Institutes
International: Foreign Educational Institutions, International Affairs
Religion: Churches, Religion-General, Jewish Causes, Religious Organizations, Religious Welfare
Social Services: Animal Protection, Camps, Child Abuse, Child Welfare, Community Centers, Community Service Organizations, Day Care, Domestic Violence, Family Services, Food/Clothing Distribution, Homes, People with Disabilities, Recreation & Athletics, Refugee Assistance, Senior Services, Shelters/Homelessness, Social Services-General, United Funds/United Ways, Volunteer Services, YMCA/YWCA/YMHA/YWHA, Youth Organizations

Application Procedures

Initial Contact: Applicants should submit a two- to three-page letter of inquiry. An applicant who knows a trustee should indicate the association in the inquiry letter, and staff will bring the application to the attention of the trustees.
Application Requirements: Letters of inquiry should include brief statement of organization's purpose and goals; if applicable, description of project, need, and target population; information about capability of leaders who will implement project; anticipated short- and long-term outcomes and plans for assessing achievements; grant amount requested; statement about total agency budget and project budget, if different; and statement about other funding sources for agency and/or project, specifying committed as well as projected sources of support.
Deadlines: None.
Review Process: Staff reviews the letter of inquiry within one month of receipt to determine whether the proposed effort fits within the fund's giving programs. If so, a staff member will call or write the applicant, requesting additional information or a full proposal. The fund will provide specific questions and a list of required attachments if it requests a full proposal. Staff members analyze each proposal for fit with the fund's program priorities and values, significance of the need being addressed, potential to add value and achieve significant and enduring impacts, capacity of the agency to accomplish its goals and objectives, appropriateness of the budget (cost efficiencies), and the capacity to track program progress and assess results. Staff members research each request through telephone inquiries, meetings, or site visits. Staff might speak with colleagues, board members, or outside experts. Staff will then submit a written grant recommendation to the trustees.
Applicants can expect a decision within four months of the date of full-proposal receipt. This time line may vary, depending on the dates of the trustee meetings and the number of proposals being considered. The board of trustees meets at least three times a year to discuss program strategies and make grant decisions.

Restrictions

The fund will not make grants for capital or endowment campaigns, major equipment, basic research, conferences, publications, films or videos, deficit or emergency funding, scholarships, direct-mail campaigns, fund-raising events, annual appeals, or aid to individuals. Exceptions may be made for requests that are a component of a larger effort in which the fund is engaged, or for an organization with a well-established relationship with the fund.

The fund supports organizations that are tax-exempt under Section 501(c)(3) of the IRS code and are not classified as private foundations under Section 509(a) of the code. In selected cases, the fund might consider support for projects sponsored by governmental entities. Organizations also can submit applications through a sponsoring organization, if the sponsor has a 501(c)(3) status, is not a private foundation under 509(a), and provides written authorization confirming its willingness to act as the fiscal sponsor.

Additional Information

Publications: Annual Report; Guidelines

Corporate Officials

Robert Douglas Haas: chairman B San Francisco, CA 1942. ED University of California at Berkeley BA (1964); Harvard University MBA (1968). PRIM CORP EMPL chairman: Levi Strauss & Co. ADD CORP EMPL chairman: Levi Strauss Associates Inc. CORP AFFIL chairman, director: Levi Strauss International. NONPR AFFIL honorary director: San Francisco AIDS Foundation; member: Trilateral Commission; member: Ron Brown Award for Corporate Leadership; member: Council Foreign Relations; member: Phi Beta Kappa; member: Conference Board; member, honorary trustee: Brookings Institution; member: California Business Roundtable; director: Bay Area Council; director: Bay Area Community.

Foundation Officials

Evelyn Danzig Haas: don, co-chairman, trustee ED Wheaton College (1939).
Robert Douglas Haas: treasurer, trustee (see above)
Walter J. Haas: co-chairman, trustee CORP AFFIL past president: Oakland A's Baseball.
Ira S. Hirschfield: president, trustee NONPR AFFIL board of directors: Council on Foundations; board of directors: Independent Sector.

Grants Analysis

Disclosure Period: calendar year ending 2002
Total Grants: $16,324,852*
Number of Grants: 389
Average Grant: $34,520*
Highest Grant: $1,000,000
Lowest Grant: $100
Typical Range: $10,000 to $50,000
***Note:** Giving excludes United Way. Average grant figure excludes three highest grants ($3,000,000)

Recent Grants

Note: Grants derived from 2002 Form 990.
General

1,000,000	Jewish Home, San Francisco, CA -- toward support of the Home's capital campaign
1,000,000	KQED, San Francisco, CA -- toward development of local programs
1,000,000	Team-Up for Youth, Oakland, CA -- for the development of youth through the power of youth sports
350,000	Museum of Modern Art, New York, NY -- toward capital project
250,000	Fine Arts Museum of San Francisco, San Francisco, CA
250,000	Jewish Community Federation of San Francisco, San Francisco, CA -- toward the annual contribution
250,000	Jewish Community Federation of San Francisco, San Francisco, CA -- toward annual contribution
250,000	Urban School of San Francisco, San Francisco, CA
225,000	Trust for Public Land, San Francisco, CA -- toward improvement of neighborhood parks and park improvement
200,000	Astraea Lesbian Action Foundation, New York, NY -- toward public education efforts to gain marriage rights for lesbians and gay men

HAFIF FAMILY FOUNDATION

Giving Contact

Herbert Hafif, Director
269 West Bonita Avenue
Claremont, CA 91711
Phone: (310)624-1671
Fax: (310)621-4851

Description

Founded: 1987
EIN: 954081964
Organization Type: Private Foundation
Giving Locations: CA: Los Angeles
Grant Types: General Support.

Donor Information

Founder: Herbert Hafif

Financial Summary

Gifts Received: $100 (1999); $4,289 (1998); $1,500,004 (1996)

Typical Recipients

Arts & Humanities: Libraries, Museums/Galleries, Music, Performing Arts
Civic & Public Affairs: Clubs, Community Foundations, Civic & Public Affairs-General, Hispanic Affairs, Law & Justice, Parades/Festivals, Professional & Trade Associations, Public Policy, Urban & Community Affairs
Education: Afterschool/Enrichment Programs, Colleges & Universities, Community & Junior Colleges, Education-General, Medical Education, Private Education (Precollege), Religious Education, Secondary Education (Private)
Health: Clinics/Medical Centers, Emergency/Ambulance Services, Health Organizations, Medical Rehabilitation, Medical Research, Mental Health, Nutrition, Prenatal Health Issues, Preventive Medicine/Wellness Organizations, Single-Disease Health Associations
International: International Organizations, International Peace & Security Issues, International Relations, Missionary/Religious Activities
Religion: Churches, Religious Organizations, Religious Welfare, Social/Policy Issues, Synagogues/Temples
Science: Scientific Organizations
Social Services: Community Centers, Community Service Organizations, Counseling, Crime Prevention, Emergency Relief, Family Services, People with Disabilities, Recreation & Athletics, Senior Services, Sexual Abuse, Shelters/Homelessness, Social Services-General, Substance Abuse, United Funds/United Ways, Volunteer Services, YMCA/YWCA/YMHA/YWHA, Youth Organizations

Application Procedures

Initial Contact: The foundation requests applications be made in writing.
Deadlines: None.

Foundation Officials

Herbert Hafif: director B Philadelphia, PA 1930. ED Pomona College BA; University of Southern California JD. OCCUPATION attorney.
Jay Rodriguez: president

Grants Analysis

Disclosure Period: calendar year ending 2000
Total Grants: $482,607*

Number of Grants: 107
Average Grant: $4,510
Highest Grant: $50,000
Typical Range: $1,000 to $10,000
***Note:** Giving excludes United Way.

Recent Grants

Note: Grants derived from 2001 Form 990.
General

50,000	University of La Verne, La Verne, CA
30,000	Center for Public Integrity, Washington, DC
30,000	State Fair Community College, Sedalia, MO
25,000	University Muslim Medical Association
20,000	Claremont School of Theology, Claremont, CA
17,950	Spanish Trails Girls Scouts, Montclair, CA
15,000	Lestonnac Clinic
13,000	Foothill Country Day School, Claremont, CA
12,500	Center for Public Integrity, Washington, DC
12,500	Pitzer College, Claremont, CA

HAGEDORN FUND

Giving Contact

Monica Neal, Vice President
c/o JP Morgan Chase Bank
345 Park Ave., 8th Fl.
New York, NY 10021
Phone: (212)464-0134
Web: http://fdncenter.org/grantmaker/hagedorn/

Description

Founded: 1953
EIN: 136048718
Organization Type: General Purpose Foundation
Giving Locations: OH: Cuyahoga County
Grant Types: General Support, Research, Scholarship.

Donor Information

Founder: Established in 1953 by the late William Hagedorn.

Financial Summary

Total Giving: $1,500,000 (2002 approx); $1,530,500 (2001)
Giving Analysis: Giving for 2001 includes: foundation scholarships ($25,500)
Assets: $31,167,003 (2001)
Gifts Received: $11,286 (1998)

Typical Recipients

Arts & Humanities: Arts Associations & Councils, Historic Preservation, Libraries, Performing Arts, Public Broadcasting
Civic & Public Affairs: Botanical Gardens/Parks, Clubs, Community Foundations, Economic Development, Housing, Inner-City Development, Legal Aid, Urban & Community Affairs, Women's Affairs
Education: Afterschool/Enrichment Programs, Colleges & Universities, Community & Junior Colleges, Education Associations, Engineering/Technological Education, Education-General, Legal Education, Literacy, Medical Education, Minority Education, Private Education (Precollege), Religious Education, Special Education, Student Aid
Environment: Environment-General, Resource Conservation
Health: AIDS/HIV, Arthritis, Cancer, Children's Health/Hospitals, Clinics/Medical Centers, Diabetes, Emergency/Ambulance Services, Eyes/Blindness, Health Policy/Cost Containment, Health Organizations, Heart, Hospices, Hospitals, Medical Rehabilita-

tion, Mental Health, Nursing Services, Respiratory
International: Health Care/Hospitals
Religion: Churches, Jewish Causes, Religious Organizations, Religious Welfare, Seminaries, Synagogues/Temples
Social Services: At-Risk Youth, Big Brothers/Big Sisters, Child Welfare, Community Centers, Community Service Organizations, Counseling, Family Planning, Family Services, Food/Clothing Distribution, Homes, People with Disabilities, Recreation & Athletics, Senior Services, Shelters/Homelessness, Social Services-General, United Funds/United Ways, YMCA/YWCA/YMHA/YWHA, Youth Organizations

Application Procedures
Initial Contact: Letter of inquiry.
Deadlines: None.

Restrictions
The fund does not make grants to individuals, or for continuing support, seed money, emergency funds, deficit financing, endowment funds, matching gifts, fellowships, research, special projects, publications, conferences, or loans.

Additional Information
Chase Manhattan Bank is corporate trustee for the fund.

Giving Program Officials
Monica Neal: contact

Foundation Officials
John J. Kindred, III: trustee ED Washington & Lee University (1952); University of Virginia (1955). NONPR AFFIL Colonial Order Acorn; Saint Nicholas Society.
Charles B. Lauren: trustee

Grants Analysis
Disclosure Period: calendar year ending 2001
Total Grants: $1,505,000*
Number of Grants: 90
Average Grant: $15,955*
Highest Grant: $85,000
Lowest Grant: $1,000
Typical Range: $5,000 to $25,000
*Note: Giving excludes scholarships. Average grant figure excludes highest grant.

Recent Grants
Note: Grants derived from 2001 Form 990.
Library-Related
25,000	New York Public Library, New York, NY -- for research

General
85,000	Wells College, Aurora, NY -- Ruth M. Hagedorn Memorial Fund
35,000	Education Broadcasting Corp, New York, NY -- general support and antenna
35,000	Rockefeller University, New York, NY -- general operating support
35,000	St. Vincent Services, New York, NY -- for American Dream Scholarship
35,000	South Bronx Overall Economic Development Corporation, Bronx, NY -- grant for general operating support for capital campaign
25,000	Big Brothers and Big Sisters, New York, NY -- general operating support
25,000	Brooklyn Botanic Garden, Brooklyn, NY -- general operating support
25,000	Cancer Research Institute, New York, NY -- general operating support
25,000	Children's AIDS Society
25,000	Community Service Society, New York, NY -- general operating support

HAIGH-SCATENA FOUNDATION

Giving Contact
Ronald W. Clement, Executive Director
PO Box 4399
Davis, CA 95617-4399
Phone: (530)758-5327

Description
Founded: 1967
EIN: 941753746
Organization Type: Private Foundation
Giving Locations: CA: Northern part of state
Grant Types: Conference/Seminar, Loan, Project, Research, Seed Money.

Donor Information
Founder: the late Isabelle Simi Haigh, Vivien Haigh

Financial Summary
Total Giving: $41,000 (fiscal year ending August 31, 2002 approx); $274,850 (fiscal 2001)
Assets: $3,095,169 (fiscal 2001)
Gifts Received: $122,225 (fiscal 1997)

Typical Recipients
Arts & Humanities: Libraries, Museums/Galleries
Civic & Public Affairs: Business/Free Enterprise, Community Foundations, Economic Development, Employment/Job Training, Civic & Public Affairs-General, Law & Justice, Legal Aid, Native American Affairs, Nonprofit Management, Philanthropic Organizations, Public Policy, Urban & Community Affairs, Women's Affairs
Education: Afterschool/Enrichment Programs, Colleges & Universities, Continuing Education, Education-General, Public Education (Precollege), Science/Mathematics Education, Special Education, Student Aid
Health: Children's Health/Hospitals
Religion: Churches, Religious Organizations, Religious Welfare
Social Services: At-Risk Youth, Child Abuse, Child Welfare, Community Service Organizations, Counseling, Day Care, Delinquency & Criminal Rehabilitation, Domestic Violence, Family Planning, Family Services, Shelters/Homelessness, Youth Organizations

Application Procedures
Initial Contact: Contact executive director to determine whether foundation is interested in project.
Deadlines: None.
Review Process: Review process from first contact to a grant award is typically six months or more.

Restrictions
Limited to organizations that benefit children or youth. Foundation does not fund political or lobbying groups, organizations outside operating areas, individuals, capital campaigns, equipment purchases, endowments, direct services, academic scholarships, or media production and distribution.

Additional Information
Foundation prefers to support efforts that emphasize advocacy and organizing strategies and favors prevention approaches rather than intervention. The foundation welcomes collaboration with other grantmakers and favors grantseekers with multiple sources of support.
Publications: Informational Brochure (including Application Guidelines)

Foundation Officials
Jean Bacigalupi: president
Ronald W. Clement: executive director
Jeanette Maddux Dunckel: director
Andrew J. Eber: director

James J. Gallagher: director
Bruce D. Goldstein: secretary
Gloria S. Hom: director
Wayne Koike: treasurer
Jan Masaoka: treasurer
Arnold X. C. Perkins: director
Gary A. Templin: director
Caroline Tower: director
Joanna Uribe de Mena: vice president

Grants Analysis
Disclosure Period: fiscal year ending August 31, 2001
Total Grants: $274,850
Number of Grants: 19
Average Grant: $14,466
Highest Grant: $52,100
Typical Range: $1,000 to $30,000

Recent Grants
Note: Grants derived from 2002 Form 990.
General
52,100	Sierra Adoption Services, Nevada City, CA -- for technical assistance
30,000	Buena Vista United Methodist Church, Alameda, CA -- for a new non-profit organization
30,000	Center on Juvenile and Criminal Justice, San Francisco, CA -- for research, technical assistance and public education
30,000	Families in Self Help, West Sacramento, CA -- support of a new community-based organization assisting immigrant and refugee families in moving to self-efficiency
30,000	Sacramento Valley Organizing Community, Sacramento, CA -- support for the Solano County Organizing Community
28,000	Youth Empowerment Center, Oakland, CA -- support of a new organization providing leadership, technical assistance and sponsorship to youth-led organizations
25,000	Immigrant Legal Resource Center, San Francisco, CA -- for training, technical assistance and advocacy efforts
8,750	Families in Self Help, West Sacramento, CA -- support of a new community-based organization assisting immigrant and refugee families in moving to self-efficiency
7,500	Sacramento Valley Organizing Community, Sacramento, CA -- support for the Solano County Organizing Community
7,000	Northern California Grantmaker, San Francisco, CA -- for Summer Youth Project

CRESCENT PORTER HALE FOUNDATION

Giving Contact
Ulla Z. Davis, Executive Director
655 Redwood Highway, Suite 301
Mill Valley, CA 94941
Phone: (415)388-2333
Fax: (415)381-4799

Description
Founded: 1961
EIN: 946093385
Organization Type: General Purpose Foundation
Giving Locations: CA: San Francisco Bay area
Grant Types: Capital, General Support, Scholarship.

Donor Information
Founder: Incorporated in 1961 by the late Elwyn C. Hale and the late M. Eugenie Hale.

Financial Summary

Total Giving: $1,120,750 (2003); $1,162,750 (2002)
Assets: $33,089,078 (2003); $28,390,782 (2002)

Typical Recipients

Arts & Humanities: Arts Festivals, Arts Institutes, Arts Outreach, Ballet, Libraries, Museums/Galleries, Music, Opera, Performing Arts, Theater

Civic & Public Affairs: Botanical Gardens/Parks, Community Foundations, Economic Development, Employment/Job Training, Ethnic Organizations, Civic & Public Affairs-General, Hispanic Affairs, Housing, Law & Justice, Municipalities/Towns, Native American Affairs, Urban & Community Affairs, Women's Affairs

Education: Afterschool/Enrichment Programs, Arts/Humanities Education, Business Education, Colleges & Universities, Education Associations, Education Funds, Education Reform, Elementary Education (Private), Environmental Education, Education-General, International Studies, Medical Education, Preschool Education, Private Education (Precollege), Public Education (Precollege), Religious Education, Science/Mathematics Education, Secondary Education (Private), Secondary Education (Public), Special Education, Student Aid

Environment: Environment-General, Protection, Wildlife Protection

Health: AIDS/HIV, Arthritis, Cancer, Children's Health/Hospitals, Health Organizations, Hospices, Hospitals, Long-Term Care, Medical Research, Nursing Services, Research/Studies Institutes, Single-Disease Health Associations

International: Foreign Educational Institutions, International Development, Missionary/Religious Activities

Religion: Churches, Religion-General, Religious Organizations, Religious Welfare, Seminaries

Science: Science Museums

Social Services: At-Risk Youth, Big Brothers/Big Sisters, Camps, Child Abuse, Child Welfare, Community Centers, Community Service Organizations, Counseling, Day Care, Domestic Violence, Family Planning, Family Services, Food/Clothing Distribution, Homes, People with Disabilities, Recreation & Athletics, Senior Services, Sexual Abuse, Shelters/Homelessness, Social Services-General, Substance Abuse, United Funds/United Ways, Volunteer Services, YMCA/YWCA/YMHA/YWHA, Youth Organizations

Application Procedures

Initial Contact: The foundation requests applications be made in writing.

Application Requirements: A concise letter of intent (up to two pages) should include the target population to be served; agency or project budget; amount requested from this foundation; purpose of funds sought; and other anticipated or committed sources of funding; and a brief statement of agency/project's history, goals and objectives.

Deadlines: None.

Review Process: The foundation will respond to inquiries within 30 days of receipt. Additional information will be requested from applicants invited to submit a full proposal. Eligibility is limited to organizations within the San Francisco Bay area.

Restrictions

No gifts will be made to individuals, for research for health projects, or to hospitals. Organizations must be tax exempt under Section 501(c)(3) of the IRS code. Grants are restricted to the San Francisco Bay area.

Additional Information

Publications: Application Guidelines; Application Letter

Foundation Officials

L. E. Alford: vice president
A. L. Ballard: director B 1934. PRIM CORP EMPL president, director: Ballard Exploration Co.
Eugene Edmund Bleck, MD: director B Milwaukee, WI 1923. ED Northwestern University; Duke University (1948-1955); University of Southern California (1960); Marquette University MD (1977). NONPR AFFIL member: San Mateo County Medicine Association; member: Western Orthopedic Association; member: Piedmont Orthopedic Society; member advisor: Rehabilitation Engineering Society North America; director: Notre Dame High School Belmont California; member: Pediatric Orthopedic Society North American; member advisor: New York Academy Science; member: California Medicine Association; member: Medicine Advisory Group State Department Rehab; member: American Orthopaedic Association; member: American Academy Orthopedic Surgeons; member: American Academy Orthopedic Surgery; member: American Academy for Cerebral Palsy and Dev Medicine.
Ulla Z. Davis: executive director
Joan Withers Dinner: director
Ephraim P. Engelman, MD: director
Robert S. Kelling, Jr.: director
Hon. Thomas J. Mellon, Jr.: president
E. William Swanson: secretary, treasurer, director

Grants Analysis

Disclosure Period: calendar year ending 2003
Total Grants: $1,120,750
Number of Grants: 106
Average Grant: $10,573
Highest Grant: $150,000
Lowest Grant: $1,000
Typical Range: $5,000 to $20,000

Recent Grants

Note: Grants derived from 2002 Form 990.
General

150,000	Family Aid Catholic Education, Oakland, CA -- for education purposes
100,000	BASIC Fund, San Francisco, CA -- toward education purposes
50,000	Notre Dame High School, Belmont, CA -- toward capital and equipment
50,000	Sacred Heart Cathedral Preparatory, San Francisco, CA -- toward capital and equipment
50,000	St. Joseph Notre Dame High School, Alameda, CA
33,000	Together in the Mission of Education, San Francisco, CA -- for education purposes
25,000	Carondelet High School, Concord, CA -- toward capital and equipment
25,000	Junipero Serra High School, San Mateo, CA -- for capital and equipment
25,000	University of San Francisco, San Francisco, CA
20,000	Catholic Charities - East Bay, Oakland, CA -- toward community services

W. B. Haley Foundation

Giving Contact

Eloise T. Haley, President
1612 Orchard Dr.
Albany, GA 31707
Phone: (229)435-3686

Description

Founded: 1973
EIN: 586113405
Organization Type: Private Foundation

Giving Locations: GA: Albany
Grant Types: General Support.

Donor Information

Founder: the late W. B. Haley, Jr.

Financial Summary

Total Giving: $104,500 (fiscal year ending February 28, 2004); $190,000 (fiscal 2002); $189,500 (fiscal 2001)
Giving Analysis: Giving for fiscal 2004 includes: foundation grants to United Way ($3,000); fiscal 2002: foundation grants to United Way ($3,000); fiscal 2001: foundation grants to United Way ($3,000)
Assets: $2,285,213 (fiscal 2004); $2,265,517 (fiscal 2002); $2,481,148 (fiscal 2001)

Typical Recipients

Arts & Humanities: Community Arts, Historic Preservation, History & Archaeology, Libraries, Museums/Galleries, Music, Opera, Theater

Civic & Public Affairs: Civic & Public Affairs-General, Housing, Women's Affairs

Education: Colleges & Universities, Education Funds

Health: Cancer, Heart, Hospitals, Medical Research, Public Health, Single-Disease Health Associations

International: International Affairs, International Relations

Religion: Religion-General, Religious Welfare

Social Services: Child Abuse, Community Centers, Community Service Organizations, Family Services, People with Disabilities, Scouts, United Funds/United Ways, YMCA/YWCA/YMHA/YWHA, Youth Organizations

Application Procedures

Initial Contact: Send a brief letter of inquiry describing program.
Deadlines: None.

Foundation Officials

Stephen J. Byrne: director
Eloise T. Haley: president
Emily Jean H. McAfee: director
G. Edmund Nobles: director
Harry Willson: director

Grants Analysis

Disclosure Period: fiscal year ending February 28, 2004
Total Grants: $101,500*
Number of Grants: 9
Average Grant: $2,688*
Highest Grant: $80,000
Lowest Grant: $500
Typical Range: $500 to $5,000
*Note: Giving excludes United Way. Average grant excludes highest grant.

Recent Grants

Note: Grants derived from fiscal 2004 Form 990.
General

80,000	Albany Museum of Art, Albany, GA
8,000	Boys and Girls Club of Albany, Albany, GA
5,000	Albany YMCA, Albany, GA
4,000	Girls Inc., Albany, GA
3,000	United Way of Southwest Georgia, Albany, GA
1,500	Darton College Foundation, Albany, GA
1,000	St. Claire's Community Center, Albany, GA
1,000	Salvation Army, Albany, GA
500	Liberty House, Albany, GA
500	Open Arms, Albany, GA

G. A. C. HALFF FOUNDATION

Giving Contact

Thomas F. Bibb, Vice President, Treasurer & Trustee
745 East Mulberry, Suite 400
San Antonio, TX 78212
Phone: (210)735-3300

Description

Founded: 1951
EIN: 746042432
Organization Type: Private Foundation
Giving Locations: TX: San Antonio
Grant Types: General Support, Research.

Donor Information

Founder: the late G. A. C. Halff

Financial Summary

Total Giving: $438,750 (fiscal year ending February 28, 2004); $490,000 (fiscal 2002); $437,340 (fiscal 2001)
Giving Analysis: Giving for fiscal 2004 includes: foundation grants to United Way ($30,000); fiscal 2002: foundation grants to United Way ($30,000); fiscal 2001: foundation grants to United Way ($30,000)
Assets: $7,065,190 (fiscal 2004); $7,773,369 (fiscal 2002); $9,251,577 (fiscal 2001)

Typical Recipients

Arts & Humanities: Arts Institutes, Ethnic & Folk Arts, Libraries, Museums/Galleries, Music, Public Broadcasting, Theater
Civic & Public Affairs: Employment/Job Training, Civic & Public Affairs-General, Hispanic Affairs, Nonprofit Management, Zoos/Aquariums
Education: Colleges & Universities, Education Funds, Education-General, Literacy, Private Education (Precollege)
Environment: Environment-General
Health: Cancer, Children's Health/Hospitals, Eyes/Blindness, Health Organizations, Hospices, Hospitals, Medical Rehabilitation, Medical Research, Mental Health, Nursing Services, Public Health, Single-Disease Health Associations
Religion: Dioceses, Religious Organizations, Religious Welfare
Social Services: At-Risk Youth, Big Brothers/Big Sisters, Camps, Child Welfare, Community Centers, Community Service Organizations, Counseling, Family Services, Food/Clothing Distribution, Homes, People with Disabilities, Scouts, Sexual Abuse, Shelters/Homelessness, Substance Abuse, United Funds/United Ways, YMCA/YWCA/YMHA/YWHA, Youth Organizations

Application Procedures

Initial Contact: Send a brief letter of inquiry describing program or project. Include proof of tax-exempt status.
Deadlines: May 15.

Restrictions

Does not support individuals.

Foundation Officials

Thomas F. Bibb: vice president, treasurer, trustee
Catherine H. Edson: trustee
Thomas H. Edson: trustee
Hugh Halff, Jr.: chairman B 1936. OCCUPATION investor. NONPR AFFIL member: McNay Friends Gallery Council; member: Order Alamo; member: Charity Ball Association. CLUB AFFIL San Antonio German Club; Giraud Club; San Antonio Country Club; Argyle Club.
Marie M. Halff: trustee
Jerry O. Street: trustee
Stephanie H. Street: trustee

Grants Analysis

Disclosure Period: fiscal year ending February 28, 2004
Total Grants: $408,750*
Number of Grants: 61
Average Grant: $6,701
Highest Grant: $10,000
Lowest Grant: $500
Typical Range: $5,000 to $10,000
*Note: Giving excludes United Way.

Recent Grants

Note: Grants derived from fiscal 2004 Form 990.
General

30,000	United Way, San Antonio, TX
10,000	Avance, San Antonio, TX
10,000	Big Brothers Big Sisters, San Antonio, TX
10,000	Cancer Therapy and Research Center, San Antonio, TX
10,000	Child Guidance Center of San Antonio, San Antonio, TX
10,000	Episcopal Diocese, Houston, TX
10,000	Family Service Association of San Antonio Inc., San Antonio, TX
10,000	Good Samaritan Center, San Antonio, TX
10,000	Nonprofit Resource Center of Texas, San Antonio, TX
10,000	Planned Parenthood of San Antonio, San Antonio, TX

THE HALL FAMILY FOUNDATION

Giving Contact

William A. Hall, President
PO Box 419580, Department 323
Kansas City, MO 64141-6580
Phone: (816)274-8515
Fax: (816)274-8547

Description

Founded: 1993
EIN: 446006291
Organization Type: Family Foundation
Giving Locations: MO: Kansas City metropolitan area
Grant Types: Capital, Endowment, General Support, Matching, Multiyear/Continuing Support, Project, Seed Money.

Donor Information

Founder: Joyce C. Hall was born in 1891, in David City, NE. In 1910, he went to Kansas City, MO, and built a business that eventually would become Hallmark Cards. With his wife, Elizabeth Ann Dilday, he began a foundation to aid and strengthen the Kansas City area.
In 1983, the Hallmark Educational Foundation of Kansas and the Hallmark Education Foundation merged into the Hall Family Foundation to reflect more accurately the source of funds and to avoid philanthropic confusion between Hallmark Cards and the Hall family.

Financial Summary

Total Giving: $39,012,002 (2002); $36,958,990 (2001)
Giving Analysis: Giving for 2002 includes: foundation grants to United Way ($95,000)
Assets: $611,394,790 (2002); $741,132,396 (2001)
Gifts Received: $90,000 (1998). Note: In 1998, contributions were received from Hallmark Cards.

Typical Recipients

Arts & Humanities: Arts Associations & Councils, Arts Institutes, Ballet, Dance, Arts & Humanities-General, History & Archaeology, Libraries, Museums/Galleries, Music, Opera, Performing Arts, Public Broadcasting, Theater, Visual Arts
Civic & Public Affairs: Botanical Gardens/Parks, Business/Free Enterprise, Community Foundations, Economic Development, Employment/Job Training, Ethnic Organizations, Civic & Public Affairs-General, Hispanic Affairs, Housing, Inner-City Development, Minority Business, Municipalities/Towns, Nonprofit Management, Parades/Festivals, Philanthropic Organizations, Urban & Community Affairs, Zoos/Aquariums
Education: Arts/Humanities Education, Business Education, Colleges & Universities, Economic Education, Education Associations, Education Reform, Environmental Education, Education-General, Health & Physical Education, Literacy, Medical Education, Minority Education, Preschool Education, Private Education (Precollege), Public Education (Precollege), School Volunteerism, Science/Mathematics Education, Vocational & Technical Education
Health: Children's Health/Hospitals, Clinics/Medical Centers, Health-General, Health Funds, Health Organizations, Home-Care Services, Hospitals, Hospitals (University Affiliated), Medical Rehabilitation, Medical Research, Mental Health, Public Health
International: International Relations
Religion: Dioceses, Ministries, Religious Welfare
Science: Science Museums, Scientific Centers & Institutes, Scientific Organizations
Social Services: At-Risk Youth, Big Brothers/Big Sisters, Camps, Child Abuse, Child Welfare, Community Centers, Community Service Organizations, Crime Prevention, Day Care, Domestic Violence, Emergency Relief, Family Services, Food/Clothing Distribution, Homes, People with Disabilities, Recreation & Athletics, Scouts, Senior Services, Sexual Abuse, Shelters/Homelessness, Social Services-General, Special Olympics, Substance Abuse, United Funds/United Ways, Volunteer Services, YMCA/YWCA/YMHA/YWHA, Youth Organizations

Application Procedures

Initial Contact: All requests must be submitted in writing. If the request falls within the foundation's areas of interest and meets the guidelines, a proposal will be requested. Only requests from the metropolitan Kansas City area are considered. Grant application guidelines are available from the foundation.
Application Requirements: If requested, proposals should contain the following information: a clear description of the project for which funds are being requested, including program goals and objectives, documentation, of need and expected outcomes; a brief background on the proposing organization or agency; a detailed expense budget for the project indicating how the funds would be spent and over what time period; an income statement showing other sources of project support, public and/or private, which have been or will be solicited, including a statement of funds which have been received or pledged to date; a financial plan showing how the project will be supported beyond the grant period; criteria and/or method by which effectiveness of the grant will be measured; information on the staff responsible for managing the project; a list of the organization's current board of directors and their terms of office; a copy of the organization's most recent 501 (c)(3) tax-exempt ruling from the Internal Revenue Service; and the organization's most recent certified audit or audited financial statement, where applicable.
Deadlines: None. However, proposals must be submitted at least eight weeks prior to when the board meets to be considered at the meeting.
Review Process: The average period of preliminary review (before a proposal is presented to the board) is six to eight weeks. The board of directors meets in March, June, September, and December. The average period of initial review is six to eight weeks.
Notes: The foundation gives preference to programs which create long-term solutions, have a positive impact on the community, are innovative, have the likelihood of future support for on-going operating costs,

are non-competing with the government, promote excellence, have the capacity to achieve the desired results, and cooperate with other community agencies.

Restrictions

Grants are not made to individuals. In addition, the foundation does not provide grants for dinners, special events, international or fraternal organizations, political and lobbying groups, international or religious organizations for sectarian purposes, goodwill advertising, past operating deficits, or travel/conference expenses.

Additional Information

Grant recipients are asked to make periodic written progress reports.

Publications: Annual Report; Guidelines and Procedures for Grant Applicants

Foundation Officials

Jeanne M. Bates: vice president, program officer PRIM CORP EMPL manager community development: Hallmark Cards Inc.

Richard C. Green: director CORP AFFIL chairman, president, chief executive officer, director: Aquila Inc. NONPR AFFIL director: Midwest Research Institute.

Donald Joyce Hall: chairman, director B Kansas City, MO July 09, 1928. ED Dartmouth College AB (1950). PRIM CORP EMPL chairman board, director: Hallmark Cards Inc. CORP AFFIL director: Target Corp. NONPR AFFIL life trustee: Midwest Research Institute; trustee: Nelson-Atkins Museum Art; director: Kansas City Symphony; member: Kansas City Chamber of Commerce; director: Kansas City Minority Suppliers Development Council; president: Civic Council Greater Kansas City; director: Friends of Art; director: American Royal Association; honorary member: American Institute Architects.

William A. Hall: president NONPR AFFIL trustee: Midwest Research Institute.

Irvine O. Hockaday: director CORP AFFIL director: Ford Motor Co.; director: Sprint Corp.; director: Estee Lauder Co.; director: Crown Media Holdings Inc.; director: Dow Jones & Co.; director: Aquila Inc..

Lucinda S. Hogle: assistant secretary

David H. Hughes: director NONPR AFFIL trustee: Midwest Research Institute.

Robert Almy Kipp: director B Lincoln, NE 1932. ED University of Kansas BScE (1952); University of Kansas MPA (1956). PRIM CORP EMPL group vice president: Hallmark Cards Inc. CORP AFFIL vice president: Hallmark Cards Inc. NONPR AFFIL fellow: National Academy Public Administration; board of directors: University of Kansas Center for Research; vice president board of directors: Kansas City Symphony; board of directors: Metro Kansas City Performing Arts Centre; member: Greater Kansas City Chamber of Commerce; board of directors: Kansas City Area Life Sciences Institute.

John Laney: vice president ED University of Kansas MA; University of Miami BA. NONPR AFFIL director: Minority Business Capital Corp.; co-chairman: SkillsUSA-VICA; board of directors: Kansas City Area Development Council; chairman: Economic Development Corp. of Kansas City; member: Greater Downtown Development Authority.

John A. MacDonald: vice president, treasurer NONPR AFFIL finance committee: Greater Kansas City Community Foundation.

John P. Mascotte: director CORP AFFIL director: LabOne Inc.; director: Wyeth Inc.; director: Hallmark Cards Inc.; director: Crown Media Holdings Inc.; director: General Life Reinsurance Co..

Terri R. Maybee: assistant treasurer

Margaret H. Pence: director

Danita M.H. Robinson: secretary

Morton Irvin Sosland: director B Kansas City, MO 1925. ED Harvard University (1946). CORP AFFIL director: H & R Block; director: Kansas City Southern Industries. NONPR AFFIL director: Greater Kansas City Community Foundation; life trustee: Midwest Research Institute.

Grants Analysis

Disclosure Period: calendar year ending 2002
Total Grants: $38,917,002*
Number of Grants: 159
Average Grant: $249,468*
Highest Grant: $12,375,000
Lowest Grant: $2,500
Typical Range: $50,000 to $500,000
*Note: Giving excludes United Way. Average grant figure excludes three highest grants ($17,275,000).

Recent Grants

Note: Grants derived from 2002 Form 990.
General

12,375,000	Children's Mercy Hospital, Kansas City, MO
2,900,000	Kansas University Endowment Association, Lawrence, KS
2,000,000	Nelson Gallery Foundation, Kansas City, MO
1,500,000	Midwest Research Foundation, Kansas City, MO
1,000,000	Missouri Development Finance Board, Jefferson City, MO
1,000,000	Missouri Development Finance Board, Jefferson City, MO
833,334	Union Station Kansas City Inc., Kansas City, MO -- toward operating support
833,333	Union Station Kansas City Inc., Kansas City, MO
833,333	Union Station Kansas City Inc., Kansas City, MO
566,000	Greater Kansas City Community Foundation, Kansas City, MO -- toward the Kansas City Community Development Initiative

HALL-PERRINE FOUNDATION

Giving Contact

Jack B. Evans, President, Chief Executive Officer
Hall-Perrine Foundation
115 3rd Street Southeast, Suite 803
Cedar Rapids, IA 52401-1222
Phone: (319)362-9079
Fax: (319)362-7220

Description

Founded: 1953
EIN: 426057097
Organization Type: Family Foundation
Giving Locations: IA: Linn County, Cedar Rapids
Grant Types: Capital, Challenge, General Support, Matching

Donor Information

Founder: The foundation originally was organized by Howard Hall under the Iowa Nonprofit Corporation Act in 1953. The incorporators were the late Margaret L. Hall and Howard Hall, Margaret D. Hall (also deceased), Irene H. Perrine, and Beahl T. Perrine (deceased). Howard Hall (d. 1971) was born in Onslow, IA. Mr. Hall was founder of the Margaret and Howard Hall Radiation Center and president and chairman of Iowa Manufacturing Co., Iowa Steel and Iron Works, and the Amana Refrigeration Co. He also was director of Iowa Electric Light and Power Co., Quaker Oats Co., and the Square D Co. of Detroit.

Financial Summary

Total Giving: $5,038,496 (2003); $5,375,967 (2002); $5,000,000 (2001 approx)
Giving Analysis: Giving for 2003 includes: foundation grants to United Way ($620,000); 2002: foundation grants to United Way ($550,000)
Assets: $108,446,319 (2003); $100,874,803 (2002)

Gifts Received: $535 (2000); $751 (1999); $573 (1998). Note: The above gifts were bequeathed from the estate of Irene H. Perrine, former chairman of the foundation.

Typical Recipients

Arts & Humanities: Arts Associations & Councils, Ethnic & Folk Arts, History & Archaeology, Libraries, Museums/Galleries, Music, Opera, Theater

Civic & Public Affairs: Botanical Gardens/Parks, Business/Free Enterprise, Chambers of Commerce, Clubs, Community Foundations, Economic Development, Employment/Job Training, Civic & Public Affairs-General, Housing, Inner-City Development, Municipalities/Towns, Nonprofit Management, Urban & Community Affairs, Women's Affairs, Zoos/Aquariums

Education: Afterschool/Enrichment Programs, Business Education, Colleges & Universities, Community & Junior Colleges, Education Funds, Leadership Training, Minority Education, Science/Mathematics Education, Student Aid

Environment: Environment-General, Protection, Resource Conservation

Health: Clinics/Medical Centers, Emergency/Ambulance Services, Geriatric Health, Health Funds, Health Organizations, Heart, Hospitals

Religion: Churches, Jewish Causes, Religious Welfare, Synagogues/Temples

Science: Science-General, Scientific Centers & Institutes

Social Services: Animal Protection, Camps, Child Welfare, Community Centers, Community Service Organizations, Counseling, Domestic Violence, Emergency Relief, Family Planning, Family Services, Food/Clothing Distribution, Homes, People with Disabilities, Recreation & Athletics, Scouts, Senior Services, Shelters/Homelessness, Substance Abuse, United Funds/United Ways, Volunteer Services, YMCA/YWCA/YMHA/YWHA, Youth Organizations

Application Procedures

Initial Contact: Applicants should make a preliminary inquiry to determine the foundation's interest in their request. This inquiry should briefly describe the organization and its purposes, and outline the goal of the proposed project. A grant application form is available upon request.

Application Requirements: Formal written proposals should include a brief description of the organization (legal name, history, activities, purpose, and governing board); purpose for grant; amount requested; other sources of financial support; audited financial statement; IRS determination letter of 501(c)(3) status; and Form 990.

Deadlines: None.

Review Process: Grant proposals are thoroughly screened by the foundation staff. Those meeting the established criteria are then considered by the board of directors or its duly authorized committee. Proposals are reviewed by the board approximately four times per year.

When a decision is reached, the foundation promptly sends a written notice advising of either the approval or disapproval of the grant proposal.

For grants that are approved, it is essential that the grantee accept the grant and the conditions set forth in an Agreement of Donee which includes financial reporting and a summary of the results obtained. This procedure enables the foundation to periodically review and evaluate its performance.

Restrictions

No grants are made to individuals. The following types of support do not have high priority: deficit financing, scholarships, fellowships, loans, endowment, continuing operating support, and basic scholarly research. Funds also are restricted for churches, elementary and secondary schools, benefits, special events, and conferences. Serves only county organizations.

Additional Information

The foundation's original name was The Hall Foundation.

Publications: Guidelines; Application Form

Foundation Officials

Dr. Dennis L. Boatman: director B 1939. ED University of Iowa MD (1965). NONPR AFFIL principal: PCI Urology.

Ernest J. Buresh: director PRIM CORP EMPL president: Citizens Savings Bank.

Kathy E. Eno: director

Jack B. Evans: president, director B 1948. ED University of Iowa MBA. PRIM CORP EMPL president, director: Sci Fin Group Inc. CORP AFFIL director: Cedar Rapids Gazette Inc.; director: United Fire Casualty Co.

Carleen M. Grandon: director

John Gabrielson Lidvall: treasurer, director B 1924.

Alex Alfred Meyer: director B Cedar Rapids, IA 1931. ED University of Iowa (1956). PRIM CORP EMPL president, chairman, chief executive officer, director: Amana Refrigeration. CORP AFFIL director: Toro Co.

Darrel Arle Morf: vice president, director B Fredericksburg, IA 1943. ED University of Iowa BA (1966); University of Iowa JD (1969). PRIM CORP EMPL partner: Simmons, Perrine, Albright. NONPR AFFIL member: Iowa Bar Association; member: Linn County Bar Association; member: American Bar Association.

Iris Muchmore: director, secretary PRIM CORP EMPL partner: Simmons, Perrine, Albright.

Charles M. Peters: director

William Perry Whipple: chairman, director B Cedar Rapids, IA November 01, 1913. ED Coe College BA (1935). PRIM NONPR EMPL chairman, director: Hall-Perrine Foundation, Inc. NONPR AFFIL director: Linn County ARC; honorary director: Methwick Manor; chairman, trustee: Coe College; trustee: Cedar Rapids Public Library. CLUB AFFIL mem: Rotary Club; mem: Elks Club.

Grants Analysis

Disclosure Period: calendar year ending 2003

Total Grants: $4,418,496*

Number of Grants: 28

Average Grant: $110,352*

Highest Grant: $1,439,000

Lowest Grant: $250

Typical Range: $25,000 to $250,000

***Note:** Giving excludes United Way. Average grant figure excludes highest grant.

Recent Grants

Note: Grants derived from 2003 Form 990.

Library-Related

250	Cedar Rapids Public Library, Cedar Rapids, IA -- toward memorial giftCity of Springville, Springville, IA -- toward the new public library

General

1,439,000	Community Health Free Clinic, Cedar Rapids, IA -- for free medical clinic
520,000	United Way of East Central Iowa, Cedar Rapids, IA
500,000	American Red Cross, Iowa City, IA -- toward new facility and modifications
500,000	City of Cedar Rapids, Cedar Rapids, IA -- toward the renovation of Paramount theatre
400,000	Science Station, Cedar Rapids, IA -- for renovations and IMAX theater
333,333	Cedar Rapids Museum of Art, Cedar Rapids, IA -- toward Grant wood studio and air conditioning
250,000	American Red Cross, Iowa City, IA -- toward funding for new facility
250,000	Cedar Rapids Symphony Orchestra, Cedar Rapids, IA -- toward the symphony center

198,812	Area Substance Abuse Council, Cedar Rapids, IA -- toward new housing for clients
180,000	City of Marion, Marion, IA -- toward Lowe Park Children's Gardens

E. L. AND R. F. HALLBERG FOUNDATION

Giving Contact

Virginia L. Winker, Co-Trustee
2705 S. Cooper St., Suite 300
Arlington, TX 76015
Phone: (817)884-4448

Description

Founded: 1986

EIN: 756356892

Organization Type: Private Foundation

Giving Locations: TX

Grant Types: General Support.

Financial Summary

Total Giving: $186,772 (fiscal year ending September 30, 2004); $168,125 (fiscal 2001)

Assets: $4,050,879 (fiscal 2004); $4,183,871 (fiscal 2001)

Typical Recipients

Arts & Humanities: Arts Funds, Libraries, Museums/Galleries, Music, Performing Arts, Theater

Civic & Public Affairs: Clubs, Civic & Public Affairs-General, Hispanic Affairs, Housing, Philanthropic Organizations

Education: Colleges & Universities, Engineering/Technological Education, Environmental Education, Health & Physical Education, Journalism/Media Education, Literacy, Minority Education, Private Education (Precollege), Religious Education, School Volunteerism, Science/Mathematics Education, Student Aid

Environment: Wildlife Protection

Health: Alzheimer's Disease, Health Funds, Hospices

International: International Organizations

Religion: Churches, Religious Welfare

Social Services: Child Welfare, Community Service Organizations, Family Services, Food/Clothing Distribution, People with Disabilities, Shelters/Homelessness, Volunteer Services

Application Procedures

Initial Contact: Send a brief letter of inquiry.

Application Requirements: Include a description of organization, amount requested, purpose of funds sought, recently audited financial statement, and proof of tax-exempt status.

Deadlines: None.

Restrictions

Does not support individuals or political or lobbying groups.

Additional Information

Trust(s): Bank One TX NA

Foundation Officials

Virginia Winkler: co-trustee

Grants Analysis

Disclosure Period: fiscal year ending September 30, 2004

Total Grants: $186,772

Number of Grants: 41

Average Grant: $4,044*

Highest Grant: $25,000

Lowest Grant: $1,000

Typical Range: $1,000 to $5,000

***Note:** Average grant figure excludes two highest grants ($59,000).

Recent Grants

Note: Grants derived from fiscal 2004 Form 990.

General

25,000	First United Methodist Church of Richardson, Richardson, TX -- for the building in faith campaign
14,272	Christian Church Foundation, Indianapolis, IN -- for the permanent fund
12,000	College of Engineering at University of Texas Austin, Austin, TX -- for teaching assistant program in electrical engineering
12,000	Van Cliburn Foundation, Ft. Worth, TX -- for 2005 international piano competition
10,000	Airline Ambassadors International Inc., Carrollton, TX -- towards children's escort program
10,000	Baylor Health Care System Foundation, Dallas, TX -- for Baylor institute for rehabilitation
10,000	Fort Worth Symphony Orchestra Association, Ft. Worth, TX
6,000	Houston Aid in Neonatal Death Inc., Houston, TX
5,000	Arlington Woman's Club Foundation, Arlington, TX
5,000	St. Barnabas United Methodist Church, Arlington, TX -- for building fund

E. W. HALLETT CHARITABLE TRUST

Giving Contact

Duane Feragen, Trust Officer
c/o US National Bank
PO Box 64713
St. Paul, MN 55164
Phone: (612)973-4485

Description

Founded: 1984

EIN: 416261160

Organization Type: Private Foundation

Giving Locations: MN

Grant Types: General Support, Scholarship.

Financial Summary

Total Giving: $443,967 (fiscal year ending November 30, 2004); $779,217 (fiscal 2001)

Giving Analysis: Giving for fiscal 2004 includes: foundation scholarships ($34,500); fiscal 2001: foundation scholarships ($18,000)

Assets: $15,626,946 (fiscal 2004); $16,411,279 (fiscal 2001)

Typical Recipients

Arts & Humanities: History & Archaeology, Libraries

Civic & Public Affairs: Community Foundations, Economic Development, Civic & Public Affairs-General, Housing, Inner-City Development, Municipalities/Towns, Urban & Community Affairs

Education: Colleges & Universities, Education Funds, Education-General, Public Education (Precollege), Religious Education, Science/Mathematics Education, Special Education, Student Aid

Environment: Protection

Health: Clinics/Medical Centers, Eyes/Blindness, Heart, Home-Care Services, Hospices, Hospitals, Medical Rehabilitation

Religion: Churches, Seminaries

Social Services: Camps, Child Welfare, Community Centers, Crime Prevention, Food/Clothing Distribution, Homes, People with Disabilities, Recreation & Athletics, Scouts, Youth Organizations

Application Procedures

Initial Contact: Send a brief letter of inquiry describing program or project.
Deadlines: None.

Restrictions

Does not support individuals.

Additional Information

Trust(s): US Bank
Trust(s): US Bank NA

Foundation Officials

A. C. Jensen: co-trustee
N. Jean Rude: co-trustee
Paul D. Schliesman: co-trustee

Grants Analysis

Disclosure Period: fiscal year ending November 30, 2004
Total Grants: $409,467*
Number of Grants: 8
Highest Grant: $187,722
Lowest Grant: $1,000
*Note: GEX scholarship.

Recent Grants

Note: Grants derived from fiscal 2004 Form 990.
Library-Related

| 187,722 | Jessie F. Hallett Memorial Library, Crosby, MN |

General

94,470	Hallett Community Center Foundation Inc., Crosby, MN
75,000	Crosby-Ironton Independent School District, Crosby, MN -- 2nd and last half of technology grant
34,500	Crosby-Ironton Independent School District 182, Crosby, MN -- 2004 scholarships
25,000	City of Ironton, Ironton, MN -- capital grant for park-playground
13,775	Long Lake Conservation Center, Palisade, MN -- for completion of schoolhouse
10,000	City of Ironton, Ironton, MN -- matching capital grant for park-playground
2,500	Bay Lake Lions Charities Inc., Deerwood, MN -- support for operation of mobility bus
1,000	Salem Church, Deerwood, MN

HALLIBURTON CO.

Company Headquarters

4100 Clinton Dr.
Houston, TX 77020-6299
Web: http://www.halliburton.com

Company Description

Founded: 1919
Ticker: HAL
Exchange: NYSE
Revenue: US$20.466 billion (2004)
Profit: (US$979 million) (2004)
Employees: 101000 (2003)
Fortune Rank: 101, per FORTUNE Magazine's list of 500 Largest U.S. Corporations (2004).
SIC(s): 1389 Oil & Gas Field Services Nec, 1541 Industrial Buildings & Warehouses, 1629 Heavy Construction Nec, 1799 Special Trade Contractors Nec.

Operating Locations

Halliburton Co. (AL--Mobile; CA--Alhambra; DC--Washington; FL--St. Petersburg; MD--Gaithersburg; OK--Davis, Duncan; PA--Pittsburgh)

Nonmonetary Support

Type: Donated Equipment; Donated Products

Halliburton Foundation, Inc.

Giving Contact

Brinda Maxwell
Halliburton Foundation
PO Box 4574
Houston, TX 77210
Phone: (713)839-4848
E-mail: fhoufoundation@halliburton.com
Web:
http://www.halliburton.com/about/community.jsp
Note: Contact for foundation giving.

Alternate Contact

Community & Governmental Affairs Manager
Halliburton Co.
PO Box 3
Houston, TX 77001-0003
Note: Contact for corporate contributions.

Description

EIN: 751212458
Organization Type: Corporate Foundation
Giving Locations: TX: Southwest.
Grant Types: Employee Matching Gifts, General Support.
Note: Employee matching gift ratio: 2 to 1.

Financial Summary

Total Giving: $1,603,035 (2003); $1,299,441 (2001).
Note: Contributes through foundation only.
Assets: $13,974,305 (2003); $14,297,951 (2002); $16,326,786 (2001)
Gifts Received: $1,000,004 (2003); $1,077,480 (2001); $1,406,603 (2000). Note: Contributions were received from Halliburton Energy Services and Brown & Root Companies.

Typical Recipients

Arts & Humanities: Arts Centers, Historic Preservation, History & Archaeology, Libraries, Museums/Galleries, Music, Opera, Performing Arts
Civic & Public Affairs: Business/Free Enterprise, Employment/Job Training, Civic & Public Affairs-General, Housing, Law & Justice, Philanthropic Organizations, Professional & Trade Associations, Public Policy, Urban & Community Affairs, Women's Affairs, Zoos/Aquariums
Education: Afterschool/Enrichment Programs, Agricultural Education, Business Education, Business-School Partnerships, Colleges & Universities, Community & Junior Colleges, Elementary Education (Public), Engineering/Technological Education, Faculty Development, Education-General, International Studies, Legal Education, Literacy, Medical Education, Minority Education, Private Education (Precollege), Public Education (Precollege), Religious Education, Science/Mathematics Education, Social Sciences Education, Student Aid, Vocational & Technical Education
Environment: Energy, Environment-General, Resource Conservation
Health: Cancer, Diabetes, Health Funds, Hospitals, Single-Disease Health Associations, Transplant Networks/Donor Banks
International: Foreign Educational Institutions
Religion: Religious Organizations, Religious Welfare, Seminaries
Science: Science Museums, Scientific Centers & Institutes, Scientific Research
Social Services: Animal Protection, Camps, Child Abuse, Child Welfare, Scouts, Shelters/Homelessness, Social Services-General, Substance Abuse, United Funds/United Ways, YMCA/YWCA/YMHA/YWHA, Youth Organizations

Application Procedures

Initial Contact: Requests for corporate contributions (either cash or in-kind support) should be in the form of a written proposal. Requests for foundation funding should be in the form of a letter.
Application Requirements: Corporate contributions requests should include description of organization to be funded, expected outcomes, program objectives with target dates, evaluation plan, and strategy to secure full funding for program. Also include 501(c)3 determination letter; list of board of directors and their business or other affiliations; audited financial statement; and current list of supporters.
Letters requesting foundation support should include amount requested and purpose of funds sought.
Deadlines: None.
Review Process: Requests are reviewed throughout the year. Decisions are based on available resources and eligibility of applying organization. Full review may take up to three months.
Evaluative Criteria: The company reports that it evaluates applications based on their ability to demonstrate Halliburton employee involvement or interest; meet critical community needs; provide solutions to critical social issues that have a demonstrated impact on children and youth; serve as a catalyst for raising additional funds from other corporations and foundations; demonstrate a specific need for Halliburton support; demonstrate sound financial management; impact or benefit key communities around the world where Halliburton has an employee and business presence. In addition, the program or activity should be recognized as a model program and have potential for replication.

Restrictions

Support is not made for individuals, scholarships for individuals, advertising campaigns, travel expenses, sporting events, or film and video projects. Also does not support religious organizations or organizations whose fundraising/administrative expenses exceed 15% of their annual budget.

Additional Information

Halliburton Co. merged with Dresser Industries effective September 1998.

Corporate Officials

David J. Lesar: chairman, president, chief executive officer B 1953. ED University of Wisconsin MBA; University of Wisconsin BS. PRIM CORP EMPL chairman president, chief executive officer: Halliburton Co. ADD CORP EMPL chairman: Kellogg Brown & Root Inc. CORP AFFIL director: Highlands Insurance Co.; director: Southern Co. Inc.; director: Cordant Technology Inc.

Foundation Officials

J. R. Blurton: treasurer
Margaret E. Carriere: trustee
David J. Lesar: president, trustee (see above)
Michele Mastream: vice president, corp. secretary
Weldon Mire: trustee
Mike Weberpal: counsel

Grants Analysis

Disclosure Period: calendar year ending 2003
Total Grants: $950,485*
Number of Grants: 357
Average Grant: $2,662
Highest Grant: $150,000
Typical Range: $1,000 to $5,000
*Note: Giving excludes scholarships; United Way.

Recent Grants

Note: Grants derived from 2003 Form 990.
General

| 100,000 | Oklahoma Centennial Commission, Oklahoma City, OK |
| 100,000 | University of Texas M. D. Anderson Cancer Center, Houston, TX |

40,500	Oklahoma State University, Norman, OK
37,500	Texas A and M University, TX
35,000	University of Houston, Houston, TX
32,000	University of Texas, Austin, TX
30,000	Junior Achievement of Southeast Texas Inc., Houston, TX
30,000	Texas Tech University, Lubbock, TX
29,500	Colorado School of Mines, Golden, CO
25,000	Southern Methodist University, Dallas, TX

EWING HALSELL FOUNDATION

Giving Contact
Gilbert M. Denman, Jr., Trustee, Chairman of the Board
711 Navarro, Suite 537
San Antonio, TX 78205
Phone: (210)223-2649
Fax: (210)271-9089

Description
Founded: 1957
EIN: 746063016
Organization Type: General Purpose Foundation
Giving Locations: TX: San Antonio
Grant Types: Capital, General Support, Operating Expenses, Project, Research, Scholarship.

Donor Information
Founder: Established in 1957 by the late Ewing Halsell and the late Grace Fortner Rider, who died in 1971. Mr. Halsell was a cattle rancher whose interests centered in Texas, Oklahoma, and Kansas.

Financial Summary
Total Giving: $4,471,366 (fiscal year ending June 30, 2004); $4,384,264 (fiscal 2002)
Giving Analysis: Giving for fiscal 2004 includes: foundation grants to United Way ($5,000); foundation scholarships ($100,000); fiscal 2002: foundation grants to United Way ($5,000); foundation scholarships ($105,000)
Assets: $103,066,348 (fiscal 2004); $83,600,071 (fiscal 2002)

Typical Recipients
Arts & Humanities: Arts Associations & Councils, Arts Centers, Arts Festivals, Arts Outreach, Ballet, Dance, Ethnic & Folk Arts, History & Archaeology, Libraries, Literary Arts, Museums/Galleries, Music, Opera, Public Broadcasting, Theater
Civic & Public Affairs: Botanical Gardens/Parks, Business/Free Enterprise, Community Foundations, Economic Development, Employment/Job Training, Civic & Public Affairs-General, Hispanic Affairs, Housing, Nonprofit Management, Philanthropic Organizations, Public Policy, Rural Affairs, Safety, Urban & Community Affairs, Zoos/Aquariums
Education: Afterschool/Enrichment Programs, Agricultural Education, Arts/Humanities Education, Colleges & Universities, Economic Education, Education Reform, Elementary Education (Public), Faculty Development, Education-General, Literacy, Medical Education, Minority Education, Private Education (Precollege), Religious Education, Science/Mathematics Education, Special Education, Student Aid, Vocational & Technical Education
Environment: Environment-General, Resource Conservation, Watershed, Wildlife Protection
Health: AIDS/HIV, Cancer, Children's Health/Hospitals, Clinics/Medical Centers, Emergency/Ambulance Services, Geriatric Health, Health Organizations, Heart, Hospitals, Medical Research, Nursing Services, Public Health, Single-Disease Health Associations

International: International Organizations
Religion: Churches, Jewish Causes, Ministries, Religious Organizations, Religious Welfare
Social Services: Camps, Child Welfare, Community Centers, Community Service Organizations, Day Care, Domestic Violence, Family Planning, Family Services, Food/Clothing Distribution, People with Disabilities, Scouts, Shelters/Homelessness, Substance Abuse, United Funds/United Ways, YMCA/YWCA/YMHA/YWHA, Youth Organizations

Application Procedures
Initial Contact: Applicants should submit a letter and a short summary of the proposed project.
Application Requirements: Proposals should include the history and purposes of the organization, proposed use of funds, anticipated results of expenditures, and explanation of financial need (including other sources of funds, if any, to be used for the project). Also include a copy of the IRS tax exemption letter and information clearly indicating that any contribution made by the foundation will be considered a qualifying distribution, not a taxable expenditure. Applications should be signed or approved in writing by the chief executive of the applicant organization.
Deadlines: None.
Review Process: The foundation's trustees meet three to four times a year. Applicants will be notified in writing of receipt of application. Interviews are conducted only at the foundation's initiative.
Notes: The foundation discourages expensive and elaborate presentations.

Restrictions
The foundation discourages proposals for general support, deficit reduction, or continuing or additional support for current or previous programs. Grants are not made to individuals.

Additional Information
Grant commitments may cover several years. Matching funding is encouraged. The foundation trustees also initiate grants, and may make challenge grants to stimulate other financial participation. In fields of special foundation interest, the foundation's program includes support for undertaking these projects. In many cases, trustees take an active part in the formation and operation of these programs as well as their support.
Because of the periodic nature of the trustees' meetings and the foundation's long-range planning process, it is suggested that applicants needing immediate help should apply to private individuals or corporations who are in a better position to make such grants to municipal, state, federal, or other public agencies.
Denman, Franklin, Denman in San Antonio, TX, provides legal and administrative services.
Publications: Application Guidelines

Foundation Officials
Edward H. Austin, Jr.: trustee B 1941. ED New York University; University of Texas; Tulane University BBA (1961). PRIM CORP EMPL partner, treasurer: Austin, Calvert & Flavin Inc. CORP AFFIL director: KN Energy Inc.
Jean Deacy: trustee emeritus
Leroy G. Denman, Jr.: trustee B San Antonio, TX 1918. ED University of Texas BA (1939); University of Texas LLB (1939). PRIM CORP EMPL attorney: Denman, Franklin & Denman. CORP AFFIL vice president, director: King Ranch Saddle Shop Inc.; vice president, director: Running W Saddle Shop; director: King Ranch Holdings Inc.
Hugh A. Fitzsimmons, Jr.: trustee

Grants Analysis
Disclosure Period: fiscal year ending June 30, 2004
Total Grants: $4,366,366*
Number of Grants: 45
Average Grant: $55,032*
Highest Grant: $1,000,000

Lowest Grant: $419
Typical Range: $10,000 to $100,000
***Note:** Giving excludes United Way and scholarships. Average grant figure excludes two highest grants ($2,000,000).

Recent Grants
Note: Grants derived from fiscal 2003 Form 990.
General

400,000	San Antonio Museum of Art, San Antonio, TX -- towards Asian art project expense
250,000	San Antonio Academy, San Antonio, TX -- towards permanent endowment
50,000	Trinity University, San Antonio, TX -- to support core knowledge office
21,400	KLRN Alamo Public Telecommunication Council, San Antonio, TX -- contribution toward sponsoring NOVA
20,000	Lyric Opera of San Antonio, San Antonio, TX -- for production underwriting
19,400	KLRN Alamo Public Telecommunication Council, San Antonio, TX -- contribution toward sponsoring NATURE
10,000	San Antonio Museum of Art, San Antonio, TX -- towards Asian art photography
5,000	San Antonio Livestock Exposition, San Antonio, TX -- towards youth scholarship program
5,000	San Antonio Museum of Art, San Antonio, TX -- towards operating services
5,000	San Antonio Symphony, San Antonio, TX -- towards classical music performance

HAMAN FAMILY FOUNDATION

Giving Contact
Larry Markworth
Huntington National Bank
232 W. Third St.
Dover, OH 44622
Phone: (614)331-9539

Description
Founded: 1998
EIN: 316565640
Organization Type: Private Foundation
Giving Locations: OH: Tuscarawas County
Grant Types: Capital, Project.

Financial Summary
Total Giving: $56,891 (fiscal year ending March 31, 2002); $61,076 (fiscal 2001)
Assets: $1,188,421 (fiscal 2002); $1,208,567 (fiscal 2001)

Typical Recipients
Arts & Humanities: Libraries, Museums/Galleries
Civic & Public Affairs: Civic & Public Affairs-General, Safety
Education: Colleges & Universities, Elementary Education (Public), Public Education (Precollege)
Health: Emergency/Ambulance Services
Social Services: Emergency Relief, YMCA/YWCA/YMHA/YWHA, Youth Organizations

Restrictions
Grants must go to charitable organizations in and for the benefit of Tuscarawas County, Ohio.

Additional Information
Trust(s): Huntington National Bank

Foundation Officials
Ruth Goertz: committee member
Ruth Goertz: committee member
Mark Heil: committee member

Mark Heill: committee member
Wilford Miller: committee member
Wilford Miller: committee member

Grants Analysis

Disclosure Period: fiscal year ending March 31, 2002
Total Grants: $56,891
Number of Grants: 19
Average Grant: $2,994
Highest Grant: $10,000
Lowest Grant: $500
Typical Range: $2,500 to $5,000

Recent Grants

Note: Grants derived from 2001 Form 990.
Library-Related

2,500	Dover Public Library, Dover, OH -- building addition

General

10,000	Kent State University, Kent, OH -- science and technology facility
6,562	Tusky Valley Youth Services -- software and television for youth center
5,500	Port Washington Police Department -- video camera for cruiser
5,000	Bolivar Volunteer Fire Department -- for portable radios
5,000	Claymont High School Library -- for library reference material
5,000	East Elementary -- for PTA and school playground renovation
5,000	New Philadelphia Fire Department, Philadelphia, PA -- equipment for trench rescue team
3,333	TUSC County YMCA -- expansion of Wellness Center
3,163	Tri County Joint Ambulance Department -- for emergency medical equipment
2,518	Dennison Railroad Depot Museum, Dennison, OH -- for photographic archival supplies

HAMER FOUNDATION

Giving Contact

Diane M. Kerly, Trustee
Hamer Foundation
2470 Fox Hill Road
State College, PA 16803-1797
Phone: (814)355-8004

Description

Founded: 1989
EIN: 251610780
Organization Type: Private Foundation
Giving Locations: PA: Centre County
Grant Types: General Support.

Donor Information

Founder: Established in 1989 by Donald W. Hamer.

Financial Summary

Total Giving: $222,550 (2003); $705,000 (2001)
Giving Analysis: Giving for 2003 includes: foundation grants to United Way ($15,000)
Assets: $4,930,901 (2003); $4,903,128 (2001)
Gifts Received: $400,000 (2003); $750,000 (2001); $1,040,440 (2000). Note: In 1996, 2001, and 2003, contributions were received from Donald W. Hamer. In 1999, contributions were received from Donald W. Hamer and Diane M. Kerly.

Typical Recipients

Arts & Humanities: Libraries, Museums/Galleries
Civic & Public Affairs: Botanical Gardens/Parks, Community Foundations, Housing, Women's Affairs
Education: Business Education, Colleges & Universities, Education Funds, Education-General, Minority Education
Environment: Environment-General, Resource Conservation, Wildlife Protection
Health: Emergency/Ambulance Services, Hospitals
Religion: Religion-General
Social Services: Community Service Organizations, Food/Clothing Distribution, Scouts, United Funds/United Ways

Application Procedures

Initial Contact: The foundation reports no specific application guidelines. Send a brief letter of inquiry.
Application Requirements: Include statement of purpose, amount requested, and proof of tax-exempt status.
Deadlines: None.

Restrictions

Focus is on environmental concerns and educational institutions in the Centre County, PA, area.

Foundation Officials

Donald W. Hamer: trustee
Diane M. Kerly: trustee
Edward J. Matosziuk: trustee

Grants Analysis

Disclosure Period: calendar year ending 2003
Total Grants: $207,550*
Number of Grants: 24
Average Grant: $6,850*
Highest Grant: $50,000
Lowest Grant: $1,500
Typical Range: $1,500 to $10,000
*Note: Giving excludes United Way. Average grant figure excludes highest grant.

Recent Grants

Note: Grants derived from 2003 Form 990.
Library-Related

10,000	Schlow Library, State College, PA

General

50,000	University of Illinois Foundation, Urbana, IL
15,000	Alpha Ambulance, State College, PA -- towards building fund
15,000	Center County United Way, State College, PA -- for annual campaign
15,000	Pennsylvania State University, University Park, PA -- towards capital fund-palmer
12,500	Center County Community Foundation, State College, PA
12,500	Nature Conservancy, Arlington, VA
11,875	University of Illinois Foundation, Urbana, IL
11,875	University of Illinois Foundation, Urbana, IL
10,000	University of Chicago Graduate School of Business, Chicago, IL

HAMILTON CHARITABLE CORP.

Giving Contact

Harold Brown, President & Treasurer
39 Brighton Avenue
Allston, MA 02134-2301
Phone: (617)783-0039

Description

Founded: 1996
EIN: 043314367
Organization Type: Private Foundation
Giving Locations: MA
Grant Types: General Support, Scholarship.

Financial Summary

Total Giving: $174,559 (2001)
Assets: $2,361,671 (2001)
Gifts Received: $160,000 (2001); $80,000 (2000); $155,725 (1999). Note: Contributions were received from Harold Brown.

Typical Recipients

Arts & Humanities: Libraries, Theater
Civic & Public Affairs: Civic & Public Affairs-General, Philanthropic Organizations, Women's Affairs
Education: Colleges & Universities, Private Education (Precollege), Public Education (Precollege), Student Aid
Health: Cancer, Heart, Hospitals, Public Health
Religion: Jewish Causes
Social Services: Community Service Organizations, Recreation & Athletics, Senior Services

Application Procedures

Initial Contact: The foundation has no formal application procedure.
Deadlines: None.

Foundation Officials

Harold Brown: president, treasurer
Harold Brown: president, treasurer, director
Sally Starr: director
Sally Starr: clerk
Luci Daley Vincent: director

Grants Analysis

Disclosure Period: calendar year ending 2001
Total Grants: $174,559
Number of Grants: 23
Average Grant: $1,169*
Highest Grant: $100,000
Lowest Grant: $89
Typical Range: $500 to $2,500
*Note: Average grant excludes two highest grants ($150,000).

Recent Grants

Note: Grants derived from 2001 Form 990.
Library-Related

1,000	Brookline Public Library, Brookline, MA
1,000	Brookline Public Library, Brookline, MA

General

100,000	MIT Scholarship Fund, Cambridge, MA
50,000	Massachusetts General Hospital, Boston, MA
6,000	American Associates Ben-Gurion University, Los Angeles, CA
2,500	Anti-Defamation League, Boston, MA
2,000	Brookline Youth Hockey, Brookline, MA
1,500	Beaver Country Day School, Brookline, MA
1,500	Whittier Street Health Clinic, Roxbury, MA
1,000	Belmont Women's Club Preservation Fund, Belmont, MA
1,000	Brookline High School 21st Century Fund, Brookline, MA
1,000	Brookline Senior Citizens, Brookline, MA

GEORGE AND MARY JOSEPHINE HAMMAN FOUNDATION

Giving Contact

E. Alan Fritsche, Executive Director
3336 Richmond, Suite 310
Houston, TX 77098

Phone: (713)522-9891
Fax: (713)522-9693
E-mail: hammanfdn@aol.com
Web: http://www.hammanfoundation.org

Description
Founded: 1954
EIN: 746061447
Organization Type: Family Foundation
Giving Locations: TX: Houston
Grant Types: Capital, Challenge, Emergency, General Support, Operating Expenses, Project, Research, Scholarship.

Donor Information
Founder: Incorporated in 1954 by George Hamman and the late Mary Josephine Hamman.

Financial Summary
Total Giving: $2,437,500 (2004); $2,599,400 (2003); $2,571,500 (2002)
Giving Analysis: Giving for 2002 includes: foundation scholarships ($117,000)
Assets: $61,621,545 (2003); $49,979,537 (2002); $56,654,713 (2001)

Typical Recipients
Arts & Humanities: Arts Centers, Ballet, Dance, History & Archaeology, Libraries, Museums/Galleries, Music, Performing Arts, Theater
Civic & Public Affairs: Botanical Gardens/Parks, Clubs, Economic Development, Civic & Public Affairs-General, Hispanic Affairs, Housing, Urban & Community Affairs, Zoos/Aquariums
Education: Arts/Humanities Education, Colleges & Universities, Education Reform, Elementary Education (Private), Faculty Development, Education-General, Health & Physical Education, Literacy, Medical Education, Minority Education, Preschool Education, Private Education (Precollege), Public Education (Precollege), Religious Education, Science/Mathematics Education, Secondary Education (Private), Special Education, Student Aid
Environment: Air/Water Quality, Environment-General, Protection, Resource Conservation, Wildlife Protection
Health: Alzheimer's Disease, Cancer, Children's Health/Hospitals, Clinics/Medical Centers, Emergency/Ambulance Services, Eyes/Blindness, Health Organizations, Heart, Hospices, Hospitals, Hospitals (University Affiliated), Medical Rehabilitation, Medical Research, Mental Health, Single-Disease Health Associations, Speech & Hearing
Religion: Churches, Ministries, Religious Organizations, Religious Welfare
Science: Science Museums, Scientific Centers & Institutes
Social Services: At-Risk Youth, Camps, Child Abuse, Child Welfare, Community Centers, Community Service Organizations, Domestic Violence, Family Planning, Family Services, Food/Clothing Distribution, Homes, People with Disabilities, Scouts, Senior Services, Shelters/Homelessness, Social Services-General, Special Olympics, Substance Abuse, Volunteer Services, YMCA/YWCA/YMHA/YWHA, Youth Organizations

Application Procedures
Initial Contact: The foundation requests applications be made in writing. Applications for scholarships must be obtained from the foundation either by downloading forms from the website or request them in writing.
Deadlines: Monthly for grant applications; February 28 for scholarship applications.

Restrictions
The foundation does not support post-graduate education or individuals. Scholarship recipients must be Houston area high school seniors.

Additional Information
Publications: Guidelines; application form. for scholarships.

Foundation Officials
Mary M. Brown: trustee
E. Alan Fritsche: executive director PRIM CORP EMPL chief financial officer: Looney & Co.
Henry R. Hamman: president, director B 1937. ED University of Texas BS (1959); University of Texas MA (1961). PRIM CORP EMPL president: Hamman Oil & Refining Co. CORP AFFIL director: Devon Energy Corp.; Hamman Aviation Inc.
Russell R. Hamman: trustee
Charles D. Milby, Jr.: treasurer
Ann H. Shepherd: secretary

Grants Analysis
Disclosure Period: calendar year ending 2004
Total Grants: $2,437,500
Number of Grants: 183
Average Grant: $13,320
Highest Grant: $85,000
Lowest Grant: $2,000
Typical Range: $5,000 to $30,000

Recent Grants
Note: Grants derived from 2003 Form 990.
General

85,000	University of Texas Houston Health Science Center, Houston, TX
65,000	Houston Museum of Natural Science, Houston, TX
50,000	Casa De Esperanza, Houston, TX
50,000	University of Texas M.D. Anderson Cancer Center, Houston, TX
35,000	Technology For All Inc., Houston, TX
35,000	University of Houston System, Houston, TX
33,000	Arbor School, Houston, TX
30,000	Texas Children's Hospital, Houston, TX
30,000	YWCA of Houston, Houston, TX
25,000	Boy Scouts of America, Houston, TX

ARMAND HAMMER FOUNDATION

Giving Contact
Michael A. Hammer, President, Chief Executive Officer & Director
2425 Olympic Boulevard, Suite 140 E
Santa Monica, CA 90404
Phone: (713)951-3303

Description
Founded: 1968
EIN: 237010813
Organization Type: General Purpose Foundation
Giving Locations: broad geographic distribution.
Grant Types: Capital, General Support, Multiyear/Continuing Support, Project, Research.

Donor Information
Founder: the late Dr. Armand Hammer

Financial Summary
Total Giving: $2,261,800 (2001)
Assets: $1,403,658 (2001)
Gifts Received: $30,000 (2001); $295,500 (2000); $826,000 (1995). Note: In 1995, 2000, and 2001, contributions were received from the Armand Hammer Living Trust.

Typical Recipients
Arts & Humanities: Arts Associations & Councils, Arts Centers, Film & Video, Historic Preservation, History & Archaeology, Libraries, Museums/Galleries, Music, Opera, Public Broadcasting, Theater
Civic & Public Affairs: Clubs, Civic & Public Affairs-General, Parades/Festivals, Philanthropic Organizations, Public Policy
Education: Business Education, Colleges & Universities, Education-General, Medical Education, Private Education (Precollege), Public Education (Precollege), Religious Education, Student Aid, Vocational & Technical Education
Health: AIDS/HIV, Cancer, Children's Health/Hospitals, Clinics/Medical Centers, Emergency/Ambulance Services, Health-General, Health Organizations, Heart, Hospices, Hospitals, Hospitals (University Affiliated), Medical Research, Medical Training, Multiple Sclerosis, Single-Disease Health Associations
International: Foreign Arts Organizations, Foreign Educational Institutions, Health Care/Hospitals, International Affairs, International Organizations, International Peace & Security Issues, Missionary/Religious Activities
Religion: Churches, Jewish Causes, Ministries, Missionary Activities (Domestic), Religious Organizations, Religious Welfare
Science: Scientific Centers & Institutes
Social Services: Child Welfare, Community Service Organizations, Crime Prevention, Day Care, Family Services, People with Disabilities, Recreation & Athletics, Scouts, Shelters/Homelessness, Social Services-General, Volunteer Services, YMCA/YWCA/YMHA/YWHA, Youth Organizations

Application Procedures
Initial Contact: The foundation has no formal grant application procedure or application form.
Deadlines: None.

Restrictions
No grants are made to individuals.

Foundation Officials
Rex Alexander: director
G. Dwight Clayton: director
Scott R. Deitrick: vice president
Dru Hammer: cfo, secretary, director
Michael A. Hammer: president, chief executive officer, director
W. Dayton Pittman: director
David Sewell: director

Grants Analysis
Disclosure Period: calendar year ending 2001
Total Grants: $2,261,800
Number of Grants: 20
Average Grant: $13,779*
Highest Grant: $2,000,000
Lowest Grant: $900
Typical Range: $10,000 to $30,000
*Note: Average grant figure excludes highest grant.

Recent Grants
Note: Grants derived from 2002 Form 990.

General

13,750	Stop Cancer, Los Angeles, CA
10,000	Partnership for the Homeless, New York, NY
10,000	Pepperdine University, Malibu, CA
8,000	Department of Recreation and Parks, Los Angeles, CA
2,500	HIV Resource Consortium, Tulsa, OK
1,500	Henry Street Settlement, New York, NY
1,200	Petersen Automotive Museum, Los Angeles, CA
1,000	Avon Products Foundation, Inc., New York, NY

EDNA AND YU-SHAN HAN CHARITABLE FOUNDATION

Giving Contact

Robert Sung, Co-Trustee
c/o Sonderbeck
6151 W. Century Blvd., Suite 1112
Los Angeles, CA 90045
Phone: (310)670-5442

Description

Founded: 1983
EIN: 953823449
Organization Type: Private Foundation
Giving Locations: CA
Grant Types: General Support, Scholarship.

Typical Recipients

Arts & Humanities: Libraries, Music, Performing Arts, Public Broadcasting
Civic & Public Affairs: Asian American Affairs, Civic & Public Affairs-General, Philanthropic Organizations
Education: Arts/Humanities Education, Colleges & Universities, Education-General, International Studies, Student Aid
Health: Clinics/Medical Centers, Emergency/Ambulance Services
International: International Relations, Missionary/Religious Activities

Application Procedures

Initial Contact: Send financial statement, scholastic record, letter of admissions from an accredited college or university, and a short essay about applicants life goals and plans.
Deadlines: None.

Additional Information

Provides assistance to needy students without restriction as to race or ethnic background to study Chinese culture, art, or history. Assistance is also provided to needy students of Asian descent, with preference given to students of Chinese ancestry, who are of good character and high scholastic achievement to pursue any field of study.

Foundation Officials

Patsy Sung: co-trustee
Robert Sung: co-trustee

Grants Analysis

Disclosure Period: calendar year ending 2000
Total Grants: $142,820
Number of Grants: 15
Average Grant: $6,630*
Highest Grant: $50,000
Typical Range: $1,000 to $10,000
*Note: Average grant figure excludes highest grant.

Recent Grants

Note: Grants derived from 2001 Form 990.
General

50,000	Stanford University, Stanford, CA
50,000	University of California Los Angeles School of Arts and Architecture, Los Angeles, CA
20,600	University of California Los Angeles College of Letter and Sciences, Los Angeles, CA
16,000	University of California Los Angeles, Los Angeles, CA -- East Asian Library
10,000	Curtis Institute of Music, Philadelphia, PA
10,000	University of California Los Angeles School of Theater, Film, and Television, Los Angeles, CA
6,244	University of California Los Angeles Film Archive, Los Angeles, CA
5,000	University of California Los Angeles, Los Angeles, CA -- annual fund
5,000	University of California Los Angeles, Los Angeles, CA -- Royce Center Circle
4,500	Henry Mancini Institute, Los Angeles, CA

JOHN HANCOCK FINANCIAL SERVICES

Company Headquarters

Boston, MA
Web: http://www.jhancock.com

Company Description

Founded: 1862
Ticker: JHF
Exchange: NYSE
Former Name: John Hancock Mutual Life (2000).
Revenue: US$10.071 billion (2003)
Profit: US$806 million (2003)
Employees: 7974 (2003)
SIC(s): 6311 Life Insurance.
Parent Company: Manulife Financial, 200 Bloor Street E., Toronto, ON, Canada

Operating Locations

John Hancock Mutual Life Insurance Co. (MA--Boston)
Note: Operates throughout the USA.

Nonmonetary Support

Value: $2,300,000 (2000)
Type: Donated Equipment; Donated Products; In-kind Services
Note: Co. also provides nonmonetary support in the form of meeting space, printing and graphic services, public relations assistance, photography, special events planning.
Volunteer Programs: Supports HERO (Hancock Employees Reaching Out), a program which organizes group volunteer projects. Outreach programs include Community Sports Initiative; educational programs, such as Operation Math Corps, Adopt-a-Class, Summer of Opportunity, and Financial Wizard Program; and community service programs, including the Incredible Sandwich Making Event (for food banks), Habitat for Humanity building projects, and holiday relief efforts.

Giving Contact

Carol Fulp, Vice President of Community Relations
Box 111, T-58
Boston, MA 02117
Phone: (617)572-0451
Fax: (617)572-6290
E-mail: cfulp@jhancock.com
Web: http://www.jhancock.com/about/community/com-relations.jsp

Description

Organization Type: Corporate Giving Program
Giving Locations: MA: Boston
Grant Types: Employee Matching Gifts, General Support, Project.
Note: Employee matching gift ratio: 1 to 1 for non-educational nonprofits and 0.5 to 1 for education institutions; program allows employees to give to non-educational nonprofits through payroll deductions and have these gifts matched.

Financial Summary

Total Giving: $6,100,000 (2002 approx); $6,100,000 (2001 approx). Note: Contributes through corporate direct giving program only.

Typical Recipients

Arts & Humanities: Arts Appreciation, Arts Associations & Councils, Arts Centers, Arts Institutes, Community Arts, Dance, Ethnic & Folk Arts, Historic Preservation, Libraries, Museums/Galleries, Music, Opera, Performing Arts, Public Broadcasting, Theater
Civic & Public Affairs: Business/Free Enterprise, Civil Rights, Economic Development, Economic Policy, Employment/Job Training, Law & Justice, Professional & Trade Associations, Public Policy, Urban & Community Affairs, Women's Affairs
Education: Business Education, Continuing Education, Economic Education, Education Funds, Medical Education, Minority Education, Science/Mathematics Education, Special Education
Environment: Environment-General
Health: Health Policy/Cost Containment, Hospitals, Medical Research, Nutrition, Public Health, Single-Disease Health Associations
Social Services: Child Welfare, Community Centers, Community Service Organizations, Counseling, Delinquency & Criminal Rehabilitation, Family Services, Food/Clothing Distribution, Homes, People with Disabilities, Recreation & Athletics, Senior Services, Shelters/Homelessness, Substance Abuse, United Funds/United Ways, Volunteer Services, Youth Organizations

Application Procedures

Initial Contact: Send a brief letter or proposal.
Application Requirements: Include objectives, services, program activities, and accomplishments of organization; purpose for which funds are sought; proof of tax-exempt status; names and affiliations of officers, trustees, and members of the board of directors; population served and their socioeconomic composition; annual budget for the project or program to be assisted, agency budget, audited financial statements, and list of current and potential funds; and method for program evaluation.
Deadlines: None.
Evaluative Criteria: Project provides innovative solutions to significant social needs; stimulates additional giving by other institutions and individuals.
Notes: All organizations receiving company grants are requested to submit periodic reports on how funds are used.

Restrictions

Does not support fraternal or political organizations, religious organizations for sectarian purposes, individuals, goodwill advertising, scholarships, conferences, or trips.

Corporate Officials

Wayne A. Budd: executive vice president, general counsel
David F. D'Alessandro: president, chief operating officer

Giving Program Officials

Carol Bolling: 2nd vice president, community relations

Grants Analysis

Disclosure Period: calendar year ending 1998
Total Grants: $3,825,000 (approx)*
Number of Grants: 2,200
Average Grant: $10,000
Typical Range: $5,000 to $20,000
*Note: Grants analysis provided by the company. Giving excludes nonmonetary support.

HANDY & HARMAN

Company Headquarters

555 Theodore Fremd Avenue
Rye, NY 10580
Web: http://www.handyharmon.com

Company Description

Employees: 2,567
SIC(s): 3300 Primary Metal Industries, 3400 Fabricated Metal Products.

Operating Locations

Handy & Harman (CT--Fairfield, South Windsor; MI--Auburn Hills; NJ--Willingboro; NY--Oriskany; OH--Dover; OK--Tulsa; WI--Cudahy)

Handy & Harman Foundation

Giving Contact

Paul E. Dixon, Trustee & Secretary
555 Theodore Fremd Avenue
Rye, NY 10580-1451
Phone: (914)921-5200

Description

EIN: 237408431
Organization Type: Corporate Foundation
Giving Locations: CT; IL; IN; ME; MA; NY; PA: principally near operating locations and to national organizations.
Grant Types: General Support.

Financial Summary

Total Giving: $125,205 (2001)
Giving Analysis: Giving for 2001 includes: foundation grants to United Way ($18,025)
Assets: $193,660 (2001)
Gifts Received: $150,000 (2000); $150,000 (1999); $150,000 (1998)

Typical Recipients

Arts & Humanities: Arts Centers, Community Arts, Arts & Humanities-General, Libraries, Museums/Galleries, Public Broadcasting
Civic & Public Affairs: Botanical Gardens/Parks, Business/Free Enterprise, Clubs, Community Foundations, Economic Development, Economic Policy, Employment/Job Training, Civic & Public Affairs-General, Inner-City Development, Law & Justice, Legal Aid, Municipalities/Towns, Professional & Trade Associations, Public Policy, Safety, Urban & Community Affairs, Women's Affairs, Zoos/Aquariums
Education: Arts/Humanities Education, Business Education, Colleges & Universities, Economic Education, Education Associations, Education Funds, Education Reform, Engineering/Technological Education, Education-General, Legal Education, Medical Education, Minority Education, Private Education (Precollege), Public Education (Precollege), Science/Mathematics Education, Secondary Education (Private), Secondary Education (Public), Student Aid
Health: Arthritis, Cancer, Children's Health/Hospitals, Clinics/Medical Centers, Diabetes, Emergency/Ambulance Services, Eyes/Blindness, Health-General, Health Organizations, Heart, Home-Care Services, Hospitals, Hospitals (University Affiliated), Medical Training, Mental Health, Nursing Services, Single-Disease Health Associations
International: Health Care/Hospitals, International Affairs, International Organizations, International Relations, International Relief Efforts
Religion: Dioceses, Religion-General, Jewish Causes, Religious Organizations
Science: Science Museums, Scientific Centers & Institutes
Social Services: Camps, Community Centers, Community Service Organizations, Crime Prevention, Domestic Violence, Emergency Relief, Recreation & Athletics, Shelters/Homelessness, Social Services-General, Substance Abuse, United Funds/United Ways, Veterans, YMCA/YWCA/YMHA/YWHA, Youth Organizations

Application Procedures

Initial Contact: Requests should be in writing on organizations letterhead.
Application Requirements: Include a description of organization, amount requested, purpose of funds sought, and proof of tax-exempt status.
Deadlines: None.

Restrictions

Does not support individuals, religious organizations for sectarian purposes, political or lobbying groups, or organizations outside operating areas.

Corporate Officials

Robert LeBlanc: president, chief operating officer PRIM CORP EMPL president, chief operating officer: Handy & Harman.

Foundation Officials

R. F. Burlinson: treasurer, trust
Paul Edward Dixon: secretary, trustee B Brooklyn, NY 1944. ED Villanova University BA (1966); Saint John's University JD (1972). PRIM CORP EMPL vice president, general counsel, secretary: Handy & Harman. CORP AFFIL chairman: Teeches Ltd. NONPR AFFIL member: New York State Bar Association; member: U.S. Supreme Court Historical Society; member: American Corporate Counsel Association; member: New York City Bar Association; member: American Bar Association. CLUB AFFIL Bedford Golf & Tennis Club.
D. C. Kelly: treasurer, trustee
D. P. Murphy, Jr.: president trustee

Grants Analysis

Disclosure Period: calendar year ending 2002
Total Grants: $107,180*
Number of Grants: 104
Average Grant: $838*
Highest Grant: $20,000
Typical Range: $100 to $2,000
*Note: Giving excludes United Way. Average grant excludes highest grant.

Recent Grants

Note: Grants derived from 2002 Form 990.
General

20,000	Alliance for Progress - National Roofing Foundation, Rosemont, IL
10,000	Boston College, Boston, MA
10,000	United Way Eastern Fairfield County, Fairfield, CT
5,000	American Lyme Disease Foundation, New York, NY
5,000	CLMB Foundation, Stockton Springs, ME
5,000	Mary Louis Academy, Jamaica Estates, NY
5,000	Mary Louis Academy, Jamaica Estates, NY
4,000	Avon Old Farms School, Avon, CT
4,000	Sisters of St. Joseph, Holyoke, MA
4,000	United Way Tri-State, New York, NY

JOHN WESLEY AND ANNA HODGIN HANES FOUNDATION

Giving Contact

Linda Tilley, Relationship Manager
c/o Wachovia Bank
100 North Main
PO Box 3099
Winston-Salem, NC 27150-7131
Phone: (336)732-5372
Fax: (336)732-6537

Description

Founded: 1947
EIN: 566037589
Organization Type: Family Foundation
Giving Locations: NC: Winston-Salem and Forsyth County area, Winston-Salem
Grant Types: Capital, General Support, Matching, Project, Research, Seed Money.

Donor Information

Founder: Established in 1947.

Financial Summary

Total Giving: $1,447,902 (2001)
Assets: $28,253,555 (2001)
Gifts Received: $284,831 (1996). Note: Contributions were received from C. Annelle Shillington.

Typical Recipients

Arts & Humanities: Arts Associations & Councils, Arts Centers, Arts Festivals, Arts Funds, Arts Institutes, Community Arts, Dance, Historic Preservation, History & Archaeology, Libraries, Museums/Galleries, Music, Performing Arts, Theater
Civic & Public Affairs: Botanical Gardens/Parks, Chambers of Commerce, Community Foundations, Economic Development, Employment/Job Training, Civic & Public Affairs-General, Housing, Municipalities/Towns, Public Policy, Rural Affairs, Urban & Community Affairs, Zoos/Aquariums
Education: Afterschool/Enrichment Programs, Arts/Humanities Education, Colleges & Universities, Community & Junior Colleges, Education Associations, Education Funds, Elementary Education (Public), Education-General, Medical Education, Private Education (Precollege), Public Education (Precollege), Religious Education, Vocational & Technical Education
Environment: Air/Water Quality, Environment-General, Protection, Resource Conservation, Wildlife Protection
Health: AIDS/HIV, Alzheimer's Disease, Clinics/Medical Centers, Emergency/Ambulance Services, Eyes/Blindness, Health Funds, Hospices, Hospitals, Hospitals (University Affiliated), Medical Rehabilitation, Preventive Medicine/Wellness Organizations, Public Health, Single-Disease Health Associations, Transplant Networks/Donor Banks
International: International Development
Religion: Churches, Religion-General, Jewish Causes, Ministries, Religious Organizations, Religious Welfare
Science: Science Museums, Scientific Centers & Institutes
Social Services: Animal Protection, Child Welfare, Community Service Organizations, Crime Prevention, Delinquency & Criminal Rehabilitation, Domestic Violence, Family Planning, Family Services, Food/Clothing Distribution, Homes, People with Disabilities, Recreation & Athletics, Scouts, Senior Services, Shelters/Homelessness, Social Services-General, Substance Abuse, United Funds/United Ways, Volunteer Services, YMCA/YWCA/YMHA/YWHA, Youth Organizations

Application Procedures

Initial Contact: Write to the foundation for a formal application.
Application Requirements: The foundation's formal application includes the name and address of the organization requesting assistance; a contact person; a brief description of the organization, including a list of trustees; major goals and purposes; range and scope of programs; properties owned and rented; and date of founding. Applicants are also requested to attach a copy of the IRS certification indicating the organization's status as tax-exempt and as a private or public foundation. Information about the project should include a three-page outline of the project's scope and purpose, a description of the geographic area to be served, the project budget, other sources of funding, and plans for future funding of the project.

Deadlines: Deadlines for submitting applications are March 15, June 15, September 15, and December 15.

Review Process: The board reviews applications in January, April, July, and October. Requests received after the deadline will be carried over for consideration at the next meeting when appropriate. Each organization completing the application form for a grant will be notified of the decision of the trustees shortly after each meeting.

Restrictions

Grants are disbursed to IRS-designated tax-exempt section 501(c)(3) organizations only and must be public foundations. The foundation reports that in order for a request to receive adequate attention from the trustees, prospective applicants must complete an application form and adhere to foundation's established procedures. No grants are made to individuals or for operating expenses. Grants are not made for typical operational costs or maintenance-oriented purposes.

Additional Information

Wachovia Bank of North Carolina, is the foundation's corporate trustee.

Publications: Program Policy Statement; Application Guidelines; Application Form

Foundation Officials

Frank Borden Hanes, Jr.: trustee B Winston-Salem, NC 1945. ED University of North Carolina BA (1942); Saint Andrew's Presbyterian College DHL (1992). CORP AFFIL member: P.E.N.; member: North Carolina Quarter Horse Association; member: North Carolina Writers Conference; director: Hanes Co.; director: Chatham Manufacturing Co. NONPR AFFIL member: Order Minotaur; member: Sigma Alpha Epsilon; member: Order Gimghoul. CLUB AFFIL Rotarian Club; Roaring Gap Club; Rainbow Springs Club; Rancheros Visitadores Club; Old Town Club.

Ralph Philip Hanes, Jr.: trustee B Winston-Salem, NC 1926. ED University of North Carolina BA (1944-1946); Yale University BA (1949). NONPR AFFIL member: Wilderness Society; member: World Business Council; member: Walpole Society; member: Isaac Walton League; member: Trout Unlimited; member: Utah Prosim Society; member: Royal Society Arts; member: Southeast Council Foundations; member: North American Mycological Association; member: Pennsylvania Academy Fine Arts; board government: National Committee for the New River; member: National Wildlife Federation; director: Jargon Society Inc.; trustee emeritus: Kennedy Center for the Arts; member: Appalachian Trail Conference; member: East African Wildlife Society; member: American League Anglers; member: Appalachian Consortium; executive committee: Ambs for the Arts. CLUB AFFIL Yale Club; Roaring Gap Club; Twin City Club; Piedmont Club; Potomac Appalachian Mountain Club; Metro Club; Peale Visual Arts Club; Currituck Club; Lotos Club; Cane River Club; Century Association; Bohemian Club.

Ralph H. Womble: trustee

Grants Analysis

Disclosure Period: calendar year ending 2001
Total Grants: $1,447,902
Number of Grants: 55
Average Grant: $19,383*
Highest Grant: $200,000
Lowest Grant: $1,000
Typical Range: $10,000 to $40,000
***Note:** Average grant figure excludes three highest grants ($440,000).

Recent Grants

Note: Grants derived from 2002 Form 990.
General

400,000	Winston-Salem Foundation, Winston-Salem, NC -- to support millennium fund
66,667	Second Harvest Food Bank of Northwest North Carolina, Winston-Salem, NC -- to assist in the expansion of the current building, add more cold storage and upgrading computer hardware
60,000	Reynolda House Inc., Winston-Salem, NC -- to assist in Expansion Project
50,000	Arts Council Inc., Winston-Salem, NC -- to assist the "Arts Ignite Festival"
50,000	Little Theatre of Winston-Salem Inc., Winston-Salem, NC -- fund to re-stabilize the organization
50,000	Old Salem Inc., Winston-Salem, NC -- fund to exhibit, design and install a Toy Museum
50,000	Wake Forest University Baptist Medical Center, Winston-Salem, NC -- fund for Nutrition Center
40,000	Piedmont Craftsmen Inc., Winston-Salem, NC -- fund to relocate a new home
40,000	Southeastern Center for Contemporary Art, Winston-Salem, NC -- to assist "The Art of Our Time 2002"
37,500	Downtown Winston-Salem Foundation, Winston-Salem, NC -- fund for revitalization of Downtown area

DANE G. HANSEN FOUNDATION

Giving Contact

Ross Beach, Trustee
110 West Main Street
PO Box 187
Logan, KS 67646
Phone: (785)689-4832
Fax: (785)689-4833
E-mail: hansentr@ruraltel.net

Description

Founded: 1965
EIN: 486121156
Organization Type: General Purpose Foundation
Giving Locations: KS: Northwestern part of state
Grant Types: General Support, Project, Scholarship.

Donor Information

Founder: The foundation was established in 1965, following the death of Dane G. Hansen, who left most of his estate to the foundation. Mr. Hansen, the son of Danish immigrants, was born in 1883, and grew up in Kansas. He entered the mercantile business with his parents and later developed interests in ranching, cattle raising, and road and bridge construction. In the 1930s, he went into oil development and became one of the largest independent oil producers in Kansas. Mr. Hansen served in the administration of President Eisenhower and later became a trustee of the Eisenhower Foundation. He was very active in civic organizations in Logan, KS, and wanted his foundation to continue his commitment to the Logan area. His charitable interests included children and education.

Financial Summary

Total Giving: $2,094,898 (fiscal year ending September 30, 2003); $2,241,200 (fiscal 2002); $2,800,841 (fiscal 2001)
Giving Analysis: Giving for fiscal 2003 includes: foundation scholarships ($588,302); fiscal 2002: foundation scholarships ($415,578) fiscal 2001: foundation scholarships ($371,756)
Assets: $51,339,537 (fiscal 2003); $40,720,709 (fiscal 2002); $53,785,422 (fiscal 2001)

Typical Recipients

Arts & Humanities: Arts Associations & Councils, Community Arts, Arts & Humanities-General, Historic Preservation, Libraries, Museums/Galleries, Music, Performing Arts, Public Broadcasting, Theater
Civic & Public Affairs: Business/Free Enterprise, Chambers of Commerce, Clubs, Community Foundations, Economic Development, Economic Policy, Employment/Job Training, Civic & Public Affairs-General, Housing, Inner-City Development, Legal Aid, Municipalities/Towns, Parades/Festivals, Professional & Trade Associations, Public Policy, Rural Affairs, Safety, Urban & Community Affairs
Education: Agricultural Education, Arts/Humanities Education, Business Education, Colleges & Universities, Community & Junior Colleges, Education Funds, Faculty Development, Education-General, Journalism/Media Education, Literacy, Medical Education, Private Education (Precollege), Public Education (Precollege), Secondary Education (Private), Student Aid, Vocational & Technical Education
Environment: Environment-General, Resource Conservation, Wildlife Protection
Health: Cancer, Children's Health/Hospitals, Clinics/Medical Centers, Emergency/Ambulance Services, Eyes/Blindness, Health-General, Health Organizations, Heart, Hospices, Hospitals, Long-Term Care, Medical Rehabilitation, Medical Research, Mental Health, Single-Disease Health Associations
Religion: Churches, Religious Welfare
Social Services: Animal Protection, At-Risk Youth, Community Centers, Community Service Organizations, Day Care, Food/Clothing Distribution, People with Disabilities, Recreation & Athletics, Scouts, Senior Services, Social Services-General, YMCA/YWCA/YMHA/YWHA, Youth Organizations

Application Procedures

Initial Contact: Grant applicants should submit seven unfolded copies of a detailed proposal to the foundation. Application forms for the scholarship program are available from either the foundation or the office of the school counselor.

Application Requirements: Detailed proposals for grants should include the name, address, and phone number of the organization and the contact person; verification of 501(c)3 tax status; concise description of the project, its significance, benefits, and objectives; amount requested; detailed financial statement (preferably audited); detailed proposal budget; project timetable; list of other sources of potential funding; list of board members; qualifications of the organization and individuals with respect to project objectives; appropriate institution, organizational or individual letter of support; evaluation procedure for the project; and method and criteria for assessing the project's effectiveness.

Deadlines: None, for grant proposals. For scholarships, all applications and six semester grades (with GPA circled) must be completed and returned no later than October 9, reference questionnaires are due no later than October 29, and letters of acceptance of scholarship should be received within thirty days after graduation from high school.

Review Process: The foundation board meets monthly. Grant applicants will be notified within two weeks of receipt of proposal. Scholarship recipients are expected to enroll in appropriate institutions of higher learning without delay and in the fall term of the awarding year.

Notes: The following rules apply to scholarship applicants: only high school seniors who are graduating in the current academic year are eligible; students who have intentions of attending an out-of-state school should not apply; students interested in the Hansen Leader of Tomorrow, the Hansen Scholar, or Hansen Student scholarships must register with their school counselor or principal and take the qualifying test (no formal application is required); students interested in Vocational Education scholarships must complete the application form.

Restrictions

The foundation does not support political projects; normal organizational operating expenses; construction projects; endowment programs; degree programs; organizations without tax-exempt status; or organizations that practice discrimination by race, color, creed, sex, or national origin.

Additional Information
Publications: Application Guidelines

Foundation Officials
Carol Bales: secretary, treasurer, trustee
Ross Beach: trustee PRIM CORP EMPL chairman, president, director: Douglas County Bank.
F. Doyle Fair: president, trustee
Charles I. Moyer: vice president, trustee PRIM CORP EMPL president: First National Bank & Trust.
Doyle Dean Rahjes: trustee B Kirwin, KS 1930. PRIM CORP EMPL president: Farm Bureau Mutual Insurance Co. CORP AFFIL president: Kansas Farm Bureau Life Insurance Co.; president: Kansas Farm Bureau Services; partner: Gus Rahjes & Sons Farms; president: Kansas Farm Bureau Insurance Co. NONPR AFFIL member: Kansas Livestock Association; director: Western Agriculture Insurance Co.; president: Kansas Farm Bureau; president: Kansas Agricultural Marketing Association; member: Kansas Association Commerce Industry.
Don Stahr: trustee

Grants Analysis
Disclosure Period: fiscal year ending September 30, 2003
Total Grants: $1,506,596*
Number of Grants: 70
Average Grant: $17,907*
Highest Grant: $271,000
Lowest Grant: $100
Typical Range: $5,000 to $30,000
*Note: Giving excludes scholarships. Average grant figure excludes highest grant.

Recent Grants
Note: Grants derived from fiscal 2003 Form 990.
General

511,802	Wichita State University, Wichita, KS -- towards interviewing
271,000	City of Logan, Logan, KS -- towards Hansen plaza
168,000	Boy Scouts of America, Salina, KS
150,000	Phillips County Development, Phillipsburg, KS -- towards regional learning center
131,201	Kansas State University, Manhattan, KS -- towards education scholarship
100,000	City of Agra, Agra, KS -- towards building materials for community center
75,000	Developmental Services of Northwest Kansas, Hays, KS -- towards programs for the handicap
71,000	Kansas State University, Manhattan, KS -- funds to be utilized according to the discretion of the president
69,250	Fort Hays State University, Hays, KS -- towards education scholarship
67,500	Smoky Hill Public Television, Bunker Hill, KS

ELLEN KNOWLES HARCOURT FOUNDATION

Giving Contact
Paul Altermatt, President
51 Main St.
New Milford, CT 06776
Phone: (860)355-2631
Fax: (860)355-9460

Description
Founded: 1982
EIN: 061068025
Organization Type: Private Foundation
Giving Locations: CT: New Milford
Grant Types: General Support.

Donor Information
Founder: the late Ellen Knowles Harcourt

Financial Summary
Total Giving: $125,750 (2001)
Giving Analysis: Giving for 2001 includes: foundation grants to United Way ($4,000); foundation scholarships ($18,000)
Assets: $4,172,340 (2001)

Typical Recipients
Arts & Humanities: Arts Associations & Councils, Arts & Humanities-General, Historic Preservation, History & Archaeology, Libraries, Literary Arts, Museums/Galleries, Music, Performing Arts, Public Broadcasting, Theater
Civic & Public Affairs: Botanical Gardens/Parks, Clubs, Employment/Job Training, Civic & Public Affairs-General, Housing, Parades/Festivals, Professional & Trade Associations, Safety, Urban & Community Affairs, Women's Affairs
Education: Afterschool/Enrichment Programs, Agricultural Education, Arts/Humanities Education, Colleges & Universities, Environmental Education, Education-General, Minority Education, Private Education (Precollege), Public Education (Precollege), Science/Mathematics Education, Secondary Education (Public), Student Aid
Environment: Environment-General, Protection, Resource Conservation, Watershed
Health: Cancer, Children's Health/Hospitals, Home-Care Services, Hospitals, Medical Rehabilitation, Nursing Services
International: Health Care/Hospitals
Religion: Religion-General, Jewish Causes
Social Services: Animal Protection, Child Welfare, Community Centers, Community Service Organizations, Recreation & Athletics, Scouts, Senior Services, Shelters/Homelessness, Social Services-General, United Funds/United Ways, Volunteer Services, YMCA/YWCA/YMHA/YWHA, Youth Organizations

Application Procedures
Initial Contact: Send a brief letter of inquiry.
Application Requirements: Include amount requested, purpose of funds sought, and proof of tax-exempt status.
Deadlines: None.

Foundation Officials
Paul B. Altermatt: president, director B New Haven, CT 1930. ED Wesleyan University BA (1951); Georgetown University LLB (1956). PRIM CORP EMPL partner: Cramer & Anderson.
Roger Chace: assistant treasurer
Barbara Chappuis: secretary, director
Adele F. Ghisalbert: director
Susan N. Kustosz: director
Nancy A. Miller: director B 1943. ED California State University; University of California; University of Nevada.
Leandro Pasqual: director
George Verenes: treasurer, director

Grants Analysis
Disclosure Period: calendar year ending 2001
Total Grants: $103,750*
Number of Grants: 23
Average Grant: $4,511
Highest Grant: $15,000
Lowest Grant: $500
Typical Range: $1,000 to $10,000

*Note: Giving excludes scholarships and United Way.

Recent Grants
Note: Grants derived from 2002 Form 990.
General

28,850	New Milford Hospital, New Milford, CT -- pulse volume recorder
21,000	J.P. Memorial Scholarship, New Milford, CT -- scholarship fund
19,582	Children's Center, New Milford, CT -- classroom equipment
10,000	Northwest Connecticut Association for the Art, Torrington, CT -- Art Education Program
8,000	DATAHR, Brookfield, CT -- group home
7,000	Cumberland College, Williamsburg, KY -- scholarship support
6,600	Healing the Children, Albuquerque, NM -- program support
6,000	Oratory of Little Way, New Milford, CT -- handicapped walkway
5,200	Sherman Chamber Ensemble, Sherman, CT -- twenty year celebration
5,000	Candlewood Lake Authority, Brookfield, CT -- environmental bulletins

HARDEN FOUNDATION

Giving Contact
Joseph C. Grainger, Executive Director
PO Box 779
Salinas, CA 93902-0779
Phone: (831)442-3005
Fax: (831)443-1429
E-mail: jgrainger@hardenfoundation.org
Web: http://www.hardenfoundation.org

Alternate Contact
Patricia Tynan-Chapman, Secretary

Description
Founded: 1963
EIN: 946098887
Organization Type: General Purpose Foundation
Giving Locations: CA: Monterey County, Salinas Valley
Grant Types: Capital, Emergency, General Support, Matching, Multiyear/Continuing Support, Operating Expenses, Project, Scholarship.

Donor Information
Founder: Established in 1963 by Eugene E. Harden and Ercia E. Harden, both deceased. Mr. Harden was born in Wyoming in 1892. He moved to California as a young man. In 1913, he married Ercia Swindle. The Hardens were active in the civic and social life of the Imperial Valley, where they formed the Zenos and Harden Farms.
In the 1930s, the Hardens moved to Salinas where Mr. Harden formed the E.E. Harden Packing Company (later known as Harden Farms of California) and Harden Farms, Inc. He also helped to found the Growers Ice and Development Company. Mr. Harden died in 1984.
Mrs. Harden was an active volunteer with local charitable and civic organizations, often bringing home grown flowers to patients' rooms at the Salinas Valley Memorial Hospital. She was also a founding member and volunteer of the Pink Lady in the Service League. Mrs. Harden died in 1986.

Financial Summary
Total Giving: $2,440,493 (fiscal year ending February 28, 2004); $2,191,871 (fiscal 2003); $1,800,000 (fiscal 2002 approx). Note: Figure for 1996 includes $773,500 in matching gifts.
Giving Analysis: Giving for fiscal 2004 includes:

foundation grants to United Way ($15,000); foundation matching gifts ($620,000); fiscal 2003: foundation grants to United Way ($15,000); foundation matching gifts ($42,000); fiscal 2001: foundation matching gifts ($24,000)

Assets: $63,247,484 (fiscal 2004); $50,251,340 (fiscal 2003); $65,167,635 (fiscal 2001)

Typical Recipients

Arts & Humanities: Arts Associations & Councils, Arts Centers, Arts Outreach, Arts & Humanities-General, History & Archaeology, Libraries, Literary Arts, Museums/Galleries, Music, Theater

Civic & Public Affairs: Chambers of Commerce, Community Foundations, Economic Development, Civic & Public Affairs-General, Housing, Legal Aid, Nonprofit Management, Philanthropic Organizations, Rural Affairs, Urban & Community Affairs, Zoos/Aquariums

Education: Agricultural Education, Arts/Humanities Education, Colleges & Universities, Community & Junior Colleges, Education Funds, Environmental Education, Faculty Development, Education-General, Literacy, Preschool Education, School Volunteerism, Student Aid

Environment: Environment-General, Resource Conservation, Watershed

Health: AIDS/HIV, Alzheimer's Disease, Cancer, Children's Health/Hospitals, Clinics/Medical Centers, Emergency/Ambulance Services, Eyes/Blindness, Health-General, Health Funds, Health Organizations, Heart, Home-Care Services, Hospices, Hospitals, Long-Term Care, Medical Rehabilitation, Medical Training, Mental Health, Multiple Sclerosis, Nursing Services, Nutrition, Outpatient Health Care, Prenatal Health Issues, Respiratory, Single-Disease Health Associations

International: Health Care/Hospitals, International Relief Efforts

Religion: Churches, Religious Welfare

Social Services: Animal Protection, At-Risk Youth, Big Brothers/Big Sisters, Child Abuse, Child Welfare, Community Centers, Community Service Organizations, Counseling, Crime Prevention, Day Care, Delinquency & Criminal Rehabilitation, Domestic Violence, Emergency Relief, Family Planning, Family Services, Food/Clothing Distribution, People with Disabilities, Recreation & Athletics, Scouts, Senior Services, Shelters/Homelessness, Social Services-General, Special Olympics, Substance Abuse, United Funds/United Ways, Veterans, Volunteer Services, YMCA/YWCA/YMHA/YWHA, Youth Organizations

Application Procedures

Initial Contact: Applicants should contact the foundation for application guidelines and procedures. Applicants are also encouraged to discuss proposals with the Executive Director before submitting an application.

Application Requirements: Applicants should keep a copy of the completed proposal for themselves and send two to the foundation. Proposal must have a cover letter which includes organization's name, address, contact, telephone and amount and purpose of funding being requested; brief history of organization including date established; number of full-time, part-time, and volunteer employees; list of officers and board members, including name, address, occupation and phone number; copies of state and federal tax-exempt letters; if an ongoing program, cite effectiveness or unique achievement; need for project; how project relates to other programs, if any; major objectives accomplished, including a time frame for each objective; how results will be evaluated; project budget, include anticipated income and expense; other grant requests pending, showing funding source and amount requested; qualification and experience of staff to accomplish project; plan for future funding; and discuss alternate plans of support if funding is rejected.

Deadlines: March 1 and September 1.

Review Process: Grants are reviewed semi-annually in June and December.

Restrictions

The foundation will not make grants for the following: to support sectarian religious programs, to support education programs, other than special projects that are related to agriculture; to support operating foundations or associations established for the benefit of an organization which receives substantial tax support; to establish or add to endowments; or to support annual events, conferences, or fundraising events. Grant requests generally should not exceed $100,000. Multiyear grants will be considered only in exceptional cases. The foundation will consider one request per calendar year per organization.

Additional Information

The foundation allows 501(c)(3) charitable organizations to use the premises of the Harden Home for events. Contact the foundation for more information. The Harden Home now serves as the Harden Foundation's headquarters.

Publications: Guidelines; Annual Report; Application Form

Foundation Officials

C. Bill Elliot: vice president

Frank E. Ferrasci: treasurer

Joseph C. Grainger: executive director

Ralph L. Kokjer, Jr.: president, director PRIM CORP EMPL CPA: Bailey Kokjer & Berry.

Thomas M. Merrill: vice president, director B 1929. PRIM CORP EMPL president, chief executive officer: Merrill Farms. CORP AFFIL president: Growers Ice Co.

Patricia Tynan-Chapman: secretary, director ED University of California at Berkeley (1949). PRIM CORP EMPL chairwoman: Tynan Lumber Co. Inc.

Grants Analysis

Disclosure Period: fiscal year ending February 28, 2004

Total Grants: $1,805,493*

Number of Grants: 110

Average Grant: $16,414

Highest Grant: $200,000

Lowest Grant: $400

Typical Range: $5,000 to $25,000

*Note: Giving excludes matching gifts, United Way.

Recent Grants

Note: Grants derived from fiscal 2003 Form 990.

General

150,000	National Steinbeck Center Foundation, Salinas, CA -- to complete the Valley of the World Agricultural History and Education Center
88,000	Salinas Police Activities League, Salinas, CA -- funding for a director at the Harden Youth Center
50,000	Central Coast YMCA, Salinas, CA -- to support youth, after school and family programs in Salinas
50,000	Foundation of California State University, Monterey Bay, Seaside, CA -- operating grant to support watershed institutes
50,000	Interim, Inc., Monterey, CA -- to support development of Lupine garden apartments
50,000	Visiting Nurse Association, Tell City, IN -- to assist with the purchase of computer hardware, software and training for the association
45,000	Easter Seals Central California, Aptos, CA -- operating expenses to expand the services of the Equestrian program for children and adults with disabilities
41,000	Soledad Community Health Care District Foundation, Soledad, CA -- to improve the laundry equipment at Eden valley Care Center nursing home
35,000	Planned Parenthood Mar Monte, San Jose, CA -- support for the Facts of Life Line project
32,000	Gateway Center of Monterey County, Inc., Pacific Grove, CA -- to provide transportation for Senior Day program

PHIL HARDIN FOUNDATION

Giving Contact

C. Thompson-Wacaster, Vice President
Phil Hardin Foundation
1921 24th Avenue
Meridian, MS 39301
Phone: (601)483-4282
Fax: (601)483-5665
E-mail: info@philhardin.org
Web: http://www.philhardin.org

Description

Founded: 1964

EIN: 646024940

Organization Type: General Purpose Foundation

Giving Locations: MS, nationally

Grant Types: Award, Capital, Challenge, Conference/Seminar, Endowment, Fellowship, General Support, Loan, Matching, Multiyear/Continuing Support, Operating Expenses, Professorship, Project, Research, Scholarship, Seed Money.

Donor Information

Founder: Incorporated in 1964 by the late Philip Bernard Hardin and Hardin's Bakeries Corp. A remarkable marketing entrepreneur, Mr. Hardin built the Hardin Bakeries Corp. into a highly successful business operation. Mr. Hardin had a strong sense of the importance of the bakeries' corporation being a good corporate citizen and responsible member of the community.

Financial Summary

Total Giving: $1,565,980 (2003 approx); $1,746,523 (2002); $2,085,222 (2001)

Giving Analysis: Giving for 2002 includes: foundation scholarships ($16,500); foundation scholarships ($263,000)

Assets: $34,625,245 (2002 approx); $43,783,715 (2001)

Typical Recipients

Arts & Humanities: Arts Associations & Councils, Arts Centers, Arts Institutes, Historic Preservation, History & Archaeology, Libraries, Literary Arts, Museums/Galleries, Opera, Public Broadcasting, Visual Arts

Civic & Public Affairs: Community Foundations, Economic Development, Economic Policy, Civic & Public Affairs-General, Hispanic Affairs, Nonprofit Management, Philanthropic Organizations, Professional & Trade Associations, Urban & Community Affairs, Women's Affairs

Education: Afterschool/Enrichment Programs, Arts/Humanities Education, Business Education, Colleges & Universities, Community & Junior Colleges, Education Associations, Education Funds, Education Reform, Elementary Education (Private), Faculty Development, Education-General, Gifted & Talented Programs, International Studies, Leadership Training, Literacy, Minority Education, Preschool Education, Private Education (Precollege), Public Education (Precollege), Religious Education, School Volunteerism, Science/Mathematics Education, Special Education, Student Aid

Environment: Environment-General, Resource Conservation

Health: Health Policy/Cost Containment, Hospitals

(University Affiliated), Medical Rehabilitation, Medical Research, Outpatient Health Care, Speech & Hearing

International: Foreign Arts Organizations, International Environmental Issues

Religion: Jewish Causes, Religious Welfare

Science: Observatories & Planetariums, Science Museums

Social Services: Child Welfare, Community Centers, Community Service Organizations, Family Services, People with Disabilities, Volunteer Services, Youth Organizations

Application Procedures

Initial Contact: The foundation requests that grant applicants submit an application form, obtainable from the foundation, and a written proposal.

Application Requirements: Proposal summaries should include a brief summary of not more than one page describing the purpose of the organization, why the organization is requesting the grant and how the grant will be spent and the aspired outcomes. Proposals, of not more than five pages, should include a statement of need for the project, the project's goals, a calendar of the project's major activities and a description of each, the names of the persons planning and implementing the uses of the grant and their qualifications, a statement of approval for the project from the organizations's chief officer, a description of how the request relates to the organization's long-range planning and priorities, and how the organization will evaluate the effectiveness of the use of the grant. Also include a line-item budget, the most recent audit or financial statement, a statement of the organization's tax-exempt status and a copy of the tax exemption letter from the IRS. Submit a list of the members of the governing board of the organization and any optional materials to supplement the proposal, if appropriate. If the request is for partial support of a project, submit the entire project budget and show the projected amounts and sources of other financial and in-kind support for the project. If the project is to continue beyond the Hardin Foundation grant, describe future plans for project funding.

Deadlines: Submit proposals at least three months in advance of the date by which a funding decision is needed.

Review Process: The directors of the foundation meet monthly but do not consider proposals each month.

Restrictions

All grants are given for projects that directly benefit education of Mississippians. No grants are made for land acquisition or deficit financing.

Additional Information

Publications: Guidelines; Program Policy Statement; Application Form

Foundation Officials

Joe S. Covington, MD: director

R. B. Deen, Jr.: secretary, director

Edwin E. Downer: director CORP AFFIL director: MIS Power Co.

Archie R. McDonnell, Sr.: treasurer, director

Stephen O. Moore: director, vice president

Lynne Taleff: director

C. Thompson Wacaster: vice president B 1941. ED Yale University BS (1963); University of Virginia MA (1965); University of Oregon PhD (1973).

Robert F. Ward: president, director B Eden, NC 1949. ED North Carolina State University BS (1970-1974); North Carolina State University BS (1977). PRIM CORP EMPL senior vice president: Mantech Environmental Technology.

Sarah W. Wile: director B 1944. ED Vanderbilt University BA (1966); Mississippi State University MEd (1975). PRIM CORP EMPL secretary, treasurer, director: Southern Cast Product Inc.

Grants Analysis

Disclosure Period: calendar year ending 2002

Total Grants: $1,467,023*

Number of Grants: 24

Average Grant: $61,126*

Highest Grant: $333,334

Lowest Grant: $2,000

Typical Range: $2,000 to $100,000

*Note: Giving excludes scholarships and fellowships

Recent Grants

Note: Grants derived from 2002 Form 990.

General

333,333	Mississippi State University Foundation, Mississippi State, MS -- for Riley Education and Performing Arts Center Endowment
153,000	Meridian Community College, Meridian, MS -- for MathFirst Distance Learning Project
141,000	Harvard University, Cambridge, MA -- for Ward Fellowships
105,940	Mississippi State University Foundation, Mississippi State, MS -- Academy for Educational Leadership
104,400	Montgomery Institute, Meridian, MS -- for Educational Policy Fellowship Program
100,000	Teach for America, Oxford, MS -- for Teach for America Expansion
100,000	University of Mississippi, University, MS -- the endowment on the Future of the South
90,000	Earthwatch, Watertown, MA -- S.A. Rosenbaum Teacher Fellow Program
75,000	Jones County Junior College, Ellisville, MS -- for information technology grant
75,000	Mississippi State University Foundation, Mississippi State, MS -- for publication of "Atlas of American Children"

HARKNESS FOUNDATION FOR DANCE

Giving Contact

Theodore S. Bartwink, Treasurer
145 East 48th St., Suite 26C
New York, NY 10017-0025
Phone: (212)755-5540
Fax: (212)755-5542

Description

Founded: 1986

EIN: 131926551

Organization Type: Private Foundation

Giving Locations: NY: New York some giving nationally.

Grant Types: General Support, Scholarship.

Donor Information

Founder: In 1986, Rebekah Harkness founded the Harkness Ballet Foundation, now known as the Harkness Foundation for Dance.

Financial Summary

Total Giving: $1,300,000 (2003 approx); $1,400,000 (2002 approx); $1,433,100 (2001)

Assets: $21,700,000 (2003 approx); $21,700,000 (2002 approx); $21,740,615 (2001)

Gifts Received: $352 (2001); $437,402 (1994); $410,943 (1993)

Typical Recipients

Arts & Humanities: Arts Centers, Arts Festivals, Arts Funds, Arts Institutes, Ballet, Community Arts, Dance, Ethnic & Folk Arts, Film & Video, Music, Opera, Performing Arts, Theater

Civic & Public Affairs: Ethnic Organizations, Civic & Public Affairs-General, Public Policy, Urban & Community Affairs

Education: Arts/Humanities Education, Colleges & Universities, Education Funds

Health: AIDS/HIV, Cancer, Hospitals

International: Foreign Arts Organizations

Science: Scientific Organizations

Social Services: At-Risk Youth, Community Centers, Community Service Organizations, YMCA/YWCA/YMHA/YWHA, Youth Organizations

Application Procedures

Initial Contact: Send a brief letter of inquiry.

Application Requirements: Provide a description of the program or project, amount requested, purpose of funds sought, budget, and copy of IRS 501 (c)(3) determination.

Deadlines: None.

Restrictions

Grants are awarded to arts organizations qualified under IRC Section 501(c)(3).

Additional Information

Publications: Guidelines

Foundation Officials

Theodore S. Bartwink: treasurer, secretary

Etta Brandman: vice president, assistant treasurer, secretary

William Alan Perlmuth: president B New York, NY 1929. ED Wilkes College AB (1951); Columbia University LLB (1953). PRIM CORP EMPL partner: Stroock & Stroock & Lavan. CORP AFFIL director: Sentry Tech Corp. NONPR AFFIL trustee: School American Ballet; trustee: Wilkes University; trustee: New York University Medical Center; member: New York City Bar Association; member: New York State Bar Association; trustee: 55th Street Theater Foundation; trustee: Hospital Joint Diseases Orthopedic Institute. CLUB AFFIL Harmonie Club.

Grants Analysis

Disclosure Period: calendar year ending 2001

Total Grants: $1,433,100

Number of Grants: 203

Average Grant: $7,060

Highest Grant: $117,000

Lowest Grant: $500

Typical Range: $500 to $10,000

Recent Grants

Note: Grants derived from 2002 Form 990.

General

115,000	Brooklyn Academy of Music, Brooklyn, NY
112,000	92nd Street Y, Manhattan, NY
110,000	Hospital for Joint Diseases, New York, NY
56,750	City Center, New York, NY
54,650	Joyce Theater Foundation, New York, NY
50,000	Lincoln Center, New York, NY
45,000	School of American Ballet, New York, NY
37,500	Spoleto Festival, Charleston, SC
32,000	American Ballet Theater Inc., New York, NY
30,000	New York City Ballet, Saratoga Springs, NY

JOHN H. AND WILHELMINA D. HARLAND CHARITABLE FOUNDATION

Giving Contact
John A. Conant, Secretary
2 Piedmont Center, Suite 106
Atlanta, GA 30305
Phone: (404)264-9912
Fax: (404)266-8834
E-mail: harland@randomc.com

Description
Founded: 1972
EIN: 237225012
Organization Type: General Purpose Foundation
Giving Locations: GA: Atlanta metropolitan area
Grant Types: Capital, Endowment, General Support, Matching, Professorship, Project, Research.

Donor Information
Founder: Established in May 1972 by Mr. John Harland and his wife, Wilhelmina D. Harland through a gift of 125,000 shares of John H. Harland Company common stock. Mr. Harland, originally from Northern Ireland, came to Atlanta in 1906. In 1923, he founded the John H. Harland Company which now operates 44 plants in the United States and Puerto Rico. Mrs. Harland was born in Atlanta, and she studied at the New England Conservatory of Music in Boston. She also offered voluntary service in France and Serbia during and immediately following World War I.

Financial Summary
Total Giving: $1,647,401 (2002); $1,619,067 (2001)
Giving Analysis: Giving for 2002 includes: foundation grants to United Way ($20,000) 2001: foundation grants to United Way ($20,000)
Assets: $24,501,651 (2002); $28,856,882 (2001)
Gifts Received: $302,640 (2002); $238,680 (2001); $214,425 (2000). Note: In 2001 and 2002, contributions were received from John A. & Miriam H. Conant.

Typical Recipients
Arts & Humanities: Arts Centers, Arts Festivals, Arts Outreach, Ballet, Film & Video, Historic Preservation, Libraries, Museums/Galleries, Opera, Performing Arts, Public Broadcasting, Theater
Civic & Public Affairs: African American Affairs, Botanical Gardens/Parks, Community Foundations, Economic Development, Employment/Job Training, Ethnic Organizations, Civic & Public Affairs-General, Housing, Law & Justice, Legal Aid, Municipalities/Towns, Philanthropic Organizations, Professional & Trade Associations, Urban & Community Affairs
Education: Arts/Humanities Education, Colleges & Universities, Economic Education, Education Funds, Education-General, International Studies, Literacy, Medical Education, Preschool Education, Private Education (Precollege), Public Education (Precollege), Religious Education, Science/Mathematics Education, Secondary Education (Private), Special Education, Student Aid, Vocational & Technical Education
Environment: Environment-General, Resource Conservation
Health: Children's Health/Hospitals, Clinics/Medical Centers, Emergency/Ambulance Services, Geriatric Health, Health Organizations, Hospitals, Long-Term Care, Medical Rehabilitation, Mental Health, Nursing Services, Nutrition, Preventive Medicine/Wellness Organizations, Public Health, Research/Studies Institutes, Single-Disease Health Associations, Speech & Hearing
International: Foreign Arts Organizations, International Organizations, International Relief Efforts
Religion: Churches, Jewish Causes, Ministries, Religious Organizations, Religious Welfare, Seminaries

Science: Science Museums, Scientific Centers & Institutes
Social Services: At-Risk Youth, Big Brothers/Big Sisters, Camps, Child Abuse, Child Welfare, Community Centers, Community Service Organizations, Counseling, Day Care, Delinquency & Criminal Rehabilitation, Domestic Violence, Emergency Relief, Family Services, Food/Clothing Distribution, Homes, People with Disabilities, Recreation & Athletics, Scouts, Senior Services, Shelters/Homelessness, Social Services-General, Substance Abuse, United Funds/United Ways, Volunteer Services, YMCA/YWCA/YMHA/YWHA, Youth Organizations

Application Procedures
Initial Contact: Send a brief letter of inquiry requesting a Grant Applicant Questionnaire.
Application Requirements: Proposals should include a letter of request and a copy of the foundation's Grant Applicant Questionnaire.
Deadlines: Proposals may be submitted at any time, but the cut-off for new proposals to be considered at the Trustees' April and October meetings is no later than March 1 and September 1.
Notes: After the trustees have considered a grant proposal from an applicant organization, there is generally a 21-month waiting period before a new grant proposal will be eligible for consideration.

Restrictions
The foundation does not make grants to private primary or secondary schools except for those serving the disabled, to individual churches for operations or capital campaigns, or to individuals, annual funds, or special events.

Additional Information
The foundation requires a written report on the use of the grant at the end of the grant period.
Publications: Annual Report; Grant Application Questionnaire

Foundation Officials
John A. Conant: secretary B 1923. NONPR AFFIL chairman: Columbia Theological Seminary.
Miriam Harland Conant: president
Winifred S. Davis: trustee
Margaret C. Dickson: vice president, treasurer
Michael M. Dickson: trustee
James Malcolm Sibley: trustee B Atlanta, GA 1919. ED Princeton University AB (1941); Woodrow Wilson School of Law (1942); Harvard University Law School (1945-1946). CORP AFFIL director: Ichauway Inc. NONPR AFFIL trustee: AG Rhodes Home; trustee emeritus: TUFF; member: Georgia Bar Association; member: American Law Institute; member: Atlanta Bar Association; member: American College Probate Counsel; member: American Bar Association; member: American Bar Foundation. CLUB AFFIL Commerce Club; Piedmont Driving Club.
Allison F. Williams: trustee

Grants Analysis
Disclosure Period: calendar year ending 2002
Total Grants: $1,627,401*
Number of Grants: 76
Average Grant: $14,973*
Highest Grant: $504,440
Lowest Grant: $1,000
Typical Range: $5,000 to $30,000
*Note: Giving excludes United Way. Average grant figure excludes highest grant.

Recent Grants
Note: Grants derived from 2002 Form 990.
General

504,440	Howard School, Atlanta, GA -- to assist in the purchase of property for new campus
50,000	Frazer Center, Atlanta, GA -- fund for facility renovation
50,000	Visiting Nurse Health System, Atlanta, GA -- fund for continuing the caring campaign
45,000	Georgia Foundation for Independent Colleges, Atlanta, GA
40,413	Emory University Center for Ethics in Public Policy and the Professions Ethics Fellowship, Atlanta, GA -- fund for Ethics Fellowship
34,877	Early Learning Property Management, Stone Mountain, GA -- fund for the construction of Atlanta Head Start facilities
30,171	Families First, Cambridge, MA -- to support Merger with Capitol Area Mosaic
30,000	Camp Sunshine, Casco, ME -- to support capital campaign
25,000	Atlanta Enterprise Center, Atlanta, GA -- to support its current operations
25,000	Bedford School Inc., East Point, GA

HARLEY-DAVIDSON CO.

Company Headquarters
Milwaukee, WI
Web: http://www.harley-davidson.com

Company Description
Founded: 1903
Ticker: HDI
Exchange: NYSE
Revenue: US$5.32 billion (2004)
Profit: US$889.8 million (2004)
Employees: 8800 (2003)
Fortune Rank: 368, per FORTUNE Magazine's list of 500 Largest U.S. Corporations (2004).
SIC(s): 2389 Apparel & Accessories Nec, 3519 Internal Combustion Engines Nec, 3714 Motor Vehicle Parts & Accessories, 3751 Motorcycles, Bicycles & Parts.

Operating Locations
Harley-Davidson Co. (PA--York)

Nonmonetary Support
Type: Donated Products; In-kind Services

Harley-Davidson Foundation

Giving Contact
Mary Ann Martiny, Manager
3700 West Juneau Avenue
Milwaukee, WI 53208
Phone: (414)343-4001

Description
Founded: 1993
EIN: 391769946
Organization Type: Corporate Foundation
Giving Locations: AL, headquarters and operating communities; MO; PA: headquarters and operating communities; WI: headquarters and operating communities
Grant Types: Employee Matching Gifts, General Support, Operating Expenses, Project, Research, Scholarship.
Note: Foundation makes a small number of contributions for capital or operating support, but this is not the priority.

Financial Summary
Total Giving: $2,236,422 (2003); $2,041,500 (2002); $2,146,038 (2001)
Giving Analysis: Giving for 2002 includes: foundation grants to United Way ($256,345)
Assets: $15,233,808 (2003); $6,683,453 (2002);

$6,797,885 (2001)
Gifts Received: $8,513,650 (2003); $2,867,391 (2002); $2,468,778 (2001). Note: Contributions were received from the Harley-Davidson Motor Co.

Typical Recipients

Arts & Humanities: Arts Centers, Arts Institutes, Dance, Film & Video, Arts & Humanities-General, History & Archaeology, Libraries, Museums/ Galleries, Music, Opera, Performing Arts, Public Broadcasting, Theater
Civic & Public Affairs: African American Affairs, Business/Free Enterprise, Chambers of Commerce, Civil Rights, Community Foundations, Economic Development, Economic Policy, Employment/Job Training, Civic & Public Affairs-General, Hispanic Affairs, Housing, Inner-City Development, Public Policy, Urban & Community Affairs, Women's Affairs, Zoos/ Aquariums
Education: Afterschool/Enrichment Programs, Arts/ Humanities Education, Business Education, Colleges & Universities, Education Funds, Education Reform, Elementary Education (Private), Engineering/ Technological Education, Education-General, Health & Physical Education, Literacy, Minority Education, Private Education (Precollege), Public Education (Precollege), Secondary Education (Public), Vocational & Technical Education
Environment: Environment-General
Health: Cancer, Children's Health/Hospitals, Clinics/ Medical Centers, Diabetes, Emergency/Ambulance Services, Health Funds, Health Organizations, Mental Health, Nursing Services, Public Health, Single-Disease Health Associations
International: International-General
Religion: Ministries
Science: Science Exhibits & Fairs, Science Museums, Scientific Centers & Institutes
Social Services: Big Brothers/Big Sisters, Child Welfare, Community Centers, Community Service Organizations, Crime Prevention, Domestic Violence, Emergency Relief, Family Planning, Family Services, Food/Clothing Distribution, People with Disabilities, Recreation & Athletics, Scouts, Shelters/ Homelessness, Substance Abuse, United Funds/ United Ways, Veterans, Volunteer Services, YMCA/ YWCA/YMHA/YWHA, Youth Organizations

Application Procedures

Initial Contact: Send a complete proposal using the Milwaukee Area Funders common grant application form.
Application Requirements: For merchandise or table sponsorship, submit a letter describing the organization and how the event will benefit the community, including what percentage of the event's budget will result in a contribution to the organization; copy of 501(c)(3) letter and federal identification number.
Deadlines: March 26, June 4, August 13, October 1, and December 10.
Evaluative Criteria: Foundation looks closely for relevance to foundation's areas of interest; clarity in expected outcomes and strategy for achieving them; and a collaborative approach to solving problems.
Decision Notification: Bimonthly.
Notes: Call the foundation's information line for a list of current dates (414)343-8047.

Restrictions

The foundation does not make grants to individuals, political causes or candidates, athletic events or teams, conferences, or religious causes unless for a major project that benefits the greater community.

Additional Information

The Harley-Davidson family of employees, dealers, and customers has raised approximately $20 million for the Muscular Dystrophy Association in the last 16 years.
The foundation's emphasis is community revitalization and education. However, other areas of interest are arts and culture, medicine, and the environment.

Because of the number of requests the foundation receives, only one request per year from an organization is considered. considered.
Publications: Guidelines

Corporate Officials

Dr. Jeffrey L. Bleustein: chief executive officer, chairman B 1939. ED Columbia University PhD; Columbia University MS; Cornell University BS. PRIM CORP EMPL chief executive officer, chairman: Harley-Davidson Inc. CORP AFFIL chairman, chief executive officer, director: Harley-Davidson Motor Co.; director: Holiday Holding Corp.; president: Harley-Davidson Holding Co.; director: Brunswick Corp.; chief executive officer: Buell Motorcycle Co.

Foundation Officials

Dr. Jeffrey L. Bleustein: director (see above)
James M. Brostowitz: vice president, assistant secretary, treasurer, director B Milwaukee, WI 1952. ED Marquette University BS (1974). PRIM CORP EMPL vice president, treasurer: Harley-Davidson Motor Co. ADD CORP EMPL vice president, treasurer, controller: Harley-Davidson Inc.; treasurer: Harley-Davidson Transportation Co.
Tonit M. Calaway: assistant secretary
Edward Krishok: assistant secretary
Kathleen A. Lawler: director
Mr. Gail A. Lione: vice president, secretary, director
Brian H. Marron: assistant treasurer
Mary Anne Martiny: assistant secretary
Cynthia A. Rooks: assistant treasurer
Harold A. Scott: director
James L. Ziemer: president, director B 1950. ED University of Wisconsin BA (1975); University of Wisconsin MBA (1986). PRIM CORP EMPL vice president, chief financial officer: Harley-Davidson Inc. CORP AFFIL vice president: Harley-Davidson Transportation Co.

Grants Analysis

Disclosure Period: calendar year ending 2003
Total Grants: $1,927,498*
Number of Grants: 320
Average Grant: $6,023
Highest Grant: $250,000
Lowest Grant: $13
Typical Range: $1,000 to $10,000
*Note: Giving excludes United Way.

Recent Grants

Note: Grants derived from 2003 Form 990.
Library-Related
20,000	Menomonee Falls Library, Menomonee Falls, WI	

General
250,000	Bradley Tech/Trade, Milwaukee, WI
220,094	United Way, Milwaukee, WI
100,000	American Freedom Center, Austin, TX
100,000	Habitat Humanity, Milwaukee, WI
84,000	Boys and Girls Club, Milwaukee, WI
83,420	United Way, York, PA
50,000	Habitat for Humanity, Americus, GA
50,000	Habitat for Humanity, York, PA
50,000	Hunger Task Force, Milwaukee, WI
50,000	Next Door Foundation, Milwaukee, WI

PEARL M. AND JULIA J. HARMON FOUNDATION

Giving Contact

George L. Hangs, Jr., Secretary & Treasurer
PO Box 52568
Tulsa, OK 74152-0568
Phone: (918)743-6191
Web: http://www.HarmonFoundation.com
Note: The foundation reported in 1997 that it is

over-distributed in funding and is not currently accepting applications.

Description

Founded: 1962
EIN: 736095893
Organization Type: General Purpose Foundation
Giving Locations: AR; KS; NM; OK: Tulsa; TX
Grant Types: Endowment, General Support, Loan, Project.

Financial Summary

Total Giving: $256,598 (fiscal year ending May 31, 2002)
Assets: $35,687,781 (fiscal 2002)
Gifts Received: $4,684 (fiscal 1999); $11,790 (fiscal 1997); $500 (fiscal 1995)

Typical Recipients

Arts & Humanities: Arts Associations & Councils, Ballet, Arts & Humanities-General, History & Archaeology, Libraries, Museums/Galleries, Music, Opera, Theater
Civic & Public Affairs: Botanical Gardens/Parks, Business/Free Enterprise, Community Foundations, Employment/Job Training, Civic & Public Affairs-General, Hispanic Affairs, Housing, Legal Aid, Municipalities/Towns, Nonprofit Management, Parades/ Festivals, Safety, Urban & Community Affairs
Education: Afterschool/Enrichment Programs, Colleges & Universities, Elementary Education (Private), Elementary Education (Public), Education-General, Leadership Training, Private Education (Precollege), Public Education (Precollege), Secondary Education (Private)
Environment: Resource Conservation
Health: Clinics/Medical Centers, Emergency/ Ambulance Services, Health-General, Health Organizations, Medical Rehabilitation, Mental Health, Nursing Services, Prenatal Health Issues, Research/ Studies Institutes
Religion: Churches, Dioceses, Ministries, Religious Organizations, Religious Welfare
Social Services: Big Brothers/Big Sisters, Child Welfare, Community Service Organizations, Crime Prevention, Domestic Violence, Emergency Relief, Family Planning, Family Services, Food/Clothing Distribution, People with Disabilities, Recreation & Athletics, Senior Services, Sexual Abuse, Shelters/ Homelessness, Substance Abuse, Volunteer Services, Youth Organizations

Application Procedures

Initial Contact: Inquiry by one page letter.

Restrictions

The foundation is restricted by trust agreement to charitable organizations in Oklahoma, Kansas, Texas, Arkansas, and New Mexico. The foundation does not fund evangelism or research, and it will not make grants to individuals or foundations.

Additional Information

The foundation operates the Harmon Science Center, an interactive science museum in Tulsa, OK.
Publications: Guidelines

Foundation Officials

Catherine H. Frederick: trustee
George L. Hangs, Jr.: secretary, treasurer, trustee, directory
Jean M. Kuntz: trustee
Charlotte Kay Owens: trustee, officer mgr

Grants Analysis

Disclosure Period: fiscal year ending May 31, 1999
Total Grants: $59,870
Number of Grants: 39
Average Grant: $1,535
Highest Grant: $5,000
Lowest Grant: $100
Typical Range: $100 to $2,500

Recent Grants

Note: Grants derived from 2002 Form 990.
Library-Related

19,380	Nowata City County Library, Nowata, OK -- maintain grounds, Nowata library
13,743	Nowata City County Library, Nowata, OK -- contribution
5,000	Tulsa City County Library, Tulsa, OK -- contribution Hardesty Library
5,000	Tulsa City County Library, Tulsa, OK -- contribution Hardesty Library
2,000	Nowata City County Library, Nowata, OK -- contribution
1,500	Nowata City County Library, Nowata, OK -- contribution

General

250,000	Big Brothers & Big Sisters, Tulsa, OK -- for Bartlesville/Nowata
104,989	Ambulance Service, Nowata, OK -- Ford Ambulance
8,468	Grand Lake Mental Health Center, Nowata, OK -- building maintenance and utilities
8,046	Ambulance Service, Nowata, OK -- equipment for new ambulance
6,480	City of Nowata, Nowata, OK -- purchase drug enforcement equipment
5,000	Living Word Family Church, Nowata, OK -- for construction
5,000	New Life Assembly of God Church, Nowata, OK -- renovation
5,000	Seventh Day Adventist Church, Nowata, OK -- renovation
5,000	Tulsa Opera, Inc., Tulsa, OK -- contribution
5,000	Tulsa Philharmonic, Tulsa, OK -- contribution

HARPER BRUSH WORKS

Company Headquarters

400 N. 2nd St.
Fairfield, IA 52556
Web: http://www.harper-brush.com

Company Description

Revenue: US$9 million (2001)
Employees: 75 (2001)
SIC(s): 3900 Miscellaneous Manufacturing Industries, 3991 Brooms & Brushes.

Harper Brush Works Foundation

Giving Contact

Wendall King, Director
Harper Brush Works Foundation
PO Box 608
Fairfield, IA 52556
Phone: (515)472-5186

Description

EIN: 421145331
Organization Type: Corporate Foundation
Giving Locations: headquarters area only.
Grant Types: Award, General Support, Scholarship.

Financial Summary

Total Giving: $29,050 (fiscal year ending August 31, 2001)
Giving Analysis: Giving for fiscal 2001 includes: foundation scholarships ($18,500).
Assets: $95,043 (fiscal 2001)
Gifts Received: $49,825 (fiscal 2001); $49,291 (fiscal 2000); $63,185 (fiscal 1999). Note: In fiscal 2000

and 2001, contributions were received from Harper Brush Works, Inc. and Harper Corp. (d/b/a Texas Feathers). In fiscal 1999, contributions were received from Harper Brush Works ($30,800) and Texas Feathers ($32,385). In fiscal 1998, contributions were received from Harper Brush Works, Inc. and Harper Corp. (d/b/a Texas Feathers). In 1996 and 1997, contributions were received from Harper Brush Works ($9,760) and Texas Feathers.

Typical Recipients

Arts & Humanities: Libraries
Civic & Public Affairs: Botanical Gardens/Parks, Clubs, Civic & Public Affairs-General, Safety, Women's Affairs
Education: Business-School Partnerships, Colleges & Universities, Education Reform, Faculty Development, Education-General, Private Education (Precollege), Public Education (Precollege), Science/Mathematics Education, Student Aid
Health: Cancer, Emergency/Ambulance Services, Hospitals
Religion: Religious Welfare
Social Services: Community Centers, Day Care, Recreation & Athletics, Shelters/Homelessness, Social Services-General, Special Olympics, Substance Abuse, Youth Organizations

Application Procedures

Initial Contact: The foundation has no formal grant application procedure or application form.
Deadlines: None.

Additional Information

Provides scholarships to IA residents for higher education.

Corporate Officials

Barry Harper: president, chief executive officer PRIM CORP EMPL president, chief executive officer: Harper Brush Works.
Dan Turtell: chief financial officer PRIM CORP EMPL chief financial officer: Harper Brush Works.

Foundation Officials

Wendall King: director
George Patten: director
Emily Reneker: director

Grants Analysis

Disclosure Period: fiscal year ending August 31, 2001
Total Grants: $8,050*
Number of Grants: 14
Average Grant: $575
Highest Grant: $2,000
Lowest Grant: $100
Typical Range: $100 to $1,000
*Note: Giving excludes scholarship.

Recent Grants

Note: Grants derived from 2002 Form 990.
Library-Related

1,000	Worth County Partnership Library, Grant City, MO

General

12,000	Jefferson County Civic Center, Inc., Fairfield, IA
2,000	City of Hope, West Bloomfield, MI
2,000	Howard Payne University, Brownwood, TX
1,000	AISD Educational Foundation, Arlington, TX
1,000	Ark, Brownwood, TX
1,000	Arlington Women's Shelter, Arlington, TX
1,000	Boys & Girls Club of Arlington, Arlington, TX
1,000	Boys & Girls Club of Brownwood, Brownwood, TX
1,000	First Night Stockton, Stockton, CA
1,000	Foundation for Excellence, Baton Rouge, LA

HARPERCOLLINS PUBLISHERS INC.

Company Headquarters

10 E. 53rd Street
New York, NY 10022
Web: http://www.harpercollins.com

Company Description

Employees: 3,500
SIC(s): 2700 Printing & Publishing.
Parent Company: News Corporation Ltd., 2 Holt St., Sydney, Australia

Operating Locations

Ballinger Publishing Co. (MA--Cambridge); Basic Books, Inc. (NY--New York); Harper Audio (NY--New York); Harper Reference (NY--New York); HarperCollins Adult Trade Division (NY--New York); HarperCollins Junior Books Division (NY--New York); HarperCollins Publishers (NY--New York); HarperCollins San Francisco (CA--San Francisco); Scott Foresman/Addison Wesley (IL--Glenview); Zondervan Corp. (MI--Grand Rapids)

Nonmonetary Support

Type: Donated Products; Workplace Solicitation
Note: Workplace solicitation is United Way only.

Giving Contact

Aimee Johnson, Corp. Communications, Asst. Director
10 E. 53rd St.
New York, NY 10022
Phone: (212)207-7555
Fax: (212)207-7909

Description

Organization Type: Corporate Giving Program
Giving Locations: principally near operating locations and to national organizations.
Grant Types: Employee Matching Gifts, General Support.

Financial Summary

Total Giving: Company does not disclose contributions figures.

Typical Recipients

Arts & Humanities: Ethnic & Folk Arts, Libraries, Literary Arts
Civic & Public Affairs: First Amendment Issues, Women's Affairs
Education: Education-General, Literacy, Minority Education
Social Services: Community Service Organizations, Family Services, Volunteer Services

Application Procedures

Initial Contact: Initial letter and proposal, addressed to Karen Berberich, may be submitted at any time and should include a description of organization, amount requested, purpose of funds sought, a recently audited financial statement, and proof of tax-exempt status.

Restrictions

Does not support fraternal organizations, individuals, member agencies of united funds, political or lobbying groups, or religious organizations for sectarian purposes.

Corporate Officials

Glenn D'Agnes: chief financial officer PRIM CORP EMPL chief financial officer: HarperCollins Publishers Inc.
Anthea Disney: president, chief executive officer B Dunstable, United Kingdom 1946. ED Queens College. PRIM CORP EMPL president, chief executive

officer: HarperCollins Publishers. NONPR AFFIL editorial director: Murdoch Mags.

Grants Analysis

Note: Grant size varies.

GLADYS AND ROLAND HARRIMAN FOUNDATION

Giving Contact

William F. Hibberd, Secretary
140 Broadway, 4th Floor
New York, NY 10005-1101
Phone: (212)493-8182
Fax: (212)493-5570

Description

Founded: 1966
EIN: 510193915
Organization Type: General Purpose Foundation
Giving Locations: NY: New York nationally.
Grant Types: General Support.

Donor Information

Founder: Established in 1966 by the late Gladys Harriman and Roland Harriman. Their trusts continue to support the foundation.

Financial Summary

Total Giving: $6,375,571 (2002)
Assets: $102,975,325 (2002)
Gifts Received: $600,000 (1994); $1,200,000 (1993); $1,200,000 (1992)

Typical Recipients

Arts & Humanities: Arts Festivals, Ballet, Arts & Humanities-General, Historic Preservation, History & Archaeology, Libraries, Literary Arts, Museums/Galleries, Music, Public Broadcasting
Civic & Public Affairs: Botanical Gardens/Parks, Business/Free Enterprise, Civil Rights, Economic Development, Employment/Job Training, Civic & Public Affairs-General, Philanthropic Organizations, Public Policy, Urban & Community Affairs
Education: Afterschool/Enrichment Programs, Arts/Humanities Education, Business Education, Colleges & Universities, Community & Junior Colleges, Education Funds, Elementary Education (Public), Engineering/Technological Education, Education-General, Leadership Training, Medical Education, Minority Education, Preschool Education, Private Education (Precollege), Public Education (Precollege), Secondary Education (Private), Student Aid
Environment: Air/Water Quality, Forestry, Environment-General, Protection, Research, Resource Conservation, Wildlife Protection
Health: Cancer, Clinics/Medical Centers, Diabetes, Emergency/Ambulance Services, Geriatric Health, Health Organizations, Hospitals, Medical Research, Speech & Hearing
International: Foreign Educational Institutions, Health Care/Hospitals, International Relief Efforts
Religion: Churches, Religious Organizations, Seminaries
Science: Science Museums, Scientific Labs
Social Services: Animal Protection, At-Risk Youth, Big Brothers/Big Sisters, Camps, Child Abuse, Child Welfare, Community Service Organizations, Domestic Violence, Emergency Relief, Family Planning, Family Services, People with Disabilities, Scouts, Social Services-General, Substance Abuse, United Funds/United Ways, Volunteer Services, YMCA/YWCA/YMHA/YWHA, Youth Organizations

Application Procedures

Initial Contact: Applicants should submit a written proposal.

Application Requirements: Proposals should be typed and include the organization's history and details of its program.
Deadlines: None.
Review Process: The directors meet twice a year.

Restrictions

There are no restrictions or limitations on grants.

Additional Information

The foundation shares office space and members of the board of directors with the Mary W. Harriman Foundation, New York, NY.

Foundation Officials

Crispin H. Connery: director
Thomas F. Dixon: vice president, director
Terrence Michael Farley: director B New York, NY 1930. ED City College of New York BBA (1955). PRIM CORP EMPL partner: Brown Brothers Harriman & Co. CORP AFFIL director: Atlantic Reinsurance Co.; director: Centennial Insurance Co.; trustee: Atlantic Mutual Insurance Co. CLUB AFFIL Wianno Club; The Links Club; University Club; Echo Lake Country Club.
Elbridge Thomas Gerry, Jr.: president, director B New York, NY 1933. ED Harvard University AB (1955). PRIM CORP EMPL general partner: Brown Brothers Harriman & Co. ADD NONPR EMPL vice president: Boys Club New York. CORP AFFIL director: Union Pacific Corp.
William F. Hibberd: secretary
Anna T. Korniczky: treasurer
Wilhem E. Northrup: director

Grants Analysis

Disclosure Period: calendar year ending 2002
Total Grants: $6,375,571
Number of Grants: 100
Average Grant: $59,349*
Highest Grant: $500,000
Lowest Grant: $1,000
Typical Range: $10,000 to $100,000
*Note: Average grant figure excludes highest grant.

Recent Grants

Note: Grants derived from 2002 Form 990.
Library-Related

50,000	Auburn Public Library, Auburn, ME
50,000	New York Public Library, New York, NY

General

500,000	American Red Cross, Washington, DC
412,000	Boys Club of New York, New York, NY
320,000	American Museum of Natural History, New York, NY
250,000	Weill Medical College of Cornell University, New York, NY
235,000	Columbia University, New York, NY
175,000	Cold Spring Harbor Laboratory, Cold Spring Harbor, NY
172,911	Goshen's Historic Track, Goshen, NY
150,000	Artrain United States of America, Ann Arbor, MI
150,000	Bates College, Lewiston, ME
150,000	Bath Area Family YMCA, Bath, ME

MARY W. HARRIMAN FOUNDATION

Giving Contact

William F. Hibberd, Secretary
140 Broadway, 4th Fl.
New York, NY 10005
Phone: (212)493-8182
Fax: (212)493-5570

Description

Founded: 1925
EIN: 237356000
Organization Type: General Purpose Foundation
Giving Locations: NY: New York metropolitan area
Grant Types: Department, General Support, Project, Research.

Donor Information

Founder: The Mary W. Harriman Foundation was established in New York in 1925 and incorporated in 1973, with funds donated by the late Mary W. Harriman, wife of Union Pacific Railroad magnate and financier Edward Henry Harriman.

Financial Summary

Total Giving: $1,440,200 (2002); $1,375,206 (2001)
Assets: $26,114,035 (2002); $30,554,099 (2001)

Typical Recipients

Arts & Humanities: Arts Centers, Arts Funds, Ballet, Film & Video, Historic Preservation, History & Archaeology, Libraries, Museums/Galleries, Music, Performing Arts, Public Broadcasting, Theater
Civic & Public Affairs: African American Affairs, Botanical Gardens/Parks, Clubs, Community Foundations, Civic & Public Affairs-General, Inner-City Development, Law & Justice, Municipalities/Towns, Native American Affairs, Public Policy, Urban & Community Affairs, Zoos/Aquariums
Education: Afterschool/Enrichment Programs, Arts/Humanities Education, Business Education, Colleges & Universities, Education Associations, Education Funds, Faculty Development, Education-General, International Studies, Leadership Training, Legal Education, Medical Education, Minority Education, Private Education (Precollege), Public Education (Precollege), Religious Education, School Volunteerism, Secondary Education (Private), Secondary Education (Public), Special Education, Student Aid, Vocational & Technical Education
Environment: Air/Water Quality, Environment-General, Protection, Research, Resource Conservation, Wildlife Protection
Health: AIDS/HIV, Cancer, Children's Health/Hospitals, Emergency/Ambulance Services, Health Policy/Cost Containment, Hospices, Hospitals, Medical Rehabilitation, Mental Health, Nursing Services
International: Foreign Educational Institutions, International Affairs, International Environmental Issues, International Relations, International Relief Efforts
Religion: Jewish Causes
Science: Science Museums
Social Services: Child Abuse, Child Welfare, Community Service Organizations, Counseling, Day Care, Emergency Relief, Family Planning, Family Services, People with Disabilities, Recreation & Athletics, Social Services-General, Volunteer Services, Youth Organizations

Application Procedures

Initial Contact: Applicants should submit a written proposal and include tax-exempt status.
Application Requirements: Proposals should be typed and include the organization's history and details of grants purposes.
Deadlines: Proposals should be submitted no later than February.
Review Process: The directors meet once a year.

Additional Information

The foundation shares office space and members of the board of directors with the Gladys and Roland Harriman Foundation.

Foundation Officials

Kathleen L.F. Ames: vice president, director
Marjorie N. Friedman: director
William F. Hibberd: secretary
David H. Mortimer: president, director
Kathleen H. Mortimer: director

Grants Analysis

Disclosure Period: calendar year ending 2002
Total Grants: $1,440,200
Number of Grants: 115
Average Grant: $12,523
Highest Grant: $98,000
Lowest Grant: $1,000
Typical Range: $5,000 to $25,000

Recent Grants

Note: Grants derived from 2002 Form 990.
Library-Related

10,000	New York Public Library, New York, NY

General

98,000	Learning Leaders Inc., New York, NY
75,000	American Assembly, Latham, NY
60,000	School for Language and Communication Development, Glen Cove, NY
51,000	Bennington College, Bennington, VT
50,000	Franklin & Eleanor Roosevelt Institute, Hyde Park, NY
45,000	World Wildlife Fund, Washington, DC
35,000	Boys' Club of New York, New York, NY
35,000	Harriman Institute/Columbia University, New York, NY
35,000	Palisades Interstate Park Commission, Bear Mountain, NY
35,000	Scenic Hudson Inc., Poughkeepsie, NY

FRANCIS A. AND JACQUELYN H. HARRINGTON FOUNDATION

Giving Contact

Sumner B. Tilton, Jr., Trustee
370 Main St., 12th Fl.
Worcester, MA 01608
Phone: (508)798-8621
Fax: (508)791-6454

Description

Founded: 1965
EIN: 046125088
Organization Type: Private Foundation
Giving Locations: MA: Worcester
Grant Types: Capital, General Support, Project.

Donor Information

Founder: Francis A. Harrington, Charles A. Harrington Foundation

Financial Summary

Total Giving: $772,000 (2001)
Giving Analysis: Giving for 2001 includes: foundation grants to United Way ($4,000); foundation scholarships ($10,000)
Assets: $13,626,489 (2001)

Typical Recipients

Arts & Humanities: Arts Centers, Historic Preservation, History & Archaeology, Libraries, Museums/Galleries, Music, Performing Arts, Public Broadcasting, Theater
Civic & Public Affairs: Botanical Gardens/Parks, Clubs, Community Foundations, Civic & Public Affairs-General, Housing, Municipalities/Towns, Native American Affairs, Philanthropic Organizations, Public Policy, Rural Affairs, Urban & Community Affairs
Education: Arts/Humanities Education, Colleges & Universities, Community & Junior Colleges, Education Funds, Education Reform, Private Education (Precollege), Religious Education, Science/Mathematics Education, Secondary Education (Private), Student Aid

Environment: Environment-General, Resource Conservation, Wildlife Protection
Health: Cancer, Clinics/Medical Centers, Health-General, Health Organizations, Hospitals (University Affiliated), Medical Research, Nursing Services, Public Health
International: Foreign Arts Organizations
Religion: Churches, Jewish Causes
Science: Science Museums, Scientific Centers & Institutes, Scientific Organizations, Scientific Research
Social Services: Big Brothers/Big Sisters, Child Welfare, Community Centers, Community Service Organizations, Crime Prevention, Family Planning, Family Services, United Funds/United Ways, YMCA/YWCA/YMHA/YWHA, Youth Organizations

Application Procedures

Initial Contact: Send a brief letter of inquiry.
Application Requirements: Provide proof of tax-exempt status. Include goals and objectives and plan.
Deadlines: June 1.

Restrictions

The foundation provides grants to health, educational, and cultural organizations that are exempt under section 51(c)(3) of the IRC.

Foundation Officials

Francis A. Harrington, Jr.: trustee
James H. Harrington: trustee
Phyllis Harrington: trustee
Sumner B. Tilton, Jr.: trustee PRIM CORP EMPL clerk: New England Newspaper Supply Co. CORP AFFIL clerk: Whitinsville Water Co.; clerk: Whiteater Inc.; clerk: NDI Inc.; clerk: R H White Co. Inc.; officer: Fletcher, Tilton & Whipple PC. NONPR AFFIL president: Greater Worcester Community Foundation.

Grants Analysis

Disclosure Period: calendar year ending 2001
Total Grants: $758,000*
Number of Grants: 45
Average Grant: $12,977*
Highest Grant: $100,000
Lowest Grant: $1,000
Typical Range: $5,000 to $25,000
***Note:** Giving excludes United Way and scholarships. Average grant figure excludes two highest grants ($200,000).

Recent Grants

Note: Grants derived from 2001 Form 990.
Library-Related

20,000	Friends of the Worcester Public Library, Worcester, MA -- expansion and renovation of library

General

100,000	Bancroft School, Worcester, MA -- building new lower middle school facility
100,000	Greater Worcester Community Foundation, Inc., Worcester, MA -- to fund F A & J H Harrington Human Service Fund
60,000	EcoTarium, Worcester, MA -- capital campaign
50,000	Clark University, Worcester, MA -- Traina Center for the Arts
40,000	Worcester Art Museum, Worcester, MA -- capital campaign
25,000	Greater Worcester Community Foundation, Inc., Worcester, MA -- December 3rd Fund
20,000	Greater Worcester Community Foundation, Inc., Worcester, MA -- United Way Endowment Fund
20,000	Massachusetts Audubon Society-Worcester, Worcester, MA -- Worcester county drive
20,000	Mechanics Hall of Worcester, Worcester, MA -- anniversary campaign
20,000	Quinsigamond Community College Foundation, Worcester, MA -- increase endowment

WILLIAM H. AND MATTIE WATTIS HARRIS FOUNDATION

Giving Contact

Marilyn Harris-Hite, Secretary
6655 W. Sahara, Suite B-118
Las Vegas, NV 89102
Phone: (702)253-1317

Description

Founded: 1960
EIN: 870405724
Organization Type: Private Foundation
Giving Locations: Western US.
Grant Types: General Support, Project.

Donor Information

Founder: the late Matte Wattis Harris, William H. Harris

Typical Recipients

Arts & Humanities: Arts Associations & Councils, Arts Centers, Arts Festivals, Arts Institutes, Ballet, Community Arts, Dance, Ethnic & Folk Arts, Film & Video, Arts & Humanities-General, Historic Preservation, History & Archaeology, Museums/Galleries, Music, Opera, Public Broadcasting, Theater
Civic & Public Affairs: Botanical Gardens/Parks, Community Foundations, Civic & Public Affairs-General, Professional & Trade Associations, Urban & Community Affairs, Zoos/Aquariums
Education: Arts/Humanities Education, Colleges & Universities, Environmental Education, Faculty Development, Education-General, Health & Physical Education, International Studies, Journalism/Media Education, Medical Education, Preschool Education, Private Education (Precollege), Science/Mathematics Education, Secondary Education (Private), Social Sciences Education, Student Aid
Environment: Air/Water Quality, Forestry, Environment-General, Protection, Research, Resource Conservation, Wildlife Protection
Health: AIDS/HIV, Eyes/Blindness, Health Organizations, Medical Research, Speech & Hearing
International: Foreign Arts Organizations, Health Care/Hospitals, International Environmental Issues, International Organizations, International Relations
Religion: Churches, Religious Welfare
Science: Science Museums, Scientific Centers & Institutes, Scientific Research
Social Services: Animal Protection, At-Risk Youth, Camps, Child Welfare, Community Centers, Community Service Organizations, Crime Prevention, Family Planning, Family Services, Food/Clothing Distribution, People with Disabilities, Recreation & Athletics, Senior Services, Shelters/Homelessness, Substance Abuse, United Funds/United Ways, YMCA/YWCA/YMHA/YWHA, Youth Organizations

Application Procedures

Initial Contact: Request application guidelines, then send four copies of proposal.
Application Requirements: Include a description of organization, purpose of funds sought, and other funding sources.
Deadlines: February 1 and August 1.

Restrictions

Does not support individuals.

Additional Information

Publications: Program Policy Statement; Application Guidelines

Foundation Officials

Henry Hite: president
James W. Hite: vice president
Marilyn Harris Hite: secretary

Sharon Lewis: trustee
William Rohrback: trustee

Grants Analysis

Disclosure Period: calendar year ending 2000
Total Grants: $455,180*
Number of Grants: 90
Average Grant: $5,058
Highest Grant: $60,000
Typical Range: $1,000 to $10,000
***Note:** Giving excludes scholarships.

Recent Grants

Note: Grants derived from 2001 Form 990.
General

55,000	Four Corners School of Outdoor Education, Inc., Monticello, UT
55,000	Hawkwatch International, Albuquerque, NM
55,000	Ocean Mammal Institute, Reading, PA
15,000	Punahou School, Honolulu, HI
14,700	YMCA of Rome - Floyd County, Rome, GA
10,000	College of Santa Fe, Santa Fe, NM
10,000	United Way of New York City, New York, NY
7,000	American Hackney Horse Society Foundation, Lexington, KY
6,000	Billfish Foundation, Ft. Lauderdale, FL
6,000	Letlotlo Animal Sanctuary

HARSCO CORP.

Company Headquarters

350 Poplar Church Rd.
Camp Hill, PA 17011
Web: http://www.harsco.com

Company Description

Founded: 1956
Ticker: HSC
Exchange: NYSE
Revenue: US$1.976 billion (2002)
Employees: 17500 (2003)
SIC(s): 2952 Asphalt Felts & Coatings, 3295 Minerals--Ground or Treated, 3494 Valves & Pipe Fittings Nec, 3743 Railroad Equipment.

Operating Locations

Harsco Corp. (AL--Birmingham, Leeds, Theodore; CA--Los Angeles, Pomona; CT--Hamden; FL--Plant City, Tampa; GA--Jesup; IL--Chicago; IN--Gary, Highland; IA--Bloomfield, Des Moines; KY--Drakesboro; LA--Crowley; MD--Baltimore; MN--Fairmont; NJ--Fort Lee, Union; NY--Lockport, Long Island City, New York; NC--Charlotte; OH--Cleveland, Columbus, Kenton, Lansing, Marysville, West Jefferson; OK--Tulsa; PA--Butler, Cheswick, East Stroudsburg, Harrisburg, York; TN--Nashville; TX--Channelview, Houston, Mineral Wells; WV--Moundsville)
Note: Also operates internationally.

Harsco Corp. Fund

Giving Contact

Robert G. Yocum, Chairman & Trustee
PO Box 8888
Camp Hill, PA 17001-8888
Phone: (717)763-7064
Web: http://www.harsco.com/Governance/gov_corp_phil.htm

Description

EIN: 236278376
Organization Type: Corporate Foundation

Giving Locations: headquarters and operating communities.
Grant Types: Capital, Department, Employee Matching Gifts, General Support, Research, Scholarship.

Financial Summary

Total Giving: $1,300,242 (2003); $1,372,776 (2002); $1,319,930 (2001). Note: Contributes through foundation only.
Assets: $3,758,652 (2003); $4,237,862 (2002); $6,114,221 (2001)
Gifts Received: $210,000 (1997); $150,000 (1996); $150,000 (1995). Note: Contributions were received from the Harsco Corp and Sordoni Enterprises.

Typical Recipients

Arts & Humanities: Arts Associations & Councils, Arts Centers, Arts Festivals, Arts Funds, Arts Institutes, Community Arts, Dance, Historic Preservation, History & Archaeology, Libraries, Museums/Galleries, Music, Opera, Performing Arts, Public Broadcasting, Theater
Civic & Public Affairs: African American Affairs, Business/Free Enterprise, Chambers of Commerce, Civil Rights, Clubs, Economic Development, Economic Policy, Employment/Job Training, Ethnic Organizations, Civic & Public Affairs-General, Hispanic Affairs, Housing, Law & Justice, Legal Aid, Philanthropic Organizations, Professional & Trade Associations, Public Policy, Safety, Urban & Community Affairs
Education: Arts/Humanities Education, Business Education, Colleges & Universities, Community & Junior Colleges, Economic Education, Education Associations, Education Funds, Engineering/Technological Education, Education-General, International Exchange, International Studies, Leadership Training, Legal Education, Literacy, Medical Education, Minority Education, Public Education (Precollege), Religious Education, Science/Mathematics Education, Student Aid, Vocational & Technical Education
Environment: Environment-General
Health: Cancer, Children's Health/Hospitals, Clinics/Medical Centers, Diabetes, Emergency/Ambulance Services, Health Funds, Health Organizations, Heart, Hospices, Hospitals, Medical Research, Mental Health, Multiple Sclerosis, Public Health, Single-Disease Health Associations
International: Foreign Arts Organizations, International Relations
Religion: Jewish Causes, Missionary Activities (Domestic), Religious Welfare, Seminaries, Social/Policy Issues
Science: Science Museums, Scientific Centers & Institutes
Social Services: Big Brothers/Big Sisters, Child Welfare, Community Centers, Community Service Organizations, Crime Prevention, Day Care, Emergency Relief, Family Planning, Family Services, Food/Clothing Distribution, Homes, People with Disabilities, Recreation & Athletics, Scouts, Sexual Abuse, Shelters/Homelessness, Social Services-General, Special Olympics, Substance Abuse, United Funds/United Ways, Volunteer Services, YMCA/YWCA/YMHA/YWHA, Youth Organizations

Application Procedures

Initial Contact: Send a brief letter or proposal; organizations in company operating locations should contact local divisions directly.
Application Requirements: Include a description of organization, amount requested, purpose of funds sought, recently audited financial statement, and proof of tax-exempt status.
Deadlines: None. For US scholarship programs, January 1 of year preceding date of entrance into college. For international scholarship program, January 31 of each year.
Evaluative Criteria: Organization must be in area where corporation has business operations.

Decision Notification: Annually, usually in January or February.

Restrictions

Does not support dinners or special events, fraternal organizations, goodwill advertising, political or lobbying groups, religious organizations for sectarian purposes, or individuals.
The fund seldom makes grants to organizations with limited purposes or for special projects that do not receive wide public support.

Foundation Officials

P. C. Coppock: trustee
Salvatore D. Fazzolari: treasurer, secretary, trustee
D. C. Hathaway: trustee
Robert G. Yocum: chairman, trustee PRIM CORP EMPL treasurer, director: Harsco Corp.

Grants Analysis

Disclosure Period: calendar year ending 2003
Total Grants: $1,224,600*
Number of Grants: 74
Average Grant: $15,337*
Highest Grant: $105,000
Lowest Grant: $200
Typical Range: $5,000 to $30,000
***Note:** Giving excludes matching gifts and United Way. Average grant figure excludes highest grant.

Recent Grants

Note: Grants derived from 2003 Form 990.
Library-Related

5,000	Butler Area Public Library, Butler, PA
5,000	Joseph T. Simpson Public Library, Mechanicsburg, PA

General

105,000	Goodwill Industries of Central PA, Harrisburg, PA
100,000	ALS Association, Ft. Washington, PA
69,167	Keystone Council Boy Scouts of America, Mechanicsburg, PA
52,000	Pinnacle Health Auxiliary, Harrisburg, PA
15,200	YMCA, Harrisburg, PA
14,548	YMCA Fund Incorporated, Chicago, IL
10,000	Davis County Hospital, Bloomfield, IA
10,000	Grove City College, Grove City, PA
6,000	United Way, Ludington, MI
5,000	Harrisburg Boys and Girls Club, Harrisburg, PA

HARTFORD COURANT FOUNDATION

Giving Contact

Kate Miller, Executive Director
285 Broad Street
Hartford, CT 06115
Phone: (860)241-6472
Fax: (860)520-6988
E-mail: hcfoundation@courant.com
Web: http://www.hartfordcourantfoundation.org

Description

Founded: 1950
EIN: 060759107
Organization Type: General Purpose Foundation
Giving Locations: CT: Central Connecticut
Grant Types: Capital, Challenge, General Support, Matching, Operating Expenses, Project, Scholarship, Seed Money.

Donor Information

Founder: The foundation was established in 1950 by The Hartford Courant newspaper. When the newspaper was purchased by Times Mirror Corporation in 1979, The Hartford Courant Foundation was restructured as a private foundation independent of the company.

Financial Summary

Total Giving: $868,181 (2001)
Giving Analysis: Giving for 2001 includes: foundation matching gifts ($70,000)
Assets: $15,781,216 (2001)
Gifts Received: $111,699 (2001); $2,000 (1999); $12,000 (1998). Note: In 2001, contributions were received from Hartford Courant.

Typical Recipients

Arts & Humanities: Arts Associations & Councils, Arts Centers, Arts Outreach, Ballet, Dance, Arts & Humanities-General, Libraries, Literary Arts, Museums/Galleries, Music, Opera, Performing Arts, Public Broadcasting, Theater
Civic & Public Affairs: African American Affairs, Botanical Gardens/Parks, Civil Rights, Community Foundations, Economic Development, Employment/Job Training, Civic & Public Affairs-General, Hispanic Affairs, Housing, Legal Aid, Nonprofit Management, Philanthropic Organizations, Public Policy, Urban & Community Affairs, Women's Affairs
Education: Afterschool/Enrichment Programs, Arts/Humanities Education, Colleges & Universities, Continuing Education, Education Associations, Education-General, Health & Physical Education, Leadership Training, Literacy, Minority Education, Preschool Education, Private Education (Precollege), Public Education (Precollege), Science/Mathematics Education, Secondary Education (Private), Special Education, Student Aid, Vocational & Technical Education
Health: Adolescent Health Issues, AIDS/HIV, Children's Health/Hospitals, Clinics/Medical Centers, Health-General, Health Organizations, Hospitals, Hospitals (University Affiliated), Medical Rehabilitation, Medical Research, Mental Health, Nursing Services, Prenatal Health Issues, Public Health
International: Health Care/Hospitals, International Development
Religion: Churches, Jewish Causes, Ministries, Religious Organizations, Religious Welfare
Science: Science Museums, Scientific Centers & Institutes
Social Services: At-Risk Youth, Big Brothers/Big Sisters, Camps, Child Abuse, Child Welfare, Community Service Organizations, Counseling, Crime Prevention, Domestic Violence, Emergency Relief, Family Planning, Family Services, Food/Clothing Distribution, Homes, People with Disabilities, Recreation & Athletics, Scouts, Shelters/Homelessness, Social Services-General, Substance Abuse, United Funds/United Ways, YMCA/YWCA/YMHA/YWHA, Youth Organizations

Application Procedures

Initial Contact: Send full proposal, including completed application. Application form is available on the foundation's web site.
Application Requirements: Completed application form must be accompanied by the following attachments: proof of tax-exempt status; list of current funders and their levels of support; most recent income and expense statement (audited, if possible); program for the most recent year; and description of program for which funds are requested including evidence of need, measurable outcomes, program activities, detailed budget, timetable, evaluation plan, and plan for future funding.
Deadlines: December 15, March 15, June 15, and September 15.
Review Process: Foundation staff reviews requests prior to submitting applications to the board of trustees. Staff review may involve meeting with the applicant, site visits, and interviews with other agencies and individuals who are knowledgeable about the need the application addresses.
Notes: Applicants are expected to be able to demonstrate compliance with anti-discrimination legislation.

Restrictions

Does not make contributions to individuals, endowments, organizations which are not tax-exempt, organizations which have IRS private foundation designation, religious institutions other than for provision of non-sectarian community services, groups engaged in activities meant to influence either legislation or the outcome of elections, capital projects related to the arts, performances, conferences, trips, one-time events, and annual campaigns. Applicants must be located in Hartford, Middlesex, or Tolland County.

Additional Information

Publications: Annual Report; Application Guidelines; Informational Brochure

Corporate Officials

Raymond Koupal: vice president, chief financial officer PRIM CORP EMPL vice president, chief financial officer: Hartford Courant Co.
Worth Loomis: president, trustee B New York, NY 1923. ED Yale University BS (1947); New York University MBA (1955). PRIM CORP EMPL president, trustee: Hartford Graduate Center. CORP AFFIL director: Spencer Turbine Co.; director: Southern New England Telephone Co.; chairman: Life Techs Inc.; trustee: Mechanics Savings Bank; director: Covenant Mutual Insurance Co.; director: Colts Manufacturing Co.; director: Connecticut Natural Gas Corp.; president board trustees: Colt Bequest Inc.; director: Chemstone Corp.; director: CIGNA Funds Group; director: Capewell Components Co. NONPR AFFIL trustee: Trinity College; trustee: Yale-Berkeley Divinity School; member, board overseers: New York University Stern School Business; member: Society Cincinnati; trustee: Morehouse College; member: National Association Manufacturers; trustee: Kazanjian Economic Foundation; trustee: Hartford Courant Foundation; visiting professor, trustee: Hartford Seminary; trustee: Hartford College Women; member: Century Association; member: Connecticut Business & Industry Association; trustee: American Institute Managing Diversity; trustee: Alpha Center.
Millard H. Pryor, Jr.: managing director B Owosso, MI 1933. ED University of Michigan (1955-1957). PRIM CORP EMPL managing director: Pryor & Clark Co. CORP AFFIL chairman: Lydall; chairman: Wiremold Corp.; director: Hartford Fund; director: Hoosier Magnetics Inc.; director: Duro-Test Corp.; director: GEO International Corp.; vice chairman: Compudyne Corp.
George A. Scott: president PRIM CORP EMPL president: Hartford West Indian Bakeries.

Foundation Officials

Dr. Eddie L. Davis: trustee
Luis Diez-Morales: trustee
Bernard Michael Fox: trustee B New York, NY 1942. ED Manhattan College BSEE (1963); Rensselaer Polytechnic Institute MSEE (1964); Harvard University Graduate School of Business Administration (1979). PRIM CORP EMPL president, chief executive officer, director, chairman: Northeast Utilities. CORP AFFIL director: Shawmut Bank Connecticut; director: Shawmut National Corp.; director: Shawmut Bank; director: Connecticut Yankee Atomic Power Co.; director: Dexter Corp.; director: CIGNA Corp. NONPR AFFIL director: Institute Nuclear Power Operations; director: Mount Holyoke College; chairman: Institute Living; director: Connecticut Business & Industry Association; sr member: Institute Electrical & Electronics Engineers; member: American Leadership Forum.
Mary E. Junck: trustee PRIM CORP EMPL president, eastern newspapers: Times Mirror Co.
Raymond Koupal: trustee (see above)
Maura L. Melley: trustee PRIM CORP EMPL senior vice president public affairs: Phoenix Home Life Mutual Insurance Co.
Marty Petty: trustee PRIM CORP EMPL vice president sales: Hartford Courant Co.

Olcott D. Smith: hon trustee
Michael E. Waller: trustee
Efram Zimbalist, III: trustee ED Harvard University MBA; Harvard University BA. PRIM CORP EMPL president, chief executive officer: Times Mirror Magazines. NONPR AFFIL member national council: House Ear Institute; chairman emeritus, trustee: Robert Louis Stevenson School.

Grants Analysis

Disclosure Period: calendar year ending 2001
Total Grants: $798,181*
Number of Grants: 115
Average Grant: $6,941
Highest Grant: $70,000
Typical Range: $5,000 to $15,000 and $250 to $3,000
*Note: Giving excludes matching gifts.

Recent Grants

Note: Grants derived from 2002 Form 990.
General

70,000	Greater Hartford Arts Council, Hartford, CT -- for challenge grant to match new or increased donations
31,972	Camp Courant, Hartford, CT -- for enclosure of the outdoor stage
30,000	TheaterWorks, Hartford, CT -- for theater works' renovation project
25,000	Real Art Ways, Hartford, CT -- for capital improvements
20,000	Local Initiatives Support Corporation, Hartford, CT -- for operating support
20,000	Northwest Catholic High School, West Hartford, CT
17,500	Center City Churches Inc., Lubbock, TX -- for after-school programming at Betances and Sanchez elementary schools
15,000	Co-Opportunity, Hartford, CT -- for the youthbuild training program
15,000	Hartford Neighborhood Development Support Collaborative/LISC, Hartford, CT -- for Hartford neighborhood collaborative grants
15,000	Marlborough Arts Center & Museum -- for the renovation of the recently acquired building

HARTFORD FINANCIAL SERVICES GROUP INC.

Company Headquarters

Hartford Plaza
690 Asylum Ave.
Hartford, CT 06115
Web: http://www.thehartford.com

Company Description

Founded: 1810
Ticker: HIG
Exchange: NYSE
Revenue: US$22.693 billion (2004)
Profit: US$2.115 billion (2004)
Employees: 29000 (2003)
Fortune Rank: 88, per FORTUNE Magazine's list of 500 Largest U.S. Corporations (2004).

Nonmonetary Support

Value: $530,000 (2002)
Type: Donated Equipment; Loaned Employees; Loaned Executives
Volunteer Programs: The company sponsors a Reading Buddies Program with a local middle elementary school. Approximately 100 employees volunteer for this program.

Giving Contact

Michael Gannon, Grants Program Specialist
The Hartford Financial Services Group, Inc.
Hartford Place
690 Asylum Avenue
T-12-56
Hartford, CT 06115
Phone: (860)547-4995
Fax: (860)547-6393
E-mail: michael.gannon@thehartford.com

Alternate Contact

Darlene Leak, corporate relations
Phone: (860)547-3133

Description

Organization Type: Corporate Giving Program
Giving Locations: CT: Hartford Greater Hartford area principally near operating locations and to national organizations, grants are allocated based on the size of the operation in the.
Grant Types: Capital, Employee Matching Gifts, General Support, Project, Scholarship.
Note: Employee matching gift ratio: 1 to 1 up to $2,000 per employee annually for education.

Financial Summary

Total Giving: $5,000,000 (2003 approx); $5,108,893 (2002); $6,928,970 (2001). Note: Contributes through corporate direct giving program only. 2001 giving includes prepaid capital commitments and United Way contributions for 2002.
Giving Analysis: Giving for 2002 includes: corporate direct giving (approx $3,460,000); 2001: corporate direct giving ($6,928,970)
Gifts Received: $1,136,066 (1997); $2,500,000 (1995); $2,200,000 (1994). Note: Contributions are received from Hartford Fire Insurance Co.

Typical Recipients

Arts & Humanities: Arts Associations & Councils, Arts Centers, Arts Funds, Community Arts, Dance, Arts & Humanities-General, History & Archaeology, Libraries, Literary Arts, Museums/Galleries, Music, Opera, Performing Arts, Public Broadcasting, Theater
Civic & Public Affairs: African American Affairs, Botanical Gardens/Parks, Business/Free Enterprise, Civil Rights, Economic Development, Employment/Job Training, Civic & Public Affairs-General, Hispanic Affairs, Housing, Law & Justice, Nonprofit Management, Parades/Festivals, Professional & Trade Associations, Public Policy, Safety, Urban & Community Affairs, Women's Affairs
Education: Agricultural Education, Arts/Humanities Education, Business Education, Colleges & Universities, Community & Junior Colleges, Continuing Education, Education Associations, Education Funds, Education-General, Health & Physical Education, International Studies, Journalism/Media Education, Legal Education, Literacy, Medical Education, Minority Education, Private Education (Precollege), Public Education (Precollege), Religious Education, Science/Mathematics Education, Special Education, Student Aid, Vocational & Technical Education
Environment: Environment-General
Health: AIDS/HIV, Children's Health/Hospitals, Clinics/Medical Centers, Eyes/Blindness, Geriatric Health, Health Policy/Cost Containment, Health Organizations, Hospices, Hospitals, Medical Rehabilitation, Medical Research, Prenatal Health Issues, Preventive Medicine/Wellness Organizations, Public Health
Religion: Ministries, Religious Welfare
Social Services: Big Brothers/Big Sisters, Camps, Child Welfare, Community Service Organizations, Crime Prevention, Day Care, Delinquency & Criminal Rehabilitation, Domestic Violence, Emergency Relief, Family Services, Food/Clothing Distribution, Homes, People with Disabilities, Recreation & Athletics, Senior Services, Shelters/Homelessness, Social

Services-General, Substance Abuse, United Funds/United Ways, YMCA/YWCA/YMHA/YWHA, Youth Organizations

Application Procedures

Initial Contact: Organizations in Hartford should send a brief two-page letter requesting application form to headquarters; organizations near the company's regional offices should send requests to the local general manager for consideration, who may forward it to Hartford depending on the size of the grant requested. Application and guidelines may also be obtained on company's web site or by calling (810) 547-4998.
Application Requirements: Submit a completed application form and required attachments.
Deadlines: January 15, April 1, July 1, and September 15.
Review Process: Committee meets in March, June, September, and November for grant considerations. Decisions are generally based on written proposals, however, a periodic site visit by Hartford or a personal interview may be required.
Evaluative Criteria: Degree to which proposal meets company's guidelines, efficient management of program funds, human service value and practicality of objectives, nonduplication of existing programs, number of individuals served, fundraising stability of organization and range of support of program, organization's track record.
Decision Notification: Quarterly.

Restrictions

Excluded from consideration are endowments, health care issues or organizations, individualss, conferences and seminars, courtesy advertising, private foundations, religious purposes, athletic outings, reducing or eliminating a pre-existing debt, one-time events including testimonial and fund-raising dinners, environmental issues/organizations, or activities such as scouting band, and little league, etc. if they are not a part of programs that fall under the specified funding categories.

Capital support is generally limited to agencies in Greater Hartford. Organizations accepted for a capital grant may not also receive operating support in the same year.

Funding is generally not provided to agencies that receive United Way funding. Special programs can be an exception, but the agency must have the permission of the United Way before it solicits funding.

Individual applications for scholarships are not accepted.

Additional Information

In 1997, the foundation was integrated into the corporate giving program.

Generally seeks to support organizations that enable individuals to help themselves and that are supported by creative and ultimately self-supporting funding initiatives.

Where possible, the Hartford will try to leverage its funds through matching and challenge grants and consider awarding multiple-year grants if appropriate and where desirable. matching and challenge grants and consider awarding multiple-year grants if appropriate and where desirable.

Corporate Officials

Ramani Ayer: chairman, president, chief executive officer B Kerala, KE India 1947. ED Indian Institute of Technology BS (1969); Drexel University MS (1973). PRIM CORP EMPL chairman, president, chief executive officer: The Hartford. CORP AFFIL chairman: Trumball Insurance Co.; chairman: Twin City Fire Insurance Co.; director: New York Stock Exchange Inc.; president: Hartford Insurance Southeast; chairman: Hartford Life Accident Insurance Co.; chairman: Hartford Insurance Midwest; president: Hartford Index Fund Inc.; chairman: Hartford Insurance Co. Illinois; chairman, chief executive officer: Hartford Financial Services Group Inc.; chairman: Hartford Ca-

sualty Insurance Co.; president: Hartford Financial Group Inc.; chairman: Hartford Accident Indemnity Co.

Joseph H. Gareau: executive vice president, chief investment officer B Westfield, MA 1947. ED University of Massachusetts BBA (1973); University of Hartford MBA (1978). PRIM CORP EMPL executive vice president, chief investment officer: The Hartford Insurance Co. ADD CORP EMPL executive vice president: Hartford Financial Services Group Inc.; senior vice president, chief investment officer, director: Hartford Insurance Midwest; executive vice president: Hartford Insurance of the Southeast; executive vice president: Hartford Accident Indemnity Co.; executive vice president, director: Hartford Casualty Insurance Co.; president, chief invest officer: Hartford Investment Management Co.; vice president,chief investment officer: Pacific Industry Co. Inc. CORP AFFIL vice president, chief investment officer: Pacific Industry Co. Inc.

Edward L. Morgan: group senior vice president B Scranton, PA 1943. ED Gettysburg College (1965). PRIM CORP EMPL group senior vice president: The Hartford ADD CORP EMPL senior vice president: Hartford Financial Services Group Inc.; senior vice president: Hartford Fire Insurance Co.

Giving Program Officials

Ann D. De Raismes: member PRIM CORP EMPL senior vice president: Hartford Life Annuity Insurance Co.
Joseph H. Gareau: investment officer (see above)
Helen G. Goodman: senior vice president B Bridgeport, CT 1941. ED Barnard College (1964); Columbia University (1979). PRIM CORP EMPL senior vice president: The Hartford. CORP AFFIL treasurer, director: Hartford Action Plan Infant Health; senior vice president: Hartford Financial Services Group Inc.
David M. Klein: vice president B Brooklyn, NY 1946. ED University of Rhode Island (1968); Temple University (1970). PRIM CORP EMPL senior vice president: The Hartford ADD CORP EMPL senior vice president: Hartford Insurance Group; executive vice president: Hartford Financial Service Group; senior vice president: Hartford Insurance Midwest.
Edward L. Morgan: member contributions committee (see above)
Edna Negron: PRIM CORP EMPL director community affairs: The Hartford.
Michael Stephen Wilder: B New Haven, CT 1941. ED Yale University BA (1963); Harvard University JD (1966). PRIM CORP EMPL senior vice president, general counsel: The Hartford Financial Services Group Inc. CORP AFFIL senior vice president: Twin City Fire Insurance Co.; vice president: ITT Hartford Insurance Group; vice president: Property Casualty Insurance; secretary: Hartford Insurance Southeast; officer: Hartford Fire Insurance Co.; officer: Hartford Insurance Midwest; secretary: Hartford Equity Sales Co.; officer: Hartford Accident Indemnity Co.; secretary: Hartford Casualty Insurance Co. NONPR AFFIL director: American Arbitration Association; member: American Bar Association.

Grants Analysis

Disclosure Period: calendar year ending 2002
Total Grants: $5,108,893
Number of Grants: 2,396
Average Grant: $2,200
Highest Grant: $680,000
Lowest Grant: $10
Typical Range: $50 to $5,000
Note: Grants analysis was provided by the foundation.

Recent Grants

Note: Grants derived from 1997 Form 990.
Library-Related
88,000   Wadsworth Athenaeum, Hartford, CT
General
383,333   United Way Capital Area

110,000	Greater Hartford Arts Council, Hartford, CT
100,000	Connecticut Children's Medical Center, Hartford, CT
100,000	St. Francis Hospital and Medical Center
40,000	Disabled Sports USA, Rockville, MD
40,000	Mark Twain House
40,000	Salvation Army, Hartford, CT
25,000	Hartford Action Plan on Infant Health, Hartford, CT
25,000	West Middle School Committee, Hartford, CT
20,000	Child Council, Hartford, CT

THE JOHN A. HARTFORD FOUNDATION, INC.

Giving Contact
James F. O'Sullivan, Program Officer
55 East 59th Street, 16th Fl.
New York, NY 10022-1178
Phone: (212)832-7788
Fax: (212)593-4913
E-mail: mail@jhartfound.org
Web: http://www.jhartfound.org

Description
Founded: 1929
EIN: 131667057
Organization Type: General Purpose Foundation
Giving Locations: nationally.
Grant Types: Employee Matching Gifts, Fellowship, General Support, Matching, Multiyear/Continuing Support, Project, Research.

Donor Information
Founder: The John A. Hartford Foundation was established in 1929 by the late John A. Hartford (d. 1951) and George L. Hartford Jr. (d. 1957). The donors were the sons of George Huntington Hartford who, with George F. Gilman, founded the Great Atlantic and Pacific Tea Company in 1869 (which became the A&P foodstore chain). Upon their father's death in 1917, George Hartford, Jr., became chairman of the company, and John Hartford, the president. The brothers left the bulk of their estates to the foundation. Although the foundation formerly held a great deal of A&P stock, its holdings have been diversified and its portfolio no longer contains A&P stock.

Financial Summary
Total Giving: $22,999,057 (2003); $25,612,754 (2002); $24,305,339 (2001)
Giving Analysis: Giving for 2003 includes: foundation matching gifts ($684,505); 2002: foundation matching gifts ($577,131).
Assets: $560,945,206 (2003); $489,172,586 (2002); $587,895,434 (2001)

Typical Recipients
Arts & Humanities: Arts Associations & Councils, Ethnic & Folk Arts, Libraries
Civic & Public Affairs: Housing, Nonprofit Management, Philanthropic Organizations, Professional & Trade Associations, Public Policy, Women's Affairs
Education: Colleges & Universities, Education Associations, Education-General, Health & Physical Education, International Studies, Medical Education, Minority Education, Private Education (Precollege), Social Sciences Education
Health: Arthritis, Cancer, Clinics/Medical Centers, Health-General, Geriatric Health, Health Policy/Cost Containment, Health Funds, Health Organizations, Home-Care Services, Hospitals, Hospitals (University Affiliated), Long-Term Care, Medical Rehabilitation, Medical Research, Medical Training, Mental Health, Public Health, Research/Studies Institutes

Religion: Religious Welfare
Science: Science-General, Scientific Labs
Social Services: At-Risk Youth, Community Service Organizations, Day Care, People with Disabilities, Senior Services, Social Services-General, Volunteer Services, Youth Organizations

Application Procedures
Initial Contact: Submit a brief letter of inquiry which summarizes the purpose and activities of the grant, the qualifications of the applicant and institution, and an estimated cost and time frame for the project.
Deadlines: None.
Review Process: Although the foundation requires no formal application, it expects applicants to be familiar with the guidelines and interests of the foundation. Current program guidelines may be obtained by contacting the foundation. The proposed project will be reviewed by members of the foundation's staff and possibly by outside reviewers. Results of this review will be sent within approximately six weeks and may be asked to supply additional information.

Restrictions
Grants are made only to organizations with tax-exempt status under IRS section 501(c)(3) and which are not private foundations under sections 509(a) or 170(c)(1). No grants are given to individuals. Support is not provided for general research. Rarely will the foundation support projects for longer than three years.

Additional Information
Publications: Annual Report; Guidelines

Foundation Officials
Anson McC. Beard, Jr.: trustee
William T. Comfort, Jr.: trustee ED New York University School of Law LLM (1964). CORP AFFIL chairman: Citicorp Venture Capital. NONPR AFFIL trustee: New York University School of Law.
James Duncan Farley: chairman emeritus, trustee B Chicago, IL 1926. ED Georgetown University BS (1949). CLUB AFFIL Valley Club; Wequetonsing Golf Club; Los Angeles Country Club; Round Hill Club; Cypress Point Club; Loblolly Pines Golf Club; Birnham Wood Golf Club.
Samuel R. Gische: fin director, controller B 1953. ED Queens College BA (1975); New York University MBA (1983).
James G. Kenan, III: trustee B Lexington, KY 1945. ED University of North Carolina (1968). PRIM CORP EMPL chairman: Flagler System Inc. CORP AFFIL chairman: Kentucky River Coal Corp. NONPR AFFIL vice chairman board of directors: Transylvania University.
William B. Matteson: secretary, trustee B New York, NY 1928. ED Yale University BA (1950); Harvard University JD (1953). PRIM CORP EMPL partner: Debevoise & Plimpton. NONPR AFFIL member: New York State Bar Association; senior trustee: USCIB; member: New York Institute; member: American Bar Association; member: New York City Bar Association. CLUB AFFIL Sky Club; Union Club; River Club; Sankaty Head Club.
Christopher T.H. Pell: trustee NONPR AFFIL advisory board: Fort Adams Trust.
Thomas A. Reynolds, Jr.: trustee B Chicago, IL 1928. ED Georgetown University AB (1948); University of Michigan JD (1951). PRIM CORP EMPL chairman emeritus: Winston & Strawn. NONPR AFFIL member: Illinois State Bar Association; life trustee: Rush University Medical Center; member: American Bar Association; member: Chicago Bar Association.
Corrine H. Rieder, EdD: executive director, treasurer
Norman Hans Volk: chairman, trustee B New York, NY 1935. ED Valparaiso University BA (1957); Marquette University MA (1959). PRIM CORP EMPL president: Chamberlain & Steward Associates. CLUB AFFIL University Club; University Glee Club New York; Doubles Club.

Kathryn Dineen Wriston: president, trustee B Syracuse, NY. ED University of Geneva (1958-1959); Smith College BA (1960); University of Michigan LLB (1963). CORP AFFIL director: Stanley Works Inc. NONPR AFFIL member: Practicing Law Institute; member visiting committee: University Michigan Law School; member: New York State Bar Association; member: National Association Accts; member: New York County Lawyers Association; member: Independent Standards Board; member executive committee: CPR Institute Dispute Resolution; member: Finance Womens Association New York; member: Association Bar New York City; member: American Bar Association.

Grants Analysis
Disclosure Period: calendar year ending 2003
Total Grants: $22,314,552*
Number of Grants: 89
Average Grant: $169,632*
Highest Grant: $2,328,390
Lowest Grant: $3,000
Typical Range: $50,000 to $300,000
*Note: Giving excludes matching gifts. Average grant figure excludes six highest grants ($8,235,134).

Recent Grants
Note: Grants derived from 2003 Form 990.
General

2,328,390	American Academy of Nursing, Washington, DC -- towards nursing initiative coordinating center and scholar stipends
1,350,743	Gerontological Society of America, Washington, DC -- towards Hartford geriatric social work faculty scholars program
1,343,744	American Federation for Aging Research Inc., New York, NY -- towards Paul Benson physician faculty scholars in aging research program
1,099,679	American Association of Colleges of Nursing, Washington, DC -- towards enhancing geriatric nursing education at baccalaureate and advanced practice levels
1,084,325	American Geriatric Society Inc., New York, NY -- towards increasing geriatrics expertise in surgical and medical specialties phase 3
1,078,253	New York University, New York, NY -- towards the John A Hartford foundation institute for geriatric nursing
701,828	Society of General Internal Medicine, Washington, DC -- towards increasing education and research capacity to improve care of older Americans
647,562	American Society of Clinical Oncology, Alexandria, VA -- towards enhancing geriatric oncology training
623,454	National Council on the Aging Inc., Washington, DC -- towards promoting vital aging through teamwork between community organizations and health care providers
567,114	American Association of Colleges of Nursing, Washington, DC -- towards creating careers in geriatric advanced practice nursing

HARTMARX CORP.

Company Headquarters
101 N. Wacker Dr.
Chicago, IL 60606
Web: http://www.hartmarx.com

Company Description
Founded: 1983
Ticker: HMX

Exchange: NYSE
Revenue: US$601.6 million (2001)
Employees: 4100 (2003)
SIC(s): 2311 Men's/Boys' Suits & Coats, 2325 Men's/Boys' Trousers & Slacks, 2329 Men's/Boys' Clothing Nec, 6719 Holding Companies Nec.

Operating Locations

Hartmarx Corp. (AL--Anniston; AR--Rector; GA--Loganville, Norcross; IL--Des Plaines; IN--Michigan City; KY--Elizabethtown, Winchester; MO--Cape Girardeau, Chaffee, Farmington, St. Louis; NY--Buffalo, New York, Rochester; PA--Easton)

Hartmarx Charitable Foundation

Giving Contact

Kay C. Nalbach, President
101 North Wacker Drive, 23rd Floor
Chicago, IL 60606
Phone: (312)357-5331
Web: http://www.hartmarx.com

Description

EIN: 366152745
Organization Type: Corporate Foundation
Giving Locations: headquarters and operating communities.
Grant Types: Capital, Employee Matching Gifts, General Support, Research.
Note: Employee matching gift ratio: 1 to 1 up to $3,000 for each individual annually for gift amounts of at least $25. Matches gifts made to institutions of higher learning. Foundation will not match bequests, dues, tuition fees, subscription fees, loan payment, or contributions not made as direct donations.

Financial Summary

Total Giving: $223,822 (fiscal year ending November 30, 2003); $228,050 (fiscal 2002); $326,593 (fiscal 2001). Note: Contributes through corporate direct giving program and foundation.
Assets: $10,005 (fiscal 2003); $14,028 (fiscal 2002); $12,279 (fiscal 2001).
Gifts Received: $266,136 (fiscal 2003); $230,000 (fiscal 2002); $314,000 (fiscal 2001). Note: In fiscal 2002, contributions were received from Hartmarx Corp.

Typical Recipients

Arts & Humanities: Arts Associations & Councils, Arts Festivals, Arts Funds, Arts Institutes, Dance, Arts & Humanities-General, Historic Preservation, History & Archaeology, Libraries, Museums/Galleries, Music, Opera, Performing Arts, Public Broadcasting, Theater
Civic & Public Affairs: African American Affairs, Botanical Gardens/Parks, Business/Free Enterprise, Civil Rights, Clubs, Community Foundations, Economic Development, Ethnic Organizations, Civic & Public Affairs-General, Housing, Law & Justice, Legal Aid, Nonprofit Management, Philanthropic Organizations, Professional & Trade Associations, Public Policy, Safety, Urban & Community Affairs, Women's Affairs, Zoos/Aquariums
Education: Afterschool/Enrichment Programs, Arts/Humanities Education, Business Education, Colleges & Universities, Community & Junior Colleges, Economic Education, Education Associations, Education Funds, Education Reform, Engineering/Technological Education, Faculty Development, Education-General, Literacy, Minority Education, Private Education (Precollege), Public Education (Precollege), Science/Mathematics Education, Social Sciences Education, Student Aid, Vocational & Technical Education
Environment: Air/Water Quality, Environment-General, Protection, Watershed, Wildlife Protection

Health: AIDS/HIV, Arthritis, Cancer, Children's Health/Hospitals, Clinics/Medical Centers, Diabetes, Emergency/Ambulance Services, Health Funds, Health Organizations, Heart, Hospitals, Multiple Sclerosis, Nursing Services, Prenatal Health Issues, Preventive Medicine/Wellness Organizations, Public Health, Respiratory, Single-Disease Health Associations, Speech & Hearing
International: Foreign Arts Organizations
Religion: Churches, Jewish Causes, Ministries, Religious Organizations, Religious Welfare
Science: Science Museums
Social Services: Animal Protection, At-Risk Youth, Camps, Child Abuse, Child Welfare, Community Centers, Community Service Organizations, Crime Prevention, Domestic Violence, Family Planning, Family Services, Food/Clothing Distribution, Homes, People with Disabilities, Recreation & Athletics, Scouts, Senior Services, Sexual Abuse, Shelters/Homelessness, United Funds/United Ways, Volunteer Services, YMCA/YWCA/YMHA/YWHA, Youth Organizations

Application Procedures

Initial Contact: Submit a written request.
Application Requirements: Include legal name of organization, summary of specific project to be supported, amount requested, latest financial statements and budget, and proof of tax-exempt status.
Deadlines: None.
Review Process: Foundation president and contributions committee review requests over $2,500, which are then submitted to board of directors for approval; grants of less than $2,500 must be approved by foundation president and the subsidiary's chief executive officer before processing.
Decision Notification: Quarterly, for contributions over $2,500.

Restrictions

Does not support goodwill advertising, fundraising benefits, political or lobbying groups, individuals, or religious organizations for sectarian purposes.
In July 2002, the foundation president reported that the foundation is not accepting proposals from any organization that is not presently being funded.

Corporate Officials

Elbert O. Hand: chairman, chief executive officer, director B 1939. ED Hamilton College BA (1961). PRIM CORP EMPL chairman, chief executive officer, director: Hartmarx Corp. CORP AFFIL director: Jaymar-Ruby Inc.
Glenn R. Morgan: executive vice president, chief financial officer, treasurer, member B Chicago, IL 1947. ED Northwestern University BS (1968); Northwestern University MBA (1970). PRIM CORP EMPL executive vice president, chief financial officer: Hartmarx Corp. CORP AFFIL vice president: Hart Schaffner & Marx. NONPR AFFIL chairman financial managing committee: American Apparel Manufacturer Association; member: Financial Executives Institute.
Homi Burjor Patel: president, chief operating officer, director B Bombay, MH India 1949. ED University of Bombay BS (1973); Columbia University MBA (1975). PRIM CORP EMPL president, chief operating officer, director: Hartmarx Corp. CORP AFFIL chairman, director: M Wile & Co.; treasurer, director: Textile Clothing Tech Corp.; director: Jaymar-Ruby Inc.; chairman: Plaid Clothing Co. Inc.; vice president: Hart Schaffner & Marx; president: Hart Services Inc. DEL. NONPR AFFIL executive vice president, member, director: Clothing Manufacturer Association America. CLUB AFFIL Chicago Club; University Club New York.

Foundation Officials

Glenn R. Morgan: vice president, director (see above)
Kay C. Nalbach: president, director B Moweaqua, IL. ED University of Illinois (1959). PRIM CORP EMPL assistant section: Hartmarx Corp. NONPR AFFIL

member: American Society of Corporate Secretaries; member: Executive Women International.
Taras R. Proczko: secretary, director
Andrew A. Zahr: treasurer

Grants Analysis

Disclosure Period: fiscal year ending November 30, 2003
Total Grants: $140,572*
Number of Grants: 97
Average Grant: $1,449
Highest Grant: $15,000
Lowest Grant: $100
Typical Range: $200 to $3,000
*Note: Giving excludes matching gifts and United Way.

Recent Grants

Note: Grants derived from fiscal 2003 Form 990.
General

38,000	United Way Crusade of Mercy, Chicago, IL
10,930	Anti Defamation League, New York, NY
9,350	United Way of LaPorte County, LaPorte, IN
8,500	United Way of Buffalo and Erie County, Buffalo, NY
7,500	Robert T. Jones Junior Memorial Scholarship Fund, New York, NY
6,800	United Way of Greater Rochester, Chicago, IL
6,100	Hull House Foundation, Chicago, IL
5,000	Chicago Christian Industrial League, Chicago, IL
5,000	Crossroads Group, Chicago, IL
5,000	Kellogg School of Management, Evanston, IL

C. FELIX HARVEY FOUNDATION

Giving Contact

C. Felix Harvey, Vice President
PO Box 189
Kinston, NC 28502
Phone: (252)523-4103

Description

EIN: 237038942
Organization Type: Private Foundation
Grant Types: General Support.

Donor Information

Founder: Felix Harvey, Margaret B. Harvey

Financial Summary

Total Giving: $416,192 (fiscal year ending August 31, 2002)
Giving Analysis: Giving for fiscal 2002 includes: foundation grants to United Way ($500); foundation scholarships ($5,000)
Assets: $10,005,705 (fiscal 2002)
Gifts Received: $263,781 (fiscal 2002); $770,757 (fiscal 1999); $260,000 (fiscal 1996). Note: In fiscal 2002, contributions were received from John O. & Leigh H. McNairy ($33,281) and Robert L. & Sunny H. Burrows Jr. ($35,500). In fiscal 1999, contributions were received from L. Harvey & Son ($100,000), Mallard Oil Co. ($10,000), Tidewater Transit Co. ($70,000), C. Felix Harvey ($321,000), John & Leigh McNairy ($169,845.75), and Sunny Burrows ($99,911.25). In fiscal 1998, contributions were received from L. Harvey & Son ($100,000), Mallard Oil Co. Tidewater Transit Co. ($70,000), L. Harvey, Inc. ($10,000), C. Felix Harvey ($321,000), John S. Leigh McNairy ($169,845.75), and Sunny Borrows ($99,911.25). North Carolina Natural Gas ($10,000), and Robert Lee Burrows ($50,000).

Typical Recipients

Arts & Humanities: Arts Associations & Councils, Arts Funds, Historic Preservation, History & Archaeology, Libraries, Museums/Galleries, Music, Performing Arts, Public Broadcasting

Civic & Public Affairs: Botanical Gardens/Parks, Community Foundations, Economic Development, Civic & Public Affairs-General, Housing, Rural Affairs, Safety, Urban & Community Affairs, Zoos/Aquariums

Education: Agricultural Education, Arts/Humanities Education, Business Education, Colleges & Universities, Community & Junior Colleges, Education Funds, Education-General, Private Education (Precollege), Science/Mathematics Education, Secondary Education (Public), Student Aid

Health: Cancer, Health Organizations, Single-Disease Health Associations, Trauma Treatment

International: International Relations, Missionary/Religious Activities

Religion: Churches, Religious Organizations, Religious Welfare, Seminaries

Science: Scientific Centers & Institutes

Social Services: Child Welfare, Community Service Organizations, Food/Clothing Distribution, Homes, Recreation & Athletics, Refugee Assistance, Scouts, Special Olympics, United Funds/United Ways, Veterans, Youth Organizations

Application Procedures

Initial Contact: The foundation has no formal grant application procedure or application form.
Deadlines: None.

Foundation Officials

Robert Lee Burrows, Jr.: vice president
Sunny Harvey Burrows: secretary, treasurer
Ann Harvey: director
C. Felix Harvey: vice president
Margaret B. Harvey: president
Ruth Heath: assistant secretary

Grants Analysis

Disclosure Period: fiscal year ending August 31, 2002
Total Grants: $410,692*
Number of Grants: 65
Average Grant: $5,167*
Highest Grant: $80,000
Lowest Grant: $250
Typical Range: $1,000 to $10,000
***Note:** Giving excludes scholarships and United Way. Average grant figure excludes highest grant.

Recent Grants

Note: Grants derived from 2002 Form 990.

General

80,000	Global Transpark Foundation, Kinston, NC -- operating expenses
26,000	Mount Olive College, Mt. Olive, NC -- operating expenses
25,000	LaGrange Development Corporation, Toledo, OH -- operating expenses
25,000	Louisburg College, Louisburg, NC -- operating expenses
25,000	Mount Olive College, Mt. Olive, NC -- debt reduction
20,000	Charis Community Housing, Atlanta, GA -- operating expenses
20,000	North Avenue Presbyterian Church, Atlanta, GA -- for operating expenses
20,000	Salvation Army -- operating expenses
20,000	University of North Carolina Education Foundation, Chapel Hill, NC -- operating expenses
15,000	Westminster Schools, Atlanta, GA -- operating expenses

HASBRO INC.

Company Headquarters

1027 Newport Avenue
Pawtucket, RI 02861
Phone: (401)431-8697
Web: http://www.hasbro.com

Company Description

Founded: 1923
Ticker: HAS
Exchange: NYSE
Revenue: US$2.816 billion (2002)
Employees: 6900 (2003)
SIC(s): 3944 Games, Toys & Children's Vehicles.

Operating Locations

Hasbro Inc. (Rhode Island) (CA--San Diego; NJ--Northvale; NY--Amsterdam; SC--Easley; TX--El Paso)

Nonmonetary Support

Value: $3,500,000 (2000 approx)
Type: Donated Products; Loaned Employees; Loaned Executives; Workplace Solicitation
Note: The foundation has several toy donation programs, including hospital and shelter playrooms, the after-school programs of the United Neighborhood Centers and Boys & Girls Clubs, children whose lives have been affected by disaster, and holiday giving to needy children. Also donates toys yearly to the Appalachian areas and to Walking Shield, the agency handling all Native American Indian reservations west of the Mississippi River. The Hasbro Orphanage program works with World Vision, an international relief agency. Each year a different country is selected for toy donations and orphanage support. The Team Hasbro volunteer program allows eligible employees to donate up to four hours a month of volunteer time to organizations that work with children.
Note: Company donates toys nationally to direct service organizations that provide services around the clock for children (see "Other Things You Should Know")

Hasbro Charitable Trust Inc.

Giving Contact

Karen Davis, Director
1027 Newport Avenue
Pawtucket, RI 02862
Phone: (401)431-8151
Fax: (401)721-7275
Web: http://www.hasbro.org

Description

EIN: 222538470
Organization Type: Corporate Foundation
Giving Locations: headquarters and operating communities.
Grant Types: Capital, Employee Matching Gifts, General Support, Multiyear/Continuing Support, Project.
Note: Employee matching gift ratio: 1 to 1 for higher education.

Financial Summary

Total Giving: $1,210,407 (2003). Note: Contributes through corporate direct giving program and foundation.
Assets: $1,969,046 (2003)
Gifts Received: $1,839,386 (2003); $1,650,000 (2000); $1,214,175 (1999). Note: Contributions were received from Hasbro Inc. and miscellaneous donors.

Typical Recipients

Arts & Humanities: Arts Centers, Arts Funds, Arts Institutes, Community Arts, History & Archaeology, Libraries, Literary Arts, Museums/Galleries, Music, Performing Arts, Theater

Civic & Public Affairs: African American Affairs, Business/Free Enterprise, Community Foundations, Economic Development, Economic Policy, Ethnic Organizations, Civic & Public Affairs-General, Hispanic Affairs, Housing, Law & Justice, Legal Aid, Minority Business, Municipalities/Towns, Professional & Trade Associations, Public Policy, Urban & Community Affairs, Women's Affairs, Zoos/Aquariums

Education: Afterschool/Enrichment Programs, Arts/Humanities Education, Business Education, Colleges & Universities, Economic Education, Education Funds, Education Reform, Elementary Education (Private), Elementary Education (Public), Education-General, Health & Physical Education, Literacy, Medical Education, Preschool Education, Private Education (Precollege), Public Education (Precollege), School Volunteerism, Special Education, Student Aid

Environment: Air/Water Quality, Forestry, Environment-General, Protection

Health: AIDS/HIV, Alzheimer's Disease, Cancer, Children's Health/Hospitals, Clinics/Medical Centers, Diabetes, Emergency/Ambulance Services, Eyes/Blindness, Geriatric Health, Health Funds, Health Organizations, Heart, Hospices, Hospitals, Hospitals (University Affiliated), Kidney, Medical Rehabilitation, Medical Research, Mental Health, Multiple Sclerosis, Nursing Services, Prenatal Health Issues, Preventive Medicine/Wellness Organizations, Public Health, Research/Studies Institutes, Single-Disease Health Associations, Transplant Networks/Donor Banks

International: Health Care/Hospitals, Human Rights, International Affairs, International Environmental Issues, International Organizations, International Peace & Security Issues, International Relations, International Relief Efforts

Religion: Jewish Causes, Religious Organizations, Religious Welfare

Science: Science Museums

Social Services: Big Brothers/Big Sisters, Child Abuse, Child Welfare, Community Centers, Community Service Organizations, Counseling, Day Care, Domestic Violence, Emergency Relief, Family Planning, Family Services, Food/Clothing Distribution, People with Disabilities, Recreation & Athletics, Refugee Assistance, Scouts, Senior Services, Sexual Abuse, Shelters/Homelessness, Social Services-General, Special Olympics, Substance Abuse, United Funds/United Ways, Volunteer Services, YMCA/YWCA/YMHA/YWHA, Youth Organizations

Application Procedures

Initial Contact: Request guidelines and application by phone.
Application Requirements: Include statement of purpose and objectives; history of organization's programs; list of board and staff, as well as record of financial commitment by board for proposed project; annual operating budget for organization and for year in which grant will occur; recently audited financial statement; description of program for which funds are requested, including its budget; amount requested; copy of tax-exempt determination letter; list of other corporations and foundations approached and level of financial support requested or received.
Deadlines: March 31 for annual review in June.
Notes: Foundation only reviews requests in communities where company has operations.

Restrictions

From time to time, unusual or special projects will alter the grant review process.
Cash contributions are limited to operating locations. Does not support religious organizations, individuals, political organizations, scholarships, loans, endowments, goodwill advertising, fund raisers, sponsorship of recreational activities, or research.

Additional Information

Hasbro also sponsors the Hasbro Children's Foundation, which contributes about $2,000,000 annually to health, social services, and educational programs for children under the age of 12. Contact is Eve Weiss, Executive Director, Hasbro Children's Foundation, 32 W 23rd Street, New York, NY 10010, (212) 645-2400. Toy requests should be submitted by October 1. If an organization receives toys for two consecutive years, company follows with a two year hiatus. No participation in fundraisers, give-a-ways, or incentives. Toys go to supervised playrooms in organizations which provide direct services to children, especially shelters and child life departments of hospitals. Donates only to 501(c)(3) organizations within the U.S. Policy holds for Hasbro and its subsidiaries: Milton Bradley, Playskool, Tonka, Kenner, and Parker.

Corporate Officials

Cynthia Reed: senior vice president, general counsel ED Wellesley College AB (1977); Northeastern University JD (1980). PRIM CORP EMPL senior vice president, general counsel: Hasbro Inc.

Alfred J. Verrecchia: executive, director B Providence, RI 1943. ED University of Rhode Island BS (1967); University of Rhode Island MBA (1972). PRIM CORP EMPL executive, director: Hasbro Inc. CORP AFFIL president, director: Hasbro Inc. NONPR AFFIL director: Bradley Hospital.

Foundation Officials

Karen Davis: director

David Hargreaves: senior vice president, chief financial officer

Alan Geoffrey Hassenfeld: president, director B Providence, RI 1948. ED University of Pennsylvania BA (1970). NONPR AFFIL trustee: Miriam Hospital; overseer: University Pennsylvania School Arts & Sciences; director: Foster Parents Plan; director: Jerusalem Foundation; trustee: Bryant College; trustee: Deerfield Academy Alumni Association; director: Association of Governing Boards of Colleges and Universities.

Joanne Haworth: assistant treasurer

Richard B. Holt: senior vice president

Barry Nagler: senior vice president, general counsel, secretary, director

Martin R. Trueb: senior vice president, treasurer

Alfred J. Verrecchia: executive vice president, director (see above)

Grants Analysis

Disclosure Period: calendar year ending 2003
Total Grants: $921,657*
Number of Grants: 111
Average Grant: $7,188*
Highest Grant: $131,000
Lowest Grant: $100
Typical Range: $1,000 to $10,000
***Note:** Giving excludes matching gifts; United Way. Average grant figure excludes highest grant.

Recent Grants

Note: Grants derived from 2003 Form 990.
Library-Related
2,500	Providence Public Library, Providence, RI -- creating readers program

General
165,000	United Way of Southeastern New England, Providence, RI
131,000	Rhode Island Community Food Bank, West Warwick, RI
123,750	United Way of Pioneer Valley, Springfield, MA
50,000	Institute for International Sport, Kingston, RI -- scholar athlete games
50,000	Teammates for Kids Foundation, Littleton, CO -- benefits teammates for kids
30,000	American Red Cross of Rhode Island, Providence, RI -- Pawtucket mill fire donation
30,000	City Year, Providence, RI -- support generation program
26,253	Women and Infants Hospital of Rhode Island, Providence, RI -- purchase of a giraffe omnibed
25,000	Friends Way, East Greenwich, RI -- station fire victims
25,000	Travelers Aid, Providence, RI

HASKELL FUND

Giving Contact

James Sekerak
1422 Euclid Avenue, Rm. 1010
Cleveland, OH 44115-2078
Phone: (216)363-6481

Description

Founded: 1955
EIN: 346513797
Organization Type: Private Foundation
Giving Locations: OH: Cleveland nationally.
Grant Types: Capital, Endowment, General Support, Multiyear/Continuing Support, Operating Expenses, Project, Scholarship.

Donor Information

Founder: the late Melville H. Haskell, Coburn Haskell, Melville H. Haskell, Jr., Mark Haskell

Financial Summary

Total Giving: $209,000 (2002)
Giving Analysis: Giving for 2002 includes: foundation scholarships ($16,000)
Assets: $3,502,626 (2002)

Typical Recipients

Arts & Humanities: Arts Associations & Councils, Arts Centers, Community Arts, History & Archaeology, Libraries, Literary Arts, Museums/Galleries, Music, Visual Arts
Civic & Public Affairs: Clubs, Civic & Public Affairs-General, Hispanic Affairs, Native American Affairs, Professional & Trade Associations, Urban & Community Affairs
Education: Arts/Humanities Education, Colleges & Universities, Education Funds, Engineering/Technological Education, International Studies, Medical Education, Minority Education, Private Education (Precollege), Public Education (Precollege), Student Aid, Vocational & Technical Education
Environment: Air/Water Quality, Environment-General, Resource Conservation, Wildlife Protection
Health: AIDS/HIV, Cancer, Children's Health/Hospitals, Clinics/Medical Centers, Emergency/Ambulance Services, Health Organizations, Hospitals, Hospitals (University Affiliated), Medical Research, Nursing Services, Public Health
International: Human Rights, International Environmental Issues, International Relief Efforts, Missionary/Religious Activities
Religion: Churches, Religion-General, Religious Organizations, Religious Welfare
Science: Scientific Centers & Institutes, Scientific Organizations
Social Services: Child Abuse, Child Welfare, Community Service Organizations, Day Care, Domestic Violence, Emergency Relief, Family Planning, Family Services, Food/Clothing Distribution, Recreation & Athletics, Shelters/Homelessness, Social Services-General, United Funds/United Ways, Youth Organizations

Application Procedures

Initial Contact: Send brief letter and proposal.
Application Requirements: Include statement of operations and proof of tax-exempt status.
Deadlines: None.

Restrictions

Does not support individuals.

Additional Information

Publications: Annual Report

Foundation Officials

Coburn Haskell: president, trustee
Eric T. Haskell: trustee
Mark Haskell: trustee
Mary E. Haskell: trustee
Melville H. Haskell, Jr.: trustee
Schuyler A. Haskell: vice president, trustee
Sarah Haskell-Green: trustee
Paulette F. Kitko: secretary, treasurer
James C. Sekerak: treasurer
Mary H. Walker: trustee

Grants Analysis

Disclosure Period: calendar year ending 2002
Total Grants: $193,000*
Number of Grants: 73
Average Grant: $2,644
Highest Grant: $16,000
Lowest Grant: $500
Typical Range: $1,000 to $5,000
***Note:** Giving excludes scholarships.

Recent Grants

Note: Grants derived from 2002 Form 990.
General
16,000	University of Arizona, Tucson, AZ -- H.M. Hanna Scholarship
12,000	Hoag Hospital, Newport Beach, CA -- Women's Pavilion capital campaign
11,500	Arizona Sonora Desert Museum, Tucson, AZ -- endowment fund
7,500	Pacolet Area Conservancy, Columbus, NC
7,000	North Kohala Community Hospital, Inc.
6,600	Direct Relief International, Santa Barbara, CA -- endowment campaign
6,000	Scripps College, Claremont, CA -- French and humanities symposia
5,000	Cleveland Scholarship Programs, Cleveland, OH
5,000	Community Arts Music Association, Santa Barbara, CA -- endowment campaign
5,000	Maritime Museum, San Diego, CA -- Educational Programs

HATHAWAY MEMORIAL CHARITABLE TRUST

Giving Contact

Augusta Haydock
c/o Fleet National Bank
PO Box 6767
Providence, RI 02940
Phone: (401)276-7239

Description

Founded: 1992
EIN: 046599655
Organization Type: Private Foundation
Giving Locations: MA: Somerset
Grant Types: General Support.

Financial Summary

Total Giving: $71,060 (fiscal year ending July 31, 2004); $89,972 (fiscal 2002)
Assets: $1,352,947 (fiscal 2004); $1,700,675 (fiscal 2002)

Typical Recipients

Arts & Humanities: Dance, History & Archaeology, Libraries

Civic & Public Affairs: Civic & Public Affairs-General

Education: Afterschool/Enrichment Programs, Elementary Education (Public), Education-General, Private Education (Precollege), Public Education (Precollege), Student Aid

Health: Health Organizations, Hospices, Nursing Services

International: Missionary/Religious Activities

Religion: Churches, Ministries, Religious Organizations, Religious Welfare

Social Services: Day Care, Delinquency & Criminal Rehabilitation, Family Services, Social Services-General, YMCA/YWCA/YMHA/YWHA, Youth Organizations

Application Procedures

Initial Contact: Send a brief letter of inquiry.
Application Requirements: Include all pertinent information for review by the advisory committee.
Deadlines: None.

Restrictions

Limited to Somerset, MA.

Additional Information

Provides scholarships to deserving students from Somerset, MA.
Trust(s): Fleet National Bank

Grants Analysis

Disclosure Period: fiscal year ending July 31, 2004
Total Grants: $71,060
Number of Grants: 17
Average Grant: $4,180
Highest Grant: $10,000
Lowest Grant: $1,000
Typical Range: $1,000 to $10,000

Recent Grants

Note: Grants derived from 2000 Form 990.
Library-Related

1,800	Somerset Public Library, Somerset, MA

General

10,000	Citizens Scholarship Foundation of Somerset, Somerset, MA
7,500	St. Vincent's, Santa Barbara, CA
7,000	Hospice Outreach, Inc.
6,250	Somerset Children's Center, Somerset, MA
6,000	Somerset Historical Society, Somerset, MA
5,000	Congregational Christian Church
5,000	Historical Commission
4,950	Congregational Christian Church
4,000	Somerset Baptist Church, Somerset, MA
3,500	YMCA of Greater Fall River

A. JOHN AND BARBARA A. HAUPTLI CHARITABLE FOUNDATION

Giving Contact

Barbara A. Hauptli, Trustee
A. John and Barbara A. Hauptli Charitable Foundation
407 E. Iron
Salina, KS 67401
Phone: (785)827-7177

Description

Founded: 1996
EIN: 481173715

Organization Type: Private Foundation
Grant Types: General Support.

Financial Summary

Total Giving: $56,590 (fiscal year ending September 30, 2004); $82,600 (fiscal 2001)
Assets: $1,105,313 (fiscal 2004); $1,147,192 (fiscal 2001)
Gifts Received: $1,896 (fiscal 2001); $1,556 (fiscal 1999); $919,600 (fiscal 1996). Note: In fiscal 2001, contributions were received from Barbara A. Hauptli. In fiscal 1996, contributions were received from A. John and Barbara A. Hauptli.

Typical Recipients

Arts & Humanities: Art History, Arts Centers, Museums/Galleries, Public Broadcasting, Theater

Civic & Public Affairs: Civic & Public Affairs-General

Education: Arts/Humanities Education, Colleges & Universities

Health: Emergency/Ambulance Services, Multiple Sclerosis

Religion: Churches, Missionary Activities (Domestic), Religious Welfare

Social Services: Child Abuse, Counseling, Domestic Violence, Emergency Relief, Food/Clothing Distribution, Social Services-General, United Funds/United Ways, YMCA/YWCA/YMHA/YWHA

Application Procedures

Initial Contact: Send a letter of request.
Deadlines: None.

Foundation Officials

Barbara A. Hauptli: trustee

Grants Analysis

Disclosure Period: fiscal year ending September 30, 2004
Total Grants: $56,590
Number of Grants: 19
Average Grant: $1,514*
Highest Grant: $15,600
Lowest Grant: $25
Typical Range: $500 to $2,000
*Note: Average grant figure excludes two highest grants ($30,850).

Recent Grants

Note: Grants derived from fiscal 2004 Form 990.
General

15,600	St. Johns Lutheran Church, Salina, KS
15,250	Kansas Wesleyan University, Salina, KS
5,300	Morrison House, Salina, KS
5,100	Focus on Faith, Salina, KS
4,100	Salina Community Theater, Salina, KS
3,000	Smoky Hill Public Television, Salina, KS
1,500	Salina Art Center, Salina, KS
1,000	American Red Cross, Salina, KS
1,000	Ellsworth County Museum, Ellsworth, KS
1,000	Salina Area United Way, Salina, KS

ROBERT Z. HAWKINS FOUNDATION

Giving Contact

William H. Wallace, Chairman
One East Liberty Street, Suite 509
Reno, NV 89501
Phone: (775)786-1105
Fax: (775)786-4886
E-mail: rzhawkins@aol.com

Description

Founded: 1980
EIN: 880162645

Organization Type: General Purpose Foundation
Giving Locations: CA; NV: Northern Nevada, Reno
Grant Types: Capital, Matching, Scholarship.
Note: Operating expenses includes equipment.

Donor Information

Founder: Robert Ziemer Hawkins was born in Boulder, CO., December 26, 1903, the eldest son of Prince A. Hawkins, Sr., and Myrtle Ziemer Hawkins. Bob Hawkins was a lawyer and an investor. He was the dominant shareholder of Security National Bank of Nevada, where he served as a member of the Board and was Chairman of the Executive Committee.

He also became interested in, and acquired several large ranches in the Marysville area where he grew the first commercially successful wild rice.

Some years prior to his death, he decided to leave the bulk of his estate in trust, for charitable purposes. He died in September, 1979. The Robert Z. Hawkins Foundation was created by his will. The Foundation is a Testamentary Trust, established on March 3, 1980, by Decree of the Second Judicial District Court of the State of Nevada. The Trust is under the supervision of the Court and renders an annual account to the Court.

Financial Summary

Total Giving: $635,928 (2001)
Assets: $22,403,419 (2001)
Gifts Received: In 1991, contributions were received from the trust fund of Kathryn Ackley Hawkins.

Typical Recipients

Arts & Humanities: Arts Festivals, Arts Funds, Ballet, Film & Video, Arts & Humanities-General, Libraries, Museums/Galleries, Music, Opera, Performing Arts, Public Broadcasting, Theater

Civic & Public Affairs: Botanical Gardens/Parks, Business/Free Enterprise, Chambers of Commerce, Clubs, Community Foundations, Employment/Job Training, Civic & Public Affairs-General, Hispanic Affairs, Housing, Law & Justice, Legal Aid, Municipalities/Towns, Native American Affairs, Urban & Community Affairs

Education: Business Education, Colleges & Universities, Community & Junior Colleges, Education Funds, Education Reform, Elementary Education (Private), Elementary Education (Public), Engineering/Technological Education, Faculty Development, Journalism/Media Education, Legal Education, Literacy, Medical Education, Private Education (Precollege), Public Education (Precollege), School Volunteerism, Science/Mathematics Education, Secondary Education (Public), Student Aid

Environment: Research, Resource Conservation

Health: Cancer, Children's Health/Hospitals, Clinics/Medical Centers, Diabetes, Emergency/Ambulance Services, Health Funds, Health Organizations, Hospitals, Long-Term Care, Mental Health, Public Health, Single-Disease Health Associations, Transplant Networks/Donor Banks

Religion: Churches, Religion-General, Religious Organizations, Religious Welfare

Science: Science Museums, Scientific Labs, Scientific Research

Social Services: Animal Protection, At-Risk Youth, Child Welfare, Community Centers, Community Service Organizations, Counseling, Crime Prevention, Delinquency & Criminal Rehabilitation, Domestic Violence, Family Services, Food/Clothing Distribution, People with Disabilities, Recreation & Athletics, Scouts, Senior Services, Shelters/Homelessness, Social Services-General, Special Olympics, Substance Abuse, United Funds/United Ways, Volunteer Services, YMCA/YWCA/YMHA/YWHA, Youth Organizations

Application Procedures

Initial Contact: The foundation requests that applicants call to obtain a request form.
Application Requirements: The grant request

should include six copies of the request form, the amount and purpose of the request, a brief history of the organization, and a description of the need and how it will be met by the proposal. The applicant should also submit financial information, including a copy of the determination letter from the IRS, stating that the organization is exempt from taxation under Section 501(c)(3), or other identification to establish eligibility to receive charitable contributions; a copy of the last annual financial statement, current budget, an d most recent operating statement; a statement of the organization's major sources of financial support; and a statement of plans to secure continuing operating funds, if the program is of an ongoing nature. In addition, the applicant should include personnel information, including biographical descriptions of those responsible for the project and a list of the directors or trustees. Also include in request any other foundations and sources which aid has been requested or received, with any reasons why grants from other sources have not been requested; and a statement t of how the applicant will judge the success of the project. Applicants are requested to report to the foundation upon completion of the project to evaluate the worth of the grant.

Deadlines: None.

Review Process: Applications received by the 30th day of any month will be considered at the board's meeting the following month, unless additional information is required. After a grant request has been initiated, a meeting, site visit or telephone discussion may be required before submitting a formal proposal.

Restrictions

The foundation reports that grants are exclusively for charitable purposes within, or directly related to, the state of Nevada. The foundation does not make grants to individuals except through its scholarship funds. The foundation does not approve requests that would require permanent or on-going support.

Additional Information

The Bank of America, Reno, NV, acts as a corporate trustee for the foundation.

The foundation generally favors projects with a recognizable and long lasting effect; projects that are not financed by public tax funds; projects that will become self-sustaining; and projects in which other donors or foundations participate.

Publications: Annual Report; Guidelines; Application Form

Foundation Officials

Carolyn K. Bernard: trustee
Prince A. Hawkins: trustee
Bill A. Ligon, Jr.: trustee
William H. Wallace: chairman B Senatobia, MS 1933. ED University of Mississippi BBA (1955); University of Mississippi MBA (1956); University of Illinois PhD (1962). PRIM NONPR EMPL professor finance: Old Dominion University College Business & Public Administration. CORP AFFIL president: Wallace Consulting Inc. NONPR AFFIL trustee: Dallas Historical Society; member executive committee: Greater Dallas Chamber of Commerce; member: Central Dallas Association; member: Dallas Committee Foreign Relations; member: American Economic Association; member: American Statistical Association. CLUB AFFIL Rotary Club.

Grants Analysis

Disclosure Period: calendar year ending 2001
Total Grants: $545,641*
Number of Grants: 71
Average Grant: $7,685
Highest Grant: $50,000
Lowest Grant: $200
Typical Range: $2,000 to $10,000
*Note: Giving excludes United Way; scholarships.

Recent Grants

Note: Grants derived from 2002 Form 990.

Library-Related
5,000	Smoky Valley Library District, Round Mountain, NV -- funding for furnishings

General
125,000	Nevada Museum of Art, Reno, NV -- funding for new construction
64,000	School Districts in Nevada -- toward high school scholarships
50,000	University of Nevada-Redfield Campus, Reno, NV -- toward general purpose computer lab
25,000	KNPB-CHANNEL 5, Reno, NV -- toward digital television capital campaign
20,000	Assistance League Reno-Sparks, Reno, NV -- assistance for food pantry/operation school bell
20,000	KNPB-CHANNEL 5, Reno, NV -- toward support of broadcasts
20,000	Truckee Meadows Community College, Reno, NV -- toward upgrade of computers for faculty members
19,400	University of Nevada-School of Medicine, Reno, NV -- toward continuing grant for research
16,000	Orvis Nursing Clinic, Reno, NV -- assistance to pay portion of patients fees
15,000	Washoe County Parks & Recreation, Reno, NV -- toward Beethoven at Bartley series artown

HAWN FOUNDATION

Giving Contact

Joe V. Hawn, Jr., President
Hawn Foundation, Inc.
5949 Sherry Lane, No. 775
Dallas, TX 75225-3553
Phone: (214)696-6595
Fax: (214)696-6596

Alternate Contact

Janey Bateman, Secretary

Description

Founded: 1962
EIN: 756036761
Organization Type: Family Foundation
Giving Locations: TX: Dallas
Grant Types: Endowment, Fellowship, General Support, Multiyear/Continuing Support, Operating Expenses, Project, Research, Scholarship, Seed Money.

Donor Information

Founder: Incorporated in 1962 by the late W.R. "Fritz" Hawn and his wife, Mildred Hawn.

Financial Summary

Total Giving: $1,615,100 (fiscal year ending August 31, 2002); $1,400,000 (fiscal 2001)
Giving Analysis: Giving for fiscal 2002 includes: foundation scholarships ($16,200)
Assets: $33,984,411 (fiscal 2002)
Gifts Received: $628,253 (fiscal 2000); $5,000 (fiscal 1998). Note: In fiscal 2000, contributions were received from the Mary C. Hawn Estate.

Typical Recipients

Arts & Humanities: Arts Associations & Councils, Arts Outreach, Community Arts, Dance, Historic Preservation, Libraries, Museums/Galleries, Music, Opera, Performing Arts, Theater
Civic & Public Affairs: Business/Free Enterprise, Civic & Public Affairs-General, Hispanic Affairs, Housing, Nonprofit Management, Professional & Trade Associations, Public Policy, Urban & Community Affairs
Education: Arts/Humanities Education, Colleges &

Universities, Literacy, Minority Education, Private Education (Precollege), Religious Education, Secondary Education (Private), Special Education, Student Aid
Environment: Wildlife Protection
Health: Alzheimer's Disease, Arthritis, Cancer, Children's Health/Hospitals, Clinics/Medical Centers, Diabetes, Emergency/Ambulance Services, Eyes/Blindness, Health-General, Health Funds, Health Organizations, Heart, Hospitals, Hospitals (University Affiliated), Long-Term Care, Medical Rehabilitation, Medical Research, Mental Health, Multiple Sclerosis, Nursing Services, Public Health, Research/Studies Institutes, Respiratory, Single-Disease Health Associations
International: Health Care/Hospitals, Missionary/Religious Activities
Religion: Churches, Religion-General, Missionary Activities (Domestic), Religious Organizations, Religious Welfare
Science: Science Museums
Social Services: Animal Protection, At-Risk Youth, Camps, Child Abuse, Child Welfare, Community Centers, Community Service Organizations, Counseling, Emergency Relief, Family Services, People with Disabilities, Recreation & Athletics, Scouts, Shelters/Homelessness, Substance Abuse, United Funds/United Ways, Volunteer Services, YMCA/YWCA/YMHA/YWHA, Youth Organizations

Application Procedures

Initial Contact: Initial approach for a grant should be through a brief narrative letter.
Application Requirements: The letter should describe the project for which funds are asked, its justification, and the type and amount requested. Also include a copy of the organization's IRS 501(c)(3) letter and a written statement that no financial support will be donated to any political cause out of funds granted from the Hawn Foundation, Inc.
Deadlines: None.
Review Process: If the project falls within the areas of the foundation's interests, purposes, and current funding policies, the board may act directly upon the original request or ask for more detailed information before making a grant decision. The board may meet at any time of the year to consider applications and approve or reject applications at these meetings. The annual meeting is held in August prior to fiscal year-end date of August 31.
Notes: If a grant is approved, it will be with stipulations that accounting for the expenditures of such grant may be required.

Restrictions

Grants are not made to individuals. No grants are made outside the foundation's main focus. Under the present policy of the board of directors, the foundation does not make loans.

Additional Information

Publications: Guidelines

Foundation Officials

Janey F. Bateman: secretary, director
Edward Alvin Copley: director B Memphis, TN 1936. ED Southern Methodist University BA (1957); Southern Methodist University JD (1960). PRIM CORP EMPL managing partner: Akin Gump Strauss Hauer & Feld LLP.
Joe Verne Hawn, Jr.: director
W. A. Hawn, Jr.: president
William Russell Hawn, Jr.: director
Grady Jordan: director

Grants Analysis

Disclosure Period: fiscal year ending August 31, 2002
Total Grants: $1,598,900*
Number of Grants: 78
Average Grant: $15,762*
Highest Grant: $264,000

Lowest Grant: $250
Typical Range: $10,000 to $75,000
*Note: Giving excludes scholarships. Average grant figure excludes two highest grants ($464,000).

Recent Grants

Note: Grants derived from 2002 Form 990.
General

264,000	Southwestern Medical Foundation, Dallas, TX -- capital campaign
200,000	Children's Medical Center, Dallas, TX -- capital campaign
100,100	Highland Park Presbyterian Church, Dallas, TX -- religious and community assistance
100,000	M.D. Anderson Cancer Center, Houston, TX -- medical research
100,000	Texas Scottish Rite Hospital, Dallas, TX -- medical assistance
75,000	Medisend, Dallas, TX -- overseas medical aid
75,000	Multiple Sclerosis, Dallas Chapter, Dallas, TX -- medical research
60,000	Dallas Center for the Performing Arts, Dallas, TX -- capital campaign
50,000	Arthritis Foundation, Dallas, TX -- medical research
50,000	Juvenile Diabetes Foundation, Dallas, TX -- medical research

CHARLES HAYDEN FOUNDATION

Giving Contact

Kenneth D. Merin, President, Chief Executive Officer
Charles Hayden Foundation
140 Broadway
New York, NY 10005
Phone: (212)785-3677
Fax: (212)785-3689
Web: http://www.fdncenter.org/grantmaker/hayden/

Alternate Contact

Mary Phillips, Boston Program Officer
Charles Hayden Foundation
c/o Grants Management Associates
77 Summer Street, 8th Floor
Boston, MA 02110-1006
Phone: (617)426-7172
Note: Organizations in the metropolitan Boston area should send second copies of requests to alternate contact.

Description

Founded: 1937
EIN: 135562237
Organization Type: General Purpose Foundation
Giving Locations: MA: Boston metropolitan area; NY: New York metropolitan area
Grant Types: Capital, Project, Seed Money.

Donor Information

Founder: Charles Hayden was born in Boston, MA, in 1870. He was the elder of the two sons of Emma A. Tirrell Hayden and Josiah Willard Hayden. After graduating from Massachusetts Institute of Technology in 1890 with an engineering degree, he began his business career as a clerk for the Boston brokerage firm of Clark, Ward and Co. Within two years he founded the Boston brokerage firm of Hayden, Stone and Company. In 1906, he opened a New York City office and later moved into the city. Charles Hayden was excellent at predicting the stock market's future, including foreseeing the stock market crash of 1929. At the time of his death, he was well known as an international businessman and was serving as a director of 58 different corporations.

During the Depression, Mr. Hayden contributed to many causes, often anonymously. In 1934, he was honored as the primary benefactor of the American Museum of Natural History's Hayden Planetarium in New York. The foundation was established in 1937 by a $45.8 million bequest from Charles Hayden.

Financial Summary

Total Giving: $12,607,732 (fiscal year ending June 30, 2003); $13,197,000 (fiscal 2002); $16,851,508 (fiscal 2001)
Assets: $287,285,179 (fiscal 2003); $286,069,116 (fiscal 2002); $311,558,536 (fiscal 2001)

Typical Recipients

Arts & Humanities: Arts Outreach, Libraries, Museums/Galleries, Performing Arts
Civic & Public Affairs: Botanical Gardens/Parks, Economic Development, Employment/Job Training, Civic & Public Affairs-General, Hispanic Affairs, Municipalities/Towns, Nonprofit Management, Public Policy, Urban & Community Affairs, Women's Affairs, Zoos/Aquariums
Education: Afterschool/Enrichment Programs, Arts/Humanities Education, Business Education, Business-School Partnerships, Colleges & Universities, Continuing Education, Education Associations, Education Funds, Education Reform, Elementary Education (Private), Elementary Education (Public), Education-General, Health & Physical Education, Leadership Training, Literacy, Minority Education, Preschool Education, Private Education (Precollege), Public Education (Precollege), Religious Education, School Volunteerism, Science/Mathematics Education, Secondary Education (Private), Secondary Education (Public), Special Education, Vocational & Technical Education
Environment: Air/Water Quality, Resource Conservation, Wildlife Protection
Health: AIDS/HIV, Hospitals, Prenatal Health Issues, Research/Studies Institutes
International: International Environmental Issues
Religion: Jewish Causes, Religious Welfare
Science: Science Museums, Scientific Centers & Institutes
Social Services: At-Risk Youth, Camps, Child Welfare, Community Centers, Community Service Organizations, Crime Prevention, Day Care, Family Planning, Family Services, Food/Clothing Distribution, Homes, People with Disabilities, Recreation & Athletics, Scouts, Shelters/Homelessness, Social Services-General, Substance Abuse, Volunteer Services, YMCA/YWCA/YMHA/YWHA, Youth Organizations

Application Procedures

Initial Contact: Applicants should send a written request. The foundation encourages applicants to use the New York area and AGM (Boston area) common application forms. Boston area agencies should send copies of proposals and all related follow-up correspondence to alternate contact as well as contact.
Application Requirements: Funding requests should include a concise description of the project and its goals, description of the youth population, including age and number of youth, to be served, total costs (based on professional estimates), sources for additional operating funds, operating budget (including breakdown of revenue sources and amounts, for current and previous years), most recent audited financial report, IRS letter stating that applicant has 501(c)(3) tax-exempt status, the project's expected outcomes, criteria the applicant prefers that the foundation apply in evaluating the completed project, and other printed material concerning the activities and history of the institution. If the request is for less than the total amount, explain the plans for raising the balance of those costs. If request is for full amount, describe how a lesser amount would be of assistance and how, in that event, the balance of funds could be raised from other sources.
Deadlines: None.

Review Process: The board of trustees meets ten times a year. If the foundation has declined a grant request, reapplication can be made six months after the denial letter. The reapplication may be for the same project or a different one.

Restrictions

Capital grants generally are not made to groups that have received funds from the foundation within the past two years, unless the applicant is a large organization with distinctly separate facilities in different locations. In addition, Grants are not made to individuals.; theological institutions; projects to raise revenue to offset operating costs; hospitals; hospices; projects that are basically medical in nature; religious organizations for sectarian purposes organisation, unless the program is oriented toward community youth; institutions of higher education, except for program support for work with pre-collegiate education; endowments; and arts exposure programs. Also, the foundation has restrictions on supporting dinners, special events, goodwill advertising, and fraternal organisation. restrictions on supporting dinners, special events, goodwill advertising, and fraternal organizations.

Additional Information

Publications: Annual Report (biennially); Application Guidelines

Foundation Officials

Maureen T. Fletcher: grants administrator, assistant secretary
Robert Howitt: treasurer, trustee PRIM NONPR EMPL officer: Door - A Center of Alternatives.
Kristen J. McCormack: vice president, trustee B 1955. PRIM NONPR EMPL executive director: Federated Dorchester.
Kenneth D. Merin: president, chief executive officer, trustee PRIM CORP EMPL partner: Purcell, Ries, Shannon, Mulcahy & O'Neill.
Dean H. Steeger: secretary, trustee
Carol Van Atten: assistant secretary
Howard G. Wachenfeld: trustee

Grants Analysis

Disclosure Period: fiscal year ending June 30, 2003
Total Grants: $12,607,732
Number of Grants: 191
Average Grant: $60,403*
Highest Grant: $1,131,157
Lowest Grant: $1,500
Typical Range: $10,000 to $100,000
*Note: Average grant figure excludes highest grant.

Recent Grants

Note: Grants derived from fiscal 2003 Form 990.
Library-Related

150,000	New York Public Library, New York, NY -- toward addition of a second floor dedicated to children's materials and programming at their Parkchester Branch

General

1,131,157	American Museum of Natural History, New York, NY -- towards creation of movable Museum on Astrophysics
728,300	Trust for Public Land, New York, NY -- toward the construction of community playgrounds in New York
600,000	YMCA, New York, NY
500,000	Fresh Air Fund, New York, NY -- towards Camp Hayden capital development program
350,000	Sports & Arts in Schools Foundation, Long Island City, NY -- toward the support of their summer school sports and arts day camps
345,540	YMCA, Boston, MA -- toward the expansion of the Allston-Brighton connect 5 Project
325,000	Madison Square Boys & Girls Club, New York, NY -- towards support of sustaining

core programs and introducing the Kids educational empowerment program

300,000	After-School Corporation, New York, NY
300,000	Children's Aid Society, New York, NY -- toward support of their community school programs
300,000	North Star Academy, Newark, NJ -- toward the purchase and renovation of their high school facility

JOHN RANDOLPH AND DORA HAYNES FOUNDATION

Giving Contact

Diane Cornwell, Administrative Director
888 West 6th Street, Suite 1150
Los Angeles, CA 90017-2737
Phone: (213)623-9151
Fax: (213)623-3951
E-mail: info@haynesfoundation.org
Web: http://www.haynesfoundation.org

Description

Founded: 1926
EIN: 951644020
Organization Type: Specialized/Single Purpose Foundation
Giving Locations: CA: Los Angeles metropolitan area
Grant Types: Award, Employee Matching Gifts, Fellowship, General Support, Research, Scholarship.

Donor Information

Founder: The Haynes Foundation was established in 1926 by Dr. John Randolph Haynes, "a distinguished physician, and his wife Dora Haynes, who were active and progressive citizens of Los Angeles during one of the city's most important developmental period (1887-1937)."

Financial Summary

Total Giving: $2,035,379 (fiscal year ending August 31, 2003); $2,728,537 (fiscal 2002); $3,064,840 (fiscal 2001)
Giving Analysis: Giving for fiscal 2003 includes: foundation matching gifts ($5,675); foundation scholarships ($425,000); foundation fellowships ($666,000); fiscal 2002: foundation matching gifts ($6,150); foundation scholarships ($475,000); foundation fellowships ($698,000); fiscal 2001: foundation scholarships ($658,000); foundation fellowships ($1,028,500)
Assets: $48,286,924 (fiscal 2003); $46,436,383 (fiscal 2002); $51,406,080 (fiscal 2001)
Gifts Received: In fiscal 1990, contributions were received from Edward Levonlan.

Typical Recipients

Arts & Humanities: Historic Preservation, History & Archaeology, Libraries, Museums/Galleries, Public Broadcasting
Civic & Public Affairs: Economic Development, Economic Policy, Civic & Public Affairs-General, Hispanic Affairs, Housing, Law & Justice, Legal Aid, Native American Affairs, Nonprofit Management, Philanthropic Organizations, Professional & Trade Associations, Public Policy, Urban & Community Affairs, Women's Affairs
Education: Arts/Humanities Education, Business Education, Colleges & Universities, Continuing Education, Economic Education, Education Reform, Environmental Education, Faculty Development, Education-General, International Studies, Medical Education, Minority Education, Religious Education, Science/Mathematics Education, Social Sciences

Education, Student Aid
Environment: Environment-General, Resource Conservation
Health: Children's Health/Hospitals, Geriatric Health, Health Policy/Cost Containment, Medical Research
International: International Affairs
Religion: Jewish Causes, Seminaries, Social/Policy Issues
Science: Science Museums
Social Services: At-Risk Youth, Community Service Organizations, Crime Prevention, Delinquency & Criminal Rehabilitation, Senior Services, Shelters/Homelessness, Substance Abuse

Application Procedures

Initial Contact: The Foundation requests that applicants notify the Foundation of their intent to apply prior to submitting a proposal. When submitting a proposal, applicants should send 15 hard copies of the proposal and one copy electronically to info@haynesfoundation.org.
Application Requirements: Proposals for Research Grants should include a main proposal that describes the project and includes objectives for the period of the proposed work, expected significance of the proposed work, problems to be dealt with and a detailed explanation of the methods which will be followed, explanation of how the proposed work relates to the present state of knowledge in the field, how the proposed work relates to the principal investigator's longer-term goals, other works in progress by the PI, other support being received by the PI for the proposed work and/or for other projects, and, if appropriate, plans for preservation, documentation, and sharing of data resulting from the project; a one-page summary of the proposed activity, written in third person in laymen's terms; a detailed budget and timeline for the project; the names and qualifications of the personnel involved; a cover letter from the college, university, or research institute, signed by an administrative officer or grants administrator; and copies of the institution's exemption letters from the IRS and California Franchise Tax Board.
Proposals for Archival Grants should include a statement of purpose for which the funds will be used; a detailed budget and time-line for the project; names and qualifications of the personnel involved; a cover letter on the institution's letterhead, signed by an administrative officer; and copies of the institution's exemption letters from the IRS and the California Franchise Tax Board.
Deadlines: January 18, March 29, May 17, September 6, and November 1.
Review Process: Grants are made quarterly. Requests for grants are considered first by the foundation's committee on research and grants, which then makes its recommendations to the foundation's board of trustees.
Notes: Applications for scholarships should be made directly to the educational institution and not to the foundation.

Restrictions

No grants are made to individuals. The foundation does not pay for equipment or for institutional overhead. Grants are made only to organizations within the United States whose endeavors are focused in or on Los Angeles.

Additional Information

Publications: Guidelines; Purposes and Program Brochure

Foundation Officials

Diane Cornwell: administrative director
Robert Ray Dockson: trustee B Quincy, IL October 06, 1917. ED Springfield Junior College AB (1937); University of Illinois BS (1939); University of Southern California MS (1940); University of Southern California PhD (1946). CORP AFFIL director: CalFed Inc. NONPR AFFIL member: Phi Kappa Phi; member, board councils: University Southern California School

Business Administration; board regents: Pepperdine University; member: Hugh O'Brian Youth Foundation; president, trustee: Orthopedic Hospital; member: Los Angeles Chamber of Commerce; member: Newcomen Society; trustee: Committee for Economic Development; trustee: California Council Economic Education; chairman housing task force: California Roundtable; member: Beta Gamma Sigma; member: California Chamber of Commerce; member: American Arbitration Association. CLUB AFFIL Thunderbird Country Club; California Club; Los Angeles Country Club; Bohemian Club; 100 Club; Birnham Wood Golf Club.

Philip Metschan Hawley: trustee B Portland, OR 1925. ED University of California at Berkeley BS (1946); Harvard University Advanced Management Program (1967). CORP AFFIL chairman, chief executive officer: Krauses Furniture Inc.; director: Weyerhaeuser Co. NONPR AFFIL member: Phi Beta Kappa; trustee: University Notre Dame; trustee: California Institute Technology; chairman, member: California Retailers Association; member: Beta Alpha Psi; member: Beta Gamma Sigma. CLUB AFFIL Newport Harbor Yacht Club; Pacific-Union Club; Los Angeles Country Club; Multnomah Athletic Club; California Club; The Links Club; Beach Club; Bohemian Club.

Kent Kresa: trustee B New York, NY 1938. ED Massachusetts Institute of Technology BSAA (1959); Massachusetts Institute of Technology MSAA (1961); Massachusetts Institute of Technology EAA (1966). PRIM CORP EMPL chairman: Northrop Grumman Corp. CORP AFFIL director: MannKind Corp.; director: Trust Co. of the West; director: General Motors Corp.; director: Eclipse Aviation Corp.; director: Fluor Corp.; director: Avery Dennison Corp. NONPR AFFIL member: Society Flight Test Engineers; director: John Tracy Clinic for the Hearing Impaired; member: Navy League; member (visiting committee): Massachusetts Institute Technology; member: Naval Aviation Museum Foundation; member: Los Angeles World Affairs Council; member: DNA New Alternative Working Group; board governors: Los Angeles Music Center; member: Department Aeronautics & Astronautics Corp.; member: Chief Naval Operations Executive Panel Washington; member: Defense Science Board; member: Association U.S. Army; member: American Defense Preparedness Association; fellow: American Institute Aeronautics & Astronautics; member: Aerospace Industries Association. CLUB AFFIL Los Angeles Country Club; National Space Club.

F. Haynes Lindley, Jr.: trustee B Los Angeles, CA 1945. ED Claremont Men's College BA (1967); Claremont Graduate School MFA (1972); Southwestern University JD (1976). NONPR AFFIL member board fellows: Claremont University Center Graduate School; member: Marin Agricultural Land Trust.

Daniel A. Mazmanian: trustee
Harry P. Pachon: trustee
Jane G. Pisano: chairman comm res & grants, trustee
Gilbert T. Ray: trustee B Mansfield, OH 1944. ED Ashland College BA (1966); University of Toledo MBA (1968); Howard University JD (1972). PRIM CORP EMPL partner: O'Melveny & Myers. CORP AFFIL director: Host Marriott Services Corp. NONPR AFFIL board directors: Automobile Club Southern California; board directors: Los Angeles Chamber of Commerce. CLUB AFFIL California Club; Louisiana Country Club.

Willis B. Wood, Jr.: trustee B Kansas City, MO 1934. ED University of Tulsa BS (1957); Harvard University (1983); Pepperdine University JD (1996). NONPR AFFIL director, member business council: Sustainable Energy Future; trustee: University Southern California; member: Society Petroleum Engineers; trustee: Southwest Museum; director: Pacific Council International Affairs; member: Pacific Energy Association; member: National Association Manufacturers; member: Pacific Coast Gas Association; trustee: Harvey Mudd College; director: Los Angeles World Affairs Council; chairman, trustee: California Medical Center Foundation; member: Chamber of Commerce California State; member: American Gas Association. CLUB AFFIL Hacienda Golf Club; California Club; Center Club.

Grants Analysis

Disclosure Period: fiscal year ending August 31, 2003
Total Grants: $938,704*
Number of Grants: 36
Average Grant: $26,075
Highest Grant: $160,799
Lowest Grant: $2,500
Typical Range: $10,000 to $50,000
***Note:** Giving excludes fellowships, matching gifts and scholarships.

Recent Grants

Note: Grants derived from 2002 Form 990.
Library-Related

25,068	Library Foundation of Los Angeles, Los Angeles, CA -- assists with electronic neighborhood
22,000	Huntington Library, San Marino, CA -- offers history fellowships
22,000	Huntington Library, San Marino, CA -- assists with early California population project
10,000	Huntington Library, San Marino, CA -- provides cataloging Edmund D. Edelman papers

General

118,146	University of Southern California, Los Angeles, CA -- provides options for alternative government
102,956	University of Southern California, Los Angeles, CA -- assists with urban participatory democracy
71,490	University of California, Los Angeles, CA -- provides economic prospects for Los Angeles
66,270	University of Southern California, Los Angeles, CA -- assists towards a sustainable Los Angeles
65,104	Los Angeles Economic Roundtable, Los Angeles, CA -- assists with working welfare parents
64,038	California Tomorrow, Oakland, CA -- provides a new look at the majority
50,000	University of Southern California, Los Angeles, CA -- offers Dockson scholarship
47,845	University of Southern California, Los Angeles, CA -- offers welfare reform and neighborhood impact study
47,465	Tomas Rivera Policy Institute, Los Angeles, CA -- provides future of inland empire
41,647	University of Southern California, Los Angeles, CA -- provides philanthropy and social capital

EDWARD W. HAZEN FOUNDATION

Giving Contact

Barbara A. Taveras, President
90 Broad Street, Suite 604
New York, NY 10004
Phone: (212)889-3034
Fax: (212)889-3039
E-mail: hazen@hazenfoundation.org
Web: http://www.hazenfoundation.org

Description

Founded: 1925
EIN: 060646671
Organization Type: General Purpose Foundation

Giving Locations: nationally.
Grant Types: General Support, Matching.

Donor Information

Founder: Incorporated in 1925 by the late Edward Warriner Hazen, the late Helen Russell Hazen, the late Lucy Abigail Hazen, and the late Mary Hazen Arnold.

Financial Summary

Total Giving: $1,900,000 (2003 approx); $1,842,241 (2002); $1,987,452 (2001)
Giving Analysis: Giving for 2002 includes: foundation matching gifts ($7,380) 2001: foundation matching gifts ($1,460)
Assets: $27,927,777 (2002); $34,888,534 (2001)

Typical Recipients

Arts & Humanities: Arts Funds, Arts Outreach, Libraries, Music, Public Broadcasting
Civic & Public Affairs: African American Affairs, Asian American Affairs, Botanical Gardens/Parks, Civil Rights, Community Foundations, Economic Development, Economic Policy, Employment/Job Training, Ethnic Organizations, Gay/Lesbian Issues, Civic & Public Affairs-General, Hispanic Affairs, Housing, Law & Justice, Legal Aid, Municipalities/Towns, Native American Affairs, Nonprofit Management, Philanthropic Organizations, Professional & Trade Associations, Public Policy, Rural Affairs, Safety, Urban & Community Affairs, Women's Affairs, Zoos/Aquariums
Education: Afterschool/Enrichment Programs, Colleges & Universities, Education Associations, Education Funds, Education Reform, Elementary Education (Private), Education-General, Leadership Training, Legal Education, Minority Education, Private Education (Precollege), Public Education (Precollege), School Volunteerism, Science/Mathematics Education, Special Education, Vocational & Technical Education
Environment: Air/Water Quality, Environment-General, Protection, Resource Conservation
Health: AIDS/HIV, Medical Research, Mental Health, Public Health, Single-Disease Health Associations
International: Foreign Arts Organizations, Human Rights, International Affairs, International Environmental Issues, International Relations
Religion: Churches, Religion-General, Ministries, Religious Organizations, Religious Welfare
Science: Scientific Labs
Social Services: At-Risk Youth, Child Welfare, Community Centers, Community Service Organizations, Crime Prevention, Delinquency & Criminal Rehabilitation, Family Planning, Family Services, Food/Clothing Distribution, Homes, Refugee Assistance, Sexual Abuse, Shelters/Homelessness, Social Services-General, United Funds/United Ways, YMCA/YWCA/YMHA/YWHA, Youth Organizations

Application Procedures

Initial Contact: Applicants should send a brief letter of inquiry (1-2 pages) to the foundation.
Application Requirements: The letter should highlight the goals, objectives, activities target population, duration, and total cost of the project for which funding is sought. If the foundation staff feel that the goals of the project address the foundation's mission and the approach is a sound one, they will mail applicants a formal application. The application should be prepared in compliance with instructions supplied by the foundation. Two copies should be submitted.
Deadlines: Deadlines for applications are January 15 and July 15 for review at the spring and fall board meetings, respectively.
Review Process: All applicants will be notified of the status of their request two to three weeks after submission. The trustees meet twice each year to set foundation policy and make grants.
Notes: Do not send articles, letters of reference, videos, audio cassettes, books, or press kits unless they

are specifically requested by foundation staff. The foundation does not accept letters of inquiry by fax.

Restrictions

The foundation does not make grants to individuals, schools, or school districts. It also does not provide funds toward ongoing operational expenses, endowments, building construction or maintenance, deficits, scholarships, or fellowships.

Additional Information

The foundation favors proposals from organizations which demonstrate a commitment to diversifying their boards and staff. In those cases where the demographics of the community served by the organization limit such diversity, the foundation encourages its grantees to collaborate with agencies or groups that work with people from other racial, ethnic, and cultural backgrounds.
Publications: Application Guidelines; Application Form; Newsletter

Foundation Officials

Arlene Adler: board chair PRIM CORP EMPL vice president: Citigroup NA.
Lori Bezahler: president, board secretary ED New York University Wagner School Public Service MPA; Oberlin College BA. NONPR AFFIL member professional education committee: New York Regional Association Grantmakers; co-chairman: Working Group Education Organizing; director: Center Community Alternatives; director: Grantmakers in Education.
Marsha Bonner: trustee
Madeline de Lone: trustee CLUB AFFIL Merion Cricket Club; Racquet & Tennis Club.
Beverly Divers-White: trustee
Earl Durham: vice chair, trustee
Arturo Vargas: trustee

Grants Analysis

Disclosure Period: calendar year ending 2002
Total Grants: $1,834,861*
Number of Grants: 96
Average Grant: $19,113
Highest Grant: $135,000
Lowest Grant: $50
Typical Range: $10,000 to $40,000
***Note:** Giving excludes matching gifts.

Recent Grants

Note: Grants derived from 2002 Form 990.

General

55,000	North Midtown Community Development Corporation, Jackson, MS -- toward neighborhood community organizing project
50,000	All Saints Catholic Community, El Paso, TX -- for the alliance scholars initiative
50,000	American Institute for Social Justice, Providence, RI
50,000	Greater Homewood Community Corporation Inc., Homewood, MD -- funding for parent organizing project
50,000	Highbridge Community Life Center, Bronx, NY
50,000	Make the Road by Walking, Brooklyn, NY -- support for parent organizing initiative
50,000	Northwest Bronx Community, Albany, NY
50,000	Pacific Institute for Community Organization, Rochester, NY -- assistance for transform schools project
50,000	Quitman County Development Organization Inc., Marks, MS -- for public education and community organizing project
50,000	Southern Echo, Greenville, MS -- assistance for education organizing initiatives

THE HEARST FOUNDATION, INC.

Giving Contact
Robert M. Frehse, Jr., Executive Director & Vice President
888 7th Avenue, 45th Floor
New York, NY 10106-0057
Phone: (212)586-5404
Fax: (212)586-1917
E-mail: hearst@fdn.org
Web: http://www.hearstfdn.org
Note: Applicants located east of the Mississippi River should mail appeals to the New York office.

Alternate Contact
Thomas Eastham, Western Director
Hearst Foundation
90 New Montgomery Street, Suite 1212
San Francisco, CA 94105
Phone: (415)543-0400
Fax: (415)348-0887
Note: Applicants located west of the Mississippi River should mail appeals to Western Director.

Description
Founded: 1945
EIN: 136161746
Organization Type: General Purpose Foundation
Giving Locations: nationally.
Grant Types: Endowment, General Support, Project, Research, Scholarship.

Financial Summary
Total Giving: $15,212,500 (2004); $13,165,000 (2002); $6,430,000 (2001 approx)
Giving Analysis: Giving for 2004 includes: foundation scholarships ($50,000)
Assets: $237,362,317 (2002)

Typical Recipients
Arts & Humanities: Arts Centers, Arts Funds, Arts Institutes, Arts Outreach, Ballet, Ethnic & Folk Arts, Historic Preservation, History & Archaeology, Libraries, Museums/Galleries, Music, Opera, Performing Arts, Public Broadcasting, Theater
Civic & Public Affairs: Community Foundations, Employment/Job Training, Civic & Public Affairs-General, Hispanic Affairs, Housing, Native American Affairs, Nonprofit Management, Philanthropic Organizations, Professional & Trade Associations, Public Policy, Safety, Urban & Community Affairs
Education: Afterschool/Enrichment Programs, Arts/Humanities Education, Business Education, Colleges & Universities, Education Associations, Education Funds, Education Reform, Engineering/Technological Education, Faculty Development, Education-General, Health & Physical Education, International Studies, Journalism/Media Education, Literacy, Medical Education, Minority Education, Preschool Education, Private Education (Precollege), Public Education (Precollege), Religious Education, Science/Mathematics Education, Social Sciences Education, Special Education, Student Aid
Environment: Environment-General, Resource Conservation
Health: AIDS/HIV, Cancer, Children's Health/Hospitals, Clinics/Medical Centers, Diabetes, Emergency/Ambulance Services, Health-General, Health Funds, Heart, Home-Care Services, Hospitals, Hospitals (University Affiliated), Medical Rehabilitation, Medical Research, Mental Health, Nursing Services, Prenatal Health Issues, Public Health, Research/Studies Institutes, Single-Disease Health Associations
International: Health Care/Hospitals
Religion: Dioceses, Ministries, Religious Organizations, Religious Welfare, Seminaries
Science: Science Museums, Scientific Centers & Institutes, Scientific Labs

Social Services: Animal Protection, Child Welfare, Community Service Organizations, Counseling, Day Care, Family Services, Food/Clothing Distribution, People with Disabilities, Recreation & Athletics, Scouts, Senior Services, Shelters/Homelessness, Substance Abuse, United Funds/United Ways, Volunteer Services, YMCA/YWCA/YMHA/YWHA, Youth Organizations

Application Procedures
Initial Contact: The foundation does not have a formal application form. The foundation prefers applicants submit a one-page executive summary accompanied by a full proposal.
Application Requirements: The one-page proposal summary should describe the organization's mission and the purpose and dollar amount of the request. The expanded proposal narrative should not exceed five pages. Additionally, the following information is required: budget showing project costs and how funds will be used; current fiscal year's operating budget; most recent audited financial report; current and potential sources of support for proposed project and for organization in general; names and primary affiliations of officers and board members; IRS documentation certifying applicant is tax-exempt under section 501(c)(3) and "not a private foundation" under section 509(a). Organizations should be listed in the current IRS cumulative list of tax-exempt organizations (Publication 78). If an organization has been omitted from this publication, further documentation of its tax-exempt status will be required. Catholic organizations should be listed in the current official Catholic directory. Colleges and universities should include a current profile or fact sheet if available.
Deadlines: None.
Review Process: Board meetings on grant decisions are held in March, June, September, and December. Only fully documented appeals will be considered. Meetings are arranged between foundation staff and applicants only if serious consideration of their appeals is anticipated. A site visit is required prior to board review.

Restrictions
Except in rare cases, the following restrictions apply: Private sector organizations are favored over those financed through taxation. Organizations serving larger geographical areas are favored over those of a neighborhood or grassroots nature. The foundation does not fund on an annual basis or make multi-year grants. Grantee organizations must wait a minimum of three years from their grant award date before the foundation will consider another request. Only one proposal from an organization will be reviewed in a calendar year. Institutions with more than one department should coordinate proposals through a central office. The foundation does not support public policy, conferences, workshops, seminars, building projects, or requests for start-up/seed funding. The foundation will not consider requests for individuals, loans, funds for radio, film television or other media related projects, or special events, tickets, tables or advertising for fundraising events.

Additional Information
Please see the related entry for the William Randolph Hearst Foundation.
The Hearst Foundation and William Randolph Hearst Foundation are independent private philanthropies operating separately from the Hearst Corporation. Charitable goals of the two foundations are the same; they are administered as one, and only one proposal need be submitted.
Supplemental material should be held to a minimum necessary to ensure a basic understanding of the organization seeking support. Video tapes should not be sent unless specifically requested.
Publications: Application Guidelines

Foundation Officials
John G. Conomikes: trustee PRIM CORP EMPL vice president, director: Hearst Corp. Broadcasting Group. CORP AFFIL director: Hearst-Argyle Television Inc.
Thomas Eastham: western director B Attleboro, MA 1923. ED Northwestern University (1952).
Robert M. Frehse, Jr.: executive director NONPR AFFIL secretary: Interchurch Center.
Virginia H. Randt: director

Grants Analysis
Disclosure Period: calendar year ending 2004
Total Grants: $15,162,500*
Number of Grants: 111
Average Grant: $136,599
Highest Grant: $500,000
Lowest Grant: $10,000
Typical Range: $25,000 to $200,000
***Note:** Giving excludes scholarships.

Recent Grants
Note: Grants derived from 2002 Form 990.
General

250,000	North Shore - Long Island Jewish Health System, Great Neck, NY
200,000	All Kinds of Minds, Chapel Hill, NC
200,000	United Way of New York City, New York, NY
200,000	University Hospital of Cleveland, Cleveland, OH
200,000	University of Minnesota Foundation, Minneapolis, MN
150,000	Emory University, Atlanta, GA
150,000	New York City Police Foundation, New York, NY
150,000	Rehabilitation Institute of Chicago, Chicago, IL
140,000	Minneapolis Heart Institute Foundation, Minneapolis, MN
100,000	Aspen Music Festival & School, Aspen, CO

WILLIAM RANDOLPH HEARST FOUNDATION

Giving Contact
Robert M. Frehse, Jr., Executive Director & Vice President
888 7th Avenue, 45th Floor
New York, NY 10106-0057
Phone: (212)586-5404
Fax: (212)586-1917
E-mail: hearst@fdn.org
Web: http://hearstfdn.org
Note: Applicants headquartered east of the Mississippi River should mail appeals to the New York office.

Alternate Contact
Thomas Eastham, Western Director
90 New Montgomery Street
Suite 1212
San Francisco, CA 94105
Phone: (415)543-0400
Fax: (415)348-0887
Note: Applicants located west of the Mississippi River should mail appeals to the Western Director.

Description
Founded: 1948
EIN: 136019226
Organization Type: General Purpose Foundation
Giving Locations: nationally.
Grant Types: Challenge, Endowment, General Support, Project, Research, Scholarship.

Financial Summary

Total Giving: $15,212,500 (2004); $30,030,000 (2003); $26,832,700 (2002)

Giving Analysis: Giving for 2004 includes: foundation scholarships ($50,000); 2003: foundation scholarships ($200,000)

Assets: $520,618,134 (2002); $624,456,279 (2001)

Typical Recipients

Arts & Humanities: Arts Associations & Councils, Arts Centers, Arts Funds, Arts Institutes, Arts Outreach, Ballet, Community Arts, Ethnic & Folk Arts, Arts & Humanities-General, Historic Preservation, History & Archaeology, Libraries, Museums/Galleries, Music, Opera, Performing Arts, Theater, Visual Arts

Civic & Public Affairs: Botanical Gardens/Parks, Business/Free Enterprise, Chambers of Commerce, Community Foundations, Employment/Job Training, Civic & Public Affairs-General, Hispanic Affairs, Housing, Municipalities/Towns, Native American Affairs, Nonprofit Management, Philanthropic Organizations, Public Policy, Safety, Women's Affairs, Zoos/Aquariums

Education: Arts/Humanities Education, Business Education, Colleges & Universities, Continuing Education, Education Funds, Engineering/Technological Education, Faculty Development, Literacy, Medical Education, Minority Education, Private Education (Precollege), Religious Education, Science/Mathematics Education, Secondary Education (Private), Special Education, Student Aid

Environment: Resource Conservation

Health: Cancer, Children's Health/Hospitals, Clinics/Medical Centers, Emergency/Ambulance Services, Eyes/Blindness, Geriatric Health, Health Funds, Health Organizations, Home-Care Services, Hospitals, Hospitals (University Affiliated), Medical Rehabilitation, Medical Research, Medical Training, Prenatal Health Issues, Public Health, Research/Studies Institutes, Single-Disease Health Associations, Transplant Networks/Donor Banks

International: Health Care/Hospitals, International Affairs, International Development, International Environmental Issues

Religion: Churches, Dioceses, Religious Welfare, Seminaries

Science: Science Museums, Scientific Centers & Institutes, Scientific Labs, Scientific Organizations, Scientific Research

Social Service: At-Risk Youth, Child Welfare, Community Service Organizations, Counseling, Family Services, People with Disabilities, Recreation & Athletics, Scouts, Senior Services, Shelters/Homelessness, Substance Abuse, Volunteer Services, YMCA/YWCA/YMHA/YWHA, Youth Organizations

Application Procedures

Initial Contact: The Foundation does not have a formal application form. Applicants should submit a one-page executive summary accompanied by a proposal narrative and attachments.

Application Requirements: The proposal narrative should include: an executive summary summarizing key points of the proposal, purpose and relevance of the request, and amount requested; organizational history and capacity, including mission, governing structure, principal activities, and population served by organization; statement of need, identifying the needs that the proposal addresses, and how those needs coincide with the goals of the Foundation; program description, identifying the program's goals and objectives, activities, numbers served, facilities, timeline and staffing plan, and anticipated outcomes; evaluation, indicating how methods for evaluating program outcomes and effectiveness, including findings from previous evaluations, if available; and a conclusion, summarizing the proposal's main points and describing the purpose, relevance, and amount requested. The following attachments must be included with a proposal: current proof of tax-exempt status and non-private foundation status; names and primarily affiliations of officers and board members; most recent audited financial statements; organizational operating budget for the previous and current fiscal years; program budget for the previous and current fiscal years, if applicable; list of foundation and corporate grants for the previous and current fiscal years for both the organization and program or project, including dollar amounts; current fair market value of endowment, if applicable; and most recent annual report. Applicants should also check the foundation's guidelines for additional information required for proposals in the specific grant category for which they are applying.

Deadlines: None.

Review Process: Board meetings on grant decisions are held in March, June, September, and December. Only fully documented appeals will be considered. Meetings are arranged between foundation staff and applicants only if serious consideration of their appeals is anticipated. A site visit is required prior to board review.

Restrictions

Grants must be used for charitable purposes within the U.S. and its territories. Except in rare cases, the following restrictions apply: private sector organizations are favored over those financed through taxation; organizations serving larger geographical areas are favored over those of a neighborhood or grassroots nature; the foundation does not provide funding for building projects; the foundation does not make grants on an annual basis or make multi-year grants; organizations must wait three years from their award date before submitting another request; only one proposal will be considered from an organization within a calendar year, institutions with more than one department should coordinate grants through appropriate central office; the foundation does not support public policy, workshops, seminars, or requests for start-ups/seed funding. No grants are made to individuals, for loans, funds for radio, film, television or other related projects, publishing projects, equipment of any kind, special events, tickets, tables or advertising for an event. Proposals sent by fax or e-mail will not be accepted.

Additional Information

In addition to general grantmaking activities, the foundation provides funds and advisors for two operating programs: United States Senate Youth Program, which allows two students from each state to travel to Washington, DC for one week to observe the federal government in action and meet key officials. For more information contact Rita A. Almon, Program Director at the foundation's San Francisco office.

The Journalism Awards Program is designed to encourage excellence in journalism education. Prizes are awarded in writing, photography, television and radio news. For more information contact Jan C. Watten, Program Director at the foundation's San Francisco office.

The Hearst Foundation and William Randolph Hearst Foundation are independent private philanthropies operating separately from the Hearst Corporation. Because the charitable goals of the two foundations are the same, they are administered as one, and only one proposal need be submitted for review.

Supplemental material should be held to a minimum necessary to ensure a basic understanding of the organization seeking support. Videotapes should not be sent unless specifically requested.

Publications: Application Guidelines

Foundation Officials

Frank Anthony Bennack, Jr.: vice president, director B San Antonio, TX 1933. ED University of Maryland (1954-1956); Saint Mary's University (1956-1958). PRIM CORP EMPL chief executive officer, president, director: Hearst Corp. CORP AFFIL director: Polo Ralph Loren Corp.; director: Wyeth; vice chairman, director: Lincoln Center for the Performing Arts; managing director: Metropolitan Opera of New York; director: Hearst Corporation; director: JP Morgan Chase and Co. NA; director: Hearst-Argyle Television Inc. NONPR AFFIL president: Texas Daily Newspaper Association; honorary trustee: Witte Memorial Museum; trustee: Our Lady Lake College; chairman: Museum Television & Radio; member, board governors: New York Presbyterian Hospital; trustee: Hearst Family Trust; chairman: Museum of Television & Radio; director: American Newspaper Publishers Association; president: Greater San Antonio Chamber of Commerce. CLUB AFFIL Rotary Club.

John G. Conomikes: vice president, director PRIM CORP EMPL vice president, director: Hearst Corp. Broadcasting Group. CORP AFFIL director: Hearst-Argyle Television Inc.

Richard Emmet Deems: vice president, director B New York, NY January 19, 1913. PRIM CORP EMPL director, consult: Hearst Corp. NONPR AFFIL member: Magazine Publishers Association. CLUB AFFIL Everglades Club; Bohemian Club.

Thomas Eastham: vice president, executive director NONPR AFFIL member: Independent Sector.

Robert M. Frehse, Jr.: vice president, executive director NONPR AFFIL secretary: Interchurch Center.

Victor F. Ganzi: vice president, secretary, director B New York, NY 1947. ED Fordham University BS (1968); Harvard University JD (1971). PRIM CORP EMPL executive vice president: Hearst Books/Business Publications Group. CORP AFFIL director: PGA Tour Inc.; director: Palm Management Corp.; chairman, director: Hearst-Argyle Television Inc.; president, chief executive officer, director: Hearst Corp.; director: Gentiva Health Services Inc.; director: ESPN. NONPR AFFIL member: Council Future Law School; director: New York City Economic Development Corp.; member: American Institute of Certified Public Accountants; member: Colorado Society of Certified Public Accountants; member: American Bar Association. CLUB AFFIL Sky Club; Cherry Valley Country Club.

George Randolph Hearst, Jr.: vice president, director B San Francisco, CA July 13, 1927. PRIM CORP EMPL chairman: Hearst Corp. NONPR AFFIL member: Veterans Foreign Wars. CLUB AFFIL Riviera Club; Jonathan Club; Burlingame Country Club; California Club.

John Randolph Hearst, Jr.: vice president, director B 1934. CORP AFFIL director: Hearst Corp.

William R. Hearst, III: president, director B Washington, DC 1949. ED Harvard University AB (1972). PRIM CORP EMPL publisher: San Francisco Examiner. CORP AFFIL director: RGB Media; director: Pictos; director: Oblix; director: OnFiber; director: Juniper Networks; general partner: Kleiner Perkins Caufiled Byers; director: Hearst-Argyle Television; director: Hearst Corp.; director: Applied Minds. NONPR AFFIL trustee: Grace Cathedral of San Francisco; trustee: Mathematical Sciences Research Institute; trustee: California Academy of Sciences; trustee: Carnegie Institute; fellow: American Assn. for the Advancement of Science.

Harvey L. Lipton: vice president, director B Brooklyn, NY 1925. ED New York University (1948); Saint John's University LLB (1951). PRIM CORP EMPL director: Hearst Corp.

Gilbert Charles Maurer: vice president, director B New York, NY 1928. ED Saint Lawrence University AB (1950); Harvard University MBA (1952). PRIM CORP EMPL executive vice president, chief operating officer, director: Hearst Corp. ADD CORP EMPL chief operating officer, director: Down East Timberlands Division; chief operating officer, director: Hearst Realties Division; chief operating officer, director: King Features Syndicate Division; chief operating officer, director: Sunical Land & Livestock Division. CORP AFFIL director: Hearst-Argyle Television Inc. NONPR AFFIL member New York advisory board: Salvation Army; president, trustee: Whitney Museum American Art; member: Magazine Publishers Association; trustee: Norton Museum Art; director: Boys & Girls Clubs America. CLUB AFFIL Harvard Club New York; Metro Club.

Mark F. Miller: vice president, director ED University of Pennsylvania Wharton School BS. PRIM CORP EMPL executive vice president, general manager, magazine division: Hearst Corp. CORP AFFIL director: Periodical Publishers Service Bureau.

Raymond Joseph Petersen: vice president, director B West Orange, NJ 1919. PRIM CORP EMPL executive vice president, director: Hearst Magazines. NONPR AFFIL director, vice president: United Service Organization Metropolitan New York; director: U.S. National Comm Libs Info Science; director: National Crime Prevention Council; member chairman committee: United Cerebral Palsy Campaign; director: Boys & Girls Clubs Madison Square; honorary advisor: Children Alcoholics Foundation; member, director: American Advertising Federation.

Virginia H. Randt: vice president, director CORP AFFIL director: Hearst-Argyle Television Inc..

Grants Analysis

Disclosure Period: calendar year ending 2004
Total Grants: $15,162,500*
Number of Grants: 111
Average Grant: $136,599*
Highest Grant: $500,000
Lowest Grant: $10,000
Typical Range: $25,000 to $200,000
***Note:** Giving excludes scholarships.

Recent Grants

Note: Grants derived from 2002 Form 990.
Library-Related
250,000	Boston Public Library Foundation, Boston, MA
250,000	New York Public Library, New York, NY

General
1,000,000	Memorial Sloan-Kettering Cancer Center, New York, NY
1,000,000	Saint Luke's-Roosevelt Hospital Center, New York, NY
1,000,000	Salk Institute for Biological Studies, San Diego, CA
500,000	Cold Spring Harbor Laboratory, Cold Spring Harbor, NY
500,000	John Wayne Cancer Institute Center, Santa Monica, CA
500,000	Metropolitan Museum of Art, New York, NY
250,000	California Academy of Sciences, San Francisco, CA
250,000	Field Museum, Chicago, IL
250,000	Museum of Modern Art, New York, NY
250,000	New York Botanical Garden, Bronx, NY

ED AND MARY HEATH FOUNDATION

Giving Contact

W. R. Smith, Chairman
PO Box 338
Tyler, TX 75710
Phone: (903)597-7436

Description

Founded: 1954
EIN: 756021506
Organization Type: Private Foundation
Giving Locations: TX: Smith County
Grant Types: General Support.

Donor Information

Founder: the late J. E. Heath, the late Mary M. Heath

Financial Summary

Total Giving: $61,750 (2001)
Giving Analysis: Giving for 2001 includes: foundation grants to United Way ($250)
Assets: $2,188,101 (2001)

Typical Recipients

Arts & Humanities: Arts Outreach, History & Archaeology, Libraries, Museums/Galleries, Music, Public Broadcasting, Theater
Civic & Public Affairs: Economic Policy, Employment/Job Training, Civic & Public Affairs-General, Hispanic Affairs, Housing, Municipalities/Towns, Native American Affairs, Philanthropic Organizations, Public Policy, Urban & Community Affairs
Education: Agricultural Education, Colleges & Universities, Community & Junior Colleges, Elementary Education (Public), Environmental Education, Faculty Development, Education-General, Literacy, Minority Education, Private Education (Precollege), Public Education (Precollege), Religious Education, Special Education, Student Aid
Health: AIDS/HIV, Alzheimer's Disease, Cancer, Children's Health/Hospitals, Clinics/Medical Centers, Emergency/Ambulance Services, Eyes/Blindness, Hospices, Medical Rehabilitation, Mental Health, Prenatal Health Issues, Respiratory, Single-Disease Health Associations, Speech & Hearing
International: Health Care/Hospitals
Religion: Churches, Ministries, Religious Organizations, Religious Welfare, Seminaries, Synagogues/Temples
Science: Science Museums, Scientific Centers & Institutes
Social Services: Animal Protection, Camps, Child Abuse, Child Welfare, Community Service Organizations, Day Care, Delinquency & Criminal Rehabilitation, Domestic Violence, Family Services, Food/Clothing Distribution, People with Disabilities, Recreation & Athletics, Scouts, Senior Services, Social Services-General, Substance Abuse, United Funds/United Ways, YMCA/YWCA/YMHA/YWHA, Youth Organizations

Application Procedures

Initial Contact: Send a brief letter of inquiry on organization letterhead.
Application Requirements: Include a description of organization and purpose of funds sought.
Deadlines: None.

Foundation Officials

Jack Jackson: vice chairman, secretary, treasurer
Mike Massar: director
Charlotte Schaeffers: program director, trustee
Margaret Smith: director
W. R. Smith: director
Charles H. White, Jr.: director

Grants Analysis

Disclosure Period: calendar year ending 2001
Total Grants: $61,500*
Number of Grants: 77
Average Grant: $799
Highest Grant: $6,000
Lowest Grant: $50
Typical Range: $200 to $1,000
***Note:** Giving excludes United Way.

Recent Grants

Note: Grants derived from 2002 Form 990.
General
7,000	First Baptist Church, Tyler, TX
2,500	Marvin United Methodist Church, Tyler, TX
2,000	Scottish Rite Children's Learning Center, Tyler, TX
1,500	Association for Retarded Citizens, Tyler, TX
1,500	Azelway Boys Ranch, Inc., Tyler, TX
1,500	Boys and Girls Club of Tyler of Smith County, Inc., Tyler, TX
1,500	Camp Tyler Foundation, Tyler, TX
1,500	Children's Weekday Ministry of Tyler, Inc., Tyler, TX
1,500	East Texas Symphony Orchestra, Tyler, TX
1,500	First Presbyterian Church, Tyler, TX

MARY HEATH FOUNDATION

Giving Contact

Jimmy J. Rogers, Vice President
c/o Old National Trust Co.
PO Box 217
Oblong, IL 62449-0217
Phone: (618)544-2960

Description

Founded: 1994
EIN: 371330907
Organization Type: Private Foundation
Giving Locations: IL
Grant Types: General Support.

Donor Information

Founder: Established in 1994 by Mary Heath Morris.

Financial Summary

Total Giving: $61,900 (2001)
Assets: $5,115,728 (2001)
Gifts Received: $1,824,105 (1996). Note: In 1996, contributions were received from the estate of Mary Heath Morris.

Typical Recipients

Arts & Humanities: Historic Preservation, History & Archaeology, Libraries, Museums/Galleries
Civic & Public Affairs: Botanical Gardens/Parks, Clubs, Community Foundations, Civic & Public Affairs-General, Housing, Municipalities/Towns, Safety, Urban & Community Affairs
Education: Education-General, Literacy, Private Education (Precollege), Public Education (Precollege), Science/Mathematics Education, Secondary Education (Public), Special Education
Environment: Air/Water Quality
Health: Emergency/Ambulance Services
Religion: Churches, Religious Welfare
Social Services: Animal Protection, Community Centers, Community Service Organizations, Crime Prevention, Emergency Relief, Food/Clothing Distribution, Recreation & Athletics, Senior Services, Social Services-General, Veterans, Youth Organizations

Application Procedures

Initial Contact: Request application form.
Application Requirements: Include six identical copies of the complete proposal. Include current financial information and tax exempt ruling determination from the Internal Revenue Service.
Deadlines: May 1 and November 1.
Evaluative Criteria: The Advisory Committee looks for applicants with a history of achievement and good management; with a current stable financial condition, supported by financial statements; whose programs and projects which encourage self-sufficiency; whose projects mean to accomplish a measurable impact in the area and for the purpose for which the applicant requests; and whose programs are consistent with the purpose of the Foundation.
Notes: Foundation will monitor the impact of all grants to help determine the Foundation's future program objectives. Committee does not permit individual contact regarding specific grant proposals.

Restrictions

Applying organizations must be located in the State of Illinois; must have received permanent, tax-exempt ruling from the IRS; and the organization's project must be for the benefit and enjoyment of the general public of the State of Illinois.

Grants are not made for individuals; organizations which use funds granted to support other organizations; endowments; deficit reductions;routine institutional expenses; general campaigns, including fundraising events, dinners, or mass mailings; efforts to carry out propaganda, or influence legislation; participation or intervention in political campaigns on behalf of any candidate for public office; or requests that do not fall within the Foundation's specific areas of interest.

Foundation Officials

Radford Burkett: adv board comm mem
Betty Cunningham: adv board comm mem
Thomas Eden: adv board committee member
Steve Holliday: adv board committee member
Myrl Littejohn: advisory board, committee member
Todd Musgrave: adv board committee member
Thomas Pearce: adv board comm mem
Gilbert Phillippe: adv board comm mem
Keith Waldrop: adv board committee member

Grants Analysis

Disclosure Period: calendar year ending 2001
Total Grants: $61,900
Number of Grants: 22
Average Grant: $2,814
Highest Grant: $9,000
Lowest Grant: $300
Typical Range: $1,000 to $5,000

Recent Grants

Note: Grants derived from 2001 Form 990.
Library-Related

2,000	Coffeen Community Library, Coffeen, IL -- purchase of books
400	Palestine Public Library District, Palestine, IL -- library lighting

General

9,000	Hutsonville Fire Protection District, Hutsonville, IL -- thermal imaging camera
7,500	Hutsonville Community Unit School District 1, Hutsonville, IL -- After School Teen Center
5,000	Oblong Community Unit School District 4, Oblong, IL -- school road extension and parking lot
4,000	Eastern Illinois Children's Home, Oblong, IL -- construction of new home
4,000	Summer Success Project, Robinson, IL -- programs for children
3,700	Illinois Oil Field Museum of Oblong, Oblong, IL -- Erect Old Wooden Derrick display
3,000	Goshen Preservation Alliance, Edwardsville, IL -- restoration of train depot
3,000	St. Michael Archangel School, Sigel, IL -- school roof repairs
2,500	Palestine Development Association, Palestine, IL -- soil and water conservation survey
2,500	Pioneer City Youth Baseball, Palestine, IL -- lights for baseball diamonds

HEBREW TECHNICAL INSTITUTE

Giving Contact

Anita Goldberg, Trust Officer
c/o REM Residential

118 East 17th Street
New York, NY 10003
Phone: (212)286-2600

Description

Founded: 1884
EIN: 135562240
Organization Type: Private Foundation
Giving Locations: NY
Grant Types: General Support, Scholarship.

Financial Summary

Gifts Received: $29,157 (2000); $18,644 (1999); $18,627 (1998). Note: In 1995, contributions were received from the Henry Stern Trust.

Typical Recipients

Arts & Humanities: Libraries, Museums/Galleries
Civic & Public Affairs: Botanical Gardens/Parks, Business/Free Enterprise, Civic & Public Affairs-General, Housing, Women's Affairs
Education: Agricultural Education, Arts/Humanities Education, Colleges & Universities, Engineering/Technological Education, Environmental Education, Education-General, Private Education (Precollege)
Environment: Environment-General, Resource Conservation
International: Missionary/Religious Activities
Religion: Jewish Causes, Religious Organizations
Science: Science Museums, Scientific Centers & Institutes, Scientific Organizations
Social Services: Community Centers, Community Service Organizations, Refugee Assistance, Youth Organizations

Application Procedures

Initial Contact: Send a brief letter of inquiry describing program.
Deadlines: None.

Restrictions

Grants are limited to IRS approved public charities involved in vocational studies.

Foundation Officials

Catherine H. Behrend: director
Lawrence A. Benenson: director
Andrew Berkman: director
Seth Harris Dubin: director B New York, NY 1933. ED Amherst College BA (1954); Harvard University LLB (1957). PRIM CORP EMPL partner: Satterlee Stephens Burke & Burke. NONPR AFFIL trustee, president: New York Hall Science; member: New York State Bar Association; chairman: Hebrew Technology Institute; member: Council Foreign Relations; fellow: Foreign Political Association; trustee: Chatham House Foundation; member advisory council: Cooper Union School Engineering; member: Association Bar New York City. CLUB AFFIL Century Association.
Irving Lipkowitz: director
Jay J. Meltzer: director
John R. Menke: director
Sandra Priest Rose: director
Herbert A. Raisler: director
Hyman B. Ritchin: director
Robert Rosenthal, Esq.: director
Bruce D. Schlechter: director
Russell O. Vernon: director
Charles Weilman: director

Grants Analysis

Disclosure Period: calendar year ending 2000
Total Grants: $246,500*
Number of Grants: 12
Average Grant: $17,864*
Highest Grant: $50,000
Typical Range: $5,000 to $30,000
*Note: Giving excludes scholarships. Average grant figure excludes highest grant.

Recent Grants

Note: Grants derived from 2001 Form 990.
General

50,000	Cooper Union, New York, NY
25,000	B'nai Zion, Pittsburgh, PA
25,000	New York Academy of Sciences, New York, NY
25,000	New York Botanical Gardens, New York, NY
25,000	New York Hall of Science, New York, NY
15,000	Mosholu Montefiore Community Center, Bronx, NY
15,000	Rockefeller University, New York, NY
10,400	Virginia Cooperative Extension, Jonesville, VA
10,000	Housing Conservation Coordinator, New York, NY
6,700	Mid Westchester JCC, New York, NY

HECHT-LEVI FOUNDATION

Giving Contact

Blanche Roche, Trust Officer
c/o Mercantile Safe Deposit and Trust Co.
2 Hopkins Plaza
Baltimore, MD 21201
Phone: (410)209-5454

Description

Founded: 1958
EIN: 526035023
Organization Type: Private Foundation
Giving Locations: MD: Baltimore metropolitan area
Grant Types: General Support.

Donor Information

Founder: the late Alexander Hecht, the late Selma H. Hecht, Robert H. Levi, Ryda H. Levi

Typical Recipients

Arts & Humanities: Arts Funds, Arts Institutes, Arts Outreach, Ballet, Dance, Historic Preservation, History & Archaeology, Libraries, Museums/Galleries, Music, Opera, Performing Arts, Public Broadcasting, Theater
Civic & Public Affairs: Civil Rights, Community Foundations, Civic & Public Affairs-General, Housing, Legal Aid, Philanthropic Organizations, Urban & Community Affairs, Zoos/Aquariums
Education: Arts/Humanities Education, Business Education, Colleges & Universities, Education Funds, Elementary Education (Public), Environmental Education, Education-General, Leadership Training, Private Education (Precollege), Religious Education, Student Aid
Environment: Environment-General, Resource Conservation
Health: Emergency/Ambulance Services, Health Organizations, Hospitals, Mental Health, Preventive Medicine/Wellness Organizations
Religion: Churches, Jewish Causes, Religious Organizations, Religious Welfare, Synagogues/Temples
Science: Science Museums, Scientific Centers & Institutes
Social Services: Child Welfare, Community Service Organizations, Family Planning, Food/Clothing Distribution, People with Disabilities, Recreation & Athletics, United Funds/United Ways, Youth Organizations

Application Procedures

Initial Contact: The foundation requests applications be made in writing.
Deadlines: None.

Additional Information

Trust(s): Mercantile Safe Deposit & Trust Co

Foundation Officials

Sandra L. Gerstung: president, director
Clementine Kaufman: officer
Alexander H. Levi: vice president, director
Richard H. Levi: vice president, treasurer, director
Ryda H. Levi: vice president, director
Blanche Roche: trust officer
Wilbert H. Sirota, Esq.: secretary, director

Grants Analysis

Disclosure Period: calendar year ending 2000
Total Grants: $748,667
Number of Grants: 58
Average Grant: $6,117*
Highest Grant: $400,000
Typical Range: $1,000 to $10,000
*Note: Average grant figure excludes highest grant.

Recent Grants

Note: Grants derived from 2001 Form 990.
Library-Related

5,000	Enoch Pratt Free Library, Baltimore, MD

General

400,000	Johns Hopkins University, Baltimore, MD -- Bioethics Chair
60,000	Baltimore Symphony Orchestra, Baltimore, MD
50,000	Associated Jewish Charities, Baltimore, MD
50,000	Baltimore Symphony Orchestra, Baltimore, MD -- Sustaining Greatness Campaign
40,000	Baltimore Museum of Art, Baltimore, MD -- garden maintenance
25,000	American Civil Liberties Union -- Bill of Rights
10,000	Jewish Museum of Maryland, Baltimore, MD
10,000	Johns Hopkins University, Baltimore, MD -- Bioethics Institute
10,000	Marlboro Music School, Philadelphia, PA
10,000	Park School, Buffalo, NY

HECKSCHER FOUNDATION FOR CHILDREN

Giving Contact

Virginia Sloane, President
17 East 47th Street
New York, NY 10017
Phone: (212)371-7775
Fax: (212)371-7787

Description

Founded: 1921
EIN: 131820170
Organization Type: Specialized/Single Purpose Foundation
Giving Locations: NY: New York
Grant Types: Capital, General Support, Multiyear/Continuing Support, Project.

Donor Information

Founder: August Heckscher, who died in 1941, was the donor of the Heckscher Foundation for Children, which was established in 1921. Mr. Heckscher made his fortune in mining and New York City real estate. He first demonstrated his interest in the welfare of children in New York City in the early twentieth century, when he donated a building and the land on which it stood to a children's home.

Financial Summary

Total Giving: $5,132,143 (2003); $5,029,887 (2002)
Assets: $170,572,900 (2003); $126,283,004 (2002)

Typical Recipients

Arts & Humanities: Arts Associations & Councils, Arts Centers, Arts Institutes, Arts Outreach, Ballet, Dance, Ethnic & Folk Arts, Arts & Humanities-General, Historic Preservation, History & Archaeology, Libraries, Museums/Galleries, Music, Opera, Performing Arts, Public Broadcasting, Theater
Civic & Public Affairs: Botanical Gardens/Parks, Clubs, Community Foundations, Economic Development, Employment/Job Training, Civic & Public Affairs-General, Hispanic Affairs, Housing, Inner-City Development, Municipalities/Towns, Philanthropic Organizations, Public Policy, Urban & Community Affairs, Women's Affairs, Zoos/Aquariums
Education: Afterschool/Enrichment Programs, Arts/Humanities Education, Colleges & Universities, Education Associations, Education Funds, Education Reform, Elementary Education (Private), Elementary Education (Public), Environmental Education, Education-General, Leadership Training, Medical Education, Minority Education, Preschool Education, Private Education (Precollege), Public Education (Precollege), Secondary Education (Private), Special Education, Student Aid, Vocational & Technical Education
Environment: Forestry, Environment-General, Wildlife Protection
Health: Adolescent Health Issues, AIDS/HIV, Cancer, Children's Health/Hospitals, Clinics/Medical Centers, Emergency/Ambulance Services, Health Organizations, Hospitals, Medical Rehabilitation, Medical Research, Mental Health, Nursing Services, Preventive Medicine/Wellness Organizations, Single-Disease Health Associations, Speech & Hearing, Transplant Networks/Donor Banks
International: Health Care/Hospitals
Religion: Churches, Jewish Causes, Religious Welfare
Social Services: At-Risk Youth, Big Brothers/Big Sisters, Camps, Child Welfare, Community Centers, Community Service Organizations, Day Care, Delinquency & Criminal Rehabilitation, Family Planning, Family Services, People with Disabilities, Recreation & Athletics, Scouts, Shelters/Homelessness, Substance Abuse, Volunteer Services, YMCA/YWCA/YMHA/YWHA, Youth Organizations

Application Procedures

Initial Contact: Applicants should send a letter to the foundation.
Application Requirements: Include a concise statement of the program or project; amount requested; a brief background of the organization; a budget for the program/project; a list of officers, director, or trustees; donor list for the past twelve months, and a copy of the IRS tax-determination letter.
Deadlines: None.

Additional Information

Publications: Application Guidelines

Foundation Officials

Phyllis Fannan: trustee
William D. Hart, Jr.: secretary, trustee B 1918. ED Yale University AB (1940); Harvard University LLB (1943). PRIM CORP EMPL vice president, director: North Shore Corp. CORP AFFIL vice president, treasurer, director: Park Lexington Co.; partner: Whitman & Ransom.
Carole Landman: trustee
Gail Meyers: trustee PRIM CORP EMPL senior vice president: Barnett Bank South Florida. NONPR AFFIL secretary: Greater Miami Jewish Federation.
Fred Obser: trustee
Howard Rosenbaum: assistant treasurer, trustee
Marlene Shyer: trustee
Howard Grant Sloane: chairman, trustee B 1922. PRIM CORP EMPL president, director: North Shore Corp. CORP AFFIL president: Anahma Realty; president: Okeechobee Inc.
Virginia Sloane: president, trustee PRIM CORP

EMPL president: Anahma Realty.
Arthur J. Smadbeck: trustee B 1949. PRIM CORP EMPL vice president, director: Park Lexington Co. CORP AFFIL vice president: Okeechobee Inc.; vice president: Anahma Realty. NONPR AFFIL selectman: Town of Edgartown, Massachusetts.
Louis Smadbeck, Jr.: trustee
Mina Smadbeck: trustee
Paul Smadbeck: vice president, trustee PRIM CORP EMPL vice president, director: Park Lexington Co. CORP AFFIL vice president, director: North Shore Corp.

Grants Analysis

Disclosure Period: calendar year ending 2003
Total Grants: $5,132,143
Number of Grants: 209
Average Grant: $24,556
Highest Grant: $300,000
Lowest Grant: $108
Typical Range: $5,000 to $50,000

Recent Grants

Note: Grants derived from 2003 Form 990.
General

300,000	Cornell University, New York, NY -- for Urban Scholars program
300,000	Teach for America, New York, NY
250,000	United Cerebral Palsy, New York, NY
200,000	Friends of Karen, Croton Falls, NY
200,000	New York Botanical Garden, Bronx, NY
200,000	Urban Assembly, New York, NY
150,000	Florida Stage, Manalapan, FL
140,000	Take the Field, New York, NY
125,000	Summer on the Hill, Riverdale, NY
100,000	Carnegie Hall, New York, NY

HEDCO FOUNDATION

Giving Contact

Mary A. Goriup, Foundation Manager
1221 Broadway, 21st Fl.
1221 Broadway, 21st Fl.
Oakland, CA 94612
Phone: (925)283-3442

Description

Founded: 1972
EIN: 237259742
Organization Type: Private Foundation
Giving Locations: CA; MN
Grant Types: Capital, Project, Scholarship.

Donor Information

Founder: Herrick Corp., Catalina Associates

Financial Summary

Total Giving: $2,557,383 (fiscal year ending November 30, 2003 approx); $3,403,028 (fiscal 2002)
Assets: $22,080,129 (fiscal 2002)
Gifts Received: $14,308,768 (fiscal 2002); $200,000 (fiscal 2000); $3,507,256 (fiscal 1999). Note: In fiscal 1999 and 2000, contributions were received from Herrick-Pacific Corp. ($3,002,350) and David Dornsife ($504,906). In fiscal 1998, contributions were received from the Herrick Corp. ($100,000); Catalina Associates II ($2,500,000). In fiscal 1997, contributions were received from the Herrick Corp., Catalina Associates II, and Dorothy Jernstedt. In fiscal 2002, contributions were received from Herrick-Pacific Corp. ($4,000,000); The Herrick Corp. ($100,000); Dorothy Jernstedt ($100,000); Dornsife Family Trust ($8,108,568); David Dornsife ($2,000,100) and James Appleton ($100).

Typical Recipients

Arts & Humanities: Libraries, Museums/Galleries
Civic & Public Affairs: Asian American Affairs, Civic

& Public Affairs-General, Housing
Education: Arts/Humanities Education, Colleges & Universities, Education Reform, Minority Education, Private Education (Precollege), Religious Education, Science/Mathematics Education, Social Sciences Education, Student Aid
Environment: Environment-General, Resource Conservation
Health: Alzheimer's Disease, Cancer, Children's Health/Hospitals, Clinics/Medical Centers, Health Organizations, Hospices, Hospitals, Medical Research, Research/Studies Institutes, Single-Disease Health Associations
International: International Relations, International Relief Efforts
Religion: Religious Welfare, Seminaries
Social Services: Community Service Organizations, Food/Clothing Distribution, Homes, Scouts, Senior Services, YMCA/YWCA/YMHA/YWHA, Youth Organizations

Application Procedures

Initial Contact: The foundation has no formal grant application procedure or application form.
Deadlines: None.

Foundation Officials

Laine Ainsworth: director
Dr. James Appleton: director
Rena Brantley: secretary, director
Allen L. Dobbins, EdD: director
David H. Dornsife: vice president, director
Ester M. Dornsife: president, director
Harold W. Dornsife: cfo, director B Mishawaka, IN 1915. ED University of Southern California (1939). PRIM CORP EMPL chairman: Peninsula Steel Product. CORP AFFIL chairman, chief executive officer: Herrick-Pacific Corp.; chairman: Peninsula Steel Products; chairman: Central Texas IW; chairman: Gillig Corp.
Mary A. Goriup: mgr
Tom Herman: director
Derek Jernstedt: director
Dorothy Jernstedt: secretary, director
James S. Little: director
Dr. William Picard: director
Roger Schwab: director

Grants Analysis

Disclosure Period: fiscal year ending November 30, 2002
Total Grants: $3,403,028
Number of Grants: 17
Average Grant: $53,872*
Highest Grant: $2,000,000
Typical Range: $25,000 to $150,000
***Note:** Average grant excludes two highest grants ($2,487,200).

Recent Grants

Note: Grants derived from fiscal 2001 Form 990.

General

2,000,000	San Francisco Theological Seminary, San Francisco, CA
487,200	World Vision, Minneapolis, MN
256,000	Children's Hospital Oakland, Oakland, CA
154,515	St. Vincent's Day Home, Oakland, CA
129,053	Oregon Health Sciences University, Portland, OR
84,115	St. Vincent's Day Home, Oakland, CA
62,078	St. Luke's Hospital Foundation, San Francisco, CA
60,000	Alzheimer's Association
35,031	East Bay Conservation Corps, Oakland, CA
33,922	St. Luke's Hospital Foundation, San Francisco, CA

JULIUS W. HEGELER II FOUNDATION

Giving Contact

Madelle G. Hegeler, Manager
Julius W. Hegeler II Foundation
1521 N. Vermilion Street
Danville, IL 61832-2370
Phone: (217)442-1521

Description

Founded: 1993
EIN: 371302455
Organization Type: Private Foundation
Grant Types: General Support.

Financial Summary

Total Giving: $301,365 (fiscal year ending June 30, 2001)
Giving Analysis: Giving for fiscal 2001 includes: foundation grants to United Way ($3,500)
Assets: $11,694,506 (fiscal 2001)
Gifts Received: $1,000 (fiscal 1996)

Typical Recipients

Arts & Humanities: Arts Institutes, Historic Preservation, Libraries, Museums/Galleries, Music
Civic & Public Affairs: Clubs, Civic & Public Affairs-General
Education: Business Education, Colleges & Universities, Community & Junior Colleges, Education Funds
Environment: Resource Conservation
Health: Single-Disease Health Associations
Social Services: Community Centers, Recreation & Athletics, United Funds/United Ways, YMCA/YWCA/YMHA/YWHA

Application Procedures

Initial Contact: The foundation has no formal grant application procedure or application form.
Deadlines: None.

Foundation Officials

R. K. Bates: director
F. Jay Foster: acct
Alix S. Hegeler: director
Julius W. Hegeler, II: director
Madelle G. Hegeler: mgr
Dolores A. Roberts: director

Grants Analysis

Disclosure Period: fiscal year ending June 30, 2001
Total Grants: $297,865*
Number of Grants: 14
Average Grant: $17,143*
Highest Grant: $75,000
Typical Range: $5,000 to $20,000
***Note:** Giving excludes United Way. Average grant figure excludes highest grant.

Recent Grants

Note: Grants derived from fiscal 2001 Form 990.
Library-Related

25,000	Westville Public Library, Westville, IL

General

75,000	Vermilion County Conservation District - Forest Glen, Danville, IL
55,000	YMCA, Danville, IL
50,000	YWCA, Danville, IL
25,000	Ambucs Playground for Everyone, Danville, IL
25,000	Cerebral Palsy Association, Chicago, IL
20,000	Vermilion Area Community Health Center, Danville, IL
6,300	Vermilion County Museum, Danville, IL
5,000	Danville Community Public School Fund, Danville, IL
5,000	Millikin University, Decatur, IL
5,000	USS LST Ship Memorial, Danville, IL

ANNA M. HEILMAIER CHARITABLE FOUNDATION

Giving Contact

Cheryl Nelson, Vice President
c/o U. S. Bank
101 E. Fifth St.
St. Paul, MN 55101
Phone: (651)466-8731

Description

Founded: 1993
EIN: 411761632
Organization Type: Private Foundation
Giving Locations: MN: Dakota County, Saint Paul; WA: Ramsey
Grant Types: General Support.

Donor Information

Founder: Founded in 1993 by the late Anna M. Heilmaier.

Financial Summary

Total Giving: $218,500 (2003). Note: Giving includes scholarships ($8,000).
Assets: $7,448,636 (2003)
Gifts Received: $4,039,850 (1994). Note: In 1994, contributions were received from the estate of Anna M. Heilmaier.

Typical Recipients

Arts & Humanities: Arts Associations & Councils, Arts Funds, Ballet, History & Archaeology, Libraries, Museums/Galleries, Music, Opera
Civic & Public Affairs: Clubs, Civic & Public Affairs-General
Education: Arts/Humanities Education, Colleges & Universities, Medical Education, Student Aid
Health: Cancer, Children's Health/Hospitals, Clinics/Medical Centers, Eyes/Blindness, Health Organizations, Hospices, Hospitals, Prenatal Health Issues, Speech & Hearing
Religion: Churches, Religious Welfare
Science: Science Museums
Social Services: Child Welfare, Community Service Organizations, Family Services, Social Services-General

Application Procedures

Initial Contact: Send a brief letter of inquiry.
Application Requirements: Include information on purpose of funds sought and proof of tax-exempt status.
Deadlines: None.

Restrictions

Does not support individuals, religious organizations for sectarian purposes, political or lobbying groups, or organizations outside operating areas.

Additional Information

Emphasis is on treatment of cancer, diseases of the eye, medical research, and support for chamber and classical music.
Trust(s): US Bank National Association Minnesota

Foundation Officials

Terence N. Doyle: co-trustee B Minneapolis, MN 1936. ED Saint Thomas College BA (1958); University of Minnesota JD (1961). NONPR AFFIL member: Minnesota Law Alumni Association; member: Order Coif; fellow: American College Trust & Estate Counsel; member: Minnesota Bar Association; director: AH South Foundation; member: American Bar Association. CLUB AFFIL Minnesota Club.

Grants Analysis

Disclosure Period: calendar year ending 2003
Total Grants: $218,500
Number of Grants: 16
Average Grant: $11,900*
Highest Grant: $40,000
Lowest Grant: $5,000
Typical Range: $5,000 to $20,000
*Note: Average grant figure excludes highest grant.

Recent Grants

Note: Grants derived from 2001 Form 990.

Library-Related

10,000	Friends of the St. Paul Public Library, St. Paul, MN

General

200,000	Schubert Club, St. Paul, MN -- for Raspberry Island Bandshell Project
62,500	Saint Paul Chamber Orchestra Society, St. Paul, MN
26,000	Minnesota Sinfonia, Minneapolis, MN
25,000	Gillette Children's Foundation, St. Paul, MN -- for focus on special children
25,000	State Services for the Blind, St. Paul, MN
20,000	Lifetrack Resources, St. Paul, MN -- support of rehabilitation therapies division services for low income and elderly
15,000	Healthstart, Inc., St. Paul, MN -- for support of school based clinics
10,000	Minnesota Historical Society, St. Paul, MN
10,000	Minnesota Opera, Minneapolis, MN
10,000	United Cambodian Association of Minnesota, Inc., St. Paul, MN

H.J. HEINZ CO.

Company Headquarters

600 Grant Street
Pittsburgh, PA 15219
Web: http://www.heinz.com

Company Description

Founded: 1869
Ticker: HNZ
Exchange: NYSE
Revenue: US$8.414 billion (2004)
Profit: US$804.3 million (2004)
Employees: 38900 (2003)
Fortune Rank: 259, per FORTUNE Magazine's list of 500 Largest U.S. Corporations (2004).
SIC(s): 2032 Canned Specialties, 2033 Canned Fruits & Vegetables, 2038 Frozen Specialties Nec, 2099 Food Preparations Nec.

Operating Locations

Alden Merrell Desserts (MA--West Newburyport); Chef Francisco, Inc. (PA--King of Prussia); Escalon Premier Brands, Inc. (CA--Escalon); Heinz Frozen Food Co. (FL--Fort Myers; ID--Pocatello; OH--Massillon; OR--Ontario; PA--West Chester); H.J. Heinz Co. (AZ--Phoenix; CA, Chatsworth, Escalon, Irvine, Stockton; FL--Jacksonville; GA--Atlanta; IL--Northbrook; IA--Cedar Rapids, Muscatine; MA--Westburyport; MI--Holland; NJ--Pennsauken; OH--Fremont, Mason; PA--King of Prussia; TX--Dallas); Portion Pac, Inc. (CA--Chatsworth; FL--Jacksonville; GA--Atlanta; OH--Mason; TX--Dallas); Quality Chef Foods, Inc. (IA--Cedar Rapids); Thermo Pac, Inc. (GA--Stone Mountain); Todds (AZ--Phoenix; CA--Irvine)
Note: Heinz also has operating locations in Italy, India, Indonesia, Singapore, China, South Korea, Hong Kong and the Philippines.

H.J. Heinz Co. Foundation

Giving Contact

Loretta M. Oken, Program Director
H.J. Heinz Co. Foundation
PO Box 57
Pittsburgh, PA 15230-0057
Phone: (412)456-5772
Fax: (412)456-7868
E-mail: heinz_foundation@hjheinz.com
Web: http://www.heinz.com/jsp/foundation.jsp

Alternate Contact

Robert Hass
Mellon Bank NA
AIM 151-3725
Pittsburgh, PA 15230

Description

Founded: 1951
EIN: 256018924
Organization Type: Corporate Foundation
Giving Locations: principally near operating locations and to national organizations.
Grant Types: Capital, Challenge, Conference/Seminar, Employee Matching Gifts, Endowment, Fellowship, General Support, Project, Scholarship.
Note: Foundation gives to scholarship funds only and does not give individual scholarships.

Donor Information

Founder: H. J. Heinz Co.

Financial Summary

Total Giving: $5,699,101 (2001). Note: Contributes through foundation only.
Assets: $1,153,903 (2001)
Gifts Received: $6,000,000 (2001); $6,000,000 (2000); $6,000,000 (1999). Note: Foundation receives contributions from the H.J. Heinz Company and various individuals.

Typical Recipients

Arts & Humanities: Arts Associations & Councils, Arts Centers, Arts Festivals, Arts Funds, Arts Outreach, Ballet, Dance, Film & Video, Arts & Humanities-General, Historic Preservation, History & Archaeology, Libraries, Literary Arts, Museums/Galleries, Music, Opera, Performing Arts, Public Broadcasting, Theater
Civic & Public Affairs: African American Affairs, Botanical Gardens/Parks, Business/Free Enterprise, Civil Rights, Community Foundations, Economic Development, Economic Policy, Employment/Job Training, Civic & Public Affairs-General, Housing, Law & Justice, Legal Aid, Philanthropic Organizations, Professional & Trade Associations, Public Policy, Rural Affairs, Safety, Urban & Community Affairs, Women's Affairs, Zoos/Aquariums
Education: Afterschool/Enrichment Programs, Agricultural Education, Arts/Humanities Education, Business Education, Colleges & Universities, Community & Junior Colleges, Continuing Education, Economic Education, Education Associations, Education Funds, Elementary Education (Private), Environmental Education, Education-General, Health & Physical Education, International Exchange, International Studies, Journalism/Media Education, Legal Education, Literacy, Medical Education, Minority Education, Private Education (Precollege), Public Education (Precollege), Religious Education, Science/Mathematics Education, Secondary Education (Private), Special Education, Student Aid
Environment: Environment-General
Health: AIDS/HIV, Cancer, Children's Health/Hospitals, Clinics/Medical Centers, Health Organizations, Heart, Home-Care Services, Hospices, Hospitals, Medical Rehabilitation, Medical Research, Nutrition, Public Health, Single-Disease Health

Associations
International: Foreign Educational Institutions, Health Care/Hospitals, Human Rights, International Affairs, International Development, International Environmental Issues, International Organizations, International Peace & Security Issues, International Relations, International Relief Efforts
Religion: Religious Organizations, Religious Welfare
Science: Science-General, Scientific Centers & Institutes, Scientific Organizations
Social Services: Animal Protection, Child Welfare, Community Centers, Community Service Organizations, Counseling, Delinquency & Criminal Rehabilitation, Family Planning, Family Services, Food/Clothing Distribution, Homes, People with Disabilities, Recreation & Athletics, Senior Services, Substance Abuse, United Funds/United Ways, Volunteer Services, YMCA/YWCA/YMHA/YWHA, Youth Organizations

Application Procedures

Initial Contact: Submit a brief letter requesting guidelines or obtain guidelines from the foundation's web site.
Application Requirements: A formal proposal should be made in writing and must include five items: Program Information, Financial Information, Volunteers, Impact, and Policy Decisions. Program Information should provide an executive summary, a description of organization, including the organization's purposes, overall goals, and plans for the current year; project description; measurable goals and objectives; target demographic; and sustainability of the project after grant funding ends. Financial Information must include the organization's current operating budget; project budget; and recently audited financial statement with management letter. Requested Volunteers information includes a description of the extent to which Heinz employees, retirees, or directors are involved with the organization and an outline of volunteer opportunities available within the organization. Impact information describes how the program will be evaluated, which may include feedback from recipients, improvements made, attendance and/or participation at events, and independent evaluation. Policy Decision describes the organization's type of governing structure. The following Attachments are required: proof of tax-exempt status; a list of board members, with affiliations; most recent annual report; and requested financial information.
Deadlines: None; board meets quarterly.
Evaluative Criteria: Priority to United Ways, scholarship programs in food-related courses of study, grants for health-related facilities in geographic areas served by the company, and organizations receiving matching gifts.

Restrictions

The foundation does not provide loans and does not support individuals, equipment, conferences, travel, general scholarships, religious programs, political campaigns, or unsolicited research projects.

Additional Information

Publications: Grant Application Information

Corporate Officials

William R. Johnson: chairman, president, chief executive officer B 1949. ED University of California, Los Angeles BBA (1971); University of Texas MBA (1974). PRIM CORP EMPL chairman, president, chief executive officer: H.J. Heinz Co. CORP AFFIL director: Amerada Hess Corp.
S. Donald Wiley: director B Pittsburgh, PA 1926. ED Westminster College BA (1950); University of Pennsylvania School of Law LLB (1953). NONPR AFFIL director: Weighco Inc.; trustee: Westminister College; trustee: Carnegie Mellon University.
David R. Williams: executive vice president, director B London, United Kingdom 1943. ED Exeter University BA (1964). PRIM CORP EMPL executive vice

president, director: H.J. Heinz Co. CORP AFFIL chief executive officer: StarKist Foods Inc. NONPR AFFIL member: Association Chartered Accts U.S.; member: Financial Executives Institute; member: Association Chartered Accts UK.

Foundation Officials
Tammy B. Aupperle: program director
Karyll A. Davis: trustee
Loretta M. Oken: program director
David R. Williams: trustee (see above)

Grants Analysis
Disclosure Period: calendar year ending 2001
Total Grants: $3,885,951*
Number of Grants: 146
Average Grant: $5,464
Highest Grant: $250,000
Lowest Grant: $115
Typical Range: $1,000 to $100,000
*Note: Giving excludes matching gifts, scholarship, and United Way.

Recent Grants
Note: Grants derived from 2001 Form 990.
General

485,000	United Way Allegheny County, Pittsburgh, PA -- for operating support
250,000	Hospital for Sick Children, North York, ON Canada -- in support of the SPRINKLES Research in Toronto
100,000	American Ireland Fund, San Francisco, CA -- in support of the Institute for Neuroscience at Trinity College
100,000	Carnegie Mellon University, Pittsburgh, PA -- for scholarships
100,000	Center for Environmental Science and Economics, Washington, DC -- for endowment support
100,000	Extra-Mile Education Foundation, Inc., Pittsburgh, PA -- funding to 4 inner-city parochial schools
100,000	Irish Educational Foundation, Cork Ireland -- in support of endowed research fellowship
100,000	National Underground Freedom Center, Cincinnati, OH -- for endow the Teacher Candidate's Summer Institute on Freedom
100,000	Robert Morris College, Moon Township, PA -- in support of the College's Communications Skills Program
100,000	United Way Allegheny County, Pittsburgh, PA -- funding to 4 inner-city parochial schools

HOWARD HEINZ ENDOWMENT

Giving Contact
Maxwell King, Executive Director
30 Dominion Tower
625 Liberty Avenue
Pittsburgh, PA 15222-3199
Phone: (412)281-5777
Fax: (412)281-5788
E-mail: info@heinz.org
Web: http://www.heinz.org

Description
Founded: 1941
EIN: 251721100
Organization Type: General Purpose Foundation
Giving Locations: PA: Southwest Pennsylvania, Pittsburgh
Grant Types: General Support.

Donor Information
Founder: Howard Heinz was born near Sharpsburg, a suburb of Pittsburgh, on August 27, 1877, the son of Henry John and Sarah Young Heinz. After graduation from Shady Side Academy and then Yale University in 1900, he entered active service with the H.J. Heinz Company, where he successfully became advertising manager, sales manager, vice president and president.

He was a director and/or trustee of the Pennsylvania Railroad, Mellon Bank, N.A., National Industrial Conference Board, Pittsburgh Regional Planning Association, Pittsburgh Chamber of Commerce, University of Pittsburgh, Carnegie Institute, Shady Side Academy, Western Pennsylvania Hospital and the Pittsburgh Symphony Society. He was ruling elder of the Shadyside Presbyterian Church.

Mr. Heinz died on February 9, 1941. He bequeathed his residual estate to the Howard Heinz Endowment for philanthropic purposes.

Financial Summary
Total Giving: $43,740,619 (2002); $55,398,822 (2001)
Giving Analysis: Giving for 2002 includes: foundation grants to United Way ($1,114,000)
Assets: $767,628,379 (2002 approx); $1,400,000,000 (2001)

Typical Recipients
Arts & Humanities: Arts Associations & Councils, Arts Festivals, Arts Funds, Arts Institutes, Arts Outreach, Ballet, Community Arts, Dance, Film & Video, Arts & Humanities-General, Historic Preservation, History & Archaeology, Libraries, Museums/Galleries, Music, Opera, Performing Arts, Public Broadcasting, Theater
Civic & Public Affairs: African American Affairs, Business/Free Enterprise, Clubs, Community Foundations, Economic Development, Economic Policy, Employment/Job Training, Civic & Public Affairs-General, Hispanic Affairs, Housing, Inner-City Development, Municipalities/Towns, Nonprofit Management, Philanthropic Organizations, Professional & Trade Associations, Public Policy, Urban & Community Affairs, Zoos/Aquariums
Education: Afterschool/Enrichment Programs, Business Education, Colleges & Universities, Community & Junior Colleges, Economic Education, Education Associations, Education Funds, Education Reform, Elementary Education (Private), Elementary Education (Public), Environmental Education, Faculty Development, Education-General, Health & Physical Education, International Studies, Leadership Training, Legal Education, Literacy, Medical Education, Minority Education, Preschool Education, Private Education (Precollege), Public Education (Precollege), School Volunteerism, Science/Mathematics Education, Secondary Education (Public), Social Sciences Education, Student Aid, Vocational & Technical Education
Environment: Air/Water Quality, Energy, Forestry, Environment-General, Protection, Resource Conservation, Watershed, Wildlife Protection
Health: Children's Health/Hospitals, Clinics/Medical Centers, Health Policy/Cost Containment, Health Organizations, Heart, Hospitals, Medical Rehabilitation, Medical Research, Mental Health, Nursing Services, Nutrition, Prenatal Health Issues, Preventive Medicine/Wellness Organizations, Public Health, Research/Studies Institutes
International: International Affairs, International Organizations
Religion: Churches
Science: Scientific Centers & Institutes
Social Services: At-Risk Youth, Child Abuse, Child Welfare, Community Centers, Community Service Organizations, Day Care, Domestic Violence, Family Planning, Family Services, Food/Clothing Distribution, Recreation & Athletics, Senior Services, Shelters/Homelessness, Substance Abuse, United Funds/United Ways, Volunteer Services, YMCA/YWCA/YMHA/YWHA, Youth Organizations

Application Procedures
Initial Contact: Applicants should request a copy of guidelines before sending letter of inquiry. If the proposed project meets the basic funding criteria of the grantmaking program, applicants are asked to submit a formal proposal.
Application Requirements: The letter of inquiry should be signed by the head of the applicant's organization and should address: the need for the proposed program; the nature of the program, including objectives, target population(s), and action plan; ways that the program is consistent with the endowment's strategy in this area; staff and organizational qualifications for carrying out program; how the program is distinguished from similar programs; estimated cost and amount of funding requested; and the method by which the project's effectiveness will be monitored and measured. The proposal should include: a list of the program's board of directors; the organization's budget, including projected income sources and average contribution per member for membership organizations; the organization's most recent audit and financial statement, IRS determination letter, and a line-item budget (revenues and expenses) for the proposed project.
Deadlines: None.
Review Process: The board of trustees meets twice annually to award grants. Written notification of decisions made on grants will be mailed within a few weeks of the meetings.
Notes: The Heinz Endowments has separate guideline brochures for each of the following program areas: Arts and Culture, Economic Opportunity, Education Environment and Health and Human Services. These are available in print format, or by accessing the website.

Restrictions
Individuals and for-profit organizations are not eligible for funding. Grants are awarded primarily to organizations in southwestern Pennsylvania, and exclusively for projects that benefit Pennsylvania and its residents.

Additional Information
The Howard Heinz Endowment operates jointly with the Vira I. Heinz Endowment.
A representative of Mellon Bank serves as a corporate trustee for the endowment.
Each program area is reviewed every five years; program guidelines are revised accordingly.
Publications: Annual Report; Guidelines; Newsletters; Special Report

Foundation Officials
Carol R. Brown: director ED Marquette University BA; University of Chicago MA. CORP AFFIL director: Mellon Bank; director: Mellon Financial Corp. NONPR AFFIL board of directors: Mid Atlantic Arts Foundation; board of directors: Pittsburgh Regional Alliance; board of directors: Greater Pittsburgh Convention and Visitors Bureau; board of directors: Duquesne University; board of directors: Governor's Council on Travel and Tourism; board of directors: Americans for the Arts; board of directors: Carnegie Mellon University.
Frank Vondell Cahouet: director B Cohasset, MA 1932. ED Harvard University BA (1954); University of Pennsylvania Wharton School MBA (1959). PRIM CORP EMPL chairman, president, chief executive officer, director: Mellon Bank NA. CORP AFFIL director: Teledyne Inc.; director: Saint-Gobain Corp.; director: Allegheny Technologies Inc.; director: Avery Dennison Corp. NONPR AFFIL board of directors: University Pennsylvania Wharton School; member: University Pittsburgh; member: The Pennsylvania Society; trustee: Extra Mile Foundation; trustee: Historical Society of Western Pennsylvania; trustee: Carnegie-Mellon University.

Judith Davenport: director ED Penn State University BA (1961).

Drue Heinz: director emeritus NONPR AFFIL honorary trustee: Carnegie Museums of Pittsburgh.

H. John Heinz, IV: director NONPR AFFIL owner: Buddhist High School.

Teresa Heinz: chairwoman B Maputo, Mozambique October 05, 1938. NONPR AFFIL director: Ovation Inc.; cons: UN Trusteeship; trustee: National Gallery Art; chairman environ policy: John F. Kennedy School Government; founder: National Council Families & Television; trustee emeritus: Brookings Institution; member advisory board: Earth Committee Office; co-founder, director: Alliance to End Childhood Lead Poisoning; director: American Institute for Public Service.

Howard McClintic Love: director B Pittsburgh, PA 1930. ED Colgate University (1952); Harvard University Graduate School of Business Administration (1956). NONPR AFFIL director: United Way of Allegheny County; trustee: University of Pittsburgh; director: Pittsburgh Symphony; trustee: The Carnegie. CLUB AFFIL Rolling Rock Club; Pittsburgh Golf Club; The Links Club; Masons Club; Fox Chapel Golf Club; member: Beta Theta Pi; Colony Club.

Shirley M. Malcom: director B Birmingham, AL September 06, 1946. ED Penn State University PhD; University of Washington BA (1967); University of California, Los Angeles MA (1968); Penn State University PhD (1974). PRIM NONPR EMPL head education and human resources programs: American Association for the Advancement of Science. NONPR AFFIL trustee: Morgan State University; director: National Center on Education & the Economy; trustee: California Institute of Technology; trustee: Adelphi University; director: American Museum of Natural History.

William H. Rea: director B Pittsburgh, PA 1912. ED Princeton University BA. PRIM CORP EMPL director: Colt Industries Inc. NONPR AFFIL trustee emeritus: University of Pittsburgh.

Barbara K. Robinson: director ED University of Pittsburgh MBA; Washington & Jefferson College BA. NONPR AFFIL treasurer: Staunton Farm Foundation; trustee: Washington & Jefferson University.

Barbara K. Robinson: director ED University of Pittsburgh MBA; Washington & Jefferson College BA. NONPR AFFIL treasurer: Staunton Farm Foundation; trustee: Washington & Jefferson University.

Frederick W. Thieman: director B Pittsburgh, PA July 16, 1951. ED Penn State University BA (1973); University of Pittsburgh JD (1977). NONPR AFFIL member: American College of Trial Lawyers; member: Pennsylvania Bar Assn.; member: Academy of Trial Lawyers of Allegheny County; member: Allegheny County Bar Assn..

Mallory Walker: director B Washington, DC 1939. ED University of Virginia (1958-1963). PRIM CORP EMPL president, director: Walker & Dunlop. CORP AFFIL chairman, president: Walker & Dunlop Service Corp.; president, chief executive officer: Green Park Financial LP; president, chief executive officer: Walker & Dunlop Multifamily Inc. NONPR AFFIL trustee: Phillips Collection; trustee: WETA; honorary trustee: National Building Museum; trustee: Greater Washington Board of Trade; trustee: Greater Washington Research Center; board of directors: Fannie Mae Foundation; trustee: Federal City Council.

Grants Analysis

Disclosure Period: calendar year ending 2002
Total Grants: $42,626,619*
Number of Grants: 347
Average Grant: $103,990*
Highest Grant: $3,750,000
Lowest Grant: $4,000
Typical Range: $50,000 to $200,000
*Note: Giving excludes United Way. Average grant figure excludes two highest grants ($6,750,000).

Recent Grants

Note: Grants derived from 2002 Form 990.

General

1,800,000	University of Pittsburgh, Pittsburgh, PA
1,500,000	Sports & Exhibition Authority of Pittsburgh and Allegheny County, Pittsburgh, PA -- towards implementation of green technology into the David L. Lawrence convention center expansion
1,000,000	Community Loan Fund of Southwestern Pennsylvania, Pittsburgh, PA -- towards green building loan fund
1,000,000	University of Pittsburgh, Pittsburgh, PA
1,000,000	University of Pittsburgh, Pittsburgh, PA -- assistance for artificial organ development
988,000	Sarah Heinz House Association, Pittsburgh, PA
977,000	Sarah Heinz House Association, Pittsburgh, PA
950,000	Historical Society of Western Pennsylvania, Pittsburgh, PA -- fund for the senator John Heinz regional history center
950,000	Pittsburgh Cultural Trust, Pittsburgh, PA
750,000	Sports & Exhibition Authority of Pittsburgh and Allegheny County, Pittsburgh, PA -- fund for North Shore Riverfront Park

VIRA I. HEINZ ENDOWMENT

Giving Contact

Maxwell King, President
30 Dominion Tower
625 Liberty Avenue
Pittsburgh, PA 15222-3199
Phone: (412)281-5777
Fax: (412)281-5788
E-mail: info@heinz.org
Web: http://www.heinz.org

Description

Founded: 1986
EIN: 251762825
Organization Type: General Purpose Foundation
Giving Locations: PA: Southwest Pennsylvania
Grant Types: Capital, General Support, Multiyear/Continuing Support, Operating Expenses.

Donor Information

Founder: In a city known for its active and concerned civic leaders, Vira Ingham Heinz was among the foremost. Born Vira M. Ingham in what is now the Brighton Heights district of Pittsburgh, in 1932 she married Clifford S. Heinz, son of Henry J. Heinz, founder of the food processing company.

Mrs. Heinz actively engaged in the philanthropic and civic work for which she is now remembered. She was vice president of the World Council of Christian Education and an active supporter of its works in Africa. She was a founder of the Civic Light Opera, president and principal benefactor of the Pittsburgh Youth Symphony, and a member of the boards of the Pittsburgh Chamber Music Society, the Pittsburgh Opera, and the Pittsburgh Symphony Society.

Mrs. Heinz received the Chancellor's Medal from the University of Pittsburgh and honorary degrees from eleven colleges and universities. She was a trustee of Chatham College and the first woman trustee of Carnegie Mellon University. She served as a member of College Hospital Administrators. As a member of the Board of Directors of the H.J. Heinz Company, she was the first woman board member of a multinational corporation headquartered in Pittsburgh. In the spirit of the generosity that characterized her life, Vira I. Heinz's will provided for the establishment Vira I. Heinz Endowment in 1986.

Financial Summary

Total Giving: $17,992,237 (2002); $18,506,696 (2001)
Giving Analysis: Giving for 2002 includes: foundation grants to United Way ($10,000)
Assets: $399,181,803 (2002); $468,932,556 (2001)

Typical Recipients

Arts & Humanities: Arts Associations & Councils, Arts Centers, Arts Funds, Arts Outreach, Ballet, Community Arts, Dance, Ethnic & Folk Arts, Arts & Humanities-General, Historic Preservation, History & Archaeology, Libraries, Museums/Galleries, Music, Opera, Performing Arts, Public Broadcasting, Theater, Visual Arts

Civic & Public Affairs: African American Affairs, Botanical Gardens/Parks, Business/Free Enterprise, Community Foundations, Economic Development, Economic Policy, Employment/Job Training, Civic & Public Affairs-General, Housing, Legal Aid, Municipalities/Towns, Nonprofit Management, Parades/Festivals, Philanthropic Organizations, Professional & Trade Associations, Public Policy, Urban & Community Affairs, Zoos/Aquariums

Education: Afterschool/Enrichment Programs, Arts/Humanities Education, Business Education, Business-School Partnerships, Colleges & Universities, Community & Junior Colleges, Economic Education, Education Associations, Education Funds, Education Reform, Elementary Education (Public), Engineering/Technological Education, Environmental Education, Faculty Development, Education-General, International Studies, Leadership Training, Literacy, Medical Education, Minority Education, Preschool Education, Private Education (Precollege), Public Education (Precollege), Religious Education, School Volunteerism, Science/Mathematics Education, Secondary Education (Public), Student Aid, Vocational & Technical Education

Environment: Energy, Forestry, Environment-General, Protection, Research, Resource Conservation, Watershed, Wildlife Protection

Health: Adolescent Health Issues, Cancer, Children's Health/Hospitals, Geriatric Health, Health Policy/Cost Containment, Health Organizations, Hospitals, Medical Research, Mental Health, Single-Disease Health Associations

International: Foreign Arts Organizations, Health Care/Hospitals, International Affairs, International Environmental Issues, International Organizations, Missionary/Religious Activities

Religion: Churches, Jewish Causes, Ministries, Religious Organizations, Religious Welfare, Seminaries

Science: Science-General, Scientific Centers & Institutes

Social Services: At-Risk Youth, Big Brothers/Big Sisters, Camps, Child Welfare, Community Service Organizations, Crime Prevention, Day Care, Delinquency & Criminal Rehabilitation, Domestic Violence, Emergency Relief, Family Planning, Family Services, Food/Clothing Distribution, Homes, People with Disabilities, Recreation & Athletics, Scouts, Senior Services, Sexual Abuse, Shelters/Homelessness, Social Services-General, Substance Abuse, United Funds/United Ways, Volunteer Services, YMCA/YWCA/YMHA/YWHA, Youth Organizations

Application Procedures

Initial Contact: Applicants should request a copy of the guidelines before sending a letter of inquiry. If the endowment feels the proposal merits further consideration, a full proposal will be requested.

Application Requirements: The letter of inquiry should be signed by the head of the applicant organization of its board and should address: the need for the proposed program; the objectives, target population(s), and action plan for the program; an explanation of how the program is consistent with the endowment's strategy for its area of significance; staff and organizational qualifications; how the program is distinguished from similar programs; the estimated cost and amount of funding requested; and the method by which the project's impact will be monitored and measured. The formal proposal should include: a list of the organization's board of directors; the organization's budget, including projected income sources, and average contribution per member for membership organizations; a recent financial statement and an independent auditor's report thereof; a letter from the IRS confirming tax exempt public charity status; and a line-item budget (revenues and expenses) for the proposed project. Proposal materials should not be included with the initial letter of inquiry.

Deadlines: None.

Review Process: The trustees meet twice annually to award grants. Written notification of decisions made on grants will be mailed within a few weeks of meeting.

Notes: Letters of inquiry will be presented to the Howard Heinz Endowment as well as the Vira I Heinz Endowment. There is no need for organizations to submit applications to each endowment separately.

Restrictions

Individuals and for-profit organizations are not eligible for funding.

Grants are awarded primarily to organizations in Southwestern Pennsylvania and exclusively for projects that benefit Pennsylvania and its residents.

Additional Information

The Vira I Heinz Endowment operates jointly with the Howard Heinz Endowment.

A representative of Mellon Bank serves as a corporate trustee for the endowment.

Publications: Annual Report

Corporate Officials

Konrad M. Weis: chairman, director B Leipzig, Germany 1928. ED University of Bonn PhD (1955). PRIM CORP EMPL chairman, director: AGFA Division Miles. CORP AFFIL director: Titan Pharmaceuticals; board of directors: Visible Genetics Inc.; board of directors: Demegen Inc.; director: PNC Equity Management Corp.; director: Michael Baker Corp. NONPR AFFIL life trustee: The Carnegie Institute; life trustee: Carnegie-Mellon University.

Foundation Officials

Franco Harris: director B Fort Dix, NJ March 07, 1950. ED Penn State University. NONPR AFFIL member: ProFootball Hall of Fame.

Andre T. Heinz: director ED Yale University School of Forestry MA.

Teresa Heinz: director B Maputo, Mozambique October 05, 1938. NONPR AFFIL director: Ovation Inc.; cons: UN Trusteeship; trustee: National Gallery Art; chairman environ policy: John F. Kennedy School Government; founder: National Council Families & Television; trustee emeritus: Brookings Institution; member advisory board: Earth Committee Office; cofounder, director: Alliance to End Childhood Lead Poisoning; director: American Institute for Public Service.

Wendy Jacobus McKenzie: director

William H. Rea: director B Pittsburgh, PA 1912. ED Princeton University BA. PRIM CORP EMPL director: Colt Industries Inc. NONPR AFFIL trustee emeritus: University of Pittsburgh.

Barbara K. Robinson: director ED University of Pittsburgh MBA; Washington & Jefferson College BA. NONPR AFFIL treasurer: Staunton Farm Foundation; trustee: Washington & Jefferson University.

James Mellon Walton: chairman B Pittsburgh, PA 1930. ED Yale University BA (1953); Harvard University MBA (1958). PRIM CORP EMPL vice chairman, director: MMC Group Inc. NONPR AFFIL member sponsoring comm: Pennsylvania Southwest Association; director: World Affairs Council Pittsburgh; director: One Hundred Friends Pittsburgh Art; member: Cultural District Development Committee; director: Irish Investment Fund Inc.; life trustee: Carnegie Library; trustee emeritus: Carnegie-Mellon University;

treasurer: Carnegie Hero Fund Commission; life trustee, president emeritus: Carnegie Institute.

Konrad M. Weis: director (see above)

S. Donald Wiley: trustee CORP AFFIL director: Weighco Inc. NONPR AFFIL trustee: Carnegie Mellon University; trustee: Westminister College.

Grants Analysis

Disclosure Period: calendar year ending 2002
Total Grants: $17,982,237*
Number of Grants: 203
Average Grant: $72,411*
Highest Grant: $1,500,000
Lowest Grant: $500
Typical Range: $20,000 to $150,000
***Note:** Giving excludes United Way. Average grant figure excludes three highest grants ($3,500,000)

Recent Grants

Note: Grants derived from 2002 Form 990.
General

1,500,000	Sports & Exhibition Authority of Pittsburgh and Allegheny County, Pittsburgh, PA
1,000,000	3 Rivers Connect, Pittsburgh, PA -- toward technology-based initiative to improve children's early success as readers
1,000,000	University of Pittsburgh, Pittsburgh, PA -- toward university initiatives in international studies, environmental studies and school improvement
500,000	Local Initiatives Support Corporation, Pittsburgh, PA
450,000	Community Loan Fund of Southwestern Pennsylvania, Pittsburgh, PA
400,000	Pittsburgh Life Sciences Greenhouse, Pittsburgh, PA
400,000	Pittsburgh Regional Alliance, Pittsburgh, PA -- toward an international business attraction and a new employee recruitment
300,000	Pittsburgh Opera Inc., Pittsburgh, PA
300,000	Riverlife Task Force, Pittsburgh, PA
250,000	Carnegie Institute, Pittsburgh, PA

HEINZ FAMILY FOUNDATION

Giving Contact

Teresa Heinz, Chairperson & Chief Executive Officer
32 Dominion Tower
625 Liberty Avenue
Pittsburgh, PA 15222
Phone: (412)497-5775

Description

Founded: 1984
EIN: 251689382
Organization Type: Private Foundation
Giving Locations: PA: some giving nationally.
Grant Types: Fellowship, General Support, Matching.

Donor Information

Founder: Teresa and H. John Heinz III Charitable Trust

Financial Summary

Total Giving: $5,510,876 (2001)
Giving Analysis: Giving for 2001 includes: foundation grants to United Way ($1,000)
Assets: $69,007,621 (2001)
Gifts Received: $7,063,955 (2000); $6,663,955 (1998); $6,663,955 (1996). Note: Contributions were received from Teresa and H. John Heinz III Charitable Trust, H. John Heinz III Charitable and Family Trust and the Howard Heinz Endowment.

Typical Recipients

Arts & Humanities: Community Arts, Dance, Film & Video, Arts & Humanities-General, History & Archaeology, Libraries, Museums/Galleries, Music, Performing Arts, Public Broadcasting

Civic & Public Affairs: Botanical Gardens/Parks, Business/Free Enterprise, Economic Development, Economic Policy, Employment/Job Training, Civic & Public Affairs-General, Municipalities/Towns, Philanthropic Organizations, Professional & Trade Associations, Public Policy, Safety, Women's Affairs

Education: Arts/Humanities Education, Business Education, Colleges & Universities, Engineering/Technological Education, Environmental Education, Faculty Development, Education-General, Gifted & Talented Programs, International Exchange, International Studies, Literacy, Medical Education, Minority Education, Private Education (Precollege), Science/Mathematics Education, Social Sciences Education

Environment: Energy, Environment-General, Resource Conservation, Wildlife Protection

Health: AIDS/HIV, Cancer, Children's Health/Hospitals, Clinics/Medical Centers, Health Policy/Cost Containment, Medical Rehabilitation, Medical Research, Prenatal Health Issues, Public Health, Research/Studies Institutes

International: Foreign Educational Institutions, Human Rights, International Affairs, International Environmental Issues, International Relations, International Relief Efforts

Religion: Jewish Causes, Religious Welfare

Science: Scientific Centers & Institutes

Social Services: At-Risk Youth, Child Welfare, Family Services, Recreation & Athletics, United Funds/United Ways

Application Procedures

Initial Contact: The foundation has no formal grant application procedure or application form. Send a brief letter of inquiry.

Application Requirements: Include a description of organization, type and amount of funding, budget information, and proof of tax-exempt status.

Deadlines: None.

Foundation Officials

Rose Gibson: assistant secretary
Andre Heinz: director
Jack E. Kime: chief financial officer
Jeffrey R. Lewis: executive director, chief operating officer
Wendy Jacobus Mackenzie: secretary
Joan D. McCauley: director
John R. Taylor: investment officer

Grants Analysis

Disclosure Period: calendar year ending 2001
Total Grants: $5,509,876*
Number of Grants: 135
Average Grant: $40,814
Highest Grant: $1,000,000
Lowest Grant: $100
Typical Range: $500 to $250,000 and $100 to $100,000
***Note:** Excludes one grant from United Way $1,000.00

Recent Grants

Note: Grants derived from 2001 Form 990.
General

1,000,000	Nantucket Historical Association, Nantucket, MA -- for campaign for the Island of Nantucket Fund
500,000	H. John Heinz III Center for Science, Economics, and Environment, Washington, DC -- for operating support
250,000	Foundation for Cognitive Therapy and Research, Bala Cynwyd, PA -- for the human condition
200,000	Pennsylvania Public School Health Care Trust, Hermitage, PA -- operating support

150,000	National Gallery of Art, Washington, DC -- educational endowment
150,000	Pennsylvania Public School Health Care Trust, Hermitage, PA -- operating support
125,000	Pennsylvania Public School Health Care Trust, Hermitage, PA -- operating support
100,000	American Computer Museum, Bozeman, MT -- for technology, the economy and employment
100,000	Carnegie Mellon University, Pittsburgh, PA -- for endowment purposes
74,300	United Negro College Fund, Fairfax, VA -- for environmental fellows program

DRUE HEINZ TRUST

Giving Contact
Julia V. Shea, Foundation Manager
c/o Drue Heinz Office
PO Box 68
FDR Station
New York, NY 10150
Phone: (212)371-5757
Fax: (212)759-0479

Description
Founded: 1954
EIN: 256018930
Organization Type: General Purpose Foundation
Giving Locations: NY: New York; United Kingdom
Grant Types: Award, General Support, Multiyear/Continuing Support, Project.

Financial Summary
Total Giving: $962,665 (2003); $2,322,696 (2001)
Assets: $34,136,337 (2003); $34,708,794 (2001)
Gifts Received: $3,836 (1995); $1,686,244 (1994); $88,537 (1993)

Typical Recipients
Arts & Humanities: Arts Appreciation, Arts Associations & Councils, Arts Centers, Arts Funds, Arts Institutes, Arts Outreach, Ballet, Community Arts, Dance, Film & Video, Arts & Humanities-General, Historic Preservation, History & Archaeology, Libraries, Literary Arts, Museums/Galleries, Music, Opera, Performing Arts, Public Broadcasting, Theater, Visual Arts
Civic & Public Affairs: African American Affairs, Botanical Gardens/Parks, Ethnic Organizations, Civic & Public Affairs-General, Law & Justice, Philanthropic Organizations, Professional & Trade Associations, Public Policy, Urban & Community Affairs, Women's Affairs, Zoos/Aquariums
Education: Afterschool/Enrichment Programs, Arts/Humanities Education, Colleges & Universities, Continuing Education, Education Reform, Elementary Education (Private), Education-General, International Studies, Literacy, Medical Education, Private Education (Precollege), Social Sciences Education, Student Aid
Environment: Air/Water Quality, Environment-General, Wildlife Protection
Health: AIDS/HIV, Cancer, Children's Health/Hospitals, Clinics/Medical Centers, Emergency/Ambulance Services, Eyes/Blindness, Geriatric Health, Hospitals, Medical Rehabilitation, Medical Research, Single-Disease Health Associations
International: Foreign Arts Organizations, Foreign Educational Institutions, International-General, Health Care/Hospitals, Human Rights, International Affairs, International Environmental Issues, International Organizations, International Peace & Security Issues, International Relations, Missionary/Religious Activities
Religion: Churches, Religious Organizations
Science: Scientific Centers & Institutes
Social Services: Animal Protection, Child Welfare, Community Service Organizations, Emergency Relief, Family Planning, People with Disabilities, Scouts, Shelters/Homelessness, United Funds/United Ways, YMCA/YWCA/YMHA/YWHA, Youth Organizations

Application Procedures
Initial Contact: All requests should be submitted by letter.

Restrictions
The foundation generally limits funding to the London, England, and New York City geographic areas.

Additional Information
Trust(s): Mellon Bank NA

Foundation Officials
James F. Dolan: trustee
Drue Heinz: trustee NONPR AFFIL honorary trustee: Carnegie Museums of Pittsburgh.

Grants Analysis
Disclosure Period: calendar year ending 2003
Total Grants: $962,665
Number of Grants: 40
Average Grant: $19,621*
Highest Grant: $197,440
Lowest Grant: $500
Typical Range: $5,000 to $50,000
*****Note:** Average grant figure excludes highest grant.

Recent Grants
Note: Grants derived from 2003 Form 990.
General

197,440	American Academy in Rome, New York, NY
150,000	Royal Shakespeare Company of America Inc.
84,000	Paris Review Foundation, New York, NY
80,000	Butrint Foundation, London United Kingdom
70,000	Royal Oak Foundation, New York, NY
50,000	Burlington Magazine, London United Kingdom
47,500	Metropolitan Museum of Art, New York, NY
45,000	CAF America, Alexandria, VA
30,000	Pittsburgh Symphony Society, Pittsburgh, PA
25,000	International Crisis Group, Brussels Belgium

EVAN AND MARION HELFAER FOUNDATION

Giving Contact
Thomas L. Smallwood, Trustee
735 North Water Street
Milwaukee, WI 53202
Phone: (414)287-7184
Fax: (414)276-0172

Description
Founded: 1971
EIN: 396238856
Organization Type: General Purpose Foundation
Giving Locations: WI: Milwaukee
Grant Types: Capital, General Support, Professorship, Research.

Donor Information
Founder: Established in 1971 by the late Evan P. Helfaer.

Financial Summary
Total Giving: $792,100 (fiscal year ending July 31, 2003); $948,760 (fiscal 2001)
Giving Analysis: Giving for fiscal 2003 includes: foundation grants to United Way ($15,000)
Assets: $22,700,770 (fiscal 2003); $26,851,186 (fiscal 2001)

Typical Recipients
Arts & Humanities: Arts Centers, Arts Festivals, Community Arts, Dance, Historic Preservation, Libraries, Museums/Galleries, Music, Opera, Performing Arts, Theater
Civic & Public Affairs: Botanical Gardens/Parks, Business/Free Enterprise, Civil Rights, Employment/Job Training, Civic & Public Affairs-General, Hispanic Affairs, Municipalities/Towns, Parades/Festivals, Urban & Community Affairs, Zoos/Aquariums
Education: Arts/Humanities Education, Business Education, Colleges & Universities, Education Funds, Engineering/Technological Education, Faculty Development, Health & Physical Education, Leadership Training, Medical Education, Private Education (Precollege), Public Education (Precollege), Secondary Education (Private), Secondary Education (Public), Student Aid
Environment: Environment-General
Health: Cancer, Children's Health/Hospitals, Clinics/Medical Centers, Geriatric Health, Health Funds, Health Organizations, Heart, Hospitals, Medical Research, Mental Health, Nursing Services, Public Health, Research/Studies Institutes, Single-Disease Health Associations, Transplant Networks/Donor Banks
International: Foreign Arts Organizations, Health Care/Hospitals, Trade
Religion: Churches, Jewish Causes, Religious Organizations, Religious Welfare
Social Services: Animal Protection, Big Brothers/Big Sisters, Child Abuse, Child Welfare, Community Centers, Community Service Organizations, Counseling, Family Services, Food/Clothing Distribution, Homes, People with Disabilities, Recreation & Athletics, Scouts, Senior Services, Shelters/Homelessness, Social Services-General, Substance Abuse, United Funds/United Ways, YMCA/YWCA/YMHA/YWHA, Youth Organizations

Application Procedures
Initial Contact: Organizations should request the foundation's application form.
Deadlines: None.

Restrictions
Grants are not made to individuals. or to organizations outside Wisconsin.

Foundation Officials
Thomas L. Smallwood: trustee

Grants Analysis
Disclosure Period: fiscal year ending July 31, 2003
Total Grants: $777,100*
Number of Grants: 102
Average Grant: $6,704*
Highest Grant: $100,000
Lowest Grant: $100
Typical Range: $1,000 to $10,000
*****Note:** Giving excludes United Way. Average grant figure excludes highest grant.

Recent Grants
Note: Grants derived from 2002 Form 990.
Library-Related

10,000	Milwaukee Public Library, Milwaukee, WI

General

100,000	Marquette University, Milwaukee, WI
25,000	Great Circus Parade, Milwaukee, WI
20,000	Boys & Girls Clubs of Greater Milwaukee, Milwaukee, WI
20,000	Janeway Children's Hospital Foundation, St. John's, NL Canada
20,000	Marquette University, Milwaukee, WI
20,000	Milwaukee Public Museum, Milwaukee, WI

17,500	United Performing Arts Fund, Milwaukee, WI
15,000	United Way of Greater Milwaukee, Milwaukee, WI
13,000	Marquette University, Milwaukee, WI
10,000	Blood Center Research Foundation, Milwaukee, WI

CLARENCE E. HELLER CHARITABLE FOUNDATION

Giving Contact
Bruce A. Hirsch, Executive Director
1 Lombard St., Suite 305
San Francisco, CA 94111
Phone: (415)989-9839
Fax: (415)989-1909

Description
Founded: 1982
EIN: 942814266
Organization Type: Private Foundation
Giving Locations: CA
Grant Types: General Support, Research, Scholarship, Seed Money.

Donor Information
Founder: the late Clarence E. Heller

Financial Summary
Total Giving: $1,676,604 (2003)
Assets: $44,794,190 (2003)
Gifts Received: $4,024,706 (1994); $6,596,349 (1993)

Typical Recipients
Arts & Humanities: Arts Centers, Arts Outreach, History & Archaeology, Libraries, Music, Theater
Civic & Public Affairs: Community Foundations, Employment/Job Training, Legal Aid, Nonprofit Management, Public Policy, Rural Affairs
Education: Agricultural Education, Arts/Humanities Education, Colleges & Universities, Education Funds, Elementary Education (Public), Environmental Education, Faculty Development, Literacy, Private Education (Precollege), Public Education (Precollege), School Volunteerism, Science/Mathematics Education, Student Aid
Environment: Energy, Forestry, Environment-General, Protection, Research, Resource Conservation
Health: AIDS/HIV, Health Organizations, Medical Research, Public Health, Research/Studies Institutes
International: International Development, International Environmental Issues, International Organizations, International Relations, Trade
Science: Scientific Organizations, Scientific Research
Social Services: Shelters/Homelessness, Youth Organizations

Application Procedures
Initial Contact: Send a brief letter of inquiry.
Application Requirements: Include project description, amount requested, both project and annual budgets, and a description of organization. Foundation will request a full proposal.
Deadlines: None; the board meets three times each year.

Foundation Officials
Peter B. Harckham: vice president, trustee
Katherine Heller: trustee
Miranda Heller: president, trustee
Bruce A. Hirsch: executive director

Grants Analysis
Disclosure Period: calendar year ending 2003
Total Grants: $1,676,604
Number of Grants: 59
Average Grant: $22,261*
Highest Grant: $200,000
Typical Range: $10,000 to $50,000
***Note:** Average grant figure excludes three highest grants ($430,000).

Recent Grants
Note: Grants derived from 2003 Form 990.
General

200,000	Trust for Conservation Innovation, San Francisco, CA -- to support the roots for change fund
130,000	Pesticide Action Network, San Francisco, CA -- for the environmental health program
100,000	Environmental Defense, New York, NY -- to support the project entitled "strategic advancement of policies to reduce toxic chemical pollution"
51,351	Stanford University, Stanford, CA -- to support "understanding and communicating the practices of equitable mathematics teaching" project
50,000	Center for Health and the Global Environment, Boston, CA -- to support its report on biodiversity and human health and its education programs for top policy makers
50,000	University of California Berkeley Foundation, Berkeley, CA -- to support the establishment of teacher cluster groups in urban bay area schools
50,000	Youth Service California, Oakland, CA -- to support professional development in service learning methods for classroom teachers
45,000	Crossroads School, Santa Monica, CA -- in support of the Elizabeth Mandell music institute
45,000	University of Santa Barbara, Santa Barbara, CA -- to support projects in Oxnard schools
35,000	Prevention Institute, Oakland, CA -- to support the project - Building bridges linking public health and the sustainable agriculture movement

HELMERICH FOUNDATION

Giving Contact
Walter H. Helmerich, III, Trustee
1437 S. Boulder
Tulsa, OK 74114
Phone: (918)742-5531

Description
Founded: 1965
EIN: 736105607
Organization Type: Family Foundation
Giving Locations: OK: Tulsa
Grant Types: Capital, Endowment, General Support, Scholarship.

Donor Information
Founder: Established in 1965 by the late W.H. Helmerich.

Financial Summary
Total Giving: $3,897,500 (fiscal year ending September 30, 2003); $4,418,000 (fiscal 2002); $4,535,000 (fiscal 2001). Note: Fiscal 1997 Giving includes scholarship ($65,000).
Giving Analysis: Giving for fiscal 2001 includes: foundation scholarships ($25,000)
Assets: $74,462,683 (fiscal 2003); $67,844,728 (fiscal 2002); $81,527,787 (fiscal 2001)

Typical Recipients
Arts & Humanities: Arts Centers, Ballet, Historic Preservation, History & Archaeology, Libraries, Literary Arts, Museums/Galleries, Music, Opera, Performing Arts
Civic & Public Affairs: African American Affairs, Botanical Gardens/Parks, Clubs, Community Foundations, Civic & Public Affairs-General, Housing, Municipalities/Towns, Parades/Festivals, Public Policy, Safety, Urban & Community Affairs, Women's Affairs, Zoos/Aquariums
Education: Business Education, Colleges & Universities, Education Funds, Education Reform, Elementary Education (Public), Education-General, International Studies, Literacy, Preschool Education, Private Education (Precollege), Public Education (Precollege), Religious Education, School Volunteerism, Science/Mathematics Education, Secondary Education (Private), Student Aid
Environment: Environment-General, Wildlife Protection
Health: Adolescent Health Issues, AIDS/HIV, Cancer, Children's Health/Hospitals, Clinics/Medical Centers, Diabetes, Emergency/Ambulance Services, Eyes/Blindness, Health Organizations, Hospices, Mental Health, Nursing Services, Preventive Medicine/Wellness Organizations, Public Health, Respiratory
International: Foreign Educational Institutions
Religion: Bible Study/Translation, Ministries, Religious Organizations, Religious Welfare, Seminaries
Social Services: Camps, Child Abuse, Child Welfare, Community Service Organizations, Crime Prevention, Day Care, Domestic Violence, Emergency Relief, Family Services, Food/Clothing Distribution, Homes, People with Disabilities, Recreation & Athletics, Scouts, Senior Services, Shelters/Homelessness, Social Services-General, YMCA/YWCA/YMHA/YWHA, Youth Organizations

Application Procedures
Initial Contact: The foundation does not publish an official grant application form. Applicants should send request letters directly to the foundation.
Deadlines: None.

Restrictions
Grants are limited to the Tulsa, OK, area and will focus primarily on large capital needs. The foundation does not make grants to individuals, matching gifts, fellowships, emergency funds, deficit financing, research, operating budgets, demonstration projects, conferences, publications, or loans.

Additional Information
Publications: Application Guidelines; Program Policy Statement

Foundation Officials
Walter Hugo Helmerich, III: trustee B Tulsa, OK 1921. ED University of Oklahoma BA (1948); Harvard University MBA (1950). PRIM CORP EMPL chairman, director: Helmerich & Payne Inc. ADD CORP EMPL chairman: Helmerich & Payne International Drilling; chairman: Helmerich & Payne Columbia Drilling Co.; chairman: Helmerich & Payne Trinidad Drilling; chairman: Helmerich & Payne de Venezuela. CORP AFFIL director: Atwood Oceanics Inc.

Grants Analysis
Disclosure Period: fiscal year ending September 30, 2003
Total Grants: $3,897,500
Number of Grants: 62
Average Grant: $35,792*
Highest Grant: $1,000,000
Lowest Grant: $5,000
Typical Range: $20,000 to $100,000

*Note: Average grant figure excludes two highest grants ($1,750,000).

Recent Grants

Note: Grants derived from fiscal 2003 Form 990.
General

1,000,000	Philbrook Museum of Art, Tulsa, OK
750,000	Hillcrest Medical Center (HMC), Tulsa, OK -- fund for women's health center
250,000	Tulsa Day Center for the Homeless, Tulsa, OK -- endowment fund
250,000	University of Oklahoma Foundation Inc., Norman, OK -- memorial stadium fund
200,000	Monte Cassino Elementary School, Tulsa, OK -- fund for building campaign/renovations
125,000	Wright Christian Academy, Tulsa, OK -- fund for new building
100,000	Oklahoma Centennial Commemoration Fund Inc., Oklahoma City, OK -- fund for capitol dome
100,000	Oral Roberts University, Tulsa, OK -- fund for sim lab units
100,000	Philbrook Museum of Art, Tulsa, OK -- fund for exhibition
100,000	Retina Research Foundation (RRF), Houston, TX -- fund for retina center

HENDERSON FOUNDATION

Giving Contact

Ernest Henderson, III, Trustee
PO Box 420
Sudbury, MA 01776
Phone: (978)449-4646

Description

Founded: 1947
EIN: 046051095
Organization Type: Private Foundation
Giving Locations: MA
Grant Types: General Support, Multiyear/Continuing Support.

Donor Information

Founder: the late Ernest Henderson, the late George B. Henderson, the late J. Brooks Fenno, Ernest Henderson III

Financial Summary

Total Giving: $758,950 (2003)
Assets: $9,198,770 (2003)

Typical Recipients

Arts & Humanities: Ballet, Dance, Historic Preservation, History & Archaeology, Libraries, Literary Arts, Music, Public Broadcasting
Civic & Public Affairs: Botanical Gardens/Parks, Clubs, Civic & Public Affairs-General, Housing, Public Policy
Education: Business Education, Colleges & Universities, Economic Education, Education Funds, Education-General, Preschool Education, Private Education (Precollege), Student Aid
Health: Health-General, Health Organizations, Hospitals, Medical Research, Nursing Services, Research/Studies Institutes
International: Foreign Arts Organizations, International Peace & Security Issues, International Relations
Religion: Religious Welfare, Synagogues/Temples
Social Services: Child Welfare, Community Centers, Family Planning, Scouts, Shelters/Homelessness, Substance Abuse, United Funds/United Ways, Volunteer Services, Youth Organizations

Application Procedures

Initial Contact: Send a brief letter of inquiry.
Application Requirements: Include purpose of funds sought and proof of tax-exempt status.
Deadlines: None.

Restrictions

Does not support individuals or provide funds for scholarships or fellowships.

Foundation Officials

Barclay G. S. Henderson: trustee
Ernest Henderson, III: trustee B Boston, MA 1924. ED Harvard University SB (1944); Harvard University MBA (1949). PRIM CORP EMPL president, chief executive officer: Fidelity Product Corp. CORP AFFIL president: Henderson Houses Am; director: Boston Biotechnology Corp. NONPR AFFIL president: Sudbury Nursing Home; director: Wellesley Community Center; member: Chief Executives Organization; treasurer, director: Boston Biomedical Research Institute.
Joseph Carlton Petrone, Jr.: trustee

Grants Analysis

Disclosure Period: calendar year ending 2003
Total Grants: $758,950
Number of Grants: 78
Average Grant: $6,547*
Highest Grant: $70,000
Lowest Grant: $1,000
Typical Range: $1,000 to $15,000
*Note: Average grant figure excludes five highest grants ($281,000).

Recent Grants

Note: Grants derived from 2003 Form 990.
General

70,000	Healthy U of Delmarva, Salisbury, MD
61,000	National Center on Family Homelessness, Newton, MA
50,000	Bard College, Annandale-on-Hudson, NY
50,000	Boston Biomedical Institute, Watertown, MA
50,000	New England Genealogical Society, Boston, MA
40,000	Northeastern University, Boston, MA
33,000	Newton Wellesley Hospital, Newton, MA
30,000	Friends of Longfellow House, Cambridge, MA
25,000	Hauptman-Woodward Medical Research Institute, Buffalo, NY
25,000	WGBH Educational Foundation, Boston, MA

GEORGE B. HENDERSON FOUNDATION

Giving Contact

Brenda Taylor
c/o Palmer & Dodge LLP
111 Huntington Avenue
Boston, MA 02199
Phone: (617)239-0556

Description

Founded: 1964
EIN: 046089310
Organization Type: Private Foundation
Giving Locations: MA: Boston
Grant Types: Capital, General Support.

Donor Information

Founder: the late George B. Henderson

Financial Summary

Total Giving: $667,503 (2001)
Assets: $11,681,901 (2001)

Typical Recipients

Arts & Humanities: Arts Associations & Councils, Arts Centers, Historic Preservation, History & Archaeology, Libraries, Museums/Galleries, Music, Public Broadcasting, Theater, Visual Arts
Civic & Public Affairs: African American Affairs, Botanical Gardens/Parks, Clubs, Economic Development, Civic & Public Affairs-General, Housing, Municipalities/Towns, Urban & Community Affairs, Women's Affairs, Zoos/Aquariums
Education: Colleges & Universities, Education Funds, Education-General, Secondary Education (Private)
Environment: Environment-General, Resource Conservation
Health: Clinics/Medical Centers, Health Organizations
Religion: Churches
Social Services: Community Centers, Community Service Organizations, Recreation & Athletics, Veterans, Youth Organizations

Application Procedures

Initial Contact: Send letter requesting application form.
Deadlines: None. Applicants are usually notified within three months.

Restrictions

Does not support individuals, endowment funds, or operating expenses. Grants solely for enhancement of physical appearance of Boston city.

Additional Information

Publications: Application Form

Foundation Officials

Thomas B. Adams: mem
Valerie Burns: secretary board designators
Robert Cormier: ex-officio member NONPR AFFIL member: Boston Art Commission.
Margaret DePopolo: mem
Henry Rice Guild, Jr.: trustee B Boston, MA 1928. ED Harvard University (1950-1953). PRIM CORP EMPL president: Guild Monrad & Oates. CORP AFFIL director: Tampa Electric Co.; director: TECO Energy Inc.
Pauline Chase Harrell: mem
Ernest Henderson, III: trustee B Boston, MA 1924. ED Harvard University SB (1944); Harvard University MBA (1949). PRIM CORP EMPL president, chief executive officer: Fidelity Product Corp. CORP AFFIL president: Henderson Houses Am; director: Boston Biotechnology Corp. NONPR AFFIL president: Sudbury Nursing Home; director: Wellesley Community Center; member: Chief Executives Organization; treasurer, director: Boston Biomedical Research Institute.
Gerald C. Henderson: trustee
John K. Herbert, III: trustee
Carol R. Johnson: chairman
Jane C. Nylander: ex-officio mem

Grants Analysis

Disclosure Period: calendar year ending 2001
Total Grants: $667,503
Number of Grants: 18
Average Grant: $24,589*
Highest Grant: $125,000
Typical Range: $10,000 to $50,000
*Note: Average grant figure excludes two highest grants ($225,000).

Recent Grants

Note: Grants derived from 2001 Form 990.

General

125,000	Allston Congregational Church, Boston, MA
100,000	Massachusetts Audubon Society, Boston, MA
65,580	Light Boston, Inc., Boston, MA
64,000	Historic Boston, Inc., Boston, MA
57,800	Union United Methodist Church, Boston, MA
50,000	Shirley Eustis House, Shirley, MA
34,600	Women's Educational and Industrial Union, Boston, MA
31,037	Christ Episcopal Church, Hyde Park, MA
29,875	Gibson House Museum, Boston, MA
18,811	Concord Square Association, Concord, MA

HENKEL CORP.

Company Headquarters

2200 Renaissance Boulevard, Suite 200
King of Prussia, PA 19406
Phone: (610)270-8100
Fax: (610)270-8104
Web: http://www.henkelcorp.com

Company Description

Employees: 3,315
SIC(s): 2819 Industrial Inorganic Chemicals Nec, 2821 Plastics Materials & Resins, 2899 Chemical Preparations Nec, 5169 Chemicals & Allied Products Nec.

Operating Locations

Emery Group Henkel Corp. (CA--Los Angeles); Henkel Adhesives Corp. (CA--Hayward); Henkel Chemical Specialities Division (PA--Ambler); Henkel Corp. (PA--Gulph Mills); Henkel Corp. Chemicals Group (OH--Cincinnati); Henkel Corp. Fine Chemicals Division (PA--Gulph Mills); Henkel Corp. Functional Products Division (IL--La Grange); Henkel Corp. Minerals Industry Division (AZ--Tucson); Henkel Corp. Polymers Division (IL--La Grange); Henkel Corp. Process Chemicals (GA--Cedartown); Henkel Corp. Textile Chemicals (NC--Charlotte); Henkel Organic Products Division (PA--Ambler); Henkel Surface Technologies (WI--Madison Heights)

Subsidiary Companies

CT: Henkel Loctite, Rocky Hill

Giving Contact

William B. Read, Vice President, Human Resources Services
The Triad, Suite 200
2200 Renaissance Blvd.
King of Prussia, PA 19406
Phone: (610)270-8100
Fax: (610)270-8102
E-mail: bill.read@henkel-americas.com
Web: http://www.henkelcorp.com

Description

Organization Type: Corporate Giving Program
Giving Locations: headquarters and operating communities.
Grant Types: General Support.

Typical Recipients

Arts & Humanities: Arts Centers, Dance, Historic Preservation, Libraries, Museums/Galleries, Music, Public Broadcasting, Theater
Civic & Public Affairs: Business/Free Enterprise, Civil Rights, Law & Justice, Municipalities/Towns, Safety, Women's Affairs, Zoos/Aquariums
Education: Colleges & Universities
Health: Hospitals

International: International Relations
Social Services: United Funds/United Ways

Application Procedures

Initial Contact: Send a brief letter of inquiry and a full proposal. Include a description of organization, amount and purpose of funds sought, and proof of tax-exempt status.

Restrictions

Program does not support political or religious organizations. Member agencies of united funds also will not be considered. Henkel Corp. divisions in Arizona, Illinois, Michigan, North Caroline, New Jersey, and Pennsylvania have independent giving programs.

Corporate Officials

John E. Knudson, Jr.: vice president, chief financial officer PRIM CORP EMPL vice president, chief financial officer: Henkel Corp.
Robert Lurcott: president, chief executive officer PRIM CORP EMPL president, chief executive officer: Henkel Corp.
Hans Dietrich Winkhaus: chairman, director PRIM CORP EMPL chairman, director: Henkel Corp.

Grants Analysis

Typical Range: $2,500 to $5,000

KEITH HENNEY TRUST

Giving Contact

Lenora Hurley, Trust Officer
PO Box 2
Eaton Center, NH 03832
Phone: (401)438-1810

Description

Founded: 1992
EIN: 026065480
Organization Type: Private Foundation
Grant Types: General Support, Scholarship.

Financial Summary

Total Giving: $20,436 (2003); $27,065 (2001)
Giving Analysis: Giving for 2003 includes: foundation scholarships ($5,000); 2001: foundation scholarships ($15,315)
Assets: $605,139 (2003); $619,543 (2001)
Gifts Received: $250 (2001); $233 (1992). Note: In 2001, contributions were received from Christopher Burns.

Typical Recipients

Arts & Humanities: Arts & Humanities-General, Historic Preservation, History & Archaeology, Libraries
Civic & Public Affairs: Municipalities/Towns, Urban & Community Affairs
Education: Colleges & Universities
Religion: Churches

Application Procedures

Initial Contact: Request application procedures.
Deadlines: April 10.

Additional Information

Provides scholarships to graduates of Kennett High School in Eaton, NH.
Trust(s): Fleet National Bank

Grants Analysis

Disclosure Period: calendar year ending 2003
Total Grants: $15,436*
Number of Grants: 5
Highest Grant: $8,500
*Note: Giving excludes scholarship.

Recent Grants

Note: Grants derived from 2000 Form 990.
Library-Related
7,601	Conway Public Library

General
2,500	Sandwich Historical Society
2,000	Freedom Historical Society
750	Colby College, Waterville, ME
750	Dartmouth College, Hanover, NH
750	University of New Hampshire, Durham, NH
694	Conway Historical Society
500	The Brownfield Historical Society
500	University of Maine Orono, Orono, ME
500	University of Maryland/Baltimore County, Baltimore, MD
500	University of South Carolina, Columbia, SC

RICHARD A. HENSON FOUNDATION

Giving Contact

Donna Ashby, Executive Director
PO Box 151
Salisbury, MD 21803
Phone: (410)742-7057
Fax: (410)742-4036

Description

Founded: 1989
EIN: 521642558
Organization Type: Private Foundation
Giving Locations: MD: Eastern Shore area, Salisbury
Grant Types: Capital, General Support, Operating Expenses, Project.

Donor Information

Founder: Richard A. Henson

Financial Summary

Total Giving: $213,603 (2001)
Giving Analysis: Giving for 2001 includes: foundation grants to United Way ($1,000)
Assets: $8,459,248 (2001)
Gifts Received: $868,332 (2001); $226,000 (2000); $1,164,162 (1999). Note: In 1998, 1999, 2000 and 2001, contributions were received from Richard A. Henson.

Typical Recipients

Arts & Humanities: Libraries, Museums/Galleries
Civic & Public Affairs: Botanical Gardens/Parks, Chambers of Commerce, Community Foundations, Civic & Public Affairs-General, Housing, Municipalities/Towns, Parades/Festivals, Professional & Trade Associations, Public Policy, Safety, Urban & Community Affairs, Zoos/Aquariums
Education: Business Education, Colleges & Universities, Community & Junior Colleges, Preschool Education, Private Education (Precollege), Public Education (Precollege), Science/Mathematics Education
Health: Alzheimer's Disease, Arthritis, Cancer, Children's Health/Hospitals, Clinics/Medical Centers, Health Organizations, Hospices, Hospitals
Religion: Churches, Religious Welfare
Social Services: Child Welfare, Community Service Organizations, Domestic Violence, Recreation & Athletics, Scouts, Shelters/Homelessness, Social Services-General, Substance Abuse, United Funds/United Ways, YMCA/YWCA/YMHA/YWHA, Youth Organizations

Application Procedures

Initial Contact: Send a brief letter of inquiry.
Application Requirements: Include a summary of

scope and acts.
Deadlines: None.

Foundation Officials

Thomas H. Evans: trustee
Gordon D. Gladden: trustee
Richard A. Henson: chairman, trustee
C. Brooks Hubbert: treasurer, trustee
Thomas F. McCarthy: chairman, trustee
Jon Sherwell: trustee
Thomas L. Trice, IV: treasurer, trustee

Grants Analysis

Disclosure Period: calendar year ending 2001
Total Grants: $212,603*
Number of Grants: 24
Average Grant: $2,775*
Highest Grant: $56,000
Lowest Grant: $250
Typical Range: $1,000 to $20,000
*Note: Giving excludes United Way. Average grant excludes three highest grants ($146,000).

Recent Grants

Note: Grants derived from 2001 Form 990.
General

56,000	Boy Scouts of America
56,000	Salisbury State University Foundation, Salisbury, MD
38,000	Dorchester County YMCA, Boston, MA
20,000	West Salisbury Youth Club, Salisbury, MD
19,000	University of Maryland Eastern Shore Foundation, Princess Office, MD
5,000	Life Crisis Center, Salisbury, MD
5,000	Salisbury Neighborhood Housing Services, Salisbury, MD
3,853	Junior Achievement of the Eastern Shore, Salisbury, MD
3,000	Salisbury Substance Abuse, Salisbury, MD
2,000	Christian Shelter, Inc., Salisbury, MD

BOB L. HERD FOUNDATION

Giving Contact

Janice Thompson, Secretary & Treasurer
3901 Manhattan
Tyler, TX 75701
Phone: (903)509-3456

Description

Founded: 1994
EIN: 752530305
Organization Type: Private Foundation
Giving Locations: TX: Tyler
Grant Types: General Support.

Donor Information

Founder: Established in 1994 by Bob L. Herd.

Financial Summary

Total Giving: $228,875 (2003)
Giving Analysis: Giving for 2003 includes: foundation grants to United Way ($26,000)
Assets: $10,008,127 (2003)
Gifts Received: $2,026,080 (2003); $4,106,149 (2000); $1,000,000 (1998). Note: In 1998, 2000, and 2003, contributions were received from Bob L. Herd.

Typical Recipients

Arts & Humanities: Libraries, Museums/Galleries, Music
Civic & Public Affairs: Clubs, Economic Policy, Civic & Public Affairs-General, Housing
Education: Business Education, Colleges & Univer-

sities, Community & Junior Colleges, Engineering/ Technological Education, Medical Education, Private Education (Precollege), Public Education (Precollege), Secondary Education (Public), Student Aid
Health: Cancer, Health-General, Heart, Hospices, Hospitals (University Affiliated), Respiratory, Single-Disease Health Associations
International: Health Care/Hospitals
Religion: Churches, Religion-General, Religious Welfare
Social Services: Camps, Child Welfare, Community Centers, Community Service Organizations, Counseling, Crime Prevention, Domestic Violence, Family Services, Food/Clothing Distribution, Recreation & Athletics, Substance Abuse, United Funds/United Ways, Youth Organizations

Application Procedures

Initial Contact: The foundation requests applications be made in writing. Include proof of tax-exempt status.
Deadlines: None.

Foundation Officials

Bob L. Herd: president
Patsy L. Herd: vice president
Janice Thompson: secretary, treasurer

Grants Analysis

Disclosure Period: calendar year ending 2003
Total Grants: $202,875*
Number of Grants: 50
Average Grant: $3,407*
Highest Grant: $35,940
Lowest Grant: $200
Typical Range: $1,000 to $5,000
*Note: Giving excludes United Way. Average grant figure excludes highest grant.

Recent Grants

Note: Grants derived from 2001 Form 990.
General

101,000	Good Shepherd Episcopal, Dallas, TX
50,000	Texas State History Museum Foundation, Austin, TX
15,000	Marvin Methodist Church, Tyler, TX
15,000	United Way of Tyler/Smith County, Tyler, TX
10,000	American Cancer Society, Tyler, TX
10,000	Junior League of Tyler, Inc., Tyler, TX
10,000	PATH, Tyler, TX
6,300	Azleway Boys Ranch, Tyler, TX
5,000	American Heart Association, Tyler, TX
5,000	Habitat for Humanity, Tyler, TX

GROVER HERMANN FOUNDATION

Giving Contact

Katheryn V. Rhoads, Executive Director
1000 Hillgrove, Suite 200
Western Springs, IL 60558
Phone: (708)246-8331
Fax: (708)246-8319

Alternate Contact

PO Box 596
Pebble Beach, CA 93953
Note: Organizations in Monterey County, CA should use the alternate address.

Description

Founded: 1955
EIN: 366064489
Organization Type: Family Foundation
Giving Locations: IL: Chicago
Grant Types: Capital, Challenge, Endowment, Fel-

lowship, General Support, Project, Research, Scholarship.

Donor Information

Founder: The Grover Hermann Foundation was established in 1955. Its donors are Grover Hermann and Sarah T. Hermann.

Financial Summary

Total Giving: $871,000 (2001)
Assets: $13,953,283 (2001)
Gifts Received: $11,027,026 (1998). Note: In 1998, contributions were received from the Estate of Sarah T. Hermann ($6,302,612); Trust A U/W Grover M. Hermann ($4,284,986); Harriet Thurmond CRAT U/W Sarah T. Hermann ($245,744); Harriet Thurmond CRAT U/W Grover Hermann ($112,627); and Ruth Pooley West CRAT ($81,057).

Typical Recipients

Arts & Humanities: Arts Institutes, Ballet, Historic Preservation, Libraries, Museums/Galleries, Music, Performing Arts, Public Broadcasting, Theater
Civic & Public Affairs: Community Foundations, Economic Policy, Employment/Job Training, Civic & Public Affairs-General, Hispanic Affairs, Law & Justice, Legal Aid, Nonprofit Management, Philanthropic Organizations, Professional & Trade Associations, Public Policy, Women's Affairs, Zoos/Aquariums
Education: Afterschool/Enrichment Programs, Arts/ Humanities Education, Colleges & Universities, Continuing Education, Education Associations, Education Funds, Education Reform, Engineering/ Technological Education, Faculty Development, Education-General, Health & Physical Education, Journalism/Media Education, Legal Education, Literacy, Medical Education, Minority Education, Preschool Education, Private Education (Precollege), Social Sciences Education, Special Education, Student Aid
Environment: Environment-General, Research
Health: AIDS/HIV, Children's Health/Hospitals, Emergency/Ambulance Services, Health-General, Health Policy/Cost Containment, Health Organizations, Hospices, Hospitals, Long-Term Care, Medical Rehabilitation, Medical Research, Mental Health, Nursing Services, Preventive Medicine/Wellness Organizations, Single-Disease Health Associations, Speech & Hearing
International: Health Care/Hospitals, International Affairs, International Organizations, International Relations
Religion: Ministries, Religious Organizations, Religious Welfare
Social Services: Animal Protection, At-Risk Youth, Child Abuse, Child Welfare, Community Centers, Community Service Organizations, Domestic Violence, Emergency Relief, Family Services, Food/ Clothing Distribution, People with Disabilities, Senior Services, Shelters/Homelessness, Social Services-General, Youth Organizations

Application Procedures

Initial Contact: Organizations should submit a brief letter to the foundation. Telephone inquiries are not considered. The foundation has no formal application form.
Application Requirements: Requests for funds should provide, in triplicate, a concise description of the proposed project or other use for requested funds; a brief history of the organization, identity of board members and their affiliations; specific objectives to be accomplished; background and qualifications of the organization and the individuals involved; the methods by which the organization will evaluate the results of the proposed project; a budget, including amount requested; latest audited financial statement; and a copy of the organization's most recent evidence of its federal tax-exempt status, accompanied by a separate representation that no change in that status has occurred or is currently anticipated since it was issued. Also include a listing of major grants from corporate and foundation contributors

during the past twelve months. The foundation discourages submission of extraneous materials such as brochures, marketing materials, and newspaper or magazine clippings or booklets containing the same.
Deadlines: None.
Review Process: The foundation's board normally meets in March, June, September, and December. Responses normally will be received from several weeks to two or three months following application.

Restrictions

The foundation will not provide funds for individuals, non-exempt organizations, general operating expenses, fraternal organizations, foreign organizations, athletic organizations, other private foundations, or political entities. Grantmaking confined to greater Chicago area.

Foundation Officials

John Hayes: director, secretary
Katheryn V. Rhoads: executive director
Paul Kelly Rhoads: president, director B La Grange, IL 1940. ED Washington & Lee University BA (1962); Loyola University JD (1967). PRIM CORP EMPL partner: Schiff Hardin & Waite. CORP AFFIL director: McKay Enterprises; director: Glen Ellyn III; director: Haymarsh Corp. NONPR AFFIL director: Philanthropy Roundtable; member: Union League; member: Illinois State Bar Association; member: Chicago Bar Association. CLUB AFFIL Salt Creek Club; Manistee Golf Club & Country Club; Portage Lake Yacht Club.

Grants Analysis

Disclosure Period: calendar year ending 2001
Total Grants: $871,000
Number of Grants: 45
Average Grant: $9,791*
Highest Grant: $250,000
Lowest Grant: $1,000
Typical Range: $5,000 to $20,000
*Note: Average grant figure excludes two highest grants ($450,000).

Recent Grants

Note: Grants derived from 2002 Form 990.
General

250,000	Community Foundation for Monterey County, Monterey, CA -- for Hermann foundation fund
200,000	Heritage Foundation, Washington, DC -- for fellow in federal budgetary affairs
45,000	Intercollegiate Studies Institute, Wilmington, DE -- for honors fellowships and student self-reliance project
30,000	Salt Creek Ballet, Westmont, IL -- for 2002-2003 performance season
25,000	Alice Lloyd College, Pippa Passes, KY -- for need-based scholarships
25,000	Cato Institute, Washington, DC -- for fiscal policies studies center
20,000	Reason Foundation, Los Angeles, CA -- for education and child welfare program
15,000	Capital Research Center, Washington, DC -- for foundation watch newsletter
15,000	Interplast Inc., Mountain View, CA -- for visiting educator program
12,000	Daniel Murphy Scholarship Foundation, Chicago, IL -- for need-based scholarships

HERRICK FOUNDATION

Giving Contact

Kenneth G. Herrick, Chairman, President, Treasurer, & Trustee
150 W. Jefferson Ave., Suite 2500
Detroit, MI 48226
Phone: (313)496-7585

Description

Founded: 1949
EIN: 386041517
Organization Type: Family Foundation
Giving Locations: MI: Primarily Michigan, occasionally Washington, D.C., Indiana, Mississippi, Ohio, Tennessee, Oklahoma and Wisconsin
Grant Types: Capital, Emergency, Endowment, Fellowship, General Support, Matching, Multiyear/Continuing Support, Operating Expenses, Professorship, Research, Scholarship, Seed Money.

Donor Information

Founder: Established in 1949 by the late Ray Wesley Herrick and his wife, the late Hazel M. Herrick. In the early days of the automotive industry in Detroit, Mr. Herrick was in charge of production for the Ford Motor Company. In the early 1930s, he moved to Tecumseh, MI, where he founded and became chairman of the board of directors of the predecessor of the Tecumseh Products Company. Through the Herrick Foundation, he helped build Adrian College in Michigan and the Howe (Indiana) Military Academy. He also gave the city of Holland, MI, a public library now bearing his name. A majority of the foundation's assets consist of shares in the Tecumseh Products Company.

Financial Summary

Total Giving: $10,119,070 (fiscal year ending September 30, 2003); $11,335,255 (fiscal 2002); $11,384,885 (fiscal 2001)
Giving Analysis: Giving for fiscal 2003 includes: foundation grants to United Way ($65,000); foundation scholarships ($100,000); fiscal 2002: foundation grants to United Way ($38,000); foundation scholarships ($95,000); fiscal 2001: foundation scholarships ($130,000); foundation grants to United Way ($135,000)
Assets: $179,502,473 (fiscal 2003); $176,698,569 (fiscal 2002); $209,098,025 (fiscal 2001)

Typical Recipients

Arts & Humanities: Arts Centers, Arts Funds, Arts & Humanities-General, Historic Preservation, History & Archaeology, Libraries, Museums/Galleries, Music, Opera, Performing Arts, Public Broadcasting, Theater
Civic & Public Affairs: Botanical Gardens/Parks, Civil Rights, Clubs, Community Foundations, Economic Development, Economic Policy, Civic & Public Affairs-General, Housing, Municipalities/Towns, Native American Affairs, Philanthropic Organizations, Public Policy, Safety, Urban & Community Affairs, Zoos/Aquariums
Education: Arts/Humanities Education, Business Education, Colleges & Universities, Community & Junior Colleges, Economic Education, Education Associations, Education Funds, Education Reform, Elementary Education (Private), Elementary Education (Public), Engineering/Technological Education, Faculty Development, Education-General, Health & Physical Education, Medical Education, Preschool Education, Private Education (Precollege), Public Education (Precollege), Religious Education, Science/Mathematics Education, Secondary Education (Private), Secondary Education (Public), Student Aid, Vocational & Technical Education
Environment: Resource Conservation
Health: Alzheimer's Disease, Cancer, Children's Health/Hospitals, Clinics/Medical Centers, Diabetes, Emergency/Ambulance Services, Health-General, Health Funds, Health Organizations, Heart, Hospices, Hospitals, Hospitals (University Affiliated), Kidney, Long-Term Care, Medical Research, Nursing Services, Preventive Medicine/Wellness Organizations, Single-Disease Health Associations, Speech & Hearing
International: Health Care/Hospitals, Missionary/Religious Activities
Religion: Churches, Ministries, Religious Organizations, Religious Welfare
Social Services: Animal Protection, At-Risk Youth, Big Brothers/Big Sisters, Child Welfare, Community Service Organizations, Crime Prevention, Delinquency & Criminal Rehabilitation, Emergency Relief, Family Services, Food/Clothing Distribution, Homes, People with Disabilities, Recreation & Athletics, Scouts, Senior Services, Special Olympics, Substance Abuse, United Funds/United Ways, YMCA/YWCA/YMHA/YWHA, Youth Organizations

Application Procedures

Initial Contact: The foundation has no formal application requirements and procedures. Prospective grantees should send the foundation a letter of request.
Application Requirements: The letter should include the amount requested, the goal to be accomplished, methods to be used, plans for evaluation, copy of the most current IRS 501(c)(3) tax-exempt ruling, name of the person to contact who will be administering the program, other organizations contributing to the project, specify name of organization and amount of contributions, and any other information that would aid the board of trustees in making their decision.
Deadlines: None.
Notes: The foundation prefers that applications be brief and to the point.

Restrictions

No grants for use outside the U.S.

Foundation Officials

Kenneth G. Herrick: chairman, trustee, president, treasurer
Todd W. Herrick: vice president, trustee
Michael A. Indenbaum: secretary, trustee

Grants Analysis

Disclosure Period: fiscal year ending September 30, 2003
Total Grants: $9,954,070*
Number of Grants: 262
Average Grant: $32,641*
Highest Grant: $500,000
Lowest Grant: $500
Typical Range: $10,000 to $100,000
*Note: Giving excludes United Way and scholarships. Average grant figure excludes three highest grants ($1,500,000).

Recent Grants

Note: Grants derived from fiscal 2003 Form 990.
General

500,000	Heritage Foundation, Washington, DC -- funding for program costs
500,000	Tecumseh Civic Auditorium, Tecumseh, MI -- funding for operating expenses
500,000	University of Notre Name, Notre Dame, IN -- toward Business School Research Grant Programs
250,000	Boysville of Michigan Inc., Clinton, MI -- toward renovation of campus infrastructure
250,000	Eastern Michigan University Foundation, Ypsilanti, MI -- funding for graduate student fellowship
250,000	Spring Arbor University, Spring Arbor, MI -- funding for new academic building to the campus
210,000	Herrick Memorial Hospital, Tecumseh, MI -- toward purchase of CCU monitors and portable x-ray units
200,000	Central American Ministries, Toledo, OH -- funding for endowment to further its programs
200,000	Michigan State University School of Music, East Lansing, MI -- funding for construction of new school building

200,000	Redeemer Lutheran Church, Jackson, MI -- funding for air-conditioning and sound-proofing of activity center

HERSHEY FAMILY FOUNDATION

Giving Contact
Barry J. Hershey, Trustee
1 International Place
Boston, MA 02110
Phone: (617)428-3414
Web: http://fdncenter.org/grantmaker/hershey

Description
Founded: 1988
EIN: 341574366
Organization Type: Private Foundation
Grant Types: General Support.

Donor Information
Founder: Barry J. Hershey

Financial Summary
Total Giving: $888,150 (2004)
Giving Analysis: Giving for 2004 includes: foundation grants to United Way ($2,500)
Assets: $57,121,097 (2003)
Gifts Received: $36,235,950 (1996); $26,000 (1995); $602,000 (1994). Note: In 1996, contributions were received from Barry J. Hershey ($35,771,200) and Walden Woods Film Co. ($464,750).

Typical Recipients
Arts & Humanities: Arts Associations & Councils, Ballet, Film & Video, Arts & Humanities-General, Historic Preservation, Libraries, Literary Arts, Museums/Galleries, Music, Theater
Civic & Public Affairs: Botanical Gardens/Parks, Civic & Public Affairs-General, Housing, Urban & Community Affairs, Women's Affairs
Education: Arts/Humanities Education, Colleges & Universities, Continuing Education, Education Associations, Education Funds, Medical Education, Private Education (Precollege), Public Education (Precollege), Religious Education, Science/Mathematics Education, Student Aid
Environment: Resource Conservation
Health: Children's Health/Hospitals, Clinics/Medical Centers, Health Organizations, Hospitals
International: Foreign Arts Organizations, International-General, Human Rights, International Development, International Organizations, International Peace & Security Issues
Religion: Jewish Causes, Religious Organizations, Religious Welfare
Social Services: Child Welfare, Community Service Organizations, Food/Clothing Distribution

Application Procedures
Initial Contact: The foundation has no formal grant application procedure or application form.
Deadlines: None.

Grants Analysis
Disclosure Period: calendar year ending 2000
Total Grants: $885,650*
Number of Grants: 37
Average Grant: $18,050*
Highest Grant: $130,000
Typical Range: $10,000 to $30,000
*Note: Giving excludes United Way. Average grant figure excludes four highest grants ($290,000).

Recent Grants
Note: Grants derived from 2003 Form 990.
General

665,000	Partners in Health, Boston, MA
200,000	Beth Israel Deaconess Medical Center, Boston, MA
140,000	Shechen Inc., New York, NY
125,000	Hunger Project, New York, NY
108,461	Expenditure Responsibility Grant
100,000	America's Second Harvest, Chicago, IL
100,000	Hershey Montessori School, Concord Township, OH
100,000	Oxfam-American Inc., Boston, MA
80,000	University of Washington School of Nursing, Seattle, WA
70,000	American Repertory Theatre, Cambridge, MA

HERSHEY FOODS CORP.

Company Headquarters
Hershey, PA
Web: http://www.hersheys.com

Company Description
Founded: 1894
Ticker: HSY
Exchange: NYSE
Revenue: US$4.429 billion (2004)
Profit: US$590.9 million (2004)
Employees: 13700 (2003)
Fortune Rank: 436, per FORTUNE Magazine's list of 500 Largest U.S. Corporations (2004).
SIC(s): 2064 Candy & Other Confectionery Products, 2066 Chocolate & Cocoa Products, 2098 Macaroni & Spaghetti.

Operating Locations
Hershey Foods Corp. (CA--Fresno, Oakdale; CT--Naugatuck; KY--Louisville; NE--Omaha; NM--Farmington; PA--Hazleton, Lebanon, Reading; VA--Stuarts Draft, Winchester)

Nonmonetary Support
Type: Cause-related Marketing & Promotion; Donated Products; Loaned Executives
Contact: Harold Miller, Senior Account Representative, Customer Service
Note: Loaned executives are for United Way only.

Giving Contact
Jennifer Goss, Corporate Contributions Representative
100 Crystal A Dr.
PO Box 810
Hershey, PA 17033-0810
Phone: (717)534-7880
Fax: (717)534-7015
E-mail: jgoss@hersheys.com
Web: html

Description
Organization Type: Corporate Giving Program
Giving Locations: limited to manufacturing site communities.
Grant Types: Capital, Employee Matching Gifts, Endowment, General Support, Operating Expenses, Project, Research.
Note: Employee matching gift ratio: 2 to 1 to colleges only.

Financial Summary
Total Giving: Contributes through corporate direct giving program only.
Assets: $4,400,000,000 (2005 approx); $4,400,000,000 (2004)
Gifts Received: $2,400,000 (1993)

Typical Recipients
Arts & Humanities: Arts Associations & Councils, Libraries, Museums/Galleries, Theater
Civic & Public Affairs: Business/Free Enterprise, Community Foundations, Economic Development, Employment/Job Training, Civic & Public Affairs-General
Education: Colleges & Universities, Community & Junior Colleges, Economic Education, Engineering/Technological Education, Literacy, Science/Mathematics Education
Environment: Resource Conservation
Health: Clinics/Medical Centers, Hospitals, Nutrition
Science: Scientific Centers & Institutes, Scientific Organizations
Social Services: Community Service Organizations, Food/Clothing Distribution, People with Disabilities, Substance Abuse, United Funds/United Ways, Volunteer Services

Application Procedures
Initial Contact: Submit a written proposal.
Application Requirements: Requests for under $5,000 should provide a description of organization and its purpose; proof of tax-exempt status; list of organization's key management and board of directors; recently audited financial statement; amount requested; brief description and proposed timeline of the project for which funding is requested; list of other funding sources and support amounts for this project (including cash, in-kind, and volunteer services); and a list of Hershey Foods Corp. employees who currently volunteer for your organization.
Requests for $5,000 and over should complete the Common Funding Application Form, available on the company's web site.
Deadlines: None; decisions generally made monthly; 60-day lead time needed.
Notes: Organizations outside the Harrisburg, PA metropolitan area should direct requests for funding to the local management of the Hershey Foods facility in their geographic area.
Organizations in the Harrisburg, PA metropolitan area, national organizations and statewide organizations should direct funding requests to the Corporate Contributions Department.

Restrictions
Does not support individuals; fraternal, veterans, or labor organizations; churches or religious organizations, including seminaries, bible colleges, and theological institutions; political contributions; organizations outside the immediate areas of Hershey Foods' manufacturing facilities, except for national and statewide organizations whose programs complement Hershey Foods' priorities; member agencies of the United Way of the Capital Region, Central Pennsylvania (Cumberland, Dauphin and Perry counties), and United Way of Lebanon County, Pennsylvania; affiliate organizations of the Allied Arts Fund in Central Pennsylvania; or organizations without 501(c)(3) nonprofit, tax exempt status.

Additional Information
The Hershey Fund is defunct; giving is now done at the discretion of the corporation.
Publications: Biennial Report

Corporate Officials
William F. Christ: executive vice president, chief operating officer PRIM CORP EMPL executive vice president, chief operating officer: Hershey Foods Corp.
Richard H. Lenny: president, chief executive officer B 1951. ED Georgia State University; Northwestern University. PRIM CORP EMPL president, chief executive officer: Hershey Foods Corp.
Kenneth L. Wolfe: chairman, director B February 15, 1939. ED Yale University BA (1961); University of Pennsylvania MBA (1967). PRIM CORP EMPL chairman, director: Hershey Foods Corp. CORP AFFIL chairman: Henry Heide Inc.; director: Hershey Trust Co.; director: Bausch & Lomb Inc.; director: Carpenter Technology Corp.

Grants Analysis

Disclosure Period: calendar year ending 1995
Total Grants: $2,358,534
Number of Grants: 250
Average Grant: $9,434
Highest Grant: $125,000
Lowest Grant: $1,000
Typical Range: $5,000 to $20,000

HERSHEY FOUNDATION

Giving Contact

Debra H. Guren, President
10229 Prouty Rd.
Painesville, OH 44077
Phone: (202)682-4780
Web: http://fdncenter.org/grantmaker/hershey/

Description

Founded: 1986
EIN: 341525626
Organization Type: Private Foundation
Giving Locations: OH: Northeastern Ohio
Grant Types: Capital, Project.

Donor Information

Founder: Jo Hershey Selden

Financial Summary

Total Giving: $818,000 (2001)
Assets: $16,762,673 (2001)
Gifts Received: $1,803,125 (1996); $214,375 (1994); $152,500 (1992). Note: In 1996, contributions were received from Debra H. Guren ($1,450,000) and Carole Walters ($353,125).

Typical Recipients

Arts & Humanities: Arts Centers, Arts Outreach, Ballet, Historic Preservation, History & Archaeology, Libraries, Museums/Galleries, Music, Opera, Performing Arts, Public Broadcasting, Theater, Visual Arts
Civic & Public Affairs: Botanical Gardens/Parks, Economic Development, Civic & Public Affairs-General, Nonprofit Management, Urban & Community Affairs, Women's Affairs, Zoos/Aquariums
Education: Arts/Humanities Education, Colleges & Universities, Community & Junior Colleges, Education Reform, Elementary Education (Private), Education-General, Leadership Training, Literacy, Minority Education, Preschool Education, Private Education (Precollege), Public Education (Precollege), Science/Mathematics Education, Special Education
Environment: Environment-General
Health: Emergency/Ambulance Services
Religion: Jewish Causes
Science: Science Museums, Scientific Centers & Institutes
Social Services: Animal Protection, Big Brothers/Big Sisters, Child Welfare, Community Service Organizations, Crime Prevention, Day Care, Family Planning, Family Services, People with Disabilities, Recreation & Athletics, Social Services-General, YMCA/YWCA/YMHA/YWHA, Youth Organizations

Application Procedures

Initial Contact: Send a brief letter of inquiry and a full proposal.
Application Requirements: Include a description of organization, amount requested, purpose of funds sought, recently audited financial statement, proof of tax-exempt status, and other funding sources.
Deadlines: None.

Restrictions

The foundation does not support individuals, religious organizations for sectarian purposes, political or lob-

bying groups, or organizations outside operating areas.

Foundation Officials

Georgia A. Froelich: treasurer
Debra S. Guren: president
Loren W. Hershey: chairman
Carole H. Walters: vice president

Grants Analysis

Disclosure Period: calendar year ending 2001
Total Grants: $818,000
Number of Grants: 38
Average Grant: $16,789*
Highest Grant: $100,000
Typical Range: $5,000 to $40,000
*Note: Average grant excludes two highest grants ($180,000).

Recent Grants

Note: Grants derived from 2001 Form 990.
General

100,000	Cleveland Botanical Garden, Cleveland, OH -- Hershey Children's Garden
80,000	Hershey Montesorri School, Concord Township, OH -- capital and farm school
63,000	Montessori Development Partnerships, Cleveland, OH -- project support and farm project
50,000	Hiram House, Chagrin Falls, OH -- capital campaign for facilities
30,000	Cuyahoga Valley Scenic Railroad, Peninsula, OH -- for curriculum revision project
30,000	Parkworks, Cleveland, OH -- for Green School Environmental Education Program
26,000	WVIZ, Cleveland, OH -- for WVIZ/PBS Kids
25,000	Boys and Girls Clubs of Cleveland, Cleveland, OH -- capital campaign for Broadway Club facility
25,000	Cuyahoga County Board of Commissioners, Cleveland, OH -- for Early Childhood Initiative
25,000	Geauga Humane Society, Novelty, OH -- for Rescue Village Capital Campaign

ALBERT AND ETHEL HERZSTEIN CHARITABLE FOUNDATION

Giving Contact

L. Michael Hajtman, President
Albert and Ethel Herzstein Charitable Foundation
6131 Westview Dr.
Houston, TX 77055
Phone: (713)681-7868
Fax: (713)681-3652
E-mail: albertandethel@herzsteinfoundation.org
Web: http://www.herzsteinfoundation.org

Description

Founded: 1965
EIN: 746070484
Organization Type: Family Foundation
Giving Locations: TX: Houston some giving nationally
Grant Types: Capital, Emergency, Endowment, General Support, Multiyear/Continuing Support, Research, Scholarship, Seed Money.

Donor Information

Founder: The foundation was established in 1965 by the Herzstein family. The estate of Ms. Sadie R. Smith, Mr. Herzstein's sister, contributed to the foundation in 1985.

Financial Summary

Total Giving: $2,811,865 (2003); $3,192,141 (2002); $3,197,000 (2001 approx)
Giving Analysis: Giving for 2003 includes: foundation scholarships ($77,000); 2002: foundation grants to United Way ($10,000); foundation matching gifts ($10,000); foundation scholarships ($161,000)
Assets: $65,567,379 (2003); $60,129,207 (2002); $69,231,000 (2001)
Gifts Received: $2,286,131 (2000); $383,570 (1998); $71,390 (1995). Note: Contributions were received from the Albert Herzstein Estate.

Typical Recipients

Arts & Humanities: Arts Associations & Councils, Arts Festivals, Arts Funds, Ballet, Historic Preservation, History & Archaeology, Libraries, Museums/Galleries, Music, Opera, Performing Arts, Public Broadcasting, Theater
Civic & Public Affairs: African American Affairs, Botanical Gardens/Parks, Chambers of Commerce, Clubs, Community Foundations, Economic Development, Economic Policy, Employment/Job Training, Ethnic Organizations, Civic & Public Affairs-General, Hispanic Affairs, Municipalities/Towns, Nonprofit Management, Parades/Festivals, Philanthropic Organizations, Public Policy, Urban & Community Affairs, Women's Affairs, Zoos/Aquariums
Education: Afterschool/Enrichment Programs, Business Education, Colleges & Universities, Education Funds, Education Reform, Faculty Development, Education-General, Medical Education, Private Education (Precollege), Public Education (Precollege), Secondary Education (Private), Secondary Education (Public), Special Education, Student Aid, Vocational & Technical Education
Environment: Energy, Environment-General, Resource Conservation, Wildlife Protection
Health: Adolescent Health Issues, AIDS/HIV, Alzheimer's Disease, Cancer, Children's Health/Hospitals, Clinics/Medical Centers, Diabetes, Emergency/Ambulance Services, Eyes/Blindness, Health-General, Health Organizations, Heart, Hospitals, Medical Research, Mental Health, Multiple Sclerosis, Prenatal Health Issues, Respiratory, Single-Disease Health Associations
International: Health Care/Hospitals, International Organizations, Missionary/Religious Activities
Religion: Churches, Dioceses, Religion-General, Jewish Causes, Ministries, Religious Organizations, Religious Welfare, Social/Policy Issues, Synagogues/Temples
Science: Science Museums, Scientific Centers & Institutes
Social Services: Animal Protection, Camps, Child Welfare, Community Centers, Community Service Organizations, Crime Prevention, Delinquency & Criminal Rehabilitation, Emergency Relief, Food/Clothing Distribution, People with Disabilities, Recreation & Athletics, Scouts, Senior Services, Shelters/Homelessness, Social Services-General, Special Olympics, Substance Abuse, United Funds/United Ways, Veterans, YMCA/YWCA/YMHA/YWHA, Youth Organizations

Application Procedures

Initial Contact: Applicants should send a written request.
Application Requirements: Include a brief description of the history and mission, and achievements of the organization; names of present officers and board members; IRS determination letter documenting tax-exempt status; and financial statements (preferably audited) and IRS Form 990 for most recent fiscal year. Also include information on the proposed project, including need for the program and population it will serve; goals and objectives for the program and timetable for their accomplishment; overall project cost and specific amount requested; project budget (revenue and expense); sources and amounts being solicited and/or received or pledged; and future fund-

ing plans, if the project is new and continuing. for which funding is sought and the amount of funding requested of the foundation; and a separate sheet showing the project budget, including projected revenue and expenses. The statement should further discuss how the project will continue to operate after the foundation's funding ceases. Also include names of present officers and board members, IRS determination letter, audited financial statements, Form 990 of the most recent fiscal year, and list of officers and board members.

Deadlines: None.

Notes: Organizations submitting proposals should limit their request to no more than one (1) in any twelve (12) month period. Lobbying of the individual directors by grant applications may result in the adverse consideration of grant application.

Restrictions

Grants are made only to nonprofit organizations that are tax exempt under sections 501(c)(3) or 170(c) of the Internal Revenue Code. Grants are not made to individuals. or provide loans.

Additional Information

Publications: Foundation brochure

Foundation Officials

L. Michael Hajtman: president
Richard J. Loewenstern: chairman, director
Emil Nakfoor: advisory director
George W. Strake, Jr.: director B Houston, TX 1935. ED University of Notre Dame AB (1957); Harvard University MBA (1961). PRIM CORP EMPL chairman, chief executive officer, founder: Strake Trading Group Inc. CORP AFFIL principal: GW Strake Co. NONPR AFFIL director: Texas Independent Producers & Royalty Board; advisory council: University Notre Dame College Arts and Sciences; director: Task Force Public Education; director: Boy Scouts America; director: Interstate Oil Compact Commission.
Nathan H. Topek, MD: director

Grants Analysis

Disclosure Period: calendar year ending 2003
Total Grants: $2,734,865*
Number of Grants: 150
Average Grant: $11,384*
Highest Grant: $550,000
Lowest Grant: $500
Typical Range: $1,000 to $20,000
*Note: Giving excludes scholarships. Average grant figure excludes two highest grants ($1,050,000).

Recent Grants

Note: Grants derived from 2003 Form 990.
General

550,000	William Marsh Rice University, Houston, TX -- for operating and maintenance endowment for the physics building
500,000	New Houston Jewish Community School Campus, Houston, TX -- for the construction of the educational campus and facilities
200,000	Jewish Community Center of Houston, Houston, TX -- to develop a family retreat center
100,000	Alley Theater, Houston, TX
100,000	University of St. Thomas, Houston, TX -- for renovation of the enrollment center
50,000	Baylor College of Medicine, Houston, TX -- for comprehensive care of patients
50,000	Center, Houston, TX -- to relocate the facilities
50,000	Hadassah Medical Relief Association Inc., New York, NY -- to support the hematology day care room
50,000	Jewish Federation of Greater Houston, Houston, TX -- for support of the Jewish chaplaincy program
50,000	Junior Achievement Inc., Houston, TX

BERNARD K. AND NORMA F. HEUERMANN FOUNDATION

Giving Contact

John B. Atkins, Treasurer & Director
c/o Wells Fargo Bank Nebraska
Private Client Services
10010 Regency Circle
Suite 300
Omaha, NE 68114

Alternate Contact

Charles L. Whitney, Secretary & Director
c/o Law Offices
Professional Building
PO Box 228
Aurora, NE 68818
Phone: (402)536-2470

Description

Founded: 1991
EIN: 470748466
Organization Type: Private Foundation
Giving Locations: NE
Grant Types: Capital, General Support, Project, Scholarship.

Donor Information

Founder: Bernard K. Heuermann, Norma F. Heuermann

Financial Summary

Total Giving: $559,692 (fiscal year ending July 31, 2002); $423,784 (fiscal 2001)
Giving Analysis: Giving for fiscal 2002 includes: foundation scholarships ($22,462)
Assets: $8,889,404 (fiscal 2002); $10,945,255 (fiscal 2001)
Gifts Received: $2,000,000 (fiscal 2001); $1,000 (fiscal 2000); $450,103 (fiscal 1998). Note: In fiscal 2001, contributions were received from Bernard K. and Norma F. Heuermann. In fiscal 1998, contributions were received from B. K. Heuermann.

Typical Recipients

Arts & Humanities: History & Archaeology, Libraries, Museums/Galleries, Public Broadcasting
Civic & Public Affairs: Chambers of Commerce, Clubs, Community Foundations, Economic Development, Civic & Public Affairs-General
Education: Agricultural Education, Colleges & Universities, Education-General, Private Education (Precollege), Science/Mathematics Education, Student Aid
Health: Alzheimer's Disease, Cancer, Children's Health/Hospitals, Hospitals, Public Health
Religion: Churches
Social Services: Child Welfare, Community Centers, Homes, People with Disabilities, Senior Services, Youth Organizations

Application Procedures

Initial Contact: Submit a proposal (limited to two pages). The foundation requests an original proposal and two copies.
Application Requirements: Identify a special need or project to which funds will be applied, including the objectives to be obtained, people or groups who will benefit, a timetable for achieving objectives, and other means of support. Include proof of tax-exempt status. Supporting documents such as a project budget, other resources and names of supporters, and background information about the organization may be attached to the proposal.
Deadlines: None.
Decision Notification: The trustees meet at least three times per year to review grant requests. All grant applicants are notified of the foundation's deci-

sion after the request has been reviewed.
Notes: Stapled proposals are preferred to bound ones.

Restrictions

The foundation does not support individuals, nor does it provide loans.

Additional Information

Publications: Grant Guidelines
Trust(s): Wells Fargo Bank NE NA

Foundation Officials

John B. Atkins: treasurer, director
Bernard K. Heuermann: president, director
Norma F. Heuermann: vice president, director
Charles L. Whitney: atty, secretary, director

Grants Analysis

Disclosure Period: fiscal year ending July 31, 2002
Total Grants: $537,230*
Number of Grants: 67
Average Grant: $8,018
Highest Grant: $41,420
Lowest Grant: $250
Typical Range: $1,000 to $25,000
*Note: Giving excludes scholarships.

Recent Grants

Note: Grants derived from 2002 Form 990.
General

41,420	Nebraska Christian Schools, Central City, NE -- for improvements and equipment
35,000	Nebraska Wesleyan University, Lincoln, NE
33,000	Hamilton County Senior Center, Aurora, NE -- pledge
30,000	Memorial Hospital Foundation, Aurora, NE -- for endowment fund
29,000	University of Nebraska Foundation, Lincoln, NE -- for Agronomy Department
25,000	Hastings College Foundation, Omaha, NE
22,000	Hamilton County Foundation Inc., Aurora, NE -- for Nebraska Wesleyan tuition
21,542	Nebraska Wesleyan University, Lincoln, NE -- for annual insurance premium
21,000	Hamilton County Foundation Inc., Aurora, NE -- for scholarships
20,000	Plainsman Museum, Aurora, NE -- for endowment

HEWIT FAMILY FOUNDATION

Giving Contact

William D. Hewit, President, Treasurer & Director
Hewit Family Foundation
621 17th St., Suite 2555
Denver, CO 80293
Phone: (303)292-0697

Description

Founded: 1985
EIN: 742397040
Organization Type: Private Foundation
Giving Locations: CO: Denver
Grant Types: General Support.

Donor Information

Founder: members of the Hewit family

Financial Summary

Total Giving: $820,000 (fiscal year ending November 30, 2004); $715,000 (fiscal 2001)
Assets: $14,755,077 (fiscal 2004); $13,812,832 (fiscal 2001)

Gifts Received: $5,754,524 (fiscal 2000); $4,290,846 (fiscal 1998); $300,000 (fiscal 1997). Note: In fiscal 1998 and 2000, contributions were received from the estate of William E. Hewit. In fiscal 1995, contributions were received from William D. Hewit ($150,000) and Betty Ruth Hewit ($150,000).

Typical Recipients

Arts & Humanities: Historic Preservation, Libraries, Museums/Galleries, Public Broadcasting
Civic & Public Affairs: Botanical Gardens/Parks, Civic & Public Affairs-General, Philanthropic Organizations, Zoos/Aquariums
Education: Afterschool/Enrichment Programs, Education Funds, Education-General, Science/Mathematics Education
Environment: Resource Conservation
Health: Cancer, Children's Health/Hospitals, Health Policy/Cost Containment, Health Organizations, Hospitals, Hospitals (University Affiliated), Preventive Medicine/Wellness Organizations, Transplant Networks/Donor Banks
Science: Science Museums, Scientific Centers & Institutes
Social Services: Big Brothers/Big Sisters, Child Abuse, Child Welfare, Community Service Organizations, Recreation & Athletics, Scouts, Youth Organizations

Application Procedures

Initial Contact: Send a brief letter of inquiry.
Application Requirements: Include a description of organization, amount requested, proof of tax-exempt status.
Deadlines: None.

Restrictions

Does not support individuals, religious organizations for sectarian purposes, political or lobbying groups, or organizations outside operating areas.

Foundation Officials

Christie F. Andrews: vice president, director
Richard J. Andrews: director
Robert S. Brown: director
Betty Ruth Hewit: vice president, director
William D. Hewit: president, treasurer, director
Jack E. Kennedy: director

Grants Analysis

Disclosure Period: fiscal year ending November 30, 2004
Total Grants: $820,000
Number of Grants: 18
Average Grant: $14,667*
Highest Grant: $300,000
Lowest Grant: $5,000
Typical Range: $5,000 to $20,000
*Note: Average grant figure excludes three highest grants ($600,000).

Recent Grants

Note: Grants derived from fiscal 2004 Form 990.
General

300,000	University of Nebraska Foundation, Lincoln, NE
200,000	PorterCare Foundation, Englewood, CO
100,000	Denver Museum of Nature and Science, Denver, CO
60,000	Billfish Foundation, Ft. Lauderdale, FL
25,000	University of Colorado Health Sciences Center, Denver, CO
15,000	Boy Scouts of America, Denver, CO
15,000	Double Angel Foundation, Parker, CO
15,000	Girl Scouts Mile High Council, Denver, CO
15,000	Kempe Children's Foundation, Denver, CO
15,000	Make-a-Wish Foundation, Eaglewood, CO

WILLIAM AND FLORA HEWLETT FOUNDATION

Giving Contact

Paul Brest, President
2121 Sand Hill Road
Menlo Park, CA 94025
Phone: (650)234-4500
Fax: (650)234-4501
E-mail: info@hewlett.org
Web: http://www.hewlett.org

Description

Founded: 1966
EIN: 941655673
Organization Type: General Purpose Foundation
Giving Locations: CA: San Francisco Bay area internationally; nationally.
Grant Types: Challenge, Department, Employee Matching Gifts, General Support, Matching, Multiyear/Continuing Support, Operating Expenses, Project.

Donor Information

Founder: The Hewlett Foundation was established in 1966 by William R. Hewlett; his late wife, Flora Lamson Hewlett; and their eldest son, Walter B. Hewlett. William Hewlett is a co-founder of the Hewlett-Packard Company, established in 1939 with his partner, David Packard. Mr. Hewlett is retired from the computer and electronics company and is chairman of the foundation. In 1977, the foundation's name changed to the William and Flora Hewlett Foundation, in memory of Mrs. Hewlett who died that year. She bequeathed $230 million in Hewlett-Packard stock to the foundation.

Financial Summary

Total Giving: $195,221,736 (2002); $119,000,000 (2001)
Assets: $5,144,254,523 (2002); $5,459,549,000 (2001)
Gifts Received: $53,125 (2002); $394,835,000 (2000); $46,880,438 (1998). Note: In 2002, 2000 and 1998, contributions were received from William R. Hewlett.

Typical Recipients

Arts & Humanities: Arts Associations & Councils, Arts Funds, Arts Institutes, Arts Outreach, Ballet, Dance, Ethnic & Folk Arts, Film & Video, Libraries, Museums/Galleries, Music, Opera, Performing Arts, Public Broadcasting, Theater
Civic & Public Affairs: Botanical Gardens/Parks, Chambers of Commerce, Community Foundations, Economic Development, Economic Policy, Employment/Job Training, Ethnic Organizations, Civic & Public Affairs-General, Housing, Inner-City Development, Law & Justice, Native American Affairs, Nonprofit Management, Philanthropic Organizations, Professional & Trade Associations, Public Policy, Urban & Community Affairs, Women's Affairs
Education: Afterschool/Enrichment Programs, Arts/Humanities Education, Business Education, Colleges & Universities, Continuing Education, Economic Education, Education Associations, Education Funds, Education Reform, Engineering/Technological Education, Environmental Education, Faculty Development, Education-General, International Studies, Legal Education, Literacy, Minority Education, Science/Mathematics Education, Social Sciences Education, Student Aid, Vocational & Technical Education
Environment: Air/Water Quality, Energy, Environment-General, Resource Conservation
Health: Adolescent Health Issues, AIDS/HIV, Health Policy/Cost Containment, Health Organizations, Public Health, Research/Studies Institutes
International: Foreign Educational Institutions, International-General, Health Care/Hospitals, Internation-

al Affairs, International Development, International Environmental Issues, International Organizations, International Peace & Security Issues, International Relations
Religion: Seminaries, Social/Policy Issues
Science: Scientific Centers & Institutes, Scientific Organizations, Scientific Research
Social Services: Child Welfare, Community Centers, Community Service Organizations, Crime Prevention, Emergency Relief, Family Planning, Family Services, Shelters/Homelessness, Volunteer Services, Youth Organizations

Application Procedures

Initial Contact: Applicants should submit a letter of inquiry addressed to the president, containing a brief statement of need for funds and sufficient factual information to enable the staff to determine whether the proposal falls within the foundation's area of preferred interest. Applicants also should provide reasons and needs for support, taking into account other possible sources of funding.
Application Requirements: Applicants who receive a favorable response to their initial inquiry will be invited to submit a formal proposal. Special supporting materials may be requested in some cases, but normally the formal proposal should include: a statement of purpose; a budget and financial statement, including an indication of other prospective funding sources, the amount requested of each, and how they would continue a successful program once support from the Hewlett Foundation ceases; the identity and qualifications of key personnel; a list of governing members; evidence of tax-exempt status; and a statement that the proposal has been reviewed and approved by the applicant's governing body, and specifically approved for submission to the foundation.
Deadlines: Applications for music programs should be submitted by January 1, for review in April. Theater program applications should be submitted by April 1, for review in July. Applications from dance programs and film and video service organizations are due by July 1, for review in October. For the Conflict Resolution program, applications from theory organizations and international organizations are due January 1, for review in April; applications from training and promotional organizations and public policy decision making organizations are due July 1, for review in October; and applications from practitioner organizations are due October 1, for review in January. Although the foundation does not expect to be able to adhere rigidly to this schedule, it will make every effort to do so.
Review Process: Letters of application will be acknowledged briefly upon receipt. Grants must be reviewed by the Board of Directors, which meets quarterly. Because the foundation prefers to conduct its affairs with a small staff, a more detailed response will be delayed in some cases. Applicants who have not received a substantive reply after a reasonable period of time should make a follow-up inquiry. All inquiries initially are reviewed by the relevant program officer who will request further information, if needed. He or she, in consultation with the president, will either decline those requests which seem unlikely to result in a project the foundation can support, or present the request to the staff for discussion.

Restrictions

The foundation recognizes that significant programs require time to demonstrate their value, and is therefore willing to consider proposals covering several years of support. While the foundation will fund specific projects in its areas of interest and will occasionally provide general support for organizations of special interest, it expects to work primarily through support of organizations active in its main programs. One exception is the regional grants program, under which the foundation will fund specific projects that meet an immediate community need.

The foundation normally will not consider grants or loans to individuals, for basic research, capital construction funds, or medical or health-related fields. It will not support general fund-raising drives or make grants intended directly or indirectly to support candidates for political office or to influence legislation. The foundation does not accept proposals by fax or e-mail.

Additional Information

The foundation reports that "in its grantmaking decisions as well as in its interests and activities, the Hewlett Foundation is wholly independent of the Hewlett-Packard Company and the Hewlett-Packard Company Foundation."
Publications: Annual Report; Guidelines

Foundation Officials

Paul Brest: president, director ED Swarthmore College (1962); Harvard University LLB (1965). NONPR AFFIL fellow: American Academy of Arts and Sciences.

Robert F. Erburu: director B Ventura, CA 1930. ED University of Southern California BA (1952); Harvard University JD (1955). CORP AFFIL director: Marsh & McLennan Companies Inc. NONPR AFFIL trustee: National Gallery Art; director: Pacific Council on International Policy; life director: Independent Colleges Southern California; member: American Bar Association; chairman board trustee: H.E. Huntington Library Art Gallery.

Harvey V. Fineberg, MD: director B Pittsburgh, PA September 15, 1945. ED Harvard University BA (1967); Harvard University MD (1972). NONPR AFFIL president: Institute of Medicine; board of directors: National Research Council.

James C. Gaither: director B Oakland, CA 1937. ED Princeton University BA (1959); Stanford University JD (1964). CORP AFFIL director: Siebel System Inc.; director: Levi Strauss & Co.; director: NVIDIA Corp. NONPR AFFIL member: San Francisco Bar Association; member executive committee, board visitors, advisory board: Stanford University School Law; member: Phi Delta Phi; member executive committee, trustee, vice chairman: Carnegie Endowment International Peace; member: Order Coif; member: California Bar Association; fellow: American Academy of Arts & Sciences; member: American Bar Association.

Eleanor Hewlett Gimon: director NONPR AFFIL treasurer: Family Foundation North America.

Walter B. Hewlett: chairman CORP AFFIL director: Agilent Technologies Inc.; chairman: Vermont Telephone Co. NONPR AFFIL director: Public Policy Institute of California; trustee: Stanford University; founder, director: Center for Computer Assisted Research in Humanities.

Mary Hewlett Jaffe: director

Herant Katchadourian, MD: director B Iskenderun, Turkey 1933. ED American University BA (1954); American University MD (1958); University of Rochester (1958-1961). PRIM NONPR EMPL dean undergraduate studies: Stanford University. NONPR AFFIL member corporate visitors committee: Massachusetts Institute Technology; professor emeritus: Stanford University; trustee: Haigazian College; member: Alpha Omega Alpha; trustee: American University of Beirut.

Richard C. Levin: director ED Stanford University BA (1968); Yale University PhD (1974). CORP AFFIL director: J-STOR. NONPR AFFIL chairman: University Alliance for Lifelong Learning; president: Yale University; director: National Academy of Sciences Board on Science.

Jean G. Stromberg: director

Grants Analysis

Disclosure Period: calendar year ending 2002
Total Grants: $195,221,736
Number of Grants: 950 (approx)
Average Grant: $205,497
Highest Grant: $5,000,000
Typical Range: $50,000 to $500,000

Recent Grants

Note: Grants derived from 2002 Form 990.
General

21,252,250	Board of Trustees of the Leland Stanford University, Stanford, CA -- fund for the undergraduate education programs
7,666,667	Bay Area School Reform Collaborative, San Francisco, CA -- fund for the Hewlett Annenberg Challenge for school reform
3,500,000	Energy Foundation, San Francisco, CA -- fund for the promotion of clean energy policies
3,500,000	Energy Foundation, San Francisco, CA -- fund for transportation program in China and renewable energy project in Rockies
2,400,000	Planned Parenthood Federation of America Inc., New York, NY
2,235,000	Energy Foundation, San Francisco, CA -- fund for work on energy and lands issues
2,200,000	Opera America Inc., Washington, DC -- fund for the music project
2,000,000	Hypercar Inc., Basalt, CO -- fund for a car design aimed at better fuel efficiency
2,000,000	KCET Community Television of Southern California, Los Angeles, CA -- fund for the public television series
2,000,000	National Energy Commission Inc., Washington, DC

HEXCEL CORP.

Company Headquarters

2 Stamford Plaza
281 Tressor Boulevard
Stamford, CT 06901
Web: http://www.hexcel.com

Company Description

Founded: 1946
Ticker: HXL
Exchange: NYSE
Revenue: US$850.8 million (2002)
Employees: 4245 (2002)
SIC(s): 2200 Textile Mill Products, 2800 Chemicals & Allied Products, 3400 Fabricated Metal Products, 3728 Aircraft Parts & Equipment Nec.

Operating Locations

Hexcel Corp. (AZ--Casa Grande, Chandler; CA--Chatsworth, City of Industry, Livermore, Pleasanton, San Francisco; MI--Zeeland; OH--Lancaster; PA--Pottsville; TX--Graham, Seguin)
Note: Includes plant locations

Hexcel Foundation

Giving Contact

Michael Bacal, Treasurer
Hexcel Foundation
281 Tresser Blvd.
Stamford, CT 06901
Phone: (203)969-0666
Fax: (925)416-7756

Description

EIN: 942972860
Organization Type: Corporate Foundation
Giving Locations: CA
Grant Types: Employee Matching Gifts, General Support, Scholarship.

Financial Summary

Total Giving: $10,810 (fiscal year ending June 30, 2003); $20,316 (fiscal 2001)
Assets: $78,088 (fiscal 2003); $119,854 (fiscal 2001)
Gifts Received: $3,000 (fiscal 1993)

Typical Recipients

Arts & Humanities: Libraries, Museums/Galleries, Music, Opera
Civic & Public Affairs: Civic & Public Affairs-General, Urban & Community Affairs
Education: Business Education, Colleges & Universities, Community & Junior Colleges, Engineering/Technological Education, Education-General, Public Education (Precollege), Religious Education, Science/Mathematics Education, Secondary Education (Public), Student Aid
Health: Cancer, Children's Health/Hospitals, Emergency/Ambulance Services, Eyes/Blindness, Health Organizations, Heart, Hospices, Hospitals, Mental Health, Prenatal Health Issues, Single-Disease Health Associations
International: International-General
Science: Science Exhibits & Fairs
Social Services: Community Service Organizations, Crime Prevention, Day Care, Food/Clothing Distribution, Homes, Recreation & Athletics, Senior Services, Shelters/Homelessness, Substance Abuse, United Funds/United Ways, YMCA/YWCA/YMHA/YWHA, Youth Organizations

Application Procedures

Initial Contact: Send a brief letter of inquiry.
Application Requirements: Include proof of tax-exempt status.
Deadlines: None.

Restrictions

Does not support individuals; religious organizations for sectarian purposes; political or lobbying groups; veterans, labor or other groups; or organizations which function only in and for the benefit of communities where Hexcel has no operations or employees.

Additional Information

Publications: Corporate Contributions Guidelines

Corporate Officials

Stephen C. Forsyth: senior vice president finance & administration, chief financial officer PRIM CORP EMPL senior vice president finance & administration, chief financial officer: Hexcel Corp.
Juergen Habermeier: vice chairman PRIM CORP EMPL vice chairman: Hexcel Corp.
John J. Lee: chairman, president, chief executive officer, director B 1933. PRIM CORP EMPL chairman, president, chief executive officer, director: Hexcel Corp. CORP AFFIL director: Playtex Products; chief executive officer: Seminole Fertilizer Corp.; director: Aviva Petroleum Co.

Foundation Officials

Michael Bacal: treasurer
Stephen C. Forsyth: president (see above)
Rodney P. Jenks, Jr.: secretary

Grants Analysis

Disclosure Period: fiscal year ending June 30, 2003
Total Grants: $10,810*
Number of Grants: 17
Average Grant: $176*
Highest Grant: $8,000
Lowest Grant: $25
Typical Range: $50 to $500
***Note:** Average grant figure excludes highest grant.

Recent Grants

Note: Grants derived from fiscal 2003 Form 990.
General

8,000	Scholarship Management Services, Wilton, CT
500	Auburn University, Auburn, AL
500	Presbyterian College, Clinton, SC
500	University of Tennessee, Knoxville, TN
250	Colorado School of Mines, Golden, CO
200	Brigham Young University, Provo, UT
150	Syracuse University, Syracuse, NY

150	University of Massachusetts, Amherst, MA
100	University of Michigan, Ann Arbor, MI
100	Utah State University, Logan, UT

NAN AND MATILDA HEYDT FUND

Giving Contact
Thea Katsounakis, Trust Officer
PO Box 6767
PO Box 6767
Providence, RI 02940-6767
Phone: (401)276-7229

Description
Founded: 1966
EIN: 046136421
Organization Type: Private Foundation
Giving Locations: MA: Hampden County
Grant Types: Capital, Project, Seed Money.

Donor Information
Founder: the late Matilda L. Heydt

Financial Summary
Total Giving: $263,115 (2002)
Assets: $5,250,990 (2002)

Typical Recipients
Arts & Humanities: Arts Associations & Councils, Arts Institutes, Ethnic & Folk Arts, Film & Video, Historic Preservation, History & Archaeology, Libraries, Literary Arts, Museums/Galleries, Music, Opera, Public Broadcasting, Theater
Civic & Public Affairs: Asian American Affairs, Botanical Gardens/Parks, Business/Free Enterprise, Community Foundations, Employment/Job Training, Civic & Public Affairs-General, Hispanic Affairs, Housing, Legal Aid, Minority Business, Public Policy, Safety, Urban & Community Affairs
Education: Business-School Partnerships, Colleges & Universities, Community & Junior Colleges, Elementary Education (Public), Education-General, International Studies, Social Sciences Education, Special Education
Environment: Energy, Environment-General, Resource Conservation, Watershed
Health: AIDS/HIV, Alzheimer's Disease, Children's Health/Hospitals, Clinics/Medical Centers, Health Funds, Hospices, Hospitals, Medical Rehabilitation, Medical Training, Mental Health, Nursing Services, Public Health
International: Human Rights, Missionary/Religious Activities
Religion: Churches, Seminaries
Science: Scientific Centers & Institutes
Social Services: At-Risk Youth, Camps, Child Welfare, Community Service Organizations, Counseling, Domestic Violence, Emergency Relief, Family Planning, Food/Clothing Distribution, People with Disabilities, Recreation & Athletics, Scouts, Senior Services, Social Services-General, United Funds/United Ways, Volunteer Services, YMCA/YWCA/YMHA/YWHA, Youth Organizations

Application Procedures
Initial Contact: Contact trust officer for application information and deadlines.

Additional Information
Publications: Informational Brochure (including Application Guidelines)
Trust(s): Fleet National Bank

Grants Analysis
Disclosure Period: calendar year ending 2002
Total Grants: $263,115

Number of Grants: 43
Average Grant: $6,119
Highest Grant: $31,000
Typical Range: $1,000 to $7,000

Recent Grants
Note: Grants derived from 2002 Form 990.
General

31,000	Hampshire Education Collaborative, Inc., Northampton, MA
10,000	Community Adolescent Resources and Education Center, Holyoke, MA
10,000	Cooperative Development Institute, Greenfield, MA
10,000	Hampshire Education Collaborative, Inc., Northampton, MA
10,000	Hampshire Education Collaborative, Inc., Northampton, MA
10,000	Holyoke Community Land Trust, Inc., Holyoke, MA
8,650	Community Foundation of Western Massachusetts, Springfield, MA
8,498	Community Foundation of Western Massachusetts, Springfield, MA
8,498	Community Foundation of Western Massachusetts, Springfield, MA
7,500	Community Adolescent Resources and Education Center, Holyoke, MA

DUBOSE AND DOROTHY HEYWARD MEMORIAL FUND

Giving Contact
Peter McDermott, Trust Officer
c/o The Bank of New York, Tax Dept.
1290 Ave. of the Americas, 5th Fl.
New York, NY 10104
Phone: (212)635-1520

Description
Founded: 1985
EIN: 136840999
Organization Type: Private Foundation
Giving Locations: NH; NY; SC
Grant Types: General Support.

Donor Information
Founder: the late Jenifer Heyward

Financial Summary
Total Giving: $478,500 (2002)
Assets: $6,719,738 (2002)
Gifts Received: $129,518 (1999); $35 (1995); $130,000 (1994). Note: In 1999, contributions were received from Patti Whitelaw Charitable Trust. In 1994, contributions were received from Elizabeth Miller Charitable Trust.

Typical Recipients
Arts & Humanities: Arts Associations & Councils, Arts Festivals, Arts Institutes, Ballet, Dance, Arts & Humanities-General, History & Archaeology, Libraries, Literary Arts, Museums/Galleries, Music, Opera, Performing Arts, Public Broadcasting, Theater
Civic & Public Affairs: Community Foundations, Civic & Public Affairs-General, Municipalities/Towns, Parades/Festivals, Urban & Community Affairs
Education: Arts/Humanities Education, Colleges & Universities, Medical Education
Health: Cancer, Hospitals, Single-Disease Health Associations
Social Services: Community Centers

Application Procedures
Initial Contact: Send a brief letter of inquiry.
Application Requirements: Include a description of organization.
Deadlines: None.

Restrictions
Provides grants for the promotion of the arts or for cancer research and treatment.

Additional Information
Trust(s): The Bank of New York

Foundation Officials
Albert J. Cardinali: trustee B New York, NY 1934. ED City College of New York BA (1955); Columbia University LLB (1958); New York University LLM (1965). PRIM CORP EMPL Partner: Thatcher Proffitt & Wood. NONPR AFFIL member: Association Bar New York City; member: New York State Bar Association; member: American Bar Association. CLUB AFFIL Shenorock Shore Club; University Club.

Grants Analysis
Disclosure Period: calendar year ending 2002
Total Grants: $478,500
Number of Grants: 41
Average Grant: $9,962*
Highest Grant: $50,000
Lowest Grant: $1,000
Typical Range: $5,000 to $20,000
*Note: Average grant figure excludes two highest grants ($90,000).

Recent Grants
Note: Grants derived from 2001 Form 990.
General

50,000	MacDowell Colony, New York, NY
40,000	MacDowell Colony, New York, NY
25,000	Carnegie Hall Society, New York, NY
25,000	Metropolitan Opera Association, New York, NY
25,000	Metropolitan Opera Association, New York, NY
25,000	Public Theatre New York Shakespeare Festival, New York, NY
20,000	City Center 55th Street Theater Foundation, New York, NY
20,000	Columbia University Cancer Center, New York, NY
20,000	Glimmerglass Opera, New York, NY
20,000	Jazz at Lincoln Center, New York, NY

HICKORY TECH CORP.

Company Headquarters
Mankato, MN
Web: http://www.hickorytech.com

Company Description
Founded: 1898
Ticker: HTCO
Exchange: NASDAQ
Revenue: US$106.6 million (2002)
Employees: 414 (2003)
SIC(s): 4813 Telephone Communications Except Radiotelephone, 4841 Cable & Other Pay Television Services.

Operating Locations
Hickory Tech Corp. (IA--Homestead; MN--St. Paul)

Hickory Tech Corp. Foundation

Giving Contact

Jane L. Rush, Administrator
221 E. Hickory St.
PO Box 3248
Mankato, MN 56002-3248
Phone: (507)387-3355
Fax: (507)625-9191

Description

Founded: 1963
EIN: 416034001
Organization Type: Corporate Foundation
Giving Locations: MN: Mankato
Grant Types: Capital, Employee Matching Gifts, General Support, Multiyear/Continuing Support, Scholarship.

Financial Summary

Total Giving: $154,805 (fiscal year ending February 28, 2003); $228,825 (fiscal 2002); $192,156 (fiscal 2001). Note: Contributes through foundation only.
Assets: $2,587,523 (fiscal 2003); $3,092,190 (fiscal 2002); $3,465,857 (fiscal 2001)
Gifts Received: $10,000 (fiscal 1996); $70,000 (fiscal 1994); $450,000 (fiscal 1993). Note: Gifts are received from Mankato Citizens Telephone Co.

Typical Recipients

Arts & Humanities: Arts Funds, Arts Outreach, Ballet, Arts & Humanities-General, Historic Preservation, Libraries, Music, Performing Arts, Public Broadcasting, Theater
Civic & Public Affairs: Botanical Gardens/Parks, Business/Free Enterprise, Chambers of Commerce, Clubs, Community Foundations, Economic Development, Economic Policy, Employment/Job Training, Civic & Public Affairs-General, Housing, Municipalities/Towns, Parades/Festivals, Public Policy, Safety, Urban & Community Affairs, Women's Affairs
Education: Afterschool/Enrichment Programs, Arts/Humanities Education, Business Education, Business-School Partnerships, Colleges & Universities, Community & Junior Colleges, Economic Education, Education Funds, Engineering/Technological Education, Faculty Development, Education-General, International Studies, Leadership Training, Minority Education, Private Education (Precollege), Public Education (Precollege), Religious Education, Science/Mathematics Education, Secondary Education (Private), Secondary Education (Public), Social Sciences Education, Student Aid, Vocational & Technical Education
Environment: Environment-General, Resource Conservation, Wildlife Protection
Health: AIDS/HIV, Alzheimer's Disease, Cancer, Children's Health/Hospitals, Clinics/Medical Centers, Diabetes, Emergency/Ambulance Services, Health-General, Heart, Hospitals, Medical Rehabilitation, Multiple Sclerosis, Prenatal Health Issues, Public Health, Single-Disease Health Associations, Trauma Treatment
International: International Organizations
Religion: Bible Study/Translation, Religious Welfare, Social/Policy Issues
Science: Observatories & Planetariums, Science Exhibits & Fairs
Social Services: At-Risk Youth, Camps, Community Service Organizations, Emergency Relief, Family Services, Food/Clothing Distribution, People with Disabilities, Recreation & Athletics, Scouts, Senior Services, Shelters/Homelessness, Social Services-General, United Funds/United Ways, Veterans, Volunteer Services, YMCA/YWCA/YMHA/YWHA, Youth Organizations

Application Procedures

Initial Contact: By telephone, to request guidelines
Application Requirements: If project meets foundation's mission: a description of project, including specific goals and completion dates; amount requested and percentage of budget it represents; current budget; audited financial statement; list of other contributors, and funding levels; a list of board of directors with affiliations; letter of tax-exempt status; description of how support will be recognized; a plan to evaluate the project's success; and any descriptive brochures or materials
Deadlines: December 15 of each fiscal year.
Evaluative Criteria: Foundation focuses on areas of Hickory Tech Corporation's subsidiaries in South Central Minnesota.

Restrictions

Does not support individuals; political activities or organizations; religious organizations for sectarian purposes; fraternal, veteran or labor groups; special occasion or goodwill advertising; general operating purposes, except United Way; loans; sports programs or events; cause-related marketing; organizations that discriminate; hospital operating funds or capital funds; and organizations without 501(c)(3) status.

Corporate Officials

Lyle T. Bosacker: director PRIM CORP EMPL director: Hickory Tech Corp.
Robert K. Else: director B 1935. ED University of Illinois MBA (1958); University of Chicago MBA (1959). PRIM CORP EMPL president: EI Microcircuits Inc. CORP AFFIL director: Hickory Technology Corp.; director: Mankato Citizens Tel Co.
James H. Holdrege: director PRIM CORP EMPL director: Hickory Tech Corp. CORP AFFIL director: Mankato Citizens Tel Co.
R. Wynn Kearney, Jr.: director PRIM CORP EMPL director: Hickory Tech Corp. CORP AFFIL director: Hickory Technology Corp.
Starr J. Kirklin: director PRIM CORP EMPL director: Hickory Tech Corp. CORP AFFIL director: Mankato Citizens Tel Co.
Brett M. Taylor, Jr.: director PRIM CORP EMPL director: Hickory Technology Corp. CORP AFFIL director: Mankato Citizens Tel Co.

Foundation Officials

Robert D. Alton, Jr.: trustee B 1948. ED Lindenwood University MBA; Iowa State University (1970). CORP AFFIL chairman: Minnesota Southern Wireless Co.
Lyle T. Bosacker: trustee (see above)
Myrita P. Craig: trustee
Robert K. Else: trustee (see above)
James H. Holdrege: trustee (see above)
Lyle Gordon Jacobson: trustee B Duluth, MN 1941. ED University of Minnesota (1963); University of Minnesota MS (1965). PRIM CORP EMPL president, chief executive officer: Katolight Corp. ADD CORP EMPL vice president: Jones Metal Products Inc.; treasurer: Winnebago Manufacturing Co. CORP AFFIL director: Mankato Citizens Tel Co.; director: Hickory Technology Corp.; director, owner: JKW Management Corp. NONPR AFFIL Kiwanis International.
R. Wynn Kearney, Jr.: president (see above)
Starr J. Kirklin: trustee (see above)
Robert E. Switz: trustee

Grants Analysis

Disclosure Period: fiscal year ending February 28, 2003
Total Grants: $68,750*
Number of Grants: 13
Average Grant: $5,288
Highest Grant: $20,000
Lowest Grant: $1,250
Typical Range: $2,500 to $15,000

*Note: Giving excludes matching gifts and scholarship.

Recent Grants

Note: Grants derived from fiscal 2004 Form 990.
General

21,500	Minnesota State University Scholarships, Mankato, MN -- scholarships to be given to school students
15,000	South Central Technical College, North Mankato, MN -- scholarships to be given to school students
15,000	YMCA, Mankato, MN -- funds for new building project
10,000	Minnesota State University College of Science Engineering & Technology, Mankato, MN -- launch of civil engineering program
10,000	Twin Valley Boy Scouts, Mankato, MN -- funds for new building project
6,000	Citizens' Scholarship Foundation, St. Peter, MN -- to employee daughter & son Program
5,000	Dakota Meadows School, North Mankato, MN -- wellness center-public achievement plus project
5,000	Educare, Mankato, MN -- funds for mini-grants to area teachers
5,000	Hope Heaven, Rock Valley, IA -- software technology update
5,000	Mankato Symphony Orchestra, Mankato, MN

JOHN W. AND CLARA C. HIGGINS FOUNDATION

Giving Contact

Sumner B. Tilton, Jr., President
370 Main St., 12th Fl.
Worcester, MA 01608
Phone: (508)798-8521
Fax: (508)794-1201

Description

Founded: 1956
EIN: 046026914
Organization Type: Private Foundation
Grant Types: Multiyear/Continuing Support, Project.

Typical Recipients

Arts & Humanities: Arts Associations & Councils, Arts Institutes, Ethnic & Folk Arts, History & Archaeology, Libraries, Literary Arts, Museums/Galleries, Music, Opera
Civic & Public Affairs: Civil Rights, Community Foundations, Ethnic Organizations, Civic & Public Affairs-General, Native American Affairs
Education: Afterschool/Enrichment Programs, Colleges & Universities, Journalism/Media Education, Private Education (Precollege)
Environment: Resource Conservation
Health: Emergency/Ambulance Services
Religion: Churches, Religion-General, Religious Welfare, Synagogues/Temples
Social Services: Animal Protection, Food/Clothing Distribution, Senior Services, Social Services-General, Youth Organizations

Application Procedures

Initial Contact: Send a brief letter of inquiry.
Application Requirements: Include proof of tax-exempt status.
Deadlines: None.

Restrictions

Recipient must be eligible for listing in the IRS cumulative list. Grants are not made to individuals.

Foundation Officials

Richard Higgins: trustee
Mary Louise Wilding White: trustee
Philip Q. Wilding White: trustee

Grants Analysis

Disclosure Period: calendar year ending 2000
Total Grants: $174,500*
Number of Grants: 61
Average Grant: $2,861
Highest Grant: $20,000
Typical Range: $1,000 to $5,000
*Note: Giving excludes United Way.

Recent Grants

Note: Grants derived from 2001 Form 990.
Library-Related
9,000	Library of Congress Trust Fund Board, Washington, DC

General
22,000	Higgins Armory Museum, Worcester, MA
19,000	Dutchess County Arts Council, Poughkeepsie, NY
14,000	Higgins Armory Museum, Worcester, MA
11,000	American Civil Liberties Union, New York, NY
7,000	Capital Area Food Bank, Washington, DC
7,000	St. Mary's College of Maryland, St. Mary's City, MD
7,000	Worcester Art Museum, Worcester, MA
5,500	Sedona Charter School, Sedona, AZ
5,000	Horizon Communications, New Haven, CT
4,000	Higgins Armory Museum, Worcester, MA

CORINA HIGGINSON TRUST

Giving Contact

Charles C. Abeles, Esq., Trustee
4339 Westover Place NW
Washington, DC 20016
Phone: (202)334-0553

Description

Founded: 1962
EIN: 526055743
Organization Type: Private Foundation
Giving Locations: DC: Washington
Grant Types: Emergency, General Support, Multiyear/Continuing Support, Operating Expenses, Project, Research, Seed Money.

Donor Information

Founder: the late Corina Higginson

Financial Summary

Total Giving: $277,000 (2003)
Assets: $5,980,690 (2003)
Gifts Received: $10,171 (1992)

Typical Recipients

Arts & Humanities: Arts Associations & Councils, Arts Centers, Arts Funds, Arts Outreach, Ballet, Community Arts, Dance, Ethnic & Folk Arts, History & Archaeology, Libraries, Museums/Galleries, Music, Opera, Performing Arts, Theater
Civic & Public Affairs: Community Foundations, Economic Development, Employment/Job Training, Civic & Public Affairs-General, Hispanic Affairs, Law & Justice, Nonprofit Management, Philanthropic Organizations, Professional & Trade Associations, Public Policy, Women's Affairs
Education: Afterschool/Enrichment Programs, Arts/Humanities Education, Environmental Education, Faculty Development, Education-General, Gifted & Talented Programs, Literacy, Minority Education,

Preschool Education, Private Education (Precollege), Science/Mathematics Education, Secondary Education (Public)
Environment: Forestry, Environment-General, Resource Conservation, Watershed, Wildlife Protection
Health: AIDS/HIV, Clinics/Medical Centers, Geriatric Health, Mental Health, Prenatal Health Issues
International: Health Care/Hospitals, International Environmental Issues
Religion: Churches, Jewish Causes, Religious Organizations, Religious Welfare, Social/Policy Issues
Social Services: Community Service Organizations, Counseling, Family Planning, Family Services, Food/Clothing Distribution, Recreation & Athletics, Refugee Assistance, Senior Services, Sexual Abuse, Shelters/Homelessness, Social Services-General, United Funds/United Ways, Volunteer Services, Youth Organizations

Application Procedures

Initial Contact: Send a concise, one-page statement summarizing the project. Submit the original and five copies.
Application Requirements: Include name and purpose of the organization, a summary of activities, names and qualifications of staff members, financial statements, amount requested, and proof of tax-exempt status.
Deadlines: March 1 and September 1.

Restrictions

Does not support individuals or provide funds for scholarships or endowments for individual schools, fixed assets, or medical or health-related programs or organizations.

Additional Information

Publications: Application Form; Guidelines

Foundation Officials

Charles Calvert Abeles: trustee B Norfolk, VA 1929. ED Harvard University AB (1952); University of Virginia JD (1958). CORP AFFIL director: D&D Ventures Corp. NONPR AFFIL member, officer: Transplant Recipients International Organization; member: Virginia Bar Association; member: District of Columbia Bar Association; trustee: Corina Higgins Trust. CLUB AFFIL Metropolitan Washington Club.
Wilton C. Corken, Jr.: trustee
Floretta Dukes McKenzie: trustee

Grants Analysis

Disclosure Period: calendar year ending 2003
Total Grants: $277,000
Number of Grants: 62
Average Grant: $4,468
Highest Grant: $12,500
Lowest Grant: $500
Typical Range: $1,000 to $10,000

Recent Grants

Note: Grants derived from 2003 Form 990.
General
12,500	Washington AIDS Partnership, Washington, DC
10,000	Christian Communities Group Homes, Washington, DC
10,000	Ellington Fund, Washington, DC
7,500	Byte Back Inc., Washington, DC
7,500	Capital Children's Museum, Washington, DC
7,500	Center for Artistry in Teaching, Washington, DC
7,500	Friends of the US National Arboretum, Washington, DC
7,500	Homeless Children's Tutorial Program, Washington, DC
7,500	Round House Theatre, Silver Spring, MD
7,500	St. Gabriel's Church, Washington, DC

HIGH FOUNDATION

Giving Contact

Richard L. High, Trustee
831 Salisbury Ct.
Lancaster, PA 17601
Phone: (717)293-4444

Description

Founded: 1980
EIN: 232149972
Organization Type: Private Foundation
Grant Types: General Support, Scholarship.

Donor Information

Founder: High Industries

Financial Summary

Total Giving: $186,600 (fiscal year ending August 31, 2004); $147,000 (fiscal 2001)
Giving Analysis: Giving for fiscal 2004 includes: foundation scholarships ($24,600); fiscal 2001: foundation scholarships ($19,000)
Assets: $4,269,579 (fiscal 2004); $3,964,761 (fiscal 2001)
Gifts Received: $100,000 (fiscal 2004); $50,000 (fiscal 2001); $30,000 (fiscal 2000). Note: In fiscal 2004, contributions were received from High Industries Inc. ($50,000) and Janet C. High ($500,000). Contributions were received from High Industries.

Typical Recipients

Arts & Humanities: Arts Centers, Community Arts, Historic Preservation, Libraries, Music, Opera, Performing Arts, Public Broadcasting, Theater
Civic & Public Affairs: Ethnic Organizations, Civic & Public Affairs-General, Housing, Parades/Festivals, Professional & Trade Associations, Urban & Community Affairs
Education: Arts/Humanities Education, Business Education, Colleges & Universities, Education Funds, Engineering/Technological Education, Education-General, Minority Education, Private Education (Precollege), Public Education (Precollege), Religious Education, Student Aid
Environment: Environment-General
Health: Children's Health/Hospitals, Clinics/Medical Centers, Heart, Hospices, Hospitals, Public Health, Single-Disease Health Associations
International: Health Care/Hospitals
Religion: Churches, Ministries, Religious Organizations, Religious Welfare, Seminaries
Social Services: Camps, Community Centers, Community Service Organizations, Family Services, Food/Clothing Distribution, People with Disabilities, Scouts, Senior Services, Social Services-General, Substance Abuse, United Funds/United Ways, Youth Organizations

Application Procedures

Initial Contact: Request application form.
Deadlines: December 15.

Additional Information

Awards scholarships to dependent children of High Industries and related companies' employees.
Publications: Application Form

Foundation Officials

Calvin G. High: trustee
Gregory A. High: trustee
Janet C. High: trustee
Richard L. High: trustee
S. Dale High: trustee B Lancaster, PA 1942. ED Elizabethtown College BSBA (1963). PRIM CORP EMPL chairman, president: High Industries. CORP AFFIL partner: High Properties; director: Lancaster Alliance; director: High Hotels Ltd.; director: High Investors Ltd.; gen ptnr: High Empls Services Ltd; director: High Food Services Ltd.; director: Educators

---

Mutual Life Insurance Co. NONPR AFFIL trustee, director: Pennsylvania Chamber Business & Industry; trustee: World President Organization; member: Lancaster Chamber of Commerce; trustee: Lancaster County Foundation; hon mem: Delta Mu Delta; trustee: Elizabethtown College. CLUB AFFIL Tuesday Club; Hamilton Club; Lancaster Country Club.

Sadie H. High: trustee
Steven D. High: trustee
Suzanne M. High: trustee
Chester A. Raber: trustee

Grants Analysis

Disclosure Period: fiscal year ending August 31, 2004
Total Grants: $162,000*
Number of Grants: 22
Average Grant: $5,600*
Highest Grant: $25,000
Lowest Grant: $500
Typical Range: $1,000 to $10,000
*Note: Giving excludes scholarships. Average grant figure excludes two highest grants ($50,000).

Recent Grants

Note: Grants derived from 2004 Form 990.
General

25,000	Water Street Rescue Mission, Lancaster, PA -- capital campaign
25,000	WITF, Harrisburg, PA -- capital campaign
20,000	Brightside Opportunities Partnership, Lancaster, PA -- capital campaign
20,000	Landis Homes, Lititz, PA -- capital campaign
10,000	Lancaster Theological Seminary, Lancaster, PA -- capital campaign
10,000	Strasburg Heritage Society, Strasburg, PA -- capital campaign
5,000	Center for Parent/Youth Understanding, Elizabethtown, PA -- capital campaign
5,000	Ephrata Performing Arts, Ephrata, PA -- capital campaign
4,000	Neffsville Mennonite Church, Lancaster, PA
4,000	New Holland Band, Lancaster, PA

HILL CREST FOUNDATION

Giving Contact

Charles R. Terry, Sr., Chairman
PO Box 530507
Birmingham, AL 35253
Phone: (205)870-0400
Fax: (205)870-0484

Description

Founded: 1988
EIN: 630516927
Organization Type: General Purpose Foundation
Giving Locations: AL: Birmingham metropolitan area
Grant Types: Capital, General Support, Operating Expenses, Project, Research, Scholarship.

Financial Summary

Total Giving: $1,601,050 (fiscal year ending June 30, 2003); $1,636,700 (fiscal 2001)
Giving Analysis: Giving for fiscal 2001 includes: foundation scholarships ($18,000)
Assets: $32,210,940 (fiscal 2003); $33,277,781 (fiscal 2001)

Typical Recipients

Arts & Humanities: Arts Associations & Councils, Arts Festivals, Arts Outreach, Ballet, Dance, History & Archaeology, Museums/Galleries, Music, Perform-

ing Arts, Theater
Civic & Public Affairs: Botanical Gardens/Parks, Clubs, Community Foundations, Economic Development, Civic & Public Affairs-General, Housing, Law & Justice, Municipalities/Towns, Nonprofit Management, Public Policy, Urban & Community Affairs
Education: Colleges & Universities, Community & Junior Colleges, Education Associations, Education Funds, Education Reform, Elementary Education (Private), Elementary Education (Public), Education-General, Gifted & Talented Programs, International Studies, Leadership Training, Literacy, Medical Education, Minority Education, Private Education (Precollege), Public Education (Precollege), Secondary Education (Private), Social Sciences Education, Special Education, Student Aid, Vocational & Technical Education
Environment: Environment-General, Resource Conservation, Wildlife Protection
Health: AIDS/HIV, Alzheimer's Disease, Cancer, Children's Health/Hospitals, Diabetes, Eyes/Blindness, Geriatric Health, Health Funds, Health Organizations, Hospitals, Hospitals (University Affiliated), Medical Rehabilitation, Mental Health, Multiple Sclerosis, Nutrition, Prenatal Health Issues, Preventive Medicine/Wellness Organizations, Public Health, Respiratory, Single-Disease Health Associations, Trauma Treatment
Religion: Churches, Jewish Causes, Ministries, Missionary Activities (Domestic), Religious Organizations, Religious Welfare, Social/Policy Issues
Science: Science Museums
Social Services: Animal Protection, At-Risk Youth, Camps, Child Welfare, Community Centers, Community Service Organizations, Counseling, Delinquency & Criminal Rehabilitation, Domestic Violence, Family Planning, Family Services, Food/Clothing Distribution, Homes, People with Disabilities, Recreation & Athletics, Scouts, Senior Services, Shelters/Homelessness, Social Services-General, Substance Abuse, YMCA/YWCA/YMHA/YWHA, Youth Organizations

Application Procedures

Initial Contact: Applicants should request guidelines prior to submitting a proposal. Organizations should submit a brief proposal of one to three pages in letter form.
Application Requirements: The proposal should contain the following: proof of IRS 501(c)(3) nonprofit status; a short history of the organization and its purpose; a description of the project goals and the qualifications of the staff involved; the amount of funding requested; and anticipated long- and short-term advantages of the project affecting the foundation as well as all others who stand to benefit.
Deadlines: None.

Restrictions

Grants are made only to tax-exempt organizations.

Additional Information

Publications: Annual Report; Guidelines

Foundation Officials

Peter G. Cowin: trustee B 1931. ED Oberlin College. PRIM CORP EMPL vice president, director: Cowin & Co. Inc. CORP AFFIL vice president, secretary: C & C Holding Inc.; chairman board, treasurer: Cowin Equipment Co. Inc.
Stanley E. Graham: trustee
Willard L. Hurley: trustee
Charles R. Terry, Sr.: chairman

Grants Analysis

Disclosure Period: fiscal year ending June 30, 2003
Total Grants: $1,601,050
Number of Grants: 72
Average Grant: $22,237
Highest Grant: $100,000
Lowest Grant: $1,000
Typical Range: $10,000 to $40,000

Recent Grants

Note: Grants derived from fiscal 2002 Form 990.
General

117,000	St Vincent's Foundation, Birmingham, AL
100,000	Alabama Children's Hospital Foundation, Birmingham, AL
100,000	UAB School Of Medicine, Tuscaloosa, AL
100,000	United Cerebral Palsy/Greater Birmingham, Washington, DC
100,000	University/Alabama School of Social Work , Tuscaloosa, AL
85,000	Lakeshore Foundation, Birmingham, AL
50,000	Oasis Women's Counseling Center, Birmingham, AL
50,000	Vulcan Park Foundation, Birmingham, AL
50,000	Vulcan Park Foundation, Birmingham, AL
30,000	Community Grief Support Service, Birmingham, AL

SANDY HILL FOUNDATION

Giving Contact

Floyd H. Rourke, Trustee
PO Box 30
Hudson Falls, NY 12839
Phone: (518)747-5805

Description

Founded: 1953
EIN: 146018954
Organization Type: Private Foundation
Giving Locations: NY: Hudson Falls including surrounding area
Grant Types: General Support.

Financial Summary

Total Giving: $237,897 (fiscal year ending August 31, 2004). Note: Fiscal 1997 Giving includes scholarships ($45,000) AND United Way ($12,000).
Giving Analysis: Giving for fiscal 2004 includes: foundation grants to United Way ($7,000); foundation scholarships ($45,000)
Assets: $8,768,054 (fiscal 2004)

Typical Recipients

Arts & Humanities: Arts Associations & Councils, History & Archaeology, Libraries, Literary Arts, Museums/Galleries, Music, Opera, Performing Arts, Theater
Civic & Public Affairs: Botanical Gardens/Parks, Chambers of Commerce, Clubs, Community Foundations, Civic & Public Affairs-General, Hispanic Affairs, Municipalities/Towns, Native American Affairs, Parades/Festivals, Urban & Community Affairs
Education: Colleges & Universities, Education Funds, Literacy, Private Education (Precollege), Public Education (Precollege), Science/Mathematics Education, Student Aid
Environment: Environment-General, Wildlife Protection
Health: AIDS/HIV, Cancer, Clinics/Medical Centers, Emergency/Ambulance Services, Health Funds, Heart, Hospitals, Public Health
International: Foreign Arts Organizations
Religion: Churches, Ministries, Religious Welfare, Synagogues/Temples
Social Services: Animal Protection, Camps, Child Welfare, Community Centers, Community Service Organizations, Counseling, Day Care, Family Services, People with Disabilities, Recreation & Athletics, Scouts, Social Services-General, United Funds/United Ways, Veterans, Volunteer Services, YMCA/YWCA/YMHA/YWHA, Youth Organizations

Application Procedures

Initial Contact: For scholarships: request application form from guidance department of high school. Return application with current academic records, letters of recommendation, and a written statement indicating academic and occupational career goals, interests and activities, and any other pertinent information.
Deadlines: April 1.

Additional Information

Provides scholarships to students from the greater Hudson Falls, NY, area.
Publications: Application Guidelines

Foundation Officials

Nancy Juckett Brown: trustee
Floyd H. Rourke: trustee

Grants Analysis

Disclosure Period: fiscal year ending August 31, 2004
Total Grants: $185,897*
Number of Grants: 117
Average Grant: $1,172*
Highest Grant: $50,000
Lowest Grant: $200
Typical Range: $500 to $5,000
*Note: Giving excludes scholarships; United Way. Average grant figure excludes highest grant.

Recent Grants

Note: Grants derived from 2004 Form 990.
General

50,000	Double H Hole in the Woods Ranch, Lake Luzerne, NY -- for capital project
15,500	Glens Falls Hospital Foundation, Glens Falls, NY
10,200	Double H Hole in the Woods Ranch, Lake Luzerne, NY
10,000	Adirondack Samaritan Counseling Center, Hudson Falls, NY -- for capital project
7,000	Tri-County United Way, Queensbury, NY
5,000	Gansevoort Cemetery, Gansevoort, NY
5,000	Hudson Falls Presbyterian Church, Hudson Falls, NY
5,000	Saratoga Care Foundation, Saratoga, NY
3,300	Hyde Collection, Glens Falls, NY
2,500	Bentley College Annual Fund, Waltham, MA

HILLCREST FOUNDATION

Giving Contact

Dan Kelly, Specialist
c/o Bank of America
PO Box 830241
Dallas, TX 75283
Phone: (214)209-1965
Fax: (214)209-1940

Description

Founded: 1959
EIN: 756007565
Organization Type: General Purpose Foundation
Giving Locations: TX: Dallas
Grant Types: Capital, General Support, Project.

Donor Information

Founder: The late Mrs. W. W. Caruth Sr., (also known as Earle Clark Caruth) established the Hillcrest Foundation in 1959. The Caruth family, by the 1900s, had amassed some 30,000 acres of land in what is now North Dallas. The late W. W. Caruth, Jr., a former trustee of the Hillcrest Foundation, developed family land over the past four decades. He is succeeded by his widow, Mabel P. Caruth. Addition-

ally, NationsBank and individuals named by the donor serve as trustees.

Financial Summary

Total Giving: $5,619,700 (fiscal year ending May 31, 2003); $6,463,332 (fiscal 2002)
Assets: $126,604,241 (fiscal 2003); $134,888,149 (fiscal 2002); $141,000,000 (fiscal 2001 approx)

Typical Recipients

Arts & Humanities: Arts Centers, Arts Outreach, Historic Preservation, History & Archaeology, Libraries, Literary Arts, Museums/Galleries, Performing Arts, Theater
Civic & Public Affairs: Botanical Gardens/Parks, Business/Free Enterprise, Clubs, Economic Development, Employment/Job Training, Civic & Public Affairs-General, Hispanic Affairs, Housing, Law & Justice, Legal Aid, Minority Business, Nonprofit Management, Public Policy, Rural Affairs, Safety, Urban & Community Affairs, Women's Affairs, Zoos/Aquariums
Education: Arts/Humanities Education, Business Education, Colleges & Universities, Community & Junior Colleges, Continuing Education, Education Associations, Education Funds, Elementary Education (Private), Engineering/Technological Education, Faculty Development, Education-General, International Studies, Legal Education, Literacy, Medical Education, Preschool Education, Private Education (Precollege), Public Education (Precollege), Religious Education, School Volunteerism, Science/Mathematics Education, Secondary Education (Private), Social Sciences Education, Special Education, Student Aid
Environment: Environment-General
Health: Alzheimer's Disease, Arthritis, Cancer, Children's Health/Hospitals, Clinics/Medical Centers, Diabetes, Emergency/Ambulance Services, Health Funds, Health Organizations, Heart, Hospitals, Long-Term Care, Medical Research, Mental Health, Nursing Services, Outpatient Health Care, Prenatal Health Issues, Public Health, Research/Studies Institutes, Respiratory, Single-Disease Health Associations
International: Foreign Educational Institutions
Religion: Bible Study/Translation, Churches, Jewish Causes, Ministries, Missionary Activities (Domestic), Religious Welfare, Seminaries
Science: Science-General, Science Museums, Scientific Centers & Institutes
Social Services: At-Risk Youth, Camps, Child Abuse, Child Welfare, Community Centers, Community Service Organizations, Counseling, Crime Prevention, Day Care, Delinquency & Criminal Rehabilitation, Domestic Violence, Emergency Relief, Family Services, Food/Clothing Distribution, Homes, People with Disabilities, Recreation & Athletics, Scouts, Senior Services, Shelters/Homelessness, Social Services-General, Substance Abuse, United Funds/United Ways, Volunteer Services, YMCA/YWCA/YMHA/YWHA, Youth Organizations

Application Procedures

Initial Contact: A formal application form, provided by the foundation, must be submitted. A copy of the full proposal is requested.
Application Requirements: The proposal should include a brief history of the organization, purpose of proposal, an explanation of how funds will be used, a list of other contributors, budget information, a copy of the organization's IRS tax-exemption letter, and a statement that the organization is not a private foundation.
Deadlines: March 31, August 31, and November 30.
Review Process: All applications are considered as long as they pertain to the purposes of the foundation. The trustees meet in January, May, and October.
Evaluative Criteria: Priority is given to organizations in the Dallas, Texas area and the majority of grants are made to organizations located in Dallas County.

Restrictions

The foundation does not fund individuals, propaganda, political campaigns, groups influencing legislation, or religious organizations. No loans are distributed. OrganizationS must be located in Texas and the purpose of the grant must be for the relief of poverty or furtherance of education or health.

Additional Information

Bank of America is the corporate trustee of the foundation.
Publications: Guidelines; Application Form
Trust(s): Bank of America

Foundation Officials

Harold Byrd, Jr.: trustee
W. W. Caruth, II: trustee
Sandra Estess: trustee
Charles Porter Storey: trustee B Austin, TX 1922. ED University of Texas BA (1947); University of Texas LLB (1948); Southern Methodist University LLM (1952). CORP AFFIL secretary, director: Hargrove Electric Co. Inc.; director: Storey Armstrong Steger & Martin Professional Corp. NONPR AFFIL member: Texas Bar Association; fellow: Texas Bar Foundation; member: Philosophers Society Texas; trustee: Southwest Legal Foundation; member: Phi Delta Phi; member: Phi Delta Theta; fellow: American College Trial Lawyers; member: Dallas Bar Association; member: American Bar Association; fellow: American Bar Foundation. CLUB AFFIL Dallas Country Club; Idlewild Club; Crescent Club.

Grants Analysis

Disclosure Period: fiscal year ending May 31, 2003
Total Grants: $5,629,700
Number of Grants: 130
Average Grant: $40,466*
Highest Grant: $250,000
Lowest Grant: $1,000
Typical Range: $10,000 to $75,000
*Note: Average grant figure excludes two highest grants ($450,000).

Recent Grants

Note: Grants derived from 2003 Form 990.
Library-Related

50,000	Friends of the Dallas Public Library, Dallas, TX
50,000	Laura Bush Foundation for America's Libraries, Washington, DC

General

200,000	Oak Hill Academy, Dallas, TX
167,000	Dallas Baptist University, Dallas, TX
167,000	Old Red Courthouse Inc., Dallas, TX
125,000	Trinity Christian Academy, Addison, TX
100,000	Dallas Center for the Performing Arts Foundation, Dallas, TX
100,000	Gilda's Club North Texas, Dallas, TX
100,000	Low Birth Weight Development Center, Dallas, TX
100,000	Methodist Hospitals of Dallas, Dallas, TX
100,000	Oak Lawn United Methodist Church, Dallas, TX
100,000	Presbyterian Healthcare Foundation, Dallas, TX

HILLIARD CORP.

Company Headquarters

PO Box 866
Elmira, NY 14902
Web: http://www.hilliardcorp.com

Company Description

Employees: 233
SIC(s): 3500 Industrial Machinery & Equipment, 3519 Internal Combustion Engines Nec, 3564 Blow-

ers & Fans, 3568 Power Transmission Equipment Nec.

Operating Locations
Hilliard Corp. (NY--Elmira)

Hilliard Foundation

Giving Contact
Nelson Mooers van den Blink, President & Trustee
100 W. 4th St.
Elmira, NY 14901
Phone: (607)733-7121

Description
EIN: 161176159
Organization Type: Corporate Foundation
Giving Locations: NY: Elmira
Grant Types: General Support.

Financial Summary
Total Giving: $165,576 (fiscal year ending April 30, 2004); $189,800 (fiscal 2002)
Giving Analysis: Giving for fiscal 2004 includes: foundation grants to United Way ($9,000); fiscal 2002: foundation grants to United Way ($9,000)
Assets: $889,373 (fiscal 2004); $1,134,803 (fiscal 2002)
Gifts Received: $10,000 (fiscal 2004); $200,000 (fiscal 2000); $200,000 (fiscal 1998). Note: Contributions were received from the Hilliard Corp.

Typical Recipients
Arts & Humanities: Arts Associations & Councils, Arts Centers, Community Arts, Arts & Humanities-General, Historic Preservation, History & Archaeology, Libraries, Literary Arts, Museums/Galleries, Music, Performing Arts, Theater
Civic & Public Affairs: Community Foundations, Civic & Public Affairs-General, Housing, Legal Aid, Urban & Community Affairs
Education: Afterschool/Enrichment Programs, Business Education, Colleges & Universities, Education Funds, Environmental Education, Education-General, Literacy, Private Education (Precollege)
Environment: Environment-General
Health: AIDS/HIV, Cancer, Clinics/Medical Centers, Emergency/Ambulance Services, Health Funds, Health Organizations, Hospices, Hospitals, Multiple Sclerosis, Nursing Services
Religion: Religious Organizations, Religious Welfare
Science: Science Museums, Scientific Centers & Institutes
Social Services: Animal Protection, At-Risk Youth, Community Centers, Community Service Organizations, Delinquency & Criminal Rehabilitation, Emergency Relief, Family Planning, Family Services, Food/Clothing Distribution, People with Disabilities, Recreation & Athletics, Scouts, United Funds/United Ways, YMCA/YWCA/YMHA/YWHA, Youth Organizations

Application Procedures
Initial Contact: Send a brief letter of inquiry.
Application Requirements: Include a description of organization and program.
Deadlines: None.

Corporate Officials
Gerald F. Schichtel: president, chief operating officer, director PRIM CORP EMPL president, chief operating officer, director: Hilliard Corp.
Nelson Mooers van den Blink: chairman, chief executive officer, treasurer, director B Elmira, NY 1934. ED Smith College (1956). PRIM CORP EMPL chairman, chief executive officer, treasurer, director: Hilliard Corp. CORP AFFIL director: Chemung Canal Trust Co.; director: Southern Tier Econ Growth; president, director: Capabilities.

Gordon Webster: chief financial officer PRIM CORP EMPL chief financial officer: Hilliard Corp.

Foundation Officials
George L. Howell: trustee
Gerald F. Schichtel: trustee (see above)
Paul A. Schweizer: trustee B New York, NY 1913. ED New York University (1935). PRIM CORP EMPL director: Schweizer Aircraft Corp. CORP AFFIL director: Harris Hill Soaring Corp. NONPR AFFIL trustee: National Soaring Museum.
Allen C. Smith: trustee
Mary Welles Mooers Smith: vice president, trustee
Finley M. Steele: trustee
Richard W. Swan: trustee CORP AFFIL director: Hilliard Corp.
Jan van den Blink: trustee
Nelson Mooers van den Blink: president, trustee (see above)
Gordon Webster: treasurer, trustee

Grants Analysis
Disclosure Period: fiscal year ending April 30, 2004
Total Grants: $151,576*
Number of Grants: 29
Average Grant: $5,227
Highest Grant: $20,000
Lowest Grant: $500
Typical Range: $1,000 to $10,000
***Note:** Giving excludes United Way.

Recent Grants
Note: Grants derived from fiscal 2004 Form 990.
General

20,000	Arnot-Ogden Medical Center, Elmira, NY -- capital campaign
17,000	Ernie Davis Campus, Elmira, NY
15,000	Bradford County Regional Arts Council, Towanda, PA -- for stage rigging
12,500	Tanglewood Nature Center and Museum, Elmira, NY -- for exhibits
10,000	Glove House Inc., Elmira, NY -- for capital project
9,000	United Way of the Southern Tier, Corning, NY
6,000	St. Joseph's Hospital Foundation, Syracuse, NY -- for charity care program
5,061	Corning Community College Foundation, Corning, NY -- for mach tool enhancement
5,000	Arnot Art Museum, Elmira, NY
5,000	Arnot-Ogden Medical Center, Elmira, NY

HILLMAN FOUNDATION

Giving Contact
Ronald W. Wertz, President
2000 Grant Building
Pittsburgh, PA 15219
Phone: (412)338-3466
Fax: (412)338-3463
E-mail: foundation@hillmanfo.com

Description
Founded: 1951
EIN: 256011462
Organization Type: General Purpose Foundation
Giving Locations: PA: Southwestern part of state, Pittsburgh
Grant Types: Capital, Endowment, General Support, Professorship, Scholarship, Seed Money.

Donor Information
Founder: The Hillman Foundation was established in 1951 by John Hartwell Hillman Jr., a transportation and coal industrialist. The Hillman Company, a private corporation, is a major venture capital firm, with additional holdings in real estate and manufacturing.

Mr. Hillman, who died in 1981, intended the foundation to benefit the city of Pittsburgh where his business interests were centered. The Hillmans had seven children, one of whom is chairman of the foundation.

Financial Summary
Total Giving: $6,070,700 (2002); $6,462,400 (2001)
Giving Analysis: Giving for 2002 includes: foundation grants to United Way ($115,000); 2001: foundation grants to United Way ($110,000)
Assets: $120,646,913 (2002); $133,410,036 (2001)
Gifts Received: $26,318 (1998). Note: In 1998, contributions were received from the John Hartwell Educational Trust.

Typical Recipients
Arts & Humanities: Arts Associations & Councils, Arts Centers, Arts Institutes, Ballet, Ethnic & Folk Arts, Film & Video, Arts & Humanities-General, Historic Preservation, History & Archaeology, Libraries, Museums/Galleries, Music, Opera, Performing Arts, Public Broadcasting, Theater
Civic & Public Affairs: African American Affairs, Botanical Gardens/Parks, Business/Free Enterprise, Clubs, Community Foundations, Economic Development, Employment/Job Training, Civic & Public Affairs-General, Housing, Minority Business, Urban & Community Affairs, Zoos/Aquariums
Education: Afterschool/Enrichment Programs, Arts/Humanities Education, Business Education, Colleges & Universities, Community & Junior Colleges, Economic Education, Education Funds, Education Reform, Elementary Education (Private), Faculty Development, Education-General, Gifted & Talented Programs, Literacy, Medical Education, Minority Education, Preschool Education, Private Education (Precollege), Public Education (Precollege), Religious Education, Science/Mathematics Education, Social Sciences Education, Special Education, Student Aid
Environment: Environment-General, Protection, Resource Conservation, Wildlife Protection
Health: AIDS/HIV, Cancer, Children's Health/Hospitals, Eyes/Blindness, Health Organizations, Long-Term Care, Medical Rehabilitation, Medical Research, Mental Health, Nursing Services, Outpatient Health Care, Research/Studies Institutes, Single-Disease Health Associations, Speech & Hearing
International: International Relief Efforts
Religion: Jewish Causes, Ministries, Religious Organizations, Religious Welfare, Seminaries
Science: Science Museums, Scientific Centers & Institutes
Social Services: At-Risk Youth, Big Brothers/Big Sisters, Child Welfare, Community Centers, Community Service Organizations, Crime Prevention, Day Care, Delinquency & Criminal Rehabilitation, Domestic Violence, Emergency Relief, Family Planning, Family Services, Food/Clothing Distribution, Homes, People with Disabilities, Recreation & Athletics, Scouts, Senior Services, Sexual Abuse, Shelters/Homelessness, Social Services-General, Substance Abuse, United Funds/United Ways, YMCA/YWCA/YMHA/YWHA, Youth Organizations

Application Procedures
Initial Contact: The foundation will accept the Common Grant Application Form of Grantmakers of Western Pennsylvania.
Application Requirements: The cover letter of the proposal should convey justification for the request and must be signed by an authorized official of the organization. The request should include an annual budget, a listing of the organization's directors or trustees, detailed information about costs of the project for which funds are sought, and a time schedule (if appropriate). Applications also must provide proof of tax-exempt status, and indicate that any grant received from the foundation will be considered a "qualifying distribution" as defined in the Internal Revenue Code Section 4942(g) rather than a "taxable expenditure" as defined in the Internal Revenue Code Sec-

tion 4945(d).
Deadlines: None.
Review Process: The board meets quarterly to consider applications.

Restrictions

The foundation does not make grants to individuals, to organizations outside the United States, for travel expenses, or for conferences or seminars.

Additional Information

Recipients are expected to provide periodic written reports concerning the project or program funded. The foundation will specify the timetable and contents of the reports when each contribution is made.
Publications: Annual Report

Foundation Officials

H. Vaughan Blaxter, III: director, secretary B 1943. PRIM CORP EMPL vice president, secretary, director: Hillman Co. CORP AFFIL secretary: Emerald Holding Co. Inc. NONPR AFFIL treasurer: Childrens Center Pittsburgh.

Carl G. Grefenstette: director, vice president B Toledo, OH 1927. ED Duquesne University (1950). PRIM CORP EMPL chairman, chief executive officer, director: Hillman Co. NONPR AFFIL member: American Institute of Certified Public Accountants; director: Duquesne University.

Elsie Hilliard Hillman: director B 1925. ED Westminster Choir College (1944-1945). CORP AFFIL director: Hillman Co.; director: Hillman Manufacturing Co. NONPR AFFIL director: Westminster Choir College; director, vice president: WQED Public TV; vice president: Squirrel Hill Urban Coalition; director, vice president: Pittsburgh Oratorio Society; director, vice president: Pittsburgh Symphony Society; trustee: Carlow College; honorary board member: Ellis School.

Henry Lea Hillman, Jr.: chairman, director B Pittsburgh, PA December 25, 1918. ED Princeton University AB (1941). PRIM CORP EMPL chairman executive committee: Hillman Co. NONPR AFFIL member: Business Council; trustee: Carnegie Institute; emeritus member executive committee: Allegheny Conference Community Development. CLUB AFFIL Seminole Golf Club; Princeton Club; Rolling Rock Club; Pittsburgh Golf Club; The Links Club; Lyford Cay Club; Laurel Valley Golf Club; Duquesne Club; Fox Chapel Golf Club; Augusta National Golf Club.

Lisa R. Johns: assistant treasurer

Lawrence M. Wagner: treasurer, director B 1939. PRIM CORP EMPL president: Hillman Co.

Ronald W. Wertz: president B 1937.

Grants Analysis

Disclosure Period: calendar year ending 2002
Total Grants: $5,955,700*
Number of Grants: 58
Average Grant: $91,328*
Highest Grant: $750,000
Lowest Grant: $4,000
Typical Range: $50,000 to $150,000
*Note: Giving excludes United Way. Average grant figure excludes highest grant.

Recent Grants

Note: Grants derived from 2002 Form 990.
Library-Related

75,000	Allegheny County Library Association, Pittsburgh, PA -- for the expansion of e network information infrastructure

General

750,000	Children's Museum of Pittsburgh, Pittsburgh, PA -- toward development of Pittsburgh Children's Center
500,000	University of Pittsburgh, Pittsburgh, PA
500,000	UPMC Shadyside, Pittsburgh, PA -- toward construction of a facility for cancer care and research
350,000	Carnegie Institution, Pittsburgh, PA
300,000	Duquesne University, Pittsburgh, PA
250,000	MPC Corporation, Pittsburgh, PA -- toward operations and program investments of the life sciences greenhouse
200,000	Carnegie Mellon University, Pittsburgh, PA -- toward an endowment
200,000	Pittsburgh Symphony, Pittsburgh, PA
150,000	Sports & Exhibition Authority, Pittsburgh, PA -- toward development of North Shore Riverfront Park
125,000	Allegheny Conference on Community Development, Pittsburgh, PA -- toward infrastructure staffing and regional improvement projects

HILLSDALE FUND

Giving Contact

E. Eloy Doolan, Vice President
Hillsdale Fund
PO Box 20124
Greensboro, NC 27420
Phone: (336)274-5471

Description

Founded: 1963
EIN: 566057433
Organization Type: Family Foundation
Giving Locations: NC: U.S. Eastern Region.
Grant Types: General Support.

Donor Information

Founder: The fund was incorporated in 1963 by the L. Richardson family.

Financial Summary

Total Giving: $1,411,831 (2003); $1,574,903 (2002)
Assets: $31,484,308 (2003); $25,177,087 (2002)
Gifts Received: $20,132 (2003); $1,556,478 (2000); $50,000 (1998). Note: In 1998 and 2003, contributions were received from Lunsford Richardson, Jr.

Typical Recipients

Arts & Humanities: Arts Associations & Councils, Arts Centers, Arts Festivals, Arts Funds, Ballet, Dance, Film & Video, Historic Preservation, History & Archaeology, Libraries, Literary Arts, Museums/Galleries, Music, Opera, Performing Arts, Public Broadcasting, Theater
Civic & Public Affairs: Botanical Gardens/Parks, Community Foundations, Economic Development, Ethnic Organizations, Civic & Public Affairs-General, Housing, Inner-City Development, Legal Aid, Municipalities/Towns, Nonprofit Management, Philanthropic Organizations, Public Policy, Rural Affairs, Safety, Urban & Community Affairs, Women's Affairs, Zoos/Aquariums
Education: Agricultural Education, Arts/Humanities Education, Colleges & Universities, Community & Junior Colleges, Economic Education, Education Funds, Education Reform, Elementary Education (Private), Engineering/Technological Education, Education-General, Health & Physical Education, Leadership Training, Legal Education, Literacy, Private Education (Precollege), Public Education (Precollege), Religious Education, Social Sciences Education, Student Aid
Environment: Forestry, Environment-General, Protection, Resource Conservation
Health: AIDS/HIV, Alzheimer's Disease, Cancer, Children's Health/Hospitals, Clinics/Medical Centers, Emergency/Ambulance Services, Health-General, Health Policy/Cost Containment, Health Funds, Health Organizations, Hospices, Hospitals, Mental Health, Multiple Sclerosis, Preventive Medicine/Wellness Organizations, Public Health, Single-Disease Health Associations
International: Foreign Arts Organizations, Health Care/Hospitals, International Relief Efforts, Missionary/Religious Activities
Religion: Churches, Ministries, Missionary Activities (Domestic), Religious Organizations, Religious Welfare, Seminaries
Science: Science Museums, Scientific Centers & Institutes, Scientific Labs
Social Services: Animal Protection, At-Risk Youth, Child Welfare, Community Centers, Community Service Organizations, Counseling, Domestic Violence, Emergency Relief, Family Planning, Family Services, Food/Clothing Distribution, Homes, People with Disabilities, Recreation & Athletics, Refugee Assistance, Scouts, Senior Services, Shelters/Homelessness, Social Services-General, Substance Abuse, United Funds/United Ways, YMCA/YWCA/YMHA/YWHA, Youth Organizations

Application Procedures

Initial Contact: Applicants should write for application form.
Application Requirements: Completed applications will include a copy of an IRS exemption letter with the application form, which asks for legal name of organization, name of contact person, summary description of project (not to exceed three double-spaced pages), total cost of project, amount requested, other principal funding sources, principal sources of funds for day-to-day operations, financial information, and signature of officer or chief staff person.
Deadlines: Set not less than two nor more than three months before the board meetings.
Review Process: The board of trustees meets twice each year--in the spring and fall. At each board meeting, the date of the next board meeting and the deadline for that meeting are established.

Restrictions

The fund does not maintain a discretionary fund nor make emergency grants. No grant funds will be made for indirect costs or overhead. Grants will not be made for routine, recurring operating expenses except in unusual circumstances, such as for pilot projects; where the need is temporary; or where more permanent funding is in sight. Pass-through grants from one organization to another will not be made unless the organizations are legally affiliated or in other unusual circumstances. Challenge grants will be limited to one year and will expire automatically after that time if the challenge is not met. Video tapes will not be accepted as part of the grant request. No grants will be made for conferences and seminars; for film or video production, or for travel for bands, sports teams, or other groups except in unusual circumstances. No grants will be made for travel and study. No grants will be made to individuals.

Additional Information

Publications: Application Form

Foundation Officials

Sion A. Boney, III: trustee B Goldsboro, NC 1923. ED University of North Carolina (1947). Harvard University Graduate School of Business Administration (1949). PRIM CORP EMPL vice president, secretary, treasurer, trustee: Hillsdale Fund Inc. CORP AFFIL director: Piedmont Finance Co.; director: Piedmont Management Co.

Sion A. Boney, Jr.: manager
Laurinda L. Douglas: trustee
Barbara Richardson Evans: trustee
John Peter Gallagher: trustee
Margaret W. Gallagher: trustee
Louise Boney McCoy: trustee
Beatrix W. Richardson: trustee
Eudora L. Richardson: trustee
Lunsford Richardson, Jr.: chairman, trustee B Greensboro, NC 1924. ED Lehigh University (1946). PRIM CORP EMPL chairman: Richardson Corp. CORP AFFIL director: Chartwell Reinsurance Co.; director: Lexington Global Asset Management Co.
Lunsford Richardson Smith: trustee
Molly R. Smith: trustee

Richard G. Smith, III: trustee
Margaret R. White: trustee

Grants Analysis
Disclosure Period: calendar year ending 2003
Total Grants: $1,411,831
Number of Grants: 86
Average Grant: $15,433*
Highest Grant: $100,000*
Lowest Grant: $606
Typical Range: $5,000 to $30,000
***Note:** Average grant figure excludes highest grant.

Recent Grants
Note: Grants derived from 2003 Form 990.
Library-Related
15,000	Greensboro Public Library, Greensboro, NC
10,000	Free Library of Northampton Township, Nassawadox, VA

General
100,000	YMCA of Norwalk, Norwalk, CT
64,000	Berkshire Country Day School, Lenox, MA
64,000	Columbus Academy, Gahanna, OH
50,000	Colorado Open Lands, Lakewood, CO
50,000	ECHO Ministry Inc., Elkin, NC
50,000	Hugh Chatham Memorial Hospital, Elkin, NC
49,200	Catholic Health Initiatives, Denver, CO
40,000	Overlook Hospital Foundation, Summit, NJ
37,000	Webb School, Bell Buckle, TN
35,000	International Rescue Committee, New York, NY

PAUL AND ANNETTA HIMMELFARB FOUNDATION

Giving Contact
Lillian Kronstadt, Executive Director
4545 42nd St. NW, Suite 203
Washington, DC 20016-4623
Phone: (202)966-3795

Description
Founded: 1947
EIN: 520784206
Organization Type: Private Foundation
Giving Locations: DC: Washington; MD; NY: New York
Grant Types: Emergency, General Support, Project, Research.

Donor Information
Founder: members of the Himmelfarb family

Financial Summary
Total Giving: $396,916 (2001)
Assets: $5,964,623 (2001)

Typical Recipients
Arts & Humanities: Arts Centers, Arts Outreach, Historic Preservation, Libraries, Museums/Galleries, Music, Opera, Performing Arts, Public Broadcasting, Theater
Civic & Public Affairs: Economic Development, Employment/Job Training, Civic & Public Affairs-General, Housing, Law & Justice, Urban & Community Affairs, Women's Affairs
Education: Arts/Humanities Education, Colleges & Universities, Preschool Education, Private Education (Precollege), Science/Mathematics Education, Secondary Education (Private), Student Aid, Vocational & Technical Education

Environment: Environment-General
Health: AIDS/HIV, Cancer, Children's Health/Hospitals, Clinics/Medical Centers, Diabetes, Emergency/Ambulance Services, Eyes/Blindness, Health-General, Heart, Hospices, Hospitals, Kidney, Long-Term Care, Medical Research, Mental Health, Research/Studies Institutes, Respiratory, Single-Disease Health Associations
International: Foreign Arts Organizations, Foreign Educational Institutions, Health Care/Hospitals, International Organizations, Missionary/Religious Activities
Religion: Churches, Religion-General, Jewish Causes, Religious Organizations, Religious Welfare, Synagogues/Temples
Science: Scientific Centers & Institutes
Social Services: Animal Protection, At-Risk Youth, Camps, Child Welfare, Community Service Organizations, Crime Prevention, Day Care, Delinquency & Criminal Rehabilitation, Domestic Violence, Emergency Relief, Family Services, Food/Clothing Distribution, Homes, People with Disabilities, Senior Services, Shelters/Homelessness, Substance Abuse, United Funds/United Ways, YMCA/YWCA/YMHA/YWHA, Youth Organizations

Application Procedures
Initial Contact: Send a brief letter describing program or project.
Application Requirements: Include annual report, proof of tax-exempt status, and amount requested.
Deadlines: None.

Restrictions
Does not provide grants to individuals.

Foundation Officials
Paul Himmelfarb: secretary, director
Annette Kronstadt: director
Lillian Kronstadt: executive director
Norma Lee Naiman: director
Carol Himmelfarb Parker: director
Carole Preston: director

Grants Analysis
Disclosure Period: calendar year ending 2001
Total Grants: $396,916
Number of Grants: 174
Average Grant: $2,218
Highest Grant: $16,666
Typical Range: $1,000 to $5,000

Recent Grants
Note: Grants derived from 2001 Form 990.
General
20,000	WETA, Washington, DC
16,666	Weizmann Institute of Science, Washington, DC
10,000	Gallaudet University, Washington, DC
10,000	Himmelfarb Mobile University - JSSA, Rockville, MD
7,500	Jewish Foundation for Group Homes, Rockville, MD
6,000	Lab School, Washington, DC
5,000	American Diabetes Association, Washington, DC
5,000	American Jewish World Services, New York, NY -- India earthquake
5,000	Bread for the City Zacchaeus Free Clinic, Washington, DC
5,000	Camp Holiday Trails, Charlottesville, VA

HINO DIESEL TRUCKS (U.S.A.)

Company Headquarters
25 Corporate Dr.
Orangeburg, NY 10962

Company Description
Employees: 44
SIC(s): 5012 Automobiles & Other Motor Vehicles.
Parent Company: Hino Motors Ltd., 1-1 Hinadai 3-chome Hino-Shi, Tokyo, Japan

Operating Locations
Hino Diesel Trucks (U.S.A.) (NY--Orangeburg)

Giving Contact
Frank Merz, Vice President
25 Corporate Dr.
Orangeburg, NY 10962
Phone: (845)365-1400
Fax: (845)365-1409
E-mail: merz@hino.com

Description
Organization Type: Corporate Giving Program
Giving Locations: headquarters and operating communities.
Grant Types: Capital.

Typical Recipients
Arts & Humanities: Libraries
Social Services: Substance Abuse, Volunteer Services, Youth Organizations

Application Procedures
Initial Contact: Applications not encouraged.

Corporate Officials
Mr. Y. Hayakawa: chairman, president, chief executive officer treasurer PRIM CORP EMPL chairman, president, chief executive officer: Hino Diesel Trucks (USA).
N. Mukai: executive vice president, secretary, treasurer PRIM CORP EMPL executive vice president, secretary, treasurer: Hino Diesel Trucks (U.S.A.).

GILBERT M. AND MARTHA H. HITCHCOCK FOUNDATION

Giving Contact
Thomas R. Burke, Attorney
10306 Regency Pky. Dr.
Omaha, NE 68114
Phone: (402)397-7300

Description
Founded: 1943
EIN: 476025723
Organization Type: Private Foundation
Giving Locations: IA: Western part of state; NE: Omaha
Grant Types: Capital, Endowment, General Support, Scholarship.

Donor Information
Founder: the late Martha H. Hitchcock

Financial Summary
Total Giving: $808,000 (2001)
Giving Analysis: Giving for 2001 includes: foundation grants to United Way ($5,000); foundation scholarships ($40,000)
Assets: $17,675,166 (2001)

Typical Recipients
Arts & Humanities: Arts Associations & Councils, Community Arts, Dance, Historic Preservation, History & Archaeology, Libraries, Museums/Galleries, Music, Opera, Performing Arts, Public Broadcasting, Theater
Civic & Public Affairs: Botanical Gardens/Parks,

Civic & Public Affairs-General, Safety, Zoos/
Aquariums
Education: Colleges & Universities, Education
Funds, Education-General, Legal Education, Private
Education (Precollege), Public Education (Precollege), Special Education, Student Aid
Environment: Forestry, Environment-General, Resource Conservation
Health: Children's Health/Hospitals, Health Organizations, Hospices, Nursing Services
Religion: Churches, Religious Welfare
Science: Science Museums
Social Services: Child Welfare, Crime Prevention,
Day Care, People with Disabilities, Scouts, United
Funds/United Ways, Volunteer Services, Youth Organizations

Application Procedures

Initial Contact: Send a brief letter of inquiry requesting application form.
Application Requirements: Include a description of
organization, amount requested, recently audited financial statement, printing, budget of project, purpose of funds sought and proof of tax-exempt status.
Deadlines: November 1.

Restrictions

Provides grants to private educational institutions, religious organizations, and arts organizations. Does
not support individuals.

Additional Information

Foundation provides scholarships for newspaper carriers.
Publications: Application Guidelines; Application
Form

Foundation Officials

Thomas R. Burke: secretary
Tyler B. Gaines: trustee
Charles Denman Kountze: trustee
Denman Kountze: president, trustee
Edward H. Kountze: trustee
Mary Kountze: trustee
Neely Kountze: trustee
Ronald R. Ruh: trustee
Paul V. Shirley, Jr.: trustee

Grants Analysis

Disclosure Period: calendar year ending 2001
Total Grants: $763,000*
Number of Grants: 34
Average Grant: $14,030*
Highest Grant: $300,000
Lowest Grant: $1,000
Typical Range: $5,000 to $30,000
*Note:** Giving excludes United Way and scholarships. Average grant figure excludes highest grant.

Recent Grants

Note: Grants derived from 2001 Form 990.
Library-Related
10,000	Kountze Library, Kountze, TX

General
300,000	Omaha Botanical Gardens, Omaha, NE
50,000	Bellevue University Foundation, Bellevue, NE
50,000	Henry Doorly Zoo Farm Endowment Fund, Omaha, NE
50,000	Henry Doorly Zoo Farm Endowment Fund, Omaha, NE
45,000	Pottawattamie Conservation Foundation, Council Bluffs, IA
40,000	Brownell Talbot, Omaha, NE
25,000	Historical Society of Douglas County, Omaha, NE
25,000	Ross Film Theater
25,000	SAC Museum Memorial Society, Omaha, NE
25,000	Stephen Center, Omaha, NE

GEORGE HOAG FAMILY FOUNDATION

Giving Contact

Charles W. Smith, Secretary/Executive Director
2665 Main St., Suite 220
Santa Monica, CA 90405
Phone: (310)664-1358

Description

Founded: 1940
EIN: 956006885
Organization Type: Family Foundation
Giving Locations: CA: Orange County
Grant Types: General Support, Project, Research.

Donor Information

Founder: The Hoag Foundation was established in
1940 with funds donated by the late George Grant
Hoag and from bequests from his estate. His widow,
Grace E. Hoag, and his son, George Grant Hoag II,
also have supported the foundation with donations.
George Grant Hoag was a prominent vice president
and director of the J.C. Penney Company. The foundation sponsored the construction of the Hoag Memorial Hospital in Newport Beach, CA.

Financial Summary

Total Giving: $2,741,600 (2003); $2,629,200 (2002);
$2,731,900 (2001)
Assets: $70,673,678 (2003); $61,354,268 (2002);
$69,250,056 (2001)

Typical Recipients

Arts & Humanities: Arts Festivals, Ballet, Libraries,
Literary Arts, Museums/Galleries, Music, Opera, Performing Arts, Public Broadcasting, Theater
Civic & Public Affairs: Business/Free Enterprise,
Civil Rights, Community Foundations, Employment/
Job Training, Civic & Public Affairs-General, Hispanic
Affairs, Housing, Law & Justice, Legal Aid, Municipalities/Towns, Public Policy, Urban & Community Affairs, Zoos/Aquariums
Education: Afterschool/Enrichment Programs, Agricultural Education, Arts/Humanities Education, Colleges & Universities, Continuing Education, Education Associations, Education Funds, Education
Reform, Elementary Education (Public), Education-General, Gifted & Talented Programs, Literacy, Preschool Education, Private Education (Precollege),
Public Education (Precollege), Science/Mathematics
Education, Secondary Education (Private), Secondary Education (Public), Special Education, Student
Aid
Environment: Environment-General, Wildlife Protection
Health: Adolescent Health Issues, AIDS/HIV, Alzheimer's Disease, Cancer, Children's Health/
Hospitals, Clinics/Medical Centers, Diabetes, Emergency/Ambulance Services, Eyes/Blindness, Health-General, Health Funds, Health Organizations, Heart,
Hospices, Hospitals, Medical Research, Mental
Health, Outpatient Health Care, Prenatal Health Issues, Preventive Medicine/Wellness Organizations,
Public Health, Research/Studies Institutes, Respiratory, Single-Disease Health Associations, Speech &
Hearing
International: International Environmental Issues,
International Relations, International Relief Efforts,
Missionary/Religious Activities
Religion: Churches, Religion-General, Religious Organizations, Religious Welfare
Science: Science Museums
Social Services: At-Risk Youth, Big Brothers/Big
Sisters, Child Abuse, Child Welfare, Community Centers, Community Service Organizations, Counseling,
Day Care, Delinquency & Criminal Rehabilitation, Domestic Violence, Emergency Relief, Family Services,
Food/Clothing Distribution, Homes, People with Disabilities, Recreation & Athletics, Scouts, Senior Ser-

vices, Shelters/Homelessness, Social Services-General, Substance Abuse, YMCA/YWCA/YMHA/
YWHA, Youth Organizations

Application Procedures

Initial Contact: Written requests, not exceeding two
pages, should be sent to the foundation to determine
eligibility and to arrange for necessary forms and any
additional information which may be needed.
Application Requirements: Requests should outline aims and specific needs. Finished applications
(nine copies) must be accompanied by IRS determination letter of tax-exempt status, California Franchise Tax Board letter, Forms 4653 or 2218, and notification of status under section 509(a). Also include
an audited financial statement; list of officers, directors, and trustees; detailed statement of request; budget; timetable; list of other funding sources; statement
of how the project would benefit California and/or Orange County residents and the need served; statement specifying when the organization will report to
the foundation on the disbursement of funds and the
results obtained; and a declaration from the governing body of the organization authorizing the application.
Deadlines: March 31 for May meeting and September 30 for November meeting.
Review Process: The foundation's grant-making
criteria include current need for proposed project and
extent to which it duplicates existing services; reasonableness of budget; evidence of efficient, economical management and experienced, competent
personnel; and assurance of practical results. Final
decisions on each application are communicated to
applicants in writing following the board meetings in
May and November.

Restrictions

The foundation does not make grants to individuals
for any purpose. It generally does not give to governmental agencies or organizations that receive substantial support from taxation; sectarian or religious
organizations in which the principal activity benefits
the members; or organizations soliciting funds in support of projects or programs operated by a party other
than the applicant. The foundation usually does not
make grants to any organization two years in succession, and prefers not to grant funds more often than
once every three or four years.

Additional Information

Communications with individual directors of the foundation will not be of assistance to the applicant, and
are discouraged.
The foundation was originally known as the HOAG
Foundation.

Foundation Officials

Albert J. Auer: director B 1924. PRIM CORP EMPL
president: Albert J. Auer Associates Inc. CORP
AFFIL director: Kearney Mesa Bowl Inc.
Gerald E. Boltz: director
John L. Curci: director CORP AFFIL general partner: Washington Plaza Associates.
George Grant Hoag, III: vice president, chief financial officer, director
Gwyn P. Parry: director
Michael B. Sedgwick: treasurer
Charles W. Smith: secretary, executive director, director
Melinda Hoag Smith: president, chief executive officer, director
Del V. Werderman: treasurer

Grants Analysis

Disclosure Period: calendar year ending 2003
Total Grants: $2,741,600
Number of Grants: 75
Average Grant: $30,292*
Highest Grant: $500,000
Lowest Grant: $5,000

Typical Range: $10,000 to $50,000
*Note: Average grant figure excludes highest grant.

Recent Grants

Note: Grants derived from 2003 Form 990.
General

500,000	Hoag Memorial Hospital Presbyterian, Newport Beach, CA
500,000	Hoag Memorial Hospital Presbyterian, Newport Beach, CA -- towards construction of women's pavilion
100,000	Saint John's Health Center, Santa Monica, CA -- towards construction of new Saint John's Health Center
75,000	Union Rescue Mission, Los Angeles, CA
70,000	John Wayne Cancer Institute (JWCI), Santa Monica, CA
60,000	City of Hope National Medical Center, Los Angeles, CA -- towards aid in developing innovative and effective treatments for cancer and other life threatening illness
55,000	Doheny Eye Institute, Los Angeles, CA -- towards purchase OCT equipment in support of research and clinical care
55,000	Greater Los Angeles Zoo, Los Angeles, CA -- towards interactive materials in the new children's discovery center learning complex
50,000	Alzheimer's Association, Orange, CA -- towards association's helpline providing individualized telephone support, information and education
50,000	Holy Family Services Adoption & Foster Care (HFS), Pasadena, CA

HOBBY FAMILY FOUNDATION

Giving Contact

Jennifer Cole, Secretary
2131 San Felipe
Houston, TX 77019-5620
Phone: (713)521-4694
Fax: (713)521-3950

Description

Founded: 1945
EIN: 746026606
Organization Type: Family Foundation
Giving Locations: TX: Houston
Grant Types: General Support.

Donor Information

Founder: Incorporated in 1945 by Oveta Culp Hobby, the late W. P. Hobby, and the Houston Post Co.

Financial Summary

Total Giving: $1,300,000 (2001)
Assets: $30,000,000 (2001)
Gifts Received: $100,000 (1993)

Typical Recipients

Arts & Humanities: Arts Associations & Councils, Arts Institutes, Ballet, Arts & Humanities-General, Historic Preservation, History & Archaeology, Libraries, Literary Arts, Museums/Galleries, Music, Opera, Theater
Civic & Public Affairs: African American Affairs, Botanical Gardens/Parks, Civic & Public Affairs-General, Hispanic Affairs, Housing, Legal Aid, Municipalities/Towns, Parades/Festivals, Philanthropic Organizations, Public Policy, Urban & Community Affairs, Women's Affairs, Zoos/Aquariums
Education: Arts/Humanities Education, Business Education, Colleges & Universities, Elementary Education (Public), Education-General, International Studies, Literacy, Minority Education, Private Education (Precollege), Science/Mathematics Education, Social Sciences Education, Special Education, Student Aid
Environment: Environment-General, Resource Conservation, Wildlife Protection
Health: AIDS/HIV, Alzheimer's Disease, Cancer, Children's Health/Hospitals, Emergency/Ambulance Services, Eyes/Blindness, Health Funds, Health Organizations, Heart, Hospices, Hospitals, Mental Health, Single-Disease Health Associations
International: International Affairs, Missionary/Religious Activities
Religion: Churches, Ministries, Religious Organizations, Religious Welfare
Science: Observatories & Planetariums, Science Museums, Scientific Centers & Institutes, Scientific Organizations
Social Services: Animal Protection, Child Welfare, Community Centers, Community Service Organizations, Domestic Violence, Emergency Relief, Family Planning, Food/Clothing Distribution, People with Disabilities, Scouts, Shelters/Homelessness, United Funds/United Ways, Volunteer Services, YMCA/YWCA/YMHA/YWHA, Youth Organizations

Application Procedures

Initial Contact: Write a proposal letter or memorandum briefly describing the need for funds.
Application Requirements: The following information should be included in the proposal: a brief background of the organization; a description of the proposed project along with a concise statement of the project; an explanation of the proposed use of funds; evidence of tax-exempt status; and a statement of approval of the request for funds signed by the chief administrator of the organization.
Deadlines: None.

Restrictions

The foundation does not make grants or award scholarships to individuals. Majority of giving is limited to Houston area.

Additional Information

In 1996 the Hobby Foundation split into two seperate foundations: Catto Charitable Foundation in San Antonio, TX, and Hobby Family Foundation in Houston, TX.
Publications: Application Guidelines

Foundation Officials

Laura H. Beckworth: vice president
Pamela L. George: secretary
Diana P. Hobby: vice president
Paul W. Hobby: vice president B Houston, TX 1960. ED University of Virginia (1982); University of Texas JD (1985). PRIM CORP EMPL chairman: Hobby Media Services Inc. CORP AFFIL director: Coastal Bancorp Inc.; director: Stewart Information Services Corp.; director: Aronex Pharmaceuticals Inc.
William Pettus Hobby: president B Houston, TX 1932. ED Rice University BA (1953). CORP AFFIL director: Southwest Airlines Co. NONPR AFFIL professor: Rice University.
Cathy Leeson: treasurer

Grants Analysis

Disclosure Period: calendar year ending 1998
Total Grants: $691,704*
Number of Grants: 144
Average Grant: $4,804
Highest Grant: $100,000
Typical Range: $1,000 to $10,000
*Note: Giving excludes United Way and $2,396,940 in stock contributions to two organizations.

Recent Grants

Note: Grants derived from 1999 Form 990.

General

1,000,000	Baylor College of Medicine, Houston, TX -- for operating expenses
100,000	Harry Ransom Humanities Research Center, Austin, TX -- for endowment fund
60,000	St. John's School, Houston, TX -- for retirement of debt and building fund
50,000	Kinkaid School, Houston, TX -- capital campaign
37,500	Wake Forest University, Winston-Salem, NC -- for scholarship fund
35,000	Houston Symphony Society, Houston, TX -- for operating expenses
30,000	Lockhart Community Recreation Center, Lockhart, TX -- for operating expenses
30,000	Willie Mae Mitchell Community Opportunity Center, San Marcos, TX -- for operating expenses
25,000	Houston Ballet, Houston, TX -- for operating expenses
25,000	Houston Grand Opera, Houston, TX -- for operating expenses

HOBLITZELLE FOUNDATION

Giving Contact

Paul W. Harris, Executive Vice President
5956 Sherry Lane, Suite 901
Dallas, TX 75225-6522
Phone: (214)373-0462
Fax: (214)750-7412
E-mail: hoblitzelle@worldnet.att.net
Web: http://www.hoblitzelle.org/pages/1/index.htm

Description

Founded: 1942
EIN: 756003984
Organization Type: General Purpose Foundation
Giving Locations: TX, Dallas
Grant Types: Capital, General Support, Matching, Multiyear/Continuing Support.

Donor Information

Founder: The foundation was established in 1942. The foundation's donors were the late Karl St. John Hoblitzelle and Esther Hoblitzelle. Karl Hoblitzelle (1879-1967) was president of Interstate Circuit, Texas Consolidated Theaters, and Hoblitzelle Properties. He was also chairman of Republic National Bank of Dallas and the Southwest Medical Foundation. In addition, he served as trustee of Texas A&M University and the Dallas Foundation.

Financial Summary

Total Giving: $5,523,358 (fiscal year ending April 30, 2004); $5,178,882 (fiscal 2002); $6,694,347 (fiscal 2001)
Assets: $115,946,439 (fiscal 2004); $116,000,000 (fiscal 2002); $131,795,263 (fiscal 2001)
Gifts Received: $26,584 (fiscal 2004); $30,140 (fiscal 2001); $27,924 (fiscal 2000). Note: In fiscal 2004, 2001, 2000 and 1999, contributions were received from the Karl Hoblitzelle Trust.

Typical Recipients

Arts & Humanities: Arts Festivals, Arts Outreach, Ballet, Community Arts, Ethnic & Folk Arts, Historic Preservation, History & Archaeology, Libraries, Museums/Galleries, Music, Opera, Performing Arts, Public Broadcasting, Theater
Civic & Public Affairs: Botanical Gardens/Parks, Chambers of Commerce, Clubs, Economic Development, Employment/Job Training, Civic & Public Affairs-General, Hispanic Affairs, Housing, Inner-City Development, Native American Affairs, Nonprofit Management, Professional & Trade Associations,

Public Policy, Safety, Urban & Community Affairs, Women's Affairs, Zoos/Aquariums

Education: Afterschool/Enrichment Programs, Agricultural Education, Business Education, Colleges & Universities, Education Funds, Education Reform, Engineering/Technological Education, Education-General, Literacy, Medical Education, Minority Education, Private Education (Precollege), Public Education (Precollege), Religious Education, Science/Mathematics Education, Secondary Education (Private), Special Education, Student Aid

Environment: Environment-General, Resource Conservation

Health: AIDS/HIV, Alzheimer's Disease, Cancer, Children's Health/Hospitals, Clinics/Medical Centers, Diabetes, Emergency/Ambulance Services, Eyes/Blindness, Health-General, Health Funds, Health Organizations, Hospices, Hospitals, Hospitals (University Affiliated), Long-Term Care, Medical Research, Medical Training, Mental Health, Multiple Sclerosis, Nursing Services, Prenatal Health Issues, Public Health, Single-Disease Health Associations, Transplant Networks/Donor Banks, Trauma Treatment

Religion: Churches, Religion-General, Ministries, Missionary Activities (Domestic), Religious Organizations, Religious Welfare

Science: Science Exhibits & Fairs, Science Museums, Scientific Centers & Institutes

Social Services: Animal Protection, At-Risk Youth, Big Brothers/Big Sisters, Camps, Child Welfare, Community Centers, Community Service Organizations, Counseling, Crime Prevention, Day Care, Emergency Relief, Family Planning, Family Services, Food/Clothing Distribution, Homes, People with Disabilities, Recreation & Athletics, Scouts, Senior Services, Shelters/Homelessness, Substance Abuse, United Funds/United Ways, Volunteer Services, YMCA/YWCA/YMHA/YWHA, Youth Organizations

Application Procedures

Initial Contact: Applicants should send a letter to the foundation.

Application Requirements: The letter should include a brief narrative describing the project, its justification, cost based on reliable estimates, funding already realized or anticipated from other sources, proof of tax-exempt status, and the amount requested. If the project falls within the foundation's areas of interest, a more detailed proposal may be requested.

Deadlines: Submit requests before January 15, May 15, or September 15.

Review Process: The board meets to consider applications in the latter part of February, June, and October.

Restrictions

No grants are made for religious purposes or to individuals. Grants are not made for operating budgets, debt retirement, research, media productions or publications, scholarships, endowments, or loans. No grants are made outside of Texas.

Additional Information

The foundation lists Nations Bank as a corporate trustee.

Publications: Annual Report

Foundation Officials

Jerry S. Farrington: director B Burkburnett, TX 1934. ED North Texas State University BBA (1955); North Texas State University MBA (1958). PRIM CORP EMPL chairman emeritus, director: Texas Utilities Co. CORP AFFIL chairman emeritus: Texas Utilities Mining Co.; chairman: TXV Corp.

Gerald W. Fronterhouse: chairman, director B Ada, OK 1936. ED University of Oklahoma (1959); Harvard University MBA (1962). CORP AFFIL director: Texas Instruments; director: Employees Casualty Co. NONPR AFFIL member: Beta Theta Pi.

Paul W. Harris: executive vice president

Caren H. Prothro: treasurer, director

George A. Shafer: president, chief executive officer,

director PRIM CORP EMPL president: Industrial Properties Corp. CORP AFFIL director: General Homes Corp.

William Tarver Solomon: director B Dallas, TX 1942. ED Southern Methodist University BScE (1965); Harvard University MBA (1967). PRIM CORP EMPL chairman, chief executive officer, director: Austin Industries. CORP AFFIL director: National Bank Texas; director: Chilton Corp.; director: Fidelity Union Life Insurance Co.; director: AH Belo Corp.; chairman: British American Insurance Co.; chairman: Austin Commercial Inc. NONPR AFFIL trustee: Southwest Medicine Foundation; member: Young President Organization; member: Salesmanship Club Dallas; trustee: Southern Methodist University; member: Dallas Chamber of Commerce; founder: Dallas Museum Art; director: Baylor University Medical Center Foundation; member: Dallas Assembly; member: American Society Civil Engineers.

Grants Analysis

Disclosure Period: fiscal year ending April 30, 2004
Total Grants: $5,523,358
Number of Grants: 77
Average Grant: $56,311*
Highest Grant: $800,000
Lowest Grant: $3,000
Typical Range: $25,000 to $100,000
*Note: Average grant figure excludes two highest grants ($1,300,000).

Recent Grants

Note: Grants derived from fiscal 2003 Form 990.

Library-Related
500,000	Friends of the Dallas Public Library, Dallas, TX -- renovation of downtown library

General
500,000	Southern Methodist church, Dallas, TX -- towards campus capital improvement
300,000	Dallas County Historical Museum, Dallas, TX -- towards development of a museum
300,000	Southwestern Medical Foundation Karl and Esther Hoblitzelle Fund, Dallas, TX -- towards campus expansion
225,000	Southwestern Legal Foundation, Plano, TX -- construction of new campus
200,000	Dallas Museum of Art, Dallas, TX -- storage area refurbishment
200,000	University of Texas Ransom Center, Austin, TX -- towards facility improvements and modernization
175,000	Episcopal School of Dallas, Dallas, TX -- towards campus infrastructure development
150,000	Hockaday School, Dallas, TX -- for classroom building renovation
150,000	Texas Christian University, Ft. Worth, TX -- towards a new media center
125,000	Sixth Floor Museum, Dallas, TX -- towards capital development

CHARLES H. HOCH FOUNDATION

Giving Contact

Richard J. Hummel, President & Treasurer
1825 Lehigh Parkway N.
Allentown, PA 18103
Phone: (610)366-9934

Description

Founded: 1956
EIN: 236265016
Organization Type: Private Foundation
Giving Locations: PA: Allentown
Grant Types: General Support.

Financial Summary

Gifts Received: $619,044 (1994)

Typical Recipients

Arts & Humanities: Arts Outreach, History & Archaeology, Libraries, Museums/Galleries, Music, Public Broadcasting, Theater

Civic & Public Affairs: Community Foundations, Hispanic Affairs, Housing

Education: Arts/Humanities Education, Business Education, Colleges & Universities, Community & Junior Colleges, Private Education (Precollege), Secondary Education (Private), Special Education, Student Aid

Environment: Resource Conservation, Wildlife Protection

Health: Emergency/Ambulance Services, Eyes/Blindness, Health Organizations

International: International Peace & Security Issues

Religion: Churches, Ministries, Religious Welfare

Social Services: Animal Protection, Camps, Family Services, Food/Clothing Distribution, People with Disabilities, Recreation & Athletics, Scouts, Senior Services, Shelters/Homelessness, Social Services-General, Special Olympics, YMCA/YWCA/YMHA/YWHA, Youth Organizations

Application Procedures

Initial Contact: Send a brief letter of inquiry.
Application Requirements: Include purpose of funds sought and proof of tax-exempt status.
Deadlines: None.

Restrictions

Grants are not made to individuals.

Foundation Officials

Alfred E. DeMott: director
James R. Feller: secretary, director
Richard J. Hummel: president, treasurer
Russell K. Laub: first vice president

Grants Analysis

Disclosure Period: calendar year ending 2000
Total Grants: $300,822*
Number of Grants: 69
Average Grant: $4,360
Highest Grant: $10,000
Typical Range: $2,000 to $10,000
*Note: Giving excludes scholarships.

Recent Grants

Note: Grants derived from 2001 Form 990.

General
15,000	Boys and Girls Club of Allentown, Allentown, PA -- Youth Program
12,000	Lehigh County Meals on Wheels, Allentown, PA -- Senior Citizens Programs
10,000	Allentown Rescue Mission, Allentown, PA -- building repairs
10,000	Allentown YMCA/ YWCA, Allentown, PA -- support Youth Programs
10,000	Cedar Crest College, Allentown, PA -- student scholarships
10,000	Lehigh County Historical Society, Allentown, PA -- new building program
10,000	Minsi Trails Boy Scouts of America, Allentown, PA -- Scouting Program
10,000	Muhlenberg College, Allentown, PA -- scholarship fund
10,000	Salvation Army, Allentown, PA -- charitable food bank
8,000	Allentown Art Museum, Allentown, PA -- educational project

HOCHE-SCOFIELD FOUNDATION

Giving Contact
Dorothy Dudley
c/o Fleet Bank
446 Main St.
Worcester, MA 01608-2302
Phone: (508)770-7292

Description
Founded: 1983
EIN: 222519554
Organization Type: Private Foundation
Giving Locations: MA: Worcester County, Worcester
Grant Types: Capital, General Support, Multiyear/Continuing Support, Project, Seed Money.

Donor Information
Founder: the late William B. Scofield

Financial Summary
Total Giving: $1,197,734 (fiscal year ending June 30, 2004); $865,647 (fiscal 2002); $1,064,351 (fiscal 2001)
Assets: $16,692,767 (fiscal 2004); $17,156,541 (fiscal 2002); $20,155,873 (fiscal 2001)

Typical Recipients
Arts & Humanities: Arts Associations & Councils, Arts Outreach, Historic Preservation, History & Archaeology, Libraries, Museums/Galleries, Music, Theater
Civic & Public Affairs: Clubs, Economic Development, Civic & Public Affairs-General, Housing, Municipalities/Towns, Professional & Trade Associations, Urban & Community Affairs, Women's Affairs
Education: Arts/Humanities Education, Colleges & Universities, Community & Junior Colleges, Education Reform, Engineering/Technological Education, Preschool Education, Private Education (Precollege), Public Education (Precollege), Science/Mathematics Education, Secondary Education (Private)
Environment: Environment-General, Resource Conservation
Health: Cancer, Children's Health/Hospitals, Clinics/Medical Centers, Diabetes, Health Policy/Cost Containment, Health Organizations, Hospitals, Medical Research, Nursing Services, Public Health
International: Foreign Arts Organizations
Religion: Jewish Causes, Religious Welfare
Science: Scientific Centers & Institutes
Social Services: At-Risk Youth, Big Brothers/Big Sisters, Child Welfare, Community Service Organizations, Counseling, Crime Prevention, Domestic Violence, Family Planning, Food/Clothing Distribution, Senior Services, Sexual Abuse, Shelters/Homelessness, Substance Abuse, United Funds/United Ways, YMCA/YWCA/YMHA/YWHA, Youth Organizations

Application Procedures
Initial Contact: Request application and guidelines. Requests are reviewed four times per year.

Additional Information
Publications: Application Form; Guidelines
Trust(s): Fleet National Bank

Foundation Officials
Henry Bowen Dewey, Esq.: co-trustee B Worcester, MA 1924. ED Williams College BA (1948); Boston University LLB (1952). PRIM CORP EMPL vice president: Clark Art Institute. NONPR AFFIL overseer: UGBA; member, director: Worcester Youth Guidance Association; member: Massachusetts Historical Society; president: Rural Cemetery; fellow: American College Estate & Turst Council; trustee: Hoche Scofield Charitable Trust; member: American Antiquarian Society. CLUB AFFIL Worcester Club.
Lois B. Green: co-trustee

Grants Analysis
Disclosure Period: fiscal year ending June 30, 2004
Total Grants: $1,197,734
Number of Grants: 133
Average Grant: $9,006
Highest Grant: $30,000
Lowest Grant: $1,000
Typical Range: $2,000 to $15,000

Recent Grants
Note: Grants derived from fiscal 2000 Form 990.
Library-Related
30,000	Worcester Public Library, Worcester, MA

General
114,781	Trustees of Clark University, Worcester, MA
111,227	Worcester Art Museum, Worcester, MA
111,227	Worcester Polytechnic Institute, Worcester, MA
92,673	City of Worcester, Worcester, MA
91,226	Music Worcester, Inc., Worcester, MA
19,000	American Antiquarian Society, Worcester, MA
15,000	United Way of Central Massachusetts, Worcester, MA
13,500	Worcester Municipal Research Bureau, Worcester, MA
13,000	Dynamy Inc., Worcester, MA
12,000	Tri - Community Young Men's Christian Association

BESS J. HODGES FOUNDATION

Giving Contact
Joyce Murchison, Executive Director
5100 E. Anaheim Rd.
Long Beach, CA 90815
Phone: (562)961-4115

Description
Founded: 1984
EIN: 330046140
Organization Type: Private Foundation
Giving Locations: CA
Grant Types: General Support.

Donor Information
Founder: the late Bess J. Hodges

Financial Summary
Total Giving: $218,288 (2004); $203,627 (2001)
Assets: $4,646,911 (2004); $4,849,941 (2001)

Typical Recipients
Arts & Humanities: Arts Centers, Arts Outreach, Community Arts, History & Archaeology, Libraries, Museums/Galleries, Music, Opera, Performing Arts, Public Broadcasting, Theater
Civic & Public Affairs: African American Affairs, Economic Development, Civic & Public Affairs-General, Hispanic Affairs, Law & Justice, Legal Aid, Nonprofit Management, Urban & Community Affairs, Women's Affairs
Education: Colleges & Universities, Education Funds, Education-General, Preschool Education, Private Education (Precollege), Religious Education, Secondary Education (Private), Student Aid
Health: Cancer, Children's Health/Hospitals, Clinics/Medical Centers, Health-General, Hospices, Hospitals, Medical Rehabilitation, Medical Research, Nursing Services
Religion: Religious Organizations, Religious Welfare, Social/Policy Issues

Social Services: At-Risk Youth, Child Abuse, Child Welfare, Community Service Organizations, Day Care, Emergency Relief, Family Services, Food/Clothing Distribution, Recreation & Athletics, Scouts, Shelters/Homelessness, Substance Abuse, Volunteer Services, YMCA/YWCA/YMHA/YWHA, Youth Organizations

Application Procedures
Initial Contact: Proposals should be submitted in duplicate, with a cover letter typed on the organization's letterhead and signed by the chief executive officer.
Deadlines: March 31.

Restrictions
Government agencies are not encouraged to apply.

Additional Information
Publications: Application Guidelines

Foundation Officials
Pierre E. Auw: trustee
George M. Murchison: trustee

Grants Analysis
Disclosure Period: calendar year ending 2004
Total Grants: $218,288
Number of Grants: 44
Average Grant: $4,961
Highest Grant: $25,152
Lowest Grant: $650
Typical Range: $1,000 to $10,000

Recent Grants
Note: Grants derived from 2002 Form 990.
General
35,939	Oral Roberts University, Tulsa, OK
17,970	Trinity Broadcasting Network, Santa Ana, CA
5,000	Carpenter Performing Arts Center, Long Beach, CA
5,000	Childnet, Long Beach, CA
5,000	Long Beach City College Foundation, Long Beach, CA
5,000	Long Beach Day Nursery, Long Beach, CA
5,000	Long Beach Nonprofit Partnership, Long Beach, CA
5,000	Musical Theatre West, Long Beach, CA
5,000	National Conference of Christian, Long Beach, CA
5,000	St. Joseph School, Long Beach, CA

H. LESLIE HOFFMAN & ELAINE S. HOFFMAN FOUNDATION

Giving Contact
J. Kristoffer Popovich, Trustee
225 South Lake Ave., Suite 1150
Pasadena, CA 91101
Phone: (626)793-0043
Fax: (626)793-0047

Description
Founded: 1952
EIN: 956048600
Organization Type: General Purpose Foundation
Giving Locations: CA: Los Angeles metro area
Grant Types: Employee Matching Gifts, General Support, Multiyear/Continuing Support.

Donor Information
Founder: Established in 1952 by the late H. Leslie Hoffman and the late Elaine S. Hoffman.

Financial Summary

Total Giving: $1,289,436 (2002); $1,419,811 (2001)
Assets: $32,715,352 (2002); $37,875,884 (2001)

Typical Recipients

Arts & Humanities: Arts Associations & Councils, Arts Centers, Arts Institutes, Arts & Humanities-General, Libraries, Museums/Galleries, Music, Opera, Performing Arts, Public Broadcasting
Civic & Public Affairs: Botanical Gardens/Parks, Business/Free Enterprise, Civil Rights, Clubs, Community Foundations, Employment/Job Training, Civic & Public Affairs-General, Law & Justice, Legal Aid, Nonprofit Management, Philanthropic Organizations, Professional & Trade Associations, Public Policy, Safety, Women's Affairs, Zoos/Aquariums
Education: Arts/Humanities Education, Business Education, Colleges & Universities, Education Funds, Elementary Education (Private), Education-General, Health & Physical Education, Medical Education, Minority Education, Preschool Education, Private Education (Precollege), Public Education (Precollege), Student Aid
Environment: Environment-General, Protection
Health: Arthritis, Cancer, Children's Health/Hospitals, Clinics/Medical Centers, Diabetes, Emergency/Ambulance Services, Eyes/Blindness, Health-General, Health Organizations, Heart, Hospices, Hospitals, Medical Research, Single-Disease Health Associations
International: International Peace & Security Issues
Religion: Churches, Dioceses, Religious Organizations, Religious Welfare
Social Services: Camps, Child Abuse, Child Welfare, Community Service Organizations, Crime Prevention, Emergency Relief, Family Services, Food/Clothing Distribution, Homes, People with Disabilities, Recreation & Athletics, Scouts, Senior Services, Special Olympics, Substance Abuse, United Funds/United Ways, Volunteer Services, YMCA/YWCA/YMHA/YWHA, Youth Organizations

Application Procedures

Initial Contact: The foundation has no formal grant application procedure or application form. Grant requests are received in any form.
Deadlines: None.

Restrictions

No grants are made to individuals.

Foundation Officials

J. Kristoffer Popovich: trustee PRIM CORP EMPL chief executive officer: Hoffman Video System.
Jane H. Popovich: trustee

Grants Analysis

Disclosure Period: calendar year ending 2002
Total Grants: $1,289,436
Number of Grants: 79
Average Grant: $6,714*
Highest Grant: $765,750
Lowest Grant: $50
Typical Range: $1,000 to $15,000
*Note: Average grant figure excludes highest grant.

Recent Grants

Note: Grants derived from 2002 Form 990.
Library-Related

15,000	Huntington Library, San Marino, CA

General

765,750	Kidspace, Pasadena, CA
151,000	Children's Hospital, Los Angeles, CA
20,481	Boy Scouts of America, Pasadena, CA
20,000	USC- School Of Business Administration, Los Angeles, CA
13,000	Huntington Memorial Hospital, Pasadena, CA
13,000	USC- Norris Cancer Center, Los Angeles, CA
11,500	San Marino Schools Foundation, San Marino, CA
11,000	YMCA of Metro Los Angeles, Los Angeles, CA
11,000	Young & Healthy, Pasadena, CA
10,000	Boys and Girls Clubs of Pasadena, Pasadena, CA

MAXIMILIAN E. AND MARION O. HOFFMAN FOUNDATION

Giving Contact

Doris C. Chaho, President
970 Farmington Avenue, Suite 203
West Hartford, CT 06107
Phone: (860)521-2949
Fax: (860)561-5082

Description

Founded: 1986
EIN: 222648036
Organization Type: General Purpose Foundation
Giving Locations: U.S. Northeastern Region.
Grant Types: Capital, Endowment, General Support, Project, Scholarship.

Donor Information

Founder: The foundation was established in 1986 in Connecticut as a successor foundation of the Maximilian E. and Marion O. Hoffman Foundation, which was established in New York in 1984 by Marion O. Hoffman.

Financial Summary

Total Giving: $2,368,364 (fiscal year ending June 30, 2004); $2,194,853 (fiscal 2002); $2,145,883 (fiscal 2001)
Assets: $55,567,093 (fiscal 2004); $38,019,247 (fiscal 2002); $52,593,918 (fiscal 2001)

Typical Recipients

Arts & Humanities: Arts Associations & Councils, Arts Centers, Ballet, Dance, Film & Video, Arts & Humanities-General, Historic Preservation, History & Archaeology, Libraries, Literary Arts, Museums/Galleries, Music, Opera, Performing Arts, Public Broadcasting, Theater
Civic & Public Affairs: Botanical Gardens/Parks, Clubs, Economic Policy, Employment/Job Training, Civic & Public Affairs-General, Housing, Law & Justice, Public Policy, Safety, Urban & Community Affairs, Women's Affairs
Education: Arts/Humanities Education, Colleges & Universities, Continuing Education, Education Funds, Elementary Education (Private), Engineering/Technological Education, Environmental Education, Education-General, Health & Physical Education, International Exchange, International Studies, Literacy, Medical Education, Minority Education, Private Education (Precollege), Public Education (Precollege), Religious Education, Science/Mathematics Education, Secondary Education (Private), Social Sciences Education, Special Education, Student Aid, Vocational & Technical Education
Environment: Air/Water Quality, Energy, Environment-General, Protection, Resource Conservation, Watershed
Health: Adolescent Health Issues, AIDS/HIV, Alzheimer's Disease, Cancer, Children's Health/Hospitals, Clinics/Medical Centers, Diabetes, Emergency/Ambulance Services, Health-General, Geriatric Health, Health Funds, Health Organizations, Heart, Home-Care Services, Hospitals, Hospitals (University Affiliated), Kidney, Medical Rehabilitation, Mental Health, Nursing Homes, Nutrition, Prenatal Health Issues, Research/Studies Institutes, Respiratory, Single-Disease Health Associations
International: Health Care/Hospitals, International Development, International Environmental Issues, International Organizations, International Relief Efforts, Missionary/Religious Activities
Religion: Churches, Dioceses, Religion-General, Jewish Causes, Ministries, Religious Organizations, Religious Welfare, Seminaries, Social/Policy Issues, Synagogues/Temples
Science: Science Museums, Scientific Centers & Institutes, Scientific Organizations, Scientific Research
Social Services: Camps, Child Abuse, Child Welfare, Community Service Organizations, Domestic Violence, Emergency Relief, Family Services, Food/Clothing Distribution, Homes, People with Disabilities, Scouts, Senior Services, Shelters/Homelessness, Social Services-General, Substance Abuse, United Funds/United Ways, Volunteer Services, YMCA/YWCA/YMHA/YWHA, Youth Organizations

Application Procedures

Initial Contact: Send letter of request for application.
Application Requirements: Applications should include a copy of the IRS tax-exempt determination letter.
Deadlines: Applications should be received by the foundation a month before board meetings.
Review Process: The board meets three times a year.

Restrictions

Does not make grants for political purposes.

Foundation Officials

Marion L. Barrak: president, director
Doris C. Chaho: director
Joseph B. Chaho: vice president, secretary
Michael B. Chaho: treasurer
Joseph J. Fauliso: director
Marie Gustin: director
Robert M. Heresaty, MD: director

Grants Analysis

Disclosure Period: fiscal year ending June 30, 2004
Total Grants: $2,368,364
Number of Grants: 68
Average Grant: $28,309*
Highest Grant: $250,000
Lowest Grant: $2,000
Typical Range: $5,000 to $50,000
*Note: Average grant figure excludes two highest grants ($500,000).

Recent Grants

Note: Grants derived from fiscal 2003 Form 990.
Library-Related

10,000	Hartford Public Library, Hartford, CT

General

375,000	Providence College, Providence, RI -- towards construction of a new arts center
250,000	Saint Francis Hospital and Medical Center Diabetes Center, Hartford, CT -- towards diabetes center reception and waiting room
250,000	Saint Joseph College, West Hartford, CT
150,000	Mark Twain House, Hartford, CT
100,000	East Catholic High School, Manchester, CT -- towards funding for handicapped accessibility
100,000	Hill Stead Museum, Farmington, CT -- towards renovations
100,000	Holy Apostles College and Seminary, Cromwell, CT -- towards technical advancements in computer education
100,000	Yale University, New Haven, CT
50,000	Asylum Boys and Girls Development Association, Hartford, CT
50,000	Bates College, Lewiston, ME -- towards Hoffman endowed fund for student research at the college

HOFFMANN-LA ROCHE INC.

Company Headquarters
Nutley, NJ
Web: http://www.roche.com

Company Description
Employees: 17,000
SIC(s): 2833 Medicinals & Botanicals, 2834 Pharmaceutical Preparations, 8071 Medical Laboratories.
Parent Company: Roche Group, Grenzacherstrasse 124, Basel, Switzerland

Operating Locations
American Roche International (NJ--Clifton); Genentech (CA--San Francisco); Givaudan-Roure Corp. (NJ--Clifton); Givaudan-Roure Corp. Flavors Division (NJ--Clifton); Givaudan-Roure Corp. Fragrances Division (NJ--Teaneck); Hoffmann-La Roche Inc. (NJ--Belleville, Belvidere, Montclair, Nutley, Paramus, Raritan, Totowa; NC--Burlington); Roche Biomedical Laboratories (NC--Burlington); Roche Diagnostic Systems (NJ--Somerville); Roche Molecular Systems (NJ--Somerville); Roche Professional Service Centers (NJ--Paramus); Syntex (CA--Palo Alto); Syntex Agribusiness (CA--Palo Alto); Syntex Chemicals (CO--Boulder)

Nonmonetary Support
Type: In-kind Services

Roche Foundation

Giving Contact
Vivian Beetle, Executive Director
PO Box 278
Nutley, NJ 07110-0278
Phone: (973)562-2055
Fax: (973)562-2999
Web: http://www.rocheusa.com

Alternate Contact
340 Kingsland Street
Nutley, NJ 07110-1199
Phone: (973)235-5000

Description
Founded: 1945
EIN: 226063790
Organization Type: Corporate Foundation
Former Name: Hoffmann-La Roche Foundation (2002).
Giving Locations: NJ
Grant Types: Employee Matching Gifts, Fellowship, General Support, Research, Scholarship, Seed Money.

Donor Information
Founder: Hoffmann-La Roche Inc.

Financial Summary
Total Giving: $728,750 (2003); $750,150 (2002); $1,338,155 (2001). Note: Contributes through corporate direct giving program and foundation.
Giving Analysis: Giving for 2001 includes: foundation grants to United Way ($500,000); foundation ($838,155)
Gifts Received: $729,000 (2003); $740,400 (2002); $1,338,405 (2001). Note: Contributions were received from Hoffmann-La Roche and Roche Laboratories, Inc.

Typical Recipients
Arts & Humanities: Libraries, Museums/Galleries, Music, Opera, Performing Arts
Civic & Public Affairs: Community Foundations, Employment/Job Training, Civic & Public Affairs-

General, Philanthropic Organizations, Professional & Trade Associations, Urban & Community Affairs, Zoos/Aquariums
Education: Arts/Humanities Education, Colleges & Universities, Economic Education, Education Funds, Education-General, International Exchange, Medical Education, Minority Education, Private Education (Precollege), Science/Mathematics Education, Secondary Education (Public), Student Aid, Vocational & Technical Education
Environment: Environment-General, Wildlife Protection
Health: AIDS/HIV, Cancer, Children's Health/Hospitals, Emergency/Ambulance Services, Health Policy/Cost Containment, Health Funds, Health Organizations, Hospices, Hospitals, Medical Research, Medical Training, Mental Health, Public Health, Single-Disease Health Associations, Transplant Networks/Donor Banks
International: Health Care/Hospitals, Human Rights, International Affairs, International Environmental Issues, International Relations
Religion: Churches, Religious Organizations
Science: Science Museums, Scientific Centers & Institutes, Scientific Labs, Scientific Organizations, Scientific Research
Social Services: Animal Protection, Community Service Organizations, People with Disabilities, Social Services-General, Substance Abuse, United Funds/United Ways, YMCA/YWCA/YMHA/YWHA

Application Procedures
Initial Contact: Send a letter of inquiry of not more than three pages.
Application Requirements: Include basic background on the organization including contact information, purpose, and mission; and a description of the program for which support is requested including proposed purpose, current status, professional personnel, anticipated length of program, and final results; and program budget information.
Deadlines: None.
Decision Notification: Applicants are notified of decisions within six to eight weeks of receipt of letter.

Restrictions
The foundation will not consider requests for: gifts to individuals, endowment or scholarship funds; international organizations or projects; political organizations, parties, candidates, or office holders; the purchase, construction, expansion or modification of facilities; equipment or other capital expenditures; goodwill advertising; sectarian groups, except for education and health programs which serve the general population without regard to religious affiliation; or labor or veterans' organizations, unless the project in question is for the general welfare of an entire community in which Roche is present or has a significant interest. Grants are focused on health and education programs with priority emphasis on health promotion (not medical delivery) and math and science education.

Additional Information
Preference is given to organizations located within the state of New Jersey and sites of Hoffmann-La Roche. Preference is also given to local chapters of national health organizations. National headquarters of health organizations are rarely funded.
Publications: Guidelines

Corporate Officials
Vivian Beetle: director community affairsrc PRIM CORP EMPL director community affairs: Hoffmann-La Roche Inc.
Frederick C. Kentz, III: vice president, secretary, general counsel B Summit, NJ 1952. ED Georgetown University (1974); Fordham University (1977). PRIM CORP EMPL vice president, secretary, general counsel: Hoffmann-La Roche Inc. CORP AFFIL officer: Roche Diagnostics System; officer: Roche Molecular System Inc.; officer: Roche Carolina Inc.

Patrick J. Zenner: president, chief executive officer, director B 1948. ED Creighton University BSBA; Fairleigh Dickinson University MBA (1969). PRIM CORP EMPL president, chief executive officer, director: Hoffmann-La Roche Inc. CORP AFFIL officer: Roche Carolina Inc.; officer: Roche Molecular System Inc.; president: HLR Service Corp.

Foundation Officials
George B. Abercrombie: trustee
Vivian Beetle: executive director (see above)
Frederick C. Kentz, III: secretary, trustee (see above)
Ivor Macleod: trustee

Grants Analysis
Disclosure Period: calendar year ending 2003
Total Grants: $640,000*
Number of Grants: 9
Average Grant: $20,833*
Highest Grant: $240,000
Lowest Grant: $5,000
Typical Range: $15,000 to $30,000
*Note: Giving excludes scholarship. Average grant figure excludes three highest grants ($515,000).

Recent Grants
Note: Grants derived from 2003 Form 990.
General

240,000	Hepatitis Foundation International, Silver Spring, MD -- towards national viral hepatitis roundtable and website
175,000	Title II Community AIDS National Network, Washington, DC -- towards HIVF/HCV co-infection Treatment Access Expansion Project
100,000	University of Texas MD Anderson Cancer Center, Houston, TX -- towards living fully with Cancer conference
51,250	Hispanic Scholarship Fund, San Francisco, CA -- towards New Horizons Scholars Program
30,000	Princeton Area Community Foundation Inc., Skillman, NJ -- towards New Jersey AIDS Partnership
25,000	Independent College Fund, Summit, NJ
25,000	National Association of People with AIDS, Washington, DC -- towards national survival training for people living with HIV/AIDS
25,000	United Negro College Fund Inc., Newark, NJ -- towards UNCF's campaign
22,500	Hispanic Scholarship Fund, San Francisco, CA -- towards New Horizons Scholars Program
15,000	Technical Training Project Inc., Newark, NJ -- towards technical training project program

HOGLUND FOUNDATION

Giving Contact
Kelly H. Compton, Executive Director
5910 N. Central Expressway, Suite 255
Dallas, TX 75206
Phone: (214)987-3605

Description
Founded: 1989
EIN: 752300978
Organization Type: Private Foundation
Giving Locations: TX
Grant Types: Capital, General Support, Project.

Donor Information
Founder: Established in 1989 by Forrest E. Hoglund.

Financial Summary

Total Giving: $2,058,110 (2003)
Giving Analysis: Giving for 2003 includes: foundation grants to United Way ($70,833)
Assets: $47,674,068 (2003)
Gifts Received: $4,576,563 (2000); $1,546,552 (1999); $250,000 (1996). Note: In 1996, 1999 and 2000, contributions were received from Forrest E. Hoglund.

Typical Recipients

Arts & Humanities: Arts Outreach, History & Archaeology, Libraries, Museums/Galleries, Performing Arts, Theater
Civic & Public Affairs: Economic Development, Civic & Public Affairs-General, Women's Affairs, Zoos/Aquariums
Education: Business Education, Colleges & Universities, Elementary Education (Private), Education-General, Medical Education, Minority Education, Private Education (Precollege), Science/Mathematics Education, Student Aid
Health: AIDS/HIV, Alzheimer's Disease, Arthritis, Cancer, Children's Health/Hospitals, Clinics/Medical Centers, Emergency/Ambulance Services, Health Organizations, Hospices, Kidney, Long-Term Care, Nursing Services, Prenatal Health Issues, Single-Disease Health Associations, Transplant Networks/Donor Banks
International: Foreign Arts Organizations
Religion: Churches, Ministries, Religious Welfare
Science: Science-General, Science Museums
Social Services: At-Risk Youth, Child Welfare, Community Centers, Community Service Organizations, Crime Prevention, Family Planning, Family Services, Food/Clothing Distribution, People with Disabilities, Recreation & Athletics, Senior Services, Shelters/Homelessness, Special Olympics, Substance Abuse, United Funds/United Ways, YMCA/YWCA/YMHA/YWHA, Youth Organizations

Application Procedures

Initial Contact: Send a brief letter of inquiry; request application guidelines
Application Requirements: a description of organization, amount requested, purpose of funds sought, recently audited financial statement, proof of tax-exempt status, list of current officers and board of trustees, current budget, budget for the proposed project (if applicable) and plans to support the project after the grant period.
Deadlines: None. Board meets quarterly to review grant applications.

Restrictions

The foundation does not support individuals.

Additional Information

Publications: Application guidelines.

Foundation Officials

Kelly Hoglund Compton: secretary, treasurer
Shelly Louise Hoglund Dee: director
Forrest Eugene Hoglund: don, president B Lawrence, KS 1933. ED University of Kansas BS (1956). PRIM CORP EMPL chairman, president, chief executive officer: Enron Oil & Gas Co. CORP AFFIL director: Texas Commerce Bancshares; director: Western Transmission Corp.; director: Marathon Oil Co. NONPR AFFIL vice president: Kansas University Endowment Association; director: Texas Research League; member: American Petroleum Institute; member: Dallas Citizens Council.
Sally Sue Roney Hoglund: vice president
Kristan Kay Hoglund Robinson: director

Grants Analysis

Disclosure Period: calendar year ending 2003
Total Grants: $1,987,277*
Number of Grants: 152
Average Grant: $10,653*

Highest Grant: $200,000
Lowest Grant: $400
Typical Range: $5,000 to $20,000
*Note: Giving excludes United Way. Average grant figure excludes three highest grants ($400,000).

Recent Grants

Note: Grants derived from 2003 Form 990.
General

200,000	University of Texas M. D. Anderson Cancer Center, Houston, TX -- for basic science research building
100,000	Reasoning Mind Inc., Houston, TX -- to support for the development of production grade system for web based math program
100,000	University of Texas M. D. Anderson Cancer Center, Houston, TX -- for basic science research building
50,000	Children's Medical Center, Dallas, TX -- to support the day surgery expansion
50,000	Dallas County Heritage Society, Dallas, TX -- capital campaign for the education and visitors center
50,000	St. Philip's School and Community Center, Dallas, TX -- capital and operating funds for science lab
50,000	Texas Children's Cancer Center, Houston, TX -- to support pediatric brain tumor research
50,000	Visiting Nurse Association, Dallas, TX -- for capital campaign - touching every life
50,000	Visiting Nurse Association, Dallas, TX -- for capital campaign - touching every life
25,000	Opportunity International, Oak Brook, IL -- funding for new trust banks in the Philippines and Mexico

HOLMBERG FOUNDATION

Giving Contact

Dr. Robert F. Wettingfeld, President
519 Washington St.
Jamestown, NY 14701
Phone: (716)483-0735

Description

Founded: 1992
EIN: 161426226
Organization Type: Private Foundation
Giving Locations: NY: Chautauqua County
Grant Types: Capital, Fellowship, General Support.

Financial Summary

Total Giving: $137,876 (fiscal year ending July 31, 2004); $160,500 (fiscal 2001)
Giving Analysis: Giving for fiscal 2004 includes: foundation grants to United Way ($2,000); fiscal 2001: foundation grants to United Way ($7,500)
Assets: $3,324,774 (fiscal 2004); $3,632,816 (fiscal 2001)
Gifts Received: $500 (fiscal 2001); $600 (fiscal 2000); $500 (fiscal 1999). Note: In fiscal 2000, contributions were received from Robert F. Wettingfeld.

Typical Recipients

Arts & Humanities: Libraries
Civic & Public Affairs: Economic Development, Civic & Public Affairs-General, Law & Justice
Education: Community & Junior Colleges, Education Funds, Environmental Education
Environment: Watershed, Wildlife Protection
Health: Hospitals, Nursing Services
Religion: Missionary Activities (Domestic)
Social Services: Camps, United Funds/United Ways, Youth Organizations

Application Procedures

Initial Contact: Send a brief letter of inquiry.
Deadlines: None.

Foundation Officials

Mary T. Bessemer: director emeritus
Leslie A. Johnson: secretary
Robert F. Wettingfeld, MD: president

Grants Analysis

Disclosure Period: fiscal year ending July 31, 2004
Total Grants: $135,876*
Number of Grants: 15
Average Grant: $5,063*
Highest Grant: $65,000
Lowest Grant: $1,500
Typical Range: $2,000 to $10,000
*Note: Giving excludes United Way. Average grant figure excludes highest grant.

Recent Grants

Note: Grants derived from 2004 Form 990.
Library-Related

7,000	James Prendergast Library, Jamestown, NY
5,000	Farnam Free Library

General

65,000	Jamestown Community College
15,000	Fredonia College Foundation, Fredonia, NY
5,000	Chautauqua Striders, Jamestown, NY
5,000	Chautauqua Watershed Conservancy, Jamestown, NY
5,000	Jamestown Audubon Society, Jamestown, NY
5,000	Jamestown Boys and Girls Club, Jamestown, NY
5,000	Robert H. Jackson Center Inc., Jamestown, NY
5,000	Roger Tory Peterson Institute, Jamestown, NY

HOLNAM INC.

Company Headquarters

6211 N. Ann Arbor Rd.
Dundee, MI 48131
Web: http://www.holcim.com/us

Company Description

Employees: 5,200
SIC(s): 3241 Cement--Hydraulic, 3273 Ready-Mixed Concrete, 3531 Construction Machinery, 6719 Holding Companies Nec.
Parent Company: Holderbank Financiere Glaris Ltd., Zurcherstrasse 156, Jona, Switzerland

Operating Locations

Braswell Concrete Products (LA--Shreveport); Braswell Industries (LA--Shreveport); Braswell Sand & Gravel Co. (AR--Wilton); Dundee Cement Co. (MI--Dundee); Graysonia, Nashville & Ashdawn Railroad Co. (AR--Nashville); Holnam Inc. (MI--Dundee); Holnam Inc. (West Division) (CO--Lakewood); Ideal Concrete (TX--Houston); Kevaland Corp. (CO--Denver); Kevaland Texas Corp. (CO--Denver); Louisiana Nevada Transit Co. (CO--Denver); Northwestern States Portland Cement (IA--Mason City); Thorstenberg Materials Co. (CO--Denver); United Cement Co. (MS--Artesia)

Nonmonetary Support

Type: Cause-related Marketing & Promotion; Donated Equipment; Donated Products; Loaned Employees

Giving Contact

Linda McCormick, Public Affairs Administrator
6211 N. Ann Arbor Rd.
PO Box 122
Dundee, MI 48131
Phone: (734)529-2411
Fax: (734)529-5268

Description

Organization Type: Corporate Giving Program
Giving Locations: headquarters and operating communities.
Grant Types: Capital, Conference/Seminar, Emergency, Employee Matching Gifts, General Support, Multiyear/Continuing Support, Project, Scholarship.

Typical Recipients

Arts & Humanities: Arts Associations & Councils, Arts Festivals, Arts & Humanities-General, Historic Preservation, Libraries, Music, Performing Arts, Public Broadcasting
Civic & Public Affairs: Chambers of Commerce, Community Foundations, Economic Development, Civic & Public Affairs-General, Parades/Festivals, Professional & Trade Associations, Safety, Urban & Community Affairs
Education: Agricultural Education, Business Education, Business-School Partnerships, Colleges & Universities, Community & Junior Colleges, Continuing Education, Education-General
Environment: Environment-General, Wildlife Protection
Health: Health-General
Science: Science-General
Social Services: Social Services-General

Application Procedures

Initial Contact: Send a full proposal.
Application Requirements: Include a description of organization, amount requested, purpose of funds sought, and proof of tax-exempt status.

Restrictions

Does not support individuals, religious organizations for sectarian purposes, political or lobbying groups, or organizations outside operating areas.

Corporate Officials

Kent Jensen: chief financial officer, treasurer, director PRIM CORP EMPL chief financial officer, treasurer: Holnam.
Paul A. Yhouse: president, chief executive officer, director B Grand Rapids, MI 1949. ED University of Michigan BBA (1971). PRIM CORP EMPL president, chief executive officer, director: Holnam. NONPR AFFIL member: Michigan Association Certified Pub Accts; advisory board: University Michigan Paton Acct Center; member: American Institute CPA's; member: Financial Executives Institute.

Grants Analysis

Typical Range: $10 to $999

HOLT FAMILY FOUNDATION

Giving Contact

Leon C. Holt, Jr., Trustee
1611 Pond Road, Suite 300
Allentown, PA 18104-2256
Phone: (610)391-0377

Description

Founded: 1988
EIN: 236906143
Organization Type: Private Foundation
Giving Locations: PA: Allentown and Lehigh Valley Area
Grant Types: General Support.

Donor Information

Founder: Leon C. and June W. Holt, Jr.

Financial Summary

Total Giving: $215,250 (2002); $234,500 (2001). Note: 1997 Giving includes United Way ($1,000).
Giving Analysis: Giving for 2002 includes: foundation grants to United Way ($1,000); 2001: foundation grants to United Way ($2,000)
Assets: $4,132,742 (2002); $4,726,431 (2001)
Gifts Received: $10,000 (2002); $142,814 (2000); $350,000 (1999). Note: Contributions were received from Leon C. and June W. Holt.

Typical Recipients

Arts & Humanities: Arts Centers, Ballet, History & Archaeology, Libraries, Museums/Galleries, Music, Theater
Civic & Public Affairs: Clubs, Economic Development, Civic & Public Affairs-General, Hispanic Affairs, Urban & Community Affairs
Education: Arts/Humanities Education, Colleges & Universities, Education Funds, Private Education (Precollege)
Environment: Environment-General, Resource Conservation, Wildlife Protection
Health: Hospitals, Prenatal Health Issues, Public Health
Religion: Churches, Religious Welfare
Science: Scientific Centers & Institutes
Social Services: Child Welfare, Community Service Organizations, Recreation & Athletics, United Funds/United Ways, YMCA/YWCA/YMHA/YWHA, Youth Organizations

Application Procedures

Initial Contact: Request funding guidelines, then send a brief letter of inquiry.
Application Requirements: Include a description of organization, amount requested, purpose of funds sought, proof of tax-exempt status, proposed project budget, including other sources of financial support, plan to measure and evaluate program results, and a summary of the proposed program along with a plan for accomplishing objectives.
Deadlines: None.

Restrictions

The foundation does not support individuals, religious organizations for sectarian purposes, political or lobbying groups, organizations outside operating areas, debt reduction, charitable or testimonial dinners, fundraising events or related advertising, or fraternal, social, or veterans organizations.

Additional Information

Publications: Funding Guidelines

Foundation Officials

June W. Holt: trustee
Leon Conrad Holt, Jr.: trustee B Reading, PA 1925. ED Lehigh University BS (1948); University of Pennsylvania JD (1951). CORP AFFIL director: VF Corp.; director: Air Products & Chemicals. NONPR AFFIL member: Tunkhannock Creek Association; member advisory board: University Pennsylvania Institute Law & Economics; trustee: Pool (Dorothy Rider) Health Care Trust; director: Pennsylvanians Modern Courts; director: Pocono Lake Preserve; member: New York City Bar Association; member: Pennsylvania Society; member executive committee: Machinery & Allied Products Institute; director: Nature Conservancy Pennsylvania Chapter; trustee: Committee for Economic Development; director: Lehigh County United Fund; member: American Bar Association; member: Allentown Chamber of Commerce; member: Alpha Tau Omega; trustee: Allentown Art Museum. CLUB AFFIL Lehigh Country Club.

Richard W. Holt, Jr.: trustee
Deborah Holt Weil: trustee

Grants Analysis

Disclosure Period: calendar year ending 2002
Total Grants: $214,250*
Number of Grants: 46
Average Grant: $3,872*
Highest Grant: $40,000
Lowest Grant: $250
Typical Range: $1,000 to $5,000
*Note: Giving excludes United Way. Average grant figure excludes highest grant.

Recent Grants

Note: Grants derived from 2004 Form 990.
General

25,000	University of Pennsylvania, Philadelphia, PA
20,000	Allentown Art Museum, Allentown, PA
15,000	Discovery Center of Science, Bethlehem, PA
15,000	Lehigh University, Bethlehem, PA
10,000	Cornell University, Ithaca, NY
10,000	Lehigh Valley Hospital, Allentown, PA
10,000	Nature Conservancy, Long Pond, PA
10,000	Teton Valley Ranch Camp Education Foundation, Jackson, WY
10,000	Zoellner Arts Center, Bethlehem, PA
7,500	Episcopal Church of the Mediator, Allentown, PA

WILLIAM KNOX HOLT FOUNDATION

Giving Contact

George M. Malti, Director
300 Aztec Ave., Suite 200
Gallup, NM 87301
Phone: (505)863-6851

Description

Founded: 1967
EIN: 746084245
Organization Type: Private Foundation
Giving Locations: CA: Northern part of state; CO; NY; TX: Southern part of state
Grant Types: Capital, Endowment, General Support, Project, Research, Scholarship.

Donor Information

Founder: the late William Knox Holt

Financial Summary

Total Giving: $553,500 (2002)
Giving Analysis: Giving for 2002 includes: foundation scholarships ($20,000)
Assets: $8,396,923 (2002)

Typical Recipients

Arts & Humanities: Arts Associations & Councils, Arts Centers, Arts Outreach, Libraries, Museums/Galleries, Music, Theater
Civic & Public Affairs: Civic & Public Affairs-General, Hispanic Affairs, Native American Affairs, Zoos/Aquariums
Education: Arts/Humanities Education, Colleges & Universities, Education Funds, Education-General, Leadership Training, Legal Education, Private Education (Precollege), Public Education (Precollege), Science/Mathematics Education, Secondary Education (Public), Student Aid
Health: Cancer, Children's Health/Hospitals, Emergency/Ambulance Services, Health-General, Health Organizations, Multiple Sclerosis, Public Health
Religion: Religious Welfare
Science: Science Museums, Scientific Centers & In-

stitutes, Scientific Labs
Social Services: At-Risk Youth, Child Welfare, Community Service Organizations, Crime Prevention, Domestic Violence, People with Disabilities, Recreation & Athletics, Scouts, Social Services-General, Youth Organizations

Application Procedures

Initial Contact: Send a brief letter of inquiry describing program or project.
Application Requirements: Include a description of organization and purpose of funds sought.
Deadlines: None.

Restrictions

Limited to science and education charities in CA, TX, CO, NM, and NY.

Foundation Officials

Judy S. Akin: assistant secretary
Geary Atherton: director
Holt Atherton: director
George M. Malti: director
Richard C. Perkins: director
Roberta S. Plummer: director

Grants Analysis

Disclosure Period: calendar year ending 2002
Total Grants: $533,500*
Number of Grants: 27
Average Grant: $16,673*
Highest Grant: $100,000
Lowest Grant: $2,500
Typical Range: $10,000 to $30,000
*__Note:__ Giving excludes scholarships. Average grant figure excludes highest grant.

Recent Grants

Note: Grants derived from 2001 Form 990.
General

100,000	Lawrence Hall of Science, Berkeley, CA -- for interactive landscape experience
65,000	Haggin Museum, Stockton, CA -- for maintenance of Holt Hall and industrial archives
33,000	Central E Austin Community Organization, Austin, TX -- for youth and women's programs
33,000	Rehoboth McKinley/Christian Health Care Services, Gallup, NM -- for women's health services
30,000	Austin Symphony Orchestra, Austin, TX -- for young peoples' concerts
30,000	Navajo Nation, Window Rock, AZ -- for educational programs
25,000	Colorado Rocky Mountain School, Carbondale, CO -- for Scholarship Program
25,000	Monterey Bay Aquarium, Monterey, CA -- for educational programs
20,000	Cancer Therapy & Research Center, San Antonio, TX -- for Cancer Institute symposium
20,000	Crime Prevention Institute, Austin, TX -- for job and resource fairs

JACOB L. AND LILLIAN HOLTZMANN FOUNDATION

Giving Contact

Howard Holtzmann, Trustee
c/o Holtzmann, Wise & Shepard
630 5th Ave., Suite 2000
New York, NY 10111-0100

Description

Founded: 1958
EIN: 136174349
Organization Type: Private Foundation
Giving Locations: NY
Grant Types: General Support.

Donor Information

Founder: the late Jacob L. Holtzmann, the late Lillian Holtzmann, Howard M. Holtzmann

Financial Summary

Gifts Received: $50,000 (2000); $50,000 (1999); $50,000 (1998). Note: Contributions received from Howard M. Holtzmann.

Typical Recipients

Arts & Humanities: Ballet, Libraries, Museums/Galleries, Music, Opera, Theater
Civic & Public Affairs: Botanical Gardens/Parks, Employment/Job Training, Civic & Public Affairs-General, Law & Justice, Legal Aid, Native American Affairs, Philanthropic Organizations, Public Policy, Women's Affairs
Education: Arts/Humanities Education, Colleges & Universities, Education Funds, Elementary Education (Private), Education-General, Legal Education, Medical Education, Private Education (Precollege), Public Education (Precollege), Religious Education
Environment: Environment-General
Health: Geriatric Health, Health Organizations, Hospitals, Medical Research, Single-Disease Health Associations
International: Foreign Arts Organizations, Foreign Educational Institutions, Health Care/Hospitals, International Affairs, International Organizations, International Relief Efforts, Missionary/Religious Activities
Religion: Churches, Jewish Causes, Missionary Activities (Domestic), Religious Organizations, Religious Welfare, Seminaries, Synagogues/Temples
Social Services: Community Centers, Community Service Organizations, People with Disabilities, Youth Organizations

Application Procedures

Initial Contact: The foundation requests applications be made in writing.
Deadlines: None.

Restrictions

Does not support individuals.

Foundation Officials

Howard Marshall Holtzmann, Esq.: trustee B New York, NY 1921. ED Yale University AB (1942); Yale University JD (1947); Saint Bonaventure University LittD (1952); Jewish Theological Seminary LLD (1990). NONPR AFFIL US del: UN Commission International Trade Law; member: World Peace Law; member: Society Professionals Dispute Resolution; director: Stockholm Arbitration Institute; trustee: Pace University School Law; trustee emeritus: Saint Bonaventure University; member: New York State Bar Association; member: New York County Lawyers Association; member: New York Law Institute; member: New York City Bar Association; vice chairman, member: Intl Council Commercial Arbitration; honorary chairman: Jewish Theological Seminary; member: International Law Association; member: International Bar Association; member, vice chairman arbitration commissioner: International Chamber of Commerce; trustee: Institute International Law; director: Bagrain Arbitration Center; member: Indus Relations Research Association; member: American Society International Law; member: American Foreign Law Association; member: American Judicature Society; member: American Bar Foundation; member: American Association International Comm Jurists; member: American Bar Association; member: American Arbitration Association.

Benjamin C. O'Sullivan, Esq.: trustee
Susan H. Richardson: trustee

Grants Analysis

Disclosure Period: calendar year ending 2000
Total Grants: $3,095,459
Number of Grants: 31
Average Grant: $7,849*
Highest Grant: $2,010,000
Typical Range: $1,000 to $15,000
*__Note:__ Average grant figure excludes two highest grants ($2,860,000).

Recent Grants

Note: Grants derived from 2001 Form 990.
General

150,000	Jewish Theological Seminary, New York, NY
50,000	Ackerman Institute for the Family, New York, NY
50,000	United Jewish Appeal - Federation of Jewish Philanthropies of New York, Greenwich, CT
25,000	Environmental Law Institute, Washington, DC
20,000	Jewish Child Care Association of New York, New York, NY
19,900	Metropolitan Opera Association, New York, NY
10,000	Classic Stage Company, New York, NY
10,000	Student Advocacy, Elmsford, NY
9,600	American Ballet Theatre, New York, NY
6,000	Yale Alumni Fund, New Haven, CT

RICHARD H. HOLZER MEMORIAL FOUNDATION

Giving Contact

Vivian K. Holzer, President
120 Sylvan Ave.
Englewood Cliffs, NJ 07632
Phone: (201)947-8810

Description

Founded: 1969
EIN: 237014880
Organization Type: Private Foundation
Giving Locations: U.S. Northeast Region.
Grant Types: General Support.

Donor Information

Founder: Erich Holzer

Financial Summary

Total Giving: $328,650 (2003)
Assets: $6,864,090 (2003)
Gifts Received: $121,869 (2003); $337,230 (2000); $311,788 (1999). Note: In 1998, 1999, and 2003, contributions were received from Eva Holzer. In 1996, major contributions were received from Eva Holzer Charitable Lead Trust ($299,224), Chickmaster International Co. ($100,000), and Victor Koenig ($50).

Typical Recipients

Arts & Humanities: Arts Associations & Councils, Arts Centers, Ballet, Community Arts, Dance, Arts & Humanities-General, Libraries, Museums/Galleries, Music, Opera, Performing Arts, Public Broadcasting, Theater
Civic & Public Affairs: Clubs, Civic & Public Affairs-General
Education: Agricultural Education, Arts/Humanities Education, Business Education, Colleges & Universities, Education Funds, Gifted & Talented Programs, Minority Education, Private Education (Precollege), Public Education (Precollege), Secondary Education

(Private), Student Aid
Health: Cancer, Clinics/Medical Centers, Health Funds, Health Organizations, Hospitals, Medical Rehabilitation, Medical Research, Single-Disease Health Associations
International: Missionary/Religious Activities
Religion: Churches, Jewish Causes, Religious Organizations, Seminaries, Synagogues/Temples
Social Services: Child Welfare, Community Centers, Community Service Organizations, Counseling, Homes, People with Disabilities

Application Procedures

Initial Contact: a brief letter of inquiry
Application Requirements: a description of organization, purpose of funds sought
Deadlines: None.

Restrictions

Grants are not made to support individuals, political or lobbying groups, or organizations outside operating areas.

Foundation Officials

Wally Dietl: secretary
Robert Holzer: vice president, treasurer
Vivian Holzer: president

Grants Analysis

Disclosure Period: calendar year ending 2003
Total Grants: $328,650
Number of Grants: 56
Average Grant: $5,066*
Highest Grant: $50,000
Lowest Grant: $200
Typical Range: $1,000 to $10,000
*Note: Average grant figure excludes highest grant.

Recent Grants

Note: Grants derived from 2003 Form 990.
General

50,000	Metropolitan Opera, New York, NY
26,000	Jewish Theological Seminary, New York, NY
25,000	JCC Thurnauer School of Music, Tenafly, NJ
20,000	Schechter Regional High School, Teaneck, NJ
20,000	Solomon Schechter Day School, New Milford, NJ
15,000	Carnegie Hall, New York, NY
15,000	Lincoln Center for the Performing Arts, New York, NY
15,000	Pascack Valley Hospital Foundation, Westwood, NJ
14,050	JCC on the Palisades, Tenafly, NJ
10,000	New Jersey Symphony Orchestra, Newark, NJ

HOME FOR AGED MEN IN THE CITY OF BROCKTON

Giving Contact

John F. Creedon, President
c/o Silverstein and Creedon
71 Legion Parkway, 3rd Fl.
Brockton, MA 02301
Phone: (508)584-4088

Description

EIN: 042103796
Organization Type: Private Foundation
Giving Locations: MA
Grant Types: General Support, Operating Expenses.

Donor Information

Founder: the late Horace Howard

Financial Summary

Total Giving: $300,000 (fiscal year ending March 31, 2001)
Assets: $5,400,353 (fiscal 2001)
Gifts Received: $6,848 (fiscal 2001); $6,943 (fiscal 1997); $6,621 (fiscal 1996). Note: In fiscal 1997, contributions were received from the Daniel W. Field Trust.

Typical Recipients

Arts & Humanities: Libraries
Civic & Public Affairs: Economic Development, Civic & Public Affairs-General, Municipalities/Towns, Parades/Festivals
Education: Colleges & Universities, Community & Junior Colleges, Student Aid
Health: Cancer, Clinics/Medical Centers, Health Organizations, Hospices, Hospitals, Long-Term Care, Medical Rehabilitation
Religion: Dioceses, Religious Welfare
Social Services: Community Service Organizations, Counseling, Family Planning, Family Services, Homes, People with Disabilities, Recreation & Athletics, Senior Services, Social Services-General, United Funds/United Ways, YMCA/YWCA/YMHA/YWHA, Youth Organizations

Application Procedures

Initial Contact: The foundation has no formal grant application procedure or application form.
Deadlines: None.

Foundation Officials

Ida Caggiano: clerk
John F. Creedon: president
Robert Prince: treasurer

Grants Analysis

Disclosure Period: fiscal year ending March 31, 2001
Total Grants: $300,000
Number of Grants: 20
Average Grant: $11,667*
Highest Grant: $50,000
Typical Range: $5,000 to $20,000
*Note: Average grant figure excludes two highest grants ($90,000).

Recent Grants

Note: Grants derived from 2002 Form 990.
Library-Related

15,000	Brockton Library, Brockton, MA

General

21,195	City of Brockton - Council on Aging, Brockton, MA
20,000	St. Joseph's Manor, Trumbull, CT
15,000	Brockton Hospital, Brockton, MA
15,000	Brockton VNA, Brockton, MA
15,000	Dana Farber Institute, Boston, MA
15,000	Helpline, Walla Walla, WA
15,000	Hospice of Greater Brockton, Brockton, MA
15,000	Old Colony Elderly Services, Brockton, MA
15,000	Salvation Army, Clearwater, FL
15,000	Vision

HOMECREST INDUSTRIES INC.

Company Headquarters

PO Box 350
Wadena, MN 56482
Web: http://www.homecrest.com

Company Description

Revenue: US$72.1 million (2001)
Employees: 680 (2001)
SIC(s): 2500 Furniture & Fixtures, 2514 Metal Household Furniture.

Operating Locations

Homecrest Industries (MN--Wadena)

Homecrest Foundation

Giving Contact

Bruce Koppenhaver, Trustee
PO Box 350
Wadena, MN 56482
Phone: (218)631-1000
Fax: (218)631-2609

Description

Founded: 1986
EIN: 411550750
Organization Type: Corporate Foundation
Giving Locations: MN
Grant Types: General Support, Scholarship.

Donor Information

Founder: Homecrest Industries

Financial Summary

Total Giving: $9,230 (fiscal year ending July 31, 2004); $20,000 (fiscal 2001). Note: Giving includes scholarship ($8,400).
Giving Analysis: Giving for fiscal 2004 includes: foundation grants to United Way ($2,250); foundation scholarships ($5,900); fiscal 2001: foundation grants to United Way ($3,750); foundation scholarships ($6,600).
Assets: $120,162 (fiscal 2004); $184,439 (fiscal 2001)
Gifts Received: $25 (fiscal 2004); $50 (fiscal 2001); $15,040 (fiscal 2000). Note: Contributions were received from Homecrest Industries.

Typical Recipients

Arts & Humanities: Arts Outreach, Arts & Humanities-General, History & Archaeology, Libraries, Museums/Galleries, Music
Civic & Public Affairs: Chambers of Commerce, Clubs, Economic Development, Civic & Public Affairs-General, Housing, Parades/Festivals, Safety
Education: Arts/Humanities Education, Economic Education, Education Funds, Preschool Education, Public Education (Precollege)
Health: Cancer, Hospitals, Multiple Sclerosis
International: Health Care/Hospitals
Religion: Religious Welfare
Social Services: Animal Protection, Child Welfare, Community Centers, Family Services, Recreation & Athletics, Scouts, Special Olympics, United Funds/United Ways

Application Procedures

Initial Contact: Request application guidelines.
Deadlines: None.

Additional Information

Provides employee-related scholarships.
Publications: Application Guidelines

Corporate Officials

Donald L. Bottemiller: president, treasurer, vice president finance PRIM CORP EMPL president: Homecrest Industries.
Lawrence E. Calhoun: secretary, treasurer, vice president finance PRIM CORP EMPL secretary, treasurer, vice president finance: Homecrest Industries.

Foundation Officials

Donald L. Bottemiller: trustee (see above)
Mark Bottemiller: secretary, treasurer

Grants Analysis

Disclosure Period: fiscal year ending July 31, 2004
Total Grants: $1,080*
Number of Grants: 6
Average Grant: $180
Highest Grant: $350
Lowest Grant: $30
Typical Range: $100 to $350
*Note:** Giving excludes scholarships and United Way.

Recent Grants

Note: Grants derived from 2004 Form 990.
General

2,250	Wadena United Way, Wadena, MN
350	Wadena Area Concert Association, Wadena, MN
250	Wadena-Deer Creek Backcourt Club, Wadena, MN
150	National Child Safety Council, Grand Forks, ND
100	American Cancer Society, Rochester, MN
30	Wadena Deer Creek Amateur Baseball Association, Wadena, MN

HOMELAND FOUNDATION (NY)

Giving Contact

E. Lisk-Wyckoff, Jr., President
c/o Wethersfield
214 Pugsley Hill Rd.
Amenia, NY 12501
Phone: (212)888-5959

Description

Founded: 1938
EIN: 136113816
Organization Type: General Purpose Foundation
Giving Locations: NY: metropolitan area internationally; nationally.
Grant Types: General Support, Scholarship.
Note: Capital and endowment grants are made on the basis of special interest.

Donor Information

Founder: The foundation was incorporated in 1938. In fiscal 1990, the foundation's assets grew to more than $75 million under a trust established by the late Chauncey Stillman.

Financial Summary

Total Giving: $2,402,197 (fiscal year ending April 30, 2003); $2,039,419 (fiscal 2002)
Giving Analysis: Giving for fiscal 2003 includes: foundation scholarships ($125,000); fiscal 2001: foundation scholarships ($120,000)
Assets: $84,478,354 (fiscal 2003); $85,969,144 (fiscal 2002)
Gifts Received: $385 (fiscal 2002); $803 (fiscal 1998); $599,098 (fiscal 1997). Note: In 1997, contributions were received from Anne G. Earhart. In 1995, contributions were received from the estate of Chauncey Stillman.

Typical Recipients

Arts & Humanities: Arts Centers, Arts Outreach, Dance, Arts & Humanities-General, Historic Preservation, History & Archaeology, Libraries, Literary Arts, Museums/Galleries, Music, Opera, Public Broadcasting
Civic & Public Affairs: Clubs, Employment/Job Training, Civic & Public Affairs-General, Philanthropic Organizations, Professional & Trade Associations, Public Policy, Urban & Community Affairs, Women's Affairs
Education: Arts/Humanities Education, Colleges & Universities, Education Funds, Faculty Development, Education-General, Legal Education, Private Education (Precollege), Public Education (Precollege), Religious Education, Secondary Education (Private), Secondary Education (Public), Social Sciences Education, Student Aid
Environment: Environment-General, Resource Conservation, Wildlife Protection
Health: Cancer, Clinics/Medical Centers, Emergency/Ambulance Services, Heart, Hospitals, Long-Term Care, Prenatal Health Issues
International: Foreign Arts Organizations, Foreign Educational Institutions, International-General, Health Care/Hospitals, Human Rights, International Environmental Issues, International Organizations, International Peace & Security Issues, International Relations, Missionary/Religious Activities
Religion: Churches, Dioceses, Religion-General, Jewish Causes, Ministries, Missionary Activities (Domestic), Religious Organizations, Religious Welfare, Seminaries, Social/Policy Issues
Social Services: Big Brothers/Big Sisters, Camps, Child Welfare, Community Service Organizations, Emergency Relief, Family Planning, Family Services, Food/Clothing Distribution, People with Disabilities, Recreation & Athletics, Shelters/Homelessness, Social Services-General, Youth Organizations

Application Procedures

Initial Contact: Send a brief letter of inquiry.
Application Requirements: Include a description of organization, amount requested, purpose of funds sought, proof of tax-exempt status, organization budget, project budget, list of board of directors, and of major donors.
Deadlines: None.
Review Process: The foundation requires a report on a grant made, indicating how the applicant used the grant together with dates and expenditure responsibility.

Restrictions

Grants are limited to support of religious, charitable, scientific, or literary purposes, or for the prevention of cruelty to children or animals. Grants are not made to individuals, private foundations, or governmental organizations. Grants for endowments, building funds, and capital development are made only on the basis of a special interest.

Foundation Officials

Rev. Rafael F. Caamano: trustee
Monsignor Eugene V. Clark: vice president, secretary, trustee
Lucy Fleming-McGrath: trustee
Carl Schmitt: trustee
Charles Scribner, III: trustee B Washington, DC 1951. ED Princeton University AB (1973); Princeton University MFA (1975); Princeton University PhD (1977). PRIM CORP EMPL editor: Charles Scribner's Sons. NONPR AFFIL trustee: Saint Pauls School; board advisors: Wethersfield Institute; member: Association Princeton University Press. CLUB AFFIL Piping Rock Club; Racquet & Tennis Club; Ivy Club.
Ed Lisk Wyckoff, Jr.: president, treasurer, trustee B Middletown, NJ 1934. ED Duke University BA (1955); University of Michigan JD (1960). PRIM CORP EMPL partner: Kramer, Levin, Naftalis, Nessen, Kamin & Frankel. NONPR AFFIL board advisors: Wildlife Conservation Society; president, director: Wyckoff House Association; trustee: Society Preservation Long Island Antiquities; member: New York State Bar Association; lecturer: Practicing Law Institute; member: International Fiscal Association; trustee: New York Historical Society; member: International Bar Association; member: Association Bar New York City; member: Concilium Sodalium to Vatican Museum; member: American Bar Association; fellow: American College Probate Counsel. CLUB AFFIL Saint Nicholas Society; Pine Plains New York Club; Racquet & Tennis Club; Knickerbocker Club; Mashomack Fish & Game Preserve Club; Essex Connecticut Yacht Club; Holland Society.

Grants Analysis

Disclosure Period: fiscal year ending April 30, 2003
Total Grants: $2,277,197*
Number of Grants: 38
Average Grant: $32,577*
Highest Grant: $855,300
Lowest Grant: $2,500
Typical Range: $10,000 to $50,000
*Note:** Giving excludes scholarships. Average grant figure excludes two highest grants ($1,104,422).

Recent Grants

Note: Grants derived from fiscal 2002 Form 990.
Library-Related

100,000	Morgan Library, New York, NY

General

600,000	Vatican Museum, Vatican City Italy
150,000	Path to Peace Foundation, New York, NY
120,000	Wildlife Conservation Society, Bronx, NY
82,000	Seminaire de la Societe JM Vianney, Ars Sur Formans France
60,000	Catholic Big Sisters, New York, NY
60,000	Society for Preservation of Long Island Antiquities, Cold Spring Harbor, NY
50,000	Barllan University, Jerusalem Israel
50,000	California International Sailing Association, Irvine, CA
50,000	Homes for the Homeless, New York, NY
50,000	Inner City Scholarship Fund, New York, NY

HON INDUSTRIES INC.

Company Headquarters

Muscatine, IA
Web: http://www.honi.com

Company Description

Founded: 1944
Ticker: HNI
Exchange: NYSE
Also Known As: Home-O-Nize.
Revenue: US$1.692 billion (2002)
Employees: 8900 (2003)
SIC(s): 2521 Wood Office Furniture, 2522 Office Furniture Except Wood, 2678 Stationery Products, 3433 Heating Equipment Except Electric.

Operating Locations

HON Industries Inc. (CA--South Gate, Van Nuys; GA--Cedartown; IA--Mount Pleasant; KY--Owensboro; NY--Avon, Wayland; NC--Louisburg; PA--Williamsport; TX--Sulphur Springs; VA--Richmond; WA--Kent)

HON Industries Charitable Foundation

Giving Contact

Susan J. Cradick, Secretary-Treasurer
414 East Third Street
Muscatine, IA 52761-0071
Phone: (563)264-7503
Fax: (563)264-7217
Web: http://www.honi.com/
CorporateResponsibility.htm

Description

Founded: 1985
EIN: 421246787
Organization Type: Corporate Foundation
Giving Locations: IA: Muscatine headquarters and operating communities.

Grant Types: Employee Matching Gifts, General Support, Matching, Project, Scholarship.

Financial Summary

Total Giving: $1,285,650 (2002); $738,198 (2001). Note: Contributes through corporate direct giving program and foundation.
Assets: $2,571,645 (2002); $2,322,644 (2001)
Gifts Received: $2,000,000 (2002); $200,000 (2000); $2,000,000 (1999). Note: Contributions are received from HON Industries Inc.

Typical Recipients

Arts & Humanities: Arts Associations & Councils, Arts Centers, Arts Outreach, Ballet, Arts & Humanities-General, History & Archaeology, Libraries, Museums/Galleries, Music, Performing Arts
Civic & Public Affairs: Business/Free Enterprise, Chambers of Commerce, Clubs, Community Foundations, Economic Development, Economic Policy, Civic & Public Affairs-General, Housing, Legal Aid, Minority Business, Municipalities/Towns, Public Policy, Safety, Urban & Community Affairs
Education: Afterschool/Enrichment Programs, Agricultural Education, Business Education, Colleges & Universities, Community & Junior Colleges, Education Funds, Education Reform, Engineering/Technological Education, Education-General, Preschool Education, Private Education (Precollege), Public Education (Precollege), Science/Mathematics Education, Secondary Education (Public), Student Aid
Environment: Environment-General, Resource Conservation
Health: Cancer, Children's Health/Hospitals, Emergency/Ambulance Services, Eyes/Blindness, Health Funds, Health Organizations, Hospitals, Preventive Medicine/Wellness Organizations, Public Health, Speech & Hearing
Religion: Churches, Religious Organizations, Religious Welfare
Science: Science Exhibits & Fairs, Scientific Centers & Institutes, Scientific Research
Social Services: Animal Protection, Camps, Community Centers, Community Service Organizations, Day Care, Domestic Violence, Emergency Relief, Family Services, Recreation & Athletics, Scouts, Senior Services, Shelters/Homelessness, Social Services-General, United Funds/United Ways, Volunteer Services, YMCA/YWCA/YMHA/YWHA, Youth Organizations

Application Procedures

Initial Contact: The foundation has no specific format for applications.
Application Requirements: Requests should include tax status and any pertinent information.
Deadlines: None.
Evaluative Criteria: Preference is given to organizations located in geographical areas in which HON Industries, Inc. or its operating companies have a presence.

Corporate Officials

A. Mosby Harvey, Jr.: vice president, secretary, general counsel B Memphis, TN 1943. ED Dartmouth College (1965); University of Texas (1969). PRIM CORP EMPL vice president, secretary, general counsel: HON Industries Inc.
Jack D. Michaels: chairman, chief executive officer, director B 1937. ED University of Cincinnati BA. PRIM CORP EMPL chairman, chief executive officer, director: HON Industries Inc. CORP AFFIL president, director: Holga Inc.; director: Snap-On Inc.

Foundation Officials

Roger Behrens: director
Susan J. Cradick: secretary, treasurer
Jeffrey D. Fick: director
Stanley M. Howe: director B Muscatine, IA 1924. ED Iowa State University (1946); Harvard University Graduate School of Business Administration (1948).

CORP AFFIL director: Pella Corp. NONPR AFFIL trustee: Iowa Wesleyan College; member: National Association Manufacturers; member: Benevolent Protectorate Elks; member: Business & Institutional Furniture Manufacturer Association. CLUB AFFIL Rotary Club; 33 Club; Elks Club.
Jack D. Michaels: chairman, director (see above)

Grants Analysis

Disclosure Period: calendar year ending 2002
Total Grants: $795,958*
Number of Grants: 165
Average Grant: $3,614*
Highest Grant: $203,185
Lowest Grant: $45
Typical Range: $200 to $10,000
*Note: Giving excludes scholarship and United Way. Average grant figure excludes highest grant.

Recent Grants

Note: Grants derived from 2003 Form 990.
General

220,050	Citizens Scholarship Foundation of America, St. Peter, MN
203,185	City of Muscatine, Muscatine, IA
106,500	United Way of Muscatine, Muscatine, IA
50,000	Muscatine Beyond 2000, Muscatine, IA
50,000	University of Northern Iowa, Cedar Falls, IA
42,997	United Way of Greater Los Angeles, South Gate, CA
38,000	St. Ambrose University, Davenport, IA
35,000	Iowa College Foundation, Des Moines, IA
35,000	Muscatine Center for Social Action, Muscatine, IA
25,000	City of Mt. Pleasant, Mt. Pleasant, IA

HONDA OF AMERICA MANUFACTURING INC.

Company Headquarters

24000 Honda Parkway
Marysville, OH 43040
Web: http://www.ohio.honda.com

Company Description

Founded: 1979
Employees: 13,000
SIC(s): 3711 Motor Vehicles & Car Bodies.
Parent Company: Honda Motor Company Ltd., 1-1, 2-chome, Minami-Aoyama, Minato-ku, Tokyo, Japan

Operating Locations

Honda of America Manufacturing (OH--Marysville)

Nonmonetary Support

Volunteer Programs: The company maintains the Honda Hero Volunteer program, through which the company will donate $200 to eligible organizations to which employees volunteer a minimum of 50 hours.

Honda of America Foundation

Giving Contact

Lourene Hoy, Administrative Coordinator, Company Communications
Honda of America Manufacturing
24000 Honda Pkwy.
Marysville, OH 43040-9251
Phone: (937)645-6883

Description

Founded: 1981
EIN: 311006130

Organization Type: Corporate Foundation
Giving Locations: OH: 15-county hiring area
Grant Types: General Support, Project, Research, Scholarship.

Donor Information

Founder: Honda of America Manufacturing

Financial Summary

Total Giving: $477,086 (2002); $403,705 (2001). Note: Figures are for foundation only. Company gives directly, but does not release information on direct giving.
Assets: $7,412,362 (2002); $6,863,027 (2001)
Gifts Received: $2,000,000 (2002). Note: In 2002, contributions were received from Honda of America.

Typical Recipients

Arts & Humanities: Arts Associations & Councils, Arts Institutes, Ethnic & Folk Arts, Arts & Humanities-General, Historic Preservation, History & Archaeology, Libraries, Literary Arts, Performing Arts, Theater, Visual Arts
Civic & Public Affairs: African American Affairs, Employment/Job Training, Civic & Public Affairs-General, Professional & Trade Associations, Zoos/Aquariums
Education: Business Education, Colleges & Universities, Community & Junior Colleges, Economic Education, Education Associations, Education Funds, Education-General, International Exchange, International Studies, Literacy, Student Aid
Environment: Environment-General, Wildlife Protection
Health: Health-General
International: Health Care/Hospitals, International Organizations, International Relations
Religion: Ministries
Science: Science Museums
Social Services: Community Centers, Community Service Organizations, Crime Prevention, Delinquency & Criminal Rehabilitation, Family Services, People with Disabilities, YMCA/YWCA/YMHA/YWHA, Youth Organizations

Application Procedures

Initial Contact: Request a grant application form by writing to:
Honda of America Mfg., Inc.
Company Communications Dept.
24000 Honda Parkway
Marysville, OH 43040. Explain request and purpose of funds sought.
Application Requirements: Completed application forms should be accompanied by a copy of the organization's 501(c)(3) certification.
Deadlines: January 31, for applications to be considered for the current year. If an application is not received by that date, it will be considered for the next fiscal year.
Decision Notification: Grants are reviewed by a Senior Management Board on a three- to four-month cycle beginning in April. Applicants will be notified in writing of the Board's decision.

Restrictions

Does not support individuals or organizations outside operating areas.

Additional Information

Honda of America's giving priorities focus on the development of programs (with emphasis on education) and not on annual operating support budgets. The company's support of area United Way campaigns is taken into account when evaluating requests.
All grants listed were made by the Honda of America Foundation; information on direct giving recipients is not available.

Giving Program Officials

Sandra Fleming: PRIM CORP EMPL administration government & committee relations: Honda of America Manufacturing.

Foundation Officials

John Adams: director PRIM CORP EMPL senior vice president, general manager: Honda of America Manufacturing.
Larry Jutte: director
Shaun McCloskey: treasurer
Ed Miller: secretary
Kay Miller: director
Ted Noguchi: director
Rick Shostek: president, director

Grants Analysis

Disclosure Period: calendar year ending 2002
Total Grants: $477,086
Number of Grants: 23
Average Grant: $16,766*
Highest Grant: $75,000
Lowest Grant: $1,000
Typical Range: $5,000 to $25,000
*Note: Average grant figure excludes two highest grants ($125,000).

Recent Grants

Note: Grants derived from 2003 Form 990.
General

75,000	Columbus Urban League, Columbus, OH
50,000	Ohio Foundation of Independent Colleges, Columbus, OH
32,682	Wilde, Cumberland, OH
30,000	International Friendship Center, Bellefontaine, OH
30,000	Jobs for Columbus Graduates, Columbus, OH
30,000	Washington Center, Washington, DC
29,044	Educators to Japan Program, Marysville, OH -- towards education program for area teachers to travel to Japan for school visits
25,000	CAPA, Columbus, OH
25,000	H Youth in Government, Columbus, OH
25,000	OCEA, Cincinnati, OH

HERBERT W. HOOVER FOUNDATION

Giving Contact

Brian Hostettler
c/o Key Bank
126 Central Plaza
Canton, OH 44702
Phone: (330)489-5427

Description

Founded: 1989
EIN: 346905388
Organization Type: Private Foundation
Giving Locations: FL: Miami; OH: Stark County
Grant Types: Capital, General Support.

Donor Information

Founder: the Hoover Foundation

Financial Summary

Total Giving: $831,020 (2002); $902,811 (2001)
Giving Analysis: Giving for 2002 includes: foundation grants to United Way ($20,000)
Assets: $20,294,250 (2002); $22,692,939 (2001)
Gifts Received: $10,184 (2001). Note: In 2001, contributions were received from Elizabeth Hoover.

Typical Recipients

Arts & Humanities: Arts Centers, Arts Institutes, Libraries, Museums/Galleries, Music, Theater
Civic & Public Affairs: African American Affairs, Chambers of Commerce, Community Foundations, Economic Development, Civic & Public Affairs-General, Housing, Minority Business, Nonprofit Management, Safety, Urban & Community Affairs, Zoos/Aquariums
Education: Business Education, Colleges & Universities, Education Funds, Education Reform, Elementary Education (Public), Education-General, Medical Education, Private Education (Precollege), Public Education (Precollege), Secondary Education (Public), Student Aid, Vocational & Technical Education
Environment: Air/Water Quality, Environment-General, Resource Conservation
Health: Cancer, Clinics/Medical Centers, Health-General, Health Organizations, Single-Disease Health Associations
Religion: Ministries, Religious Organizations, Religious Welfare
Science: Scientific Centers & Institutes
Social Services: Animal Protection, Camps, Child Welfare, Community Centers, Community Service Organizations, Crime Prevention, Domestic Violence, Family Services, Food/Clothing Distribution, People with Disabilities, Recreation & Athletics, Scouts, United Funds/United Ways, YMCA/YWCA/YMHA/YWHA, Youth Organizations

Application Procedures

Initial Contact: Send a brief letter of inquiry.
Application Requirements: Include a description of organization, amount requested, purpose of funds sought, background information on organization, proof of tax-exempt status, and other organizations funding the project.
Deadlines: None.

Restrictions

Foundation does not support individuals, religious organizations for sectarian purposes, political or lobbying groups, or organizations outside operating areas.

Additional Information

Trust(s): Key Trust Co OH NA

Foundation Officials

Ruth H. Basner: mem
Mrs. Carl Good Hoover: member
Elizabeth Lacy Hoover: chairman
Robert S. O'Brien: mem
Blair C. Woodside, Jr.: member

Grants Analysis

Disclosure Period: calendar year ending 2002
Total Grants: $811,020*
Number of Grants: 35
Average Grant: $19,276*
Highest Grant: $100,000
Lowest Grant: $2,500
Typical Range: $10,000 to $50,000
*Note: Giving excludes United Way. Average grant figure excludes two highest grants ($175,000).

Recent Grants

Note: Grants derived from 2001 Form 990.
Library-Related

75,000	National First Ladies Library, Canton, OH
25,000	Minerva Public Library, Minerva, OH

General

75,000	North Canton Community Building, North Canton, OH
75,000	Walsh University, Canton, OH
50,000	Kent State University, Kent, OH
50,000	North Canton Medical Foundation, North Canton, OH
50,000	Spinal Cord Society, Fergus Falls, MN
49,740	Tropical Audubon Society, Miami, FL

42,750	Minority Development Services, Canton, OH
33,000	Stark State College Foundation, Canton, OH
30,000	Cultural Center for the Arts, Canton, OH
30,000	Neighbors For Neighbors, Miami, FL

THE HOOVER FOUNDATION

Giving Contact

Lawrence R. Hoover, Chairman
101 East Maple Street
North Canton, OH 44720
Fax: (216)497-5857

Description

Founded: 1945
EIN: 346510994
Organization Type: General Purpose Foundation
Giving Locations: OH: Stark County
Grant Types: Capital, Challenge, General Support, Multiyear/Continuing Support, Research, Scholarship, Seed Money.

Donor Information

Founder: Established in 1945 by members of the Hoover family.

Financial Summary

Total Giving: $2,587,650 (2003); $2,779,400 (2002). Note: The figure for 1995 includes $62,400 in matching gifts and scholarships.
Giving Analysis: Giving for 2003 includes: foundation grants to United Way ($202,650); 2002: foundation matching gifts ($15,700); foundation scholarships ($50,000); foundation grants to United Way ($233,000)
Assets: $50,261,854 (2003); $45,565,173 (2002)
Gifts Received: $332,500 (1993)

Typical Recipients

Arts & Humanities: Arts Centers, Arts Funds, Arts Institutes, Arts Outreach, Ballet, Arts & Humanities-General, Historic Preservation, History & Archaeology, Libraries, Museums/Galleries, Music, Opera, Performing Arts, Public Broadcasting, Theater
Civic & Public Affairs: African American Affairs, Botanical Gardens/Parks, Chambers of Commerce, Clubs, Economic Development, Employment/Job Training, Ethnic Organizations, Civic & Public Affairs-General, Housing, Minority Business, Municipalities/Towns, Philanthropic Organizations, Professional & Trade Associations, Safety, Urban & Community Affairs, Zoos/Aquariums
Education: Agricultural Education, Business Education, Colleges & Universities, Economic Education, Education Funds, Education Reform, Education-General, Leadership Training, Minority Education, Preschool Education, Private Education (Precollege), Public Education (Precollege), Religious Education, Science/Mathematics Education, Secondary Education (Public), Special Education, Student Aid
Environment: Forestry, Resource Conservation
Health: Cancer, Children's Health/Hospitals, Clinics/Medical Centers, Emergency/Ambulance Services, Eyes/Blindness, Health Funds, Health Organizations, Heart, Hospitals, Medical Research, Mental Health, Multiple Sclerosis, Prenatal Health Issues, Respiratory, Transplant Networks/Donor Banks
International: International Relations, Missionary/Religious Activities
Religion: Churches, Ministries, Missionary Activities (Domestic), Religious Organizations, Religious Welfare
Social Services: Animal Protection, At-Risk Youth, Camps, Child Welfare, Community Centers, Commu-

nity Service Organizations, Counseling, Day Care, Delinquency & Criminal Rehabilitation, Domestic Violence, Family Planning, Family Services, Food/Clothing Distribution, Homes, People with Disabilities, Recreation & Athletics, Scouts, Senior Services, Shelters/Homelessness, Substance Abuse, United Funds/United Ways, YMCA/YWCA/YMHA/YWHA, Youth Organizations

Application Procedures

Initial Contact: Send a brief letter of inquiry.
Application Requirements: Include purpose for which grant is requested, amount requested, and proof of 501(c)(3) status.
Deadlines: None.

Restrictions

The foundation primarily supports organizations located in the Stark County, OH, area. It does not make grants to individuals.

Additional Information

The Key Trust of Ohio, N.A. acts as a corporate trustee for the foundation.
Trust(s): Unizan Financial Services Group

Foundation Officials

Ronald Kent Bennington: committee member B Circleville, OH 1936. ED Kenyon College BA (1958); Ohio State University JD (1961). PRIM CORP EMPL partner: Black McCuskey Souers & Arbaugh. CORP AFFIL director: United Hard Chrome Inc. NONPR AFFIL board associates: Union College; fund-raising director: United Way Fund Drive; trustee: Timken Mercy Medical Center; member: Stark County Bar Association; president: Stark County Law Library Association; member: Ohio State Bar Foundation; steering committee: Pro Football Hall Fame; ambassador: Ohio Foundation Independent Colleges; trustee: Malone College; member: Ohio Bar Association; member advisory committee: Kenyon College; member: Leadership Canton; trustee: Greater Canton Chamber of Commerce; ofcl: Big Ten Football; president: Eastern Ohio Football Officials Association; member: American Bar Foundation; director: American Red Cross Canton; member: American Bar Association; board associate: Alliance.
Lawrence Richard Hoover: chairman, trustee B Canton, OH 1935. ED Massachusetts Institute of Technology (1957). PRIM CORP EMPL vice president: Ohio Power Co. CORP AFFIL vice president: Columbus Southern Power Co. NONPR AFFIL Free Accepted Masons:.
Thomas H. Hoover: committee member B 1921. ED Cornell University (1947). PRIM CORP EMPL president: Stark Co. Womens Clinic.
Joyce U. Niffenegger: committee member
Dr. Timothy D. Schiltz: committee member NONPR AFFIL president: North Canton Board Education.

Grants Analysis

Disclosure Period: calendar year ending 2003
Total Grants: $2,385,000*
Number of Grants: 84
Average Grant: $22,988*
Highest Grant: $300,000
Lowest Grant: $100
Typical Range: $10,000 to $50,000
*Note: Giving excludes United Way. Average grant figure excludes two highest grants ($500,000).

Recent Grants

Note: Grants derived from 2003 Form 990.
General

300,000	Walsh University, Canton, OH
200,000	North Canton Community Building YMCA, Canton, OH
180,000	YMCA of Western Stark County, Canton, OH
110,000	Cultural Center for the Arts, Canton, OH
97,000	First Tee of Canton, Canton, OH
85,000	Buckeye council, Boy Scouts, Canton, OH
83,000	Stark Education Partnership, Canton, OH
75,000	Buckeye Council, Boy Scouts, Canton, OH
75,000	Christian Church in Ohio, Elyria, OH
75,000	North Canton City Schools, Canton, OH

W. HENRY HOOVER TRUST FUND

Giving Contact

Kim Mayle
c/o Key Trust Co. OH NA
4495 Everhand Road North West
Canton, OH 44718
Phone: (330)497-3604

Description

Founded: 1945
EIN: 346573738
Organization Type: Private Foundation
Giving Locations: OH
Grant Types: General Support.

Donor Information

Founder: the late W. Henry Hoover

Financial Summary

Total Giving: $280,000 (2002); $308,000 (2001)
Giving Analysis: Giving for 2002 includes: foundation grants to United Way ($50,000)
Assets: $4,831,008 (2002); $5,979,535 (2001)
Gifts Received: $1,000 (1995)

Typical Recipients

Arts & Humanities: Arts Centers, Arts Funds, Arts Institutes, Arts & Humanities-General, Historic Preservation, History & Archaeology, Libraries, Museums/Galleries, Performing Arts, Theater
Civic & Public Affairs: Clubs, Civic & Public Affairs-General, Municipalities/Towns, Urban & Community Affairs
Education: Colleges & Universities, Education Funds, Education Reform, Engineering/Technological Education, Education-General, Minority Education, Private Education (Precollege), Student Aid
Environment: Resource Conservation
Health: Cancer, Emergency/Ambulance Services, Heart, Medical Research, Respiratory, Single-Disease Health Associations
International: Health Care/Hospitals, International Relations
Religion: Churches, Religious Organizations, Religious Welfare
Social Services: Animal Protection, At-Risk Youth, Child Welfare, Community Service Organizations, Family Planning, Family Services, People with Disabilities, Scouts, United Funds/United Ways, YMCA/YWCA/YMHA/YWHA, Youth Organizations

Application Procedures

Initial Contact: Send a brief letter of inquiry.
Application Requirements: Include amount requested and purpose of funds sought.
Deadlines: None.

Additional Information

Trust(s): Key Trust Co OH NA

Grants Analysis

Disclosure Period: calendar year ending 2002
Total Grants: $230,000*
Number of Grants: 30
Average Grant: $6,207*
Highest Grant: $50,000
Lowest Grant: $1,000
Typical Range: $1,000 to $10,000
*Note: Giving excludes United Way. Average grant figure excludes highest grant.

Recent Grants

Note: Grants derived from 2001 Form 990.
General

50,000	Cultural Center for the Arts, Canton, OH
50,000	Ohio Wesleyan University, Delaware, OH
50,000	United Way of Central Stark County, Canton, OH
15,000	Central American Medical, Orrville, OH
15,000	United Arts Fund, Canton, OH
10,000	Goodwill Industries, Canton, OH
10,000	Pathway Caring for Children, Canton, OH
10,000	Pegasus Farm, Hartville, OH
10,000	Wilderness Center, Wilmot, OH
8,000	Museum Guild, Canton, OH

HOPEDALE FOUNDATION

Giving Contact

Dr. Vincent J. Arone, Treasurer & Trustee
43 Hope St.
PO Box 123
Hopedale, MA 01747
Phone: (508)473-2871

Description

Founded: 1946
EIN: 046044779
Organization Type: Private Foundation
Giving Locations: MA: Hopedale
Grant Types: Capital, General Support, Loan, Scholarship.

Donor Information

Founder: Draper Corp., the late Thomas H. West, the late John D. Gannett

Financial Summary

Total Giving: $439,978 (fiscal year ending October 31, 2004); $415,405 (fiscal 2001)
Giving Analysis: Giving for fiscal 2001 includes: foundation scholarships ($145,405)
Assets: $8,344,679 (fiscal 2004); $8,438,197 (fiscal 2001)

Typical Recipients

Arts & Humanities: Arts Associations & Councils, Historic Preservation, History & Archaeology, Libraries, Museums/Galleries, Music, Public Broadcasting, Theater
Civic & Public Affairs: Botanical Gardens/Parks, Economic Development, Civic & Public Affairs-General, Municipalities/Towns, Safety, Zoos/Aquariums
Education: Arts/Humanities Education, Colleges & Universities, Education Funds, Elementary Education (Private), Elementary Education (Public), Education-General, Medical Education, Science/Mathematics Education, Secondary Education (Public)
Health: Children's Health/Hospitals, Clinics/Medical Centers, Health Organizations, Hospitals, Hospitals (University Affiliated), Nursing Services
Religion: Religious Welfare
Science: Science Museums
Social Services: Child Welfare, Community Centers, Community Service Organizations, Crime Prevention, Food/Clothing Distribution, People with Disabilities, Recreation & Athletics, Scouts, Senior Services, United Funds/United Ways, Veterans, YMCA/YWCA/YMHA/YWHA, Youth Organizations

Application Procedures

Initial Contact: Send a written request.
Deadlines: June 1 for student loans; no deadline for

other grants.
Review Process: Board meets in February, June, and October.

Restrictions

Grants to charitable organizations are restricted to those having an impact on the local area.

Additional Information

Provides student loans to graduates of Hopedale High School.

Foundation Officials

Dr. Vincent J. Arone: treasurer, director
W. Gregory Burrill: secretary, director
Peter S. Ellis: vice chairman, director
William B. Gannett: chairman, director
Alfred H. Sparling, Jr.: director

Grants Analysis

Disclosure Period: fiscal year ending October 31, 2004
Total Grants: $439,978*
Typical Range: $1,000 to $10,000
*Note: Complete grant list not available for 2004.

Recent Grants

Note: Grants derived from 2004 Form 990.
General

5,000	Hopedale Friends of Music, Hopedale, MA -- towards music event
2,500	Whitin Community Center, Whitinsville, MA
2,000	WGBH, Boston, MA -- towards Ralph Lowell society
1,000	Worcester Children's Friend Society, Worcester, MA

JOSEPHINE LAWRENCE HOPKINS FOUNDATION

Giving Contact

Ivan Obolensky, President, Treasurer & Director
61 Broadway, Suite 2100
New York, NY 10006
Phone: (212)480-0400

Description

Founded: 1968
EIN: 136277593
Organization Type: Private Foundation
Giving Locations: NY
Grant Types: General Support.

Donor Information

Founder: the late Josephine H. Graeber

Financial Summary

Total Giving: $156,000 (2001)
Assets: $3,947,217 (2001)
Gifts Received: $100 (1995)

Typical Recipients

Arts & Humanities: Arts Centers, Community Arts, Libraries, Literary Arts, Music, Performing Arts, Public Broadcasting
Civic & Public Affairs: Clubs, Civic & Public Affairs-General, Municipalities/Towns, Philanthropic Organizations, Professional & Trade Associations, Zoos/Aquariums
Education: Colleges & Universities, Education-General, Medical Education, Private Education (Precollege), Science/Mathematics Education, Secondary Education (Private), Secondary Education (Public), Special Education
Environment: Air/Water Quality, Environment-General, Resource Conservation

Health: Cancer, Children's Health/Hospitals, Emergency/Ambulance Services, Geriatric Health, Health Organizations, Hospitals, Long-Term Care, Medical Research
International: Missionary/Religious Activities
Religion: Churches, Missionary Activities (Domestic), Religious Organizations, Religious Welfare
Social Services: Animal Protection, Child Welfare, Community Centers, Community Service Organizations, Counseling, Emergency Relief, People with Disabilities, Recreation & Athletics, YMCA/YWCA/YMHA/YWHA, Youth Organizations

Application Procedures

Initial Contact: Send written request.
Deadlines: None.
Notes: Foundation mainly supports pre-selected organizations and rarely chooses to fund unsolicited requests.

Restrictions

Foundation does not support individuals.

Foundation Officials

Vera L. Colage: vice president, director
Lee Harrison Corbin: assistant secretary, assistant treasurer, director
William P. Hurley: vice president, secretary, assistant treasurer, director
John G. Ledes: assistant treasurer, assistant secretary, director
Ivan Obolensky: president, treasurer, director B London, United Kingdom 1925. ED Yale University BA (1947). PRIM CORP EMPL senior vice president: Josephthal & Co. CORP AFFIL vice president: Shields & Co.; general partner: Astor Capital Management Associates. NONPR AFFIL director: Un Service Organization; member: West Point Society; director: Tolstoy Foundation; member: Saint Elmo Society; president, director: Soldiers Sailors & Airmens Club; member: Military Order Loyal Museum Art; member: New England Society; member: Metropolitan Museum Art; director: Childrens Blood Foundation New York Hospital; grand treasurer, member: Masons; member: American Legion; director: Audubon Canyon Ranch. CLUB AFFIL Saint Georges Society; Navy League US; New York Yacht Club; Knickerbocker Club; Army-Navy Country Club; Explorers Club.
Gerald C. Tobin: assistant treasurer, assistant secretary, director

Grants Analysis

Disclosure Period: calendar year ending 2001
Total Grants: $156,000
Number of Grants: 26
Average Grant: $6,000
Highest Grant: $20,000
Lowest Grant: $1,000
Typical Range: $1,000 to $10,000

Recent Grants

Note: Grants derived from 2001 Form 990.
General

20,000	Archbishop of New York, New York, NY
10,000	American Red Cross, West Palm Beach, FL
10,000	American Red Cross, Ft. Lauderdale, FL
10,000	Audubon Canyon Ranch, Glen Ellen, CA
10,000	Children's Blood Foundation, New York, NY
10,000	Christopher Reeves Paralysis Foundation, Springfield, NJ
10,000	Inner-city Scholarship Fund, New York, NY
10,000	Soldiers', Sailors', Marines & Airmen's Club, Inc., New York, NY
10,000	Yale University Medical School, New Haven, CT
7,500	Cornell University, Ithaca, NY -- science - education

JOHN M. HOPWOOD CHARITABLE TRUST

Giving Contact

John M. Hopwood Charitable Trust
c/o PNC Advisors
2 PNC Plaza
620 Liberty Ave.
Pittsburgh, PA 15222-2705
Phone: (412)762-3785
Fax: (412)705-1043

Description

Founded: 1948
EIN: 256022634
Organization Type: Family Foundation
Giving Locations: PA: Western part of state
Grant Types: Challenge, Endowment, Loan, Matching, Project, Research, Seed Money.

Donor Information

Founder: Established in 1948 by the late John M. Hopwood.

Financial Summary

Total Giving: $1,210,500 (2002)
Giving Analysis: Giving for 2002 includes: foundation grants to United Way ($20,000); foundation scholarships ($255,000)
Assets: $26,824,260 (2002)
Gifts Received: In 1990, contributions were received from Mary Hopwood.

Typical Recipients

Arts & Humanities: Arts Centers, Ballet, Dance, Arts & Humanities-General, History & Archaeology, Libraries, Museums/Galleries, Music, Opera, Public Broadcasting, Theater
Civic & Public Affairs: Botanical Gardens/Parks, Clubs, Community Foundations, Employment/Job Training, Civic & Public Affairs-General, Housing, Parades/Festivals, Professional & Trade Associations, Public Policy, Urban & Community Affairs, Women's Affairs, Zoos/Aquariums
Education: Business Education, Colleges & Universities, Community & Junior Colleges, Education Funds, Education-General, Legal Education, Literacy, Medical Education, Private Education (Precollege), Public Education (Precollege), Science/Mathematics Education, Student Aid
Environment: Air/Water Quality, Energy, Environment-General, Resource Conservation
Health: Cancer, Children's Health/Hospitals, Clinics/Medical Centers, Emergency/Ambulance Services, Health Organizations, Hospices, Hospitals, Kidney, Long-Term Care, Medical Rehabilitation, Mental Health, Multiple Sclerosis, Nursing Services, Public Health, Single-Disease Health Associations, Speech & Hearing
International: Health Care/Hospitals
Religion: Churches, Religion-General, Ministries, Religious Organizations, Religious Welfare
Social Services: Big Brothers/Big Sisters, Camps, Child Welfare, Community Centers, Community Service Organizations, Day Care, Domestic Violence, Family Services, Homes, People with Disabilities, Recreation & Athletics, Scouts, Senior Services, Social Services-General, Substance Abuse, United Funds/United Ways, Veterans, YMCA/YWCA/YMHA/YWHA, Youth Organizations

Application Procedures

Initial Contact: The trust requests that applications be made in writing.
Deadlines: None.

Restrictions

The trust reports grants are made only to corporations or associations organized and operated exclusively for religious, charitable, scientific, literary, medical, or educational purposes. Funding is limited to southwestern Pennsylvania.

Additional Information

The PNC Bank acts as a corporate trustee for the John M. Hopwood Charitable Trust.
Publications: Guidelines
Trust(s): PNC Advisors

Foundation Officials

William T. Hopwood: trustee

Grants Analysis

Disclosure Period: calendar year ending 2002
Total Grants: $935,500*
Number of Grants: 29
Average Grant: $18,448*
Highest Grant: $200,000
Lowest Grant: $1,000
Typical Range: $1,000 to $50,000
*Note: Giving excludes United Way; scholarships. Average grant figure excludes four highest grants totaling $400,000.

Recent Grants

Note: Grants derived from 2002 Form 990.
General

255,000	Citizen's Scholarship Foundation, Santa Ana, CA
200,000	Pittsburgh Children's Museum, Pittsburgh, PA
100,000	Shadyside Hospital Foundation, Pittsburgh, PA
100,000	United Cerebral Palsy, Washington, PA
70,000	Washington Hospital, Washington, PA
50,000	Allegheny Valley School, Coraopolis, PA
50,000	Amateur Astronomers Association of Pittsburgh, Inc., Glenshaw, PA
40,000	Northeast Health Foundation, Rockland, ME
40,000	Pennsylvania Future, Harrisburg, PA
40,000	University of Pittsburgh, Pittsburgh, PA

HENRY HORNBLOWER FUND

Giving Contact

Nathan N. Withington, President
PO Box 2365
Boston, MA 02107
Phone: (617)589-3286

Description

Founded: 1945
EIN: 237425285
Organization Type: Private Foundation
Giving Locations: MA: Boston
Grant Types: General Support, Research.

Donor Information

Founder: Hornblower and Weeks - Hemphill, Noyes

Typical Recipients

Arts & Humanities: Community Arts, Arts & Humanities-General, Historic Preservation, History & Archaeology, Libraries, Museums/Galleries, Music, Public Broadcasting
Civic & Public Affairs: Community Foundations, Employment/Job Training, Civic & Public Affairs-General, Parades/Festivals, Philanthropic Organizations, Urban & Community Affairs, Women's Affairs
Education: Colleges & Universities, Private Education (Precollege), Secondary Education (Private), Secondary Education (Public), Special Education
Environment: Environment-General, Resource Conservation, Wildlife Protection
Health: Cancer, Children's Health/Hospitals, Clinics/

Medical Centers, Hospices, Hospitals, Medical Research, Nursing Services, Single-Disease Health Associations, Trauma Treatment
International: Health Care/Hospitals
Religion: Religious Organizations, Religious Welfare
Science: Science Museums
Social Services: Child Welfare, Community Centers, Community Service Organizations, Emergency Relief, Homes, People with Disabilities, Recreation & Athletics, Scouts, United Funds/United Ways, Youth Organizations

Application Procedures

Initial Contact: Foundation requests applications be made in writing. Send a brief letter of inquiry.
Application Requirements: Include a description of organization, amount requested, purpose of funds sought, and proof of tax-exempt status.
Deadlines: None.

Restrictions

Does not support individuals, or political or lobbying groups.

Foundation Officials

Dudley H. Bradlee, II: director B Medford, MA 1915. ED Harvard University (1938). PRIM CORP EMPL consultant: Shearson American Express. CORP AFFIL treasurer: Franklin Square House; director: Winchester Co-operative Bank; vice president, director: Charlesbank Homes.
Elaine Renzi: secretary
Nathan N. Withington: president

Grants Analysis

Disclosure Period: calendar year ending 2000
Total Grants: $357,500*
Number of Grants: 28
Average Grant: $5,833*
Highest Grant: $200,000
Typical Range: $100 to $10,000
*Note: Giving excludes matching gifts. Average grant excludes highest grant.

Recent Grants

Note: Grants derived from 2001 Form 990.
Library-Related

5,000	Plymouth Public Library, Plymouth, MA

General

100,000	Eel River Watershed, Redway, CA
25,000	Plimouth Plantation, Plymouth, MA
20,000	Jordan Hospital Club, Plymouth, MA
5,000	Children's Hospital, Boston, MA
5,000	Cura Visiting Nurse Association, Plymouth, MA
5,000	Eel River Watershed, Redway, CA
5,000	Friends of Cranberry Hospice, Kingston, MA
5,000	Governor Dummer Academy, Byfield, MA
5,000	Jimmy Fund, Brookline, MA
5,000	Kenyon College, Gambier, OH

ERVIN G. HOUCHENS FOUNDATION

Giving Contact

Suel Houchens, Director
Ervin G. Houchens Foundation
PO Box 90009
Bowling Green, KY 42102-9009
Phone: (270)843-3252

Description

Founded: 1954
EIN: 610623087
Organization Type: Private Foundation
Giving Locations: KY: Bowling Green
Grant Types: General Support.

Donor Information

Founder: Houchens Markets, Inc., B.G. Wholesale

Financial Summary

Total Giving: $326,994 (2001)
Giving Analysis: Giving for 2001 includes: foundation grants to United Way ($10,200)
Assets: $3,369,196 (2001)
Gifts Received: $16,236 (2001); $8,547 (2000); $13,994 (1996). Note: In 2001, contributions were received from E. G. Houchens Foundation Charitable Trust. In 1995 and 2000, contributions were received from the Houchens-Ervin G. Houchens Foundation.

Typical Recipients

Arts & Humanities: Arts Associations & Councils, Arts Centers, Arts Festivals, Arts Funds, Historic Preservation, History & Archaeology, Libraries, Museums/Galleries, Music, Theater
Civic & Public Affairs: Clubs, Employment/Job Training, Civic & Public Affairs-General, Housing, Parades/Festivals, Safety, Urban & Community Affairs, Women's Affairs
Education: Business Education, Colleges & Universities, Economic Education, Education Funds, Elementary Education (Public), Literacy, Private Education (Precollege), Secondary Education (Public), Student Aid
Environment: Environment-General
Health: Children's Health/Hospitals, Clinics/Medical Centers, Eyes/Blindness, Single-Disease Health Associations
Religion: Churches, Missionary Activities (Domestic), Religious Organizations, Religious Welfare
Science: Science Museums
Social Services: At-Risk Youth, Big Brothers/Big Sisters, Child Welfare, Community Service Organizations, Homes, Recreation & Athletics, Scouts, United Funds/United Ways, YMCA/YWCA/YMHA/YWHA, Youth Organizations

Application Procedures

Initial Contact: Send a brief letter of inquiry with comprehensive details.
Deadlines: None.

Additional Information

Provides interest-free and low-interest rate loans to churches and public charities.

Foundation Officials

Lou Beckner: assistant secretary
Covella H. Biggers: treasurer
Erin Biggers: director
Gil E. Biggers: director
Gil M. Biggers: president
George Suel Houchens: director
C. Cecil Martin: director
Lois Lynne Martin: secretary
Tara Biggers Parker: director

Grants Analysis

Disclosure Period: calendar year ending 2001
Total Grants: $316,794*
Number of Grants: 53
Average Grant: $3,186*
Highest Grant: $151,119
Lowest Grant: $60
Typical Range: $500 to $10,000
*Note: Giving excludes United Way. Average grant figure excludes highest grant.

Recent Grants

Note: Grants derived from 2001 Form 990.
General

151,119	State Street United Methodist Church, Bowling Green, KY
25,000	Salvation Army, Bowling Green, KY
16,000	Big Brothers Big Sisters, Inc., Bowling Green, KY
14,365	Girls Inc., Bowling Green, KY

13,479	Western Kentucky University Foundation, Bowling Green, KY
10,200	United Way of Southern Kentucky, Bowling Green, KY
7,500	State Street United Methodist Church, Bowling Green, KY
5,000	Court Appointed Special Advocates of Warren County, Bowling Green, KY
5,000	Horse Cave Theatre, Bowling Green, KY
5,000	Lindsey Wilson College, Columbia, KY

MAY KAY HOUCK FOUNDATION

Giving Contact
John Germany
Holland & Knight
PO Box 1288
Tampa, FL 33601
Phone: (813)227-8500

Description
Founded: 1955
EIN: 590777857
Organization Type: Private Foundation
Giving Locations: FL: Sarasota, Tampa; NY: Albany, Genesee, Greenwich, Rochester
Grant Types: General Support.

Financial Summary
Total Giving: $117,600 (fiscal year ending April 30, 2004); $97,000 (fiscal 2001)
Assets: $2,648,168 (fiscal 2004); $2,725,916 (fiscal 2001)

Typical Recipients
Arts & Humanities: Arts Funds, History & Archaeology, Libraries, Museums/Galleries, Music, Public Broadcasting, Theater
Civic & Public Affairs: Botanical Gardens/Parks, Community Foundations, Housing, Philanthropic Organizations, Urban & Community Affairs
Education: Afterschool/Enrichment Programs, Business Education, Education Funds, Public Education (Precollege)
Environment: Air/Water Quality, Resource Conservation, Watershed
Science: Scientific Centers & Institutes
Social Services: Community Centers, Community Service Organizations, Counseling, Domestic Violence, Homes, People with Disabilities, Recreation & Athletics, Sexual Abuse, Shelters/Homelessness, United Funds/United Ways, YMCA/YWCA/YMHA/YWHA, Youth Organizations

Application Procedures
Initial Contact: Request Application Form.
Deadlines: None.

Foundation Officials
Karen Hargrave: trustee
F. Wesley Moffett, Jr.: trustee
David Robison: trustee

Grants Analysis
Disclosure Period: fiscal year ending April 30, 2004
Total Grants: $117,600
Number of Grants: 13
Average Grant: $6,950*
Highest Grant: $34,200
Lowest Grant: $2,000
Typical Range: $3,000 to $10,000
*Note: Average grant excludes highest grant.

Recent Grants
Note: Grants derived from fiscal 2004 Form 990.
Library-Related

16,600	J. Germany Public Library, Tampa, FL

General

34,200	Junior Achievement, Colorado Springs, CO
13,000	Albany Symphony, Albany, NY
10,000	Nature Conservancy, Albany, NY
7,000	Battenkill Conservancy, Cambridge, NY
6,900	Habitat for Humanity, Sarasota, FL
6,900	Lighthouse for the Blind, Sarasota, FL
6,900	Safe Place and Rape Crisis, Sarasota, FL
6,900	Southeastern Guide Dogs, Sarasota, FL
3,000	Boys and Girls Clubs, Albany, NY

HOUSTON ENDOWMENT

Giving Contact
H. Joe Nelson, III, President
600 Travis, Suite 6400
Houston, TX 77002-3000
Phone: (713)238-8100
Fax: (713)238-8101
E-mail: info@houstonendowment.org
Web: http://www.houstonendowment.org

Description
Founded: 1937
EIN: 746013920
Organization Type: General Purpose Foundation
Giving Locations: TX: some statewide giving, Harris County, Houston
Grant Types: Capital, Endowment, Fellowship, General Support, Operating Expenses, Professorship, Project, Scholarship.

Donor Information
Founder: The Houston Endowment was established in 1937 by the late Mr. and Mrs. Jesse H. Jones. Mr. Jones was a Houston financier, owner-publisher of the *Houston Chronicle*, and a builder and real estate developer. In addition to his local leadership in civic affairs, Mr. Jones was nationally prominent as head of the Reconstruction Finance Corporation during the Depression, and Secretary of Commerce from 1940 to 1945.

Financial Summary
Total Giving: $61,555,873 (2004); $41,092,512 (2003 approx); $68,425,909 (2002)
Assets: $1,181,339,181 (2002); $1,340,803,428 (2001)

Typical Recipients
Arts & Humanities: Arts Associations & Councils, Arts Outreach, Ballet, Ethnic & Folk Arts, Arts & Humanities-General, Historic Preservation, History & Archaeology, Libraries, Literary Arts, Museums/Galleries, Music, Opera, Performing Arts, Public Broadcasting, Theater, Visual Arts
Civic & Public Affairs: African American Affairs, Asian American Affairs, Botanical Gardens/Parks, Community Foundations, Economic Development, Employment/Job Training, Civic & Public Affairs-General, Hispanic Affairs, Housing, Inner-City Development, Law & Justice, Municipalities/Towns, Professional & Trade Associations, Public Policy, Safety, Urban & Community Affairs, Women's Affairs, Zoos/Aquariums
Education: Afterschool/Enrichment Programs, Arts/Humanities Education, Business Education, Colleges & Universities, Economic Education, Education Associations, Education Funds, Education Reform, Elementary Education (Public), Engineering/Technological Education, Environmental Education, Faculty Development, Education-General, Gifted & Talented Programs, Health & Physical Education, International Studies, Legal Education, Literacy, Medical Education, Minority Education, Preschool Education, Private Education (Precollege), Public Education (Precollege), Religious Education, Science/Mathematics Education, Secondary Education (Private), Social Sciences Education, Special Education, Student Aid, Vocational & Technical Education
Environment: Environment-General, Protection, Research, Resource Conservation, Wildlife Protection
Health: AIDS/HIV, Alzheimer's Disease, Cancer, Children's Health/Hospitals, Clinics/Medical Centers, Diabetes, Emergency/Ambulance Services, Geriatric Health, Health Policy/Cost Containment, Health Funds, Health Organizations, Heart, Hospices, Hospitals, Medical Rehabilitation, Medical Research, Medical Training, Mental Health, Nursing Services, Outpatient Health Care, Research/Studies Institutes, Single-Disease Health Associations, Transplant Networks/Donor Banks
Religion: Churches, Jewish Causes, Ministries, Religious Organizations, Religious Welfare
Science: Science Museums, Scientific Centers & Institutes
Social Services: Animal Protection, At-Risk Youth, Child Abuse, Child Welfare, Community Centers, Community Service Organizations, Counseling, Crime Prevention, Day Care, Domestic Violence, Family Planning, Family Services, Food/Clothing Distribution, Homes, People with Disabilities, Recreation & Athletics, Scouts, Senior Services, Shelters/Homelessness, Substance Abuse, United Funds/United Ways, Volunteer Services, YMCA/YWCA/YMHA/YWHA, Youth Organizations

Application Procedures
Initial Contact: An application for a grant should be presented in written form. A specific application form is not required.
Application Requirements: Applications should contain a cover letter signed by the chief executive officer of the organization stating that he or she has approved the request. The letter should provide the name, title, and telephone number of the contact person; amount requested; a statement that no change occurred in the tax exempt status, purpose, character, or method of the organization's operation since the organization received its tax-exempt status from the IRS; and a statement indicating whether the organization has in the past or is now operated under any name other than the name on the organization's IRS determination letter. In addition, an application should include a three- to five-page proposal that provides a description of organization, the nature of its work, its mission, and its achievements; a statement about the issue being addressed by the proposed project; a list of names and qualifications of the people who will be in charge of the project; a description of the proposed project, including answers to the following questions: How will the project address the identified issues? Where will the project make a difference? Who will it target? How will it impact them? When will the project begin and end? If the project already is underway, what has been accomplished so far? How will the project be evaluated? What are the expected milestones and outcomes? How much will the project cost? How much does the organization need from Houston Endowment and over what period of time? If the project is ongoing, how will it be sustained after the Endowment's funding ends?

The following attachments should be provided: proof of tax-exempt status; recently audited financial statement; a complete copy of the organization's most recently filed IRS Form 990; a current list of the organization's board of directors or trustees; and the organization's current annual operating budget. If request is for a multi-year grant, also include the organization's projected annual operating budget for the years covered by the request. If request is for a specific project, include a project budget including the amounts and sources of committed and pending funds, including amounts. Also indicate the percentage of board members and/or trustees who financially supported the organization during the last fiscal year and the aggregate amount they donated. Budgets should include a narrative describing each major item in the budget and should explain how each was determined.

Deadlines: None.

Review Process: The review and decision process typically takes three to six months. The board of directors usually meet six times a year to consider grant requests. Applicant will be notified if additional information is requested, or an interview or site visit is planned. All applicants are notified in writing of the action taken by the directors on their requests.

Notes: Elaborate presentations are not necessary. Proposals should be unbound and on 8.5" by 11" paper.

Restrictions

The endowment does not make grants to individuals; for loans of any kind; galas or gala-like events, testimonial or fund raising luncheons or dinners, advertising in programs, or similar fund raising activity; organizations that in turn make grants to others; activities that promote or support a religion, a denomination or church; purchase of uniforms, equipment or trips for school-related organizations or amateur sports teams; honoraria for guest speakers; charities operated by service clubs; memorials to individuals; activities that are typically the responsibility of the government, including public schools; or a second request for a capital support that has been previously funded. No grants are made to organizations outside the U.S.

Additional Information

Publications: Annual Report; Guidelines

Foundation Officials

D. Kent Anderson: chairman, director ED University of Virginia MBA; Rice University BA (1962). CORP AFFIL board of directors: Sam Houston Race Park Ltd.; board of directors: Pulte Homes Inc. NONPR AFFIL trustee: Rice University.

Anthony W. Hall, Jr.: director ED Howard University BA; Texas Southern University JD. CORP AFFIL director: El Paso Corp. NONPR AFFIL trustee: Museum of Fine Arts Houston; chairman: United Negro College Fund; trustee: Junior Achievement Inc.; trustee: Junior Achievement of SE Texas; chief administrative officer: City of Houston; trustee: Houston Symphony Society; trustee: Boule Foundation.

Sheryl Lightfoot Johns: vice president, treasurer, chief financial officer B Pasadena, TX 1956. ED University of Houston BS (1986).

Melissa A. Jones: director CORP AFFIL director: Austin Trust Company. NONPR AFFIL board of directors: Settlement Club of Austin.

Harold Metts: director ED University of Texas JD; University of Texas BA. NONPR AFFIL trustee: Grace Presbyterian Church; development board: University of Texas Health Science Center. CLUB AFFIL past president: Houston Club.

David L. Nelson: vice president, grant director

H. Joe Nelson, III: president, director ED Rice University BA. NONPR AFFIL director: Houston Forum; professor: Rice University; director: Central Houston Civic Improvement Inc.; director: Central Houston Inc..

Laurence E. Simmons: director B Salt Lake City, UT 1946. ED University of Utah BA; Harvard University Graduate School of Business Administration MBA (1972). PRIM CORP EMPL chairman: Tuboscope Inc. ADD CORP EMPL chairman: Tuboscope Vetco International. CORP AFFIL owner, partner: SCF Partner LP; partner: Simmons Media Group; partner: SCF-II LP; president: SCF-III LP; chairman: Oil States International; director: ExpressJet Holdings Inc.; director: Integrated Productions Services. NONPR AFFIL director: National Parks Conservation Association; chairman: Texas Children's Hospital; director: Gordon & Mary Cain Pediatric Neurology Research Foundation.

Rosie Zamora: director B Elsa, TX 1935. ED Pan American University (1955); University of Texas, Austin (1955-1958). PRIM CORP EMPL president, treasurer, director: Telesurveys TX Inc. CORP AFFIL president: Telesurveys Research Associates.

NONPR AFFIL advisory board member: University Houston College Law Health Law & Policy Institute; director: Women's Museum; president: Houston Wilderness; board member: United Way Texas Gulf Coast; director: Greater Houston Partnership; advisory council: Hogg Foundation for Mental Health; director: Center for Houston's Future.

Grants Analysis

Disclosure Period: calendar year ending 2004
Total Grants: $61,555,873
Number of Grants: 675 (approx)
Average Grant: $76,379*
Highest Grant: $10,000,000
Typical Range: $5,000 to $100,000 and $200,000 to $1,000,000
*Note: Average grant figure excludes highest grant.

Recent Grants

Note: Grants derived from 2002 Form 990.
General

5,000,000 University of Houston, Houston, TX -- fund for the expansion and renovation of the Anderson Library

4,000,000 Alley Theater, Houston, TX -- fund for costs associated with the Staging the Future campaign

2,000,000 Central Houston Civic Improvement Inc., Houston, TX -- fund for the development of a major pedestrian space

2,000,000 William Marsh Rice University, Houston, TX -- fund for the enhancement of the Jesse H. Jones Graduate School of Management

1,500,000 Texas State University System, Austin, TX -- towards the Novice Teacher Induction Program

1,215,000 Houston Independent School District, Houston, TX -- scholarship assistance

1,000,000 Memorial Hermann Foundation, Houston, TX -- fund for flood recovery and restoration at Memorial Hermann Hospital

1,000,000 Texas A & M Foundation, College Station, TX -- fund for graduate and undergraduate scholarships and program to provide quality teachers

1,000,000 Texas Southern University, Houston, TX -- fund for early childhood education

1,000,000 United Way of the Texas Gulf Coast, Houston, TX -- fund for new headquarters building

HOWARD AND BUSH FOUNDATION

Giving Contact
Deborah Byers
2 Bekke Avenue
Troy, NY 12180
Phone: (518)271-1134

Description
EIN: 066059063
Organization Type: General Purpose Foundation
Giving Locations: NY: Rensselaer County
Grant Types: Challenge, General Support, Project.

Donor Information
Founder: the late Edith Mason Howard, the late Julia Howard Bush

Financial Summary
Total Giving: $308,780 (2001)
Assets: $4,063,371 (2001)
Gifts Received: $75,553 (1999); $97,855 (1995); $116,758 (1994)

Typical Recipients

Arts & Humanities: Arts Associations & Councils, Arts Centers, Dance, Arts & Humanities-General, Historic Preservation, History & Archaeology, Libraries, Museums/Galleries, Music, Performing Arts, Public Broadcasting, Theater, Visual Arts

Civic & Public Affairs: African American Affairs, Botanical Gardens/Parks, Business/Free Enterprise, Community Foundations, Economic Development, Civic & Public Affairs-General, Hispanic Affairs, Housing, Law & Justice, Legal Aid, Municipalities/Towns, Public Policy, Safety, Urban & Community Affairs

Education: Afterschool/Enrichment Programs, Arts/Humanities Education, Colleges & Universities, Elementary Education (Private), Elementary Education (Public), Engineering/Technological Education, Education-General, Literacy, Medical Education, Minority Education, Private Education (Precollege), Public Education (Precollege), Secondary Education (Public), Student Aid

Environment: Environment-General, Resource Conservation

Health: AIDS/HIV, Emergency/Ambulance Services, Health Organizations, Home-Care Services, Hospices, Hospitals, Medical Rehabilitation, Nursing Services, Prenatal Health Issues

Religion: Churches, Ministries, Religious Organizations, Religious Welfare

Social Services: Camps, Child Welfare, Community Centers, Community Service Organizations, Family Planning, Family Services, Food/Clothing Distribution, Recreation & Athletics, Senior Services, Shelters/Homelessness, YMCA/YWCA/YMHA/YWHA, Youth Organizations

Application Procedures

Initial Contact: Send letter requesting application guidelines and the annual report, or call for information.

Deadlines: None.

Restrictions

The foundation ordinarily does not make grants to government agencies; churches or schools not associated with the founders, except for nondenominational community projects; organizations that have received grants from the foundation within the past two years; operating deficits; endowment funds; municipalities or other tax-supported institutions; reserve or revolving funds; or to individuals.

Additional Information

In 1991, the foundation contributed approximately $4 million, about half of the foundation's assets, to the Hartford Foundation for Public Giving. The funds supported approximately 27 advised grants made by the Hartford Foundation's main fund and created two permanent funds--Tomlinson Fund for Philanthropy and Endowment Fund for Architecture Conservancy of Hartford. Both are administered by the Hartford Foundation.

Publications: Application Guidelines.

Foundation Officials

Judith A. Barnes: director
Donald C. Bowes: director
Sarah H. Catlin: president
David Sands Haviland: director B Rome, NY 1942. ED Rensselaer Polytechnic Institute BS (1964); Rensselaer Polytechnic Institute BArch (1965); Rensselaer Polytechnic Institute MArch (1967). PRIM CORP EMPL dean student life, professor architect: Rensselaer Polytechnic Institute. NONPR AFFIL trustee: Troy Music Hall; vis professor: University Reading United Kingdom; trustee: Rensselaer Newman Foundation; member: New York Saint Association Architects; member: Project Management Institute; member: Association Collegiate Schs; member: Council Education Facility Planners; treasurer: Architectural Research Centers Consortium; member facil-

ities committee: Albany Medical Center; member: American Institute Architects.
Margaret Mochon: director
David W. Parmelee: trustee

Grants Analysis
Disclosure Period: calendar year ending 2001
Total Grants: $308,780
Number of Grants: 18
Average Grant: $15,222*
Highest Grant: $50,000
Lowest Grant: $2,500
Typical Range: $5,000 to $30,000
*Note: Average grant figure excludes highest grant.

Recent Grants
Note: Grants derived from 2002 Form 990.
Library-Related
8,500 New Brunswick Community Library, New Brunswick, NJ -- for updated computers
General
28,000 Capital District Community Gardens -- to service immigrant victims of domestic violence
25,000 Ark Community Charter School -- for second year of operation
25,000 Arts Center of the Capital Region, Troy, NY -- for salary for youth programs director
25,000 Friends of Washington Park
15,000 Habitat for Humanity
15,000 Home Aide Service of Eastern New York, Inc., NY -- for care teams for the elderly
12,500 Jewish Family Services of Northeastern New York, NY
11,981 Upper Hudson Planned Parenthood -- for outreach educator
10,000 Albany Symphony Orchestra, Albany, NY -- for capital region heritage commissions
10,000 Capital District Community Gardens -- for outreach to hard to reach populations

LUCILLE HORTON HOWE AND MITCHELL B. HOWE FOUNDATION

Giving Contact
Mitchell B. Howe, Jr., President & Treasurer
180 S. Lake Ave.
Pasadena, CA 91101
Phone: (626)792-2771

Description
Founded: 1964
EIN: 956081945
Organization Type: Private Foundation
Giving Locations: CA: Pasadena
Grant Types: General Support.

Donor Information
Founder: the late Mitchell B. Howe

Financial Summary
Total Giving: $109,000 (2001)
Assets: $1,894,222 (2001)

Typical Recipients
Arts & Humanities: Arts Centers, Historic Preservation, Libraries, Museums/Galleries, Music
Civic & Public Affairs: Employment/Job Training, Civic & Public Affairs-General, Law & Justice, Legal Aid, Municipalities/Towns
Education: Business Education, Colleges & Universities, Community & Junior Colleges, Private Education (Precollege), Public Education (Precollege), Secondary Education (Private), Student Aid, Vocational

& Technical Education
Health: Children's Health/Hospitals, Health Organizations, Hospitals, Kidney, Medical Research, Prenatal Health Issues, Public Health, Research/Studies Institutes, Single-Disease Health Associations
Religion: Churches, Religious Organizations, Religious Welfare
Social Services: Animal Protection, Child Welfare, Community Service Organizations, Family Services, Homes, People with Disabilities, Recreation & Athletics, Substance Abuse, United Funds/United Ways, Volunteer Services, YMCA/YWCA/YMHA/YWHA, Youth Organizations

Application Procedures
Initial Contact: Send brief letter describing program.
Application Requirements: Include purpose of funds sought, indicate whether the donee is a new applicant, and include proof of tax-exempt status.
Deadlines: February.

Restrictions
Does not support: individuals, political or lobbying groups, or organizations outside operating areas.

Foundation Officials
John C. Cushman: secretary
James J. Howe: director
Mitchell B. Howe, Jr.: president, treasurer
Hugh V. Hunter: director
Lynn Howe Myers: chairman, vice president
Mitchell C. Myers: director

Grants Analysis
Disclosure Period: calendar year ending 2001
Total Grants: $109,000
Number of Grants: 10
Average Grant: $5,444*
Highest Grant: $60,000
Lowest Grant: $1,000
Typical Range: $2,000 to $10,000
*Note: Average grant figure excludes highest grant.

Recent Grants
Note: Grants derived from 2001 Form 990.
General
60,000 Huntington Medical Research Institute, Pasadena, CA
12,000 Pasadena Guild Children's Hospital, Pasadena, CA
10,000 Maranatha High School, Sierra Madre, CA
10,000 Santa Fe Christian Schools, Solana Beach, CA
5,000 Azusa Pacific University, Azusa, CA
4,000 Door of Hope, Newark, DE
3,000 Los Angeles Philharmonic Association, Los Angeles, CA
2,000 Hillsides Home for Children, Pasadena, CA
2,000 Sam Schmidt Paralysis Foundation, Indianapolis, IN
1,000 Huntington Medical Research Institute, Pasadena, CA

HRK FOUNDATION

Giving Contact
Kathleen Fluegel, Foundation Director
345 Saint Peter Street, Suite 1200
St. Paul, MN 55102
Phone: (651)293-9001
Fax: (651)298-0551
E-mail: heidi@hrkfoundation.org
Web: http://www.hrkfoundation.org

Description
Founded: 1962
EIN: 416020911
Organization Type: Family Foundation
Former Name: Mary Anderson Foundation MAHADH Foundation (1994).
Former Name: MAHADH Foundation to HRK Foundation (1998).
Giving Locations: MN: Twin Cities metropolitan area; WI: St. Croix Valley and Ashland and Bayfield Counties
Grant Types: Capital, Endowment, General Support, Matching, Operating Expenses, Project, Scholarship.

Donor Information
Founder: The HRK Foundation, formerly the MAHADH Foundation, began in 1962 as the Mary Anderson Hulings Foundation, established by members of the Anderson and Hulings families.

Financial Summary
Total Giving: $1,800,000 (2004 approx); $2,418,400 (2003); $2,271,580 (2002)
Assets: $28,277,424 (2003); $24,605,559 (2002); $33,463,486 (2001)
Gifts Received: $755,391 (2003); $99,946 (2002); $2,101,715 (1999). Note: In 2003, contributions were received from Martha H. Kaemmer ($580,682), Katherine D. Hayes ($94,901), Frederick C. Kaemmer ($46,672), and Julia Hynnek ($33,135). In 2002, contributions were received from Katherine D. Rice.

Typical Recipients
Arts & Humanities: Arts Associations & Councils, Arts Centers, Arts Institutes, Arts & Humanities-General, Historic Preservation, History & Archaeology, Libraries, Museums/Galleries, Music, Opera, Performing Arts, Public Broadcasting
Civic & Public Affairs: Business/Free Enterprise, Clubs, Community Foundations, Economic Development, Employment/Job Training, Civic & Public Affairs-General, Housing, Inner-City Development, Municipalities/Towns, Professional & Trade Associations, Rural Affairs, Urban & Community Affairs, Women's Affairs
Education: Colleges & Universities, Community & Junior Colleges, Education Funds, Education-General, International Exchange, Medical Education, Minority Education, Private Education (Precollege), Public Education (Precollege), Religious Education, Student Aid
Environment: Environment-General, Protection, Resource Conservation, Watershed, Wildlife Protection
Health: AIDS/HIV, Children's Health/Hospitals, Clinics/Medical Centers, Emergency/Ambulance Services, Health Funds, Health Organizations, Hospitals, Medical Rehabilitation, Mental Health, Public Health, Single-Disease Health Associations, Transplant Networks/Donor Banks
International: Health Care/Hospitals, International Environmental Issues, International Relief Efforts
Religion: Churches, Religious Welfare, Seminaries
Science: Science Museums
Social Services: Child Welfare, Community Service Organizations, Day Care, Family Planning, Family Services, Homes, People with Disabilities, Scouts, Shelters/Homelessness, Social Services-General, Substance Abuse, United Funds/United Ways, Volunteer Services, YMCA/YWCA/YMHA/YWHA, Youth Organizations

Application Procedures
Initial Contact: Prior to submitting a proposal (at least two weeks before the deadline), call the Foundation's Director to discuss your request.
Application Requirements: The foundation requests that applicants include one copy of an unbound proposal of six pages or less exclusive of attachments. Include a cover sheet; copy of IRS 501(c)(3) determination letter; recently audited financial statement; and organizational or project budget;

organizational information, including history, mission and goals, description of current programs and activities, service statistics, board members and key staff, and relationship with other organizations working to meet the same needs or providing similar services; brief summary highlighting the situation, specific activities, goals, and timeframe; summary of how you define success and who will be involved in evaluating the potential outcomes. specific activities, and impact of the activities; and methods of evaluation. Required attachments include a copy of most recent audit and/or IRS Form 990 and unaudited financial statements; organizational and/or project budget; description of any future plans your organization has for a capital or endowment campaign; one-paragraph description of key staff, including qualifications; a listing of the board of directors and affiliations; and a letter from your fiscal agent, if not a 501(c)(3), explaining that you have been incorporated as a program or project of the sponsoring organization and are governed by its board of directors. If the request is for capital support, include a projected operating budget which
Deadlines: March 15 and October 15.
Review Process: Requests are generally reviewed in May and November. Final funding decisions will be mailed within three weeks of board meeting.
Notes: The foundation also accepts the Minnesota Common Grant Form. The foundation will not consider videos.

Restrictions
The foundation does not support individuals or businesses. The foundation reports that most of its resources are committed to organizations that have received support in the past. New applicants will be considered for single-year funding in the areas of AIDS issues, children's health, and community-specific projects only.

Additional Information
The Foundation has a commitment to long-term relationships with grantees and accepts only a limited number of new, capital, or project requests in each calendar year.
Publications: Annual Report (including Application Guidelines)

Foundation Officials
Julia L. Hynnek: director
Arthur W. Kaemmer, MD: chairman, treasurer NONPR AFFIL chairman: National Medicine Fellowships.
Frederick C. Kaemmer: director
Martha H. Kaemmer: vice president, director CORP AFFIL director: Andersen Corp.
Katherine D. Rice: director
Mary E. Rice: director
Mary H. Rice: vice president, director

Grants Analysis
Disclosure Period: calendar year ending 2003
Total Grants: $2,418,400
Number of Grants: 181
Average Grant: $9,274*
Highest Grant: $750,000
Lowest Grant: $100
Typical Range: $1,000 to $20,000
*Note: Average grant figure excludes highest grant.

Recent Grants
Note: Grants derived from 2003 Form 990.
General

750,000	Northland College, Ashland, WI
200,000	Carleton College, Northfield, MN
82,500	Saint Paul Chamber Orchestra, St. Paul, MN
75,000	Vocal Essence, Minneapolis, MN
70,000	Saint Paul Riverfront Corporation, St. Paul, MN
50,000	Friends of the St. Paul Farmers Market, St. Paul, MN
50,000	Lake Superior Big Top Chautauqua, Washburn, WI
50,000	Saint Paul Chamber Orchestra, St. Paul, MN
50,000	United Theological Seminary, Dayton, OH
45,000	Minnesota Opera Company, Minneapolis, MN

HUBBARD BROADCASTING INC.

Company Headquarters
3415 University Ave., W
St. Paul, MN 55114
Web: http://www.kstp.com

Company Description
Employees: 1,200
SIC(s): 4832 Radio Broadcasting Stations, 4833 Television Broadcasting Stations, 7812 Motion Picture & Video Production.

Operating Locations
Hubbard Broadcasting, Inc. (CA--Montego Bay; FL--Cyprus Gardens, Dade County, Miami Beach, Pinellas Park, St. Petersburg, Tampa; MN--Maplewood, Minneapolis, St. Croix, White Bear Lake; NM--Albuquerque; WA--Spokane)

Hubbard Foundation

Giving Contact
Kathryn Hubbard-Rominski, Executive Director
3415 University Avenue
St. Paul, MN 55114
Phone: (651)642-4305
Fax: (612)642-4103

Alternate Contact
Phone: (651)642-4300

Description
EIN: 416022291
Organization Type: Corporate Foundation
Giving Locations: nationally; principally near operating locations and to national organizations.
Grant Types: Capital, Operating Expenses.

Financial Summary
Total Giving: $3,397,725 (2003); $1,095,718 (2002); $1,179,690 (2001)
Assets: $19,576,102 (2003); $19,444,849 (2002); $23,053,819 (2001)

Typical Recipients
Arts & Humanities: Arts Associations & Councils, Arts Centers, Arts Funds, Arts Institutes, Arts Outreach, Ballet, Community Arts, Historic Preservation, History & Archaeology, Libraries, Museums/Galleries, Music, Opera, Performing Arts, Public Broadcasting, Theater, Visual Arts
Civic & Public Affairs: African American Affairs, Botanical Gardens/Parks, Civil Rights, Clubs, Community Foundations, Economic Development, Civic & Public Affairs-General, Housing, Municipalities/Towns, Nonprofit Management, Philanthropic Organizations, Professional & Trade Associations, Public Policy, Safety, Zoos/Aquariums
Education: Arts/Humanities Education, Business Education, Colleges & Universities, Economic Education, Education Funds, Elementary Education (Private), Elementary Education (Public), Engineering/Technological Education, Education-General, Journalism/Media Education, Legal Education, Literacy, Medical Education, Minority Education, Private Education (Precollege), Public Education (Precollege), Secondary Education (Private), Secondary Education (Public), Special Education, Student Aid, Vocational & Technical Education
Environment: Air/Water Quality, Environment-General, Research
Health: Arthritis, Cancer, Children's Health/Hospitals, Diabetes, Health Funds, Health Organizations, Heart, Hospitals, Kidney, Medical Rehabilitation, Medical Research, Mental Health, Preventive Medicine/Wellness Organizations, Research/Studies Institutes, Single-Disease Health Associations, Speech & Hearing
International: International Environmental Issues, International Organizations
Religion: Churches, Jewish Causes, Religious Organizations, Religious Welfare
Science: Science Museums, Scientific Centers & Institutes
Social Services: Camps, Child Welfare, Community Centers, Community Service Organizations, Counseling, Day Care, Emergency Relief, Family Planning, Family Services, Food/Clothing Distribution, Homes, People with Disabilities, Recreation & Athletics, Scouts, Social Services-General, Substance Abuse, United Funds/United Ways, Volunteer Services, YMCA/YWCA/YMHA/YWHA, Youth Organizations

Application Procedures
Application Requirements: Send a summary of history and a description of organization, copy of IRS section 501(c)(3) status letter, purpose of funds sought, and whether funds are intended to be used for operating or non-operating expenses.
Deadlines: November 30.
Decision Notification: Most foundation activity takes place before the end of the calendar year.

Restrictions
The foundation typically does not accept unsolicited proposals.

Corporate Officials
Stanley S. Hubbard: chairman, president, chief executive officer B Saint Paul, MN 1933. ED University of Minnesota BA (1955). PRIM CORP EMPL chairman, president, chief executive officer: Hubbard Broadcasting, Inc. ADD CORP EMPL vice president: F & F Productions LLC. CORP AFFIL director: Fingerhut Co. Inc.; chairman, president, chief executive officer, director: US Satellite Broadcasting Co. Inc. NONPR AFFIL director: University Saint Thomas; member: World Business Council; director: University Minnesota Foundation; member: Society Professional Journalists; member: Society Satellite Professionals International; member: Royal Television Society London; chairman: Saint Croix Valley Youth Center; director: Ramsey County Ice Arena Committee; chairman, president, chief executive officer: Minnesota Business Partnership; member: Minnesota Executives Organization; member: Metropolitan Airports Public Foundation Advisory Board; director: Minneapolis American Friends Jamaica; member: International Radio & Television Society; director: Broadcast Pioneers Library; member: Broadcasters Foundation; director: Baptist Hospital Fund Sponsor Board; member: Broadcast Pioneers; director: Association Maximum Service Telecasters.

Foundation Officials
Julia D. Coyte: director
Gerald D. Deeney: secretary
Constance L. Eckert: assistant secretary
Robert W. Hubbard: director
Stanley E. Hubbard: director
Stanley S. Hubbard: president, director (see above)
Kathryn Hubbard Rominski: executive director, director ADD CORP EMPL secretary: F & F Productions LLC. CORP AFFIL secretary: D Diamond Sports Inc.
Virginia H. Morris: director

Grants Analysis

Disclosure Period: calendar year ending 2003
Total Grants: $3,380,725*
Number of Grants: 246
Average Grant: $6,196*
Highest Grant: $750,000
Lowest Grant: $100
Typical Range: $1,000 to $10,000
*Note: Giving excludes United Way. Average grant figure excludes three highest grants ($1,875,000).

Recent Grants

Note: Grants derived from 2003 Form 990.
Library-Related

50,000	Friends of the St. Paul Public Library, St. Paul, MN
11,000	Friends of the Minneapolis Public Library, Minneapolis, MN

General

750,000	University of Minnesota, Minneapolis, MN
625,000	United Hospital Foundation, St. Paul, MN
500,000	Gustavus Adolphus College, St. Peter, MN
200,000	Children's Cancer Research Funds, Los Angeles, CA
150,000	Saint Paul Academy and Summit School, St. Paul, MN
100,000	Breck School, Minneapolis, MN
75,000	Gillette Childrens Hospital Foundation, St. Paul, MN
50,000	Mounds Park Academy, St. Paul, MN
50,000	Saint Ambrose of Woodbury, Woodbury, MN
35,000	Intrepid Museum Foundation, New York, NY

R. D. AND JOAN DALE HUBBARD FOUNDATION

Giving Contact

James A. Stoddard, Executive Director
PO Box 2498
Ruidoso, NM 88355-2498
Phone: (505)258-5919
Fax: (505)258-3749

Description

Founded: 1986
EIN: 752266308
Organization Type: Family Foundation
Giving Locations: CA; KS; NM; TX
Grant Types: Challenge, Endowment, Fellowship, General Support, Matching, Multiyear/Continuing Support, Professorship, Research, Scholarship.

Donor Information

Founder: The foundation was founded by R. D. Hubbard and Joan Dale Hubbard of Ft. Worth, TX, in 1986. Today, Mr. Hubbard is chairman of the board of AFG Industries, the second largest glass manufacturer in North America. His primary business interest is an extensive involvement in the racing industry. In addition to his horse breeding operations in Kentucky and New Mexico, he is the owner or major stockholder in four race tracks. Mr. Hubbard is owner and chairman of Ruidoso Downs Racing, a quarterhorse track in Ruidoso, NM; majority owner and chairman of the Woodlands, a dual horse and dog racing operation in Kansas City, KS; chairman and chief executive officer of Hollywood Park, a thoroughbred racing facility in California; and owner and chairman of Multnomah Kennel Club, a greyhound track in Portland, OR.

Financial Summary

Total Giving: $933,898 (2003); $1,000,000 (2002 approx)
Giving Analysis: Giving for 2003 includes: founda-

tion scholarships ($194,325)
Assets: $36,686,063 (2003)
Gifts Received: $1,000 (1998). Note: In 1998, contributions were received from David Shepherd.

Typical Recipients

Arts & Humanities: Arts Associations & Councils, Arts Funds, Dance, Historic Preservation, History & Archaeology, Libraries, Museums/Galleries, Music, Performing Arts, Theater
Civic & Public Affairs: Business/Free Enterprise, Chambers of Commerce, Clubs, Community Foundations, Civic & Public Affairs-General, Municipalities/Towns, Nonprofit Management, Philanthropic Organizations, Safety, Urban & Community Affairs, Women's Affairs
Education: Agricultural Education, Arts/Humanities Education, Business Education, Colleges & Universities, Community & Junior Colleges, Education Funds, Elementary Education (Private), Elementary Education (Public), Faculty Development, Education-General, Legal Education, Medical Education, Private Education (Precollege), Public Education (Precollege), Science/Mathematics Education, Secondary Education (Public), Social Sciences Education, Student Aid
Environment: Wildlife Protection
Health: AIDS/HIV, Alzheimer's Disease, Cancer, Children's Health/Hospitals, Clinics/Medical Centers, Emergency/Ambulance Services, Health Funds, Heart, Home-Care Services, Medical Research, Medical Training, Single-Disease Health Associations
International: Foreign Arts Organizations, Foreign Educational Institutions
Religion: Religion-General, Religious Organizations, Religious Welfare
Social Services: Animal Protection, At-Risk Youth, Big Brothers/Big Sisters, Community Centers, Community Service Organizations, Domestic Violence, People with Disabilities, Recreation & Athletics, Scouts, Senior Services, Social Services-General, Youth Organizations

Application Procedures

Initial Contact: Send a brief letter describing the organization.
Application Requirements: The specific program to be considered, budget summary, and amount requested.
Deadlines: None.
Review Process: Applicants are informed of the decision within two months.

Additional Information

Publications: Application Guidelines; Annual Report; Program Policy Statement

Foundation Officials

Edward A. Burger: secretary, treasurer, director CLUB AFFIL secretary-treasurer, director: Multnomah Kennel Club.
Joan Dale Hubbard: vice president, director
Randall Dee Hubbard: president, director B Smith Center, KS 1935. ED Butler County Community College BA (1956). PRIM CORP EMPL chairman board: AFG Industries Inc. CORP AFFIL president, chief executive officer, director: Turf Paradise Inc.; chief executive officer, director: Sunflower Racing Inc.; director: Hollywood Park Realty Enterprises; president, director, co-owner: Ruidoso Downs Racing Inc.; chief executive officer, director: Hollywood Park Inc.; chairman, director: Hollywood Park Operation Co.; chief executive officer, director: Hollywood Park Food Service; director: America Flat Glass Distributors. NONPR AFFIL member: International Association Businessmen & Professionals Foundation. CLUB AFFIL chairman, director, co-owner: Multnomah Kennel Club.
Jennings Jay Newcom: assistant secretary, director B Saint Joseph, MO 1941. ED Graceland College BA (1964); Harvard University JD (1968). PRIM CORP

EMPL partner: Shook Hardy & Bacon. NONPR AFFIL member: Kansas City Bar Association; member: Lawyers Association Kansas City; chairman board: Graceland College.
James A. Stoddard: executive director

Grants Analysis

Disclosure Period: calendar year ending 2003
Total Grants: $739,573*
Number of Grants: 66
Average Grant: $4,455*
Highest Grant: $350,000
Lowest Grant: $200
Typical Range: $1,000 to $10,000
*Note: Giving excludes scholarships. Average grant excludes two highest grant ($450,000).

Recent Grants

Note: Grants derived from 2002 Form 990.
General

341,667	Hubbard Museum, Ruidoso Downs, NM -- towards arts education
150,000	Scripps Foundation, La Jolla, CA -- towards medical and science research
50,000	McCallum Theater & The Bob Hope Cultural Center, Palm Desert, CA -- towards arts education
30,000	AIDS Assistance Program, Palm Springs, CA -- fund for AIDS assistance
29,795	Smith Center Public Schools, Smith Center, KS -- fund for scholarships
25,000	Cap Cure, Santa Monica, CA -- fund for cancer research
25,000	University of California, San Diego, CA -- fund for scholarships
25,000	University of Kentucky, Lexington, KY -- towards library endowment fund
20,000	California State University, Palm Desert, CA -- towards beautification of new campus facility
20,000	Friends of Utah Golf, Park City, UT

HUBER FOUNDATION

Giving Contact

Lorraine Barnhart, Executive Director
PO Box 277
Rumson, NJ 07760
Phone: (732)933-7700

Description

Founded: 1949
EIN: 210737062
Organization Type: Family Foundation
Giving Locations: nationally.
Grant Types: General Support, Project.

Donor Information

Founder: The Huber Foundation was established in 1949 in New Jersey. Since then, the foundation has received personal contributions from various members of the Huber family.

Financial Summary

Total Giving: $1,907,000 (2002)
Assets: $39,931,428 (2002)
Gifts Received: $864 (1999); $991,259 (1995); $270,000 (1994). Note: The foundation receives contributions from the estate of Catherine G. Huber.

Typical Recipients

Arts & Humanities: Libraries
Civic & Public Affairs: African American Affairs, Civil Rights, Civic & Public Affairs-General, Legal Aid, Nonprofit Management, Philanthropic Organizations, Professional & Trade Associations, Public Policy, Urban & Community Affairs, Women's Affairs
Education: Colleges & Universities, Education

Funds, Social Sciences Education
Environment: Environment-General
Health: Clinics/Medical Centers, Health Organizations, Hospitals, Public Health
International: Health Care/Hospitals, International Environmental Issues, International Peace & Security Issues
Religion: Social/Policy Issues
Social Services: Family Planning, Family Services, Youth Organizations

Application Procedures

Initial Contact: Applications should take the form of a typewritten letter.
Application Requirements: Letters of application should describe the proposed project, and include a project budget, and proof of the applicant's tax-exempt status. The foundation will request more information if needed.
Deadlines: None.
Review Process: The trustees meet four times a year. The dates for these meetings are not fixed.
Notes: The foundation's interest lies in funding organizations that will impact issues on a national level. Therefore, the foundation does not encourage proposal submission from projects that are local or regional in scope.

Restrictions

Grants are made only to tax-exempt organizations. The foundation does not consider grants to individuals, foreign organizations, capital campaigns, scholarships, research, international projects, or film productions.

Additional Information

Publications: Annual Report

Foundation Officials

Lorraine Barnhart: vice president, trustee
Jennifer Curry: trustee
Lisa Goodspeed: trustee
Hans A. Huber: president, trustee CORP AFFIL director: J M Huber Corp.
Michael W. Huber: secretary, trustee B 1926. PRIM CORP EMPL director: J.M. Huber Corp. CORP AFFIL director: Crompton & Knowles Corp.
Julia Ann Nagy: treasurer
Christopher W. Seely: trustee
Catherine Weiss: trustee

Grants Analysis

Disclosure Period: calendar year ending 2000
Total Grants: $2,087,000
Number of Grants: 32
Average Grant: $65,219
Highest Grant: $225,000
Typical Range: $40,000 to $400,000

Recent Grants

Note: Grants derived from 2002 Form 990.
General

225,000	Planned Parenthood Federation of America, New York, NY -- for general support
150,000	American Civil Liberties Union Foundation, New York, NY -- for reproductive rights project
150,000	Center for Reproductive Law & Policy, New York, NY -- for general support
150,000	NARAL Foundation, Washington, DC -- for general support
100,000	Alan Guttmacher Institute, New York, NY -- for general support
60,000	N.A.A.C.P. Legal Defense and Educational Fund, New York, NY -- for Herbert Lehman educational fund and reproductive rights work
50,000	Advocates for Youth, Washington, DC -- for general support
50,000	Catholics for a Free Choice, Washington, DC -- for general support
50,000	Choice USA, Washington, DC -- for general support
50,000	Feminist Majority Foundation, Arlington, VA -- for national clinic access project

HUDSON RIVER BANCORP INC.

Company Headquarters

1 Hudson City Cir.
Hudson, NY 12534
Web: http://www.hudsonriver.com

Company Description

Founded: 1998
Ticker: HRBT
Exchange: NASDAQ
Assets: US$2.508 billion (2001)
Employees: 571 (2001)
SIC(s): 6036 Savings Institutions Except Federal, 6719 Holding Companies Nec.

Hudson River Bancorp Inc. Foundation

Giving Contact

Holly Rappleyea, Secretary & Treasurer
One Hudson City Centre
PO Box 76
Hudson, NY 12534
Phone: (518)828-4600
Web: http://www.hudsonriverbank.com/html/foundation_hrbt.html
Note: Ms. Rappleyea is available at extension 303.

Description

Founded: 1999
EIN: 223595668
Organization Type: Corporate Foundation
Giving Locations: NY
Grant Types: General Support.

Financial Summary

Total Giving: $452,038 (fiscal year ending 1, 2003); $328,642 (fiscal 2002); $251,055 (fiscal 2001)
Giving Analysis: Giving for fiscal 2003 includes: foundation grants to United Way ($3,691); fiscal 2002: foundation grants to United Way ($3,447); foundation ($325,195); fiscal 2001: foundation ($251,055)
Assets: $11,729,107 (fiscal 2003); $12,500,915 (fiscal 2002); $6,839,775 (fiscal 2001)
Gifts Received: $3,917 (fiscal 2003); $888,814 (fiscal 2002); $5,200,120 (fiscal 1999). Note: In fiscal 2002 and 2003, contributions were received from the Estate of Arthur L. Hegarty. In fiscal 1999, contributions were received from Hudson River Bank & Trust.

Typical Recipients

Arts & Humanities: Arts Associations & Councils, Arts Centers, Film & Video, Historic Preservation, History & Archaeology, Libraries, Music, Opera, Theater
Civic & Public Affairs: Asian American Affairs, Clubs, Economic Development, Ethnic Organizations, Civic & Public Affairs-General, Housing, Inner-City Development, Legal Aid, Parades/Festivals, Professional & Trade Associations, Rural Affairs, Safety, Urban & Community Affairs, Women's Affairs
Education: Afterschool/Enrichment Programs, Colleges & Universities, Community & Junior Colleges, Education Funds, Elementary Education (Private), Legal Education, Literacy, Preschool Education, Private Education (Precollege), Public Education (Precollege)

Environment: Air/Water Quality
Health: Alzheimer's Disease, Cancer, Clinics/Medical Centers, Emergency/Ambulance Services, Health-General, Health Funds, Heart, Hospices, Hospitals, Preventive Medicine/Wellness Organizations, Single-Disease Health Associations
Religion: Churches, Ministries, Religious Welfare
Science: Science Exhibits & Fairs
Social Services: At-Risk Youth, Community Service Organizations, Emergency Relief, Food/Clothing Distribution, Homes, People with Disabilities, Recreation & Athletics, Social Services-General, Special Olympics, United Funds/United Ways, YMCA/YWCA/YMHA/YWHA, Youth Organizations

Application Procedures

Initial Contact: Submit a letter to request a grant request for less than $1,000. Requests for more than $1,000 should be submitted using the New York/New Jersey Area Common Grant Application Format. A copy of this application may be obtained by contacting the foundation.
Application Requirements: Requests for less than $1,000 should include a cover letter on the applicant's letterhead which describes the amount requested, purpose of funds sought, and name and telephone number of the contact person. The following attachments should be included: a brief description of the organization's purpose, history and accomplishments; the current year's operating budget; a list of organizations and foundations that support the applicant organization, including the most recent amounts contributed; proof of tax-exempt status; a list of the names and affiliations of the board of directors; and the purpose and amount of the last grant received from Hudson River Bank & Trust Company or the Hudson City Savings Institution (if applicable).
Deadlines: None.

Restrictions

Does not typically support individuals; political organizations; debt liquidation; religious groups for sectarian purposes; or memberships for which the company receives a benefit.

Corporate Officials

Timothy Blow: chief financial officer
Carl A. Florio: president, chief executive officer
Tony Jones: chairman

Foundation Officials

Carl A. Florio: director (see above)
Marilyn A. Herrington: president
William H. Jones: vice president
Holly Rappleyea: secretary, treasurer

Grants Analysis

Total Grants: $448,347*
Number of Grants: 197
Average Grant: $2,276
Highest Grant: $26,500
Lowest Grant: $25
Typical Range: $500 to $5,000
*Note: Giving excludes United Way.

Recent Grants

Note: Grants derived from fiscal 2004 Form 990.
General

40,000	St. Mary's Hospital, Leonardtown, MD -- equipment and renovation
25,000	Columbia-Greene Hospital Foundation, Hudson, NY -- to support the renovation and expansion of the intensive care unit
18,000	Gilda's, Royal Oak, MI -- cancer patient support
15,000	Albany Medical Center, Albany, NY -- renovation and expansion
15,000	Amsterdam Memorial Hospital, Amsterdam, NY -- equipment and renovation
12,500	Columbia County Agricultural Society, Chatham, NY -- support the renovations to the stage

10,000	C-G Hospital Foundation, Washington, DC -- hospital improvement
10,000	Hudson Opera House, Hudson, NY -- assist in the exterior restoration project
10,000	Olana Partnership, Hudson, NY -- support the museum
10,000	University at Albany Foundation, Albany, NY -- to support the contract management project

HUDSON-WEBBER FOUNDATION

Giving Contact

David O. Egner, President
333 West Fort Street, Suite 1310
Detroit, MI 48226
Phone: (313)963-7777
Fax: (313)963-2818

Description

Founded: 1943
EIN: 386052131
Organization Type: General Purpose Foundation
Giving Locations: MI: Oakland County, Southeastern Michigan, Wayne County, Detroit
Grant Types: Award, Challenge, Employee Matching Gifts, General Support, Matching, Multiyear/Continuing Support, Project, Research, Scholarship, Seed Money.

Donor Information

Founder: The Hudson-Webber Foundation was organized in 1943, with funds donated by the J. L. Hudson Company and by Richard Webber, Joseph Webber, and Oscar Webber. Significant contributions also were provided by company employees and other members of the family. At the close of 1983, the foundation merged with two other foundations: the Eloise and Richard Webber Foundation (established in 1939, with Richard and Eloise Webber; their daughters, Jean Webber Sutphin and Mary Webber Parker; and Richard Webber's sister, Louise Webber O'Brien as donors) and the Richard H. and Eloise Jenks Webber Charitable Fund (established in 1960, with Richard and Eloise Webber; their daughters, Jean and Mary; and Richard Webber's brother, Joseph L. Webber, as donors).
Joseph L. Hudson, Jr., chairman of the foundation, and Gilbert Hudson, its president and chief executive, are grandnephews of Joseph L. Hudson (1846-1912), who founded J. L. Hudson Company (1881), a major Detroit merchandiser. Joseph L. Hudson was a generous benefactor of local charities and a leader of civic boards and committees. The Webber family's relationship to the company derives from the founder's sister, Mary, who married Joseph T. Webber. When Mr. Hudson died, his four nephews inherited the majority of the company's stock, and Richard Hudson Webber became president of J. L. Hudson Company.

Financial Summary

Total Giving: $5,747,979 (2003); $6,524,832 (2002). Note: Giving includes United Way, gifts to individuals.
Giving Analysis: Giving for 2002 includes: foundation gifts to individuals ($16,928); foundation scholarships ($35,000); foundation grants to United Way ($150,000); foundation matching gifts ($1,533,654)
Assets: $138,459,347 (2003); $114,944,188 (2002)
Gifts Received: $1,003,641 (2003); $974,421 (2002); $1,000,000 (1999 approx). Note: In 2002 and 2003, contributions were received from Mary Webber Parker.

Typical Recipients

Arts & Humanities: Arts Associations & Councils, Arts Centers, Arts Funds, Arts Institutes, Ethnic & Folk Arts, Arts & Humanities-General, Historic Preservation, History & Archaeology, Libraries, Museums/Galleries, Music, Opera, Performing Arts, Public Broadcasting, Theater
Civic & Public Affairs: African American Affairs, Botanical Gardens/Parks, Business/Free Enterprise, Chambers of Commerce, Community Foundations, Economic Development, Economic Policy, Employment/Job Training, Civic & Public Affairs-General, Hispanic Affairs, Housing, Inner-City Development, Law & Justice, Minority Business, Municipalities/Towns, Nonprofit Management, Parades/Festivals, Philanthropic Organizations, Public Policy, Safety, Urban & Community Affairs, Women's Affairs, Zoos/Aquariums
Education: Afterschool/Enrichment Programs, Arts/Humanities Education, Business Education, Colleges & Universities, Continuing Education, Education Associations, Education Funds, Education Reform, Education-General, Legal Education, Minority Education, Private Education (Precollege), Public Education (Precollege), Secondary Education (Public), Social Sciences Education, Student Aid, Vocational & Technical Education
Environment: Environment-General
Health: Alzheimer's Disease, Cancer, Children's Health/Hospitals, Clinics/Medical Centers, Health Funds, Health Organizations, Hospitals, Hospitals (University Affiliated), Kidney, Nursing Services, Prenatal Health Issues, Public Health, Transplant Networks/Donor Banks
International: International Development, International Peace & Security Issues
Religion: Churches, Dioceses, Religious Organizations, Religious Welfare, Social/Policy Issues
Science: Scientific Centers & Institutes
Social Services: At-Risk Youth, Child Abuse, Community Service Organizations, Counseling, Crime Prevention, Delinquency & Criminal Rehabilitation, Domestic Violence, Family Planning, Family Services, Food/Clothing Distribution, Homes, People with Disabilities, Recreation & Athletics, Shelters/Homelessness, Substance Abuse, United Funds/United Ways, Volunteer Services, YMCA/YWCA/YMHA/YWHA, Youth Organizations

Application Procedures

Initial Contact: Applicants should send a brief letter, signed by a senior officer of the requesting organization.
Application Requirements: The letter of request should include a brief description of organization; description of the proposed program, including an explanation of its importance and a clear statement of its goals; detailed income and expense budget for the program; potential sources of other funding; and amount requested and time period during which the funds will be used. Proof of the organization's tax-exempt status is required.
Deadlines: Grant requests should be submitted by April 15, August 15, or December 15. Requests received after these dates are reviewed during the next period.
Notes: Only one copy of the proposal should be submitted.

Restrictions

The foundation does not make grants for endowments, fundraising social events, conferences, or exhibits. Also, the foundation does not fund individuals, except under the Hudson-Webber program for Hudsonians. Programs outside the foundation's geographical area of interest are not supported.

Additional Information

Publications: Annual Report (annually); Guidelines

Foundation Officials

William C. Brooks: trustee PRIM CORP EMPL chairman: Brooks Group International. CORP AFFIL director: Louisiana-Pacific Corp.; chairman: Brooks Group International; director: DTE Energy Co. NONPR AFFIL chairman: Greater Detroit Chamber of Commerce.
Matthew P. Cullen: trustee
Stephen R. D'Arcy: trustee
David O. Egner: president, trustee ED Western Michigan University MS.
W. Frank Fountain: trustee
Alfred Robinson Glancy, III: trustee, treasurer B Detroit, MI 1938. ED Princeton University BA (1960); Harvard University MA (1962). PRIM CORP EMPL chairman, president, chief executive officer: MCN Corp. CORP AFFIL vice chairman: UNICO Properties; chairman, president, chief executive officer: MCN Energy Group Inc.; director: Morton Industrial Group Inc. NONPR AFFIL chairman: Detroit Symphony Orchestra; director: New Detroit Inc.; chairman: Detroit Renaissance Inc.; chairman: Detroit Medical Center. CLUB AFFIL Princeton Michigan Club; Country Club Detroit; Detroit Club.
Frank Martin Hennessey: trustee B Lynn, MA 1938. ED Northeastern University BS (1964). PRIM CORP EMPL vice chairman, chief executive officer: MascoTech Inc. ADD CORP EMPL chairman: Emco Ltd.; chairman, director: Metcraft Inc. CORP AFFIL director: MCN Corp.; director: MCN Energy Group Inc.
Hudson Holland, Jr.: secretary, trustee B Springfield, MA 1939. ED Williams College BA (1961). NONPR AFFIL trustee: Cottage Hospital Massachusetts; president: Nantucket House. CLUB AFFIL Fontinalis Club; Nantucket Yacht Club.
Gilbert Hudson: chairman, trustee
Joseph L. Hudson, IV: trustee CORP AFFIL director: Masco Corp.
Joseph Lowthian Hudson, Jr.: trustee CORP AFFIL director: Masco Corp.
John E. Lobbia: trustee B Chicago, IL 1941. ED University of Detroit BSEE (1964). PRIM CORP EMPL chairman, chief executive officer, director: Detroit Edison Co. CORP AFFIL chairman, chief executive officer, director: DTE Energy Co.; director: Rouge Steel Co.
Jennifer H. Parke: vice chairman, trustee
Reginald M. Turner: trustee
Amanda Vandusen: trustee

Grants Analysis

Disclosure Period: calendar year ending 2003
Total Grants: $5,747,979*
Highest Grant: $500,000
Lowest Grant: $100
Typical Range: $10,000 to $100,000
*Note: Grants list incomplete for 2003.

Recent Grants

Note: Grants derived from 2003 Form 990.

General

500,000	Barbara Ann Karmanos Cancer Institute, Detroit, MI -- cancer research center
250,000	Detroit Institute of Arts, Detroit, MI
250,000	Detroit Science Center Inc., Detroit, MI -- Capital Campaign
250,000	Goodwill Industries of Greater Detroit, Detroit, MI -- reducing chronic unemployment
200,000	Community Foundation for Southeastern Michigan, Detroit, MI -- Greenways initiative
200,000	Detroit Institute of Arts, Detroit, MI -- for funding additional building
200,000	Detroit Symphony Orchestra Hall Inc., Detroit, MI
200,000	Detroit Symphony Orchestra Hall Inc., Detroit, MI
200,000	Operation ABLE of Michigan, Southfield, MI -- to reduce chronic unemployment
200,000	Starfish Family Services (f.n.a. Youth Living Centers), Inkster, MI -- to reduce chronic unemployment

GEOFFREY C. HUGHES FOUNDATION

Giving Contact

John R. Young, President & Director
c/o Cahill, Gordon & Reindel
80 Pine Street, Suite 1701
New York, NY 10005
Phone: (212)701-3400

Description

Founded: 1991
EIN: 133622255
Organization Type: Private Foundation
Giving Locations: CA; KY; NY: northeastern states.
Grant Types: General Support.

Donor Information

Founder: the late Geoffrey C. Hughes

Financial Summary

Total Giving: $2,218,072 (fiscal year ending March 31, 2001)
Assets: $35,464,221 (fiscal 2001)
Gifts Received: $47,481 (fiscal 2000); $60,573 (fiscal 1997); $642,663 (fiscal 1996). Note: In fiscal 1996 and 2000, contributions were received from the estate of Geoffrey C. Hughes.

Typical Recipients

Arts & Humanities: Ballet, Ethnic & Folk Arts, History & Archaeology, Music, Opera, Theater
Civic & Public Affairs: Urban & Community Affairs, Zoos/Aquariums
Education: Arts/Humanities Education, Colleges & Universities, Literacy, Medical Education
Environment: Environment-General, Resource Conservation, Wildlife Protection
International: Foreign Arts Organizations

Application Procedures

Initial Contact: Send a brief letter of inquiry.
Application Requirements: Include a description of organization, amount requested, purpose of funds sought, and proof of tax-exempt status.
Deadlines: None.

Restrictions

Awards are generally concentrated in the areas of environmental protection, opera, and ballet.

Foundation Officials

Ursula Cliff: director
Joan Murtagh Frankel: assistant secretary, assistant treasurer
June McCandless: director
O. Carlysle McCandless: executive vice president, assistant secretary, treasurer, director
John R. Young: president, director B Milwaukee, WI 1934. ED University of Chicago AB (1953); University of Chicago JD (1956). PRIM CORP EMPL Cahill Gordon & Reindel.
Mary K. Young: director

Grants Analysis

Disclosure Period: fiscal year ending March 31, 2001
Total Grants: $2,218,072
Number of Grants: 35
Average Grant: $63,373
Highest Grant: $226,938
Lowest Grant: $1,000
Typical Range: $5,000 to $400,000

Recent Grants

Note: Grants derived from 2001 Form 990.
General

226,938	Hancock Shaker Village, Pittsfield, MA -- for HSV New England Heritage Breeds Conservancy Collaborations
200,000	Nature Conservancy, Boston, MA
200,000	Nature Conservancy, Middletown, CT -- for GCH land preservation fund
200,000	New York City Ballet, New York, NY -- for artist in residence program
150,000	San Francisco Opera, San Francisco, CA -- for showcase performances by Adler Fellows
120,000	Engremont Environmental Action and Land Trust
100,000	American Friends of the Paris Opera and Ballet -- for San Francisco Ballet appearance in Paris
100,000	Long Island Sound Keeper Fund, Monterey, CA -- for Yankee Oyster Project
100,000	Nature Conservancy, Concord, NH -- for preserving lands
100,000	New York City Opera, New York, NY

HOWARD HUGHES MEDICAL INSTITUTE

Giving Contact

Office of Grants and Special Programs
4000 Jones Bridge Road
Chevy Chase, MD 20815-6789
Phone: (301)215-8500
Fax: (301)215-8888
E-mail: webmaster@hhmi.org
Web: http://www.hhmi.org

Description

Founded: 1954
EIN: 590735717
Organization Type: Specialized/Single Purpose Foundation
Giving Locations: internationally; nationally.
Grant Types: Award, Fellowship, Multiyear/ Continuing Support, Research, Scholarship.

Donor Information

Founder: The Howard Hughes Medical Institute was established as a medical research organization in 1953 by aviator-industrialist Howard R. Hughes. The institute was funded through its ownership of the Hughes Aircraft Company whose sole trustee was Mr. Hughes until his death in 1976. New trustees were appointed in 1984, and, in 1985, they sold Hughes Aircraft Company to General Motors Corporation. The proceeds of that sale represent the basis of the institute's present endowment.

Financial Summary

Total Giving: $486,129,571 (fiscal year ending August 31, 2003); $582,000,000 (fiscal 2002 approx); $103,278,000 (fiscal 2001)
Assets: $12,820,000,000 (fiscal 2004 approx); $11,376,573,656 (fiscal 2003); $10,291,341,000 (fiscal 2002)
Gifts Received: $47,481 (fiscal 2000)

Typical Recipients

Arts & Humanities: Arts Outreach, Ballet, Museums/ Galleries, Opera, Theater
Civic & Public Affairs: Botanical Gardens/Parks, Nonprofit Management, Zoos/Aquariums
Education: Colleges & Universities, Engineering/ Technological Education, Faculty Development, Education-General, Medical Education, Minority Education, Science/Mathematics Education, Student Aid, Vocational & Technical Education
Environment: Environment-General, Protection, Resource Conservation, Wildlife Protection
Health: Arthritis, Cancer, Health Funds, Hospitals, Hospitals (University Affiliated), Medical Research, Research/Studies Institutes, Respiratory
International: Foreign Arts Organizations

Science: Science Museums, Scientific Centers & Institutes, Scientific Labs, Scientific Organizations, Scientific Research

Application Procedures

Initial Contact: For Grants and Special Programs, each of the programs in graduate, undergraduate, and pre-college, and international research has individual eligibility requirements, criteria for support, and methods of application. Informational brochures, program announcements, and application forms should be consulted prior to contact. These materials are available upon request from the Office of Grants and Special Programs.
Deadlines: For Grants and Special Programs, deadlines vary according to the particular program. Program announcements should be consulted for the exact dates.
Review Process: Graduate fellowships, grants for undergraduate and pre-college science education, and grants for research in selected countries abroad are awarded on the basis of applications or proposals reviewed by outside panels of scientists and educators. The panels' evaluations are reviewed by an internal committee, which makes recommendations to the institute's trustees for authorization of funding. The trustees and institute management annually review current grants policies, initiatives, and possible directions for program development.

Restrictions

The institute does not award scholarships or funds to students directly. The grantee colleges and universities award and distribute the funds on their own. The institute does not award grants for research in the United States. It does not award institutional training grants or support conferences or publications.

Additional Information

Information on specific programs may be obtained from the following contact persons: Barbara Filner, PhD., graduate science education; Stephen A. Barkanic, undergraduate science education; Jill G. Conley, PhD, international and pre-college science education, as well as the international program; and Dennis WC. Liu, PhD., research resource and public science education.
Publications: Annual Report; Guidelines; Application Form; Directories; Fact Sheets

Foundation Officials

James Addison Baker, III: trustee B Houston, TX April 28, 1930. ED Princeton University BA (1952); University of Texas JD (1957). PRIM CORP EMPL senior partner: Baker & Botts, LLP ADD CORP EMPL senior counselor: Carlyle Group. NONPR AFFIL director: Rice University; member: Texas Bar Association; vice president: Professional Development Institute; honorary chairman: James A. Baker III Institute Public Policy; member: Phi Delta Phi; member: Council on Foreign Relations; member: Houston Bar Association; member: American Bar Association; member: American Judicature Society.
Stephen M. Cohen: vice president, chief financial officer B Harrisburg, PA 1952. ED Pennsylvania State University BA (1974); New York University MBA (1976). PRIM NONPR EMPL dean: Yale University, School of Medicine. NONPR AFFIL director: Medicine Centre Industry Co. Ltd.; director: Tech Council of Maryland; mem: America Israel Public Affairs Committee; mem: Association American Medical Colleges.
Frank William Gay: trustee B Provo, UT. ED Brigham Young University; Colorado College. PRIM CORP EMPL former president, former chief executive officer: Summa Corp.
Joseph L. Goldstein, MD: trustee B Sumter, SC April 18, 1940. ED Washington & Lee University BS (1962); Southwestern Medical School MD (1966). NONPR AFFIL member: National Academy of Sciences; chairman: University of Texas, Dept. of Molecular Genetics; member: American Society for Clinical

Investigation; member: American Society of Human Genetics; member: American Society of Biological Chemists; member: American Society for Cell Biology; member: American Academy of Arts and Sciences; member: American Federation for Clinical Research.

Garnett L. Keith: trustee B Atlanta, GA 1935. ED Georgia Institute of Technology (1957); Harvard University Graduate School of Business Administration MA (1962). PRIM CORP EMPL chairman, chief executive officer: SeaBridge Investment Advisors. CORP AFFIL director: Supervalu Inc.; director: Whitecap Capital LLC; chairman, chief executive officer: SeaBridge Investment Advisors, LLC; director: Pan-Holding Societe Anonyme; director: Philippe Investment Management.

Jeremy R. Knowles, PhD: trustee B Rugby, United Kingdom 1935. ED Oxford University BA (1958); Balliol College BA (1959); Christ Church University MA (1961); Christ Church University MA (1961). PRIM NONPR EMPL dean arts & sciences, Amory Houghton professor: Harvard University. NONPR AFFIL member: Royal Chemistry Society London; fellow: Royale Society; foreign associate: National Academy of Sciences; fellow: Harvard University; member: NAS; member: American Society Biological Chemists; member: Biochemistry Society London; fellow: American Philosophical Society; Dean emeritus: American Academy of Arts & Sciences; member: American Chemical Society.

Joan S. Leonard, Esq.: vice president, general counsel PRIM NONPR EMPL secretary, general counsel: Howard Hughes Medical Institute. NONPR AFFIL member: AAMC Task Force on Financial Conflicts of Interest.

William R. Lummis, Esq.: trustee B Houston, TX 1929. ED University of Texas BA (1951); University of Texas LLB (1953). PRIM CORP EMPL chairman: Summa Corp. CORP AFFIL director: Stewart & Stevenson Services Inc.; director: Rouse Co. Inc. NONPR AFFIL member: Texas State Historical Association.

Grants Analysis

Disclosure Period: fiscal year ending August 31, 2003
Total Grants: $486,129,571*
Number of Grants: 1,000 (approx)
Average Grant: $461,129*
Highest Grant: $25,000,000
Lowest Grant: $35,000
Typical Range: $100,000 to $1,000,000
*Note: Average grant figure excludes highest grant. The typical range for the graduate program fellowships is $29,000 to $106,000, and for the institutional grants in the undergraduate program, $500,000 to $2,200,000.

Recent Grants

Note: Grants derived from 2003 Form 990.

General
539,970	University of Rochester SOM, Rochester, NY
539,787	University of Texas, Arlington, TX
539,779	Jackson Laboratory, Bar Harbor, ME
539,671	University of California, San Francisco, CA
539,602	Fred Hutchinson Cancer, Seattle, WA
539,352	Wake Forest University, Winston-Salem, NC
539,111	Penn State University, University Park, PA
538,650	Oklahoma Medical Research Foundation, Oklahoma City, OK
538,574	University of Michigan, Dearborn, MI
538,307	Duke University SOM, Durham, NC

HUGOTON FOUNDATION

Giving Contact

Joan K. Stout, President
900 Park Ave.
New York, NY 10021
Phone: (212)734-5447
Fax: (212)734-5448

Description

Founded: 1981
EIN: 341351062
Organization Type: Family Foundation
Giving Locations: FL: Miami; NY: New York
Grant Types: General Support, Project, Research.
Note: The foundation also reports equipment contributions.

Donor Information

Founder: Established in 1981 by the late Wallace Gilroy.

Financial Summary

Total Giving: $1,686,700 (2002); $1,941,100 (2001)
Assets: $36,558,380 (2002); $41,234,974 (2001)

Typical Recipients

Arts & Humanities: Historic Preservation, History & Archaeology, Libraries, Museums/Galleries, Music, Performing Arts
Civic & Public Affairs: Botanical Gardens/Parks, Clubs, Civic & Public Affairs-General, Public Policy
Education: Business Education, Colleges & Universities, Education-General, Legal Education, Medical Education, Private Education (Precollege), Public Education (Precollege), Religious Education, Science/Mathematics Education, Secondary Education (Private), Student Aid, Vocational & Technical Education
Environment: Resource Conservation
Health: Alzheimer's Disease, Cancer, Children's Health/Hospitals, Clinics/Medical Centers, Emergency/Ambulance Services, Eyes/Blindness, Geriatric Health, Health Funds, Health Organizations, Heart, Hospitals, Hospitals (University Affiliated), Medical Rehabilitation, Medical Research, Mental Health, Nursing Services, Research/Studies Institutes, Respiratory, Single-Disease Health Associations, Speech & Hearing, Transplant Networks/Donor Banks
International: Foreign Educational Institutions, International Organizations
Religion: Churches, Dioceses, Religion-General, Religious Organizations, Religious Welfare
Science: Science Museums
Social Services: Animal Protection, Big Brothers/Big Sisters, Child Welfare, Community Service Organizations, Emergency Relief, Food/Clothing Distribution, Homes, People with Disabilities, Recreation & Athletics, Scouts, Senior Services, Social Services-General, YMCA/YWCA/YMHA/YWHA

Application Procedures

Initial Contact: The foundation requests applications be made in writing.
Application Requirements: Written request must include a description of organization, proof of tax-exempt status, brief statement of need, date request is needed by, and a detailed cost analysis. Requests should not exceed three pages.
Deadlines: None. Requests are received and reviewed throughout the calendar year.

Restrictions

Foundation mainly gives in the New York, NY area and in Miami, FL to improve health care.

Foundation Officials

Frank S. Fejes: director
Jean C. Stout: treasurer, director
Joan K. Stout: president, managing director

Joan M. Stout: secretary, director
John K. Stout: director
Ray E. Stout, III: vice president, director

Grants Analysis

Disclosure Period: calendar year ending 2002
Total Grants: $1,686,700
Number of Grants: 85
Average Grant: $19,844
Highest Grant: $125,000
Lowest Grant: $1,000
Typical Range: $10,000 to $40,000

Recent Grants

Note: Grants derived from 2002 Form 990.
Library-Related
10,000	New York Public Library, New York, NY -- for preservation and restoration

General
125,000	Weill-Cornell Center of New York, New York, NY -- for rhinology research lab
100,000	Society of Gynecologic Oncologists, Chicago, IL -- for endowed lectureship
100,000	South Florida Center for Theological Studies, Miami, FL -- for library expansion
75,000	Lenox Hill Hospital, New York, NY -- for spine fellowship
60,000	Barry University School of Nursing, Miami Shores, FL -- for clinical simulation nursing lab
60,000	St. John Medical Center, Tulsa, OK -- for medical equipment
50,000	Archdiocese of Miami, Miami Shores, FL -- for ecumenical support
50,000	Cathedral of St. Mary, Miami, FL -- for work with poor
50,000	Epiphany Parish, New York, NY -- for church and school
50,000	Lenox Hill Hospital, New York, NY -- for equipment

HUISKING FOUNDATION

Giving Contact

Frank R. Huisking, Treasurer & Director
PO Box 368
Botsford, CT 06404-0353
Phone: (203)426-8618

Description

Founded: 1946
EIN: 136117501
Organization Type: Private Foundation
Giving Locations: nationally.
Grant Types: Operating Expenses, Project, Research.

Donor Information

Founder: members of the Huisking family and family-related corporations

Financial Summary

Gifts Received: In 1991, contributions in the form of stocks were received from Charles A. Huisking.

Typical Recipients

Arts & Humanities: History & Archaeology, Libraries, Museums/Galleries, Music
Civic & Public Affairs: Botanical Gardens/Parks, Municipalities/Towns, Urban & Community Affairs
Education: Arts/Humanities Education, Colleges & Universities, Education Funds, Engineering/Technological Education, Education-General, Legal Education, Private Education (Precollege), Secondary Education (Private), Student Aid
Environment: Resource Conservation
Health: Cancer, Children's Health/Hospitals, Clinics/Medical Centers, Emergency/Ambulance Services,

Hospices, Hospitals, Long-Term Care, Medical Research, Multiple Sclerosis, Nursing Services, Single-Disease Health Associations
International: International Relief Efforts, Missionary/Religious Activities
Religion: Churches, Dioceses, Religion-General, Jewish Causes, Religious Organizations, Religious Welfare, Seminaries, Social/Policy Issues
Social Services: Animal Protection, At-Risk Youth, Community Centers, Community Service Organizations, Day Care, Family Services, Homes, People with Disabilities, Social Services-General, United Funds/United Ways, YMCA/YWCA/YMHA/YWHA, Youth Organizations

Application Procedures
Initial Contact: Send brief letter describing program.
Deadlines: None.

Restrictions
Does not support individuals.

Foundation Officials
Helen Crawford: director
Robert P. Daly: director
John E. Haigney: president, director
Claire F. Hanavan: director
Taylor W. Hanavan: director
Frank R. Huisking: treasurer, director
Richard V. Huisking, Sr.: director
Richard V. Huisking, Jr.: secretary, director
William W. Huisking, Jr.: vice president, director
Jean M. Steinschneider: director

Grants Analysis
Disclosure Period: calendar year ending 2000
Total Grants: $813,000*
Number of Grants: 284
Average Grant: $2,608*
Highest Grant: $75,000
Typical Range: $1,000 to $5,000
***Note:** Giving excludes United Way. Average grant figure excludes highest grant.

Recent Grants
Note: Grants derived from 2001 Form 990.
Library-Related
20,000	Larchmont Public Library, Larchmont, NY -- operating needs

General
60,000	St. Mary's College, Notre Dame, IN -- Tech Center construction
35,000	Sound Shore Medical Center, Larchmont, NY -- operating needs
31,700	University of Notre Dame, Notre Dame, IN -- operating needs
30,000	St. Augustine's Roman Catholic Church, Larchmont, NY -- operating needs
30,000	Spring Hill College, Mobile, AL -- library upgrade
25,000	Ringling Museum Foundation, Venice, FL -- operating needs
25,000	St. Mary's Roman Catholic Church, Manhasset, NY -- operating needs
20,000	Christ the King Monastery -- operating needs
20,000	Florida West Coast Symphony, Sarasota, FL -- operating needs
20,000	Vincent R. Saurino Fellowship -- scholarship

NILA B. HULBERT FOUNDATION

Giving Contact
Henry L. Hulbert, Trustee
6 Ford Avenue
Oneonta, NY 13820
Phone: (607)432-6720

Description
Founded: 1971
EIN: 237039996
Organization Type: Private Foundation
Giving Locations: NY: Oneonta
Grant Types: General Support.

Donor Information
Founder: Nila B. Hulbert

Financial Summary
Total Giving: $269,756 (2002); $257,358 (2001)
Giving Analysis: Giving for 2002 includes: foundation grants to United Way ($1,000); foundation scholarships ($13,000)
Assets: $5,753,699 (2002); $7,149,132 (2001)
Gifts Received: $14,021 (1992)

Typical Recipients
Arts & Humanities: Historic Preservation, History & Archaeology, Libraries, Museums/Galleries, Music
Civic & Public Affairs: Housing, Philanthropic Organizations
Education: Colleges & Universities, Public Education (Precollege)
Health: Children's Health/Hospitals, Health Organizations, Hospices, Hospitals
Religion: Churches, Religious Organizations, Religious Welfare
Social Services: Family Services, Food/Clothing Distribution, Recreation & Athletics, Social Services-General, United Funds/United Ways, YMCA/YWCA/YMHA/YWHA, Youth Organizations

Application Procedures
Initial Contact: Send a brief letter of inquiry with supporting documentation.
Deadlines: September 30.

Foundation Officials
Henry L. Hulbert: trustee
J. Burton Hulbert: trustee
William H. Hulbert: trustee

Grants Analysis
Disclosure Period: calendar year ending 2002
Total Grants: $255,756*
Number of Grants: 20
Average Grant: $8,198*
Highest Grant: $100,000
Lowest Grant: $500
Typical Range: $5,000 to $10,000
***Note:** Giving excludes United Way and scholarships. Average grant figure excludes highest grant.

Recent Grants
Note: Grants derived from 2001 Form 990.
General
100,000	Hartwick College, Oneonta, NY
25,000	A.O. Fox Memorial Hospital Foundation, Oneonta, NY
20,000	Catskill Symphony Orchestra, Oneonta, NY
16,458	Huntington Memorial Library Foundation, Oneonta, NY
10,000	Catskill Area Hospice, Oneonta, NY -- for operations
10,000	First United Presbyterian Society, Oneonta, NY -- annual operation
10,000	St. Lawrence University, Canton, NY -- for operation
10,000	Volunteers in Medicine, Hilton Head, SC -- annual operation
8,000	Morris Central School, Morris, NY -- for scholarships
7,500	Oneonta Family YMCA, Oneonta, NY -- annual operation

MILTON G. HULME CHARITABLE FOUNDATION

Giving Contact
519 Frick Bldg.
Pittsburgh, PA 15219
Phone: (412)281-2007

Description
Founded: 1960
EIN: 256062896
Organization Type: Private Foundation
Giving Locations: PA
Grant Types: General Support.

Donor Information
Founder: Glove, Inc. and MacGregor

Financial Summary
Gifts Received: $417,000 (1999); $285,600 (1998).
Note: In 1999, contributions were received from Jocelyn H. MacConnell ($137,500), Natalie H. Curry ($129,625), and Holiday H. Shoup ($149,875). In 1998, contributions were received from Helen C. Hulme.

Typical Recipients
Arts & Humanities: Arts Associations & Councils, Ballet, Community Arts, Historic Preservation, History & Archaeology, Libraries, Museums/Galleries, Music, Opera, Performing Arts, Public Broadcasting, Theater
Civic & Public Affairs: Business/Free Enterprise, Civic & Public Affairs-General, Urban & Community Affairs
Education: Colleges & Universities, Preschool Education, Private Education (Precollege), Special Education, Student Aid
Environment: Resource Conservation
Health: Children's Health/Hospitals, Emergency/Ambulance Services, Geriatric Health, Hospices, Hospitals, Medical Rehabilitation, Nursing Services, Single-Disease Health Associations
Religion: Churches, Ministries, Religious Organizations, Religious Welfare
Science: Scientific Centers & Institutes
Social Services: Child Welfare, Community Centers, Community Service Organizations, Family Planning, Family Services, Food/Clothing Distribution, Homes, People with Disabilities, Recreation & Athletics, Scouts, Senior Services, Shelters/Homelessness, United Funds/United Ways, Youth Organizations

Application Procedures
Initial Contact: Send a brief letter of inquiry.
Application Requirements: Include a description of organization, purpose of funds sought, and proof of tax-exempt status.
Deadlines: June 30.

Foundation Officials
Natalie H. Curry: trustee
Aura P. Hulme: trustee
Helen C. Hulme: trustee
Jocelyn H. MacConnell: trustee
Helen H. Shoup: trustee

Grants Analysis
Disclosure Period: calendar year ending 2000
Total Grants: $410,000*
Number of Grants: 45
Average Grant: $8,227*
Highest Grant: $48,000
Typical Range: $1,000 to $15,000
***Note:** Giving excludes United Way. Average grant excludes highest grant.

Recent Grants

Note: Grants derived from 2001 Form 990.

Library-Related

12,000	Carnegie Second Century Fund, Pittsburgh, PA
12,000	Lauri Ann West Memorial Library, Pittsburgh, PA
10,000	Carnegie Library for the Blind and Physically Handicapped, Pittsburgh, PA

General

49,000	Shadyside Hospital Foundation, Pittsburgh, PA
34,000	Pittsburgh Cultural Trust, Pittsburgh, PA
25,000	Family Resources, Pittsburgh, PA
23,000	Salvation Army, Pittsburgh, PA
20,000	United Way of Southwestern Pennsylvania, Pittsburgh, PA
20,000	WQED & WQED-FM, Pittsburgh, PA
15,200	Coalition for Christian Outreach, Pittsburgh, PA
15,000	Shadyside Presbyterian Church, Pittsburgh, PA
15,000	Three Rivers Rowing Association, Pittsburgh, PA
13,500	Shadyside Academy, Pittsburgh, PA

HULTQUIST FOUNDATION

Giving Contact

Thomas J. Flowers, President
PO Box 1219
Jamestown, NY 14701
Phone: (716)664-5210

Description

Founded: 1965
EIN: 160907729
Organization Type: Private Foundation
Giving Locations: NY: Chautauqua County
Grant Types: General Support.

Financial Summary

Total Giving: $346,958 (fiscal year ending June 30, 2004); $1,191,339 (fiscal 2002); $640,145 (fiscal 2001). Note: Fiscal 1999 Giving includes.
Giving Analysis: Giving for fiscal 2004 includes: foundation grants to United Way ($25,000); fiscal 2002: foundation grants to United Way ($22,000)
Assets: $14,834,836 (fiscal 2004); $13,783,958 (fiscal 2002); $16,299,991 (fiscal 2001)
Gifts Received: $71,359 (fiscal 1992)

Typical Recipients

Arts & Humanities: Arts Associations & Councils, Arts Funds, Arts & Humanities-General, Historic Preservation, History & Archaeology, Libraries, Music, Performing Arts
Civic & Public Affairs: Civic & Public Affairs-General, Urban & Community Affairs
Education: Arts/Humanities Education, Colleges & Universities, Community & Junior Colleges, Education Funds, Education-General, Literacy, Student Aid
Environment: Environment-General, Wildlife Protection
Health: Cancer, Children's Health/Hospitals, Hospitals
Religion: Religious Welfare
Social Services: Animal Protection, Child Welfare, Community Service Organizations, Emergency Relief, Family Services, Food/Clothing Distribution, Homes, Recreation & Athletics, Scouts, United Funds/United Ways, YMCA/YWCA/YMHA/YWHA, Youth Organizations

Application Procedures

Initial Contact: Send a written description of the capital improvement or replacement project including an estimate of the cost.
Deadlines: approximately June 1 and December 1.

Restrictions

Emphasis is on religious, charitable, and educational organizations in Chautauqua County, NY, which the Hultquist family supported during their lifetimes.

Foundation Officials

Thomas J. Flowers: president
Charles H. Price: vice president
Robert F. Rohm, Jr.: secretary, treasurer
William L. Wright: vice president

Grants Analysis

Disclosure Period: fiscal year ending June 30, 2004
Total Grants: $321,958*
Number of Grants: 13
Average Grant: $16,308*
Highest Grant: $126,259
Lowest Grant: $3,500
Typical Range: $5,000 to $30,000
*Note: Giving excludes United Way. Average grant figure excludes three highest grants ($700,000).

Recent Grants

Note: Grants derived from fiscal 2004 Form 990.

Library-Related

41,987	James Prendergast Library, Jamestown, NY -- for literary program/building
17,935	Chautauqua Cattaraugus Library System, Jamestown, NY

General

126,259	Woman's Christian Association Hospital, Jamestown, NY -- towards building fund
28,000	Chautauqua Striders Inc., Jamestown, NY -- for educational purposes
25,000	Chautauqua Institution, Chautauqua, NY
25,000	United Way of Southern Chautauqua County, Jamestown, NY
15,000	American Red Cross
15,000	Robert H. Jackson Center, Jamestown, NY -- towards building fund
12,000	YMCA, Jamestown, NY -- for building
9,803	Family Service of Jamestown, Jamestown, NY

HUMANA INC.

Company Headquarters

Louisville, KY
Web: http://www.humana.com

Company Description

Founded: 1961
Ticker: HUM
Exchange: NYSE
Revenue: US$13.104 billion (2004)
Profit: US$280 million (2004)
Employees: 13700 (2003)
Fortune Rank: 162, per FORTUNE Magazine's list of 500 Largest U.S. Corporations (2004).
SIC(s): 6321 Accident & Health Insurance, 6324 Hospital & Medical Service Plans, 6411 Insurance Agents, Brokers & Service, 8062 General Medical & Surgical Hospitals.

Operating Locations

Humana, Inc. (AL; AZ; DC; FL--Jacksonville; KS; KY--Lexington, Louisville; MO; OH; TX--San Antonio)

Humana Foundation

Giving Contact

Virginia Kelly-Judd, Executive Director
500 West Main Street
Louisville, KY 40202

Phone: (502)580-3613
Fax: (502)580-1256
E-mail: BWright@Humana.com
Web: http://www.humanafoundation.org

Alternate Contact

PO Box 740026
Louisville, KY 40201-7426

Description

EIN: 611004763
Organization Type: Corporate Foundation
Giving Locations: AL: Birmingham; CA: Claremont; CO: Pine; CT: New Haven; DC: Washington; KY: Lexington, Louisville, Murray; MN: St. Peter; NJ: Princeton; NY: New York; NC: Chapel Hill; SC: Columbia; TN: Memphis; VT: Middlebury; WI: Green Bay principally near operating locations and to national organizations.
Grant Types: Capital, Conference/Seminar, Department, Employee Matching Gifts, Endowment, General Support, Project, Research, Scholarship.
Note: Employee matching gift ratio: 1 to 1 for contributions made by officers and board of directors members only.

Financial Summary

Total Giving: $5,500,000 (2004 approx); $4,110,888 (2003); $4,522,904 (2002). Note: Contributes through corporate direct giving program and foundation.
Giving Analysis: Giving for 2002 includes: foundation grants to United Way ($218,000); foundation scholarships ($600,960).
Assets: $51,868,713 (2003); $37,423,051 (2002); $47,434,063 (2001)
Gifts Received: $3,600,000 (2003); $2,400,000 (2002); $4,500,000 (2000). Note: Contributions were received from Humana Inc.

Typical Recipients

Arts & Humanities: Arts Associations & Councils, Arts Centers, Arts Festivals, Arts Funds, Ballet, Community Arts, Dance, Historic Preservation, History & Archaeology, Libraries, Literary Arts, Museums/Galleries, Music, Opera, Performing Arts, Public Broadcasting, Theater, Visual Arts
Civic & Public Affairs: African American Affairs, Asian American Affairs, Botanical Gardens/Parks, Business/Free Enterprise, Civil Rights, Clubs, Community Foundations, Economic Development, Ethnic Organizations, Civic & Public Affairs-General, Hispanic Affairs, Housing, Legal Aid, Municipalities/Towns, Nonprofit Management, Philanthropic Organizations, Professional & Trade Associations, Public Policy, Rural Affairs, Urban & Community Affairs, Women's Affairs, Zoos/Aquariums
Education: Business Education, Colleges & Universities, Community & Junior Colleges, Continuing Education, Education Associations, Education Funds, Education Reform, Elementary Education (Private), Education-General, Health & Physical Education, Leadership Training, Legal Education, Literacy, Medical Education, Minority Education, Preschool Education, Private Education (Precollege), Public Education (Precollege), Science/Mathematics Education, Secondary Education (Private), Special Education, Student Aid
Environment: Environment-General, Resource Conservation
Health: AIDS/HIV, Cancer, Children's Health/Hospitals, Clinics/Medical Centers, Diabetes, Emergency/Ambulance Services, Eyes/Blindness, Health-General, Health Funds, Health Organizations, Heart, Hospitals, Medical Research, Mental Health, Nursing Services, Prenatal Health Issues, Preventive Medicine/Wellness Organizations, Public Health, Respiratory, Single-Disease Health Associations
International: Foreign Educational Institutions, Human Rights, International Relations, International Relief Efforts
Religion: Churches, Dioceses, Religious Organizations, Religious Welfare

Science: Science Exhibits & Fairs, Science Museums, Scientific Centers & Institutes, Scientific Organizations

Social Services: Animal Protection, Child Welfare, Community Centers, Community Service Organizations, Emergency Relief, Family Planning, Family Services, Food/Clothing Distribution, Homes, People with Disabilities, Recreation & Athletics, Scouts, Senior Services, United Funds/United Ways, YMCA/YWCA/YMHA/YWHA, Youth Organizations

Application Procedures

Initial Contact: Request an application from the foundation or obtain one from the foundation's web site.

Application Requirements: Include a description of organization amount requested, purpose of funds sought, other funding commitments to date, and copy of IRS tax-exemption letter. Scholarship applications should be submitted directly to Citizens Scholarship Foundation of America Inc. and are available from the foundation.

Deadlines: Applications accepted January 1 to November 15, except for February 1 application deadline for Humana Foundation Scholarship Program.

Evaluative Criteria: The foundation evaluates applicants on their ability to improve the quality of life in communities where Humana has a business presence and the organization's level of community support.

Decision Notification: The foundation responds promptly to applications, either rejecting them or requesting full proposals; final decisions are made by the contributions committee within about three months.

Notes: Applications from organizations in the Louisville, KY area should be directed to the foundation's corporate office in Louisville. Applications from organizations outside of the Louisville area should be submitted to a local Humana market office; a list of market office mailing addresses is available on the foundation's web site (www.humana.com/agent/localsales.asp).

Restrictions

Does not support requests for seed money; social, labor, political, veterans, or fraternal organizations; religious organizations, except for fully accredited public or private religious educational institutions that possess 501(c)(3) status; requests to be used solely for an organization's salary or other administrative costs; or lobbying efforts or political action committees.

Recipient organizations must be 501(c)3 according to IRS regulations.

Additional Information

Scholarships are awarded to children of full-time Humana employees.

Publications: Application Form

Corporate Officials

David Allen Jones: co-founder, chairman, director B Louisville, KY 1931. ED University of Louisville BS (1954); Yale University JD (1960). PRIM CORP EMPL co-founder, chairman, director: Humana, Inc. CORP AFFIL director: Abbott Laboratories. NONPR AFFIL member: Louisville Chamber of Commerce.

Foundation Officials

George G. Bauernfeind: vice president ADD CORP EMPL vice president: Humana Health Insurance Co. of Florida.

James H. Bloem: senior vice president

Michael E. Gellert: director

Arthur J. Hipwell: senior vice president

David A. Jones, Jr.: director

David Allen Jones: president, director (see above)

Virginia Kelly-Judd: executive director

Joan O. Lenahan: secretary

Grants Analysis

Disclosure Period: calendar year ending 2003
Total Grants: $3,264,938*
Number of Grants: 81
Average Grant: $28,769*
Highest Grant: $653,000
Lowest Grant: $2,500
Typical Range: $10,000 to $50,000
***Note:** Giving excludes scholarship and United Way. Average grant figure excludes two highest grants ($992,200).

Recent Grants

Note: Grants derived from 2003 Form 990.
General

653,000	Actors Theatre of Louisville, Louisville, KY -- towards human festival
561,410	Scholarship America, St. Peter, MN -- for the scholarship for children of Humana Inc. employees
339,200	Greater Louisville Fund for the Arts, Louisville, KY
224,540	Metro United Way, Louisville, KY
200,000	University of Kentucky, Lexington, KY -- towards W T Young Library
166,200	University Pediatrics Foundation, Louisville, KY -- towards pediatric program
112,000	University of Louisville Foundation, Louisville, KY -- towards salary support for international projects
100,000	Bellarmine University, Louisville, KY -- for the science center
100,000	Community Foundation of Louisville, Louisville, KY -- towards bicentennial celebrations
100,000	Georgetown College, Georgetown, KY -- towards professorship

GEORGE M. AND PAMELA S. HUMPHREY FUND

Giving Contact

Jackie A. Horning, Secretary & Treasurer
c/o Advisory Services, Inc.
1422 Euclid Ave., Suite 1010
Cleveland, OH 44115-2078
Phone: (216)363-6483

Description

Founded: 1951
EIN: 346513798
Organization Type: Private Foundation
Giving Locations: FL; GA; MA; OH
Grant Types: Capital, Emergency, Endowment, General Support, Multiyear/Continuing Support, Operating Expenses, Professorship, Research.

Donor Information

Founder: George M. Humphrey, the late Pamela S. Humphrey

Financial Summary

Total Giving: $612,370 (2001)
Giving Analysis: Giving for 2001 includes: foundation grants to United Way ($36,000)
Assets: $13,433,192 (2001)

Typical Recipients

Arts & Humanities: Arts Associations & Councils, Historic Preservation, History & Archaeology, Libraries, Museums/Galleries, Music, Opera, Public Broadcasting, Theater

Civic & Public Affairs: Botanical Gardens/Parks, Economic Development, Employment/Job Training, Civic & Public Affairs-General, Housing, Municipalities/Towns, Parades/Festivals, Philanthropic Organizations, Urban & Community Affairs, Women's Affairs

Education: Arts/Humanities Education, Colleges & Universities, Education-General, Medical Education, Private Education (Precollege), Special Education, Student Aid

Environment: Forestry, Environment-General, Research, Resource Conservation, Wildlife Protection

Health: AIDS/HIV, Cancer, Children's Health/Hospitals, Emergency/Ambulance Services, Eyes/Blindness, Hospitals, Hospitals (University Affiliated), Long-Term Care, Medical Rehabilitation, Medical Research, Multiple Sclerosis, Nursing Services, Single-Disease Health Associations, Speech & Hearing

Religion: Churches, Jewish Causes, Religious Welfare

Science: Science Museums, Scientific Centers & Institutes, Scientific Research

Social Services: Camps, Child Welfare, Community Centers, Community Service Organizations, Family Planning, Family Services, Food/Clothing Distribution, People with Disabilities, Recreation & Athletics, Senior Services, Substance Abuse, United Funds/United Ways, Volunteer Services

Application Procedures

Initial Contact: Send a brief letter of inquiry.
Application Requirements: Include amount requested and purpose of funds sought.
Deadlines: Prior to meetings held in September each year.

Restrictions

Does not support individuals or provide loans.

Additional Information

Publications: Annual Report

Foundation Officials

Peter Webster Adams: trustee B Cleveland, OH 1939. ED Yale University (1961). PRIM CORP EMPL senior vice president: Alliance Capital Management Corp.

Alice B. Burnham: trustee

Carol H. Butler: president, trustee

Jackie A. Horning: secretary, treasurer

Pamela B. Keefe: trustee

Grants Analysis

Disclosure Period: calendar year ending 2001
Total Grants: $576,370*
Number of Grants: 28
Average Grant: $7,549*
Typical Range: $1,000 to $30,000
***Note:** Giving excludes United Way. Average grant excludes two highest grants ($365,000).

Recent Grants

Note: Grants derived from 2001 Form 990.
General

275,000	Hathaway Brown School, Shaker Heights, OH -- capital campaign
90,000	Benjamin Rose Institute, Cleveland, OH -- capital campaign
50,000	Rainbow Babies and Children's Hospital, Cleveland, OH -- pediatric surgical facilities
35,000	Cleveland Botanical Garden, Cleveland, OH -- operating support
31,000	United Way Services, Cleveland, OH -- operating support
25,000	University Hospitals of Cleveland, Cleveland, OH -- Department of Ophthalmology
20,000	Cleveland Museum of Natural History, Cleveland, OH -- planetarium facility
10,000	Foundation Center, Cleveland, OH -- endowment fund
10,000	Miss Hall's School, Pittsfield, MA -- capital campaign
10,000	Tall Timbers Research, Tallahassee, FL -- quail research initiative

H. P. AND ANNE S. HUNNICUTT FOUNDATION

Giving Contact
William Stafford, Jr.
c/o First Community Bank
PO Box 309
Princeton, WV 24740
Phone: (304)425-9259

Description
Founded: 1987
EIN: 550670462
Organization Type: Private Foundation
Giving Locations: WV: Southern West Virginia
Grant Types: General Support.

Donor Information
Founder: the late H. P. Hunnicutt, the late Anne S. Hunnicutt

Financial Summary
Total Giving: $1,754,700 (fiscal year ending June 30, 2004); $1,046,857 (fiscal 2001)
Assets: $44,818,258 (fiscal 2004); $37,067,432 (fiscal 2001)
Gifts Received: $7,115,860 (fiscal 1995)

Typical Recipients
Arts & Humanities: Libraries, Performing Arts
Civic & Public Affairs: Business/Free Enterprise, Community Foundations, Employment/Job Training, Civic & Public Affairs-General, Municipalities/Towns, Safety, Urban & Community Affairs
Education: Education Funds, Private Education (Precollege), Public Education (Precollege), Science/Mathematics Education, Secondary Education (Private), Secondary Education (Public)
Health: Emergency/Ambulance Services, Medical Research, Public Health
Religion: Churches, Ministries, Religious Welfare
Social Services: Child Welfare, Community Service Organizations, Recreation & Athletics, Substance Abuse, Youth Organizations

Application Procedures
Initial Contact: Send a brief letter of inquiry describing program or project.
Deadlines: None.

Additional Information
Trust(s): First Community Bank

Foundation Officials
James H. Sarver, II: treasurer
James H. Sarver: vice president
William Stafford, II: secretary
William P. Stafford: president

Grants Analysis
Disclosure Period: fiscal year ending June 30, 2004
Total Grants: $1,754,700
Number of Grants: 15
Average Grant: $17,823*
Highest Grant: $1,275,000
Lowest Grant: $227
Typical Range: $10,000 to $40,000
***Note:** Average grant figure excludes two highest grants ($1,523,000).

Recent Grants
Note: Grants derived from fiscal 2003 Form 990.
General

500,000	Charles T. Mathena II Foundation, Princeton, WV
460,000	First United Methodist Church, Princeton, WV
385,000	City of Princeton, Princeton, WV
150,000	Community Foundation of the Virginias Inc., Bluefield, WV
100,000	Greater Princeton Little League, Princeton, WV
60,000	Mercer Christian Academy Foundation Inc., Princeton, WV
55,000	Child Protect of Mercer County Inc., Princeton, WV
50,000	Princeton Area Business Development Corporation, Princeton, WV
35,000	Heaven Sent Ministries Inc., Princeton, WV
35,000	Peterstown Middle School, Peterstown, WV

C. GILES HUNT CHARITABLE TRUST

Giving Contact
c/o Wells Fargo Bank of Oregon NA
PO Box 53456
Eugene, OR 97401
Phone: (541)465-5952

Description
Founded: 1974
EIN: 237428278
Organization Type: Private Foundation
Giving Locations: OR: Douglas County
Grant Types: Capital, Endowment, General Support.

Donor Information
Founder: the late C. Giles Hunt

Financial Summary
Total Giving: $308,166 (2002); $305,934 (2001)
Assets: $5,434,618 (2002); $6,375,935 (2001)

Typical Recipients
Arts & Humanities: Arts Associations & Councils, Community Arts, Arts & Humanities-General, Historic Preservation, History & Archaeology, Libraries, Music, Theater
Civic & Public Affairs: Botanical Gardens/Parks, Clubs, Community Foundations, Economic Development, Civic & Public Affairs-General, Municipalities/Towns, Parades/Festivals, Safety, Urban & Community Affairs
Education: Afterschool/Enrichment Programs, Agricultural Education, Community & Junior Colleges, Elementary Education (Public), Education-General, Literacy, Private Education (Precollege), Public Education (Precollege), Science/Mathematics Education, Secondary Education (Private), Secondary Education (Public)
Environment: Forestry, Environment-General, Wildlife Protection
Health: AIDS/HIV, Clinics/Medical Centers, Emergency/Ambulance Services, Health Organizations, Hospitals, Mental Health, Prenatal Health Issues
International: International Environmental Issues
Religion: Churches, Missionary Activities (Domestic), Religious Welfare
Science: Science Museums
Social Services: Camps, Child Welfare, Community Centers, Community Service Organizations, Counseling, Crime Prevention, Day Care, Domestic Violence, Family Planning, Family Services, Food/Clothing Distribution, People with Disabilities, Recreation & Athletics, Scouts, Senior Services, Shelters/Homelessness, Substance Abuse, Volunteer Services, YMCA/YWCA/YMHA/YWHA, Youth Organizations

Application Procedures
Initial Contact: Send letter requesting application form.
Deadlines: February 28.

Additional Information
Publications: Application Guidelines
Trust(s): Wells Fargo OR NA

Grants Analysis
Disclosure Period: calendar year ending 2001
Total Grants: $305,934
Number of Grants: 60
Average Grant: $5,099
Highest Grant: $15,000
Typical Range: $2,000 to $15,000

Recent Grants
Note: Grants derived from 2001 Form 990.
Library-Related

6,800	Winston Branch Library, Winston, OR
6,425	Glendale Library Branch of the Douglas County, Glendale, OR
6,000	Reedsport Branch Library, Reedsport, OR

General

15,000	Cobb Street Children's Learning Center, Roseburg, OR
15,000	Sutherlin Lions Club, Sutherlin, OR
11,232	Umpqua Community College, Roseburg, OR
10,750	Safarj Game Search Foundation, Winston, OR
10,000	South Umpqua School District 19, Roseburg, OR
10,000	Friendly Kitchen, Roseburg, OR
10,000	Myrtle Creek Volunteer Fire Department, Myrtle Creek, OR
8,000	Umpqua Valley Endowment Foundation, Winchester, OR
8,000	Wilani Council Camp Fire Boys and Girls, Roseburg, OR
7,500	Umpqua Discovery Center, Reedsport, OR

HUNT CORP.

Company Headquarters
1 Commerce Sq.
2005 Market St.
Philadelphia, PA 19103-7085
Web: http://www.hunt-corp.com

Company Description
Ticker: HUN
Exchange: OTC
Former Name: Hunt Manufacturing Co..
Revenue: US$160.9 million (2001)
Employees: 900 (2001)
SIC(s): 2522 Office Furniture Except Wood, 2679 Converted Paper Products Nec, 2893 Printing Ink, 3579 Office Machines Nec.

Operating Locations
Hunt Manufacturing Co. (AL--Florence; CA--Fresno; CT--Naugatuck; KY--Florence; PA--Philadelphia; TX--Laredo; WI--Cottage Grove)

Nonmonetary Support
Value: $5,000 (1998)
Type: Donated Products

Giving Contact
Cheryl M. Walmsley, Grant Administrator
1 Commerce Sq.
2005 Market St.
Philadelphia, PA 19103-7085
Phone: (215)841-2398
Fax: (215)656-3714
E-mail: cheryl_walmsley@Hunt-Corp.com

Description

Organization Type: Corporate Giving Program
Giving Locations: headquarters.
Grant Types: Capital, Employee Matching Gifts, General Support, Project, Seed Money.

Financial Summary

Total Giving: Contributes through corporate direct giving program only. Foundation became defunct as of 1997. 1995 Giving includes foundation($302,525); matching gifts ($70,660).

Typical Recipients

Arts & Humanities: Arts Appreciation, Arts Associations & Councils, Arts Centers, Ballet, Community Arts, Dance, Arts & Humanities-General, Libraries, Museums/Galleries, Music, Opera, Performing Arts, Public Broadcasting, Theater, Visual Arts
Civic & Public Affairs: Clubs, Economic Development, Economic Policy, Employment/Job Training, Legal Aid, Safety, Urban & Community Affairs
Education: Afterschool/Enrichment Programs, Arts/Humanities Education, Business-School Partnerships, Colleges & Universities, Community & Junior Colleges, Elementary Education (Private), Literacy, Public Education (Precollege), Secondary Education (Public), Student Aid, Vocational & Technical Education
Health: AIDS/HIV, Children's Health/Hospitals
International: International Affairs
Religion: Ministries
Science: Scientific Centers & Institutes
Social Services: Big Brothers/Big Sisters, Child Abuse, Child Welfare, Counseling, Domestic Violence, Family Services, Food/Clothing Distribution, Senior Services, United Funds/United Ways, YMCA/YWCA/YMHA/YWHA, Youth Organizations

Application Procedures

Initial Contact: brief letter or proposal
Application Requirements: name of organization and contact person; a description of organization and its programs; copy of current year budget and most recently audited financial statements; copy of IRS determination letter; NAA number, if organization has received designation as a Neighborhood Assistance Act organization; and if requesting project support, include description of project including objectives, methodology, budget, key staff, sources of funding, and expected results
Deadlines: March 15 and September 15
Decision Notification: at Contributions Committee meetings held twice a year, usually during April and October
Notes: Does not make contributions in response to telephone solicitations. Grantees are required to submit applications on an annual basis.

Restrictions

Company generally does not provide general support, endowment funds or building funds to schools, colleges or universities. However, grants may be made to both educational institutions and non-profit educational organizations for specific educational programs.
Support for national appeals is minimal. Contributions to fund-raising dinners, testimonials, and courtesy advertising strictly limited. Grants are not made to individuals or for religious, social, or political purposes. Grants for building and capital campaigns, general support for education and health care institutions, and endowments are made only in exceptional cases.
No telephone or fax solicitations.

Additional Information

Company's goal is to donate 3% of pretax profits to charitable organizations.
Favors applications that leverage company funds with monies from other sources. Encourages propos-

als for specific projects instead of general operating support.
In 1998, the company reported that the foundation is inactive.
The company only funds a project for three consecutive years. Organization must wait one year before reapplying for grants.

Corporate Officials

William Everett Chandler: senior vice president finance, secretary, chief financial officer B Chattanooga, TN 1943. ED University of Florida BSBA (1965); University of Florida (1966). PRIM CORP EMPL senior vice president finance, secretary, chief financial officer: Hunt Co. CORP AFFIL treasurer: Hunt Holdings Inc.; secretary: Hunt Graphics America Corp. NONPR AFFIL member: Financial Executives Institute.
Kathleen Essex: vice president human resources PRIM CORP EMPL vice president human resources: Hunt Manufacturing Co.
Donald L. Thompson: chairman, chief executive officer B 1941. ED University of Vermont (1962); State University of New Jersey (1971). PRIM CORP EMPL chairman, chief executive officer, president: Hunt Corp.

Giving Program Officials

William Everett Chandler: secretary (see above)
Kathleen Essex: member (see above)
Donald L. Thompson: (see above)
Cheryl M. Walmsley: grant administrator

Grants Analysis

Disclosure Period: fiscal year ending November 30, 1999
Total Grants: $300,000*
Number of Grants: 30
Average Grant: $2,000
Highest Grant: $20,000
Typical Range: $1,000 to $5,000
*Note: Grants analysis provided by the co. A more recent grants list was unavailable.

Recent Grants

Note: Grants derived from fiscal 1996 Form 990.
General

9,000	United Way Southeastern Pennsylvania, Philadelphia, PA
4,000	Family Services, Philadelphia, PA
4,000	Village of Arts and Humanities, Philadelphia, PA
3,000	Philadelphia Futures, Philadelphia, PA
2,000	AIDS Law Project, Philadelphia, PA
2,000	Brandywine Workshop, Philadelphia, PA
2,000	Print Club, Philadelphia, PA
2,000	Settlement Music School, Philadelphia, PA

ROY A. HUNT FOUNDATION

Giving Contact

Torrence M. Hunt, Jr., President & Trustee
One Bigelow Square, Suite 630
Pittsburgh, PA 15219-3030
Phone: (412)281-8734
Fax: (412)255-0522
E-mail: info@rahuntfdn.org
Web: http://www.rahuntfdn.org

Description

Founded: 1966
EIN: 256105162
Organization Type: Family Foundation
Giving Locations: MA: Boston; PA: Pittsburgh limited national giving.

Grant Types: Capital, General Support, Operating Expenses.

Donor Information

Founder: The Roy A. Hunt Foundation was established in 1966, with funds bequeathed by Roy A. Hunt, former president and chairman of the executive committee of Alcoa. Mr. Hunt was an alumnus of Shady Side Academy and Yale University, and a trustee of the Carnegie Institute of Technology (now Carnegie-Mellon University). Each of these institutions traditionally receives support from the foundation.
Mr. Hunt and his wife founded the Hunt Institute for Botanical Documentation at Carnegie-Mellon in 1961. This institute was formed to receive and supervise Mrs. Hunt's large botanical collections, and remains a substantial recipient of the foundation's annual grants. The late Mr. Hunt and members of his family also set up the Hunt Foundation in 1951.

Financial Summary

Total Giving: $3,123,523 (fiscal year ending May 31, 2004); $3,018,447 (fiscal 2003); $3,790,039 (fiscal 2002)
Giving Analysis: Giving for fiscal 2004 includes: foundation scholarships ($7,000); foundation grants to United Way ($25,000); fiscal 2002: foundation scholarships ($5,000); foundation grants to United Way ($35,500)
Assets: $76,133,748 (fiscal 2004); $81,535,907 (fiscal 2002); $94,754,273 (fiscal 2001)

Typical Recipients

Arts & Humanities: Arts Associations & Councils, Arts Centers, Arts Festivals, Arts Institutes, Dance, Film & Video, Arts & Humanities-General, Historic Preservation, History & Archaeology, Libraries, Museums/Galleries, Music, Opera, Performing Arts, Public Broadcasting, Theater
Civic & Public Affairs: Botanical Gardens/Parks, Business/Free Enterprise, Civil Rights, Clubs, Civic & Public Affairs-General, Housing, Inner-City Development, Municipalities/Towns, Native American Affairs, Philanthropic Organizations, Professional & Trade Associations, Public Policy, Rural Affairs, Urban & Community Affairs, Zoos/Aquariums
Education: Afterschool/Enrichment Programs, Agricultural Education, Arts/Humanities Education, Business Education, Colleges & Universities, Education Funds, Elementary Education (Private), Environmental Education, Education-General, International Exchange, International Studies, Private Education (Precollege), Public Education (Precollege), School Volunteerism, Science/Mathematics Education, Secondary Education (Private), Social Sciences Education, Special Education
Environment: Air/Water Quality, Environment-General, Protection, Resource Conservation, Watershed, Wildlife Protection
Health: AIDS/HIV, Alzheimer's Disease, Cancer, Children's Health/Hospitals, Clinics/Medical Centers, Health-General, Health Organizations, Hospitals, Medical Rehabilitation, Mental Health, Single-Disease Health Associations
International: Foreign Arts Organizations, Foreign Educational Institutions, International Environmental Issues, International Relations
Religion: Churches, Dioceses, Ministries, Religious Welfare
Science: Science Museums, Scientific Centers & Institutes, Scientific Research
Social Services: Animal Protection, At-Risk Youth, Big Brothers/Big Sisters, Camps, Child Welfare, Community Centers, Community Service Organizations, Domestic Violence, Emergency Relief, Family Planning, Family Services, Recreation & Athletics, Shelters/Homelessness, Social Services-General, Substance Abuse, United Funds/United Ways, YMCA/YWCA/YMHA/YWHA, Youth Organizations

Application Procedures

Initial Contact: Contact foundation for application guidelines and deadlines.

Restrictions

The foundation does not support gifts to individuals.

Foundation Officials

Dr. Helen Hunt Bouscaren: trustee
Susan Hunt Hollingsworth: trustee
Andrew McQ. Hunt: trustee PRIM CORP EMPL president: Fitness & Exercise Supply Co.
Christopher M. Hunt, MD: trustee
Daniel K. Hunt: trustee
John Bankson Hunt: trustee B Pittsburgh, PA 1956. ED Boston University BS (1979). CORP AFFIL treasurer: Micro Serve New England. NONPR AFFIL treasurer, director: Rindge Historical Society; chairman: Rindge Rep Town Budget Committee; member: New Hampshire State House Representatives.
Dr. Richard M. Hunt: trustee, donor son
Dr. Roy A. Hunt, III: trustee
Torrence M. Hunt, Jr.: president, trustee B 1948. ED University of North Carolina (1970). PRIM CORP EMPL vice president, director: Elmhurst Corp. CORP AFFIL treasurer: Dahlia Development Corp. CLUB AFFIL Rolling Rock Club; Fox Chapel Golf Club; Pittsburgh Club.
William Edwards Hunt: trustee B Columbus, OH 1921. ED Ohio State University BA (1943); Ohio State University MD (1945). PRIM NONPR EMPL mem attending staff: Ohio State University Hospitals. CORP AFFIL president: Elmhurst Corp. NONPR AFFIL member: Society International Chirurgie; member: Society Neuroscience; member: Royal Society Medicine; member: Sigma Xi; member: Ohio State Medicine Association; member: Phi Beta Kappa; member: Neurosurgical Society America; member: Ohio Saint Neurosurgical Society; member: American Surgical Association; member: Congress Neurological Surgeons; member: American College Surgeons; member: American Medical Association; member: Academy Medicine Columbus & Franklin County; member: Alpha Omega Alpha.
Marion Hunt Badiner: trustee
Rachel Hunt Knowles: trustee

Grants Analysis

Disclosure Period: fiscal year ending May 31, 2004
Total Grants: $3,091,523*
Number of Grants: 488
Average Grant: $6,335
Highest Grant: $72,152
Lowest Grant: $500
Typical Range: $1,000 to $10,000
***Note:** Giving excludes scholarships and United Way.

Recent Grants

Note: Grants derived from 2004 Form 990.
General

72,152	One Hundred Seventh Field Artillery Battalion, Pittsburgh, PA -- grant for Drill Hall refurbishment
50,000	Carnegie Institute, Pittsburgh, PA
50,000	Carnegie Mellon University, Pittsburgh, PA -- to assist security technology education, for library resources in security technology
50,000	Trust for Public Land, Boston, MA -- fund for Neighborhood Backyard Project
40,000	Allegheny Cemetery Historical Association, Pittsburgh, PA
40,000	Dorchester Bay Economic Development Corporation, Dorchester, MA -- for affordable homeownership program
27,000	Tellus Institute, Boston, MA -- for development of educational material on climate change vulnerability
25,000	Animal Rescue League of Western Pennsylvania, Pittsburgh, PA -- to support No Kill Initiative final implementation and general operating support
25,000	Carnegie Institute, Pittsburgh, PA -- for 'Playing with Nature: Flowers Observed, Flowers Transformed' exhibit at the Warhol
25,000	Clean Air-Cool Planet, New Canaan, NJ

SAMUEL P. HUNT FOUNDATION

Giving Contact

Janet P. Magee
Wall Street Tower, Suite 710
555 Canal Street
Manchester, NH 03101
Phone: (603)627-1121

Description

Founded: 1951
EIN: 026004471
Organization Type: Private Foundation
Giving Locations: NH: Manchester
Grant Types: Capital, Conference/Seminar, Emergency, General Support, Multiyear/Continuing Support, Project, Research, Seed Money.

Donor Information

Founder: the late Samuel P. Hunt

Financial Summary

Total Giving: $628,178 (fiscal year ending September 30, 2004); $725,980 (fiscal 2001)
Assets: $12,148,416 (fiscal 2004); $14,067,287 (fiscal 2001)

Typical Recipients

Arts & Humanities: Arts Associations & Councils, Arts Centers, Arts Funds, Arts Institutes, Community Arts, Historic Preservation, History & Archaeology, Libraries, Museums/Galleries, Music, Opera, Performing Arts, Public Broadcasting, Theater, Visual Arts
Civic & Public Affairs: Community Foundations, Ethnic Organizations, Hispanic Affairs, Housing, Law & Justice, Municipalities/Towns, Parades/Festivals, Urban & Community Affairs, Women's Affairs
Education: Afterschool/Enrichment Programs, Agricultural Education, Arts/Humanities Education, Business Education, Colleges & Universities, Environmental Education, Education-General, International Studies, Leadership Training, Private Education (Precollege), Public Education (Precollege), Science/Mathematics Education, Secondary Education (Public)
Environment: Forestry, Environment-General, Resource Conservation, Watershed, Wildlife Protection
Health: AIDS/HIV, Alzheimer's Disease, Cancer, Children's Health/Hospitals, Clinics/Medical Centers, Emergency/Ambulance Services, Health Organizations, Hospices, Hospitals, Hospitals (University Affiliated), Medical Rehabilitation, Medical Research, Mental Health, Nursing Services, Public Health, Respiratory, Single-Disease Health Associations
Religion: Churches, Religious Welfare
Science: Observatories & Planetariums, Science Museums, Scientific Centers & Institutes
Social Services: Animal Protection, At-Risk Youth, Child Welfare, Community Centers, Community Service Organizations, Domestic Violence, Family Services, Food/Clothing Distribution, Homes, People with Disabilities, Recreation & Athletics, Scouts, Senior Services, Shelters/Homelessness, Social Services-General, Substance Abuse, United Funds/United Ways, YMCA/YWCA/YMHA/YWHA, Youth Organizations

Application Procedures

Initial Contact: Send a brief letter requesting guidelines and grant application.
Deadlines: February 15 and August 15.

Restrictions

Does not support individuals or provide funds for scholarships or fellowships.

Additional Information

Publications: Program Policy Statement; Application Guidelines; Application Form
Trust(s): Citizens Bank NH

Foundation Officials

Douglas A. McIninch: co-trustee
James C. Tyrie: co-trustee

Grants Analysis

Disclosure Period: fiscal year ending September 30, 2004
Total Grants: $628,178
Number of Grants: 49
Average Grant: $12,820
Highest Grant: $30,000
Lowest Grant: $500
Typical Range: $5,000 to $20,000

Recent Grants

Note: Grants derived from fiscal 2004 Form 990.
General

30,000	Manchester Police Athletic League, Manchester, NH -- towards rehabilitation of St. Cecilia's hall
26,000	Unitarian Universalist Church of Manchester, Manchester, NH -- for repairs and renovations
25,000	Avis Goodwin Health Center, Dover, NH -- for equipment
25,000	Families in Transition, Manchester, NH -- for building development
25,000	Girls Incorporated of New Hampshire, Manchester, NH -- for firebox
25,000	Manchester Community Health Center and Child Health Services, Manchester, NH -- towards healthy kids program
25,000	New Hampshire Public Television, Durham, NH -- for transition to digital technology
21,000	New Hampshire Humanities Council, Concord, NH -- for Blackbaud Raiser's Edge software
20,000	Society for the Protection of New Hampshire Forests, Concord, NH -- contribution for land conservation
20,000	Trust for Public Land, Concord, NH -- for Merrimack river conservation

HUNTINGTON BANCSHARES INC.

Company Headquarters

Huntington Center
41 South High Street, 34th Floor
Columbus, OH 43287
Web: http://www.huntington.com

Company Description

Founded: 1866
Ticker: HBAN
Exchange: NASDAQ
Assets: US$27.578 billion (2002)
Employees: 7983 (2003)
SIC(s): 6021 National Commercial Banks, 6022 State Commercial Banks, 6035 Federal Savings Institutions, 6712 Bank Holding Companies.

Operating Locations

Huntington Bancshares Inc. (FL--Orlando; IN--Indianapolis; KY--Covington; MI--Grand Rapids)

Nonmonetary Support

Type: Cause-related Marketing & Promotion; Donated Equipment; In-kind Services; Loaned Employees; Loaned Executives

Giving Contact

Ms. Elfi DiBella, Executive Vice President, Director of Community Affairs
41 S. High St.
Columbus, OH 43215
Phone: (614)480-8300
Fax: (614)480-4973
E-mail: elfi.dibella@huntington.com

Alternate Contact

Sandy Romano, Executive Assistant

Description

Organization Type: Corporate Giving Program
Giving Locations: headquarters area only; States where company has business locations.
Grant Types: Award, Capital, Challenge, Emergency, Endowment, Employment/Job Training, Operating Expenses, Professorship, Project, Research, Scholarship, Seed Money.

Financial Summary

Total Giving: $4,000,000 (2001). Note: Contributes through corporate direct giving program only. Total giving is approximately 2% of Huntington's annual pre-tax earnings.

Typical Recipients

Arts & Humanities: Arts Associations & Councils, Arts Institutes, Ballet, Ethnic & Folk Arts, Arts & Humanities-General, Libraries, Museums/Galleries, Opera, Performing Arts, Theater, Visual Arts
Civic & Public Affairs: African American Affairs, Asian American Affairs, Business/Free Enterprise, Chambers of Commerce, Community Foundations, Economic Development, Employment/Job Training, Ethnic Organizations, Civic & Public Affairs-General, Housing, Inner-City Development, Minority Business, Nonprofit Management, Parades/Festivals, Philanthropic Organizations, Urban & Community Affairs, Women's Affairs, Zoos/Aquariums
Education: Agricultural Education, Business Education, Business-School Partnerships, Colleges & Universities, Community & Junior Colleges, Economic Education, Elementary Education (Private), Education-General, Health & Physical Education, International Exchange, Employment/Job Training, International Studies, Minority Education, Science/Mathematics Education, Student Aid, Vocational & Technical Education
Health: Alzheimer's Disease, Arthritis, Cancer, Children's Health/Hospitals, Eyes/Blindness, Health-General, Geriatric Health, Heart, Hospices, Hospitals, Hospitals (University Affiliated), Long-Term Care, Medical Research, Multiple Sclerosis, Respiratory, Speech & Hearing
International: International Affairs, International Development, Trade
Religion: Jewish Causes
Science: Science-General, Science Museums
Social Services: Animal Protection, Camps, Homes, Shelters/Homelessness, Social Services-General, United Funds/United Ways, Volunteer Services, Youth Organizations

Application Procedures

Initial Contact: Send a brief letter of inquiry.
Application Requirements: Include a description of organization, amount requested, purpose of funds sought, recently audited financial statement, and proof of tax-exempt status.
Deadlines: None. Company prefers to receive re-

quests in summer for fall consideration of the following year's budget.

Restrictions

Does not support individuals, religious organizations for sectarian purposes, political or lobbying groups, or organizations outside operating areas.

Corporate Officials

Frank Wobst: chairman, director B Dresden, Germany 1933. ED University of Erlangen (1956); University of Goettingen (1958); Rutgers University MBA (1964). PRIM CORP EMPL chairman, director: Huntington Bancshares Inc. CORP AFFIL director: Midland Mutual Life Insurance Co.; member: Robert Morris Associates; chairman: Huntington Trust Co. NONPR AFFIL member: Greater Columbus Chamber of Commerce; member: Newcomen Society; member: American Institute Banking; member: Association Reserve City Bankers. CLUB AFFIL Sciotto Country Club.

HUNTINGTON FOUNDATION

Giving Contact

Arlene Aurthor, Executive Secretary
Huntington Foundation
401 11th Street, Suite 306
Huntington, WV 25701
Phone: (304)522-0611

Description

Founded: 1988
EIN: 550370129
Organization Type: Private Foundation
Giving Locations: WV
Grant Types: General Support.

Financial Summary

Total Giving: $460,297 (2003)
Assets: $6,808,067 (2003)
Gifts Received: $4,208 (1998); $3,410 (1997); $8,033 (1995)

Typical Recipients

Arts & Humanities: Libraries, Museums/Galleries, Music
Civic & Public Affairs: Civic & Public Affairs-General, Municipalities/Towns, Professional & Trade Associations, Safety
Education: Colleges & Universities, Education Funds, Education-General, Medical Education, Public Education (Precollege), Science/Mathematics Education
Environment: Environment-General
Health: Geriatric Health, Health Funds, Hospices, Hospitals, Research/Studies Institutes
Social Services: At-Risk Youth, Child Welfare, Community Centers, Community Service Organizations, Domestic Violence, Family Services, People with Disabilities, Scouts, Shelters/Homelessness, Social Services-General, Special Olympics, Volunteer Services, YMCA/YWCA/YMHA/YWHA, Youth Organizations

Application Procedures

Initial Contact: Request application form.
Deadlines: None.

Additional Information

Publications: Application Form

Foundation Officials

Frank E. Hanshaw, Jr.: vice president
John E. Jenkins, Jr.: director
Dr. Winfield C. John: director

Kermit E. McGinnis: secretary, treasurer
C. H. McKown: director
Cecil H. Underwood: president B Josephs Mills, WV 1922. ED Salem College BA (1943); West Virginia University MA (1952). PRIM CORP EMPL president: Morgantown Industrial Park. CORP AFFIL chairman: West Virginia Council Vocational Education; chairman,director: West Virginia Foundation Independent Coll; member: Sigma Phi Epsilon; chairman,director: Salem Teikyo University; member: Shriners; member: Rotary; president,member: National Association State Council Vocational Education; member: Pi Kappa Delta; member: Masons; member: Elks; secretary,director: Huntington Federal Savings & Loan Association; chairman,director: Applachian Regional Hospital.

Grants Analysis

Disclosure Period: calendar year ending 2003
Total Grants: $460,297
Number of Grants: 14
Average Grant: $20,030*
Highest Grant: $100,000
Lowest Grant: $2,500
Typical Range: $5,000 to $25,000
***Note:** Average grant figure excludes four highest grants ($260,000).

Recent Grants

Note: Grants derived from 2003 Form 990.
General

100,000	Ebenezer Medical Outreach, Huntington, WV -- for the renovation of building
60,431	Frank E. Hanshaw Geriatric Center, Huntington, WV -- for challenge grant
50,000	Huntington City Mission, Huntington, WV -- for renovating men's shelter and building new services center
50,000	Tri-State Area Council, Boy Scouts of America, Huntington, WV -- maintenance for camp pool/bathhouse
25,000	American Foundation for the Blind, Huntington, WV -- for mentor program
25,000	Hospital Hospitality House of Huntington, Huntington, WV -- for challenge grant
25,000	Mission West Virginia Inc., Huntington, WV -- funding for technology for tri state fire academy
23,281	Huntington Symphony Orchestra, Huntington, WV -- for purchase of percussion instruments
15,984	J W Scott Community Center Inc., Huntington, WV -- for purchase of 13 computer systems
5,000	Hospice of Huntington, Huntington, WV -- for bereavement camp for children

HURST FOUNDATION

Giving Contact

Anthony P. Hurst, President
675 Robinson Rd.
Jackson, MI 49203
Phone: (517)788-8600

Description

Founded: 1955
EIN: 386089457
Organization Type: Private Foundation
Giving Locations: MI: Jackson County
Grant Types: Capital, Operating Expenses, Project.

Donor Information

Founder: the late Peter F. Hurst, Elizabeth S. Hurst

Typical Recipients

Arts & Humanities: History & Archaeology, Libraries, Museums/Galleries, Music, Public Broadcasting

Civic & Public Affairs: Botanical Gardens/Parks, Business/Free Enterprise, Clubs, Community Foundations, Employment/Job Training, Civic & Public Affairs-General, Housing, Municipalities/Towns, Parades/Festivals, Philanthropic Organizations, Professional & Trade Associations, Public Policy, Safety, Urban & Community Affairs

Education: Arts/Humanities Education, Business Education, Business-School Partnerships, Colleges & Universities, Community & Junior Colleges, Education Funds, Education Reform, Elementary Education (Public), Environmental Education, Education-General, International Studies, Preschool Education, Private Education (Precollege), Public Education (Precollege), Secondary Education (Private)

Environment: Environment-General

Health: AIDS/HIV, Alzheimer's Disease, Health-General, Health Organizations, Hospices, Prenatal Health Issues, Respiratory, Speech & Hearing

International: International Organizations

Religion: Churches, Religious Organizations, Religious Welfare

Science: Observatories & Planetariums

Social Services: Animal Protection, At-Risk Youth, Camps, Child Welfare, Community Centers, Community Service Organizations, Crime Prevention, Day Care, Family Services, Homes, People with Disabilities, Recreation & Athletics, Shelters/Homelessness, Substance Abuse, United Funds/United Ways, Youth Organizations

Application Procedures

Initial Contact: Send a brief letter of inquiry and full proposal (two copies).

Application Requirements: Include a description of organization, amount requested, purpose of funds sought, recently audited financial statement, and proof of tax-exempt status. Also list of directors.

Deadlines: October 1.

Restrictions

Does not support individuals or loans.

Foundation Officials

Anthony P. Hurst: president
Ronald F. Hurst: vice president

Grants Analysis

Disclosure Period: calendar year ending 2000
Total Grants: $399,500*
Number of Grants: 42
Average Grant: $9,512
Highest Grant: $65,000
Typical Range: $5,000 to $20,000
*Note: Giving excludes United Way.

Recent Grants

Note: Grants derived from 2001 Form 990.
General

204,200	Lily Missionary Baptist Church, Jackson, MI -- building fund
50,000	Spring Arbor College, Spring Arbor, MI -- building project
44,000	Community Respite Center, Jackson, MI -- building project
30,000	Cascade Humane Society, Jackson, MI -- building project
25,000	United Way of Jackson County, Jackson, MI -- endowment fund raising
20,000	Jackson Intermediate School, Jackson, MI -- Beaman Art Project
15,000	Disability Connection, Jackson, MI -- remodel facilities
10,000	Columbia School District, Brooklyn, MI -- joint star
10,000	Columbia School District, Brooklyn, MI -- staffing enrichment
10,000	Great Sauk Trails Boy Scout Council, Jackson, MI -- Camp facilities maintenance

STEWART HUSTON CHARITABLE TRUST

Giving Contact

Scott G. Huston, Executive Director
Lukens Historic District
50 S. 1st Avenue, 2nd Floor
Coatesville, PA 19320
Phone: (610)384-2666
Fax: (610)384-3396
E-mail: admin@stewarthuston.org
Web: http://www.stewarthuston.org

Description

Founded: 1989
EIN: 232612599
Organization Type: Family Foundation
Giving Locations: GA: Savannah; PA: Chester County
Grant Types: Capital, Challenge, General Support, Matching, Operating Expenses, Project, Seed Money.

Donor Information

Founder: The foundation was established in 1989 in accordance with provisions left by Stewart Huston (d. 1971) in his will. He was the great-grandson of Rebecca Lukens, member of the founding family of Lukens Iron and Steel, Inc., of Coatesville, PA. Mr. Huston was an executive at Lukens Steel, and active with numerous community groups, small local business, and his church. He also was interested in Savannah, GA, the birthplace of his mother, and home of his wife, Harriet Lawrence Huston, who was an artist and a poet. The Trust has allotted money specifically for Trinitarian Evangelical activities and for secular activities, primarily for programs in Chester County, PA, and in Savannah, GA.

Financial Summary

Total Giving: $675,898 (2003); $1,099,581 (2002); $1,183,610 (2001)
Assets: $21,777,477 (2003); $17,792,228 (2002); $20,829,418 (2001)

Typical Recipients

Arts & Humanities: Arts Funds, Arts Outreach, Dance, Ethnic & Folk Arts, Arts & Humanities-General, Historic Preservation, History & Archaeology, Libraries, Museums/Galleries, Music, Public Broadcasting, Theater, Visual Arts

Civic & Public Affairs: Chambers of Commerce, Community Foundations, Economic Development, Economic Policy, Employment/Job Training, Civic & Public Affairs-General, Housing, Nonprofit Management, Philanthropic Organizations, Public Policy, Urban & Community Affairs, Women's Affairs, Zoos/Aquariums

Education: Afterschool/Enrichment Programs, Arts/Humanities Education, Business Education, Colleges & Universities, Community & Junior Colleges, Continuing Education, Elementary Education (Public), Faculty Development, Education-General, International Studies, Literacy, Private Education (Precollege), Public Education (Precollege), Religious Education, Science/Mathematics Education, Secondary Education (Private), Special Education, Student Aid

Environment: Resource Conservation

Health: AIDS/HIV, Children's Health/Hospitals, Clinics/Medical Centers, Health-General, Geriatric Health, Medical Rehabilitation, Mental Health, Nursing Services, Trauma Treatment

International: International Peace & Security Issues, Missionary/Religious Activities

Religion: Bible Study/Translation, Churches, Religion-General, Jewish Causes, Ministries, Missionary Activities (Domestic), Religious Organizations, Religious Welfare, Seminaries, Social/Policy Issues

Science: Observatories & Planetariums, Scientific Centers & Institutes, Scientific Labs

Social Services: Animal Protection, Child Abuse, Child Welfare, Community Centers, Community Service Organizations, Crime Prevention, Delinquency & Criminal Rehabilitation, Emergency Relief, Family Planning, Family Services, Food/Clothing Distribution, Homes, People with Disabilities, Recreation & Athletics, Refugee Assistance, Scouts, Senior Services, Shelters/Homelessness, Social Services-General, Substance Abuse, Volunteer Services, YMCA/YWCA/YMHA/YWHA, Youth Organizations

Application Procedures

Initial Contact: Organizations should contact the trust to request a Grant Request form. Organizations are encouraged to discuss projects with trust staff before submitting an application.

Application Requirements: A completed Grant Request form should be accompanied by a brief summary (4-6 pages) of the proposal; charitable organization registration CPA only; by-laws; most recent financial audit; list of board of directors, with community and professional affiliations; current operating budget; annual report; other sources solicited for funds; detailed project budget; media reviews of the program; other sources of funds; and a copy of the applicant's IRS tax-exempt determination letter.

Deadlines: March 1 and September 1 for religious grants; January 15 for secular grants.

Review Process: Notices of approval, rejection, or requests for additional information are sent out semi-annually in June and December.

Restrictions

The trust does not make grants to individuals, for endowments, for purchases of tickets or advertising, for operating deficits, or for publications costs. Groups such as fraternal organizations, political parties or candidates, veterans labor or local civic groups, volunteer fire companies, and groups influencing legislation will not receive support.

Additional Information

Publications: Application Form

Foundation Officials

Samuel A. Cann: trustee
Charles Lukens Huston, III: trustee B Dayton, OH 1934. ED University of Virginia; Spring Garden College (1956).
Scott G. Huston: executive director
Louis N. Seltzer: trustee

Grants Analysis

Disclosure Period: calendar year ending 2003
Total Grants: $675,898
Number of Grants: 80
Average Grant: $8,448
Highest Grant: $60,239
Lowest Grant: $1,000
Typical Range: $1,000 to $15,000

Recent Grants

Note: Grants derived from 2002 Form 990.
General

80,564	Graystone Society Inc., Coatesville, PA
51,639	Calvary Baptist Day School, Savannah, GA -- fund for mini bus and architectural fees for new building
35,000	Calvary Baptist Day School, Savannah, GA -- fund for security systems
33,000	Boy Scouts of America Chester County Council, West Chester, PA
20,000	Bridges for Peace Inc., Tulsa, OK -- fund for food bank, dental equipment and upgrading the phones
20,000	Chester County Economic Development Foundation, Exton, PA
20,000	Eastern University, St. Davids, PA -- fund for emergency aid program
20,000	Life Transforming Ministries, Coatesville, PA

20,000	Life Transforming Ministries, Coatesville, PA
20,000	North Fayette United Methodist Church, Fayetteville, GA

HUSTON FOUNDATION

Giving Contact

Susan B. Heilman, Executive Assistant
1 Fayette Street, Suite 190
Conshohocken, PA 19428-2064
Phone: (610)832-4949
Fax: (610)832-4960
E-mail: hustonfndn@aol.com

Description

Founded: 1957
EIN: 236284125
Organization Type: General Purpose Foundation
Giving Locations: PA: Eastern Pennsylvania nationally.
Grant Types: Capital, General Support, Matching, Operating Expenses, Project, Seed Money.
Note: The foundation also makes officer and director matching gift grants.

Donor Information

Founder: The foundation was established in 1957 by the late Charles Lukens Huston Jr. and the late Ruth Huston, as a tribute to their parents, Charles Lukens Huston, a Protestant Evangelical Christian philanthropic industrialist, and Anne Stewart Huston, a Protestant Evangelical Christian community leader.

Financial Summary

Total Giving: $1,104,243 (2002); $1,515,777 (2001)
Giving Analysis: Giving for 2002 includes: foundation matching gifts ($1,000); 2001: foundation matching gifts ($1,000)
Assets: $27,937,259 (2002); $34,698,636 (2001)

Typical Recipients

Arts & Humanities: Arts Associations & Councils, Arts Centers, Arts Institutes, Arts Outreach, Film & Video, Arts & Humanities-General, Historic Preservation, Libraries, Museums/Galleries, Music, Performing Arts, Public Broadcasting, Theater
Civic & Public Affairs: Chambers of Commerce, Community Foundations, Economic Development, Employment/Job Training, Civic & Public Affairs-General, Hispanic Affairs, Housing, Law & Justice, Municipalities/Towns, Nonprofit Management, Philanthropic Organizations, Professional & Trade Associations, Public Policy, Urban & Community Affairs, Zoos/Aquariums
Education: Afterschool/Enrichment Programs, Colleges & Universities, Education Funds, Education Reform, Elementary Education (Private), Education-General, Health & Physical Education, International Studies, Leadership Training, Legal Education, Literacy, Medical Education, Minority Education, Preschool Education, Private Education (Precollege), Religious Education, Secondary Education (Private), Secondary Education (Public), Social Sciences Education, Special Education, Student Aid, Vocational & Technical Education
Environment: Environment-General
Health: Children's Health/Hospitals, Clinics/Medical Centers, Emergency/Ambulance Services, Eyes/Blindness, Health Organizations, Hospices, Hospitals, Medical Rehabilitation, Medical Research, Nursing Services, Prenatal Health Issues, Public Health, Respiratory, Single-Disease Health Associations
International: Foreign Educational Institutions, Health Care/Hospitals, International Organizations, Missionary/Religious Activities
Religion: Bible Study/Translation, Churches, Religion-General, Ministries, Missionary Activities (Domestic), Religious Organizations, Religious Welfare, Seminaries
Science: Observatories & Planetariums, Scientific Centers & Institutes
Social Services: Animal Protection, At-Risk Youth, Big Brothers/Big Sisters, Camps, Child Abuse, Child Welfare, Community Service Organizations, Counseling, Family Planning, Family Services, Food/Clothing Distribution, Homes, People with Disabilities, Recreation & Athletics, Sexual Abuse, Shelters/Homelessness, Social Services-General, Substance Abuse, United Funds/United Ways, YMCA/YWCA/YMHA/YWHA, Youth Organizations

Application Procedures

Initial Contact: Send a brief letter of inquiry outlining the request. Applicants are also encouraged to call the foundation office to discuss potential projects with a program executive, and to have a Request Packet sent.
Application Requirements: 2-4 page grant proposal; IRS 990PF tax exemption letter and employee identification number; a history of the organization; a statement of faith (Protestant Evangelical Christian missions only); names of supporting organizations providing public and private funding sources, in general or for this specific project; a list of the Board of Directors; the organization's current operating budget and a detailed project budget; most recent annual/financial report; statement verifying there has been no change in purpose, character, or method of operation since the latest IRS tax letter was issued; and, where applicable, present project goals in quantifiable objectives.
Deadlines: Applicants should submit proposals by April 1 and October 1.

Restrictions

The foundation reports grants are made to religious, charitable, scientific, literary, and educational organizations. No grants are made to individuals, or for multi-year projects, grant-making organizations, endowment funds, organizations for individual or group travel purposes, fraternal organizations, political candidates or parties, veterans organizations, labor groups, social clubs, coverage of continuing operating deficits, document publication costs, for ticket purchases or benefit advertising, research, fellowships, or loans.

Additional Information

Publications: Annual Report; Informational Brochure; Application Guidelines

Foundation Officials

Nancy Huston Hansen: vice president evangelical relations B 1936.
Charles L. Huston, IV: treasurer
Elinor Huston Lashley: vice president ed and cultural rels

Grants Analysis

Disclosure Period: calendar year ending 2002
Total Grants: $1,103,243*
Number of Grants: 166
Average Grant: $6,646
Highest Grant: $30,000
Lowest Grant: $1,000
Typical Range: $1,000 to $10,000
*****Note:** Giving excludes matching gifts.

Recent Grants

Note: Grants derived from 2002 Form 990.
General

30,000	Damaris Project, Dallas, TX
25,000	Fourteen Four Group, Verdugo City, CA -- towards development of countries by way of strategic plans among broad-based ministry partnerships
25,000	Inter Varsity Christian Fellowship, Upper Darby, PA
25,000	Life Transforming Ministries, Coatesville, PA
25,000	Sentinel Group, Lynnwood, WA
20,000	Fairview Cemetery Association, Coatesville, PA -- towards emergency partial funding for audit
20,000	Impact Ministries Inc., Atlanta, GA -- fund for Georgia Service Network
20,000	Life Ministries, San Dimas, CA
20,000	Team Faith Racing Ministry, Knoxville, TN -- towards Gospel of Jesus Christ
17,000	Focus, West Tisbury, MA -- fund for two full time staff workers for ministry to teenagers

HUTHSTEINER FINE ARTS TRUST

Giving Contact

Joe Sayklay, Trust Officer
c/o Bank of the West
PO Box 99102
El Paso, TX 79999
Phone: (915)747-1644

Description

Founded: 1980
EIN: 746308412
Organization Type: Private Foundation
Giving Locations: TX: West Texas
Grant Types: Emergency, Endowment, General Support, Multiyear/Continuing Support, Operating Expenses.

Donor Information

Founder: Robert and Pauline Huthsteiner Trust

Financial Summary

Total Giving: $129,250 (fiscal year ending July 31, 2004)
Assets: $2,974,313 (fiscal 2004)
Gifts Received: $416 (fiscal 1999); $500 (fiscal 1996). Note: In fiscal 1996, contributions were received from Burton Patterson.

Typical Recipients

Arts & Humanities: Arts Associations & Councils, Arts Funds, Ballet, Community Arts, Dance, Arts & Humanities-General, Libraries, Literary Arts, Museums/Galleries, Music, Opera, Performing Arts, Public Broadcasting, Theater
Civic & Public Affairs: Professional & Trade Associations
Education: Arts/Humanities Education, Colleges & Universities
International: Foreign Arts Organizations
Religion: Churches
Social Services: Community Service Organizations, Youth Organizations

Application Procedures

Initial Contact: Send a brief letter of inquiry.
Application Requirements: a description of organization, amount requested, and proof of tax-exempt status.
Deadlines: None.

Restrictions

Grants awarded to support the fine arts.

Additional Information

Trust(s): Bank of the West

Grants Analysis

Disclosure Period: fiscal year ending July 31, 2004
Total Grants: $129,250
Number of Grants: 14

Average Grant: $9,232
Highest Grant: $21,000
Lowest Grant: $1,250
Typical Range: $2,500 to $20,000

Recent Grants

Note: Grants derived from 2004 Form 990.
General

28,000	El Paso Symphony, El Paso, TX
21,000	Art Museum Foundation, El Paso, TX
20,000	El Paso Opera, El Paso, TX
20,000	University of Texas at El Paso, El Paso, TX -- funds for music department
14,000	El Paso Pro Musica, El Paso, TX
6,000	El Paso Wind Symphony, El Paso, TX
2,500	KCOS, El Paso, TX -- funds for programming
2,500	KRWG TV, El Paso, TX
2,500	KSCE TV, El Paso, TX
2,500	KTEP FM, El Paso, TX

HYDE AND WATSON FOUNDATION

Giving Contact

Hunter W. Corbin, President
Hyde and Watson Foundation
437 Southern Boulevard
Chatham, NJ 07928
Phone: (973)966-6024
Fax: (973)966-6404
Web: http://www.fdncenter.org/grantmaker/hydeandwatson

Description

Founded: 1983
EIN: 222425725
Organization Type: General Purpose Foundation
Giving Locations: NJ: Essex County, Morris County, Union County; NY: New York metropolitan area
Grant Types: Capital, General Support, Research.
Note: Funds for research are very limited.

Donor Information

Founder: The Hyde and Watson Foundation was established in 1983 through the consolidation of The Lillia Babbitt Hyde Foundation and The John Jay and Eliza Jane Watson Foundation.

Lillia Babbitt Hyde (1856-1939) was the daughter of Benjamin Talbot Babbitt, a businessman and inventor who made his fortune in the chemical industry and with mechanical products. Upon his death, he left to Lillia one-half of his estate and controlling interest in B.T. Babbitt, Inc. Lillia's name is derived from her marriage to Clarence Hyde, a New York lawyer. Lillia established The Lillia Babbitt Hyde Foundation in 1924, served as its president until her death, and left the bulk of her estate to the foundation.

John Jay Watson (1874-1939) headed two subsidiaries of U.S. Rubber Co. and organized Lee Tire and Rubber Co., which he later merged with Republic Tire and Rubber. Later in his career he headed International Minerals and Chemicals Corp., where he established a potash mine in New Mexico, freeing the United States from dependence on foreign sources. Eliza Jane Watson, John's wife, created The John Jay and Eliza Jane Watson Foundation as a tribute to her husband upon his death. The bulk of Eliza Jane's estate was donated to the foundation upon her own death in 1957.

Financial Summary

Total Giving: $4,560,550 (2003); $4,497,750 (2002); $4,849,400 (2001)
Assets: $111,581,768 (2003); $99,604,186 (2002); $106,913,170 (2001)

Typical Recipients

Arts & Humanities: Arts Associations & Councils, Arts Funds, Ethnic & Folk Arts, Historic Preservation, History & Archaeology, Libraries, Literary Arts, Museums/Galleries, Music, Opera, Performing Arts, Public Broadcasting, Theater, Visual Arts
Civic & Public Affairs: African American Affairs, Botanical Gardens/Parks, Business/Free Enterprise, Clubs, Economic Development, Employment/Job Training, Civic & Public Affairs-General, Hispanic Affairs, Inner-City Development, Municipalities/Towns, Nonprofit Management, Philanthropic Organizations, Public Policy, Safety, Urban & Community Affairs
Education: Afterschool/Enrichment Programs, Arts/Humanities Education, Business Education, Colleges & Universities, Education Funds, Education Reform, Elementary Education (Private), Engineering/Technological Education, Education-General, International Studies, Literacy, Medical Education, Minority Education, Private Education (Precollege), Public Education (Precollege), Religious Education, Science/Mathematics Education, Secondary Education (Private), Special Education, Student Aid
Environment: Air/Water Quality, Forestry, Environment-General, Protection, Resource Conservation, Watershed, Wildlife Protection
Health: Adolescent Health Issues, Alzheimer's Disease, Cancer, Children's Health/Hospitals, Clinics/Medical Centers, Emergency/Ambulance Services, Eyes/Blindness, Health-General, Geriatric Health, Health Funds, Health Organizations, Heart, Hospices, Hospitals, Hospitals (University Affiliated), Medical Rehabilitation, Medical Research, Nursing Services, Prenatal Health Issues, Public Health, Research/Studies Institutes, Respiratory, Single-Disease Health Associations, Speech & Hearing, Transplant Networks/Donor Banks, Trauma Treatment
International: International Affairs
Religion: Churches, Jewish Causes, Religious Organizations, Religious Welfare, Seminaries
Science: Science Museums, Scientific Centers & Institutes, Scientific Labs
Social Services: Animal Protection, At-Risk Youth, Camps, Child Abuse, Child Welfare, Community Centers, Community Service Organizations, Counseling, Day Care, Domestic Violence, Emergency Relief, Family Services, Food/Clothing Distribution, Homes, People with Disabilities, Scouts, Senior Services, Shelters/Homelessness, Social Services-General, Substance Abuse, United Funds/United Ways, YMCA/YWCA/YMHA/YWHA, Youth Organizations

Application Procedures

Initial Contact: Acquire the Grant Application Information Sheet from foundation or the foundation website, then send a full proposal.
Application Requirements: Full proposals will include completed Grant Application Information Sheet; a brief narrative (no more than three pages), signed by an appropriate officer, summarizing the background or the organization and constituency served, purpose of funds sought, project total and amount requested, and anticipated timeframe; project budget with line items, including amount raised and balance needed; operating budget for current fiscal year; list of supporters for the most recent fiscal year; list of board of directors/trustees, with affiliations; copy of most recent audited financial report or Form 990; proof of tax-exempt status. The foundation also accepts the New York/New Jersey Area Common Application Form.
Deadlines: February 15 for review during the spring meetings and September 15 for the fall meetings.
Review Process: The foundation attempts to respond to each application. Appeals are preliminarily evaluated on an ongoing basis; therefore, early submission of appeals is encouraged.

Restrictions

The foundation does not make grants to individuals nor to applicants located outside the United States. Requests for endowment or operating support or from fiscal agents are not likely to receive favorable responses.

Additional Information

The foundation reports that it also provides investment advice and board and volunteer services to nonprofit organizations.

The foundation reports that it is affiliated with the Charles E. and Joy C. Pettinos Foundation in New Jersey.

Publications: Annual Report; Grant Application Information Sheet

Foundation Officials

Nancy A. Allocco: vice president
Loretta J. Becht: assistant secretary
Thomas W. Berry: director, treasurer
Jennifer Chandler-Hauge: director
Hunter W. Corbin: director, president
Elizabeth R. Curry: director
H. Corbin Day: director B Orange, NJ 1937. ED Brown University BA (1959); University of Pennsylvania MBA (1963). CORP AFFIL director: Jemison Steel Co. LLC; director: Schreiber Corp. Inc.; chairman, chief executive officer, director: Jemison Investment Co. Inc.; director: Altec Industries Inc.; director: Hughes Supply Inc.
William V. Engel, Esq.: director, secretary
John W. Holman, III: director
John W. Holman, Jr.: chairman, director PRIM CORP EMPL managing director: Triak Services Corp.
G. Morrison Hubbard, Jr.: director emeritus
Anke Lofrese: assistant secretary
Brunilda Moriarty: vice president
Robert W. Parsons, Jr.: director, assistant treasurer, assistant section
Roger B. Parsons: director
Kate B. Wood: director NONPR AFFIL vice chairman: New Jersey Historical Society.

Grants Analysis

Disclosure Period: calendar year ending 2003
Total Grants: $4,560,550*
Number of Grants: 343
Average Grant: $12,788*
Highest Grant: $100,000
Lowest Grant: $4,000
Typical Range: $5,000 to $25,000
*Note: Average grant figure excludes two highest grants ($200,000).

Recent Grants

Note: Grants derived from 2003 Form 990.
Library-Related

100,000	Library of the Chatham, Chatham, NJ -- fund for purchase of computer & office equipment to enhance its library expansion project

General

100,000	Learning Circle, Summit, NJ -- fund for the expansion and modernization of its child care facilities
75,000	Frost Valley YMCA, Claryville, NY -- fund for the modifications and expansion of its camp facilities to enhance its environmental education programs
75,000	Newark Museum, Newark, NJ -- fund for the construction of a science gallery
75,000	YMCA of Greater New York, New York, NY -- fund for alterations, improvements & expansion of YMCA buildings
50,000	Boys Club of New York, New York, NY -- fund for the construction of a new clubhouse facility

50,000	Camp Speers-Eljabar YMCA, Westfield, NJ -- fund for the construction of a new community and performing arts center
50,000	Gill St. Bernard's School, Gladstone, NJ -- fund for the construction of a new athletic center and modernization of its facilities
50,000	Paper Mill Playhouse, Millburn, NJ -- fund for replacement of the HVAC system in its main facility
50,000	Trinitas Hospital, Elizabeth, NJ -- fund for the purchase of radiology equipment
50,000	University of Medicine and Dentistry of New Jersey (UMDNJ), Somerset, NJ -- fund for the purchase of equipment for its FOCUS community health center in Newark

HYDE MANUFACTURING CO.

Company Headquarters
54 Eastford Road
Southbridge, MA 01550
Web: http://www.hudetools.com

Company Description
Employees: 500
SIC(s): 3421 Cutlery, 3423 Hand & Edge Tools Nec, 3545 Machine Tool Accessories.

Operating Locations
Hyde Manufacturing Co. (MA--Southbridge)

Hyde Charitable Foundation

Giving Contact
Richard B. Hardy, Chairman & Chief Executive Officer
Hyde Charitable Foundation
54 Eastford Rd.
Southbridge, MA 01550-3604
Phone: (508)764-4344
Fax: (508)765-9929

Description
EIN: 042752893
Organization Type: Corporate Foundation
Giving Locations: MA: Worcester County
Grant Types: Capital, General Support.

Financial Summary
Total Giving: $182,000 (2003); $184,250 (2001)
Assets: $3,811,233 (2003); $3,558,189 (2001)
Gifts Received: $112,400 (2003); $166,000 (2001); $138,500 (2000). Note: In 2003, contributions were received from Hyde Manufacturing Co. ($46,100), Dexter-Russell Inc. ($64,100), and Wilson Machine Knife Co., Inc. ($2,200). In 2001, contributions were received from Hyde Manufacturing Co. ($74,500), Dexter-Russell Inc. ($86,300), and Wilson Machine Knife Co., Inc. ($5,200). In 2000, contributions were received from Hyde Manufacturer ($54,600), Russell Harrington Cutlery ($78,500), and Wilson Machine Knife Co. ($5,400). In 1999, contributions were received from Hyde Manufacturer ($76,900), Russell Harrington Cutlery ($80,100), and Wilson Machine Knife Co. ($6,500). In 1998, contributions were received from Hyde Manufacturing Co. ($66,300), Russell Harrington Cutlery ($69,100), and Wilson Machine Knife Co. ($5,600). In 1996, contributions were received from Hyde Manufacturing Co. ($39,000), Russell Harrington Cutlery ($54,000), and Wilson Machine Knife Co. ($3,000).

Typical Recipients
Arts & Humanities: Arts Centers, Historic Preservation, History & Archaeology, Libraries, Museums/Galleries, Public Broadcasting, Theater
Civic & Public Affairs: Business/Free Enterprise, Clubs, Civic & Public Affairs-General, Public Policy, Safety
Education: Arts/Humanities Education, Business Education, Colleges & Universities, Education Funds, Education Reform, Elementary Education (Public), Engineering/Technological Education, Education-General, Private Education (Precollege), Science/Mathematics Education, Secondary Education (Public), Vocational & Technical Education
Health: Health Organizations, Hospices, Hospitals
Religion: Churches
Science: Science Museums, Scientific Centers & Institutes
Social Services: Child Welfare, Community Service Organizations, Counseling, Family Services, Food/Clothing Distribution, Recreation & Athletics, Scouts, Shelters/Homelessness, YMCA/YWCA/YMHA/YWHA, Youth Organizations

Application Procedures
Initial Contact: The foundation requests applications be made in writing. Include a description of organization, purpose of funds sought, amount requested, budget, and tax status of the organization.
Application Requirements: Include a description of organization, purpose of funds sought, amount requested, budget, and tax status of the organization.
Deadlines: None.

Restrictions
Does not support individuals or organizations outside operating areas.

Additional Information
Company reports approximately 25% of contributions support arts and humanities; 40% to education; 5% to health and human services; and 30% to civic and public affairs.

Corporate Officials
Richard B. Hardy: chairman, chief executive officer, director B Worcester, MA 1932. ED Rice University (1954). PRIM CORP EMPL chairman, chief executive officer, director: Hyde Manufacturing Co. CORP AFFIL chairman: Russell Harrington Cutlery; director: Mechanics Bank; chairman: Gutmann Cutlery Co.; director: Load Controls. NONPR AFFIL member: Shriners.
Ralph Lawrence: president, chief operating officer PRIM CORP EMPL president, chief operating officer: Hyde Manufacturing Co.

Foundation Officials
Ronald P. Carlson: trustee
Richard R. Clemence: trustee B Southbridge, MA 1939. PRIM CORP EMPL executive vice president, secretary, director: Hyde Manufacturing Co. CORP AFFIL vice chairman, director: Savers Cooperative Bank; president, director: Wilson Machine Knife Co.; clerk, director: Russell Harrington Cutlery Co.; secretary, director: Beaut-Ease; secretary, director: Gutmann Cutlery Co.
Richard B. Hardy: trustee (see above)
Alan S. Peppel: trustee
John P. Rawls: trustee

Grants Analysis
Disclosure Period: calendar year ending 2003
Total Grants: $182,000
Number of Grants: 25
Average Grant: $7,280
Highest Grant: $31,000
Lowest Grant: $500
Typical Range: $500 to $10,000

Recent Grants
Note: Grants derived from 2003 Form 990.
Library-Related
| 20,000 | Charlton Public Library, Charlton, MA |

General
31,000	Tri-Community YMCA, Southbridge, MA
27,000	Nichols College, Dudley, MA
21,500	Ecotarium, Worcester, MA
20,000	Federated Church of Sturbridge, Sturbridge, MA
15,000	St. Mary's Building Fund, Brush, CO
14,500	Worcester Academy, Worcester, MA
10,000	Trinity Catholic Academy, Southbridge, MA
5,000	ELM Street Congregational Church, Fitchburg, MA
3,000	Old Sturbridge Village, Sturbridge, MA
3,000	St. Nicholas Albanian Orthodox Church, Jamaica Estates, NY

IBP

Company Headquarters
800 Stevens Port Dr.
Dakota Dunes, SD 57049
Web: http://www.ibpinc.com

Company Description
Employees: 41000 (2003)
SIC(s): 2011 Meat Packing Plants.
Parent Company: Tyson Foods Inc., Springdale, AR, United States

Operating Locations
IBP (NE--Dakota City)

Nonmonetary Support
Type: Donated Equipment; Donated Products; Loaned Executives

IBP Foundation

Giving Contact
Archie Schaffer, Director
2210 W. Oaklawn Dr.
Springdale, AR 72762
Phone: (479)290-4000

Description
Founded: 1979
EIN: 476014039
Organization Type: Corporate Foundation
Giving Locations: ID: Boise; IL: Joslin; IN: Logansport; IA: Columbus Junction, Denison, Perry, Sioux City, Storm Lake, Waterloo; KS: Emporia, Garden City; NE: Dakota City, Lexington, Madison, South Sioux City, West Point; TX: Amarillo; WA: Pasco
Grant Types: Award, Capital, Challenge, General Support.

Donor Information
Founder: IBP, Inc.

Financial Summary
Total Giving: $55,000 (2003)
Assets: $3,874,285 (2003); $3,305,581 (2002); $3,830,559 (2001)
Gifts Received: $74,334 (2003); $1,000,000 (1999); $1,000,000 (1994). Note: Contributions were received from IBP, Inc. In 1994, substantial contributions were received from IBP.

Typical Recipients
Arts & Humanities: Libraries, Public Broadcasting, Theater
Civic & Public Affairs: Employment/Job Training,

Civic & Public Affairs-General, Housing, Law & Justice, Municipalities/Towns, Native American Affairs, Philanthropic Organizations, Professional & Trade Associations, Rural Affairs, Safety, Urban & Community Affairs
Education: Afterschool/Enrichment Programs, Business Education, Colleges & Universities, Community & Junior Colleges, Elementary Education (Public), Education-General, Preschool Education, Public Education (Precollege), Secondary Education (Public)
Health: Children's Health/Hospitals, Clinics/Medical Centers, Emergency/Ambulance Services, Hospitals, Prenatal Health Issues
International: International-General
Religion: Churches, Religious Welfare
Social Services: Big Brothers/Big Sisters, Child Welfare, Community Centers, Community Service Organizations, Family Centers, Recreation & Athletics, United Funds/United Ways, YMCA/YWCA/YMHA/YWHA, Youth Organizations

Application Procedures
Initial Contact: Contact the foundation to request an application form.
Deadlines: None.

Additional Information
Publications: Application Form

Corporate Officials
Robert L. Peterson: chairman, chief executive officer, director B NE 1932. ED University of Nebraska. PRIM CORP EMPL chairman, chief executive officer, director: IBP. CLUB AFFIL Sioux City Country Club.
Larry Shipley: chief financial officer PRIM CORP EMPL chief financial officer: IBP.

Foundation Officials
Les Baledge: director
Richard Bond: director
Greg Lee: director
Archie Schaffer: director
John Tyson: director
Robin A. Wages: secretary

Grants Analysis
Disclosure Period: calendar year ending 2003
Total Grants: $55,000
Number of Grants: 5
Highest Grant: $25,000
Lowest Grant: $5,000
Typical Range: $5,000 to $10,000

Recent Grants
Note: Grants derived from 2003 Form 990.
General

25,000	Arkansas Sheriffs' Youth Ranches, Batesville, AR
10,000	Storm Lake Police Department, Storm Lake, IA
10,000	Wilkes Regional Medical Center, NC
5,000	Amarillo College, Amarillo, TX
5,000	Big Brothers Big Sisters

CARL C. ICAHN FOUNDATION

Giving Contact
Gail Golden-Icahn, Vice President
767 5th Avenue, Suite 4700
New York, NY 10153-0023
Phone: (212)702-4300

Description
Founded: 1980
EIN: 133091588
Organization Type: Private Foundation

Giving Locations: NY: New York
Grant Types: General Support.

Donor Information
Founder: Carl C. Icahn

Financial Summary
Total Giving: $537,000 (fiscal year ending November 30, 2003); $2,225,650 (fiscal 2001)
Assets: $11,565,587 (fiscal 2003); $12,833,905 (fiscal 2001)
Gifts Received: $100 (fiscal 2000)

Typical Recipients
Arts & Humanities: Arts Associations & Councils, Ballet, Community Arts, Historic Preservation, History & Archaeology, Libraries, Museums/Galleries, Music, Opera, Performing Arts, Public Broadcasting
Civic & Public Affairs: Civil Rights, Clubs, Community Foundations, Ethnic Organizations, Civic & Public Affairs-General, Municipalities/Towns, Philanthropic Organizations, Safety, Urban & Community Affairs, Women's Affairs
Education: Arts/Humanities Education, Colleges & Universities, Education Funds, Education-General, Medical Education, Minority Education, Private Education (Precollege), Student Aid
Environment: Air/Water Quality, Environment-General
Health: Alzheimer's Disease, Cancer, Children's Health/Hospitals, Clinics/Medical Centers, Diabetes, Health Organizations, Heart, Hospitals, Long-Term Care, Medical Rehabilitation, Medical Research, Mental Health, Multiple Sclerosis, Single-Disease Health Associations
International: Foreign Arts Organizations, Health Care/Hospitals, Human Rights, International Development, International Environmental Issues, International Organizations, International Relief Efforts, Missionary/Religious Activities
Religion: Jewish Causes, Religious Welfare
Science: Scientific Research
Social Services: Animal Protection, Big Brothers/Big Sisters, Child Welfare, Community Centers, Community Service Organizations, Counseling, Crime Prevention, Day Care, Domestic Violence, Food/Clothing Distribution, People with Disabilities, Recreation & Athletics, Refugee Assistance, Shelters/Homelessness, Social Services-General, Substance Abuse, United Funds/United Ways, Youth Organizations

Application Procedures
Initial Contact: Send a brief letter of inquiry describing program or project. Include basic budget and proof of tax-exempt status.
Deadlines: None.

Foundation Officials
Gail Golden-Icahn: vice president
Susan Gordon: assistant treasurer
Carl Celian Icahn: president, director B Queens, NY 1936. ED New York University School of Medicine; Princeton University BA (1957). PRIM CORP EMPL owner, chairman, director: Icahn & Co. CORP AFFIL chairman: XO Communications Inc.; chairman: Stratosphere Corp.; chairman, president, chief executive officer: Trans World Airlines; Samsonite Corp.; chairman, chief executive officer: Starfire Holding Corp.; president: Riverdale Investors Corp., Inc.; president: Foxfield Thoroughbreds Inc.; chairman, president: Icahn Holding Corp.; director: Fairchild Corp.; chairman: Bayswater Realty & Capital; director: Cadus Corp.; chairman: American RE Holdings LP. NONPR AFFIL Jewish Guild for the Blind Inc.

Grants Analysis
Disclosure Period: fiscal year ending November 30, 2003
Total Grants: $537,000
Number of Grants: 5
Highest Grant: $500,000

Lowest Grant: $1,000
Typical Range: $5,000 to $30,000

Recent Grants
Note: Grants derived from fiscal 2004 Form 990.
General

4,000,000	Randall's Island Sports Foundation, New York, NY
2,125,000	Mount Sinai School of Medicine, New York, NY
95,000	Children's Rescue Fund, New York, NY

IDEAL INDUSTRIES INC.

Company Headquarters
1 Becker Place
Sycamore, IL 60178
Web: http://www.idealindustries.com

Company Description
Employees: 480
SIC(s): 3546 Power-Driven Handtools, 3548 Welding Apparatus, 3549 Metalworking Machinery Nec, 3569 General Industrial Machinery Nec.

Operating Locations
Ideal Industries (IL--Sycamore)

Ideal Industries Foundation

Giving Contact
Jim Pfotenhauer, Treasurer
Becker Place
Sycamore, IL 60178
Phone: (815)895-5181
Fax: (815)895-6973
E-mail: wjablow@wirenot.com

Description
Founded: 1987
EIN: 363449960
Organization Type: Corporate Foundation
Giving Locations: IL
Grant Types: General Support.

Financial Summary
Total Giving: $164,107 (2003); $169,975 (2001)
Giving Analysis: Giving for 2001 includes: foundation grants to United Way ($5,000)
Assets: $159,860 (2003); $232,216 (2001)
Gifts Received: $117,000 (2003); $152,000 (2001); $192,000 (2000). Note: Contributions were received from Ideal Industries.

Typical Recipients
Arts & Humanities: Libraries, Music, Public Broadcasting
Civic & Public Affairs: Clubs, Community Foundations, Economic Development, Civic & Public Affairs-General, Hispanic Affairs, Housing, Legal Aid, Professional & Trade Associations, Safety, Urban & Community Affairs
Education: Afterschool/Enrichment Programs, Business Education, Colleges & Universities, Economic Education, Education Associations, Education Funds, Engineering/Technological Education, Faculty Development, Education-General, Private Education (Precollege), Public Education (Precollege), Secondary Education (Public), Student Aid
Health: Cancer, Children's Health/Hospitals, Clinics/Medical Centers, Heart, Hospices, Multiple Sclerosis, Public Health, Single-Disease Health Associations
International: International Organizations
Religion: Religious Welfare
Science: Science Museums

Social Services: Big Brothers/Big Sisters, Child Welfare, Community Service Organizations, Day Care, Family Planning, Family Services, Food/Clothing Distribution, Recreation & Athletics, Scouts, Shelters/Homelessness, Social Services-General, Special Olympics, Substance Abuse, United Funds/United Ways, Volunteer Services, YMCA/YWCA/YMHA/YWHA, Youth Organizations

Application Procedures

Initial Contact: Initial inquiry should be a brief letter indicating the nature of the project for which support is sought.
Deadlines: None.

Corporate Officials

David W. Juday: chairman, director PRIM CORP EMPL chairman, director: Ideal Industries.
Robert Lane: president PRIM CORP EMPL president: Ideal Industries.
James Pfotenhauer: chief financial officer PRIM CORP EMPL chief financial officer: Ideal Industries.

Foundation Officials

Margaret Baack: vice president
Wendy Joblow: director
David W. Juday: president (see above)
Chris Lomb: director
James Pfotenhauer: treasurer (see above)

Grants Analysis

Disclosure Period: calendar year ending 2003
Total Grants: $159,107*
Number of Grants: 34
Average Grant: $3,306*
Highest Grant: $50,000
Lowest Grant: $50
Typical Range: $1,000 to $5,000
*Note: Giving excludes United Way. Average grant figure excludes highest grant.

Recent Grants

Note: Grants derived from 2003 Form 990.
General

50,000	Museum of Natural History, Dekalb, IL
13,000	Sycamore United Fund, Sycamore, IL
12,000	Court Appointed Special Advocates, Dekalb, IL
10,000	Tri County Community Health Center, Dekalb, IL
7,500	Dekalb County Economic Development Corporation, Dekalb, IL
7,500	Habitat for Humanity International, Bloomington, IL
7,500	Kishwaukee Family YMCA, Dekalb, IL
7,000	Junior Achievement, Sycamore, IL
6,000	Northern Illinois University, Dekalb, IL
5,000	Dekalb United Way, Dekalb, IL

IF HUMMINGBIRD FOUNDATION

Giving Contact

Jill Iscol, President, Treasurer & Director
63 Lyndel Road
Pound Ridge, NY 10576
Phone: (914)764-8477
Fax: (914)966-0639

Description

Founded: 1990
EIN: 061314468
Organization Type: Private Foundation
Former Name: Iscol Family Foundation (2002).
Giving Locations: New England.
Grant Types: General Support.

Donor Information

Founder: Established in 1990 by Kenneth Iscol.

Financial Summary

Total Giving: $267,910 (fiscal year ending June 30, 2004); $610,925 (fiscal 2001)
Assets: $1,988,664 (fiscal 2004); $4,212,790 (fiscal 2001)
Gifts Received: $1,000 (fiscal 1994); $5,700 (fiscal 1993); $55,249 (fiscal 1992)

Typical Recipients

Arts & Humanities: Historic Preservation, History & Archaeology, Libraries, Museums/Galleries, Music, Visual Arts
Civic & Public Affairs: Economic Development, Civic & Public Affairs-General, Philanthropic Organizations, Public Policy, Rural Affairs
Education: Colleges & Universities, Education Funds, Leadership Training, Literacy, Minority Education, Private Education (Precollege), Science/Mathematics Education, Student Aid
Environment: Environment-General, Resource Conservation, Wildlife Protection
Health: AIDS/HIV, Alzheimer's Disease, Cancer, Clinics/Medical Centers, Diabetes, Emergency/Ambulance Services, Health Organizations, Hospices, Hospitals, Hospitals (University Affiliated), Medical Research, Respiratory, Single-Disease Health Associations, Speech & Hearing, Trauma Treatment
International: International Environmental Issues, International Peace & Security Issues, International Relief Efforts
Religion: Jewish Causes, Synagogues/Temples
Science: Science Museums
Social Services: Child Welfare, Community Service Organizations, Crime Prevention, Delinquency & Criminal Rehabilitation, Domestic Violence, Food/Clothing Distribution, Recreation & Athletics, Shelters/Homelessness, Youth Organizations

Application Procedures

Initial Contact: Send a brief letter of inquiry.
Application Requirements: Include amount requested, need, and purpose of funds sought.
Deadlines: None.

Foundation Officials

Samuel Hurwitz: assistant secretary
Jill Iscol: president, treasurer, director
Kenneth H. Iscol: vice president, secretary, director

Grants Analysis

Disclosure Period: fiscal year ending June 30, 2004
Total Grants: $267,910
Number of Grants: 110
Average Grant: $2,436
Highest Grant: $35,000
Lowest Grant: $50
Typical Range: $1,000 to $5,000

Recent Grants

Note: Grants derived from fiscal 2004 Form 990.
General

56,000	Bank Street College of Education, New York, NY
35,000	Facing History and Ourselves, Brookline, MA
25,000	City Year, New York, NY
15,000	Acumen Fund, New York, NY
15,000	Teachers College Fund, New York, NY
10,000	Bob Hope Chrysler Classic, Rancho Mirage, CA
10,000	Israel Policy Forum, New York, NY
10,000	Kayne Eras Center, Culver City, CA
5,000	Naral Pro Choice America Fund, New York, NY
5,000	Prep for Prep, New York, NY

ILLINOIS TOOL WORKS INC.

Company Headquarters

3600 W. Lake Avenue
Glenview, IL 60025-5811
Phone: (847)724-7500
Fax: (847)657-4392
Web: http://www.itwinc.com

Company Description

Founded: 1912
Ticker: ITW
Exchange: NYSE
Acquired: Premark International (1999).
Revenue: US$11.731 billion (2004)
Profit: US$1.338 billion (2004)
Employees: 47500 (2003)
Fortune Rank: 183, per FORTUNE Magazine's list of 500 Largest U.S. Corporations (2004).
SIC(s): 2899 Chemical Preparations Nec, 3082 Unsupported Plastics Profile Shapes, 3089 Plastics Products Nec, 3429 Hardware Nec.

Operating Locations

Illinois Tool Works, Inc. (AR--Pine Bluff; CA--Hawthorne; CO--Colorado Springs; CT--Waterbury; IL--Des Plaines, Downers Grove, Elk Grove Village, Elmhurst, Glenview, Itasca, Lincolnshire, Lincolnwood, Wood Dale; MA--Danvers; MI--Detroit, Ferndale; NJ--Piscataway; NY--Orangeburg; OH--Loveland; PA--Montgomeryville; TN--Erin; TX--Arlington, Irving; VA--Lynchburg)

Nonmonetary Support

Type: Donated Equipment; Donated Products; Loaned Employees

Illinois Tool Works Foundation

Giving Contact

Mary Ann Mallahan, Manager, Community Relations
3600 West Lake Avenue
Glenview, IL 60025-5811
Phone: (847)657-4092
Fax: (847)657-4505
E-mail: mmallahan@itw.com
Web: http://itw.com/itw_foundation.html

Alternate Contact

Phone: (847)724-7500

Description

EIN: 366087160
Organization Type: Corporate Foundation
Giving Locations: IL: principally near operating locations and to national organizations.
Grant Types: Capital, Employee Matching Gifts, General Support, Multiyear/Continuing Support.
Note: Employee matching gift ratio: 3 to 1 for donations to nonprofit charitable organisation not already sponsored by company.

Financial Summary

Total Giving: $6,916,376 (fiscal year ending February 28, 2003); $7,248,657 (fiscal 2002); $6,070,358 (fiscal 2001)
Giving Analysis: Giving for fiscal 2001 includes: foundation scholarships ($254,964); foundation grants to United Way ($1,139,276); foundation grants ($2,093,691); foundation matching gifts ($2,582,427)
Assets: $13,736,827 (fiscal 2003); $2,201,385 (fiscal 2002); $5,524,801 (fiscal 2001)
Gifts Received: $18,600,000 (fiscal 2003); $4,000,000 (fiscal 2002). Note: In fiscal 2003, Contributions were received from Illinois Tool Works Inc.

Typical Recipients

Arts & Humanities: Arts Associations & Councils, Arts Festivals, Arts Institutes, Dance, Historic Preservation, History & Archaeology, Libraries, Museums/Galleries, Music, Opera, Performing Arts, Public Broadcasting, Theater

Civic & Public Affairs: Botanical Gardens/Parks, Business/Free Enterprise, Civil Rights, Clubs, Community Foundations, Economic Development, Employment/Job Training, Civic & Public Affairs-General, Hispanic Affairs, Housing, Inner-City Development, Law & Justice, Legal Aid, Nonprofit Management, Professional & Trade Associations, Public Policy, Urban & Community Affairs, Women's Affairs, Zoos/Aquariums

Education: Business Education, Colleges & Universities, Community & Junior Colleges, Economic Education, Education Associations, Education Funds, Engineering/Technological Education, Faculty Development, Education-General, Literacy, Minority Education, Private Education (Precollege), Science/Mathematics Education, Student Aid, Vocational & Technical Education

Health: Cancer, Children's Health/Hospitals, Clinics/Medical Centers, Diabetes, Health Funds, Health Organizations, Heart, Hospitals, Medical Rehabilitation, Medical Research, Mental Health, Nursing Services

International: Foreign Educational Institutions

Religion: Bible Study/Translation, Jewish Causes, Religious Welfare

Science: Observatories & Planetariums, Science Exhibits & Fairs, Science Museums, Scientific Centers & Institutes

Social Services: Child Welfare, Community Centers, Domestic Violence, Family Planning, Family Services, Food/Clothing Distribution, Homes, People with Disabilities, Scouts, Senior Services, Substance Abuse, United Funds/United Ways, Volunteer Services, YMCA/YWCA/YMHA/YWHA, Youth Organizations

Application Procedures

Initial Contact: Send a brief letter or proposal.

Application Requirements: Provide a description of organization; amount requested and purpose of funds sought; recently audited financial statement; and proof of tax-exempt status.

Deadlines: May and December 1.

Corporate Officials

W. James Farrell: chairman, chief executive officer B New York, NY 1942. ED University of Detroit BA (1965). PRIM CORP EMPL chairman, chief executive officer: IL Tool Works Inc. CORP AFFIL director: Quaker Oats Co.; director: Sears, Roebuck & Co.; director: Morton International Inc.; director: Premark International Inc.

Foundation Officials

John Carpin: director

Stewart Skinner Hudnut: director B Cincinnati, OH 1939. ED Princeton University AB (1961); Oxford University JD (1962); Harvard University JD (1965); Pace University (1991). PRIM CORP EMPL senior vice president, general counsel, secretary: Illinois Tool Works, Inc. NONPR AFFIL member: Illinois Bar Association; member: Phi Beta Kappa; member: American Bar Association; director: Guild Lyric Opera Chicago.

Michael Lynch: director

Mary Ann Mallahan: secretary

Ted McDougal: secretary, treasurer, director

Michael J. Robinson: treasurer

Harold Byron Smith, Jr.: president

Stephen Byron Smith: director

Grants Analysis

Disclosure Period: fiscal year ending February 28, 2001

Total Grants: $1,793,885*

Number of Grants: 89

Average Grant: $17,010*

Highest Grant: $297,044

Lowest Grant: $1,000

Typical Range: $1,000 to $50,000

*Note: Giving excludes matching gifts, scholarship, United Way. Average grant figure excludes highest grant.

Recent Grants

Note: Grants derived from fiscal 2004 Form 990.

General

723,710	United Way, Chicago, IL
314,700	Scholarship America, Minneapolis, MN
200,000	Northwestern University, Evanston, IL
112,682	United Way Fox Cities Inc., Menasha, WI
100,000	Smith Museum of Stained Glass Windows, Chicago, IL
100,000	United Way, Chicago, IL
84,263	United Way of Central Texas, Temple, TX
83,030	National Merit Scholarship Corporation, Evanston, IL
57,504	Ralph Wilson Youth Clubs of Temple Inc., Temple, TX
57,504	Ralph Wilson Youth Clubs of Temple Inc., Temple, TX

INASMUCH FOUNDATION

Giving Contact

Nancy Woodson, Adv Committee Member
120 N. Robinson, Suite 723 West
Oklahoma City, OK 73102
Phone: (405)235-1356
Fax: (405)235-2340
E-mail: inasmuchfdn@coxinet.net

Description

Founded: 1983

EIN: 731167188

Organization Type: Private Foundation

Giving Locations: CO; OK

Grant Types: General Support, Research, Seed Money.

Donor Information

Founder: Edith Gaylord Harper

Financial Summary

Total Giving: $968,077 (fiscal year ending June 30, 2003); $179,500 (fiscal 2001)

Giving Analysis: Giving for fiscal 2003 includes: foundation grants to United Way ($9,000) fiscal 2001: foundation grants to United Way ($1,000)

Assets: $258,380,549 (fiscal 2003); $5,708,715 (fiscal 2001)

Gifts Received: $243,995,604 (fiscal 2003); $1,020,108 (fiscal 2001); $364,375 (fiscal 1997). Note: In 2003, contributions were received from Edith Gaylord Harper Revocable Trusts. Contributions were received from the Edith G. Harper and Edith G. Harper Estate.

Typical Recipients

Arts & Humanities: Arts Associations & Councils, Arts Institutes, Arts Outreach, Ethnic & Folk Arts, History & Archaeology, Libraries, Literary Arts, Museums/Galleries, Music, Opera, Performing Arts, Public Broadcasting, Theater

Civic & Public Affairs: Botanical Gardens/Parks, Community Foundations, Hispanic Affairs, Nonprofit Management

Education: Arts/Humanities Education, Colleges & Universities, Education Funds, Elementary Education (Public), Faculty Development, Education-General, Literacy, Preschool Education, Private Education (Precollege), Special Education, Student Aid

Environment: Environment-General, Protection, Resource Conservation, Wildlife Protection

Health: Clinics/Medical Centers, Diabetes, Health Organizations, Hospices, Mental Health, Preventive Medicine/Wellness Organizations, Speech & Hearing

Science: Science Museums

Social Services: At-Risk Youth, Child Abuse, Child Welfare, Community Service Organizations, Domestic Violence, Family Planning, Family Services, People with Disabilities, Scouts, Senior Services, Shelters/Homelessness, YMCA/YWCA/YMHA/YWHA, Youth Organizations

Application Procedures

Initial Contact: Submit a concept paper of no more than three pages.

Application Requirements: Include a description of the project and the specific expected outcomes. Also send a description of organization, proof of tax-exempt status, other sources of funding, proposed budget for project, amount requested, and a timetable for the project.

Deadlines: February 15 and August 15.

Restrictions

Contributions are not generally made to individuals or for regular operating expenses. Giving is limited to organizations in Oklahoma and Colorado Springs, CO.

Foundation Officials

David O. Hogan: director

Cathy O. Robbins: advisory committee member

John Hugh Roff, Jr.: director B Wewoka, OK 1931. ED University of Oklahoma AB (1954); University of Oklahoma LLB (1955). PRIM CORP EMPL chairman: PetroUnited Terminals. NONPR AFFIL member: Phi Beta Kappa; chairman advisory board: Salvation Army; member: Order Coif; member advisory board: Center Strategic & International Studies; member council overseers: Jones School Business Administration; trustee: Baylor College Medicine; member: Beta Theta Pi. CLUB AFFIL Houstonian Club; Coronado Club; Houston Country Club.

Patrick T. Rooney: advisory committee member

Robert J. Ross: director

William Jarboe Ross: director B Oklahoma City, OK 1930. ED University of Oklahoma BBA (1952); University of Oklahoma LLB (1954). PRIM CORP EMPL partner: Rainey, Ross, Rice & Binns. CORP AFFIL member admissions & grievences committee: US District Court; director: PetroUnited Terminals. NONPR AFFIL member: Rotary; director: Saint Anthony Hospital Foundation; chairman education committee, member: OK Heritage Association; member: Phi Alpha Delta; member: Newcomen Society; member: OK Bar Association; member: Knights of Columbus; member: Beta Theta Phi; director: Harn Homestead. CLUB AFFIL Oklahoma City Golf & Country Club; Economic Club.

Jeanne H. Smith: adv comm mem

Barbara L. Yalich: advisory committee member

Grants Analysis

Disclosure Period: fiscal year ending June 30, 2003

Total Grants: $959,077*

Number of Grants: 110

Average Grant: $7,927*

Highest Grant: $95,000

Lowest Grant: $200

Typical Range: $5,000 to $10,000

*Note: Giving excludes United Way. Average grant figure excludes highest grant.

Recent Grants

Note: Grants derived from fiscal 2003 Form 990.

General

95,000	Oklahoma Philharmonic Society Inc., Oklahoma City, OK
86,500	Rocky Mountain National Park Associates, Estes Park, CO -- funding to pay off the final note on the miller tract land
63,000	University of Oklahoma Foundation Inc., Oklahoma City, OK -- to establish interdisciplinary training program in child

abuse and neglect as a model program for interdisciplinary training in child maltreatment

50,000	Oklahoma Philharmonic Society Inc., Oklahoma City, OK -- for education concerts
35,000	Oklahoma City University, Oklahoma City, OK -- towards the production cost for "the let's pretend players" and cost of videotaping a performance for schools unable to schedule a live performance
30,000	Young Women's Christian Association of Tulsa, Tulsa, OK -- for east center enhancement project and children's mental health project
25,000	Lyric Theatre of Oklahoma Inc., Oklahoma City, OK -- seed money for feasibility study for fundraising plan for complete renovation of plaza theatre
25,000	Oklahoma Arts Institute Inc., Oklahoma City, OK -- to teach and mentor 275 students
25,000	Oklahoma Chapter of Nature Conservancy, Oklahoma City, OK -- to establish a water use plan for southeastern Oklahoma rivers
20,000	University of Oklahoma Foundation Inc., Norman, OK -- capital campaign for the humanities center at the world literature today

INDEPENDENCE FOUNDATION

Giving Contact

Susan E. Sherman, President
Offices at the Bellevue
200 South Broad Street, Suite 1101
Philadelphia, PA 19102
Phone: (215)985-4009
Fax: (215)985-3989
E-mail: ssherman@independencefoundation.org
Web: http://www.independencefoundation.org

Description

Founded: 1932
EIN: 231352110
Organization Type: Specialized/Single Purpose Foundation
Giving Locations: , Bucks County, PA , Chester County , Delaware County , Montgomery County, Philadelphia metropolitan area
Grant Types: Capital, Challenge, Fellowship, General Support, Matching, Multiyear/Continuing Support, Operating Expenses, Project, Scholarship.

Donor Information

Founder: The Independence Foundation was established in 1932 by William H. Donner, but was originally named the International Cancer Research Foundation. In 1962, the foundation was split to form the William H. Donner Foundation and the Independence Foundation. Mr. Donner (1864-1953) was chairman of the Pennsylvania Steel Company and the Otis Hidden Company, and president of Union Steel Company, Cambria Steel Company, and Donner Steel Company. He was also a founder of the towns of Donora and Monessen, PA.

Financial Summary

Total Giving: $7,613,169 (2003); $7,480,779 (2002); $9,100,000 (2001 approx)
Assets: $99,466,837 (2003); $104,608,608 (2002)

Typical Recipients

Arts & Humanities: Arts Associations & Councils, Arts Centers, Arts Festivals, Arts Funds, Arts Institutes, Ballet, Film & Video, Arts & Humanities-General, Historic Preservation, History & Archaeology, Libraries, Museums/Galleries, Music, Opera, Performing Arts, Public Broadcasting, Theater
Civic & Public Affairs: Botanical Gardens/Parks, Business/Free Enterprise, Civil Rights, Clubs, Community Foundations, Economic Development, Civic & Public Affairs-General, Hispanic Affairs, Housing, Law & Justice, Legal Aid, Professional & Trade Associations, Public Policy, Rural Affairs, Urban & Community Affairs, Women's Affairs, Zoos/Aquariums
Education: Arts/Humanities Education, Colleges & Universities, Community & Junior Colleges, Faculty Development, Education-General, Health & Physical Education, International Studies, Legal Education, Medical Education, Private Education (Precollege), Student Aid
Environment: Wildlife Protection
Health: AIDS/HIV, Cancer, Children's Health/Hospitals, Clinics/Medical Centers, Emergency/Ambulance Services, Eyes/Blindness, Health Policy/Cost Containment, Health Organizations, Hospitals, Hospitals (University Affiliated), Medical Rehabilitation, Medical Research, Mental Health, Nursing Services, Prenatal Health Issues, Preventive Medicine/Wellness Organizations, Public Health, Research/Studies Institutes
International: Human Rights, International Relations
Religion: Religious Welfare
Science: Science Museums, Scientific Centers & Institutes
Social Services: Child Welfare, Community Service Organizations, Domestic Violence, Emergency Relief, Family Planning, Homes, People with Disabilities, Senior Services, Shelters/Homelessness, United Funds/United Ways, YMCA/YWCA/YMHA/YWHA, Youth Organizations

Application Procedures

Initial Contact: Each year, the foundation sends out Request For Proposals packets under the following categories: Nurse Managed Primary Health Care Initiatives; Health and Human Services Initiatives; Legal Aid Initiatives; Culture and Arts Initiatives; the Public Interest Law Fellowship Program; and fellowships in the visual and performing arts. Please contact the foundation for RFP packets and submission deadlines.
Deadlines: Indicated in the Request for Proposal packets.
Review Process: If an application is within the scope of the foundation's interests, the board of directors may grant interviews.

Restrictions

The foundation generally does not give to individuals; building and development projects; or grants for travel, research, or publication.

Additional Information

The foundation requires grant recipients to submit annual written progress reports and financial statements. Site visits and presentations to the board may also be required.
Publications: Annual Report; Guidelines; Request for Proposal Packets; Application Form

Foundation Officials

Hon. Phyllis Whitman Beck: chairman, director B Bronx, NY 1927. ED Brown University AB (1949); Temple University JD (1967). PRIM NONPR EMPL judge: Pennsylvania Superior Court. NONPR AFFIL member, board consultors: Villanova Law School; member: Women in the Profession; director: Temple University Law School; member, board overseers: University Pennsylvania School Nursing; member: Pennsylvania Bar Association; member: Pennsylvanians Modern Courts; member: National Association Women Judges; director: Free Library Philadelphia; member: Joint State Government Committee Domestic Relations Law; president: Foundation Cognitive Therapy; member: American Judicature Society; member: American Law Institute; member: American Bar Foundation.
Andre L. Dennis, Esq.: director
Eugene C. Fish, Esq.: vice president, director B 1910. ED University of Pennsylvania Wharton School (1931); University of Pennsylvania School of Law (1934). PRIM CORP EMPL chairman, secretary, director: Eastern Foundry Co. CORP AFFIL chairman: Peerless Industries Inc.
Andre Mengel, PhD: director
Susan Elizabeth Sherman: president, chief executive officer B Salem, MA 1945. ED Rhode Island Hospital School of Nursing (1966); University of Rhode Island BSN (1969); New York University MA (1971). NONPR AFFIL member: Organization Advancement Adn; member: Sigma Theta Tau; consult: National League Nursing; head department nursing: Community College Philadelphia; instructor: Hunter College; member: American Society Aging; assistant professor: Bronx Community College; member: American Association Community College; member: American Gerontological Society Higher Education.
Theodore Kugler Warner, Jr.: secretary, treasurer B Philadelphia, PA September 13, 1909. ED University of Pennsylvania AB (1931); University of Pennsylvania LLB (1934). PRIM CORP EMPL counsel: Harper & Driver. NONPR AFFIL member: Pennsylvania Bar Association; member: Tau Kappa Epsilon; member: Order Coif; life member: American Law Institute; member: National Tax Association; member: American Bar Association. CLUB AFFIL Union League Club; Aronimink Golf Club; Masons Club.

Grants Analysis

Disclosure Period: calendar year ending 2003
Total Grants: $7,613,169
Number of Grants: 325
Average Grant: $23,425
Highest Grant: $250,000
Lowest Grant: $500
Typical Range: $5,000 to $50,000

Recent Grants

Note: Grants derived from 2003 Form 990.
General

250,000	Regional Performing Arts Center, Philadelphia, PA
200,000	National Nursing Centers Consortium, Philadelphia, PA
190,000	National Nursing Centers Consortium, Philadelphia, PA
150,000	Resources for Human Development Inc., Philadelphia, PA
125,000	La Comunidad Hispana Inc., Kennett Square, PA
125,000	La Comunidad Hispana Inc., Kennett Square, PA
125,000	Mural Arts Advocates, Philadelphia, PA
125,000	Philadelphia Health Management Corporation, Philadelphia, PA
115,000	Community College of Philadelphia, Philadelphia, PA
115,000	Temple University College of Allied Health Professions, Philadelphia, PA

INDIANA MILLS & MANUFACTURING

Company Headquarters

18881 U.S. Hwy. 31 N
Westfield, IN 46074
Web: http://www.imconet.com

Company Description

Revenue: US$117.2 million (2001)
Employees: 650 (2001)
SIC(s): 2399 Fabricated Textile Products Nec, 3429 Hardware Nec.

IMMI Word and Deed Foundation

Giving Contact
Donald C. Boyle, Director
IMMI Word and Deed Foundation, Inc.
PO Box 408
18881 US Hwy 31 North
Westfield, IN 46074-0408
Phone: (317)896-9531
Fax: (317)867-0311
E-mail: dboyle@imminet.com
Web: http://www.imminet.com

Description
Founded: 1991
EIN: 351859427
Organization Type: Corporate Foundation
Grant Types: Fellowship, General Support.

Financial Summary
Total Giving: $1,044,900 (fiscal year ending November 30, 2003); $847,400 (fiscal 2002); $987,625 (fiscal 2001)
Assets: $1,921,486 (fiscal 2003); $1,091,243 (fiscal 2002); $1,509,654 (fiscal 2001)
Gifts Received: $1,714,058 (fiscal 2003); $616,332 (fiscal 2002); $664,429 (fiscal 2001). Note: In fiscal 2003, contributions were received from Uniform Hood Lace ($6,500) IMMI ($2,000), and James R. and Beverly S. Anthony ($1,705,558). In fiscal 2002, contributions were received from Uniform Hood Lace ($5,000) and James R. and Beverly S. Anthony ($611,332). In fiscal 2001, contributions were received from Indiana Mills & Manufacturing Inc. ($532,000) and James R. and Beverly S. Anthony ($132,429). In fiscal 2000, contributions were received from Indiana Mills & Manufacturing, Inc. ($898,000), James R. and Beverly S. Anthony ($117,892), and Uniform Hood Lace, Inc. ($20,000). In fiscal 1999, contributions were received from Indiana Mills & Manufacturing, Inc. ($1,220,000), James R. and Beverly S. Anthony ($893,748), Uniform Hood Lace Co. ($10,000) and Mary Elizabeth Gordon ($10,000).

Typical Recipients
Arts & Humanities: Public Broadcasting
Civic & Public Affairs: African American Affairs, Business/Free Enterprise, Civic & Public Affairs-General, Professional & Trade Associations, Public Policy
Education: Colleges & Universities, Student Aid
Health: Health Organizations, Long-Term Care
International: Foreign Educational Institutions, International Affairs, International Organizations, International Relief Efforts, Missionary/Religious Activities
Religion: Bible Study/Translation, Churches, Religion-General, Jewish Causes, Ministries, Missionary Activities (Domestic), Religious Organizations, Religious Welfare
Social Services: Child Abuse, Community Service Organizations, Emergency Relief, Family Services, Recreation & Athletics, Social Services-General, Youth Organizations

Application Procedures
Initial Contact: Request application form.
Deadlines: None.

Restrictions
Grants are not made to individuals.

Additional Information
Contributions are made to religious organizations for the purpose of assisting them in spreading the gospel of Jesus Christ in Word & Deed.

Corporate Officials
Beverly S. Anthony: secretary B 1934. PRIM CORP EMPL secretary: Indiana Mills & Manufacturing.
James R. Anthony: chairman PRIM CORP EMPL chairman: Indiana Mills & Manufacturing.

Foundation Officials
Beverly S. Anthony: secretary (see above)
James R. Anthony: president (see above)
James T. Anthony: director
Donald C. Boyle: director
Mary Elizabeth Gordan: director
Suzanne Anthony Wilhelm: director

Grants Analysis
Disclosure Period: fiscal year ending November 30, 2003
Total Grants: $1,044,900
Number of Grants: 109
Average Grant: $3,580*
Highest Grant: $559,500
Lowest Grant: $50
Typical Range: $1,000 to $5,000
*Note: Average grant figure excludes two highest grants ($661,800).

Recent Grants
Note: Grants derived from fiscal 2003 Form 990.
General

559,500	Campus Crusade for Christ, Orlando, FL
102,300	River Oaks Community Church, Carmel, IN
50,000	Campus Crusade for Christ, San Clemente, CA
12,000	Insight for Living, Indianapolis, IN
12,000	Lighthouse Ministries Inc., Indianapolis, IN
12,000	Samaritan's Purse, Boone, NC
11,000	WGNR Radio, Anderson, IN
10,100	Northway Christian Community Church, Fishers, IN
7,400	Adelaide College Ministries, Doylestown, PA
6,100	Russian Ministries Inc., Wheaton, IL

INDIANAPOLIS NEWSPAPERS INC.

Company Headquarters
307 N. Pennsylvania St.
Indianapolis, IN 46204

Company Description
Employees: 1,400
SIC(s): 2700 Printing & Publishing.
Parent Company: Central Newspapers Inc., 200 E. Van Buren Street, Phoenix, AZ, United States
Parent Revenue: US$7,381,300,000 (2004)

Operating Locations
Indianapolis Newspapers, Inc. (IN--Indianapolis)

Giving Contact
Jennifer Gombach, Marketing Communications Manager
307 N. Pennsylvania St.
Indianapolis, IN 46204
Phone: (317)444-7023

Description
Organization Type: Corporate Giving Program
Giving Locations: headquarters area only.
Grant Types: General Support, Operating Expenses, Project.

Typical Recipients
Arts & Humanities: Arts Centers, Arts Festivals, Arts Funds, Arts Institutes, Arts Outreach, Ballet, Community Arts, Arts & Humanities-General, Historic Preservation, Libraries, Museums/Galleries, Music, Opera, Performing Arts, Public Broadcasting, Theater, Visual Arts
Civic & Public Affairs: Botanical Gardens/Parks, Business/Free Enterprise, Chambers of Commerce, Economic Development, Employment/Job Training, First Amendment Issues, Civic & Public Affairs-General, Housing, Inner-City Development
Education: Afterschool/Enrichment Programs, Arts/Humanities Education, Education-General, Journalism/Media Education, Literacy, Minority Education, Preschool Education
Environment: Environment-General
Health: Alzheimer's Disease, Eyes/Blindness, Public Health, Speech & Hearing
Social Services: At-Risk Youth, Camps, Child Welfare, Community Centers, Community Service Organizations, Counseling, Day Care, Delinquency & Criminal Rehabilitation, Domestic Violence, Family Planning, Family Services, Food/Clothing Distribution, Homes, Recreation & Athletics, Refugee Assistance, Senior Services, Shelters/Homelessness, Social Services-General, Substance Abuse, United Funds/United Ways, Volunteer Services, Youth Organizations

Application Procedures
Initial Contact: send a brief leter of inquiry
Application Requirements: a description of organization, amount requested, purpose of funds sought, recently audited financial statement, and proof of tax-exempt status

Restrictions
Does not support religious organizations for sectarian purposes, political or lobbying groups, or organizations outside operating areas.

Corporate Officials
Eugene S. Pulliam: senior vice president, publisher PRIM CORP EMPL senior vice president, publisher: Indianapolis Newspapers Inc.
Jeffrey B. Rogers: chief financial officer PRIM CORP EMPL chief financial officer: Indianapolis Newspapers Inc.

Grants Analysis
Typical Range: $2,500 to $5,000

ING NORTH AMERICA INSURANCE CORP.

Company Headquarters
Atlanta, GA
Web: http://www.ing-usa.com

Company Description
Former Name: Life Insurance Co. of Georgia.
Employees: 3,600
SIC(s): 6081 Foreign Banks--Branches & Agencies, 6300 Insurance Carriers.
Parent Company: ING Americas, 57800 Powers Ferry Rd. NW, Atlanta, GA, United States
Parent Assets: US$759,978,700,000 (2001)

Operating Locations
ING North America Atlanta Operations (GA--Atlanta); ING North America Insurance Corp. (GA--Atlanta)

Nonmonetary Support
Type: In-kind Services; Loaned Executives

Giving Contact

Karen Burnsed, Manager
PO Box 105006
Atlanta, GA 30348-5006
Phone: (770)980-5100
Fax: (770)850-7608

Description

Organization Type: Corporate Giving Program
Giving Locations: GA: southeastern states.
Grant Types: Employee Matching Gifts, General Support, Operating Expenses, Project.

Typical Recipients

Arts & Humanities: Arts Associations & Councils, Arts Centers, Dance, Ethnic & Folk Arts, Historic Preservation, Libraries, Museums/Galleries, Music, Theater
Civic & Public Affairs: Business/Free Enterprise, Employment/Job Training, Professional & Trade Associations, Safety, Zoos/Aquariums
Education: Business Education, Colleges & Universities, Economic Education, Education Associations, Literacy, Minority Education, Science/Mathematics Education
Health: Health Policy/Cost Containment, Health Organizations, Medical Research, Mental Health, Single-Disease Health Associations
Religion: Religious Welfare
Social Services: Child Welfare, Community Service Organizations, Domestic Violence, Family Services, Senior Services, Substance Abuse, United Funds/United Ways, Youth Organizations

Application Procedures

Initial Contact: Send proposal any time, including a description and history of organization, amount and purpose of funds sought, a recently audited financial statement, proof of tax-exempt status, a list of directors and officers, and a budget breakdown including administrative expenses. The National Charities Information Bureau's review of organization will be heavily considered in determining soundness of contribution.

Additional Information

Company reports contributions level and value of nonmonetary support are confidential.

Corporate Officials

Michael W. Cunningham: chief financial officer, chief executive officer PRIM CORP EMPL chief financial officer: ING North American Atlanta.
Robert Glenn Hilliard: chairman B Anderson, SC 1943. ED Clemson University (1965); George Washington University (1968). PRIM CORP EMPL chairman: ING North American Insurance Corp. CORP AFFIL chairman: Netherlands Insurance Co.; director: Liberty Corp.; president, director: Liberty Life Insurance Co.; director: Cosmos Broadcasting Corp.; chairman: ING North America Atlanta; director: Carolina First. NONPR AFFIL director: SC Life Health Insurance Guarantee Association; director, vice chairman: YMCA Camp Greenville Management Board; director: North Carolina Life Health Insurance Guarantee Association; member: SC Bar Association; director: Greenville Association Retarded Children; member: Greenville County Bar Association; st vice president: American Council Life Insurance; member: American Society of Corporate Secretaries; member: American Bar Association.
Jim Thompson: president, chief executive officer PRIM CORP EMPL president, chief executive officer: ING North American Atlanta.

Grants Analysis

Typical Range: $1,000 to $2,500

LOUISE H. AND DAVID S. INGALLS FOUNDATION

Giving Contact

Jane Watson
20600 Chagrin Boulevard, Suite 301
Shaker Heights, OH 44122
Phone: (216)921-6000
Fax: (216)921-7709
E-mail: wwwatson@visnet.com

Description

Founded: 1953
EIN: 346516550
Organization Type: General Purpose Foundation
Giving Locations: CA: Ohio, Connecticut, Virginia, and New York; NY; OH; VT
Grant Types: Capital, General Support, Project.

Donor Information

Founder: Incorporated in 1953 by Edith Ingalls Vignos, Louise Ingalls Brown, David S. Ingalls Jr., Jane I. Davison, Anne I. Lawrence, the late Louise H. Ingalls, and the late David S. Ingalls.

Financial Summary

Total Giving: $902,000 (2002); $1,800,000 (2001)
Giving Analysis: Giving for 2002 includes: foundation scholarships ($4,400)
Assets: $24,327,920 (2002)

Typical Recipients

Arts & Humanities: Arts Centers, Arts Funds, Arts Institutes, Arts Outreach, Ballet, Film & Video, Historic Preservation, History & Archaeology, Libraries, Museums/Galleries, Music, Performing Arts, Public Broadcasting, Theater
Civic & Public Affairs: Botanical Gardens/Parks, Community Foundations, Employment/Job Training, Civic & Public Affairs-General, Municipalities/Towns, Philanthropic Organizations, Public Policy, Urban & Community Affairs, Zoos/Aquariums
Education: Arts/Humanities Education, Colleges & Universities, Education Funds, Faculty Development, Education-General, International Studies, Legal Education, Medical Education, Private Education (Precollege), Public Education (Precollege), Student Aid
Environment: Forestry, Environment-General, Resource Conservation, Wildlife Protection
Health: Children's Health/Hospitals, Clinics/Medical Centers, Emergency/Ambulance Services, Eyes/Blindness, Health Organizations, Hospitals, Long-Term Care, Medical Rehabilitation, Nursing Services, Single-Disease Health Associations, Transplant Networks/Donor Banks
International: Foreign Educational Institutions
Religion: Churches, Religion-General
Science: Science Museums, Scientific Centers & Institutes, Scientific Labs, Scientific Research
Social Services: Camps, Child Welfare, Community Centers, Community Service Organizations, Counseling, Family Planning, Family Services, People with Disabilities, Recreation & Athletics, Senior Services, Social Services-General, United Funds/United Ways, YMCA/YWCA/YMHA/YWHA, Youth Organizations

Application Procedures

Initial Contact: The foundation has no formal grant application procedure or application form.
Deadlines: None.

Restrictions

The foundation makes grants to public charities only. Grants are not made to individuals.

Foundation Officials

James R. Bright: assistant secretary
Barbara Brown: president
Endicott P. Davidson: trustee
Rebekah Ingalls: secretary, trustee

Anne I. Lawrence: vice president
John T. Lawrence, Jr.: treasurer CORP AFFIL director: America Annuity Group Inc.
Caren Sturges: trustee
Jane W. Watson: assistant secretary, assistant treasurer

Grants Analysis

Disclosure Period: calendar year ending 2002
Total Grants: $897,600
Number of Grants: 35
Average Grant: $18,450*
Highest Grant: $275,000
Lowest Grant: $4,400
Typical Range: $5,000 to $50,000 and $10,000 to $25,000
*Note: Average grant excludes highest grant.

Recent Grants

Note: Grants derived from 2002 Form 990.
General

275,000	Cleveland Museum of Art, Cleveland, OH
100,000	Taft Museum of Art, Cincinnati, OH
80,000	Cleveland Botanical Garden, Cleveland, OH
50,000	Cleveland Botanical Garden, Cleveland, OH
50,000	Connecticut River Museum, Essex, CT
50,000	University School, Hunting Valley, OH
25,000	Gulf of Maine Aquarium, Portland, ME
25,000	Princeton Symphony Orchestra, Princeton, NJ
20,000	Cleveland Zoological Society, Cleveland, OH
20,000	Hopewell Inn, Mesopotamia, OH

INTEGRA BANK

Company Headquarters

201 N. Main Street
Bridgeport, IL 62417-1521
Web: http://www.integrabank.com

Company Description

Former Name: Gallatin National Bank.
Assets: US$16 million (2001)
Employees: 5 (2001)
SIC(s): 6000 Depository Institutions.
Parent Company: Integra Financial Group, 14901 Park Lake Dr., No. PH6, Fort Myers, FL, United States

Operating Locations

Integra Bank of Uniontown/National City (PA--Uniontown)

Nonmonetary Support

Type: Loaned Employees

Giving Contact

Leo Krantez, President & Chief Executive Officer
2 W. Main St.
Uniontown, PA 15401
Phone: (412)438-3551

Description

Organization Type: Corporate Giving Program
Giving Locations: headquarters area only.
Grant Types: Capital, Emergency, Employee Matching Gifts, General Support, Operating Expenses, Project, Seed Money.

Typical Recipients

Arts & Humanities: Arts & Humanities-General, Historic Preservation, Libraries, Performing Arts, Theater
Civic & Public Affairs: Botanical Gardens/Parks, Chambers of Commerce, Clubs, Economic Develop-

ment, Employment/Job Training, Civic & Public Affairs-General, Housing
Education: Colleges & Universities, Community & Junior Colleges, Education Associations, Education-General
Health: Cancer, Health-General, Hospitals
Social Services: Community Centers, Community Service Organizations, Shelters/Homelessness, Social Services-General, United Funds/United Ways

Application Procedures
Initial Contact: Send a full proposal. Include a description of organization, amount requested, purpose of funds sought, and proof of tax-exempt status. Also, include a list of board members.

Restrictions
Does not support individuals, religious organizations for sectarian purposes, or political or lobbying groups.

Corporate Officials
Leo Krantez: president, chief executive officer PRIM CORP EMPL president, chief executive officer: Integra Bank of Uniontown/National City.

Grants Analysis
Typical Range: $1,000 to $2,500

INTERKAL INC.

Company Headquarters
5981 E. Cork St.
PO Box 2107
Kalamazoo, MI 49003
Web: http://www.interkal.com

Company Description
Revenue: US$16.9 million (2001)
Employees: 160 (2001)
SIC(s): 2531 Public Building & Related Furniture.
Parent Company: Kotobuki Corp., 1-22-5 Sumitomo Seimei Bldg. 3F, Hamamatsu-cho, Minato-ku, Tokyo, Japan

Operating Locations
Interkal, Inc. (MI--Kalamazoo)

Nonmonetary Support
Type: Donated Equipment; Donated Products

Giving Contact
Dick Patterson, Pres./CEO
PO Box 2107
Kalamazoo, MI 49003
Phone: (616)349-1521
Fax: (616)349-6530
E-mail: dpatterson@interkal.com

Description
Organization Type: Corporate Giving Program
Giving Locations: headquarters and operating communities.
Grant Types: General Support.

Typical Recipients
Arts & Humanities: Arts Associations & Councils, Arts Centers, Community Arts, Libraries, Music, Performing Arts
Civic & Public Affairs: Economic Development
Education: Business Education, Colleges & Universities, International Exchange, International Studies
Social Services: Family Services, United Funds/United Ways

Application Procedures
Initial Contact: Send brief letter of inquiry, including a description of organization and purpose of funds sought.

Restrictions
Does not support dinners or special events, fraternal organizations, goodwill advertising, individuals, political or lobbying groups, or religious organizations for sectarian purposes.

Corporate Officials
Minoru Amemiya: chairman, chief executive officer B 1942. PRIM CORP EMPL president: GDS Seating Inc. ADD CORP EMPL chairman, chief executive officer: Interkal.
Brian Gould: controller, treasurer PRIM CORP EMPL controller, treasurer: Interkal.
Richard L. Patterson: president PRIM CORP EMPL president: Interkal.

Grants Analysis
Typical Range: $250 to $500

INTERMOUNTAIN GAS CO.

Company Headquarters
555 S. Cole Rd.
Boise, ID 83709

Company Description
Employees: 315
SIC(s): 4900 Electric, Gas & Sanitary Services, 4924 Natural Gas Distribution.
Parent Company: Intermountain Industries Inc., 555 S. Cole Road, Boise, ID, United States

Operating Locations
Intermountain Gas Co. (ID--Boise)

Nonmonetary Support
Type: Donated Equipment; In-kind Services; Loaned Employees; Loaned Executives

Intermountain Gas Industries Foundation

Giving Contact
James E. Simmerman, Manager, Human Resources
PO Box 7608
Boise, ID 83707
Phone: (208)377-6000
Fax: (208)377-6097

Description
EIN: 820431608
Organization Type: Corporate Foundation
Giving Locations: headquarters and operating communities.
Grant Types: General Support.

Financial Summary
Total Giving: $184,355 (fiscal year ending September 30, 2003); $211,897 (fiscal 2001)
Giving Analysis: Giving for fiscal 2001 includes: foundation scholarships ($9,600); foundation grants to United Way ($19,250)
Assets: $309,106 (fiscal 2003); $248,040 (fiscal 2002); $342,566 (fiscal 2001)
Gifts Received: $175,000 (fiscal 2003); $175,000 (fiscal 2001); $132,500 (fiscal 2000). Note: In fiscal 2001 and 2003, contributions were received from Intermountain Gas Co. In fiscal 1996 and 2000, contributions were received from Intermountain Gas Co. ($150,000) and IGI Resources ($50,000).

Typical Recipients
Arts & Humanities: Arts Associations & Councils, Arts Centers, Arts Festivals, Libraries, Museums/Galleries, Music, Performing Arts, Public Broadcast-

ing, Theater
Civic & Public Affairs: Business/Free Enterprise, Clubs, Community Foundations, Economic Development, Civic & Public Affairs-General, Housing, Legal Aid, Parades/Festivals, Philanthropic Organizations, Public Policy, Rural Affairs, Urban & Community Affairs, Zoos/Aquariums
Education: Afterschool/Enrichment Programs, Agricultural Education, Arts/Humanities Education, Business Education, Colleges & Universities, Economic Education, Education Funds, Engineering/Technological Education, Private Education (Precollege), Public Education (Precollege), Secondary Education (Private), Student Aid, Vocational & Technical Education
Environment: Environment-General, Protection, Resource Conservation, Watershed
Health: Clinics/Medical Centers, Diabetes, Emergency/Ambulance Services, Health Funds, Heart, Hospitals
International: Health Care/Hospitals, International Organizations, Missionary/Religious Activities
Religion: Churches, Religious Welfare
Social Services: Animal Protection, Child Welfare, Community Service Organizations, Emergency Relief, Family Services, Food/Clothing Distribution, People with Disabilities, Recreation & Athletics, Scouts, Special Olympics, Substance Abuse, United Funds/United Ways, YMCA/YWCA/YMHA/YWHA, Youth Organizations

Application Procedures
Initial Contact: Request application form.
Deadlines: None.

Corporate Officials
William C. Glynn: president, chief executive officer, director administration, treasurer B Monticello, IA 1944. ED Loras College (1968); Boise State University (1979). PRIM CORP EMPL president, chief executive officer, director: Intermountain Gas Co. CORP AFFIL president: Intermountain Industries. NONPR AFFIL member: American Gas Association; director: Pacific Coast Gas Association.
N. Charles Hedemark: executive vice president, chief operating officer, director B Boise, ID 1942. ED College of Idaho (1964). PRIM CORP EMPL executive vice president, chief operating officer, director: Intermountain Gas Co. CORP AFFIL director: Home Federal Savings & Loan. NONPR AFFIL director: Blue Cross ID.
Richard Hokin: chairman, director PRIM CORP EMPL chairman, director: Intermountain Gas Co.
Jeffrey Kent Lebens: senior vice president financial & administration, treasurer B Minneapolis, MN 1944. ED University of Washington (1972). PRIM CORP EMPL senior vice president financial & administration, treasurer: Intermountain Gas Co. CORP AFFIL vice president,treasurer,chief financial officer: IGI Resources; vice president,treasurer,chief financial officer: Intermountain Industries.

Foundation Officials
William C. Glynn: director (see above)
N. Charles Hedemark: director (see above)
Richard Hokin: director (see above)
Paul Powell: director
S. Kennard Smith: director

Grants Analysis
Disclosure Period: fiscal year ending September 30, 2003
Total Grants: $151,805*
Number of Grants: 116
Average Grant: $1,052*
Highest Grant: $30,800
Lowest Grant: $25
Typical Range: $500 to $5,000
*Note: Giving excludes scholarships; United Way. Average grant figure excludes highest grant.

Recent Grants

Note: Grants derived from fiscal 2003 Form 990.
General

30,800	Idaho State University Foundation, Pocatello, ID
14,000	United Way of Treasure Valley, Boise, ID
9,738	Boy Scouts of America, Irving, TX
7,000	Boise Philharmonic Association Inc., Boise, ID
6,790	Boise State University, Boise, ID
5,233	Idaho Public Television, Boise, ID
5,000	Boys and Girls Clubs of Ada County, Garden City, ID
5,000	Idaho Governor's Challenge, Boise, ID
5,000	Project S.H.A.R.E., Carlisle, PA
5,000	Project Warmth, Kansas City, MO

INTERNATIONAL BUSINESS MACHINES (IBM)

Company Headquarters

1133 Westchester Ave.
White Plains, NY 10604
Web: http://www.ibm.com

Company Description

Ticker: IBM
Exchange: NYSE
Acquired: Sequent Computer Systems (2001).
Revenue: US$96.293 billion (2004)
Profit: US$8.43 billion (2004)
Employees: 319,876 (2002)
Fortune Rank: 10, per FORTUNE Magazine's list of 500 Largest U.S. Corporations (2004).

Nonmonetary Support

Value: $86,700,000 (2000); $82,000,000 (1999); $79,000,000 (1998 approx)
Type: Donated Equipment; Donated Products; In-kind Services
Volunteer Programs: The IBM Fund for Community Service recognizes and encourages the involvement of IBM employees and their spouses as volunteers in their local communities. Through the Fund, IBM makes financial and IBM product grants to specific projects of eligible community organizations and schools, provided an employee, retiree or spouse is actively involved on a continuing basis.
Note: Contact for nonmonetary support: Corporate Community Relations local or corporate staff. Nonmonetary figures are calculated at retail value.

IBM International Foundation

Giving Contact

Stanley S. Litow, President, Director
IBM Corp.
New Orchard Road
Armonk, NY 10504
Phone: (914)765-1900
Fax: (914)499-7624
Web: http://www.ibm.com/ibm/ibmgives

Alternate Contact

Note: For local projects, contact the Corporate Relations Manager at the local IBM office.

Description

Founded: 1985
EIN: 133267906
Organization Type: Corporate Foundation
Former Name: IBM South Africa Project Fund.
Giving Locations: principally near operating locations and to national organizations.
Grant Types: Emergency, Employee Matching Gifts, Fellowship, General Support, Multiyear/Continuing Support.
Note: Matching Grant Program: There is a maximum of $5,000 cash per donor per institution, up to $10,000 in gifts annually. Cash match: Active employee 1 to 1; retirees 0.5 to 1. Equipment match for higher education: Active employees 3 to 1; retirees 1.5 to 1. Equipment match for hospitals, hospices, nursing homes, cultural and environmental institutions: active employees 2 to 1; retirees 1 to 1. The company also sponsors a K-12 Matching Grant Program for donation of equipment to K-12 schools.

Financial Summary

Total Giving: $10,209,092 (2003); $126,000,000 (2002 approx); $11,292,796 (2001). Note: 2000 figure given by foundation.
Assets: $155,189,058 (2003); $139,204,116 (2002); $153,475,604 (2001)
Gifts Received: $3,350,000 (2003); $28,100,000 (2001); $10,614,843 (2000). Note: Contributions were received from IBM Corp.

Typical Recipients

Arts & Humanities: Arts Associations & Councils, Arts Centers, Arts Funds, Arts Institutes, Community Arts, Dance, Ethnic & Folk Arts, Historic Preservation, Libraries, Museums/Galleries, Music, Opera, Performing Arts, Public Broadcasting, Theater, Visual Arts
Civic & Public Affairs: Civil Rights, Employment/Job Training, Civic & Public Affairs-General, Nonprofit Management, Public Policy, Urban & Community Affairs, Women's Affairs, Zoos/Aquariums
Education: Afterschool/Enrichment Programs, Business Education, Colleges & Universities, Community & Junior Colleges, Education Associations, Education Funds, Education Reform, Engineering/Technological Education, Faculty Development, Education-General, Literacy, Minority Education, Preschool Education, Private Education (Precollege), Public Education (Precollege), Science/Mathematics Education, Special Education, Student Aid
Environment: Environment-General
Health: Health Policy/Cost Containment, Health Organizations, Hospitals, Mental Health, Single-Disease Health Associations
International: Foreign Arts Organizations, Foreign Educational Institutions, International-General, Health Care/Hospitals, International Organizations, International Peace & Security Issues
Science: Science Exhibits & Fairs, Science Museums, Scientific Organizations
Social Services: Child Welfare, Community Service Organizations, Delinquency & Criminal Rehabilitation, Emergency Relief, Family Services, People with Disabilities, Senior Services, Substance Abuse, United Funds/United Ways, Veterans, Volunteer Services, Youth Organizations

Application Procedures

Initial Contact: Send a two-page letter.
Application Requirements: Send a brief statement fully describing the mission of the organization, the amount requested, and purpose of contribution; description of problem to be addressed, proposed solution and how IBM technology and volunteers will be incorporated (if appropriate); proof of tax-exempt status; name, address, and telephone number of the project contact; project budget with anticipated sources of income; past managerial experiences; controls to ensure funds are used as described; and a plan to measure results.
Deadlines: None.
Review Process: Unsolicited proposals are reviewed on an ongoing basis, but funding is limited. Notification is usually sent within one month.
Evaluative Criteria: Priority given to requests involving IBM technology or employee volunteers; consideration is also given to organizations currently receiving other types of company support.
Decision Notification: Rejections or additional information requests usually given within one month.
Notes: Majority of funding is initiated by IBM and does not stem from unsolicited proposals. Videotapes and supplemental materials are strongly discouraged at initial stage.

Restrictions

Does not support individuals; political, labor, religious, or fraternal organizations; sports groups; organizations without tax-exempt status; operating cost requests from United Way member organizations; raffles or telethons; auctions; capital campaigns; chairs; construction and renovation; endowments; scholarships; and company generally does not underwrite conferences, sports competitions, symposia, or controversial organizations or projects.

Additional Information

Publications: Corporate Support Programs Guidelines; Reinventing Education Guidelines

Corporate Officials

Paula W. Baker: director corporate community relations PRIM CORP EMPL director corporate support plans & programs: International Business Machines Corp.
Nicholas M. Donofrio: senior vice president technology & manufacturing ED Rensselaer Polytechnic Institute BS (1967); Syracuse University MS (1971). PRIM CORP EMPL senior vice president technology manufacturing: International Business Machines Corp. CORP AFFIL director: Bank of New York. NONPR AFFIL trustee: Rensselaer Polytechnic Institute; fellowship: Royal Academy of Engineering-UK; member: National Academy of Engineering; member: American Academy of Arts and Sciences; fellowship: Institute of Electrical & Electronics Engineers.
Abby V. Kohnstamm: senior vice president, marketing B Los Angeles, CA 1954. ED New York University MA; New York University MBA; Tufts University BA; Tufts University BA. CORP AFFIL director: Tiffany & Co. NONPR AFFIL board of overseers: NY University Stern School of Business; trustee: Tufts University; director: Association of National Advertisers Inc..
Stanley S. Litow: vice president PRIM CORP EMPL vice president community relations: International Business Machines Corp. NONPR AFFIL director: Albert Shanker Institute.
Samuel J. Palmisano: chairman, president, chief operating officer, director ED Johns Hopkins University. PRIM CORP EMPL president, chief operating officer, director: International Business Machines Corp.
Robert F. Woods: vice president, controller ED Villanova University Bs; Widener University MBA. CORP AFFIL senior vice president, chief financial officer: IKON Office Solutions Inc..

Giving Program Officials

Robin Willner: member ED Columbia University BS. PRIM CORP EMPL director corporate social policy & programs: International Business Machines Corp. NONPR AFFIL director: Grantmakers for Education; director: National Center for Educational Accountability; director: Center for Education Policy; director: City Project in New York City.

Foundation Officials

Paula W. Baker: vice president
Paula W. Baker: vice president (see above)
A. Bonzani: secretary
Cassio A. Calil: treasurer
R. J. Carroll: controller
Gregory C. Hubertus: assistant treasurer
Abby V. Kohnstamm: vice chairman, director (see above)
Stanley S. Litow: president, director (see above)
Samuel J. Palmisano: director, chairman (see above)
John Torkildsen: assistant controller

Robin Willner: director (see above)
Robert F. Woods: director (see above)

Grants Analysis
Disclosure Period: calendar year ending 2003
Total Grants: $1,588,613*
*Note: Giving excludes fellowship; matching gifts.

Recent Grants
Note: Grants derived from 2003 Form 990.
General

3,208,415	IBM United Kingdom Trust, Portsmouth United Kingdom -- cash grant to deliver educational programs
1,607,000	IBM Fellowship Grants, White Plains, NY -- to provide funds for students
705,000	IBM Italy Foundation, White Plains, NY -- cash grant to support educational initiative
419,000	Kidsmart Early Learning Program, White Plains, NY -- to provide educational materials
155,000	United Way of Canada, Ottawa, ON Canada -- cash grant to support local initiatives
100,000	Reinventing Education, White Plains, NY -- towards reinventing education
60,000	TryScience and Reinventing Education, Queens, NY -- towards teacher training
24,000	Non Profit Open Source Initiative -- cash grant to educate the non profit community
15,000	Latin American Basic Education Initiative, Washington, DC -- cash grant to pay annual dues for IIF

INTERNATIONAL MULTIFOODS CORP.

Company Headquarters
Minnetonka, MN
Web: http://www.multifoods.com

Company Description
Ticker: IMC
Exchange: OTC
Employees: 6,807
SIC(s): 2045 Prepared Flour Mixes & Doughs, 5145 Confectionery, 5149 Groceries & Related Products Nec.

Operating Locations
International Multifoods Corp. (CA--La Mirada, Los Angeles, Rialto, Riverside; CO--Denver; CT--East Windsor; FL--Orlando; GA--Atlanta; IL--Melrose Park, Woodridge; IN--Noblesville; KS--Bonner Springs; KY--Louisville; MA--Billerica, Malden; MI--Belleville; MN--Motley, Rice; MO--Carthage, Piedmont; NJ--Parsippany, Paulsboro; NM--Albuquerque; NY--Lockport, New Rochelle; NC--Greensboro; OH--Elyria, Twinsburg; TX--Dallas, Grand Prairie, Houston; WA--Seattle)

Nonmonetary Support
Type: Donated Products
Volunteer Programs: Company donates to nonprofit organizations where employees volunteer through its Employee Volunteer Bonus program. Additionally, the company sponsors the Employee Board Member Bonus where employees serve on nonprofit boards.
Note: Products are donated through the Second Harvest Food Bank network. Annual nonmonetary support approximately $100,000.

International Multifoods Charitable Foundation

Giving Contact
Karen Anderson, Foundation Administrator
110 Cheshire Ln., Suite 300
Minnetonka, MN 55305-1060
Phone: (952)594-3568
Fax: (952)594-3377

Description
EIN: 237064628
Organization Type: Corporate Foundation
Giving Locations: MN: Minneapolis, St. Paul Major principally near operating locations and to national organizations.
Grant Types: Capital, Employee Matching Gifts, General Support, Matching, Operating Expenses.
Note: Employee matching gift ratio: 1 to 1 for higher education only.

Financial Summary
Total Giving: $140,462 (fiscal year ending February 28, 2003); $221,600 (fiscal 2001)
Giving Analysis: Giving for fiscal 2003 includes: foundation matching gifts ($3,150); foundation grants to United Way ($137,312); fiscal 2002: foundation ($240,150); fiscal 2001: foundation ($224,560)
Assets: $167,724 (fiscal 2003); $240,150 (fiscal 2002); $224,560 (fiscal 2001)
Gifts Received: $300,000 (fiscal 2003); $200,000 (fiscal 2000); $200,000 (fiscal 1998). Note: Foundation receives contributions from International Multifoods Corporation.

Typical Recipients
Arts & Humanities: Arts Institutes, Community Arts, Ethnic & Folk Arts, Libraries, Museums/Galleries, Music, Opera, Theater
Civic & Public Affairs: Botanical Gardens/Parks, Clubs, Civic & Public Affairs-General, Hispanic Affairs, Municipalities/Towns
Education: Agricultural Education, Business Education, Colleges & Universities, Economic Education, Education Funds, Elementary Education (Public), Faculty Development, Education-General, Leadership Training, Medical Education, Minority Education, Private Education (Precollege), Public Education (Precollege), Religious Education, Science/Mathematics Education, Special Education, Student Aid
Environment: Environment-General
Health: Diabetes
Religion: Churches
Science: Science Museums
Social Services: At-Risk Youth, Big Brothers/Big Sisters, Child Welfare, Community Service Organizations, Crime Prevention, Family Services, Food/Clothing Distribution, People with Disabilities, Recreation & Athletics, Scouts, Substance Abuse, United Funds/United Ways, Volunteer Services, YMCA/YWCA/YMHA/YWHA, Youth Organizations

Application Procedures
Initial Contact: Request guidelines from the foundation, then send written proposal.
Application Requirements: Include name, history, and purpose of organization; proof of tax-exempt status; statement of current objectives, priorities, how organization fits Multifoods' priorities, and summary of past two years' accomplishments; list of board of directors; copy of recent annual report; copy of IRS Form 990 and current year's operating budget.
Deadlines: May 31.
Review Process: Applications are screened by community affairs staff and reviewed by contributions committee.
Evaluative Criteria: Proximity of service area to company operating locations. For funding for a specific project, include a description of organization, in-

cluding reasons for it, problem addressed, timetable and expected results; detailed budget including sources of income; method of evaluation; plans for sustaining project support; statement of how project fits company's giving priorities.
Decision Notification: Contributions committee meets biannually; notification usually within 90 days of receipt.

Restrictions
The company does not support religious groups for sectarian purposes; political or lobbying organizations; individuals; loans or investments; fundraisers such as luncheons, dinners, special events, or advertisements; industry, trade or professional association memberships; organizations receiving more than 25% of their support from the United Way or government agencies; or medical research, treatment, or equipment. No grants are made to endowment funds, and no more than 10% to 12% of the annual contributions budget will be designated to capital grants.
The company does not consider requests for support through telephone solicitation or form letters.

Additional Information
Grantees are required to provide periodic progress reports; site visits by company staff also may be requested. Company gives 2% of its pretax profits for charitable activities. Foundation strives for a 30/70 ratio between the Twin Cities and other major company locations.
Publications: Multifoods Community Connection

Corporate Officials
Frank W. Bonvino: vice president, secretary, general counsel B Mount Vernon, NY 1941. ED Coe College BA (1963); William Mitchell College of Law JD (1968). PRIM CORP EMPL vice president, secretary, general counsel: International Multifoods Corp. CORP AFFIL secretary: Multifoods Distribution Group Inc. NONPR AFFIL member: American Bar Association; member: Minnesota State Bar Association.
John E. Byom: chief financial officer
Gary E. Costley: chairman, president, chief executive officer, director B 1943. ED Oregon State University PhD; Oregon State University MS (1970). PRIM CORP EMPL chairman, president, chief executive officer, director: International Multifoods Corp. CORP AFFIL director: Bush Brothers; chairman: Multifoods Distribution Group Inc.
Ralph Hargrow: senior vice president Human Resources
Jill W. Schmidt: vice president communications B 1958. PRIM CORP EMPL vice president communications: International Multifoods Corp.
Dan C. Swander: president, chief operating officer

Foundation Officials
John E. Byom: vice president, director (see above)
Gary E. Costley: chief executive officer, director (see above)
Dan C. Swander: president, director (see above)

Grants Analysis
Disclosure Period: fiscal year ending February 28, 2003
Total Grants: $322,838*
Number of Grants: 21
Average Grant: $15,370
Typical Range: $500 to $5,000
*Note: Grants analysis provided by foundation.

Recent Grants
Note: Grants derived from fiscal 2004 Form 990.
General

110,857	United Way of Minneapolis Area, Minneapolis, MN
11,594	Pettis County United Way, Sedalia, MO
42	Eastern Niagara United Way, Lockport, NY

INTERNATIONAL PAPER CO.

Company Headquarters
400 Atlantic St.
Stamford, CT 06921
Web: http://www.ipaper.com

Company Description
Ticker: IP
Exchange: NYSE
Acquired: Champion International Corp..
Revenue: US$26.722 billion (2004)
Profit: (US$35 million) (2004)
Employees: 83000 (2003)
Fortune Rank: 70, per FORTUNE Magazine's list of 500 Largest U.S. Corporations (2004).

Nonmonetary Support
Value: $500,000 (2002 approx)
Type: Donated Equipment; Donated Products
Note: For nonmonetary support contact the local facility.

International Paper Co. Foundation

Giving Contact
Phyllis Epp, Executive Director
400 Atlantic Street
Stamford, CT 06921
Phone: (901)763-6000
Web: http://www.internationalpaper.com
Note: In communities where company maintains facilities, contact mill or plant manager, or communications, human resources, or public affairs manager.

Alternate Contact
Phyllis Epp, Executive Director
International Paper Co. Foundation
400 Atlantic Street
Stamford, CT 06921
Phone: (914)397-1500

Description
EIN: 136155080
Organization Type: Corporate Foundation
Giving Locations: nationally; principally near operating locations and to national organizations.
Grant Types: Award, Employee Matching Gifts, General Support.
Note: Employee matching gift ratio: 2 to 1 for employee gifts up to $200 each year; 1 to 1 for gifts over $200. Minimum gift foundation will match is $25, the maximum amount is $1,000 per employee annually. The foundation also supports specific educational and environmental programs.

Financial Summary
Total Giving: $7,341,973 (2002); $7,189,151 (2001).
Note: Contributes through corporate direct giving program and foundation.
Giving Analysis: Giving for 2001 includes: foundation ($6,897,000); corporate direct giving ($7,189,000).
Assets: $38,766,263 (2002); $45,983,617 (2001)
Gifts Received: $5,343,492 (2002); $530,173 (2001); $353,695 (2000). Note: Contributions are received from International Paper Co.

Typical Recipients
Arts & Humanities: Arts Associations & Councils, Arts Centers, Arts Festivals, Arts Funds, Dance, Arts & Humanities-General, Historic Preservation, History & Archaeology, Libraries, Museums/Galleries, Music, Opera, Performing Arts, Public Broadcasting, The-

ater
Civic & Public Affairs: Botanical Gardens/Parks, Business/Free Enterprise, Chambers of Commerce, Community Foundations, Civic & Public Affairs-General, Municipalities/Towns, Philanthropic Organizations, Professional & Trade Associations, Public Policy, Safety, Urban & Community Affairs, Women's Affairs, Zoos/Aquariums
Education: Agricultural Education, Business Education, Colleges & Universities, Community & Junior Colleges, Economic Education, Education Funds, Education Reform, Elementary Education (Private), Elementary Education (Public), Engineering/Technological Education, Environmental Education, Education-General, Literacy, Minority Education, Preschool Education, Private Education (Precollege), Public Education (Precollege), Science/Mathematics Education, Secondary Education (Private), Secondary Education (Public), Student Aid
Environment: Energy, Forestry, Environment-General, Protection, Resource Conservation, Wildlife Protection
Health: Children's Health/Hospitals, Clinics/Medical Centers, Emergency/Ambulance Services, Health Organizations, Hospitals
International: International Environmental Issues
Religion: Dioceses, Religious Organizations, Religious Welfare
Science: Science-General, Science Museums, Scientific Centers & Institutes, Scientific Labs
Social Services: Child Welfare, Community Centers, Community Service Organizations, Day Care, Emergency Relief, Family Services, Food/Clothing Distribution, Homes, Recreation & Athletics, Senior Services, Shelters/Homelessness, Social Services-General, Substance Abuse, United Funds/United Ways, Veterans, Volunteer Services, YMCA/YWCA/YMHA/YWHA, Youth Organizations

Application Procedures
Initial Contact: Request application form from local facility; send to manager of local International Paper Co. facility.
Application Requirements: Include a brief background of organization, including board of directors; concise description of program, budget, and objectives; audited financial statement; IRS tax-exemption letter; current funding sources and specific amounts; current annual report; including amount requested requested.
Deadlines: Check with local facilities for local deadlines; if submitting directly to foundation, applications are accepted from January 1 through November 30.
Decision Notification: Usually within two months of receipt.

Restrictions
Does not support individuals; programs for gifted students; general operating expenses; endowments; capital expenses; veterans or labor groups; athletic organizations; religious, political, or lobbying groups; organizations located outside or whose contributed funds are distributed outside the United States and its territories; tables at charitable functions or courtesy advertising; organizations which discriminate on the basis of sex, race, or creed; or groups that do not have 501(c)(3) tax-exempt status. Major emphasis is on communities where International Paper Company operates mills and plants, also in Memphis, Tennessee.

Corporate Officials
John T. Dillon: chairman, chief executive officer, director B Schroon Lake, NY 1938. ED University of Hartford (1965); Columbia University (1971). PRIM CORP EMPL chairman, chief executive officer, director: International Paper Co. CORP AFFIL director: Caterpillar Inc.; director: Capital Formation Inc.; director: Carter Holt Harvey Ltd. NONPR AFFIL trustee: Economic Education.
James Patrick Melican, Jr.: executive vice president B Worcester, MA 1940. ED Fordham University

BA (1962); Harvard University JD (1965); Michigan State University MBA (1971). PRIM CORP EMPL executive vice president legal & external affairs: International Paper Co. CORP AFFIL director: Scitex Corp. Ltd. NONPR AFFIL member: Industries Sector Advisory Comm Paper Products for Trade Policy Matters; chairman finance & management policy committee: National Association Manufacturers; member: Association General Counsel; trustee: Fordham Prep School; member: American Law Institute; member: Association Bar New York City; member: American Bar Association.
Marianne M. Parrs: executive vice president B 1944. ED Brown University (1965). PRIM CORP EMPL executive vice president: International Paper Co.

Foundation Officials
Phyllis Epp: executive director
John V. Faraci: director
Marianne Parrs: director
Ken Reeves: vice president, administrator, director
Dennis Thomas: director
Carol Tusch: treasurer
Elizabeth Walenczyk: assistant secretary
Sandra C. Wilson: vice president administration, director B 1949.

Grants Analysis
Disclosure Period: calendar year ending 2002
Total Grants: $6,788,531*
Number of Grants: 1,063
Average Grant: $6,400
Highest Grant: $400,000
Lowest Grant: $85
Typical Range: $1,000 to $5,000
*Note: Giving includes matching gifts.

Recent Grants
Note: Grants derived from 2003 Form 990.
General

500,000	National Geographic, Washington, DC
250,000	National Civil Rights Museum, Memphis, TN
100,000	Paul D Camp Community College, Franklin, VA
100,000	Paul Smith's College, Paul Smiths, NY
100,000	RISE Foundation Inc., Memphis, TN
85,000	Memphis Brooks Museum of Art, Memphis, TN
50,000	Atlantic Salmon Federation, Calais, ME
50,000	Earth's Birthday Project
50,000	Memphis Zoo, Memphis, TN
50,000	Northfield Mount Hermon School, Northfield, MA

IOWA SAVINGS BANK

Company Headquarters
118 5th Ave.
Coon Rapids, IA 50058

Company Description
Employees: 23

Operating Locations
Iowa Savings Bank (IA--Coon Rapids)

Iowa Savings Bank Charitable Foundation

Giving Contact
William C. Hess, Chief Executive Officer
PO Box 967
Carroll, IA 51401
Phone: (712)792-9772

Description

Founded: 1988
EIN: 421329826
Organization Type: Corporate Foundation
Giving Locations: IA
Grant Types: General Support, Scholarship.

Financial Summary

Total Giving: $85,235 (2003)
Giving Analysis: Giving for 2003 includes: foundation grants to United Way ($1,655)
Assets: $134,611 (2003)
Gifts Received: $250,536 (2000); $72,740 (1999); $426,100 (1997). Note: Contributions were received from Iowa Savings Bank.

Typical Recipients

Arts & Humanities: Arts Associations & Councils, History & Archaeology, Libraries, Music, Public Broadcasting
Civic & Public Affairs: Botanical Gardens/Parks, Business/Free Enterprise, Chambers of Commerce, Clubs, Community Foundations, Civic & Public Affairs-General, Housing, Municipalities/Towns, Parades/Festivals, Professional & Trade Associations, Rural Affairs, Safety, Urban & Community Affairs, Women's Affairs
Education: Agricultural Education, Colleges & Universities, Education Associations, Education Funds, Private Education (Precollege), Public Education (Precollege), Secondary Education (Private), Secondary Education (Public)
Environment: Environment-General, Resource Conservation, Wildlife Protection
Health: Alzheimer's Disease, Cancer, Children's Health/Hospitals, Emergency/Ambulance Services, Heart, Hospices, Hospitals, Multiple Sclerosis, Public Health
Religion: Churches, Religion-General, Religious Organizations, Religious Welfare
Science: Scientific Centers & Institutes, Scientific Organizations
Social Services: Child Welfare, Community Service Organizations, Day Care, Family Planning, Food/Clothing Distribution, People with Disabilities, Recreation & Athletics, United Funds/United Ways

Application Procedures

Initial Contact: Send a brief letter with an explanation as to the purpose or need.
Deadlines: None.

Corporate Officials

John Chrystal: chairman PRIM CORP EMPL chairman: Iowa Savings Bank.
Richard Fulton: chief financial officer PRIM CORP EMPL chief financial officer: Iowa Savings Bank.
William C. Hess: chief executive officer PRIM CORP EMPL chief executive officer: Iowa Savings Bank.

Foundation Officials

Tom Chrystal: vice president, director
William C. Hess: president, secretary, treasurer, director (see above)

Grants Analysis

Disclosure Period: calendar year ending 2003
Total Grants: $83,580*
Number of Grants: 66
Average Grant: $850*
Highest Grant: $10,000
Lowest Grant: $35
Typical Range: $250 to $2,000
*Note: Giving excludes United Way. Average grant excludes three highest grants ($30,000).

Recent Grants

Note: Grants derived from 2003 Form 990.
General

10,000	Carroll County Conservation Foundation, Carroll, IA
10,000	Carroll Depot Centre, Carroll, IA
10,000	St. Anthony - Alzheimer's Unit, Carroll, IA
5,250	Coon Rapids-Bayard Community School District, Coon Rapids, IA
5,000	Chapter Farm and Fruit Association, Lake City, IA
5,000	Habitat for Humanity, Carroll, IA
5,000	New Hope Village, Carroll, IA
2,500	Bayard Betterment Foundation, Bayard, IA
2,500	World Food Prize Foundation, Des Moines, IA
2,350	Iowa State University Foundation, Ames, IA

THE JAMES IRVINE FOUNDATION

Giving Contact

One Market, Steuart Tower, Suite 2500
San Francisco, CA 94105
Phone: (415)777-2244
Fax: (415)777-0869
Web: http://www.irvine.org

Alternate Contact

James Irvine Foundation
865 South Figueroa Street
Suite 2308
Los Angeles, CA 90017
Phone: (213)236-0552
Fax: (213)236-0537
Note: Above address provides contact information for the foundation's Los Angeles office.

Description

Founded: 1937
EIN: 941236937
Organization Type: General Purpose Foundation
Giving Locations: CA
Grant Types: Capital, Employee Matching Gifts, General Support, Multiyear/Continuing Support, Operating Expenses, Project, Seed Money, Dissemination of Technical Information.

Donor Information

Founder: Established by James Irvine in 1937 "to promote the general welfare of the people of California." Mr. Irvine (d. 1947) was president of the Irvine Land and Orchard Company, Napa Valley Railroad, and Moraga Land Company. The original trust property was a significant portion of Irvine Company stock, whose primary asset was approximately 100,000 acres of land in Orange County, CA, known as Irvine Ranch.

Financial Summary

Total Giving: $51,000,000 (2003 approx); $73,455,310 (2002)
Giving Analysis: Giving for 2002 includes: foundation grants to United Way ($25,000); foundation scholarships ($30,000)
Assets: $1,132,589,948 (2002)
Gifts Received: $2,500 (2002); $2,000 (1996)

Typical Recipients

Arts & Humanities: Arts Centers, Arts Institutes, Arts Outreach, Ballet, Community Arts, Dance, Ethnic & Folk Arts, Film & Video, Arts & Humanities-General, History & Archaeology, Libraries, Literary Arts, Museums/Galleries, Music, Opera, Performing Arts, Public Broadcasting, Theater
Civic & Public Affairs: African American Affairs, Asian American Affairs, Business/Free Enterprise, Community Foundations, Economic Development, Economic Policy, Employment/Job Training, Ethnic Organizations, Civic & Public Affairs-General, Hispanic Affairs, Housing, Law & Justice, Legal Aid, Native American Affairs, Nonprofit Management, Philanthropic Organizations, Professional & Trade Associations, Public Policy, Rural Affairs, Urban & Community Affairs, Women's Affairs, Zoos/Aquariums
Education: Afterschool/Enrichment Programs, Agricultural Education, Arts/Humanities Education, Business Education, Colleges & Universities, Education Associations, Education Funds, Education Reform, Engineering/Technological Education, Faculty Development, Education-General, International Studies, Journalism/Media Education, Leadership Training, Minority Education, Religious Education, Science/Mathematics Education, Student Aid, Vocational & Technical Education
Environment: Air/Water Quality, Forestry, Environment-General, Resource Conservation, Watershed, Wildlife Protection
Health: AIDS/HIV, Children's Health/Hospitals, Clinics/Medical Centers, Health-General, Health Policy/Cost Containment, Health Organizations, Hospitals, Hospitals (University Affiliated), Medical Research, Nursing Services, Prenatal Health Issues, Preventive Medicine/Wellness Organizations, Public Health, Research/Studies Institutes
International: Foreign Arts Organizations, Human Rights, International Affairs, International Development, International Environmental Issues
Religion: Churches, Jewish Causes, Religious Welfare, Social/Policy Issues
Science: Science Museums, Scientific Centers & Institutes
Social Services: At-Risk Youth, Child Abuse, Child Welfare, Community Service Organizations, Crime Prevention, Day Care, Domestic Violence, Family Planning, Family Services, People with Disabilities, Recreation & Athletics, Refugee Assistance, Shelters/Homelessness, Social Services-General, United Funds/United Ways, Volunteer Services, YMCA/YWCA/YMHA/YWHA, Youth Organizations

Application Procedures

Initial Contact: Send a two-page letter of inquiry or use online inquiry form, after reviewing the foundation's annual report and/or website.
Application Requirements: The letter should include a brief background of organization, amount requested and a one-sentence summary of the proposed project, overview of issue being addressed, summary of goals and objectives of proposed project.
Deadlines: None.
Review Process: Letters of inquiry are accepted year-round and are reviewed promptly. Applicants will receive a response within three to six weeks. The foundation then invites proposals from qualifying organizations. Following review of the proposals, the foundation conducts site visits and interviews. Final decisions may take up to six months.

Restrictions

The foundation only supports programs and organizations that benefit the State of California. The foundation does not fund agencies of the government, tax-supported organizations, or groups that primarily benefit public entities. The foundation primarily supports organizations that are classified as tax-exempt under section 501(c)(3) under the Internal Revenue Code. Grants are not made to individuals.

Additional Information

Publications: Annual Report; Guidelines

Foundation Officials

Greg Avis: director ED Harvard University MBA; Williams College BA (1980). CORP AFFIL founding managing partner: Summit Partners. NONPR AFFIL director: San Jose Repertory Theatre Co.; director: Williams College; director: National Outdoor Leadership School; director: Community Foundation Silicon Valley.
Elisa Crystal Callow: program director ED California

State University, Los Angeles MA; San Jose State University BFA.

Martha S. Campbell: vice president program ED Dartmouth College BA; Princeton University MA. NONPR AFFIL director: Lucile Packard Foundation for Children's Health.

James E. Canales: president, chief executive officer, director B San Francisco, CA 1966. ED Stanford University BA (1988); Stanford University MA (1989). NONPR AFFIL member board: Southern California Grantmakers; chairman: Stanford Alumni Association; honorary director: Larkin Street Youth Center; member: Independent Sector; chairman: KQED Public Broadcasting; member: Hispanics in Philanthropy.

Frank H. Cruz: director ED University of Southern California BA; University of Southern California MS. PRIM CORP EMPL president: Cruz & Associates. CORP AFFIL founder: Telemundo. NONPR AFFIL member: Public Interest Obligations of Digital Television Broadcasters; trustee: University of Southern California; vice chairman, director: Corp. for Public Broadcasting.

John R. Jenks: treasurer, chief information officer ED Washington State University MA; Washington State University BA. NONPR AFFIL director: Contra Costs Crisis Center; member: Security Analysts of San Francisco; member: Association for Investment Management & REsearch.

Davis Mas Masumoto: director ED University of California at Berkeley BA; University of California, Davis MS. OCCUPATION author. NONPR AFFIL director: California Council for the Humanities.

Regina L. Muehlhauser: director CORP AFFIL president: On Lok Inc. NONPR AFFIL director: Golden Gate National Parks Conservancy; director: San Francisco Symphony; director: Committee on Jobs; director: Bay Area Council.

Molly Munger: director ED Harvard University Law School JD; Radcliffe College. PRIM CORP EMPL attorney: English, Munger & Rice. CORP AFFIL co-founder, partner: English, Munger & Rice. NONPR AFFIL director: Southern California Association of Philanthropy; director: Westridge School for Girls; trustee: Occidental College; member: Rand Corp. Committee on K-12 Education; co-founder, director: The Advancement Project; director: Children Now.

Patricia S. Pineda: director ED University of California at Berkeley JD; Mills College BA (1974). PRIM CORP EMPL general counsel, assistant corporate secretary: New United Motor Manufacturing Inc. CORP AFFIL trustee: Rand Corp.; director: Levi Strauss & Co.; vice president, secretary: New United Motor Manufacturing Inc. NONPR AFFIL director: California Manufacturing Association; director: Mills College.

Gary B. Pruitt: vice chairman, director ED University of California at Berkeley JD; University of California at Berkeley MA; University of Florida BA. CORP AFFIL director: Mutual Insurance Co.; president, chief executive officer, chairman: The McClatchy Co. NONPR AFFIL board of directors: Newspaper Assn. of America.

Toby Rosenblatt: director ED Yale University BA; Stanford University MBA (1964). PRIM CORP EMPL president, general partner: Founders Investments Ltd PRIM NONPR EMPL board chairman: The Presidio Trust. CORP AFFIL director: Premier Pacific Vineyards; director: State Street Research Mutual Funds; director: MetLife Series Mutual Funds; director: Pherin Corp.; director: AP Pharma Inc.; president, general partner: Founders Investments Ltd. NONPR AFFIL chairman: Presidio Trust; trustee: Thacher School.

Anne B. Stanton: program director youth ED New York University MSW; New York University BFA. NONPR AFFIL director: Association for Corporate Growth; director: Federal Emergency Management Agency.

Peter J. Taylor: director ED Claremont Graduate School MS; University of California, Los Angeles BA. CORP AFFIL managing director: Lehman Brothers Inc. NONPR AFFIL president: UCLA Foundation.

Grants Analysis

Disclosure Period: calendar year ending 2002
Total Grants: $73,400,310*
Number of Grants: 405 (approx)
Average Grant: $163,501*
Highest Grant: $2,000,000
Lowest Grant: $500
Typical Range: $5,000 to $15,000 and $100,000 to $500,000
***Note:** Giving excludes United Way and scholarships. Average grant excludes five highest grants ($8,000,000).

Recent Grants

Note: Grants derived from 2002 Form 990.
General

2,250,000	Great Valley Center Inc., Modesto, CA -- towards supporting youth leadership programs
2,000,000	Community Television of Southern California, Los Angeles, CA -- fund for KCET for the initial production of a television and Internet series California Connected
2,000,000	New Vision Partners Inc., Pasadena, CA -- towards continued support for the Communities Organizing Resources to Advancing Learning Initiative in Pasadena
2,000,000	United Way of Fresno County, Fresno, CA -- towards Communities Organizing Resources to Advancing Learning Initiative in Fresno
2,000,000	Young Men's Christian Association of Greater Long Beach, Long Beach, CA -- towards Communities Organizing Resources to Advancing Learning Initiative in Long Beach
1,200,000	University of Southern California, Los Angeles, CA -- towards enhancing campus diversity by establishing the Center for American Study and Ethnicity
1,000,000	New Vision Partners Inc., Pasadena, CA -- towards implementing the Communities Organizing Resources to Advancing Learning Initiative in Pasadena
1,000,000	Occidental College, Los Angeles, CA -- fund for academic and capital program and re-dedicating the Admission Building
968,000	California Institute of Technology, Pasadena, CA
937,500	Sacramento Children's Home, Sacramento, CA -- towards implementation of the Communities Organizing Resources to Advancing Learning Initiative in Sacramento

WILLIAM G. IRWIN CHARITY FOUNDATION

Giving Contact

Michael R. Gorman, Executive Director
William G. Irwin Charity Foundation
235 Montgomery Street, Suite 711
San Francisco, CA 94104-2996
Phone: (415)362-6954

Description

Founded: 1919
EIN: 946069873
Organization Type: General Purpose Foundation
Giving Locations: CA; HI
Grant Types: Capital, General Support, Project, Research.

Donor Information

Founder: Established in 1919 by Mrs. Fannie M. Irwin. The foundation received contributions from Mrs. Fannie M. Irwin and Mrs. Helene Irwin Fagan, both deceased.

Financial Summary

Total Giving: $5,482,000 (2003); $6,374,600 (2002)
Giving Analysis: Giving for 2003 includes: foundation grants to United Way ($40,000); 2002: foundation grants to United Way ($40,000)
Assets: $110,412,682 (2003); $101,294,124 (2002)

Typical Recipients

Arts & Humanities: Ballet, Dance, Ethnic & Folk Arts, Historic Preservation, History & Archaeology, Libraries, Museums/Galleries, Music, Opera, Performing Arts, Theater

Civic & Public Affairs: Asian American Affairs, Botanical Gardens/Parks, Civic & Public Affairs-General, Law & Justice, Urban & Community Affairs, Women's Affairs, Zoos/Aquariums

Education: Afterschool/Enrichment Programs, Arts/Humanities Education, Colleges & Universities, Elementary Education (Private), Education-General, Medical Education, Preschool Education, Private Education (Precollege), Public Education (Precollege), Religious Education, Science/Mathematics Education, Secondary Education (Private), Secondary Education (Public)

Environment: Resource Conservation

Health: Alzheimer's Disease, Arthritis, Cancer, Children's Health/Hospitals, Clinics/Medical Centers, Emergency/Ambulance Services, Eyes/Blindness, Geriatric Health, Health Funds, Health Organizations, Heart, Hospitals, Long-Term Care, Medical Rehabilitation, Medical Research, Multiple Sclerosis, Research/Studies Institutes, Single-Disease Health Associations, Speech & Hearing, Transplant Networks/Donor Banks

Religion: Churches, Religious Organizations, Religious Welfare, Seminaries

Science: Science Museums

Social Services: Animal Protection, Child Welfare, Community Service Organizations, Day Care, Food/Clothing Distribution, People with Disabilities, Scouts, Shelters/Homelessness, Social Services-General, United Funds/United Ways, YMCA/YWCA/YMHA/YWHA, Youth Organizations

Application Procedures

Initial Contact: The foundation has no application forms. Prospective applicants should submit a summary letter to the foundation.

Application Requirements: Grant proposals should include a summary letter, current financial information (audited, if possible, with a balance sheet and statement of revenue and expenses), budget, list of officers, directors and/or trustees, complete justification for request, history of organization, description of activities, and proof of federal and state tax-exempt status.

Deadlines: None. However, applications should be submitted approximately four to six weeks prior to a meeting date which are held every two months.

Review Process: Meetings are held approximately every two months.

Notes: The foundation does not accept video or audio tapes.

Restrictions

The foundation does not give grants for scholarships or to individuals, and limits grants to charitable uses in California and Hawaii.

Additional Information

A waiting period of twelve months is required between proposal submissions.

Foundation Officials

Jane Olds Bogart: vice president, trustee
Michael R. Gorman: executive director
William Lee Olds, III: trustee ED Lewis & Clark College (1981).
William Lee Olds, Jr.: president, trustee ED Univer-

sity of San Francisco (1970).
Anthony Olds Zanze: trustee ED Dartmouth College (1982); University of Wisconsin (1988).
James F. Zanze: trustee

Grants Analysis

Disclosure Period: calendar year ending 2003
Total Grants: $5,442,000*
Number of Grants: 34
Average Grant: $123,188*
Highest Grant: $1,000,000
Lowest Grant: $15,000
Typical Range: $30,000 to $200,000
*Note: Giving excludes United Way. Average grant figure excludes two highest grants ($1,500,000).

Recent Grants

Note: Grants derived from 2003 Form 990.
General

1,000,000	Scared Heart Cathedral Preparatory, San Francisco, CA -- capital campaign
500,000	St. Hilary School, Tiburon, CA -- new gymnasium
300,000	Oceanic Institute, Waimanalo, HI -- facility expansion
300,000	St. Elizabeth Elementary, Oakland, CA -- renovation project
250,000	Bay Area Discovery Museum, Sausalito, CA -- capital campaign
250,000	Cate School, Carpinteria, CA -- faculty housing
250,000	East Bay Zoological Society, Oakland, CA -- Capital campaign
250,000	St. Luke's Hospital, San Francisco, CA -- x-ray machine
200,000	French American International School, San Francisco, CA -- capital campaign
200,000	Mid-Pacific Institute, Honolulu, HI -- math/science complex

ISHIYAMA FOUNDATION

Giving Contact

Margaret Raffin
Ishiyama Foundation
465 California St., No. 800
San Francisco, CA 94104
Phone: (415)392-0800
Fax: (415)392-1268

Description

Founded: 1968
EIN: 941659373
Organization Type: Private Foundation
Giving Locations: CA; Japan
Grant Types: General Support, Scholarship.

Donor Information

Founder: George S. Ishiyama

Financial Summary

Total Giving: $538,950 (2002)
Assets: $47,841,305 (2002)
Gifts Received: $3,000,000 (2002); $1,000,000 (2000); $1,000,000 (1999). Note: In 2002 a contribution was received from JR Limited.

Typical Recipients

Arts & Humanities: Arts Centers, Ethnic & Folk Arts, Libraries, Museums/Galleries, Music
Civic & Public Affairs: Community Foundations, Ethnic Organizations, Civic & Public Affairs-General, Philanthropic Organizations, Urban & Community Affairs
Education: Colleges & Universities, Education Associations, Education-General, International Studies, Legal Education, Private Education (Precollege), Public Education (Precollege), Religious Education,

Science/Mathematics Education, Student Aid
Environment: Air/Water Quality, Environment-General, Resource Conservation, Wildlife Protection
Health: Children's Health/Hospitals, Clinics/Medical Centers, Health Organizations, Heart, Hospitals, Medical Rehabilitation, Research/Studies Institutes, Single-Disease Health Associations, Speech & Hearing
International: Foreign Arts Organizations, Foreign Educational Institutions, International Peace & Security Issues, International Relations
Religion: Jewish Causes, Religious Organizations
Science: Science Museums, Scientific Centers & Institutes
Social Services: Child Welfare, Community Service Organizations, Delinquency & Criminal Rehabilitation, Family Services, Senior Services

Application Procedures

Initial Contact: The foundation has no formal grant application procedure or application form.
Deadlines: None.

Restrictions

Preference is given to educational institutions. Does not support individuals.

Foundation Officials

Ralph Bardoff: vice president, director
George I. Ishiyama: president, director
Jean Ishiyama: assistant secretary
Setsuko Ishiyama: secretary, treasurer, director
Margaret Raffin: director

Grants Analysis

Disclosure Period: calendar year ending 2002
Total Grants: $538,950*
Number of Grants: 24
Average Grant: $7,087*
Highest Grant: $375,950
Lowest Grant: $1,000
Typical Range: $2,000 to $25,000 and $100,000 to $500,000
*Note: Giving includes scholarship. Average grant figure excludes highest grant.

Recent Grants

Note: Grants derived from 2002 Form 990.
General

375,950	International University of Japan, Niigata Japan
35,000	National Fish and Wildlife Foundation, Washington, DC
20,000	Trout Unlimited, Arlington, VA
15,000	Jewish Community Federation
12,000	Castelleja School
10,000	California Academy of Science, San Francisco, CA
10,000	Palo Alto Medical Center, Palo Alto, CA
10,000	Sitka Arts Southwest, Inc.
8,000	Palo Alto Community Fund
5,000	Cardiac Therapy Foundation

ISLAND FOUNDATION (MA)

Giving Contact

Jo-Ann Watson, President
589 Mill Street
Marion, MA 02738-1553
Phone: (508)748-2809
Fax: (508)748-0991
E-mail: islandfdn@earthlink.net

Description

Founded: 1979
EIN: 042670567

Organization Type: General Purpose Foundation
Giving Locations: MA: New Bedford
Grant Types: General Support, Multiyear/Continuing Support, Project, Research.

Donor Information

Founder: The Island Foundation was founded in 1980 by Van Alan Clark and Mary Aland and is perhaps the strongest expression of their activism. Van Clark was dedicated to change. He was constantly rethinking and the range of his inquiry was truly impressive. In his life, he sought to affect fields as far ranging as tropical disease, higher education, art in inner city, electronics, oceanography, anti-submarine warfare, low speed aerodynamics, and positive alternatives for troubled youth.

In her seventies, Mary Clark is anything but retiring. After Van's death in 1983, she led the Foundation through years of expanding vision and capacity. She no longer serves on the board yet dynamically pursues a wide variety of other interests.

Van's goal was always to change the ground rules. He ardently believed that one should never accept an unsatisfactory status quo if one has the means of changing it. This would be admirable in itself, but what made Van and Mary remarkable was their willingness to put ideas to the test. They were singularly courageous. They understood that it takes money, vision, hard work and endurance to make ideas into reality.

Thus, the charge of the Island Foundation is to foster those visions and provide the capital, guidance, and support to bring about a better reality.

Financial Summary

Total Giving: $1,600,000 (2002)
Giving Analysis: Giving for 2002 includes: foundation grants to United Way ($30,000)
Assets: $32,050,080 (2002)
Gifts Received: $271,808 (1994); $5,490 (1993)

Typical Recipients

Arts & Humanities: Arts Associations & Councils, Arts Centers, Arts Festivals, Arts & Humanities-General, Historic Preservation, Museums/Galleries, Music, Theater
Civic & Public Affairs: Botanical Gardens/Parks, Business/Free Enterprise, Civil Rights, Community Foundations, Economic Development, Employment/Job Training, Civic & Public Affairs-General, Hispanic Affairs, Law & Justice, Municipalities/Towns, Nonprofit Management, Philanthropic Organizations, Professional & Trade Associations, Public Policy, Urban & Community Affairs, Women's Affairs, Zoos/Aquariums
Education: Afterschool/Enrichment Programs, Arts/Humanities Education, Business Education, Colleges & Universities, Economic Education, Education Reform, Elementary Education (Public), Environmental Education, Faculty Development, Education-General, Health & Physical Education, Leadership Training, Preschool Education, Private Education (Precollege), Public Education (Precollege), Science/Mathematics Education, Secondary Education (Private), Secondary Education (Public), Special Education, Student Aid
Environment: Air/Water Quality, Environment-General, Protection, Research, Resource Conservation, Watershed, Wildlife Protection
Health: Adolescent Health Issues, AIDS/HIV, Kidney, Medical Rehabilitation
International: Foreign Educational Institutions, International Affairs, International Environmental Issues, International Relations, Trade
Religion: Religious Welfare, Social/Policy Issues
Science: Science Museums, Scientific Centers & Institutes, Scientific Research
Social Services: At-Risk Youth, Community Centers, Community Service Organizations, Counseling, Day Care, Delinquency & Criminal Rehabilitation, Domestic Violence, Emergency Relief, Family Planning, Family Services, People with Disabilities, Recreation

& Athletics, Senior Services, Shelters/Homelessness, Social Services-General, Substance Abuse, United Funds/United Ways, YMCA/YWCA/YMHA/YWHA, Youth Organizations

Application Procedures

Initial Contact: The foundation requests an initial letter or phone call to determine the interest and appropriateness of a full proposal.

Application Requirements: A formal proposal should include the following: a cover letter; a narrative of the specific goals, intended beneficiaries, timetable, procedure, and current status of the project; a history and background of the organization; methods of assessment and evaluation; an income and expense budget for the organization and the project for past, current and proposed years; an IRS tax-determination letter indicating section 501(c)(3) status; the most recent year-end fiscal statement or audit; the background of key personnel and a list of directors; and any supplementary materials. Research proposals should be formatted to include a one-page abstract summarizing the question(s) asked, methods used, results expected, and justification.

Deadlines: None.

Review Process: Decisions are made by the board on an ongoing basis. Site visits are often made by the foundation, and grantees are expected to submit semiannual reports.

Notes: The foundation accepts proposals that use the Common Proposal Format as developed by the Associated Grantmakers of Massachusetts. The foundation asks that proposals be submitted in an environmentally sensitive manner. One copy will suffice.

Restrictions

All applicants must be tax-exempt organizations. No grants are made to individuals, sectarian religious activities, or candidates for public office. Grants made only in the New Bedford Area.

Additional Information

Publications: Annual Report; Application Guidelines

Foundation Officials

Kim N. Clark: vice president

Stephen H. Clark: president, director B 1953. ED Cornell University BA (1975); Cornell University MA (1976). PRIM CORP EMPL chairman: Quartermoon Inc.

Julie A. Early: executive director

Hannah T. C. Moore: treasurer

Michael J. Moore: director

Peter J. Nesbeda: corporator B 1950. PRIM CORP EMPL chairman, president, chief executive officer, director: Xyplex Inc.

Christopher N. Tupper: corporator

JoAnn Watson: corporator

Grants Analysis

Disclosure Period: calendar year ending 2002

Total Grants: $1,570,000*

Number of Grants: 64

Average Grant: $17,302*

Highest Grant: $480,000

Lowest Grant: $1,000

Typical Range: $10,000 to $40,000

*Note: Giving excludes United Way. Average grant figure excludes highest grant.

Recent Grants

Note: Grants derived from 2002 Form 990.

General

480,000	YMCA Southcoast, New Bedford, MA -- towards Wareham YMCA capital campaign
50,000	Community Foundation of South East Massachusetts, New Bedford, MA -- general operating assistance
50,000	Education Development Center, Newton, MA -- towards curricula development for the New Bedford Global Learning Center
50,000	New England Aquarium, Boston, MA -- general assistance for S. Kraus' right whale research
50,000	Quebec-Labrador Foundation, Ipswich, MA -- towards education and bioregional programs
40,000	Penikese Island School, Woods Hole, MA -- towards aftercare and community service programs
40,000	PKR Foundation, Kansas City, MO -- general research assistance
35,000	ArtWorks at Dover Street, New Bedford, MA -- towards professional exhibits curator
35,000	Save the Bay, Providence, RI -- general assistance
30,000	Cape Cod Stranding Network, Buzzards Bay, MA -- for Cape Cod Stranding Network

ITTLESON FOUNDATION

Giving Contact

Anthony C. Wood, Executive Director
15 East 67th Street
New York, NY 10021
Phone: (212)794-2008
Fax: (212)794-0351
Web: http://www.ittlesonfoundation.org

Description

Founded: 1932
EIN: 510172757
Organization Type: Family Foundation
Giving Locations: nationally.
Grant Types: Project, Seed Money.

Donor Information

Founder: The Ittleson Foundation was established in New York in 1932 by the late Henry Ittleson, founder and past chairman of C.I.T. Financial Corporation. After his death in 1948, the foundation received a substantial bequest from his estate. Mr. Ittleson's widow, Blanche F. Ittleson, former trustee of the foundation (until her death in 1975), directed the focus of the foundation toward health and welfare, particularly mental health care and research.

Financial Summary

Total Giving: $731,965 (2003); $948,583 (2002); $969,021 (2001). Note: 1998 Giving includes membership grants ($15,755) and miscellaneous grants totaling ($143,276). 1997 Giving includes membership grants totaling ($10,130). 1996 Giving includes memberships ($10,130).

Assets: $18,339,177 (2003); $16,523,286 (2002); $21,710,168 (2001)

Gifts Received: $3,000 (2000); $25,000 (1998); $175,000 (1992). Note: Contributions were received from the estate of Nancy S. Ittleson.

Typical Recipients

Arts & Humanities: Arts Associations & Councils, Arts Centers, Arts Outreach, Dance, Film & Video, Historic Preservation, History & Archaeology, Libraries, Museums/Galleries, Opera, Public Broadcasting, Theater

Civic & Public Affairs: Botanical Gardens/Parks, Chambers of Commerce, Civil Rights, Community Foundations, Economic Development, Employment/Job Training, Gay/Lesbian Issues, Civic & Public Affairs-General, Housing, Law & Justice, Legal Aid, Minority Business, Native American Affairs, Nonprofit Management, Philanthropic Organizations, Professional & Trade Associations, Public Policy, Safety, Urban & Community Affairs, Women's Affairs, Zoos/Aquariums

Education: Arts/Humanities Education, Business Education, Colleges & Universities, Education Associations, Education Reform, Elementary Education (Private), Environmental Education, Faculty Development, Education-General, Medical Education, Private Education (Precollege), Social Sciences Education

Environment: Air/Water Quality, Forestry, Environment-General, Protection, Resource Conservation, Watershed, Wildlife Protection

Health: AIDS/HIV, Cancer, Children's Health/Hospitals, Emergency/Ambulance Services, Health-General, Geriatric Health, Health Organizations, Hospitals, Hospitals (University Affiliated), Medical Rehabilitation, Medical Research, Mental Health, Nutrition, Prenatal Health Issues, Preventive Medicine/Wellness Organizations, Public Health, Research/Studies Institutes, Single-Disease Health Associations

International: Health Care/Hospitals, Human Rights, International Affairs, International Environmental Issues, International Organizations, International Peace & Security Issues, International Relations, International Relief Efforts

Religion: Churches, Jewish Causes, Religious Welfare, Synagogues/Temples

Social Services: Animal Protection, At-Risk Youth, Child Abuse, Child Welfare, Community Centers, Community Service Organizations, Counseling, Crime Prevention, Delinquency & Criminal Rehabilitation, Family Planning, Family Services, Food/Clothing Distribution, Homes, People with Disabilities, Refugee Assistance, Senior Services, Shelters/Homelessness, Social Services-General, Substance Abuse, United Funds/United Ways, Volunteer Services, Youth Organizations

Application Procedures

Initial Contact: The foundation does not supply application forms. Applicants should send a brief letter.

Application Requirements: The letter should include a a description of organization and project for which funds are sought, organization's budget, an annual report, if available, and evidence of tax-exempt status.

Deadlines: April 1 for the spring meeting, and September 1 for the fall meeting.

Review Process: Grant requests are reviewed on a continuing basis. If the grant proposal fits within the foundation's current scope of interest, additional information will be required. If the foundation declines a proposal, applicants must wait at least one year before reapplying for any purpose.

Restrictions

The foundation generally does not provide funding for general support, capital building projects, endowments, grants to individuals, scholarships or internships (except as part of a program), biomedical research, or continuing support to existing programs. Support also is not given for direct service programs, especially when outside New York City, or for projects with a local focus or constituency. The foundation does not make international grants.

Additional Information

The foundation reports that it supports pilot programs or the start-up of new services when the service or project is truly innovative, there are practical plans for evaluation, there appears to be an audience for the results, and there is a credible plan for dissemination to those audiences.

In 1995, the foundation reported that it had dropped its crime and justice program area.

Publications: Annual Report

Foundation Officials

Henry Anthony Ittleson: chairman, president, director B New York, NY 1937. ED Brown University BA (1960). PRIM CORP EMPL chairman: Travent Ltd. NONPR AFFIL board fellows: Brown University;

member: Phi Gamma Delta; trustee: Brooks School. CLUB AFFIL Regency Whist Club; Shinnecock Hills Golf Club; Long Island Wyandanch Club; Meadow Club; Links America; Brown University Club; Deepdale Golf Club.

Lionel Irwin Pincus: director B Philadelphia, PA 1931. ED University of Pennsylvania BA (1953); Columbia University School of Business Administration MBA (1956). PRIM CORP EMPL chairman, chief executive officer, director: EM Warburg, Pincus & Co. Inc. ADD CORP EMPL managing partner: Warburg Pincus Capital Partners LP; president: Warburg Pincus Asset Management; managing partner: Warburg Pincus Ventures Inc. CORP AFFIL managing partner: Warburg Pincus Investors LP. NONPR AFFIL member: New York City Partnership Chamber of Commerce; trustee: School American Ballet; director: National Park Foundation; member: Council Foreign Relations; trustee: Montefiore Hospital Medical Center; trustee, chairman emeritus: Columbia University; member, board overseers: Columbia University Graduate School Business. CLUB AFFIL Meadow Club; National Golf Links America Club.

Pamela L. Syrmis: vice president, director
Victor P. Syrmis, MD: director B 1943.
Anthony C. Wood: executive director, secretary

Grants Analysis

Disclosure Period: calendar year ending 2002
Total Grants: $948,583
Number of Grants: 55
Average Grant: $12,937*
Highest Grant: $250,000
Lowest Grant: $100
Typical Range: $1,000 to $25,000
*Note: Average grant figure excludes highest grant.

Recent Grants

Note: Grants derived from 2002 Form 990.
General

250,000	Brown University, Providence, RI
60,000	Generation Five, San Francisco, CA
55,000	New England Science Center Collaborative, Bethlehem, NH
50,000	Center for Public Representation, Northampton, MA
50,000	McLean Hospital, Belmont, MA
40,000	Matrix Research Institute, Philadelphia, PA
30,000	Child & Adolescent Bipolar Foundation, Wilmette, IL
30,000	Oregon Water Trust, Portland, OR
30,000	Scenarios USA, New York, NY
30,000	SIECUS, New York, NY

J&L SPECIALTY STEEL INC.

Company Headquarters

PO Box 3373
Pittsburgh, PA 15230
Web: http://www.jlspecialty.com

Company Description

Former Name: J&L Specialty Products Corp.
Employees: 1,200
SIC(s): 3300 Primary Metal Industries.
Parent Company: Ugine Stainless & Alloys Inc., 370 Franklin Turnpike, Mahwah, NJ, United States

Operating Locations

Edgcomb Metals (PA--Bensalem); Edgcomb Metals of New England (NH--Nashua); Francosteel Corp. (NY--New York); Hood & Co. (PA--Hamburg); Interstate Steel Co. (IL--Des Plaines); J&L Specialty Steel (PA--Pittsburgh); Metron Steel (IL--Chicago); Rahns Specialty Metals (PA--Collegeville); Techalloy Co. (NJ--Mahwah)

J&L Specialty Steel Charitable Foundation

Giving Contact

Joseph Kusic, Chairman & Administrator
J&L Specialty Steel, Inc
1550 Coraopolis Heights Rd.
Coraopolis, PA 15108
Phone: (412)375-1600

Description

Founded: 1989
EIN: 256311251
Organization Type: Corporate Foundation
Giving Locations: headquarters and operating communities.
Grant Types: Employee Matching Gifts, General Support, Scholarship.

Financial Summary

Total Giving: $1,085,400 (2004)
Assets: $767,629 (2004)
Gifts Received: $300,000 (1994). Note: In 1994, contributions were received from J&L Specialty Steel.

Typical Recipients

Arts & Humanities: Arts Centers, Arts Outreach, Libraries, Museums/Galleries, Music, Public Broadcasting, Theater
Civic & Public Affairs: Economic Development, Employment/Job Training, Civic & Public Affairs-General, Municipalities/Towns, Urban & Community Affairs, Zoos/Aquariums
Education: Afterschool/Enrichment Programs, Business Education, Colleges & Universities, Community & Junior Colleges, Education Funds, Education Reform, Education-General, Preschool Education, Public Education (Precollege), Secondary Education (Public), Special Education, Student Aid
Health: Cancer, Children's Health/Hospitals, Diabetes, Emergency/Ambulance Services, Health Funds, Heart, Hospitals, Kidney, Mental Health, Single-Disease Health Associations
Religion: Religious Welfare
Science: Science Exhibits & Fairs
Social Services: At-Risk Youth, Big Brothers/Big Sisters, Child Welfare, Community Service Organizations, Family Services, Homes, People with Disabilities, Recreation & Athletics, Scouts, Sexual Abuse, Shelters/Homelessness, United Funds/United Ways, YMCA/YWCA/YMHA/YWHA, Youth Organizations

Application Procedures

Initial Contact: Send a letter describing organization and program or project for which funding is requested. Include a copy of 501(c)(3) certification letter and recent financial statements.
Deadlines: Submission should be made in the calendar year in which funds are requested.

Restrictions

Does not support individuals, religious organizations for sectarian purposes, political or lobbying groups, or organizations outside operating areas.

Additional Information

Trust(s): Mellon Bank NA NA

Corporate Officials

Guy Dolle: chairman vice president PRIM CORP EMPL chairman: J&L Specialty Steel.
Eugene Anthony Salvadore: president, chief executive officer B Pittsburgh, PA 1949. ED Carnegie Mellon University (1970); University of Pittsburgh (1975). PRIM CORP EMPL president, chief executive officer: J&L Specialty Steel. CORP AFFIL director: Midland Terminal Co.
Kirk F. Vincent: executive vice president PRIM CORP EMPL executive vice president: J&L Specialty Steel.

Foundation Officials

Joseph Kusic: chairman, administrator

Grants Analysis

Disclosure Period: calendar year ending 2004
Total Grants: $1,085,400
Number of Grants: 11
Average Grant: $16,300*
Highest Grant: $400,000
Lowest Grant: $5,000
Typical Range: $5,000 to $35,000
*Note: Average grant figure excludes three highest grants ($955,000).

Recent Grants

Note: Grants derived from 2003 Form 990.
Library-Related

1,000	Carnegie Library of Midland, Midland, PA

General

20,880	United Way of Beaver County, Monaca, PA
20,460	United Way of Stark County, Canton, OH
14,400	United Way of Columbiana County, East Liverpool, OH
12,500	Robert Morris University, Moon Township, PA
7,200	Midland Borough School District, Midland, PA
4,800	United Way of Allegheny County, Pittsburgh, PA
3,500	Midland Borough, Midland, PA
2,000	McGuire Memorial Home, New Brighton, PA
2,000	Pittsburgh Regional Science Fair, Pittsburgh, PA
2,000	Tri-State Area Citizen's Scholarship Fund, East Liverpool, OH

ANN JACKSON FAMILY FOUNDATION

Giving Contact

Palmer G. Jackson, President
PO Box 5580
Santa Barbara, CA 93150
Phone: (805)969-2258
Fax: (805)969-0315

Description

Founded: 1978
EIN: 953367511
Organization Type: Family Foundation
Giving Locations: CA: Santa Barbara and surrounding areas
Grant Types: Capital, General Support, Project.

Donor Information

Founder: The foundation was established in 1978 by Ann G. Jackson and the Ann Jackson Family Charitable Trust.

Financial Summary

Total Giving: $2,201,100 (fiscal year ending May 31, 2004); $3,125,100 (fiscal 2002); $2,927,933 (fiscal 2001)
Giving Analysis: Giving for fiscal 2001 includes: foundation grants to United Way ($15,000)
Assets: $48,402,890 (fiscal 2004); $49,202,170 (fiscal 2002); $56,373,702 (fiscal 2001)
Gifts Received: $262,500 (fiscal 1999); $350,000 (fiscal 1998); $350,000 (fiscal 1997). Note: Contributions were received from the Ann Jackson Charitable Trust.

Typical Recipients

Arts & Humanities: Arts Associations & Councils, Arts Centers, Arts Institutes, Arts Outreach, Community Arts, Arts & Humanities-General, Historic Preservation, History & Archaeology, Libraries, Museums/Galleries, Music, Opera, Performing Arts, Theater

Civic & Public Affairs: Botanical Gardens/Parks, Clubs, Community Foundations, Economic Development, Employment/Job Training, Hispanic Affairs, Nonprofit Management, Philanthropic Organizations, Professional & Trade Associations, Urban & Community Affairs, Zoos/Aquariums

Education: Agricultural Education, Arts/Humanities Education, Business Education, Business-School Partnerships, Colleges & Universities, Community & Junior Colleges, Education Funds, Education Reform, Education-General, Minority Education, Private Education (Precollege), Public Education (Precollege), Religious Education, Secondary Education (Private), Social Sciences Education, Special Education, Student Aid, Vocational & Technical Education

Environment: Air/Water Quality, Environment-General, Resource Conservation

Health: Cancer, Clinics/Medical Centers, Emergency/Ambulance Services, Eyes/Blindness, Geriatric Health, Health Funds, Health Organizations, Heart, Home-Care Services, Hospices, Hospitals, Medical Rehabilitation, Medical Research, Mental Health, Multiple Sclerosis, Nursing Services, Prenatal Health Issues, Respiratory

International: Foreign Arts Organizations, Health Care/Hospitals, International Relief Efforts

Religion: Churches, Religious Organizations, Religious Welfare

Science: Science Museums

Social Services: Child Abuse, Child Welfare, Community Service Organizations, Emergency Relief, Family Planning, Family Services, Food/Clothing Distribution, People with Disabilities, Recreation & Athletics, Scouts, Senior Services, Shelters/Homelessness, Social Services-General, Special Olympics, Substance Abuse, United Funds/United Ways, Volunteer Services, YMCA/YWCA/YMHA/YWHA, Youth Organizations

Application Procedures

Initial Contact: Applications should be in the form of a letter.

Application Requirements: The letter should detail the grant request and its proposed uses. A copy of the State and Federal ruling under Section 509(a)(1), (2), or (3) must be included, as well as a statement from an officer of the organization that the IRS exempt ruling has not changed since its issuance and that a grant from the foundation will not change the applicant's public charity status.

Deadlines: None.

Review Process: Applications are reviewed by the board of trustees.

Restrictions

Grants are not made to individuals.

Foundation Officials

Charles A. Jackson: vice president, director
James H. Jackson: vice president, director
Palmer G. Jackson, Jr.: secretary, director
Palmer G. Jackson: president, director B 1930. PRIM CORP EMPL president, director: Alisal Properties. NONPR AFFIL chief financial officer, director: Santa Barbara Cottage Hospital.
William L. Jackson: chief financial officer, director

Grants Analysis

Disclosure Period: fiscal year ending May 31, 2004
Total Grants: $2,201,100
Number of Grants: 194
Average Grant: $9,823*
Highest Grant: $25,000
Lowest Grant: $1,000
Typical Range: $1,000 to $20,000
*Note: Average grant figure excludes three highest grants ($325,000).

Recent Grants

Note: Grants derived from 2004 Form 990.
General

125,000	Santa Barbara Cottage Hospital Foundation, Santa Barbara, CA -- for building campaign
100,000	Girls Inc., Santa Barbara, CA
100,000	Santa Barbara Center for the Performing Arts, Santa Barbara, CA -- for building campaign
75,000	Braille Institute, Santa Barbara, CA -- for capital campaign
50,000	Boys and Girls Club Westside, Santa Barbara, CA
50,000	Crane Country Day School, Santa Barbara, CA -- for library and fine arts center
50,000	Laguna Blanca School, Santa Barbara, CA -- for capital campaign
50,000	Laguna Cottages for Seniors, Santa Barbara, CA -- for capital campaign
50,000	Lobero Theater Foundation, Santa Barbara, CA -- for capital campaign
50,000	Nonprofit Support Center of Santa Barbara County, Santa Barbara, CA

JACKSON FOUNDATION (OR)

Giving Contact

Robert H. Depew, Trust Officer
c/o US National Bank of Oregon
PO Box 3168
Portland, OR 97208
Phone: (503)275-6574

Description

Founded: 1960
EIN: 936020752
Organization Type: General Purpose Foundation
Giving Locations: OR: Portland
Grant Types: Capital, Endowment, Matching, Multiyear/Continuing Support, Project, Research.

Donor Information

Founder: Maria C. Jackson

Financial Summary

Total Giving: $497,530 (fiscal year ending June 30, 2004); $793,460 (fiscal 2001)
Assets: $12,945,775 (fiscal 2004); $16,116,768 (fiscal 2001)

Typical Recipients

Arts & Humanities: Arts Associations & Councils, Arts Festivals, Arts Funds, Arts Institutes, Ballet, Dance, Historic Preservation, History & Archaeology, Libraries, Museums/Galleries, Music, Opera, Performing Arts, Public Broadcasting, Theater

Civic & Public Affairs: Botanical Gardens/Parks, Clubs, Community Foundations, Economic Development, Employment/Job Training, Civic & Public Affairs-General, Hispanic Affairs, Housing, Legal Aid, Urban & Community Affairs, Women's Affairs, Zoos/Aquariums

Education: Afterschool/Enrichment Programs, Arts/Humanities Education, Colleges & Universities, Community & Junior Colleges, Education-General, Medical Education, Preschool Education, Private Education (Precollege), Public Education (Precollege), Science/Mathematics Education, Student Aid

Environment: Environment-General, Resource Conservation, Wildlife Protection

Health: AIDS/HIV, Alzheimer's Disease, Children's Health/Hospitals, Clinics/Medical Centers, Emergency/Ambulance Services, Health Funds, Health Organizations, Hospices, Hospitals, Long-Term Care, Medical Rehabilitation, Medical Research, Mental

Health, Public Health, Speech & Hearing
International: Health Care/Hospitals
Religion: Jewish Causes, Religious Organizations, Religious Welfare
Science: Science Museums
Social Services: At-Risk Youth, Camps, Child Welfare, Community Centers, Community Service Organizations, Counseling, Day Care, Domestic Violence, Family Planning, Family Services, Food/Clothing Distribution, Homes, People with Disabilities, Recreation & Athletics, Scouts, Senior Services, Shelters/Homelessness, Social Services-General, Substance Abuse, United Funds/United Ways, Volunteer Services, YMCA/YWCA/YMHA/YWHA, Youth Organizations

Application Procedures

Initial Contact: A formal application is available upon request.
Deadlines: None; applications are reviewed at the spring, fall, and winter meetings.

Restrictions

Grants are not made to individuals or private businesses, and generally not to a K-12 school. Grants are made only to organizations whose exemption letter shows them to be Oregon organizations.

Additional Information

The foundation reports, "Funds requested for operating purposes, staff salaries and the like do not, generally, have the priority that funds for one-time, special projects or developmental projects enjoy."
Publications: Annual Report; Application Form
Trust(s): US Natl Bank OR

Foundation Officials

Milo E. Ormseth: co-trustee
Julie Vigeland: co-trustee

Grants Analysis

Disclosure Period: fiscal year ending June 30, 2004
Total Grants: $497,530
Number of Grants: 123
Average Grant: $4,045
Highest Grant: $25,000
Lowest Grant: $1,000
Typical Range: $1,000 to $10,000

Recent Grants

Note: Grants derived from fiscal 2004 Form 990.
General

16,000	Portland Center State, Portland, OR
15,000	Nature Conservancy, Portland, OR
15,000	Oregon Food Bank Inc., Portland, OR
11,450	Journal of Public Welfare, Portland, OR
11,000	Oregon Children's Foundation, Portland, OR
11,000	Oregon Community Foundation, Portland, OR
10,000	Cascade Aids Project Inc., Portland, OR
10,000	Doernbecher Children's Hospital, Portland, OR
10,000	Marylhurst University, Marylhurst, OR
10,000	Oregon Ballet School, Portland, OR

MARGARET G. JACOBS CHARITABLE TRUST

Giving Contact

William R. Levy, Co-Trustee
PO Box 58910
6114 Ensley Drive
Flourtown, PA 19031
Phone: (215)587-6311

Description
Founded: 1994
EIN: 232743317
Organization Type: Private Foundation
Giving Locations: PA
Grant Types: General Support.

Donor Information
Founder: Established in 1994 by Margaret G. Jacobs.

Financial Summary
Gifts Received: $1,459,214 (fiscal year ending June 30, 1993). Note: In fiscal 1993, contributions were received from Margaret G. Jacobs.

Typical Recipients
Arts & Humanities: Libraries
Civic & Public Affairs: Botanical Gardens/Parks, Clubs, Civic & Public Affairs-General, Urban & Community Affairs, Women's Affairs
Education: Private Education (Precollege)
Health: Children's Health/Hospitals, Diabetes, Emergency/Ambulance Services, Hospices, Single-Disease Health Associations
International: International Relief Efforts
Religion: Churches, Jewish Causes, Religious Welfare
Social Services: Child Welfare, Community Service Organizations, Crime Prevention, Family Services, Food/Clothing Distribution, People with Disabilities, Shelters/Homelessness, Special Olympics, YMCA/YWCA/YMHA/YWHA

Application Procedures
Initial Contact: Send a brief letter of inquiry.
Deadlines: None.

Foundation Officials
Philip Brown: co-trustee
William R. Levy: co-trustee

Grants Analysis
Disclosure Period: fiscal year ending June 30, 2001
Total Grants: $139,050
Number of Grants: 43
Average Grant: $2,392*
Highest Grant: $27,500
Lowest Grant: $1,000
Typical Range: $1,000 to $5,000
*Note: Average grant figure excludes two highest grants ($41,000).

Recent Grants
Note: Grants derived from fiscal 2001 Form 990.

Library-Related
2,500	William Jeanes Memorial Library, Lafayette Hill, PA

General
27,500	American Red Cross, Philadelphia, PA
13,500	Germantown Friends School, Philadelphia, PA
5,000	Carson Valley School, Flourtown, PA
5,000	Congregation Kol Ami, New York, NY
5,000	Green Tree School, Philadelphia, PA
5,000	Juvenile Diabetes Foundation, Philadelphia, PA
5,000	Salvation Army, Philadelphia, PA
5,000	Special Olympics, Norristown, PA
3,000	Academy of Notre Dame De Namur, Villanova, PA
3,000	St. Christopher's Hospital for Children, Philadelphia, PA

BERNARD H. AND BLANCHE E. JACOBSON FOUNDATION

Giving Contact
John L. Ray, Trustee
109 Capitol St., Suite 700
Charleston, WV 25301
Phone: (304)342-1141

Description
Founded: 1952
EIN: 556014902
Organization Type: Private Foundation
Giving Locations: WV: Kanawha Valley, Charleston
Grant Types: General Support.

Donor Information
Founder: Bernard H. Jacobson, Blanche E. Jacobson

Financial Summary
Total Giving: $394,500 (2003); $448,500 (2001). Note: 1997 Giving includes United Way (50,000).
Giving Analysis: Giving for 2001 includes: foundation grants to United Way ($50,000)
Assets: $7,244,560 (2003); $7,427,208 (2001)

Typical Recipients
Arts & Humanities: Arts Associations & Councils, Arts Centers, Community Arts, Film & Video, Historic Preservation, History & Archaeology, Libraries, Museums/Galleries, Music, Opera, Public Broadcasting, Theater
Civic & Public Affairs: Business/Free Enterprise, Chambers of Commerce, Community Foundations, Economic Development, Ethnic Organizations, Civic & Public Affairs-General, Housing, Philanthropic Organizations, Professional & Trade Associations, Urban & Community Affairs, Women's Affairs
Education: Arts/Humanities Education, Business Education, Colleges & Universities, Continuing Education, Education Funds, Education Reform, Faculty Development, Education-General, Literacy, Minority Education, Public Education (Precollege), Science/Mathematics Education, Secondary Education (Private), Vocational & Technical Education
Environment: Environment-General, Research
Health: Clinics/Medical Centers, Emergency/Ambulance Services, Health Organizations, Hospices, Mental Health
International: International Affairs, Missionary/Religious Activities
Religion: Churches, Jewish Causes, Religious Organizations, Religious Welfare, Synagogues/Temples
Science: Science-General, Scientific Centers & Institutes, Scientific Research
Social Services: At-Risk Youth, Camps, Child Welfare, Community Service Organizations, Counseling, Family Services, Food/Clothing Distribution, Homes, Recreation & Athletics, Scouts, Shelters/Homelessness, United Funds/United Ways, Volunteer Services, YMCA/YWCA/YMHA/YWHA, Youth Organizations

Application Procedures
Initial Contact: The foundation has no formal grant application procedure or application form.
Application Requirements: Include description of project, budget, amount requested, other funding sources and amount requested from them, proof of tax-exempt status, name, address, and telephone number of contact person.
Deadlines: None.
Review Process: The trustees generally meet in March, June, September, and December to review applications.

Additional Information
Trust(s): Branch Banking & Trust Company

Foundation Officials
John L. Ray: trustee
L. Newton Thomas, Jr.: trustee

Grants Analysis
Disclosure Period: calendar year ending 2003
Total Grants: $369,500*
Number of Grants: 38
Average Grant: $7,284*
Highest Grant: $100,000
Lowest Grant: $500
Typical Range: $5,000 to $15,000
*Note: Giving excludes United Way. Average grant figure excludes highest grant.

Recent Grants
Note: Grants derived from 2003 Form 990.
General
100,000	Clay Center for Arts and Sciences, Charleston, WV
25,000	LifeBridge Inc., Charleston, WV
25,000	United Way of Kanawha Valley, Charleston, WV
18,000	Federated Jewish Charities of Charleston Inc., Charleston, WV
15,000	West Virginia Symphony Orchestra, Charleston, WV
15,000	YWCA of Charleston, Charleston, WV
13,000	Scottie's Place, Peterstown, WV
11,250	Business and Industrial Development Corporation, Charleston, WV
10,000	Boy Scouts of America Buckskin Council, Charleston, WV
10,000	Greater Kanawha Valley Foundation, Charleston, WV

JAFFE FOUNDATION

Giving Contact
Holly Seagrave, Executive Secretary
PO Box 307
Stockbridge, MA 01262
Phone: (413)298-0000
Fax: (413)298-3199

Description
Founded: 1962
EIN: 046049261
Organization Type: Private Foundation
Giving Locations: MA
Grant Types: General Support.

Donor Information
Founder: the late Meyer Jaffe, Edwin A. Jaffe

Financial Summary
Total Giving: $298,189 (fiscal year ending June 30, 2004); $453,734 (fiscal 2001)
Giving Analysis: Giving for fiscal 2004 includes: foundation grants to United Way ($10,000)
Assets: $1,932,950 (fiscal 2004); $4,314,493 (fiscal 2001)
Gifts Received: $250 (fiscal 1997); $15,371 (fiscal 1994). Note: In fiscal 1997, contributions were received from Edwin A. Jaffe.

Typical Recipients
Arts & Humanities: Arts Associations & Councils, Arts Centers, Arts Outreach, Dance, Arts & Humanities-General, Libraries, Museums/Galleries, Music, Opera, Performing Arts, Public Broadcasting, Theater
Civic & Public Affairs: African American Affairs, Economic Policy, Ethnic Organizations, Civic & Public Affairs-General, Law & Justice, Urban & Communi-

ty Affairs
Education: Arts/Humanities Education, Colleges & Universities, Community & Junior Colleges, Education-General, International Studies, Private Education (Precollege)
Environment: Environment-General, Resource Conservation
Health: AIDS/HIV, Cancer, Children's Health/Hospitals, Health Organizations, Hospices, Hospitals, Medical Research, Mental Health, Nursing Services, Public Health, Single-Disease Health Associations
International: Foreign Arts Organizations, Foreign Educational Institutions, Health Care/Hospitals, Human Rights, International Peace & Security Issues, International Relations, International Relief Efforts, Missionary/Religious Activities
Religion: Jewish Causes, Religious Organizations, Religious Welfare, Synagogues/Temples
Social Services: Child Welfare, Community Centers, Community Service Organizations, Family Planning, Food/Clothing Distribution, People with Disabilities, Recreation & Athletics, Sexual Abuse, United Funds/United Ways, Youth Organizations

Application Procedures

Initial Contact: Send a brief letter of inquiry.
Application Requirements: amount requested and purpose of funds sought.
Deadlines: None.

Restrictions

Does not support individuals.

Additional Information

Publications: Mission Statement (including General Guidelines)

Foundation Officials

David S. Greer: trustee B Brooklyn, NY 1925. ED University of Notre Dame BS (1948); University of Chicago MD (1953); Brown University MA (1975); Southeastern Massachusetts University LHD (1981). PRIM CORP EMPL professor community health: Brown University. NONPR AFFIL member: RI Governments Task Force Institute Mental Health; member: RI Medicine Society; founding director: International Physicians Prevention Nuclear War; member: International Society Rehabilitation Medicine; member: Institute Medicine; member: Institute Mental Health Rhode Island; member: American Congress Rehabilitation Medicine; director: Association Home Health Agencies.
Edwin A. Jaffe: chairman
Lola Jaffe: vchairman
Robert Jaffe: trustee

Grants Analysis

Disclosure Period: fiscal year ending June 30, 2004
Total Grants: $288,189*
Number of Grants: 58
Average Grant: $3,361*
Highest Grant: $50,000
Lowest Grant: $250
Typical Range: $1,000 to $5,000
*Note: Giving excludes United Way. Average grant figure excludes two highest grants ($100,000).

Recent Grants

Note: Grants derived from fiscal 2004 Form 990.
General

50,000	Berkshire South Regional Community Center, Stockbridge, MA -- towards capital campaign building
50,000	Mahaiwe Performing Arts Center, Great Barrington, MA -- funds for arts and cultural activities
17,500	Manhattan Theatre Club's Outreach Program, New York, NY
15,000	Berkshire Theatre Festival, Stockbridge, MA -- towards youth outreach programs
13,500	Austen Riggs Center, Stockbridge, MA

10,000	Berkshire United Way, Pittsfield, MA
10,000	Brown University, Providence, RI
10,000	Human Rights Watch, New York, NY
10,000	Jewish Federation of the Berkshires, Pittsfield, MA
7,500	Coffee Kids, Santa Fe, NM

JAFFEE FOUNDATION

Giving Contact

Glenn A. Schwartz, Trustee
111 W. Washington St., Rm. 1025
Chicago, IL 60602-2705
Phone: (312)346-6650

Description

Founded: 1992
EIN: 367001569
Organization Type: Private Foundation
Grant Types: General Support.

Financial Summary

Total Giving: $25,000 (2001)
Assets: $654,240 (2001)
Gifts Received: $691,886 (1992)

Typical Recipients

Arts & Humanities: Arts Festivals, Arts Institutes, Historic Preservation, Libraries, Museums/Galleries, Music, Opera, Public Broadcasting
Civic & Public Affairs: Botanical Gardens/Parks, Zoos/Aquariums
Education: Colleges & Universities
Environment: Environment-General
Health: AIDS/HIV, Arthritis, Cancer, Children's Health/Hospitals, Clinics/Medical Centers, Diabetes, Emergency/Ambulance Services, Hospitals, Medical Research, Single-Disease Health Associations
Religion: Jewish Causes
Science: Science Museums

Application Procedures

Initial Contact: The foundation has no formal grant application procedure or application form. Send a brief letter of inquiry.
Deadlines: None.

Foundation Officials

Sidney F. Jarrow: trustee
Glenn A. Schwartz: trustee

Grants Analysis

Disclosure Period: calendar year ending 2001
Total Grants: $25,000
Number of Grants: 51
Average Grant: $340*
Highest Grant: $8,000
Lowest Grant: $50
Typical Range: $100 to $500
*Note: Average grant figure excludes highest grant.

Recent Grants

Note: Grants derived from 2002 Form 990.
Library-Related

500	Glencoe Public Library, Glencoe, IL

General

8,000	Jewish United Fund of Metropolitan Chicago, Chicago, IL
1,850	North Shore Congregation Israel, Glencoe, IL
500	Alder Planetarium and Astronomy Museum, Chicago, IL
500	Art Institute of Chicago, Chicago, IL
500	Arthritis Foundation Greater Chicago Chapter, Chicago, IL
500	Chicago Symphony Orchestra, Chicago, IL

500	Epilepsy Foundation of Greater Chicago, Chicago, IL
500	Field Museum of Natural History, Chicago, IL
500	Lyric Opera of Chicago, Chicago, IL
500	Parkinson's Disease Foundation, New York, NY

LEE AND JOSEPH D. JAMAIL FOUNDATION

Giving Contact

Robert L. Jamail, Secretary & Treasurer
1200 Smith St., Suite 1135
Houston, TX 77002
Phone: (713)650-8544

Description

Founded: 1986
EIN: 760181247
Organization Type: Private Foundation
Giving Locations: TX
Grant Types: General Support.

Donor Information

Founder: Joseph D. Jamail, Lillie H. Jamail

Financial Summary

Total Giving: $440,000 (2003); $626,918 (2001)
Assets: $15,356,176 (2003); $14,527,096 (2001)
Gifts Received: $34,724 (1998); $200,000 (1996)

Typical Recipients

Arts & Humanities: Arts Centers, History & Archaeology, Libraries, Museums/Galleries, Music, Theater, Visual Arts
Civic & Public Affairs: Botanical Gardens/Parks, Clubs, Civic & Public Affairs-General, Hispanic Affairs, Housing, Law & Justice, Municipalities/Towns, Parades/Festivals, Urban & Community Affairs, Women's Affairs, Zoos/Aquariums
Education: Agricultural Education, Arts/Humanities Education, Colleges & Universities, Education Funds, Education Reform, Education-General, Legal Education, Literacy, Medical Education, Minority Education, Preschool Education, Private Education (Precollege), Religious Education, Secondary Education (Private), Special Education, Student Aid
Environment: Environment-General, Protection
Health: AIDS/HIV, Cancer, Children's Health/Hospitals, Clinics/Medical Centers, Emergency/Ambulance Services, Eyes/Blindness, Heart, Hospices, Hospitals, Medical Rehabilitation, Mental Health, Multiple Sclerosis, Public Health, Single-Disease Health Associations, Speech & Hearing
International: International Environmental Issues, International Relief Efforts
Religion: Churches, Ministries, Religious Welfare
Science: Science Museums
Social Services: At-Risk Youth, Camps, Child Abuse, Child Welfare, Community Service Organizations, Domestic Violence, Family Planning, Family Services, People with Disabilities, Senior Services, Social Services-General, Special Olympics, Youth Organizations

Application Procedures

Initial Contact: Send a brief letter of inquiry on organization's letterhead.
Application Requirements: Include proof of tax-exempt status.
Deadlines: None.

Foundation Officials

Denise S. Davidson: secretary
Joseph D. Jamail, III: vice president
Lee H. Jamail: president

Randall Hage Jamail: vice president
Robert Lee Jamail: secretary, treasurer

Grants Analysis

Disclosure Period: calendar year ending 2003
Total Grants: $440,000
Number of Grants: 41
Average Grant: $8,975*
Highest Grant: $81,000
Lowest Grant: $1,000
Typical Range: $1,000 to $15,000
*Note: Average grant excludes highest grant.

Recent Grants

Note: Grants derived from 2003 Form 990.
General

81,000	Kinkaid School, Houston, TX
30,000	St. Stephen's Episcopal School, Houston, TX
28,000	Museum of Fine Arts, Houston, TX
25,000	Alley Theatre, Houston, TX
25,000	University of Texas at Austin-C Huber Teaching Foundation, Houston, TX
24,000	Houston Arboretum and Nature Conservancy, Houston, TX
22,500	Contemporary Arts Museum, Houston, TX
18,500	Houston Museum of Natural Science, Houston, TX
13,000	St. John's School, Houston, TX
12,500	Center for Hearing and Speech, Houston, TX

J. W. AND IDA M. JAMESON FOUNDATION

Giving Contact

Les M. Huhn, President
PO Box 397
Sierra Madre, CA 91024
Phone: (626)355-3020

Description

Founded: 1955
EIN: 956031465
Organization Type: Private Foundation
Giving Locations: CA
Grant Types: General Support, Research, Scholarship.

Donor Information

Founder: J. W. Jameson Corp., the late Ida May Jameson

Financial Summary

Total Giving: $775,000 (fiscal year ending June 30, 2004); $855,000 (fiscal 2001)
Assets: $14,505,009 (fiscal 2004); $15,269,748 (fiscal 2001)
Gifts Received: $990,000 (fiscal 1996); $973,000 (fiscal 1995); $1,008,851 (fiscal 1994)

Typical Recipients

Arts & Humanities: Arts Associations & Councils, Community Arts, Arts & Humanities-General, Libraries, Museums/Galleries, Music, Public Broadcasting, Visual Arts
Civic & Public Affairs: Botanical Gardens/Parks, Civic & Public Affairs-General, Law & Justice, Legal Aid, Philanthropic Organizations, Public Policy, Safety, Zoos/Aquariums
Education: Colleges & Universities, Community & Junior Colleges, Education Funds, Education-General, Legal Education, Medical Education, Preschool Education, Private Education (Precollege), Public Education (Precollege), Religious Education, Secondary Education (Public), Special Education,

Student Aid
Health: Children's Health/Hospitals, Emergency/Ambulance Services, Geriatric Health, Health Organizations, Hospitals, Long-Term Care, Medical Research, Preventive Medicine/Wellness Organizations, Research/Studies Institutes, Single-Disease Health Associations
International: International Peace & Security Issues
Religion: Churches, Missionary Activities (Domestic), Religious Organizations, Religious Welfare
Social Services: Community Service Organizations, People with Disabilities, Recreation & Athletics, Senior Services, Social Services-General, Substance Abuse, Youth Organizations

Application Procedures

Initial Contact: Send a brief letter of inquiry.
Application Requirements: Include a description of organization, purpose of funds sought, amount requested, and proof of tax-exempt status.
Deadlines: February 1.
Decision Notification: The Directors meet in March to decide grant recipients.

Foundation Officials

Bill B. Betz: secretary, director
Les M. Huhn: president
Frederick Leroy Leydorf: vice president, director B Toledo, OH 1930. ED University of Toledo (1948-1949); University of Michigan BBA (1953); University of California, Los Angeles JD (1958). NONPR AFFIL member: Phi Delta Theta; member: University California Los Angeles Law Alumni Association; member: Los Angeles World Affairs Council; member: Phi Delta Phi; member: Los Angeles County Bar Association; member: Los Angeles County Bar Foundation; member: Life Insurance & Trust Council; member: California Bar Association; member: Intl Academy Estate & Trust Law; member: American Bar Association; member: American College Trust & Estate Counsel. CLUB AFFIL Jonathan Club; Laguna Hills Golf Club; Chancery Club.
Pauline Vetrovec: treasurer

Grants Analysis

Disclosure Period: fiscal year ending June 30, 2004
Total Grants: $775,000
Number of Grants: 51
Average Grant: $15,196
Highest Grant: $51,000
Lowest Grant: $5,000
Typical Range: $5,000 to $30,000

Recent Grants

Note: Grants derived from fiscal 2004 Form 990.
General

51,000	University of California Los Angeles Foundation, Los Angeles, CA
50,000	Huntington Medical Research Institute, Pasadena, CA
50,000	University of South Carolina School of Internal Medicine, Los Angeles, CA
50,000	World Institute of Disability, Oakland, CA
40,000	Union Station Foundation, Pasadena, CA
40,000	University of Michigan, Ann Arbor, MI
34,000	Zoological Society of San Diego, San Diego, CA
30,000	Paraclete Mission Group Inc., Colorado Springs, CO
25,000	Pasadena City College, Pasadena, CA
25,000	Reason Foundation, Los Angeles, CA

OLEONDA JAMESON TRUST

Giving Contact

Malcolm McLane, Trustee
c/o Orr & Reno

1 Eagle Sq.
PO Box 3550
Concord, NH 03302-3550
Phone: (603)224-2381
Fax: (603)224-2318

Description

Founded: 1977
EIN: 026048930
Organization Type: Private Foundation
Giving Locations: NH: Concord and Merrimack County
Grant Types: General Support.

Financial Summary

Total Giving: $333,962 (2001)
Giving Analysis: Giving for 2001 includes: foundation grants to United Way ($30,000)
Assets: $6,189,490 (2001)

Typical Recipients

Arts & Humanities: Arts Appreciation, Arts Associations & Councils, Arts Centers, Arts Institutes, History & Archaeology, Libraries, Museums/Galleries, Music, Public Broadcasting
Civic & Public Affairs: Civil Rights, Community Foundations, Civic & Public Affairs-General, Housing, Law & Justice, Legal Aid, Municipalities/Towns, Parades/Festivals, Philanthropic Organizations, Professional & Trade Associations, Public Policy, Urban & Community Affairs, Women's Affairs, Zoos/Aquariums
Education: Arts/Humanities Education, Colleges & Universities, Medical Education, Minority Education, Private Education (Precollege), Public Education (Precollege), Science/Mathematics Education, Student Aid
Environment: Air/Water Quality, Environment-General, Resource Conservation
Health: AIDS/HIV, Clinics/Medical Centers, Hospitals, Mental Health, Nursing Services, Public Health, Respiratory, Single-Disease Health Associations
Religion: Churches, Religious Organizations, Religious Welfare
Social Services: Animal Protection, Child Welfare, Community Centers, Community Service Organizations, Day Care, Domestic Violence, Emergency Relief, Family Planning, Family Services, Food/Clothing Distribution, Homes, People with Disabilities, Recreation & Athletics, Scouts, United Funds/United Ways, YMCA/YWCA/YMHA/YWHA, Youth Organizations

Application Procedures

Initial Contact: Send a brief letter of inquiry.
Application Requirements: Include amount requested, purpose of funds sought, and a description of organization.
Deadlines: None.

Restrictions

Grantmaking is limited to charitable organizations or individuals in the Concord, NH area.

Foundation Officials

Charles F. Leahy: trustee
Malcolm McLane: trustee
Robert H. Reno: trustee
Ronald Snow: trustee

Grants Analysis

Disclosure Period: calendar year ending 2001
Total Grants: $303,962*
Number of Grants: 27
Average Grant: $11,258
Highest Grant: $30,000
Typical Range: $1,000 to $25,000
*Note: Giving excludes United Way.

Recent Grants

Note: Grants derived from 2001 Form 990.

Library-Related

20,000   Concord Public Library Foundation, Concord, NH -- children's Room Project

General

30,000   United Way of Merrimack County, Concord, NH -- provide community services

25,000   Bishop Brady High School, Concord, NH -- building improvements

25,000   Concord Community Music School, Concord, NH -- develop new music programs for community

25,000   New Hampshire Center Public Policy Study, Durham, NH -- study of issues affecting New Hampshire persons

25,000   New Hampshire Charitable Foundation, Concord, NH -- scholarship fund

20,000   Fellowship Housing Opportunities, Concord, NH -- rehabilitation of low income housing

20,000   Initiative for a 20/20 Vision for Concord, Concord, NH -- vision guidelines

13,667   Rolfz and Rumford Home, Concord, NH -- repairs

12,500   Canterbury Shaker Village, Canterbury, NH -- building restoration

12,000   Concord Area Trust for Community Housing, Concord, MA -- education center

JANIRVE FOUNDATION

Giving Contact

Met Ray Poston, Chairman, Director
One North Pack Square, Suite 416
Asheville, NC 28801
Phone: (828)258-1877
Fax: (828)258-1837

Description

Founded: 1964
EIN: 596147678
Organization Type: General Purpose Foundation
Giving Locations: FL: Palm Beach, West Palm Beach; NC: Western North Carolina
Grant Types: Capital, Challenge, General Support, Matching, Operating Expenses, Project.

Donor Information

Founder: Established in 1964 by the late Irving J. Reuter, a General Motors executive. Upon the death of his widow, Jeannett Reuter, in 1984, the foundation became active on a full-time basis.

In 1985, the foundation received $25 million from the estate of Irving and Jeannett Reuter. Financial records are kept in Palm Beach, FL, the location of the Reuter's residence. The grant-making office is located in Asheville, NC, where the Reuters kept a summer home.

Financial Summary

Total Giving: $3,779,310 (2003); $5,185,319 (2002)
Giving Analysis: Giving for 2003 includes: foundation grants to United Way ($35,000)
Assets: $53,614,081 (2003); $50,678,992 (2002)

Typical Recipients

Arts & Humanities: Arts Associations & Councils, Arts Centers, Arts Festivals, Arts Funds, Arts Institutes, Ethnic & Folk Arts, Arts & Humanities-General, Historic Preservation, History & Archaeology, Libraries, Literary Arts, Museums/Galleries, Music, Opera, Public Broadcasting, Theater
Civic & Public Affairs: Botanical Gardens/Parks, Business/Free Enterprise, Chambers of Commerce, Community Foundations, Employment/Job Training, Civic & Public Affairs-General, Hispanic Affairs, Housing, Inner-City Development, Law & Justice, Legal Aid, Philanthropic Organizations, Professional & Trade Associations, Public Policy, Safety, Urban &

Community Affairs
Education: Afterschool/Enrichment Programs, Arts/Humanities Education, Colleges & Universities, Community & Junior Colleges, Education Associations, Education Funds, Education Reform, Education-General, Leadership Training, Literacy, Medical Education, Preschool Education, Private Education (Precollege), Public Education (Precollege), Special Education, Student Aid, Vocational & Technical Education
Environment: Air/Water Quality, Environment-General, Protection, Resource Conservation
Health: Adolescent Health Issues, Alzheimer's Disease, Cancer, Children's Health/Hospitals, Clinics/Medical Centers, Emergency/Ambulance Services, Health-General, Geriatric Health, Health Organizations, Hospices, Hospitals, Long-Term Care, Medical Rehabilitation, Preventive Medicine/Wellness Organizations, Public Health, Single-Disease Health Associations, Transplant Networks/Donor Banks
International: Foreign Educational Institutions
Religion: Bible Study/Translation, Religion-General, Jewish Causes, Ministries, Religious Organizations, Religious Welfare
Science: Science Museums, Scientific Centers & Institutes
Social Services: Animal Protection, Big Brothers/Big Sisters, Camps, Child Abuse, Child Welfare, Community Centers, Community Service Organizations, Counseling, Day Care, Domestic Violence, Emergency Relief, Family Planning, Family Services, Food/Clothing Distribution, Homes, People with Disabilities, Recreation & Athletics, Scouts, Senior Services, Social Services-General, Special Olympics, Substance Abuse, United Funds/United Ways, YMCA/YWCA/YMHA/YWHA, Youth Organizations

Application Procedures

Initial Contact: Prospective applicants may call or write the foundation for an application.
Application Requirements: Applicants should send a written proposal, no longer than three single-spaced pages, including a detailed description of the organization's activities, amount requested, grant purpose, financial information, and a list of governing members. Four copies of the proposal, with a completed application form and IRS tax-exemption letter, should be sent to the foundation's office.
Deadlines: Proposals should be received by December 1 for the first quarter, by March 1 for the second quarter, by June 1 for the third quarter, and by September 1 for the fourth quarter.
Review Process: Proposals are considered quarterly by a five-person advisory committee. Applicants will be notified of the committee's decision following the final meeting of the quarter.

Restrictions

Grants are not made to individuals.

Additional Information

All accepted applicants are expected to furnish a progress report(s) as well as a project completion report accounting for the use of the Janirve Foundation grant. The foundation makes single-year grants as opposed to multiple-year awards. It gives low priority to projects proposed by government groups or those operated primarily with tax funds.

First National Bank in Palm Beach, a division of First Union National Bank is the corporate trustee of the foundation.
Publications: Guidelines; Application Form; Information Sheet for Applicants
Trust(s): First National in Palm Beach

Foundation Officials

E. Charles Dyson: director
John W. Erichson: director
Met R. Poston: chairman, director
James Woollcott: director
Richard B. Wynne: director

Grants Analysis

Disclosure Period: calendar year ending 2003
Total Grants: $3,744,310*
Number of Grants: 71
Average Grant: $47,019*
Highest Grant: $250,000
Lowest Grant: $5,000
Typical Range: $10,000 to $100,000
*Note: Giving excludes United Way. Average grant figure excludes two highest grants ($500,000).

Recent Grants

Note: Grants derived from 2003 Form 990.
General

300,000   Community Foundation of Western North Carolina, Asheville, NC

250,000   Daniel Boone Council Inc. Boy Scouts of America, Asheville, NC

250,000   North Carolina Center for Creative Retirement, Asheville, NC

250,000   Warren Wilson College, Asheville, NC

166,000   Nature Conservancy North Carolina Chapter, Durham, NC

150,000   Mars Hill College, Mars Hill, NC

150,000   Our Next Generation Inc., Asheville, NC

150,000   Tri-County Community College Foundation, Murphy, NC

120,000   Asheville Area Chamber of Commerce Community Betterment Foundation, Asheville, NC

100,000   Community Arts Council of Western North Carolina, Asheville, NC

JAQUA FOUNDATION

Giving Contact

Eli Hoffman, Chairman
100 Campus Drive
PO Box 944
Florham Park, NJ 07932
Phone: (973)593-7010
Fax: (973)593-7070

Description

Founded: 1977
EIN: 222086399
Organization Type: Private Foundation
Giving Locations: NJ; NY
Grant Types: Endowment, General Support, Scholarship.

Donor Information

Founder: the late George R. Jaqua

Financial Summary

Total Giving: $2,338,966 (2003); $4,540,714 (2001)
Giving Analysis: Giving for 2003 includes: foundation scholarships ($176,000); 2001: foundation scholarships ($220,000)
Assets: $5,766,767 (2003); $11,466,113 (2001)
Gifts Received: $22,974 (1996); $21,500 (1995); $27,550 (1994)

Typical Recipients

Arts & Humanities: Historic Preservation, History & Archaeology, Libraries, Museums/Galleries, Music, Performing Arts
Civic & Public Affairs: Economic Development, Civic & Public Affairs-General, Housing, Professional & Trade Associations
Education: Arts/Humanities Education, Colleges & Universities, Education Associations, Elementary Education (Private), Engineering/Technological Education, Medical Education, Private Education (Precollege), Public Education (Precollege), Science/Mathematics Education, Student Aid
Environment: Resource Conservation
Health: Cancer, Children's Health/Hospitals, Clinics/

Medical Centers, Emergency/Ambulance Services, Geriatric Health, Health Organizations, Heart, Hospitals, Hospitals (University Affiliated), Long-Term Care, Medical Research, Public Health, Single-Disease Health Associations, Speech & Hearing
International: Foreign Educational Institutions
Religion: Churches, Jewish Causes, Ministries, Religious Organizations, Religious Welfare, Synagogues/Temples
Social Services: Animal Protection, At-Risk Youth, Child Welfare, Community Service Organizations, Family Services, Food/Clothing Distribution, Homes, People with Disabilities, Recreation & Athletics, Scouts, United Funds/United Ways, Volunteer Services, YMCA/YWCA/YMHA/YWHA, Youth Organizations

Application Procedures

Initial Contact: Submit a brief letter of inquiry.
Application Requirements: Include a description of organization, amount requested, and purpose of funds sought.
Deadlines: None.

Restrictions

Does not support individuals or private foundations.

Foundation Officials

W. Fletcher Hock, Jr.: secretary
Eli Hoffman: chairman

Grants Analysis

Disclosure Period: calendar year ending 2003
Total Grants: $2,162,966*
Number of Grants: 47
Average Grant: $25,282*
Highest Grant: $1,000,000
Lowest Grant: $1,000
Typical Range: $10,000 to $50,000
*Note: Giving excludes scholarship. Average grant figure excludes highest grant.

Recent Grants

Note: Grants derived from 2003 Form 990.
General

1,000,000	New Jersey Symphony Orchestra, Newark, NJ
200,000	Valley Hospital, Ridgewood, NJ
100,000	Animal Medical Center, New York, NY
100,000	New Jersey Performing Arts Center, Newark, NJ
100,000	St. Barnabas Development Foundation, Livingston, NJ
83,000	Newark Museum, Newark, NJ
50,000	Cornell University, Ithaca, NY
50,000	Rutgers the Sate University, New Brunswick, NJ -- for scholarships
50,000	School in Rose Valley, Rose Valley, PA
35,000	Lafayette College, Easton, PA -- for scholarships

JARSON KAPLAN FOUNDATION

Giving Contact

Stanley M. Kaplan, Trustee
9435 Waterstone Blvd., Suite 390
Cincinnati, OH 45249
Phone: (513)785-6060

Alternate Contact

Myron J. Kaplan

Description

Founded: 1955
EIN: 316033453
Organization Type: Private Foundation

Former Name: Isaac N. and Esther M. Jarson Charitable Trust.
Former Name: Isaac and Esther Jarson-Stanley and Mickey Kaplan Foundation (2000).
Giving Locations: OH: Cincinnati The greater Cincinnati area
Grant Types: General Support.

Financial Summary

Total Giving: $37,750 (2002)
Assets: $1,840,850 (2002)

Typical Recipients

Arts & Humanities: Arts Associations & Councils, Arts Centers, Arts Festivals, Arts Funds, Arts Institutes, Arts Outreach, Ballet, Community Arts, Dance, Arts & Humanities-General, Historic Preservation, Libraries, Museums/Galleries, Music, Opera, Performing Arts, Public Broadcasting, Theater
Civic & Public Affairs: African American Affairs, Botanical Gardens/Parks, Community Foundations, Civic & Public Affairs-General, Housing, Parades/Festivals, Philanthropic Organizations, Urban & Community Affairs, Women's Affairs
Education: Afterschool/Enrichment Programs, Arts/Humanities Education, Business Education, Colleges & Universities, Education Funds, Engineering/Technological Education, Literacy, Medical Education, Minority Education, Private Education (Precollege), Public Education (Precollege), Religious Education, Secondary Education (Public), Student Aid
Environment: Air/Water Quality
Health: AIDS/HIV, Cancer, Children's Health/Hospitals, Clinics/Medical Centers, Diabetes, Emergency/Ambulance Services, Health Organizations, Hospices, Hospitals, Kidney, Medical Rehabilitation, Medical Research, Mental Health, Prenatal Health Issues, Preventive Medicine/Wellness Organizations, Single-Disease Health Associations
International: Foreign Arts Organizations, Health Care/Hospitals
Religion: Churches, Religion-General, Jewish Causes, Religious Organizations, Religious Welfare, Synagogues/Temples
Science: Science Museums
Social Services: Animal Protection, At-Risk Youth, Child Welfare, Community Centers, Community Service Organizations, Emergency Relief, Food/Clothing Distribution, People with Disabilities, Recreation & Athletics, Senior Services, Shelters/Homelessness, Substance Abuse, United Funds/United Ways, YMCA/YWCA/YMHA/YWHA, Youth Organizations

Application Procedures

Initial Contact: Send a brief letter of inquiry.
Application Requirements: Include proof of tax-exempt status.
Deadlines: None.

Foundation Officials

Myran J. Kaplan: trustee
Stanley Meisel Kaplan, MD: trustee B Cincinnati, OH 1922. ED University of Cincinnati BS (1943); University of Cincinnati MD (1946); Institute of Psychoanalysis (1962-1967). PRIM NONPR EMPL professor, faculty department psychiatry: University of Cincinnati. CORP AFFIL chairman, director: G&J Pepsi Cola. NONPR AFFIL member: Sigma Xi; professor: University Cincinnati; director: Contemporary Arts Center Ohio; director: Friends College Conservatory Music; director: Cincinnati Art Museum; director: Cincinnati Ballet; director: Bonds Israel; member: American Psychoanalytic Association; member: American Psychosomatic Society; fellow: American Psychiatric Association; member: American Association University Professors; member: American Medical Association.

Grants Analysis

Disclosure Period: calendar year ending 2002
Total Grants: $37,750
Number of Grants: 5

Highest Grant: $18,000
Typical Range: $250 to $18,000

Recent Grants

Note: Grants derived from 2002 Form 990.
General

18,000	Adath Israel Congregation, Cincinnati, OH
10,000	Free Store Food Bank, Cincinnati, OH
6,500	Fine Arts Fund, Cincinnati, OH
3,000	Playhouse in the Park, Cincinnati, OH
250	WGUC, Cincinnati, OH

JELD-WEN INC.

Company Headquarters

3250 Lakeport Blvd.
Klamath Falls, OR 97601
Web: http://www.jeld-wen.com

Company Description

Founded: 1960
SIC(s): 2431 Millwork, 3442 Metal Doors, Sash & Trim.

Jeld-wen Foundation

Giving Contact

Carol Chesnut
JELD-WEN Foundation
PO Box 1329
Klamath Falls, OR 97601
Phone: (541)882-3451
Fax: (541)885-7454

Description

EIN: 936054272
Organization Type: Corporate Foundation
Giving Locations: major principally near operating locations and to national organizations.
Grant Types: Capital, Challenge, General Support, Project, Scholarship, Seed Money.

Financial Summary

Total Giving: $6,981,786 (2003); $7,496,346 (2001). Note: Contributes through foundation only. 1996 Giving includes scholarship ($117,600); United Way ($371,519).
Assets: $46,974,063 (2003); $33,014,422 (2002); $37,976,455 (2001)
Gifts Received: $13,456,000 (2003); $1,000,000 (2000); $2,989,000 (1998). Note: Contributions were received from JELD-WEN Inc.

Typical Recipients

Arts & Humanities: Arts Associations & Councils, Arts Centers, Arts Festivals, Film & Video, Historic Preservation, History & Archaeology, Libraries, Museums/Galleries, Music, Opera, Public Broadcasting, Theater
Civic & Public Affairs: Botanical Gardens/Parks, Business/Free Enterprise, Chambers of Commerce, Clubs, Community Foundations, Economic Development, Employment/Job Training, Civic & Public Affairs-General, Housing, Municipalities/Towns, Native American Affairs, Parades/Festivals, Philanthropic Organizations, Professional & Trade Associations, Public Policy, Safety, Urban & Community Affairs, Women's Affairs
Education: Arts/Humanities Education, Business Education, Colleges & Universities, Community & Junior Colleges, Education Associations, Education Funds, Education Reform, Elementary Education (Public), Engineering/Technological Education, Environmental Education, Education-General, Literacy, Preschool Education, Private Education (Precollege),

Public Education (Precollege), Science/Mathematics Education, Student Aid, Vocational & Technical Education

Environment: Forestry, Environment-General, Wildlife Protection

Health: Cancer, Children's Health/Hospitals, Clinics/Medical Centers, Emergency/Ambulance Services, Health-General, Health Policy/Cost Containment, Health Organizations, Hospices, Hospitals, Medical Rehabilitation, Medical Research, Prenatal Health Issues, Public Health

Religion: Ministries, Religious Organizations, Religious Welfare

Science: Science Museums

Social Services: Animal Protection, At-Risk Youth, Child Welfare, Community Centers, Community Service Organizations, Crime Prevention, Day Care, Domestic Violence, People with Disabilities, Recreation & Athletics, Scouts, Senior Services, Social Services-General, Substance Abuse, United Funds/United Ways, Volunteer Services, YMCA/YWCA/YMHA/YWHA, Youth Organizations

Application Procedures

Initial Contact: Write to request funding application.

Application Requirements: Applicants are encouraged to meet with a company manager in the area to discuss proposal. The completed application form should be submitted to this manager, who will forward it to the foundation.

Deadlines: Write to request deadline dates.

Review Process: Foundation board generally meets on a quarterly basis; receipt is acknowledged, and proposal may be accepted, rejected, or referred for modification within two weeks; proposals accepted for consideration are then reviewed at trustees' meeting in March, June, September, or December; proposal contact persons are notified within two weeks after meeting.

Evaluative Criteria: Location of organization relative to company operating areas, value of project to company employees and families, involvement of employees in organization and project proposed, few previous requests, proposed project planning, sources and uses of funds, and tax exempt status.

Notes: Foundation meeting dates vary due to requests received and scheduling logistics of foundation trustees.

Restrictions

Foundation does not fund projects related to religious purposes; proposals which duplicate government or private agency programs; projects which serve a very narrow segment of the community; proposals that the foundation feels are not clearly defined, not feasible, not cost effective, or inappropriate to meet existing needs. Funds must be used within the United States. Foundation generally discourages requests for annual support outside of United Way giving.

Rejected proposals may not be resubmitted during the same calendar year.

Additional Information

The foundation may fund an outstanding organization more than once in a short period of time, but is cautious not to let organizations become dependent on regular giving.

Corporate Officials

William Bernard Early: senior vice president, assistant secretary, director B Mexico, MO 1936. ED Stanford University (1958); Harvard University (1964). PRIM CORP EMPL senior vice president, assistant secretary, director: Jeld-Wen, Inc. NONPR AFFIL member: Initiative for Global Development.

Richard L. Wendt: chief executive officer, chairman B Dubuque, IA 1931. PRIM CORP EMPL chief executive officer, chairman: Jeld-Wen, Inc. CORP AFFIL director: Columbia Forest Products Inc.; director: Windmill Inns America Inc.; chairman: Avanti Industries Inc.; chairman: Bend Millwork System Inc.

Roderick C. Wendt: president, director B 1954. ED

Willamette University Law School JD (1980). PRIM CORP EMPL president, director: Jeld-Wen, Inc. CORP AFFIL treasurer: Windmill Inns America Inc.; president: 3D Industries Inc.; president: Bend Millwork System Inc. NONPR AFFIL trustee: National Park Foundation.

Larry V. Wetter: vice chairman, director B Rockwell City, IA 1933. ED Iowa State University of Science & Technology (1955). PRIM CORP EMPL vice chairman, director: Jeld-Wen, Inc.

Foundation Officials

William Bernard Early: trustee (see above)

R. F. Turner: trustee

Nancy Wendt: trustee B Dubuque, IA. NONPR AFFIL trustee: Oregon Tech Foundation.

Richard L. Wendt: trustee (see above)

Roderick C. Wendt: trustee (see above)

Grants Analysis

Disclosure Period: calendar year ending 2003

Total Grants: $5,725,065*

Number of Grants: 214

Average Grant: $26,753

Highest Grant: $200,000

Lowest Grant: $250

Typical Range: $5,000 to $50,000

*Note: Giving excludes scholarship and United Way.

Recent Grants

Note: Grants derived from 2003 Form 990.

Library-Related

121,500	Hawkins Area Library, Hawkins, WI	

General

726,081	Merle West Cancer Center, Klamath Falls, OR
500,000	Oregon Health and Science Center, Portland, OR
214,404	Merle West Cancer Center, Klamath Falls, OR
200,000	Chiloquin Visions in Progress, Chiloquin, OR
200,000	Grinnell Regional Medical Center, Grinnell, IA
200,000	University of Oregon - Lundquist College of Business, Eugene, OR
167,000	National Parks Foundation, Washington, DC
150,000	Chiloquin Visions in Progress, Chiloquin, OR
125,000	Tender Learning Center, Ladysmith, WI
115,000	Tulelake Community, Tulelake, CA

JENJO FOUNDATION

Giving Contact

Alan Alda, Trustee
c/o Morris Pliskow, PC
641 Lexington Ave., No. 1400
New York, NY 10022
Phone: (212)421-6161

Description

Founded: 1990

EIN: 136944768

Organization Type: Private Foundation

Giving Locations: NY: New York

Grant Types: General Support, Research.

Donor Information

Founder: Established in 1990 by Alan Alda.

Financial Summary

Total Giving: $64,010 (2001)

Assets: $1,845,453 (2001)

Typical Recipients

Arts & Humanities: Arts Outreach, Libraries, Public Broadcasting

Civic & Public Affairs: Business/Free Enterprise, Civil Rights, Civic & Public Affairs-General, Housing, Municipalities/Towns, Philanthropic Organizations, Public Policy, Urban & Community Affairs, Women's Affairs

Education: Education Reform, Education-General, Literacy, Private Education (Precollege), Public Education (Precollege)

Environment: Environment-General

Health: AIDS/HIV, Single-Disease Health Associations

International: Missionary/Religious Activities

Social Services: At-Risk Youth, Child Welfare, Community Centers, Community Service Organizations, Counseling, Crime Prevention, Day Care, Domestic Violence, Family Services, Food/Clothing Distribution, Recreation & Athletics, Youth Organizations

Application Procedures

Initial Contact: Send a brief letter of inquiry.

Application Requirements: proof of tax-exempt status.

Deadlines: None.

Restrictions

Grants will generally be given to causes relating to health, education, the environment, and other critical areas that affect the quality of life for all people.

Foundation Officials

Alan Alda: trustee B New York, NY 1936. ED Fordham University BS (1956). OCCUPATION actor, writer, director. NONPR AFFIL member: Screen Actors Guild; member: Writers Guild America; member: Directors Guild America; member: Actors Equity Association; member: American Federation Television & Radio Artists.

Arlene Alda: trustee

Beatrice Alda: trustee

Elizabeth Alda: trustee

Mark Caligiuri: trustee

Eve Alda Coffey: trustee

James Coffey: trustee

Grants Analysis

Disclosure Period: calendar year ending 2001

Total Grants: $64,010

Number of Grants: 1

Recent Grants

Note: Grants derived from 2001 Form 990.

General

64,010	Philanthropic Initiative, Boston, MA -- health, education and environment

MARTHA HOLDEN JENNINGS FOUNDATION

Giving Contact

Dr. William T. Hiller, Executive Director
The Halle Building
1228 Euclid Avenue, Suite 710
Cleveland, OH 44115
Phone: (216)589-5700
Fax: (216)589-5730
Web: http://www.mhjf.org

Description

Founded: 1958

EIN: 340934478

Organization Type: General Purpose Foundation

Giving Locations: OH: Cuyahoga County

Grant Types: Award, Conference/Seminar, General Support, Project, Research.

Donor Information

Founder: Martha Holden Jennings established the foundation bearing her name in 1959, three years before her death. Mrs. Jennings made her home in Cleveland after living for many years in Europe with her husband, Andrew R. Jennings. She was known for her love of children, art, animals, and traveling. She hoped that her foundation would "foster the development of individual capabilities of young people to the maximum extent through improving the quality of teaching in secular primary and secondary schools and by furnishing incentives thereto." She supported elementary and secondary education because, although various foundations were committed to higher education, less attention was being paid to the earlier stages of learning, especially in public schools.

Financial Summary

Total Giving: $7,021,132 (2003); $9,065,927 (2002); $10,885,188 (2001)
Giving Analysis: Giving for 2002 includes: foundation grants to United Way ($15,000); foundation scholarships ($42,000)
Assets: $82,438,284 (2003); $76,919,463 (2002); $103,079,737 (2001)
Gifts Received: $21,710 (2002); $3,800 (1993). Note: In 2002, contributions were received from the estate of Grace E. Huntley.

Typical Recipients

Arts & Humanities: Arts Associations & Councils, Arts Centers, Arts Institutes, Arts Outreach, Ballet, Dance, Arts & Humanities-General, Historic Preservation, History & Archaeology, Libraries, Literary Arts, Museums/Galleries, Music, Opera, Performing Arts, Public Broadcasting, Theater
Civic & Public Affairs: African American Affairs, Botanical Gardens/Parks, Civic & Public Affairs-General, Hispanic Affairs, Nonprofit Management, Parades/Festivals, Public Policy, Zoos/Aquariums
Education: Afterschool/Enrichment Programs, Arts/Humanities Education, Business Education, Colleges & Universities, Education Associations, Education Funds, Education Reform, Elementary Education (Private), Faculty Development, Education-General, Gifted & Talented Programs, Health & Physical Education, International Studies, Leadership Training, Literacy, Minority Education, Preschool Education, Private Education (Precollege), Public Education (Precollege), School Volunteerism, Science/Mathematics Education, Secondary Education (Public), Special Education, Student Aid
Environment: Environment-General, Resource Conservation
Health: Adolescent Health Issues, Heart, Mental Health, Preventive Medicine/Wellness Organizations
International: Foreign Educational Institutions
Religion: Religious Welfare
Science: Science Museums, Scientific Centers & Institutes
Social Services: At-Risk Youth, Child Welfare, Community Centers, Community Service Organizations, Family Services, People with Disabilities, Substance Abuse, Youth Organizations

Application Procedures

Initial Contact: Application forms for Grants to Educators are available from the website. There are no forms for other grant applications.
Application Requirements: Submit an original proposal. Applications must include a cover letter signed by the chief executive of the organization requesting funds and a listing of all enclosures. A one-page summary of the proposed project, listing the amount requested, specific purpose of and need for the project, proposed plan of action and projected outcome, number of participants or schools to be involved, and other sources of funding, should be included. A detailed budget must be enclosed indicating how the requested funds will be used and the amount, if any, of other funds to be used to support the project. Applica-

tions also must include a copy of the organization's tax-exempt classification under IRS section 501(c)(3).
Institutions which provide services to schools should enclose a letter indicating the need for such services, signed by the superintendent of schools.
A succinct (limited to six pages) proposal must be included. The proposal should indicate how the project will help elementary or secondary teachers and students attain a higher level of excellence; how the project is innovative or original; how the project will be evaluated; how the results will be disseminated to others; who will direct the project; what the project's immediate and long-term objectives are; what the projects timetable is; and, if the project is successful, what plans there are for funding it after the grant has ended. The full request should not exceed ten pages.
Deadlines: None.
Review Process: Proposals must be received by the 20th of each month to be considered for the following month's committee meeting (committee does not meet in July or December). Applicants are notified within two months of their submission.

Restrictions

The foundation does not make grants for capital improvements, equipment, travel, or graduate study. A grant must be spent solely for the purpose for which it was made. Requests should be for one year only. You may reapply if your project is successful.

Additional Information

Besides making grants, the foundation also supports conferences, seminars/workshops, and offers proposal writing assistance. Reports are required from the grantees on how the funds were spent and the results achieved.
Publications: Annual Report; Guidelines; Application Form; Pro Excellentia Bulletin

Foundation Officials

Dr. Jeanette Grasselli Brown: trustee B Cleveland, OH 1928. ED Ohio University BS (1950); Case Western Reserve University MS (1958). ADD CORP EMPL director corporate research: BP America. CORP AFFIL director: BDM International Inc.; director: USX Corp. NONPR AFFIL trustee: Musical Arts Association/Cleveland Orchestra; chairperson: Ohio Board Regents.
Roy Church: trustee
Julian M. Earls: trustee
Russell R. Gifford: trustee
Dr. William T. Hiller: executive director ED Indiana University of Pennsylvania BS (1969); Indiana University of Pennsylvania MS (1972); University of Pittsburgh PhD (1979).
Arthur S. Holden, Jr.: chairman emeritus, trustee
George B. Milbourn: chairman, president
Karen R. Nestor: trustee
Jon Outcalt: trustee
Deborah Z. Read: secretary, trustee

Grants Analysis

Disclosure Period: calendar year ending 2003
Total Grants: $7,021,132
Number of Grants: 183
Average Grant: $28,729*
Highest Grant: $1,071,182
Lowest Grant: $4,000
Typical Range: $10,000 to $50,000
*Note: Average grant figures excludes two highest grants ($1,821,182).

Recent Grants

Note: Grants derived from 2003 Form 990.
General

1,071,183	University Partnership/ Urban Initiative, Cleveland, OH -- fund for improving urban schools
770,076	Jennings Grants-to-Educators Program, OH
688,770	University Partnership/ Urban Initiative, Cleveland, OH -- fund for improving Urban Schools
404,468	Ohio Department of Education, Columbus, OH -- to assist Ohio Learning First Alliance/Jennings Initiative
203,600	Ohio Department of Education, Columbus, OH -- grant for Ohio Learning First Alliance
150,588	Kent State University Foundation Inc., Kent, OH -- to support Urban Fellows Program
145,045	Kent State University Foundation Inc., Kent, OH -- to assist Educational Excellence through Technological Innovation and Collaboration
101,773	Ohio Department of Education, Columbus, OH -- to support Early Childhood Initiative Program
101,485	Ohio Department of Education, Columbus, OH -- to support Early Childhood Initiative Program
100,383	Kent State University Foundation Inc., Kent, OH -- grant for Literacy Alliance

MARY HILLMAN JENNINGS FOUNDATION

Giving Contact

Paul Euwer, Jr., Executive Director
2203 Allegheny Tower
625 Stanwix St.
Pittsburgh, PA 15222
Phone: (412)434-5606
Fax: (412)434-5907

Description

Founded: 1968
EIN: 237002091
Organization Type: General Purpose Foundation
Giving Locations: PA: Pittsburgh
Grant Types: Capital, Department, Emergency, Endowment, Fellowship, General Support, Multiyear/Continuing Support, Project, Seed Money.

Donor Information

Founder: The foundation was established in 1968 by the late Mary Hillman Jennings.

Financial Summary

Total Giving: $2,684,000 (2002); $3,404,958 (2001)
Giving Analysis: Giving for 2002 includes: foundation grants to United Way ($15,000); 2001: foundation grants to United Way ($15,000)
Assets: $27,454,420 (2002); $41,429,036 (2001)

Typical Recipients

Arts & Humanities: Arts Associations & Councils, Arts Centers, Ballet, Ethnic & Folk Arts, Film & Video, Arts & Humanities-General, Historic Preservation, History & Archaeology, Libraries, Museums/Galleries, Music, Opera, Public Broadcasting, Theater, Visual Arts
Civic & Public Affairs: Botanical Gardens/Parks, Business/Free Enterprise, Community Foundations, Economic Development, Employment/Job Training, Civic & Public Affairs-General, Housing, Parades/Festivals, Philanthropic Organizations, Professional & Trade Associations, Urban & Community Affairs, Zoos/Aquariums
Education: Arts/Humanities Education, Business Education, Colleges & Universities, Community & Junior Colleges, Economic Education, Education Funds, Education Reform, Elementary Education (Public), Environmental Education, Faculty Development, Education-General, Literacy, Minority Education, Preschool Education, Private Education (Precol-

lege), Public Education (Precollege), Science/ Mathematics Education, Social Sciences Education, Special Education

Environment: Environment-General, Protection, Resource Conservation, Wildlife Protection

Health: Alzheimer's Disease, Cancer, Children's Health/Hospitals, Clinics/Medical Centers, Diabetes, Emergency/Ambulance Services, Health Funds, Health Organizations, Hospices, Hospitals, Long-Term Care, Medical Rehabilitation, Medical Research, Nursing Services, Outpatient Health Care, Public Health, Single-Disease Health Associations, Trauma Treatment

Religion: Churches, Jewish Causes, Ministries, Religious Organizations, Religious Welfare

Science: Science-General, Science Museums, Scientific Centers & Institutes

Social Services: At-Risk Youth, Camps, Child Welfare, Community Centers, Community Service Organizations, Delinquency & Criminal Rehabilitation, Domestic Violence, Emergency Relief, Family Planning, Family Services, Food/Clothing Distribution, Homes, People with Disabilities, Recreation & Athletics, Sexual Abuse, Shelters/Homelessness, Social Services-General, Substance Abuse, United Funds/United Ways, YMCA/YWCA/YMHA/YWHA, Youth Organizations

Application Procedures

Initial Contact: Submit a letter of proposal or common grant application form.

Application Requirements: The application should describe the organization, amount requested, and the intended use of the grant.

Deadlines: May 31 and October 1.

Review Process: The foundation's board of trustees meets twice a year to consider grant applications.

Additional Information

Trust(s): Evan D. Jennings II

Foundation Officials

Paul Euwer, Jr.: executive director NONPR AFFIL vice president-treasurer, director: Allegheny Valley School.

Evan D. Jennings, II: president

Irving A. Wechsler: treasurer PRIM CORP EMPL partner: Wechsler Myers & Wolsh. CORP AFFIL director: Merchandise Service Division; director: Music Network Division; director: Comcast Corp.; director: Cablevision Communication Division; director: Comcast Cellular Communication.

Andrew L. Weil: secretary ED Chatham College (1949).

Grants Analysis

Disclosure Period: calendar year ending 2002

Total Grants: $2,669,000*

Number of Grants: 123

Average Grant: $17,029*

Highest Grant: $408,500

Lowest Grant: $1,000

Typical Range: $1,000 to $30,000

*Note: Giving excludes United Way. Average grant figure excludes two highest grants ($608,500).

Recent Grants

Note: Grants derived from 2002 Form 990.

Library-Related

20,000	Sewickley Public Library, Sewickley, PA

General

408,500	Shadyside Hospital Foundation, Pittsburgh, PA
200,000	Allegheny Valley School, Coraopolis, PA
200,000	George Washington's Mt. Vernon, Mt. Vernon, VA
100,000	Allegheny General Hospital, Pittsburgh, PA
100,000	Pittsburgh Glass Center, Pittsburgh, PA
100,000	Pittsburgh Leadership Foundation, Pittsburgh, PA
75,000	Avon Old Farms School, Avon, CT

50,000	Boulder Community Family Resources, Boulder, CO
50,000	Juvenile Diabetes Foundation, Pittsburgh, PA
50,000	Manchester Craftsmen's Guild, Pittsburgh, PA

GEORGE FREDERICK JEWETT FOUNDATION

Giving Contact

Ann D. Gralnek, Senior Advisor
Russ Building
235 Montgomery Street, Suite 612
San Francisco, CA 94104
Phone: (415)421-1351
Fax: (415)421-0721
E-mail: tfbjewettf@aol.com

Description

Founded: 1957

EIN: 046013832

Organization Type: Family Foundation

Giving Locations: CA: San Francisco; WA: Eastern Washington, Spokane

Grant Types: Capital, Endowment, Fellowship, General Support, Multiyear/Continuing Support, Project.

Donor Information

Founder: The George Frederick Jewett Foundation was established on December 2, 1957, under the will of George Frederick Jewett (1896-1956), whose mother was the former Margaret Weyerhaeuser. Mr. Jewett was chairman of Potlatch Corporation and a trustee of the American University of Cairo.

Financial Summary

Total Giving: $1,480,000 (2002); $1,560,500 (2001)

Giving Analysis: Giving for 2002 includes: foundation grants to United Way ($25,000)

Assets: $32,630,028 (2002); $36,837,552 (2001)

Gifts Received: $289,644 (1998); $128,499 (1994); $7,944 (1992). Note: In 1998, contributions were received from W.G. & E.S. Cooper. The foundation receives gifts from Berkshire Hathaway, Omaha, NE, and M. J. Gaiser House, Spokane, WA.

Typical Recipients

Arts & Humanities: Arts Associations & Councils, Arts Centers, Arts Festivals, Arts Funds, Arts Institutes, Arts Outreach, Ballet, Community Arts, Dance, Film & Video, Historic Preservation, History & Archaeology, Libraries, Literary Arts, Museums/ Galleries, Music, Opera, Performing Arts, Public Broadcasting, Visual Arts

Civic & Public Affairs: Botanical Gardens/Parks, Community Foundations, Economic Development, Economic Policy, Civic & Public Affairs-General, Housing, Nonprofit Management, Philanthropic Organizations, Public Policy, Zoos/Aquariums

Education: Afterschool/Enrichment Programs, Arts/ Humanities Education, Business Education, Colleges & Universities, Economic Education, Elementary Education (Private), Elementary Education (Public), Faculty Development, Education-General, International Studies, Medical Education, Minority Education, Private Education (Precollege), Public Education (Precollege), Religious Education, Science/ Mathematics Education, Secondary Education (Private), Social Sciences Education, Special Education, Student Aid

Environment: Air/Water Quality, Forestry, Environment-General, Protection, Resource Conservation, Watershed, Wildlife Protection

Health: Cancer, Clinics/Medical Centers, Diabetes, Emergency/Ambulance Services, Health Funds, Hospitals, Medical Rehabilitation, Nursing Services,

Prenatal Health Issues, Public Health, Speech & Hearing

International: Foreign Arts Organizations, Foreign Educational Institutions, Health Care/Hospitals, International Affairs, International Environmental Issues, International Relations

Religion: Churches, Religious Organizations, Religious Welfare

Science: Science-General, Science Museums, Scientific Centers & Institutes, Scientific Labs

Social Services: Child Welfare, Community Service Organizations, Family Planning, Family Services, Food/Clothing Distribution, People with Disabilities, Recreation & Athletics, Senior Services, Shelters/Homelessness, Substance Abuse, United Funds/United Ways, YMCA/YWCA/YMHA/YWHA, Youth Organizations

Application Procedures

Initial Contact: Verbal requests will not be accepted. Before making a formal proposal, however, an applicant is welcome to make written inquiries regarding foundation policies and programs.

Application Requirements: Proposals should include the name and address of applicant, names of chief administrative officers, statement of private foundation status, and a letter from an officer endorsing the proposal and agreeing that the applicant will assume full fiscal management and accounting responsibility for any funds received. The statement must be supported either by a copy of an IRS letter regarding private foundation status; a copy of completed form 4653, with a statement from a principal officer providing date filed and IRS response; a n opinion of legal status; or a copy of an IRS letter of tax exemption. An applicant should also provide a statement attesting that no portion of a Jewett grant will be used to employ, compensate, or benefit a government official.

The foundation also requires specific information for project proposals. Proposals must contain a brief description of the project, with background information; development plan; e valuation method; expected results; constituency served; and information on key personnel administering the project. Applicants must provide budgetary information on salaries, rent, supplies for technicians, clerical services, equipment, expendable supplies, and travel. They also must indicate amounts of "in-kind" or cash contributions, sources of income, and amounts received from other philanthropic agencies. The foundation prefers to have a three-year projected budget. Prospective grantees also should indicate start and completion dates, and whether or not the proposal has been submitted to other grant-making organizations, including federal and state agencies.

Deadlines: None.

Review Process: Proposals are reviewed quarterly, and many are held for final processing at the foundation's annual meeting at the end of the year. Staff notify, within a reasonable period, applicants whose proposals fall outside the foundation's scope. The foundation prefers to participate with other donors, and not to assume a major portion of the amount to be raised. A high priority is given to organizations receiving little or no support from public tax funds.

Restrictions

The foundation limits its grants largely to requests from eastern Washington and San Francisco, CA. No grants are made to individuals. Support occasionally may be given to scholarship, fellowship, or research programs of established institutions. Grants generally are not given to other private or operating foundations. While the foundation will not support activities that influence legislation, it may support research on and studies of problems of public concern. Emergency petitions are not favored except when they involve disaster and human suffering. It is the intent of the trustees to keep the foundation's program flexible at all times by making no long-term commitments. No uninvited proposals will be accepted. No funds will be given for the purchase of tickets or for the support of fundraising events.

Additional Information

The administrative officers of each recipient organization must agree in writing to administer the grant in accordance with its stated terms, to submit interim financial and progress reports, to advise the foundation of any changes, to request the termination of a project if the program as approved becomes impossible to carry out, and to refund any unused amounts. When grants are made to organizations in states that require annual reporting of receipts and expenditures by organizations soliciting general support, the foundation requires evidence that its grant has been reported properly.

No plaques or memorials relating to the foundation can be used without prior approval.

Publications: Annual Report; Application Guidelines

Foundation Officials

Ann D. Gralnek: senior advisor
Margaret Weyerhaeuser Jewett Greer: trustee ED Harvard University (1952).
William Hershey Greer, Jr.: trustee B Owensboro, KY 1928. ED Yale University BA (1951); Harvard University JD (1954).
George Frederick Jewett, Jr.: chairman B Spokane, WA 1927. ED Dartmouth College BA (1950); Harvard University MBA (1952). PRIM CORP EMPL vice chairman, director: Potlatch Corp.
Lucille Winifred McIntyre Jewett: trustee B Saint Louis, MO 1929.

Grants Analysis

Disclosure Period: calendar year ending 2002
Total Grants: $1,455,000*
Number of Grants: 82
Average Grant: $17,744
Highest Grant: $50,000
Lowest Grant: $300
Typical Range: $5,000 to $30,000
*Note: Giving excludes United Way.

Recent Grants

Note: Grants derived from 2002 Form 990.
General

65,000	St. Luke's Chamber Ensemble, New York, NY
50,000	Planned Parenthood of the Inland Northwest, Spokane, WA
50,000	San Francisco Ballet, San Francisco, CA -- restricted grant for donor development effort
50,000	San Francisco Foundation, San Francisco, CA
50,000	San Francisco Foundation, San Francisco, CA
50,000	San Francisco General Hospital Foundation, San Francisco, CA
40,000	California College of Arts and Crafts, San Francisco, CA
40,000	Inland Northwest Land Trust, Spokane, WA -- support of conservation organization's community outreach education
35,000	Chinese Historical Society, San Francisco, CA
30,000	Planned Parenthood Association of Metropolitan Washington, Washington, DC

JEWISH HEALTHCARE FOUNDATION

Giving Contact

Karen Wolk-Feinstein, President
Center City Tower, Suite 2330
650 Smithfield Street
Pittsburgh, PA 15222

Phone: (412)594-2550
Fax: (412)232-6240
E-mail: info@jhf.org
Web: http://www.jhf.org

Description

Founded: 1991
EIN: 251624347
Organization Type: Specialized/Single Purpose Foundation
Giving Locations: PA: Western Pennsylvania
Grant Types: Challenge, Conference/Seminar, General Support, Matching, Multiyear/Continuing Support, Project, Research, Seed Money.

Donor Information

Founder: In 1991, Presbyterian University Hospital in Pittsburgh, PA, endowed a $75 million foundation as a health care resource after assuming control of Montefiore Hospital, which was also located in Pittsburgh.

Financial Summary

Total Giving: $4,270,935 (2002)
Giving Analysis: Giving for 2002 includes: foundation grants to United Way ($45,000)
Assets: $102,062,728 (2002)
Gifts Received: $5,242,523 (2002); $2,273,792 (2000); $1,868,964 (1998). Note: In 2002, contributions were received from the Commonwealth of Pennsylvania AIDS Grant ($2,433,112), the City of Pittsburgh AIDS Grant ($611,4650), Pittsburgh Regional Healthcare Init ($2,082,657), and miscellaneous donors. In 2000, contributions were received from the Commonwealth of Pennsylvania AIDS Grant ($1,743,609), the City of Pittsburgh AIDS Grant ($529,702), and miscellaneous donors.

Typical Recipients

Arts & Humanities: Arts Outreach, Arts & Humanities-General, Libraries, Public Broadcasting, Theater
Civic & Public Affairs: African American Affairs, Asian American Affairs, Business/Free Enterprise, Community Foundations, Economic Development, Ethnic Organizations, Civic & Public Affairs-General, Housing, Municipalities/Towns, Public Policy, Urban & Community Affairs, Women's Affairs
Education: Colleges & Universities, Education Funds, Education Reform, Education-General, Leadership Training, Medical Education, Preschool Education, Private Education (Precollege), Public Education (Precollege), Science/Mathematics Education, Special Education, Student Aid
Environment: Air/Water Quality, Environment-General
Health: Adolescent Health Issues, AIDS/HIV, Alzheimer's Disease, Cancer, Children's Health/Hospitals, Clinics/Medical Centers, Health-General, Geriatric Health, Health Policy/Cost Containment, Health Funds, Health Organizations, Heart, Home-Care Services, Hospitals, Hospitals (University Affiliated), Kidney, Long-Term Care, Medical Research, Medical Training, Mental Health, Nursing Services, Nutrition, Prenatal Health Issues, Preventive Medicine/Wellness Organizations, Public Health, Research/Studies Institutes, Single-Disease Health Associations, Transplant Networks/Donor Banks
International: Foreign Educational Institutions, Health Care/Hospitals, Missionary/Religious Activities, Trade
Religion: Jewish Causes, Religious Welfare, Social/Policy Issues
Social Services: At-Risk Youth, Child Welfare, Community Service Organizations, Crime Prevention, Day Care, Delinquency & Criminal Rehabilitation, Domestic Violence, Family Services, Food/Clothing Distribution, People with Disabilities, Scouts, Senior Services, Social Services-General, Substance Abuse, United Funds/United Ways, Volunteer Services, YMCA/YWCA/YMHA/YWHA, Youth Organizations

Application Procedures

Initial Contact: Applicants should send four copies of a preliminary letter of intent that does not exceed six pages.
Application Requirements: The letter should describe the problem and the program objectives, include a budget, list of board of directors, IRS tax-determination letter, name and address of contact person, institutional and personnel qualifications, the most recent auditor's report (if available), and recent financial statements showing amounts and sources of current income. In addition, the letter should include information on partnerships; a timetable; proposed intervention; anticipated outcome; innovative aspects; likelihood of success; long-term plans; and community education, research, and/or evaluation components.
Deadlines: None.
Evaluative Criteria: The Foundation honors certain values: faculty for creation partnerships and building community awareness; going beyond individual program breakthroughs to systems, policy, and practice changes; skill and determination to translate medical and scientific advances into new protocols and best practices.

Restrictions

Generally, the foundation does not fund organizations without IRS tax-exempt status, organizations outside western Pennsylvania, programs without a health care component, general operations, capital needs, operating deficits, debt retirement, political campaigns, scholarships, fellowships, individual research, or individual travel.

Additional Information

Foundation also sponsors conferences, and provides proposal writing assistance, and technical assistance in planning.
Publications: Annual Report; Guidelines; Branches Newsletter

Foundation Officials

Karen Wolk Feinstein, PhD: president B 1945.
Stephen Halpern: treasurer NONPR AFFIL treasurer, director: United Jewish Federation.
Leon L. Netzer: trustee B 1923. ED University of Pittsburgh. PRIM CORP EMPL president: Federation Alloy Corp. CORP AFFIL president, director: Nicroloy Co. Inc.
Robert Arthur Paul: vice chairman B New York, NY 1937. ED Cornell University AB (1959); Harvard University JD (1962); Harvard University MBA (1964). PRIM CORP EMPL president, chief executive officer, director: Ampco-Pittsburgh Corp. CORP AFFIL partner: Romar Trading Co.; partner: National City Corp.; executive vice president, assistant secretary, director, trustee: Louis Berkman Co. NONPR AFFIL member: Massachusetts Bar Association; trustee: Presbyterian University Hospital; trustee: Cornell University; member: American Bar Association. CLUB AFFIL Pittsburgh Athletic Association; Harvard Club; Concordia Club; Duquesne Club.

Grants Analysis

Disclosure Period: calendar year ending 2002
Total Grants: $4,225,935*
Number of Grants: 46
Average Grant: $20,193*
Highest Grant: $900,000
Lowest Grant: $434
Typical Range: $10,000 to $50,000
*Note: Giving excludes United Way. Average grant figure excludes five highest grants ($3,398,040).

Recent Grants

Note: Grants derived from 2002 Form 990.
General

900,000	United Jewish Federation, Pittsburgh, PA
671,313	Pittsburgh Foundation, Pittsburgh, PA
623,954	Renaissance Expense

612,773	Patient Safety, Plano, TX
590,000	Joint Aviation Authorities
492,937	PRHI Partial Core, Newark, NJ
443,792	Technical Assistance
249,620	Renaissance 2
200,000	UJF Israel Emergency Campaign
200,000	UPMC Shadyside, Pittsburgh, PA -- complementary medecine

JJJ FOUNDATION

Giving Contact

Keith W. Wegen, President & Director
287 Century Circle, Suite 100
Louisville, CO 80027-9439
Phone: (303)926-1111

Description

Founded: 1985
EIN: 133379770
Organization Type: Private Foundation
Giving Locations: CO
Grant Types: General Support, Project, Seed Money.

Donor Information

Founder: John R. Butler

Financial Summary

Total Giving: $67,400 (fiscal year ending September 30, 2004); $76,450 (fiscal 2001)
Assets: $1,701,222 (fiscal 2004); $1,772,526 (fiscal 2001)
Gifts Received: $1,000 (fiscal 1994); $1,000 (fiscal 1993); $1,000 (fiscal 1992)

Typical Recipients

Arts & Humanities: Arts Centers, Arts Festivals, Arts Outreach, Dance, Museums/Galleries, Music
Civic & Public Affairs: Community Foundations, Civic & Public Affairs-General, Housing, Nonprofit Management, Philanthropic Organizations, Safety
Education: Afterschool/Enrichment Programs, Colleges & Universities, Education Funds, Environmental Education, Education-General, Leadership Training, Minority Education, Preschool Education, Private Education (Precollege), Secondary Education (Public), Special Education, Student Aid
Environment: Environment-General, Resource Conservation, Wildlife Protection
Health: AIDS/HIV, Cancer, Children's Health/Hospitals, Health-General, Geriatric Health, Hospitals, Medical Rehabilitation, Multiple Sclerosis, Prenatal Health Issues, Single-Disease Health Associations
International: Foreign Educational Institutions, Missionary/Religious Activities
Religion: Churches, Ministries, Religious Welfare
Science: Science Museums
Social Services: At-Risk Youth, Big Brothers/Big Sisters, Child Abuse, Child Welfare, Community Service Organizations, Crime Prevention, Day Care, Delinquency & Criminal Rehabilitation, Domestic Violence, Emergency Relief, Family Services, People with Disabilities, Shelters/Homelessness, Social Services-General, Substance Abuse, Veterans, YMCA/YWCA/YMHA/YWHA

Application Procedures

Initial Contact: Send a one-page letter of inquiry.
Application Requirements: Include amount requested, description of project, purpose of funds sought, annual budget, government support, and a description of organization.
Deadlines: None.

Restrictions

Foundation limits contributions to only one grant per year.

Foundation Officials

John R. Butler: chairman
Stuart Lemle: director
Jennifer A. Wegen: vice president, secretary, director
Keith W. Wegen: president, director

Grants Analysis

Disclosure Period: fiscal year ending September 30, 2004
Total Grants: $67,400
Number of Grants: 31
Average Grant: $2,174
Highest Grant: $10,000
Lowest Grant: $250
Typical Range: $1,000 to $5,000

Recent Grants

Note: Grants derived from fiscal 2004 Form 990.
General

10,000	World of Wonder Children's Museum, Louisville, CO -- building fund for family discovery museum
7,000	Freedom Service Dogs, Lakewood, CO -- for dog rescue to train and match special needs individuals
5,000	Social Venture Partners, Boulder, CO -- to connect business professionals with non-profit organizations to effect social change
4,000	Front Range Center for Assault Prevention, Arvada, CO -- for child assault prevention program
4,000	Kim Robards Dance, Denver, CO -- towards educational outreach dance programs for youth
3,000	Heads Up, Washington, DC -- for learning opportunities for low-income children and families
3,000	Hotchkiss School Annual Fund, Lakeville, CT
3,000	Leaders Challenge, Denver, CO -- for leadership training for high school students
2,500	Rebuilding Together, Colorado Springs, CO -- towards volunteer program to repair and maintain homes for low income, elderly and disabled
2,500	Suicide Education & Support Services, Evans, CO -- for suicide prevention Hispanic youth project

JM FOUNDATION

Giving Contact

Carl Helstrom, Assistant Secretary
60 East 42nd Street, Room 1651
New York, NY 10165
Phone: (212)687-7735
Fax: (212)697-5495

Description

Founded: 1936
EIN: 136068340
Organization Type: General Purpose Foundation
Grant Types: General Support, Project, Research.

Donor Information

Founder: Jeremiah Milbank was engaged, throughout his life, in philanthropic activities. Mr. Milbank was born in New York City on January 24, 1887. After graduating from Yale University in 1909, Mr. Milbank established his own investment firm in 1916. A believer in free enterprise, Mr. Milbank was a director of several companies and had long-term investments in private corporations.

Mr. Milbank's belief that persons with disabilities could lead independent and meaningful lives was to become a subject of major national importance. His conviction that the Red Cross was a viable organization led him to found the Red Cross Institution for Crippled Soldiers and Sailors in 1917. This was the first American organization to address the needs of physically disabled veterans. In 1919, he founded the Institute for the Crippled and Disabled (ICD). It was at this Institute that vocational education, medical service, and psychosocial support were integrated to form a new comprehensive rehabilitation approach for people with physical disabilities.

In 1928, Mr. Milbank founded and financed the International Committee for the Study of Infantile Paralysis. As a result of this active interest in the subject of polio, President Roosevelt asked him to be the acting chairman of the organization that preceded the National Foundation for Infantile Paralysis.

Mr. Milbank personally contributed to a collaborative effort with Metropolitan Life Insurance Company to finance a research project to combat diphtheria. In addition, he worked with President Hoover to form the Boys and Girls Clubs of America, and served as its treasurer for 25 years. Mr. Milbank also had personal interests in recovering and converting acres of swampland in South Carolina for agricultural use. His spiritual beliefs led to his financing the first film on the life of Jesus Christ, Cecil B. DeMille's "King of Kings." Mr. Milbank died on March 22, 1972.

Financial Summary

Total Giving: $1,000,000 (2003 approx); $858,335 (2002); $1,072,270 (2001)
Giving Analysis: Giving for 2002 includes: foundation matching gifts ($58,335); 2001: foundation matching gifts ($79,270)
Assets: $21,301,743 (2002); $24,942,788 (2001)

Typical Recipients

Arts & Humanities: Arts & Humanities-General, Historic Preservation, History & Archaeology, Libraries, Public Broadcasting, Theater
Civic & Public Affairs: African American Affairs, Botanical Gardens/Parks, Business/Free Enterprise, Civil Rights, Community Foundations, Economic Development, Economic Policy, Employment/Job Training, Ethnic Organizations, Civic & Public Affairs-General, Housing, Law & Justice, Legal Aid, Native American Affairs, Nonprofit Management, Philanthropic Organizations, Professional & Trade Associations, Public Policy, Safety, Urban & Community Affairs, Women's Affairs, Zoos/Aquariums
Education: Afterschool/Enrichment Programs, Arts/Humanities'Education, Business Education, Colleges & Universities, Continuing Education, Education Associations, Education Funds, Education Reform, Environmental Education, Faculty Development, Education-General, Journalism/Media Education, Leadership Training, Legal Education, Medical Education, Minority Education, Preschool Education, Private Education (Precollege), Religious Education, Secondary Education (Public), Social Sciences Education, Student Aid
Environment: Forestry, Environment-General, Wildlife Protection
Health: AIDS/HIV, Cancer, Children's Health/Hospitals, Clinics/Medical Centers, Eyes/Blindness, Health-General, Geriatric Health, Health Policy/Cost Containment, Health Organizations, Heart, Hospitals, Medical Rehabilitation, Medical Research, Prenatal Health Issues, Preventive Medicine/Wellness Organizations, Public Health, Research/Studies Institutes, Single-Disease Health Associations, Speech & Hearing, Trauma Treatment
International: International-General, Health Care/Hospitals, International Development, International Organizations
Religion: Religious Organizations, Religious Welfare, Social/Policy Issues

Social Services: Child Welfare, Community Centers, Community Service Organizations, Crime Prevention, Day Care, Emergency Relief, Family Planning, Family Services, People with Disabilities, Recreation & Athletics, Scouts, Senior Services, Shelters/Homelessness, Social Services-General, Substance Abuse, Volunteer Services, Youth Organizations

Application Procedures

Initial Contact: The foundation invites written proposals. The foundation requests that applicants do not send video or audio tapes unless requested.
Application Requirements: Applications should contain a brief abstract of the proposed project (one page or less); proposal, outlining purpose of project, plan of action, board and staff involvement, financing, plans for evaluation, and anticipated results; vitae of authors, researchers, or project officers; project budget, current organizational budget, promotional brochure, and most recent annual report; most recent audited financial statements; list of governing and advisory board members; copy of IRS 501(c)(3) tax-exemption letter; list of organization's current donors, current funders of the proposed project, and grantmakers with whom proposals are pending.
Deadlines: None.
Review Process: The foundation does not have a printed application form or a rigid format for requests. Applicants will be notified of a decision within three to four weeks. Proposals that are consistent with the capacity and interests of the foundation are examined further, and forwarded to the directors who meet in early May and late October.

Restrictions

The foundation usually declines support to annual appeals, dinner events, endowments, or operating funds; arts, music, or theater; capital campaigns, renovations, or building funds; equipment, including computers and biomedical devices; government agencies or public schools; grants to individuals, including scholarships and financial aid; or international projects.

Additional Information

The foundation collaborates with like-minded foundations and is closely affiliated with the Milbank Foundation for Rehabilitation.
Publications: Application Guidelines; Annual Report

Foundation Officials

Jeremiah Milbank Bogert: member B New York, NY 1941. ED Yale University BA (1963); University of Connecticut MBA (1973). PRIM CORP EMPL chairman board, director: James C. Edwards & Co. Inc.
Margaret Milbank Bogert: vice president, director
William Lee Hanley, Jr.: treasurer, director ED Yale University (1964).
Jeremiah Milbank, III: mem ED Trinity College BA (1970); Stanford University MBA (1973); University of Virginia JD (1980). PRIM CORP EMPL chairman: Milbank Associate ADD CORP EMPL vice president: Cypress Woods Corp.; vice president: Turkey Hill Plantation; president: Winthrop Milbank & Co.
Jeremiah Milbank, Jr.: president, director B New York, NY March 24, 1920. ED Yale University BA (1942); Harvard University MBA (1948). PRIM CORP EMPL president: Cypress Woods Corp. ADD CORP EMPL president: Turkey Hill Corp. CORP AFFIL director: International Minerals & Chemicals Corp. NONPR AFFIL chairman emeritus: Boys & Girls Club Greenwich; honorary president: International Center Disabled. CLUB AFFIL Yale Club; River Club; Round Hill Club; Brook Club.
Peter C. Morse: director CORP AFFIL director: America Guardian Life Assurance Co.; director: PFG Inc.
Chris K. Olander: executive director, assistant treasurer
Michael Sanger: director
Daniel Gleason Tenney, Jr.: secretary, director B

New York, NY 1913. ED Yale University BA (1935); Yale University LLB (1938).

Grants Analysis

Disclosure Period: calendar year ending 2002
Total Grants: $800,000*
Number of Grants: 36
Average Grant: $20,000*
Highest Grant: $100,000
Lowest Grant: $5,000
Typical Range: $10,000 to $25,000
*Note: Giving excludes matching gifts. Average grant figure excludes highest grant.

Recent Grants

Note: Grants derived from 2002 Form 990.
General

100,000	Boys & Girls Clubs of America, Atlanta, GA
40,000	Center for Security Policy, Washington, DC
40,000	Institute for Humane Studies, Arlington, VA
35,000	American Enterprise Institute for Public Policy Research, Washington, DC
30,000	Fund for American Studies, Washington, DC
25,000	America's Future Foundation, Washington, DC
25,000	Federalist Society for Law and Public Policy Studies, Phoenix, AZ
25,000	Foundation for Community and Faith-Centered Enterprise, Phoenix, AZ
25,000	Hoover Institution, Stanford, CA
25,000	Institute for Policy Innovation, Lewisville, TX

JOCKEY HOLLOW FOUNDATION

Giving Contact

Betsy S. Michel, President
PO Box 462
Bernardsville, NJ 07924
Phone: (973)425-3212

Description

Founded: 1960
EIN: 221724138
Organization Type: Private Foundation
Giving Locations: MA; NJ
Grant Types: General Support, Scholarship.

Donor Information

Founder: Carl Shirley, Mrs. Carl Shirley

Financial Summary

Total Giving: $1,212,215 (fiscal year ending March 31, 2004); $1,078,271 (fiscal 2001)
Giving Analysis: Giving for fiscal 2004 includes: foundation grants to United Way ($1,000); foundation scholarships ($50,000); fiscal 2001: foundation grants to United Way ($1,000); foundation scholarships ($50,000)
Assets: $25,744,277 (fiscal 2004); $23,890,904 (fiscal 2001)
Gifts Received: $206,000 (fiscal 1996); $206,000 (fiscal 1995); $206,000 (fiscal 1994)

Typical Recipients

Arts & Humanities: Arts Associations & Councils, Arts Funds, Ethnic & Folk Arts, Historic Preservation, History & Archaeology, Libraries, Museums/Galleries, Music, Opera, Performing Arts, Theater
Civic & Public Affairs: African American Affairs, Employment/Job Training, Civic & Public Affairs-General, Safety, Urban & Community Affairs

Education: Business Education, Colleges & Universities, Education Funds, Education-General, Medical Education, Minority Education, Private Education (Precollege), Public Education (Precollege), Secondary Education (Private), Student Aid
Environment: Air/Water Quality, Environment-General, Resource Conservation
Health: Clinics/Medical Centers, Emergency/Ambulance Services, Health Funds, Health Organizations, Hospitals, Medical Research, Nursing Services, Public Health, Trauma Treatment
Religion: Churches
Social Services: Child Welfare, Community Centers, Community Service Organizations, Domestic Violence, Family Planning, Family Services, Recreation & Athletics, Shelters/Homelessness, Social Services-General, United Funds/United Ways, Youth Organizations

Application Procedures

Initial Contact: Send a brief letter of inquiry.
Application Requirements: Include a description of organization, amount requested, purpose of funds sought, recently audited financial statement, and proof of tax-exempt status.
Deadlines: None.

Foundation Officials

Joanne S. Gill: vice president
Clifford Lloyd Michel: treasurer B New York, NY 1939. ED Princeton University AB (1961); Yale University JD (1964). PRIM CORP EMPL partner: Cahill Gordon & Reindel. CORP AFFIL director: Wenonah Development Co.; director: Placer Dome Inc.; director: Alliance Capital Management Mutual Funds; director: Faber-Castell Corp. NONPR AFFIL member: New York State Bar Association; director: Saint Marks School; member: New York County Lawyers Association; member: Fed Bar Association; director: Morristown Memorial Hospital; member: American Society International Law; member: American Bar Association.
Betsy B. Shirley: vice president

Grants Analysis

Disclosure Period: fiscal year ending March 31, 2004
Total Grants: $1,211,215*
Number of Grants: 142
Average Grant: $7,259*
Highest Grant: $100,000
Lowest Grant: $30
Typical Range: $1,000 to $10,000
*Note: Giving excludes scholarships and United Way. Average grant figure excludes two highest grants ($195,000).

Recent Grants

Note: Grants derived from 2004 Form 990.

General

100,000	Morristown Memorial Health Foundation, Morristown, NJ
95,000	Newark Museum, Newark, NJ
85,000	Museum of Fine Arts, Boston, MA
75,000	Conservatory Lab Charter School, Boston, MA
60,000	Nantucket Cottage Hospital, Nantucket, MA
55,000	Morristown Neighborhood House, Morristown, NJ
50,500	Boston Lyric Opera, Boston, MA
50,000	Bernard's Area Scholarship Assistance Inc., Gladstone, NJ
25,000	Epiphany Charter School, Dorchester, MA
20,000	Big Tree Boating Association, Islesboro, ME

JOCO FOUNDATION

Giving Contact
Raymond D. Smoot, Jr., Treasurer
c/o Virginia Tech
312 Burruss Hall, No. 0142
Blacksburg, VA 24061
Phone: (540)231-5751

Description
Founded: 1990
EIN: 541552388
Organization Type: Private Foundation
Giving Locations: VA: Bedford, Roanoke Valley
Grant Types: General Support.

Donor Information
Founder: Reid Jones, Jr.

Financial Summary
Total Giving: $390,000 (2001)
Assets: $2,387,229 (2001)
Gifts Received: $3,000 (2001); $683,636 (1997); $1,967,727 (1992). Note: In 1997, contributions were received from the estate of Reid Jones, Jr.

Typical Recipients
Arts & Humanities: Arts Funds, History & Archaeology, Libraries, Museums/Galleries
Civic & Public Affairs: Botanical Gardens/Parks, Clubs, Community Foundations, Civic & Public Affairs-General, Housing, Municipalities/Towns, Safety
Education: Agricultural Education, Colleges & Universities, Education Funds, Elementary Education (Public), Engineering/Technological Education, Literacy, Private Education (Precollege), Student Aid
Environment: Air/Water Quality, Environment-General, Wildlife Protection
Health: Cancer, Children's Health/Hospitals, Emergency/Ambulance Services, Multiple Sclerosis, Public Health
International: International Organizations
Religion: Churches, Religious Welfare, Social/Policy Issues
Social Services: Animal Protection, At-Risk Youth, Community Centers, Crime Prevention, Family Planning, Recreation & Athletics, Senior Services, United Funds/United Ways, Volunteer Services, YMCA/YWCA/YMHA/YWHA, Youth Organizations

Application Procedures
Initial Contact: Send a written application.
Application Requirements: Include description of charitable purpose and brief history of charitable activities.
Deadlines: None.

Restrictions
The foundation does not support individuals, religious organizations or political or lobbying groups.

Foundation Officials
Judy Jarrells: director
William Killinger: director
Diane E. H. Wilcox, Esq.: director

Grants Analysis
Disclosure Period: calendar year ending 2001
Total Grants: $390,000
Number of Grants: 2
Average Grant: $195,000
Highest Grant: $240,000
Typical Range: $1,000 to $5,000 and $100,000 to $400,000

Recent Grants
Note: Grants derived from 2001 Form 990.
General

240,000	Smith Mountain Lake 4 H Center, Inc., Wirtz, VA
150,000	Rescue Mission, Roanoke, VA

JOHNS MANVILLE

Company Headquarters
PO Box 5108
Denver, CO 80217-5108
Web: http://www.johnsmanville.com

Company Description
Former Name: Schuller International.
Revenue: US$2 billion (2002)
Employees: 9000 (2002)
SIC(s): 1499 Miscellaneous Nonmetallic Minerals, 2952 Asphalt Felts & Coatings, 3296 Mineral Wool, 5039 Construction Materials Nec.
Parent Company: Berkshire Hathaway Inc., 1440 Kiewit Plaza, Omaha, NE, United States

Operating Locations
Johns Manville (AZ--Tucson; CA--Pittsburg, Santa Ana, Willows; IL--Rockdale, Waukegan; KS--McPherson; ME--Lewiston; NJ--Edison, Penbryn; NC--Laurinburg; OH--Defiance; TN--Etowah; TX--Cleburne, Ennis, Fort Worth; VA--Shenandoah; WV--Parkersburg)

Nonmonetary Support
Type: Donated Equipment; Donated Products; In-kind Services; Loaned Executives; Workplace Solicitation

Johns Manville Fund

Giving Contact
PO Box 5108
Denver, CO 80217-5108
Phone: (303)978-3863
Fax: (303)978-3547
Web: http://www.jm.com/AboutUs/JMFund/default.asp

Description
Founded: 1952
EIN: 136034039
Organization Type: Corporate Foundation
Giving Locations: company operating locations.
Grant Types: Award, Challenge, Emergency, Employee Matching Gifts, General Support, Scholarship, Seed Money.

Donor Information
Founder: Manville Corp.

Financial Summary
Total Giving: $163,412 (2002). Note: Figures represent fund contributions for foundation only; company does not distribute direct giving information. 1997 Giving includes matching gifts ($20,957).
Giving Analysis: Giving for 2002 includes: foundation matching gifts ($17,190)
Assets: $398,579 (2002)
Gifts Received: $300,000 (1997); $475,000 (1996); $475,000 (1995). Note: In 1997, contributions were received from Johns Manville International, Inc.

Typical Recipients
Arts & Humanities: Arts Associations & Councils, Arts Centers, Arts Outreach, Ballet, Community Arts, Arts & Humanities-General, Historic Preservation, History & Archaeology, Libraries, Literary Arts, Museums/Galleries, Opera, Performing Arts, Theater, Visual Arts
Civic & Public Affairs: Botanical Gardens/Parks, Clubs, Economic Development, Employment/Job Training, Civic & Public Affairs-General, Housing, Inner-City Development, Legal Aid, Safety, Urban & Community Affairs, Women's Affairs, Zoos/Aquariums
Education: Business Education, Colleges & Universities, Community & Junior Colleges, Elementary Ed-ucation (Public), Education-General, Literacy, Public Education (Precollege)
Environment: Environment-General, Wildlife Protection
Health: AIDS/HIV, Cancer, Children's Health/Hospitals, Emergency/Ambulance Services, Eyes/Blindness, Health Organizations, Heart, Hospitals, Medical Rehabilitation, Mental Health, Multiple Sclerosis, Respiratory, Single-Disease Health Associations, Transplant Networks/Donor Banks
Religion: Religion-General, Religious Welfare
Social Services: Animal Protection, At-Risk Youth, Child Abuse, Child Welfare, Community Centers, Community Service Organizations, Counseling, Crime Prevention, Domestic Violence, Emergency Relief, Family Services, Food/Clothing Distribution, Homes, People with Disabilities, Recreation & Athletics, Scouts, Senior Services, Sexual Abuse, Shelters/Homelessness, Social Services-General, Substance Abuse, United Funds/United Ways, Volunteer Services, YMCA/YWCA/YMHA/YWHA, Youth Organizations

Application Procedures
Initial Contact: Send letter requesting guidelines.
Deadlines: None.

Restrictions
The fund does not give to hospitals, organizations involved in private education, religious activities, organizations without 501(c)(3) tax-exempt status, special events, or organizations that receive more than 20% of their annual income from the United Way or similar community fund drives.
Organizations that have previously been awarded a grant from the fund may not reapply until two years after the application date of the funded request.

Additional Information
Religious institutions may receive funding for programs that are secular and not religious or ceremonial in nature.
In 1997, the Schuller Fund was renamed as the Johns Manville Fund. Its program description includes the following areas: (1) Community Grants: Supports a range of organizations involved with the arts, culture, and social service activities. Recent recipients include child recreation groups, training for the handicapped, and health organizations; (2) Education Grants: Grants are available to high school seniors with a parent or guardian who has been a company employee for at least one year; and (3) Matching Grants: The fund matches dollar-for-dollar personal donations of $50 to $249 by company employees or their families to colleges and universities. Program details, including budgets, deadlines, procedures, and forms can be obtained from representatives at company sites or from headquarters in Denver, CO.
Fund officers give preference to proposals that reflect company's employee's volunteerism at all levels and all locations.
Priority will be given to applicants for matching funds, challenge grants, and proposals that yield some significant multiple effect.

Corporate Officials
C. L. Henry: chairman, president, chief executive officer PRIM CORP EMPL chairman, president, chief executive officer: Johns Manville.
Kenneth L. Jensen: chief financial officer PRIM CORP EMPL chief financial officer: Johns Manville.

Foundation Officials
R. Arant: vice president, trustee
Joni E. Baird: vice president, fund administrator PRIM CORP EMPL community relations manager: Johns Manville.
D. A. Forte: vice president
J. J. Gebert: vice president, treasurer, trustee
M. Mitchell: vice president, trustee
Dave E. Pullen: president

M. K. Rhinehart: treasurer PRIM CORP EMPL director finance & administration: Johns Manville.
William G. Spink: secretary

Grants Analysis

Disclosure Period: calendar year ending 2002
Total Grants: $146,222*
Number of Grants: 54
Average Grant: $2,708*
Highest Grant: $31,100
Lowest Grant: $250
Typical Range: $1,000 to $5,000
*Note: Giving excludes matching gifts. Average grant figure excludes highest grant.

Recent Grants

Note: Grants derived from 2002 Form 990.
General

10,000	American Red Cross Denver Chapter, Denver, CO -- for Colorado wild fires
10,000	Harbor House, Waterville, NH
10,000	JM Charity Christmas Fund, Etowah, GA -- 50th initial major grant
5,000	Habitat for Humanity, Richmond, VA
5,000	Lost Valley Handicapped Ski Association, Lewiston, ID
5,000	National Multiple Sclerosis Society, Denver, CO
4,000	Richmond Community Schools, Richmond, IN
3,000	Arbor House, Ann Arbor, MI
3,000	Auglaize Volunteer Firemen's Association, Defiance, OH
3,000	Interfaith Hospital Network, Indianapolis, IN

James Hervey Johnson Charitable Educational Trust

Giving Contact

Kevin Munnelly, Trustee
James Hervey Johnson Charitable Educational Trust
PO Box 16160
San Diego, CA 92176
Phone: (619)283-8016

Description

Founded: 1989
EIN: 336081439
Organization Type: Private Foundation
Giving Locations: CA
Grant Types: General Support.

Financial Summary

Total Giving: $30,000 (fiscal year ending July 31, 2001)
Assets: $11,783,739 (fiscal 2001)

Typical Recipients

Arts & Humanities: Ethnic & Folk Arts, History & Archaeology, Libraries, Museums/Galleries
Civic & Public Affairs: Clubs, Community Foundations, First Amendment Issues, Gay/Lesbian Issues, Professional & Trade Associations, Public Policy
Education: Faculty Development, Education-General, Health & Physical Education, Religious Education
Health: Health-General, Health Organizations, Public Health, Respiratory
International: International Organizations
Religion: Jewish Causes, Religious Organizations, Religious Welfare, Social/Policy Issues
Social Services: Shelters/Homelessness, Substance Abuse

Application Procedures

Initial Contact: Request guidelines and application form.
Application Requirements: Include IRS 501(c)(3) status, an itemized breakdown of grant fund expenditures, annual budget, IRS Form 990.
Deadlines: April 15.

Additional Information

Publications: Application Form; Instructions

Foundation Officials

Lawrence Y. True: trustee

Grants Analysis

Disclosure Period: fiscal year ending July 31, 2001
Total Grants: $30,000
Number of Grants: 2

Recent Grants

Note: Grants derived from 2001 Form 990.
General

15,000	American Natural Hygiene Society, Inc. -- donate subscriptions to Health Science magazine to various public libraries
15,000	San Diego Museum of Man, San Diego, CA

Keith Wold Johnson Charitable Trust

Giving Contact

Robert W. Johnson, IV, Trustee
c/o Johnson Co.
630 5th Ave., Suite 1510
New York, NY 10111
Phone: (212)872-7903

Description

Founded: 1986
EIN: 112845826
Organization Type: Private Foundation
Giving Locations: CO; NJ; NY
Grant Types: General Support.

Donor Information

Founder: Betty Wold Johnson

Financial Summary

Total Giving: $285,000 (2002)
Assets: $3,332,504 (2002)

Typical Recipients

Arts & Humanities: Ballet, Dance, Libraries, Public Broadcasting
Civic & Public Affairs: Civic & Public Affairs-General, Zoos/Aquariums
Education: Colleges & Universities, Faculty Development, Private Education (Precollege)
Health: Clinics/Medical Centers, Health Organizations, Hospitals, Medical Rehabilitation, Nursing Services, Public Health, Single-Disease Health Associations
Religion: Religious Organizations, Religious Welfare
Social Services: Crime Prevention, Food/Clothing Distribution, People with Disabilities

Application Procedures

Initial Contact: The foundation has no formal grant application procedure or application form.
Deadlines: None.

Restrictions

OrganizationS must be listed under section 501 (C) (3) of The Internal Revenue Code.

Foundation Officials

Christopher W. Johnson: trustee
Elizabeth Ross Johnson: trustee
Robert Wood Johnson, IV: trustee

Grants Analysis

Disclosure Period: calendar year ending 2002
Total Grants: $285,000
Number of Grants: 4
Highest Grant: $200,000
Lowest Grant: $25,000

Recent Grants

Note: Grants derived from 2002 Form 990.
General

200,000	Autism Research Institute, San Diego, CA
30,000	New School University, New York, NY
30,000	Princeton Friends School, Princeton, NJ
25,000	Vail Valley Medical Center Foundation, Vail, CO

Johnson Controls Inc.

Company Headquarters

Milwaukee, WI
Web: http://www.johnsoncontrols.com

Company Description

Founded: 1885
Ticker: JCI
Exchange: NYSE
Revenue: US$26.553 billion (2004)
Profit: US$817.5 million (2004)
Employees: 112000 (2003)
Fortune Rank: 71, per FORTUNE Magazine's list of 500 Largest U.S. Corporations (2004).
SIC(s): 2531 Public Building & Related Furniture, 3081 Unsupported Plastics Film & Sheet, 3085 Plastics Bottles, 3822 Environmental Controls.

Operating Locations

Johnson Controls Inc. (AL--Tuscaloosa; AR--Texarkana; CA--City of Industry, Fullerton, Los Angeles, Milpitas, Modesto, Stockton; DE--Middletown, New Castle; FL--Cape Canaveral, Orlando; GA--Atlanta, Cumming; IL--Geneva, Itasca; IN--Franklin, Goshen, Greencastle, Ossian; KS--Lenexa; KY--Bardstown, Cadiz, Florence, Glasgow, Harrodsburg, Lexington, Louisville, Nicholasville; LA--Shreveport; MD--Belcamp; MA--East Longmeadow; MI--Ann Arbor, Lapeer, Madison Heights, Mount Clemens, Novi, Owosso, Plymouth, Saline, Whitmore Lake, Williamston; MO--Jefferson City, St. Joseph; NH--Merrimack; NJ--Edison, Pine Brook, Somerville; OH--Columbus, Greenfield, Strongsville, Toledo; OK--Poteau; OR--Canby; PA--Erie, Pittsburgh; SC--Oconee; TN--Athens, Lewisburg, Lexington, Murfreesboro, Pulaski; TX--Carrollton, Fort Worth, Garland, New Braunfels; VT--Bennington; WA--Tacoma; WI--Watertown)

Nonmonetary Support

Note: Co. provides nonmonetary support.

Johnson Controls Foundation

Giving Contact

Valerie Adisek, Foundation Coordinator
5757 N. Green Bay Avenue
PO Box 591
Milwaukee, WI 53201-0591
Phone: (414)524-2296
Fax: (414)524-3200

Web: http://www.johnsoncontrols.com/corpvalues/foundation.htmfoundation

Description

EIN: 396036639
Organization Type: Corporate Foundation
Giving Locations: in areas where company has a significant presence.
Grant Types: Capital, General Support, Multiyear/Continuing Support.
Note: Employee matching gift ratio: 1 to 1 for gifts to education, the arts, and the United Way.

Financial Summary

Total Giving: $6,334,651 (2003); $6,332,355 (2002); $5,958,094 (2001). Note: Contributes through corporate direct giving program and foundation.
Giving Analysis: Giving for 2002 includes: foundation grants to United Way ($1,026,661)
Assets: $43,958,927 (2003); $35,444,637 (2002); $39,043,033 (2001)
Gifts Received: $6,500,000 (2003); $6,000,000 (2002); $5,000,000 (2001). Note: Contributions were received from Johnson Controls, Inc.

Typical Recipients

Arts & Humanities: Arts Associations & Councils, Arts Centers, Arts Festivals, Arts Funds, Arts Institutes, Ballet, Dance, Film & Video, Historic Preservation, Libraries, Museums/Galleries, Music, Opera, Performing Arts, Public Broadcasting, Theater
Civic & Public Affairs: Botanical Gardens/Parks, Business/Free Enterprise, Civil Rights, Economic Development, Employment/Job Training, Civic & Public Affairs-General, Housing, Municipalities/Towns, Nonprofit Management, Parades/Festivals, Professional & Trade Associations, Urban & Community Affairs, Women's Affairs, Zoos/Aquariums
Education: Afterschool/Enrichment Programs, Agricultural Education, Arts/Humanities Education, Business Education, Colleges & Universities, Community & Junior Colleges, Continuing Education, Economic Education, Education Associations, Education Funds, Education Reform, Elementary Education (Private), Engineering/Technological Education, Education-General, Literacy, Medical Education, Minority Education, Private Education (Precollege), Public Education (Precollege), Science/Mathematics Education, Secondary Education (Private), Student Aid, Vocational & Technical Education
Environment: Energy, Environment-General, Protection, Resource Conservation
Health: Cancer, Children's Health/Hospitals, Clinics/Medical Centers, Health Organizations, Heart, Hospices, Hospitals, Medical Research, Public Health, Single-Disease Health Associations, Transplant Networks/Donor Banks
International: Health Care/Hospitals, International Organizations, International Relations
Religion: Ministries, Missionary Activities (Domestic), Religious Welfare
Science: Science Museums, Scientific Centers & Institutes
Social Services: Animal Protection, At-Risk Youth, Big Brothers/Big Sisters, Camps, Child Welfare, Community Centers, Community Service Organizations, Counseling, Emergency Relief, Family Services, Food/Clothing Distribution, People with Disabilities, Recreation & Athletics, Scouts, Senior Services, Shelters/Homelessness, Social Services-General, Substance Abuse, United Funds/United Ways, YMCA/YWCA/YMHA/YWHA, Youth Organizations

Application Procedures

Initial Contact: Send a clear, concise letter on organization letterhead.
Application Requirements: Include a description of the organization's structure, purpose, history, and programs; a list of current officers and governing board members, including their outside affiliations; summary of need for support and its intended use;

geographic area served; current income and expense budget, and copy of most recent audited financial statement; statement of other funding sources, community support and involvement; copy of 501 (c)(3) status letter.
Deadlines: None.
Evaluative Criteria: Organization's general structure, objectives, management capacity, relationship to community, population to be served, position relative to other organizations performing similar functions.
Decision Notification: Advisory board meets approximately three times per year in March, September, and November; allow up to 120 days for decision.
Notes: In preliminary stage, personal visits, phone calls to the foundation, and video tapes are discouraged.

Restrictions

Foundation does not support organizations which are not tax-exempt; individuals; private foundations or endowment funds; political or lobbying groups; fraternal or veterans groups; or organizations based or located outside the United States. The foundation does not generally support precollege education; medical or scientific research; religious groups for sectarian purposes; testimonials, fundraising events, tickets to benefits or shows; or travel, tours, seminars, conferences, or publications. The foundation does not donate equipment, products or labor.

Additional Information

Grants are not automatically renewed.
Publications: Giving Guidelines

Corporate Officials

John M. Barth: president, chief executive officer
Denise M. Zutz: vice president corporate communications B Milwaukee, WI 1951. ED University of Wisconsin (1973). PRIM CORP EMPL vice president corporate communications: Johnson Controls Inc.

Foundation Officials

Valerie Adisek: admin secretary
John M. Barth: member advisory board (see above)
Robert Cornog: member advisory board
James Henry Keyes: member advisory board B LaCrosse, WI 1940. ED Marquette University BS (1962); Northwestern University MBA (1963). ADD CORP EMPL president: Johnson Controls International; president: Johnson Controls Battery Group; president: Johnson Controls Interiors Inc.; vice president: Johnson Controls World Services Inc.; president: Prince Holding Corp. CORP AFFIL director: Pitney Bowes Inc.; director: Universal Foods Corp.; director: Federal Reserve Bank Chicago. NONPR AFFIL member: Manufacturers Alliance Productivity & Innovation; member: National Association Manufacturers; member: American Institute CPAs.
Blaine Rieke: member advisory board
Denise M. Zutz: member advisory board (see above)

Grants Analysis

Disclosure Period: calendar year ending 2003
Total Grants: $5,321,107*
Number of Grants: 1,200 (approx)
Average Grant: $4,355*
Highest Grant: $100,000
Lowest Grant: $50
Typical Range: $1,000 to $5,000
*Note: Giving excludes United Way. Average grant figure excludes highest grant.

Recent Grants

Note: Grants derived from 2003 Form 990.
General

350,000	United Performing Arts Fund, Mahwah, NJ
266,750	United Way of Greater Milwaukee, Milwaukee, WI
100,000	Children's Centre, ON Canada
100,000	Corpus Christi Schools, Corpus Christi, TX
100,000	Marquette University, Milwaukee, WI
100,000	Milwaukee School of Engineering, Milwaukee, WI
86,733	United Way of West Tennessee, Jackson, TN
83,000	National Underground Railroad Freedom Centre, Columbus, OH
81,244	United Way of Forsyth County, Winston-Salem, NC
75,000	Milwaukee Symphony Orchestra, Milwaukee, WI

JOHNSON FOUNDATION

Giving Contact

Barbara Schmidt, Program Secretary
33 E. Four Mile Rd.
Racine, WI 53402
Phone: (262)681-3343
Fax: (262)681-3325
E-mail: bschmidt@johnsonfdn.org
Web: http://www.johnsonfdn.org

Description

Founded: 1958
EIN: 390958255
Organization Type: Private Foundation
Grant Types: Conference/Seminar, General Support.

Donor Information

Founder: S. C. Johnson and Son, the late H. F. Johnson, and descendants of the late H. F. Johnson

Financial Summary

Assets: $35,201,908 (fiscal year ending June 30, 2001)
Gifts Received: $4,456,907 (fiscal 2001); $2,352,275 (fiscal 1994); $1,808,657 (fiscal 1992). Note: In fiscal 2001, contributions were received from S.C. Johnson & Son Inc. ($2,300,000), Mr. & Mrs. Samuel C. Johnson ($9,187), The David and Lucile Packard Foundation ($47,107), and S.C. Johnson & Son Commercial Markets Inc. ($500,000). In fiscal 1994, contributions were received from S. C. Johnson and Sons ($2,100,000), Mr. and Mrs. S. C. Johnson ($50,000), William and Flora Hewlett Fdn. ($43,588), Pew Charitable Trust ($89,156), Lilly Endowment ($65,381), and miscellaneous ($4,150).

Typical Recipients

Arts & Humanities: Arts Associations & Councils, Libraries, Museums/Galleries, Music
Civic & Public Affairs: Civil Rights, Hispanic Affairs, Minority Business, Nonprofit Management, Public Policy
Education: Business Education, Colleges & Universities, Community & Junior Colleges, Engineering/Technological Education, Education-General, Leadership Training, Medical Education, Preschool Education, Private Education (Precollege), Secondary Education (Private), Student Aid
International: International Development, International Relief Efforts
Social Services: Family Services

Application Procedures

Initial Contact: Send a brief letter of inquiry requesting application guidelines.
Deadlines: None.

Restrictions

Does not make grants to individuals.

Additional Information

Publications: Application Guidelines

Foundation Officials

Lois Berg: secretary
Boyd M. Gibbons, III: president
Patricia Albjerg Graham, PhD: vice president B Lafayette, IN 1935. ED Purdue University BS (1955); Purdue University MS (1957); Columbia University PhD (1964). CORP AFFIL trustee: Northwestern Mutual Life Insurance Co. NONPR AFFIL member: Phi Beta Kappa; member: Science Research Associates; member: National Academy Education; council: American Association Advancement Science; member: American Historical Association.
Helen P. Johnson-Leipold: trustee
Janice C. Kreamer: trustee
Charles Selden McNeer: treasurer B Gilbert, WV 1926. ED Berea College (1947); Northwestern University BSEE (1950). CORP AFFIL chairman, chief executive officer, director: WI Natural Gas Co.; director: WI Electric Power Co.; director: WI Energy Co.; director: Metro Milwaukee Inc.; director: Universal Foods Corp.; chairman: Bradley Center Corp.; chairman: Federal Reserve Bank Chicago; director: Association Edison Illuminating Companies; president, director: Badger Service Co. NONPR AFFIL director: WI Utilities Association; director: YMCA Metropolitan Milwaukee; chairman executive committee: WI Upper Michigan Systems; director: WI Electric Utilities Research Foundation; member: WI Society Prof Engineers; member advisory council: University Wisconsin School Business Administration; director: WI Chapter Nature Conservancy; director: Sinai Samaritan Medical Center; member: Tau Beta Pi; member: Sigma Pi Sigma; member: Sigma Xi; member: Pi Mu Epsilon; director: Milwaukee Redevelopment Corp.; member: National Society Professional Engineers; member executive committee: Mid-American Interpool Network; director: Milwaukee Innovation Center; member council: Medical College Wisconsin; vice chairman (urban affairs): Metropolitan Milwaukee Association Commerce; director: Greater Milwaukee Comm; member: Kiwanis; director: Forward Wisconsin; member: Edison Electric Institute; member: Eta Kappa Nu; trustee: Berea College; director: Competitive Wisconsin; chairman: American Comm Radwaste Disposal.
William J. Raspberry: trustee
John M. Richman: trustee
Paula Wolff: trustee CORP AFFIL director: Ariel Capital Management Inc. NONPR AFFIL director: University of Chicago; chairman: University of Chicago Hospitals Board; director: Golden Apple Foundation.

Grants Analysis

Disclosure Period: fiscal year ending June 30, 2000
Total Grants: $39,500
Number of Grants: 12
Average Grant: $3,375
Highest Grant: $6,000
Lowest Grant: $1,000
Typical Range: $1,000 to $5,000

Recent Grants

Note: Grants derived from fiscal 2001 Form 990.

General

6,000	Arts Council of Metropolitan Kansas City, Kansas City, MO
6,000	Institute for the Transformation of Learning, Milwaukee, WI
6,000	Resources for the Future, Washington, DC
6,000	University of Chicago, Chicago, IL
3,000	Harvard University, Cambridge, MA
2,500	Foundation Center, New York, NY
2,000	Berea College Alumni Association, Berea, KY
2,000	Grantmakers for Children, Youth, and Families, Washington, DC
2,000	Medical College of Wisconsin, Milwaukee, WI
2,000	National Lighthouse Museum, Staten Island, NY

A.D. Johnson Foundation

Giving Contact

Wayne J. Johnson, President & Treasurer
1 N. LaSalle St., Suite 3000
1 N. LaSalle St., Suite 3000
Chicago, IL 60602-4003
Phone: (312)782-7320
Fax: (312)782-7131

Description

Founded: 1965
EIN: 366124270
Organization Type: Private Foundation
Giving Locations: FL; IL
Grant Types: General Support, Research.

Donor Information

Founder: the late A. D. Johnson

Financial Summary

Total Giving: $110,000 (2001)
Giving Analysis: Giving for 2001 includes: foundation grants to United Way ($10,000)
Assets: $2,717,700 (2001)

Typical Recipients

Arts & Humanities: Arts Festivals, Arts Outreach, Community Arts, Libraries, Music
Civic & Public Affairs: Parades/Festivals
Education: Arts/Humanities Education, Colleges & Universities, Medical Education, Private Education (Precollege), Science/Mathematics Education
Health: Clinics/Medical Centers, Diabetes, Health-General, Hospices, Hospitals, Long-Term Care, Medical Research, Mental Health, Single-Disease Health Associations
Religion: Churches
Social Services: Animal Protection, Child Welfare, Community Service Organizations, People with Disabilities, Shelters/Homelessness, United Funds/United Ways, Youth Organizations

Application Procedures

Initial Contact: Send a brief letter of inquiry describing program.
Deadlines: None.

Restrictions

Does not support individuals or political or lobbying groups.

Foundation Officials

Diane T. Johnson: vice president, secretary
Wayne J. Johnson: president, treasurer
Herbert J. Theisen: assistant secretary, general counsel

Grants Analysis

Disclosure Period: calendar year ending 2001
Total Grants: $110,000*
Number of Grants: 8
Highest Grant: $20,000
Lowest Grant: $5,000
Typical Range: $5,000 to $20,000
*Note: Giving includes United Way.

Recent Grants

Note: Grants derived from 2001 Form 990.
General

25,000	Cystic Fibrosis Gold Coast, Ft. Lauderdale, FL
20,000	Evanston Northwestern Healthcare Corporation, Evanston, IL
15,000	Henderson Mental Health Center, Ft. Lauderdale, FL
15,000	Humane Society of Broward County, Ft. Lauderdale, FL
10,000	Ravinia Festival, Inc., Chicago, IL
10,000	Ravinia Festival Young Artist Endowment Fund, Chicago, IL
10,000	United Way of Skokie Valley, Skokie, IL
5,000	St. Mark's Episcopal School, Ft. Lauderdale, FL

Burdine Johnson Foundation

Giving Contact

Robert C. Giberson, Trustee
PO Box 1230
Buda, TX 78610-1230
Phone: (512)312-1336
Fax: (512)295-4773

Description

Founded: 1960
EIN: 746036669
Organization Type: Family Foundation
Giving Locations: TX
Grant Types: General Support.

Donor Information

Founder: Established in 1960 by Burdine C. Johnson and J. M. Johnson.

Financial Summary

Total Giving: $1,358,000 (2003); $1,800,000 (2002 approx); $1,713,750 (2001)
Assets: $32,690,312 (2003); $35,295,400 (2001)

Typical Recipients

Arts & Humanities: Arts & Humanities-General, Historic Preservation, Libraries, Museums/Galleries, Performing Arts, Theater
Civic & Public Affairs: Community Foundations, Civic & Public Affairs-General, Municipalities/Towns, Women's Affairs, Zoos/Aquariums
Education: Arts/Humanities Education, Colleges & Universities, Community & Junior Colleges, Education Funds, Elementary Education (Private), Elementary Education (Public), Education-General, Literacy, Medical Education, Private Education (Precollege), Public Education (Precollege), Religious Education, Student Aid
Environment: Environment-General, Resource Conservation
Health: Cancer, Children's Health/Hospitals, Emergency/Ambulance Services, Medical Research, Multiple Sclerosis, Single-Disease Health Associations, Transplant Networks/Donor Banks
International: Health Care/Hospitals
Religion: Churches, Religion-General, Religious Welfare
Science: Scientific Centers & Institutes
Social Services: Animal Protection, Child Abuse, Child Welfare, Community Service Organizations, Crime Prevention, Domestic Violence, Emergency Relief, Family Planning, Family Services, Food/Clothing Distribution, Recreation & Athletics, Scouts, Senior Services, Sexual Abuse, Shelters/Homelessness, Substance Abuse, Volunteer Services

Application Procedures

Initial Contact: The foundation has no formal grant application procedure or application form.
Application Requirements: Applicants must submit full details about the applying organization and the use of the proposed grant. The foundation also requests applicants attach a copy of the IRS ruling or

determination letter.
Deadlines: None.

Restrictions

Grants made by the foundation are limited to religious, charitable, scientific, literary, or educational purposes.

Foundation Officials

Robert C. Giberson: trustee
William T. Johnson: trustee
Martha L. Mattox: trustee

Grants Analysis

Disclosure Period: calendar year ending 2003
Total Grants: $1,358,000
Number of Grants: 36
Average Grant: $37,722
Highest Grant: $150,000
Lowest Grant: $2,000
Typical Range: $15,000 to $50,000

Recent Grants

Note: Grants derived from 2002 Form 990.
Library-Related

2,500	Friends of the Public Library of Buda, Buda, TX

General

200,000	James Dick Foundation for the Performing Arts, Round Top, TX
200,000	James Dick Foundation for the Performing Arts, Round Top, TX
200,000	St. Stephen's Episcopal School, Austin, TX
150,000	St. Stephen's Episcopal School, Wimberley, TX
125,000	University of Texas at Austin, Austin, TX
90,000	North Hays County Optimist Foundation, Buda, TX
75,000	Hays Consolidated Independent School District, Kyle, TX
50,000	Children's Hospital Foundation of Austin, Austin, TX
50,000	Planned Parenthood of the Texas Capital Region, Austin, TX
50,000	St. Stephen's Episcopal School, Austin, TX

CHARLES AND ANN JOHNSON FOUNDATION

Giving Contact

Charles B. Johnson, Trustee
c/o Franklin Resources Inc.
One Franklin Pkwy., Bldg. 920, 4th Floor
San Mateo, CA 94403
Phone: (650)312-3000

Description

Founded: 1986
EIN: 943026398
Organization Type: Private Foundation
Giving Locations: CA
Grant Types: General Support.

Donor Information

Founder: Ann L. Johnson, Charles B. Johnson

Financial Summary

Total Giving: $1,445,793 (2003); $1,530,623 (2002); $1,357,071 (2001)
Assets: $50,401,177 (2003); $32,560,181 (2002); $27,292,913 (2001)
Gifts Received: $6,317,250 (2003); $6,016,885 (2002); $1,216,805 (2001). Note: In 2000, 2001, 2002, and 2003, contributions were received from Charles and Ann Johnson. In 1994 and 1999, contributions were received from Charles Johnson.

Typical Recipients

Arts & Humanities: Historic Preservation, History & Archaeology, Libraries, Museums/Galleries, Music, Opera, Public Broadcasting
Civic & Public Affairs: Botanical Gardens/Parks, Community Foundations, Civic & Public Affairs-General, Housing, Municipalities/Towns, Parades/Festivals, Public Policy, Urban & Community Affairs, Zoos/Aquariums
Education: Colleges & Universities, Education Funds, Education Reform, Education-General, International Exchange, Private Education (Precollege), Public Education (Precollege), Student Aid
Environment: Air/Water Quality, Environment-General
Health: Cancer, Clinics/Medical Centers, Health Funds, Hospices, Hospitals, Single-Disease Health Associations
International: International Affairs, International Peace & Security Issues
Religion: Churches, Religious Organizations, Religious Welfare
Science: Science-General, Scientific Centers & Institutes
Social Services: Community Service Organizations, Domestic Violence, Family Planning, People with Disabilities, Recreation & Athletics, United Funds/United Ways, Volunteer Services

Application Procedures

Initial Contact: Send a brief letter of inquiry.
Deadlines: Contact foundation for deadline information.

Foundation Officials

Ann L. Johnson: trustee
Charles Bartlett Johnson: trustee B Montclair, NJ 1933. ED Yale University BA (1954). PRIM CORP EMPL chairman, chief executive officer, president: Franklin Resources. CORP AFFIL director: Res Capital Fund; director: Res Equity Fund; director: General Host Corp.; director: Franklin Money Fund; director: Franklin Option Fund; director: Franklin California Tax Free Income Fund; director: Franklin Custodian Funds. NONPR AFFIL chairman board governors: National Association Securities Directors; director: San Francisco Symphony; trustee: Crystal Springs Uplands School; 97 board overseers: Hoover Institution. CLUB AFFIL Commonwealth Club California; director: Pacific-Union Club; Burlingame Country Club.

Grants Analysis

Disclosure Period: calendar year ending 2003
Total Grants: $1,445,793
Number of Grants: 64
Average Grant: $7,111*
Highest Grant: $445,067
Lowest Grant: $200
Typical Range: $1,000 to $20,000
*Note: Average grant figure excludes four highest grants ($1,019,153).

Recent Grants

Note: Grants derived from 2003 Form 990.
General

445,067	San Mateo County Historical Association, Redwood City, CA
368,826	Yale University/Development, New Haven, CT
103,260	California Academy of Sciences, San Francisco, CA
102,090	New York Botanical Garden, Bronx, NY
30,720	St. Paul's Episcopal Church
30,000	Cathedral School for Boys, San Francisco, CA
25,815	Asian Art Museum, San Francisco, CA
25,815	New de Young, San Francisco, CA
25,522	Salvation Army, Los Angeles, CA
20,418	Hillsborough School Foundation, Hillsborough, CA

HELEN K. AND ARTHUR E. JOHNSON FOUNDATION

Giving Contact

John H. Alexander, Jr., President
1700 Broadway, Suite 1100
Denver, CO 80290-1039
Phone: (303)861-4127
Fax: (303)861-0607
E-mail: info@johnsonfoundation.org
Web: http://www.johnsonfoundation.org

Alternate Contact

Phone: 800-232-9931

Description

Founded: 1948
EIN: 846020702
Organization Type: General Purpose Foundation
Giving Locations: CO
Grant Types: Capital, Challenge, General Support, Matching, Operating Expenses, Project, Scholarship.

Donor Information

Founder: Incorporated in 1948 as the Arthur E. Johnson Foundation, the foundation became the Helen K. and Arthur E. Johnson Foundation in 1975.

Financial Summary

Total Giving: $6,554,176 (2003); $7,408,607 (2002); $8,078,427 (2001)
Giving Analysis: Giving for 2003 includes: foundation scholarships ($704,648); 2002: foundation grants to United Way ($40,000); foundation scholarships ($682,570)
Assets: $158,043,391 (2003); $165,493,498 (2002); $168,432,125 (2001)

Typical Recipients

Arts & Humanities: History & Archaeology, Libraries, Museums/Galleries, Music, Opera, Public Broadcasting
Civic & Public Affairs: Botanical Gardens/Parks, Business/Free Enterprise, Community Foundations, Employment/Job Training, Civic & Public Affairs-General, Hispanic Affairs, Housing, Inner-City Development, Native American Affairs, Urban & Community Affairs, Women's Affairs, Zoos/Aquariums
Education: Afterschool/Enrichment Programs, Colleges & Universities, Community & Junior Colleges, Economic Education, Education Funds, Elementary Education (Private), Faculty Development, Education-General, Leadership Training, Literacy, Minority Education, Private Education (Precollege), Public Education (Precollege), Science/Mathematics Education, Secondary Education (Private), Student Aid, Vocational & Technical Education
Environment: Air/Water Quality, Environment-General, Resource Conservation, Wildlife Protection
Health: AIDS/HIV, Alzheimer's Disease, Cancer, Children's Health/Hospitals, Clinics/Medical Centers, Eyes/Blindness, Health-General, Health Funds, Health Organizations, Heart, Home-Care Services, Hospices, Hospitals, Long-Term Care, Medical Rehabilitation, Medical Research, Medical Training, Multiple Sclerosis, Nursing Services, Public Health, Research/Studies Institutes, Single-Disease Health Associations, Speech & Hearing, Transplant Networks/Donor Banks
Religion: Churches, Religion-General, Religious Welfare, Seminaries
Science: Science Museums, Scientific Centers & Institutes
Social Services: Animal Protection, At-Risk Youth, Child Welfare, Community Centers, Community Service Organizations, Day Care, Emergency Relief, Family Planning, Family Services, Food/Clothing Distribution, Homes, People with Disabilities, Recreation

& Athletics, Scouts, Senior Services, Sexual Abuse, Shelters/Homelessness, Social Services-General, Substance Abuse, United Funds/United Ways, Volunteer Services, YMCA/YWCA/YMHA/YWHA, Youth Organizations

Application Procedures

Initial Contact: Applicants should send a brief preliminary letter of no more than two pages outlining the project. If interested, the foundation will request a full proposal.

Application Requirements: A full proposal: a cover letter that states the amount requested and objective of the project, signed by the Chief Executive Officer and the President of the Board; a narrative stating the relevance of project to others, timetable for accomplishing goals, history of organization; current board members; list of other funding agencies; operating and project budget; a description of organization's programs and those they serve; financial statements for last two years, including balance sheet and statement of revenue and expenses; proposed evaluation plan; plans for possible long-term funding; a completed Tax Exempt Status Certificate; a completed Board and Community Support Form; and IRS tax exemption letter.

Deadlines: January 1 for the spring meeting; April 1 for summer meeting; July 1 for fall meeting; and October 1 for winter meeting.

Restrictions

The foundation does not support organizations whose purpose is to influence the legislative or judicial process in any manner or for any cause; it does not contribute to loans; endowments; purchase of blocks of tickets; individual scholarships; grants that pass through the nominal grant recipient to another organization; or support for conferences. The foundation makes grants primarily to Colorado organizations. Re-applicants must wait a full twelve months after submitting a proposal to re-apply.

Additional Information

Publications: Annual Report; Application Guidelines

Foundation Officials

John H. Alexander, Jr.: president, assistant treasurer

Ashley C. Campion: treasurer, trustee
Berit K. Campion: secretary, trustee
Lynn H. Campion: vice chairman, trustee
Thomas B. Campion, Jr.: trustee
Brigit Ann Davis: vice president, assistant secretary
Barbara Hartley: chairperson, trustee
Charles R. Hazelrigg: trustee emeritus
Gerald R. Hillyard, Jr.: trustee
Ronald L. Lehr: trustee
Stanley Duane Neeleman: trustee B Salt Lake City, UT 1943. ED Westminster College BA (1967); George Washington University MA (1969); University of Denver JD (1972). PRIM NONPR EMPL professor: Brigham Young University, J. Reuben Clark Law School. CORP AFFIL counsel: Holme Roberts Owen. NONPR AFFIL founder: Utah Lawyers Arts; member: Utah State Bar Association; member: Governors Task Force Income Tax Reform Utah; member: Utah Citizens Arts; fellow: American College Trust & Estate Counsel; trustee: Beren Foundation.
Matthew D. Semler: trustee
Richard G. Wohlgenant: trustee

Grants Analysis

Disclosure Period: calendar year ending 2003
Total Grants: $5,849,528*
Number of Grants: 235
Average Grant: $24,892
Highest Grant: $260,000
Lowest Grant: $500
Typical Range: $5,000 to $50,000
*Note: Giving excludes scholarship.

Recent Grants

Note: Grants derived from 2003 Form 990.
General

260,000	YMCA, Denver, CO -- compass outreach program
250,000	Children's Hospital Foundation, Denver, CO
200,000	Clinica Campesina, Lafayette, CO -- for expansion of facilities
200,000	Idaho Community Foundation, Boise, ID -- deer creek fund
200,000	St. Joseph Hospital Foundation, Houston, TX -- education assistance program
199,680	University of Colorado Foundation, Boulder, CO -- accelerated nursing program
179,582	Planned Parenthood of the Rocky Mountains, Denver, CO
140,568	University of Denver, Denver, CO -- Johnson scholars
139,040	Colorado College, Colorado Springs, CO -- Johnson scholars
119,780	Regis University, Denver, CO -- Johnson scholars

HOWARD JOHNSON FOUNDATION

Giving Contact

Lisa Franciscovich, Trustee Officer
c/o U.S. Trust Co. of New York
114 W. 47th St.
New York, NY 10036
Phone: (212)852-3834

Description

Founded: 1961
EIN: 046060965
Organization Type: Private Foundation
Giving Locations: AK; ID; LA; MT; OR; WV
Grant Types: General Support.

Donor Information

Founder: the late Howard D. Johnson

Financial Summary

Total Giving: $168,500 (2003)
Assets: $4,407,043 (2003)
Gifts Received: $28,307 (2003); $9,225 (1999); $24,725 (1997). Note: In 2003, contributions were received from William Howard Weeks. In 1998, contributions were received from Dorothy Johnson Henry.

Typical Recipients

Arts & Humanities: Historic Preservation, Museums/Galleries, Music
Civic & Public Affairs: Botanical Gardens/Parks, Civic & Public Affairs-General, Zoos/Aquariums
Education: Business Education, Colleges & Universities, Elementary Education (Private), Gifted & Talented Programs, Medical Education, Minority Education, Private Education (Precollege), Public Education (Precollege), Religious Education
Environment: Air/Water Quality, Forestry, Environment-General, Resource Conservation, Wildlife Protection
Health: Cancer, Children's Health/Hospitals, Clinics/Medical Centers, Health Organizations, Hospitals, Hospitals (University Affiliated), Medical Research, Single-Disease Health Associations
International: International Environmental Issues
Religion: Churches, Religious Organizations, Seminaries
Social Services: Animal Protection, Community Service Organizations, Family Planning, People with Disabilities, Scouts, United Funds/United Ways, Youth Organizations

Application Procedures

Initial Contact: Send a brief letter of inquiry.
Deadlines: None.

Restrictions

Does not support individuals. Funds are committed for the foreseeable future. No unsolicited proposals are being accepted at this time.

Foundation Officials

Marissa J. Brock: trustee
Patricia Bates Crawford: trustee
Dorothy J. Henry: trustee
Howard Bates Johnson: trustee
Howard Brennan Johnson: trustee
Joshua J. Weeks: trustee
William H. Weeks: trustee

Grants Analysis

Disclosure Period: calendar year ending 2003
Total Grants: $168,500
Number of Grants: 37
Average Grant: $4,554
Highest Grant: $25,000
Lowest Grant: $1,000
Typical Range: $1,000 to $10,000

Recent Grants

Note: Grants derived from 2003 Form 990.
General

25,000	Greens Farms Academy, Greens Farms, CT
20,000	Duke University Markets and Management Studies Program, Durham, NC -- for Howard Johnson foundation entrepreneur in residence
15,000	Foxcroft School, Middleburg, VA
10,000	American Society for the Prevention of Cruelty to Animals, New York, NY
10,000	Spence School, New York, NY
10,000	Spence School, New York, NY
5,000	Buckley School in the City of New York, New York, NY
5,000	Dana Hall School, Wellesley, MA -- for second installment for the campaign for athletics
5,000	Danbury Hospital, Danbury, CT
5,000	Duke University Markets and Management Studies Program, Durham, NC -- for Howard Johnson foundation entrepreneur in residence

M. G. AND LILLIE A. JOHNSON FOUNDATION

Giving Contact

Robert Halepeska, Executive Vice President
PO Box 2269
Victoria, TX 77902
Phone: (361)575-7970
Fax: (361)575-2264
E-mail: mgj@cox-internet.com

Description

Founded: 1958
EIN: 746076961
Organization Type: General Purpose Foundation
Giving Locations: TX: Gulf Coast between San Patricio and Wharton.
Grant Types: Capital, Challenge, Endowment, General Support, Matching, Project, Scholarship.

Donor Information

Founder: The foundation was established in 1958, with contributions from M. G. Johnson and Lillie A. Johnson.

Financial Summary

Total Giving: $2,410,867 (fiscal year ending November 30, 2003); $2,433,387 (fiscal 2002); $2,781,905 (fiscal 2001)

Assets: $48,503,920 (fiscal 2003); $46,492,541 (fiscal 2002); $51,612,794 (fiscal 2001)

Gifts Received: $50,000 (fiscal 1999 approx); $1,800,000 (fiscal 1998 approx); $500,000 (fiscal 1997 approx)

Typical Recipients

Arts & Humanities: Historic Preservation, History & Archaeology, Libraries, Museums/Galleries, Performing Arts

Civic & Public Affairs: Botanical Gardens/Parks, Chambers of Commerce, Community Foundations, Civic & Public Affairs-General, Inner-City Development, Municipalities/Towns, Parades/Festivals, Safety, Urban & Community Affairs

Education: Colleges & Universities, Community & Junior Colleges, Continuing Education, Literacy, Medical Education, Religious Education, Science/Mathematics Education, Student Aid, Vocational & Technical Education

Environment: Wildlife Protection

Health: Children's Health/Hospitals, Clinics/Medical Centers, Emergency/Ambulance Services, Eyes/Blindness, Health Policy/Cost Containment, Health Funds, Health Organizations, Heart, Hospices, Hospitals, Long-Term Care, Medical Rehabilitation, Mental Health, Nursing Services, Nutrition, Public Health, Research/Studies Institutes, Transplant Networks/Donor Banks, Trauma Treatment

International: International-General, International Organizations

Religion: Bible Study/Translation, Churches, Ministries, Religious Organizations, Religious Welfare

Science: Science-General, Science Museums, Scientific Centers & Institutes

Social Services: Animal Protection, At-Risk Youth, Child Abuse, Child Welfare, Community Centers, Community Service Organizations, Counseling, Day Care, Domestic Violence, Emergency Relief, Family Services, Food/Clothing Distribution, Homes, People with Disabilities, Recreation & Athletics, Senior Services, Sexual Abuse, Social Services-General, Substance Abuse, Volunteer Services, YMCA/YWCA/YMHA/YWHA, Youth Organizations

Application Procedures

Initial Contact: Submit one copy of a detailed written proposal.

Application Requirements: Applications should include biographical information, proof of tax-exempt status, amount requested, purpose of funds sought, and anticipated length of time within which the funds will be expended.

Deadlines: None. Proposals should be received no later than one month prior to a meeting for consideration.

Review Process: The board of trustees usually meets in March, July and October. Applicants whose proposals are not approved will be informed only if the proposal conforms to the foundation's stated criteria.

Restrictions

Grants are seldom provided for operational expenses. The foundation does not fund national charities, fellowship programs, or organizations outside its geographic area of interest.

Additional Information

Publications: Application Guidelines

Foundation Officials

James A. Bouligny: trustee CORP AFFIL director: Prosperity Bancshares Inc.

M. H. Brock: chairman, trustee CORP AFFIL chairman: Maurco Corp.

Robert L. Halepeska: executive vice president

CORP AFFIL director: First Victoria National Bank.

Dick W. Koop: trustee CORP AFFIL director: Jackson Electric Co-op.

Jack Morrison, Jr.: assistant secretary PRIM CORP EMPL partner: Bumgardner Morrison & Co.

Terrell Mullins: trustee

Judge Lloyd Rust: vice chairman, trustee

M. Munson Smith: trustee, secretary PRIM CORP EMPL secretary, treasurer, director: Texas Concrete Co.

Grants Analysis

Disclosure Period: fiscal year ending November 30, 2003

Total Grants: $2,410,867

Number of Grants: 48

Average Grant: $42,954*

Highest Grant: $250,000

Lowest Grant: $4,400

Typical Range: $10,000 to $60,000

*Note: Average grant figure excludes two highest grants ($435,000).

Recent Grants

Note: Grants derived from fiscal 2003 Form 990.

Library-Related

11,000	Jackson County Memorial Library, Edna, TX -- to purchase microfilm viewing equipment

General

250,000	Wharton County Junior College, Wharton, TX -- to purchase instructional equipment for the academic programs
185,000	Citizens Medical Center, Victoria, TX
100,750	Jackson County Hospital District, Marianna, FL
100,000	City of El Campo, El Campo, TX -- for the construction of swimming pool
100,000	El Campo Medical Foundation, El Campo, TX
100,000	Lavaca Exposition -- to construct a covered youth facility
100,000	Sweeny Community Hospital, Sweeny, TX -- to purchase equipment for its operating room
90,000	Victoria College, Victoria, TX -- E-0480
88,532	Brownson Home Inc., Victoria, TX
75,000	Habitat for Humanity, Victoria, BC Canada -- as a challenge grant to purchase a building

SAMUEL S. JOHNSON FOUNDATION

Giving Contact

Elizabeth Hill Johnson, President
PO Box 356
Redmond, OR 97756-0079
Phone: (541)548-8104
Fax: (541)548-8104
E-mail: ssjohnson@empnet.com

Description

Founded: 1995
EIN: 946062478
Organization Type: Private Foundation
Giving Locations: OR
Grant Types: General Support.

Financial Summary

Total Giving: $418,158 (fiscal year ending May 31, 2004); $584,266 (fiscal 2001)

Giving Analysis: Giving for fiscal 2004 includes: foundation grants to United Way ($3,000); foundation gifts to individuals ($9,000); fiscal 2001: foundation grants to United Way ($3,250); foundation gifts to individuals ($3,506)

Assets: $9,257,094 (fiscal 2004); $11,374,391 (fiscal 2001)

Gifts Received: $16,985 (fiscal 2001); $17,000 (fiscal 1995); $61,267 (fiscal 1994). Note: In fiscal 1995, contributions were received from Elizabeth Hill Johnson.

Typical Recipients

Arts & Humanities: Historic Preservation, History & Archaeology, Museums/Galleries, Music, Public Broadcasting

Civic & Public Affairs: Community Foundations, Civic & Public Affairs-General, Public Policy, Safety

Education: Arts/Humanities Education, Colleges & Universities, Legal Education, Literacy, Medical Education, Preschool Education, Special Education

Environment: Resource Conservation

Health: Cancer, Health-General, Home-Care Services, Hospices, Preventive Medicine/Wellness Organizations

International: Health Care/Hospitals

Religion: Religion-General, Religious Welfare

Social Services: Animal Protection, Camps, Child Welfare, Community Service Organizations, Domestic Violence, Emergency Relief, People with Disabilities, Scouts, Senior Services, Shelters/Homelessness, Volunteer Services, YMCA/YWCA/YMHA/YWHA, Youth Organizations

Application Procedures

Initial Contact: The foundation has no formal grant application procedure or application form. Send a brief letter of inquiry.

Application Requirements: Include a description of organization, amount requested, purpose of funds sought, recently audited financial statement, and proof of tax-exempt status.

Deadlines: January 15 and June 15. The Foundation Board of Directors meet twice a year, in mid-February and mid-July.

Decision Notification: Applicants are notified in writing of the action taken by the board of directors relative to grant proposals usually within two weeks of the meeting of the Board of Directors.

Restrictions

Does not fund individuals, political or lobbying groups, endowments, capital expenditures, large equipment purchases, or building funds.

Foundation Officials

Karen K. Creason: director
John Helm: director
Elizabeth Hill Johnson: president, director
Patricia C. Johnson: cfo, director
Elizabeth K. Johnson-Helm: vice president, director

Grants Analysis

Disclosure Period: fiscal year ending May 31, 2004
Total Grants: $406,158*
Number of Grants: 179
Average Grant: $2,269
Highest Grant: $25,000
Lowest Grant: $100
Typical Range: $1,000 to $5,000
*Note: Giving excludes scholarships, United Way.

Recent Grants

Note: Grants derived from 2004 Form 990.

General

25,000	Hospice of Redmond, Sisters & Grant County, Redmond, OR -- in support of office expansion
20,000	Children's Cancer Association, Portland, OR -- in support of the caring cabin construction
15,000	Community Action Team Inc., St. Helens, OR -- in support of St. Helens family resource center
10,000	Boys and Girls Aid Society of Oregon, Bend, OR -- in support of adoption services

10,000	Boys and Girls Clubs of Central Oregon, Redmond, OR -- support in coordination with other youth groups
10,000	Friends of the Metolius, Camp Sherman, OR -- for the area of greatest need
10,000	Linfield College, McMinnville, OR -- for the president's discretionary fund
10,000	Oregon Health Sciences University, Portland, OR -- for the director's chair endowment
10,000	Oregon Health Sciences University, Portland, OR -- for the director's chair endowment
10,000	Scappoose Senior Citizens Inc., Scappoose, OR -- for administrative and accounting support services

THOMAS PHILLIPS AND JANE MOORE JOHNSON FOUNDATION

Giving Contact

Jane T. Johnson, Trustee
101 State Farm Pl.
Ballston Spa, NY 12020
Phone: (518)884-7922

Description

Founded: 1991
EIN: 256357015
Organization Type: Private Foundation
Giving Locations: CO; PA: nationally.
Grant Types: General Support.

Financial Summary

Total Giving: $926,733 (2003); $585,900 (2001)
Assets: $78,980,884 (2003); $51,438,098 (2001)
Gifts Received: $30,283,066 (2003); $48,808,751 (2001); $43,660 (2000). Note: In 2000, 2001, and 2003, contributions were received from the Estate of Thomas Johnson. In 1996 and 1999, contributions were received from Thomas P. Johnson.

Typical Recipients

Arts & Humanities: Film & Video, History & Archaeology, Libraries, Museums/Galleries, Music, Performing Arts, Public Broadcasting
Civic & Public Affairs: Community Foundations, Gay/Lesbian Issues, Civic & Public Affairs-General, Housing, Philanthropic Organizations, Public Policy
Education: Arts/Humanities Education, Colleges & Universities, Community & Junior Colleges, Environmental Education, Faculty Development, Private Education (Precollege), Student Aid
Environment: Air/Water Quality, Environment-General
Health: AIDS/HIV, Health-General, Hospitals
Religion: Churches, Religious Welfare
Science: Scientific Centers & Institutes

Application Procedures

Initial Contact: Send a brief letter of inquiry.
Application Requirements: Include amount requested, purpose of funds sought, and proof of tax-exempt status.
Deadlines: None.

Foundation Officials

James M. Johnson: president, trustee
Jane T. Johnson: trustee
Jesse D. Johnson: treasurer
Thomas P. Johnson, Jr.: chairman, trustee

Grants Analysis

Disclosure Period: calendar year ending 2003
Total Grants: $926,733

Number of Grants: 46
Average Grant: $18,344*
Highest Grant: $101,250
Lowest Grant: $200
Typical Range: $5,000 to $30,000
*Note: Average grant figure excludes highest grant.

Recent Grants

Note: Grants derived from 2003 Form 990.
General

101,250	Gay, Lesbian and Straight Education Network, New York, NY
75,000	Liberty Hill Foundation, Santa Monica, CA
70,000	Yale University, New Haven, CT
60,000	Teak Fellowship, New York, NY
50,000	Bethany College, Bethany, WV
50,000	International Film Seminars, New York, NY
50,000	Neighborhood Academy, Pittsburgh, PA
50,000	Telluride Historical Museum, Telluride, CO
50,000	Vermont Community Foundation, Middlebury, VT
45,000	National Environmental Education and Training Foundation, Washington, DC

WILLARD T. C. JOHNSON FOUNDATION

Giving Contact

Robert W. Johnson, IV, President
630 5th Avenue, Suite 1510
New York, NY 10111
Phone: (212)332-7500
Fax: (212)332-7510
E-mail: tjici1@tjinc.com

Description

Founded: 1979
EIN: 132993310
Organization Type: Family Foundation
Giving Locations: DC: Washington; NJ; NY: New York
Grant Types: General Support.

Donor Information

Founder: Incorporated in 1979 by the late Willard T. C. Johnson and the late Keith W. Johnson.

Financial Summary

Total Giving: $2,805,000 (2003); $3,215,000 (2002); $3,362,000 (2001)
Assets: $58,928,346 (2003); $51,924,580 (2002); $63,364,979 (2001)
Gifts Received: $1,124,456 (1992)

Typical Recipients

Arts & Humanities: Arts Funds, Libraries, Music, Opera, Public Broadcasting
Civic & Public Affairs: African American Affairs, Botanical Gardens/Parks, Business/Free Enterprise, Community Foundations, Civic & Public Affairs-General, Parades/Festivals, Safety
Education: Afterschool/Enrichment Programs, Colleges & Universities, Continuing Education, Education Funds, Education Reform, Faculty Development, Education-General, Private Education (Precollege), Student Aid
Environment: Wildlife Protection
Health: AIDS/HIV, Arthritis, Diabetes, Emergency/Ambulance Services, Health Organizations, Hospitals, Long-Term Care, Medical Research, Single-Disease Health Associations
International: Health Care/Hospitals
Religion: Religious Organizations, Religious Welfare
Science: Scientific Centers & Institutes

Social Services: Community Service Organizations, Crime Prevention, Family Planning, Senior Services, Youth Organizations

Application Procedures

Initial Contact: Send a brief letter of inquiry and a full proposal.
Deadlines: None.

Restrictions

Grants are made to organizations listed under section 501(c)(3) of the IRS code. Grants are not made to individuals.

Foundation Officials

Betty Wold Johnson: chairman, director
Robert Wood Johnson, IV: president, director
Robert J. Mortimer: vice president, secretary, treasurer, director

Grants Analysis

Disclosure Period: calendar year ending 2003
Total Grants: $2,805,000
Number of Grants: 8
Average Grant: $174,286*
Highest Grant: $1,585,000
Lowest Grant: $20,000
Typical Range: $75,000 to $500,000
*Note: Average grant figure excludes highest grant.

Recent Grants

Note: Grants derived from 2003 Form 990.
Library-Related

200,000	Princeton Public Library Foundation Inc., Princeton, NJ

General

1,585,000	Princeton Area Community Foundation, Lawrenceville, NJ
500,000	Robin Hood Foundation, New York, NY
275,000	Juvenile Diabetes Foundation International, New York, NY
100,000	Student/Sponsor Partnership Inc., New York, NY
75,000	Opera Festival of New Jersey, New Jersey, NJ
50,000	Best Friends Foundation, Washington, DC
20,000	New York City Police Foundation Inc., New York, NY

EDWARD C. JOHNSON FUND

Giving Contact

Anne-Marie Soulliere, Foundation Director
Fidelity Investments
82 Devonshire Street, F9A3
Boston, MA 02109
Phone: (617)563-6806
Web: http://www.fidelityfoundation.org

Description

Founded: 1964
EIN: 046108344
Organization Type: Family Foundation
Giving Locations: New England.
Grant Types: Capital, Endowment, General Support, Project.

Donor Information

Founder: The fund was established in 1964 by Edward C. Johnson III and the late Edward C. Johnson II.

Financial Summary

Total Giving: $19,368,388 (2003); $15,840,618 (2002); $20,987,524 (2001)

Assets: $302,842,948 (2003); $234,653,859 (2002); $280,101,038 (2001)
Gifts Received: $14,939,679 (2003); $996,212 (2002); $1,637,361 (2001). Note: In 2003, contributions were received from Abel Partners ($744,846), Edward C. Johnson Trust ($313,200), FMR Corp. ($13,881,633). In 2002, contributions were received from Fidelity Ventures Ltd ($275,792), the Edward C. Johnson III Charitable Lead Trust ($313,200), and Abel Partners ($407,220). In 2001, contributions were received from Fidelity Investors ($242,093), FMR Corp. ($749,911), the Edward C. Johnson II Charitable Lead Trust ($308,001), the Edward C. Johnson III Charitable Lead Trust ($313,200), and Abel Partners ($23,716). In 1999, contributions were received from the Edward C. Johnson II Charitable Lead Trust ($621,201) and FMR Corp. ($6,468,665). In 1998, contributions were received from the Edward C. Johnson III and Edward C. Johnson II Charitable Lead Trusts.

Typical Recipients

Arts & Humanities: Art History, Arts Associations & Councils, Ethnic & Folk Arts, Film & Video, Arts & Humanities-General, Historic Preservation, History & Archaeology, Libraries, Museums/Galleries, Music, Opera
Civic & Public Affairs: Botanical Gardens/Parks, Clubs, Economic Development, Economic Policy, Civic & Public Affairs-General, Municipalities/Towns, Native American Affairs, Parades/Festivals, Philanthropic Organizations, Public Policy, Urban & Community Affairs, Zoos/Aquariums
Education: Arts/Humanities Education, Business Education, Colleges & Universities, Environmental Education, Education-General, International Studies, Leadership Training, Medical Education, Private Education (Precollege), Public Education (Precollege), Science/Mathematics Education, Secondary Education (Private), Vocational & Technical Education
Environment: Environment-General, Resource Conservation
Health: Alzheimer's Disease, Cancer, Children's Health/Hospitals, Clinics/Medical Centers, Emergency/Ambulance Services, Eyes/Blindness, Health-General, Health Organizations, Home-Care Services, Hospitals, Medical Research, Mental Health, Nursing Services, Preventive Medicine/Wellness Organizations, Single-Disease Health Associations
International: Foreign Arts Organizations, Foreign Educational Institutions, Health Care/Hospitals, International Environmental Issues, International Organizations
Religion: Churches, Religious Organizations, Religious Welfare
Science: Science Museums, Scientific Centers & Institutes, Scientific Labs, Scientific Research
Social Services: Animal Protection, Camps, Child Welfare, Community Centers, Community Service Organizations, Family Services, Recreation & Athletics, Senior Services, Shelters/Homelessness, Social Services-General, YMCA/YWCA/YMHA/YWHA, Youth Organizations

Application Procedures

Initial Contact: Contact the fund for a summary of request form.
Application Requirements: A full application is made in a letter of request with supporting materials including the following: an organizational history and the organization's objectives; current audited financial statements; a project budget; a list of officers and directors; an IRS 501(c)(3) determination letter; reports on previous Edward C. Johnson Fund grants; and a brief development summary, including a list of other foundations and corporations receiving proposals.
Deadlines: Applications should be received by March 30 or October 30.
Review Process: Applications are considered in June or December, respectively.

Restrictions

The fund does not make multiyear pledges and does not normally award grants to any organization in successive years. No grants are made to individuals or for scholarships.
Applicants to the Edward C. Johnson Fund may not submit proposals simultaneously to the Fidelity Foundation, nor to the Fidelity Non-Profit Management Foundation.

Additional Information

Publications: Application Guidelines; Summary of Request Form

Corporate Officials

Edward Crosby Johnson, III: chairman, president, chief executive officer, director B Boston, MA 1930. ED Harvard University AB (1954). PRIM CORP EMPL chairman, president, chief executive officer, director: FMR Corp. ADD CORP EMPL president: Fidelity Government Securities Fund; chairman: Fidelity Management Research Co.; president: Fidelity Management Trust Co.; president: Fidelity Cash Reserve Fund; director: Fidelity Distributors Corp.; chairman: Fidelity Magellan Fund; president: Fidelity Trend Fund OCCUPATION Fidelity Intermediate Bond Fund. NONPR AFFIL director: Center Neurologic Diseases; member: Massachusetts Historical Society; fellow: American Academy of Arts & Sciences; honorary trustee: Boston Museum Fine Arts.

Foundation Officials

Patricia R. Harley: secretary
Abigail P. Johnson: director B 1961. PRIM CORP EMPL executive vice president: Fidelity Investments.
Edward Crosby Johnson, IV: director
Edward Crosby Johnson, III: president, director (see above)
Elizabeth L. Johnson: director
Anne-Marie Soulliere: foundation director NONPR AFFIL advisory board: Center for Effective Philanthropy; board of directors: New England Conservatory of Music.

Grants Analysis

Disclosure Period: calendar year ending 2003
Total Grants: $19,368,388
Number of Grants: 82
Average Grant: $109,869*
Highest Grant: $3,500,000
Lowest Grant: $400
Typical Range: $20,000 to $200,000
*Note: Average grant figure excludes six highest grants ($11,018,324).

Recent Grants

Note: Grants derived from 2002 Form 990.

General

5,000,000	Brookfield Arts Foundation
1,500,000	Proctor Academy, Andover, NH
675,888	Bermuda Underwater Exploration Institute Bermuda
600,000	Bermuda Underwater Exploration Institute Bermuda
455,145	Peabody Essex Museum, Salem, MA
440,469	Peabody Essex Museum, Salem, MA
415,500	Foundation for Neurological Diseases, New York, NY
412,157	Museum of Fine Arts of Boston, Boston, MA
301,136	Alzheimer's Research Forum Foundation
269,695	Alzheimer's Research Forum Foundation

JOHN ALFRED AND OSCAR JOHNSON MEMORIAL TRUST

Giving Contact

Carole W. Sellstrom, Foundation Coordinator
9-11 E. Fourth St.
PO Box 50
Jamestown, NY 14702
Phone: (716)484-7190

Description

Founded: 1996
EIN: 166438291
Organization Type: Private Foundation
Giving Locations: NY: Jamestown
Grant Types: General Support.

Financial Summary

Total Giving: $438,104 (fiscal year ending January 31, 2002); $460,092 (fiscal 2001)
Giving Analysis: Giving for fiscal 2002 includes: foundation grants to United Way ($1,000)
Assets: $7,499,286 (fiscal 2002); $9,312,213 (fiscal 2001)
Gifts Received: $25 (fiscal 2000)

Typical Recipients

Arts & Humanities: Libraries, Music
Civic & Public Affairs: Urban & Community Affairs
Education: Environmental Education, Private Education (Precollege)
Environment: Environment-General
Health: Hospitals, Medical Research, Speech & Hearing
Social Services: Child Welfare, Family Services, Food/Clothing Distribution, Social Services-General, YMCA/YWCA/YMHA/YWHA, Youth Organizations

Application Procedures

Initial Contact: Submit a written request.
Application Requirements: Include a description of project; project budget; recently audited financial statement; proof of tax-exempt status; list of board members and officers and their names and telephone numbers; a report of the organization's public and private funding sources, and a copy of the organization's most recent IRS Form 990.
Deadlines: June 1 and December 1.

Restrictions

No grants to individuals.

Additional Information

Trust(s): M&T Trust Co.

Foundation Officials

John L. Sellstrom: co-trustee

Grants Analysis

Disclosure Period: fiscal year ending January 31, 2002
Total Grants: $437,104*
Number of Grants: 19
Average Grant: $12,728*
Highest Grant: $208,000
Lowest Grant: $100
Typical Range: $5,000 to $20,000
*Note: Giving excludes United Way. Average grant excludes highest grant.

Recent Grants

Note: Grants derived from 2001 Form 990.
Library-Related

14,500	James Prendergast Library, Jamestown, NY -- for computer resources and senior services

General

232,000	Salvation Army, Jamestown, NY -- for grant
47,000	Jamestown Center City Development Corporation, Jamestown, NY -- for Ice Arena Project
30,000	Jamestown New York YMCA, Jamestown, NY -- for Camp Scandinavia 2000 Program
23,592	Chautauqua Lake Association, Lakewood, NY -- purchase shore conveyor
14,000	Chautauqua Striders, Chautauqua, NY -- for Lighted Schoolhouse Program
12,000	Jamestown Audubon Society, Jamestown, NY -- for Rural pre-school Program and After School Nature
10,000	National Multiple Sclerosis Society, New York, NY -- for grant
10,000	Roger Tory Peterson Institute, Jamestown, NY -- for gift photographic exhibit
10,000	WBFO/FM 88, Jamestown, NY -- gift to improve area signal
9,000	Chautauqua Institute, Chautauqua, NY -- for underwriting Sunday amphitheater

S.C. JOHNSON & SON

Company Headquarters
Racine, WI
Web: http://www.scjohnsonwax.com

Company Description
Former Name: S.C. Johnson Wax Fun (1998).
Revenue: US$5.895 billion (2002)
Employees: 12000 (2003)
SIC(s): 2841 Soap & Other Detergents, 2842 Polishes & Sanitation Goods, 2844 Toilet Preparations, 2879 Agricultural Chemicals Nec.

Operating Locations
S.C. Johnson & Son (AR--Rogers; CA--Brea; GA--Atlanta; IL--Downers Grove; MD--Columbia, Millersville, Silver Spring; NJ--Hammonton; OH--Cleveland; TX--Dallas, Houston; WA--Issaquah)

Nonmonetary Support
Type: Donated Equipment; Donated Products; Inkind Services; Loaned Executives
Contact: Kari Iselin, Community Relations Administrator

S.C. Johnson Fund

Giving Contact
Colleen Cribari, Program Administrator
S.C. Johnson Fund
1525 Howe Street
Racine, WI 53403
Phone: (262)260-2119
Fax: (262)260-2652
Web: http://www.scjohnson.com/community/

Description
EIN: 396052089
Organization Type: Corporate Foundation
Former Name: S.C. Johnson Wax Fund, Inc. (1998).
Giving Locations: WI: Racine headquarters and operating communities.
Grant Types: Employee Matching Gifts, Fellowship, General Support, Project, Scholarship, Seed Money.
Note: Employee matching gift ratio: 1 to 1 for gifts to education and the United Way.

Financial Summary
Total Giving: $9,454,114 (fiscal year ending June 30, 2004); $9,533,251 (fiscal 2003); $15,014,000 (fis-

cal 2002). Note: Contributes through corporate direct giving program and foundation.
Giving Analysis: Giving for fiscal 2002 includes: foundation grants to United Way ($10,000); foundation matching gifts ($1,339,726); corporate direct giving (approx $4,879,227); foundation ($8,785,047); fiscal 2001: foundation matching gifts ($1,507,371); foundation ($6,632,654); corporate direct giving (approx $7,806,975)
Assets: $8,402,156 (fiscal 2004); $5,991,791 (fiscal 2003); $7,781,185 (fiscal 2002)
Gifts Received: $12,109,276 (fiscal 2004); $7,617,009 (fiscal 2003); $11,301,798 (fiscal 2002). Note: In 2002, 2003, and 2004, contributions were received from S.C. Johnson & Son and JohnsonDiversey, Inc. In 2001, contributions were received from S.C. Johnson & Son and S.C. Johnson Commercial Markets, Inc. In 2000, contributions were received from S.C. Johnson & Son.

Typical Recipients
Arts & Humanities: Arts Associations & Councils, Arts Centers, Arts Funds, Arts Institutes, Community Arts, Dance, Ethnic & Folk Arts, Arts & Humanities-General, Historic Preservation, History & Archaeology, Libraries, Museums/Galleries, Music, Performing Arts, Public Broadcasting, Theater
Civic & Public Affairs: Botanical Gardens/Parks, Business/Free Enterprise, Civil Rights, Community Foundations, Economic Development, Employment/Job Training, Civic & Public Affairs-General, Hispanic Affairs, Housing, Law & Justice, Minority Business, Municipalities/Towns, Professional & Trade Associations, Public Policy, Safety, Urban & Community Affairs, Women's Affairs, Zoos/Aquariums
Education: Afterschool/Enrichment Programs, Arts/Humanities Education, Business Education, Colleges & Universities, Economic Education, Education Associations, Education Funds, Elementary Education (Public), Engineering/Technological Education, Education-General, Health & Physical Education, International Exchange, International Studies, Leadership Training, Literacy, Medical Education, Minority Education, Private Education (Precollege), Public Education (Precollege), Religious Education, Science/Mathematics Education, Secondary Education (Private), Secondary Education (Public), Social Sciences Education, Special Education, Student Aid, Vocational & Technical Education
Environment: Air/Water Quality, Environment-General, Protection, Resource Conservation, Wildlife Protection
Health: AIDS/HIV, Cancer, Children's Health/Hospitals, Clinics/Medical Centers, Health Funds, Health Organizations, Hospitals, Medical Research, Medical Training, Nutrition, Public Health, Single-Disease Health Associations
International: International Environmental Issues, International Relations
Religion: Religion-General, Ministries, Religious Welfare
Social Services: Animal Protection, At-Risk Youth, Child Welfare, Community Centers, Community Service Organizations, Crime Prevention, Day Care, Delinquency & Criminal Rehabilitation, Emergency Relief, Family Services, Food/Clothing Distribution, Homes, People with Disabilities, Recreation & Athletics, Scouts, Senior Services, Social Services-General, Substance Abuse, United Funds/United Ways, Veterans, Volunteer Services, YMCA/YWCA/YMHA/YWHA, Youth Organizations

Application Procedures
Initial Contact: Send a brief letter of inquiry.
Application Requirements: Include proof of tax-exempt status, statement of purpose and brief history of the organization, description of overall program, explanation regarding the specific request for support, itemized annual and project budget, copy of most recent audited financial statements, and list of other corporate and foundation donors.
Deadlines: March 1, July 1, and November 1.

Review Process: Process involves four advisory committees in program areas, who make recommendations to the trustees. Proposals are acknowledged upon receipt; if within guidelines and interest of fund, follow-up contact is made by the foundation.
Evaluative Criteria: Project reflects favorably on company's public image; employee involvement; nonduplication or overlap of services and programs provided by organizations already receiving funds or corporate support, either directly or indirectly through united funds; broad support within community; impacts a community where employees live and work. Most S.C. Johnson Fund grants are made to private organizations; contributions to tax-supported organizations are considered only for projects in which the Fund has a specific interest.
Decision Notification: Committees review proposals prior to each board meeting, which are held in February, June, and October. All grant seekers are informed of the board's decision on their applications.

Restrictions
The fund does not support individuals; social, athletic, veterans, labor, or fraternal organizations, or religious institutions. (A program may be considered if it is not restricted to organization members and is available to the community as a whole.) The fund also does not support political actions or lobbying efforts; national health fund drives or national health organizations; or salary or wage support. Fund does not make individual grants to United Way agencies for operating expenses, but will consider major capital requests. The fund should not be the only funding source for an organization. (Sole source funding may be given for special, one-time projects.) Grants are given for one year to discourage dependence of the recipient on this source, with the exception of major capital drives. The fund makes grants only to programs in the United States.

The Johnson Foundation, Inc., an entirely separate institution, operates the Wingspread Conference Center and also receives contributions from S.C. Johnson & Son, Inc. Therefore, the fund generally does not support conferences, workshops, or seminars.

Additional Information
Corporation contributes at least 5% of pre-tax profit to nonprofit organizations.
Publications: Social Responsibility Report; Application Form; Contributions Policy and Guidelines (Pamphlet)

Corporate Officials
Jane M. Hutterly: vice president, North American Professional
H. Fisk Johnson: chairman ED Cornell University BA (1979); Cornell University MA (1980); Cornell University MS (1982); Cornell University MBA (1984); Cornell University PhD (1986). NONPR AFFIL director: Grocery Manufacturer's Association; member: World Business Council for Sustainable Development; director: Conservation International; trustee emeritus: Cornell University.
Helen P. Johnson-Leipold: chairman, chief executive officer, Johnson Outdoors Inc. ED Cornell University BA (1978). CORP AFFIL chairman: Johnson Financial Group. NONPR AFFIL director: Racine Charter One; director: Sustainable Racine; director: Prairie School; founder, chairman: Next Generation Now.
William D. Perez: president, chief executive officer, director ED American Graduate School of International Management MA; Cornell University BA. CORP AFFIL president, chief executive officer, director: Nike Inc.; director: Hallmark Cards Inc.; director: Kellogg Co. NONPR AFFIL director: Grocery Manufacturers of America.
J. Gary Raley: president, North American Professional

Foundation Officials

Gregory F. Clark: trustee
Richard S. Hutchings: trustee
Jane M. Hutterly: executive vice president (see above)
H. Fisk Johnson: trustee (see above)
Helen P. Johnson-Leipold: trustee (see above)
William D. Perez: vice chairman, trustee (see above)
Susan E. Perszyk: trustee
J. Gary Raley: trustee (see above)
Thomas J. Reigle: vice president, executive director, secretary
Jeffrey M. Waller: treasurer, trustee ED Carroll College BA (1973). NONPR AFFIL trustee: Carroll College.
Thomas M. Wierzba: trustee

Grants Analysis

Disclosure Period: fiscal year ending June 30, 2004
Total Grants: $7,661,931*
Number of Grants: 67
Average Grant: $92,605*
Highest Grant: $1,550,000
Lowest Grant: $1,000
Typical Range: $5,000 to $50,000
***Note:** Giving excludes matching gifts, scholarship, and United Way. Average grant figure excludes highest grant.

Recent Grants

Note: Grants derived from fiscal 2004 Form 990.
General

1,550,000	Cornell University, Ithaca, NY
1,088,100	Racine Charter One Inc., Racine, WI
1,000,000	Prairie School, Racine, WI
400,000	Mound Properties Inc., Racine, WI
352,930	Sons and Daughters Scholarship Program, St. Peter, MN
305,000	Lincoln Lutheran of Racine Inc., Racine, WI
250,000	Conservation International, Washington, DC
250,000	Norfolk Academy, Norfolk, VA
250,000	World Resources Institute, Washington, DC
250,000	World Wildlife Fund Inc., Washington, DC

JOHNSTON-HANSON FOUNDATION

Giving Contact

Elizabeth J. Hanson, Chairperson & Secretary-Treasurer
5118 S. Perry St.
Spokane, WA 99223
Phone: (509)448-4708

Description

Founded: 1948
EIN: 943077091
Organization Type: Private Foundation
Giving Locations: CA; FL; ID; KY; NE; RI; WA: Spokane
Grant Types: Endowment, Multiyear/Continuing Support, Scholarship.

Donor Information

Founder: the late Eric Johnston

Financial Summary

Total Giving: $105,000 (2002 approx); $242,650 (2001)
Giving Analysis: Giving for 2002 includes: foundation scholarships (approx $163,000); 2001: foundation scholarships ($128,950)
Assets: $4,739,031 (2001)

Typical Recipients

Arts & Humanities: Arts Associations & Councils, Ballet, Community Arts, Arts & Humanities-General, Historic Preservation, History & Archaeology, Museums/Galleries, Music, Opera, Performing Arts, Public Broadcasting, Theater
Civic & Public Affairs: Civic & Public Affairs-General, Housing, Urban & Community Affairs
Education: Arts/Humanities Education, Business Education, Colleges & Universities, Education-General, Private Education (Precollege), Religious Education, Secondary Education (Private), Student Aid
Religion: Churches, Dioceses, Religious Organizations, Religious Welfare
Science: Scientific Centers & Institutes
Social Services: Big Brothers/Big Sisters, Community Service Organizations, Food/Clothing Distribution, People with Disabilities, Scouts, United Funds/United Ways, YMCA/YWCA/YMHA/YWHA, Youth Organizations

Application Procedures

Initial Contact: The foundation has no formal grant application procedure or application form. Submit inquiry by phone or mail.
Application Requirements: Provide a description of organization, amount requested, purpose of funds sought, recently audited financial statement, and proof of tax-exempt status.
Deadlines: None.

Restrictions

Does not support individuals, public institutions, or the medical field. Grants are generally restricted to the Spokane, WA area.

Foundation Officials

Herbert Johnston Butler: director
Victoria Butler Carney: director
Elizabeth J. Hanson: chp, secretary, treasurer
Eric Hanson: director
Fred L. Hanson: vice president
Maage E. LaCounte: director
Scott Lukins: assistant treasurer, assistant secretary
Ann Hanson Scarborough: director
Gil A. Zwetsch: director

Grants Analysis

Disclosure Period: calendar year ending 2001
Total Grants: $113,700*
Number of Grants: 15
Average Grant: $4,580*
Highest Grant: $45,000
Typical Range: $1,000 to $10,000
***Note:** Giving excludes Scholarship. Average grant figure excludes highest grant.

Recent Grants

Note: Grants derived from 2001 Form 990.
General

45,000	Museum of Arts and Culture, Miami, FL -- for the auditorium
32,000	Saint Georges School, Newport, RI -- for scholarships
25,000	Gonzaga University, Spokane, WA -- for scholarships
15,000	Habitat for Humanity, Spokane, WA -- to help people build homes and independence
15,000	MIT University -- for scholarships
15,000	Work for Education, Peducah, KY -- for scholarships
12,950	Gonzaga Preparatory School, Spokane, WA -- for scholarships
10,000	Cathedral and the Arts, Spokane, WA
10,000	Whitworth College, Spokane, WA -- for scholarships
5,000	Cathedral of St. John the Evangelist, Spokane, WA

CYRUS W. AND AMY F. JONES AND BESSIE D. PHELPS FOUNDATION

Giving Contact

Aram H. Tellalian, Jr., President & Treasurer
c/o Tellalian & Tellalian
211 State St.
Bridgeport, CT 06604
Phone: (203)336-5566

Description

EIN: 060943204
Organization Type: Private Foundation
Giving Locations: CT: Bridgeport
Grant Types: General Support, Operating Expenses, Project.

Donor Information

Founder: the late Amy F. Jones

Financial Summary

Total Giving: $148,000 (fiscal year ending September 30, 2004); $210,000 (fiscal 2001)
Assets: $4,204,959 (fiscal 2004); $4,862,997 (fiscal 2001)

Typical Recipients

Arts & Humanities: Arts Centers, Community Arts, Libraries, Museums/Galleries, Music, Opera, Performing Arts, Public Broadcasting, Theater
Civic & Public Affairs: Ethnic Organizations, Housing, Inner-City Development, Municipalities/Towns, Parades/Festivals, Philanthropic Organizations, Urban & Community Affairs
Education: Colleges & Universities, Education-General, Legal Education, Private Education (Precollege), Public Education (Precollege), Secondary Education (Private), Student Aid, Vocational & Technical Education
Environment: Environment-General
Health: Cancer, Children's Health/Hospitals, Clinics/Medical Centers, Health Funds, Heart, Hospices, Hospitals, Prenatal Health Issues, Research/Studies Institutes, Single-Disease Health Associations
International: International Affairs
Religion: Churches, Religious Organizations, Religious Welfare
Social Services: Big Brothers/Big Sisters, Child Welfare, Community Centers, Community Service Organizations, Family Planning, Family Services, Food/Clothing Distribution, People with Disabilities, Senior Services, YMCA/YWCA/YMHA/YWHA, Youth Organizations

Application Procedures

Initial Contact: Send brief letter describing program. Include history, current function, and needs as a tax exempt organization.
Deadlines: None.

Restrictions

Preference is given to local religious organizations.

Foundation Officials

Alexander R. Nestor: vice president, trustee
Aram H. Tellalian, Jr.: president, treasurer, trustee
Robert S. Tellalian: vice president, secretary, trustee

Grants Analysis

Disclosure Period: fiscal year ending September 30, 2004
Total Grants: $148,000
Number of Grants: 36
Average Grant: $4,111
Highest Grant: $20,000
Lowest Grant: $1,000
Typical Range: $1,000 to $10,000

Recent Grants

Note: Grants derived from fiscal 2004 Form 990.
General

20,000	Greater Bridgeport Symphony, Bridgeport, CT
10,000	Bridgeport Hospital Foundation Inc., Bridgeport, CT
10,000	Connecticut Grand Opera & Orchestra Inc., Stamford, CT
10,000	Olivet Congregational Church, Bridgeport, CT
10,000	St. Vincent's Medical Center Foundation, Bridgeport, CT
9,500	Council of Churches of Greater Bridgeport Inc., Bridgeport, CT
9,000	Sacred Heart University, Fairfield, CT -- for graduate program in occupational therapy
6,000	Armenian Church of Holy Ascension, Trumbull, CT
5,000	Goodwill Industries of Western Connecticut, Bridgeport, CT
5,000	Music & Arts Center for Humanity Inc., Bridgeport, CT

DAISY MARQUIS JONES FOUNDATION

Giving Contact

Roger L. Gardner, President & Trustee
1600 South Avenue, Suite 250
Rochester, NY 14620
Phone: (585)461-4950
Fax: (585)461-9752
E-mail: mail@dmjf.org
Web: http://www.dmjf.org

Description

Founded: 1968
EIN: 237000227
Organization Type: General Purpose Foundation
Giving Locations: NY: Monroe County, Yates County
Grant Types: Capital, Challenge, General Support, Matching, Project, Seed Money.

Donor Information

Founder: "The Daisy Marquis Jones Foundation is a not-for-profit, private foundation created in 1968 by the late Daisy Marquis Jones. Daisy Marquis Jones was born in Pennsylvania and came to Rochester around 1909. She married Nelson Jones, a Himrod dairy farmer in the 1940s. The years they operated the dairy farm together formed the basis for her special interest in Yates County. She gave her Himrod farmhouse to the fledgling volunteer fire department and continued to support them in building a firehouse and purchasing equipment. After her husband's death in 1961 she returned to Rochester. Daisy was a shrewd investor and an astute businesswoman. She had the admiration and respect of the bankers and brokers of the downtown area, but was little known in the community until after her death in 1971. She left a multi-million dollar estate to the Foundation she had set up three years before her death."

Financial Summary

Total Giving: $1,441,485 (2002); $3,100,000 (2001)
Assets: $45,724,447 (2002); $48,000,000 (2001)
Gifts Received: $650,000 (1998); $3,754,757 (1997); $200,000 (1996). Note: In 1998, contributions were received from Leo M. Lyons.

Typical Recipients

Arts & Humanities: Arts Associations & Councils, Arts Outreach, Dance, Arts & Humanities-General, Historic Preservation, History & Archaeology, Libraries, Literary Arts, Museums/Galleries, Music, Opera, Performing Arts, Public Broadcasting, Visual Arts
Civic & Public Affairs: African American Affairs, Botanical Gardens/Parks, Civil Rights, Community Foundations, Economic Development, Employment/Job Training, Ethnic Organizations, Gay/Lesbian Issues, Civic & Public Affairs-General, Housing, Law & Justice, Legal Aid, Municipalities/Towns, Native American Affairs, Nonprofit Management, Philanthropic Organizations, Professional & Trade Associations, Public Policy, Safety, Urban & Community Affairs, Women's Affairs, Zoos/Aquariums
Education: Afterschool/Enrichment Programs, Arts/Humanities Education, Business Education, Colleges & Universities, Community & Junior Colleges, Continuing Education, Education Funds, Education-General, Health & Physical Education, Legal Education, Literacy, Medical Education, Preschool Education, Science/Mathematics Education, Secondary Education (Public), Special Education, Student Aid, Vocational & Technical Education
Environment: Environment-General
Health: Adolescent Health Issues, AIDS/HIV, Alzheimer's Disease, Cancer, Children's Health/Hospitals, Clinics/Medical Centers, Emergency/Ambulance Services, Geriatric Health, Health Funds, Health Organizations, Hospices, Hospitals, Hospitals (University Affiliated), Long-Term Care, Medical Rehabilitation, Mental Health, Nursing Services, Nutrition, Outpatient Health Care, Prenatal Health Issues, Preventive Medicine/Wellness Organizations, Public Health, Research/Studies Institutes, Speech & Hearing
International: Foreign Arts Organizations, Health Care/Hospitals
Religion: Churches, Jewish Causes, Religious Organizations, Religious Welfare
Science: Science Museums, Scientific Centers & Institutes, Scientific Organizations
Social Services: At-Risk Youth, Big Brothers/Big Sisters, Child Welfare, Community Centers, Community Service Organizations, Crime Prevention, Day Care, Delinquency & Criminal Rehabilitation, Domestic Violence, Emergency Relief, Family Planning, Family Services, Food/Clothing Distribution, Homes, People with Disabilities, Recreation & Athletics, Scouts, Senior Services, Shelters/Homelessness, Substance Abuse, United Funds/United Ways, Veterans, Volunteer Services, YMCA/YWCA/YMHA/YWHA, Youth Organizations

Application Procedures

Initial Contact: A short letter of inquiry should be sent to the foundation.
Application Requirements: The letter should describe the project, list the amount requested, and include an intended starting date. If the foundation is interested in the proposal, an application form will be sent. The form should include a detailed program description, work plan, qualifications of staff, itemized program budget, plans for evaluation, and coordination with related organizations and programs.
Deadlines: None. Early submission of requests is encouraged.
Review Process: A decision generally takes two to three months. The board meets monthly, except during July and August, to review proposals.

Restrictions

The foundation does not make grants in the following areas: arts, endowments, local chapters of national health-related organizations, private schools, religious projects, research, scholarships, and projects by or for individuals.

Additional Information

HSBC and M&T Bank, both of Rochester, NY, serve as corporate trustees for the foundation.
Publications: Annual Report; Guidelines

Foundation Officials

Roger L. Gardner: president, director
Pearl W. Rubin: trustee
Donald W. Whitney: chairman, trustee

Grants Analysis

Disclosure Period: calendar year ending 2003
Total Grants: $1,441,485
Number of Grants: 68
Average Grant: $18,530*
Highest Grant: $200,000
Lowest Grant: $350
Typical Range: $10,000 to $50,000
*Note: Average grant figure excludes highest grant.

Recent Grants

Note: Grants derived from 2003 Form 990.
General

200,000	Children's Institute Inc., Rochester, NY -- to assist the Rochester Early Enhancement Project
106,153	Lifespan of Greater Rochester Inc., Rochester, NY -- to support the Geriatric Addictions programs
100,000	Rochester Children's Nursery, Rochester, NY -- grant for classroom renovation and facility improvement
75,000	Enterprise Foundation Inc., Columbia, MD -- to assist the Rochester Community Development Collaborative
75,000	Genesee Country Museum, Mumford, NY -- grant for History Bus & Summer Enrichment program
75,000	YMCA of Greater Rochester, Rochester, NY -- to support the construction of camp Northpoint
65,000	Ibero-American Development Corporation, Rochester, NY -- fund for Buena Vista Centro De Oro Project, to provide services to the elderly
50,000	Community Health Network Inc., Wallingford, CT -- grant to relocate Community Health Network into a larger, upgraded facility
50,000	University of Rochester Medical Center, Rochester, NY -- grant for Health-E-Access, to provide high quality medical examination
40,000	Flower City Habitat For Humanity Inc., Rochester, NY -- for the construction of a single family home on Fulton avenue

FLETCHER JONES FOUNDATION

Giving Contact

Christine W. Sisley, Executive Director
523 W. Sixth Street, Suite 301
Los Angeles, CA 90014
Phone: (213)943-4646
Fax: (213)943-4648
E-mail: chris@fletcherjonesfdn.org

Description

Founded: 1969
EIN: 237030155
Organization Type: General Purpose Foundation
Giving Locations: CA
Grant Types: Award, Challenge, Endowment, Fellowship, Loan, Matching, Scholarship.

Donor Information

Founder: In 1969, the Jones Foundation was established by the will of Fletcher Jones with a bequest of approximately $30 million. Mr. Jones was the co-founder, chairman, and chief executive officer of Computer Services Corporation, a computer software services company. He was a collector of fine art, and possessed a large collection of Impressionist paintings. He also assembled one of the West's preeminent stables of thoroughbred racehorses. Mr. Jones died in 1972 at the age of 41. The first distribution of funds from the Jones estate was given to the foundation in 1977; the final distribution of the estate was made in 1981. The foundation donated its first grants in 1974. In March of 1987, the Jones Foundation was renamed the Fletcher Jones Foundation.

Financial Summary

Total Giving: $5,265,750 (2003); $7,000,000 (2002 approx); $5,828,000 (2001)

Giving Analysis: Giving for 2003 includes: foundation scholarships ($195,000); foundation fellowships ($425,000)

Assets: $153,701,155 (2003); $130,000,000 (2002 approx); $132,632,230 (2001)

Typical Recipients

Arts & Humanities: Arts Institutes, Arts Outreach, Ballet, Arts & Humanities-General, History & Archaeology, Libraries, Museums/Galleries, Music, Opera, Performing Arts, Public Broadcasting

Civic & Public Affairs: Botanical Gardens/Parks, Community Foundations, Civic & Public Affairs-General, Law & Justice, Legal Aid, Professional & Trade Associations, Public Policy, Zoos/Aquariums

Education: Afterschool/Enrichment Programs, Arts/Humanities Education, Business Education, Colleges & Universities, Continuing Education, Education Associations, Education Funds, Engineering/Technological Education, Faculty Development, Education-General, Gifted & Talented Programs, International Studies, Leadership Training, Legal Education, Private Education (Precollege), Public Education (Precollege), Religious Education, Science/Mathematics Education, Secondary Education (Private), Social Sciences Education, Special Education, Student Aid, Vocational & Technical Education

Environment: Environment-General, Wildlife Protection

Health: Children's Health/Hospitals, Clinics/Medical Centers, Eyes/Blindness, Health-General, Health Funds, Health Organizations, Hospices, Hospitals, Medical Research, Mental Health, Multiple Sclerosis, Nursing Services, Public Health, Research/Studies Institutes, Single-Disease Health Associations, Speech & Hearing

International: International Affairs, International Development, International Peace & Security Issues, International Relations, International Relief Efforts

Religion: Religious Organizations, Religious Welfare

Science: Observatories & Planetariums, Science Museums, Scientific Centers & Institutes, Scientific Research

Social Services: Child Welfare, Day Care, Domestic Violence, Food/Clothing Distribution, Homes, People with Disabilities, Recreation & Athletics, Scouts, United Funds/United Ways, Volunteer Services, Youth Organizations

Application Procedures

Initial Contact: The foundation urges organizations to read the application guidelines carefully to ensure that only qualified applicants apply. Organizations may submit a short "test letter" to the foundation before preparing a formal grant application. There is no special grant application format.

Application Requirements: For a full proposal, include a fact sheet summarizing significant statistics and background information about the organization's qualifications, objectives, current programs and services, sources of support, purpose, goals, expense budget, funding, and method of evaluation, and include most recent financial report, proof of nonprofit status, most recent IRS Form 990, list of officers with professional affiliations, and most recent annual report. Also include the name, address, and telephone number of the organization's attorney. A short cover letter summarizing the request should accompany

the proposal. The foundation requests that proposals be typewritten on 8 1/2 x 11 white paper, and places no limit on the number of attachments.

Deadlines: None.

Review Process: Each test letter will be acknowledged with either a denial or an invitation to submit a formal application.

Decision Notification: Grant decisions are made once in each calendar quarter.

Restrictions

Grants are not made to individuals, political candidates; projects which are financed by government agencies, or K-12 schools; or for deficit financing, operating funds, contingencies; conferences, seminars, or workshops; travel exhibits or surveys; elections, campaigns, voter registration, or propaganda.

Additional Information

Publications: Annual Report

Foundation Officials

Peter Keefe Barker: vice president, trustee B Chicago, IL 1948. ED Colgate University (1966-1968); Claremont McKenna College (1968-1970); University of Chicago MBA (1971). PRIM CORP EMPL partner: Goldman Sachs & Co. CORP AFFIL director: Avery Dennison Inc.; director: Stone Energy. NONPR AFFIL chairman: Claremont McKenna College; director: Performing Arts Center of Los Angeles County.

Samuel P. Bell: vice president, trustee

Robert F. Erburu: vice president, trustee B Ventura, CA 1930. ED University of Southern California BA (1952); Harvard University JD (1955). CORP AFFIL director: Marsh & McLennan Companies Inc. NONPR AFFIL trustee: National Gallery Art; director: Pacific Council on International Policy; life director: Independent Colleges Southern California; member: American Bar Association; chairman board trustee: H.E. Huntington Library Art Gallery.

Houston I. Flournoy: vice president B New York, NY 1929. ED Cornell University BA (1950); Princeton University MA (1952); Princeton University PhD (1956). CORP AFFIL director: Tosco Refining Co.; director: Tosco Corp.; director: Tosco Marketing Co.; director: Lockheed Martin Corp.; director: Lockheed Martin Financial Corp.; director: Fremont General Corp.; director: LFC. NONPR AFFIL special assistant president government affairs: University Southern California Sacramento.

Parker S. Kennedy: vice president, trustee

Robert W. Kummer, Jr.: vice president, trustee B Pittsburgh, PA 1936. ED Oberlin College (1958); University of California (1960). PRIM CORP EMPL chairman, chief executive officer: First Business Bank. CORP AFFIL chairman, chief executive officer: First Business Corp.; chairman: Mellon First Business Corp.

Dan Lundgren: vice president, trustee

Michael D. McKee: vice president, director

Donald E. Nickelson: vice president, trustee

John Phleger Pollock: president B Sacramento, CA April 28, 1920. ED Stanford University AB (1942); Harvard University JD (1948). PRIM CORP EMPL officer counsel: Rodi, Pollock, Pettker, Galbraith & Phillips. NONPR AFFIL trustee: Good Hope Medicine Foundation; member: Los Angeles County Bar Association; member: American Bar Association; active: Boy Scouts America.

Dickinson C. Ross: vice president, trustee B Los Angeles, CA 1923. ED University of Southern California (1947). CORP AFFIL director: Westmark Realty Advisors; director: Xybernet Inc.; director: Assoc Travel Corp.; director: Fremont General Corp.

Grants Analysis

Disclosure Period: calendar year ending 2003

Total Grants: $4,645,750*

Number of Grants: 69

Average Grant: $54,414*

Highest Grant: $500,000

Lowest Grant: $1,000

Typical Range: $25,000 to $100,000

*****Note:** Giving excludes scholarships and fellowships. Average grant figure excludes two highest grants ($1,000,000).

Recent Grants

Note: Grants derived from 2003 Form 990.

Library-Related

25,000	Huntington Library, San Marino, CA
20,000	Huntington Library, San Marino, CA

General

500,000	Mount Saint Mary's College, Los Angeles, CA -- to renovate chemical laboratory
500,000	University of the Pacific, Stockton, CA -- to create FJF wing at university library
425,000	Scripps Research Institute, San Diego, CA -- to establish fellowship for graduate students
250,000	Art Center College of Design, Pasadena, CA -- to develop new south campus
250,000	California Science Center, Los Angeles, CA
250,000	Claremont McKenna College, Claremont, CA
250,000	Claremont University Consortium, Claremont, CA -- to construct health and wellness center
250,000	Dominican University, San Rafael, CA -- for microbiology lab in new center
250,000	Keck Graduate Institute, Claremont, CA -- towards support of FJF assistant professor awards
250,000	Loma Linda University, Loma Linda, CA -- towards technical upgrades

HELEN JONES FOUNDATION

Giving Contact

Louise Arnold, President & Director
4603 92nd St.
Lubbock, TX 79424
Phone: (806)794-8078

Description

Founded: 1984

EIN: 751977748

Organization Type: Private Foundation

Giving Locations: TX: Lubbock

Grant Types: General Support, Operating Expenses, Scholarship.

Donor Information

Founder: Helen DeVitt Jones

Financial Summary

Total Giving: $4,354,550 (2001)

Giving Analysis: Giving for 2001 includes: foundation grants to United Way ($30,000)

Assets: $89,222,932 (2001)

Typical Recipients

Arts & Humanities: Arts Associations & Councils, Arts Centers, Ballet, Ethnic & Folk Arts, Historic Preservation, History & Archaeology, Libraries, Museums/Galleries, Music, Public Broadcasting, Theater

Civic & Public Affairs: Clubs, Civic & Public Affairs-General, Housing, Philanthropic Organizations

Education: Agricultural Education, Arts/Humanities Education, Colleges & Universities, Education Reform, Elementary Education (Private), Engineering/Technological Education, Journalism/Media Education, Preschool Education, Public Education (Precollege), Science/Mathematics Education, Secondary Education (Public), Social Sciences Education, Student Aid

Environment: Environment-General

Health: Alzheimer's Disease, Hospitals, Medical Research
International: International Relations
Religion: Churches, Religious Welfare
Science: Science Museums, Scientific Centers & Institutes, Scientific Organizations
Social Services: Child Welfare, Community Service Organizations, Food/Clothing Distribution, Homes, People with Disabilities, Scouts, Shelters/Homelessness, Social Services-General, Substance Abuse, United Funds/United Ways, YMCA/YWCA/YMHA/YWHA, Youth Organizations

Application Procedures

Initial Contact: Send a brief letter of inquiry.
Application Requirements: Include amount requested and purpose of funds sought.
Deadlines: None.

Restrictions

Does not support individuals. Grantmaking is generally restricted to the Lubbock, TX area.

Foundation Officials

James C. Arnold: vice president
Louise Willson Arnold: president, executive secretary, director
Robert Neff Arnold: vice president, secretary, director
Helen DeVitt Jones: director
Marianna Markham: director
L. Edwin Smith: treasurer, director
Randy L. Wright: treasurer

Grants Analysis

Disclosure Period: calendar year ending 2001
Total Grants: $4,324,550*
Number of Grants: 65
Average Grant: $21,364*
Highest Grant: $1,000,000
Lowest Grant: $500
Typical Range: $15,000 to $50,000
***Note:** Giving excludes United Way. Average grant figure excludes three highest grants ($3,000,000).

Recent Grants

Note: Grants derived from 2001 Form 990.
General

1,000,000	Museum of Texas Tech University, Lubbock, TX -- Curator of Art
1,000,000	Texas Tech University College of Education, Lubbock, TX
1,000,000	Texas Tech University, College of Human Sciences, Lubbock, TX
103,000	O.L. Slaton Junior High School, LISD, Lubbock, TX
100,000	San Angelo Museum of Fine Arts, San Angelo, TX
67,000	Ballet Lubbock, Lubbock, TX
62,500	Lubbock Regional Arts Center, Lubbock, TX
61,000	Museum Association of Texas Tech University, Lubbock, TX
57,000	Museum of Texas Tech University, Lubbock, TX
54,000	Lubbock Women's Club, Lubbock, TX

MARY RANKEN JORDAN AND ETTIE A. JORDAN CHARITABLE FOUNDATION

Giving Contact

Fred E. Arnold, Chairman, Advisory Committee
1 US BankPlaza, Suite 3500
St. Louis, MO 63101

Phone: (314)552-6000
Fax: (314)552-7000
E-mail: farnold@thompsoncoburn.com

Description

Founded: 1958
EIN: 436020554
Organization Type: General Purpose Foundation
Giving Locations: MO: emphasis on St. Louis area
Grant Types: Capital, Endowment, General Support.

Donor Information

Founder: Established in 1957 by the late Mary Ranken Jordan and Ettie A. Jordan.

Financial Summary

Total Giving: $1,100,000 (2003 approx); $1,236,120 (2002); $1,300,714 (2001 approx)
Assets: $23,431,233 (2001)
Gifts Received: $10,000 (1996)

Typical Recipients

Arts & Humanities: Arts Associations & Councils, Arts Centers, Arts Funds, Arts Outreach, Dance, Ethnic & Folk Arts, Arts & Humanities-General, Historic Preservation, History & Archaeology, Libraries, Literary Arts, Museums/Galleries, Music, Opera, Performing Arts, Public Broadcasting, Theater
Civic & Public Affairs: Botanical Gardens/Parks, Clubs, Employment/Job Training, Civic & Public Affairs-General, Hispanic Affairs, Inner-City Development, Urban & Community Affairs, Zoos/Aquariums
Education: Arts/Humanities Education, Colleges & Universities, Medical Education, Private Education (Precollege), Science/Mathematics Education, Secondary Education (Private), Secondary Education (Public), Special Education, Vocational & Technical Education
Health: Children's Health/Hospitals, Clinics/Medical Centers, Diabetes, Emergency/Ambulance Services, Hospitals, Mental Health, Respiratory, Single-Disease Health Associations, Speech & Hearing
International: International Relations
Religion: Churches, Jewish Causes, Ministries, Religious Welfare
Science: Scientific Centers & Institutes, Scientific Organizations
Social Services: Animal Protection, At-Risk Youth, Child Abuse, Child Welfare, Community Centers, Community Service Organizations, Day Care, Emergency Relief, Family Services, Food/Clothing Distribution, Homes, People with Disabilities, Scouts, Shelters/Homelessness, United Funds/United Ways, Volunteer Services, YMCA/YWCA/YMHA/YWHA, Youth Organizations

Application Procedures

Initial Contact: The foundation requests that applications be made in writing and that three copies be furnished.
Deadlines: December 31.
Review Process: Grants are made annually in the spring.

Restrictions

Grants are not made to individuals. The foundation makes grants only to charitable organizations.

Additional Information

The foundation lists the Mercantile Trust Co. NA as a corporate trustee.

Foundation Officials

Fred E. Arnold: chairman advisory committee B Mexico 1930. ED Harvard University AB (1960); Harvard University AB (1963). PRIM CORP EMPL partner: Thompson Coburn. NONPR AFFIL member board curators: Ctrl Meth College; member: Missouri Bar Association; member: American College Real Estate Lawyers; member: American Bar Association. CLUB AFFIL Racquet Club; Noonday Club.
W. Stanley Walch: mem adv comm B Sedalia, MO

1934. ED Kenyon College AB (1956); University of Michigan JD (1959). PRIM CORP EMPL partner: Thompson & Mitchell. CORP AFFIL director: Precision Stainless Co.; director: Orion Capital Corp.; director: Central Street Diversified Corp.; director: Morgan-Wrightmann Supply Co. NONPR AFFIL member: Saint Louis Bar Association; member campaign committee: United Way Saint Louis; member: Missouri Bar Association; member: American Law Institute; director: Downtown Saint Louis Inc.; member: American Bar Association; member: Algonquin Chamber of Commerce. CLUB AFFIL Noonday Club.
W. David Wells: mem adv comm

Grants Analysis

Disclosure Period: calendar year ending 2001
Total Grants: $1,300,714
Number of Grants: 79
Average Grant: $16,465
Highest Grant: $100,000
Lowest Grant: $800
Typical Range: $5,000 to $60,000
Note: Grants analysis provided by foundation.

Recent Grants

Note: Grants derived from 2002 Form 990.
General

125,000	St Louis Symphony Orchestra, St. Louis, MO
100,000	Washington University, St. Louis, MO
75,000	Missouri Botanical Garden, St. Louis, MO
75,000	St Louis Art Museum, St. Louis, MO
60,000	Ranken Jordan Home for Convalescent Crippled Children, St. Louis, MO
50,000	Forest Park Forever, St. Louis, MO
50,000	St Louis Zoo Foundation, St. Louis, MO
45,000	Ranken Technical College, St. Louis, MO
35,000	Shakespeare Festival of St Louis, St. Louis, MO
30,000	Center of Contemporary Arts, St. Louis, MO

JOSLIN-NEEDHAM FAMILY FOUNDATION

Giving Contact

Judy Gunnon
PO Box 324
Brush, CO 80723
Phone: (970)842-5101
Fax: (970)842-5105

Description

EIN: 846038670
Organization Type: Private Foundation
Giving Locations: CO: Brush
Grant Types: General Support.

Donor Information

Founder: the late Gladys Joslin

Financial Summary

Total Giving: $272,356 (2001)
Giving Analysis: Giving for 2001 includes: foundation grants to United Way ($2,000).
Assets: $5,240,307 (2001)

Typical Recipients

Arts & Humanities: Libraries
Civic & Public Affairs: Clubs, Civic & Public Affairs-General, Municipalities/Towns, Parades/Festivals, Safety, Urban & Community Affairs
Education: Afterschool/Enrichment Programs, Agricultural Education, Public Education (Precollege), Secondary Education (Public)
Health: Clinics/Medical Centers, Emergency/Ambulance Services, Health Organizations, Hospi-

tals, Long-Term Care
Religion: Churches, Ministries, Religious Organizations, Religious Welfare
Social Services: Camps, Community Service Organizations, Food/Clothing Distribution, Recreation & Athletics, Scouts, United Funds/United Ways, Volunteer Services, Youth Organizations

Application Procedures
Initial Contact: Send a brief letter of inquiry describing need and any pertinent information.
Deadlines: None.

Restrictions
Grantmaking is limited to the Brush, CO area.

Additional Information
Trust(s): Farmers State Bank

Foundation Officials
Robert V. Hansen: director
Robert Petteys: director

Grants Analysis
Disclosure Period: calendar year ending 2001
Total Grants: $270,356*
Number of Grants: 10
Average Grant: $27,036
Highest Grant: $60,000
Lowest Grant: $300
Typical Range: $5,000 to $60,000
*Note: Giving excludes United Way.

Recent Grants
Note: Grants derived from 2001 Form 990.
Library-Related

43,800	East Morgan County Library, Brush, CO

General

60,000	East Morgan County Hospital Foundation, Brush, CO -- for challenge campaign
58,700	City of Brush, Brush, CO -- for recreation
57,046	Eben Ezer Lutheran Care Center, Brush, CO
39,650	East Morgan County Hospital Foundation, Brush, CO -- equipment
5,000	Brush High School, Brush, CO -- grants, summer workshops
3,000	Brush Area Churches, Brush, CO
3,000	Brush Boy Scout Troop 28, Brush, CO
2,260	Northeastern County Transportation Authority, Ft. Morgan, CO -- for van trip
2,000	Morgan County United Way, Ft. Morgan, CO -- 2001 campaign donation
600	Brush Girl Scouts, Brush, CO

JOSTENS INC.

Company Headquarters
Minneapolis, MN
Web: http://www.jostens.com

Company Description
Founded: 1897
Ticker: JOSEA
Exchange: OTC
Revenue: US$756 million (2002)
Employees: 6700 (2003)
SIC(s): 2389 Apparel & Accessories Nec, 2741 Miscellaneous Publishing, 2752 Commercial Printing--Lithographic, 3911 Jewelry & Precious Metal.

Operating Locations
Jostens, Inc. (CA--Porterville, Visalia; IL--Princeton; KS--Topeka; MN--Burnsville, Owatonna, Red Wing; NY--Webster; PA--State College; SC--Laurens; TN--Clarksville, Shelbyville; TX--Denton)

Nonmonetary Support
Value: $40,000 (2001)
Type: Donated Products; In-kind Services
Note: Co. provides nonmonetary support.

The Jostens Foundation Inc.

Giving Contact
Lynda Michielutti, Executive Director
5501 American Boulevard
Minneapolis, MN 55437
Phone: (952)830-3302
Fax: (952)897-4116
Web: http://www.jostens.com

Description
EIN: 411280587
Organization Type: Corporate Foundation
Giving Locations: principally near operating locations and to national organizations.
Grant Types: Emergency, Employee Matching Gifts, General Support, Multiyear/Continuing Support, Project.

Financial Summary
Total Giving: $553,573 (2003); $576,510 (2002); $489,875 (2001). Note: Contributes through corporate direct giving program and foundation.
Giving Analysis: Giving for 2002 includes: foundation (approx $500,000); 2001: foundation (approx $500,000)
Assets: $29,733 (2003); $303,845 (2002); $399,875 (2001)
Gifts Received: $300,000 (2003); $500,000 (2002); $500,000 (2001). Note: Contributions were received from Jostens, Inc.

Typical Recipients
Arts & Humanities: Arts Associations & Councils, Arts Centers, Arts Institutes, Dance, Ethnic & Folk Arts, Arts & Humanities-General, History & Archaeology, Libraries, Museums/Galleries, Music, Opera, Performing Arts, Public Broadcasting, Theater
Civic & Public Affairs: Asian American Affairs, Business/Free Enterprise, Community Foundations, Economic Development, Employment/Job Training, Civic & Public Affairs-General, Housing, Law & Justice, Legal Aid, Nonprofit Management, Philanthropic Organizations, Public Policy, Urban & Community Affairs, Women's Affairs, Zoos/Aquariums
Education: Arts/Humanities Education, Business Education, Colleges & Universities, Economic Education, Education Associations, Education Funds, Education Reform, Engineering/Technological Education, Education-General, Gifted & Talented Programs, International Studies, Leadership Training, Literacy, Medical Education, Minority Education, Private Education (Precollege), Public Education (Precollege), Science/Mathematics Education, Secondary Education (Public), Student Aid, Vocational & Technical Education
Environment: Environment-General
Health: AIDS/HIV, Arthritis, Cancer, Children's Health/Hospitals, Clinics/Medical Centers, Diabetes, Emergency/Ambulance Services, Eyes/Blindness, Health-General, Heart, Hospices, Hospitals, Mental Health, Multiple Sclerosis, Prenatal Health Issues, Public Health, Research/Studies Institutes, Single-Disease Health Associations, Trauma Treatment
International: Foreign Educational Institutions
Religion: Religion-General, Religious Organizations, Religious Welfare
Science: Science Museums
Social Services: Animal Protection, At-Risk Youth, Big Brothers/Big Sisters, Camps, Child Abuse, Child Welfare, Community Centers, Community Service Organizations, Day Care, Family Services, Food/Clothing Distribution, Homes, People with Disabili-

ties, Recreation & Athletics, Scouts, Senior Services, Social Services-General, Special Olympics, Substance Abuse, United Funds/United Ways, YMCA/YWCA/YMHA/YWHA, Youth Organizations

Application Procedures
Initial Contact: Submit a written application.
Application Requirements: Applicants may use the Minnesota Common Grant form or submit an application the includes the following information: Organizational Information, Purpose of Grant, Evaluation, and Financial Information. Organizational Information should include the history, mission and goals of the organization, current programs, activities, service statistics, and accomplishments; the organization's relationship with other organizations that provide similar services; the reason that your organization is appropriate to address the problem; and a list of board members and the number of full- and part-time paid staff and volunteers. The Purpose of Grant section should describe the community need the proposal addresses and how the focus was determined; the specific activities for which funding is sought and who will carry them out; the overall goals and how they will be met; and how the proposed activities will benefit the community, including a long-term plan for sustaining them. Evaluation should state how effectiveness of the activities will be measured and the results that are expected by the end of the funding period. Financial Information must include financial statements from the most recently completed fiscal year, organizational and/or project budget, and proof of tax-exempt status.
Deadlines: In 2004, March 22, June 21, September 20, and December 13 for Jostens Community Grants; May 1 for the Renaissance Program.
Review Process: The board of directors meets quarterly to review applications.
Evaluative Criteria: The foundation gives preference to organizations that provide services in communities where Jostens facilities and employees are located, and to nonprofit organizations that involve Jostens employees.

Restrictions
The foundation does not provide grants to schools or school districts; organizations involved in highly political or controversial issues; churches, religious groups, or programs primarily sponsored by religious organizations; individuals or groups for personal needs or travel expenses; political or lobbying groups; benefit fundraisers or tickets to fundraisers; recognition or testimonial events; fundraising campaigns to eliminate or control specific diseases; fraternal, veterans or professional associations; athletic scholarships or activities; advertising sponsorships; or endowments.
Foundation gives grants only to 501(c)(3) organizations.

Additional Information
Jostens Community Grants program offers funding to organizations that "enhance the lives of youth and promote educational opportunities that positively impact children from birth through college". Community Grants typically range from $500 to $10,000. Grants for this program should be sent directly to the Jostens Foundation.
Program grants generally made during the current year and not in installments for future years.
In 1987, Jostens organized GIVE employee contributions committees in several operating locations across the country. These committees make charitable grants for special community president within employees' local communities from dollars allocated by the foundation.
Publications: Annual Report; Application Form; Guidelines

Corporate Officials
Robert C. Buhrmaster: president, chief executive officer, chairman B Schenectady, NY 1947. ED Rens-

selaer Polytechnic Institute BS (1969); Dartmouth College MBA (1974). PRIM CORP EMPL president, chief executive officer, chairman: Jostens, Inc. ADD CORP EMPL president: American Yearbook Co.; president, director: Jostens Photography Inc. CORP AFFIL director: Toro Co.

Foundation Officials

M. J. Bauer: director
Mark Cassutt: director
Kent Gilmore: president
Julie Goetz: director
Paula Johnson: director
Mary Klimek: director
Claire Kraus: director
Tim Larson: director
Charley Nelson: director
Lance Novak: director
Al Nuness: director
Bonnie Severson: director
William Sheahan: secretary
Ron Somerville: treasurer
Kris Thompson: director
Tim Wolfe: director

Grants Analysis

Disclosure Period: calendar year ending 2003
Total Grants: $364,235*
Number of Grants: 97
Average Grant: $3,755
Highest Grant: $25,000
Lowest Grant: $100
Typical Range: $1,000 to $5,000
***Note:** Giving excludes matching gifts, scholarship, and United Way.

Recent Grants

Note: Grants derived from 2003 Form 990.
General

50,000	Search Institute, Minneapolis, MN
45,000	United Way, St. Paul, MN
25,000	Twin Cities Public Television, St. Paul, MN
25,000	Twin Cities Public Television, St. Paul, MN
20,000	Abington Foundation, Cleveland, OH
20,000	Ohio County Together We Care, Hartford, KY
20,000	United Way of Northwest Michigan, Traverse City, MI
5,000	Casselton Youth Task Force, Casselton, ND
5,000	Council on Crime and Justice, Minneapolis, MN
5,000	Jeremiah Program, Minneapolis, MN

JOURNAL-GAZETTE CO.

Company Headquarters

701 S. Clinton St., Ste. 104
Fort Wayne, IN 46802

Company Description

Employees: 600
SIC(s): 2711 Newspapers.

Journal-Gazette Foundation, Inc.

Giving Contact

Jerry D. Fox, Secretary & Treasurer
701 South Clinton Street, Suite 104
Ft. Wayne, IN 46802-1806
Phone: (260)424-5257
Fax: (219)426-0949

Description

Founded: 1985
EIN: 311134237
Organization Type: Corporate Foundation
Giving Locations: IN: Northeast Indiana; OH: Northwest Ohio
Grant Types: Capital, General Support, Operating Expenses.

Donor Information

Founder: Journal-Gazette Co., Richard G. Inskeep

Financial Summary

Total Giving: $553,174 (2003); $632,191 (2002); $545,782 (2001). Note: Contributes through foundation only.
Giving Analysis: Giving for 2002 includes: foundation grants to United Way ($155,000)
Assets: $12,700,468 (2003); $7,095,127 (2002); $8,620,941 (2001)
Gifts Received: $648,504 (2003); $54,994 (2002); $103,281 (2001). Note: In 2003, contributions were received from Richard G. Inskeep ($26,368), Harriett J. Inskeep ($76,363), and Julie Inskeep Simpson ($21,956). In 2002, contributions were received from Richard G. Inskeep ($41,040), Harriett J. Inskeep ($41,040), and Julie Inskeep Simpson ($18,961). In 2001, contributions were received from Richard G. Inskeep ($14,439), Harriett J. Inskeep ($5,164), and Journal Gazette Company ($83,678). In 2000, contributions were received from Journal-Gazette Co. ($122,049); Richard G. and Harriett J. Inskeep ($49,204); and Stephen S. Inskeep ($3,081).In 1998 and 1997, contributions were received from Richard G. Inskeep and Harriett J. Inskeep.

Typical Recipients

Arts & Humanities: Arts Appreciation, Arts Associations & Councils, Arts Centers, Arts Funds, Arts Outreach, Historic Preservation, History & Archaeology, Libraries, Museums/Galleries, Music, Performing Arts, Public Broadcasting, Theater
Civic & Public Affairs: African American Affairs, Botanical Gardens/Parks, Business/Free Enterprise, Chambers of Commerce, Clubs, Community Foundations, Employment/Job Training, Civic & Public Affairs-General, Hispanic Affairs, Municipalities/Towns, Parades/Festivals, Professional & Trade Associations, Public Policy, Rural Affairs, Urban & Community Affairs, Women's Affairs, Zoos/Aquariums
Education: Afterschool/Enrichment Programs, Agricultural Education, Business Education, Colleges & Universities, Continuing Education, Economic Education, Education Associations, Education Funds, Elementary Education (Private), Engineering/Technological Education, Education-General, Journalism/Media Education, Literacy, Medical Education, Private Education (Precollege), Public Education (Precollege), Secondary Education (Private), Secondary Education (Public), Special Education, Student Aid, Vocational & Technical Education
Environment: Air/Water Quality, Environment-General, Resource Conservation, Watershed
Health: AIDS/HIV, Cancer, Children's Health/Hospitals, Clinics/Medical Centers, Emergency/Ambulance Services, Health-General, Geriatric Health, Health Organizations, Hospices, Hospitals, Kidney, Mental Health, Research/Studies Institutes, Single-Disease Health Associations
Religion: Churches, Jewish Causes, Ministries, Religious Organizations, Religious Welfare
Science: Science Museums, Scientific Centers & Institutes
Social Services: Animal Protection, At-Risk Youth, Big Brothers/Big Sisters, Camps, Child Abuse, Child Welfare, Community Service Organizations, Counseling, Crime Prevention, Day Care, Family Planning, Family Services, Food/Clothing Distribution, People with Disabilities, Recreation & Athletics, Scouts, Senior Services, Shelters/Homelessness, Social Services-General, Substance Abuse, United Funds/

United Ways, Volunteer Services, YMCA/YWCA/YMHA/YWHA, Youth Organizations

Application Procedures

Initial Contact: Send a brief letter.
Application Requirements: Include the need for financial assistance, timeframe and proof of tax-exempt status.
Deadlines: None.
Decision Notification: Committee meets quarterly.

Restrictions

Recipient organization must be in the general geographic area of northeast Indiana or northwest Ohio and qualify under the IRS code as a 501(c)(3) organization.

Corporate Officials

Richard G. Inskeep: owner, president, public B 1925. PRIM CORP EMPL owner: Journal-Gazette Co.
Craig Klugman: editor B Fargo, ND 1945. PRIM CORP EMPL editor: Journal-Gazette Co. NONPR AFFIL member: American Newspaper Editors.

Foundation Officials

Jerry D. Fox: secretary, treasurer, director B 1952. PRIM CORP EMPL secretary, treasurer, director: Journal-Gazette Co.
Harriet J. Inskeep: director
Richard G. Inskeep: president, director (see above)
Thomas R. Inskeep: director
Julie Inskeep Simpson: director PRIM CORP EMPL vice president, director: Journal-Gazette Co.

Grants Analysis

Disclosure Period: calendar year ending 2003
Total Grants: $553,174*
Typical Range: $1,000 to $5,000
***Note:** Incomplete grants list for 2003.

Recent Grants

Note: Grants derived from 2003 Form 990.
Library-Related

5,000	Ligonier Public Library, Ligonier, IN

General

112,000	United Way of Allen County, Ft. Wayne, IN
25,000	Embassy Centre, Ft. Wayne, IN
20,000	Arts Plaza Project, Ft. Wayne, IN
18,000	Big Brothers Big Sisters of Northeast Indiana, Ft. Wayne, IN
16,000	Fort Wayne Zoological Society, Ft. Wayne, IN
15,200	Arts United of Greater Fort Wayne, Ft. Wayne, IN
15,000	431 Foundation Inc.
15,000	Fort Wayne Urban League, Ft. Wayne, IN
15,000	Vera Bradley Foundation, Ft. Wayne, IN
11,200	Indiana University Foundation, Indianapolis, IN

JOY FAMILY FOUNDATION

Giving Contact

Marsha J. Sullivan, Exec. Dir.
5436 Main St.
Williamsville, NY 14221
Phone: (716)633-6600
E-mail: info@joyfamilyfoundation.org
Web: http://www.joyfamilyfoundation.org

Description

Founded: 1990
EIN: 166335211
Organization Type: Private Foundation
Giving Locations: NY: Erie County, Niagra County

Grant Types: Capital, Department, General Support, Matching.

Donor Information

Founder: Established in 1990 by Paul W. Joy.

Financial Summary

Total Giving: $452,685 (2002)

Giving Analysis: Giving for 2002 includes: foundation grants to United Way ($12,000); 2001: foundation grants to United Way ($10,000)

Gifts Received: $29,904 (2002); $43,201 (2000); $115,552 (1998). Note: In 1998, 2000, and 2002 contributions were received from Paul Joy. In 1993, contributions were received from Paul W. Joy ($177,205) and miscellaneous ($4,670).

Typical Recipients

Arts & Humanities: Arts Associations & Councils, Arts Centers, Historic Preservation, Libraries, Music, Public Broadcasting

Civic & Public Affairs: Civic & Public Affairs-General, Housing, Law & Justice, Municipalities/Towns, Urban & Community Affairs, Women's Affairs, Zoos/Aquariums

Education: Afterschool/Enrichment Programs, Arts/Humanities Education, Business Education, Colleges & Universities, Community & Junior Colleges, Faculty Development, Education-General, Leadership Training, Literacy, Private Education (Precollege), Science/Mathematics Education, Secondary Education (Private), Secondary Education (Public), Special Education, Student Aid

Health: Alzheimer's Disease, Cancer, Children's Health/Hospitals, Eyes/Blindness, Geriatric Health, Hospices, Hospitals, Medical Research, Nursing Services, Speech & Hearing

Religion: Churches, Religious Organizations, Religious Welfare, Seminaries

Social Services: Animal Protection, At-Risk Youth, Camps, Child Welfare, Community Centers, Community Service Organizations, Counseling, Day Care, Family Services, Food/Clothing Distribution, People with Disabilities, Recreation & Athletics, Scouts, Substance Abuse, United Funds/United Ways, YMCA/YWCA/YMHA/YWHA, Youth Organizations

Application Procedures

Initial Contact: Request application form.

Deadlines: None.

Additional Information

Publications: Application Form

Foundation Officials

Joan H. Joy: trustee
Paul W. Joy: don, trustee
Stephen T. Joy: trustee
Paula Joy Reinhold: trustee
Marsha Joy Sullivan: trustee

Grants Analysis

Disclosure Period: calendar year ending 2002
Total Grants: $440,685*
Number of Grants: 98
Average Grant: $4,732
Highest Grant: $25,000
Typical Range: $1,000 to $10,000
*Note: Giving excludes United Way.

Recent Grants

Note: Grants derived from 2002 Form 990.

General

25,000	Bison Fund, Buffalo, NY -- children's scholarship fund
25,000	Burchfield-Penney Art Center, Buffalo, NY -- building campaign
25,000	Catholic Charities of Buffalo New York, Buffalo, NY
25,000	Catholic Charities of Buffalo New York, Buffalo, NY
20,000	Alcohol and Drug Dependency Services Foundation, West Seneca, NY -- addition of two buildings
20,000	Center for Joy, Niagara Falls, MI -- annual support
17,000	Nardin Academy High School, Buffalo, NY -- scholarship
16,000	Foundation of the RC Diocese of Buffalo, Buffalo, NY -- construct a new catholic middle school
15,000	Buffalo Philharmonic Orchestra Society, Buffalo, NY
15,000	Heart and Soul, Inc., Niagara Falls, NY -- building fund

JOY GLOBAL INC.

Company Headquarters

100 E. Wisconsin Avenue, Suite 2780
Milwaukee, WI 53201-0554
Web: http://www.harnischfeger.com

Company Description

Founded: 1884
Ticker: JOYG
Exchange: NASDAQ
Revenue: US$1.15 billion (2002)
Employees: 7200 (2003)
SIC(s): 3532 Mining Machinery, 3536 Hoists, Cranes & Monorails, 3554 Paper Industries Machinery, 3599 Industrial Machinery Nec.

Operating Locations

Harnischfeger Industries (WI--Milwaukee)

Joy Global Foundation, Inc.

Giving Contact

Sandy McKenzie, Executive Assistant
PO Box 554
Milwaukee, WI 53201-0554
Phone: (414)671-7430
Fax: (414)319-8520

Description

Founded: 1989
EIN: 391659070
Organization Type: Corporate Foundation
Giving Locations: AZ; DC; IL; MD; MI; MN; NY; PA; TX; VA; WI
Grant Types: Employee Matching Gifts, General Support, Operating Expenses, Project.

Donor Information

Founder: Established in 1989 by Harnishfeger Industries.

Financial Summary

Total Giving: $807,322 (fiscal year ending October 31, 2004); $790,732 (fiscal 2003); $473,568 (fiscal 2002)

Giving Analysis: Giving for fiscal 2003 includes: foundation grants to United Way ($85,000); foundation ($705,732); fiscal 2002: foundation (approx $750,000); fiscal 2001: foundation ($644,135)

Assets: $10,617,509 (fiscal 2004); $10,473,718 (fiscal 2003); $10,475,500 (fiscal 2002)

Gifts Received: $20,000 (fiscal 2004); $2,256,024 (fiscal 1992). Note: In fiscal 2004, contributions were received from Joy Technologies Inc. ($10,000) and Harnischfeger Corp. ($10,000). In fiscal 1992, major contributions were received from Harnischfeger Foundation.

Typical Recipients

Arts & Humanities: Arts Associations & Councils, Libraries, Museums/Galleries, Music, Opera, Performing Arts

Civic & Public Affairs: Botanical Gardens/Parks, Chambers of Commerce, Clubs, Community Foundations, Economic Development, Ethnic Organizations, Civic & Public Affairs-General, Hispanic Affairs, Housing, Municipalities/Towns, Nonprofit Management, Parades/Festivals, Philanthropic Organizations, Professional & Trade Associations, Public Policy, Urban & Community Affairs, Women's Affairs, Zoos/Aquariums

Education: Afterschool/Enrichment Programs, Arts/Humanities Education, Business Education, Colleges & Universities, Education Funds, Education Reform, Engineering/Technological Education, Environmental Education, Education-General, Leadership Training, Literacy, Medical Education, Minority Education, Private Education (Precollege), Public Education (Precollege), Science/Mathematics Education, Secondary Education (Private)

Environment: Air/Water Quality, Energy, Environment-General, Protection, Resource Conservation, Wildlife Protection

Health: AIDS/HIV, Cancer, Children's Health/Hospitals, Clinics/Medical Centers, Diabetes, Emergency/Ambulance Services, Eyes/Blindness, Health Funds, Health Organizations, Heart, Long-Term Care, Medical Research, Mental Health, Prenatal Health Issues, Preventive Medicine/Wellness Organizations, Single-Disease Health Associations

Religion: Dioceses, Religious Organizations, Religious Welfare

Science: Science Museums, Scientific Centers & Institutes

Social Services: At-Risk Youth, Big Brothers/Big Sisters, Camps, Child Welfare, Community Centers, Community Service Organizations, Counseling, Crime Prevention, Domestic Violence, Emergency Relief, Family Services, Food/Clothing Distribution, People with Disabilities, Recreation & Athletics, Scouts, Social Services-General, United Funds/United Ways, Veterans, Volunteer Services, YMCA/YWCA/YMHA/YWHA, Youth Organizations

Application Procedures

Initial Contact: Apply in writing, with proof of tax-exempt status attached.

Application Requirements: Requests for $1,000 or more should include a description of the organization's structure, purpose, history and programs; a list of current officers and directors and their affiliations; current income and expense budget; recently audited financial statement; summary of the proposed program(s) for which support is requested, including the specific objectives to be achieved, total amount to be raised, amount requested, and other anticipated sources of funding; population and geographic location to be served; and evidence of need for the programs to be funded.

Decision Notification: The foundation will communicate its funding decision in writing within 90 days of application receipt.

Notes: Do not submit videotapes unless requested to do so by the foundation. Phone calls and personal visits to the foundation are discouraged.

Restrictions

The foundation does not contribute to religious organizations or institutions primarily supported by taxes or public funds. Contributions are limited to 501(c)(3) organizations in communities where Joy Global Inc. has a significant employee presence. Contributions will not be made for use in foreign countries.

Additional Information

Publications: Guidelines; Grant Request Form

Corporate Officials

John Nils Hanson: chairman, president, chief executive officer treasurer ED Carnegie Mellon University PhD; Massachusetts Institute of Technology BS; Massachusetts Institute of Technology MS. PRIM CORP EMPL chairman, president, chief executive officer: Joy Global Inc. CORP AFFIL board member: Arrow Electronics Inc.

Donald C. Roof: executive vice president, chief financial officer, treasurer ED Eastern Michigan University BS. PRIM CORP EMPL executive vice president, chief financial officer, treasurer: Joy Global Inc.

Foundation Officials

James A. Chokey: vice president
Eric B. Fonstad: secretary
John Nils Hanson: president (see above)
Donald C. Roof: vice president (see above)
Kenneth J. Stark: treasurer
Dennis R. Winkleman: vice president

Grants Analysis

Disclosure Period: fiscal year ending October 31, 2004
Total Grants: $744,822*
Number of Grants: 100
Average Grant: $6,463*
Highest Grant: $105,000
Lowest Grant: $200
Typical Range: $1,000 to $10,000
*Note: Giving excludes United Way. Average grant figure excludes highest grant.

Recent Grants

Note: Grants derived from 2003 Form 990.
General

100,000	United Performing Arts Fund, Milwaukee, WI
85,000	United Way of Greater Milwaukee Incorporated, Milwaukee, WI
60,000	Milwaukee Women's Center, Milwaukee, WI
42,500	Boys and Girls Clubs of Greater Milwaukee, Milwaukee, WI
32,350	Milwaukee Symphony Orchestra, Milwaukee, WI
30,000	American Cancer Society, Pewaukee, WI
25,000	Habitat for Hunanity, Milwaukee, WI
25,000	Milwaukee School of Engineering, Milwaukee, WI
20,000	Milwaukee Immediate Care Center, Milwaukee, WI
15,000	Milwaukee Public Museum, Milwaukee, WI

JOYCE FAMILY FOUNDATION

Giving Contact

Kim Williams, Trust Officer
Joyce Family Foundation
Care of SunTrust Bank Nashville NA
PO Box 305110
Nashville, TN 37230-5110
Phone: (615)748-5813

Description

Founded: 1991
EIN: 626225946
Organization Type: Private Foundation
Grant Types: General Support.

Financial Summary

Total Giving: $244,985 (2001)
Assets: $2,460,509 (2001)
Gifts Received: $344,982 (2001); $334,565 (1999);

$312,925 (1998). Note: In 1998 and 1996, contributions were received from Margaret Henry Wood.

Typical Recipients

Arts & Humanities: Arts Centers, Historic Preservation, Libraries, Opera
Civic & Public Affairs: Botanical Gardens/Parks, Civic & Public Affairs-General, Public Policy, Safety, Zoos/Aquariums
Education: Colleges & Universities, Education-General, Private Education (Precollege)
Environment: Resource Conservation
Health: Cancer, Children's Health/Hospitals, Multiple Sclerosis, Speech & Hearing
Religion: Churches, Religion-General, Religious Organizations, Religious Welfare
Social Services: Community Service Organizations, Food/Clothing Distribution, Sexual Abuse, Social Services-General

Application Procedures

Initial Contact: Send a brief letter of inquiry.
Deadlines: None.

Additional Information

Trust(s): SunTrust Bank Nashville NA

Foundation Officials

Dr. Benjamin F. Byrd, Jr.: director
Douglas Henry: director
Margaret Henry Wood: chairperson
Richard D. Holton, Esq.: director
Alexis Jones Joyce: director

Grants Analysis

Disclosure Period: calendar year ending 2001
Total Grants: $244,985
Number of Grants: 18
Average Grant: $8,529*
Highest Grant: $100,000
Lowest Grant: $100
Typical Range: $1,000 to $15,000
*Note: Average grant figure excludes highest grant.

Recent Grants

Note: Grants derived from 2001 Form 990.
Library-Related

50,000	Metropolitan Nashville Library, Nashville, TN

General

100,000	Vanderbilt Cancer Center, Nashville, TN
50,000	Second Harvest Food Bank, Allentown, PA
15,000	Wofford College, Spartanburg, SC
8,800	Woodberry Forest School, Woodberry Forest, VA
6,000	TJ Martell Foundation for Cancer, New York, NY
5,000	Bill Wilkerson Center, Nashville, TN
2,000	Percy Priest School
1,210	Cheekwood, Nashville, TN
1,000	All Saints Episcopal Church
1,000	Bethlehem House, El Dorado, KS

JSJ CORP.

Company Headquarters

700 Robbins Rd.
Grand Haven, MI 49417
Web: http://www.jsjcorp.com

Company Description

Employees: 15 (2003)
SIC(s): 2522 Office Furniture Except Wood, 3089 Plastics Products Nec, 3364 Nonferrous Die-Castings Except Aluminum, 3469 Metal Stampings Nec.

Operating Locations

JSJ Corp. (MI--Grand Rapids; WI--La Crosse)

Nonmonetary Support

Value: $21,100 (2000)
Type: Donated Equipment; Workplace Solicitation
Note: NOT NOT Workplace solicitation is for United Way only.

JSJ Foundation

Giving Contact

Lynne Sherwood, Secretary & Trustee
700 Robbins Road
Grand Haven, MI 49417-2603
Phone: (616)842-6350
Fax: (616)847-3112
E-mail: sherwoodl@jsjcorp.com

Description

EIN: 382421508
Organization Type: Corporate Foundation
Giving Locations: FL; MI; TX; WI
Grant Types: Capital, Endowment, General Support, Multiyear/Continuing Support, Operating Expenses, Scholarship.

Financial Summary

Total Giving: $249,776 (2003); $303,334 (2002); $357,900 (2001)
Assets: $210,271 (2003); $441,185 (2002); $698,108 (2001)
Gifts Received: $300,000 (2001); $275,000 (2000); $275,000 (1999). Note: Contributions were received from JSJ Corp.

Typical Recipients

Arts & Humanities: Arts Associations & Councils, Arts Centers, Arts Festivals, Arts Funds, Arts Institutes, Community Arts, Arts & Humanities-General, Libraries, Museums/Galleries, Music, Opera, Performing Arts, Public Broadcasting, Theater
Civic & Public Affairs: Community Foundations, Economic Policy, Ethnic Organizations, Civic & Public Affairs-General, Housing, Municipalities/Towns, Parades/Festivals, Philanthropic Organizations, Public Policy, Urban & Community Affairs, Women's Affairs, Zoos/Aquariums
Education: Afterschool/Enrichment Programs, Arts/Humanities Education, Business Education, Colleges & Universities, Community & Junior Colleges, Continuing Education, Economic Education, Education Associations, Education Funds, Elementary Education (Public), Engineering/Technological Education, Education-General, Minority Education, Private Education (Precollege), Student Aid
Health: Cancer, Health Policy/Cost Containment, Health Organizations, Hospices, Transplant Networks/Donor Banks
International: Foreign Arts Organizations
Religion: Churches, Ministries, Religious Organizations, Religious Welfare
Social Services: Animal Protection, Child Welfare, Community Centers, Community Service Organizations, Counseling, Day Care, Domestic Violence, Family Services, Homes, People with Disabilities, Recreation & Athletics, Scouts, Shelters/Homelessness, Social Services-General, Substance Abuse, United Funds/United Ways, Volunteer Services, YMCA/YWCA/YMHA/YWHA, Youth Organizations

Application Procedures

Initial Contact: No specific format required.
Deadlines: None.
Decision Notification: Applicants are notified within 60 days.

Restrictions

Limited to the geographic areas where JSJ Corp. has facilities.

Corporate Officials

F. Martin Johnson: chairman, director PRIM CORP EMPL chairman, chief executive officer, director: JSJ Corp.

Michael D. Metzger: vice president, chief financial officer B Buchanan, MI 1947. ED Western Michigan University (1969); Seidman Graduate School MBA (1977). PRIM CORP EMPL vice president, chief financial officer: JSJ Corp. NONPR AFFIL member: Financial Executives Institute.

Edward L. Ozark: vice president administration, assistant secretary B Buffalo, NY 1944. ED Canisius College (1967); Aquinas College (1994). PRIM CORP EMPL vice president, treasurer, assistant secretary: JSJ Corp. NONPR AFFIL director: Priority Health; member: Risk & Insurance Management Society.

Lynne Sherwood: corporate secretary PRIM CORP EMPL secretary: JSJ Corp.

Philip E. Taylor: president, chief executive officer ED Ball State University BS (1968); University of Wisconsin MBA (1980). PRIM CORP EMPL president: JSJ Corp.

Foundation Officials

Nelson C. Jacobson: trustee
Donald A. Johnson: chairman, trustee
F. Martin Johnson: trustee (see above)
John P. Richardson, Jr.: trustee CORP AFFIL director: JSJ Corp.
Lynne Sherwood: secretary, treasurer, trustee (see above)

Grants Analysis

Disclosure Period: calendar year ending 2003
Total Grants: $218,359*
Number of Grants: 33
Average Grant: $6,617
Highest Grant: $25,000
Lowest Grant: $360
Typical Range: $1,000 to $10,000
*Note: Giving excludes scholarship; United Way.

Recent Grants

Note: Grants derived from 2003 Form 990.

Library-Related

25,000	Spring Lake District Library, Spring Lake, MI

General

28,578	Greater Ottawa County United Way, Holland, MI
25,000	Tri-Cities Family YMCA, Grand Haven, MI
20,000	Grand Valley University Foundation, Grand Rapids, MI -- toward Grand Rapids campus
15,000	Center for Women in Transition, Holland, MI
15,000	Michigan Colleges Foundation, Southfield, MI -- funding for scholarships
10,000	Citizens Research Council of Michigan, Livonia, MI
10,000	Grand Rapids Symphony, Grand Rapids, MI
9,500	Alma College, Alma, MI
8,000	Alliance for Health, Grand Rapids, MI
8,000	Tri-Cities Family YMCA, Grand Haven, MI

ALFRED JURZYKOWSKI FOUNDATION

Giving Contact

Bluma D. Cohen, Executive Director & Vice President
15 East 65th Street
New York, NY 10021
Phone: (212)535-8930

Description

Founded: 1960
EIN: 136192256
Organization Type: Family Foundation
Giving Locations: NY: New York metropolitan area; Brazil; Poland
Grant Types: General Support, Operating Expenses, Project.

Donor Information

Founder: Incorporated in 1960 by the late Alfred Jurzykowski.

Financial Summary

Total Giving: $1,376,100 (2003); $2,102,050 (2002); $2,650,243 (2001)
Giving Analysis: Giving for 2003 includes: foundation fellowships ($217,278); 2002: foundation fellowships ($349,688)
Assets: $35,332,213 (2003); $32,004,159 (2002); $39,202,860 (2001)

Typical Recipients

Arts & Humanities: Arts Associations & Councils, Arts Centers, Arts Outreach, Ethnic & Folk Arts, Arts & Humanities-General, History & Archaeology, Libraries, Museums/Galleries, Music, Performing Arts, Public Broadcasting, Theater, Visual Arts
Civic & Public Affairs: Botanical Gardens/Parks, Business/Free Enterprise, Community Foundations, Employment/Job Training, Ethnic Organizations, Civic & Public Affairs-General, Nonprofit Management, Philanthropic Organizations, Public Policy, Women's Affairs, Zoos/Aquariums
Education: Afterschool/Enrichment Programs, Arts/Humanities Education, Colleges & Universities, Education Funds, Environmental Education, Faculty Development, Education-General, International Exchange, International Studies, Journalism/Media Education, Literacy, Medical Education, Minority Education, Private Education (Precollege), Science/Mathematics Education, Secondary Education (Public), Student Aid
Environment: Environment-General, Research, Resource Conservation
Health: AIDS/HIV, Cancer, Children's Health/Hospitals, Clinics/Medical Centers, Health Organizations, Home-Care Services, Hospices, Hospitals
International: Foreign Arts Organizations, Foreign Educational Institutions, Health Care/Hospitals, Human Rights, International Affairs, International Development, International Environmental Issues, International Organizations, International Relations, International Relief Efforts, Missionary/Religious Activities
Religion: Religion-General, Jewish Causes, Religious Organizations, Religious Welfare, Social/Policy Issues, Synagogues/Temples
Science: Science Museums, Scientific Centers & Institutes
Social Services: Big Brothers/Big Sisters, Child Welfare, Community Centers, Community Service Organizations, Delinquency & Criminal Rehabilitation, Family Planning, Family Services, Food/Clothing Distribution, People with Disabilities, Shelters/Homelessness, United Funds/United Ways, Youth Organizations

Application Procedures

Initial Contact: The foundation requests applications be made in writing.
Application Requirements: Applications must include a statement of the purposes and objectives of the organization, an explanation of the current financial needs of the organization and any special projects requiring aid, a project budget and any other sources of support, a copy of the most recent audited financial statement, and a formal statement from the IRS as to the organization's tax-exempt status and that it is not a private foundation. Applicants are encouraged to include any other information that might be helpful in processing the application.
Deadlines: None.

Restrictions

The foundation does not make grants for endowment funds or loans.

Additional Information

The foundation's awards program has been discontinued.
Publications: Application Guidelines

Foundation Officials

Bluma D. Cohen: vice president, executive director, foundation manager, trustee
Karin Falencki: trustee
M. Christine Jurzykowski: secretary, treasurer, trustee B New York, NY 1952. ED Boston University BA (1968). PRIM NONPR EMPL president: Fossil Rim Wildlife Center. NONPR AFFIL president: Conservation Connection.
Yolande L. Jurzykowski: executive vice president, trustee

Grants Analysis

Disclosure Period: calendar year ending 2003
Total Grants: $1,158,822*
Number of Grants: 21
Average Grant: $40,269*
Highest Grant: $353,451
Lowest Grant: $1,000
Typical Range: $20,000 to $50,000
*Note: Giving excludes fellowships. Average grant figure excludes highest grants.

Recent Grants

Note: Grants derived from 2003 Form 990.

Library-Related

10,000	New York Public Library, New York, NY -- support research libraries

General

353,451	Ashoka, Arlington, VA -- support public entrepreneurship program in Brazil
217,278	Kosciusko Foundation, New York, NY -- polish exchange grant and fellowship program
196,704	Ashoka, Arlington, VA -- support public entrepreneurship program in Poland
194,700	Ashoka, Arlington, VA -- support for public entrepreneurship program in United States
99,167	Cornell University, Ithaca, NY -- support international agricultural program
90,000	Kosciusko Foundation, New York, NY -- establishment of environmental science department in University at Poland
40,000	Peacemaker Community, Montague, MA -- to support of their affiliate Peacemaker Polaska
20,000	Kosciusko Foundation, New York, NY -- maintenance of office in Warsaw Poland
20,000	Tides Center, Washington, DC -- support building circles of change a project of spirit in action
20,000	World Learning, Brattleboro, VT -- new ecological preservation engaging cross cultural educational challenge

EDITH C. JUSTUS TRUST

Giving Contact
Stephen P. Kosak
PO Box 374
Oil City, PA 16301
Phone: (814)677-5085

Description
Founded: 1931
EIN: 256031057
Organization Type: Private Foundation
Giving Locations: PA: Oil City Venango County
Grant Types: General Support.

Donor Information
Founder: the late Edith C. Justus

Financial Summary
Total Giving: $249,944 (2004)
Giving Analysis: Giving for 2004 includes: foundation grants to United Way ($10,500)
Assets: $5,863,751 (2004)

Typical Recipients
Arts & Humanities: Arts Appreciation, Arts Associations & Councils, Arts Centers, Film & Video, Historic Preservation, History & Archaeology, Libraries, Museums/Galleries, Music, Opera, Theater
Civic & Public Affairs: Botanical Gardens/Parks, Community Foundations, Economic Development, Employment/Job Training, Civic & Public Affairs-General, Housing, Municipalities/Towns, Safety, Urban & Community Affairs
Education: Agricultural Education, Arts/Humanities Education, Colleges & Universities, Education-General, Literacy, Private Education (Precollege), Public Education (Precollege), Vocational & Technical Education
Environment: Environment-General
Health: Clinics/Medical Centers, Health-General, Health Organizations, Mental Health, Nursing Services
Religion: Churches, Religious Organizations, Religious Welfare
Science: Science Museums
Social Services: Child Welfare, Community Service Organizations, Day Care, Family Services, Food/Clothing Distribution, People with Disabilities, Recreation & Athletics, Senior Services, Shelters/Homelessness, United Funds/United Ways, Volunteer Services, YMCA/YWCA/YMHA/YWHA, Youth Organizations

Application Procedures
Initial Contact: Send a brief letter of inquiry.
Application Requirements: Include purpose of funds sought and proof of tax-exempt status.
Deadlines: None.

Additional Information
Trust(s): National City Bank of PA

Grants Analysis
Disclosure Period: calendar year ending 2004
Total Grants: $239,444*
Number of Grants: 23
Average Grant: $9,066*
Highest Grant: $40,000
Lowest Grant: $25
Typical Range: $1,000 to $20,000
*Note: Giving excludes United Way. Average grant figure excludes highest grant.

Recent Grants
Note: Grants derived from 2001 Form 990.
Library-Related
20,000   Oil City Library, Oil City, PA
General
38,750   Oil City YMCA, Oil City, PA

32,500	Family Service and Children's Aid Society, Oil City, PA
27,250	Community Services of Venango County, Oil City, PA
22,000	Salvation Army, Oil City, PA
17,490	Oil City Civic Center, Inc., Oil City, PA
16,667	City of Oil City, Oil City, PA
15,845	Youth Alternatives, Oil City, PA
15,000	Venango Museum of Art Science, Oil City, PA
13,000	Oil Valley Center for the Arts, Oil City, PA
11,000	Venango Center for Creative Development, Franklin, PA

KAHN, LUCAS-LANCASTER INCORPORATED CHILDREN'S WEAR

Company Headquarters
100 W. 33rd St., Ste. 921
New York, NY 10001

Company Description
Employees: 940
SIC(s): 2300 Apparel & Other Textile Products.

Operating Locations
Kahn-Lucas-Lancaster (NY--New York; PA--Columbia)

Kahn Foundation

Giving Contact
Andrew Kahn, Director
100 West 33rd Street, Suite 921
New York, NY 10001
Phone: (717)684-6911

Description
Founded: 1987
EIN: 236343794
Organization Type: Corporate Foundation
Grant Types: General Support.

Financial Summary
Gifts Received: $44,153 (2000); $12,000 (1997); $5,000 (1996). Note: In 2000, contributions were received from Andrew Kahn. In 1997, contributions were received from Kahn-Lucas-Lancaster.

Typical Recipients
Arts & Humanities: Community Arts, Libraries
Civic & Public Affairs: Civic & Public Affairs-General, Urban & Community Affairs
Education: Business Education, Colleges & Universities, Continuing Education, Engineering/Technological Education, Literacy, Private Education (Precollege), Public Education (Precollege), Science/Mathematics Education, Secondary Education (Public)
Environment: Environment-General
Health: AIDS/HIV, Cancer, Children's Health/Hospitals, Diabetes, Emergency/Ambulance Services, Geriatric Health, Health Organizations, Heart, Hospices, Hospitals (University Affiliated), Prenatal Health Issues, Single-Disease Health Associations
Religion: Churches, Jewish Causes, Religious Organizations
Social Services: Child Welfare, Crime Prevention, Food/Clothing Distribution, People with Disabilities, Recreation & Athletics, United Funds/United Ways

Application Procedures
Initial Contact: The foundation requests applications be made in writing.
Deadlines: None.

Corporate Officials
Andrew Kahn: chief executive officer PRIM CORP EMPL chief executive officer: Kahn-Lucas-Lancaster.
Donald E. McKonly: chief financial officer PRIM CORP EMPL chief financial officer: Kahn-Lucas-Lancaster.
Stanley Silver: president PRIM CORP EMPL president: Kahn-Lucas-Lancaster.

Foundation Officials
Andrew Kahn: director (see above)
Peggy Anne Kahn: director
Donald E. McKonly: director (see above)

Grants Analysis
Disclosure Period: calendar year ending 2000
Total Grants: $10,550
Number of Grants: 19
Average Grant: $555
Typical Range: $100 to $1,000

Recent Grants
Note: Grants derived from 2001 Form 990.
General

5,100	University of Pennsylvania, Philadelphia, PA
5,000	Yale Cancer Center, New Haven, CT
2,500	Gilda's Club, New York, NY
2,500	MDA, Wichita, KS
2,500	Rye County Day School, Rye, NY
1,000	Cure for Lymphoma Foundation, New York, NY
1,000	New York University Medical Center, New York, NY
600	Cancer Research Institute, New York, NY
350	Sports for a Cure Foundation, New York, NY
300	UJA-Federation, New York, NY

KAJIMA ENGINEERING AND CONSTRUCTION INC.

Company Headquarters
901 Corporate Center Dr., Ste. 201
Monterey Park, CA 91754

Company Description
Founded: 1984
SIC(s): 6552 Subdividers & Developers Nec.
Parent Company: Kajima Corp., 2-7, Motoakasaka 1-chome, Minato-ku, Tokyo, Japan

Giving Contact
Itsuko Kosai, Office Manager
901 Corporate Center Dr., Suite 104
Monterey Park, CA 91754
Phone: (323)262-8484
Fax: (323)262-8893

Description
Organization Type: Corporate Giving Program
Giving Locations: CA: Monterey Park

Financial Summary
Gifts Received: $4,246 (1993)

Typical Recipients
Arts & Humanities: Ballet, Historic Preservation, Libraries, Museums/Galleries, Music, Opera, Performing Arts
Civic & Public Affairs: Housing, Urban & Community Affairs, Zoos/Aquariums

Education: Colleges & Universities, Engineering/ Technological Education, International Studies, Minority Education, Secondary Education (Public), Student Aid, Vocational & Technical Education
Health: AIDS/HIV, Cancer, Children's Health/ Hospitals, Emergency/Ambulance Services, Multiple Sclerosis, Single-Disease Health Associations
International: Foreign Educational Institutions
Social Services: Big Brothers/Big Sisters, Child Welfare, Community Service Organizations, Recreation & Athletics, Scouts, United Funds/United Ways, YMCA/YWCA/YMHA/YWHA

Corporate Officials

Eiichi Motoshige: chairman, president, chief executive officer PRIM CORP EMPL chairman, president, chief executive officer: Kajima Development Corp.

Recent Grants

Library-Related

2,500	Museum of Modern Art, New York, NY

General

5,000	Princeton in Asia, Princeton, NJ -- for internships
5,000	University of Michigan, Ann Arbor, MI -- for scholarships
2,500	Cancer Care, Inc., New York, NY -- to provide guidance, information and referrals
2,500	New Jersey Institute of Technology, Newark, NY -- for scholarship
2,500	Ohio Wesleyan University, Delaware, OH -- for a conference
2,000	Habitat for Humanity, Stone Mountain, GA -- to provide funds to construct single family residences
2,000	Long Beach Junior Crew, Long Beach, CA -- for equipment and scholarships
2,000	Long Island University, Brookville, NY
1,500	Cystic Fibrosis Foundation, New York, NY
1,000	Boy Scouts of America Northeast Georgia Council, Athens, GA -- to continue and expand programs

KAJIMA INTERNATIONAL INC.

Company Headquarters

Englewood Cliffs, NJ
Web: http://www.kajimausa.com

Company Description

Employees: 457
SIC(s): 1542 Nonresidential Construction Nec, 1711 Plumbing, Heating & Air-Conditioning, 7812 Motion Picture & Video Production.
Parent Company: Kajima Corp., 2-7, Motoakasaka 1-chome, Minato-ku, Tokyo, Japan

Operating Locations

Kajima Engineering & Construction (CA--Pasadena); Kajima International (GA; IL; NJ--Englewood Cliffs; NY; TX); Kajima U.S.A. (NY--New York)

Kajima Foundation

Giving Contact

Kent Stolzman
395 W. Passaic St.
Rochelle Park, NJ 07662
Phone: (201)518-2100

Description

EIN: 521675796
Organization Type: Corporate Foundation

Giving Locations: headquarters and operating communities.
Grant Types: Emergency, Employee Matching Gifts, Multiyear/Continuing Support, Project, Research.

Financial Summary

Total Giving: $50,000 (2001)
Giving Analysis: Giving for 2001 includes: foundation scholarships ($7,500)
Assets: $894,994 (2001)
Gifts Received: $4,246 (1993); $3,650 (1992)

Typical Recipients

Arts & Humanities: Ballet, Historic Preservation, Libraries, Literary Arts, Museums/Galleries, Music, Opera, Performing Arts
Civic & Public Affairs: Chambers of Commerce, Community Foundations, Civic & Public Affairs-General, Housing, Zoos/Aquariums
Education: Colleges & Universities, Community & Junior Colleges, Economic Education, Engineering/ Technological Education, Faculty Development, International Exchange, International Studies, Leadership Training, Minority Education, Private Education (Precollege), Science/Mathematics Education, Secondary Education (Public), Student Aid
Health: AIDS/HIV, Cancer, Heart, Hospitals
International: Foreign Arts Organizations, Foreign Educational Institutions, International Relations, International Relief Efforts
Religion: Jewish Causes, Religious Welfare
Social Services: At-Risk Youth, Big Brothers/Big Sisters, Child Welfare, Emergency Relief, Family Services, Recreation & Athletics, Scouts, United Funds/United Ways, Volunteer Services, YMCA/ YWCA/YMHA/YWHA, Youth Organizations

Application Procedures

Initial Contact: Application form required. Send a brief letter of inquiry and a full proposal. Include a description of organization, amount requested, purpose of funds sought, recently audited financial statement, and proof of tax-exempt status.
Deadlines: on a bimonthly basis.

Restrictions

Contributions are limited to the 40 states in which Kajima International conducts business. Major U.S. headquarters for Kajima operating companies are listed above. Contributions also are restricted to organizations in which employees volunteer.

Corporate Officials

Hiroaki Hoshino: president, chief executive officer PRIM CORP EMPL president, chief executive officer: Kajima International.
Kiyoshi Sugasawa: chief financial officer PRIM CORP EMPL chief financial officer: Kajima International ADD CORP EMPL treasurer: Commercial Development International East Inc.; chief financial officer: Kajima Construction Services; vice president: Kajima Real Estate Development; vice president: Kajima United States of America Inc.

Foundation Officials

Hiroaki Hoshino: treasurer, trustee (see above)
Ayao Katayama: president, trustee
Marvin J. Suomi: secretary

Grants Analysis

Disclosure Period: calendar year ending 2001
Total Grants: $42,500*
Number of Grants: 23
Average Grant: $1,848
Highest Grant: $5,000
Typical Range: $1,000 to $5,000
*Note: Giving excludes scholarship.

Recent Grants

Note: Grants derived from 2001 Form 990.

General

5,000	Japanese Community World Trade Center Relief, New York, NY -- aid victims of World Trade Center attacks
5,000	Long Beach Aquarium, Long Beach, CA -- aquarium fundraising
5,000	University of Michigan College of Literature, Science and the Arts, Ann Arbor, MI -- Kajima Dean's Merit Scholarship
5,000	William Paterson University of New Jersey Foundation Inc., Wayne, NJ -- needy student in the College of Education
4,000	Jewish Federation of Southern New Jersey, Cherry Hill, NJ -- early literacy conference
3,000	Habitat for Humanity, Stone Mountain, GA -- construct single family residences
3,000	Woodrow Wilson National Fellowship Foundation, Princeton, NJ -- support ongoing programs
2,500	California State University, Long Beach, CA -- scholarships for National Merit Scholars and Valedictorians
2,500	Emmaus House, Atlanta, GA -- "The Study Hall"
2,000	Avon Breast Cancer 3-Day Walk, Chicago, IL -- Breast Health Programs

KALKUS FOUNDATION

Giving Contact

Lara Purchase, Vice President
Kalkus Foundation
Care of Lamar Companies
365 South Street
Morristown, NJ 07960
Phone: (973)285-0010

Description

Founded: 1992
EIN: 650258064
Organization Type: Private Foundation
Grant Types: General Support.

Financial Summary

Total Giving: $96,140 (2001)
Assets: $1,094,465 (2001)
Gifts Received: $4,000 (1996); $85,000 (1994)

Typical Recipients

Arts & Humanities: Libraries, Music, Opera, Theater
Civic & Public Affairs: Community Foundations, Civic & Public Affairs-General, Public Policy, Safety, Urban & Community Affairs, Zoos/Aquariums
Education: Colleges & Universities, Education Funds, Education-General, Private Education (Precollege), Student Aid
Environment: Air/Water Quality, Environment-General
Health: Cancer, Clinics/Medical Centers, Health Organizations, Hospitals, Medical Research, Single-Disease Health Associations
International: International-General
Religion: Churches
Social Services: Child Welfare, Community Service Organizations, Domestic Violence, People with Disabilities, Recreation & Athletics, Social Services-General, United Funds/United Ways

Application Procedures

Initial Contact: The foundation requests applications be made in writing.
Application Requirements: Include a description of organization.
Deadlines: None.

Foundation Officials

June Kalkus: vice president
Mark Kalkus: secretary
Peter Kalkus: president B 1959. CORP AFFIL vice president, treasurer, director: Cyprus Foote Mineral Co.
Lara Purchase: vice president

Grants Analysis

Disclosure Period: calendar year ending 2001
Total Grants: $96,140
Number of Grants: 36
Average Grant: $2,175*
Highest Grant: $20,000
Lowest Grant: $100
Typical Range: $1,000 to $5,000
***Note:** Average grant figure excludes highest grant.

Recent Grants

Note: Grants derived from 2001 Form 990.
General

20,000	St. Clare of Assisi Parish, Edwards, CO
14,190	Metropolitan Opera Association, Vail, CO
12,500	Vail Valley Foundation, Vail, CO
10,000	Eisenhower Medical Center, Rancho Mirage, CA
10,000	Morristown Memorial Hospital, Morristown, NJ
8,000	Bravo Colorado, Vail, CO
5,000	Betty Ford Center, Rancho Mirage, CA
2,700	Vail Valley Medical Center, Vail, CO
2,350	CASA of the Continental Divide, Vail, CO
2,000	American Friends of Czech Republic

KANSAS CITY SOUTHERN RAILWAY

Company Headquarters

114 W. 11th Street
Kansas City, MO 64105-1804
Web: http://www.kcsi.com

Company Description

Revenue: US$512 million (2002)
Employees: 2711 (2002)
SIC(s): 4000 Railroad Transportation, 6700 Holding & Other Investment Offices.

Operating Locations

Kansas City Southern Industries (LA--Shreveport; MS--Jackson; MO--Kansas City)

Nonmonetary Support

Type: Donated Equipment; In-kind Services; Loaned Employees; Loaned Executives

Giving Contact

Jan Armstrong, Director, Community Relations
114 West 11th Street
Kansas City, MO 64105
Phone: (816)983-1303
Fax: (816)983-1192

Description

Organization Type: Corporate Giving Program
Giving Locations: headquarters and operating communities.
Grant Types: Capital, Challenge, Emergency, Employee Matching Gifts, Endowment, General Support, Multiyear/Continuing Support, Operating Expenses, Project.

Financial Summary

Total Giving: Company does not disclose contributions figures.

Typical Recipients

Arts & Humanities: Arts Associations & Councils, Arts Centers, Arts Festivals, Arts Funds, Arts Institutes, Arts Outreach, Ballet, Community Arts, Dance, Ethnic & Folk Arts, Film & Video, Arts & Humanities-General, Historic Preservation, History & Archaeology, Libraries, Literary Arts, Museums/Galleries, Music, Opera, Performing Arts, Public Broadcasting, Theater, Visual Arts

Civic & Public Affairs: African American Affairs, Asian American Affairs, Botanical Gardens/Parks, Business/Free Enterprise, Chambers of Commerce, Civil Rights, Community Foundations, Economic Development, Economic Policy, Ethnic Organizations, Civic & Public Affairs-General, Hispanic Affairs, Housing, Inner-City Development, Municipalities/Towns, Native American Affairs, Nonprofit Management, Parades/Festivals, Philanthropic Organizations, Public Policy, Safety, Urban & Community Affairs, Women's Affairs, Zoos/Aquariums

Education: Afterschool/Enrichment Programs, Agricultural Education, Arts/Humanities Education, Business Education, Business-School Partnerships, Colleges & Universities, Community & Junior Colleges, Continuing Education, Economic Education, Education Funds, Elementary Education (Public), Education-General, Literacy, Minority Education, Preschool Education, Private Education (Precollege), Public Education (Precollege), Science/Mathematics Education, Secondary Education (Private), Secondary Education (Public), Social Sciences Education, Special Education

Environment: Environment-General, Resource Conservation, Wildlife Protection

Health: Adolescent Health Issues, AIDS/HIV, Alzheimer's Disease, Arthritis, Cancer, Children's Health/Hospitals, Clinics/Medical Centers, Diabetes, Eyes/Blindness, Health-General, Geriatric Health, Health Organizations, Heart, Home-Care Services, Hospices, Hospitals, Hospitals (University Affiliated), Long-Term Care, Medical Rehabilitation, Nursing Services, Single-Disease Health Associations

Science: Science-General, Science Exhibits & Fairs, Science Museums, Scientific Centers & Institutes, Scientific Research

Social Services: Animal Protection, At-Risk Youth, Camps, Child Welfare, Community Centers, Community Service Organizations, Counseling, Day Care, Delinquency & Criminal Rehabilitation, Domestic Violence, Emergency Relief, Family Planning, Family Services, Food/Clothing Distribution, Homes, People with Disabilities, Recreation & Athletics, Refugee Assistance, Senior Services, Sexual Abuse, Shelters/Homelessness, Social Services-General, Substance Abuse, United Funds/United Ways, Volunteer Services, YMCA/YWCA/YMHA/YWHA, Youth Organizations

Application Procedures

Initial Contact: Send a brief letter of inquiry and a full proposal.
Application Requirements: Include a description of organization, amount requested, purpose of funds sought, recently audited financial statement, proof of tax-exempt status, and a list of the board of directors.

Restrictions

Does not support individuals, religious organizations for sectarian purposes, political or lobbying groups, or organizations outside operating areas.

Corporate Officials

Joseph D. Monello: vice president financeo, director B New York, NY 1945. ED Trenton State College (1973). PRIM CORP EMPL vice president finance: Kansas City Southern Industries.
Landon Hill Rowland: president, chief executive officer, director B Fuquay Springs, NC 1937. ED Dartmouth College BA (1959); Harvard University LLB (1962). PRIM CORP EMPL president, chief executive officer, director: Kansas City Southern Industries.

CORP AFFIL chairman: Kansas City Southern Railway Co.; chief executive officer: Louisiana & Northwest Railroad Co.; chairman: DST Systems. NONPR AFFIL member: Phi Beta Kappa; chairman board director: Swope Ridge Health Care Center; trustee: Midwest Research Institute; member: Missouri Bar Association; director: Lyric Opera Kansas City; chairman: Metropolitan Performing Arts Fund; director: Jacob L & Ella C Loose Foundation; member: American Bar Association; director: American Royal Association. CLUB AFFIL River Club; Kansas City Country Club.

Grants Analysis

Typical Range: $1,000 to $2,500

KANSAS HEALTH FOUNDATION

Giving Contact

Nancy Claassen, Grants Manager
309 East Douglas
Wichita, KS 67202-3405
Phone: (316)262-7676
Fax: (316)262-2044
E-mail: info@khf.org
Web: http://www.kansashealth.org

Alternate Contact

Phone: 800-373-7681

Description

Founded: 1978
EIN: 480873431
Organization Type: Private Foundation
Giving Locations: KS
Grant Types: Award, Conference/Seminar, Employee Matching Gifts, Endowment, General Support, Matching, Multiyear/Continuing Support, Project, Research.

Financial Summary

Total Giving: $14,912,952 (2003); $11,871,669 (2002); $16,300,000 (2001)
Giving Analysis: Giving for 2003 includes: foundation grants to United Way ($119,634) 2002: foundation grants to United Way ($55,356)
Assets: $442,428,252 (2003); $375,703,185 (2002); $438,900,000 (2001)
Gifts Received: $12,500 (2003); $20,000 (2002); $183,843 (2000). Note: In 2002 and 2003, contributions were received from Sterling Trust. In 1998, contributions were received from the George E. and Blanche Sterling Trust ($38,828), the Mrs. H.C. Wear Charitable Remainder Annuity Trust 1 ($1,000,00), and the Turner Investment Partners, Inc ($18,000).

Typical Recipients

Arts & Humanities: Arts Centers, Arts Outreach, Libraries, Public Broadcasting
Civic & Public Affairs: African American Affairs, Botanical Gardens/Parks, Community Foundations, Civic & Public Affairs-General, Nonprofit Management, Parades/Festivals, Safety
Education: Afterschool/Enrichment Programs, Colleges & Universities, Education Funds, Elementary Education (Public), Faculty Development, Education-General, Health & Physical Education, Literacy, Medical Education, Preschool Education, Public Education (Precollege), Religious Education, Secondary Education (Public), Social Sciences Education, Special Education, Student Aid
Environment: Air/Water Quality, Environment-General
Health: Adolescent Health Issues, AIDS/HIV, Alzheimer's Disease, Cancer, Children's Health/Hospitals, Clinics/Medical Centers, Emergency/

Ambulance Services, Health-General, Geriatric Health, Health Policy/Cost Containment, Health Organizations, Heart, Home-Care Services, Hospices, Hospitals, Hospitals (University Affiliated), Medical Rehabilitation, Medical Research, Medical Training, Nursing Services, Nutrition, Prenatal Health Issues, Preventive Medicine/Wellness Organizations, Public Health, Research/Studies Institutes, Respiratory
International: International Relief Efforts
Religion: Churches, Ministries, Religious Welfare
Science: Science Museums, Scientific Centers & Institutes
Social Services: At-Risk Youth, Big Brothers/Big Sisters, Camps, Child Abuse, Child Welfare, Community Service Organizations, Counseling, Crime Prevention, Domestic Violence, Emergency Relief, Family Services, Food/Clothing Distribution, People with Disabilities, Scouts, Senior Services, Sexual Abuse, Social Services-General, Substance Abuse, Volunteer Services, YMCA/YWCA/YMHA/YWHA, Youth Organizations

Application Procedures
Initial Contact: Applications are available for the Recognition Grant program, and can be obtained by visiting www.kansashealth.org.
Application Requirements: Letters of inquiry should include summary of need, explanation of plan and address that need, and estimated cost.
Deadlines: March 15 and September 15 for the Recognition Grants.
Notes: The foundation reports that, with the exception of the Recognition Grant program, relatively few grants are awarded through unsolicited requests.

Restrictions
Grants are not made to individuals., clinical research, capital campaigns, operating deficits, endowments, construction, or vehicle purchases. Grants typically made only to preselected organizations.

Additional Information
Publications: Annual Report; Guidelines for Making Grants (Brochure); Newsletter

Foundation Officials
Eric T. Knorr: director CORP AFFIL director: Intrust Bank Park.
Timothy E. McKee: director PRIM CORP EMPL partner: Triplett Woolf & Garretson.
Judge Deanell Reece Tacha: vice chairman, director B 1946. ED University of Kansas BA (1968); University of Michigan JD (1971). PRIM NONPR EMPL judge: U.S. Court Appeals Denver. NONPR AFFIL member: United States Sentencing Commission.
Marni Vliet: president, chief executive officer, director
Kermit Wedel, MD: chairman, director PRIM CORP EMPL partner: Wedel Barker & Burnett Medical Practice.

Grants Analysis
Disclosure Period: calendar year ending 2003
Total Grants: $14,793,318*
Number of Grants: 255
Average Grant: $44,874*
Highest Grant: $1,530,000
Lowest Grant: $300
Typical Range: $10,000 to $75,000
*Note: Giving excludes United Way. Average grant figure excludes four highest grants ($3,530,000).

Recent Grants
Note: Grants derived from 2002 Form 990.
General
4,000,000 Kansas Health Institute, Topeka, KS -- provides four years of support to the Kansas health institute
384,456 Wichita State University Foundation, Wichita, KS -- offers funding for a three-year project

309,793 Kansas Department of Health and Environment, Topeka, KS -- develops statewide capacity for implementing and evaluating community interventions
301,319 Kansas University Endowment Association, Lawrence, KS -- provides funds for the benefit of the university
300,000 Abilene Community Foundation Inc., Abilene, TX -- provides sustained funding to the Abilene community
266,453 Kansas Action for Children Inc., Topeka, KS -- to plan and implement a statewide report card reflecting the health status
250,000 Legacy, a Regional Community Foundation, Winfield, KS -- to build and strengthen community foundations
250,000 Thomas County Community Foundation, Colby, KS -- to build and strengthen community foundations
224,337 Kansas Department of Health and Environment, Topeka, KS -- creates the public health workforce development coordinator position
200,000 McPherson County Community Foundation, McPherson, KS -- to build and strengthen community foundations

KANTZLER FOUNDATION

Giving Contact
Robert D. Sarow, Secretary
900 Center Ave.
Bay City, MI 48708
Phone: (989)892-4549

Description
Founded: 1974
EIN: 237422733
Organization Type: Private Foundation
Giving Locations: MI: Bay City including the greater Bay City area
Grant Types: Capital, General Support, Operating Expenses, Seed Money.

Donor Information
Founder: Leopold I. Kantzler

Financial Summary
Total Giving: $297,514 (2002); $329,166 (2001)
Assets: $4,943,712 (2002); $5,828,542 (2001)
Gifts Received: $19,263 (1998)

Typical Recipients
Arts & Humanities: Arts Associations & Councils, Community Arts, Historic Preservation, History & Archaeology, Libraries, Performing Arts, Theater, Visual Arts
Civic & Public Affairs: Botanical Gardens/Parks, Chambers of Commerce, Community Foundations, Civic & Public Affairs-General, Housing, Municipalities/Towns, Nonprofit Management, Urban & Community Affairs, Women's Affairs
Education: Colleges & Universities, Public Education (Precollege), Science/Mathematics Education, Student Aid
Environment: Environment-General, Resource Conservation, Wildlife Protection
Health: Health Funds, Health Organizations, Hospitals
Religion: Ministries
Science: Observatories & Planetariums
Social Services: Big Brothers/Big Sisters, Community Service Organizations, Day Care, Family Services, People with Disabilities, Recreation & Athletics, Scouts, Senior Services, United Funds/United Ways, YMCA/YWCA/YMHA/YWHA, Youth Organizations

Application Procedures
Initial Contact: Request application guidelines.
Deadlines: two weeks prior to each scheduled board meeting.

Additional Information
Publications: Application Guidelines

Foundation Officials
Meade A. Gougeon: trustee
Linda R. Heemstra: trustee
Ruth M. Jaffe: trustee
D. Brian Law: trustee
D. Brian Law: trustee
Mr. Dominic Monastiere: president
Robert D. Sarrow: secretary
Joseph Sasiela: vice president
Clifford D. Van Dyke: vice president B Fort Madison, IA 1929. ED Knox College BA (1951); Harvard University MBA (1955). PRIM CORP EMPL senior vice president: First American Bank of Mid Michigan. NONPR AFFIL director: Delta College Foundation; trustee: Kantzler Foundation; president, director: Bay County Growth Alliance; member: Bay Area Chamber of Commerce. CLUB AFFIL Saginaw Valley Torch Club; Rotary Club; Saginaw Bay Yacht Club; Bay City Country Club; Elks Club.
Jerome Yantz: treasurer

Grants Analysis
Disclosure Period: calendar year ending 2002
Total Grants: $297,514
Number of Grants: 14
Average Grant: $16,468*
Highest Grant: $50,000
Lowest Grant: $1,000
Typical Range: $5,000 to $30,000
*Note: Average grant figure excludes two highest grants ($100,000).

Recent Grants
Note: Grants derived from 2001 Form 990.
General
100,000 Studio 23, Bay City, MI -- to renovate art gallery
75,000 Bay County Women's Center, Bay City, MI -- to construct a women's shelter
50,000 Saginaw Valley State University, University Center, MI -- to endow scholarship funds
25,000 County of Bay City, Bay City, MI -- to construct skate park
20,000 Saginaw Basin Land Conservation, Bay City, MI -- to purchase shoreline land
16,666 Bay Area Community Foundation, Bay City, MI -- for construction of ice arena
12,500 Bay Sail, Bay City, MI -- sails for schooner appledore
10,000 Hidden Harvest, Saginaw, MI -- to expand food program
7,500 Bay Area Chamber Commerce, Bay City, MI -- to fund family support program
7,500 Bay Sail, Bay City, MI -- to fund environmental scholarship

J. M. KAPLAN FUND

Giving Contact
Peter Davidson, Chairman
261 Madison Avenue, 19th Floor
New York, NY 10016
Phone: (212)767-0630
Fax: (212)767-0639
E-mail: info@jmkfund.org
Web: http://www.jmkfund.org

Description
Founded: 1945
EIN: 136090286
Organization Type: Family Foundation
Giving Locations: NY: New York
Grant Types: General Support, Multiyear/Continuing Support, Operating Expenses, Project, Research, Seed Money.

Donor Information
Founder: Jacob Merrill Kaplan (1891-1987) established the fund in 1945 with proceeds from the Welch Grape Juice Company, which he headed for many years. His daughter, Joan K. Davidson, was president of the fund between 1977 and 1993. Mr. Kaplan worked imaginatively in responding to human need and the improvement of American social service institutions. Today, Mr. Kaplan's ideas and values govern the work of the fund, as they have for over fifty years.

Financial Summary
Total Giving: $8,766,428 (2002); $8,854,895 (2001)
Assets: $127,797,834 (2002); $146,189,671 (2001)
Gifts Received: $4,627,454 (2000)

Typical Recipients
Arts & Humanities: Arts Associations & Councils, Arts Centers, Arts Festivals, Arts Funds, Arts Outreach, Ethnic & Folk Arts, Film & Video, Historic Preservation, History & Archaeology, Libraries, Literary Arts, Museums/Galleries, Performing Arts, Public Broadcasting, Theater

Civic & Public Affairs: Asian American Affairs, Botanical Gardens/Parks, Business/Free Enterprise, Civil Rights, Clubs, Community Foundations, Economic Development, Economic Policy, Employment/Job Training, Civic & Public Affairs-General, Hispanic Affairs, Housing, Inner-City Development, Law & Justice, Legal Aid, Municipalities/Towns, Nonprofit Management, Philanthropic Organizations, Professional & Trade Associations, Public Policy, Rural Affairs, Urban & Community Affairs, Women's Affairs

Education: Afterschool/Enrichment Programs, Arts/Humanities Education, Business Education, Colleges & Universities, Economic Education, Education Funds, Education Reform, Elementary Education (Public), Education-General, International Exchange, International Studies, Leadership Training, Literacy, Minority Education, Private Education (Precollege), Science/Mathematics Education, Secondary Education (Private), Secondary Education (Public), Social Sciences Education, Student Aid

Environment: Air/Water Quality, Forestry, Environment-General, Protection, Resource Conservation, Wildlife Protection

Health: AIDS/HIV, Cancer, Children's Health/Hospitals, Health Organizations, Respiratory

International: Foreign Arts Organizations, Foreign Educational Institutions, International-General, Human Rights, International Development, International Environmental Issues, International Relief Efforts

Religion: Churches, Jewish Causes

Science: Scientific Centers & Institutes, Scientific Labs

Social Services: At-Risk Youth, Child Welfare, Community Centers, Community Service Organizations, Day Care, Family Planning, Family Services, Food/Clothing Distribution, Recreation & Athletics, Senior Services, Shelters/Homelessness, Social Services-General

Application Procedures
Initial Contact: Applicants are strongly encouraged to complete the pre-application questionnaire which can be obtained from the fund, or send a clear, concise letter (two to three pages) describing the organization and project for which support is requested.
Application Requirements: Proposals should include a one-page summary and be fewer than ten pages. They should include a history of the organiza-

tion, its mission, current programs and accomplishments, statement of purpose, beneficiaries served and how they will be involved, what qualities or advantages the organization has to be successful in purpose, planned approach and strategy, time frame for project, results anticipated, how program will be evaluated, recent annual report, IRS tax exemption letter, latest financial statement or 990 Form, operating budget including year-to-date income and expenses as source of income, list of Board and staff members, and, if funding is for a specific project, include a description and project budget.
Deadlines: None, however proposals received after October 1 may be carried over to the next year.
Review Process: All requests are acknowledged. A request for further information or a decision in writing is generally made within three months. A site visit or meeting is often helpful.
Notes: Fund accepts the New York Area Common Grant Application.
Fund asks that applicants do not send audio or video tapes unless requested to do so.

Restrictions
The fund generally does not contribute to: operating budgets of educational and medical, institutions; endowment funds, building programs or construction; individuals; films or video; individual scholarships or fellowships; and/or for the personal sponsorship of books, dances, plays or works of art.

Additional Information
Applicants should not fax proposals.
Applicants for the fund's Furthermore program should submit applications to: Furthermore, PO Box 667, Hudson, NY 12534, (518) 828-8900.

Foundation Officials
Brad Davidson: trustee
Peter W. Davidson: chairman, trustee B Portland, OR 1959. ED Stanford University BA (1981); Harvard University MBA (1986). PRIM CORP EMPL founder, chief executive officer, president: Latin Community Group.
William Falahee: controller
Caio Fonseca: trustee
Elizabeth K. Fonseca: trustee
Isabel Fonseca: trustee
Quina Fonseca: trustee
Mary E. Kaplan: trustee
Richard D. Kaplan: trustee

Grants Analysis
Disclosure Period: calendar year ending 2002
Total Grants: $8,766,428
Number of Grants: 348
Average Grant: $20,917*
Highest Grant: $550,000
Lowest Grant: $75
Typical Range: $5,000 to $50,000
*Note: Average grant figure excludes three highest grants ($1,550,0000).

Recent Grants
Note: Grants derived from 2002 Form 990.
General

600,000	Isamu Noguchi Foundation Inc., Long Island City, NY -- towards Martha Graham dance sets
550,000	Migration Policy Institute, Washington, DC -- towards development of migration information source a web based resource for migration news data and analysis
500,000	Nature Conservancy, Arlington, VA -- towards legal services for Mexican land conservation strategies of local enviro coalitions
400,000	Nature Conservancy, Arlington, VA -- towards challenge grant to the nature conservancy of New Mexico for protection of grasslands in NW Chihuahua
300,000	World Monuments Fund Inc., New York, NY -- towards a special J M Kaplan Fund at WMF
250,000	Conservation Law Foundation, NY -- towards marine protected areas initiative in the gulf of Maine
250,000	Nature Conservancy, Arlington, VA -- towards matching grant for operational and maintenance fees for the South Fork shelter island chapter headquarters
200,000	New York Foundation for the Arts, New York, NY -- towards artists fund
200,000	World Wildlife Fund, Washington, DC -- towards general support for marine systems work to protect the waters off North America
160,000	Essential Information Inc., Washington, DC -- towards general support

KAPLEN FOUNDATION

Giving Contact
Wilson R. Kaplen, Trustee
Kaplen Foundation
PO Box 792
Tenafly, NJ 07670-0792
Phone: (201)227-0722

Description
Founded: 1963
EIN: 226048152
Organization Type: Private Foundation
Giving Locations: NJ
Grant Types: General Support.

Donor Information
Founder: Wilson R. Kaplen

Financial Summary
Total Giving: $4,904,725 (fiscal year ending July 31, 2003); $6,223,740 (fiscal 2002); $6,018,239 (fiscal 2001)
Assets: $123,700,513 (fiscal 2003); $123,163,876 (fiscal 2002); $133,943,900 (fiscal 2001)
Gifts Received: $50,000 (fiscal 2003); $1,000 (fiscal 2001); $4,500 (fiscal 2000). Note: In 2003, contributions were received from the Estate of Ted Kaplen ($40,000) and Russell Berrie Foundation ($10,000). In 1998, contributions were received from Wilson R. Kaplen ($54,723,392), Andrew V. Schnurr ($1,000), Alexander Kaplan ($500), and Lawrence Kaplan ($500). In fiscal 1996, contributions were received from Wilson R. Kaplen ($1,000,000) and Evelyn Surloff ($100).

Typical Recipients
Arts & Humanities: Arts Centers, Film & Video, Arts & Humanities-General, Historic Preservation, Libraries, Literary Arts, Museums/Galleries, Music, Public Broadcasting, Theater

Civic & Public Affairs: Botanical Gardens/Parks, Civil Rights, Employment/Job Training, Ethnic Organizations, Civic & Public Affairs-General, Law & Justice, Legal Aid, Women's Affairs

Education: Afterschool/Enrichment Programs, Colleges & Universities, Community & Junior Colleges, Environmental Education, Education-General, Leadership Training, Legal Education, Medical Education, Preschool Education, Private Education (Precollege), Public Education (Precollege), Special Education

Environment: Air/Water Quality, Environment-General

Health: Cancer, Children's Health/Hospitals, Clinics/Medical Centers, Diabetes, Emergency/Ambulance Services, Health Funds, Hospitals, Medical Rehabilitation, Medical Research, Mental Health, Public Health, Single-Disease Health Associations

International: Foreign Educational Institutions, Inter-

national Relations, International Relief Efforts
Religion: Religion-General, Jewish Causes, Religious Organizations, Religious Welfare, Seminaries, Synagogues/Temples
Social Services: Community Centers, Community Service Organizations, Day Care, Family Services, Food/Clothing Distribution, Homes, People with Disabilities, Recreation & Athletics, Scouts, Senior Services, Shelters/Homelessness, Substance Abuse, United Funds/United Ways, YMCA/YWCA/YMHA/YWHA, Youth Organizations

Application Procedures

Initial Contact: The foundation requests applications be made in writing.
Application Requirements: Information and materials should include organization's history, financial status, purpose, and the percentage of contributions actually applied to purpose.
Deadlines: None.

Foundation Officials

Alexander Kaplen: trustee
Lawrence Kaplen: trustee
Margaret Kaplen: fdn mgr, trustee
Wilson R. Kaplen: trustee
Andrew V. Schnurr, Jr.: trustee

Grants Analysis

Disclosure Period: fiscal year ending July 31, 2003
Total Grants: $4,904,725
Number of Grants: 97
Average Grant: $40,605*
Highest Grant: $1,006,600
Lowest Grant: $25
Typical Range: $10,000 to $75,000
*Note: Average grant figure excludes highest grant.

Recent Grants

Note: Grants derived from 2003 Form 990.
General

1,006,600	Jewish Home Foundation, RockLeigh, NJ
375,000	National Yiddish Book Center, Amherst, MA
365,050	United Jewish Community, River Edge, NJ
357,500	WNYC Communications Group, New York, NY
330,000	PEN American Center, New York, NY
280,000	New York Philharmonic, New York, NY
265,750	Jewish Community Center on the Palisades, Tenafly, NJ
251,540	Anti Defamation League, New York, NY
250,000	American Jewish Committee, New York, NY
225,000	Roundabout Theatre Company, New York, NY

MORRIS J. AND BETTY KAPLUN FOUNDATION

Giving Contact

Moshe Sheinbaum, Vice President
225 W. 34th St., Suite 320
New York, NY 10122
Phone: (212)594-8155

Description

Founded: 1955
EIN: 136096009
Organization Type: Private Foundation
Giving Locations: NY: New York
Grant Types: General Support, Research.

Donor Information

Founder: the late Morris J. Kaplun

Financial Summary

Total Giving: $177,469 (fiscal year ending August 31, 2004); $201,912 (fiscal 2001)
Assets: $3,050,102 (fiscal 2004); $3,722,445 (fiscal 2001)
Gifts Received: $18 (fiscal 2001); $18 (fiscal 2000)

Typical Recipients

Arts & Humanities: Arts Festivals, Film & Video, Libraries, Literary Arts, Performing Arts, Public Broadcasting, Theater
Civic & Public Affairs: Civil Rights, Civic & Public Affairs-General, Public Policy, Women's Affairs
Education: Arts/Humanities Education, Colleges & Universities, Education Funds, Education-General, Literacy, Medical Education, Private Education (Precollege), Religious Education
Health: AIDS/HIV, Cancer, Children's Health/Hospitals, Clinics/Medical Centers, Eyes/Blindness, Health Organizations, Hospitals, Medical Research, Prenatal Health Issues, Public Health, Single-Disease Health Associations
International: Foreign Educational Institutions, Health Care/Hospitals, International Peace & Security Issues, International Relations, International Relief Efforts, Missionary/Religious Activities
Religion: Religion-General, Jewish Causes, Religious Organizations, Religious Welfare
Social Services: At-Risk Youth, Child Welfare, Community Service Organizations, Crime Prevention, Delinquency & Criminal Rehabilitation, Family Services, Homes, People with Disabilities, Refugee Assistance, Senior Services, Social Services-General, United Funds/United Ways, Youth Organizations

Application Procedures

Initial Contact: The foundation has no formal grant application procedure or application form.
Deadlines: None.

Foundation Officials

Glorie Isakower: vice president
Lawrence Marin: vice president
Aaron Seligson: president
Moshe Sheinbaum: vice president

Grants Analysis

Disclosure Period: fiscal year ending August 31, 2004
Total Grants: $177,469
Number of Grants: 109
Average Grant: $1,321*
Highest Grant: $34,799
Lowest Grant: $100
Typical Range: $500 to $3,000
*Note: Average grant figure excludes highest grant.

Recent Grants

Note: Grants derived from 2004 Form 990.

General

34,799	PEF-Israel Endowment Funds Inc., New York, NY
5,000	American Friends of Sanz Medical Center, New York, NY
5,000	Torah Mitzion, North Merrick, NY
5,000	Yeshiva Torah Mitzion, North Merrick, NY
4,500	Maine Jewish Film Festival, South Portland, ME
4,000	Re'uth Medical Center, New York, NY
3,500	Boys Town National Research Hospital, New York, NY
3,000	Bar-Ilan University, Carlstadt, NJ
3,000	Center for Deaf-Blind Persons, Milwaukee, WI
3,000	Israel Guide Dog Center for the Blind, Warrington, PA

SAMUEL AND REBECCA KARDON FOUNDATION

Giving Contact

David Kitter, President &Trustee
c/o MAJ
18 Sentry Park West, Suite 300
Blue Bell, PA 19422-2240
Phone: (215)643-3900

Description

Founded: 1952
EIN: 236278123
Organization Type: Private Foundation
Giving Locations: PA
Grant Types: General Support.

Donor Information

Founder: Emanuel S. Kardon, American Bag and Paper Corp.

Financial Summary

Total Giving: $1,465,250 (2003)
Assets: $6,955,401 (2003)

Typical Recipients

Arts & Humanities: Arts Associations & Councils, Arts Institutes, Arts Outreach, Libraries, Museums/Galleries, Music, Opera
Civic & Public Affairs: Ethnic Organizations, Civic & Public Affairs-General, Professional & Trade Associations
Education: Arts/Humanities Education, Colleges & Universities, Legal Education, Medical Education, Private Education (Precollege)
Health: Alzheimer's Disease, Cancer, Health-General, Health Funds, Heart, Hospitals, Medical Rehabilitation, Medical Research, Nursing Services
International: International Affairs, Missionary/Religious Activities
Religion: Jewish Causes, Religious Welfare, Synagogues/Temples
Social Services: Community Service Organizations, People with Disabilities, Scouts, Social Services-General, United Funds/United Ways, Volunteer Services, YMCA/YWCA/YMHA/YWHA

Application Procedures

Initial Contact: Send a brief letter of inquiry.
Application Requirements: Include a description of organization and purpose of funds sought.
Deadlines: None.

Foundation Officials

David Kittner: president, trustee

Grants Analysis

Disclosure Period: calendar year ending 2003
Total Grants: $1,465,250*
Typical Range: $1,000 to $20,000
*Note: No grants list available for 2003.

Recent Grants

Note: Grants derived from 2003 Form 990.
General

1,000,000	Constance S. Kittner Foundation, Blue Bell, PA
70,000	Jewish Federation of Greater Philadelphia, Philadelphia, PA
48,000	Kardon Institute for Arts Therapy, Philadelphia, PA
31,000	Settlement Music School, Philadelphia, PA
27,500	Friends of Akim USA Inc., New York, NY
25,000	Goodspeed Opera, East Haddam, CT
25,000	Jefferson Medical College, Philadelphia, PA
25,000	Philadelphia Chamber Music Society, Philadelphia, PA
25,000	Temple Sinai, Sarasota, FL

20,000   Holy Family College, Philadelphia, PA

KATZ FAMILY FOUNDATION

Giving Contact

Cheryl Kurz, Grants Administrator
409 Summit
Mill Valley, CA 94941
Phone: (415)381-4800

Description

Founded: 1986
EIN: 042947276
Organization Type: Private Foundation
Grant Types: General Support.

Donor Information

Founder: Bruce R. Katz

Financial Summary

Total Giving: $111,970 (fiscal year ending November 30, 2002); $283,000 (fiscal 2001). Note: Fiscal 1997 Giving includes United Way ($1,000).
Assets: $4,440,613 (fiscal 2002); $4,444,823 (fiscal 2001)
Gifts Received: $2,194,695 (fiscal 2000); $52,350 (fiscal 1998); $50,000 (fiscal 1997). Note: In fiscal 2000, contributions were received from Bruce R. Katz. In 1998, contributions were received from Steve Mayer.

Typical Recipients

Arts & Humanities: Arts Institutes, Ballet, Film & Video, Arts & Humanities-General, Historic Preservation, Libraries, Music, Opera
Civic & Public Affairs: Botanical Gardens/Parks, Community Foundations, Economic Development, Civic & Public Affairs-General, Housing, Native American Affairs, Public Policy, Safety, Urban & Community Affairs
Education: Afterschool/Enrichment Programs, Agricultural Education, Arts/Humanities Education, Colleges & Universities, Private Education (Precollege), Public Education (Precollege), Science/Mathematics Education
Environment: Environment-General, Resource Conservation, Wildlife Protection
Health: AIDS/HIV, Clinics/Medical Centers, Hospices, Hospitals, Mental Health, Preventive Medicine/Wellness Organizations
International: Human Rights, International Environmental Issues, International Organizations, International Peace & Security Issues, International Relations, International Relief Efforts
Religion: Churches, Religious Organizations
Social Services: Camps, Child Welfare, Community Service Organizations, Day Care, Family Services, Food/Clothing Distribution, People with Disabilities, Social Services-General, Special Olympics, United Funds/United Ways, Youth Organizations

Application Procedures

Initial Contact: Send a brief letter of inquiry, including statement of purpose, amount requested, and proof of tax-exempt status.
Deadlines: None.

Foundation Officials

Bruce Katz: trustee B 1948.
Roger Katz: trustee
Saul Katz: trustee

Grants Analysis

Disclosure Period: fiscal year ending November 30, 2002
Total Grants: $111,970

Number of Grants: 15
Average Grant: $4,075*
Highest Grant: $39,000
Lowest Grant: $220
Typical Range: $1,000 to $10,000
***Note:** Average grant figure excludes two highest grants ($59,000).

Recent Grants

Note: Grants derived from fiscal 2002 Form 990.
General

20,000	Farm and Wilderness Camp, Plymouth, VT
15,000	Film Institute of Northern California, Mill Valley, CA
10,000	Entrepreneurs Foundation and NRDC
5,000	California Pacific Medical Center, San Francisco, CA
5,000	Sundance Institute
4,000	Two/Ten International Footware Foundation
4,000	Youth for Environmental Sanity, Soquel, CA
3,000	Delance Street Foundation, San Francisco, CA
2,500	Film Odyssey
1,000	Camphill

KATZENBERGER FOUNDATION

Giving Contact

Abner J. Golieb, President, Director & Member
200 Park Avenue S, Suite 1700
New York, NY 10003
Phone: (212)315-5575

Description

Founded: 1952
EIN: 136094434
Organization Type: Private Foundation
Giving Locations: IL: IL, MA, NJ, and NY; MA; NJ; NY
Grant Types: General Support.

Donor Information

Founder: the late Walter B. Katzenberger, the late Helen Katherine Katzenberger, The Advertising Checking Bureau

Financial Summary

Total Giving: $830,000 (fiscal year ending November 30, 2003); $655,000 (fiscal 2001)
Assets: $16,447,675 (fiscal 2003); $17,749,496 (fiscal 2001)
Gifts Received: $5,000 (fiscal 2003). Note: In fiscal 2003, contributions were received from The Advertising Checking Bureau Inc.

Typical Recipients

Arts & Humanities: Arts Associations & Councils, Arts Funds, Arts Institutes, Arts Outreach, Community Arts, Libraries, Museums/Galleries, Performing Arts
Civic & Public Affairs: Community Foundations, Economic Development, Civic & Public Affairs-General, Hispanic Affairs, Housing, Inner-City Development, Philanthropic Organizations
Education: Arts/Humanities Education, Business Education, Colleges & Universities, Community & Junior Colleges, Education Funds, Education-General, Minority Education, Private Education (Precollege), Special Education, Vocational & Technical Education
Environment: Resource Conservation
Health: Children's Health/Hospitals, Mental Health
International: International Organizations
Religion: Churches, Ministries, Religious Organizations, Religious Welfare
Science: Science Museums, Scientific Centers & Institutes
Social Services: Animal Protection, Camps, Child Abuse, Child Welfare, Community Service Organizations, Counseling, Domestic Violence, Food/Clothing Distribution, People with Disabilities, Recreation & Athletics, Scouts, Shelters/Homelessness, United Funds/United Ways, YMCA/YWCA/YMHA/YWHA, Youth Organizations

Application Procedures

Initial Contact: Send a brief letter of inquiry describing program or project.
Deadlines: September 1.

Restrictions

Does not support individuals or provide scholarships, grants or awards.

Foundation Officials

Margaret G. Axelrod: treasurer, director, mem
Edward Davis: secretary, director, mem PRIM CORP EMPL president: Advertising Checking Bur.
Richard Eason: director, mem
Abner J. Golieb: president, director, mem
George Haibloom: director, member
Earl Swanson: director, member

Grants Analysis

Disclosure Period: fiscal year ending November 30, 2003
Total Grants: $830,000
Number of Grants: 46
Average Grant: $15,333*
Highest Grant: $140,000
Lowest Grant: $1,000
Typical Range: $5,000 to $30,000
***Note:** Average grant figure excludes highest grants.

Recent Grants

Note: Grants derived from fiscal 2004 Form 990.
General

135,000	Fox River Country Day School, Elgin, IL
70,000	Lincoln Center for the Performing Arts Inc., New York, NY
35,000	New York University, Manhattan, NY
30,000	Lighthouse, Kansas City, MO
30,000	Second Harvest, Toronto, ON Canada
30,000	United Negro College Fund, Fairfax, VA
28,000	Smithsonian Institute, Washington, DC
25,000	Hadley School for the Blind, Winnetka, IL
20,000	Juilliard School, New York, NY
15,000	Point Sebago Camp Sunshine Inc., South Casco, ME

EWING MARION KAUFFMAN FOUNDATION

Giving Contact

Sharon Cohen, Chief Communications Officer
4801 Rockhill Road
Kansas City, MO 64110-2046
Phone: (816)932-1000
Fax: (818)932-1440
E-mail: info@emkf.org
Web: http://www.emkf.org

Alternate Contact

Web: http://www.entreworld.org

Description

Founded: 1966
EIN: 436064859
Organization Type: Private Foundation
Giving Locations: MO: Kansas City
Grant Types: Award, Employee Matching Gifts, Fel-

lowship, General Support, Multiyear/Continuing Support, Operating Expenses, Project, Research.

Donor Information

Founder: The foundation was established in 1966 by the late Ewing Marion Kauffman, who died in August 1993 of bone cancer. Kauffman's wealth was estimated at $2 billion, with more than half to be awarded to the foundation upon his death.

Kauffman, born on a southern Missouri farm, began his career as a pharmaceutical salesman. In 1950, he started his own pharmaceutical company, Marion Laboratories. The company merged in 1989 with Merrell Dow Pharmaceuticals. He served on the board of the Merrell Dow subsidiary Marion Merrell Dow as chairman emeritus and director until his death.

Kauffman devoted many of his later years to major league baseball and the foundation. He owned the Kansas City Royals, and in 1993 created a trust to keep his team in Kansas City after his death. Kauffman was too ill to attend a July 1993 ceremony to rename the Royals Stadium as Kauffman Stadium.

Financial Summary

Total Giving: $58,476,276 (fiscal year ending June 30, 2003); $48,276,062 (fiscal 2002); $90,652,000 (fiscal 2001 approx)

Giving Analysis: Giving for fiscal 2003 includes: foundation gifts to individuals ($114,210); foundation grants to United Way ($127,968)

Assets: $1,575,461,763 (fiscal 2003); $1,687,454,656 (fiscal 2002); $2,034,722,000 (fiscal 2001)

Gifts Received: $25,866 (fiscal 2003); $41,628 (fiscal 2002); $135,000 (fiscal 2001 approx)

Typical Recipients

Arts & Humanities: Public Broadcasting
Civic & Public Affairs: Business/Free Enterprise, Clubs, Community Foundations, Economic Policy, Employment/Job Training, Civic & Public Affairs-General, Hispanic Affairs, Housing, Inner-City Development, Nonprofit Management, Philanthropic Organizations, Professional & Trade Associations, Public Policy, Urban & Community Affairs, Women's Affairs, Zoos/Aquariums
Education: Afterschool/Enrichment Programs, Agricultural Education, Business Education, Colleges & Universities, Community & Junior Colleges, Continuing Education, Economic Education, Education Associations, Education Funds, Education Reform, Elementary Education (Private), Engineering/Technological Education, Faculty Development, Education-General, Leadership Training, Literacy, Preschool Education, Public Education (Precollege), Science/Mathematics Education, Special Education, Student Aid, Vocational & Technical Education
Environment: Resource Conservation
Health: Clinics/Medical Centers, Health Policy/Cost Containment, Mental Health, Outpatient Health Care, Prenatal Health Issues
Religion: Dioceses, Jewish Causes, Religious Welfare
Science: Science Museums, Scientific Organizations, Scientific Research
Social Services: At-Risk Youth, Camps, Child Abuse, Child Welfare, Community Service Organizations, Counseling, Day Care, Family Services, Scouts, Senior Services, Social Services-General, Substance Abuse, United Funds/United Ways, Volunteer Services, YMCA/YWCA/YMHA/YWHA, Youth Organizations

Application Procedures

Initial Contact: Applicants should request the foundation's Guidelines for Grantseekers, either in writing or via email (info@emkf.org).
Application Requirements: Proposals should describe how the proposed project complements the missions and goals of the foundation and its youth development projects and entrepreneurship, describe the organization, and indicate the level of support requested. The letter should be on the organization's letterhead, and contain the following information: a brief description of the problem or opportunity to be addressed; a brief statement of the project's primary goals; a brief statement of the rationale for the project and how it fits within the foundation's focus areas; a time estimate for the project, and the project's expected outcome; a compressed budget estimate for the project, including the amount requested from the foundation and other anticipated sources of support; a brief statement describing how the program will be sustained after grant funding expires; the name of the primary contact person for follow-up; and verification that the applicant organization has a tax-exempt status under the Internal Revenue Code.
Deadlines: None.
Review Process: Acknowledgments of all grant requests are sent within four weeks of their receipt. When the foundation needs additional information for thorough consideration of a request, the foundation will contact the organization.

Restrictions

The foundation does not make grants to individuals, secular or fraternal organizations, political organizations or campaigns, social clubs, or organizations which do not have 501(c)(3) tax-exempt status. The foundation also does not make grants for endowments, capital campaigns, or special events. The foundation generally does not seek unsolicited proposals. Most grants develop out of relationships with key partners who are pursuing mutual goals.

Additional Information

The foundation is primarily an operating foundation which uses its research for education of at-risk youth to become self-sufficient and productive members of society and to support the understanding of the free enterprise system and the spirit of entrepreneurship for future generations.
Publications: Annual Report; Guidelines

Foundation Officials

Thomas M. Hoenig: trustee B Fort Madison, IA 1946. ED Benedictine College BA; Iowa State University MA; Iowa State University PhD; Iowa State University MA. PRIM CORP EMPL president, chief executive officer: Federal Reserve Bank Kansas City. CORP AFFIL president, chief executive officer: Federal Reserve Bank; member: Federal Reserve Bank System's Open Market Committee. NONPR AFFIL director: Midwest Research Institute; director: Union Station Kansas City; chairman: Benedictine College.
John A. "Tony" Mayer, Jr.: chairman, trustee ED Princeton University BA; Harvard University MBA (1964). CORP AFFIL partner: Cove Harbor Partners.
Thomas A. McDonnell: trustee ED Rockhurst University BSBA (1966); University of Pennsylvania Wharton School MBA (1968). PRIM CORP EMPL president, chief executive officer, director: DST Systems Inc. CORP AFFIL director: Wall Street Access; director: Garmin Ltd.; director: Kansas City Southern; president, chief executive officer: DST Systems Inc.; director: Euronet Worldwide Inc.; director: Commerce Bancshares Inc.; director: Computer Sciences Corp.; director: BHA Group Holdings Inc.; director: Blue Valley Bank Corp. NONPR AFFIL chairman: Harry S. Truman Library Institute; director: Union Station Project Consultants; director: Midwest Research Institute; chairman, trustee: Rockhurst University; chairman: Great Kansas City Community Foundation; co-chairman: Greater Downtown Development Authority; member: Civic Council.
Dr. Anne Hodges Morgan: trustee ED Columbia University MA; North Texas State University BA; University of Texas PhD.
Siobhan Nicolau: trustee ED Goucher College BA. NONPR AFFIL member: Public/Private Ventures.
Thomas J. Rhone: trustee ED University of Denver MA.
Carl J. Schramm: president, chief executive officer, trustee ED Georgetown University JD; Le Moyne College BA; University of Wisconsin PhD; University of Wisconsin PhD; University of Wisconsin MA. CORP AFFIL vice chairman: Patient Choice Health Care Inc. NONPR AFFIL batten fellow: Darden Graduate School, University Virginia.

Grants Analysis

Disclosure Period: fiscal year ending June 30, 2003
Total Grants: $58,234,098*
Number of Grants: 650 (approx)*
Average Grant: $85,878*
Highest Grant: $2,500,000
Lowest Grant: $100
Typical Range: $50,000 to $100,000
*Note: Giving excludes gifts to individuals; United Way. Average grant figure excludes highest grant.

Recent Grants

Note: Grants derived from fiscal 2003 Form 990.
General

2,500,000	Greater Kansas City Community Foundation, Kansas City, MO -- funding to support grant making by the Ewing Kaufman fund
2,276,126	Kansas Unified School District, Kansas City, MO -- a five-year grant to provide support for first things first initiative
2,100,000	Institute for Education in Entrepreneurship and Venture Creation, Shawnee Mission, KS -- funding to support the transition of the Kaufman fellows program
2,000,000	Union Station Kansas City Inc., Kansas City, MO -- funding to enable the transition to substantiate financial operation
1,500,000	Midwest Research Institute, Kansas City, MO -- funding for research and technology development in life sciences
1,397,831	Curators of the University of Missouri, Columbia, MO -- to support project linking professional development and compensation based on wages
1,152,664	Kansas Association of Child Care Resources and Referral Agencies, Salina, KS -- to support project linking professional development, quality services and increased compensation for early educators
1,000,000	Greater Kansas City Community Foundation, Kansas City, MO -- funding for program enhancement, outreach and state of the art technology
876,217	Greater Kansas City Community Foundation, Kansas City, MO -- to support the Kansas city community development initiative
793,333	National Commission on Entrepreneurship, Washington, DC -- to support the national commission on entrepreneurship

LOUIS G. KAUFMAN ENDOWMENT FUND

Giving Contact

Jim Duranceau, Vice President & Trust Officer
c/o Wells Fargo
101 West Washington
PO Box 580
Marquette, MI 49855
Phone: (906)228-1243
Fax: (906)228-1479

Description

Founded: 1927
EIN: 386048505
Organization Type: Private Foundation
Giving Locations: MI: Marquette

Grant Types: Emergency, General Support, Operating Expenses, Project, Scholarship, Seed Money.

Donor Information
Founder: L. G. Kaufman Trust

Financial Summary
Total Giving: $132,902 (fiscal year ending December 01, 2001)
Giving Analysis: Giving for fiscal 2001 includes: foundation scholarships ($62,000)
Assets: $3,252,695 (fiscal 2001)

Typical Recipients
Arts & Humanities: Arts & Humanities-General, History & Archaeology, Museums/Galleries, Music, Public Broadcasting
Civic & Public Affairs: Municipalities/Towns, Safety
Education: Afterschool/Enrichment Programs, Private Education (Precollege), Public Education (Precollege), Science/Mathematics Education, Secondary Education (Public), Student Aid
Environment: Resource Conservation
Health: Health Organizations, Public Health
Science: Scientific Centers & Institutes
Social Services: Camps, Community Service Organizations, Crime Prevention, Family Planning, Family Services, Recreation & Athletics, Scouts, Substance Abuse, United Funds/United Ways, YMCA/YWCA/YMHA/YWHA, Youth Organizations

Application Procedures
Initial Contact: Send a brief letter of inquiry.
Application Requirements: Include the history and purpose of requesting organization, statement of financial condition, proof of tax-exempt status, purpose of funds sought, and amount requested.
Deadlines: April 30.

Restrictions
Limited to the advancements of the moral, physical, and mental development of youth.

Additional Information
Trust(s): Wells Fargo

Foundation Officials
Henry J. Bothwell: fund comm mem
Don Grisham: fund committee member
Harold N. Herlich, Jr.: secretary
Ann K. Jordan: fund comm mem
Michael Kaufman: fund committee member
Peter Kaufman: chairman, fund comm mem
Ellwood Mattson: fund comm mem
Donald Parsons, Esq.: director
Melvin Rossway: fund comm mem

Grants Analysis
Disclosure Period: fiscal year ending December 01, 2001
Total Grants: $70,902*
Number of Grants: 18
Average Grant: $1,818*
Highest Grant: $40,000
Lowest Grant: $400
Typical Range: $500 to $5,000
*Note: Giving excludes scholarships. Average grant figure excludes highest grant.

Recent Grants
Note: Grants derived from 2001 Form 990.
General

40,000	Marquette Area Public Schools, Marquette, MI -- high school scholarship program
40,000	Peter White Public Library, Marquette, MI
11,000	Marquette Area Public Schools, Marquette, MI -- middle school scholarship program
7,000	Marquette Junior Hockey, Marquette, MI -- scholarship programs
5,000	Bay Cliff Health Camp, Marquette, MI
5,000	City of Marquette, Marquette, MI -- Sesquicentennial Pavilion Project
4,152	Marquette Area Public Schools, Marquette, MI -- Lyceum Program
4,000	Marquette Area Public Schools, Marquette, MI -- special incentive programs
3,000	YMCA of Marquette County, Marquette, MI -- strong kids scholarship program
2,000	YMCA of Marquette County, Marquette, MI

KAUFMAN FOUNDATION

Giving Contact
Richard Kaufman, Trustee
297 West Clay Avenue, Suite 106
Muskegon, MI 49440
Phone: (231)727-3415

Description
Founded: 1959
EIN: 386091556
Organization Type: Private Foundation
Grant Types: General Support.

Financial Summary
Total Giving: $172,790 (fiscal year ending October 31, 2002); $195,086 (fiscal 2001)
Giving Analysis: Giving for fiscal 2002 includes: foundation grants to United Way ($1,000)
Assets: $2,905,812 (fiscal 2002); $3,139,373 (fiscal 2001)
Gifts Received: $25,000 (fiscal 1994). Note: In fiscal 1994, contributions were received from Amstore Corp.

Typical Recipients
Arts & Humanities: Arts Associations & Councils, Arts Centers, Arts Institutes, Dance, Arts & Humanities-General, Libraries, Museums/Galleries, Music, Public Broadcasting, Theater
Civic & Public Affairs: Community Foundations, Employment/Job Training, Civic & Public Affairs-General, Nonprofit Management, Philanthropic Organizations, Public Policy, Women's Affairs
Education: Arts/Humanities Education, Business Education, Colleges & Universities, Education Funds, Environmental Education, Education-General, Minority Education, Private Education (Precollege), Religious Education, Secondary Education (Public), Special Education
Health: Children's Health/Hospitals, Heart, Hospices, Medical Research
International: Foreign Educational Institutions, International Affairs, International Relief Efforts, Missionary/Religious Activities
Religion: Churches, Religion-General, Jewish Causes, Religious Organizations, Religious Welfare, Synagogues/Temples
Science: Scientific Centers & Institutes
Social Services: Child Welfare, Community Service Organizations, Family Planning, Scouts, United Funds/United Ways, YMCA/YWCA/YMHA/YWHA

Application Procedures
Initial Contact: Send a brief letter of inquiry.
Deadlines: None.

Foundation Officials
Richard F. Kaufman: trustee
Sylvia C. Kaufman: trustee

Grants Analysis
Disclosure Period: fiscal year ending October 31, 2002
Total Grants: $171,790*
Number of Grants: 72
Average Grant: $954*

Highest Grant: $80,000
Lowest Grant: $50
Typical Range: $100 to $3,000
*Note: Giving excludes United Way. Average grant figure excludes two highest grants ($105,000).

Recent Grants
Note: Grants derived from 2001 Form 990.
General

8,333	Grand Valley State University, Allendale, MI
7,500	Cleveland Clinic Foundation, Cleveland, OH
2,394	Aspen Museum of Art, Aspen, CO
1,667	Aspen Museum of Art, Aspen, CO
1,000	Blossoming Rose, Cedar Springs, MI
1,000	Congregation B'nai Israel, Northampton, MA
1,000	United Way of Muskegon County, Muskegon, MI
550	Aitz Chayim Synagogue
250	Abraham Fund, New York, NY
250	Amherst Parent's Fund, Amherst, OH

HUGH KAUL FOUNDATION TRUST

Giving Contact
Karla Gayle, Vice President & Trust Officer
Care of AmSouth Bank
PO Box 11426
Birmingham, AL 35202
Phone: (205)326-5382
Fax: (205)581-7433

Description
Founded: 1990
EIN: 636158725
Organization Type: Family Foundation
Giving Locations: AL: Coosa County, Jefferson County, Birmingham Clay County
Grant Types: Capital, Fellowship, General Support, Matching, Multiyear/Continuing Support, Research.

Donor Information
Founder: Established in 1990 by the late Mr. Hugh Kaul.

Financial Summary
Total Giving: $2,712,200 (2003); $2,977,592 (2002)
Assets: $59,213,681 (2003); $52,925,039 (2002)
Gifts Received: $7,176,129 (1998); $21,212,494 (1992). Note: Contributions were received from the estate of Hugh Kaul.

Typical Recipients
Arts & Humanities: Arts Associations & Councils, Arts Festivals, Arts Funds, Ballet, Dance, History & Archaeology, Libraries, Museums/Galleries, Music, Opera, Performing Arts, Public Broadcasting, Theater
Civic & Public Affairs: Asian American Affairs, Botanical Gardens/Parks, Business/Free Enterprise, Civil Rights, Clubs, Community Foundations, Civic & Public Affairs-General, Housing, Law & Justice, Municipalities/Towns, Nonprofit Management, Philanthropic Organizations, Professional & Trade Associations, Public Policy, Urban & Community Affairs, Women's Affairs, Zoos/Aquariums
Education: Afterschool/Enrichment Programs, Arts/Humanities Education, Business Education, Colleges & Universities, Economic Education, Education Reform, Environmental Education, Education-General, Gifted & Talented Programs, Leadership Training, Literacy, Medical Education, Minority Education, Preschool Education, Private Education (Precollege), Public Education (Precollege), Religious Education,

Special Education, Student Aid

Environment: Air/Water Quality, Environment-General, Resource Conservation, Wildlife Protection
Health: Cancer, Children's Health/Hospitals, Eyes/Blindness, Health-General, Hospitals, Medical Research, Mental Health, Preventive Medicine/Wellness Organizations, Public Health, Single-Disease Health Associations, Speech & Hearing
International: International Development, International Organizations
Religion: Churches, Ministries, Missionary Activities (Domestic), Religious Organizations, Religious Welfare
Science: Science Museums, Scientific Centers & Institutes
Social Services: Child Welfare, Community Centers, Community Service Organizations, Crime Prevention, Family Planning, Family Services, People with Disabilities, Recreation & Athletics, Scouts, Senior Services, Shelters/Homelessness, Social Services-General, Substance Abuse, United Funds/United Ways, YMCA/YWCA/YMHA/YWHA, Youth Organizations

Application Procedures

Initial Contact: Applicants should submit grant requests to the foundation in written form.
Application Requirements: Grant requests should include a one-page cover letter, with the name and address of the organization which is requesting funds, as well as a designation of the individual filing the request and his/her relationship to the organization, amount requested, and succinct summary of project (no more than one paragraph); a full proposal of no more than four pages, with agency's history including major programs and accomplishments, links with similar organizations, need or issue project addresses, total cost of program and amount requested, goals and objectives, activities that will be carried out, qualifications of key personnel, and other organizations involved in project. Documentation of the tax-exempt status of the organization is also required.
Deadlines: Requests must be received by March 15 and September 15 in order to be considered at the June and December meetings of the trustees.
Review Process: Applicants are notified within a reasonable period following the meeting of the trustees.

Additional Information

Trust(s): AmSouth Bank, NA

Foundation Officials

William Houston Blount: director B Union Springs, AL 1922. ED Harvard University; University of Alabama (1942). PRIM CORP EMPL chairman emeritus: Vulcan Materials Co. CORP AFFIL director: VF Corp.; director: Blount International Inc. NONPR AFFIL Rotary International. CLUB AFFIL member: Rotary Club of Birmingham; member: Shoal Creek; member: Mountain Brook Country Club; member: National Golf Club; member: The Club; member: Elk River Club.
Nancy E. Dunlap: director
Karla Gayle: vice president, trust officer
John K. Greene: director B Birmingham, AL 1929. ED Yale University (1951). PRIM CORP EMPL special principal: William Blair & Co. LLC. CORP AFFIL director: Vulcan Materials Co.
Beverly P. Head, III: director PRIM CORP EMPL chairman: Giles & Kendall Inc. CORP AFFIL vice president: Mantlecraft; chairman: Pacific Rim Manufacturing.
Hillery Head: director
Don James: director
John J. McMahan, Jr.: director
Samuel E. Yates: director

Grants Analysis

Disclosure Period: calendar year ending 2003
Total Grants: $2,712,200
Number of Grants: 39

Average Grant: $42,216*
Highest Grant: $650,000
Lowest Grant: $6,000
Typical Range: $20,000 to $50,000
*Note: Average grant figure excludes two highest grants ($1,150,000).

Recent Grants

Note: Grants derived from 2003 Form 990.
General

500,000	Children's Hospital of Alabama, Birmingham, AL
150,000	Birmingham Zoo, Birmingham, AL
120,000	Children's Health System, Birmingham, AL
100,000	Alabama Symphonic Association, Birmingham, AL
100,000	Aldridge Gardens, Hoover, AL
100,000	Birmingham Museum of Art, Birmingham, AL
100,000	Boy Scouts of America, Irving, TX
100,000	Civic Club Foundation Poland
100,000	Entrepreneurial Center, Birmingham, AL
69,200	Birmingham Botanical Society, Birmingham, AL

T. JAMES KAVANAGH FOUNDATION

Giving Contact

Thomas Kavanagh, Trustee
234 E. State Street
Sharon, PA 16146
Phone: (724)347-5215

Description

Founded: 1968
EIN: 236442981
Organization Type: Private Foundation
Giving Locations: NJ: southern NJ; PA, Philadelphia PA, Sharon
Grant Types: Capital, Emergency, General Support, Multiyear/Continuing Support, Project, Research.

Donor Information

Founder: T. James Kavanagh

Financial Summary

Total Giving: $429,736 (2003)
Giving Analysis: Giving for 2003 includes: foundation grants to United Way ($5,000)
Assets: $14,405,271 (2003)

Typical Recipients

Arts & Humanities: Ballet, Historic Preservation, Libraries, Music, Opera, Performing Arts, Theater
Civic & Public Affairs: Clubs, Civic & Public Affairs-General, Safety
Education: Arts/Humanities Education, Colleges & Universities, Elementary Education (Private), Elementary Education (Public), Literacy, Medical Education, Private Education (Precollege), Religious Education, Science/Mathematics Education, Secondary Education (Private), Student Aid, Vocational & Technical Education
Environment: Environment-General
Health: Emergency/Ambulance Services, Health Organizations, Hospices, Hospitals, Long-Term Care, Medical Research, Nursing Services, Single-Disease Health Associations
Religion: Churches, Missionary Activities (Domestic), Religious Organizations, Religious Welfare, Synagogues/Temples
Social Services: Camps, Community Service Organizations, Day Care, Family Services, Food/Clothing Distribution, Recreation & Athletics, Shelters/Homelessness, Social Services-General, United

Funds/United Ways, YMCA/YWCA/YMHA/YWHA, Youth Organizations

Application Procedures

Initial Contact: Applications must be accompanied by proper identification and proof of tax-exempt status.
Deadlines: None.

Restrictions

Grants are not made to individuals.

Additional Information

Publications: Application Guidelines

Foundation Officials

Louis J. Esposito: trustee
Thomas E. Kavanagh: trustee

Grants Analysis

Disclosure Period: calendar year ending 2003
Total Grants: $424,736*
Number of Grants: 103
Average Grant: $4,124
Highest Grant: $20,000
Lowest Grant: $1,000
Typical Range: $1,000 to $10,000
*Note: Giving excludes United Way.

Recent Grants

Note: Grants derived from 2003 Form 990.
General

20,000	Buhl Farm Trust, Sharon, PA
20,000	Delaware Valley College of Science and Agriculture, Doylestown, PA
20,000	Prince of Peace Center, Farrell, PA
20,000	Sisters of the Holy Child, Drexel Hill, PA
16,000	Saint Joseph School, Sharon, PA
15,000	Church of Notre Dame, Hermitage, PA
10,396	Sisters of the Holy Child Jesus Convent, Sea Isle City, NJ
10,000	Opera Company of Philadelphia, Philadelphia, PA
5,000	South Philadelphia Lions Club, Philadelphia, PA
5,000	United Way of Mercer County, Sharon, PA

KAWABE MEMORIAL FUND

Giving Contact

Margaret Liu, Trust Officer
Kawabe Memorial Fund
Care of Bank of America
PO Box 24565
Seattle, WA 98124
Phone: (206)358-3144

Description

Founded: 1972
EIN: 916116549
Organization Type: Private Foundation
Giving Locations: WA: Seattle including metropolitan area
Grant Types: Capital, Emergency, Multiyear/Continuing Support, Operating Expenses, Seed Money.

Donor Information

Founder: the late Tomo Kawabe, the late Harry Kawabe

Financial Summary

Total Giving: $208,000 (2001)
Giving Analysis: Giving for 2001 includes: foundation scholarships ($6,000)

Assets: $4,140,101 (2001)
Gifts Received: $200 (1999)

Typical Recipients

Arts & Humanities: Libraries, Museums/Galleries, Opera
Civic & Public Affairs: Asian American Affairs, Civic & Public Affairs-General, Housing, Parades/ Festivals, Urban & Community Affairs, Women's Affairs
Education: Colleges & Universities, Education-General, International Studies, Literacy, Minority Education, Religious Education, Student Aid
Health: AIDS/HIV, Children's Health/Hospitals, Clinics/Medical Centers, Emergency/Ambulance Services, Geriatric Health, Health Organizations, Long-Term Care, Nursing Services, Nutrition, Trauma Treatment
International: International Relations, International Relief Efforts
Religion: Churches, Jewish Causes, Ministries, Religious Organizations, Religious Welfare, Synagogues/Temples
Social Services: Child Welfare, Community Centers, Community Service Organizations, Domestic Violence, Family Services, Food/Clothing Distribution, Homes, People with Disabilities, Refugee Assistance, Senior Services, Shelters/Homelessness, Substance Abuse, United Funds/United Ways, Youth Organizations

Application Procedures

Initial Contact: Send a brief project proposal.
Application Requirements: Include expenses, income summary, and proof of tax-exempt status.
Deadlines: None.
Review Process: Requests are reviewed quarterly.

Restrictions

Support is given to institutions and social service agencies devoted to the care of children, the indigent, and aged people, and for capital grants to churches for improvement of physical facilities.

Additional Information

Provides scholarships to graduating students of Seward High School, AK.
Publications: Application Guidelines
Trust(s): Bank of America

Foundation Officials

Yasue Brevig: mem allocations comm NONPR AFFIL member: Permian Basin Petroleum Association.
Rev. Donald Castro: mem allocations comm
Tsuyoshi Horike: mem allocations comm
Ruth S. Iwata: mem allocations comm
Aizo Kosai: mem allocations comm
Takashi Matsui: mem allocations comm
Tsuyoshi Nakano: mem allocations comm
Rev. Sadamori Ouichi: mem allocations comm
Toru Sakahara: mem allocations comm
Chiyoko Yasutake: member allocations committee
Webster T. Yasutake: member allocations committee

Grants Analysis

Disclosure Period: calendar year ending 2001
Total Grants: $202,000*
Number of Grants: 38
Average Grant: $4,316
Highest Grant: $40,500
Lowest Grant: $500
Typical Range: $1,000 to $10,000
*Note: Giving excludes scholarships.

Recent Grants

Note: Grants derived from 2002 Form 990.
General

30,000	Seattle Buddhist Church
26,800	Kawabe Memorial House, Seattle, WA
25,500	Seattle Betsuin Buddhist Temple, Seattle, WA -- for repairs and maintenance projects
10,000	Nikkei Concerns, Seattle, WA -- resident bed replacement project
5,000	Asian Counseling and Referral Service, Seattle, WA -- food bank
5,000	Chinatown International District
5,000	Family Services, Seattle, WA -- homeless children's services
5,000	Seattle Cherry Blossom Festival, Seattle, WA -- for scholarship awards
5,000	Senior Services, Kalamazoo, MI -- Senior Programs
3,500	Seattle Betsuin Buddhist Temple, Seattle, WA -- replace fence

KAWASAKI MOTORS MANUFACTURING CORPORATION U.S.A.

Company Headquarters

Lincoln, NE
Web: http://www.kawasaki.com

Company Description

Employees: 800
SIC(s): 3751 Motorcycles, Bicycles & Parts, 3799 Transportation Equipment Nec.
Parent Company: Kawasaki Heavy Industries Ltd., Kobe Crystal Tower, 1-3 Higashikawasaki-cho 1-chome, Chuo-ku, Kobe, Japan

Operating Locations

Kawasaki Heavy Industries U.S.A. (NY--New York); Kawasaki Loaders Manufacturing Corp. U.S.A. (GA--Newnan); Kawasaki Motors Manufacturing Corp. U.S.A. (CA--Irvine); Kawasaki Rail Car (NY--Yonkers); Kawasaki Robotics U.S.A. (MI--Farmington Hills)

Kawasaki Good Times Foundation

Giving Contact

Steve Becker
PO Box 81469
Lincoln, NE 68501
Phone: (402)476-6600
Fax: (402)476-4735

Description

Founded: 1993
EIN: 363879896
Organization Type: Corporate Foundation
Giving Locations: DC: Washington; GA: Atlanta; MO: Maryville; NE: Lincoln; NJ: New Brunswick; NY: New York, Yonkers; PA: Warrendale

Financial Summary

Total Giving: $61,200 (2003)
Assets: $3,058,564 (2003)
Gifts Received: $229,000 (2003); $241,000 (1999); $69,000 (1998). Note: In 2003, contributions were received from Kawasaki Motors Manufacturing Corporation ($78,500), Kawasaki Motors Corp ($50,000), Kawasaki Heavy Industries ($3,500) and Kawasaki Rail Car Inc. ($97,000). In 1999, contributions were received from Kawasaki Motors Manufacturing Corporation ($70,000), Kawasaki Robotics ($15,000), Kawasaki Motors Corp ($117,000), Kawasaki Heavy Industries ($9,000) and Kawasaki Loaders Mfg. Corp. ($30,000). In 1998, contributions were received from Kawasaki Motors Manufacturing Corporation ($60,000) and Kawasaki Robotics ($9,000).

Typical Recipients

Arts & Humanities: Arts Associations & Councils, Arts Centers, Ethnic & Folk Arts, History & Archaeology, Libraries, Museums/Galleries, Music
Civic & Public Affairs: Civic & Public Affairs-General, Professional & Trade Associations, Zoos/ Aquariums
Education: Colleges & Universities, Engineering/ Technological Education
Health: Cancer
International: Foreign Arts Organizations, International Relief Efforts
Science: Scientific Organizations, Scientific Research

Application Procedures

Initial Contact: Send proposal in written form.
Application Requirements: Include amount requested, purpose of funds sought, time needed, expected benefits to the public, and any other information related to the request.
Deadlines: None.

Corporate Officials

Steve Becker: chief executive officer, chief financial officer PRIM CORP EMPL chief executive officer, chief financial officer: Kawasaki Motors Manufacturing Corp. U.S.A.
Stan Hanson: vice president PRIM CORP EMPL vice president: Kawasaki Motors Manufacturing Corp. U.S.A.
Takehiko Saeki: president PRIM CORP EMPL president: Kawasaki Motors Manufacturing Corp. U.S.A.

Grants Analysis

Disclosure Period: calendar year ending 2003
Total Grants: $61,200
Number of Grants: 8
Average Grant: $4,457*
Highest Grant: $30,000
Lowest Grant: $1,000
Typical Range: $1,000 to $10,000
*Note: Average grant figure excludes highest grant.

Recent Grants

Note: Grants derived from 2003 Form 990.
General

30,000	University of Nebraska, Lincoln, NE
10,000	Metropolitan Museum of Art, New York, NY
10,000	New York Transit Museum, New York, NY
5,000	Jane Voorhees Zimmerli Art Museum, New Brunswick, NJ
3,000	Indue Chamber Ensemble, New York, NY
1,200	Jassi, New York, NY
1,000	Memorial Sloan-Kettering Cancer Center, New York, NY
1,000	Midori and Friends, New York, NY

KAYSER FOUNDATION

Giving Contact

R. Bruce LaBoon, President
600 Travis, Suite 3500
Houston, TX 77002
Phone: (713)226-1393

Description

Founded: 1961
EIN: 746050591
Organization Type: Private Foundation
Giving Locations: DC; SC; TX
Grant Types: Emergency, General Support, Research.

Donor Information

Founder: Paul Kayser, Mrs. Paul Kayser

Financial Summary

Total Giving: $267,189 (2001)
Giving Analysis: Giving for 2001 includes: foundation scholarships ($5,000)
Assets: $4,886,127 (2001)

Typical Recipients

Arts & Humanities: Arts Outreach, Ballet, History & Archaeology, Libraries, Museums/Galleries, Music, Performing Arts, Theater
Civic & Public Affairs: Botanical Gardens/Parks, Employment/Job Training, Law & Justice, Safety, Women's Affairs
Education: Afterschool/Enrichment Programs, Business Education, Colleges & Universities, Education-General, Legal Education, Medical Education, Private Education (Precollege), Public Education (Precollege), Secondary Education (Private), Student Aid
Environment: Forestry, Environment-General, Wildlife Protection
Health: AIDS/HIV, Alzheimer's Disease, Arthritis, Cancer, Children's Health/Hospitals, Clinics/Medical Centers, Diabetes, Emergency/Ambulance Services, Eyes/Blindness, Health Organizations, Heart, Hospices, Hospitals, Hospitals (University Affiliated), Medical Rehabilitation, Medical Research, Mental Health, Multiple Sclerosis, Prenatal Health Issues, Public Health, Single-Disease Health Associations
International: Health Care/Hospitals
Religion: Religion-General, Jewish Causes, Ministries, Religious Organizations, Religious Welfare, Social/Policy Issues
Social Services: Animal Protection, At-Risk Youth, Child Abuse, Child Welfare, Community Service Organizations, Crime Prevention, Day Care, Emergency Relief, Family Planning, Family Services, Food/Clothing Distribution, Homes, People with Disabilities, Scouts, Shelters/Homelessness, Special Olympics, Substance Abuse, United Funds/United Ways, YMCA/YWCA/YMHA/YWHA, Youth Organizations

Application Procedures

Initial Contact: Send a brief letter of inquiry.
Application Requirements: Outline the purpose of funds sought.
Deadlines: None.

Restrictions

Does not support individuals. Must be organized under IRS Section 501(c) (3).

Foundation Officials

Robert Bruce La Boon: vice president B Saint Louis, MO 1941. ED Texas Christian University BSc (1963); Southern Methodist University LLB (1965). PRIM CORP EMPL partner: Liddell, Sapp, Zivley, Hill & La-Boon. CORP AFFIL director: Texas Commerce Bankshares; director: Texas Med Center Board; director: Gamma Biological; director: Big Three Industries. NONPR AFFIL member: Texas State Bar; member, board visitors: University Cancer Foundation Maryland Anderson Cancer Center; trustee: Texas Christian University; advisor director: Retina Research Foundation; fellow: Texas Bar Foundation; trustee: Kayser Foundation; director: Institute Rehabilitation & Research; director: International Center Arbitration; director: Houston International Festival; director: Greater Houston Partnership & Community Schools Houston; member: Houston Bar Association; member: Association Bank Counsel; director: Greater Houston Community Foundation; member: American Law Institute; member: American Bar Association; fellow: American College Probate Counsel. CLUB AFFIL Houston River Oaks Country Club.
Jeff Love: vice president
Charles Sapp: vice president
Kenneth Simon: secretary, treasurer
Henry O. Weaver: president

Grants Analysis

Disclosure Period: calendar year ending 2001
Total Grants: $262,189*
Number of Grants: 36
Average Grant: $5,894*
Highest Grant: $50,000
Typical Range: $2,000 to $10,000
*Note: Giving excludes scholarship. Average grant figure excludes highest grant.

Recent Grants

Note: Grants derived from 2001 Form 990.
General

50,000	Retina Research Foundation, Houston, TX -- for research on vision related items
25,000	American Red Cross, Denison, TX -- for disaster assistance services
21,689	University of Texas at Austin, Austin, TX -- for law school
10,000	Boys and Girls Club of America, Richardson, TX -- for community services to less fortunate youth
10,000	Dallas Bar Foundation, Dallas, TX -- for legal assistance to the poor
10,000	Houston Eye Associates Foundation, Houston, TX -- for research on vision related items
10,000	Kent Waldrep National Paralysis Foundation, Dallas, TX -- for research on paralysis related items
10,000	University of Houston Law Foundation, Houston, TX -- for law school
7,500	Hobby Center for the Performing Arts, Houston, TX -- for the arts
5,000	American Judicature Society, Washington, DC -- for legal assistance to the poor

KEATS FAMILY FOUNDATION

Giving Contact

Robert M. Keats, President & Treasurer
4800 Hampden Lane, 650
Bethesda, MD 20814
Phone: (301)652-5032

Description

Founded: 1989
EIN: 521645642
Organization Type: Private Foundation
Grant Types: General Support.

Financial Summary

Total Giving: $25,615 (fiscal year ending June 30, 2001)
Assets: $150,067 (fiscal 2001)
Gifts Received: $29,000 (fiscal 2000). Note: In fiscal 1998 and 2000, contributions were received from Robert M. Keats.

Typical Recipients

Arts & Humanities: Libraries, Performing Arts, Public Broadcasting
Civic & Public Affairs: Civil Rights, Civic & Public Affairs-General, Women's Affairs
Education: Education-General, Private Education (Precollege), Student Aid
Health: Cancer, Clinics/Medical Centers, Long-Term Care
International: International Development, Missionary/Religious Activities
Religion: Religion-General, Jewish Causes, Religious Organizations, Synagogues/Temples
Social Services: Homes, Recreation & Athletics, Social Services-General, United Funds/United Ways

Application Procedures

Initial Contact: Send a brief letter of inquiry.
Application Requirements: Include a description of organization, amount requested, purpose of funds sought, recently audited financial statement, and proof of tax-exempt status.
Deadlines: None.

Foundation Officials

Gregory A. Keats: director
Karen H. Keats: vice president, secretary
Robert M. Keats: president, treasurer
Dale K. Lipnick: director

Grants Analysis

Disclosure Period: fiscal year ending June 30, 2001
Total Grants: $25,615
Number of Grants: 27
Average Grant: $949
Highest Grant: $6,000
Typical Range: $500 to $2,500

Recent Grants

Note: Grants derived from fiscal 2002 Form 990.
Library-Related

400	B'nai Israel

General

5,400	B'nai Israel, Rockville, MD
2,500	Israel Emergency Fund, West Palm Beach, FL
1,550	Jewish Council for the Aging, Rockville, MD
1,500	Jewish Federation of Palm Beach, Palm Beach, FL
1,500	Jewish Social Services Agency, Rockville, MD
1,250	AIPAC, Washington, DC
1,131	Palm Beach Orthodox Synagogue, Palm Beach, FL
1,000	American Friends of Aish HaTorah, Potomac, MD
1,000	Melvin J. Berman Hebrew Academy, Rockville, MD
800	JINSA, Washington, DC

W. M. KECK FOUNDATION

Giving Contact

Dr. Maria Pellegrini, Program Director
550 South Hope Street, Suite 2500
Los Angeles, CA 90071
Phone: (213)680-3833
Fax: (213)614-0934
E-mail: info@wmkeck.org
Web: http://www.wmkeck.org
Note: Contact person handles requests concerning higher education in science, engineering, and liberal arts.

Alternate Contact

Roxanne Ford, Program Director, medical research.

Description

Founded: 1954
EIN: 956092354
Organization Type: General Purpose Foundation
Giving Locations: CA: southern CA nationally.
Grant Types: Capital, Challenge, General Support, Project, Research.

Donor Information

Founder: The W. M. Keck Foundation was established in 1954 by William M. Keck, founder of Superior Oil Company, one of the nation's largest independent producers of oil and gas. He also established the W. M. Keck Trust for the sole benefit of the foundation. In 1984, the W. M. Keck Foundation and the W. M. Keck Trust benefited from the sale of Superior Oil stock to Mobil Corporation. The sale produced combined assets for the trust and foundation of more than $500 million, and raised its ranking nationwide to twenty-first by asset size in 1991. Mr. Keck also established within his will charitable trusts for the benefit of several colleges and his family church.

Mr. Keck's son, Howard B. Keck, was chairman of the foundation until his death in 1996, and several of Mr. Keck's grandchildren are officers and directors of the foundation. Mr. Keck died in 1964.

Financial Summary

Total Giving: $49,513,360 (2002); $70,624,731 (2001)

Giving Analysis: Giving for 2002 includes: foundation grants to United Way ($1,000)

Assets: $1,012,746,341 (2002); $1,263,938,337 (2001)

Gifts Received: $7,024,808 (1998). Note: Gifts received from W.M. Keck Trust.

Typical Recipients

Arts & Humanities: Arts Associations & Councils, Arts Centers, Arts Institutes, Dance, Libraries, Museums/Galleries, Music, Performing Arts, Public Broadcasting

Civic & Public Affairs: Botanical Gardens/Parks, Civil Rights, Community Foundations, Housing, Inner-City Development, Zoos/Aquariums

Education: Agricultural Education, Arts/Humanities Education, Business Education, Colleges & Universities, Education Funds, Education Reform, Engineering/Technological Education, Faculty Development, Education-General, Gifted & Talented Programs, International Studies, Legal Education, Literacy, Medical Education, Preschool Education, Private Education (Precollege), Science/Mathematics Education, Secondary Education (Private), Social Sciences Education, Student Aid, Vocational & Technical Education

Environment: Forestry, Research, Resource Conservation

Health: Cancer, Children's Health/Hospitals, Clinics/Medical Centers, Geriatric Health, Health Funds, Hospitals, Hospitals (University Affiliated), Medical Rehabilitation, Medical Research, Outpatient Health Care, Speech & Hearing

International: Foreign Educational Institutions

Religion: Churches

Science: Observatories & Planetariums, Science Museums, Scientific Centers & Institutes, Scientific Labs, Scientific Organizations, Scientific Research

Social Services: Child Abuse, Child Welfare, Community Service Organizations, Day Care, Family Services, People with Disabilities, Scouts, Shelters/Homelessness, Social Services-General, Substance Abuse, Youth Organizations

Application Procedures

Initial Contact: Applicants should call or write the foundation for detailed application instructions.

Application Requirements: The application process is divided into two phases. After reviewing the foundation's materials, organizations may submit a letter of inquiry, which must contain a narrative, no longer than three pages, with a description of the project; statement of the amount sought from the foundation; brief statement of the institution's background; cost summary of the project or program for which funds are sought; current, certified, audited financial statement; and copy of the organization's IRS determination letter showing 501(c)(3) and not 509(a) status. If the institution is located within the state of California, or is operating in the state, evidence is required showing that the institution is tax-exempt under Section 23701(d) of the California Revenue and Taxation Code. Both federal and California tax exemptions must be permanent.

Phase II involves submitting a full proposal upon invitation from the foundation. Unsolicited proposals are

never accepted. The foundation will provide all necessary guidelines and materials.

Deadlines: Phase I inquiries are due by May 15 for consideration in the December grant cycle, and by November 15 for consideration in the June grant cycle; full proposals, if invited, are due by September 15 for consideration at the December board meeting, and by March 15 for consideration at the June board meeting.

Review Process: The foundation will reply to initial inquiries within six weeks. Grants are made in June and December.

Restrictions

Funding will not be considered for the following purposes: routine institutional or general operating expenses, general endowments, deficit reduction, or general or administrative overhead expenses; general and federated campaigns, including fundraising events, dinners, or mass mailings; direct aid to individuals; support for conduit organizations, unified funds, or organizations that use grant funds to support other organizations or individuals; sponsorship for conferences or seminars; publication of books or the production of films or theater; public policy research or activities of any kind; organizations or projects to be undertaken outside the United States; or requests that do not fall within the foundation's areas of interest.

Additional Information

Publications: Annual Report; Statement of Policies & Procedures

Foundation Officials

Dr. Lew Allen, Jr.: director, member directors grant program committee B Miami, FL 1925. ED United States Military Academy BS (1946); University of Illinois MS (1952); University of Illinois PhD (1954); University of Illinois PhD (1954). NONPR AFFIL member: President's Foreign Intelligence Advisory Board; member: Sigma Xi; member: Council Foreign Relations; member: National Academy Engineering; member: American Geophysical Union; fellow: American Physical Society. CLUB AFFIL Alfalfa Club; Sunset Club.

Norman Barker, Jr.: director, member audit committee, member grant committee B San Diego, CA 1922. ED University of Chicago BA (1947); University of Chicago MBA (1953). NONPR AFFIL trustee emeritus: Occidental College; life trustee: University Chicago.

Peter Keefe Barker: treasurer, director, member executive committee, member grant B Chicago, IL 1948. ED Colgate University (1966-1968); Claremont McKenna College (1968-1970); University of Chicago MBA (1971). PRIM CORP EMPL partner: Goldman Sachs & Co. CORP AFFIL director: Avery Dennison Inc.; director: Stone Energy. NONPR AFFIL chairman: Claremont McKenna College; director: Performing Arts Center of Los Angeles County.

John E. Bryson: director B New York, NY 1943. ED Stanford University BA (1965); Freie University Berlin (1965-1966); Yale University Law School JD (1969). PRIM CORP EMPL chairman, chief executive officer: Edison International. CORP AFFIL director: The Walt Disney Co.; trustee: Western Asset Funds; director: Pacific America Income Shares Inc.; chairman, chief executive officer: Southern California Edison Co.; chairman: Edison Mission Energy; director: Mission Group Inc.; director: Boeing Co. NONPR AFFIL member: Phi Beta Kappa; member: Stanford University Alumni Association; member: District of Columbia Bar Association; member: Oregon Bar Association; member: California Water Rights Law Review Committee; trustee: Claremont University Center; member: California Bar Association; member: California Pollution Control Financing Authority.

Marsh Alexander Cooper: vice president, director, member grant program committee B Toronto, ON Canada October 08, 1912. ED University of Toronto MSc (1935); University of Toronto BSc (1935); Har-

vard University (1938-1939). PRIM CORP EMPL president, chief executive officer: M.A. Cooper Consultants Inc. NONPR AFFIL director: Keck Graduate Institute; fellow: Society Economic Geologists; member: Engineering Institute Canada; fellow: Geological Association of Canada; member: Association Professional Engineers Ontario; member: Canadian Institute Mining & Metallurgy; member: American Institute Mining Metallurgical Petroleum Engineers.

Howard M. Day: vice president, director, member director grant program committee PRIM CORP EMPL general partner: Crescent Investment Co.

Robert A. Day, Jr.: chairman, president, chief executive officer, director B 1945. ED Claremont McKenna College (1965). PRIM CORP EMPL founder, chairman, chief executive officer: TCW Asset Management Co. CORP AFFIL chairman, chief executive officer, director: Trust Co. West; director: Fisher Scientific International Inc. NONPR AFFIL chairman investments committee, trustee: Claremont McKenna College.

Tammis M. Day: director PRIM CORP EMPL general partner: Crescent Investment Co.

Theodore J. Day: director, member audit committee PRIM CORP EMPL general partner: Crescent Investment Co. CORP AFFIL senior partner: Hale Day Gallagher; director: Sierra Pacific Resources.

Thomas Joseph Deegan-Day: director

Richard N. Foster: director CORP AFFIL chief executive officer: Caxton Health Holdings LLC; director: Trust Company of the West. NONPR AFFIL member, ceo council: New York Academy of Science; advisory board: Whitehead Institute for Biomedical Research; member: Memorial Sloan Kettering Hospital.

Lucinda Fournier: director NONPR AFFIL board of governors: Boys & Girls Club of Central Oregon.

Walter Bland Gerken: vice president, director, chairman audit comm B New York, NY 1922. ED Wesleyan University BA (1948); Syracuse University MPA (1958). NONPR AFFIL trustee emeritus: Occidental College; trustee emeritus: Wesleyan University; member: Maxwell School Citizenship & Public Affairs; director: Nature Conservancy California; director: Executive Service Corps; director: Hoag Memorial Presbyterian Hospital; member: California Commission Higher Education; director: Edison International; member: California Citizens Budget Commission; member: California Commission Campaign Finance Reform. CLUB AFFIL Dairymens Country Club; Pauma Valley Country Club; Balboa Bay Yacht Club; California Club; director: Automobile Club Southern California.

Jonathan D. Jaffrey: vice president, chief admin officer NONPR AFFIL chairman: USC Hillel Foundation.

Howard B. Keck, Jr.: director, member audit & executive committees CORP AFFIL president: Brighton Distributing Co.; trustee emeritus: Keck Graduate Institute.

William M. Keck, II: vice president, director, membership audit & executive committee B 1942. PRIM CORP EMPL president, director: Coalinga Corp. CORP AFFIL president: Coalinga Corp. NONPR AFFIL life trustee: University Southern California.

William M. Keck, III: director

John E. Kolb: director, mem executive committee, chairman legal committee B Argenta, TX 1928. ED University of Texas BBA (1949); University of Texas LLB (1955). NONPR AFFIL development board of directors: University Texas Health Science Center.

Kent Kresa: director B New York, NY 1938. ED Massachusetts Institute of Technology BSAA (1959); Massachusetts Institute of Technology MSAA (1961); Massachusetts Institute of Technology EAA (1966). PRIM CORP EMPL chairman: Northrop Grumman Corp. CORP AFFIL director: MannKind Corp.; director: Trust Co. of the West; director: General Motors Corp.; director: Eclipse Aviation Corp.; director: Fluor Corp.; director: Avery Dennison Corp. NONPR AFFIL member: Society Flight Test Engineers; director: John Tracy Clinic for the Hearing Impaired; member: Navy League; member (visiting committee): Massachusetts Institute Technology; member: Naval Aviation Museum Foundation; member: Los Angeles World Affairs Council; member: DNA New Alternative Working Group; board governors: Los Angeles Music Center; member: Department Aeronautics & Astronautics Corp.; member: Chief Naval Operations Executive Panel Washington; member: Defense Science Board; member: Association U.S. Army; member: American Defense Preparedness Association; fellow: American Institute Aeronautics & Astronautics; member: Aerospace Industries Association. CLUB AFFIL Los Angeles Country Club; National Space Club.

James Paul Lower: director, mem legal comm B Los Angeles, CA 1943. ED Claremont McKenna College BA (1965); Loyola University JD (1968). PRIM CORP EMPL partner: Hanna & Morton. NONPR AFFIL member: California Bar Association; member: Los Angeles City Bar Association; member: American Bar Association. CLUB AFFIL director: California State Club Association; director: National Club Association.

Judith A. Lower: secretary ED Stanford University AB (1963); Loyola Law School JD (1984). NONPR AFFIL member: Los Angeles County Bar Association; trustee, finance committee: Westminster Seminary; member: California State Bar Association; member: Commercial Real Estate Women.

Kerry K. Mott: director

Dr. Stephen J. Ryan: director, member executive committee, member grant committee B Honolulu, HI. ED Johns Hopkins University MD. NONPR AFFIL president: Doheny Eye Institute; director: Pasadena Hospital Association.

Dr. Edward Carroll Stone, Jr.: director, chairman science engineering liberal arts committee B Knoxville, IA 1936. ED Burlington Junior College AA (1956); University of Chicago MS (1959); University of Chicago PhD (1964). NONPR AFFIL member: Space Studies Board, The National Academies; scientist: Voyager; member: National Academy Sciences; member, board governors: National Space Club; member: International Academy Astronautics; fellow: International Astronomical Union; member: California Association Research Astronomy; member: California Council Science & Technology; fellow: American Physics Society; honorary member: Astronomical Society Pacific; fellow: American Institute Aeronautics & Astronautics; member: American Philosophical Society; member: American Astronomical Society; fellow: American Geophysical Union; fellow: American Association Advancement Science; member: American Association Physics Teachers.

Hon. David A. Thomas: director, member legal committee PRIM CORP EMPL chief executive officer, director: Execusoft Inc. NONPR AFFIL honorary member: Children's Hospital Los Angeles.

James R. Ukropina: director, member legal committee B Fresno, CA 1937. ED Stanford University BA (1959); Stanford University MBA (1961); University of Southern California Law School JD (1965). PRIM CORP EMPL partner: O'Melveny & Myers. CORP AFFIL director: Central Natural Resources Inc.; director: Indymac Bancorp Inc. NONPR AFFIL member: Los Angeles County Bar Association; trustee: Stanford University; member: American Bar Association; member: Beta Theta Pi. CLUB AFFIL Annandale Golf Club; California Club.

C. William Verity, Jr.: director emeritus B Middletown, OH January 26, 1917. ED Yale University BA (1939). CORP AFFIL director emeritus: First Financial Bancorp.

Julian Onesime von Kalinowski: director, member legal committee B Saint Louis, MO May 19, 1916. ED Mississippi College BA (1937); University of Virginia JD (1940). PRIM CORP EMPL attorney, advisor partner: Gibson, Dunn & Crutcher. CORP AFFIL chairman emeritus: Dispute Dynamics. NONPR AFFIL member: University Virginia Law School Alumni Association; member: Virginia Bar Association; member: Phi Alpha Delta; member: Phi Kappa Psi; member: California Bar Association; member: Los Angeles County Bar Association; fellow: American College Trial Lawyers; member: American Bar Asso-

ciation; fellow: American Bar Foundation. CLUB AFFIL member: Sky Club; member: La Jolla Beach & Tennis Club; member: Los Angeles Country Club; member: California Club.

Grants Analysis
Disclosure Period: calendar year ending 2002
Total Grants: $49,512,360*
Number of Grants: 230 (approx)
Average Grant: $190,010*
Highest Grant: $6,000,000
Lowest Grant: $25
Typical Range: $50,000 to $500,000
*Note: Giving excludes United Way. Average grant figure excludes highest grant.

Recent Grants
Note: Grants derived from 2002 Form 990.
General
6,000,000 University of Southern California, Los Angeles, CA -- towards support of Neurogenetic initiative at the health sciences campus and to endow the Keck School of medicine
1,500,000 Baylor College of Medicine, Houston, TX -- for Gulf Coast consortium strengthening research in computational & structural biology of 6 Houston universities and training programs at Keck Center
1,500,000 University of Colorado at Boulder, Boulder, CO -- towards establishing a center for ultracold molecular research
1,500,000 University of Minnesota Twin Cities, Minneapolis, MN -- towards purchase of a 9.4 Tesla 65cm MRI for the center for magnetic resonance research
1,350,000 Mayo Foundation, Rochester, MN -- towards construction of a highly sensitive mass spectrometer for protein analysis for the Mayo Proteomics research center
1,250,000 University of California Riverside, Riverside, CA -- towards purchase of proteomics instruments for the Genomics institute
1,200,000 University of California Santa Barbara, Santa Barbara, CA -- towards support of an interdisciplinary ecotechnology initiative
1,200,000 Yale University, New Haven, CT -- towards support of interdisciplinary project in coherence control and noise in quantum information systems
1,197,556 Performing Arts Center of Los Angeles County, Los Angeles, CA -- towards construction of the children's amphitheater at the new Disney concert hall
1,000,000 Duke University, Durham, NC -- towards the WM Keck Center for Neuroncology Genomics

WILLIAM M. KECK, JR. FOUNDATION

Giving Contact
Hilda Avanesian
12575 Beatrice St.
Los Angeles, CA 90066-7001
Phone: (310)578-5900
Fax: (310)578-5900

Description
Founded: 1958
EIN: 136097874
Organization Type: Private Foundation
Giving Locations: CA: southern California area
Grant Types: General Support.

Donor Information
Founder: William M. Keck, Jr.

Financial Summary
Total Giving: $755,000 (2001)
Assets: $14,772,600 (2001)
Gifts Received: $175,000 (2001); $175,000 (2000); $175,000 (1999). Note: In 1995, 1997, 1999, and 2001, contributions were received from the trust for the benefit of W. M. Keck, Jr. Foundation.

Typical Recipients
Arts & Humanities: Arts Centers, Libraries, Music, Theater
Civic & Public Affairs: Economic Policy, Civic & Public Affairs-General, Zoos/Aquariums
Education: Arts/Humanities Education, Colleges & Universities, Education Funds, Education Reform, Education-General, Legal Education, Minority Education, Private Education (Precollege), Public Education (Precollege), School Volunteerism, Secondary Education (Private), Secondary Education (Public)
Environment: Environment-General
Health: Clinics/Medical Centers, Emergency/Ambulance Services, Health-General, Public Health
International: International Development, International Relations
Religion: Churches, Religious Welfare
Social Services: Child Welfare, Counseling, Family Planning, Food/Clothing Distribution, People with Disabilities, Shelters/Homelessness, Substance Abuse, United Funds/United Ways

Application Procedures
Initial Contact: Send a brief letter of inquiry. Include a description of organization.
Deadlines: November 30.

Foundation Officials
Carl D. Hasting: vice president, secretary, treasurer, director

Grants Analysis
Disclosure Period: calendar year ending 2001
Total Grants: $755,000
Number of Grants: 4
Highest Grant: $490,000
Lowest Grant: $15,000

Recent Grants
Note: Grants derived from 2002 Form 990.
General
250,000 Institute of International Economics, Washington, DC -- for economic policy
100,000 Loyola Marymount University, Los Angeles, CA -- for education
50,000 Midnight Mission, Los Angeles, CA -- for Homeless Programs
50,000 Student Health Services, Los Angeles, CA -- for Student Health Programs
50,000 United Negro College Fund, Fairfax, VA -- for education
10,000 Church of the Good Shepherd, Beverly Hills, CA -- for property education choir fund

KEEL FOUNDATION

Giving Contact
Diane Gilchrist, Executive Director
c/o Testa, Hurwitz & Thibeault
125 High Street
Boston, MA 02110-2725
Phone: (617)248-7412

Description
Founded: 1992
EIN: 043166698

Organization Type: Private Foundation
Giving Locations: MA
Grant Types: General Support.

Donor Information
Founder: Established in 1992 by Kenneth H. Olsen.

Financial Summary
Total Giving: $380,000 (2001)
Assets: $5,010,820 (2001)
Gifts Received: $3,500,000 (1992)

Typical Recipients
Arts & Humanities: Libraries, Literary Arts
Civic & Public Affairs: Zoos/Aquariums
Education: Colleges & Universities, Education-General, Minority Education, Preschool Education
Health: Cancer
Social Services: Community Service Organizations, Youth Organizations

Application Procedures
Initial Contact: Application may be requested of the executive director.
Deadlines: None.

Restrictions
Limited to tax-exempt organizations other than religious and political organizations.

Foundation Officials
Kenneth Harry Olsen: trustee B Bridgeport, CT 1926. ED Massachusetts Institute of Technology BSEE (1950); Massachusetts Institute of Technology MS (1952). CORP AFFIL director: Polaroid Corp.; chairman: Advanced Modular Solutions Inc. NONPR AFFIL director: Corporate MIT.
Richard J. Testa: trustee B Marlboro, MA 1939. ED Assumption College AB (1959); Harvard University LLB (1962). PRIM CORP EMPL managing partner: Testa Hurwitz & Thibeault ADD CORP EMPL vice president: Granite State Phoenix Co. NONPR AFFIL member: American Bar Association.
Peter A. Wilson: trustee PRIM CORP EMPL senior vice president: Shawmut Bank Boston. NONPR AFFIL treasurer, director MA division: American Cancer Society.

Grants Analysis
Disclosure Period: calendar year ending 2001
Total Grants: $380,000
Number of Grants: 4
Average Grant: $95,000
Highest Grant: $200,000
Lowest Grant: $30,000
Typical Range: $30,000 to $200,000

Recent Grants
Note: Grants derived from 2001 Form 990.
General

200,000	Assumption College, Worcester, MA
100,000	Connecticut College, New London, CT
50,000	A Different September, Boston, MA
30,000	Teen Ink

KEELER FOUNDATION

Giving Contact
Miner S. Keeler, Jr., Trustee
200 Monroe Ave. NW, Suite 340
Grand Rapids, MI 49503
Phone: (616)774-0422

Alternate Contact
Mary Ann Keeler

Description
Founded: 1985
EIN: 382625402
Organization Type: Private Foundation
Former Name: Miner S. and Mary Ann Keeler Fund.
Giving Locations: MI
Grant Types: General Support.

Donor Information
Founder: Keeler Fund

Financial Summary
Total Giving: $624,550 (fiscal year ending July 31, 2004); $988,073 (fiscal 2001)
Giving Analysis: Giving for fiscal 2004 includes: foundation grants to United Way ($20,000); fiscal 2001: foundation grants to United Way ($20,000)
Assets: $2,314,477 (fiscal 2004); $3,996,447 (fiscal 2001)
Gifts Received: $200,000 (fiscal 2004); $43,799 (fiscal 2001); $47,926 (fiscal 1994). Note: In fiscal 2004, contributions were received from Mary Ann Keeler. In fiscal 2001, contributions were received from Miner S. Keeler II & Mary Ann Keeler. In fiscal 1994, contributions were received from M. S. Keeler, II.

Typical Recipients
Arts & Humanities: Arts Associations & Councils, Historic Preservation, History & Archaeology, Libraries, Museums/Galleries, Music, Opera, Public Broadcasting, Theater, Visual Arts
Civic & Public Affairs: Botanical Gardens/Parks, Chambers of Commerce, Clubs, Community Foundations, Economic Policy, Civic & Public Affairs-General, Law & Justice, Nonprofit Management, Parades/Festivals, Philanthropic Organizations, Urban & Community Affairs, Zoos/Aquariums
Education: Business Education, Colleges & Universities, Environmental Education, Private Education (Precollege), Science/Mathematics Education, Secondary Education (Public)
Environment: Environment-General, Resource Conservation, Wildlife Protection
Health: Eyes/Blindness, Health Organizations, Hospices, Hospitals, Medical Rehabilitation, Single-Disease Health Associations
International: Foreign Arts Organizations, International Affairs
Religion: Churches, Ministries, Religious Welfare
Social Services: Camps, Community Service Organizations, Family Services, Food/Clothing Distribution, Recreation & Athletics, Scouts, Senior Services, United Funds/United Ways, YMCA/YWCA/YMHA/YWHA, Youth Organizations

Application Procedures
Initial Contact: Send a brief letter of inquiry.
Deadlines: None.

Restrictions
Contributions generally are artistic or scholastic in nature.

Foundation Officials
Issac S. Keeler: vice president
Mary Ann Keeler: president

Grants Analysis
Disclosure Period: fiscal year ending July 31, 2004
Total Grants: $604,550*
Number of Grants: 69
Average Grant: $3,972*
Highest Grant: $255,000
Lowest Grant: $100
Typical Range: $1,000 to $5,000
***Note:** Giving excludes United Way. Average grant figure excludes three highest grants ($342,425).

Recent Grants
Note: Grants derived from 2004 Form 990.

Library-Related

255,000	Ryerson Library Foundation, Grand Rapids, MI

General

44,000	Grand Action Foundation, Grand Rapids, MI
43,425	Frederik Meijer Gardens and Sculpture Park, Grand Rapids, MI
27,000	Grand Rapids Symphony, Grand Rapids, MI
25,280	Grand Rapids Art Museum, Grand Rapids, MI
25,000	St. John's Home
25,000	St. Stephens Church
20,000	United Way of West Michigan, Grand Rapids, MI
10,000	Hospice of Michigan, Detroit, MI
10,000	Mel Trotter Ministries, Grand Rapids, MI

KELLER FAMILY FOUNDATION

Giving Contact
Mary K. Zervigon, President
PO Box 13625
New Orleans, LA 70185-3625
Phone: (504)861-3391

Description
Founded: 1949
EIN: 726027426
Organization Type: Private Foundation
Giving Locations: LA: New Orleans
Grant Types: General Support.

Donor Information
Founder: Charles Keller, Jr., Rosa F. Keller

Financial Summary
Gifts Received: $1,156,892 (1999); $140,475 (1996). Note: In 1996 and 1999, contributions were received from the estate of Charles Keller, Jr.

Typical Recipients
Arts & Humanities: Arts Centers, Ballet, Community Arts, Historic Preservation, Libraries, Museums/Galleries, Music, Public Broadcasting
Civic & Public Affairs: Botanical Gardens/Parks, Clubs, Community Foundations, Economic Development, Civic & Public Affairs-General, Housing, Philanthropic Organizations, Public Policy, Urban & Community Affairs, Women's Affairs, Zoos/Aquariums
Education: Afterschool/Enrichment Programs, Arts/Humanities Education, Colleges & Universities, Education Reform, Education-General, Minority Education, Private Education (Precollege), Science/Mathematics Education, Special Education, Student Aid
Environment: Environment-General, Resource Conservation
Health: Geriatric Health, Hospitals
International: International Peace & Security Issues
Religion: Churches, Ministries, Religious Organizations, Religious Welfare, Seminaries
Social Services: Camps, Child Welfare, Community Service Organizations, Food/Clothing Distribution, Recreation & Athletics, Scouts, United Funds/United Ways, YMCA/YWCA/YMHA/YWHA, Youth Organizations

Application Procedures
Initial Contact: Send two copies of a two-page proposal on letter size paper or 2 copies of the Common application form. of the Southeast Louisiana Association of grantmakers.
Application Requirements: Include the legal name

and address of the organization, the name of the contact person including a telephone number, purpose of funds sought, amount requested, total cost of the program or project, other sources of funding, and references. Also attach recently audited fiancial statement, the first two pages of organizations Form 990, and proof of tax-exempt status.

Deadlines: Between January 1 and October 1.

Restrictions

Preference is given to organizations devoted to education, civic affairs, and social services. Grants are not made to individuals.

Additional Information

Publications: Application Guidelines

Foundation Officials

Julie F. Breitmeyer: trustee
Caroline K. Loughlin: treasurer, trustee
Elizabeth M. Loughlin: director
Luis C. Zervigon: secretary, director
Mary K. Zervigon: secretary, trustee

Grants Analysis

Disclosure Period: calendar year ending 2000
Total Grants: $992,743
Number of Grants: 1

Recent Grants

Note: Grants derived from 2001 Form 990.
Library-Related

| 12,500 | Grand Rapids Public Library, Grand Rapids, MI |

General

15,750	United Methodist Community House, Grand Rapids, MI
15,500	St. Cecilia Music Society, Grand Rapids, MI
15,000	Grand Rapids Symphony, Grand Rapids, MI
12,500	Camp Blodgett, Grand Rapids, MI
12,500	YMCA, Grand Rapids, MI
10,250	Gilda's Club, Grand Rapids, MI
10,000	Garrett Evangelical Seminary, Evanston, IL
10,000	Grand Rapids Ballet, Grand Rapids, MI
10,000	In the Image, Grand Rapids, MI
9,700	Delta Strategy, Grand Rapids, MI

KELLER FOUNDATION

Giving Contact

Anne Williamson, Executive Director
5225 33rd St. SE
Grand Rapids, MI 49512
Phone: (616)949-2220
Fax: (616)949-2796

Description

Founded: 1985
EIN: 382331693
Organization Type: Private Foundation
Giving Locations: MI: Grand Rapids

Donor Information

Founder: Cascade Engineering Co., Paragon Die & Engineering Co.

Financial Summary

Total Giving: $217,050 (fiscal year ending June 30, 2002)
Assets: $4,508,920 (fiscal 2002)
Gifts Received: $360,741 (fiscal 1999); $379,698 (fiscal 1997); $397,554 (fiscal 1996). Note: In fiscal 1999, contributions were received from Paragon Die & Engineering ($76,741) and Fred and Bernedine Keller ($284,000). In fiscal 1997, contributions were

received from Paragon Die & Engineering and David Muir. In fiscal 1996, contributions were received from Paragon Die & Engineering.

Typical Recipients

Arts & Humanities: Arts Associations & Councils, Ballet, Libraries, Museums/Galleries, Music, Opera, Performing Arts, Theater
Civic & Public Affairs: Botanical Gardens/Parks, Clubs, Civic & Public Affairs-General, Housing, Urban & Community Affairs, Zoos/Aquariums
Education: Business Education, Colleges & Universities, Community & Junior Colleges, Education-General, Public Education (Precollege), Special Education
Health: AIDS/HIV, Health Organizations, Long-Term Care
Religion: Churches, Ministries, Religious Organizations, Religious Welfare, Seminaries
Social Services: Camps, Child Welfare, Community Service Organizations, Counseling, Family Planning, Food/Clothing Distribution, People with Disabilities, Scouts, Senior Services, Youth Organizations

Application Procedures

Initial Contact: Send a brief letter of inquiry.
Application Requirements: Include a description of organization; a brief description of the program to be funded, including its importance and goals; amount requested and the time period in which funds would be used; a detailed income and expense budget for the proposed program; and proof of tax-exempt status.
Deadlines: None.
Review Process: Grant requests are reviewed quarterly in March, June, September, and December.

Restrictions

Grants are not made to individuals.

Additional Information

Trust(s): Fifth-Third Bank

Foundation Officials

Bernedine J. Keller: vice president
Fred M. Keller: president
Frederick P. Keller: treasurer
Linn Maxwell Keller: director
Lorissa K. Keller: director
Susan Keller: director
David F. Muir: director
Elizabeth M. Muir: director
Kathleen K. Muir: secretary
William M. Muir: director
William W. Muir, Jr.: director B Grand Rapids, MI 1936. ED Bowling Green State University (1958). PRIM CORP EMPL chairman, president, director: Grand Rapids Label Co. CORP AFFIL director: First America Bank West Michigan; director: Paragon Die & Engineering; director: Alpena Power Co.; secretary, treasurer, director: Cascade Sales Associates.
Anne Williamson: executive director

Grants Analysis

Disclosure Period: fiscal year ending June 30, 2002
Total Grants: $217,050
Number of Grants: 65
Average Grant: $3,339
Highest Grant: $15,300
Typical Range: $250 to $10,000

Recent Grants

Note: Grants derived from fiscal 2002 Form 990.
General

15,300	Gilda's Club of Grand Rapids, Grand Rapids, MI
15,000	Grand Rapids Symphony, Grand Rapids, MI
11,250	United Methodist Community House, Grand Rapids, MI
10,000	Garrett-Evangelical Seminary, Evanston, IL

10,000	Grand Rapids Ballet, Grand Rapids, MI
10,000	In the Image, Grand Rapids, MI
10,000	Progressions, Grand Rapids, MI
10,000	Spectrum Health Care Foundation, Grand Rapids, MI
6,050	First United Methodist Church, Grand Rapids, MI
5,100	John Ball Zoo Society, Grand Rapids, MI

EDWARD BANGS KELLEY AND ELZA KELLEY FOUNDATION

Giving Contact

Henry L. Murphy, Jr., President & Director
243 Station Street
PO Box M
Hyannis, MA 02601
Phone: (508)775-3117
Fax: (508)775-3720

Description

Founded: 1954
EIN: 046039660
Organization Type: Private Foundation
Giving Locations: MA: Barnstable County
Grant Types: Capital, Emergency, General Support, Operating Expenses, Project, Research, Scholarship.

Donor Information

Founder: the late Edward Bangs Kelley, the late Elza deHorvath Kelley

Financial Summary

Total Giving: $214,000 (2002); $236,771 (2001). Note: 1997 Giving includes scholarship ($53,375).
Assets: $4,863,002 (2002); $5,376,699 (2001)
Gifts Received: $7,500 (2002); $16,715 (2001); $16,000 (2000). Note: In 2002, contributions were received from Harriett Schluter. In 2001, contributions were received from Harriett Schluter ($5,000) and Ann Renner Trust ($10,615). In 2000, contributions were received from Harriett Schluter ($5,000) and Ann Renner Trust ($10,000). In 1998, contributions were received from Christmas Tree Shops. In 1996, contributions were received from the Carlotta Casey Coyne Trust.

Typical Recipients

Arts & Humanities: Arts Centers, Arts Festivals, Arts Funds, Arts Institutes, Arts Outreach, Community Arts, Arts & Humanities-General, Historic Preservation, History & Archaeology, Libraries, Literary Arts, Museums/Galleries, Music, Performing Arts, Theater
Civic & Public Affairs: Civic & Public Affairs-General, Housing, Legal Aid, Philanthropic Organizations, Professional & Trade Associations, Urban & Community Affairs
Education: Arts/Humanities Education, Colleges & Universities, Community & Junior Colleges, Private Education (Precollege), Secondary Education (Private), Student Aid, Vocational & Technical Education
Environment: Air/Water Quality, Environment-General, Resource Conservation, Wildlife Protection
Health: AIDS/HIV, Alzheimer's Disease, Cancer, Emergency/Ambulance Services, Eyes/Blindness, Hospices, Hospitals, Medical Rehabilitation, Medical Research, Mental Health, Nursing Services, Prenatal Health Issues, Preventive Medicine/Wellness Organizations, Public Health, Research/Studies Institutes, Single-Disease Health Associations
International: International Organizations
Religion: Churches, Religious Welfare
Science: Science Museums, Scientific Centers & Institutes

Social Services: Animal Protection, Big Brothers/Big Sisters, Child Welfare, Community Service Organizations, Day Care, Family Services, Homes, Recreation & Athletics, Senior Services, Substance Abuse, Youth Organizations

Application Procedures

Initial Contact: Send letter requesting application form.
Deadlines: April 30 for scholarships; no deadline for grants.
Review Process: The Executive Committee meets once or twice each quarter to interview grant applications and the Board of DirectorS meets quarterly to act on Executive Committee recommendations.

Additional Information

Publications: Annual Report (includes Application Guidelines)

Foundation Officials

Adm. John F. Aylmer: director
Doreen Bilezikian: director
Jocelyn Bowman: director
Palmer Davenport: director
R. Bruce Hammatt, Jr.: clerk, director
Robert B. Hirschman: director
Townsend Hornor: director
John M. Kayajan: director
Ruth B. Kelley: hon director
Kenneth S. MacAffer, Jr.: director
Stephen W. Malaquias, MD: director
Mary Louise Montgomery: clerk, director
Henry L. Murphy, Jr.: vice president, admin mgr, director
E. Carlton Nickerson: hon director
Frank L. Nickerson: hon director
Joshua A. Nickerson, Jr.: director
Thomas S. Olsen: treasurer, director
Milton L. Penn: president, director
Charles N. Robinson: director
Walter G. Robinson: hon director
Barbara H. Sheaffer: director
Hamilton N. Shepley: director

Grants Analysis

Disclosure Period: calendar year ending 2002
Total Grants: $214,000
Number of Grants: 26
Average Grant: $7,208*
Highest Grant: $25,000
Lowest Grant: $150
Typical Range: $1,000 to $15,000
*Note: Average grant figure excludes two highest grants ($41,000).

Recent Grants

Note: Grants derived from 2001 Form 990.
Library-Related
6,850	Hyannis Public Library Association -- air conditioning of the facility

General
25,000	Hospice Foundation of Cape Cod, Yarmouth Port, MA -- campaign for Hospice House
15,000	Cape Cod Community College Educational Foundation, Inc., Barnstable, MA -- Smart Classroom
12,500	Rehabilitation Hospital of Cape and Islands -- capital gift
12,500	Sandwich Historical Society -- renovation, expansion
12,500	Three Bays Preservation, Inc, Osterville, MA -- Volunteer Monitoring Program
12,000	Cape Cod Symphony Orchestra Association, Inc., Yarmouth Port, MA -- education and access plan
10,000	Dennis Memorial Library -- library expansion
10,000	Latham Centers, Inc., Brewster, MA -- renovation of Latham Schoolhouse
7,500	Cape Cod Museum of Natural History, Brewster, MA -- A Naturalist in the Schools
7,000	Big Brothers and Big Sisters of Cape Cod and the Islands, MA -- health and human services, community development

KELLY FOUNDATION

Giving Contact

Scott G. Nichols, Treasurer
3610 American River Dr., Suite 190
PO Box 255868
Sacramento, CA 95864
Phone: (916)978-4892

Description

Founded: 1989
EIN: 680175739
Organization Type: Private Foundation
Grant Types: General Support, Scholarship.

Financial Summary

Total Giving: $287,500 (fiscal year ending September 30, 2004); $280,000 (fiscal 2001)
Giving Analysis: Giving for fiscal 2004 includes: foundation scholarships ($5,000); foundation fellowships ($45,000); fiscal 2001: foundation scholarships ($7,400); foundation fellowships ($45,000)
Assets: $5,929,820 (fiscal 2004); $5,392,648 (fiscal 2001)
Gifts Received: $2,685,000 (fiscal 2000); $387,488 (fiscal 1996); $525,000 (fiscal 1995). Note: In fiscal 2000, contributions were received from G.G. Kelly, LLC and J.S. Kelly, LLC.

Typical Recipients

Arts & Humanities: Arts Outreach, Ballet, Libraries
Civic & Public Affairs: Civic & Public Affairs-General, Housing, Urban & Community Affairs
Education: Afterschool/Enrichment Programs, Business Education, Education Funds, Education Reform, Education-General, Literacy, Preschool Education, Private Education (Precollege), Public Education (Precollege), School Volunteerism, Science/Mathematics Education, Student Aid
Environment: Wildlife Protection
Health: Alzheimer's Disease, Heart, Hospices, Mental Health, Single-Disease Health Associations
Religion: Bible Study/Translation, Churches, Religious Welfare
Science: Scientific Centers & Institutes
Social Services: Animal Protection, At-Risk Youth, Child Welfare, Community Service Organizations, Crime Prevention, Food/Clothing Distribution, People with Disabilities, Recreation & Athletics, Senior Services, Social Services-General, Special Olympics, Volunteer Services, Youth Organizations

Application Procedures

Initial Contact: Send a a brief letter of inquiry. Request application form.
Application Requirements: Submit application form.; proof of tax-exempt status; budget; recently audited financial statement; and list of Board of Directorss.
Deadlines: October 15; January 15; April 15; July 15 for foundation.

Restrictions

Foundation does not support religious organizations for religious activities, as distinguished from social or educational activities; political or lobbying groups; fraternal organizations, labor, societies or orders, telephone societies, or national fundraising efforts. An organization may only apply once a year. Primarily funds preselected organizations.

Foundation Officials

Jon S. Kelly: director
Scott G. Nichols: treasurer

Grants Analysis

Disclosure Period: fiscal year ending September 30, 2004
Total Grants: $237,500*
Number of Grants: 22
Average Grant: $10,795
Highest Grant: $20,000
Lowest Grant: $2,500
Typical Range: $5,000 to $20,000
*Note: Giving excludes scholarships and fellowship.

Recent Grants

Note: Grants derived from fiscal 2004 Form 990.
General
70,000	Center For Equine Health, Davis, CA -- to be used towards the purchase of an MRI diagnostic unit
45,000	University of California Davis Center for Equine Health, Davis, CA -- fellowship for equine studies
20,000	Ronald McDonald Community Grants Program, Sacramento, CA -- for WIND, Sierra adoption and other youth oriented programs
10,000	California Wildlife Foundation, Oakland, CA -- for Fishy Playscapes project at Nimbus Hatchery
10,000	Community Care Investment Services, Sacramento, CA
10,000	Cystic Fibrosis Foundation, San Diego, CA -- for therapeutics development program
10,000	Fremont Presbyterian Church, Sacramento, CA -- for Fremont family life center project
10,000	Senior Gleaners, Sacramento, CA -- to be used towards their new building loan fund
10,000	Special Olympics of Northern California, Sacramento, CA -- fund for their athletes to compete in the Special Olympics
10,000	Stanford Home, North Highlands, CA -- for family alliance program

WILLIAM T. KEMPER FOUNDATION

Giving Contact

Michael D. Fields, Executive Director
Care of Commerce Bank
922 Walnut St., Suite 200
Kansas City, MO 64106
Phone: (816)234-2112
Fax: (816)234-8690

Description

Founded: 1989
EIN: 436345116
Organization Type: General Purpose Foundation
Giving Locations: MO
Grant Types: Capital, Challenge, Conference/Seminar, General Support, Matching, Multiyear/Continuing Support, Operating Expenses, Project.

Donor Information

Founder: The foundation was established in 1989, following the death of William T. Kemper. Kemper was associated with the former First National Bank of Independence, as their president, chairman, chairman of the executive committee, and director. He was involved in the development and improvement of downtown Kansas City and was active in social service and community organizations like the American Red Cross, Boy Scouts of America, and American

Royal Association. He was an avid art collector and he founded the Charlotte Crosby Kemper Gallery at the Kansas City Art Institute, in memory of his mother. Kemper was associated with Commerce Bank of Kansas City by family ties, and gave the majority of his estate to the William T. Kemper Foundation, with Commerce Bank as co-trustee, at his death.

Financial Summary

Total Giving: $10,634,143 (fiscal year ending October 31, 2003); $11,030,053 (fiscal 2002); $13,267,045 (fiscal 2001)
Giving Analysis: Giving for fiscal 2003 includes: foundation grants to United Way ($9,000); fiscal 2002: foundation grants to United Way ($9,000)
Assets: $242,618,951 (fiscal 2003); $220,109,543 (fiscal 2002); $240,896,887 (fiscal 2001)
Gifts Received: $6,730,120 (fiscal 2002); $89,546 (fiscal 2000); $625,000 (fiscal 1999). Note: Contributions were received from the William T. Kemper Trust.

Typical Recipients

Arts & Humanities: Arts Associations & Councils, Arts Centers, Arts Institutes, Ballet, Historic Preservation, Libraries, Museums/Galleries, Music, Opera, Public Broadcasting, Theater, Visual Arts
Civic & Public Affairs: Botanical Gardens/Parks, Chambers of Commerce, Clubs, Community Foundations, Economic Development, Employment/Job Training, Ethnic Organizations, Civic & Public Affairs-General, Housing, Law & Justice, Municipalities/Towns, Nonprofit Management, Philanthropic Organizations, Rural Affairs, Urban & Community Affairs, Zoos/Aquariums
Education: Agricultural Education, Arts/Humanities Education, Business Education, Colleges & Universities, Education Associations, Education Funds, Elementary Education (Public), Education-General, Medical Education, Private Education (Precollege), Public Education (Precollege), Secondary Education (Public), Vocational & Technical Education
Environment: Environment-General, Resource Conservation
Health: Cancer, Children's Health/Hospitals, Clinics/Medical Centers, Eyes/Blindness, Health Funds, Health Organizations, Hospitals, Hospitals (University Affiliated), Medical Research, Mental Health, Nursing Services, Research/Studies Institutes
International: International Development, International Relations
Religion: Churches, Dioceses, Jewish Causes, Religious Organizations, Religious Welfare
Science: Science Museums, Scientific Research
Social Services: At-Risk Youth, Big Brothers/Big Sisters, Camps, Child Welfare, Community Centers, Community Service Organizations, Domestic Violence, Family Planning, Homes, People with Disabilities, Scouts, Senior Services, Sexual Abuse, Substance Abuse, United Funds/United Ways, YMCA/YWCA/YMHA/YWHA, Youth Organizations

Application Procedures

Initial Contact: All proposals must be submitted in writing; guidelines available on request.
Application Requirements: A complete proposal must include a clear statement of the problem or need, what will be accomplished by a particular date, background of organization and staff, general plan for evaluation, proof of tax-exempt status, amount requested, program budget, recently audited financial statement, and letter from chairman or chief administrative officer indicating endorsement of proposal.
Deadlines: None.
Evaluative Criteria: Preference is given to projects in the Midwest, with particular emphasis on the state of Missouri and surrounding areas.

Restrictions

The foundation does not fund private foundations, individuals, tickets for benefits, exhibits, or other event activities, advertisements, endowment funds, politically partisan purposes, loans or investment funds,

fraternal or veteran organizations, or research unrelated to current priorities. Although the foundation typically makes one-year grants, requests for up to five years of funding for special projects may be considered.

Additional Information

Publications: Application Guidelines; Brochure
Trust(s): Commerce Bank, N.A. trustee

Grants Analysis

Disclosure Period: fiscal year ending October 31, 2003
Total Grants: $10,625,143*
Number of Grants: 386
Average Grant: $18,045*
Highest Grant: $1,000,000
Lowest Grant: $200
Typical Range: $5,000 to $50,000
*Note: Giving excludes United Way. Average grant figure excludes five highest grants ($3,750,000).

Recent Grants

Note: Grants derived from 2003 Form 990.

Library-Related

1,000,000	Downtown Kansas City Public Library Fund, Kansas City, MO
62,500	Harry S. Truman Library Institute, Independence, MO

General

1,000,000	Nelson Gallery Foundation, Kansas City, MO
950,000	Missouri Botanical Garden Board of Trustees, St. Louis, MO
400,000	Archdiocese of St. Louis, St. Louis, MO
400,000	Kansas City Art Institute, Kansas City, MO
250,000	Barstow School, Kansas City, MO
250,000	Kansas City Art Institute, Kansas City, MO
250,000	Vashon Education Compact, St. Louis, MO
200,000	Grace and Holy Trinity Cathedral, Kansas City, MO
187,500	Saint Louis Symphony Orchestra, St. Louis, MO
150,000	Kansas City Symphony, Kansas City, MO

KEMPER NATIONAL INSURANCE COS.

Company Headquarters

Long Grove, IL
Web: http://www.kemperinsurance.com

Company Description

Former Name: Kemper Corp.
Employees: 9,000
SIC(s): 6331 Fire, Marine & Casualty Insurance.

Operating Locations

Kemper National Insurance Companies (CA--Los Angeles, Menlo Park, Pasadena; CO--Denver; IL--Chicago; OH--Cleveland; WI--Milwaukee)

Nonmonetary Support

Type: In-kind Services
Note: Company contributes printing and creative support in the way of writing and design.

James S. Kemper Foundation

Giving Contact

Dr. Thomas Hellie, Executive Director
20 N. Wacker Dr., Suite 1823
Chicago, IL 60606
Phone: (312)332-3114
E-mail: thellie@kemperinsurance.com

Description

EIN: 366007812
Organization Type: Corporate Foundation
Giving Locations: IL: Chicago including metropolitan area nationally.
Grant Types: Fellowship, General Support, Multiyear/Continuing Support, Professorship, Research, Scholarship, Seed Money.

Financial Summary

Total Giving: $1,059,962 (fiscal year ending July 31, 2004); $1,336,112 (fiscal 2003); $1,509,605 (fiscal 2002). Note: Contributes through corporate direct giving program and foundation.
Assets: $37,758,585 (fiscal 2004); $38,419,776 (fiscal 2003); $34,804,504 (fiscal 2002)
Gifts Received: $300 (fiscal 2004); $6,161 (fiscal 2003); $10,376 (fiscal 2002). Note: Contributions were received from James S. Kemper, Jr.

Typical Recipients

Arts & Humanities: Arts Festivals, Arts Funds, Arts Outreach, Ballet, Community Arts, Dance, Libraries, Museums/Galleries, Music, Opera, Public Broadcasting, Theater
Civic & Public Affairs: Business/Free Enterprise, Community Foundations, Civic & Public Affairs-General, Parades/Festivals, Philanthropic Organizations, Public Policy
Education: Afterschool/Enrichment Programs, Arts/Humanities Education, Business Education, Colleges & Universities, Community & Junior Colleges, Continuing Education, Economic Education, Education Associations, Education Funds, Engineering/Technological Education, Faculty Development, Education-General, International Studies, Legal Education, Medical Education, Minority Education, Science/Mathematics Education, Student Aid, Vocational & Technical Education
Environment: Wildlife Protection
Health: Emergency/Ambulance Services, Hospitals, Medical Rehabilitation, Medical Research, Single-Disease Health Associations
International: International Affairs
Science: Science Museums
Social Services: People with Disabilities, Recreation & Athletics, Shelters/Homelessness, Substance Abuse, YMCA/YWCA/YMHA/YWHA, Youth Organizations

Application Procedures

Initial Contact: Send a brief letter.
Application Requirements: Include a concise description of project, realistic time-frame, mission statement, detailed project budget, statement of how future funding needs will be met, amount needed to complete project, amount requested, information about personnel involved, and method of evaluation.
Deadlines: Applications must be received by November 1.
Decision Notification: Decisions are made annually, in late February or early March.
Notes: The foundation identifies colleges and universities and invites them to participate in the Kemper Scholars program. If they choose to do so, the institution conducts a selection process which leads to the identification of individuals from the freshman class who are the institutional nominees for the program. The foundation then selects one of the nominees as a Kemper Scholar.

Restrictions

Does not support dinners or special events, fraternal organizations, good-will advertising, member agencies of united funds, political or lobbying groups, or religious organizations for sectarian purposes. The foundation rarely supports multi-year grants.

Additional Information

Publications: Foundation Annual Report

Corporate Officials

General John T. Chain, Jr.: president PRIM CORP EMPL president: Quarterdeck Equity Partners Inc. CORP AFFIL director: RJR Nabisco Inc.; director: Thomas Group Inc.; director: RJR Nabisco Holdings Corp.; director: Nabisco Inc.; director: Northrop Grumman Corp.; director: American Motorists Insurance Co.

Foundation Officials

General John T. Chain, Jr.: trustee (see above)

J. Reed Coleman: trustee CORP AFFIL director: Regal-Beloit Corp.

John K. Conway: secretary

Robert A. Daniel: assistant treasurer

James R. Edgar: trustee

Michael A. Finelli, Jr.: treasurer

Peter Bannerman Hamilton: trustee B Philadelphia, PA 1946. ED Princeton University AB (1968); Yale University JD (1971). PRIM CORP EMPL vice president, president: Brunswick Corp. CORP AFFIL director: Fidelity Life Association; director: Kemper National Insurance Companies; director: American Motorists Insurance Co.

Thomas L. Hellie: executive director NONPR AFFIL trustee: Lenoir-Rhyne College.

Robert S. Karmel: trustee B Chicago, IL 1937. ED Radcliffe College BA; New York University LLB (1962). PRIM CORP EMPL partner: Kelly, Drye & Warren LLP PRIM NONPR EMPL professor: Brooklyn Law School. CORP AFFIL director: Mallinckrodt Inc. NONPR AFFIL member: Financial Womens Association; trustee: Practicing Law Institute; member: Association Bar New York City; co-director: Center Study International Business Law; fellow: American Bar Foundation; member: American Law Institute; member: American Bar Association.

George Ralph Lewis: trustee B Burgess, VA 1941. ED Hampton University BS (1963); Iona College MBA (1966). CORP AFFIL director: Ceridian Corp.

Katharine Culbert Lyall: trustee B Lancaster, PA 1941. ED Cornell University BA (1963); New York University MBA (1965); Cornell University PhD (1969). PRIM NONPR EMPL president: University of Wisconsin System. CORP AFFIL director: Kemper National Insurance Companies; director: Marshall & Ilsley Corp.; director: Heartland Development Corp.; director: Interstate Energy Corp. NONPR AFFIL member: Phi Beta Kappa; professor: University Wisconsin Madison; member board: Carnegie Foundation Advancement Teaching; member: American Economic Association; member: Association American Universities.

David B. Mathis: trustee, chairman B Atlanta, GA 1938. ED Lake Forest College BA (1960). PRIM CORP EMPL chairman, chief executive officer: Kemper Insurance Companies. CORP AFFIL director: TMC Global Inc.; chairman: Lumbermens Mutual Casualty Co.; chairman, chief executive officer: Kemper Corp.; director: Kemper Income Capital Prese; director: Fidelity Life Association; director: IMC Global Inc.; chief executive officer: American Manufacturer Mutual Insurance Co.; chairman: American Motorists Insurance Co. NONPR AFFIL director: Evanston Hospital Corp.

John E. Porter: trustee

Grants Analysis

Disclosure Period: fiscal year ending July 31, 2004
Total Grants: $678,376*
Number of Grants: 39

Average Grant: $17,394
Highest Grant: $100,000
Lowest Grant: $900
Typical Range: $10,000 to $25,000
*Note: Giving excludes scholarship and fellowships.

Recent Grants

Note: Grants derived from 2003 Form 990.
General

100,000	Boys and Girls Club of America
100,000	Gerald L. Maatman Fellowship Worcester Polytechnic Institute, Worcester, MA
100,000	Rehabilitation Institute, Chicago, IL
75,000	Chicago Symphony Orchestra, Chicago, IL
75,000	Lyric Opera, Chicago, IL
65,000	Association of Governing Boards, Washington, DC
54,960	Washington University, St. Louis, MO
50,000	La Salle University, Philadelphia, PA
50,000	Rehabilitation Institute of Chicago, Chicago, IL
48,000	Manchester College

HARRIS AND ELIZA KEMPNER FUND

Giving Contact

Elaine Perachio, Executive Director
2201 Market Street, Suite 601
Galveston, TX 77550-1529
Phone: (409)762-1603
Fax: (409)762-5435
E-mail: information@kempnerfund.org
Web: http://kempnerfund.org

Description

Founded: 1946
EIN: 746042458
Organization Type: Family Foundation
Giving Locations: TX: Galveston county
Grant Types: Award, Capital, Challenge, Conference/Seminar, Endowment, Fellowship, General Support, Matching, Multiyear/Continuing Support, Operating Expenses, Project, Research, Seed Money.
Note: Also provides family matching gifts.

Donor Information

Founder: The Kempner family established the "Galveston Fund" in 1946 with an initial donation of $38,500. In 1950 the name was changed to the Harris and Eliza Kempner Fund to honor the family's first American generation and founder of the family's business interests.

Harris Kempner, a Jewish refugee from Poland, served in the Confederate Army and shortly after the war he started a general mercantile business in Galveston, TX. The following generations developed extensive interests in banking, farming, ranching, cotton, and sugar refining. In the early 1900s, the family bought a bank, which today is known as the United States National Bank in Galveston. The bank is a subsidiary of Cullen/Frost Bankers located in San Antonio, TX. Harris L. Kempner, Jr., and Isaac Herbert Kempner III, both serve on the boards of directors of Cullen/Frost and the Imperial Holly Corporation, which contributed $75,000 to the foundation in 1990. Isaac H. Kempner III, also serves as the chairman of the Imperial Holly Corporation.

Financial Summary

Total Giving: $1,500,000 (2002); $1,000,000 (2001). Note: 1995 Giving includes matching gifts and scholarship ($246,765).
Assets: $35,590,000 (2002); $40,000,000 (2001)
Gifts Received: $84,947 (2000); $500 (1999);

$50,000 (1998). Note: Foundation receives gifts from Daniel K. Thorne.

Typical Recipients

Arts & Humanities: Arts Associations & Councils, Arts Centers, Historic Preservation, History & Archaeology, Libraries, Literary Arts, Museums/Galleries, Music, Opera, Public Broadcasting, Theater, Visual Arts

Civic & Public Affairs: Botanical Gardens/Parks, Chambers of Commerce, Civil Rights, Community Foundations, Economic Development, Employment/Job Training, Civic & Public Affairs-General, Law & Justice, Municipalities/Towns, Public Policy, Urban & Community Affairs, Zoos/Aquariums

Education: Colleges & Universities, Elementary Education (Public), Engineering/Technological Education, Environmental Education, Faculty Development, International Exchange, Legal Education, Literacy, Medical Education, Preschool Education, Private Education (Precollege), Public Education (Precollege), Religious Education, Science/Mathematics Education, Student Aid, Vocational & Technical Education

Environment: Environment-General, Resource Conservation

Health: Adolescent Health Issues, AIDS/HIV, Alzheimer's Disease, Cancer, Children's Health/Hospitals, Clinics/Medical Centers, Emergency/Ambulance Services, Health Organizations, Heart, Hospices, Mental Health, Nursing Services, Prenatal Health Issues, Research/Studies Institutes, Single-Disease Health Associations

International: Health Care/Hospitals, International Development, International Environmental Issues, International Relations, International Relief Efforts

Religion: Churches, Jewish Causes, Religious Welfare, Synagogues/Temples

Social Services: Big Brothers/Big Sisters, Child Abuse, Child Welfare, Community Centers, Community Service Organizations, Crime Prevention, Domestic Violence, Emergency Relief, Family Planning, People with Disabilities, Recreation & Athletics, Scouts, Special Olympics, Substance Abuse, United Funds/United Ways, Youth Organizations

Application Procedures

Initial Contact: Applicants should send a grant proposal to the fund.

Application Requirements: Include a cover letter signed by the executive directory and the board chair or president that includes a brief a description of organization of need and amount requested. Project or program information should include name and telephone number of contact person, a description of organization, timeline budget (income and expenses), list of sources and amounts solicited and/or pleged, future funding plans if program is new and continuing, and plans for evaluation. Organizational information should include statement of purpose and brief history; list of current officers and board members; operating budget (revenue and expenses) for year for which funds are sought; financial statements, audit, and/or 990 for most recent fiscal year; proof of tax-exempt status; and statement on organization letterhead that there has been no change in IRS status since issuance of ruling letter.

Deadlines: March 15, June 15, October 15, for primary grant programs; December 1 for grants regarding the environment and population control; March 31 for student loan program.

Review Process: Proposals are reviewed three times a year at trustee meetings in April, July, and December. Requests of a national/international nature related to the areas of education, environment, population control, and Third World development will be reviewed at the April meeting.

Restrictions

The Kempner Fund does not participate in fundraising benefits, direct-mail solicitations, or make grants to individuals, or organizations not based in the United States.

Additional Information

Publications: Biennial Report (includes Application Guidelines)

Foundation Officials

John Thornton "Jack" Currie: vice chairman, trustee B Houston, TX 1928. ED University of Texas BA (1949); University of Texas BBA (1950). CORP AFFIL director: Triflex Fund; director: American Indemnity Financial Corp.; director: Stewart & Stevenson Services Inc.; director: America National Growth Fund; director: America National Income Fund. NONPR AFFIL member devel board: University Texas Medicine Branch; member chancellors council: University Texas System. CLUB AFFIL Krewe Momus Galveston Club; Galveston Artillery Club; Houston Country Club.

Hetta Ellen Towler Kempner: trustee

Isaac Herbert Kempner, III: trustee B Houston, TX 1932. ED Stanford University BA (1955); Stanford University MBA (1959). PRIM CORP EMPL chairman, director: Imperial Holly Corp. CORP AFFIL president: Foster Farms Inc. NONPR AFFIL trustee: Methodist Health Care System; trustee: U.S. Cane Sugar Refiners Association; trustee: H. Kempner Trust Association; trustee, treasurer: Contemporary Art Museum; chairman, director: Federal Reserve Bank Dallas-Houston. CLUB AFFIL Coronado Club; Bayou Club; Camden Ale & Quail Club.

Rabbi James Lee Kessler: trustee B Houston, TX 1945. ED University of Texas BA (1967); Hebrew Union College MA (1972); Hebrew Union College (1988). PRIM NONPR EMPL rabbi: Temple B'nai Israel. NONPR AFFIL member: Texas Jewish Historical Society; member rev board: University Texas Medicine Board; member: Siebel Loan Fund; member: Kallah Texas Rabbis; chairman: Lipson Scholarship Fund; member: Central Conference American Rabbis; advisor: Handbook Texas; member: B'nai B'rith. CLUB AFFIL member: Masons Club.

Robert L. K. Lynch: chairman CORP AFFIL director: Imperial Holly Corp.

Elaine Perachio: executive director

Barbara Weston Sasser: secretary B 1953. ED University of Texas, Galveston Medical School PhD. PRIM CORP EMPL manager: XVI Ltd. Co. CORP AFFIL secretary: ABA/Zack Inc.; manager: EMZ Ltd.

Lyda Ann Quinn Thomas: trustee

Leonora Kempner Thompson: chairman emeritus

Peter K. Thompson, MD: treasurer

Daniel Kempner Thorne: trustee PRIM CORP EMPL president: Star Lake Cattle Co. ADD CORP EMPL president: Star Lake Properties. CORP AFFIL director: Imperial Holly Corp.; director: Imperial Sugar Co.

Grants Analysis

Disclosure Period: calendar year ending 2000
Total Grants: $1,064,214*
Number of Grants: 182
Average Grant: $5,847
Highest Grant: $37,500
Typical Range: $2,500 to $10,000
*Note: Giving excludes United Way, scholarships, fellowship, matching gifts.

Recent Grants

Note: Grants derived from 1999 Form 990.
General

100,000	Galveston College Foundation, Galveston, TX -- Universal Access Program
75,000	University of Texas Medical Branch, Galveston, TX -- Jeane B. Kempner Fellowship Program
75,000	University of Texas Medical Branch, Galveston, TX -- Jeane B. Kempner Fellowship Program
60,000	United Way of Galveston, Galveston, TX -- operations
58,000	City of Galveston, Galveston, TX -- water truck purchase

37,500	Grand 1894 Opera House, Galveston, TX -- operations support
30,000	Galveston College Foundation, Galveston, TX -- Harris L. Kempner Award for Universal Access Endowment
30,000	United Way of Galveston, Galveston, TX -- operations
30,000	United Way of Galveston, Galveston, TX -- operations
30,000	United Way of Galveston, Galveston, TX -- operations

HENRY P. KENDALL FOUNDATION

Giving Contact

Theodore M. Smith, Executive Director
176 Federal Street
Boston, MA 02110
Phone: (617)951-2525
Fax: (617)443-1977
E-mail: jpatrick@kendall.org
Web: http://www.kendall.org

Description

Founded: 1957
EIN: 046029103
Organization Type: Family Foundation
Giving Locations: AK; New England and the Pacific Northwest; Canada: maritime provinces; western Canada.
Grant Types: General Support.

Donor Information

Founder: The foundation was established in 1957. Donors to the foundation are members of the Henry P. Kendall family.

Financial Summary

Total Giving: $2,236,813 (2003); $2,462,321 (2002); $3,322,395 (2001)
Assets: $78,373,487 (2003); $70,530,845 (2002); $79,448,455 (2001)
Gifts Received: $27,790 (2003); $42,575 (2002); $5,890,000 (2000). Note: In 2002 and 2003, contributions were received from Henry W. Kendall Trust.

Typical Recipients

Arts & Humanities: Art History, Arts & Humanities-General, Historic Preservation, History & Archaeology, Libraries, Museums/Galleries, Public Broadcasting
Civic & Public Affairs: Botanical Gardens/Parks, Community Foundations, Economic Development, Civic & Public Affairs-General, Public Policy, Urban & Community Affairs, Zoos/Aquariums
Education: Colleges & Universities, Environmental Education, Journalism/Media Education, Legal Education, Medical Education, Private Education (Precollege), Secondary Education (Public)
Environment: Air/Water Quality, Energy, Forestry, Environment-General, Protection, Research, Resource Conservation, Watershed, Wildlife Protection
International: Foreign Educational Institutions, Health Care/Hospitals, International Affairs, International Environmental Issues, International Peace & Security Issues, International Relations, Trade
Science: Science Museums, Scientific Centers & Institutes, Scientific Labs, Scientific Organizations
Social Services: Food/Clothing Distribution

Application Procedures

Initial Contact: Brief proposals of no more than two pages should be sent to the foundation.
Application Requirements: Proposals should include amount and purpose of funds sought in the first paragraph; background of the issue to be addressed,

the strategy being employed, the timetable, and the budget; organization's mission statement; organization's total annual budget; other sources of financing sought; staff personnel and a list of board members, including the curriculum vitae of the chief executive; and a copy of the organization's IRS determination letter of tax-exempt status.
Deadlines: February1; May 1; October 1.
Review Process: Decisions are made in three cycles, requests postmarked by February 1 made in March; by May 1 made in June; by October 1 in November. Requests are usually acknowledged within two to three weeks.

Restrictions

The foundation does not fund the following: waste clean-ups, toxics or air/water pollution prevention or pollution monitoring initiatives, land trusts, or species-specific preservation efforts; endowments or capital fund campaigns; building construction/operation; capital equipment; routine institutional operating costs; conference participation/travel unrelated to current foundation institutional grants; debt reduction; basic research; or individual fellowships. E-mail requests and audio/video tapes are not acceptable.

Additional Information

The foundation admits to a preference for concise, well-organized, jargon-free letters printed on high post-consumer content recycled paper. Grants are usually given for a two-year period.
Publications: Annual Report; Guidelines

Foundation Officials

John P. Kendall: trustee PRIM CORP EMPL officer: Faneuil Hall Associates Inc. CORP AFFIL director: Colgate-Palmolive Co.
Theodore M. Smith: executive director

Grants Analysis

Disclosure Period: calendar year ending 2003
Total Grants: $2,236,813
Number of Grants: 57
Average Grant: $34,997*
Highest Grant: $277,000
Lowest Grant: $5,000
Typical Range: $10,000 to $75,000
*Note: Average grant figure excludes highest grant.

Recent Grants

Note: Grants derived from 2002 Form 990.

General

455,000	Kendall Whaling Museum, New Bedford, MA
115,000	Canadian Parks & Wilderness Society, ON Canada
115,000	Tufts University, Somerville, MA
91,446	Henry P. Kendall Foundation, Boston, MA
80,000	University of Calgary Miistakis Institute, Calgary, AB Canada
77,500	Nature Conservancy Northeastern Landscape, Arlington, VA
75,000	Canadian Parks & Wilderness Society-BC Chapter, Vancouver, BC Canada
75,000	St. Francis Xavier University-Centre for Community-based Management, NS Canada
75,000	Sierra Club of Canada Foundation, ON Canada
75,000	Yellowstone to Yukon Conservation Initiative, Canmore, AB Canada

ETHEL AND W. GEORGE KENNEDY FAMILY FOUNDATION

Giving Contact
Kathleen Kennedy-Olsen, President
1550 Madruga Ave., Suite 225
Coral Gables, FL 33146
Phone: (305)666-6226
Fax: (605)666-2441
E-mail: admin@kennedyfamilyfdn.org
Web: http://www.kennedyfamilyfdn.org

Description
Founded: 1968
EIN: 596204880
Organization Type: Private Foundation
Giving Locations: FL: Miami
Grant Types: Capital, Endowment, General Support, Matching, Multiyear/Continuing Support.

Donor Information
Founder: the late W. George Kennedy

Financial Summary
Total Giving: $1,192,667 (2001)
Assets: $26,462,585 (2001)

Typical Recipients
Arts & Humanities: Arts Associations & Councils, Arts Centers, Arts Festivals, Ballet, Arts & Humanities-General, History & Archaeology, Libraries, Museums/Galleries, Opera, Performing Arts, Theater
Civic & Public Affairs: Botanical Gardens/Parks, Chambers of Commerce, Community Foundations, Civic & Public Affairs-General, Nonprofit Management, Safety, Zoos/Aquariums
Education: Arts/Humanities Education, Colleges & Universities, Community & Junior Colleges, Education Funds, Education-General, Medical Education, Private Education (Precollege), Public Education (Precollege), Secondary Education (Public), Student Aid
Environment: Wildlife Protection
Health: Cancer, Children's Health/Hospitals, Emergency/Ambulance Services, Hospices, Hospitals, Long-Term Care, Medical Research, Preventive Medicine/Wellness Organizations, Single-Disease Health Associations, Speech & Hearing, Transplant Networks/Donor Banks
International: International Organizations
Religion: Churches, Religion-General, Jewish Causes, Missionary Activities (Domestic), Religious Welfare, Synagogues/Temples
Science: Science Museums, Scientific Centers & Institutes
Social Services: Child Welfare, Community Service Organizations, Emergency Relief, Food/Clothing Distribution, People with Disabilities, Recreation & Athletics, Sexual Abuse, Social Services-General, Special Olympics, Youth Organizations

Application Procedures
Initial Contact: Send a brief letter of inquiry outlining program for which funding is sought.
Application Requirements: For a full proposal, include 8 copies of proposal on 3 hole punches letter-sized paper. Proposals not to exceed five pages in length. Include a description of organization, amount requested, purpose of funds sought, recently audited financial statement, list of Board of Directors, project and organization budgets, plan for sustaining project after the grant funding expires, and proof of tax-exempt status.
Deadlines: February 1 for March meeting and September 15 for October meeting.
Review Process: Board meets to consider requests in March and October.
Notes: Video material not to exceed ten minutes in length. Provide self-addressed stamped manila envelope for the return of supporting documents or visual aids.

Restrictions

Foundation Officials
Alvena Allen: director
Kendal Kennedy Dobkin: director
Karen Kennedy Herterich: director
Kimberly Kennedy: director
Wayne G. Kennedy: president, director
William Kennedy: director
Kathleen P. Kennedy Olsen: director
Forrest I. Mulcahey: director
Martin Nash: director
Guy Rizzo: director

Grants Analysis
Disclosure Period: calendar year ending 2001
Total Grants: $1,192,667
Number of Grants: 87
Average Grant: $9,255*
Highest Grant: $194,000
Lowest Grant: $250
Typical Range: $1,000 to $20,000
*Note: Average grant figure excludes three highest grants ($415,250).

Recent Grants
Note: Grants derived from 2001 Form 990.
General

194,000	Miami City Ballet, Miami, FL
110,650	Bay Point Schools, Miami, FL
110,600	American Red Cross, Idaho Falls, ID
70,000	University of Miami Pediatric Mobile Clinic, Miami, FL
48,000	House of Hope, Anaheim, CA
43,240	PACE Center for Girls, Orlando, FL
30,775	Blowing Rock Stage Company, Blowing Rock, NC
30,000	Neat Stuff, Miami, FL
30,000	Temple Emanu EL, Palm Beach, FL
25,500	Shake-A-Leg, Miami, FL

ETHEL KENNEDY FOUNDATION

Giving Contact
Ethel K. Marran, President & Treasurer
271 Johns Island Dr.
Vero Beach, FL 32963
Phone: (561)231-2971

Description
Founded: 1986
EIN: 112768682
Organization Type: Private Foundation
Giving Locations: NY
Grant Types: General Support.

Typical Recipients
Arts & Humanities: Arts Centers, Arts & Humanities-General, History & Archaeology, Libraries, Museums/Galleries, Music, Public Broadcasting, Theater
Civic & Public Affairs: Economic Development, Employment/Job Training, Ethnic Organizations, Civic & Public Affairs-General, Housing, Legal Aid, Urban & Community Affairs, Women's Affairs
Education: Business Education, Colleges & Universities, Education Funds, Faculty Development, Medical Education, Minority Education, Private Education (Precollege), Public Education (Precollege), School Volunteerism, Science/Mathematics Education, Student Aid
Environment: Air/Water Quality, Environmental, Resource Conservation
Health: Alzheimer's Disease, Arthritis, Cancer, Clinics/Medical Centers, Health Organizations, Hospices, Hospitals, Medical Research, Single-Disease Health Associations
International: Health Care/Hospitals, Human Rights, International Relief Efforts
Religion: Religious Organizations, Religious Welfare
Social Services: Animal Protection, At-Risk Youth, Camps, Child Welfare, Community Centers, Community Service Organizations, Domestic Violence, Family Planning, Family Services, Food/Clothing Distribution, Homes, People with Disabilities, Recreation & Athletics, Senior Services, Shelters/Homelessness, Social Services-General, Special Olympics, United Funds/United Ways, Youth Organizations

Application Procedures
Initial Contact: The foundation requests applications be made in writing. Include proof of tax-exempt status, purpose of funds sought, a description of organization, and activities in general.
Deadlines: None.

Restrictions
Does not support individuals.

Foundation Officials
Elizabeth Marran: vice president
Ethel K. Marran: president, treasurer
Laura Marran: secretary

Grants Analysis
Disclosure Period: calendar year ending 2000
Total Grants: $538,972
Number of Grants: 46
Average Grant: $5,441*
Highest Grant: $105,000
Typical Range: $1,000 to $10,000
*Note: Average grant figure excludes three highest grants ($305,000).

Recent Grants
Note: Grants derived from 2001 Form 990.
General

150,000	Habitat of Vero Beach, Vero Beach, CA
100,000	Hanne Fenishil Center for Child Development
50,000	Coalition for the Homeless, New York, NY
25,000	Buckingham Browne and Nichols School, Cambridge, MA
20,000	Brigham and Women's Hospital, Boston, MA -- Department of Urology
20,000	Buckingham Browne and Nichols School, Cambridge, MA
20,000	Dollars for Scholars
20,000	Exeter Academy
20,000	Hamilton College Scholarship, Clinton, NY
20,000	Hampton Day School, Bridgehampton, NY

JOSEPH P. KENNEDY, JR. FOUNDATION

Giving Contact
Susan Swenson, Executive Director
1133 19th Street, Northwest, 12th Fl.
Washington, DC 20036
Phone: (202)393-1250
Fax: (202)824-0351
E-mail: info@jpkf.org
Web: http://www.jpkf.org

Description
Founded: 1946
EIN: 136083407

Organization Type: Family Foundation
Giving Locations: nationally.
Grant Types: General Support, Project, Seed Money.

Donor Information

Founder: Joseph P. Kennedy, Jr., the oldest son of Joseph P. Kennedy and Rose Kennedy, was born in Massachusetts on July 28, 1915. He graduated from Choate School in Connecticut and attended the London School of Economics for one year before entering Harvard Law School in 1934. Joseph P. Kennedy Jr. left Harvard before his final year to volunteer as a Navy flyer. In May 1942, he was awarded his wings, and in 1943, was sent to England with the first naval squadron to fly B-24s with the British Naval Command. He died on August 12, 1944.
The Joseph P. Kennedy, Jr. Foundation was established in 1946 by Ambassador and Mrs. Joseph P. Kennedy, in honor of their son.

Financial Summary

Total Giving: $1,568,029 (fiscal year ending June 30, 2003); $2,524,492 (fiscal 2002); $2,379,854 (fiscal 2001)
Assets: $15,536,630 (fiscal 2003); $17,780,104 (fiscal 2002); $24,135,253 (fiscal 2001)
Gifts Received: $912,004 (fiscal 2000); $34,439 (fiscal 1998); $1,720 (fiscal 1997). Note: In fiscal 2000, contributions were received from Simon Grimault.

Typical Recipients

Arts & Humanities: Arts Institutes, Arts Outreach, Ballet, Community Arts, Film & Video, Arts & Humanities-General, History & Archaeology, Libraries, Performing Arts
Civic & Public Affairs: Botanical Gardens/Parks, Civil Rights, Economic Development, Employment/Job Training, Civic & Public Affairs-General, Housing, Law & Justice, Legal Aid, Nonprofit Management, Philanthropic Organizations, Public Policy, Women's Affairs
Education: Colleges & Universities, Education Reform, Faculty Development, Education-General, Health & Physical Education, Medical Education, Private Education (Precollege), Public Education (Precollege), Social Sciences Education, Special Education, Student Aid, Vocational & Technical Education
Environment: Environment-General, Resource Conservation, Watershed
Health: AIDS/HIV, Children's Health/Hospitals, Clinics/Medical Centers, Health Policy/Cost Containment, Hospitals, Medical Rehabilitation, Medical Research, Medical Training, Mental Health, Prenatal Health Issues, Preventive Medicine/Wellness Organizations, Single-Disease Health Associations
International: Foreign Educational Institutions, International-General, Health Care/Hospitals, Human Rights, International Organizations
Religion: Churches, Missionary Activities (Domestic), Religious Welfare
Social Services: Child Welfare, Community Service Organizations, Counseling, Day Care, Family Planning, People with Disabilities, Recreation & Athletics, Shelters/Homelessness, Special Olympics, Substance Abuse, Youth Organizations

Application Procedures

Initial Contact: The foundation solicits its own grantees and also accepts applications from others. Applicants should direct letters of interest to Jill Sosse, Grants Manager.
Application Requirements: The proposal should include a five-page description of the project including description of problem, relevance of the proposal to the subject population, its goal, identify collaboration with other systems, and a statement of how the project will advance the present state of knowledge. Other items to include are the following: plan of work, including timelines, work methodology, and the identification of target population; training activities for various audiences (e.g., people with mental retarda-

tion, their families, caregivers, etc.); dissemination of results; description of organization and management, including qualifications of the personnel involved (full curriculum vitae of each person affiliated with the proposal are to be filed) and explanation of how the program builds on existing services; references including any literature discussed in the proposals and future funding; and budget information.
Deadlines: Short concept letters of intent can be accepted at any time. Proposals are accepted from July 1 through December 1.
Review Process: All applicants undergo initial screening; those suitable for further consideration are requested to prepare a more detailed proposal based on consultation with foundation staff. Scientific applications are reviewed by the Scientific Advisory Board and other applications are reviewed by experts in an area related to the grant proposal. Recommendations for funding are presented to the board of trustees, which makes the final funding decisions. Final decisions are made by July 1.

Restrictions

The foundation only works in the area of mental retardation and is only interested in innovative projects that are not supported elsewhere by public funds. The foundation does not fund capital costs or equipment for projects, nor does it pay for ongoing support or operations of existing programs.

Additional Information

The foundation also provides technical assistance and consultation services, including policy consultation, to assist in writing local and governmental policies for health and education programs for adolescents; operational consultation, to help schools and agencies access and develop supportive, caring environments for students, clients, and staff; financial consultation, to aid in fund raising, grant writing, and management; and program evaluation, to provide expert assistance in assessing community needs and program effectiveness.
Responding to the pressing need for change in the area of physical education for persons with mental retardation, the foundation created the Special Olympics program as a model for greatly expanded sports and recreation opportunities in schools, communities, and institutions throughout the world. Sanctioned by the United States Olympic Committee, recognized by the International Olympic Committee, and endorsed by most major organizations of special educators, recreation specialists, coaches, and athletes, Special Olympics International is the largest year around sports organization in the world for children and adults with mental retardation.
Publications: Grant Policy Statement; Grant Guidelines; Brochures

Foundation Officials

Caroline Kennedy: trustee
Hon. Edward Moore Kennedy: president, trustee B Boston, MA 1932. ED Harvard University AB (1956); The Hague Academy of International Law (1958); University of Virginia LLB (1959). PRIM NONPR EMPL senator: U.S. Senate. NONPR AFFIL member: NAACP; member: Technology Assessment Board; member: Martin Luther King Junior Federal Holiday Commission; trustee: Massachusetts General Hospital; trustee: John F. Kennedy Library; trustee: Robert F. Kennedy Memorial Foundation; trustee: John F. Kennedy Center Performing Arts; member: Commission Bicentennial U.S. Constitution; member: Congressional Friends Ireland; trustee emeritus: Boston Symphony Orchestra; trustee: Childrens Hospital Medical Center; member: Biomedical Ethics Board; trustee: Boston College; member: Arms Control Observer Group.
Rory Kennedy: trustee
Patricia Kennedy Lawford: trustee
Eunice Kennedy Shriver: executive vice president, trustee B Brookline, MA 1921. ED Manhattanville College of Sacred Heart; Stanford University BS

(1943). NONPR AFFIL founder: Special Olympics International.
William Kennedy Smith: trustee
Susan Swenson: executive director

Grants Analysis

Disclosure Period: fiscal year ending June 30, 2003
Total Grants: $1,568,029
Number of Grants: 38
Average Grant: $28,658*
Highest Grant: $200,000
Lowest Grant: $5,000
Typical Range: $10,000 to $50,000
***Note:** Average grant figures excludes three highest grants ($565,000).

Recent Grants

Note: Grants derived from fiscal 2003 Form 990.
Library-Related
200,000	John Fitzgerald Kennedy Library, Boston, MA

General
190,000	Park Foundation, Washington, DC -- donation
175,000	Community of Care, Washington, DC -- contribution for operating expenses
70,000	Arizona Center for Disability Law, Phoenix, AZ -- fellowship for Julianne carter
70,000	Association of University Centers on Disabilities, Silver Spring, MD -- fellowship for Aaron Bishop
70,000	University of Massachusetts, Boston, MA -- fellowship for Evelyn Milorin
69,750	Arc of the United States, Silver Spring, MD -- fellowship for Daniel Mont
50,000	Wisconsin Initiatives in Sustainable Housing, Madison, WI -- creation of housing trust
48,000	Oregon Health and Science University, Portland, OR -- voter education training voters for mental retardation
47,400	Many Voices Inc, Brooklyn, NY -- plight of the world's mentally disabled photo reportage
46,000	Westchester Institute for Human Development, Valhalla, NY -- consulting services from Dr. Ansley Bacon

KENRIDGE FUND

Giving Contact

Paulette F. Kitko, Secretary & Treasurer
c/o Advisory Services
1422 Euclid Ave., Rm. 1010
Cleveland, OH 44115-2078
Phone: (216)363-6485

Description

Founded: 1989
EIN: 341616683
Organization Type: Private Foundation
Giving Locations: AL; FL; GA; IL; KY; ME; MA; NJ; OH; VA
Grant Types: Emergency, General Support, Operating Expenses, Research.

Donor Information

Founder: Established in 1989 by Fanny H. Bolton and Claire H. B. Jonklass.

Financial Summary

Total Giving: $164,000 (2001). Note: 1997 Giving includes United Way ($5,000).
Giving Analysis: Giving for 2001 includes: foundation grants to United Way ($3,000); foundation scholarships ($9,000).
Assets: $3,741,622 (2001)
Gifts Received: $40 (1996)

Typical Recipients

Arts & Humanities: Arts Centers, History & Archaeology, Museums/Galleries, Music
Civic & Public Affairs: Civic & Public Affairs-General
Education: Colleges & Universities, Faculty Development, Medical Education, Minority Education, Private Education (Precollege), Public Education (Precollege), Science/Mathematics Education, Special Education, Student Aid
Environment: Forestry, Environment-General, Research, Resource Conservation
Health: Cancer, Emergency/Ambulance Services, Hospitals, Medical Rehabilitation, Medical Research, Nursing Services, Prenatal Health Issues, Public Health, Respiratory, Single-Disease Health Associations
International: Foreign Arts Organizations, International Environmental Issues
Religion: Churches, Religious Welfare
Science: Science-General, Scientific Research
Social Services: Child Welfare, Emergency Relief, Recreation & Athletics, Scouts, Shelters/Homelessness, Substance Abuse, United Funds/United Ways, YMCA/YWCA/YMHA/YWHA, Youth Organizations

Application Procedures

Initial Contact: The foundation requests applications be made in writing.
Application Requirements: Include proof of tax-exempt status.
Deadlines: None.

Restrictions

Grants are not made to individuals.

Foundation Officials

Kenneth G. Hochman: vice president
Jackie A. Horning: assistant secretary
Anthony Jonklaas: trustee
Clair Hanna B. Jonklaas: president, trustee
Paulette F. Kitko: secretary, treasurer

Grants Analysis

Disclosure Period: calendar year ending 2001
Total Grants: $152,000*
Number of Grants: 31
Average Grant: $3,935*
Highest Grant: $30,000
Lowest Grant: $1,000
Typical Range: $1,000 to $10,000
*Note: Giving excludes United Way, scholarships. Average grant figure excludes highest grant.

Recent Grants

Note: Grants derived from 2001 Form 990.
General

30,000	Friends of the Bermuda Aquarium, Ltd, Wharton, NJ -- Bermuda Biodiversity Project
25,000	YMCA of Thomasville, Thomasville, GA -- Remington Park Project
6,000	Halcyon Home, Thomasville, GA -- child abuse counseling
5,000	American Red Cross - Thomas County Chapter -- operations
5,000	Auburn University Foundation, Auburn University, AL -- Scott Richey Research Center - sports medicine one day program
5,000	Christian Children's Fund, Richmond, VA -- United States aid
5,000	Cradle Society, Evanston, IL -- operations
5,000	Dana Hall School, Wellesley, MA -- operations
5,000	Hanna Perkins School, Cleveland, OH
5,000	Hearts Adaptive Riding Program, Santa Barbara, CA -- current operations

KENT-LUCAS FOUNDATION

Giving Contact

Elizabeth K. Van Alen, President, Treasurer & Trustee
101 Springer Bldg.
3411 Silverside Rd.
Wilmington, DE 19810
Phone: (302)478-4383

Description

Founded: 1968
EIN: 237010084
Organization Type: Private Foundation
Giving Locations: FL; ME; PA: Philadelphia including metropolitan area
Grant Types: Capital, General Support, Multiyear/Continuing Support, Operating Expenses.

Donor Information

Founder: Atwater Kent Foundation

Typical Recipients

Arts & Humanities: Arts Associations & Councils, Historic Preservation, History & Archaeology, Libraries, Museums/Galleries, Public Broadcasting, Theater
Civic & Public Affairs: Botanical Gardens/Parks, Clubs, Employment/Job Training, Civic & Public Affairs-General, Municipalities/Towns, Philanthropic Organizations, Public Policy, Safety, Urban & Community Affairs
Education: Arts/Humanities Education, Colleges & Universities, Education-General, International Exchange, International Studies, Medical Education, Private Education (Precollege), Religious Education, Special Education, Student Aid
Environment: Environment-General, Resource Conservation
Health: Cancer, Children's Health/Hospitals, Clinics/Medical Centers, Emergency/Ambulance Services, Eyes/Blindness, Heart, Hospices, Hospitals, Medical Research, Nursing Services
International: Foreign Educational Institutions, International Environmental Issues, International Organizations, International Relief Efforts
Religion: Churches, Religion-General, Religious Organizations, Religious Welfare
Science: Scientific Centers & Institutes, Scientific Labs
Social Services: Animal Protection, Child Welfare, Community Service Organizations, Crime Prevention, Family Services, Food/Clothing Distribution, Recreation & Athletics, Shelters/Homelessness, Youth Organizations

Application Procedures

Initial Contact: Send a full proposal. Describe the general activities of the organization and the specific need for and purpose of the requested grant. Include the complete legal name and address of the organization, proof of tax-exempt status, most recent annual report and certified financial statements, and a detailed project budget.
Application Requirements: Describe the general activities of the organization and the specific need for and purpose of the requested grant. Include the complete legal name and address of the organziation, proof of tax-exempt status, most recent annual report and certified financial statements, and a detailed project budget.
Deadlines: None.

Restrictions

Does not support individuals.

Additional Information

Publications: Application Procedures

Foundation Officials

Cassandra V. A. Ludington: trustee
Elizabeth K. Van Alen: president, treasurer, trustee
James L. Van Alen, II: trustee
William L. Van Alen: vice president, trustee
James R. Weaver: secretary
Stella R. Williams: assistant secretary

Grants Analysis

Disclosure Period: calendar year ending 2000
Total Grants: $87,125
Number of Grants: 33
Average Grant: $1,773*
Highest Grant: $30,400
Typical Range: $500 to $5,000
*Note: Average grant excludes highest grant.

Recent Grants

Note: Grants derived from 2001 Form 990.
General

30,450	Children's Hospital of Philadelphia, Philadelphia, PA
19,550	University of Pennsylvania, Philadelphia, PA
15,000	Bascom Palmer Eye Institute, Miami, FL
5,400	Willistown Conservation Trust, Newtown Square, PA
5,000	Lost Tree Charitable Foundation, North Palm Beach, FL
3,500	Fellowship Christians University, West Tisbury, CT
1,250	Dream Chasers, Inc.
1,250	O'Gorman Garden Center, New York, NY
1,000	Barry Telecommunications, West Palm Beach, FL
1,000	Community Television Foundation of South Florida, Miami, FL

KERN FOUNDATION TRUST

Giving Contact

Dale Rudy, Contact
Northern Trust Co.
50 S. LsSalle St., L-5
Chicago, IL 60675
Phone: (312)630-6000
Fax: (312)444-4122
E-mail: dgr@ntrs.com
Note: Dale Rudy can also be reached at (312)444-3796.

Description

Founded: 1959
EIN: 366107250
Organization Type: Specialized/Single Purpose Foundation
Giving Locations: CA; IL
Grant Types: Fellowship, General Support, Project, Scholarship.
Note: The foundation reports that scholarships and fellowships are made to qualified persons interested in utilizing the theosophical world view and paid through their universities/colleges.

Donor Information

Founder: Established in 1959 by the late Herbert A. Kern, who felt that the basic theosophical concepts such as the essential unity of all in manifestation was a critical starting point for changing peoples' attitudes about race, culture, responsibility towards one another and the environment. It became operational in 1966 and is not affiliated with or related to any other charitable trust or foundation.

Financial Summary

Total Giving: $1,454,894 (2001)
Assets: $11,383,185 (2001)

Typical Recipients

Arts & Humanities: Libraries, Museums/Galleries
Education: Arts/Humanities Education, Colleges & Universities, Continuing Education, Private Education (Precollege), Public Education (Precollege)
Religion: Religious Organizations, Religious Welfare
Social Services: Child Welfare, People with Disabilities

Application Procedures

Initial Contact: The foundation has no formal grant application procedure or application form.
Deadlines: None.
Review Process: Upon receipt of a proposal which includes sufficient detail to make a case for support, the proposal is routed to a qualified professional to evaluate it.

Restrictions

The foundation reports that it limits grantmaking to religious foundations chartered to advance the cause of theosophy. Grants are not made to individuals.

Additional Information

The Northern Trust Company of Chicago operates as a corporate trustee.

The foundation reports that it provides all types of services to its principal theosophical organizations receiving grants. It gives only financial support to universities and colleges to which a grant has been made to assist a graduate student or faculty member.
Publications: Program Policy Statement

Foundation Officials

John C. Kern: trustee
Dale Rudy: corporate trustee rep

Grants Analysis

Disclosure Period: calendar year ending 2001
Total Grants: $1,454,894
Number of Grants: 5
Highest Grant: $1,253,184
Lowest Grant: $4,710
Typical Range: $5,000 to $75,000

Recent Grants

Note: Grants derived from 2001 Form 990.
General

1,253,184	Theosophical Society in America, Wheaton, IL
120,000	Krotona Institute of Theosophy, Ojai, CA
72,000	Happy Valley School, Ojai, CA
5,000	Theosophical Book Gift Institute, Wheaton, IL
4,710	Shimer College, Waukegan, IL

KERR FOUNDATION, INC.

Giving Contact

Mrs. Robert S. Kerr, Jr., Chairman & President
12501 North May Avenue
Oklahoma City, OK 73120
Phone: (405)749-7991
Fax: (405)749-2877
E-mail: ccastle@thekerrfoundation.org
Web: http://www.thekerrfoundation.org

Description

Founded: 1963
EIN: 731256122
Organization Type: General Purpose Foundation
Giving Locations: AR; CO; DC; KS; MO; NM; OK; TX

Grant Types: Capital, Challenge, General Support, Project, Research, Seed Money.

Donor Information

Founder: The foundation was established in 1963, with the late Grayce B. Kerr Flynn as donor.

Financial Summary

Total Giving: $789,627 (2002); $768,860 (2001)
Assets: $23,514,831 (2002); $27,870,754 (2001)
Gifts Received: $1,344 (1995); $6,480 (1994); $6,565 (1993)

Typical Recipients

Arts & Humanities: Arts Associations & Councils, Arts Centers, Arts Festivals, Arts Funds, Arts Institutes, Arts Outreach, Ballet, Dance, Ethnic & Folk Arts, Film & Video, Arts &'Humanities-General, Historic Preservation, History & Archaeology, Libraries, Museums/Galleries, Music, Opera, Performing Arts, Public Broadcasting, Theater
Civic & Public Affairs: Botanical Gardens/Parks, Community Foundations, Economic Development, Economic Policy, Employment/Job Training, Civic & Public Affairs-General, Housing, Inner-City Development, Native American Affairs, Nonprofit Management, Parades/Festivals, Philanthropic Organizations, Professional & Trade Associations, Public Policy, Safety, Urban & Community Affairs, Women's Affairs, Zoos/Aquariums
Education: Agricultural Education, Arts/Humanities Education, Business Education, Business-School Partnerships, Colleges & Universities, Community & Junior Colleges, Education Funds, Engineering/Technological Education, Environmental Education, Faculty Development, Education-General, Health & Physical Education, Legal Education, Literacy, Medical Education, Private Education (Precollege), Public Education (Precollege), School Volunteerism, Science/Mathematics Education, Secondary Education (Private), Secondary Education (Public), Social Sciences Education, Special Education, Student Aid
Environment: Energy, Forestry, Environment-General, Protection, Resource Conservation, Wildlife Protection
Health: AIDS/HIV, Cancer, Children's Health/Hospitals, Clinics/Medical Centers, Emergency/Ambulance Services, Health-General, Geriatric Health, Health Funds, Health Organizations, Hospitals (University Affiliated), Medical Research, Mental Health, Prenatal Health Issues, Public Health, Research/Studies Institutes, Single-Disease Health Associations, Transplant Networks/Donor Banks
International: Foreign Arts Organizations, Foreign Educational Institutions, Health Care/Hospitals, International Affairs, International Development, International Environmental Issues
Religion: Churches, Ministries, Religious Welfare
Science: Science Museums, Scientific Organizations
Social Services: At-Risk Youth, Child Abuse, Child Welfare, Community Service Organizations, Counseling, Delinquency & Criminal Rehabilitation, Domestic Violence, Emergency Relief, Family Planning, Family Services, Food/Clothing Distribution, People with Disabilities, Scouts, Senior Services, Shelters/Homelessness, Social Services-General, Substance Abuse, Veterans, Volunteer Services, YMCA/YWCA/YMHA/YWHA, Youth Organizations

Application Procedures

Initial Contact: Applicants should request the foundation's application forms.
Application Requirements: Requests for funding should include a cover letter with summary request, completed institutional profile and proposal summary forms, copy of the IRS determination letter of tax-exempt status, a proposal, and other documentation appropriate to the request. The foundation asks that applicants send an original and two duplicates.
Deadlines: None, but the foundation should receive applications at least forty-five days prior to quarterly trustee meetings to allow time for review for consideration at the meetings. Meetings are generally held in the third month of the quarter. Applicants should contact the foundation for specific dates.
Review Process: Upon acceptance of a proposal, the applicant will be informed as to when action by the trustees may be anticipated. Grant awards will be made contingent upon signing a grant contract which includes provision for project evaluation. Foundation trustees and/or staff often conduct site visits to organizations being considered for a grant.
Notes: Favorable consideration of a proposal will normally be in the form of a challenge grant.

Restrictions

The foundation does not make grants to individuals or provide operating dollars.

Additional Information

Publications: Annual Report; Guidelines; Application Form

Foundation Officials

Royce Mitchell Hammons: treasurer B Hallettsville, TX 1945. ED University of Oklahoma BBA (1969); Southern Methodist University (1976); Stanford University (1990). PRIM CORP EMPL president, chairman, chief executive officer: UMB Oklahoma Bank. CORP AFFIL director: UMB Financial Corp. NONPR AFFIL trustee: Oklahoma City University; trustee: University Oklahoma Associate Council; member: Oklahoma Bankers Association; trustee: Arthritis Foundation; financial committee: City Nichols Hills. CLUB AFFIL Whitehall Club; Oklahoma City Golf & Country Club; Galveston Country Club; Oklahoma City Dinner Club.
Cody T. Kerr: trustee
Mrs. Robert Samuel Kerr, Jr.: president, chairman, trustee B Ada, OK 1926. ED University of Oklahoma (1951); University of Oklahoma (1955). PRIM CORP EMPL attorney, chairman: Kerr, Irvine & Rhodes. CORP AFFIL director: Kerr-McGee Corp.; director: Bank Oklahoma Tulsa. NONPR AFFIL member: American Bar Association.
Sharon Kerr: assistant secretary, trustee
Steven Kerr: assistant secretary, trustee
Ray Klein: trustee
Laura Kerr Ogle: trustee
Elmer Boyd Staats: trustee B Richfield, KS June 06, 1914. ED McPherson College AB (1935); University of Kansas MA (1936); University of Minnesota PhD (1939). PRIM NONPR EMPL chairman: Harry S Truman Scholarship Foundation. CORP AFFIL director: Computer Data System; emeritus member: Metro Life Insurance Co. NONPR AFFIL member visiting committee: University California Los Angeles Graduate School Management; member: University Chicago Comm Public Policy Studies; member: Pi Sigma Alpha; member: National Academy Public Administration; member: Phi Beta Kappa; chairman: Federal Accounting Standards Advisory Board; director: George C. Marshall Foundation; member: Association Government Accountants; member: Beta Gamma Sigma; member: American Management Association; member: American Society Public Administration; member: Alpha Kappa Psi; member, director: American Academy Political & Social Science. CLUB AFFIL Chevy Chase Club; Cosmos Club.

Grants Analysis

Disclosure Period: calendar year ending 2002
Total Grants: $789,627
Number of Grants: 36
Average Grant: $18,989*
Highest Grant: $125,000
Lowest Grant: $1,000
Typical Range: $5,000 to $25,000
*Note: Average grant figure excludes highest grant.

Recent Grants

Note: Grants derived from 2002 Form 990.

Library-Related

15,000   Cartwright Memorial Library Inc., Oklahoma City, OK -- towards helping a new facility to replace the current facility that is now far beyond economic repair

General

250,000   University of Oklahoma Foundation, Norman, OK -- towards building a library in the college of law and provide a new auditorium and computer laboratory

195,000   Lyric Theater of Oklahoma City, Oklahoma City, OK -- towards renovation of the 16th street plaza Theater project

125,000   Franklin & Eleanor Roosevelt Institute, Hyde Park, NY -- towards construction and landscaping of the Senator Robert Kerr Memorial garden

70,000   On the Chisholm Trait Association, Street Duncan, OK -- towards construction of a children's gallery in the expanded heritage center

50,000   National Academy of Public Administration, Oklahoma City, OK -- towards making a state of the art conference facility that will be named after Elmer B Staats the founding member

50,000   National Cowboy and Western Heritage Museum, Oklahoma City, OK -- towards establishment and endowment for preserving and conserving the Native American collection

50,000   Oklahoma Area United Methodist Church, Oklahoma City, OK -- in helping construction furnishing and equipping of a new conference office building

50,000   Oklahoma Arts Institute, Oklahoma City, OK -- for OAI operating budget during the return to Quartz mountain for scholarships & portable flooring for dance space for visual arts and music equipment

50,000   Oklahoma Centennial Commemoration Fund Inc., Oklahoma City, OK -- towards completion of the construction of the dome on Oklahoma's state capitol

50,000   Oklahoma State Senate Historical Preservation Fund Inc., Oklahoma City, OK -- towards painting by artist Wayne Cooper which will be displayed in the Oklahoma House of Representatives

GRAYCE B. KERR FUND

Giving Contact

Sheryl V. Kerr, President & Secretary
117 Bay Street
Easton, MD 21601
Phone: (410)822-6652
Fax: (410)822-4546
E-mail: gbkf@bluecrab.org

Description

Founded: 1986
EIN: 731256124
Organization Type: Family Foundation
Grant Types: Award, Capital, Challenge, Employee Matching Gifts, Endowment, General Support, Matching, Multiyear/Continuing Support, Project, Research.

Donor Information

Founder: Established in 1986 by Breene M. Kerr and the late Grayce B. Kerr Flynn. Grayce Flynn was the widow of Robert S. Kerr, a former governor of Oklahoma and a former U.S. Senator. The Grayce B. Kerr Fund is one of the four successor foundations of the Kerr Foundation managed by Mrs. Kerr's children after her death in 1965.

Financial Summary

Total Giving: $1,147,750 (2002); $1,075,032 (2001)
Assets: $30,485,176 (2002); $34,159,355 (2001)
Gifts Received: $2,767 (1998); $1,344 (1995); $6,480 (1994)

Typical Recipients

Arts & Humanities: Arts Associations & Councils, Arts Institutes, Arts Outreach, Community Arts, Historic Preservation, History & Archaeology, Libraries, Museums/Galleries, Music, Performing Arts, Theater

Civic & Public Affairs: Asian American Affairs, Botanical Gardens/Parks, Community Foundations, Employment/Job Training, Ethnic Organizations, Civic & Public Affairs-General, Hispanic Affairs, Housing, Law & Justice, Municipalities/Towns, Nonprofit Management, Professional & Trade Associations, Public Policy, Safety, Urban & Community Affairs

Education: Arts/Humanities Education, Business-School Partnerships, Colleges & Universities, Education Funds, Elementary Education (Public), Engineering/Technological Education, Faculty Development, Education-General, Gifted & Talented Programs, International Studies, Leadership Training, Legal Education, Literacy, Medical Education, Private Education (Precollege), Public Education (Precollege), Science/Mathematics Education, Secondary Education (Private), Social Sciences Education

Environment: Air/Water Quality, Forestry, Environment-General, Resource Conservation, Watershed, Wildlife Protection

Health: Cancer, Children's Health/Hospitals, Hospices, Hospitals, Medical Research, Mental Health, Public Health

International: Human Rights

Religion: Churches, Ministries, Religious Organizations

Science: Science Museums, Scientific Centers & Institutes, Scientific Research

Social Services: At-Risk Youth, Camps, Community Service Organizations, Counseling, Crime Prevention, Day Care, Family Planning, Family Services, Recreation & Athletics, United Funds/United Ways, Youth Organizations

Application Procedures

Initial Contact: Applicants should submit a letter of inquiry.

Restrictions

Proposals which commit the fund to continued support of operations generally are not approved. The fund does not award grants to individuals.

Additional Information

Publications: Annual Report; Application Guidelines; Application Form

Foundation Officials

Breene M. Kerr: chairman, treasurer, life trustee B 1929. ED Massachusetts Institute of Technology MA (1951). CORP AFFIL director: Chesapeake Energy Corp.; vice chairman: Seven Seas Petroleum Inc.
Sheryl V. Kerr: president, secretary B 1953. PRIM CORP EMPL executive vice president: Kerr Consolidated Inc.
Marcy S. Kerr Yuknat: trustee
James F. Moffitt: vice president, trustee
Collin Wesley Scarborough: vice chairman
John R. Valliant: trustee

Grants Analysis

Disclosure Period: calendar year ending 2002
Total Grants: $1,147,750
Number of Grants: 13
Average Grant: $34,775*
Highest Grant: $500,000
Lowest Grant: $100
Typical Range: $10,000 to $50,000

*Note: Average grant figure excludes three highest grants ($800,000).

Recent Grants

Note: Grants derived from 2002 Form 990.

General

250,000   Chesapeake Bay Maritime Museum, St. Michaels, MD

200,000   Dana Farber Cancer Institute, Boston, MA

100,000   Chesapeake Bay Foundation, Annapolis, MD

100,000   Johns Hopkins Medicine, Baltimore, MD

60,000   Evergreen Cove, Easton, MD

55,000   Phillips Academy, Andover, MA

50,000   Bay Hundred Community Pool, St. Michaels, MD

50,000   Country School, Easton, MD

50,000   National Wildlife Art Museum, Jackson Hole, WY

50,000   Salisbury State University, Salisbury, MD

KETROW FOUNDATION

Giving Contact

Thomas H. Graber, Jr., Trustee
507 S. Broadway
Greenville, OH 45331
Phone: (937)548-1157

Description

Founded: 1991
EIN: 341667300
Organization Type: Private Foundation
Giving Locations: OH: Darke County
Grant Types: General Support, Scholarship.

Financial Summary

Total Giving: $18,000 (fiscal year ending September 30, 2004); $18,000 (fiscal 2001)
Assets: $449,884 (fiscal 2004); $458,602 (fiscal 2001)

Typical Recipients

Arts & Humanities: Arts Centers, Arts Outreach, Historic Preservation, History & Archaeology, Libraries, Music

Civic & Public Affairs: Botanical Gardens/Parks, Employment/Job Training, Civic & Public Affairs-General, Housing, Parades/Festivals

Education: Arts/Humanities Education, Elementary Education (Private), Elementary Education (Public), Medical Education, Private Education (Precollege)

Health: Cancer, Hospices, Hospitals, Mental Health

Religion: Religious Organizations, Religious Welfare

Social Services: Community Service Organizations, Emergency Relief, Recreation & Athletics, Senior Services, Shelters/Homelessness, Substance Abuse, Volunteer Services, YMCA/YWCA/YMHA/YWHA, Youth Organizations

Application Procedures

Initial Contact: Send a brief letter of inquiry.
Application Requirements: Include purpose of funds sought and charitable purpose of organization.
Deadlines: None.

Restrictions

Restricted to Darke County, OH.

Foundation Officials

Thomas H. Graber, II: trustee

Grants Analysis

Disclosure Period: fiscal year ending September 30, 2004
Total Grants: $18,000
Number of Grants: 12

Average Grant: $1,500
Highest Grant: $2,500
Lowest Grant: $500
Typical Range: $500 to $2,500

Recent Grants

Note: Grants derived from fiscal 2004 Form 990.
Library-Related

2,100	New Madison Public Library, New Madison, OH -- for replacing the children's computer

General

2,500	Cancer Association of Darke County, Greenville, OH -- for purchasing patient education materials
2,500	Darke County Center for the Arts, Greenville, OH -- to support family theatre series and arts in education programming
2,500	Wayne Hospital, Greenville, OH -- for the purchase of a sports art elliptical machine
2,000	Boys and Girls Club of Greenville, Greenville, OH -- to support serving youth additional hours of the week
1,500	State of the Heart Home Health and Hospice, Greenville, OH -- towards the expenses for the camp bearable
1,000	Community Action Partnership, Greenville, OH -- to replace and update equipment
1,000	Darke County Youth for Christ, Greenville, OH -- for purchasing sound system
1,000	REACH, Greenville, OH -- to assist the organization
900	Retired and Senior Volunteer Program, Greenville, OH -- to purchase instruments for advance science and math and supplemental materials to be used by the tutors

KETTERING FUND

Giving Contact

Judy Thompson, Executive Director
1560 Kettering Tower
Dayton, OH 45423
Phone: (937)228-1021
Fax: (937)449-7239
E-mail: ketteringfund@aol.com

Description

Founded: 1958
EIN: 316027115
Organization Type: General Purpose Foundation
Giving Locations: OH: especially Dayton
Grant Types: General Support.

Donor Information

Founder: Established in 1958 by Charles F. Kettering who died in the same year. Mr. Kettering was a principal stockholder in General Motors Corporation, which acquired his automotive engineering laboratory. Mr. Kettering's inventions include the modern automotive ignition system and the electric cash register. He worked with National Cash Register Company and General Motors, and organized Dayton Engineering Laboratories Company (Delco), Dayton Metal Products Company, and the Dayton-Wright Airplane Company. He was president of the Thomas A. Edison Foundation; co-founder of Moraine Park School; a trustee of Ohio State University, Antioch College, College of Wooster (OH), Miami University (OH), and Southern Research Institute; and a director of the Memorial Sloan-Kettering Institute of Cancer Research.

Financial Summary

Total Giving: $4,252,500 (fiscal year ending June 30, 2004)

Assets: $87,544,304 (fiscal 2004)
Gifts Received: $8,492 (fiscal 2000)

Typical Recipients

Arts & Humanities: Arts Associations & Councils, Arts Centers, Arts Festivals, Arts Funds, Arts Institutes, Ballet, Community Arts, Dance, Historic Preservation, History & Archaeology, Libraries, Museums/ Galleries, Music, Performing Arts, Public Broadcasting, Theater, Visual Arts
Civic & Public Affairs: African American Affairs, Botanical Gardens/Parks, Clubs, Community Foundations, Economic Development, Employment/Job Training, Civic & Public Affairs-General, Hispanic Affairs, Housing, Law & Justice, Municipalities/Towns, Nonprofit Management, Parades/Festivals, Professional & Trade Associations, Rural Affairs, Urban & Community Affairs, Women's Affairs, Zoos/ Aquariums
Education: Business Education, Colleges & Universities, Education Associations, Education Funds, Education Reform, Engineering/Technological Education, Faculty Development, Education-General, International Studies, Journalism/Media Education, Literacy, Medical Education, Private Education (Precollege), Student Aid
Environment: Environment-General, Resource Conservation
Health: Arthritis, Children's Health/Hospitals, Clinics/ Medical Centers, Emergency/Ambulance Services, Health Organizations, Hospices, Hospitals, Long-Term Care, Nursing Services, Public Health, Transplant Networks/Donor Banks
International: Health Care/Hospitals, International Affairs, International Development
Religion: Churches, Religious Welfare, Synagogues/Temples
Science: Science Museums
Social Services: Animal Protection, At-Risk Youth, Big Brothers/Big Sisters, Child Welfare, Community Centers, Community Service Organizations, Crime Prevention, Family Planning, Family Services, Food/ Clothing Distribution, Homes, People with Disabilities, Scouts, Senior Services, YMCA/YWCA/YMHA/ YWHA, Youth Organizations

Application Procedures

Initial Contact: Proposals should be sent to the fund. No specific application form is required.
Application Requirements: The proposal should include the amount requested, reason for request, a brief description of project or program, description and dates of previous Kettering Fund support, names of other foundations which have given support, project and organization budget, brief statement of the organization's long-range plans, a copy of IRS tax-exempt letter, and an audited financial statement.
Deadlines: Applications should be submitted by March 15 and September 15.
Review Process: The Distribution Committee meets in May and November.

Restrictions

The fund does not support individuals, partisan political causes or candidates, elementary or secondary schools. No scholarships are awarded directly through grants or loans. No travel for any purpose is funded. Organizations must be located in Ohio.

Additional Information

The Kettering Fund is affiliated with the Kettering Family Foundation, which is located at the same address.
The fund lists Bank One Trust Company, NA, as a corporate trustee.

Foundation Officials

Susan K. Beck: member distribution committee, trustee
Terri Hurd: administrator
Virginia W. Kettering: trustee CORP AFFIL director emeritus: Bank One Dayton NA; director: C F Kettering.
Jane K. Lombard: mem distribution comm, trustee
Susan K. Williamson: mem distribution comm, trustee

Grants Analysis

Disclosure Period: fiscal year ending June 30, 2004
Total Grants: $4,252,500
Number of Grants: 35
Average Grant: $74,318*
Highest Grant: $500,000
Lowest Grant: $2,000
Typical Range: $20,000 to $150,000
*Note: Average grant figure excludes four highest grants ($1,800,000).

Recent Grants

Note: Grants derived from fiscal 2001 Form 990.
General

1,000,000	Dayton Foundation, Dayton, OH
575,000	University of Dayton, Dayton, OH
500,000	Wright State University, Dayton, OH
380,000	Kettering University, Flint, MI
300,000	Ohio State University, Columbus, OH
279,000	Dayton Ballet, Dayton, OH
250,000	Kettering Medical Center, Dayton, OH
200,000	Dakota Center, Dayton, OH
200,000	Downtown Dayton Riverscape Fund, Dayton, OH
200,000	Hathaway Brown School, Shaker Heights, OH

KEY BANK N.A.

Company Headquarters

127 Public Sq.
Cleveland, OH 44114
Web: http://www.keybank.com

Company Description

Former Name: Society National Bank.
Assets: US$75.032 billion (2001)
Employees: 19285 (2001)
SIC(s): 6021 National Commercial Banks.
Parent Company: KeyCorp, 127 Public Square, Cleveland, OH, United States

Operating Locations

Key Bank of Cleveland (OH--Ahtabula, Akron, Canton, Celina, Columbus, Dayton, Defiance, Mansfield, Mentor, Sandusky, Springfield, Youngstown)

Nonmonetary Support

Type: In-kind Services
Volunteer Programs: Company employees volunteer at Neighbors Make The Difference Day, a program where key closes its office for one afternoon and send its employees to perform volunteer services.

Key Foundation

Giving Contact

Margot Copeland
KeyBank of Cleveland
127 Public Square
Mailcode OH-01-27-0705
Cleveland, OH 44114-1306
Phone: (216)689-4724
E-mail: key_foundation@keybank.com
Web: http://keybank.com/templates/t-ak2.jhtml?nodeID=A-12

Description

EIN: 237036607
Organization Type: Corporate Foundation

Giving Locations: primarily service area.
Grant Types: Capital, Conference/Seminar, Employee Matching Gifts, General Support, Matching, Multiyear/Continuing Support, Operating Expenses.

Financial Summary

Total Giving: $9,989,998 (2003); $11,602,727 (2002); $16,639,981 (2001). Note: Contributes through corporate direct giving program and foundation.
Assets: $21,619,218 (2003); $24,308,119 (2002); $38,127,646 (2001)
Gifts Received: $24,242 (2003); $1,241,156 (2002); $16,137 (2001). Note: In 2003, contributions were received from Key Capital Corp. ($60,448) and KeyCorp ($2,701,251). In 2002, contributions were received from KeyBank National Association ($10,291,003) and individuals (under $2,000 each).

Typical Recipients

Arts & Humanities: Arts Associations & Councils, Arts Centers, Arts Funds, Ballet, Libraries, Museums/Galleries, Music, Opera, Performing Arts, Public Broadcasting, Theater
Civic & Public Affairs: African American Affairs, Business/Free Enterprise, Clubs, Community Foundations, Economic Development, Civic & Public Affairs-General, Housing, Legal Aid, Municipalities/Towns, Urban & Community Affairs
Education: Afterschool/Enrichment Programs, Arts/Humanities Education, Business Education, Colleges & Universities, Community & Junior Colleges, Education Funds, Engineering/Technological Education, Leadership Training, Minority Education, Private Education (Precollege), Student Aid
Health: Alzheimer's Disease, Cancer, Children's Health/Hospitals, Clinics/Medical Centers, Health Funds, Hospitals, Hospitals (University Affiliated), Mental Health, Multiple Sclerosis, Prenatal Health Issues
Religion: Churches, Dioceses, Religious Welfare
Social Services: Child Welfare, Community Centers, Community Service Organizations, Emergency Relief, People with Disabilities, Recreation & Athletics, Scouts, United Funds/United Ways, Youth Organizations

Application Procedures

Initial Contact: Submit a written proposal.
Application Requirements: Include history and purpose of the organization; amount requested and purpose of funds sought; budget information; list of officers, directors, or trustees; complete budget for the project period; last annual financial statement; proof of tax-exempt status; and any additional information that will aid the foundation in making its decision.
Deadlines: None.
Review Process: Local contributions committees review requests throughout the year; annual budget is approved in December.
Evaluative Criteria: Programs and objectives must benefit communities served by the company. The organization should enhance the civic, cultural, or educational goals of the community, or provide for the health and welfare of its citizens. The organization must demonstrate sound fiscal management, nonduplication of services, and evidence of broad community support.
Decision Notification: Decisions are made locally.
Notes: Requests should be directed to the nearest KeyBank office.

Restrictions

Company does not support political organizations or programs that are sensitive, controversial, harmful, or which pose a potential conflict of interest; churches or religious programs, preschool or primary educational institutions, fraternal, social, labor or veterans organizations unless for a significant project of benefit to the entire community regardless of race, religion, or sex; individualss, private foundations, trade or professional associations or organizations whose prima-

ry purpose is the support of athletic activities; international or foreign organizations.

Additional Information

In 1994, Society Corp. merged with KeyCorp and changed its name to Society National Bank Society National Bank changed its name to Key Bank of Cleveland in 1995.
Publications: Guidelines for Giving

Foundation Officials

Patrick V. Auletta: trustee
Steven N. Bulloch: assistant secretary
John M. Burmaster: treasurer
Margot J. Copeland: trustee
Linda M. Friedlander: vice president
Karen R. Haefling: trustee
Paul N. Harris: trustee
Robert B. Heisler, Jr.: president, trustee
Thomas E. Helfrich: trustee
Robert G. Jones: trustee
Jack L. Kopnisky: trustee
Michael J. Monroe: trustee
Bruce D. Murphy: trustee
Michael J. Thacker: secretary

Grants Analysis

Disclosure Period: calendar year ending 2003
Total Grants: $6,656,593*
Number of Grants: 996
Average Grant: $6,683
Highest Grant: $250,000
Lowest Grant: $250
Typical Range: $1,000 to $10,000
*Note: Giving excludes matching gifts, scholarships, and United Way.

Recent Grants

Note: Grants derived from 2003 Form 990.

General
1,318,250	United Way Services, Cleveland, OH
250,000	Cuyahoga Community College Foundation, Cleveland, OH
126,000	University Hospitals Health System Inc., Cleveland, OH
100,000	Cleveland Clinic Foundation, Cleveland, OH
100,000	Musical Arts Association, Cleveland, OH
95,500	United Way of Greater Toledo, Toledo, OH
85,000	United Way of Northeastern New York, Albany, NY
78,000	United Way of Buffalo & Erie County, Buffalo, NY
76,000	Urban League of Greater Cleveland, Cleveland, OH
71,430	Kent State University Foundation, Kent, OH

KEY BANK OF MAINE

Company Headquarters

1 Canal Plz., No. 1
Portland, ME 04101

Company Description

Employees: 1,231
SIC(s): 6000 Depository Institutions.
Parent Company: KeyCorp, 127 Public Square, Cleveland, OH, United States

Key Bank of Maine Foundation

Giving Contact

Key Bank of Maine
800 Superior, Trust Tax
Cleveland, OH 44114
Phone: (216)828-9536

Description

EIN: 016017321
Organization Type: Corporate Foundation
Giving Locations: ME
Grant Types: Capital, General Support, Scholarship.

Financial Summary

Total Giving: $30,000 (fiscal year ending November 30, 2002). Note: Company gives directly and through the foundation. Figures for 1994 and 1995 represent foundation contributions.
Assets: $0 (fiscal 2002)

Typical Recipients

Arts & Humanities: Libraries, Museums/Galleries
Civic & Public Affairs: Economic Development, Civic & Public Affairs-General
Education: Arts/Humanities Education, Colleges & Universities, Medical Education, Private Education (Precollege), Student Aid
Environment: Environment-General, Protection
Health: Children's Health/Hospitals, Clinics/Medical Centers, Health Organizations, Hospitals, Mental Health, Prenatal Health Issues
Social Services: Big Brothers/Big Sisters, Child Welfare, Community Centers, Community Service Organizations, Recreation & Athletics, Scouts, Youth Organizations

Application Procedures

Initial Contact: The foundation requests applications be made in writing.
Deadlines: None.

Restrictions

Does not support religious organizations for sectarian purposes.

Additional Information

Trust(s): KeyBank NA

Corporate Officials

Michael William McNamara: chairman, president, chief executive officer, director B Saint Stephen, NB Canada 1945. ED University of Maine (1967). PRIM CORP EMPL chairman, president, chief executive officer, director: Key Bank of Maine.
Richard A. Molyneux: chairman, director PRIM CORP EMPL chairman, director: Key Bank of Maine.

Grants Analysis

Disclosure Period: fiscal year ending November 30, 2002
Total Grants: $30,000
Number of Grants: 1

Recent Grants

Note: Grants derived from fiscal 2002 Form 990.
General
30,000	Nature Conservancy, Arlington, VA

KEYSPAN CORP.

Company Headquarters

1 MetroTech Center
Brooklyn, NY 11201
Web: http://www.keyspanenergy.com

Company Description

Founded: 1998
Ticker: KSE
Exchange: NYSE
Revenue: US$6.989 billion (2004)
Profit: US$463.7 million (2004)
Employees: 11300 (2003)
Fortune Rank: 302, per FORTUNE Magazine's list of 500 Largest U.S. Corporations (2004).
SIC(s): 4911 Electric Services.

KeySpan Foundation

Giving Contact

Robert G. Keller, Executive Director
175 East Old Country Road
Hicksville, NY 11801
Phone: (516)545-6182
E-mail: foundation@keyspanenergy.com
Web: http://www.keyspanenergy.com/corpinfo/community/index_all_all.jsp

Description

Founded: 1998
EIN: 113466416
Organization Type: Corporate Foundation
Grant Types: Challenge, General Support, Matching, Project.

Donor Information

Founder: Established in 1998 by KeySpan Corp.

Financial Summary

Total Giving: $737,500 (2003); $1,435,835 (2002); $2,029,023 (2001)
Giving Analysis: Giving for 2002 includes: foundation grants to United Way ($505,000)
Assets: $23,020,671 (2003); $23,087,957 (2002); $24,913,152 (2001)
Gifts Received: $48,000 (2002); $51,033 (2001); $10,000,000 (2000). Note: In 2000 and 2002, contributions were received from KeySpan Corp.

Typical Recipients

Arts & Humanities: Arts Centers, Arts Institutes, Historic Preservation, Libraries, Literary Arts, Museums/Galleries, Music, Performing Arts, Public Broadcasting, Theater
Civic & Public Affairs: African American Affairs, Botanical Gardens/Parks, Community Foundations, Economic Development, Employment/Job Training, Civic & Public Affairs-General, Housing, Inner-City Development, Legal Aid, Nonprofit Management, Philanthropic Organizations, Zoos/Aquariums
Education: Business-School Partnerships, Colleges & Universities, Education Funds, Engineering/Technological Education, Environmental Education, Education-General, Health & Physical Education, Leadership Training, Literacy, Public Education (Precollege), Religious Education, Special Education, Student Aid, Vocational & Technical Education
Environment: Air/Water Quality, Forestry, Environment-General, Protection, Research, Resource Conservation, Sanitary Systems, Wildlife Protection
Health: Cancer, Clinics/Medical Centers, Health Funds, Health Organizations, Heart, Hospices, Hospitals, Kidney, Mental Health, Prenatal Health Issues, Single-Disease Health Associations
Religion: Religion-General
Science: Scientific Centers & Institutes
Social Services: Community Centers, Community Service Organizations, Emergency Relief, Family Services, People with Disabilities, Recreation & Athletics, Scouts, Sexual Abuse, Shelters/Homelessness, Social Services-General, Substance Abuse, United Funds/United Ways, YMCA/YWCA/YMHA/YWHA, Youth Organizations

Application Procedures

Initial Contact: Submit a letter of request.
Application Requirements: Include purpose for which funds are requested and how the funds will be appropriated for the specific venture; project objectives and anticipated outcomes; detailed project budget, including a cost estimate for each item for which funds are requested; a description of organization, including geographic reach, number of clients served, and existing programs; a list of other potential sources of funding; proof of tax-exempt status; most current audited financial statements and/or Form 990; list of the organization's board of directors and affiliations; and the organization's annual report or brochures, if applicable. The foundation reports that they will also accept the New York/New Jersey Common Application Form in place of the above outline.
Deadlines: None.
Review Process: The board of directors meets on a quarterly basis to review requests.
Evaluative Criteria: Organization's mission should directly support one of the foundation's main focus areas (health and human services, education, environment, community development, or arts and culture). Organization should provide services within KeySpan's service territory or in areas where the company plans to operate in the future. Only one grant proposal request per organization will be evaluated in each calendar year.
Decision Notification: Proposal review is generally completed within 60 days.

Restrictions

Grants generally will not be made to individuals; to sectarian and religious organizations that do not serve the general public on a non-denominational basis; to organizations requesting funds for capital or endowment campaigns; to organizations requesting funds for advertisements, tables or tickets at dinners or other functions; to political, fraternal, social or other membership organizations providing services mainly to their own constituencies; or to organizations whose combined administrative, management and fundraising expenses exceed 30% of the organization's total operating budget.

Corporate Officials

Robert Barry Catell: chairman, chief executive officer B Brooklyn, NY February 01, 1937. ED City University of New York BME (1958); City University of New York MME (1964). PRIM CORP EMPL chairman, chief executive officer: KeySpan Corp. CORP AFFIL chairman, chief executive officer, director: MarketSpan Corp.; director: Star Energy Inc.; director: The Houston Exploration Co.; trustee: Independence Savings Bank; director: Fuel Resources Inc.; director: Gas Energy Inc.; director: Alberta Northeast Inc.; chairman: Boundary Gas Inc. NONPR AFFIL member: New York State Business Council; member: Society Gas Lighting; member: New York Serda Board; director: New York Energy Research & Development Authority; member executive committee: New York Gas Group; director: Gas Research Institute; member: New York City Partnership; director: American Gas Association; chairman: Business Council for a Sustainable Energy Future.

Foundation Officials

Pamela Adamo: director
Donald H. Elliott: vice chairman
Carmen Fields: director
Robert G. Keller: executive director
Basil A. Paterson: chairman
Michael J. Taunton: treasurer
Colin P. Watson: vice chairman
Elaine Weinstein: director

Grants Analysis

Disclosure Period: calendar year ending 2003
Total Grants: $737,500
Number of Grants: 46

Average Grant: $8,314*
Highest Grant: $200,000
Lowest Grant: $1,000
Typical Range: $5,000 to $10,000
*Note: Average grant figure excludes three highest grants ($380,000).

Recent Grants

Note: Grants derived from 2003 Form 990.
Library-Related

10,000	Brooklyn Public Library Foundation, Brooklyn, NY

General

300,000	New York City Partnership Foundation, New York, NY
262,500	United Way New York City and Long Island, New York, NY
120,000	Prospect Park Alliance, Brooklyn, NY
100,000	Fund for Public Schools, New York, NY
45,000	Salvation Army, Baltimore, MD
30,000	Audubon Society of New Hampshire, Concord, NH
25,000	Brooklyn Academy of Music, Brooklyn, NY
25,000	City College of New York City, New York, NY
25,000	Take the Field, New York, NY
20,000	INFORM Inc., New York, NY

J. W. KIECKHEFER FOUNDATION

Giving Contact

Eugene P. Polk, Administrative Officer, Trustee
PO Box 1151
Prescott, AZ 86302
Phone: (928)445-4010
Fax: (928)445-4012

Description

Founded: 1953
EIN: 866022877
Organization Type: General Purpose Foundation
Giving Locations: AZ: nationally.
Grant Types: Capital, Emergency, Endowment, General Support, Multiyear/Continuing Support, Project, Research, Seed Money.

Donor Information

Founder: The foundation was established in 1953, with funds provided by John W. Kieckhefer, the founder of Kieckhefer Container Company. In 1957, the family firm and its affiliate, Eddy Paper Corporation, were merged into Weyerhaeuser Company.

Financial Summary

Total Giving: $966,501 (2002); $891,250 (2001)
Giving Analysis: Giving for 2002 includes: foundation scholarships ($4,000)
Assets: $16,605,055 (2002); $18,742,863 (2001)
Gifts Received: $58,090 (2001). Note: In 2001, contributions were received from Robert H. Kieckhefer Charitable Remainder Trust.

Typical Recipients

Arts & Humanities: Arts Associations & Councils, Arts Centers, Ballet, Community Arts, Film & Video, Arts & Humanities-General, Historic Preservation, History & Archaeology, Libraries, Literary Arts, Museums/Galleries, Music, Performing Arts, Public Broadcasting, Theater, Visual Arts
Civic & Public Affairs: Botanical Gardens/Parks, Community Foundations, Economic Development, Economic Policy, Civic & Public Affairs-General, Hispanic Affairs, Housing, Law & Justice, Legal Aid, Municipalities/Towns, Philanthropic Organizations, Professional & Trade Associations, Public Policy,

Women's Affairs, Zoos/Aquariums

Education: Agricultural Education, Business Education, Colleges & Universities, Continuing Education, Environmental Education, Education-General, Literacy, Medical Education, Preschool Education, Private Education (Precollege), Public Education (Precollege), Science/Mathematics Education, Student Aid
Environment: Environment-General, Resource Conservation, Wildlife Protection
Health: Alzheimer's Disease, Cancer, Children's Health/Hospitals, Clinics/Medical Centers, Eyes/Blindness, Geriatric Health, Health Funds, Health Organizations, Heart, Hospices, Hospitals, Kidney, Medical Rehabilitation, Medical Research, Mental Health, Prenatal Health Issues, Preventive Medicine/Wellness Organizations, Public Health, Research/Studies Institutes, Respiratory, Single-Disease Health Associations
International: Health Care/Hospitals, International Environmental Issues, International Organizations, International Peace & Security Issues
Religion: Churches, Missionary Activities (Domestic), Religious Welfare
Science: Science Museums, Scientific Centers & Institutes
Social Services: Animal Protection, At-Risk Youth, Big Brothers/Big Sisters, Camps, Child Abuse, Child Welfare, Community Centers, Community Service Organizations, Counseling, Day Care, Domestic Violence, Emergency Relief, Family Planning, Family Services, Food/Clothing Distribution, People with Disabilities, Recreation & Athletics, Senior Services, Shelters/Homelessness, Special Olympics, Substance Abuse, Volunteer Services, YMCA/YWCA/YMHA/YWHA, Youth Organizations

Application Procedures

Initial Contact: Send a brief letter of inquiry and a full proposal.
Application Requirements: The letter should include a description of the problem addressed, nature of the project, and objectives of the program. A copy of tax-exempt ruling also should be enclosed.
Deadlines: The foundation prefers to receive applications from May to November.
Review Process: The foundation acknowledges the receipt of all proposals and grants interviews with applicants during the secondary stage of the application process.
Notes: Final notification is made within six months.

Restrictions

Grants or loans are not made to individuals. Internally initiated grants are usually all of the current grant making of the foundation. Informal letters will be accepted, but may not be responded to.

Foundation Officials

John I. Kieckhefer: trustee PRIM CORP EMPL president, chief executive officer: Kieckhefer Associatess Inc. CORP AFFIL director: Weyerhaeuser Co.
Robert H. Kieckhefer: trustee B 1918.

Grants Analysis

Disclosure Period: calendar year ending 2002
Total Grants: $962,501*
Number of Grants: 60
Average Grant: $15,334*
Highest Grant: $57,800
Lowest Grant: $750
Typical Range: $5,000 to $25,000
*Note: Giving excludes scholarships. Average grant figure excludes highest grant.

Recent Grants

Note: Grants derived from 2002 Form 990.
General

250,000	Mayo Foundation, Scottsdale, AZ -- funds in support of Mayo clinic-Scottsdale comprehensive cancer center
57,800	Sharlot Hall Museum, Prescott, AZ -- funds in support of the cowboy project, current capital drive
35,000	Phoenix Children's Hospital, Phoenix, AZ -- funds towards "building better care for kids" capital campaign
25,000	Arizona Friends of Foster Children Foundation, Sedona, AZ -- funds towards permanent endowment fund
25,000	Camp Fire Boys and Girls, Phoenix, AZ -- funds towards save a memory-share a dream campaign for restoration of camp Wamatochick
25,000	Phoenix Art Museum, Phoenix, AZ -- funds towards exhibition
25,000	Phoenix Zoo, Phoenix, AZ -- funds towards permanent endowment fund for the animal care center
25,000	Sterling Ranch, Inc., Skull Valley, AZ -- funds towards construction of a new residential facility for mentally challenged adult women
22,500	Arizona Aerospace Foundation, Scottsdale, AZ -- funds towards the purchase and installation of museum display cases
20,000	Adult Day Care Services, Inc., Prescott, AZ -- funds towards capital campaign for a new facility in Prescott valley

PETER KIEWIT FOUNDATION

Giving Contact

Lyn Wallin Ziegenbein, Executive Director
8805 Indian Hills Drive, Suite 225
Omaha, NE 68114
Phone: (402)344-7890
Fax: (402)344-8099

Alternate Contact

Trust Tax Service
PO Box 64713
St. Paul, MN 55164-0713
Phone: (402)348-6548

Description

Founded: 1980
EIN: 476098282
Organization Type: General Purpose Foundation
Giving Locations: CA: Rancho Mirage; IA: the portion of Iowa which is within a 100-mile radius of Omaha, NE; NE, Omaha; WY: Sheridan
Grant Types: Capital, General Support, Professorship, Project, Scholarship, Seed Money.

Donor Information

Founder: Established in Nebraska in 1975 by the late Peter Kiewit (1900-1979), president of Peter Kiewit Sons, a construction company. He successively worked as a mason tender, hod carrier, and bricklayer for his family business during his summer vacations and throughout high school. He completed one year of study at Dartmouth College before entering the construction business full-time at the age of 19. After he joined the business, Mr. Kiewit began buying company stock from his brothers. When Mr. Kiewit assumed leadership in 1931, the company's total assets were less than $125,000. Hard work, dedication to the principle of good relations with owners and their representatives, the ability to recognize contracting opportunities, and a farsighted plan of rewarding key employees with stock ownership in the company made Peter Kiewit Sons a multi-million dollar firm and one of the largest construction companies in the world. The present foundation is the result of Mr. Kiewit's personal philanthropy, and has no affiliation with the Kiewit Company.

Mr. Kiewit was committed to "building the character of men and good things for a better, more meaningful world." His commitment extended to civil rights, as he believed that "the competitive construction business allows no room for prejudice in employment practices." In 1963, he headed the employment subcommittee of the Mayors Bi-Racial Committee in Omaha, and in 1967, the National Conference of Christians and Jews presented him with its Brotherhood Award. Peter Kiewit was also committed to philanthropy. At the time of his death, he had contributed $15 million to various causes, and had pledged an additional $5 million. The foundation which bears his name is a continuing reflection of Peter Kiewit's philanthropic interests.

Financial Summary

Total Giving: $23,421,633 (fiscal year ending June 30, 2003); $25,656,429 (fiscal 2002); $28,735,420 (fiscal 2001)
Giving Analysis: Giving for fiscal 2001 includes: foundation gifts to individuals ($127,356); foundation grants to United Way ($450,000); foundation scholarships ($2,480,638)
Assets: $332,489,280 (fiscal 2003); $349,247,678 (fiscal 2002); $462,612,397 (fiscal 2001)
Gifts Received: $275,751 (fiscal 1997); $2,800 (fiscal 1992). Note: Fiscal 1997 contributions consist of scholarship refunds, endowment refunds, and registration fees for fundraising seminars.

Typical Recipients

Arts & Humanities: Arts Appreciation, Arts Associations & Councils, Arts Centers, Arts Funds, Arts Outreach, Historic Preservation, History & Archaeology, Libraries, Museums/Galleries, Music, Opera, Performing Arts, Theater
Civic & Public Affairs: Botanical Gardens/Parks, Chambers of Commerce, Community Foundations, Economic Development, Employment/Job Training, Civic & Public Affairs-General, Housing, Inner-City Development, Municipalities/Towns, Native American Affairs, Parades/Festivals, Philanthropic Organizations, Safety, Urban & Community Affairs, Zoos/Aquariums
Education: Agricultural Education, Colleges & Universities, Community & Junior Colleges, Education Associations, Education Funds, Elementary Education (Private), Faculty Development, Education-General, International Studies, Journalism/Media Education, Literacy, Minority Education, Preschool Education, Public Education (Precollege), Science/Mathematics Education, Special Education, Student Aid
Environment: Environment-General, Protection, Resource Conservation
Health: AIDS/HIV, Cancer, Clinics/Medical Centers, Emergency/Ambulance Services, Health Organizations, Hospitals, Medical Rehabilitation, Mental Health, Nutrition, Trauma Treatment
International: International Peace & Security Issues
Religion: Religious Organizations, Religious Welfare
Science: Science Museums
Social Services: Animal Protection, Child Welfare, Community Centers, Community Service Organizations, Crime Prevention, Day Care, Family Planning, Family Services, Food/Clothing Distribution, Homes, People with Disabilities, Recreation & Athletics, Scouts, Senior Services, Shelters/Homelessness, United Funds/United Ways, Volunteer Services, YMCA/YWCA/YMHA/YWHA, Youth Organizations

Application Procedures

Initial Contact: Contact the foundation office to obtain standard application forms. Personal interviews are not a part of the normal application process, and are not encouraged.
Deadlines: April 1 and October 1 for general grants in excess of $10,000; March 1, June 1, September 1, and December 1 for small grants. Nebraska Teacher Achievement Awards applications are due February 1; scholarship applications are due March 1.

Review Process: The board of trustees meets in March, June, September, and December.

Notes: Organizations whose applications have been denied must wait one full year before resubmitting. Grants are made only on a matching fund basis, except in situations involving dire need where matching funds cannot be made available. The foundation will also consider granting seed money for innovative programs. Priority consideration is given to organizations which are not tax-supported. At least equal matching funds are required of organizations which are not tax-supported, and at least a three-to-one match is required of organizations which receive tax support. Any grants made for the purposes of capital construction are conditioned upon the actual completion of such improvement. Applicants are encouraged to develop other sources of support for a particular project prior to approaching the foundation.

Restrictions

The foundation does not make grants to individuals or private, non-operating foundations. The foundation generally does not consider support for endowment funds; elementary and secondary schools; churches and similar groups; or construction, renovation, or operations of normally tax-supported public facilities. A low priority is given to applications for normal operating budgets or contributions to annual fund-raising campaigns. No more than two applications from the same organization will be considered in any calendar year.

Additional Information

Trust(s): U.S. Bank National Association

Foundation Officials

Mogens C. Bay: trustee CORP AFFIL director: Peter Kiewit Sons' Inc.; chairman, chief executive officer: Valmont Industries Inc.; director: ConAgra Foods Inc.; director: Level 3 Communications Inc..

Michael L. Gallagher: vice chairman, trustee CORP AFFIL director: Suncor Development Co.; presiding director: Pinnacle West Capital Corp.; director: El Dorado Investment Co.; director: Omaha-World Herald Co.; director: Arizona Public Service Co. NONPR AFFIL fellow: International Academy of Trial Lawyers.

John W. Hancock: chairman, trustee

G. Richard Russell: trustee NONPR AFFIL immediate past chairman: United Way of the Midlands.

Lyn Wallin Ziegenbein: executive director, secretary B 1952. ED University of Kansas BS (1974); Creighton University JD (1977). CORP AFFIL director: Assurity Security Group Inc..

Grants Analysis

Disclosure Period: fiscal year ending June 30, 2003

Total Grants: $19,534,742*

Number of Grants: 179

Average Grant: $81,655*

Highest Grant: $5,000,000

Lowest Grant: $100

Typical Range: $10,000 to $250,000

*Note: Giving excludes scholarships, gifts to individuals, and United Way. Average grant figure excludes highest grant.

Recent Grants

Note: Grants derived from fiscal 2003 Form 990.

General

5,000,000 City of Omaha, Omaha, NE -- towards convention center arena

3,500,000 University of Nebraska Foundation, Lincoln, NE -- towards the institute of information science technology and engineering

2,059,096 University of Nebraska, Lincoln, NE

875,000 Bellevue University, Bellevue, NE

750,000 University of Arizona Foundation, Tucson, AZ -- towards the Arizona cancer center

500,000 Boy Scouts of American Comhusker Council, Omaha, NE

500,000 Dana College, Blari, NE

500,000 Nebraska Game and Parks Foundation, Lincoln, NE

500,000 Omaha Zoological Foundation, Omaha, NE -- towards aquarium

500,000 Omaha Zoological Foundation, Omaha, NE -- towards program support

PETER KIEWIT SONS' INC.

Company Headquarters

1000 Kiewit Plaza
Omaha, NE 68131-3374
E-mail: miscellaneous@kiewit.com
Web: http://www.kiewit.com

Company Description

Revenue: US$3.375 billion (2003)
Profit: US$157 million (2003)
Employees: 15000 (2003)
SIC(s): 6719 Holding Companies Nec.

Operating Locations

Peter Kiewit Sons' Inc. (MD--Aberdeen)

Nonmonetary Support

Type: Loaned Employees; Loaned Executives; Workplace Solicitation
Note: Co. provides nonmonetary support.

Kiewit Companies Foundation

Giving Contact

Michael L. Faust, Foundation Administrator
1000 Kiewit Plaza
Omaha, NE 68131-3374
Phone: (402)271-2950
Fax: (402)943-1302
E-mail: mike.faust@kiewit.com
Web: http://www.kiewit.com

Description

Founded: 1963
EIN: 476029996
Organization Type: Corporate Foundation
Giving Locations: NE: Omaha operating locations.
Grant Types: Capital, General Support, Multiyear/Continuing Support, Operating Expenses, Project, Scholarship.

Financial Summary

Total Giving: Contributes through foundation only.
Gifts Received: $2,500,000 (2000); $2,000,000 (1999). Note: In 1999 and 2000, contributions were received from Peter Kiewit Sons', Inc.

Typical Recipients

Arts & Humanities: Arts Associations & Councils, Arts Centers, Dance, Historic Preservation, Libraries, Museums/Galleries, Music, Opera, Performing Arts, Theater

Civic & Public Affairs: Botanical Gardens/Parks, Business/Free Enterprise, Community Foundations, Economic Development, Housing, Inner-City Development, Parades/Festivals, Philanthropic Organizations, Safety, Urban & Community Affairs, Zoos/Aquariums

Education: Business Education, Colleges & Universities, Community & Junior Colleges, Economic Education, Education Funds, Engineering/Technological Education, Legal Education, Minority Education, Private Education (Precollege), Science/Mathematics Education, Special Education, Student Aid

Environment: Environment-General, Protection, Wildlife Protection

Health: Arthritis, Children's Health/Hospitals, Clinics/Medical Centers, Health Organizations

Religion: Religious Welfare

Social Services: Animal Protection, Child Welfare, Community Centers, Community Service Organizations, Emergency Relief, Food/Clothing Distribution, Homes, People with Disabilities, Recreation & Athletics, Scouts, United Funds/United Ways, YMCA/YWCA/YMHA/YWHA, Youth Organizations

Application Procedures

Initial Contact: Send brief letter or proposal.
Application Requirements: Include a description of organization, mission statement explaining how it makes a positive impact on the quality of life in a Kiewit community, amount requested, purpose of funds sought, recently audited financial statement, proof of tax-exempt status.
Deadlines: None.
Review Process: Decisions are made approximately every eight weeks.

Restrictions

The foundation generally does not support endowment funds, grant-making organizations, social or fraternal organizations, conferences or seminars, study or travel, academic or medical research, advocacy organizations or controversial causes, churches or religious organizations, production of films or sponsorship of television programming, elementary schools, or sponsorship of athletic teams or athletic events.

Additional Information

The majority of funding is repeat grants to local organizations in Omaha, NE. Limited funding is available to new grant seekers.

Corporate Officials

Kenneth E. Stinson: chairman, chief executive officer, director B 1942. ED University of Notre Dame BS (1964); Stanford University MS (1970). PRIM CORP EMPL chairman, chief executive officer, director: Peter Kiewit Sons' Inc. CORP AFFIL director: MFS Communications Co.; director: United Metro Materials Inc.; director: Kiewit Western Co.; director: Kiewit Industrial Co.; executive vice president: Peter Kiewit Sons Inc.; chairman, chief executive officer, director: Kiewit Construction Group Inc.; director: Kiewit Diversified Group Inc.; director: Kiewit Construction Co.; director: ConAgra Inc.; director: Global Surety & Insurance Co.

Foundation Officials

Michael L. Faust: administrator PRIM CORP EMPL assistant to chairman: Peter Kiewit Sons' Inc.

Walter Scott, Jr.: chairman emeritus B Omaha, NE 1931. ED Colorado State University BS (1953). PRIM CORP EMPL director: Peter Kiewit Sons' Inc. CORP AFFIL director: MidAmerica Holdings Co.; director: Level 3 Telecommunications Holdings Inc.; director: MidAmerica Energy Holdings Co.; chairman: Level 3 Communications Inc.; president: Kiewit Coal Properties Inc.; director: Kiewit Mining Group Inc.; director: ConAgra Inc.; director: Burlington Resources Inc.; director: CalEnergy Co. Inc.; director: Berkshire Hathaway Inc. NONPR AFFIL director: Hastings College Foundation; president: Joslyn Art Museum; chairman: Creighton University.

Kenneth E. Stinson: member contributions committee (see above)

Grants Analysis

Disclosure Period: calendar year ending 2000
Total Grants: $5,400,000*
Number of Grants: 255
Average Grant: $9,486*
Highest Grant: $2,000,000
Typical Range: $1,000 to $10,000
*Note: Giving includes matching gifts to United Way by employees and scholarships. Average grant figure excludes two highest grants totaling $3,000,000.

Recent Grants

Note: Grants derived from 2003 Form 990.
General

1,000,000	Donors Trust, Alexandria, VA -- towards civic arena project
400,000	Omaha Performing Arts Society, Omaha, NE -- towards concert hall project
300,000	Creighton University, Omaha, NE -- towards science complex project
250,000	Omaha Zoo Foundation, Omaha, NE -- towards gorilla valley project
150,000	New Community Development Corporation, Newark, NJ -- for gift to inner city redevelopment project
115,000	United Way of the Midlands, Omaha, NE
100,000	Beavers Charitable Trust, Los Altos, CA -- to engineering scholarship fund
100,000	College of Saint Mary, Notre Dame, IN
100,000	Greater Omaha Chamber Foundation, Omaha, NE -- to target Omaha program
100,000	YMCA of Omaha Council Bluffs, Omaha, NE

KIKKOMAN FOODS

Company Headquarters

PO Box 69
Walworth, WI 53184
Web: http://www.kikkoman.com

Company Description

Revenue: US$60.4 million (2001)
Employees: 145 (2001)
SIC(s): 2035 Pickles, Sauces & Salad Dressings.
Parent Company: Kikkoman Corp., 250 Noda, Chiba, Japan

Kikkoman Foundation

Giving Contact

Robert V. Conover, Director
PO Box 69
Walworth, WI 53184
Phone: (262)275-6181

Description

Founded: 1993
EIN: 391763633
Organization Type: Corporate Foundation
Giving Locations: WI: internationally; nationally.
Grant Types: General Support.

Financial Summary

Total Giving: $400,695 (2003)
Assets: $7,217,573 (2003)
Gifts Received: $1,400,000 (2000); $600,000 (1999); $700,000 (1997). Note: In 1996, 1999, and 2000, contributions were received from Kikkoman Foods.

Typical Recipients

Arts & Humanities: Arts Festivals, Dance, Arts & Humanities-General, Historic Preservation, History & Archaeology, Libraries, Museums/Galleries, Performing Arts, Public Broadcasting
Civic & Public Affairs: Asian American Affairs, Botanical Gardens/Parks, Business/Free Enterprise, Chambers of Commerce, Community Foundations, Economic Development, Economic Policy, Employment/Job Training, Civic & Public Affairs-General, Municipalities/Towns, Public Policy, Urban & Community Affairs
Education: Business Education, Colleges & Universities, Economic Education, Education Funds, Education Reform, Engineering/Technological Education, International Exchange, Medical Education,
Minority Education, Public Education (Precollege), Secondary Education (Public), Student Aid
Environment: Air/Water Quality
Health: Cancer, Health Funds
International: International-General, International Development, Trade
Religion: Ministries
Social Services: Child Welfare, Family Services, People with Disabilities, Recreation & Athletics, Scouts, Shelters/Homelessness, YMCA/YWCA/ YMHA/YWHA, Youth Organizations

Application Procedures

Initial Contact: Request application form in writing.
Application Requirements: Include the following information: organization's name, address, and phone number along with the name of the contact person familiar with the details of the program; the type of program being funded, the target population, amount requested, and the date by which funds are needed; a budget specifically outlining when and how the funding will be spent; the expected long-term and short-term results of the program; information on amounts committed or pending from other sources for the program; a brief overview of the organization, including its history, purpose, number of members, the constituents it serves, geographic service area, volunteers, and general accomplishments to date; and a copy of the organization's determination letter from the IRS proving tax-exemption. If necessary, the foundation may request more detailed information about the organization, its proposal, and overall objectives of the project.
Review Process: Proposals are reviewed and evaluated by the foundation's board of directors.

Restrictions

Does not support individual persons one private organizations; raffle tickets, product purchases, etc.; political organizations, campaign committees, or lobbying groups; religious or sectarian organizations; performing or graphic art associations not in the state of Wisconsin; athletic events outside the foundation's interests; scientific or developmental research outside the food area; travel or lodging for individuals or groups; promotional events; organizations without 501(c)(3) status; organizations that discriminate on the basis of color, sex, religion, national origin, age, handicap, or veteran's status; or organizations or purposes that might in any way be inconsistent with the company's goals, programs, products, or employees.

Additional Information

Publications: Guidelines Sheet

Corporate Officials

Kuniki Hatayama: chief financial officer PRIM CORP EMPL chief financial officer: Kikkoman Foods.
Yuzaburo Mogi: chairman, president, chief executive officer PRIM CORP EMPL chairman, president, chief executive officer: Kikkoman Foods.
William E. Nelson: vice president PRIM CORP EMPL vice president: Kikkoman Foods.

Foundation Officials

Robert V. Conover: director
Hiroshi Futamura: director
Kuniki Hatayama: director (see above)
Masaaki Hirose: director
Yuzaburo Mogi: director (see above)
William E. Nelson: director (see above)
Milton E. Neshek: director
Yoshiyuki Nogi: director
Malcolm Pennington: director
Mitsuo Someya: director
Shigeomi Ushijima: director

Grants Analysis

Disclosure Period: calendar year ending 2003
Total Grants: $328,525*
Number of Grants: 64
Average Grant: $3,627*
Highest Grant: $100,000
Lowest Grant: $100
Typical Range: $1,000 to $5,000
***Note:** Giving excludes scholarships; United Way. Average grant figure excludes highest grant.

Recent Grants

Note: Grants derived from 2003 Form 990.
General

100,000	University of Wisconsin Foundation, Madison, WI -- for annual payment on pledge agreement for microbial sciences building fund Kikkoman laboratory of microbial fermentation
32,970	Youth for Understanding USA, Bethesda, MD -- for American overseas summer scholarships to Japan for six students
25,000	Wisconsin Foundation for Independent Colleges Inc., Milwaukee, WI -- to support Wisconsin Foundation Independent Colleges' annual campaign
20,000	University of Wisconsin Foundation, Madison, WI -- annual contribution to promote and support educational and cultural programs and projects
15,000	Institute for International Economics, Washington, DC -- for the study of agricultural trade policy and creation of advisory group
15,000	Jose Limon Dance Foundation Inc., New York, NY -- memorial contribution in the name of Malcolm W. Pennington
15,000	University of Wisconsin Economic Summit Fund, Milwaukee, WI -- for financial assistance for 4th annual economic development conference
15,000	University of Wisconsin Foundation, Madison, WI -- for chancellor's fund
10,000	Institute for International Economics, Washington, DC -- for the study of international economic policy
10,000	International House, New York, NY -- for 75th anniversary campaign

WILLIAM H. KILCAWLEY FUND

Giving Contact

Myra Vito
c/o National City Bank
PO Box 450
Youngstown, OH 44501
Phone: (330)742-4289

Description

Founded: 1946
EIN: 346515643
Organization Type: Private Foundation
Giving Locations: OH
Grant Types: Capital, General Support.

Financial Summary

Total Giving: $2,003,795 (2001)
Assets: $1,679,037 (2001)

Typical Recipients

Arts & Humanities: Arts Centers, Arts Institutes, Arts & Humanities-General, History & Archaeology, Libraries, Music, Performing Arts, Public Broadcasting
Civic & Public Affairs: Botanical Gardens/Parks, Business/Free Enterprise, Civic & Public Affairs-General, Municipalities/Towns, Urban & Community Affairs
Education: Business Education, Colleges & Universities, Community & Junior Colleges, Education Funds, Private Education (Precollege)
Health: AIDS/HIV, Children's Health/Hospitals,

Health Organizations, Home-Care Services, Hospices, Research/Studies Institutes, Speech & Hearing
Religion: Churches, Religious Organizations, Religious Welfare
Social Services: Animal Protection, Child Welfare, Community Service Organizations, Food/Clothing Distribution, People with Disabilities, Senior Services, United Funds/United Ways, YMCA/YWCA/YMHA/YWHA, Youth Organizations

Application Procedures
Initial Contact: The foundation requests applications be made in writing.
Deadlines: None.

Restrictions
Does not support individuals.

Additional Information
Trust(s): Natl City Bank

Foundation Officials
Anne K. Christman: trustee

Grants Analysis
Disclosure Period: calendar year ending 2001
Total Grants: $2,003,795
Number of Grants: 1

Recent Grants
Note: Grants derived from 2002 Form 990.
General
2,003,796   Youngstown Foundation, Cleveland, OH
       -- for distribution per governing document

CONSTANCE KILLAM TRUST

Giving Contact
Thomas P. Jalkut, Trustee
Constance Killam Trust
Care of Nutter, McClennen & Fish
1 International Pl.
Boston, MA 02110-2699
Phone: (617)439-2000
Fax: (617)973-9748

Description
Founded: 1977
EIN: 046420685
Organization Type: Private Foundation
Giving Locations: MA
Grant Types: Multiyear/Continuing Support, Scholarship.

Donor Information
Founder: the late Constance Killam

Financial Summary
Total Giving: $222,322 (fiscal year ending April 30, 2001)
Assets: $6,330,585 (fiscal 2001)
Gifts Received: $79,377 (fiscal 1995). Note: In fiscal 1995, contributions were received from the Constance Killam Trust.

Typical Recipients
Arts & Humanities: Libraries, Museums/Galleries, Music
Civic & Public Affairs: Native American Affairs, Zoos/Aquariums
Education: Arts/Humanities Education, Colleges & Universities, Health & Physical Education, Science/Mathematics Education
Environment: Environment-General

Application Procedures
Initial Contact: Send brief letter describing program and proposed use of funds requested.
Deadlines: None.

Foundation Officials
Thomas P. Jalkut: trustee
John Breed Newhall: trustee B Salem, MA 1932. ED Harvard University (1954); Harvard University JD (1959). CORP AFFIL chairman: D B Gurney Co. NONPR AFFIL member: American Bar Association.

Grants Analysis
Disclosure Period: fiscal year ending April 30, 2001
Total Grants: $222,322
Number of Grants: 9
Average Grant: $9,286*
Highest Grant: $100,000
Typical Range: $5,000 to $10,000
*Note: Average grant figure excludes two highest grants ($157,322).

Recent Grants
Note: Grants derived from fiscal 2001 Form 990.
Library-Related
10,000   Boston Athenaeum, Boston, MA
General
100,000   Brown University, Providence, RI
57,322   Massachusetts Audubon Society, Lincoln, MA
10,000   Appalachian Mountain Club, Boston, MA
10,000   Boston Symphony Orchestra, Boston, MA
10,000   Bowdoin College, Bowdoin, ME
10,000   Harvard College, Cambridge, MA
10,000   Peabody Museum of Salem and Essex Institute, Salem, MA
5,000   Trustees of Reservations, Beverly, MA

KILMARTIN INDUSTRIES

Company Headquarters
Walton St.
Attleboro, MA 02703

Company Description
Employees: 100
SIC(s): 3900 Miscellaneous Manufacturing Industries.

Kilmartin Industries Charitable Foundation

Giving Contact
David F. Kilmartin, Chairman, President & Chief Executive Officer
247 Farnum Road
Glocester, RI 02814
Phone: (401)949-1166

Description
EIN: 222727613
Organization Type: Corporate Foundation
Giving Locations: headquarters area only.
Grant Types: General Support.

Financial Summary
Total Giving: $18,100 (fiscal year ending February 28, 2004)
Giving Analysis: Giving for fiscal 2004 includes: foundation scholarships ($8,500)
Assets: $520,936 (fiscal 2004)
Gifts Received: $17,000 (fiscal 2004); $32,252 (fiscal 2000); $3,000 (fiscal 1997). Note: In fiscal 2000 and 2004, contributions were received from David Kilmartin. In fiscal 1997, contributions were received from Kilmartin Industries.

Typical Recipients
Arts & Humanities: Ballet, History & Archaeology, Libraries, Music, Public Broadcasting
Civic & Public Affairs: Safety, Zoos/Aquariums
Education: Arts/Humanities Education, Colleges & Universities, Legal Education, Medical Education, Private Education (Precollege), Special Education, Student Aid, Vocational & Technical Education
Health: Cancer, Children's Health/Hospitals, Diabetes, Mental Health, Single-Disease Health Associations
Religion: Churches, Dioceses, Religious Organizations, Religious Welfare
Social Services: Animal Protection, Community Service Organizations, Scouts, Social Services-General

Application Procedures
Initial Contact: Send typed, double-spaced letter containing statement of need.
Deadlines: None.

Corporate Officials
David F. Kilmartin: chairman, president, chief executive officer, director PRIM CORP EMPL chairman, president, chief executive officer, director: Kilmartin Industries.

Foundation Officials
David F. Kilmartin: president, director (see above)

Grants Analysis
Disclosure Period: fiscal year ending February 28, 2004
Total Grants: $9,600*
Number of Grants: 14
Average Grant: $686
Highest Grant: $2,000
Lowest Grant: $50
Typical Range: $200 to $1,000
*Note: Giving excludes scholarship.

Recent Grants
Note: Grants derived from fiscal 2004 Form 990.

General
2,500   University of the South, Sewanee, TN -- for scholarship assistance
2,000   Cardinal Cushing School, Hanover, MA -- for handicapped children
2,000   Saint Mary's Academy-Bay View, East Providence, RI -- for scholarship assistance
2,000   Washington and Lee University School of Law, Lexington, VA -- towards scholarship assistance
1,000   Angell Memorial, Boston, MA -- for animal hospital
1,000   Bryant College, North Smithfield, RI -- for scholarship assistance
1,000   Harmony Fire District, Harmony, RI -- for support of ongoing operations
1,000   Providence College, Providence, RI -- scholarship assistance
1,000   Rhode Island Ballet Theatre, Providence, RI -- for cultural support ongoing operations
1,000   RI Zoological Society, Providence, RI -- for support of ongoing operations

WILLIAM S. AND LORA JEAN KILROY FOUNDATION

Giving Contact
Lora Jean Kilroy, Jr., Trustee
3700 Buffalo Speedway, Ste. 750
Houston, TX 77098
Phone: (713)621-8221

Description
Founded: 1985
EIN: 760169904
Organization Type: Private Foundation
Giving Locations: CA; CT; TX
Grant Types: Capital, Endowment, Multiyear/Continuing Support, Operating Expenses, Research.

Donor Information
Founder: William S. Kilroy, Lora Jean Kilroy

Financial Summary
Total Giving: $478,192 (2001)
Assets: $10,499,132 (2001)
Gifts Received: In 1991, contributions were received from W. S. and L. J. Kilroy.

Typical Recipients
Arts & Humanities: Arts Funds, Community Arts, Dance, Historic Preservation, History & Archaeology, Libraries, Museums/Galleries
Civic & Public Affairs: Municipalities/Towns, Professional & Trade Associations, Public Policy, Urban & Community Affairs, Women's Affairs, Zoos/Aquariums
Education: Colleges & Universities, Elementary Education (Public), Medical Education, Private Education (Precollege), Religious Education, Science/Mathematics Education, Special Education, Student Aid
Environment: Resource Conservation
Health: Children's Health/Hospitals, Eyes/Blindness, Heart, Hospitals, Medical Rehabilitation, Medical Research, Mental Health, Single-Disease Health Associations
International: Health Care/Hospitals
Religion: Religious Organizations, Religious Welfare
Science: Science Museums
Social Services: Animal Protection, Child Abuse, Child Welfare, Community Service Organizations, Day Care, Family Services, People with Disabilities, Senior Services, YMCA/YWCA/YMHA/YWHA, Youth Organizations

Application Procedures
Initial Contact: Send a brief letter of inquiry.
Application Requirements: any information relevant to the request. There are no deadlines.

Foundation Officials
Lora Jean Kilroy: trustee
Mari Angela Kilroy: trustee
William S. Kilroy: trustee

Grants Analysis
Disclosure Period: calendar year ending 2001
Total Grants: $478,192
Number of Grants: 20
Average Grant: $11,228*
Highest Grant: $153,630
Typical Range: $5,000 to $20,000
***Note:** Average grant figure excludes two highest grants ($253,630).

Recent Grants
Note: Grants derived from 2001 Form 990.

General
153,630	University School, Hunting Valley, OH -- for faculty excellence fund and the annual fund
100,000	Museum of Fine Arts, Houston, TX -- capital campaign pledge
75,000	Brookwood Community, Brookshire, TX -- to fund endowment of Kilroy House
44,462	Kinkaid School, Houston, TX -- for computer lab equipment
20,000	Texas Heart Institute, Houston, TX -- for pledge in honor of Denton Cooley
20,000	Texas Heart Institute, Houston, TX
10,000	Texas Children's Hospital, Houston, TX -- building for children capital campaign
10,000	University of Texas Houston Health Science Center, Houston, TX -- donor funds
10,000	University of Texas Medical School, Houston, TX -- for lung disease cellular research
10,000	Yale University, New Haven, CT -- for Trumbull fund

FLORENCE B. KILWORTH CHARITABLE TRUST

Giving Contact
Michael W. Steadman, Assistant Vice President & Trust Officer
c/o Key Trust Co., NW
800 Superior, 4th Fl.
Cleveland, OH 44114
Phone: (216)828-9535

Description
Founded: 1977
EIN: 916221495
Organization Type: Private Foundation
Giving Locations: WA: Tacoma and Pierce counties and surrounding area
Grant Types: Capital, Emergency, General Support, Project, Research, Scholarship.

Financial Summary
Total Giving: $296,000 (2001)
Assets: $5,957,120 (2001)

Typical Recipients
Arts & Humanities: Arts Associations & Councils, Ballet, Community Arts, History & Archaeology, Libraries, Museums/Galleries, Music, Opera, Performing Arts, Public Broadcasting, Theater
Civic & Public Affairs: African American Affairs, Botanical Gardens/Parks, Clubs, Community Foundations, Employment/Job Training, Civic & Public Affairs-General, Hispanic Affairs, Housing, Public Policy, Urban & Community Affairs, Women's Affairs, Zoos/Aquariums
Education: Arts/Humanities Education, Colleges & Universities, Community & Junior Colleges, Faculty Development, Literacy, Minority Education, Private Education (Precollege), Public Education (Precollege), Religious Education, Science/Mathematics Education, Secondary Education (Public), Special Education
Environment: Environment-General, Wildlife Protection
Health: Arthritis, Cancer, Children's Health/Hospitals, Clinics/Medical Centers, Emergency/Ambulance Services, Health-General, Health Policy/Cost Containment, Health Organizations, Hospitals, Mental Health, Single-Disease Health Associations, Transplant Networks/Donor Banks, Trauma Treatment
International: Missionary/Religious Activities
Religion: Churches, Religion-General, Ministries, Religious Organizations, Religious Welfare
Social Services: At-Risk Youth, Child Welfare, Community Service Organizations, Crime Prevention, Day Care, Family Planning, Family Services, Food/Clothing Distribution, People with Disabilities, Recreation & Athletics, Scouts, Senior Services, Shelters/Homelessness, Social Services-General, United Funds/United Ways, YMCA/YWCA/YMHA/YWHA, Youth Organizations

Application Procedures
Initial Contact: The foundation requests applications be made in writing.
Deadlines: None.

Additional Information
Trust(s): KeyBank N.A.

Foundation Officials
Michael W. Steadman: assistant vice president

Grants Analysis
Disclosure Period: calendar year ending 2001
Total Grants: $296,000
Number of Grants: 73
Average Grant: $4,055
Highest Grant: $15,000
Typical Range: $1,000 to $10,000

Recent Grants
Note: Grants derived from 2001 Form 990.
General
15,000	Tacoma Symphony Orchestra, Tacoma, WA
12,500	Tacoma Art Museum, Tacoma, WA
10,000	Annie Wright School, Tacoma, WA
10,000	Associated Ministries, Tacoma, WA
10,000	Boys and Girls Clubs of Pierce County, Tacoma, WA
10,000	Emergency Food Network, Tacoma, WA
10,000	Pacific Lutheran University, Tacoma, WA
10,000	Tacoma Actors Guild, Tacoma, WA
10,000	Tacoma Art Museum, Tacoma, WA
10,000	University of Puget Sound, Tacoma, WA

HORACE A. KIMBALL AND S. ELLA KIMBALL FOUNDATION

Giving Contact
Thomas F. Black, III, President
130 Woodville Rd.
Hope Valley, RI 02832
Phone: (401)364-3565
Fax: (401)364-3565
Web: http://www.hkimballfoundation.org

Description
Founded: 1956
EIN: 056006130
Organization Type: Private Foundation
Giving Locations: RI
Grant Types: Capital, General Support, Operating Expenses.

Donor Information
Founder: the late H. Earle Kimball

Financial Summary
Total Giving: $289,897 (fiscal year ending September 30, 2001)
Giving Analysis: Giving for fiscal 2001 includes: foundation scholarships ($20,000); foundation matching gifts ($60,660)
Assets: $6,937,338 (fiscal 2001)
Gifts Received: $100 (fiscal 2001); $1,180 (fiscal 2000)

Typical Recipients

Arts & Humanities: Arts Centers, Arts Funds, Arts & Humanities-General, Historic Preservation, History & Archaeology, Libraries, Museums/Galleries, Performing Arts, Theater

Civic & Public Affairs: Botanical Gardens/Parks, Civic & Public Affairs-General, Legal Aid, Municipalities/Towns, Parades/Festivals, Safety, Urban & Community Affairs, Women's Affairs

Education: Afterschool/Enrichment Programs, Colleges & Universities, International Studies, Literacy, Preschool Education, Private Education (Precollege), School Volunteerism, Science/Mathematics Education, Secondary Education (Private), Student Aid

Environment: Environment-General, Resource Conservation, Watershed

Health: Children's Health/Hospitals, Clinics/Medical Centers, Emergency/Ambulance Services, Health-General, Health Organizations, Hospitals, Long-Term Care, Medical Rehabilitation, Medical Research, Nursing Services, Public Health, Single-Disease Health Associations

International: International Peace & Security Issues

Religion: Religious Organizations, Religious Welfare

Social Services: Animal Protection, Big Brothers/Big Sisters, Camps, Child Welfare, Community Service Organizations, Crime Prevention, Day Care, Food/Clothing Distribution, Homes, Recreation & Athletics, Scouts, Senior Services, Shelters/Homelessness, Volunteer Services, YMCA/YWCA/YMHA/YWHA, Youth Organizations

Application Procedures

Initial Contact: Send a brief letter of inquiry. or apply online at the website.

Deadlines: None.

Foundation Officials

Norman D. Baker, Jr.: secretary, treasurer, trustee PRIM CORP EMPL senior vice president: Allendale Insurance.

Thomas F. Black, III: president, trustee

F. Thomas Lenihan, Esq.: trustee

Grants Analysis

Disclosure Period: fiscal year ending September 30, 2001

Total Grants: $219,277*

Number of Grants: 23

Average Grant: $9,534

Highest Grant: $36,000

Lowest Grant: $100

Typical Range: $2,000 to $15,000

*Note: Giving excludes scholarships and matching gifts.

Recent Grants

Note: Grants derived from fiscal 2002 Form 990.

Library-Related

15,000	John Carter Brown Library, Providence, RI -- scholarship fund

General

26,500	Granite Theatre, Inc., Westerly, RI -- debt retirement
25,000	Dorcas Place, Providence, RI -- operational
25,000	Rhode Island Bar Association, RI -- scholarship fund
25,000	St. Mary's Home for Children, Providence, RI -- Campus Renovation Project
20,000	Westerly Education Endowment Fund -- educational
15,500	Granite Theatre Corporation, Westerly, RI -- mortgage reduction
15,000	Arcadia YMCA -- gym equipment
15,000	Westerly Hospital Foundation, Westerly, RI -- capital campaign
13,000	Wood Pawcatuck Watershed Association, Pawcatuck, RI -- building improvements

10,000	Frank A. Olean Regional Center -- administrative

KIMBERLY-CLARK CORP.

Company Headquarters

Dallas, TX

Web: http://www.kimberly-clark.com

Company Description

Founded: 1872

Ticker: KMB

Exchange: NYSE

Revenue: US$15.4 billion (2004)

Profit: US$1.8 billion (2004)

Employees: 63900 (2003)

Fortune Rank: 135, per FORTUNE Magazine's list of 500 Largest U.S. Corporations (2004).

SIC(s): 2621 Paper Mills, 2676 Sanitary Paper Products.

Operating Locations

Kimberly-Clark Corp. (AL--Aliceville, Birmingham, Boligee, Calvert, Coosa Pines, Excel, Gilbertown, Goodwater, Heflin, Huxford, Jacksons Gap, Lineville, Mobile, Monroeville, Oxford, Pine Hill, Quinton, Saraland, Weogufka, Westover; AZ--Scottsdale; AR--Little Rock, Maumelle; CA--Dublin, Fullerton; CO--Englewood, Golden, Littleton; DE--Dover; DC--Washington; FL--Jacksonville; GA--Dunwoody, Roswell; HI--Waipahu; ID--Santa; IL--Des Plaines; ME--Guilford; MD--Woodstock; MA--Feeding Hills; MI--Munising; MS--Corinth, Dennis, Hattiesburg, Pearlington, State Line, Waynesboro; MO--Chesterfield; NJ--Kirkwood Voorhees, Spotswood; NY--Ancram, Melville; NC--Charlotte, Hendersonville, Lexington; OH--Chagrin Falls, Columbus; OK--Jenks; PA--Gibsonia, Media, Newtown Square; SC--Jackson; TN--Collierville, Knoxville, Loudon; TX--Dallas, Irving, Paris; UT--Ogden; WA--Everett; WI--Appleton, Elm Grove, Marinette, Oconto Falls, Oshkosh)

Nonmonetary Support

Type: Donated Products

Volunteer Programs: Foundation makes grants to organizations where employees and their spouses volunteer through the Community Partners program.

Note: Co. provides nonmonetary support in the form of donated products for disaster relief only.

Kimberly-Clark Foundation

Giving Contact

Carolyn Mentesana, Vice President

Kimberly-Clark Foundation

PO Box 619100

Dallas, TX 75261-9100

Phone: (972)281-1200

Fax: (972)281-1490

Web: http://www.kimberly-clark.com/aboutus/comm_involvement.asp

Note: Contact local plant manager for information on corporate direct giving.

Description

EIN: 396044304

Organization Type: Corporate Foundation

Giving Locations: nationally; operating locations.

Grant Types: Capital, Employee Matching Gifts, General Support, Operating Expenses, Project.

Note: Employee matching gift ratio: 1 to 1.

Financial Summary

Total Giving: $5,965,018 (2003); $7,765,116 (2001).

Note: Contributes through corporate direct giving program and foundation.

Assets: $3,015,730 (2003); $8,081,821 (2002); $6,019,856 (2001). Note: Assets pertain to Foundation only.

Gifts Received: $698,094 (2003); $7,398,694 (2001); $10,335,947 (2000). Note: Contributions were received from Kimberly-Clark Corporation.

Typical Recipients

Arts & Humanities: Arts Appreciation, Arts Associations & Councils, Arts Centers, Arts Funds, Community Arts, Dance, Arts & Humanities-General, Historic Preservation, History & Archaeology, Libraries, Museums/Galleries, Music, Opera, Performing Arts, Public Broadcasting, Theater

Civic & Public Affairs: African American Affairs, Botanical Gardens/Parks, Business/Free Enterprise, Chambers of Commerce, Civil Rights, Clubs, Community Foundations, Economic Development, Economic Policy, Civic & Public Affairs-General, Law & Justice, Legal Aid, Municipalities/Towns, Parades/Festivals, Philanthropic Organizations, Professional & Trade Associations, Public Policy, Safety, Urban & Community Affairs, Women's Affairs, Zoos/Aquariums

Education: Arts/Humanities Education, Business Education, Colleges & Universities, Community & Junior Colleges, Economic Education, Education Associations, Education Funds, Education Reform, Engineering/Technological Education, Environmental Education, Faculty Development, Education-General, International Studies, Leadership Training, Legal Education, Literacy, Medical Education, Minority Education, Private Education (Precollege), School Volunteerism, Science/Mathematics Education, Special Education, Student Aid

Environment: Air/Water Quality, Energy, Environment-General, Resource Conservation, Wildlife Protection

Health: Adolescent Health Issues, Cancer, Children's Health/Hospitals, Clinics/Medical Centers, Diabetes, Emergency/Ambulance Services, Health-General, Geriatric Health, Health Funds, Health Organizations, Hospitals, Hospitals (University Affiliated), Medical Research, Multiple Sclerosis, Nursing Services, Preventive Medicine/Wellness Organizations, Public Health, Single-Disease Health Associations

International: Foreign Educational Institutions, International-General, International Relations, International Relief Efforts

Religion: Religious Welfare

Science: Science Museums, Scientific Research

Social Services: Animal Protection, Child Welfare, Community Centers, Community Service Organizations, Counseling, Crime Prevention, Delinquency & Criminal Rehabilitation, Domestic Violence, Emergency Relief, Family Services, Food/Clothing Distribution, People with Disabilities, Recreation & Athletics, Senior Services, Shelters/Homelessness, Substance Abuse, United Funds/United Ways, Volunteer Services, YMCA/YWCA/YMHA/YWHA, Youth Organizations

Application Procedures

Initial Contact: Send a written proposal.

Application Requirements: Include amount requested, purpose of grant, and proof of tax-exempt 501(c)(3) status.

Deadlines: None; proposals reviewed as received.

Restrictions

The foundation does not make grants to sports or athletic activities; dinners or special events; individuals; fraternal organizations; state or secondary schools (except through matching gifts); religious organizations; goodwill advertising; member agencies of united funds; or political parties or candidates.

Additional Information

Kimberly-Clark Corp. annually budgets 1% of pre-tax domestic income averaged from preceding three years for charitable contributions, which may be given directly to qualified recipients or to the Kimberly-Clark Foundation for distribution. Since 1952, the foundation has served as the principal means through which the corporation supports tax-exempt charitable organizations.

In 1995, Kimberly-Clark Corp. acquired Scott Paper Co. currently being considered by the Kimberly-Clark Foundation.

Publications: Annual Report

Corporate Officials

Tina S. Barry: senior vice president corporate communications PRIM CORP EMPL vice president corporate communications: Kimberly-Clark Corp.

Mark A. Buthman: senior vice president, chief financial officer ED University of Iowa BA.

Thomas J. Falk: chairman, president, chief executive officer ED Stanford University MS; University of Wisconsin BA (1980). CORP AFFIL director: Centex Corp. NONPR AFFIL director: Grocery Manufacturers of America; trustee: University of Wisconsin; director: Boys & Girls Clubs of America.

W. Anthony Gamron: vice president B Seymour, IN 1948. ED Indiana State University BS (1971); Indiana University MBA (1977). PRIM CORP EMPL vice president, treasurer: Kimberly-Clark Corp. ADD CORP EMPL treasurer: Kimberly Clark Tissue Co.

Ronald D. McCray: vice president ED Cornell University BA (1979); Harvard University JD (1983). CORP AFFIL director: Knight-Ridder Inc. NONPR AFFIL director: Hockaday School.

Foundation Officials

Tina S. Barry: president (see above)
Mark A. Buthman: vice president (see above)
Timothy C. Everett: secretary, director
Thomas J. Falk: director (see above)
Carolyn A. Mentesana: vice president
Jolene L. Varney: treasurer

Grants Analysis

Disclosure Period: calendar year ending 2003
Total Grants: $2,861,000*
Number of Grants: 57
Average Grant: $25,375*
Highest Grant: $1,440,000
Lowest Grant: $200
Typical Range: $10,000 to $50,000
*Note: Giving excludes matching gifts; scholarship; United Way. Average grant figure excludes highest grant.

Recent Grants

Note: Grants derived from 2003 Form 990.

General

1,786,250	Bright Futures Scholarship Program, Tallahassee, FL
1,440,000	Community Partners, Los Angeles, CA
250,000	Marquette University, Milwaukee, WI
200,000	Visiting Nurse Association of Texas, Dallas, TX
100,000	Dallas County Community College District Foundation, Dallas, TX
75,000	MedShare International Inc., Lithonia, GA
71,072	United Way of Metropolitan Dallas, Dallas, TX
50,000	Dallas Arboretum & Botanical Society Inc., Dallas, TX
50,000	Foundation for Women's Resources Inc., Austin, TX
50,000	Friends of the CEELI Institute, Prague Czech Republic

KINDER MORGAN

Company Headquarters

1301 McKinney, Suite 3400
Houston, TX 77010
Phone: (713)844-9500
Web: http://www.kindermorgan.com

Company Description

Founded: 1936
Ticker: KMI
Exchange: NYSE
Former Name: KN Energy Co. (1999).
Revenue: US$7.932 billion (2004)
Profit: US$831.6 million (2004)
Employees: 5530 (2003)
Fortune Rank: 271, per FORTUNE Magazine's list of 500 Largest U.S. Corporations (2004).
SIC(s): 4900 Electric, Gas & Sanitary Services, 4923 Gas Transmission & Distribution, 5172 Petroleum Products Nec, 5983 Fuel Oil Dealers.

Operating Locations

KN Energy (CO--Lakewood; NE--Hastings; WY--Casper)

Nonmonetary Support

Type: Donated Equipment
Note: NOT Company provides nonmonetary support.
Volunteer Programs: The Foundation funds the KM for Kids program, through which youth programs throughout Kinder Morgan's retail communities receive funding and volunteer support.

Kinder Morgan Foundation

Giving Contact

Maureen Bulkley, Foundation Administrator
PO Box 281304
Lakewood, CO 80228
Phone: (303)763-3471
Fax: (303)984-3306
E-mail: maureen_bulkley@kindermorgan.com
Web: http://www.kindermorgan.com/community/km_foundation.cfm

Description

Founded: 1990
EIN: 841148161
Organization Type: Corporate Foundation
Giving Locations: AR; CO; IL; IA; KS; LA; MO; MT; NE; NM; ND; OK; TX; UT; WY
Grant Types: Capital, Employee Matching Gifts, General Support, Project.
Note: Employee matching gift ratio: 1 to 1, up to $1,000 per employee each year.

Donor Information

Founder: KN Energy, Inc.

Financial Summary

Total Giving: $768,605 (2003); $811,000 (2002); $755,752 (2001)
Giving Analysis: Giving for 2001 includes: foundation grants to United Way ($6,941); foundation matching gifts ($23,692)
Assets: $2,770,800 (2003); $2,983,136 (2002); $4,216,599 (2001)

Typical Recipients

Arts & Humanities: Arts Associations & Councils, Arts Centers, Arts Funds, Arts Outreach, Dance, Arts & Humanities-General, Historic Preservation, History & Archaeology, Libraries, Museums/Galleries, Music, Opera, Performing Arts, Public Broadcasting, Theater

Civic & Public Affairs: African American Affairs, Botanical Gardens/Parks, Business/Free Enterprise, Chambers of Commerce, Clubs, Community Foundations, Economic Development, Civic & Public Affairs-General, Housing, Municipalities/Towns, Parades/Festivals, Rural Affairs, Safety, Urban & Community Affairs, Women's Affairs, Zoos/Aquariums

Education: Afterschool/Enrichment Programs, Agricultural Education, Business Education, Colleges & Universities, Community & Junior Colleges, Economic Education, Education Associations, Education Funds, Elementary Education (Private), Engineering/Technological Education, Education-General, Leadership Training, Minority Education, Private Education (Precollege), Public Education (Precollege), Secondary Education (Private), Secondary Education (Public), Special Education, Student Aid

Environment: Air/Water Quality, Energy, Environment-General, Wildlife Protection

Health: Children's Health/Hospitals, Clinics/Medical Centers, Emergency/Ambulance Services, Health-General, Health Organizations, Hospices, Hospitals, Multiple Sclerosis, Nutrition, Public Health

Religion: Jewish Causes, Religious Welfare, Seminaries

Science: Science-General, Science Museums, Scientific Centers & Institutes

Social Services: Big Brothers/Big Sisters, Camps, Child Welfare, Community Centers, Community Service Organizations, Delinquency & Criminal Rehabilitation, Emergency Relief, Family Planning, Family Services, Homes, People with Disabilities, Recreation & Athletics, Scouts, Senior Services, Social Services-General, United Funds/United Ways, YMCA/YWCA/YMHA/YWHA, Youth Organizations

Application Procedures

Initial Contact: Request guidelines and organization summary form from the foundation. Send a brief letter of inquiry. not more than three pages in length.
Application Requirements: Proposals should include a completed organization summary form, and a cover letter/proposal narrative of three pages or less. Include a description of organization, amount requested and total amount sought in campaign, and purpose of funds sought; statement of rationale for proposal including an indication of its goal, the need for such a program, any unique element, population benefited, and geographical reach; list of other collaborative agencies, and their role in the program to be funded; timeline for implementation; expected goals, objectives, and tactics; plans for project evaluation; itemized budget for the program or project; list of officers and directors, with affiliations; detailed organizational budget for the current year, with income and expenses; recently audited financial statement, and proof of tax-exempt status.
Deadlines: None.
Decision Notification: Awards are typically announced on a quarterly basis.

Restrictions

Foundation will not fund individuals; political causes, candidates, or lobbying efforts; programs or organizations outside of the U.S.; operating expenses; projects of religious denominations; advertising; athletic team sponsorships; or elementary or secondary schools (unless submitted through an educational foundation).

Applicants must have 501(c)(3) status and proposals must reflect the purpose of the Kinder Morgan Foundation.

Foundation Officials

Maureen Bulkley: foundation administrator
Larry S. Pierce: director
C. Park Shaper: director
James E. Street: director
Daniel E. Watson: director

Grants Analysis

Disclosure Period: calendar year ending 2003
Total Grants: $730,175*

Number of Grants: 400 (approx)
Average Grant: $1,825*
Highest Grant: $30,000
Lowest Grant: $50
Typical Range: $500 to $5,000
*Note: Giving excludes matching gifts and United Way.

Recent Grants

Note: Grants derived from 2003 Form 990.
Library-Related
2,000	Campbell County Public Library, Newport, KY

General
7,500	Council of Energy Resource Tribes, Denver, CO
7,500	Roland McDonald House, Houston, TX
7,500	University of Wyoming Foundation, Laramie, WY
5,000	CA State University Dominguez Hills, Carson, CA
5,000	Children's Fund, Houston, TX
5,000	Children's Hospital Foundation of Austin, Austin, TX
5,000	Crow Canyon Archaeological Center, Cortez, CO
5,000	Da Camera of Houston, Houston, TX
5,000	Houston Livestock Show and Rodeo, Houston, TX
5,000	Josephinum, Chicago, IL

CHARLES AND LUCILLE KING FAMILY FOUNDATION

Giving Contact

Karen Kennedy, Assistant Educational Director
366 Madison Avenue, 10th Floor
New York, NY 10017-3122
Phone: (212)682-2459
Fax: (212)949-0728
E-mail: info@kingfoundation.org
Web: http://www.kingfoundation.org

Description

Founded: 1988
EIN: 133489257
Organization Type: Private Foundation
Giving Locations: nationally.
Grant Types: Scholarship.

Donor Information

Founder: Diana King

Financial Summary

Total Giving: $385,762 (2001)
Giving Analysis: Giving for 2001 includes: foundation grants to United Way ($12,500); foundation scholarships ($74,850)
Assets: $5,366,741 (2001)
Gifts Received: $155,220 (2001); $57,305 (2000); $87,869 (1999). Note: In 2001, contributions were received from Diana King ($95,200) and Karen Rabe ($60,000). In 1999, contributions were received from Diana King.

Typical Recipients

Arts & Humanities: Film & Video, Arts & Humanities-General, History & Archaeology, Libraries, Museums/Galleries, Performing Arts, Theater
Civic & Public Affairs: Civic & Public Affairs-General, Safety
Education: Arts/Humanities Education, Colleges & Universities, Journalism/Media Education, Minority Education, Special Education, Student Aid
Environment: Watershed, Wildlife Protection

Health: Cancer, Children's Health/Hospitals, Diabetes, Emergency/Ambulance Services, Home-Care Services, Hospitals, Public Health
International: International Affairs, International Organizations
Religion: Churches, Religious Organizations, Religious Welfare
Social Services: Child Welfare, Crime Prevention, Food/Clothing Distribution, Recreation & Athletics, Shelters/Homelessness, Special Olympics, United Funds/United Ways, Veterans, Youth Organizations

Application Procedures

Initial Contact: Request application form.
Deadlines: April 15.

Restrictions

Student applicants must be currently enrolled in a four-year university in the United States.

Additional Information

Provides scholarships to television and film undergraduate students.
Publications: Application Form

Foundation Officials

Charles J. Brucia: vice president, treasurer, director
Michael Collyer, Esq.: director
Diana King: president, director B 1949. PRIM CORP EMPL vice president, secretary, director: King World Productions.
Eugene V. Kokot: secretary, director

Grants Analysis

Disclosure Period: calendar year ending 2001
Total Grants: $298,412*
Number of Grants: 73
Average Grant: $4,088
Highest Grant: $60,000
Typical Range: $500 to $10,000
*Note: Giving excludes scholarships; United Way.

Recent Grants

Note: Grants derived from 2001 Form 990.
General
60,000	Blairsden Association, New York, NY
50,000	New York University, New York, NY -- millennium grant
15,000	New York University, New York, NY -- Heinemann grant
13,000	American Red Cross, Morristown, NJ
12,500	United Way, New York, NY
10,000	Columbia College-Chicago, Chicago, IL
10,000	International Council of Natas Foundation, New York, NY
10,000	Kips Bay Boys and Girls Club, Bronx, NY
10,000	Salvation Army, New York, NY
10,000	University of California Los Angeles, Los Angeles, CA

CARL B. AND FLORENCE E. KING FOUNDATION

Giving Contact

Dr. Mary Sias, Contact
Board of Directors
5956 Sherry Lane, Suite 620
Dallas, TX 75225
Phone: (214)750-1884
Fax: (214)750-1651

Description

Founded: 1966
EIN: 756052203
Organization Type: General Purpose Foundation
Giving Locations: TX: Dallas including metropolitan area

Grant Types: Capital, General Support, Multiyear/Continuing Support, Project, Scholarship.

Donor Information

Founder: Incorporated in 1966 by the late Carl B. King and the late Florence E. King. Mr. King formed the Carl B. King Drilling Company during the oil boom in Oklahoma. The foundation was created a year before his death in 1967.

Financial Summary

Total Giving: $1,793,622 (2002). Note: 1996 Giving includes scholarships ($39,500); 1995 scholarships ($15,500).
Giving Analysis: Giving for 2002 includes: foundation scholarships ($373,132)
Assets: $37,599,609 (2002)
Gifts Received: $484,377 (1995). Note: In 1995, contributions were received from the D.E. King estate.

Typical Recipients

Arts & Humanities: Arts Associations & Councils, Arts Festivals, Arts Institutes, Arts Outreach, Ballet, Ethnic & Folk Arts, Historic Preservation, History & Archaeology, Libraries, Museums/Galleries, Music, Opera, Public Broadcasting
Civic & Public Affairs: Botanical Gardens/Parks, Clubs, Community Foundations, Employment/Job Training, Civic & Public Affairs-General, Hispanic Affairs, Inner-City Development, Law & Justice, Municipalities/Towns, Nonprofit Management, Philanthropic Organizations, Professional & Trade Associations, Public Policy, Rural Affairs, Safety, Urban & Community Affairs, Women's Affairs, Zoos/Aquariums
Education: Afterschool/Enrichment Programs, Agricultural Education, Arts/Humanities Education, Colleges & Universities, Education Associations, Education Funds, Education Reform, Elementary Education (Private), Engineering/Technological Education, Faculty Development, Education-General, Legal Education, Literacy, Medical Education, Private Education (Precollege), Public Education (Precollege), Science/Mathematics Education, Secondary Education (Private), Social Sciences Education, Special Education, Student Aid
Environment: Environment-General, Resource Conservation, Wildlife Protection
Health: Cancer, Children's Health/Hospitals, Clinics/Medical Centers, Diabetes, Emergency/Ambulance Services, Eyes/Blindness, Health Funds, Health Organizations, Heart, Hospices, Hospitals, Medical Rehabilitation, Medical Research, Nursing Services, Prenatal Health Issues, Research/Studies Institutes
Religion: Churches, Jewish Causes, Religious Organizations, Religious Welfare
Science: Science Museums, Scientific Organizations
Social Services: Animal Protection, Camps, Child Welfare, Community Service Organizations, Counseling, Crime Prevention, Delinquency & Criminal Rehabilitation, Family Planning, Family Services, People with Disabilities, Recreation & Athletics, Scouts, Shelters/Homelessness, Social Services-General, Substance Abuse, United Funds/United Ways, Veterans, Volunteer Services, YMCA/YWCA/YMHA/YWHA, Youth Organizations

Application Procedures

Initial Contact: The foundation welcomes introductory inquiries.
Application Requirements: Formal grant proposals should include an IRS tax-exempt form; a description of the applicant organization, a history of the organization's activities, and its purpose; a summary of the proposed program, its goals and objectives, and plans for implementation; the purpose of the grant; the specific amount requested from the foundation, as well as all other sources of funding; a financial statement and proposed budget a copy of the IRS determination letters; and a statement of approval, signed by the organization's chief administrator, for requesting funds.

Deadlines: None.
Review Process: Once the application has been received and reviewed, the foundation may call upon the applicant for additional information. The directors will then study the request and convey their decision directly to the applicant.
Notes: The foundation accepts no responsibility for keeping any part of a request confidential and reserves the right to discuss a proposal with outside consultants.

Restrictions

As a general policy, the foundation refrains from extending grants for individuals, organisation outside Texas, organization which are not tax-exempt, religious organizations for sectarian purposes, deficit financing or ongoing operating expenses, and loan financing. ScholarshipS are awarded to Texas High School graduates and/or to college students majoring in science, math, or English education. (1998 Form 990)

Additional Information

Publications: Program Policy Statement; Brochure and Guidelines

Foundation Officials

Thomas W. Vett: secretary, treasurer
Carl L. Yeckel: president, director

Grants Analysis

Disclosure Period: calendar year ending 2002
Total Grants: $1,420,490*
Number of Grants: 34
Average Grant: $31,890*
Highest Grant: $180,000
Lowest Grant: $400
Typical Range: $10,000 to $50,000
***Note:** Giving excludes scholarships. Average grant figure excludes two highest grants ($400,000).

Recent Grants

Note: Grants derived from 2002 Form 990.
General

220,000	YMCA of Metropolitan Dallas, Dallas, TX -- towards general endowment
200,000	Texas A&M University, College Station, TX -- towards deanship in veterinary medicine
180,000	Kera Channel 13, Dallas, TX -- towards Sesame Street
144,632	Texas Interscholastic League, Austin, TX -- towards scholarships
115,500	Siloam Springs High School, Siloam Springs, AR -- towards scholarships
100,000	Midland Memorial Foundation, Midland, TX -- towards new medical office
76,500	YMCA Urban Services, Dallas, TX -- towards scholarships
75,000	Gladney Fund, Ft. Worth, TX -- towards center for adoption construction
50,000	children's Medical Center of Dallas, Dallas, TX -- towards pediatric cardiac ICU expansion
50,000	Dallas Symphony Orchestra, Dallas, TX -- towards Dallas symphony orchestra academy

KENNETH KENDAL KING FOUNDATION

Giving Contact

Robert Sweeney, President & Director
Kenneth Kendal King Foundation
900 Pennsylvania Street
Denver, CO 80203-3163

Phone: (303)832-3200
Fax: (303)832-4176
E-mail: info@kennethkingfoundation.org
Web: http://www.kennethkingfoundation.org

Description

Founded: 1990
EIN: 841148157
Organization Type: Private Foundation
Grant Types: Capital, Emergency, General Support, Matching, Project, Research.

Donor Information

Founder: Established in 1990 by the late Kenneth Kendal King.

Financial Summary

Total Giving: $1,330,240 (2002); $1,500,000 (2001 approx)
Assets: $40,266,998 (2002); $64,198,965 (2001)
Gifts Received: $500 (2002); $500 (1999); $2,494 (1997)

Typical Recipients

Arts & Humanities: Arts Centers, Libraries, Museums/Galleries, Opera
Civic & Public Affairs: African American Affairs, Botanical Gardens/Parks, Employment/Job Training, Civic & Public Affairs-General, Housing, Women's Affairs, Zoos/Aquariums
Education: Arts/Humanities Education, Colleges & Universities, Community & Junior Colleges, Economic Education, Engineering/Technological Education, Education-General, Gifted & Talented Programs, Private Education (Precollege), Religious Education, Secondary Education (Private), Special Education, Student Aid, Vocational & Technical Education
Environment: Environment-General, Resource Conservation
Health: Cancer, Children's Health/Hospitals, Eyes/Blindness, Hospices, Hospitals, Mental Health, Multiple Sclerosis, Research/Studies Institutes, Speech & Hearing, Transplant Networks/Donor Banks
International: Health Care/Hospitals
Religion: Churches, Religious Welfare
Science: Science Museums
Social Services: At-Risk Youth, Child Welfare, Community Centers, Community Service Organizations, Counseling, Family Services, Food/Clothing Distribution, People with Disabilities, Recreation & Athletics, Refugee Assistance, Senior Services, YMCA/YWCA/YMHA/YWHA, Youth Organizations

Application Procedures

Initial Contact: Request application.
Application Requirements: Complete application will include proof of tax-exempt status and last two years balance sheet and income and expense statement are mandatory.
Deadlines: March 1.

Additional Information

Publications: Application Form; Annual Report

Foundation Officials

Matthew R. Banner, III: director
Bernice A. Bettis: secretary, director
Peter Hoke: director
Joseph Kelly: director
Minnie P. Lundberg: treasurer, director
Eaton Smith: director
Robert Sweeney: president, director
T. E. Welker: director

Grants Analysis

Disclosure Period: calendar year ending 2002
Total Grants: $1,330,240
Number of Grants: 233
Average Grant: $4,027*
Highest Grant: $200,000
Lowest Grant: $300
Typical Range: $1,000 to $10,000

***Note:** Average grant figure excludes two highest grants.

Recent Grants

Note: Grants derived from 2002 Form 990.
Library-Related

20,000	Auraria Library, Denver, CO -- for purchasing additional equipment for the computer commons area

General

200,000	Auraria Foundation, Denver, CO -- for King Center multi year commitment
200,000	University of Colorado Foundation, Boulder, CO -- for multi year commitment
56,000	Iliff School of Technology, Denver, CO -- for operating support
25,000	Goodwill Industries of Denver, Denver, CO -- for School to Work Program
25,000	Little Voice Productions, Denver, CO -- for operating support
25,000	Metropolitan State College Denver, Denver, CO -- for purchasing specialized hardware and software
25,000	Sigma Chi Foundation, Evanston, IL -- commitment
18,000	Sigma Chi Foundation, Evanston, IL -- commitment
16,000	Sigma Chi Foundation, Evanston, IL -- for operating support
15,000	Liberty Day Colorado, Centennial, CO -- to support Liberty Day

KINGSBURY CORP.

Company Headquarters

80 Laurel St.
Keene, NH 03431
Web: http://www.kingsburycorp.com

Company Description

Revenue: US$47.2 million (2001)
Employees: 165 (2003)
SIC(s): 3541 Machine Tools--Metal Cutting Types, 3542 Machine Tools--Metal Forming Types.

Operating Locations

Kingsbury Corp. (NH--Keene)

Nonmonetary Support

Type: Donated Equipment; Donated Products; In-kind Services; Loaned Employees

Kingsbury Fund

Giving Contact

James E. O'Neil, Executive Trustee
Kingsbury Fund
Box 2020
80 Laurel Street
Keene, NH 03431-7020
Phone: (603)352-5212
Fax: (603)357-1955
Web: http://www.kingsburycorp.com

Description

Founded: 1952
EIN: 026004465
Organization Type: Corporate Foundation
Giving Locations: ME; MA; NH: especially Cheshire County; VT
Grant Types: Capital, Multiyear/Continuing Support, Operating Expenses, Project, Scholarship, Seed Money.
Note: Matches gifts to educational institutions.

Donor Information

Founder: Kingsbury Corp., Kingsbury Manufacturing Co., Fitchburg Foundry

Financial Summary

Total Giving: $132,354 (2003); $152,460 (2002); $154,590 (2001). Note: Contributes through foundation only.

Assets: $3,366,740 (2003); $3,096,210 (2002); $3,555,626 (2001)

Gifts Received: $10,000 (1998); $88,105 (1997); $20,000 (1996). Note: In 1998, contributions were received from an anonymous donor. In 1997, contributions were received from Kingsbury Corp.

Typical Recipients

Arts & Humanities: Arts Appreciation, Arts Associations & Councils, Arts Centers, Arts Festivals, Arts Funds, Arts Institutes, Ballet, Community Arts, Dance, Ethnic & Folk Arts, Arts & Humanities-General, Historic Preservation, History & Archaeology, Libraries, Museums/Galleries, Music, Opera, Performing Arts, Public Broadcasting, Theater, Visual Arts

Civic & Public Affairs: Botanical Gardens/Parks, Chambers of Commerce, Clubs, Economic Development, Civic & Public Affairs-General, Housing, Inner-City Development, Parades/Festivals, Safety, Urban & Community Affairs, Women's Affairs

Education: Arts/Humanities Education, Business Education, Colleges & Universities, Community & Junior Colleges, Continuing Education, Education Funds, Elementary Education (Public), Engineering/Technological Education, Education-General, International Studies, Private Education (Precollege), Public Education (Precollege), Religious Education, School Volunteerism, Science/Mathematics Education, Student Aid, Vocational & Technical Education

Environment: Air/Water Quality, Environment-General, Protection, Resource Conservation

Health: AIDS/HIV, Cancer, Children's Health/Hospitals, Clinics/Medical Centers, Emergency/Ambulance Services, Health Funds, Health Organizations, Heart, Hospices, Medical Research

Religion: Religious Welfare

Science: Observatories & Planetariums

Social Services: Animal Protection, Camps, Child Welfare, Community Centers, Community Service Organizations, Crime Prevention, Day Care, Emergency Relief, Family Services, Food/Clothing Distribution, Homes, People with Disabilities, Recreation & Athletics, Scouts, Senior Services, Social Services-General, Special Olympics, Substance Abuse, United Funds/United Ways, Volunteer Services, YMCA/YWCA/YMHA/YWHA, Youth Organizations

Application Procedures

Initial Contact: Request application guidelines for scholarship grants. Submit a brief letter of inquiry for grant requests.

Application Requirements: Scholarship application forms include contact information, high school or college background, transcripts, estimated budget, evaluation form, and financial statement.

Deadlines: April 19.

Notes: There are no formal application procedures or deadlines for grant requests.

Additional Information

Provides scholarships for higher education to the children of Kingsbury Machine employees.

Trust(s): State Street Bank & Trust Co. of New Hampshire

Corporate Officials

James E. O'Neil: vice president technology PRIM CORP EMPL vice president corporate relations: Kingsbury Corp.

Foundation Officials

William Cogger: executive trustee
James E. O'Neil: executive trustee (see above)

Grants Analysis

Disclosure Period: calendar year ending 2003
Total Grants: $96,618*
Number of Grants: 111
Average Grant: $870
Highest Grant: $10,000
Lowest Grant: $25
Typical Range: $100 to $3,000
*Note: Giving excludes matching gifts; scholarship; United Way.

Recent Grants

Note: Grants derived from 2002 Form 990.
Library-Related

2,500	Keene Public Library, Keene, NH -- towards expansion of reading programs

General

15,000	Harris Center, Hancock, NH -- towards pledge payments
12,500	Keene State College, Keene, NH -- towards soccer stadium press box
10,000	Cedarcrest Foundation, Keene, NH -- towards pledge payments
10,000	Home Healthcare, Hospice & Community Services, Keene, NH -- towards pledge payments
8441	Monadnock United Way, Keene, NH -- towards corporate match
8,441	Monadnock United Way, Keene, NH
8,441	Monadnock United Way, Keene, NH
8,441	Monadnock United Way, Keene, NH
8,000	Colonial Theater, Boston, MA -- towards corporate sponsorship for Swan Lake ballet
7,500	Monadnock Humane Society, West Swanzey, NH -- towards pledge payments for Adoption & Learning Center

KINGTON FOUNDATION, INC.

Giving Contact

Mark J. Kington, Secretary & Director
201 North Union Street, Suite 300
Alexandria, VA 22314-2642
Phone: (703)519-3599

Description

Founded: 1997
EIN: 541831668
Organization Type: Private Foundation
Grant Types: General Support.

Financial Summary

Total Giving: $298,000 (fiscal year ending November 30, 2001)
Assets: $1,885,247 (fiscal 2001)
Gifts Received: $27,765 (fiscal 2000); $94,572 (fiscal 1997). Note: In 1997 and 2000, contributions were received from Mark and Ann Kington.

Typical Recipients

Arts & Humanities: Arts Centers, Historic Preservation, History & Archaeology, Museums/Galleries, Visual Arts

Civic & Public Affairs: Civic & Public Affairs-General, Philanthropic Organizations

Education: Arts/Humanities Education, Colleges & Universities, International Studies, Private Education (Precollege)

Environment: Environment-General

Religion: Churches

Social Services: Senior Services, Youth Organizations

Foundation Officials

Allison W. Cryor: president
Ann A. Kington: director
Ann A. Kington: director
Helen Kington: director
Mark J. Kington: director
Mark J. Kington: secretary, director
Allison W. Kryor: president

Grants Analysis

Disclosure Period: fiscal year ending November 30, 2001
Total Grants: $298,000
Number of Grants: 36
Average Grant: $5,657*
Highest Grant: $100,000
Lowest Grant: $500
Typical Range: $1,000 to $10,000
*Note: Average grant excludes highest grant.

Recent Grants

Note: Grants derived from fiscal 2002 Form 990.
General

150,000	National Gallery of Art, Washington, DC -- gallery for acquisition of American art
25,000	Christ Church, Alexandria, VA -- capital campaign
20,000	St. Stephens and St. Agnes School, Alexandria, VA -- capital campaign
15,000	Alexandria Seaport Foundation, Alexandria, VA -- challenge grant
15,000	National Public Radio, Washington, DC -- annual gift
15,000	Piedmont Environmental Council, Warrenton, VA -- annual gift
10,000	Gadsby's Tavern Museum, Alexandria, VA -- challenge grant
10,000	National Gallery of Art, Washington, DC -- annual gift
10,000	National Trust for Historic Preservation, Washington, DC -- for annual fund
10,000	University of Virginia, Charlottesville, VA -- annual gift

KINNEY-LINDSTROM FOUNDATION

Giving Contact

Lowell K. Hall, Secretary/Treasurer
PO Box 520
Mason City, IA 50401
Phone: (515)896-3888

Description

Founded: 1957
EIN: 426037351
Organization Type: General Purpose Foundation
Giving Locations: IA
Grant Types: Capital, General Support, Scholarship.

Donor Information

Founder: the late Ida Lindstrom Kinney

Financial Summary

Total Giving: $212,651 (2001)
Giving Analysis: Giving for 2001 includes: foundation scholarships ($4,000); foundation grants to United Way ($30,000)
Assets: $4,206,229 (2001)

Typical Recipients

Arts & Humanities: Arts Associations & Councils, Arts Festivals, Historic Preservation, History & Archaeology, Libraries, Museums/Galleries, Music,

Performing Arts, Public Broadcasting, Theater

Civic & Public Affairs: Botanical Gardens/Parks, Community Foundations, Employment/Job Training, Civic & Public Affairs-General, Municipalities/Towns, Parades/Festivals, Safety, Urban & Community Affairs

Education: Agricultural Education, Colleges & Universities, Community & Junior Colleges, Public Education (Precollege), Science/Mathematics Education, Special Education, Student Aid

Environment: Environment-General, Resource Conservation

Health: Cancer, Children's Health/Hospitals, Emergency/Ambulance Services, Health-General, Heart

International: International Environmental Issues

Religion: Churches, Religious Welfare

Science: Science Museums

Social Services: Camps, Community Service Organizations, Counseling, Day Care, Emergency Relief, People with Disabilities, Recreation & Athletics, Scouts, Senior Services, Substance Abuse, United Funds/United Ways, YMCA/YWCA/YMHA/YWHA, Youth Organizations

Application Procedures

Initial Contact: Send a brief letter of inquiry.
Deadlines: None.

Foundation Officials

John H. Greve: trustee
Lowell K. Hall: secretary
Everett J. Hermanson: trustee
Thor J. Jenson: trustee

Grants Analysis

Disclosure Period: calendar year ending 2001
Total Grants: $178,651*
Number of Grants: 30
Average Grant: $4,436*
Highest Grant: $50,000
Lowest Grant: $250
Typical Range: $1,000 to $10,000
*Note: Giving excludes scholarship and United Way. Average grant figure excludes highest grant.

Recent Grants

Note: Grants derived from 2001 Form 990.
General

50,000	Iowa College Foundation, Des Moines, IA -- library challenge
30,000	United Way of North Central Iowa, Mason City, IA -- annual fund drive
20,000	Iowa College Foundation, Des Moines, IA -- Net Library
12,000	Clear Lake, Clear Lake, IA -- public library
10,000	American Red Cross, Idaho Falls, ID -- New York Disaster Fund
8,500	Boy Scouts of America - Winnebago Council-- log cabin
8,000	Francis Lauer Youth Services, Mason City, IA -- equipment
7,500	Fertile Fire Department, Fertile, IA -- new fire truck funds
7,200	Pioneer Museum and Historical Society, IA -- museum repairs
6,000	Mason City, Mason City, IA -- parks and recreation beautification

KINNEY MEMORIAL FOUNDATION

Giving Contact

Thomas W. Bindert, Vice President & Trust Officer
c/o Bank of New York, Tax Dept.
1290 Ave. of the Americas
New York, NY 10104
Phone: (212)635-1520

Description

Founded: 1992
EIN: 136968427
Organization Type: Private Foundation
Giving Locations: no restrictions.
Grant Types: General Support.

Financial Summary

Total Giving: $243,143 (2002)
Assets: $3,780,134 (2002)
Gifts Received: $100 (1992)

Typical Recipients

Arts & Humanities: Arts & Humanities-General, Historic Preservation, History & Archaeology, Libraries, Theater

Civic & Public Affairs: Botanical Gardens/Parks, Clubs, Civic & Public Affairs-General, Housing, Law & Justice, Public Policy, Safety, Urban & Community Affairs

Education: Arts/Humanities Education, Colleges & Universities, Community & Junior Colleges, International Studies, Legal Education, Minority Education, Preschool Education, Private Education (Precollege), Science/Mathematics Education, Secondary Education (Private), Special Education

Environment: Environment-General, Resource Conservation

Health: AIDS/HIV, Clinics/Medical Centers, Diabetes, Eyes/Blindness, Heart, Hospitals, Medical Research, Mental Health

International: Foreign Educational Institutions, International Relief Efforts

Religion: Churches, Religion-General, Religious Organizations, Religious Welfare

Social Services: At-Risk Youth, Child Welfare, Community Service Organizations, Crime Prevention, Emergency Relief, Food/Clothing Distribution, People with Disabilities, Recreation & Athletics, Senior Services, Youth Organizations

Application Procedures

Initial Contact: Send a brief letter of inquiry.
Deadlines: None.

Additional Information

Trust(s): The Bank New York

Foundation Officials

Edward Holloway, Jr.: trustee
George R. Kinney: trustee
Josephine J. Kinney: trustee

Grants Analysis

Disclosure Period: calendar year ending 2002
Total Grants: $243,143
Number of Grants: 25
Average Grant: $6,754*
Highest Grant: $81,048
Lowest Grant: $1,000
Typical Range: $1,000 to $10,000
*Note: Average grant figure excludes highest grant.

Recent Grants

Note: Grants derived from 2002 Form 990.
General

81,047	Flatbush Tompkins Congregation Church of Brooklyn, Brooklyn, NY
25,000	Estes Park Volunteer Fire Department, Inc., Estes Park, CO
10,000	Bucknell University, Lewisburg, PA
10,000	Canadensis United Methodist Church
10,000	Carroll College, Milwaukee, WI
10,000	Estes Park Medical Center Foundation, Inc., Estes Park, CO
10,000	Estes Park Senior Citizen Center, Inc., Estes Park, CO
10,000	Freedom From Hunger, Davis, CA
10,000	Lucille Packard Children's Fund, Stanford, CA
10,000	Presbyterian Church of Sunnydale

KIPLINGER FOUNDATION

Giving Contact

Andrea Wilkes, Secretary
1729 H Street, Northwest
Washington, DC 20006
Phone: (202)887-6559
Fax: (202)496-1817

Description

Founded: 1948
EIN: 520792570
Organization Type: Family Foundation
Giving Locations: DC: Washington including metropolitan area
Grant Types: Capital, Challenge, Employee Matching Gifts, Endowment, General Support, Multiyear/Continuing Support, Project.

Donor Information

Founder: The foundation was incorporated in 1948 by the late Willard M. Kiplinger.

Financial Summary

Total Giving: $1,307,831 (2002); $1,670,970 (2001). Note: 1997 Giving includes matching gifts ($86,603).
Giving Analysis: Giving for 2002 includes: foundation matching gifts ($93,481)
Assets: $16,793,669 (2002); $19,598,144 (2001)
Gifts Received: $250,000 (1993). Note: Contributions were received from the Kiplinger Washington Editors, Inc.

Typical Recipients

Arts & Humanities: Arts Associations & Councils, Arts Centers, Arts Institutes, Ballet, Arts & Humanities-General, Historic Preservation, History & Archaeology, Libraries, Literary Arts, Museums/Galleries, Music, Opera, Performing Arts, Public Broadcasting, Theater, Visual Arts

Civic & Public Affairs: Business/Free Enterprise, Civil Rights, Community Foundations, Economic Development, Employment/Job Training, Civic & Public Affairs-General, Hispanic Affairs, Housing, Law & Justice, Legal Aid, Nonprofit Management, Philanthropic Organizations, Professional & Trade Associations, Public Policy, Safety, Urban & Community Affairs, Women's Affairs

Education: Arts/Humanities Education, Business Education, Colleges & Universities, Community & Junior Colleges, Economic Education, Education Funds, Elementary Education (Public), Engineering/Technological Education, Faculty Development, Education-General, International Exchange, Journalism/Media Education, Legal Education, Literacy, Minority Education, Private Education (Precollege), Public Education (Precollege), Science/Mathematics Education, Secondary Education (Private), Secondary Education (Public), Student Aid

Environment: Environment-General

Health: Cancer, Children's Health/Hospitals, Emergency/Ambulance Services, Health Organizations, Hospices, Hospitals, Medical Rehabilitation, Mental Health, Nursing Services, Public Health, Research/Studies Institutes

International: Foreign Arts Organizations, International Relations

Religion: Churches, Dioceses, Religion-General, Jewish Causes, Religious Organizations, Religious Welfare

Science: Science Exhibits & Fairs, Science Museums

Social Services: Child Welfare, Community Centers, Community Service Organizations, Family Planning, Family Services, Food/Clothing Distribution, Homes, People with Disabilities, Recreation & Athletics, Senior Services, Sexual Abuse, Shelters/Homelessness, Substance Abuse, United Funds/United Ways, Volunteer Services, Youth Organizations

Application Procedures

Initial Contact: The foundation requests applications be made in writing.

Application Requirements: Written proposals must state the purpose and the background of the organization, and provide proof of tax-exempt status.

Deadlines: None.

Review Process: The board meets four to five times a year. Decisions are made within three to six months.

Restrictions

Grants are limited to education, health, welfare, civic, and cultural organizations. No grants or scholarships are made to individuals.

Additional Information

The foundation reported that it was not considering any new proposals at the end of 1997.

On-going obligations and proposals from organizations that have been funded in the past have priority over applications for new programs.

Publications: Application Guidelines

Foundation Officials

David M. Daugherty: treasurer

Lucinda P. Janke: trustee

Austin Huntington Kiplinger: president, trustee B Washington, DC September 19, 1918. ED Cornell University AB (1939); Harvard University (1939-1940). PRIM CORP EMPL chairman, director: Kiplinger Washington Editors Inc. CORP AFFIL chairman: Fairview Properties; director: Outlook Inc.; chairman, director: Editors Press Service Inc.

Knight Austin Kiplinger: trustee B Washington, DC 1948. ED Cornell University BA (1969); Princeton University (1969-1970). PRIM CORP EMPL president, publisher, director: Kiplinger Washington Editors Inc. CORP AFFIL director: Fairview Properties. NONPR AFFIL member: Society American Business Editors & Writers; member: Society Professional Journalists; member advisory board: Mount Vernon Ladies Association; director: Oratorio Society; trustee: Greater Washington Research Center; member advisory board: Levine School Music. CLUB AFFIL National Press Club.

Todd Lawrence Kiplinger: trustee PRIM CORP EMPL vice chairman, director: Kiplinger Washington Editors Inc.

Andrea Wilkes: secretary, trustee

Grants Analysis

Disclosure Period: calendar year ending 2002

Total Grants: $1,214,350*

Number of Grants: 95

Average Grant: $9,493*

Highest Grant: $322,000

Lowest Grant: $500

Typical Range: $5,000 to $20,000

*Note: Giving excludes matching gifts. Average grant figure excludes highest grant.

Recent Grants

Note: Grants derived from 2002 Form 990.

General

322,000	Historical Society of Washington, Washington, DC
100,000	Stone Ridge School of the Sacred Heart, Bethesda, MD
88,000	National Press Foundation, Washington, DC
50,000	Ohio State University Kiplinger Fellows, Columbus, OH
35,000	National Symphony Orchestra, Washington, DC
30,000	Independent College Fund of Maryland, Baltimore, MD
30,000	University of Maryland Foundation, College Park, MD
25,000	American University WAMU 88.5, Washington, DC
25,000	Cedar Lane Unitarian Church, Bethesda, MD
25,000	Saint Stephen's & Saint Agnes Schools, Alexandria, VA

KIPLINGER WASHINGTON EDITORS INC.

Company Headquarters

1729 H Street NW
Washington, DC 20006
Web: http://www.kiplinger.com

Company Description

Revenue: US$34.5 million (2001)
Employees: 150 (2001)
SIC(s): 2700 Printing & Publishing, 7300 Business Services.

Operating Locations

Kiplinger Washington Editors (DC--Washington; MD--Hyattsville)

Giving Contact

Todd Kiplinger, Vice Chairman and Director
1729 H St. NW
Washington, DC 20006
Phone: (202)887-6400
Fax: (202)887-6655
E-mail: tkiplinger@kiplinger.com

Description

Organization Type: Corporate Giving Program
Giving Locations: DC: Washington metro area
Grant Types: Employee Matching Gifts, Project.

Application Procedures

Initial Contact: Send a brief letter of inquiry.

Application Requirements: Include a description of organization, amount requested, purpose of funds sought, and proof of tax-exempt status.

Restrictions

Does not fund individuals, religious organizations for sectarian purposes, political or lobbying groups, or organizations outside operating areas.

Additional Information

Company gives through the Kiplinger Foundation.

Corporate Officials

Austin Huntington Kiplinger: chairman, director B Washington, DC September 19, 1918. ED Cornell University AB (1939); Harvard University (1939-1940). PRIM CORP EMPL chairman, director: Kiplinger Washington Editors Inc. CORP AFFIL chairman: Fairview Properties; director: Outlook Inc.; chairman, director: Editors Press Service Inc.

Knight Austin Kiplinger: president, publisher, director B Washington, DC 1948. ED Cornell University BA (1969); Princeton University (1969-1970). PRIM CORP EMPL president, publisher, director: Kiplinger Washington Editors Inc. CORP AFFIL director: Fairview Properties. NONPR AFFIL member: Society American Business Editors & Writers; member: Society Professional Journalists; member advisory board: Mount Vernon Ladies Association; director: Oratorio Society; trustee: Greater Washington Research Center; member advisory board: Levine School Music. CLUB AFFIL National Press Club.

Todd Lawrence Kiplinger: vice chairman, director PRIM CORP EMPL vice chairman, director: Kiplinger Washington Editors Inc.

James Otis Mayo: vice chairman, secretary, director B Philadelphia, MS 1920. ED Mississippi State University (1941); George Washington University (1961). PRIM CORP EMPL vice chairman, secretary, direc-

tor: Kiplinger Washington Editors. CORP AFFIL director: Outlook; president: Shadow Lake Groves; director: May Properties Inc.; director: Fairview Properties; director: Magazine Services.

Corbin M. Wilkes: vice president finance B Washington, DC 1946. ED Hampden-Sydney College (1968); Rutgers University (1972). PRIM CORP EMPL vice president finance: Kiplinger Washington Editors. CORP AFFIL chairman: Magazine Services; treasurer: Outlook; treasurer: KCMississippi Inc.; treasurer: Editors Press; treasurer: Fairview Properties.

Grants Analysis

Typical Range: $100 to $1,000

F. M. KIRBY FOUNDATION

Giving Contact

S. Dillard Kirby, Executive Director
17 DeHart Street
PO Box 151
Morristown, NJ 07963-0151
Phone: (973)538-4800
Web: http://fdncenter.org/grantmaker/kirby/

Description

Founded: 1931
EIN: 516017929
Organization Type: Family Foundation
Giving Locations: NJ: Morristown; NC: Hillsborough; PA: Wilkes-Barre some giving nationally.
Grant Types: Capital, Conference/Seminar, Endowment, Fellowship, General Support, Project.

Donor Information

Founder: Established in 1931 by the late Fred M. Kirby (1861-1940). In 1912, Mr. Kirby merged his interest in a chain of variety stores with F. W. Woolworth Company. He was a trustee of Lafayette College and a director of Wilkes-Barre Hospital, Wilkes-Barre YMCA, and the Wyoming Seminary. Mr. Kirby's son, Allan P. Kirby, was also a major contributor to the foundation, endowing it with approximately $10 million in Allegheny Corporation stock through his will in 1973. The Kirby family's fortune also stems from holdings in such companies as Allegheny Corporation, Investors Diversified Services, and Pittston Company.

Financial Summary

Total Giving: $17,713,500 (2003); $19,866,828 (2002); $21,871,720 (2001)
Giving Analysis: Giving for 2003 includes: foundation grants to United Way ($425,000); 2002: foundation grants to United Way ($395,000)
Assets: $433,616,051 (2003); $342,067,001 (2002); $465,996,621 (2001)

Typical Recipients

Arts & Humanities: Arts Associations & Councils, Arts Festivals, Community Arts, Ethnic & Folk Arts, Historic Preservation, History & Archaeology, Libraries, Museums/Galleries, Opera, Performing Arts, Public Broadcasting, Theater

Civic & Public Affairs: African American Affairs, Botanical Gardens/Parks, Civil Rights, Economic Policy, Civic & Public Affairs-General, Law & Justice, Legal Aid, Philanthropic Organizations, Professional & Trade Associations, Public Policy, Urban & Community Affairs, Zoos/Aquariums

Education: Business Education, Colleges & Universities, Education Associations, Education Funds, Education Reform, Elementary Education (Private), Education-General, International Exchange, International Studies, Journalism/Media Education, Leadership Training, Medical Education, Private Education (Precollege), Public Education (Precollege), Religious Education, Science/Mathematics Education, Special Education, Student Aid

Environment: Air/Water Quality, Environment-General, Protection, Resource Conservation

Health: AIDS/HIV, Alzheimer's Disease, Arthritis, Cancer, Children's Health/Hospitals, Emergency/Ambulance Services, Eyes/Blindness, Health-General, Geriatric Health, Health Funds, Health Organizations, Heart, Hospices, Hospitals, Medical Rehabilitation, Medical Research, Nursing Services, Public Health, Respiratory, Single-Disease Health Associations, Transplant Networks/Donor Banks

International: Health Care/Hospitals, International Affairs, International Organizations

Religion: Churches, Missionary Activities (Domestic), Religious Organizations, Religious Welfare, Seminaries

Science: Science Museums, Scientific Centers & Institutes

Social Services: Animal Protection, At-Risk Youth, Child Welfare, Community Centers, Community Service Organizations, Domestic Violence, Emergency Relief, Family Planning, Family Services, Food/Clothing Distribution, People with Disabilities, Recreation & Athletics, Shelters/Homelessness, Substance Abuse, United Funds/United Ways, YMCA/YWCA/YMHA/YWHA, Youth Organizations

Application Procedures

Initial Contact: Applications must be in written form, signed by an official, and addressed to the foundation. There is no formal application form.

Application Requirements: Proposals should include a report on the use of previous grants, if applicable; a report on current activities; a declaration of the amount sought; a full description of the reasons for the current solicitation; an assertion as to whether it is for general operations, a specific project, capital needs, or endowment; a roster of directors (trustees) and principal officers; a copy of the audited financial statement; and a copy of the valid IRS tax exemption letter.

Deadlines: Proposals are considered throughout the year. Proposals received after October 31 are filed for consideration in the following year.

Review Process: The foundation does not grant interviews to grant applicants. Unsuccessful applicants do not receive notification.

Restrictions

The foundation does not fund organizations which have applied for tax-exempt status, but have not as yet received it; organizations outside the IRS regulations; or public foundations. No grants are made to individuals, fund-raising or underwriting of events such as benefits, charitable dinners, or sporting events. No loans are made.

Additional Information

Grants usually are reflective of personal interest by one or more members of the Kirby family.

Publications: Information Brochure

Foundation Officials

Thomas J. Bianchini: secretary, treasurer
William H. Byrnes, Jr.: director
Alice Kirby Horton: director NONPR AFFIL trustee: Wake Forest University School of Medicine.
Fred Morgan Kirby: president, director B Wilkes-Barre, PA November 23, 1919. ED Lafayette College BA (1942); Harvard University (1947); Saint Joseph's University LLD (1981); Lafayette College LLD (1984). PRIM CORP EMPL chairman, member executive committee, director: Alleghany Corp. NONPR AFFIL director: United Cerebal Palsy Research & Education Foundation Inc.; member: Zeta Psi; vice chairman: College Hall Fame Inc.; director: National Football Foundation. CLUB AFFIL Treyburn Country Club; Westmoreland Country Club; Morris County Golf Club; Spring Valley Hunt Club.
Jefferson Walker Kirby: director B Summit, NJ

1961. ED Lafayette College BA (1984); Duke University MBA (1987). PRIM CORP EMPL vice president: Alleghany Corp. NONPR AFFIL trustee: The Peck School; member: Zeta Psi; director: National Football Foundation; volunteer: Green Village Volunteer Fire Department; director: Museum of Early Trades & Crafts; director: College Hall Fame Inc. CLUB AFFIL University Club; Mendham Valley Gun Club; Morris County Golf Club.
S. Dillard Kirby: executive vice president, executive director, director NONPR AFFIL trustee: Shakespeare Theatre of New Jersey.
Walker D. Kirby: vice president, director NONPR AFFIL honorary trustee: The Seeing Eye.
Laura H. Virkler: director

Grants Analysis

Disclosure Period: calendar year ending 2003
Total Grants: $17,288,500*
Number of Grants: 332
Average Grant: $38,338*
Highest Grant: $1,332,000
Lowest Grant: $1,000
Typical Range: $10,000 to $50,000
*Note: Giving excludes United Way. Average grant figure excludes five highest grants ($4,752,000).

Recent Grants

Note: Grants derived from 2003 Form 990.
General

1,332,000	Mount Vernon Ladies Association of the Union, Mt. Vernon, VA -- towards F M Kirby gallery for changing exhibitions
1,000,000	Franklin Institute, Philadelphia, PA
1,000,000	Lawrenceville School, Lawrenceville, NJ -- towards future decision and restoration of upper house
750,000	Lafayette College Athletics Enhancement Endowment Funds, Easton, PA -- towards athletics enhancement endowment funds
670,000	Lafayette College Future Decisions, Easton, PA -- towards future decision
350,000	United Way of Morris County, Morristown, NJ -- towards general allocations to member agencies only
250,000	Alzheimer's Disease and Related Disorders Association Inc., Chicago, IL -- towards Alzheimer's research
250,000	American Cancer Society Foundation, Atlanta, GA -- towards cancer research
250,000	American Red Cross National headquarters, Washington, DC -- towards national disaster relief fund
250,000	Memorial Sloan Kettering Cancer Center, New York, NY

KIRKPATRICK FOUNDATION, INC.

Giving Contact

Joan E. Kirkpatrick, President
1200 N.W. 63rd, Suite 500
PO Box 268822
Oklahoma City, OK 73126-8822
Phone: (405)840-2882
Fax: (405)840-2946

Description

Founded: 1955
EIN: 730701736
Organization Type: Family Foundation
Former Name: Kirkpatrick Foundation.
Giving Locations: OK: Oklahoma City including metropolitan area
Grant Types: General Support, Matching, Project, Seed Money.

Donor Information

Founder: Incorporated in 1955 by Eleanor B. Kirkpatrick, John E. Kirkpatrick, and Joan E. Kirkpatrick.

Financial Summary

Total Giving: $1,635,240 (2002); $2,452,670 (2001)
Assets: $27,724,128 (2002); $34,601,964 (2001)
Gifts Received: $9,931,250 (1999); $159,557 (1998); $10,305,625 (1997)

Typical Recipients

Arts & Humanities: Arts Associations & Councils, Arts Centers, Arts Festivals, Arts Funds, Arts Institutes, Ballet, Dance, Ethnic & Folk Arts, Film & Video, Arts & Humanities-General, Historic Preservation, History & Archaeology, Libraries, Museums/Galleries, Music, Opera, Performing Arts, Public Broadcasting, Theater

Civic & Public Affairs: Asian American Affairs, Community Foundations, Economic Development, Ethnic Organizations, Civic & Public Affairs-General, Housing, Legal Aid, Municipalities/Towns, Nonprofit Management, Public Policy, Urban & Community Affairs, Zoos/Aquariums

Education: Arts/Humanities Education, Colleges & Universities, Community & Junior Colleges, Education Funds, Education-General, Gifted & Talented Programs, International Studies, Literacy, Medical Education, Private Education (Precollege), Public Education (Precollege), Science/Mathematics Education, Secondary Education (Private)

Environment: Environment-General, Protection, Resource Conservation

Health: Children's Health/Hospitals, Clinics/Medical Centers, Emergency/Ambulance Services, Heart, Hospitals, Medical Research, Public Health, Single-Disease Health Associations

International: International Relations, Missionary/Religious Activities

Religion: Churches, Religion-General, Ministries, Religious Organizations, Religious Welfare, Synagogues/Temples

Science: Science Museums, Scientific Centers & Institutes

Social Services: Animal Protection, Big Brothers/Big Sisters, Camps, Child Welfare, Community Centers, Community Service Organizations, Crime Prevention, Domestic Violence, Family Planning, Family Services, Food/Clothing Distribution, People with Disabilities, Recreation & Athletics, Senior Services, Social Services-General, United Funds/United Ways, Volunteer Services, Youth Organizations

Application Procedures

Initial Contact: Send a brief letter of inquiry.
Application Requirements: Grant proposals should include the following information: a two-page preliminary letter summarizing the request is required no later than 5:00 p.m. on February 15, May 15, August 15 and November 15. The preliminary letter must include the amount to be requested, a brief summary of the project or program for which funding is needed, and your e-mail address if applicable. All mailed proposals must be sent to the Post Office Box.
Deadlines: Grant proposals are due on the 15th of February, May, and August for consideration in March, June, and September, respectively.
Review Process: The foundation's board of trustees makes funding decisions at quarterly meetings.

Restrictions

Grants are not made to individuals. Health care, mental health, social welfare, lobbying organizations, and school trips.

Additional Information

The foundation reports an affiliation with the Oklahoma City Community Foundation.
Faxed requests are not accepted.
Publications: Annual Report; Application Guidelines

Foundation Officials

Nancy Anthony: advisor

Donald Balaban: director B Caldwell, KS 1932. ED Kansas State University (1953); Oklahoma City University (1961). PRIM CORP EMPL senior vice president, senior trustee officer: Liberty Bank & Trust Oklahoma City NA. NONPR AFFIL director: Lyric Theatre; trustee: Omniplex; member: Lions International; member: American Bar Association; director: Goodwill Industries.

John L. Belt: director PRIM CORP EMPL secretary: Capital Mortgage Co. CORP AFFIL treasurer: Kirkpatrick Oil Co. Inc.; director: Texas Guaranty National Bank.

Douglas R. Cummings: honorary director B 1929. PRIM CORP EMPL chairman: Cummings Oil Co.

Dan Hogan: director B 1933. PRIM CORP EMPL chairman, director: Hogan Publishing Co. CORP AFFIL chairman: Hogan Information Services.

Joe Howell: director

Christian Kirkpatrick Keesee: vice president, director B Oklahoma City, OK 1961. ED Menlo College AA (1983); Harvard University (1985); Pepperdine University (1984-1985); University of Central Oklahoma BS (1991). PRIM CORP EMPL president, director: American Bancorp Oklahoma. CORP AFFIL chairman, director: American Bank & Trust.

Joan E. Kirkpatrick: chairman PRIM CORP EMPL chairman, president, chief executive officer, director: Kirkpatrick Oil Co. Inc.

John Elson Kirkpatrick: honorary chairman, director B Oklahoma City, OK February 13, 1908. ED United States Military Academy (1925-1926); United States Naval Academy BS (1931); Harvard University Graduate School of Business Administration (1935-1936); Oklahoma City University LLD (1963); Bethany Nazarene College HHD (1967). PRIM CORP EMPL chairman: Kirkpatrick Oil Co. Inc. NONPR AFFIL honorary chairman board director: Presbyterian Home; honorary consult: Republic of Korea; honorary director: Oklahoma State Fair; life trustee: Oklahoma Zoological Society; member: Oklahoma Heritage Association; director emeritus: Oklahoma Historical Society; member advisory board: Oklahoma Health Sciences Center; founder, director: Oklahoma City Community Foundation; member: Oklahoma County Historical Society; life director: Oklahoma City Chamber of Commerce; director, president: Oklahoma Center Science & Arts; member, life board member: Oklahoma City Art Museum; director emeritus, honorary life trustee: National Cowboy Hall of Fame Western Heritage Center; director: Kirkpatrick Science Air Space Museum Omniplex; honorary chairman: Lyric Theatre Oklahoma; member: Industrial Petroleum Association; trustee: Falcon Foundation; member: Harvard Area Group; member: Asia Society Oklahoma; honorary life director: 45th Infantry Division Museum; member: Allied Arts Foundation. CLUB AFFIL Rotary Club; Men's Dinner Club; Oklahoma City Petroleum Club; Economic Club.

Eleanor Johnson Maurer: treasurer, director B Milan, MO 1914. ED Stephens College (1930-1931); Southwestern University (1932); Draughons Business College (1933). NONPR AFFIL director Oklahoma City chapter: English Speaking Union. CLUB AFFIL member: Rotary Club.

Susan McCalmont: executive director

Kathy McCord: secretary

Marilyn B. Myers: adv

Charles E. Nelson: chairman, director B 1944. ED Oklahoma State University (1965). PRIM CORP EMPL chairman emeritus: Bank One Oklahoma.

George Jeffrey Records: director B Saint Louis, MO 1934. ED Dartmouth College (1956). PRIM CORP EMPL chairman: Midland Mortgage. CORP AFFIL director: Wilson Foods Corp.; chairman: Midfirst Bank; chairman: Midland Financial Co.; director: Bonray Energy Corp. NONPR AFFIL director: Sunbeam Family Services Association; director: United Way Greater Oklahoma City; director: Oklahoma Chamber of Commerce.

Robert E. Torray: director PRIM CORP EMPL president: Robert E. Torray & Co. Inc.

Max Weitzenhoser: director

Grants Analysis

Disclosure Period: calendar year ending 2002
Total Grants: $1,635,240
Number of Grants: 57
Average Grant: $28,688
Highest Grant: $274,750
Lowest Grant: $1,000
Typical Range: $5,000 to $50,000

Recent Grants

Note: Grants derived from 2002 Form 990.
General

274,750	Da Vinci Institute, Edmond, OK
216,000	Oklahoma City Art Museum, Oklahoma City, OK
144,000	University of Central Oklahoma, Edmond, OK
101,000	Ballet Oklahoma, Oklahoma City, OK
75,000	Canterbury Choral Society, Oklahoma City, OK
75,000	Oklahoma City University, Oklahoma City, OK
75,000	Oklahoma Philharmonic Society, Oklahoma City, OK
70,000	Mid-America Arts Alliance, Kansas City, MO
63,130	Oklahoma City Public School Foundation, Oklahoma City, OK
50,000	Urban Impact Foundation, Oklahoma City, OK

KITZMILLER/BALES TRUST

Giving Contact

Robert U. Hansen, Trustee
PO Box 96
Wray, CO 80758
Phone: (970)332-3484

Description

Founded: 1984
EIN: 846178085
Organization Type: Private Foundation
Giving Locations: CO: East Yuma County School District
Grant Types: Capital, Operating Expenses, Project.

Donor Information

Founder: the late Edna B. Kitzmiller

Financial Summary

Total Giving: $431,003 (2001)
Assets: $9,578,910 (2001)

Typical Recipients

Arts & Humanities: Arts Associations & Councils, History & Archaeology, Libraries, Museums/ Galleries, Performing Arts
Civic & Public Affairs: Civic & Public Affairs-General, Municipalities/Towns, Safety, Urban & Community Affairs
Education: Elementary Education (Public), Education-General, Literacy, Public Education (Precollege), Science/Mathematics Education, Secondary Education (Public)
Environment: Environment-General
Health: Emergency/Ambulance Services, Eyes/ Blindness, Health Organizations, Hospices, Hospitals, Medical Rehabilitation
Social Services: Child Welfare, Community Centers, Community Service Organizations, Family Services, Recreation & Athletics, Scouts, Senior Services, Substance Abuse, Youth Organizations

Application Procedures

Initial Contact: Send a brief letter of inquiry and a full proposal in writing.
Deadlines: None.

Restrictions

Benefit vicinity of Yuma County within East Yuma County S.D. RJ-2.

Additional Information

Trust(s): Farmers State Bank

Foundation Officials

Duard Fix: trustee
Robert U. Hansen: trustee

Grants Analysis

Disclosure Period: calendar year ending 2001
Total Grants: $431,003
Number of Grants: 10
Highest Grant: $123,290
Lowest Grant: $2,000

Recent Grants

Note: Grants derived from 2001 Form 990.
General

123,290	City of Wray, Wray, CO -- for improvements and projects
91,492	Wray Rehabilitation and Public Activities Center, Wray, CO -- for improvements and projects
87,145	Wray Community District Hospital, Wray, CO -- equipment
83,963	East Yuma County School District, Wray, CO -- for improvements and projects
25,000	Renotta Health Care Systems, Inc., Wray, CO -- furniture
5,113	Baby Bear Hugs, Inc., Wray, CO -- Visitor Program
5,000	Hospice of the Plains, Inc., Wray, CO -- operating funds
5,000	Yuma County Fire Protection District, Wray, CO -- vehicle purchase
3,000	Yuma County Youth Center, Wray, CO -- improvements
2,000	Northeast Colorado Bookmobile Services, Wray, CO -- books

ROBERT J. KLEBERG, JR. AND HELEN C. KLEBERG FOUNDATION

Giving Contact

Robert L. Washington, Grants Coordinator
700 North Saint Mary's Street, Suite 1200
San Antonio, TX 78205
Phone: (210)271-3691
Fax: (210)271-9089

Description

Founded: 1950
EIN: 746044810
Organization Type: Family Foundation
Giving Locations: TX: nationally.
Grant Types: Capital, General Support, Multiyear/ Continuing Support, Operating Expenses, Project, Research.

Donor Information

Founder: The foundation was established in Texas in 1950 with funds donated by Robert J. Kleberg Jr., and his wife, Helen C. Kleberg. Mr. Kleberg was the grandson of Richard King, the founder of King Ranch, and he served as executive officer of the ranch for 56 years. He originated the Santa Gertrudis breed of beef cattle, bred horses, championed wildlife conservation, and initiated worldwide agricultural research. His wife shared these interests, and she participated in a variety of cultural and civic activities.

Financial Summary

Total Giving: $8,952,682 (2003); $9,673,734 (2002)
Assets: $197,325,740 (2003); $167,063,548 (2002)

Typical Recipients

Arts & Humanities: Arts Associations & Councils, Arts Institutes, Ballet, Ethnic & Folk Arts, Arts & Humanities-General, Historic Preservation, History & Archaeology, Libraries, Museums/Galleries, Music, Performing Arts, Public Broadcasting, Theater, Visual Arts
Civic & Public Affairs: Botanical Gardens/Parks, Economic Development, Civic & Public Affairs-General, Housing, Municipalities/Towns, Nonprofit Management, Rural Affairs, Urban & Community Affairs, Zoos/Aquariums
Education: Agricultural Education, Arts/Humanities Education, Business Education, Colleges & Universities, Education Funds, Elementary Education (Private), Engineering/Technological Education, Faculty Development, International Studies, Literacy, Medical Education, Private Education (Precollege), Public Education (Precollege), Science/Mathematics Education, Secondary Education (Private), Special Education, Student Aid
Environment: Environment-General, Resource Conservation, Watershed, Wildlife Protection
Health: Alzheimer's Disease, Cancer, Children's Health/Hospitals, Clinics/Medical Centers, Emergency/Ambulance Services, Eyes/Blindness, Health-General, Health Funds, Health Organizations, Heart, Hospitals, Kidney, Medical Rehabilitation, Medical Research, Nursing Services, Research/Studies Institutes, Respiratory, Speech & Hearing, Transplant Networks/Donor Banks, Trauma Treatment
International: Health Care/Hospitals
Religion: Religious Welfare
Science: Observatories & Planetariums, Scientific Centers & Institutes, Scientific Research
Social Services: Camps, Community Centers, Community Service Organizations, Counseling, Crime Prevention, Domestic Violence, Family Planning, Family Services, Food/Clothing Distribution, People with Disabilities, Recreation & Athletics, Scouts, Shelters/Homelessness, Social Services-General, Youth Organizations

Application Procedures

Initial Contact: Send a brief letter of inquiry full proposal on organization's letterhead.
Application Requirements: A full proposal should include a brief history of the organization, profile of the proposed project illustrating the need for such a project, outline of how the funds will be used and the specific amount requested, proof of tax-exempt status, a letter of approval signed by the organization's chief administrator, and a copy of the organizations exemption letter from the I.R.S.
Deadlines: None.
Review Process: The board meets in June and December.

Restrictions

The governing instrument directs that contributions be made to support biomedical research, veterinary science, and wildlife. Grants for other purposes favor organizations in south Texas. The foundation does not fund individuals, endowments, deficit financing, ongoing operating expenses, community organizations outside of Texas, organizations limited by race or religion, or groups that are not tax-exempt. The Foundation does not fund indirect costs or overhead for research projects.

Additional Information

Recipients must submit periodic progress reports and a financial record to the foundation.
Publications: Information Brochure; Annual Report

Foundation Officials

Helen C. Alexander: vice president, director
John D. Alexander, Jr.: secretary, vice president B 1954. PRIM CORP EMPL president: Alexander Production Co.
John Boyd Carter, Jr.: director B Fort Worth, TX 1924. ED Kemper Military School (1941-1943); University of Texas (1943-1946); Babson College (1946-1947). CORP AFFIL director: Sterling Bancshares; president, director: High Prairie Ranch Co.; director: Pogo Producing Co.; chairman: BCM Tech Inc. NONPR AFFIL member: Sigma Alpha Epsilon; member: U.S. Seniors Golf Association; member: Houston Society Financial Analysts; director: Private Enterprise Research Corp. Texas A&M University; trustee: Baylor College Medicine Howard Florey Institute; member: Houston Committee Foreign Relations. CLUB AFFIL Pilgrims Club; Brook Club; Houston Country Club; Bayou Club.
Caroline A. Forgason: director
Henrietta A. George: director
Helen K. Groves: president, director
Emory A. Hamilton: vice president, treasurer
Dorothy A. Matz: director PRIM NONPR EMPL assistant secretary, director: U.S. Equestrian Team.
Hugh Virgil Sherrill: director B Long Beach, CA 1920. ED Yale University (1942); Yale University JD (1948). PRIM CORP EMPL senior director: Prudential Securities Inc.

Grants Analysis

Disclosure Period: calendar year ending 2003
Total Grants: $8,952,682
Number of Grants: 42
Average Grant: $116,735*
Highest Grant: $2,000,000
Lowest Grant: $3,000
Typical Range: $20,000 to $200,000
*Note: Average grant excludes three highest grants ($4,400,000).

Recent Grants

Note: Grants derived from 2003 Form 990.
General

2,000,000	Baylor College of Medicine, Houston, TX -- towards Bovine Genome project phase 1
1,000,000	Vanderbilt-Ingram Cancer Center, Nashville, TN -- towards Genomic Wing final installment
656,250	San Antonio Museum of Art, San Antonio, TX -- towards land acquisition
500,000	Baylor College of Medicine, Houston, TX -- towards Pediatric Cancer center
500,000	Christus Spohn Health System, Kingsville, TX -- towards Computer Tomagraphy Scanner
500,000	San Antonio Academy, San Antonio, TX
350,000	Salk Institute, San Diego, CA -- towards Neuropeptide research
300,000	Howard Florey Biomedical Foundation, San Antonio, TX -- towards Neuroendocrinology research
220,000	U.T. Health Science Center, San Antonio, TX -- towards Fellowships
205,000	Webb-Waring Institute, Denver, CO -- towards Breast Cancer and Tuberculosis research

CONRAD AND VIRGINIA KLEE FOUNDATION

Giving Contact

Clayton M. Axtell, Jr., President
700 Security Mutual Bldg.
80 Exchange St.
Binghamton, NY 13901

Phone: (607)754-2504

Description

Founded: 1957
EIN: 156019821
Organization Type: Private Foundation
Giving Locations: NY: especially Broome County and Guilford
Grant Types: General Support, Operating Expenses.

Donor Information

Founder: the late Conrad C. Klee, the late Virginia Klee

Financial Summary

Total Giving: $919,693 (2002); $992,318 (2001)
Giving Analysis: Giving for 2002 includes: foundation grants to United Way ($115,566)
Assets: $15,950,372 (2002); $18,289,283 (2001)
Gifts Received: $1,017,130 (1992). Note: In 1992, contributions were received from Elise Coons ($791,184) and Margaret Bratton ($225,946).

Typical Recipients

Arts & Humanities: Arts Associations & Councils, Arts Centers, Historic Preservation, History & Archaeology, Libraries, Museums/Galleries, Music, Opera, Public Broadcasting
Civic & Public Affairs: Clubs, Economic Development, Civic & Public Affairs-General, Housing, Municipalities/Towns, Public Policy, Rural Affairs, Safety, Urban & Community Affairs, Zoos/Aquariums
Education: Arts/Humanities Education, Colleges & Universities, Education Funds, Education-General, Health & Physical Education, Religious Education, Science/Mathematics Education
Health: Emergency/Ambulance Services, Health-General, Health Organizations, Hospices, Hospitals, Public Health
Religion: Churches, Religious Organizations, Religious Welfare
Science: Science Museums, Scientific Centers & Institutes
Social Services: Animal Protection, Community Centers, Community Service Organizations, Counseling, Crime Prevention, Family Planning, Family Services, Food/Clothing Distribution, Homes, People with Disabilities, Recreation & Athletics, Scouts, Shelters/Homelessness, Social Services-General, United Funds/United Ways, YMCA/YWCA/YMHA/YWHA, Youth Organizations

Application Procedures

Initial Contact: Send a brief letter of inquiry and a full proposal.
Application Requirements: Include a description of organization, amount requested, purpose of funds sought, and proof of tax-exempt status.
Deadlines: None.

Restrictions

Does not support individuals.

Foundation Officials

Wells Allen, Jr.: director
Clayton M. Axtell, III: director
Clayton M. Axtell, Jr.: president
Linda Biemer: director
David Birchenough: vice president
John E. Gwyn: director
Floyd Lawson: director
Robert Nash: director
David K. Patterson: secretary

Grants Analysis

Disclosure Period: calendar year ending 2002
Total Grants: $804,127*
Number of Grants: 52
Average Grant: $12,558*
Highest Grant: $90,533
Lowest Grant: $1,263

Typical Range: $1,000 to $20,000
*****Note:** Giving excludes United Way. Average grant figure excludes two highest grants ($176,244).

Recent Grants

Note: Grants derived from 2001 Form 990.
General

113,300	Broome County United Way, Binghamton, NY -- operations
83,333	WSKG, Binghamton, NY -- capital project
60,000	Our Lady of Lourdes Hospital, Norfolk, NE -- capital project
50,000	Broome County of Churches, Binghamton, NY -- capital projects
50,000	Center for Health and Healing, Inc., New York, NY -- create a positive place for those touched by AD/HD
50,000	Phelps Mansion Foundation, Binghamton, NY -- capital projects
50,000	Roberson Museum and Science Center, Binghamton, NY -- building expansion
50,000	Sheltered Workshop for The Disabled -- operations
50,000	Tri-Cities Opera, Binghamton, NY -- expansion of set and costume construction and rental department
39,286	Samaritan Counseling Center -- operations

CHARLES AND FIGA KLINE FOUNDATION

Giving Contact

Fabian I. Fraenkel, Director
626 N. Main St.
Allentown, PA 18104
Phone: (610)437-4077

Description

Founded: 1957
EIN: 236262315
Organization Type: Private Foundation
Giving Locations: PA: Allentown
Grant Types: General Support.

Donor Information

Founder: the late Charles Kline, the late Figa Cohen Kline

Financial Summary

Total Giving: $380,500 (fiscal year ending October 31, 2003); $385,840 (fiscal 2001)
Giving Analysis: Giving for fiscal 2003 includes: foundation grants to United Way ($20,000); fiscal 2001: foundation grants to United Way ($10,000)
Assets: $8,297,151 (fiscal 2003); $8,462,768 (fiscal 2001)

Typical Recipients

Arts & Humanities: Libraries, Museums/Galleries
Civic & Public Affairs: Civil Rights, Ethnic Organizations, Law & Justice
Education: Arts/Humanities Education, Colleges & Universities, International Studies, Private Education (Precollege), Religious Education
Health: Hospitals, Medical Rehabilitation
International: Missionary/Religious Activities
Religion: Churches, Religion-General, Jewish Causes, Religious Organizations, Religious Welfare, Synagogues/Temples
Social Services: Community Centers, Community Service Organizations, Family Services, People with Disabilities, Scouts, United Funds/United Ways, Youth Organizations

Application Procedures

Initial Contact: The foundation has no formal grant application procedure or application form.
Deadlines: September 30.

Restrictions

Does not support individuals.

Foundation Officials

Fabian I. Fraenkel: director
Stewart Furmansky: director
Leonard Rapoport: director

Grants Analysis

Disclosure Period: fiscal year ending October 31, 2003
Total Grants: $360,500*
Number of Grants: 16
Average Grant: $7,214*
Highest Grant: $185,000
Lowest Grant: $500
Typical Range: $5,000 to $10,000
*****Note:** Giving excludes United Way. Average grant excludes two highest grants ($259,500).

Recent Grants

Note: Grants derived from 2003 Form 990.
General

185,000	Jewish Federation of Lehigh Valley, Allentown, PA
74,500	Jewish Community Center of Allentown, Allentown, PA
26,000	Jewish Day School of Allentown, Allentown, PA
25,000	Temple Beth El, Allentown, PA
20,000	United Way of the Greater Lehigh Valley
10,000	Anti-Defamation League
10,000	Congregation Keneseth Israel, Allentown, PA
10,000	Jewish Family Services of Allentown, Allentown, PA
4,000	Association for the Blind and Visually Impaired
2,500	Muhlenberg College, Allentown, PA

JOSIAH W. AND BESSIE H. KLINE FOUNDATION

Giving Contact

John A. Obrock, Secretary
515 S. 29th St.
Harrisburg, PA 17104
Phone: (717)561-4373
Fax: (717)561-0826

Description

Founded: 1952
EIN: 236245783
Organization Type: General Purpose Foundation
Giving Locations: PA
Grant Types: Capital, Challenge, General Support, Loan, Matching, Multiyear/Continuing Support.

Donor Information

Founder: Incorporated in 1952 by the late Josiah W. Kline and the late Bessie H. Kline.

Financial Summary

Total Giving: $916,750 (2003); $1,276,290 (2001)
Giving Analysis: Giving for 2003 includes: foundation grants to United Way ($30,000)
Assets: $21,810,106 (2003); $23,580,713 (2001)

Typical Recipients

Arts & Humanities: Arts Associations & Councils, Arts Centers, Ballet, Historic Preservation, History & Archaeology, Libraries, Museums/Galleries, Music,

Opera, Performing Arts, Public Broadcasting, Theater
Civic & Public Affairs: Botanical Gardens/Parks, Business/Free Enterprise, Clubs, Economic Policy, Employment/Job Training, Civic & Public Affairs-General, Hispanic Affairs, Housing, Professional & Trade Associations, Public Policy, Safety
Education: Afterschool/Enrichment Programs, Business Education, Colleges & Universities, Community & Junior Colleges, Education Associations, Education Funds, Education Reform, Environmental Education, Education-General, Legal Education, Literacy, Minority Education, Public Education (Precollege), Religious Education, Science/Mathematics Education, Student Aid
Environment: Forestry, Environment-General, Resource Conservation, Wildlife Protection
Health: Alzheimer's Disease, Arthritis, Cancer, Children's Health/Hospitals, Clinics/Medical Centers, Diabetes, Emergency/Ambulance Services, Health-General, Health Funds, Health Organizations, Heart, Hospices, Hospitals, Kidney, Medical Rehabilitation, Medical Research, Mental Health, Multiple Sclerosis, Nursing Services, Outpatient Health Care, Public Health, Single-Disease Health Associations
International: Foreign Arts Organizations
Religion: Churches, Jewish Causes, Ministries, Religious Welfare
Science: Science Museums, Scientific Centers & Institutes
Social Services: Animal Protection, Big Brothers/Big Sisters, Camps, Child Welfare, Community Centers, Community Service Organizations, Emergency Relief, Family Planning, Family Services, Food/Clothing Distribution, People with Disabilities, Recreation & Athletics, Scouts, Shelters/Homelessness, Social Services-General, Special Olympics, Substance Abuse, United Funds/United Ways, Volunteer Services, YMCA/YWCA/YMHA/YWHA, Youth Organizations

Application Procedures

Initial Contact: The foundation requests applications be made in writing.
Application Requirements: Written applications should include the name, location, and purpose of the organization requesting assistance, qualifications of requesting organization budget, any support that will be received from other sources, amount requested and dates of need, and proof of tax-exempt status.
Deadlines: None.
Review Process: Board of Directors review requests in May and November.

Restrictions

The foundation only makes grants to tax-exempt charities; organization must provide documentation of IRS 501(c)(3) status. The foundation does not support individuals, endowment funds, operating budgets, special projects, publications, conferences, fellowships, or loans. Normally, grants are not made to State or Federal affiliated schools, colleges, or universities.

Additional Information

Publications: Guidelines

Foundation Officials

Derek C. Hathaway: director B 1944. ED Aston University BS (1965). PRIM CORP EMPL chairman, chief executive officer: Harsco Corp.
William Joseph King: vice president, treasurer, director B Philadelphia, PA 1929. ED University of Pennsylvania Wharton School (1954); LaSalle University MBA (1979). PRIM CORP EMPL chairman, chief executive officer: Dauphin Deposit Bank & Trust Co. CORP AFFIL director: Hempt Brothers; director: Millers Mutual Insurance Co.
James Earl Marley: director B Marietta, PA 1935. ED Pennsylvania State University BS (1957); Drexel Institute of Technology MS (1963). PRIM CORP EMPL chairman, director: AMP Inc. CORP AFFIL director:

Harsco Corp.; director: Armstrong World Industries Inc. NONPR AFFIL member: Institute Electrical & Electronics Engineers; member: Manufacturing Council Machinery & Allied Products Institute; member: American Society Mechanical Engineers; member: Harrisburg Chamber of Commerce; member: American Management Association. CLUB AFFIL Harrisburg Country Club.

Robert F. Nation: president, director B 1926. ED Elizabethtown College (1947). PRIM CORP EMPL former president, director: Penn Harris Co. CORP AFFIL treasurer: Sun Enterprises Inc.; treasurer: Sun Motor Cars Inc.; director: Phico Insurance Co.; director: Phico Service Co.; treasurer: Mansun North Inc.; director: Phico Group Inc.; director: Harsco Corp.

Samuel D. Ross, Jr.: director B 1933. ED Susquehanna University. PRIM NONPR EMPL president, chief executive officer, director: Medical Service Association of Pennsylvania. CORP AFFIL chairman: Highmark Inc.

John A. Russell: director
David A. Smith: director

Grants Analysis

Disclosure Period: calendar year ending 2003
Total Grants: $886,750*
Number of Grants: 40
Average Grant: $18,891*
Highest Grant: $150,000
Lowest Grant: $500
Typical Range: $10,000 to $40,000
*Note: Giving excludes United Way. Average grant figure excludes highest grant.

Recent Grants

Note: Grants derived from 2002 Form 990.
Library-Related
52,000	Marysville Rye Library Association, Marysville, PA -- towards replacing 31 wooden bookcases with custom built new ones
50,000	Dauphin County Library System, Harrisburg, PA -- for construction of a new uptown branch library and partial renovation of historical downtown branch library

General
150,000	Pinnacle Health Foundation, Harrisburg, PA
100,000	Harrisburg Area YMCA, Harrisburg, PA -- for renovation and improvement of the YMCA facilities to meet needs of the communities
50,000	Boy Scouts of America Keystone Area Council, Mechanicsburg, PA -- towards annual eagle scout recognition dinner
50,000	Boys & Girls Club of Central Pennsylvania, Inc., Harrisburg, PA -- towards renovation of playground outside basketball court community park and adjacent fields the Berryhill street clubhouse
50,000	Gettysburg College, Gettysburg, PA -- towards establishing a new science complex at the college
50,000	Gettysburg National Battlefield Museum Foundation, Gettysburg, PA -- towards financing the building of a new museum and visitor center at Gettysburg national military park
50,000	Goodwill Industries of Central Pennsylvania Inc., Harrisburg, PA -- towards building program
50,000	Lebanon Valley College, Annville, PA -- for the finishing and equipping classroom lab suite
50,000	Messiah College, Grantham, PA -- towards building a student union on the campus of the college
50,000	Susquehanna University, Selinsgrove, PA -- support of equipment technology and instrumentation upgrades for the university's science programs

ESTHER A. AND JOSEPH KLINGENSTEIN FUND, INC.

Giving Contact

John Klingenstein, President
Care of Tanton & Co.
37 W. 57th St., 5th Fl.
New York, NY 10019
Phone: (212)583-1100

Description

Founded: 1946
EIN: 136028788
Organization Type: Family Foundation
Giving Locations: nationally.
Grant Types: Fellowship, General Support, Multiyear/Continuing Support, Operating Expenses, Project, Research, Scholarship.

Donor Information

Founder: The Esther A. and Joseph Klingenstein Fund was established in 1946 with the late Esther Adler Klingenstein and Joseph Klingenstein as donors. Mr. and Mrs. Klingenstein were contributors to Mount Sinai Hospital, with gifts including a chair in psychiatry and contributions toward a clinical center. They were also founding sponsors of the Mount Sinai School of Medicine. Mr. Klingenstein was chairman emeritus of the Mount Sinai Medical Center and was a senior partner in the investment banking firm of Wertheim and Company.

Financial Summary

Total Giving: $5,214,920 (fiscal year ending September 30, 2003); $5,818,213 (fiscal 2002)
Giving Analysis: Giving for fiscal 2002 includes: foundation scholarships ($1,445,000)
Assets: $118,153,079 (fiscal 2003); $107,987,979 (fiscal 2002)
Gifts Received: $47,047 (fiscal 2002); $16,819 (fiscal 2000); $271,869 (fiscal 1997)

Typical Recipients

Arts & Humanities: Historic Preservation, History & Archaeology, Libraries, Museums/Galleries
Civic & Public Affairs: Botanical Gardens/Parks, Business/Free Enterprise, Civil Rights, Ethnic Organizations, First Amendment Issues, Gay/Lesbian Issues, Civic & Public Affairs-General, Philanthropic Organizations, Public Policy, Urban & Community Affairs, Women's Affairs
Education: Colleges & Universities, Education Associations, Education Funds, Education Reform, Engineering/Technological Education, Environmental Education, Faculty Development, Education-General, Health & Physical Education, Medical Education, Minority Education, Private Education (Precollege), Public Education (Precollege), Science/Mathematics Education
Environment: Environment-General, Protection, Research
Health: Adolescent Health Issues, Cancer, Children's Health/Hospitals, Clinics/Medical Centers, Hospitals, Hospitals (University Affiliated), Medical Research, Mental Health, Preventive Medicine/Wellness Organizations, Public Health, Research/Studies Institutes, Single-Disease Health Associations
International: Foreign Educational Institutions, International Environmental Issues
Religion: Churches, Jewish Causes, Religious Organizations, Religious Welfare, Social/Policy Issues
Science: Science Museums, Scientific Centers & Institutes, Scientific Labs, Scientific Organizations, Scientific Research
Social Services: Child Welfare, Family Planning, People with Disabilities, Youth Organizations

Application Procedures

Initial Contact: The fund has no specific application form. The proposal should be in writing. For the annual Klingenstein Fellowship Awards in the Neurosciences, contact the fund for application form and brochure.
Application Requirements: Proposals should include the following: a description of the proposed project or program its purpose, desired outcome, and how these outcomes will be evaluated; amount requested; project and/or organizational budget and other sources of support received or being sought; information about the organization, its latest audited financial statement, and a copy of its IRS tax-exemption letter.
Deadlines: None for general grants; December for Klingenstein neuroscience fellowships.
Review Process: The fund's directors meet four or five times a year to review proposals.
Notes: All applicants are informed in writing of the action taken by the fund, whether the proposal is approved or not.

Restrictions

The fund rarely contributes to endowments, buildings, or other types of capital projects.

Additional Information

Recipients must submit substantive and financial reports annually and at the conclusion of the grant period, and maintain a systematic record of payments and receipts, available to the fund on request.
Publications: Descriptive Brochure; Application for Fellowship Program

Foundation Officials

Kenneth H. Fields: assistant treasurer
Frederick A. Klingenstein: vice president B New York, NY 1931. ED Yale University BA (1953); Harvard University Graduate School of Business Administration (1953-1954); Saint Lawrence University LHD (1986). PRIM CORP EMPL chairman, partner: Klingenstein Fields & Co. LP ADD CORP EMPL president: Sherry-Netherland Inc. CORP AFFIL director: Whitley Products Inc.; director: Arch Petroleum Inc.; director: Pogo Producing Co. NONPR AFFIL trustee: American Museum Natural History; chairman: Mount Sinai Medical Center.
John Klingenstein: president, treasurer, director PRIM CORP EMPL general partner: Klingenstein Fields & Co. LP.
Patricia Klingenstein: director
Sharon Klingenstein: director

Grants Analysis

Disclosure Period: fiscal year ending September 30, 2003
Total Grants: $5,214,920
Number of Grants: 96
Average Grant: $42,679*
Highest Grant: $803,120
Lowest Grant: $600
Typical Range: $10,000 to $100,000
*Note: Average grant figure excludes two highest grants ($1,203,120).

Recent Grants

Note: Grants derived from fiscal 2003 Form 990.
Library-Related
250,000	New York Public Library, Manhattan, NY

General
803,120	Teachers College, Columbia University, New York, NY
400,000	Mt. Sinai Medical Center, New York, NY
400,000	Teachers College, Columbia University, New York, NY
350,000	UJA - Federation of New York, New York, NY
300,000	Deerfield Academy, Deerfield, MA
75,000	Rensselaerville Institute, Rensselaerville, NY

70,000	American Jewish Committee, New York, NY
60,000	Klingenstein Third Generation Foundation, New York, NY
55,000	Trustees of Columbia University, New York, NY
50,000	Board of Regents of University of Wisconsin, Madison, WI

KLINGESTEIN FUND

Giving Contact
Lee P. Klingestein, President
31 Oxford Rd.
Scarsdale, NY 10583
Phone: (212)476-9000

Description
Founded: 1940
EIN: 136077894
Organization Type: Private Foundation
Giving Locations: CA; CO; CT; MA; NJ; NY; NC; VT
Grant Types: Emergency, Fellowship, General Support, Multiyear/Continuing Support, Project, Research.

Donor Information
Founder: Lee Paul Klingestein, Paul H. Klingestein

Financial Summary
Total Giving: $910,430 (2001)
Assets: $5,618,606 (2001)
Gifts Received: $540,490 (2001); $438,688 (1999); $1,462,316 (1998). Note: In 2001, contributions were received from direct public support. In 1999, contributions were received from Paul H. Klingestein. In 1998, contributions were received from Lee P. Klingenstein ($1,321,938) and Frances Klingenstein ($140,377). In 1996, contributions were received from Paul H. Klingestein.

Typical Recipients
Arts & Humanities: Arts Associations & Councils, Arts Institutes, Ballet, History & Archaeology, Libraries, Museums/Galleries, Music, Public Broadcasting
Civic & Public Affairs: Botanical Gardens/Parks, Civic & Public Affairs-General, Legal Aid, Philanthropic Organizations, Public Policy, Urban & Community Affairs, Women's Affairs
Education: Afterschool/Enrichment Programs, Colleges & Universities, Leadership Training, Minority Education, Preschool Education, Private Education (Precollege), Public Education (Precollege)
Environment: Environment-General, Resource Conservation, Wildlife Protection
Health: AIDS/HIV, Cancer, Children's Health/Hospitals, Clinics/Medical Centers, Hospices, Hospitals, Long-Term Care, Medical Research
International: International Environmental Issues, International Peace & Security Issues, International Relief Efforts
Religion: Churches, Jewish Causes, Religious Welfare
Social Services: Camps, Child Welfare, Community Service Organizations, Delinquency & Criminal Rehabilitation, Family Planning, Family Services, United Funds/United Ways, Veterans, YMCA/YWCA/YMHA/YWHA

Application Procedures
Initial Contact: Submit a letter stating charitable purpose and proof of tax-exempt status.
Deadlines: None.

Additional Information
The Klingestein Fund primarily supports a private school and a wilderness program. In addition, the fund gives support for universities and other education and Jewish organizations.

Foundation Officials
Alan L. Klingestein: treasurer
Lee P. Klingestein: president
Paul H. Klingestein: vice president
Joanne K. Ziesing: secretary

Grants Analysis
Disclosure Period: calendar year ending 2001
Total Grants: $914,430
Number of Grants: 188
Average Grant: $1,859*
Highest Grant: $250,000
Typical Range: $500 to $5,000
*Note: Average grant figure excludes three highest grants ($565,000).

Recent Grants
Note: Grants derived from 2001 Form 990.
General

250,000	Juma Ventures, San Francisco, CA
215,000	Outward Bound, Asheville, NC
100,000	Taft School, Watertown, CT
50,000	Juma Ventures, San Francisco, CA
25,000	African Elephant Conservation Trust
25,000	Outward Bound, Asheville, NC
25,000	Vermont Academy, Saxtons River, VT
15,000	Harbor Schools, Newbury, MA
15,000	Princeton University, Princeton, NJ
11,000	Vail Valley Institute, Vail Valley, CO

ERNEST CHRISTIAN KLIPSTEIN FOUNDATION

Giving Contact
Marion C. White, Secretary
Village Rd.
PO Box 278
New Vernon, NJ 07976
Phone: (973)538-4445

Description
Founded: 1954
EIN: 226028529
Organization Type: Private Foundation
Giving Locations: CA; CT; IL; MA; NJ
Grant Types: Emergency, General Support, Project.

Donor Information
Founder: Kenneth H. Klipstein

Financial Summary
Total Giving: $178,045 (2001)
Assets: $3,792,562 (2001)

Typical Recipients
Arts & Humanities: Arts Associations & Councils, Arts Centers, Arts Funds, Community Arts, Libraries, Museums/Galleries, Music, Opera, Performing Arts, Public Broadcasting, Theater
Civic & Public Affairs: Community Foundations, Civic & Public Affairs-General, Public Policy, Safety, Urban & Community Affairs
Education: Business Education, Colleges & Universities, Education Reform, Engineering/Technological Education, Education-General, Legal Education, Private Education (Precollege), Public Education (Precollege), School Volunteerism, Science/Mathematics Education, Secondary Education (Public), Student Aid
Environment: Air/Water Quality, Environment-General, Resource Conservation, Watershed
Health: AIDS/HIV, Cancer, Children's Health/Hospitals, Clinics/Medical Centers, Emergency/Ambulance Services, Health Funds, Health Organizations, Hospitals, Medical Rehabilitation, Medical Research, Nursing Services, Prenatal Health Issues, Public Health, Research/Studies Institutes
International: International Environmental Issues, International Organizations
Religion: Churches, Jewish Causes, Religious Organizations
Science: Scientific Centers & Institutes, Scientific Labs
Social Services: Animal Protection, Camps, Community Centers, Community Service Organizations, Domestic Violence, Family Planning, Homes, Recreation & Athletics, Scouts, United Funds/United Ways, YMCA/YWCA/YMHA/YWHA, Youth Organizations

Application Procedures
Initial Contact: The foundation has no formal grant application procedure or application form.
Deadlines: None.

Restrictions
Does not support individuals.

Foundation Officials
David C. Klipstein: vice president
David H. Klipstein: president
Pamela Klipstein: treasurer
Pamela Klipstein Smith: vice president
Marion C. White: secretary

Grants Analysis
Disclosure Period: calendar year ending 2001
Total Grants: $178,045
Number of Grants: 67
Average Grant: $2,135*
Highest Grant: $35,000
Lowest Grant: $100
Typical Range: $500 to $5,000
*Note: Average grant figure excludes highest grant.

Recent Grants
Note: Grants derived from 2001 Form 990.
General

35,000	Women's Crisis Services, Flemington, NJ
30,000	Earth Justice Legal Defense Fund, San Francisco, CA
25,000	MIT, Cambridge, MA
25,000	Princeton University, Princeton, NJ
10,525	Rutgers Preparatory School, Somerset, NJ
5,200	Rutgers University Foundation, New Brunswick, NJ
5,000	Community Coalition, Chester Springs, PA
3,000	Upper Raritan Watershed Association, Gladstone, NJ
2,600	San Diego State University, San Diego, CA -- KPBS
2,500	Far Hills Country Day School, Far Hills, NJ

JAY E. KLOCK AND LUCIA KLOCK KINGSTON FOUNDATION

Giving Contact
Meri Beth Cummings, Assistant Vice President
c/o Key Trust Co.
2637 Wall St.
Kingston, NY 12401
Phone: (914)339-6752

Description
Founded: 1966
EIN: 146038479
Organization Type: Private Foundation

Giving Locations: NY: Kingston and Ulster counties
Grant Types: General Support.

Financial Summary

Total Giving: $239,450 (2003)
Giving Analysis: Giving for 2003 includes: foundation grants to United Way ($12,500)
Assets: $4,961,734 (2003)

Typical Recipients

Arts & Humanities: Libraries, Music, Performing Arts
Civic & Public Affairs: Civic & Public Affairs-General, Philanthropic Organizations
Education: Business Education, Community & Junior Colleges, Education-General, Literacy, Student Aid
Health: Cancer, Children's Health/Hospitals, Health-General, Health Organizations, Heart, Hospices, Hospitals, Medical Research, Mental Health
Science: Science Museums, Scientific Centers & Institutes
Social Services: Child Welfare, Community Service Organizations, Family Services, Homes, People with Disabilities, Scouts, Social Services-General, Substance Abuse, United Funds/United Ways, YMCA/YWCA/YMHA/YWHA, Youth Organizations

Application Procedures

Initial Contact: Send a brief letter of inquiry. with a full proposal.
Application Requirements: Include a description of organization, amount requested, purpose of funds sought, recently audited financial statement, and proof of tax-exempt status.
Deadlines: Applications are due at the end of each calendar quarter.

Restrictions

Does not fund administrative purposes or expenses.

Additional Information

Trust(s): KeyBank NA

Grants Analysis

Disclosure Period: calendar year ending 2003
Total Grants: $226,950*
Number of Grants: 45
Average Grant: $5,043*
Highest Grant: $20,000
Typical Range: $1,000 to $10,000
*Note: Giving excludes United Way.

Recent Grants

Note: Grants derived from 1999 Form 990.

Library-Related
8,000	Kingston Area Library, Kingston, NY

General
10,000	UCCC Foundation
8,000	United Way, Dubuque, IA
5,000	Benedictine Health Foundation, Kingston, NY
5,000	Benedictine Health Foundation, Kingston, NY
5,000	Benedictine Health Foundation, Kingston, NY
5,000	Benedictine Health Foundation, Kingston, NY
5,000	Kingston Hospital Foundation, Kingston, NY
5,000	Kingston Hospital Foundation, Kingston, NY
5,000	Kingston Hospital Foundation, Kingston, NY
5,000	YMCA

ROSE AND LOUIS KLOSK FUND

Giving Contact

Nathan R. Cooper, co-Trustee
PO Box 31412 S-5
Rochester, NY 14603
Phone: (716)258-5330

Description

Founded: 1970
EIN: 136328994
Organization Type: Private Foundation
Giving Locations: CT; NM; NY; NC
Grant Types: Emergency, General Support, Multi-year/Continuing Support, Research.

Donor Information

Founder: the late Louis Klosk

Financial Summary

Total Giving: $320,000 (2001)
Assets: $6,558,628 (2001)

Typical Recipients

Arts & Humanities: Arts Associations & Councils, Libraries, Music, Opera
Civic & Public Affairs: Community Foundations, Civic & Public Affairs-General, Women's Affairs
Education: Colleges & Universities, Medical Education, Private Education (Precollege), Science/Mathematics Education
Health: Cancer, Children's Health/Hospitals, Clinics/Medical Centers, Geriatric Health, Health Organizations, Home-Care Services, Hospitals, Kidney, Long-Term Care, Medical Research, Multiple Sclerosis, Single-Disease Health Associations
International: International-General, Health Care/Hospitals, International Relations, Missionary/Religious Activities
Religion: Jewish Causes, Religious Organizations, Synagogues/Temples
Social Services: Child Abuse, Community Service Organizations, Domestic Violence, Homes, People with Disabilities, Senior Services, United Funds/United Ways

Application Procedures

Initial Contact: The foundation has no formal grant application procedure or application form.
Deadlines: None.

Additional Information

Trust(s): JPMorgan Chase Bank

Foundation Officials

Barry Cooper: trustee
Nathan Cooper: trustee

Grants Analysis

Disclosure Period: calendar year ending 2001
Total Grants: $320,000
Number of Grants: 38
Average Grant: $8,421
Highest Grant: $35,000
Lowest Grant: $1,000
Typical Range: $1,000 to $15,000

Recent Grants

Note: Grants derived from 2001 Form 990.

General
35,000	Columbia University College of Physicians and Surgeons, New York, NY
35,000	United Jewish Appeal, New York, NY
35,000	Weill Medical College of Cornell University, New York, NY
25,000	Sid Jacobson Jewish Community Center, New York, NY
20,000	Hadassah, New York, NY
20,000	Hebrew Home for the Aged in Riverdale, Riverdale, NY
20,000	Laura Rosenberg Foundation, Hewlett, NY
18,000	Women's League for Israel, New York, NY
15,000	Bar-Ilan University, New York, NY
10,000	Hebrew Hospital Home, Inc., West Hartford, CT

KNAPP FOUNDATION (CA)

Giving Contact

Janis Minton, Senior Program Advisor
10100 Santa Monica Blvd., Suite 2000
Los Angeles, CA 90067-4003
Phone: (310)553-7810
Fax: (310)553-7688

Description

Founded: 1993
EIN: 954416658
Organization Type: Private Foundation
Giving Locations: CA; MA; NM; NY
Grant Types: General Support.

Donor Information

Founder: Established in 1993 by Cleon T. Knapp.

Financial Summary

Total Giving: $3,755,649 (fiscal year ending September 30, 2001)
Assets: $4,171,294 (fiscal 2001)
Gifts Received: $461,272 (fiscal 1996); $1,365,000 (fiscal 1993)

Typical Recipients

Arts & Humanities: Ethnic & Folk Arts, Libraries, Museums/Galleries, Music, Opera
Education: Arts/Humanities Education, Colleges & Universities, Education Funds, Education-General, Health & Physical Education, Private Education (Precollege)
Environment: Forestry
Health: Alzheimer's Disease, Cancer, Children's Health/Hospitals, Clinics/Medical Centers, Health-General, Kidney, Medical Research, Prenatal Health Issues
Religion: Religious Welfare
Social Services: Child Welfare, Community Service Organizations

Application Procedures

Initial Contact: Send a brief letter of inquiry.
Application Requirements: Include purpose of organization, geographic area and population served, brief description of project, amount requested, budget, and proof of tax-exempt status.
Deadlines: August

Restrictions

Foundation does not support individuals, religious activities, political or lobbying groups, publiclic policy research, fund-raising, or general endowments.

Foundation Officials

H. Stephen Cranston: secretary
Cleon Talboys Knapp: president B Los Angeles, CA 1937. ED University of California, Los Angeles (1955-1958). PRIM CORP EMPL president: Talwood Corp. NONPR AFFIL director, trustee: Sante Fe Opera; board visitors: University California Los Angeles John E Anderson Graduate School Management; director, trustee: Museum Contemporary Art; director, trustee: Fulfillment Fund; director, trustee: Los Angeles County Museum; chairman, trustee: Craft & Folk Art Museum; chairman, trustee: Art Center College Design. CLUB AFFIL Regency Club; Eagle Springs Golf Club;

Bel-Air Country Club; Country Club Rockies.
Elizabeth W. Knapp: vice president
Karl H. Loring, CPA: chief financial officer

Grants Analysis

Disclosure Period: fiscal year ending September 30, 2001
Total Grants: $3,755,649
Number of Grants: 10
Highest Grant: $1,422,885
Lowest Grant: $1,370
Typical Range: $300,000 to $1,000,000

Recent Grants

Note: Grants derived from fiscal 2002 Form 990.
General

1,498,823	Wellesley College, Wellesley, MA
50,000	Art Center College of Design, Pasadena, CA
25,710	UCLA Foundation, Los Angeles, CA
25,000	Young Black Scholars, Inglewood, CA
6,000	Bravo Vail Valley Music Festival, Vail, CO
100	Pan Mass Challenge, Wellesley, MA

KNAPP FOUNDATION, INC. (MD)

Giving Contact

Antoinette P. Vojvoda, President
PO Box O
St. Michaels, MD 21663
Phone: (410)745-5660

Description

Founded: 1929
EIN: 136001167
Organization Type: General Purpose Foundation
Giving Locations: East-coast states.
Grant Types: Matching.

Donor Information

Founder: Incorporated in 1929 by the late Joseph Palmer Knapp.

Financial Summary

Total Giving: $490,923 (2001)
Assets: $25,694,413 (2001)

Typical Recipients

Arts & Humanities: Film & Video, Historic Preservation, History & Archaeology, Libraries, Museums/ Galleries
Civic & Public Affairs: Botanical Gardens/Parks, Civil Rights, Civic & Public Affairs-General, Municipalities/Towns, Public Policy, Safety, Urban & Community Affairs, Zoos/Aquariums
Education: Arts/Humanities Education, Colleges & Universities, Elementary Education (Private), Elementary Education (Public), Engineering/ Technological Education, Environmental Education, Education-General, Health & Physical Education, Legal Education, Literacy, Medical Education, Private Education (Precollege), Public Education (Precollege), Religious Education, Science/Mathematics Education, Secondary Education (Public), Social Sciences Education, Special Education, Student Aid, Vocational & Technical Education
Environment: Environment-General, Research, Resource Conservation, Watershed, Wildlife Protection
Health: Cancer, Children's Health/Hospitals, Emergency/Ambulance Services, Hospitals, Research/ Studies Institutes, Single-Disease Health Associations
Science: Science-General, Science Museums, Scientific Centers & Institutes, Scientific Labs
Social Services: Child Welfare, Community Service Organizations, People with Disabilities, United Funds/United Ways, Youth Organizations

Application Procedures

Initial Contact: The foundation requests detailed letters of application.
Deadlines: Quarterly.

Restrictions

The foundation does not support individuals or international organizations, or provide funds for loans, scholarships, fellowships, research, endowment or building funds, or operating budgets. The foundation reports that giving to arts and humanities, civic and public affairs, and health and social services organizations is done so by a predetermined list of recipients for annual contribution purposes only.

Additional Information

Publications: Guidelines

Foundation Officials

Ruth M. Capranica: vice president
Steven F. Capranica: treasurer
Krista L. Hodgkin: trustee
Margaret P. Newcombe: trustee
Sylvia V. Penny: trustee PRIM CORP EMPL secretary: George L. Penny Inc.
Antoinette P. Vojvoda: president

Grants Analysis

Disclosure Period: calendar year ending 2001
Total Grants: $490,923
Number of Grants: 31
Average Grant: $16,380*
Highest Grant: $99,530
Lowest Grant: $2,000
Typical Range: $10,000 to $20,000
***Note:** Average grant figure excludes highest grant.

Recent Grants

Note: Grants derived from 2002 Form 990.
General

1,000,000	University of North Carolina, Chapel Hill, NC -- funds for library
110,000	Chesapeake College, Wye Mills, MD -- toward library resource center technology acquisitions
100,000	Washington College, Chestertown, MD -- toward purchase of equipment for Trans-GIS Program
52,000	University of Hartford, CT -- funds for equipment acquisitions
25,000	Horry-Georgetown Technical College, Conway, SC -- toward digital database purchases
19,000	University of North Carolina, Chapel Hill, NC -- toward acquisition of reference material for University Satellite Location
18,400	Living Classroom Foundation, Baltimore, MD -- funds for the acquisition of textbooks and equipment for Wetland Restoration Programs
17,500	Virginia Polytechnic Institute, Blacksburg, VA -- funds for library acquisitions
16,520	Pickering Creek Audubon, Easton, MD -- funds for Wetlands restoration equipment and supplies
12,400	New Jersey Institute of Technology, Newark, NJ -- toward equipment for digital imaging center in Architecture Library

JOHN S. AND JAMES L. KNIGHT FOUNDATION

Giving Contact

Alberto Ibarguen, President & Chief Executive Officer
Wachovia Financial Center, Suite 3300
200 Biscayne Boulevard
Miami, FL 33131

Phone: (305)908-2600
Fax: (305)908-2698
E-mail: publications@knightfdn.org
Web: http://www.knightfdn.org
Note: Grant proposals should be addressed: Attn: Grant Request.

Description

Founded: 1950
EIN: 650464177
Organization Type: Private Foundation
Giving Locations: nationally.
Grant Types: Award, Capital, Challenge, Emergency, Endowment, Fellowship, General Support, Matching, Multiyear/Continuing Support, Operating Expenses, Project.
Note: The foundation also funds program-related investments.

Donor Information

Founder: The John S. and James L. Knight Foundation was established in Akron, OH, on December 29, 1950. Its forerunner was the Charles Landon Knight Memorial Education Fund. Upon the death of John S. Knight in 1981, his brother James was elected chairman of the foundation and served in that capacity until his death in February 1991. Foundation funds have been provided by the estates of John S. and James L. Knight and their mother, Clara I. Knight.

Financial Summary

Total Giving: $85,617,981 (2002); $85,000,000 (2001 approx)
Giving Analysis: Giving for 2002 includes: foundation grants to United Way ($760,000)
Assets: $1,718,236,238 (2002); $1,900,829,942 (2001)
Gifts Received: $2,028,923 (2002); $300,000 (2001 approx); $400,000 (2000 approx). Note: Since 1991, the foundation has received almost $200,000,000 from the estate of James L. Knight.

Typical Recipients

Arts & Humanities: Arts Associations & Councils, Arts Centers, Arts Funds, Arts Institutes, Arts Outreach, Ballet, Community Arts, Dance, Ethnic & Folk Arts, Film & Video, Arts & Humanities-General, Historic Preservation, History & Archaeology, Libraries, Museums/Galleries, Music, Opera, Performing Arts, Public Broadcasting, Theater
Civic & Public Affairs: African American Affairs, Botanical Gardens/Parks, Clubs, Community Foundations, Economic Development, Employment/Job Training, First Amendment Issues, Civic & Public Affairs-General, Hispanic Affairs, Housing, Municipalities/Towns, Nonprofit Management, Philanthropic Organizations, Professional & Trade Associations, Public Policy, Urban & Community Affairs, Women's Affairs, Zoos/Aquariums
Education: Afterschool/Enrichment Programs, Arts/Humanities Education, Business Education, Colleges & Universities, Community & Junior Colleges, Education Associations, Education Funds, Education Reform, Elementary Education (Public), Engineering/Technological Education, Environmental Education, Faculty Development, Education-General, International Exchange, International Studies, Journalism/Media Education, Legal Education, Literacy, Minority Education, Public Education (Precollege), Science/Mathematics Education, Social Sciences Education, Student Aid, Vocational & Technical Education
Environment: Air/Water Quality, Protection
Health: Cancer, Children's Health/Hospitals, Emergency/Ambulance Services, Health Organizations, Hospices, Hospitals, Medical Research, Mental Health, Prenatal Health Issues
International: Foreign Educational Institutions, Human Rights, International Organizations, International Relations, International Relief Efforts
Religion: Ministries, Religious Welfare, Seminaries
Science: Observatories & Planetariums, Science Museums, Scientific Centers & Institutes, Scientific

Labs
Social Services: At-Risk Youth, Child Welfare, Community Service Organizations, Day Care, Delinquency & Criminal Rehabilitation, Family Services, Food/Clothing Distribution, Recreation & Athletics, Refugee Assistance, Shelters/Homelessness, Social Services-General, Substance Abuse, United Funds/United Ways, Volunteer Services, YMCA/YWCA/YMHA/YWHA, Youth Organizations

Application Procedures

Initial Contact: Submit a brief letter of inquiry (two pages or less).
Application Requirements: All letters of inquiry should include a description of organization; contact information; amount requested and over what time period the funds are needed; purpose of funds sought and how it fills a public need; the organization's total income and expenditures for the most recent year; and proof of tax-exempt status. In addition to the above information, inquiries submitted to the National Venture Fund or the Knight Community Partners Program should describe the community need(s) addressed; the relationship of the project to the Foundation's funding priorities for the specific community; anticipated results and how they will benefit people in need; the organization's qualifications to carry out the project; the project's relation to the applicant's mission and programmatic goals; the role of any other organizations in planning the project and the nature of their participation.
Deadlines: None, with the exception of special initiatives. Proposals are accepted throughout the year and are reviewed on a rolling basis. If a proposal is considered appropriate and complete, it will be scheduled for board review.
Review Process: Organizations will be contacted if their inquiry has been approved for development into a proposal. Generally, it is approximately six months between proposal submission and board review, but the times may vary depending on the circumstances and timing of a proposal. The board of trustees meets quarterly in March, June, September, and December. Applicants are usually notified of the foundation's decisions in writing within two weeks after the trustees' meeting.

Restrictions

The Foundation prefers not to support fundraising events; operating deficits; charities operated by service clubs; activities that are normally the responsibility of government; medical research, single-disease associations, or hospitals (unless for a community-wide capital campaign with a stated goal and beginning and ending dates, or for specific projects that meet Foundation goals); religious organizations for sectarian purposes; political candidates; memorials; international programs and organizations, except U.S.-based organizations supporting a free press around the world; and conferences, group travel, or honoraria for distinguished guests (except in Foundation initiatives). The Foundation will not generally accept a second request for a capital campaign for which the Foundation has previously approved a grant, or a second proposal from an organization that has applied for support in the last twelve months.
Applications for the National Venture Fund and Knight Community Partners Program must benefit one or more of the Foundation's 26 communities located in the states of California, Colorado, Florida, Georgia, Indiana, Kansas, Kentucky, Minnesota, Mississippi, North Carolina, North Dakota, Ohio, Pennsylvania, South Carolina, and South Dakota. A complete list of the communities is available on the Foundation's web site. needed.

Additional Information

A major portion of the proposals are rejected because they fail to meet published criteria.
Education and Arts and Culture programs award grants nationally and locally (27 communities). Although the journalism program is national in focus,

U.S. organizations funded by the foundation may support international journalism organizations.
Publications: Annual Report; Guidelines; Application Form; Quarterly Newsletter

Foundation Officials

Cesar L. Alvarez: trustee ED University of Florida JD; University of Florida BA; University of Florida MS. PRIM CORP EMPL president, chief executive officer: Greenberg Traurig. CORP AFFIL director: NASDAQ; director: New York Stock Exchange; president, chief executive officer: Greenberg Traurig LLP. NONPR AFFIL trustee: Our Kids, Inc.; trustee: Vizcaya Foundation; trustee: Miami Art Museum; trustee: National Foundation for the Advancement of the Arts; co-chairman: International Diplomacy Committee for the Florida Free Trade Area; trustee: Manhattanville College; trustee: Florida International University Foundation; member: Facts About Cuban Exiles; member: Florida Bar Association; member: American Bar Association; member: Cuban Bar Association.

W. Gerald Austen, MD: trustee, trustee B Akron, OH 1930. ED Massachusetts Institute of Technology BS (1951); Harvard University MD (1955). CORP AFFIL director: Abiomed Inc. NONPR AFFIL fellow: Royal College Surgeons; member: Society University Surgeons; trustee: North Shore Medical Center; member: National Academy of Sciences Institute Medicine; member: New England Cardiovascular Society; member: Massachusetts Heart Association; life trustee: Massachusetts Institute Technology; honorary trustee: Massachusetts General Hospital; professor surgery: Harvard University Medical School; trustee: Massachusetts Eye & Ear Infirmary; member: Association Academy of Surgery; trustee: Dana Farber Partners Cancer Care; member: American Heart Association; director, member: American Board Thoracic Surgery; member, residency review surgery: American College Surgeons; member: American Association Thoracic Surgery; member: American Board Surgery; fellow: American Academy of Arts & Sciences; member: Accreditation Council Graduate Medicine Education.

Leslie Mayo Baker, Jr.: trustee B Brunswick, MD 1942. ED University of Richmond BA (1964); University of Virginia MBA (1969). NONPR AFFIL board member: National Humanities Center; member: North Carolina Arboretum; member: American Bankers Council; founder: Marine Corps Heritage Foundation.

Creed Carter Black: trustee B Harlan, KY 1925. ED Northwestern University BS (1949); University of Chicago MA (1952). PRIM CORP EMPL president, chief executive officer: Knight Ridder Inc. NONPR AFFIL member: Newspapers Association America; president, member: Southern Newspaper Publishers Association; member: Lambda Chi Alpha; life member: National Conference Editorial Writers; member: Kappa Tau Alpha; member: Kentucky Journalism Hall of Fame. CLUB AFFIL member: Bankers Club; member: Riviera Country Club.

Robert Briggs: trustee ED Duke University BA; Ohio State University JD. NONPR AFFIL trustee: Northeast Ohio Council on Higher Education; trustee: Northeast Ohio Technology Coalition; trustee: Musical Arts Association; chairman, trustee: National Inventors Hall of Fame; trustee: Catholic Diocese of Cleveland Foundation; chairman: Fund for Our Economic Future; co-chairman, board of overseers: Blossom Music Center.

Hodding Carter, III: president, chief executive officer, trustee ED Princeton University BA (1957). NONPR AFFIL member, editorial board: Southern Cultures; director: Twentieth Century Fund.

Mary Sue Coleman: trustee ED Grinnell College BS; University of North Carolina PhD. CORP AFFIL president: University Michigan. NONPR AFFIL fellow: American Association Advancement of Science; member: Institute of Medicine; fellow: American Academy Arts and Sciences.

Jill Kathryn Ker Conway: vice chairman, trustee B Hillston, NW Australia October 09, 1934. ED University of Sydney BA (1958); Harvard University PhD (1969). PRIM NONPR EMPL president emeritus: Smith Colorado. CORP AFFIL director: Nike Inc.; director: Merrill Lynch & Co. Inc.; director: Colgate-Palmolive Co.; director: Arthur D Little Inc. NONPR AFFIL visiting scholar: Massachusetts Institute Technology.

Marjorie Knight Crane: trustee B Miami, FL. ED Queens University BA. NONPR AFFIL director: Queens University Library; president: RibbonWalk Conservancy Inc.; member: Crown Society of Carolinas Concert Association; member: Opera Guild of Charlotte.

Timothy J. Crowe: vice president, chief financial officer ED Holy Cross College BA; Pennsylvania State University MBA; United States International University MS. NONPR AFFIL member: Association for Investment Management; investment council: Pennsylvania State University.

Paul S. Grogan: trustee ED Harvard University MA; Williams College BA. PRIM NONPR EMPL vice president government community & public affairs: Harvard University. NONPR AFFIL president: Boston Foundation.

Belinda Turner Lawrence: vice president, chief administrative officer B Louisville, KY. ED Barry University BA.

Jorge Martinez: director information NONPR AFFIL member: Hispanics in Philanthropy.

Lawrence H. (Bud) Meyer: vice president commun NONPR AFFIL committee member: Council on Foundations; committee member: Living Cities; director: Communications Network.

Rolfe Neill: trustee B Mount Airy, NC 1932. ED University of North Carolina AB (1954). PRIM CORP EMPL chairman, publisher: Charlotte Observer ADD CORP EMPL chairman, publ: Knight Publishing Co. Inc.

Mariam C. Noland: trustee ED Case Western Reserve University BA; Harvard University MS. NONPR AFFIL president: Community Foundation for Southeastern Michigan.

Beverly Knight Olson: trustee NONPR AFFIL director: Macon Rescue Mission; director: Wesleyan College-Macon; advisory board: Children's Hospital of the Medicine Center of Central Georgia.

John W. Rogers, Jr.: trustee ED Princeton University AB (1980). CORP AFFIL director: McDonald's Corp.; director: Exelon Corp.; director: GATX Corp.; director: Bank One Corp.; director: Burrell Communications Group; director: Aon Corp.; chairman, chief executive officer: Ariel Capital Management LLC. NONPR AFFIL chairman: Chicago Urban League; trustee: University Chicago.

Grants Analysis

Disclosure Period: calendar year ending 2002
Total Grants: $84,857,981*
Number of Grants: 747
Average Grant: $113,598
Highest Grant: $1,580,000
Typical Range: $20,000 to $200,000
*Note: Giving excludes United Way.

Recent Grants

Note: Grants derived from 2002 Form 990.
General
9,000,000 International Center for Journalists, Washington, DC -- towards support of the fourth phase of the knight international press fellowship program
5,000,000 Cornell University, Ithaca, NY -- towards strengthening the John S Knight Writing program and to expand program outreach to other colleges and universities
4,830,000 American Society of Newspaper Editors, Reston, VA -- for revitalizing high school journalism and emphasize the role of the First Amendment
4,000,000 Akron Art Museum, Akron, OH -- towards partial challenge grant to plan and build

3,750,000 an addition to the museum and increase endowment for community cultural center

3,750,000 Community Foundation for Southeastern Michigan, Detroit, MI -- towards community foundation donor advised funds

3,750,000 Foundation for the Carolinas, Duluth, MN -- towards community foundation donor advised funds

3,400,000 Akron Community Foundation, Akron, OH -- towards community foundation donor advised funds

3,100,000 Committee to Protect Journalists, New York, NY -- towards partial challenge grant to support operations and build an endowment

2,750,000 Massachusetts Institute of Technology, Cambridge, MA -- towards the museum loan network

2,750,000 Massachusetts Institute of Technology, Cambridge, MA -- towards the museum loan network

KNIGHT RIDDER INC.

Company Headquarters
San Jose, CA
Web: http://www.kri.com

Company Description
Founded: 1974
Ticker: KRI
Exchange: NYSE
Revenue: US$2.841 billion (2002)
Employees: 18000 (2003)
SIC(s): 2711 Newspapers.

Operating Locations
Knight Ridder (CA--Long Beach, Palo Alto, San Jose; CO--Boulder; FL--Boca Raton, Bradenton, Marathon, Miami; GA--Columbus, Macon, Milledgeville; IN--Fort Wayne; KS--Wichita; KY--Lexington; MI--Detroit; MN--St. Paul; MS--Biloxi; NJ--Bridgewater; NC--Charlotte; ND--Grand Forks; OH--Akron; PA--Philadelphia, State College; SC--Columbia; SD--Aberdeen)

Nonmonetary Support
Type: Loaned Executives
Volunteer Programs: The company sponsors a variety of employee-led volunteer efforts.

Knight Ridder Fund

Giving Contact
Polk Laffoon, Vice President & Corporate Secretary
Knight Ridder, Inc.
50 West San Fernando Street, Suite 1500
San Jose, CA 95113
Phone: (408)938-7838
Fax: (408)938-7766

Alternate Contact
Lorraine Brenner
Phone: (408)938-7857

Description
EIN: 592610440
Organization Type: Corporate Foundation
Giving Locations: headquarters and operating communities.
Grant Types: Employee Matching Gifts, General Support.

Financial Summary
Total Giving: $2,033,678 (2003); $2,041,124 (2002); $2,068,333 (2001). Note: Contributes through foun-

dation only.
Giving Analysis: Giving for 2002 includes: foundation grants to United Way ($312,500); 2001: foundation grants to United Way ($363,883)
Assets: $1,659,903 (2003); $3,671,274 (2002); $5,647,599 (2001)
Gifts Received: $6,000,000 (2000); $850,000 (1997). Note: Contributions were received from Knight Ridder, Inc.

Typical Recipients
Arts & Humanities: Arts Institutes, Arts Outreach, Ballet, Film & Video, Arts & Humanities-General, History & Archaeology, Libraries, Museums/Galleries, Music, Opera, Theater
Civic & Public Affairs: African American Affairs, Asian American Affairs, Chambers of Commerce, Civil Rights, Clubs, Community Foundations, First Amendment Issues, Civic & Public Affairs-General, Municipalities/Towns, Philanthropic Organizations, Professional & Trade Associations, Public Policy, Urban & Community Affairs, Women's Affairs, Zoos/Aquariums
Education: Business Education, Colleges & Universities, Education-General, International Studies, Journalism/Media Education, Private Education (Precollege), Social Sciences Education, Student Aid
Environment: Forestry
Health: Cancer, Children's Health/Hospitals, Health Organizations, Kidney, Medical Rehabilitation
Science: Science Museums
Social Services: Emergency Relief, Recreation & Athletics, Social Services-General, Substance Abuse, United Funds/United Ways, Veterans, Volunteer Services, YMCA/YWCA/YMHA/YWHA, Youth Organizations

Application Procedures
Initial Contact: Call to request proposal coversheet and proposal checklist.
Application Requirements: Proposal cover sheet; letter of application; project budget; organization's current operating budget; list of governing body/officers; audited financial statements; IRS documentation of current tax exempt status.
Deadlines: None.
Decision Notification: Contributions committee meets quarterly.

Restrictions
Does not contribute to individuals or single-disease health organizations.

Additional Information
Knight Ridder's newspapers also have contributions programs to support activities in their individual markets.

Corporate Officials
Polk Laffoon, IV: vice president corporate relations, corporate secretary ED Pennsylvania State University MBA; Yale University (1967). PRIM CORP EMPL vice president corporate relations, corporate secretary: Knight Ridder.
Paul Anthony Ridder: chairman, chief executive officer, director B Duluth, MN 1940. ED University of Michigan BA (1962). PRIM CORP EMPL chairman, chief executive officer, director: Knight Ridder, Inc. CORP AFFIL director: Seattle Times Co.; director: Newspaper First. NONPR AFFIL director: United Way America; member president advisory board: University Michigan; member: Florida Chamber of Commerce; member advisory board: Center Economic Policy Development. CLUB AFFIL Pine Valley Golf Club; Cypress Point Club; Indian Creek Country Club.

Foundation Officials
Jerome Ceppos: director
Mary Jean Connors: director
Garry Effren: vice president, treasurer, director
Lynda Hauswirth: assistant vice president

Polk Laffoon, IV: secretary (see above)
Adrienne Lilly: assistant secretary
Sharon Orlando: assistant secretary
Margaret Randazzo: assistant treasurer
Paul Anthony Ridder: president, director (see above)
Steve Rossi: director
Hilary A. Schneider: director
Joseph Visci: director
Gordon Yamate: director

Grants Analysis
Disclosure Period: calendar year ending 2003
Total Grants: $1,695,678*
Number of Grants: 65
Average Grant: $17,379*
Highest Grant: $200,000
Lowest Grant: $100
Typical Range: $5,000 to $30,000
***Note:** Giving excludes United Way. Average grant figure excludes four highest grants ($635,569).

Recent Grants
Note: Grants derived from 2003 Form 990.
Library-Related

500	San Jose Public Library Partners in Reading, Willow Glen, CA

General

100,000	San Jose Repertory Theatre, San Jose, CA
75,000	CADCA, Alexandria, VA
75,000	National Constitution Center, Philadelphia, PA
50,000	Heart of America United Way, Kansas City, MO
50,000	Robert McGruder Memorial Scholarship Fund, Detroit, MI
50,000	San Jose Downtown Association, San Jose, CA
10,000	Belleville YMCA, Belleville, ON Canada
10,000	Stanford University, Stanford, CA
7,500	AAJA, San Francisco, CA
5,000	American Red Cross, Everett, WA

MARION I. AND HENRY J. KNOTT FOUNDATION

Giving Contact
M. Gregory Cantori, Exec. Dir.
3904 Hickory Avenue
Baltimore, MD 21211-1834
Phone: (410)235-7068
Fax: (410)889-2577
E-mail: knott@knottfoundation.org
Web: http://www.knottfoundation.org

Description
Founded: 1986
EIN: 521517876
Organization Type: Family Foundation
Giving Locations: CA; MD
Grant Types: Capital, Challenge, Endowment, General Support, Matching, Operating Expenses, Project.

Donor Information
Founder: Established in 1978 by Marion I. Knott and Henry J. Knott Sr.

Financial Summary
Total Giving: $1,752,506 (2002)
Giving Analysis: Giving for 2002 includes: foundation fellowships ($284,129)
Assets: $37,691,396 (2002)
Gifts Received: $281,090 (1997)

Typical Recipients
Arts & Humanities: Arts Centers, Arts Festivals, Arts Outreach, History & Archaeology, Libraries, Muse-

ums/Galleries, Music, Opera, Public Broadcasting, Theater

Civic & Public Affairs: African American Affairs, Botanical Gardens/Parks, Business/Free Enterprise, Economic Development, Employment/Job Training, Civic & Public Affairs-General, Housing, Legal Aid, Native American Affairs, Parades/Festivals, Professional & Trade Associations, Urban & Community Affairs, Women's Affairs, Zoos/Aquariums

Education: Afterschool/Enrichment Programs, Arts/Humanities Education, Business Education, Colleges & Universities, Continuing Education, Elementary Education (Public), Education-General, Health & Physical Education, Literacy, Medical Education, Minority Education, Preschool Education, Private Education (Precollege), Public Education (Precollege), Religious Education, Science/Mathematics Education, Secondary Education (Private), Special Education, Student Aid

Environment: Environment-General

Health: AIDS/HIV, Alzheimer's Disease, Cancer, Children's Health/Hospitals, Clinics/Medical Centers, Eyes/Blindness, Health Funds, Health Organizations, Hospices, Medical Rehabilitation, Medical Research, Mental Health, Multiple Sclerosis, Nutrition, Prenatal Health Issues, Preventive Medicine/Wellness Organizations, Public Health, Single-Disease Health Associations, Speech & Hearing, Trauma Treatment

Religion: Churches, Dioceses, Religion-General, Ministries, Religious Organizations, Religious Welfare

Science: Scientific Centers & Institutes

Social Services: At-Risk Youth, Big Brothers/Big Sisters, Child Welfare, Community Centers, Community Service Organizations, Counseling, Day Care, Delinquency & Criminal Rehabilitation, Emergency Relief, Family Services, Food/Clothing Distribution, People with Disabilities, Recreation & Athletics, Scouts, Senior Services, Shelters/Homelessness, Special Olympics, Substance Abuse, YMCA/YWCA/YMHA/YWHA, Youth Organizations

Application Procedures

Initial Contact: The foundation requests that applicants call or write the foundation for formal application guidelines. The request must be presented by telephone to the foundation's executive director before submitting a fully developed written proposal.

Application Requirements: Two copies of the full proposal must be submitted as a formal application. The proposal should include: a cover letter including amount requested; purpose of the program, and a contact name and phone number; concise history, mission statement, current programs, description of volunteers (number and duties); funding request/purpose of grant, statement of need, target population, project outcomes, impact, timetable, project budget, list of key staff, expected results, outcomes and how measured, description of project evaluation, cost effectiveness, funding sources (anticipated, pending, and awarded); list of Board of Directors, description of organizational structure; current IRS Form 990, budget for previous two years, current annual operating budget, two-year projections, current audited financial statement including income expenses, and balance sheet; copy of IRS determination letter; and directions to organization.

Deadlines: February 1 and August 1.

Review Process: The board meets in June and December. Onsite visits are performed for all proposals.

Notes: Foundation does not accept proposals by fax or e-mail. Organizations are required to complete post-grant report one year after receipt of funding.

Restrictions

The foundation does not support individuals, public education, scholarships for education, "pro-choice activities," reproductive health, or political organizations. It does not support organizations that have not been in operation for at least one year, annual giving, one-time only events/seminars/workshops, legal services, the environment, medical research, day care

centers, endowment funds for arts/humanities, national/local chapters for specific diseases, agencies that redistribute grants to other nonprofits, or government agencies that form 501 (c)(3) nonprofits to fund public sector projects. Multi-year grants are generally not awarded. awarded. awarded.

Additional Information

There are no extensions of the grant deadlines, under any circumstances.

Publications: Annual Report; Application Guidelines

Foundation Officials

Daniel J. Gallagher: member PRIM CORP EMPL vice president, director: Liberty Federal Savings & Loan Association. CORP AFFIL treasurer, director: Gallagher Asphalt Corp.

Lindsay R. Gallagher: member

Marty Voelkel Hanssen: vice president

Kelly L. Harris: secretary

Lindsay Harris: member

Thomas K. Harris: member

Carlisle V. Hashim: member

Marion I. Knott: chairman

Martin G. Knott, Jr.: member B 1949. PRIM CORP EMPL president, director: Martin G. Knott & Associates.

Patty L. Knott: member

Teresa A. Knott: member B 1949. ED Johns Hopkins University (1971). PRIM CORP EMPL vice president: Martin G. Knott & Associates.

Joann O. Porter: member

Martin F. Porter: member

Margaret K. Riehl: member B 1934. CORP AFFIL partner: Northern Village Apartments; partner: Riehl Estate Management Co.; partner: Beechfield Apartments.

Geralynn D. Smyth: member

John C. Smyth: president

Patricia K. Smyth: member NONPR AFFIL chairman, director: Good Samaritan Hospital Maryland.

Alice K. Voelkel: member

Grants Analysis

Disclosure Period: calendar year ending 2002

Total Grants: $1,468,377*

Number of Grants: 114

Average Grant: $12,741*

Highest Grant: $200,000

Lowest Grant: $33

Typical Range: $15,000 to $50,000

*Note: Giving excludes fellowships. Average grant excludes two highest grants.

Recent Grants

Note: Grants derived from 2002 Form 990.

General

125,000	St. Bernardine School, Baltimore, MD -- capital projects
100,000	Mercy High School, Baltimore, MD -- construction of auditorium
100,000	New All Saints School, Baltimore, MD -- educational programming
75,000	St. Bernardine School, Baltimore, MD -- educational programming
67,624	Good Samaritan Hospital Foundation, Baltimore, MD -- equipment for Good Health Center
60,000	Maryvale Preparatory School, Brookland-ville, MD
55,000	St. Philip and St. James School, Baltimore, MD -- install two vertical lifts
51,100	Maryland Food Bank, Baltimore, MD
50,000	Archbishop Curley High School, Baltimore, MD -- replace windows
50,000	Mount Saint Joseph High School, Baltimore, MD -- computers

SEYMOUR H. KNOX FOUNDATION

Giving Contact

James F. Wendel, Assistant Secretary & Assistant Treasurer
1 HSBC Center Suite 3840
Buffalo, NY 14203
Phone: (716)854-6811
Fax: (716)856-0517
E-mail: kbojw@aol.com

Description

Founded: 1945
EIN: 160839066
Organization Type: Family Foundation
Giving Locations: NY: Buffalo nationally.
Grant Types: General Support.

Donor Information

Founder: Incorporated in 1945 by the late Seymour H. Knox, the late Marjorie K. C. Klopp, and the late Dorothy K. G. Rogers.

Financial Summary

Total Giving: $703,969 (2001)
Assets: $21,197,169 (2001)
Gifts Received: $1,089,474 (1994)

Typical Recipients

Arts & Humanities: Arts Associations & Councils, Arts Centers, Arts Institutes, Arts & Humanities-General, Historic Preservation, History & Archaeology, Libraries, Museums/Galleries, Music, Performing Arts, Public Broadcasting, Theater

Civic & Public Affairs: Botanical Gardens/Parks, Business/Free Enterprise, Chambers of Commerce, Clubs, Economic Development, Employment/Job Training, Civic & Public Affairs-General, Municipalities/Towns, Nonprofit Management, Philanthropic Organizations, Professional & Trade Associations, Urban & Community Affairs, Women's Affairs, Zoos/Aquariums

Education: Arts/Humanities Education, Colleges & Universities, Education Funds, Elementary Education (Private), Environmental Education, Education-General, Gifted & Talented Programs, Medical Education, Private Education (Precollege), Public Education (Precollege), Secondary Education (Private), Special Education, Student Aid

Environment: Air/Water Quality, Forestry, Environment-General, Protection, Resource Conservation, Wildlife Protection

Health: Alzheimer's Disease, Cancer, Children's Health/Hospitals, Health Funds, Hospices, Medical Rehabilitation, Medical Research, Research/Studies Institutes, Speech & Hearing, Trauma Treatment

International: International Organizations

Religion: Churches, Religious Organizations, Religious Welfare, Seminaries

Science: Scientific Centers & Institutes, Scientific Organizations

Social Services: Animal Protection, Community Service Organizations, Day Care, Family Planning, Family Services, Food/Clothing Distribution, Homes, People with Disabilities, Recreation & Athletics, Substance Abuse, United Funds/United Ways, YMCA/YWCA/YMHA/YWHA, Youth Organizations

Application Procedures

Initial Contact: Send a letter of inquiry to the foundation.

Deadlines: None.

Restrictions

Grants are not made to individuals.

Foundation Officials

Benjamin K. Campbell: vice president, treasurer
Hazard K. Campbell: chairman, treasurer
Northrup Rand Knox, Jr.: president ED Yale University (1984).
Seymour Horace Knox, IV: vice president, secretary B 1920. CORP AFFIL chairman: Buffalo Sabres Hockey Club.
Randolph A. Marks: director B Rome, NY 1935. ED Lehigh University (1957). CORP AFFIL director: Computer Task Group Inc.; director: Modern-Tek Shops; director: America Brass Co.; director: Columbus McKinnon Corp.
Henry Zellar Urban: director B Buffalo, NY July 11, 1920. ED Yale University BS (1943). NONPR AFFIL member: Buffalo Chamber of Commerce; member: New York State Publishers Association. CLUB AFFIL Tennis & Squash Club; Sankaty Head Golf Club; Saturn Club; Nantucket Yacht Club; Pack Club; Mid-Day Club; Buffalo Club; Buffalo Country Club.
James F. Wendell: assistant secretary, assistant treasurer

Grants Analysis

Disclosure Period: calendar year ending 2001
Total Grants: $661,469*
Number of Grants: 105
Average Grant: $5,476*
Highest Grant: $92,000
Lowest Grant: $250
Typical Range: $1,000 to $10,000
*Note: Giving excludes United Way. Average grant figure excludes highest grant.

Recent Grants

Note: Grants derived from 2002 Form 990.
General

125,650	Buffalo Fine Arts Academy, Buffalo, NY
60,000	Elmwood-Franklin School, Buffalo, NY
50,000	Ducks Unlimited, Memphis, TN
50,000	Elmwood-Franklin School, Buffalo, NY
42,000	United way of Buffalo and Eire County, Buffalo, NY
40,000	Forest Lawn Heritage Foundation, Buffalo, NY
25,000	Buffalo and Erie County Historical Society, Buffalo, NY
25,000	Buffalo Seminary, Buffalo, NY
25,000	YMCA of Greater Buffalo, Buffalo, NY
20,000	Zoological Society of Buffalo Inc., Buffalo, NY

ROBERT W. KNOX, SR., AND PEARL WALLIS KNOX CHARITABLE FOUNDATION

Giving Contact

Jacky Ducote, Trust Officer
c/o Bank of America
PO Box 2518
Houston, TX 77252-2518
Phone: (713)247-7432

Description

Founded: 1964
EIN: 746064974
Organization Type: Private Foundation
Giving Locations: TX: Galveston, Houston
Grant Types: General Support, Scholarship.

Donor Information

Founder: Robert W. Knox, Jr.

Financial Summary

Total Giving: $201,295 (fiscal year ending August 31, 2004); $282,925 (fiscal 2001)
Giving Analysis: Giving for fiscal 2004 includes: foundation grants to United Way ($1,000); foundation scholarships ($7,500); fiscal 2001: foundation grants to United Way ($5,000); foundation scholarships ($7,500)
Assets: $5,021,782 (fiscal 2004); $5,434,479 (fiscal 2001)

Typical Recipients

Arts & Humanities: Arts Associations & Councils, Arts Centers, Arts Institutes, Community Arts, Ethnic & Folk Arts, Historic Preservation, History & Archaeology, Libraries, Museums/Galleries, Music, Opera, Theater, Visual Arts
Civic & Public Affairs: Asian American Affairs, Botanical Gardens/Parks, Clubs, Civic & Public Affairs-General, Hispanic Affairs, Housing, Law & Justice, Municipalities/Towns, Parades/Festivals, Urban & Community Affairs, Women's Affairs, Zoos/Aquariums
Education: Business Education, Colleges & Universities, Education-General, Legal Education, Literacy, Medical Education, Minority Education, Private Education (Precollege), Student Aid
Health: AIDS/HIV, Alzheimer's Disease, Cancer, Children's Health/Hospitals, Clinics/Medical Centers, Emergency/Ambulance Services, Heart, Hospices, Mental Health, Prenatal Health Issues, Transplant Networks/Donor Banks, Trauma Treatment
International: International Environmental Issues, International Relations
Religion: Churches, Ministries, Religious Organizations, Religious Welfare
Science: Science Museums
Social Services: Big Brothers/Big Sisters, Camps, Child Abuse, Child Welfare, Community Centers, Community Service Organizations, Crime Prevention, Day Care, Delinquency & Criminal Rehabilitation, Family Services, Food/Clothing Distribution, People with Disabilities, Recreation & Athletics, Scouts, Senior Services, Shelters/Homelessness, Substance Abuse, United Funds/United Ways, Volunteer Services, YMCA/YWCA/YMHA/YWHA, Youth Organizations

Application Procedures

Initial Contact: Send a brief letter of inquiry and a full proposal.
Application Requirements: Include a description of organization, amount requested, purpose of funds sought, recently audited financial statement, and proof of tax-exempt status.
Deadlines: August 31, November 30, February 28, and June 30.

Additional Information

Trust(s): Bank of America

Grants Analysis

Disclosure Period: fiscal year ending August 31, 2004
Total Grants: $192,795*
Number of Grants: 63
Average Grant: $3,060
Highest Grant: $25,000
Lowest Grant: $1,000
Typical Range: $1,000 to $5,000
*Note: Giving excludes scholarships and United Way.

Recent Grants

Note: Grants derived from 2004 Form 990.
General

25,000	Goodwill Industries of Houston, Houston, TX -- for Moreton achievement lunch and golf tournament
15,000	Miller Outdoor Theatre, Houston, TX -- for facility construction
10,000	Galveston Historical Foundation, Dallas, TX -- for Galveston Historical Homes tour
7,500	Austin College, Sherman, TX -- for scholarships
5,000	First Presbyterian Church, Dallas, TX
5,000	Houston Grand Opera, Houston, TX -- to support 'serious fun'
5,000	Houston Museum of Natural Science, Houston, TX -- for educational programs
4,000	University of Houston Law Center, Houston, TX -- for law gala and auction
3,500	Boys and Girls Country of Houston, Hockley, TX -- for athletic equipment for kids
3,500	Partnership for Baylor, Houston, TX -- for a multi-organ transplant center

EARL KNUDSEN CHARITABLE FOUNDATION

Giving Contact

Judith D. Morrison, Secretary
PO Box 22070
Pittsburgh, PA 15222

Description

Founded: 1975
EIN: 256062530
Organization Type: Private Foundation
Giving Locations: PA
Grant Types: General Support.

Donor Information

Founder: the late Earl Knudsen

Financial Summary

Gifts Received: $1,000 (1995); $2,765 (1994); $1,638 (1993)

Typical Recipients

Arts & Humanities: Arts Centers, Ballet, Community Arts, Arts & Humanities-General, Historic Preservation, Libraries, Museums/Galleries, Music
Civic & Public Affairs: Community Foundations, Employment/Job Training, Civic & Public Affairs-General, Municipalities/Towns, Urban & Community Affairs, Women's Affairs
Education: Colleges & Universities, Education Funds, Education-General, Preschool Education, Private Education (Precollege), Science/Mathematics Education, Special Education, Student Aid
Health: Children's Health/Hospitals, Clinics/Medical Centers, Emergency/Ambulance Services, Eyes/Blindness, Health-General, Hospices, Hospitals, Hospitals (University Affiliated), Long-Term Care, Medical Rehabilitation, Mental Health, Public Health, Research/Studies Institutes, Single-Disease Health Associations
Religion: Churches, Ministries, Religious Organizations, Religious Welfare
Social Services: Big Brothers/Big Sisters, Child Welfare, Community Centers, Community Service Organizations, Crime Prevention, Day Care, Family Services, Food/Clothing Distribution, People with Disabilities, Scouts, Senior Services, United Funds/United Ways, YMCA/YWCA/YMHA/YWHA, Youth Organizations

Application Procedures

Initial Contact: Send brief letter describing program.
Application Requirements: Include purpose of funds sought and proof of tax-exempt status.
Deadlines: None.

Additional Information

Trust(s): National City Bank of PA, Clark & Peelor.

Foundation Officials
Roy Thomas Clark, Esq.: co-trustee
Pamela K. Peelor, Esq.: co-trustee

Grants Analysis
Disclosure Period: calendar year ending 2000
Total Grants: $406,000
Number of Grants: 67
Average Grant: $6,060
Highest Grant: $25,000
Typical Range: $1,000 to $10,000

Recent Grants
Note: Grants derived from 2001 Form 990.
General

30,000	Pittsburgh Leadership Foundation, Pittsburgh, PA
25,000	Wells College, Aurora, NY
20,000	Extra-Mile Education Foundation, Inc., Pittsburgh, PA
20,000	Family Hospice, Pittsburgh, PA
15,000	Coalition for Christian Outreach, Pittsburgh, PA
15,000	DePaul Institute, Pittsburgh, PA
15,000	Family House, Pittsburgh, PA
10,000	Baptist Homes of Western Pennsylvania, Pittsburgh, PA
10,000	Focus on Renewal, McKees Rocks, PA
10,000	Intervarsity Christian Fellowship, Lexington, KY

KOCH FOUNDATION, INC.

Giving Contact
Michael A. Marconi, Executive Director
2830 Northwest 41st Street, Suite H
Gainesville, FL 32606
Phone: (352)373-7491
Fax: (352)337-1548

Description
Founded: 1979
EIN: 591885997
Organization Type: Family Foundation
Giving Locations: internationally; nationally.
Grant Types: Capital, Conference/Seminar, General Support, Matching, Project, Seed Money.

Donor Information
Founder: The Koch Foundation was established in 1979 with funds donated by Carl Koch and Paula Koch.

Financial Summary
Total Giving: $8,294,503 (fiscal year ending March 31, 2004); $11,126,958 (fiscal 2002); $10,756,718 (fiscal 2001)
Assets: $136,314,558 (fiscal 2004); $130,799,599 (fiscal 2002); $128,812,214 (fiscal 2001)
Gifts Received: $2,350,001 (fiscal 2001); $15,946 (fiscal 1993)

Typical Recipients
Arts & Humanities: Film & Video, Libraries, Public Broadcasting
Civic & Public Affairs: Civil Rights, Civic & Public Affairs-General, Hispanic Affairs
Education: Colleges & Universities, Education Associations, Education Funds, Education Reform, Elementary Education (Private), Education-General, Minority Education, Preschool Education, Private Education (Precollege), Religious Education, Secondary Education (Private)
Health: Emergency/Ambulance Services, Health-General, Hospitals, Prenatal Health Issues
International: Foreign Educational Institutions, International-General, Health Care/Hospitals, International Development, International Relief Efforts, Mission-ary/Religious Activities
Religion: Churches, Dioceses, Religion-General, Ministries, Missionary Activities (Domestic), Religious Organizations, Religious Welfare, Seminaries
Science: Scientific Research
Social Services: Child Welfare, Community Service Organizations, Refugee Assistance, Shelters/Homelessness, Social Services-General

Application Procedures
Initial Contact: Prospective applicants should submit a brief letter describing the project and requesting an application form.
Application Requirements: Provide a budget and statement of the impact on evangelization that the project would accomplish. If the program is outside the United States, include the country or diocese where it will take place and a verification letter from a U.S. fiscal stating that they will be assisting in the distribution of funds. If the funds are for a continuing project, include a report describing the progress of the project with the application.
Deadlines: Requests for application forms are received from January 1 to May 31. Letters of request for an application must be postmarked no later than May 31. Completed applications must be returned within 90 days of the date of the application cover letter.
Review Process: All applications are reviewed by the grant committee on a regular basis. Final decisions are made by the board at the annual meeting, and applicants will be notified by late March.
Notes: All requests must be made in English and may not be faxed.

Restrictions
Koch Foundation grants are limited to Roman Catholic activities that propagate the faith. Financial support is not provided to individuals or for individual scholarships.

Additional Information
Applicants are encouraged to seek matching or collaborative funding.
Publications: Annual Report; Guidelines

Foundation Officials
Carolyn L. Bomberger: president
Dorothy C. Bomberger: assistant treasurer, director
Matthew A. Bomberger: director
Michelle H. Bomberger: director
Rachel A. Bomberger: secretary, director
William A. Bomberger: assistant secretary, director
Michael A. Marconi: executive director
Charlotte Spacinsky: director
Inge Vraney: vice president, director
Lawrence Vraney: treasurer
Maura J. Vraney: director

Grants Analysis
Disclosure Period: fiscal year ending March 31, 2004
Total Grants: $8,294,503
Number of Grants: 684
Average Grant: $12,126
Highest Grant: $100,000
Lowest Grant: $1,500
Typical Range: $5,000 to $25,000

Recent Grants
Note: Grants derived from 2003 Form 990.
General

300,000	Society for the Propagation of the Faith, New York, NY -- for international development
26,150	Casa Jesus, Chicago, IL -- for training of Hispanic aspirants for the priesthood
25,000	Benedictine Sisters of the Sacred Heart, Lisle, IL -- for missionary activities
25,000	Diocese of Mandeville, Mandeville Jamaica
25,000	St. Ann's School, Carthage, MO
25,000	St.Anthony of Padua Catholic School, Greenville, SC -- for constructing additional classrooms
25,000	Saint Luke Institute, Silver Spring, MD -- for religious welfare
25,000	Sign Me Up Evangelization Project, Detroit, MI -- for supporting seminarians
25,000	University of St. Mary of the Lake, Mundelein, IL -- for the expansion seminary
24,000	St.Cecila Catholic School, Dallas, TX -- for religious welfare

KOCH INDUSTRIES INC.

Company Headquarters
Wichita, KS
Web: http://www.kochind.com

Company Description
Revenue: US$38.93 billion (2002)
Employees: 11000 (2002)
SIC(s): 0212 Beef Cattle Except Feedlots, 1311 Crude Petroleum & Natural Gas, 1321 Natural Gas Liquids, 2911 Petroleum Refining.

Operating Locations
Koch Industries, Inc. (KS--Wichita)

Nonmonetary Support
Type: Donated Equipment; In-kind Services
Note: NOT NOT The company provides nonmonetary support to schools, community groups, emergency response agencies, and charitable organizations near company facilities.

Fred C. and Mary R. Koch Foundation, Inc.

Giving Contact
Roger Ramseyer, Director, Community Relations
Koch Industries, Inc.
PO Box 2256
Wichita, KS 67201
Phone: (316)828-7483
Fax: (316)828-5739
E-mail: ramseyer@kochind.com
Web: http://www.kochind.com/community/default.asp
Note: Visit company website for further giving contact information.

Description
EIN: 486113560
Organization Type: Corporate Foundation
Giving Locations: KS
Grant Types: Capital, Endowment, General Support, Operating Expenses, Project, Scholarship.
Note: Also provides grants for special needs.

Financial Summary
Total Giving: $1,099,803 (2003); $880,550 (2002); $887,500 (2001). Note: Contributes through foundation only.
Giving Analysis: Giving for 2002 includes: foundation scholarships ($97,000)
Assets: $24,908,437 (2003); $24,464,571 (2002); $20,735,423 (2001)
Gifts Received: $570,000 (2003); $97,000 (2002); $481,000 (2001). Note: Contributions were received from Koch Industries, Inc. and the Charles G. Koch Charitable Foundation.

Typical Recipients
Arts & Humanities: Arts Associations & Councils, Arts Centers, Ballet, Dance, Ethnic & Folk Arts, Historic Preservation, Libraries, Museums/Galleries,

Music, Opera, Performing Arts, Theater
Civic & Public Affairs: Botanical Gardens/Parks, Business/Free Enterprise, Clubs, Economic Development, Employment/Job Training, Philanthropic Organizations, Rural Affairs, Zoos/Aquariums
Education: Arts/Humanities Education, Business Education, Colleges & Universities, Education Funds, Education-General, Legal Education, Religious Education, Special Education, Student Aid
Environment: Environment-General
Health: Cancer, Children's Health/Hospitals, Clinics/Medical Centers, Hospices, Mental Health, Preventive Medicine/Wellness Organizations, Single-Disease Health Associations
Religion: Religious Welfare
Science: Science-General, Science Museums
Social Services: At-Risk Youth, Big Brothers/Big Sisters, Child Welfare, Community Service Organizations, Family Services, Food/Clothing Distribution, People with Disabilities, Scouts, Senior Services, Social Services-General, United Funds/United Ways, YMCA/YWCA/YMHA/YWHA, Youth Organizations

Application Procedures

Initial Contact: Send a brief letter describing project.
Application Requirements: Include a list of board of directors, tax status, project budget, and annual report or audited financial statements.
Deadlines: None.

Restrictions

Grants limited to tax-exempt organizations. Scholarships are limited to children of Koch Industries employees. Does not support individuals, religious organizations for sectarian purposes, political or lobbying groups, or organizations outside operating areas.

Corporate Officials

Joseph W. Moeller: president, chief operating officer
Roger Ramseyer: director community relations

Foundation Officials

Tye Darland: secretary
Richard H. Fink: director PRIM CORP EMPL executive vice president, director: Koch Industries, Inc.
Vonda Holliman: treasurer
Charles G. Koch: director
David Hamilton Koch: director B Wichita, KS 1940. ED Massachusetts Institute of Technology BS (1962); Massachusetts Institute of Technology MS (1963). PRIM CORP EMPL executive vice president: Koch Industries, Inc. ADD CORP EMPL executive vice president: Koch Industries Chemical Technology Group. CORP AFFIL overseers: WGBH Channel 2; director: Koch Engineering Company Inc. NONPR AFFIL trustee: New York University Hospital Medical Center Fund; member: Whitehead Institute; trustee: Memorial Sloan-Kettering Cancer Center; governor, chairman development committee: New York University Downtown Hospital; trustee: Guggenheim Museum; director: Institute Human Origins; director: Citizens for Sound Economy; director: Earthwatch; director: Aspen Institute; director: Cato Institute; director: American Museum Natural History. CLUB AFFIL River Club; Explorers Club; Racquet & Tennis Club.
Elizabeth B. Koch: president, director
Michael Morgan: director
Roger Ramseyer: vice president (see above)

Grants Analysis

Disclosure Period: calendar year ending 2003
Total Grants: $990,803*
Number of Grants: 30
Average Grant: $12,622*
Highest Grant: $300,000
Lowest Grant: $1,000
Typical Range: $5,000 to $25,000
***Note:** Giving excludes scholarships. Average grant figure excludes three highest grants ($650,000).

Recent Grants

Note: Grants derived from 2003 Form 990.
General

300,000	Youth Entrepreneurs of Kansas Inc., Wichita, KS -- Program Support
250,000	Sedgwick County Zoo, Wichita, KS -- Koch Primate Education Program
100,000	YMCA, Wichita, KS -- South Branch Programs
50,000	Kansas State University Foundation, Wichita, KS -- Center for Economic Education
29,500	Wichita Symphony, Wichita, KS -- 2003 Koch Fall Pope Concert
25,000	Cerebral Palsy Research Foundation, Wichita, KS -- Improvements to Skill/Job Training Development
25,000	Wichita Art Museum, Wichita, KS -- Underwriting Murdock Exhibition
19,625	Wichita Center for the Arts, Wichita, KS -- 2003 Wichita National All Medical Exhibition
17,000	Friends University, Wichita, KS -- 2003 Production of "The Nutcracker"
15,000	Washburn University, Wichita, KS -- Koch Leadership Scholarship Program

MARCIA AND OTTO KOEHLER FOUNDATION

Giving Contact

Jerry A. Higginson, Jr., Vice President & Trust Officer
Bank of America
PO Box 831041
Dallas, TX 75283-1041
Phone: (214)508-2422

Description

Founded: 1980
EIN: 742131195
Organization Type: Private Foundation
Giving Locations: TX: San Antonio
Grant Types: Capital, General Support, Operating Expenses, Research.

Donor Information

Founder: the late Marcia Koehler

Financial Summary

Total Giving: $465,000 (fiscal year ending July 31, 2003); $522,100 (fiscal 2002)
Giving Analysis: Giving for fiscal 2002 includes: foundation grants to United Way ($25,000)
Assets: $7,609,262 (fiscal 2003); $7,503,952 (fiscal 2002)

Typical Recipients

Arts & Humanities: Arts Associations & Councils, Arts Centers, Arts Institutes, Arts Outreach, Community Arts, Ethnic & Folk Arts, Arts & Humanities-General, Libraries, Museums/Galleries, Music, Opera, Performing Arts, Public Broadcasting, Theater
Civic & Public Affairs: Botanical Gardens/Parks, Clubs, Economic Development, Civic & Public Affairs-General, Hispanic Affairs, Municipalities/Towns, Nonprofit Management, Urban & Community Affairs, Zoos/Aquariums
Education: Arts/Humanities Education, Business Education, Business-School Partnerships, Colleges & Universities, Community & Junior Colleges, Education Funds, Education Reform, Education-General, Literacy, Private Education (Precollege), Public Education (Precollege), Student Aid
Health: Children's Health/Hospitals, Geriatric Health, Health Organizations, Hospitals, Hospitals (University Affiliated), Medical Research, Mental Health, Single-Disease Health Associations
Religion: Jewish Causes, Religious Welfare
Social Services: Big Brothers/Big Sisters, Child Welfare, Community Centers, Community Service Organizations, Day Care, Family Services, Homes, People with Disabilities, Recreation & Athletics, Senior Services, Substance Abuse, United Funds/United Ways, YMCA/YWCA/YMHA/YWHA, Youth Organizations

Application Procedures

Initial Contact: The foundation has no formal grant application procedure or application form.
Deadlines: None.

Restrictions

Does not support individuals.

Additional Information

The purpose of the foundation is to award charitable and education grants.
Trust(s): Bank of America

Grants Analysis

Disclosure Period: fiscal year ending July 31, 2003
Total Grants: $465,000
Number of Grants: 44
Average Grant: $10,568
Highest Grant: $50,000
Lowest Grant: $2,500
Typical Range: $5,000 to $20,000

Recent Grants

Note: Grants derived from 2003 Form 990.
General

50,000	Baptist Children's Ministries, San Antonio, TX
30,000	KLRN, San Antonio, TX
30,000	San Antonio Education, San Antonio, TX
30,000	San Antonio Zoological Society, San Antonio, TX
25,000	The Alameda, Museo Americana, San Antonio, TX
25,000	Alamo Community College, San Antonio, TX
15,000	Alamo Public Telecommunications, San Antonio, TX
15,000	Christus Santa Rosa Children's Hospital, San Antonio, TX
15,000	Marion Koogler McNay Art Museum, San Antonio, TX
15,000	Transplants for Children, San Antonio, TX

KOHLER FOUNDATION

Giving Contact

Terri Yoho, Executive Director
725 Woodlake Road, Suite X
Kohler, WI 53044
Phone: (920)458-1972
Fax: (920)458-4280
E-mail: Terri.Yoho@kohler.com
Web: http://www.kohlerfoundation.org

Description

Founded: 1940
EIN: 390810536
Organization Type: Specialized/Single Purpose Foundation
Giving Locations: CA; CO; IL; IN; MN; NJ; NY; NC; WI
Grant Types: Award, Conference/Seminar, Endowment, Fellowship, General Support, Matching, Multiyear/Continuing Support, Project, Scholarship.

Donor Information

Founder: Incorporated in 1940 by the late Herbert V. Kohler, the late Marie C. Kohler, the late Evangeline Kohler, the late Lillie B. Kohler, and the late O. A. Kroos.

Financial Summary

Total Giving: $5,512,791 (2002)
Giving Analysis: Giving for 2002 includes: foundation scholarships ($193,959)
Assets: $138,784,012 (2002)

Typical Recipients

Arts & Humanities: Arts Associations & Councils, Arts Centers, Arts Festivals, Arts Funds, Arts Institutes, Arts Outreach, Ballet, Community Arts, Dance, Ethnic & Folk Arts, Film & Video, Arts & Humanities-General, Historic Preservation, History & Archaeology, Libraries, Literary Arts, Museums/Galleries, Music, Opera, Performing Arts, Theater, Visual Arts
Civic & Public Affairs: Asian American Affairs, Botanical Gardens/Parks, Chambers of Commerce, Civic & Public Affairs-General, Hispanic Affairs, Municipalities/Towns, Rural Affairs, Urban & Community Affairs, Women's Affairs
Education: Arts/Humanities Education, Business Education, Colleges & Universities, Continuing Education, Education Funds, Education Reform, Elementary Education (Private), Elementary Education (Public), Engineering/Technological Education, Environmental Education, Education-General, Medical Education, Preschool Education, Private Education (Precollege), Public Education (Precollege), Science/Mathematics Education, Secondary Education (Private), Secondary Education (Public), Student Aid
Environment: Forestry, Environment-General, Wildlife Protection
Health: Children's Health/Hospitals, Heart, Medical Rehabilitation, Mental Health, Nursing Services, Single-Disease Health Associations
International: International Organizations
Religion: Religious Organizations
Social Services: At-Risk Youth, Big Brothers/Big Sisters, Child Abuse, Community Service Organizations, Family Planning, Family Services, People with Disabilities, Recreation & Athletics, Scouts, Social Services-General, YMCA/YWCA/YMHA/YWHA, Youth Organizations

Application Procedures

Initial Contact: The foundation requests applications be made in writing.
Application Requirements: Copies of two designations of organization: 501(c) and 509(a) 1, 2 or 3. Also include a description of the project including why the grant is needed and how many people will benefit from the grant; a budget of how much the project will cost, other funding sources, and a timetable of when the money is actually needed; and credentials of the project manager.
Deadlines: May 1 and November 1.
Review Process: The Grants Committee convenes in June and December to review grant requests.

Restrictions

The foundation does not make grants to individuals, except for scholarships in Sheboygan County, WI. No grants are made for health care or medical programs, operating budgets, or annual fundraising drives. The foundation does not make loans.

Additional Information

Publications: Application Guidelines

Foundation Officials

Natalie A. Black: vice president, director B Bakersfield, CA 1949. ED Stanford University AB (1972); Marquette University JD (1978). PRIM CORP EMPL general counsel, secretary, vice president: Kohler Co. CORP AFFIL secretary, director: Sterling Plumbing Group Inc.; secretary, director, vice chairman: Mc-Guire Furniture Co.; vice president: Kohler Ltd.; secretary, director: Kohler Sanimex; vice president, secretary, director: Kohler of France; president, director: Kohler Interiors Group Ltd.; director: Johnson Controls Inc.; vice chairman, chief executive officer, director, secretary, president: Baker, Knapp & Tubbs Inc.; president, secretary, director: Dapha Ltd. NONPR AFFIL member: American Bar Association.
Jeffrey P. Cheney: vice president, treasurer ED Marquette University MBA; University of Wisconsin. NONPR AFFIL director: Friendship House.
Ruth DeYoung Kohler, II: president, chief operating officer, director B Chicago, IL 1941. ED Smith College; University of Hamburg; University of Wisconsin. NONPR AFFIL principal: Sheboygan Arts Foundation Inc.
Paul H. Ten Pas: secretary, director

Grants Analysis

Disclosure Period: calendar year ending 2002
Total Grants: $5,318,832*
Number of Grants: 65
Average Grant: $56,237*
Highest Grant: $2,385,000
Lowest Grant: $100
Typical Range: $5,000 to $100,000
*Note: Giving excludes scholarships. Average grant figure excludes two highest grants ($3,542,874).

Recent Grants

Note: Grants derived from 2002 Form 990.
Library-Related

5,000	Mead Library, Sheboygan, WI
1,000	Lakeview Community Library, Random Lake, WI

General

111,200	Sheboygan Arts Foundation Inc.
70,834	Kohler Foundation Incentive Scholarships
47,625	Herbert V Kohler Scholarships, Kohler, WI
40,500	Ruth D Kohler Scholarships
32,000	Kohler Foundation Four-Year Scholarships
20,000	University of Wisconsin, Madison, WI
12,300	UW Madison Graduate School, Madison, WI
9,500	Wade House
5,000	Safe Harbor, Los Angeles, CA
4,710	Sheboygan County Historical Research Center, Sheboygan Falls, WI

KOHN-JOSELOFF FOUNDATION

Giving Contact

Bernhard L. Kohn, Jr., President
125 LaSalle Rd., Rm. 304
West Hartford, CT 06107
Phone: (860)236-5051

Description

Founded: 1936
EIN: 136062846
Organization Type: Private Foundation
Giving Locations: CT; DC: Washington; IL; NY
Grant Types: General Support.

Donor Information

Founder: the late Lillian L. Joseloff, Morris Joseloff Foundation Trust

Financial Summary

Total Giving: $447,965 (2003)
Assets: $10,409,611 (2003)

Typical Recipients

Arts & Humanities: Arts Associations & Councils, History & Archaeology, Libraries, Literary Arts, Museums/Galleries, Music, Opera, Performing Arts, Public Broadcasting, Theater
Civic & Public Affairs: Botanical Gardens/Parks, Clubs, Ethnic Organizations, Civic & Public Affairs-General, Native American Affairs, Women's Affairs, Zoos/Aquariums
Education: Arts/Humanities Education, Colleges & Universities, Faculty Development, Minority Education, Private Education (Precollege), Public Education (Precollege), Special Education, Student Aid
Environment: Environment-General, Watershed
Health: Cancer, Children's Health/Hospitals, Emergency/Ambulance Services, Health Organizations, Home-Care Services, Hospices, Hospitals, Medical Research, Nursing Services, Respiratory, Single-Disease Health Associations
International: Health Care/Hospitals
Religion: Jewish Causes, Religious Organizations, Religious Welfare
Social Services: Camps, Child Welfare, Community Service Organizations, Family Services, People with Disabilities, Recreation & Athletics, Scouts, Senior Services, Shelters/Homelessness, United Funds/United Ways, Youth Organizations

Application Procedures

Initial Contact: The foundation has no formal grant application procedure or application form.
Deadlines: None.

Restrictions

Does not support individuals. Awards limited to organizations qualifying under IRC SEC 501(c)(3).

Foundation Officials

Bernhard L. Kohn, Jr.: president
Joan J. Kohn: secretary, treasurer
Kathryn K. Rieger: vice president

Grants Analysis

Disclosure Period: calendar year ending 2003
Total Grants: $447,965*
Number of Grants: 101
Average Grant: $2,000*
Highest Grant: $200,000
Lowest Grant: $20
Typical Range: $500 to $5,000
*Note: Giving excludes United Way. Average grant figure excludes two highest grants ($250,000).

Recent Grants

Note: Grants derived from 2003 Form 990.

General

200,000	Wadsworth Atheneum, Hartford, CT
50,000	Renbrook School, West Hartford, CT
33,300	Kingswood Oxford School, West Hartford, CT
20,000	Connecticut Golf Foundation, Rocky Hill, CT
20,000	Connecticut Institute for the Blind, Hartford, CT
20,000	Jewish Federation Greater Hartford, West Hartford, CT
10,000	Equistride, Granby, CT
10,000	United Way, Hartford, CT
7,000	Gray Lodge Shelter for Women, Hartford, CT
5,000	Jewish Federation Greater Hartford, West Hartford, CT

KONGSGAARD-GOLDMAN FOUNDATION

Giving Contact
Anna Agee, Administration
1932 1st Avenue, Suite 602
Seattle, WA 98101-1040
Phone: (206)448-1874
E-mail: kgf@kongsgaard-goldman.org
Web: http://www.kongsgaard-goldman.org

Description
Founded: 1989
EIN: 943088217
Organization Type: Private Foundation
Giving Locations: AK; ID; MT; OR; WA; Canada : BC
Grant Types: General Support.

Financial Summary
Total Giving: $746,740 (2003); $885,698 (2001)
Assets: $10,292 (2003); $86,291 (2001)
Gifts Received: $818,166 (2003); $1,002,142 (2001); $1,131,839 (2000). Note: Contributions were received from Peter Goldman and Martha Kongsgaard.

Typical Recipients
Arts & Humanities: Arts & Humanities-General, Libraries, Museums/Galleries, Music
Civic & Public Affairs: Community Foundations, Ethnic Organizations, Civic & Public Affairs-General, Inner-City Development, Law & Justice, Urban & Community Affairs, Women's Affairs, Zoos/Aquariums
Education: Education Reform, Legal Education, Private Education (Precollege), Secondary Education (Private)
Environment: Air/Water Quality, Forestry, Environment-General, Protection, Resource Conservation, Wildlife Protection
International: Health Care/Hospitals, International Environmental Issues, International Peace & Security Issues, Missionary/Religious Activities
Religion: Jewish Causes, Religious Organizations
Social Services: Community Service Organizations, Domestic Violence, Family Services, Recreation & Athletics, Youth Organizations

Application Procedures
Initial Contact: Send a preliminary letter of no more than two pages. The organization and the proposed project. Include amount requested, purpose of funds sought, proof of tax-exempt status, and budget.
Deadlines: March 16 and September 16.

Restrictions
Does not support individuals, religious organizations for sectarian purposes, or organizations outside operating areas.

Foundation Officials
Peter Goldman: vice president
Martha Kongsgaard: president

Grants Analysis
Disclosure Period: calendar year ending 2003
Total Grants: $746,740
Number of Grants: 92
Average Grant: $8,117
Highest Grant: $41,666
Lowest Grant: $500
Typical Range: $1,000 to $10,000

Recent Grants
Note: Grants derived from 2003 Form 990.
General

41,666	Delridge Neighborhoods Development Association, Seattle, WA -- capital campaign
40,000	Earthjustice, Seattle, WA -- fish-trees-water: safeguarding and restoring the Pacific Northwest
26,000	Jewish Federation of Greater Seattle, Seattle, WA
25,000	Confluence Project, Vancouver, WA
25,000	Pinchot Institute for Conservation, Washington, DC -- pilot certifications on public lands in Washington
25,000	Rails-to-Trails Conservancy, Washington, DC -- for support of legal defense fund
20,000	Bicycle Alliance of Washington, Seattle, WA
20,000	Jewish Family Service, Seattle, WA
18,000	Washington Environmental Council, Seattle, WA
16,666	Seattle Academy, Seattle, WA -- capital campaign

KOOPMAN FUND

Giving Contact
Georgette Koopman, President
17 Brookside Blvd.
West Hartford, CT 06107
Phone: (860)232-6406

Description
Founded: 1963
EIN: 066050431
Organization Type: Private Foundation
Giving Locations: CT
Grant Types: Capital, Emergency, Endowment, General Support, Multiyear/Continuing Support, Scholarship.

Donor Information
Founder: the late Richard Koopman, Georgette Koopman

Financial Summary
Total Giving: $856,655 (2002); $1,206,939 (2001)
Assets: $9,559,687 (2002); $11,480,985 (2001)

Typical Recipients
Arts & Humanities: Arts Centers, Community Arts, Dance, Historic Preservation, History & Archaeology, Libraries, Museums/Galleries, Music, Public Broadcasting, Theater
Civic & Public Affairs: Civil Rights, Community Foundations, Economic Development, Civic & Public Affairs-General, Hispanic Affairs, Housing, Nonprofit Management, Philanthropic Organizations, Safety, Urban & Community Affairs, Women's Affairs, Zoos/Aquariums
Education: Agricultural Education, Arts/Humanities Education, Colleges & Universities, Engineering/Technological Education, Education-General, Leadership Training, Preschool Education, Private Education (Precollege), Secondary Education (Private), Special Education, Student Aid
Environment: Environment-General, Resource Conservation
Health: AIDS/HIV, Clinics/Medical Centers, Emergency/Ambulance Services, Health Organizations, Hospices, Hospitals, Long-Term Care, Medical Rehabilitation, Medical Research, Nursing Services, Prenatal Health Issues, Preventive Medicine/Wellness Organizations, Public Health, Single-Disease Health Associations
International: International Affairs, International Peace & Security Issues, International Relations
Religion: Jewish Causes, Religious Organizations, Religious Welfare, Synagogues/Temples
Science: Scientific Centers & Institutes, Scientific Organizations
Social Services: At-Risk Youth, Camps, Child Welfare, Community Service Organizations, Crime Prevention, Emergency Relief, Family Planning, Family Services, Food/Clothing Distribution, Homes, People with Disabilities, United Funds/United Ways, YMCA/YWCA/YMHA/YWHA, Youth Organizations

Application Procedures
Initial Contact: The foundation has no formal grant application procedure or application form. Send a brief letter of inquiry detailing purpose of funds sought and proof of tax-exempt status.
Deadlines: None.

Foundation Officials
Beatrice F. Koopman: trustee
Dorothy B. Koopman: trustee
Georgette A. Koopman: president, trustee
Rena B. Koopman: secretary, trustee
Richard Koopman, Jr.: trustee

Grants Analysis
Disclosure Period: calendar year ending 2002
Total Grants: $856,655
Number of Grants: 103
Average Grant: $466*
Highest Grant: $809,089
Lowest Grant: $35
Typical Range: $100 to $2,000
*Note: Average grant figure excludes highest grant.

Recent Grants
Note: Grants derived from 2001 Form 990.
Library-Related

1,000	Alexandria Library, Alexandria, VA

General

4,100	Tripod School, Burbank, CA
3,000	Kenyon College, Gambler, OH
2,000	Kingswood Oxford School, West Hartford, CT
1,200	Deaf West Theatre Company, Los Angeles, CA
1,150	Hartford Art School, Hartford, CT -- HAS, Inc.
1,000	Alexandria United Way Community Services Fund, Alexandria, VA -- annual fund
1,000	American Red Cross Mile High Chapter, Denver, CO
1,000	Anderson Ranch Arts Center, Snowmass Village, CO
1,000	Boulder Community Hospital Foundation, Boulder, CO
1,000	Boulder County Safe House, Boulder, CO

KORET FOUNDATION

Giving Contact
33 New Montgomery Street, Suite 1090
San Francisco, CA 94105-4509
Phone: (415)882-7740
Fax: (415)882-7775
E-mail: info@koretfoundation.org
Web: http://www.koretfoundation.org

Description
Founded: 1966
EIN: 941624987
Organization Type: General Purpose Foundation
Giving Locations: CA: San Francisco including Bay area
Grant Types: Award, Capital, Challenge, Endowment, General Support, Multiyear/Continuing Support, Operating Expenses, Professorship, Project, Research, Scholarship, Seed Money.

Donor Information
Founder: The Koret Foundation was established in 1966, with the late Stephanie Koret and the late Joseph Koret as donors.

Financial Summary

Total Giving: $17,058,963 (2002); $16,699,871 (2001)

Assets: $285,051,272 (2003); $301,661,493 (2002); $315,112,125 (2001)

Gifts Received: $2,500 (2001); $892 (1995); $100,000 (1993)

Typical Recipients

Arts & Humanities: Arts Centers, Arts Funds, Ballet, Ethnic & Folk Arts, History & Archaeology, Libraries, Literary Arts, Museums/Galleries, Music, Opera, Performing Arts, Public Broadcasting, Theater, Visual Arts

Civic & Public Affairs: Asian American Affairs, Botanical Gardens/Parks, Community Foundations, Economic Development, Economic Policy, Ethnic Organizations, Civic & Public Affairs-General, Housing, Public Policy, Urban & Community Affairs, Zoos/Aquariums

Education: Afterschool/Enrichment Programs, Colleges & Universities, Continuing Education, Economic Education, Education Funds, Environmental Education, Education-General, Gifted & Talented Programs, International Exchange, International Studies, Journalism/Media Education, Literacy, Medical Education, Preschool Education, Public Education (Precollege), Religious Education, Science/Mathematics Education, Secondary Education (Private), Social Sciences Education, Student Aid

Environment: Resource Conservation

Health: Emergency/Ambulance Services, Geriatric Health, Health Funds, Hospitals (University Affiliated), Long-Term Care, Research/Studies Institutes

International: Foreign Educational Institutions, International-General, Health Care/Hospitals, International Affairs, International Development, International Environmental Issues, International Organizations, International Peace & Security Issues, Missionary/Religious Activities

Religion: Jewish Causes

Science: Science Museums

Social Services: Animal Protection, Camps, Child Welfare, Community Centers, Community Service Organizations, Family Services, Food/Clothing Distribution, Recreation & Athletics, Senior Services, Shelters/Homelessness, Social Services-General, United Funds/United Ways, Volunteer Services, Youth Organizations

Application Procedures

Initial Contact: Applicants must first submit a one- to three-page preliminary letter to the foundation's executive director or program officer.

Application Requirements: The preliminary letter should include a description of the project for which support is requested; information about the applicant organization, including experience, programs or services, and population and geographic area served; summary budget for the proposed project, including amount sought from the foundation and other sources; a list of the board of directors with professional affiliations; an evaluation plan; and copy of the IRS determination letter of tax-exempt status. If the foundation is interested, an application for funding package will be sent; if not, the applicant will be notified in writing within 90 days.

Deadlines: None.

Review Process: Completed applications for funding are reviewed by a program officer, who may request additional information, an interview, or a visit. The review process may take up to six months. All grants are subject to the approval of the foundation's board of directors. Once a grant is awarded, a grantee is required to provide narrative and financial reports at specified times detailing accomplishments, problems, and the use of funds.

Restrictions

The foundation reports that it will only make grants to organizations which have proof of tax-exempt status under Section 501(c)(3) of the IRS Code and which are not private foundations as described in Section 509(a). No grants will be made to fiscal agents soliciting funds in support of programs which are not conducted by the applicant, for propaganda or lobbying activities, or to organizations which have not fulfilled all the terms of a previous grant. Grants generally will not be made for a request in which there are no other sources of funding; for deficit funding, endowments, or emergency funding; for general fund-raising campaigns; for the purchase of equipment or furnishings; or to sectarian, veterans, fraternal, military, religious, or similar groups whose principal activity is for the benefit of their own membership.

Foundation Officials

Michael J. Boskin: director B New York, NY 1945. ED University of California at Berkeley AB (1967); University of California at Berkeley MA (1968); University of California at Berkeley PhD (1971). PRIM NONPR EMPL professor: Stanford University. CORP AFFIL director: First Health Group; director: Oracle Corp.; president, chief executive officer: Boskin & Co.; director: ExxonMobil Corp. NONPR AFFIL research associate: National Bureau Economic Research; professor: Stanford University; fellow: National Association Business Economists; scholar: American Enterprise Institute; chairman: Congressional Advisory Commission Consumer Price Index.

William Kraemer Coblentz: director B San Francisco, CA 1922. ED University of California at Berkeley BA (1943); Yale University (1947). PRIM CORP EMPL senior partner: Coblentz, Cahen, McCabe & Breyer. CORP AFFIL director: Pacific Telesis Group; director: Sacramento Bee; director: Modesto Bee; director: Pacific Bell; director: McClatchy Co. Inc.; director: McClatchy Newspapers Inc.; director: Fresno Bee.

Eugene L. Friend: vice chairman, director B 1916. PRIM CORP EMPL chairman, director: Kutler Clothiers Inc.

Richard L. Greene: director

Stanley Herzstein: director CORP AFFIL director: Software Logistics Corp.

Susan Koret: chairman, director

Thaddeus N. Taube: president, director B 1931. ED Stanford University BS (1954); Stanford University MS (1957). PRIM CORP EMPL chairman, director: Woodmont Companies.

Grants Analysis

Disclosure Period: calendar year ending 2002

Total Grants: $17,058,963

Number of Grants: 330

Average Grant: $38,101*

Highest Grant: $2,000,000

Lowest Grant: $535

Typical Range: $20,000 to $50,000

*Note: Average grant figure excludes three highest grants ($4,600,000).

Recent Grants

Note: Grants derived from 2002 Form 990.

General

2,000,000	University of California San Francisco, San Francisco, CA
1,600,000	Jewish Community Center of San Francisco, San Francisco, CA
1,000,000	Campus for Jewish Life, San Francisco, CA
600,000	Alameda County Health Care Foundation, Oakland, CA
600,000	Friends of Recreation and Parks, San Francisco, CA
500,000	Exploratorium, San Francisco, CA
500,000	Peninsula Jewish Community Center, Foster City, CA
400,000	Jewish Community Federation of San Francisco, San Francisco, CA
325,000	Korean Center, San Francisco, CA
300,000	San Francisco Museum of Modern Art, San Francisco, CA

EMILY DAVIE AND JOSEPH S. KORNFELD FOUNDATION

Giving Contact

Karen R. Berry, Secretary
Patterson Belknap Webb & Tyler LLP
1133 Avenue. of the Americans, Suite 2200
New York, NY 10036-6710
Phone: (212)336-2000
E-mail: office@kornfeldfdn.org
Web: http://fdncenter.org/grantmaker/kornfeld

Description

Founded: 1979
EIN: 133042360
Organization Type: Private Foundation
Giving Locations: NY
Grant Types: General Support.

Donor Information

Founder: the late Emily Davie Kornfeld

Typical Recipients

Arts & Humanities: Arts Associations & Councils, Arts Outreach, Arts & Humanities-General, Libraries, Museums/Galleries, Music

Civic & Public Affairs: Botanical Gardens/Parks, Economic Development, Civic & Public Affairs-General, Hispanic Affairs, Philanthropic Organizations, Professional & Trade Associations, Public Policy, Urban & Community Affairs

Education: Afterschool/Enrichment Programs, Arts/Humanities Education, Colleges & Universities, Education Funds, Education Reform, Environmental Education, Faculty Development, Education-General, Leadership Training, Literacy, Medical Education, Minority Education, Private Education (Precollege), Public Education (Precollege), Special Education

Health: Adolescent Health Issues, AIDS/HIV, Cancer, Clinics/Medical Centers, Geriatric Health, Health Organizations, Hospitals, Hospitals (University Affiliated), Medical Research, Mental Health, Public Health

International: International-General, Human Rights, Missionary/Religious Activities

Religion: Jewish Causes

Social Services: At-Risk Youth, Child Welfare, Community Centers, Community Service Organizations, People with Disabilities, Youth Organizations

Application Procedures

Initial Contact: Send a brief letter of inquiry.
Deadlines: None.

Restrictions

Emphasis is on research and other activities concerning the right of the individual to choose the time and manner of his or her death without undue interference by doctors, hospitals, courts, churches, families, or society and the advancement of the understanding of physical pain in human beings and, in particular, chronic and intractable pain, including the mechanism, causes, control, treatment, and prevention of such pain. The foundation also supports programs that teach reading, writing, and other subjects to students who attend New York City public schools. Grants are not awarded to individuals or for scholarships.

Foundation Officials

Christopher C. Angell: president, director
Karen R. Berry: secretary
Peter Bokor: director
Emme Levin Deland: director
Patricia Llosa: director
Morris S. Roberts: treasurer, director
William J. Welch: vice president, director
John P. White: chairman, director

Grants Analysis

Disclosure Period: calendar year ending 2000
Total Grants: $1,787,937*
Number of Grants: 20
Average Grant: $55,637*
Highest Grant: $730,832
Typical Range: $25,000 to $100,000
*Note: Giving excludes fellowships. Average grant figure excludes highest grant.

Recent Grants

Note: Grants derived from 2001 Form 990.
General

268,944	Johns Hopkins University School of Medicine, Baltimore, MD
126,540	Fund for Public Schools, Inc., Long Island City, NY
100,000	Neighborhood Initiatives Development Corporation, Bronx, NY
100,000	Partnership for After School Education, New York, NY
100,000	Project Reach Youth, Brooklyn, NY
62,000	Henry Street Settlement, New York, NY
50,000	Learning Project, New York, NY
50,000	New York Academy of Medicine, New York, NY
45,000	Forest Hills Community House, Forest Hills, NY
40,000	Claremont Neighborhood Centers, Bronx, NY

KORTE CONSTRUCTION CO.

Company Headquarters

12441 US Hwy. 40
PO Box 146
Highland, IL 62249
Web: http://www.korteco.com

Company Description

Employees: 300
SIC(s): 1500 General Building Contractors, 6700 Holding & Other Investment Offices.

Operating Locations

Korte Construction Co. (IL--Highland; MO--St. Louis)

Ralph and Donna Korte Family Charitable Foundation

Giving Contact

William Boudouris, Chief Financial Officer
700 St. Louis Union Station
St. Louis, MO 63103
Phone: (314)241-3327

Description

Founded: 1989
EIN: 431475774
Organization Type: Corporate Foundation
Giving Locations: IL; MO
Grant Types: Employee Matching Gifts, Endowment, General Support.

Financial Summary

Total Giving: $211,919 (2003); $238,332 (2002); $629,866 (2001)
Giving Analysis: Giving for 2001 includes: foundation grants to United Way ($10,000)
Assets: $226,567 (2003); $403,999 (2002); $725,263 (2001)
Gifts Received: $365,309 (1999); $125,500 (1998);

$395,000 (1997). Note: In 1996, 1998 and 1999, contributions were received from Ralph Korte.

Typical Recipients

Arts & Humanities: Arts Associations & Councils, History & Archaeology, Libraries, Museums/Galleries, Music, Public Broadcasting, Theater
Civic & Public Affairs: Botanical Gardens/Parks, Business/Free Enterprise, Clubs, Community Foundations, Civic & Public Affairs-General, Housing, Municipalities/Towns, Urban & Community Affairs, Women's Affairs, Zoos/Aquariums
Education: Business Education, Business-School Partnerships, Colleges & Universities, Continuing Education, Education Funds, Environmental Education, Education-General, Private Education (Precollege), Public Education (Precollege), Secondary Education (Public), Special Education
Environment: Forestry
Health: Children's Health/Hospitals, Diabetes, Geriatric Health, Health Organizations, Hospices, Hospitals, Multiple Sclerosis, Prenatal Health Issues
International: Missionary/Religious Activities
Religion: Churches, Dioceses, Religion-General, Religious Organizations, Religious Welfare
Social Services: Animal Protection, Big Brothers/Big Sisters, Camps, Child Welfare, Community Service Organizations, Family Services, Homes, Scouts, Shelters/Homelessness, Social Services-General, Special Olympics, United Funds/United Ways, YMCA/YWCA/YMHA/YWHA, Youth Organizations

Corporate Officials

William Boudouris: chief financial officer PRIM CORP EMPL chief financial officer: Korte Construction Co.
Vernon Eardley: president, chief executive officer PRIM CORP EMPL president, chief executive officer: Korte Construction Co.
Ralph F. Korte: chairman PRIM CORP EMPL chairman: Korte Construction Co.

Foundation Officials

Susan D. Bowman: secretary, director
Greg O. Korte: director
Ralph F. Korte: president, director (see above)
Todd J. Korte: vice president, director
Vicki Korte Solheim: director

Grants Analysis

Disclosure Period: calendar year ending 2003
Total Grants: $211,919
Number of Grants: 36
Average Grant: $4,769*
Highest Grant: $45,000
Lowest Grant: $400
Typical Range: $1,000 to $10,000
*Note: Average grant figure excludes highest grant.

Recent Grants

Note: Grants derived from 2003 Form 990.
General

45,000	School Sisters of Notre Dame, St. Louis, MO
45,000	School Sisters of St Francis, Milwaukee, WI
30,000	Diocese of Springfield in Illinois, Springfield, IL
20,000	Chestnut Health, Bloomington, IL
17,500	Alexis de Tocqueville Society, St. Louis, MO
15,000	Regional Business Council, St. Louis, MO
11,000	Missouri Botanical Garden, St. Louis, MO
11,000	Muny, St. Louis, MO
10,000	Highland School Foundation, Highland, IL
8,244	St Paul Catholic Church, Highland, IL

HENRY P. KOVARIK FOUNDATION FOR POETRY

Giving Contact

Lawrence J. Holt, Director
Henry P. Kovarik Foundation for Poetry
810 Middle Country Road
Selden, NY 11784
Phone: (631)732-6600

Description

Founded: 1988
EIN: 112781923
Organization Type: Private Foundation
Grant Types: General Support, Scholarship.

Financial Summary

Total Giving: $4,950 (fiscal year ending April 30, 2001)
Giving Analysis: Giving for fiscal 2001 includes: foundation scholarships ($1,000)
Assets: $163,798 (fiscal 2001)

Typical Recipients

Arts & Humanities: Libraries
Education: Secondary Education (Public)

Application Procedures

Initial Contact: Contact foundation for scholarship application.
Deadlines: April 1.

Additional Information

Provides scholarships for higher education to graduates of Longwood High School in Middle Island, NY.
Publications: Scholarship Application

Foundation Officials

Eugene Dooley: director
Lawrence J. Holt: director
Karen Mouzakas: director

Grants Analysis

Disclosure Period: fiscal year ending April 30, 2001
Total Grants: $3,950*
Number of Grants: 1
*Note: Giving excludes scholarships.

Recent Grants

Note: Grants derived from fiscal 2001 Form 990.
Library-Related

3,950	Longwood Public Library, Middle Island, NY

KOVLER FAMILY FOUNDATION

Giving Contact

H. Jonathan Kovler, President
875 North Michigan Avenue, Suite 3400
Chicago, IL 60611
Phone: (312)664-5050
Fax: (312)664-8983

Description

Founded: 1967
EIN: 366152744
Organization Type: Family Foundation
Former Name: Harry and Maribel G. Blum Foundation (2000).
Giving Locations: IL: nationally.
Grant Types: General Support.

Donor Information

Founder: Established in 1967 by the late Harry Blum.

Financial Summary

Total Giving: $1,736,025 (2003); $2,090,600 (2002); $2,306,275 (2001)
Assets: $40,100,182 (2003); $32,447,257 (2002); $38,587,445 (2001)

Typical Recipients

Arts & Humanities: Arts Centers, Arts Funds, Arts Institutes, Film & Video, Historic Preservation, History & Archaeology, Libraries, Museums/Galleries, Music, Theater
Civic & Public Affairs: Community Foundations, Employment/Job Training, Gay/Lesbian Issues, Civic & Public Affairs-General, Urban & Community Affairs, Women's Affairs, Zoos/Aquariums
Education: Afterschool/Enrichment Programs, Business Education, Business-School Partnerships, Colleges & Universities, Education Funds, Education Reform, Elementary Education (Private), Education-General, Gifted & Talented Programs, Legal Education, Medical Education, Private Education (Precollege), Religious Education
Environment: Environment-General
Health: AIDS/HIV, Cancer, Children's Health/Hospitals, Clinics/Medical Centers, Diabetes, Health Funds, Health Organizations, Hospitals, Kidney, Medical Rehabilitation, Medical Research, Mental Health, Prenatal Health Issues, Research/Studies Institutes, Single-Disease Health Associations, Transplant Networks/Donor Banks
Religion: Churches, Jewish Causes, Religious Organizations, Synagogues/Temples
Social Services: Animal Protection, At-Risk Youth, Child Welfare, Community Centers, Community Service Organizations, Day Care, Family Services, Food/Clothing Distribution, People with Disabilities, Recreation & Athletics, Scouts, Social Services-General, United Funds/United Ways, Youth Organizations

Application Procedures

Initial Contact: The foundation reports that no specific application form is required.
Deadlines: None.

Foundation Officials

Hymen H. Bregar: secretary, director
H. Jonathan Kovler: president
Peter Kovler: assistant secretary

Grants Analysis

Disclosure Period: calendar year ending 2003
Total Grants: $1,736,025
Number of Grants: 27
Average Grant: $20,251*
Highest Grant: $750,000
Lowest Grant: $500
Typical Range: $5,000 to $40,000
*Note: Average grant figure excludes three highest grants ($1,250,000).

Recent Grants

Note: Grants derived from 2003 Form 990.
Library-Related
1,000	Chicago Public Library Foundation, Chicago, IL

General
750,000	American Diabetes Association, Alexandria, VA
300,000	Washington University School of Memorial, St. Louis, MO
200,000	Jewish United Fund of Metro, Chicago, IL
125,000	CINN Foundation, Chicago, IL
125,000	Northwestern Memorial Hospital, Chicago, IL
100,000	Franklin and Marshall College, Lancaster, PA
39,950	Museum of Contemporary Art, Chicago, IL
25,000	Menomonee Club, Chicago, IL
20,000	Survivors of the Shoah, Los Angeles, CA
15,000	Artadia, New York, NY

SIDNEY AND JUDITH KRANES CHARITABLE TRUST

Giving Contact

Thomas J. Sweeney, Co-Trustee
420 Lexington Avenue, Suite 626
New York, NY 10170
Phone: (212)599-1892

Description

Founded: 1993
EIN: 136981197
Organization Type: Private Foundation
Giving Locations: NY: New York
Grant Types: General Support.

Financial Summary

Total Giving: $140,000 (2003); $57,500 (2001)
Assets: $2,348,343 (2003); $2,667,212 (2001)

Typical Recipients

Arts & Humanities: Arts Outreach, Historic Preservation, History & Archaeology, Libraries, Music, Opera
Civic & Public Affairs: Botanical Gardens/Parks, Community Foundations, Law & Justice, Legal Aid, Professional & Trade Associations, Urban & Community Affairs
Education: Colleges & Universities, Science/Mathematics Education, Special Education
Environment: Air/Water Quality, Environment-General
Health: Clinics/Medical Centers, Emergency/Ambulance Services, Health-General, Geriatric Health, Health Organizations, Hospitals, Speech & Hearing
Religion: Religion-General, Jewish Causes, Religious Welfare
Science: Scientific Centers & Institutes
Social Services: Child Welfare, Community Service Organizations, Emergency Relief, Food/Clothing Distribution, People with Disabilities, Senior Services, Shelters/Homelessness, Substance Abuse, Youth Organizations

Application Procedures

Initial Contact: Send a brief letter of inquiry.
Application Requirements: Include an outline of the proposed project, a statement of its significance, and the proposed budget.
Deadlines: None.

Foundation Officials

Thomas J. Hubbard, Esq.: co-trustee
Thomas Joseph Sweeney, Jr.: co-trustee B New York, NY 1923. ED New York University BA (1947); Columbia University JD (1949). PRIM CORP EMPL partner: Decker, Hubbard, Welden & Sweeney. CORP AFFIL chairman inst trustee & investment committee: Morgan Guaranty Trust Co. New York. NONPR AFFIL director: WR Kenan Fund; member: New York State Bar Association.

Grants Analysis

Disclosure Period: calendar year ending 2003
Total Grants: $140,000
Number of Grants: 32
Average Grant: $4,375
Highest Grant: $6,000
Lowest Grant: $1,000
Typical Range: $2,000 to $6,000

Recent Grants

Note: Grants derived from 2003 Form 990.
General
6,000	Association of the Bar of the City of New York Fund Inc., New York, NY -- for community outreach law program
6,000	Food for Survival, New York, NY
6,000	Legal Aid Society, New York, NY
6,000	Lexington Center for the Deaf, Jackson Heights, NY
6,000	New York League for the Hard of Hearing, New York, NY
6,000	New York Times Neediest Cases Fund, New York, NY
5,000	Dorot Inc., New York, NY -- for homeless prevention program
5,000	Fresh Air Fund, New York, NY
5,000	Madison Square Boys and Girls Club, New York, NY -- for summer youth development program
5,000	Neighborhood Coalition for Shelter Center, New York, NY

KREITLER FOUNDATION

Giving Contact

Hobart C. Kreitler, President
2537 Post Rd.
Southport, CT 06890
Phone: (203)259-8585

Description

Founded: 1991
EIN: 061311676
Organization Type: Private Foundation
Giving Locations: CT
Grant Types: General Support.

Donor Information

Founder: Established in 1991 by Hobart C. Kreitler and Sally S. Kreitler.

Financial Summary

Total Giving: $222,288 (2003)
Giving Analysis: Giving for 2003 includes: foundation grants to United Way ($250); foundation scholarships ($11,390)
Assets: $4,368,421 (2003)
Gifts Received: $9,884 (1999). Note: In 1991 and 1999, contributions were received from Hobart C. and Sally S. Kreitler.

Typical Recipients

Arts & Humanities: Arts Outreach, Arts & Humanities-General, Historic Preservation, History & Archaeology, Libraries, Museums/Galleries, Performing Arts
Civic & Public Affairs: Community Foundations, Employment/Job Training, Civic & Public Affairs-General, Housing, Public Policy, Rural Affairs, Safety, Urban & Community Affairs, Women's Affairs, Zoos/Aquariums
Education: Afterschool/Enrichment Programs, Arts/Humanities Education, Business Education, Colleges & Universities, Community & Junior Colleges, Education Funds, Education-General, Private Education (Precollege), Public Education (Precollege), Student Aid
Environment: Environment-General
Health: Children's Health/Hospitals, Diabetes, Home-Care Services, Hospices, Hospitals, Long-Term Care, Medical Rehabilitation, Prenatal Health Issues
International: Health Care/Hospitals, International Relief Efforts
Religion: Churches, Ministries, Religious Organiza-

tions, Religious Welfare

Science: Science Museums, Scientific Centers & Institutes

Social Services: Child Welfare, Community Centers, Community Service Organizations, Crime Prevention, Family Services, Food/Clothing Distribution, People with Disabilities, Recreation & Athletics, Senior Services, Shelters/Homelessness, United Funds/United Ways, YMCA/YWCA/YMHA/YWHA, Youth Organizations

Application Procedures

Initial Contact: Send a summary of grant request including proof of tax-exempt status.

Deadlines: None.

Foundation Officials

Katherine K. Hodge: treasurer
Hobart C. Kreitler: president
James S. Kreitler: director
John M. Kreitler: director
Karen R. Kreitler: director
Sally S. Kreitler: secretary
Thomas S. Kreitler: vice president

Grants Analysis

Disclosure Period: calendar year ending 2003
Total Grants: $210,648*
Number of Grants: 62
Average Grant: $3,043*
Highest Grant: $25,000
Lowest Grant: $40
Typical Range: $1,000 to $5,000
*Note: Giving excludes United Way; scholarships. Average grant figure excludes highest grant.

Recent Grants

Note: Grants derived from 2003 Form 990.
General

25,000	Greens Farms Academy, Greens Farms, CT -- to support horizons program at Greens farms academy
15,100	Wellesley College, Wellesley, MA
11,000	First Church Congregational, Fairfield, CT
10,000	Center for Creative Youth, Middletown, CT -- scholarship support for Bridgeport high school students to attend program
10,000	Habitat for Humanity, Benton Harbor, MI
10,000	Hamilton College, Clinton, NY
7,000	Horizons Student Enrichment Program, New Canaan, CT
6,000	Children's Community School, Van Nuys, CA
5,500	Stuart Congregational Church, Stuart, FL
5,000	Norwalk Community College, Norwalk, CT -- to support a summer school program for children primarily from Stamford and Norwalk

KRESGE FOUNDATION

Giving Contact

John E. Marshall, III, President & Chief Executive Officer
2701 Troy Center Dr.
Troy, MI 48084
Phone: (248)643-9630
Fax: (248)643-0588
Web: http://www.kresge.org

Description

Founded: 1924
EIN: 381359217
Organization Type: Private Foundation
Giving Locations: nationally; Canada; England; Republic of South Africa

Grant Types: Capital, Challenge, General Support, Scholarship.

Donor Information

Founder: The foundation was established in 1924 by Sebastian S. Kresge (1867-1966), the founder of the Kresge chain of retail stores now known as the Kmart Corporation. As owner of S. S. Kresge Company, Mr. Kresge amassed a fortune of $100 million by 1924. He established the foundation with an initial personal contribution of almost $2 million. Family representation is continued on the board of trustees through Dr. Bruce A. Kresge. The charity is an independent, private foundation and has never been affiliated with Kmart Corporation.

Financial Summary

Total Giving: $107,699,101 (2003); $107,008,508 (2002); $123,292,500 (2001)
Giving Analysis: Giving for 2003 includes: foundation matching gifts ($828,501); 2001: foundation matching gifts ($299,590); foundation grants to United Way ($1,500,000)
Assets: $2,504,554,217 (2003); $2,164,478,054 (2002); $2,415,971,841 (2001)

Typical Recipients

Arts & Humanities: Arts Centers, Arts Festivals, Arts Institutes, Arts Outreach, Ballet, Historic Preservation, History & Archaeology, Libraries, Museums/Galleries, Music, Opera, Performing Arts, Public Broadcasting, Theater, Visual Arts

Civic & Public Affairs: African American Affairs, Botanical Gardens/Parks, Clubs, Community Foundations, Economic Development, Gay/Lesbian Issues, Civic & Public Affairs-General, Housing, Nonprofit Management, Professional & Trade Associations, Public Policy, Zoos/Aquariums

Education: Agricultural Education, Arts/Humanities Education, Business Education, Colleges & Universities, Education Associations, Education Reform, Engineering/Technological Education, Faculty Development, International Studies, Journalism/Media Education, Legal Education, Medical Education, Minority Education, Preschool Education, Private Education (Precollege), Religious Education, Science/Mathematics Education, Social Sciences Education, Special Education, Student Aid

Environment: Air/Water Quality, Forestry, Environment-General, Resource Conservation, Wildlife Protection

Health: AIDS/HIV, Alzheimer's Disease, Cancer, Children's Health/Hospitals, Clinics/Medical Centers, Diabetes, Emergency/Ambulance Services, Eyes/Blindness, Health Organizations, Hospices, Hospitals, Long-Term Care, Medical Rehabilitation, Medical Research, Mental Health, Nursing Services, Outpatient Health Care, Preventive Medicine/Wellness Organizations, Research/Studies Institutes, Single-Disease Health Associations, Trauma Treatment

International: Foreign Arts Organizations, Foreign Educational Institutions, Health Care/Hospitals, International Environmental Issues, International Relations, International Relief Efforts

Religion: Jewish Causes, Ministries, Religious Organizations, Religious Welfare, Seminaries

Science: Science Museums, Scientific Centers & Institutes

Social Services: Animal Protection, At-Risk Youth, Camps, Child Abuse, Child Welfare, Community Centers, Community Service Organizations, Domestic Violence, Family Planning, Family Services, Food/Clothing Distribution, People with Disabilities, Recreation & Athletics, Scouts, Senior Services, Sexual Abuse, Shelters/Homelessness, Substance Abuse, YMCA/YWCA/YMHA/YWHA, Youth Organizations

Application Procedures

Initial Contact: The foundation accepts telephone calls or meetings from grantseekers prior to sending an application. Applicants should submit a completed proposal after reviewing application guidelines.

Application Requirements: Submit a type-written, double-spaced cover letter (signed by the senior administrative official) describing the project's purpose, impact, and priority; proposal narrative including a Fact Sheet form (provided by foundation); a brief history of the organization; description of the services provided and persons served, along with external evidence of their quality and distinctiveness; a description of major affiliations with other nonprofit organizations; extent to which organization demonstrates through governance, staff and individuals served, a commitment to serving a diverse population; policy for maintaining the current facilities; and a listing of the governing board with professional affiliations. Project information should include a description of the project; expected impact on the organization; status of architectural plans; project cost estimates; effect of completed project on organization's budget; and photograph or drawing of project (no blueprints). Fundraising information should include a brief a description of organization's previous fund-raising track record; total dollar goal for each category listed on Fact Sheet; Identification of the five largest gifts shown on Fact Sheet; amount of fund raising expected while the four to six months that the proposal is under consideration by foundation; description of constituencies likely to respond to a challenge grant; description of campaign committee and role of volunteers; how a successfully completed campaign will strengthen ongoing fund-raising programs; and if project is part of a larger campaign, outline campaign goals and priorities. The proposal should include the following attachments: a most recent audit; description of any long-term financing for project shown on Fact Sheet; a copy of the most recent accreditation and/or licensure report; and IRS ruling letter indicating tax-exempt status. The Science Initiative is a challenge grant program to upgrade and endow scientific equipment and laboratories in colleges and universities, teaching hospitals, medical schools, and research institutions. The Science Initiative application and the proposal for the capital projects program should be considered two separate and unique applications.

Deadlines: None.

Review Process: A decision is made within five to six months after submission.

Notes: The foundation does not accept videos or architectural renderings. Limit one proposal per institution in any twelve-month period. Foundation encourages grant recipients to wait two years from payment before submitting another proposal.

Restrictions

The foundation does not give grants to religious organizations, elementary and secondary schools, community colleges, private foundations, or individuals. The foundation does not make grants toward projects that are substantially completed at the time of application, or toward the retirement of long-term debt. Minor equipment, furnishings, operating/program support, and endowment by themselves are not eligible (but may be funded as part of an eligible project). Projects that are eligible for funding include: construction and renovation of facilities, purchase of major equipment or an integrated system at a cost of at least $300,000, and the purchase of real estate.

Additional Information

Publications: Annual Report; Informational Pamphlets

Foundation Officials

Sandra McAlister Ambrozy: senior program officer
Lee C. Bollinger: trustee B Santa Rosa, CA. ED Columbia Law School JD. NONPR AFFIL president: Columbia University; director: Royal Shakespeare Co. of Great Britain; fellow: American Academy of Arts and Sciences; member: American Philosophical Society.
Jane L. Delgado: trustee B Havana, Cuba 1953. ED State University of New York College New Paltz BA (1973); New York University MA (1975); State Univer-

sity of New York College Stony Brook PhD (1981); W Averell Harriman School MS (1981). PRIM CORP EMPL president, chief executive officer: COSSHMO PRIM NONPR EMPL chief executive officer: National Coalition for Hispanic Health & Human Services. NONPR AFFIL president, chief executive officer, director: National Coalition Hispanic Health & Human Services; trustee: SUNY New Paltz Foundation; member: Hispanics Philanthropy; member, national advisory council: Carter Center Mental Health Task Force; member, advisory council: EPA Clean Air Act.

Richard Lowell Dunlap: program director, information systems B Passaic, NJ 1950. ED Southern Methodist University BA (1972); Southern Methodist University MFA (1974). ADD NONPR EMPL music director: Presbyterian Church Utica. NONPR AFFIL member, trustee: Detroit Department Cultural Affairs Advisory Committee; member: Sterling Heights Cultural Community; member: Concerned Citizens Arts Michigan.

Ernest B. Gutierrez, Jr.: senior program officer

Steve K. Hamp: trustee NONPR AFFIL president: Henry Ford Museum.

Irene Y. Hirano: chairman, trustee ED University of Southern California MS; University of Southern California BA. CORP AFFIL member, diversity advisory board: Toyota North American. NONPR AFFIL secretary, treasurer: LA Inc.-Convention & Visitors Bureau; president, chief executive officer: National Center for the Preservation of Democracy; president, chief executive officer: Japanese American National Museum; vice chairman: California Japanese American Community Leadership Council.

Robert C. Larson: trustee CORP AFFIL chairman: Larson Realty Group; chairman: United Dominion Realty; director: Brandywine Realty Trust; director: Intercontinental Hotels Group plc.

John Elbert Marshall, III: president, chief executive officer, trustee B Providence, RI 1942. ED Brown University BA (1964). NONPR AFFIL director: Detroit Symphony Orchestra Hall Inc.; director: Independent Sector; member, advisory cabinet: Council Michigan Foundations.

Deborah E. McDowell: trustee B Bessemer, AL.

William F. L. Moses: senior program officer NONPR AFFIL member, international committee: Council on Foundations.

David Keith Page: vice chairman, trustee B Detroit, MI 1933. ED Dartmouth College AB (1955); Harvard University LLB (1958). PRIM CORP EMPL senior partner: Honigman, Miller, Schwartz & Cohn. CORP AFFIL director: Meadowbrook Insurance Group.

Robert Davis Storey: trustee B Tuskegee, AL 1936. ED Harvard University AB (1958); Case Western Reserve University JD (1964). PRIM CORP EMPL partner: Thompson Hine LLP. CORP AFFIL director: Verizon Communications Inc.; director: Procter & Gamble Co. NONPR AFFIL member: Society Benchers; trustee: Spelman College; member: Cleveland Bar Association; member: Alpha Phi Alpha Fraternity; trustee: Case Western Reserve University. CLUB AFFIL University Club; Union Club; Ponce de Leon Club; Rowfant Club.

Elizabeth C. Sullivan: vice president, program ED Michigan State University MA; Michigan State University BA. PRIM NONPR EMPL chairman development council: New Steps. NONPR AFFIL trustee: University Liggett School.

Grants Analysis

Disclosure Period: calendar year ending 2003
Total Grants: $106,870,600*
Number of Grants: 172
Average Grant: $530,078*
Highest Grant: $7,500,000
Typical Range: $50,000 to $1,000,000
***Note:** Giving excludes matching gifts. Average grant figure excludes three highest grants ($17,287,500).

SAMUEL H. KRESS FOUNDATION

Giving Contact

Lisa M. Ackerman, Vice President
174 East 80th Street
New York, NY 10021
Phone: (212)861-4993
Fax: (212)628-3146
E-mail: lisa@kressfoundation.org
Web: http://www.kressfoundation.org

Description

Founded: 1929
EIN: 131624176
Organization Type: Specialized/Single Purpose Foundation
Giving Locations: nationally.
Grant Types: Conference/Seminar, Employee Matching Gifts, Fellowship, General Support, Matching, Multiyear/Continuing Support, Research, Scholarship.

Donor Information

Founder: The Samuel H. Kress Foundation was established in 1929, with three brothers, Samuel H. Kress (1863-1955), Claude W. Kress (1876-1940), and Rush H. Kress (1877-1963), as donors. Samuel H. Kress, a native Pennsylvanian, was the founder of the S. H. Kress and Company stores. Although Samuel was known for his extensive collection of Italian Renaissance art, the brothers expanded the Kress Collection to contain works of European masters in a variety of mediums. This vast collection of more than 3,000 pieces was eventually donated to 50 museums in 38 states. Samuel was a trustee of the Metropolitan Museum of Art and the National Gallery of Art, which received a significant portion of his art collection and named him as a Founding Benefactor.

Financial Summary

Total Giving: $4,074,477 (fiscal year ending June 30, 2003); $5,000,000 (fiscal 2002 approx); $4,873,012 (fiscal 2001)
Giving Analysis: Giving for fiscal 2003 includes: foundation matching gifts ($160,000); foundation fellowships ($889,000).
Assets: $85,657,587 (fiscal 2003); $110,000,000 (fiscal 2002 approx); $103,691,174 (fiscal 2001)

Typical Recipients

Arts & Humanities: Art History, Arts Associations & Councils, Arts Centers, Arts Funds, Arts Institutes, Ethnic & Folk Arts, Film & Video, Arts & Humanities-General, Historic Preservation, History & Archaeology, Libraries, Museums/Galleries, Music, Visual Arts
Civic & Public Affairs: Botanical Gardens/Parks, Ethnic Organizations, Civic & Public Affairs-General, Professional & Trade Associations, Public Policy, Urban & Community Affairs
Education: Arts/Humanities Education, Colleges & Universities, International Exchange, International Studies
International: Foreign Arts Organizations, Foreign Educational Institutions, International-General, International Development, International Environmental Issues, International Organizations, International Peace & Security Issues, Missionary/Religious Activities, Trade
Religion: Religious Organizations, Religious Welfare
Social Services: Community Service Organizations

Application Procedures

Initial Contact: Applicants should contact the foundation by letter. Fellowship applicants require an application form.
Application Requirements: Letters should include a description of the project, its budget, curriculum vitae of the principal investigator, an IRS determination letter, and the funds to be requested.

Deadlines: None. Proposals for projects within the standard funding programs may be submitted any time. Contact the foundation for specific program deadlines.

Restrictions

The foundation awards grants to U.S. charitable organizations only. The foundation does not support art history programs below the predoctoral level or the purchase of works of art. No grants are given to artists, operating budgets, annual campaigns, endowments, deficit financing, capital funds, films, or loans. The foundation does not accept applications via fax or e-mail.

Additional Information

Application forms for fellowships in art history and conservation are required. Applications are to be addressed: Kress Fellowship Program, Samuel H. Kress Foundation, 174 E 80th Street, New York, NY 10021. The foundation does not accept applications by fax or email.
Publications: Annual Report; Guidelines

Foundation Officials

Lisa Marilyn Ackerman: vice president B Danville, PA 1960. ED Middlebury College BA (1982); New York University MBA (1986). NONPR AFFIL member: Middlebury College Alumni Association; member: Museum Modern Art Education Department; member: College Art Association; member: Jewish Heritage Council.
Frederick William Beinecke: secretary, treasurer, trustee B Stamford, CT 1943. ED Yale University BA (1966); University of Virginia JD (1972); Harvard University PMD (1977). PRIM CORP EMPL president, director: Antaeus Enterprises Inc.
John C. Fontaine: chairman, trustee B 1932. ED University of Michigan BA (1953); Harvard University LLB (1956). CORP AFFIL director: Twin Cities Newspaper Service; director: Wichita Eagle & Beacon Publishing Co.; director: State Newspaper; director: State-Record Co. Inc.; director: Pioneer Press Inc.; director: Saint Paul Pioneer Press; director: Northwest Publications Inc.; director: Miami Herald; director: Nittany Printing & Publishing Co. Inc.; partner: Hughes Hubbard & Reed LLP; president: Knight-Ridder Inc.; director: Columbia Newspaper; director: Detroit Free Press Inc.; director: Centre Daily Times.
Marilyn Perry: president, trustee B 1940. ED University of North Carolina (1970).
Inmaculada von Habsburg-Lothringen: trustee
Walter L. Weisman: trustee B Chicago, IL 1935. ED Stanford University BA (1956); Stanford University JD (1959). PRIM NONPR EMPL president, chief executive officer: American Medicine International Inc.

Grants Analysis

Disclosure Period: fiscal year ending June 30, 2003
Total Grants: $3,025,477*
Number of Grants: 300 (approx)
Average Grant: $10,085*
Highest Grant: $250,000
Lowest Grant: $700
Typical Range: $1,000 to $25,000
***Note:** Giving excludes matching gifts; fellowships.

VERNON K. KRIEBLE FOUNDATION

Giving Contact

Helen E. Krieble, President
1777 S. Harrison St., Suite 807
Denver, CO 80210

Description

Founded: 1985
EIN: 222538914

Organization Type: Private Foundation
Giving Locations: DC: Washington nationally.
Grant Types: General Support.

Donor Information

Founder: Established by Gladys V. K. Delmas.

Financial Summary

Total Giving: $340,751 (2003); $1,083,800 (2001)
Assets: $12,406,702 (2003); $8,888,045 (2001)

Typical Recipients

Arts & Humanities: Arts Funds, Arts Institutes, Ballet, Historic Preservation, Libraries, Museums/Galleries, Music, Performing Arts, Public Broadcasting, Theater
Civic & Public Affairs: Business/Free Enterprise, Civil Rights, Economic Policy, Civic & Public Affairs-General, Law & Justice, Legal Aid, Professional & Trade Associations, Public Policy, Safety, Urban & Community Affairs
Education: Arts/Humanities Education, Colleges & Universities, Economic Education, Education Associations, Education Funds, Education-General, Journalism/Media Education, Leadership Training, Legal Education, Private Education (Precollege), Science/Mathematics Education, Student Aid
Environment: Environment-General
Health: Hospitals
International: Foreign Educational Institutions, International-General, International Affairs, International Peace & Security Issues, International Relations
Science: Scientific Organizations
Social Services: Child Welfare, Community Service Organizations, Recreation & Athletics, United Funds/United Ways, Youth Organizations

Application Procedures

Initial Contact: Send a brief letter of inquiry.
Application Requirements: Include a summary of the project, project budget, amount requested, qualifications of individuals involved, and proof of tax-exempt status.
Deadlines: None.

Restrictions

Awards are made only to 501(c)(3) organizations.

Foundation Officials

Amanda C. Fusscas: secretary
Christopher P. Fusscas: treasurer
Frederick B. Fusscas: director
Frederick K. Krieble: vice president B Camden, NJ 1941. ED Yale University (1967). PRIM CORP EMPL chairman financial committee, director: Loctite Corp. CORP AFFIL president: Management I Ltd.; president: Management II Ltd.
Helen E. Krieble: president

Grants Analysis

Disclosure Period: calendar year ending 2003
Total Grants: $340,751
Number of Grants: 46
Average Grant: $6,350*
Highest Grant: $55,000
Lowest Grant: $500
Typical Range: $1,000 to $15,000
*Note: Average grant excludes highest grant.

Recent Grants

Note: Grants derived from 2003 Form 990.
General

55,000	Center for the Study of Popular Culture, Los Angeles, CA
30,000	Turks and Caicos Islands Education Foundation, Providenciales Turks and Caicos Islands
30,000	Turks and Caicos National Trust, Providenciales Turks and Caicos Islands
25,000	Citizens for a Sound Economy Foundation, Washington, DC
25,000	Intercollegiate Studies Institute, Wilmington, DE
25,000	Leadership Program of the Rockies, Denver, CO
15,000	Ivoryton Playhouse Foundation Inc., Ivoryton, CT
15,000	Wadsworth Atheneum, Hartford, CT
10,000	American Foreign Policy Council, Washington, DC
10,000	Bill of Rights Foundation, Chicago, IL

KROGER CO.

Company Headquarters

Cincinnati, OH
Web: http://www.kroger.com

Company Description

Founded: 1883
Ticker: KR
Exchange: NYSE
Revenue: US$56.434 billion (2004)
Profit: (US$128 million) (2004)
Employees: 288000 (2003)
Fortune Rank: 21, per FORTUNE Magazine's list of 500 Largest U.S. Corporations (2004).
SIC(s): 2000 Food & Kindred Products, 5300 General Merchandise Stores, 5400 Food Stores, 5900 Miscellaneous Retail.

Operating Locations

Kroger Co. (AZ--Phoenix; CO--Denver; GA--Atlanta; IN--Indianapolis; MI--Detroit; OH--Cincinnati, Columbus; TN--Memphis; TX--Dallas, Houston; VA--Roanoke)

Nonmonetary Support

Note: For nonmonetary support contact local store manager.

The Kroger Co. Foundation

Giving Contact

Lynn Marmer, President
1014 Vine Street
Cincinnati, OH 45202-1100
Phone: (513)762-4449
Fax: (513)762-1295
Web: http://www.kroger.com/corpnewsinfo_charitablegiving.htm

Description

EIN: 311192929
Organization Type: Corporate Foundation
Former Name: Kroger Co. Foundation.
Giving Locations: headquarters and operating communities.
Grant Types: Award, Capital, General Support, Operating Expenses, Seed Money.

Financial Summary

Total Giving: $2,491,783 (fiscal year ending February 01, 2004); $2,500,000 (fiscal 2003 approx); $3,167,322 (fiscal 2001). Note: Contributes through foundation only.
Giving Analysis: Giving for fiscal 2001 includes: foundation ($3,167,322)
Assets: $8,014,900 (fiscal 2004); $9,944,345 (fiscal 2003); $11,638,184 (fiscal 2001)

Typical Recipients

Arts & Humanities: Arts Associations & Councils, Arts Centers, Arts Festivals, Arts Funds, Ballet, Dance, Historic Preservation, History & Archaeology, Libraries, Museums/Galleries, Music, Opera, Performing Arts, Public Broadcasting, Theater, Visual Arts
Civic & Public Affairs: African American Affairs, Botanical Gardens/Parks, Business/Free Enterprise, Chambers of Commerce, Civil Rights, Community Foundations, Economic Development, Employment/Job Training, Civic & Public Affairs-General, Housing, Minority Business, Municipalities/Towns, Parades/Festivals, Philanthropic Organizations, Professional & Trade Associations, Public Policy, Rural Affairs, Safety, Urban & Community Affairs, Women's Affairs, Zoos/Aquariums
Education: Afterschool/Enrichment Programs, Agricultural Education, Arts/Humanities Education, Business Education, Business-School Partnerships, Colleges & Universities, Community & Junior Colleges, Economic Education, Education Associations, Education Funds, Elementary Education (Private), Education-General, Literacy, Medical Education, Minority Education, Private Education (Precollege), Public Education (Precollege), Science/Mathematics Education, Student Aid
Environment: Environment-General
Health: Arthritis, Cancer, Children's Health/Hospitals, Clinics/Medical Centers, Diabetes, Emergency/Ambulance Services, Eyes/Blindness, Health-General, Health Funds, Health Organizations, Heart, Hospices, Hospitals, Medical Rehabilitation, Medical Research, Mental Health, Nutrition, Prenatal Health Issues, Single-Disease Health Associations
International: Foreign Arts Organizations, International Relations
Religion: Churches, Religious Organizations, Religious Welfare
Science: Science Exhibits & Fairs
Social Services: Animal Protection, Big Brothers/Big Sisters, Camps, Child Abuse, Child Welfare, Community Centers, Community Service Organizations, Day Care, Delinquency & Criminal Rehabilitation, Domestic Violence, Emergency Relief, Family Services, Food/Clothing Distribution, Homes, People with Disabilities, Recreation & Athletics, Scouts, Senior Services, Shelters/Homelessness, Social Services-General, Special Olympics, Substance Abuse, United Funds/United Ways, YMCA/YWCA/YMHA/YWHA, Youth Organizations

Application Procedures

Initial Contact: Submit a brief letter or proposal.
Application Requirements: Include a description of organization, statement of goals and objectives, amount requested, purpose of funds sought, recently audited financial statement, proof of tax-exempt status, list of board of trustees.
Deadlines: None.
Review Process: Requests are reviewed by foundation trustees on a monthly basis.
Evaluative Criteria: Ability to address an identified need in the community; clearly defined goals and objectives; strong base of community support.
Decision Notification: Decisions usually made within four to six weeks.

Restrictions

The foundation does not assist religious institutions or organizations for sectarian purposes; individuals; endowment campaigns; program or journal advertisements; event sponsorships; medical researchl national organizations.

Additional Information

Certain national and regional groups are supported, but an important part of evaluating grant requests is the extent to which agency provides services to areas where the company operates.
The foundation was created in 1987.

Corporate Officials

David Brian Dillon: chief executive officer B Hutchinson, KS 1951. ED University of Kansas BS (1973); Southern Methodist University JD (1976). PRIM CORP EMPL chief executive officer: The Kroger Co.

CORP AFFIL director: Jackson Ice Cream Co. Inc.; director: First National Hutchinson; director: Fry's Food Stores Arizona Inc.; director: City Market Inc. NONPR AFFIL board: University Kansas Business School; trustee: University Kansas Endowment Association; member: University Kansas Alumni Association; member: Sigma Chi; trustee: University Circle Foundation; member: Order Coif; director: Bethesda Hospital; den board council: Boy Scouts America.

Joseph A. Pichler: chairman B Saint Louis, MO 1939. ED University of Notre Dame BBA (1961); University of Chicago MBA (1963); University of Chicago PhD (1966). PRIM CORP EMPL chairman: Kroger Co. CORP AFFIL director: Milacron Inc.; president: Pace Dairy Foods Co.; director: Federated Department Stores Inc. NONPR AFFIL chairman national board: National Alliance Business; director: Tougaloo College; director: Cincinnati Opera; national board director: Boys Hope; member: Business Roundtable. CLUB AFFIL Commercial Club Cincinnati; Queen City Club.

Foundation Officials

Don Becker: trustee
Geoff Covert: trustee
David Brian Dillon: trustee (see above)
Paul Heldman: secretary
Scott Henderson: treasurer
Lynn Marmer: president
Marnette Perry: trustee
Bob Zinkle: trustee

Grants Analysis

Disclosure Period: fiscal year ending February 01, 2004
Total Grants: $1,696,212*
Number of Grants: 1,000 (approx)
Average Grant: $1,696
Highest Grant: $50,000
Lowest Grant: $250
Typical Range: $1,000 to $5,000
*Note: Giving excludes United Way.

Recent Grants

Note: Grants derived from fiscal 2004 Form 990.
General

106,250	United Way Community Chest, Cincinnati, OH
106,250	United Way Community Chest, Cincinnati, OH
106,250	United Way Community Chest, Cincinnati, OH
106,250	United Way Community Chest, Cincinnati, OH
103,550	First Data Western Union Foundation, Greenwood Village, OH
60,000	Habitat for Humanity of Greater Indianapolis, Indianapolis, IN
60,000	United Way of Central Ohio, Columbus, OH
50,000	Mercer University Southern School of Pharmacy, Atlanta, GA
50,000	University of Georgia College of Pharmacy, Athens, GA
35,821	Mile High United Way, Denver, CO

CHARLES W. KUHNE FOUNDATION TRUST

Giving Contact

Alice Kopfer
c/o Wells Fargo Bank
PO Box 960
Ft. Wayne, IN 46801
Phone: (219)461-6451

Description

EIN: 356011137
Organization Type: Private Foundation
Giving Locations: IN: Allen City
Grant Types: Capital, General Support, Project.

Financial Summary

Total Giving: $265,372 (fiscal year ending July 31, 2004). Note: Fiscal 1997 Giving includes United Way ($60,500).
Assets: $6,880,878 (fiscal 2004)

Typical Recipients

Arts & Humanities: Arts Associations & Councils, Arts Funds, Historic Preservation, History & Archaeology, Libraries, Museums/Galleries, Music, Public Broadcasting, Theater
Civic & Public Affairs: African American Affairs, Botanical Gardens/Parks, Community Foundations, Economic Development, Ethnic Organizations, Civic & Public Affairs-General, Hispanic Affairs, Urban & Community Affairs, Zoos/Aquariums
Education: Business Education, Colleges & Universities, Education Funds, Engineering/Technological Education, Education-General, Literacy, Private Education (Precollege), Public Education (Precollege), Science/Mathematics Education, Student Aid, Vocational & Technical Education
Environment: Air/Water Quality, Resource Conservation
Health: Cancer, Children's Health/Hospitals, Health Funds, Health Organizations, Mental Health, Public Health, Single-Disease Health Associations
Religion: Churches, Ministries, Religious Organizations, Religious Welfare
Social Services: Child Welfare, Community Service Organizations, Day Care, Family Services, Food/Clothing Distribution, Homes, People with Disabilities, Recreation & Athletics, Scouts, Senior Services, Shelters/Homelessness, Substance Abuse, United Funds/United Ways, YMCA/YWCA/YMHA/YWHA, Youth Organizations

Application Procedures

Initial Contact: Send a brief letter of inquiry.
Application Requirements: Include a description of organization, amount requested, purpose of funds sought, recently audited financial statement, and proof of tax-exempt status.
Deadlines: None.

Restrictions

Does not fund individuals, political or lobbying groups, religious organizations for sectarian purposes, or organizations outside operating areas.

Additional Information

Trust(s): Wells Fargo Bank

Grants Analysis

Disclosure Period: fiscal year ending July 31, 2004
Total Grants: $265,372
Number of Grants: 22
Average Grant: $12,062
Highest Grant: $30,000
Lowest Grant: $1,000
Typical Range: $5,000 to $15,000

Recent Grants

Note: Grants derived from 2004 Form 990.
General

30,000	Fort Wayne Urban League, Ft. Wayne, IN -- capital campaign
25,000	Arts United, Ft. Wayne, IN -- for arts plaza project
25,000	Children's Hope, Ft. Wayne, IN
20,000	Arc, Ft. Wayne, IN
20,000	Indiana Institute of Technology, Ft. Wayne, IN
19,000	United Hispanic-Americans, Ft. Wayne, IN
15,500	Cancer Services of Allen County, Ft. Wayne, IN
12,000	Independent Colleges of Indiana, Indianapolis, IN
10,000	Crossroad Children's Home, Ft. Wayne, IN -- towards purchase of a car
10,000	Fort Wayne Clubhouse Inc., Ft. Wayne, IN -- for carriage house-copies and notes

KULAS FOUNDATION

Giving Contact

Nancy W. McCann, President
50 Public Square, Suite 924
Cleveland, OH 44113-2203
Phone: (216)623-4770
Fax: (216)623-4773
E-mail: azambie@gateway.net
Web: http://fdncenter.org/grantmaker/kulas/

Description

Founded: 1938
EIN: 340770687
Organization Type: General Purpose Foundation
Giving Locations: OH: Cleveland including metropolitan area
Grant Types: Award, Capital, General Support, Matching, Multiyear/Continuing Support.

Donor Information

Founder: The Kulas Foundation was established in 1937 by Mrs. Fynette Kulas, whose husband, E. J. Kulas, headed Otis Steel and Midland Steel Products Co. Both Mr. and Mrs. Kulas took an active interest in music, music education, and other cultural organizations in Cleveland, OH. This interest in music and musical organizations is reflected today by the foundation, which continues to allocate funds to music institutions for a variety of programs and purposes.

Financial Summary

Total Giving: $2,523,046 (2003); $2,829,000 (2002); $2,518,135 (2001)
Giving Analysis: Giving for 2003 includes: foundation grants to United Way ($45,000); 2002: foundation grants to United Way ($45,000)
Assets: $33,870,797 (2003); $30,531,964 (2002); $37,246,781 (2001). Note: As of January 1, 1997, the foundation became the trustee of the Elroy J. Kulas Trust No. 1; that trust's assets are included in the figures above.
Gifts Received: $740,295 (2003); $380,449 (2002); $404,619 (2001). Note: Contributions were received from the Elroy J. Kulas Trust.

Typical Recipients

Arts & Humanities: Arts Associations & Councils, Arts Centers, Arts Festivals, Arts Funds, Arts Institutes, Arts Outreach, Ballet, Community Arts, Dance, Arts & Humanities-General, History & Archaeology, Libraries, Museums/Galleries, Music, Opera, Performing Arts, Public Broadcasting, Theater, Visual Arts
Civic & Public Affairs: Botanical Gardens/Parks, Business/Free Enterprise, Community Foundations, Economic Development, Employment/Job Training, Civic & Public Affairs-General, Hispanic Affairs, Municipalities/Towns, Parades/Festivals, Rural Affairs, Urban & Community Affairs, Women's Affairs
Education: Arts/Humanities Education, Colleges & Universities, Community & Junior Colleges, Education Associations, Education Funds, Education Reform, Elementary Education (Private), Education-General, Medical Education, Private Education (Precollege), Public Education (Precollege), Special Education, Student Aid
Health: Cancer, Children's Health/Hospitals, Clinics/Medical Centers, Eyes/Blindness, Health Funds,

Health Organizations, Hospices, Hospitals, Hospitals (University Affiliated), Long-Term Care, Medical Research, Mental Health, Nursing Services
International: Foreign Arts Organizations, International Affairs
Religion: Churches, Dioceses, Jewish Causes, Ministries, Religious Organizations, Religious Welfare
Science: Science Museums, Scientific Centers & Institutes
Social Services: Child Welfare, Community Service Organizations, Counseling, Food/Clothing Distribution, Homes, People with Disabilities, Recreation & Athletics, Senior Services, Social Services-General, United Funds/United Ways, Volunteer Services, Youth Organizations

Application Procedures

Initial Contact: Applicants should submit a letter stating the purpose of request and asking for a formal application form.
Application Requirements: Five copies of the completed application are required, with proof of tax-exempt and non-foundation status. Also include most recent financial statement, names of board members, and names and qualifications of staff responsible for project.
Deadlines: Foundation must receive proposals six weeks to two months prior to quarterly board meetings.
Review Process: Grant decisions are made at meetings which usually take place in February, May, August, and November.

Restrictions

No grants are given for endowments, including scholarships.

Additional Information

Publications: Guidelines; Application Form; Brochure; Annual Report

Foundation Officials

Ellen E. Halfon: assistant secretary
Nancy W. McCann: president
Patrick F. McCartan, Esq.: trustee, vice president
Richard Welch Pogue: chairman, vice president, trustee B Cambridge, MA 1928. ED Cornell University BA (1950); University of Michigan JD (1953). PRIM CORP EMPL senior partner: Jones, Day, Reavis & Pogue. CORP AFFIL director: TRW Inc.; director: Redland PLC Reigate Engineer; director: Rotek Inc.; director: Massachusetts Hanna Co.; director: OHM Corp.; director: Key Corp.; director: Continental Airlines Inc.; director: Derlan Industries Inc. NONPR AFFIL member: Ohio Bar Association; trustee: Rock & Roll Hall Fame Museum; member: Council Foreign Relations; member: American Bar Association; trustee: Case Western Reserve University; co-chairman: 1996 Cleveland Bicentennial Commission. CLUB AFFIL Metro Club; Union Club; Bohemian Club; The Links Club.
Allan John Zambie: vice president, secretary B Cleveland, OH 1935. ED Ohio University (1953-1954); Denison University BA (1957); Case Western Reserve University LLB (1960). NONPR AFFIL trustee, treasurer: Cleveland Music School Settlement; member: Ohio Bar Association; member, national vice president: American Society of Corporate Secretaries; member: Cleveland Bar Association.

Grants Analysis

Disclosure Period: calendar year ending 2003
Total Grants: $2,478,046*
Number of Grants: 116
Average Grant: $19,374*
Highest Grant: $250,000
Lowest Grant: $118
Typical Range: $10,000 to $50,000
*Note: Giving excludes United Way. Average grant figure excludes highest grant.

Recent Grants

Note: Grants derived from 2003 Form 990.
General
250,000	Musical Arts Association, Cleveland, OH
125,000	Musical Arts Association, Cleveland, OH
125,000	University Hospitals Health System, Cleveland, OH
101,000	Cleveland Institute of Music, Cleveland, OH
100,000	Cleveland Institute of Music, Cleveland, OH
92,300	Case Western Reserve University, Cleveland, OH
80,000	Children's Hospital Medical Center of Akron, Akron, OH -- for music therapy
75,000	University Circle Inc., Cleveland, OH
60,000	University Hospitals Health System, Cleveland, OH -- music therapy
50,000	Beech Brook, Pepper Pike, OH -- for music therapy

JOHN CRAIN KUNKEL FOUNDATION

Giving Contact

Nancy W. Berget, Trustee
PO Box 658
Camp Hill, PA 17001-0658
Phone: (717)763-1284

Description

Founded: 1965
EIN: 237026914
Organization Type: Private Foundation
Giving Locations: PA
Grant Types: General Support, Project.

Financial Summary

Total Giving: $630,000 (2002 approx); $444,010 (2001)
Giving Analysis: Giving for 2001 includes: foundation grants to United Way ($20,000)
Assets: $13,052,337 (2001)

Typical Recipients

Arts & Humanities: Arts Associations & Councils, Arts Centers, Arts Funds, Ballet, Community Arts, Historic Preservation, History & Archaeology, Libraries, Museums/Galleries, Public Broadcasting, Theater
Civic & Public Affairs: Botanical Gardens/Parks, Clubs, Civic & Public Affairs-General, Housing, Municipalities/Towns, Safety, Urban & Community Affairs, Zoos/Aquariums
Education: Colleges & Universities, Community & Junior Colleges, Medical Education, Preschool Education, Private Education (Precollege), Public Education (Precollege), Secondary Education (Private)
Health: Alzheimer's Disease, Cancer, Clinics/Medical Centers, Emergency/Ambulance Services, Health Organizations, Hospitals, Kidney, Long-Term Care, Mental Health, Public Health, Single-Disease Health Associations
Religion: Churches, Religious Welfare
Social Services: Community Service Organizations, Family Planning, Family Services, Substance Abuse, United Funds/United Ways, YMCA/YWCA/YMHA/YWHA, Youth Organizations

Application Procedures

Initial Contact: The foundation requests applications be made in writing. Include specific requests.
Deadlines: None.

Foundation Officials

Nancy W. Bergent: trustee
Elizabeth K. Davis: trustee

Deborah L. Facini: trustee
John C. Kunkel, II: trustee
Paul A. Kunkel: trustee
W. Minster Kunkel, MD: trustee
Jay W. Stark: trustee
John K. Stark: trustee
K. R. Stark: trustee
Hasbrouck S. Wright: executive trustee
William T. Wright, II: trustee

Grants Analysis

Disclosure Period: calendar year ending 2001
Total Grants: $424,010*
Number of Grants: 13
Average Grant: $15,155*
Highest Grant: $120,000
Lowest Grant: $4,000
Typical Range: $5,000 to $50,000
*Note: Giving excludes United Way. Average grant figure excludes two highest grants ($227,000).

Recent Grants

Note: Grants derived from 2001 Form 990.
Library-Related
50,000	Fredrickson Public Library, Camp Hill, PA -- for building fund

General
120,000	Pinnacle Health Foundation, Harrisburg, PA
107,000	National Civil War Museum, Harrisburg, PA
50,000	Whitaker Center for the Arts, Harrisburg, PA
30,000	Allied Arts, Harrisburg, PA
20,000	United Way, Harrisburg, PA
15,000	Harrisburg Cemetery Association, Harrisburg, PA
12,000	Planned Parenthood, Harrisburg, PA
10,000	American Red Cross, Harrisburg, PA
10,000	Gaudenzia, Harrisburg, PA
10,000	Theatre Harrisburg, Harrisburg, PA

KURZ FAMILY FOUNDATION

Giving Contact

69 Lydecker St.
Nyack, NY 10960
Phone: (845)358-2300

Description

Founded: 1992
EIN: 133680855
Organization Type: Private Foundation
Grant Types: General Support.

Donor Information

Founder: Established in 1992 by Herbert Kurz.

Financial Summary

Total Giving: $341,250 (2002); $345,463 (2001)
Assets: $7,160,672 (2002); $13,702,394 (2001)
Gifts Received: $496,500 (2002); $525,500 (2001); $1,000,000 (1994). Note: In 1994, 2001, and 2002, , contributions were received from Herbert Kurz.

Typical Recipients

Arts & Humanities: Libraries, Music, Opera, Theater
Civic & Public Affairs: African American Affairs, Civil Rights, Economic Development, Economic Policy, Civic & Public Affairs-General, Law & Justice, Philanthropic Organizations, Professional & Trade Associations, Public Policy, Urban & Community Affairs, Women's Affairs
Education: Arts/Humanities Education, Colleges & Universities, Education Associations, Education Reform, Environmental Education, Education-General,

Medical Education, Private Education (Precollege), Public Education (Precollege), Student Aid
Environment: Environment-General, Resource Conservation
Health: Cancer, Clinics/Medical Centers, Health-General, Health Organizations, Heart, Hospitals
International: International Affairs, International Peace & Security Issues, Trade
Religion: Jewish Causes
Social Services: Child Welfare, Community Service Organizations, Family Planning, Family Services, Food/Clothing Distribution, Recreation & Athletics

Application Procedures

Initial Contact: Send a written request including amount requested and a brief summary of the purpose of funds sought.
Deadlines: None.

Foundation Officials

Ellen Kurz: director
Herbert Kurz: president B New York, NY 1920. ED City University of New York (1941). PRIM CORP EMPL chairman, president, chief executive officer, director: Presidential Life Insurance Co. CORP AFFIL president, director: Presidential Life Corp.
Leonard Kurz: director
Brenda Noel: director
Lewis Wechsley: director

Grants Analysis

Disclosure Period: calendar year ending 2002
Total Grants: $341,250
Number of Grants: 184
Average Grant: $1,855
Highest Grant: $12,000
Lowest Grant: $36
Typical Range: $500 to $5,000

Recent Grants

Note: Grants derived from 2001 Form 990.
General

30,000	Alaska Wilderness League, Anchorage, AK
30,000	Center for Environmental Citizenship, Washington, DC
30,000	ProChoice Resource Center, Mamaroneck, NY
15,000	Public Policy and Education Fund, New York, NY
10,000	Westchester Jewish Community Center, Westchester, NY
5,000	Althea Gibson Foundation, Newark, NJ
5,000	CAP Cure, Santa Monica, CA
5,000	Children's Defense Fund
5,000	FIVF
5,000	Inner City Scholarship Fund, New York, NY

MILTON AND HATTIE KUTZ FOUNDATION

Giving Contact

Executive Director
Jewish Federation of Delaware
100 West 10th Street
Suite 301
Wilmington, DE 19801-1628
Phone: (302)427-2100

Description

Founded: 1955
EIN: 510187055
Organization Type: Private Foundation
Giving Locations: DE
Grant Types: Capital, Emergency, General Support, Operating Expenses, Project, Scholarship, Seed Money.

Donor Information

Founder: Milton Kutz, Hattie Kutz

Financial Summary

Total Giving: 1997 Giving includes scholarships ($7,500).

Typical Recipients

Arts & Humanities: Libraries
Civic & Public Affairs: Botanical Gardens/Parks, Community Foundations, Economic Development, Employment/Job Training, Housing, Urban & Community Affairs
Education: Colleges & Universities, Literacy, Medical Education, Preschool Education, Private Education (Precollege), Secondary Education (Private), Student Aid
Environment: Resource Conservation
Health: Clinics/Medical Centers, Health Organizations, Single-Disease Health Associations
International: Missionary/Religious Activities
Religion: Churches, Jewish Causes, Missionary Activities (Domestic), Religious Organizations, Religious Welfare, Synagogues/Temples
Social Services: At-Risk Youth, Child Welfare, Community Centers, Community Service Organizations, Crime Prevention, Day Care, Family Planning, Family Services, Food/Clothing Distribution, Homes, People with Disabilities, Scouts, Senior Services, Social Services-General, YMCA/YWCA/YMHA/YWHA, Youth Organizations

Application Procedures

Initial Contact: Send a brief letter of inquiry.
Application Requirements: Include a description of organization, amount requested, purpose of funds sought, proof of tax-exempt status, individuals served, program planning mechanism, budget, other funding sources, and program evaluation.
Deadlines: March 31.

Restrictions

Individual scholarships are no longer given. Funds go directly to Delaware colleges for distribution. No grants made outside Delaware. Grants made to Delaware nonsectarian not-for-profit organizations for educational and/or social projects.

Additional Information

Publications: Application Form

Foundation Officials

John A. Elzufon, Esq.: director
Dr. Bennett N. Epstein: secretary
Rolf F. Eriksen: treasurer
Clara Hollander: director
Dr. Barry Kayne: director
Donald Parsons: director
Barbara H. Schoenberg: director
Jeremiah Patrick Shea: vice president B Philadelphia, PA 1926. ED Yale University BA (1946); Catholic University America MA (1950). PRIM CORP EMPL chairman, chief executive officer, director: Bank of Delaware Wilmington. CORP AFFIL assistant secretary, treasurer: Santa Fe Natural Resources; president: Wilmington Financial Co.; chairman: Bank DE Corp. Wilmington; treasurer, director: Santa Fe Industries. NONPR AFFIL director: Saint Marks High School; vice president: United Way; member: Robert Morris Associates; member: American Bankers Association; member: National Alliance Businessmen.
Bernard L. Siegel: president
Judy B. Wortman: executive secretary
Toni P. Young: director
Dr. Leo Zeftel: director

Grants Analysis

Disclosure Period: fiscal year ending June 30, 2000
Total Grants: $128,100*
Number of Grants: 17
Average Grant: $4,256*

Highest Grant: $60,000
Lowest Grant: $1,000
Typical Range: $1,000 to $10,000
*Note: Giving excludes scholarships. Average grant figure excludes highest grant.

Recent Grants

Note: Grants derived from fiscal 2002 Form 990.
General

50,000	Jewish Federation of Delaware, Wilmington, DE -- grant
10,000	Salesianum School, Wilmington, DE -- grant
10,000	University of Delaware, Newark, DE -- scholarship
5,000	Albert Einstein Academy, Wilmington, DE -- grant
5,000	Jewish Community Center, Wilmington, DE -- grant
5,000	Lutheran Community Services, Wilmington, DE -- grant
5,000	United Cerebral Palsy of Delaware, Wilmington, DE -- grant
5,000	Way Home Program, Georgetown, DE -- for scholarship
4,000	Delaware Gratz Hebrew High School, Wilmington, DE -- grant
4,000	Hillel Center, Newark, DE -- grant

PETER H. AND E. LUCILLE GAASS KUYPER FOUNDATION

Giving Contact

Mary Van Zante, Secretary & Treasurer
c/o Pella Corp.
102 Main St.
Pella, IA 50219
Phone: (641)628-6224

Description

Founded: 1970
EIN: 237068402
Organization Type: Private Foundation
Giving Locations: IA: Pella
Grant Types: General Support.

Donor Information

Founder: Peter H. Kuyper, E. Lucille Gaass Kuyper

Financial Summary

Total Giving: $698,551 (2001)
Giving Analysis: Giving for 2001 includes: foundation scholarships ($185,000); foundation matching gifts ($222,915)
Assets: $11,638,422 (2001)

Typical Recipients

Arts & Humanities: Arts Associations & Councils, Arts Centers, Ballet, Historic Preservation, History & Archaeology, Libraries, Museums/Galleries, Music, Opera, Public Broadcasting
Civic & Public Affairs: Botanical Gardens/Parks, Chambers of Commerce, Clubs, Community Foundations, Civic & Public Affairs-General, Municipalities/Towns, Parades/Festivals, Urban & Community Affairs, Women's Affairs, Zoos/Aquariums
Education: Arts/Humanities Education, Colleges & Universities, Private Education (Precollege), Public Education (Precollege), Religious Education, Secondary Education (Public), Student Aid
Environment: Environment-General, Research, Resource Conservation
Health: Children's Health/Hospitals, Emergency/Ambulance Services, Health Organizations, Hospices, Hospitals, Public Health, Single-Disease

Health Associations
Religion: Churches, Religion-General, Ministries, Religious Organizations, Religious Welfare, Seminaries
Social Services: At-Risk Youth, Child Welfare, Community Centers, Community Service Organizations, Day Care, Family Services, People with Disabilities, Recreation & Athletics, Special Olympics, United Funds/United Ways, Youth Organizations

Application Procedures

Initial Contact: The foundation has no formal grant application procedure or application form.
Deadlines: None.

Restrictions

Does not support individuals, religious organizations for sectarian purposes, political or lobbying groups, or organizations outside operating areas.

Additional Information

In 1996, the foundation changed from a fiscal year ending April 30 to a calendar year.

Foundation Officials

William J. Anderson: treasurer B Fort Dodge, IA 1946. ED Northeast Missouri State University (1969).
Charles Farver: vice president
Joan Kuyper Farver: president, director B 1919. ED Grinnell College BA (1941). PRIM CORP EMPL chairman emeritus, director: Pella Corp.
Chip Griffith: vice president
Mary Griffith: vice president
Ann Lennartz: vice president
Mary Van Zante: secretary, treasurer

Grants Analysis

Disclosure Period: calendar year ending 2001
Total Grants: $290,636*
Number of Grants: 33
Average Grant: $6,582*
Highest Grant: $80,000
Typical Range: $1,000 to $10,000
*Note: Giving excludes matching gifts and scholarships. Average grant figure excludes highest grant.

Recent Grants

Note: Grants derived from 2001 Form 990.
General

175,000	Central College, Pella, IA -- scholarship fund
80,000	Pella Historical Society, Pella, IA -- Windmill Project
39,056	Central College, Pella, IA -- scholarship fund
25,000	Nature Conservancy, St. Louis, MO
25,000	Pella Opera House, Pella, IA -- programming
20,012	Community Health Service of Marion County, Knoxville, IA -- van service
20,000	Carbondale Clay Center, Carbondale, CO
15,000	All Seasons Center, Sioux Center, IA -- expansion project
15,000	Aspen Country Day School, Aspen, CO
15,000	Kuemper High School, Carroll, IA -- expansion project

L AND L FOUNDATION

Giving Contact

Mildred C. Brinn, President, Treasurer & Director
570 Park Ave.
New York, NY 10021
Phone: (212)758-7764

Description

Founded: 1963
EIN: 136155758
Organization Type: Private Foundation
Giving Locations: NY
Grant Types: General Support.

Donor Information

Founder: Lawrence E. Brinn

Financial Summary

Total Giving: $495,850 (2001)
Assets: $9,628,975 (2001)

Typical Recipients

Arts & Humanities: Arts Appreciation, Arts Associations & Councils, Arts Centers, Ballet, Dance, Ethnic & Folk Arts, Arts & Humanities-General, Historic Preservation, History & Archaeology, Libraries, Literary Arts, Museums/Galleries, Music, Opera, Performing Arts, Theater, Visual Arts
Civic & Public Affairs: Botanical Gardens/Parks, Civic & Public Affairs-General, Safety, Urban & Community Affairs, Women's Affairs
Education: Arts/Humanities Education, Colleges & Universities, Medical Education, Private Education (Precollege), Religious Education, School Volunteerism
Health: AIDS/HIV, Cancer, Children's Health/Hospitals, Health-General, Health Organizations, Heart, Hospices, Hospitals, Kidney, Long-Term Care, Single-Disease Health Associations
International: Foreign Educational Institutions, International Affairs, International Organizations, International Relations
Religion: Churches, Jewish Causes, Religious Organizations, Religious Welfare, Seminaries
Social Services: Animal Protection, Child Welfare, Community Service Organizations, Counseling, Crime Prevention, Homes, People with Disabilities, Recreation & Athletics, Veterans, Volunteer Services, Youth Organizations

Application Procedures

Initial Contact: Send a brief letter of inquiry.
Application Requirements: a description of organization and purpose of funds sought.
Deadlines: None.

Restrictions

Does not support individuals.

Foundation Officials

Mildred Cunningham Brinn: president, treasurer, director
Peter F. DeGaetano: secretary, director

Grants Analysis

Disclosure Period: calendar year ending 2001
Total Grants: $495,850
Number of Grants: 34
Average Grant: $7,121*
Highest Grant: $150,000
Typical Range: $1,000 to $15,000
*Note: Average grant figure excludes two highest grants ($253,750).

Recent Grants

Note: Grants derived from 2001 Form 990.
General

150,000	Parrish Art Museum, New York, NY
103,750	Ballet Theatre Foundation, New York, NY
100,000	St. Bartholomew's Church, New York, NY
50,000	Lenox Hill Hospital, New York, NY
10,100	Skowhegan School of Painting and Sculpture, New York, NY
10,000	Cat Macrae Fund, New York, NY
8,000	St. John's Episcopal Church
7,000	Metropolitan Opera Association, New York, NY
5,000	God's Love We Deliver, New York, NY

5,000	Harlem School of the Arts, New York, NY

LA-Z-BOY INC.

Company Headquarters

1284 N. Telegraph Road
Monroe, MI 48162-3390
Web: http://www.lazyboy.com

Company Description

Founded: 1928
Ticker: LZB
Exchange: NYSE
Former Name: La-Z-Boy Chair Co.
Revenue: US$2.111 billion (2003)
Employees: 16800 (2003)
SIC(s): 2512 Upholstered Household Furniture, 2514 Metal Household Furniture, 2521 Wood Office Furniture, 2522 Office Furniture Except Wood.

Operating Locations

La-Z-Boy Inc. (AR--Siloam Springs; CA--Redlands; MI--Grand Rapids, Monroe; MS--Leland, Newton; NC--Hudson, Lenoir; SC--Florence; TN--Dayton; UT--Tremonton)

La-Z-Boy Foundation

Giving Contact

Donald E. Blohm, Administrator/Trustee
La-Z-Boy Foundation
1284 N. Telegraph Road
Monroe, MI 48162
Phone: (734)242-1444
Fax: (734)457-2005
Note: Mr. Blohm's extension is 3680.

Description

Founded: 1953
EIN: 386087673
Organization Type: Corporate Foundation
Giving Locations: AR: Siloam Springs; CA: Redlands; MI: Monroe; MS: Leland, Newton; MO: Neosho; NC: Lincolnton; SC: Florence; TN: Dayton; UT: Tremonton operating locations.
Grant Types: General Support.

Donor Information

Founder: E. M. Knabusch, the late Edwin J. Shoemaker, H. F. Gertz, and La-Z-Boy Chair Co.

Financial Summary

Total Giving: $979,500 (2003); $974,850 (2002); $1,019,480 (2001). Note: Contributes through foundation only.
Assets: $20,758,484 (2003); $17,225,954 (2002); $19,760,434 (2001)

Typical Recipients

Arts & Humanities: Arts Associations & Councils, Arts Centers, Community Arts, Historic Preservation, History & Archaeology, Libraries, Museums/Galleries, Music, Public Broadcasting, Theater
Civic & Public Affairs: Business/Free Enterprise, Community Foundations, Economic Development, Civic & Public Affairs-General, Housing, Municipalities/Towns, Safety, Urban & Community Affairs, Women's Affairs
Education: Business Education, Colleges & Universities, Community & Junior Colleges, Education Funds, Elementary Education (Public), Education-General, Public Education (Precollege), Religious Education, Science/Mathematics Education, Secondary Education (Public), Special Education
Environment: Resource Conservation
Health: Children's Health/Hospitals, Clinics/Medical

Centers, Diabetes, Emergency/Ambulance Services, Health Funds, Health Organizations, Hospices, Hospitals, Single-Disease Health Associations
International: Health Care/Hospitals
Religion: Churches, Ministries, Religious Welfare
Social Services: Animal Protection, At-Risk Youth, Child Welfare, Community Centers, Community Service Organizations, Crime Prevention, Day Care, Emergency Relief, Family Services, People with Disabilities, Recreation & Athletics, Senior Services, Shelters/Homelessness, Social Services-General, United Funds/United Ways, Veterans, YMCA/YWCA/YMHA/YWHA, Youth Organizations

Application Procedures

Initial Contact: Send a letter of request.
Application Requirements: Briefly describe the basic need; include a description of organization, amount requested, purpose of funds sought, recently audited financial statement, the organization's budget, and list of directors, proof of 501(c)(3) tax-exempt status, project time span and estimated costs, and benefits of the project to the community.
Deadlines: February 15, May 15, August 15, November 15.
Decision Notification: The board of trustees meets quarterly in March, June, September, and December.
Notes: Personal interviews are arranged upon the foundation's initiative only. Sufficient funding must be assured for successful completion of the project.

Restrictions

Foundation does not make direct grants to individuals; or for loans, travel or conferences, nor does it provide startup funds or seed money. The geographic areas for grant consideration are normally limited to the communities where La-Z-Boy Inc. production plants are located, and within a fifteen mile radius of corporate headquarters.

Corporate Officials

David K. Hehl: director B 1947. ED Michigan State University BA. PRIM CORP EMPL partner: Cooley, Hehl, Wohlgamuth & Carlton. CORP AFFIL director: La-Z-Boy Chair Co.; director: La-Z-Boy Inc.
James W. Johnston: director
Gerald L. Kiser: president, chief executive officer, director ED Western Carolina University BBA (1969). PRIM CORP EMPL president, chief executive officer, director: La-Z-Boy Inc.
Dr. H. George Levy: director PRIM CORP EMPL director: La-Z-Boy Inc.
Patrick H. Norton: chairman, director B 1923. PRIM CORP EMPL chairman, director: La-Z-Boy Inc. CORP AFFIL director: Culp Inc.; director: England/Corsair Inc.
Lorne G. Stevens: director
John F. Weaver: director PRIM CORP EMPL vice chairman: Monroe Bank & Trust Co.

Foundation Officials

Marvin J. Baumann: secretary, trustee
Donald E. Blohm: administrator
Gene M. Hardy: director B Selma, AL 1937. ED University of Alabama (1959). PRIM CORP EMPL secretary, treasurer, director: La-Z-Boy Inc. NONPR AFFIL member: Financial Executives Institute.
June E. Knabusch-Taylor: president, trustee

Grants Analysis

Disclosure Period: calendar year ending 2003
Total Grants: $744,500*
Number of Grants: 131
Average Grant: $5,683
Highest Grant: $25,000
Lowest Grant: $250
Typical Range: $1,000 to $10,000
*Note: Giving excludes United Way.

Recent Grants

Note: Grants derived from 2003 Form 990.

Library-Related
15,000 Ida Township (Library), Monroe, MI
15,000 Ida Township (Library), Monroe, MI
7,000 Leland Public Library, Leland, MS
General
50,000 High Point University KSISHF Endowment, Monroe, MI
50,000 Monroe Public Schools LEEOP BHMSC, Monroe, MI
41,000 United Way of Monroe County, Monroe, MI
40,000 Neosho United Fund, Neosho, MO
25,000 Bedford Community YMCA, Monroe, MI
25,000 City of Neosho, Neosho, MO
25,000 Newton United Givers Fund, Neosho, MO
25,000 Rhea County Department Education, Dayton, TN
25,000 Rhea County United Way, Dayton, TN
25,000 United Way Northern Utah, Ogden, UT

HELEN AND GEORGE LADD CHARITABLE CORP.

Giving Contact

Charles A. Rosebrock, Director
c/o Nutter, McClennen & Fish
PO Box 51400
Boston, MA 02205
Phone: (617)439-2498
Fax: (617)973-9748
E-mail: car@nutter.com

Description

Founded: 1984
EIN: 042767890
Organization Type: Private Foundation
Giving Locations: ME
Grant Types: General Support.

Donor Information

Founder: George E. Ladd, Jr. Charitable Trust

Financial Summary

Total Giving: $559,095 (2002); $566,751 (2001)
Giving Analysis: Giving for 2002 includes: foundation grants to United Way ($500)
Assets: $9,894,124 (2002); $11,363,726 (2001)
Gifts Received: $167,500 (2001); $420,188 (2000); $420,188 (1999). Note: In 1999, 2000, and 2001, contributions were received from George E. Ladd Jr. Charitable Trust. In 1998 contributions were received from George E. Ladd, Jr. ($420,188) and Helen F. Ladd Charitable Trust ($84,699). In 1996, contributions were received from George E. Ladd, Jr. ($420,188) and the Helen F. Ladd Charitable Trust ($100,000).

Typical Recipients

Arts & Humanities: Community Arts, History & Archaeology, Libraries, Literary Arts, Music, Performing Arts, Public Broadcasting, Theater
Civic & Public Affairs: African American Affairs, Economic Development, Employment/Job Training, Civic & Public Affairs-General, Municipalities/Towns, Nonprofit Management, Parades/Festivals, Public Policy, Rural Affairs, Safety, Urban & Community Affairs, Women's Affairs, Zoos/Aquariums
Education: Colleges & Universities, Elementary Education (Public), Faculty Development, Leadership Training, Literacy, Minority Education, Private Education (Precollege), Special Education
Environment: Forestry, Environment-General, Resource Conservation
Health: Arthritis, Clinics/Medical Centers, Hospices, Hospitals, Mental Health, Public Health, Single-Disease Health Associations
International: International Affairs

Religion: Churches, Ministries, Religious Welfare
Social Services: Big Brothers/Big Sisters, Child Welfare, Community Centers, Community Service Organizations, Counseling, Crime Prevention, Domestic Violence, Family Planning, Food/Clothing Distribution, People with Disabilities, Recreation & Athletics, Social Services-General, Veterans, YMCA/YWCA/YMHA/YWHA, Youth Organizations

Application Procedures

Initial Contact: Send brief letter describing program. Include purpose of funds sought.
Deadlines: None.

Foundation Officials

George E. Ladd, III: director
Lincoln F. Ladd: director
Robert M. Ladd: director
Charles A. Rosebrock: director

Grants Analysis

Disclosure Period: calendar year ending 2002
Total Grants: $558,595*
Number of Grants: 64
Average Grant: $5,973*
Highest Grant: $80,235
Lowest Grant: $50
Typical Range: $1,000 to $10,000
*Note: Giving excludes United Way. Average grant figure excludes three highest grants ($194,235).

Recent Grants

Note: Grants derived from 2001 Form 990.
Library-Related
10,000 Lubec Memorial Library
General
62,000 Skidmore College, Saratoga Springs, NY
57,000 Bates College, Lewiston, ME
53,175 Town of Wayne, ME
27,500 Rural Action Community Ministry, Athens, OH
25,000 Kennebec Valley Mental Health Center, Waterville, ME
22,500 Opportunity Farm, New Gloucester, ME
20,000 Russell Medical Center
18,350 Maine Public Broadcasting Corp, Lewiston, ME
17,500 YMCA of Central Maine, ME
15,000 Good Shepherd Food Bank

LAFFEY-MCHUGH FOUNDATION

Giving Contact

David Sysko
PO Box 2286
Wilmington, DE 19899
Phone: (302)654-1680
Fax: (302)654-1681

Description

Founded: 1949
EIN: 516015095
Organization Type: General Purpose Foundation
Grant Types: Capital, General Support, Project, Scholarship.

Donor Information

Founder: The principal donor of the Laffey-McHugh Foundation was Frank A. McHugh, who died in 1949. Mr. McHugh was secretary to Pierre S. du Pont at the E. I. du Pont de Nemours Company. Other donors to the foundation included the late Alice L. McHugh and the late Marie Louise McHugh.

Financial Summary

Total Giving: $3,414,040 (2003); $4,500,000 (2002); $4,916,190 (2001)

Assets: $66,213,669 (2003); $76,604,098 (2001)
Gifts Received: $23,736 (1997)

Typical Recipients

Arts & Humanities: Arts Centers, Arts Funds, Arts Institutes, Ballet, Historic Preservation, History & Archaeology, Libraries, Museums/Galleries, Public Broadcasting, Visual Arts

Civic & Public Affairs: African American Affairs, Botanical Gardens/Parks, Civil Rights, Clubs, Community Foundations, Employment/Job Training, Civic & Public Affairs-General, Housing, Law & Justice, Legal Aid, Public Policy, Urban & Community Affairs, Zoos/ Aquariums

Education: Arts/Humanities Education, Business Education, Colleges & Universities, Education Associations, Education Funds, Elementary Education (Private), Elementary Education (Public), Education-General, Leadership Training, Legal Education, Medical Education, Minority Education, Preschool Education, Private Education (Precollege), Public Education (Precollege), Science/Mathematics Education, Secondary Education (Private), Student Aid

Environment: Environment-General, Resource Conservation, Watershed

Health: AIDS/HIV, Alzheimer's Disease, Cancer, Children's Health/Hospitals, Clinics/Medical Centers, Health-General, Geriatric Health, Health Funds, Heart, Hospices, Hospitals, Long-Term Care, Medical Research, Nursing Services, Outpatient Health Care, Preventive Medicine/Wellness Organizations, Public Health, Single-Disease Health Associations

Religion: Churches, Dioceses, Religion-General, Jewish Causes, Ministries, Religious Organizations, Religious Welfare, Seminaries, Social/Policy Issues

Social Services: Animal Protection, At-Risk Youth, Camps, Child Abuse, Child Welfare, Community Centers, Community Service Organizations, Counseling, Day Care, Emergency Relief, Family Planning, Family Services, Food/Clothing Distribution, Homes, People with Disabilities, Recreation & Athletics, Scouts, Senior Services, Sexual Abuse, Shelters/ Homelessness, Special Olympics, Substance Abuse, United Funds/United Ways, YMCA/YWCA/YMHA/ YWHA, Youth Organizations

Application Procedures

Initial Contact: There are no application forms. Applicants should send a succinct two-page letter.

Application Requirements: Application letters should include background information on the organization and project, goals of the project, amount requested, listing of other funding sources, and indication of IRS tax-exempt status. The foundation will request any additional information.

Deadlines: Applications should be submitted by April 1 or October 1.

Review Process: The directors normally meet in May and November.

Restrictions

Grants are not made to individuals.

Additional Information

Trustees prefer capital investments/improvements rather than studies or projects.

Foundation Officials

Arthur Gould Connolly, Jr.: president B Wilmington, DE. ED Georgetown University BSS (1959); Georgetown University LLB (1962). PRIM CORP EMPL attorney: Connolly, Bove, Lodge & Hutz.

Grants Analysis

Disclosure Period: calendar year ending 2003
Total Grants: $3,414,040*
Number of Grants: 91
Average Grant: $35,712*
Highest Grant: $200,000
Lowest Grant: $5,000
Typical Range: $10,000 to $50,000
***Note:** Average grant figure excludes highest grant.

Recent Grants

Note: Grants derived from 2002 Form 990.
Library-Related

35,000	Friends of Concord Pike Library, Wilmington, DE

General

200,000	Children's Hospital for Philadelphia, Philadelphia, PA
175,000	United Way of Delaware Inc., Wilmington, DE
100,000	Children's Hospital of Philadelphia, Philadelphia, PA
100,000	Tower Hill School, Wilmington, DE
100,000	Wilmington Friends School, Wilmington, DE
100,000	Wilmington Friends School, Wilmington, DE
90,000	Johns Hopkins Medicine, Baltimore, MD
75,000	College of Human Services, Education & Public Policy / University of Delaware, Newark, DE
75,000	College of Human Services, Education & Public Policy / University of Delaware, Newark, DE
75,000	Saint Francis Foundation, Wilmington, DE

LAKE PLACID EDUCATION FOUNDATION

Giving Contact

John S. Lansing, Executive Director
157 Saranac Avenue
Lake Placid, NY 12946
Phone: (518)523-4433

Description

Founded: 1922
EIN: 510243919
Organization Type: Private Foundation
Giving Locations: NY
Grant Types: Fellowship, General Support, Matching, Scholarship.

Donor Information

Founder: the late Melvil Dewey

Financial Summary

Total Giving: $2,392,110 (fiscal year ending June 30, 2001)
Giving Analysis: Giving for fiscal 2001 includes: foundation scholarships ($5,500)
Assets: $6,572,237 (fiscal 2001)
Gifts Received: $1,000 (fiscal 2001); $6,200 (fiscal 1997); $152,315 (fiscal 1996). Note: In fiscal 1997, contributions were received from various individuals for SL Youth AA.

Typical Recipients

Arts & Humanities: Arts Associations & Councils, Arts Centers, Arts Outreach, History & Archaeology, Libraries, Museums/Galleries, Music

Civic & Public Affairs: Clubs, Economic Development, Civic & Public Affairs-General, Philanthropic Organizations, Public Policy

Education: Arts/Humanities Education, Colleges & Universities, Faculty Development, Education-General, Literacy, Private Education (Precollege), Public Education (Precollege), Science/Mathematics Education, Student Aid

Religion: Churches

Social Services: Camps, Counseling, Day Care, Shelters/Homelessness

Application Procedures

Initial Contact: The foundation has no formal grant application procedure or application form. Send a brief letter of inquiry.
Deadlines: November 1.

Restrictions

Grants are generally limited to educational purposes.

Foundation Officials

Henry M. Bonner: director
Fred E. Brown: director
William J. Bumsted: director
Frederick C. Calder: vice president
Walter W. Curley: president
W. John Friedlander: director
George G. Hart: secretary
John S. Lansing: executive director
Meredith Prime: director
Peter F. Roland: director

Grants Analysis

Disclosure Period: fiscal year ending June 30, 2001
Total Grants: $2,386,610*
Number of Grants: 35
Average Grant: $8,577*
Highest Grant: $2,095,000
Typical Range: $1,000 to $25,000
***Note:** Giving excludes scholarships. Average grant figure excludes highest grant.

Recent Grants

Note: Grants derived from fiscal 2001 Form 990.
Library-Related

25,500	Lake Placid Public Library, Lake Placid, NY -- debt servicing
20,000	New York Library Association, Albany, NY -- library purposes and fellowships
7,410	Long Lake Library, Long Lake, NY -- education

General

2,095,000	Adirondack Community Crestview Plaza, Lake Placid, NY -- Dewey Endowment
50,000	National Sports Academy, Lake Placid, NY -- education
40,000	Northwood School, Lake Placid, NY -- education
35,000	Lake Placid Center for Arts, Lake Placid, NY -- arts and humanities
20,000	North Country School, Lake Placid, NY -- education
10,000	Adirondack Explorer, Saranac Lake, NY -- operations
10,000	Lake Placid Institute, Lake Placid, NY -- arts and humanities
10,000	Samaritan Family Counseling, Keene, NY -- social service
9,080	Lake Placid Central School, Lake Placid, NY -- education
9,050	Saranac Lake Central School, Saranac Lake, NY -- education

LAMB FOUNDATION

Giving Contact

Frank Lamb, Director
PO Box 1705
Lake Oswego, OR 97035-0575
Phone: (503)635-8010

Description

Founded: 1971
EIN: 237120564
Organization Type: Private Foundation
Giving Locations: OR
Grant Types: Emergency, General Support, Project, Seed Money.

Donor Information

Founder: members of the Lamb family

Financial Summary

Total Giving: $242,400 (2002); $180,110 (2001)
Assets: $4,713,649 (2002); $5,618,838 (2001)

Typical Recipients

Arts & Humanities: Arts Associations & Councils, Arts Festivals, Ballet, Community Arts, History & Archaeology, Libraries, Literary Arts, Museums/Galleries, Music, Public Broadcasting, Theater
Civic & Public Affairs: Botanical Gardens/Parks, Clubs, Economic Development, Civic & Public Affairs-General, Hispanic Affairs, Housing, Municipalities/Towns, Native American Affairs, Public Policy, Urban & Community Affairs
Education: Afterschool/Enrichment Programs, Arts/Humanities Education, Business Education, Colleges & Universities, Community & Junior Colleges, Continuing Education, Economic Education, Education-General, Literacy, Private Education (Precollege), Religious Education, Student Aid
Environment: Air/Water Quality, Forestry, Environment-General, Resource Conservation, Wildlife Protection
Health: Cancer, Children's Health/Hospitals, Clinics/Medical Centers, Diabetes, Emergency/Ambulance Services, Health Organizations, Hospices, Hospitals
Religion: Religious Welfare
Social Services: Animal Protection, At-Risk Youth, Camps, Child Welfare, Community Centers, Community Service Organizations, Crime Prevention, Day Care, Delinquency & Criminal Rehabilitation, Family Planning, Family Services, Food/Clothing Distribution, People with Disabilities, Recreation & Athletics, Shelters/Homelessness, Social Services-General, Youth Organizations

Application Procedures

Initial Contact: Send a brief letter of inquiry.
Application Requirements: Include amount requested, purpose of funds sought and any additional information or brochures applicable.
Deadlines: None.

Restrictions

Does not support individuals.

Additional Information

Publications: Annual Report

Foundation Officials

Anita Lamb Bailey: director
Ben Bailey: director
Toff Bailey: director
Barbara Lamb: director
Carl Lamb: director
Dorothy Lamb: director
Frank Lamb: chairman
Greg Lamb: director
Helen Lamb: director
Maryann Lamb: treasurer
Paula L. Lamb: vchairman
Peter Lamb: director

Grants Analysis

Disclosure Period: calendar year ending 2002
Total Grants: $242,400
Number of Grants: 82
Average Grant: $2,956
Highest Grant: $12,500
Lowest Grant: $250
Typical Range: $1,000 to $5,000

Recent Grants

Note: Grants derived from 2001 Form 990.
General

7,500	Caldera
5,000	Center for Watershed and Community Health, Springfield, OR
5,000	Eastern Oregon Regional Arts Council, La Grande, OR
5,000	Heart of Oregon Corps, OR
5,000	Jackson Bottom Wetland Preservation
5,000	Mother Oak's Child
5,000	Nature Conservancy of Oregon, Portland, OR
5,000	Portland House of Umoja, Portland, OR
5,000	Pregnancy Centers
5,000	Shangri-La Corporation, Salem, OR

LAMCO COMMUNICATIONS

Company Headquarters

Williamsport, PA

Operating Locations

Lamco Communications (PA--Williamsport)

Lamco Foundation

Giving Contact

Andrew Stabler, Jr., Relationship Banking Leader
Care of M & T Trust
101 W. Third St.
Williamsport, PA 17701
Phone: (670)327-2174

Description

EIN: 246012727
Organization Type: Corporate Foundation
Giving Locations: PA
Grant Types: Award, Capital, Emergency, Employee Matching Gifts, Endowment, Fellowship, General Support, Operating Expenses, Project, Scholarship.

Financial Summary

Total Giving: $54,500 (2003)
Assets: $777,846 (2003)
Gifts Received: $5,000 (2003); $25,000 (1998).
Note: In 1989, contributions were received from LamCo. Communications.

Typical Recipients

Arts & Humanities: Art History, Arts Appreciation, Community Arts, Arts & Humanities-General, History & Archaeology, Libraries, Museums/Galleries, Music, Public Broadcasting
Civic & Public Affairs: Business/Free Enterprise, Chambers of Commerce, Community Foundations, Economic Development, Civic & Public Affairs-General, Housing, Inner-City Development, Urban & Community Affairs, Women's Affairs
Education: Business Education, Colleges & Universities, Economic Education, Education Funds, Education-General, Medical Education
Environment: Air/Water Quality
Health: Alzheimer's Disease, Cancer, Diabetes, Emergency/Ambulance Services, Eyes/Blindness, Health-General, Health Funds, Hospitals, Medical Research, Preventive Medicine/Wellness Organizations
International: Health Care/Hospitals, Missionary/Religious Activities
Religion: Churches, Religion-General, Ministries, Religious Organizations, Religious Welfare
Science: Science-General, Science Museums, Scientific Centers & Institutes
Social Services: Animal Protection, Camps, Child Welfare, Community Centers, Community Service Organizations, Emergency Relief, Family Services, Homes, People with Disabilities, Recreation & Athletics, Scouts, Shelters/Homelessness, Social Services-General, United Funds/United Ways, YMCA/YWCA/YMHA/YWHA, Youth Organizations

Application Procedures

Initial Contact: Send a full proposal. Include a description of organization, amount requested, and purpose of funds sought.
Deadlines: None.

Restrictions

Does not support organizations outside operating areas.

Additional Information

Trust(s): M & T Trust Co.

Corporate Officials

Frank Concino, Jr.: president, chief executive officer
PRIM CORP EMPL president, chief executive officer: Lamco Communications.

Foundation Officials

Andrew Stabler: adv comm

Grants Analysis

Disclosure Period: calendar year ending 2003
Total Grants: $54,500
Number of Grants: 17
Average Grant: $2,469*
Highest Grant: $15,000
Lowest Grant: $200
Typical Range: $1,000 to $5,000
***Note:** Average grant figure excludes highest grant.

Recent Grants

Note: Grants derived from 2003 Form 990.
General

15,000	Little League Baseball, Williamsport, PA -- funds for program activities
10,000	Hope Enterprises, Williamsport, PA -- funds for service activities
6,000	American Rescue Workers, Williamsport, PA -- funds for program activities
5,000	Repasz Band, Williamsport, PA -- funds for service activities
3,400	American Red Cross, Williamsport, PA -- funds for service activities
3,000	Lycoming County Historical Society, Williamsport, PA -- funds for program activities
2,000	Children's Development CE, Williamsport, PA -- funds for service activities
2,000	Hemlock Girl Scout Council, Williamsport, PA -- funds for service activities
2,000	Williamsport Hospital Foundation, Williamsport, PA -- funds for service activities
1,000	Salvation Army, Williamsport, PA -- funds for service activities

LAND O'LAKES INC.

Company Headquarters

4001 Lexington Ave. N.
St. Paul, MN 55126
Web: http://www.landolakesinc.com

Company Description

Founded: 1921
Revenue: US$7.742 billion (2004)
Profit: US$21.4 million (2004)
Employees: 8000 (2003)
Fortune Rank: 279, per FORTUNE Magazine's list of 500 Largest U.S. Corporations (2004).
SIC(s): 2021 Creamery Butter, 5143 Dairy Products Except Dried or Canned, 5451 Dairy Products Stores.

Operating Locations

Land O'Lakes, Inc. (CA--Orland; FL--Orange City; ID; IA--Audubon; MN--Browerville, Luverne, Minneapolis; MT; NE--Hardy, Reynolds, Superior; OR; SD--

Sioux Falls, Volga; UT; WA; WI--Kiel, Pulaski, Spencer; WY)

Nonmonetary Support

Value: $450,000 (1998)
Type: Donated Products; Loaned Executives
Volunteer Programs: Supports a Dollars for Doers program, which provides cash donations to organizations where employees volunteer. At many company plants and offices, Community Involvement Councils organize and coordinate community activities for employees. The company also supports Expanding Community and Horizon Outreach for Seniors (ECHOS), a volunteer program for company retirees.
Note: Food donations are made only through Second Harvest Foodbank Network.

Land O'Lakes Foundation

Giving Contact

Bonnie Bassett, Executive Director
Land O'Lakes Foundation
PO Box 64150
St. Paul, MN 55164-0150
Phone: (651)481-2212
Fax: (651)481-2000
E-mail: bbbass@landolakes.com
Web: http://www.foundation.landolakes.com

Description

EIN: 411864977
Organization Type: Corporate Foundation
Giving Locations: AR; CA; CO; ID; IN; IA; MD; MI; MN; MT; NE; ND; OH; OR; PA; SD; VA; WA; WI
Grant Types: Capital, Employee Matching Gifts, Endowment, General Support, Operating Expenses, Professorship, Project, Seed Money.
Note: Employee matching gift ratio: 1 to 1 for gifts to post-secondary education, ranging from $25 to $500 annually. Also offers a cooperative match program (for member cooperatives).

Financial Summary

Total Giving: $995,835 (2003); $1,404,239 (2002); $1,368,958 (2001)
Giving Analysis: Giving for 2001 includes: foundation matching gifts ($77,913); foundation ($1,443,260)
Assets: $2,000,000 (2004 approx); $2,719,728 (2003); $2,495,864 (2002)
Gifts Received: $925,000 (2003); $2,380,000 (2002); $1,145,165 (2001). Note: Contributions were received from Land O'Lakes, Inc.

Typical Recipients

Arts & Humanities: Arts Associations & Councils,' Arts Centers, Arts Funds, Arts Institutes, Community Arts, Ethnic & Folk Arts, Arts & Humanities-General, Historic Preservation, History & Archaeology, Libraries, Literary Arts, Museums/Galleries, Music, Opera, Performing Arts, Public Broadcasting, Theater
Civic & Public Affairs: African American Affairs, Business/Free Enterprise, Clubs, Community Foundations, Economic Policy, Employment/Job Training, Civic & Public Affairs-General, Housing, Municipalities/Towns, Native American Affairs, Parades/Festivals, Professional & Trade Associations, Public Policy, Rural Affairs, Safety, Urban & Community Affairs, Zoos/Aquariums
Education: Agricultural Education, Business Education, Colleges & Universities, Continuing Education, Economic Education, Education Funds, Elementary Education (Public), Faculty Development, Education-General, Leadership Training, Minority Education, Private Education (Precollege), Public Education (Precollege), Secondary Education (Public), Social Sciences Education, Student Aid

Environment: Environment-General, Resource Conservation, Wildlife Protection
Health: Cancer, Children's Health/Hospitals, Clinics/Medical Centers, Emergency/Ambulance Services, Geriatric Health, Health Funds, Health Organizations
International: International-General, International Development, International Relief Efforts
Religion: Religion-General, Religious Welfare
Science: Science Museums, Scientific Centers & Institutes
Social Services: Big Brothers/Big Sisters, Child Welfare, Community Centers, Crime Prevention, Day Care, Domestic Violence, Emergency Relief, Family Services, Food/Clothing Distribution, People with Disabilities, Recreation & Athletics, Senior Services, Shelters/Homelessness, Social Services-General, Special Olympics, United Funds/United Ways, Volunteer Services, YMCA/YWCA/YMHA/YWHA, Youth Organizations

Application Procedures

Initial Contact: For direct company grants toward programs of local interest, send a brief letter on organization's stationery to facility manager at nearest Land O'Lakes facility; for other corporate grants and for foundation grants, write or see website for application form.
Application Requirements: Include completed application, a copy of the most recent annual report with financial information included, or a brief history and current activities of the organization; a current operating budget and proposed budget; a copy of the organization's tax-exempt ruling, or description of organization's ownership and/or management.
Deadlines: April 1, July 1, September 1, and December 1 for general grants; for arts grants over $5,000, April 1.
Review Process: For direct company giving: operating locations are responsible for budgeting contributions strictly benefiting their communities; requests with broad applications are submitted to headquarters. For foundation giving: requests will be reviewed by foundation board for grants of over $5,000, and by the foundation staff for grants of less than $5,000.
Evaluative Criteria: The foundation looks for quality delivery of a needed service; potential benefit to a substantial segment of community; results which are predictable and can be evaluated; broad-based community support; competent, qualified staff and board; fiscal and management capability to carry out program.
Decision Notification: The foundation board meets in January, May, August, and October.

Restrictions

Does not support individuals; lobbying, political, or religious organizations; veteran, fraternal, or labor organizations; advertising; fund-raising events, dinners, or benefits; scholarships, or private colleges or universities; travel expenses; disease/medical research or treatment; or racing/sports sponsorships.

Additional Information

Because Land O'Lakes is a farmer-owned cooperative, rural and agriculture-related programs receive special consideration. About 80% of donations are made to rural areas, and 20% to urban communities. Special consideration also is given to organizations in which company employees are involved.
In December 1996, "Land O'Lakes, Inc., officially created and endowed the Land O'Lakes Foundation...with an initial donation of $2,000,000. The foundation continues Land O'Lakes' well-established corporate giving program and focuses on improving the quality of life in rural America."
Land O'Lakes dedicates 2% of pre-tax earnings to charitable giving, with 1.5% going to the Foundation and .5% into direct corporate giving.
The company and the foundation continue to focus on the North Central, Northwest and Eastern United States, where most of their operating facilities are located; also on rural areas.

The Foundation also matches dollar for dollar grants made by member co-operatives. Organizations should apply directly to the local co-op, which can request a match from the foundation.
Publications: Community Grants Program Guidelines

Corporate Officials

Lydia Botham: director test kitchens PRIM CORP EMPL director test kitchens: Land O'Lakes, Inc.
John E. Gherty: president, chief executive officer B New Richmond, WI 1944. ED University of Wisconsin BBA (1965); University of Wisconsin JD (1970); University of Wisconsin MA (1970). PRIM CORP EMPL president, chief executive officer: Land O'Lakes, Inc. CORP AFFIL member executive committee: CF Industries Inc.; director: Recovery Engineering Inc.; director: Alpine Lace Brands Inc.; director: Cenex/Land O Lakes Agronomy Co. NONPR AFFIL member, director: National Council Farmer Coops; director: National Parenting Association; director: Minnesota Business Partnership; member: American Bar Association; director: Graduate Institute Coop Leadership.

Foundation Officials

Bonnie Bassett: executive director
Don Berg: director
Lydia Botham: treasurer (see above)
Lawrence Hooks: director
Jane Kleinkramer: director
Manuel Maciel, Jr.: chairman
Bonnie Neuenfeldt: executive director PRIM CORP EMPL director community relations: Land O'Lakes, Inc.
Dave Reinders: vice chairman, secretary
Bob Winner: director

Grants Analysis

Disclosure Period: calendar year ending 2003
Total Grants: $989,224*
Number of Grants: 625 (approx)
Average Grant: $1,583
Highest Grant: $50,000
Lowest Grant: $100
Typical Range: $100 to $3,000
*Note: Giving excludes United Way. Giving includes matching gifts.

Recent Grants

Note: Grants derived from 2003 Form 990.
General

110,000	Greater Twin Cities United Way, Minneapolis, MN
60,000	National 4-H Council, Chevy Chase, MD
60,000	National FFA Foundation, Indianapolis, IN
25,000	Friends of the St. Paul Farmers' Market, Shoreview, MN
20,000	Children's Theatre Company and School, Minneapolis, MN
10,000	Farm Safety 4 Just Kids, Earlham, IA
10,000	Holstein Foundation, Brattleboro, VT
7,500	American Cancer Society, Pewaukee, WI
7,500	Second Harvest Heartland, Maplewood, MN
6,000	Child Nutrition Foundation, Alexandria, VA

LANDEGGER CHARITABLE FOUNDATION

Giving Contact

Jewell L. Fair, Secretary
2090 S. Nova Rd., Suite B-221
South Daytona, FL 32119
Phone: (386)763-9220

Description

Founded: 1975
EIN: 510180544
Organization Type: Private Foundation
Giving Locations: DC: Washington
Grant Types: General Support, Multiyear/Continuing Support.

Financial Summary

Total Giving: $783,500 (fiscal year ending October 31, 2001)
Assets: $13,322,229 (fiscal 2001)

Typical Recipients

Arts & Humanities: Arts Centers, Dance, Historic Preservation, Libraries, Museums/Galleries
Civic & Public Affairs: Civic & Public Affairs-General, Urban & Community Affairs
Education: Colleges & Universities, Community & Junior Colleges, Education-General, International Studies, Literacy, Private Education (Precollege), Religious Education, Secondary Education (Private), Student Aid
Health: Clinics/Medical Centers, Hospitals
International: Foreign Educational Institutions, International Affairs, International Relief Efforts, Missionary/Religious Activities
Religion: Churches, Religion-General, Jewish Causes, Religious Welfare
Social Services: Child Welfare, Community Service Organizations, Family Services, Recreation & Athletics

Application Procedures

Initial Contact: Send a brief letter of inquiry describing program or project.
Deadlines: None.

Foundation Officials

John F. Bolt: secretary
Jewell L. Fair: secretary
Carl Clement Landegger: treasurer, director B Vienna, Austria 1930. ED Georgetown University BS (1951). PRIM CORP EMPL chairman, director: Black Clawson Co. CORP AFFIL vice chairman: Parsons & Whittemore; chairman: Saint Anne Nackawic Pulp & Paper Co.; chairman: AlabamaRiver Pulp Co.; director: Downingtown Manufacturing Co. NONPR AFFIL director: Georgetown University; trustee: New York Historical Society. CLUB AFFIL Explorers Club; Road Runners Club.
George Francis Landegger: president, director B 1938. PRIM CORP EMPL chairman, chief executive officer, director: Parsons & Whittemore Enterprises Corp.
Arthur L. Schwartz: vice president PRIM CORP EMPL president, director: Parsons & Whittemore Enterprises Corp.

Grants Analysis

Disclosure Period: fiscal year ending October 31, 2001
Total Grants: $783,500
Number of Grants: 76
Average Grant: $5,493*
Highest Grant: $277,000
Lowest Grant: $250
Typical Range: $1,000 to $10,000
*Note: Average grant figure excludes two highest grants ($377,000).

Recent Grants

Note: Grants derived from 2001 Form 990.
General

277,000	Georgetown University, Washington, DC
100,000	Association of Jesuit Colleges and Universities, Washington, DC
54,000	Americares Foundation
50,000	Gregorian University Foundation
27,500	Interaid, Inc., Washington, DC
27,500	Taft School, Watertown, CT
25,000	Lifewater International, Arcadia, CA
25,000	Louise H & Arthur Schwartz Foundation, Inc.
22,500	Lenox Hill Neighborhood House, New York, NY
20,000	Abraham House

LANDMARK COMMUNICATIONS INC.

Company Headquarters

150 W. Brambleton Ave.
Norfolk, VA 23510
Web: http://www.landmarkcom.com

Company Description

Revenue: US$732 million (2002)
Employees: 5000 (2003)
SIC(s): 2711 Newspapers, 2752 Commercial Printing--Lithographic, 2759 Commercial Printing Nec, 4833 Television Broadcasting Stations.

Operating Locations

Landmark Communications Inc. (NV--Las Vegas; NC--Greensboro; VA--Norfolk, Roanoke)

Nonmonetary Support

Type: Cause-related Marketing & Promotion; In-kind Services; Loaned Executives

Landmark Communications Foundation

Giving Contact

Linda Hyatt, Executive Director
150 W. Brambleton Avenue
Norfolk, VA 23510
Phone: (757)446-2016
Fax: (757)446-2489
E-mail: Lhyatt@Lcimedia.com

Description

EIN: 546038902
Organization Type: Corporate Foundation
Giving Locations: MD; NV: Las Vegas; NC; SC; TN; VA
Grant Types: Capital, Conference/Seminar, Emergency, Endowment, Fellowship, Multiyear/Continuing Support.
Note: Also offers leadership gifts.

Financial Summary

Total Giving: $1,982,249 (2002); $2,401,361 (2001). Note: Contributes through corporate direct giving program and foundation.
Assets: $46,704,887 (2002); $53,481,734 (2001)
Gifts Received: $797,497 (2002); $786,423 (2001); $1,048,505 (1999). Note: Foundation receives contributions from Landmark Communications, Inc., and its subsidiaries.

Typical Recipients

Arts & Humanities: Arts Associations & Councils, Arts Centers, Arts Funds, Ballet, Ethnic & Folk Arts, Arts & Humanities-General, Historic Preservation, History & Archaeology, Museums/Galleries, Music, Opera, Public Broadcasting, Theater
Civic & Public Affairs: African American Affairs, Asian American Affairs, Civil Rights, Clubs, Community Foundations, Civic & Public Affairs-General, Housing, Nonprofit Management, Philanthropic Organizations, Professional & Trade Associations, Public Policy, Urban & Community Affairs, Zoos/Aquariums

Education: Business Education, Colleges & Universities, Community & Junior Colleges, Education Associations, Education Funds, Faculty Development, Education-General, Journalism/Media Education, Literacy, Minority Education, Preschool Education, Public Education (Precollege), Science/Mathematics Education, Social Sciences Education, Special Education, Student Aid
Environment: Resource Conservation
Health: Emergency/Ambulance Services, Health-General, Hospitals, Research/Studies Institutes
Religion: Bible Study/Translation, Ministries, Religious Welfare
Science: Science Museums, Scientific Centers & Institutes
Social Services: Child Welfare, Community Service Organizations, Crime Prevention, Day Care, Family Services, Food/Clothing Distribution, People with Disabilities, Scouts, Shelters/Homelessness, Social Services-General, United Funds/United Ways, Volunteer Services, YMCA/YWCA/YMHA/YWHA, Youth Organizations

Application Procedures

Initial Contact: Send one-page letter to the president of the nearest subsidiary.
Application Requirements: Include a description of organization, amount requested, purpose of funds sought, impact foundation funds would have on the program and community, evidence of other support, program timetable, expected sources of future revenue, program budget, and proof of tax-exempt status.
Deadlines: None.
Review Process: Applications are screened by local company and, if approved, forwarded to the foundation for further screening and possible inclusion in the foundation's annual budget.
Evaluative Criteria: Priority given to projects that reach a broad section of the community; yield substantial benefits to the community for costs involved; promote cooperation among agencies within their fields of interest; project seeks funds for new innovative programs, or to expand an innovative program to other parts of the community; demonstrates major support from other donors and can use foundation support to attract greater community support; is part of a capital campaign; demonstrates in-kind services; has not received foundation funding for a similar program.

Restrictions

Foundation does not make grants to organizations not tax-exempt under IRS standards, individuals, or any organization that has received a capital pledge from the foundation within the preceding two years. Foundation does not give for religious or political purposes; fundraising events; deficit financing; projects normally the responsibility of a government agency; health care; or medical education or research.

Additional Information

Individual budgets from participating Landmark companies are submitted to corporate headquarters in November each year, where they are reviewed and receive final approval during the month of January. Capital pledges are made with the provision that a campaign meets its goal and that the project goes forward as proposed.
Programs supportive of the broadcasting and publishing industries on a national scale occasionally receive grants from corporate headquarters.
Publications: Foundation Guidelines

Corporate Officials

Frank Batten, Sr.: chairman vice president B Norfolk, VA 1927. ED University of Virginia BA (1950); Harvard University MBA (1952). PRIM CORP EMPL chairman: Landmark Communications Inc. CORP AFFIL chairman: Roanoke Times; chairman, founder: Weather Channel; chairman: Norfolk Virginian-Pilot & Ledger Star; chairman: Greensboro Daily News & Record; chairman: KLAS-TV Las Vegas; director:

Capital Gazette Communication Inc. NONPR AFFIL trustee: U.S. Naval Academy Foundation; trustee: University Virginia Colgate Business School; trustee: Southern Newspaper Publishers Association Foundation; member: Delta Kappa; member: Newspaper Association America; trustee: Culver Education Foundation.

Frank Batten, Jr.: executive vice president B 1958. PRIM CORP EMPL executive vice president: Landmark Communications Inc. ADD CORP EMPL president: Commonwealth Printing Co.

Foundation Officials

Frank Batten, Jr.: president, director (see above)
Frank Batten, Sr.: chairman, director (see above)
Linda S. Hyatt: vice president, executive director

Grants Analysis

Disclosure Period: calendar year ending 2002
Total Grants: $1,548,374*
Number of Grants: 189
Average Grant: $8,192
Highest Grant: $113,000
Lowest Grant: $500
Typical Range: $1,000 to $25,000
***Note:** Giving excludes United Way.

Recent Grants

Note: Grants derived from 2003 Form 990.
General

182,000	United Way of South Hampton Roads, Norfolk, VA
113,000	Business Consortium for Arts Support, Norfolk, VA -- towards arts and museums
75,000	United Way of Roanoke Valley, Roanoke, VA
60,000	Ferrum College, Norfolk, VA -- towards education
52,550	United Way of Greater Greensboro, Greensboro, NC
50,000	Chrysler Museum of Art, Norfolk, VA -- towards arts and museums
50,000	Hollins University, Roanoke, VA -- towards education
50,000	YMCA of South Hampton Roads, Norfolk, VA -- towards human services
39,579	Clark County Public Education Foundation, Las Vegas, NV -- towards special initiatives
36,624	Clark County Public Education Foundation, Las Vegas, NV -- towards education

LANE FAMILY CHARITABLE TRUST

Giving Contact

R&J Lane
Lane Family Charitable Trust
500 Almer Rd., No. 301
Burlingame, CA 94010
Phone: (415)348-4026

Description

EIN: 946585396
Organization Type: Private Foundation
Giving Locations: CA: San Francisco, San Mateo
Grant Types: General Support.

Financial Summary

Total Giving: $640,000 (fiscal year ending June 30, 2004); $478,075 (fiscal 2001)
Assets: $3,465,442 (fiscal 2004); $4,310,910 (fiscal 2001)
Gifts Received: $510,150 (fiscal 2000); $648,595 (fiscal 1997); $150,000 (fiscal 1996). Note: In fiscal 1996 and 2000, contributions were received from Ralph and Joan Lane.

Typical Recipients

Arts & Humanities: Arts Associations & Councils, Film & Video, Libraries, Literary Arts, Theater
Civic & Public Affairs: Community Foundations, Economic Development, Employment/Job Training, Ethnic Organizations, Civic & Public Affairs-General, Hispanic Affairs, Law & Justice, Philanthropic Organizations, Urban & Community Affairs
Education: Colleges & Universities, Community & Junior Colleges, Education Funds, Education-General, Preschool Education, Public Education (Precollege), Religious Education, Secondary Education (Private), Student Aid
Environment: Environment-General, Resource Conservation
Health: AIDS/HIV, Cancer, Clinics/Medical Centers, Health Organizations
International: International Affairs
Religion: Churches, Religion-General, Religious Organizations, Religious Welfare, Social/Policy Issues
Social Services: Child Abuse, Child Welfare, Community Service Organizations, Counseling, Domestic Violence, Family Planning, Family Services, Food/Clothing Distribution, Recreation & Athletics, Shelters/Homelessness, YMCA/YWCA/YMHA/YWHA, Youth Organizations

Application Procedures

Initial Contact: Send a brief letter of inquiry.
Application Requirements: Include purpose of funds sought and manner of expending funds.

Foundation Officials

Joan Lane: trustee
Ralph Lane: trustee

Grants Analysis

Disclosure Period: fiscal year ending June 30, 2004
Total Grants: $640,000
Number of Grants: 39
Average Grant: $10,263*
Highest Grant: $250,000
Lowest Grant: $3,000
Typical Range: $5,000 to $20,000
***Note:** Average grant figure excludes highest grant.

Recent Grants

Note: Grants derived from fiscal 2004 Form 990.
General

250,000	University of San Francisco, San Francisco, CA
25,000	Central Coast Interfaith, Watsonville, CA
25,000	San Francisco Unified Schools, San Francisco, CA
25,000	San Mateo County Community College Foundation, San Mateo, CA
25,000	Transport for Livable City, San Francisco, CA
20,000	Sierra Pac Soroptimist Foundation, Watsonville, CA
15,000	Peninsula Interfaith Action, San Carlos, CA
15,000	Peninsula Interfaith Action, San Carlos, CA
15,000	Youth and Family Enrichment Services, San Carlos, CA
10,000	Sunset Youth Services, San Francisco, CA

MINNIE AND BERNARD LANE FOUNDATION

Giving Contact

R. L. Short, Trustee
414 Washington Street
Altavista, VA 24517
Phone: (804)369-6663

Alternate Contact

Bernard Lane, Trustee

Description

EIN: 546052404
Organization Type: Private Foundation
Giving Locations: VA
Grant Types: General Support.

Donor Information

Founder: Bernard B. Lane, Minnie B. Lane

Financial Summary

Total Giving: $815,590 (fiscal year ending March 31, 2001)
Giving Analysis: Giving for fiscal 2001 includes: foundation grants to United Way ($500)
Assets: $8,719,109 (fiscal 2001)
Gifts Received: $270,880 (fiscal 2001); $294,371 (fiscal 2000); $5,994 (fiscal 1997). Note: In fiscal 2001, contributions were received from Crestar Bank ($262,924) and Bernard B. Lane, Jr. ($7,956). In fiscal 2000, contributions were received from Crestar Bank. In fiscal 1997, contributions were received from Bernard B. Lane, Jr.

Typical Recipients

Arts & Humanities: Arts & Humanities-General, Historic Preservation, Libraries, Music, Public Broadcasting
Civic & Public Affairs: Employment/Job Training, Civic & Public Affairs-General, Municipalities/Towns, Philanthropic Organizations, Professional & Trade Associations, Urban & Community Affairs
Education: Arts/Humanities Education, Colleges & Universities, Community & Junior Colleges, Education Funds, Engineering/Technological Education, International Exchange, Minority Education, Private Education (Precollege), Public Education (Precollege)
Environment: Forestry
Health: Clinics/Medical Centers, Emergency/Ambulance Services, Eyes/Blindness, Health Organizations, Hospitals, Medical Research, Prenatal Health Issues, Single-Disease Health Associations
International: Health Care/Hospitals, International Relief Efforts, Missionary/Religious Activities
Religion: Churches, Religion-General, Ministries, Missionary Activities (Domestic), Religious Organizations, Religious Welfare, Seminaries
Social Services: Animal Protection, Community Centers, Community Service Organizations, Emergency Relief, Food/Clothing Distribution, People with Disabilities, Scouts, Shelters/Homelessness, United Funds/United Ways, YMCA/YWCA/YMHA/YWHA, Youth Organizations

Application Procedures

Initial Contact: Send a brief letter of inquiry.
Application Requirements: Include applicant's name and address, a description of organization, amount requested, and purpose of funds sought.
Deadlines: None.

Restrictions

Does not support individuals.

Foundation Officials

Cindy Jester: administrative assistant
Bernard Bell Lane: director B Lynchburg, VA 1928. ED United States Naval Academy BS (1950). NONPR AFFIL member: Board Project Concern International; member: Virginia Manufacturers Association.
Minnie B. Lane: director

Grants Analysis

Disclosure Period: fiscal year ending March 31, 2001
Total Grants: $815,090*
Number of Grants: 142

Average Grant: $5,740
Highest Grant: $84,000
Typical Range: $100 to $25,000
*Note: Giving excludes United Way.

Recent Grants

Note: Grants derived from 2001 Form 990.
General
84,000	Altavista Area YMCA, Altavista, VA
58,350	Lane Memorial Methodist Church, Altavista, VA
50,000	Randolph Macon Academy, Front Royal, VA
46,000	New Covenant School, Lynchburg, VA
45,170	Project Concern International, San Diego, CA
40,000	Food for the Hungry, Scottsdale, AZ
25,000	Hickory Christian Academy, Hickory, NC
25,000	Princeton University, Princeton, NJ
25,000	SEMILLA, Chesapeake, VA
25,000	United Methodist Foundation, Richmond, VA

EUGENE M. LANG FOUNDATION

Giving Contact
Eugene M. Lang, Contact
Eugene M. Lang Foundation
535 5th Avenue, Suite 906
New York, NY 10017
Phone: (212)949-4100
Fax: (212)286-8964

Description
Founded: 1963
EIN: 136153412
Organization Type: General Purpose Foundation
Giving Locations: NY: New York, nationally nationally.
Grant Types: General Support, Scholarship.

Donor Information
Founder: The foundation was established in 1968 by Eugene M. Lang. Mr. Lang is the founder and president of REFAC Technology Development Corporation, which licenses and promotes new technologies. He is most well-known for his offer to pay college tuition for a sixth-grade class at New York City's P.S. 121, which he attended as a youth. The I Have a Dream Foundation offers programs to motivate disadvantaged grade school students to attend college by offering scholarships, reading materials, support groups, and counseling services.

Financial Summary
Total Giving: $1,796,068 (2002)
Assets: $36,770,040 (2002)
Gifts Received: $75,000 (2002); $150,000 (2000); $5,489,896 (1998). Note: In 1998, stock contributions were received from Eugene M. Lang. In 1996, the foundation received contributions from Eugene M. Lang. In previous years, the foundation received contributions from Susan Safer.

Typical Recipients
Arts & Humanities: Arts Festivals, Libraries, Museums/Galleries, Music, Opera, Performing Arts, Public Broadcasting, Theater
Civic & Public Affairs: African American Affairs, Botanical Gardens/Parks, Civic & Public Affairs-General, Law & Justice, Legal Aid, Philanthropic Organizations, Public Policy, Urban & Community Affairs, Women's Affairs, Zoos/Aquariums
Education: Arts/Humanities Education, Business Education, Colleges & Universities, Community & Junior Colleges, Education Funds, Education Reform,

Elementary Education (Public), Education-General, Legal Education, Literacy, Minority Education, Private Education (Precollege), Public Education (Precollege), Science/Mathematics Education, Secondary Education (Private), Social Sciences Education, Student Aid
Health: AIDS/HIV, Cancer, Children's Health/Hospitals, Clinics/Medical Centers, Health Organizations, Hospitals, Medical Rehabilitation, Mental Health
International: Foreign Arts Organizations, International Organizations, International Peace & Security Issues, International Relations, International Relief Efforts, Missionary/Religious Activities
Religion: Churches, Jewish Causes, Religious Welfare, Synagogues/Temples
Science: Science Museums
Social Services: Child Welfare, Community Service Organizations, Family Services, Recreation & Athletics, Shelters/Homelessness, Social Services-General, Youth Organizations

Application Procedures
Initial Contact: The foundation does not have a formal application. Grant requests should be submitted in letter form.
Deadlines: None.

Foundation Officials
David Lang: trustee
Eugene Michael Lang: donor, trustee B New York, NY March 16, 1919. ED Swarthmore College BA (1938); Columbia University School of Business Administration MS (1940); Polytechnic Institute Brooklyn (1941-1942). PRIM CORP EMPL founder, chairman: Refac Technology Development Corp. ADD CORP EMPL chairman emeritus: Refac International Ltd. CORP AFFIL director: Gough Econ Inc. NONPR AFFIL vice chairman, trustee: New School Social Research; chairman emeritus: Swarthmore College; director: Mannes College Music; director: Columbia University Graduate School Business; member: Licensing Executive Society; advisor director: Carnegie-Mellon University Graduate School Business Administration. CLUB AFFIL Yale Club; University Club; Century Country Club; Golden Key Club.
Jane Lang: trustee B 1947. ED Swarthmore College BA (1967); University of Pennsylvania JD (1970). PRIM CORP EMPL partner, attorney: Sprenger & Lang. NONPR AFFIL member: District of Columbia Bar Association; member: Minnesota State Bar Association.
Stephen Lang: trustee
Theresa Lang: trustee B Hochhausen, Germany 1952. ED Fordham University BA (1974); University of California, Los Angeles MBA (1982). PRIM CORP EMPL senior vice president, treasurer: Merrill Lynch & Co., Inc. ADD CORP EMPL president, treasurer: Merrill Lynch Group Inc. CORP AFFIL president, treasurer: Merrill Lynch Group Inc.
Paul Sprenger: member B 1940. ED University of Michigan BBA (1962); University of Michigan JD (1965). PRIM CORP EMPL partner, attorney: Sprenger & Lang. NONPR AFFIL member: District of Columbia Bar Association; member: Minnesota Bar Association.

Grants Analysis
Disclosure Period: calendar year ending 2002
Total Grants: $1,796,068*
Number of Grants: 138
Average Grant: $5,941*
Highest Grant: $350,000
Lowest Grant: $100
Typical Range: $1,000 to $25,000
*Note: Giving includes scholarships. Average grant figure excludes four highest grantss ($1,000,000).

Recent Grants
Note: Grants derived from 2002 Form 990.
Library-Related
5,000	New York Public Library, New York, NY

General
350,000	New York Presbyterian Hospital, New York, NY
250,000	New School University, New York, NY
250,000	New York Hospital Medical Center, Queens, NY
250,000	Project Pericles Inc.
100,000	Atlas Performing Arts Center, Washington, DC
50,000	Atlas Performing Arts Center, Washington, DC
33,000	Columbia Business School, New York, NY
32,500	Baruch College, New York, NY
25,000	I Have a Dream Foundation, New York, NY
25,000	Pace University, New York, NY

STANLEY S. LANGENDORF FOUNDATION

Giving Contact
Richard J. Guggenhime, President
3701 Sacramento Street
PMB377
San Francisco, CA 94118
Phone: (415)263-0780

Description
Founded: 1982
EIN: 942861512
Organization Type: Private Foundation
Giving Locations: CA: San Francisco
Grant Types: Fellowship, Operating Expenses, Project.

Donor Information
Founder: the late Stanley S. Langendorf

Financial Summary
Total Giving: $377,500 (2002 approx); $610,333 (2001)
Giving Analysis: Giving for 2001 includes: foundation scholarships ($40,000)
Assets: $16,448,948 (2001)
Gifts Received: $443,007 (1995)

Typical Recipients
Arts & Humanities: Arts Associations & Councils, Ballet, Community Arts, Dance, Ethnic & Folk Arts, History & Archaeology, Libraries, Museums/Galleries, Music, Opera, Performing Arts, Theater
Civic & Public Affairs: Botanical Gardens/Parks, Civic & Public Affairs-General, Housing, Public Policy, Urban & Community Affairs, Zoos/Aquariums
Education: Afterschool/Enrichment Programs, Colleges & Universities, International Studies, Leadership Training, Literacy, Minority Education, Private Education (Precollege), Secondary Education (Private), Secondary Education (Public), Student Aid
Health: Cancer, Geriatric Health, Health Organizations, Hospitals
International: International Affairs
Science: Science Museums, Scientific Centers & Institutes
Social Services: Big Brothers/Big Sisters, Camps, Child Welfare, Community Service Organizations, Family Services, Food/Clothing Distribution, People with Disabilities, Recreation & Athletics, Senior Services, Veterans, YMCA/YWCA/YMHA/YWHA, Youth Organizations

Application Procedures
Initial Contact: Submit a one-page letter.
Application Requirements: Include a description of the organization, amount requested, purpose of funds sought, project budget, organization budget.

Send six sets. Send one copy of recently audited financial statement and proof of tax-exempt status.
Deadlines: March 1, and October 1.

Restrictions

Does not support individuals. Limits funding primarily to the city and county of San Francisco

Additional Information

Publications: Application Guidelines

Foundation Officials

Charles H. Clifford, Jr.: director
Charles H. Clifford: treasurer
Richard Johnson Guggenhime: president, trustee B San Francisco, CA 1940. ED Stanford University AB (1961); Harvard University JD (1964). PRIM CORP EMPL partner: Heller, Ehrman, White & McAuliffe. CORP AFFIL director, member: North America Trust Co. NONPR AFFIL trustee: Saint Ignatius College Prep School; director, member: San Francisco Opera Association; member: American College Probate Counsel. CLUB AFFIL Wine & Food Society Club; Olympic Club; Thunderbird Country Club; Bohemian Club; Chevaliers du Tastevin Club.
Lisa G. Hauswirth: director
Ann Wagner: secretary, trustee

Grants Analysis

Disclosure Period: calendar year ending 2001
Total Grants: $570,333*
Number of Grants: 61
Average Grant: $7,984*
Highest Grant: $83,333
Typical Range: $5,000 to $25,000
*Note: Giving excludes scholarship. Average grant figure excludes highest grant.

Recent Grants

Note: Grants derived from 2001 Form 990.
General

83,333	San Francisco Zoological Society, San Francisco, CA -- for new amphitheater for educational programs
40,500	Marin Academy, San Rafael, CA -- for building campaign
30,000	Lick-Wilmerding High School, San Francisco, CA -- for scholarships
26,000	Coro Foundation, San Francisco, CA -- for Fellow Program
25,000	John Wayne Cancer Institute, Santa Monica, CA -- for operations
25,000	Marin City Children's Program, Marin City, CA -- for operations
25,000	San Francisco General Hospital, San Francisco, CA -- for Women's Imaging Center
25,000	San Francisco Opera Association, San Francisco, CA -- for In-school Program and performance attendance
25,000	World Affairs Council of Northern California, San Francisco, CA -- for Asilomar Conference
20,000	California Pacific Medical Center, San Francisco, CA -- for children with developmental disabilities

WALTER LANTZ FOUNDATION

Giving Contact

Edward A. Landry, Trustee
4444 Lakeside Dr., Ste. 310
Burbank, CA 91505
Phone: (818)842-1616
Fax: (818)842-1943

Description

Founded: 1984
EIN: 953994420
Organization Type: Private Foundation
Giving Locations: CA
Grant Types: General Support.

Donor Information

Founder: the late Grace T. Lantz, the late Walter Lantz

Financial Summary

Total Giving: $1,107,798 (fiscal year ending November 30, 2003); $1,468,130 (fiscal 2001)
Assets: $14,125,858 (fiscal 2003); $17,613,582 (fiscal 2001)
Gifts Received: $568,904 (fiscal 1997); $301,634 (fiscal 1996); $11,634,067 (fiscal 1995). Note: In fiscal 1994, contributions were received from Walter Lantz.

Typical Recipients

Arts & Humanities: Arts Associations & Councils, Arts Funds, Arts Institutes, Film & Video, Arts & Humanities-General, Libraries, Opera, Public Broadcasting
Civic & Public Affairs: Botanical Gardens/Parks, Civic & Public Affairs-General, Parades/Festivals, Philanthropic Organizations
Education: Arts/Humanities Education, Business Education, Colleges & Universities, Economic Education, Education Funds, Education Reform, Education-General, Private Education (Precollege), Special Education
Health: AIDS/HIV, Children's Health/Hospitals, Clinics/Medical Centers, Emergency/Ambulance Services, Eyes/Blindness
Religion: Religious Welfare
Science: Scientific Organizations
Social Services: Child Abuse, Child Welfare, Community Service Organizations, Crime Prevention, Emergency Relief, People with Disabilities, Recreation & Athletics, Special Olympics, Veterans, YMCA/YWCA/YMHA/YWHA

Application Procedures

Initial Contact: Send a brief letter of inquiry.
Deadlines: None.

Restrictions

Does not support individuals, religious organizations for sectarian purposes, political or lobbying groups, or organizations outside area.

Foundation Officials

Susan J. Hazard: trustee
Peggy E. Jackson: trustee
Edward A. Landry: trustee B New Orleans, LA 1939. ED Louisiana State University BA (1961); University of California, Los Angeles JD (1964). PRIM CORP EMPL attorney: Musick, Peeler & Garrett.

Grants Analysis

Disclosure Period: fiscal year ending November 30, 2003
Total Grants: $1,107,798
Number of Grants: 29
Average Grant: $23,937*
Highest Grant: $260,000
Lowest Grant: $1,000
Typical Range: $10,000 to $50,000
*Note: Average grant figure excludes three highest grants ($485,432).

Recent Grants

Note: Grants derived from fiscal 2003 Form 990.
General

260,000	Los Angeles Opera, Los Angeles, CA
125,432	Rancho Santa Ana Botanic Gardens, Claremont, CA
100,000	Western Foundation of Vertebrate Zoology, Camarillo, CA
50,000	Cathedral Building Foundation, Los Angeles, CA
50,000	Motion Picture and Television Fund, Woodland Hills, CA
50,000	Teach for America, Los Angeles, CA
50,000	Woodbury University, Burbank, CA
25,000	American Red Cross, Burbank, CA
25,000	Foundation for Teaching Economics, Davis, CA
25,000	Los Angeles County High School for the Arts, Los Angeles, CA

MARY POTISHMAN LARD TRUST

Giving Contact

Walker C. Friedman, Co-Trustee
Mary Potishman Lard Trust
604 E. 4th St., Suite 200
Ft. Worth, TX 76102
Phone: (817)884-4448

Description

Founded: 1968
EIN: 756210697
Organization Type: Private Foundation
Giving Locations: TX: especially Fort Worth area
Grant Types: General Support, Research.

Donor Information

Founder: the late Mary P. Lard

Financial Summary

Total Giving: $624,666 (2003); $598,750 (2001)
Giving Analysis: Giving for 2003 includes: foundation grants to United Way ($5,000); 2001: foundation grants to United Way ($10,000)
Assets: $12,923,569 (2003); $13,057,077 (2001)

Typical Recipients

Arts & Humanities: Arts Associations & Councils, Arts Centers, Arts Festivals, Ballet, Dance, Ethnic & Folk Arts, Libraries, Museums/Galleries, Music, Opera, Performing Arts
Civic & Public Affairs: Business/Free Enterprise, Clubs, Civic & Public Affairs-General, Hispanic Affairs, Parades/Festivals, Philanthropic Organizations, Urban & Community Affairs, Women's Affairs, Zoos/Aquariums
Education: Business Education, Colleges & Universities, Education Reform, Private Education (Precollege), Public Education (Precollege), Special Education, Student Aid
Environment: Air/Water Quality
Health: AIDS/HIV, Alzheimer's Disease, Cancer, Emergency/Ambulance Services, Health Funds, Health Organizations, Heart, Hospitals, Medical Research, Medical Training, Mental Health, Nursing Services, Prenatal Health Issues, Public Health, Research/Studies Institutes, Respiratory, Single-Disease Health Associations
International: Foreign Arts Organizations
Religion: Churches, Jewish Causes, Social/Policy Issues
Science: Science Museums
Social Services: Child Welfare, Community Centers, Community Service Organizations, Counseling, Crime Prevention, Family Planning, Family Services, Food/Clothing Distribution, People with Disabilities, Recreation & Athletics, Scouts, Substance Abuse, United Funds/United Ways, Volunteer Services, YMCA/YWCA/YMHA/YWHA, Youth Organizations

Application Procedures

Initial Contact: Send a brief letter of inquiry describing program or project.

Application Requirements: Include name and location of organization, its purpose and the purpose of funds sought, and amount requested.
Deadlines: None.

Restrictions

Does not support individuals.

Additional Information

Trust(s): Bank One TX NA

Foundation Officials

Alan D. Friedman: co-trustee
Walker C. Friedman: co-trustee

Grants Analysis

Disclosure Period: calendar year ending 2003
Total Grants: $619,666*
Number of Grants: 69
Average Grant: $6,204*
Highest Grant: $144,000
Lowest Grant: $500
Typical Range: $1,000 to $10,000
*Note: Giving excludes United Way. Average grant figure excludes two highest grants ($204,000).

Recent Grants

Note: Grants derived from 2003 Form 990.
General

144,000	Texas Christian University, Ft. Worth, TX
60,000	Fort Worth Symphony Orchestra, Ft. Worth, TX
25,000	All Saints Foundation, Ft. Worth, TX
25,000	All Saints Health Foundation, Ft. Worth, TX
25,000	Modern Art Museum of Fort Worth, Ft. Worth, TX
20,000	Amon Carter Museum, Ft. Worth, TX
20,000	Fort Worth Museum of Science and History, Ft. Worth, TX
16,666	University of Texas, Austin, TX -- for Hogg Auditorium renovation
15,000	Cistercian Preparatory School, Irving, TX
15,000	Salesmanship Club of Dallas, Dallas, TX

LARSEN FUND

Giving Contact

Patricia S. Palmer, Grants Administrator
2537 Post Road, Suite 224
Southport, CT 06890
Phone: (203)255-5318
Fax: (203)255-6206

Description

Founded: 1941
EIN: 136104430
Organization Type: Private Foundation
Giving Locations: CT; MA; MN: Minneapolis including metropolitan area; NY: New York including metropolitan area
Grant Types: Capital, Conference/Seminar, Endowment, Fellowship, General Support, Project, Research, Scholarship.

Donor Information

Founder: the late Roy E. Larsen

Financial Summary

Total Giving: $543,750 (2003); $693,233 (2001)
Assets: $11,837,488 (2003); $12,869,339 (2001)
Gifts Received: $3,904 (2000). Note: In 2000, contributions were received from Margaret Z. Larsen.

Typical Recipients

Arts & Humanities: Arts Centers, Arts Institutes, History & Archaeology, Libraries, Museums/Galleries, Music, Performing Arts, Theater

Civic & Public Affairs: Civic & Public Affairs-General, Professional & Trade Associations, Urban & Community Affairs, Zoos/Aquariums
Education: Colleges & Universities, Education-General, Journalism/Media Education, Minority Education, Private Education (Precollege), Science/Mathematics Education, Secondary Education (Public)
Environment: Air/Water Quality, Environment-General, Resource Conservation, Wildlife Protection
Health: Health Organizations, Hospitals, Hospitals (University Affiliated), Outpatient Health Care, Single-Disease Health Associations
International: Health Care/Hospitals, International Affairs, International Organizations
Religion: Churches, Seminaries
Science: Science Museums, Scientific Centers & Institutes
Social Services: Camps, Child Welfare, Community Centers, Community Service Organizations, Domestic Violence, Family Planning, Recreation & Athletics, YMCA/YWCA/YMHA/YWHA, Youth Organizations

Application Procedures

Initial Contact: Send a brief letter of inquiry accompanied by a brief proposal.
Application Requirements: Include history of project, project goals, methods, budget, and schedule for implementation. Attach a copy of organization's most recent annual financial statement, list board members, current grants, and proof of tax-exempt status.
Deadlines: None.
Review Process: Grant applications are circulated quarterly to board members. Board members advise the grants administrator which applications should be considered at the upcoming board meeting. Those who submitted an application that will not be considered will be notified at least three weeks prior to the board meeting. Board meetings are generally held in June and December.
Decision Notification: Applicants whose proposals are considered at a board meeting will be notified by mail of the board's decision within three weeks of the meeting.

Restrictions

Does not support individuals.

Additional Information

Publications: Annual Report (including Application Guidelines)

Foundation Officials

Christopher Larsen: president
Jonathan Zerbe Larsen: vice president B New York, NY 1940. ED Harvard University BA (1961); Harvard University MAT (1963). PRIM CORP EMPL editor in chief: Village Voice. NONPR AFFIL trustee: Cambridge College; trustee: Natural Resources Defense Council.
Patricia S. Palmer: grants admin
Anne Larsen Simonson: vice president

Grants Analysis

Disclosure Period: calendar year ending 2003
Total Grants: $543,750
Number of Grants: 31
Average Grant: $15,129*
Highest Grant: $55,000
Lowest Grant: $1,000
Typical Range: $5,000 to $25,000
*Note: Average grant figure excludes two highest grants ($105,000).

Recent Grants

Note: Grants derived from 2003 Form 990.
General

20,000	Sarah Lawrence College, Bronxville, NY -- capital campaign
10,000	Breck School, Minneapolis, MN
10,000	Children's Theatre Company and School, Minneapolis, MN

10,000	Minneapolis Institute of Arts, Minneapolis, MN -- for patrons circle
10,000	Nantucket Conservation Foundation, Nantucket, MA -- for land acquisition program
7,000	Yellow Brick Road Project, Rockland, MA -- annual funding for teachers' salaries
5,000	American Museum of Asmat Art, St. Paul, MN
5,000	American Rivers, Coloma, CA
5,000	Breck School, Minneapolis, MN
5,000	Sarah Lawrence College, Bronxville, NY

WILLIAM AND MILDRED LASDON FOUNDATION

Giving Contact

Nanette L. Laitman, Trustee
575 Madison Avenue, Suite 1006
New York, NY 10022-2588
Phone: (212)935-3916

Description

Founded: 1947
EIN: 237380362
Organization Type: Private Foundation
Giving Locations: NY.
Grant Types: General Support.

Donor Information

Founder: Jacob S. Lasdon, William S. Lasdon, Mildred D. Lasdon, Nanetta L. Leitman

Financial Summary

Total Giving: $2,196,412 (2003)
Assets: $33,625,417 (2003)
Gifts Received: $1,694,707 (2003); $4,283,813 (1998); $10,000 (1996). Note: In 1998, contributions were received from N.L. Laitman ($383,813) and Estate of M.D. Lasdon ($3,900,000). In 1995, contributions were received from Mildred D. Lasdon.

Typical Recipients

Arts & Humanities: Arts Associations & Councils, Ballet, Dance, Ethnic & Folk Arts, Film & Video, Arts & Humanities-General, Historic Preservation, Libraries, Museums/Galleries, Music, Opera, Performing Arts, Public Broadcasting, Theater
Civic & Public Affairs: Botanical Gardens/Parks, Ethnic Organizations, Civic & Public Affairs-General
Education: Arts/Humanities Education, Colleges & Universities, Leadership Training, Medical Education
Environment: Resource Conservation
Health: Cancer, Clinics/Medical Centers, Health-General, Hospitals, Nursing Services
International: Foreign Arts Organizations, International Organizations, Missionary/Religious Activities
Religion: Jewish Causes, Seminaries, Synagogues/Temples
Social Services: People with Disabilities, Youth Organizations

Application Procedures

Initial Contact: Send a brief letter of inquiry.
Application Requirements: current financial statements and purpose of funds sought.
Deadlines: None.

Foundation Officials

Bonnie Eletz: trustee
Nanette L. Laitman: trustee
Cathy Sorkin Seligman: trustee

Grants Analysis

Disclosure Period: calendar year ending 2003
Total Grants: $2,196,412
Number of Grants: 110

Average Grant: $6,413*
Highest Grant: $1,497,384
Lowest Grant: $100
Typical Range: $1,000 to $10,000
*Note: Average grant figure excludes high grant.

Recent Grants

Note: Grants derived from 2003 Form 990.
General

129,282	Weill Medical College, New York, NY -- for child bereavement program
100,000	Smithsonian Archives of American Art, New York, NY
50,000	American Craft Museum, New York, NY
50,000	American Craft Museum, New York, NY
37,500	Westchester County Department of Parks
37,500	Westchester County Department of Parks, Mt. Kisco, NY
25,000	Museum of Arts and Design, New York, NY
25,000	United Jewish Appeal Federation of New York, New York, NY
25,000	United Jewish Appeal Federation of New York, New York, NY
12,000	New York Weill Cornell Medical Center, New York, NY

HERBERT AND GERTRUDE LATKIN CHARITABLE FOUNDATION

Giving Contact

John Berryhill, Co-Trustee
1505 E. Valley Road, Suite B
Santa Barbara, CA 93150

Alternate Contact

Janice Gibbons
Care of Pacific Capital Bank NA
PO Box 2340
Santa Barbara, CA 93120-2340
Phone: (805)899-8407
Note: Applications may be submitted to either address.

Description

Founded: 1992
EIN: 776070540
Organization Type: Private Foundation
Giving Locations: CA: Santa Barbara
Grant Types: General Support, Scholarship.

Donor Information

Founder: Established in 1992 from the Herbert and Gertrude Latkin Trust.

Financial Summary

Total Giving: $271,543 (2003); $434,545 (2001)
Giving Analysis: Giving for 2003 includes: foundation scholarships ($19,000); 2001: foundation scholarships ($20,500)
Assets: $5,809,794 (2003); $7,253,373 (2001)
Gifts Received: $3,544,205 (1992)

Typical Recipients

Arts & Humanities: Libraries
Civic & Public Affairs: Ethnic Organizations, Civic & Public Affairs-General, Urban & Community Affairs, Women's Affairs
Education: Minority Education, Student Aid
Health: AIDS/HIV, Alzheimer's Disease, Cancer, Children's Health/Hospitals, Health Organizations, Hospices, Hospitals, Medical Rehabilitation, Multiple Sclerosis, Nursing Services

Religion: Jewish Causes, Religious Organizations, Religious Welfare
Social Services: Animal Protection, At-Risk Youth, Camps, Child Abuse, Community Service Organizations, Day Care, Domestic Violence, Family Planning, Family Services, Food/Clothing Distribution, Senior Services, Sexual Abuse, Shelters/Homelessness, YMCA/YWCA/YMHA/YWHA, Youth Organizations

Application Procedures

Initial Contact: Send a brief letter of inquiry.
Application Requirements: Include organization's name and purpose, and describe how the grant would be used.
Deadlines: April 1 and October 1.

Additional Information

Trust(s): Pacific Capital Bank NA

Foundation Officials

John Berryhill: co-trustee

Grants Analysis

Disclosure Period: calendar year ending 2003
Total Grants: $250,543*
Number of Grants: 53
Average Grant: $4,727
Highest Grant: $10,000
Lowest Grant: $750
Typical Range: $1,000 to $10,000
*Note: Giving excludes scholarship.

Recent Grants

Note: Grants derived from 2003 Form 990.
General

16,000	Scholarship Foundation of Santa Barbara, Santa Barbara, CA -- grant for higher education scholarships for economically disadvantaged and deserving students from Santa Barbara
10,500	Domestic Violence Solutions for Santa Barbara County, Santa Barbara, CA -- for partial program support for Mariposa house, a new transitional housing program serving domestic violence survivors and their children
10,000	Channel Islands YMCA, Santa Barbara, CA -- to assist with funding the position of extended care case manager of the youth shelter program for runaway, homeless, and troubled youth
10,000	Coalition to Provide Shelter and Support to Santa Barbara Homeless, Santa Barbara, CA -- to support for the Cacique street homeless shelter
10,000	Friendship Adult Day Care Center, Santa Barbara, CA -- to help with the cost of a full time, on-site nurse
10,000	Santa Barbara Jewish Federation, Santa Barbara, CA -- to assist with funding for senior programs provided by Jewish family services
9,000	Transition House, Santa Barbara, CA -- to support the operation of the infant care center for homeless children
8,000	Catholic Charities of the Santa Barbara Region, Santa Barbara, CA -- grant for the 'oasis program', which serves the frail elderly of all faiths at risk of premature institutionalization
8,000	Visiting Nurse and Hospice Care of Santa Barbara, Santa Barbara, CA -- grant to provide direct patient care for elderly community members who are unable to pay or are uninsured
7,500	Foodbank of Santa Barbara County, Santa Maria, CA -- for North county brown bag program

FORREST C. LATTNER FOUNDATION

Giving Contact

Susan L. Lloyd, President & Secretary
777 East Atlantic Avenue, Suite 317
Delray Beach, FL 33483
Phone: (561)278-3781

Alternate Contact

Martha L. Walker, Chairman

Description

Founded: 1982
EIN: 592147657
Organization Type: General Purpose Foundation
Giving Locations: FL: Midwest.
Grant Types: General Support.

Donor Information

Founder: Incorporated in 1981 by Mrs. Forrest C. Lattner, Mrs. Frances H. Lattner, and the late Forrest C. Lattner.

Financial Summary

Total Giving: $7,129,400 (2002); $7,185,200 (2001)
Assets: $138,028,193 (2002); $156,635,067 (2001)
Gifts Received: $2,690,497 (1998). Note: In 1998, contributions were received from the Francis H. Lattner Trust.

Typical Recipients

Arts & Humanities: Arts Associations & Councils, Community Arts, Arts & Humanities-General, Historic Preservation, Libraries, Museums/Galleries, Music, Performing Arts, Public Broadcasting, Theater
Civic & Public Affairs: African American Affairs, Botanical Gardens/Parks, Clubs, Community Foundations, Employment/Job Training, Civic & Public Affairs-General, Housing, Municipalities/Towns, Philanthropic Organizations, Professional & Trade Associations, Public Policy, Women's Affairs, Zoos/Aquariums
Education: Afterschool/Enrichment Programs, Arts/Humanities Education, Business Education, Colleges & Universities, Community & Junior Colleges, Education Associations, Education Reform, Elementary Education (Public), Education-General, Leadership Training, Literacy, Medical Education, Preschool Education, Private Education (Precollege), Public Education (Precollege), Science/Mathematics Education, Secondary Education (Private), Special Education, Student Aid, Vocational & Technical Education
Environment: Air/Water Quality, Forestry, Environment-General, Protection, Research, Resource Conservation, Wildlife Protection
Health: AIDS/HIV, Alzheimer's Disease, Cancer, Children's Health/Hospitals, Clinics/Medical Centers, Emergency/Ambulance Services, Eyes/Blindness, Health-General, Health Funds, Heart, Home-Care Services, Hospices, Hospitals, Hospitals (University Affiliated), Medical Research, Mental Health, Public Health, Research/Studies Institutes, Single-Disease Health Associations, Trauma Treatment
International: Health Care/Hospitals
Religion: Churches, Ministries, Religious Organizations, Religious Welfare
Science: Science Museums, Scientific Centers & Institutes, Scientific Research
Social Services: Animal Protection, Big Brothers/Big Sisters, Child Welfare, Community Service Organizations, Counseling, Crime Prevention, Day Care, Domestic Violence, Family Planning, Family Services, Food/Clothing Distribution, Homes, People with Disabilities, Recreation & Athletics, Scouts, Senior Services, Shelters/Homelessness, Social Services-General, Substance Abuse, YMCA/YWCA/YMHA/YWHA, Youth Organizations

Application Procedures

Initial Contact: Send an initial letter of request to the foundation.

Application Requirements: Initial proposal should include the applicant's name, address, and phone number; the name of person to be contacted, with title; a brief statement of the history of the applicant and the purpose of the grant request; and supplemental information about the applicant, including a list of officers and directors, an audited financial statement (receipts and disbursements and a balance sheet) for the most recent fiscal year, a budget for the current fiscal year, and an IRS tax-exempt letter.

Deadlines: Grant proposals are accepted in May and October.

Review Process: If the request falls within the foundation's guidelines, it will be acknowledged. If necessary, supplemental information will be requested. The foundation's grant review committee meets to consider final proposals. If the request is approved and a grant is awarded, the applicant will be notified in June or December following the grant review committee's meeting.

Foundation Officials

Forrest C. Brown, MD: trustee B 1940.
Richard M. Harris: trustee
Douglas W. Hollenbeck: trustee
Susan L. Lloyd: president, trustee
Martha L. Walker: chairman, trustee

Grants Analysis

Disclosure Period: calendar year ending 2002
Total Grants: $7,129,400
Number of Grants: 295
Average Grant: $22,549*
Highest Grant: $500,000
Lowest Grant: $1,000
Typical Range: $5,000 to $40,000
*Note: Average grant amount excludes highest grant.

Recent Grants

Note: Grants derived from 2002 Form 990.
Library-Related
100,000	Delray Beach Public Library, Delray Beach, FL

General
170,000	Wichita Community Foundation, Wichita, KS
150,000	Bethesda Memorial Hospital Foundation, Bethesda, MD
125,000	Save America's Forests Fund, Washington, DC
120,000	Surf Rider Foundation, San Clemente, CA
100,000	Bethesda Memorial Hospital Foundation, Bethesda, MD
100,000	Denton Parks Foundation, Denton, TX
100,000	Eden's Promise
100,000	Independent Resource Center
100,000	Kansas Humane Society, Wichita, KS
100,000	NARSAD, Great Neck, NY

LAUDER FOUNDATION

Giving Contact

J. Krupskas, Administrator
767 5th Ave., 40th Fl.
New York, NY 10153
Phone: (212)572-4426

Description

Founded: 1962
EIN: 136153743
Organization Type: Family Foundation
Giving Locations: NY: New York
Grant Types: General Support.

Donor Information

Founder: The Lauder Foundation was incorporated in New York in 1962, with funds donated by the Lauder family. Estee Lauder and her husband, Joseph H. Lauder, founded the cosmetics firm, Estee Lauder, in 1946. Most of the company stock is still owned by members of the Lauder family, including Estee Lauder's two sons, Ronald S. Lauder and Leonard A. Lauder.

Financial Summary

Total Giving: $3,901,290 (fiscal year ending November 30, 2003); $6,165,305 (fiscal 2001)
Assets: $17,830,078 (fiscal 2003); $18,096,216 (fiscal 2001)
Gifts Received: $2,400,000 (fiscal 2003); $2,400,000 (fiscal 2001); $2,400,000 (fiscal 2000). Note: In fiscal 2003, 2001, 2000, contributions were received from Estee Lauder. In fiscal 1996, contributions were received from Estee Lauder and Leonard Lauder.

Typical Recipients

Arts & Humanities: Art History, Arts Associations & Councils, Arts Centers, Arts Funds, Arts Institutes, Ballet, Dance, Arts & Humanities-General, Historic Preservation, History & Archaeology, Libraries, Museums/Galleries, Music, Performing Arts, Theater, Visual Arts

Civic & Public Affairs: Botanical Gardens/Parks, Community Foundations, Economic Policy, Employment/Job Training, Ethnic Organizations, Civic & Public Affairs-General, Inner-City Development, Philanthropic Organizations, Professional & Trade Associations, Public Policy, Urban & Community Affairs, Women's Affairs, Zoos/Aquariums

Education: Afterschool/Enrichment Programs, Arts/Humanities Education, Colleges & Universities, Education Funds, Education Reform, Education-General, Leadership Training, Literacy, Medical Education, Private Education (Precollege), Science/Mathematics Education, Secondary Education (Private), Social Sciences Education, Student Aid

Environment: Forestry, Environment-General, Resource Conservation, Wildlife Protection

Health: AIDS/HIV, Cancer, Children's Health/Hospitals, Clinics/Medical Centers, Eyes/Blindness, Health Funds, Heart, Hospices, Hospitals, Hospitals (University Affiliated), Medical Research, Multiple Sclerosis, Public Health, Research/Studies Institutes

International: Foreign Arts Organizations, International-General, International Peace & Security Issues, International Relations, International Relief Efforts, Missionary/Religious Activities

Religion: Jewish Causes, Religious Welfare, Synagogues/Temples

Science: Science Museums

Social Services: Child Welfare, Community Centers, Community Service Organizations, Crime Prevention, Emergency Relief, Family Planning, Family Services, Homes, People with Disabilities, Recreation & Athletics, Senior Services, Substance Abuse, United Funds/United Ways, YMCA/YWCA/YMHA/YWHA, Youth Organizations

Application Procedures

Initial Contact: Prospective applicants should send a letter to the foundation describing the organization and the project for which funds are sought.
Deadlines: None.

Restrictions

No grants are given to individuals.

Foundation Officials

Estee Lauder: president, director B Queens, NY July 01, 1908. PRIM CORP EMPL founder, chairman board: Estee Lauder Co.
Leonard Alan Lauder: secretary-treasurer, director B New York, NY 1933. ED University of Pennsylvania BS (1954). PRIM CORP EMPL chairman: Estee Lau-

der Co.s. NONPR AFFIL board governors: Joseph H Lauder Institute Management International Studies; president: Whitney Museum American Art; member: French-American Chamber of Commerce U.S.; trustee: Aspen Institute Humanistic Studies; member: Chief Executives Organization.
Ronald Stephen Lauder: vice president, director B New York, NY 1944. ED University of Paris (1964); University of Pennsylvania BS (1965). PRIM CORP EMPL chairman: Clinique Laboratorys Inc. CORP AFFIL founder, chairman: Central European Development Co.; chairman, president: Lauder Investments. NONPR AFFIL trustee: Mt Sinai Medical Center; trustee: Museum Modern Art.

Grants Analysis

Disclosure Period: fiscal year ending November 30, 2003
Total Grants: $3,901,290
Number of Grants: 62
Average Grant: $4,683*
Highest Grant: $3,200,000
Lowest Grant: $100
Typical Range: $1,000 to $10,000
*Note: Average grant figure excludes three highest grants ($3,625,000).

Recent Grants

Note: Grants derived from fiscal 2002 Form 990.
General
1,400,000	Leonard & Evelyn Lauder Foundation, New York, NY
678,300	Breast Cancer Research Foundation, New York, NY
252,750	Lenox Hill hospital, New York, NY
129,500	Nightingale Bamford School, New York, NY
125,000	United Jewish Appeal, New York, NY
112,850	Bronx High School of Science, Bronx, NY
110,000	New Yorkers for Parks, New York, NY
100,000	Whitney Museum of American Art, New York, NY
52,000	Jewish Museum, New York, NY
50,000	American Friends of Kiev Jewish Community, Brooklyn, NY

LAUREL FOUNDATION

Giving Contact

Donna M. Panazzi, Vice President
603 Stanwix St., Suite 1800
Pittsburgh, PA 15222
Phone: (412)765-2400
Fax: (412)765-2407

Description

Founded: 1951
EIN: 256008073
Organization Type: General Purpose Foundation
Giving Locations: PA: Pittsburgh including southwestern PA
Grant Types: General Support, Matching, Operating Expenses, Project.

Donor Information

Founder: Incorporated in 1951 by Cordelia S. May.

Financial Summary

Total Giving: $1,665,902 (2003); $2,339,900 (2002); $1,842,343 (2001)
Assets: $37,940,913 (2003); $33,709,123 (2002); $39,230,870 (2001)

Typical Recipients

Arts & Humanities: Arts Associations & Councils, Arts Centers, Arts Festivals, Arts Funds, Arts Institutes, Arts Outreach, Community Arts, Dance, Ethnic & Folk Arts, Film & Video, Arts & Humanities-General,

Historic Preservation, History & Archaeology, Libraries, Literary Arts, Museums/Galleries, Music, Opera, Performing Arts, Public Broadcasting, Theater

Civic & Public Affairs: Botanical Gardens/Parks, Business/Free Enterprise, Civil Rights, Clubs, Community Foundations, Economic Development, Employment/Job Training, Civic & Public Affairs-General, Legal Aid, Nonprofit Management, Philanthropic Organizations, Professional & Trade Associations, Public Policy, Rural Affairs, Safety, Urban & Community Affairs, Women's Affairs, Zoos/Aquariums

Education: Afterschool/Enrichment Programs, Arts/Humanities Education, Business Education, Colleges & Universities, Community & Junior Colleges, Education Associations, Education Funds, Engineering/Technological Education, Environmental Education, Faculty Development, Education-General, Journalism/Media Education, Literacy, Medical Education, Private Education (Precollege), Public Education (Precollege), School Volunteerism, Science/Mathematics Education, Secondary Education (Private), Secondary Education (Public), Social Sciences Education, Student Aid

Environment: Air/Water Quality, Energy, Environment-General, Protection, Resource Conservation, Watershed, Wildlife Protection

Health: Alzheimer's Disease, Children's Health/Hospitals, Clinics/Medical Centers, Emergency/Ambulance Services, Health Funds, Hospices, Hospitals, Medical Research, Nursing Services, Public Health

International: Foreign Educational Institutions, Health Care/Hospitals, International Affairs, International Development, International Environmental Issues, International Relations

Religion: Churches, Ministries, Religious Welfare

Science: Science Museums, Scientific Centers & Institutes

Social Services: Animal Protection, At-Risk Youth, Big Brothers/Big Sisters, Child Welfare, Community Service Organizations, Counseling, Day Care, Delinquency & Criminal Rehabilitation, Emergency Relief, Family Planning, Family Services, Homes, People with Disabilities, Recreation & Athletics, Senior Services, Shelters/Homelessness, Social Services-General, Substance Abuse, United Funds/United Ways, Volunteer Services, YMCA/YWCA/YMHA/YWHA, Youth Organizations

Application Procedures

Initial Contact: Applicants are encouraged to carefully review the annual report to gauge whether their project is likely to be funded.

Application Requirements: The foundation accepts the common Grant Application of the Grantmakers of Western Pennsylvania. With the complete application, include a narrative of less than 300 words and a proposal summary stating the specific purpose of the requested grant and the amount requested; a brief description of the applying organization and its mission, and a brief summary of the project and goals for the period of time during which the funds will be used; and the key staff who will be involved. The full proposal should also include a list of the board of directors with affiliations; a current operating budget and annual financial statements for the past two years; a list of any major contributors, with amounts, and a summary of the balance of contributions; the names of the organization's executive staff and the total number of paid staff; an annual report, if available; and an IRS determination letter.

Deadlines: Formal submission deadlines are April 1 and October 1 for consideration at trustee meetings held in June and December, respectively. Applicants are encouraged to submit applications early, however, as applications received late in the cycle necessarily receive less intensive review.

Review Process: Proposals are acknowledged promptly and applicants are advised of the meeting at which their request will be considered. Every effort is made to consider all proposals which have been timely submitted, but occasionally it is necessary to defer until the following meeting. If this occurs, applicants are promptly advised and given an opportunity to revise or withdraw their request, as appropriate.

Restrictions

Cultural organizations whose service areas fall outside the Greater Pittsburgh area ordinarily are not funded. The foundation does not accept proposals from individuals or from for-profit organizations. Multi-year grants are not usually approved.

Additional Information

Special preference is given to financially responsible organizations, i.e. those that direct 70% or more of funds to client services and limit administrative costs to less than 30%. The trustees also favor collaborations between art organizations and social service groups that pool resources to address common problems and programs.

Publications: Annual Report

Foundation Officials

Nancy C. Fales: trustee

Timothy M. Inglis: vice president, treasurer

Cordelia Scaife May: chairman, trustee, donor B Pittsburgh, PA 1928. ED University of Pittsburgh.

Roger F. Meyer: president, trustee B 1939. PRIM CORP EMPL treasurer, director: Commercial Electric Product Corp.

Donna M. Panazzi: vice president, secretary

Curtis S. Scaife: trustee ED University of Arizona (1956).

Thomas Mellon Schmidt: trustee B Pittsburgh, PA 1940. ED Princeton University AB (1962); Harvard University JD (1965). PRIM NONPR EMPL sr vice president law: Fallingwater & Urban Conservation. NONPR AFFIL vice chairman: Pittsburgh Historical Review Commission; trustee: Saint Barnabas Health Systems; trustee: Morris Arboretum; trustee: Carnegie Museum Natural History; advisor: Land Conservation Law Institute; member: American Bar Association; member: Allegheny County Bar Association; member: American Association Museums. CLUB AFFIL Rolling Rock Club; Anglers New York Club; Pittsburgh Golf Club.

Grants Analysis

Disclosure Period: calendar year ending 2003
Total Grants: $1,665,902
Number of Grants: 75
Average Grant: $20,039*
Highest Grant: $183,000
Lowest Grant: $1,000
Typical Range: $10,000 to $40,000
*Note: Average grant figure excludes highest grant.

Recent Grants

Note: Grants derived from 2003 Form 990.
Library-Related

20,000	CC Mellor Memorial Library & Edgewood Community House, Edgewood, PA -- toward renovation project

General

183,000	Allegheny Conference on Community Development, Pittsburgh, PA
100,000	Pennsylvania Environmental Council Inc., Harrisburg, PA
60,000	Westmoreland Museum of Art, Greensburg, PA
50,000	Allegheny Conference on Community Development, Pittsburgh, PA
50,000	Carnegie Institute, Pittsburgh, PA -- toward the Hudson river school project
50,000	National Aviary Pittsburgh Inc., Pittsburgh, PA
50,000	Penn State Public Broadcasting WPSX, University Park, PA
50,000	Phipps Conservatory Inc., Pittsburgh, PA
50,000	Sports & Exhibition Authority of Pittsburgh and Allegheny County, Pittsburgh, PA
50,000	Three Rivers Employment Service Inc., Pittsburgh, PA

RICHARD AND RUTH LAVINE FAMILY FOUNDATION

Giving Contact

Ruth J. Lavine, President & Director
121 S. Beverly Drive
Beverly Hills, CA 90212
Phone: (310)275-5132

Description

Founded: 1991
EIN: 954300271
Organization Type: Private Foundation
Giving Locations: CA: Beverly Hills, Los Angeles
Grant Types: General Support.

Financial Summary

Total Giving: $188,625 (fiscal year ending June 30, 2001)
Giving Analysis: Giving for fiscal 2001 includes: foundation grants to United Way ($2,000)
Assets: $4,841,295 (fiscal 2001)
Gifts Received: $2,912,506 (fiscal 1997). Note: In fiscal 1997, contributions were received from Ruth J. Lavine.

Typical Recipients

Arts & Humanities: Arts Centers, Arts Festivals, Libraries, Music, Public Broadcasting, Theater

Civic & Public Affairs: Civic & Public Affairs-General, Law & Justice, Legal Aid, Minority Business, Philanthropic Organizations, Professional & Trade Associations

Education: Colleges & Universities, Education Funds, Legal Education

Health: Arthritis, Cancer, Medical Research

Religion: Jewish Causes, Religious Organizations, Synagogues/Temples

Social Services: Family Planning, Recreation & Athletics, Senior Services, United Funds/United Ways, Youth Organizations

Application Procedures

Initial Contact: Send a brief letter of inquiry.
Application Requirements: Include proof of tax-exempt status.
Deadlines: None.
Notes: The foundation reports that its funds are committed for the foreseeable future and it is therefore not soliciting proposals at this time.

Restrictions

Grants are not made to individuals.

Foundation Officials

Ruth J. Lavine: president, director
Leonard Unger: secretary, treasurer, director

Grants Analysis

Disclosure Period: fiscal year ending June 30, 2001
Total Grants: $186,625*
Number of Grants: 17
Average Grant: $6,775*
Highest Grant: $50,000
Lowest Grant: $250
Typical Range: $500 to $10,000
*Note: Giving excludes United Way. Average grant figure excludes two highest grants ($85,000).

Recent Grants

Note: Grants derived from fiscal 2001 Form 990.

General

50,000	University of Southern California Law School, Los Angeles, CA
35,000	KCET, Los Angeles, CA
28,000	Planned Parenthood, Los Angeles, CA
20,000	Arthritis Foundation Southern California Chapter, Los Angeles, CA
10,000	Women Lawyers Association of Los Angeles, Los Angeles, CA
9,500	American Jewish Committee, Los Angeles, CA
8,500	United Jewish Fund, Los Angeles, CA
7,000	Los Angeles Philharmonic, Los Angeles, CA
5,000	Jewish Family Service, Los Angeles, CA
3,000	Benefactors of the Jewish Club of 1933, Inc., Los Angeles, CA

LAZARUS CHARITABLE TRUST

Giving Contact

Charles Lazarus, President
c/o Toys 'R' Us
One Geoffrey Way
Wayne, NJ 07470
Phone: (973)617-5660

Description

Founded: 1986
EIN: 133360876
Organization Type: Private Foundation
Giving Locations: DC: Washington; NY
Grant Types: General Support.

Donor Information

Founder: Charles Lazarus

Financial Summary

Total Giving: $327,455 (fiscal year ending May 31, 2004); $263,388 (fiscal 2001)
Assets: $3,812,084 (fiscal 2004); $3,618,681 (fiscal 2001)
Gifts Received: $851,224 (fiscal 2004); $1,938,600 (fiscal 1995). Note: In fiscal 1995 and fiscal 2004, contributions were received from Charles P. Lazarus.

Typical Recipients

Arts & Humanities: Arts Associations & Councils, Arts Funds, Ballet, Community Arts, Dance, Arts & Humanities-General, History & Archaeology, Libraries, Literary Arts, Museums/Galleries, Music, Performing Arts, Public Broadcasting
Civic & Public Affairs: Botanical Gardens/Parks, Clubs, Civic & Public Affairs-General, Municipalities/Towns, Public Policy, Urban & Community Affairs, Women's Affairs
Education: Colleges & Universities, Education-General, Health & Physical Education, Medical Education, Private Education (Precollege), Science/Mathematics Education, Student Aid
Environment: Environment-General, Resource Conservation
Health: AIDS/HIV, Cancer, Children's Health/Hospitals, Clinics/Medical Centers, Diabetes, Emergency/Ambulance Services, Health Organizations, Hospices, Hospitals, Kidney, Medical Research, Mental Health, Multiple Sclerosis, Single-Disease Health Associations
International: Foreign Educational Institutions, Health Care/Hospitals, Human Rights, International Peace & Security Issues, Missionary/Religious Activities
Religion: Churches, Jewish Causes, Religious Organizations, Religious Welfare

Science: Scientific Centers & Institutes
Social Services: At-Risk Youth, Child Welfare, Community Centers, Community Service Organizations, Family Planning, Family Services, Food/Clothing Distribution, Recreation & Athletics, Scouts, Shelters/Homelessness, YMCA/YWCA/YMHA/YWHA, Youth Organizations

Application Procedures

Initial Contact: Send brief letter describing program.
Deadlines: None.

Foundation Officials

Charles P. Lazarus: president B Washington, DC 1923. PRIM CORP EMPL chairman, director: Toys R Us. CORP AFFIL director: Automatic Data Processing Corp.; director: Wal Mart Stores.

Grants Analysis

Disclosure Period: fiscal year ending May 31, 2004
Total Grants: $327,455
Number of Grants: 39
Average Grant: $1,428*
Highest Grant: $239,637
Lowest Grant: $50
Typical Range: $500 to $3,000
*Note: Average grant figure excludes two highest grants ($274,637).

Recent Grants

Note: Grants derived from 2004 Form 990.

General

239,637	New Museum, New York, NY
35,000	Women in Need, New York, NY
20,200	Dalton School, New York, NY
5,000	Facing History, Brookline, MA
5,000	Sidwell Friends School Rowing, Washington, DC
4,248	Congregation Har Hashem, Boulder, CO
2,000	Central Park Conservancy, New York, NY
1,670	Win Affair-Fifth Seventy Seven
1,500	Dana Farber Cancer Institute, Boston, MA
1,250	Jewish Arts Foundation, Palm Beach, FL

HELEN SPERRY LEA FOUNDATION

Giving Contact

Sperry Lea, President & Director
3534 Fulton Street NW
Washington, DC 20007
Phone: (202)337-5448
Fax: (202)337-6722

Description

Founded: 1940
EIN: 136161749
Organization Type: Private Foundation
Giving Locations: DC: Washington
Grant Types: General Support.

Donor Information

Founder: the late Helen Sperry Lea

Financial Summary

Total Giving: $97,270 (2003)
Assets: $2,522,770 (2003)
Gifts Received: $18,000 (2003). Note: In 2003, contributions were received from Sperry and Helen Lea.

Typical Recipients

Arts & Humanities: Arts Associations & Councils, Ballet, Dance, Film & Video, Historic Preservation, History & Archaeology, Libraries, Museums/Galleries, Music, Opera, Performing Arts, Public

Broadcasting, Theater
Civic & Public Affairs: Ethnic Organizations, Civic & Public Affairs-General, Nonprofit Management, Philanthropic Organizations, Public Policy, Urban & Community Affairs
Education: Afterschool/Enrichment Programs, Agricultural Education, Arts/Humanities Education, Colleges & Universities, Education Reform, International Exchange, International Studies, Legal Education, Private Education (Precollege), Public Education (Precollege), School Volunteerism, Secondary Education (Private), Secondary Education (Public)
Environment: Environment-General, Protection
Health: Hospitals
International: Foreign Educational Institutions, International Affairs, International Organizations, International Peace & Security Issues, International Relations
Religion: Religious Welfare
Science: Scientific Labs
Social Services: Community Service Organizations, Shelters/Homelessness

Application Procedures

Initial Contact: The foundation has no formal grant application procedure or application form.
Deadlines: None.

Foundation Officials

Anna L. Lea: vice president, treasurer, director
Helena A. Lea: vice president, director
R. Brooke Lea, II: vice president, director
Sperry Lea: president, director

Grants Analysis

Disclosure Period: calendar year ending 2003
Total Grants: $97,270
Number of Grants: 19
Average Grant: $5,119
Highest Grant: $15,000
Lowest Grant: $250
Typical Range: $1,000 to $10,000

Recent Grants

Note: Grants derived from 2003 Form 990.

General

15,000	St. Joseph Ballet Company, Santa Ana, CA
15,000	St. Paul Arts College, St. Paul, MN
10,000	Save the Bay Inc., Santa Monica, CA
10,000	Sidwell Friends School, Washington, DC
10,000	WAMU-FM American University Radio, Washington, DC
5,596	American Farm School, New York, NY
5,000	National Gallery of Art, Washington, DC
5,000	SEED Public Charter School, Washington, DC
5,000	Society for the Preservation of Greek Heritage, Washington, DC
5,000	Stanislavsky Theater, Washington, DC

THOMAS AND DOROTHY LEAVEY FOUNDATION

Giving Contact

The Trustees McCarthy, President
Thomas & Dorothy Leavey Foundation
10100 Santa Monica Boulevard, Suite 610
Los Angeles, CA 90067
Phone: (310)551-9936
Fax: (310)551-9938

Description

Founded: 1952
EIN: 956060162
Organization Type: Family Foundation
Giving Locations: CA: Southern California

Grant Types: Capital, Endowment, General Support, Research, Scholarship.

Donor Information
Founder: The Thomas and Dorothy Leavey Foundation was established in California in 1952 by Thomas E. Leavey and his wife, Dorothy Leavey.

Financial Summary
Total Giving: $10,149,540 (2003); $10,693,563 (2002)
Giving Analysis: Giving for 2003 includes: foundation scholarships ($332,530); 2002: foundation matching gifts ($100,000); foundation scholarships ($313,260)
Assets: $233,226,144 (2003); $199,947,331 (2002)
Gifts Received: $1,566,594 (1997). Note: Contributions were received from Dorothy E. Leavey.

Typical Recipients
Arts & Humanities: Arts Associations & Councils, Arts Outreach, Ballet, Arts & Humanities-General, History & Archaeology, Libraries, Music, Performing Arts, Public Broadcasting, Theater
Civic & Public Affairs: Clubs, Economic Policy, Gay/Lesbian Issues, Civic & Public Affairs-General, Hispanic Affairs, Housing, Legal Aid, Philanthropic Organizations, Professional & Trade Associations, Public Policy, Women's Affairs
Education: Afterschool/Enrichment Programs, Agricultural Education, Arts/Humanities Education, Colleges & Universities, Education Associations, Education Funds, Education Reform, Faculty Development, Education-General, International Exchange, Legal Education, Medical Education, Minority Education, Private Education (Precollege), Public Education (Precollege), Religious Education, Science/Mathematics Education, Secondary Education (Private), Special Education, Student Aid, Vocational & Technical Education
Environment: Resource Conservation
Health: AIDS/HIV, Cancer, Children's Health/Hospitals, Clinics/Medical Centers, Emergency/Ambulance Services, Eyes/Blindness, Health Policy/Cost Containment, Health Funds, Health Organizations, Hospitals, Long-Term Care, Medical Research, Nursing Services, Prenatal Health Issues, Public Health, Respiratory, Single-Disease Health Associations
International: Foreign Educational Institutions, Health Care/Hospitals, International Organizations, International Peace & Security Issues, Missionary/Religious Activities
Religion: Churches, Dioceses, Religion-General, Ministries, Religious Organizations, Religious Welfare, Social/Policy Issues
Science: Science Museums, Scientific Research
Social Services: Animal Protection, At-Risk Youth, Camps, Child Abuse, Child Welfare, Community Service Organizations, Counseling, Domestic Violence, Emergency Relief, Family Planning, Family Services, Food/Clothing Distribution, People with Disabilities, Recreation & Athletics, Scouts, Senior Services, Shelters/Homelessness, Social Services-General, Special Olympics, Substance Abuse, Volunteer Services, YMCA/YWCA/YMHA/YWHA, Youth Organizations

Application Procedures
Initial Contact: Applicants should submit a letter to the foundation.
Application Requirements: The letter should include descriptions of the organization and the project for which funds are sought, and proof of tax-exempt status.
Deadlines: None.
Review Process: If the application is accepted, a full proposal will be requested. Grants are made quarterly.

Restrictions
The foundation reports that scholarships are provided only to children of employees of agents of Farmers Insurance Group and its subsidiaries.

Foundation Officials
Louis M. Castruccio: trustee
Leo E. Denlea, Jr.: trustee
Michael Enright: trustee
Joseph James Leavey: trustee B Oakland, CA 1930. ED University of San Francisco AB (1952); Stanford University LLB (1955). PRIM CORP EMPL attorney: Early Maslach Leavey & Nutt.
Mark C. Lemons: trustee
Thomas Lemons: trustee
John McCarthy: trustee
Kathleen Leavey McCarthy: chairman B Beverly Hills, CA 1935. ED University of Southern California BS (1957).
Marie McDonough: trustee
Colleen Pennell: trustee

Grants Analysis
Disclosure Period: calendar year ending 2003
Total Grants: $9,817,010*
Number of Grants: 68
Average Grant: $33,339*
Highest Grant: $2,000,000
Lowest Grant: $1,000
Typical Range: $10,000 to $75,000
*Note: Giving excludes scholarships. Average grant figure excludes six highest grantss ($7,750,000).

Recent Grants
Note: Grants derived from 2003 Form 990.
General

2,000,000	Campaign for Saint John's, Santa Monica, CA
2,000,000	Georgetown University Student Reasidence, Washington, DC
1,000,000	Disney Hall, Los Angeles, CA
1,000,000	Loyola Marymount University, Los Angeles, CA
1,000,000	Santa Clara University, Santa Clara, CA
750,000	Loyola High School, Los Angeles, CA
250,000	Mount St. Mary's College, Los Angeles, CA
133,010	California 4H Foundation Awards and Incentives, Davis, CA
125,000	Marymount High School, Los Angeles, CA
125,000	Regis University, Denver, CO

LEBANON MUTUAL INSURANCE CO.

Company Headquarters
137 W. Penn Ave.
Cleona, PA 17042

Company Description
Employees: 31
SIC(s): 6300 Insurance Carriers.

Operating Locations
Lebanon Mutual Insurance Co. (PA--Cleona)

Lebanon Mutual Foundation

Giving Contact
Rollin Rissinger, Jr., Director
137 W. Penn Ave.
PO Box 2005
Cleona, PA 17042

Phone: (717)272-6655

Description
EIN: 222521649
Organization Type: Corporate Foundation
Giving Locations: PA: Lebanon
Grant Types: General Support.

Financial Summary
Total Giving: 1997 Giving includes United Way ($2,300).
Gifts Received: $50,000 (1999). Note: In 1991 and 1999, contributions were received from Lebanon Mutual Insurance Company.

Typical Recipients
Arts & Humanities: Historic Preservation, Libraries, Performing Arts, Public Broadcasting
Civic & Public Affairs: Clubs, Civic & Public Affairs-General, Parades/Festivals, Philanthropic Organizations, Public Policy, Safety
Education: Business Education, Colleges & Universities, Community & Junior Colleges, Education Associations, Education-General, Health & Physical Education, Secondary Education (Public), Student Aid
Environment: Environment-General
Health: Cancer, Children's Health/Hospitals, Health-General, Hospitals, Public Health
Religion: Churches, Ministries
Social Services: Community Service Organizations, Crime Prevention, Scouts, Special Olympics, United Funds/United Ways, YMCA/YWCA/YMHA/YWHA

Application Procedures
Initial Contact: Send a written request specifying purpose of funds sought and affirmation of tax-exempt status.
Deadlines: None.

Corporate Officials
Samuel G. Kurtz: chairman, director PRIM CORP EMPL chairman, director: Lebanon Mutual Insurance Co.
Rollin Rissinger: president, director PRIM CORP EMPL president, director: Lebanon Mutual Insurance Co.

Foundation Officials
Milton Garrison: director B Doylesville, VA 1933. PRIM CORP EMPL senior vice president, secretary: Lebanon Mutual Insurance Co. NONPR AFFIL member: Lions; member: Masons.
Darwin Glick: director
Samuel B. Kurtz: director
Joseph Lauck: director
Warren Lewis: director
Rollin Rissinger, Jr.: director
William Schadler: director
Mark Randolph Tice: director B Harrisburg, PA 1941. ED Pennsylvania State University (1963); Pennsylvania State University (1969). PRIM CORP EMPL president: APR Supply Co. CORP AFFIL director: Lebanon Valley National Bank; director: Lebanon Mutual Insurance Co. NONPR AFFIL member: American Institute Heating Refrigeration & Air Conditioning Engineers.

Grants Analysis
Disclosure Period: calendar year ending 2000
Total Grants: $13,525*
Number of Grants: 13
Average Grant: $710*
Highest Grant: $5,000
Typical Range: $100 to $1,000
*Note: Giving excludes United Way. Average grant excludes highest grant.

Recent Grants
Note: Grants derived from 2001 Form 990.
General

5,000	Lebanon Valley College, Annville, PA

3,000	Harrisburg Area Community College, Harrisburg, PA
2,500	United Way of Lebanon County, Lebanon, PA
1,500	Lebanon Valley Rails-to-Trails, Cleona, PA
1,000	American Cancer Society, Hershey, PA
1,000	GSH Health Services Foundation, Lebanon, PA
1,000	Insurance Education Foundation, Indianapolis, IN
1,000	Lebanon Valley Education Partnership, Annville, PA
350	Special Olympics, Orwigsburg, PA
250	Cleona Fire Company 1, Cleona, PA

LEBOVITZ FUND

Giving Contact
Herbert C. Lebovitz, President & Treasurer
3050 Tremont St.
Allentown, PA 18104
Phone: (610)820-5053

Description
Founded: 1944
EIN: 236270079
Organization Type: Private Foundation
Giving Locations: MI
Grant Types: General Support, Scholarship.

Donor Information
Founder: Peter Lebovitz

Financial Summary
Total Giving: $147,495 (fiscal year ending July 31, 2004); $204,400 (fiscal 2001)
Giving Analysis: Giving for fiscal 2001 includes: foundation scholarships ($1,000)
Assets: $4,501,097 (fiscal 2004); $4,026,204 (fiscal 2001)
Gifts Received: $70,047 (fiscal 2004); $70,000 (fiscal 2001); $21,150 (fiscal 2000). Note: In fiscal 2001 and 2004, contributions were received from Beth Ann Segal Trust. In fiscal 1995 and 2000, contributions were received from Peter Lebovitz.

Typical Recipients
Arts & Humanities: Arts Associations & Councils, Arts Centers, Arts Institutes, Community Arts, Libraries, Museums/Galleries, Music, Opera, Public Broadcasting, Theater
Civic & Public Affairs: Botanical Gardens/Parks, Civic & Public Affairs-General, Municipalities/Towns, Public Policy, Safety, Women's Affairs
Education: Arts/Humanities Education, Business Education, Colleges & Universities, Engineering/Technological Education, Legal Education, Private Education (Precollege), Science/Mathematics Education, Secondary Education (Private), Student Aid
Environment: Environment-General, Resource Conservation, Wildlife Protection
Health: Children's Health/Hospitals, Health-General, Health Organizations, Home-Care Services, Hospitals, Long-Term Care, Medical Research, Single-Disease Health Associations
International: Human Rights
Religion: Religion-General, Jewish Causes, Ministries, Religious Organizations, Religious Welfare, Synagogues/Temples
Science: Science Museums
Social Services: Camps, Child Welfare, Community Service Organizations, Family Services, Food/Clothing Distribution, People with Disabilities, Recreation & Athletics, Social Services-General, United Funds/United Ways, YMCA/YWCA/YMHA/YWHA, Youth Organizations

Application Procedures
Initial Contact: Send brief letter describing program.
Deadlines: None.

Foundation Officials
Jonathan Javitch: director
Herbert C. Lebovitz: president, treasurer, director
James Lebovitz: director
Beth Ann Segal: vice president, secretary, director

Grants Analysis
Disclosure Period: fiscal year ending July 31, 2004
Total Grants: $147,495
Number of Grants: 79
Average Grant: $1,867
Highest Grant: $20,000
Lowest Grant: $25
Typical Range: $500 to $3,000

Recent Grants
Note: Grants derived from 2004 Form 990.
General

20,000	Chrysalis-A Center for Women, Minneapolis, MN
10,700	Baldwin School, Bryn Mawr, PA
10,000	Amos Tuck School of Business, Hanover, NH
10,000	Southern Poverty Law Center, Montgomery, AL
9,000	Minneapolis Federation for Jewish Service, Minneapolis, MN
5,000	Jewish Community Center, Allentown, PA
5,000	Jewish Federation of Lehigh Valley, Allentown, PA
5,000	National Audubon Puffin Project, Ithaca, NY
5,000	Trustee of Columbia University, New York, NY
5,000	Wheaton College, Norton, MA

FRANCIS L. LEDERER FOUNDATION

Giving Contact
Robert I. Ury, Vice President, Secretary & Director
120 S. Riverside Plz., Suite 1200
Chicago, IL 60606-3913
Phone: (312)876-7100
Fax: (312)876-0277

Description
Founded: 1966
EIN: 362594937
Organization Type: Private Foundation
Giving Locations: IL: Chicago
Grant Types: Endowment, General Support, Operating Expenses, Scholarship.

Financial Summary
Total Giving: $1,580,000 (2002 approx); $842,000 (2001)
Giving Analysis: Giving for 2002 includes: foundation scholarships ($750,000); 2001: foundation scholarships ($250,000)
Assets: $6,211,685 (2001)

Typical Recipients
Arts & Humanities: Arts Institutes, Arts Outreach, Historic Preservation, History & Archaeology, Libraries, Museums/Galleries, Music, Opera, Performing Arts, Public Broadcasting, Theater
Civic & Public Affairs: Botanical Gardens/Parks, Housing, Native American Affairs, Professional & Trade Associations, Public Policy, Urban & Community Affairs
Education: Colleges & Universities, Education

Funds, Medical Education, Private Education (Precollege), Religious Education, Science/Mathematics Education, Student Aid
Health: AIDS/HIV, Alzheimer's Disease, Cancer, Children's Health/Hospitals, Clinics/Medical Centers, Health Organizations, Medical Research, Multiple Sclerosis, Prenatal Health Issues, Public Health, Single-Disease Health Associations, Speech & Hearing
International: Foreign Arts Organizations
Religion: Religion-General, Jewish Causes, Religious Organizations, Synagogues/Temples
Science: Science-General, Science Museums
Social Services: At-Risk Youth, Child Abuse, Child Welfare, Community Service Organizations, Crime Prevention, Domestic Violence, Family Planning, Family Services, Homes, People with Disabilities, Scouts, Shelters/Homelessness, YMCA/YWCA/YMHA/YWHA, Youth Organizations

Application Procedures
Initial Contact: Send a brief letter of inquiry.
Application Requirements: Include a description of organization, purpose of funds sought, and proof of tax-exempt status.
Deadlines: None.

Foundation Officials
Adrienne Lederer: president, director
Lawrence D. Silverman: treasurer, director
Robert I. Ury: vice president, secretary, director

Grants Analysis
Disclosure Period: calendar year ending 2001
Total Grants: $592,000*
Number of Grants: 32
Average Grant: $12,250*
Highest Grant: $200,000
Typical Range: $8,000 to $40,000
*Note: Giving excludes scholarship. Average grant excludes highest grant.

Recent Grants
Note: Grants derived from 2001 Form 990.
General

250,000	University of Chicago School of Medicine, Chicago, IL -- scholarship endowment
200,000	Millennium Park, Inc., Chicago, IL -- Founders' Program
50,000	National Community for Prevention of Child Abuse, Chicago, IL
40,000	Chicago Opera Theater, Chicago, IL
40,000	Jewish United Fund of Metropolitan Chicago, Chicago, IL
25,000	Emanuel Congregation, Chicago, IL -- building renovation
25,000	Goodman Theatre, Chicago, IL -- campaign for new Goodman Theatre
20,000	Art Institute of Chicago, Chicago, IL
20,000	Chicago Children's Museum, Chicago, IL -- Dinosaur Discovery Program
20,000	Museum of Contemporary Art, Chicago, IL

LEE ENDOWMENT FOUNDATION

Giving Contact
Bill Feller, Trust Officer
c/o First Citizens Trust Co. NA
2601 4th Street SW
PO Box 1708
Mason City, IA 50402-1708
Phone: (641)423-1600
Fax: (641)423-4600
Web: http://www.firstcitizens.com

Alternate Contact

Dr. David L. Buettner, Chairman, Nominating Committee, Muse Scholar
N. Iowa Area Community College
500 College Dr.
Mason City, IA 50401
Phone: (641)422-4050

Description

Founded: 1978
EIN: 421074052
Organization Type: Private Foundation
Giving Locations: IA
Grant Types: General Support, Scholarship.

Donor Information

Founder: the late Elizabeth Norris

Typical Recipients

Arts & Humanities: Arts Festivals, Community Arts, Libraries, Museums/Galleries, Music, Performing Arts, Theater
Civic & Public Affairs: Botanical Gardens/Parks, Clubs, Community Foundations, Economic Development, Employment/Job Training, Civic & Public Affairs-General, Housing, Municipalities/Towns, Parades/Festivals, Rural Affairs, Safety, Urban & Community Affairs
Education: Arts/Humanities Education, Colleges & Universities, Community & Junior Colleges, Education-General, Minority Education, Preschool Education, Private Education (Precollege), Public Education (Precollege), Secondary Education (Public)
Environment: Environment-General
Health: Emergency/Ambulance Services, Health Organizations, Hospices, Hospitals, Public Health
Religion: Churches, Religious Organizations, Religious Welfare
Social Services: Camps, Child Welfare, Community Service Organizations, Counseling, Delinquency & Criminal Rehabilitation, Family Services, Food/Clothing Distribution, People with Disabilities, Recreation & Athletics, Scouts, Senior Services, Shelters/Homelessness, United Funds/United Ways, YMCA/YWCA/YMHA/YWHA, Youth Organizations

Application Procedures

Initial Contact: Application form required for scholarships.
Deadlines: March 1. There are no deadlines for charitable fund applications, but funds are usually awarded once a year in February.

Additional Information

Provides scholarships for residents of IA for higher education.

Foundation Officials

Donald G. Harrer: president
Lloyd Loers: vice president
Robert D. Ross: vice president
Mr. Douglas F. Sherwin: vice president
J. Martin Wolman: vice president, treasurer B Elizabeth, NJ March 08, 1919. ED University of Wisconsin (1937-1942). CORP AFFIL director: Madison Newspapers Inc. NONPR AFFIL member: WI Daily Newspaper League; member: WI Newspaper Association; director, trustee: WI Clinical Cancer Center; member: Madison Art Association; trustee: University Wisconsin Hospital & Clinic; trustee: Island Daily Press Association; trustee: Children & Youth Services; member: Edgewood College; member: Chamber of Commerce Madison; member: B'nai B'rith; member: Central Madison Comm.

Grants Analysis

Disclosure Period: calendar year ending 2000
Total Grants: $975,045*
Number of Grants: 69
Average Grant: $10,075*
Highest Grant: $200,000

Typical Range: $1,000 to $20,000
***Note:** Giving excludes scholarships. Average grant figure excludes two highest grants ($300,000).

Recent Grants

Note: Grants derived from 2001 Form 990.
General

200,000	Mason City Foundation, Mason City, IA
100,000	North Iowa Area Community College, Mason City, IA
75,709	City of Mason City, Mason City, IA
55,000	YMCA and Rehabilitation Center
50,000	North Iowa Vocational Center, IA
31,776	Mason City High School, Mason City, IA
30,000	Opportunity Village, Clear Lake, IA
27,000	Francis Lauer Youth Services, Mason City, IA
25,000	North Iowa Area Community College, Mason City, IA
25,000	North Iowa Area Community College, Mason City, IA

LEE ENTERPRISES INC.

Company Headquarters

215 N. Main Street
Davenport, IA 52801-1924
Phone: (563)383-2100
Fax: (563)323-9609
Web: http://www.lee.net

Company Description

Founded: 1890
Ticker: LEE
Exchange: NYSE
Revenue: US$525.9 million (2002)
Employees: 6700 (2003)
SIC(s): 2711 Newspapers, 4813 Telephone Communications Except Radiotelephone, 4833 Television Broadcasting Stations.

Operating Locations

Lee Enterprises (AZ--Tucson; CA--San Marcos; HI--Honolulu; IL--Carbondale, Decatur; IA--Mason City, Ottumwa, Rapid City; MN--Winona; MT--Billings, Butte, Helena; NE--Lincoln, Omaha; NM--Albuquerque; ND--Bismarck; OR--Portland; WV--Huntington; WI--La Crosse, Racine)

Lee Foundation

Giving Contact

Carl Schmidt, Secretary & Director
215 North Main Street
Davenport, IA 52801
Phone: (319)383-2100
Fax: (319)326-2972

Description

Founded: 1962
EIN: 426057173
Organization Type: Corporate Foundation
Giving Locations: headquarters and operating communities.
Grant Types: Capital, Endowment, General Support.

Donor Information

Founder: Lee Enterprises

Financial Summary

Total Giving: $329,711 (fiscal year ending September 30, 2003); $503,123 (fiscal 2002); $534,372 (fiscal 2001). Note: Contributes through foundation only.
Giving Analysis: Giving for fiscal 2001 includes: foundation scholarships ($22,500); foundation grants to United Way ($40,039) foundation ($471,833)

Assets: $6,910,853 (fiscal 2003); $5,617,813 (fiscal 2002); $6,461,121 (fiscal 2001)
Gifts Received: $1,000,000 (fiscal 2003); $500,000 (fiscal 1992). Note: Contributions were received from Lee Enterprises, Inc.

Typical Recipients

Arts & Humanities: Arts Centers, Arts & Humanities-General, Historic Preservation, History & Archaeology, Libraries, Literary Arts, Museums/Galleries, Music, Public Broadcasting, Theater, Visual Arts
Civic & Public Affairs: Asian American Affairs, Botanical Gardens/Parks, Business/Free Enterprise, Clubs, Community Foundations, Economic Development, Employment/Job Training, Civic & Public Affairs-General, Inner-City Development, Law & Justice, Municipalities/Towns, Nonprofit Management, Parades/Festivals, Philanthropic Organizations, Professional & Trade Associations, Public Policy, Rural Affairs, Urban & Community Affairs, Women's Affairs, Zoos/Aquariums
Education: Afterschool/Enrichment Programs, Agricultural Education, Business Education, Colleges & Universities, Community & Junior Colleges, Economic Education, Education Funds, Environmental Education, Education-General, International Studies, Journalism/Media Education, Literacy, Medical Education, Minority Education, Private Education (Precollege), Public Education (Precollege), Science/Mathematics Education, Secondary Education (Private), Secondary Education (Public), Social Sciences Education, Student Aid, Vocational & Technical Education
Environment: Environment-General, Resource Conservation, Wildlife Protection
Health: Cancer, Children's Health/Hospitals, Clinics/Medical Centers, Emergency/Ambulance Services, Health-General, Geriatric Health, Health Organizations, Hospitals, Nursing Services, Public Health, Single-Disease Health Associations
International: Human Rights
Religion: Religion-General, Jewish Causes, Missionary Activities (Domestic), Religious Welfare
Science: Science Museums, Scientific Organizations
Social Services: Animal Protection, Big Brothers/Big Sisters, Child Welfare, Community Centers, Community Service Organizations, Day Care, Emergency Relief, Family Planning, Family Services, Food/Clothing Distribution, Homes, Recreation & Athletics, Scouts, Senior Services, Shelters/Homelessness, Social Services-General, Special Olympics, United Funds/United Ways, YMCA/YWCA/YMHA/YWHA, Youth Organizations

Application Procedures

Initial Contact: Send a brief letter of inquiry.
Application Requirements: Include a description of organization and purpose of funds sought.
Deadlines: None.
Notes: The foundation has no formal grant application procedure or application form.

Restrictions

Foundation does not support individuals or outside of geographic area of Lee Enterprises, Inc.

Corporate Officials

Larry L. Bloom: chief financial officer B 1949. ED DePaul University BS. PRIM CORP EMPL senior vice president finance, treasurer, chief financial officer: Lee Enterprises Inc.

Foundation Officials

Mary Junck: president
Greg Schermer: director
Carl Schmidt: secretary
Greg Veon: director

Grants Analysis

Disclosure Period: fiscal year ending September 30, 2003
Total Grants: $304,071*

Number of Grants: 36
Average Grant: $8,446
Highest Grant: $50,000
Lowest Grant: $300
Typical Range: $1,000 to $10,000
*****Note:** Giving excludes United Way.

Recent Grants

Note: Grants derived from fiscal 2003 Form 990.
General

50,000	Davenport One, Davenport, IA
25,640	United Way of the Quad Cities, Davenport, IA
15,000	University of Nebraska, Lincoln, NE
12,500	Lincoln Children's Museum, Lincoln, NE
12,000	Center for Active Seniors Inc., Davenport, IA
10,000	Butte Family YMCA, Butte, MT
10,000	Friends of Brady Street, Davenport, IA
10,000	Gilda's Club of Quad Cities, Davenport, IA
10,000	Girl Scouts of the Mississippi Valley, Davenport, IA
10,000	University of Nebraska Athletic Department, Lincoln, NE

WHILMA B. LEE SCHOLARSHIP FUND TRUST

Giving Contact

Donald R. France, Trustee
PO Box 247
Marcellus, MI 49067-0247
Phone: (269)646-5345

Description

Founded: 1989
EIN: 386547465
Organization Type: Private Foundation
Giving Locations: MI: Cass County, Kalamazoo County, St. Joseph County, Van Buren County
Grant Types: Scholarship.

Financial Summary

Total Giving: $11,575 (2003); $12,075 (2001)
Giving Analysis: Giving for 2003 includes: foundation scholarships ($11,575); 2001: foundation scholarships ($12,075)
Assets: $134,614 (2003); $146,227 (2001)
Gifts Received: $2,000 (1994); $2,000 (1993). Note: In 1994, contributions were received from Jack and Rita Bradtke.

Typical Recipients

Education: Colleges & Universities, Education-General, Medical Education, Minority Education, Special Education, Student Aid
Social Services: Child Welfare, Community Service Organizations, Counseling, Family Services, Food/Clothing Distribution, United Funds/United Ways, YMCA/YWCA/YMHA/YWHA

Application Procedures

Initial Contact: Request application form.
Deadlines: April 15.

Additional Information

Provides scholarships for higher education to high school graduates from Van Buren, Cass, Kalamazoo, and St. Joseph counties, MI.

Foundation Officials

Donald R. France: trustee

Grants Analysis

Disclosure Period: calendar year ending 2003
Total Grants: $11,575*
Number of Grants: 22
Average Grant: $526
Highest Grant: $1,275
Lowest Grant: $300
Typical Range: $300 to $500
*****Note:** Giving includes scholarships.

Recent Grants

Note: Grants derived from 1997 Form 990.
Library-Related

3,000	Atlanta Fulton Public Library, Atlanta, GA

General

40,000	Woodruff Arts Center, Atlanta, GA
30,000	Foundation of Public Broadcasting
25,000	Scottish Rite Children's Hospital
20,000	Harris College
20,000	Shorter College
12,500	Eagle Ranch, Chestnut Mountain, GA
12,500	United Way, Atlanta, GA
10,000	Juvenile Diabetes Foundation, New York, NY
10,000	State YMCA, Atlanta, GA
7,500	Devereaux Center, GA

LEF FOUNDATION

Giving Contact

Marina Drummer, Grants Administrator
LEF Foundation
1095 Lodi Lane
St. Helena, CA 94574
Phone: (707)963-9591
Fax: (707)963-2109
E-mail: marina@lef-foundation.org
Web: http://www.lef-foundation.org

Alternate Contact

Lyda Kuth, Director
PO Box 382866
Cambridge, MA 02238-2866
Phone: (617)492-5333
Fax: (617)868-5603

Description

Founded: 1985
EIN: 680070194
Organization Type: Private Foundation
Giving Locations: CA: New England.
Grant Types: General Support, Project, Scholarship, Seed Money.

Donor Information

Founder: Lyda Ebert Trust

Financial Summary

Total Giving: $1,332,250 (fiscal year ending June 30, 2002); $1,240,700 (fiscal 2001)
Giving Analysis: Giving for fiscal 2002 includes: foundation scholarships ($25,000)
Assets: $13,784,123 (fiscal 2002); $15,330,239 (fiscal 2001)
Gifts Received: $400,008 (fiscal 2002); $413,439 (fiscal 1997); $70,017 (fiscal 1994). Note: In fiscal 2002, contributions were received from Lyda Kuth. In fiscal 1994, contributions were received from Lyda Kuth ($50,034) and Marion Green ($19,983).

Typical Recipients

Arts & Humanities: Arts Associations & Councils, Arts Centers, Arts Festivals, Arts Funds, Dance, Ethnic & Folk Arts, Film & Video, Arts & Humanities-General, History & Archaeology, Libraries, Museums/Galleries, Music, Opera, Performing Arts, Theater, Visual Arts
Civic & Public Affairs: African American Affairs, Asian American Affairs, Clubs, Economic Development, Civic & Public Affairs-General, Native American Affairs, Urban & Community Affairs, Women's Affairs
Education: Arts/Humanities Education, Colleges & Universities, Engineering/Technological Education, Education-General, Private Education (Precollege), Public Education (Precollege)
Environment: Environment-General, Wildlife Protection
Health: AIDS/HIV, Emergency/Ambulance Services
International: Foreign Arts Organizations, International Organizations
Religion: Churches, Religious Organizations
Social Services: Camps, Community Service Organizations, Family Services, Recreation & Athletics, Youth Organizations

Application Procedures

Initial Contact: Telephone the foundation and submit a brief letter of inquiry.
Application Requirements: Include a description of organization, amount requested, purpose of funds sought.
Deadlines: Check website for current deadlines.
Review Process: Announcements made within two months of application deadlines.

Restrictions

The foundation funds projects, programs, and services that encourage a positive interchange between the arts and the natural and urban environment.

Additional Information

"Past grantees may reapply for one funding cycle per year, Spring or Fall, for two additional years, provided all final reports have been filed. After a third year of funding, the Foundation requests that grantees allow a two-year hiatus prior to reapplication." Guidelines.
Publications: Application Guidelines

Foundation Officials

Laurey Finneran: trustee
Marion E. Greene: president
Byron Kuth: vice president
Lyda Ebert Kuth: cfo, secretary

Grants Analysis

Disclosure Period: fiscal year ending June 30, 2002
Total Grants: $1,307,250*
Number of Grants: 155
Average Grant: $8,434
Highest Grant: $35,000
Lowest Grant: $500
Typical Range: $3,000 to $15,000
*****Note:** Giving excludes scholarships.

Recent Grants

Note: Grants derived from fiscal 2002 Form 990.
General

35,000	Center for Land Use Interpretation, Culver City, CA -- in support of the development of CLUI's Interactive Landscape Environment
25,000	Spoleto Festival USA, Charleston, SC -- in support of six artists
20,000	African Services Committee, New York, NY -- in support of Global AIDS Alliance Medication for All Initiative
20,000	Center for Independent Documentary Inc., Sharon, MA -- in support of Project Touched
20,000	Drawing Center, New York, NY -- in support of your joint exhibition
20,000	President and Fellows of Harvard, Cambridge, MA -- in support of Robb Moss's project The Same River Twice
20,000	Puppet Showplace Theater, Brookline, MA -- in support of Puppets at Night
20,000	Theater Offensive, Boston, MA -- in support of Plays at Work Laboratory

18,000 Trustees of Phillips Academy, Andover, MA -- in support of Art on Main Program

15,000 California College of Arts and Crafts, San Francisco, CA -- in support of a residency and installation at the Capp Street Project

AL PAUL LEFTON CO.

Company Headquarters
100 Independence Mall W.
Philadelphia, PA 19106-2399
Web: http://www.lefton.com

Company Description
Revenue: US$70 million (2001)
Employees: 60 (2001)
SIC(s): 7300 Business Services.

Al Paul Lefton Co. Foundation

Giving Contact
Al Paul Lefton, Jr.
100 Independence Mall W., 4th Fl.
Philadelphia, PA 19106
Phone: (215)923-9600
Fax: (215)351-4298

Description
EIN: 236298693
Organization Type: Corporate Foundation
Giving Locations: PA: Philadelphia
Grant Types: General Support.

Financial Summary
Gifts Received: $20,000 (2000); $15,000 (1999); $20,000 (1995)

Typical Recipients
Arts & Humanities: Arts Associations & Councils, Arts Centers, Arts Institutes, Arts & Humanities-General, History & Archaeology, Libraries, Museums/Galleries, Music, Opera
Civic & Public Affairs: Botanical Gardens/Parks, Civic & Public Affairs-General, Parades/Festivals, Public Policy, Urban & Community Affairs, Zoos/Aquariums
Education: Arts/Humanities Education, Business Education, Colleges & Universities, Student Aid
Environment: Resource Conservation
Health: Hospitals, Hospitals (University Affiliated), Multiple Sclerosis
Religion: Churches, Jewish Causes
Social Services: United Funds/United Ways, Youth Organizations

Application Procedures
Initial Contact: Send a brief letter of inquiry.
Deadlines: None.

Corporate Officials
Al Paul Lefton, Jr.: president, chief executive officer, director B Wilmington, DE 1928. ED Yale University BA (1950). PRIM CORP EMPL president, chief executive officer, director: Al Paul Lefton Co. CORP AFFIL member: Mayors Comm Culture Arts; director: University Arts; director: Mann Music Center.
Raymond D. Scanlon: vice president, chief financial officer, director PRIM CORP EMPL vice president, chief financial officer, director: Al Paul Lefton Co.

Foundation Officials
Al Paul Lefton, Jr.: trustee (see above)
Raymond D. Scanlon: trustee (see above)

Grants Analysis
Disclosure Period: calendar year ending 2000
Total Grants: $20,570*
Number of Grants: 20
Average Grant: $1,029
Highest Grant: $5,000
Typical Range: $500 to $2,600
***Note:** Giving excludes United Way.

Recent Grants
Note: Grants derived from 2001 Form 990.
General

7,500 University of the Arts, Philadelphia, PA -- annual fund drive

5,600 Institute of Contemporary Art, Philadelphia, PA -- annual benefit fund

1,800 Union for Traditional Judaism, Teaneck, NJ -- for Ad in dinner journal

1,700 United Way of Southeastern Pennsylvania, Philadelphia, PA -- annual fund drive

1,050 Yale University, New Haven, CT -- for alumni fund

1,000 Main Line Art Center, Haverford, PA -- annual operating fund

750 Sconset Trust, Siasconset, MA -- for annual conservation

400 Japan America Society of Philadelphia, Philadelphia, PA -- annual sponsorship

170 Philadelphia Museum of Art, Philadelphia, PA -- for Craft Show and subscriber

LEHIGH CEMENT CO.

Company Headquarters
7660 Imperial Way, 4th Fl
Allentown, PA 18195

Company Description
Employees: 225 (2003)
SIC(s): 3241 Cement--Hydraulic, 3272 Concrete Products Nec.
Parent Company: HeidelbergCement A.G., Berliner Strasse 6, Heidelberg, Germany

Operating Locations
Lehigh Cement Co. (AL--Birmingham; CA--Los Angeles; IN--Glastonbury; MN; VA--Mannassas, Norfolk); Lehigh Portland Cement Co. (PA--Allentown)

Nonmonetary Support
Type: Donated Products; In-kind Services; Loaned Employees

Giving Contact
Corliss Bachman, communications coordinator
7660 Imperial Way
Allentown, PA 18195
Phone: (610)366-4764
Fax: (610)366-4684
E-mail: cbachman@lehighcement.com

Description
Organization Type: Corporate Giving Program
Former Name: Lehigh Portland Cement Co. (1999).
Giving Locations: headquarters and operating communities.
Grant Types: Employee Matching Gifts, General Support, Project, Scholarship.

Financial Summary
Total Giving: $250,000 (2005 approx); $250,000 (2004); $200,000 (2003 approx). Note: The Co.'s corporate office location has a funding budget of approximately $200,000. Each economic base unit, or sales office location, has a funding budget of $50,000 to $100,000.
Gifts Received: $225,000 (1995)

Typical Recipients
Arts & Humanities: Arts Funds, Historic Preservation, History & Archaeology, Libraries, Museums/Galleries, Music, Performing Arts, Public Broadcasting, Theater
Civic & Public Affairs: Business/Free Enterprise, Community Foundations, Employment/Job Training, Civic & Public Affairs-General, Municipalities/Towns, Native American Affairs, Professional & Trade Associations, Urban & Community Affairs, Zoos/Aquariums
Education: Business Education, Business-School Partnerships, Colleges & Universities, Community & Junior Colleges, Continuing Education, Economic Education, Education Associations, Education Funds, Elementary Education (Public), Engineering/Technological Education, Education-General, Literacy, Preschool Education, Private Education (Precollege), Public Education (Precollege), Science/Mathematics Education, Secondary Education (Public), Special Education, Student Aid, Vocational & Technical Education
Environment: Environment-General
Health: Cancer, Children's Health/Hospitals, Emergency/Ambulance Services, Health-General, Health Organizations, Heart, Hospices, Hospitals, Prenatal Health Issues, Transplant Networks/Donor Banks
Religion: Churches
Science: Scientific Organizations
Social Services: At-Risk Youth, Camps, Child Welfare, Community Service Organizations, Counseling, Day Care, Domestic Violence, Emergency Relief, Family Services, People with Disabilities, Recreation & Athletics, Scouts, Sexual Abuse, Shelters/Homelessness, Social Services-General, Substance Abuse, United Funds/United Ways, YMCA/YWCA/YMHA/YWHA, Youth Organizations

Application Procedures
Initial Contact: Send a brief letter of inquiry.
Deadlines: None.

Restrictions
Funding is provided to organization's in operating locations only. Tax exempt only.

Additional Information
The Lehigh Portland Cement Co. Charitable Trust dissolved in 1999.

Corporate Officials
Jeffry H. Brozyna: vice president, general counsel B Schenectady, NY 1952. ED Hobart College (1974); Albany Law School (1977). PRIM CORP EMPL vice president, general counsel: Lehigh Portland Cement Co. CORP AFFIL secretary: Addiment Inc. NONPR AFFIL director: American Portland Cement Alliance.
Helmut Erhard: president, chief executive officer

Foundation Officials
Jeffry H. Brozyna: trustee (see above)

Grants Analysis
Disclosure Period: calendar year ending 1996
Total Grants: $149,485*
Number of Grants: 250 (approx)
Average Grant: $598
Highest Grant: $19,755
Typical Range: $50 to $1,000
***Note:** Giving excludes matching gifts.

Recent Grants
Note: Grants derived from 1999 Form 990.
General

8,138 Habitat for Humanity, Allentown, PA

500 United Way of Greater Lehigh, Bethlehem, PA

OTTO W. LEHMANN FOUNDATION

Giving Contact
Richard J. Peterson, Trustee
680 Lake Shore Dr.
420 Tower Res.
Chicago, IL 60611
Phone: (312)587-0762

Description
Founded: 1967
EIN: 366160836
Organization Type: Private Foundation
Giving Locations: IL: Chicago
Grant Types: General Support.

Donor Information
Founder: the late Otto W. Lehmann

Financial Summary
Total Giving: $200,000 (fiscal year ending July 31, 2004); $200,000 (fiscal 2002); $200,000 (fiscal 2001)
Giving Analysis: Giving for fiscal 2004 includes: foundation scholarships ($46,000); fiscal 2002: foundation scholarships ($47,000); fiscal 2001: foundation scholarships ($47,000)
Assets: $2,020,599 (fiscal 2004); $1,970,507 (fiscal 2002); $2,212,827 (fiscal 2001)

Typical Recipients
Arts & Humanities: Arts Institutes, History & Archaeology, Libraries, Music, Opera
Civic & Public Affairs: Clubs, Employment/Job Training, Philanthropic Organizations, Zoos/Aquariums
Education: Colleges & Universities, Engineering/Technological Education, Private Education (Precollege), Special Education, Student Aid, Vocational & Technical Education
Health: Alzheimer's Disease, Cancer, Children's Health/Hospitals, Emergency/Ambulance Services, Eyes/Blindness, Health Organizations, Hospitals, Medical Rehabilitation, Medical Research, Nursing Services, Outpatient Health Care, Single-Disease Health Associations
Religion: Religious Organizations, Religious Welfare
Science: Observatories & Planetariums, Science Museums
Social Services: Child Welfare, Community Service Organizations, Domestic Violence, Food/Clothing Distribution, Homes, People with Disabilities, Shelters/Homelessness, United Funds/United Ways, Youth Organizations

Application Procedures
Initial Contact: Send brief letter describing program.
Application Requirements: Include a description of organization, amount requested, purpose of funds sought, recently audited financial statement, and proof of tax-exempt status.
Deadlines: June 15.

Restrictions
Does not support individuals, religious organizations for sectarian purposes, political or lobbying groups, or organizations outside operating areas.

Foundation Officials
Mary E. Peterson: trustee
Richard J. Peterson: trustee

Grants Analysis
Disclosure Period: fiscal year ending July 31, 2004
Total Grants: $154,000*
Number of Grants: 46
Average Grant: $3,348
Highest Grant: $9,000
Lowest Grant: $1,000

Typical Range: $1,000 to $5,000
***Note:** Giving excludes scholarships.

Recent Grants
Note: Grants derived from 2004 Form 990.
General
15,000	Loyola University, Chicago, IL -- towards education/scholarships
15,000	Northwestern University, Evanston, IL -- towards education/scholarships
10,000	Lincoln Park Zoological Society, Chicago, IL -- to support civic and public affairs
9,000	Shedd Aquarium, Chicago, IL -- to support civic and public affairs
8,000	Chicago Zoological Society, Brookfield, IL -- to support civic and public affairs
7,000	DePaul University, Chicago, IL -- towards education/scholarships
7,000	Field Museum of Natural History, Chicago, IL -- to support arts and humanities
6,000	Museum of Science and Industry, Chicago, IL -- for science
5,000	Hundred Club of Cook County, Chicago, IL -- for human services
5,000	Illinois Institute of Technology, Chicago, IL -- towards education/scholarships

JOHN J. LEIDY FOUNDATION

Giving Contact
W. Michel Pierson, President
201 E. Baltimore St., Suite 1420
Baltimore, MD 21202
Phone: (410)727-4136
E-mail: leidyfd@attglobal.net

Description
Founded: 1957
EIN: 526034785
Organization Type: Private Foundation
Giving Locations: MD: Baltimore including metropolitan area
Grant Types: General Support, Scholarship.

Donor Information
Founder: the late John J. Leidy

Financial Summary
Total Giving: $603,679 (2001)
Giving Analysis: Giving for 2001 includes: foundation scholarships ($125,540)
Assets: $12,429,603 (2001)

Typical Recipients
Arts & Humanities: Arts Institutes, Community Arts, Historic Preservation, Libraries, Museums/Galleries, Music, Opera
Civic & Public Affairs: Clubs, Economic Development, Employment/Job Training, Civic & Public Affairs-General, Housing, Legal Aid, Philanthropic Organizations, Public Policy, Urban & Community Affairs
Education: Arts/Humanities Education, Colleges & Universities, Education Reform, Elementary Education (Private), Education-General, Legal Education, Literacy, Private Education (Precollege), Special Education, Student Aid
Health: AIDS/HIV, Clinics/Medical Centers, Emergency/Ambulance Services, Health Organizations, Heart, Hospitals, Medical Research, Public Health, Single-Disease Health Associations
Religion: Churches, Jewish Causes, Ministries, Religious Organizations, Religious Welfare
Science: Science Museums, Scientific Research
Social Services: Big Brothers/Big Sisters, Child Welfare, Community Service Organizations, Emergency

Relief, Family Services, Food/Clothing Distribution, People with Disabilities, Senior Services, United Funds/United Ways, Veterans, Youth Organizations

Application Procedures
Initial Contact: Send full proposal.
Application Requirements: Include an original and four copies which contains complete details of need and amount requested, proof of tax-exempt status, budget, a description of organization and its activities in general, list of board members, and an explanation of whether the applicant is controlled by, related to, connected with, or sponsored by another organization.
Deadlines: None.

Restrictions
Preference is given to educational and health care organizations. Does not support individuals.

Foundation Officials
Henry E. Pear: treasurer
Ruth C. Pear: vice president
Robert L. Pierson: secretary
W. Michel Pierson: president

Grants Analysis
Disclosure Period: calendar year ending 2001
Total Grants: $478,139*
Number of Grants: 73
Average Grant: $6,550*
Highest Grant: $27,500
Lowest Grant: $500
Typical Range: $1,000 to $10,000
***Note:** Giving excludes scholarships.

Recent Grants
Note: Grants derived from 2001 Form 990.
Library-Related
25,000	Enoch Pratt Free Library, Baltimore, MD

General
50,000	Maryland Institute College of Art, Baltimore, MD
50,000	Walters Art Museum, Baltimore, MD
27,500	Associated Jewish Charities, Baltimore, MD
20,000	Maryland Center for Veterans, Baltimore, MD
19,000	Preservation Society, Newport, RI
15,000	American Red Cross, Baltimore, MD
15,000	Govans Ecumenical Development, Baltimore, MD
12,500	Edward A. Myerberg Northwest Senior Center, Inc., Baltimore, MD
11,000	Baltimore Symphony Orchestra, Baltimore, MD
10,000	American Red Cross, Baltimore, MD

LEMBERG FOUNDATION

Giving Contact
John Usdan, Treasurer
60 E. 42nd St., Rm. 1814
New York, NY 10165
Phone: (212)682-9595

Description
Founded: 1945
EIN: 136082064
Organization Type: Private Foundation
Giving Locations: NY: New York
Grant Types: Capital, Endowment, Fellowship, Project, Research, Scholarship.

Donor Information
Founder: the late Samuel Lemberg

Financial Summary

Total Giving: $770,480 (2001)
Giving Analysis: Giving for 2001 includes: foundation scholarships ($40,500)
Assets: $32,208,117 (2001)
Gifts Received: $75,000 (2000)

Typical Recipients

Arts & Humanities: Arts Associations & Councils, Arts Centers, Arts Funds, Community Arts, Dance, Film & Video, Historic Preservation, Libraries, Museums/Galleries, Music, Opera, Performing Arts, Public Broadcasting, Theater, Visual Arts
Civic & Public Affairs: Botanical Gardens/Parks, Economic Development, Civic & Public Affairs-General, Professional & Trade Associations, Public Policy
Education: Arts/Humanities Education, Colleges & Universities, Economic Education, Education Funds, Education-General, Health & Physical Education, Literacy, Minority Education, Private Education (Precollege), Public Education (Precollege), Religious Education, Science/Mathematics Education, Student Aid
Health: Cancer, Clinics/Medical Centers, Health Organizations, Hospitals, Hospitals (University Affiliated), Medical Research, Multiple Sclerosis, Single-Disease Health Associations
International: Foreign Arts Organizations, Human Rights
Religion: Jewish Causes, Religious Organizations, Seminaries, Synagogues/Temples
Social Services: Animal Protection, Child Welfare, Community Service Organizations, Family Services, People with Disabilities, United Funds/United Ways, YMCA/YWCA/YMHA/YWHA

Application Procedures

Initial Contact: Send a brief letter of inquiry describing program or project.
Deadlines: None.

Restrictions

No grants for matching gifts.

Foundation Officials

Adam Usdan: vice president
John Usdan: treasurer
Suzanne Usdan: president

Grants Analysis

Disclosure Period: calendar year ending 2001
Total Grants: $729,980*
Number of Grants: 155
Average Grant: $4,710
Highest Grant: $75,000
Lowest Grant: $50
Typical Range: $100 to $50,000
***Note:** Giving excludes scholarships.

Recent Grants

Note: Grants derived from 2001 Form 990.

General

75,000	United Jewish Appeal Federation, New York, NY
65,600	Lincoln Center Institute, New York, NY
55,000	WNET/Channel 13, New York, NY
50,000	Multiple Sclerosis Research Fund
50,000	Usdan Center for Performing Arts, New York, NY
44,550	92nd Street "Y", New York, NY
40,500	Samuel Lemberg Scholarship Loan Fund, New York, NY
33,700	WNYC, New York, NY
28,000	Carnegie Hall Society, New York, NY
25,000	Bronx House, Bronx, NY

REGINALD A. AND ELIZABETH S. LENNA FOUNDATION

Giving Contact

Randy Ordines, Treasurer
Reginald A. and Elizabeth S. Lenna Foundation
214 W. Fifth St.
Jamestown, NY 14701
Phone: (716)484-2402

Description

Founded: 1985
EIN: 112800733
Organization Type: Private Foundation
Giving Locations: NY: Jamestown
Grant Types: General Support.

Donor Information

Founder: Reginald A. Lenna

Financial Summary

Total Giving: $435,000 (2003); $230,000 (2001)
Assets: $8,774,524 (2003); $9,448,550 (2001)
Gifts Received: $8,681,017 (1998)

Typical Recipients

Arts & Humanities: Arts Associations & Councils, Arts Funds, Arts Institutes, Ballet, Arts & Humanities-General, History & Archaeology, Libraries, Music, Performing Arts, Public Broadcasting
Civic & Public Affairs: Community Foundations, Economic Development, Employment/Job Training, Civic & Public Affairs-General, Public Policy, Safety, Urban & Community Affairs
Education: Arts/Humanities Education, Colleges & Universities, Community & Junior Colleges, Education-General, Public Education (Precollege)
Environment: Environment-General, Wildlife Protection
Health: Emergency/Ambulance Services, Hospices, Hospitals
Religion: Churches, Religious Welfare
Science: Science Museums
Social Services: Animal Protection, Community Centers, Food/Clothing Distribution, Homes, Recreation & Athletics, Scouts, United Funds/United Ways, YMCA/YWCA/YMHA/YWHA, Youth Organizations

Application Procedures

Initial Contact: Send a brief letter of inquiry and a full proposal.
Application Requirements: Include purpose of funds sought, amount requested, a description of organization, and proof of tax-exempt status.
Deadlines: None.

Foundation Officials

Elizabeth S. Lenna: president, director

Grants Analysis

Disclosure Period: calendar year ending 2003
Total Grants: $435,000
Number of Grants: 3
Highest Grant: $360,000
Lowest Grant: $25,000

Recent Grants

Note: Grants derived from 2003 Form 990.
General

360,000	WCA Hospital, Jamestown, NY
50,000	Reg Lenna Civic Center, Jamestown, NY
25,000	Chautauqua Institution, Chautauqua, NY

MARTHA, DAVID AND BAGBY LENNOX FOUNDATION

Giving Contact

William P. Streng, President & Treasurer
228 6th St. SE
Paris, TX 75460
Phone: (903)784-4316

Description

Founded: 1985
EIN: 760157945
Organization Type: Private Foundation
Giving Locations: TX: northeast area
Grant Types: General Support, Scholarship.

Donor Information

Founder: the late Martha Lennox, the late David Lennox, the late Bagby Lennox

Financial Summary

Total Giving: $791,625 (2002)
Giving Analysis: Giving for 2002 includes: foundation scholarships ($22,500)
Assets: $11,612,662 (2002)
Gifts Received: $2,500 (1999); $3,514,610 (1994).
Note: In 1994, contributions were received from the estate of Martha Lennox.

Typical Recipients

Arts & Humanities: History & Archaeology, Libraries, Museums/Galleries
Civic & Public Affairs: African American Affairs, Community Foundations, Civic & Public Affairs-General, Legal Aid, Municipalities/Towns, Public Policy, Urban & Community Affairs
Education: Agricultural Education, Colleges & Universities, Education-General, Gifted & Talented Programs, Science/Mathematics Education, Special Education, Student Aid
Environment: Resource Conservation
Health: Arthritis, Mental Health
International: International Organizations
Religion: Churches, Ministries, Religious Welfare
Social Services: Animal Protection, Camps, Child Welfare, Crime Prevention, Family Services, Scouts, Shelters/Homelessness, Youth Organizations

Application Procedures

Initial Contact: Send a brief letter of inquiry.
Deadlines: None.

Restrictions

Grants are not made to individuals.

Foundation Officials

Mary W. Clark: director
Sam L. Hocker: director
Hardy Moore: president
William Paul Streng: secretary, treasurer B Sterling, IL 1937. ED Wartburg College BA (1959); Northwestern University JD (1962). PRIM CORP EMPL law professor: Vision & Elkins. CORP AFFIL lecturer: Practicing Law Institute; lecturer: World Trade Institute; consult: Braceurell & Patterson; lecturer: International Fiscal Association; lecturer: America Law Institute. NONPR AFFIL member: American Bar Association; member: Texas State Bar.

Grants Analysis

Disclosure Period: calendar year ending 2002
Total Grants: $769,125*
Number of Grants: 28
Average Grant: $22,824*
Highest Grant: $100,000
Lowest Grant: $1,000
Typical Range: $10,000 to $50,000

*Note: Giving excludes scholarships. Average grant figure excludes two highest grants ($175,700).

Recent Grants

Note: Grants derived from 2002 Form 990.

Library-Related

15,000	Civil War Preservation Trust, Arlington, TX -- support for the Land and Water Conservation Fund

General

100,000	Christus St. Joseph's Health System, Paris, TX -- support for Lennox Health Resource Center
100,000	Nature Conservancy of Texas, Houston, TX -- support for acquisition of the Hancock land
75,700	Clarksville Independent School District, Clarksville, TX -- support towards implementing an electronic curriculum system
45,000	Red River County Firefighters Association, Detroit, TX -- to promote fire prevention
32,800	Avery Independent School District, Avery, TX -- to support the Laptop Learning Project
32,144	City of Detroit, Detroit, MI -- for construction of a new ball field
31,644	Rivercrest Independent School District, Bogata, TX -- for foreign language lab and technology upgrade to the high school library
30,000	Family Haven Crisis & Resource Center, Inc., Paris, TX -- to establish Crisis Center Programs
25,000	Detroit Independent School District, Detroit, TX -- for media center materials
21,715	City of Clarksville, Clarksville, TX -- support for the Historic Creek Walk Project

DEAN AND MARGARET LESHER FOUNDATION

Giving Contact

Kathleen Odne, Executive Director
Dean and Margaret Lesher Foundation
1333 N. California Boulevard, Suite 510
Walnut Creek, CA 94596
Phone: (925)935-9988
Fax: (925)935-7459

Description

Founded: 1994
EIN: 680208980
Organization Type: Private Foundation
Giving Locations: CA: Contra Costa County
Grant Types: General Support, Matching, Scholarship.

Donor Information

Founder: Established in 1994 by Dean S. Lesher.

Financial Summary

Total Giving: $1,939,200 (2003)
Assets: $78,438,224 (2003)
Gifts Received: $34,163,288 (2003); $914,652 (2000); $10,207,579 (1995). Note: In 2003, contributions were received from M.L. Lesher Trust. In 1995, contributions were received from the estate of Dean S. Lesher.

Typical Recipients

Arts & Humanities: Arts Associations & Councils, Arts Centers, Ballet, Arts & Humanities-General, History & Archaeology, Libraries, Museums/Galleries, Music, Theater, Visual Arts
Civic & Public Affairs: Clubs, Housing, Municipalities/Towns, Parades/Festivals, Urban & Community

Affairs, Women's Affairs
Education: Arts/Humanities Education, Colleges & Universities, Community & Junior Colleges, Education Funds, Elementary Education (Public), Private Education (Precollege), Public Education (Precollege), Secondary Education (Public)
Environment: Resource Conservation
Health: AIDS/HIV, Children's Health/Hospitals, Emergency/Ambulance Services, Heart, Mental Health, Prenatal Health Issues, Preventive Medicine/Wellness Organizations
Religion: Religious Organizations, Religious Welfare
Social Services: Animal Protection, Big Brothers/Big Sisters, Child Welfare, Community Centers, Community Service Organizations, Counseling, Day Care, Domestic Violence, Family Services, Food/Clothing Distribution, Homes, People with Disabilities, Recreation & Athletics, Scouts, Sexual Abuse, Shelters/Homelessness, Substance Abuse, Volunteer Services, YMCA/YWCA/YMHA/YWHA

Application Procedures

Initial Contact: Return completed application form with a brief letter of inquiry.
Application Requirements: Include a description of organization, amount requested, purpose of funds sought, recently audited financial statement, and proof of tax-exempt status.
Deadlines: None.

Restrictions

Foundation does not support individuals, political or lobbying groups, or organizations outside operating areas.

Foundation Officials

Cynthia Lesher: director
Melinda Lesher: director
Stephen Lesher: director

Grants Analysis

Disclosure Period: calendar year ending 2003
Total Grants: $1,939,200
Number of Grants: 74
Average Grant: $17,538*
Highest Grant: $250,000
Lowest Grant: $300
Typical Range: $5,000 to $25,000
*Note: Average grant figure excludes three highest grants ($694,000).

Recent Grants

Note: Grants derived from 2001 Form 990.

General

250,000	Battered Women's Alternatives, San Francisco, CA
244,000	Contra Costa County Office of Education, Contra Costa, CA
200,000	City of Walnut Creek, Walnut Creek, CA -- arts endowment grant
100,000	Cambridge Community Center, Concord, CA
100,000	Concord Pavilion Association, Concord, CA
100,000	Contra Costa Community College District, Contra Costa, CA
70,000	New Connections, Concord, CA
50,000	Diablo Ballet, Walnut Creek, CA
50,000	East Bay Habitat for Humanity, Oakland, CA
50,000	Rape Crisis Center, Beaufort, SC

LEVITT FOUNDATION (NY)

Giving Contact

Barbara Greenberg
Levitt Foundation

Care of The Philanthropic Group
630 Fifth Ave., 20th Fl.
New York, NY 10111
Phone: (212)476-9000

Description

Founded: 1949
EIN: 136128226
Organization Type: Private Foundation
Giving Locations: NY: Suffolk and Nassau counties, New York
Grant Types: General Support.

Donor Information

Founder: Levitt and Sons, the late Abraham Levitt, the late Alfred Levitt, William Levitt

Financial Summary

Total Giving: $596,608 (fiscal year ending April 30, 2004); $707,449 (fiscal 2001)
Assets: $13,693,852 (fiscal 2004); $18,607,783 (fiscal 2001)

Typical Recipients

Arts & Humanities: Arts Appreciation, Arts Funds, Arts Outreach, Dance, Arts & Humanities-General, History & Archaeology, Libraries, Museums/Galleries, Music, Opera, Performing Arts
Civic & Public Affairs: African American Affairs, Botanical Gardens/Parks, Business/Free Enterprise, Civil Rights, Economic Development, Gay/Lesbian Issues, Civic & Public Affairs-General, Hispanic Affairs, Housing, Legal Aid, Municipalities/Towns, Philanthropic Organizations, Urban & Community Affairs
Education: Afterschool/Enrichment Programs, Arts/Humanities Education, Colleges & Universities, Elementary Education (Public), Education-General, International Studies, Leadership Training, Preschool Education, Private Education (Precollege)
Environment: Air/Water Quality, Environment-General
Health: Clinics/Medical Centers, Geriatric Health, Hospitals (University Affiliated), Mental Health, Prenatal Health Issues
International: International Relations, International Relief Efforts
Religion: Dioceses, Jewish Causes, Ministries, Religious Organizations
Science: Science Museums, Scientific Centers & Institutes
Social Services: At-Risk Youth, Child Welfare, Community Centers, Community Service Organizations, Day Care, Domestic Violence, Family Planning, Family Services, Social Services-General, United Funds/United Ways, Youth Organizations

Application Procedures

Initial Contact: Send brief letter describing program.
Deadlines: None.

Restrictions

Does not support individuals.

Foundation Officials

Robert J. Appel: treasurer, trustee
Prudence Brown: trustee
Dr. Farrell Jones: president, trustee
Stephen Jon Mathes, Esq.: secretary, trustee B New York, NY 1945. ED University of Pennsylvania BA (1967); University of Pennsylvania JD (1970). NONPR AFFIL member: Philadelphia Bar Association; member: Thanatopsis Society; member: American Bar Association; member: Pennsylvania Bar Association; director: Academy Vocal Arts. CLUB AFFIL Racquet Club; Germantown Cricket Club.
May W. Newburger: trustee

Grants Analysis

Disclosure Period: fiscal year ending April 30, 2004
Total Grants: $596,608
Number of Grants: 44
Average Grant: $10,102*

Highest Grant: $97,308
Lowest Grant: $1,000
Typical Range: $5,000 to $20,000
*Note: Average grant figure excludes two highest grants ($172,308).

Recent Grants

Note: Grants derived from fiscal 2004 Form 990.
General

97,308	Rocking the Boat Inc., Bronx, NY
75,000	Point Community Development Corporation, Bronx, NY
50,000	Brooklyn Center for the Urban Environment, Brooklyn, NY
50,000	Green Guerillas Inc., New York, NY
50,000	United Puerto Rican Organization of Southeast Park Inc., Brooklyn, NY
42,500	Youth Ministries for Peace and Justice, Bronx, NY
40,500	Five Towns Community Center, Lawrence, NY
25,000	United Neighborhood Houses of New York Inc., New York, NY
20,000	Groundswell Community Mural Project Inc., Brooklyn, NY
10,000	New Cassel-Westbury Youth Services, Westbury, NY

JUNE ROCKWELL LEVY FOUNDATION

Giving Contact

Jonathan Loring, President
Sherry Trust Co.
175 Federal Street
Boston, MA 02110
Phone: (617)482-5270

Description

Founded: 1947
EIN: 046074284
Organization Type: General Purpose Foundation
Giving Locations: MA; RI
Grant Types: Capital, General Support, Research, Scholarship, Seed Money.

Donor Information

Founder: Incorporated in 1947 by the late Austin T. Levy.

Financial Summary

Total Giving: $1,301,999 (2001)
Assets: $29,129,634 (2001)

Typical Recipients

Arts & Humanities: Arts Associations & Councils, Arts Centers, Arts Festivals, Ballet, Dance, Historic Preservation, History & Archaeology, Libraries, Museums/Galleries, Music, Opera, Performing Arts, Public Broadcasting, Theater
Civic & Public Affairs: African American Affairs, Economic Development, Civic & Public Affairs-General, Hispanic Affairs, Housing, Legal Aid, Municipalities/Towns, Nonprofit Management, Philanthropic Organizations, Public Policy, Safety, Urban & Community Affairs, Women's Affairs, Zoos/Aquariums
Education: Afterschool/Enrichment Programs, Agricultural Education, Arts/Humanities Education, Colleges & Universities, Engineering/Technological Education, Education-General, Health & Physical Education, Leadership Training, Literacy, Medical Education, Minority Education, Private Education (Precollege), Public Education (Precollege), Secondary Education (Private), Secondary Education (Public), Special Education, Student Aid
Environment: Air/Water Quality, Environment-General, Resource Conservation

Health: AIDS/HIV, Cancer, Children's Health/Hospitals, Clinics/Medical Centers, Diabetes, Emergency/Ambulance Services, Geriatric Health, Health Funds, Health Organizations, Home-Care Services, Hospices, Hospitals, Long-Term Care, Medical Rehabilitation, Medical Research, Mental Health, Nursing Services, Public Health, Single-Disease Health Associations
International: International Affairs, International Organizations, International Relations
Religion: Religious Welfare, Social/Policy Issues
Science: Science Museums
Social Services: Animal Protection, At-Risk Youth, Camps, Child Welfare, Community Centers, Community Service Organizations, Domestic Violence, Family Planning, Family Services, Food/Clothing Distribution, Homes, People with Disabilities, Recreation & Athletics, Refugee Assistance, Scouts, Senior Services, Sexual Abuse, Social Services-General, Substance Abuse, United Funds/United Ways, Volunteer Services, YMCA/YWCA/YMHA/YWHA, Youth Organizations

Application Procedures

Initial Contact: The foundation requests applications be made in letter form.
Application Requirements: The application should include any materials the organization feels are necessary for a complete review.
Deadlines: None.

Restrictions

The foundation does not make grants for religious purposes or to individuals.

Foundation Officials

James K. Edwards: trustee
Paul F. Greene: trustee
George T. Helm: trustee
Raymond G. Leveille, Jr.: trustee
Jonathan B. Loring: president, trustee
Raymond N. Menard: trustee
James W. Noonan: secretary, trustee
Edward H. Osgood: trustee B Wenham, MA 1916. ED Harvard University (1938). CORP AFFIL director: Fiduciary Trust Co. International.
Nancy DuVergne Smith: treasurer, trustee B Meridian, MS 1951. ED Tulane University BFA (1973); Harvard University MA (1989). PRIM NONPR EMPL education director, public affairs office: Wellesley College. NONPR AFFIL member: National Writers Union; member: National Writers Union Services Organization; member: Council Advancement & Support Education; director: Artists Foundation; member: Boston Women Communicators.
James M. White, Jr.: trustee NONPR AFFIL assistant clerk, director: Nebraska Health Services.

Grants Analysis

Disclosure Period: calendar year ending 2001
Total Grants: $1,236,999*
Number of Grants: 88
Average Grant: $14,057
Highest Grant: $50,000
Lowest Grant: $1,000
Typical Range: $10,000 to $20,000
*Note: Giving excludes United Way.

Recent Grants

Note: Grants derived from 2002 Form 990.
Library-Related

20,000	Providence Public Library, Providence, RI -- for operating support

General

65,000	United Way of Rhode Island Inc., Providence, RI -- for annual contribution
50,000	Landmark Medical Center, North Smithfield, RI -- for cardiac cath lab
50,000	Medical Foundation Inc., Boston, MA -- for medical research
30,000	Miriam Hospital Foundation, Providence, RI -- for equipment for cardiac center
30,000	Rhode Island Hospital Foundation, Providence, RI -- for endoscopy unit equipment
25,000	ARC of Northern Rhode Island Inc., Woonsocket, RI -- for operating support
25,000	Boy Scouts of America-Narragansett Council, Providence, RI -- for operating support
25,000	Dorcas Place Parent Literacy Center, Providence, RI -- for capital campaign
25,000	Elizabeth Buffum Chase House, Warwick, RI -- for capital campaign
25,000	Massachusetts General Hospital, Boston, MA -- for medical research

LG&E ENERGY CORP.

Company Headquarters

Louisville, KY
Web: http://www.lgeenergy.com

Company Description

Assets: US$2.707 billion (2001)
Employees: 5403 (2001)
SIC(s): 4911 Electric Services, 4922 Natural Gas Transmission, 6719 Holding Companies Nec.

Operating Locations

LG&E Energy Corp. (KY--Louisville)

LG&E Energy Foundation

Giving Contact

Elaine Ashcraft, Grants Administrator
LG&E Energy Foundation
PO Box 32030
Louisville, KY 40232
Phone: (502)627-4037
Fax: (502)217-2672
Web: http://www.lgeenergy.com/foundation/default.asp

Description

Founded: 1994
EIN: 611257368
Organization Type: Corporate Foundation
Giving Locations: KY: Louisville headquarters and operating communities.
Grant Types: Award, Capital, Employee Matching Gifts, Endowment, General Support, Matching, Multiyear/Continuing Support, Operating Expenses, Scholarship.

Donor Information

Founder: Established in 1994 by Louisville Gas and Electric Co.

Financial Summary

Total Giving: $1,185,293 (2003); $2,158,323 (2002); $2,206,912 (2001)
Assets: $14,199,181 (2003); $13,666,761 (2002); $17,541,353 (2001)
Gifts Received: $4,882 (1997); $15,000,000 (1994)

Typical Recipients

Arts & Humanities: Arts Associations & Councils, Arts Centers, Arts Funds, Ballet, Ethnic & Folk Arts, History & Archaeology, Libraries, Museums/Galleries, Music, Public Broadcasting, Theater
Civic & Public Affairs: African American Affairs, Botanical Gardens/Parks, Community Foundations, Economic Development, Employment/Job Training, Civic & Public Affairs-General, Housing, Law & Justice, Minority Business, Parades/Festivals, Urban & Community Affairs, Women's Affairs, Zoos/

Aquariums
Education: Afterschool/Enrichment Programs, Agricultural Education, Business Education, Colleges & Universities, Education Associations, Education Funds, Education Reform, Engineering/Technological Education, Environmental Education, Education-General, Leadership Training, Literacy, Minority Education, Private Education (Precollege), Public Education (Precollege), Religious Education, School Volunteerism, Science/Mathematics Education, Special Education, Student Aid, Vocational & Technical Education
Environment: Environment-General, Resource Conservation
Health: Children's Health/Hospitals, Emergency/Ambulance Services, Geriatric Health, Heart, Transplant Networks/Donor Banks
Religion: Churches, Religious Organizations, Religious Welfare
Science: Science Exhibits & Fairs, Scientific Centers & Institutes
Social Services: At-Risk Youth, Child Welfare, Community Centers, Community Service Organizations, Counseling, Day Care, Emergency Relief, Family Services, Food/Clothing Distribution, Homes, Recreation & Athletics, Scouts, Shelters/Homelessness, Social Services-General, United Funds/United Ways, Veterans, YMCA/YWCA/YMHA/YWHA, Youth Organizations

Application Procedures

Initial Contact: Request a corporate contributions application form.
Application Requirements: Include a description of organization, amount requested, purpose of funds sought, recently audited financial statement, proof of tax-exempt status, and list of board of directors.
Deadlines: None.

Restrictions

Does not support individuals, religious organizations for sectarian purposes, political or lobbying groups, or organizations outside operating areas. Applicant must be a 501(c)(3) organization.

Additional Information

Publications: Application Form; Guidelines

Corporate Officials

Roger W. Hale: chairman, chief executive officer, director B Baltimore, MD 1943. ED University of Maryland BA (1965); Massachusetts Institute of Technology MS (1979). PRIM CORP EMPL chairman, chief executive officer, director: LG&E Energy Corp. CORP AFFIL director: PNC Bank Corp.; director: H & R Block. NONPR AFFIL director: Edison Electric Institute.
Charles A. Markel, III: vice president finance, treasurer PRIM CORP EMPL vice president finance, treasurer: LG&E Energy Corp.
Stephen R. Wood: president

Foundation Officials

Rudolph W. Keeling: vice president
John R. McCall: vice president, secretary, director
S. Bradford Rives: vice president, treasurer, director
Victor A. Staffieri: president, director

Grants Analysis

Disclosure Period: calendar year ending 2003
Total Grants: $615,000*
Number of Grants: 30
Average Grant: $18,621*
Highest Grant: $75,000
Lowest Grant: $500
Typical Range: $1,000 to $30,000
*Note: Giving excludes matching gifts, scholarship, and United Way. Average grant figure excludes highest grant.

Recent Grants

Note: Grants derived from 2003 Form 990.

Library-Related
15,000	Louisville Free Public Library Foundation Inc., Louisville, KY

General
75,000	Cabbage Patch Settlement House, Louisville, KY
58,000	Partnerships in Education Inc., Lexington, KY
57,725	United Way of the Bluegrass, Lexington, KY
50,813	Greater Louisville Fund for the Arts Inc., Louisville, KY
50,000	Bellarmine College, Louisville, KY
50,000	University of Louisville Foundation Inc., Louisville, KY
40,000	Lexington Partnership for Workforce, Lexington, KY
39,636	United Way of Henderson, Henderson, KY
31,500	University of Kentucky Research Foundation, Lexington, KY
30,000	Louisville Science Center, Louisville, KY

BERTHA AND ISAAC LIBERMAN FOUNDATION

Giving Contact

Jeffrey Klein, President
480 Park Avenue
New York, NY 10022

Description

Founded: 1947
EIN: 136119056
Organization Type: Private Foundation
Giving Locations: NY: New York City
Grant Types: General Support.

Donor Information

Founder: the late Isaac Liberman

Financial Summary

Total Giving: $339,900 (fiscal year ending June 30, 2004); $278,550 (fiscal 2001)
Assets: $7,769,151 (fiscal 2004); $7,225,857 (fiscal 2001)
Gifts Received: $19,504 (fiscal 1998); $910,606 (fiscal 1997). Note: In fiscal 1997, contributions were received from the Estate of Seymour Klein and the from the Estate of Ruth Klein.

Typical Recipients

Arts & Humanities: Arts Centers, Libraries, Museums/Galleries, Music, Opera, Theater
Civic & Public Affairs: Inner-City Development, Law & Justice, Philanthropic Organizations, Professional & Trade Associations, Urban & Community Affairs
Education: Business Education, Colleges & Universities, Education-General, Private Education (Precollege), Science/Mathematics Education, Secondary Education (Private)
Environment: Environment-General
Health: Cancer, Clinics/Medical Centers, Hospitals, Prenatal Health Issues, Single-Disease Health Associations
Religion: Jewish Causes, Religious Organizations
Social Services: Community Service Organizations, Crime Prevention, Delinquency & Criminal Rehabilitation, Food/Clothing Distribution, Scouts, YMCA/YWCA/YMHA/YWHA, Youth Organizations

Application Procedures

Initial Contact: Send a brief letter of inquiry describing program or project. Include purpose of funds sought and proof of tax-exempt status.
Deadlines: None.

Restrictions

Does not support individuals.

Foundation Officials

Jeffrey Klein: president

Grants Analysis

Disclosure Period: fiscal year ending June 30, 2004
Total Grants: $339,900
Number of Grants: 67
Average Grant: $4,226*
Highest Grant: $61,000
Lowest Grant: $250
Typical Range: $1,000 to $10,000
*Note: Average grant figure excludes highest grant.

Recent Grants

Note: Grants derived from fiscal 2004 Form 990.
General
61,000	Museum of Modern Art, New York, NY
25,000	Lab School of Washington, Washington, DC
25,000	New Museum of Contemporary Art, New York, NY
20,000	92nd Street Young Men's and Young Women's Hebrew Association, New York, NY
20,000	Dia Center for the Arts, New York, NY
15,000	Hundred Year Association, New York, NY
15,000	Mount Sinai Medical Center, New York, NY
15,000	New Museum of Contemporary Art, New York, NY
12,000	Whitney Museum of American Art, New York, NY
10,000	New York City Opera, New York, NY

LIBERTY CORP.

Company Headquarters

Greenville, SC
Web: http://www.libertycorp.com

Company Description

Founded: 1968
Ticker: LC
Exchange: NYSE
Revenue: US$206.4 million (2002)
Employees: 1500 (2003)
SIC(s): 4833 Television Broadcasting Stations, 6311 Life Insurance, 6321 Accident & Health Insurance, 6552 Subdividers & Developers Nec.

Operating Locations

Liberty Corp. (AL--Montgomery; AR--Jonesboro; IN--Evansville; KY--Louisville; OH--Toledo; SC--Columbia, Greenville)

Nonmonetary Support

Type: Donated Equipment; Loaned Executives

Liberty Corp. Foundation

Giving Contact

Sophia Vergas, Secretary
PO Box 135
South Main Street
Greenville, SC 29602
Phone: (864)241-5496
Fax: (864)241-5401
E-mail: svergas@libertycorp.com

Alternate Contact

PO Box 502
Greenville, SC 29602

Phone: (864)241-5443

Description

EIN: 570468195
Organization Type: Corporate Foundation
Giving Locations: SC: nationally.
Grant Types: Award, Capital, General Support, Multiyear/Continuing Support, Scholarship.

Financial Summary

Total Giving: $709,637 (fiscal year ending August 31, 2003); $371,507 (fiscal 2002); $1,725,880 (fiscal 2001). Note: Contributes through foundation only.
Giving Analysis: Giving for fiscal 2002 includes: foundation scholarships ($51,200); foundation grants to United Way ($100,300)
Assets: $20,762 (fiscal 2003); $430,785 (fiscal 2002); $895,706 (fiscal 2001)
Gifts Received: $300,000 (fiscal 2003); $2,500,000 (fiscal 2001); $100,000 (fiscal 2000). Note: Contributions were received from Liberty Corporation; and Cosmos Broadcasting Corp.

Typical Recipients

Arts & Humanities: Arts Associations & Councils, Arts Centers, Arts Festivals, Arts Funds, Community Arts, Arts & Humanities-General, History & Archaeology, Libraries, Museums/Galleries, Music, Performing Arts, Theater
Civic & Public Affairs: African American Affairs, Botanical Gardens/Parks, Business/Free Enterprise, Chambers of Commerce, Community Foundations, Economic Development, Employment/Job Training, Civic & Public Affairs-General, Housing, Legal Aid, Municipalities/Towns, Philanthropic Organizations, Professional & Trade Associations, Urban & Community Affairs, Women's Affairs, Zoos/Aquariums
Education: Arts/Humanities Education, Business Education, Colleges & Universities, Education Associations, Education Funds, Education Reform, Elementary Education (Public), Engineering/Technological Education, Education-General, Leadership Training, Literacy, Private Education (Precollege), Public Education (Precollege), Science/Mathematics Education, Special Education, Student Aid
Environment: Environment-General, Resource Conservation, Wildlife Protection
Health: Cancer, Children's Health/Hospitals, Clinics/Medical Centers, Diabetes, Emergency/Ambulance Services, Health Organizations, Hospices, Hospitals, Research/Studies Institutes, Single-Disease Health Associations
International: Foreign Educational Institutions, International Relations
Religion: Churches, Ministries, Religious Welfare
Science: Scientific Centers & Institutes
Social Services: Animal Protection, Child Welfare, Community Centers, Community Service Organizations, Emergency Relief, Family Services, Food/Clothing Distribution, People with Disabilities, Recreation & Athletics, Scouts, Shelters/Homelessness, United Funds/United Ways, Volunteer Services, YMCA/YWCA/YMHA/YWHA, Youth Organizations

Application Procedures

Initial Contact: Send a brief letter.
Application Requirements: Include proof of tax-exempt status of organization.
Deadlines: None.

Restrictions

Awards are not made to individuals.
Contributions are made only to organizations exempt from Federal income tax under 501(c)(3).

Additional Information

Matching gifts program discontinued in 1999.
Publications: Policies Fact Sheet

Corporate Officials

Mary Anne Bunton: vice president public relations PRIM CORP EMPL vice president: Liberty Corp. treasurer: Press Printing International.
William Hayne Hipp: president, chief executive officer, director B Greenville, SC 1940. ED Washington & Lee University BA (1962); University of Pennsylvania Wharton School MBA (1965). PRIM CORP EMPL president, chief executive officer, director: Liberty Corp. CORP AFFIL director: SCANA Corp.; director: Wachovia Corp.; director: American Council Life Insurance; chairman: Pierce National Life Insurance Co. NONPR AFFIL member: Greenville Chamber of Commerce; director: South Carolina Research Authority; chairman, trustee: Alliance for Quality Education; trustee: Communication Economic Development New York.
Kenneth W. Jones: controller PRIM CORP EMPL controller: Liberty Corp.
Carry Price: director public relations PRIM CORP EMPL director public relations: Liberty Corp.

Foundation Officials

William Hayne Hipp: chairman, president, director (see above)
Sophia G. Vergas: secretary, administrator
Mark D. Wesson: treasurer, controller

Grants Analysis

Disclosure Period: fiscal year ending August 31, 2003
Total Grants: $581,396*
Number of Grants: 73
Average Grant: $6,200*
Highest Grant: $135,000
Lowest Grant: $1,000
Typical Range: $1,000 to $10,000
*Note: Giving excludes United Way and scholarships. Average grant figure excludes highest grant.

Recent Grants

Note: Grants derived from 2002 Form 990.
General

37,500	Southern Environmental Law Center, Charlottesville, VA -- capital contribution
36,000	Urban League of the Upstate, Inc., Greenville, SC -- capital campaign
25,000	Cannon Memorial Hospital, Pickens, SC -- capital campaign
25,000	Center for Development Services -- capital campaign
25,000	Tuskegee University, St. Louis, MO -- building fund
25,000	Upstate Forever, Greenville, SC -- capital campaign
22,500	University of South Carolina Development Foundation, Columbia, SC -- law school and business school contribution
20,000	Alliance for Quality Education, Greenville, SC -- capital contribution
15,000	Palmetto Project, Charleston, SC -- Voter Project 2002
15,000	United Way Greenville County, Greenville, SC -- capital campaign

LIED FOUNDATION TRUST

Giving Contact

Christina M. Hixson, Trustee
Lied Foundation Trust
3907 West Charleston Boulevard
Las Vegas, NV 89102
Phone: (702)878-1559
Fax: (702)878-6469

Description

Founded: 1972
EIN: 237282946
Organization Type: General Purpose Foundation
Giving Locations: IA; NE; NV
Grant Types: Capital, General Support, Operating Expenses, Scholarship.

Financial Summary

Total Giving: $14,038,826 (2003); $12,842,904 (2002)
Giving Analysis: Giving for 2002 includes: foundation scholarships ($1,000,000)
Assets: $76,630,338 (2003); $99,516,907 (2002)
Gifts Received: $459,090 (1994); $19,027,367 (1993); $96,088,670 (1992)

Typical Recipients

Arts & Humanities: Arts Centers, Arts Institutes, Ballet, Dance, History & Archaeology, Libraries, Museums/Galleries, Performing Arts, Public Broadcasting
Civic & Public Affairs: Economic Development, Employment/Job Training, Housing, Law & Justice, Municipalities/Towns, Parades/Festivals, Zoos/Aquariums
Education: Business Education, Colleges & Universities, Community & Junior Colleges, Education Funds, Faculty Development, Education-General, Private Education (Precollege), Public Education (Precollege), School Volunteerism, Science/Mathematics Education, Secondary Education (Private), Special Education, Student Aid
Environment: Forestry, Environment-General
Health: Children's Health/Hospitals, Health Funds, Health Organizations, Hospitals (University Affiliated), Research/Studies Institutes, Speech & Hearing, Transplant Networks/Donor Banks
Religion: Bible Study/Translation, Churches, Religious Organizations, Religious Welfare
Science: Science-General, Science Museums
Social Services: Animal Protection, Child Welfare, Community Centers, Community Service Organizations, Day Care, Family Services, Food/Clothing Distribution, People with Disabilities, Recreation & Athletics, Senior Services, Shelters/Homelessness, Social Services-General, Youth Organizations

Application Procedures

Initial Contact: The foundation has no formal grant application procedure or application form.
Deadlines: None.

Foundation Officials

Christina M. Hixson: trustee

Grants Analysis

Disclosure Period: calendar year ending 2003
Total Grants: $14,038,826
Number of Grants: 18
Average Grant: $148,622*
Highest Grant: $6,000,000
Lowest Grant: $3,000
Typical Range: $25,000 to $250,000
*Note: Average grants figure excludes four highest grantss ($11,958,118).

Recent Grants

Note: Grants derived from 2003 Form 990.
Library-Related

190,206	Clarinda Foundation Inc., Clarinda, IA -- funding for library construction

General

6,000,000	University of Nebraska Foundation, Lincoln, NE -- funding for Hixson-Lied College of Fine and Performing Arts
2,500,000	Athletic Association of the University of Nevada, Reno, NV -- toward property purchase for athletics
2,458,118	Lied Learning and Technology, Omaha, NE -- funding for construction

1,000,000	Creighton University, Omaha, NE -- funding for Hixson-Lied science building
667,227	National Arbor Day Foundation, Lincoln, NE -- toward construction of lied greenhouse
400,000	Palm Spring Boys and Girls Club, Palm Springs, CA -- funding for lake renovation project
251,275	City of Council Bluffs, Council Bluffs, IA -- toward renovation of Carnegie Museum
130,000	University of Nebraska Foundation, Lincoln, NE -- toward Lied main street program
100,000	Lied Discovery Children's Museum, Las Vegas, NV
100,000	Nevada Ballet Theatre, Las Vegas, NV -- toward future dance program

ELI LILLY & CO.

Company Headquarters
Indianapolis, IN
Web: http://www.lilly.com

Company Description
Founded: 1876
Ticker: LLY
Exchange: NYSE
Revenue: US$13.857 billion (2004)
Profit: US$1.81 billion (2004)
Employees: 46100 (2003)
Fortune Rank: 152, per FORTUNE Magazine's list of 500 Largest U.S. Corporations (2004).
SIC(s): 2833 Medicinals & Botanicals, 2834 Pharmaceutical Preparations.

Operating Locations
Eli Lilly & Co. (AL--Birmingham; AZ--Phoenix; CA--Fresno, Sacramento, Solana Beach, Woodland Hills; CO--Englewood; CT--Enfield; FL--Jacksonville, Tampa; GA--Atlanta; IN--Clinton, Greenfield, Indianapolis, Lafayette; IA--Cedar Rapids; KY--St. Matthews; LA--Metairie; MD--Rockville; MA--Braintree; MN--Bloomington; MS--Brandon; MO--St. Louis; NE--Omaha; NJ--Parsippany; NY--Albany, Melville; NC--Charlotte; OH--Cincinnati, Cleveland; PA--Bala-Cynwyd, Pittsburgh; TN--Knoxville, Memphis, Nashville; TX--Dallas; WA--Kirkland, Spokane; WV--Charleston)

Nonmonetary Support
Value: $176,576,789 (2001); $120,000,000 (2000); $96,000,000 (1999)
Type: Donated Products
Contact: Pat Gibson, Product Contributions Specialist
Note: Donations are in the form of pharmaceuticals (wholesale cost) to nonprofit organizations for disaster assistance.

Eli Lilly Foundation

Giving Contact
Thomas A. King, President
Eli Lilly Co. Foundation
Tax Division
Lilly Corporate Center
Indianapolis, IN 46285
Phone: (317)276-3743
Fax: (317)277-6719
E-mail: tom@lilly.com
Web: http://www.lilly.com/about/responsible/

Alternate Contact
Kendy Smith, Senior Contributions Assistant

Description
EIN: 356202479
Organization Type: Corporate Foundation
Giving Locations: headquarters and operating communities; international organizations; national organizations.
Grant Types: Capital, Employee Matching Gifts, General Support, Multiyear/Continuing Support.
Note: Employee matching gift ratio: 1 to 1.

Financial Summary
Total Giving: $273,500,000 (2003); $233,542,420 (2001)
Giving Analysis: Giving for 2001 includes: corporate direct giving (approx $12,500); foundation grants to United Way ($4,475,004); foundation matching gifts ($5,689,835); foundation ($9,026,234); international subsidiaries ($9,077,737); domestic subsidiaries ($28,684,321); nonmonetary support ($176,576,789)
Assets: $75,761,852 (2003); $88,280,528 (2002); $115,325,584 (2001)
Gifts Received: $232,881 (2002); $23,750,000 (1998); $16,540,606 (1997). Note: Gifts are received from Eli Lilly & Co.

Typical Recipients
Arts & Humanities: Arts Associations & Councils, Arts Funds, Arts Outreach, Ballet, Community Arts, Dance, Ethnic & Folk Arts, Historic Preservation, History & Archaeology, Libraries, Museums/Galleries, Music, Opera, Performing Arts, Public Broadcasting, Theater
Civic & Public Affairs: African American Affairs, Botanical Gardens/Parks, Business/Free Enterprise, Chambers of Commerce, Civil Rights, Community Foundations, Economic Development, Economic Policy, Employment/Job Training, Civic & Public Affairs-General, Hispanic Affairs, Housing, Law & Justice, Municipalities/Towns, Parades/Festivals, Professional & Trade Associations, Public Policy, Rural Affairs, Urban & Community Affairs, Zoos/Aquariums
Education: Business Education, Business-School Partnerships, Colleges & Universities, Education Associations, Education Funds, Education Reform, Engineering/Technological Education, Faculty Development, Education-General, Health & Physical Education, International Studies, Leadership Training, Medical Education, Minority Education, Private Education (Precollege), Public Education (Precollege), Religious Education, Science/Mathematics Education, Secondary Education (Private), Student Aid
Environment: Environment-General
Health: AIDS/HIV, Cancer, Children's Health/Hospitals, Diabetes, Emergency/Ambulance Services, Health Policy/Cost Containment, Health Funds, Health Organizations, Heart, Medical Research, Mental Health, Prenatal Health Issues, Public Health, Research/Studies Institutes, Single-Disease Health Associations, Trauma Treatment
International: Health Care/Hospitals, International Affairs
Religion: Ministries, Religious Welfare
Science: Science Exhibits & Fairs
Social Services: Camps, Child Welfare, Community Service Organizations, Homes, People with Disabilities, Recreation & Athletics, Scouts, United Funds/United Ways, YMCA/YWCA/YMHA/YWHA, Youth Organizations

Application Procedures
Initial Contact: Submit a written proposal.
Application Requirements: Include letter from IRS stating 501(c)(3) tax-exempt status, apartment, explanation of amount requested and purpose of request, and purpose of organization (see guidelines at www.lilly.com).
Deadlines: June 30 and December 31.
Review Process: A postcard will be sent upon receipt of proposal which will indicate the quarter in which the proposal will be reviewed. Applicants are notified in writing as soon as possible after the pro-

posal has been reviewed to explain what action has been taken on the request.
Notes: Grants are offered in four areas: health and welfare, education, cultural, and civic.

Restrictions
Does not support individuals; organizations without 501(c)(3) status; endowments; debt reduction; religious or sectarian programs for religious purposes; fraternal, labor, athletic, bands, or veterans organizations; political contributions; beauty or talent contests; fundraising activities related to individual sponsorship; conferences or media productions (though such proposals relating to Lilly products or research may be directed to the company's appropriate product or operating group); non-accredited educational groups; or memorials.

Additional Information
Products, including insulin and anticancer agents, are donated throughout the developing world, to Eastern Europe, summer camp programs for children with diabetes, and emergency relief agencies.
Physician requests for the Lilly Cares--Indigent Patient Program should contact Lilly Cares Program Administrator, PO Box 9105, McLean, VA 22102-0105, (800)545-6962. of victims, families, and relief workers during times of disaster. of victims, families, and relief workers during times of disaster.
Publications: Charitable Contributions Report

Corporate Officials
Charles E. Golden: executive vice president, chief financial officer ED Lafayette College BA (1968); Lehigh University MBA (1970). PRIM CORP EMPL executive vice president, chief financial officer: Eli Lilly & Co. NONPR AFFIL advisory board: INSEAD; steering committee: Pharmaceutical Research and Manufacturers of America; director: Clarian Health Partners; finance committee: Indianapolis Museum of Art.
Pedro P. Granadillo: senior vice president CORP AFFIL director: Haemonetics Corp.; director: Noven Pharmaceuticals Inc.; director: First Indiana Bank NA; senior vice president: First Indiana Corp.
John C. Lechleiter: executive vice president ED Xavier University BS (1975); Harvard University MS (1980); Harvard University PhD (1980). CORP AFFIL director: Great Lakes Chemical Corp. NONPR AFFIL member: American Chemical Society; trustee: Xavier University.
Sidney Taurel: chairman, president, chief executive officer B Casablanca, Morocco February 09, 1949. ED Columbia University MBA (1971). PRIM CORP EMPL chairman, president, chief executive officer: Eli Lilly & Co. CORP AFFIL director: McGraw-Hill Companies Inc.; director: IBM Corp. NONPR AFFIL member: President's Export Council; director: RCA Tennis Championships; trustee: Indianapolis Museum of Art; director: Pharmaceutical Research and Manufacturers of America; member, board of overseers: Columbia Business School.

Foundation Officials
Charles E. Golden: director (see above)
Pedro P. Granadillo: director (see above)
Rebecca O. Kendall: director ED Indiana University JD (1975). NONPR AFFIL chairman: Central Indiana Community Foundation.
Thomas A. King: president NONPR AFFIL director: Indy Partnership; trustee: Sigma Theta Tau International Honor Soc. for Nursing.
John C. Lechleiter: director (see above)
Gerhard N. Mayr: director ED Swiss Federal Institute of Technology MS (1969); Stanford University MBA (1972). CORP AFFIL director: OMV AG; director: Bank Austria-Creditanstalt A.G.; advisory board: Guidant Corp. NONPR AFFIL director: Project Hope; member: U.S.-Egypt President's Council.
Sidney Taurel: director (see above)
August M. Watanabe, MD: director CORP AFFIL director: Ambrix Inc.; director: Guidant Corp. NONPR

AFFIL director: Damon Runyon Cancer Research Foundation; trustee: Indiana University Foundation.

Grants Analysis

Disclosure Period: calendar year ending 2003
Total Grants: $273,500,000 (approx)
Number of Grants: 7,000
Average Grant: $39,071
Typical Range: $10,000 to $50,000

Recent Grants

Note: Grants derived from 2003 Form 990.
Library-Related

200,000	Indianapolis - Marion County Public Library Foundation, Indianapolis, IN -- for renovation and expansion of the Indianapolis-Marion county central library

General

2,055,253	United Way Central Indiana, Indianapolis, IN
2,055,253	United Way Central Indiana, Indianapolis, IN
1,030,000	National Alliance for the Mentally ill, Arlington, VA -- to assist mental health advocacy relations
1,030,000	National Alliance for the Mentally ill, Arlington, VA -- for mental health advocacy relations
650,000	National Mental Health Association (NAMA), Alexandria, VA
430,000	National Alliance for the Mentally ill, Arlington, VA -- fund for mental health advocacy relations
350,000	European Foundation for the Study of Diabetes, Dusseldorf Germany -- to support the new European research grant program
333,000	American College of Chest Physicians, Northbrook, IL -- for the expansion of critical care family assistance program
250,000	University of Michigan, Ann Arbor, MI -- to assist the newly established depression center
238,396	United Way of Greater Lafayette, Lafayette, IN

LILLY ENDOWMENT

Giving Contact

Sue Ellen Walker
Grant Services Office
2801 North Meridian Street
PO Box 88068
Indianapolis, IN 46208-0068.
Phone: (317)924-5471
Fax: (317)926-4431
Web: http://www.lilly.org/

Description

Founded: 1937
EIN: 350868122
Organization Type: Family Foundation
Giving Locations: IN: statewide, Indianapolis nationally.
Grant Types: Award, Capital, Challenge, Conference/Seminar, Emergency, Endowment, Fellowship, General Support, Matching, Multiyear/Continuing Support, Operating Expenses, Project, Research.

Donor Information

Founder: The endowment was created in Indianapolis in 1937 with gifts of Eli Lilly and Company stock from the personal holdings of the late Josiah Kirby Lilly Sr. and his two sons, the late Eli Lilly and the late Josiah Kirby Lilly Jr. J. K. Lilly, Sr., was the son of Colonel Eli Lilly who, in 1876, founded what became one of the world's largest pharmaceutical firms. J. K. Lilly, Sr., strongly supported the YMCA, the Episcopal Church, and the Red Cross. His son, Eli Lilly, contributed large amounts of money to the Episcopal Church, the United Way, and colleges in Indiana. He left a majority of his estate to charity. J. K. Lilly, Jr., was especially interested in museums, libraries, and historical societies. The foundation still owns about 18 percent of Eli Lilly and Company stock, and its board of directors includes one family member.

Financial Summary

Total Giving: $462,336,723 (2003); $571,857,974 (2002); $598,001,582 (2001)
Giving Analysis: Giving for 2003 includes: foundation grants to United Way ($35,191,422); 2002: foundation fellowships ($797,580); foundation grants to United Way ($8,325,075)
Assets: $10,849,402,388 (2003); $10,053,479,797 (2002); $12,814,397,581 (2001)
Gifts Received: $14,364,325 (2003); $137,493 (2002); $137,468 (2001). Note: In 2003, contributions were received from Ruth Lilly Trusts ($14,222,362) and Voris Lyons Trust ($137,468). In 2001 and 2002, contributions were received from Voris Lyons Trust. In 1999, contributions were received from the Estate of Phoebe B. Comer ($221,695) and the Voris Lyons Trust ($137,468).

Typical Recipients

Arts & Humanities: Arts Associations & Councils, Arts Centers, Arts Festivals, Community Arts, Dance, Ethnic & Folk Arts, Historic Preservation, History & Archaeology, Libraries, Museums/Galleries, Music, Opera, Performing Arts, Public Broadcasting, Theater, Visual Arts
Civic & Public Affairs: African American Affairs, Asian American Affairs, Botanical Gardens/Parks, Community Foundations, Economic Development, Economic Policy, Employment/Job Training, Civic & Public Affairs-General, Housing, Nonprofit Management, Philanthropic Organizations, Public Policy, Rural Affairs, Urban & Community Affairs, Women's Affairs, Zoos/Aquariums
Education: Arts/Humanities Education, Business Education, Business-School Partnerships, Colleges & Universities, Economic Education, Education Associations, Education Funds, Education Reform, Elementary Education (Private), Engineering/Technological Education, Environmental Education, Faculty Development, Education-General, Leadership Training, Literacy, Medical Education, Minority Education, Private Education (Precollege), Public Education (Precollege), Religious Education, Science/Mathematics Education, Secondary Education (Private), Secondary Education (Public), Social Sciences Education, Student Aid
Environment: Environment-General, Resource Conservation, Wildlife Protection
Health: Emergency/Ambulance Services, Health Organizations
International: Foreign Educational Institutions, International Development, Trade
Religion: Churches, Dioceses, Jewish Causes, Ministries, Religious Organizations, Religious Welfare, Seminaries, Social/Policy Issues
Science: Science-General
Social Services: Child Welfare, Community Centers, Community Service Organizations, Crime Prevention, Day Care, Delinquency & Criminal Rehabilitation, Emergency Relief, Family Planning, Family Services, Homes, People with Disabilities, Recreation & Athletics, Scouts, Social Services-General, Substance Abuse, United Funds/United Ways, YMCA/YWCA/YMHA/YWHA, Youth Organizations

Application Procedures

Initial Contact: Applicants should submit a preliminary letter of no more than two pages describing the organization, project, and amount requested.
Application Requirements: Preliminary letter should include description of organization and project, and amount requested. The Endowment responds to all preliminary inquiries, and will request a full proposal if appropriate.
Deadlines: None.
Review Process: Grant proposals are reviewed by a program director. Proposals meeting the criteria for consideration are reviewed by the appropriate division or committee, then by the corporate officers, and finally by members of the board of directors. The process generally takes from three to six months; all grantseekers receive written notification of decisions. Grants are considered in February, March, May, June, July, September, November, and December.
Decision Notification: All requests receive written notification of decision.

Restrictions

The endowment generally will not make loans or grants to individuals; for healthcare projects; mass media projects; endowments or endowed chairs; libraries; or outside Indiana.

Additional Information

The endowment's concentration on Indianapolis and Indiana applies primarily to grants for community development and elementary/secondary education. The endowment's interest in higher education extends to Indiana colleges, and historically to black colleges nationwide. Religious and philanthropic support is given nationally.
Publications: Annual Report; Grant Guidelines; Progressions Magazine

Foundation Officials

David D. Biber: secretary, treasurer
Otis R. Bowen, MD: director B Rochester, IN February 26, 1918. ED Indiana University AB (1939); Indiana University MD (1942).
Daniel P. Carmichael: director ED University of Cincinnati BS (1965); University of Cincinnati JD (1968). NONPR AFFIL director: Indianapolis Legal Aid Society; board of visitors: University Cincinnati College of Law; board of directors: Indiana University Public and Environment Affairs; member: Indianapolis Bar Association; editorial board: Food, Drug and Cosmetic Law Journal; member: Indiana State Bar Association; member: American Bar Association; member: American Society for Pharmacy Law.
Sara B. Cobb: vice president education
Rev. Craig Richard Dykstra: vice president rel B Detroit, MI 1947. ED University of Michigan BA (1969); Princeton Theological Seminary MDiv (1973); Princeton Theological Seminary PhD (1978). NONPR AFFIL member: Phi Kappa Phi; member: Religion Education Association; member: American Academy Religion; member: Association Professors Research Religious Education.
Rev. William Gerald Enright: director B Peoria, IL 1935. ED Wheaton College BA (1958); Fuller Theological Seminary MDiv (1961); McCormick Theological Seminary ThM (1965); University of Edinburgh PhD (1968). PRIM NONPR EMPL pastor: 2nd Presbyterian Church of Indianapolis. NONPR AFFIL director: Wishard Hospital Foundation; director: YMCA Indianapolis; member: Society Science Study Religion; director: Saint Vincent Hospital; member: Society American Church History; member: Police Chiefs Advisor Board; director: Indiana Center Advanced Research; director, senior fellow: Lake Family Institute on Faith and Giving; advisory board: Hanover College; chairman task force on ethics & values: City of Indianapolis. CLUB AFFIL member: Rotary Club.
William Maxwell Goodwin: vice president commun devel B Muncie, IN February 19. ED Indiana University AB (1961); Indiana University MBA (1966). NONPR AFFIL member: Indiana Association Certified Public Accountants; member: Kappa Delta Rho; director: Greater Indianapolis Progress Committee; member: Beta Gamma Sigma; member: Delta Phi Alpha; member: American Institute of Certified Public Accountants.
Earl Binkley Herr, Jr.: director B Lancaster, PA 1928. ED Franklin and Marshall College BS (1948); University of Delaware MS (1950); University of Dela-

ware PhD (1953); Cornell University (1953-1955). CORP AFFIL director: Ipalco Enterprises; director: Indianapolis Power & Light Co. NONPR AFFIL director: Indiana Science Education Foundation; member: Sigma Xi; member: American Chemical Society; member: American Association Advancement Science.

Eli Lilly, II: director B IN 1930. ED Philadelphia College of Pharmacy BS. CLUB AFFIL member: Woodhill Country Club.

Mary K. Lisher: director

Thomas M. Lofton: chairman, director B Indianapolis, IN 1929. ED Indiana University BS (1951); Indiana University JD (1954). NONPR AFFIL member, board visitors: Indiana University Law School; member: Order Coif; honorary director: Indiana University Foundation; member: Beta Gamma Sigma. CLUB AFFIL Masons Club.

Eugene F. Ratliff: director ED University of Florida BA. NONPR AFFIL trustee emeritus: Butler University.

N. Clay Robbins: president, director B Indianapolis, IN 1957. ED Wabash College BA (1979); Vanderbilt University JD (1982). NONPR AFFIL member: Indiana State Bar Association; director: United Way Central Indiana; member: Indiana Chamber of Commerce; member: American Bar Association; member: Corporate Community Council.

Grants Analysis
Disclosure Period: calendar year ending 2003
Total Grants: $427,145,301*
Number of Grants: 600 (approx)
Average Grant: $676,094*
Highest Grant: $15,000,885
Lowest Grant: $500
Typical Range: $25,000 to $2,000,000
*Note: Giving excludes United Way. Average grant figure excludes three highest grants ($23,517,438).

Recent Grants
Note: Grants derived from 2003 Form 990.

Library-Related
25,000,000 Indianapolis Marion County Public Library Foundation, Indianapolis, IN

General
20,000,000 United Way of Central Indiana Inc., Indianapolis, IN
15,000,885 University of Evansville, Evansville, IN -- fund for Institute of Global Enterprise in Indiana
14,000,000 Independent Colleges of Indiana Inc., Indianapolis, IN -- towards scholarship program
11,452,404 Trustees of Hanover College, Hanover, IN -- towards creation of The Rivers Institute
10,700,422 Indiana Association of United Ways Inc., Indianapolis, IN
10,564,149 Louisville Presbyterian Theological Seminary, Louisville, KY -- support for the Louisville Institute project
7,500,000 Indianapolis Zoological Society Inc., Indianapolis, IN
7,383,275 Wabash College, Crawfordsville, IN -- fund for Wabash Center for Teaching and Learning in Theology and Religion
6,275,000 Educational Broadcasting Corporation, New York, NY -- assistance for seventh season of Religion & Ethics NewsWeekly
6,000,000 Fund for Theological Education Inc., Atlanta, GA -- support for FTE programs

RICHARD COYLE LILLY FOUNDATION

Giving Contact
Jeffrey T. Peterson, Secretary & Treasurer
c/o US Bank NA
101 E. Fifth Street
St. Paul, MN 55101
Phone: (651)466-8735

Description
Founded: 1941
EIN: 416038717
Organization Type: Private Foundation
Giving Locations: MN: St. Paul
Grant Types: Capital, Endowment, General Support, Multiyear/Continuing Support, Project, Research, Seed Money.

Donor Information
Founder: the late Richard C. Lilly

Financial Summary
Total Giving: $441,300 (2002); $625,050 (2001)
Giving Analysis: Giving for 2002 includes: foundation matching gifts ($2,000); foundation grants to United Way ($22,000)
Assets: $8,902,992 (2002); $10,265,962 (2001)

Typical Recipients
Arts & Humanities: Arts Associations & Councils, Arts Centers, Arts Institutes, Community Arts, Dance, Arts & Humanities-General, Historic Preservation, History & Archaeology, Libraries, Literary Arts, Museums/Galleries, Music, Opera, Public Broadcasting, Theater, Visual Arts
Civic & Public Affairs: Botanical Gardens/Parks, Business/Free Enterprise, Clubs, Economic Development, Civic & Public Affairs-General, Municipalities/ Towns, Urban & Community Affairs, Women's Affairs, Zoos/Aquariums
Education: Arts/Humanities Education, Colleges & Universities, Education Funds, Education Reform, Elementary Education (Private), Faculty Development, Preschool Education, Private Education (Precollege), Public Education (Precollege), Student Aid
Environment: Environment-General, Resource Conservation
Health: Hospitals
International: Human Rights, International Peace & Security Issues
Religion: Churches, Religious Welfare
Social Services: Camps, Child Welfare, Community Centers, Community Service Organizations, Day Care, Family Planning, Family Services, Food/ Clothing Distribution, United Funds/United Ways, YMCA/YWCA/YMHA/YWHA, Youth Organizations

Application Procedures
Initial Contact: Submit full proposal
Application Requirements: Include proof of tax-exempt status and any other supporting materials necessary to consider the request
Deadlines: None.

Restrictions
Does not make grants to individuals, for scholarships, or to organizations that would require expenditure responsibility.

Foundation Officials
Suzanne Lilly Hutcheson: director
Bruce A. Lilly: director
David M. Lilly, Jr.: president
David M. Lilly: president
Elizabeth M. Lilly: vice president
Jeffrey T. Peterson: secretary, treasurer

Grants Analysis
Disclosure Period: calendar year ending 2002
Total Grants: $417,300*
Number of Grants: 67
Average Grant: $6,228
Highest Grant: $35,000
Lowest Grant: $500
Typical Range: $1,000 to $10,000
*Note: Giving excludes United Way; matching gifts.

Recent Grants
Note: Grants derived from 2001 Form 990.
General
50,000 Guthrie Theatre, Minneapolis, MN -- capital campaign
50,000 Minnesota Public Radio, St. Paul, MN
40,000 Family and Children's Services of Minneapolis, Minneapolis, MN -- capital campaign
35,000 St. Paul Academy, St. Paul, MN
30,000 St. Paul Foundation, St. Paul, MN
25,000 Compatible Technology International, St. Paul, MN -- capital campaign
25,000 Nantucket Maria Mitchell Association, Nantucket, MA -- new aquarium
25,000 Planned Parenthood of Minnesota and South Dakota, St. Paul, MN
22,000 University of Minnesota, Minneapolis, MN
20,000 United Way Twin Cities, Minneapolis, MN

T. Y. LIN FOUNDATION

Giving Contact
Robert B. Yee, Treasurer
T. Y. Lin Foundation
315 Bay St.
San Francisco, CA 94133
Phone: (415)989-3100

Description
Founded: 1991
EIN: 943107208
Organization Type: Private Foundation
Grant Types: General Support.

Financial Summary
Total Giving: $4,200 (2003); $20,100 (2001)
Assets: $449,728 (2003); $431,410 (2001)
Gifts Received: $17,000 (1999); $88,511 (1998); $41,226 (1996). Note: In 1999, contributions were received from T. Y. and Margaret Lin. In 1998, contributions were received from Y.C. and 1/a-Chen Yang ($60,000), U. and Margaret Lin ($26,000), and James and Alice Tai ($2,500). In 1996, contributions were received from T. Y. Lin-Taiwan ($2,500), T. Y. and Margaret Lin ($33,500), and T. Y. Lin-Hong Kong ($5,000).

Typical Recipients
Arts & Humanities: Ballet, Libraries
Education: Colleges & Universities, Engineering/ Technological Education
International: Foreign Educational Institutions, International Peace & Security Issues
Science: Science Museums

Application Procedures
Initial Contact: Send a brief letter of inquiry.
Application Requirements: a description of organization, amount requested, and proof of tax-exempt status.
Deadlines: None.

Foundation Officials
Claudia Berger: secretary
Philip Chow: director
Y. C. Yang: chairman
Robert B. Yee: treasurer

Grants Analysis

Disclosure Period: calendar year ending 2003
Total Grants: $4,200
Number of Grants: 1

Recent Grants

Note: Grants derived from 2003 Form 990.
General
4,200   University of California, Berkeley, CA

LINGNAN FOUNDATION

Giving Contact

Jane S. Permaul, Chairman & Trustee
PO Box 208340
New Haven, CT 06520
Phone: (203)432-1063
Fax: (203)432-7246
E-mail: leslie.stone@yale.edu
Web: http://www.lingnanfoundation.org/

Description

Founded: 1893
EIN: 136400470
Organization Type: Private Foundation
Giving Locations: People's Republic of China; Hong Kong
Grant Types: Conference/Seminar, General Support, Operating Expenses, Professorship, Research, Seed Money.

Financial Summary

Total Giving: $948,525 (fiscal year ending June 30, 2004); $1,349,850 (fiscal 2001)
Assets: $19,966,752 (fiscal 2004); $22,404,957 (fiscal 2001)
Gifts Received: $70,563 (fiscal 2004); $94,465 (fiscal 2001); $1,972,795 (fiscal 2000). Note: In fiscal 2004, contributions were received from Anna Luk Liu ($57,813) and Pausang and Huey Wong ($10,500). In fiscal 2000 and 2001, contributions were received from the estate of Yue Shuen Lee. In fiscal 1998, contributions were received from Yi-Faai Laai Bequest and Ying-Lam Lee Foundation. In fiscal 1997, contributions were received from Joseph Lai, Max Saffiath and Marshall Sanders. In fiscal 1996, contributions were received from the estate of J. Ackerman Coles ($828,239) and from the estate of King Y. Laai ($160,000); miscellaneous contributions totaling $100 also were received.

Typical Recipients

Arts & Humanities: Libraries
Civic & Public Affairs: Civic & Public Affairs-General
Education: Arts/Humanities Education, Colleges & Universities, Education Associations, Education-General, International Studies, Minority Education
International: Foreign Educational Institutions, International Peace & Security Issues, International Relations

Application Procedures

Initial Contact: Send a brief letter of inquiry.
Deadlines: None.

Restrictions

Grants are made to institutions contributing to the advancement of the formal education of Chinese students. As a general rule, grants are limited to selected colleges and universities in the People's Republic of China and in Hong Kong and to similar organizations in the U.S. that are engaged in cooperative programs with these colleges and universities. Does not support individuals or provide loans.

Additional Information

Publications: Program Policy Statement

Foundation Officials

Ralph E. Lerner: secretary B New York, NY 1943. ED Bucknell University BS (1964); Boston University JD (1967); New York University LLM (1969). PRIM CORP EMPL assistant professor paralegal studies: New York University. NONPR AFFIL member: New York State Bar Association; adj assistant professor: New York University; member: Intl Bar Association; member: American Bar Association; member: Association New York City Bar.
Jane S. Permaul: chairman PRIM CORP EMPL assistant vice chancellor student affairs administration: University CA.

Grants Analysis

Disclosure Period: fiscal year ending June 30, 2004
Total Grants: $948,525
Number of Grants: 15
Average Grant: $89,990
Highest Grant: $453,000
Lowest Grant: $3,000
Typical Range: $50,000 to $150,000

Recent Grants

Note: Grants derived from fiscal 2004 Form 990.
General
453,000   Lingnan University, Hong Kong People's Republic of China
186,000   Lingan (University) Development Fund
162,800   Sun Yat-sen University, Guangzhou People's Republic of China
66,000   University of California Los Angeles Bruin Corps University of California Regents, Los Angeles, CA
43,225   Yale-China Association, New Haven, CT
25,000   Institute of International Education, New York, NY
9,500   University of California Berkeley Cal Corps, Berkeley, CA
3,000   Yale University, New Haven, CT

GEORGE LINK, JR. FOUNDATION

Giving Contact

Michael J. Cantanzaro, Vice President & Director
Bank of New York
1290 Avenue of the Americas, 5th Floor
New York, NY 10104
Phone: (201)846-8481

Description

Founded: 1980
EIN: 133041396
Organization Type: General Purpose Foundation
Giving Locations: NJ; NY: Northeast.
Grant Types: Capital, Endowment, Fellowship, General Support, Scholarship.

Donor Information

Founder: The foundation was established in 1980 by the late George Link Jr.

Financial Summary

Total Giving: $2,101,957 (2003); $2,495,615 (2002); $2,625,575 (2001)
Assets: $33,863,197 (2003); $31,391,346 (2002); $40,488,172 (2001)
Gifts Received: $142,797 (2001); $14,088 (1995); $55,273 (1994). Note: In 2001, contributions were received from the estate of Eleanor Link.

Typical Recipients

Arts & Humanities: Arts Associations & Councils, Arts Centers, Ethnic & Folk Arts, Historic Preservation, Libraries, Museums/Galleries, Opera, Performing Arts, Public Broadcasting, Theater

Civic & Public Affairs: African American Affairs, Botanical Gardens/Parks, Business/Free Enterprise, Community Foundations, Economic Development, Ethnic Organizations, Civic & Public Affairs-General, Housing, Inner-City Development, Law & Justice, Philanthropic Organizations
Education: Afterschool/Enrichment Programs, Arts/Humanities Education, Business Education, Business-School Partnerships, Colleges & Universities, Community & Junior Colleges, Education Associations, Education Funds, Education Reform, Elementary Education (Public), Education-General, Legal Education, Medical Education, Private Education (Precollege), Public Education (Precollege), Religious Education, Secondary Education (Private), Secondary Education (Public), Special Education, Student Aid
Health: Cancer, Children's Health/Hospitals, Clinics/Medical Centers, Health Funds, Health Organizations, Heart, Hospitals, Hospitals (University Affiliated), Long-Term Care, Medical Rehabilitation, Medical Research, Mental Health, Public Health, Single-Disease Health Associations
International: Health Care/Hospitals, International Affairs, International Development, International Organizations, Missionary/Religious Activities
Religion: Bible Study/Translation, Churches, Dioceses, Religion-General, Ministries, Missionary Activities (Domestic), Religious Organizations, Religious Welfare, Seminaries
Science: Scientific Centers & Institutes
Social Services: At-Risk Youth, Big Brothers/Big Sisters, Child Welfare, Community Centers, Community Service Organizations, Counseling, Family Services, Homes, People with Disabilities, Recreation & Athletics, Scouts, Senior Services, Shelters/Homelessness, Social Services-General, Volunteer Services, YMCA/YWCA/YMHA/YWHA, Youth Organizations

Application Procedures

Initial Contact: A letter of inquiry should be sent to the foundation.
Application Requirements: Letter should include a brief description of the project objective and the area(s) for which assistance is being requested.
Deadlines: None.

Foundation Officials

Kevin J. Bannon: treasurer, director
Michael J. Catanzaro: vice president, director
Bernard F. Joyce: vice president, director
Robert Emmett Link: vchairman, director
J. Michael Shepherd: secretary, director

Grants Analysis

Disclosure Period: calendar year ending 2003
Total Grants: $2,101,957
Number of Grants: 176
Average Grant: $11,297*
Highest Grant: $125,000
Lowest Grant: $500
Typical Range: $5,000 to $20,000
*Note: Average grant figure excludes highest grant.

Recent Grants

Note: Grants derived from 2003 Form 990.
General
125,000   Museum of Modern Art, New York, NY
50,000   College of Saint Elizabeth, Morristown, NJ
50,000   Common Good Institute, New York, NY
50,000   Neighborhood Housing Services of New York City Inc., New York, NY
47,200   Downtown Hospital, New York, NY
44,000   Education and Research Foundation, New York, NY
41,666   New York City Partnership Foundation, New York, NY
40,000   New York Province Jesuit Seminary, New York, NY

30,000	Junior Achievement of New York Inc., New York, NY
30,000	Local Initiatives Support Corporation, New York, NY

LIPTON CO.

Company Headquarters
Englewood Cliffs, NJ
Web: http://www.unilever.com

Company Description
Former Name: Thomas J. Lipton Co.
Employees: 7,400
SIC(s): 2034 Dehydrated Fruits, Vegetables & Soups, 2035 Pickles, Sauces & Salad Dressings, 2099 Food Preparations Nec.
Parent Company: Unilever PLC, Unilever House, Blackfriars, London, United Kingdom

Operating Locations
Lipton Co. (CA--Los Angeles, Santa Cruz; FL--Jacksonville; IA--Sioux City; NJ--Englewood Cliffs, Fairfield, Flemington, Moonachie; PA--Harrisburg; VA--Suffolk)

Lipton Foundation

Giving Contact
Suzanne Cuff, Contact
800 Sylvan Avenue
Englewood Cliffs, NJ 07632
Phone: (201)894-7405
Fax: (201)871-8198

Description
Founded: 1952
EIN: 226063094
Organization Type: Corporate Foundation
Giving Locations: primarily near corporate headquarters and plant locations.
Grant Types: Employee Matching Gifts, General Support.

Donor Information
Founder: Thomas J. Lipton Inc., Calvin Klein Cosmetics

Financial Summary
Total Giving: Contributes through foundation only. 1995 Giving includes foundation ($300,135); matching gifts ($23,351); United Way ($23,500).
Gifts Received: $443,795 (1995); $402,296 (1994); $993,750 (1992). Note: In 1995, the foundation received contributions from value of Colgate stock ($351,006) and from Conopco Inc. ($92,789).

Typical Recipients
Arts & Humanities: Arts Associations & Councils, Arts Centers, Arts Festivals, Dance, Historic Preservation, Libraries, Museums/Galleries, Music, Performing Arts, Public Broadcasting, Theater
Civic & Public Affairs: Business/Free Enterprise, Civil Rights, Economic Development, Civic & Public Affairs-General, Law & Justice, Legal Aid, Philanthropic Organizations, Public Policy, Safety, Urban & Community Affairs, Women's Affairs, Zoos/Aquariums
Education: Business Education, Colleges & Universities, Community & Junior Colleges, Economic Education, Education Associations, Education Funds, Education Reform, Health & Physical Education, Legal Education, Literacy, Medical Education, Minority Education, Private Education (Precollege), Public Education (Precollege), Science/Mathematics Education, Student Aid

Environment: Environment-General
Health: Cancer, Children's Health/Hospitals, Clinics/Medical Centers, Diabetes, Health Funds, Health Organizations, Heart, Hospices, Hospitals, Medical Rehabilitation, Medical Research, Medical Training, Mental Health, Multiple Sclerosis, Nutrition, Prenatal Health Issues, Single-Disease Health Associations
International: International Organizations, International Relations
Religion: Missionary Activities (Domestic), Religious Organizations, Religious Welfare
Science: Scientific Organizations
Social Services: At-Risk Youth, Big Brothers/Big Sisters, Community Centers, Community Service Organizations, Emergency Relief, Family Planning, Food/Clothing Distribution, People with Disabilities, Recreation & Athletics, Scouts, Special Olympics, Substance Abuse, United Funds/United Ways, Volunteer Services, Youth Organizations

Application Procedures
Initial Contact: write for guidelines; then a letter or proposal
Application Requirements: description of the organization and its purpose, amount requested, purpose of funds sought, recently audited financial statement, proof of tax-exempt status, list of current sponsors and amount each contributes, past record of support, description of programs offered and their geographical scope, annual report, name of agency executive and phone number, methods to be used for evaluating program or project
Deadlines: to be included in next year's budget, no later than December; some late applications are approved if proposal meets requirements and funds are available; many are held over to the next year
Notes: Currently funded organizations wishing continued support should send letter by end of year with updated information.

Restrictions
Does not support individuals, dinners, tours, or special events.
Restricted from supporting international giving where funds will be spent overseas.

Additional Information
Publications: Guidelines

Corporate Officials
Patrick Cescau: president, chief executive officer PRIM CORP EMPL president, chief executive officer: Lipton Co.

Grants Analysis
Disclosure Period: calendar year ending 1995
Total Grants: $300,135*
Number of Grants: 65
Average Grant: $4,617
Highest Grant: $75,000
Typical Range: $100 to $5,000 and $10,000 to $20,000
*Note: Giving excludes matching gifts; United Way.

LISLE CORP.

Company Headquarters
807 E. Main St.
Clarinda, IA 51632
Web: http://www.lislecorp.com

Company Description
Revenue: US$32.2 million (2001)
Employees: 246 (2001)
SIC(s): 3400 Fabricated Metal Products, 3700 Transportation Equipment.

Operating Locations
Lisle Corp. (IA--Clarinda)

Lisle Foundation

Giving Contact
John C. Lisle, Trustee
PO Box 89
Clarinda, IA 51632
Phone: (712)542-5101

Description
EIN: 426056080
Organization Type: Corporate Foundation
Giving Locations: IA: Clarinda, Des Moines
Grant Types: General Support.

Donor Information
Founder: Lisle Corp.

Financial Summary
Total Giving: $24,396 (fiscal year ending November 30, 2004); $14,225 (fiscal 2001)
Assets: $185,333 (fiscal 2004); $219,653 (fiscal 2001)

Typical Recipients
Arts & Humanities: Historic Preservation, History & Archaeology, Libraries, Music, Theater
Civic & Public Affairs: Business/Free Enterprise, Community Foundations, Civic & Public Affairs-General, Housing, Municipalities/Towns, Parades/Festivals, Safety
Education: Colleges & Universities, Community & Junior Colleges, Education Funds, Education-General, Minority Education, Preschool Education, Secondary Education (Public)
Environment: Environment-General, Resource Conservation, Watershed, Wildlife Protection
Health: Cancer, Children's Health/Hospitals, Clinics/Medical Centers, Diabetes, Emergency/Ambulance Services, Eyes/Blindness, Heart, Prenatal Health Issues, Single-Disease Health Associations
International: Health Care/Hospitals
Religion: Churches, Religious Welfare
Social Services: Big Brothers/Big Sisters, Community Centers, Community Service Organizations, Day Care, Family Planning, Family Services, Food/Clothing Distribution, People with Disabilities, Scouts, Veterans

Application Procedures
Initial Contact: The foundation requests applications be made in writing.
Deadlines: None.

Restrictions
Grants are not made to individuals.

Corporate Officials
Edwin Lisle: chairman PRIM CORP EMPL chairman: Lisle Corp.
John C. Lisle: president, chief executive officer PRIM CORP EMPL president, chief executive officer: Lisle Corp.
Marty Williams: chief financial officer PRIM CORP EMPL chief financial officer: Lisle Corp.

Foundation Officials
John C. Lisle: trustee (see above)

Grants Analysis
Disclosure Period: fiscal year ending November 30, 2004
Total Grants: $24,396
Number of Grants: 23
Average Grant: $595*
Highest Grant: $11,300
Lowest Grant: $100

Typical Range: $100 to $1,000
***Note:** Average grant figure excludes highest grant.

Recent Grants

Note: Grants derived from fiscal 2004 Form 990.
General

11,300	Iowa Western Community College, Clarinda, IA -- for educational purposes
5,000	Aerial Firetruck Project, Clarinda, IA
1,800	Grandma's House Day Care, Clarinda, IA
1,000	Peace With Christ Lutheran Church, Aurora, CO
900	Iowa College Foundation, Des Moines, IA -- for educational purposes
500	American Cancer Society, Clarinda, IA
500	Bethel Presbyterian Church, Staunton, VA
500	Iowa Western Community College Foundation, Clarinda, IA
325	Ducks Unlimited, Clarinda, IA
300	Big Brothers & Big Sisters, Philadelphia, PA

LUCIUS N. LITTAUER FOUNDATION

Giving Contact

William Lee Frost, President
60 East 42nd Street, Suite 2910
New York, NY 10165
Phone: (212)697-2677

Alternate Contact

Pamela Ween-Brumberg, Program Officer

Description

Founded: 1929
EIN: 131688027
Organization Type: General Purpose Foundation
Giving Locations: NY: New York internationally; nationally.
Grant Types: Challenge, Conference/Seminar, Employee Matching Gifts, Endowment, Fellowship, General Support, Project, Research, Scholarship.
Note: The foundation also supports the production of publications.

Donor Information

Founder: The foundation was established by Lucius N. Littauer in 1929. The late Mr. Littauer was president of Littauer Brothers, a family-owned glove manufacturing company, and president or director of several public utilities, and transportation and banking firms. He also served as a U.S. congressman.
Mr. Littauer was an active philanthropist. Aside from the charitable activities of the Littauer Foundation, he donated over $2.25 million to Harvard University for the Littauer Center and Graduate School in Public Administration, and established the Nathan Littauer Hospital in Gloversville, NY.

Financial Summary

Total Giving: $1,300,000 (2002 approx); $1,337,396 (2001)
Giving Analysis: Giving for 2001 includes: foundation grants to United Way ($4,000); foundation scholarships ($21,666)
Assets: $39,600,000 (2002 approx); $41,011,478 (2001)
Gifts Received: $3,332,084 (2001); $944,350 (1998); $2,649,235 (1997)

Typical Recipients

Arts & Humanities: Arts Outreach, Ethnic & Folk Arts, Historic Preservation, History & Archaeology, Libraries, Literary Arts, Museums/Galleries, Music, Theater
Civic & Public Affairs: Botanical Gardens/Parks, Community Foundations, Employment/Job Training, Ethnic Organizations, Civic & Public Affairs-General, Philanthropic Organizations
Education: Arts/Humanities Education, Colleges & Universities, Education Funds, Education Reform, Engineering/Technological Education, Education-General, International Exchange, International Studies, Journalism/Media Education, Legal Education, Literacy, Medical Education, Private Education (Precollege), Religious Education, School Volunteerism, Social Sciences Education, Student Aid
Environment: Forestry, Environment-General
Health: Clinics/Medical Centers, Geriatric Health, Health Policy/Cost Containment, Health Organizations, Hospitals, Hospitals (University Affiliated)
International: Foreign Arts Organizations, Foreign Educational Institutions, Health Care/Hospitals, International Environmental Issues, International Organizations, International Relations, Missionary/Religious Activities
Religion: Bible Study/Translation, Churches, Religion-General, Jewish Causes, Missionary Activities (Domestic), Religious Organizations, Religious Welfare, Seminaries
Science: Scientific Centers & Institutes, Scientific Research
Social Services: Child Welfare, Community Centers, Family Services, People with Disabilities, Recreation & Athletics, Senior Services, Social Services-General

Application Procedures

Initial Contact: Send a brief proposal.
Application Requirements: Include description of project, budget request, timetable for completion, curriculum vitae of key personnel, and proof of tax exempt status. Requests for a Book Fund should include a description of the library and its collections, details about any existing book fund program, current budget for Judaica, a list of holdings in Judaica as well as projected needs, and background information about the institution and the Jewish Studies program on campus.
Deadlines: None. The officers and directors meet as needed to decide on grants.
Notes: All grants must be administered without deductions for overhead and/or administration.

Restrictions

Grants are seldom made for endowments (except for book funds), operating budgets, or capital projects.

Additional Information

The foundation awards grants for travel purposes.
Publications: Guidelines

Foundation Officials

Charles Berlin, PhD: director B Boston, MA 1936. ED Hebrew College (1956); Harvard University AB (1958); Hebrew College (1959); Harvard University PhD (1963); Simmons College MLS (1964). NONPR AFFIL consult: University Florida; consult: University Texas; trustee: Hebrew College; member, executive secretary: Association Jewish Studies; head Judaica division: Harvard College; member: Association Jewish Libraries.
Berthold Bilski: director PRIM CORP EMPL officer: Lepercq De Neuflize & Co. Inc. CORP AFFIL director: Lepercq 99 First Management.
Pamela Ween Brumberg: program officer
Robert D. Frost: director
William Lee Frost: president, treasurer, director B Larchmont, NY 1926. ED Harvard University BA (1947); Yale University LLB (1951); Harvard University MPA (1958). OCCUPATION private law practice. CORP AFFIL director: Overseas Shipholding Group. NONPR AFFIL member: New York County Bar Association; member: New York State Bar Association; member: Harvard University Alumni Association; member: New York City Bar Association. CLUB AFFIL Yale Club; Harvard Club.
George Harris: assistant secretary, assistant treasurer, director
Henry A. Lowet: vice president, secretary, director
Mark Milski: director
Peter J. Solomon: director B New York, NY 1938. ED Harvard University BA (1960); Harvard University MBA (1963). PRIM CORP EMPL chairman, chief executive officer: Peter J Solomon Co. Ltd. CORP AFFIL director: Office Depot Inc.; director: Phillips-Van Heusen Corp.

Grants Analysis

Disclosure Period: calendar year ending 2001
Total Grants: $1,313,230*
Number of Grants: 147
Average Grant: $8,934
Highest Grant: $125,000
Typical Range: $1,000 to $15,000
***Note:** Giving excludes scholarships and United Way.

Recent Grants

Note: Grants derived from 2002 Form 990.
Library-Related

20,000	Queens Library Foundation, Jamaica, NY -- to support Cultural Program for Russian & Jewish Communities
10,000	American Friends of the Medem, New York, NY -- fund for Archives Project

General

40,000	Brooklyn College - B'nai B'rith Hillel Foundation, Brooklyn, NY -- to support center for Russian Jewish Life
30,000	Jewish Child Care Association of New York, New York, NY -- fund for Milk & Honey Day Care Program Reading Readiness Enrichment for Bukharan Caregivers
30,000	New York University - Medical Center, New York, NY -- to support Palliative Care Program, Rabbinic Bereavement Counselor
27,500	Center for Judaic Studies, University of Pennsylvania, Philadelphia, PA -- fund for Lucius N. Littauer Fellow
25,000	Jewish Museum, New York, NY -- to support exhibition "The Power of Conversation Jewish Women their Salons"
25,000	National Foundation for Jewish Culture, New York, NY -- fund for Doctoral Dissertation Fellowship Program
25,000	Yale University - Yale Law School, New Haven, CT -- Fund for Littauer Public Interest Career Assistance
20,000	Johns Hopkins University, Baltimore, MD -- to support the Lucius N. Littauer Judaica Book Fund
17,500	Federation Employment Guidance Service (FEGS), New York, NY -- to support Partners in Citizenship
16,667	American Society for Technion, New York, NY -- to assist Lucius N. Littauer Scholarship Fund

MILTON S. AND CORINNE N. LIVINGSTON FOUNDATION

Giving Contact

Yale Richards, Executive Director
11605 Miracle Hills Dr., Suite 300
Omaha, NE 68154-4487
Phone: (402)492-9800
Fax: (402)492-9336

Description

Founded: 1948
EIN: 476027670

Organization Type: Private Foundation
Giving Locations: DC; NE: Omaha; NJ; NY
Grant Types: Capital, General Support, Multiyear/Continuing Support.

Donor Information
Founder: the late Milton S. Livingston

Financial Summary
Total Giving: $537,625 (2001)
Giving Analysis: Giving for 2001 includes: foundation grants to United Way ($5,000)
Assets: $4,059,157 (2001)
Gifts Received: $2,200 (1993)

Typical Recipients
Arts & Humanities: Arts Funds, Ballet, Libraries, Museums/Galleries, Music, Opera
Civic & Public Affairs: Civic & Public Affairs-General, Municipalities/Towns, Philanthropic Organizations, Public Policy
Education: Colleges & Universities, Education Funds, Education-General, International Studies, Medical Education, Minority Education, Public Education (Precollege), Special Education, Student Aid
Health: AIDS/HIV, Cancer, Health Organizations, Nursing Services, Public Health
International: Foreign Educational Institutions, International-General, Missionary/Religious Activities
Religion: Jewish Causes, Religious Organizations, Social/Policy Issues, Synagogues/Temples
Social Services: Big Brothers/Big Sisters, Child Welfare, Family Planning, Food/Clothing Distribution, People with Disabilities, Scouts, Social Services-General, United Funds/United Ways, Youth Organizations

Application Procedures
Initial Contact: Send a brief letter of inquiry describing program or project.
Application Requirements: Include a description of organization, amount requested, purpose of funds sought, recently audited financial statement, and proof of tax-exempt status.
Deadlines: None.
Review Process: Board meets in 2–May and 2–December.

Restrictions
Does not support individuals.

Foundation Officials
Gerald A. Hoberman: trustee
Robert I. Kully: president, trust
Murray H. Newman: vice president, trust
Dr. Patricia Newman: trustee
Yale Richards: asst secy
Suzanne Singer: secretary, trust
Stanley J. Slosburg: trust

Grants Analysis
Disclosure Period: calendar year ending 2001
Total Grants: $532,625*
Number of Grants: 34
Average Grant: $8,250*
Highest Grant: $252,125
Typical Range: $1,000 to $20,000
*Note: Giving excludes United Way. Average grant figure excludes highest grant.

Recent Grants
Note: Grants derived from 2001 Form 990.
General

252,125	Jewish Federation Foundation, Omaha, NE
73,000	Jewish Federation, Omaha, NE
60,500	Temple Israel, Omaha, NE
20,000	Omaha Schools Foundation, Omaha, NE
17,500	Nebraska Jewish Historical Society, Omaha, NE
12,500	Chabad of Nebraska, Omaha, NE
11,500	National Conference For Community & Justice, Omaha, NE
10,000	Anti-Defamation League of B'Nai B'Rith, New York, NY
10,000	Girl Scouts, Omaha, NE
10,000	Planned Parenthood of Omaha/Council Bluffs, Omaha, NE

LOCKHART VAUGHAN FOUNDATION

Giving Contact
John B. Powell, Jr., Executive Director
2 E. Read Street, Suite 100
Baltimore, MD 21202
Phone: (410)837-9400

Description
EIN: 521693184
Organization Type: Private Foundation
Giving Locations: MD
Grant Types: General Support.

Financial Summary
Total Giving: $1,346,250 (2002)
Assets: $26,411,756 (2002)

Typical Recipients
Arts & Humanities: Dance, Libraries, Theater
Civic & Public Affairs: Botanical Gardens/Parks, Community Foundations, Economic Development, Employment/Job Training, Civic & Public Affairs-General, Housing, Inner-City Development, Legal Aid, Philanthropic Organizations, Public Policy, Urban & Community Affairs, Women's Affairs, Zoos/Aquariums
Education: Afterschool/Enrichment Programs, Colleges & Universities, Education Funds, Elementary Education (Public), Faculty Development, Education-General, Leadership Training, Legal Education, Literacy, Medical Education, Preschool Education, Private Education (Precollege), Science/Mathematics Education, Social Sciences Education
Environment: Air/Water Quality, Forestry, Environment-General, Protection, Resource Conservation
Health: Cancer, Children's Health/Hospitals, Clinics/Medical Centers, Emergency/Ambulance Services, Health-General, Health Organizations, Hospitals, Medical Research, Mental Health, Public Health, Speech & Hearing
Religion: Churches, Ministries, Religious Welfare
Science: Science Museums, Scientific Centers & Institutes
Social Services: At-Risk Youth, Big Brothers/Big Sisters, Camps, Child Abuse, Child Welfare, Community Centers, Community Service Organizations, Crime Prevention, Family Planning, Family Services, Food/Clothing Distribution, People with Disabilities, Recreation & Athletics, Scouts, Shelters/Homelessness, Social Services-General, Substance Abuse, United Funds/United Ways, YMCA/YWCA/YMHA/YWHA, Youth Organizations

Application Procedures
Initial Contact: Submit a completed grant application. The foundation accepts the Association of Baltimore Area Grantmakers (ABAG) Common Grant Application Format, which can be obtained at www.abagmd.org.
Application Requirements: The application should be submitted in duplicate, and should include a cover letter, proposal narrative, and attachments as outlined in the ABAG Application Format.
Deadlines: February 20, June 20, and October 20.
Decision Notification: Applicants will be notified of the foundation's decision within approximately 60 days.

Restrictions
The foundation does not support organizations involved in the arts.

Additional Information
Publications: Application Procedures

Foundation Officials
Benjamin M. Baker, III: director
Julia Baker Menzies: director
Julia P. O'Brien: trustee
Brentnall M. Powell: trustee
John Brentnall Powell, Jr.: director
Susan Baker Powell: director
Julia B. Schnupp: trustee
Kevin A. Schnupp: trustee

Grants Analysis
Disclosure Period: calendar year ending 2002
Total Grants: $1,346,250
Number of Grants: 66
Average Grant: $20,398
Highest Grant: $150,000
Typical Range: $5,000 to $30,000

Recent Grants
Note: Grants derived from 2002 Form 990.
Library-Related

40,000	Roland Park Library Initiative, Inc., Baltimore, MD -- for community development

General

150,000	Maryland Zoological Society, Baltimore, MD -- for community development and capital campaign for Baltimore Zoo
100,000	Maryland Zoological Society, Baltimore, MD -- for community development and capital campaign for Baltimore Zoo
55,000	Hearing and Speech Agency, Baltimore, MD -- for health care and capital campaign
50,000	Baltimore Community Foundation, Baltimore, MD -- for Youth Program and A-Teams
50,000	Rice University, Houston, TX -- for education
35,000	Environmental Defense, Inc., Baltimore, MD -- for Community Development Baltimore Regional Partnership for Vision
30,000	Midtown Community Fund, Baltimore, MD -- for community development and operation of vacuum vehicle
30,000	St. Vincent de Paul, Baltimore, MD -- for community development
30,000	Shepherd's Clinic, Baltimore, MD -- for capital campaign and health care
25,000	Baltimore Museum of Industry, Baltimore, MD -- for Youth Program After-school and Weekend Educational Programs

LOEWS CORP.

Company Headquarters
667 Madison Ave.
New York, NY 10021-8087
Web: http://www.loews.com

Company Description
Ticker: LTR
Exchange: NYSE
Revenue: US$14.584 billion (2004)
Profit: US$1.231 billion (2004)
Employees: 22700 (2003)
Fortune Rank: 144, per FORTUNE Magazine's list of 500 Largest U.S. Corporations (2004).

Nonmonetary Support
Type: Donated Products

Loews Foundation

Giving Contact

John J. Kenny, Trustee
Loews Foundation
655 Madison Avenue
New York, NY 10021-8043
Phone: (212)521-2650
Fax: (212)521-2329

Description

Founded: 1957
EIN: 136082817
Organization Type: Corporate Foundation
Giving Locations: NY: operating locations.
Grant Types: Employee Matching Gifts, General Support, Matching, Scholarship.

Financial Summary

Total Giving: $842,198 (2003); $738,850 (2002); $1,824,476 (2001). Note: Contributes through foundation only.
Assets: $106,265 (2003); $943,996 (2002); $1,662,345 (2001)
Gifts Received: $2,119,390 (2001); $2,986,383 (2000); $1,735,000 (1999). Note: Contributions were received from Loews Corporation and its subsidiaries.

Typical Recipients

Arts & Humanities: Arts Associations & Councils, Arts Festivals, Arts Funds, Arts Institutes, Arts Outreach, Dance, Arts & Humanities-General, Historic Preservation, Libraries, Museums/Galleries, Music, Opera, Performing Arts, Public Broadcasting, Theater, Visual Arts
Civic & Public Affairs: African American Affairs, Botanical Gardens/Parks, Business/Free Enterprise, Chambers of Commerce, Civil Rights, Clubs, Economic Development, Employment/Job Training, Ethnic Organizations, Civic & Public Affairs-General, Housing, Law & Justice, Legal Aid, Municipalities/Towns, Parades/Festivals, Philanthropic Organizations, Professional & Trade Associations, Public Policy, Safety, Urban & Community Affairs, Women's Affairs, Zoos/Aquariums
Education: Afterschool/Enrichment Programs, Arts/Humanities Education, Business Education, Colleges & Universities, Education Associations, Education Funds, Education Reform, Education-General, International Studies, Leadership Training, Legal Education, Literacy, Medical Education, Minority Education, Public Education (Precollege), Secondary Education (Private), Social Sciences Education, Special Education, Student Aid, Vocational & Technical Education
Environment: Forestry, Environment-General, Resource Conservation, Wildlife Protection
Health: AIDS/HIV, Cancer, Children's Health/Hospitals, Clinics/Medical Centers, Diabetes, Emergency/Ambulance Services, Health-General, Geriatric Health, Health Organizations, Hospitals, Hospitals (University Affiliated), Medical Rehabilitation, Medical Research, Mental Health, Multiple Sclerosis, Nutrition, Prenatal Health Issues, Public Health, Research/Studies Institutes, Single-Disease Health Associations, Speech & Hearing
International: Foreign Arts Organizations, Health Care/Hospitals, Human Rights, International Organizations, International Peace & Security Issues, International Relations, International Relief Efforts, Missionary/Religious Activities
Religion: Jewish Causes, Religious Welfare, Synagogues/Temples
Science: Science Museums
Social Services: Animal Protection, Camps, Child Welfare, Community Centers, Community Service Organizations, Delinquency & Criminal Rehabilitation, Family Planning, Food/Clothing Distribution, People with Disabilities, Recreation & Athletics, Scouts, Social Services-General, Substance Abuse, United Funds/United Ways, Volunteer Services, YMCA/YWCA/YMHA/YWHA, Youth Organizations

Application Procedures

Initial Contact: Contact foundation by letter; foundation does not accept phone calls.
Application Requirements: Include a description of organization and project, budget, and proof of tax exemption.
Deadlines: None.
Notes: Applications for employee-related sponsorships are available from the foundation. Scholarships are provided only for children of Loews Corporation through the National Merit Scholarship Corp.

Restrictions

Foundation does not make grants to individuals.

Additional Information

All charitable giving is through the foundation. Subsidiaries do not make contributions independent of Loews Foundation, except for CNA Insurance Co., which is affiliated with CNA Financial Corp., a Loews Corp. joint venture.

Corporate Officials

John J. Kenny: treasurer, chief executive officer, director B Jersey City, NJ 1938. ED New York University (1965); Saint John's University School of Law (1972). PRIM CORP EMPL treasurer: Loews Corp. ADD CORP EMPL treasurer, director: 48th Street & 8th Avenue Corp.; treasurer: Lowes Hotels Inc. NONPR AFFIL trustee: Loews Foundation.
James S. Tisch: president, chief executive officer, director B Atlantic City, NJ January 02, 1953. ED Cornell University BS (1975); University of Pennsylvania Wharton School MBA (1976). PRIM CORP EMPL president, chief executive officer, director: Loews Corp. CORP AFFIL chairman: Diamond Offshore Drilling Inc.; director: Vail Resorts Inc.; director: CNA Financial Corp. NONPR AFFIL trustee: Mount Sinai Medical Center New York; president elect: United Jewish Appeal Federation New York; trustee: Dalton School New York; director: Federation Employment & Guidance Service.

Foundation Officials

Peter Keegan: senior vice president B Providence, RI 1944. ED Brown University BA (1966); Columbia University MBA (1970). PRIM CORP EMPL senior vice president, chief financial officer: Loews Corp.
John J. Kenny: secretary, treasurer, trustee (see above)
Andrew H. Tisch: trustee
Preston R. Tisch: trustee

Grants Analysis

Disclosure Period: calendar year ending 2003
Total Grants: $704,128*
Number of Grants: 64
Average Grant: $9,986*
Highest Grant: $75,000
Lowest Grant: $250
Typical Range: $1,000 to $20,000
*Note: Giving excludes matching gifts, scholarships, and United Way. Average grant figure excludes highest grant.

Recent Grants

Note: Grants derived from 2003 Form 990.
Library-Related

10,000	Dorot Jewish Division of the New York Public Library, New York, NY
10,000	Laura Bush Foundation for American Libraries, Washington, DC

General

75,000	New York City 2012, New York, NY
43,010	National Merit Scholarship Corporation, Evanston, IL
37,156	City Parks Foundation, New York, NY
35,000	Advertising Council Inc., New York, NY
35,000	American Museum of Natural History, Washington, DC
30,000	American Express Carnegie Hall, New York, NY
30,000	Camp Heartland, Milwaukee, WI
30,000	Smithsonian Cooper Hewitt National Design Museum, New York, NY
25,000	Boys and Girls Clubs of America, Atlanta, GA
25,000	Common Good, New York, NY

LOEWY FAMILY FOUNDATION

Giving Contact

John P. Reiner, Treasurer & Director
80 Wall Street, Suite 1018
New York, NY 10005-3601
Phone: (212)269-2466

Description

Founded: 1966
EIN: 136225288
Organization Type: Private Foundation
Giving Locations: NY: New York
Grant Types: General Support, Scholarship.

Donor Information

Founder: the late Alfred Loewy, the late Edna Loewy Butler

Financial Summary

Total Giving: $443,000 (fiscal year ending June 30, 2004); $505,000 (fiscal 2001)
Giving Analysis: Giving for fiscal 2004 includes: foundation scholarships ($18,000); fiscal 2001: foundation scholarships ($25,000)
Assets: $9,587,767 (fiscal 2004); $10,328,814 (fiscal 2001)

Typical Recipients

Arts & Humanities: Arts Associations & Councils, Libraries, Performing Arts, Public Broadcasting, Theater
Education: Colleges & Universities, Education Funds, Medical Education, Minority Education, Private Education (Precollege), Science/Mathematics Education, Student Aid
Health: Hospitals, Medical Research, Mental Health, Transplant Networks/Donor Banks
Social Services: Child Welfare, Youth Organizations

Application Procedures

Initial Contact: Send proposal in letter form.
Deadlines: None.

Restrictions

No grants to individuals.

Foundation Officials

Michael Green: vice president, director
Erik A. Hanson: vice president, director
John P. Reiner: treasurer, director
Mischa A. Zabotin: vice president, director

Grants Analysis

Disclosure Period: fiscal year ending June 30, 2004
Total Grants: $425,000*
Number of Grants: 6
Highest Grant: $200,000
Lowest Grant: $15,000
*Note: Giving excludes scholarships.

Recent Grants

Note: Grants derived from fiscal 2004 Form 990.
General

200,000	Columbia University, New York, NY -- for advancement of transplant medicine

75,000	Trinity School, New York, NY -- towards Tercentennial history project
50,000	Georgetown University, Washington, DC -- lectureship program in science, technology and international
50,000	San Diego Blood Bank Foundation, San Diego, CA -- research funding on blood disorders
35,000	Lehigh University, Bethlehem, PA -- graduate fellowship assistance
18,000	Catching the Dream, Albuquerque, NM -- to provide scholarship assistance
15,000	Association for Development of Dramatic Arts Inc., New York, NY -- grant for student matinee series

GEORGE A. AND GRACE LONG FOUNDATION

Giving Contact

Marjorie Alexander-Davis, Co-Trustee
Care of Fleet Bank
777 Main Street
Providence, RI 02904-5703
Phone: (203)728-2274

Description

Founded: 1960
EIN: 066030953
Organization Type: Private Foundation
Giving Locations: CT: Hartford greater Hartford
Grant Types: General Support, Project, Scholarship.

Donor Information

Founder: George A. Long, the late Grace L. Long

Financial Summary

Total Giving: $620,766 (2002)
Giving Analysis: Giving for 2002 includes: foundation scholarships ($20,300)
Assets: $9,601,127 (2002)

Typical Recipients

Arts & Humanities: Arts Centers, Community Arts, Dance, History & Archaeology, Libraries, Museums/Galleries, Music, Opera, Performing Arts, Public Broadcasting, Theater
Civic & Public Affairs: Botanical Gardens/Parks, Clubs, Community Foundations, Economic Development, Employment/Job Training, Civic & Public Affairs-General, Hispanic Affairs, Housing, Parades/Festivals, Professional & Trade Associations, Public Policy, Rural Affairs, Urban & Community Affairs, Women's Affairs
Education: Agricultural Education, Arts/Humanities Education, Colleges & Universities, Education Associations, Education Reform, Engineering/Technological Education, Leadership Training, Literacy, Minority Education, Preschool Education, Private Education (Precollege), Public Education (Precollege), Special Education, Student Aid, Vocational & Technical Education
Environment: Environment-General, Resource Conservation
Health: Adolescent Health Issues, AIDS/HIV, Alzheimer's Disease, Children's Health/Hospitals, Clinics/Medical Centers, Emergency/Ambulance Services, Home-Care Services, Hospitals, Long-Term Care, Nursing Services, Prenatal Health Issues, Single-Disease Health Associations
International: International Relief Efforts
Religion: Churches, Ministries, Religious Organizations, Religious Welfare
Science: Scientific Centers & Institutes
Social Services: Animal Protection, At-Risk Youth, Big Brothers/Big Sisters, Camps, Child Welfare, Community Centers, Community Service Organiza-

tions, Counseling, Domestic Violence, Emergency Relief, Family Planning, Family Services, Food/Clothing Distribution, Homes, People with Disabilities, Recreation & Athletics, Scouts, Senior Services, Shelters/Homelessness, Social Services-General, United Funds/United Ways, YMCA/YWCA/YMHA/YWHA, Youth Organizations

Application Procedures

Initial Contact: Request application form.
Deadlines: March 15 and September 15.

Restrictions

Does not support individuals.

Additional Information

Publications: Application Form; Guidelines
Trust(s): Fleet National Bank

Foundation Officials

Charles R. Moore, Jr.: trustee

Grants Analysis

Disclosure Period: calendar year ending 2002
Total Grants: $600,466*
Number of Grants: 161
Average Grant: $3,730
Highest Grant: $10,000
Lowest Grant: $750
Typical Range: $1,000 to $5,000
*Note: Giving excludes scholarships.

Recent Grants

Note: Grants derived from 2002 Form 990.
General

10,000	Almada Lodge Times Farm Camp Corporation, Andover, CT
10,000	Connecticut Children's Medical Center Foundation, Hartford, CT
8,627	Hartford Camp Courant, Hartford, CT
8,000	Connecticut Humane Society, Newington, CT
7,500	Equistrides Therapeutic Riding Center, Inc.
6,000	City Slicker Farm Program
6,000	Community Foundation of Southeastern Connecticut, New London, CT
6,000	Connecticut Forum, Hartford, CT
6,000	Hartford Interval House, Hartford, CT
5,800	Trinity College Community Child Center, Hartford, CT

J. M. LONG FOUNDATION

Giving Contact

Robert M. Long, President & Trustee
2700 Ygnacio Valley Rd., Suite 172
Walnut Creek, CA 94598
Phone: (925)935-4138

Description

Founded: 1966
EIN: 941643626
Organization Type: Private Foundation
Giving Locations: CA
Grant Types: General Support, Scholarship.

Donor Information

Founder: the late Joseph M. Long

Financial Summary

Total Giving: $2,274,283 (2002); $1,764,600 (2001)
Assets: $47,993,889 (2002); $37,254,412 (2001)
Gifts Received: $13,745,127 (2002); $1,388,243 (1993); $8,066,684 (1992). Note: In 2002, contributions were received from Joseph M. Long Marital Trust.

Typical Recipients

Arts & Humanities: Arts Associations & Councils, Historic Preservation, History & Archaeology, Libraries, Museums/Galleries, Music, Performing Arts
Civic & Public Affairs: Botanical Gardens/Parks, Economic Development, Employment/Job Training, Municipalities/Towns, Safety, Urban & Community Affairs, Women's Affairs, Zoos/Aquariums
Education: Agricultural Education, Arts/Humanities Education, Business Education, Colleges & Universities, Community & Junior Colleges, Education Funds, Education Reform, Elementary Education (Public), Environmental Education, Education-General, Health & Physical Education, Medical Education, Private Education (Precollege), Public Education (Precollege), School Volunteerism, Science/Mathematics Education, Secondary Education (Public), Social Sciences Education, Student Aid
Environment: Environment-General, Research, Resource Conservation, Wildlife Protection
Health: Arthritis, Cancer, Children's Health/Hospitals, Clinics/Medical Centers, Diabetes, Emergency/Ambulance Services, Health-General, Health Funds, Health Organizations, Hospices, Hospitals, Medical Rehabilitation, Medical Research, Mental Health, Nursing Services, Preventive Medicine/Wellness Organizations, Public Health, Single-Disease Health Associations
Religion: Jewish Causes, Religious Organizations, Religious Welfare
Science: Science Museums, Scientific Centers & Institutes, Scientific Research
Social Services: Camps, Community Centers, Community Service Organizations, Counseling, Day Care, Family Services, Food/Clothing Distribution, People with Disabilities, Recreation & Athletics, Scouts, Senior Services, Social Services-General, Veterans, YMCA/YWCA/YMHA/YWHA, Youth Organizations

Application Procedures

Initial Contact: Send letter requesting application and guidelines. Deadline information is listed in the guidelines.

Restrictions

Grants are not awarded to individuals.

Foundation Officials

W. G. Combs: vice president, trustee
O. D. Jones: trustee
Milton Long: trustee
Robert Merrill Long: president, trustee B Oakland, CA 1938. ED Brown University (1956-1958); Claremont Men's College BA (1960). PRIM CORP EMPL chairman emeritus: Longs Drug Stores Corp. NONPR AFFIL director: National Association Chain Drug Stores.
S. D. Roath: trustee
M. J. Souyoultzis: trustee
C. Tessler: secretary

Grants Analysis

Disclosure Period: calendar year ending 2002
Total Grants: $2,274,283
Number of Grants: 153
Average Grant: $9,771*
Highest Grant: $418,182
Typical Range: $1,000 to $20,000
*Note: Average grant figure excludes five highest grants ($828,182).

Recent Grants

Note: Grants derived from 2001 Form 990.
General

250,000	University of the Pacific School of Pharmacy and Health Sciences, Stockton, CA
50,000	City of Hope, Los Angeles, CA
50,000	John Muir Memorial Association, Martinez, CA
38,800	Isla Vista School, Isla Vista, CA
38,100	Milestones of Development, Vallejo, CA

35,000	Enloe Medical Center, Chico, CA
28,000	Community Action Marin, San Rafael, CA
25,000	Alameda Hospital Foundation, Alameda, CA
25,000	Arthritis Foundation
25,000	California Waterfowl Association, San Francisco, CA

JOHN F. LONG FOUNDATION

Giving Contact
John F. Long, Director
5035 W. Camelback Rd.
Phoenix, AZ 85031
Phone: (602)272-0421
Fax: (602)846-7208
E-mail: webmaster@jflong.com
Web: http://www.jflong.com/foundation.htm

Description
Founded: 1959
EIN: 866052431
Organization Type: Private Foundation
Giving Locations: AZ
Grant Types: General Support.

Donor Information
Founder: John F. Long

Financial Summary
Total Giving: $370,915 (fiscal year ending April 30, 2002); $266,528 (fiscal 2001)
Assets: $6,190,500 (fiscal 2002); $6,216,000 (fiscal 2001)
Gifts Received: $76,057 (fiscal 2001); $1,565 (fiscal 1994)

Typical Recipients
Arts & Humanities: History & Archaeology, Libraries, Music, Public Broadcasting, Theater, Visual Arts
Civic & Public Affairs: Botanical Gardens/Parks, Clubs, Community Foundations, Civic & Public Affairs-General, Inner-City Development, Municipalities/Towns, Parades/Festivals, Urban & Community Affairs, Women's Affairs, Zoos/Aquariums
Education: Colleges & Universities, Education Reform, Elementary Education (Public), Education-General, Literacy, Medical Education, Preschool Education, Private Education (Precollege), Public Education (Precollege), School Volunteerism, Secondary Education (Public)
Environment: Air/Water Quality, Environment-General
Health: AIDS/HIV, Cancer, Children's Health/Hospitals, Clinics/Medical Centers, Health Organizations, Research/Studies Institutes, Single-Disease Health Associations
International: International Environmental Issues, International Organizations
Religion: Churches, Jewish Causes, Ministries, Religious Organizations, Religious Welfare
Science: Science Museums
Social Services: Child Welfare, Community Centers, Crime Prevention, Emergency Relief, Family Planning, Family Services, Food/Clothing Distribution, Homes, People with Disabilities, Recreation & Athletics, Scouts, Shelters/Homelessness, Social Services-General, Substance Abuse, Youth Organizations

Application Procedures
Initial Contact: Send a brief letter of inquiry.
Application Requirements: Include purpose of funds sought and Better Business Bureau approval.
Deadlines: None.

Foundation Officials
Jacob F. Long: trustee
John F. Long: director
Mary P. Long: director
Bonnie O'Hara: admin

Grants Analysis
Disclosure Period: fiscal year ending April 30, 2002
Total Grants: $370,915
Number of Grants: 156
Average Grant: $1,748*
Highest Grant: $100,000
Lowest Grant: $100
Typical Range: $500 to $3,000
*Note: Average grant figure excludes highest grant.

Recent Grants
Note: Grants derived from fiscal 2003 Form 990.
General

25,000	Grand Canyon University, Phoenix, AZ
20,310	Milwaukee Brewers, Milwaukee, WI
20,145	West Maricopa Education Center, Phoenix, AZ
20,000	University of Arizona Foundation, Tucson, AZ
15,950	Brophy College, Phoenix, AZ
13,100	West Valley Child Crisis Center, Phoenix, AZ
10,000	Denver Health Reading Program, Denver, CO
10,000	Reserve Components Emergency Relief Fund, Phoenix, AZ
8,000	Historical League, Tempe, AZ
6,300	Alhambra School District 68, Phoenix, AZ

LONG ISLAND LIGHTING CO.

Company Headquarters
600 Doctors Path
Riverhead, NY 11901

Company Description
Employees: 5,403
SIC(s): 4900 Electric, Gas & Sanitary Services.

Operating Locations
Long Island Lighting Co. (NY--Hicksville)

Nonmonetary Support
Type: Donated Equipment; In-kind Services; Loaned Employees; Loaned Executives; Workplace Solicitation

Giving Contact
James M. Cunningham, Public Affairs
175 E. Old Country Rd.
Hicksville, NY 11801
Phone: (516)755-6650

Description
Organization Type: Corporate Giving Program
Giving Locations: service area.

Typical Recipients
Arts & Humanities: Arts Associations & Councils, Arts Centers, Arts Festivals, Arts Funds, Community Arts, Ethnic & Folk Arts, Historic Preservation, Libraries, Literary Arts, Museums/Galleries, Music, Opera, Performing Arts, Public Broadcasting, Theater, Visual Arts
Civic & Public Affairs: Economic Development, Employment/Job Training, Nonprofit Management, Professional & Trade Associations, Safety, Urban & Community Affairs, Women's Affairs, Zoos/Aquariums
Education: Business Education, Colleges & Universities, Community & Junior Colleges, Continuing Education, Elementary Education (Private), Engineering/Technological Education, Faculty Development, Literacy, Minority Education, Public Education (Precollege), Science/Mathematics Education, Social Sciences Education, Special Education
Environment: Environment-General
Health: Geriatric Health, Nutrition, Single-Disease Health Associations
Science: Science Exhibits & Fairs, Scientific Centers & Institutes, Scientific Organizations
Social Services: Community Centers, Family Services, Food/Clothing Distribution, People with Disabilities, Senior Services, Shelters/Homelessness, United Funds/United Ways, Volunteer Services, Youth Organizations

Application Procedures
Initial Contact: Send inquiry letter.

Corporate Officials
James T. Flynn: executive vice president, chief operating officer chief financial officer PRIM CORP EMPL executive vice president, chief operating officer: Long Island Lighting Co.
Anthony Nozzolillo: senior vice president financial, chief financial officer B Marcone, Italy 1948. ED Brooklyn Polytechnic Institute (1972); Long Island University (1978). PRIM CORP EMPL senior vice president financial, chief financial officer: Long Island Lighting Co.

LONGWOOD FOUNDATION

Giving Contact
Peter C. Morrow, Executive Director
100 West 10th Street, Suite 1109
Wilmington, DE 19801
Phone: (302)654-2477
Fax: (302)654-2323

Description
Founded: 1937
EIN: 510066734
Organization Type: General Purpose Foundation
Giving Locations: DE; PA: Southern Chester County
Grant Types: Capital, Challenge, General Support, Multiyear/Continuing Support, Seed Money.

Donor Information
Founder: The Longwood Foundation was created in 1937 by Pierre Samuel du Pont and became the principal beneficiary of his estate upon his death in 1954.

Financial Summary
Total Giving: $28,036,718 (fiscal year ending September 30, 2003); $39,872,605 (fiscal 2002); $33,128,076 (fiscal 2001)
Giving Analysis: Giving for fiscal 2003 includes: foundation grants to United Way ($529,000); fiscal 2002: foundation grants to United Way ($391,000) fiscal 2001: foundation grants to United Way ($416,000)
Assets: $645,198,897 (fiscal 2003); $600,786,854 (fiscal 2002); $651,327,269 (fiscal 2001)
Gifts Received: $919,510 (fiscal 1997); $552,560 (fiscal 1996)

Typical Recipients
Arts & Humanities: Arts Centers, Arts Funds, Arts Institutes, Dance, Arts & Humanities-General, Historic Preservation, History & Archaeology, Libraries, Museums/Galleries, Music, Opera, Public Broadcasting, Theater, Visual Arts
Civic & Public Affairs: African American Affairs, Botanical Gardens/Parks, Clubs, Community Foundations, Economic Development, Employment/Job

Training, Civic & Public Affairs-General, Housing, Inner-City Development, Municipalities/Towns, Non-profit Management, Parades/Festivals, Professional & Trade Associations, Public Policy, Rural Affairs, Safety, Urban & Community Affairs, Women's Affairs, Zoos/Aquariums

Education: Business Education, Colleges & Universities, Economic Education, Education Funds, Education Reform, Environmental Education, Education-General, Literacy, Minority Education, Preschool Education, Private Education (Precollege), Public Education (Precollege), Religious Education, Science/Mathematics Education, Secondary Education (Private), Special Education, Student Aid

Environment: Air/Water Quality, Forestry, Environment-General, Protection, Resource Conservation, Watershed, Wildlife Protection

Health: AIDS/HIV, Cancer, Children's Health/ Hospitals, Clinics/Medical Centers, Emergency/ Ambulance Services, Health-General, Geriatric Health, Health Funds, Health Organizations, Hospices, Hospitals, Long-Term Care, Medical Research, Multiple Sclerosis, Preventive Medicine/ Wellness Organizations, Public Health

Religion: Religion-General, Jewish Causes, Ministries, Religious Welfare

Science: Science Museums, Scientific Centers & Institutes, Scientific Organizations

Social Services: Animal Protection, At-Risk Youth, Camps, Child Welfare, Community Centers, Community Service Organizations, Counseling, Day Care, Family Planning, Family Services, Food/Clothing Distribution, Homes, People with Disabilities, Recreation & Athletics, Scouts, Senior Services, Shelters/ Homelessness, Social Services-General, Special Olympics, Substance Abuse, United Funds/United Ways, Veterans, YMCA/YWCA/YMHA/YWHA, Youth Organizations

Application Procedures
Initial Contact: Prospective applicants should send a two-page letter to the foundation.
Application Requirements: The letter of inquiry should include reason for the grant, pertinent financial statements, and a copy of the IRS 501(c)(3) tax-exempt status letter.
Deadlines: Proposals should be submitted by March 15 and September 15.

Restrictions
Grants are generally not made to fraternal organizations or to political or lobbying groups, or for special projects and/or events. Limited to the Delaware and Southern Chester County, PA area.

Additional Information
About 10% of the grantees in any given year are first-time recipients of foundation aid.

Foundation Officials
Charles T.L. Copeland: trustee
Gerret van Sweringen Copeland: trustee CORP AFFIL chairman: Bouchaine Vineyards. NONPR AFFIL trustee: Delaware Art Museum.
David Leigh Craven: trustee B Winston-Salem, NC 1953. ED Davidson College BA (1975); Wake Forest University JD (1978). PRIM CORP EMPL senior vice president: BB & T Corp.
Eleuthere I. DuPont: trustee
Pierre S. DuPont, IV: trustee
Irenee du Pont May, Jr.: secretary, trustee
Hugh Rodney Sharp, III: president, trustee CORP AFFIL director: E.I. du Pont de Nemours & Co.; director: Wilmington Trust Corp.; trustee: Christiana Care Corp..
Henry Harper Silliman, Jr.: treasurer, trustee NONPR AFFIL trustee emeritus: St. Andrews School.

Grants Analysis
Disclosure Period: fiscal year ending September 30, 2003
Total Grants: $27,507,718*

Number of Grants: 72
Average Grant: $101,683*
Highest Grant: $13,000,000
Lowest Grant: $1,500
Typical Range: $25,000 to $200,000
***Note:** Giving excludes United Way. Average grant figure excludes eight highest grants ($21,000,000).

Recent Grants
Note: Grants derived from fiscal 2003 Form 990.
Library-Related
500,000	Friends of Concord Park Library, Concord, MA
100,000	Friends of Milton Public Library, Milton, PA

General
13,000,000	Longwood Gardens Inc., Kennett Square, PA
1,500,000	Independence School, Newark, DE
1,500,000	St. Francis Hospital Foundation, Wilmington, DE
1,000,000	Bayhealth Foundation, Dover, DE
1,000,000	Delaware State University, Dover, DE
1,000,000	Easter Seals Delaware & Maryland Eastern Shore, New Castle, DE
1,000,000	Innovative Schools Development Corporation, Wilmington, DE
1,000,000	University of Delaware, Newark, DE
600,500	Delaware Wild Lands, Townsend, DE
500,000	Boy Scouts of America Chester County, West Chester, PA

HARRY WILSON LOOSE TRUST

Giving Contact
Dalene Dradford
c/o Greater Kansas City Community Foundation
1010 Broadway, Suite 130
Kansas City, MO 64105
Phone: (816)842-0944
Fax: (816)842-0944
Web: http://www.gkccf.org

Description
Founded: 1927
EIN: 446009245
Organization Type: Private Foundation
Giving Locations: MO: Kansas City
Grant Types: Project, Research.

Donor Information
Founder: the late Harry Wilson Loose

Typical Recipients
Arts & Humanities: Arts Outreach, Libraries, Music
Civic & Public Affairs: Community Foundations, Economic Development, Nonprofit Management, Urban & Community Affairs, Zoos/Aquariums
Education: Business Education, Colleges & Universities, Community & Junior Colleges, Education Funds, Faculty Development, Education-General, International Exchange, Minority Education, Public Education (Precollege)
Environment: Environment-General
Health: Cancer, Clinics/Medical Centers, Health Organizations, Hospitals, Kidney, Public Health
Religion: Religious Welfare
Social Services: Child Welfare, Community Centers, Community Service Organizations, Day Care, Family Services, Recreation & Athletics, United Funds/ United Ways, Youth Organizations

Application Procedures
Initial Contact: Request grant guidelines.
Deadlines: Applications must be received four months prior to full board meetings.

Review Process: Board meets in March, June, September, and December.
Decision Notification: Decisions are made within two weeks of board meeting.

Restrictions
Does not support individuals or provide funds for general support, matching gifts, or scholarships.

Additional Information
Publications: Annual Report; Application Guidelines
Trust(s): Bank of America, N.A.

Foundation Officials
Donald Herbert Chisholm: trustee B Kansas City, MO September 25, 1917. ED Kansas City Junior College AA (1935); University of Missouri JD (1938); Park College LLD (1979). PRIM CORP EMPL officer counsel: Stinson, Mag & Fizzell PC. CORP AFFIL director: Kansas City Bridge Co. NONPR AFFIL director: Truman Medical Center; trustee: University Kansas City; trustee: Harry South Truman Library Institute; trustee: Saint Lukes Hospital Foundation; trustee: Victor East & Caroline East Schuttle Foundation; trustee emeritus: Park College; trustee: Midwest Research Institute; member: Order Coif; trustee: Mag Foundation; trustee: Illa C & Jacob Loose Foundation; trustee: Harry Wilson Loose Trust; member: Kansas City Bar Association; member: Lawyers Association Kansas City; chairman: Childrens Mercy Hospital; fellow: American College Trust & Estate Counsel; member: American Judicature Society; member: American Bar Association; fellow: American Bar Foundation. CLUB AFFIL Mission Hills Country Club; University Club.

Grants Analysis
Disclosure Period: calendar year ending 2000
Total Grants: $250,602
Number of Grants: 7
Highest Grant: $30,000
Lowest Grant: $5,000
Typical Range: $10,000 to $20,000

Recent Grants
Note: Grants derived from 2001 Form 990.
General
100,000	Swope Parkway Health Center, Kansas City, MO
82,804	Greater Kansas City Community Foundation, Kansas City, MO
10,000	Greater Kansas City Sports Commission and Foundation, Kansas City, MO -- national events and membership
10,000	Learning Exchange, Kansas City, MO -- support charter school evaluation study

L'OREAL U.S.A.

Company Headquarters
575 5th Avenue, Suite 14
New York, NY 10017
Web: http://www.lancome.com

Company Description
Employees: 585
SIC(s): 2844 Toilet Preparations.
Parent Company: L'Oreal S.A., 41 rue Martre, Clichy, France

Operating Locations
Bivona (IN--Gary); Cosmair, Inc. (NY--New York); Cosmair, Ralph Lauren Fragrance Division (NY--New York); ELA Medical (MN--Minnetonka); Galderma Laboratories (TX--Fort Worth); Maybelline (TN--Memphis); Parbel (FL--Miami); Sylamerica (NY--Tarrytown); Yardley of London (TN--Memphis)

Nonmonetary Support
Type: Donated Products

Giving Contact
Susan Davidowitz, Vice President, Corporate Public Relations
575 5th Ave., 33rd Floor
New York, NY 10017
Phone: (212)984-4105
Fax: (212)984-4150

Description
Organization Type: Corporate Giving Program
Giving Locations: NY: New York including metropolitan area and New Jersey

Financial Summary
Total Giving: Company does not disclose contributions figures.

Typical Recipients
Arts & Humanities: Dance, Ethnic & Folk Arts, Arts & Humanities-General, Historic Preservation, Libraries, Literary Arts, Museums/Galleries, Music, Opera, Performing Arts, Public Broadcasting, Theater, Visual Arts
Civic & Public Affairs: Civic & Public Affairs-General, Housing, Philanthropic Organizations, Urban & Community Affairs
Education: Education-General
Health: Health-General, Hospitals, Medical Research, Nursing Services, Single-Disease Health Associations
Religion: Churches, Religion-General, Missionary Activities (Domestic), Religious Organizations, Synagogues/Temples
Science: Science-General
Social Services: Animal Protection, Child Welfare, Emergency Relief, Senior Services, Shelters/Homelessness, Social Services-General, Substance Abuse, United Funds/United Ways, Volunteer Services, Youth Organizations

Application Procedures
Initial Contact: Send a brief letter of inquiry.
Application Requirements: Include a description of organization, amount requested, and purpose of funds sought.

Restrictions
Does not support individuals or political or lobbying groups.

Corporate Officials
Jean-Paul Agon: president, chief executive officer, director PRIM CORP EMPL president, chief executive officer, director: L'Oreal USA Inc.
Roger Dolden: chief financial officer PRIM CORP EMPL chief financial officer: Cosmair.
Mr. Lindsay Owen-Jones: chairman, director PRIM CORP EMPL chairman, director: Cosmair.
Michel Somnolet: chief operating officer, director, executive, vice president B Chateaurenault, France 1940. ED Faculte de Droit et Science Economique; Paris Law School (1963); Hautes Etudes Commerciales MBA (1964). PRIM CORP EMPL chief operating officer, director, executive, vice president: Cosmair Inc. CORP AFFIL director: France-Growth Fund. NONPR AFFIL member: French Chamber of Commerce New York; member: French Reserve Officers United States of America; director: Chevalier de la Legion d'Honneur. CLUB AFFIL Millbrook Country Club; Paris American Club; CYCL de Saint Briac; Mashomack Club.

Grants Analysis
Typical Range: $1,000 to $5,000

MARY AND DANIEL LOUGHRAN FOUNDATION

Giving Contact
F. William Burke, Executive Director & Secretary
4910 Massachusetts Avenue, NW, Suite 215
Washington, DC 20016-4300
Phone: (202)434-7005
Fax: (202)347-4866

Alternate Contact
Tawawna Williams, Grant Coordinator

Description
Founded: 1967
EIN: 521095883
Organization Type: General Purpose Foundation
Giving Locations: DC; MD; VA
Grant Types: Operating Expenses.

Donor Information
Founder: Incorporated in 1967 by the late John Loughran.

Financial Summary
Total Giving: $883,900 (fiscal year ending July 31, 2002); $819,900 (fiscal 2001)
Assets: $12,937,202 (fiscal 2002); $17,010,011 (fiscal 2001)

Typical Recipients
Arts & Humanities: Arts Centers, Dance, Historic Preservation, History & Archaeology, Libraries, Museums/Galleries, Music, Performing Arts, Theater
Civic & Public Affairs: Community Foundations, Civic & Public Affairs-General, Housing, Law & Justice, Nonprofit Management, Philanthropic Organizations, Public Policy, Safety, Urban & Community Affairs, Women's Affairs, Zoos/Aquariums
Education: Agricultural Education, Arts/Humanities Education, Business Education, Colleges & Universities, Economic Education, Education Funds, Elementary Education (Public), Engineering/Technological Education, Education-General, International Studies, Legal Education, Medical Education, Minority Education, Private Education (Precollege), Religious Education, Science/Mathematics Education, Secondary Education (Private), Special Education, Student Aid, Vocational & Technical Education
Health: Adolescent Health Issues, Cancer, Children's Health/Hospitals, Clinics/Medical Centers, Emergency/Ambulance Services, Eyes/Blindness, Health Funds, Heart, Hospitals, Long-Term Care, Medical Rehabilitation, Medical Research, Prenatal Health Issues, Single-Disease Health Associations
International: International Affairs
Religion: Churches, Dioceses, Ministries, Religious Welfare, Seminaries
Science: Scientific Centers & Institutes
Social Services: Animal Protection, At-Risk Youth, Community Service Organizations, Crime Prevention, Emergency Relief, Family Planning, Family Services, Food/Clothing Distribution, Homes, People with Disabilities, Recreation & Athletics, Scouts, Senior Services, Sexual Abuse, Shelters/Homelessness, Social Services-General, Youth Organizations

Application Procedures
Initial Contact: Applicants should submit a brief letter
Application Requirements: The letter should state the purpose of your organization, the specific amount requested, the use of the grant, IRS certification of tax-exempt status, financial reports, and list of directors and officers.
Deadlines: May 1.
Review Process: All grant requests are considered by the board during the July meeting.

Restrictions
The foundation does not make grants to individuals or for capital, endowment funds, or loans.

Additional Information
Trust(s): NationsBank Trust Co.

Foundation Officials
Richard K.A. Becker: assistant secretary PRIM CORP EMPL executive vice president: James Madison Mortgage.
F. William Burke: director, secretary
Walter Robert Fatzinger, Jr.: director B Northampton, PA 1942. ED George Washington University (1965); American University (1970). PRIM CORP EMPL president: Security Trust Co. NA.
Carl L. Gell: director
John T. Hazel, Jr.: director B 1930. ED Harvard University BA (1951); University of Virginia (1951-1952); Harvard University LLB (1954). PRIM CORP EMPL chairman, partner: Hazel & Thomas ADD CORP EMPL president: Flint Hill School.
A. Linwood Holton, Jr.: director B Big Stone Gap, VA 1923. ED Washington & Lee University BA (1944); Harvard University LLB (1949); Virginia State College LLD (1971); Virginia Union University LLD (1972); Washington & Lee University LLD (1972); College of William & Mary LLD (1973). PRIM CORP EMPL partner: Mezzulo & McCandlish. CORP AFFIL director: Interstate Railroad Co. NONPR AFFIL member: Virginia Bar Association; member: Virginia State Bar; member: Roanoke Bar Association; chairman: University Virginia Burket Miller Center Public Affairs; member: District of Columbia Bar Association; member: Omicron Delta Kappa; member: American Bar Association.
M. Langhorne Keith: assistant secretary B Washington, DC 1936. ED University of Virginia BA (1958); University of Virginia JD (1970). PRIM CORP EMPL lawyer: Hogan & Hartson. NONPR AFFIL member: Raven Society; member: Virginia Bar Association; member: District of Columbia Bar Association. CLUB AFFIL member: Omicron Delta Kappa.
R. Robert Linowes: director
Joseph L. Whyte: director

Grants Analysis
Disclosure Period: fiscal year ending July 31, 2002
Total Grants: $883,900
Number of Grants: 85
Average Grant: $10,399
Highest Grant: $40,000
Lowest Grant: $2,500
Typical Range: $5,000 to $20,000

Recent Grants
Note: Grants derived from 2002 Form 990.

General

40,000	Corcoran, Washington, DC
30,000	University of Maryland Foundation Inc., Adelphi, MD
25,000	Community Foundation for the National Capital Region, Washington, DC
25,000	George Mason University Foundation Inc., Fairfax, VA
20,000	Children's National Medical Center, Washington, DC
20,000	Paramount Theater Community Center, Charlottesville, VA
20,000	Phillips Collection, Washington, DC
15,000	Catholic University of America, Washington, DC
15,000	Keswick Equestrian Foundation Inc., Keswick, VA
15,000	Randolph-Macon Academy, Front Royal, VA

LOUTIT FOUNDATION

Giving Contact
c/o Standard Federal Bank
PO Box 1707
Grand Rapids, MI 49501-1707
Phone: (616)451-7736

Description
Founded: 1957
EIN: 386053445
Organization Type: Private Foundation
Giving Locations: MI
Grant Types: Capital, Emergency, Endowment, General Support, Project, Seed Money.

Donor Information
Founder: the late William R. Loutit

Financial Summary
Total Giving: $100,164 (fiscal year ending June 30, 2004); $250,802 (fiscal 2001)
Giving Analysis: Giving for fiscal 2004 includes: foundation grants to United Way ($19,000)
Assets: $938,818 (fiscal 2004); $1,124,195 (fiscal 2001)
Gifts Received: $45,810 (fiscal 2004); $136,265 (fiscal 2001); $136,265 (fiscal 2000). Note: Contributions were received from the William Loutit Memorial Trust.

Typical Recipients
Arts & Humanities: Arts Associations & Councils, Libraries, Museums/Galleries, Music, Public Broadcasting, Theater
Civic & Public Affairs: Community Foundations, Economic Development, Civic & Public Affairs-General, Housing, Municipalities/Towns, Parades/Festivals, Philanthropic Organizations, Urban & Community Affairs
Education: Colleges & Universities, Community & Junior Colleges, Education Associations, Education Funds, Education-General, Medical Education, Minority Education, Private Education (Precollege), Public Education (Precollege)
Health: Cancer, Emergency/Ambulance Services, Health Policy/Cost Containment, Health Organizations, Hospices, Hospitals, Public Health
International: International Relief Efforts
Religion: Churches, Ministries, Religious Organizations, Religious Welfare
Social Services: Animal Protection, Camps, Child Welfare, Community Centers, Community Service Organizations, Scouts, Senior Services, United Funds/United Ways, YMCA/YWCA/YMHA/YWHA, Youth Organizations

Application Procedures
Initial Contact: Send brief letter describing program. Include any information deemed relevant to the request, amount requested, and proof of tax-exempt status. Further information may be requested.
Deadlines: None.

Restrictions
Does not support individuals.

Additional Information
Publications: Biennial Report
Trust(s): Standard Federal Bank

Foundation Officials
Thomas Boven: vice president
Kennard Creason: trustee
Jon W. Eshleman: president
Bari Johnson: trustee

Grants Analysis
Disclosure Period: fiscal year ending June 30, 2004
Total Grants: $81,164*
Number of Grants: 31

Average Grant: $1,387*
Highest Grant: $20,750
Lowest Grant: $100
Typical Range: $500 to $5,000
*Note: Giving excludes United Way. Average grant figure excludes two highest grants ($40,950).

Recent Grants
Note: Grants derived from fiscal 2004 Form 990.
General

20,750	Tri-Cities Historical Museum, Grand Haven, MI -- for Akeley Project
20,200	Seventh-Day Adventist Community Service Center, Grand Haven, MI
19,000	Tri-Cities Area United Fund, Grand Rapids, MI
10,000	Hope College, Holland, MI
7,500	Girl Scouts of Michigan Trails, Grand Rapids, MI
5,000	Grand Rapids Art Museum, Grand Rapids, MI
4,000	Grand Haven Area Community Foundation, Grand Haven, MI -- musical fountain fund Dewey hill restoration
2,814	Greater Ottawa County United Way and Volunteer Center, Grand Haven, MI
1,400	Tuesday Musicale, Grand Haven, MI
1,300	Grand Haven Area Community Foundation, Grand Haven, MI -- towards YMCA endowment fund

GEORGE H. AND MARGARET MCCLINTIC LOVE FOUNDATION

Giving Contact
Helen Collins, Trust Officer
c/o Mellon Bank NA
1 Mellon Bank Center, Rm. 3815
Pittsburgh, PA 15258
Phone: (412)234-4695

Description
Founded: 1952
EIN: 256018655
Organization Type: Private Foundation
Giving Locations: nationally.
Grant Types: Capital, General Support.

Donor Information
Founder: George H. Love

Financial Summary
Total Giving: $712,500 (2001)
Giving Analysis: Giving for 2001 includes: foundation grants to United Way ($30,000)
Assets: $6,186,986 (2001)
Gifts Received: $52,558 (2001); $56,967 (2000); $56,967 (1996). Note: In 1996, 2000, and 2001, contributions were received from the Charitable Trust No. 2.

Typical Recipients
Arts & Humanities: Arts Associations & Councils, Community Arts, Libraries, Music, Opera
Civic & Public Affairs: Civic & Public Affairs-General, Urban & Community Affairs, Women's Affairs
Education: Arts/Humanities Education, Colleges & Universities, Education Funds, Education-General, Private Education (Precollege), Public Education (Precollege), Religious Education, Science/Mathematics Education
Environment: Environment-General
Health: Children's Health/Hospitals, Clinics/Medical Centers, Hospices, Hospitals, Medical Research,

Mental Health, Nursing Services, Single-Disease Health Associations
International: International Relations, International Relief Efforts
Religion: Churches, Religious Welfare
Social Services: Camps, Child Welfare, Community Service Organizations, Domestic Violence, Emergency Relief, Family Services, Food/Clothing Distribution, People with Disabilities, Shelters/Homelessness, Substance Abuse, United Funds/United Ways, YMCA/YWCA/YMHA/YWHA, Youth Organizations

Application Procedures
Initial Contact: Send a brief letter of inquiry describing program.
Deadlines: None.

Additional Information
Trust(s): Mellon Bank NA

Foundation Officials
Howard McClintic Love: director B Pittsburgh, PA 1930. ED Colgate University (1952); Harvard University Graduate School of Business Administration (1956). NONPR director: United Way of Allegheny County; trustee: University of Pittsburgh; director: Pittsburgh Symphony; trustee: The Carnegie. CLUB AFFIL Rolling Rock Club; Pittsburgh Golf Club; The Links Club; Masons Club; Fox Chapel Golf Club; member: Beta Theta Pi; Colony Club.

Grants Analysis
Disclosure Period: calendar year ending 2001
Total Grants: $682,500*
Number of Grants: 26
Average Grant: $16,630*
Highest Grant: $200,000
Lowest Grant: $2,000
Typical Range: $7,500 to $30,000
*Note: Giving excludes United Way. Average grant excludes two highest grants ($300,000).

Recent Grants
Note: Grants derived from 2001 Form 990.
General

200,000	Shady Lane School, Pittsburgh, PA -- educational
38,000	Phillips Exeter Academy, Exeter, NH -- educational
35,000	Pittsburgh Opera, Pittsburgh, PA -- for public assistance
34,000	Little Sisters of the Assumption Family Center, New York, NY -- for family counseling
34,000	Westminister Choir College, Princeton, NJ -- religious
30,000	Greater Pittsburgh Chapter of National Parkinson Foundation, Pittsburgh, PA -- medical
30,000	Horizon Hospice, Chicago, IL -- for medical assistance
30,000	United Way of Allegheny County, Pittsburgh, PA -- for public assistance
25,000	Pitzer College, Claremont, CA -- educational
25,000	Winnie Palmer Nature Rescue, Latrobe, PA -- for public assistance

LOWE FAMILY FOUNDATION

Giving Contact
John W. Yates, CPA
228 East Primrose
Springfield, MO 65807-5206
Phone: (417)883-8176

Description

Founded: 1999
EIN: 431799494
Organization Type: Private Foundation
Grant Types: General Support.

Financial Summary

Total Giving: $116,840 (fiscal year ending September 30, 2001)
Assets: $878,267 (fiscal 2001)
Gifts Received: $38,000 (fiscal 2000). Note: In 2000, contributions were received from Derrick and Sonja Lowe.

Typical Recipients

Arts & Humanities: Libraries, Public Broadcasting
Civic & Public Affairs: Community Foundations
Environment: Air/Water Quality
International: International Environmental Issues, International Peace & Security Issues, Missionary/ Religious Activities
Religion: Churches, Ministries, Missionary Activities (Domestic), Religious Organizations, Religious Welfare
Social Services: Child Welfare, Family Planning, Food/Clothing Distribution, Homes

Foundation Officials

Derrick C. Lowe: vice president
Kimberly Lowe Root: secretary

Grants Analysis

Disclosure Period: fiscal year ending September 30, 2001
Total Grants: $116,840
Number of Grants: 12
Average Grant: $8,804*
Highest Grant: $20,000
Lowest Grant: $540
Typical Range: $5,000 to $15,000
*Note: Average grant figure excludes highest grant.

Recent Grants

Note: Grants derived from fiscal 2002 Form 990.
Library-Related

10,000	Lebanon Public Library, Lebanon, MO -- library project

General

38,000	New Tribes Mission, Sanford, FL -- support of missionaries
36,000	Life Outreach International, Ft. Worth, TX -- to provide fresh water wells for seven people in Africa
30,000	Fellowship Christian Athletes, Springfield, MO -- for office in Columbia
15,000	Fellowship Christian Athletes, Springfield, MO -- for budgetary needs
10,000	First Baptist Church, Lebanon, MO -- Jared Hilton Fund
10,000	First Baptist Church, Lebanon, MO -- for Ray Tan ministry
10,000	Vitae Society, Jefferson City, MO -- benefit of children
9,000	Christian Ministry, Wichita, KS -- budgetary
8,000	Lebanon Area Foundation, Lebanon, MO -- for share with Christmas
8,000	Lebanon Area Foundation, Lebanon, MO -- for crosslines

JOE AND EMILY LOWE FOUNDATION

Giving Contact

Ellen Liman, President
249 Royal Palm Way, Suite 502
Palm Beach, FL 33480

Fax: (561)655-7130

Description

Founded: 1949
EIN: 136121361
Organization Type: Family Foundation
Giving Locations: FL: Palm Beach; NY: New York metropolitan area
Grant Types: Challenge, Conference/Seminar, General Support, Matching, Multiyear/Continuing Support, Operating Expenses, Project, Research.

Typical Recipients

Arts & Humanities: Arts Associations & Councils, Arts Centers, Arts Funds, Arts Outreach, Ballet, Dance, Ethnic & Folk Arts, Film & Video, History & Archaeology, Libraries, Museums/Galleries, Music, Opera, Performing Arts, Public Broadcasting, Theater, Visual Arts
Civic & Public Affairs: Civil Rights, Ethnic Organizations, Civic & Public Affairs-General, Law & Justice, Legal Aid, Municipalities/Towns, Professional & Trade Associations, Rural Affairs, Safety, Urban & Community Affairs, Women's Affairs
Education: Afterschool/Enrichment Programs, Arts/ Humanities Education, Business Education, Colleges & Universities, Community & Junior Colleges, Education Reform, Faculty Development, Education-General, Legal Education, Literacy, Medical Education, Minority Education, Private Education (Precollege), Public Education (Precollege), Special Education, Student Aid
Environment: Environment-General, Resource Conservation, Wildlife Protection
Health: Cancer, Children's Health/Hospitals, Clinics/ Medical Centers, Emergency/Ambulance Services, Eyes/Blindness, Heart, Hospices, Hospitals, Hospitals (University Affiliated), Kidney, Medical Rehabilitation, Mental Health, Single-Disease Health Associations
International: Foreign Arts Organizations, Foreign Educational Institutions, Human Rights
Religion: Jewish Causes, Religious Welfare, Social/ Policy Issues, Synagogues/Temples
Social Services: Animal Protection, At-Risk Youth, Child Abuse, Child Welfare, Community Centers, Community Service Organizations, Emergency Relief, Family Planning, Family Services, Food/Clothing Distribution, Homes, People with Disabilities, Shelters/Homelessness, Social Services-General, Substance Abuse, YMCA/YWCA/YMHA/YWHA, Youth Organizations

Application Procedures

Initial Contact: Applicants should submit a letter.
Application Requirements: A brief description and need for the proposed project or activity; objectives; timetable; overall costs; amount requested from the foundation; the status of additional support; a project budget, including projected revenue and expenses; current annual operating budget; list of governing body and officers; IRS letter determining tax-exempt status; most recent audited financial statements; and any relevant promotional publications.
Deadlines: None.
Review Process: Letters are generally acknowledged within two months.

Restrictions

The foundation does not give grants to individuals or award scholarships, fellowships, loans, prizes, or similar benefits.

Additional Information

The foundation has a revolving presidency.

Foundation Officials

David Hauben: vice president, treasurer
Ellen Liman: president ED Barnard College BA (1957); New York School Interior Design (1959).
Henry Stern: vice president, secretary

Grants Analysis

Disclosure Period: calendar year ending 1999
Total Grants: $1,800,000
Number of Grants: 206
Average Grant: $8,738
Highest Grant: $100,000
Lowest Grant: $500
Typical Range: $1,000 to $35,000

Recent Grants

Note: Grants derived from 1999 Form 990.
Library-Related

12,500	Randall Library, Stow, MA
10,000	Darien Library, Darien, CT

General

100,000	United Jewish Appeal of South Palm Beach, New York, NY
50,000	Bascom Palmer Eye Institute, Miami, FL
50,000	Beth Israel Deaconess Medical Center, Boston, MA
50,000	Boca Raton Community Hospital, Boca Raton, FL
50,000	Creative Capital Foundation, New York, NY
50,000	United Jewish Appeal of Bergen County, River Edge, NJ
35,000	WGBH Educational Foundation, Boston, MA
30,000	American Federation of the Arts, New York, NY
30,000	Jewish Museum, New York, NY
25,000	Ascent Funding Organization, Inc., Muttontown, NY

LEON LOWENSTEIN FOUNDATION

Giving Contact

John Van Gorder, Executive Director
126 East 56th Street, 28th Floor
New York, NY 10022
Phone: (212)319-0670
Fax: (212)319-0670

Description

Founded: 1941
EIN: 136015951
Organization Type: General Purpose Foundation
Giving Locations: NY: New York metropolitan area
Grant Types: General Support.

Donor Information

Founder: The foundation was established in 1941, with the late Leon Lowenstein as donor. Mr. Lowenstein's fortune stemmed from M. Lowenstein Corporation, a textile firm, now a subsidiary of Springs Industries.

Financial Summary

Total Giving: $6,637,200 (2003); $6,712,600 (2002)
Giving Analysis: Giving for 2003 includes: foundation grants to United Way ($20,000); 2002: foundation grants to United Way ($25,000)
Assets: $140,316,956 (2003); $122,456,012 (2002)
Gifts Received: $2,441,585 (1992)

Typical Recipients

Arts & Humanities: Arts Associations & Councils, Arts Institutes, Dance, History & Archaeology, Libraries, Literary Arts, Museums/Galleries, Music, Performing Arts, Public Broadcasting
Civic & Public Affairs: Botanical Gardens/Parks, Business/Free Enterprise, Community Foundations, Economic Development, Ethnic Organizations, Civic & Public Affairs-General, Housing, Law & Justice, Municipalities/Towns, Nonprofit Management, Philanthropic Organizations, Public Policy, Zoos/

Aquariums

Education: Afterschool/Enrichment Programs, Arts/Humanities Education, Business Education, Colleges & Universities, Community & Junior Colleges, Education Associations, Education Funds, Education Reform, Elementary Education (Private), Elementary Education (Public), Engineering/Technological Education, Faculty Development, Education-General, International Studies, Leadership Training, Literacy, Medical Education, Minority Education, Private Education (Precollege), Public Education (Precollege), Secondary Education (Private), Social Sciences Education, Special Education, Student Aid

Environment: Air/Water Quality, Environment-General, Wildlife Protection

Health: Arthritis, Cancer, Children's Health/Hospitals, Clinics/Medical Centers, Emergency/Ambulance Services, Eyes/Blindness, Health Funds, Health Organizations, Hospitals, Hospitals (University Affiliated), Medical Rehabilitation, Medical Research, Mental Health, Nursing Services, Research/Studies Institutes, Single-Disease Health Associations

International: Health Care/Hospitals, International Development, International Peace & Security Issues

Religion: Jewish Causes, Religious Welfare

Science: Science Museums

Social Services: At-Risk Youth, Big Brothers/Big Sisters, Child Welfare, Community Centers, Community Service Organizations, Emergency Relief, Family Services, Food/Clothing Distribution, Homes, People with Disabilities, Recreation & Athletics, Scouts, Social Services-General, Substance Abuse, United Funds/United Ways, Volunteer Services, YMCA/YWCA/YMHA/YWHA, Youth Organizations

Application Procedures

Initial Contact: Applications should be in letter form.
Deadlines: None.
Evaluative Criteria: Applications from the New York City area are given preference.

Foundation Officials

Andrew Bendheim: director
John M. Bendheim, Jr.: director
John M. Bendheim: vice president, director B New York, NY June 18, 1918. PRIM CORP EMPL director: M. Lowenstein Corp.
Kim Bendheim: director
Robert Austin Bendheim: president, director B New York, NY August 05, 1916. ED Princeton University AB (1937); Harvard University (1942). PRIM CORP EMPL director: M. Lowenstein Corp. NONPR AFFIL member national campaign committee: Princeton University; director: United Way New York City; member education committee: New York City Partnership; trustee: Mount Sinai Hospital. CLUB AFFIL Union League Club; Round Hill Club; Stanwich Club; Princeton Club; Century Club; Lyford Cay Club.
Thomas L. Bendheim: director
Lynn Bendheim-Thoman: director
Bernard R. Rapaport: secretary, treasurer B New York, NY 1919. ED Cornell University (1939); Cornell University JD (1941). PRIM CORP EMPL secretary, treasurer, general counsel, director: M. Lowenstein Corp.
Joanna Schulman: director
John Frederic Van Gorder: executive director B Jacksonville, FL 1943. ED Dover College (1961); Dartmouth College AB (1965); United States Air Force Institute of Technology (1967-1968); George Washington University MS (1973); Fordham University School of Law JD (1981). NONPR AFFIL advisory committee: Toshiba American Foundation; member: U.S. Jaycees; member: Society Mayflower Descendants; member: Sons American Revolution; member: New Jersey Bar Association; member: New York City Jaycees; member: International Jaycees; member: American Bar Association; member: District of Columbia Jaycees; member: Alpha Delta Phi. CLUB AFFIL Masons Club; Toastmasters Club; Lions

Club.
Thomas H. Wright: director

Grants Analysis

Disclosure Period: calendar year ending 2003
Total Grants: $6,617,200*
Number of Grants: 162
Average Grant: $19,982*
Highest Grant: $950,000
Lowest Grant: $100
Typical Range: $5,000 to $50,000
*Note: Giving excludes United Way. Average grant figure excludes six highest grants ($3,500,000).

Recent Grants

Note: Grants derived from 2003 Form 990.
Library-Related
25,000	Wilton Library Association Inc., Wilton, CT
17,700	Wilton Library Association Inc., Wilton, CT

General
950,000	Columbia University, New York, NY
550,000	Mount Sinai Medical Center, FL
500,000	Long Island Jewish Health System Federation, Huntington, NY
500,000	Memorial Sloan-Kettering Cancer Center, New York, NY
500,000	Princeton University, Princeton, NJ
500,000	Western Greenwich Civic Center Federation
250,000	Columbia University, New York, NY
250,000	Memorial Sloan-Kettering Cancer Center, New York, NY
250,000	University of Pennsylvania, Philadelphia, PA
250,000	Western Greenwich Civic Center Federation

LOWE'S COS.

Company Headquarters

North Wilkesboro, NC
Web: http://www.lowes.com

Company Description

Founded: 1957
Ticker: LOW
Exchange: NYSE
Revenue: US$36.464 billion (2004)
Profit: US$2.176 billion (2004)
Employees: 123000 (2003)
Fortune Rank: 43, per FORTUNE Magazine's list of 500 Largest U.S. Corporations (2004).
SIC(s): 5211 Lumber & Other Building Materials, 5251 Hardware Stores.

Operating Locations

Lowe's Companies (NC--North Wilkesboro)
Note: Company has 303 stores in 290 communities in 20 southeastern states.

Lowe's Charitable and Educational Foundation

Giving Contact

Cindy Williams
Lowe's Companies
1000 Lowes Blvd.
Mooresville, NC 28117
Phone: (336)658-4221

Description

EIN: 566061689
Organization Type: Corporate Foundation
Giving Locations: headquarters and operating communities.
Grant Types: General Support, Scholarship.

Donor Information

Founder: Lowe's Companies, Inc.

Financial Summary

Total Giving: $114,300 (fiscal year ending January 31, 2004); $988,128 (fiscal 2002); $1,177,996 (fiscal 2001). Note: Fiscal 1997 Giving includes United Way ($2,000).
Giving Analysis: Giving for fiscal 2002 includes: foundation scholarships ($77,500).
Assets: $436,329 (fiscal 2004); $1,192,671 (fiscal 2002); $1,168,433 (fiscal 2001)
Gifts Received: $7,500 (fiscal 2004); $1,000,000 (fiscal 2002); $792,381 (fiscal 2001). Note: In fiscal 2004, contributions were received from ADT Security Services. In fiscal 2002, contributions were received from Lowe's Companies. In fiscal 2001, contributions were received from Lowe's Companies and Wilkes Educational Foundation. In fiscal 1998, contributions were received from Lowe's Companies and Thomas E. Whiddon.

Typical Recipients

Arts & Humanities: Arts & Humanities-General, Historic Preservation, Libraries

Civic & Public Affairs: Asian American Affairs, Botanical Gardens/Parks, Clubs, Community Foundations, Economic Development, Civic & Public Affairs-General, Housing, Inner-City Development, Law & Justice, Municipalities/Towns, Philanthropic Organizations, Public Policy, Safety, Urban & Community Affairs, Women's Affairs

Education: Arts/Humanities Education, Business Education, Colleges & Universities, Community & Junior Colleges, Education Funds, Elementary Education (Public), Engineering/Technological Education, Education-General, Medical Education, Private Education (Precollege), Public Education (Precollege), Secondary Education (Private), Secondary Education (Public), Student Aid, Vocational & Technical Education

Environment: Environment-General, Protection, Resource Conservation

Health: Cancer, Children's Health/Hospitals, Diabetes, Emergency/Ambulance Services, Health-General, Hospices, Hospitals, Medical Rehabilitation, Preventive Medicine/Wellness Organizations

International: International Relief Efforts

Religion: Religion-General, Ministries, Religious Organizations, Religious Welfare

Social Services: At-Risk Youth, Big Brothers/Big Sisters, Child Welfare, Community Centers, Community Service Organizations, Domestic Violence, Family Services, Food/Clothing Distribution, Homes, People with Disabilities, Recreation & Athletics, Senior Services, Social Services-General, Special Olympics, Substance Abuse, United Funds/United Ways, Volunteer Services, YMCA/YWCA/YMHA/YWHA, Youth Organizations

Application Procedures

Initial Contact: All applications must be in written form.
Deadlines: None.
Notes: Grants will only be considered for qualified charitable and educational purposes.

Restrictions

Does not support individuals, religious organizations for sectarian purposes, political or lobbying groups, or organizations outside operating areas.

Corporate Officials

Robert L. Tillman: chairman, president, chief executive officer PRIM CORP EMPL chairman, president, chief executive officer: Lowes Companies.

Foundation Officials

Gregory M. Bridgeford: trustee
Marshall A. Croom: trustee
Darryl K. Henderson: trustee
Perry G. Jennings: trustee
N. Brian Peace: secretary
Dale C. Pond: trustee
Larry W. Stanley: treasurer
Larry D. Stone: chairman

Grants Analysis

Disclosure Period: fiscal year ending January 31, 2004
Total Grants: $66,300*
Number of Grants: 37
Average Grant: $1,792
Highest Grant: $12,000
Lowest Grant: $1,000
Typical Range: $1,000 to $10,000
*Note: Giving excludes scholarship; United Way.

Recent Grants

Note: Grants derived from 2004 Form 990.
General

18,000	Asnuntuck Community College, Enfield, CT
12,000	North Vernon Parks & Recreation Department, North Vernon, IN
10,800	Lake Washington Technical College, Kirkland, WA
10,400	John Tyler Community College, Chester, VA
8,500	Parkway Partners Program, New Orleans, LA
2,000	Cincinnati State Technical College, Cincinnati, OH
2,000	College of the Mainland, Texas City, TX
1,000	Advocates Against Violence Against, Caldwell, ID
1,000	Best Buddies-North Penn HS, Miami, FL
1,000	Big Brothers/Big Sisters of the Bluegrass, Lexington, KY

LSR FUND

Giving Contact

Clayton W. Frye, Jr., Trustee
LSR Fund
Care of Rockefeller Trust Co.
30 Rockefeller Plz., Rm. 5600
New York, NY 10112
Phone: (212)649-5979

Description

Founded: 1994
EIN: 137039108
Organization Type: Private Foundation
Giving Locations: nationally.
Grant Types: General Support.

Donor Information

Founder: Established in 1994 by Laurance S. Rockefeller.

Financial Summary

Total Giving: $1,963,933 (2001)
Assets: $27,390,633 (2001)
Gifts Received: $1,887,500 (1999); $1,000,000 (1997); $630,000 (1996). Note: In 1997 and 1999, contributions were received from from Laurance S. Rockefeller.

Typical Recipients

Arts & Humanities: Arts Associations & Councils, Ethnic & Folk Arts, Historic Preservation, History & Archaeology, Libraries, Public Broadcasting
Civic & Public Affairs: Civic & Public Affairs-General, Nonprofit Management, Parades/Festivals

---

Education: Arts/Humanities Education, Colleges & Universities, Education Reform, Legal Education
Environment: Environment-General, Protection, Resource Conservation, Wildlife Protection
Health: Health-General, Hospitals, Public Health, Single-Disease Health Associations
International: Foreign Arts Organizations
Religion: Religion-General
Science: Scientific Centers & Institutes
Social Services: Youth Organizations

Application Procedures

Initial Contact: Send a brief letter of inquiry.
Deadlines: None.

Foundation Officials

Clayton Wesley Frye, Jr.: trustee B Los Angeles, CA 1930. ED Stanford University AB (1953); Stanford University MBA (1959). PRIM CORP EMPL senior associate: Laurance S. Rockefeller. CORP AFFIL chairman, director: Woodstock Resort Corp.; director: Times Mirror Co.; partner: Rockefeller & Associates Realty; director: Tejon Ranch Co.; partner: Pacific Property Services; director: Colonial Williamsburg Hotel Properties Inc.; director: King Ranch Inc. NONPR AFFIL member: Urban Land Institute; trustee: White House Historical Association; trustee, chairman: Jackson Hole Preserve Inc.; trustee: Historic Hudson Valley.
Donal Clare O'Brien, Jr.: trustee B New York, NY 1934. ED Williams College BA (1956); University of Virginia LLB (1959). PRIM CORP EMPL partner: Milbank, Tweed, Hadley & McCloy. NONPR AFFIL trustee: Wendell Gilley Museum; trustee: Winthrop Rockefeller Charitable Trust; trustee: Trust Mutual Understanding; trustee: Waterfowl Research Foundation; chairman: Quebec Labrador Foundation; member council: Rockefeller University; trustee: North American Wildlife Foundation; trustee: JDR 3rd Fund; chairman: National Audubon Society; member: Council Environmental Quality; board directors: Greenacre Foundation; trustee: American Bird Conservancy; chairman board directors: Atlantic Salmon Federation. CLUB AFFIL mem: Century Association Anglers Club.
Ellen R.C. Pomeroy: trustee
James S. Sligar: trustee

Grants Analysis

Disclosure Period: calendar year ending 2001
Total Grants: $1,963,933
Number of Grants: 38
Average Grant: $31,292*
Highest Grant: $260,000
Lowest Grant: $5,000
Typical Range: $10,000 to $50,000
*Note: Average grant figure excludes four highest grants ($860,000).

Recent Grants

Note: Grants derived from 2001 Form 990.
Library-Related

75,000	Norman Williams Public Library, Woodstock, VT

General

260,000	Hawaii Community Foundation, Honolulu, HI
200,000	Center for Special Studies
200,000	Mind Brain Body and Health Initiative, Chicago, IL
200,000	Vermont Institute of Natural Science, Woodstock, VT
100,000	Center for Special Studies
100,000	Council on the Environment, New York, NY
60,000	Henry M. Jackson Foundation, Rockville, MD
60,000	New York Hall of Science, Corona Park, NY
50,000	Central Park Conservancy, New York, NY
50,000	Classroom, Inc., New York, NY

HENRY LUCE FOUNDATION

Giving Contact

Michael Gilligan, President & Director
111 West 50th Street, Suite 4601
New York, NY 10020-1202
Phone: (212)489-7700
Fax: (212)581-9541
E-mail: hlf@hluce.org
Web: http://www.hluce.org

Description

Founded: 1936
EIN: 136001282
Organization Type: General Purpose Foundation
Giving Locations: nationally; East and Southeast Asia.
Grant Types: Capital, Challenge, Conference/Seminar, Fellowship, General Support, Professorship, Project, Research, Seed Money.

Donor Information

Founder: The Henry Luce Foundation was established in 1936 by the late Henry R. Luce, co-founder and editor-in-chief of *Time Magazine.* Mr. Luce created the foundation as a tribute to his parents, the Reverend Dr. Henry Winters Luce and Elizabeth Root Luce. Dr. Luce, a Presbyterian minister, went to China as a missionary and educator in the late nineteenth century. He helped found Yenching University in 1916 and served as its vice president. His name is still linked to several sites on the campus of what is now the University of Beijing. Upon the death of Henry R. Luce in 1967, the foundation was a major beneficiary of his estate. The founder's son, Henry Luce III, has been chairman of the foundation since 1958.

Financial Summary

Total Giving: $33,328,893 (2002); $54,275,009 (2001)
Assets: $696,004,872 (2002); $905,305,357 (2001)
Gifts Received: $223,207 (2002); $1,995,493 (1996); $199,910 (1994)

Typical Recipients

Arts & Humanities: Art History, Arts Appreciation, Arts Associations & Councils, Arts Institutes, Ethnic & Folk Arts, Film & Video, Arts & Humanities-General, Historic Preservation, History & Archaeology, Libraries, Literary Arts, Museums/Galleries, Music, Public Broadcasting, Visual Arts
Civic & Public Affairs: Asian American Affairs, Botanical Gardens/Parks, Civic & Public Affairs-General, Law & Justice, Philanthropic Organizations, Public Policy
Education: Arts/Humanities Education, Business Education, Colleges & Universities, Economic Education, Education Associations, Education Reform, Engineering/Technological Education, Environmental Education, Faculty Development, Education-General, International Exchange, International Studies, Legal Education, Medical Education, Minority Education, Private Education (Precollege), Religious Education, Science/Mathematics Education, Secondary Education (Private), Social Sciences Education, Student Aid
Environment: Environment-General, Protection, Research, Wildlife Protection
Health: Geriatric Health, Public Health
International: Foreign Arts Organizations, Foreign Educational Institutions, Health Care/Hospitals, Human Rights, International Affairs, International Development, International Environmental Issues, International Organizations, International Peace & Security Issues, International Relations, Missionary/Religious Activities
Religion: Bible Study/Translation, Churches, Religion-General, Jewish Causes, Ministries, Religious

---

Organizations, Religious Welfare, Seminaries, Social/Policy Issues, Synagogues/Temples
Science: Science Museums, Scientific Centers & Institutes, Scientific Organizations
Social Services: Crime Prevention, Recreation & Athletics

Application Procedures

Initial Contact: Contact foundation for guidelines or visit the website.
Deadlines: November 1 for the Henry R. Luce Professorship Program; the first Monday in December for Luce Scholarship Program institutional nominations. The Henry Luce III Fellows in Theology are selected through the Association of Theological Schools in Pittsburgh. Individual scholars should contact the ATS for application information.
Review Process: Awards for grants are determined by the board of directors, which meets three times a year.

Restrictions

The foundation does not provide funds for endowments, capital campaigns, construction projects, general operating support or annual fund drives. Outside of specifically designated programs, no grants are made to individuals.

Additional Information

Terrill E. Lautz is the Secretary and Program Director for Asia and Higher Education Programs.
Evelyn Benjamin is the Program Director for the Clare Boothe Luce and Public Affairs Programs.
Ellen Holtzman is the Program Director for the Arts.
Helene E. Redell is the Program Director for the Luce Scholars Program.
Michael Gilligan is the Program Directory for the Theology Program.
H. Christopher Luce is the Program Directory for Public Policy and the Environment Program.
Publications: Annual Report (biennially)

Foundation Officials

Robert E. Armstrong: director B Omaha, NE 1932. ED University of Illinois BA (1954); Princeton University (1955). NONPR AFFIL member: National Theatre Deaf.
Anne d'Harnoncourt: director, administration committee ED Radcliffe College BA (1965); University of London Courtauld Institute of Art MA (1967). PRIM NONPR EMPL George D. Widener director: Philadelphia Music of Art. NONPR AFFIL chief executive officer, director: Philadelphia Museum of Art; member advisory committee: Stuart Foundation; member: Pennsylvania Council Arts; member visitors committee: J Paul Getty Museum; member: Mayor's Cultural Advisory Council Philadelphia; trustee: Fairmont Park Art Association; member: Association Art Museum Directors; member: The Fabric Workshop; director: ARTstor; fellow: American Academy of Arts & Sciences; member: American Philosophical Society.
John C. Evans: vice president, treasurer, director B 1943. ED Kearney State College BA (1978); University of Nebraska JD (1981). CORP AFFIL president, director: Hauser Communication Inc. NONPR AFFIL member: Pennsylvania Bar Association; member: Pennsylvania Trial Lawyers Association; member: Association of Trial Lawyers of American; treasurer, director: DIA Center Arts; member: Academy of Trial Lawyers of Allegheny County; member: Allegheny County Bar Association.
Margaret Boles Fitzgerald: chairperson, director ED Bucknell University BA (1977).
Claire L. Gaudiani: director ED Indiana University PhD; Connecticut College BA (1966); Indiana University MA (1969); Indiana University PhD (1975). PRIM NONPR EMPL president: Connecticut College. NONPR AFFIL member, fellow: Phi Beta Kappa Society; trustee: Worcester Polytechnic Institute; fellow: American Academy of Arts and Sciences.
Dr. Michael F. Gilligan: president, director NONPR AFFIL trustee: General Theological Seminary.

Kenneth T. Jackson: director ED University of Memphis BA (1961); University of Chicago MA (1963); University of Chicago PhD (1966). NONPR AFFIL general editor: Columbia History of Urban Life; president, chief executive officer: New York Historical Society.
James Thomas Laney: director B Wilson, AR 1927. ED Yale University BA (1950); Yale University BD (1954); Yale University PhD (1966); Yale University PhD (1966). NONPR AFFIL member: Phi Beta Kappa; member tercentenary steering committee: Yale University; president emeritus: Emory University; member: Omicron Delta Kappa; trustee: Atlanta Chamber of Commerce; member: Council Foreign Relations; member: American Society Christian Ethics. CLUB AFFIL Commerce Club.
Terrill E. Lautz: vice president, secretary, program director Asia NONPR AFFIL advisory council: Center for U.S.-China Arts Exchange.
H. Christopher Luce: director, program director public policy & environment ED Yale University BA (1972).
Henry Luce, III: chairman emeritus, director B New York, NY 1925. ED Yale University BA (1948). NONPR AFFIL director: Foreign Policy Associate; director: National Committee on US-China Relations; trustee: College Wooster; trustee: Eisenhower Exchange Fellowships; trustee: Center Theological Inquiry; trustee: Christian Ministry National Parks; member: American Russian Young Artists Orchestra; trustee: Brooklyn Museum Art; member: American Council United Nations University. CLUB AFFIL director: University Club; Hay Harbor Club; Pilgrims Club; Explorers Club New York; Fishers Island Country Club New York; Brook Club.
Thomas Leffingwell Pulling: director B New York, NY 1939. ED Princeton University BA (1961). PRIM CORP EMPL managing director: Citigroup Asset Management. CORP AFFIL managing director: Citigroup Asset Management. NONPR AFFIL trustee: South Street Seaport Museum; director: Woodlawn Cemetery; member: Pilgrims U.S.; board of governors: Franklin & Eleanor Roosevelt Institute; trustee: Long Island University; member: Council Foreign Relations; member: Century Association. CLUB AFFIL University Club; Piping Rock Club; Surf Club.

Grants Analysis

Disclosure Period: calendar year ending 2002
Total Grants: $33,328,893
Number of Grants: 279
Average Grant: $112,694*
Highest Grant: $2,000,000
Lowest Grant: $2,000
Typical Range: $25,000 to $200,000
*Note: Average grant figure excludes highest grant.

Recent Grants

Note: Grants derived from 2002 Form 990.
Library-Related
185,000	Library of Congress, Washington, DC -- towards support of acquisition and fellowship program to strengthen the Asia collection
175,000	Library of Congress, Washington, DC -- towards an orientation seminar for new House Members of 108th congress

General
2,000,000	Brooklyn Museum of Art, Brooklyn, NY -- for reinstalling the American art collection and create the Luce Art Center for American art
1,000,000	Educational Broadcasting Corporation, New York, NY -- towards PBS television series "Becoming American The Chinese Experience"
695,000	Association of Theological Schools in United States and Canada, Pittsburgh, PA -- towards renewal of Henry Luce III Fellows in Technology program
500,000	Princeton Theological Seminary, Princeton, NJ

489,663	Luce Scholars Program, New York, NY -- towards Luce scholars' stipends
400,000	Brown University, Providence, RI -- towards the project Catalyzing the Flow of North-South Environmental program
400,000	Stanford University, Stanford, CA -- towards "Interdisciplinary Environmental Studies Graduate Program"
400,000	Yale University, New Haven, CT -- towards "Collaborative Industrial Ecology in Asia" project
349,854	Asia Foundation, San Francisco, CA -- towards placement and support services for the Luce Scholars program in Asia
285,000	Boston University, Boston, MA -- towards CBL program

LUCK STONE

Company Headquarters

PO Box 29682
Richmond, VA 23242
Web: http://www.luckstone.com

Company Description

Employees: 500
SIC(s): 1400 Nonmetallic Minerals Except Fuels.

Luck Stone Foundation

Giving Contact

Charles S. Luck, III
Luck Stone Foundation
PO Box 29682
Richmond, VA 23229
Phone: (804)784-3335

Description

Founded: 1966
EIN: 546064982
Organization Type: Corporate Foundation
Giving Locations: VA
Grant Types: Capital, General Support, Multiyear/Continuing Support.

Donor Information

Founder: Luck Stone Corp.

Financial Summary

Total Giving: $456,892 (fiscal year ending October 31, 2003); $378,008 (fiscal 2002); $378,008 (fiscal 2001)
Giving Analysis: Giving for fiscal 2002 includes: foundation grants to United Way ($3,000); foundation scholarships ($10,775); fiscal 2001: foundation grants to United Way ($3,000)
Assets: $6,493,283 (fiscal 2003); $4,828,605 (fiscal 2002); $5,767,691 (fiscal 2001)
Gifts Received: $1,510,000 (fiscal 2002); $1,510,000 (fiscal 2001); $450,000 (fiscal 1999). Note: In 2002, contributions were received from Luck Stone Corporation.

Typical Recipients

Arts & Humanities: Arts Centers, Arts Funds, Ballet, Arts & Humanities-General, Historic Preservation, History & Archaeology, Libraries, Museums/Galleries, Music, Performing Arts
Civic & Public Affairs: Botanical Gardens/Parks, Business/Free Enterprise, Clubs, Civic & Public Affairs-General, Law & Justice, Philanthropic Organizations, Rural Affairs, Safety, Urban & Community Affairs
Education: Afterschool/Enrichment Programs, Agricultural Education, Business Education, Colleges & Universities, Community & Junior Colleges, Educa-

tion Funds, Faculty Development, Education-General, Literacy, Private Education (Precollege), Public Education (Precollege), Science/Mathematics Education, Student Aid
Environment: Air/Water Quality, Environment-General, Resource Conservation, Watershed, Wildlife Protection
Health: Cancer, Children's Health/Hospitals, Clinics/Medical Centers, Emergency/Ambulance Services, Health-General, Health Organizations, Multiple Sclerosis, Public Health
International: International Relations
Religion: Churches, Religious Organizations, Religious Welfare
Social Services: Animal Protection, Child Abuse, Community Service Organizations, Emergency Relief, Family Services, Homes, Recreation & Athletics, Scouts, Social Services-General, United Funds/United Ways, Volunteer Services, YMCA/YWCA/YMHA/YWHA, Youth Organizations

Application Procedures

Initial Contact: Send a brief letter of inquiry.
Deadlines: None.

Corporate Officials

Joseph Andrews, Jr.: vice president corporate relations PRIM CORP EMPL vice president corporate relations: Luck Stone.
C. S. Luck, III: chairman, chief executive officer PRIM CORP EMPL chairman, chief executive officer: Luck Stone.

Foundation Officials

Joseph Andrews, Jr.: secretary (see above)
C. S. Luck, III: president (see above)
J. H. Parker, III: treasurer

Grants Analysis

Disclosure Period: fiscal year ending October 31, 2003
Total Grants: $453,892*
Number of Grants: 63
Average Grant: $3,506*
Highest Grant: $120,000
Lowest Grant: $100
Typical Range: $1,000 to $5,000
*Note: Giving excludes United Way. Average grant figure excludes two highest grants ($240,000).

Recent Grants

Note: Grants derived from 2003 Form 990.

Library-Related

4,000	Fauquier County Library, Warrenton, VA

General

120,000	Goochland YMCA, Richmond, VA
120,000	VMI Alumni Education Fund, Lexington, VA
35,000	St Catherine's School Foundation, Richmond, VA
33,333	Hand Workshop Art Center, Richmond, VA
20,000	Children's Museum of Richmond, Richmond, VA
5,000	George C Marshall International Center, Leesburg, VA
5,000	Powhatan YMCA, Powhatan, VA
5,000	VMI Alumni Education Fund, Lexington, VA
4,000	Virginia Foundation for Independent Colleges, Richmond, VA
3,500	Virginia Museum of Fine Arts Foundation, Richmond, VA

LUDWICK FAMILY FOUNDATION

Giving Contact

Arthur J. Ludwick, Chief Financial Officer, Director
PO Box 1796
Glendora, CA 91740
Phone: (626)852-0092
E-mail: ludwickfndn@ludwick.org
Web: http://www.ludwick.org

Description

Founded: 1990
EIN: 954296315
Organization Type: Private Foundation
Giving Locations: CA: nationally.
Grant Types: Capital, General Support.

Donor Information

Founder: Arthur J. Ludwick, Sarah Lynne Ludwick, Rain Bird Corporate Services

Financial Summary

Gifts Received: $1,562,683 (2000); $1,310,403 (1999); $805,063 (1996). Note: In 2000, contributions were received from Arthur J. and Sarah L. Ludwick. In 1996, contributions were received from Arthur J. and Sarah L. Ludwick ($505,063) and Rain Bird Corporate Services ($300,000).

Typical Recipients

Arts & Humanities: Arts Centers, Film & Video, Historic Preservation, History & Archaeology, Libraries, Museums/Galleries, Music, Opera, Theater
Civic & Public Affairs: Clubs, Economic Development, Employment/Job Training, Civic & Public Affairs-General, Hispanic Affairs, Housing, Legal Aid, Women's Affairs
Education: Arts/Humanities Education, Business Education, Colleges & Universities, Education Reform, Education-General, School Volunteerism, Special Education, Vocational & Technical Education
Environment: Air/Water Quality, Environment-General, Resource Conservation, Wildlife Protection
Health: AIDS/HIV, Children's Health/Hospitals, Clinics/Medical Centers, Emergency/Ambulance Services, Hospitals, Prenatal Health Issues, Research/Studies Institutes
International: Health Care/Hospitals
Religion: Missionary Activities (Domestic), Religious Organizations
Science: Scientific Labs
Social Services: Animal Protection, At-Risk Youth, Child Welfare, Community Centers, Community Service Organizations, Day Care, Domestic Violence, Family Services, Food/Clothing Distribution, People with Disabilities, Recreation & Athletics, Scouts, Senior Services, Substance Abuse, Volunteer Services, YMCA/YWCA/YMHA/YWHA, Youth Organizations

Application Procedures

Initial Contact: Send a brief letter of inquiry.
Application Requirements: Include a description of organization, amount requested, purpose of funds sought, and proof of tax-exempt status.
Deadlines: None.

Restrictions

Does not support individuals or political or lobbying groups.

Foundation Officials

Arthur J. Ludwick: cfo, director
Erik Arthur Ludwick: director
Heidi Ann Ludwick: director
Sarah Lynne Ludwick: president, director
Sharon Lynne Ludwick Warner: secretary, director

Grants Analysis

Disclosure Period: calendar year ending 2000
Total Grants: $550,900
Number of Grants: 20
Average Grant: $27,545
Highest Grant: $50,000
Typical Range: $10,000 to $50,000

Recent Grants

Note: Grants derived from 2001 Form 990.
Library-Related

50,000	Rapid City Library Foundation, Inc., Rapid City, SD -- for expansion of services

General

50,000	Cal Poly Pomona University, Pomona, CA -- for Guardian Scholars Program
50,000	Matilda Joslyn Gage Foundation, Fayetteville, NY -- for office equipment that assists the educational outreach program
50,000	Mount San Antonio College, Walnut, CA -- for renovation of Wildlife Sanctuary
50,000	World Bird Sanctuary, St. Louis, MO -- for construction of a new Wildlife Rehabilitation Hospital
45,000	Books for the Barrios, Inc., Walnut Creek, CA -- for a heavy-duty truck and forklift
42,000	Behavior Management Systems, Rapid City, SD -- for computer hardware and software
40,000	Wheels for Humanity, North Hollywood, CA -- to purchase a Ford Box Truck
30,000	Oregon Food Bank, Portland, OR -- to purchase a refrigerated trailer
25,000	Claremont Community School of Music, Claremont, CA -- to help with furnishing the new recital hall
25,000	Helen Woodward Animal Care Center, Rancho Santa Fe, CA -- for a new ultrasound machine

CHRISTOPHER LUDWICK FOUNDATION

Giving Contact

Christopher Ludwick Foundation
First Union National Bank
Broad and Walnut Sts., PA 1308
Philadelphia, PA 19109-1199
Phone: (215)985-8930
Web: http://www.ludwickfoundation.org/

Description

Founded: 1899
EIN: 236256408
Organization Type: Private Foundation
Giving Locations: PA: Philadelphia
Grant Types: Project, Scholarship.

Donor Information

Founder: Christopher Ludwick

Financial Summary

Total Giving: $250,000 (fiscal year ending April 30, 2001)
Assets: $5,541,736 (fiscal 2001)

Typical Recipients

Arts & Humanities: Arts & Humanities-General, History & Archaeology, Museums/Galleries, Theater
Civic & Public Affairs: Civic & Public Affairs-General, Hispanic Affairs, Urban & Community Affairs, Zoos/Aquariums
Education: Arts/Humanities Education, Colleges & Universities, Private Education (Precollege), Public Education (Precollege), Science/Mathematics Education, Secondary Education (Public), Special Edu-

cation
Religion: Churches, Religious Welfare
Science: Scientific Centers & Institutes

Application Procedures

Initial Contact: Contact foundation for application form.
Deadlines: March 31

Restrictions

Does not support individuals, religious organizations for sectarian purposes, political or lobbying groups, organizations outside operating areas.

Additional Information

Supports the Voyager Program in the Philadelphia School District.
Publications: Application Form
Trust(s): First Union National Bank

Foundation Officials

Susan Williams Catherwood: vice president, mgr CORP AFFIL director: PECO Energy Co. NONPR AFFIL director: Monell Chemical Senses Center; vice chairman: University Pennsylvania; vice chairman: Executive Service Corps..
Alan Crawford, Jr.: mgr
Henry E. Crouter: mgr
William M. Davidson, IV: treasurer, mgr
Dr. Roger Moss, Jr.: secretary, mgr
Hugh A. A. Sargent, Esq.: president, mgr
Dr. L. Wilbur Zimmerman: office, vice president, mgr

Grants Analysis

Disclosure Period: fiscal year ending April 30, 2001
Total Grants: $250,000
Number of Grants: 40
Average Grant: $6,250
Highest Grant: $50,000
Typical Range: $5,000 to $10,000

Recent Grants

Note: Grants derived from fiscal 2001 Form 990.
General

50,000	School District, Philadelphia, PA
7,500	Academy of Natural Sciences, Philadelphia, PA
7,500	Academy of Natural Sciences, Philadelphia, PA
7,500	Academy of Natural Sciences, Philadelphia, PA
7,500	Academy of Natural Sciences, Philadelphia, PA
7,500	Episcopal Community Services, Philadelphia, PA
7,500	Historic Bartram's Gardens, Philadelphia, PA
7,500	Wagner Free Institute of Science, Philadelphia, PA
7,500	William Penn Charter School, Philadelphia, PA
6,250	School District, Philadelphia, PA

LUNDA CHARITABLE TRUST

Giving Contact

Carl Holmquist, Trustee
620 Gebhardt Rd.
PO Box 669
Black River Falls, WI 54615-0669
Phone: (715)284-9491

Description

Founded: 1988
EIN: 396491037

Organization Type: Private Foundation
Giving Locations: WI: Jackson County and surrounding area
Grant Types: General Support, Scholarship.

Donor Information

Founder: Milton Lunda

Financial Summary

Total Giving: $475,691 (2001)
Giving Analysis: Giving for 2001 includes: foundation scholarships ($4,000); foundation matching gifts ($176,283)
Assets: $9,243,936 (2001)
Gifts Received: $128,547 (2000); $229,673 (1999); $1,004,340 (1998). Note: In 2000, contributions were received from Larry Lunda. In 1999, contributions were received from Larry Lunda ($139,673) and Marlee Slifka ($90,000). In 1998,, contributions were received from Milton Lunda ($463,500), Larry Lunda ($99,150), and Marlee Slifka ($200,000). In 1996, contributions were received from Milton Lunda ($880,849), Larry Lunda ($100,000), and Marlee Slifka ($104,500).

Typical Recipients

Arts & Humanities: History & Archaeology, Libraries
Civic & Public Affairs: Botanical Gardens/Parks, Clubs, Civic & Public Affairs-General, Housing, Municipalities/Towns, Rural Affairs, Safety, Urban & Community Affairs
Education: Agricultural Education, Arts/Humanities Education, Education-General, Student Aid, Vocational & Technical Education
Environment: Environment-General
Health: Health-General, Hospitals, Long-Term Care
Religion: Religion-General
Social Services: Animal Protection, Camps, Child Welfare, Community Service Organizations, Day Care, Emergency Relief, People with Disabilities, Recreation & Athletics, Scouts, Social Services-General

Application Procedures

Initial Contact: a brief letter of inquiry
Application Requirements: Include purpose of funds sought, amount requested, and proof of tax-exempt status.
Deadlines: July 31.

Restrictions

Foundation supports tax-exempt educational, scientific, and other charitable institutions, as the trustees select.

Additional Information

The foundation reports no specific application guidelines.
Trust(s): Firstar Bank

Foundation Officials

Carl Holmquist: trustee
Larry Lunda: trustee
Lydia Lunda: trustee
Milton Lunda: trustee
Marlee Slifka: trustee
Mary Van Gorden: trustee
Bill Waughtal: trustee

Grants Analysis

Disclosure Period: calendar year ending 2001
Total Grants: $295,408*
Number of Grants: 95
Average Grant: $3,110
Highest Grant: $25,000
Lowest Grant: $100
Typical Range: $1,000 to $5,000
*Note: Giving excludes matching gifts; scholarships.

Recent Grants

Note: Grants derived from 2001 Form 990.

General

176,283	City of Black River Falls, Black River Falls, WI -- Park Project
25,000	Black River Youth Hockey, Black River Falls, WI -- ice arena improvements and upkeep
15,000	Hixton Volunteer Fire Department, Hixton, WI -- equipment update and replacement
14,257	Pine View Home Health, Black River Falls, WI -- EZ stand and food service heating systems
10,444	Pine View Nursing Home, Black River Falls, WI -- Parker tub
10,000	Alma Center Play Ground Committee -- playground equipment upgrade
10,000	Jackson County Habitat for Humanity, Black River Falls, WI -- house with contingency
9,852	City of Black River Falls, Black River Falls, WI -- Karner Blue Garden Club 2000 operations
6,685	Partners of Black River Memorial Hospital, Black River Falls, WI
6,420	City of Black River Falls, Black River Falls, WI -- bleachers

GEORGES LURCY CHARITABLE AND EDUCATIONAL TRUST

Giving Contact

Seth E. Frank, Trustee
125 W. 55th St.
New York, NY 10019
Phone: (212)424-8000

Description

EIN: 136372044
Organization Type: Specialized/Single Purpose Foundation
Giving Locations: nationally.
Grant Types: Fellowship.

Donor Information

Founder: the late Georges Lurcy

Financial Summary

Total Giving: $1,106,624 (fiscal year ending June 30, 2004)
Assets: $32,095,539 (fiscal 2004)

Typical Recipients

Arts & Humanities: Arts Centers, Ballet, Libraries, Museums/Galleries, Music, Opera, Public Broadcasting, Theater
Civic & Public Affairs: Civic & Public Affairs-General, Public Policy
Education: Arts/Humanities Education, Colleges & Universities, Continuing Education, Engineering/Technological Education, Education-General, International Exchange, International Studies, Minority Education, Private Education (Precollege), Science/Mathematics Education, Student Aid
Environment: Environment-General
Health: Cancer, Hospitals, Single-Disease Health Associations
International: Foreign Arts Organizations, Foreign Educational Institutions, International Organizations, International Relations, Missionary/Religious Activities
Religion: Jewish Causes, Religious Welfare, Synagogues/Temples
Science: Science-General
Social Services: Camps, Community Service Organizations, Youth Organizations

Application Procedures

Initial Contact: Universities are requested to recommend a candidate for its fellowship. Applicants from France must apply to the FrancoAmerican Commission for Educational Exchange. Applicants cannot apply directly to the foundation.
Deadlines: None.

Additional Information

Provides fellowship grants to outstanding American students to study in French colleges and universities, and fellowships to outstanding French students to study in American colleges and universities.
Publications: Application Guidelines

Foundation Officials

Alan S. Bernstein: trustee
Daniel Lewis Bernstein: trustee B Durham, NC 1937. ED Amherst College BA (1959); Harvard University LLB (1962). CORP AFFIL pntr: Law Office Daniel L Bernstein. NONPR AFFIL member: International Bar Association; trustee: Georges Lucy Charitable & Education Trust; member: Bar Association New York City; director: Collegeeen Giblin Endowment Fund Child Neurology Research; member: American Bar Association; director: Arts & Sciences Foundation.
George Lurcy Bernstein: trustee PRIM NONPR EMPL associate professor: Tulane University, Department History.
Seth E. Frank: trustee

Grants Analysis

Disclosure Period: fiscal year ending June 30, 2004
Total Grants: $1,106,624
Number of Grants: 76
Average Grant: $12,833*
Highest Grant: $82,000
Lowest Grant: $1,000
Typical Range: $5,000 to $20,000
*Note: Average grant figure excludes two highest grants ($157,000).

Recent Grants

Note: Grants derived from fiscal 2004 Form 990.
General

506,000	Brought Forward
82,000	University of Chicago, Chicago, IL
75,000	Louis August Jonas Foundation Inc., Rhinebeck, NY
50,000	University of Chicago, Chicago, IL
50,000	Walnut Hill School, Natick, MA
45,000	Harvard University, Cambridge, MA
40,300	University of California, Berkeley, CA
35,000	Tulane University, New Orleans, LA
35,000	Yale University, New Haven, CT
30,524	University of North Carolina, Chapel Hill, NC

W. P. AND BULAH LUSE FOUNDATION

Giving Contact

Bill Arrington, Trust Officer
c/o Bank of America, NA
PO Box 831041
Dallas, TX 75283-1041
Phone: (214)209-1989

Description

Founded: 1947
EIN: 756007639
Organization Type: Private Foundation
Giving Locations: TX
Grant Types: General Support.

Financial Summary

Total Giving: $253,887 (2003)
Assets: $5,723,721 (2003)
Gifts Received: $248 (2003); $839 (2000); $888 (1999). Note: In 1999, 2000, and 2003, contributions were received from W. P. Luse Employees Trust.

Typical Recipients

Civic & Public Affairs: Civic & Public Affairs-General, Housing, Women's Affairs, Zoos/Aquariums
Education: Colleges & Universities, Education Funds, Education Reform, Engineering/Technological Education, Education-General, Literacy, Medical Education, Preschool Education, Private Education (Precollege), Special Education
Environment: Environment-General
Health: Cancer, Diabetes, Eyes/Blindness, Health-General, Health Funds, Health Organizations, Medical Research, Mental Health, Nursing Services, Public Health, Single-Disease Health Associations
Religion: Religious Welfare
Social Services: Big Brothers/Big Sisters, Camps, Child Welfare, Counseling, Domestic Violence, Family Planning, Family Services, Food/Clothing Distribution, People with Disabilities, Scouts, Senior Services, Shelters/Homelessness, Volunteer Services, Youth Organizations

Application Procedures

Initial Contact: The Foundation has no formal grant application procedure or application form. Send a brief letter of inquiry and a full proposal.
Application Requirements: Include a description of organization, amount requested, purpose of funds sought, and proof of tax-exempt status.
Deadlines: None. Requests are reviewed at the end of each year.

Restrictions

Request must be for educational or medical purposes or for the alleviation of poverty. Does not support individuals.

Additional Information

Trust(s): Bank of America NA

Foundation Officials

Jack L. Burrell, Jr.: co-trustee
George Wilkin: co-trustee

Grants Analysis

Disclosure Period: calendar year ending 2003
Total Grants: $253,887
Number of Grants: 32
Average Grant: $7,934
Highest Grant: $20,000
Lowest Grant: $3,887
Typical Range: $5,000 to $10,000

Recent Grants

Note: Grants derived from 2003 Form 990.
General

20,000	Texas A&M University Development Foundation, College Station, TX
20,000	Visiting Nurses Association, Dallas, TX
15,000	Salvation Army, Dallas, TX -- for relief of poverty
14,000	Metroplex Food Bank, Ft. Worth, TX -- for food collection and distribution
14,000	North Texas Food Bank, Dallas, TX -- for hunger relief
10,000	Episcopal School of Dallas, Dallas, TX
10,000	Family Place, Dallas, TX
10,000	Genesis Women's Shelter, Dallas, TX -- for relief of poverty
10,000	Mi Escuelita Preschools Inc., Dallas, TX
10,000	Presbyterian Healthcare Foundation, Dallas, TX

MIRANDA LUX FOUNDATION

Giving Contact

Kenneth J. Blum, Executive Director
57 Post St., Suite 510
San Francisco, CA 94104
Phone: (415)981-2966
E-mail: admin@mirandalux.org
Web: http://www.mirandalux.org/

Description

Founded: 1908
EIN: 941170404
Organization Type: Private Foundation
Giving Locations: CA: San Francisco
Grant Types: Fellowship, General Support, Multi-year/Continuing Support, Operating Expenses, Project, Scholarship, Seed Money.

Donor Information

Founder: the late Miranda W. Lux

Financial Summary

Total Giving: $409,200 (fiscal year ending June 30, 2004); $474,300 (fiscal 2002); $521,800 (fiscal 2001)
Giving Analysis: Giving for fiscal 2004 includes: foundation scholarships ($10,000); fiscal 2002: foundation scholarships ($10,000); fiscal 2001: foundation scholarships ($25,810)
Assets: $9,536,561 (fiscal 2004); $9,348,861 (fiscal 2002); $10,478,366 (fiscal 2001)

Typical Recipients

Arts & Humanities: Arts Institutes, Film & Video, Arts & Humanities-General, Libraries, Music, Opera, Performing Arts, Public Broadcasting, Theater
Civic & Public Affairs: Asian American Affairs, Botanical Gardens/Parks, Business/Free Enterprise, Employment/Job Training, Hispanic Affairs, Nonprofit Management, Urban & Community Affairs, Zoos/Aquariums
Education: Afterschool/Enrichment Programs, Arts/Humanities Education, Business Education, Business-School Partnerships, Colleges & Universities, Education Funds, Education-General, Journalism/Media Education, Leadership Training, Literacy, Minority Education, Preschool Education, Private Education (Precollege), Public Education (Precollege), Science/Mathematics Education, Secondary Education (Private), Secondary Education (Public), Student Aid, Vocational & Technical Education
Environment: Forestry, Protection, Resource Conservation
Health: Children's Health/Hospitals, Clinics/Medical Centers, Health Organizations, Mental Health
Religion: Jewish Causes, Religious Organizations, Religious Welfare
Science: Science Museums, Scientific Centers & Institutes
Social Services: At-Risk Youth, Child Welfare, Community Centers, Community Service Organizations, Counseling, Family Services, People with Disabilities, Recreation & Athletics, Shelters/Homelessness, Social Services-General, YMCA/YWCA/YMHA/YWHA, Youth Organizations

Application Procedures

Initial Contact: Send a full proposal.
Application Requirements: Include a description of organization; amount requested; purpose of funds sought; total project budget; other funding sources; number of participants; age range and distribution of participants; term and goals of the project; staff, and apartments.
Deadlines: None.

Restrictions

Foundation supports promising proposals for preschool through junior college in the fields of prevocational and vocational training in San Francisco. Does not support individuals or provide funds for annual campaigns, deficit financing, land acquisition, loans, renovations, publications, or conferences.

Additional Information
Publications: Annual Report

Foundation Officials
Beatrice Bowles: secretary, treasurer
Robert Cappelloni: trustee
Betsy Keller: trustee
Philip F. Spalding: vice president
David Wisnom, Jr.: president

Grants Analysis
Disclosure Period: fiscal year ending June 30, 2004
Total Grants: $399,200*
Number of Grants: 41
Average Grant: $9,737
Highest Grant: $25,000
Lowest Grant: $1,500
Typical Range: $5,000 to $15,000
*Note: Giving excludes scholarships.

Recent Grants
Note: Grants derived from fiscal 2004 Form 990.
General

25,000	Bay Area Video Coalition, San Francisco, CA -- to support youth link
17,500	San Francisco Art Institute, San Francisco, CA -- to support the young artist program
15,000	Bernal Heights Neighborhood Center, San Francisco, CA -- to support the youth employment services program
15,000	GirlSource, San Francisco, CA -- to support the young women's technology and leadership program
12,500	Archbishop Riordan High School, San Francisco, CA -- to support the video technology production program
12,500	California Academy of Sciences, San Francisco, CA -- to support the careers in science program
12,500	Community Learning Center, Bakersfield, CA -- to support the homework club
11,000	Math/Science Network, Oakland, CA -- to support the San Francisco Expanding Your Horizons in Science and Mathematics conference
10,000	Better Chance, New York, NY -- to support the college preparatory schools program
10,000	Marine Mammal Center, Sausalito, CA -- to support the science discovery and education programs

LYDALL INC.

Company Headquarters
PO Box 151
Manchester, CT 06045-0151
Web: http://www.lydall.com

Company Description
Founded: 1879
Ticker: LDL
Exchange: NYSE
Revenue: US$253.5 million (2002)
Employees: 0 (2002)
SIC(s): 3900 Miscellaneous Manufacturing Industries.

Operating Locations
Lydall, Inc. (NH--Rochester; NY--Green Island; NC--Hamptonville; VA--Richmond)

Nonmonetary Support
Type: Donated Equipment; Loaned Employees; Loaned Executives

Giving Contact
Charlene Cefarattir, Executive Assistant
PO Box 151
Manchester, CT 06045-0151
Phone: (860)646-1233
Fax: (860)646-8847

Description
Organization Type: Corporate Giving Program
Giving Locations: headquarters and operating communities.
Grant Types: Capital, Emergency, Employee Matching Gifts, General Support, Multiyear/Continuing Support, Operating Expenses, Project, Research, Scholarship.

Typical Recipients
Arts & Humanities: Arts Associations & Councils, Arts Centers, Arts Funds, Arts Institutes, Ballet, Community Arts, Arts & Humanities-General, Historic Preservation, Libraries, Literary Arts, Museums/Galleries, Music, Opera, Performing Arts, Public Broadcasting, Theater
Civic & Public Affairs: Chambers of Commerce, Economic Development, Civic & Public Affairs-General, Housing, Nonprofit Management, Philanthropic Organizations, Urban & Community Affairs
Education: Business Education, Business-School Partnerships, Colleges & Universities, Community & Junior Colleges, Continuing Education, Economic Education, Education-General, Literacy
Environment: Air/Water Quality, Resource Conservation
Health: Alzheimer's Disease, Arthritis, Cancer, Children's Health/Hospitals, Eyes/Blindness, Health-General, Health Policy/Cost Containment, Health Organizations, Heart, Hospices, Hospitals, Medical Rehabilitation, Medical Research, Mental Health, Multiple Sclerosis, Nursing Services, Nutrition, Public Health, Single-Disease Health Associations
Social Services: Child Welfare, Community Centers, Community Service Organizations, Counseling, Domestic Violence, Emergency Relief, Family Services, Food/Clothing Distribution, Homes, People with Disabilities, Shelters/Homelessness, Social Services-General, Special Olympics, Substance Abuse, United Funds/United Ways, Youth Organizations

Application Procedures
Initial Contact: Send a brief letter of request. Include a description of organization, amount requested, purpose of funds sought, recently audited financial statement, and proof of tax-exempt status.
Deadlines: September/October for the following year.

Restrictions
Does not support individuals, religious organizations for sectarian purposes, or political or lobbying groups.

Corporate Officials
John E. Hanley: chief financial officer, vice president finance, treasurerc PRIM CORP EMPL chief financial officer, vice president finance, treasurer: Lydall.
Leonard R. Jaskol: chairman, president, chief executive officer, director B New Rochelle, NY 1937. ED American University (1958); City University of New York (1969). PRIM CORP EMPL chairman, president, chief executive officer, director: Lydall.

Grants Analysis
Typical Range: $500 to $1,000

Recent Grants
Note: Grants derived from 1998 Form 990.
General
American Cancer Society, Hartford, CT

Connecticut Association for Human Services, Hartford, CT
Connecticut Special Olympics, Hartford, CT
Habitat for Humanity, Hartford, CT
Hartford College for Women, Hartford, CT
Jimmy Fund, Hartford, CT
Lutz Children's Museum, Manerostoe, CT
Manchester Symphony Orchestra and Chorale, Manchester, CT
United Way, Hartford, CT
Greater Hartford Arts Council, Hartford, CT

LYNDHURST FOUNDATION

Giving Contact
Jack Murrah, President
517 East Fifth Street
Chattanooga, TN 37403-1826
Phone: (423)756-0767
Fax: (423)756-0770
Web: http://www.lyndhurstfoundation.org

Description
Founded: 1938
EIN: 626044177
Organization Type: General Purpose Foundation
Giving Locations: TN: Chattanooga Southeastern USA.
Grant Types: Employee Matching Gifts, General Support, Matching, Multiyear/Continuing Support, Operating Expenses.

Donor Information
Founder: The Lyndhurst Foundation was established in Delaware in 1938 as the Memorial Welfare Foundation, with funds donated by the late Thomas Cartter Lupton and the Central Shares Corporation. Mr. Lupton was a pioneer in the development of the Coca-Cola bottling industry. The estate of Mr. Lupton transferred about $45 million to the foundation from 1977 to 1979.

Financial Summary
Total Giving: $6,223,357 (2003); $5,565,171 (2002); $10,052,081 (2001)
Giving Analysis: Giving for 2003 includes: foundation matching gifts ($38,485); foundation grants to United Way ($125,000); 2002: foundation matching gifts ($44,886); foundation grants to United Way ($150,000); foundation scholarships ($240,000)
Assets: $162,000,000 (2003 approx); $149,620,257 (2002); $157,202,266 (2001)

Typical Recipients
Arts & Humanities: Arts Appreciation, Arts Associations & Councils, Arts Centers, Arts Festivals, Arts Funds, Arts Institutes, Community Arts, Ethnic & Folk Arts, Film & Video, Arts & Humanities-General, Historic Preservation, Libraries, Literary Arts, Museums/Galleries, Music, Performing Arts, Public Broadcasting, Theater, Visual Arts
Civic & Public Affairs: Botanical Gardens/Parks, Chambers of Commerce, Community Foundations, Economic Development, Civic & Public Affairs-General, Housing, Inner-City Development, Law & Justice, Municipalities/Towns, Nonprofit Management, Parades/Festivals, Philanthropic Organizations, Professional & Trade Associations, Public Policy, Rural Affairs, Urban & Community Affairs, Zoos/Aquariums
Education: Afterschool/Enrichment Programs, Arts/Humanities Education, Colleges & Universities, Education Funds, Education Reform, Elementary Education (Private), Engineering/Technological Education, Environmental Education, Education-General, Leadership Training, Private Education (Precollege), Public Education (Precollege), School Volunteerism, Student Aid

Environment: Air/Water Quality, Energy, Forestry, Environment-General, Protection, Research, Resource Conservation, Sanitary Systems, Watershed, Wildlife Protection
Health: Clinics/Medical Centers, Mental Health
International: International Environmental Issues
Religion: Churches, Religious Welfare
Social Services: Animal Protection, Child Abuse, Child Welfare, Community Centers, Community Service Organizations, Day Care, Family Services, Food/Clothing Distribution, Homes, People with Disabilities, Recreation & Athletics, Sexual Abuse, Shelters/Homelessness, Substance Abuse, United Funds/United Ways, Volunteer Services, Youth Organizations

Application Procedures

Initial Contact: The foundation does not have an application form. Applicants should submit a letter of not more than three pages describing the project for which the grant is being sought.
Application Requirements: An application and a letter a description of organization, list of directors and staff, copy of the organization's annual budget, copy of the organization's tax-exempt ruling from the IRS, and an estimated project budget with tentative line items.
Deadlines: Proposals are considered on a quarterly basis. Contact the foundation for specific deadlines.
Review Process: All grant requests are reviewed and researched by the foundation's staff before presentation to the board of trustees. Applicants will be notified of the board's decision following regular meetings, generally held in January, April, July, and October.

Restrictions

The foundation reports that it does not award grants to individuals except under the Lyndhurst Prize. The Lyndhurst Prizes are given solely at the initiative of the board of trustees, never in response to applications, requests, or nominations.

The foundation generally does not accept unsolicited requests for funds. The only category the foundation does accept unsolicited requests for grants supporting environmental improvement programs in the southern Appalachian Mountain region of Tennessee, North Carolina, South Carolina, Georgia, Alabama, and Mississippi.

Additional Information

Publications: Annual Report; Guidelines

Foundation Officials

Nelson D. Campbell: trustee
Benic M. Clark, III: vice president, secretary, treasurer
George R. Fontaine: trustee
Margaret L. Gerber: trustee
Katherine Crosland Juett: trustee
T. Cartter Lupton, II: trustee
Allen L. McCallie: chairman, trustee
Jack Murrah: president, trustee
Alice Smith: trustee

Grants Analysis

Disclosure Period: calendar year ending 2003
Total Grants: $6,059,872*
Number of Grants: 47
Average Grant: $73,713*
Highest Grant: $1,183,000
Lowest Grant: $750
Typical Range: $25,000 to $100,000
*Note: Giving excludes United Way; matching gifts. Average grant figure excludes three highest grants ($2,816,488).

Recent Grants

Note: Grants derived from 2002 Form 990.
General

500,000	Chattanooga Neighborhood Enterprise, Chattanooga, TN
500,000	RiverCity Company, Chattanooga, TN -- for the 4th street boulevard project
500,000	RiverCity Company, Chattanooga, TN -- for planning and design costs associated with 21st century waterfront project
500,000	Rural School and Community Trust, Washington, DC
431,500	Allied Arts of Greater Chattanooga, Chattanooga, TN
250,000	Community Foundation of Greater Chattanooga, Chattanooga, TN -- towards support of community information service for Chattanooga
250,000	Cumberland Trail Conference, Crossville, TN -- towards support of pathways for people - People for Nature campaign
250,000	Southern Appalachian Forest Coalition, Asheville, NC -- towards implementation of Great Forest campaign and related activities
250,000	Tennessee River Gorge Trust, Chattanooga, TN -- towards purchase of 768 acre "McGlothlin" tracts
240,000	Lyndhurst Prizes -- for individuals whose work has been interesting, creative and significant for a number of years

LYON FOUNDATION

Giving Contact

James W. Connor, President
PO Box 546
Bartlesville, OK 74005
Phone: (918)336-0066

Description

Founded: 1975
EIN: 237299980
Organization Type: General Purpose Foundation
Giving Locations: OK: Bartlesville
Grant Types: Capital, General Support, Scholarship.

Donor Information

Founder: Established in 1975 by the late E. H. Lyon and the late Melody Lyon.

Financial Summary

Total Giving: $955,946 (2002)
Assets: $18,925,386 (2002)
Gifts Received: $352,779 (2002); $378,167 (2000); $376,719 (1999). Note: In 2002, 2000, 1999, and 1998, contributions were received from E. H. Lyon Trust.

Typical Recipients

Arts & Humanities: Arts Centers, Arts Festivals, Ballet, Community Arts, Arts & Humanities-General, Historic Preservation, History & Archaeology, Libraries, Museums/Galleries, Music, Theater, Visual Arts
Civic & Public Affairs: Botanical Gardens/Parks, Clubs, Community Foundations, Economic Development, Civic & Public Affairs-General, Law & Justice, Legal Aid, Municipalities/Towns, Native American Affairs, Nonprofit Management, Parades/Festivals, Professional & Trade Associations, Public Policy, Safety
Education: Colleges & Universities, Faculty Development, Education-General, Literacy, Medical Education, Private Education (Precollege), Public Education (Precollege), Special Education, Vocational & Technical Education
Health: Alzheimer's Disease, Clinics/Medical Centers, Emergency/Ambulance Services, Health-General, Geriatric Health, Health Funds, Health Organizations, Hospitals, Medical Rehabilitation, Mental Health, Nutrition, Public Health
Religion: Churches, Ministries, Religious Welfare
Social Services: Animal Protection, Big Brothers/Big Sisters, Child Welfare, Community Centers, Community Service Organizations, Family Services, Homes, People with Disabilities, Recreation & Athletics, Scouts, Senior Services, Substance Abuse, YMCA/YWCA/YMHA/YWHA, Youth Organizations

Application Procedures

Initial Contact: Submit a written application of no more than four double-spaced pages.
Application Requirements: An application should contain the following information about the project: formal name of organization; brief description of history and purpose; address and phone number; name and title of person responsible for grant application; amount of grant requested; period for which grant is requested; purpose of grant; copy of most current IRS determination letter; copy of most recently filed IRS Form 990; applicant's budget for current year and year(s) for which grant is requested; identification of other organizations solicited for same purpose; names, titles, and affiliations of officers and members of governing body; and certification that applicant's exempt status has not changed since initial IRS determination letter.
Deadlines: None.
Review Process: After reviewing the application, foundation staff may request additional information.

Restrictions

Policy guidelines established by the board of directors normally preclude grants for ongoing general operating expenses or existing deficits, endowment funds, direct support to individuals, and projects or programs outside the Bartlesville area. In addition, no grants will be made for computers or computer-related items. (However, grants in the past have been made for endowment funds and computers.)

Foundation Officials

Walter W. Allison: vice president, assistant treasurer PRIM NONPR EMPL chief accountant: City of Norman, Oklahoma.
James W. Connor: president
Don Donaldson: vice president, assistant secretary PRIM CORP EMPL president: Community Bank. CORP AFFIL director: Community State Bank.
John F. Kane: treasurer
Larry G. Markel, MD: assistant secretary PRIM CORP EMPL director: Weststar Bank.
Charles W. Selby: secretary, director

Grants Analysis

Disclosure Period: calendar year ending 2002
Total Grants: $955,946
Number of Grants: 26
Average Grant: $15,476*
Highest Grant: $200,000
Lowest Grant: $166
Typical Range: $2,000 to $30,000
*Note: Average grant excludes three highest grants ($600,000).

Recent Grants

Note: Grants derived from 2002 Form 990.
General

200,000	Bluestem Regional Medical Foundation, Bartlesville, OK -- hospital facility
200,000	City of Bartlesville, Bartlesville, OK -- industrial development
200,000	Price Tower Arts Center, Bartlesville, OK -- renovate price tower
110,000	City of Bartlesville, Bartlesville, OK -- memorial stadium upgrading
110,000	Collingsworth General Hospital, Wellington, TX -- assisted living project
50,000	Bluestem Regional Medical Foundation, Bartlesville, OK -- enlarge emergency care facility
50,000	Boys & Girls Club of Nowata
40,000	Washington County Elder Care, Bartlesville, OK
25,000	Ochelata Volunteer Fire Department, Ochelata, OK -- build new firehouse

15,000   Bluestem Therapeutic Horseback Riding, Bartlesville, OK -- purchase equipment to maintain property

BERTHA RUSS LYTEL FOUNDATION

Giving Contact

George Hindley, Manager
PO Box 893
Ferndale, CA 95536
Phone: (707)786-4682

Description

Founded: 1974
EIN: 942271250
Organization Type: Private Foundation
Giving Locations: CA: Humboldt County
Grant Types: Capital, General Support, Multiyear/Continuing Support, Operating Expenses, Scholarship, Seed Money.

Donor Information

Founder: the late Bertha Russ Lytel, L. D. O'Rourke

Financial Summary

Total Giving: $746,534 (fiscal year ending September 30, 2004); $802,526 (fiscal 2001)
Assets: $16,995,340 (fiscal 2004); $17,091,191 (fiscal 2001)
Gifts Received: $823,991 (fiscal 2000); $82,628 (fiscal 1998); $115 (fiscal 1992). Note: In fiscal 1998, contributions were received from the late Bertha Lytel.

Typical Recipients

Arts & Humanities: Arts Associations & Councils, Libraries, Museums/Galleries, Public Broadcasting, Theater
Civic & Public Affairs: Civil Rights, Clubs, Employment/Job Training, Civic & Public Affairs-General, Municipalities/Towns, Nonprofit Management, Parades/Festivals, Safety, Urban & Community Affairs
Education: Agricultural Education, Colleges & Universities, Education Associations, Engineering/Technological Education, Preschool Education, Private Education (Precollege), Public Education (Precollege), Science/Mathematics Education, Secondary Education (Public), Student Aid
Environment: Environment-General, Resource Conservation
Health: Arthritis, Children's Health/Hospitals, Clinics/Medical Centers, Emergency/Ambulance Services, Health Organizations, Heart, Home-Care Services, Hospitals, Long-Term Care, Nursing Services, Public Health
Religion: Churches, Religious Welfare
Science: Scientific Organizations
Social Services: Child Welfare, Community Service Organizations, Family Planning, Family Services, Food/Clothing Distribution, People with Disabilities, Recreation & Athletics, Scouts, Senior Services, Special Olympics, Substance Abuse, Veterans, Volunteer Services, Youth Organizations

Application Procedures

Initial Contact: Send a letter requesting an application form for scholarships or grants.
Deadlines: April 1.

Restrictions

Does not provide funds for annual campaigns, emergency or deficit financing, land acquisition, loans, renovations, demonstration projects, or publications. Grants are awarded to organizations in Humboldt County that generally support programs that deal with the elderly.

Additional Information

Awards scholarships to students entering a four-year agricultural college. Priority is given to graduates of Ferndale High School. If no Ferndale High School graduates apply, graduates of Fortuna High School are given consideration. Applicants are judged on grade point average; rigor of course of study in high school; letters of recommendation; non-academic activities including leadership activities, age-related activities and work experience and an essay.
Publications: Application Guidelines; Application Form

Foundation Officials

Betty Diehl: vice president
Charles Lakin: director
Charles M. Lawrence: president
James K. Morrison: secretary
Tom Renner: director
Jack Russ: director
Jack Smith: director

Grants Analysis

Disclosure Period: fiscal year ending September 30, 2004
Total Grants: $746,534
Number of Grants: 33
Average Grant: $18,485*
Highest Grant: $155,000
Lowest Grant: $222
Typical Range: $5,000 to $30,000
***Note:** Average grant figure excludes highest grant.

Recent Grants

Note: Grants derived from fiscal 2004 Form 990.
General
155,000   Senior Resource Center, Denver, CO
87,650   Ferndale Cemetery District, Ferndale, CA
85,200   Ferndale Community Church, Ferndale, CA
45,000   Southern Humboldt Senior Care
40,000   William Russ Scholarships
37,440   Retired Senior Volunteer Program
25,000   City of Ferndale, Ferndale, CA
25,000   Our Savior's Lutheran Church, Lake Oswego, OR
24,674   Ferndale Repertory, Ferndale, CA
19,293   Ferndale Unified School District, Ferndale, CA

M.E. FOUNDATION

Giving Contact

Grace McCrane, Administrative Assistant
PO Box 20266
Washington, DC 20041
Phone: (703)478-0100

Description

Founded: 1966
EIN: 136205356
Organization Type: Private Foundation
Giving Locations: nationally.
Grant Types: General Support.

Donor Information

Founder: Margaret Brown Trimble, Frances Carroll Brown

Financial Summary

Gifts Received: $440 (1993)

Typical Recipients

Arts & Humanities: Libraries, Music, Public Broadcasting
Civic & Public Affairs: Economic Development, Civic & Public Affairs-General
Education: Colleges & Universities, International Ex-

change, Private Education (Precollege), Religious Education, Special Education, Student Aid
Health: Health-General, Health Organizations
International: Foreign Educational Institutions, International Development, International Organizations, International Peace & Security Issues, International Relations, International Relief Efforts, Missionary/Religious Activities
Religion: Churches, Ministries, Missionary Activities (Domestic), Religious Organizations, Religious Welfare, Seminaries, Social/Policy Issues
Social Services: At-Risk Youth, Community Service Organizations, Family Services, Homes, People with Disabilities, Social Services-General, Substance Abuse, Youth Organizations

Application Procedures

Initial Contact: Submit a statement describing how organization has participated in the furtherance of educational and religious beliefs and studies.
Deadlines: None.

Foundation Officials

Dr. Sharon Berry: director
Frances Carroll Brown: vice president, treasurer, director
Charles Wendell Colson: acting president B Boston, MA 1931. ED Brown University AB (1953); George Washington University JD (1959). NONPR AFFIL member: Order Coif; associate: Prison Fellowship; member: Beta Theta Pi.
Dr. Carl F.H. Henry: director
Calvin E. Howe: director

Grants Analysis

Disclosure Period: calendar year ending 2000
Total Grants: $2,607,929*
Typical Range: $1,000 to $25,000
***Note:** No grant list available for 2000.

Recent Grants

Note: Grants derived from 2001 Form 990.
General
309,000   Prison Fellowship International, Washington, DC
130,000   Prison Fellowship International, Washington, DC
60,000   Fleming-Hunter Foundation, Inc., Randallstown, MD
60,000   Gordon Conwell Theological Seminary, South Hamilton, MA
53,000   Campus Crusade for Christ International, Orlando, FL
52,000   Walter Hoving Home, Garrison, NY
50,000   LeTourneau University, Longview, TX
48,000   World Reach, Birmingham, AL
41,000   Truth Ministries, Baltimore, MD
40,000   Spanish World Gospel Mission, Winona Lake, IN

J. E. AND L. E. MABEE FOUNDATION, INC.

Giving Contact

John H. Conway, Jr., Vice Chairman & Trustee
401 South Boston Avenue, Suite 3001
Tulsa, OK 74103-4017
Phone: (918)584-4286
Fax: (918)584-5540

Description

Founded: 1948
EIN: 736090162
Organization Type: Family Foundation
Giving Locations: AR; KS; MO; NM; OK; TX
Grant Types: Capital, General Support.
Note: Most of the foundation's grants are made for

building construction, renovations, and to purchase major medical capital equipment. Normally, capital grants are made on a challenge or conditional basis for leveraging purposes. The challenge is to raise the balance needed to assure complete project funding within the challenge period. There is no set rule to determine what percentage of the total project cost may be the subject of a challenge grant.

Donor Information

Founder: The J. E. and L. E. Mabee Foundation was established in 1948 by Mr. and Mrs. J. E. Mabee (both deceased), who lived in the southwestern United States and made their fortune in oil. The foundation formed its grant-making policies to reflect the interests of the founders.

Financial Summary

Total Giving: $35,716,704 (fiscal year ending August 31, 2003); $28,759,122 (fiscal 2002); $28,550,263 (fiscal 2001)
Giving Analysis: Giving for fiscal 2003 includes: foundation grants to United Way ($175,000); fiscal 2001: foundation grants to United Way ($275,000)
Assets: $728,819,060 (fiscal 2003); $696,114,826 (fiscal 2002); $735,208,451 (fiscal 2001)

Typical Recipients

Arts & Humanities: Art History, Arts Associations & Councils, Arts Centers, Dance, Ethnic & Folk Arts, History & Archaeology, Libraries, Museums/Galleries, Opera, Performing Arts, Public Broadcasting, Theater
Civic & Public Affairs: Botanical Gardens/Parks, Clubs, Civic & Public Affairs-General, Hispanic Affairs, Housing, Minority Business, Urban & Community Affairs
Education: Business Education, Colleges & Universities, Education-General, Medical Education, Private Education (Precollege), Public Education (Precollege), Religious Education, Science/Mathematics Education, Special Education, Student Aid
Health: Alzheimer's Disease, Cancer, Children's Health/Hospitals, Clinics/Medical Centers, Diabetes, Health-General, Health Funds, Health Organizations, Heart, Hospices, Hospitals, Long-Term Care, Medical Rehabilitation, Medical Research, Mental Health, Nursing Services, Preventive Medicine/Wellness Organizations, Public Health, Research/Studies Institutes, Respiratory, Single-Disease Health Associations
Religion: Bible Study/Translation, Churches, Dioceses, Religion-General, Jewish Causes, Ministries, Religious Organizations, Religious Welfare, Seminaries
Science: Science Museums, Scientific Centers & Institutes, Scientific Research
Social Services: At-Risk Youth, Big Brothers/Big Sisters, Camps, Child Welfare, Community Centers, Community Service Organizations, Day Care, Domestic Violence, Emergency Relief, Family Services, Food/Clothing Distribution, Homes, People with Disabilities, Recreation & Athletics, Scouts, Senior Services, Shelters/Homelessness, Social Services-General, Substance Abuse, United Funds/United Ways, Volunteer Services, YMCA/YWCA/YMHA/YWHA, Youth Organizations

Application Procedures

Initial Contact: The foundation does not require a standard application form.
Application Requirements: To be evaluated by the foundation, all proposals must contain the legal name and address of the applicant; name, title, address, and phone number of the appropriate contact person; a brief description of the organization, including a summary of its qualifications and background in the field in which funds are sought; a description of the project with its goals, significance, and benefiting population; substantiation of the extent of need for those benefits; and comments on past or present attempts by the applicant or others to meet this need.

Applicants also should submit a detailed expenditure budget for the project which explains how major portions were estimated, and how and when the funds will be spent; description of other possible sources of support which have been or will be solicited, including funds previously received or pledged for the project; amount requested from the foundation; time schedule for the construction and commencement of the project; and an explanation of how the project will be sustained after the requested support period. If a challenge grant is requested, the period of time within which the challenge must be met needs to be included (not in excess of one year).

In addition to the proposal, the foundation requires an applicant to include copies of the most recent IRS 501(c)(3) tax-exempt status letter (if there is any variance between the name on the IRS letter and the applicant's letter, this must be fully explained and documented); a statement on organization letterhead, signed by its chief executive officer, that there has been no change in the purpose, character, or method of operation subsequent to the IRS ruling letter(s); a copy of the organization's audited financial statement for the most recently completed fiscal year (if not audited, include a copy of the latest IRS Form 990); and an interim financial statement for the current fiscal period. Applicants also should include a listing of names of the primary professional affiliations, members of the applicant's governing body, and names and titles of the officers.

Deadlines: December 1; March 1; June 1; and September 1.
Review Process: Applications should be as brief as possible, but must contain all the required information. The trustees send a written decision on the proposal usually within one week of their meeting.

Restrictions

The foundation ordinarily does not make grants for deficit financing, initial funds, total project costs, operating funds, annual fundraising campaigns, reserve purposes, dinners or special events, fraternal organizations, individuals, political or lobbying groups, goodwill advertising, projects that are likely to be delayed, endowments, religious organizations for sectarian purposes, tax supported organizations, government-owned or operated institutions and facilities (such as state universities, municipal parks, and libraries), or precollege educational institutions. The foundation requests that only one proposal be submitted per twelve month period, unless a tremendous change in circumstances has occurred. If a grant has been previously issued to an applicant, there should be a two year period between the final payment for the previous grant and the request for another. New proposals must include all required information without relying on previously submitted information.

Additional Information

The foundation prefers to participate with other donors, so it is suggested that the applicant seek support from other foundations and donors before submitting a proposal. The typical recipient has previously raised some funds before applying and has outlined a fund-raising strategy which incorporates the use of a Mabee Foundation challenge grant for securing the balance of funds needed to complete the project.

Challenge grants are paid after the foundation is supplied with substantiation that the applicant has raised the balance of funds required to complete the project by the challenge deadline. A list of principal contributors is needed. If building is involved, construction must have begun and the foundation notified of project costs; these costs must be within the available resources. If asset acquisition is involved, the purchase order or similar information must be executed.

Publications: Application Guidelines

Foundation Officials

Thomas R. Brett: assistant secretary, trustee B Oklahoma City, OK 1931. ED University of Oklahoma

BBA (1953); University of Oklahoma LLB (1957); University of Oklahoma JD (1971). PRIM NONPR EMPL federal judge: U.S. District Court, Tulsa. NONPR AFFIL member: Phi Delta Alpha; member: Tulsa County Bar Association; trustee: Oklahoma Bar Foundation; member: Order Coif; member: American Judicature Society; member: Oklahoma Bar Association; fellow: American Bar Foundation; fellow: American College Trial Lawyers.
John H. Conway, Jr.: vice chairman, trustee
James L. Houghton: assistant secretary, trustee ED University of Kansas JD; University of Kansas BS. CORP AFFIL director: Pioneer Natural Resources. NONPR AFFIL member: American Institute of Certified Public Accountants; member: Oklahoma Society of Certified Public Accountants.
James E. Jones: trustee
Dr. Kathleen A. Kastelic: assistant secretary
Joseph G. Mabee: chairman, trustee PRIM CORP EMPL president, director: Mabee Petroleum Corp.
Joseph Guy Mabee, Jr.: trustee
Raymond L. Tullius, Jr.: assistant secretary, trustee NONPR AFFIL member: Oklahoma Society of CPAs.

Grants Analysis

Disclosure Period: fiscal year ending August 31, 2003
Total Grants: $35,541,704*
Number of Grants: 87
Average Grant: $305,736*
Highest Grant: $2,000,000
Lowest Grant: $20,000
Typical Range: $50,000 to $500,000
*Note: Giving excludes United Way. Average grant figure excludes ten highest grants ($12,000,000).

Recent Grants

Note: Grants derived from 2003 Form 990.
General
2,000,000 St. John's Medical Center, Tulsa, OK
2,000,000 Southern Methodist University, Dallas, TX
1,750,000 John Brown University, Siloam Springs, AR
1,500,000 Arkansas Children's Hospital, Little Rock, AR
1,500,000 Central Methodist College, Fayette, MO
1,500,000 Daughters of Charity Health Services, Austin, TX
1,500,000 Ottawa University, Ottawa, KS
1,500,000 Recreation Center for Physically Limited, Tulsa, OK
1,500,000 University of Mary-Hardin Baylor, Belton, TX
1,200,000 Baptist Child & Family Services, San Antonio, TX

JOHN D. AND CATHERINE T. MACARTHUR FOUNDATION

Giving Contact

140 South Dearborn Street
Chicago, IL 60603-5285
Phone: (312)726-8000
Fax: (312)920-6258
E-mail: 4answers@macfound.org
Web: http://www.macfound.org
Note: In Chicago metropolitan area.

Alternate Contact

John D. and Catherine T. MacArthur Foundation
550 Heritage Drive, Suite 160
Jupiter, FL 33458

Phone: (561)626-4800
Fax: (561)624-4948
Note: In the Palm Beach County area.

Description

Founded: 1970
EIN: 237093598
Organization Type: General Purpose Foundation
Giving Locations: FL: Palm Beach County: human and community development grants; IL: Chicago education reform grants, human and community development grants; internationally; nationally; Brazil: global security and sustainability grants; India: global security and sustainability grants; Mexico: global security and sustainability grants; Nigeria: global security and sustainability grants.
Grant Types: Fellowship, General Support, Matching, Multiyear/Continuing Support, Project, Research.

Donor Information

Founder: The foundation was incorporated in 1970 in Illinois, with funds donated by John D. MacArthur. Mr. MacArthur, who died in 1978, built his fortune through the Bankers Life and Casualty Company of Chicago, of which he was the sole owner. He also owned an array of related companies and over 100,000 acres of land, primarily in the Palm Beach, FL, area. He left the assets of his insurance fortune and real estate holdings, ultimately valued at more than $3 billion, to the foundation. His wife, Catherine T. MacArthur, was a board member of both Bankers Life and Casualty and the foundation prior to her death in 1981. Mr. MacArthur left the selection of areas of interest, programs, and guidelines for the foundation entirely up to its board of trustees.

Financial Summary

Total Giving: $194,114,644 (2003); $203,652,697 (2002); $226,600,000 (2001)
Giving Analysis: Giving for 2003 includes: foundation matching gifts ($2,456,582); foundation gifts to individuals ($12,928,200)
Assets: $4,530,410,640 (2003); $3,836,621,632 (2002)

Typical Recipients

Arts & Humanities: Arts Associations & Councils, Arts Centers, Arts Festivals, Arts Funds, Arts Institutes, Community Arts, Dance, Ethnic & Folk Arts, Film & Video, Historic Preservation, History & Archaeology, Libraries, Literary Arts, Museums/Galleries, Music, Opera, Performing Arts, Public Broadcasting, Theater, Visual Arts
Civic & Public Affairs: African American Affairs, Business/Free Enterprise, Civil Rights, Community Foundations, Economic Development, Economic Policy, Employment/Job Training, Civic & Public Affairs-General, Hispanic Affairs, Housing, Law & Justice, Legal Aid, Minority Business, Municipalities/Towns, Nonprofit Management, Philanthropic Organizations, Professional & Trade Associations, Public Policy, Safety, Urban & Community Affairs, Women's Affairs, Zoos/Aquariums
Education: Arts/Humanities Education, Business Education, Colleges & Universities, Economic Education, Education Associations, Education Funds, Education Reform, Environmental Education, Faculty Development, Education-General, Health & Physical Education, International Exchange, International Studies, Journalism/Media Education, Legal Education, Literacy, Medical Education, Minority Education, Public Education (Precollege), Science/Mathematics Education, Social Sciences Education
Environment: Air/Water Quality, Energy, Environment-General, Resource Conservation, Wildlife Protection
Health: Clinics/Medical Centers, Geriatric Health, Health Policy/Cost Containment, Health Organizations, Medical Research, Mental Health, Preventive Medicine/Wellness Organizations, Public Health, Research/Studies Institutes, Single-Disease Health Associations

International: Foreign Educational Institutions, Health Care/Hospitals, Human Rights, International Affairs, International Development, International Environmental Issues, International Organizations, International Peace & Security Issues, International Relations, Missionary/Religious Activities
Religion: Religious Welfare, Seminaries, Social/Policy Issues
Science: Observatories & Planetariums, Scientific Centers & Institutes, Scientific Organizations, Scientific Research
Social Services: Child Welfare, Community Service Organizations, Crime Prevention, Family Planning, Family Services, Senior Services, United Funds/United Ways, Volunteer Services, Youth Organizations

Application Procedures

Initial Contact: Submit a one-page summary accompanied by a two- to three-page letter of inquiry.
Application Requirements: The summary should include information regarding who will carry out the work; name of the organization (and acronym if commonly used); name of parent organization, if applicable; name of chief executive officer or similar person; organization's address, phone number, fax number, and e-mail address; name and title of principal contact person; and web address, if any.
Although the foundation has no set format for letters of inquiry, they should generally include the name or topic of the proposed project; a brief statement (two or three sentences) of the purpose and nature of the proposed work; the significance of the issue addressed and how it relates to a MacArthur program strategy; how the work will address the issue; how the issue relates to the applicant organization; why applicant organization is qualified to undertake the project; geographic area or country where the work will take place; time period for which funding is requested; information about those who will be helped by and interested in the work and how you will communicate with them; amount requested; and total estimated cost. The foundation welcomes attachments that the applicant feels will help the foundation understand the proposal.
Deadlines: None for most grant programs. However, the Special Grant Competitions do have varying deadlines; contact the Office of Grants Management for further information.
Review Process: Applicants will be acknowledged promptly.
Notes: Letters of Inquiry may be submitted by mail or may be emailed to: LOI@macfound.org. Faxed inquiries are not accepted.

Restrictions

The foundation does not support political activities or attempts to influence action on specific legislation, nor does it provide scholarships. Annual fundraising drives, institutional benefits, honorary functions, or similar projects are not supported.

Additional Information

Although not a prerequisite, the Foundation explores the possibility of including support for communications as part of the consideration of all proposals and welcomes proposals that have incorporated communication plans.
Publications: Annual Report; Programs and Policies; Individual Booklets Concerning Each Program as Well as Program-Related Investments

Foundation Officials

Lloyd Axworthy: director ED United College BA (1961); Princeton University MA (1963); Princeton University PhD (1972). PRIM NONPR EMPL director Liu Centre Study Global Issues: University of British Columbia. NONPR AFFIL board of directors: Pacific Council on International Policy; president: University Winnipeg; director: Liu Centre for the Study of Global Issues; board of directors: Human Rights Watch; board of directors: Lester B. Pearson College; board

of directors: College of the Arctic.
Herman Brewer: program director ED Illinois Institute of Technology BA.
John Seely Brown: director ED Brown University BA (1962); University of Michigan MS (1964); University of Michigan PhD (1972). CORP AFFIL director: Varian Medical Systems; director: Corning Inc.; director: Polycom Inc. NONPR AFFIL trustee: Brown University; trustee: In-Q-Tel.
Drew Saunders Days, III: director B Atlanta, GA August 29, 1941. ED Hamilton College BA (1963); Yale University LLB (1966). PRIM NONPR EMPL Alfred M. Rankin Professor of Law: Yale University, Law School. NONPR AFFIL member: U.S. Citizen Committee Monitor Helsinki Accords; solicitor general: U.S. Department Justice; director, member executive committee: Lawyers Committee Civil Rights Under Law; member: American Law Institute; member: Council on Foreign Relations.
Robert E. Denham: director B Abilene, TX. ED Harvard University MA; Harvard University JD; Harvard University JD; University of Texas BA (1966). PRIM CORP EMPL attorney: Munger, Tolles & Olson LLP. CORP AFFIL drc: Wesco Financial Corp.; director: U.S. Trust Co.; director: Fomento Economico Mexicano S.A. de CV; director: Lucent Technologies Inc. NONPR AFFIL chairman, president: Financial Accounting Foundation.
Jonathan Foster Fanton: president, director B Mobile, AL 1943. ED Yale University BA (1965); Yale University MA (1977); Yale University PhD (1978). NONPR AFFIL trustee: New York Commission Inc. Colleges & Universities; co-chairman: Taynbee Foundation; director: Living Cities; chairman: Helsinki Watch Committee; co-chairman: International Committee Academic Freedom; member: Council Foreign Relations; board directors: Foundation Civil Society; member: American Historical Association; board directors: American Ditchley Foundation. CLUB AFFIL Economic Club.
Mark D. Fitzsimmons: associate director fellows program
William H. Foege, MD: director B Decorah, IA 1936. ED Pacific Lutheran University BA (1957); University of Washington MD (1961); Harvard University MPh (1965); Harvard University MPH (1965). PRIM NONPR EMPL distinguished professor: Emory University, Rollins School Public Health. NONPR AFFIL director: Kaiser Foundation Hospitals; director: Kaiser Permanente; department field coord: International Red Cross Joint Relief Action; director: Kaiser Foundation Health Plan.
Jamie Gorelick: director B New York, NY August 19. ED Harvard University JD; Harvard University BA. PRIM CORP EMPL vice chair: Fannie Mae. CORP AFFIL partner: Wilmer, Cutler, Pickering, Hale & Dorr; director: Schlumberger Ltd.; director: United Technologies Corp. NONPR AFFIL director: Washington Legal Clinic for Homeless; member: Women's Bar Association; member: National Women's Law Center; member: National Legal Center Public Interest; director: National Park Foundation; director: Local Initiatives Support Corp.; member: National Community Support Law Enforcement; board of overseers: Harvard University; member: Council Foreign Relations; member: District of Columbia College Access; member: Bazelon Center Mental Health Law; director: Carnegie Endowment for International Peace; director: American Promise - Alliance for Youth; fellow: American Bar Foundation; member: American Law Institute; member: 9/11 Commission.
Mary Graham: director PRIM NONPR EMPL research fellow: Harvard University, Kennedy School Government. NONPR AFFIL visiting fellow: Brookings Institution; co-director, transparency project: Kennedy School of Government, Harvard University.
Judith F. Helzner: director population & reprod health ED Tufts University BA; University of Pennsylvania MS.
John Paul Holdren: director B Sewickley, PA 1944. ED Massachusetts Institute of Technology SB (1965); Massachusetts Institute of Technology SM

(1966); Stanford University PhD (1970). NONPR AFFIL member: President Committee Advisory Science & Technology; chairman, member executive committee: Pugwash Conference Science & World Affairs; member: National Academy Sciences; professor envir policy: Harvard University; consult: Lawrence Livermore National Laboratory; member: Federation American Scientists; chairman: Committee on International Security & Arms Control; chairman: Committee on International Security and Arms Control; member: California Academy Sciences; fellow: American Association Advancement Science; member: American Physics Society; fellow: American Academy of Arts & Sciences.

Richard J. Kaplan: assistant vice president institutional research & grants management CLUB AFFIL pres: Standard Club.

Sara Lawrence Lightfoot: chairman, director ED Harvard University EdD. PRIM NONPR EMPL professor: Harvard University, Graduate School of Education. NONPR AFFIL director: Bright Horizons Childrens Centers; professor: Harvard University.

Susan E. Manske: vice president, chief investment officer ED Marquette University MBA; University of Wisconsin, Milwaukee BA. NONPR AFFIL director: Educational District 181 Foundation; member: Investment board of United Way.

Dr. Walter Eugene Massey: director B Hattiesburg, MS April 05, 1938. ED Morehouse College BS (1958); Washington University PhD (1966); Washington University MA (1966); Washington University PHD (1966). PRIM NONPR EMPL president: Morehouse College. CORP AFFIL director: McDonalds Corp.; director: Motorola Inc.; director: Conoco Corp.; director: BankAmerica Corp.; director: BP Amoco Corp. NONPR AFFIL member: Sigma Xi; member: United Way of Chicago; trustee: Rand Corp.; president: Morehouse College; member: National Science Foundation; president: American Association Advancement Science.

Mario J. Molina: director B Mexico City, Mexico. ED Universidad Nacional Autonoma de Mexico BS (1965); University of California at Berkeley PhD (1972). PRIM NONPR EMPL institute professor: Massachusetts Institute Technology. NONPR AFFIL member: Pontifical Academy of Sciences; member: US National Academy of Sciences; member: Institute of Medicine; professor: MIT.

Mary E. Petrites: grant administrator

George A. Ranney, Jr.: director B Chicago, IL 1940. ED Harvard University BA (1962); University of Chicago JD (1966). PRIM CORP EMPL partner: Mayer, Brown & Platt PRIM NONPR EMPL president, chief executive officer: Chicago Metropolis 2020. NONPR AFFIL chairman: Task Force on the Future of Illinois; trustee: University Chicago; member: Commerce Counsel Network; trustee: Newberry Library; past president: Chicago Metropolis 2020; trustee: Chicago Public Television; member: American Bar Association; member: Chicago Bar Association.

Elspeth Revere: director general program

J. Stephen Richards: grant department administrator ED Carleton University BA (1979).

Daniel J. Socolow: director fellows program

Thomas Charles Theobald: director B Cincinnati, OH 1937. ED College of the Holy Cross BA (1958); Harvard University MBA (1960). PRIM CORP EMPL partner: Blair Capital Partners, LLC. CORP AFFIL director: Ventas Inc.; chairman: Columbia Funds; director: Jones Lange LaSalle Inc.; director: Ambac Financial Group Inc.; director: Anixter International Inc. NONPR AFFIL life trustee: Northwestern University; trustee: Northwestern University; member commission architecture: Art Institute of Chicago.

Marc P. Yanchura: treasurer

Grants Analysis
Disclosure Period: calendar year ending 2003
Total Grants: $178,729,862*
Number of Grants: 1,640 (approx)
Average Grant: $97,822*
Highest Grant: $18,400,000

Lowest Grant: $2,500
Typical Range: $50,000 to $500,000
***Note:** Giving excludes gifts to individuals; matching gifts. Average grant figure excludes highest grant.

Recent Grants
Note: Grants derived from 2001 Form 990.
General

2,650,000 Social Science Research Council, New York, NY -- for training and research fellowships program on global security and cooperation

2,500,000 Conservation International Foundation, Washington, DC -- for creation of the critical Ecosystems Partnership Fund

2,296,000 Conservation International Foundation, Washington, DC -- towards conservation of threatened areas that are rich in biodiversity

2,240,000 Judge David L. Bazelon Center for Mental Health Law, Washington, DC -- towards endowment fund

2,240,000 Metropolitan Planning Council, Chicago, IL -- towards endowment fund

1,560,000 President and Fellows of Harvard College, Boston, MA -- for the Project on Human Development in Chicago Neighborhoods

1,500,000 Chicago Community Foundation, Chicago, IL -- to support the design and delivery of effective social services

1,380,000 Regents of the University of Michigan, Ann Arbor, MI -- for the Network on Successful Paths through middle Childhood Program

1,370,000 Temple University, Philadelphia, PA -- for the Network on Adolescent Development and Juvenile Justice program

1,220,000 Washington University, St. Louis, MO -- for Network on the Family and the Economy program

JOSIAH MACY, JR. FOUNDATION

Giving Contact
Martha Wolfgang, Vice President & Treasurer
44 East 64th Street
New York, NY 10021
Phone: (212)486-2424
Fax: (212)644-0765
E-mail: jmacyinfo@josiahmacyfoundation.org
Web: http://www.josiahmacyfoundation.org/jmacy1.html

Description
Founded: 1930
EIN: 135596895
Organization Type: General Purpose Foundation
Giving Locations: nationally.
Grant Types: Conference/Seminar, Project.

Donor Information
Founder: Established in 1930 by Mrs. Kate Macy Ladd (1863-1945) in honor of her father. The Macy family made its fortune in the whaling industry, shipping (both coastal and transoceanic), and oil. Mrs. Ladd directed the foundation to devote its attention to the advancement of medicine and health in the United States and abroad.

Financial Summary
Total Giving: $5,181,077 (fiscal year ending June 30, 2004); $7,251,917 (fiscal 2001)
Giving Analysis: Giving for fiscal 2004 includes: foundation matching gifts ($359,177) fiscal 2001: foundation matching gifts ($273,045)

Assets: $148,124,330 (fiscal 2004); $164,169,681 (fiscal 2001)

Typical Recipients
Arts & Humanities: Film & Video, Historic Preservation, Libraries, Museums/Galleries, Public Broadcasting

Civic & Public Affairs: Economic Policy, Civic & Public Affairs-General, Housing, Law & Justice, Nonprofit Management, Philanthropic Organizations, Public Policy, Women's Affairs

Education: Business Education, Colleges & Universities, Education Reform, Faculty Development, Gifted & Talented Programs, Health & Physical Education, Medical Education, Minority Education, Public Education (Precollege), Science/Mathematics Education, Social Sciences Education, Student Aid

Health: AIDS/HIV, Cancer, Children's Health/Hospitals, Clinics/Medical Centers, Health-General, Health Policy/Cost Containment, Health Funds, Health Organizations, Hospitals, Hospitals (University Affiliated), Medical Research, Medical Training, Nursing Services, Public Health, Single-Disease Health Associations

International: Foreign Educational Institutions, Health Care/Hospitals, Human Rights, International Development, International Relief Efforts

Religion: Religion-General, Social/Policy Issues

Science: Scientific Centers & Institutes, Scientific Labs

Social Services: Family Planning, Family Services, Substance Abuse

Application Procedures
Initial Contact: Send a full proposal.
Application Requirements: Brief summary should include the name of the sponsoring organization or institution, description of the project, names and qualifications of the persons in charge of the project, expected costs and duration of the project (including an itemized budget), letter of endorsement from the head of the sponsoring organization, and proof of current tax-exempt status.
Deadlines: None.
Review Process: Proposals are evaluated on their relevance to the foundation's current programs, the likelihood of the project's continued success after foundation support ceases, and the grantee's record of achievement in the proposed area of endeavor.

Restrictions
Grants are not made to individuals. The foundation does not fund medical research, general support, or construction or renovation projects.

Additional Information
The foundation also sponsors conferences and seminars/workshops.
Publications: Annual Report; Occasional Monographs

Foundation Officials
Lawrence Kimball Altman, MD: director B Quincy, MA 1937. ED Harvard University AB (1958); Tufts University MD (1962). PRIM CORP EMPL medicine corr columnist: New York Times Co. PRIM NONPR EMPL associate professor medicine: New York University. NONPR AFFIL fellow: New YorkAcademy of Medicine; member: Society Epidemiology; associate professor medicine: New York University; member: American Society Tropical Medicine Hygiene; member: National Academy of Sciences Institute Medicine; fellow: American College Epidemiology; fellow: American College Physicians; member: American Board Medicine Specialties. CLUB AFFIL Century Club; Harvard Club.

Louis Stanton Auchincloss: honorary director B Lawrence, NY September 27, 1917. ED Yale University (1939); University of Virginia LLB (1941). NONPR AFFIL member: Century Association; chairman: Museum City New York; member: American Academy of Arts & Letters; member: Association Bar New York

City.

John Carter Bacot: director B Utica, NY 1933. ED Hamilton College AB (1955); Cornell University LLB (1958). CORP AFFIL director: Time Warner Inc.; director: Venator Group Inc.; director: Centennial Insurance Co.; director: Phoenix Home Life Mutual Insurance Co.; director: Atlantic Reinsurance Co.; director: Associates First Capital Corp.; trustee: Atlantic Mutual Insurance Co. NONPR AFFIL member: New York State Bar Association; member: Pilgrims U.S.; chairman, trustee: New York Clearing House Association; director: Federal Reserve Bank New York; chairman board trustees: Hamilton College; member: Association Reserve City Bankers; member: Council Foreign Relations. CLUB AFFIL Montclair Golf Club; Union Club; Economic Club New York; The Links Club.

Jordan J. Cohen, MD: director

E. Virgil Conway: director

Rina Forlini: secretary

John W. Frymoyer, MD: director PRIM CORP EMPL dean: University of Vermont College Medicine. CORP AFFIL president, chief executive officer, director: Medical Center Hospital Vermont; president, chief executive officer, director: University Health Center; president, chief executive officer, director: Fanny Allen Hospital; president, chief executive officer, director: Fletcher Allen Health Care.

S. Parker Gilbert: director B New York, NY 1933. ED Yale University BA (1956). CORP AFFIL director: Taubman Centers Inc.; director: Burlington Resources Inc.; advisory director: Morgan Stanley Group Inc. NONPR AFFIL member: Better Business Bureau; president board trustee: Pierpont Morgan Library.

Patricia Albjerg Graham: director

Bernard W. Harleston: director

Dr. Arthur H. Hayes, Jr.: director B Highland Park, MI 1933. ED University of Santa Clara AB (1955); Oxford University MA (1957); Georgetown University (1957-1960); Cornell University MD (1964). PRIM CORP EMPL president: MediSci Associates. CORP AFFIL director: Myriad Genetics Inc.; director: Napro Biotherapeutics Inc.; director: Celgene Corp. NONPR AFFIL board regents: Santa Clara University; member: Sigma Xi; member editorial board: Prescribers Newsletter; fellow: Royal Society Medicine; director: Peace Foundation; member: Phi Beta Kappa; professor: New York Medicine College; fellow: New York Academy Medicine; member: New York Academy Science; member: Medical Society New York State; fellow: College Physicians Philadelphia; member: Harvey Society; member, council deans, council academic socs: Association American Medical Colleges; honorary member: American Pharmacological Association; member: American Society Clinical Pharmacology & Therapeutics; member: American Federation Clinical Research; member: American Medical Association; fellow: American College Cardiology; fellow: American College Chest Physicians; fellow: American Academy Pharmacy Physicians; member: Alpha Omega Alpha; member: Alpha Sigma Nu; fellow: Academy Pharmacology Scientists.

John Jay Iselin, PhD: director B Greenville, SC 1933. ED Harvard University AB (1956); Cambridge University Corpus Christi College BA (1958); Cambridge University Corpus Christi College MA (1963); Harvard University PhD (1965). PRIM CORP EMPL president: Cooper Union for the Advancement of Science & Art. NONPR AFFIL member: Ventures Education; member: Waterford Institute; trustee: Public Education Association; member: Council Foreign Relations; member: National Geographic Society; member: Academy Political Science; member: American Friends University Cambridge. CLUB AFFIL Metro District of Columbia Club; Century Club; Harvard Club New York.

David Lincoln Luke, III: honorary director B Tyrone, PA 1923. ED Yale University AB (1945). NONPR AFFIL trustee emeritus: Cold Spring Harbor Laboratory; trustee emeritus: Hotchkiss School. CLUB AFFIL River Club; Megantic Fish & Game Club; Piping Rock Club; Johns Island Club.

Mary Patterson McPherson, PhD: director B Abington, PA 1935. ED Smith College AB (1957); University of Delaware MA (1960); Bryn Mawr College PHD (1969). member: American Academy of Arts & Sciences NONPR AFFIL member: American Philosophical Society; director: Philadelphia Contributionship. CLUB AFFIL Cosmopolitan Club.

Clarence F. Michalis: chairman, director B New York, NY 1922. ED Harvard University BS (1944). CORP AFFIL director: Schroeder Capital Funds. NONPR AFFIL trustee: Cooper Union; honorary chairman, trustee: Saint Lukes Roosevelt Hospital Center. CLUB AFFIL Masons Club.

June Elaine Osborn, MD: president, director B Endicott, NY 1937. ED Oberlin College BA (1957); Case Western Reserve University MD (1961). PRIM NONPR EMPL professor: University of Michigan. NONPR AFFIL member: National Vaccine Advisory Centre; professor emerita: University Michigan School Public Health & Medical School; member: National Institute on Drug Abuse; fellow: Infectious Diseases Society America; member: Institute Medicine; member: American Association Immunologists; director: Corporate Supportive Housing; fellow: American Academy Pediatrics; fellow: American Academy of Arts & Sciences; fellow: American Academy Microbiology.

Martha Wolfgang: vice president, treasurer

Grants Analysis

Disclosure Period: fiscal year ending June 30, 2004
Total Grants: $4,821,900*
Number of Grants: 40
Average Grant: $112,255*
Highest Grant: $443,948
Lowest Grant: $3,000
Typical Range: $50,000 to $200,000
*Note: Giving excludes matching gifts. Average grant figure excludes highest grant.

Recent Grants

Note: Grants derived from fiscal 2003 Form 990.
General

1,000,002	Columbia University Mailman School of Public Health, New York, NY
468,000	University of California Los Angeles School of Medicine, Los Angeles, CA
450,000	Institute of Medicine of the National Academics, Washington, DC
351,970	University of Pennsylvania School of Medicine, Philadelphia, PA
314,000	Associated Medical Schools, New York, NY
270,911	University of Washington, Seattle, WA
269,525	Case Western Reserve University, Cleveland, OH
243,161	University of Pennsylvania, Philadelphia, PA
225,143	Massachusetts Institute of Technology, Cambridge, MA
179,824	University of California San Francisco, San Francisco, CA

MACY'S EAST INC.

Company Headquarters

151 W. 34th St.
New York, NY 10001
Web: http://www.macys.com

Company Description

Revenue: US$4.943 billion (2001)
Employees: 33200 (2001)
SIC(s): 5311 Department Stores.
Parent Company: Federated Department Stores Inc., 7 W. Seventh St., Cincinnati, OH, United States

Operating Locations

Bloomingdale's (NY--New York); Bon Marche (WA--Seattle); Burdines (FL--Miami); Federated Department Stores, Inc. (OH--Cincinnati); Macy's East Inc. (CA--Los Angeles, Newark, San Francisco, San Jose, Sunnyvale; GA--Decatur; KS--Mission; NJ--Cranford, Lawrenceville, Paramus; NY--Bay Shore, Brooklyn); Rich's/Lazarus/Goldsmith's (GA--Atlanta); Stern's Department Stores (NJ--Paramus)

Giving Contact

Tom Zapf, Director, Consumer Affairs & Charitable Contributions
151 West 34th Street, Room 1825
New York, NY 10001
Phone: (212)494-5669

Description

Organization Type: Corporate Giving Program
Giving Locations: company operating locations.
Grant Types: Employee Matching Gifts, General Support, Project.

Financial Summary

Total Giving: Contributes through corporate direct giving program only.

Typical Recipients

Arts & Humanities: Arts Associations & Councils, Arts Centers, Arts Festivals, Arts Funds, Arts Institutes, Community Arts, Dance, Historic Preservation, Libraries, Literary Arts, Museums/Galleries, Music, Opera, Performing Arts, Public Broadcasting, Visual Arts

Civic & Public Affairs: Business/Free Enterprise, Civil Rights, Economic Policy, Employment/Job Training, Law & Justice, Legal Aid, Professional & Trade Associations, Public Policy, Safety, Urban & Community Affairs, Women's Affairs, Zoos/Aquariums

Education: Business Education, Colleges & Universities, Community & Junior Colleges, Continuing Education, Economic Education, Education Funds, Legal Education, Medical Education, Minority Education, Private Education (Precollege), Social Sciences Education, Special Education

Health: Emergency/Ambulance Services, Health Funds, Health Organizations, Hospitals, Medical Rehabilitation, Medical Research, Medical Training, Mental Health, Public Health

Social Services: Child Welfare, Community Centers, Community Service Organizations, Counseling, Delinquency & Criminal Rehabilitation, Emergency Relief, Homes, People with Disabilities, Recreation & Athletics, Senior Services, Substance Abuse, United Funds/United Ways, Volunteer Services, Youth Organizations

Application Procedures

Initial Contact: letter and proposal
Application Requirements: a description of organization, amount requested, purpose of funds sought, recently audited financial statement, last year's operating budget, list of major corporate contributors, copy of IRS determination letter
Deadlines: None.
Decision Notification: notification of funding decision will be made in writing
Notes: The company is unable to provide a status report on applications.

Restrictions

No merchandise, fashion shows, individuals, per answering machine message.

Additional Information

Although the company is now in Chapter 11, it is continuing its contributions. However, requests are being reviewed more carefully.
The company's objective is to donate 1% of pretax earnings to charitable activities.

Corporate Officials

James E. Gray: president, chief operating officer PRIM CORP EMPL president, chief operating officer: Macy's East Inc.

Giving Program Officials

Edward Jay Goldberg: vice president PRIM CORP EMPL vice president consumer affairs: R.H. Macy & Co. Inc.

J. F. MADDOX FOUNDATION

Giving Contact

Robert J. Reid, Executive Director
J.F. Maddox Foundation
PO Box 2588
Hobbs, NM 88241-2588
Phone: (505)393-6338
Fax: (505)397-7266
E-mail: bobreid@leaco.net
Web: http://www.jfmaddox.org/

Description

Founded: 1963
EIN: 756023767
Organization Type: General Purpose Foundation
Giving Locations: NM: Southeast New Mexico; TX: West Texas
Grant Types: Capital, Emergency, General Support, Loan, Matching, Project, Scholarship.
Note: Preference to capital programs and one-time programs.

Donor Information

Founder: The foundation was established in 1963 by the late J. F. Maddox and the late Mabel S. Maddox.

Financial Summary

Total Giving: $5,577,385 (2002); $6,433,159 (2001)
Giving Analysis: Giving for 2002 includes: foundation grants to United Way ($132,684); foundation scholarships ($1,053,664) 2001: foundation grants to United Way ($187,352)
Assets: $137,379,345 (2002); $157,524,045 (2001). Note: NOTE: In 1998 the foundation moved from a fiscal year ending on June 30 to a calendar year.

Typical Recipients

Arts & Humanities: Arts & Humanities-General, Libraries, Museums/Galleries, Music, Opera, Performing Arts, Public Broadcasting, Theater
Civic & Public Affairs: Botanical Gardens/Parks, Community Foundations, Employment/Job Training, Civic & Public Affairs-General, Hispanic Affairs, Housing, Law & Justice, Legal Aid, Municipalities/Towns, Nonprofit Management, Parades/Festivals, Professional & Trade Associations, Safety, Urban & Community Affairs, Zoos/Aquariums
Education: Arts/Humanities Education, Colleges & Universities, Community & Junior Colleges, Education Associations, Education Funds, Education Reform, Engineering/Technological Education, Education-General, Leadership Training, Literacy, Private Education (Precollege), Public Education (Precollege), Science/Mathematics Education, Student Aid
Environment: Environment-General, Resource Conservation
Health: Alzheimer's Disease, Cancer, Diabetes, Emergency/Ambulance Services, Hospices, Hospitals, Hospitals (University Affiliated), Nursing Services, Nutrition
International: Missionary/Religious Activities
Religion: Churches, Religion-General, Jewish Causes, Ministries, Religious Organizations, Religious Welfare
Social Services: At-Risk Youth, Child Abuse, Child

Welfare, Community Centers, Community Service Organizations, Counseling, Crime Prevention, Day Care, Domestic Violence, Emergency Relief, Family Services, Food/Clothing Distribution, Homes, People with Disabilities, Recreation & Athletics, Scouts, Senior Services, Shelters/Homelessness, Social Services-General, Substance Abuse, United Funds/United Ways, Youth Organizations

Application Procedures

Initial Contact: Potential applicants should request guidelines before making formal proposals.
Application Requirements: The foundation will request further information if the proposal is considered to fall within the scope of the foundation. Include description of agency, list of agency's directors, officers, and key managers, description of proposed project, proof of tax-exempt status, and the agency's prior years Form 990
Deadlines: None.

Restrictions

The foundation does not ordinarily approve grants for individuals, operating budgets, other foundations, or endowment funds. Funding is restricted to Southeast New Mexico and Texas. The student loan and scholarship programs are limited to students in Lea County, New Mexico.

Additional Information

The foundation reports that projects that are ongoing must have a high probability of self-sustaining capability within a defined time frame in order to be funded.
Publications: Application Guidelines; Annual Report; Student Loan application form.

Foundation Officials

Harry H. Lynch: director B 1939. PRIM CORP EMPL principal: Sun Valley Partners Ltd. ADD CORP EMPL president: Lynch Properties Inc.; chairman, director: Sun Valley Fruit Co. Inc. CORP AFFIL director: Fleetwood Transportation Services.
Don Maddox: vice president PRIM CORP EMPL director: Maddox Law Firm PC. CORP AFFIL director: Southwest Public Service Co.
James M. Maddox: president
Thomas M. Maddox: director
Robert J. Reid: executive director
Ann M. Utterback: director

Grants Analysis

Disclosure Period: calendar year ending 2002
Total Grants: $4,391,037*
Number of Grants: 174
Average Grant: $16,433*
Highest Grant: $1,548,161
Lowest Grant: $100
Typical Range: $5,000 to $30,000
*Note: Giving excludes United Way; scholarships. Average grant figure excludes highest grant.

Recent Grants

Note: Grants derived from 2002 Form 990.
Library-Related

92,980	Estacado Library Information Network, Hobbs, NM

General

1,548,161	College of the Southwest, Hobbs, NM
951,733	College of the Southwest, Hobbs, NM
575,000	Hobbs Municipal Schools, Hobbs, NM -- fund towards 'advanced placement (AP)' program
281,004	Hobbs Municipal Schools, Hobbs, NM -- fund towards 'core knowledge (grade K-6)'
200,000	Lea County Community Improvement Corporation, Hobbs, NM
103,699	College of the Southwest, Hobbs, NM
91,677	United Way of Lea County, Hobbs, NM
90,061	Southwest Symphony Inc., Hobbs, NM
74,179	College of the Southwest, Hobbs, NM -- fund towards distinguished lecture series (2002)
65,000	Lea County Community Improvement Corporation, Hobbs, NM -- fund towards economic assessment study

MAGNA INTERNATIONAL OF AMERICA INC.

Company Headquarters

600 Wilshire Drive
Troy, MI 48084
Web: http://www.magnaint.com

Company Description

Former Name: Douglas & Lomason Co.
Revenue: US$120 million (2001)
Employees: 400 (2001)
SIC(s): 3465 Automotive Stampings, 3714 Motor Vehicle Parts & Accessories.
Parent Company: Magna International Inc., 337 Magna Dr., Aurora, ON, Canada

Operating Locations

Bloomington-Normal Seating Co. (IL--Normal); Chantland Co. Division (IA--Humboldt); Douglas & Lomason Co. (AR--Marianna; GA--Carrollton; IA--Red Oak; MO--Excelsior Springs, Troy; NE--Columbus; TN--Milan; TX--Del Rio); Magna International of America (MI--Southfield); Magna Lomason Corp. (AR--Marianna; GA--Carrollton, Columbus, La Grange; IL--Normal; IA--Humboldt, Red Oak; MI--Farmington Hills; MS--Amory; MO--Kansas City, Troy; NE--Columbus; TX--Del Rio)

Nonmonetary Support

Type: Donated Products; Workplace Solicitation

Giving Contact

Dick Banfield, President
24600 Hallwood Ct.
Farmington Hills, MI 48335-1671
Phone: (248)478-7800

Description

Organization Type: Corporate Giving Program
Giving Locations: MI
Grant Types: Capital, Challenge, Emergency, General Support, Operating Expenses, Project, Research, Scholarship.

Typical Recipients

Arts & Humanities: Arts Associations & Councils, Arts Institutes, Arts & Humanities-General, Historic Preservation, Libraries, Museums/Galleries, Music, Opera, Public Broadcasting, Theater
Civic & Public Affairs: Business/Free Enterprise, Economic Development, Civic & Public Affairs-General, Professional & Trade Associations, Public Policy, Safety, Urban & Community Affairs, Zoos/Aquariums
Education: Business Education, Colleges & Universities, Community & Junior Colleges, Education Associations, Engineering/Technological Education, Education-General, Minority Education
Health: Eyes/Blindness, Health-General, Hospices, Hospitals, Medical Research, Mental Health, Single-Disease Health Associations
Science: Science Exhibits & Fairs
Social Services: Animal Protection, Child Welfare, Community Centers, Community Service Organizations, Family Services, Recreation & Athletics, United Funds/United Ways, Volunteer Services, Youth Organizations

Application Procedures

Initial Contact: Send a full proposal. Include a description of organization, amount requested, purpose of funds sought, recently audited financial statements, proof of tax-exempt status, and how support benefits company associates.
Deadlines: None.

Restrictions

Does not support individuals, religious organizations for sectarian purposes, or political or lobbying groups.

Corporate Officials

Dick Banfield: president PRIM CORP EMPL president: Magna Lomason Corp.

Grants Analysis

Typical Range: $500 to $1,000
Note: A more recent grants list was unavailable.

Recent Grants

Note: Grants derived from fiscal 1996 grants list.
GeneralBoy Scouts of America, Detroit, MIDetroit Historical Society, Detroit, MIDetroit Institute of Arts, Detroit, MIDetroit Institute for Children, Detroit, MIDetroit Symphony Orchestra, Detroit, MIFarmington Philharmonic, Farmington, MIGirl Scouts Council of Michigan, Pontiac, MIMichigan Opera Theater, Detroit, MIYMCA Farmington, Farmington, MIConcerned Citizens for Arts, Detroit, MI

CHESLEY G. MAGRUDER FOUNDATION

Giving Contact

Board of Trustees
c/o SunTrust
PO Box 3838
Orlando, FL 32802
Phone: (407)237-5319
Fax: (407)237-5346

Description

Founded: 1979
EIN: 591920736
Organization Type: Private Foundation
Giving Locations: FL: emphasis is on central FL
Grant Types: General Support, Multiyear/Continuing Support.

Donor Information

Founder: Chesley G. Magruder Trust

Financial Summary

Total Giving: $785,200 (fiscal year ending June 30, 2001)
Assets: $14,791,092 (fiscal 2001)

Typical Recipients

Arts & Humanities: Arts Associations & Councils, Dance, Historic Preservation, History & Archaeology, Libraries, Museums/Galleries, Opera, Public Broadcasting, Theater
Civic & Public Affairs: Clubs, Employment/Job Training, Civic & Public Affairs-General, Housing, Safety, Zoos/Aquariums
Education: Business Education, Colleges & Universities, Community & Junior Colleges, Education-General, Literacy, Preschool Education, Private Education (Precollege), Vocational & Technical Education
Environment: Resource Conservation
Health: Alzheimer's Disease, Cancer, Clinics/Medical Centers, Eyes/Blindness, Health-General, Geriatric Health, Health Organizations, Hospices, Hospitals, Kidney, Single-Disease Health Associa-

tions
Religion: Churches, Ministries, Religious Organizations, Religious Welfare
Science: Scientific Centers & Institutes
Social Services: Camps, Child Welfare, Community Centers, Community Service Organizations, Counseling, Crime Prevention, Day Care, Emergency Relief, Family Planning, Family Services, Food/Clothing Distribution, Scouts, YMCA/YWCA/YMHA/YWHA, Youth Organizations

Application Procedures

Initial Contact: Request application guidelines and grant proposal form.

Restrictions

Does not support individuals.

Additional Information

Publications: Application Guidelines; Grant Proposal Form
Trust(s): Suntrust Bank, Central Florida, NA

Foundation Officials

Robert N. Blackford: trustee
Leon Hunter Handley: trustee B Lakeland, FL 1927. ED University of Florida BSBA (1949). PRIM CORP EMPL president: Gurney & Handley. CORP AFFIL director: Claude H Wolfe; director: Mine & Mill Supply Co.; director: Southern Industries Savings Bank; chairman, director: Beneficial Savings Bank. NONPR AFFIL member: Trial Attorneys America; chairman, trustee: WMFE-TV; membere: Shriners; member: Rotary; member: Scottish Rite; member: Phi Kappa Phi; member: Press Society; director: Orlando/Tampa; member: Phi Delta Phi; member: Masons; member: Orange County Bar Association; member: Intl Associate Defense Counsel; member: Florida Bar Association; member: Florida Blue Key; director: Cracker Groves; member: Fed Insurance & Corp. Counsel; member: Beta Gamma Sigma; general counsel, life director: Central Florida Fair; member: American Judicature Society; member: Association Defense Trial Attys; fellow: American College Trial Lawyers; nen: American Board Trial Advocates; member: American Board Trial Attys; member: Alpha Tau Omega; member: American Bar Association; member: Alpha Kappa Psi. CLUB AFFIL University Club; Orlando Country Club; Travelers Club; Century Club; Citrus Club.
Dr. Allen R. Holcomb: trustee
Ernest M. Kelly: trustee
Dr. G. Brock Magruder: trustee

Grants Analysis

Disclosure Period: fiscal year ending June 30, 2001
Total Grants: $785,200
Number of Grants: 64
Average Grant: $12,269
Highest Grant: $50,000
Lowest Grant: $3,657
Typical Range: $5,000 to $25,000

Recent Grants

Note: Grants derived from fiscal 2002 Form 990.
General

30,000	St. John Lutheran Church, New Orleans, LA
25,000	Christ School
25,000	Downtown Orlando YMCA Family Center
25,000	Health Alliance Campaign
25,000	Orlando Museum of Art, Orlando, FL
25,000	Orlando Science Center, Orlando, FL
25,000	Rollins College, Winter Park, FL
20,000	Edgewood Children's Ranch, Orlando, FL
20,000	Habitat for Humanity of Greater Orlando, Orlando, FL
13,000	Boy Scouts of America Central Florida Council, Orlando, FL

A. L. MAILMAN FAMILY FOUNDATION

Giving Contact

Luba H. Lynch, Executive Director
707 Westchester Avenue
White Plains, NY 10604
Phone: (914)683-8089
Fax: (914)686-5519
E-mail: almf@mailman.org
Web: http://www.mailman.org

Description

Founded: 1980
EIN: 510203866
Organization Type: Family Foundation
Giving Locations: nationally.
Grant Types: Project, Research.

Donor Information

Founder: The foundation was created by the late Abraham L. Mailman and the Mailman Foundation, Inc. A. L. Mailman was a financier from Hollywood, FL, who had a lifelong commitment to philanthropy. In 1943, with his brother Joseph, A. L. Mailman established the Mailman Foundation, which supported universities, hospitals, and Jewish causes in the United States and Israel. The brothers also contributed to the Mailman Child Development Center at the University of Miami, The Mailman Family Center at Nova Southeastern University, and the Mailman Research Center at McLean Hospital.
The A. L. Mailman Family Foundation was established in 1980 when the assets of the original Mailman Foundation were divided between the families of the two brothers. Marilyn M. Segal, A. L. Mailman's daughter, then became the chairman of the foundation and continued her father's philanthropic tradition.

Financial Summary

Total Giving: $1,532,569 (2001)
Assets: $25,869,540 (2001)
Gifts Received: $5,052 (1993); $15,000 (1992)

Typical Recipients

Arts & Humanities: Arts Centers, History & Archaeology, Libraries, Museums/Galleries, Music, Performing Arts, Public Broadcasting
Civic & Public Affairs: African American Affairs, Civil Rights, Community Foundations, Economic Development, Economic Policy, Civic & Public Affairs-General, Hispanic Affairs, Housing, Law & Justice, Municipalities/Towns, Philanthropic Organizations, Professional & Trade Associations, Public Policy, Urban & Community Affairs, Women's Affairs, Zoos/Aquariums
Education: Arts/Humanities Education, Colleges & Universities, Continuing Education, Education Associations, Education Reform, Education-General, Health & Physical Education, International Studies, Leadership Training, Medical Education, Preschool Education, Public Education (Precollege), Religious Education, Social Sciences Education, Vocational & Technical Education
Environment: Environment-General
Health: Alzheimer's Disease, Cancer, Children's Health/Hospitals, Clinics/Medical Centers, Health Organizations, Mental Health, Nutrition, Prenatal Health Issues, Public Health, Research/Studies Institutes
International: Health Care/Hospitals, International Development, International Relief Efforts
Religion: Jewish Causes, Religious Welfare, Social/Policy Issues
Social Services: At-Risk Youth, Camps, Child Welfare, Community Service Organizations, Counseling, Crime Prevention, Day Care, Delinquency & Criminal Rehabilitation, Domestic Violence, Family Planning, Family Services, Food/Clothing Distribution, People with Disabilities, Shelters/Homelessness, United Funds/United Ways, Youth Organizations

Application Procedures

Initial Contact: All potential applicants are encouraged to write a two- to three-page letter of inquiry before writing a full proposal. The letter should include a summary of the project's goals and target audience, its fit with the foundation's objectives, an estimated budget and timeframe, and plans for evaluation and dissemination of results. If the proposed project is of interest to the foundation, the applicant will be invited to send a full proposal.

Application Requirements: The full proposal should include the following: full contact information; a two-page executive summary; statement of need; description of the project and rationale for the approach; workplan, including a timeline and staffing plan; anticipated outcomes, benchmarks, products, and long-term impact; evaluation plan; plans for disseminating the product or communicating lessons learned to key constituencies; a description of organization and staff qualifications, including past performance on similar projects; project budget, showing committed and anticipated funds; organization's current operating budget; list of board members and/or advisors; letters of support from board and collaborating organizations; proof of tax-exempt status; and reasons for seeking partnership with a national funder (for state-focused proposals).

Deadlines: Proposals are due by January 15 for April review and by June 15 for October review. Letters of inquiry should be submitted at least four weeks prior to the proposal deadline.

Review Process: The directors of the foundation meet twice a year in April and October to set policy and to authorize grants.

Notes: Applicants are encouraged to submit letters of inquiry and proposals by e-mail rather than by hard copy, and to fax or mail the requested attachments. The foundation does not accept unsolicited proposals for health-related grants under The Love Jen Fund.

Restrictions

The foundation does not give grant support for ongoing direct services, general operating expenses, individual support, capital expenditures, or endowment campaigns. The foundation does not fund local services or programs.

Additional Information

The foundation reports that they conduct seminars and workshops.

The foundation is interested in projects that extend knowledge, make linkages between research and improved practice and policies, and communicate knowledge gained through research and practice to the broader public.

Publications: Annual Report (including Application Guidelines)

Foundation Officials

Betty S. Bardige: chairman, director PRIM CORP EMPL stockholder, director: Puritan Investment Corp.
Jonathan R. Gordon: director
Jay B. Langner: director B 1930. ED University of Pennsylvania BS; University of Pennsylvania Wharton School (1950). PRIM CORP EMPL chairman, president, chief executive officer, director: Hudson General Corp. CORP AFFIL president, director: Hudson Aviation Services Delaware.
Patricia S. Leiberman: vice chair PRIM CORP EMPL stockholder, director: Puritan Investment Corp.
Luba H. Lynch: executive director, secretary B Regensburg, Germany 1947. ED Royal Conservatory of Music (Toronto) AA (1967); University of Toronto BA (1968). NONPR AFFIL member: National Association Education Young Children; board member: New York Regional Association Grantmakers; board member: Family Resource Coalition; member: American Orthopsychiatric Association; board member: Viola W Bernard Foundation.
Wendy S. Masi: vice president PRIM CORP EMPL stockholder, director: Puritan Investment Corp.

Marilyn Mailman Segal: chairman emeritus B Utica, NY 1927. ED Wellesley College BA (1948); McGill University BS (1949); Nova University PhD (1970). CORP AFFIL stockholder, director: Puritan Investment Corp. NONPR AFFIL trustee: University Miami; chairman national visiting committee: University Miami School Nursing; dean: Nova University Family School Center; member: Society Research Child Development; member: American Psychological Association; member: Delta Kappa Gamma.
Richard D. Segal: president, director PRIM CORP EMPL stockholder, director: Puritan Investment Corp.
Donna Tookmanian: treasurer PRIM CORP EMPL controller: Seavest Partners.

Grants Analysis

Disclosure Period: calendar year ending 2001
Total Grants: $1,502,569*
Number of Grants: 64
Average Grant: $19,247*
Highest Grant: $290,000
Lowest Grant: $250
Typical Range: $5,000 to $50,000
*Note: Giving excludes United Way. Average grant figure excludes highest grant.

Recent Grants

Note: Grants derived from 2002 Form 990.
Library-Related

5,000	Libraries for the Future, New York, NY -- charitable fund

General

290,000	Nova Southeastern University, Ft. Lauderdale, FL -- capital fund
80,000	Nova Southeastern University, Ft. Lauderdale, FL -- capital fund
50,000	Erikson Institute, Chicago, IL -- fund for education
50,000	Institute for Civil Society Inc., Newton Center, MA -- fund for education
50,000	National Association for the Education of Young Children, Washington, DC -- fund for education
50,000	United Way of New York City, New York, NY -- fund for education
50,000	United Ways of Florida Inc., Tallahassee, FL -- fund for education
30,000	Brandeis University, Waltham, MA -- fund for education
30,000	Chicago Health Connection, Chicago, IL -- fund for education
30,000	College University Resource Institute Inc., Washington, DC -- fund for education

MANAGEMENT COMPENSATION GROUP/ DULWORTH INC.

Company Headquarters

Los Angeles, CA

Company Description

Employees: 135
SIC(s): 8700 Engineering & Management Services.

Operating Locations

Management Compensation Group/Dulworth Inc. (TX--Houston)

Nonmonetary Support

Type: Donated Equipment

Giving Contact

Pat Bratcher, Office Manager
1021 Main St. Suite 1300
Houston, TX 77002

Phone: (713)222-8383
Fax: (713)222-8831
E-mail: pbratcher@mcghouston.com

Description

Organization Type: Corporate Giving Program
Giving Locations: headquarters area only.
Grant Types: Award, Employee Matching Gifts, Multiyear/Continuing Support.
Note: Also provides officer discretionary gifts.

Typical Recipients

Arts & Humanities: Arts Appreciation, Arts Associations & Councils, Arts Centers, Arts Funds, Arts Institutes, Ballet, Community Arts, Arts & Humanities-General, Libraries, Museums/Galleries, Music, Performing Arts, Public Broadcasting, Theater, Visual Arts
Civic & Public Affairs: Business/Free Enterprise, Civil Rights, Ethnic Organizations, Civic & Public Affairs-General, Inner-City Development, Philanthropic Organizations, Professional & Trade Associations
Education: Arts/Humanities Education, Business Education, Colleges & Universities, Education-General
Health: Cancer, Health-General, Geriatric Health, Multiple Sclerosis
Religion: Jewish Causes
Social Services: Animal Protection, At-Risk Youth, Camps, Family Planning, Social Services-General, United Funds/United Ways, Youth Organizations

Application Procedures

Initial Contact: Send a brief letter of inquiry.
Application Requirements: Include a description of organization, purpose of funds sought, and proof of tax-exempt status.

Restrictions

Does not support political or lobbying groups, fraternal or social organizations, or organizations outside operating areas.

Corporate Officials

Chuck Bracht: president PRIM CORP EMPL president: Management Compensation Group/Dulworth.
James Phillips: chief executive officer PRIM CORP EMPL chief executive officer: Management Compensation Group/Dulworth.

Grants Analysis

Typical Range: $10 to $1,000

JACK N. AND LILYAN MANDEL FOUNDATION

Giving Contact

Jack N. Mandel, President, Trustee
2829 Euclid Avenue
Cleveland, OH 44115
Phone: (216)875-6500
Fax: (216)875-6580

Description

Founded: 1963
EIN: 346546418
Organization Type: Private Foundation
Giving Locations: OH
Grant Types: General Support.

Donor Information

Founder: Jack N. Mandel and the late Lilyan Mandel

Financial Summary

Total Giving: $9,534,465 (2002); $8,793,428 (2001)
Giving Analysis: Giving for 2002 includes: foundation grants to United Way ($25,000); 2001: foundation-

tion grants to United Way ($25,000)
Assets: $183,737,749 (2002); $190,768,270 (2001)
Gifts Received: $2,719,017 (2002); $4,735,700 (2000); $857,852 (1998). Note: In 2002, contributions were received from Jack N. Mandel. In 1998, contributions were received from John N. Mandel ($801,038) and Sheldon Mandel ($56,814). In 1996, contributions were received from John N. Mandel ($97,500,000), Courtland Associates ($33,509,375) and Lilyan Mandel Irrevocable Trust ($700,000). In 1993, contributions were received from Courtland Associates ($9,595,846) and Lilyan Mandel Trust ($500,000).)

Typical Recipients

Arts & Humanities: Arts Funds, Arts Outreach, Ballet, Dance, History & Archaeology, Libraries, Museums/Galleries, Music, Opera, Performing Arts, Public Broadcasting, Theater
Civic & Public Affairs: Asian American Affairs, Civil Rights, Community Foundations, Economic Development, Ethnic Organizations, Civic & Public Affairs-General, Housing, Law & Justice, Municipalities/Towns, Nonprofit Management, Philanthropic Organizations, Professional & Trade Associations, Public Policy, Safety, Urban & Community Affairs, Women's Affairs
Education: Arts/Humanities Education, Business-School Partnerships, Colleges & Universities, Education Funds, Elementary Education (Private), Elementary Education (Public), Education-General, International Studies, Leadership Training, Literacy, Medical Education, Private Education (Precollege), Religious Education, Secondary Education (Private), Student Aid
Health: AIDS/HIV, Alzheimer's Disease, Children's Health/Hospitals, Clinics/Medical Centers, Diabetes, Emergency/Ambulance Services, Eyes/Blindness, Geriatric Health, Health Funds, Heart, Medical Rehabilitation, Medical Research, Multiple Sclerosis, Public Health, Single-Disease Health Associations
International: Foreign Arts Organizations, Health Care/Hospitals, International Organizations, International Peace & Security Issues, Missionary/Religious Activities
Religion: Bible Study/Translation, Churches, Dioceses, Religion-General, Jewish Causes, Religious Organizations, Religious Welfare, Social/Policy Issues, Synagogues/Temples
Science: Scientific Organizations
Social Services: Child Welfare, Community Centers, Community Service Organizations, Emergency Relief, Food/Clothing Distribution, Homes, People with Disabilities, Recreation & Athletics, Senior Services, Social Services-General, United Funds/United Ways, Volunteer Services, YMCA/YWCA/YMHA/YWHA, Youth Organizations

Application Procedures

Initial Contact: The foundation has no formal grant application procedure or application form. Send written request.
Application Requirements: Include description of project and justification for grant, amount requested and term of grant, pertinent financial information, proof of tax-exempt status, and an appraisal of the requesting organization by a standard-setting organization, if available.
Deadlines: None.

Foundation Officials

Jack N. Mandel: trustee B Austria July 16, 1911. ED Cleveland College; Fenn College (1930-1933). PRIM CORP EMPL director: Premier Farnell PLC. CORP AFFIL founder, chairman finance committee: Premier Industries Corp. NONPR AFFIL trustee: Tel Aviv University Museum Diaspora; trustee: Temple Woodruff Foundation; member executive committee: National Conference Christians & Jews; life trustee: South Broward Jewish Federation; honorary trustee: Hebrew University; president: Montefiore Home Aged; member executive committee: Florida Society Blind;

life trustee: Cleveland Jewish Welfare Foundation; trustee: Cleveland Playhouse; president advisory board: Barry University. CLUB AFFIL Commede Club; Emerald Hills Country Club; Beachmont Country Club.

Grants Analysis

Disclosure Period: calendar year ending 2002
Total Grants: $9,509,465*
Number of Grants: 52
Average Grant: $11,356*
Highest Grant: $8,600,000
Lowest Grant: $11
Typical Range: $1,000 to $20,000
*Note: Giving excludes United Way. Average grant figure excludes two highest grants ($8,941,667).

Recent Grants

Note: Grants derived from 2002 Form 990.
General

8,600,000	Mandel Foundation, Cleveland, OH
341,667	Jewish Community Federation of Cleveland, Cleveland, OH
73,358	Jewish Community Center Association, New York, NY
52,000	Cleveland Clinic Foundation, Cleveland, OH
51,667	Montefiore Foundation, Beachwood, OH
41,667	Peter F. Drucker Foundation for Nonprofit Management, New York, NY
27,500	Middle East Forum, Philadelphia, PA
27,000	Temple-Tifereth Israel, Beachwood, OH
25,000	American Friends of Kedumim, Union, NJ
25,000	Bezalel Academy of Art and Design, Jerusalem Israel

MANDEVILLE FOUNDATION

Giving Contact

Hubert T. Mandeville, President, Treasurer & Director
c/o Joseph W. Roskos & Co.
P.O. Box A
Wayne, PA 19087

Description

Founded: 1963
EIN: 066043343
Organization Type: Private Foundation
Giving Locations: CT; NY
Grant Types: General Support.

Donor Information

Founder: Ernest W. Mandeville

Financial Summary

Total Giving: $28,536 (2001)
Assets: $673,059 (2001)
Gifts Received: $22,000 (1995). Note: In 1995, contributions were received from the Ernest W. Mandeville Trust.

Typical Recipients

Arts & Humanities: Arts Associations & Councils, Community Arts, Ethnic & Folk Arts, Arts & Humanities-General, Historic Preservation, History & Archaeology, Libraries, Museums/Galleries, Music, Theater
Civic & Public Affairs: Botanical Gardens/Parks, Chambers of Commerce, Employment/Job Training, Civic & Public Affairs-General, Nonprofit Management, Public Policy, Safety, Urban & Community Affairs
Education: Colleges & Universities, Education Associations, Environmental Education, Faculty Development, Medical Education, Minority Education, Preschool Education, Private Education (Precollege), Public Education (Precollege), Student Aid

Environment: Air/Water Quality, Environment-General, Resource Conservation
Health: Cancer, Clinics/Medical Centers, Emergency/Ambulance Services, Heart, Hospitals, Medical Research, Single-Disease Health Associations
International: Foreign Educational Institutions, International Organizations, International Relations
Religion: Churches, Ministries
Social Services: Animal Protection, Camps, Child Welfare, Community Centers, Community Service Organizations, Recreation & Athletics, Youth Organizations

Application Procedures

Initial Contact: The foundation has no formal grant application procedure or application form.
Deadlines: None.
Decision Notification: Replies are usually made in 90 days.

Foundation Officials

Maurice Coleman Greenbaum: secretary, director B Detroit, MI April 03, 1918. ED Wayne State University BA (1938); University of Michigan JD (1941); New York University LLM (1948). PRIM CORP EMPL counsel: Rosenman & Colin. CORP AFFIL director: Scrambler Inc.; member advisory committee: Great Neck Senior Citizens Center. NONPR AFFIL member: Village Justice; director: World Rehabilitation Fund; member visitors committee: University Miami School Marine & Atmospheric Science; associate trustee: North Shore University Hospital.
Meredith H. Hollis: director
Hubert T. Mandeville: president, treasurer, director
Matthew T. Mandeville: director
P. Kempton Mandeville: vice president, director

Grants Analysis

Disclosure Period: calendar year ending 2001
Total Grants: $28,536
Number of Grants: 13
Average Grant: $828*
Highest Grant: $18,600
Lowest Grant: $100
Typical Range: $500 to $5,000
*Note: Average grant figure excludes highest grant.

Recent Grants

Note: Grants derived from 2001 Form 990.
General

18,600	Westover School, Middleburg, CT
2,600	Sherman Chamber Ensemble, Sherman, TX
2,377	Andrew Glover Youth Program, Inc., New York, NY
1,250	Yale University, New Haven, CT
1,000	Hotchkiss School, Lakeville, CT
1,000	Ridley College, St. Catharines, ON Canada
500	Holland Society of New York, NY
500	Sherman Soccer, Sherman, CT
250	Jewish Community Center, Sherman, CT
134	Naromi Land Trust, Inc.

MANEELY FUND

Giving Contact

James E. O'Donnell, Vice President & Treasurer
900 Haddon Ave., Suite 432
Collingswood, NJ 08108
Phone: (856)854-5400
Fax: (856)854-5578

Description

Founded: 1952
EIN: 231569917
Organization Type: Private Foundation

Giving Locations: PA: limited grantmaking nationally.
Grant Types: General Support.

Donor Information

Founder: the late Edward F. Maneely

Financial Summary

Total Giving: $220,805 (2001)
Giving Analysis: Giving for 2001 includes: foundation grants to United Way ($19,500)
Assets: $3,487,162 (2001)

Typical Recipients

Arts & Humanities: Arts Associations & Councils, Ballet, Historic Preservation, History & Archaeology, Libraries, Museums/Galleries, Music, Opera, Public Broadcasting
Civic & Public Affairs: African American Affairs, Botanical Gardens/Parks, Business/Free Enterprise, Clubs, Economic Development, Economic Policy, Employment/Job Training, Ethnic Organizations, Civic & Public Affairs-General, Housing, Public Policy, Safety
Education: Arts/Humanities Education, Business Education, Colleges & Universities, Education Funds, Elementary Education (Public), Education-General, Legal Education, Preschool Education, Private Education (Precollege), Religious Education, Secondary Education (Private), Student Aid, Vocational & Technical Education
Health: AIDS/HIV, Cancer, Children's Health/Hospitals, Emergency/Ambulance Services, Geriatric Health, Health Organizations, Hospices, Hospitals, Long-Term Care, Medical Rehabilitation, Medical Research, Nursing Services, Single-Disease Health Associations
International: International Relief Efforts, Missionary/Religious Activities
Religion: Churches, Dioceses, Missionary Activities (Domestic), Religious Organizations, Religious Welfare
Social Services: At-Risk Youth, Child Welfare, Community Service Organizations, Delinquency & Criminal Rehabilitation, Domestic Violence, Family Planning, Family Services, Homes, People with Disabilities, United Funds/United Ways, Youth Organizations

Application Procedures

Initial Contact: Send a letter of request on organization's letterhead.
Application Requirements: Include a description of organization, purpose of funds sought, and proof of tax-exempt status.
Deadlines: None.

Foundation Officials

Elizabeth J. Boylan: vice president
Betty DiPilla: secretary
Marie E. Dooner: secretary
James E. O'Donnell: president, treasurer

Grants Analysis

Disclosure Period: calendar year ending 2001
Total Grants: $201,305*
Number of Grants: 169
Average Grant: $1,191
Highest Grant: $14,000
Typical Range: $500 to $5,000
*Note: Giving excludes United Way.

Recent Grants

Note: Grants derived from 2001 Form 990.
General

14,000	United Way of Mercer County, Sharon, PA -- annual campaign
10,000	Project H.O.M.E., Philadelphia, PA -- operating expenses
5,000	Archdiocese of Philadelphia, Philadelphia, PA -- Catholic Heritage Center

5,000	Christopher Dock Mennonite High School, Lansdale, PA -- capital campaign
5,000	Holy Redeemer Health System, Huntington Valley, PA -- Drueding Center
5,000	Mercy Hospice, Philadelphia, PA -- operating expenses
5,000	Mount Tamalpais School, Mill Valley, CA -- annual giving and building fund and faculty endowment
5,000	Penn Northwest Development Corp., Mercer, PA -- economic development marketing and industrial outreach
5,000	Philadelphia Museum of Art, Philadelphia, PA -- operating expenses
5,000	Philadelphia Museum of Art, Philadelphia, PA -- operating expenses

MARBROOK FOUNDATION

Giving Contact

Conley Brooks, Jr., Trustee
730 Second Ave. S., Suite 1450
Minneapolis, MN 55402
Phone: (612)752-1783

Description

Founded: 1948
EIN: 416019899
Organization Type: Private Foundation
Giving Locations: MN: Minneapolis, St. Paul
Grant Types: Capital, Conference/Seminar, Emergency, Endowment, General Support, Multiyear/Continuing Support, Operating Expenses, Professorship, Project, Research, Seed Money.

Donor Information

Founder: the late Edward Brooks, the late Markell C. Brooks, Markell C. Brooks Charitable Trust

Financial Summary

Total Giving: $778,500 (2002); $860,000 (2001)
Giving Analysis: Giving for 2002 includes: foundation grants to United Way ($17,500)
Assets: $17,192,046 (2002); $13,055,675 (2001)
Gifts Received: $1,600 (2001); $1,298,443 (2000); $150,380 (1999). Note: In 2001, contributions were received from Katherine S. Brooks. In 2000, contributions were received from the Dwight F. Brooks Estate. In 1999, contributions were received from Corey Gibson. In 1997, contributions were received from Markell Brooks.

Typical Recipients

Arts & Humanities: Arts Centers, Arts Institutes, Community Arts, History & Archaeology, Libraries, Museums/Galleries, Music, Public Broadcasting, Theater
Civic & Public Affairs: African American Affairs, Botanical Gardens/Parks, Business/Free Enterprise, Community Foundations, Economic Policy, Employment/Job Training, Civic & Public Affairs-General, Native American Affairs, Nonprofit Management, Philanthropic Organizations, Public Policy, Urban & Community Affairs, Zoos/Aquariums
Education: Colleges & Universities, Economic Education, Education Funds, Leadership Training, Private Education (Precollege)
Environment: Air/Water Quality, Environment-General, Resource Conservation
Health: Cancer, Hospitals
Religion: Religious Organizations, Seminaries
Science: Science Museums, Scientific Centers & Institutes
Social Services: Child Welfare, Community Service Organizations, Day Care, Family Planning, Family Services, Recreation & Athletics, Social Services-General, United Funds/United Ways, YMCA/YWCA/YMHA/YWHA, Youth Organizations

Application Procedures

Initial Contact: full proposal
Application Requirements: Includes a description of organization, amount requested, budget, other possible sources of support, purpose of funds sought, and proof of tax-exempt status.
Deadlines: None.
Review Process: Trustee meetings are generally held in June/July and November/December.

Restrictions

Grants are not made to support individuals, political or lobbying groups, or organizations outside operating areas.

Additional Information

Publications: Annual Report (including Application Guidelines)

Foundation Officials

Conley Brooks, Sr.: trustee
Conley Brooks, Jr.: trustee
Markell Brooks: trustee
William R. Humphrey, Jr.: trustee

Grants Analysis

Disclosure Period: calendar year ending 2002
Total Grants: $761,000*
Number of Grants: 123
Average Grant: $6,187
Highest Grant: $25,000
Lowest Grant: $1,000
Typical Range: $1,000 to $10,000
*Note: Giving excludes United Way.

Recent Grants

Note: Grants derived from 2001 Form 990.
General

30,000	Guthrie Theater, Minneapolis, MN
30,000	Minnesota Parks and Trails Council, St. Paul, MN
25,000	Minneapolis Foundation, Minneapolis, MN
25,000	University of Minnesota, St. Paul, MN
18,000	National Center for Social Entrepreneurs, Minneapolis, MN
17,500	Greater Twin Cities United Way, Minneapolis, MN
15,000	Amherst College, Amherst, MA
15,000	Minnesota Historical Society, St. Paul, MN
15,000	Minnetonka Center for the Arts, Minneapolis, MN
15,000	St. Paul Academy and Summit School, St. Paul, MN

MARCUS CORP.

Company Headquarters

Milwaukee, WI
Web: http://www.marcuscorp.com

Company Description

Founded: 1935
Ticker: MCS
Exchange: NYSE
Operating Revenue: US$389.8 million (2002)
Employees: 7000 (2003)
SIC(s): 5812 Eating Places, 7011 Hotels & Motels, 7832 Motion Picture Theaters Except Drive-In.

Operating Locations

Marcus Corp. (CT; FL; IL; IN; IA; KY; MA; MI; MN; MO; NE; NM; NC; OH; SC; TN; TX; WI--Milwaukee)

Marcus Corp. Foundation

Giving Contact

Stephen H. Marcus, President, Treasurer & Director
100 East Wisconsin Avenue, Suite 1900
Milwaukee, WI 53202-4125
Phone: (414)905-1503

Description

EIN: 396046268
Organization Type: Corporate Foundation
Giving Locations: WI: Milwaukee
Grant Types: General Support, Project, Research.

Financial Summary

Total Giving: $652,290 (2003); $619,818 (2002); $595,755 (2001). Note: Contributes through foundation only.
Assets: $1,351,549 (2003); $1,609,563 (2002); $1,623,792 (2001)
Gifts Received: $358,217 (2003); $569,219 (2002); $606,323 (2001). Note: Contributions were received from the Marcus Corporation.

Typical Recipients

Arts & Humanities: Arts Centers, Arts Festivals, Arts Funds, Arts Institutes, Ballet, Community Arts, Dance, Film & Video, Arts & Humanities-General, Historic Preservation, History & Archaeology, Libraries, Museums/Galleries, Music, Opera, Performing Arts, Theater
Civic & Public Affairs: African American Affairs, Civil Rights, Clubs, Community Foundations, Economic Development, Employment/Job Training, Ethnic Organizations, Civic & Public Affairs-General, Hispanic Affairs, Housing, Law & Justice, Municipalities/Towns, Nonprofit Management, Parades/Festivals, Philanthropic Organizations, Professional & Trade Associations, Public Policy, Urban & Community Affairs, Zoos/Aquariums
Education: Afterschool/Enrichment Programs, Arts/Humanities Education, Business Education, Colleges & Universities, Education Associations, Education Funds, Engineering/Technological Education, Faculty Development, Education-General, Leadership Training, Medical Education, Minority Education, Private Education (Precollege), Student Aid
Environment: Wildlife Protection
Health: AIDS/HIV, Alzheimer's Disease, Arthritis, Cancer, Children's Health/Hospitals, Clinics/Medical Centers, Diabetes, Health Organizations, Heart, Hospitals, Kidney, Medical Research, Multiple Sclerosis, Prenatal Health Issues, Public Health, Respiratory, Single-Disease Health Associations, Speech & Hearing, Transplant Networks/Donor Banks, Trauma Treatment
International: Foreign Arts Organizations, Foreign Educational Institutions, International Development
Religion: Churches, Jewish Causes, Ministries, Religious Organizations, Religious Welfare
Science: Science Museums, Scientific Centers & Institutes
Social Services: Big Brothers/Big Sisters, Child Abuse, Child Welfare, Community Centers, Community Service Organizations, Crime Prevention, Day Care, Domestic Violence, Family Services, People with Disabilities, Recreation & Athletics, Scouts, Shelters/Homelessness, Social Services-General, United Funds/United Ways, Volunteer Services, YMCA/YWCA/YMHA/YWHA, Youth Organizations

Application Procedures

Initial Contact: The foundation requests applications be made in writing.
Application Requirements: Include name, address, project/program objectives, and reason for the request.
Deadlines: None.
Decision Notification: Late May and late November

Corporate Officials

Stephen Howard Marcus: chairman, chief executive officer B Minneapolis, MN 1935. ED University of Wisconsin BBA (1957); University of Michigan LLB (1960). PRIM CORP EMPL chairman, chief executive officer: Marcus Corp. ADD CORP EMPL president: Centre Theatres Corp.; president: Marcus Restaurants Inc.; president: Marcus Cinemas Inc.; president: Vending Corp. CORP AFFIL chairman: Budgetel Inns Inc.; trustee: Marc Plz Corp.; chairman: Baymont Inns Suites.

Foundation Officials

Thomas F. Kissinger: secretary, director
Gregory S. Marcus: director
Stephen Howard Marcus: president, treasurer, director (see above)

Grants Analysis

Disclosure Period: calendar year ending 2003
Total Grants: $577,290*
Number of Grants: 99
Average Grant: $4,819*
Highest Grant: $105,000
Lowest Grant: $50
Typical Range: $1,000 to $10,000
*Note: Giving excludes United Way. Average grant figure excludes highest grant.

Recent Grants

Note: Grants derived from 2003 Form 990.
General

105,000	Medical College of Wisconsin, Milwaukee, WI
75,000	United Way of Greater Milwaukee, Milwaukee, WI
50,000	Great Circus Parade, Milwaukee, WI -- towards community betterment
43,000	Childrens Hospital Foundation, Milwaukee, WI
26,250	United Performing Arts Fund UPAF, Milwaukee, WI
25,000	Florentine Opera, Milwaukee, WI
25,000	Genuine American Inc. NACO, Washington, DC -- towards community betterment
25,000	Marcus Center for the Performing Arts, Milwaukee, WI
25,000	UWM Architecture School, Milwaukee, WI
25,000	UWM Business Administration, Milwaukee, WI

MARDAG FOUNDATION

Giving Contact

Joe Garman, Grants Manager
55 Fifth St. East, Suite 600
St. Paul, MN 55101-1797
Phone: (651)224-5463
Fax: (651)224-8123
E-mail: inbox@mardag.org
Web: http://www.mardag.org/

Description

Founded: 1969
EIN: 411698990
Organization Type: General Purpose Foundation
Giving Locations: MN
Grant Types: Capital, Challenge, General Support, Matching, Multiyear/Continuing Support, Project.

Donor Information

Founder: The Mardag Foundation was established in 1969. Originally known as the Ober Charitable Foundation, it was created by the estate of Agnes E. Ober. Mrs. Ober, who died at the age of eighty-two in 1969, was interested in the education of youth and in securing the welfare of the elderly. She served on the boards of trustees of several charitable foundations in St. Paul. Much of her estate was left to benefit charitable foundations in Minnesota.
The Mardag Foundation continues to distribute grants that reflect the philanthropic interests of Mrs. Ober.

Financial Summary

Total Giving: $2,054,506 (2003); $2,413,725 (2002); $1,703,725 (2001)
Assets: $50,535,303 (2003); $42,359,745 (2002); $52,236,978 (2001)

Typical Recipients

Arts & Humanities: Arts Associations & Councils, Arts Centers, Ballet, Arts & Humanities-General, Historic Preservation, History & Archaeology, Libraries, Literary Arts, Museums/Galleries, Music, Opera, Performing Arts, Public Broadcasting, Theater
Civic & Public Affairs: African American Affairs, Asian American Affairs, Botanical Gardens/Parks, Business/Free Enterprise, Community Foundations, Economic Development, Employment/Job Training, Ethnic Organizations, Civic & Public Affairs-General, Hispanic Affairs, Housing, Inner-City Development, Legal Aid, Municipalities/Towns, Native American Affairs, Nonprofit Management, Philanthropic Organizations, Public Policy, Rural Affairs, Urban & Community Affairs, Women's Affairs, Zoos/Aquariums
Education: Colleges & Universities, Continuing Education, Education Funds, Education Reform, Elementary Education (Private), Faculty Development, Education-General, Literacy, Minority Education, Preschool Education, Private Education (Precollege), Public Education (Precollege), School Volunteerism, Special Education, Student Aid
Environment: Air/Water Quality, Environment-General
Health: Alzheimer's Disease, Emergency/Ambulance Services, Geriatric Health, Health Organizations, Hospices, Hospitals, Long-Term Care, Mental Health, Public Health, Single-Disease Health Associations
International: International Environmental Issues
Religion: Churches, Dioceses, Jewish Causes, Religious Welfare
Science: Science Museums
Social Services: Animal Protection, Big Brothers/Big Sisters, Camps, Child Abuse, Child Welfare, Community Centers, Community Service Organizations, Counseling, Crime Prevention, Day Care, Delinquency & Criminal Rehabilitation, Domestic Violence, Emergency Relief, Family Planning, Family Services, Food/Clothing Distribution, Homes, People with Disabilities, Refugee Assistance, Scouts, Senior Services, Sexual Abuse, Shelters/Homelessness, Social Services-General, Substance Abuse, United Funds/United Ways, Volunteer Services, YMCA/YWCA/YMHA/YWHA, Youth Organizations

Application Procedures

Initial Contact: The foundation has a full set of application requirements available upon request. Applicants may wish to submit a brief summary (three to four pages, and less detailed than a full proposal) of their projects to determine whether or not they meet the interests of the foundation.
Application Requirements: A full proposal should include the name and address of the applicant, amount requested, project objective, proof of tax-exempt status, and (if applicable) the estimated number of Minnesota citizens who will benefit from the project. Applicants should also include the position of the individual signing the application, detailed budget, other sources of funding, statement that applicant will spend the funds awarded solely for the purpose stated, length of time for which support will be needed, detailed income statement, and a description of each staff member assigned to the project.
Deadlines: December 31, May 1, and August 1.
Review Process: The board meets in April, August, and November.

Notes: Proposals will not be returned to the applicant.

Restrictions

Normally, the foundation will not make grants for the west metro area of Minnesota; make grants to individuals; make annual grants; support sectarian religious programs; make grants for federated campaigns; or make grants for events, development offices or officers, medical research, conservation, or scholarship programs.

Additional Information

Publications: Annual Report

Foundation Officials

Richard C. Broeker: director
John G. Couchman: assistant secretary, director
Gretchen D. Davidson: director
Cornelia Eberhart: director
Gayle M. Ober: vice president, director
Richard B. Ober: treasurer, director
Timothy M. Ober: president, director
Jack H. Pohl: assistant treasurer, director
Carleen Rhodes: secretary, director
Wilhelmina M. Wright: director

Grants Analysis

Disclosure Period: calendar year ending 2003
Total Grants: $2,054,506
Number of Grants: 77
Average Grant: $23,393*
Highest Grant: $200,000
Lowest Grant: $5,000
Typical Range: $10,000 to $50,000
***Note:** Average grant figure excludes two highest grants ($300,000).

Recent Grants

Note: Grants derived from 2003 Form 990.
Library-Related
50,000	Pioneerland Library System, Willmar, MN	

General
200,000	Neighborhood House, St. Paul, MN
100,000	Minnesota Public Radio, St. Paul, MN
75,000	Amherst H. Wilder Foundation, St. Paul, MN
75,000	Saint Paul Foundation, St. Paul, MN
61,218	Goodwill Industries Inc., St. Paul, MN
60,000	Saint Paul Riverfront Corporation, St. Paul, MN
50,000	American Composers Forum, St. Paul, MN
50,000	Cathedral of St. Paul, St. Paul, MN
50,000	Catholic Charities of the Archdiocese of St. Paul and Minneapolis, Minneapolis, MN
50,000	Children's Home Society & Family Services, St. Paul, MN

MARITZ INC.

Company Headquarters

Fenton, MO
Web: http://www.maritz.com

Company Description

Revenue: US$15 billion (2001)
Employees: 6000 (2001)
SIC(s): 8740 Management & Public Relations.

Operating Locations

Maritz Inc. (IL--Chicago; KS--Kansas City; MI--Detroit; MO--St. Louis; NY--New York; TX--Dallas)

Nonmonetary Support

Type: Donated Equipment; Donated Products; In-kind Services; Loaned Employees; Loaned Executives

Giving Contact

Beth Rusert, Corporate Communications
1375 North Highway Drive
Fenton, MO 63099
Phone: (636)827-4000
Fax: (636)827-8605
E-mail: beth.rusert@maritz.com

Description

Organization Type: Corporate Giving Program
Giving Locations: headquarters and operating communities.
Grant Types: Award, Capital, Conference/Seminar, Emergency, Employee Matching Gifts, General Support, Matching, Multiyear/Continuing Support.
Note: Employee matching gift ratio: 1 to 1. The company also awards one-time grants.

Financial Summary

Total Giving: Contributes through corporate direct giving program and foundation.

Typical Recipients

Arts & Humanities: Arts Associations & Councils, Arts Funds, Arts Institutes, Community Arts, Dance, Ethnic & Folk Arts, Historic Preservation, Libraries, Museums/Galleries, Music, Opera, Performing Arts, Public Broadcasting, Theater, Visual Arts
Civic & Public Affairs: Business/Free Enterprise, Civil Rights, Economic Development, Employment/Job Training, Municipalities/Towns, Philanthropic Organizations, Public Policy, Women's Affairs, Zoos/Aquariums
Education: Colleges & Universities, Community & Junior Colleges, Economic Education, Elementary Education (Private), Literacy, Minority Education, Preschool Education, Public Education (Precollege)
Environment: Environment-General
Health: Health-General, Hospitals, Mental Health
Social Services: Child Welfare, Delinquency & Criminal Rehabilitation, Domestic Violence, Emergency Relief, Food/Clothing Distribution, People with Disabilities, Shelters/Homelessness, Social Services-General, Substance Abuse, United Funds/United Ways, Youth Organizations

Application Procedures

Initial Contact: Send a brief letter of inquiry and a full proposal.
Application Requirements: Include a description of organization, amount requested, purpose of funds sought, and recently audited financial statement.
Deadlines: None.

Restrictions

Does not support individuals or religious organizations for sectarian purposes.

Corporate Officials

James W. Kienker: senior vice president, chief financial officer
W. Stephen Maritz: president, chief executive officer B 1958. PRIM CORP EMPL president, chief executive officer: Maritz Inc.
Jeffrey D. Reinberg: senior vice president

Grants Analysis

Disclosure Period: calendar year ending 1999
Total Grants: $900,000 (approx)
Typical Range: $500 to $2,000

JOHN C. MARKEY CHARITABLE FUND

Giving Contact

John C. Markey, Jr., Treasurer
PO Box 623
Bryan, OH 43506
Phone: (419)636-4475

Description

Founded: 1966
EIN: 346572724
Organization Type: Private Foundation
Giving Locations: OH: nationally
Grant Types: General Support.

Donor Information

Founder: the late John C. Markey

Financial Summary

Total Giving: $63,000 (fiscal year ending June 30, 2004); $150,550 (fiscal 2001)
Assets: $3,316,076 (fiscal 2004); $3,565,392 (fiscal 2001)

Typical Recipients

Arts & Humanities: Arts Associations & Councils, Arts Centers, Community Arts, History & Archaeology, Libraries, Museums/Galleries, Music, Opera, Public Broadcasting, Theater
Civic & Public Affairs: Chambers of Commerce, Clubs, Community Foundations, Civic & Public Affairs-General, Parades/Festivals, Professional & Trade Associations, Public Policy, Safety, Urban & Community Affairs, Women's Affairs
Education: Afterschool/Enrichment Programs, Colleges & Universities, Education Funds, Elementary Education (Public), Engineering/Technological Education, Education-General, Medical Education, Private Education (Precollege), Public Education (Precollege), Secondary Education (Public), Student Aid
Environment: Protection, Wildlife Protection
Health: Alzheimer's Disease, Cancer, Clinics/Medical Centers, Diabetes, Emergency/Ambulance Services, Heart, Hospices, Hospitals, Medical Research, Multiple Sclerosis, Nursing Services, Preventive Medicine/Wellness Organizations, Public Health
International: Health Care/Hospitals, International Peace & Security Issues, Missionary/Religious Activities
Religion: Churches, Religion-General, Ministries, Religious Organizations
Social Services: Animal Protection, Community Centers, Community Service Organizations, Crime Prevention, Domestic Violence, Emergency Relief, Family Planning, Homes, People with Disabilities, Recreation & Athletics, Senior Services, United Funds/United Ways, YMCA/YWCA/YMHA/YWHA, Youth Organizations

Application Procedures

Initial Contact: Send a brief letter of inquiry.
Application Requirements: Include a description of organization and proof of tax-exempt status.
Deadlines: None.

Foundation Officials

Carl T. Anderson: president, secretary
Larry D. Lisle: trustee
Lorance W. Lisle: vice president
John Clifton Markey, II: treasurer

Grants Analysis

Disclosure Period: fiscal year ending June 30, 2004
Total Grants: $63,000
Number of Grants: 7
Average Grant: $9,000
Highest Grant: $20,000
Lowest Grant: $500
Typical Range: $500 to $20,000

Recent Grants

Note: Grants derived from fiscal 2004 Form 990.

General

20,000	Bryan Senior Center, Bryan, OH
20,000	Choate Rosemary Hall Foundation, Wallingford, CT
20,000	Grand Traverse Regional Land Conservancy, Traverse City, MI
1,500	Fraternal Order of Police Captain Custar Lodge No. 181, Bryan, OH
500	Bryan Chamber of Commerce, Bryan, OH
500	Bryan High School, Bryan, OH
500	Junior Achievement of Northwestern Ohio, Bryan, OH

MARMOT FOUNDATION

Giving Contact

Charles F. Gummey, Jr., Secretary (For Delaware OrganizationS)
1100 N. Market Street
Wilmington, DE 19890
Phone: (302)651-1000

Alternate Contact

Willis H. duPont, Chairman (For Florida OrganizationS)
Marmot Foundation
PO Box 2468
Palm Beach, FL 33480

Description

Founded: 1968
EIN: 516022487
Organization Type: General Purpose Foundation
Giving Locations: DE; FL
Grant Types: Capital, General Support, Matching, Research.

Donor Information

Founder: Established in 1968 by the Margaret F. duPont Trust.

Financial Summary

Total Giving: $1,795,000 (2002); $1,978,000 (2001)
Giving Analysis: Giving for 2002 includes: foundation grants to United Way ($70,000)
Assets: $27,039,994 (2002); $33,185,646 (2001)

Typical Recipients

Arts & Humanities: Arts Associations & Councils, Arts Centers, Arts Funds, Ballet, Arts & Humanities-General, Historic Preservation, History & Archaeology, Libraries, Museums/Galleries, Opera, Performing Arts, Visual Arts
Civic & Public Affairs: Community Foundations, Economic Development, Employment/Job Training, Civic & Public Affairs-General, Housing, Philanthropic Organizations, Professional & Trade Associations, Public Policy, Safety, Urban & Community Affairs, Zoos/Aquariums
Education: Arts/Humanities Education, Business Education, Colleges & Universities, Economic Education, Elementary Education (Private), Elementary Education (Public), Education-General, Medical Education, Preschool Education, Private Education (Precollege), Public Education (Precollege), Religious Education, Science/Mathematics Education, Secondary Education (Private), Social Sciences Education, Special Education, Vocational & Technical Education
Environment: Air/Water Quality, Environment-General, Protection, Resource Conservation
Health: Arthritis, Cancer, Children's Health/Hospitals, Clinics/Medical Centers, Diabetes, Emergency/Ambulance Services, Eyes/Blindness, Health Funds, Health Organizations, Heart, Hospices, Hospitals, Hospitals (University Affiliated), Mental Health, Outpatient Health Care, Preventive Medicine/Wellness Organizations, Public Health, Research/Studies Institutes, Single-Disease Health Associations, Trauma Treatment
Religion: Churches, Dioceses, Religion-General, Jewish Causes, Ministries, Religious Organizations, Religious Welfare
Science: Science Museums, Scientific Centers & Institutes
Social Services: Animal Protection, Child Welfare, Community Centers, Community Service Organizations, Day Care, Emergency Relief, Family Planning, Family Services, Food/Clothing Distribution, Homes, People with Disabilities, Recreation & Athletics, Scouts, Senior Services, Social Services-General, Special Olympics, Substance Abuse, United Funds/United Ways, YMCA/YWCA/YMHA/YWHA, Youth Organizations

Application Procedures

Initial Contact: The foundation has no formal grant application procedure or application form.
Deadlines: April 30 and October 31.
Review Process: The board meets in May and November to review Delaware grants, and only in November to review Florida grants. Decisions are reported within two weeks after the board meeting. Applicants should have established track records of meeting objectives. Appeals should be summarized in cover letter not longer than two pages.

Restrictions

The foundation does not support individuals, operating budgets, or scholarships, and does not make loans. No support is given to religious organizations.

Foundation Officials

Lammot Joseph du Pont: trustee
Miren de Amezola du Pont: trustee
Willis Harrington du Pont: president, trustee B Wilmington, DE 1936. ED Wesleyan University (1958); Cornell University (1960). NONPR AFFIL trustee: Miami Science Museum.
George S. Harrington: trustee

Grants Analysis

Disclosure Period: calendar year ending 2002
Total Grants: $1,725,000*
Number of Grants: 110
Average Grant: $15,682
Highest Grant: $70,000
Lowest Grant: $3,000
Typical Range: $10,000 to $25,000
*Note: Giving excludes United Way.

Recent Grants

Note: Grants derived from 2002 Form 990.

Library-Related

20,000	Georgetown Public Library, Georgetown, DE
15,000	Selbyville Public Library, Selbyville, DE

General

70,000	Rollins College, Winter Park, FL
60,000	Baptist Health South Florida, Miami, FL
60,000	Society of Memorial Sloan-Kettering Cancer Center, New York, NY
60,000	United Way of Delaware, Wilmington, DE
50,000	Bascom Palmer Eye Institute, Miami, FL
35,000	Brandywine Conservancy, Chadds Ford, PA
35,000	Presbyterian Hospital, New York, NY
35,000	Tri-County TEC Foundation, Stuart, FL
35,000	Winterthur Museum, Williamstown, MA
30,000	Delaware Financial Literacy Institute, Dover, DE

MARPAT FOUNDATION

Giving Contact

Joan Follin Koven, Secretary, Treasurer & Director
PO Box 1769
Silver Spring, MD 20915
E-mail: jkoven@marpatfoundation.org
Web: http://fdncenter.org/grantmaker/marpat/

Description

Founded: 1985
EIN: 521358159
Organization Type: Private Foundation
Giving Locations: DC: Washington metropolitan area
Grant Types: General Support, Operating Expenses, Research.

Donor Information

Founder: Marvin Breckinridge Patterson

Financial Summary

Total Giving: $1,747,500 (2004); $1,197,593 (2003)
Assets: $11,804,996 (2003)
Gifts Received: $1,528,840 (2003); $119,978 (2000). Note: In 2003, contributions were received from the estate of Marvin B. Patterson. In 2000, contributions were received from Marvin B. Patterson Unitrust.

Typical Recipients

Arts & Humanities: Arts Associations & Councils, Arts Outreach, Dance, Ethnic & Folk Arts, Arts & Humanities-General, Historic Preservation, History & Archaeology, Libraries, Literary Arts, Museums/Galleries, Music, Performing Arts, Public Broadcasting, Theater
Civic & Public Affairs: Asian American Affairs, Botanical Gardens/Parks, Employment/Job Training, Civic & Public Affairs-General, Law & Justice, Safety, Women's Affairs
Education: Arts/Humanities Education, Colleges & Universities, Education Reform, Environmental Education, International Exchange, International Studies, Preschool Education, Private Education (Precollege), Science/Mathematics Education, Special Education
Environment: Air/Water Quality, Environment-General, Protection, Research, Resource Conservation, Watershed
Health: Adolescent Health Issues, AIDS/HIV, Children's Health/Hospitals, Clinics/Medical Centers, Health-General, Health Organizations, Home-Care Services, Hospitals, Long-Term Care, Nursing Services, Prenatal Health Issues, Preventive Medicine/Wellness Organizations, Public Health
International: International-General, International Organizations
Science: Science Museums, Scientific Centers & Institutes, Scientific Labs, Scientific Organizations
Social Services: At-Risk Youth, Child Abuse, Child Welfare, Community Service Organizations, Domestic Violence, Family Planning, Food/Clothing Distribution, Homes, Scouts, Senior Services, Shelters/Homelessness, Volunteer Services, YMCA/YWCA/YMHA/YWHA

Application Procedures

Initial Contact: Send a brief, one or two page letter. Include the completed summary sheet provided by the foundation, the correct legal name and address of the organization, a description of the need to be addressed by the program and how the need will be met, who will be served, amount requested, project budget, other sources of funding, plans for future funding, list of officers and directors, staff involved in the project and their qualifications, proof of tax-exempt status, and most recent annual report.
Deadlines: September 15.

Restrictions

Does not make grants to individuals, projects or organizations involved in weapons development, or to establish or add to endowment funds.

Additional Information

Publications: Informational Brochure (including Summary Sheet); Application Guidelines (annually)

Foundation Officials

Mrs. William H. Bozman: vice president, director
Isabella Breckenridge: president, director
Joan Follin Koven: secretary, treasurer, director B Washington, DC 1937. ED Scarritt College (1959); West Virginia University BS (1959); University of Salisbury (1961); Sorbonne University (1962-1963); American University (1973); George Washington University (1979). PRIM CORP EMPL director, treasurer, secretary: Marpat Foundation. NONPR AFFIL member: Society Women Geographers; member: Women & Fisheries Network; member: Sea Plane Pilots Association; member: Pacific Science Association; member: Phi Upsilon Omicron; researchcollaborator: National Museum Natural History; member: Omicron Nu; member: Intl Society Reef Studies; director: Marine Environmental Institute; member: Conchologists America; president coral reef res: Fiji Islands Astrolabe; member: American Malacological Union; member: American Institute Biological Sciences; member: American Litoral Society; member: Aircraft Owners & Pilots Association; member: American Academy Underwater Research Scientists. CLUB AFFIL Hawaiian Shell Club; National Capital Shell Club.
Christine Minter-Dowd: vice president, director
Thomas W. Richards: vice president, director emeritus
Samuel N. Stokes: vice president, director

Grants Analysis

Disclosure Period: calendar year ending 2004
Total Grants: $1,747,500
Number of Grants: 153
Average Grant: $11,422
Highest Grant: $35,000
Lowest Grant: $5,000
Typical Range: $5,000 to $20,000

Recent Grants

Note: Grants derived from 2003 Form 990.
General

25,000	Historical Society of Washington DC and City Museum, Washington, DC -- to support the development of program materials for young people, particularly school children in the DC metropolitan area
20,000	Arlington Free Clinic, Arlington, VA
20,000	Atlas Performing Arts Center, Washington, DC -- to support the renovation of the atlas complex for theatre, dance, music, film and education in the performing arts and stagecraft
20,000	Round House Theatre, Bethesda, MD -- to support the capital campaign and help in matching a Kresge foundation grant
17,500	Calvary Bilingual Multicultural Learning Center, Washington, DC -- to support the early childhood and school age
15,000	Cacapon Institute, High View, WV -- for generating operating support for environmental science and education
15,000	DC Wheel Productions - Dance Place, Washington, DC
15,000	Marine Environmental Research Institute, Blue Hill, ME -- to support the coastal awareness program
15,000	Phillips Collection, Washington, DC -- to support the creation of a digital archive of works from the museums permanent collection by important American artists over the internet and CD-ROM

15,000   Potomac Conservancy, Arlington, VA

MARSHALL FOUNDATION

Giving Contact

Ron Mumford
PO Box 3306
Tucson, AZ 85722
Phone: (520)622-8613

Description

Founded: 1930
EIN: 860102198
Organization Type: Private Foundation
Giving Locations: AZ: Tuscon and Pima County
Grant Types: General Support.

Donor Information

Founder: the late Louise F. Marshall

Financial Summary

Total Giving: $263,545 (2001)
Assets: $18,393,246 (2001)

Typical Recipients

Arts & Humanities: Arts Associations & Councils, Historic Preservation, History & Archaeology, Libraries, Literary Arts, Museums/Galleries, Music
Civic & Public Affairs: Botanical Gardens/Parks, Civic & Public Affairs-General, Hispanic Affairs, Housing, Law & Justice, Legal Aid, Parades/Festivals, Philanthropic Organizations, Urban & Community Affairs
Education: Business Education, Colleges & Universities, Community & Junior Colleges, Continuing Education, Education Funds, Elementary Education (Public), Education-General, Health & Physical Education, Public Education (Precollege), Science/Mathematics Education, Student Aid
Environment: Resource Conservation
Health: AIDS/HIV, Clinics/Medical Centers, Diabetes, Health Organizations, Heart, Hospitals, Medical Research, Public Health, Single-Disease Health Associations
Religion: Churches, Religion-General, Jewish Causes, Ministries, Religious Welfare
Social Services: At-Risk Youth, Camps, Child Welfare, Community Service Organizations, Family Services, Food/Clothing Distribution, Homes, People with Disabilities, Recreation & Athletics, Scouts, Shelters/Homelessness, Social Services-General, Special Olympics, United Funds/United Ways, Veterans, YMCA/YWCA/YMHA/YWHA, Youth Organizations

Application Procedures

Initial Contact: a brief letter of inquiry
Application Requirements: a description of organization, purpose of funds sought, and proof of tax-exempt status
Deadlines: February 1, May 1, August 1, November 1. Board meets in March, June, September and December.

Restrictions

Grants are not made to support individuals, religious organizations for sectarian purposes, political or lobbying groups, or organizations outside operating areas.

Foundation Officials

Mr. Charles Jackson: president
Anne Nelson: secretary, treasurer
Jonathan Schmitt: vice president
George Steele: vice president
Elizabeth Sugges: student board mem
Christine Thompson: secretary

Grants Analysis

Disclosure Period: calendar year ending 2001
Total Grants: $263,545
Number of Grants: 20
Average Grant: $4,607*
Highest Grant: $176,012
Lowest Grant: $100
Typical Range: $1,000 to $10,000
***Note:** Average grant figure excludes highest grant.

Recent Grants

Note: Grants derived from 2001 Form 990.
General

1,000,000	Arizona State University, Tempe, AZ
348,000	Nature Conservancy, Phoenix, AZ
50,000	Arizona Center for Law in the Public Interest, Phoenix, AZ
20,000	Teenage Parenting School, Tucson, AZ
10,000	Community Outreach, Tucson, AZ
10,000	Handi-Dogs, Tucson, AZ
10,000	NRDC, New York, NY
7,500	Shoebox Ministry, Scottsdale, AZ
4,000	Neighbor to Neighbor, Prescott, AZ

MARSHALL & ILSLEY CORP.

Company Headquarters

770 N. Water St.
Milwaukee, WI 53202
Web: http://www.micorp.com

Company Description

Founded: 1847
Ticker: MI
Exchange: NYSE
Also Known As: Marshall & Ilsley Bank;
Acquired: National City Bancorporation.
Assets: US$26.37 billion (2001)
Employees: 12244 (2003)
SIC(s): 6021 National Commercial Banks, 6712 Bank Holding Companies.

Operating Locations

Marshall & Ilsley Corp. (WI--Adams, Beloit, Cambridge, Coloma, Dodgeville, Green Bay, Lancaster, Madison, Marshfield, Mayville, Merrill, Middleton, New Holstein, Racine, Rhinelander, Ripon, Stevens Point, Watertown, Wauwatosa, West Bend, Westfield)

Marshall & Ilsley Foundation, Inc.

Giving Contact

Rebecca Lonergan, Assistant Secretary
Marshall & Ilsley Foundation
770 North Water Street
Milwaukee, WI 53202
Phone: (414)765-7805
Fax: (414)765-7899

Description

Founded: 1958
EIN: 396043185
Organization Type: Corporate Foundation
Giving Locations: WI: emphasis on Milwaukee
Grant Types: Capital, General Support, Scholarship.

Financial Summary

Total Giving: $2,442,950 (2003); $2,206,250 (2002); $1,900,250 (2001). Note: Contributes through foundation only.
Giving Analysis: Giving for 2001 includes: founda-

tion scholarships ($47,000); foundation grants to United Way ($280,000); foundation ($1,573,250)
Assets: $224,120 (2003); $163,374 (2002); $123,285 (2001)
Gifts Received: $2,500,000 (2003); $2,250,000 (2002); $1,900,000 (2001). Note: Contributions are received from M&I Corp. and M&I Bank.

Typical Recipients
Arts & Humanities: Arts Associations & Councils, Arts Centers, Arts Festivals, Arts Funds, Arts Institutes, Film & Video, Historic Preservation, History & Archaeology, Libraries, Museums/Galleries, Music, Performing Arts, Public Broadcasting, Theater, Visual Arts
Civic & Public Affairs: Botanical Gardens/Parks, Community Foundations, Economic Development, Employment/Job Training, Ethnic Organizations, Civic & Public Affairs-General, Hispanic Affairs, Housing, Professional & Trade Associations, Urban & Community Affairs, Women's Affairs, Zoos/ Aquariums
Education: Arts/Humanities Education, Business Education, Colleges & Universities, Community & Junior Colleges, Education Associations, Education Funds, Education Reform, Elementary Education (Private), Elementary Education (Public), Engineering/Technological Education, Education-General, Leadership Training, Literacy, Medical Education, Minority Education, Private Education (Precollege), Science/Mathematics Education, Secondary Education (Private), Secondary Education (Public), Student Aid
Environment: Environment-General, Protection, Resource Conservation, Wildlife Protection
Health: Cancer, Children's Health/Hospitals, Clinics/ Medical Centers, Health Funds, Health Organizations, Hospitals, Hospitals (University Affiliated), Long-Term Care, Medical Research, Medical Training, Mental Health, Multiple Sclerosis, Nursing Services, Research/Studies Institutes, Single-Disease Health Associations, Transplant Networks/Donor Banks, Trauma Treatment
International: International Relations
Religion: Ministries, Religious Organizations, Religious Welfare
Science: Science Museums
Social Services: Animal Protection, Child Welfare, Community Centers, Community Service Organizations, Crime Prevention, Day Care, Family Planning, Family Services, Food/Clothing Distribution, People with Disabilities, Recreation & Athletics, Scouts, Senior Services, Shelters/Homelessness, Social Services-General, United Funds/United Ways, Volunteer Services, YMCA/YWCA/YMHA/YWHA, Youth Organizations

Application Procedures
Initial Contact: Send a brief letter or proposal.
Application Requirements: Include a a description of organization, amount requested, purpose of funds sought, recently audited financial statement, and proof of tax-exempt status.
Deadlines: None.

Restrictions
Scholarships are for sons and daughters of permanent, full-time employees of M&I Corp.

Corporate Officials
Dennis J. Kuester: president, director B 1942. ED University of Milwaukee BBA (1966). PRIM CORP EMPL president, director: Marshall & Ilsley Corp. CORP AFFIL director: Modine Manufacturing Co.; director: Super Steel Products Corp.; president: Marshall & Ilsley Bank; director: Krueger International Inc.; chairman, chief executive officer: M & I Data Services Inc.
James B. Wigdale: chairman, director B 1936. PRIM CORP EMPL chairman, director: Marshall & Ilsley Corp. CORP AFFIL chairman, chief executive officer: Marshall & Ilsley Bank; chairman: M & I Marshall & Ilsley Bank; director: M & I Mortgage Corp.; director:

M & I Capital Markets Group; director: M & I First National Leasing; director: Columbia Health System Inc.; director: Green Bay Packaging Inc. NONPR AFFIL chairman: Medical College Wisconsin; vice chairman: Metropolitan Milwaukee Association.

Foundation Officials
Richard A. Abdoo: director
Thomas Bolger: director
Bruce E. Jacobs: director
Dennis J. Kuester: vice president, director (see above)
Becky Lonergan: assistant secretary
James A. Urdan: director
George E. Wardeberg: director
James B. Wigdale: president, director (see above)

Grants Analysis
Disclosure Period: calendar year ending 2003
Total Grants: $2,012,950*
Number of Grants: 145
Average Grant: $13,007*
Highest Grant: $140,000
Lowest Grant: $1,000
Typical Range: $1,000 to $25,000
*Note: Giving excludes scholarships and United Way. Average grant figure excludes highest grant.

Recent Grants
Note: Grants derived from 2003 Form 990.
Library-Related

25,000	Milwaukee Public Library, Milwaukee, WI
25,000	Whitefish Bay Library Fund Inc., Whitefish Bay, WI

General

140,000	United Performing Arts Fund, Milwaukee, WI
93,750	United Way of Greater Milwaukee, Milwaukee, WI
93,750	United Way of Greater Milwaukee, Milwaukee, WI
93,750	United Way of Greater Milwaukee, Milwaukee, WI
93,750	United Way of Greater Milwaukee, Milwaukee, WI
50,000	Aurora Health Care, Aurora, CO
50,000	Children's Hospital Foundation
50,000	Fox Cities Performing Arts Center, Appleton, WI
50,000	Milwaukee Public Museum, Milwaukee, WI
50,000	Milwaukee School of Engineering, Milwaukee, WI

MARGARET LEE MARTIN CHARITABLE TRUST

Giving Contact
James M. Floyd, Sr., Trustee
PO Box 1009
Hinesville, GA 31310

Description
Founded: 1995
EIN: 586305150
Organization Type: Private Foundation

Financial Summary
Total Giving: $331,203 (2003); $295,000 (2001)
Giving Analysis: Giving for 2003 includes: foundation grants to United Way ($8,896); foundation scholarships ($220,000); 2001: foundation grants to United Way ($10,400); foundation scholarships ($165,000)
Assets: $9,172,043 (2003); $10,325,011 (2001)
Gifts Received: $23,949 (1998); $1,470,000 (1996).
Note: In 1998, contributions were received from the estate of Margaret L. Martin.

Typical Recipients
Arts & Humanities: Arts Associations & Councils, Historic Preservation, History & Archaeology, Libraries, Museums/Galleries
Civic & Public Affairs: Botanical Gardens/Parks, Chambers of Commerce
Education: Student Aid
Religion: Churches
Science: Science-General
Social Services: Scouts, United Funds/United Ways, Youth Organizations

Application Procedures
Initial Contact: Applications should be submitted on the forms provided to the high school guidance counselors. Also, counselors should provide a transcript, class ranking, and verification of S.A.T. or A.C.T. scores.
Deadlines: May 1.

Additional Information
Provides scholarships to residents of Liberty County, GA, who are in the top 10% of his or her class, score a minimum of 1,000 on the SAT or equivalent on the ACT, and have been accepted by a regionally accredited college, university, or nursing school.
Trust(s): Bank of America

Foundation Officials
James M. Floyd, Sr.: trustee

Grants Analysis
Disclosure Period: calendar year ending 2003
Total Grants: $102,307*
Number of Grants: 9
Average Grant: $11,367
Highest Grant: $22,241
Lowest Grant: $2,224
Typical Range: $5,000 to $20,000
*Note: Giving excludes United Way; scholarships.

Recent Grants
Note: Grants derived from 2003 Form 990.
Library-Related

22,241	Liberty County Public Library, Hinesville, GA

General

220,000	Bank of America
22,241	Flemington Presbyterian Church, Hinesville, GA
22,241	Hinesville Arts Council, Hinesville, GA
8,896	Liberty County Historical Society, Hinesville, GA
8,896	Midway Church and Society, Hinesville, GA
8,896	Midway Museum Inc., Midway, GA
8,896	United Way of Liberty County, Hinesville, GA
4,448	LeConte Woodmanston Foundation Inc., Midway, GA
2,224	Coastal Empire Council Boy Scouts of America, Savannah, GA

MARTIN FOUNDATION

Giving Contact
Geraldine Martin, President
Martin Foundation, Inc.
Castillo Square
5051 Castillo Drive, Suite 204
Naples, FL 34103-8982
Phone: (239)649-4543

Description
Founded: 1954
EIN: 351070929
Organization Type: Family Foundation
Giving Locations: nationally.

Grant Types: Challenge, Conference/Seminar, Endowment, General Support, Matching, Professorship, Project, Research, Scholarship, Seed Money.

Donor Information

Founder: Incorporated in 1953 by Lee Martin, Geraldine F. Martin, the late Ross Martin, the late Esther Martin, and NIBCO, Inc.

Financial Summary

Total Giving: $2,348,189 (fiscal year ending June 30, 2003); $3,524,400 (fiscal 2002); $2,758,420 (fiscal 2001)

Giving Analysis: Giving for fiscal 2003 includes: foundation fellowships ($935,000); fiscal 2001: foundation scholarships ($16,500); foundation fellowships ($1,490,000)

Assets: $25,934,492 (fiscal 2003); $25,877,585 (fiscal 2002); $68,901,780 (fiscal 2001)

Typical Recipients

Arts & Humanities: Arts Appreciation, Arts Associations & Councils, Arts Centers, Arts Festivals, Arts Institutes, Ethnic & Folk Arts, Historic Preservation, History & Archaeology, Libraries, Museums/Galleries, Music, Performing Arts, Public Broadcasting, Theater

Civic & Public Affairs: Botanical Gardens/Parks, Clubs, Community Foundations, Economic Development, Civic & Public Affairs-General, Hispanic Affairs, Housing, Law & Justice, Legal Aid, Municipalities/ Towns, Public Policy, Rural Affairs, Safety, Urban & Community Affairs, Women's Affairs, Zoos/ Aquariums

Education: Agricultural Education, Arts/Humanities Education, Business Education, Colleges & Universities, Community & Junior Colleges, Continuing Education, Education Funds, Elementary Education (Private), Engineering/Technological Education, Environmental Education, Legal Education, Literacy, Medical Education, Minority Education, Preschool Education, Private Education (Precollege), Public Education (Precollege), Secondary Education (Private), Special Education, Student Aid, Vocational & Technical Education

Environment: Air/Water Quality, Energy, Forestry, Environment-General, Protection, Research, Resource Conservation, Wildlife Protection

Health: AIDS/HIV, Alzheimer's Disease, Cancer, Clinics/Medical Centers, Diabetes, Emergency/ Ambulance Services, Health-General, Health Organizations, Hospices, Hospitals, Medical Research, Medical Training, Mental Health, Nursing Services, Public Health, Single-Disease Health Associations

International: Health Care/Hospitals, International Development, International Environmental Issues, International Peace & Security Issues, International Relations, Missionary/Religious Activities

Religion: Churches, Ministries, Missionary Activities (Domestic), Religious Organizations, Religious Welfare, Social/Policy Issues

Science: Science Museums, Scientific Centers & Institutes, Scientific Organizations, Scientific Research

Social Services: Animal Protection, At-Risk Youth, Child Abuse, Child Welfare, Community Centers, Community Service Organizations, Counseling, Crime Prevention, Day Care, Delinquency & Criminal Rehabilitation, Domestic Violence, Family Planning, Family Services, Food/Clothing Distribution, Homes, People with Disabilities, Recreation & Athletics, Scouts, Senior Services, Shelters/Homelessness, Social Services-General, Substance Abuse, United Funds/United Ways, YMCA/YWCA/YMHA/YWHA, Youth Organizations

Application Procedures

Initial Contact: Write the foundation for guidelines and annual report.

Application Requirements: A written proposal should include the following: the legal name, address and telephone number of the organization; a copy of the IRS tax exempt determination letter; a brief description of the history of the organization including goals, objectives and activities; a statement describing in detail the project or activities for which grant was requested; a copy of the latest annual report and an audited financial statement or Form 990 for the most recent fiscal year; a list of other funding sources contacted and results; an itemized budget for the organization and project showing both projected revenue and expenses for the current fiscal year; time frame of the project and future funding plans; and a list of names of the current Board of Directors.

Deadlines: None.

Review Process: Proposals are reviewed by the board approximately four to six times a year.

Restrictions

The foundation does not support gifts to individuals.

Additional Information

Since its founding, the Martin Foundation has been managed by directors who were related by blood or marriage. Over time, the interests of the directors with respect to the Foundation's management and goals diverged. Believing that the Martin Foundation's charitable purposes would be better served by allowing four of its directors to start private foundations with separate boards, in 2001 the Martin Foundation transferred assets equaling about 64.5% of total assets to each of the four new foundations. The four new foundations and the assets transferred are: Rex and Alice A. Martin Foundation, Inc. ($9,354,953); Foundation M ($9,594,954); Martin Fabert Foundation ($9,594,954); and Martin and Brown Foundation ($9,603,582).

Foundation Officials

Casper Martin: treasurer, secretary, director CORP AFFIL officer: NIBCO Inc.

Elizabeth Martin: director

Geraldine F. Martin: president, director

Jennifer Martin: director

Grants Analysis

Disclosure Period: fiscal year ending June 30, 2003

Total Grants: $1,413,189*

Number of Grants: 90

Average Grant: $15,813

Highest Grant: $150,000

Lowest Grant: $500

Typical Range: $5,000 to $40,000

*Note: Giving excludes fellowships.

Recent Grants

Note: Grants derived from fiscal 2003 Form 990.

General

925,000	MIT, Cambridge, MA -- toward graduate fellows support	
150,000	Middlesex School, Concord, MA -- toward new math classroom for high school	
100,000	Organix Exchange -- toward environment	
64,000	Westover School, Middlebury, CT -- funding for summer sabbatical fund	
50,000	Lowe's Home Safety Council, Wilkesboro, NC -- toward sponsor of safety programs for children	
40,000	Sustainable Cotton Project, Davis, CA -- toward environment	
33,000	New England Wildlife Center, Hingham, MA	
28,000	Loveway Inc., Middlebury, IN -- for building horseback riding arena for handicapped children	
25,364	Empowerment Alliance for Southwest Florida, Naples, FL -- funding for housing coordinator	
25,000	Appalachian Mountain Club, Boston, MA -- toward capital campaign	

NICHOLAS MARTINI FOUNDATION

Giving Contact

777 Passaic Avenue
Clifton, NJ 07012
Phone: (973)594-1899

Description

Founded: 1986
EIN: 222756049
Organization Type: Private Foundation
Giving Locations: NJ: Bergen County, Essex County, Passaic County
Grant Types: General Support.

Donor Information

Founder: the late Nicholas Martini

Financial Summary

Total Giving: $365,850 (2001)

Giving Analysis: Giving for 2001 includes: foundation grants to United Way ($4,000)

Assets: $13,345,465 (2001)

Gifts Received: $295,000 (1995); $3,550,961 (1993). Note: In 1995, contributions were received from the estate of Nicholas Martini.

Typical Recipients

Arts & Humanities: Arts Associations & Councils, Dance, Ethnic & Folk Arts, Film & Video, History & Archaeology, Libraries, Museums/Galleries, Music, Performing Arts, Public Broadcasting

Civic & Public Affairs: Clubs, Economic Development, Ethnic Organizations, Civic & Public Affairs-General, Hispanic Affairs, Housing, Parades/ Festivals, Public Policy, Safety

Education: Arts/Humanities Education, Colleges & Universities, Education Funds, Elementary Education (Private), Education-General, Gifted & Talented Programs, Journalism/Media Education, Legal Education, Medical Education, Preschool Education, Private Education (Precollege), Public Education (Precollege), Secondary Education (Private), Secondary Education (Public), Student Aid, Vocational & Technical Education

Environment: Air/Water Quality

Health: Cancer, Clinics/Medical Centers, Emergency/Ambulance Services, Health Organizations, Heart, Hospices, Hospitals, Hospitals (University Affiliated), Long-Term Care, Mental Health, Prenatal Health Issues, Single-Disease Health Associations

International: International Relief Efforts, Missionary/Religious Activities

Religion: Churches, Dioceses, Religious Organizations, Religious Welfare, Synagogues/Temples

Science: Scientific Centers & Institutes

Social Services: At-Risk Youth, Camps, Child Welfare, Community Service Organizations, Crime Prevention, Day Care, Family Services, Homes, People with Disabilities, Recreation & Athletics, Scouts, Senior Services, Social Services-General, United Funds/United Ways, YMCA/YWCA/YMHA/YWHA, Youth Organizations

Application Procedures

Initial Contact: Send a brief letter of inquiry.

Application Requirements: Include a description of organization, qualifications of the people involved, the nature and scope of the proposed project and the anticipated results, a preliminary timetable, proposed budget, recently audited financial statement, proof of tax-exempt status, and a list of board members.

Deadlines: None.

Restrictions

Does not provide grants to individuals.

Foundation Officials

Gloria Martini: vice president
William J. Martini: trustee B Passaic, NJ. ED Villanova University (1968); Rutgers University JD (1972). PRIM CORP EMPL congressman: U.S. House Reps. NONPR AFFIL trustee: Center Italian American Culture; trustee: United Way Passaic County; trustee: Boy Scouts America Passaic Valley Council.
Fannie Rosta: trustee
Marie Salanitri: trustee

Grants Analysis

Disclosure Period: calendar year ending 2001
Total Grants: $361,850*
Number of Grants: 70
Average Grant: $5,169
Highest Grant: $30,200
Typical Range: $1,000 to $10,000
*Note: Giving excludes United Way.

Recent Grants

Note: Grants derived from 2001 Form 990.
General

30,200	Hackensack University Medical Center Foundation, Hackensack, NJ
25,350	NIAF, Washington, DC
25,000	John Cabot University, DE
25,000	Rutgers University Law School, New Brunswick, NJ
22,500	Boys & Girls Club of Clifton, Clifton, NJ
15,000	Montclair Art Museum, Montclair, NJ
15,000	Scholarship Fund for Inner-City Children, New York, NY
15,000	Tri-County Scholarship Fund, Paterson, NJ
12,500	Ripon Education Fund, Washington, DC
10,000	Boy Scouts of America Northern New Jersey Council, Fair Lawn, NJ

VIRGINIA AND LEONARD MARX FOUNDATION

Giving Contact

Jennifer Gruenberg, Secretary
708 Third Avenue
New York, NY 10017
Phone: (212)557-1400

Description

Founded: 1959
EIN: 136162557
Organization Type: Private Foundation
Giving Locations: NY: New York
Grant Types: General Support.

Donor Information

Founder: The late Leonard Marx, Virginia Marx.

Financial Summary

Total Giving: $491,300 (2001)
Giving Analysis: Giving for 2001 includes: foundation grants to United Way ($5,000)
Assets: $35,716,416 (2001)
Gifts Received: $1,233,768 (2001); $15,172,810 (2000); $1,082,046 (1999). Note: In 2001, contributions were received from Leonard Marx ($500,000); Dollar Land ($274,749); Rier Realty Co. ($140,850); and miscellaneous other donors who contributed less than $100,000 each. In 2000, contributions were received from the estate of Virginia Marx ($14,227,637), Leonard Marx ($500,000), Dollar Land Syndicate ($167,188), and miscellaneous other donors who contributions less than $100,000 each. Marx Co., Inc. ($79,325), Kesmar Realty Co., ($5,088), Leonard Marx ($500,000), Merchants National Properties, Inc. ($31,488), Promar Realty Co.,

Inc. ($46,081), Rier Realty Co., Inc. ($47,050), and Virginia Marx ($500,000). In 1996, contributions were received from 17 West Orange Realty Co. ($9,600), 26 East Realty Co. ($27,881), Argin Realty Co. ($21,900), Darb Realty Co. ($35,000), Dollar Land Syndicate ($267,385), Guest Realty Co. ($80,000), Joseph E. Marx Co. ($37,750), Kesmar Realty Co. ($6,138), Leonard Marx ($500,000), Merchants National Properties ($31,318), Promar Realty Co. ($60,437), Rier Realty Co. ($46,850), and Virginia Marx ($500,000).

Typical Recipients

Arts & Humanities: Arts Associations & Councils, Arts Funds, Historic Preservation, History & Archaeology, Libraries, Museums/Galleries, Music, Performing Arts, Public Broadcasting, Theater
Civic & Public Affairs: Civic & Public Affairs-General, Legal Aid, Philanthropic Organizations, Women's Affairs
Education: Arts/Humanities Education, Colleges & Universities, Community & Junior Colleges, Education Associations, Education-General, Minority Education, Public Education (Precollege)
Environment: Environment-General
Health: Alzheimer's Disease, Cancer, Clinics/Medical Centers, Hospitals, Medical Research, Mental Health, Public Health, Research/Studies Institutes, Single-Disease Health Associations
Religion: Jewish Causes, Religious Organizations, Religious Welfare
Social Services: Camps, Child Welfare, Counseling, Crime Prevention, Family Planning, Family Services, United Funds/United Ways, YMCA/YWCA/YMHA/YWHA, Youth Organizations

Application Procedures

Initial Contact: Send a brief letter of inquiry describing program or project.
Application Requirements: Include complete information regarding grant requested.
Deadlines: None.

Foundation Officials

Jennifer Gruenberg: director
Leonard Marx, Jr.: treasurer
Leonard Marx: vice president B New York, NY 1932. ED Yale University (1954); Harvard University (1956). PRIM CORP EMPL president, director: Merchants National Properties.
Virginia Marx: president
John E. Tuchler: president

Grants Analysis

Disclosure Period: calendar year ending 2001
Total Grants: $491,300
Number of Grants: 43
Average Grant: $11,426
Highest Grant: $100,000
Lowest Grant: $200
Typical Range: $5,000 to $25,000

Recent Grants

Note: Grants derived from 2001 Form 990.
Library-Related

10,000	White Plains Public Library Foundation, White Plains, NY

General

100,000	UJA Federation, New York, NY
55,000	Jewish Board of Family and Children's Services, New York, NY
45,000	Westchester Jewish Community Services, Westchester, NY
25,000	American Jewish Committee
25,000	Thirteen-WNET, Brooklyn, NY
25,000	White Plains Hospital, White Plains, NY
25,000	Yale University Child Study Center, New Haven, CT
20,000	Mental Health Association of Westchester, Westchester, NY
16,000	Yale Alumni Fund, New Haven, CT
10,000	Hypertension Education Foundation, Inc.

MASCOMA SAVINGS BANK

Company Headquarters

67 N. Park St.
Lebanon, NH 03766

Company Description

Employees: 85
SIC(s): 6000 Depository Institutions.

Nonmonetary Support

Type: Donated Equipment

Mascoma Savings Bank Foundation

Giving Contact

Thomas F. Terry, Trustee
Mascoma Savings Bank Foundation
PO Box 435
Lebanon, NH 03766

Description

EIN: 222816632
Organization Type: Corporate Foundation
Giving Locations: operating communities.
Grant Types: Capital, General Support, Project.

Financial Summary

Total Giving: $104,405 (2001)
Giving Analysis: Giving for 2001 includes: foundation grants to United Way ($1,500); foundation ($102,905)
Assets: $2,327,121 (2001)
Gifts Received: $153,625 (2001); $162,698 (2000); $155,275 (1999). Note: In 2000 and 2001, contributions were received from Mascoma Savings Bank. In 1999, contributions were received from Mascoma Savings Bank ($155,025) and Stephen Christy ($250).

Typical Recipients

Arts & Humanities: Arts & Humanities-General, Historic Preservation, History & Archaeology, Libraries, Museums/Galleries, Music, Opera, Public Broadcasting
Civic & Public Affairs: Botanical Gardens/Parks, Business/Free Enterprise, Clubs, Community Foundations, Civic & Public Affairs-General, Housing, Municipalities/Towns, Parades/Festivals, Safety, Urban & Community Affairs, Women's Affairs
Education: Colleges & Universities, Education Associations, Elementary Education (Public), Faculty Development, Education-General, Medical Education, Preschool Education, Private Education (Precollege), Public Education (Precollege), Science/Mathematics Education, Special Education, Student Aid
Environment: Air/Water Quality, Energy, Environment-General, Protection, Resource Conservation
Health: AIDS/HIV, Cancer, Emergency/Ambulance Services, Health-General, Health Funds, Health Organizations, Hospices, Medical Rehabilitation, Nursing Services, Public Health
International: International Affairs
Religion: Churches
Science: Science Museums
Social Services: Animal Protection, Camps, Child Welfare, Community Centers, Community Service Organizations, Crime Prevention, Day Care, Delinquency & Criminal Rehabilitation, Family Planning, Family Services, Food/Clothing Distribution, Recreation & Athletics, Scouts, Senior Services, Social Services-General, Substance Abuse, United Funds/United Ways, Veterans, Volunteer Services, YMCA/YWCA/YMHA/YWHA, Youth Organizations

Application Procedures

Initial Contact: Send a one- to three-page letter describing the organization and the program for which grant is sought.

Application Requirements: Include name, address, and phone number of contact person, amount requested, annual report, recently audited financial statement, proof of tax-exempt status, details of current sources of support, and plans for future funding.

Deadlines: April 1 and October 1.

Restrictions

Does not support individuals, religious organizations for sectarian purposes, political or lobbying groups, or organizations outside operating areas.

Corporate Officials

Stephen Christy: president, chief executive officer PRIM CORP EMPL president, chief executive officer: Mascoma Savings Bank.

Clark A. Griffiths: chairman PRIM CORP EMPL chairman: Mascoma Savings Bank.

Foundation Officials

Elizabeth L. Crory: trustee
Charles M. Harrington: trustee
Raymond A. Lagasse: chairman
Joseph M. Longacre: trustee
Barry E. McCabe: executive vice president, chief operating officer
Thomas T. Terry: trustee

Grants Analysis

Disclosure Period: calendar year ending 2001
Total Grants: $102,905*
Number of Grants: 88
Average Grant: $1,169
Highest Grant: $5,000
Typical Range: $500 to $2,000
***Note:** Giving excludes United Way.

Recent Grants

Note: Grants derived from 2001 Form 990.
Library-Related

2,300	Fairlee Public Library, Fairlee, VT -- for renovations

General

5,000	Cooperative Preschool of Lebanon, Lebanon, OH -- for renovations
4,500	Friends of Veterans -- for Veteran's Aid and Assistance Programs
3,000	Northern Stage, White River Junction, VT -- for new rehearsal hall
3,000	Thompson Senior Center, Woodstock, VT -- for new computers
2,500	Saint Barnabas Church of Central Vermont Community Action, VT -- for the Good Wheels Program
2,150	Windsor School District, Boston, MA -- for LCD projector and laptop computer
2,000	Hampshire Cooperative Nursery School -- for facility improvements
2,000	Opera North, Hanover, NH -- for Opera Scenes Program
2,000	Wolf and Wild Canine Sanctuary, Inc., White River Junction, VT -- for upgrade to kennel roof
1,750	Child and Family Services -- for Mascoma Student Assistance Program

MAURICE H. MASLAND TRUST NO. 2

Giving Contact

Phyllis W. Smith, Trustee
3932 Druid Hills Rd.
Louisville, KY 40207

Phone: (502)721-8982

Description

Founded: 1994
EIN: 237733774
Organization Type: Private Foundation
Giving Locations: CO; FL; IL; MI; PA
Grant Types: General Support.

Financial Summary

Total Giving: $128,000 (2001)
Assets: $22,685 (2001)

Typical Recipients

Arts & Humanities: Arts & Humanities-General, Libraries

Civic & Public Affairs: Civic & Public Affairs-General

Education: Colleges & Universities, Education-General, Leadership Training, Religious Education

Health: Clinics/Medical Centers, Health Organizations

International: Foreign Arts Organizations, Foreign Educational Institutions, International Development, Missionary/Religious Activities

Religion: Bible Study/Translation, Churches, Religion-General, Ministries, Missionary Activities (Domestic), Religious Organizations, Religious Welfare

Application Procedures

Initial Contact: Send a brief letter of inquiry.
Application Requirements: State project, funds requested, and background information.
Deadlines: None.

Foundation Officials

Phyllis W. Smith: trustee

Grants Analysis

Disclosure Period: calendar year ending 2001
Total Grants: $128,000
Number of Grants: 8
Average Grant: $9,000*
Highest Grant: $65,000
Lowest Grant: $3,000
Typical Range: $5,000 to $15,000
***Note:** Average grant figure excludes highest grant.

Recent Grants

Note: Grants derived from 2001 Form 990.
General

65,000	Church of the Nazarene International Board of Education, Kansas City, MO
15,000	Philadelphia College of Bible, Langhorne, PA
10,000	Adelaide College of Ministries, Doylestown, PA
10,000	Christar, Reading, PA
10,000	SEND International, Farmington, MI
10,000	Stephen's Children Ministries, Atlanta, GA
5,000	ACMC, Atlanta, GA
3,000	Campus Crusade for Christ, Orlando, FL

MASSACHUSETTS MUTUAL LIFE INSURANCE CO.

Company Headquarters

1295 State Street
Springfield, MA 01111
Web: http://www.massmutual.com

Company Description

Revenue: US$23.159 billion (2004)
Profit: US$677 million (2004)

Employees: 31000 (2003)
Fortune Rank: 83, per FORTUNE Magazine's list of 500 Largest U.S. Corporations (2004).
SIC(s): 6311 Life Insurance, 6321 Accident & Health Insurance.

Operating Locations

Massachusetts Mutual Life Insurance Co. (CT--Hartford)

Subsidiary Companies

NY: Oppenheimer Fund, Rochester

Nonmonetary Support

Type: Donated Equipment; Donated Products
Volunteer Programs: Company sponsors volunteer activities, such as Junior Achievement, literacy, and tutor/mentor programs. Supports the volunteers in Action Program, which awards cash grants to organizations where employees actively volunteer.
Contact: Portia Allen, Administrative Assistant, Corporate Communications
Note: Company provides nonmonetary support.

The MassMutual Foundation for Hartford, Inc.

Giving Contact

Ronald A. Copes, Executive Director
140 Garden Street
ATTN: H356
Hartford, CT 06154
Phone: (860)987-2085
Fax: (860)987-2493
E-mail: rcopes@massmutual.com
Web: http://massmutual.com/mmfg/about/community.html

Description

EIN: 510192500
Organization Type: Corporate Foundation
Giving Locations: CT: Hartford and surrounding area
Grant Types: Capital, General Support, Multiyear/Continuing Support, Scholarship.
Note: Employee matching gift ratio: 1 to 1, up to $1,000 for employees and up to $2,500 for directors.

Financial Summary

Total Giving: $1,262,076 (2003); $1,846,233 (2002); $1,418,203 (2001). Note: Contributes through corporate direct giving program and foundation.
Assets: $5,433,520 (2003); $5,700,723 (2002); $8,412,720 (2001)
Gifts Received: $3,400 (2000); $153,213 (1998). Note: Contributions were received from Massachusetts Mutual Life Insurance Company.

Typical Recipients

Arts & Humanities: Arts Associations & Councils, Dance, Arts & Humanities-General, Historic Preservation, History & Archaeology, Libraries, Literary Arts, Museums/Galleries, Music, Opera, Performing Arts, Public Broadcasting, Theater

Civic & Public Affairs: African American Affairs, Botanical Gardens/Parks, Community Foundations, Economic Development, Employment/Job Training, Civic & Public Affairs-General, Housing, Parades/Festivals, Public Policy, Safety, Urban & Community Affairs, Women's Affairs

Education: Afterschool/Enrichment Programs, Business Education, Colleges & Universities, Community & Junior Colleges, Continuing Education, Education Associations, Education Funds, Elementary Education (Public), Education-General, Leadership Training, Legal Education, Literacy, Private Education (Precollege), Public Education (Precollege), Student Aid, Vocational & Technical Education

Environment: Environment-General
Health: AIDS/HIV, Children's Health/Hospitals, Clinics/Medical Centers, Health Funds, Hospitals, Medical Research, Multiple Sclerosis, Preventive Medicine/Wellness Organizations
Religion: Religious Organizations, Religious Welfare
Social Services: Animal Protection, At-Risk Youth, Big Brothers/Big Sisters, Camps, Child Welfare, Community Service Organizations, Emergency Relief, Family Services, Food/Clothing Distribution, Homes, People with Disabilities, Shelters/Homelessness, Social Services-General, Substance Abuse, United Funds/United Ways, Volunteer Services, YMCA/YWCA/YMHA/YWHA, Youth Organizations

Application Procedures

Initial Contact: Request copies of application and contribution guidelines, then submit a written proposal.
Application Requirements: Include a description of organization or program to be funded, including a clear statement of goals and objectives; budget; proof of tax-exempt status; a list of the organization's board of directors. tax-exemption letter. tax-exemption letter.
Deadlines: None.
Review Process: Applications are reviewed quarterly.
Decision Notification: Applicants are generally notified of the foundation's decision within two months of application.
Notes: The foundation prefers that applicants use the common grant application form developed by the Coordinating Council for Foundations in Hartford.

Restrictions

Contributions will not be made for: individuals; operating costs and expenses, such as transportation, refreshments and promotional items; deficit reduction campaigns; fraternal societies, labor organizations and veterans' groups; independent fundraising activities of United Way agencies, other than selected capital fund campaigns; organizations which are not tax-exempt; religious or political organizations; or fundraising activities such as golf tournaments, auctions, walkathons, etc.

Additional Information

Company has operations in nearly all 50 states.
Mass Mutual merged with Connecticut Mutual in 1996. The Connecticut Mutual Foundation became the MassMutual Foundation for Hartford; the Massachusetts Mutual Contributions Program continues its support for the Springfield, MA area.
Those organizations which receive support are required to provide a status report of the program funded at the end of the grant period, usually within six months of funding. A MassMutual report form will be provided for this purpose when the grant is awarded. Any future support will be contingent on MassMutual's receipt of this information in a timely manner.
Publications: Social Report; Guidelines; Application Form

Corporate Officials

Frances Emerson: senior vice president, Corporate Communications MassMutual

Giving Program Officials

Ronald Adrian Copes: second vice president B Hartford, CT 1941. ED Lincoln University BS (1963); Atlanta University MBA (1973). NONPR AFFIL member: Omega Psi Phi Fraternity Inc.

Foundation Officials

John L. Abbott: director
Suzanne M. Bergin: director
Michael Chong: director
Constance Clayton: president, director
Ronald Adrian Copes: executive director, director (see above)

William B. Ellis: director
Frances Emerson: director (see above)
Beverly Holmes: director
James M. Lynch: treasurer
James E. Miller: director
James P. Puhala, III: secretary, director
Kevin M. Sweeney: director
Eustis Walcott: vice president, director

Grants Analysis

Disclosure Period: calendar year ending 2003
Total Grants: $643,659*
Number of Grants: 61
Average Grant: $9,061*
Highest Grant: $100,000
Lowest Grant: $750
Typical Range: $1,000 to $20,000
*Note: Giving excludes scholarships; United Way. Average grant figure excludes highest grant.

Recent Grants

Note: Grants derived from 2003 Form 990.
Library-Related

33,000	Hartford Public Library, Hartford, CT

General

100,000	University of Connecticut Foundation, Storrs, CT
50,000	Greater Hartford Arts Council, Hartford, CT
50,000	Hartford Public Schools, Hartford, CT
50,000	United Way of the Capital Area, Hartford, CT
50,000	University of Hartford, Hartford, CT
45,000	Hartford Stage, Hartford, CT
35,000	Hartford Area Habitat for Humanity, Hartford, CT
34,786	Bushnell Center for the Performing Arts, Hartford, CT
25,000	Connecticut Historical Society, Hartford, CT
25,000	Hartford Hospital, Hartford, CT

MASSEY CHARITABLE TRUST

Giving Contact

Walter J. Carroll, Managing Trustee
PO Box 1178
Coraopolis, PA 15108
Phone: (412)262-5992

Description

Founded: 1968
EIN: 237007897
Organization Type: Family Foundation
Giving Locations: PA: emphasis on Southwest Pennsylvania, Pittsburgh
Grant Types: General Support, Research.

Donor Information

Founder: The trust was established in 1968 by Doris J. Massey, the late H. B. Massey, and Massey Rental.

Financial Summary

Total Giving: $1,274,538 (2003); $2,116,580 (2001)
Assets: $37,138,380 (2003); $38,433,065 (2001)

Typical Recipients

Arts & Humanities: Arts Associations & Councils, Arts Centers, Ballet, Historic Preservation, History & Archaeology, Libraries, Museums/Galleries, Music, Opera, Performing Arts, Public Broadcasting, Theater, Visual Arts
Civic & Public Affairs: Botanical Gardens/Parks, Clubs, Employment/Job Training, Civic & Public Affairs-General, Legal Aid, Professional & Trade Associations, Public Policy, Urban & Community Affairs, Zoos/Aquariums
Education: Arts/Humanities Education, Colleges & Universities, Continuing Education, Education Funds, Education-General, Literacy, Medical Education, Minority Education, Private Education (Precollege), Public Education (Precollege), Science/Mathematics Education, Special Education
Environment: Resource Conservation
Health: Alzheimer's Disease, Arthritis, Cancer, Children's Health/Hospitals, Clinics/Medical Centers, Diabetes, Emergency/Ambulance Services, Eyes/Blindness, Health Funds, Health Organizations, Hospices, Hospitals, Hospitals (University Affiliated), Kidney, Long-Term Care, Medical Rehabilitation, Medical Research, Mental Health, Nursing Services, Preventive Medicine/Wellness Organizations, Public Health, Single-Disease Health Associations
International: Foreign Arts Organizations, International Peace & Security Issues, International Relations
Religion: Churches, Dioceses, Ministries, Religious Organizations, Religious Welfare, Synagogues/Temples
Science: Scientific Centers & Institutes, Scientific Research
Social Services: At-Risk Youth, Big Brothers/Big Sisters, Child Welfare, Community Centers, Community Service Organizations, Counseling, Family Planning, Family Services, Food/Clothing Distribution, Homes, People with Disabilities, Scouts, Senior Services, Sexual Abuse, Shelters/Homelessness, Substance Abuse, United Funds/United Ways, Volunteer Services, YMCA/YWCA/YMHA/YWHA, Youth Organizations

Application Procedures

Initial Contact: The trust has no formal grant application procedure or application form.
Application Requirements: Applications should include the amount requested and purpose, and documentation of exempt and non-private foundation status.
Deadlines: None.

Restrictions

Grants are not made to individuals.

Foundation Officials

Daniel B. Carroll: trustee
Walter J. Carroll: managing trustee
Robert M. Connolly: trustee
Joe B. Massey: trustee

Grants Analysis

Disclosure Period: calendar year ending 2003
Total Grants: $1,274,538
Number of Grants: 101
Average Grant: $12,619
Highest Grant: $125,000
Lowest Grant: $1,000
Typical Range: $5,000 to $25,000

Recent Grants

Note: Grants derived from 2002 Form 990.
General

125,000	Robert Morris University, Moon Township, PA
90,000	High Museum of Art, Atlanta, GA
75,000	Atlanta Symphony Orchestra, Atlanta, GA
75,000	Pittsburgh Leadership Foundation, Pittsburgh, PA
30,000	Families First Inc., Atlanta, GA
30,000	Family Guidance Inc., Sewickley, PA
25,000	Atlanta Contemporary Art Center, Atlanta, GA
25,000	Atlanta Historical Society Inc., Atlanta, GA
25,000	Belmont University, Nashville, TN
25,000	Carlow College, Pittsburgh, PA

DAVID MEADE MASSIE TRUST

Giving Contact
PO Box 41
Chillicothe, OH 45601
Phone: (740)772-5070

Description
EIN: 316022292
Organization Type: Private Foundation
Giving Locations: OH: Chillicothe County, Ross County
Grant Types: General Support.

Financial Summary
Total Giving: $290,176 (2001)
Assets: $5,262,183 (2001)

Typical Recipients
Arts & Humanities: Historic Preservation, History & Archaeology, Libraries, Music, Performing Arts, Theater
Civic & Public Affairs: African American Affairs, Botanical Gardens/Parks, Clubs, Civic & Public Affairs-General, Housing, Law & Justice, Municipalities/Towns, Parades/Festivals, Professional & Trade Associations, Rural Affairs, Safety, Urban & Community Affairs
Education: Agricultural Education, Arts/Humanities Education, Business Education, Colleges & Universities, Education Funds, Elementary Education (Private), Elementary Education (Public), Education-General, Private Education (Precollege), Public Education (Precollege), School Volunteerism, Science/Mathematics Education, Secondary Education (Public), Student Aid, Vocational & Technical Education
Health: Cancer, Children's Health/Hospitals, Clinics/Medical Centers, Emergency/Ambulance Services, Health-General, Health Organizations, Heart, Home-Care Services, Hospitals, Medical Research, Mental Health, Public Health, Respiratory, Single-Disease Health Associations, Speech & Hearing
International: International Relations
Religion: Churches, Religious Organizations, Religious Welfare
Social Services: Animal Protection, At-Risk Youth, Camps, Child Welfare, Community Centers, Community Service Organizations, Day Care, Delinquency & Criminal Rehabilitation, Domestic Violence, Emergency Relief, Food/Clothing Distribution, Homes, People with Disabilities, Recreation & Athletics, Senior Services, Substance Abuse, Veterans, Volunteer Services, YMCA/YWCA/YMHA/YWHA, Youth Organizations

Application Procedures
Initial Contact: Request application form.
Application Requirements: Return completed application form along with proof of tax-exempt status, an itemization of the cost breakdown of the project, a copy of the minutes of executive committee meeting stating that the organization authorizes the filing of the application and assumes responsibility for the grant if it is awarded, and current financial statements. Application materials must be submitted in quadruplicate.
Deadlines: March 1, June 1, September 1, and December 1.

Restrictions
Grants are made to educational, charitable, and community service organizations to be used exclusively for the purpose of helping to provide for the health, happiness, and welfare of the citizens of Chillicothe and Roso County, OH.

Additional Information
Publications: Program Policy Statement; Application Form; Guidelines

Foundation Officials
Joseph G. Kear: trustee
Thomas M. Spetnagel: trustee
Joseph P. Sulzer: trustee B Chillicothe, OH 1947. ED Ohio University BGS (1972); Capital University JD (1982). PRIM CORP EMPL state rep: Ohio House of Representatives. CORP AFFIL member environmental advisor board: Martin Marietta Energy Systems; member environmental advisor board: Goodyear Atomic Corp. NONPR AFFIL trustee: Juvenile Detention Center. CLUB AFFIL Kiwanis; KofC.

Grants Analysis
Disclosure Period: calendar year ending 2001
Total Grants: $290,176
Number of Grants: 37
Average Grant: $6,271*
Highest Grant: $64,424
Typical Range: $2,000 to $5,000 and $10,000 to $25,000
***Note:** Average grant figure excludes highest grant.

Recent Grants
Note: Grants derived from 2001 Form 990.
General

64,424	YMCA, Chillicothe, OH -- for sidewalks and sewer repairs
26,982	Bishop Flaget Schools, Chillicothe, OH -- for heating system
25,000	Chillicothe Education Foundation, Chillicothe, OH -- for scholarships
16,517	Frontier Community Service, Chillicothe, OH -- for electronic communications and voice mail system
10,000	City of Chillicothe Community Affairs, Chillicothe, OH -- for Manor Park Project
5,000	Adena Local Schools, Frankfort, OH -- to equip science lab and junior high school
5,000	American Red Cross, Chillicothe, OH -- for manikins for training CPR
5,000	Chillicothe Area Artist Series, Inc, Chillicothe, OH -- for concert in October
5,000	City of Chillicothe Community Affairs, Chillicothe, OH -- for Chautauqua performance
5,000	God's Community Church, Chillicothe, OH -- for hymnals and screen

MASTERPOOL FOUNDATION

Giving Contact
James M. Hughes, Trustee
1432 Post Rd.
Fairfield, CT 06824
Phone: (203)256-1977

Description
Founded: 1989
EIN: 066323079
Organization Type: Private Foundation
Grant Types: General Support.

Financial Summary
Total Giving: $32,000 (fiscal year ending July 31, 2004)
Assets: $293,961 (fiscal 2004); $423,816 (fiscal 2001)
Gifts Received: $5,000 (fiscal 1994); $10,000 (fiscal 1993). Note: In fiscal 1994, contributions were received from Michael D. Masterpool.

Typical Recipients
Arts & Humanities: Arts Centers, Libraries, Museums/Galleries, Music, Opera, Performing Arts, Theater
Civic & Public Affairs: Civic & Public Affairs-General, Native American Affairs, Zoos/Aquariums
Education: Colleges & Universities, Education Funds, Education-General, Secondary Education (Public), Student Aid
Environment: Environment-General
Health: Cancer, Diabetes, Health Organizations, Medical Research, Mental Health, Single-Disease Health Associations
Religion: Churches, Religion-General, Religious Organizations, Religious Welfare
Science: Scientific Centers & Institutes
Social Services: Child Welfare, Community Service Organizations, Family Services, People with Disabilities, Substance Abuse, Youth Organizations

Application Procedures
Initial Contact: Send a brief letter of inquiry.
Application Requirements: EIN number and financial data.
Deadlines: None.

Foundation Officials
James M. Hughes: trustee

Grants Analysis
Disclosure Period: fiscal year ending July 31, 2004
Total Grants: $32,000
Number of Grants: 16
Average Grant: $2,000
Highest Grant: $6,500
Lowest Grant: $500
Typical Range: $1,000 to $5,000

Recent Grants
Note: Grants derived from 2004 Form 990.
General

6,500	Metropolitan Opera, New York, NY
5,000	Fairfield High School, Fairfield, OH
5,000	Rose Hill Center, Holly, MI
4,000	St. Matthews Church, Wilton, CT
1,500	Catholic Near East, New York, NY
1,500	Fairfield Rotary Fund, Fairfield, OH
1,500	Maritime Center of Norwalk, Norwalk, CT
1,500	Sr. Marion Rielly Memorial
1,000	Stepping Stones Museum, Norwalk, CT
1,000	Swim Across the Sound, Bridgeport, CT

MASTERS FAMILY FOUNDATION

Giving Contact
Micky Jo Masters, Chairman
433 E. Las Colinas Blvd., No. 1290
Irving, TX 75039
Phone: (972)556-1190

Description
Founded: 1991
EIN: 752323131
Organization Type: Private Foundation
Grant Types: General Support, Scholarship.

Financial Summary
Total Giving: $0 (2003)
Assets: $154,133 (2003)
Gifts Received: $250 (1995); $10,513 (1993). Note: In 1993, contributions were received from James L. Masters.

Typical Recipients
Arts & Humanities: Libraries
Health: Cancer, Children's Health/Hospitals, Emer-

gency/Ambulance Services, Hospitals
Religion: Churches, Ministries, Religious Organizations, Religious Welfare
Social Services: Community Service Organizations, Food/Clothing Distribution, Homes, Substance Abuse, Youth Organizations

Application Procedures
Initial Contact: Request application guidelines.
Deadlines: March 13 for scholarships.

Additional Information
Provides scholarships to Hopkins County seniors who maintain a 3.0 grade point average and show financial need.
Publications: Application Form

Foundation Officials
James L. Masters, IV: president
Mickey Jo Masters: chairman
Chad Young: director

Grants Analysis
Disclosure Period: calendar year ending 2003
Total Grants: $0
Note: No grants awarded in 2003.

Recent Grants
Note: Grants derived from 1999 Form 990.
General
58,333	Hopkins County Medical Hospital, Sulphur Springs, TX
600	St. James Catholic Church, IL

ELIZABETH RING MATHER AND WILLIAM GWINN MATHER FUND

Giving Contact
James D. Ireland, III, President
1111 Superior Ave., Suite 1000
Cleveland, OH 44114
Phone: (216)696-4200

Description
Founded: 1954
EIN: 346519863
Organization Type: Private Foundation
Giving Locations: OH: emphasis on the greater Cleveland area
Grant Types: Capital, Endowment, General Support.

Donor Information
Founder: the late Elizabeth Ring Mather

Financial Summary
Total Giving: $1,088,644 (2001)
Giving Analysis: Giving for 2001 includes: foundation grants to United Way ($10,000)
Assets: $9,711,729 (2001)
Gifts Received: $315,713 (2001); $532,511 (2000); $651,906 (1999). Note: Contributions are made by James D. Ireland III, Lucy I. Weller, Cornelia I. Hallinan, George R. Ireland, and the United States Trust Co.

Typical Recipients
Arts & Humanities: Arts Associations & Councils, Arts Centers, Arts Institutes, Ballet, Community Arts, Historic Preservation, History & Archaeology, Libraries, Museums/Galleries, Music, Opera, Performing Arts, Public Broadcasting
Civic & Public Affairs: Botanical Gardens/Parks, Business/Free Enterprise, Clubs, Community Foundations, Civic & Public Affairs-General, Municipalities/Towns, Nonprofit Management, Parades/

Festivals, Philanthropic Organizations, Professional & Trade Associations, Urban & Community Affairs, Women's Affairs, Zoos/Aquariums
Education: Arts/Humanities Education, Colleges & Universities, Economic Education, Education Funds, Environmental Education, Faculty Development, Education-General, Leadership Training, Legal Education, Medical Education, Private Education (Precollege), Public Education (Precollege), Science/Mathematics Education, Social Sciences Education, Student Aid
Environment: Air/Water Quality, Forestry, Environment-General, Resource Conservation, Wildlife Protection
Health: Cancer, Children's Health/Hospitals, Health Organizations, Hospitals, Medical Rehabilitation, Medical Research, Mental Health, Nursing Services, Public Health
Religion: Churches
Science: Science Museums, Scientific Centers & Institutes
Social Services: Child Welfare, Community Service Organizations, Day Care, Domestic Violence, Family Planning, Food/Clothing Distribution, People with Disabilities, Senior Services, United Funds/United Ways, Youth Organizations

Application Procedures
Initial Contact: Send a brief letter of inquiry.
Application Requirements: Include a description of organization, amount requested, purpose of funds sought, recently audited financial statement, and proof of tax-exempt status.
Deadlines: None.

Restrictions
Does not support individuals or provide scholarships or loans.

Foundation Officials
Cornelia I. Hallinan: secretary
Cornelia W. Ireland: trustee
George R. Ireland: treasurer
James D. Ireland, III: president CORP AFFIL director: Cleveland-Cliffs Inc.
Jane J. Masters: assistant secretary, assistant treasurer
Kathleen K. Riley: assistant secretary, assistant treasurer
Lucy I. Weller: vice president

Grants Analysis
Disclosure Period: calendar year ending 2001
Total Grants: $1,078,644*
Number of Grants: 43
Average Grant: $15,759*
Highest Grant: $416,760
Lowest Grant: $50
Typical Range: $10,000 to $30,000
***Note:** Giving excludes United Way. Average grant figure excludes highest grant.

Recent Grants
Note: Grants derived from 2001 Form 990.
Library-Related
12,500	Cleveland Health Science Library

General
416,760	University Circle Incorporated, Cleveland, OH -- operations
132,000	Musical Arts, Cleveland, OH
100,000	Cleveland Botanical Garden, Cleveland, OH
100,000	Kenyon College, Gambier, OH
50,000	Hathaway Brown School, Cleveland, OH
50,000	Phillips Academy, Andover, MA
35,833	Great Lakes Science Center, Cleveland, OH
25,000	Hopewell Inn, Cleveland, OH
15,000	Saginaw Art Museum, Saginaw, MI
15,000	University Circle Incorporated, Cleveland, OH

S. LIVINGSTON MATHER CHARITABLE TRUST

Giving Contact
Janet Havener
One Corporate Exchange
25825 Science Park Dr., Suite 110
Beachwood, OH 44122
Phone: (216)828-9770

Description
Founded: 1953
EIN: 346505619
Organization Type: Private Foundation
Giving Locations: OH: Northeastern Ohio
Grant Types: General Support.

Donor Information
Founder: the late S. Livingston Mather

Financial Summary
Total Giving: $181,250 (2003)
Assets: $5,482,937 (2003)
Gifts Received: $125,000 (2003); $1,766 (1993).
Note: In 2003, contributions were received from the estate of S. Sterling McMillan.

Typical Recipients
Arts & Humanities: Arts Associations & Councils, Arts Centers, Arts Institutes, Arts Outreach, Arts & Humanities-General, Historic Preservation, History & Archaeology, Libraries, Museums/Galleries, Music, Opera, Performing Arts, Public Broadcasting, Theater
Civic & Public Affairs: Botanical Gardens/Parks, Clubs, Employment/Job Training, Civic & Public Affairs-General, Parades/Festivals, Urban & Community Affairs
Education: Afterschool/Enrichment Programs, Arts/Humanities Education, Colleges & Universities, Education Funds, Education Reform, Environmental Education, Faculty Development, Education-General, Medical Education, Minority Education, Private Education (Precollege), Public Education (Precollege), Student Aid
Environment: Environment-General, Protection, Resource Conservation
Health: AIDS/HIV, Clinics/Medical Centers, Emergency/Ambulance Services, Health Organizations, Hospices, Medical Rehabilitation, Mental Health
Science: Science Museums, Scientific Centers & Institutes
Social Services: Camps, Child Abuse, Child Welfare, Community Centers, Community Service Organizations, Day Care, Domestic Violence, Family Planning, Family Services, Food/Clothing Distribution, Homes, Sexual Abuse, Substance Abuse, United Funds/United Ways, Volunteer Services, Youth Organizations

Application Procedures
Initial Contact: Submit a a brief letter of inquiry.
Application Requirements: Submit a statement defining the purpose of funds sought, the project's significance to the community, sponsorship, budget for the project, other sources of support in hand and solicited, and staffing.
Deadlines: None.
Review Process: The Distribution Committee meets as needed, at least four times during the year.

Restrictions
Grants are made for operating support, building funds, and special purposes, but not ordinarily for scientific and medical programs or research, or in areas appropriately supported by the government and the United Way. Does not support individuals, provide deficit financing or loans, or award grants in response to mass mailings or telephone solicitations.

Additional Information

Publications: Biennial Report (including Application Guidelines)
Trust(s): Glenmede Trust Co OH NA

Grants Analysis

Disclosure Period: calendar year ending 2003
Total Grants: $181,250
Number of Grants: 41
Average Grant: $4,421
Highest Grant: $12,500
Lowest Grant: $1,000
Typical Range: $1,000 to $10,000

Recent Grants

Note: Grants derived from 2003 Form 990.
General

12,500	Cleveland Botanical Garden, Cleveland, OH
10,000	Beechbrook, Cleveland, OH -- family life education program
10,000	Goodrich Gannett Neighborhood Center, Cleveland, OH
10,000	Great Lakes Science Center, Cleveland, OH
9,500	Yellowstone Park Foundation, Bozeman, MT
9,000	Cleveland Museum of Art, Cleveland, OH -- collaboration and education program
8,000	Holden Arboretum, Kirtland, OH
5,000	Chagrin River Land Conversancy, Novelty, OH
5,000	Chardon Extracurricular Foundation, Chardon, OH
5,000	Cleveland Museum of Natural History, Cleveland, OH -- x-ray machine

RICHARD MATHER FUND

Giving Contact

Michele Draper
Care of M&T Bank
101 S. Salina St.
Syracuse, NY 13202
Phone: (716)842-5506

Description

Founded: 1955
EIN: 156018423
Organization Type: Private Foundation
Giving Locations: NY: Central New York, Syracuse
Grant Types: Endowment, General Support, Project.

Donor Information

Founder: the late Flora Mather Hosmer, the late R. C. Hosmer, Jr., Hosmer Descendants Trust

Financial Summary

Total Giving: $333,300 (2001)
Giving Analysis: Giving for 2001 includes: foundation grants to United Way ($16,000)
Assets: $4,335,333 (2001)
Gifts Received: $10,438 (2000); $10,067 (1999); $10,837 (1998). Note: In 1994, 1999 and 2000, contributions were received from Hosmer Trust.

Typical Recipients

Arts & Humanities: Arts Associations & Councils, Community Arts, Arts & Humanities-General, History & Archaeology, Libraries, Museums/Galleries, Music, Opera, Performing Arts, Public Broadcasting, Theater
Civic & Public Affairs: Community Foundations, Civic & Public Affairs-General, Municipalities/Towns, Nonprofit Management, Public Policy, Urban & Community Affairs, Women's Affairs, Zoos/Aquariums
Education: Arts/Humanities Education, Colleges & Universities, Literacy, Private Education (Precollege),
School Volunteerism
International: International Development, International Organizations
Religion: Missionary Activities (Domestic), Religious Welfare
Science: Science Museums, Scientific Centers & Institutes
Social Services: Camps, Child Welfare, Community Centers, Community Service Organizations, Family Planning, Family Services, United Funds/United Ways, Youth Organizations

Application Procedures

Initial Contact: Send a brief letter of inquiry in writings.
Application Requirements: Include proof of tax-exempt status.
Deadlines: None.

Restrictions

Limited to central NY cultural fields.

Additional Information

Publications: Informational Brochure (including Application Guidelines)

Foundation Officials

Stephen E. Chase: trustee
S. Sterling McMillan, PhD: trustee
Gay M. Pomeroy: trustee
Elizabeth H. Schaefer: trustee

Grants Analysis

Disclosure Period: calendar year ending 2001
Total Grants: $317,300*
Number of Grants: 20
Average Grant: $11,700*
Highest Grant: $95,000
Lowest Grant: $600
Typical Range: $5,000 to $20,000
*Note: Giving excludes United Way. Average grant figure excludes highest grant.

Recent Grants

Note: Grants derived from 2001 Form 990.
Library-Related

2,000	Syracuse Children's Chorus, Inc., Syracuse, NY

General

95,000	Syracuse Symphony Orchestra, Syracuse, NY
50,000	Everson Museum of Art, Syracuse, NY
32,500	Syracuse Symphony Foundation, Syracuse, NY
29,750	Syracuse Symphony Orchestra, Syracuse, NY
25,000	Syracuse Stage, Syracuse, NY
16,000	United Way of Central New York, Syracuse, NY
15,000	International Center of Syracuse, Syracuse, NY
15,000	Syracuse Opera, Syracuse, NY
10,000	Boys and Girls Club of Syracuse, Syracuse, NY
10,000	Cazenovia College, Cazenovia, NY

G. HAROLD AND LEILA Y. MATHERS CHARITABLE FOUNDATION

Giving Contact

James H. Handelman, Executive Director
188 N. Bedford Rd., Suite 203
Mt. Kisco, NY 10549
Phone: (914)242-0465
Fax: (914)242-0665
E-mail: mathers@mathersfoundation.org
Web: http://www.mathersfoundation.org

Description

Founded: 1975
EIN: 237441901
Organization Type: Specialized/Single Purpose Foundation
Giving Locations: nationally.
Grant Types: General Support, Research.

Donor Information

Founder: The G. Harold and Leila Y. Mathers Charitable Foundation was established in 1975.

Financial Summary

Total Giving: $10,012,227 (2003); $10,074,106 (2002); $9,900,000 (2001)
Assets: $150,595,782 (2003); $133,289,830 (2002); $176,000,000 (2001)

Typical Recipients

Arts & Humanities: Arts Associations & Councils, Libraries, Theater
Civic & Public Affairs: Economic Development
Education: Business Education, Colleges & Universities, Education-General, Health & Physical Education, Medical Education, Science/Mathematics Education
Environment: Environment-General, Protection
Health: Cancer, Children's Health/Hospitals, Clinics/Medical Centers, Emergency/Ambulance Services, Health-General, Health Organizations, Heart, Hospices, Hospitals, Hospitals (University Affiliated), Medical Research, Public Health, Research/Studies Institutes, Single-Disease Health Associations
International: Foreign Educational Institutions, International-General, Health Care/Hospitals, International Relief Efforts
Science: Scientific Centers & Institutes, Scientific Labs, Scientific Research
Social Services: Child Welfare, Emergency Relief, Family Services, Food/Clothing Distribution, Social Services-General

Application Procedures

Initial Contact: There is no formal application form. Initial contact should be in the form of a concise query letter.
Application Requirements: Letters should describe the research to be pursued; place the proposed research in a context of the current or historical efforts by other researchers addressing the problem; indicate the individuals conducting the research (with credentials); state whether the request has been, or is being submitted elsewhere, and if so, its status; and detail the funds required in the form of a simple budget statement.
Deadlines: None.
Review Process: Applications are reviewed initially by the foundation's executive director and, subsequently, by the executive committee. Additionally, applications often are examined by outside reviewers. A response, in the form of approval, rejection, or request for additional information, can be expected within ninety days. A request should state that an earlier response is desired if circumstances so require.

Restrictions

The foundation makes contributions only to organizations having tax-exempt status under section 501(c)(3) of the Internal Revenue Code and to those that are not private foundations within section 509(a) of the Code, or in the absence of such a determination, to a state or any political subdivision thereof within the meaning of section 170(c)(1) of the Code, or a state college or university. The foundation does not make grants to individuals, and rarely provides support for longer than three years.

Foundation Officials

Don Fizer: secretary, director
Donald E. Handelman: president, director B 1927.

ED New York University MBA (1950). PRIM CORP EMPL partner: Meyer Handelman Co.

James H. Handelman: executive director

Joseph W. Handelman: treasurer, assistant secretary, director B 1930. ED New York University MBA; Princeton University (1952). PRIM CORP EMPL partner: Meyer Handelman Co.

William R. Handelman: vice president, director PRIM CORP EMPL partner: Meyer Handelman Co.

John R. Young: director B Milwaukee, WI 1934. ED University of Chicago AB (1953); University of Chicago JD (1956). PRIM CORP EMPL Cahill Gordon & Reindel.

Grants Analysis

Disclosure Period: calendar year ending 2003
Total Grants: $10,012,227
Number of Grants: 55
Average Grant: $159,530*
Highest Grant: $616,667
Lowest Grant: $1,000
Typical Range: $30,000 to $300,000
***Note:** Average grant figure excludes three highest grants ($1,716,667).

Recent Grants

Note: Grants derived from 2003 Form 990.
Library-Related

20,000	Friends of the Montecito Library, Santa Barbara, CA

General

616,667	Salk Institute, San Diego, CA -- towards stem cell initiative
600,000	Columbia University, New York, NY -- towards molecular approaches to higher order aspects of cognition
562,026	University of California, San Francisco, CA -- towards attempts to produce synthetic prions causing brain degeneration
550,000	Memorial Sloan-Kettering Cancer Center, New York, NY -- towards regulation of vesicle transport pathways
417,401	M. D. Anderson Cancer Center, Houston, TX -- towards study of protein differentiation
384,800	University of Iowa College of Medicine, Iowa City, IA -- towards neurobiology of consciousness
377,956	University of Washington, Seattle, WA -- towards identification and quantitative analysis of regulatory networks in living systems
321,202	Einstein College of Medicine, Bronx, NY -- towards application of chemical genetics
314,990	Scripps Research Institute, La Jolla, CA -- towards cellular and molecular processes in the development of the nervous system
289,170	Columbia University, New York, NY -- towards research in schizophrenia

MATHIS-PFOHL FOUNDATION

Giving Contact

James M. Pfohl, President
5-46 46th Ave.
Long Island City, NY 11101
Phone: (718)784-4800

Description

Founded: 1947
EIN: 116013764
Organization Type: Private Foundation
Giving Locations: IA; MA; NY; NC
Grant Types: General Support, Scholarship.

Donor Information

Founder: members of the Pfohl family and associated companies

Financial Summary

Total Giving: $365,450 (fiscal year ending November 30, 2003)
Assets: $5,871,685 (fiscal 2003)
Gifts Received: $41,900 (fiscal 1994); $15,000 (fiscal 1993); $22,543 (fiscal 1992). Note: In fiscal 1994, contributions were received from William J. Kirby ($40,400) and miscellaneous ($1,500).

Typical Recipients

Arts & Humanities: Ballet, Community Arts, Historic Preservation, History & Archaeology, Libraries, Museums/Galleries, Music, Opera, Public Broadcasting
Civic & Public Affairs: Civic & Public Affairs-General, Municipalities/Towns, Urban & Community Affairs, Zoos/Aquariums
Education: Arts/Humanities Education, Colleges & Universities, Continuing Education, Education Funds, Education Reform, Education-General, Legal Education, Private Education (Precollege), Public Education (Precollege), Science/Mathematics Education, Secondary Education (Private), Secondary Education (Public), Special Education, Student Aid
Environment: Air/Water Quality
Health: Alzheimer's Disease, Cancer, Clinics/Medical Centers, Health Funds, Health Organizations, Hospitals, Mental Health, Nursing Services, Public Health, Single-Disease Health Associations
International: International Relations, International Relief Efforts
Religion: Churches, Religious Organizations, Religious Welfare
Science: Science Museums, Scientific Organizations
Social Services: At-Risk Youth, Child Welfare, Community Centers, Community Service Organizations, Homes, Social Services-General, YMCA/YWCA/YMHA/YWHA, Youth Organizations

Application Procedures

Initial Contact: Send a brief letter of inquiry describing program or project.
Deadlines: None.

Foundation Officials

James M. Pfohl: president

Grants Analysis

Disclosure Period: fiscal year ending November 30, 2003
Total Grants: $365,450
Number of Grants: 248
Average Grant: $1,342*
Highest Grant: $34,000
Lowest Grant: $100
Typical Range: $500 to $3,000
***Note:** Average grant figure excludes highest grant.

Recent Grants

Note: Grants derived from fiscal 2003 Form 990.

General

34,000	Duke University, Durham, NC
25,000	Duke University, Durham, NC
10,000	Neuroscience, Washington, DC
10,000	St. Matthias, North Bellmore, NY
10,000	St. Vincent's Hospital, Birmingham, AL
6,000	Mary Louis Academy, Jamaica, NY
5,000	Calvary Fund, Bronx, NY
5,000	Catholic Near East Welfare Association, New York, NY
5,000	Harvard College, Cambridge, MA
5,000	Rhodes College, Memphis, TN

MATTEL INC.

Company Headquarters

333 Continental Avenue
El Segundo, CA 90245-3802
Web: http://www.mattelmedia.com

Company Description

Founded: 1944
Ticker: MAT
Exchange: NYSE
Revenue: US$5.102 billion (2004)
Profit: US$572.7 million (2004)
Employees: 25000 (2003)
Fortune Rank: 383, per FORTUNE Magazine's list of 500 Largest U.S. Corporations (2004).
SIC(s): 3942 Dolls & Stuffed Toys, 3944 Games, Toys & Children's Vehicles.

Operating Locations

Mattel Inc. (CA--City of Industry; IL--Des Plaines; NY--East Aurora, New York; TX--Fort Worth)

Nonmonetary Support

Value: $500,000 (1998)
Type: In-kind Services
Volunteer Programs: Employees may apply for Employee Volunteer Grants. Grants amounts are linked to the length of service of requesting employee, and by number of other Mattel employees volunteering within the organization.
The Foundation coordinates more than 30 volunteer activities annually to encourage employee volunteerism.
Contact: Regina Rodman, Toy Donations Coordinator

Mattel Foundation

Giving Contact

Paul R. Millman, Foundation Directory
333 Continental Blvd.
Mail Stop M1-1418
El Segundo, CA 90245-5012
Phone: (310)252-3530
Fax: (310)252-3802
Web: http://www.mattel.com

Description

EIN: 953263647
Organization Type: Corporate Foundation
Giving Locations: CA: Los Angeles Southern California and Western New York.
Grant Types: Capital, Employee Matching Gifts, General Support, Matching, Scholarship.
Note: Employee matching gift ratio: 1 to 1 up to $5,000 per employee annually.

Financial Summary

Total Giving: $5,924,165 (2003); $4,966,638 (2001). Note: Contributes through corporate direct giving program and foundation.
Assets: $765,194 (2003); $761,081 (2002); $707,767 (2001)
Gifts Received: $5,944,000 (2003); $5,095,439 (2001); $3,997,000 (2000). Note: Contributions were received from Mattel, Inc.

Typical Recipients

Arts & Humanities: Arts Funds, Arts Institutes, Arts Outreach, Ballet, Dance, Libraries, Museums/Galleries, Music, Performing Arts, Theater
Civic & Public Affairs: African American Affairs, Botanical Gardens/Parks, Business/Free Enterprise, Civil Rights, Clubs, Community Foundations, Economic Development, Economic Policy, Employment/Job Training, Gay/Lesbian Issues, Civic & Public Affairs-General, Housing, Philanthropic Organizations, Public Policy, Urban & Community Affairs, Women's

Affairs

Education: Afterschool/Enrichment Programs, Business Education, Colleges & Universities, Economic Education, Education Funds, Education Reform, Elementary Education (Private), Elementary Education (Public), Engineering/Technological Education, Education-General, Leadership Training, Literacy, Medical Education, Minority Education, Private Education (Precollege), Public Education (Precollege), Science/Mathematics Education, Secondary Education (Public), Special Education, Student Aid

Environment: Air/Water Quality, Forestry, Environment-General

Health: AIDS/HIV, Cancer, Children's Health/Hospitals, Clinics/Medical Centers, Diabetes, Geriatric Health, Health Funds, Health Organizations, Heart, Hospitals, Medical Rehabilitation, Multiple Sclerosis, Prenatal Health Issues, Public Health, Single-Disease Health Associations

International: Health Care/Hospitals, International Development, International Relief Efforts

Religion: Religious Welfare

Science: Scientific Centers & Institutes, Scientific Organizations

Social Services: Animal Protection, Big Brothers/Big Sisters, Camps, Child Welfare, Community Centers, Community Service Organizations, Crime Prevention, Day Care, Delinquency & Criminal Rehabilitation, Emergency Relief, Family Services, People with Disabilities, Recreation & Athletics, Scouts, Social Services-General, Special Olympics, Substance Abuse, United Funds/United Ways, Volunteer Services, YMCA/YWCA/YMHA/YWHA, Youth Organizations

Application Procedures

Initial Contact: For toy donations, send a written request.

Application Requirements: Application must be on the organization's letterhead and include a mission statement, contact person, and mailing address (no Post Office boxes); include proof of tax-exempt status. For silent auction items, include description of the event and the date that the item must arrive.

Deadlines: September 30 for holiday toy donation requests.

Evaluative Criteria: Ability of program to alleviate hardships, provide opportunities for better lives for children, or strengthen family life.

Decision Notification: Quarterly; meetings are in February, May, August, and November.

Notes: The foundation has a large commitment to the Mattel Children's Hospital at UCLA; because of this commitment, applications for grant support will not be accepted through 2004.

Restrictions

Foundation generally does not support capital facilities; religious activities; research activities; endowments; individuals; religious, fraternal, political, athletic, social, or veterans organizations; labor groups; programs receiving substantial financial support; federal, state, or local government agencies; or courtesy advertising. Toys will not be donated to third-party requests or to schools.

Only gives to nonprofit organizations that benefit children.

Additional Information

Fischer-Price is now part of Mattel, Inc.

Corporate Officials

Robert A. Eckert: chairman, chief executive officer B August 14, 1954. ED University of Arizona BS (1976); Northwestern University MBA (1977). PRIM CORP EMPL chairman, chief executive officer: Mattel Inc.

Foundation Officials

Harold Brown, PhD: chairman, director B New York, NY September 19, 1927. ED Columbia University AB (1945); Columbia University AM (1946); Columbia

University PhD (1949). PRIM CORP EMPL partner: Warburg, Pincus & Co. PRIM NONPR EMPL counsel: Center Strategic International Studies. CORP AFFIL partner: Warburg Pincus & Co. Inc.; trustee: Rand Corp.; trustee: Trilateral Community; director: Evergreen Holdings INC; director: Mattel Inc.; director: Alumax Inc.; director: Cummins Engine Co. Inc.; director: Altria Group Inc. NONPR AFFIL member: National Academy Sciences; member: Phi Beta Kappa; member: American Physical Society; member: National Academy Engineering; member: American Academy of Arts & Sciences. CLUB AFFIL River Club; Bohemian Club; Metro Club.

Robert John Normile: secretary

William Stavro: treasurer

Grants Analysis

Disclosure Period: calendar year ending 2003

Total Grants: $5,606,377*

Number of Grants: 89

Average Grant: $6,891*

Highest Grant: $5,000,000

Lowest Grant: $500

Typical Range: $1,000 to $10,000

*Note: Giving excludes matching gifts, United Way, and scholarships. Average grant figure excludes highest grant.

Recent Grants

Note: Grants derived from 2001 Form 990.

General

4,000,000	Mattel Children's Hospital at UCLA, Los Angeles, CA -- for operating support
100,000	United Way, Los Angeles, CA -- operating budget
50,000	Foundation for Technology Access, San Rafael, CA -- for operating support
50,000	United Fund of Buffalo and Erie County, Buffalo, NY -- operating support
37,500	Children Affected by AIDS Foundation, El Segundo, CA -- operating support
31,045	American Red Cross
30,000	Citizens Scholarship Foundation, St. Peter, MN -- support of scholarship awards for Mattel Employee children
25,000	Every Person Influences Children, Inc. (EPIC), Buffalo, NY -- for operating support
23,635	United Way of New York, New York, NY
21,310	NYCPPI, New York, NY

KATHARINE MATTHIES FOUNDATION

Giving Contact

Marjorie Alexander-Davis, Trust Officer
c/o Fleet Bank
777 Main St., CT EH 40222B
Hartford, CT 06115
Phone: (860)952-7405
Web: http://electronicvalley.org/matthies/

Description

Founded: 1987

EIN: 066261860

Organization Type: Private Foundation

Giving Locations: CT: Ansonia, Beacon Falls, Derby, Oxford, Seymour

Grant Types: General Support.

Donor Information

Founder: the late Katharine Matthies

Financial Summary

Total Giving: $856,760 (2002); $788,563 (2001)

Giving Analysis: Giving for 2002 includes: foundation grants to United Way ($45,000)

Assets: $18,352,334 (2001)

Gifts Received: $71,375 (1999)

Typical Recipients

Arts & Humanities: Arts Outreach, Arts & Humanities-General, History & Archaeology, Libraries, Music, Theater

Civic & Public Affairs: Botanical Gardens/Parks, Chambers of Commerce, Community Foundations, Economic Development, Civic & Public Affairs-General, Housing, Legal Aid, Municipalities/Towns, Nonprofit Management, Safety, Urban & Community Affairs, Zoos/Aquariums

Education: Afterschool/Enrichment Programs, Business Education, Environmental Education, Faculty Development, Education-General, Literacy, Student Aid

Environment: Environment-General, Resource Conservation, Wildlife Protection

Health: Adolescent Health Issues, Emergency/Ambulance Services, Health Organizations, Hospitals, Long-Term Care, Medical Rehabilitation, Public Health

International: Missionary/Religious Activities

Religion: Churches, Religious Organizations, Religious Welfare

Science: Scientific Centers & Institutes

Social Services: Child Welfare, Community Service Organizations, Crime Prevention, Day Care, People with Disabilities, Recreation & Athletics, Scouts, Senior Services, Social Services-General, Substance Abuse, United Funds/United Ways, Veterans, YMCA/YWCA/YMHA/YWHA, Youth Organizations

Application Procedures

Initial Contact: The foundation has no formal grant application procedure or application form. Applications are reviewed quarterly.

Additional Information

Trust(s): Fleet Bank

Grants Analysis

Disclosure Period: calendar year ending 2002

Total Grants: $811,760*

Number of Grants: 50

Average Grant: $14,866*

Highest Grant: $83,333

Lowest Grant: $2,500

Typical Range: $5,000 to $30,000

*Note: Giving excludes United Way. Average grant figure excludes highest grant.

Recent Grants

Note: Grants derived from 2001 Form 990.

General

95,333	Griffin Hospital, Derby, CT
57,189	Boys and Girls Club of Lower Naugatuck Valley, Shelton, CT -- for two vans and expenses
50,000	Lower Naugatuck Valley Parent Child Resource, Shelton, CT -- support capital campaign project
39,900	Catholic Family Services of Ansonia, Ansonia, CT -- to implement Stop it Now Youth Violence
39,125	Valley United Way, Ansonia, CT
35,000	Seymour Ambulance Association -- purchase of a safekids vehicle van
30,000	St. Joseph Parish -- for salary of coordinator
27,119	Southern Connecticut State University, New Haven, CT -- to provide violence prevention and serve the middle schools
24,850	Hewitt Foundation, Inc., Shelton, CT -- implement Clinical Education Program
24,365	TEAM, Wheaton, IL -- to deliver home meals and homemaking visits

May Department Stores Co.

Company Headquarters
611 Olive St.
St. Louis, MO 63101
Web: http://www.mayco.com

Company Description
Founded: 1877
Ticker: MAY
Exchange: NYSE
Revenue: US$14.441 billion (2004)
Profit: US$524 million (2004)
Employees: 110000 (2003)
Fortune Rank: 147, per FORTUNE Magazine's list of 500 Largest U.S. Corporations (2004).

Nonmonetary Support
Type: Cause-related Marketing & Promotion

The May Department Stores Co. Foundation

Giving Contact
Jan Kniffen
The May Department Stores Co. Foundation
611 Olive Street
St. Louis, MO 63101
Phone: (314)342-6299
Fax: (314)342-4461

Description
Founded: 1945
EIN: 436028949
Organization Type: Corporate Foundation
Giving Locations: operating locations.
Grant Types: Capital, Employee Matching Gifts, Operating Expenses.
Note: Employee matching gift ratio: 1 to 1 to eligible schools, colleges, cultural organisation, and hospitals.

Financial Summary
Total Giving: Contributes through corporate direct giving program and foundation.
Gifts Received: $20,946,947 (2000); $8,378,082 (1998); $7,210,132 (1996). Note: Contributions are received from the May Department Store Company.

Typical Recipients
Arts & Humanities: Arts Associations & Councils, Arts Centers, Arts Funds, Ballet, Community Arts, Ethnic & Folk Arts, Historic Preservation, Libraries, Museums/Galleries, Music, Performing Arts, Public Broadcasting, Theater
Civic & Public Affairs: African American Affairs, Botanical Gardens/Parks, Civil Rights, Clubs, Economic Development, Employment/Job Training, Civic & Public Affairs-General, Housing, Municipalities/Towns, Parades/Festivals, Public Policy, Safety, Urban & Community Affairs, Zoos/Aquariums
Education: Agricultural Education, Arts/Humanities Education, Business Education, Colleges & Universities, Continuing Education, Education Associations, Education Funds, Education Reform, Engineering/Technological Education, Education-General, Literacy, Medical Education, Minority Education, Public Education (Precollege), Science/Mathematics Education, Student Aid
Environment: Environment-General
Health: AIDS/HIV, Cancer, Children's Health/Hospitals, Clinics/Medical Centers, Emergency/Ambulance Services, Health Funds, Health Organizations, Heart, Hospitals, Multiple Sclerosis, Respiratory
Religion: Churches, Dioceses, Jewish Causes, Ministries, Religious Organizations, Religious Welfare, Synagogues/Temples
Science: Scientific Centers & Institutes
Social Services: Child Welfare, Community Centers, Community Service Organizations, Counseling, Food/Clothing Distribution, People with Disabilities, Scouts, Substance Abuse, United Funds/United Ways, YMCA/YWCA/YMHA/YWHA, Youth Organizations

Application Procedures
Initial Contact: Letter.
Application Requirements: Description of organization, including history, goals, and breadth of support it receives from constituents; amount requested, and purpose of funds sought; recently audited financial statement; proof of tax-exempt status.
Deadlines: None.

Restrictions
Foundation does not give to individuals.

Additional Information
Associated companies of May Department Stores are Lord & Taylor, Hecht's, Strawbridge's, Foley's, Robinsons-May, Kaufmann's, Filene's, Famous-Barr, L.S. Ayres, The Jones Store, and Meier & Frank. Some associated companies have their own giving programs.

Corporate Officials
Jan Rogers Kniffen: senior vice president, treasurer B Herrin, IL 1948. ED University of Illinois (1966-1968); Southern Illinois University BS (1968-1971); Lindenwood College MBA (1978); Saint Louis University (1985). PRIM CORP EMPL senior vice president, treasurer: The May Department Stores Co. ADD CORP EMPL treasurer, director: May Department Stores International ADD NONPR EMPL adj professor, director: Lindenwood College. CLUB AFFIL Media Club; Noonday Club.

Foundation Officials
Jan Rogers Kniffen: vice president, secretary, treasurer, director (see above)

Grants Analysis
Disclosure Period: calendar year ending 1999
Total Grants: $10,676,773*
Number of Grants: 1,135
Average Grant: $8,421*
Highest Grant: $1,127,308
Typical Range: $1,000 to $5,000
*Note: Giving excludes scholarships, matching gifts, and United Way. Average grant excludes highest grant.

Recent Grants
Note: Grants derived from 1998 Form 990.

General
1,127,308	OASIS, St. Louis, MO
1,007,900	United Way, St. Louis, MO
441,668	United Way of Los Angeles, Los Angeles, CA
355,262	National Merit Scholarship Corporation, Evanston, IL
342,000	OASIS Intergenerational Tutoring Program, St. Louis, MO
327,553	YMCA, St. Louis, MO
250,515	United Way New England, Boston, MA
212,350	Washington University, St. Louis, MO
200,000	Forest Park Forever, St. Louis, MO
195,640	YMCA, St. Louis, MO

James And Eva Mayer Foundation

Giving Contact
Gene V. Owen, Trustee
PO Box 328
Plainview, TX 79073-0328
Phone: (806)296-6304

Description
Founded: 1988
EIN: 756360908
Organization Type: Private Foundation
Giving Locations: TX
Grant Types: Capital, Matching, Project.

Donor Information
Founder: the late Eva H. Mayer

Financial Summary
Total Giving: $24,500 (2001)
Assets: $4,884,337 (2001)

Typical Recipients
Arts & Humanities: Community Arts, Libraries, Music
Civic & Public Affairs: Clubs, Civic & Public Affairs-General
Education: Colleges & Universities, Legal Education, Literacy, Science/Mathematics Education, Secondary Education (Public)
Health: Cancer, Children's Health/Hospitals, Diabetes, Health Organizations, Hospices, Hospitals, Public Health, Single-Disease Health Associations
Religion: Religious Welfare
Social Services: Child Welfare, Community Centers, Community Service Organizations, Day Care, Recreation & Athletics, Senior Services, United Funds/United Ways, Youth Organizations

Application Procedures
Initial Contact: Send a brief letter of inquiry, not more than two pages.
Application Requirements: Include the nature and brief history of the organization; the circumstances leading to the need for the grant; amount requested; intended use/purpose of funds sought; date that funds are needed and when they will be expended; and what public recognition, if any, would be given to the Mayer Foundation. Requests should include proof of tax-exempt status.
Deadlines: None.

Restrictions
Does not support individuals, religious organizations for sectarian purposes, political or lobbying groups, or organizations outside operating areas.

Additional Information
Grants are made only to organizations operated exclusively for religious, charitable, educational, literary, or scientific purposes, no substantial part of the activities of which is carrying on propaganda, or otherwise attempting to influence legislation or the election of public officials. Grants are made only for use within the United States or its possessions.
Publications: Application Guidelines

Foundation Officials
Paul Lyle: trustee
Gene V. Owen: trustee
David Wilder: trustee

Grants Analysis
Disclosure Period: calendar year ending 2001
Total Grants: $24,500
Number of Grants: 5
Average Grant: $4,900
Highest Grant: $6,000

Lowest Grant: $3,500
Typical Range: $3,500 to $5,000

Recent Grants

Note: Grants derived from 2001 Form 990.
General

6,000	American Heart Association, Lubbock, TX -- implement CPR training in schools
5,000	Share A Warm Hug, Plainview, TX -- purchase winter coats for elementary school children
5,000	Soroptimist, Plainview, TX -- purchase shoes for needy school children
5,000	Southwest Diabetic Foundation, Gainesville, TX -- build activity center
3,500	Ronald McDonald House, Lubbock, TX -- furnish and decorate television room

MANUEL D. AND RHODA MAYERSON FOUNDATION

Giving Contact

Dr. Neal H. Mayerson, President
Manuel D. and Rhoda Mayerson Foundation
312 Walnut Street, Suite 3600
Cincinnati, OH 45202
Phone: (513)621-7500
E-mail: contact@mayersonfoundation.org
Web: http://www.mayersonfoundation.org/

Description

Founded: 1986
EIN: 311310431
Organization Type: Private Foundation
Giving Locations: OH: Cincinnati
Grant Types: Capital, Emergency, General Support, Project, Seed Money.

Donor Information

Founder: Manuel D. Mayerson, Rhoda Mayerson

Financial Summary

Total Giving: $861,319 (fiscal year ending October 31, 2004); $2,423,028 (fiscal 2001)
Giving Analysis: Giving for fiscal 2004 includes: foundation grants to United Way ($11,000); fiscal 2001: foundation grants to United Way ($31,000)
Assets: $32,740,920 (fiscal 2004); $20,919,827 (fiscal 2001)
Gifts Received: $1,093,847 (fiscal 2004); $7,528,774 (fiscal 2001); $1,399,168 (fiscal 2000). Note: In fiscal 2004, contributions were received from the Manuel D. Mayerson Charitable Lead Trust ($100,000), Rhoda & Manuel Mayerson Charitable Lead Trust ($303,714), and 2002 Arlene and Neal Mayerson Charitable Lead Trust ($110,955). In fiscal 2001, contributions were received from the Manuel D. Mayerson Charitable Lead Trust ($200,000), Rhoda & Manuel Mayerson Charitable Lead Trust ($303,714), and Manuel and Rhoda Mayerson ($7,025,060). In 2000, contributions were received from Manuel D. Mayerson ($213,886) and Rhoda & Manuel Mayerson ($1,185,282). In 1999, contributions were received from Manuel D. Mayerson ($568,896) and Rhoda Mayerson ($147,800). In fiscal 1998, contributions were received from the Manuel D. Mayerson Charitable Lead Trust ($200,000) and Rhoda Mayerson ($597,832).

Typical Recipients

Arts & Humanities: Arts Associations & Councils, Arts Centers, Arts Funds, Ballet, History & Archaeology, Museums/Galleries, Music, Performing Arts, Public Broadcasting, Theater, Visual Arts
Civic & Public Affairs: Civil Rights, Community Foundations, Employment/Job Training, Ethnic Organizations, Civic & Public Affairs-General, Legal Aid,

Professional & Trade Associations, Public Policy, Urban & Community Affairs
Education: Arts/Humanities Education, Colleges & Universities, Education-General, Private Education (Precollege), Public Education (Precollege), Religious Education, Science/Mathematics Education, Secondary Education (Public), Student Aid
Environment: Environment-General
Health: Children's Health/Hospitals, Clinics/Medical Centers, Hospices, Hospitals, Medical Research, Multiple Sclerosis, Preventive Medicine/Wellness Organizations, Speech & Hearing
International: International Relations, Missionary/Religious Activities
Religion: Jewish Causes, Religious Organizations, Social/Policy Issues, Synagogues/Temples
Social Services: At-Risk Youth, Camps, Child Welfare, Community Service Organizations, Counseling, Domestic Violence, Family Planning, Family Services, Food/Clothing Distribution, People with Disabilities, Recreation & Athletics, Refugee Assistance, Senior Services, Shelters/Homelessness, Social Services-General, United Funds/United Ways, Youth Organizations

Application Procedures

Initial Contact: The foundation requests applications be made in writing.
Application Requirements: Include a description of organization, amount requested, purpose of funds sought, recently audited financial statement, and proof of tax-exempt status.
Deadlines: None.
Evaluative Criteria: Responsive to strategic planning, grantee stability and leadership ability, creativity, entrepreneurial visioning, leveraging of resources, and collaboration and empowerment of people.

Restrictions

Preference to improving the lives of children and people with disabilities, important community institutions and efforts aimed at preserving cultural heritage.

Additional Information

Publications: Application Guidelines

Foundation Officials

Arlene B. Mayerson: vice president
Donna Mayerson: secretary
Fred Mayerson: trustee
Manuel D. Mayerson: trustee
Neal H. Mayerson: president, treasurer
Rhoda Mayerson: trustee

Grants Analysis

Disclosure Period: fiscal year ending October 31, 2004
Total Grants: $850,319*
Number of Grants: 142
Average Grant: $3,120*
Highest Grant: $123,573
Lowest Grant: $26
Typical Range: $1,000 to $5,000
*Note: Giving excludes United Way. Average grant figure excludes four highest grants ($419,736).

Recent Grants

Note: Grants derived from 2004 Form 990.
General

118,830	Cincinnati Art Museum, Cincinnati, OH
100,000	Contemporary Arts Center, Cincinnati, OH
47,000	Jewish Family Services, Cincinnati, OH
32,000	Jewish Federation of Cincinnati, Cincinnati, OH
30,000	Cincinnati Ballet, Cincinnati, OH
24,000	Mayerson High School, Cincinnati, OH -- community service program
16,376	Children's Hospital Medical Center, Cincinnati, OH
13,998	Mayerson High School, Cincinnati, OH -- funds for summer 2004 program

11,000	United Way and Community Chest, Cincinnati, OH
10,000	American Jewish Archives, Cincinnati, OH

OLIVER DEWEY MAYOR FOUNDATION

Giving Contact

Regina Pruitt, Governor
c/o Bank of Texas Trust Co. NA
307 W. Washington
Sherman, TX 75090
Phone: (903)813-5100

Description

Founded: 1983
EIN: 751864630
Organization Type: Private Foundation
Giving Locations: OK: Mayes County; TX: Grayson County
Grant Types: General Support.

Donor Information

Founder: the late Oliver Dewey Mayor

Financial Summary

Total Giving: $1,653,755 (fiscal year ending June 30, 2004); $854,380 (fiscal 2001)
Giving Analysis: Giving for fiscal 2004 includes: foundation grants to United Way ($5,000)
Assets: $25,403,660 (fiscal 2004); $18,793,637 (fiscal 2001)

Typical Recipients

Arts & Humanities: Community Arts, Historic Preservation, History & Archaeology, Libraries, Museums/Galleries, Music, Performing Arts, Theater
Civic & Public Affairs: Chambers of Commerce, Clubs, Community Foundations, Economic Development, Civic & Public Affairs-General, Inner-City Development, Legal Aid, Municipalities/Towns, Native American Affairs, Parades/Festivals, Rural Affairs, Safety, Urban & Community Affairs
Education: Arts/Humanities Education, Colleges & Universities, Community & Junior Colleges, Continuing Education, Education Reform, Leadership Training, Literacy, Medical Education, Public Education (Precollege), Science/Mathematics Education, Secondary Education (Public), Student Aid
Health: Cancer, Children's Health/Hospitals, Clinics/Medical Centers, Emergency/Ambulance Services, Health Funds, Hospices, Hospitals, Medical Rehabilitation, Nursing Services, Nutrition, Prenatal Health Issues, Public Health, Speech & Hearing, Transplant Networks/Donor Banks
Religion: Ministries, Religious Welfare
Social Services: At-Risk Youth, Community Centers, Community Service Organizations, Crime Prevention, Family Services, Recreation & Athletics, Scouts, Senior Services, Shelters/Homelessness, United Funds/United Ways, Youth Organizations

Application Procedures

Initial Contact: The foundation requests applications be made in writing.
Application Requirements: Include purpose of funds sought.
Deadlines: None.

Restrictions

Does not support individuals.

Additional Information

Publications: Application Guidelines

Foundation Officials
Samuel W. Graber: gov
Tony J. Lyons: gov

Grants Analysis
Disclosure Period: fiscal year ending June 30, 2004
Total Grants: $1,648,755*
Number of Grants: 91
Average Grant: $14,518*
Highest Grant: $156,616
Lowest Grant: $200
Typical Range: $5,000 to $30,000
*Note: Giving excludes United Way. Average grant figure excludes three highest grants ($356,616).

Recent Grants
Note: Grants derived from fiscal 2004 Form 990.
General

156,616	Mayes County Commissioners, Pryor, OK -- for fair grounds improvement
100,000	Gunter Volunteer Fire and Rescue, Gunter, TX -- fire station/community center
100,000	Pryor Fire Department, Pryor, OK -- for fire truck
75,000	Chouteau Volunteer Fire Department, Chouteau, OK -- for rescue truck
55,600	Thunderbird Challenge Inc., Pryor, OK -- for Thunderbird trades academy
50,000	Pryor Youth Baseball Organization, Pryor, OK -- for concession building
50,000	Texoma Medical Center Foundation, Denison, TX -- for emergency department
50,000	Wilson N. Jones Medical Center Foundation, Sherman, TX -- for heart of excellence
41,667	Grayson County Women's Crisis Line, Sherman, TX -- building a new shelter
37,500	Hilltop Haven Christian Care Center, Gunter, TX -- campus improvement

MAYS FOUNDATION

Giving Contact
Troy M. Mays, Director
914 S. Tyler St.
Amarillo, TX 79101
Phone: (806)376-5417

Description
Founded: 1965
EIN: 751213346
Organization Type: Private Foundation
Giving Locations: AR; TX
Grant Types: General Support.

Donor Information
Founder: W. A. Mays

Financial Summary
Total Giving: $410,898 (fiscal year ending July 31, 2004); $338,924 (fiscal 2002); $461,286 (fiscal 2001)
Giving Analysis: Giving for fiscal 2004 includes: foundation grants to United Way ($1,000); fiscal 2002: foundation grants to United Way ($1,000); fiscal 2001: foundation grants to United Way ($1,350)
Assets: $7,946,277 (fiscal 2004); $7,360,347 (fiscal 2002); $7,317,137 (fiscal 2001)
Gifts Received: $64,782 (fiscal 2004); $79,895 (fiscal 2002); $3,844 (fiscal 2001). Note: In fiscal 2002 and fiscal 2004, contributions were received from the Mays Trusts. In fiscal 1997, contributions were received from the W. A. and Agnes Mays Trust No. 2. In fiscal 1996, contributions were received from Mays Trusts ($1,298) and the W. A. and Agnes Mays Trust No. 2 ($79,861).

Typical Recipients
Arts & Humanities: Arts Centers, Ballet, History & Archaeology, Libraries, Music, Public Broadcasting
Civic & Public Affairs: Botanical Gardens/Parks, Business/Free Enterprise, Community Foundations, Civic & Public Affairs-General, Urban & Community Affairs
Education: Colleges & Universities, Community & Junior Colleges, Elementary Education (Public), Engineering/Technological Education, Environmental Education, Education-General, Private Education (Precollege), Public Education (Precollege), Religious Education, Secondary Education (Public), Student Aid
Health: Alzheimer's Disease, Cancer, Clinics/Medical Centers, Health Organizations, Hospitals, Prenatal Health Issues, Public Health, Single-Disease Health Associations
International: Missionary/Religious Activities
Religion: Bible Study/Translation, Churches, Ministries, Religious Welfare, Social/Policy Issues
Science: Science Museums
Social Services: Child Welfare, Community Centers, Community Service Organizations, Day Care, Food/Clothing Distribution, Recreation & Athletics, Scouts, Senior Services, United Funds/United Ways, YMCA/YWCA/YMHA/YWHA, Youth Organizations

Application Procedures
Initial Contact: The foundation requests applications be made in writing. Send a full proposal.
Deadlines: None.

Restrictions
Does not support individuals, religious organizations for sectarian purposes, political or lobbying groups, or organizations outside operating areas.

Foundation Officials
Karra Mays Hill: director
Troy M. Mays: director

Grants Analysis
Disclosure Period: fiscal year ending July 31, 2004
Total Grants: $409,898*
Number of Grants: 81
Average Grant: $2,137*
Highest Grant: $131,307
Lowest Grant: $100
Typical Range: $1,000 to $5,000
*Note: Giving excludes United Way. Average grant figure excludes two highest grants ($241,107).

Recent Grants
Note: Grants derived from 2004 Form 990.

General

131,307	Wayland Baptist University, Plainview, TX
109,800	Baylor University, Waco, TX
30,000	Hawaii Baptist Academy, Honolulu, HI
7,667	Harrington Regional Medical Center, Amarillo, TX
7,500	Amarillo Symphony, Amarillo, TX
7,125	Baptist St. Anthony's Foundation, Amarillo, TX
5,125	First Baptist Church of Amarillo, Amarillo, TX
5,000	Don Harrington Discovery Center, Amarillo, TX
5,000	Wildcat Bluff Nature Center, Amarillo, TX
4,833	Center for Texas Culture, Borger, TX

JACOB AND RUTH MAZER FOUNDATION

Giving Contact
David Mazer, Vice President & Treasurer
66 Mooreland Road
Greenwich, CT 06831
Phone: (203)661-9733

Description
Founded: 1961
EIN: 136115875
Organization Type: Private Foundation
Giving Locations: CT; NY: New York metro area
Grant Types: General Support.

Donor Information
Founder: Abraham Mazer Foundation

Financial Summary
Total Giving: $222,635 (2001)
Giving Analysis: Giving for 2001 includes: foundation grants to United Way ($7,500)
Assets: $1,499,741 (2001)

Typical Recipients
Arts & Humanities: Arts Centers, History & Archaeology, Libraries, Museums/Galleries, Music, Opera, Public Broadcasting
Civic & Public Affairs: Business/Free Enterprise, Civil Rights, Economic Development, Civic & Public Affairs-General, Philanthropic Organizations, Public Policy, Urban & Community Affairs
Education: Colleges & Universities, Education-General, Medical Education, Minority Education, Private Education (Precollege), Religious Education
Health: Cancer, Clinics/Medical Centers, Geriatric Health, Health Organizations, Hospitals, Medical Research, Research/Studies Institutes, Single-Disease Health Associations
International: Foreign Arts Organizations, International Peace & Security Issues, Missionary/Religious Activities
Religion: Jewish Causes, Religious Organizations, Synagogues/Temples
Social Services: Animal Protection, Community Service Organizations, Counseling, Family Planning, United Funds/United Ways, YMCA/YWCA/YMHA/YWHA, Youth Organizations

Application Procedures
Initial Contact: The foundation requests applications be made in writing.
Deadlines: None.

Restrictions
Does not give grants to individuals, religious organizations for sectarian purposes, or political or lobbying groups.

Foundation Officials
David Mazer: vice president, treasurer
Richard Mazer: vice president, secretary

Grants Analysis
Disclosure Period: calendar year ending 2001
Total Grants: $215,135*
Number of Grants: 72
Average Grant: $2,523*
Highest Grant: $36,000
Lowest Grant: $160
Typical Range: $500 to $5,000
*Note: Giving excludes United Way. Average grant figure excludes highest grant.

Recent Grants
Note: Grants derived from 2001 Form 990.
General

36,000	United Jewish Appeal of Greenwich, Greenwich, CT

25,000	United Jewish Appeal of Greenwich, Greenwich, CT
25,000	United Jewish Appeal of Greenwich, Greenwich, CT
10,000	Academy for Jewish Religion, New York, NY
10,000	Yale University, New Haven, CT
7,500	Connecticut Civil Liberties Union Foundation, Hartford, CT
7,500	Connecticut Civil Liberties Union Foundation, Hartford, CT
7,500	United Way of Greenwich, Greenwich, CT
7,000	Chamah, New York, NY
6,000	Beth Israel Deaconess Medical Center, Boston, MA

MBIA INC.

Company Headquarters
Armonk, NY
Web: http://www.mbia.com

Company Description
Founded: 1974
Ticker: MBI
Exchange: NYSE
Assets: US$18.852 billion (2002)
Employees: 701 (2003)
SIC(s): 6399 Insurance Carriers Nec.

Nonmonetary Support
Type: Donated Equipment; In-kind Services
Note: The company also offers the use of its auditorium.

Giving Contact
Susan Voltz, president of foundation
113 King Street
Armonk, NY 10504
Phone: (914)273-4545
Fax: (914)765-3375
E-mail: sue.voltz@mbia.com

Description
Organization Type: Corporate Giving Program
Giving Locations: generally in tri-state area where employees live.
Grant Types: Emergency, Employee Matching Gifts, Endowment.
Note: Employee matching gift ratio: 2 to 1 up to $1,000; 1 to 1 from $1,001 to $1,500. Employee matching gifts are for higher education only.

Financial Summary
Total Giving: $1,600,000 (2005 approx); $1,600,000 (2004); $800,000 (2001). Note: Contributes through corporate direct giving program only.

Typical Recipients
Arts & Humanities: Arts Associations & Councils, Arts & Humanities-General, Historic Preservation, Libraries, Museums/Galleries, Performing Arts
Civic & Public Affairs: Employment/Job Training, Civic & Public Affairs-General, Housing, Municipalities/Towns, Women's Affairs
Education: Business Education, Colleges & Universities, Elementary Education (Private), Education-General, Legal Education
Health: Health-General, Geriatric Health, Health Organizations, Medical Research, Single-Disease Health Associations
Social Services: Community Centers, Community Service Organizations, Counseling, Day Care, Family Planning, Family Services, Food/Clothing Distribution, Homes, People with Disabilities, Recreation & Athletics, Senior Services, Shelters/Homelessness,

Social Services-General, Substance Abuse, Volunteer Services, Youth Organizations

Application Procedures
Initial Contact: Call or write for application, then full proposal
Application Requirements: a description of organization, program description, budget information, needs assessment, amount requested, purpose of funds sought, audited financial statements and Form 990's for past three years, and proof of tax-exempt status
Deadlines: None.
Review Process: requests reviewed by the Charitable Contributions Committee
Evaluative Criteria: employee volunteer involvement; impact on the trio-state area; focus on the cause of a problem; organization serves society's neediest; project improves quality of life; highest priority to organizations that will benefit most from contribution

Restrictions
The company does not support individuals, religious organizations for sectarian purposes, umbrella agencies, for general operating support, or for sponsorships or table purchases (unless there is a clear business reason).

Additional Information
Publications: Guidelines; Application Form

Corporate Officials
Joseph Warner Brown, Jr.: chairman, chief executive officer B Evanston, IL 1949. ED Northern Illinois University (1974). PRIM CORP EMPL chairman, chief executive officer: MBIA Inc. ADD CORP EMPL chairman: Industries Indemnity Holdings Inc.; chairman: Apprise Corp.; chairman: Constitution Re corp.; chairman: Coregis Group Inc.; chairman: Crum & Forster Holdings Inc.; chairman: Enuision Claims Management Corp.; chairman: Resolution Group Inc.; chairman, president, chief executive officer: Viking Insurance Holdings Inc.; chairman: Westchester SPLty Group Inc. CORP AFFIL director: First Quadrant Corp. NONPR AFFIL trustee: Insurance Institute America; member: Society Chartered Property & Casualty Underwriters; trustee: American Institute Chartered Property & Casualty Underwriters; member: American Academy of Actuaries.
Gary C. Dunton: president, chief operating officer B 1955. ED Northeastern University BA (1978); Harvard University MBA (1980). PRIM CORP EMPL vice president, chief financial officer: MBIA Inc. CORP AFFIL director: MBIA Inc.; president: USF&G Corp.

Grants Analysis
Typical Range: $2,500 to $7,500

MBNA CORP.

Company Headquarters
1100 N. King St.
Wilmington, DE 19884-0341
Web: http://www.mbnainternational.com

Company Description
Founded: 1990
Ticker: KRB
Exchange: NYSE
Revenue: US$12.327 billion (2004)
Profit: US$2.677 billion (2004)
Employees: 28000 (2003)
Fortune Rank: 171, per FORTUNE Magazine's list of 500 Largest U.S. Corporations (2004).
SIC(s): 6712 Bank Holding Companies.

Nonmonetary Support
Type: In-kind Services; Loaned Executives
Volunteer Programs: The Community Partnership Program matches MBNA businesses with charitable organizations and schools for volunteer opportunities. The company provides financial contributions to nonprofit organizations for which MBNA employees have volunteered more than 40 hours of their personal time during a calendar year. MBNA also sponsors the Francis X. Norton Community Service award to recognize outstanding volunteerism among MBNA employees.

The MBNA Foundation

Giving Contact
Victor P. Manning, Executive Director
MBNA Foundation
1100 N. King St.
Wilmington, DE 19884
Phone: 800-441-7048
Web: http://www.mbnafoundation.org
Note: Dial ext. 25205 for information on the Community Grants Program and volunteer programs; dial ext. 25288 for information on Helen F. Graham Grants program.

Description
Founded: 2000
EIN: 522191136
Organization Type: Corporate Foundation
Giving Locations: DE; ME; OH: Cleveland
Grant Types: General Support, Scholarship.

Financial Summary
Total Giving: $40,376,557 (2003); $50,933,355 (2002); $46,740,190 (2001)
Giving Analysis: Giving for 2001 includes: foundation grants to United Way ($172,250); foundation scholarships ($5,301,280) foundation ($41,266,660)
Assets: $66,681,995 (2003); $41,505,644 (2002); $69,529,857 (2001)
Gifts Received: $61,416,949 (2003); $26,633,172 (2002); $63,978,715 (2001). Note: Substantial contributions were received from MBNA America Bank, NA; The Cawley Family Foundation.

Typical Recipients
Arts & Humanities: Arts Institutes, Libraries, Museums/Galleries, Music, Opera, Performing Arts, Public Broadcasting
Civic & Public Affairs: African American Affairs, Botanical Gardens/Parks, Employment/Job Training, Civic & Public Affairs-General, Municipalities/Towns
Education: Afterschool/Enrichment Programs, Colleges & Universities, Education-General, Preschool Education, Private Education (Precollege), Science/Mathematics Education, Secondary Education (Private)
Environment: Environment-General, Resource Conservation
Health: Children's Health/Hospitals, Clinics/Medical Centers, Health Funds, Health Organizations, Hospitals, Long-Term Care
Religion: Dioceses, Ministries
Social Services: Community Centers, Community Service Organizations, Counseling, Family Services, Recreation & Athletics, YMCA/YWCA/YMHA/YWHA, Youth Organizations

Application Procedures
Initial Contact: To apply to the Community Grants Program, call (302) 432-5205 or (800) 441-7048, ext. 25205. To apply to the Helen F. Graham Grants Program, download a grant application from the foundation's web site. To apply for either a grant through the Excellence in Education program or a college scholarship from the Scholars Program, download the appropriate application form for your geographic area from the foundation's web site.

Deadlines: None for the Helen F. Graham Grants program and the Excellence in Education program. Scholarship deadlines vary by region.

Restrictions

The Community Grants Program does not support organizations located outside of MBNA operating communities; travel for individuals or groups; sports-related sponsorships; sectarian activities of religious groups; or political causes or candidates. The Helen F. Graham Grants Program does not support salaries for additional staff, benefits, or tuition reimbursement for required courses or professional accreditation; capital projects, major repairs to buildings or equipment, and routine operating expenses; housing costs, tuition assistance, or other financial aid for individuals; private-employer work programs; or research projects. Excellence in Education Grants are not made to fund salaries for additional permanent staff, benefits, or tuition reimbursements for required courses or professional accreditation programs; capital projects and repairs to school buildings or equipment; large purchases of personal computers, networks, or upgrades in hardware and operating software (smaller purchases will be considered if they are an integral part of a well-developed program); routine school operating expenses and maintenance; or new or replacement textbooks, uniforms, band instruments, sports equipment, and other school supplies generally provided by school budgets.

Corporate Officials

Charles M. Cawley: chief executive officer, president, director ED Georgetown University BA (1962).
John R. Cochran, III: president; chief executive officer MBNA America Bank ED Loyola College BA. CORP AFFIL chairman, president, chief executive officer, director: MBNA America Bank.
Michael C. Ford, Esq.: senior executive vice president, MBNA American Bank
Randolph D. Lerner, Esq.: chairman, director CORP AFFIL co-owner: Cleveland Browns. NONPR AFFIL member: NFL Business Ventures Committee; co-chairman: US Marine Corps Heritage Foundation; trustee: Hospital for Special Surgery.
Frank H. Murphy: executive vice president NONPR AFFIL director: Maine Public Broadcasting.
John W. Scheflen: senior vice chairman, secretary
David W. Spartin: vice chairman ED George Washington University MBA (1985). NONPR AFFIL director: Metropolitan Wilmington Urban League; director: Opera Delaware; member, board of advisors: George Washington University, School of Business.
Lance L. Weaver: executive vice chairman, chief administrative officer ED Georgetown University BA. CORP AFFIL chairman board of directors: MasterCard International. NONPR AFFIL director: Tower Hill School; director: Wilmington Renaissance Corp.; trustee: Grand Opera House; chairman: Helen F. Graham Cancer Center; trustee: Christiana Care Corp.; trustee: Georgetown University Board of Regents.
Vernon H.C. Wright: executive vice chairman, chief financial officer, director NONPR AFFIL charter member: European Securitization Forum; director: University of Baltimore Board of Visitors; chairman, founder: American Securitization Forum.

Foundation Officials

Nancy Beck: trustee CORP AFFIL co-owner: Cleveland Browns.
Kenneth F. Boehl: treasurer, trustee ED Loyola University (1976); Loyola University MBA (1981).
Claire Z. Carey, PhD: trustee CORP AFFIL associate dean: Georgetown University.
C. Michael Cawley: trustee
Charles M. Cawley: trustee (see above)
John R. Cochran, III: trustee (see above)
Phillip W. Conkling: trustee NONPR AFFIL founder, president, director: Island Institute.
William B. DeLauder: trustee ED Morgan State College BS; Wayne State University PhD. NONPR

AFFIL director: Partnership to Cut Hunger and Poverty in Africa; director: United Way Delaware; chairman: NASULGC Task Force on International Education; president emeritus: Delaware State University; director: International Food and Agriculture Development.
Lanny Edelson, MD: trustee
Michael C. Ford, Esq.: trustee (see above)
David Ley Hamilton, Esq.: trustee
Vaughn C. Hardin: trustee
Frederick E. Hutchinson, PhD: trustee NONPR AFFIL president emeritus: University of Maine.
David B. Kedash: chief financial officer
Rev. Edwin D. Leahy, OSB: trustee NONPR AFFIL headmaster: St. Benedict's Preparatory School.
Victor P. Manning: president, executive director, trustee
Elizabeth A. Moran: trustee NONPR AFFIL chairman: Maine Library Commission.
Frank H. Murphy: trustee (see above)
Tern C. Murphy: trustee
David P. Roselle, PhD: trustee B May 30, 1939. ED West Chester State College BS (1961); Duke University PhD (1965). NONPR AFFIL president: University of Delaware.
John W. Scheflen: secretary (see above)
W. Craig Schroeder: trustee
David W. Spartin: trustee (see above)
Penelope J. Taylor: trustee ED College of Notre Dame of Maryland MA; College of Notre Dame of Maryland BA. NONPR AFFIL life member: NAACP; member: Urban Finance Services Coalition; director: Metropolitan Urban League-Wilmington; trustee: Christiana Care Corp.; charter member: Maryland Association of Urban Bankers.
Lance L. Weaver: chairman, trustee (see above)

Grants Analysis

Disclosure Period: calendar year ending 2003
Total Grants: $35,531,370*
Number of Grants: 2,700 (approx)
Average Grant: $13,160
Highest Grant: $1,000,000
Lowest Grant: $100
Typical Range: $5,000 to $25,000
*Note: Giving excludes scholarships and United Way.

Recent Grants

Note: Grants derived from 2003 Form 990.
Library-Related
300,000   George Bush Presidential Library Foundation, College Station, TX
General
1,400,000   Christiana Care Health System, New Castle, DE
1,100,000   St. Benedict's Preparatory School, Newark, NJ
1,000,000   Cleveland Clinic Foundation, Cleveland, OH
1,000,000   Loyola College in Maryland, Baltimore, MD
1,000,000   Maine Medical Center, Portland, ME
1,000,000   University of Delaware, Newark, DE
800,000   Ministry of Caring, Wilmington, DE
665,000   Grand Opera House, Wilmington, DE
600,000   Texas A&M University, College Station, TX
500,000   America's Promise, Alexandria, VA

HAROLD MCALISTER CHARITABLE FOUNDATION

Giving Contact

4801 Wilshire Boulevard, Suite 232
Los Angeles, CA 90010

Phone: (323)937-0927
Fax: (323)937-4727

Description

Founded: 1959
EIN: 956050036
Organization Type: Family Foundation
Giving Locations: CA: Los Angeles
Grant Types: General Support.

Donor Information

Founder: The foundation was incorporated in 1959 by Fern Smith McAlister and the late Harold McAlister.

Financial Summary

Total Giving: $1,400,605 (fiscal year ending May 31, 2004); $1,647,018 (fiscal 2002); $1,745,000 (fiscal 2001)
Assets: $31,793,115 (fiscal 2004); $30,843,346 (fiscal 2002); $34,538,157 (fiscal 2001)
Gifts Received: $50,000 (fiscal 1992)

Typical Recipients

Arts & Humanities: Arts Associations & Councils, Arts Outreach, Community Arts, Arts & Humanities-General, Libraries, Museums/Galleries, Music
Civic & Public Affairs: Business/Free Enterprise, Civic & Public Affairs-General, Nonprofit Management, Public Policy, Urban & Community Affairs
Education: Colleges & Universities, Education Funds, Education-General, Private Education (Precollege), Science/Mathematics Education, Special Education, Student Aid
Environment: Environment-General, Wildlife Protection
Health: Arthritis, Cancer, Children's Health/Hospitals, Clinics/Medical Centers, Emergency/Ambulance Services, Eyes/Blindness, Health-General, Geriatric Health, Health Funds, Health Organizations, Heart, Hospitals, Kidney, Long-Term Care, Medical Research, Mental Health, Nutrition, Public Health, Research/Studies Institutes, Respiratory, Single-Disease Health Associations, Speech & Hearing
International: Health Care/Hospitals, International Relief Efforts
Religion: Churches, Religious Organizations, Religious Welfare
Social Services: Animal Protection, Camps, Child Abuse, Child Welfare, Community Centers, Community Service Organizations, Counseling, Day Care, Family Services, Food/Clothing Distribution, Homes, People with Disabilities, Recreation & Athletics, Senior Services, Sexual Abuse, Substance Abuse, YMCA/YWCA/YMHA/YWHA, Youth Organizations

Application Procedures

Initial Contact: The foundation does not require a formal application form. Applicants should request funding by writing a letter to the board of trustees.
Application Requirements: The letter should detail the amount requested and for what purpose the money will be used. Any other information will be considered, but is not necessary.
Deadlines: None.
Review Process: Priority is given to organizations located in the Los Angeles area.

Restrictions

Grants are not made to individuals.

Foundation Officials

David B. Heyler, Jr.: trustee
James P. McAlister: president, trustee

Grants Analysis

Disclosure Period: fiscal year ending May 31, 2004
Total Grants: $1,400,605
Number of Grants: 40
Average Grant: $23,221*
Highest Grant: $495,000

Lowest Grant: $105
Typical Range: $5,000 to $50,000
*Note: Average grant figure excludes highest grant.

Recent Grants

Note: Grants derived from 2003 Form 990.
General
500,000	St. John's Health Center Foundation, Santa Monica, CA
150,000	Children's Hospital Los Angeles, Los Angeles, CA
150,000	Stanford University, Stanford, CA
100,000	University of Southern California, Los Angeles, CA
75,000	Assistance League of Southern California, Hollywood, CA
75,000	John Wayne Cancer Institute, Santa Monica, CA
75,000	Los Angeles Heart Institute, Los Angeles, CA
40,000	House Ear Institute, Los Angeles, CA
30,000	El Rodeo School, Beverly Hills, CA
25,000	University of California Los Angeles Foundation, Los Angeles, CA

ALLETTA MORRIS MCBEAN CHARITABLE TRUST

Giving Contact

Charlene Kleiner, Assistant Secretary
Alletta Morris McBean Charitable Trust
400 S. El Camino Real, Suite 777
San Mateo, CA 94402
Phone: (650)558-8480
Fax: (650)558-8481
E-mail: mcbeancharitabletrust@att.net

Description

Founded: 1986
EIN: 943019660
Organization Type: General Purpose Foundation
Giving Locations: RI: Aquidneck Island, Newport
Grant Types: Capital, Challenge, Endowment, General Support, Multiyear/Continuing Support, Operating Expenses, Project.

Donor Information

Founder: Established in 1986 by the late Alletta Morris McBean.

Financial Summary

Total Giving: $1,416,500 (2003); $2,760,923 (2002); $2,593,500 (2001)
Assets: $50,009,915 (2003); $42,168,897 (2002); $55,196,085 (2001)

Typical Recipients

Arts & Humanities: Arts Associations & Councils, Arts Centers, Historic Preservation, History & Archaeology, Libraries, Museums/Galleries
Civic & Public Affairs: Economic Development, Civic & Public Affairs-General, Professional & Trade Associations, Urban & Community Affairs, Zoos/Aquariums
Education: Arts/Humanities Education, Colleges & Universities, Education Funds, Environmental Education, Private Education (Precollege), Public Education (Precollege)
Environment: Air/Water Quality, Forestry, Environment-General, Protection, Resource Conservation, Watershed, Wildlife Protection
Health: Emergency/Ambulance Services, Health-General, Home-Care Services, Hospices, Hospitals, Mental Health, Nursing Services
Religion: Churches, Religious Organizations, Religious Welfare
Social Services: Animal Protection, Community Service Organizations, Family Services, Recreation & Athletics, Senior Services, Youth Organizations

Application Procedures

Initial Contact: The trust requests that applications be made in writing.
Application Requirements: Written proposals should thoroughly explain the program and the project for which the organization is seeking funding. Proposals should include budget information, along with other sources of funding, list of board of directors, and proof of 501 (c)(s) status. The board meets in May and October.
Deadlines: February 28 and July 31.

Restrictions

The trust does not make grants to individuals.

Additional Information

Publications: Application Guidelines

Foundation Officials

Donald Christ: secretary, trustee
Noreen Drexel: president, trustee
Hariett Reed: trustee
Gladys V. Szapary: trustee
John A. van Beuren: trustee

Grants Analysis

Disclosure Period: calendar year ending 2003
Total Grants: $1,416,500
Number of Grants: 14
Average Grant: $70,500*
Highest Grant: $500,000
Lowest Grant: $12,500
Typical Range: $25,000 to $100,000
*Note: Average grant figure excludes highest grants.

Recent Grants

Note: Grants derived from 2003 Form 990.

Library-Related
| 500,000 | Company of the Redwood Library and Athenaeum, Newport, RI -- renovation and restoration of the library |
| 200,000 | Newport Public Library, Newport, RI -- towards renovation project |

General
200,000	Norman Bird Sanctuary Trust, Middletown, RI -- for the acquisition of lands
100,000	Newport Art Museum and Art Association, Newport, RI -- towards renovation of Griswold House
100,000	Save the Bay Inc., Providence, RI -- to explore the bay campaign
60,000	Visiting Nurse Services of Newport and Bristol Counties, Portsmouth, RI -- towards charitable care
50,000	Aquidneck Island Land Trust, Middletown, RI
50,000	Naval War College Foundation Inc., Newport, RI -- for study group endowment
45,000	Preservation Society of Newport County, Newport, RI -- towards restoration and replacement of gas lamp
34,000	Friends of Cardines Field Ltd., Portsmouth, RI -- for restoration of building
25,000	New England Aquarium Corporation, Boston, MA -- towards exploration centre
25,000	Save the Bay Inc., Providence, RI -- towards habitat restoration work

MCBEAN FAMILY FOUNDATION

Giving Contact

Charlene Kleiner, Secretary
400 S. El Camino Real, Suite 777
San Mateo, CA 94402
Phone: (650)558-8480
Fax: (605)558-8481
E-mail: mcbeanfamilyfoundation@att.net

Description

Founded: 1955
EIN: 946062239
Organization Type: Private Foundation
Giving Locations: CA: San Francisco Bay area
Grant Types: Capital, Endowment, General Support, Multiyear/Continuing Support.

Donor Information

Founder: Established in 1955 by the late Atholl McBean.

Financial Summary

Total Giving: $1,200,000 (2004 approx); $1,000,000 (2003 approx); $978,500 (2002)
Assets: $16,000,000 (2004 approx); $15,000,000 (2003 approx); $12,946,983 (2002)

Typical Recipients

Arts & Humanities: Arts Centers, Arts Institutes, Community Arts, Arts & Humanities-General, Historic Preservation, History & Archaeology, Libraries, Museums/Galleries, Music, Opera, Performing Arts
Civic & Public Affairs: Botanical Gardens/Parks, Business/Free Enterprise, Community Foundations, Civic & Public Affairs-General, Nonprofit Management, Philanthropic Organizations, Public Policy, Urban & Community Affairs, Zoos/Aquariums
Education: Colleges & Universities, Education Associations, Education Funds, Elementary Education (Private), Faculty Development, Education-General, Medical Education, Minority Education, Private Education (Precollege), Public Education (Precollege), Religious Education, Science/Mathematics Education, Special Education, Student Aid
Environment: Resource Conservation, Wildlife Protection
Health: AIDS/HIV, Alzheimer's Disease, Cancer, Children's Health/Hospitals, Clinics/Medical Centers, Eyes/Blindness, Health Organizations, Hospices, Hospitals, Long-Term Care, Medical Research, Prenatal Health Issues, Speech & Hearing
International: International Relations, Missionary/Religious Activities
Religion: Churches, Religion-General, Ministries, Religious Organizations, Religious Welfare
Science: Science Museums, Scientific Centers & Institutes, Scientific Organizations
Social Services: Animal Protection, At-Risk Youth, Big Brothers/Big Sisters, Child Abuse, Child Welfare, Community Service Organizations, Family Services, Food/Clothing Distribution, People with Disabilities, Recreation & Athletics, Scouts, Sexual Abuse, Shelters/Homelessness, Social Services-General, United Funds/United Ways, Youth Organizations

Application Procedures

Initial Contact: The foundation decided in 1999 to no longer accept unsolicited proposals from organizations that have been previously received support from the foundation. Proposals are accepted, however, from previously supported organizations and from organizations that have been researched and endorsed by a board member prior to proposal submission.

Restrictions

Does not support individuals or fund scholarships, fellowships, or loans.

Foundation Officials

Judith McBean Cosper: vice president, director
Peter Folger: director
Deidra Head: director
Sheila McBean Head: director
Natasha Hunt: director
Charlene Kleiner: secretary
Nancy H. McBean: director
Clark Nelson: treasurer
Edith McBean Newberry: president, director
Henry K. Newhall: director

Grants Analysis

Disclosure Period: calendar year ending 2002
Total Grants: $978,500
Number of Grants: 27
Average Grant: $29,942*
Highest Grant: $200,000
Lowest Grant: $5,000
Typical Range: $10,000 to $50,000
*Note:** Average grant figure excludes highest grant.

Recent Grants

Note: Grants derived from 2002 Form 990.
General

200,000	Exploratorium, San Francisco, CA
100,000	Corporation of the Fine Arts Museums, San Francisco, CA -- provides New de Young construction
100,000	Regents of the University of California, San Francisco, CA -- provides McBean fellowship in Alzheimer's disease research
60,000	Asian Art Foundation of San Francisco, San Francisco, CA -- offers the new Asian capital campaign
50,000	Friends of the Recreation and Park Corporation, San Francisco, CA -- provides development of plant collections and interpretive stations
50,000	United Religions Initiative, San Francisco, CA -- provides strategic growth support
38,000	California Academy of Sciences, San Francisco, CA -- offers logistics center facility
30,000	Regents of the University of California, Davis, CA -- provides equine reproductive research
30,000	University of California San Francisco Foundation, San Francisco, CA -- assists with socio demographic profile of participants
30,000	Wildlife Conservation Society, Bronx, NY -- provides coral molecular ecology research program

FAYE MCBEATH FOUNDATION

Giving Contact

Scott E. Gelzer, Executive Director
1020 North Broadway, Suite 112
Milwaukee, WI 53202
Phone: (414)272-2626
Fax: (414)272-6235
E-mail: info@fayemcbeath.org
Web: http://www.fayemcbeath.org

Description

Founded: 1964
EIN: 396074450
Organization Type: General Purpose Foundation
Giving Locations: WI: particularly the Milwaukee metropolitan area
Grant Types: Capital, General Support, Operating Expenses, Project.

Donor Information

Founder: Faye McBeath was born in Milwaukee, WI, in 1882. She graduated from the University of Wisconsin in 1913, and taught in a local school for three years. In 1916, her uncle Lucius W. Nieman, founder of The Milwaukee Journal, invited her to join the Journal staff. She worked there for the next twenty years, and upon her uncle's death in 1935, inherited half of his estate. Throughout the last thirty years of her life, Miss McBeath became involved in a variety of local causes. In 1964, she created the Faye McBeath Foundation which received the bulk of her estate upon her death in 1967.

Financial Summary

Total Giving: $1,597,728 (2003); $1,683,830 (2001)
Assets: $12,324,644 (2003); $15,001,253 (2001)
Gifts Received: $2,000 (2003); $2,000 (2001); $2,000 (2000)

Typical Recipients

Arts & Humanities: Arts Centers, Arts Festivals, Libraries, Museums/Galleries, Music
Civic & Public Affairs: Botanical Gardens/Parks, Business/Free Enterprise, Community Foundations, Economic Development, Employment/Job Training, Gay/Lesbian Issues, Civic & Public Affairs-General, Hispanic Affairs, Housing, Inner-City Development, Law & Justice, Legal Aid, Minority Business, Native American Affairs, Nonprofit Management, Public Policy, Urban & Community Affairs, Women's Affairs
Education: Afterschool/Enrichment Programs, Arts/Humanities Education, Colleges & Universities, Continuing Education, Education Funds, Education Reform, Elementary Education (Private), Environmental Education, Faculty Development, Education-General, Health & Physical Education, Leadership Training, Literacy, Medical Education, Minority Education, Private Education (Precollege), Public Education (Precollege), Science/Mathematics Education, Secondary Education (Private), Social Sciences Education, Special Education
Environment: Environment-General
Health: AIDS/HIV, Alzheimer's Disease, Children's Health/Hospitals, Clinics/Medical Centers, Eyes/Blindness, Geriatric Health, Health Policy/Cost Containment, Health Funds, Health Organizations, Hospices, Hospitals, Long-Term Care, Medical Rehabilitation, Mental Health, Nursing Services, Public Health, Single-Disease Health Associations, Speech & Hearing, Transplant Networks/Donor Banks
Religion: Dioceses, Jewish Causes, Ministries, Religious Welfare, Social/Policy Issues
Science: Science Museums, Scientific Centers & Institutes
Social Services: At-Risk Youth, Big Brothers/Big Sisters, Camps, Child Abuse, Child Welfare, Community Centers, Community Service Organizations, Counseling, Crime Prevention, Day Care, Delinquency & Criminal Rehabilitation, Domestic Violence, Family Planning, Family Services, Food/Clothing Distribution, People with Disabilities, Recreation & Athletics, Scouts, Senior Services, Shelters/Homelessness, Social Services-General, Substance Abuse, United Funds/United Ways, Volunteer Services, YMCA/YWCA/YMHA/YWHA, Youth Organizations

Application Procedures

Initial Contact: Applicants must complete a letter of intent application form, which can be obtained from the foundation offices.
Application Requirements: The preliminary application form should include basic information about the applying organization and its tax-exempt status; summary of the proposed project, its objectives, significance, and anticipated costs. If the proposed project falls within the scope of the foundation's activities, a formal proposal will be requested. At that time, a formal grant application and review schedule will be provided. When submitting a formal application, ap-

plicants must use the Milwaukee Area Common Grant Application. The formal proposal must include specific objectives and measures for assessing the project's success; detailed budget, including total costs and amount sought; a description of the agency qualifications and of key personnel; a statement that the request is made by the organization's governing body; and support statements from planning agencies underscoring the need for the project and the capability of the organization to complete it.
Deadlines: The board of trustees meet 5 times each year to consider proposals, with application deadlines in January (preliminary applications only), April, June, September, and November (formal applications only). Contact foundation for exact deadlines.
Review Process: Applicants are notified in writing within ten days of the trustee meeting. The following guidelines are used in considering grant proposals: the relevance of the proposal to the foundation's areas of interest; clearly-stated project or program outcomes and the strategy for achieving them; commitment to continue successful programs after the foundation's support ceases; the extent to which the proposal involves the people being served and other organizations in a collective approach to solve a problem or address an issue; the ability of the organization, its leadership, and staff to carry out the project; and the clarity and completeness of the grant application.
Notes: Proposals must be received by noon on the deadline date. General solicitation letters are not considered. Grants are paid out four times each year during the big week of each calendar quarter.

Restrictions

Grants are made to nonprofit, federally tax-exempt organizations created under the laws of Wisconsin. In any year, no more than 20 percent of grants will support construction or other capital programs. Grants are not made for annual fund drives, endowment funds, individuals, scholarships, specific scientific or medical research inquiries, emergency assistance, or operating expenses of established agencies. Grants will be made only within Wisconsin and principally to support projects having primary focus on the welfare of the residents of the greater Milwaukee community. Grants made to agencies located in other regions of the state will be limited to the support of projects which clearly have a state-wide focus. Capital grant awards will not be released until the construction or renovation project is about to get underway. Commitments will not be undertaken by the foundation for payment of grants beyond a period of three years from the time the grant was originally approved.

Additional Information

In 1997, the foundation modified its capital giving policy. Trustees will consider capital grant requests, but only for projects with significant community-wide impact. Few capital grants will be awarded each year. The Nonprofit Management Fund, established in 1993 in collaboration with the Milwaukee and Helen Bader Foundations, awards small grants to improve the management capabilities and provide technical assistance to Milwaukee County nonprofit organizations.
In 1991, the foundation began an awards program to "recognize excellence and leadership among nonprofit organizations" which have been recipients of foundation funds within the past five years. The purpose of this program is "to stimulate all nonprofits to strive for a greater degree of excellence in programming and management" and also to provide agencies with "unencumbered operating dollars." Admission to the awards program is by nomination. Final decision for the annual award, which will be in the range of $25,000 to $50,000, is made by the trustees.
Publications: Annual Report
Trust(s): US Bank NA

Foundation Officials

Charles A. Krause: vice chairman, trustee PRIM CORP EMPL president: Krause Consultants Ltd.
Steve C. Smith: trustee B Hutchinson, MN 1949. ED University of Minnesota BA (1972); Oklahoma City University JD (1975). PRIM NONPR EMPL legislator: State of Minnesota.
Bonnie R. Weigell: trustee

Grants Analysis

Disclosure Period: calendar year ending 2003
Total Grants: $1,597,728
Number of Grants: 102
Average Grant: $13,839*
Highest Grant: $200,000
Lowest Grant: $1,000
Typical Range: $5,000 to $30,000
*Note: Average grant figure excludes highest grant.

Recent Grants

Note: Grants derived from 2003 Form 990.
General

200,000	Greater Milwaukee Foundation, Milwaukee, WI -- to support McBeath Community Partners endowment program
55,000	Greater Milwaukee Foundation, Milwaukee, WI -- for Nonprofit Management fund
50,000	Marquette University, Milwaukee, WI -- to assist the Wisconsin Nursing Redesign Project
50,000	University of Wisconsin, Milwaukee, WI -- to support Helen Bader Institute
50,000	University of Wisconsin, Milwaukee, WI -- fund for Helen Bader Institute
40,000	Westside Healthcare Association, Madison, WI -- fund for dental clinic
37,500	St. John's Home of Milwaukee, Milwaukee, WI -- fund for renovation/expansion of the health care center
37,178	Older Adult Service Providers' Consortium in Milwaukee County, Milwaukee, WI -- fund for Interfaith Older Adult Programs
35,000	Women's Center of Waukesha, Waukesha, WI -- fund for indoor & outdoor child play area equipment
30,000	Hunger Task Force of Milwaukee Inc., Milwaukee, WI -- fund for Commodity Supplemental Food Program

B. C. McCabe
Foundation

Giving Contact

James D. Shepard, Trustee
B.C. McCabe Foundation
8152 Painter Avenue, Suite 201
Whittier, CA 90602
Phone: (562)696-1433
Fax: (562)698-5508

Description

Founded: 1976
EIN: 510192036
Organization Type: General Purpose Foundation
Giving Locations: CA
Grant Types: General Support.

Financial Summary

Total Giving: $6,263,047 (2003); $4,422,938 (2002); $4,875,363 (2001)
Assets: $116,306,550 (2003); $99,357,221 (2002)
Gifts Received: $160,000 (1998); $10,000 (1996); $10,000 (1994). Note: In 1998, contributions were received from B.C. McCabe Trust.

Typical Recipients

Arts & Humanities: Arts Centers, Arts Institutes, Libraries, Museums/Galleries, Music
Civic & Public Affairs: Botanical Gardens/Parks, Civil Rights, Civic & Public Affairs-General, Hispanic Affairs, Housing, Law & Justice, Urban & Community Affairs, Women's Affairs
Education: Afterschool/Enrichment Programs, Arts/Humanities Education, Business Education, Colleges & Universities, Education Associations, Education-General, Medical Education, Private Education (Precollege), Public Education (Precollege), Religious Education, Special Education, Student Aid, Vocational & Technical Education
Health: AIDS/HIV, Children's Health/Hospitals, Clinics/Medical Centers, Diabetes, Emergency/Ambulance Services, Health Organizations, Hospitals, Nursing Services, Nutrition, Trauma Treatment
International: International Affairs
Religion: Churches, Religion-General, Religious Organizations, Religious Welfare
Social Services: At-Risk Youth, Camps, Child Welfare, Community Centers, Community Service Organizations, Crime Prevention, Day Care, Delinquency & Criminal Rehabilitation, Emergency Relief, Family Services, Food/Clothing Distribution, Homes, People with Disabilities, Recreation & Athletics, Scouts, Senior Services, Shelters/Homelessness, Social Services-General, Substance Abuse, Volunteer Services, YMCA/YWCA/YMHA/YWHA, Youth Organizations

Application Procedures

Initial Contact: A brief phone call of inquiry.
Application Requirements: Provide a complete summary grant request (explained upon phone call) of the proposed project or purpose.
Deadlines: None.

Foundation Officials

Roy D. Miller: trustee
James D. Shepard: trustee

Grants Analysis

Disclosure Period: calendar year ending 2003
Total Grants: $6,263,047
Number of Grants: 92
Average Grant: $51,196*
Highest Grant: $654,250
Lowest Grant: $3,553
Typical Range: $10,000 to $100,000
*Note: Average grant figure excludes three highest grants ($1,706,603).

Recent Grants

Note: Grants derived from 2003 Form 990.

Library-Related

35,000	Library Foundation of Los Angeles, Los Angeles, CA

General

654,250	Hathaway Children and Family Services, Sylmar, CA
586,000	Boys & Girls Club of Troy, Troy, MI
466,353	Claremont School of Theology, Claremont, CA
275,000	Salvation Army, Whittier, CA
234,000	Boys & Girls Club of Truckee Meadows, Reno, NV
200,000	Boys & Girls Clubs of America, Atlanta, GA
175,000	Whittier Area First Day Coalition, Whittier, CA
150,000	Long Beach Museum of Art, Long Beach, CA
150,000	Volunteers of America, Alexandria, VA
147,076	Woman Haven, Inc., El Centro, CA

McCann Foundation

Giving Contact

John J. Gartland, Jr., Trustee
35 Market Street
Poughkeepsie, NY 12601
Phone: (245)452-3085
Fax: (245)452-3093

Description

Founded: 1969
EIN: 146050628
Organization Type: General Purpose Foundation
Giving Locations: NY: Dutchess County, Poughkeepsie
Grant Types: Capital, Fellowship, Multiyear/Continuing Support.

Donor Information

Founder: The McCann Foundation was established in New York in 1969 following the death of James J. McCann, the foundation's benefactor. Mr. McCann, a grain merchant, was a lifetime resident of Poughkeepsie, NY. He owned and operated a feed and grain store; however, he amassed his fortune through shrewd understanding of and success with the stock market. His deep ties with the Catholic Church underlie one of the main focuses of the McCann Foundation.

Financial Summary

Total Giving: $800,000 (2002 approx); $914,766 (2001). Note: Figure for 1996 represents the combined giving of both the McCann Foundation and the James J. McCann Trust.
Assets: $33,000,000 (2002 approx); $33,308,891 (2001)

Typical Recipients

Arts & Humanities: Arts Associations & Councils, Arts Centers, Film & Video, Arts & Humanities-General, Historic Preservation, History & Archaeology, Libraries, Music, Opera, Performing Arts, Public Broadcasting
Civic & Public Affairs: African American Affairs, Botanical Gardens/Parks, Community Foundations, Economic Development, Employment/Job Training, Civic & Public Affairs-General, Housing, Law & Justice, Legal Aid, Municipalities/Towns, Nonprofit Management, Philanthropic Organizations, Professional & Trade Associations, Public Policy, Safety, Urban & Community Affairs, Zoos/Aquariums
Education: Colleges & Universities, Community & Junior Colleges, Continuing Education, Education Funds, Elementary Education (Public), Engineering/Technological Education, Environmental Education, Legal Education, Private Education (Precollege), Public Education (Precollege), Religious Education, Secondary Education (Private), Student Aid
Environment: Air/Water Quality, Environment-General, Research, Resource Conservation
Health: Cancer, Children's Health/Hospitals, Emergency/Ambulance Services, Hospices, Hospitals, Single-Disease Health Associations, Trauma Treatment
International: Foreign Arts Organizations, Missionary/Religious Activities
Religion: Churches, Dioceses, Religion-General, Jewish Causes, Religious Organizations, Religious Welfare, Seminaries, Synagogues/Temples
Science: Science Exhibits & Fairs
Social Services: Animal Protection, Big Brothers/Big Sisters, Child Welfare, Community Centers, Community Service Organizations, Crime Prevention, Day Care, Delinquency & Criminal Rehabilitation, Emergency Relief, Food/Clothing Distribution, Homes, People with Disabilities, Recreation & Athletics, Senior Services, Shelters/Homelessness, United Funds/United Ways, Volunteer Services, YMCA/YWCA/YMHA/YWHA, Youth Organizations

Application Procedures

Initial Contact: The foundation has no formal application guidelines or forms.
Application Requirements: All applications for grants must be made in writing and addressed to the trustees, who meet regularly every January and July.
Deadlines: None. Applications should be received as far in advance as possible before trustees' meetings.

Restrictions

The foundation makes no grants to individuals or for operating budgets, emergency funds, endowment funds, deficit financing, matching gifts, or loans.

Additional Information

The McCann Foundation and the James J. McCann Charitable Trust are separate legal entities which act as a single unit. Most of the assets are held in the trust. For convenience, the activities of both organizations are referred to as the McCann Foundation.

Foundation Officials

Richard V. Corbally: secretary, director
John J. Gartland, Jr.: president, director B 1914. ED Georgetown University BA (1935); Fordham University LLB (1939); Saint John's University JSD (1941). PRIM CORP EMPL partner: Corbally Gartland & Rappleyea.
Michael G. Gartland: assistant secretary, director ADD CORP EMPL partner: Corbally Gartland & Rappleyea.

Grants Analysis

Disclosure Period: calendar year ending 2001
Total Grants: $914,766
Number of Grants: 58
Average Grant: $11,306*
Highest Grant: $181,651
Lowest Grant: $104
Typical Range: $1,000 to $20,000
*Note: Average grant figure excludes two highest grants ($281,651).

Recent Grants

Note: Grants derived from 2002 Form 990.

Library-Related

10,000	Poughkeepsie Public Library, Poughkeepsie, NY -- toward capital campaign for facilities expansion
2,500	Millbrook Free Library, Millbrook, NY -- toward capital campaign

General

105,108	Mount Carmel Church, Poughkeepsie, NY -- funding for meeting hall
100,000	Institute of Ecosystems Studies, Millbrook, NY -- toward campaign for ecosystems studies
100,000	St. Martin DePorres, Poughkeepsie, NY -- assistance for school expansion project
90,000	St. Francis Hospital, Poughkeepsie, NY -- funding for new imaging center
84,062	Mid-Hudson Civic Center, Poughkeepsie, NY -- assistance for expansion project
75,500	Manst College, Poughkeepsie, NY -- toward scholarship
50,000	Hudson Valley Philharmonic, Poughkeepsie, NY -- funding for pops series
45,000	Our Lady of the Way Chapel, Hyde Park, NY -- assistance for renovations
33,750	Ebenezer Baptist Church, Poughkeepsie, NY -- funding for new heating and cooling system
27,160	Franklin & Eleanor Roosevelt Institute, New York, NY -- toward red house renovation

CATHERINE MCCARTHY MEMORIAL TRUST FUND

Giving Contact

PO Box 898
Lawrence, MA 01842
Phone: (978)435-7256

Description

Founded: 1984
EIN: 222549008
Organization Type: Private Foundation
Giving Locations: MA: and surrounding areas
Grant Types: General Support.

Donor Information

Founder: the late John J. McCarthy

Financial Summary

Total Giving: $306,320 (fiscal year ending June 30, 2004); $143,419 (fiscal 2002); $316,119 (fiscal 2001). Note: Fiscal 1997 Giving includes United Way ($2,000).
Assets: $4,882,253 (fiscal 2004); $4,896,871 (fiscal 2002); $5,235,243 (fiscal 2001)

Typical Recipients

Arts & Humanities: Arts Associations & Councils, Arts Centers, Ethnic & Folk Arts, Arts & Humanities-General, History & Archaeology, Libraries, Museums/Galleries, Music
Civic & Public Affairs: Botanical Gardens/Parks, Chambers of Commerce, Clubs, Community Foundations, Civic & Public Affairs-General, Hispanic Affairs, Housing, Municipalities/Towns, Philanthropic Organizations, Safety, Urban & Community Affairs, Women's Affairs
Education: Arts/Humanities Education, Colleges & Universities, Legal Education, Private Education (Precollege), Public Education (Precollege), Secondary Education (Private), Student Aid
Health: Cancer, Geriatric Health, Health Organizations, Hospitals, Mental Health, Prenatal Health Issues, Public Health
Religion: Churches, Dioceses, Jewish Causes, Ministries, Religious Organizations, Religious Welfare, Synagogues/Temples
Social Services: Child Welfare, Community Centers, Community Service Organizations, Day Care, Family Services, Food/Clothing Distribution, Homes, People with Disabilities, Recreation & Athletics, Shelters/Homelessness, United Funds/United Ways, YMCA/YWCA/YMHA/YWHA, Youth Organizations

Application Procedures

Initial Contact: The foundation has no formal grant application procedure or application form.
Deadlines: None.

Additional Information

Trust(s): Fleet National Bank

Foundation Officials

Thomas F. Caffrey, Esq.: co-trustee

Grants Analysis

Disclosure Period: fiscal year ending June 30, 2004
Total Grants: $306,320
Number of Grants: 49
Average Grant: $5,173*
Highest Grant: $58,000
Lowest Grant: $500
Typical Range: $1,000 to $10,000
*Note: Average grant figure excludes highest grant.

Recent Grants

Note: Grants derived from fiscal 2000 Form 990.
Library-Related

7,550	Brooks School, North Andover, MA

General

25,500	Merrimack Valley Community Foundation, North Andover, MA
21,500	St. Mary Immaculate Conception, Lawrence, MA
12,500	Essex Art Center, Essex, MA
10,000	St. Augustine Parish, Lawrence, MA
10,000	St. Michael's Parish, Litchfield, CT
10,000	Summer in Greater Lawrence, Lawrence, MA
7,500	Addison Gallery of American Art, Andover, MA
7,500	Lawrence Boys and Girls Club, Lawrence, MA
7,500	Massachusetts Caring for Children Foundation, Boston, MA
5,000	American Textile History Museum, Lowell, MA

JOHN AND MARGARET MCCARTY FOUNDATION

Giving Contact

William H. Cheney, Sr., President
358 Hill Road
Highlands, NC 28741-6568

Description

Founded: 1989
EIN: 581867301
Organization Type: Private Foundation
Grant Types: General Support.

Donor Information

Founder: Established in 1989 by the late John McCarty and the late Margaret McCarty.

Financial Summary

Total Giving: $396,900 (2002); $556,150 (2001)
Assets: $8,914,620 (2002); $9,357,405 (2001)

Typical Recipients

Arts & Humanities: Film & Video, Historic Preservation, History & Archaeology, Libraries, Museums/Galleries, Music, Public Broadcasting
Civic & Public Affairs: Civil Rights, Community Foundations, Civic & Public Affairs-General, Housing, Law & Justice, Municipalities/Towns, Native American Affairs, Public Policy, Urban & Community Affairs
Education: Colleges & Universities, Education-General, Private Education (Precollege), Religious Education, Secondary Education (Private), Student Aid
Environment: Resource Conservation
Health: Alzheimer's Disease, Children's Health/Hospitals, Health Organizations, Hospitals, Mental Health, Nursing Services, Single-Disease Health Associations
International: International Organizations, Missionary/Religious Activities
Religion: Churches, Dioceses, Religion-General, Ministries, Religious Organizations, Religious Welfare, Seminaries
Social Services: Camps, Community Service Organizations, Family Services, Social Services-General, United Funds/United Ways, YMCA/YWCA/YMHA/YWHA

Application Procedures

Initial Contact: Send a brief letter of inquiry.
Application Requirements: Include purpose of funds sought and proof of tax-exempt status.
Deadlines: None.

Foundation Officials

Eleanor M. Cheney: secretary
William H. Cheney, Sr.: president

Grants Analysis

Disclosure Period: calendar year ending 2002
Total Grants: $396,900
Number of Grants: 13
Average Grant: $16,408*
Highest Grant: $200,000
Lowest Grant: $1,000
Typical Range: $5,000 to $25,000
*Note: Average grant figure excludes highest grant.

Recent Grants

Note: Grants derived from 2001 Form 990.

General

200,000	Visiting Nurse Association, Atlanta, GA -- Alzheimer's care
154,500	Community Bible Church, Highlands, NC
50,000	Heritage School, Newnan, GA -- for capital campaign
25,000	Capital Area YMCA, Arapahoe, NC -- for Camp Seagull
25,000	Highlands Cashiers Hospital Foundation, Highlands, NC
25,000	Kennesaw State University, Kennesaw, GA -- for building fund
25,000	Northwest Georgia Community Foundation, Dalton, GA -- for Alzheimer's issues
15,000	Raleigh MCCBG, Raleigh, NC
8,500	Atlanta Classic Foundation, Inc., Atlanta, GA
7,950	Anglican Mission in America

MCCASLAND FOUNDATION

Giving Contact

Barbara Braught, Executive Director
PO Box 400
Duncan, OK 73534
Phone: (580)252-5580
Fax: (580)252-5791

Description

Founded: 1952
EIN: 736096032
Organization Type: General Purpose Foundation
Giving Locations: OK: primarily Oklahoma
Grant Types: Challenge, Endowment, General Support, Operating Expenses, Professorship, Scholarship.

Donor Information

Founder: The foundation was established in 1952. The donors include members of the McCasland family as well as Mack Oil Company, where Thomas H. McCasland, Jr., a foundation trustee, serves as chairman and chief executive officer.

Financial Summary

Total Giving: $2,070,472 (2003); $2,324,201 (2002); $2,175,300 (2001)
Giving Analysis: Giving for 2003 includes: foundation grants to United Way ($20,000); 2002: foundation grants to United Way ($20,000)
Assets: $44,903,206 (2003); $37,615,490 (2002); $47,095,706 (2001)

Typical Recipients

Arts & Humanities: Arts Associations & Councils, Arts Centers, Arts Funds, Arts Institutes, Arts Outreach, Ethnic & Folk Arts, Arts & Humanities-General, Historic Preservation, History & Archaeology, Libraries, Museums/Galleries, Music, Public Broadcasting, Theater
Civic & Public Affairs: Botanical Gardens/Parks, Business/Free Enterprise, Chambers of Commerce, Clubs, Community Foundations, Economic Development, Employment/Job Training, Civic & Public Affairs-General, Housing, Municipalities/Towns, Native American Affairs, Nonprofit Management, Parades/Festivals, Philanthropic Organizations, Professional & Trade Associations, Public Policy, Urban & Community Affairs
Education: Afterschool/Enrichment Programs, Arts/Humanities Education, Business Education, Business-School Partnerships, Colleges & Universities, Community & Junior Colleges, Education Associations, Education Funds, Education Reform, Faculty Development, Education-General, Literacy, Medical Education, Private Education (Precollege), Public Education (Precollege), Religious Education, Science/Mathematics Education, Special Education, Student Aid, Vocational & Technical Education
Environment: Environment-General, Research, Wildlife Protection
Health: Alzheimer's Disease, Cancer, Children's Health/Hospitals, Clinics/Medical Centers, Emergency/Ambulance Services, Health Organizations, Heart, Hospices, Hospitals, Long-Term Care, Medical Rehabilitation, Medical Research, Single-Disease Health Associations
International: Foreign Educational Institutions
Religion: Churches, Religion-General, Ministries, Religious Organizations, Religious Welfare
Science: Science Exhibits & Fairs, Science Museums, Scientific Centers & Institutes, Scientific Organizations
Social Services: At-Risk Youth, Camps, Child Welfare, Community Centers, Community Service Organizations, Emergency Relief, Family Services, Food/Clothing Distribution, Homes, People with Disabilities, Recreation & Athletics, Scouts, Senior Services, Shelters/Homelessness, Social Services-General, Special Olympics, Substance Abuse, United Funds/United Ways, Veterans, Volunteer Services, YMCA/YWCA/YMHA/YWHA, Youth Organizations

Application Procedures

Initial Contact: The foundation requests applications be made in writing.
Application Requirements: The letter should include brief a description of organization, the amount and purpose of the grant, names of contact persons, and proof of tax-exempt status.
Deadlines: None.
Review Process: The board of trustees generally meets on a quarterly basis. Applicants receive notification following the board meeting.
Notes: An application form is available, but the foundation reports that use of the form is optional.

Foundation Officials

Barbara Braught: executive director
Thomas H. McCasland, Jr.: trustee B Duncan, OK 1933. ED University of Oklahoma BPOE (1956). PRIM CORP EMPL chairman, chief executive officer: Mack Energy Co. ADD CORP EMPL vice president, director: M&M Supply Co.; vice president, director: Mack Oil Co.; vice president, director: Thomas Drilling Co. CORP AFFIL president, director: Investors Trust Co.; chairman: AmQuest Bank Co.; manager: Enerwest Trading Co. NONPR AFFIL member: Benevolent Protectorate Elks.
Mary F. Michaelis: trustee
W. H. Phelps: trustee

Grants Analysis

Disclosure Period: calendar year ending 2003
Total Grants: $2,050,472*
Number of Grants: 91
Average Grant: $16,297*
Highest Grant: $350,000
Lowest Grant: $500
Typical Range: $5,000 to $30,000
*Note: Giving excludes United Way. Average grant figure excludes two highest grants ($600,000).

Recent Grants

Note: Grants derived from 2002 Form 990.

General

575,000	On the Chisholm Trail Association, Duncan, OK -- towards operating expense
225,000	University of Oklahoma Foundation, Norman, OK -- towards installment on pledge
168,000	Communities Foundation of Okla, Oklahoma City, OK -- towards scholarship fund for 2002
150,000	On the Chisholm Trail Association, Duncan, OK -- towards operating expense
100,000	Cameron University Foundation, Lawton, OK -- towards installment on pledge
100,000	National Cowboy Museum, Oklahoma City, OK -- towards installment pledge
100,000	Oklahoma Communities Foundation, Oklahoma City, OK -- for On the Chisholm Trail Endow
100,000	Oklahoma Medical Research Foundation, Oklahoma City, OK -- towards installment on pledge
50,000	Oklahoma Arts Institute, Oklahoma City, OK -- towards installment on pledge (capital expense)
50,000	Oklahoma Baptist University, Shawnee, OK -- towards installment on pledge

MCCAUSLAND FOUNDATION

Giving Contact

Bonnie McCausland, President
PO Box 6675
Radnor, PA 19087-8675
Phone: (610)687-5253

Description

Founded: 1994
EIN: 232776475
Organization Type: Private Foundation
Giving Locations: MA: Nantucket; PA: Philadelphia
Grant Types: General Support.

Financial Summary

Total Giving: $164,480 (2003); $56,000 (2001)
Assets: $90,018 (2003); $80,693 (2001)
Gifts Received: $4,482 (1995); $1,500,032 (1994).
Note: In 1995, contributions were received from Peter McCausland.

Typical Recipients

Arts & Humanities: Libraries, Museums/Galleries, Music
Civic & Public Affairs: Botanical Gardens/Parks, Business/Free Enterprise, Economic Development, Employment/Job Training, Civic & Public Affairs-General
Education: Community & Junior Colleges, Education-General, International Exchange, Private Education (Precollege)
Environment: Environment-General, Resource Conservation, Wildlife Protection
Health: Cancer, Clinics/Medical Centers, Hospices, Hospitals, Public Health
Social Services: Child Welfare, Family Planning, People with Disabilities, Social Services-General

Application Procedures

Initial Contact: Send a brief letter of inquiry.
Application Requirements: a description of organization and purpose of funds sought.
Deadlines: None.

Foundation Officials

Cornelia B. Gross: secretary, treasurer
Gordon L. Keen, Jr.: director
Bonnie McCausland: president
Peter McCausland: vice president

Grants Analysis

Disclosure Period: calendar year ending 2003
Total Grants: $164,480
Number of Grants: 20
Average Grant: $2,529*
Highest Grant: $50,907
Lowest Grant: $500
Typical Range: $1,000 to $5,000
*Note: Average grant figure excludes three highest grants ($121,480).

Recent Grants

Note: Grants derived from 2003 Form 990.
Library-Related

10,000	Nantucket Atheneum, Nantucket, MA

General

50,907	Nantucket Land Council Inc., Nantucket, MA
50,573	Nantucket Land Council Inc., Nantucket, MA
20,000	Philadelphia Museum of Art, Philadelphia, PA
15,000	Independence Seaport Museum, Philadelphia, PA
5,000	Independence Seaport Museum, Philadelphia, PA
5,000	National Center for American Revolution, Wayne, PA
1,000	Baker Industries, Malvern, PA
1,000	Inglis Foundation, Philadelphia, PA
500	Wissahickon Hospice, Philadelphia, PA

MCCLATCHY CO.

Company Headquarters

2100 Q Street
Sacramento, CA 95816
Phone: (916)321-1846
Fax: (916)321-1964
Web: http://www.mcclatchy.com

Company Description

Founded: 1857
Ticker: MNI
Exchange: NYSE
Former Name: Cowles Media Co.
Revenue: US$1.08 billion (2001)
Employees: 9093 (2003)
SIC(s): 2711 Newspapers, 2721 Periodicals.

Operating Locations

McClatchy Media Co. (AZ--Scottsdale; CT--Stamford; MN--Minneapolis; PA--Harrisburg)

Subsidiary Companies

MN: Star Tribune Co., Minneapolis

Star Tribune Foundation

Giving Contact

Sandra K. Fleitman, Secretary
Star Tribune Foundation
425 Portland Avenue
Minneapolis, MN 55488-0002
Phone: (612)673-7051
Fax: (612)673-7020
E-mail: sfleitman@startribune.com

Description

EIN: 416031373
Organization Type: Corporate Foundation
Former Name: Cowles Media Foundation.
Giving Locations: MN: Minneapolis-St. Paul
Grant Types: Capital, Employee Matching Gifts, Endowment, General Support.
Note: Employee matching gift ratio: 1 to 1 for schools, colleges, and civic and cultural organisation.

Financial Summary

Total Giving: $3,000,000 (2003); $3,000,000 (2001).
Note: Contributes through corporate direct giving program and foundation.
Giving Analysis: Giving for 2001 includes: foundation scholarships ($17,500); foundation matching gifts ($202,510); foundation grants to United Way ($355,000); foundation ($2,424,990)
Assets: $15,043,597 (2003); $19,644,790 (2001)
Gifts Received: $500,000 (2003); $200 (2001); $10,089,651 (1998). Note: In 2003, contributions were received from McClatchy Co. In 1998, contributions were received from Cowles Media Co.

Typical Recipients

Arts & Humanities: Arts Associations & Councils, Arts Centers, Arts Festivals, Arts Funds, Arts Institutes, Arts Outreach, Community Arts, Dance, Ethnic & Folk Arts, Arts & Humanities-General, Historic Preservation, History & Archaeology, Libraries, Literary Arts, Museums/Galleries, Music, Opera, Performing Arts, Public Broadcasting, Theater, Visual Arts
Civic & Public Affairs: African American Affairs, Botanical Gardens/Parks, Chambers of Commerce, Civil Rights, Community Foundations, Economic Development, Employment/Job Training, First Amendment Issues, Civic & Public Affairs-General, Hispanic Affairs, Housing, Law & Justice, Native American Affairs, Nonprofit Management, Professional & Trade Associations, Public Policy, Urban & Community Affairs, Women's Affairs, Zoos/Aquariums
Education: Afterschool/Enrichment Programs, Arts/Humanities Education, Business Education, Colleges & Universities, Community & Junior Colleges, Continuing Education, Economic Education, Education Associations, Education Funds, Education Reform, Elementary Education (Private), Elementary Education (Public), Engineering/Technological Education, Faculty Development, Education-General, Journalism/Media Education, Leadership Training, Literacy, Minority Education, Preschool Education, Private Education (Precollege), Public Education (Precollege), Science/Mathematics Education, Secondary Education (Public), Social Sciences Education, Vocational & Technical Education
Environment: Air/Water Quality, Resource Conservation
Health: AIDS/HIV, Emergency/Ambulance Services, Medical Rehabilitation
International: Foreign Educational Institutions, Human Rights
Religion: Churches, Jewish Causes, Missionary Activities (Domestic), Religious Welfare
Science: Science Exhibits & Fairs, Science Museums
Social Services: At-Risk Youth, Child Abuse, Child Welfare, Community Centers, Community Service Organizations, Crime Prevention, Day Care, Delinquency & Criminal Rehabilitation, Domestic Violence, Emergency Relief, Family Planning, Family Services, Food/Clothing Distribution, People with Disabilities, Recreation & Athletics, Refugee Assistance, Shelters/Homelessness, Social Services-General, Substance Abuse, United Funds/United Ways, Volunteer Services, YMCA/YWCA/YMHA/YWHA, Youth Organizations

Application Procedures

Initial Contact: Request application guidelines, then send a brief letter or proposal.
Application Requirements: Include purpose of funds being sought; total project budget; a description of organization, its objectives, and how program will be administered; information about organization's officers and directors, current finances, and current contributors; and copy of current IRS tax-exempt ruling.
Deadlines: For general grants, None; for annual operating grants, January.
Review Process: General support is committed at the beginning of the fiscal year (April); large grants

and capital requests are considered at the quarterly meetings of the board of directors.
Evaluative Criteria: The proposal must meet company objectives in one of the funding categories.
Decision Notification: Applications are considered on a quarterly basis; a response is made generally within three months.
Notes: Preliminary inquiries by phone or fax may be useful in determining the extent to which a proposed project relates to guidelines and existing commitments. The foundation now accepts the Minnesota Common Grant Application Form.

Restrictions

Generally does not support organizations principally related to medicine and specific diseases, substance abuse, rehabilitation, and related research; religious or international programs; development of low-income housing; dinners or special events; publications or films; recreation, athletic groups and sporting events; individuals, including travel; conferences and writing or performing; fund raising events; or political or lobbying groups. Preference is given to Minnesota charitable organizations.

Additional Information

A stipulation of the 1998 merger between McClatchy and Cowles Media provided for an annual contribution of at least $3 million to Twin Cities community causes for at least 10 years.
Publications: Contributions Report

Corporate Officials

Randy Miller Lebedoff: vice president, general counsel B Washington, DC 1949. ED Smith College BA (1971); Indiana University JD (1975). PRIM CORP EMPL vice president, general counsel: Star Tribune. CORP AFFIL assistant secretary: Star Tribune Cowles Media Co. NONPR AFFIL director: Minnesota Newspapers Association; member: Newspaper Association America.
John R. Schueler: publisher, president PRIM CORP EMPL publisher, president: Star Tribune Co.
Robert J. Weil: vice president operations ED Indiana University. PRIM CORP EMPL vice president operations: The McClatchy Co. ADD CORP EMPL vice president operations: McClatchy Newspapers Inc.

Foundation Officials

Sandra K. Fleitman: secretary, director
Keith Moyer: director
Philip S. Sherburne: assistant treasurer, director
Pat Talamantes: treasurer, director
Benjamin Taylor: chairman, director
Robert J. Weil: director (see above)

Grants Analysis

Disclosure Period: calendar year ending 2003
Total Grants: $2,640,000*
Number of Grants: 400
Average Grant: $6,600
Highest Grant: $200,000
Typical Range: $1,000 to $10,000
*Note: Giving includes matching gifts; scholarships. Giving excludes United Way.

Recent Grants

Note: Grants derived from 2003 Form 990.
Library-Related

250,000	Minneapolis Central Library, Minneapolis, MN

General

360,000	United Way of Minneapolis and Saint Paul, Minneapolis, MN
200,000	Children's Theatre Company, Minneapolis, MN -- towards capital camp expansion
200,000	Guthrie Theater Foundation, Minneapolis, MN
100,000	Goodwill/Easter Seals, St. Paul, MN
100,000	Minnesota Computer for Schools, Mendota Heights, MN -- towards prisons refurbishing computers for schools

100,000	Walker Art Center, Minneapolis, MN
50,000	Catholic Charities, Minneapolis, MN -- to assist in basic children's services
50,000	Twin Cities RISE!, Minneapolis, MN
50,000	University of Minnesota Foundation, Minneapolis, MN -- to educate young leaders in public policy
43,000	Minnesota Children's Museum, St. Paul, MN

MCCONNELL FOUNDATION

Giving Contact

Ana Diaz Bachman, Program Associate
McConnell Foundation
PO Box 492050
Redding, CA 96049-2050
Phone: (530)226-6200
Fax: (530)226-6210
E-mail: info@mcconnellfoundation.org
Web: http://www.mcconnellfoundation.org

Description

Founded: 1964
EIN: 946102700
Organization Type: General Purpose Foundation
Giving Locations: CA: Shasta County, Siskiyou County
Grant Types: General Support, Matching, Project, Scholarship.

Donor Information

Founder: The McConnell Foundation was established in 1964 by Carl R. McConnell and Leah F. McConnell.

Financial Summary

Total Giving: $8,632,884 (2003); $9,192,755 (2002); $3,650,773 (2001)
Giving Analysis: Giving for 2003 includes: foundation matching gifts ($149,686); foundation scholarships ($213,178); 2002: foundation scholarships ($124,475); foundation matching gifts ($147,211)
Assets: $349,358,031 (2003); $302,579,597 (2002); $350,000,000 (2001)
Gifts Received: $72,020 (2000); $315,871 (1998); $11,315,311 (1994). Note: In 2000, contributions were received from Myrle and Peggy Lema. In 1998, contributions were received from from Leah F. McConnell 1992 Trust.

Typical Recipients

Arts & Humanities: Arts Festivals, Arts & Humanities-General, Historic Preservation, History & Archaeology, Libraries, Museums/Galleries, Music, Performing Arts, Public Broadcasting, Theater
Civic & Public Affairs: Asian American Affairs, Botanical Gardens/Parks, Clubs, Community Foundations, Economic Development, Employment/Job Training, Civic & Public Affairs-General, Housing, Law & Justice, Municipalities/Towns, Nonprofit Management, Parades/Festivals, Philanthropic Organizations, Public Policy, Safety, Urban & Community Affairs, Women's Affairs
Education: Arts/Humanities Education, Colleges & Universities, Education Funds, Environmental Education, Faculty Development, Education-General, Literacy, Minority Education, Preschool Education, Private Education (Precollege), Public Education (Precollege), Science/Mathematics Education, Secondary Education (Private), Secondary Education (Public), Student Aid
Environment: Air/Water Quality, Forestry, Environment-General, Research, Resource Conservation, Watershed, Wildlife Protection
Health: Clinics/Medical Centers, Emergency/Ambulance Services, Hospices, Hospitals, Medical Rehabilitation, Medical Research, Medical Training, Nutrition, Public Health
International: International-General, International Relief Efforts
Religion: Religious Welfare
Science: Science Exhibits & Fairs
Social Services: Child Welfare, Community Centers, Community Service Organizations, Crime Prevention, Day Care, Domestic Violence, Family Planning, Family Services, People with Disabilities, Recreation & Athletics, Senior Services, Substance Abuse, Volunteer Services, YMCA/YWCA/YMHA/YWHA, Youth Organizations

Application Procedures

Initial Contact: Send an application letter of not more than five pages. Applicants should contact the foundation to obtain a grant application cover sheet.
Application Requirements: Applicants should include the following: the grant application cover sheet; the history and purpose of the organization; the amount requested and specific use of the proposed grant; description of why this project is needed and how it would make a difference; the project's goals and how progress will be measured; description of how volunteers will be utilized; the project timeline, including a projected completion date; personnel responsible for carrying out the project; and a list of board members. The following attachments are also required (in addition to the five page maximum proposal): for nonprofits, a copy of the organization's IRS determination letter (a letter from the State of California will not satisfy this requirement) and a current Income and Expense Statement and Balance Sheet; for schools and government agencies, a department budget; an itemized total project budget; a list of anticipated project funds and/or in-kind services, including all sources which applicant has approached or intends to approach (or an explanation of why your organization has not applied for other funding sources); for proposals requesting purchase of equipment, vehicles or services, list brand names, model numbers, specifications and name and address of vendors.
Deadlines: Foundation must receive the letter of intent and cover sheet by the first Thursday of February; May; August; and November.
Review Process: Letters of intent will be reviewed and all applicants will be notified by mail within 60 days. Successful applicants will be invited to submit a full proposal.

Restrictions

The foundation does not make grants to individuals, endowment funds, annual fund drives, sectarian religious purposes, construction or purchase of buildings, for salaries, administrative costs, operating costs, or budget deficits.

Additional Information

The foundation reports that the distribution of funds in the Foundation's areas of interest changes from year to year depending on the number of suitable proposals received and favorably reviewed by the Board of Directors
Publications: Annual Report; Grant Policies and Procedures; Community Connection

Foundation Officials

Robert P. Blankenship: chairman, director
Doreta J. Domke: treasurer, director
John A. Mancasola: executive vice president, secretary, director
William B. Nystrom: director emeritus
Lee W. Salter: president, chief executive officer, director
Richard J. Stimpel: director

Grants Analysis

Disclosure Period: calendar year ending 2003
Total Grants: $8,270,130*
Number of Grants: 39
Average Grant: $62,180*
Highest Grant: $5,031,636
Lowest Grant: $500
Typical Range: $10,000 to $100,000 and $200,000 to $750,000
*Note: Giving excludes matching gifts; scholarship. Average grant figure excludes three highest grants ($6,031,636).

Recent Grants

Note: Grants derived from 2003 Form 990.
General

5,031,636	City of Redding, Redding, CA -- fund for Pedestrian Bridge
500,000	Anderson Union High School District, Anderson, CA -- to assist New Technology High School
500,000	Turtle Bay Exploration Park, Redding, CA -- grant for general support
450,000	Turtle Bay Exploration Park, Redding, CA -- for endowment interest
270,000	Shasta Regional Community, Redding, CA -- to support Shasta and Siskiyou Counties
200,000	Shasta Regional Community, Redding, CA -- for Community Foundation Funding
184,568	Mountain Resource Management, Kathmandu India -- fund for Arghakhanchi Sustainable Villages Project
120,000	Mountain Resource Management, Kathmandu India -- to assist Mustang Development Project
116,782	University of California, Berkeley, CA -- fund for Math and Science Teacher Training Program
100,000	JPR Foundation Inc., Redding, CA -- grant for Cascade Theater Restoration Project

MARGARET OGILVIE MCCORMICK CHARITABLE TRUST

Giving Contact

Larry A. Hartman, Trust Officer
Allfirst Bank
PO Box 2961
Harrisburg, PA 17105
Phone: (717)255-2046

Description

Founded: 1991
EIN: 236216167
Organization Type: Private Foundation
Giving Locations: PA: Harrisburg and surrounding area
Grant Types: General Support.

Financial Summary

Total Giving: $201,220 (2001). Note: 1997 Giving includes United Way ($7,560).
Assets: $3,629,599 (2001)

Typical Recipients

Arts & Humanities: Arts Associations & Councils, History & Archaeology, Libraries, Music, Public Broadcasting, Theater
Civic & Public Affairs: Civic & Public Affairs-General, Municipalities/Towns
Education: Colleges & Universities, Private Education (Precollege), Science/Mathematics Education
Health: Cancer, Hospices, Kidney, Mental Health, Public Health
Religion: Churches
Science: Science Museums

Social Services: Camps, Community Service Organizations, Family Services, Food/Clothing Distribution, Senior Services, Social Services-General, Special Olympics, United Funds/United Ways, YMCA/YWCA/YMHA/YWHA, Youth Organizations

Application Procedures
Initial Contact: Send a letter stating purpose or scope of project.
Deadlines: None.

Additional Information
Trust(s): Allfirst Bank

Grants Analysis
Disclosure Period: calendar year ending 2001
Total Grants: $201,220
Number of Grants: 10
Average Grant: $12,653*
Highest Grant: $50,000
Lowest Grant: $2,500
Typical Range: $1,000 to $15,000
*Note: Average grant figure excludes two highest grants ($100,000).

Recent Grants
Note: Grants derived from 2001 Form 990.
General

50,000	Allfirst Charitable Gift Fund, Inc., Harrisburg, PA
50,000	Messiah College, Grantham, PA
38,220	Pinnacle Health Hospice, Harrisburg, PA
17,000	Historical Society of Dauphin County, Harrisburg, PA
15,000	WITF TV-33, Harrisburg, PA
10,000	Military Heritage Foundation, Carlisle, PA
10,000	Project SHARE, Harrisburg, PA
5,000	Jump Street, Harrisburg, PA
3,500	Area M Special Olympics, Harrisburg, PA
2,500	Kidney Foundation of Central Pennsylvania, Harrisburg, PA

MCCORMICK & COMPANY INC.

Company Headquarters
Sparks, MD
Web: http://www.mccormick.com

Company Description
Founded: 1889
Ticker: MKC
Exchange: NYSE
Revenue: US$2.32 billion (2002)
Employees: 8000 (2003)
SIC(s): 2079 Edible Fats & Oils Nec, 2087 Flavoring Extracts & Syrups Nec, 2099 Food Preparations Nec, 3085 Plastics Bottles.

Operating Locations
McCormick & Co. Inc. (AZ--Chandler; CA--Arbuckle, City of Industry, Irvine, Salinas, Stockton; CT--Bristol; FL--Tampa; IL--Aurora, Elmhurst; IN--South Bend; KS--Shawnee Mission; MD--Hunt Valley; MI--Belmont; MO--St. Louis; NJ--Rochelle Park; PA--Camp Hill; RI--North Providence; TX--Dallas, Salt Lake City, San Antonio, Spring; VT--Bradford; VA--Richmond; WA--Bellevue)

Nonmonetary Support
Type: Donated Products

Giving Contact
Allen M. Barrett, Jr., Vice President, Corporate Communications
18 Loveton Circle
Sparks, MD 21152-6000

Phone: (410)771-7310
Fax: (410)527-8289

Description
Organization Type: Corporate Giving Program
Giving Locations: headquarters and operating communities.
Grant Types: Capital, Employee Matching Gifts, Scholarship.
Note: Employee matching gift ratio: 1 to 1 for education institutions and cultural organisation.

Financial Summary
Total Giving: $1,175,000 (2002); $1,500,000 (2001).
Note: Company gives directly through the McCormick Fund.

Typical Recipients
Arts & Humanities: Historic Preservation, Libraries, Museums/Galleries, Music, Public Broadcasting, Theater
Civic & Public Affairs: Business/Free Enterprise, Economic Development, Law & Justice, Professional & Trade Associations, Urban & Community Affairs
Education: Business Education, Colleges & Universities, Economic Education, Minority Education, Science/Mathematics Education, Student Aid
Environment: Environment-General
Health: Health Organizations, Medical Research, Nutrition
Science: Scientific Organizations
Social Services: Community Service Organizations, Family Planning, Family Services, Food/Clothing Distribution, United Funds/United Ways, Volunteer Services, Youth Organizations

Application Procedures
Initial Contact: call or write for guidelines, then written proposal
Application Requirements: a one-page, written summary statement, including: amount requested and funding periods, key deadline dates, program/project needs, organization's goals and objectives, mission statement, project fit with McComick's business operations; organization's name, address, phone number, and name of contact; current operating budget and project budget; sources of financial support; amounts committed or pending; statement of administrative, fundraising, and general expenses; audited financial statements; annual report; proof of tax-exempt status; and list of officers and board members, with affiliations
Deadlines: None.
Review Process: Charitable Donations Committee allocates donations from the fund and makes recommendations to the company; personal interviews are often requested
Evaluative Criteria: priority given to food-related causes, projects in communities with company operations, and McCormick representation on board of directors

Restrictions
Company does not support individuals; fraternal, veterans', or labor organizations; religious and sectarian organizations; political or lobbying groups; secondary schools; travel funds; organizations that might pose a conflict with company goals; or promotional activities, such as goodwill advertising or benefit events.

Additional Information
The McCormick Fund is a vehicle through which the company makes direct contributions.
Publications: Guidelines

Corporate Officials
Allen M. Barrett, Jr.: vice president corporate communications B Baltimore, MD 1949. ED Dartmouth College (1971); Loyola College (1983). PRIM CORP EMPL vice president corporate communications: McCormick & Co. Inc. NONPR AFFIL member: Public Relations Society America.

Francis A. Contino: executive vice president, chief financial officer B 1944. PRIM CORP EMPL executive vice president, chief financial officer: McCormick & Co. Inc.
Robert J. Lawless: chairman, president, chief executive officer, chief operating officer, director B Guelph, ON Canada 1946. ED University of Windsor. PRIM CORP EMPL chairman, president, chief executive officer, chief operating officer, director: McCormick & Co. Inc. CORP AFFIL director: Carpenter Technology Corp. NONPR AFFIL director: Grocery Manufacturers of America; director: Kennedy Krieger Institute.
Carroll D. Nordhoff: executive vice president

Giving Program Officials
Allen M. Barrett, Jr.: chairman (see above)

Grants Analysis
Typical Range: $5,000 to $10,000

CHAUNCEY AND MARION DEERING MCCORMICK FOUNDATION

Giving Contact
Lawson E. Whitesides, Jr., President, Trustee
410 North Michigan Avenue, Room 590
Chicago, IL 60611
Phone: (312)644-6720
Fax: (312)644-7555

Description
Founded: 1957
EIN: 366054815
Organization Type: General Purpose Foundation
Giving Locations: IL: Chicago metropolitan area
Grant Types: Capital, Endowment, General Support, Project, Scholarship.

Donor Information
Founder: The Chauncey and Marion Deering McCormick Foundation was established in 1957 by Brooks McCormick (b. 1917), and named after his parents. Mr. McCormick was the last member of his family to run International Harvester; he stepped down in 1977. International Harvester was formed through the merger of the McCormick and Deering Harvester Companies. The McCormick Company was founded in 1831 by Cyrus McCormick, inventor of the reaper.

Financial Summary
Total Giving: $9,370,655 (fiscal year ending July 31, 2003); $4,777,592 (fiscal 2002); $3,682,167 (fiscal 2001)
Giving Analysis: Giving for fiscal 2003 includes: foundation grants to United Way ($5,000); fiscal 2002: foundation grants to United Way ($5,000); fiscal 2001: foundation grants to United Way ($5,000)
Assets: $59,248,738 (fiscal 2003); $60,657,043 (fiscal 2002); $71,461,331 (fiscal 2001)
Gifts Received: $5,015,000 (fiscal 2003); $2,500,000 (fiscal 2002); $30,000 (fiscal 2001). Note: In 2003, contributions were received from Nancy H. McCormick ($5,000,000), Hillary H. McCutcheon ($5,000) and Blair Collins Maus ($10,000). In 1999 and 2002, contributions were received from Nancy H. McCormick. In fiscal 2001, contributions were received from Fiona Hunt. In 1997, $2,908,437 was given by the Miami Corp.

Typical Recipients
Arts & Humanities: Arts Festivals, Arts Funds, Arts Institutes, Dance, Ethnic & Folk Arts, Historic Preservation, History & Archaeology, Libraries, Museums/

Galleries, Music, Opera, Performing Arts, Public Broadcasting, Theater, Visual Arts

Civic & Public Affairs: African American Affairs, Botanical Gardens/Parks, Community Foundations, Economic Development, Civic & Public Affairs-General, Philanthropic Organizations, Public Policy, Rural Affairs, Urban & Community Affairs, Women's Affairs, Zoos/Aquariums

Education: Agricultural Education, Arts/Humanities Education, Business Education, Colleges & Universities, Education Associations, Education Funds, Faculty Development, Education-General, Leadership Training, Medical Education, Minority Education, Private Education (Precollege), Public Education (Precollege), Secondary Education (Private), Secondary Education (Public), Student Aid

Environment: Air/Water Quality, Forestry, Environment-General, Protection, Resource Conservation, Wildlife Protection

Health: Cancer, Clinics/Medical Centers, Emergency/Ambulance Services, Health Funds, Health Organizations, Hospices, Hospitals, Hospitals (University Affiliated), Medical Rehabilitation, Medical Research, Mental Health, Prenatal Health Issues, Research/Studies Institutes, Single-Disease Health Associations

International: Foreign Educational Institutions, Health Care/Hospitals, International Environmental Issues, Trade

Religion: Churches, Ministries, Religious Welfare, Seminaries

Science: Observatories & Planetariums, Science Museums, Scientific Centers & Institutes

Social Services: Animal Protection, Child Abuse, Child Welfare, Family Planning, Homes, People with Disabilities, Scouts, United Funds/United Ways, YMCA/YWCA/YMHA/YWHA, Youth Organizations

Application Procedures

Initial Contact: The foundation has no formal application procedure.
Deadlines: None.

Restrictions

Grants, scholarships, fellowships loans, etc. are generally not made based upon an application.
Recipients are limited to organizations described in Section 170(c) IRS Code and are determined by the foundation's board of directors.

Additional Information

In addition to giving grants, the foundation owns a 500-acre plot of land that is made available to various charitable organizations for conferences and meetings.

Foundation Officials

Christopher Hunt: trustee
Fiona M. Hunt: trustee
Ian C. Hunt: trustee
David E. Mates: assistant treasurer, assistant secretary
Blair Collins Maus: trustee
Brooks McCormick: chairman, director B Chicago, IL 1917. ED Yale University BA (1940). CORP AFFIL stockholder: Megabyte International Corp. CLUB AFFIL Racquet & Tennis Club; Casino Club; Chicago Club.
Charlotte Deering McCormick: vice president, trustee
Nancy V.T. McCormick: trustee
Hilary H. McCutcheon: trustee
Lisa Collins Meaney: trustee
Abby McCormick O'Neil: trustee
John Rau: secretary, treasurer, trustee
Charles Edgar Schroeder: president, director B Chicago, IL 1935. ED Dartmouth College BA (1957); Dartmouth College Amos Tuck Graduate School of Business Administration MBA (1958). PRIM CORP EMPL president, director: Miami Corp. CORP AFFIL president: Cutler Oil & Gas Corp.; director: National Standard Co. NONPR AFFIL member: Financial Ana-

lysts Society Chicago; trustee: Northwestern University. CLUB AFFIL Glen View Golf Club; Michigan Shores Club; Chicago Club; Commercial Club.

Grants Analysis

Disclosure Period: fiscal year ending July 31, 2003
Total Grants: $9,365,655*
Number of Grants: 65
Average Grant: $37,550*
Highest Grant: $5,000,000
Lowest Grant: $2,500
Typical Range: $10,000 to $50,000
*Note: Giving excludes United Way. Average grant figure excludes two highest grants ($7,000,000).

Recent Grants

Note: Grants derived from 2003 Form 990.
Library-Related

200,000	Groton School Library, Groton, MA
20,000	Newberry Library, Chicago, IL

General

5,000,000	Northwestern Memorial Women's Hospital, Chicago, IL
2,000,000	Art Institute of Chicago, Chicago, IL
250,000	Kellogg School of Management, Northwestern University, Evanston, IL
150,000	Lyric Opera of Chicago, Chicago, IL
150,000	Music and Dance Theater Chicago Inc. (MADTC), Chicago, IL
127,822	Rush University Medical Center, Chicago, IL
110,000	Lincoln Park Zoological Society, Chicago, IL
100,000	DuPage Community Foundation, Wheaton, IL
100,000	Groton School - Marion D. Campbell Performing Arts Center, Groton, MA
100,000	Holton-Arms School, Bethesda, MD

ROBERT R. MCCORMICK TRIBUNE FOUNDATION

Giving Contact

Communications Department
435 North Michigan Avenue, Suite 770
Chicago, IL 60611
Phone: (312)222-3512
Fax: (312)222-3523
E-mail: rrmtf@tribune.com
Web: http://www.rrmtf.org

Description

Founded: 1990
EIN: 363689171
Organization Type: General Purpose Foundation
Former Name: Robert R. McCormick Charitable Trust.
Giving Locations: IL: Chicago metropolitan area varies by program area.
Grant Types: Award, Employee Matching Gifts, General Support, Matching.

Donor Information

Founder: The foundation was funded out of income from the estate of Colonel Robert R. McCormick (d. 1955), editor, publisher, and principal owner of the Chicago Tribune. The foundation was established, as directed in his will, for "religious, charitable, scientific, literary or educational purposes or for the prevention of cruelty to children or animals."

Financial Summary

Total Giving: $82,396,944 (2003); $98,851,665 (2002); $112,048,773 (2001)
Assets: $2,025,651,254 (2003); $2,000,000,000 (2002 approx); $1,599,796,701 (2001)
Gifts Received: $41,639,215 (1998); $24,226 (1997); $16,079,628 (1996)

Typical Recipients

Arts & Humanities: Historic Preservation, History & Archaeology, Libraries, Museums/Galleries, Music, Opera, Performing Arts, Public Broadcasting, Theater

Civic & Public Affairs: African American Affairs, Asian American Affairs, Botanical Gardens/Parks, Clubs, Community Foundations, Economic Development, Economic Policy, Employment/Job Training, Ethnic Organizations, First Amendment Issues, Civic & Public Affairs-General, Hispanic Affairs, Housing, Law & Justice, Legal Aid, Municipalities/Towns, Native American Affairs, Nonprofit Management, Philanthropic Organizations, Professional & Trade Associations, Public Policy, Urban & Community Affairs, Women's Affairs, Zoos/Aquariums

Education: Afterschool/Enrichment Programs, Arts/Humanities Education, Business Education, Colleges & Universities, Economic Education, Education Associations, Education Funds, Education Reform, Engineering/Technological Education, Faculty Development, Education-General, Health & Physical Education, Journalism/Media Education, Literacy, Medical Education, Minority Education, Preschool Education, Private Education (Precollege), Public Education (Precollege), Special Education, Student Aid, Vocational & Technical Education

Health: AIDS/HIV, Cancer, Children's Health/Hospitals, Clinics/Medical Centers, Emergency/Ambulance Services, Eyes/Blindness, Health Organizations, Heart, Hospices, Hospitals, Medical Rehabilitation, Medical Research, Mental Health, Multiple Sclerosis, Nursing Services, Prenatal Health Issues, Public Health, Respiratory, Single-Disease Health Associations

International: Human Rights, International Affairs, International Organizations, International Relations

Religion: Churches, Jewish Causes, Ministries, Religious Organizations, Religious Welfare

Science: Science Museums, Scientific Centers & Institutes

Social Services: Animal Protection, At-Risk Youth, Camps, Child Welfare, Community Service Organizations, Crime Prevention, Day Care, Delinquency & Criminal Rehabilitation, Domestic Violence, Emergency Relief, Family Services, Food/Clothing Distribution, Homes, People with Disabilities, Recreation & Athletics, Refugee Assistance, Scouts, Senior Services, Shelters/Homelessness, Social Services-General, Special Olympics, Substance Abuse, United Funds/United Ways, Volunteer Services, YMCA/YWCA/YMHA/YWHA, Youth Organizations

Application Procedures

Initial Contact: The foundation suggests visiting their website prior to initiating a grant inquiry. Inquiries and proposals should then be addressed to the foundation.
Application Requirements: Guidelines for grant applications under the communities program may be obtained from participating corporate entities or from the McCormick Tribune Foundation. To initiate a grant request for the journalism, education, or citizenship programs, send a short letter describing the proposal.

Additional Information

Foundation trustees are active or retired officers of the Tribune Company and Chicago Tribune Company, with the exception of certain officers of the Society of the First Division, who are also board members of the Cantigny First Division Foundation.
Besides making grants, the foundation also conducts seminars for the benefit of nonprofit organizations.
Publications: Annual Report; Information Reports on Contingency Conferences

Foundation Officials

Richard A. Behrenhausen: president, chief executive officer B Reading, PA August 30, 1939. ED George Washington University MS; United States

Military Academy BS. CORP AFFIL director: Associated Bank Chicago. NONPR AFFIL director: U.S. Military Academy; director: US Naval Institute Foundation; director: Chicago Council on Foreign Relations; director: National Strategy Forum; vice president, secretary, chief operating officer: Cantigny Foundation; director: Center on Philanthropy at Indiana University. CLUB AFFIL member: Commercial Club of Chicago.

Catherine Brown: director communities programs
Charles T. Brumback: director B Toledo, OH 1928. ED Princeton University BA (1950); University of Toledo (1953-1954). PRIM CORP EMPL director: Tribune Co. CORP AFFIL director: Avid Technology Inc.; director: Spyglass Inc. NONPR AFFIL trustee: Northwestern Memorial Hospital; life trustee: Northwestern University; member: Florida Press Association; member: Newspaper Association America; trustee: Chicago Symphony Orchestra; trustee: Culver Education Foundation; trustee: Chicago Historical Society; member: American Institute of Certified Public Accountants; trustee: American Newspaper Publishers Association. CLUB AFFIL member: Commercial Club Chicago; member: Tavern Club; member: Chicago Club.

James C. Dowdle: director B Chicago, IL March 12, 1934. ED University of Notre Dame BA (1956). PRIM CORP EMPL executive vice president, director: Tribune Co. CORP AFFIL director: Maximum Service Television, Inc.; president, chief executive officer, director: Tribune Broadcasting Co. NONPR AFFIL trustee: Museum of Science and Industry; director: Television Operators Caucus; director: Museum of Broadcast Communications; director: Junior Achievement of Chicago; director: Loyola University; director: Catholic Charities Big Shoulders Campaign; director: Chicago Center for Peace Studies; director: Advertising Council.

Dennis J. FitzSimons: director B NY June 26, 1950. ED Fordham University BA. NONPR AFFIL vice president: Off the Street Club; director: United Way of Metro Chicago; director: Newspaper Associate of American; trustee: Northwestern University; director: Big Shoulders Fund; member: Business Council. CLUB AFFIL member: Commercial Club of Chicago.

Jack W. Fuller: director B Chicago, IL October 12, 1946. ED Northwestern University BS (1968); Yale University JD (1973). PRIM CORP EMPL president, chief executive officer, publisher: Tribune Publishing Co. CORP AFFIL president, director: Tribune Publishing Co. NONPR AFFIL member: Pulitzer Prize Board; trustee: University Chicago; member: Newspaper Association America; member: International American Dialogue; director: International American Press Association; member: American Society Newspaper Editors; director: Field Museum Natural History; fellow: American Academy of Arts & Sciences. CLUB AFFIL member: Commercial Club Chicago.

Brig. Gen. David L. Grange: secretary, chief operating officer B Long Island, NY December 29, 1947. ED North George College BA; Western Kentucky University MA.

John W. Madigan: chairman, director B Chicago, IL 1937. ED University of Michigan BBA (1958); University of Michigan MBA (1959). PRIM CORP EMPL president, chief executive officer, director: Tribune Co. CORP AFFIL director: Morgan Stanley. NONPR AFFIL trustee: Rush-Presbyterian-Saint Lukes Medical Center; member visiting committee: University Michigan School Business Administration; trustee: Northwestern University; trustee: Illinois Institute Technology; trustee: Museum Television & Radio New York; director: Chicago Council Foreign Relations; board of overseers: Hoover Institute. CLUB AFFIL Commercial Club Chicago; Economic Club Chicago.

Wanda Y. Newell: director education programs
John Sirek: director citizenship programs ED George Washington University MA; University of Minnesota BA. NONPR AFFIL member: International Visitors Center of Chicago; director: Philanthropy for Active Civic Engagement; director: Famous Door

Theater Co.; director: Alfred Friendly Press Fellowships; member: Chicago Council on Foreign Relations.

Vivian Vahlberg: journalism program director B Oklahoma City, OK 1948. ED Rice University BS. NONPR AFFIL member: Oklahoma Journalism Hall of Fame; member: Society Professional Journalists; member: Donors Forum. CLUB AFFIL member: National Press Club.

Grants Analysis

Disclosure Period: calendar year ending 2003
Total Grants: $82,396,944
Number of Grants: 1,800 (approx)
Average Grant: $45,776
Highest Grant: $3,000,000
Typical Range: $10,000 to $50,000 and $150,000 to $450,000

Recent Grants

Note: Grants derived from 2001 Form 990.
General

2,500,000	Millennium Park Incorporated, Chicago, IL -- skating rink
2,000,000	Big Shoulders Fund, Chicago, IL -- Act of Faith campaign
2,000,000	University of Chicago, Chicago, IL -- Program for Urban and Community Leadership
1,775,000	Voices for Illinois Children, Chicago, IL
1,250,000	Northwestern University Medill School of Journalism, Evanston, IL -- for construction, renovation and equipping of journalism buildings
1,000,000	Loyola University of Chicago, Chicago, IL -- for Center for Urban Research and Learning (CURL)
1,000,000	Partnership for Child Care Accreditation, Chicago, IL
798,000	University of Chicago Center for Early Childhood Research, Chicago, IL -- for the new Center on Early Childhood Research
625,000	YMCA of Metropolitan Chicago, Chicago, IL -- for the construction of new YMCA facilities in Logan Square and Pilsen
600,000	Civitas Initiative, Chicago, IL -- production and distribution of grandparent videos and companion book

ANNE MCCORMICK TRUST

Giving Contact

Larry A. Hartman, Trust Officer
c/o M & T Trust Co.
PO Box 2961
Harrisburg, PA 17105
Phone: (717)565-2672

Description

Founded: 1989
EIN: 236471389
Organization Type: Private Foundation
Giving Locations: PA: Dauphin, Cumberland, Perry and Franklin counties
Grant Types: General Support.

Donor Information

Founder: Established in 1989 by the late Anne McCormick.

Financial Summary

Total Giving: $362,200 (2003). Note: 1997 Giving includes United Way ($2,000).
Assets: $7,796,947 (2003)

Typical Recipients

Arts & Humanities: Arts Associations & Councils, Arts Funds, Arts Outreach, Community Arts, Dance, Arts & Humanities-General, History & Archaeology, Libraries, Literary Arts, Museums/Galleries, Music, Opera, Public Broadcasting, Theater
Civic & Public Affairs: Botanical Gardens/Parks, Civic & Public Affairs-General, Municipalities/Towns, Philanthropic Organizations
Education: Business Education, Colleges & Universities, Community & Junior Colleges, Education Funds, Education-General, Literacy, Medical Education, Public Education (Precollege), Religious Education, Science/Mathematics Education
Environment: Environment-General
Health: Arthritis, Cancer, Children's Health/Hospitals, Clinics/Medical Centers, Emergency/Ambulance Services, Eyes/Blindness, Heart, Hospices, Hospitals, Medical Research, Multiple Sclerosis, Public Health, Single-Disease Health Associations
Religion: Churches, Religious Welfare
Social Services: Big Brothers/Big Sisters, Child Welfare, Community Service Organizations, Counseling, Crime Prevention, Emergency Relief, Family Services, Food/Clothing Distribution, People with Disabilities, Scouts, Special Olympics, Substance Abuse, United Funds/United Ways, YMCA/YWCA/YMHA/YWHA, Youth Organizations

Application Procedures

Initial Contact: Send a brief letter of inquiry.
Application Requirements: Include recently audited financial statement and proof of tax-exempt status.
Deadlines: None.

Restrictions

Support is limited to Dauphin, Cumberland, Pery, and Franklin counties of Pennsylvania.

Additional Information

Trust(s): M. & T. Trust Co.

Grants Analysis

Disclosure Period: calendar year ending 2003
Total Grants: $362,200
Number of Grants: 12
Average Grant: $10,400*
Highest Grant: $198,200
Lowest Grant: $1,000
Typical Range: $1,000 to $20,000
***Note:** Average grant figure excludes two highest grants ($258,200).

Recent Grants

Note: Grants derived from 2003 Form 990.

Library-Related

20,000	Dauphin County Library System, Harrisburg, PA
10,000	Mechanicsburg Area Public Library, Mechanicsburg, PA

General

198,200	McCormick Family Foundation, Vincennes, IN
60,000	Harrisburg Area YMCA, Harrisburg, PA
20,000	Allied Arts Fund, Harrisburg, PA
20,000	Susquehanna Art Museum, Harrisburg, PA
15,000	Keystone Area Council Boy Scouts of America, Mechanicsburg, PA
10,000	Perry County Council of the Arts, Newport, PA
4,000	American Literacy Corporation, Palm Springs, CA
2,500	Shalom House, Portland, ME

MARSHALL L. AND PERRINE D. MCCUNE CHARITABLE FOUNDATION

Giving Contact

Frances R. Sowers, Associate Director
345 E. Alameda St.
Santa Fe, NM 87501-2229
Phone: (505)983-8300
Fax: (505)983-7887
E-mail: info@nmmccune.org
Web: http://www.nmmccune.org

Description

Founded: 1988
EIN: 850429439
Organization Type: Private Foundation
Giving Locations: NM
Grant Types: General Support, Project.

Donor Information

Founder: the late Perrine Dixon McCune

Financial Summary

Total Giving: $6,827,100 (2003); $6,348,000 (2002)
Assets: $134,663,355 (2003); $230,385,729 (2002)
Gifts Received: $2,600 (1993)

Typical Recipients

Arts & Humanities: Arts Associations & Councils, Ethnic & Folk Arts, Libraries, Literary Arts, Museums/Galleries, Music, Opera, Public Broadcasting
Civic & Public Affairs: Business/Free Enterprise, Community Foundations, Economic Development, Civic & Public Affairs-General, Hispanic Affairs, Housing, Legal Aid, Municipalities/Towns, Native American Affairs, Urban & Community Affairs, Women's Affairs
Education: Afterschool/Enrichment Programs, Colleges & Universities, Community & Junior Colleges, Faculty Development, Education-General, International Studies, Leadership Training, Preschool Education, Public Education (Precollege), Science/Mathematics Education, Secondary Education (Public), Student Aid, Vocational & Technical Education
Environment: Forestry, Environment-General, Resource Conservation
Health: AIDS/HIV, Children's Health/Hospitals, Clinics/Medical Centers, Diabetes, Hospices, Hospitals, Nursing Services, Prenatal Health Issues, Preventive Medicine/Wellness Organizations, Public Health
Religion: Churches, Religious Organizations, Religious Welfare
Science: Science Museums
Social Services: At-Risk Youth, Big Brothers/Big Sisters, Child Welfare, Community Centers, Community Service Organizations, Crime Prevention, Family Services, Food/Clothing Distribution, Sexual Abuse, Shelters/Homelessness, United Funds/United Ways, Volunteer Services, Youth Organizations

Application Procedures

Initial Contact: Request current application guideline since deadlines vary.

Restrictions

Does not support: individuals, religious organizations for sectarian purposes, political or lobbying groups, organizations outside operating areas, or deficits.

Foundation Officials

James M. Edwards: member ED University of Illinois BA (1953); Institute des Sciences Politiques (1955); Yale University (1960). CORP AFFIL director: Lockhart Chemical; director: Lockhart. NONPR AFFIL director: Childrens Hospital Pittsburgh.
Owen M. Lopez: executive director

Sarah McCune Losinger: chairman
John R. McCune, VI: director
Frances Sowers: associate director

Grants Analysis

Disclosure Period: calendar year ending 2002
Total Grants: $6,348,000
Number of Grants: 363
Average Grant: $17,488
Highest Grant: $263,000
Lowest Grant: $1,000
Typical Range: $5,000 to $50,000

JOHN R. MCCUNE CHARITABLE TRUST

Giving Contact

James M. Edwards, Executive Director
PO Box 1749
Pittsburgh, PA 15230
Phone: (412)644-7796
Fax: (412)644-8059

Description

Founded: 1972
EIN: 256160722
Organization Type: General Purpose Foundation
Giving Locations: PA: Pittsburgh including western Pennsylvania
Grant Types: Capital, General Support, Project, Scholarship.

Donor Information

Founder: The trust was established in 1972 with funds donated by the late John R. McCune IV. The trust reports that it is affiliated with the McCune Foundation, which is also located in Pittsburgh, PA.

Financial Summary

Total Giving: $6,259,875 (fiscal year ending November 30, 2003); $7,018,354 (fiscal 2002); $6,000,000 (fiscal 2001)
Giving Analysis: Giving for fiscal 2002 includes: foundation scholarships ($13,000)
Assets: $120,492,627 (fiscal 2003); $114,120,104 (fiscal 2002); $140,000,000 (fiscal 2001)

Typical Recipients

Arts & Humanities: Arts Associations & Councils, Arts & Humanities-General, History & Archaeology, Libraries, Museums/Galleries, Music, Public Broadcasting
Civic & Public Affairs: Botanical Gardens/Parks, Business/Free Enterprise, Community Foundations, Economic Development, Employment/Job Training, Civic & Public Affairs-General, Nonprofit Management, Philanthropic Organizations, Public Policy, Urban & Community Affairs, Women's Affairs
Education: Afterschool/Enrichment Programs, Arts/Humanities Education, Colleges & Universities, Education Funds, Education Reform, Elementary Education (Public), Education-General, Journalism/Media Education, Minority Education, Preschool Education, Private Education (Precollege), Public Education (Precollege), Religious Education, Secondary Education (Private), Social Sciences Education, Special Education, Vocational & Technical Education
Environment: Environment-General, Resource Conservation, Wildlife Protection
Health: Alzheimer's Disease, Cancer, Children's Health/Hospitals, Clinics/Medical Centers, Diabetes, Geriatric Health, Health Funds, Health Organizations, Hospitals, Medical Research, Mental Health, Multiple Sclerosis, Prenatal Health Issues, Public Health, Research/Studies Institutes, Single-Disease Health Associations, Transplant Networks/Donor Banks
International: Health Care/Hospitals, International

Relations
Religion: Jewish Causes, Ministries, Religious Organizations, Religious Welfare, Seminaries
Science: Science Museums, Scientific Centers & Institutes, Scientific Research
Social Services: Animal Protection, Camps, Child Abuse, Child Welfare, Community Service Organizations, Counseling, Crime Prevention, Delinquency & Criminal Rehabilitation, Family Services, Food/Clothing Distribution, Homes, People with Disabilities, Recreation & Athletics, Senior Services, Shelters/Homelessness, Social Services-General, Substance Abuse, Volunteer Services, YMCA/YWCA/YMHA/YWHA, Youth Organizations

Application Procedures

Initial Contact: Applicants should submit a brief proposal no more than two pages.
Application Requirements: The inquiry should include the following: project description, including budget; amount of funding requested; copy of IRS tax-determination letter verifying the applicant's status as a nonprofit organization, and an annual report.
Deadlines: May 1.
Review Process: The dispensing committee meets annually in June to authorize grants.

Restrictions

The trust does not make grants to individuals nor pledges beyond one year.

Additional Information

National City Bank of PA, N.A., serves as a corporate trustee of the foundation.
Although the John R. McCune Charitable Trust and the McCune Foundation are co-housed, share staff and have overlapping board members, they operate as separate organizations with unique missions.

Foundation Officials

James M. Edwards: executive director ED University of Illinois BA (1953); Institute des Sciences Politiques (1955); Yale University (1960). CORP AFFIL director: Lockhart Chemical; director: Lockhart. NONPR AFFIL director: Childrens Hospital Pittsburgh.

Grants Analysis

Disclosure Period: fiscal year ending November 30, 2003
Total Grants: $6,259,875
Number of Grants: 157
Average Grant: $39,872
Highest Grant: $180,000
Lowest Grant: $5,000
Typical Range: $20,000 to $75,000

Recent Grants

Note: Grants derived from fiscal 2002 Form 990.

General

176,000	Wheeler School, Providence, RI
167,454	University of Oklahoma, Oklahoma City, OK -- Women's Cancer Center
155,000	Shady Side Academy, Pittsburgh, PA
150,000	Casady School, Oklahoma City, OK
150,000	Colorado State University, Ft. Collins, CO
150,000	Oklahoma City Philharmonic Orchestra, Oklahoma City, OK
137,000	Westminster College, New Wilmington, PA
125,000	Greater Oklahoma Hunter Jumper Association, Norman, OK
125,000	Jews for Jesus, San Francisco, CA
125,000	Rancho Santa Fe Community School Endowment Fund, Rancho Santa Fe, CA

MCCUNE FOUNDATION

Giving Contact

Henry S. Beukema, Executive Director
750 Six PPG Place
Pittsburgh, PA 15222
Phone: (412)644-8779
Fax: (412)644-8059
E-mail: info@mccune.org
Web: http://www.mccune.org

Description

Founded: 1979
EIN: 256210269
Organization Type: General Purpose Foundation
Giving Locations: CT; NM; OK; PA: Southwestern Pennsylvania, Pittsburgh
Grant Types: Capital, Endowment, Fellowship, General Support, Multiyear/Continuing Support, Project, Research, Scholarship, Seed Money.

Donor Information

Founder: The McCune Foundation was established in 1979 by the will of Charles Lockhart McCune (1895-1979) in memory of his parents, Janet Lockhart McCune and John Robison McCune. The Charles L. McCune Charitable Trust was absorbed into the McCune Foundation in 1980. Charles L. Mc-Cune was president of Union National Bank of Pittsburgh (which was founded by his grandfather in 1857) from 1945 to 1972, and then served as chairman of the board until his death. Mr. McCune also was an oil-man and a corporate director of such companies as Texaco, Armstrong Cork Co., Sharon Steel Corp., Cyclops Steel Corp., and Joseph Horne Co.
The foundation became fully funded in 1984. According to terms of the donor's will, the foundation will terminate in 2029. The foundation is governed by a three-member distribution committee which meets at least twice a year.

Financial Summary

Total Giving: $23,635,991 (fiscal year ending September 30, 2003); $23,524,031 (fiscal 2002)
Assets: $527,551,350 (fiscal 2003); $498,040,395 (fiscal 2002); $564,422,495 (fiscal 2001)

Typical Recipients

Arts & Humanities: Arts Associations & Councils, Arts Centers, Arts Festivals, Arts Funds, Arts Institutes, Arts Outreach, Ballet, Community Arts, Dance, Ethnic & Folk Arts, Film & Video, Arts & Humanities-General, Historic Preservation, History & Archaeology, Libraries, Museums/Galleries, Music, Opera, Performing Arts, Public Broadcasting, Theater
Civic & Public Affairs: African American Affairs, Botanical Gardens/Parks, Business/Free Enterprise, Chambers of Commerce, Community Foundations, Economic Development, Employment/Job Training, Civic & Public Affairs-General, Housing, Inner-City Development, Municipalities/Towns, Nonprofit Management, Philanthropic Organizations, Professional & Trade Associations, Public Policy, Rural Affairs, Urban & Community Affairs, Women's Affairs, Zoos/Aquariums
Education: Afterschool/Enrichment Programs, Arts/Humanities Education, Business Education, Colleges & Universities, Economic Education, Education Funds, Education Reform, Elementary Education (Private), Engineering/Technological Education, Environmental Education, Faculty Development, Education-General, Health & Physical Education, International Studies, Literacy, Medical Education, Minority Education, Preschool Education, Private Education (Precollege), Religious Education, Secondary Education (Public), Social Sciences Education, Special Education, Student Aid, Vocational & Technical Education
Environment: Energy, Environment-General, Protection, Resource Conservation

Health: AIDS/HIV, Cancer, Children's Health/Hospitals, Clinics/Medical Centers, Geriatric Health, Health Policy/Cost Containment, Health Funds, Health Organizations, Hospices, Hospitals, Hospitals (University Affiliated), Medical Rehabilitation, Medical Research, Medical Training, Mental Health, Nursing Services, Nutrition, Prenatal Health Issues, Public Health, Single-Disease Health Associations, Speech & Hearing
International: Health Care/Hospitals, Human Rights, International Relations
Religion: Churches, Dioceses, Jewish Causes, Ministries, Religious Organizations, Religious Welfare, Seminaries
Science: Science Museums, Scientific Centers & Institutes, Scientific Research
Social Services: Animal Protection, At-Risk Youth, Camps, Child Abuse, Child Welfare, Community Centers, Community Service Organizations, Counseling, Crime Prevention, Day Care, Delinquency & Criminal Rehabilitation, Domestic Violence, Emergency Relief, Family Services, Food/Clothing Distribution, Homes, People with Disabilities, Recreation & Athletics, Scouts, Senior Services, Shelters/Homelessness, Social Services-General, Substance Abuse, United Funds/United Ways, YMCA/YWCA/YMHA/YWHA, Youth Organizations

Application Procedures

Initial Contact: Applicants should send a brief letter of inquiry addressed to the foundation's Executive Director. Contact foundation for detailed application guidelines.
Application Requirements: The summary should provide an overview of and rationale for the project along with a description of the constituencies served, the total cost of the project, the amount sought from the McCune Foundation, and the anticipated income from and information about other funders. A copy of the organization's IRS 501(c)(3) letter should also be included with the brief proposal.
Deadlines: Proposals should be submitted at least 90 days prior to scheduled Distribution Committee meetings, usually held in March, July, September, and December.
Review Process: If the proposal meets the foundation's current funding criteria, a request for a meeting at the foundation's office will be arranged to discuss the project. After a site visit, if necessary, the organization will receive further guidance regarding additional information needed for a formal proposal.
Evaluative Criteria: Potential for high impact on the health, growth and prosperity of the region; organizational capacity to render key services and programs in an increasingly complex environment; or research development, and experimental aspects to influence and improve the operation of individual organizations as well as clusters of related organizations.
Notes: The foundation requests that recipients make no public acknowledgement of grants from the foundation.

Restrictions

No grants are made to individuals. No pledges are made for more than one year. An applicant should have a realistic strategy for financing the project following foundation support. The foundation does not consider grants intended to support operations, special projects, or programs that rely on future support from the foundation.

Additional Information

Unsolicited proposals from outside the foundation's geographical focus area are rarely considered. National City Bank serves as a corporate trustee for the foundation.
Publications: Annual Report; Guidelines

Foundation Officials

Henry S. Beukema: executive director
James M. Edwards: chairman
John R. McCune, VI: member distribution committee

Grants Analysis

Disclosure Period: fiscal year ending September 30, 2003
Total Grants: $23,635,991*
Number of Grants: 197
Average Grant: $105,826*
Highest Grant: $2,000,000
Lowest Grant: $1,000
Typical Range: $10,000 to $250,000
*Note: Average grant figure excludes two highest grants ($3,000,000).

Recent Grants

Note: Grants derived from fiscal 2003 Form 990.
Library-Related
500,000	Carnegie Library of Pittsburgh, Pittsburgh, PA -- towards capital campaign
250,000	Allegheny County Library Association, Pittsburgh, PA -- towards Seamless education environment

General
2,000,000	Pittsburgh Life Sciences Greenhouse Inc., Pittsburgh, PA -- towards exchange and renovation of library and art classrooms
1,000,000	Historical Society of Western Pennsylvania, Pittsburgh, PA -- towards endowment and new facility campaign
650,000	Pittsburgh Partnership for Neighborhood Development, Pittsburgh, PA
500,000	Chatham College, Pittsburgh, PA -- towards athletic and fitness center
500,000	Greater Pittsburgh Literacy Council, Pittsburgh, PA -- towards 20th anniversary capital campaign
500,000	Historical Society of Western Pennsylvania, Pittsburgh, PA -- towards campaign and endowment facility
500,000	Mattress Factory Ltd., Pittsburgh, PA -- towards education and administrative facilities and visitor amenity improvements
500,000	Pittsburgh Children's Museum, Pittsburgh, PA -- towards children's campus
500,000	Pittsburgh Children's Museum, Pittsburgh, PA -- towards children's campus
450,000	Hamden Hall Country Day School, Hamden, CT -- towards nucleus fund

THE EUGENE MCDERMOTT FOUNDATION

Giving Contact

Mary McDermott-Cook, President
3808 Euclid
Dallas, TX 75205
Phone: (214)521-2924

Alternate Contact

Patricia Brown, Assistant Secretary

Description

Founded: 1972
EIN: 237237919
Organization Type: General Purpose Foundation
Giving Locations: TX: Dallas
Grant Types: Award, Capital, Challenge, Endowment, General Support, Matching, Operating Expenses, Professorship, Project, Research, Scholarship.

Donor Information

Founder: Founded by Eugene McDermott (d. 1973), a geophysicist and a founder of Texas Instruments.

Financial Summary

Total Giving: $5,140,500 (fiscal year ending August 31, 2003); $8,009,790 (fiscal 2002 approx); $8,991,902 (fiscal 2001 approx). Note: 1999 Giving includes United Way ($15,000). 1996 Giving includes scholarships ($521,000).
Giving Analysis: Giving for fiscal 2003 includes: foundation scholarships ($3,500)
Assets: $102,517,304 (fiscal 2003)

Typical Recipients

Arts & Humanities: Arts Associations & Councils, Arts Centers, Arts Festivals, Arts Funds, Arts Institutes, Arts Outreach, Ballet, Dance, Ethnic & Folk Arts, Film & Video, Arts & Humanities-General, Historic Preservation, History & Archaeology, Libraries, Museums/Galleries, Music, Opera, Performing Arts, Public Broadcasting, Theater, Visual Arts
Civic & Public Affairs: Asian American Affairs, Botanical Gardens/Parks, Chambers of Commerce, Community Foundations, Economic Development, Civic & Public Affairs-General, Housing, Legal Aid, Municipalities/Towns, Nonprofit Management, Parades/Festivals, Philanthropic Organizations, Professional & Trade Associations, Urban & Community Affairs, Women's Affairs, Zoos/Aquariums
Education: Arts/Humanities Education, Business Education, Colleges & Universities, Community & Junior Colleges, Education Funds, Education Reform, Engineering/Technological Education, Education-General, Health & Physical Education, Literacy, Medical Education, Preschool Education, Private Education (Precollege), Public Education (Precollege), Religious Education, Secondary Education (Private), Student Aid
Environment: Environment-General, Protection, Research, Resource Conservation, Wildlife Protection
Health: AIDS/HIV, Cancer, Children's Health/Hospitals, Clinics/Medical Centers, Emergency/Ambulance Services, Geriatric Health, Hospitals, Hospitals (University Affiliated), Nursing Services, Prenatal Health Issues, Preventive Medicine/Wellness Organizations, Public Health, Single-Disease Health Associations, Speech & Hearing, Transplant Networks/Donor Banks
International: Foreign Arts Organizations, Health Care/Hospitals, International Organizations
Religion: Churches, Ministries, Religious Organizations, Religious Welfare
Science: Science Museums, Scientific Centers & Institutes
Social Services: Child Abuse, Child Welfare, Community Centers, Community Service Organizations, Counseling, Domestic Violence, Family Planning, Family Services, Food/Clothing Distribution, People with Disabilities, Recreation & Athletics, Scouts, Senior Services, Shelters/Homelessness, Substance Abuse, United Funds/United Ways, Volunteer Services, YMCA/YWCA/YMHA/YWHA, Youth Organizations

Application Procedures

Initial Contact: The foundation has no set application form or guidelines. Applicants should send a letter of inquiry and submit one copy of a proposal.
Application Requirements: The proposal should include a copy of the organization's 501(c)(3) letter.
Deadlines: None.
Review Process: The board of trustees meets quarterly.
Notes: The foundation will acknowledge letters of inquiry and provide applicants with an initial assessment of the likelihood of its consideration for a grant. The applicant will be notified approximately three months after the application is received.

Restrictions

Grants are not made to individuals.

Additional Information

NationsBank of Texas, N.A. serves as an agent to the foundation.

Foundation Officials

Patricia Brown: assistant secretary
Mary McDermott Cook: president, trustee
Charles E. Cullum: vice president, trustee B Dallas, TX August 26, 1916. ED Southern Methodist University BS (1936); Texas College LLD (1982). PRIM CORP EMPL chairman executive committee, director: Cullum Companies.
Margaret M. McDermott: trustee
C. J. Thomsen: trustee

Grants Analysis

Disclosure Period: fiscal year ending August 31, 2003
Total Grants: $5,137,000*
Number of Grants: 120
Average Grant: $22,347*
Highest Grant: $1,500,000
Lowest Grant: $1,000
Typical Range: $5,000 to $50,000
*Note: Giving excludes scholarships. Average grant figure excludes two highest grants ($2,500,000).

Recent Grants

Note: Grants derived from 2003 Form 990.
General

1,500,000	Dallas Symphony Association Inc., Dallas, TX
1,000,000	Dallas Center for the Performing Arts, Dallas, TX -- fund for capital campaign
300,000	Communities Foundation of Texas Inc., Dallas, TX -- for the building design of Booker T Washington Arts Magnet School
250,000	African American Museum, Dallas, TX -- to support The Real McCoy Learning Center
250,000	Dallas Black Dance Theater, Dallas, TX -- fund for capital campaign
250,000	Visiting Nurse Association, Dallas, TX
100,000	Child Care Group, Dallas, TX -- for challenge grant
100,000	Community Foundation for the National Capital Region, Washington, DC -- fund for the Laura Bush foundation for American Libraries
100,000	Dallas Museum of Art, Dallas, TX -- to assist in 100th anniversary celebration
100,000	Dallas Symphony Association Inc., Dallas, TX

ARMSTRONG MCDONALD FOUNDATION

Giving Contact

James M. McDonald, III, Trustee
PO Box 900
Cortaro, AZ 85652-0900
Phone: (602)949-0974

Description

Founded: 1987
EIN: 363458711
Organization Type: Private Foundation
Giving Locations: nationally.
Grant Types: Emergency, General Support, Research.

Financial Summary

Total Giving: $789,150 (2003); $1,098,355 (2001)
Giving Analysis: Giving for 2001 includes: foundation grants to United Way ($35,000)
Assets: $17,411,634 (2003); $19,800,768 (2001)

Typical Recipients

Arts & Humanities: Ballet, Libraries, Museums/Galleries, Music, Public Broadcasting
Civic & Public Affairs: Botanical Gardens/Parks, Employment/Job Training, Civic & Public Affairs-General, Housing, Zoos/Aquariums
Education: Colleges & Universities, Education Associations, Education-General, Private Education (Precollege), Secondary Education (Private), Special Education, Student Aid
Environment: Protection
Health: Cancer, Children's Health/Hospitals, Clinics/Medical Centers, Emergency/Ambulance Services, Health-General, Health Organizations, Hospices, Hospitals, Long-Term Care, Medical Research, Prenatal Health Issues, Respiratory, Single-Disease Health Associations
Religion: Jewish Causes, Religious Organizations, Religious Welfare
Science: Observatories & Planetariums, Scientific Research
Social Services: Animal Protection, At-Risk Youth, Camps, Child Welfare, Community Service Organizations, Domestic Violence, Family Services, Food/Clothing Distribution, Homes, People with Disabilities, Senior Services, Substance Abuse, Youth Organizations

Application Procedures

Initial Contact: Send a brief letter of inquiry.
Application Requirements: Include purpose of funds sought, budget, time frame, future findings, and other sources of income.
Deadlines: April 15 and September 15.

Restrictions

Grants are not made to individuals.

Foundation Officials

Mike Bouchard: secretary, treasurer
Ryan Bouchard: vice president
Laurie Bourchard: president
James McDonald, IV: vice president
James M. McDonald, III: trustee
Katherine McDonald: trustee

Grants Analysis

Disclosure Period: calendar year ending 2003
Total Grants: $789,150
Number of Grants: 36
Average Grant: $18,651*
Highest Grant: $80,000
Lowest Grant: $2,500
Typical Range: $5,000 to $30,000
*Note: Average grant figure excludes two highest grants ($155,000).

Recent Grants

Note: Grants derived from 2001 Form 990.

General

100,000	National Jewish Research and Medical Center, Denver, CO
60,000	College of St. Mary, Omaha, NE
50,000	Hastings College Foundation, Hastings, NE
50,000	Radio Talking Book Services, Omaha, NE
30,000	Bellevue University Foundation, Bellevue, NE
30,000	San Diego Zoo Center for the Reproduction of Endangered Species, San Diego, CA
28,000	Easter Seals Arizona, AZ
25,000	Arizona's Children Foundation, Phoenix, AZ
25,000	Canine Companions
25,000	Esperanza, Phoenix, AZ

J. M. MCDONALD FOUNDATION

Giving Contact
Donald R. McJunkin, President
PO Box 3219
Evergreen, CO 80439
Phone: (303)674-9300
Fax: (303)674-9216

Description
Founded: 1952
EIN: 471431059
Organization Type: Family Foundation
Giving Locations: Northeast USA; primarily upstate NY.
Grant Types: Capital, General Support, Operating Expenses, Project.

Donor Information
Founder: James M. McDonald Sr., founder of the J. M. McDonald Company, a department store chain, incorporated the foundation in 1952. The foundation received several gifts from Mr. McDonald during his lifetime and a bequest from his estate at the time of his death in 1956. Mr. McDonald's home was in Cortland, NY, where several of the foundation's recipients are located.

Financial Summary
Total Giving: $1,300,300 (2001)
Assets: $24,378,215 (2001)

Typical Recipients
Arts & Humanities: Ethnic & Folk Arts, Arts & Humanities-General, Libraries, Museums/Galleries, Opera, Public Broadcasting, Theater
Civic & Public Affairs: Botanical Gardens/Parks, Community Foundations, Civic & Public Affairs-General, Women's Affairs, Zoos/Aquariums
Education: Afterschool/Enrichment Programs, Arts/Humanities Education, Business Education, Colleges & Universities, Education Funds, Education-General, Leadership Training, Literacy, Medical Education, Private Education (Precollege), Public Education (Precollege), Science/Mathematics Education, Special Education, Student Aid, Vocational & Technical Education
Environment: Air/Water Quality, Environment-General, Resource Conservation
Health: Adolescent Health Issues, Cancer, Children's Health/Hospitals, Clinics/Medical Centers, Emergency/Ambulance Services, Geriatric Health, Health Funds, Health Organizations, Heart, Hospices, Hospitals, Hospitals (University Affiliated), Medical Rehabilitation, Medical Research, Mental Health, Outpatient Health Care, Public Health, Research/Studies Institutes, Single-Disease Health Associations, Speech & Hearing
International: International Affairs
Religion: Churches, Religion-General, Ministries, Missionary Activities (Domestic), Religious Organizations, Religious Welfare
Science: Scientific Centers & Institutes, Scientific Research
Social Services: At-Risk Youth, Camps, Child Abuse, Child Welfare, Community Centers, Community Service Organizations, Delinquency & Criminal Rehabilitation, Domestic Violence, Emergency Relief, Family Planning, Family Services, Food/Clothing Distribution, Homes, People with Disabilities, Recreation & Athletics, Scouts, Senior Services, Shelters/Homelessness, Social Services-General, Substance Abuse, United Funds/United Ways, Volunteer Services, YMCA/YWCA/YMHA/YWHA, Youth Organizations

Application Procedures
Initial Contact: Prospective applicants should send a letter to the foundation.

Application Requirements: The letter should include purpose of funds sought, budget, time frame, future funding and sources of income, and IRS Form 509A.
Deadlines: April 15 and September 15.
Review Process: Applicants may call the foundation to check on their status.

Restrictions
No grants are made to individuals or to organizations outside the United States. No grants can be made to projects that influence legislation or elections. No grants are awarded for conferences, seminars, workshops, travel or exhibits.

Additional Information
Grant payments are made only during October and May.
Publications: Guidelines

Foundation Officials
Donald C. Berry, Jr.: treasurer, trustee
Donald R. McJunkin: president, trustee
Eleanor F. McJunkin: vice president, trustee
Reed L. McJunkin: secretary, trustee

Grants Analysis
Disclosure Period: calendar year ending 2001
Total Grants: $1,300,300
Number of Grants: 44
Average Grant: $29,552
Highest Grant: $130,000
Lowest Grant: $300
Typical Range: $10,000 to $50,000

Recent Grants
Note: Grants derived from 2002 Form 990.
Library-Related
40,000	Lamont Memorial Free Library, McGraw, NY
25,000	Mynderese Library, Seneca Falls, NY

General
100,000	Northwood School, Lake Placid, NY
52,000	Cortland Rural Cemetery Foundation, Cortland, NY
50,000	Franziska Racker Centers, Ithaca, NY
50,000	St. Joseph's Hospital Health Center Foundation, Syracuse, NY
40,000	Clarkson University, Potsdam, NY
40,000	University of Rochester Medical Center, Rochester, NY
30,000	1890 House, Cortland, NY
30,000	Sage Colleges, Albany, NY
25,000	Every Person Influences, Buffalo, NY
25,000	Heritage Farms Inc., Spanaway, WA

BERNARD MCDONOUGH FOUNDATION

Giving Contact
Mark C. Kury, President & Director
311 Fourth Street
Parkersburg, WV 26101
Phone: (304)424-6280
Fax: (304)424-6281

Description
Founded: 1961
EIN: 556023693
Organization Type: Private Foundation
Giving Locations: WV
Grant Types: Capital, Emergency, General Support, Multiyear/Continuing Support, Operating Expenses, Project.

Donor Information
Founder: Established in 1961 by the late Bernard P. McDonough.

Financial Summary
Total Giving: $1,405,904 (2003); $1,456,643 (2001)
Giving Analysis: Giving for 2003 includes: foundation grants to United Way ($71,200)
Assets: $35,350,448 (2003); $35,788,904 (2001)

Typical Recipients
Arts & Humanities: Arts Associations & Councils, Arts Centers, History & Archaeology, Libraries, Museums/Galleries, Music, Theater
Civic & Public Affairs: Business/Free Enterprise, Chambers of Commerce, Community Foundations, Civic & Public Affairs-General, Hispanic Affairs, Housing, Legal Aid, Minority Business, Municipalities/Towns, Zoos/Aquariums
Education: Agricultural Education, Arts/Humanities Education, Colleges & Universities, Education Funds, Education-General, Legal Education, Medical Education, Minority Education, Preschool Education, Private Education (Precollege), Public Education (Precollege), Secondary Education (Public), Special Education, Student Aid
Environment: Environment-General, Protection, Resource Conservation, Wildlife Protection
Health: Alzheimer's Disease, Cancer, Children's Health/Hospitals, Clinics/Medical Centers, Emergency/Ambulance Services, Eyes/Blindness, Health-General, Health Funds, Health Organizations, Heart, Hospices, Hospitals, Hospitals (University Affiliated), Mental Health, Multiple Sclerosis, Research/Studies Institutes
International: Foreign Educational Institutions, Health Care/Hospitals
Religion: Dioceses, Ministries, Religious Welfare
Science: Science Museums
Social Services: At-Risk Youth, Child Welfare, Community Centers, Community Service Organizations, Day Care, Emergency Relief, Family Services, Food/Clothing Distribution, Homes, People with Disabilities, Recreation & Athletics, Scouts, Senior Services, Shelters/Homelessness, Social Services-General, Special Olympics, United Funds/United Ways, Volunteer Services, YMCA/YWCA/YMHA/YWHA, Youth Organizations

Application Procedures
Initial Contact: Send a brief letter describing the program.
Deadlines: None.

Restrictions
The foundation does not support religious activities or individuals.

Foundation Officials
Robert E. Evans: director B 1935. PRIM CORP EMPL vice chairman: TCF Financial Corp.
Dale Knight: director
Mark C. Kury: president, director
Francis C. McCusker: treasurer B Pittsburgh, PA 1937. ED Gannon University (1961). PRIM CORP EMPL senior vice president, chief financial officer: McDonough Corp.
George F. Partridge, Jr.: director
Mary Riccobene: vice president, director
Katrina A. Valentine: secretary
James T. Wakley: past president, director B Springfield, OH 1921. NONPR AFFIL trustee: Ohio Valley Improvement Association; trustee: West Virginia Foundation Indiana Colleges; trustee: Marietta College; member: National Sand & Gravel Association.

Grants Analysis
Disclosure Period: calendar year ending 2003
Total Grants: $1,334,704*
Number of Grants: 158
Average Grant: $8,447
Highest Grant: $60,000
Lowest Grant: $50
Typical Range: $1,000 to $20,000
***Note:** Giving excludes United Way.

Recent Grants

Note: Grants derived from 2002 Form 990.
General

93,750	Ohio Valley College, Vienna, WV -- fund for Baccalaureate program
75,000	West Virginia University School of Medicine, Morgantown, WV
62,000	United Way of the Mid Ohio Valley, Parkersburg, WV
50,000	Smoot Theater, Parkersburg, WV -- fund for McDonough Wakley Hall
50,000	Social Worker's Resources, New York, NY
40,000	Mayo Foundation, Rochester, MN
39,309	Smoot Theater, Parkersburg, WV
38,750	Artsbridge, Irvine, CA
34,000	Ohio Valley Rowing Club, Parkersburg, WV
33,750	West Virginia Independent Colleges & Universities, Charleston, WV

RUTH CAMP MCDOUGALL CHARITABLE TRUST

Giving Contact

Donald E. Koonce, First Vice President & Trust Officer
c/o Bank of America
PO Box 26903
Richmond, VA 23261
Phone: (804)788-2573

Description

Founded: 1976
EIN: 546162697
Organization Type: Private Foundation
Giving Locations: VA
Grant Types: General Support.

Donor Information

Founder: the late Ruth Camp McDougall

Financial Summary

Total Giving: $602,500 (2003); $746,800 (2001)
Giving Analysis: Giving for 2003 includes: foundation scholarships ($91,000); 2001: foundation scholarships ($95,500)
Assets: $10,788,233 (2003); $12,338,255 (2001)
Gifts Received: $17,000 (2000); $1,000 (1998); $3,953 (1996). Note: In fiscal 1992, contributions were received from the Ruth Camp McDougall Charitable Trust.

Typical Recipients

Arts & Humanities: Arts Associations & Councils, Arts Centers, Arts Funds, Ballet, Ethnic & Folk Arts, Arts & Humanities-General, Historic Preservation, History & Archaeology, Libraries, Museums/Galleries, Opera, Performing Arts, Theater
Civic & Public Affairs: Botanical Gardens/Parks, Business/Free Enterprise, Community Foundations, Civic & Public Affairs-General, Housing, Municipalities/Towns, Parades/Festivals, Philanthropic Organizations, Public Policy, Safety, Urban & Community Affairs
Education: Agricultural Education, Business Education, Colleges & Universities, Community & Junior Colleges, Education Funds, Faculty Development, Education-General, Gifted & Talented Programs, Medical Education, Private Education (Precollege), Public Education (Precollege), Science/Mathematics Education, Student Aid
Environment: Resource Conservation, Wildlife Protection
Health: Cancer, Children's Health/Hospitals, Emergency/Ambulance Services, Heart, Hospices, Hospitals, Nursing Services
International: International Development
Religion: Churches, Dioceses, Missionary Activities (Domestic), Religious Welfare, Seminaries
Science: Science Museums, Scientific Centers & Institutes
Social Services: Child Welfare, Community Service Organizations, Day Care, Family Services, Homes, Recreation & Athletics, Scouts, Volunteer Services, YMCA/YWCA/YMHA/YWHA, Youth Organizations

Application Procedures

Initial Contact: The foundation requests applications be made in writing.
Deadlines: None.

Restrictions

The majority of funds are limited to charitable organizations in Virginia.

Additional Information

Trust(s): Bank of America

Foundation Officials

John M. Camp, Jr.: director
Paul D. Camp, III: director
Paul Camp Marks: director
Harry Webster Walker, II: director B Bridgeport, CT 1921. PRIM CORP EMPL president, chief executive officer, director: Sunsweet Fruit Inc. CORP AFFIL president: Indian River Elite Citrus Inc.; director: Walker Group Inc.; director: Carpenter Technology Corp. NONPR AFFIL director: Vero Beach YMCA; devel board: Yale University; member: United States Yacht Racing Union; chairman: Piedmont College; member: Rotary Club; chairman: Olympic International Star Class Yacht Racing Association; director: Blue Ridge Assemblies, Inc.; member: National Boating Safety; member: Association Yale University Alumni.

Grants Analysis

Disclosure Period: calendar year ending 2003
Total Grants: $511,500*
Number of Grants: 103
Average Grant: $3,701*
Highest Grant: $134,000
Lowest Grant: $1,000
Typical Range: $1,000 to $5,000
*Note: Giving excludes scholarships. Average grant figure excludes highest grant.

Recent Grants

Note: Grants derived from 2003 Form 990.
General

134,000	Elms Foundation, Waltham, MA
45,000	Southampton Academy, Courtland, VA
29,500	University of Virginia, Charlottesville, VA -- for scholarship and student aid
13,500	North Carolina Museum of Art Foundation Inc., Raleigh, NC
12,500	Carolina Ballet Inc., Raleigh, NC
12,000	Virginia Polytechnic Institute, Blacksburg, VA -- for scholarships
11,000	Texie Camp Marks, Franklin, VA
10,500	College of William and Mary, Williamsburg, VA -- for scholarships
10,000	St. Andrews Presbyterian College, Laurinburg, NC
10,000	University of North Carolina at Chapel Hill, Chapel Hill, NC

R. J. MCELROY TRUST

Giving Contact

Linda L. Klinger, Executive Director
500 KWWL Building
Suite 318
Waterloo, IA 50703
Phone: (319)287-9102
Fax: (319)287-9105
E-mail: klinger@mcelroytrust.org
Web: http://www.mcelroytrust.org

Description

Founded: 1965
EIN: 426173496
Organization Type: General Purpose Foundation
Giving Locations: IA: Black Hawk County and rural counties in the Waterloo area, Waterloo
Grant Types: Capital, Challenge, Endowment, Fellowship, General Support, Project, Scholarship, Seed Money.

Donor Information

Founder: The trust was founded in 1965 with funds from the estate of Ralph J. McElroy, the owner of Black Hawk Broadcasting. McElroy's company included television and radio stations throughout Iowa and southern Minnesota.
McElroy started his career at the age of thirteen, when he left home, took off on a freight train, and worked the wheat fields. In 1935, McElroy became a salesman and air personality for WMT in Waterloo, IA. Twelve years later, he founded the Black Hawk Broadcasting Company.
McElroy died in 1965 and his will established a trust fund, the proceeds of which are to be used for the educational benefit of deserving youth. "It is ironic that McElroy's own accomplishments were achieved without the benefit of higher education, and he had no natural children of his own. Yet his strong commitment to youth and education has extended far beyond his lifetime to the enormous benefit of many, many young people."

Financial Summary

Total Giving: $1,699,515 (2002); $2,599,964 (2001)
Giving Analysis: Giving for 2002 includes: foundation grants to United Way ($10,000); foundation gifts to individuals ($34,975); foundation fellowships ($56,500); foundation scholarships ($249,536)
Assets: $39,869,713 (2002); $46,886,215 (2001)
Gifts Received: $26,099 (1998); $60,000 (1996). Note: In 1998, contributions were received from the estate of T.H. Williams. In 1996, gifts were given by T.H. Williams Family Trust.

Typical Recipients

Arts & Humanities: Arts Associations & Councils, Arts Centers, Arts Outreach, Historic Preservation, Libraries, Museums/Galleries, Music, Performing Arts, Public Broadcasting, Theater
Civic & Public Affairs: Botanical Gardens/Parks, Chambers of Commerce, Community Foundations, Employment/Job Training, Civic & Public Affairs-General, Municipalities/Towns, Philanthropic Organizations, Rural Affairs, Urban & Community Affairs, Women's Affairs
Education: Afterschool/Enrichment Programs, Arts/Humanities Education, Business Education, Colleges & Universities, Community & Junior Colleges, Economic Education, Education Funds, Elementary Education (Private), Faculty Development, Education-General, Gifted & Talented Programs, Health & Physical Education, International Exchange, Journalism/Media Education, Leadership Training, Literacy, Medical Education, Minority Education, Preschool Education, Private Education (Precollege), Public Education (Precollege), School Volunteerism, Science/Mathematics Education, Secondary Education (Public), Student Aid
Environment: Environment-General, Resource Conservation, Wildlife Protection
Health: AIDS/HIV, Children's Health/Hospitals, Clinics/Medical Centers, Hospices, Hospitals, Medical Training, Prenatal Health Issues, Research/Studies Institutes
Religion: Ministries, Religious Welfare
Science: Science Museums, Scientific Centers & Institutes

Social Services: Big Brothers/Big Sisters, Child Abuse, Child Welfare, Community Centers, Community Service Organizations, Crime Prevention, Day Care, Domestic Violence, Family Planning, Family Services, Food/Clothing Distribution, People with Disabilities, Recreation & Athletics, Scouts, Substance Abuse, United Funds/United Ways, Volunteer Services, YMCA/YWCA/YMHA/YWHA, Youth Organizations

Application Procedures

Initial Contact: Applicants should send a proposal to the trust.

Application Requirements: Proposals should contain general information including the following: name of organization and project, address, names and qualifications of persons who will administer the grant, contact person including title and phone number, a copy of 501(c)(3) determination letter, and the articles of incorporation. Background information should include a statement of purpose and a description of organization of the organization and its activities. A project description should explain community need and benefits to be derived by the community, long-term goals of the project, specific short-term measurable objectives, specific activities planned, number of young people to be served and from what age group, timetable for the project, and project evaluation plan. Financial information should include a copy of the organization's most recently audited financial statement, a copy of project budget including: payroll (hourly rate), payroll taxes and fringes, materials and supplies, taxes, rent, transportation, utilities, and miscellaneous; amount requested from McElroy Trust and desired timing of grant payment; amount requested from all other funding sources; and plans for ongoing funding.

Deadlines: Applications should be received on or before March 1, June 1, September 1, and December 1.

Review Process: Requests for funds are voted upon by the board; the trust will send written notice of the trustees' decision. Decisions are made by the first of May, August, November and February.

Restrictions

The trust does not make grants to individuals.

Additional Information

Publications: Application Guidelines

Foundation Officials

Raleigh D. Buckmaster: trustee
Ross D. Christensen: trustee B 1940. ED University of Iowa. PRIM CORP EMPL vice president, director: Heartland Midwest Management OCCUPATION orthodontist. CORP AFFIL partner: Jo Ro General Partnership; director: MidAmerican Energy Holdings Co.
Linda L. Klinger: executive director
James B. Waterbury: trustee, chairman B Waterloo, IA 1947. ED Princeton University (1969). PRIM CORP EMPL general manager: KWWL TV.
Richard C. Young: trustee B 1948. ED University of Colorado (1970). PRIM CORP EMPL president: Young Plumbing & Heating. CORP AFFIL principal: Park Avenue Plumbing & Heating; principal: Young Development.

Grants Analysis

Disclosure Period: calendar year ending 2002
Total Grants: $1,348,504*
Number of Grants: 74
Average Grant: $18,223
Highest Grant: $200,000
Lowest Grant: $50
Typical Range: $5,000 to $40,000
*Note: Giving excludes scholarships; fellowships; gifts to individuals; and United Way.

Recent Grants

Note: Grants derived from 2002 Form 990.

General

200,000	University of Northern Iowa, Cedar Falls, IA -- toward the Early Childhood Education Program
112,000	R.J. McElroy Trust, Waterloo, IA -- toward high school scholarships
100,000	America's Agricultural/Industrial Heritage, Waterloo, IA -- funds for the Camp Silos and Country Heritage Community
100,000	East Side Ministerial Alliance, Waterloo, IA
50,000	Hawkeye Community College, Waterloo, IA -- toward the African-American Scholarship Fund
41,168	Area Education Agency VII, Cedar Falls, IA
41,168	Keystone Area Education Agency I, Elkader, IA
40,000	University of Iowa, Iowa City, IA
35,000	YWCA of Black Hawk County, Waterloo, IA
30,000	City of Monona, Monona, IA -- toward the family aquatic center

MILDRED H. MCEVOY FOUNDATION

Giving Contact

Sumner B. Tilton, Jr., Trustee
370 Main Street
12th Floor
Worcester, MA 01608
Phone: (508)798-8621
Fax: (508)791-1201

Description

Founded: 1963
EIN: 046069958
Organization Type: General Purpose Foundation
Giving Locations: ME: Boothbay Harbor
Grant Types: Capital, General Support.

Donor Information

Founder: Established in 1963 by the late Mildred H. McEvoy.

Financial Summary

Total Giving: $1,480,663 (2001)
Assets: $25,715,494 (2001)

Typical Recipients

Arts & Humanities: Arts Appreciation, Arts Associations & Councils, Ethnic & Folk Arts, Film & Video, Historic Preservation, History & Archaeology, Libraries, Museums/Galleries, Music, Performing Arts, Public Broadcasting
Civic & Public Affairs: Botanical Gardens/Parks, Clubs, Community Foundations, Economic Development, Employment/Job Training, Civic & Public Affairs-General, Housing, Municipalities/Towns, Professional & Trade Associations, Public Policy, Rural Affairs, Safety, Urban & Community Affairs
Education: Arts/Humanities Education, Colleges & Universities, Community & Junior Colleges, Education Funds, Education Reform, Engineering/Technological Education, Education-General, Medical Education, Private Education (Precollege), Public Education (Precollege), Science/Mathematics Education, Secondary Education (Private), Secondary Education (Public), Student Aid
Environment: Environment-General
Health: Cancer, Children's Health/Hospitals, Clinics/Medical Centers, Diabetes, Emergency/Ambulance Services, Hospitals, Hospitals (University Affiliated), Long-Term Care, Medical Research, Nursing Services, Public Health, Single-Disease Health Associations

International: Foreign Arts Organizations, International Environmental Issues
Religion: Bible Study/Translation, Churches, Jewish Causes, Missionary Activities (Domestic), Religious Organizations, Religious Welfare
Science: Science Museums, Scientific Centers & Institutes, Scientific Research
Social Services: Big Brothers/Big Sisters, Camps, Child Welfare, Community Centers, Community Service Organizations, Day Care, Emergency Relief, Family Planning, Family Services, Senior Services, Social Services-General, Substance Abuse, United Funds/United Ways, YMCA/YWCA/YMHA/YWHA, Youth Organizations

Application Procedures

Initial Contact: Submit a proposal in letter form.
Application Requirements: Proposals should include the goals and objectives of the request. It should include the project plan and budget and a copy of the organization's federal determination letter.
Deadlines: Requests should be received prior to June 1.
Review Process: The trustees meet twice a year, once in late summer to review requests received to date and to make tentative allocation of the funds, and again in December to review requests and confirm or reject tentative grants made at their summer meeting. If a request gains tentative approval it will be moved to the December agenda for further action at that time.

Restrictions

The foundation does not make grants for general operating expenses or for individual scholarship assistance. Grantees must qualify for federal cumulative listing. Grants made in the Boothbay area only.

Additional Information

The latest annual report is available for inspection at the offices of Fletcher, Tilton & Whipple, P.C., 370 Main Street, Worchester, MA.

Foundation Officials

George H. McEvoy: trustee
Paul Robert Rossley: trustee B Worcester, MA 1938. ED Clark University BSBA (1960). PRIM CORP EMPL State Mutual Life Assurance Co. America. CORP AFFIL trustee: Leicester Savings Bank.
Sumner B. Tilton, Jr.: trustee PRIM CORP EMPL clerk: New England Newspaper Supply Co. CORP AFFIL clerk: Whitinsville Water Co.; clerk: Whiteater Inc.; clerk: NDI Inc.; clerk: R H White Co. Inc.; officer: Fletcher, Tilton & Whipple PC. NONPR AFFIL president: Greater Worcester Community Foundation.

Grants Analysis

Disclosure Period: calendar year ending 2001
Total Grants: $1,430,663*
Number of Grants: 52
Average Grant: $27,513
Highest Grant: $220,000
Typical Range: $10,000 to $50,000
*Note: Giving excludes matching gifts.

Recent Grants

Note: Grants derived from 2002 Form 990.

Library-Related

500,000	American Antiquarian Society, Worcester, MA -- towards capital campaign

General

10,000,000	Worcester Academy, Worcester, MA -- to the furthering of the goals and mission of the academy
7,500,000	Grand Banks Schooner Museum Trust, Boothbay, ME -- towards restoration of the Scherman Zwicker
7,000,000	Worcester Arts Museum, Worcester, MA -- towards support of the 30 million dollar centennial campaign

6,000,000   Ecotarium, Worcester, MA -- for its capital campaign

6,000,000   Grand Banks Schooner Museum Trust, Boothbay, ME -- towards restoration of the Scherman Zwicker

6,000,000   Grand Banks Schooner Museum Trust, Boothbay, ME -- towards restoration of the Scherman Zwicker

6,000,000   Grand Banks Schooner Museum Trust, Boothbay, ME -- towards restoration of the Scherman Zwicker

6,000,000   Maine Maritime Museum, Bath, ME -- towards capital campaign

5,500,000   Boothbay Railway Village Museum, Boothbay, ME -- towards operating expenses

5,500,000   Boothbay Railway Village Museum, Boothbay, ME -- towards operating expenses

H. RICHARD MCFARLAND CHARITABLE TRUST

Giving Contact
Gail S. McLain, Trust Officer
c/o Fountain Trust Co.
PO Box 8
Covington, IN 47932
Phone: (765)793-2237

Description
Founded: 1989
EIN: 356479692
Organization Type: Private Foundation
Grant Types: Capital, General Support, Scholarship.

Financial Summary
Total Giving: $70,000 (2001)
Giving Analysis: Giving for 2001 includes: foundation scholarships ($70,000)
Assets: $1,285,375 (2001)

Typical Recipients
Arts & Humanities: Libraries
Education: Colleges & Universities, Student Aid
Religion: Churches, Seminaries

Application Procedures
Initial Contact: Request application form.
Deadlines: None.

Additional Information
Provides scholarships for students primarily attending colleges and universities in Indiana and Illinois.
Trust(s): Fountain Trust Co.

Foundation Officials
H. Richard McFarland: trustee
Sarah F. McFarland: trustee

Grants Analysis
Disclosure Period: calendar year ending 2001
Total Grants: $70,000*
Number of Grants: 1
*Note: Giving includes scholarships.

Recent Grants
Note: Grants derived from 2001 Form 990.
General
70,000   University of Illinois, Bloomington, IL

L. SISLER MCFAWN-THE SISLER MCFAWN FOUNDATION

Giving Contact
Charlotte M. Stanley-Jowers, Grants Manager
PO Box 149
Richfield, OH 44286-0149
Phone: (216)828-9770

Description
Founded: 1956
EIN: 346508111
Organization Type: Private Foundation
Giving Locations: OH: Summit County, Akron
Grant Types: Capital, Endowment, General Support, Operating Expenses, Project.

Donor Information
Founder: Lois Sisler McFawn

Financial Summary
Total Giving: $1,020,904 (2001)
Giving Analysis: Giving for 2001 includes: foundation grants to United Way ($150,000)
Assets: $20,345,715 (2001)

Typical Recipients
Arts & Humanities: Arts Associations & Councils, Arts Outreach, Ballet, Community Arts, Dance, Arts & Humanities-General, Historic Preservation, History & Archaeology, Libraries, Museums/Galleries, Music, Performing Arts, Public Broadcasting, Theater
Civic & Public Affairs: Business/Free Enterprise, Clubs, Economic Development, Employment/Job Training, Civic & Public Affairs-General, Housing, Nonprofit Management, Parades/Festivals, Professional & Trade Associations, Urban & Community Affairs, Women's Affairs, Zoos/Aquariums
Education: Business Education, Colleges & Universities, Education Funds, Environmental Education, Education-General, Literacy, Private Education (Precollege), Science/Mathematics Education, Secondary Education (Private), Special Education, Student Aid
Health: AIDS/HIV, Arthritis, Cancer, Children's Health/Hospitals, Clinics/Medical Centers, Emergency/Ambulance Services, Eyes/Blindness, Hospices, Hospitals, Medical Research, Mental Health, Nursing Services, Prenatal Health Issues, Public Health
International: International Development
Religion: Ministries
Science: Science Museums, Scientific Centers & Institutes
Social Services: Big Brothers/Big Sisters, Camps, Child Welfare, Community Centers, Community Service Organizations, Counseling, Domestic Violence, Family Planning, Family Services, Food/Clothing Distribution, People with Disabilities, Refugee Assistance, Scouts, Senior Services, Shelters/Homelessness, United Funds/United Ways, Volunteer Services, YMCA/YWCA/YMHA/YWHA, Youth Organizations

Application Procedures
Initial Contact: Send a brief letter of inquiry and one copy of an unbound 199 on agency letterhead (4-6 numbered pages) including Executive summary or a proposal letter (4-6 pages) including an Executive summary as an advertising.
Application Requirements: Include a description of organization, history, missions, operating expenses, sources of income, budget, and IRS determinations letter.
Deadlines: March 15; July 15; and October 15.

Restrictions
Does not support individuals, church, general units of government, private foundations, annual campaigns, special events, or provide loans.

Additional Information
The foundation has no formal grant application form.
Publications: Application Guidelines
Trust(s): KeyBank National Association

Grants Analysis
Disclosure Period: calendar year ending 2001
Total Grants: $870,904*
Number of Grants: 80
Average Grant: $10,886
Highest Grant: $100,000
Typical Range: $5,000 to $25,000
*Note: Giving excludes United Way.

Recent Grants
Note: Grants derived from 2001 Form 990.
General
100,000   Akron Art Museum, Akron, OH -- capital campaign for new museum

75,000   Musical Arts Association, Cleveland, OH -- capital campaign

75,000   United Way of Summit County, Akron, OH -- leadership challenge grant

75,000   United Way of Summit County, Akron, OH -- annual campaign

75,000   University of Akron, Akron, OH -- music and dance

65,000   Ohio Foundation of Independent Colleges, Columbus, OH -- Scholarship Program

25,000   Walsh Jesuit High School, Cleveland, OH -- capital campaign

21,000   Ohio Federation of Independent Colleges, Columbus, OH

15,000   Ashland University, Ashland, OH -- capital campaign

15,000   Battered Women's Shelter, Akron, OH -- operating

MCFEELY-ROGERS FOUNDATION

Giving Contact
James R. Okonak, Executive Director, Secretary & Trustee
PO Box 110
Latrobe, PA 15650-0110
Phone: (724)537-5588

Description
Founded: 1953
EIN: 251120947
Organization Type: Private Foundation
Giving Locations: PA: Latrobe including surrounding area, Pittsburgh metropolitan area
Grant Types: Capital, Emergency, Endowment, General Support, Multiyear/Continuing Support, Operating Expenses, Scholarship.

Donor Information
Founder: the late James H. Rogers, the late Nancy K. McFeely, the late Nancy M. Rogers

Financial Summary
Total Giving: $894,245 (2001)
Giving Analysis: Giving for 2001 includes: foundation grants to United Way ($4,900)
Assets: $20,910,497 (2001)

Typical Recipients
Arts & Humanities: Arts Funds, Ballet, Libraries, Museums/Galleries, Music, Theater

Civic & Public Affairs: African American Affairs, Chambers of Commerce, Civic & Public Affairs-General, Municipalities/Towns, Nonprofit Management, Philanthropic Organizations, Professional & Trade Associations, Urban & Community Affairs, Women's Affairs, Zoos/Aquariums

Education: Arts/Humanities Education, Colleges & Universities, Education Funds, Education-General, Literacy, Minority Education, Private Education (Precollege), Public Education (Precollege), Science/Mathematics Education, Student Aid

Environment: Environment-General, Resource Conservation, Watershed

Health: Cancer, Children's Health/Hospitals, Clinics/Medical Centers, Emergency/Ambulance Services, Health-General, Health Organizations, Hospices, Hospitals, Single-Disease Health Associations

Religion: Churches, Religion-General, Religious Organizations, Religious Welfare

Social Services: At-Risk Youth, Camps, Community Service Organizations, Crime Prevention, Delinquency & Criminal Rehabilitation, Domestic Violence, Family Services, Homes, People with Disabilities, Recreation & Athletics, Scouts, Senior Services, United Funds/United Ways, YMCA/YWCA/YMHA/YWHA, Youth Organizations

Application Procedures

Initial Contact: Send a brief letter of inquiry and a full proposal.

Application Requirements: a description of organization, amount requested, purpose of funds sought, recently audited financial statement, proof of tax-exempt status and a list of names on the Board of Directors.

Deadlines: April 15 and November 1

Restrictions

Does not support individuals.

Additional Information

Publications: Application Guidelines

Foundation Officials

William P. Barker: trustee
Daniel G. Crozier, Jr.: trustee
James Brooks Crozier: trustee
Nancy R. Crozier: vice president, trustee
Catherine G. Keefe: assistant secretary, treasurer
Douglas R. Nowicki: trustee
James R. Okonak: executive director, secretary, trustee
Fred McFeely Rogers: president, trustee B Latrobe, PA 1928. ED Rollins College MusB (1951); Pittsburgh Theological Seminary MDiv (1962); Thiel College DHL (1969); Christian Theological Seminary DD (1973); Eastern Michigan University HHD (1973); Saint Vincent College LiHD (1973); Yale University LHD (1974). PRIM CORP EMPL executive producer, host: Mister Rogers' Neighborhood. NONPR AFFIL member: Luxor Ministerial Association; chairman child devel & mass media forum: White House Conference on Children; member: Esther Island Preserve Association.
James B. Rogers: trustee
John F. Rogers: trustee

Grants Analysis

Disclosure Period: calendar year ending 2001
Total Grants: $889,345*
Number of Grants: 87
Average Grant: $7,818*
Highest Grant: $217,000
Lowest Grant: $245
Typical Range: $1,000 to $15,000
*Note: Giving excludes United Way. Average grant figure excludes three highest grants ($530,350).

Recent Grants

Note: Grants derived from 2001 Form 990.
Library-Related
59,200   Adams Memorial Library, Latrobe, PA

General
217,000   Latrobe Foundation, Latrobe, PA
71,100   Greater Latrobe School District, Latrobe, PA
55,300   Saint Vincent College, Latrobe, PA -- scholarship fund
55,000   Rollins College, Winter Park, FL
40,500   American Red Cross Chestnut Ridge Chapter, Latrobe, PA
35,000   Latrobe Area Hospital Charitable Foundation, Latrobe, PA
30,000   Saint Vincent Archabbey, Latrobe, PA
25,250   Roanoke College, Salem, VA
25,000   Pittsburgh Youth Symphony Orchestra Association, Pittsburgh, PA
20,000   Family Communications, Pittsburgh, PA

MCGEE FOUNDATION (MO)

Giving Contact
Carrie Lenahan
709 W. 50th St.
Kansas City, MO 64112
Phone: (816)421-0050

Description
Founded: 1951
EIN: 446006285
Organization Type: Private Foundation
Giving Locations: MO: Kansas City metropolitan area
Grant Types: Capital, General Support, Multiyear/Continuing Support, Operating Expenses, Project, Scholarship.

Donor Information
Founder: the late Joseph J. McGee, the late Mrs. Joseph I. McGee, the late Frank McGee, the late Mrs. Frank McGee, the late Louis B. McGee, Old American Insurance Co., Thomas McGee and Sons, Joseph I. McGee, Jr.

Financial Summary
Total Giving: $581,000 (2004); $429,300 (2001)
Assets: $13,450,402 (2004); $12,725,082 (2001)
Gifts Received: $25,000 (2004); $2,000 (2001); $2,720 (2000). Note: In 2004, contributions were received from the estate of Joseph J. McGee Jr.

Typical Recipients
Arts & Humanities: Libraries, Museums/Galleries
Civic & Public Affairs: Clubs, Civic & Public Affairs-General, Hispanic Affairs, Native American Affairs, Nonprofit Management, Public Policy, Urban & Community Affairs, Zoos/Aquariums
Education: Business Education, Colleges & Universities, Education Funds, Education Reform, Elementary Education (Public), Education-General, International Exchange, Private Education (Precollege), Religious Education, Science/Mathematics Education, Secondary Education (Public), Special Education, Student Aid
Health: AIDS/HIV, Cancer, Children's Health/Hospitals, Clinics/Medical Centers, Geriatric Health, Health Organizations, Home-Care Services, Hospices, Hospitals, Medical Rehabilitation, Mental Health, Nursing Services, Prenatal Health Issues, Trauma Treatment
International: Missionary/Religious Activities
Religion: Churches, Dioceses, Missionary Activities (Domestic), Religious Organizations, Religious Welfare
Social Services: Camps, Child Welfare, Community Service Organizations, Emergency Relief, Family Services, Food/Clothing Distribution, Homes, People with Disabilities, Senior Services, Shelters/Homelessness, Youth Organizations

Application Procedures
Initial Contact: Send a brief letter of inquiry. Include a description of organization, amount requested, purpose of funds sought, recently audited financial statement, and proof of tax-exempt status., one or two pages.
Deadlines: None.

Restrictions
Primary support to greater metropolitan Kansas City area. Does not support visual and performing arts, preservation of historic places, or with exception of applied research, scholarly research projects and programs.

Additional Information
Publications: Annual Report (including Application Guidelines)

Foundation Officials
Robert A. Long: director
Thomas R. McGee, Jr.: vice president

Grants Analysis
Disclosure Period: calendar year ending 2004
Total Grants: $581,000
Number of Grants: 32
Average Grant: $12,259*
Highest Grant: $50,000
Lowest Grant: $500
Typical Range: $3,000 to $25,000
*Note: Average grant figure excludes five highest grants ($250,000).

Recent Grants
Note: Grants derived from 2004 Form 990.
General
50,000   Central City School Fund, Kansas City, MO -- for scholarships and tuition assistance for disadvantaged youths
50,000   Notre Dame de Slon, Kansas City, MO -- capital campaign
50,000   Rockhurst High School, Kansas City, MO -- scholarships and tuition assistance
50,000   Rockhurst University, Kansas City, MO
50,000   St. Teresa's Academy, Kansas City, MO -- for building renovations
41,500   Operation Breakthrough Inc., Kansas City, MO -- emergency relief
30,000   Little Sisters of the Poor, Kansas City, MO -- for building repair
25,000   Avila University, Kansas City, MO -- for facility expansion
25,000   Sisters Servants of Mary, Kansas City, KS -- for vehicle purchase
15,000   Donnelly College, Kansas City, KS

DEXTRA BALDWIN MCGONAGLE FOUNDATION

Giving Contact
Jonathan G. Spanier, President & Chief Executive Officer
PO Box 709
South Salem, NY 10590
Phone: (914)694-3493

Description
Founded: 1967
EIN: 136219236
Organization Type: Private Foundation
Giving Locations: CA; NY
Grant Types: Capital, Endowment, General Support, Research, Seed Money.

Donor Information
Founder: the late Mrs. Dextra Baldwin McGonagle

Financial Summary
Total Giving: $617,028 (2001)
Giving Analysis: Giving for 2001 includes: foundation grants to United Way ($1,000)
Assets: $12,375,372 (2001)

Typical Recipients
Arts & Humanities: Art History, Arts Associations & Councils, Community Arts, Historic Preservation, History & Archaeology, Libraries, Museums/Galleries, Music, Opera, Performing Arts, Public Broadcasting
Civic & Public Affairs: Botanical Gardens/Parks, Civic & Public Affairs-General, Legal Aid, Municipalities/Towns, Nonprofit Management, Philanthropic Organizations, Public Policy, Safety, Urban & Community Affairs, Zoos/Aquariums
Education: Colleges & Universities, Education Funds, Education-General, Legal Education, Medical Education, Preschool Education, Private Education (Precollege), Science/Mathematics Education, Student Aid
Environment: Environment-General
Health: Cancer, Children's Health/Hospitals, Clinics/Medical Centers, Emergency/Ambulance Services, Health-General, Geriatric Health, Hospices, Hospitals, Hospitals (University Affiliated), Long-Term Care, Medical Research, Mental Health, Prenatal Health Issues, Research/Studies Institutes, Single-Disease Health Associations, Speech & Hearing
International: Foreign Educational Institutions, International Environmental Issues, International Organizations, International Relations, Missionary/Religious Activities
Religion: Jewish Causes, Religious Organizations, Religious Welfare, Synagogues/Temples
Science: Science Museums, Scientific Centers & Institutes, Scientific Labs
Social Services: Child Welfare, Community Service Organizations, Family Services, People with Disabilities, Senior Services, Social Services-General, United Funds/United Ways, Youth Organizations

Application Procedures
Initial Contact: The foundation has no formal grant application procedure or application form. Submit a one-page summary of request.
Deadlines: None.
Review Process: The foundation will request additional information if interested in the proposal.

Foundation Officials
David B. Spanier: president
Helen G. Spanier: vice president
Jonathan Spanier: president, chief executive officer
Maury L. Spanier: chairman B New York, NY August 13, 1916. ED City University of New York (1936). PRIM CORP EMPL chairman emeritus: Un Aircraft Product. CORP AFFIL chairman executive committee: Baldwin Investment Co.

Grants Analysis
Disclosure Period: calendar year ending 2001
Total Grants: $616,028*
Number of Grants: 93
Average Grant: $5,881*
Highest Grant: $75,000
Lowest Grant: $15
Typical Range: $1,000 to $10,000
*Note: Giving excludes United Way. Average grant figure excludes highest grant.

Recent Grants
Note: Grants derived from 2001 Form 990.
Library-Related
75,000	South Salem Library Association, South Salem, NY

General
52,500	Columbia University School of Law, New York, NY
50,000	Purchase College Foundation, Purchase, NY
45,000	Young Adult Institute and Workshop, New York, NY
40,000	Tahoe Tallac Association, South Lake Tahoe, CA
35,000	Beth Israel Medical Center Foundation, New York, NY
35,000	Montefiore Medical Center, Bronx, NY
25,000	Central Synagogue, New York, NY
20,000	Federation of Jewish Philanthropies, New York, NY
15,000	American Lyme Disease Foundation, Somers, NY
15,000	Camphill Village, Copake, NY

JOHN P. MCGOVERN FOUNDATION

Giving Contact
Dr. John P. McGovern, President
2211 Norfolk, Suite 900
Houston, TX 77098-4044
Phone: (713)524-5255
Fax: (713)661-3031

Alternate Contact
Gay Collette, Secretary

Description
Founded: 1961
EIN: 746053075
Organization Type: General Purpose Foundation
Giving Locations: TX: Houston some giving nationally.
Grant Types: General Support, Research, Scholarship.

Donor Information
Founder: The foundation was established in 1961 by John P. McGovern M.D.

Financial Summary
Total Giving: $7,547,145 (fiscal year ending August 31, 2003); $9,361,525 (fiscal 2002); $9,451,286 (fiscal 2001)
Giving Analysis: Giving for fiscal 2003 includes: foundation grants to United Way ($75,000)
Assets: $191,046,555 (fiscal 2003); $193,043,587 (fiscal 2002); $197,269,019 (fiscal 2001)
Gifts Received: $373,700 (fiscal 2003); $2,560,653 (fiscal 2001); $4,410,914 (fiscal 1999). Note: Contributions were received from John P. McGovern, MD.

Typical Recipients
Arts & Humanities: Arts & Humanities-General, History & Archaeology, Libraries, Museums/Galleries, Music, Performing Arts, Theater
Civic & Public Affairs: Botanical Gardens/Parks, Clubs, Economic Development, Civic & Public Affairs-General, Municipalities/Towns, Professional & Trade Associations, Public Policy, Women's Affairs, Zoos/Aquariums
Education: Afterschool/Enrichment Programs, Colleges & Universities, Education Funds, Environmental Education, Education-General, International Studies, Literacy, Medical Education, Private Education (Precollege), Social Sciences Education, Student Aid
Environment: Environment-General
Health: Cancer, Children's Health/Hospitals, Clinics/Medical Centers, Eyes/Blindness, Health-General, Health Funds, Health Organizations, Heart, Hospitals, Medical Rehabilitation, Medical Research, Men-

tal Health, Public Health, Research/Studies Institutes
International: Health Care/Hospitals
Religion: Religion-General, Jewish Causes, Ministries, Religious Organizations, Religious Welfare
Science: Science Museums
Social Services: At-Risk Youth, Camps, Child Abuse, Child Welfare, Community Centers, Community Service Organizations, Domestic Violence, Emergency Relief, Family Services, Food/Clothing Distribution, Homes, Scouts, Shelters/Homelessness, Social Services-General, Substance Abuse, United Funds/United Ways, Volunteer Services

Application Procedures
Initial Contact: Applicants should submit a letter to the foundation.
Application Requirements: There is no particular application form. Applicants should include information concerning the type of research to be conducted.
Deadlines: None.

Restrictions
The foundation reports no specific restrictions or limitations on giving to organizations. No grants are made to individuals, except for research purposes and honorariums. Generally, grants are foundation-initiated.

Foundation Officials
Gay Collette: secretary
Kathrine G. McGovern: vice president, treasurer

Grants Analysis
Disclosure Period: fiscal year ending August 31, 2003
Total Grants: $7,472,145*
Number of Grants: 377
Average Grant: $15,617*
Highest Grant: $1,600,000
Lowest Grant: $70
Typical Range: $5,000 to $30,000
*Note: Giving excludes United Way. Average grant figure excludes highest grant.

Recent Grants
Note: Grants derived from 2003 Form 990.
General
1,600,000	University of Texas Medical Branch, Galveston, TX -- to assist John P McGovern Academy for Oslerian Medicine endowment fund
350,000	DeLay Foundation Inc., Sugar Land, TX -- for John P McGovern Assessment Center
275,000	Duke School of Medicine, Durham, NC -- fund for Pediatrics Exchange Program to be named McGovern-Oxford-Duke Pediatric Program
171,000	Houston Academy of Medicine - Texas Medical Center Library, Houston, TX -- to assist John P McGovern Historical Collections and Research Center
150,000	Salvation Army, Houston, TX -- fund for Harbor Light Center Emergency Restoration Project
125,000	Institute for Behavior & Health Inc., Rockville, MD
100,000	Barbara Bush Foundation for Family Literacy, Washington, DC
100,000	Council on Alcohol and Drugs, Houston, TX -- fund for John P McGovern Center for Aftercare Services
100,000	University of Texas Health Science - Houston Medical Science, Houston, TX -- fund to establish professorship titled John P McGovern, M D Professorship in Oslerian Medicine
80,000	Act for 8, Houston, TX -- fund for Women's Health Conference, Golf Classics, and anniversary gala

MCGOVERN FUND

Giving Contact
Dr. John P. McGovern, President
2211 Norfolk, Suite 900
Houston, TX 77098
Phone: (713)524-5255

Description
Founded: 1979
EIN: 742086867
Organization Type: Private Foundation
Giving Locations: TX
Grant Types: Capital, General Support, Multiyear/Continuing Support.

Donor Information
Founder: the John P. McGovern Foundation

Financial Summary
Total Giving: $15,000 (fiscal year ending November 30, 2004); $461,200 (fiscal 2001)
Assets: $700,391 (fiscal 2004); $745,000 (fiscal 2001)
Gifts Received: $277,000 (fiscal 2000); $6,992,000 (fiscal 1998); $3,835,500 (fiscal 1996). Note: In fiscal 1998 and 2000, contributions were received from John P. McGovern, M.D.

Typical Recipients
Arts & Humanities: Arts & Humanities-General, Libraries, Museums/Galleries, Music
Civic & Public Affairs: Botanical Gardens/Parks, Clubs, Community Foundations, Economic Development, Employment/Job Training, Civic & Public Affairs-General, Hispanic Affairs, Municipalities/Towns, Nonprofit Management, Philanthropic Organizations, Public Policy, Safety, Urban & Community Affairs, Zoos/Aquariums
Education: Arts/Humanities Education, Colleges & Universities, Engineering/Technological Education, Environmental Education, Education-General, Health & Physical Education, Medical Education, Private Education (Precollege), Public Education (Precollege), Religious Education, Social Sciences Education, Special Education, Student Aid
Environment: Environment-General
Health: Cancer, Clinics/Medical Centers, Emergency/Ambulance Services, Eyes/Blindness, Health Organizations, Hospices, Hospitals, Hospitals (University Affiliated), Medical Rehabilitation, Medical Research, Public Health, Single-Disease Health Associations, Speech & Hearing
International: Foreign Educational Institutions, Health Care/Hospitals, International Organizations, International Relations
Religion: Churches, Religious Organizations, Religious Welfare
Science: Science Museums, Scientific Centers & Institutes, Scientific Labs, Scientific Organizations
Social Services: At-Risk Youth, Big Brothers/Big Sisters, Camps, Child Welfare, Community Service Organizations, Day Care, Domestic Violence, Family Services, Scouts, Shelters/Homelessness, Substance Abuse, United Funds/United Ways, Volunteer Services, Youth Organizations

Application Procedures
Initial Contact: Send a brief letter of inquiry.
Application Requirements: Include purpose of funds sought.
Deadlines: None.

Foundation Officials
John Phillip McGovern, MD: president B Washington, DC 1921. ED Duke University MD (1945); Duke University BS (1945). NONPR AFFIL professor: University Texas; professor: University Texas School Public Health; member: Southern Medicine Association; member: Texas Pediatric Society; honorary

member: Sociedad de Algeria y Ciencias Afines; member: Society Experimental Biology & Medicine; member: Sigma Xi; member: Sigma Kappa Alpha; member: Sigma Pi Sigma; editor: Psychosomatics Headaches International Corresponding Society Allergists; member: Royal College Physicians; member: Phi Beta Kappa; member: Pi Kappa Alpha; member: Osler Club London; diplomate: National Board Medicine Examiners; consult: National Library Medicine; director: McGovern Fund Behavioral Sciences; member: National Advisory Council Alcohol Abuse; honorary member: La Sociedad Mexicana de Alergia e Immunologia; regional consult: Lackland Air Force Base; adj professor: Kent State University; fellow: Green College; associate editor: Journal Asthma Research; member: Duke University Medicine Alumni Association; honorary member: Canadian Allergy Socs; editorial board: The Classics Medicine Libraries; adj professor: Baylor College Medicine; member: Association Research Nervous & Mental Diseases; regional consult, national medical advisory council: Asthmatic Childrens Foundation; honorary member: Asociacion Argentina de Alergia e Inmunologia; member: Association Convalescent Homes & Hospitals Asthmatic Children; member: American School Health Association; adj professor: Maryland Anderson Hospital & Tumor Institute; member: American Osler Society; member: American Medical Association; member: American Medicine Writers Association; member: American College Physicians; fellow: American College Allergy & Immunology; fellow: American College Chest Physicians; diplomate: American Board Pediatrics; fellow: American Association Study Headaches; diplomate: American Board Allergy & Immunology; member: American Association History Medicine; member: American Association Immunologists; fellow: American Academy Pediatrics; member: American Association Certified Allergists; fellow: American Academy Allergy & Immunology; member: Alpha Omega Alpha. CLUB AFFIL Westchester Club; Vintage Club; Cosmos Club; Osler Club; Army-Navy Country Club.

Grants Analysis
Disclosure Period: fiscal year ending November 30, 2004
Total Grants: $15,000
Number of Grants: 1

Recent Grants
Note: Grants derived from fiscal 2004 Form 990.
General
15,000   Family Services of Greater Houston, Houston, TX

WILLIAM G. MCGOWAN CHARITABLE FUND

Giving Contact
Bernard A. Goodrich, Executive Director
William G. McGowan Charitable Fund, Inc.
PO Box 40515
Washington, DC 20016-0515
Phone: (202)364-5030
Fax: (202)364-3382
E-mail: goodric@aol.com
Web: http://www.mcgowanfund.org

Description
Founded: 1992
EIN: 521829785
Organization Type: Private Foundation
Giving Locations: DC: Central, North of San Luis; IL: Chicago; MD: Baltimore; NY: Western; PA: Northern
Grant Types: General Support, Matching, Project, Research, Scholarship.

Donor Information
Founder: Established in 1992 by the late William G. McGowan.

Financial Summary
Total Giving: $6,034,844 (fiscal year ending June 30, 2003); $8,086,546 (fiscal 2002)
Giving Analysis: Giving for fiscal 2003 includes: foundation grants to United Way ($7,800)
Assets: $129,721,320 (fiscal 2003); $127,193,389 (fiscal 2002)
Gifts Received: $2,010,502 (fiscal 2002); $171,065 (fiscal 1996); $1,089,179 (fiscal 1994). Note: In 2002, contributions were received from the Estate of William McGowen.

Typical Recipients
Arts & Humanities: Libraries
Civic & Public Affairs: Community Foundations, Civic & Public Affairs-General, Housing
Education: Business Education, Colleges & Universities, Education Associations, Education Funds, Environmental Education, Faculty Development, International Studies, Legal Education, Medical Education, Minority Education, Preschool Education, Private Education (Precollege), Public Education (Precollege), School Volunteerism, Science/Mathematics Education, Secondary Education (Private), Special Education, Student Aid, Vocational & Technical Education
Health: Cancer, Children's Health/Hospitals, Clinics/Medical Centers, Diabetes, Health-General, Health Funds, Heart, Hospices, Hospitals, Hospitals (University Affiliated), Public Health, Research/Studies Institutes, Single-Disease Health Associations, Speech & Hearing, Transplant Networks/Donor Banks
International: International Peace & Security Issues, International Relief Efforts
Religion: Churches, Religious Organizations, Religious Welfare
Social Services: At-Risk Youth, Child Welfare, Community Service Organizations, Domestic Violence, Family Services, Food/Clothing Distribution, Homes, People with Disabilities, YMCA/YWCA/YMHA/YWHA, Youth Organizations

Application Procedures
Initial Contact: The foundation requests applications be made in writing.
Application Requirements: Obtain a formal grant application from the foundation or its Web site. Submit two (2) copies of the following (should be attached) in support of your application: Grant proposal, not more than five pages in length, including: program summary, reason why the problems to be addressed were selected, description of how the program was developed, list of specific objectives for the program and brief discussion of how each will be realized, and how the program will be evaluated; detailed budget for project and current agency budget, to include projected sources of income as well as expense; qualifications of personnel assigned to project, if special talents or skills are required; audited financial statements for latest fiscal year, list of principal officers and directors; and copy of Internal Revenue Service determination that applicant is an exempt organization under Section 501(c)(3) of the IRS Code. Name of applying organization must be identical with that on exemption letter.
Deadlines: January 2, May 1, September 1.
Review Process: The board of directors considers grant requests at three board sessions each year (February, June, and October).
Notes: The fund prefers that applications be plain and unbound. The fund discourages direct inquiries of board of directors members.

Restrictions
In general, the fund will not consider requests for funding of arts, theatrical activities, building funds, or church renovation campaigns. The fund does not

make grants to individuals or to endowment funds of organisation or educational institutions.

Additional Information

Publications: Application Guidelines; Informational Brochure

Foundation Officials

Michael N. Cachine, Sr.: director CORP AFFIL director: Trustworthy Communications; director: IS3 Inc.; chief operating officer, director: IceWEB Inc.; director: Information Networks Inc. NONPR AFFIL founder, chief executive officer: Fathers Forever.
Kenneth Cox: director
Calvin Gin: director
Sue Gin McGowan: president, director
Bernard Goodrich: executive director
Sherilyn Kingsbury: director
Msgr. Andrew J. McGowan: chairman, director
Gertrude McGowan: director
Leo McGowan: director
Tim McGowan: director
A. Joseph Rosica: director
Daniel Rosica: director
Kathryn Rosica: director
Lenore M. Rosica: director
Mark Rosica: director
Mary Pat Swartz: director

Grants Analysis

Disclosure Period: fiscal year ending June 30, 2003
Total Grants: $6,027,044*
Number of Grants: 176
Average Grant: $23,413*
Highest Grant: $700,000
Lowest Grant: $1,500
Typical Range: $5,000 to $50,000
*Note: Giving includes scholarships; Giving excludes United Way. Average grant figure excludes four highest grants ($2,000,000.)

Recent Grants

Note: Grants derived from fiscal 2003 Form 990.

Library-Related
25,000	Oakland Public Library Foundation, Oakland, CA -- to support the PASSI program

General
700,000	McGowan Institute for Regenerative Medicine, Pittsburgh, PA -- fund for the Institute and its research
500,000	Georgetown University, Washington, DC -- fund for William G. McGowan Chair in Chemistry
400,000	Canisius College, Buffalo, NY -- for prepayment of McGowan Learning Program
400,000	Chicago Community Trust, Chicago, IL -- for funds being held in donor-advised account
250,000	Baylor Health Care System Foundation, Dallas, TX -- to support Cardiac Robotics Surgery Program
200,000	Canisius College, Buffalo, NY -- fund for McGowan Learning Program
200,000	Canisius College, Buffalo, NY -- to support McGowan Learning Program
150,000	University of Texas Southwestern Medical Center, Dallas, TX -- for research to identify "master control" genes for embryonic heart development
100,000	Big Shoulders Fund, Chicago, IL -- fund to provide tuition assistance and support for Catholic schools of Chicago
100,000	St. John the Apostle Catholic Church, Virginia Beach, VA -- to assist phase two of the school's technology

MCGRAW-HILL COMPANIES INC.

Company Headquarters

1221 Avenue of the Americas
New York, NY 10020
Web: http://www.mcgraw-hill.com

Company Description

Founded: 1925
Ticker: MHP
Exchange: NYSE
Revenue: US$5.254 billion (2004)
Profit: US$755.8 million (2004)
Employees: 16505 (2003)
Fortune Rank: 375, per FORTUNE Magazine's list of 500 Largest U.S. Corporations (2004).
SIC(s): 2721 Periodicals, 2731 Book Publishing.

Nonmonetary Support

Type: Donated Products

Giving Contact

Susan A. Wallman, Manager, Corporate Contributions
1221 Avenue of the Americas, 47th Floor
New York, NY 10020-1095
Phone: (212)512-6480
Fax: (212)512-3611
E-mail: susan_wallman@mcgraw-hill.com
Web: http://www.mcgraw-hill.com/community/community/html

Description

Organization Type: Corporate Giving Program
Giving Locations: NY: New York nationally; primarily headquarters and operating communities.
Grant Types: Employee Matching Gifts, General Support.
Note: Employee matching gift ratio: 2 to 1.

Financial Summary

Total Giving: $4,800,000 (2005 approx); $4,800,000 (2004); $3,600,000 (2003). Note: Contributes through corporate direct giving program only, as of 1997. 1996 Giving includes foundation ($761,749); matching gifts ($1,198,505); United Way ($479,840).
Gifts Received: $2,400,000 (1996); $2,300,000 (1995); $2,650,000 (1994).

Typical Recipients

Arts & Humanities: Arts Centers, Dance, Libraries, Museums/Galleries, Music, Performing Arts, Public Broadcasting
Civic & Public Affairs: African American Affairs, Business/Free Enterprise, Civil Rights, Economic Development, Employment/Job Training, First Amendment Issues, Hispanic Affairs, Housing, Law & Justice, Professional & Trade Associations, Public Policy, Women's Affairs
Education: Business Education, Colleges & Universities, Education Associations, Education Funds, Education Reform, Engineering/Technological Education, Education-General, Journalism/Media Education, Literacy, Minority Education, Private Education (Precollege), Student Aid
Environment: Air/Water Quality
Health: AIDS/HIV, Clinics/Medical Centers, Eyes/Blindness, Health Organizations, Hospitals, Hospitals (University Affiliated), Transplant Networks/Donor Banks
International: International Development
Religion: Religious Welfare
Social Services: Community Service Organizations, Family Services, People with Disabilities, Substance Abuse, United Funds/United Ways, Volunteer Services, YMCA/YWCA/YMHA/YWHA

Application Procedures

Initial Contact: Send preliminary proposal letter.
Application Requirements: Brief background of your organization, including its goals and objectives, staff, and board of directors; a concise description of the program and objectives for which funds are sought; a copy of most recent audited financial statement and annual report; current year's budget and the sources of funding; the budget for the program for which you support is sought, and the sum requested; and evidence of your public charity status under the U.S. Internal Revenue Code.
Deadlines: None.
Review Process: If request fits current priorities, meeting may be arranged and on-site visits conducted.
Evaluative Criteria: Organization staffed by people with demonstrated competence and experience in the field; project addresses problems affecting communities the company serves; contribution supports projects that can be evaluated and serve as models elsewhere; project extends reach globally, and utilizes unique applications of new and developing technologies.
Decision Notification: Corporate Contributions and Community Relations Committee meets quarterly.

Restrictions

The organization does not support political activities or groups established to influence legislation; individuals; publication of books, magazines, videos, or films; member organizations of United Way funds; sectarian or religious organizations; endowment funds; loans; or institutions and agencies clearly outside McGraw-Hill's primary geographic concerns and interests.
McGraw-Hill does not subscribe to tables or tickets for charitable events, sponsor courtesy advertisements, or pledge support for walk-a-thons or similar activities.

Additional Information

Grants are not renewed automatically; new requests must be submitted each year.
Recipients are asked to submit periodic reports on, and evaluation of, progress and an annual financial report.
Foundation ceased operations in 1997; all contributions are now made through Corporate Contributions and Community Relations.
Publications: Giving Guidelines

Corporate Officials

Barbara A. Munder: senior vice president new initiatives B New York, NY 1945. ED Elmira College (1967); New York University Leonard N. Stern School of Business MBA (1980). PRIM CORP EMPL senior vice president new initiatives: McGraw-Hill Companies, Inc. NONPR AFFIL member: Information Industry Association; director: Lighthouse.
Louise Raymond: director corporate contributions
Donald S. Rubin: senior vice president investor relations B Chicago, IL 1934. ED Columbia University; University of Miami AB (1956). PRIM CORP EMPL senior vice president investor relations: McGraw-Hill Companies, Inc.
Susan A. Wallman: manager corporate contributions

Grants Analysis

Disclosure Period: calendar year ending 1996
Total Grants: $761,749*
Number of Grants: 174
Average Grant: $4,378
Highest Grant: $109,710
Typical Range: $1,000 to $20,000
*Note: Giving excludes matching gifts; United Way. A more recent grants list was unavailable.

Recent Grants

Note: Grants derived from 1996 Form 990.

Library-Related

25,000	New York Public Library, New York, NY
10,000	Library Foundation, San Francisco, CA

General

361,680	United Way Tri-State Area, New York, NY
109,710	National Merit Scholarship Corporation, Evanston, IL
50,000	National Organization on Disability, Washington, DC
50,000	National Organization on Disability, Washington, DC
50,000	Salvation Army, New York, NY
30,400	United Way Burlington County, Mt. Holly, NJ
30,000	Cornell University Knight-Baghot Fellowship, New York, NY
25,000	A Better Chance, New York, NY
25,000	Lincoln Center for Performing Arts, New York, NY
20,000	Hartley House, New York, NY

THOMAS AND FRANCES MCGREGOR FOUNDATION

Giving Contact

Robert W. Smith
Thomas and Frances McGregor Foundation
PO Box 40
York, AL 36925
Phone: (601)485-8305

Description

Founded: 1961
EIN: 526041498
Organization Type: Private Foundation
Giving Locations: DC: Washington metropolitan area
Grant Types: General Support.

Donor Information

Founder: Thomas W. McGregor, McGregor Printing Corp.

Financial Summary

Total Giving: $18,050 (fiscal year ending February 28, 2004); $203,719 (fiscal 2001)
Assets: $1,091,461 (fiscal 2004); $1,963,848 (fiscal 2001)
Gifts Received: $300,000 (fiscal 1992). Note: In 1992, contributions were received from McGregor Printing Corporation.

Typical Recipients

Arts & Humanities: Arts Associations & Councils, Arts Centers, Arts Institutes, Arts Outreach, Ballet, Libraries, Museums/Galleries, Music, Public Broadcasting, Theater
Civic & Public Affairs: African American Affairs, Botanical Gardens/Parks, Business/Free Enterprise, Clubs, Community Foundations, Economic Development, Employment/Job Training, Civic & Public Affairs-General, Hispanic Affairs, Housing, Municipalities/Towns, Public Policy, Urban & Community Affairs, Zoos/Aquariums
Education: Arts/Humanities Education, Colleges & Universities, Education Funds, Education Reform, Education-General, Private Education (Precollege), Secondary Education (Private)
Environment: Environment-General, Wildlife Protection
Health: AIDS/HIV, Cancer, Children's Health/Hospitals, Clinics/Medical Centers, Diabetes, Emergency/Ambulance Services, Health Organizations, Heart, Hospitals, Medical Rehabilitation, Medical Research, Multiple Sclerosis, Prenatal Health Issues, Research/Studies Institutes, Single-Disease Health Associations

International: Health Care/Hospitals, Missionary/Religious Activities
Religion: Churches, Jewish Causes, Religious Organizations, Religious Welfare, Synagogues/Temples
Social Services: Camps, Child Welfare, Community Service Organizations, Emergency Relief, Family Planning, Family Services, Food/Clothing Distribution, Refugee Assistance, Scouts, Shelters/Homelessness, United Funds/United Ways, YMCA/YWCA/YMHA/YWHA, Youth Organizations

Application Procedures

Initial Contact: No specific form of application is required.
Deadlines: None.

Grants Analysis

Disclosure Period: fiscal year ending February 28, 2004
Total Grants: $18,050
Number of Grants: 10
Average Grant: $1,805
Highest Grant: $5,000
Lowest Grant: $200
Typical Range: $500 to $5,000

Recent Grants

Note: Grants derived from fiscal 2000 Form 990.

Library-Related

1,500	Hitower Library

General

72,244	Helen Keller
60,000	Helen Keller
16,000	University of North Caroline Arts & Sciences, NC
12,000	University of North Carolina Education Foundation, Chapel Hill, NC
10,000	NL Missions
10,000	University of North Carolina Education Foundation, Chapel Hill, NC
5,000	American Cancer Society
5,000	Cathedral Fund
5,000	Hazelton Foundation
5,000	Lewisburg College

MCGREGOR FUND

Giving Contact

C. David Campbell, President & Assistant Secretary
333 West Fort Street, Suite 2090
Detroit, MI 48226-3134
Phone: (313)963-3495
Fax: (313)963-3512
E-mail: info@mcgregorfund.org
Web: http://www.mcgregorfund.org

Description

Founded: 1925
EIN: 380808800
Organization Type: General Purpose Foundation
Giving Locations: MI: Detroit metropolitan area
Grant Types: Capital, Emergency, Endowment, General Support, Multiyear/Continuing Support, Operating Expenses, Project.

Donor Information

Founder: The McGregor Fund was established in 1925 by the late Tracy W. McGregor, and it was funded by Mr. McGregor and his wife, Katherine Whitney McGregor. Tracy McGregor was president of Whitney Realty Company, LaSalle Land Company, Provident Loan and Savings, Merrill-Palmer School, Detroit Community Fund, and the Training School of the Feeble Minded, as well as trustee of the Goodwill Farm School. The McGregors were dedicated "to relieving the misfortunes and promoting the well-being of mankind." Among their specific interests were the McGregor Institute (for homeless men), the McGregor Home

(for children), Bay Court (for underprivileged mothers), and the Detroit Community Fund (a forerunner of the United Foundation). Mr. McGregor was also a member of the "Thursday Group" of influential men in Detroit who gathered to find solutions to the problems of their time. The McGregors' gifts to the fund from their estates totaled approximately $10 million.

Financial Summary

Total Giving: $5,608,047 (fiscal year ending June 30, 2004); $7,757,207 (fiscal 2003); $7,429,552 (fiscal 2002)
Giving Analysis: Giving for fiscal 2004 includes: foundation scholarships ($40,000); foundation matching gifts ($95,797); foundation grants to United Way ($172,000); fiscal 2003: foundation scholarships ($40,000); foundation grants to United Way ($49,500); foundation matching gifts ($87,582); fiscal 2001: foundation matching gifts ($85,007); foundation grants to United Way ($166,500); foundation scholarships ($225,000)
Assets: $169,688,848 (fiscal 2004); $155,065,124 (fiscal 2003); $159,265,246 (fiscal 2002)

Typical Recipients

Arts & Humanities: Arts Associations & Councils, Arts Centers, Arts Institutes, Ethnic & Folk Arts, Historic Preservation, History & Archaeology, Libraries, Museums/Galleries, Music, Opera, Performing Arts, Public Broadcasting, Theater
Civic & Public Affairs: Chambers of Commerce, Community Foundations, Economic Development, Employment/Job Training, Civic & Public Affairs-General, Hispanic Affairs, Housing, Inner-City Development, Municipalities/Towns, Nonprofit Management, Philanthropic Organizations, Professional & Trade Associations, Urban & Community Affairs, Women's Affairs, Zoos/Aquariums
Education: Afterschool/Enrichment Programs, Arts/Humanities Education, Business Education, Colleges & Universities, Education Associations, Education Funds, Education Reform, Elementary Education (Public), Engineering/Technological Education, Environmental Education, Faculty Development, Education-General, Minority Education, Private Education (Precollege), Public Education (Precollege), Science/Mathematics Education, Secondary Education (Private), Social Sciences Education, Student Aid, Vocational & Technical Education
Health: AIDS/HIV, Children's Health/Hospitals, Clinics/Medical Centers, Emergency/Ambulance Services, Health Organizations, Hospitals, Long-Term Care, Mental Health, Nursing Services, Prenatal Health Issues
Religion: Churches, Dioceses, Religious Welfare, Seminaries, Social/Policy Issues
Science: Scientific Centers & Institutes, Scientific Research
Social Services: At-Risk Youth, Big Brothers/Big Sisters, Child Welfare, Community Service Organizations, Counseling, Crime Prevention, Delinquency & Criminal Rehabilitation, Emergency Relief, Family Planning, Family Services, Food/Clothing Distribution, People with Disabilities, Recreation & Athletics, Scouts, Senior Services, Sexual Abuse, Shelters/Homelessness, Substance Abuse, United Funds/United Ways, Volunteer Services, YMCA/YWCA/YMHA/YWHA, Youth Organizations

Application Procedures

Initial Contact: Applicants should request grant guidelines from the fund's office. Separate guidelines for private schools, colleges, and universities are available from the fund office. After reviewing the information, applicants are encouraged to speak with the staff of the Fund to discuss eligibility and purpose.
Application Requirements: Each grant request should include a brief cover letter signed by the chief executive officer, stating the specific purpose, time period, amount of request, proof of tax-exempt status under Internal Revenue Code Section 501(c)(3) and classification under Section 509(a) of the code. Also,

please include a copy of Form 4653, an audited financial statement and balance sheet of income and expenses, detailed budget statement for the proposed project, and an explanation about the reasonable financial potential to achieve and sustain the project. The organization's most recent IRS Form 990 and a listing of the organization's officers and directors should also be included. If the organization is classified as a public charity, a written statement that the requested grant will not result in the loss of such organization's classification must be signed and submitted by an officer. A description of organization, including history, current programs, and future plans, is required as well. Include details of the request, including: name and description of the proposed program or project, indicating whether it is a new program or part of an ongoing activity; description of the purpose of the program and the need it addresses; an indication of other known organizations offering such a program; amount of request; geographic area and target population to be served; description of the work plan and timeline to carry out the activity; expected measurable results, and how they will be evaluated; details about other sources of funding; whether any other funding sources have declined a request for support of this activity, and identify those sources; a plan for proceeding if only part of the funding sought is granted; an outline of a plan to secure continued support for the program after the conclusion of Mcgregor Fund support; and the names and qualifications of the individuals who will implement the program or project (resumes are acceptable). A copy of an annual report, if available, should be included.

Deadlines: None. Applications may be submitted anytime. Trustee meetings are scheduled four times a year, in February, May, September, and November. Applicants are encouraged to submit proposals well in advance of the trustee meeting where the proposal is to be considered, as proposals may take up to 3 months for staff review.

Restrictions

The fund does not provide loans; direct grants to students for scholarships; grants for travel, conferences, seminars, or workshops; or grants to individuals. The principal interest of the fund is the Detroit metropolitan area, although requests will be considered from organizations located elsewhere for programs or projects significantly benefiting the Detroit metropolitan area. The geographic area for educational programs at the private college level is limited to the states of Michigan and Ohio. Occasional grants are made as individual trustee selections to higher educational institutions elsewhere in the United States. National and local chapters of disease-specific organizations are no longer funded.

Additional Information

The Matching Gifts Program of the McGregor fund matches trustee and employee contributions to nonprofit organizations dollar-for-dollar with certain conditions and limitations. Matching gifts totaling $69,168 were paid during the 1998 fiscal year.
Publications: Annual Report; Guidelines

Foundation Officials

Dave Bing: trustee B Washington, DC 1943. ED Syracuse University BA (1966). PRIM CORP EMPL chief executive officer, chairman: Bing Group. CORP AFFIL owner: Heritage 21; chief executive officer, chairman: Superb Manufacturing; director: Detroit Edison Co.; founder: Alpha Capital Management; chairman, president: Bing Steel.
C. David Campbell: president, assistant secretary, trustee
Cynthia N. Ford: trustee
Ruth R. Glancy: trustee
Ira J. Jaffe: trustee
Eugene A. Miller: chairman, trustee
James B. Nicholson: trustee
William W. Shelden, Jr.: trustee
Bruce W. Steinhauer, MD: trustee, vice chairman B

1933. ED Amherst College BS (1955); Harvard University Medical School MD (1959). CORP AFFIL director: Analogic Corp. NONPR AFFIL chief executive officer, director: Lahey-Hitchcock Clinic.
Peter Palms Thurber: trustee emeritus B Detroit, MI 1928. ED Williams College BA (1950); Harvard University Law School JD (1953). PRIM CORP EMPL council: Miller, Canfield, Paddock & Stone. NONPR AFFIL trustee: Council Michigan Foundations; member: Michigan Bar Association; trustee: Community Foundation Southeast Michigan; member: American Bar Association; fellow: American Bar Foundation. CLUB AFFIL mem: Country Club Detroit.

Grants Analysis

Disclosure Period: fiscal year ending June 30, 2004
Total Grants: $5,300,250*
Number of Grants: 69
Average Grant: $76,815
Highest Grant: $300,000
Typical Range: $25,000 to $150,000
*Note: Giving excludes matching gifts, scholarships, United Way.

Recent Grants

Note: Grants derived from fiscal 2003 Form 990.
General

500,000	Community Foundation for South-eastern Michigan, Detroit, MI -- to assist the Green Ways Initiative
500,000	Community Foundation for Southeastern Michigan, Detroit, MI -- to assist the GreenWays Initiative
500,000	Community Foundation for Southeastern Michigan, Detroit, MI -- to assist the GreenWays Initiative
500,000	Local Initiatives Support Corporation, Detroit, MI -- to assist a collaborative, public/private partnership to continue revitalizing Detroit's neighborhoods
500,000	Wayne State University, Detroit, MI -- for the renovation of McGregor Memorial Conference Center
500,000	Wayne State University, Detroit, MI -- for the renovation of McGregor Memorial Conference Center
500,000	Wayne State University, Detroit, MI -- grant to renovate McGregor Memorial Conference Center
500,000	Wayne State University, Detroit, MI -- for the renovation of McGregor Memorial Conference Center
400,000	University of Detroit Mercy, Detroit, MI -- grant to improve the University's information technology
335,000	YMCA of Metropolitan Detroit, Detroit, MI -- fund to construct new YMCA in downtown Detroit

MCINERNY FOUNDATION

Giving Contact

Paula Boyce, Grants Administration Officer
c/o Pacific Century Trust
PO Box 3170
Honolulu, HI 96802-3170
Phone: (808)538-4545
Fax: (808)538-4006
E-mail: pboyce@boh.com

Description

Founded: 1937
EIN: 996002356
Organization Type: General Purpose Foundation
Giving Locations: HI
Grant Types: Capital, Challenge, General Support, Matching, Project, Seed Money.

Donor Information

Founder: The McInerny Foundation was established in 1937, by William H. McInerny and James D. McInerny and their sister, Ella McInerny. They were descendants of Patrick Michael McInerny who arrived in the Hawaiian Islands from Ireland during the mid-nineteenth century whaling period. The first distribution committee of the McInerny Foundation consisted of James and William McInerny. After the death of James in 1945, William constituted the distribution committee until his death in 1947. Since then, as provided in the trust indenture, the distribution committee has consisted of three members appointed by the board of directors of Pacific Century Trust, corporate trustee of the foundation.

Financial Summary

Total Giving: $2,731,849 (fiscal year ending September 30, 2003); $3,435,144 (fiscal 2002); $2,997,811 (fiscal 2001)
Giving Analysis: Giving for fiscal 2002 includes: foundation grants to United Way ($6,900)
Assets: $54,766,199 (fiscal 2003); $51,333,980 (fiscal 2002); $59,686,036 (fiscal 2001)

Typical Recipients

Arts & Humanities: Arts Centers, Arts Festivals, Arts Funds, Arts Institutes, Community Arts, Dance, Arts & Humanities-General, Historic Preservation, History & Archaeology, Libraries, Literary Arts, Museums/Galleries, Music, Opera, Performing Arts, Public Broadcasting, Theater, Visual Arts
Civic & Public Affairs: Asian American Affairs, Botanical Gardens/Parks, Business/Free Enterprise, Community Foundations, Economic Development, Employment/Job Training, Civic & Public Affairs-General, Housing, Legal Aid, Nonprofit Management, Parades/Festivals, Rural Affairs, Women's Affairs, Zoos/Aquariums
Education: Afterschool/Enrichment Programs, Arts/Humanities Education, Colleges & Universities, Economic Education, Education Funds, Education Reform, Elementary Education (Private), Elementary Education (Public), Environmental Education, Faculty Development, Education-General, Gifted & Talented Programs, International Studies, Literacy, Medical Education, Minority Education, Preschool Education, Private Education (Precollege), Public Education (Precollege), Science/Mathematics Education, Secondary Education (Private), Social Sciences Education, Special Education, Student Aid, Vocational & Technical Education
Environment: Environment-General, Protection, Resource Conservation
Health: AIDS/HIV, Cancer, Children's Health/Hospitals, Clinics/Medical Centers, Emergency/Ambulance Services, Health Funds, Health Organizations, Home-Care Services, Hospices, Hospitals, Long-Term Care, Medical Rehabilitation, Mental Health, Prenatal Health Issues, Public Health, Single-Disease Health Associations
International: Foreign Arts Organizations, Foreign Educational Institutions, International Affairs
Religion: Jewish Causes, Ministries, Religious Welfare
Science: Science Exhibits & Fairs, Science Museums, Scientific Centers & Institutes
Social Services: Animal Protection, At-Risk Youth, Child Welfare, Community Centers, Community Service Organizations, Day Care, Domestic Violence, Family Planning, Family Services, Food/Clothing Distribution, People with Disabilities, Recreation & Athletics, Scouts, Senior Services, Shelters/Homelessness, Substance Abuse, United Funds/United Ways, Veterans, Volunteer Services, YMCA/YWCA/YMHA/YWHA, Youth Organizations

Application Procedures

Initial Contact: Applicants seeking capital grants, tuition aid, or scholarship programs (schools only) should contact the foundation to obtain required questionnaires. Organizations requesting general support should submit a written proposal.

Application Requirements: The proposal should include a letter of not more than three pages, signed by the presiding officer of the board of directors, containing a description of organization; summary of the proposed activity, including a statement of need or problem to be addressed, how the activity is to be carried out, population to be served, and plan for evaluating the activity's effectiveness; total cost of the project/program, amount requested from the McInerny Foundation and from other funding sources, and plans for future support; statement regarding the qualifications of personnel responsible for carrying out the project; statement as to active participation by board members; and name and telephone number of board members. The letter should be accompanied by a project/program budget and an organizational budget showing projected income and expenditures; a list of the governing board members and their professional of business affiliations; and two or three letters of endorsement for the proposed activity. Applicants should submit an original and six copies of the proposal, avoiding elaborate or bulky binding.

Additionally, one copy of the following should be included with the proposal: proof of tax-exempt status, organization's financial statements for its last accounting period (preferably audited); the organization's charter and bylaws; and any other information and material pertinent to the request.

Deadlines: None, for applications for general support; July 15 for major capital projects; and January 15 for scholarship programs.

Review Process: The distribution committee meets frequently to consider grant proposals. Requests for capital fund drives are considered only at the committee's September meetings. Requests from schools for tuition aid and scholarships are considered only at the committee's March meetings.

Sixty days are required to process proposals, allowing for a possible visit to the site and for studying the proposal in relation to other foundation activities.

Decision Notification: Applicants are notified in writing of the distribution committee's decision.

Restrictions

Under the deed of trust, the foundation does not give grants or scholarships to individuals, nor does it provide grants for deficit funding or endowments, or to religious organizations.

Additional Information

Grantees are required to submit narrative and financial reports to the foundation.

The foundation will consider one grant request per organization per year, with the exception of scholarship/tuition aid requests.

Publications: Annual Report (including Guidelines)

Grants Analysis

Disclosure Period: fiscal year ending September 30, 2003
Total Grants: $2,731,849
Number of Grants: 135
Average Grant: $20,236
Highest Grant: $120,000
Lowest Grant: $1,000
Typical Range: $5,000 to $50,000

Recent Grants

Note: Grants derived from fiscal 2003 Form 990.
General

120,000	Punahou School, Honolulu, HI -- middle school capital campaign project
100,000	Institute for Human Services, Honolulu, HI -- unsolicited award for housing program
100,000	YMCA of Honolulu, Honolulu, HI -- reaching for tomorrow
75,000	Bishop Museum, Honolulu, HI -- toward science learning center
75,000	Enterprise Honolulu, Honolulu, HI -- implementation of business plan
61,000	Punahou School, Honolulu, HI -- tuition aid program
50,000	Assistance League of Hawaii, Honolulu, HI -- purchase and renovate new property site
50,000	Boys & Girls Club of Hawaii, Honolulu, HI -- towards completion of full service facility at Ewa beach clubhouse
50,000	Hanahauoli School, Honolulu, HI -- capital campaign
50,000	Hawaii Public Television Foundation, Honolulu, HI -- toward digital broadcasting equipment and tower collaboration

MCKAY FAMILY FOUNDATION

Giving Contact

C. Bruce Kilen, Trustee
2350 Oakmont Way, Rm. 206
PO Box 70313
Eugene, OR 97401-0117
Phone: (541)686-5963

Description

Founded: 1986
EIN: 930935036
Organization Type: Private Foundation
Giving Locations: OR: Lane County
Grant Types: Capital, General Support, Scholarship.

Donor Information

Founder: the late Miles E. McKay, the late Eleanor P. McKay

Financial Summary

Total Giving: $177,189 (2002); $169,820 (2001)
Giving Analysis: Giving for 2002 includes: foundation scholarships ($10,000)
Assets: $3,900,639 (2002); $3,742,403 (2001)
Gifts Received: $553 (2000); $550 (1999); $595 (1997)

Typical Recipients

Arts & Humanities: Arts & Humanities-General, Libraries, Museums/Galleries, Opera
Civic & Public Affairs: Botanical Gardens/Parks, Civic & Public Affairs-General, Housing, Women's Affairs
Education: Business Education, Engineering/Technological Education, Education-General, Leadership Training, Science/Mathematics Education, Student Aid
Health: Children's Health/Hospitals, Clinics/Medical Centers, Emergency/Ambulance Services, Heart, Mental Health, Prenatal Health Issues
Religion: Religious Welfare
Science: Scientific Centers & Institutes
Social Services: At-Risk Youth, Camps, Child Abuse, Child Welfare, Community Service Organizations, Counseling, Day Care, Emergency Relief, Family Services, Food/Clothing Distribution, People with Disabilities, Senior Services, Shelters/Homelessness, Youth Organizations

Application Procedures

Initial Contact: Send a brief letter of inquiry.
Application Requirements: Include a description of organization, amount requested, proof of tax-exempt status, list of board of governors.
Deadlines: March 15 and September 15.

Foundation Officials

Philip F. Baird, Jr.: trustee
C. Bruce Kilen: trustee
Tracie M. Shojai: trustee
Kelly L. Thakkar: trustee
Dale Williams: trustee

Grants Analysis

Disclosure Period: calendar year ending 2002
Total Grants: $167,189*
Number of Grants: 25
Average Grant: $6,688
Highest Grant: $20,000
Lowest Grant: $1,000
Typical Range: $1,000 to $10,000
*****Note:** Giving excludes scholarships.

Recent Grants

Note: Grants derived from 2001 Form 990.
General

15,000	Relief Nursery, Eugene, OR -- Outreach Connections Program
15,000	St. Vincent de Paul Society, Eugene, OR -- The Boy's Group Program
10,000	American Red Cross, Eugene, OR -- capital grant for renovation
10,000	Casa of Lane County, Eugene, OR -- Capacity Building Project
10,000	Cottage Grove Habitat for Humanity -- acquisition of land
10,000	Eugene Mission, Eugene, OR -- upgrading shelter building
10,000	Lane County Legal Aid Service, Inc., Eugene, OR -- Supervised Parenting Time Program
10,000	Looking Glass Youth and Family Services, Eugene, OR -- Violence Intervention Project
10,000	Pearl Buck Center, Eugene, OR -- Family with Special Needs program
7,500	Food for Lane County, Eugene, OR -- Youth Farm Project

THOMAS M. MCKEE CHARITABLE TRUST

Giving Contact

Lynn A. Hammond, Trustee
200 E. 7th St., Suite 418
Loveland, CO 80537-4871
Phone: (970)667-1023
Fax: (970)669-9380

Description

Founded: 1992
EIN: 846228546
Organization Type: Private Foundation
Giving Locations: CO: Loveland
Grant Types: General Support, Project.

Financial Summary

Total Giving: $218,566 (2003); $309,345 (2001)
Assets: $3,616,395 (2003); $3,902,308 (2001)

Typical Recipients

Arts & Humanities: Arts Centers, Libraries
Civic & Public Affairs: Employment/Job Training, Housing, Municipalities/Towns
Education: Colleges & Universities, Community & Junior Colleges, Education-General, Preschool Education, Public Education (Precollege)
Health: Clinics/Medical Centers, Health Funds, Heart, Hospices, Medical Rehabilitation, Public Health
Religion: Churches
Social Services: Community Service Organizations, Counseling, Day Care, Food/Clothing Distribution, People with Disabilities, Recreation & Athletics, Substance Abuse, Volunteer Services, Youth Organizations

Application Procedures

Initial Contact: Send a brief letter of inquiry.
Application Requirements: Include supporting financial information, purpose of funds sought, and proof of tax-exempt status.
Deadlines: None.

Restrictions

Grants limited to Loveland, CO and Colorado College.

Foundation Officials

Lynn A. Hammond: trustee

Grants Analysis

Disclosure Period: calendar year ending 2003
Total Grants: $218,566
Number of Grants: 5
Highest Grant: $150,000
Lowest Grant: $15,114

Recent Grants

Note: Grants derived from 2003 Form 990.
General

150,000	Respite Care Inc., Ft. Collins, CO -- for medical rehabilitation
23,224	Boys and Girls Clubs, Loveland, CO
15,114	Colorado College, Colorado Springs, CO
15,114	Foothills Gateway Foundation, Ft. Collins, CO
15,114	McKee Medical Center Foundation, Loveland, CO

ROBERT E. AND EVELYN MCKEE FOUNDATION

Giving Contact

Louis B. McKee, President, Treasurer & Trustee
PO Box 220599
El Paso, TX 79913-2599
Phone: (915)581-4025
E-mail: McKee_Foundation@msn.com
Web: http://www.mckeefoundation.org

Description

Founded: 1952
EIN: 746036675
Organization Type: Private Foundation
Giving Locations: TX: emphasis on El Paso
Grant Types: Capital, Emergency, General Support, Multiyear/Continuing Support, Operating Expenses, Research, Scholarship, Seed Money.

Donor Information

Founder: the late Robert E. McKee, the late Evelyn McKee, Robert E. McKee, Inc., the Zia Co.

Financial Summary

Gifts Received: $10,075 (1996); $10,000 (1995); $196,244 (1994). Note: In 1996, contributions were received from Elizabeth McKee Lund ($10,000) and Michael and Lillian Bidal ($75).

Typical Recipients

Arts & Humanities: Arts & Humanities-General, History & Archaeology, Libraries, Museums/Galleries, Music, Public Broadcasting
Civic & Public Affairs: Clubs, Civic & Public Affairs-General, Hispanic Affairs, Parades/Festivals, Urban & Community Affairs, Women's Affairs, Zoos/Aquariums
Education: Afterschool/Enrichment Programs, Agricultural Education, Business Education, Colleges & Universities, Education Funds, Elementary Education (Public), Engineering/Technological Education, Health & Physical Education, Medical Education, Private Education (Precollege), Public Education (Precollege), Science/Mathematics Education, Secondary Education (Public), Student Aid
Health: Alzheimer's Disease, Cancer, Children's Health/Hospitals, Clinics/Medical Centers, Emergency/Ambulance Services, Eyes/Blindness, Heart, Hospices, Hospitals, Medical Rehabilitation, Medical Research, Mental Health, Nursing Services, Single-Disease Health Associations, Trauma Treatment
International: Health Care/Hospitals
Religion: Churches, Religious Welfare
Science: Science Museums
Social Services: Animal Protection, Camps, Child Abuse, Child Welfare, Community Centers, Community Service Organizations, Counseling, Crime Prevention, Domestic Violence, Food/Clothing Distribution, People with Disabilities, Scouts, Senior Services, Shelters/Homelessness, Substance Abuse, United Funds/United Ways, YMCA/YWCA/YMHA/YWHA, Youth Organizations

Application Procedures

Initial Contact: Send a brief letter of inquiry.
Application Requirements: Include a description of organization, purpose of funds sought, list of governing board and chief administrator of organization, recently audited financial statement, and proof of tax-exempt status.
Deadlines: December 15.

Restrictions

Does not support individuals.

Additional Information

Publications: Annual Report; Application Guidelines

Foundation Officials

Charlotte McKee Cohen: vice president, trustee
Frances McKee Hays: senior vice president
Robert L. Hazelton: senior vice president
Sharon Hays Herrera: vice president, trustee
Margaret McKee Lund: senior vice president
C. Steven McKee: trustee
David C. McKee: secretary, assistant treasurer, trustee
John S. McKee: senior vice president
Louis B. McKee: president-treasurer, trustee
Nelson D. McKee: vice president, trustee
Philip Russell McKee: vice president, trustee
R. Brian McKee: trustee
Robert E. McKee, III: trustee, treasurer ED Colorado School of Mines; Massachusetts Institute of Technology. PRIM CORP EMPL executive vice president corporate strategy & development: Conoco, Inc. CORP AFFIL senior vice president corporate strategy & development: El du Pont de Nemours & Co. NONPR AFFIL director: American Petroleum Institute; member: Society Petroleum Engineers.
Susan J. McKee: vice president, trustee
H. A. (Al) Woods: trustee
Helen Lund Yancey: vice president, trustee

Grants Analysis

Disclosure Period: calendar year ending 2000
Total Grants: $439,221*
Number of Grants: 140
Average Grant: $3,137
Highest Grant: $40,425
Typical Range: $1,000 to $5,000
*Note: Giving excludes scholarship; United Way.

Recent Grants

Note: Grants derived from 2001 Form 990.
General

149,534	XII Travelers Memorial of the Southwest, El Paso, TX
25,000	University of Texas at El Paso, El Paso, TX -- for Centennial Museum
15,990	El Paso Lighthouse for the Blind, El Paso, TX
15,000	New Mexico State University, Las Cruces, NM -- electric utility management program
15,000	University of Texas at El Paso, El Paso, TX -- for women's basketball
13,200	EPISD Fund, El Paso, TX
12,442	Carlos Rivera Elementary School, El Paso, TX
12,400	YMCA of Greater El Paso, El Paso, NM
12,000	Candlelighters of El Paso Area, El Paso, NM
11,000	Hospice of El Paso, El Paso, TX

KATHERINE MABIS MCKENNA FOUNDATION

Giving Contact

Linda M. Boxx, Chairman
Mellon Bank NA
PO Box 185
Latrobe, PA 15650-0185
Phone: (724)537-6900
Fax: (724)537-6906

Description

Founded: 1969
EIN: 237042752
Organization Type: Family Foundation
Giving Locations: PA: Eastern Westmoreland County
Grant Types: Capital, Endowment, General Support, Operating Expenses, Project, Scholarship, Seed Money.

Donor Information

Founder: Incorporated in 1969 by the late Katherine M. McKenna.

Financial Summary

Total Giving: $2,980,967 (2002)
Giving Analysis: Giving for 2002 includes: foundation grants to United Way ($85,000)
Assets: $61,773,283 (2002)
Gifts Received: $25,881,829 (1993). Note: In 1991, contributions were received from the estate of Katherine Mabis McKenna. In 1993, contributions were also received from this estate as well as from property transferred from agency account for Alex McKenna, executor for Kathryn Mabis McKenna.

Typical Recipients

Arts & Humanities: Arts Associations & Councils, Arts Festivals, Arts Funds, Arts Institutes, Ethnic & Folk Arts, Arts & Humanities-General, Historic Preservation, History & Archaeology, Libraries, Museums/Galleries, Music, Opera, Performing Arts, Public Broadcasting, Theater
Civic & Public Affairs: Botanical Gardens/Parks, Business/Free Enterprise, Chambers of Commerce, Civil Rights, Clubs, Community Foundations, Economic Development, Economic Policy, Civic & Public Affairs-General, Housing, Law & Justice, Legal Aid, Municipalities/Towns, Nonprofit Management, Parades/Festivals, Philanthropic Organizations, Public Policy, Safety, Urban & Community Affairs, Women's Affairs, Zoos/Aquariums
Education: Arts/Humanities Education, Business Education, Colleges & Universities, Community & Junior Colleges, Economic Education, Education Associations, Education Funds, Education Reform, Environmental Education, Education-General, Legal Education, Literacy, Minority Education, Private Education (Precollege), Public Education (Precollege), Religious Education, Science/Mathematics Education, Social Sciences Education, Student Aid
Environment: Environment-General, Resource Conservation, Watershed
Health: Arthritis, Cancer, Emergency/Ambulance Services, Hospitals, Medical Rehabilitation, Research/Studies Institutes, Single-Disease Health As-

sociations

International: International Affairs, International Organizations

Religion: Bible Study/Translation, Churches, Religion-General, Religious Welfare, Social/Policy Issues

Science: Science Exhibits & Fairs, Science Museums, Scientific Centers & Institutes

Social Services: Big Brothers/Big Sisters, Community Centers, Community Service Organizations, Crime Prevention, Emergency Relief, Family Services, People with Disabilities, Recreation & Athletics, Scouts, Social Services-General, United Funds/United Ways, Volunteer Services, YMCA/YWCA/YMHA/YWHA, Youth Organizations

Application Procedures

Initial Contact: The foundation does not have a specific application form.

Application Requirements: All requests should briefly describe the requesting organization and the particular project for which funding is sought. Foundation will provide requirements for a full proposal after initial inquiry. Proposals should include budgets for both the organization and the project, a list of donors and trustees or directors, the organization's IRS tax-exempt letter, and its most recent audited financial statements.

Deadlines: Contact the foundation for deadlines.

Restrictions

The foundation does not support individuals, matching funds, or loans.

Additional Information

Mellon Bank, NA, Pittsburgh, PA, is corporate agent. In 1993, the foundation made a non-cash gift of $1,500 in tangible property to the Westmoreland Symphony Orchestra.

Publications: Program Policy Statement

Foundation Officials

Linda McKenna Boxx: chairman, director
T. William Boxx: treasurer
Wilma F. McKenna: vchairman, director
Zan McKenna Rich: director

Grants Analysis

Disclosure Period: calendar year ending 2002
Total Grants: $2,895,967*
Number of Grants: 74
Average Grant: $32,821*
Highest Grant: $500,000
Lowest Grant: $500
Typical Range: $1,000 to $50,000
*Note: Giving excludes United Way. Average grant figure excludes highest grant.

Recent Grants

Note: Grants derived from 2002 Form 990.
Library-Related

25,000	Adams Memorial Library, Latrobe, PA -- funding for community network interactive web site

General

500,000	Saint Vincent College, Latrobe, PA -- support for school of business, economics and Government
229,800	Holy Trinity Catholic Church, Ligonier, PA -- funding for capital campaign
225,000	Fort Ligonier Association, Ligonier, PA -- assist in new exhibition capital campaign
175,000	Friends of National Parks at Gettysburg, Gettysburg, PA -- funding for purchase of property
125,000	Regional Trail Corporation, West Newton, PA -- funding to rehabilitate big savage tunnel
100,000	Gettysburg National Battlefield Museum Foundation, Gettysburg, PA -- toward support of new museum and visitor center
100,000	Indian Creek Valley Christian Family & Children's Center, Champion, PA -- funding to complete the Donegal Center
100,000	Phipps Conservatory and Botanical Gardens, Pittsburgh, PA -- toward tropical forest education demonstration area
100,000	University of Pittsburgh, Greensburg, PA -- funding of smart growth partnership
90,000	Westmoreland Trust, Greensburg, PA -- support for general operations

PHILIP M. MCKENNA FOUNDATION

Giving Contact

T. William Boxx, Chairman
PO Box 186
Latrobe, PA 15650
Phone: (724)537-6900
Fax: (724)537-6906

Description

Founded: 1967
EIN: 256082635
Organization Type: General Purpose Foundation
Giving Locations: PA: Southwestern Pennsylvania for community and civic programs nationally for public policy.
Grant Types: Capital, General Support, Operating Expenses, Research, Scholarship, Seed Money.

Donor Information

Founder: Incorporated in 1967 by the late Philip M. McKenna.

Financial Summary

Total Giving: $1,101,000 (2003 approx); $1,101,000 (2002 approx); $1,363,590 (2001)
Assets: $17,429,656 (2001)
Gifts Received: $100,000 (2001); $325,000 (2000); $325,000 (1998). Note: Contributions were received from Katherine M. McKenna Foundation.

Typical Recipients

Arts & Humanities: Arts Centers, Libraries, Museums/Galleries, Public Broadcasting, Theater

Civic & Public Affairs: Business/Free Enterprise, Civil Rights, Community Foundations, Economic Development, Economic Policy, Ethnic Organizations, Civic & Public Affairs-General, Law & Justice, Legal Aid, Nonprofit Management, Philanthropic Organizations, Professional & Trade Associations, Public Policy

Education: Business Education, Colleges & Universities, Continuing Education, Economic Education, Education Associations, Education Funds, Education Reform, Environmental Education, Education-General, Journalism/Media Education, Legal Education, Minority Education, Religious Education, Science/Mathematics Education, Social Sciences Education, Student Aid

Environment: Environment-General, Watershed

Health: Health Policy/Cost Containment, Hospitals, Research/Studies Institutes

International: Foreign Educational Institutions, Health Care/Hospitals, International Relations

Religion: Religious Welfare, Social/Policy Issues

Science: Science Museums, Scientific Centers & Institutes, Scientific Research

Social Services: Animal Protection, Community Service Organizations, Emergency Relief, Family Services, Food/Clothing Distribution, Recreation & Athletics, United Funds/United Ways, Veterans, Youth Organizations

Application Procedures

Initial Contact: Send a letter to the chairman explaining grant request and copy of 501(c).

Application Requirements: Include description of the organization, purpose of funds sought, operating budget, project budget, annual report, list of members of the governing board with affiliations, list of major donors, recently audited financial statement, and proof of tax-exempt status.

Deadlines: April1 and October 1.

Restrictions

The foundation does not make grants to individuals, foreign organizations, or for matching gifts or loans.

Foundation Officials

T. William Boxx: secretary, treasurer, officer
Zan McKenna Rich: director
Norbert Tail: secretary, director

Grants Analysis

Disclosure Period: calendar year ending 2001
Total Grants: $1,363,590
Number of Grants: 30
Average Grant: $29,577*
Highest Grant: $300,000
Lowest Grant: $2,500
Typical Range: $10,000 to $50,000
*Note: Average grant figure excludes three highest grants ($565,000).

Recent Grants

Note: Grants derived from 2001 Form 990.
Library-Related

25,000	Adams Memorial Library, Latrobe, PA

General

300,000	Saint Vincent College, Latrobe, PA
165,000	Intercollegiate Studies Institute Inc., Wilmington, DE
100,000	Heritage Foundation, Washington, DC
96,540	Commonwealth Foundation for Public Policy Alternatives, Harrisburg, PA
40,000	Allegheny Institute for Public Policy, Pittsburgh, PA
40,000	Claremont Institute for the Study of Statesmanship and Political Philosophy, Claremont, CA
39,500	Saint Vincent College - Center for Economic & Policy Education, Latrobe, PA -- funding of economic education series
35,000	Capital Research Center, Washington, DC
35,000	Federalist Society for Law and Public Policy Studies, Washington, DC
30,000	Pacific Research Institute for Public Policy, San Francisco, CA

CARL AND ALLEEN MCKINNEY CHARITABLE TRUST

Giving Contact

c/o Arvest Trust Co., NA
PO Box 1229
Bentonville, AR 72712-1229
Phone: (479)271-1254

Description

Founded: 1997
EIN: 716167536
Organization Type: Private Foundation
Giving Locations: AR
Grant Types: General Support, Scholarship.

Financial Summary

Total Giving: $177,406 (2003); $250,108 (2001)
Giving Analysis: Giving for 2003 includes: foundation scholarships ($44,385); 2001: foundation scholarships ($10,397)

Assets: $3,661,222 (2003); $3,764,392 (2001)
Gifts Received: $49,952 (1998); $2,909,669 (1997).
Note: In 1998, contributions were received from the McKinney Charitable Trust.

Typical Recipients

Civic & Public Affairs: Clubs, Housing
Education: Colleges & Universities, Elementary Education (Public), Education-General, Preschool Education, Student Aid, Vocational & Technical Education
Religion: Churches
Social Services: Child Welfare, Emergency Relief, Senior Services, Shelters/Homelessness, Social Services-General

Application Procedures

Initial Contact: Request scholarship application from NWACC Financial Aid Office.
Application Requirements: Include application, essay, letters of recommendation, copy of transcripts or GED test scores and/or grade transcript from post-secondary schools.

Additional Information

Trust(s): Arvest Trust Company

Foundation Officials

Ed Clifford: trustee
Gary Compton: board
Doylene Fuqua: board
Blaine Jackson: trustee
Donna Scanlan: trustee
Alice Stephens: trustee
T. Diane Wells: trustee

Grants Analysis

Disclosure Period: calendar year ending 2003
Total Grants: $133,021*
Number of Grants: 15
Average Grant: $8,868
Highest Grant: $20,000
Lowest Grant: $570
Typical Range: $1,000 to $15,000
*Note: Giving excludes scholarships.

Recent Grants

Note: Grants derived from 2001 Form 990.

General

35,559	Helen R. Walton Children's Center, Bentonville, AR -- for classroom repairs and furniture purchases
31,795	Northwest Arkansas Children's Shelter, Bentonville, AR -- to purchase storage building and 2 freezers
30,200	Youth Bridge, Inc., Centerton, AR -- for van and furnishings for shelter and recreation
28,582	Boys and Girls Club of Benton County, Bentonville, AR -- to replace gym floors
25,000	First United Methodist Church, Bentonville, AR -- for youth and children's building
25,000	Rocky Creek Horses Help, Rogers, AR -- for 50 riding scholarships
23,325	Bella Vista Leadership Class, Bentonville, AR -- for construction of state park in Bentonville
20,000	Our Farm, Inc., Rogers, AR -- for new windows for May House for Boys
7,000	Havenwood, Bentonville, AR -- for therapy and activity equipment and dental fund
5,650	Boys and Girls Club of Benton County, Bentonville, AR -- to replace bathroom stalls at McKinney Unit

MCLEAN CONTRIBUTIONSHIP

Giving Contact

Sandra L. McLean, Executive Director
945 Haverford Road, Suite A
Bryn Mawr, PA 19010-3814
Phone: (610)527-6330
Fax: (610)527-9733
Web: http://fdncenter.org/grantmaker/mclean

Description

Founded: 1951
EIN: 236396940
Organization Type: General Purpose Foundation
Giving Locations: PA: primarily metropolitan Philadelphia
Grant Types: Capital, Endowment, Multiyear/Continuing Support.

Donor Information

Founder: Established in 1951 by the late Robert McLean, the late William L. McLean Jr., and Bulletin Co.

Financial Summary

Total Giving: $2,392,500 (2003); $2,269,240 (2001)
Giving Analysis: Giving for 2003 includes: foundation grants to United Way ($56,000)
Assets: $50,983,039 (2003); $47,265,519 (2001)
Gifts Received: $87,483 (2003); $89,457 (2001); $177,222 (2000). Note: In 2003, contributions were received from Independence Communications, Inc. ($85,000); William & Elizabeth McLean, III ($2,143); and Elizabeth McLean ($340). In 2001, contributions were received from Independence Communications, Inc. ($80,000); William & Elizabeth McLean, III ($6,527); William McLean, IV ($2,048); and miscellaneous donors. In 1999 and 2000, substantial contributions were received from from Independence Communications, Inc. and William McLean, III.

Typical Recipients

Arts & Humanities: Arts Associations & Councils, Arts Centers, Ballet, Dance, Arts & Humanities-General, Historic Preservation, History & Archaeology, Libraries, Museums/Galleries, Music, Opera, Performing Arts, Theater
Civic & Public Affairs: Botanical Gardens/Parks, Business/Free Enterprise, Civil Rights, Clubs, Economic Development, Employment/Job Training, Civic & Public Affairs-General, Housing, Urban & Community Affairs, Women's Affairs, Zoos/Aquariums
Education: Afterschool/Enrichment Programs, Agricultural Education, Arts/Humanities Education, Colleges & Universities, Continuing Education, Education Funds, Education Reform, Elementary Education (Private), Environmental Education, Education-General, Health & Physical Education, Journalism/Media Education, Literacy, Medical Education, Minority Education, Private Education (Precollege), Science/Mathematics Education, Social Sciences Education, Special Education, Student Aid, Vocational & Technical Education
Environment: Air/Water Quality, Environment-General, Protection, Resource Conservation, Watershed, Wildlife Protection
Health: AIDS/HIV, Cancer, Children's Health/Hospitals, Diabetes, Emergency/Ambulance Services, Eyes/Blindness, Health-General, Geriatric Health, Health Organizations, Hospitals, Long-Term Care, Medical Rehabilitation, Medical Research, Mental Health, Nursing Services, Prenatal Health Issues, Public Health, Research/Studies Institutes, Single-Disease Health Associations, Transplant Networks/Donor Banks
International: International Affairs, International Environmental Issues
Religion: Churches, Religious Welfare
Science: Science Museums, Scientific Centers & Institutes, Scientific Organizations
Social Services: Animal Protection, Camps, Child Welfare, Community Centers, Community Service Organizations, Day Care, Domestic Violence, Emergency Relief, Family Planning, Family Services, Food/Clothing Distribution, Homes, People with Disabilities, Recreation & Athletics, Scouts, Senior Services, Social Services-General, United Funds/United Ways, YMCA/YWCA/YMHA/YWHA, Youth Organizations

Application Procedures

Initial Contact: The foundation requests applications be made in writing.
Application Requirements: The Contributionship accepts the Delaware Valley Grantmakers Association Common Grant Application Form. Application may also be made by letter, including a project description and justification, budget and timetable, and strategy for securing funding. Applications should be accompanied by a financial statement for the most recent fiscal year, interim operating statements or budgets for future periods (if appropriate), proof of tax-exempt status, and a list of officers and directors.
Deadlines: None. Proposals are accepted throughout the year.
Review Process: The foundation reports that trustees meet three or four times per year.
Notes: The recipient of the grant is expected to submit periodic reports.

Restrictions

The Contributionship does not fund the costs or expenses of existing staff allocated to a project.

Additional Information

Publications: Application Guidelines

Foundation Officials

Jean G. Bodine: trustee
Leila Gordon Dyer: advisory trustee
Hunter R. Gordon: advisory trustee
Joseph K. Gordon: trustee B Philadelphia, PA 1925. ED Princeton University (1948); University of Pennsylvania School of Law (1951). PRIM CORP EMPL attorney: Montgomery, McCracken, Walker & Rhoads LLP. CORP AFFIL director: Independent Publications Inc.; chairman, director: Main Line Health Inc.
Sandra L. McLean: executive drc, advisory trustee
William L. McLean, IV: vice chairman, trustee PRIM CORP EMPL secretary: Independent Publications Inc.
William L. McLean, III: chairman, trustee B Philadelphia, PA 1927. ED Princeton University (1949). PRIM CORP EMPL president, director: Finger Lakes Printing Co. ADD CORP EMPL president, director: Independent Publications Inc.; president: Finger Lakes Times; president: Telegraph.
Carolyn M. Raymond: trustee

Grants Analysis

Disclosure Period: calendar year ending 2003
Total Grants: $2,336,500*
Number of Grants: 108
Average Grant: $21,634
Highest Grant: $100,000
Lowest Grant: $1,000
Typical Range: $5,000 to $50,000
*Note: Giving excludes United Way.

Recent Grants

Note: Grants derived from 2002 Form 990.

Library-Related

50,000	Library Company of Philadelphia, Philadelphia, PA -- funding for creation of endowment fund
50,000	Pioneer Library System, Canandaigua, NY -- funding for creation of online catalog and circulation system

General

100,000	Academy of Natural Sciences, Philadelphia, PA -- funding to help endow the position of archivist
100,000	Lankenau Hospital, Wynnewood, PA -- toward renovation and development of emergency room in hospital
55,000	Philadelphia Protestant Home, Philadelphia, PA -- toward renovation of suites and units
50,000	Academy of Music, Philadelphia, PA -- funding for raising the roof campaign
50,000	Bryn Mawr Rehab Hospital, Malvern, PA -- funding for construction of new stroke unit
50,000	Coriell Institute of Medical Research, Camden, NJ -- funding for inventory tracking system
50,000	Devereux Foundation, West Chester, PA -- funding for capital and expansion needs
50,000	Drexel University, Philadelphia, PA -- funding for organization's programs
50,000	Highlands, Ft. Washington, PA -- toward restoration of greenhouse and garden walls
50,000	Historic Bartrams Garden, Philadelphia, PA -- toward design and construction costs for building

CATHERINE L. AND ROBERT O. MCMAHAN FOUNDATION

Giving Contact
Neal W. McMahan, Executive Director
PO Box 221580
Carmel, CA 93922
Phone: (831)625-6444

Description
EIN: 946061273
Organization Type: Private Foundation
Giving Locations: CA: primarily Monterey County
Grant Types: Capital, General Support, Matching, Scholarship.

Donor Information
Founder: Robert O. McMahan

Typical Recipients
Arts & Humanities: Arts Centers, Arts & Humanities-General, History & Archaeology, Libraries, Museums/Galleries, Music, Public Broadcasting, Theater
Civic & Public Affairs: Clubs, Community Foundations, Civic & Public Affairs-General, Housing, Legal Aid, Municipalities/Towns, Parades/Festivals, Public Policy, Rural Affairs, Urban & Community Affairs, Zoos/Aquariums
Education: Colleges & Universities, Education-General, International Studies, Private Education (Precollege), Public Education (Precollege), School Volunteerism, Student Aid
Environment: Forestry, Resource Conservation, Wildlife Protection
Health: AIDS/HIV, Alzheimer's Disease, Clinics/Medical Centers, Emergency/Ambulance Services, Eyes/Blindness, Heart, Home-Care Services, Medical Rehabilitation, Mental Health, Multiple Sclerosis, Nursing Services, Respiratory
Religion: Religious Welfare
Science: Science Museums
Social Services: Animal Protection, At-Risk Youth, Big Brothers/Big Sisters, Child Welfare, Community Service Organizations, Counseling, Emergency Relief, Family Planning, Family Services, Food/Clothing

Distribution, People with Disabilities, Recreation & Athletics, Senior Services, Sexual Abuse, Shelters/Homelessness, Social Services-General, Substance Abuse, Volunteer Services, YMCA/YWCA/YMHA/YWHA, Youth Organizations

Application Procedures
Initial Contact: Send a brief letter of inquiry.
Application Requirements: Include a description of organization, current budget, list of board members, proof of tax-exempt status, purpose of funds sought, amount requested.
Deadlines: March 31 and September 30

Restrictions
Preference is given to education and healthcare organizations. No grants are made to individuals, religious purposes, religious organizations, or public schools.

Foundation Officials
Michael L. McMahan: chief financial officer
Neal W. McMahan: executive director
Nicki Wilson McMahan: director
Marsha Zelus: director

Grants Analysis
Disclosure Period: calendar year ending 2000
Total Grants: $374,700*
Number of Grants: 58
Average Grant: $4,905*
Highest Grant: $50,000
Typical Range: $1,000 to $10,000
*Note: Giving excludes scholarships. Average grant figure excludes two highest grants ($100,000).

Recent Grants
Note: Grants derived from 2001 Form 990.
General

50,000	Campaign for Sunset, Carmel, CA -- expansion and enhancement of Sunset Theater
30,000	Big Sur Land Trust, Carmel, CA -- Notley's Landing
25,000	York School, Monterey, CA -- capital campaign
15,000	Food Bank for Monterey County, Salinas, CA -- expand distribution center
10,000	Boys and Girls Club of Monterey County, Seaside, CA -- fund the intercession period
10,000	Central Coast YMCA, Salinas, CA -- Alisal Community Friends Program
10,000	Coalition of Homeless Services Providers, Marina, CA -- develop programs
10,000	Community Partnership for Youth, Monterey, CA -- after-school mentor/tutor program
10,000	Landwatch Monterey County, Monterey, CA
10,000	Planned Parenthood Mar Monte, Monterey, CA -- Expanded Service Program

MCMAHON FOUNDATION

Giving Contact
James F. Wood, Director
PO Box 2156
Lawton, OK 73502
Phone: (580)355-4622
Fax: (580)357-3248

Description
Founded: 1940
EIN: 730664314
Organization Type: General Purpose Foundation
Giving Locations: OK: Comanche County, only Oklahoma, Lawton

Grant Types: Capital, General Support, Matching, Multiyear/Continuing Support, Project, Scholarship.

Donor Information
Founder: The McMahon Foundation was established in Oklahoma in 1940, with funds donated by the estate of the late Eugene D. McMahon. The purpose of the foundation is to benefit the city of Lawton and Comanche County, OK.

Financial Summary
Total Giving: $2,361,343 (fiscal year ending March 31, 2003); $2,882,584 (fiscal 2002); $2,976,431 (fiscal 2001). Note: Figure for 1996 includes $157,200 in scholarships.
Giving Analysis: Giving for fiscal 2003 includes: foundation grants to United Way ($25,500); foundation scholarships ($178,939)
Assets: $53,890,500 (fiscal 2003); $56,383,430 (fiscal 2002); $56,383,430 (fiscal 2001)

Typical Recipients
Arts & Humanities: Arts Associations & Councils, Arts Festivals, Arts Funds, Arts Institutes, Community Arts, Dance, Ethnic & Folk Arts, Historic Preservation, History & Archaeology, Libraries, Museums/Galleries, Music, Public Broadcasting, Theater
Civic & Public Affairs: Botanical Gardens/Parks, Community Foundations, Civic & Public Affairs-General, Housing, Inner-City Development, Municipalities/Towns, Parades/Festivals, Professional & Trade Associations, Safety, Urban & Community Affairs
Education: Arts/Humanities Education, Business-School Partnerships, Colleges & Universities, Education Funds, Education Reform, Education-General, Gifted & Talented Programs, Journalism/Media Education, Literacy, Public Education (Precollege), Secondary Education (Private), Special Education, Student Aid, Vocational & Technical Education
Environment: Wildlife Protection
Health: Emergency/Ambulance Services, Health Funds, Hospices, Nursing Services, Transplant Networks/Donor Banks
Religion: Religion-General, Religious Welfare
Social Services: Child Welfare, Community Centers, Community Service Organizations, Counseling, Crime Prevention, Food/Clothing Distribution, Homes, Recreation & Athletics, Substance Abuse, United Funds/United Ways, YMCA/YWCA/YMHA/YWHA, Youth Organizations

Application Procedures
Initial Contact: The foundation does not issue specific guidelines for applications. Send an initial letter of inquiry.
Application Requirements: The initial letter should describe the nature of the organization and the purpose of the grant requested.
Deadlines: None.
Review Process: The board meets on the first Monday of each month.

Restrictions
The foundation does not make grants to recipients outside of Oklahoma. Primary consideration in Comanche County, Oklahoma. No grants to individuals.

Foundation Officials
Kenneth Bridges: trustee
Ronald E. Cagle, MD: trustee
Kenneth Easton: trustee PRIM CORP EMPL secretary, director: Easton's Inc. CORP AFFIL secretary, director: Easton's Ace Hardware; secretary, director: Easton's Marine.
Charles S. Graybill, MD: chairman, trustee
Manville Redman: vchairman
Gale Sadler: secretary, treasurer PRIM CORP EMPL secretary, treasurer, director: Sunnyside Farm Store Inc.
Orville D. Smith: trustee
James F. Wood: director

Grants Analysis

Disclosure Period: fiscal year ending March 31, 2003
Total Grants: $2,210,904*
Number of Grants: 23
Average Grant: $49,191*
Highest Grant: $450,000
Lowest Grant: $1,000
Typical Range: $25,000 to $100,000
***Note:** Giving excludes scholarships and United Way. Average grant excludes four highest grants ($1,276,276).

Recent Grants

Note: Grants derived from 2004 Form 990.
Library-Related

5,000	Lawton Area Reading Council, Lawton, OK -- to support special program

General

450,000	Lawton Evening Optimist Soccer Association, Lawton, OK -- for construction of a sports complex
300,276	City of Lawton, Lawton, OK -- for park improvements
300,000	American Choral Directors Association, Lawton, OK -- for building construction
226,000	Lawton Public Schools, Lawton, OK -- to support special program
150,000	Comanche County Health Department, Lawton, OK -- for building improvement
143,780	Cameron University, Lawton, OK -- for scholarships
142,300	Cameron University Foundation, Lawton, OK -- for capital improvements and support educational radio station
125,000	University of Oklahoma Foundation, Norman, OK -- scholarships and journalism building fund
95,632	Center for Creative Living, Lawton, OK -- for building improvements
70,000	McMahon Auditorium Authority, Lawton, OK -- for building renovation

HAROLD AND HELEN MCMASTER FOUNDATION

Giving Contact

Scott Savage, Trust Officer
6711 Monroe St., Building 4 Suite A
Sylvania, OH 43560-2538
Phone: (419)885-2626

Description

Founded: 1988
EIN: 341576110
Organization Type: Private Foundation
Giving Locations: OH
Grant Types: General Support.

Donor Information

Founder: Harold A. McMaster, Helen E. McMaster

Financial Summary

Total Giving: $1,289,392 (fiscal year ending November 30, 2003); $1,505,282 (fiscal 2001)
Giving Analysis: Giving for fiscal 2003 includes: foundation gifts to individuals ($3,600); foundation scholarships ($10,000); foundation grants to United Way ($10,000); fiscal 2001: foundation gifts to individuals ($3,600); foundation grants to United Way ($10,000); foundation scholarships ($20,000)
Assets: $9,470,992 (fiscal 2003); $7,478,855 (fiscal 2001)
Gifts Received: $416,432 (fiscal 1998); $4,058,640 (fiscal 1997); $10,000 (fiscal 1996). Note: In 1997 and 1998, contributions were received from Harold and Helen McMaster. In 1996, contributions were re-

ceived from Harold A. McMaster Trust. In 1993, contributions were received from Harold and Helen McMaster.

Typical Recipients

Arts & Humanities: Arts Associations & Councils, Libraries, Museums/Galleries, Music, Public Broadcasting
Civic & Public Affairs: Business/Free Enterprise, Civic & Public Affairs-General
Education: Colleges & Universities, Education Funds, Education Reform, Education-General, Preschool Education, Private Education (Precollege), Religious Education, Science/Mathematics Education, Secondary Education (Private), Student Aid, Vocational & Technical Education
Health: Hospices, Prenatal Health Issues
Religion: Ministries, Religious Welfare
Science: Observatories & Planetariums, Scientific Centers & Institutes
Social Services: Community Centers, Family Planning, Recreation & Athletics, United Funds/United Ways, YMCA/YWCA/YMHA/YWHA, Youth Organizations

Application Procedures

Initial Contact: Send a brief letter of inquiry.
Application Requirements: Include explanation of needs and wants.
Deadlines: None.

Additional Information

Provides grants to individuals.

Foundation Officials

Frank D. Jacobs: assistant secretary
Helen E. McMaster: vice president, secretary
Ronald A. McMaster: trustee

Grants Analysis

Disclosure Period: fiscal year ending November 30, 2003
Total Grants: $1,265,792*
Number of Grants: 24
Average Grant: $24,515*
Highest Grant: $300,000
Lowest Grant: $1,000
Typical Range: $5,000 to $50,000
***Note:** Giving excludes scholarships; United Way; gifts to individuals. Average grant figure excludes five highest grants ($800,000).

Recent Grants

Note: Grants derived from fiscal 2003 Form 990.
General

300,000	Defiance College, Defiance, OH -- towards McMaster Institute
200,000	WGTE Public Broadcasting, Toledo, OH
100,000	Defiance College, Defiance, OH -- for Serrick Center
100,000	Toledo Museum of Art, Toledo, OH -- capital campaign
100,000	West Side Montessori Center, Toledo, OH
85,000	University of Toledo Foundation, Toledo, OH -- for bio medical chair fund
50,000	Bowling Green State University, Bowling Green, OH -- towards college of arts & sciences
50,000	Bowling Green State University, Bowling Green, OH -- towards college of musical arts
50,000	Bowling Green State University, Bowling Green, OH -- for student union meeting room
50,000	Perkins Observatory, Delaware, OH -- for Ohio Wesleyan University fund

BRUCE MCMILLAN, JR. FOUNDATION

Giving Contact

Ralph Ward, Jr., President, Treasurer & Director
PO Box 9
Overton, TX 75684
Phone: (903)834-3148
Fax: (903)834-3947

Description

Founded: 1951
EIN: 750945924
Organization Type: Family Foundation
Giving Locations: TX: emphasis on the Overton area
Grant Types: Endowment, General Support, Scholarship.

Donor Information

Founder: Established in 1951 by the late V. Bruce McMillan M.D. and the late Mary Moore McMillan.

Financial Summary

Total Giving: $918,950 (fiscal year ending June 30, 2002); $1,050,191 (fiscal 2001). Note: 1997 Giving includes scholarship ($126,267).
Giving Analysis: Giving for fiscal 2002 includes: foundation scholarships ($53,850); fiscal 2001: foundation scholarships ($70,648)
Assets: $17,640,689 (fiscal 2002); $20,306,968 (fiscal 2001)

Typical Recipients

Arts & Humanities: Film & Video, Libraries, Museums/Galleries
Civic & Public Affairs: Business/Free Enterprise, Economic Development, Housing, Law & Justice, Legal Aid, Municipalities/Towns, Public Policy, Rural Affairs, Safety, Urban & Community Affairs
Education: Afterschool/Enrichment Programs, Agricultural Education, Arts/Humanities Education, Business Education, Colleges & Universities, Community & Junior Colleges, Economic Education, Education Funds, Education Reform, Elementary Education (Private), Engineering/Technological Education, Faculty Development, Education-General, Literacy, Minority Education, Private Education (Precollege), Public Education (Precollege), Religious Education, Science/Mathematics Education, Special Education, Student Aid
Environment: Resource Conservation
Health: Cancer, Children's Health/Hospitals, Emergency/Ambulance Services, Health Organizations, Heart, Medical Rehabilitation, Prenatal Health Issues, Public Health, Single-Disease Health Associations, Transplant Networks/Donor Banks
Religion: Churches, Missionary Activities (Domestic), Religious Organizations, Religious Welfare, Seminaries
Social Services: Child Abuse, Child Welfare, Crime Prevention, Domestic Violence, Family Planning, Family Services, Food/Clothing Distribution, Scouts, Sexual Abuse, Substance Abuse, Youth Organizations

Application Procedures

Initial Contact: Applicants for grants and scholarships should contact the foundation for a formal application.
Deadlines: June 15. For churches and noneducational institutions is May 1.
Review Process: All other applications are reviewed in June and October.

Restrictions

Scholarship awards are generally limited to applications from the following high schools; West Rusk, Overton, Henderson, Leverett Chapel, Kilgore, Troup, Arp, Troup Hill and Carlisle.

Grants are limited to Overton, TX.

Additional Information
Publications: Application Guidelines

Foundation Officials
Drew R. Heard: chairman B Lockhart, TX 1950. ED Baylor University BA (1972); Baylor University JD (1975). PRIM CORP EMPL attorney: Jenkens Gilchrist PC. NONPR AFFIL member: Phi Eta Sigma; member: State Bar Texas; member: Phi Alpha Theta; member: Dallas Bar Association; member: Phi Alpha Delta; member: American Bar Association.
Pamela M. Merritt: secretary
John Rogers Pope: vice chairman
Ralph Ward, Jr.: president, treasurer B 1947. ED Austin College (1968-1970); Texas A&M University (1970-1973).

Grants Analysis
Disclosure Period: fiscal year ending June 30, 2002
Total Grants: $865,201*
Number of Grants: 62
Average Grant: $12,380*
Highest Grant: $110,000
Lowest Grant: $500
Typical Range: $5,000 to $25,000
*Note: Giving excludes scholarships. Average grant figure excludes highest grant.

Recent Grants
Note: Grants derived from fiscal 2002 Form 990.
General

110,000	Kilgore College, Kilgore, TX
75,000	Baylor University, Waco, TX
65,000	Texas A&M University Foundation, College Station, TX
40,000	Austin Presbyterian Theological Seminary, Austin, TX
40,000	Buckner Children & Family Services, Longview, TX
38,000	University of Texas MD Anderson Cancer Center, Smithville, TX
30,000	East Texas Treatment Center, Kilgore, TX
30,000	Kilgore College Demo Farm, Kilgore, TX
25,000	Austin College, Sherman, TX
25,000	Centenary College, Shreveport, LA

MCMILLEN FOUNDATION

Giving Contact
John F. McMillen, President
6610 Mutual Drive
Ft. Wayne, IN 46825
Phone: (260)484-8631
Fax: (260)483-0474

Description
Founded: 1947
EIN: 356021003
Organization Type: Family Foundation
Giving Locations: IN: Allen County, Ft. Wayne
Grant Types: Capital, General Support, Scholarship.

Donor Information
Founder: Incorporated in 1947 by the late Dale W. McMillen and members of the McMillen family.

Financial Summary
Total Giving: $1,000,000 (2003 approx); $1,242,765 (2002); $1,016,529 (2001)
Giving Analysis: Giving for 2002 includes: foundation scholarships ($20,000)
Assets: $30,000,000 (2003 approx); $20,944,553 (2002); $28,000,000 (2001 approx)

Typical Recipients
Arts & Humanities: Arts Associations & Councils, Arts Funds, Historic Preservation, Music, Public Broadcasting, Theater
Civic & Public Affairs: Botanical Gardens/Parks, Business/Free Enterprise, Chambers of Commerce, Community Foundations, Economic Development, Civic & Public Affairs-General, Housing, Municipalities/Towns, Public Policy, Women's Affairs, Zoos/Aquariums
Education: Afterschool/Enrichment Programs, Business Education, Colleges & Universities, Continuing Education, Education Funds, Engineering/Technological Education, Education-General, Health & Physical Education, International Exchange, Literacy, Private Education (Precollege), Public Education (Precollege), Religious Education, Secondary Education (Private), Student Aid
Environment: Air/Water Quality
Health: AIDS/HIV, Clinics/Medical Centers, Health-General, Geriatric Health, Health Organizations, Hospices, Public Health
Religion: Ministries, Religious Organizations, Religious Welfare
Science: Scientific Centers & Institutes
Social Services: Big Brothers/Big Sisters, Child Welfare, Community Centers, Community Service Organizations, Day Care, Delinquency & Criminal Rehabilitation, Domestic Violence, Emergency Relief, Family Planning, Family Services, Food/Clothing Distribution, Homes, People with Disabilities, Recreation & Athletics, Scouts, Sexual Abuse, Shelters/Homelessness, Substance Abuse, United Funds/United Ways, YMCA/YWCA/YMHA/YWHA, Youth Organizations

Application Procedures
Initial Contact: The foundation requests applications be made in writing. To be eligible for support, organizations must be operated for public purposes and qualify as not-for-profit and tax-exempt status under the regulations of the United States Internal Revenue Services 501 (c) (3). The Foundation does not use a specific form. Written request should include: A description of the organization and its history. The purpose, objective and the amount of the request. A list of officers and directors of the organization. Proof tax-exempt status under Section 501 (c) (3) of the IRS Code. A recent annual report, audited financial statement and operating budget. A three-year history of donors and funding sources and the amount of grants received (detail by donor $1,000 and over) plus grants and outstanding grant requests for current project request.

Foundation Officials
Dale W. McMillen, III: director
John F. McMillen: president, director B 1945. PRIM CORP EMPL chairman: DuCharme McMillen & Associates.
Thomas Mitchell Shoaff: director, vice president B Fort Wayne, IN 1941. ED Williams College BA (1964); Vanderbilt University JD (1967). PRIM CORP EMPL partner: Baker & Daniels. CORP AFFIL director: Weaver Popcorn Co. Inc.; director: Fort Wayne National Bank; director: Fort Wayne National Corp.; director: America Steel Investment Corp.; director: Dreibelbiss Title Co. NONPR AFFIL director: Fort Wayne Park Foundation; member: Indiana Bar Association; member: American Bar Association; member: Allen County Bar Association.
Linda Crowe Tate: director

Grants Analysis
Disclosure Period: calendar year ending 2002
Total Grants: $1,222,765*
Number of Grants: 22
Average Grant: $37,376*
Highest Grant: $200,000
Lowest Grant: $2,000
Typical Range: $10,000 to $50,000

*Note: Giving excludes scholarships. Average grant figure excludes four highest grants ($550,000).

Recent Grants
Note: Grants derived from 2002 Form 990.
General

200,000	Girl Scouts of Limberlost Council, Ft. Wayne, IN -- assistance for capital campaign
150,000	Indiana Purdue Foundation, Ft. Wayne, IN -- funding for soccer field improvements
100,000	Fort · Wayne Parks Foundation, Ft. Wayne, IN -- assistance for capital campaign
100,000	YMCA of Greater Fort Wayne, Ft. Wayne, IN -- assistance for family capital campaign
89,691	Wildcats -- toward funding for 2002
89,691	Wildcats -- toward funding for 2002
89,691	Wildcats -- toward funding for 2002
89,691	Wildcats -- toward funding for 2002
50,000	Fort Wayne Neighborhood Housing, Ft. Wayne, IN -- toward US Treasury challenge grant
50,000	Junior Achievement of Northern Indiana, Ft. Wayne, IN -- funding for economics 2001-2002 school year

MCNEELY FOUNDATION

Giving Contact
Karen Reynolds, Foundation Manager
444 Pine St.
St. Paul, MN 55101-2453
Phone: (651)228-4500
E-mail: kreynolds@meritexenterprises.com

Description
Founded: 1981
EIN: 411392221
Organization Type: Private Foundation
Giving Locations: MN: Minneapolis metropolitan area, St. Paul metropolitan area
Grant Types: General Support.

Donor Information
Founder: Lee and Rose Warner Foundation

Financial Summary
Total Giving: $1,333,946 (2001)
Giving Analysis: Giving for 2001 includes: foundation grants to United Way ($18,796)
Assets: $18,156,157 (2001)
Gifts Received: $252,810 (2000); $150,000 (1999); $833,444 (1998). Note: In 1999, contributions were received from Meritex Enterprises Inc. In 1998, contributions were received from Center Enterprises ($700,000), Armor Archbold ($99,728), and Shannon McNeely Whitaker ($33,716).

Typical Recipients
Arts & Humanities: Arts Associations & Councils, Community Arts, Libraries, Museums/Galleries, Music, Public Broadcasting, Theater
Civic & Public Affairs: Asian American Affairs, Botanical Gardens/Parks, Business/Free Enterprise, Community Foundations, Economic Development, Employment/Job Training, Civic & Public Affairs-General, Native American Affairs, Urban & Community Affairs
Education: Business Education, Colleges & Universities, Economic Education, Education Funds, Environmental Education, Education-General, Legal Education, Minority Education, Private Education (Precollege), Public Education (Precollege), Special Education
Environment: Environment-General, Resource

Conservation, Wildlife Protection
Health: Children's Health/Hospitals, Health Organizations
International: International-General
Religion: Churches, Religious Organizations, Religious Welfare
Social Services: At-Risk Youth, Camps, Child Welfare, Community Centers, Community Service Organizations, Day Care, Delinquency & Criminal Rehabilitation, Domestic Violence, Family Services, People with Disabilities, Recreation & Athletics, United Funds/United Ways, YMCA/YWCA/YMHA/YWHA, Youth Organizations

Application Procedures

Initial Contact: The foundation requests applications be made in writing.
Application Requirements: Include a description of organization, amount requested, purpose of funds sought, recently audited financial statement, and proof of tax-exempt status.
Deadlines: None.

Restrictions

Grants are not made to individuals.

Additional Information

Meritex Foundation has been merged with McNeely Foundation.

Foundation Officials

Armar A. Archbold: trustee
W. E. Bye Barsness: vice chairman, trustee B 1941. ED Northwestern University MBA (1969). PRIM CORP EMPL president, chief executive officer, director: Pink Supply Corp. CORP AFFIL director: Faribault Woolen Mill Co.; president: Pink Business Interiors.
Malcolm W. McDonald: secretary, treasurer, trustee NONPR AFFIL director: Amherst H. Wilder Foundation.
Gregory McNeely: trustee
Harry G. McNeely, III: trustee
Harry G. McNeely, Jr.: chairman, trustee PRIM CORP EMPL president: Meritex.
Karen M. Reynolds: manager
Shannon McNeely Whitaker: trustee

Grants Analysis

Disclosure Period: calendar year ending 2001
Total Grants: $1,315,150*
Number of Grants: 72
Average Grant: $8,741*
Highest Grant: $450,000
Typical Range: $1,000 to $15,000
*Note: Giving excludes United Way. Average grant figure excludes three highest grants ($712,000).

Recent Grants

Note: Grants derived from 2001 Form 990.
General

450,000	Children's Hospital and Clinic Foundation, Minneapolis, MN
150,000	University of Saint Thomas, St. Paul, MN
112,000	Saint Peter Claver Catholic School, St. Paul, MN
50,000	Amherst H. Wilder Foundation, St. Paul, MN
30,000	Friends of the Saint Paul Public Library, St. Paul, MN
30,000	Wilderness Inquiry, Minneapolis, MN
25,000	Goodwill/Easter Seals, St. Paul, MN
25,000	YMCA of Greater Saint Paul, St. Paul, MN
20,000	Minnesota Business Academy, Minneapolis, MN
17,500	Minnesota Children's Museum, St. Paul, MN

AMY SHELTON MCNUTT CHARITABLE TRUST

Giving Contact

Carol Bruehler, Trust Secretary
153 Treeline Park, Suite 300
San Antonio, TX 78209-1880
Phone: (210)829-1800

Description

Founded: 1983
EIN: 742298675
Organization Type: Private Foundation
Giving Locations: TX: Corpus Christi, San Antonio
Grant Types: General Support, Operating Expenses.

Donor Information

Founder: the late Amy Shelton McNutt

Financial Summary

Total Giving: $724,816 (fiscal year ending September 30, 2002)
Giving Analysis: Giving for fiscal 2002 includes: foundation grants to United Way ($27,000)
Assets: $11,067,115 (fiscal 2002)

Typical Recipients

Arts & Humanities: Arts Associations & Councils, Arts Centers, Ethnic & Folk Arts, Historic Preservation, History & Archaeology, Libraries, Museums/Galleries, Music, Performing Arts, Public Broadcasting, Theater
Civic & Public Affairs: Botanical Gardens/Parks, Clubs, Community Foundations, Economic Development, Economic Policy, Civic & Public Affairs-General, Hispanic Affairs, Philanthropic Organizations, Professional & Trade Associations, Public Policy, Urban & Community Affairs, Women's Affairs, Zoos/Aquariums
Education: Agricultural Education, Arts/Humanities Education, Business Education, Colleges & Universities, Education Reform, Engineering/Technological Education, Private Education (Precollege), Public Education (Precollege), Science/Mathematics Education, Secondary Education (Private), Social Sciences Education, Student Aid
Environment: Environment-General, Wildlife Protection
Health: Alzheimer's Disease, Cancer, Emergency/Ambulance Services, Eyes/Blindness, Geriatric Health, Health Organizations, Hospices, Hospitals, Medical Rehabilitation, Medical Research, Mental Health, Nursing Services, Single-Disease Health Associations
International: Human Rights, International Peace & Security Issues, Missionary/Religious Activities
Religion: Churches, Ministries, Religious Organizations, Religious Welfare
Science: Scientific Centers & Institutes, Scientific Research
Social Services: Animal Protection, Community Centers, Community Service Organizations, Counseling, Day Care, Family Planning, Family Services, Homes, People with Disabilities, Recreation & Athletics, Senior Services, Substance Abuse, United Funds/United Ways, YMCA/YWCA/YMHA/YWHA, Youth Organizations

Application Procedures

Initial Contact: Submit a letter of application not exceeding three pages.
Application Requirements: Include purpose of funds sought, proof of tax-exempt status, and an indication of whether any of the organization's activities are considered lobbying activities under the Internal Revenue Code (and, if so, include copies of the past three years' tax returns).
Deadlines: February 28 and July 31 to ensure that proposal arrives prior to trustee meetings in March

and August.
Decision Notification: Applicants are notified of the board of trustee's decisions after each meeting.
Notes: Newsletters and other supporting materials should not be submitted and will not be reviewed by the foundation.

Restrictions

Does not support individuals.

Foundation Officials

Carol Bruehler: secretary
Randall Brower Cutlip: trustee B Clarksburg, WV October 01, 1916. ED Bethany College BA (1940); East Texas State University MA (1949); University of Houston EdD (1953); Bethany College LLD (1965); Drury College LHD (1975); Southwestern Baptist University ScD (1978); Columbia College LLD (1980); William Woods College LittD (1981). NONPR AFFIL member: Phi Delta Kappa; trustee: William Woods College; member: Kappa Delta Pi; elder emeritus: Life Christian Church; member: Alpha Sigma Phi; member: American Personal Guidance Association; member: Alpha Chi.
Jack Egon Guenther: trustee B San Antonio, TX 1934. ED University of Texas, Austin BBA (1956); Saint Mary's University LLB (1959); New York University LLM (1960). CORP AFFIL chairman: Volvo & Porcshe Center; chairman: Rivergate Toyota; chairman: Performance Toyota; chairman: Performance Toyota Plano; chairman: Lexus Nashville; chairman: BMW Center; of coun: Cox & Smith; chairman: Bell Ford LP. NONPR AFFIL member: Texas Bar Association; member: Texas Society CPA's; member: Phi Delta Phi; member: Sigma Chi; member: American Bar Association.
Edward D. Muir: trustee
Courtney Johnson Walker: trustee

Grants Analysis

Disclosure Period: fiscal year ending September 30, 2002
Total Grants: $697,816*
Number of Grants: 125
Average Grant: $4,821
Highest Grant: $100,000
Typical Range: $1,000 to $5,000
*Note: Giving excludes United Way.

Recent Grants

Note: Grants derived from fiscal 2002 Form 990.

General

100,000	National Center for American Western Art, Kerrville, TX -- for building project
55,000	William Woods University, Fulton, MO -- for renovation project
50,000	Alamo Public Telecommunications Council, San Antonio, TX -- for digital conversion campaign
50,000	Texas State Aquarium, Corpus Christi, TX -- for environmental discovery component of Dolphin Bay Project
36,000	Wildlife Rescue and Rehabilitation, Inc., Boerne, TX -- for construction
25,000	South Texas Public Broadcasting System, Corpus Christi, TX -- for digital conversion campaign
25,000	United Way of San Antonio and Bexar Counties, San Antonio, TX
25,000	University of Texas at San Antonio, San Antonio, TX -- for San Antonio Center for Water Research
25,000	USS Lexington Museum Association, Corpus Christi, TX
20,000	Cancer Therapy & Research Center, San Antonio, TX -- for campaign to purchase nuclear gamma camera

ADELINE AND GEORGE MCQUEEN FOUNDATION

Giving Contact
Robert Lansford, Trust Officer
c/o Bank One Texas NA
PO Box 2050
Ft. Worth, TX 76113
Phone: (817)884-4151

Description
Founded: 1960
EIN: 756014459
Organization Type: Private Foundation
Giving Locations: TX
Grant Types: General Support.

Financial Summary
Total Giving: $1,280,950 (fiscal year ending June 30, 2004); $589,000 (fiscal 2001)
Assets: $14,718,946 (fiscal 2004); $14,577,712 (fiscal 2001)

Typical Recipients
Arts & Humanities: Ballet, Libraries, Museums/Galleries, Music, Opera, Theater
Civic & Public Affairs: Clubs, Community Foundations, Economic Development, Civic & Public Affairs-General, Parades/Festivals, Urban & Community Affairs, Women's Affairs, Zoos/Aquariums
Education: Afterschool/Enrichment Programs, Business Education, Colleges & Universities, Education-General, Health & Physical Education, Medical Education, Minority Education, Private Education (Precollege), Religious Education, Special Education
Health: AIDS/HIV, Cancer, Children's Health/Hospitals, Clinics/Medical Centers, Health Funds, Health Organizations, Hospitals, Hospitals (University Affiliated), Preventive Medicine/Wellness Organizations, Public Health, Single-Disease Health Associations
Religion: Religion-General, Jewish Causes, Ministries, Religious Organizations, Religious Welfare, Seminaries
Science: Science Museums
Social Services: Big Brothers/Big Sisters, Community Service Organizations, Counseling, Day Care, Family Services, Food/Clothing Distribution, Homes, People with Disabilities, Recreation & Athletics, Shelters/Homelessness, YMCA/YWCA/YMHA/YWHA, Youth Organizations

Application Procedures
Initial Contact: The foundation requests applications be made in writing. Include a description of organization, purpose of funds sought, amount requested, and list of directors.
Deadlines: None.

Additional Information
Trust(s): Bank One TX NA

Grants Analysis
Disclosure Period: fiscal year ending June 30, 2004
Total Grants: $1,280,950
Number of Grants: 52
Average Grant: $21,041*
Highest Grant: $100,000
Lowest Grant: $1,000
Typical Range: $10,000 to $40,000
*Note: Average grant figure excludes three highest grants ($250,000).

Recent Grants
Note: Grants derived from fiscal 2004 Form 990.
General
100,000	Dallas Theological Seminary, Dallas, TX
100,000	Fort Worth Museum of Science and History, Ft. Worth, TX
100,000	Museum of Science and History, Ft. Worth, TX
100,000	Ronald McDonald House, Wauwatosa, WI
50,000	All Saints Health Foundation, Ft. Worth, TX
30,000	Tarrant County Access for the Homeless, Ft. Worth, TX
25,000	All Saints School, Denmark, WI
25,000	Fort Worth Christian School, Ft. Worth, TX
25,000	Jewel Charity Ball
25,000	Texas Refuges Centennial Celebration, Ft. Worth, TX

MCWANE CORP.

Company Headquarters
2900 Hwy. 280, Ste. 300
Birmingham, AL 35223
Phone: (205)414-3100
Fax: (205)414-3180

Company Description
Founded: 1921
Revenue: US$1.5 billion (2002)
Employees: 5200 (2002)
SIC(s): 3321 Gray & Ductile Iron Foundries, 3491 Industrial Valves.

Operating Locations
McWane Corp. (IL--Oak Brook; IA--Oskaloosa; OH--Coshocton)

McWane Foundation

Giving Contact
C. Phillip McWane
PO Box 43327
Birmingham, AL 35243
Phone: (205)414-3100
Fax: (205)414-3180

Description
Founded: 1961
EIN: 636044384
Organization Type: Corporate Foundation
Giving Locations: AL
Grant Types: Capital, General Support, Scholarship.

Financial Summary
Total Giving: $2,034,500 (2003); $4,256,000 (2002); $756,400 (2001)
Giving Analysis: Giving for 2002 includes: foundation ($4,256,000)
Assets: $446,056 (2003); $457,167 (2002); $491,362 (2001)
Gifts Received: $1,982,000 (2003); $4,180,000 (2002); $715,000 (2001). Note: Contributions were received from McWane, Inc.

Typical Recipients
Arts & Humanities: Arts Associations & Councils, Arts Centers, Arts Festivals, Arts Funds, Ballet, Dance, Historic Preservation, History & Archaeology, Libraries, Museums/Galleries, Music, Performing Arts, Public Broadcasting, Theater
Civic & Public Affairs: African American Affairs, Botanical Gardens/Parks, Business/Free Enterprise, Civil Rights, Clubs, Community Foundations, Economic Development, Civic & Public Affairs-General, Housing, Inner-City Development, Law & Justice, Municipalities/Towns, Philanthropic Organizations, Safety, Urban & Community Affairs, Zoos/Aquariums
Education: Afterschool/Enrichment Programs, Arts/Humanities Education, Business Education, Colleges & Universities, Education Funds, Education Reform, Engineering/Technological Education, Education-General, Leadership Training, Literacy, Private Education (Precollege), Public Education (Precollege), Student Aid
Environment: Environment-General, Protection, Resource Conservation
Health: Arthritis, Cancer, Children's Health/Hospitals, Diabetes, Emergency/Ambulance Services, Health Organizations, Heart, Hospitals, Medical Research, Mental Health, Multiple Sclerosis, Single-Disease Health Associations
Religion: Churches, Dioceses, Jewish Causes, Ministries, Religious Welfare, Social/Policy Issues
Science: Science Museums, Scientific Centers & Institutes
Social Services: Animal Protection, At-Risk Youth, Big Brothers/Big Sisters, Community Service Organizations, Counseling, Crime Prevention, Family Services, People with Disabilities, Recreation & Athletics, Scouts, Social Services-General, Substance Abuse, YMCA/YWCA/YMHA/YWHA, Youth Organizations

Application Procedures
Initial Contact: Send written request.
Deadlines: None.

Corporate Officials
Glenda Burson: vice president, treasurer, chief executive officer, treasurer PRIM CORP EMPL vice president, treasurer: McWane.
John J. McMahon, Jr.: chairman, president, chief executive officer, treasurer PRIM CORP EMPL chairman, president, chief executive officer, treasurer: McWane Inc. CORP AFFIL director: John H. Harland Co.; director: Protective Life Corp.; director: Birmingham Airport Authority; chief executive officer: Clow Corp.

Foundation Officials
John J. McMahon, Jr.: trustee (see above)
C. Phillip McWane: trustee

Grants Analysis
Disclosure Period: calendar year ending 2003
Total Grants: $2,034,500*
Number of Grants: 36
Average Grant: $11,703*
Highest Grant: $600,000
Lowest Grant: $500
Typical Range: $1,000 to $20,000
*Note: Average grant figure excludes four highest grants ($1,660,000).

Recent Grants
Note: Grants derived from 2003 Form 990.

General
600,000	A Education for Alabama, Birmingham, AL
600,000	McWane Center, Birmingham, AL
260,000	Vulcan Park, Birmingham, AL
200,000	University of Alabama at Birmingham, Birmingham, AL
85,000	AAR Counseling Services, Naples, FL
52,000	Birmingham Southern College, Birmingham, AL
50,000	Childrens Hospital, AL
30,000	Alabama Symphony Orchestra, Birmingham, AL
24,000	Auburn University, Auburn, AL
20,000	Birmingham Episcopal Campus Ministries, Birmingham, AL

MDU RESOURCES GROUP INC.

Company Headquarters

PO Box 5650
Bismarck, ND 58506-5650
Web: http://www.mdures.com

Company Description

Founded: 1924
Ticker: MDU
Exchange: NYSE
Assets: US$2.937 billion (2002)
Employees: 7797 (2003)
SIC(s): 1221 Bituminous Coal & Lignite--Surface, 1442 Construction Sand & Gravel, 4911 Electric Services.

Nonmonetary Support

Type: Loaned Employees; Loaned Executives

MDU Resources Foundation

Giving Contact

Robert E. Wood, President
PO Box 5650
Bismarck, ND 58506-5650
Phone: (701)222-7828
Fax: (701)222-7607
E-mail: robert.wood@mduresources.com
Web: http://www.mdu.com/the_vision/vision_foundation.htm

Description

EIN: 450378937
Organization Type: Corporate Foundation
Giving Locations: near operating locations.
Grant Types: Award, Capital, Challenge, General Support, Multiyear/Continuing Support, Operating Expenses.

Financial Summary

Total Giving: $834,657 (2003); $732,557 (2002); $525,897 (2001)
Giving Analysis: Giving for 2002 includes: foundation grants to United Way ($38,650); foundation scholarships ($91,930); 2001: foundation grants to United Way ($32,322); foundation scholarships ($52,350); foundation ($441,225).
Assets: $2,526,840 (2003); $2,286,419 (2002); $2,009,633 (2001)
Gifts Received: $1,059,960 (2003); $955,287 (2002); $674,445 (2001). Note: In 2003, contributions were received from MDU Resources Group, Inc. ($154,008), Utiltiy Services, Inc. ($81,644), Knife River Corp. ($294,088), and Williston Basin Interstate Pipeline Co. ($530,220). In 2002, contributions were received from MDU Resources Group, Inc. ($173,096), Utility Services, Inc. ($78,560), Knife River Corp. ($236,200), Williston Basin Interstate Pipeline Company ($466,624), and Prairielands Energy Marketing, Inc. ($807). In 2001, contributions were received from MDU Resources Group, Inc. ($139,820), Utility Services, Inc. ($47,912), Knife River Corp. ($211,588), Williston Basin Interstate Pipeline Company ($138,540), WBI Production, Inc. ($26,670), Prairielands Energy Marketing, Inc. ($2,421), and Fidelity Oil Co. ($107,404). In 1999, contributions were received from MDU Resources Group ($129,252), Utility Services Inc. ($10,018), Knife River Corp. ($104,342), WBI Energy Services Inc. ($4,863), and Fidelity Oil Co. ($85,777). In 1996, contributions were received from MDU Resources Group ($69,453), Williston Basin Interstate Pipeline Co. ($47,074), Knife River Coal Mining Co. ($60,467), KRC Holdings ($6,452), and Fidelity Oil Co. ($133,918).

Typical Recipients

Arts & Humanities: Arts Associations & Councils, Arts Centers, Ballet, Arts & Humanities-General, Historic Preservation, History & Archaeology, Libraries, Museums/Galleries, Music, Opera, Performing Arts, Public Broadcasting
Civic & Public Affairs: Botanical Gardens/Parks, Business/Free Enterprise, Community Foundations, Civic & Public Affairs-General, Housing, Municipalities/Towns, Parades/Festivals, Urban & Community Affairs, Zoos/Aquariums
Education: Business Education, Colleges & Universities, Community & Junior Colleges, Education Funds, Elementary Education (Private), Elementary Education (Public), Engineering/Technological Education, Education-General, Leadership Training, Medical Education, Private Education (Precollege), Public Education (Precollege), Religious Education, Science/Mathematics Education, Student Aid
Environment: Protection, Resource Conservation, Watershed, Wildlife Protection
Health: Alzheimer's Disease, Children's Health/Hospitals, Clinics/Medical Centers, Emergency/Ambulance Services, Eyes/Blindness, Health-General, Health Policy/Cost Containment, Health Funds, Health Organizations, Hospitals, Long-Term Care, Medical Rehabilitation, Mental Health, Public Health, Research/Studies Institutes
Religion: Churches, Religious Welfare
Science: Scientific Research
Social Services: Animal Protection, Camps, Child Welfare, Community Centers, Community Service Organizations, Domestic Violence, Family Services, Food/Clothing Distribution, Homes, People with Disabilities, Recreation & Athletics, Scouts, Senior Services, Social Services-General, Special Olympics, United Funds/United Ways, YMCA/YWCA/YMHA/YWHA, Youth Organizations

Application Procedures

Initial Contact: Request application form.
Application Requirements: Include proof of tax-exempt status.
Deadlines: None.

Restrictions

Does not support individuals, athletics, labor, fraternal organizations, veterans, political or lobbying groups, religious organizations, economic development, or requests for loans, venture capital, or loan pool participation.

Additional Information

Provides scholarships to children and spouses of active, full-time employees of MDU Resources Group and its subsidiaries and divisions.
Publications: Application Form; Guidelines

Corporate Officials

Douglas C. Kane: executive vice president, chief operating officer, director PRIM CORP EMPL executive vice president, chief operating officer, director: MDU Resources Group.
Warren L. Robinson: executive vice president, treasurer, chief financial officer B Logan, UT 1950. ED Brigham Young University (1974); Boise State University (1976). PRIM CORP EMPL vice president, treasurer, chief financial officer: MDU Resources Group. CORP AFFIL treasurer, assistant secretary: Fidelity Oil Holdings; treasurer, assistant secretary: Centennial Energy Holdings; treasurer, assistant secretary: Fidelity Oil Co. NONPR AFFIL member: National Investor Relations Institute; secretary, treasurer: Prairielands Energy Marketing; member: Financial Executives Institute. CLUB AFFIL Elks Club; Rotary Club.

Foundation Officials

Wanda Benz: assistant secretary
Dennis W. Boyd: vice president, secretary
John K. Castleberry: director

Terry Dean Hildestad: director B Dickinson, ND 1949. ED Dickinson State University (1971). PRIM CORP EMPL president, chief executive officer: Knife River Coal Mining Co. CORP AFFIL president, chief executive officer: KRC Aggregate. CLUB AFFIL mem: Elks Club.
Lester H. Loble, II: director
Douglass A. Mahowald: assistant treasurer
Warren L. Robinson: secretary, treasurer, director (see above)
Ronald D. Tipton: director
Robert Elkington Wood, II: president, director B Houston, TX 1938. ED Princeton University (1960).

Grants Analysis

Disclosure Period: calendar year ending 2003
Total Grants: $733,341*
Number of Grants: 365
Average Grant: $2,009
Highest Grant: $25,000
Lowest Grant: $50
Typical Range: $500 to $5,000
*Note: Giving excludes scholarships and United Way.

Recent Grants

Note: Grants derived from 2003 Form 990.
Library-Related
10,000	Library Foundation, Bismarck, ND

General
25,000	Bismarck State College Foundation, Bismarck, ND
25,000	Northern Plains Ballet, Bismarck, ND
20,000	CentraCare Health Foundation, St. Cloud, MN
20,000	Dickinson Building Authority, Dickinson, ND
20,000	SCTC Foundation, St. Cloud, MN
17,500	ND Lewis and Clark Bicentennial Foundation, Washburn, ND
15,000	Bis-Mdn Orchestral Association, Bismarck, ND
11,150	Missouri Slope Areawide United Way, Bismarck, ND
10,000	Aloha United Way, Honolulu, HI
10,000	Dickinson State University Foundation Inc., Dickinson, ND

GILBERT AND JAYLEE MEAD FAMILY FOUNDATION

Giving Contact

Linda Smith, Grants Manager
2700 Virginia Ave. NW, No. 701
Washington, DC 20037
Phone: (202)338-0398
Fax: (202)338-4407
E-mail: jayleemead@aol.com

Description

Founded: 1989
EIN: 521646030
Organization Type: Private Foundation
Giving Locations: DC: Washington; MD: Montgomery County
Grant Types: General Support.

Donor Information

Founder: Established in 1989 by Gilbert D. Mead and Jaylee M. Mead.

Financial Summary

Total Giving: $891,100 (2001)
Assets: $18,253,213 (2001)
Gifts Received: $50,014 (2001); $7,346,859 (2000);

$740,000 (1999). Note: In 2001, contributions were received from Gilbert and Jaylee Mead ($20,000); Elizabeth Mead ($10,007); Diana Mead-Siohan ($10,000); and Marilyn Mead ($10,007). In 2000, contributions were received from Gilbert and Jaylee Mead ($7,314,644), Elizabeth Mead ($10,0005), Diana Mead-Siohan ($12,210) and Marilyn Mead ($10,000). In 1998 and 1999, contributions were received from Gilbert and Jaylee Mead, Elizabeth Mead ($10,000), and Diane Mead-Siohan ($10,000).

Typical Recipients

Arts & Humanities: Arts Associations & Councils, Arts Centers, Arts Funds, Arts Outreach, Dance, Libraries, Museums/Galleries, Music, Opera, Performing Arts, Theater, Visual Arts
Civic & Public Affairs: Asian American Affairs, Economic Development, Employment/Job Training, Civic & Public Affairs-General, Housing, Inner-City Development, Safety, Urban & Community Affairs
Education: Afterschool/Enrichment Programs, Arts/Humanities Education, Education Associations, Education-General, International Exchange, International Studies, Leadership Training, Literacy, Minority Education, Preschool Education, Private Education (Precollege), Science/Mathematics Education, Secondary Education (Public), Student Aid
Environment: Environment-General
Health: AIDS/HIV, Children's Health/Hospitals, Eyes/Blindness, Hospices, Mental Health, Single-Disease Health Associations
International: Foreign Arts Organizations, Foreign Educational Institutions, International-General, Health Care/Hospitals, International Organizations, International Relief Efforts
Religion: Ministries, Religious Welfare
Social Services: At-Risk Youth, Child Abuse, Child Welfare, Community Service Organizations, Crime Prevention, Day Care, Family Planning, Family Services, Food/Clothing Distribution, Homes, Recreation & Athletics, Sexual Abuse, Substance Abuse, Youth Organizations

Application Procedures

Initial Contact: New applicants should first send a brief letter of inquiry describing the organization, the intended project, anticipated costs, and proof of tax-exempt status at least four weeks before the deadlines. A board member will contact the organization regarding the inquiry.
Application Requirements: Proposals must contain a cover sheet that includes contact information, amount requested, and purpose of funds sought. Also include a detailed budget; copy of IRS determination letter; financial statements from the previous year; a full description of the purpose of funds sought and expected accomplishments and means of evaluation; a list of officers; and a list of foundations who made grants in the previous fiscal year, including amounts. Include any additional information, such as brochures, newsletters, or newspaper clippings.
Deadlines: June 15 and December 15 for proposals; May 1 and November 1 for letters of inquiry.
Evaluative Criteria: Grants manager will respond to letters of inquiry. Once a proposal is submitted (with approval), applicants will be notified of status in August (those who submit by June 15) or February (those who submit by December 15).

Restrictions

Grants are not made to individuals. Do not submit proposals or letters via fax or e-mail. First-time grants are in the $5,000 range and are restricted to Washington, DC, and Montgomery County, MD. Previous grantees may request up to $10,000.

Additional Information

Publications: Proposal Guidelines

Foundation Officials

Elizabeth Mead: president, treasurer, director
Gilbert Dunbar Mead: chairman, director B Madi-

son, WI 1930. ED Yale University BS (1952); University of California at Berkeley PhD (1962); University of Maryland JD (1991). CORP AFFIL director, chairman audit committee: Consolidated Papers. NONPR AFFIL member: American Geophysics Union; member: Maryland State Bar Association.
Jaylee M. Mead: vice president, director
Marilyn K. Mead: director
Diana Mead-Siohan: secretary, director

Grants Analysis

Disclosure Period: calendar year ending 2001
Total Grants: $891,100
Number of Grants: 96
Average Grant: $9,282
Highest Grant: $30,000
Typical Range: $1,000 to $15,000

Recent Grants

Note: Grants derived from 2001 Form 990.
General

50,000	Food for the Hungry, Scottsdale, AZ -- school dormitory and library expansion in Bolivia
30,000	Community Development Support Collaborative, Washington, DC -- revitalization of DC neighborhoods
25,000	Hospice Caring, Gaithersburg, MD -- staff to develop and direct model hospice day program in new facility
25,000	Mercy Ships, Garden Valley, TX -- improvement of school facilities for children of crew on medical ship in Africa
12,000	Center for Artistry in Teaching, Washington, DC -- general operating expenses to support innovative teaching in public schools
12,000	For Love of Children, Washington, DC -- expansion of after-school tutoring program
12,000	Heads Up, Washington, DC -- mentoring/tutoring program partnering university students with teens living in public housing
12,000	KHI Services, Rockville, MD -- wilderness challenge program for troubled youth
12,000	Lutheran Social Services of the National Capital Area - Family Friends Program, Washington, DC -- family respite program pairing seniors and families of children with disabilities
12,000	Martha's Table, Washington, DC -- programs for low-income children and families

GILES W. AND ELISE G. MEAD FOUNDATION

Giving Contact

Ms. Parry W. Mead, Vice President
PO Box 2218
Napa, CA 94558
Phone: (707)226-2164
Web: http://www.gileswmeadfoundation.org

Description

Founded: 1961
EIN: 956040921
Organization Type: Private Foundation
Giving Locations: Western North America.
Grant Types: General Support.

Donor Information

Founder: the late Elise G. Mead

Financial Summary

Total Giving: $866,723 (fiscal year ending October 31, 2004); $1,309,790 (fiscal 2001)

Assets: $20,929,949 (fiscal 2004); $19,693,731 (fiscal 2001)

Typical Recipients

Arts & Humanities: Museums/Galleries
Civic & Public Affairs: Botanical Gardens/Parks, Civic & Public Affairs-General, Housing, Law & Justice, Public Policy
Education: Colleges & Universities, Environmental Education, Private Education (Precollege), Public Education (Precollege), Science/Mathematics Education
Environment: Air/Water Quality, Forestry, Environment-General, Protection, Research, Resource Conservation, Watershed, Wildlife Protection
Health: Diabetes
International: Health Care/Hospitals, International Environmental Issues
Religion: Churches, Religious Welfare
Science: Science Museums, Scientific Centers & Institutes, Scientific Organizations
Social Services: Child Welfare, Senior Services, Youth Organizations

Application Procedures

Initial Contact: Send a brief letter of inquiry.
Application Requirements: Include information on a description of organization, amount requested, time frame of project, other funding sources, proof of tax-exempt status, list of staff directors associated with project (including affiliation or expertise), and recently audited financial statement.
Deadlines: The Board meets in January, June, and October to review proposals.

Restrictions

Does not support individuals, provide loans, local or regional environmental organizations outside the Western U.S., individuals or for general operating expenses.

Additional Information

Supports environmentally oriented organizations with an emphasis on problems in western North America. Funding in areas such as science, education, and the arts is limited to grants proposals initiated by individual Board members.
Publications: Application and program guidelines.

Foundation Officials

Clader M. Mackay: president
Richard N. Mackay: secretary, treasurer
Jane W. Mead: vice president
Parry W. Mead: vice president

Grants Analysis

Disclosure Period: fiscal year ending October 31, 2004
Total Grants: $866,723
Number of Grants: 33
Average Grant: $19,636*
Highest Grant: $150,000
Lowest Grant: $915
Typical Range: $10,000 to $50,000
*Note: Average grant figure excludes two highest grants ($258,000).

Recent Grants

Note: Grants derived from 2004 Form 990.
General

150,000	Epiphany School, Seattle, WA
108,000	Juvenile Diabetes Research Foundation International, New York, NY
75,000	Juvenile Justice Network, Napa, CA
75,000	Land Trust of Napa County, Napa, CA
50,000	Little Sisters of the Poor, San Pedro, CA
50,000	University of Utah, Salt Lake City, UT
30,000	Amigos Bravos, Taos, NM
27,500	Ecotrust of Canada, Portland, OR
25,000	Point Reyes National Seashore, Pt. Reyes Station, CA

25,000   River Network for Canadian Parks, Portland, OR

THE MEADOWS FOUNDATION

Giving Contact

Bruce H. Esterline, Vice President, Grants
3003 Swiss Avenue
Dallas, TX 75204-6049
Phone: (214)826-9431
Fax: (214)827-7042
E-mail: grants@mfi.org
Web: http://www.mfi.org

Alternate Contact

Phone: 800-826-9431
Note: Toll-free number for calls from outside the Dallas, TX area.

Description

Founded: 1948
EIN: 756015322
Organization Type: Family Foundation
Giving Locations: TX: emphasis on Dallas
Grant Types: Award, Capital, Challenge, Emergency, Employee Matching Gifts, Endowment, General Support, Loan, Matching, Multiyear/Continuing Support, Operating Expenses, Project, Research.

Donor Information

Founder: The Meadows Foundation was incorporated in 1948 by the late Algur Hurtle Meadows and his first wife, the late Virginia Meadows. Mr. Meadows helped found the General American Oil Company of Texas in 1936 and diversified its corporate empire into mortgage banking, insurance, real estate, and crude oil and gas development. Mr. Meadows was named chairman of General American Oil in 1950, and most of the foundation's original assets were securities of the company. The company was purchased by Phillips Petroleum in 1983 and dissolved as a corporate entity.

Mr. Meadows was interested in art, and over the years donated millions of dollars to Southern Methodist University for the Meadows Museum (developed as a memorial to his first wife) for art acquisitions, the museum's endowment, and for Southern Methodist University's School of Arts. Until his death in 1978, Mr. Meadows was the foundation's president.

Financial Summary

Total Giving: $25,500,000 (2004 approx); $29,402,539 (2002); $35,298,406 (2001)
Giving Analysis: Giving for 2002 includes: foundation matching gifts ($79,212); foundation grants to United Way ($242,000)
Assets: $779,225,004 (2003); $694,602,074 (2002); $796,146,859 (2001)

Typical Recipients

Arts & Humanities: Arts Associations & Councils, Arts Centers, Arts Funds, Arts Institutes, Arts Outreach, Ballet, Community Arts, Dance, Ethnic & Folk Arts, Historic Preservation, History & Archaeology, Libraries, Museums/Galleries, Music, Opera, Performing Arts, Public Broadcasting, Theater, Visual Arts
Civic & Public Affairs: Asian American Affairs, Botanical Gardens/Parks, Business/Free Enterprise, Community Foundations, Economic Development, Employment/Job Training, Civic & Public Affairs-General, Hispanic Affairs, Housing, Law & Justice, Legal Aid, Minority Business, Municipalities/Towns, Native American Affairs, Nonprofit Management, Parades/Festivals, Philanthropic Organizations, Public Policy, Safety, Urban & Community Affairs, Women's Affairs, Zoos/Aquariums

Education: Afterschool/Enrichment Programs, Arts/Humanities Education, Colleges & Universities, Community & Junior Colleges, Continuing Education, Education Associations, Education Funds, Education Reform, Elementary Education (Private), Elementary Education (Public), Engineering/Technological Education, Faculty Development, Education-General, Health & Physical Education, Literacy, Medical Education, Minority Education, Preschool Education, Private Education (Precollege), Public Education (Precollege), Science/Mathematics Education, Secondary Education (Private), Secondary Education (Public), Special Education, Student Aid, Vocational & Technical Education
Environment: Air/Water Quality, Forestry, Environment-General, Protection, Research, Resource Conservation, Wildlife Protection
Health: AIDS/HIV, Alzheimer's Disease, Cancer, Children's Health/Hospitals, Clinics/Medical Centers, Diabetes, Emergency/Ambulance Services, Eyes/Blindness, Health-General, Geriatric Health, Health Policy/Cost Containment, Health Funds, Health Organizations, Heart, Home-Care Services, Hospices, Hospitals, Hospitals (University Affiliated), Kidney, Long-Term Care, Medical Training, Mental Health, Outpatient Health Care, Preventive Medicine/Wellness Organizations, Public Health, Single-Disease Health Associations, Speech & Hearing, Transplant Networks/Donor Banks
Religion: Churches, Dioceses, Jewish Causes, Ministries, Religious Organizations, Religious Welfare
Science: Science Museums, Scientific Centers & Institutes, Scientific Research
Social Services: Animal Protection, At-Risk Youth, Camps, Child Abuse, Child Welfare, Community Centers, Community Service Organizations, Counseling, Crime Prevention, Day Care, Delinquency & Criminal Rehabilitation, Domestic Violence, Emergency Relief, Family Planning, Family Services, Food/Clothing Distribution, Homes, People with Disabilities, Recreation & Athletics, Refugee Assistance, Scouts, Senior Services, Shelters/Homelessness, Social Services-General, Special Olympics, Substance Abuse, United Funds/United Ways, Volunteer Services, YMCA/YWCA/YMHA/YWHA, Youth Organizations

Application Procedures

Initial Contact: Contact the foundation or its web site for application guidelines. Applicants should submit one, unbound copy of a proposal describing the project and organization for which funds are sought. The foundation accepts applications submitted over the Internet, but cannot guarantee the confidentiality of information contained in electronic submittals. Applicants for the Charitable Schools Program should contact the foundation or visit the foundation web site to obtain an application form.
Application Requirements: The proposal should include a brief history of the organization and description of existing services; a description of the proposed program, including a statement of need, program components and logistics, and population and number to be served; amount requested and date funds are needed; a list anticipated and committed sources of funding including dollar amounts; project budget listing income and expenses; plans to support the project after the grant period; methods of evaluating the project, including measurable, time-specific goals, a description of information to be collected to measure progress, how that information will be gathered, and (if available) current or baseline levels; a list of trustees or directors and officers including titles for board of directors, profession, ethnicity, and gender; names and qualifications of staff involved with project; organization's current operating budget and year-to-date financial statements; most recent certified audit; and proof of tax-exempt status.
Deadlines: None for general proposals; October 1 for Charitable Schools Program applications.
Review Process: A concise and brief proposal will speed the foundation's processing of a grant applica-

tion. All requests are reviewed as soon as possible after their receipt. The foundation will acknowledge receipt of all applications within a week. The time required to process a proposal is generally three to four months.
Evaluative Criteria: The foundation finds special value in a proposal in which one or more of the following conditions are present: foundation support would be vital or catalytic to a proposed project's success; the project impact is enhanced through a collaborative network; adequate community and other support exists to ensure that the project will be implemented and continue after the grant period; the proposal makes innovative and efficient use of funds; resources are shared with other agencies or groups to reduce expenses; the project is well-planned; the project promotes better human relationships and a sense of community; and the project involves volunteers where appropriate.
Notes: Submit Internet grant applications to grants@mfi.org (no file attachments). A printed copy of the application should follow all electronic submittals.

Restrictions

The foundation's charter requires that the foundation only distribute grants to qualified public entities or 501(c)(3) charities serving the people of Texas. The foundation generally does not favor contributions for church or seminary construction projects, annual fund-raising drives or general sustentation drives, professional conferences and symposia, or out-of-state performances or competition expenses. The foundation does not make grants or loans to individuals, and reports that endowment gifts are rare.

Additional Information

The foundation maintains a twenty-two acre nonprofit agency campus with over twenty-five tenant agencies and a conference center where seminars, workshops, conferences, and proposal writing assistance are available. community; and the program would enhance the capabilities of families and/or foster traditional family values.

The foundation maintains a twenty-two acre nonprofit agency campus with over twenty-five tenant agencies and a conference center where seminars, workshops, conferences, and proposal writing assistance are available.
Publications: Annual Report; Guidelines in English and Spanish and on Audio-Cassette

Foundation Officials

Evelyn Meadows Acton: director emeritus
John W. Broadfoot, Jr.: director CLUB AFFIL member: 99 Club.
Daniel H. Chapman: director, trustee NONPR AFFIL member, estate planning council: Southwestern Medical Foundation.
Judy B. Culbertson: director, trustee
Bruce H. Esterline: vice president grants
Linda Perryman Evans: president, chief executive officer, trustee, director B Dallas, TX 1950. ED University of Texas BS (1972); East Texas State University (1975); Southern Methodist University (1976). NONPR AFFIL director: Equest; director: Texas Business Hall FAME Foundation; member: Dallas Assembly; director: Dallas Citizens Council.
John A. Hammack: trustee, director
Virginia Wilson Hanson: trustee, director
Emily J. Jones: assistant vice president, corporate secretary
Sally Rhodus Lancaster, PhD: director emeritus B Gladewater, TX 1938. ED Southern Methodist University BA (1960); Southern Methodist University MA (1979); East Texas State University PhD (1983). NONPR AFFIL member: Phi Beta Kappa; member: Philosophers Society Texas; director: Institute Nautical Archaeology; member advisory board: Communication Foundation Texas; secretary, amelia island chapter: DAR.
P. Michael McCullough: director, trustee NONPR

AFFIL advisory council: LEAP Foundation.

Curtis W. Meadows, Jr.: director emeritus B 1938. ED University of Texas JD; University of Texas BBA (1962). NONPR AFFIL fellow: American Academy of Arts and Sciences; director: RGK Center for Philanthropy & Community Service.

Eric R. Meadows: director

John M. Meadows: trustee, director

Mark A. Meadows: trustee, director

Robert A. Meadows: chairman, trustee, vice president, director

Sally C. Miller: director emeritus NONPR AFFIL member, honor roll: Carolina Bell Ringers.

William A. Nesbitt: trustee, director NONPR AFFIL chairman, chief executive officer: Central National Bank.

Michael E. Patrick: vice president, chief investment officer CORP AFFIL director: Cooper Energy Services; director: Cooper Turbo Compressor; director: Cooper Cameron Valves; director: BJ Services Co.; director: Cooper Cameron Corp.

G. Tomas Rhodus: director, trustee

Evy Kay Ritzen: director NONPR AFFIL planning director: Target: Kids in Court; advisory panel: Transition Resource Action Center.

Eloise Meadows Rouse: director emeritus B Shreveport, LA 1931. NONPR AFFIL blue ribbon panel: OneStar Foundation.

Robert E. Weiss: vice president admin ED Michigan State University; University of Detroit Law School JD. NONPR AFFIL trustee emeritus: Michigan State University; trustee: Michigan State University-Detroit College of Law.

Dorothy Cheney Wilson: director emeritus B Gardiner, ME 1904. ED Bates College AB (1925).

Grants Analysis

Disclosure Period: calendar year ending 2002
Total Grants: $29,081,327*
Number of Grants: 331*
Average Grant: $80,549*
Highest Grant: $2,500,000
Lowest Grant: $400
Typical Range: $25,000 to $150,000
*Note: Giving excludes United Way and matching gifts. Number of grants excludes awards for charitable schools projects. Average grant figure excludes highest grant.

Recent Grants

Note: Grants derived from 2002 Form 990.
General

2,500,000	Southern Methodist University, Dallas, TX -- funding for constructing a new meadows museum
1,174,125	Lyndon Baines Johnson Foundation, Austin, TX -- toward endowment and start-up funds for education and research
500,000	National Wildlife Federation, Austin, TX -- funding for collaborative, multi-year project
350,000	National Center for Educational Accountability, Austin, TX -- funding for expanding a program for improving the schools
350,000	North Texas Public Broadcasting (KERA-Channel 13), Dallas, TX -- funding for development of curriculum and materials
345,000	Nature Conservancy of Texas, San Antonio, TX -- funding for utility and janitorial expenses
320,000	Texas Scottish Rite Hospital for Crippled Children, Dallas, TX -- toward expanding a pilot program to reduce child abuse
300,000	Dallas Children's Theater, Dallas, TX -- funding for renovating the facility
300,000	Southern Methodist University, Dallas, TX -- funding for mounting temporary exhibits in the museum
275,500	Texas A&M University, College Station, TX -- toward emergency operating support

MORRIS A. MECHANIC FOUNDATION

Giving Contact

Clarisse B. Mechanic, President
PO Box 1623
Baltimore, MD 21203
Phone: (410)837-3913

Description

Founded: 1942
EIN: 526034753
Organization Type: Private Foundation
Giving Locations: MD: Baltimore
Grant Types: General Support.

Donor Information

Founder: the late Morris A. Mechanic

Financial Summary

Total Giving: $169,500 (2002); $176,750 (2001)
Assets: $3,686,345 (2002); $3,812,066 (2001)
Gifts Received: $103,333 (2001); $48,000 (1998); $40,000 (1996). Note: In 1998 and 2001, contributions were received from the estate of Morris A. Mechanic.

Typical Recipients

Arts & Humanities: Arts Associations & Councils, Arts Outreach, Community Arts, Ethnic & Folk Arts, History & Archaeology, Libraries, Museums/Galleries, Music, Opera, Public Broadcasting
Civic & Public Affairs: Civic & Public Affairs-General, Public Policy
Education: Arts/Humanities Education, Colleges & Universities, Economic Education, Education Funds, Education Reform, Elementary Education (Private), Elementary Education (Public), Education-General, Legal Education, Literacy, Private Education (Precollege), Special Education, Student Aid
Health: Arthritis, Cancer, Children's Health/Hospitals, Emergency/Ambulance Services, Health Organizations, Heart, Hospitals, Respiratory, Single-Disease Health Associations
International: International Organizations
Religion: Churches, Religion-General, Religious Organizations, Religious Welfare
Social Services: Child Abuse, Child Welfare, Community Service Organizations, Crime Prevention, Day Care, Domestic Violence, Family Planning, Family Services, Food/Clothing Distribution, People with Disabilities, Scouts, Shelters/Homelessness, United Funds/United Ways, Youth Organizations

Application Procedures

Initial Contact: Requests should be in narrative form explaining in detail the specific programs to which grants would apply and the nature of the organization applying for a grant.
Deadlines: None.

Restrictions

Maximum grant will not exceed $50,000.

Foundation Officials

Blue Baron: secretary
Clarisse B. Mechanic: president

Grants Analysis

Disclosure Period: calendar year ending 2002
Total Grants: $169,500
Number of Grants: 23
Average Grant: $7,370
Highest Grant: $15,000
Lowest Grant: $1,000
Typical Range: $2,000 to $15,000

Recent Grants

Note: Grants derived from 2001 Form 990.

General

21,250	Harbor Hospital, Baltimore, MD
15,000	Baltimore Child Abuse Center, Inc., Baltimore, MD
15,000	Baltimore Mentoring, Baltimore, MD
15,000	Baltimore Symphony, Baltimore, MD
15,000	Lancers Boys Club, Baltimore, MD
15,000	Maryland Public Television, Baltimore, MD
10,000	College of Notre Dame, Baltimore, MD
10,000	Florence Crittenton Services, Baltimore, MD
10,000	Florida Grand Opera, Palm Beach, FL
10,000	Signal 13 Foundation, Baltimore, MD

MEDINA FOUNDATION

Giving Contact

Patricia G. McKay, Executive Director
801 2nd Avenue, Suite 1300
Seattle, WA 98104
Phone: (206)652-8783
Fax: (206)652-8791
E-mail: info@medinafoundation.org
Web: http://www.medinafoundation.org

Description

Founded: 1948
EIN: 910745225
Organization Type: Family Foundation
Giving Locations: WA: greater Puget Sound region
Grant Types: Capital, General Support, Project.

Donor Information

Founder: Norton Clapp, president of the foundation, and other members of the Clapp family incorporated the Medina Foundation in the state of Washington in 1948. Several Clapp family members serve as trustees. The Clapp family are descendants of Matthew G. Clapp, one of the founders of the Weyerhaeuser Company.

Financial Summary

Total Giving: $3,728,945 (2003); $3,453,881 (2001)
Giving Analysis: Giving for 2003 includes: foundation grants to United Way ($50,000)
Assets: $88,611,948 (2003); $91,034,729 (2001)
Gifts Received: $17,693,367 (1998)

Typical Recipients

Arts & Humanities: Libraries, Public Broadcasting
Civic & Public Affairs: Asian American Affairs, Business/Free Enterprise, Clubs, Community Foundations, Economic Development, Employment/Job Training, First Amendment Issues, Civic & Public Affairs-General, Hispanic Affairs, Housing, Legal Aid, Municipalities/Towns, Native American Affairs, Nonprofit Management, Philanthropic Organizations, Professional & Trade Associations, Public Policy, Urban & Community Affairs, Women's Affairs, Zoos/Aquariums
Education: Afterschool/Enrichment Programs, Business Education, Continuing Education, Education Associations, Education Reform, Elementary Education (Private), Education-General, Literacy, Medical Education, Preschool Education, Private Education (Precollege), Public Education (Precollege), Science/Mathematics Education, Secondary Education (Private), Secondary Education (Public), Special Education, Student Aid
Health: Cancer, Children's Health/Hospitals, Clinics/Medical Centers, Emergency/Ambulance Services, Geriatric Health, Health Organizations, Hospitals, Medical Rehabilitation, Mental Health, Preventive Medicine/Wellness Organizations, Single-Disease Health Associations
Religion: Dioceses, Ministries, Religious Organizations, Religious Welfare

Science: Scientific Centers & Institutes

Social Services: At-Risk Youth, Big Brothers/Big Sisters, Child Abuse, Child Welfare, Community Centers, Community Service Organizations, Counseling, Day Care, Delinquency & Criminal Rehabilitation, Domestic Violence, Emergency Relief, Family Services, Food/Clothing Distribution, Homes, People with Disabilities, Recreation & Athletics, Refugee Assistance, Scouts, Senior Services, Shelters/Homelessness, Social Services-General, Substance Abuse, Volunteer Services, YMCA/YWCA/YMHA/YWHA, Youth Organizations

Application Procedures

Initial Contact: Submit a brief letter.

Application Requirements: The letter should include a description of the proposed project and request.

Deadlines: None.

Review Process: The foundation gives preference to direct service delivery programs over capital requests. If the program falls within the foundation's interests, an application form will be sent.

Restrictions

Grants are not made to individuals. The foundation limits its grantmaking to the greater Puget Sound region. The foundation lists the following top limits on individual grants in a single year: 10% of project operating budget, including private and government funds; 15% of start-up or program expansion budget, including private and government funds; 10% of an applicant's capital budget including private and government funds not to exceed a total of $25,000 (normally made on a contingency basis); and in no event more than 25% of total private funding.

Additional Information

Publications: Application Guidelines

Foundation Officials

Jacqueline Clapp: trustee

James N. Clapp, II: trustee

Matthew N. Clapp, Jr.: trustee CORP AFFIL officer: Pioneer Broadcasting Co.

Tamsin O. Clapp: trustee

Marion Hand: trustee

Patricia M. Henry: secretary, trustee

Gary MacLeod: treasurer PRIM CORP EMPL chairman: Norton Laird Trust Co. CORP AFFIL director: Northwest Building Corp.

Grants Analysis

Disclosure Period: calendar year ending 2003

Total Grants: $3,678,945*

Number of Grants: 134

Average Grant: $24,083*

Highest Grant: $300,000

Lowest Grant: $1,500

Typical Range: $5,000 to $50,000

*Note: Giving excludes United Way. Average grant figure excludes two highest grants ($500,000).

Recent Grants

Note: Grants derived from 2002 Form 990.

General

300,000	One Childhood
150,000	Seattle Foundation, Seattle, WA
100,000	First Place
100,000	NPower, Seattle, WA
100,000	YMCA of Tacoma-Pierce County, Tacoma, WA
90,000	Boy Scouts of America-Pacific Harbors Council, Tacoma, WA
85,000	Vision House, Renton, WA
81,000	Coalition Community
80,000	Salvation Army-Tacoma Pierce County, Seattle, WA
77,000	Northwest Harvest, Seattle, WA

MEDTRONIC INC.

Company Headquarters

710 Medtronic Parkway NE
Minneapolis, MN 55432-5604
Web: http://www.medtronic.com

Company Description

Founded: 1949

Ticker: MDT

Exchange: NYSE

Revenue: US$9.087 billion (2004)

Profit: US$1.959 billion (2004)

Employees: 30000 (2003)

Fortune Rank: 246, per FORTUNE Magazine's list of 500 Largest U.S. Corporations (2004).

Nonmonetary Support

Value: $2,357,000 (2002); $1,300,000 (1998)

Type: Donated Products

Volunteer Programs: The foundation's Medtronic Time-n-Talent Fund donates $500 to qualifying nonprofit organizations at which an employee or retiree volunteers at least 40 hours per year. If a volunteer who has donated 40 hours and also makes a financial contribution of $25 to $500 to the same organization, the foundation will match the contribution.

Note: Medtronic businesses make decisions regarding product donations.

Medtronic Foundation

Giving Contact

Penny Hunt, Foundation Executive Director & Vice President, Community Affairs
Medtronic Foundation
710 Medtronic Parkway
MS LC110
Minneapolis, MN 55432-5604
Phone: (763)505-2640
Fax: (763)505-2648
Web: http://www.medtronic.com/foundation

Description

EIN: 411306950

Organization Type: Corporate Foundation

Giving Locations: MN: Minneapolis metropolitan area, St. Paul metropolitan area internationally in Medtronic plant communities; nationally in Medtronic plant communities.

Grant Types: Employee Matching Gifts, Fellowship, General Support, Multiyear/Continuing Support, Project, Scholarship.

Note: The foundation matches gifts to educational institutions up to $7,000 per employee annually.

Donor Information

Founder: Organized by the company in 1978.

Financial Summary

Total Giving: $17,644,568 (fiscal year ending April 30, 2004); $16,564,610 (fiscal 2003); $15,134,120 (fiscal 2002). Note: Contributes through corporate direct giving program and foundation.

Giving Analysis: Giving for fiscal 2001 includes: foundation ($14,045,759)

Assets: $23,355,016 (fiscal 2004); $41,484,986 (fiscal 2003); $58,790,098 (fiscal 2002)

Gifts Received: $5,000 (fiscal 2003); $47,580,000 (fiscal 2002); $20,400,000 (fiscal 2001). Note: Contributions are received from Medtronic, Inc. In 2003, contributions were received from Georgia Institute of Technology.

Typical Recipients

Arts & Humanities: Arts Centers, Arts Institutes, Arts Outreach, Community Arts, Arts & Humanities-General, Libraries, Museums/Galleries, Music, Opera, Performing Arts, Public Broadcasting, Theater, Visual Arts

Civic & Public Affairs: African American Affairs, Botanical Gardens/Parks, Community Foundations, Economic Development, Employment/Job Training, Civic & Public Affairs-General, Hispanic Affairs, Housing, Municipalities/Towns, Safety, Urban & Community Affairs, Zoos/Aquariums

Education: Arts/Humanities Education, Business Education, Colleges & Universities, Community & Junior Colleges, Education Associations, Education Funds, Education Reform, Elementary Education (Private), Engineering/Technological Education, Faculty Development, Education-General, Health & Physical Education, International Exchange, Literacy, Medical Education, Minority Education, Private Education (Precollege), Public Education (Precollege), Science/Mathematics Education, Secondary Education (Public), Social Sciences Education, Student Aid

Health: Adolescent Health Issues, AIDS/HIV, Cancer, Children's Health/Hospitals, Clinics/Medical Centers, Diabetes, Emergency/Ambulance Services, Health-General, Geriatric Health, Health Policy/Cost Containment, Health Funds, Health Organizations, Heart, Hospices, Hospitals, Hospitals (University Affiliated), Long-Term Care, Medical Rehabilitation, Medical Research, Multiple Sclerosis, Nursing Services, Preventive Medicine/Wellness Organizations, Public Health, Research/Studies Institutes, Single-Disease Health Associations, Trauma Treatment

International: Foreign Educational Institutions, International-General, Health Care/Hospitals, Human Rights, International Affairs, International Development, International Environmental Issues, International Relief Efforts

Religion: Religious Welfare

Science: Science Exhibits & Fairs, Science Museums, Scientific Centers & Institutes

Social Services: At-Risk Youth, Community Centers, Community Service Organizations, Emergency Relief, Family Services, Food/Clothing Distribution, People with Disabilities, Senior Services, Social Services-General, United Funds/United Ways, Volunteer Services, YMCA/YWCA/YMHA/YWHA, Youth Organizations

Application Procedures

Initial Contact: See the foundation's web site for application form and guidelines (or apply using the Minnesota Common Application Form), then send written proposal.

Application Requirements: Submit a description of organization; all previous Medtronic Foundation grants received by organization; current requested amount of funds and purpose for their use; project description, including constituents served, geographic area, use of volunteers, and major accomplishments; implementation timetable; evaluation criteria; organization's current operating budget, including income (with top five donors and amounts given), and anticipated expenses; budget for proposed project, including income, expenses and grants pending; for requests for renewal of support provide brief but specific report on results of grant; copy of IRS 501(c)(3) nonprofit determination letter; list of officers and directors and their affiliations; latest annual report; most recent audited financial statement; any other information that aids in understanding how the organization or program operates.

Deadlines: None for employee committees outside the Twin Cities; January 15, July 15, and October 15 for Twin Cities and national programs; July 18 for Community Arts Program requests; October 15 for HeartRescue requests.

Review Process: Requests are reviewed by staff, then go to appropriate committee and, if necessary, to the foundation board; the board is comprised of members of Medtronic's management; and foundation has four standing committees, comprised of company employees and the board members; employee committees in communities outside Minneapolis-St. Paul determine grants up to $20,000 in their communities.

Evaluative Criteria: Programs that receive funds usually support a Medtronic focus area of emphasis; are innovative, yet simple in design; address factors causing problems in lives of people; are developed or implemented with assistance of Medtronic employees; and serve as a model that could be replicated in other communities.
Decision Notification: Generally within 90 days of receipt.

Restrictions

The foundation does not support capital or capital projects; fiscal agents; fundraising events/activities; social events, or goodwill advertising; general operating support; general support of educational institutions; Greater Twin Cities United Way-supported programs; individuals, including scholarships for individuals; lobbying, political, or fraternal activities; long-term counseling or personal development; program endowments; purchases of automatic external defibrillators (AEDs); religious groups for religious purposes.

Additional Information

Company is committed to contributing at least 2% of pretax profits to charitable organizations.
Company sponsors employee volunteer programs and supports minority vendors whenever possible.
For direct gifts, a committee--comprised of the company's president and CEO, company's vice-chairman, and the foundation's chairman--considers grant requests. Most contributions are for one-time projects or events and to organizations supported by employees in their communities. Some corporate contributions are leveraged with additional support from public relations, employee relations, or customer relations. Medtronic facilities also provide some contributions to projects and programs in their immediate vicinity and are generally less than $250.
Publications: Medtronic Community Affairs Annual Report; Application Form; Medtronic Foundation Matching Gifts to Education Programs; Foundation Guidelines; Matching Gifts to Education Form

Corporate Officials

Arthur D. Collins, Jr.: chairman, chief executive officerhuman resources B December 10, 1947. ED Duke University BA (1969); University of Virginia MBA (1973). PRIM CORP EMPL chairman, chief executive officer: Medtronic Inc. CORP AFFIL director: Cargill Inc.; director: U.S. Bancorp. NONPR AFFIL chairman: Advanced Medicine Technology Industry Association; board overseers: Wharton School at University of Pennsylvania.
Janet S. Fiola: senior vice president human resources PRIM CORP EMPL senior vice president human resources: Medtronic Inc. NONPR AFFIL trustee: College of St. Benedict & St. John's University.

Giving Program Officials

Penny A. Hunt: executive director staff ED Carleton College BA; Duke University MA; William Mitchell College of Law JD. PRIM CORP EMPL executive director community affairs: Medtronic, Inc.

Foundation Officials

Arthur D. Collins, Jr.: director (see above)
David Etzwiler: director
Janet S. Fiola: director NONPR AFFIL trustee: College of St. Benedict & St. John's University.
Douglas Hoekstra: treasurer
Penny A. Hunt: executive director, secretary (see above)
Steven B. Kelmer: director
Steve Mahle: director
Steve Oesterle: director
Scott Ward: director

Grants Analysis

Disclosure Period: fiscal year ending April 30, 2004
Total Grants: $12,798,197*

Number of Grants: 615 (approx)
Average Grant: $20,810
Highest Grant: $550,000
Lowest Grant: $250
Typical Range: $1,000 to $50,000 and $100,000 to $250,000
*Note: Giving excludes matching gifts, scholarship, nonmonetary support, and United Way.

Recent Grants

Note: Grants derived from fiscal 2004 Form 990.
Library-Related

75,000	Bakken Library and Museum, Minneapolis, MN

General

730,441	United Way International, Alexandria, VA
550,000	North American Society of Pacing and Electrophysiology, Washington, DC
350,000	Project Health Opportunities for People Everywhere, Millwood, VA
300,000	Minnesota Medical Foundation, Minneapolis, MN
255,000	Morehouse School of Medicine, Atlanta, GA
250,600	National Organization for Rare Disorders, Danbury, CT
246,000	National Black Women's Health Project, Washington, DC
238,000	Guthrie Theater, Minneapolis, MN
222,654	Valley of the Sun United Way, Phoenix, AZ
221,000	Public Radio International, Minneapolis, MN

RICHARD MEIER FOUNDATION

Giving Contact

Richard Meier, Trustee
475 Tenth Avenue, Floor 6
New York, NY 10018-1120
Phone: (212)967-6060

Description

Founded: 1997
EIN: 133978415
Organization Type: Private Foundation
Giving Locations: CT; MA; NY
Grant Types: General Support.

Financial Summary

Total Giving: $56,625 (2001)
Assets: $1,292,540 (2001)
Gifts Received: $1,047,750 (1997). Note: In 1997, contributions were received from Richard Meier.

Typical Recipients

Arts & Humanities: Arts & Humanities-General, History & Archaeology, Libraries, Museums/Galleries, Public Broadcasting
Civic & Public Affairs: Civic & Public Affairs-General
Education: Arts/Humanities Education, Colleges & Universities, International Exchange
Social Services: Community Service Organizations, Social Services-General, Substance Abuse

Application Procedures

Initial Contact: Send a brief letter of inquiry.
Deadlines: None.

Restrictions

Foundation does not support organizations that are not 501(c)3 organizations.

Foundation Officials

Sanford B. Ehrenkranz: trustee
Richard Meier: trustee

Grants Analysis

Disclosure Period: calendar year ending 2001
Total Grants: $56,625
Number of Grants: 17
Average Grant: $2,412*
Highest Grant: $10,000
Lowest Grant: $125
Typical Range: $500 to $5,000
*Note: Average grant excludes two highest grants ($20,000).

Recent Grants

Note: Grants derived from 2001 Form 990.
Library-Related

2,500	Museum of Modern Art, New York, NY
500	Pencil, Inc., New York, NY

General

10,000	Cooper Hewitt national Design Museum, New York, NY
10,000	Huggy Bears, New York, NY
8,500	National Design Museum, New York, NY
5,000	American Academy in Rome, New York, NY
5,000	Cornell University, Ithaca, NY
5,000	Cornell University, Ithaca, NY
5,000	Yale University, Hartford, CT
1,000	American Academy of Arts and Science, Cambridge, MA
1,000	MUSE Film & Television, New York, NY
1,000	National Center on Addiction and Substance Abuse, New York, NY

MEINDERS FOUNDATION

Giving Contact

Mo Grotjohn, Executive Director & Treasurer
4101 Perimeter Ctr. Drive, Suite 210
Oklahoma City, OK 73112
Phone: (405)947-2422

Description

Founded: 1994
EIN: 731438459
Organization Type: Private Foundation
Giving Locations: OK
Grant Types: General Support.

Donor Information

Founder: Established in 1994 by Herman Meinders.

Financial Summary

Total Giving: $2,763,864 (2003); $843,899 (2001)
Assets: $6,946,745 (2003); $11,981,459 (2001)
Gifts Received: $395,800 (2000); $800,000 (1995); $7,029,550 (1994). Note: In 1995 and 2000, contributions were received from Herman Meinders.

Typical Recipients

Arts & Humanities: Arts Associations & Councils, Museums/Galleries, Music
Civic & Public Affairs: Botanical Gardens/Parks, Civic & Public Affairs-General, Housing
Education: Agricultural Education, Business Education, Colleges & Universities, Faculty Development, Education-General, Science/Mathematics Education
Environment: Forestry, Environment-General
Health: Clinics/Medical Centers, Emergency/Ambulance Services
Religion: Churches, Ministries, Religious Welfare, Seminaries
Science: Science Museums
Social Services: Child Welfare, Family Services, Social Services-General, YMCA/YWCA/YMHA/YWHA

Application Procedures

Initial Contact: Send a brief letter of inquiry. Include a description of organization, amount requested, purpose of funds sought, recently audited financial state-

ment, and proof of tax-exempt status. There are no deadlines.
Deadlines: None.

Foundation Officials
Mo Grotjohn: executive director, treasurer
Herman Meinders: president, trustee
LaDonna Meinders: vice president, trustee
Robert Meinders: secretary, trustee

Grants Analysis
Disclosure Period: calendar year ending 2003
Total Grants: $2,763,864
Number of Grants: 21
Average Grant: $32,955*
Highest Grant: $1,453,631
Lowest Grant: $1,000
Typical Range: $10,000 to $50,000
*Note:** Average grant figure excludes four highest grants ($2,203,631).

Recent Grants
Note: Grants derived from 2003 Form 990.
General
1,453,631	Oklahoma City University, Oklahoma City, OK -- for Meinders school of business technology and furnishings
400,000	Phillips Theological Seminary, Tulsa, OK -- to build chapel
250,000	Pipestone - Jasper School District, Pipestone, MN -- for new library
100,000	Concordia Seminary, St. Louis, MO
72,183	Oklahoma City University, Oklahoma City, OK -- for campus expansion program
40,000	YMCA of Oklahoma City, Oklahoma City, OK
30,000	Lutheran Hour Ministries, St. Louis, MO
30,000	Oklahoma City University, Oklahoma City, OK -- for nursing school
25,000	Canterbury Choral Society, Oklahoma City, OK
25,000	Phillips Theological Seminary, Tulsa, OK

EDWARD ARTHUR MELLINGER EDUCATIONAL FOUNDATION

Giving Contact
Selection Committee
1025 E. Broadway
PO Box 770
Monmouth, IL 61462
Phone: (309)734-2419
Fax: (309)734-4435
E-mail: info@mellinger.org
Web: http://www.mellinger.org

Description
Founded: 1959
EIN: 362428421
Organization Type: Private Foundation
Giving Locations: limited to students residing in western Illinois and eastern Iowa.
Grant Types: Loan, Scholarship.

Donor Information
Founder: the late Mrs. Inez M. Hensleigh

Financial Summary
Gifts Received: $50 (2000); $493 (1999); $23,189 (1998). Note: In 1998, contributions were received from Jeffrey's Trust ($22,803).

Typical Recipients
Arts & Humanities: Libraries
Education: Colleges & Universities, Medical Education, Science/Mathematics Education

Application Procedures
Initial Contact: Request application form.
Deadlines: May 1.

Additional Information
Provides scholarships to individuals for higher education.
Publications: Application Guidelines; Program Policy Statement

Foundation Officials
David D. Fleming: president
Tom Johnson: trustee, secretary
Wyatt Thomas Johnson, Jr.: secretary, trustee B Macon, GA 1941. ED University of Georgia AB (1963); Harvard University MBA (1965). PRIM CORP EMPL president, director: Cable News Network. NONPR AFFIL director: Mayo Foundation; member: Sigma Nu; chairman: John S. & James Knight Foundation; member: Georgia Alumni Society; chairman: Lyndon B. Johnson Foundation; member: Council Foreign Relations.
Mary Frances Miller: trustee
Arthur W. Murray: trustee
Charles Slamar, Jr.: trustee
Gary Willhardt, PhD: trustee
Merle R. Yontz: vice president, trustee

Grants Analysis
Disclosure Period: calendar year ending 2000
Total Grants: $366,700*
Number of Grants: 5
Highest Grant: $360,000
Lowest Grant: $700
*Note:** Giving excludes scholarships.

Recent Grants
Note: Grants derived from 2001 Form 990.
General
3,750	Illinois College of Optometry, Chicago, IL
2,500	Harvard Radcliffe, Cambridge, MA
2,500	Illinois Institute of Technology, Chicago, IL
2,500	Midwestern University, Glendale, AZ
2,500	Northern Illinois University, De Kalb, IL
2,500	Purdue University West Lafayette, West Lafayette, IN
2,500	Southern College of Optometry, Memphis, TN
2,500	Southern Illinois University School of Medicine, Carbondale, IL
2,500	University of Cincinnati, Cincinnati, OH
2,500	University of Illinois, Chicago, IL

R. K. MELLON FAMILY FOUNDATION

Giving Contact
Michael Watson, Vice President, Trustee
One Mellon Center
500 Grant Street, Suite 4106
Pittsburgh, PA 15219-2502
Phone: (412)392-2800
Fax: (412)392-2849
Web: http://www.fdncenter.org/grantmaker/rkmellon

Description
Founded: 1978
EIN: 251356145
Organization Type: Family Foundation
Giving Locations: PA: Western Pennsylvania, Pittsburgh

Grant Types: Capital, Challenge, Emergency, General Support, Matching, Operating Expenses, Research, Seed Money.

Donor Information
Founder: The R.K. Mellon Family Foundation was established in 1978 after the merger of the Loyalhanna, Rachelwood, Cassandra Mellon Henderson, and Landfall Foundations. The four predecessor foundations were created, respectively, by donors Richard P. Mellon, the late Constance B. Mellon, Cassandra Mellon Milbury, and Seward Prosser Mellon, all children of Richard King Mellon. Richard King Mellon was the chairman of Mellon National Bank from 1946 to 1966 and a director of Alcoa and Gulf Oil. R.K. Mellon was also governor and president of T. Mellon and Sons. He handled his family's financial empire until his death in 1970.

Financial Summary
Total Giving: $1,719,595 (2002); $1,944,550 (2001)
Assets: $32,682,211 (2002); $39,571,913 (2001)

Typical Recipients
Arts & Humanities: Arts Associations & Councils, Arts Centers, Arts Funds, Arts Institutes, Arts Outreach, Ballet, Ethnic & Folk Arts, Film & Video, Arts & Humanities-General, Historic Preservation, History & Archaeology, Libraries, Museums/Galleries, Music, Performing Arts, Theater
Civic & Public Affairs: Botanical Gardens/Parks, Business/Free Enterprise, Community Foundations, Economic Development, Economic Policy, Employment/Job Training, Civic & Public Affairs-General, Inner-City Development, Philanthropic Organizations, Professional & Trade Associations, Rural Affairs, Safety, Urban & Community Affairs, Women's Affairs, Zoos/Aquariums
Education: Afterschool/Enrichment Programs, Business Education, Colleges & Universities, Community & Junior Colleges, Economic Education, Education Funds, Education Reform, Engineering/Technological Education, Environmental Education, Education-General, Gifted & Talented Programs, International Studies, Medical Education, Minority Education, Preschool Education, Private Education (Precollege), Public Education (Precollege), Science/Mathematics Education, Special Education, Student Aid
Environment: Forestry, Environment-General, Protection, Resource Conservation, Watershed, Wildlife Protection
Health: AIDS/HIV, Cancer, Clinics/Medical Centers, Emergency/Ambulance Services, Health-General, Health Funds, Health Organizations, Hospitals, Hospitals (University Affiliated), Long-Term Care, Medical Rehabilitation, Medical Research, Medical Training, Mental Health, Nursing Services, Preventive Medicine/Wellness Organizations, Single-Disease Health Associations, Transplant Networks/Donor Banks
International: Foreign Arts Organizations, Health Care/Hospitals, International Environmental Issues, International Organizations, International Relief Efforts
Religion: Churches, Jewish Causes, Ministries, Religious Organizations, Religious Welfare
Science: Science Museums, Scientific Centers & Institutes, Scientific Labs, Scientific Research
Social Services: Animal Protection, Child Welfare, Community Centers, Community Service Organizations, Delinquency & Criminal Rehabilitation, Domestic Violence, Emergency Relief, Family Services, Homes, People with Disabilities, Recreation & Athletics, Sexual Abuse, Shelters/Homelessness, Substance Abuse, United Funds/United Ways, Volunteer Services, YMCA/YWCA/YMHA/YWHA, Youth Organizations

Application Procedures
Initial Contact: Contact the foundation to obtain an application form, or download the form from the foun-

dation's web site. The foundation also accepts the Common Grant Application Format (with foundation's required attachments), available at www.cmu.edu/develop/infoserv/prop/cgaf.html.

Application Requirements: Proposals must include the completed application form, proof of tax-exempt status, an executive summary providing an overview of the organization and describing the proposed program or project, how it will benefit the community, and the organization's capacity and plan to operate the project; a description of the plan to document progress and results; project budget; organization's history, including goals, current programs and activities, and accomplishments; a list of board of directors and officers, with affiliations, addresses and telephone numbers; audited financial statements for the last two years with corresponding operating budgets; and other sources of funding and financial plan to sustain project. copy of the IRS determination letter indicating tax-exempt status under Section 509(a) and 501(c)(3), and audited financial statements for the most recent two years, must be submitted. Include any printed material on the organization, such as annual reports or catalogs, if available.

Deadlines: None.

Evaluative Criteria: The foundation prefers projects and programs that have a clearly defined evaluation component.

Decision Notification: All proposals are acknowledged in writing.

Restrictions

Proposals are not considered unless accompanied by a copy of IRS classification. The foundation does not give to individuals or to conduit organizations which pass on funds to other organizations, nor does it make grants outside of the United States.

Additional Information

Publications: Guidelines; Application Form

Foundation Officials

Seward Prosser Mellon: don, director, trustee B Chicago, IL 1942. ED Susquehanna University BA (1965). PRIM CORP EMPL president: Richard K. Mellon & Sons. CORP AFFIL director: Mellon Bank NA; president: Rolling Rock Farms; director: Mellon Bank Corp. NONPR AFFIL director: Susquehanna University; life member: W Pennsylvania Conservancy; member: Phi Mu Delta. CLUB AFFIL Rolling Rock Westmoreland Hunt Club; Vintage Club; Rolling Rock Club; Duquesne Club; Laurel Valley Golf Club.

Mason Walsh, Jr.: vice chairman, trustee B Philadelphia, PA 1935. ED Pennsylvania State University BS (1957); Harvard University LLB (1960). PRIM CORP EMPL executive vice president, general counsel: Richard K. Mellon & Sons. NONPR AFFIL director: Childrens Hospital Pittsburgh.

Michael B. Watson: vice president, director

Grants Analysis

Disclosure Period: calendar year ending 2002
Total Grants: $1,719,595
Number of Grants: 67
Average Grant: $22,181*
Highest Grant: $150,000
Lowest Grant: $500
Typical Range: $10,000 to $50,000
***Note:** Average grant figure excludes two highest grants ($300,000).

Recent Grants

Note: Grants derived from 2002 Form 990.
Library-Related

105,000	Pierpont Morgan Library, New York, NY -- fund for concert and lecture

General

150,000	Falmouth Academy Inc., Falmouth, MA -- to assist in the capital campaign for construction of new wing
150,000	University of Pittsburgh, Pittsburgh, PA -- fund for George H Taber General Internal

Medicine within the Department of Medicine at the University of Pittsburgh School of Medicine

105,000	National Gallery of Art, Washington, DC -- fund for the acquisition of photography produced by women
65,000	Penn's Corner Conservancy Charitable Trust Inc., Greensburg, PA -- to assist in the Pennsylvania Switchgrass for Energy Alternative project
50,650	Valley School of Ligonier, Ligonier, PA -- fund for the rebuild of tennis court at Rector playground
50,000	Brandywine Conservancy, Chadds Ford, PA
50,000	Healthcare Foundation of Cape Cod Inc., Falmouth, MA
50,000	Loyalhanna Association Inc., Ligonier, PA
50,000	Mill Reef Fund, Lafayette, CO -- to assist in scholarships for Antiquan children only-in honor of Mrs. Bernadetta Sherman and Miss Rika Bird
50,000	Trustees of the University of Pennsylvania, Pittsburgh, PA -- fund to purchase laser surgery equipment, an ultra sound unit, digital camera equipment and brain biopsy system needed for neurology

MELLON FINANCIAL CORP.

Company Headquarters

1 Mellon Center
Pittsburgh, PA 15258-0001
Web: http://www.mellon.com

Company Description

Founded: 1869
Ticker: MEL
Exchange: NYSE
Revenue: US$4.96 billion (2004)
Profit: US$796 million (2004)
Employees: 20900 (2003)
Fortune Rank: 391, per FORTUNE Magazine's list of 500 Largest U.S. Corporations (2004).
SIC(s): 6100 Nondepository Institutions, 6200 Security & Commodity Brokers, 6700 Holding & Other Investment Offices, 6719 Holding Companies Nec.

Operating Locations

Boston Co., Inc. (MA--Boston)

Nonmonetary Support

Value: $16,200,000 (2001 approx); $5,498,500 (1999)
Type: Donated Equipment; In-kind Services; Loaned Employees; Loaned Executives; Workplace Solicitation
Note: NOT Company provides nonmonetary support. Company also provides below-market rate financing and technical assistance and advice.
Volunteer Programs: Mellon Volunteer Professionals - a volunteer program that supports nonprofit initiatives at certain Mellon communities. Mellon also has an active Retiree Volunteer program in its Pittsburgh location.

Mellon Financial Corp. Foundation

Giving Contact

James P. McDonald, President
PO Box 185
Pittsburgh, PA 15230-9897

Phone: (412)234-1443
Fax: (412)234-0831
Web: http://www.mellon.com/communityaffairs/charitablegiving.html

Alternate Contact

One Mellon Ctr., Suite 1830
Pittsburgh, PA 15258
Phone: (412)234-2732

Description

EIN: 237423500
Organization Type: Corporate Foundation
Giving Locations: DE; MA: Boston; PA: Philadelphia, Pittsburgh retail location areas.
Grant Types: Capital, Employee Matching Gifts, General Support, Matching, Operating Expenses, Project.
Note: Employee matching gift ratio: 1 to 1. Company matches employee cash contributions to colleges, universities, secondary schools and cultural organisation up to a maximum of $1,000/year.

Financial Summary

Total Giving: $3,317,487 (2003); $4,699,600 (2001). Note: Contributes through corporate direct giving program and foundation.
Giving Analysis: Giving for 2001 includes: corporate direct giving (approx $6,850,000); foundation ($7,653,900); nonmonetary support (approx $16,200,000)
Assets: $55,300,276 (2003); $47,464,967 (2002); $57,111,129 (2001). Note: Above figures reflect foundation assets.
Gifts Received: $64,500 (2003); $100 (2001). Note: In 2001, contributions were received from Mellon Financial Corporation.

Typical Recipients

Arts & Humanities: Arts Associations & Councils, Arts Centers, Arts Festivals, Arts Funds, Community Arts, Dance, Arts & Humanities-General, Historic Preservation, History & Archaeology, Libraries, Museums/Galleries, Music, Opera, Performing Arts, Public Broadcasting, Theater
Civic & Public Affairs: Botanical Gardens/Parks, Business/Free Enterprise, Chambers of Commerce, Community Foundations, Economic Development, Employment/Job Training, Civic & Public Affairs-General, Housing, Nonprofit Management, Philanthropic Organizations, Urban & Community Affairs, Women's Affairs
Education: Business Education, Colleges & Universities, Education Funds, Education Reform, Education-General, Literacy, Minority Education, Secondary Education (Private), Secondary Education (Public), Student Aid
Environment: Environment-General, Resource Conservation
Health: AIDS/HIV, Cancer, Children's Health/Hospitals, Emergency/Ambulance Services, Health-General, Health Funds, Health Organizations, Hospices, Hospitals, Single-Disease Health Associations, Speech & Hearing
Religion: Dioceses, Jewish Causes, Religious Welfare
Science: Science Museums, Scientific Organizations
Social Services: Community Centers, Community Service Organizations, Family Services, People with Disabilities, Shelters/Homelessness, United Funds/United Ways, YMCA/YWCA/YMHA/YWHA, Youth Organizations

Application Procedures

Initial Contact: Local organizations should submit grant requests in letter form directly to the Mellon Financial Corp. office located in the requesting organization's area of operation. In addition to the company's headquarters in Pittsburgh, the following Mellon offices will accept grant requests:
For organizations in Miami-Dade, Broward, and Palm Beach counties, FL: Mellon United National Bank,

Community Affairs, 1399 SW First Ave., Miami, FL 33130-4388.

For organizations in Suffolk and Middlesex counties, MA: Mellon Financial Corp., Community Affairs--Mellon New England, One Boston Place, Boston, MA 02108-4402.

For organizations located in the Western United States: Mellon Financial Corp., Corp. Affairs--Mellon West, 400 South Hope Street, 5th floor, Los Angeles, CA 90071-2806.

For organizations in Allegheny, Bucks, Chester, Delaware, Montgomery, and Philadelphia counties, PA: Mellon Financial Corp., Corporate Affairs--One Mellon Center, Suite 1830, Pittsburgh, PA 15258.

Application Requirements: Requests should include a description of the project or program; purpose and objectives; itemized budget, including income, expenses, and other sources of income (both potential and committed); a list of board members; most recent audited financial statement; and a copy of the organization's latest IRS determination letter indicating 501(c)(3) status.

Deadlines: None; requests are considered upon receipt.

Evaluative Criteria: Proposals should support community development in one of the following ways: business and job development, affordable housing, literacy and education, art and culture, technical assistance for nonprofit organizations and fundraising and advertising to promote nonprofit groups as well as the company; also considers active board leadership, comprehensive resource development plan that includes in-kind support, income-generating activities, resource sharing with other nonprofit groups, support from individuals, and efficient and effective administration of funds and programs.

Notes: Grant requests submitted to Mellon's Pittsburgh Community Affairs office may be prepared using the Common Grant Application Format, available from the following web site: http://www.gwpa.org.

Restrictions

Does not support individuals, religious or other sectarian groups, fraternal orders of police or fire associations, scholarships, fellowships, travel grants, conferences and seminars, specialized health campaigns, political or lobbying organizations, or individual United Way agencies that already benefit from Mellon's gift to the United Way.

Additional Information

Mellon Bank Community Development Corporation, formed as a separate subsidiary in 1987, provides special bank loans and technical assistance for community development.

Copies of Mellon Community Affairs publications, Discover Total Resources: A Guide for Nonprofits and Neighbors Helping Neighbors: A Directory for Nonprofit Organizations, can be obtained by writing to Mellon Community Affairs, Room 1830, One Mellon Center, Pittsburgh, PA 15258-0001.

Since consolidation of Mellon's Pennsylvania banks, proposals that have a statewide impact in priority areas should be sent to corporate headquarters in Pittsburgh. Proposals in priority areas that are region-specific should be sent to the nearest regional office.

Publications: Opportunities and Accomplishments; Mellon Bank Corp. Community Report (annually)

Corporate Officials

Steven G. Elliot: executive managemento B 1946. PRIM CORP EMPL chief financial officer: Mellon Bank Corp.

Jeffrey L. Leininger: vice chairman ED Pennsylvania State University (1967); Rutgers University (1982). PRIM CORP EMPL vice chairman specialized commercial banking: Mellon Bank Corp. ADD CORP EMPL director: Mellon Ventures Inc. CORP AFFIL director: Tuscarora Inc.

Martin Gregory McGuinn: chairman, chief executive officer B Philadelphia, PA 1942. ED Villanova Univer-

sity AB (1964); Villanova University JD (1967). PRIM CORP EMPL chairman, chief executive officer: Mellon Financial Corp. CORP AFFIL chairman, chief executive officer: Mellon Bank NA; director: Regl Industries Development Corp.; director: General Reinsurance Corp.; director: MasterCard International. NONPR AFFIL director: University Pittsburgh Medical Center; director, consult: Villanova Law School; member: Pennsylvania Bar Association; director: Pennsylvania Chamber Business & Industry; trustee: Historical Society Western Pennsylvania; member: New York State Bar Association; member: Bankers Roundtable; trustee: Carnegie Museum Art; member: American Law Institute; member: American Society of Corporate Secretaries; member: Allegheny County Bar Association; member: American Bar Association.

Giving Program Officials

Paul S. Beideman: PRIM CORP EMPL member corporate review committee: Mellon Bank Corp. NONPR AFFIL vice president: Boy Scouts America Philadelphia Council.

Walter R. Day, III

Jeffrey L. Leininger: membership, corporate review committee (see above)

Sandra J. McLaughlin: member corporate review commission PRIM CORP EMPL senior vice president: Mellon Bank Corp.

Foundation Officials

Michael E. Bleier: trustee
Rose M. Cotton: chairman
Walter R. Day, III: trustee (see above)
Steven G. Elliot: trustee (see above)
Carlene E. Garrity: secretary
Paul M. Kochis: trustee
Jeffrey L. Leininger: trustee (see above)
James P. McDonald: president PRIM CORP EMPL member corporate review committee: Mellon Bank Corp.
Martin Gregory McGuinn: trustee (see above)
James P. Palermo: trustee
Lisa B. Peters: trustee
Robert Skena: treasurer

Grants Analysis

Disclosure Period: calendar year ending 2003
Total Grants: $2,427,966*
Number of Grants: 950 (approx)
Average Grant: $2,556
Highest Grant: $150,000
Lowest Grant: $100
Typical Range: $1,000 to $5,000
*Note: Giving excludes United Way.

Recent Grants

Note: Grants derived from 2003 Form 990.

Library-Related

275	Public Library Foundation, Pittsburgh, PA

General

200,000	Conference on Community Development, Pittsburgh, PA
150,000	Way of Massachusetts Bay, Boston, MA
150,000	Way of Southeastern Pennsylvania, Philadelphia, PA
117,500	United Way of Allegheny, Pittsburgh, PA
117,500	United Way of Allegheny County, Pittsburgh, PA
117,500	United Way of Allegheny County, Pittsburgh, PA
117,500	United Way of Allegheny County, Pittsburgh, PA
100,000	Constitution Center, Philadelphia, PA
100,000	Museums of Pittsburgh, Pittsburgh, PA
100,000	Society of Western Pennsylvania, Pittsburgh, PA

ANDREW W. MELLON FOUNDATION

Giving Contact

Michele S. Warman, General Counsel & Secretary
140 East 62nd Street
New York, NY 10021
Phone: (212)838-8400
Fax: (212)223-2778
Web: http://www.mellon.org

Description

Founded: 1969
EIN: 131879954
Organization Type: General Purpose Foundation
Giving Locations: nationally.
Grant Types: Award, Challenge, Endowment, Fellowship, Matching, Multiyear/Continuing Support, Research.

Donor Information

Founder: The Andrew W. Mellon Foundation is the product of the 1969 consolidation of two previously independent foundations: the Avalon Foundation, established by Ailsa Mellon Bruce, and the Old Dominion Foundation, established by her brother, Paul Mellon. As the children of Pittsburgh financier Andrew W. Mellon, Paul and Ailsa inherited one of the nation's largest fortunes, including substantial holdings in the Mellon National Bank and Trust Co., Gulf Oil Corp., Aluminum Co. of America, Koppers Co., and Carborundum Co. The foundation received additional funds from the estate of Mrs. Ailsa Mellon Bruce upon her death in 1969.

Financial Summary

Total Giving: $222,662,386 (2002); $205,870,148 (2001)
Assets: $3,610,368,866 (2002); $4,135,567,000 (2001 approx)
Gifts Received: In 1989, contributions were received from the estate of Margaret Meehan.

Typical Recipients

Arts & Humanities: Arts Associations & Councils, Arts Centers, Arts Institutes, Ballet, Dance, Historic Preservation, History & Archaeology, Libraries, Literary Arts, Museums/Galleries, Music, Opera, Performing Arts, Theater

Civic & Public Affairs: Botanical Gardens/Parks, Economic Policy, Civic & Public Affairs-General, Hispanic Affairs, Nonprofit Management, Philanthropic Organizations, Professional & Trade Associations, Public Policy, Women's Affairs, Zoos/Aquariums

Education: Arts/Humanities Education, Business Education, Colleges & Universities, Continuing Education, Economic Education, Education Associations, Education Funds, Education Reform, Engineering/Technological Education, Environmental Education, Faculty Development, Education-General, International Studies, Legal Education, Literacy, Medical Education, Minority Education, Science/Mathematics Education, Social Sciences Education, Student Aid, Vocational & Technical Education

Environment: Environment-General, Protection, Research, Resource Conservation

Health: Medical Research, Public Health

International: Foreign Arts Organizations, Foreign Educational Institutions, International-General, Health Care/Hospitals, International Affairs, International Development, International Environmental Issues, International Organizations, International Peace & Security Issues, International Relations, Trade

Science: Science Museums, Scientific Centers & Institutes, Scientific Organizations, Scientific Research

Social Services: Family Planning

Application Procedures

Initial Contact: Letter of request of a page or less is sufficient.
Application Requirements: Include the need, the nature, and the amount of the request and the justification for it. Evidence of classification by the IRS should be included. Supplementary exhibits may be submitted.
Deadlines: None.

Restrictions

The foundation does not give grants to individuals or to primarily local organizations.

Additional Information

Prospective applicants are encouraged to explore their ideas informally with foundation staff (preferably in writing) before submitting formal proposal.
Publications: Annual Report

Foundation Officials

William O. Baker: chairman emeritus NONPR AFFIL member: National Academy of Sciences.
Lewis W. Bernard: trustee CORP AFFIL director: Marsh & McLennan Co's. NONPR AFFIL chairman: American Museum of Natural History; chairman: Classroom Inc..
William G. Bowen: president, trustee ED Denison University AB (1955); Princeton University PhD (1958). CORP AFFIL director: American Express; director: Merck & Co. Inc. NONPR AFFIL board of overseers: Teachers Insurance and Annuity Association; director: University Corp for Advanced Internet Development; director: JSTOR.
Drew G. Faust: trustee
John E. Hull: vice president finance, chief investment officer
Patricia L. Irvin: vice president, operations and planning ED Princeton University BA (1976); Harvard University JD (1979). NONPR AFFIL member: New York State Bar Association; member: Washington DC Bar Association; board of directors: Immigration & Refugee Services of American; board of directors: Council on Foreign Relations; advisory committee, arms division: Human Rights Watch; member: American Law Institute.
Paul LeClerc: trustee NONPR AFFIL president: New York Public Library.
Colin Lucas: trustee NONPR AFFIL vice chancellor: Oxford University; trustee: Rhodes Trust; board of directors: The British Library.
Dr. Walter Eugene Massey: trustee B Hattiesburg, MS April 05, 1938. ED Morehouse College BS (1958); Washington University PhD (1966); Washington University MA (1966); Washington University PHD (1966). PRIM NONPR EMPL president: Morehouse College. CORP AFFIL director: McDonalds Corp.; director: Motorola Inc.; director: Conoco Corp.; director: BankAmerica Corp.; director: BP Amoco Corp. NONPR AFFIL member: Sigma Xi; member: United Way of Chicago; trustee: Rand Corp.; president: Morehouse College; member: National Science Foundation; president: American Association Advancement Science.
Walter Taylor Reveley, III: trustee B Churchville, VA 1943. ED Princeton University AB (1965); University of Virginia JD (1968). PRIM NONPR EMPL dean: College of William & Mary School of Law. NONPR AFFIL member: Virginia Bar Foundation; trustee: Virginia Museum Fine Arts; member: Virginia Bar Association; member: Raven Society; member: Richmond Bar Association; member: Phi Beta Kappa; board directors, member: Princeton Association Virginia; member: Order Coif; director: JSTOR; member: Omicron Delta Kappa; member: Edn Lawyers; elder: Grace Covenent Presbyterian Church; member: District of Columbia Bar Association; member: American Judicature Society; member: American Society International Law; member: American Bar Association; member: American Bar Foundation. CLUB AFFIL Knickerbocker Club; Country Club Virginia; Down-

town Club.
Anne M. Tatlock: chairman, trustee B White Plains, NY 1939. ED Vassar College BA (1961); New York University MA Economics (1968). CORP AFFIL director: Merck & Co. Inc.; chairman, chief executive officer, director: Fiduciary Trust Company International; director: Fortune Brands Inc. NONPR AFFIL chairman nominating committee, trustee: American Ballet Theater; trustee: Vassar College.
Anne M. Tatlock: chairman, trustee B White Plains, NY 1939. ED Vassar College BA (1961); New York University MA Economics (1968). PRIM CORP EMPL chairman, chief executive officer: Fiduciary Trust Co. International. CORP AFFIL director: Fortune Brands Inc.; director: Merck & Co. Inc.; chairman, chief executive officer, director: Fiduciary Trust Company International. NONPR AFFIL trustee: Mayo Foundation; trustee: Vassar College; chairman nominating committee, trustee: American Ballet Theater.
Michele S. Warman: secretary, general counsel ED Princeton University AB (1982); University of Oxford BA (1985); Harvard University Law School JD (1988). NONPR AFFIL member: Washington DC Bar Association; member, advisory council: Woodrow Wilson School of Public & International Affairs; member: Massachusetts State Bar Association; member: New York State Bar Association.
John C. Whitehead: chairman emeritus B Evanston, IL. ED Haverford College BA (1943). NONPR AFFIL chairman emeritus: Brookings Institute; chairman: Lower Manhattan Dev. Corp..
Harriet Zuckerman: vice president B New York, NY 1937. ED Vassar College AB (1958); Columbia University PhD (1965). CORP AFFIL director: Annual Reviews Inc. NONPR AFFIL trustee: Center Advanced Study Behavioral Science; professor emerita, sr res scholar: Columbia University; member: American Philosophical Society; member: American Academy of Arts & Sciences.

Grants Analysis

Disclosure Period: calendar year ending 2002
Total Grants: $222,662,386
Number of Grants: 525 (approx)
Average Grant: $42,412
Highest Grant: $4,050,000
Typical Range: $10,000 to $100,000

Recent Grants

Note: Grants derived from 2002 Form 990.
Library-Related
1,201,972 New York Public Library, New York, NY -- towards preservation of the general research collections
1,185,000 New York Public Library, New York, NY -- towards covering the losses the public branch library systems have incurred due to the reduction of government support after September 11
General
4,050,000 Social Science Research Council, New York, NY -- fund for the International Dissertation Field Research Program
4,000,000 Massachusetts Institute of Technology, Cambridge, MA -- fund for web based initiative to free worldwide access to the educational materials
3,600,000 Woodrow Wilson National Fellowship Foundation, Princeton, NJ -- fund for the Fellowships in Humanistic Studies
2,500,000 Philadelphia Museum of Art, Philadelphia, PA -- fund for scholarly publications
2,500,000 Smith College, Northampton, MA -- fund for faculty career enhancement
2,500,000 Virginia Polytechnic Institute and State University, Blacksburg, VA -- fund for the artistic initiatives and organizational development
2,166,000 Princeton University, Princeton, NJ -- towards a survey on the effects of Foundations Graduate Education Initiative

2,096,639 Columbia University, New York, NY -- fund for improving the effectiveness of graduate education in the humanities
2,000,000 American Philosophical Society, Philadelphia, PA -- towards fellowships for college and university faculty members
1,900,000 Appalachian College Association, Berea, KY -- fund for expansion of electronic collections in the library

RICHARD KING MELLON FOUNDATION

Giving Contact
Michael Watson, Vice President and Trustee
One Mellon Center
500 Grant Street, Suite 4106
Pittsburgh, PA 15219-2502
Phone: (412)392-2800
Web: http://fdncenter.org/grantmaker/rkmellon/

Description
Founded: 1947
EIN: 251127705
Organization Type: General Purpose Foundation
Giving Locations: PA: Southwestern Pennsylvania, Pittsburgh nationally for conservation programs.
Grant Types: Capital, Challenge, General Support, Project, Seed Money.

Donor Information
Founder: The Richard King Mellon Foundation was established in 1947 by Richard King Mellon, son of Richard Beatty Mellon, and nephew of Andrew Mellon. Mr. Mellon, a lieutenant general in the United States Army Reserve, managed his family's many interests from the 1930s until his death on June 3, 1970. He served as president of the Mellon National Bank and chairman of the board of Mellon National Bank and Trust Company. He was also a director of many of the companies closely linked to the Mellon family, including the Aluminum Company of America and Gulf Oil Corporation. Mr. Mellon played a leading role in the movement to revitalize Pittsburgh and was active in civic and philanthropic affairs in Pittsburgh and Ligonier, PA. He married Constance Mary Prosser, who served as the foundation's chairman of the board of trustees from its inception in 1947 until her death in 1980.

Financial Summary
Total Giving: $69,304,274 (2003); $61,836,738 (2002); $58,608,007 (2001). Note: Nonmonetary support is in the form of land donations provided through the Foundation's American Land Conservation Program.
Giving Analysis: Giving for 2003 includes: foundation grants to United Way ($1,170,000); 2002: foundation grants to United Way ($2,110,000)
Assets: $1,623,390,780 (2003); $1,392,254,809 (2002); $1,661,153,320 (2001)

Typical Recipients
Arts & Humanities: Arts Associations & Councils, Arts Centers, Arts Institutes, Arts Outreach, Ballet, Community Arts, Dance, Ethnic & Folk Arts, Film & Video, Arts & Humanities-General, Historic Preservation, History & Archaeology, Libraries, Museums/Galleries, Music, Opera, Performing Arts, Public Broadcasting, Theater
Civic & Public Affairs: African American Affairs, Botanical Gardens/Parks, Business/Free Enterprise, Community Foundations, Economic Development, Economic Policy, Employment/Job Training, Civic & Public Affairs-General, Housing, Inner-City Development, Law & Justice, Municipalities/Towns, Nonprofit Management, Philanthropic Organizations, Profes-

sional & Trade Associations, Rural Affairs, Safety, Urban & Community Affairs, Women's Affairs, Zoos/ Aquariums

Education: Afterschool/Enrichment Programs, Agricultural Education, Arts/Humanities Education, Business Education, Colleges & Universities, Community & Junior Colleges, Economic Education, Education Associations, Education Funds, Education Reform, Elementary Education (Private), Elementary Education (Public), Environmental Education, Faculty Development, Education-General, Gifted & Talented Programs, International Studies, Leadership Training, Literacy, Medical Education, Minority Education, Preschool Education, Private Education (Precollege), Public Education (Precollege), Religious Education, Science/Mathematics Education, Special Education, Student Aid, Vocational & Technical Education

Environment: Air/Water Quality, Forestry, Environment-General, Protection, Research, Resource Conservation, Watershed, Wildlife Protection

Health: AIDS/HIV, Cancer, Children's Health/ Hospitals, Clinics/Medical Centers, Emergency/ Ambulance Services, Geriatric Health, Health Policy/ Cost Containment, Health Organizations, Hospices, Hospitals, Long-Term Care, Medical Rehabilitation, Medical Research, Medical Training, Mental Health, Nursing Services, Prenatal Health Issues, Preventive Medicine/Wellness Organizations, Public Health, Research/Studies Institutes, Single-Disease Health Associations

International: International Environmental Issues, International Relief Efforts

Religion: Churches, Dioceses, Jewish Causes, Ministries, Religious Organizations, Religious Welfare, Seminaries, Synagogues/Temples

Science: Science Museums, Scientific Centers & Institutes, Scientific Labs, Scientific Research

Social Services: Animal Protection, Camps, Child Welfare, Community Centers, Community Service Organizations, Day Care, Delinquency & Criminal Rehabilitation, Domestic Violence, Emergency Relief, Family Planning, Family Services, Food/Clothing Distribution, Homes, People with Disabilities, Recreation & Athletics, Scouts, Senior Services, Sexual Abuse, Shelters/Homelessness, Social Services-General, Substance Abuse, United Funds/United Ways, Volunteer Services, YMCA/YWCA/YMHA/ YWHA, Youth Organizations

Application Procedures

Initial Contact: Obtain an application form either from the foundation's web site or through a letter requesting application materials.

Application Requirements: Proposals should include an executive summary describing the sponsoring organization, proposed project, the problems it seeks to address, the population it will serve, and how it will be operated. Background information on the requesting organization should include its history, purpose, the types of programs it offers, and the names and affiliations of members of the board and Chairman and/or President. Financial information must include an operating budget and timetable for the proposed project, and audited financial statements for the most recent two years. A copy of the latest IRS determination letter of tax-exempt status under sections 501(c)(3) and 509(a) is required. Information on the proposed project should include its specific purpose and objective, budget, and timetable. Include a description of the proposed methods of operation and evaluation, and the qualifications of the individuals who will conduct the undertaking. A statement of other sources of support for the project should also be included, with an explanation of how the project will be financed at the expiration of the proposed grant. Supporting printed material, including annual reports, pamphlets, and brochures may be included.

Deadlines: None.

Review Process: The board of trustees meets twice a year, usually in June and December.

Notes: The foundation shows preference for projects and programs that have a clearly defined evaluation component.

Restrictions

Will not consider requests on behalf of individuals, and normally does not consider requests for grants to conduit organizations that pass on funds to other organizations. The foundations does not make grants outside the United States.

Additional Information

Publications: Annual Report; Fact Sheet; Grant Application; Special Program Publications

Foundation Officials

Robert B. Burr, Jr.: treasurer, trustee
Lawrence S. Busch: trustee, assistant treasurer
Ann Marie Helms: program officer, assistant secretary
Scott D. Izzo: associate director, secretary NONPR AFFIL director: SCA National Council; director: Western Pennsylvania Conservancy; director: Latrobe Area Hospital.
Richard Prosser Mellon: chairman, trustee B Chicago, IL 1939. ED University of Pittsburgh (1958-1960). NONPR AFFIL member national executive committee life member: Ducks Unlimited Inc.; coordinator: Western Pennsylvania School Blind; director: Ducks Unlimited Foundation; trustee emeritus: Carnegie Museum of Pittsburgh. CLUB AFFIL Rolling Rock Westmoreland Hunt Club; National Steeplechase & Hunt Association; Rolling Rock Club; The Links New York City Club; Duquesne Club; Laurel Valley Golf Club.
Seward Prosser Mellon: president, chairman executive comm, trustee B Chicago, IL 1942. ED Susquehanna University BA (1965). PRIM CORP EMPL president: Richard K. Mellon & Sons. CORP AFFIL director: Mellon Bank NA; president: Rolling Rock Farms; director: Mellon Bank Corp. NONPR AFFIL director: Susquehanna University; life member: W Pennsylvania Conservancy; member: Phi Mu Delta. CLUB AFFIL Rolling Rock Westmoreland Hunt Club; Vintage Club; Rolling Rock Club; Duquesne Club; Laurel Valley Golf Club.
John J. Turcik: controller
Michael B. Watson: vice president, trustee

Grants Analysis

Disclosure Period: calendar year ending 2003
Total Grants: $68,134,274*
Number of Grants: 210
Average Grant: $178,239*
Highest Grant: $5,012,200
Lowest Grant: $5,000
Typical Range: $50,000 to $300,000
*Note: Giving excludes United Way. Average grant figure excludes thirteen highest grants ($33,021,200).

Recent Grants

Note: Grants derived from 2002 Form 990.
General

24,621,176 Brevard County, Florida-Parks and Recreation Department, Melbourne, FL -- toward environmentally endangered land program

5,284,425 Sustainable Conservation Inc., Arlington, VA -- toward gift of land

2,942,834 RIDC Fund for Economic Growth, Pittsburgh, PA -- funding for purchase of property

2,000,000 Fort Ligonier Association, Ligonier, PA -- funding for capital support

2,000,000 Pittsburgh Life Sciences Greenhouse, Pittsburgh, PA -- toward operating support

2,000,000 United Way of Allegheny County, Pittsburgh, PA -- toward early childhood initiative

1,981,910 Conservation Fund, Arlington, VA -- funding for purchase of litke tract

1,250,000 McGowan Institute of Regenerative Medicine, Pittsburgh, PA -- funding for securing fit-out of lab space

1,000,000 Coordinated Care Network, Pittsburgh, PA -- toward new prescription discount program

1,000,000 Duquesne University of the Holy Ghost, Pittsburgh, PA -- funding in honor of John Murray

MEMORIAL FOUNDATION FOR THE BLIND

Giving Contact

Roger W. Greene, President
Memorial Foundation for the Blind
51 Harvard Street
Worcester, MA 01609
Phone: (508)752-3053

Description

EIN: 041611615
Organization Type: Private Foundation
Giving Locations: MA: Worcester including surrounding area
Grant Types: General Support.

Financial Summary

Total Giving: $238,306 (fiscal year ending March 31, 2002); $234,548 (fiscal 2001). Note: Fiscal 1997 Giving includes scholarship ($1,000).
Giving Analysis: Giving for fiscal 2002 includes: foundation gifts to individuals ($11,217); fiscal 2001: foundation gifts to individuals ($1,000)
Assets: $4,333,777 (fiscal 2002); $4,576,618 (fiscal 2001)
Gifts Received: $1,233 (fiscal 2002); $79,372 (fiscal 2001); $1,175 (fiscal 1997)

Typical Recipients

Arts & Humanities: Libraries, Public Broadcasting, Theater
Civic & Public Affairs: Municipalities/Towns, Urban & Community Affairs
Education: Colleges & Universities, Special Education
Health: Eyes/Blindness, Health Organizations, Hospitals, Kidney, Single-Disease Health Associations
Social Services: People with Disabilities

Application Procedures

Initial Contact: Send a brief letter of inquiry.
Application Requirements: Include a description of organization.
Deadlines: None.

Foundation Officials

Eleanor Brockway: director
Stephanie S. Burnett: treasurer
Kleber A. Campbell, III: director
Gilbert S. Davis: director
T. Ashley Edwards: assistant treasurer
Helen D. Fifield: director
Janet B. Foley: director
Roger W. Greene: director
Barbara Higgins: director
Nancy S. Hudson: director
Nancy Jeppson: director
Helen Koskinas: director
Diane MacConnell: director
Gary MacConnell: director
Larry Raymond: vice president
Janet Reidy: director
Joseph Reidy: director
Dr. C. Reid Roberts: director
Judy Savageau: director
Betty Simpson: clerk

Alice Taylor: director
Wyatt R. Wade: president

Grants Analysis

Disclosure Period: fiscal year ending March 31, 2002
Total Grants: $227,089*
Number of Grants: 7
Highest Grant: $113,856
Lowest Grant: $2,588
Typical Range: $4,000 to $30,000
*Note: Giving excludes gifts to individuals.

Recent Grants

Note: Grants derived from 2002 Form 990.
General

113,856	Massachusetts Association for the Blind, Worcester, MA
57,500	Audio Journal, Worcester, MA
32,564	Greater Boston Aid to the Blind, Boston, MA
9,737	Foothills Theater, Worcester, MA
6,844	Central Massachusetts Bay State, Worcester, MA
4,000	Fidelco Guide Dog Foundation, Worcester, MA
2,588	Kidney Dialysis Unit, Memorial Hospital, Worcester, MA -- transportation for the blind

MEMTON FUND

Giving Contact

Lillian I. Daniels, Secretary
515 Madison Avenue
Suite 3702
New York, NY 10022
Phone: (212)644-4915

Description

Founded: 1936
EIN: 136096608
Organization Type: Private Foundation
Giving Locations: Northeast USA.
Grant Types: Capital, Endowment, General Support, Scholarship.

Donor Information

Founder: the late Albert G. Milbank, the late Charles M. Cauldwell

Financial Summary

Total Giving: $481,100 (2001)
Assets: $10,847,121 (2001)

Typical Recipients

Arts & Humanities: Arts Associations & Councils, Arts Funds, Ballet, Community Arts, Dance, Film & Video, Arts & Humanities-General, Historic Preservation, Libraries, Museums/Galleries, Music, Performing Arts, Public Broadcasting, Theater
Civic & Public Affairs: Botanical Gardens/Parks, Business/Free Enterprise, Community Foundations, Employment/Job Training, Civic & Public Affairs-General, Hispanic Affairs, Housing, Philanthropic Organizations, Professional & Trade Associations, Public Policy, Urban & Community Affairs, Women's Affairs, Zoos/Aquariums
Education: Afterschool/Enrichment Programs, Arts/Humanities Education, Colleges & Universities, Engineering/Technological Education, Education-General, Leadership Training, Legal Education, Literacy, Medical Education, Private Education (Precollege), Public Education (Precollege), Science/Mathematics Education, Secondary Education (Private), Special Education, Student Aid
Environment: Environment-General, Resource Conservation, Wildlife Protection

Health: AIDS/HIV, Cancer, Children's Health/Hospitals, Clinics/Medical Centers, Hospices, Hospitals, Long-Term Care, Medical Rehabilitation, Medical Research, Mental Health, Nursing Services, Public Health, Single-Disease Health Associations
International: Foreign Arts Organizations, Health Care/Hospitals, International Relief Efforts, Missionary/Religious Activities
Religion: Churches
Science: Scientific Centers & Institutes
Social Services: Animal Protection, Community Centers, Community Service Organizations, Crime Prevention, Delinquency & Criminal Rehabilitation, Family Services, Food/Clothing Distribution, People with Disabilities, Recreation & Athletics, Scouts, Social Services-General, United Funds/United Ways, Youth Organizations

Application Procedures

Initial Contact: Send a brief letter of inquiry.
Application Requirements: Include a description of organization and its activities.
Deadlines: None, although decisions on major requests are only made at the annual board of directors meeting in May. Applications should be received at least six weeks prior to that date.

Restrictions

Does not support individuals.

Foundation Officials

Lillian I. Daniels: secretary, treasurer
Elenita M. Drumwright: president
Elizabeth Drumwright: director
Robert V. Edgar: director
Elizabeth S. Farrar: director
Marjorie M. Farrar: vice president
Olivia Farrar-Wellman: director
Alexandra Giordano: director
David L. Milbank: director
Michelle Milbank: director
Samuel L. Milbank: director
Thomas L. Milbank: director
Karen Quackenbush: director
Pamela White: director

Grants Analysis

Disclosure Period: calendar year ending 2001
Total Grants: $481,100
Number of Grants: 146
Average Grant: $3,295
Highest Grant: $15,000
Typical Range: $1,000 to $10,000

Recent Grants

Note: Grants derived from 2001 Form 990.
Library-Related

15,000	Folger Shakespeare Library, Washington, DC -- operating support
15,000	Folger Shakespeare Library, Washington, DC -- operating support

General

15,000	Foundation for Advanced Education in the Sciences, Bethesda, MD -- operating support
15,000	Suicide Prevention and Crisis, San Francisco, CA -- operating support
10,000	Horse Cave Theatre, Bowling Green, KY -- operating support
10,000	Hospice of Northern Virginia, Falls Church, VA -- operating support
10,000	International Center for Photography, New York, NY -- operating support
10,000	King Manor Museum, Jamaica, NY -- operating support
10,000	Princeton University, Princeton, NJ -- operating support
10,000	Recordings for the Blind and Dyslexic, Denver, CO -- operating support
10,000	St. Mark's Church, New Canaan, CT -- Bell Restoration Project

10,000	Tompkins County Society for the Prevention of Cruelty to Animals, Ithaca, NY -- operating support

MENASHA CORP.

Company Headquarters

Neenah, WI
Web: http://www.menasha.com

Company Description

Revenue: US$990 million (2002)
Employees: 5500 (2003)
SIC(s): 2421 Sawmills & Planing Mills--General, 2631 Paperboard Mills, 2653 Corrugated & Solid Fiber Boxes, 2759 Commercial Printing Nec.

Operating Locations

Menasha Corp. (IA--Manchester, Monticello; MA--Monson; MI--Coloma, Otsego; MN--Hopkins; MS--Olive Branch; NJ--Farmingdale, Monmouth; OH--Columbus; OR--North Bend; PA--Delmont, Scranton, Yukon; VA--Danville; WA--Olympia; WI--Dane, Green Lake, Menasha, Milwaukee, Watertown)
Note: Includes plant locations.

Nonmonetary Support

Volunteer Programs: Foundation gives Employee Volunteer Awards, donating cash grants to select organizations where employees volunteer.

Menasha Corp. Foundation

Giving Contact

Kevin Schuh, Treasurer
Menasha Corp. Foundation
PO Box 367
Neenah, WI 54957-0367
Phone: (920)751-1217
Fax: (920)751-1236

Alternate Contact

Phone: 800-558-5073

Description

EIN: 396047384
Organization Type: Corporate Foundation
Giving Locations: headquarters and operating communities.
Grant Types: Emergency, Employee Matching Gifts, General Support, Multiyear/Continuing Support, Project, Scholarship.
Note: Employee matching gift ratio: 2 to 1 up to $1,500 per employee annually, to private colleges and universities.

Financial Summary

Total Giving: $406,460 (2003); $526,069 (2002); $864,167 (2001). Note: Contributes through corporate direct giving program and foundation. 2000 giving includes $30,000 in administrative expenses. 2001 giving includes $32,659 in administrative expenses.
Assets: $690,060 (2003); $690,998 (2002); $936,614 (2001)
Gifts Received: $300,000 (2003); $317,000 (2002); $1,043,000 (2001). Note: Contributions were received from the Menasha Corporation.

Typical Recipients

Arts & Humanities: Community Arts, Film & Video, Arts & Humanities-General, Historic Preservation, History & Archaeology, Libraries, Museums/Galleries, Music, Opera, Performing Arts, Public Broadcasting, Theater

Civic & Public Affairs: African American Affairs, Botanical Gardens/Parks, Business/Free Enterprise, Community Foundations, Economic Development, Civic & Public Affairs-General, Hispanic Affairs, Housing, Municipalities/Towns, Philanthropic Organizations, Professional & Trade Associations, Safety, Urban & Community Affairs, Women's Affairs, Zoos/Aquariums
Education: Arts/Humanities Education, Business Education, Colleges & Universities, Economic Education, Education Funds, Education Reform, Elementary Education (Private), Engineering/Technological Education, Environmental Education, Education-General, Literacy, Private Education (Precollege), Religious Education, Secondary Education (Private), Vocational & Technical Education
Environment: Environment-General, Protection, Research, Resource Conservation, Watershed, Wildlife Protection
Health: Adolescent Health Issues, Cancer, Children's Health/Hospitals, Clinics/Medical Centers, Diabetes, Emergency/Ambulance Services, Health-General, Health Funds, Health Organizations, Hospices, Hospitals, Nursing Services, Public Health, Single-Disease Health Associations
Religion: Ministries, Religious Organizations, Religious Welfare
Social Services: Animal Protection, Child Abuse, Child Welfare, Community Service Organizations, Counseling, Domestic Violence, Family Services, Food/Clothing Distribution, People with Disabilities, Recreation & Athletics, Scouts, Senior Services, Sexual Abuse, Shelters/Homelessness, Social Services-General, Substance Abuse, United Funds/United Ways, Volunteer Services, YMCA/YWCA/YMHA/YWHA, Youth Organizations

Application Procedures

Initial Contact: Submit a brief written request (not more than 3 pages).
Application Requirements: Include amount requested, a brief explanation of purpose of funds sought, information regarding any proposed funding available from other sources for this purpose, and proof of tax-exempt status.
Deadlines: None.
Decision Notification: Board meetings held quarterly in February, May, September and December.

Restrictions

Does not support individuals, religious organizations for sectarian purposes, or political or lobbying groups.

Additional Information

Recipients of grants over $1,000 are subject to evaluation.
Grants to private colleges and universities are made under the foundation's matching gift program and the scholarship program, which is limited to employees' children.
Publications: Application Guidelines

Foundation Officials

Angie Burns: secretary
Anne Des Marais Vought: co-president, director
Katherine Gosin Gansner: director
Katharine Holzman: director
Edward Norris: director
Thomas J. Prosser: director
James J. Sarosiek: director
Kevin Schuh: treasurer
Nancy B. Sensebrenner: director
Charles E. Shepard: director
Kim Smith: director
Lydia B. Smith: director
Oliver C. Smith: chairman, director CORP AFFIL director: First National Bank Fox Valley.
Marc Vaccaro: director
Lucas Vought: director
Julie Shepard Waite: co-president, director
Margie Weiss: director

Grants Analysis

Disclosure Period: calendar year ending 2003
Total Grants: $296,717*
Number of Grants: 189
Average Grant: $1,570
Highest Grant: $25,000
Lowest Grant: $30
Typical Range: $300 to $3,000
***Note:** Giving excludes matching gifts, scholarships, and United Way.

Recent Grants

Note: Grants derived from 2003 Form 990.
General

25,000	Fox Cities Performing Arts Center, Appleton, WI
11,250	United Way, Menasha, WI
11,250	United Way Fox Cities, Menasha, WI
11,250	United Way Fox Cities Inc., Menasha, WI
10,000	Appleton Medical Center Foundation, Appleton, WI
10,000	Neenah-Menasha YMCA, Neenah, WI
10,000	Theda Clark Medical Center Foundation Inc., Neenah, WI
10,000	Tri-County Community Dental Clinic, Appleton, WI
10,000	Tri-County Community Dental Clinic, Appleton, WI
10,000	Tri-County Community Dental Clinic, Appleton, WI

MENDEL FOUNDATION

Giving Contact

Herbert Mendel, President
1401 W. 22nd St., Sunset Island IV
Miami Beach, FL 33140-2501
Phone: (305)868-3600

Description

Founded: 1964
EIN: 386099787
Organization Type: Private Foundation
Giving Locations: MI
Grant Types: General Support.

Donor Information

Founder: Herbert D. Mendel

Financial Summary

Total Giving: $45,500 (fiscal year ending April 30, 2004); $20,000 (fiscal 2001)
Assets: $8,752 (fiscal 2004); $31,571 (fiscal 2001)
Gifts Received: $50,000 (fiscal 1997). Note: In 1990, contributions were received from Herbert D. Mendel. Fiscal 1997, contributions were received from Herbert D. Mendel.

Typical Recipients

Arts & Humanities: Arts Associations & Councils, Arts Centers, Ballet, Community Arts, Dance, Arts & Humanities-General, History & Archaeology, Libraries, Music, Opera, Performing Arts, Public Broadcasting, Theater
Civic & Public Affairs: Community Foundations, Civic & Public Affairs-General, Urban & Community Affairs, Women's Affairs
Education: Arts/Humanities Education, Colleges & Universities, Minority Education, Private Education (Precollege)
Health: AIDS/HIV, Alzheimer's Disease, Clinics/Medical Centers, Emergency/Ambulance Services, Health Organizations, Medical Research, Prenatal Health Issues, Single-Disease Health Associations
International: Foreign Educational Institutions, International Relief Efforts, Missionary/Religious Activities
Religion: Jewish Causes, Religious Organizations, Synagogues/Temples

Social Services: Child Welfare, Community Service Organizations, Family Planning, Senior Services, United Funds/United Ways, Youth Organizations

Application Procedures

Initial Contact: The foundation has no formal grant application procedure or application form.
Deadlines: None.

Foundation Officials

Audre D. Mendel: vice president
Herbert D. Mendel: president B Chicago, IL 1922. ED University of Illinois (1947). PRIM CORP EMPL chairman, president: MSA IndustriesCorp. CORP AFFIL director: Peoples State Bank.
Julie Mendel: director

Grants Analysis

Disclosure Period: fiscal year ending April 30, 2004
Total Grants: $45,500
Number of Grants: 7
Average Grant: $6,500
Highest Grant: $15,000
Lowest Grant: $1,000
Typical Range: $1,500 to $10,000

Recent Grants

Note: Grants derived from fiscal 2004 Form 990.
General

15,000	Wedgewood Society
10,000	International Shakespeare Globe, Delray Beach, FL
10,000	Miami City Ballet, Miami, FL
5,000	Children's Resources
3,000	Dance Visions, Miami, FL
1,500	Alliance Francaise, Miami, FL
1,000	WKAT Classical, Miami, FL

GLENN AND RUTH MENGLE FOUNDATION

Giving Contact

D. Edward Chaplin, Vice President & Trust Officer
c/o First Commonwealth Trust Co.
PO Box 1046
Du Bois, PA 15801
Phone: (814)371-0660

Description

Founded: 1956
EIN: 256067616
Organization Type: Private Foundation
Giving Locations: PA: Brockway, Dubois, Erie
Grant Types: General Support, Scholarship.

Donor Information

Founder: the late Glenn A. Mengle, the late Ruth E. Mengle Blake

Financial Summary

Total Giving: 1997 Giving includes United Way ($30,000).
Gifts Received: $415,161 (1995)

Typical Recipients

Arts & Humanities: Arts Associations & Councils, Arts Funds, Arts & Humanities-General, Libraries, Museums/Galleries, Public Broadcasting
Civic & Public Affairs: Clubs, Civic & Public Affairs-General, Municipalities/Towns, Philanthropic Organizations, Professional & Trade Associations, Urban & Community Affairs
Education: Arts/Humanities Education, Business Education, Colleges & Universities, Education Funds, Leadership Training, Literacy, Private Education (Precollege), Science/Mathematics Education, Secondary Education (Private), Special Education, Stu-

dent Aid

Environment: Air/Water Quality, Environment-General, Resource Conservation
Health: Children's Health/Hospitals, Clinics/Medical Centers, Hospitals, Long-Term Care, Nursing Services
Religion: Churches, Religion-General, Religious Organizations, Religious Welfare
Social Services: At-Risk Youth, Child Welfare, Community Centers, Community Service Organizations, Family Services, Food/Clothing Distribution, Homes, People with Disabilities, Recreation & Athletics, Scouts, United Funds/United Ways, YMCA/YWCA/YMHA/YWHA, Youth Organizations

Application Procedures

Initial Contact: Send cover letter and full proposal.
Application Requirements: Include current financial statements, financial statements for the past three years, and the budget for next operating year.
Deadlines: September 1.

Additional Information

Trust(s): First Commonwealth Trust Co

Foundation Officials

DeVere L. Sheesley: trustee

Grants Analysis

Disclosure Period: calendar year ending 2000
Total Grants: $523,594*
Number of Grants: 50
Average Grant: $10,472
Highest Grant: $50,000
Typical Range: $5,000 to $20,000
*Note: Giving excludes United Way, scholarships, and matching gifts.

Recent Grants

Note: Grants derived from 2001 Form 990.
Library-Related

35,000	Mengle Memorial Library, DuBois, PA

General

57,000	DuBois Area YMCA, DuBois, PA
52,500	Bucktail Council B.S.A., DuBois, PA
45,000	Free Medical Clinic of DuBois, DuBois, PA
30,000	DuBois Area United Way, DuBois, PA
25,000	Alfred University, Alfred, NY -- renovation of Kanakadea Hall
25,000	Brockway Volunteer Hose Company, Brockway, PA -- purchase truck
25,000	DuBois Senior and Community Center, DuBois, PA
22,000	YMCA of Greater Erie, Erie, PA -- for capital improvements to Camp Sherwin
17,500	WPSX Public Television, University Park, PA
16,000	Christ the King Manor, DuBois, PA

MERCK FAMILY FUND

Giving Contact

Jenny D. Russell, Executive Director
303 Adams Street
Milton, MA 02186
Phone: (617)696-3580
Fax: (617)696-7262
E-mail: merck@merckff.org
Web: http://www.merckff.org

Description

Founded: 1954
EIN: 226063382
Organization Type: Family Foundation
Giving Locations: MA: Boston community-building program; NY: New York community-building program; RI: Providence community-building program,

community-building program Northern forests, Southern Appalachians, and Southern Coastal Plain for the Eastern Ecosystems program.
Grant Types: General Support, Multiyear/Continuing Support, Project.

Donor Information

Founder: The fund was incorporated in 1954 by members of the Merck family.

Financial Summary

Total Giving: $2,790,855 (2003); $3,362,916 (2002); $3,655,712 (2001)
Assets: $62,467,617 (2003); $55,774,320 (2002); $72,000,000 (2001 approx)
Gifts Received: $16,874 (2003); $4,857,443 (2002); $1,004,387 (2000). Note: In 2000, contributions were received from Josephine Merck.

Typical Recipients

Arts & Humanities: Arts Associations & Councils, Arts Funds, History & Archaeology, Libraries, Museums/Galleries, Music, Public Broadcasting, Theater
Civic & Public Affairs: Asian American Affairs, Botanical Gardens/Parks, Business/Free Enterprise, Clubs, Community Foundations, Economic Development, Economic Policy, Employment/Job Training, Gay/Lesbian Issues, Civic & Public Affairs-General, Hispanic Affairs, Housing, Minority Business, Municipalities/Towns, Nonprofit Management, Philanthropic Organizations, Public Policy, Urban & Community Affairs, Women's Affairs, Zoos/Aquariums
Education: Colleges & Universities, Environmental Education, Education-General, Leadership Training, Literacy, Public Education (Precollege), Science/Mathematics Education, Secondary Education (Public)
Environment: Air/Water Quality, Forestry, Environment-General, Protection, Research, Resource Conservation, Watershed
Health: Clinics/Medical Centers, Home-Care Services, Hospitals, Long-Term Care, Preventive Medicine/Wellness Organizations
International: International Affairs, International Environmental Issues
Religion: Religious Welfare
Science: Scientific Centers & Institutes, Scientific Organizations
Social Services: At-Risk Youth, Child Welfare, Community Service Organizations, Crime Prevention, Day Care, Family Planning, Family Services, Food/Clothing Distribution, People with Disabilities, Recreation & Athletics, Shelters/Homelessness, Social Services-General, Youth Organizations

Application Procedures

Initial Contact: The fund requests initial contact be made through a brief letter of inquiry (not to exceed two pages) rather than by a full proposal, phone call, or meeting.
Application Requirements: Inquiries should describe the project, its purpose, and its likely impact. The letter should also briefly describe the organization and its goals and specify the amount of funds requested. A member of the foundation's staff will review the letter and decide whether to invite a full proposal.
Deadlines: Complete, invited proposals are due February 30 for the May meeting and July 30 for the October meeting.
Review Process: Letters of inquiry are acknowledged as soon as possible. Unsolicited full proposals are not acknowledged.

Restrictions

The fund awards grants only to tax-exempt organizations in the United States. It does not make grants to individuals or for-profit organizations. It does not fund governmental Organizations, endowments, debt reduction, annual fund-raising campaigns, capital construction, purchase of equipment, acquisition of land, or film or video projects. The fund does not generally

support academic research or books. It does not make grants intended to support candidates for political office.

Additional Information

Publications: Annual Report; Grant Guidelines

Foundation Officials

Sharman Altshuler: treasurer, trustee
Nat Chamberlin: trustee
Patience Chamberlin: trustee
Oona Coy: trustee
Antony M. Merck: secretary, trustee
Josephine A. Merck: trustee
Wilhelm M. Merck: president, trustee
Jenny D. Russell: executive director
Serena H. Whitridge: vice president, trustee

Grants Analysis

Disclosure Period: calendar year ending 2003
Total Grants: $2,790,855
Number of Grants: 108
Average Grant: $25,841
Highest Grant: $65,000
Lowest Grant: $200
Typical Range: $10,000 to $50,000

Recent Grants

Note: Grants derived from 2003 Form 990.
General

65,000	Forest Society of Maine, Bangor, ME
52,288	Center for a New American Dream, Takoma Park, MD -- for sustainable economics
51,767	Chelsea Creek Action Group -- to support green space
50,193	Appalachian Mountain Club, Boston, MA -- for Eastern ecosystems
50,000	Natural Resources Defense Council, New York, NY
50,000	Northern Forest Alliance
50,000	Rocky Mountain Institute, Snowmass, CO
50,000	Worldwatch Institute, Washington, DC
49,147	Yale School of Forestry and Environmental Studies, New Haven, CT -- for Eastern Ecosystems
41,414	Redefining Progress, Oakland, CA -- to assist sustainable economics

MERCURY AIRCRAFT INC.

Company Headquarters

PO Box 338
Hammondsport, NY 14840
Web: http://www.mercuryaircraft.com

Company Description

Employees: 600
SIC(s): 3444 Sheet Metal Work, 3449 Miscellaneous Metal Work, 3469 Metal Stampings Nec.

Mercury Aircraft Foundation

Giving Contact

Gregory Hintz, Manager
17 Wheeler Ave.
Hammondsport, NY 14840-9566
Phone: (607)569-4200

Description

EIN: 166028162
Organization Type: Corporate Foundation
Giving Locations: NY: Western New York
Grant Types: Capital, General Support.

Financial Summary

Total Giving: $139,500 (2001)
Giving Analysis: Giving for 2001 includes: foundation grants to United Way ($8,500); foundation ($131,000)
Assets: $2,374,021 (2001)
Gifts Received: $40,000 (2001); $50,000 (2000); $58,750 (1999). Note: In 2001, contributions were received from Mercury Minnesota.

Typical Recipients

Arts & Humanities: Arts Associations & Councils, Arts & Humanities-General, Libraries, Museums/Galleries
Civic & Public Affairs: Chambers of Commerce, Clubs, Economic Development, Civic & Public Affairs-General, Housing, Safety, Urban & Community Affairs
Education: Colleges & Universities
Health: Cancer, Clinics/Medical Centers, Emergency/Ambulance Services, Health-General, Health Organizations, Heart, Hospitals, Respiratory
Religion: Churches, Religious Welfare
Science: Science-General, Science Museums, Scientific Centers & Institutes, Scientific Organizations
Social Services: Animal Protection, Emergency Relief, Family Planning, Food/Clothing Distribution, Homes, People with Disabilities, Recreation & Athletics, Scouts, United Funds/United Ways, Youth Organizations

Application Procedures

Initial Contact: The foundation has no formal grant application procedure or application form.
Deadlines: None.

Corporate Officials

Gregory J. Hintz: treasurer PRIM CORP EMPL treasurer: Mercury Aircraft.
Joseph F. Meade, Jr.: chairman, director B Freeport, NY 1921. ED Alfred University (1943). PRIM CORP EMPL chairman, director: Mercury Aircraft. CORP AFFIL director: Bath National Bank; chairman: Mercury Minnesota; president, director: Atlas Metla Industries; director: Bath & Hammondsport Railroad.
Joseph F. Meade, III: president PRIM CORP EMPL president: Mercury Aircraft.

Foundation Officials

Marcia M. Coon: trustee
Gregory J. Hintz: mgr (see above)
Joseph F. Meade, III: trustee (see above)
Joseph F. Meade, Jr.: trustee (see above)

Grants Analysis

Disclosure Period: calendar year ending 2001
Total Grants: $131,000*
Number of Grants: 45
Average Grant: $2,911
Highest Grant: $30,000
Typical Range: $1,000 to $5,000
*Note: Giving excludes United Way.

Recent Grants

Note: Grants derived from 2001 Form 990.
Library-Related
5,000	Hammondsport Public Library, Hammondsport, NY

General
30,000	Alfred University, Alfred, NY
20,500	Glenn H. Curtis Museum, Hammondsport, NY
10,000	J.E. Meade Memorial Science Fund
10,000	Keuka Health Care, Keuka Park, NY
8,500	United Way of Chemung and Steuben Counties, Corning, NY
6,000	Keuka College, Keuka Park, IN -- community association campaign
4,000	Hammondsport - Methodist Church, Hammondsport, NY
4,000	Hammondsport - Presbyterian Church, Hammondsport, NY
4,000	Hammondsport St. Gabriels Catholic Church, Hammondsport, NY
4,000	Hammondsport - St. James Episcopal Church, Hammondsport, NY

MEREDITH CORP.

Company Headquarters

1716 Locust St.
Des Moines, IA 50309-3023
Web: http://www.meredith.com

Company Description

Founded: 1902
Ticker: MDP
Exchange: NYSE
Revenue: US$1.08 billion (2003)
Employees: 2633 (2003)

Nonmonetary Support

Volunteer Programs: Employees who volunteer a minimum of 20 hours at one agency within a 12-month period between July 1 and June 30 are eligible to apply for a grant to that agency. Matches range from a minimum of $200 for 20 to 29 volunteer hours, to a maximum of $500 for 50 or more hours. A maximum of $1,500 is awarded to any one nonprofit within each fiscal year, regardless of the number of employees or hours volunteered. An employee may request one grant per year, and must apply within three months of the last day he or she volunteered.

Meredith Corp. Foundation

Giving Contact

Art Slusark, Foundation Manager
1716 Locust Street
Des Moines, IA 50309-3023
Phone: (515)284-2656
Fax: (515)284-3153

Description

EIN: 421426258
Organization Type: Corporate Foundation
Giving Locations: IA: Des Moines metropolitan area
Grant Types: Capital, Emergency, Employee Matching Gifts, General Support, Loan, Project.
Note: Employee matching gift ratio: 1 to 1 for contributions to nonprofit human service or arts organisation and to public educational institutions. Employee matching gift ratio: 2 to 1 for contributions to private secondary and post-secondary educational institutions.

Financial Summary

Total Giving: $1,363,947 (fiscal year ending June 30, 2004); $1,422,979 (fiscal 2003); $1,180,108 (fiscal 2002). Note: Contributes through corporate direct giving program and foundation.
Giving Analysis: Giving for fiscal 2002 includes: foundation grants to United Way ($190,000); fiscal 2001: foundation grants to United Way ($115,000)
Assets: $11,358,253 (fiscal 2004); $10,589,986 (fiscal 2003); $9,250,178 (fiscal 2002)
Gifts Received: $850,000 (fiscal 2004); $2,500,000 (fiscal 2003); $99,573 (fiscal 2002). Note: Contributions were received from the Meredith Corp.

Typical Recipients

Arts & Humanities: Arts Associations & Councils, Arts Centers, Arts Festivals, Arts Institutes, Arts & Humanities-General, Historic Preservation, History & Archaeology, Libraries, Literary Arts, Museums/Galleries, Music, Opera, Performing Arts, Theater, Visual Arts
Civic & Public Affairs: Clubs, Community Foundations, Economic Development, Civic & Public Affairs-General, Housing, Professional & Trade Associations, Safety, Urban & Community Affairs, Women's Affairs, Zoos/Aquariums
Education: Arts/Humanities Education, Business Education, Colleges & Universities, Economic Education, Education Funds, Elementary Education (Private), Education-General, Journalism/Media Education, Preschool Education, Private Education (Precollege), Religious Education, Secondary Education (Private), Student Aid
Environment: Environment-General, Protection
Health: Arthritis, Cancer, Children's Health/Hospitals, Emergency/Ambulance Services, Hospices, Mental Health, Single-Disease Health Associations
Religion: Ministries, Religious Organizations
Science: Scientific Centers & Institutes
Social Services: Child Welfare, Community Service Organizations, Counseling, Emergency Relief, Family Services, Homes, People with Disabilities, Social Services-General, United Funds/United Ways, Volunteer Services, Youth Organizations

Application Procedures

Initial Contact: Send a written proposal.
Application Requirements: Include name, address, and telephone number of the person submitting the application; copy of the 501(c)(3) tax-exempt letter given by the IRS; a summary of the organization's objectives, a statement of how the organization meets an identified community need, and an indication of the population served by the organization; the specific amount of money being requested and an explanation of how the funds would be used; two-year budget, clearly illustrating earnings and revenues; a list of the organization's board of directors, executive director, and number of staff employed; and an audited financial statement for the most recently completed year of operation.
Deadlines: None.
Review Process: The manager of community relations reviews and researches all grant proposals, then makes recommendations to the corporate contributions committee, which is composed of corporate officers.
Decision Notification: Executives meet quarterly to make contribution decisions.
Notes: If the request is for a capital drive or a specific project, a related budget should be included in the proposal, along with an explanation of the need for the drive and a timetable for the campaign.

Restrictions

Does not support individuals, religious organizations for sectarian purposes, organizations outside operating areas, or political or lobbying groups.

Additional Information

The corporation established The Meredith Corporation Foundation in September 1994. The foundation operates separately, but has policies and guidelines similar to the corporate giving program.
Publications: Guidelines Brochure

Corporate Officials

William T. Kerr: chairman, chief executive officer, director B Seattle, WA April 17, 1941. ED Oxford University BA (1962); University of Washington BA (1963); Oxford University MA (1965); Harvard University MBA (1967); Harvard University Graduate School of Business Administration MBA (1969). PRIM CORP EMPL chairman, chief executive officer, director: Meredith Corp. CORP AFFIL director: Storage Technology Corp.; director: Principal Financial Group; director: Principal Mutual Life Insurance Co.; chairman: Golf Digest/Tennis Inc.; director: Maytag Corp. NONPR AFFIL director: International Federation Periodical Press; member: Magazine Publishers America; member: Century Association. CLUB AFFIL Union Club; Wakonda Golf Club; Quogue Field Club; Reform Club; Des Moines Club; Litchfield Country Club; Brook Club.

Suku V. Radia: vice president, chief financial officer ED Iowa State University BS (1974).

Foundation Officials

Sandra Cooney: treasurer
Mell Meredith Frazier: chairman, director
William T. Kerr: president, director (see above)
Stephen Lacy: vice president, director
Suku V. Radia: director (see above)
Arthur J. Slusark: secretary, foundation manager
John S. Zieser: director

Grants Analysis

Disclosure Period: fiscal year ending June 30, 2004
Total Grants: $1,254,831*
Number of Grants: 625 (approx)
Average Grant: $2,008*
Highest Grant: $100,000
Lowest Grant: $25
Typical Range: $1,000 to $5,000
*Note: Giving excludes scholarship and United Way.

Recent Grants

Note: Grants derived from fiscal 2004 Form 990.
Library-Related

100,460	Public Library of Des Moines, Des Moines, IA

General

115,000	United Way of Central Iowa, Des Moines, IA
112,845	Science Center of Iowa, Des Moines, IA
105,650	Drake University, Des Moines, IA
100,000	Greater Des Moines Community Foundation, Des Moines, IA
63,050	Rebuilding Together, Des Moines, IA
51,325	Des Moines Symphony, Des Moines, IA
28,600	American Red Cross, Des Moines, IA
25,000	Des Moines Higher Education Center, Des Moines, IA
22,390	Blank Park Zoo, Des Moines, IA
21,625	Civic Center of Greater Des Moines, Des Moines, IA

MERKLEY CHARITABLE TRUST

Giving Contact

Dawn Bentley, Trust Officer
c/o Citizens Bank, Trust Div.
328 S. Saginaw Street
Flint, MI 48502-2412
Phone: (810)342-7390

Description

Founded: 1990
EIN: 386528749
Organization Type: Private Foundation
Giving Locations: MI: Genesee County
Grant Types: General Support.

Financial Summary

Total Giving: $212,280 (fiscal year ending November 30, 2003); $377,512 (fiscal 2001)
Assets: $4,437,584 (fiscal 2003); $4,539,670 (fiscal 2001)
Gifts Received: $230 (fiscal 1992). Note: In fiscal 1992, contributions were received from the family of Dorothy Church.

Typical Recipients

Arts & Humanities: Arts Centers, Arts Institutes, Ballet, Arts & Humanities-General, Libraries, Museums/Galleries, Music, Theater

Civic & Public Affairs: African American Affairs, Botanical Gardens/Parks, Chambers of Commerce, Community Foundations, Urban & Community Affairs
Education: Colleges & Universities, Education Reform, Public Education (Precollege), Vocational & Technical Education
Environment: Environment-General
Health: Alzheimer's Disease, Clinics/Medical Centers, Emergency/Ambulance Services, Geriatric Health, Respiratory
Religion: Churches, Jewish Causes, Religious Welfare
Science: Science Exhibits & Fairs
Social Services: Animal Protection, Big Brothers/Big Sisters, Child Welfare, Community Service Organizations, Food/Clothing Distribution, Recreation & Athletics, Scouts, Senior Services, YMCA/YWCA/YMHA/YWHA, Youth Organizations

Application Procedures

Initial Contact: The foundation requests applications be made in writing.
Application Requirements: Include a description of organization, amount requested, purpose of funds sought, recently audited financial statement, and proof of tax-exempt status.
Deadlines: None.

Restrictions

Provides grants to organizations providing services to youth or the elderly in Genesee County, MI.

Additional Information

Trust(s): Citizens Bank

Grants Analysis

Disclosure Period: fiscal year ending November 30, 2003
Total Grants: $212,280
Number of Grants: 17
Average Grant: $5,107*
Highest Grant: $101,756
Lowest Grant: $1,000
Typical Range: $3,000 to $8,000
*Note: Average grant figure excludes two highest grants ($135,675).

Recent Grants

Note: Grants derived from fiscal 2003 Form 990.
General

101,756	Genesee County Parks & Recreation Departments, Batavia, NY
33,919	Genesee Humane Society, Burton, MI
16,500	Jewish Community Services
12,000	Flint YMCA, Flint, MI
8,000	Food Bank of Eastern Michigan, Flint, MI
7,500	Valley Area Agency on Aging, Flint, MI
5,000	Alzheimer's Association, MI
5,000	Community Presbyterian Church, Flint, MI
5,000	Kettering University, Flint, MI
4,000	Genesee Chamber Foundation

MERRICK FOUNDATION

Giving Contact

Johnnie L. Rolen, Executive Secretary
2932 NW 122nd St., Suite D
Oklahoma City, OK 73120-1955
Phone: (405)755-5571
E-mail: fwmerrick@foundationmanagementinc.com

Description

Founded: 1947
EIN: 736111622
Organization Type: Private Foundation
Giving Locations: OK: emphasis on Southern Oklahoma

Grant Types: Capital, General Support, Seed Money.

Donor Information

Founder: the late Mrs. Frank W. Merrick

Financial Summary

Total Giving: $386,343 (2003); $524,400 (2001)
Giving Analysis: Giving for 2003 includes: foundation grants to United Way ($15,000); 2001: foundation grants to United Way ($16,000)
Assets: $12,028,640 (2003); $12,281,623 (2001)

Typical Recipients

Arts & Humanities: Arts Associations & Councils, Arts Centers, Arts Funds, Arts Institutes, Historic Preservation, History & Archaeology, Libraries, Literary Arts, Museums/Galleries, Music, Performing Arts
Civic & Public Affairs: African American Affairs, Botanical Gardens/Parks, Chambers of Commerce, Clubs, Community Foundations, Economic Development, Civic & Public Affairs-General, Municipalities/Towns, Nonprofit Management, Philanthropic Organizations, Public Policy, Urban & Community Affairs
Education: Business Education, Colleges & Universities, Economic Education, Education Associations, Education Funds, Education Reform, Education-General, Literacy, Private Education (Precollege), Public Education (Precollege), Science/Mathematics Education, Special Education, Student Aid
Health: Children's Health/Hospitals, Clinics/Medical Centers, Diabetes, Emergency/Ambulance Services, Health Organizations, Hospitals, Medical Research, Mental Health, Transplant Networks/Donor Banks
Religion: Churches, Ministries, Religious Organizations, Religious Welfare
Science: Science Museums, Scientific Centers & Institutes
Social Services: Animal Protection, At-Risk Youth, Child Welfare, Community Centers, Community Service Organizations, Day Care, Domestic Violence, Family Services, Food/Clothing Distribution, People with Disabilities, Recreation & Athletics, Scouts, Social Services-General, Substance Abuse, United Funds/United Ways, YMCA/YWCA/YMHA/YWHA, Youth Organizations

Application Procedures

Initial Contact: Send a brief letter of inquiry.
Application Requirements: Include documentation stating need and purpose of funds sought.
Deadlines: August 15 for letters summarizing projects; September 30 for grant applications.
Review Process: Proposals considered at trustees' November meeting.
Decision Notification: A response will be made to each request.

Restrictions

Does not support individuals, endowments, or provide operating funds. Limited to 501(c)(3) institutes.

Additional Information

Publications: Annual Report; Grant Policies and Procedures

Foundation Officials

Valda M. Buchanan: secretary
Michael A. Cawley: trustee B 1947. PRIM NONPR EMPL president, trustee: Samuel Roberts Noble Foundation Inc. CORP AFFIL director: Noble Affiliates Inc.
Laura Clay: trustee
Robert B. Merrick: trustee
Ward S. Merrick, Jr.: trustee

Grants Analysis

Disclosure Period: calendar year ending 2003
Total Grants: $371,343*
Number of Grants: 64
Average Grant: $4,529*
Highest Grant: $86,000

Lowest Grant: $100
Typical Range: $1,000 to $10,000
***Note:** Giving excludes United Way. Average grant figure excludes highest grant.

Recent Grants

Note: Grants derived from 2003 Form 990.
General

25,000	Ardmore Chamber of Commerce, Ardmore, OK
10,500	Arbuckle Life Solutions, Ardmore, OK
7,500	Ardmore Payne Education Center, Ardmore, OK
5,000	Ardmore Animal Care Inc., Ardmore, OK
5,000	Ardmore Public Schools Foundation, Ardmore, OK
5,000	Arts Council of Oklahoma City, Oklahoma City, OK
5,000	Calm Waters, Oklahoma City, OK
5,000	A Chance to Change, Oklahoma City, OK
4,743	Center for Nonprofits, Oklahoma City, OK
2,500	Communities Foundation of Oklahoma, Oklahoma City, OK

MERRILL LYNCH & COMPANY INC.

Company Headquarters

New York, NY
Web: http://www.ml.com

Company Description

Founded: 1885
Ticker: MER
Exchange: NYSE
Revenue: US$32.467 billion (2004)
Profit: US$4.436 billion (2004)
Employees: 48100 (2003)
Fortune Rank: 53, per FORTUNE Magazine's list of 500 Largest U.S. Corporations (2004).
SIC(s): 6211 Security Brokers & Dealers, 6719 Holding Companies Nec.

Nonmonetary Support

Type: Donated Equipment; In-kind Services
Volunteer Programs: The company sponsors an Employee Community Involvement Program, which provides grants of $100 to $1,000 to organizations where employees volunteer.
Contact: Bettina Lauf, Assistant Vice President, Corporate Responsibility
Note: Company donates equipment when available.

Merrill Lynch & Co. Foundation Inc.

Giving Contact

Eddy Bayardelle, Director, Philanthropic Programs
100 Union Ave.
Cresskill, NJ 07626
Phone: (201)871-0350
Web: http://www.ml.com/philanthropy

Alternate Contact

Merrill Lynch & Co. Foundation, Inc.
Phone: (212)614-4260

Description

Founded: 1950
EIN: 136139556
Organization Type: Corporate Foundation
Giving Locations: NY: New York metropolitan area national organizations; primarily in areas where Merrill Lynch & Co. maintains offices.
Grant Types: Capital, Employee Matching Gifts,

General Support, Multiyear/Continuing Support.
Note: Employee matching gift ratio: 1 to 1 up to $1,500 annually to employee-chosen causes in the areas of the art/culture, environment, independent college funds, private elementary schools, secondary or private high schools, special education, universities/colleges, health care, and hospitals.

Financial Summary

Total Giving: $15,872,883 (2003); $15,980,319 (2002); $23,464,499 (2001). Note: Contributes through corporate direct giving program and foundation. The corporate direct giving amount includes giving by domestic and international subsidiaries.
Giving Analysis: Giving for 2001 includes: foundation ($13,275,361); corporate direct giving ($21,648,680)
Assets: $32,238,161 (2003); $35,485,924 (2002); $43,989,135 (2001)
Gifts Received: $8,132,325 (2003); $7,200,000 (2002); $25,470,000 (2001). Note: Contributions are received from Merrill Lynch and Company, Inc.

Typical Recipients

Arts & Humanities: Arts Associations & Councils, Arts Centers, Arts Institutes, Arts Outreach, Ethnic & Folk Arts, Film & Video, Historic Preservation, History & Archaeology, Libraries, Museums/Galleries, Music, Opera, Performing Arts, Public Broadcasting, Theater
Civic & Public Affairs: African American Affairs, Asian American Affairs, Botanical Gardens/Parks, Business/Free Enterprise, Civil Rights, Community Foundations, Economic Development, Employment/Job Training, Ethnic Organizations, Civic & Public Affairs-General, Hispanic Affairs, Housing, Law & Justice, Municipalities/Towns, Professional & Trade Associations, Public Policy, Safety, Urban & Community Affairs, Women's Affairs, Zoos/Aquariums
Education: Afterschool/Enrichment Programs, Business Education, Business-School Partnerships, Colleges & Universities, Economic Education, Education Associations, Education Funds, Education Reform, Education-General, Health & Physical Education, International Studies, Journalism/Media Education, Leadership Training, Legal Education, Literacy, Medical Education, Minority Education, Private Education (Precollege), Public Education (Precollege), Science/Mathematics Education, Special Education, Student Aid
Environment: Environment-General, Wildlife Protection
Health: AIDS/HIV, Cancer, Children's Health/Hospitals, Clinics/Medical Centers, Emergency/Ambulance Services, Eyes/Blindness, Geriatric Health, Health Funds, Health Organizations, Heart, Hospitals, Hospitals (University Affiliated), Medical Research, Research/Studies Institutes, Single-Disease Health Associations, Transplant Networks/Donor Banks
International: Foreign Educational Institutions, International-General, Health Care/Hospitals, International Affairs, International Development, International Peace & Security Issues, International Relations, International Relief Efforts
Religion: Jewish Causes, Religious Welfare
Science: Science Museums, Scientific Centers & Institutes, Scientific Labs
Social Services: At-Risk Youth, Child Welfare, Community Centers, Community Service Organizations, Crime Prevention, Day Care, Emergency Relief, Family Services, Food/Clothing Distribution, People with Disabilities, Recreation & Athletics, Scouts, Senior Services, Shelters/Homelessness, Substance Abuse, United Funds/United Ways, Veterans, YMCA/YWCA/YMHA/YWHA, Youth Organizations

Application Procedures

Initial Contact: Send a proposal in letter form (no more than two to three pages in length); if outside greater New York area, apply directly to local branch office.

Application Requirements: Include organization's mission; history and current activities of the organization; goals and timelines for implementing the program; explanation of how the program relates to the goals of the foundation; objectives for the program and how they would be measured; the specific activities to be carried out to meet the objectives; groups and neighborhoods to be served and how they will benefit from the program; how short-term and long-term program results will be measured; organization and program budgets; and how the program will be sustained. The following documents should accompany the proposal: proof of tax-exempt status; list of the board of directors, with their affiliations (schools must submit a list of members of the board of education or PTA board); annual report and/or current operating budget; recently audited financial statement; list of current corporate and foundation funding sources, including amounts contributed within the most recent 12 months or last fiscal year. See Web site at: www.ml.com/philanthropy.
Deadlines: None.
Review Process: Proposals reviewed by manager of corporate contributions and foundation president for recommendation to board of trustees; decision to decline request made immediately; trustees meet quarterly.
Evaluative Criteria: Priority given to national organizations and organizations located in the greater New York metropolitan area. Preference is given to specific programs and projects (as opposed to general operating support) that are innovative, sustainable, creating opportunities for employees to volunteer, easily expanded from a local to a global perspective, and having a measurable impact.
Decision Notification: Decisions for direct gifts are generally made within 30 days of receipt.

Restrictions

The company will not make grants to the following: private foundations; individuals; fundraising activities related to individual sponsorship, such as walk-a-thons; seed money for new organizations; political causes, candidates and campaigns, and organizations designed specifically for lobbying; religious, fraternal, social or other membership organizations that provide services mainly to their own constituencies; athletic events and tournaments; fundraising events; endowments, construction and renovation projects, special purpose campaigns, chairs, or purchase of major equipment; conferences, workshops, or seminars; research; video/film production; United Way-supported agencies, except in the case of an emergency relief effort; or for-profit entities.
The company will not make grants for the reduction of an operating deficit or to liquidate a debt.

Additional Information

The company will consider support of capital needs when the specific project submitted has distinctive importance or the promise of a unique contribution to the field.
Since the company has a predetermined limit on multiyear commitments, grants usually are of a one-year duration. Requests for continuing support are considered using the company's priorities for the proposed grant year.
Publications: Responsible Citizenship Annual Report

Corporate Officials

Rosemary T. Berkery: executive vice president, general counseloo B 1954. ED Mount Saint Vincent College BA; Saint John's University JD. PRIM CORP EMPL executive vice president, general counsel: Merrill Lynch & Co.
Paul W. Critchlow: counselor to chairman, vice chairman, public markets ED University of Nebraska BA (1971); Columbia University MA (1972). PRIM CORP EMPL senior vice president marketing & communications: Merrill Lynch & Co., Inc.
Westina Lomax Matthews Shatteen: senior direc-

tor, first vice president corporate respons B Yellow Springs, OH 1948. ED University of Dayton BS (1970); University of Dayton MS (1974); University of Chicago PhD (1980). PRIM CORP EMPL senior director, first vice president corporate respons: Merrill Lynch & Co., Inc.

E. Stanley O'Neal: chairman, chief executive officer, president, chief operating officer B 1952. ED Kettering University BS; Harvard University MBA (1978). PRIM CORP EMPL chairman, chief executive officer, president: Merrill Lynch & Co. CORP AFFIL director: General Motors Corp.

Foundation Officials

Eddy Bayardelle: secretary
William L. Burke: trustee ED Harvard University BA (1964); University of Virginia LLB (1967). CORP AFFIL partner: Pillsbury Winthrop Shaw Pittman LLP. NONPR AFFIL member: ABA Committee on US Activities of Foreign Taxpayers; member: New York Bar Association.
Paul W. Critchlow: chairman (see above)
Terry Kassel: trustee
Thomas J. Lombardi: treasurer NONPR AFFIL treasurer: Win Smith Foundation.
Westina Lomax Matthews Shatteen: trustee (see above)
E. Stanley O'Neal: trustee (see above)

Grants Analysis

Disclosure Period: calendar year ending 2003
Total Grants: $6,117,356*
Number of Grants: 101*
Average Grant: $60,568
Highest Grant: $500,000
Lowest Grant: $5,000
Typical Range: $1,000 to $20,000
*Note: Giving excludes matching gifts, scholarships, and United Way.

Recent Grants

Note: Grants derived from 2003 Form 990.
General

1,198,417	Scholarship Builders Program, New York, NY
1,029,355	Scholarship Builders Program, New York, NY
750,000	United Way of Tri-State Inc., New York, NY
500,000	New York Presbyterian Hospital Fund Inc., New York, NY
390,300	Citizens Scholarship Foundation of America Inc., St. Peter, MN
320,700	Citizens Scholarship Foundation of America Inc., St. Peter, MN
300,000	New York City Police Foundation Inc., New York, NY
250,125	McCarthy Scholarship Program, New York, NY
250,000	Friends of Bronx Preparatory Charter School, Bronx, CA
250,000	International Youth Foundation, Baltimore, MD

MESSING FAMILY CHARITABLE FOUNDATION

Giving Contact

Wilma E. Messing, Trustee
30 Westwood Country Club
St. Louis, MO 63131
Phone: (314)432-8898

Description

Founded: 1961
EIN: 436034863

Organization Type: Private Foundation
Giving Locations: MO: St. Louis
Grant Types: General Support, Research.

Donor Information

Founder: Roswell Messing, Jr., Mrs. Roswell Messing, Jr.

Financial Summary

Total Giving: $207,872 (2001)
Giving Analysis: Giving for 2001 includes: foundation grants to United Way ($2,000)
Assets: $4,999,066 (2001)
Gifts Received: $130,775 (2001); $58,670 (2000); $157,587 (1999). Note: In 2001, contributions were received from Wilma Messing ($100,593) and ($30,182). In 2000, contributions were received from Noel Hefty ($28,535), Roswell Messing III ($30,135). In 1999, contributions were received from Wilma Messing ($99,526), Noel Hefty ($28,294), Roswell Messing III ($29,767). In 1995, contributions were received from Noel and Terry Hefty.

Typical Recipients

Arts & Humanities: Arts Associations & Councils, Dance, Arts & Humanities-General, Libraries, Music, Opera, Performing Arts, Public Broadcasting, Theater
Civic & Public Affairs: Civic & Public Affairs-General, Urban & Community Affairs, Women's Affairs, Zoos/Aquariums
Education: Arts/Humanities Education, Business Education, Colleges & Universities, Education-General, International Studies, Medical Education, Private Education (Precollege), Public Education (Precollege), Student Aid
Environment: Resource Conservation
Health: AIDS/HIV, Children's Health/Hospitals, Clinics/Medical Centers, Health Organizations, Hospices, Hospitals, Medical Research, Single-Disease Health Associations
Religion: Jewish Causes, Religious Organizations, Religious Welfare, Synagogues/Temples
Social Services: Animal Protection, Camps, Community Service Organizations, Day Care, Family Planning, Substance Abuse, United Funds/United Ways, Youth Organizations

Application Procedures

Initial Contact: The foundation has no formal grant application procedure or application form.
Deadlines: None.

Foundation Officials

Harold S. Goodman: trustee B Saint Louis, MO 1937. ED University of Missouri AB (1960); Washington University JD (1963); Washington University LLB (1963). PRIM CORP EMPL partner: Gallop, Johnson & Neuman. NONPR AFFIL member: Washington University Law Alumni Association; member: Zeta Beta Tau; member: Phi Delta Phi; member: Saint Louis Bar Association; member: Laumeier Sculpture Park; member: Missouri Bar Association; member: American Bar Association; trustee: Cystic Fibrosis Foundation.
Noel M. Hefty: trustee
Terrance Hefty: trustee
Roswell Messing, III: trustee
Wilma E. Messing: trustee
Arlene M. Naschke: trustee

Grants Analysis

Disclosure Period: calendar year ending 2001
Total Grants: $205,872*
Number of Grants: 59
Average Grant: $2,408*
Highest Grant: $38,115
Lowest Grant: $250
Typical Range: $500 to $5,000
*Note: Giving excludes United Way. Average grant figure excludes two highest grants ($68,615).

Recent Grants

Note: Grants derived from 2001 Form 990.
General

38,115	Perry Mansfield Dance School, Steamboat Springs, CO
30,500	Synergy School, Memphis, TN
10,000	Family Education Center, Petaluma, CA
10,000	Nature Conservancy
10,000	St. Louis Zoo, St. Louis, MO
10,000	University of Missouri, St. Louis, MO
7,500	Colorado Dance Festival, Denver, CO
7,000	Temple Emanu EL
5,000	Dance St. Louis, St. Louis, MO
5,000	MICDS, St. Louis, MO

METAL INDUSTRIES INC.

Company Headquarters

PO Box 4490
Clearwater, FL 33758
Web: http://www.metalaire.com

Company Description

Employees: 2,200
SIC(s): 3442 Metal Doors, Sash & Trim.

Metal Industries Foundation

Giving Contact

Sarah Walker Guthrie, Trustee
861 N. Hercules Avenue
Clearwater, FL 33765-1922
Phone: (727)461-0501
Fax: (727)442-4291

Alternate Contact

Brenda Brannon, Corporate Contributions
Phone: (813)441-2651
Note: Ms. Brannon may be reached at ext. 460.

Description

Founded: 1971
EIN: 237098483
Organization Type: Corporate Foundation
Giving Locations: FL
Grant Types: General Support.

Donor Information

Founder: Metal Industries, Inc.

Financial Summary

Total Giving: $47,850 (fiscal year ending October 31, 2004); $134,195 (fiscal 2001)
Assets: $3,006,344 (fiscal 2004); $3,014,017 (fiscal 2001)

Typical Recipients

Arts & Humanities: History & Archaeology, Libraries, Museums/Galleries, Public Broadcasting
Civic & Public Affairs: Business/Free Enterprise, Chambers of Commerce, Clubs, Civic & Public Affairs-General, Housing, Legal Aid, Municipalities/Towns, Philanthropic Organizations, Professional & Trade Associations, Safety, Urban & Community Affairs
Education: Business Education, Colleges & Universities, Community & Junior Colleges, Elementary Education (Private), Elementary Education (Public), Education-General, Private Education (Precollege), Secondary Education (Public)
Environment: Environment-General, Resource Conservation, Wildlife Protection
Health: Alzheimer's Disease, Cancer, Children's Health/Hospitals, Health-General, Geriatric Health,

Health Organizations, Heart, Hospices, Hospitals, Medical Research, Multiple Sclerosis, Preventive Medicine/Wellness Organizations, Public Health, Research/Studies Institutes, Single-Disease Health Associations, Transplant Networks/Donor Banks
International: Health Care/Hospitals
Religion: Churches, Religion-General, Jewish Causes, Ministries, Religious Welfare, Synagogues/Temples
Science: Science Museums
Social Services: Animal Protection, At-Risk Youth, Child Welfare, Community Service Organizations, Day Care, Emergency Relief, Family Services, Food/Clothing Distribution, People with Disabilities, Recreation & Athletics, Social Services-General, United Funds/United Ways, Volunteer Services, YMCA/YWCA/YMHA/YWHA, Youth Organizations

Application Procedures

Initial Contact: Send brief letter of inquiry.
Application Requirements: Describe project or request application for student loan program.
Deadlines: None.

Restrictions

Recipients must be worthy or needy. Does not support political or lobbying groups.

Corporate Officials

Pete DeSoto: chairman, president, chief executive officer B Boston, MA 1939. ED University of Florida BSBA (1962). PRIM CORP EMPL chairman, president, chief executive officer: Metal Industries. NONPR AFFIL member: Elizabethville Rotary; member: Screen Manufacturer Association.
Janet Fasenmyer: controller PRIM CORP EMPL controller: Metal Industries.

Foundation Officials

Sarah Walker Cuthrie: trustee
Pete DeSoto: trustee (see above)
Jay K. Poppleton: trustee

Grants Analysis

Disclosure Period: fiscal year ending October 31, 2004
Total Grants: $47,850
Number of Grants: 8
Average Grant: $5,981
Highest Grant: $12,000
Lowest Grant: $100
Typical Range: $500 to $10,000

Recent Grants

Note: Grants derived from 2004 Form 990.
General

12,000	Gator Boosters, Gainesville, FL
10,000	American Red Cross, FL
10,000	Mount Zion United Methodist Church, Clearwater, FL
5,000	Cystic Fibrosis Foundation, Tampa, FL
500	Volunteer Home Care, Sanford, FL
250	St. Rita Catholic Church, Boca Raton, FL
100	Auxiliary of Mease Health Care, Dunedin, FL

METRIS COMPANIES INC.

Company Headquarters

10900 Wayzata Blvd.
Minnetonka, MN 55305-1534
Web: http://www.metriscompanies.com

Company Description

Founded: 1996
Ticker: MXT
Exchange: NYSE
Assets: US$2.594 billion (2002)

Employees: 2900 (2003)
SIC(s): 6141 Personal Credit Institutions.

Nonmonetary Support

Volunteer Programs: The company participates in volunteer programs with charities in its operating communities.

Metris Companies Foundation

Giving Contact

Anne Morrow, Director of Community Relations
Metris Companies, Inc.
10900 Wayzata Blvd., Suite 7W
Minnetonka, MN 55305-1534
Phone: (652)525-5020
Web: http://www.metriscompanies.com/page11108.html

Description

Founded: 2000
EIN: 411949946
Organization Type: Corporate Foundation
Giving Locations: AZ: Scottsdale; FL: Jacksonville, Orlando; MD: White Marsh; MN: Duluth; OK: Tulsa
Grant Types: General Support.

Financial Summary

Total Giving: $662,902 (2003); $713,980 (2002); $897,644 (2001)
Giving Analysis: Giving for 2002 includes: foundation ($713,980); 2001: foundation ($897,644)
Assets: $1,175,353 (2003); $1,830,117 (2002); $2,502,078 (2001)
Gifts Received: $1,000,000 (2001); $1,200,000 (2000). Note: Contributions were received from the Metris Companies Inc.

Typical Recipients

Arts & Humanities: Libraries, Museums/Galleries, Public Broadcasting, Theater
Civic & Public Affairs: African American Affairs, Business/Free Enterprise, Economic Development, Ethnic Organizations, Civic & Public Affairs-General, Hispanic Affairs, Housing, Municipalities/Towns, Nonprofit Management, Urban & Community Affairs, Women's Affairs
Education: Afterschool/Enrichment Programs, Business Education, Colleges & Universities, Economic Education, Education Funds, Elementary Education (Public), Education-General, Private Education (Precollege), Religious Education, Special Education, Student Aid
Health: AIDS/HIV, Arthritis, Children's Health/Hospitals, Diabetes, Health Funds, Health Organizations, Hospitals, Multiple Sclerosis, Public Health, Respiratory, Single-Disease Health Associations
Religion: Churches, Religious Welfare
Social Services: Animal Protection, Big Brothers/Big Sisters, Camps, Child Abuse, Child Welfare, Community Service Organizations, Emergency Relief, Family Services, Food/Clothing Distribution, People with Disabilities, Recreation & Athletics, Refugee Assistance, Scouts, Shelters/Homelessness, Social Services-General, Special Olympics, Substance Abuse, United Funds/United Ways, Volunteer Services, YMCA/YWCA/YMHA/YWHA, Youth Organizations

Application Procedures

Initial Contact: Contact the foundation to obtain guidelines and an application form.
Application Requirements: Proposals should include a cover letter; completed application form; proposal narrative of no more than 5 pages describing the organization's background, need, how the program fits the foundation's areas of interest, activities to be carried out, qualifications of staff involved in the activities, and anticipated outcomes; organization

budget for current year; project budget; recently audited financial statement; proof of tax-exempt status; and list of board of directors and their affiliations.
Deadlines: The first Friday in February, May, August, and November.

Restrictions

Does not support individuals; fraternal organizations; religious organizations for sectarian purposes; political parties, candidates, campaigns, or organizations where the majority of activity is lobbying; fundraising events; or requests conferring direct benefits, such as auctions, raffles, dues, reduced tuition, conference fees, etc.

Corporate Officials

Dan N. Piteleski: executive vice president, chief information officer
David D. Wesselink: chairman, chief executive officer
John A. Witham: executive vice president, chief financial officer

Foundation Officials

John D. Armbruster: treasurer, director
Tern C. Dill: director
Richard G. Evans: secretary
Carolyn R. Morehead: director
Dan N. Piteleski: director (see above)
David D. Wesselink: president, director (see above)

Grants Analysis

Disclosure Period: calendar year ending 2003
Total Grants: $662,902
Number of Grants: 218
Average Grant: $1,233*
Highest Grant: $225,000
Lowest Grant: $25
Typical Range: $500 to $5,000
*Note: Average grant figure excludes three highest grants ($397,900).

Recent Grants

Note: Grants derived from 2003 Form 990.
General

225,000	United Hospital Foundation, St. Paul, MN -- for college and university education
96,000	Uptown Association, Minneapolis, MN -- for youth art program
76,900	Pacer Center Inc., Minneapolis, MN -- for family services
35,000	Gillette Children's Foundation, St. Paul, MN -- for medical, children's care
15,250	Big Brothers, Big Sisters, Minneapolis, MN
13,000	Children's Home Society of Minnesota, St. Paul, MN
8,475	Second Harvest Heartland, St. Paul, MN -- for food shelf
6,225	Muscular Dystrophy Association, Minneapolis, MN -- for medical, muscular dystrophy
5,500	Minnesota Brigade Camp Association, Brooklyn Center, MN -- for summer program for boys
5,200	Longview Elementary, Osborn School District, Phoenix, AZ -- for elementary & secondary education

METROPOLITAN LIFE INSURANCE CO.

Company Headquarters

1 Madison Avenue
New York, NY 10010-3690
Phone: (212)578-2211
Fax: (212)578-3320
Web: http://www.metlife.com

Company Description

Ticker: MET
Exchange: OTC
Also Known As: MetLife.
Revenue: US$39.535 billion (2004)
Profit: US$2.758 billion (2004)
Employees: 42,300
Fortune Rank: 37, per FORTUNE Magazine's list of 500 Largest U.S. Corporations (2004).
SIC(s): 6311 Life Insurance, 6371 Pension, Health & Welfare Funds.

Operating Locations

Metropolitan Life Insurance Co. (CA--Orange, Walnut Creek; CT--Guilford; FL--Clearwater; HI--Honolulu; IL--Lisle, Mount Prospect, Naperville, Niles, Rockford; KS--Overland Park; MI--Jackson; NJ--Cherry Hill, Iselin; NY--Brooklyn, Flushing, New Hyde Park; OK--Sallisaw; OR--Lake Oswego; PA--Wayne; TX--Round Rock; WV--Summersville)

Subsidiary Companies

MO: GenAmerica Financial Corp., St. Louis

Nonmonetary Support

Type: Donated Equipment; In-kind Services; Loaned Employees; Loaned Executives
Volunteer Programs: Recognizes company volunteers with the MetLife Volunteer ServiceAwards; also sponsors an employee volunteer program that helps employees find volunteer opportunities with nonprofits, schools, and other public agencies. There is a full-time volunteer coordinator at the headquarters location, and several branch offices have structured volunteer programs. Company makes small grants to organizations where employees actively volunteer, through the Volunteer Ventures program.
Contact: Dennis White, Vice President
Note: The company also offers select use of facilities by nonprofits.

MetLife Foundation

Giving Contact

Sibyl C. Jacobson, President & Chief Executive Officer
MetLife Foundation
27-01 Queens Plaza North, Suite 6D
Long Island City, NY 11101
Phone: (212)578-4852
Fax: (212)685-1435
Web: http://www.metlife.org

Alternate Contact

Dennis White
MetLife Social Investment Program
Corporate Investments Department
334 Madison Avenue
Convent Station, NJ 07961

Description

EIN: 132878224
Organization Type: Corporate Foundation
Giving Locations: nationally; special consideration to communities in which Metropolitan has a major presence.
Grant Types: Employee Matching Gifts, General Support, Loan, Multiyear/Continuing Support, Project, Research, Scholarship, Seed Money.
Note: Employee matching gift ratio: 1 to 1. Scholarships are for employees children only.

Financial Summary

Total Giving: $25,803,530 (2003); $24,991,068 (2002); $23,513,915 (2001). Note: Contributes through corporate direct giving program and foundation.
Giving Analysis: Giving for 2001 includes: foundation grants to United Way ($1,412,710); corporate direct giving ($5,285,471); foundation ($16,815,734)

Assets: $142,980,401 (2003); $133,925,872 (2002); $181,570,141 (2001)
Gifts Received: $12,510,156 (2003); $53,000 (1998); $144,833,024 (1996)

Typical Recipients

Arts & Humanities: Arts Associations & Councils, Arts Centers, Arts Institutes, Arts Outreach, Ballet, Dance, Ethnic & Folk Arts, Film & Video, Arts & Humanities-General, Historic Preservation, History & Archaeology, Libraries, Museums/Galleries, Music, Opera, Performing Arts, Public Broadcasting, Theater, Visual Arts
Civic & Public Affairs: African American Affairs, Botanical Gardens/Parks, Business/Free Enterprise, Civil Rights, Community Foundations, Economic Development, Economic Policy, Employment/Job Training, Civic & Public Affairs-General, Hispanic Affairs, Housing, Law & Justice, Municipalities/Towns, Nonprofit Management, Professional & Trade Associations, Public Policy, Rural Affairs, Safety, Urban & Community Affairs, Women's Affairs, Zoos/Aquariums
Education: Afterschool/Enrichment Programs, Agricultural Education, Arts/Humanities Education, Business Education, Colleges & Universities, Community & Junior Colleges, Economic Education, Education Associations, Education Funds, Education Reform, Engineering/Technological Education, Faculty Development, Education-General, Health & Physical Education, Leadership Training, Literacy, Medical Education, Minority Education, Preschool Education, Public Education (Precollege), Science/Mathematics Education, Student Aid
Environment: Environment-General
Health: AIDS/HIV, Alzheimer's Disease, Cancer, Children's Health/Hospitals, Clinics/Medical Centers, Health-General, Geriatric Health, Health Policy/Cost Containment, Health Funds, Health Organizations, Heart, Hospitals, Hospitals (University Affiliated), Medical Research, Medical Training, Mental Health, Nursing Services, Nutrition, Prenatal Health Issues, Preventive Medicine/Wellness Organizations, Public Health, Research/Studies Institutes, Respiratory, Transplant Networks/Donor Banks
International: Foreign Arts Organizations, Foreign Educational Institutions, Health Care/Hospitals, International Organizations, International Peace & Security Issues, International Relief Efforts
Religion: Religious Welfare
Science: Science Museums, Scientific Centers & Institutes, Scientific Labs
Social Services: At-Risk Youth, Big Brothers/Big Sisters, Child Welfare, Community Service Organizations, Counseling, Crime Prevention, Delinquency & Criminal Rehabilitation, Emergency Relief, Family Services, Food/Clothing Distribution, Homes, Scouts, Senior Services, Shelters/Homelessness, Substance Abuse, United Funds/United Ways, Volunteer Services, YMCA/YWCA/YMHA/YWHA, Youth Organizations

Application Procedures

Initial Contact: Send a written request.
Application Requirements: Include a description of organization (legal name, history, activities, purpose, and governing board), purpose for which grant is requested, amount requested and list of other sources of financial support, most recently audited financial statement, copy of IRS determination letter indicating 501(c)(3) tax-exempt status, and Form 990; requests for funds to support a specific project or program should include fully defined need, objective, benefits, plans (including time frame and evaluative criteria), staff, and budget (including sources of financial support committed and pending).
Deadlines: None; requests reviewed throughout year.
Evaluative Criteria: Considers organization's general structure, history, objectives, and management capability, relationship to community and population served, position and service relative to similar organizations, financial position and sources of income; projects are evaluated on goals and implementation plans, time frame, ultimate disposition of project, staff capabilities, benefits of the project, and sources of financial and other support.
Notes: If request falls under foundation guidelines and program priorities, organization may be asked to provide more complete information before a decision is made. Foundation occasionally issues requests for proposals.

Restrictions

Grants are not made to individuals; private foundations; hospitals; organizations receiving support from United Way; organizations whose activities are mainly international; local chapters of national organizations; disease-specific organizations; organizations primarily engaged in patient care or direct treatment; drug treatment centers or community health clinics; elementary or secondary schools; endowments; courtesy advertising or festival participation; labor organizations; or religious, fraternal, political, athletic, social, or veterans organizations.

Additional Information

Occasionally, foundation establishes particular areas of interest for emphasis within a program area. When this is done, foundation actively seeks opportunities for providing grants and may issue requests for proposals.

Grant renewals are not automatic and cannot be guaranteed from year to year.

In addition to Metropolitan Life's grant programs, the company and foundation sponsor the Metlife Social Investment Program. This program provides loans, guarantees, equity investments and other financial programs to community ventures that do not meet the traditional investment criteria of private and institutional investors. The program typically underwrites projects relating to affordable housing, commercial revitalization, land preservation, health and rehab treatment centers, business development arts, and education. Although most investments are for nonprofit organizations, for-profit entities that have a clear social purpose are also considered.
Publications: Contributions Report

Corporate Officials

C. Robert Henrikson: president, chief operating officervidual business ED Emory University JD; University of Pennsylvania BA. CORP AFFIL director: MetLife Bank NA.
Catherine Amelia Rein: senior executive vice president B Lebanon, PA 1943. ED Pennsylvania State University BA (1965); New York University JD (1968). PRIM CORP EMPL vice president: Metropolitan Life Insurance Co. ADD CORP EMPL president, chief executive officer: Metropolitan Property Casualty Insurance Co.
William J. Toppeta: president, international
Lisa M. Weber: president, individual business ED State University of New York-Stony Brook BA. CORP AFFIL director: Reinsurance Group of America Inc..

Foundation Officials

Daniel Cavanagh: director
C. Robert Henrikson: director (see above)
Sibyl C. Jacobson: president, chief executive officer, director PRIM CORP EMPL senior vice president external affairs: Metropolitan Life Insurance Co. NONPR AFFIL member: Phi Beta Kappa.
James L. Lipscomb: director NONPR AFFIL director: Life Insurance Council of New York.
Deborah Mandel: assistant treasurer
Joseph A. Reali: secretary, counsel ED Fordham University JD; New York University. CORP AFFIL director: Reinsurance Group of American.
Catherine Amelia Rein: director, chairman (see above)
Jonathan Rosenthal: treasurer, director
Robert C. Tarnok: controller
William J. Toppeta: director (see above)

Lisa M. Weber: director (see above)
A. Dennis White: vice president

Grants Analysis

Disclosure Period: calendar year ending 2003
Total Grants: $22,205,226*
Number of Grants: 582
Average Grant: $38,153
Highest Grant: $1,500,000
Lowest Grant: $1,000
Typical Range: $10,000 to $100,000
*****Note:** Giving excludes United Way.

Recent Grants

Note: Grants derived from 2003 Form 990.
Library-Related

250,000	Libraries for the Future, New York, NY -- MLF reading America program

General

975,560	Young & Rubicam, New York, NY -- parenting skills
700,000	United Way of Tri-State, New York, NY
600,000	Twin Cities Public Television, St. Paul, MN -- Alzheimer's disease documentary
500,000	Boys & Girls Clubs of America, Atlanta, GA -- second phase of MLF leverage for learning fund
500,000	Harvard School of Public Health, Boston, MA -- Harvard mentoring initiative
400,000	Twin Cities Public Television, St. Paul, MN -- Alzheimer's disease documentary
380,000	Public Education Network, Washington, DC -- MLF civic engagement initiative
306,821	Young & Rubicam, New York, NY -- parenting skills radio campaign
300,000	Big Brothers Big Sisters of America, Philadelphia, PA -- MetLife foundation partnership for school based mentoring
300,000	New York City Leadership Academy, New York, NY

MEX-AM CULTURAL FOUNDATION

Giving Contact

Andrew M. Klinger, Trustee
c/o Grant, Herrmann, Schwartz and Klinger
675 Third Avenue
New York, NY 10017
Phone: (212)682-1800

Description

Founded: 1985
EIN: 133328723
Organization Type: Private Foundation
Giving Locations: NY: New York nationally.
Grant Types: General Support, Scholarship.

Donor Information

Founder: the Wolfgang Schoenborn Trust

Financial Summary

Total Giving: $93,500 (fiscal year ending September 30, 2004); $155,000 (fiscal 2001)
Giving Analysis: Giving for fiscal 2004 includes: foundation scholarships ($29,500); fiscal 2001: foundation scholarships ($30,000)
Assets: $1,781,084 (fiscal 2004); $2,017,022 (fiscal 2001)

Typical Recipients

Arts & Humanities: Arts Festivals, Arts Funds, Arts Institutes, Dance, Ethnic & Folk Arts, Film & Video, Arts & Humanities-General, Libraries, Museums/Galleries, Music, Opera, Theater, Visual Arts
Civic & Public Affairs: Civic & Public Affairs-General, Parades/Festivals

Education: Arts/Humanities Education, International Studies, Legal Education, Medical Education, Minority Education, Student Aid
International: Foreign Arts Organizations, Health Care/Hospitals, Human Rights, International Organizations
Religion: Religious Welfare
Social Services: Community Service Organizations

Application Procedures

Initial Contact: Send a brief letter of inquiry.
Application Requirements: Detail specific need for which request is made.
Deadlines: None.

Foundation Officials

William J. Brown: president
Andrew M. Klinger: trustee

Grants Analysis

Disclosure Period: fiscal year ending September 30, 2004
Total Grants: $64,000*
Number of Grants: 8
Average Grant: $5,571*
Highest Grant: $25,000
Lowest Grant: $1,500
Typical Range: $2,500 to $15,000
*****Note:** Giving excludes scholarships. Average grant figure excludes highest grant.

Recent Grants

Note: Grants derived from fiscal 2004 Form 990.
General

25,000	US- Mexico Fund for Culture, Col Jaurez Mexico -- towards program Mexico-gateway to the America in New York
15,000	Duke University, Durham, NC -- in support of Mexican undergraduate scholarships
15,000	Guggenheim Museum, New York, NY -- for exhibition Aztec Empire
12,500	Cornell University Medical College, New York, NY -- in support of Mexican- related research scholarships
7,500	Pro Mujer International, New York, NY
5,000	Mexican Fine Arts Center Museum, Chicago, IL -- for exhibition Treasures from Ancient Veracruz
3,750	Central de Projectos, Brasilla Brazil -- in support of the Foto Arte festival
3,750	Fundacion Luz Austral, Buenos Aires Argentina -- in support of the Encuentros Abiertos festival
2,500	Guild Hall, East Hampton, NY -- support of program Ballet Folklonco de Veracruz
2,000	Tisch School of Arts, New York, NY -- in support of performance scholarship for a Mexican student

ALICE KLEBERG REYNOLDS MEYER FOUNDATION

Giving Contact

Sherry McGillicuddy
Care of Frost National Bank
401 Congress Ave.
Austin, TX 78701
Phone: (512)473-4804

Description

Founded: 1978
EIN: 742847652
Organization Type: Private Foundation
Giving Locations: TX
Grant Types: Capital, General Support.

Donor Information

Founder: Alice K. Meyer

Financial Summary

Total Giving: $894,017 (2003)
Assets: $21,434,251 (2003)
Gifts Received: $577,348 (2003); $28,473 (1996); $100,000 (1995). Note: In 2003, contributions were received from the estate of Alice K. Meyer. In 1996, contributions were received from Alice K. Meyer.

Typical Recipients

Arts & Humanities: Arts Centers, Arts Institutes, Arts Outreach, Community Arts, Historic Preservation, Libraries, Literary Arts, Museums/Galleries, Music, Performing Arts, Public Broadcasting, Theater
Civic & Public Affairs: Botanical Gardens/Parks, Economic Policy, Civic & Public Affairs-General, Hispanic Affairs, Inner-City Development, Nonprofit Management, Public Policy, Urban & Community Affairs, Women's Affairs, Zoos/Aquariums
Education: Colleges & Universities, Education Funds, Education Reform, Environmental Education, Minority Education, Private Education (Precollege), Science/Mathematics Education, Special Education, Student Aid, Vocational & Technical Education
Environment: Environment-General
Health: Cancer, Children's Health/Hospitals, Clinics/Medical Centers, Emergency/Ambulance Services, Health Organizations, Long-Term Care, Medical Rehabilitation, Medical Research, Nursing Services, Public Health, Respiratory
International: Foreign Arts Organizations
Religion: Ministries, Religious Organizations
Science: Science Museums, Scientific Organizations, Scientific Research
Social Services: Child Welfare, Community Service Organizations, Counseling, Family Planning, Food/Clothing Distribution, Homes, Scouts, Special Olympics, Substance Abuse, United Funds/United Ways, Volunteer Services, Youth Organizations

Application Procedures

Initial Contact: Send a brief letter on organization's letterhead signed by a member of the board of directors or an officer of the organization. Include specific information about the purpose of funds sought, a copy of the organization's charter and by-laws, and proof of tax-exempt status.
Deadlines: None.

Grants Analysis

Disclosure Period: calendar year ending 2003
Total Grants: $894,017
Number of Grants: 83
Average Grant: $10,771
Highest Grant: $60,000
Lowest Grant: $1,500
Typical Range: $5,000 to $20,000
Note: No grants list available for 1999.

Recent Grants

Note: Grants derived from 2004 Form 990.
General

100,000	Greater Austin Performing Arts Center, Austin, TX -- towards long center for performing arts
100,000	Texas Agricultural and Mechanical University, Kingsville, TX -- towards education/training
60,000	Texas Agricultural and Mechanical University, Kingsville, TX -- towards quail fellowship
40,000	University of Texas MD Anderson Cancer Center, Houston, TX -- for proton therapy center
30,000	People's Community Clinic, Austin, TX -- for capacity clinic
30,000	Planned Parenthood of Texas, Austin, TX
25,241	Town Lake Trail Foundation, Austin, TX -- for trail signage

25,000	Fuerza Unida, San Antonio, TX
25,000	San Antonio Urban, San Antonio, TX -- for fair weather family lodge/jumpstart
25,000	Santuaria Sister Farm, Boerne, TX -- for eco-spiritual retreats

EUGENE AND AGNES E. MEYER FOUNDATION

Giving Contact

Julie L. Rogers, President
1400 16th Street Northwest, Suite 360
Washington, DC 20036-2217
Phone: (202)483-8294
Fax: (202)328-6850
E-mail: meyer@meyerfdn.org
Web: http://www.meyerfoundation.org

Description

Founded: 1944
EIN: 530241716
Organization Type: General Purpose Foundation
Giving Locations: DC: Washington metropolitan area; MD: suburban Maryland; VA: Northern Virginia
Grant Types: General Support, Loan, Operating Expenses.

Donor Information

Founder: The Meyer Foundation was established in December 1944. The foundation's donors, Mr. and Mrs. Eugene Meyer, were active in national affairs as well as community affairs in Washington, D.C. Mr. Meyer, who died in 1959, was a Wall Street investment banker, governor of the Federal Reserve, first president of the World Bank, and chairman of the board of the Washington Post, which he purchased in 1933. Agnes E. Meyer, who died in 1970, founded the Urban Service Corps in 1961 and the National Committee for Support of Public Schools in 1962. Mrs. Meyer was a journalist and author interested in public education, urban renewal, social action, and the arts. The AEM Foundation in New York City, founded by Mrs. Meyer in 1960, supports organizations in which she was interested.

Financial Summary

Total Giving: $6,577,055 (2002)
Assets: $143,336,661 (2002)
Gifts Received: $3,100 (2002); $214,943 (1998); $128,417 (1997). Note: In 1998, contributions were received from Intergroup Fund Revenue ($205,478) and Advancement Fund contributions ($9,465).

Typical Recipients

Arts & Humanities: Arts Associations & Councils, Arts Centers, Arts Outreach, Ballet, Community Arts, Dance, Ethnic & Folk Arts, Film & Video, Arts & Humanities-General, Historic Preservation, History & Archaeology, Literary Arts, Museums/Galleries, Music, Performing Arts, Public Broadcasting, Theater
Civic & Public Affairs: Asian American Affairs, Botanical Gardens/Parks, Business/Free Enterprise, Civil Rights, Community Foundations, Economic Development, Employment/Job Training, Civic & Public Affairs-General, Hispanic Affairs, Housing, Law & Justice, Legal Aid, Nonprofit Management, Philanthropic Organizations, Public Policy, Urban & Community Affairs, Women's Affairs
Education: Afterschool/Enrichment Programs, Arts/Humanities Education, Colleges & Universities, Community & Junior Colleges, Education Funds, Elementary Education (Private), Faculty Development, Education-General, Health & Physical Education, International Studies, Legal Education, Literacy, Minority Education, Preschool Education, Public Education (Precollege), Science/Mathematics Education, Special Education, Student Aid

Environment: Protection, Resource Conservation
Health: AIDS/HIV, Children's Health/Hospitals, Clinics/Medical Centers, Health-General, Health Funds, Health Organizations, Hospices, Long-Term Care, Mental Health, Prenatal Health Issues, Public Health
International: International Development
Religion: Religion-General, Jewish Causes, Ministries, Religious Welfare
Social Services: At-Risk Youth, Child Welfare, Community Centers, Community Service Organizations, Counseling, Crime Prevention, Delinquency & Criminal Rehabilitation, Domestic Violence, Family Planning, Family Services, Food/Clothing Distribution, Homes, People with Disabilities, Recreation & Athletics, Refugee Assistance, Senior Services, Shelters/Homelessness, Social Services-General, Substance Abuse, United Funds/United Ways, Volunteer Services, YMCA/YWCA/YMHA/YWHA, Youth Organizations

Application Procedures

Initial Contact: Applicants are urged to submit a preliminary letter of inquiry of no more than two pages in length to the program officer.
Application Requirements: The letter of inquiry should include: summary of proposal; primary mission and activities; amount requested, total proposed budget, and funding committed to date; annual operating budget; contact person and telephone number.
Deadlines: The letter of inquiry should be sent to the foundation at least six weeks before proposals are due. Deadlines for full proposals are March 15 for the June board meeting, July 15 for the October meeting, and November 15 for the February meeting.
Review Process: Receipt of proposals will be acknowledged in writing. The foundation staff will review the preliminary letter and contact the applicant with their best judgment whether or not the project would be of interest to the board.
Notes: The foundation does not accept faxed proposals or proposals by e-mail. If a staff member advises the applicant to send a full proposal, the foundation will provide specific details on what must be covered in the written narrative. Full proposals are reviewed upon receipt. If a proposal is considered, the project and organization are researched and an interview may be requested. All proposals are reviewed by the board, and the decision is sent in writing by the end of the month. The foundation discourages phone calls.

Restrictions

The foundation prefers not to provide continuing support to organizations. It does not contribute to programs intended to serve constituencies outside the Washington metropolitan area. The foundation does not make grants to individuals, award scholarships or financial assistance, make grants to projects which are primarily sectarian in nature, endowment drives, scientific or medical research, or special events or conferences.

Additional Information

Publications: Annual Report; Guidelines

Foundation Officials

Edward H. Bersoff, PhD: vice chairman B 1942. PRIM CORP EMPL chairman: BTG Inc.
Thomas W. Chapman: secretary, treasurer PRIM CORP EMPL vice president finance, treasurer: Qualchoice of Arkansas Inc. CORP AFFIL board member: Rooney, Ida, Nolt & Ahern.
Newman T. Halvorson, Jr.: assistant secretary, assistant treasurer B Detroit, MI 1936. ED Princeton University AB (1958); Harvard University LLB (1961). PRIM CORP EMPL partner: Covington & Burling. NONPR AFFIL member: District of Columbia Bar Association; board trustee, member executive committee: Greater Washington Research Center; trustee: Cleveland Park Historical Society; member: Committee 100 Federal City; member: American Bar Association. CLUB AFFIL Metro Club; Chevy Chase Country Club.

Boisfeuillet Jones, Jr.: director B Atlanta, GA 1946. ED Harvard University AB (1968); Harvard University JD (1974); Oxford University DPhil (1981). PRIM CORP EMPL president, general manager: Washington Post Co. CORP AFFIL director: Bowater Mersey Paper Co.; director: Robinson Terminal Warehouse Corp. NONPR AFFIL director: Greater Washington Board Trade; director: Saint Albans School; director: Federal City Council.
James W. Jones: chairman B Texarkana, TX 1945. ED Trinity University BA (1967); New York University JD (1970). PRIM CORP EMPL managing partner: Arnold & Porter.
Patricia A. McGuire: director B Philadelphia, PA 1952. ED Trinity College BA (1974); Georgetown University JD (1977). PRIM NONPR EMPL president, trustee: Trinity College. NONPR AFFIL member dollar coin design advisory committee: United States Mint; director: Women's College Coalition; member advisory board: National College Access Network; member: Trinity College Alumnae Association; commissioner: Mid-State Commission Higher Education; director: National Association Independent Colleges & Universities; board visitors: Joint Military Intelligence College; member advisory board: Merion Mercy Academy & Sisters Mercy; director: Elderhostel Inc.; adj professor law: Georgetown University Law Center; director: Association Catholic Colleges & Universities; member: Council Advancement & Support Education; member commission government relations: American Council Education; member: Association American Law Schools; director: Acacia Group; member: American Bar Association.
Mallory Walker: chairman, trustee B Washington, DC 1939. ED University of Virginia (1958-1963). PRIM CORP EMPL president, director: Walker & Dunlop. CORP AFFIL chairman, president: Walker & Dunlop Service Corp.; president, chief executive officer: Green Park Financial LP; president, chief executive officer: Walker & Dunlop Multifamily Inc. NONPR AFFIL trustee: Phillips Collection; trustee: WETA; honorary trustee: National Building Museum; trustee: Greater Washington Board of Trade; trustee: Greater Washington Research Center; board of directors: Fannie Mae Foundation; trustee: Federal City Council.
Francey Lim Youngberg: director

Grants Analysis

Disclosure Period: calendar year ending 2002
Total Grants: $6,577,055
Number of Grants: 288
Average Grant: $22,837
Highest Grant: $200,000
Lowest Grant: $1,000
Typical Range: $5,000 to $50,000

Recent Grants

Note: Grants derived from 2002 Form 990.
General

200,000	District of Columbia College Access Program, Washington, DC -- funding for organization's programs
200,000	Technology Works for Good, Washington, DC -- funding for general operations
150,000	Local Initiatives Support Corporation, Washington, DC -- toward community facilities fund and general operations
125,000	Washington AIDS Partnership, Washington, DC -- toward grantmaking and general operations support
100,000	Asian American LEAD Leadership Empowerment and Development for youth and Family, Washington, DC -- funding for capital campaign
100,000	Food & Friends, Washington, DC -- funding to support capital campaign
100,000	Historical Society of Washington, Washington, DC -- funding to support the city museum capital campaign

75,000	Building Bridges Across the River, Washington, DC -- toward capital campaign for education, arts and recreation center
75,000	Carlos Rosario International Career Center, Washington, DC -- funding for capital campaign
75,000	Community Foundation for the National Capital Region, Washington, DC -- funding for organization's programs

PAUL J. MEYER FOUNDATION

Giving Contact

Paul J. Meyer, Sr., President & Director
PO Box 7411
Waco, TX 76714-7411
Phone: (254)776-0034

Description

Founded: 1985
EIN: 742357421
Organization Type: Private Foundation
Former Name: Paul J. Meyer Family Foundation.
Giving Locations: TX
Grant Types: General Support.

Donor Information

Founder: Paul J. Meyer, Alice Jane Meyer

Financial Summary

Total Giving: $1,793,929 (2003)
Giving Analysis: Giving for 2003 includes: foundation grants to United Way ($9,000)
Assets: $27,087,227 (2003)
Gifts Received: $2,458,544 (2003); $1,986,093 (1999); $431,426 (1998). Note: In 2003, contributions were received from Cayhesse ($1,821,494), Paul J. Meyer ($51,000) and L-K Marketing ($580,000). In 1999, contributions were received from Cayhesse ($1,636,975), Paul J. Meyer ($46,545), L-K Marketing ($205,000), Rappoport ($20,000), Leslie Jane Meyer Trust ($70,447), and others less than $5,000 each ($7,126). In 1998, contributions were received from Janna Trust. In 1996, contributions were received from Japale, Ltd. ($686,500), Kim Lund ($42,869), and Paul J. Meyer ($23,440); miscellaneous contributions of less than $5,000 each totaling $4,065 also were received.

Typical Recipients

Arts & Humanities: History & Archaeology, Libraries, Museums/Galleries, Theater
Civic & Public Affairs: Clubs, Community Foundations, Economic Policy, Employment/Job Training, Civic & Public Affairs-General, Hispanic Affairs, Housing, Public Policy, Urban & Community Affairs, Zoos/Aquariums
Education: Colleges & Universities, Education-General, Private Education (Precollege), Public Education (Precollege), Religious Education, Secondary Education (Private), Student Aid
Health: Arthritis, Cancer, Eyes/Blindness, Heart, Long-Term Care, Prenatal Health Issues
International: International Peace & Security Issues, Missionary/Religious Activities
Religion: Churches, Religion-General, Jewish Causes, Ministries, Missionary Activities (Domestic), Religious Organizations, Religious Welfare, Seminaries, Social/Policy Issues
Social Services: Child Welfare, Community Service Organizations, Domestic Violence, Family Services, People with Disabilities, Recreation & Athletics, Scouts, Shelters/Homelessness, Social Services-General, United Funds/United Ways, YMCA/YWCA/YMHA/YWHA, Youth Organizations

Application Procedures

Initial Contact: Send a brief letter.
Application Requirements: Include a a description of organization and purpose of funds sought.
Deadlines: None.

Foundation Officials

Joe E. Baxter: secretary, treasurer, director
Alice Jane Meyer: vice president, director
Paul J. Meyer, Sr.: president, director B San Mateo, CA 1928. PRIM CORP EMPL founder, chairman, director: SMI/USA. CORP AFFIL founder, chairman, director: Leadership Management. NONPR AFFIL member: National Republican Finance Committee; member: National Speakers Bureau; member: International Franchise Association; member: American Management Association; director: Boys Club Waco.

Grants Analysis

Disclosure Period: calendar year ending 2003
Total Grants: $1,784,929*
Number of Grants: 73
Average Grant: $18,124*
Highest Grant: $480,000
Lowest Grant: $100
Typical Range: $10,000 to $25,000
*Note: Giving excludes United Way. Average grant figure excludes highest grant.

Recent Grants

Note: Grants derived from 2003 Form 990.
General

550,500	Haggai Institute, Atlanta, GA
235,300	Friends for Life, Waco, TX
110,927	Texas Christian Academy, Waco, TX
103,875	Christian Stewardship Association, Indianapolis, IN
100,000	University of Mary Hardin Baylor, Belton, TX
88,000	Rick Caywood Ministries
78,400	Mission Waco, Waco, TX
70,374	Faith Walk
66,000	First Baptist Church, Woodway, WA
49,194	Caritas

ROBERT R. MEYER FOUNDATION

Giving Contact

Carla B. Gale, Vice President & Trustee
AmSouth Bank of Alabama
PO Box 11426
Birmingham, AL 35202
Phone: (205)326-5382
Fax: (205)581-7433

Description

Founded: 1949
EIN: 636019645
Organization Type: General Purpose Foundation
Giving Locations: AL: Birmingham metropolitan area
Grant Types: Capital, General Support, Multiyear/Continuing Support, Research, Scholarship.

Donor Information

Founder: The Robert R. Meyer Foundation was established in 1923 by John E. Meyer and the late Robert R. Meyer (d. 1947).

Financial Summary

Total Giving: $1,781,333 (2003); $1,954,889 (2002)
Giving Analysis: Giving for 2003 includes: foundation grants to United Way ($127,500); 2002: foundation matching gifts ($23,300)
Assets: $40,567,766 (2003); $36,124,647 (2002)

Typical Recipients

Arts & Humanities: Arts Associations & Councils, Arts Festivals, Ballet, Dance, Historic Preservation, History & Archaeology, Libraries, Literary Arts, Museums/Galleries, Music, Theater
Civic & Public Affairs: Botanical Gardens/Parks, Business/Free Enterprise, Civil Rights, Clubs, Community Foundations, Employment/Job Training, Civic & Public Affairs-General, Hispanic Affairs, Housing, Nonprofit Management, Urban & Community Affairs, Zoos/Aquariums
Education: Arts/Humanities Education, Business Education, Colleges & Universities, Education Reform, Elementary Education (Private), Education-General, Gifted & Talented Programs, Literacy, Medical Education, Minority Education, Private Education (Precollege), Public Education (Precollege), Secondary Education (Private), Special Education
Environment: Air/Water Quality, Environment-General, Resource Conservation, Wildlife Protection
Health: AIDS/HIV, Cancer, Children's Health/Hospitals, Clinics/Medical Centers, Eyes/Blindness, Health Organizations, Hospitals, Long-Term Care, Mental Health, Nursing Services, Public Health, Research/Studies Institutes, Single-Disease Health Associations, Speech & Hearing
International: International Organizations
Religion: Churches, Jewish Causes, Ministries, Religious Welfare
Science: Scientific Centers & Institutes
Social Services: At-Risk Youth, Big Brothers/Big Sisters, Camps, Child Welfare, Community Centers, Community Service Organizations, Crime Prevention, Day Care, Domestic Violence, Family Planning, Family Services, Homes, People with Disabilities, Recreation & Athletics, Scouts, Senior Services, Social Services-General, Substance Abuse, United Funds/United Ways, Volunteer Services, YMCA/YWCA/YMHA/YWHA, Youth Organizations

Application Procedures

Initial Contact: There are no specific application forms. Proposals should be sent with an original and five copies.
Application Requirements: A one-page cover letter, signed by the director and board chair, should include name, address, phone and fax numbers of the applying organization; name and title of contact person if other than director; amount of funds requested; and a one-paragraph summary of the project. The full proposal, no longer than four pages, should include organization's background and history, including major programs or accomplishments and any links with similar organisation; a description of the project, including the qualifications of key personnel and any other organisation involved; project continuation and evaluation details; and complete financial information. Include a list of directors with their affiliations, three references, and the organization's tax-exempt letter.
Deadlines: March 15 and September 15.
Review Process: The board of trustees meets in the spring and fall.
Notes: Do not send binders, notebooks, or folders.

Restrictions

No grants are made to individuals, or organizations not classified as 501(c)(3) by the IRS. Grants are made only in the greater Birmingham, AL, area.

Additional Information

AmSouth Bank in Birmingham, AL, is listed as corporate trustee of the foundation.
Trust(s): Amsouth Bank

Foundation Officials

William M. Spencer, III: member advisory committee B Birmingham, AL December 10, 1920. ED University of the South (1941); Harvard University (1947). PRIM CORP EMPL chairman: Molecular Engineering Associates. CORP AFFIL director: Biocryst Pharmaceuticals Inc.; director: Porter, White & Co.

Grants Analysis

Disclosure Period: calendar year ending 2003
Total Grants: $1,653,800*
Number of Grants: 61
Average Grant: $21,251*
Highest Grant: $200,000
Lowest Grant: $2,000
Typical Range: $5,000 to $40,000
***Note:** Giving excludes United Way. Giving includes scholarships. Average grant figure excludes two highest grants ($400,000).

Recent Grants

Note: Grants derived from 2002 Form 990.
General

200,000	Birmingham Zoo, Inc., Birmingham, AL
200,000	Children's Hospital of Alabama, Birmingham, AL
135,000	Alexis De Tocqueville Society
125,000	University of Alabama Birmingham, Birmingham, AL
100,000	Metropolitan Arts Council, Birmingham, AL
100,000	Nature Conservancy of Alabama, Birmingham, AL
100,000	University of Alabama Birmingham, Birmingham, AL
50,000	Alabama Symphony Orchestra, Birmingham, AL
50,000	Birmingham Early Learning Center, Birmingham, AL
50,000	Birmingham Museum of Art, Birmingham, AL

MEYER MEMORIAL TRUST

Giving Contact

Doug Stamm, Executive Director
425 NW 10th Ave., Suite 400
Portland, OR 97209
Phone: (503)228-5512
E-mail: mmt@mmt.org
Web: http://www.mmt.org

Description

Founded: 1982
EIN: 930806316
Organization Type: General Purpose Foundation
Giving Locations: OR; WA: Clark County
Grant Types: Capital, General Support, Matching, Multiyear/Continuing Support.

Donor Information

Founder: The trust is the residuary beneficiary of the estate of Fred G. Meyer, and was established in 1978. Fred Meyer, who died in 1978, bequeathed the trust approximately two million shares of stock in Fred Meyer, Inc. Mr. Meyer was born in 1886 into a family of Brooklyn grocers. After working his way through the wheat fields of the Dakotas and Montana and the gold fields of Alaska, he moved to Portland, OR, in 1909. He then became successful at peddling coffee and managing a downtown street market. Later he invested all of his assets in an "all package" grocery store, and began a chain of stores throughout the Pacific Northwest. By 1979, his stores employed more than 13,000 people and had over $1 billion in annual sales.

Fred Meyer's wife of 41 years, Eva, was an integral part of this success. She managed several store departments in the early years and became a director and the secretary-treasurer of Fred Meyer, Inc.

Fred Meyer's life and career exemplified ingenuity, hard work, and a commitment to the communities where he built his stores. He introduced innovative

marketing concepts to the Northwest, including the packaging of bulk goods, one-stop shopping, cash-and-carry purchasing, self-service drug stores, and other creative and convenient services. He also supported economic development of the Northwest. He bought local products whenever possible, and he fostered the production of new crops in the region. He helped finance new business ventures as well as some in danger of failing.

Financial Summary

Total Giving: $23,000,000 (fiscal year ending March 31, 2005 approx); $17,372,822 (fiscal 2003); $24,735,559 (fiscal 2002)
Giving Analysis: Giving for fiscal 2003 includes: foundation matching gifts ($55,505)
Assets: $532,000,000 (fiscal 2004 approx); $402,122,936 (fiscal 2003); $475,246,555 (fiscal 2002)

Typical Recipients

Arts & Humanities: Arts Associations & Councils, Arts Centers, Arts Festivals, Arts Funds, Arts Institutes, Arts Outreach, Ballet, Community Arts, Dance, Ethnic & Folk Arts, Arts & Humanities-General, Historic Preservation, History & Archaeology, Libraries, Museums/Galleries, Music, Opera, Performing Arts, Public Broadcasting, Theater, Visual Arts
Civic & Public Affairs: African American Affairs, Asian American Affairs, Botanical Gardens/Parks, Chambers of Commerce, Community Foundations, Economic Development, Employment/Job Training, Ethnic Organizations, Civic & Public Affairs-General, Hispanic Affairs, Housing, Inner-City Development, Law & Justice, Legal Aid, Municipalities/Towns, Native American Affairs, Nonprofit Management, Philanthropic Organizations, Public Policy, Rural Affairs, Safety, Urban & Community Affairs, Zoos/Aquariums
Education: Afterschool/Enrichment Programs, Arts/Humanities Education, Business Education, Business-School Partnerships, Colleges & Universities, Community & Junior Colleges, Continuing Education, Education Associations, Education Reform, Elementary Education (Private), Elementary Education (Public), Environmental Education, Faculty Development, Education-General, International Exchange, International Studies, Leadership Training, Literacy, Medical Education, Minority Education, Preschool Education, Private Education (Precollege), Public Education (Precollege), Religious Education, School Volunteerism, Science/Mathematics Education, Secondary Education (Private), Special Education
Environment: Air/Water Quality, Forestry, Environment-General, Protection, Resource Conservation, Watershed, Wildlife Protection
Health: AIDS/HIV, Alzheimer's Disease, Cancer, Children's Health/Hospitals, Clinics/Medical Centers, Diabetes, Emergency/Ambulance Services, Geriatric Health, Health Policy/Cost Containment, Health Organizations, Heart, Home-Care Services, Hospices, Hospitals, Long-Term Care, Medical Rehabilitation, Medical Research, Medical Training, Mental Health, Nursing Services, Prenatal Health Issues, Public Health, Single-Disease Health Associations
International: International Affairs
Religion: Jewish Causes, Ministries, Religious Organizations, Religious Welfare, Seminaries
Science: Science Museums, Scientific Centers & Institutes
Social Services: At-Risk Youth, Child Abuse, Child Welfare, Community Centers, Community Service Organizations, Counseling, Day Care, Delinquency & Criminal Rehabilitation, Domestic Violence, Family Planning, Family Services, Food/Clothing Distribution, Homes, People with Disabilities, Recreation & Athletics, Refugee Assistance, Senior Services, Sexual Abuse, Shelters/Homelessness, Social Services-General, Substance Abuse, YMCA/YWCA/YMHA/YWHA, Youth Organizations

Application Procedures

Initial Contact: A grant application guidelines packet should be requested before submitting a proposal.
Application Requirements: The applicant should submit a completed application cover sheet (part of the packet); the organization's legal name and address; name, title, address, and telephone number of the person in charge of the project; a description of organization, including a summary of its background and its qualifications in the area for which funds are sought; list of names and primary affiliations of the organization's board of directors; organization's most recent financial statement; and a copy of the IRS tax-exemption letter. Only one copy of these materials should be submitted. The proposal itself should contain a statement from the chief operating officer that the project has been reviewed and recommended for submission by the governing board; description of the project and why it is important to undertake; description of the people, organizations, or groups expected to benefit from the project's outcome and the ways they would benefit; substantiation of the extent of need for these benefits; explanation of why the applicant organization is the appropriate one to conduct the project; description of the plan of action and a timetable for implementation; methods and criteria for assessing the project's effectiveness; qualifications of people involved in implementing the project; detailed descriptions of previous budgets, if the project is already in operation; detailed current budget for the project; description of other possible sources of support; and an explanation of how the project could be sustained after the period for which support has been requested.
Deadlines: None, for general proposals; January 15, April 15, and October 15 for the Small Grants program; and February 1 for the Support our Teacher Initiatives program.
Review Process: If a proposal submitted under the General Purpose guidelines passes a first review by the trustees, a staff member will contact the applicant for additional information. Final action on proposals passing first review will be made three to five months after submission. If a proposal is outside the field of interest of the trust, notification is given within two months. An applicant will be notified shortly after a decision has been reached on a proposal. Under the Small Grants program, a final decision will normally be made about twelve weeks after a deadline; incomplete proposals will not be considered. Under the Support for Teacher Initiatives program guidelines, applications submitted for the February 1 deadline are reviewed, and grantss will be announced in May.

Restrictions

The trust does not favor proposals seeking funds for direct grants, scholarships, or fellowships to individuals; endowments; general fund drives or annual appeals; general ongoing operating budgets; indirect or overhead costs (except as specifically and essentially related to the grant project); debt retirement or operational deficits; projects of sectarian or religious organizations whose principal benefit is for their own members; or propagandizing or influencing elections or legislation.

The trust will not replace funding for activities or materials previously provided by federal, state, or school district funds.

Additional Information

Applications are invited only from Oregon and Clark County, WA.
Publications: Annual Report; Grant Application Guidelines; Support for Teacher Initiatives Program Guidelines; General Purpose Grants Program Guidelines; Small Grants Program Guidelines

Foundation Officials

Debbie F. Craig: trustee
Marie Deatherage: program officer
John Emrick: trustee CORP AFFIL chairman, chief

executive officer: Norm Thompson Outfitters.
Orcilia Zuniga Forbes: trustee NONPR AFFIL director: Chalk Board Project.
Charline McDonald: program officer
Victor Merced: program officer ED Georgetown University.
Warne Harry Nunn: trustee
Wayne George Pierson: chief financial officer, treasurer ED California State University BS (1973). NONPR AFFIL member: Oregon Society CPAs; member: Portland Society Financial Analysts; member: Institute Chartered Financial Analysts Federation; member: American Institute of Certified Public Accountants; member: Association Investment Management & Research.
G. Gerald Pratt: trustee CORP AFFIL director: CenterSpan Communications Corp..
Doug Stamm: executive director

Grants Analysis

Disclosure Period: fiscal year ending March 31, 2003
Total Grants: $17,317,317*
Number of Grants: 306
Average Grant: $50,386*
Highest Grant: $1,000,000
Lowest Grant: $1,000
Typical Range: $10,000 to $100,000
Note: Giving excludes matching gifts. Average grant figure excludes two highest grants ($2,000,000).

Recent Grants

Note: Grants derived from 2003 Form 990.

Library-Related

150,000	Library Foundation of Milton-Freewater, Milton-Freewater, OR -- for building a new library
120,000	Hood River County Library Foundation, Hood River, OR -- toward renovating the community public library

General

1,000,000	Central Catholic High School, Portland, OR -- towards capital campaign to renovate and upgrade its aging facility
1,000,000	Linfield College, McMinnville, OR -- for renovating a building for a library and theater on this liberal arts college campus
600,000	Portland Center Stage, Portland, OR -- towards supporting the growth and artistic evolution of this theater company
500,000	Cathedral School, Portland, OR -- for helping build a new library at this catholic elementary school
500,000	Lakewood Center for the Arts, Lakewood, OR -- for building a new stage house for theater activities
400,000	Jack Will and Rob Kids Foundation, Camas, WA -- towards construction of a local youth center
400,000	Oregon State University, Corvallis, OR -- for support of the Willamette basin conservation project
350,000	Community Health Center, Medford, OR -- towards purchasing and renovating the organizations health and clinic facility
350,000	Tower Theater Foundation, Bend, OR -- towards purchase and renovation of Tower theater
300,000	Neighborhood Partnership Fund, Portland, OR -- toward support of a statewide initiative to help build the capacity of community development organizations

MEYERS CHARITABLE FAMILY FUND

Giving Contact

David R. Meyers, President
8748 S. Kells Dr.
Hickory Hills, IL 60457
Phone: (708)598-8111

Description

Founded: 1988
EIN: 363610777
Organization Type: Private Foundation
Grant Types: General Support.

Financial Summary

Total Giving: $199,370 (2001)
Assets: $2,325,416 (2001)

Typical Recipients

Arts & Humanities: Arts Centers, Ballet, Historic Preservation, Libraries, Music, Opera, Public Broadcasting, Theater
Civic & Public Affairs: Civic & Public Affairs-General, Native American Affairs, Public Policy, Urban & Community Affairs, Zoos/Aquariums
Education: Arts/Humanities Education, Colleges & Universities, International Studies, Medical Education, Private Education (Precollege), Secondary Education (Private), Special Education, Student Aid
Environment: Environment-General, Resource Conservation, Wildlife Protection
Health: AIDS/HIV, Children's Health/Hospitals, Clinics/Medical Centers, Medical Rehabilitation, Research/Studies Institutes
International: International Environmental Issues, International Organizations, International Peace & Security Issues
Religion: Churches, Religious Welfare, Social/Policy Issues
Science: Science Museums
Social Services: Animal Protection, At-Risk Youth, Child Welfare, Community Service Organizations, Family Services, Homes, People with Disabilities, Recreation & Athletics

Application Procedures

Initial Contact: The foundation has no formal grant application procedure or application form. Send a brief letter of inquiry.
Deadlines: None.

Restrictions

Grants are not made to individuals.

Foundation Officials

Margery McGrew: director
David R. Meyers: president, director
Frederick C. Meyers: secretary, treasurer

Grants Analysis

Disclosure Period: calendar year ending 2001
Total Grants: $199,370
Number of Grants: 141
Average Grant: $1,414
Highest Grant: $9,500
Typical Range: $1,000 to $5,000

Recent Grants

Note: Grants derived from 2001 Form 990.
General

9,500	Metropolitan Opera Association, New York, NY
7,500	Presbyterian College, Clinton, SC
7,400	Chicago Zoological Society, Chicago, IL
6,900	Sun Valley Summer Symphony, Sun Valley, ID
5,700	Cook Children's Hospital, Ft. Worth, TX
5,500	San Francisco Jazz Organization, San Francisco, CA
5,350	American Ballet Theater, New York, NY
5,000	Dennis Keller Scholarship Fund, Hinsdale, IL
5,000	NPR Foundation, San Francisco, CA
5,000	Roundabout Theater, New York, NY

MGE ENERGY INC.

Company Headquarters

133 S. Blair St.
Madison, WI 53788
Web: http://www.mge.com

Company Description

Ticker: MGEE
Exchange: AMEX
Former Name: Madison Gas & Electric Co. (2001).
Assets: US$541.5 million (2001)
Employees: 691 (2003)
SIC(s): 4939 Combination Utility Nec.

Madison Gas & Electric Foundation

Giving Contact

Bonnie Juul, Grants Coordinator
PO Box 1231
Madison, WI 53701-1231
Phone: (608)252-7279

Description

Founded: 1966
EIN: 396098118
Organization Type: Corporate Foundation
Giving Locations: WI
Grant Types: General Support.

Donor Information

Founder: Madison Gas And Electric Co.

Financial Summary

Total Giving: $318,353 (2003); $399,064 (2002); $654,752 (2001)
Giving Analysis: Giving for 2001 includes: foundation scholarships ($2,000); foundation grants to United Way ($73,625); foundation ($579,127)
Assets: $10,174,763 (2003); $6,931,003 (2002); $6,685,757 (2001)
Gifts Received: $750,000 (2003); $1,250,000 (2001); $140,550 (1997). Note: Contributions were received from Madison Gas & Electric Co.

Typical Recipients

Arts & Humanities: Arts Associations & Councils, Arts Centers, Community Arts, Arts & Humanities-General, History & Archaeology, Libraries, Museums/Galleries, Music, Opera, Public Broadcasting, Theater
Civic & Public Affairs: African American Affairs, Asian American Affairs, Botanical Gardens/Parks, Business/Free Enterprise, Chambers of Commerce, Clubs, Community Foundations, Economic Development, Civic & Public Affairs-General, Housing, Municipalities/Towns, Nonprofit Management, Parades/Festivals, Philanthropic Organizations, Public Policy, Safety, Urban & Community Affairs, Women's Affairs, Zoos/Aquariums
Education: Business Education, Business-School Partnerships, Colleges & Universities, Education Associations, Education Funds, Elementary Education (Public), Engineering/Technological Education, Education-General, Gifted & Talented Programs, Literacy, Minority Education, Preschool Education, Private Education (Precollege), Public Education (Precollege), Secondary Education (Public), Special Education, Student Aid

Environment: Environment-General, Resource Conservation
Health: AIDS/HIV, Cancer, Children's Health/ Hospitals, Clinics/Medical Centers, Emergency/ Ambulance Services, Health Funds, Health Organizations, Heart, Hospices, Hospitals, Hospitals (University Affiliated), Medical Rehabilitation, Medical Research, Prenatal Health Issues, Public Health, Single-Disease Health Associations
International: International-General, International Development
Religion: Ministries, Religious Organizations, Religious Welfare
Science: Scientific Centers & Institutes
Social Services: At-Risk Youth, Camps, Child Abuse, Child Welfare, Community Centers, Community Service Organizations, Day Care, Domestic Violence, Emergency Relief, Family Services, Food/ Clothing Distribution, Homes, People with Disabilities, Recreation & Athletics, Scouts, Senior Services, Shelters/Homelessness, Social Services-General, Special Olympics, United Funds/United Ways, Veterans, YMCA/YWCA/YMHA/YWHA, Youth Organizations

Application Procedures
Initial Contact: Scholarship application forms and deadline information are published in company newsletter. For organization grants, send a brief letter of inquiry.
Application Requirements: Include name, address, amount requested, and purpose of funds sought.
Deadlines: None.

Restrictions
Organizations must be located within Madison Gas & Electric Co.'s service territory in order to be considered.

Corporate Officials
Mr. Terry A. Hanson: chief financial officer vice president administration PRIM CORP EMPL chief financial officer: Madison Gas & Electric Co.
David Cummins Mebane: chairman, president, chief executive officer, director B Toledo, OH 1933. ED Arizona State University (1957); University of Wisconsin (1960). PRIM CORP EMPL chairman, president, chief executive officer, director: Madison Gas & Electric Co. CORP AFFIL director: First Federal Savings Bank Madison/LaCrosse; director: First Capital Investment Corp. Madison; director: First Federal Capital Corp. NONPR AFFIL director: Madison Gas & Electric Foundation Madison; trustee: University Wisconsin Research Park Corp.
Carol A. Wiskowski: assistant vice president administration PRIM CORP EMPL assistant vice president administration: Madison Gas & Electric Co.
Gary J. Wolter: senior vice president administration PRIM CORP EMPL senior vice president administration: Madison Gas & Electric Co.

Foundation Officials
Mr. Terry A. Hanson: secretary, treasurer (see above)
Lynn K. Hobbie: vice president
Thomas R. Krull: vice president
Gary J. Wolter: president (see above)

Grants Analysis
Disclosure Period: calendar year ending 2003
Total Grants: $240,977*
Number of Grants: 66
Average Grant: $2,938*
Highest Grant: $50,000
Lowest Grant: $75
Typical Range: $1,000 to $5,000
*Note: Giving excludes United Way. Average grant figure excludes highest grant.

Recent Grants
Note: Grants derived from 2003 Form 990.

Library-Related
15,000	Rosemary Garfoot Public Library, Cross Plains, WI
5,000	Middleton Public Library, Middleton, WI

General
77,376	United Way of Dane County, Madison, WI
50,000	Madison Great Performances Campaign, Madison, WI
20,000	Madison Symphony Orchestra, Madison, WI
15,000	Madison Opera-Opera in the Park, Madison, WI
13,278	University of Wisconsin Foundation, Madison, WI
10,000	Fund for Women, San Francisco, CA
10,000	Recycle Worlds Cosulting, Madison, WI
10,000	University of Wisconsin College of Engineering Vision 2000, Madison, WI
7,500	Camp Gay, Chicago, IL
5,000	American Red Cross Badger Division, Madison, WI

HERBERT I. AND ELSA B. MICHAEL FOUNDATION

Giving Contact
Laura Houston
c/o US Bank National Association
PO Box 3058
Salt Lake City, UT 84110-3058
Phone: (801)534-6085

Description
Founded: 1950
EIN: 876122556
Organization Type: Private Foundation
Giving Locations: UT
Grant Types: General Support, Scholarship.

Donor Information
Founder: the late Elsa B. Michael

Financial Summary
Total Giving: $457,800 (fiscal year ending September 30, 2004); $487,677 (fiscal 2001). Note: Fiscal 1997 Giving includes matching gifts ($6,000); scholarship ($2,500).
Giving Analysis: Giving for fiscal 2004 includes: foundation grants to United Way ($50,000); foundation scholarships ($65,000); fiscal 2001: foundation scholarships ($44,500).
Assets: $6,777,709 (fiscal 2004); $7,028,683 (fiscal 2001)

Typical Recipients
Arts & Humanities: Arts Associations & Councils, Arts Centers, Ballet, Dance, Historic Preservation, History & Archaeology, Libraries, Museums/ Galleries, Music, Opera, Public Broadcasting
Civic & Public Affairs: Botanical Gardens/Parks, Civil Rights, Clubs, Law & Justice, Legal Aid, Urban & Community Affairs
Education: Arts/Humanities Education, Business Education, Colleges & Universities, Education Funds, Education-General, International Exchange, Legal Education, Literacy, Medical Education, Preschool Education, Science/Mathematics Education, Student Aid
Environment: Resource Conservation, Wildlife Protection
Health: AIDS/HIV, Alzheimer's Disease, Children's Health/Hospitals, Clinics/Medical Centers, Emergency/Ambulance Services, Health Organizations, Hospices, Hospitals, Medical Training, Prenatal Health Issues, Public Health, Respiratory, Single-Disease Health Associations, Speech & Hearing, Trauma Treatment

International: Foreign Arts Organizations
Religion: Religious Organizations, Religious Welfare, Social/Policy Issues
Social Services: At-Risk Youth, Child Welfare, Community Service Organizations, Crime Prevention, Day Care, Domestic Violence, Family Planning, Family Services, Food/Clothing Distribution, People with Disabilities, Substance Abuse, United Funds/United Ways, YMCA/YWCA/YMHA/YWHA, Youth Organizations

Application Procedures
Initial Contact: The foundation requests applications be made in writing. Include purpose of funds sought.
Deadlines: None.

Additional Information
Trust(s): US Bank National Association

Foundation Officials
Tracy D. Smith: trustee

Grants Analysis
Disclosure Period: fiscal year ending September 30, 2004
Total Grants: $354,300*
Number of Grants: 75
Average Grant: $4,724
Highest Grant: $20,000
Lowest Grant: $1,000
Typical Range: $1,000 to $10,000
*Note: Giving excludes scholarships; United Way.

Recent Grants
Note: Grants derived from fiscal 2004 Form 990.
General
50,000	United Way of Salt Lake Area, Salt Lake City, UT -- school based dental sealant program
15,000	U of U College of Law, Salt Lake City, UT -- for volunteer students pro bono program
10,000	Guadalupe Center, Salt Lake City, UT -- for instructional costs for early learning center
10,000	Kostopulos Dream Foundation, Salt Lake City, UT -- scholarship for residential summer camp
10,000	Odyssey House, Salt Lake City, UT -- infants scholarships to attend child care
10,000	Rowland Hall- St. Marks, Salt Lake City, UT -- towards scholarship
10,000	Salt Lake Legal Aid Society, Salt Lake City, UT -- for family law clinic
10,000	Scottish Rite Foundation of Utah, Ogden, UT -- scholarships for low income students
10,000	Utah Symphony and Opera, Salt Lake City, UT -- for community outreach program
10,000	Westminister College, Salt Lake City, UT -- scholarships for students with academic achievement and financial need

MICROSOFT CORP.

Company Headquarters
Redmond, WA
Web: http://www.microsoft.com

Company Description
Founded: 1975
Ticker: MSFT
Exchange: NASDAQ
Revenue: US$36.835 billion (2004)
Profit: US$8.168 billion (2004)
Employees: 50500 (2003)
Fortune Rank: 41, per FORTUNE Magazine's list of

500 Largest U.S. Corporations (2004).
SIC(s): 7371 Computer Programming Services, 7372 Prepackaged Software.

Operating Locations

Microsoft Corp. (CA--Foster City, Sacramento; CO--Boulder; CT--Farmington; DC--Washington; FL--Fort Lauderdale; IL--Villa Park; IN--Indianapolis; MA--Newton, Waltham; MN--Bloomington; MO--Kansas City, St. Louis; NY--New York, Rochester; NC--Charlotte; OH--Chagrin Falls, Cincinnati; TX--Dallas, Houston; WA--Bothell)
Note: Operates in 21 countries.

Nonmonetary Support

Value: $179,023,000 (2001); $199,456,000 (2000); $79,013,000 (1999)
Type: Donated Products
Note: NOT Product donations recorded at estimated retail value.
Contact: Jane Meseck, Program Manager

Giving Contact

Bruce M. Brooks, Director, Community Affairs
One Microsoft Way
Redmond, WA 98052-6399
Phone: (425)882-8080
Fax: (425)936-7329
E-mail: giving@microsoft.com
Web: http://www.microsoft.com/Giving

Description

Organization Type: Corporate Giving Program
Giving Locations: WA: some national initiatives.
Grant Types: Capital, Emergency, Employee Matching Gifts, General Support, Matching, Scholarship.
Note: Employee matching gift ratio: 1 to 1 for contributions of cash, stock, or software up to $12,000 per employee annually.

Financial Summary

Total Giving: $264,000,000 (fiscal year ending June 31, 2003 approx); $246,900,000 (fiscal 2002 approx); $215,777,000 (fiscal 2001). Note: Contributes through corporate direct giving program only.
Giving Analysis: Giving for fiscal 2001 includes: foundation scholarships ($453,000); corporate direct giving ($18,722,000); corporate matching gifts ($44,707,000); nonmonetary support ($151,895,000)

Typical Recipients

Arts & Humanities: Arts Associations & Councils, Arts & Humanities-General, Historic Preservation, Libraries, Museums/Galleries
Civic & Public Affairs: African American Affairs, Business/Free Enterprise, Civic & Public Affairs-General, Hispanic Affairs, Zoos/Aquariums
Education: Colleges & Universities, Education Associations, Education Reform, Education-General, Minority Education, Private Education (Precollege)
Environment: Environment-General, Protection, Wildlife Protection
Health: AIDS/HIV, Cancer, Children's Health/Hospitals, Emergency/Ambulance Services, Kidney, Medical Rehabilitation, Single-Disease Health Associations, Transplant Networks/Donor Banks
International: Foreign Educational Institutions, International Relief Efforts, Missionary/Religious Activities
Religion: Jewish Causes, Religious Organizations, Religious Welfare
Science: Science Museums, Scientific Centers & Institutes
Social Services: Child Welfare, Community Service Organizations, Domestic Violence, Family Services, Food/Clothing Distribution, People with Disabilities, Social Services-General, YMCA/YWCA/YMHA/YWHA, Youth Organizations

Application Procedures

Initial Contact: Contact community relations to request guidelines or review them on the Microsoft giving web site. Nonprofit organizations located in Washington State may submit a full proposal for cash donations. Washington organizations wishing to apply for a software donation should request an application form. Nonprofit organizations located outside of Washington State and wishing to apply for a cash or product donation should contact its local Microsoft field office, as each office has its own set of guidelines. A list of field offices is available at the following web site: www.microsoft.com/usa/map.asp.
Application Requirements: Washington State proposals should include a description of organization, including mission, major accomplishments, governance, area and population served; amount requested and a detailed description of the project or activity for which support is being requested; operating budget for the current fiscal year, including fund sources; list of funding sources for the current fiscal year, including amounts received; project budget (if applicable); list of current board members and key staff; recently audited financial statement; and copy of IRS tax-exempt determination letter.
Deadlines: For community support grants, tax-exempt organizations may submit requests throughout the year. However, internal grantmaking deadlines are the 15th of February, May, or October.
Decision Notification: Applicants will be notified approximately one month after the deadline.
Notes: Proposal materials cannot be returned. Company will request further information, if necessary.

Restrictions

The following are not eligible for Microsoft donations of cash or software: individuals; private foundations; nonprofit organizations without 501(c)(3) status; hospitals; conferences of symposia; sponsorship of events, tables, exhibitions, or performances; fundraising events such as luncheons, dinners, walks, runs, or sports; U.S.-based organizations serving people and communities outside the country; K-12 schools; political, labor and fraternal organizations; and religious organizations without a secular community designation.

Additional Information

Publications: Annual Report; Guidelines

Corporate Officials

Steven Anthony Ballmer: chief executive officer, president, director b Detroit, MI March 24, 1956. ED Stanford University Graduate School of Business Administration; Harvard University Graduate School of Business Administration BS (1977). PRIM CORP EMPL president, chief executive officer, director: Microsoft Corp.
John G. Connors: senior vice president, chief financial officer ED University of Montana BA. PRIM CORP EMPL senior vice president finance & administration, chief financial officer: Microsoft Corp. CORP AFFIL Ignition Partners LLC; director: Nike Inc..

Giving Program Officials

Rodney Hines: program manager
Heidi Salstrom: program manager
Linda Testa: program manager
Jane Meseck Yeager: program manager, community affairs ED Evans School of Public Affairs, University of Washington (1994).

Grants Analysis

Disclosure Period: fiscal year ending June 31, 2001
Total Grants: $170,617,000*
Number of Grants: 5,000 (approx)
Average Grant: $34,123 (approx)
Typical Range: $5,000 to $25,000
*Note: Giving excludes matching gifts. Giving includes nonmonetary support.

Recent Grants

Note: Grants derived from 2001 Annual Report.
Library-Related
Milwaukee Public Library, Milwaukee, WI
Albany Public Library, Albany, NY

General
AIDS Project Los Angeles, Los Angeles, CA
Adler Planetarium, Chicago, IL
American Council on Education, Washington, DC
Arizona Center for the Blind and Visually Impaired, Phoenix, AZ
Association for Cultural Exchange, New York, NY
Battered Women's Alternatives, San Francisco, CA
Boys and Girls Clubs of Greater Dallas, Inc., Dallas, TX
California Health Collaborative Foundation, Fresno, CA
Catholic Charities, Syracuse, NY
Catholic Community Services of Western Washington, Bremerton, WA

MID-IOWA HEALTH FOUNDATION

Giving Contact

Kathryn Bradley, Principal Manager
550 39th St., Suite 104
Des Moines, IA 50312
Phone: (515)277-6411
Fax: (515)274-4188

Description

Founded: 1984
EIN: 421235348
Organization Type: Private Foundation
Giving Locations: IA: Polk County and the eight surrounding counties
Grant Types: Capital, General Support, Operating Expenses, Scholarship.

Financial Summary

Total Giving: $599,725 (2002)
Assets: $14,479,291 (2002)

Typical Recipients

Arts & Humanities: Arts & Humanities-General, Libraries, Public Broadcasting
Civic & Public Affairs: Business/Free Enterprise, Community Foundations, Employment/Job Training, Civic & Public Affairs-General, Housing, Women's Affairs
Education: Afterschool/Enrichment Programs, Agricultural Education, Colleges & Universities, Community & Junior Colleges, Health & Physical Education, Medical Education, Preschool Education, Public Education (Precollege), Student Aid
Health: AIDS/HIV, Alzheimer's Disease, Arthritis, Cancer, Children's Health/Hospitals, Clinics/Medical Centers, Diabetes, Emergency/Ambulance Services, Health-General, Geriatric Health, Health Organizations, Home-Care Services, Hospices, Hospitals, Medical Rehabilitation, Mental Health, Nursing Services, Nutrition, Prenatal Health Issues, Public Health, Respiratory, Trauma Treatment
Religion: Churches, Ministries, Religious Welfare
Social Services: At-Risk Youth, Big Brothers/Big Sisters, Child Abuse, Child Welfare, Community Service Organizations, Counseling, Day Care, Family Planning, Family Services, Food/Clothing Distribution, People with Disabilities, Recreation & Athletics, Scouts, Senior Services, Shelters/Homelessness, Special Olympics, Substance Abuse, United Funds/United Ways, YMCA/YWCA/YMHA/YWHA, Youth Organizations

Application Procedures

Initial Contact: Send a brief letter of inquiry.
Application Requirements: Request application form.
Deadlines: None. Applications are reviewed quarterly.

Restrictions

Grants are awarded for health service programs.

Additional Information

Publications: Application Guidelines

Foundation Officials

Rex Burns: vice chairman
Terry Caldwell-Johnson: director
Simon Casady: director
Nolden Gentry: director
Don C. Green: secretary, treasurer
Rob Hayes: director
Thomas Jeschke: director
Ivan Johnson: chairman
Sally Pederson: director
T. Ward Phillips: director
Judith Vogel: director

Grants Analysis

Disclosure Period: calendar year ending 2002
Total Grants: $599,725
Number of Grants: 47
Average Grant: $12,760
Highest Grant: $50,000
Lowest Grant: $1,000
Typical Range: $5,000 to $25,000

Recent Grants

Note: Grants derived from 2002 Form 990.
General

50,000	Center for Healthy Communities, Des Moines, IA -- Robert Wood Johnson Neighborhood Health Access Initiative
45,000	Des Moines Health Center, Des Moines, IA -- Dental Sealant and Education Program
35,000	Heart and Hands Inc. -- expansion of clinic services
30,000	La Clinica de la Esperanza -- Centering Pregnancy Program
25,000	Convalescent Home for Children, Ames, IA -- Child Serve campaign
25,000	Des Moines Health Center, Des Moines, IA -- oral health mobile van
25,000	Greater Des Moines Community Foundation, Des Moines, IA -- Number One Quest campaign
25,000	Primary Health Care, Inc. -- emergency funding
16,500	Young Women's Resource Center, Des Moines, IA -- health programs
15,000	Creative Visions, Des Moines, IA -- support for outreach liaison

MIDCONTINENT MEDIA INC.

Company Headquarters

7900 Xerxes Avenue S., Suite 1100
Minneapolis, MN 55431
Web: http://www.midcocomm.com

Company Description

Employees: 1,100
SIC(s): 4800 Communications, 4832 Radio Broadcasting Stations, 4833 Television Broadcasting Stations, 4841 Cable & Other Pay Television Services.

Operating Locations

Midcontinent Media Inc. (SD--Aberdeen, Sioux Falls; WI--Madison)

Nonmonetary Support

Type: Donated Equipment; In-kind Services

Midcontinent Media Foundation

Giving Contact

Steven E. Grosser, Vice President & Director
Midcontinent Media Foundation
3600 Minnesota Dr., Suite 700
Minneapolis, MN 55435
Phone: (952)844-2600
Fax: (952)844-2660
Web: http://www.midcocomm.com/foundation.php

Description

Founded: 1987
EIN: 363556764
Organization Type: Corporate Foundation
Giving Locations: operating locations.
Grant Types: Employee Matching Gifts, General Support, Operating Expenses, Project.

Donor Information

Founder: Midcontinent Media

Financial Summary

Total Giving: $171,512 (fiscal year ending August 31, 2004); $176,561 (fiscal 2003); $135,446 (fiscal 2001)
Giving Analysis: Giving for fiscal 2004 includes: foundation matching gifts ($13,456); fiscal 2001: foundation grants to United Way ($4,702)
Assets: $60,388 (fiscal 2004); $39,833 (fiscal 2003); $103,262 (fiscal 2001)
Gifts Received: $196,667 (fiscal 2004); $203,333 (fiscal 2003); $100,000 (fiscal 1999). Note: Contributions were received from Midcontinent Media Inc.

Typical Recipients

Arts & Humanities: Arts Centers, Ethnic & Folk Arts, Film & Video, Arts & Humanities-General, Historic Preservation, History & Archaeology, Libraries, Museums/Galleries, Music, Performing Arts, Public Broadcasting, Theater
Civic & Public Affairs: Botanical Gardens/Parks, Clubs, Community Foundations, Economic Development, Employment/Job Training, Civic & Public Affairs-General, Housing, Legal Aid, Municipalities/Towns, Native American Affairs, Philanthropic Organizations, Professional & Trade Associations, Public Policy, Safety, Urban & Community Affairs, Women's Affairs, Zoos/Aquariums
Education: Afterschool/Enrichment Programs, Agricultural Education, Business Education, Colleges & Universities, Education Funds, Elementary Education (Public), Education-General, Literacy, Private Education (Precollege), Public Education (Precollege), Secondary Education (Public), Special Education
Environment: Resource Conservation
Health: Cancer, Children's Health/Hospitals, Clinics/Medical Centers, Emergency/Ambulance Services, Health Organizations, Heart, Hospitals, Medical Rehabilitation, Multiple Sclerosis, Prenatal Health Issues, Research/Studies Institutes
International: International-General
Religion: Ministries, Religious Organizations, Religious Welfare
Social Services: At-Risk Youth, Camps, Child Welfare, Community Centers, Community Service Organizations, Day Care, Domestic Violence, Emergency Relief, Family Services, Food/Clothing Distribution, People with Disabilities, Recreation & Athletics, Scouts, Senior Services, Social Services-General, Special Olympics, United Funds/United Ways, Volunteer Services, YMCA/YWCA/YMHA/YWHA, Youth Organizations

Application Procedures

Initial Contact: Obtain and complete a "Requestor Form" from a company employee. Attach additional literature that will assist the board in its consideration

of the request.
Deadlines: August 1 and February 1.

Restrictions

Only requests submitted and sponsored by an employee of a Midcontinent Media operating company are considered. Preference is given to special projects rather than general operating funds.

Additional Information

The guidelines brochure includes the foundation's evaluative criteria and a list of operating companies.
Publications: Guidelines; Requestor Form

Corporate Officials

Nathan L. Bentson: chairman, chief executive officer, director PRIM CORP EMPL chairman, chief executive officer, director: Midcontinent Media.
Joseph H. Floyd: president, director PRIM CORP EMPL president, director: Midcontinent Media.

Foundation Officials

Larry Bentson: assistant secretary, director
Rod Carlson: vice president, director
Joseph H. Floyd: vice president, director (see above)
Steven E. Grosser: director, vice president
Jerry Hasbrouck: director
Judy Johnson: vice president, director
Butch Moteberg: vice president, director
Gary Reimer: director
Doreen West: director

Grants Analysis

Disclosure Period: fiscal year ending August 31, 2003
Total Grants: $157,400*
Number of Grants: 75
Average Grant: $2,099
Highest Grant: $10,000
Lowest Grant: $1,000
Typical Range: $1,000 to $5,000
*Note: Giving excludes matching gifts.

Recent Grants

Note: Grants derived from 2004 Form 990.
General

2,000	Axtell Park Middle School, Sioux Falls, SD
2,000	Junior Achievement of South Dakota, Sioux Falls, SD
1,519	Senior Companions, Minneapolis, MN
1,500	American Cancer Society
1,500	Fellowship of Christian Athletes, Morris, MN
612	Make-A-Wish Foundation of South Dakota, Sioux Falls, SD
400	Make-A-Wish Foundation of South Dakota, Sioux Falls, SD
320	American Heart Association, Minneapolis, MN
266	Sioux Empire American Red Cross, Sioux Falls, SD
250	Maryhill Manor, Enderlin, ND

MIDDENDORF FOUNDATION

Giving Contact

E. Phillips Hathaway, President & Trustee
2 East Read Street
Baltimore, MD 21202
Phone: (410)752-7088
Fax: (410)625-5728

Description

Founded: 1953
EIN: 526048944

Organization Type: General Purpose Foundation
Giving Locations: MD
Grant Types: Endowment, General Support, Matching, Professorship.

Donor Information

Founder: Incorporated in 1953 by the late J. William Middendorf Jr. and the late Alice C. Middendorf.

Financial Summary

Total Giving: $1,000,000 (fiscal year ending March 31, 2002 approx); $1,675,500 (fiscal 2001)
Giving Analysis: Giving for fiscal 2001 includes: foundation grants to United Way ($15,000)
Assets: $27,000,000 (fiscal 2002 approx); $32,100,226 (fiscal 2001)

Typical Recipients

Arts & Humanities: Arts Centers, Arts Institutes, Arts Outreach, Dance, Historic Preservation, History & Archaeology, Libraries, Museums/Galleries, Music, Opera, Public Broadcasting, Theater
Civic & Public Affairs: Asian American Affairs, Botanical Gardens/Parks, Community Foundations, Economic Development, Employment/Job Training, Civic & Public Affairs-General, Legal Aid, Philanthropic Organizations, Professional & Trade Associations, Zoos/Aquariums
Education: Agricultural Education, Arts/Humanities Education, Colleges & Universities, Education Funds, Education Reform, Education-General, Medical Education, Private Education (Precollege), Science/Mathematics Education, Special Education, Student Aid
Environment: Air/Water Quality, Environment-General, Protection, Wildlife Protection
Health: Arthritis, Cancer, Clinics/Medical Centers, Emergency/Ambulance Services, Eyes/Blindness, Health-General, Geriatric Health, Health Organizations, Heart, Hospices, Hospitals, Medical Research, Mental Health, Prenatal Health Issues, Preventive Medicine/Wellness Organizations, Public Health, Respiratory, Single-Disease Health Associations, Trauma Treatment
International: Health Care/Hospitals, International Organizations, International Relief Efforts
Religion: Churches, Dioceses, Religion-General, Ministries, Religious Organizations, Religious Welfare
Science: Scientific Centers & Institutes
Social Services: Child Abuse, Child Welfare, Community Service Organizations, Crime Prevention, Emergency Relief, Family Planning, Family Services, Food/Clothing Distribution, People with Disabilities, Recreation & Athletics, Scouts, Senior Services, Shelters/Homelessness, Social Services-General, Special Olympics, Substance Abuse, United Funds/United Ways, YMCA/YWCA/YMHA/YWHA, Youth Organizations

Application Procedures

Initial Contact: The foundation requests applications be made in writing.
Application Requirements: The foundation requests that applicants include all supporting documentation in the initial proposal.
Deadlines: None.

Restrictions

Grants are not made to individuals.

Foundation Officials

Forrest F. Bramble, Jr.: vice president, trustee PRIM CORP EMPL partner: Barton & Wilmer Niles. CORP AFFIL director: C R Daniels Inc.; secretary: Crosby Marketing Communications.
Sealy H. Hopkinson: trustee
Theresa N. Knell: secretary, trustee
Craig Lewis: treasurer, trustee B 1930. PRIM NONPR EMPL principal, director: Investment Counsel Maryland.

Grants Analysis

Disclosure Period: fiscal year ending March 31, 2001
Total Grants: $1,660,500*
Number of Grants: 41
Average Grant: $20,554*
Highest Grant: $250,000
Typical Range: $10,000 to $40,000
*Note: Giving excludes United Way. Average grant excludes four highest grants ($900,000).

Recent Grants

Note: Grants derived from 2003 Form 990.
General

500,000	Greater Baltimore Medical Center, Baltimore, MD -- towards community resource center
50,000	Kennedy Krieger Institute, Baltimore, MD -- towards main street project
50,000	Nature Conservancy, Bethesda, MD -- towards funding mountains to marshes campaign
25,000	Baltimore Maritime Museum, Baltimore, MD -- towards save America's treasures campaign
25,000	Baltimore Museum of Art, Baltimore, MD -- towards acquisition fund American wing
25,000	Garrison Forest School, Owings Mills, MD -- towards campus core completion
25,000	Gilman School, Baltimore, MD -- towards centennial campaign
25,000	Greater Baltimore Medical Center, Baltimore, MD -- towards capital campaign
25,000	Hospice of Queen Anne's, Queenstown, MD
25,000	St. Joseph Medical Center, Towson, MD -- towards M/SICU endowment

GEORGE H. AND JANE A. MIFFLIN MEMORIAL FUND

Giving Contact

Peter B. Loring, Trustee
c/o Loring, Wolcott & Coolidge
230 Congress St.
230 Congress St.
Boston, MA 02110
Phone: (617)523-6531

Description

EIN: 046384983
Organization Type: Private Foundation
Giving Locations: MA
Grant Types: Project, Scholarship.

Donor Information

Founder: George H. Mifflin, Jane A. Mifflin

Financial Summary

Total Giving: $1,975,000 (fiscal year ending September 30, 2002)
Giving Analysis: Giving for fiscal 2002 includes: foundation grants to United Way ($45,000)
Assets: $27,412,359 (fiscal 2002 approx)
Gifts Received: $22,639 (fiscal 1997); $1,563,602 (fiscal 1996); $78,741 (fiscal 1992)

Typical Recipients

Arts & Humanities: Historic Preservation, Libraries, Literary Arts, Museums/Galleries, Music, Theater
Civic & Public Affairs: Botanical Gardens/Parks, Economic Development, Employment/Job Training, Civic & Public Affairs-General, Hispanic Affairs, Housing, Law & Justice, Legal Aid, Municipalities/Towns, Public Policy, Urban & Community Affairs, Women's Affairs, Zoos/Aquariums
Education: Colleges & Universities, Continuing Education, Education Reform, Environmental Education, Education-General, Leadership Training, Minority Education, Preschool Education, Private Education (Precollege), Public Education (Precollege), Secondary Education (Private), Student Aid, Vocational & Technical Education
Environment: Forestry, Environment-General, Resource Conservation, Wildlife Protection
Health: AIDS/HIV, Clinics/Medical Centers, Health-General, Health Organizations, Mental Health, Public Health, Single-Disease Health Associations
International: International Affairs, International Environmental Issues
Religion: Ministries, Religious Organizations, Social/Policy Issues
Social Services: Animal Protection, Community Service Organizations, Counseling, Crime Prevention, Domestic Violence, Family Services, Food/Clothing Distribution, Recreation & Athletics, Senior Services, Shelters/Homelessness, Volunteer Services, Youth Organizations

Application Procedures

Initial Contact: Contact foundation by phone or in writing.
Deadlines: None.

Restrictions

Does not support individuals.

Foundation Officials

John G. Brooks, Esq.: trustee
Lawrence Coolidge: trustee B Boston, MA 1936. ED Harvard University Graduate School of Business Administration (1962). PRIM CORP EMPL chairman: Seven Islands Land Co. CORP AFFIL director: Hollingsworth & Vose Co.; trustee: Loring Wolcott & Co.ology Office; director: Big Sandy Co.
Peter B. Loring: trustee

Grants Analysis

Disclosure Period: fiscal year ending September 30, 2002
Total Grants: $1,930,000*
Number of Grants: 103
Average Grant: $18,738
Highest Grant: $70,000
Lowest Grant: $4,000
Typical Range: $5,000 to $50,000
*Note: Giving excludes United Way.

Recent Grants

Note: Grants derived from fiscal 2002 Form 990.
General

70,000	Greater Boston Legal Services, Boston, MA -- for operating funds
65,000	Massachusetts Audubon Society, Lincoln, MA -- to establish a land protection fund
50,000	Boston Museum Project, Boston, MA -- toward the Boston Museum and History Center Project
50,000	Holyoke Community Charter School, Holyoke, MA -- to support the schools pre-opening expenses
50,000	Jobs for Youth Boston, Boston, MA -- to support the JFY Net Program
50,000	Just A Start, Cambridge, MA -- for support of various programs focusing on basic urban community needs
40,000	Charles River Conservancy, Newton, MA -- toward a pilot parkland maintenance program
40,000	Massachusetts Charter School Association, Haydenville, MA -- for operating expenses
35,000	Boston Latin School Association, Boston, MA -- toward the Headmasters Fund

35,000   Morehouse College, Atlanta, GA -- for scholarships

MILLBROOK TRIBUTE GARDEN

Giving Contact
Kathy Shanks, Secretary
PO Box AC
Millbrook, NY 12545
Phone: (845)677-6823

Description
Founded: 1943
EIN: 141340079
Organization Type: General Purpose Foundation
Giving Locations: NY: Millbrook and vicinity
Grant Types: Capital, General Support, Project, Scholarship.

Financial Summary
Total Giving: $1,482,498 (fiscal year ending September 30, 2002); $1,437,809 (fiscal 2001)
Assets: $35,634,628 (fiscal 2002); $36,760,397 (fiscal 2001)

Typical Recipients
Arts & Humanities: Art History, Arts Associations & Councils, Arts Festivals, Arts Institutes, Ballet, Film & Video, History & Archaeology, Libraries, Music, Public Broadcasting, Theater
Civic & Public Affairs: Botanical Gardens/Parks, Clubs, Community Foundations, Civic & Public Affairs-General, Municipalities/Towns, Zoos/Aquariums
Education: Colleges & Universities, Environmental Education, Literacy, Minority Education, Private Education (Precollege), Secondary Education (Private), Secondary Education (Public), Student Aid
Environment: Environment-General, Protection, Research, Resource Conservation, Wildlife Protection
Health: AIDS/HIV, Hospices, Hospitals, Medical Rehabilitation, Single-Disease Health Associations
International: International Environmental Issues
Religion: Churches, Religious Organizations, Religious Welfare
Social Services: Animal Protection, Big Brothers/Big Sisters, Child Abuse, Child Welfare, Community Centers, Community Service Organizations, Family Planning, Family Services, Homes, Recreation & Athletics, Scouts, Senior Services, Social Services-General, Volunteer Services, Youth Organizations

Application Procedures
Initial Contact: The foundation requests applications be made in writing.
Application Requirements: Written proposals should include supporting materials explaining the purpose of the request and a financial statement.
Deadlines: None.

Restrictions
The foundation makes grants only to public charities under section 501(c)(3) of the IRS code, in the immediate vicinity of Millbrook, NY. Grants are not made to individuals.

Foundation Officials
Felicitas Selter Thorne: vice president
Oakleigh Thorne: trustee B 1957. ED Boston University BS (1980); Columbia University MBA (1986). PRIM CORP EMPL president, chief executive officer: CCH Inc. CORP AFFIL director: Connecticut Corp. System.
Oakleigh Blakeman Thorne: president, trustee B Santa Barbara, CA 1932. ED Harvard University BA (1954). PRIM NONPR EMPL chairman, president legal info: Commerce Clearing House. CORP AFFIL

director: Bank Millbrook; chairman, director: Connecticut Corp. System.
Vincent N. Turletes: secretary CORP AFFIL director: Bank Millbrook.
George T. Whalen, Jr.: treasurer PRIM CORP EMPL president, director: Bank Millbrook.
Robert W. Whalen: trustee

Grants Analysis
Disclosure Period: fiscal year ending September 30, 2002
Total Grants: $1,482,498
Number of Grants: 89
Average Grant: $10,005*
Highest Grant: $200,000
Lowest Grant: $100
Typical Range: $5,000 to $25,000
Note: Averge grant figure excludes four highest grants ($592,000).

Recent Grants
Note: Grants derived from fiscal 2002 Form 990.
Library-Related
120,000   Millbrook Free Library, Millbrook, NY
General
200,000   Dutchess Day School, Millbrook, NY
157,000   Village of Millbrook, Millbrook, NY
115,000   Millbrook School, Millbrook, NY
75,000   Institute of Ecosystem Studies, Millbrook, NY
65,000   Cardinal Hayes Home, Millbrook, NY
55,000   Lyall Memorial Federated Church, Millbrook, NY
50,000   Bard College, Annandale-on-Hudson, NY
47,000   St. Joseph's Church, Millbrook, NY
41,000   WBEZ Public Television, Chicago, IL
40,000   Millbrook Central School, Millbrook, NY

MILLER BREWING CO. (EDEN, NC)

Company Headquarters
863 E. Meadow Rd.
Eden, NC 27288
Web: http://www.millerbrewingcompany.com

Company Description
Employees: 900
SIC(s): 2000 Food & Kindred Products.
Parent Company: Altria Group Inc., 120 Park Ave., New York, NY, United States

Nonmonetary Support
Type: Donated Equipment; Donated Products; Loaned Employees

Giving Contact
Brenda Williams, Community Relations
PO Box 3327
Eden, NC 27289
Phone: (336)627-2100

Description
Organization Type: Corporate Giving Program
Giving Locations: principally near operating locations and to national organizations.
Grant Types: Emergency, General Support, Multi-year/Continuing Support.

Typical Recipients
Arts & Humanities: Arts Appreciation, Arts Associations & Councils, Arts Festivals, Arts Funds, Arts Outreach, Community Arts, Dance, Ethnic & Folk Arts, Arts & Humanities-General, Historic Preservation, Libraries, Museums/Galleries, Music, Performing Arts, Theater, Visual Arts
Civic & Public Affairs: African American Affairs,

Business/Free Enterprise, Chambers of Commerce, Civil Rights, Clubs, Economic Development, Employment/Job Training, Ethnic Organizations, Gay/Lesbian Issues, Civic & Public Affairs-General, Hispanic Affairs, Municipalities/Towns, Parades/Festivals, Philanthropic Organizations, Rural Affairs, Safety, Women's Affairs
Education: Afterschool/Enrichment Programs, Agricultural Education, Arts/Humanities Education, Business-School Partnerships, Colleges & Universities, Community & Junior Colleges, Elementary Education (Private), Engineering/Technological Education, Education-General, Literacy
Environment: Environment-General, Resource Conservation, Wildlife Protection
Health: AIDS/HIV, Emergency/Ambulance Services, Health-General, Health Policy/Cost Containment, Hospices, Nutrition
International: Health Care/Hospitals
Science: Science-General
Social Services: Animal Protection, At-Risk Youth, Camps, Community Centers, Community Service Organizations, Counseling, Delinquency & Criminal Rehabilitation, Food/Clothing Distribution, Homes, Shelters/Homelessness, Social Services-General, Substance Abuse, United Funds/United Ways

Application Procedures
Initial Contact: Send a brief letter of inquiry.
Application Requirements: a description of organization, amount requested, purpose of funds sought, and proof of tax-exempt status.

Restrictions
Does not support religious organizations for sectarian purposes or political or lobbying groups.

Additional Information
Profile reflects the charitable priorities of the Eden, NC, plant location. Contributions are limited to organizations within a 150-mile radius of the plant. National organizations should contact corporate headquarters (see separate entry).

Corporate Officials
Patricia Henry: plant manager PRIM CORP EMPL plant manager: Miller Brewing Co./Eden North Carolina.

Grants Analysis
Typical Range: $1,000 to $2,500

MILLER FOUNDATION

Giving Contact
Rebecca A. Engelhardt, Secretary, Treasurer & Trustee
Miller Foundation
310 WahWahTaySee Way
Battle Creek, MI 49015
Phone: (616)964-3542
Fax: (616)964-8455
Web: http://www.willard.lib.mi.us/npa/miller/

Description
Founded: 1963
EIN: 386064925
Organization Type: Private Foundation
Giving Locations: MI: Battle Creek and surrounding area
Grant Types: Capital, Emergency, Endowment, General Support, Loan, Scholarship, Seed Money.

Donor Information
Founder: the late Louise B. Miller, Robert B. Miller

Financial Summary

Total Giving: $976,875 (2001)
Giving Analysis: Giving for 2001 includes: foundation grants to United Way ($121,825)
Assets: $33,246,004 (2001)
Gifts Received: $115,000 (1997); $5,162 (1995); $76,836 (1994). Note: In 1995, contributions were received from an anonymous donor.

Typical Recipients

Arts & Humanities: Arts Associations & Councils, Arts Centers, History & Archaeology, Libraries, Music
Civic & Public Affairs: Botanical Gardens/Parks, Community Foundations, Economic Development, Civic & Public Affairs-General, Housing, Municipalities/Towns, Nonprofit Management, Parades/Festivals, Philanthropic Organizations, Professional & Trade Associations, Urban & Community Affairs, Zoos/Aquariums
Education: Arts/Humanities Education, Business Education, Colleges & Universities, Community & Junior Colleges, Education Funds, International Exchange, Preschool Education, Public Education (Precollege), Science/Mathematics Education, Special Education, Student Aid
Environment: Resource Conservation
Health: Clinics/Medical Centers, Emergency/Ambulance Services, Hospices, Nursing Services, Public Health
Religion: Ministries, Religious Organizations, Religious Welfare
Social Services: Big Brothers/Big Sisters, Community Centers, Community Service Organizations, Counseling, Crime Prevention, Day Care, Domestic Violence, Family Planning, Family Services, Food/Clothing Distribution, People with Disabilities, Scouts, Senior Services, Social Services-General, Substance Abuse, United Funds/United Ways, YMCA/YWCA/YMHA/YWHA, Youth Organizations

Application Procedures

Initial Contact: Request application guidelines and form.
Application Requirements: Include a description of organization, including history, mission, goals, current activities, and current collaborations; purpose of funds sought, including name of program, amount requested, specific purpose of funds, how program will be staffed, who will benefit, and involvement in program planning of persons benefiting from said program; description of any coordination or collaboration of organization, including similar or complimentary organizations and programs, and future plans for coordination; a one page logic model for programs over $100,000, including inputs, activities, outputs, and outcomes; detailed budget, including expenses, revenue sources, current status of other proposals, and in-kind items; annual operating statements; and explanation of future need after Miller Foundation grant is expended.
Deadlines: January 1, April 1, July 1, or October 1.

Additional Information

Publications: Annual Report; Application Form; Guidelines

Foundation Officials

Arthur W. Angood: president, chief executive officer, trustee
Barbara L. Comai: trustee
Gary Edward Costley: trustee B Caldwell, ID 1943. ED Oregon State University MS; Oregon State University BS (1966); Oregon State University PhD (1970). PRIM CORP EMPL executive vice president: Kellogg Co. CORP AFFIL president: Kellogg U.S.A. Inc. NONPR AFFIL trustee: Duke University Medicine School- Sarah W Stedman Center; trustee: Youth Understanding International Exchange; member: American Institute Nutrition; trustee: American Health Foundation.
Rebecca A. Engelhardt: secretary, treasurer, trustee
Rance Leaders: secretary, treasurer, trustee
W. James McQuiston: chairman, trustee
Allen L. Miller: trustee
Robert Branson Miller, Jr.: trustee B Battle Creek, MI 1935. ED Michigan State University BA (1959). PRIM CORP EMPL publisher: Battle Creek Enquirer. NONPR AFFIL director Battle Creek MI chapter: American Red Cross.
Robert Branson Miller, Sr.: trustee emeritus B Ottawa, KS June 25, 1906. ED Williams College BA (1929).
Paul Ohm: trustee
Gloria J. Robertson: trustee
Fred M. Woodruff, Jr.: trustee

Grants Analysis

Disclosure Period: calendar year ending 2001
Total Grants: $855,050*
Highest Grant: $100,000
***Note:** Giving excludes United Way.

Recent Grants

Note: Grants derived from 2001 Form 990.
General

100,000	Kellogg Community College, Battle Creek, MI -- for Capstone Project
100,000	Leila Arboretum Society, Battle Creek, MI -- for BC Green Project
100,000	Neighborhoods, Inc., Battle Creek, MI -- for ongoing operational cost
100,000	United Way of Greater Battle Creek, Battle Creek, MI -- for 2001 capital campaign
100,000	Y Family Center, Battle Creek, MI -- for Health Enhancement Center
55,578	Neighborhoods, Inc., Battle Creek, MI -- for development director
42,847	Calhoun Area Millennium Partnership, LLC, Battle Creek, MI -- to put operational structure in place
25,000	Girl Scouts, Kalamazoo, MI -- capital campaign
21,825	United Way of Greater Battle Creek, Battle Creek, MI -- for matching grant
20,000	Calhoun Intermediate School District, Marshall, MI -- network for young children

EARL B. AND LORAINE H. MILLER FOUNDATION

Giving Contact

Walter M. Florie, Jr., President & Chief Executive Officer
111 W. Ocean Boulevard, 22nd Floor
Long Beach, CA 90802
Phone: (562)491-3187

Description

Founded: 1967
EIN: 952500545
Organization Type: Private Foundation
Giving Locations: CA: Long Beach
Grant Types: General Support, Project.

Financial Summary

Total Giving: $1,472,660 (fiscal year ending June 30, 2004); $1,832,909 (fiscal 2002); $1,485,346 (fiscal 2001)
Assets: $37,933,597 (fiscal 2004); $34,425,850 (fiscal 2002); $35,191,515 (fiscal 2001)

Typical Recipients

Arts & Humanities: Arts Centers, Libraries, Museums/Galleries, Music
Civic & Public Affairs: African American Affairs, Nonprofit Management, Urban & Community Affairs
Education: Afterschool/Enrichment Programs, Education-General, Leadership Training, Preschool Education
Health: Children's Health/Hospitals, Clinics/Medical Centers, Eyes/Blindness, Health Funds, Mental Health, Respiratory
Social Services: Child Welfare, Community Service Organizations, Day Care, Delinquency & Criminal Rehabilitation, Scouts, YMCA/YWCA/YMHA/YWHA, Youth Organizations

Application Procedures

Initial Contact: Send a brief letter of inquiry, not exceeding 3 pages, succinctly describing project and amount needed.
Application Requirements: Include a description of organization, amount requested, and purpose of funds sought. Also indicate how the request relates to foundation's areas of giving.
Deadlines: June 30.

Restrictions

Special consideration is given to children's education, family and development, moral citizenship, and the arts. Does not support individuals, political initiatives, or activities outside of Long Beach, CA.

Additional Information

Publications: Application Form

Foundation Officials

Ron R. Arias: trustee
Walter M. Florie, Jr.: president, chief executive officer
Jeanne Karatsu: secretary, trustee
William H. Marmion: trustee
Harlan Miller: treasurer, trustee
Warren R. Schulten: vice president, trustee

Grants Analysis

Disclosure Period: fiscal year ending June 30, 2004
Total Grants: $1,472,660
Number of Grants: 39
Average Grant: $18,596*
Highest Grant: $250,000
Lowest Grant: $500
Typical Range: $5,000 to $30,000
***Note:** Average grant figure excludes six highest grants ($859,000).

Recent Grants

Note: Grants derived from fiscal 2004 Form 990.
General

250,000	Memorial Medical Center Foundation, Long Beach, CA -- for children's hospital expansion
200,000	Children's Clinic, Long Beach, CA -- for health education, promotion augmentation, and support for pine avenue clinic universal preschool symposium
109,000	Long Beach Symphony, Long Beach, CA -- for elementary ensemble program and family concert
100,000	Boys and Girls Clubs of Long Beach, Long Beach, CA
100,000	YMCA of Greater Long Beach, Long Beach, CA -- for safe and renaissance program
62,500	Long Beach Museum of Art, Long Beach, CA -- for education center
50,000	Leadership Long Beach, Long Beach, CA -- Long Beach youth leadership program
45,000	Blast - Better Learning After School Today, Long Beach, CA -- for after school educational program
40,000	Long Beach Nonprofit Partnership, Long Beach, CA -- for management assistance for Long Beach nonprofit community
10,000	Guidance Center, Long Beach, CA -- for custom software - MIS system

STEVE J. MILLER FOUNDATION

Giving Contact
Thomas N. Tuttle, Jr., Secretary, Treasurer
1000 N. Water St., 13th Floor
Milwaukee, WI 53202
Phone: (414)287-7184

Description
Founded: 1946
EIN: 396051879
Organization Type: Private Foundation
Giving Locations: AZ: Tucson; WI
Grant Types: General Support.

Donor Information
Founder: Central Cheese Co., Inc., the late Steve Miller

Typical Recipients
Arts & Humanities: Community Arts, Dance, History & Archaeology, Libraries, Museums/Galleries, Music, Opera, Performing Arts, Theater
Civic & Public Affairs: Clubs, Employment/Job Training, Civic & Public Affairs-General, Women's Affairs
Education: Agricultural Education, Arts/Humanities Education, Colleges & Universities, Environmental Education, Education-General, Literacy, Medical Education, Minority Education, Private Education (Precollege), Public Education (Precollege), Science/Mathematics Education, Student Aid
Environment: Environment-General
Health: Children's Health/Hospitals, Clinics/Medical Centers, Health Organizations, Hospitals, Medical Research, Mental Health, Multiple Sclerosis, Nursing Services, Prenatal Health Issues
Religion: Churches, Religious Organizations, Religious Welfare
Social Services: Child Abuse, Child Welfare, Community Service Organizations, Food/Clothing Distribution, People with Disabilities, Scouts, Social Services-General, United Funds/United Ways, YMCA/YWCA/YMHA/YWHA, Youth Organizations

Application Procedures
Initial Contact: Send a brief letter of inquiry and a full proposal.
Deadlines: None.

Restrictions
Does not support individuals.

Foundation Officials
Isabelle E. Black: vice president
William Thomas Gaus: treasurer B Berlin, Germany 1928. ED Marquette University (1951); Marquette University JD (1954). PRIM CORP EMPL senior vice president, chief trustee officer: Marshall & Ilsley Trust Co.
Norman C. Miller: president
Theodore W. Miller: trustee
Kurt Spreyer: trustee
Harvey D. TeStrake: mgr, secretary
Thomas N. Tuttle, Jr.: treasurer, secretary

Grants Analysis
Disclosure Period: calendar year ending 2000
Total Grants: $344,500*
Number of Grants: 42
Average Grant: $6,207*
Highest Grant: $90,000
Typical Range: $1,000 to $15,000
*Note: Average grant figure excludes highest grant.

Recent Grants
Note: Grants derived from 2001 Form 990.

General

40,000	St. Andrew's Crippled Children's Clinic, Nogales, AZ
25,000	Lura Turner Homes, Inc., Phoenix, AZ
20,000	Milwaukee Center for Independence, Milwaukee, WI
20,000	Thomas Jefferson School, St. Louis, MO
15,000	Opportunity Development Center, Marshfield, WI
10,000	Sacred Heart Catholic Church, Shawano, WI
10,000	SOS Children's Village of Wisconsin, Milwaukee, WI
10,000	United Performing Arts, Milwaukee, WI
10,000	University of Wisconsin, Madison, WI -- agriculture and life sciences
8,000	Richmond Educational Learning Center, Richmond, CA

MILLER-MELLOR ASSOCIATION

Giving Contact
James Ludlow-Miller, Secretary & Treasurer
708 E. 47th St.
Kansas City, MO 64110
Phone: (816)561-4307

Description
Founded: 1950
EIN: 446011906
Organization Type: Private Foundation
Giving Locations: MO: Kansas City
Grant Types: General Support.

Financial Summary
Total Giving: $157,015 (fiscal year ending June 30, 2001)
Giving Analysis: Giving for fiscal 2001 includes: foundation grants to United Way ($5,200)
Assets: $4,232,391 (fiscal 2001)

Typical Recipients
Arts & Humanities: Arts Associations & Councils, Arts Institutes, Community Arts, Arts & Humanities-General, History & Archaeology, Libraries, Literary Arts, Museums/Galleries, Music, Performing Arts, Public Broadcasting, Theater
Civic & Public Affairs: Community Foundations, Civic & Public Affairs-General, Law & Justice, Municipalities/Towns, Safety, Urban & Community Affairs
Education: Colleges & Universities, Education-General, Private Education (Precollege), Secondary Education (Private), Secondary Education (Public)
Environment: Environment-General, Wildlife Protection
Health: Children's Health/Hospitals, Emergency/Ambulance Services, Health Policy/Cost Containment, Health Organizations, Heart, Hospitals, Nursing Services, Prenatal Health Issues, Preventive Medicine/Wellness Organizations, Public Health, Research/Studies Institutes
Religion: Churches, Dioceses, Religious Organizations, Religious Welfare
Science: Scientific Labs
Social Services: Animal Protection, Child Welfare, Community Service Organizations, Crime Prevention, Delinquency & Criminal Rehabilitation, Family Planning, Food/Clothing Distribution, People with Disabilities, Recreation & Athletics, Scouts, Senior Services, Shelters/Homelessness, Social Services-General, United Funds/United Ways, YMCA/YWCA/YMHA/YWHA, Youth Organizations

Application Procedures
Initial Contact: The foundation has no formal grant application procedure or application form. Send a brief letter of inquiry.
Deadlines: None.

Foundation Officials
James Ludlow Miller: secretary, treasurer
JoZach Miller, IV: vice president
Helena Miller Norquist: president

Grants Analysis
Disclosure Period: fiscal year ending June 30, 2001
Total Grants: $151,815*
Number of Grants: 43
Average Grant: $3,531
Highest Grant: $20,000
Typical Range: $1,000 to $5,000
*Note: Giving excludes United Way.

Recent Grants
Note: Grants derived from fiscal 2002 Form 990.
General

22,000	Mary Atkins Trust, Kansas City, MO
15,000	St. Luke's Hospital Foundation, Kansas City, MO
7,300	St. Elizabeth Catholic Church, Tecumseh, MI
7,000	Friends of Chamber Music, Kansas City, MO
6,500	Visitation Parish, Kansas City, MO
5,500	Harvard University, Bedford, MA
5,000	Avila College, Kansas City, MO
5,000	Barstow School, Kansas City, MO
5,000	Catholic Diocese of Kansas City - St. Joseph, Kansas City, MO
5,000	LCRC Foundation, Minneapolis, MN

MILLIPORE CORP.

Company Headquarters
Bedford, MA
Web: http://www.millipore.com

Company Description
Founded: 1954
Ticker: MIL
Exchange: NYSE
Revenue: US$704.2 million (2002)
Employees: 4300 (2003)
SIC(s): 3081 Unsupported Plastics Film & Sheet, 3089 Plastics Products Nec, 3826 Analytical Instruments.

Operating Locations
Millipore Corp. (MA--Marlboro, Milford; NH--Jaffrey; PA--Pittsburgh; PR--Cidra)

Nonmonetary Support
Type: Donated Equipment; Donated Products
Volunteer Programs: Under the Voluntary Service Grant Program, employees who are currently doing volunteer work in their communities can petition the foundation for funds to support a special need or program of the organization where they volunteer. The program now provides a grant of up to $5,000 to support specific projects of eligible community organizations in which the Millipore employee is actively involved. The SkillsBank program is open to current employees, retirees, and family members who want to get involved in volunteer work. SkillsBank is a computerized program linked to the United Way's Voluntary Action Center, The Massachusetts Volunteer Network, and local charitable organizations. It acts as a clearinghouse between 500 agencies and the volunteers. Employees and others are matched with nonprofit agencies and organizations that can benefit from their specific skills, talent and knowledge.
Note: Nonmonetary support is provided by both the company and the foundation.

The Millipore Foundation

Giving Contact

Charleen Johnson, Executive Director
290 Concord Road
Billerica, MA 01821
Phone: (978)715-1268
E-mail: Charleen_Johnson@millipore.com
Web: http://www.millipore.com/foundation

Description

EIN: 222583952
Organization Type: Corporate Foundation
Giving Locations: MA: cash grants made primarily in Massachusetts matching gifts awarded nationally.
Grant Types: Capital, Employee Matching Gifts, General Support, Matching, Multiyear/Continuing Support.
Note: Employee matching gift ratio: 2 to 1 up to $5,000 annually per employee.

Financial Summary

Total Giving: $1,359,122 (fiscal year ending September 30, 2004); $1,468,281 (fiscal 2002); $1,414,387 (fiscal 2001). Note: Contributes through foundation only.
Giving Analysis: Giving for fiscal 2001 includes: foundation matching gifts ($520,874); foundation ($893,513)
Assets: $153,314 (fiscal 2004); $128,264 (fiscal 2002); $133,766 (fiscal 2001)
Gifts Received: $1,385,795 (fiscal 2003); $1,485,828 (fiscal 2002); $1,418,364 (fiscal 2001). Note: Contributions are received from Millipore Corp.

Typical Recipients

Arts & Humanities: Arts Associations & Councils, Arts Centers, Arts Funds, Arts Outreach, Ballet, Arts & Humanities-General, Libraries, Museums/Galleries, Music, Performing Arts, Public Broadcasting
Civic & Public Affairs: African American Affairs, Clubs, Employment/Job Training, Ethnic Organizations, Civic & Public Affairs-General, Hispanic Affairs, Housing, Law & Justice, Legal Aid, Municipalities/Towns, Native American Affairs, Nonprofit Management, Philanthropic Organizations, Professional & Trade Associations, Public Policy, Urban & Community Affairs, Zoos/Aquariums
Education: Afterschool/Enrichment Programs, Business Education, Business-School Partnerships, Colleges & Universities, Community & Junior Colleges, Education Associations, Education Reform, Elementary Education (Public), Engineering/Technological Education, Education-General, Leadership Training, Literacy, Medical Education, Minority Education, Preschool Education, Private Education (Precollege), Public Education (Precollege), Religious Education, Science/Mathematics Education, Secondary Education (Private), Secondary Education (Public), Special Education, Student Aid, Vocational & Technical Education
Environment: Forestry, Environment-General, Wildlife Protection
Health: AIDS/HIV, Cancer, Children's Health/Hospitals, Clinics/Medical Centers, Diabetes, Emergency/Ambulance Services, Eyes/Blindness, Health Organizations, Home-Care Services, Hospitals, Medical Research, Medical Training, Mental Health, Multiple Sclerosis, Public Health, Respiratory, Single-Disease Health Associations
International: Foreign Educational Institutions, International Relief Efforts
Religion: Jewish Causes
Science: Science Exhibits & Fairs, Science Museums, Scientific Centers & Institutes, Scientific Organizations, Scientific Research
Social Services: At-Risk Youth, Child Abuse, Child Welfare, Community Service Organizations, Delin-
quency & Criminal Rehabilitation, Domestic Violence, Emergency Relief, Family Services, Food/Clothing Distribution, Homes, People with Disabilities, Recreation & Athletics, Shelters/Homelessness, Social Services-General, Substance Abuse, United Funds/United Ways, Youth Organizations

Application Procedures

Initial Contact: Send written inquiries and proposals.
Application Requirements: Application should include summary of proposed program or project, including specific goals and objectives; dollar amount or nature of request; purpose of requested funds; background; itemized budget for project; financial statements for most recently completed fiscal year; proof of tax-exempt status; history and accomplishments of requesting organization; list of staff and board of directors; other sources of support; and current contact name, address, and phone number.
Deadlines: None.
Decision Notification: The board meets quarterly to evaluate proposals.
Notes: Foundation accepts the Associated Grantmakers of Massachusetts Common Proposal format.

Restrictions

The foundation does not support religious or political programs.

Additional Information

The foundation will support new projects or new nonprofit organizations in certain cases.
The foundation conducts periodic evaluations and does not guarantee continuing support for a project or program.
Publications: Foundation Annual Report

Corporate Officials

Francis Lunger: chief financial officer, corporate vice president B Erie, PA 1945. ED Gannon University BS (1968). PRIM CORP EMPL chief financial officer, corporate vice president: Millipore Corp. CORP AFFIL director: Stormedia Inc.
Jeffrey Rudin: vice president, general counsel PRIM CORP EMPL vice president, general counsel: Millipore Corp.

Foundation Officials

Charleen Johnson: executive director
Jeffrey Rudin: trustee (see above)
Kathy Stearns: trustee

Grants Analysis

Disclosure Period: fiscal year ending September 30, 2004
Total Grants: $902,456*
Number of Grants: 124
Average Grant: $7,278
Highest Grant: $40,000
Lowest Grant: $300
Typical Range: $1,000 to $25,000
*Note: Giving excludes matching gifts and scholarships.

Recent Grants

Note: Grants derived from fiscal 2004 Form 990.
Library-Related

7,500	New York Public Library, New York, NY

General

40,000	Italian Home for Children, Jamaica Plain, MA
40,000	Scholarship America, St. Peter, MN
35,000	City Year Inc., Boston, MA
25,000	Boston Partners in Education Inc., Boston, MA
25,000	Boston Renaissance Charter School, Boston, MA
25,000	City on a Hill Charter School, Boston, MA
25,000	Museum of Science, Boston, MA
20,000	Roxbury Preparatory Charter School, Roxbury, MA
18,899	Bedford Public Schools, Bedford, MA

16,600	University of Massachusetts, Boston, MA

FRANCES GOLL MILLS FUND

Giving Contact

Helen James
c/o Citizens Bank Saginaw
101 N. Washington Ave.
Saginaw, MI 48607
Phone: (989)776-7368

Description

Founded: 1982
EIN: 382434002
Organization Type: Private Foundation
Giving Locations: MI: Saginaw County
Grant Types: Capital, General Support, Multiyear/Continuing Support, Operating Expenses, Seed Money.

Donor Information

Founder: the late Frances Goll Mills

Financial Summary

Total Giving: $245,458 (fiscal year ending September 30, 2004); $272,570 (fiscal 2001). Note: 1997 Giving includes United Way ($19,500).
Giving Analysis: Giving for fiscal 2004 includes: foundation grants to United Way ($10,000); fiscal 2001: foundation grants to United Way ($11,000)
Assets: $5,058,058 (fiscal 2004); $4,699,924 (fiscal 2001)

Typical Recipients

Arts & Humanities: History & Archaeology, Libraries, Museums/Galleries, Music
Civic & Public Affairs: African American Affairs, Community Foundations, Economic Development, Civic & Public Affairs-General, Housing, Legal Aid, Municipalities/Towns, Parades/Festivals, Urban & Community Affairs, Zoos/Aquariums
Education: Agricultural Education, Business Education, Colleges & Universities, Engineering/Technological Education, Public Education (Precollege), Science/Mathematics Education, Student Aid
Health: Children's Health/Hospitals, Clinics/Medical Centers, Emergency/Ambulance Services, Health-General
International: International Relations
Religion: Churches, Religious Organizations, Religious Welfare
Social Services: At-Risk Youth, Community Centers, Community Service Organizations, Emergency Relief, Family Services, People with Disabilities, Scouts, Special Olympics, United Funds/United Ways, YMCA/YWCA/YMHA/YWHA, Youth Organizations

Application Procedures

Initial Contact: Request application guidelines.
Deadlines: None.

Additional Information

Publications: Application Guidelines
Trust(s): Citizens Bank NA

Grants Analysis

Disclosure Period: fiscal year ending September 30, 2004
Total Grants: $235,458*
Number of Grants: 15
Average Grant: $10,420*
Highest Grant: $50,000
Lowest Grant: $1,668
Typical Range: $1,000 to $20,000
*Note: Giving excludes United Way. Average grant figure excludes two highest grants ($100,000).

Recent Grants

Note: Grants derived from fiscal 2000 Form 990.
General

50,000	Saginaw Valley State University, University Center, MI
49,350	Saginaw Zoological Society, Saginaw, MI
45,000	First Congregation Church, Saginaw, MI
28,000	Covenant Health Care, Saginaw, MI
25,000	YMCA, Saginaw, MI
25,000	YMCA of Saginaw, Saginaw, MI -- health enhancement program
20,000	Boysville/St. Vincent Home, Saginaw, MI
20,000	Lutheran Child and Family Services, Bay City, MI
15,000	Boys and Girls Clubs of Bay County, Bay City, MI
15,000	City Rescue Mission, Saginaw, MI

MINE SAFETY APPLIANCES CO.

Company Headquarters

Pittsburgh, PA
Web: http://www.msanet.com

Company Description

Founded: 1914
Ticker: MSA
Exchange: AMEX
Revenue: US$564.4 million (2002)
Employees: 4300 (2003)
SIC(s): 3823 Process Control Instruments, 3842 Surgical Appliances & Supplies.

Operating Locations

Mine Safety Appliances Co. (RI--Esmond)
Note: Operates internationally.

Mine Safety Appliances Co. Charitable Foundation

Giving Contact

Dennis L. Zeitler, Vice President
MSA Company
PO Box 426
Pittsburgh, PA 15230
Phone: (412)967-3000
Fax: (412)967-3367
Web: http://www.msanet.com

Description

EIN: 256023104
Organization Type: Corporate Foundation
Giving Locations: PA: Pittsburgh operating location communities.
Grant Types: Capital, Conference/Seminar, General Support, Project.

Financial Summary

Total Giving: $763,272 (2003); $680,000 (2002); $950,850 (2001)
Giving Analysis: Giving for 2001 includes: foundation grants to United Way ($326,000); foundation ($624,850)
Assets: $1,765,873 (2003); $1,539,168 (2002); $2,496,598 (2001)
Gifts Received: $750,000 (2003); $500,000 (2001); $1,706 (2000). Note: Contributions are received from Mine Safety Appliances Co.

Typical Recipients

Arts & Humanities: Arts Associations & Councils, Arts Centers, Arts Festivals, Arts Outreach, Ballet, Dance, Arts & Humanities-General, Libraries, Museums/Galleries, Music, Opera, Performing Arts, Public Broadcasting, Theater
Civic & Public Affairs: African American Affairs, Botanical Gardens/Parks, Clubs, Community Foundations, Economic Development, Economic Policy, Civic & Public Affairs-General, Law & Justice, Philanthropic Organizations, Professional & Trade Associations, Public Policy, Safety, Urban & Community Affairs, Zoos/Aquariums
Education: Business Education, Colleges & Universities, Community & Junior Colleges, Economic Education, Education Associations, Education Funds, Engineering/Technological Education, Education-General, International Studies, Literacy, Minority Education, Preschool Education, Private Education (Precollege), Public Education (Precollege), Science/Mathematics Education, Special Education, Student Aid
Environment: Environment-General
Health: AIDS/HIV, Alzheimer's Disease, Children's Health/Hospitals, Diabetes, Emergency/Ambulance Services, Health Funds, Health Organizations, Hospices, Hospitals, Kidney, Long-Term Care, Medical Rehabilitation, Mental Health, Multiple Sclerosis, Respiratory, Single-Disease Health Associations
International: International Affairs, International Peace & Security Issues, International Relations, International Relief Efforts
Religion: Dioceses, Ministries, Religious Organizations, Religious Welfare, Seminaries
Science: Observatories & Planetariums, Science Museums, Scientific Centers & Institutes
Social Services: Animal Protection, Big Brothers/Big Sisters, Child Welfare, Community Service Organizations, Emergency Relief, Family Services, Food/Clothing Distribution, People with Disabilities, Recreation & Athletics, Scouts, Senior Services, Social Services-General, Special Olympics, United Funds/United Ways, YMCA/YWCA/YMHA/YWHA, Youth Organizations

Application Procedures

Initial Contact: Send brief letter of introduction.
Application Requirements: Include a description of organization, amount requested, purpose of funds sought, recently audited financial statement, proof of tax-exempt status.
Deadlines: None.

Restrictions

Foundation does not award scholarships or provide grants to individuals.

Additional Information

Trust(s): PNC Bank

Corporate Officials

James E. Herald: vice president financeo PRIM CORP EMPL vice president finance: Mine Safety Appliances Co.
John Thomas Ryan, III: chairman, chief executive officer B Pittsburgh, PA 1943. ED University of Notre Dame AB (1965); Harvard University MBA (1969). PRIM CORP EMPL chairman, chief executive officer: Mine Safety Appliances Co. CORP AFFIL director: Penns Southwest; director: Auergesellschaft GmbH; chairman: Federal Reserve Bank Cleveland. NONPR AFFIL member: Council Foreign Relations; vice chairman, director: Industrial Safety Equipment Association.

Foundation Officials

James E. Herald: secretary (see above)

Grants Analysis

Disclosure Period: calendar year ending 2003
Total Grants: $413,272*
Number of Grants: 77
Average Grant: $5,367
Highest Grant: $25,000
Lowest Grant: $500

Typical Range: $1,000 to $5,000
***Note:** Giving excludes United Way.

Recent Grants

Note: Grants derived from 2003 Form 990.
Library-Related

2,500	Evans City Public Library, Evans City, PA

General

250,000	United Way of Allegheny County, Pittsburgh, PA
60,000	Three Rivers, One Future Allegheny Conference on Community Development, Pittsburgh, PA
55,000	United Way of Butler County, Butler, PA
45,000	United Way of Westmoreland County, Greensburg, PA
30,000	Pittsburgh Ballet Theater, Pittsburgh, PA
25,000	Oratory, Pittsburgh, PA
20,822	Onslow County United Way, Jacksonville, NC
17,500	Pittsburgh Symphony Orchestra, Pittsburgh, PA -- for Heinz hall for the performing arts
16,600	Mile High United Way, Denver, CO
15,000	Council on Foreign Relations, New York, NY

JULIA J. MINGENBACK FOUNDATION

Giving Contact

Don C. Steffes, President
1008 Turkey Creek Drive
McPherson, KS 67460
Phone: (620)241-0700

Description

Founded: 1959
EIN: 486109567
Organization Type: Private Foundation
Giving Locations: KS: McPherson County
Grant Types: Capital, Operating Expenses.

Donor Information

Founder: the late E. C. Mingenback

Financial Summary

Total Giving: $221,500 (2001)
Assets: $4,651,137 (2001)

Typical Recipients

Arts & Humanities: Arts Associations & Councils, Community Arts, Libraries, Museums/Galleries, Opera
Civic & Public Affairs: Municipalities/Towns
Education: Colleges & Universities, Private Education (Precollege), Religious Education
Health: Hospitals
Social Services: Community Centers, Family Services, Food/Clothing Distribution, Homes, Senior Services, Social Services-General, YMCA/YWCA/YMHA/YWHA, Youth Organizations

Application Procedures

Initial Contact: Send a brief letter of inquiry.
Application Requirements: Include specific needs.
Deadlines: None.

Restrictions

Generally limited to educational and cultural activities of organizations in McPherson County, KS.

Additional Information

Trust(s): Peoples Bank and Trust IV KS NA

Foundation Officials

Bev Hess: secretary, treasurer
James Lee Ketcherside: director B Topeka, KS

1935. PRIM CORP EMPL chairman, president: Farmers Alliance Mutual Insurance Co.
Edwin T. Pyle: director
Brett Reber: director
Don C. Steffes: president
B. Carver Swindoll: director

Grants Analysis

Disclosure Period: calendar year ending 2001
Total Grants: $221,500
Number of Grants: 7
Average Grant: $31,643
Highest Grant: $50,000
Lowest Grant: $1,500
Typical Range: $25,000 to $50,000

Recent Grants

Note: Grants derived from 2001 Form 990.
General

50,000	Central Christian College, McPherson, KS -- capital improvements
50,000	McPherson College, McPherson, KS -- capital improvements
40,000	Memorial Hospital, McPherson, KS -- capital improvements
30,000	City of McPherson, McPherson, KS -- capital improvements
25,000	Elyria Christian School, McPherson, KS -- capital improvements
25,000	McPherson Opera House, McPherson, KS -- capital improvements
1,500	McPherson Family Life, McPherson, KS -- for operations and programs

MINNESOTA MINING & MANUFACTURING CO.

Company Headquarters

St. Paul, MN
Web: http://www.mmm.com

Company Description

Founded: 1902
Ticker: MMM
Exchange: NYSE
Also Known As: 3M.
Revenue: US$16.332 billion (2002)
Employees: 67072 (2003)
SIC(s): 2672 Coated & Laminated Paper Nec, 2834 Pharmaceutical Preparations, 2891 Adhesives & Sealants, 2899 Chemical Preparations Nec.

Operating Locations

Minnesota Mining & Manufacturing Co. (AL--Birmingham, Decatur, Guin; AK--Anchorage; AZ--Phoenix, Tucson; CA--Camarillo, Chico, Costa Mesa, Fresno, Irvine, Los Angeles, Northridge, Ontario, Petaluma, San Francisco, Tustin, Unitek; CO--Denver; CT--Wallingford; DC; FL--Pompano Beach, Sanford; GA--Atlanta; HI--Honolulu; IL--Chicago, Cordova, DeKalb, Hinsdale; IN--Indianapolis; IA--Ames, Forest City, Knoxville; KY--Cynthiana; MD--Westminster; MA, Cambridge, Chelmsford; MI, Detroit, Midland; MN, Cottage Grove, Eagan, Fairmont, Hutchinson, Park Rapids, Pine City, St. Paul, Staples; MO--Nevada, Springfield, St. Louis; NE--Valley; NJ--Belle Mead, Eatontown, Freehold, West Deptford; NY--Honeoye, Lennox Hill, Rochester; NC--Charlotte, High Point; OH--Baltimore, Cincinnati, Cleveland, Columbus, Mentor; OK--Weatherford; OR--Eugene, White City; PA--Philadelphia; SC--Greenville, North Charleston; SD--Aberdeen; TN--Nashville; TX--Austin, Brownwood, El Paso, Fort Worth, Houston, Rio Grande; UT--Salt Lake City; WA--Seattle; WV--Middleway; WI--Cumberland, Menomonee, Nekoosa, Wausau, Wisconsin Rapids)

Nonmonetary Support

Value: $18,100,000 (2000); $16,608,454 (1998)
Type: Donated Products; In-kind Services
Volunteer Programs: The 3M GIVES (Grants Initiated by Volunteer Service) program matches 25 hours of employee/retiree volunteer service with $200 to the volunteer's designated nonprofit organization. The company also supports a Community Volunteer Award program through which it selects 25 exceptional employee/retiree volunteers annually and awards $1,000 to a nonprofit organization selected by each winner. Volunteer programs contact is Anne E. Mazurowski.
Contact: Richard E. Hanson, Director Community Affairs; Vice President
3M Foundation
Note: Donated equipment at fair market value.

3M Foundation

Giving Contact

Cynthia F. Kleven, Manager Contributions
3M Community Affairs
Contributions Program
3M Center, Bldg. 224-5N-40
St. Paul, MN 55144
Phone: (651)736-1135
Fax: (651)737-3061
E-mail: cfkleven@mmm.com
Web: http://www.3M.com/about3m/community

Alternate Contact

Richard E. Hanson, Contact
3M Foundation
St. Paul, MN 55144
Phone: (651)733-8335

Description

Founded: 1953
EIN: 416038262
Organization Type: Corporate Foundation
Giving Locations: headquarters and operating communities.
Grant Types: General Support, Operating Expenses, Project.
Note: Employee matching gift ratio: 1 to 1.

Financial Summary

Total Giving: $15,794,460 (2003); $17,586,331 (2002); $16,553,268 (2001). Note: Contributes through corporate direct giving program and foundation.
Giving Analysis: Giving for 2001 includes: foundation matching gifts ($1,674,331); corporate direct giving (approx $3,625,669); foundation (approx $16,500,000); nonmonetary support (approx $25,300,000)
Assets: $38,724,763 (2003); $32,510,270 (2002); $54,259,082 (2001)
Gifts Received: $3,232,020 (1996)

Typical Recipients

Arts & Humanities: Arts Associations & Councils, Arts Centers, Arts Institutes, Arts Outreach, Ethnic & Folk Arts, Historic Preservation, History & Archaeology, Libraries, Museums/Galleries, Music, Opera, Performing Arts, Public Broadcasting, Theater
Civic & Public Affairs: African American Affairs, Business/Free Enterprise, Chambers of Commerce, Community Foundations, Economic Development, Employment/Job Training, Civic & Public Affairs-General, Hispanic Affairs, Legal Aid, Municipalities/Towns, Native American Affairs, Nonprofit Management, Parades/Festivals, Professional & Trade Associations, Safety, Urban & Community Affairs
Education: Afterschool/Enrichment Programs, Business Education, Colleges & Universities, Economic Education, Education Associations, Education Funds, Engineering/Technological Education, Faculty Development, Education-General, International

Exchange, Journalism/Media Education, Medical Education, Minority Education, Private Education (Precollege), Public Education (Precollege), Science/Mathematics Education, Social Sciences Education, Student Aid, Vocational & Technical Education
Environment: Environment-General, Protection, Resource Conservation
Health: Clinics/Medical Centers, Emergency/Ambulance Services, Geriatric Health, Health Policy/Cost Containment, Health Organizations, Hospices, Hospitals, Medical Rehabilitation, Mental Health, Public Health, Transplant Networks/Donor Banks
International: Foreign Educational Institutions
Religion: Religious Welfare, Social/Policy Issues
Science: Science Museums, Scientific Centers & Institutes, Scientific Research
Social Services: Child Welfare, Community Centers, Community Service Organizations, Counseling, Crime Prevention, Day Care, Delinquency & Criminal Rehabilitation, Domestic Violence, Emergency Relief, Family Services, Food/Clothing Distribution, Homes, People with Disabilities, Recreation & Athletics, Scouts, Senior Services, Shelters/Homelessness, Social Services-General, Substance Abuse, United Funds/United Ways, Volunteer Services, YMCA/YWCA/YMHA/YWHA, Youth Organizations

Application Procedures

Initial Contact: Submit a brief letter of inquiry. Telephone requests are not accepted, but requests may be submitted by mail, fax, or e-mailed using the link at www.3m.com/about3m/contact.
Application Requirements: Include brief organizational history, project description, evaluation and impact, targeted group of people who will be benefit, specific amount requested, and proof of tax-exempt status.
Deadlines: September 30 and January 31 for formal requests.
Review Process: If letter of inquiry demonstrates your organization meet 3M criteria, and geographic restrictions and funding priorities are met, you may be invited to submit a formal grant application.
Evaluative Criteria: Preference is given to proposals and programs that have broad-based community support, a reputation for high-quality service delivery, and measurable results.

Restrictions

Grants are not considered for advocacy and lobbying efforts to influence legislation; individuals; religious, fraternal, social, veterans, or military organizations; travel for individuals or groups; purchase of equipment not manufactured by 3M; for-profit organizations; endowment funds; disease-specific organizations; film/video productions; or scholarship funds.
Generally, grants are not made to organizations outside of 3M communities; conferences, seminars, symposiums or workshops or publications of their proceedings; fund-raising, testimonial, athletic, or special events; emergency operating support; funding for more than 10 percent of an organization's annual budget or campaign goal; funding programs beyond three years; individual K-12 schools; or hospitals. Letters of inquiry are accepted only from 501(c)(3) organizations located in 3M communities.

Additional Information

In countries where 3M has subsidiary operations, requests should be directed to that location. For more information regarding international giving, contact Richard Hanson, director, Community Affairs, and vice president, 3M Foundation.
Inquiries from the Minneapolis/St. Paul, MN area should be addressed to the designated staff person at the above address or may directed at one of the following program-specific contact people: Cynthia F. Kleven, Health & Human Services/Arts and Culture/Environment at (651) 733-1721, cfkleven@mmm.com; Anne E. Mazurowski, Volunteer Programs at (651) 733-1421, aemazurowski1@

mmm.com; and Barbara W. Kaufmann, Education at (651) 733-1241, bkaufmann@mmm.com. For locations outside of St. Paul where 3M has an operation, contact Cynthia Kleven at 613-733-1721 or your local 3M facility.

Publications: Giving Guidelines

Corporate Officials

M. Kay Grenz: senior vice president human resourcesrc B Owatonna, MN December 16, 1946. ED University of North Dakota BA (1969). PRIM CORP EMPL vice president human resources: Minnesota Mining & Manufacturing Co. NONPR AFFIL member: Human Resources Planning Society; member: Human Resources Roundtable Group; member: Human Resources Executive Council; member: The Conference Board; member: The Cowdrick Group.

W. James McNerney, Jr.: chairman, chief executive officer, director B Providence, RI August 22, 1949. ED Yale University BA (1971); Harvard University MBA (1975). PRIM CORP EMPL chairman, chief executive officer, director: Minnesota Mining & Manufacturing Co. CORP AFFIL director: The Boeing Co.; director: Procter & Gamble Co. NONPR AFFIL trustee: University of Minnesota Foundation; director: World Business Council for Sustainable Development; trustee: Northwestern University; director: Greater Twin Cities United Way; member: Minnesota Business Partnership; member: Business Council; member: Capital City Partnership; member: American Society of Corporate Executives.

Mohamed S. Nozari: executive vice president B June 12, 1942. ED Hope College BA (1965); University of Detroit PhD (1969). PRIM CORP EMPL executive vice president: Minnesota Mining & Manufacturing Co.

Charles Reich: executive vice president B Minneapolis, MN August 02, 1942. ED University of Michigan BS (1964); University of Wisconsin PhD (1968). PRIM CORP EMPL executive vice president: Minnesota Mining & Manufacturing Co. CORP AFFIL director: Imation Corp.

Harold J. Wiens: executive vice president B Dallas, OR August 04, 1946. ED Michigan Tech University BS (1968). PRIM CORP EMPL executive vice president: Minnesota Mining & Manufacturing Co. NONPR AFFIL advisory board: Michigan Tech University; member: National Association of Manufacturers.

Giving Program Officials

John W. Benson: director B Saint James, MN 1944. ED University of Minnesota BS (1966); University of Washington MS (1968). PRIM CORP EMPL executive vice president health care: Minnesota Mining & Manufacturing Co. CORP AFFIL director: SurModics Inc. NONPR AFFIL trustee: St. Olaf College.

Foundation Officials

J. Mark Borseth: treasurer
Fred Harris: vice president
Cynthia F. Kleven: secretary PRIM CORP EMPL director community affairs: Minnesota Mining & Manufacturing Co.
David Powell: president
William Schmoll: treasurer
Donna Schorr: assistant secretary

Grants Analysis

Disclosure Period: calendar year ending 2003
Total Grants: $10,437,704*
Number of Grants: 1,139
Average Grant: $5,669*
Highest Grant: $2,442,306
Typical Range: $1,000 to $25,000
*Note: Giving excludes matching gifts; United Way; scholarship. Average grant figure excludes two highest grants ($3,992,306).

Recent Grants

Note: Grants derived from 2003 Form 990.
General
10,029,119 Community and Education, St. Paul, MN

2,337,050 Social Services, St. Paul, MN
1,207,793 Education Aids, St. Paul, MN
320,200 3M Gives, St. Paul, MN
88,385 Junior Achievement, St. Paul, MN

MINNESOTA MUTUAL LIFE INSURANCE CO.

Company Headquarters

St. Paul, MN
Web: http://www.minnesotamutual.com

Company Description

Employees: 4,000
SIC(s): 6311 Life Insurance, 6321 Accident & Health Insurance.

Nonmonetary Support

Value: $1,068,000 (2001 approx); $500,000 (2000)
Type: Donated Equipment; In-kind Services; Loaned Employees; Loaned Executives; Workplace Solicitation
Note: NOT NOT Company also allows organizations the use of buildings and facilities.
Volunteer Programs: Company conducts a special program that recognizes employee volunteerism with $100 donations to organizations where employees volunteer their time.

Minnesota Mutual Foundation

Giving Contact

Lori J. Koutsky, Manager
Minnesota Mutual Foundation
400 Robert St. North
St. Paul, MN 55101-2015
Phone: (651)665-3501
Fax: (651)665-3551
E-mail: lori.koutsky@minnesotamutual.com
Web: http://www.minnesotamutual.com/about/community.asp

Description

EIN: 363608619
Organization Type: Corporate Foundation
Giving Locations: MN: Minneapolis metropolitan area, St. Paul metropolitan area
Grant Types: Capital, Employee Matching Gifts, General Support, Multiyear/Continuing Support, Scholarship.
Note: Employee matching gift ratio: 1 to 1 for gifts to higher education, arts and cultural organizations, and hospitals.

Financial Summary

Total Giving: $1,257,285 (2003); $1,415,451 (2002); $2,930,523 (2001 approx). Note: Contributes through corporate direct giving program and foundation.
Giving Analysis: Giving for 2001 includes: corporate direct giving ($422,615); nonmonetary support ($1,068,000); foundation ($1,439,908)
Assets: $33,031,109 (2003); $30,405,104 (2002); $30,321,833 (2001)
Gifts Received: $1,800,014 (2001); $1,642,875 (2000); $1,537,500 (1999). Note: In 2001, contributions were received from Securian Holding Company. In 2000, contributions were received from Cisco Systems, Inc. In 1999, contributions were received from Ciena Corp.

Typical Recipients

Arts & Humanities: Arts Centers, Arts Funds, Arts Institutes, Arts & Humanities-General, Historic Preservation, History & Archaeology, Libraries, Museums/ Galleries, Music, Opera, Public Broadcasting, Theater

Civic & Public Affairs: Asian American Affairs, Business/Free Enterprise, Clubs, Economic Development, Employment/Job Training, Civic & Public Affairs-General, Housing, Law & Justice, Legal Aid, Minority Business, Nonprofit Management, Parades/ Festivals, Philanthropic Organizations, Professional & Trade Associations, Public Policy, Urban & Community Affairs, Women's Affairs, Zoos/Aquariums

Education: Afterschool/Enrichment Programs, Arts/ Humanities Education, Business Education, Business-School Partnerships, Colleges & Universities, Economic Education, Education Funds, Education Reform, Elementary Education (Private), Education-General, Leadership Training, Literacy, Minority Education, Private Education (Precollege), Science/ Mathematics Education, Special Education, Vocational & Technical Education

Health: AIDS/HIV, Children's Health/Hospitals, Emergency/Ambulance Services, Health-General, Health Funds, Health Organizations, Hospices, Hospitals, Long-Term Care, Medical Rehabilitation, Medical Research, Nursing Services, Prenatal Health Issues, Public Health, Research/Studies Institutes

International: Human Rights, International Organizations

Religion: Churches, Religion-General, Jewish Causes, Religious Organizations, Religious Welfare

Science: Science Museums

Social Services: Child Abuse, Child Welfare, Community Service Organizations, Crime Prevention, Day Care, Domestic Violence, Emergency Relief, Family Services, Food/Clothing Distribution, People with Disabilities, Refugee Assistance, Scouts, Senior Services, Shelters/Homelessness, Social Services-General, Substance Abuse, United Funds/United Ways, YMCA/YWCA/YMHA/YWHA, Youth Organizations

Application Procedures

Initial Contact: Call or write for guidelines and applications, then send a written proposal.
Application Requirements: A cover letter, a completed Minnesota Common Grant Application, and the following attachments: financial statements from most recent fiscal year, organization and project budgets, list of funding sources with dollar amounts, a copy of the applicant's most recent IRS Form 990, list of board members with affiliations, and proof of tax-exempt status.
Deadlines: February 15, May 15, August 15, and November 15.
Evaluative Criteria: Supports direct gifts rather than benefit activities; organizations must meet either requirements of Minnesota Charitable Solicitation Act of the National Information Bureau, meet guidelines of foundation, or meet an important need not otherwise met; program has reasonable chance of success; program is not a duplication of effort; substantial support from other sources.

Restrictions

Does not support political, lobbying or fraternal activities; start-up funding for new organizations; religious organizations for sectarian purposes; organizations that do not possess 501(c)(3) tax-exempt status; fundraising events, benefits, sponsorships or advertising support; individuals or individual scholarships; endowment campaigns; athletic, recreation or sports-related organizations; services traditionally supported by government agencies; international organizations; veteran and fraternal organizations; trips or tours; hospitals or health care services that are generally supported by third party mechanisms (hospitals are eligible for matching gifts); conferences, seminars, workshops or symposiums; and public and private K-12 schools (schools are eligible for matching gifts).

Additional Information

Publications: Corporate Contributions Policy

Corporate Officials

Dennis E. Prohofsky: senior vice president, general counsel, secretary B Saint Paul, MN 1940. ED University of Minnesota (1965); William Mitchell College of Law (1972). PRIM CORP EMPL senior vice president, general counsel, secretary: Minnesota Mutual Life Insurance Co. ADD CORP EMPL secretary: Mimlic Sales Corp. CORP AFFIL director: Sargasso Mutual.

Robert L. Senkler: chairman, president, chief executive officer B Saint Paul, MN 1952. ED University of Minnesota, Duluth College BA (1979). PRIM CORP EMPL chairman, president, chief executive officer: Minnesota Mutual Life Insurance Co. NONPR AFFIL member, fellow: Society Actuaries.

Gregory S. Strong: vice president actuary B 1944. PRIM CORP EMPL vice president actuary: Minnesota Mutual Life Insurance Co.

Foundation Officials

Keith M. Campbell: vice president, director B 1945. PRIM CORP EMPL vice president: Minnesota Mutual Life Insurance Co.

Lori J. Koutsky: foundation manager
Dennis E. Prohofsky: secretary (see above)
Robert L. Senkler: president, director (see above)
Gregory S. Strong: treasurer (see above)

Grants Analysis

Disclosure Period: calendar year ending 2003
Total Grants: $753,025*
Number of Grants: 79
Average Grant: $7,090*
Highest Grant: $200,000
Lowest Grant: $500
Typical Range: $1,000 to $32,000
*Note: Giving excludes matching gifts, scholarships, and United Way. Average grant figure excludes highest grant.

Recent Grants

Note: Grants derived from 2003 Form 990.
General

355,000	United Way, St. Paul, MN
200,000	University of Minnesota - Carlson School of Management, Minneapolis, MN
110,000	Saint Paul Chamber Orchestra, St. Paul, MN
82,000	Ordway Music Theater, St. Paul, MN
30,000	KTCA/Twin Cities Public Television Inc., St. Paul, MN
27,500	Guthrie Theater, Minneapolis, MN
25,000	Minnesota Orchestra, Minneapolis, MN
21,000	Minnesota Private College Council Fund and Research Foundation, St. Paul, MN
14,000	Minnesota Public Radio, St. Paul, MN
13,000	Junior Achievement, St. Paul, MN

MINSTER MACHINE CO.

Company Headquarters

PO Box 120
Minster, OH 45865
Web: http://www.minster.com

Company Description

Employees: 775
SIC(s): 3542 Machine Tools--Metal Forming Types, 3714 Motor Vehicle Parts & Accessories.

Minster Machine Co. Foundation

Giving Contact

Robert Sudhoff, Vice President, Finance & Chief Financial Officer

240 W. 5th St.
Minster, OH 45865-1027
Phone: (419)628-2331

Description

EIN: 346559271
Organization Type: Corporate Foundation
Giving Locations: OH
Grant Types: General Support.

Financial Summary

Total Giving: $60,800 (fiscal year ending November 30, 2001)
Assets: $854,991 (fiscal 2001)
Gifts Received: $16,100 (fiscal 2001); $160,000 (fiscal 2000); $250,000 (fiscal 1994). Note: Contributions were received from the Minster Machine Co.

Typical Recipients

Arts & Humanities: Arts Associations & Councils, Arts Institutes, Community Arts, History & Archaeology, Libraries, Museums/Galleries, Opera, Public Broadcasting
Civic & Public Affairs: Clubs, Community Foundations, Civic & Public Affairs-General, Professional & Trade Associations, Public Policy, Safety, Urban & Community Affairs
Education: Agricultural Education, Arts/Humanities Education, Colleges & Universities, Education Associations, Education Funds, Engineering/Technological Education, Education-General, Special Education, Student Aid
Health: Alzheimer's Disease, Cancer, Children's Health/Hospitals, Clinics/Medical Centers, Emergency/Ambulance Services, Heart, Hospices, Hospitals, Medical Research, Nursing Services, Prenatal Health Issues, Single-Disease Health Associations
Religion: Religious Organizations, Religious Welfare
Science: Scientific Organizations
Social Services: Big Brothers/Big Sisters, Child Welfare, Community Service Organizations, Counseling, Crime Prevention, Domestic Violence, People with Disabilities, Recreation & Athletics, Scouts, Social Services-General, Special Olympics, Substance Abuse, YMCA/YWCA/YMHA/YWHA, Youth Organizations

Application Procedures

Initial Contact: Send brief letter explaining need and wants. There are no deadlines.
Deadlines: None.

Corporate Officials

Robert J. Sudhoff: vice president financial, chief financial officerc B Coldwater, OH 1955. ED Wright State University (1977). PRIM CORP EMPL vice president financial, chief financial officer: Minster Machine Co.
John Winch: president, chief operating officer, director B Lima, OH 1962. ED Southern Methodist University (1984); Ohio State University (1988). PRIM CORP EMPL president, chief operating officer, director: Minster Machine Co. CLUB AFFIL Rotary Club.

Foundation Officials

Robert J. Sudhoff: vice president, secretary (see above)
David C. Winch: treasurer
Harold S. Winch: president
Heather E. Winch: secretary
John Winch: vice president (see above)
Nancy E. Winch: president

Grants Analysis

Disclosure Period: fiscal year ending November 30, 2001
Total Grants: $60,800
Number of Grants: 32
Average Grant: $1,062*
Highest Grant: $10,000
Lowest Grant: $50
Typical Range: $250 to $2,000

*Note: Average grant figure excludes three highest grants ($30,000).

Recent Grants

Note: Grants derived from fiscal 2001 Form 990.
General

10,000	BMH Foundation, Muncie, IN
10,000	Boonshoft Museum of Discovery, Dayton, OH
10,000	PMA Educational Foundation, Independence, OH
5,000	Dayton Art Institute, Dayton, OH
5,000	Hospice of Darke and Mercer Counties, Greenville, OH
5,000	JTD Hospital Foundation, St. Marys, OH
2,000	Minster High School Scholarship Fund, Minster, OH
2,000	Village of Minster Fire Department, Minster, OH
1,500	National Child Safety Council, Minster, OH
1,000	Knights of Columbus 2158, Minster, OH

MITSUBISHI ELECTRIC AND ELECTRONICS USA

Company Headquarters

1050 E. Arques Avenue
Sunnyvale, CA 94086
Phone: (408)730-5900
Fax: (408)732-9382
Web: http://www.mitsubishichips.com

Company Description

Founded: 1980
Former Name: Mitsubishi Electric America.
Employees: 60
SIC(s): 3571 Electronic Computers, 3694 Engine Electrical Equipment.
Parent Company: Mitsubishi Electric Corp., Mitsubishi Denki Bldg., 2-3, Marunouchi 2-chome, Chiyoda-ku, Tokyo, Japan

Operating Locations

Diamond Vision (NY--New York); Mitsubishi Consumer Electronics America (CA--Santa Ana); Mitsubishi Electric & Electronics U.S.A. (CA--Cypress, Nevada City, Santa Ana, Sunnyvale; FL--Lake Mary; GA--Braselton, Norcross; MA--Cambridge, Waltham; MI--Plymouth; NY--White Plains; NC--Durham; OH--Mason; PA--Warrendale; TX--Irving); Mitsubishi Electric & Electronics U.S.A. Sales (CA--Cypress); Mitsubishi Electric Industrial Control (IL--Mount Prospect); Mitsubishi Electric Manufacturing (OH--Mason); Mitsubishi Semiconductor America (NC--Durham); Optrex Glass (MI--Plymouth); Powerex (PA--Youngwood)

Nonmonetary Support

Type: Donated Equipment; Donated Products
Volunteer Programs: To recognize growing interest in volunteerism among Mitsubishi Electric America employees, the foundation administers the MEA Foundation Starfish Enterprise Award program. The foundation also donates $10 per volunteer hour contributed to eligible projects by employees, their friends, and family members.

Mitsubishi Electric America Foundation

Giving Contact

Rayna Aylward, Executive Director
1560 Wilson Boulevard, Suite 1150
Arlington, VA 22209

Phone: (703)276-8240
Fax: (703)276-8260
E-mail: rayna.aylward@meus.mea.com
Web: http://www.meaf.org

Description

Founded: 1991
EIN: 521700855
Organization Type: Corporate Foundation
Giving Locations: nationally; operating locations.
Grant Types: Employee Matching Gifts, General Support, Matching, Project, Seed Money.
Note: Employee matching gift ratio: 1 to 1, up to $500 per employee per year to disability organizations or educational institutions that education disabled students.

Donor Information

Founder: Established in 1991 by Mitsubishi Electronics America, Mitsubishi Consumer Electronics America, Mitsubishi Semiconductor America, Mitsubishi Electric Manufacturing Cincinnati, Horizon Research, Mitsubishi Electric Industrial Controls, Mitsubishi Electric Power Products, Diamond Vision, Astronet Corp. and Mitsubishi Electric Corp.

Financial Summary

Total Giving: $406,748 (2003); $750,000 (2002 approx); $700,000 (2001 approx). Note: Contributes through foundation only.
Giving Analysis: Giving for 2002 includes: foundation (approx $750,000); 2001: foundation (approx $700,000)
Assets: $19,629,956 (2003); $19,800,000 (2002 approx); $19,657,039 (2001)
Gifts Received: $72,123 (2001); $750,026 (1996); $814,248 (1995). Note: In 1995, contributions were received from Mitsubishi Electronics Inc. ($345,300); Mitsubishi Consumer Electronics America, Inc. ($231,200); Mitsui Semiconductor America, Inc. Funds ($78,000); Mitsubishi Electric Manufacturing Cincinnati, Inc. ($41,700); Mitsubishi Electric Industrial Controls, Inc. ($21,100); Mitsubishi Electric Power Products, Inc. ($7,100); Mitsubishi Electric Research Laboratories, Inc. ($6,100); Astronet Corp. ($8,900); and other sources less than $5,000 each ($74,848).

Typical Recipients

Arts & Humanities: Arts Associations & Councils, Arts Funds, Arts Outreach, Community Arts, Film & Video, Music, Public Broadcasting
Civic & Public Affairs: Botanical Gardens/Parks, Business/Free Enterprise, Community Foundations, Employment/Job Training, Civic & Public Affairs-General, Housing, Nonprofit Management, Philanthropic Organizations, Women's Affairs
Education: Arts/Humanities Education, Colleges & Universities, Education Funds, Elementary Education (Private), Elementary Education (Public), Engineering/Technological Education, Education-General, International Studies, Legal Education, Preschool Education, Private Education (Precollege), Public Education (Precollege), School Volunteerism, Science/Mathematics Education, Social Sciences Education, Special Education, Student Aid
Environment: Environment-General, Resource Conservation
Health: AIDS/HIV, Cancer, Children's Health/Hospitals, Diabetes, Eyes/Blindness, Health Organizations, Heart, Medical Rehabilitation, Prenatal Health Issues, Preventive Medicine/Wellness Organizations, Single-Disease Health Associations, Speech & Hearing, Transplant Networks/Donor Banks
International: Health Care/Hospitals
Religion: Religious Welfare
Science: Scientific Centers & Institutes
Social Services: Animal Protection, Child Welfare, Community Service Organizations, Emergency Relief, Family Services, Food/Clothing Distribution, Homes, People with Disabilities, Recreation & Athletics, Scouts, Senior Services, Social Services-General, Special Olympics, United Funds/United Ways, Volunteer Services, YMCA/YWCA/YMHA/YWHA, Youth Organizations

Application Procedures

Initial Contact: Submit a short (not to exceed three pages) concept paper to the foundation.
Application Requirements: Concept paper should include explanation of the need and objectives for funds requested; description of the national impact of the project/organization; plans for project evaluation and dissemination of results; how this project will build on similar work being carried out in the field, and what factors make the organization's work unique; how this project will make use of information technology; and a budget summary.
Deadlines: None.
Review Process: Concept papers are reviewed throughout the year. Applicants whose concept papers pass preliminary review will be invited to submit a full proposal. New grants are announced in the fall, with funding to begin the following January.
Notes: Concept papers may be submitted online at the foundation's web site.
Due to MEA Foundation's small staff size, phone calls are discouraged during the application process.

Restrictions

Does not support: individuals; intermediary organizations such as the United Way; organizations whose Services are limited to a particular ethnic, fraternal, labor, or political constituency; organizations that discriminate by disability, race, color, creed, religion, veteran status, or national origin; religious organizations for religious purposes; organizations engaged exclusively in political activities or lobbying; organizations or programs connected with controversial social or political issues; loans of money for any purpose; endowments, capital campaigns, or annual fundraising drives; projects or events that are already completed; locally-based activities without national impact; individual schools or school districts; equipment or devices for individual users; or projects exclusively benefiting individuals or groups outside the United States.
Grants are made only to nonprofit organizations that have been granted exemption from federal income tax under Section 501(c)(3) of the Internal Revenue Code.

Additional Information

In February 1991, the Mitsubishi Electric America (MEA) group of companies established the Mitsubishi Electric America Foundation.
Foundation grants are provided to national organizations and matching grants are given to organizations within the Foundation's mission for general operating support and project support.
Publications: Foundation Guidelines; Annual Report

Corporate Officials

Cayce Blanchard: director corporate communicationsotive
Kathy Dozal: administrative assistant
John Henry: production engineer
Akira Katayama: chairman, chief executive officer PRIM CORP EMPL chairman, chief executive officer: Mitsubishi Electric of America.
Kiyoshi Kawakami: president, chief executive officer
Mickey Kurisaki: group president automotive
Art Lewis: senior vice president automotive
Ichiro Taniguchi: chairman PRIM CORP EMPL president: Mitsubishi Electric America.

Foundation Officials

Rayna Aylward: executive director
Cayce Blanchard: director (see above)
David Chang: assistant treasurer PRIM CORP EMPL controller: Mitsubishi Electric America.
Kathy Dozal: director, employee representative (see above)
John Henry: director, employee representative (see above)
Shoji Hibara: treasurer
Kiyoshi Kawakami: president, director (see above)
Mickey Kurisaki: director (see above)
Art Lewis: director (see above)
Colleen Maher: program officer
Tamotsu Nomakuchi: director
Alan P. Olschwang, Esq.: executive vice president B Chicago, IL 1942. ED University of Illinois BS (1963); University of Illinois JD (1966). PRIM CORP EMPL executive vice president, general counsel, director: Mitsubishi Electric of America. CORP AFFIL secretary, director: Astronet Corp.; secretary: Mitsubishi Consumer Electric America. NONPR AFFIL member: Illinois Bar Association; member: New York Bar Association; member: Chicago Bar Association; member: Association Bar New York City; member: California Bar Association; member: American Bar Association; member: American Corporate Counsel Association; member: American Arbitration Association.
Perry Pappous: director
David Rebmann: director
Peter Salavantis: assistant secretary-treasurer
Ichiro Taniguchi: director (see above)
Akira Tasaki: director, president
Richard Waters: director

Grants Analysis

Disclosure Period: calendar year ending 2003
Total Grants: $305,376*
Number of Grants: 38
Average Grant: $8,036
Highest Grant: $45,000
Lowest Grant: $40
Typical Range: $2,500 to $20,000
*Note: Giving excludes matching gifts.

Recent Grants

Note: Grants derived from 2003 Form 990.

General

45,000	Half the Planet Foundation, Washington, DC -- national grant for "Beyond Participation" disability and inclusion training program; Support for the project for the Project DEVELOP
35,000	Manhattan New Music Project Inc., New York, NY -- funding for NYC-based organization's creative music educators project (CME) to develop and test assistive digital technologies
33,775	American Association of People with Disabilities, Washington, DC -- funds for congressional internship video and support for Paul Hearne leadership awards
27,000	WETA, Arlington, VA -- funding for LD online, website for learning disabilities
25,000	Chabot Space and Science Center Foundation, Oakland, CA -- support of the Techbridge project-reaching out to students with visual impairments
25,000	Computer Technology Program, Berkeley, CA
20,000	Girl Scout Council of Orange County, Costa Mesa, CA -- national grant to implement "Starfish Troops" in the Orange county area
20,000	Recording for the Blind and Dyslexic, Princeton, NJ -- library of the future project
12,500	Gallaudet University, Washington, DC -- funding to support the TecEds program
10,000	Washington Very Special Arts, Washington, DC -- support for the Saori weaving project

MITSUBISHI MOTOR SALES OF AMERICA INC.

Company Headquarters
6400 Katella Avenue
Cypress, CA 90630-5208
Web: http://www.mitsubishicars.com

Company Description
Revenue: US$25.939 billion (2001)
Employees: 1100 (2001)
SIC(s): 5012 Automobiles & Other Motor Vehicles.
Parent Company: Mitsubishi Corp., 6-3, Marunouchi 2-chome, Chiyoda-ku, Tokyo, Japan
Parent Revenue: US$32,689,000,000 (2001)

Operating Locations
Mitsubishi Fuso Truck of America (NJ--Bridgeport); Mitsubishi Motor Sales of America, Inc. (CA--Orange; FL--Orlando; IL--Itasca; TX--Irving); Mitsubishi Motors America (MI--Southfield); Mitsubishi Motors Credit of America (CA--Cypress; NY--Purchase)

Nonmonetary Support
Type: Cause-related Marketing & Promotion; Donated Equipment; Donated Products; In-kind Services; Workplace Solicitation
Note: Cause-related marketing and promotion is handled by the marketing services department. Company also sponsors an employee volunteer program.

Giving Contact
Stephanie Martin, Corp. Relations
6400 Katella Ave.
Cypress, CA 90630
Phone: (714)372-6454
Fax: (714)934-7656

Description
Organization Type: Corporate Giving Program
Giving Locations: Communities where company has a major presence.
Grant Types: General Support, Multiyear/Continuing Support, Operating Expenses, Scholarship, Seed Money.

Financial Summary
Total Giving: Company does not disclose contributions figures.

Typical Recipients
Arts & Humanities: Libraries, Performing Arts, Theater
Civic & Public Affairs: African American Affairs, Asian American Affairs, Chambers of Commerce, Civil Rights, Employment/Job Training, Ethnic Organizations, Civic & Public Affairs-General, Hispanic Affairs, Safety, Women's Affairs
Environment: Environment-General

Application Procedures
Initial Contact: Send a full proposals.
Application Requirements: Inlcude a brief overview of the organization, including the specific project for which funding is requested; the exact amount requested; a short background of the organization, including the number of paid and volunteer employees; specific project information, including the purpose for desired funds, time period of proposed program, goals and how they will be attained, projected results and how they will be assessed, how the organization will report and evaluate results, geographical area served and number of people who will benefit; financial disclosure including full budget for current year, current sources of funding, ratio of administrative costs to total budget, and proportion of funding to be derived from contributions. Additional information required is a copy of IRS tax-exempt document per Section 501(c)(3); copy of current Form 990; audited financial statements from the previous two years; list of present board of directors; and support documents such as an annual report, catalogs, brochures, news clippings, and any other pertinent information.

Restrictions
Does not support political parties, candidates, or lobbying organizations; organizations that are not tax-exempt; individuals; or organizations whose major area of influence is outside the United States.

Additional Information
Company has formulated a series of guidelines by which it reviews all requests. To be considered, applicant organizations must promote safe driving or fall within other areas of support; be focused within communities where company has a major presence; allow company to review its list of contributors; show a specific use for contributions of $10,000 or less; and be able to exist independently of company's contribution. Additionally, the organization should enjoy the support of its local constituency, including community leaders. Financial support is granted on a one-time basis, and further support or renewal is not implied. However, additional orfuture funding may be available pending submission of a new request.
Publications: Guidelines for Corporate Giving

Corporate Officials
Pierre Gagnon: chief operating officer, president PRIM CORP EMPL chief operating officer, president: Mitsubishi Motor Sales America.
Hirao Iijima: chairman PRIM CORP EMPL chairman: Mitsubishi Motor Sales of America, Inc.
Takashi Sanobe: senior chief executive officer, chairman PRIM CORP EMPL senior chief executive officer, chairman: Mitsubishi Motor Sales of America.

Grants Analysis
Typical Range: $2,500 to $5,000

MITSUBISHI SILICON AMERICA

Company Headquarters
1351 Tandem Ave., NE
Salem, OR 97303
Web: http://www.mitsubishisilicon.com

Company Description
Revenue: US$196.8 million (2001)
Employees: 200
SIC(s): 3674 Semiconductors & Related Devices.
Parent Company: Mitsubishi Materials Corp., 1-5-1 Otemachi, Chiyoda-ku, Tokyo, Japan

Operating Locations
Mitsubishi Materials (NY--New York); Mitsubishi Silicon America (CA--Palo Alto; OR--Salem); Mitsubishi Silicon America - Eastern Regional Sales Office (CT--Westport); Mitsubishi Silicon America - Southwest Regional Sales Office (TX--Dallas); MMC Electronics America (IL--Rolling Meadows); Salem Manufacturing Facility (OR--Salem)

Nonmonetary Support
Type: Donated Equipment; Loaned Executives

Giving Contact
Judy Nix, Vice President, Human Resources
PO Box 7748
Salem, OR 97303-4199
Phone: (503)371-0041
Fax: (503)361-3539
E-mail: judy.nix@mitsubishisilicon.com
Web: http://www.mitsubishisilicon.com

Alternate Contact
1351 Tandem Avenue NE
Salem, OR 97303

Description
Organization Type: Corporate Giving Program
Giving Locations: operating locations.
Grant Types: Multiyear/Continuing Support, Operating Expenses, Project, Scholarship.

Typical Recipients
Arts & Humanities: Arts Festivals, Arts & Humanities-General, Historic Preservation, Libraries, Museums/Galleries, Music
Civic & Public Affairs: Community Foundations, Economic Development, Civic & Public Affairs-General, Women's Affairs
Education: Afterschool/Enrichment Programs, Education Funds, Elementary Education (Public), Education-General, Public Education (Precollege), Special Education
Health: Hospices
Social Services: Child Welfare, Community Centers, Domestic Violence, People with Disabilities, Recreation & Athletics, Shelters/Homelessness, Social Services-General, Substance Abuse, United Funds/United Ways, Volunteer Services

Application Procedures
Initial Contact: Submit a brief letter of inquiry.
Application Requirements: Include a description of the organization and purpose of funds sought.

Restrictions
Does not support organizations outside operating area

Corporate Officials
Shigeru Masuda: chairman, directorvice president administration PRIM CORP EMPL chairman, director: Mitsubishi Silicon of America.
Stanley Thomas Myers: president, chief executive officer, director B McPherson, KS 1936. ED University of Kansas (1960). PRIM CORP EMPL president, chief executive officer, director: Mitsubishi Silicon of America. CORP AFFIL director: Semiconductor Equip & Materials International; president: Siltec Expitaxial Corp.; director: CYBEQ System.
Hisashi Uchida: senior executive vice president administration PRIM CORP EMPL senior executive vice president administration: Mitsubishi Silicon of America.

Grants Analysis
Typical Range: $1,000 to $2,500

MOLDAW FAMILY FOUNDATION

Giving Contact
Stuart G. Moldaw, President
1550 El Camino Real, Suite 290
Menlo Park, CA 94025
Phone: (650)696-7489
Fax: (650)696-7585

Description
Founded: 1977
EIN: 942450734
Organization Type: Private Foundation
Giving Locations: CA: gives nationally
Grant Types: General Support.

Donor Information
Founder: members of the Moldaw Family

Financial Summary

Total Giving: $188,181 (fiscal year ending November 30, 2003); $231,150 (fiscal 2001). Note: $101,514 (fiscal year ending November 30, 1996); $1,049,845 (fiscal 1995); $141,787 (fiscal 1994).
Giving Analysis: Giving for fiscal 2001 includes: foundation grants to United Way ($10,000)
Assets: $2,656,504 (fiscal 2003); $2,828,419 (fiscal 2001)

Typical Recipients

Arts & Humanities: Arts Associations & Councils, Arts Festivals, Arts Institutes, Arts Outreach, Ballet, Ethnic & Folk Arts, Historic Preservation, History & Archaeology, Libraries, Museums/Galleries, Music, Opera, Public Broadcasting, Theater
Civic & Public Affairs: Civic & Public Affairs-General, Municipalities/Towns, Women's Affairs
Education: Colleges & Universities, Education Reform, Education-General, Private Education (Precollege), Public Education (Precollege), Student Aid
Health: Cancer, Children's Health/Hospitals, Heart, Hospitals, Hospitals (University Affiliated), Long-Term Care, Medical Research, Single-Disease Health Associations, Speech & Hearing
International: Human Rights, International Affairs, International Relations, Missionary/Religious Activities
Religion: Churches, Jewish Causes, Religious Organizations
Science: Science Museums
Social Services: Community Service Organizations, Crime Prevention, Domestic Violence, Food/Clothing Distribution, People with Disabilities, Recreation & Athletics, United Funds/United Ways, Youth Organizations

Application Procedures

Initial Contact: The foundation has no formal grant application procedure or application form.
Deadlines: April 15.

Additional Information

Publications: Application Form

Foundation Officials

Carol A. Moldaw: director
Phyllis Moldaw: vice president, treasurer
Stuart G. Moldaw: president
Susan J. Moldaw: director

Grants Analysis

Disclosure Period: fiscal year ending November 30, 2003
Total Grants: $188,181
Number of Grants: 47
Average Grant: $4,004
Highest Grant: $25,000
Lowest Grant: $50
Typical Range: $1,000 to $10,000

Recent Grants

Note: Grants derived from fiscal 2003 Form 990.
General

25,000	San Francisco Museum of Modern Art, San Francisco, CA -- towards Marc Chagall exhibition
25,000	San Francisco Museum of Modern Art, San Francisco, CA
25,000	San Francisco Museum of Modern Art, San Francisco, CA -- towards Marc Chagall exhibition
15,000	Boys and Girls Club of the Peninsula, Menlo Park, CA
14,683	San Francisco Museum of Modern Art, San Francisco, CA
10,000	Hoover Institution, Stanford University, Stanford, CA
10,000	KQED Signal Society, San Francisco, CA
10,000	San Francisco Symphony, San Francisco, CA
6,500	Achievement Rewards for College Scientists Foundation, San Francisco, CA -- towards scholarship awards
6,500	San Francisco Opera, San Francisco, CA

MONADNOCK PAPER MILLS INC.

Company Headquarters

117 Antrim Road
Bennington, NH 03442
Web: http://www.monadnockpaper.com

Company Description

Revenue: US$77.5 million (2001)
Employees: 232 (2001)
SIC(s): 2621 Paper Mills, 2672 Coated & Laminated Paper Nec, 2676 Sanitary Paper Products, 2678 Stationery Products.

Gilbert Verney Foundation

Giving Contact

Richard G. Verney, Chairman & Chief Executive Officer
117 Antrim Rd.
Bennington, NH 03442-4205
Phone: (603)588-3311
Fax: (603)588-3561

Description

EIN: 026007363
Organization Type: Corporate Foundation
Giving Locations: MA; NH
Grant Types: Capital, Endowment, General Support, Operating Expenses, Project, Research.

Donor Information

Founder: Monadnock Paper Mills

Financial Summary

Total Giving: $256,770 (2003)
Assets: $3,110,253 (2003)
Gifts Received: $125,000 (2000); $125,000 (1999); $100,000 (1998). Note: In 1998 and 2000, contributions were received from Monadnock Paper Mills.

Typical Recipients

Arts & Humanities: Arts Associations & Councils, Arts Centers, Arts Festivals, Arts Funds, Arts Institutes, Arts Outreach, Dance, Arts & Humanities-General, Historic Preservation, History & Archaeology, Libraries, Literary Arts, Museums/Galleries, Music, Opera, Performing Arts, Public Broadcasting, Theater, Visual Arts
Civic & Public Affairs: Community Foundations, Civic & Public Affairs-General, Native American Affairs, Professional & Trade Associations, Public Policy, Urban & Community Affairs, Women's Affairs
Education: Agricultural Education, Business Education, Colleges & Universities, Economic Education, Environmental Education, Education-General, Leadership Training, Private Education (Precollege), Science/Mathematics Education, Secondary Education (Private), Special Education
Environment: Forestry, Environment-General, Resource Conservation
Health: Health-General, Home-Care Services, Hospices, Hospitals, Medical Rehabilitation, Public Health
International: Health Care/Hospitals
Religion: Churches, Religion-General, Religious Organizations, Religious Welfare
Science: Science Museums, Scientific Centers & Institutes, Scientific Labs
Social Services: Animal Protection, At-Risk Youth, Child Welfare, Day Care, Domestic Violence, Emergency Relief, Family Services, People with Disabilities, Recreation & Athletics, Senior Services, Social Services-General, YMCA/YWCA/YMHA/YWHA, Youth Organizations

Application Procedures

Initial Contact: Send a brief letter of inquiry, including a description of organization, amount requested, purpose of funds sought, recently audited financial statement, and proof of tax-exempt status.
Deadlines: None.

Restrictions

Does not make contributions to individuals or to organizations carrying on propoganda or otherwise attempting to influence legislation.

Corporate Officials

Andrew Manns: vice president financial, treasurerc PRIM CORP EMPL vice president financial, treasurer: Monadnock Paper Mills.
Richard Greville Verney: chairman, chief executive officer, director B Providence, RI 1946. ED Brown University AB (1968). PRIM CORP EMPL chairman, chief executive officer, director: Monadnock Paper Mills. CORP AFFIL director: Sales Association Paper Industry; director: Business Indiana Association New Hampshire; director: American Forest & Paper Association; director: Boston Paper Trade Association. NONPR AFFIL vice president trustee: Nantucket Consult Foundation; hon trustee: Saint Georges School; trustee: Monadnock County Hosp; trustee: Crotched Mt Foundation. CLUB AFFIL New York Yacht Club; Algonquin Club; Nantucket Yacht Club.

Foundation Officials

Lumina V. Greenway: trustee
E. Geoffrey Verney: trustee PRIM CORP EMPL vice president business development & corporate communications: Monadnock Paper Mills.
Richard Greville Verney: president (see above)

Grants Analysis

Disclosure Period: calendar year ending 2003
Total Grants: $256,770
Number of Grants: 63
Average Grant: $2,125*
Highest Grant: $125,000
Lowest Grant: $250
Typical Range: $500 to $5,000
*Note: Average grant figure excludes highest grant.

Recent Grants

Note: Grants derived from 2003 Form 990.
Library-Related

5,000	Stephenson Memorial Library, Greenfield, NH -- towards building fund
2,500	Nantucket Atheneum, Nantucket, MA

General

125,000	Nantucket Conservation Foundation, Nantucket, MA -- for capital campaign
12,500	Nantucket Historical Association, Nantucket, MA -- as endowment fund
10,000	Crotched Mountain Foundation, Greenfield, NH -- for a master plan project
10,000	Harris Center, Hancock, NH -- for building campaign
7,500	All Saints' Parish, Beverly Hills, CA -- for capital fund
7,400	Well School, Peterborough, NH
6,250	Canterbury Shaker Village, Canterbury, NH
6,250	Nantucket Cottage Hospital, Nantucket, MA -- for 21st century campaign
5,000	American Red Cross, Washington, DC -- for capital fund
5,000	Monadnock Community Hospital, Peterborough, NH -- for capital campaign

MONFORT FAMILY FOUNDATION

Giving Contact
Dave Evans, Administrator
Monfort Family Foundation
PO Box 337300
Greeley, CO 80633
Phone: (970)454-1357
Fax: (970)454-2535

Description
Founded: 1970
EIN: 237068253
Organization Type: Family Foundation
Giving Locations: CO: Northern Colorado, especially Weld County
Grant Types: General Support, Scholarship.

Donor Information
Founder: Established in 1970 by Margery Monfort Wilson and Richard L. Monfort.

Financial Summary
Total Giving: $2,301,601 (2002); $1,923,581 (2001)
Giving Analysis: Giving for 2002 includes: foundation scholarships ($1,500); foundation grants to United Way ($350,000); 2001: foundation scholarships ($2,000); foundation grants to United Way ($250,000)
Assets: $41,475,521 (2002); $46,337,564 (2001)
Gifts Received: $3,160 (2002); $14,208,119 (2001); $54,963 (1992). Note: In 2001, contributions were received from the Estate of Kenneth W. Monfort.

Typical Recipients
Arts & Humanities: Ballet, Historic Preservation, History & Archaeology, Libraries, Museums/Galleries, Music, Performing Arts, Public Broadcasting, Theater
Civic & Public Affairs: African American Affairs, Botanical Gardens/Parks, Business/Free Enterprise, Clubs, Community Foundations, Economic Development, Economic Policy, Civic & Public Affairs-General, Hispanic Affairs, Housing, Municipalities/Towns, Parades/Festivals, Philanthropic Organizations, Professional & Trade Associations, Rural Affairs, Women's Affairs, Zoos/Aquariums
Education: Afterschool/Enrichment Programs, Agricultural Education, Arts/Humanities Education, Business Education, Colleges & Universities, Community & Junior Colleges, Economic Education, Education Associations, Education Funds, Education Reform, Elementary Education (Public), Engineering/Technological Education, Education-General, International Studies, Literacy, Minority Education, Private Education (Precollege), Public Education (Precollege), School Volunteerism, Secondary Education (Private), Student Aid, Vocational & Technical Education
Environment: Environment-General
Health: AIDS/HIV, Arthritis, Cancer, Children's Health/Hospitals, Clinics/Medical Centers, Health Funds, Hospitals, Medical Rehabilitation, Multiple Sclerosis, Prenatal Health Issues, Preventive Medicine/Wellness Organizations, Public Health, Respiratory, Single-Disease Health Associations, Speech & Hearing, Trauma Treatment
Religion: Churches, Ministries, Religious Welfare
Social Services: Animal Protection, At-Risk Youth, Child Welfare, Community Centers, Community Service Organizations, Counseling, Crime Prevention, Family Services, Food/Clothing Distribution, People with Disabilities, Recreation & Athletics, Scouts, Senior Services, Shelters/Homelessness, Social Services-General, Special Olympics, Substance Abuse, United Funds/United Ways, Veterans, Volunteer Services, Youth Organizations

Application Procedures
Initial Contact: Contact the foundation for application guidelines.
Application Requirements: Applications should include the organization's name, project name and contact information, total budget of the organization, total project budget, amount requested, summary of proposal, other sources of funding, future funding, and list of board members.
Deadlines: Deadlines for applications are May 1 and October 1.
Review Process: The trustees meet twice a year to review applications and determine which programs meet the objectives of the foundation.

Foundation Officials
Kyle Monfort Futo: vice president
Myra Monfort Runyan: secretary
Kaye C. Monfort Ward: president PRIM CORP EMPL president, director: High County Investor Inc.

Grants Analysis
Disclosure Period: calendar year ending 2002
Total Grants: $1,950,101*
Number of Grants: 45
Average Grant: $22,405*
Highest Grant: $636,690
Lowest Grant: $500
Typical Range: $5,000 to $50,000 and $100,000 to $350,000
*Note: Giving excludes scholarships and United Way. Average grant figure excludes two highest grants ($986,690).

Recent Grants
Note: Grants derived from 2002 Form 990.
General

636,690	Colorado State university Foundation, Ft. Collins, CO
350,000	United Way Weld County, Greeley, CO
250,000	Craig Hospital, Denver, CO
139,171	Colorado University Foundation, Denver, CO
134,400	Habitat for Humanity, Greeley, CO
125,000	Alternative Homes for Youth, Wheat Ridge, CO
100,000	Island Grove Regional Treatment Center, Greeley, CO
100,000	Poudre River Trail, Greeley, CO
60,000	National W W II Memorial, Denver, CO
35,000	Boys and Girls Club of Greeley, Greeley, CO

MONSANTO CO.

Company Headquarters
800 N. Lindbergh Blvd.
St. Louis, MO 63167
Web: http://www.monsanto.com

Company Description
Founded: 1933
Ticker: MON
Exchange: NYSE
Acquired: Dekalb Genetics Corp. (1998).
Revenue: US$5.478 billion (2004)
Profit: US$267 million (2004)
Employees: 13200 (2003)
Fortune Rank: 357, per FORTUNE Magazine's list of 500 Largest U.S. Corporations (2004).
SIC(s): 2821 Plastics Materials & Resins, 2834 Pharmaceutical Preparations.

Nonmonetary Support
Type: Donated Equipment

Monsanto Fund

Giving Contact
Deborah J. Patterson, President
Monsanto Fund
800 N. Lindbergh Boulevard
St. Louis, MO 63167
Phone: (314)694-4391
Fax: (314)694-7658
E-mail: monsanto.fund@monsanto.com
Web: http://www.monsantofund.org

Description
EIN: 436044736
Organization Type: Corporate Foundation
Giving Locations: operating facilities.
Grant Types: Employee Matching Gifts, Project.
Note: Employee matching gift ratio: 1 to 1, up to $5,000 per employee per year.

Financial Summary
Total Giving: $8,336,475 (2003); $14,408,200 (2002); $18,631,009 (2001 approx). Note: Contributes through corporate direct giving program and foundation.
Giving Analysis: Giving for 2001 includes: foundation matching gifts ($875,016); foundation grants to United Way ($1,769,020); corporate direct giving (approx $2,400,000); foundation ($13,586,973)
Assets: $1,500,427 (2003); $7,385,607 (2002); $22,643,547 (2001)
Gifts Received: $24,670 (2002); $127,526 (2001); $47,552,201 (2000). Note: In 2001 and 2002, contributions were received from Monsanto Co. In 2000 and 1999, contributions were received from Monsanto Co. and the Searle Patients in Need Foundation.

Typical Recipients
Arts & Humanities: Arts Associations & Councils, Arts Centers, Arts Institutes, Dance, Ethnic & Folk Arts, Arts & Humanities-General, Historic Preservation, History & Archaeology, Libraries, Museums/Galleries, Music, Opera, Performing Arts, Public Broadcasting, Theater
Civic & Public Affairs: African American Affairs, Botanical Gardens/Parks, Business/Free Enterprise, Clubs, Community Foundations, Economic Development, Employment/Job Training, Civic & Public Affairs-General, Housing, Municipalities/Towns, Nonprofit Management, Professional & Trade Associations, Public Policy, Rural Affairs, Safety, Urban & Community Affairs, Women's Affairs, Zoos/Aquariums
Education: Afterschool/Enrichment Programs, Arts/Humanities Education, Business Education, Colleges & Universities, Community & Junior Colleges, Economic Education, Education Funds, Education Reform, Engineering/Technological Education, Education-General, Journalism/Media Education, Minority Education, Private Education (Precollege), Public Education (Precollege), Science/Mathematics Education, Secondary Education (Private), Secondary Education (Public), Student Aid, Vocational & Technical Education
Environment: Environment-General, Protection, Resource Conservation, Watershed
Health: AIDS/HIV, Alzheimer's Disease, Cancer, Children's Health/Hospitals, Clinics/Medical Centers, Diabetes, Emergency/Ambulance Services, Health Policy/Cost Containment, Health Organizations, Hospitals, Medical Research, Research/Studies Institutes
International: Foreign Educational Institutions, International-General, International Development, International Environmental Issues, International Organizations
Religion: Dioceses, Jewish Causes, Religious Welfare, Social/Policy Issues
Science: Observatories & Planetariums, Science Museums, Scientific Centers & Institutes, Scientific Organizations

Social Services: Child Welfare, Community Service Organizations, Crime Prevention, Day Care, Domestic Violence, Emergency Relief, Family Services, Food/Clothing Distribution, Scouts, Shelters/Homelessness, Social Services-General, Substance Abuse, United Funds/United Ways, YMCA/YWCA/YMHA/YWHA, Youth Organizations

Application Procedures

Initial Contact: Organizations near a Monsanto manufacturing facility should contact local manager. Other organizations should contact the fund or see website for application information, then submit a Preliminary Funding Request (PFR).

Application Requirements: PFR may not exceed three pages, and should include: name and mission of the organization; description of the project and how it relates to one of the priority giving areas (Agricultural Abundance, the Environment, Science Education, and Our Communities); estimated budget; amount requested; methods for evaluating project's results; contact name, phone, mailing address and email; names of any Monsanto employees associated with the organization; attach proof of 501(c)(3) tax-exempt status. PFR should not include any extraneous materials, should be on standard-sized white paper with a font no smaller than 12 points, should not be in a folder or binder, and should be mailed (faxed or emailed PFR's are not accepted).

Deadlines: PFR's are due January 1 and July 1.

Evaluative Criteria: Applicants must be tax-exempt charities; project must fit within one of the priority giving areas; nonprofit must be experienced, established, and reputable (foundation does not work with start-ups); nonprofit must be financially sound, have a diverse funding base, and be audited annually.

Decision Notification: Fund attempts to respond to written requests within three months; proposals that do not meet guidelines are turned down immediately.

Restrictions

Unsolicited proposals are rarely considered.

Long-term commitments are rarely made. Fund occasionally makes grants for two years at most. Organizations repeating a request in the same year are not considered for additional funding.

Fund does not support individuals; religious, politically partisan, or similar organizations; fraternal, labor, or veterans groups, unless project benefits the general public; benefits, dinners, or goodwill advertising; underwriting of deficits; endowments; activities that directly support marketing programs; projects in which Monsanto Company has a financial interest or could derive a financial benefit through cash or rights to intellectual property; organizations that discriminate based on race, creed, ethnicity, religion, sex, age, or national origin.

Additional Information

Decisions concerning organizations near a Monsanto facility are made by that particular facility; plant locations establish giving priorities autonomously.

Grant requests must be resubmitted on an annual basis unless otherwise stipulated.

In the 1990s, the fund continued to sharpen its focus on supporting programs with measurable results. It funded more "catalyst" projects and fewer "maintenance" programs; it looked for creative partnerships with nonprofit organizations; and awarded fewer but more sizable grants. In future years, the fund will play a greater role in supporting communities outside the United States, a reflection of the company's growing international identity.

Monsanto Co. merged with Pharmacia & Upjohn in January 2000.$13,586,973

Corporate Officials

Hugh Grant: president, chief executive officer B Larkhall, Scotland March 23, 1958. ED Edinburgh University MS; International Management Centre MBA; University of Glasgow BS. PRIM CORP EMPL president, chief executive officer: Monsanto Co.

NONPR AFFIL board of directors: International Policy Council; international advisory board member: Scottish Enterprise; trustee: Donald Danforth Plant Science Center.

Foundation Officials

Hakan Astrom: director CORP AFFIL senior vice president: Pharmacia.
Brett D. Begemann: director
Phillip C. Cara: director CORP AFFIL vice president: Pharmacia.
Carl M. Casale: chairman, director ED Oregon State University BS; Washington University, St. Louis MBA.
Philippe Castaing: director
Francisco Diaz: director
Janet Holloway: director
Kathryn S. Kissam: director
Kathleen L. Klepfer: director
Pamela S. Moench: assistant treasurer
Robert A. Paley: treasurer ED Purdue University BS. NONPR AFFIL director: Opera Theatre of St. Louis.
Deborah J. Patterson: president NONPR AFFIL director: Sisters of Mercy Ministries.
Gerald A. Steiner: director

Grants Analysis

Disclosure Period: calendar year ending 2003
Total Grants: $6,721,210*
Number of Grants: 220
Average Grant: $26,124*
Highest Grant: $1,000,000
Lowest Grant: $175
Typical Range: $500 to $100,000
*Note: Giving excludes matching gifts and United Way. Average grant figure excludes highest grant.

Recent Grants

Note: Grants derived from 2003 Form 990.
General

1,000,000	Missouri Development Finance Board, Jefferson City, MO
343,750	National Audubon Society, Ivyland, PA
260,000	St. Louis Symphony Orchestra, St. Louis, MO
191,000	Nature Conservancy, Arlington, VA
125,000	Cardinal Ritter College Preparatory School, St. Louis, MO
124,000	European Development Corporation Netherlands
114,646	Food Health and Hope Foundation Republic of South Africa
114,000	St. Louis Science Center, St. Louis, MO
104,000	Lindenwood University, St. Charles, MO
90,000	Center of Emerging Technologies, St. Louis, MO

MONY Group Inc.

Company Headquarters

New York, NY
Web: http://www.mony.com

Company Description

Founded: 1843
Ticker: MNY
Exchange: NYSE
Former Name: The Mutual Life Insurance Co. of New York.
Assets: US$19.925 billion (2002)
Employees: 3717 (2003)
SIC(s): 6311 Life Insurance, 6321 Accident & Health Insurance.

Operating Locations

MONY Group (NJ--Teaneck; NY--Syracuse)

Nonmonetary Support

Value: $280,000 (1999)
Type: Donated Equipment; In-kind Services; Workplace Solicitation
Volunteer Programs: The company sponsors the Volunteer Incentive at MONY (VIM) program, which encourages employee volunteerism at nonprofit organizations by providing semi-annual grants to those served by MONY Group volunteers. Another program, the Volunteer Incentive Award Program (VIP), makes an annual monetary award to a nonprofit social service agency in the community of each of its two major sites to encourage volunteer programs that effectively maximize their recourses by creatively utilizing employed volunteers.

MONY Foundation

Giving Contact

Lynn Stekas, President
MONY Foundation
1740 Broadway, MD 10-36
New York, NY 10019
Phone: (212)708-2468
Fax: (212)708-2001
Web: http://www.mony.com/AboutMONY/InsideMONY/Foundation

Description

EIN: 133398852
Organization Type: Corporate Foundation
Former Name: MONY Life Insurance of New York.
Giving Locations: NY: New York, Syracuse headquarters and operating communities.
Grant Types: Award, Employee Matching Gifts, General Support, Project.
Note: Employee matching gift ratio: 1 to 1. Company matches gifts up to $1,000 in contributions made by eligible employees, financial professionals, and retirees throughout the U.S. Matching gifts are open to nonprofit, tax-exempt organizations and post-secondary educational institutions. Political, sectarian, religious, or United Way organization are not eligible for matching gifts.

Financial Summary

Total Giving: $850,390 (2003); $942,728 (2002); $1,006,977 (2001). Note: Contributes through corporate direct giving program and foundation.
Giving Analysis: Giving for 2002 includes: foundation matching gifts ($205,976); foundation grants to United Way ($222,250); 2001: foundation grants to United Way ($190,750); foundation matching gifts ($276,270); foundation ($539,957)
Assets: $246,735 (2003); $295,163 (2002); $272,407 (2001)
Gifts Received: $805,138 (2003); $975,157 (2002); $1,032,500 (2001). Note: Contributions are received from The MONY Life Insurance Co.

Typical Recipients

Arts & Humanities: Art History, Arts Centers, Arts Funds, Arts Institutes, Dance, Libraries, Literary Arts, Museums/Galleries, Music, Opera, Performing Arts, Public Broadcasting, Theater
Civic & Public Affairs: African American Affairs, Asian American Affairs, Botanical Gardens/Parks, Business/Free Enterprise, Community Foundations, Economic Development, Economic Policy, Employment/Job Training, Ethnic Organizations, Gay/Lesbian Issues, Civic & Public Affairs-General, Hispanic Affairs, Housing, Inner-City Development, Law & Justice, Legal Aid, Minority Business, Nonprofit Management, Philanthropic Organizations, Public Policy, Urban & Community Affairs, Women's Affairs
Education: Afterschool/Enrichment Programs, Business Education, Colleges & Universities, Economic Education, Education Funds, Education-General, Leadership Training, Literacy, Minority Education, Preschool Education, Private Education (Precollege),

Public Education (Precollege), Social Sciences Education, Special Education
Environment: Environment-General
Health: AIDS/HIV, Cancer, Clinics/Medical Centers, Emergency/Ambulance Services, Health-General, Health Organizations, Hospices, Kidney, Medical Research, Mental Health, Prenatal Health Issues, Public Health, Research/Studies Institutes, Single-Disease Health Associations
International: International Development
Religion: Churches, Ministries, Religious Organizations, Religious Welfare
Science: Science Museums
Social Services: At-Risk Youth, Big Brothers/Big Sisters, Child Abuse, Child Welfare, Community Centers, Community Service Organizations, Counseling, Day Care, Domestic Violence, Emergency Relief, Family Planning, Family Services, Food/Clothing Distribution, People with Disabilities, Recreation & Athletics, Refugee Assistance, Scouts, Senior Services, Shelters/Homelessness, Social Services-General, Substance Abuse, United Funds/United Ways, Volunteer Services, YMCA/YWCA/YMHA/YWHA, Youth Organizations

Application Procedures

Initial Contact: Submit a brief written proposal.
Application Requirements: Proposals must include organizational, and grant information, and attached documentation. Organization information should include name and address of the organization; contact person, title, a phone number; history and background of organization; and geographic area and target population served by the organization. Grant information should include amount requested, specifics on how funds will be used; project description, including target population, needs addressed, planned activities; objectives, staff, qualifications, and proposed timetable; and a proposed line-item budget. Required documentation includes proof of tax-exempt status; recently audited financial statement; IRS 990 tax form; current list of board of directors; current list of project funders, including grant amounts; and, if available, the organization's most recent annual report, brochure, and newsletter.
Deadlines: None.
Evaluative Criteria: Funding goes to well-defined programs that conform to the company's giving priorities; well-managed organizations, with ability to achieve specific objectives; organizations within company operating areas requesting reasonable amounts.
Decision Notification: Please call each site for timelines.
Notes: After reviewing the material, the foundation requests additional information if necessary. Contributions guidelines should be reviewed before submitting request.

Restrictions

The MONY Foundation makes grants only to organizations that are classified as tax exempt under 501(c)(3). In general, MONY will not consider requests for the following: capital fund drives; private foundations; research activities; fully participating members of the United Way; religious, fraternal, political, athletic, social, or veterans organizations; endowments, memorials, or contingency funds; individuals; fundraising activities such as benefits, charitable dinners, or sporting events; legislative or lobbying efforts; books, magazines, articles, film/video productions or advertising; or organizations with a financial deficit.
Foundation gives to colleges and universities in the form of matching funds only.

Additional Information

In addition to direct grants given through the Corporate Social Policy Division in New York, NY, a portion of the contributions budget is disbursed through the Syracuse Operations Center, Syracuse, NY; and Glenpointe Marketing Center, Teaneck, NJ.

Corporate Officials

Samuel J. Foti: president, chief operating officer, director B 1952. ED University of Pennsylvania Wharton School BS; University of Pennsylvania Wharton School MA. PRIM CORP EMPL president, chief operating officer, director: The Mutual Life Insurance Co. of New York Inc. CORP AFFIL president, director: Mony Life Insurance of America Arizona Corp.
Kenneth M. Levine: executive vice president, chief investment officer, director B Bronx, NY 1946. ED City University of New York (1968). PRIM CORP EMPL executive vice president, chief investment officer, director: The Mutual Life Insurance Co. of New York ADD CORP EMPL director: 1740 Advisors Inc.; president: 1740 Ventures Inc.; executive vice president: MONY Group Inc.; executive vice president: MONY Life Insurance Co.; executive vice president: MONY Life Insurance of American Arizona Corp.; president: MONY Realty Partners Inc. NONPR AFFIL member: Society Actuaries.
Michael I. Roth: chairman, chief executive officer, director B Brooklyn, NY 1945. ED City College of New York BS (1967); Boston University JD (1971); New York University LLM (1973). PRIM CORP EMPL chairman, chief executive officer, director: The Mutual Life Insurance Co. of New York. CORP AFFIL director: Promus Hotel Corp.; chairman: Mony Life Insurance of America Arizona Corp.; director: Pitney Bowes Inc. NONPR AFFIL director: Life Insurance Council; director: Metropolitan Development Association; director: Insurance Marketplace Standards Association; director: Enterprise Foundation; director: Enterprise Group; director: Committee for Economic Development; member: American Council Life Insurance; member: American Institute CPAs.

Foundation Officials

Richard M. Daddario: chief financial officer B Hartford, CT 1947. ED University of Hartford BS (1969); University of Hartford MS (1975). CORP AFFIL vice president: 1740 Advisors Inc.; director finance: Mony Life Insurance of America Arizona Corp.
Samuel J. Foti: director (see above)
Kenneth M. Levine: director (see above)
Michael I. Roth: director (see above)
Lee M. Smith: director
Lynn Stekas: president
David S. Waldman: secretary
David V. Weigel: treasurer B Hartford, CT 1946. ED Gettysburg College (1969). CORP AFFIL treasurer, director: 1740 Advisors Inc.; vice president, treasurer: Mutual Life Insurance Co. of New York.

Grants Analysis

Disclosure Period: calendar year ending 2003
Total Grants: $492,881*
Number of Grants: 71
Average Grant: $6,942
Highest Grant: $20,000
Lowest Grant: $1,080
Typical Range: $5,000 to $10,000
*Note: Giving excludes matching gifts and United Way.

Recent Grants

Note: Grants derived from 2003 Form 990.
General

102,570	United Way of Tri-State
61,550	United Way of Central New York Inc., Syracuse, NY
20,000	Partnership for After School Education (PASE), New York, NY
17,500	Lincoln Center Corporate Fund, New York, NY
15,000	Citizens Committee for New York City, New York, NY
15,000	Enterprise Foundation, Columbia, MD
15,000	Fresh Youth Initiatives (FYI), New York, NY
15,000	Medicare Rights Center, New York, NY
15,000	Young Citizens in Action

12,500	Children for Children Foundation, New York, NY

MOODY FOUNDATION

Giving Contact

Peter M. Moore, Grants Director
2302 Postoffice Street, Suite 704
Galveston, TX 77550
Phone: (409)763-5333
Fax: (409)763-5564
E-mail: pmoore@moodyf.org
Web: http://www.moodyf.org

Alternate Contact

Sandy Griffin, Scholarship Administrator
704 Moody National Bank Building
Galveston, TX 77550
Note: Contact to request information on the Moody Scholars program.

Description

Founded: 1942
EIN: 741403105
Organization Type: Family Foundation
Giving Locations: TX, Dallas, Galveston
Grant Types: Capital, Department, Endowment, Fellowship, General Support, Research, Scholarship.

Donor Information

Founder: In 1942, William Lewis Moody Jr. (1865-1954), and his wife, Libbie Rice Shearn Moody (1869-1943), established the Moody Foundation "for the perpetual benefit of present and future generations of Texans." Their financial interests included banks, newspapers, ranches, hotels, and the American National Insurance Company. William Moody was involved in cotton, railroad, and banking enterprises. Today, their daughter-in-law, Mrs. Frances Moody Newman, chairs the board of trustees; their grandson, Robert L. Moody, and great-grandson, Ross R. Moody, are trustees of the foundation.

Financial Summary

Total Giving: $9,329,196 (2002); $600,000 (2001)
Giving Analysis: Giving for 2002 includes: foundation scholarships ($135,740)
Assets: $967,301,681 (2002); $428,000,000 (2001)
Gifts Received: $19,266,170 (2002); $18,363,736 (2000); $18,181,360 (1999). Note: Contributions were received from The Libby Shearn Moody Trust.

Typical Recipients

Arts & Humanities: Arts Associations & Councils, Arts Centers, Arts Festivals, Ballet, Film & Video, Historic Preservation, History & Archaeology, Libraries, Museums/Galleries, Music, Opera, Performing Arts, Public Broadcasting, Theater
Civic & Public Affairs: Botanical Gardens/Parks, Community Foundations, Economic Development, Employment/Job Training, Civic & Public Affairs-General, Housing, Inner-City Development, Municipalities/Towns, Nonprofit Management, Parades/Festivals, Philanthropic Organizations, Safety, Urban & Community Affairs, Zoos/Aquariums
Education: Arts/Humanities Education, Colleges & Universities, Continuing Education, Education Funds, Elementary Education (Private), Engineering/Technological Education, Faculty Development, Education-General, International Exchange, Leadership Training, Medical Education, Minority Education, Private Education (Precollege), Public Education (Precollege), Religious Education, Science/Mathematics Education, Social Sciences Education, Student Aid, Vocational & Technical Education
Environment: Environment-General, Research, Resource Conservation, Wildlife Protection
Health: AIDS/HIV, Cancer, Children's Health/

Hospitals, Emergency/Ambulance Services, Eyes/Blindness, Geriatric Health, Health Policy/Cost Containment, Health Funds, Health Organizations, Heart, Hospices, Hospitals, Hospitals (University Affiliated), Kidney, Long-Term Care, Medical Rehabilitation, Medical Research, Mental Health, Nursing Services, Prenatal Health Issues, Preventive Medicine/Wellness Organizations, Research/Studies Institutes, Respiratory, Single-Disease Health Associations, Speech & Hearing, Transplant Networks/Donor Banks

International: Foreign Arts Organizations, International Environmental Issues, International Relief Efforts

Religion: Churches, Dioceses, Ministries, Religious Organizations, Religious Welfare, Seminaries

Science: Science Museums, Scientific Research

Social Services: Animal Protection, Big Brothers/Big Sisters, Camps, Child Abuse, Child Welfare, Community Centers, Community Service Organizations, Crime Prevention, Day Care, Domestic Violence, Emergency Relief, Family Planning, Family Services, People with Disabilities, Recreation & Athletics, Scouts, Senior Services, Shelters/Homelessness, Social Services-General, Special Olympics, Substance Abuse, United Funds/United Ways, YMCA/YWCA/YMHA/YWHA, Youth Organizations

Application Procedures

Initial Contact: Submit a one-page letter of inquiry or call the foundation to request the foundation's guidelines.

Application Requirements: Inquiries should describe the project and its intended purpose. If the project falls within the scope of the foundation, a detailed and complete application may be presented when the foundation sends a written guideline.

Deadlines: Six weeks prior to quarterly meetings.

Review Process: After the application has been received and studied by the foundation's staff, who may request further information either written or by interview, the board will review the application at a formal meeting, and a decision will be conveyed to the applicant. Applicants should allow two to three months for the application to be processed.

Notes: Direct or personal presentations to the board are not the practice.

Restrictions

Applicants must be tax-exempt nonprofit organizations located in Texas. No grants are given to individuals (except students covered by a scholarship program in Galveston County); the foundation generally does not give funds toward operating budgets, continuing support, annual campaigns, debt financing, or loans.

Additional Information

Currently, the foundation is concentrating its resources on projects in Galveston and Dallas, TX. Also provides advice to grant seekers.

Publications: Annual Report; Guidelines; Format for Grant Application

Foundation Officials

Sandy Griffin: scholarship administration

Harold C. MacDonald: comptroller B 1933. ED University of Houston BBA (1960). CORP AFFIL director: Seal Fleet Inc.; director: American National Insurance Co.; director: American National Property & Casualty Co. NONPR AFFIL vice president, director: Transitional Learning Center.

Wayne E. Magee: grants analyst

Allan Matthews: program officer

E. Douglas McLeod: director/development B Galveston, TX 1941. ED North Texas State University BBA (1965); Southern Methodist University (1965-1966); South Texas College of Law JD (1990); University of Houston LLM (1993). PRIM CORP EMPL president, owner: McLeod Properties & Co. CORP AFFIL director: National Western Life Insurance Co.; board director: Anrem Corp.; vice president, board di-

rector: Colonel Inc.; board director: American National Insurance Co. NONPR AFFIL chairman, director: Palm Beach at Moody Gardens; director: Saint Stephen's School; chairman, board director: Moody Gardens Inc.; chairman, director: Hope Therapy Program; member: Marine Corps League; member: Granaderos De Galvez; board director: Center Transportation & Commerce; board member: Chamber of Commerce.

Frances A. Moody: executive director CORP AFFIL director: American National Insurance Co.; director: National Western Life Insurance Co.

Ross R. Moody: trustee B 1962. ED Harvard University MBA (1986). PRIM CORP EMPL president, chief operating officer, director: National Western Life Insurance Co. CORP AFFIL director: American National Property & Casualty Co.

Peter M. Moore: grants director B Kansas City, MO 1939. ED University of the South BA (1963). NONPR AFFIL member advisory board: Galveston Historical Foundation; member advisory board: Grand 1894 Opera House; committee chairman, management consult: Conference Southwest Foundations; speaker: Funding Information Center.

Frances Moody Newman: chairman, trustee B 1912.

Gerald J. Smith: program officer CORP AFFIL director: Seal Fleet Inc.

Bernice C. Torregrossa: grants analyst

Jean Wylie: regional grants director

Grants Analysis

Disclosure Period: calendar year ending 2002

Total Grants: $9,193,456*

Number of Grants: 42

Average Grant: $40,421*

Highest Grant: $3,946,784

Lowest Grant: $1,592

Typical Range: $5,000 to $100,000

*Note: Giving excludes scholarships. Average grant figure excludes two highest grants ($7,576,602).

Recent Grants

Note: Grants derived from 2002 Form 990.

General

3,946,784	Transitional Learning Community, Galveston, TX
3,629,818	Transitional Learning Community, Galveston, TX -- towards educational programs for the neurologically impaired individuals
528,467	Transitional Learning Community, Galveston, TX -- fund for constructing and furnishing an additional building
281,228	Moody Gardens Inc., Galveston, TX -- fund for construction of an aquarium, Discovery Museum & hotel in the Moody Gardens
135,682	Moody Hospitality Institute, Galveston, TX -- fund for the certificate programs in the hospitality industry
100,000	Austin Christian Fellowship, Austin, TX -- fund for purchasing and constructing a multipurpose facility
100,000	St. Andrew's Episcopal School, Austin, TX -- towards expansion of school library
55,265	University of Texas Medical Branch, Galveston, TX -- fund for the School of Allied Health Sciences for developing cardiopulmonary exercise tests and maintaining fitness levels for brain injured persons
42,213	University of Texas Medical Branch, Galveston, TX -- fund for the School of Allied Health Sciences towards research on cardio respiratory functions in brain injured persons
36,485	Moody Gardens Inc., Galveston, TX -- fund for the acquisition of animal specimens for the aquarium

KENNETH S. MOORE AND ARLETTA E. MOORE FOUNDATION

Giving Contact

Paul Bliss, Secretary, Advisory Committee
Care of Schuneman Agency
343 Washington St.
Prophetstown, IL 61277
Phone: (309)659-7947

Description

Founded: 1993
EIN: 366914860
Organization Type: Private Foundation
Grant Types: General Support.

Financial Summary

Total Giving: $95,043 (fiscal year ending June 30, 2004); $137,917 (fiscal 2001)
Assets: $1,882,713 (fiscal 2004); $2,191,079 (fiscal 2001)

Typical Recipients

Arts & Humanities: History & Archaeology, Libraries

Civic & Public Affairs: Botanical Gardens/Parks, Civic & Public Affairs-General, Inner-City Development, Municipalities/Towns, Safety, Urban & Community Affairs

Education: Arts/Humanities Education, Public Education (Precollege)

Health: Emergency/Ambulance Services

Religion: Churches

Social Services: Animal Protection, Scouts, Social Services-General, Youth Organizations

Application Procedures

Initial Contact: The foundation has no formal grant application procedure or application form. Send a brief letter of inquiry.

Deadlines: None.

Foundation Officials

Paul Bliss: secretary, adv comm mem
Neil Castelyn: adv comm mem
A. Dean Decker: adv comm mem, trustee
Darryl R. Gibson: adv comm mem
David Matthews: adv comm mem
Glenda Sampson: adv comm mem

Grants Analysis

Disclosure Period: fiscal year ending June 30, 2004
Total Grants: $95,043
Number of Grants: 10
Highest Grant: $63,000
Lowest Grant: $500
Typical Range: $1,000 to $5,000

Recent Grants

Note: Grants derived from fiscal 2004 Form 990.

Library-Related

3,500	H C Adams Memorial Library -- for equipment

General

63,000	City of Prophetstown, Prophetstown, IL -- for eclipse square
5,400	Prophetstown Community Park District -- for equipment
5,000	Prophetstown Fire Protection District -- for equipment
5,000	Prophetstown Main Street, Prophetstown, IL -- for budget
4,620	Prophetstown-Lyndon-Tampico CUSD 3 -- for computer lab
4,523	City of Prophetstown, Prophetstown, IL -- for equipment
2,500	City of Prophetstown, Prophetstown, IL -- for cannon restoration

1,000   Prophetstown Fire Protection District -- for budget

500   Prophetstown-Lyndon-Tampico CUSD 3 -- for fine arts

MARJORIE MOORE CHARITABLE FOUNDATION

Giving Contact

Marjorie Alexander-Davis
777 Main St.
Hartford, CT 06115
Phone: (860)986-7696

Description

Founded: 1958
EIN: 066050196
Organization Type: Private Foundation
Giving Locations: CT: Kensington
Grant Types: Capital, Endowment, General Support, Multiyear/Continuing Support, Operating Expenses, Project, Scholarship, Seed Money.

Donor Information

Founder: the late Marjorie Moore

Financial Summary

Total Giving: $146,500 (fiscal year ending July 31, 2004); $307,457 (fiscal 2002); $197,078 (fiscal 2001)
Giving Analysis: Giving for fiscal 2002 includes: foundation scholarships ($25,000)
Assets: $3,315,796 (fiscal 2004); $3,207,245 (fiscal 2002); $3,873,112 (fiscal 2001)

Typical Recipients

Arts & Humanities: Arts Associations & Councils, History & Archaeology, Libraries, Museums/Galleries, Music
Civic & Public Affairs: Chambers of Commerce, Clubs, Civic & Public Affairs-General, Law & Justice, Municipalities/Towns, Safety, Urban & Community Affairs
Education: Elementary Education (Public), Literacy, Preschool Education, Private Education (Precollege), Public Education (Precollege), Science/Mathematics Education, Secondary Education (Public), Special Education, Student Aid
Health: AIDS/HIV, Emergency/Ambulance Services, Health Organizations, Hospices, Hospitals, Medical Research, Mental Health, Nursing Services, Public Health, Single-Disease Health Associations
Religion: Churches
Social Services: Camps, Child Welfare, Community Centers, Community Service Organizations, Crime Prevention, Delinquency & Criminal Rehabilitation, Family Services, People with Disabilities, Recreation & Athletics, Scouts, Senior Services, United Funds/United Ways, YMCA/YWCA/YMHA/YWHA, Youth Organizations

Application Procedures

Initial Contact: The foundation requests applications be made in writing.
Deadlines: None.

Restrictions

The foundation limits grants to charities that will benefit Kensington, CT area residents.

Additional Information

Trust(s): Fleet National Bank

Grants Analysis

Disclosure Period: fiscal year ending July 31, 2004
Total Grants: $146,500

Number of Grants: 7
Average Grant: $9,300*
Highest Grant: $50,000
Lowest Grant: $500
Typical Range: $1,000 to $20,000
*Note: Average grant figure excludes two highest grants ($100,000).

Recent Grants

Note: Grants derived from 2004 Form 990.
Library-Related

10,500   Berlin-Peck Memorial Library, Berlin, CT -- to replace books and computers

General

50,000   Berlin-Kensington YMCA, Kensington, CT -- for renovation of child center

50,000   Kensington Fire Rescue, Kensington, CT -- support the live in program

25,000   Kensington Baptist Church, Kensington, CT -- for kitchen facility program

7,000   YWCA of New Britain, New Britain, CT -- for the fitness program and equipment

3,500   Berlin Children's Fund, Berlin, CT -- provide campership to Berlin children

500   Family Services of Central Connecticut, CT -- support the caring Connection program

B.C. MOORE & SONS

Company Headquarters

101 S. Green St.
Wadesboro, NC 28170

Company Description

Employees: 1,300
SIC(s): 5300 General Merchandise Stores.

B.C. Moore & Sons Foundation

Giving Contact

Carl E. Bennett, Secretary
PO Drawer 72
Wadesboro, NC 28170
Phone: (704)694-2171
Fax: (704)694-6748

Description

EIN: 566062082
Organization Type: Corporate Foundation
Giving Locations: Southeast USA.
Grant Types: General Support.

Financial Summary

Total Giving: $89,000 (fiscal year ending January 31, 2004); $135,500 (fiscal 2002); $126,060 (fiscal 2001)
Assets: $1,934,403 (fiscal 2004); $2,228,103 (fiscal 2002); $2,864,617 (fiscal 2001)
Gifts Received: $100,000 (fiscal 1993); $100,000 (fiscal 1992)

Typical Recipients

Arts & Humanities: Arts Associations & Councils, Arts Centers, History & Archaeology, Libraries, Opera, Performing Arts, Theater
Civic & Public Affairs: Botanical Gardens/Parks, Civic & Public Affairs-General, Municipalities/Towns, Safety, Urban & Community Affairs
Education: Colleges & Universities, Community & Junior Colleges, Education Funds, Minority Education, Religious Education, Secondary Education (Public), Student Aid, Vocational & Technical Education
Environment: Resource Conservation

Health: Alzheimer's Disease, Emergency/Ambulance Services, Health Funds, Hospices, Hospitals, Long-Term Care, Research/Studies Institutes
Religion: Churches, Ministries, Missionary Activities (Domestic), Religious Organizations, Religious Welfare
Social Services: Community Centers, Food/Clothing Distribution, People with Disabilities, Recreation & Athletics, Scouts, Special Olympics, YMCA/YWCA/YMHA/YWHA

Application Procedures

Initial Contact: Send brief letter describing program.
Deadlines: None.

Additional Information

Trust(s): Compass Bank

Corporate Officials

James C. Crawford, Jr.: chairman, president, chief executive officer, director PRIM CORP EMPL chairman, president, chief executive officer, director: B.C. Moore & Sons.
Kirk Crawford: chief financial officer PRIM CORP EMPL chief financial officer: B.C. Moore & Sons.

Grants Analysis

Disclosure Period: fiscal year ending January 31, 2004
Total Grants: $89,000
Number of Grants: 44
Average Grant: $2,023
Highest Grant: $10,000
Lowest Grant: $500
Typical Range: $500 to $5,000

Recent Grants

Note: Grants derived from 2004 Form 990.
General

10,000   McCallie School Dining Hall

5,000   Alabama Independent Colleges, Montgomery, AL

5,000   Dizzy Gillespie Memorial Fund

5,000   Georgia Foundation for Independent College, Atlanta, GA

5,000   Independent College Fund of North Carolina, Raleigh, NC

5,000   Independent Colleges and Universities of South Carolina

5,000   McCallie School's Honors Scholarship Program

5,000   South Piedmont Community College Foundation

5,000   United Negro College Fund, Fairfax, VA

4,500   Spartanburg Methodist College, Spartanburg, SC

MARIETTA MCNEILL MORGAN AND SAMUEL TATE MORGAN, JR. FOUNDATION

Giving Contact

Elizabeth D. Seaman, Advisor
Bank of America
10 Light St.
Baltimore, MD 21202
Phone: (410)605-1105

Description

Founded: 1967
EIN: 546069447
Organization Type: Private Foundation
Giving Locations: VA
Grant Types: Capital, General Support.

Donor Information

Founder: the late Marietta McNeill Morgan and the late Samuel T. Morgan, Jr.

Financial Summary

Total Giving: $865,500 (fiscal year ending June 30, 2004); $815,000 (fiscal 2002); $1,639,200 (fiscal 2001)
Assets: $18,807,887 (fiscal 2004); $17,929,859 (fiscal 2002); $21,719,740 (fiscal 2001)
Gifts Received: $8,666 (fiscal 1996); $10,000 (fiscal 1995); $1,389 (fiscal 1994). Note: In fiscal 1994, contributions were received from S.T. Morgan Trust.

Typical Recipients

Arts & Humanities: Arts Centers, Ballet, Community Arts, Dance, Historic Preservation, History & Archaeology, Libraries, Literary Arts, Museums/Galleries, Music, Theater
Civic & Public Affairs: Botanical Gardens/Parks, Economic Development, Civic & Public Affairs-General, Housing, Nonprofit Management, Urban & Community Affairs, Women's Affairs, Zoos/Aquariums
Education: Arts/Humanities Education, Colleges & Universities, Education Funds, Medical Education, Private Education (Precollege), Public Education (Precollege), Secondary Education (Private), Secondary Education (Public), Special Education
Environment: Forestry, Wildlife Protection
Health: AIDS/HIV, Children's Health/Hospitals, Clinics/Medical Centers, Emergency/Ambulance Services, Health Organizations, Heart, Hospitals, Long-Term Care, Medical Research, Research/Studies Institutes
Religion: Ministries, Religious Organizations, Religious Welfare, Seminaries
Science: Observatories & Planetariums, Science Museums
Social Services: Animal Protection, Camps, Child Welfare, Community Service Organizations, Day Care, Domestic Violence, Family Services, Food/Clothing Distribution, Homes, People with Disabilities, Recreation & Athletics, Scouts, Senior Services, United Funds/United Ways, YMCA/YWCA/YMHA/YWHA, Youth Organizations

Application Procedures

Initial Contact: Submit a full proposal.
Application Requirements: Include a concise description of the project, detailed project budget and schedule, a description of organization, current balance sheet and operating statement, list of qualifications of project personnel, names and affiliations of organization's trustees or directors, and proof of tax-exempt status.
Deadlines: Applications may be submitted any time; however, proposals must be received by May 1 for the June meeting of the allocations committee, and by November 1 for the February meeting. The foundation strongly encourages matching or challenge grants.

Restrictions

Does not support individuals.

Additional Information

Publications: Informational Brochure (including Application Guidelines)
Trust(s): Bank of America

Foundation Officials

Elizabeth D. Seaman: consult

Grants Analysis

Disclosure Period: fiscal year ending June 30, 2004
Total Grants: $865,500
Number of Grants: 33
Average Grant: $26,227
Highest Grant: $65,000

Lowest Grant: $10,000
Typical Range: $15,000 to $50,000

Recent Grants

Note: Grants derived from fiscal 2004 Form 990.
General

65,000	Boys and Girls Clubs of Metro Richmond, Richmond, VA -- for the construction of capital one boys and girls club
50,000	Cross Over Ministry, Richmond, VA -- for the renovation of the health center
50,000	University of Richmond, Richmond, VA -- for the renovation of Gottawald science center
35,000	Mary Baldwin College, Richmond, VA -- for the construction of peg residence hall
35,000	St. Mary's Home for Disabled, Richmond, VA -- for the construction of a new facility
35,000	Trinity Episcopal School, Richmond, VA -- for the construction of science discovery center
35,000	Virginia University of Lynchburg, Lynchburg, VA -- for the roof replacement on humbles hall
30,000	Hanover Arts and Activities Center, Hanover, VA -- for building repairs and renovation
30,000	Richmond Ballet, Richmond, VA -- for the construction of parking facilities
25,000	Paramount Theater, Richmond, VA -- for restoration of the theatre building

W. AND E. MORGAN CHARITABLE RESIDUAL TRUST

Giving Contact

Jerry Moore, President & Trust Officer
c/o Citizens Bank and Trust
PO Box 70
Rock Port, MO 64482
Phone: (660)744-5333
Fax: (660)744-2565

Description

Founded: 1989
EIN: 436347180
Organization Type: Private Foundation
Giving Locations: MO
Grant Types: Department, General Support.

Financial Summary

Total Giving: $218,898 (2003)
Assets: $4,664,084 (2003)

Typical Recipients

Arts & Humanities: Arts Institutes, History & Archaeology, Libraries, Public Broadcasting
Civic & Public Affairs: Botanical Gardens/Parks, Clubs, Civic & Public Affairs-General, Municipalities/Towns, Parades/Festivals, Safety, Urban & Community Affairs
Education: Colleges & Universities, Faculty Development, Education-General, Minority Education, Preschool Education, Private Education (Precollege), Public Education (Precollege), Religious Education, Science/Mathematics Education, Special Education, Student Aid
Environment: Environment-General
Health: Children's Health/Hospitals, Emergency/Ambulance Services, Eyes/Blindness, Hospitals, Nutrition
International: Missionary/Religious Activities
Religion: Churches, Ministries, Missionary Activities (Domestic), Religious Organizations, Religious Welfare

Social Services: Camps, Community Centers, Community Service Organizations, Crime Prevention, Emergency Relief, Recreation & Athletics, Scouts, Social Services-General, Substance Abuse, YMCA/YWCA/YMHA/YWHA, Youth Organizations

Application Procedures

Initial Contact: The foundation has no formal grant application procedure or application form.
Deadlines: None.

Additional Information

Trust(s): Citizens Bank & Trust

Foundation Officials

Jody Ellison: trustee
Sharon Gaines: trust
Kay Gibson: trustee
Tim Whelan: trustee

Grants Analysis

Disclosure Period: calendar year ending 2003
Total Grants: $218,898
Number of Grants: 82
Average Grant: $2,669
Highest Grant: $30,000
Lowest Grant: $200
Typical Range: $1,000 to $5,000

Recent Grants

Note: Grants derived from 1999 Form 990.
Library-Related

3,500	Atchison County Library, Atchison, KS -- audio books

General

10,000	Atchison County Sheriff's Department, Atchison, KS -- equipment
10,000	Rockport Christian Church, Rockport, ME -- building project
10,000	Rockport Park Board, Rockport, ME -- fencing and helmets
7,700	Rockport School, Rockport, ME -- playground equipment, drama club, teacher of year award, etc.
7,500	Fairfax R-II Schools -- for 25 teachers
7,500	NWMO Learning Center -- lawnmower
5,000	Atchison County Salvation Army, Atchison, KS
5,000	NoWeMo -- land
5,000	Rockport School, Rockport, ME -- track project
4,000	Atchison Holt Ambulance, Atchison, KS

J.P. MORGAN CHASE & CO.

Company Headquarters

270 Park Ave.
New York, NY 10017
Web: http://www.jpmorganchase.com

Company Description

Founded: 2000
Ticker: JPM
Exchange: NYSE
Formed by Merger of: Chase Manhattan Corp (2000); J.P. Morgan & Company (2000).
Revenue: US$56.931 billion (2004)
Profit: US$4.466 billion (2004)
Employees: 93453 (2003)
Fortune Rank: 20, per FORTUNE Magazine's list of 500 Largest U.S. Corporations (2004).
SIC(s): 6000 Depository Institutions, 6021 National Commercial Banks, 6712 Bank Holding Companies.

Operating Locations

Chase Manhattan Bank, NA (AZ--Phoenix; CA--Los Angeles, San Diego, San Francisco; DE--Newark,

Wilmington; FL--Boca Raton, Palm Beach, St. Petersburg, Tampa; IL--Chicago; MD--Baltimore; NY--Rochester; TX--Dallas, Houston); J.P. Morgan & Co. (CA--Los Angeles, San Francisco; DE--Wilmington; FL--Palm Beach)

Nonmonetary Support

Range: $300,000 - $400,000
Type: Donated Equipment; In-kind Services
Volunteer Programs: Several thousand company employees volunteer in programs serving the communities in which they live and work, in a diverse set of activities that range from serving as mentors for at-risk teenagers to working as "huggers" for hospital boarder babies, from delivering meals to the homebound elderly to serving on numerous nonprofit boards.
Note: Co. donates equipment and surplus furniture, and supplies *pro bono* printing.

J.P. Morgan Chase Foundation

Giving Contact

Steven W. Gelston, Secretary
J.P. Morgan Chase Foundation
Care of The Corporate Tax Department
245 Park Ave., 8th Floor
New York, NY 10167
Phone: (212)270-8055
Web: http://www.jpmorganchase.com/cm/cs?pagename=Chase/Href&urlname=jpmc/community

Description

EIN: 237049738
Organization Type: Corporate Foundation
Giving Locations: AZ; CA; CT; DE; FL; MA; NJ; NY; OH: internationally; nationally; primarily headquarters and operating communities.
Grant Types: Award, Capital, Challenge, Department, Employee Matching Gifts, Fellowship, General Support, Multiyear/Continuing Support, Operating Expenses, Professorship, Project.
Note: Employee matching gifts are made to educational and cultural institutions, and for health and human services, housing, and the environment.

Financial Summary

Total Giving: $55,481,497 (2003); $62,844,738 (2002); $64,209,919 (2001). Note: Contributes through corporate direct giving program and foundation.
Giving Analysis: Giving for 2002 includes: foundation grants to United Way ($5,975,422); foundation matching gifts ($12,247,899); 2001: foundation grants to United Way ($5,852,050); foundation matching gifts ($15,191,397); foundation ($53,069,489)
Assets: $62,236,615 (2003); $57,509,497 (2002); $83,071,014 (2001)
Gifts Received: $61,760,673 (2003); $38,017,976 (2002); $16,680,882 (2001). Note: In 2003, contributions were received from CMRCC, Inc. ($16,226,315), JP Morgan Chase Bank ($36,000,000), Chase Manhattan Corporation Life Insurance Trust ($9,529,992), Pool Participation Fund ($16,226,315), shares of Prudential Financial Inc. ($5,256,876), shares of Metlife Inc. ($4,273,116), and miscellaneous other contributions ($4,366). In 2002, contributions were received from CMRCC Inc. (17,856,391) and J.P. Morgan Chase Bank ($20,000,000). Foundation receives funds from Chemical Investments Inc., Glazier Food Company, and individual contributors.

Typical Recipients

Arts & Humanities: Arts Appreciation, Arts Associations & Councils, Arts Centers, Arts Festivals, Arts Funds, Community Arts, Dance, Ethnic & Folk Arts, Historic Preservation, Libraries, Literary Arts, Museums/Galleries, Music, Opera, Performing Arts, Public Broadcasting, Theater, Visual Arts
Civic & Public Affairs: African American Affairs, Asian American Affairs, Botanical Gardens/Parks, Business/Free Enterprise, Civil Rights, Community Foundations, Economic Development, Economic Policy, Employment/Job Training, Civic & Public Affairs-General, Hispanic Affairs, Housing, Inner-City Development, Law & Justice, Legal Aid, Municipalities/Towns, Nonprofit Management, Philanthropic Organizations, Professional & Trade Associations, Public Policy, Rural Affairs, Safety, Urban & Community Affairs, Women's Affairs
Education: Arts/Humanities Education, Business Education, Business-School Partnerships, Colleges & Universities, Community & Junior Colleges, Economic Education, Education Associations, Education Funds, Education Reform, Elementary Education (Private), Elementary Education (Public), Engineering/Technological Education, Faculty Development, Education-General, Health & Physical Education, International Studies, Leadership Training, Literacy, Medical Education, Minority Education, Preschool Education, Private Education (Precollege), Public Education (Precollege), School Volunteerism, Science/Mathematics Education, Secondary Education (Private), Special Education, Student Aid, Vocational & Technical Education
Environment: Environment-General, Research, Wildlife Protection
Health: AIDS/HIV, Cancer, Children's Health/Hospitals, Clinics/Medical Centers, Diabetes, Emergency/Ambulance Services, Eyes/Blindness, Geriatric Health, Health Policy/Cost Containment, Health Organizations, Hospitals, Hospitals (University Affiliated), Medical Rehabilitation, Mental Health, Prenatal Health Issues, Public Health, Transplant Networks/Donor Banks
International: Foreign Arts Organizations, Foreign Educational Institutions, International-General, Health Care/Hospitals, International Affairs, International Development, International Organizations, International Peace & Security Issues, International Relations, International Relief Efforts, Missionary/Religious Activities
Religion: Churches, Dioceses, Religion-General, Jewish Causes, Ministries, Religious Organizations, Religious Welfare, Seminaries
Science: Science Museums, Scientific Centers & Institutes, Scientific Organizations
Social Services: At-Risk Youth, Big Brothers/Big Sisters, Camps, Child Welfare, Community Centers, Community Service Organizations, Counseling, Day Care, Delinquency & Criminal Rehabilitation, Domestic Violence, Emergency Relief, Family Planning, Family Services, Food/Clothing Distribution, Homes, People with Disabilities, Recreation & Athletics, Scouts, Senior Services, Sexual Abuse, Shelters/Homelessness, Social Services-General, Special Olympics, Substance Abuse, United Funds/United Ways, Volunteer Services, YMCA/YWCA/YMHA/YWHA, Youth Organizations

Application Procedures

Initial Contact: Send written requests to Steven W. Gelston, Secretary, JPMCF, 270 Park Avenue, 46th Floor, New York, New York 10017. Requests for funding in New York, New Jersey, or Connecticut contact (212)552-1112 or from Web site www.chase.com/cdg; requests in eight other states call (212)622-2025.
Application Requirements: Requests for funding from organizations in New York, New Jersey, or Connecticut should submitted on the application form, which lists additional materials requested; requests from eight other states require one-page application which requires copy of applicant's IRS determination letter aka 501(c)(3), requests for funding programs for national programs or programs serving overseas locations should send a brief letter outlining project and amount sought, letter should include IRS determination letter as appropriate - additional information may be sought from organizations of interest.
Deadlines: Deadlines vary for different focus areas in New York, New Jersey and Connecticut, Committees in other states meet periodically, National programs are on a rolling deadline, and International grants are generally reviewed in early summer.
Decision Notification: Foundation board meets three times per year; final notification is within six months, or for competitive grants, within three or four months.

Restrictions

Focus areas include Community Development and Human Services, Pre-Collegiate Education, Arts and Culture, Public Issues, International Programs. Geographic limitations: Arizona, California, Connecticut, Delaware, Florida, Illinois, Louisiana, Massachusetts, New Jersey, New York, Ohio, and developing countries overseas where JPMorgan Chase has a significant presence. All organizations in the United States must have ruling from IRS showing them to be public charity under 501 (c)(3) ruling and not a private foundation.

Additional Information

In 2001, Chase Manhattan Bank and J.P. Morgan merged under the name JPMorgan Chase. The foundation was renamed the J.P. Morgan Chase Foundation. The Foundation announced that they would review all philanthropic activities in order to develop the most effective programs for the new firm.
In 1995, Chase Manhattan Bank and Chemical Bank merged under the name Chase Manhattan Bank.
Contributions are made through several programs: The Foundation makes grants through its signature programs of corporate social responsibility, with a focus on community revitalization, education, human services (specifically child care), and the arts and culture.
The Foundation contributes to organizations outside the tri-state area (New York, New Jersey, and Connecticut) in areas where the company maintains a significant business presence.
The corporate responsibility office provides philanthropic and technical support under the Competitive Grants Program to nonprofit organizations in the tri-state area (New York, New Jersey, Connecticut). Areas of concern include culture and art, community revitalization, and pre-college education. Contact: 600 5th Ave., 3rd Fl., New York, NY 10020, (212)332-4100, fax: (212)332-4080.
The community relations office develops programs to address community needs and provides assistance to community-based organizations.
Foundation may make grants to foreign-based organizations that have never applied for, or received, an IRS tax-exempt ruling if applicant organization provides information sufficient to prove that it is a charitable, educational, or scientific organization within the meaning of Section 501(c)(3).
Community-based nonprofit 501(c)(3) organizations located in New York City, Long Island, Duchess County, Orange County, Putnam County, Rockland County, or Westchester County are eligible for the Neighborhood Grants Program, which provides funds for projects in culture and the arts, education, health and human services, and housing and economic development. The application deadline is mid-February.

Corporate Officials

James W. Zeigon: executive vice president ED Adelphi University MBA; Hofstra University BS. PRIM CORP EMPL executive vice president: Chase Manhattan Bank, NA. CORP AFFIL director: Avistar Communication Corp..

Foundation Officials

L. Thomas Block: trustee
Kim B. Christiansen: trustee
David A. Coulter: vice chairman

Grants Analysis

Disclosure Period: calendar year ending 2003
Total Grants: $38,283,472*
Number of Grants: 1,650 (approx)
Average Grant: $23,202
Highest Grant: $1,282,400
Lowest Grant: $500
Typical Range: $5,000 to $50,000
***Note:** Giving excludes matching gifts, scholarship, and United Way.

Recent Grants

Note: Grants derived from 2003 Form 990.
General

3,000,000	United Way of Tri State Inc., Poughkeepsie, NY -- towards new year programs
1,500,000	United Way of Tri State Inc., Bloomfield, NJ -- towards New Jersey programs
1,000,000	Aspen Institute, Queenstown, MD
1,000,000	Brandeis University, Waltham, MA -- towards the international center for ethics justice and public life and scholarships for needy students
750,000	Local Initiatives Support Corporation, New York, NY
660,000	Enterprise Foundation, Columbia, MD
500,000	Borough of Manhattan Community College, New York, NY
500,000	Public Education Network, Washington, DC -- towards programs outside of the tri state region
500,000	United Way of Tri State Inc., Darien, CT -- for the current year campaign
400,000	New York and Presbyterian Hospitals Inc., New York, NY -- towards children's hospital of New York

BURTON D. MORGAN FOUNDATION

Giving Contact

John V. Frank, President
PO Box 1500
Akron, OH 44309-1500
Phone: (330)258-6512
Fax: (330)258-6559
Web: http://www.bdmorganfdn.org

Description

Founded: 1967
EIN: 346598971
Organization Type: General Purpose Foundation
Giving Locations: OH: Summit County

Grant Types: Capital, General Support, Scholarship, Seed Money.

Donor Information

Founder: Established in 1967 by Burton D. Morgan.

Financial Summary

Total Giving: $10,030,800 (2003); $11,671,100 (2002)
Giving Analysis: Giving for 2003 includes: foundation fellowships ($50,000); foundation scholarships ($87,500); 2002: foundation scholarships ($5,000); foundation fellowships ($50,000)
Assets: $111,505,250 (2003); $55,197,104 (2002)
Gifts Received: $39,584,967 (2003); $1,500,000 (2002); $350,000 (1998). Note: Contributions were received from the estate of Burton D. Morgan. Contributions were received from Burton D. Morgan.

Typical Recipients

Arts & Humanities: Arts Outreach, Ballet, Dance, Historic Preservation, History & Archaeology, Libraries, Museums/Galleries, Music, Performing Arts, Public Broadcasting
Civic & Public Affairs: Botanical Gardens/Parks, Business/Free Enterprise, Clubs, Community Foundations, Economic Development, Civic & Public Affairs-General, Legal Aid, Municipalities/Towns, Nonprofit Management, Parades/Festivals, Philanthropic Organizations, Professional & Trade Associations, Safety, Women's Affairs, Zoos/Aquariums
Education: Arts/Humanities Education, Business Education, Colleges & Universities, Economic Education, Education Funds, Elementary Education (Public), Engineering/Technological Education, Faculty Development, Education-General, Health & Physical Education, Leadership Training, Medical Education, Private Education (Precollege), Public Education (Precollege), Religious Education, Science/Mathematics Education, Secondary Education (Private), Secondary Education (Public), Social Sciences Education, Student Aid
Environment: Environment-General, Research
Health: Cancer, Children's Health/Hospitals, Emergency/Ambulance Services, Health Organizations, Heart, Hospices, Hospitals, Mental Health, Nursing Services, Public Health, Research/Studies Institutes
International: Missionary/Religious Activities
Religion: Churches, Religious Organizations, Religious Welfare
Science: Science Museums, Scientific Centers & Institutes
Social Services: Big Brothers/Big Sisters, Child Welfare, Community Centers, Community Service Organizations, Counseling, Delinquency & Criminal Rehabilitation, Domestic Violence, Family Planning, Family Services, People with Disabilities, Recreation & Athletics, Scouts, Senior Services, Shelters/Homelessness, Substance Abuse, United Funds/United Ways, YMCA/YWCA/YMHA/YWHA, Youth Organizations

Application Procedures

Initial Contact: Foundation presently is not accepting applications. They will begin accepting applications after December 31, 2004.
Application Requirements: The foundation requests proposals be made in writing, not to exceed three pages. The letter must give a clear and concise description of the purpose for the request. Attachments to the letter must include a copy of the IRS tax-determination letter, a separate nonprofit determination letter, a list of the current board of trustees, and a copy of the organization's most recent financial statement or audited report. Additional material may be submitted to supplement the application.
Deadlines: May 1 and October 1. Requests for health and mental health grants are considered once a year at the January meeting and must be submitted by September 1.
Review Process: The board meets two times per year during July and January. Requests that do not

fall within the trustees' interests are declined within 30 days. Requests from the same organization can only be considered once every 12 months.

Restrictions

The foundation primarily makes grants to educational, research, mental health, and charitable organizations. Grants are not made to individuals., annual fund drives, units of government, and tax-supported organizations.

Additional Information

Publications: Application Guidelines; ANN Report

Foundation Officials

Keith A. Brown: trustee B 1951. ED Purdue University (1974). PRIM CORP EMPL president: Chimera Corp. CORP AFFIL president: PolyShades Corp.; director: USG Corp.; president: Global Film & Packaging Corp.
Richard A. Chenoweth: trustee PRIM CORP EMPL principal: Buckingham, Doolittle & Burroughs. CORP AFFIL director: Caliber System Inc.; director: Roadway Services.
J. Martin Erbaugh: trustee B 1948. ED Case Western Reserve University Law School (1973); Denison University (1969-1973); Kent State University MBA (1978). PRIM CORP EMPL chairman board, president, director: Erbaugh Corp. CORP AFFIL director: Lesco Inc.
John V. Frank: president, trustee B Cleveland, OH 1936. ED Babson College (1956-1957); University of Miami BBA (1960). PRIM CORP EMPL president: Summit Capital Management Co. NONPR AFFIL trustee: Rectory School; member finance committee: University Akron; member: Cleveland Society Security Analysts; board overseers: Blossom Music Center; councilman: City Akron; member: Akron Emergency Medical Advisory Board; trustee: Akron Rural Cemetery; president, trustee: Akron Civil War Memorial Society. CLUB AFFIL Hillsboro Club; Portage Country Club.
Stanley Carleton Gault: trustee B Wooster, OH 1926. ED College of Wooster BA (1948). PRIM CORP EMPL chairman, chief executive officer: Goodyear Tire & Rubber Co. CORP AFFIL director: Rubbermaid; director: Timken Co.; director: PPG Industries; director: Little Tikes Co.; director: New York Stock Exchange Inc.; director: Kelly-Springfield Tire Co.; director: Avon Products Inc.; director: International Paper Co. NONPR AFFIL director: National Association Manufacturers; member executive board: National Business Council Consumer Affairs; chairman board: College Wooster.
Mark D. Robeson: trustee
Richard N. Seaman: trustee

Grants Analysis

Disclosure Period: calendar year ending 2003
Total Grants: $8,893,300*
Number of Grants: 33
Average Grant: $31,571*
Highest Grant: $5,500,000
Lowest Grant: $500
Typical Range: $10,000 to $50,000
***Note:** Giving excludes scholarships; fellowships. Average grant excludes two highest grants ($7,914,600).

Recent Grants

Note: Grants derived from 2003 Form 990.
General

5,500,000	Purdue University, West Lafayette, IN -- toward Burton D. Morgan Center for Entrepreneurship
2,414,600	Denison University, Granville, OH -- funding for the Burton D. Morgan Center
800,000	Ashland University, Ashland, OH -- funding of Center for entrepreneurial studies
500,000	College of Wooster, Wooster, OH -- toward Burton D. Morgan Hall

100,000	Akron Community Foundation, Akron, OH -- toward Richard A. and Dorothy C. Chenoweth Fund
100,000	College of Wooster, Wooster, OH -- toward capital campaign
86,300	Kent State University Foundation, Kent, OH -- support for School of Fashion Design and Merchandising
75,000	Hopewell Inn, Mesopotamia, OH -- funding for general operating support
55,000	Foundation for Teaching Economics, Davis, CA -- toward Northeast Ohio Economic for Leaders program
50,000	Akron Bar Association, Akron, OH -- toward challenge grant for endowment

LOUIE R. AND GERTRUDE MORGAN FOUNDATION

Giving Contact
Robert Summerall, Jr., Vice President & Treasurer
PO Box 550
Arcadia, FL 34265
Phone: (941)494-1551

Description
Founded: 1960
EIN: 596142359
Organization Type: Private Foundation
Giving Locations: FL
Grant Types: General Support.

Donor Information
Founder: the late Louie R. Morgan, the late Mildred Morgan, Gertrude Morgan, Eleanor Morgan

Typical Recipients
Arts & Humanities: Libraries
Civic & Public Affairs: Hispanic Affairs, Municipalities/Towns
Education: Secondary Education (Public)
Health: Hospitals
Religion: Churches, Religion-General, Religious Organizations, Religious Welfare
Social Services: Community Service Organizations, People with Disabilities, Senior Services

Application Procedures
Initial Contact: Send a written description of the project and purpose of funds sought.
Deadlines: None.

Foundation Officials
George E. Bellamy: director
Bobby C. Mixon: president
Lewis W. Smith: director
Robert Summerall, Jr.: director
Richard Wertich: secretary
James R. Wierichs: secretary

Grants Analysis
Disclosure Period: calendar year ending 2000
Total Grants: $110,000
Number of Grants: 21
Highest Grant: $5,000
Lowest Grant: $5,000

Recent Grants
Note: Grants derived from 2001 Form 990.
General

5,000	Arcadia Church of God, Arcadia, FL
5,000	Arcadia Spanish Church of God, Arcadia, FL
5,000	Assembly of Praise, Arcadia, FL
5,000	Elizabeth Baptist Church, Arcadia, FL
5,000	First Presbyterian Church, Arcadia, FL
5,000	Fort Ogden Church of God, Ft. Ogden, FL
5,000	Friendship Missionary Baptist, Arcadia, FL
5,000	Heritage Baptist Church, Arcadia, FL
5,000	House of God, Arcadia, FL
5,000	Ivey Chapel Afro Methodist, Arcadia, FL

MORIAH FUND, INC.

Giving Contact
Janice Edwards, Grants Manager
Moriah Fund, Inc.
1634 I Street Northwest, Suite 1000
Washington, DC 20006-4003
Phone: (202)783-8488
Fax: (202)783-8499
E-mail: jedwards@moriahfund.org

Alternate Contact
Susan Feit
PO Box 2788
60190 Neve Monosson, Israel
Note: For projects in Israel.

Description
Founded: 1985
EIN: 311129589
Organization Type: General Purpose Foundation
Giving Locations: DC: Washington; MD; NY
Grant Types: General Support, Matching, Multiyear/Continuing Support.
Note: Also provides grants for technical assistance.

Donor Information
Founder: The Moriah Fund was established in 1985 by the late Clarence W. Efroymson and the late Robert A. Efroymson, both lifelong philanthropic contributors, who held the Jewish values and concern for the disadvantaged that the fund emulates today. The Gershon Ben-Ephraim Fund and the Gustave Aaron Efroymson Fund were also donors.

Financial Summary
Total Giving: $8,600,000 (2003 approx); $9,757,500 (2002); $32,686,944 (2001). Note: In 2001 a grant in the amount of $22,395,944 was made to create the Efroymson Fund to support programs in the environment and the Indianapolis community.
Assets: $130,611,740 (2002); $170,111,239 (2001).
Gifts Received: $165,592 (2002); $175,282 (2001); $7,421,286 (2000). Note: In 2002, contributions were received from Debra Efroymson.

Typical Recipients
Arts & Humanities: Libraries
Civic & Public Affairs: Asian American Affairs, Civil Rights, Community Foundations, Economic Development, Economic Policy, Employment/Job Training, Ethnic Organizations, Civic & Public Affairs-General, Hispanic Affairs, Housing, Law & Justice, Legal Aid, Native American Affairs, Philanthropic Organizations, Public Policy, Urban & Community Affairs, Women's Affairs
Education: Colleges & Universities, Education Funds, Education-General, International Studies, Leadership Training, Preschool Education, Private Education (Precollege), Public Education (Precollege), Social Sciences Education, Vocational & Technical Education
Environment: Air/Water Quality, Energy, Forestry, Environment-General, Protection, Research, Resource Conservation, Wildlife Protection
Health: Adolescent Health Issues, Children's Health/Hospitals, Clinics/Medical Centers, Health-General, Health Policy/Cost Containment, Health Organizations, Long-Term Care, Medical Training, Mental Health, Nutrition, Prenatal Health Issues, Public Health

International: Foreign Educational Institutions, Health Care/Hospitals, Human Rights, International Affairs, International Development, International Environmental Issues, International Organizations, International Peace & Security Issues, International Relations, International Relief Efforts, Missionary/Religious Activities
Religion: Jewish Causes, Religious Organizations, Religious Welfare, Seminaries, Social/Policy Issues
Social Services: Child Welfare, Community Centers, Community Service Organizations, Crime Prevention, Day Care, Delinquency & Criminal Rehabilitation, Family Planning, Family Services, Food/Clothing Distribution, People with Disabilities, Recreation & Athletics, Shelters/Homelessness, Social Services-General, United Funds/United Ways, Youth Organizations

Application Procedures
Initial Contact: A first-time applicant must send a short two- to three-page letter of inquiry at least one month prior to proposal deadlines. Based on the letter, the fund will decide whether or not to invite a full proposal.
Application Requirements: The letter of inquiry should include an outline of the organization's history, purpose, and goals; amount of funding requested; purpose and activities of specific project; and the total budgets for the project and the organization.

A full proposal should include the following: a cover sheet including the name, address, and phone/fax number(s) of the organization; the contact person's and Chief Executive Officer's names; the purpose of the organization; organization and total project budgets for the past, current, and projected years; dates of fiscal year; purpose, amount and period of time for which grant is requested; and other sources of income committed and pending for the period in which support is requested. The narrative for general support (ten pages maximum), should include details the history, purpose, goals, major programs and accomplishments of the organization; plans and priorities; qualifications to complete project; and methods of evaluation. If requesting a project grant, narrative should include history of organization; major programs and accomplishments; description of activities to be supported with specific goals and measurable objectives; recent and anticipated accomplishments; project goals and plan of action with timeline; qualifications of organization to accomplish project; method of evaluation; and long-term project plans including future financing. All proposals should include the following financial information: revenue and expense statements for the past, current and future years; list of organization's major institutional funders with amounts; and an audit if available. Other information that should be included: proof of IRS tax-exemption 501c(3) and non-private foundation 509(a) status; list of the board of directors and their affiliations; and an annual report if available.
Deadlines: For letters of inquiry, are February 1 and July 1. Proposals must be received by March 1 and August 1.
Review Process: Letters of inquiry are reviewed throughout the year. Proposals are reviewed by the board of directors for spring or fall grant cycle depending on the date they are received.

Restrictions
The Moriah Fund does not consider grants for individuals, arts organizations, private foundations, medical research, lobbying, non-U.S. organizations, or political campaigns.

Additional Information
Publications: Annual Report; Guidelines; Proposal Checklist

Foundation Officials
Geeta Rao Gupta: director
Judith Lichtman: 1st vice president, treasurer B 1940. ED Hofstra University (1963); University of

Wisconsin Law School (1965). PRIM NONPR EMPL president: Women's Legal Defense Fund.
Karl Mathiasen: secretary
Mary Ann Efroymson Stein: president

Grants Analysis

Disclosure Period: calendar year ending 2002
Total Grants: $9,757,500
Number of Grants: 191
Average Grant: $37,366*
Highest Grant: $2,658,000
Lowest Grant: $2,000
Typical Range: $10,000 to $50,000
*Note: Average grant figure excludes highest grant.

Recent Grants

Note: Grants derived from 2002 Form 990.
General

2,652,000	New Israel Fund, Washington, DC
210,000	Philanthropic Ventures Foundation, Oakland, CA -- fund for center for support of native lands, center for women's research and center for human rights legal action
195,000	American Jewish World Service, New York, NY
195,000	Center on Budget and Policy Priorities, Washington, DC
125,000	North American Conference on Ethiopian Jewry, New York, NY -- fund for educational & food distribution programs to families awaiting emigration to Israel and Israel dissemination program
110,000	Rights Action, Washington, DC
105,000	Center for Health and Gender Equity, Takoma Park, MD
100,000	Fund for Global Human Rights, Washington, DC
95,000	Appalachian Mountain Club, Boston, MA -- support for the northern forest campaign
95,000	Eco Logic Development Fund, Cambridge, MA -- fund for Guatemala project

MORLEY FOUNDATION

Giving Contact

Robert S. Morley, President
PO Box 2485
Saginaw, MI 48605-2485
Phone: (989)753-3438

Description

Founded: 1948
EIN: 386055569
Organization Type: Private Foundation
Giving Locations: MI: Saginaw greater Saginaw area
Grant Types: General Support, Multiyear/Continuing Support, Operating Expenses, Project, Research, Seed Money.

Donor Information

Founder: the late Ralph Chase Morley, the late Mrs. Ralph Chase Morley, Sr.

Financial Summary

Total Giving: $342,288 (2001)
Giving Analysis: Giving for 2001 includes: foundation grants to United Way ($9,200); foundation scholarships ($37,500)
Assets: $6,162,422 (2001)
Gifts Received: $2,018 (2001); $1,242 (2000); $68,391 (1999). Note: In 1992, contributions were received from Charles W. Morley Trust.

Typical Recipients

Arts & Humanities: Arts Centers, Arts Festivals, Dance, Arts & Humanities-General, Historic Preservation, History & Archaeology, Libraries, Literary Arts, Museums/Galleries, Music, Performing Arts, Public Broadcasting, Theater
Civic & Public Affairs: Botanical Gardens/Parks, Business/Free Enterprise, Chambers of Commerce, Community Foundations, Economic Development, Employment/Job Training, Civic & Public Affairs-General, Housing, Law & Justice, Parades/Festivals, Professional & Trade Associations, Public Policy, Safety, Urban & Community Affairs, Zoos/Aquariums
Education: Arts/Humanities Education, Business Education, Colleges & Universities, Education Funds, Environmental Education, Education-General, Minority Education, Private Education (Precollege), Public Education (Precollege), Science/Mathematics Education, Secondary Education (Private), Student Aid
Environment: Forestry, Resource Conservation
Health: AIDS/HIV, Emergency/Ambulance Services, Eyes/Blindness, Health-General, Hospitals, Long-Term Care, Medical Research, Nursing Services, Single-Disease Health Associations
Religion: Churches, Religious Welfare
Science: Science Exhibits & Fairs
Social Services: At-Risk Youth, Big Brothers/Big Sisters, Camps, Child Abuse, Child Welfare, Community Centers, Community Service Organizations, Crime Prevention, Day Care, Delinquency & Criminal Rehabilitation, Domestic Violence, Emergency Relief, Family Services, Food/Clothing Distribution, Recreation & Athletics, Scouts, Senior Services, Shelters/Homelessness, Substance Abuse, United Funds/United Ways, YMCA/YWCA/YMHA/YWHA, Youth Organizations

Application Procedures

Initial Contact: Send a brief letter of inquiry and a full proposal.
Application Requirements: Include an outline of the program, amount requested, description of organization, and proof of tax-exempt status, lists of board members, and other organizations contacted for funding.
Deadlines: None.

Restrictions

Does not support individuals or provide funds for deficit financing, land acquisition, or renovation projects.

Foundation Officials

Michael M. Brand: trustee
Lois K. Guttowsky: secretary
Burrows Morley, Jr.: trustee
Christopher Morley: trustee
David H. Morley: trustee
Edward B. Morley, Jr.: past president, trustee
George B. Morley, Jr.: trustee
Katharyn M. Morley: trustee
Mark B. Morley: treasurer
Peter B. Morley, Jr.: trustee
Robert S. Morley: president
Carol Morley Beck: trustee
Lucy M. Thomson: vice president, trustee
Richard B. Thomson, Jr.: trustee

Grants Analysis

Disclosure Period: calendar year ending 2001
Total Grants: $295,588*
Number of Grants: 56
Average Grant: $5,278
Highest Grant: $25,000
Lowest Grant: $500
Typical Range: $1,000 to $10,000
*Note: Giving excludes United Way and scholarship.

Recent Grants

Note: Grants derived from 2001 Form 990.

General

25,000	Saginaw Art Museum, Saginaw, MI -- capital campaign
25,000	Saginaw County Historical Society, Saginaw, MI -- Morley Room
25,000	Saginaw Valley State University, University Center, MI -- scholarships
21,108	Saginaw Children's Zoo, Saginaw, MI -- expansion
15,000	Saginaw Art Museum, Saginaw, MI
15,000	Saginaw Art Museum, Saginaw, MI -- salary support
14,000	Michigan Colleges Foundation, Inc., Southfield, MI -- endowment fund
13,750	WUCM - TV Delta College, University Center, MI -- weekly program
10,000	Interlochen Center for the Arts, Interlochen, RI -- building improvements
10,000	Saginaw City Rescue Mission, Saginaw, MI -- building expansion

MORRILL CHARITABLE FOUNDATION

Giving Contact

Tom James
Northern Trust Co.
50 S. LaSalle, L-5
Chicago, IL 60675
Phone: (312)630-6000

Description

Founded: 1983
EIN: 351584396
Organization Type: Private Foundation
Giving Locations: IN: Ft. Worth
Grant Types: Capital, General Support.

Financial Summary

Total Giving: $361,321 (fiscal year ending November 30, 2003); $427,902 (fiscal 2001)
Assets: $5,163,704 (fiscal 2003); $6,029,239 (fiscal 2001)
Gifts Received: $72,918 (fiscal 2003); $72,918 (fiscal 2001); $72,918 (fiscal 2000). Note: Contributions were received from the Morrill Charitable Annuity Trust.

Typical Recipients

Arts & Humanities: Arts Associations & Councils, Community Arts, History & Archaeology, Libraries, Museums/Galleries, Music, Performing Arts, Public Broadcasting, Theater
Civic & Public Affairs: Botanical Gardens/Parks, Chambers of Commerce, Community Foundations, Civic & Public Affairs-General, Urban & Community Affairs
Education: Afterschool/Enrichment Programs, Business Education, Colleges & Universities, Engineering/Technological Education, Gifted & Talented Programs, Private Education (Precollege), Religious Education, Student Aid, Vocational & Technical Education
Health: Cancer, Clinics/Medical Centers, Health Organizations, Public Health
Religion: Churches, Ministries, Religious Organizations, Religious Welfare
Science: Scientific Centers & Institutes
Social Services: Big Brothers/Big Sisters, Child Welfare, Community Service Organizations, Crime Prevention, Homes, People with Disabilities, Recreation & Athletics, Scouts, United Funds/United Ways, YMCA/YWCA/YMHA/YWHA, Youth Organizations

Application Procedures

Initial Contact: Send brief letter describing program.
Application Requirements: Include purpose of

funds sought and proof of tax-exempt status.
Deadlines: None.

Foundation Officials
Amy B. Morrill: trustee

Grants Analysis
Disclosure Period: fiscal year ending November 30, 2003
Total Grants: $361,321
Number of Grants: 31
Average Grant: $11,656
Highest Grant: $35,024
Lowest Grant: $2,522
Typical Range: $5,000 to $20,000

Recent Grants
Note: Grants derived from fiscal 2003 Form 990.
General

35,024	Junior Achievement
30,014	Indiana Institute of Technology, Ft. Wayne, IN
25,025	WFWA
25,013	Junior Achievement
25,011	Fort Wayne Philharmonic, Ft. Wayne, IN
18,012	SCAN
15,021	Big Brothers Big Sisters of Northeast Indiana, Ft. Wayne, IN
15,005	Fort Wayne Museum of Art, Ft. Wayne, IN
15,002	Early Childhood Alliance, Ft. Wayne, IN
15,000	Fellowship of Christians in Universities and Schools, Charlottesville, VA

CHARLES M. MORRIS CHARITABLE TRUST

Giving Contact
Joanna M. Mayo, Vice President
c/o National City Bank
20 Stanwix St., 16th Floor
Loc 25-162
Pittsburgh, PA 15222-4802
Phone: (412)644-8002
E-mail: joanna.mayo@nationalcity.com
Web: http://www.morrisfoundation.org

Description
Founded: 1988
EIN: 256312920
Organization Type: Private Foundation
Giving Locations: PA
Grant Types: General Support.

Donor Information
Founder: the late Charles M. Morris

Financial Summary
Total Giving: $1,746,960 (2002); $1,412,854 (2001)
Giving Analysis: Giving for 2002 includes: foundation grants to United Way ($25,000)
Assets: $26,979,308 (2002); $33,935,480 (2001)
Gifts Received: $135,000 (1993); $5,079,245 (1992). Note: In 1993, contributions were received from the estate of Charles M. Morris.

Typical Recipients
Arts & Humanities: Ballet, Arts & Humanities-General, Libraries, Museums/Galleries, Music, Theater
Civic & Public Affairs: African American Affairs, Employment/Job Training, Housing
Education: Colleges & Universities, Community & Junior Colleges, Education Funds, Education-General, Preschool Education, Private Education (Precollege), Religious Education
Health: Children's Health/Hospitals, Clinics/Medical Centers, Health Organizations, Medical Rehabilita-

tion, Single-Disease Health Associations
Religion: Churches, Religion-General, Jewish Causes, Ministries, Religious Organizations, Religious Welfare, Synagogues/Temples
Social Services: Child Welfare, Community Service Organizations, Crime Prevention, Day Care, Delinquency & Criminal Rehabilitation, Family Planning, Family Services, Food/Clothing Distribution, Senior Services, Social Services-General, Substance Abuse, United Funds/United Ways, YMCA/YWCA/YMHA/YWHA, Youth Organizations

Application Procedures
Initial Contact: Send a brief letter of inquiry requesting application form.
Deadlines: None.

Restrictions
Grants are not made to support individuals, political or lobbying groups, or multiple year request.

Additional Information
Publications: Application form.
Trust(s): Natl City Bank PA

Foundation Officials
Arthur Fidel: dist committee member
Arthur Fiedl: dist committee member
Charles Perlow: dist committee member

Grants Analysis
Disclosure Period: calendar year ending 2002
Total Grants: $1,721,960
Number of Grants: 49
Average Grant: $21,291*
Highest Grant: $700,000
Typical Range: $10,000 to $40,000
*Note: Average grant figure excludes highest grant.

Recent Grants
Note: Grants derived from 2002 Form 990.
General

700,000	United Jewish Federation, Pittsburgh, PA -- annual appeal
50,000	City Theatre Company, Inc., Pittsburgh, PA -- for renovations
50,000	Jewish University of Pittsburgh, Pittsburgh, PA -- capital campaign
50,000	Kollel Jewish Learning Center, Pittsburgh, PA -- capital campaign
50,000	North Tahoe Hebrew Congregation, Incline Village, NV -- capital campaign
50,000	Pittsburgh Children's Museum, Pittsburgh, PA -- capital campaign
50,000	United Jewish Federation, Pittsburgh, PA -- for Israel emergency appeal
50,000	United Jewish Federation, Pittsburgh, PA -- for Squirrel Hill Revitalization Committee
30,000	Hillel Academy, Pittsburgh, PA -- for computers and printers
30,000	Jewish Education Institute, Pittsburgh, PA -- for holocaust memorial

MORRIS COMMUNICATIONS CORP.

Company Headquarters
825 Broad Street
Augusta, GA 30903
Phone: (706)724-0851
Web: http://www.morriscomm.com

Company Description
Former Name: Stauffer Communications.
Revenue: US$578 million (2001)
Employees: 6000 (2003)
SIC(s): 2711 Newspapers, 2721 Periodicals.

Operating Locations
Morris Communications Corp. (FL--Winter Haven; KS--Topeka; MN--Brainerd; MO--Independence; SD--Brookings)

Stauffer Communications Foundation

Giving Contact
William S. Morris, IV, Trustee
PO Box 936
Augusta, GA 30903-0936
Phone: (706)823-3462
Fax: (785)295-1144
Note: Mr. Stauffer's direct line is: (785)295-1118.

Description
EIN: 486212412
Organization Type: Corporate Foundation
Giving Locations: KS; OK
Grant Types: Employee Matching Gifts, General Support.

Financial Summary
Total Giving: $2,172,192 (2003); $118,057 (2001).
Note: Contributes through foundation only.
Assets: $1,024,351 (2003); $1,160,241 (2001)
Gifts Received: $2,113,167 (2003); $99,250 (2001); $106,000 (1998). Note: Contributions were received from Morris Communications Corp.

Typical Recipients
Arts & Humanities: Ballet, Community Arts, Arts & Humanities-General, Historic Preservation, History & Archaeology, Libraries, Literary Arts, Museums/Galleries, Music, Performing Arts, Public Broadcasting, Theater
Civic & Public Affairs: Botanical Gardens/Parks, Chambers of Commerce, Civil Rights, Clubs, Community Foundations, Economic Development, Employment/Job Training, Civic & Public Affairs-General, Law & Justice, Legal Aid, Municipalities/Towns, Philanthropic Organizations, Professional & Trade Associations, Public Policy, Rural Affairs, Urban & Community Affairs, Women's Affairs, Zoos/Aquariums
Education: Arts/Humanities Education, Business Education, Colleges & Universities, Community & Junior Colleges, Economic Education, Education Associations, Education Funds, Engineering/Technological Education, Education-General, Journalism/Media Education, Legal Education, Medical Education, Private Education (Precollege), Religious Education, Science/Mathematics Education, Secondary Education (Public), Social Sciences Education, Student Aid, Vocational & Technical Education
Environment: Resource Conservation, Wildlife Protection
Health: Alzheimer's Disease, Cancer, Children's Health/Hospitals, Clinics/Medical Centers, Emergency/Ambulance Services, Health Organizations, Hospitals, Public Health
International: Foreign Arts Organizations, Human Rights
Religion: Religious Organizations, Religious Welfare
Science: Scientific Research
Social Services: Animal Protection, Child Abuse, Child Welfare, Community Centers, Community Service Organizations, Family Services, People with Disabilities, Recreation & Athletics, Scouts, Shelters/Homelessness, United Funds/United Ways, YMCA/YWCA/YMHA/YWHA, Youth Organizations

Application Procedures
Initial Contact: There is no specific application form.
Deadlines: None.

Corporate Officials

William A. Herman, III: secretary, treasurer, director B Augusta, GA 1938. ED University of Georgia (1963). PRIM CORP EMPL secretary, treasurer, director: Morris Communications Corp. CORP AFFIL secretary, treasurer, director: Southeastern Newspaper Corp.; secretary, treasurer, director: Stauffer Communications Inc.; secretary, treasurer, director: Mill Haven Co. Inc.; secretary, treasurer, director: Shivers Trading & Operating Co.; secretary, treasurer, director: Azalea Development Co.; treasurer, director: Broadcaster Press Inc.; secretary, treasurer, director: Athens Newspapers Inc. CLUB AFFIL Knights of Columbus.

William Shivers Morris, III: founder, chairman, chief executive officer, director B Augusta, GA 1934. ED University of Georgia AB (1956). PRIM CORP EMPL founder, chairman, chief executive officer, director: Morris Communications Corp. CORP AFFIL chairman, chief executive officer: Southwest Newspapers Corp.; chairman: Stauffer Communications Inc.; director: Southern Co. Inc.; chief executive officer: Shivers Trading & Operating Co.; chairman, chief executive officer: Southeastern Newspaper Corp.; director: Georgia Power Co.; chairman, chief executive officer: North America Publs Inc.; chairman, chief executive officer: Florida Publishing Co.; publ, chairman, chief executive officer: Augusta Chronicle; chairman: Broadcaster Press Inc.; chairman, chief executive officer: Athens Newspapers Inc. NONPR AFFIL member: Southeastern Newspaper Publisher's Association; member: Southern Newspaper Publishers Association; member: International Press Institute; member: American Newspaper Publishers Association; trustee: Augusta College Foundation. CLUB AFFIL University Club; Pinnacle Club; Commerce Club; Oglethorpe Club.

William Shivers Morris, IV: president, director B 1938. PRIM CORP EMPL president, director: Morris Communications Corp. CORP AFFIL president: Southeastern Newspaper Corp.; president: Stauffer Communications Inc.; president: Shivers Trading & Operating Co.; president: Athens Newspapers Inc.; president: Broadcaster Press Inc.

Foundation Officials

John Fish: trustee
Gregg A. Ireland: trustee
William Shivers Morris, III: trustee (see above)
William Shivers Morris, IV: trustee (see above)
John H. Stauffer: trustee B Arkansas City, KS 1928. ED University of Kansas BS (1949). PRIM CORP EMPL director: Morris Communications Corp. CORP AFFIL chairman: Topeka-Capital Journal; director: Mercantile Bank Topeka. NONPR AFFIL member: Top Tower; member: Topeka Chamber of Commerce; member: Phi Delta Theta; member: Kansas City Chamber of Commerce; member: Kansas Press Association; member: Inland Press Association. CLUB AFFIL Topeka Country Club.

Grants Analysis

Disclosure Period: calendar year ending 2003
Total Grants: $2,172,192
Number of Grants: 55
Average Grant: $32,818*
Highest Grant: $400,000
Lowest Grant: $100
Typical Range: $10,000 to $100,000
*Note: Average grant figure excludes highest grant.

Recent Grants

Note: Grants derived from 2003 Form 990.
Library-Related
50,000	Jacksonville Public Library, Jacksonville, FL
6,000	Harry S. Truman Library & Museum, Independence, MO

General
400,000	Jacksonville Zoo, Jacksonville, FL
332,042	Darlington School Development, Rome, GA
300,000	Globe-News Center for Performing Arts, Jacksonville, FL
100,000	Episcopal Day School, Lake Charles, LA
100,000	Fore! Augusta Foundation Inc., Augusta, GA
100,000	Jacksonville YMCA, Jacksonville, FL
100,000	Southern Newspaper Publishers Association SNPA, Atlanta, GA
90,000	United Way of CSRA, Augusta, GA
50,000	Fore! Augusta Foundation Inc., Augusta, GA
50,000	Historic Augusta, Augusta, GA

MARGARET T. MORRIS FOUNDATION

Giving Contact

Eugene P. Polk, Trustee
PO Box 592
Prescott, AZ 86302
Phone: (928)445-4010

Description

Founded: 1967
EIN: 866057798
Organization Type: General Purpose Foundation
Giving Locations: nationally.
Grant Types: Capital, General Support, Matching, Operating Expenses, Project, Scholarship.

Donor Information

Founder: The foundation was established in 1967 by the late Margaret T. Morris.

Financial Summary

Total Giving: $820,850 (2003); $2,532,835 (2002); $3,609,964 (2001)
Giving Analysis: Giving for 2003 includes: foundation scholarships ($25,000); 2002: foundation scholarships ($148,000)
Assets: $12,933,563 (2003); $12,753,091 (2002); $16,073,717 (2001)
Gifts Received: $4,050 (1994)

Typical Recipients

Arts & Humanities: Art History, Arts Associations & Councils, Arts Centers, Arts Festivals, Arts Funds, Arts Institutes, Arts Outreach, Ballet, Dance, Film & Video, Arts & Humanities-General, Historic Preservation, History & Archaeology, Libraries, Museums/Galleries, Music, Opera, Performing Arts, Public Broadcasting, Theater, Visual Arts

Civic & Public Affairs: Botanical Gardens/Parks, Business/Free Enterprise, Community Foundations, Economic Development, Economic Policy, Employment/Job Training, Civic & Public Affairs-General, Hispanic Affairs, Housing, Law & Justice, Legal Aid, Municipalities/Towns, Native American Affairs, Philanthropic Organizations, Professional & Trade Associations, Public Policy, Urban & Community Affairs, Women's Affairs, Zoos/Aquariums

Education: Arts/Humanities Education, Business Education, Colleges & Universities, Continuing Education, Education Associations, Education Funds, Education-General, Health & Physical Education, Medical Education, Private Education (Precollege), Public Education (Precollege), Science/Mathematics Education, Student Aid

Environment: Environment-General, Protection, Resource Conservation, Wildlife Protection

Health: AIDS/HIV, Alzheimer's Disease, Cancer, Children's Health/Hospitals, Clinics/Medical Centers, Emergency/Ambulance Services, Health-General, Geriatric Health, Health Policy/Cost Containment, Health Organizations, Home-Care Services, Hospices, Hospitals, Long-Term Care, Medical Research, Mental Health, Prenatal Health Issues, Preventive Medicine/Wellness Organizations, Public Health, Research/Studies Institutes, Single-Disease Health Associations, Transplant Networks/Donor Banks

International: Foreign Arts Organizations, Health Care/Hospitals, International Development, International Environmental Issues, International Organizations, International Peace & Security Issues, International Relief Efforts

Religion: Jewish Causes, Religious Organizations, Religious Welfare, Social/Policy Issues

Science: Science Museums, Scientific Centers & Institutes, Scientific Organizations

Social Services: At-Risk Youth, Big Brothers/Big Sisters, Child Welfare, Community Centers, Community Service Organizations, Counseling, Crime Prevention, Day Care, Emergency Relief, Family Planning, Family Services, Food/Clothing Distribution, Homes, People with Disabilities, Recreation & Athletics, Scouts, Senior Services, Shelters/Homelessness, Social Services-General, Special Olympics, Volunteer Services, YMCA/YWCA/YMHA/YWHA, Youth Organizations

Application Procedures

Initial Contact: Submit a brief letter of inquiry.
Application Requirements: Letter should include a description of the problem to be addressed, the nature of the project, and the objectives of the program. A copy of the IRS tax-exempt ruling and appropriate documentation should also be included.
Deadlines: Foundation prefers to receive applications between May and November.
Notes: The foundation reports that nearly all grants are internally initiated. Information letters of inquiry will be accepted, but may not receive a response.

Restrictions

The foundation does not make grants to individuals or sectarian religious organizations.

Foundation Officials

Richard L. Menschel: trustee
Eugene P. Polk: trustee
Thomas E. Polk: trustee

Grants Analysis

Disclosure Period: calendar year ending 2003
Total Grants: $795,850*
Number of Grants: 45
Average Grant: $13,857*
Highest Grant: $100,000
Lowest Grant: $350
Typical Range: $5,000 to $40,000
*Note: Giving excludes scholarships. Average grant figure excludes two highest grants ($200,000).

Recent Grants

Note: Grants derived from 2003 Form 990.
Library-Related
1,500	Prescott Public Library, Prescott, AZ

General
100,000	Harvard Business School, Boston, MA
100,000	Yavapai Regional Medical Center, Prescott, AZ
75,000	Arizona Science Center, Phoenix, AZ
50,000	Hospital for Special Surgery, New York, NY -- towards research endowments
50,000	Phipps Community Development Corporation, New York, NY -- towards low-income housing
50,000	Stepping Stones Agencies, Prescott, AZ -- towards community center campaign
35,000	Children's Hospital Auxiliary Rancho Santa Fe Unit, Rancho Santa Fe, CA
30,000	Adult Care Services Inc., Prescott, AZ -- for project strolling garden at Alzheimer's patient center
25,000	Arizona State University Foundation, Tempe, AZ

25,000   Cornell University, Ithaca, NY -- for Arizona students' scholarship endowment

NORMAN M. MORRIS FOUNDATION

Giving Contact
Wendy Aglietti
9 Rustling Lane
Bedford, NY 10506
Phone: (914)694-2000

Description
Founded: 1947
EIN: 136119134
Organization Type: Private Foundation
Giving Locations: NY
Grant Types: General Support.

Donor Information
Founder: Norman M. Morris

Financial Summary
Total Giving: $404,761 (2004); $334,826 (2001)
Giving Analysis: Giving for 2004 includes: foundation grants to United Way ($300); 2001: foundation grants to United Way ($300)
Assets: $11,858,056 (2004); $9,746,229 (2001)
Gifts Received: $1,174,599 (2004); $442,502 (2001); $442,502 (2000). Note: In 2001 and 2004, contributions were received from Norman M. Morris Trust. In 1999 and 2000, contributions were received from Norman M. Morris.

Typical Recipients
Arts & Humanities: Community Arts, Historic Preservation, Libraries, Museums/Galleries, Public Broadcasting
Civic & Public Affairs: Botanical Gardens/Parks, Clubs, Ethnic Organizations, Civic & Public Affairs-General, Legal Aid, Municipalities/Towns, Public Policy
Education: Arts/Humanities Education, Colleges & Universities, Medical Education, Preschool Education, Private Education (Precollege), Religious Education, Student Aid
Health: Alzheimer's Disease, Arthritis, Cancer, Clinics/Medical Centers, Geriatric Health, Health Funds, Health Organizations, Home-Care Services, Hospitals, Hospitals (University Affiliated), Long-Term Care, Medical Research, Mental Health, Nursing Services, Prenatal Health Issues, Respiratory, Single-Disease Health Associations, Transplant Networks/Donor Banks
International: International Peace & Security Issues, Missionary/Religious Activities
Religion: Jewish Causes, Religious Organizations, Religious Welfare, Seminaries, Social/Policy Issues, Synagogues/Temples
Science: Scientific Centers & Institutes
Social Services: Animal Protection, Community Service Organizations, Delinquency & Criminal Rehabilitation, People with Disabilities, Recreation & Athletics, Senior Services, United Funds/United Ways, Youth Organizations

Application Procedures
Initial Contact: Send a brief letter of inquiry. Include a description of organization and amount requested and purpose of funds sought.
Deadlines: None.

Foundation Officials
Arline J. Lubin: president
Kenneth A. Lubin: trustee
Marvin Lubin: vice president
Leland M. Morris: trustee
Robert E. Morris: secretary, treasurer

Grants Analysis
Disclosure Period: calendar year ending 2004
Total Grants: $404,461*
Number of Grants: 75
Average Grant: $2,207*
Highest Grant: $50,000
Lowest Grant: $100
Typical Range: $1,000 to $5,000
*Note: Giving excludes United Way. Average grant figure excludes five highest grants ($250,000).

Recent Grants
Note: Grants derived from 2004 Form 990.
General

50,000	Hebrew Home for the Aged at Riverdale, Riverdale, NY
50,000	Hospital for Joint Diseases, New York, NY
50,000	Memorial Sloan-Kettering Cancer Center, New York, NY
50,000	United Jewish Appeal Federation of Greenwich, Greenwich, CT
50,000	White Plains Hospital, White Plains, NY
25,000	Temple Sholom, Greenwich, CT
20,000	Boca Raton Community Hospital Foundation, Boca Raton, FL
10,000	Guiding Eyes for the Blind, Yorktown Heights, NY
10,000	Israel at Heart, New York, NY
10,000	St Andrew's School, Boca Raton, FL

WILLIAM T. MORRIS FOUNDATION

Giving Contact
Edward A. Antonelli, President, Chief Executive Officer & Director
230 Park Avenue, Suite 622
New York, NY 10169-0622
Phone: (212)986-8036
Fax: (212)370-1962

Description
Founded: 1937
EIN: 131600908
Organization Type: General Purpose Foundation
Giving Locations: NY; PA
Grant Types: Department, Fellowship, General Support, Project, Research, Scholarship.

Donor Information
Founder: The William T. Morris Foundation was established in 1937, with the late William T. Morris as donor.

Financial Summary
Total Giving: $1,880,000 (fiscal year ending June 30, 2002)
Assets: $51,333,357 (fiscal 2002)

Typical Recipients
Arts & Humanities: Arts Centers, Ballet, Dance, Historic Preservation, History & Archaeology, Libraries, Literary Arts, Museums/Galleries, Music, Opera, Performing Arts, Theater
Civic & Public Affairs: Botanical Gardens/Parks, Clubs, Civic & Public Affairs-General, Inner-City Development, Philanthropic Organizations, Public Policy, Urban & Community Affairs, Zoos/Aquariums
Education: Arts/Humanities Education, Colleges & Universities, Education Funds, Education-General, Health & Physical Education, Medical Education, Minority Education, Private Education (Precollege), Student Aid
Environment: Air/Water Quality, Environment-General, Resource Conservation, Wildlife Protection
Health: Alzheimer's Disease, Arthritis, Cancer, Clin-

ics/Medical Centers, Emergency/Ambulance Services, Eyes/Blindness, Health Funds, Heart, Hospitals, Medical Rehabilitation, Medical Research, Multiple Sclerosis, Respiratory, Single-Disease Health Associations, Speech & Hearing
Religion: Religious Welfare
Science: Science Museums
Social Services: People with Disabilities, Recreation & Athletics, Scouts, United Funds/United Ways, YMCA/YWCA/YMHA/YWHA, Youth Organizations

Application Procedures
Initial Contact: Requests should be submitted in writing.
Application Requirements: There is no prescribed form of application.
Deadlines: None.

Restrictions
No restrictions.

Foundation Officials
Edward A. Antonelli: president, chief executive officer, director
Bruce A. August: secretary, director
Edward W. Burns: director
Arthur Charles Laske, Jr.: treasurer, director
Wilmot Fitch Wheeler, Jr.: vice president, director B Southport, CT 1923. ED Yale University BA (1945); New York University postgrad (1947-1948). PRIM CORP EMPL chairman, director: Jelliff Corp. CORP AFFIL trustee: Peoples Mutual Holdings; director: Sormir Petroleum Inc.; director: Peoples Bank Connecticut. CLUB AFFIL Sky Club; Yale Club; Fairfield Country Club.

Grants Analysis
Disclosure Period: fiscal year ending June 30, 2002
Total Grants: $1,880,000
Number of Grants: 28
Average Grant: $60,370*
Highest Grant: $250,000
Lowest Grant: $15,000
Typical Range: $10,000 to $50,000
*Note: Average grant figure excludes highest grant.

Recent Grants
Note: Grants derived from fiscal 2002 Form 990.
General

250,000	Metropolitan Opera Association, Inc., New York, NY
135,000	Memorial Sloan-Kettering Cancer Center, New York, NY
110,000	Arthritis Foundation, Atlanta, GA
100,000	Assumption College, Worcester, MA
100,000	Boston College, Chestnut Hill, MA
100,000	Bowdoin College, South Portland, ME
100,000	Dartmouth College, Hanover, NH
100,000	Fairfield University, Fairfield, CT
100,000	Roger Williams University, Providence, RI
100,000	Simmons College, Boston, MA

HARRY W. MORRISON FOUNDATION

Giving Contact
Velma V. Morrison, President
3505 Crescent Rim Dr.
Boise, ID 83706
Phone: (208)345-5225

Description
Founded: 1952
EIN: 826008111
Organization Type: Private Foundation
Giving Locations: ID: Boise
Grant Types: Capital, General Support.

Donor Information

Founder: the late Harry W. Morrison

Financial Summary

Gifts Received: $29,000 (1999). Note: In 1999, contributions were received from Estate of Edith Miller Klein.

Typical Recipients

Arts & Humanities: Arts Associations & Councils, Ballet, Historic Preservation, History & Archaeology, Libraries, Museums/Galleries, Music, Opera, Performing Arts, Public Broadcasting, Theater
Civic & Public Affairs: Botanical Gardens/Parks, Civil Rights, Housing, Municipalities/Towns, Parades/Festivals, Zoos/Aquariums
Education: Arts/Humanities Education, Business Education, Colleges & Universities, Elementary Education (Public), Engineering/Technological Education, Literacy, Medical Education, Secondary Education (Public), Student Aid
Environment: Resource Conservation, Wildlife Protection
Health: Arthritis, Cancer, Children's Health/Hospitals, Clinics/Medical Centers, Diabetes, Emergency/Ambulance Services, Health-General, Health Organizations, Heart, Hospices, Hospitals, Kidney, Long-Term Care, Medical Research, Nursing Services, Single-Disease Health Associations
International: Health Care/Hospitals, International Affairs, International Environmental Issues, International Relief Efforts, Missionary/Religious Activities
Religion: Churches, Religion-General, Missionary Activities (Domestic), Religious Organizations, Religious Welfare
Social Services: Animal Protection, At-Risk Youth, Child Welfare, Community Centers, Community Service Organizations, Family Services, Food/Clothing Distribution, People with Disabilities, Recreation & Athletics, Scouts, Senior Services, Shelters/Homelessness, Social Services-General, Special Olympics, United Funds/United Ways, YMCA/YWCA/YMHA/YWHA, Youth Organizations

Application Procedures

Initial Contact: Send a brief letter of inquiry.
Application Requirements: Applications should include a statement of the organization's background and its purposes, objectives, and past activities; explanation of current financial status, latest balance sheet showing assets and liabilities, and a list of officers and directors and their affiliations; statement of major sources of financial support including any form of federal or state aid and if support has been received from this foundation in past years; explanation of current financial needs and any special projects or programs requiring aid; proof of tax-exempt status; and employer identification number.
Deadlines: Feb. 28.

Restrictions

Does not support individuals.

Additional Information

Publications: Application Guidelines

Foundation Officials

John J. Hockberger: director
Edith Miller Klein: director
Linda Klingner: secretary, treasurer
Velma V. Morrison: president B Woodville, CA 1920. PRIM CORP EMPL director: Morrison-Knudsen Corp. NONPR AFFIL director: Saint Lukes Hospital; trustee: Sansum Medicine Clinic; director: Pepperdine University; director: College ID; president: Morrison Center Performing Arts. CLUB AFFIL Hillcrest Country Club.
Judith V. Roberts: vice president
Michael E. Thomas: director
Frank Winsor: director

Grants Analysis

Disclosure Period: calendar year ending 2000
Total Grants: $520,839*
Number of Grants: 33
Average Grant: $6,995*
Highest Grant: $210,982
Typical Range: $1,000 to $12,500
*Note: Giving excludes scholarships. Average grant figure excludes three highest grants ($310,982).

Recent Grants

Note: Grants derived from 2001 Form 990.
General

200,000	Boise State University Foundation, Boise, ID -- Harry W. Morrison Scholl of Civil Engineering
50,000	Fred Hutchinson Cancer Research, Seattle, WA -- for patient care research fund
37,500	Idaho Anne Frank Human Rights Education Center, Boise, ID -- for reflective chasm
33,333	Bogus Basin Lifetime Sports, Boise, ID -- for Frontier Point Lodge Project
25,000	Council Community Hospital, Council, ID -- for Save the Hospital fund
25,000	First United Methodist Church, Boise, ID -- capital building fund
25,000	University of Idaho Foundation, Moscow, ID -- for the Albertson building fund
15,000	World Center for Birds of Prey, Boise, ID -- for renovations
10,000	Velma V. Morrison Center for Performing Arts, Boise, ID -- for Music Week
7,720	Minnidoka County Senior Center, Rupert, ID -- for repairs to Senior Center facility

HENRY AND LUCY MOSES FUND, INC.

Giving Contact

Irving Sitnick, President & Director
Moses and Singer
1301 Avenue of the Americas, 40th Fl.
New York, NY 10019-6076
Phone: (212)554-7800
Fax: (212)554-7700

Description

Founded: 1942
EIN: 136092967
Organization Type: General Purpose Foundation
Giving Locations: NY: New York metropolitan area some funding nationally.
Grant Types: Capital, Endowment, General Support, Operating Expenses.

Donor Information

Founder: Established in New York in 1942 by Mr. Henry L. Moses and his wife, Lucy Moses. Mr. Moses, an attorney and banker, was a partner in the law firm of Moses and Singer. He also was chairman of the Public National Bank and Trust Company and, upon its merger with Bankers Trust Company, a director of that bank. Mr. Moses was a noted philanthropist, with a special interest in hospitals. He served as president and chairman of the board of Montefiore Hospital and as director of the planning commission of the Hospital Council of Greater New York and the United Hospital Fund.

Financial Summary

Total Giving: $1,618,220 (2002)
Assets: $1,133,293 (2002)
Gifts Received: $1,505,000 (2002); $1,165,000 (2000); $1,155,000 (1998). Note: Contributions were received from the Henry and Lucy Moses Foundation Trust, and the Lucy G. Moses Trust.

Typical Recipients

Arts & Humanities: Arts Associations & Councils, Arts Centers, Arts Institutes, Ballet, Dance, Arts & Humanities-General, Libraries, Museums/Galleries, Music, Opera, Performing Arts, Public Broadcasting, Theater
Civic & Public Affairs: African American Affairs, Botanical Gardens/Parks, Civil Rights, Economic Development, Civic & Public Affairs-General, Housing, Legal Aid, Philanthropic Organizations, Public Policy, Urban & Community Affairs, Zoos/Aquariums
Education: Arts/Humanities Education, Colleges & Universities, Education Associations, Education Funds, Education Reform, Legal Education, Literacy, Medical Education, Minority Education, School Volunteerism, Special Education, Student Aid
Environment: Environment-General, Protection, Resource Conservation, Wildlife Protection
Health: Cancer, Clinics/Medical Centers, Health Organizations, Hospitals, Long-Term Care, Medical Research, Nursing Services, Research/Studies Institutes, Single-Disease Health Associations
International: Foreign Educational Institutions
Religion: Jewish Causes, Religious Organizations, Religious Welfare
Social Services: Child Welfare, Community Centers, Community Service Organizations, Family Planning, Family Services, Food/Clothing Distribution, People with Disabilities, Recreation & Athletics, Senior Services, Shelters/Homelessness, Social Services-General, Volunteer Services, YMCA/YWCA/YMHA/YWHA

Application Procedures

Initial Contact: Send a brief letter of inquiry.
Application Requirements: Include a description of organization, and project, and proof of tax-exempt status.

Restrictions

The foundation does not make grants to individuals, or for loans, film production, or travel.

Additional Information

The foundation reported that it is closely affiliated with the Henry and Lucy Moses Foundation Trust, the Henry L. Moses Trust, and the Lucy G. Moses Trust. All are located in the state of New York.
The foundation states that "the annual amount available for grants generally is committed to the activities supported in previous years by the foundation."

Foundation Officials

Joseph L. Fishman: vice president, director, treasurer, secretary PRIM CORP EMPL partner: Moses & Singer.
Jacqueline Schneider: vice president, director
Irving Sitnick: president, director PRIM CORP EMPL partner: Moses & Singer.

Grants Analysis

Disclosure Period: calendar year ending 2002
Total Grants: $1,618,220
Number of Grants: 88
Average Grant: $14,747*
Highest Grant: $250,000
Lowest Grant: $2,500
Typical Range: $5,000 to $25,000
*Note: Average grant figure excludes two highest grants ($350,000).

Recent Grants

Note: Grants derived from 2002 Form 990.
Library-Related

15,000	Brooklyn Public Library, Brooklyn, NY

General

250,000	New York Lawyers for Public Interest, New York, NY
100,000	Federation of Jewish Philanthropies, New York, NY
100,000	Montefiore Medical center, Bronx, NY

50,000	Central Park Conservancy, New York, NY
50,000	Columbia Law School, New York, NY
30,000	Prospect Park Alliance Inc., Brooklyn, NY
25,000	Brooklyn Museum, Brooklyn, NY
25,000	City College Fund, New York, NY
25,000	Educational Alliance, Providence, RI
25,000	Isaacs Stanley M Neighbourhood Center

SAMUEL B. & MARGARET C. MOSHER FOUNDATION

Giving Contact
Edward E. Birch, President
PO Box 1079
Santa Barbara, CA 93102
Phone: (805)962-1700

Description
Founded: 1951
EIN: 956037266
Organization Type: Private Foundation
Former Name: Samuel B. Mosher Foundation.
Giving Locations: AZ; CA
Grant Types: Capital, General Support, Operating Expenses, Scholarship.

Donor Information
Founder: the late Samuel B. Mosher, Goodwin I. Pelissero, Deborah S. Pelissero

Financial Summary
Total Giving: $1,129,100 (fiscal year ending August 31, 2004); $253,300 (fiscal 2001)
Assets: $27,354,980 (fiscal 2004); $8,966,594 (fiscal 2001)
Gifts Received: $5,170,668 (fiscal 2004); $1,280,000 (fiscal 2001). Note: In fiscal 2004, contributions were received from the estate of Margaret C. Mosher.

Typical Recipients
Arts & Humanities: Arts Festivals, Libraries, Museums/Galleries, Music, Opera
Civic & Public Affairs: Botanical Gardens/Parks, Civic & Public Affairs-General, Public Policy, Zoos/Aquariums
Education: Arts/Humanities Education, Colleges & Universities, Education Associations, Education Funds, Education-General, Private Education (Precollege), Religious Education, Student Aid
Health: Clinics/Medical Centers, Eyes/Blindness, Hospitals, Medical Research, Research/Studies Institutes, Single-Disease Health Associations
Religion: Churches, Religion-General, Religious Welfare, Seminaries
Social Services: Child Welfare, Community Service Organizations, Family Services, Social Services-General, Youth Organizations

Application Procedures
Initial Contact: Send a brief letter of inquiry.
Application Requirements: Include a description of organization, amount requested, and purpose of funds sought.
Deadlines: None.
Notes: Submissions are retained for one year.

Restrictions
Most grants are made for educational purposes. Does not support individuals or provide scholarships.

Foundation Officials
Edward E. Birch: president
Robert R. Fredrickson: director
R. Bruce McFadden: director

Grants Analysis
Disclosure Period: fiscal year ending August 31, 2004
Total Grants: $1,129,100
Number of Grants: 32
Average Grant: $2,728*
Highest Grant: $500,000
Lowest Grant: $100
Typical Range: $1,000 to $5,000
*Note: Average grant figure excludes three highest grants ($1,050,000).

Recent Grants
Note: Grants derived from 2004 Form 990.
General

500,000	UCSB Foundation, Santa Barbara, CA -- support for construction of alumni house
250,000	Wilmer Eye Institute, Baltimore, MD -- support for Mosher center for cataract & corneal disease
200,000	Marymount School, Santa Barbara, CA -- for new science building
26,000	Community Music Arts Association, Santa Barbara, CA
26,000	Goleta Valley Cottage Hospital, Santa Barbara, CA -- sponsorship for tournament
25,800	Opera Santa Barbara, Santa Barbara, CA -- sponsorship for production of Faust and other event
20,000	Halderman Endowment Fund, Goleta, CA -- capital campaign for La Patera school
20,000	Santa Barbara Symphony, Santa Barbara, CA -- sponsorship for philharmonic concert
15,000	United Boys & Girls Club of Santa Barbara, Goleta, CA -- sponsorship for golf tournament
10,000	Westmont College Foundation, Santa Barbara, CA -- sponsorship for fund raising event

FINIS M. MOSS CHARITABLE TRUST

Giving Contact
Donald B. Russell, Co-Trustee
108 W. Walnut
Nevada, MO 64772
Phone: (417)667-6616
Fax: (417)667-3013

Description
Founded: 1975
EIN: 237451729
Organization Type: Private Foundation
Giving Locations: MO; NV
Grant Types: Capital, Operating Expenses.

Donor Information
Founder: the late Finis M. Moss

Financial Summary
Gifts Received: $64,116 (fiscal year ending March 31, 1997)

Typical Recipients
Arts & Humanities: Historic Preservation, History & Archaeology, Libraries
Civic & Public Affairs: Chambers of Commerce, Clubs, Economic Development, Civic & Public Affairs-General, Municipalities/Towns, Safety, Urban & Community Affairs
Education: Arts/Humanities Education, Business Education, Colleges & Universities, Education-General, Literacy, Preschool Education, Private Education (Precollege), Public Education (Precollege), Science/Mathematics Education, Student Aid
Environment: Environment-General, Resource Conservation, Wildlife Protection
Health: Cancer, Children's Health/Hospitals, Clinics/Medical Centers, Emergency/Ambulance Services, Health Organizations, Hospitals, Nursing Services
Religion: Religious Welfare
Social Services: Animal Protection, Child Welfare, Community Service Organizations, Crime Prevention, Day Care, Delinquency & Criminal Rehabilitation, Emergency Relief, Family Services, Food/Clothing Distribution, People with Disabilities, Recreation & Athletics, Scouts, Social Services-General, United Funds/United Ways, YMCA/YWCA/YMHA/YWHA

Application Procedures
Initial Contact: Application form required.
Deadlines: January 31.

Foundation Officials
Lee Gilbert: co-trustee
Robert Lasley: co-trustee
Donald B. Russell: co-trustee PRIM CORP EMPL chairman, director: Farm & Home Savings Association.

Grants Analysis
Disclosure Period: fiscal year ending March 31, 2000
Total Grants: $367,196*
Number of Grants: 30
Average Grant: $5,971*
Highest Grant: $100,000
Typical Range: $1,000 to $10,000
*Note: Giving excludes United Way. Average grant excludes 2 highest grants ($200,000).

Recent Grants
Note: Grants derived from 2001 Form 990.
General

130,000	City of Nevada, Nevada, MO -- for capital improvements
100,000	YMCA, Nevada, MO -- for capital improvements
55,000	Crowder College, Neosho, MO -- for scholarships
50,000	Vernon County Ambulance, Nevada, MO -- for capital improvements
40,025	Stockton Nursing Home, Stockton, MO -- for capital improvement
25,000	Bronaugh Com Fire Protection Association, Bronaugh, MO -- for capital improvement
14,000	Cottey College, Nevada, MO -- for scholarships
11,358	Council on Families in Crisis, Nevada, MO -- for capital improvements
10,500	Ozark Area Girl Scout Council, Joplin, MO -- for capital improvements
10,000	Chamber of Commerce, Nevada, MO -- for public address system

MOTOROLA INC.

Company Headquarters
1303 E. Algonquin Rd.
Schaumburg, IL 60196
Web: http://www.mot.com

Company Description
Founded: 1928
Ticker: MOT
Exchange: NYSE
Revenue: US$35.349 billion (2004)
Profit: US$1.532 billion (2004)
Employees: 97000 (2003)

Fortune Rank: 49, per FORTUNE Magazine's list of 500 Largest U.S. Corporations (2004).

Nonmonetary Support

Type: Donated Equipment; Donated Products
Note: NOT NOT Nonmonetary support is provided by the company.
Volunteer Programs: The company sponsors volunteer programs that enable employees to support local organizations and schools in their communities. The foundation sponsors a volunteer grants program.

Motorola Foundation

Giving Contact

Judy Adkins, Program Administrator
1303 E Algonquin Rd.
Schaumburg, IL 60196
Phone: (847)576-6200
Fax: (847)576-3997
Web: http://fdncenter.org

Description

EIN: 366109323
Organization Type: Corporate Foundation
Giving Locations: headquarters community, plant locations, and to select national organizations.
Grant Types: Capital, Employee Matching Gifts, General Support, Multiyear/Continuing Support, Project, Scholarship.
Note: The foundation offers employee matching gift programs.

Financial Summary

Total Giving: $9,078,537 (2003); $8,953,407 (2002); $11,014,049 (2001). Note: Contributes through corporate direct giving program and foundation.
Assets: $75,346,301 (2003); $71,735,721 (2002); $92,648,562 (2001)
Gifts Received: $10,293,125 (1993); $5,107,670 (1992). Note: Contributions are received from Motorola, Inc.

Typical Recipients

Arts & Humanities: Arts Associations & Councils, Arts Funds, Arts Institutes, Dance, Ethnic & Folk Arts, Libraries, Museums/Galleries, Music, Opera, Performing Arts, Public Broadcasting, Theater
Civic & Public Affairs: African American Affairs, Asian American Affairs, Business/Free Enterprise, Civil Rights, Clubs, Economic Development, Economic Policy, Employment/Job Training, Civic & Public Affairs-General, Hispanic Affairs, Housing, Law & Justice, Legal Aid, Nonprofit Management, Philanthropic Organizations, Professional & Trade Associations, Public Policy, Safety, Urban & Community Affairs, Women's Affairs, Zoos/Aquariums
Education: Afterschool/Enrichment Programs, Agricultural Education, Business Education, Colleges & Universities, Community & Junior Colleges, Continuing Education, Economic Education, Education Associations, Education Funds, Elementary Education (Private), Engineering/Technological Education, Education-General, Gifted & Talented Programs, Literacy, Minority Education, Private Education (Precollege), Public Education (Precollege), Science/Mathematics Education, Student Aid, Vocational & Technical Education
Environment: Environment-General, Protection, Research
Health: Clinics/Medical Centers, Emergency/Ambulance Services, Hospices, Hospitals, Single-Disease Health Associations
International: Foreign Educational Institutions, International-General, Health Care/Hospitals, International Affairs, International Organizations, International Relief Efforts
Religion: Ministries, Religious Welfare
Science: Science-General, Observatories & Planetariums, Science Exhibits & Fairs, Science Museums,

Scientific Centers & Institutes
Social Services: Child Welfare, Community Service Organizations, Counseling, Crime Prevention, Domestic Violence, Emergency Relief, Family Services, Food/Clothing Distribution, People with Disabilities, Recreation & Athletics, Senior Services, Shelters/Homelessness, Substance Abuse, United Funds/United Ways, Volunteer Services, YMCA/YWCA/YMHA/YWHA, Youth Organizations

Application Procedures

Initial Contact: Submit a query letter of no more than two pages. An Eligibility Quiz is available at www.cybergrants.com/motorola/quiz.
Application Requirements: Query letters should provide a description of goals and objectives of the organization or program; geographic and demographics served by the organization; name, address, and telephone number of the chief executive officer; amount requested; and proof of tax-exempt status.
Deadlines: June 30 for Illinois and national programs; local operating locations have various deadlines.
Notes: Specific deadlines for local requests can be obtained by contacting the Community Relations Representative at the following operating locations:
1303 E. Algonquin Road, Schaumburg, IL 60196; (847) 576-6200 (National headquarters).
1301 N. Algonquin Road, Schaumburg, IL 60196; (847) 538-4041 (Northwest suburbs).
1475 W. Shure Drive, Arlington Heights, IL 60004; (847) 632-6021.
3102 N. 56th Street, Phoenix, AZ 85018; (602) 952-4022.
1500 Gateway Blvd., Boynton Beach, FL 33426; (561) 739-8658.
8000 W. Sunrise Blvd., Plantation, FL 33322; (954) 739-2238.
6501 Wm. Gannon Drive, Austin, TX 78735; (512) 895-8866.
5555 N. Beach Street, Ft. Worth, TX 76137; (817) 245-2102.
National requests should be sent to the foundation; regional requests should be sent to operating facility in area.
International requests are accepted. However, the Motorola Foundation only accepts international grant requests from the Motorola facility within that country. A global giving priority is to fund in those areas where Motorola has a significant presence. If a Community Relations Representative from an area is not listed above, contact Schaumburg National Headquarters at the above phone number for more information.

Restrictions

Foundation does not fund individuals, including scholarship or other forms of financial assistance; political or lobbying groups, candidates or campaigns; endowment funds; sports sponsorships; fund-raising events, conferences or benefits, including sponsorships, dinners, tickets, or courtesy advertising; national health organizations or their local chapters; single-disease health organizations; capital fund drives; trade schools; or private foundations described under IRS Code Section 509(a).
The foundation does not lease or donate Motorola products or equipment.

Additional Information

Grants are made on an annual basis only with no renewals implied.
Publications: Guidelines

Corporate Officials

Edward J. Zander: chairman, chief executive officer B 1947. ED Boston University MS; Rensselaer Polytechnic Institute BS. PRIM CORP EMPL chairman, chief executive officer: Motorola Inc. NONPR AFFIL director: Jason Foundation for Education; science advisory board: Rensselaer Polytechnic Institute; director: The Executives Club of Chicago; member advisory

board: Boston University School Management; director: The Economics Club of Chicago.

Foundation Officials

Gene Delaney: vice president
Steve Earhart: vice president
Carol Forsyte: assistant secretary ED Rutgers University BA; University of California JD.
Glenn Gienko: vice president
Anthony Knapp: vice president
A. Peter Lawson: secretary ED Cartmough College AB; Columbia University JD. NONPR AFFIL member: Illinois State Bar; member: New York State Bar Association; member: Association of General Counsel; member: Chief Legal Officer Roundtable.
Garth Leroy Milne: president, treasurer B Saint George, UT 1942. ED University of Utah BS (1966); Harvard University MBA (1968).
Dennis A. Roberson: vice president, director ED Washington State University BS (1971); Stanford University MS (1974). CORP AFFIL director: Zarlink. NONPR AFFIL advisory board: A STAR; member: TCC Technology Advisory Council; advisory board: National Institute of Information and Communications Technology; director: FIRST; vice provost: Illinois Institute of Technology.
Caroline T. Swinney: assistant secretary, foundation manager

Grants Analysis

Disclosure Period: calendar year ending 2003
Total Grants: $6,350,280*
Number of Grants: 507
Average Grant: $5,557*
Highest Grant: $900,000
Lowest Grant: $150
Typical Range: $1,000 to $25,000 and $100,000 to $900,000
*Note: Giving excludes matching gifts, scholarship and United Way. Average grant excludes four highest grants ($3,600,000).

Recent Grants

Note: Grants derived from 2003 Form 990.
Library-Related
20,000	California State Library Foundation: Governor's Book Fund, Sacramento, CA

General
900,000	MIT, Cambridge, MA
900,000	MIT, Cambridge, MA
900,000	MIT, Cambridge, MA
900,000	MIT, Cambridge, MA
500,000	United Way/Crusade of Mercy Inc., Chicago, IL
300,000	Georgia Tech Foundation, Atlanta, GA
250,000	China Youth Development Foundation
200,000	Arizona State University, Tempe, AZ
189,135	National Merit Scholarship Corporation, Evanston, IL
125,000	Junior Achievement of Chicago, Chicago, IL

CHARLES STEWART MOTT FOUNDATION

Giving Contact

Office of Proposal Entry
Mott Foundation Building
503 S. Saginaw Street, Suite 1200
Flint, MI 48502-1851
Phone: (810)238-5651
Fax: (810)766-1753
E-mail: info@mott.org
Web: http://www.mott.org

Alternate Contact

Charles Stewart Mott Foundation
100 Cambridge Grove

Fifth Floor, Cambridge House
Hammersmith
London W6 OLE, United Kingdom

Description

Founded: 1926
EIN: 381211227
Organization Type: General Purpose Foundation
Giving Locations: MI: Flint internationally; nationally.
Grant Types: Conference/Seminar, General Support, Matching, Multiyear/Continuing Support, Operating Expenses, Seed Money.
Note: Also provides technical assistance.

Donor Information

Founder: Charles Stewart Mott, an industrialist, established the foundation in Flint, MI, in 1926. From his earliest years in his adopted community, Mr. Mott was concerned with the city's welfare, and served two years as mayor. He also served as chairman of U.S. Sugar Corporation, president of the Northern Illinois Water Company, director of and one of the largest individual stockholders in General Motors, a principal stockholder in the Continental Water Company, and a trustee of Stevens Institute of Technology. Mr. Mott also started a medical and dental clinic for children and helped establish the YMCA and the Boy Scouts in Flint, as well as the Whaley Children's Center. Mr. Mott died in 1973. His son, Charles Stewart Harding Mott, guided the foundation from its earliest days until his death in 1989.

Financial Summary

Total Giving: $99,979,943 (2003); $109,110,205 (2002); $129,745,474 (2001)
Assets: $2,373,230,912 (2003); $2,013,895,612 (2002); $2,470,000,000 (2001 approx)
Gifts Received: $6,714 (1998). Note: In 1998, contributions were received from Herold W. Parker.

Typical Recipients

Arts & Humanities: Arts Centers, Arts & Humanities-General, Libraries, Public Broadcasting
Civic & Public Affairs: African American Affairs, Business/Free Enterprise, Civil Rights, Community Foundations, Economic Development, Economic Policy, Employment/Job Training, Civic & Public Affairs-General, Hispanic Affairs, Housing, Inner-City Development, Law & Justice, Legal Aid, Native American Affairs, Nonprofit Management, Philanthropic Organizations, Professional & Trade Associations, Public Policy, Rural Affairs, Safety, Urban & Community Affairs, Women's Affairs
Education: Afterschool/Enrichment Programs, Business Education, Colleges & Universities, Community & Junior Colleges, Education Associations, Education Funds, Education Reform, Engineering/Technological Education, Faculty Development, Education-General, International Exchange, International Studies, Leadership Training, Minority Education, Public Education (Precollege), Science/Mathematics Education, Social Sciences Education, Vocational & Technical Education
Environment: Energy, Environment-General, Protection, Resource Conservation, Watershed
Health: AIDS/HIV, Health Policy/Cost Containment, Health Funds, Home-Care Services, Public Health, Research/Studies Institutes
International: Foreign Educational Institutions, International-General, Human Rights, International Affairs, International Development, International Environmental Issues, International Organizations, International Peace & Security Issues, International Relations, International Relief Efforts
Religion: Religious Welfare
Science: Scientific Centers & Institutes
Social Services: At-Risk Youth, Child Welfare, Community Centers, Community Service Organizations, Crime Prevention, Day Care, Emergency Relief, Family Planning, Family Services, People with Disabilities, Scouts, Social Services-General, Substance Abuse, United Funds/United Ways, Volunteer Services, Youth Organizations

Application Procedures

Initial Contact: The foundation has no formal grant application procedure or application form. Letters of inquiry, including a brief description of the project and the range of the needed funding, are acceptable for initial contact.
Application Requirements: Formal proposals should contain the following: a cover letter detailing the amount of money requested for a specified grant period that is signed by the person ultimately responsible for signing grant contracts on behalf of grant applicant; the project description, including an explanation of why the project is needed, who will be served, and what will be accomplished during a specific period; information on the feasibility and sustainability of the proposed grant activity; information on lasting benefits to the organization, program participants, the community, or other organizations working in the field; an appropriate plan for evaluation, reporting, and dissemination; a documented line-item budget and projected sources of funds for the proposed grant period; information about the organization seeking funds, including its staff, board of directors, legal classification, and history and accomplishments. Applicants will also be required to submit copies of their annual report and audited financial statements or IRS Form 990.
Deadlines: None. The foundation strongly encourages applicants to submit proposals during the first quarter of the year for which funding is requested. Grant funds for any year are committed by September 1 of that year.
The entire review process takes up to four months from proposal receipt; therefore, proposals should be submitted at least four months prior to the start of the proposed grant period.
Review Process: Proposals are reviewed by program staff for initial recommendation of denial or approval. The proposal review committee, composed of senior management, makes the final recommendation. The proposal may then be approved by the president under delegated authority or referred to the board of trustees, which meets quarterly, for further action.
Notes: To prevent conflict-of-interest problems, grant applicants should not route proposals through trustees or solicit their assistance. Trustees are prohibited from voting on grant proposals where they have a conflict of interest. Because of the large number of requests, foundation visits, unless by invitation, are discouraged. Requests for meetings with foundation trustees and staff will be initiated only by the foundation.
Video tapes are discouraged and will not be returned.

Restrictions

The foundation does not make grants or loans to individuals or for religious activities or programs that serve a specific religious group. Outside the Flint, MI, area, the foundation makes capital and endowment grants only when necessary to carry out other foundation objectives, and grants are not made for local projects unless the projects are part of a national demonstration or foundation-planned network of grants and have clear and significant implications for replication in other communities. The foundation does not support research except when it is instrumental for other grant-making purposes or for strengthening relevant public policy. It does not provide ongoing support for projects normally supported or which should be supported by taxpayers. The foundation also does not grant scholarships.

Additional Information

The foundation occasionally considers activities of a non-grant nature that help to achieve program objectives. These may include program-related investments, direct technical or fund-raising assistance, research, and the dissemination of findings. Most foundation grants are for up to one year, although applicants may submit multi-year proposals.
To receive publications without charge, call the hotline at (800) 645-1766 (US/Canada) or (414) 273-6943 (elsewhere).
Publications: Annual Report; Facts on Grants; Guidelines; Quarterly Newsletter; Grant Listings by Program

Foundation Officials

A. Marshall Acuff, Jr.: trustee ED University of Michigan MBA. CORP AFFIL director: Owens & Minor Inc. NONPR AFFIL director: Virginia Foundation for Independent Colleges; director: Virginia Theological Seminary; director: Lewis Ginter Botanical Garden; director: Sweet Briar College; director: Endowment Association of the College of William & Mary; director: Jamestown-Yorktown Foundation Inc.; director: Community Foundation of Richmond.
Gavin T. Clabaugh: vice president information services ED University of Houston MS; University of Kansas BA.
Donald F. Dahlstrom: senior communications officer
Lois R. DeBacker: program director, environment
Neal R. Hegarty: program officer
Rushworth Moulton Kidder: trustee B Providence, RI 1944. ED Amherst College BA (1965); Columbia University MA (1966); Columbia University PhD (1969). NONPR AFFIL president, founder: Institute Global Ethics; member board director: Principia College; member values & ethics committee: Independent Sector; advisor counselor: Character Education Partnership; member advisory council: Friends of the University of Natal.
Jimmy L. Krause: director grants administration, assistant treasurer
Marilyn Stein LeFeber: vice president communications ED Benedictine University MA; Ohio University BA. NONPR AFFIL member, media & public affairs committee: Council on Foundations Inc..
Tiffany W. Lovett: trustee
Webb Franklin Martin: trustee B Flint, MI 1944. ED Michigan State University (1966); Wayne State University JD (1969). PRIM CORP EMPL senior vice president: Bank One Corp. NONPR AFFIL trustee: Mott's Children Health Center; member: MSU Beaumont Tower Society.
Olivia P. Maynard: trustee ED George Washington University BA (1959); University of Michigan MSW (1971). NONPR AFFIL president: Planned Parenthood of Michigan; board of regents: University Michigan; president: The Michigan Prospect.
John Morning: trustee B Cleveland, OH 1932. ED Pratt Institute BFA (1955). PRIM CORP EMPL president: John Morning Design. NONPR AFFIL member, board director: New York Landmarks Conservancy; chairman: Vivian Beaumont Theater; member education committee: Museum Modern Art; vice chairman: New York City Cultural Affairs Advisory Committee; director: Association Government Boards, Colleges & Universities; trustee: City University New York; member: American Academy Dramatic Arts; member: American Institute Graphic Arts.
Maryanne T. Mott: trustee NONPR AFFIL director: Trout Headwaters Inc..
Phillip Peters: vice president administration, secretary-treasurer
William H. Piper: vice chairman, trustee B Flint, MI 1933. ED Yale University BA (1955). NONPR AFFIL member advisory board professional corporate: University Michigan Flint. CLUB AFFIL University Club; Flint Golf Club.
John W. Porter: trustee B Fort Wayne, IN 1931. ED Albion College BA (1953); Michigan State University MA (1957); Michigan State University PhD (1962). PRIM NONPR EMPL chief executive officer: Urban Education Alliance Inc. NONPR AFFIL member: Sigma Pi Phi; member: Tuskeegee Airmen; member: National Measurement Council; member: Phi Delta Kappa; honorary life member: Michigan Parent Teachers Association; life member: NAACP; member: Michigan Martin Luther King Junior Holiday Com-

mission; director: Michigan Congress Parents & Teachers; member: Michigan Governments Blue Ribbon Commission Welfare Reform; member: Catherine McAuley Health Systems Board; trustee: East Lansing Edgewood United Church; member: East Lansing Human Relations Commission. CLUB AFFIL Economic Club.

Jean Simi: executive assistant, corporate assistant secretary

Michael J. Smith: assistant vice president investments

Maureen H. Smyth: vice president programs NONPR AFFIL member, advisory cabinet: Council of Michigan Foundations.

Marise M.M. Stewart: trustee

Robert E. Swaney, Jr.: vice president, chief investment officer

Claire Mott White: trustee

William Samuel White: chairman, president, chief executive officer, trustee B Cincinnati, OH 1937. ED Dartmouth College BA (1959); Dartmouth College MBA (1960). CORP AFFIL chairman: US Sugar Corp.; director: American Water Works Co. Inc. NONPR AFFIL chairman: Flint Area Focus Council; director: Independent Sector; director: European Foundation Center; director: Civicus.

Grants Analysis

Disclosure Period: calendar year ending 2003
Total Grants: $99,979,943
Number of Grants: 501
Average Grant: $199,561
Highest Grant: $4,000,000
Lowest Grant: $5,000
Typical Range: $25,000 to $500,000

Recent Grants

Note: Grants derived from 2002 Form 990.

General

2,000,000	Community Foundation of Greater Flint, Flint, MI -- to improve the quality of life
2,000,000	Conservation Fund, Arlington, VA -- towards conservation of costal and fresh water
1,881,584	National Center for Community Education, Flint, MI -- to support training and technical assistance
1,646,218	Flint Cultural Center Corporation Inc., Flint, MI -- to support a complex of performing and visual arts
1,580,500	Afterschool Alliance, Washington, DC -- towards afterschool program
1,248,541	Public/Private Ventures, Philadelphia, PA -- towards responsible fatherhood among young and low-income fathers
1,051,050	Children's Aid Society, New York, NY -- towards teen pregnancy prevention program
1,020,000	Mathematica Policy Research Inc., Princeton, NJ -- towards afterschool program
1,000,000	Focus HOPE, Detroit, MI -- to establish a fund to provide tuition loans
975,000	Regents of the University of Michigan, Flint, MI -- towards land acquisition for university campus

MUCHNIC FOUNDATION

Giving Contact

David C. Mize, Secretary
104 S. Cascade Ave., Suite 202
Colorado Springs, CO 80903-5102
Phone: (913)367-4164

Alternate Contact

704 North 4th Street
PO Box 329
Atchison, KS 66002

Description

Founded: 1946
EIN: 486102818
Organization Type: Private Foundation
Giving Locations: CO
Grant Types: General Support.

Donor Information

Founder: Valley Co., the late Helen Q. Muchnic, the late H. E. Muchnic

Financial Summary

Total Giving: $381,000 (fiscal year ending November 30, 2004); $407,700 (fiscal 2001). Note: 1997 Giving includes United Way ($10,000).
Giving Analysis: Giving for fiscal 2001 includes: foundation grants to United Way ($10,000)
Assets: $8,801,319 (fiscal 2004); $9,221,320 (fiscal 2001)

Typical Recipients

Arts & Humanities: Arts Associations & Councils, Arts Funds, History & Archaeology, Libraries, Museums/Galleries, Performing Arts
Civic & Public Affairs: Clubs, Municipalities/Towns, Urban & Community Affairs
Education: Agricultural Education, Arts/Humanities Education, Colleges & Universities, Education Funds, Education Reform, Engineering/Technological Education, Environmental Education, Education-General, International Studies, Literacy, Preschool Education, Private Education (Precollege), Public Education (Precollege), Religious Education, Student Aid
Environment: Environment-General, Resource Conservation, Wildlife Protection
Health: Alzheimer's Disease, Arthritis, Cancer, Children's Health/Hospitals, Hospitals, Prenatal Health Issues, Research/Studies Institutes, Single-Disease Health Associations
International: Health Care/Hospitals, International Environmental Issues, International Organizations, International Relief Efforts
Religion: Churches, Ministries, Religious Welfare
Science: Science Museums
Social Services: Animal Protection, Child Welfare, Community Centers, Community Service Organizations, Scouts, Substance Abuse, United Funds/United Ways, YMCA/YWCA/YMHA/YWHA, Youth Organizations

Application Procedures

Initial Contact: The foundation has no formal grant application procedure or application form. Send a brief letter of inquiry.
Deadlines: October 31.

Foundation Officials

Elizabeth M. Elicker: trustee
Ann Mize: director
David C. Mize: secretary
Daphne Nan Muchnic: director

Grants Analysis

Disclosure Period: fiscal year ending November 30, 2004
Total Grants: $381,000
Number of Grants: 61
Average Grant: $5,271*
Highest Grant: $35,000
Lowest Grant: $1,000
Typical Range: $1,000 to $10,000
***Note:** Average grant figure excludes two highest grants ($70,000).

Recent Grants

Note: Grants derived from fiscal 2004 Form 990.
General

35,000	Kansas University Endowment Association, Lawrence, KS
20,000	Saint Francis Academy, Atchison, KS
15,000	African Wildlife, Washington, DC
15,000	Benedictine College, Atchison, KS
15,000	Kansas State Engineering Department, Manhattan, KS
10,000	Atchison Area United Way, Atchison, KS
10,000	Colorado University Foundation, Boulder, CO
10,000	Cystic Fibrosis Foundation, Colorado Springs, CO
10,000	Duke University, Durham, NC
10,000	Komen Breast Cancer Foundation, Dallas, TX

JANE T. MUHLETHALER FOUNDATION, INC.

Giving Contact

James D. Funnell, Jr., Secretary
Care of Hermenze & Marcantonio
19 Ludlow Road, Suite 101
Westport, CT 06880
Phone: (203)226-6552

Description

Founded: 1997
EIN: 061481432
Organization Type: Private Foundation
Giving Locations: CT: Lower Fairfield County, Norwalk, Wilton
Grant Types: Operating Expenses.

Financial Summary

Total Giving: $101,800 (2003); $120,269 (2001)
Assets: $2,174,571 (2003); $1,952,787 (2001)
Gifts Received: $250,000 (2003); $1,924,401 (1997)

Typical Recipients

Arts & Humanities: Libraries
Civic & Public Affairs: Civic & Public Affairs-General
Education: Colleges & Universities, Education Funds
Health: Cancer, Emergency/Ambulance Services, Health Funds, Home-Care Services, Hospitals, Long-Term Care
Social Services: People with Disabilities, Social Services-General, YMCA/YWCA/YMHA/YWHA

Application Procedures

Initial Contact: Send a brief letter of inquiry and a full proposal
Application Requirements: Include a description of organization, amount requested, and purpose of funds sought.
Deadlines: November 1; preference for October submissions.

Restrictions

The foundation restricts its giving to nonprofit organizations located in lower Fairfield County, CT, with preference given to organizations serving Wilton and Norwalk, CT.

Foundation Officials

James D. Funnell, Jr.: secretary
William P. Middeleer: vice president
Jane T. Muhlethaler: president

Grants Analysis

Disclosure Period: calendar year ending 2003
Total Grants: $101,800

Number of Grants: 10
Average Grant: $8,533*
Highest Grant: $25,000
Lowest Grant: $2,500
Typical Range: $5,000 to $15,000
*****Note:** Average grant figure excludes highest grant.

Recent Grants

Note: Grants derived from 2003 Form 990.
Library-Related
5,100	Mark Twain Library, Redding, CT
5,100	Wilton Library Association Inc., Wilton, CT

General
25,000	Nursing & Home Care Inc., Wilton, CT
15,000	Fidelco Guide Dog Foundation Inc., Bloomfield, CT
15,000	University of Connecticut Foundation Inc., Storrs, CT
14,500	Wilton Ambulance Corps., Wilton, CT
9,500	Planned Lifetime Assistance Network of Connecticut Inc., West Hartford, CT
5,100	Wilton Interfaith Council, Wilton, CT
5,000	Norwalk Hospital Foundation, Norwalk, CT
2,500	Redding Social Service, Redding, CT

MULCAHY FOUNDATION

Giving Contact
Robert D. Lohse, President
2440 E. Broadway
Tucson, AZ 85719
Phone: (520)791-3939

Description
Founded: 1957
EIN: 866053461
Organization Type: Private Foundation
Giving Locations: AZ: emphasis on the Tucson area
Grant Types: Capital, Emergency, Endowment, General Support, Multiyear/Continuing Support, Operating Expenses, Project, Research.

Donor Information
Founder: the late John A. Mulcahy, Mulcahy Lumber Co.

Financial Summary
Total Giving: $120,940 (fiscal year ending June 30, 2002); $131,300 (fiscal 2001)
Assets: $2,193,579 (fiscal 2002); $2,138,335 (fiscal 2001)
Gifts Received: $125,000 (fiscal 1999); $25,000 (fiscal 1992). Note: In fiscal 1999, contributions were received from Calistri Foundation.

Typical Recipients
Arts & Humanities: Community Arts, History & Archaeology, Libraries, Museums/Galleries, Opera, Performing Arts, Theater
Civic & Public Affairs: Clubs, Civic & Public Affairs-General, Hispanic Affairs
Education: Arts/Humanities Education, Colleges & Universities, Community & Junior Colleges, Economic Education, Education Reform, Environmental Education, Education-General, Medical Education, Public Education (Precollege), Religious Education, Science/Mathematics Education, Student Aid
Health: Cancer
Religion: Churches, Religious Welfare
Social Services: Community Service Organizations, Crime Prevention, Food/Clothing Distribution, United Funds/United Ways, YMCA/YWCA/YMHA/YWHA, Youth Organizations

Application Procedures
Initial Contact: Requests should be brief and informal with a proposed budget and a copy of the organization's IRS determination letter attached.
Deadlines: None.

Restrictions
Most grants are for educational purposes. Does not support individuals.

Foundation Officials
Ashby I. Lohse: secretary
Florence Lohse: vice president
Kathy Lohse: treasurer
Linda Lohse: secretary, treasurer
Robert D. Lohse: president
Carmen Moline: treasurer

Grants Analysis
Disclosure Period: fiscal year ending June 30, 2002
Total Grants: $120,940
Number of Grants: 11
Average Grant: $4,721*
Highest Grant: $73,735
Lowest Grant: $1,000
Typical Range: $1,000 to $10,000
*****Note:** Average grant figure excludes highest grant.

Recent Grants
Note: Grants derived from fiscal 2002 Form 990.
General
73,735	University of Arizona, Tucson, AZ -- education
14,125	Pima Community College Foundation, Tucson, AZ -- education
10,000	Fox Tucson Theatre Foundation, Tucson, AZ -- for community historic preservation
6,380	Northern Arizona University, Flagstaff, AZ -- education
4,200	Pima Community College, Tucson, AZ -- education
2,500	Afro-American Historical and Genealogical Society, Green Valley, AZ -- education
2,500	Arizona State University, Tempe, AZ -- education
2,500	Barbea Williams Performing Company, Tucson, AZ -- education
2,000	Educational Enrichment Foundation, Tucson, AZ -- education
2,000	Life Long Learning, Inc., Phoenix, AZ -- education

CLARENCE E. MULFORD TRUST

Giving Contact
David R. Hastings, Jr., Trustee
PO Box 290
Fryeburg, ME 04037
Phone: (207)935-2061
Fax: (207)935-3939
E-mail: hlo@landmarknet.net

Description
Founded: 1950
EIN: 010247548
Organization Type: Private Foundation
Giving Locations: ME: Fryeburg and neighboring towns
Grant Types: General Support.

Donor Information
Founder: the late Clarence E. Mulford

Typical Recipients
Arts & Humanities: Arts Institutes, Historic Preservation, History & Archaeology, Libraries, Music

Civic & Public Affairs: Clubs, Civic & Public Affairs-General, Municipalities/Towns, Urban & Community Affairs, Women's Affairs
Education: Business Education, Colleges & Universities, Education-General, Literacy, Private Education (Precollege), Public Education (Precollege)
Environment: Resource Conservation
Health: Health Organizations, Hospices, Hospitals
Religion: Churches, Religious Organizations
Social Services: Animal Protection, Community Service Organizations, Recreation & Athletics, Scouts, Senior Services, Youth Organizations

Application Procedures
Initial Contact: Send a brief letter of inquiry. Include a description of organization, amount requested, purpose of funds sought, recently audited financial statement, and proof of tax-exempt status.
Deadlines: January 10 and July 10.

Restrictions
Does not support individuals or provide loans, matching gifts, or scholarships.

Foundation Officials
David R. Hastings, II: trustee
Peter G. Hastings: trustee

Grants Analysis
Disclosure Period: calendar year ending 2000
Total Grants: $441,360
Number of Grants: 30
Average Grant: $5,616*
Highest Grant: $278,510
Typical Range: $1,000 to $10,000
*****Note:** Average grant figure excludes highest grant.

Recent Grants
Note: Grants derived from 2001 Form 990.
Library-Related
3,300	Library Club of Lovell, Lovell, ME -- for public library purposes

General
289,311	Fryeburg Academy, Fryeburg, ME -- for educational purposes
97,650	Town of Fryeburg, Fryeburg, ME -- municipal purposes
12,500	Fryeburg Rescue Association, Inc., Fryeburg, ME -- for charitable purposes
5,000	Paugus Grange 540, Fryeburg, ME -- for charitable purposes
5,000	First Congregational Church of Fryeburg, Fryeburg, ME -- for religious purposes
5,000	St. Elizabeth Ann Seton Church, Fryeburg, ME -- for religious purposes
4,500	Frank W. Shaw Post 137 American Legion, Fryeburg, ME -- for charitable purposes
3,000	Brownfield Community Church, Brownfield, ME -- for religious purposes
3,000	Gibson Center for Senior Services, Inc., North Conway, NH -- for charitable purposes
2,500	Church of the New Jerusalem, Fryeburg, ME -- for religious purposes

J. K. MULLEN FOUNDATION

Giving Contact
John F. Malo, President & Director
333 Logan St., Suite 100
Denver, CO 80203
Phone: (303)722-3557

Description
Founded: 1924
EIN: 846002475

Organization Type: Private Foundation
Giving Locations: CO: Denver
Grant Types: General Support.

Donor Information

Founder: the late John K. Mullen, the late Catherine S. Mullen, the J. K. Mullen Co.

Financial Summary

Total Giving: $303,075 (fiscal year ending July 31, 2002)
Assets: $4,523,200 (fiscal 2002); $5,252,432 (fiscal 2001)

Typical Recipients

Arts & Humanities: Arts Associations & Councils, Libraries, Museums/Galleries, Music, Opera, Public Broadcasting
Civic & Public Affairs: Botanical Gardens/Parks, Employment/Job Training, Civic & Public Affairs-General, Native American Affairs, Public Policy, Women's Affairs, Zoos/Aquariums
Education: Business Education, Colleges & Universities, Economic Education, Education-General, Health & Physical Education, Leadership Training, Private Education (Precollege), Public Education (Precollege), Religious Education, Secondary Education (Public)
Environment: Environment-General
Health: AIDS/HIV, Children's Health/Hospitals, Health Organizations, Hospices, Hospitals, Hospitals (University Affiliated), Medical Rehabilitation, Mental Health, Multiple Sclerosis, Preventive Medicine/Wellness Organizations, Public Health, Single-Disease Health Associations
Religion: Churches, Religious Organizations, Religious Welfare, Seminaries, Social/Policy Issues
Science: Science Museums
Social Services: Animal Protection, Big Brothers/Big Sisters, Child Welfare, Community Service Organizations, Domestic Violence, Food/Clothing Distribution, Homes, People with Disabilities, Senior Services, Substance Abuse, Volunteer Services, Youth Organizations

Application Procedures

Initial Contact: Send a letter of application.
Application Requirements: Include a description of organization, amount requested, purpose of funds sought, current financial statements, and proof of tax-exempt status.
Deadlines: June 1.

Restrictions

Does not support individuals or organizations that do not have federally approved tax-exempt status.

Foundation Officials

J. Kenneth Malo, Jr.: director
John F. Malo: president, director
Kathleen Malo: director
Timothy M. O'Connor: secretary, director
Sheila Sevier: director
Heather Weckbaugh: director
John K. Weckbaugh: vice president, director
Walter S. Weckbaugh: treasurer, director

Grants Analysis

Disclosure Period: fiscal year ending July 31, 2002
Total Grants: $303,075
Number of Grants: 60
Average Grant: $5,051
Highest Grant: $30,000
Lowest Grant: $1,000
Typical Range: $1,000 to $10,000

Recent Grants

Note: Grants derived from 2002 Form 990.
General

30,000	Regis High School, Aurora, CO
25,000	Denver Academy, Denver, CO
20,000	J.K. Mullen High School, Denver, CO
15,000	St. Mary's Academy, Denver, CO
10,000	Bayaud Industries, Denver, CO
10,000	Colorado Academy, Denver, CO
10,000	Graland Country Day School, Denver, CO
10,000	Havern Center, Lakewood, CO
10,000	Kent Denver School, Cherry Hills Village, CO
10,000	Little Sisters of the Poor, Denver, CO

W. B. MUNSON FOUNDATION TRUST

Giving Contact

Norma Farrer
c/o Bank One, Texas, NA
200 N. Travis
Sherman, TX 75090-5961
Phone: (903)868-0701

Description

Founded: 1943
EIN: 756015068
Organization Type: Private Foundation
Giving Locations: TX: Grayson County with focus on Denison
Grant Types: Capital, Endowment, Operating Expenses, Scholarship.

Typical Recipients

Arts & Humanities: Arts Outreach, Community Arts, Film & Video, Historic Preservation, History & Archaeology, Libraries, Museums/Galleries, Music, Performing Arts
Civic & Public Affairs: Clubs, Community Foundations, Civic & Public Affairs-General, Housing, Municipalities/Towns, Urban & Community Affairs
Education: Arts/Humanities Education, Business Education, Colleges & Universities, Engineering/Technological Education, Education-General, Literacy, Public Education (Precollege), Science/Mathematics Education, Student Aid
Health: Cancer, Clinics/Medical Centers, Diabetes, Emergency/Ambulance Services, Geriatric Health, Health Organizations, Heart, Hospitals, Medical Rehabilitation, Medical Research
International: International Development, International Organizations
Religion: Churches, Religious Welfare
Social Services: At-Risk Youth, Big Brothers/Big Sisters, Camps, Community Centers, Community Service Organizations, Day Care, Delinquency & Criminal Rehabilitation, Emergency Relief, Family Planning, Food/Clothing Distribution, Homes, Recreation & Athletics, Scouts, Shelters/Homelessness, United Funds/United Ways, Volunteer Services, Youth Organizations

Application Procedures

Initial Contact: Send a brief letter of inquiry describing program or project.
Application Requirements: Include amount requested and purpose of funds sought.
Deadlines: None.

Restrictions

Grants are limited to educational, medical, and cultural organizations.

Additional Information

Trust(s): Bank One

Foundation Officials

Margaret Bishop: gov
Steve Jones: gov
Ben Munson, IV: gov
David Munson, Jr.: gov
David M. Munson, Sr.: gov
John K. Munson: gov
Peter Munson: gov

Grants Analysis

Disclosure Period: calendar year ending 2000
Total Grants: $263,265
Typical Range: $1,000 to $20,000
Note: Complete grant list not available for 2000.

Recent Grants

Note: Grants derived from 2001 Form 990.
General

38,318	Denison Community Foundation, Denison, TX -- for Ballpark Field improvement
36,500	Denison Public Library, Denison, TX -- for Read to Win Program
32,500	Denison Sister Cities, Denison, TX
26,073	Denison Community Foundation, Denison, TX -- for Ballpark Field improvement
24,500	Grayson County College, Denison, TX -- for capital improvements to TV Munson Memorial
17,000	American Red Cross, Denison, TX -- for full size van
15,000	Austin College, Sherman, TX -- to sponsor Pat Mitchell as keynote speaker
10,000	American Heart Association, Dallas, TX -- for CPR training
10,000	Grayson County Shelter, Denison, TX -- for operating expenses
10,000	Locust Volunteer Fire Department, Pottsboro, TX -- for equipment purchase

M. J. MURDOCK CHARITABLE TRUST

Giving Contact

John Van Zytveld, Senior Program Director
PO Box 1618
Vancouver, WA 98668
Phone: (360)694-8415
Fax: (360)694-1819
Web: http://www.murdock-trust.org

Description

Founded: 1975
EIN: 237456468
Organization Type: General Purpose Foundation
Giving Locations: AK; ID; MT; OR; WA: Pacific Northwest USA.
Grant Types: Capital, Matching.

Donor Information

Founder: M. J. (Jack) Murdock was born in Portland, OR, in 1917. Upon completion of high school, he opened a shop for the sale and service of radio and electrical appliances. In 1937, he began an association with Howard Vollum which culminated in the founding of Tektronix. He served as secretary-treasurer until 1960 when he was elected chairman of the board. Mr. Murdock died in 1971. The trust was established in 1975 by the terms of his will.

Financial Summary

Total Giving: $21,079,111 (2003); $34,450,640 (2002); $33,509,080 (2001)
Assets: $511,254,097 (2002); $619,066,798 (2001)

Typical Recipients

Arts & Humanities: Arts Centers, Arts Festivals, Arts Outreach, Ballet, Historic Preservation, History & Archaeology, Libraries, Museums/Galleries, Music, Opera, Performing Arts, Public Broadcasting, Theater
Civic & Public Affairs: Botanical Gardens/Parks, Business/Free Enterprise, Clubs, Community Foun-

dations, Economic Development, Economic Policy, Employment/Job Training, Ethnic Organizations, Civic & Public Affairs-General, Housing, Legal Aid, Native American Affairs, Philanthropic Organizations, Professional & Trade Associations, Public Policy, Rural Affairs, Urban & Community Affairs, Zoos/Aquariums

Education: Afterschool/Enrichment Programs, Arts/Humanities Education, Business Education, Colleges & Universities, Community & Junior Colleges, Education Funds, Education Reform, Engineering/Technological Education, Environmental Education, Faculty Development, Education-General, Health & Physical Education, International Exchange, Leadership Training, Medical Education, Private Education (Precollege), Public Education (Precollege), Religious Education, Science/Mathematics Education, Secondary Education (Private), Special Education, Student Aid

Environment: Environment-General, Research, Resource Conservation, Wildlife Protection

Health: Alzheimer's Disease, Cancer, Children's Health/Hospitals, Clinics/Medical Centers, Emergency/Ambulance Services, Eyes/Blindness, Health Policy/Cost Containment, Health Funds, Health Organizations, Hospitals, Hospitals (University Affiliated), Medical Rehabilitation, Medical Research, Mental Health, Preventive Medicine/Wellness Organizations, Public Health, Research/Studies Institutes

International: Health Care/Hospitals, International Environmental Issues, International Peace & Security Issues, International Relief Efforts

Religion: Bible Study/Translation, Churches, Ministries, Religious Organizations, Religious Welfare, Seminaries

Science: Science-General, Science Museums, Scientific Centers & Institutes, Scientific Research

Social Services: Camps, Child Abuse, Child Welfare, Community Centers, Community Service Organizations, Emergency Relief, Family Services, Food/Clothing Distribution, Homes, People with Disabilities, Recreation & Athletics, Scouts, Shelters/Homelessness, Social Services-General, United Funds/United Ways, YMCA/YWCA/YMHA/YWHA, Youth Organizations

Application Procedures

Initial Contact: If the proposal represents a major priority of the trust, an applicant should send an initial letter of inquiry summarizing the main elements of the proposal in order to determine whether a formal application would be within the trust's interests.

Application Requirements: Letters of inquiry should provide a brief background on the organization, a description of the project for which funds are sought, a proposed budget for the total cost of the project, and reasons for approaching the trust for this project. If the proposed project appears eligible for consideration, a grant application packet containing an application form will be sent. Proposals should be written and presented in a concise manner. Tables, charts, and appendices may be used. Elaborate and bulky bindings should be avoided.

Deadlines: None.

Review Process: The full proposal, including staff summary and analysis, is submitted to the trustees for their consideration and review. Review of proposals may take six to nine months.

Restrictions

The foundation does not consider grants to individuals; for loans; for conduit organizations, for political purposes; to institutions that discriminate on the basis of race, ethnic origin, sex, creed, or religion; to sectarian or religious organizations whose principal activity is for the benefit of their own members; or for projects requiring a financial obligation over a period of several years. Organizations outside the United States also are excluded from consideration.

In addition, the foundation will not consider funding requests for endowment; grant making organizations; debt retirement; continuation of programs previously financed by external sources; general fund drives or annual charitable appeals; emergency funding; and requests from organizations whose priorities do not match the foundation's major priorities. Requests from organizations and projects normally financed by tax funds are not favored.

Additional Information

Publications: Grant Application Packet; Annual Report; Guidelines

Foundation Officials

John W. Castles: trustee B Portland, OR 1947. ED University of Washington (1966-1967); Linfield College (1968); Portland State University (1969-1972). PRIM CORP EMPL chairman: Oregon Resource & Technology Development Account. CORP AFFIL director: Oregon Growth Account; director: SupplyChainge Inc.; chairman: Good Neighbor Care Centers Inc. CLUB AFFIL Multnomah Athletic Club; West Hills Racquet Club.

Christopher J. Gillem: program director

Janice W. Kennedy: program director

Terry Stokesbary: program director

Lynwood W. Swanson: trustee B 1934. ED University of the Pacific BS (1956); University of California, Davis PhD (1959). PRIM CORP EMPL FEI Co. CORP AFFIL chairman, founder: FEI Co..

Neal O. Thorpe: executive director, trustee ED University of Wisconsin PhD.

John Van Zytveld: senior program director ED PhD.

Grants Analysis

Disclosure Period: calendar year ending 2003

Total Grants: $21,079,111

Number of Grants: 154

Average Grant: $114,762*

Highest Grant: $1,500,000

Lowest Grant: $10,000

Typical Range: $50,000 to $200,000

*Note: Average grant figure excludes three highest grants ($3,750,000).

Recent Grants

Note: Grants derived from 2002 Form 990.

Library-Related

250,000   Friends of the Haines Borough Public Library, Haines, AK -- towards new community facility

General

1,375,000   Mission Aviation Fellowship, Redlands, CA -- towards new aircraft development

750,000   George Fox University, Newberg, OR -- towards construction of Edward F Stevens center

500,000   Community Foundation for Southwest Washington, Vancouver, WA -- towards community center construction

500,000   Linfield College, McMinnville, OR -- towards new library technology

500,000   Whitman College Board of Trustees, Walla Walla, WA -- towards science building renovation and expansion

499,500   University of Washington, Seattle, WA -- towards laser equipment purchase

475,000   Portland State University Foundation, Portland, OR -- towards acquisition of scanning transmission electron Microscope

417,000   Montana State University, Bozeman, MT -- towards purchase of mass spectrometer

414,000   Institute of Systems Biology, Seattle, WA -- towards acquisition of laboratory equipment

410,000   University of Oregon Foundation, Eugene, OR -- towards acquisition of equipments

LLUELLA MOREY MURPHEY FOUNDATION

Giving Contact

Alfred B. Hastings, Jr., Trustee
47-176 El Agadir
Palm Desert, CA 92260
Phone: (760)837-9177

Description

Founded: 1967

EIN: 956152669

Organization Type: Private Foundation

Giving Locations: CA: southern

Grant Types: Capital, General Support, Matching, Research, Scholarship.

Donor Information

Founder: the late Lluella Morey Murphey

Financial Summary

Total Giving: $154,300 (2003); $92,290 (2001)

Giving Analysis: Giving for 2003 includes: foundation scholarships ($3,500); 2001: foundation scholarships ($9,500)

Assets: $5,205,075 (2003); $5,682,795 (2001)

Typical Recipients

Arts & Humanities: Arts, Associations & Councils, Arts Funds, Arts & Humanities-General, Historic Preservation, History & Archaeology, Libraries, Museums/Galleries, Music

Civic & Public Affairs: Botanical Gardens/Parks, Community Foundations, Employment/Job Training, Civic & Public Affairs-General, Hispanic Affairs, Housing, Law & Justice, Urban & Community Affairs, Women's Affairs

Education: Afterschool/Enrichment Programs, Arts/Humanities Education, Colleges & Universities, Education Reform, Engineering/Technological Education, Education-General, Leadership Training, Legal Education, Literacy, Minority Education, Preschool Education, Private Education (Precollege), Public Education (Precollege), Religious Education, Science/Mathematics Education, Special Education, Student Aid, Vocational & Technical Education

Environment: Forestry

Health: Cancer, Children's Health/Hospitals, Clinics/Medical Centers, Emergency/Ambulance Services, Eyes/Blindness, Health-General, Health Organizations, Heart, Hospitals, Kidney, Long-Term Care, Medical Research, Mental Health, Multiple Sclerosis, Prenatal Health Issues, Preventive Medicine/Wellness Organizations, Public Health, Research/Studies Institutes, Respiratory, Speech & Hearing

International: Health Care/Hospitals, International Environmental Issues, Missionary/Religious Activities

Religion: Churches, Religious Organizations, Religious Welfare

Social Services: Animal Protection, At-Risk Youth, Child Welfare, Community Service Organizations, Counseling, Crime Prevention, Domestic Violence, Emergency Relief, Family Planning, Family Services, Food/Clothing Distribution, People with Disabilities, Recreation & Athletics, Scouts, Senior Services, Shelters/Homelessness, Social Services-General, Special Olympics, Substance Abuse, United Funds/United Ways, YMCA/YWCA/YMHA/YWHA, Youth Organizations

Application Procedures

Initial Contact: Send a brief letter of inquiry.

Application Requirements: Include a a description of organization, amount requested, and purpose of funds sought.

Deadlines: None.

Restrictions

Does not support individuals, political or lobbying groups, or organizations outside operating areas.

Foundation Officials

Alfred B. Hastings, Jr.: trustee
Leonard M. Marangi: trustee
Corene L. Pindroh: trustee

Grants Analysis

Disclosure Period: calendar year ending 2003
Total Grants: $150,800*
Number of Grants: 43
Average Grant: $3,507
Highest Grant: $5,000
Lowest Grant: $1,500
Typical Range: $1,500 to $5,000
*Note: Giving excludes scholarships.

Recent Grants

Note: Grants derived from 2003 Form 990.
Library-Related
5,000   Henry E. Huntington Library & Art Gallery, San Marino, CA -- to support education and school tour programs
General
5,000   Girl Scouts-MT Wilson Vista, Arcadia, CA -- to support pathway to promises program for girls
5,000   Lymphoma Research Foundation, New York, NY -- to help Stanford research program
5,000   Pasadena Police Foundation, Pasadena, CA -- support for youth accountability program to intervene
5,000   SGV Council Boy Scouts, Pasadena, CA -- towards programs in 2 housing projects
5,000   Tools for Tomorrow, Palm Desert, CA -- funding of an instructor at desert sands unified school district
5,000   Union State Foundation, Pasadena, CA -- support the family program
5,000   USC/Norris Comprehensive Cancer Center, Los Angeles, CA -- towards Dr. Kohn research on bone marrow
5,000   Wellness Community, Pasadena, CA -- towards English language support groups for caregivers of cancer patients
5,000   Women at Work, Pasadena, CA -- to partially fund the free job information program

G.C. Murphy Co. Foundation

Giving Contact

Edwin W. Davis, Secretary, Administrator & Director
211 Oberdick Dr.
McKeesport, PA 15135
Phone: (412)751-6649

Description

Founded: 1952
EIN: 256028651
Organization Type: Private Foundation
Giving Locations: PA: Southeastern Allegheny County, McKeesport
Grant Types: General Support.

Financial Summary

Total Giving: $233,000 (2001)
Assets: $4,325,107 (2001)

Typical Recipients

Arts & Humanities: Arts Centers, History & Archaeology, Libraries, Music, Theater
Civic & Public Affairs: Chambers of Commerce,

Clubs, Community Foundations, Economic Development, Employment/Job Training, Civic & Public Affairs-General, Housing, Municipalities/Towns, Safety, Urban & Community Affairs, Women's Affairs
Education: Business Education, Colleges & Universities, Engineering/Technological Education, Education-General, Preschool Education, Special Education, Student Aid
Environment: Environment-General
Health: Cancer, Clinics/Medical Centers, Geriatric Health, Health Organizations, Hospices, Hospitals, Medical Rehabilitation, Mental Health, Multiple Sclerosis, Public Health, Single-Disease Health Associations
Religion: Churches, Ministries, Religious Organizations, Religious Welfare
Social Services: Child Welfare, Community Service Organizations, Counseling, Emergency Relief, Family Services, Food/Clothing Distribution, Homes, People with Disabilities, Scouts, Senior Services, Social Services-General, Special Olympics, Volunteer Services, YMCA/YWCA/YMHA/YWHA, Youth Organizations

Application Procedures

Initial Contact: The foundation requests applications be made in writing.
Application Requirements: Include a description of organization with some background information as to the organization's charitable purpose and the purpose of funds sought.
Deadlines: None.

Additional Information

The G.C. Murphy Co. Foundation is independently administered and is not affiliated with G.C. Murphy Co. or McCrory Corp.

Foundation Officials

Charles Breckenridge: vice president, director
Edwin W. Davis: secretary, administrator, director
Alice J. Hajduk: vice president, director
Thomas F. Hudak: president, treasurer, director B Dunora, PA 1942. ED Saint Vincent College BS (1963); Ohio State University MBA (1968). PRIM CORP EMPL treasurer: Mack Realty Co. CORP AFFIL president, director: Terry Farris Stores; director: RXI Corp.; treasurer: Spotsylvania Realty Co.; member advisory board: Liberty Mutual Insurance; treasurer: Murphy Development Corp.; chairman, president: Continental Plastics; treasurer: Court House Village Co. NONPR AFFIL member: Spice Traders Association; member: U.S. Chamber of Commerce; member: Risk & Insurance Management Society; member: National Retail Merchants Association; member: Peanut Butter & National Processors Association; fin council, member: Machinery & Allied Products Institute; member: National Association Corp. Divs; member: Financial Executives Institute; president, director: GC Murphy Co. Foundation; member: American Institute of CPA's; member: Dressing & Sauces.
C.A. McElhinny: vice president, director
Robert T. Messner: vice president, director B McKeesport, PA 1938. ED Dartmouth College BA (1960); University of Pennsylvania LLB (1963). PRIM CORP EMPL vice president, secretary, general counsel: Dollar Bank. CORP AFFIL secretary: G C Murphy Co. NONPR AFFIL member: Theta Delta Chi; director: YMCA McKeesport; chairman corporate law department committee, member: Pennsylvania Bar Association; fin advisor: Pennsylvania Legis; member: American Society of Corporate Secretaries; director: Braddocks Field Historical Society; member: American Corporate Counsel Association; member: Allegheny Bar Association; member: American Bar Association. CLUB AFFIL Gateway Center Pittsburgh Club; Rivers Club; Dartmouth Western Pennsylvania Club.

Grants Analysis

Disclosure Period: calendar year ending 2001
Total Grants: $233,000
Number of Grants: 37
Average Grant: $6,297
Highest Grant: $20,000
Typical Range: $1,000 to $15,000

Recent Grants

Note: Grants derived from 2001 Form 990.
General
20,000   South Hills Interfaith Ministries, Pittsburgh, PA -- program support
15,000   McKeesport Heritage Center, McKeesport, PA -- for building fund
15,000   Outreach Teen and Family Service, Pittsburgh, PA -- program support
10,000   Braddock's Field Historical Society, Braddock, PA -- program support
10,000   Central Food Pantry of Elizabeth Township, Buena Vista, PA -- building fund
10,000   Greater Pittsburgh Community Food Bank, McKeesport, PA -- operations
10,000   LaRosa Boys and Girls Club of McKeesport, McKeesport, PA -- for program support
10,000   Penn State McKeesport, McKeesport, PA -- student union building fund
10,000   Ventures in People, Mckeesport, IA -- program support
6,000   Otterbein College, Westerville, OH -- for scholarship fund

Murphy Foundation

Giving Contact

Edward W. Marsh, Secretary & Treasurer
200 N. Jefferson St., Suite 400
Union Bldg.
El Dorado, AR 71730
Phone: (870)862-4961

Description

Founded: 1958
EIN: 716049826
Organization Type: General Purpose Foundation
Giving Locations: AR: Southern Arkansas
Grant Types: Capital, Endowment, General Support, Scholarship.

Donor Information

Founder: The foundation was established in Arkansas in 1958 by Charles Haywood Murphy, Jr., and other members of the Murphy family. Mr. Murphy is chairman of Murphy Oil Corporation.

Financial Summary

Total Giving: $1,138,991 (fiscal year ending April 30, 2002); $1,006,534 (fiscal 2001). Note: Fiscal 1997 Giving includes scholarship ($109,836), United Way ($65,250).
Giving Analysis: Giving for fiscal 2002 includes: foundation grants to United Way ($40,222); foundation scholarships ($133,142); fiscal 2001: foundation grants to United Way ($40,196) foundation scholarships ($133,553)
Assets: $33,278,772 (fiscal 2002); $29,443,785 (fiscal 2001)
Gifts Received: $3,000 (fiscal 2002); $6,000 (fiscal 2001); $424,096 (fiscal 1997). Note: In fiscal 1997 and 2000, contributions were received from C.N. Murphy.

Typical Recipients

Arts & Humanities: Arts Centers, Historic Preservation, History & Archaeology, Libraries, Museums/Galleries, Music, Performing Arts, Public Broadcasting

Civic & Public Affairs: Economic Development, Civic & Public Affairs-General, Public Policy
Education: Arts/Humanities Education, Colleges & Universities, Economic Education, Elementary Education (Private), Education-General, Literacy, Medical Education, Public Education (Precollege), Secondary Education (Public), Student Aid
Health: Respiratory
International: International Development
Religion: Churches, Religious Welfare
Social Services: Animal Protection, Crime Prevention, Recreation & Athletics, Scouts, United Funds/United Ways, YMCA/YWCA/YMHA/YWHA, Youth Organizations

Application Procedures

Initial Contact: For general giving program, send a brief letter of inquiry describing the program, individual student aid, request for foundation's standard application form.
Application Requirements: For student aid program, include a copy of the applicant's scholastic record.
Deadlines: August 1.
Notes: Educational grants are restricted to students from the southern Arkansas area.

Restrictions

Educational grants are restricted to students from the southern Arkansas area.

Foundation Officials

Edward W. Marsh: secretary, treasurer
Charles H. Murphy, Jr.: director
Johnie W. Murphy: president, director
R. Madison Murphy: president, director
Lucy A. Ring: director
Perry Silliman: secretary-treasurer

Grants Analysis

Disclosure Period: fiscal year ending April 30, 2002
Total Grants: $965,627*
Number of Grants: 46
Average Grant: $17,115*
Highest Grant: $112,445
Lowest Grant: $80
Typical Range: $5,000 to $30,000
***Note:** Giving excludes scholarship and United Way. Average grant figure excludes two highest grants ($212,551).

Recent Grants

Note: Grants derived from fiscal 2002 Form 990.

Library-Related
30,222	Barton Library, El Dorado, AR -- operating budget

General
112,445	El Dorado Public Schools, El Dorado, AR -- for stock
100,165	Hendrix College, Conway, AR -- for stock
78,896	El Dorado Public Schools, El Dorado, AR -- for stock
75,000	Next Step Foundation -- operating budget
62,500	American Lung Association, El Dorado, AR -- operating budget
50,077	Arkansas Council on Economic Education, Little Rock, AR -- operating budget
34,540	Boys and Girls Club of El Dorado, El Dorado, AR -- for stock
32,382	Hendrix College, Conway, AR -- for stock
30,222	Boy Scouts of America, Desota Area Council -- operating budget
30,222	South Arkansas Arts Center, El Dorado, AR -- for stock

R. C. AND KATHARINE M. MUSSON CHARITABLE FOUNDATION

Giving Contact

Ben D. Segars, Jr., Trustee
PO Box 7038
Akron, OH 44306
Phone: (330)773-7651

Description

Founded: 1984
EIN: 341549070
Organization Type: Private Foundation
Giving Locations: OH: Summit County
Grant Types: General Support, Scholarship.

Donor Information

Founder: the late R. C. Musson

Financial Summary

Total Giving: $227,780 (fiscal year ending June 30, 2004); $313,690 (fiscal 2002); $259,813 (fiscal 2001). Note: Fiscal 1997 Giving includes contribution returned by Summa ($10,000).
Giving Analysis: Giving for fiscal 2004 includes: foundation scholarships ($39,000); foundation grants to United Way ($40,000) fiscal 2001: foundation grants to United Way ($40,000)
Assets: $4,069,898 (fiscal 2004); $4,447,345 (fiscal 2002); $4,672,273 (fiscal 2001)

Typical Recipients

Arts & Humanities: Arts Institutes, Ballet, Historic Preservation, History & Archaeology, Libraries, Music, Performing Arts, Theater
Civic & Public Affairs: Botanical Gardens/Parks, Community Foundations, Economic Development, Employment/Job Training, Civic & Public Affairs-General, Housing, Inner-City Development, Legal Aid, Municipalities/Towns, Urban & Community Affairs, Zoos/Aquariums
Education: Arts/Humanities Education, Colleges & Universities, Education Funds, Education Reform, Education-General, Private Education (Precollege), Religious Education, Secondary Education (Public), Special Education, Student Aid
Health: Cancer, Children's Health/Hospitals, Clinics/Medical Centers, Diabetes, Geriatric Health, Health Funds, Health Organizations, Heart, Hospices, Hospitals, Long-Term Care, Medical Rehabilitation, Multiple Sclerosis, Nursing Services, Prenatal Health Issues, Public Health
Religion: Churches, Ministries, Religious Welfare
Science: Science Museums
Social Services: At-Risk Youth, Big Brothers/Big Sisters, Child Welfare, Community Service Organizations, Counseling, Crime Prevention, Delinquency & Criminal Rehabilitation, Domestic Violence, Family Planning, Family Services, Food/Clothing Distribution, Homes, People with Disabilities, Scouts, Senior Services, Shelters/Homelessness, Substance Abuse, United Funds/United Ways, Volunteer Services, YMCA/YWCA/YMHA/YWHA, Youth Organizations

Application Procedures

Initial Contact: Submit a narrative, a brief letter of inquiry, and a full proposal.
Application Requirements: Include a description of organization, amount requested, purpose of funds sought, recently audited financial statement, and proof of tax-exempt status.
Deadlines: None.

Restrictions

Does not support individuals, religious organizations for sectarian purposes, political or lobbying groups, or organizations outside operating areas.

Foundation Officials

Irvin J. Musson, III: trustee
Irvin J. Musson, Jr.: trustee
Ben Segers: trustee
Robert S. Segers: trustee B Akron, OH 1960. ED University of Akron (1984). PRIM CORP EMPL vice president: RC Musson Rubber Co.

Grants Analysis

Disclosure Period: fiscal year ending June 30, 2004
Total Grants: $148,780*
Number of Grants: 51
Average Grant: $2,917
Highest Grant: $7,500
Lowest Grant: $250
Typical Range: $1,000 to $5,000
***Note:** Giving excludes United Way; scholarship.

Recent Grants

Note: Grants derived from fiscal 2004 Form 990.
General
40,000	United Way, Akron, OH
30,000	University of Akron, Akron, OH -- for scholarships
7,500	Cascade Locks Park, Akron, OH
7,200	Peace Together of Akron, Akron, OH
7,000	Battered Women's Shelter, Akron, OH -- towards utility costs
6,000	Interval Brotherhood Home, Akron, OH
6,000	Ohio Foundation of Independent Colleges, Columbus, OH -- for scholarships
5,000	Hattie Larlham Foundation, Mantua, OH -- for permanent endowment
5,000	Keep Akron Beautiful, Akron, OH
5,000	Victim Assistance, Akron, OH

MYERS CHARITABLE TRUST

Giving Contact

J. Scott Raes, Trust Officer
Wells Fargo Bank Illinois NA
121 West First Street
Geneseo, IL 61254-1341
Phone: (309)944-5361

Description

Founded: 1997
EIN: 367233377
Organization Type: Private Foundation
Giving Locations: IL: Geneseo area of Henry County
Grant Types: General Support, Scholarship.

Financial Summary

Total Giving: $46,728 (2003); $57,178 (2001)
Giving Analysis: Giving for 2003 includes: foundation scholarships ($23,040); 2001: foundation scholarships ($28,684)
Assets: $1,357,073 (2003); $1,337,606 (2001)

Typical Recipients

Arts & Humanities: Libraries
Civic & Public Affairs: African American Affairs
Education: Arts/Humanities Education, Faculty Development, Medical Education, Student Aid
Health: Hospitals

Application Procedures

Initial Contact: For scholarships, request application form.
Deadlines: None.

Additional Information

Provides scholarships only to students who attend or have attended the Geneseo schools and are attending or have been accepted by an accredited college

or university in medical, dentistry, law or registered nurse programs.
Trust(s): Wells Fargo Bank IL NA

Grants Analysis
Disclosure Period: calendar year ending 2003
Total Grants: $23,688*
Number of Grants: 2
Highest Grant: $11,844
Lowest Grant: $11,844
***Note:** Giving excludes scholarship.

Recent Grants
Note: Grants derived from 2003 Form 990.
Library-Related
11,844	Geneseo Public Library District, Geneseo, IL -- for equipment

General
11,844	Hammond-Henry District Hospital, Geneseo, IL -- for equipment

E. NAKAMICHI FOUNDATION

Giving Contact
Ray Privette, Secretary/Treasurer
E. Nakamichi Foundation
446 S. Anaheim Hills Road, Suite 221
Anaheim Hills, CA 92807
Phone: (714)771-9677
Fax: (714)282-8179
E-mail: admin@enfoundation.com
Web: http://www.enfoundation.com

Description
Founded: 1985
EIN: 953870341
Organization Type: Specialized/Single Purpose Foundation
Giving Locations: no geographic restrictions.
Grant Types: Award, Project.

Donor Information
Founder: The foundation was endowed in 1985 by the founder of Nakamichi Corporation of Japan, the manufacturer of high-quality stereo equipment used by professional musicians and audiophiles. Mr. E. Nakamichi developed a love for music while designing his first equipment in his garage. He found Baroque music to have the most precise rhythm and tone to test the quality of his products. As his company grew, so did his love for Baroque music. Toward the end of his life, Mr. Nakamichi held weekly concerts in his home. He maintained his Japanese citizenship, but kept a home in Southern California, near the headquarters of Nakamichi, U.S.A. and Nakamichi America.

Financial Summary
Total Giving: $174,147 (2004); $6,562 (2001)
Assets: $7,712,852 (2004); $7,665,584 (2001)

Typical Recipients
Arts & Humanities: Arts Festivals, Arts & Humanities-General, Libraries, Music, Opera, Performing Arts, Public Broadcasting
Civic & Public Affairs: Nonprofit Management, Professional & Trade Associations
Education: Arts/Humanities Education, Colleges & Universities, Private Education (Precollege)
International: Foreign Arts Organizations

Application Procedures
Initial Contact: Applicants should submit initial proposal via website.
Application Requirements: a description of organization, summary of proposed grant, and amount re-

quested. If asked to submit a full proposal, include IRS tax-exempt letter and a copy of the most recent annual financial statement.
Deadlines: February 1 and September 15.
Review Process: Board of Directors meet in the spring and in the autumn to decide on grants. Applicants who appear to match the foundation's interests may be asked to submit a full proposal.
Notes: The foundation commits its grant dollars approximately twelve to eighteen months in advance, so applicants are encouraged to apply well in advance of the date funding is needed.

Restrictions
Grants are not made to individuals for independent study, research, travel, or participation in a musical event. The Foundation does not award grants toward capital campaigns, endowments, or deficit operations, nor does it make grants for the construction or maintenance of buildings, or for the purchase of equipment. Furthermore, public broadcasting grants are awarded only to the broadcaster. Consequently, inquiries and applications must come directly from the television/radio station. The foundation does not administer activities for which it awards grants, nor does it administer its own programs. The foundation does not make multi-year grants.

Additional Information
The foundation only considers requests from 501(c)(3) organizations. The Nakamichi Foundation has no special grant application forms or guidelines.
Publications: Information Package Containing Grants List; Program Statement; List of Officers and Directors

Foundation Officials
Ray Privette: secretary, treasurer, director PRIM CORP EMPL director human resources: Shimano American Corp.
Shunji Shinoda: director PRIM CORP EMPL president: Shinoda Construction Management.
Ken Yamasaki: director
Yashiro Yamazaki: president, director PRIM CORP EMPL president: CEM Inc.

Grants Analysis
Disclosure Period: calendar year ending 2004
Total Grants: $174,147
Number of Grants: 23
Average Grant: $6,531*
Highest Grant: $20,000
Lowest Grant: $750
Typical Range: $1,000 to $10,000
***Note:** Average grant figure excludes two highest grants ($37,000).

Recent Grants
Note: Grants derived from 2004 Form 990.
General
20,000	San Francisco Symphony, San Francisco, CA -- for promotion of baroque and classical music
17,000	Da Camera Society, Los Angeles, CA -- for promotion of baroque and classical music
10,000	Carmel Bach Festival, Carmel, CA -- for promotion of baroque and classical music
10,000	Lincoln Center for the Performing Arts, New York, NY -- for promotion of baroque and classical music
10,000	Los Angeles Chamber Orchestra, Los Angeles, CA -- for promotion of baroque and classical music
10,000	Orange County Performing Arts Center, Costa Mesa, CA -- for promotion of baroque and classical music
10,000	Philharmonic Symphony Society of New York, New York, NY -- for promotion of baroque and classical music
10,000	Public Radio International, Minneapolis, MN -- for promotion of baroque and classical music
10,000	University of California Los Angeles Performing Arts, Los Angeles, CA -- for promotion of baroque and classical music
7,500	Chamber Music Northwest, Portland, OR -- for promotion of baroque and classical music

NATIONAL CITY CORP.

Company Headquarters
1900 E. 9th Street
Cleveland, OH 44114-3404
Web: http://www.nationalcity.com

Company Description
Founded: 1845
Ticker: NCC
Exchange: NYSE
Holding Company for: National City Bank.
Revenue: US$10.559 billion (2004)
Profit: US$2.779 billion (2004)
Employees: 33331 (2003)
Fortune Rank: 211, per FORTUNE Magazine's list of 500 Largest U.S. Corporations (2004).
SIC(s): 6021 National Commercial Banks, 6712 Bank Holding Companies.

Operating Locations
National City Corp. (KY--Ashland, Louisville; OH--Akron, Ashland, Norwalk, Sandusky, Toledo, Youngstown)

National City Corp. Charitable Foundation II

Giving Contact
Michael Galland
c/o National City Bank Cleveland
1900 East Ninth Street
Cleveland, OH 44101
Phone: (216)222-2736

Alternate Contact
NCC Charitable Foundation
PO Box 94651
Cleveland, OH 44101-4651
Phone: (216)222-2934

Description
Founded: 1996
EIN: 347050989
Organization Type: Corporate Foundation
Grant Types: General Support.

Financial Summary
Total Giving: $19,061,444 (fiscal year ending June 30, 2004); $17,972,965 (fiscal 2003); $17,707,736 (fiscal 2002)
Giving Analysis: Giving for fiscal 2002 includes: foundation grants to United Way ($2,391,538)
Assets: $80,783,571 (fiscal 2004); $96,632,553 (fiscal 2003); $70,984,878 (fiscal 2002)
Gifts Received: $40,089,291 (fiscal 2003); $52,736,492 (fiscal 2002); $1,368 (fiscal 2001). Note: In fiscal 2002 and 2003, contributions were received from National City Corp. In fiscal 1998, contributions were received from National City Bank NY.

Typical Recipients
Arts & Humanities: Arts Associations & Councils, Arts Funds, Arts Institutes, Arts Outreach, Ballet,

Dance, Arts & Humanities-General, Historic Preservation, History & Archaeology, Libraries, Museums/Galleries, Music, Performing Arts, Public Broadcasting

Civic & Public Affairs: African American Affairs, Botanical Gardens/Parks, Chambers of Commerce, Community Foundations, Economic Development, Economic Policy, Employment/Job Training, Civic & Public Affairs-General, Housing, Municipalities/Towns, Philanthropic Organizations, Public Policy, Urban & Community Affairs, Women's Affairs, Zoos/Aquariums

Education: Arts/Humanities Education, Colleges & Universities, Community & Junior Colleges, Education Associations, Education Funds, Education Reform, Education-General, Medical Education, Private Education (Precollege)

Environment: Environment-General, Research

Health: Cancer, Children's Health/Hospitals, Emergency/Ambulance Services, Health Funds, Health Organizations, Heart, Hospitals, Hospitals (University Affiliated)

Religion: Dioceses, Ministries

Science: Science Museums

Social Services: Community Service Organizations, Counseling, Emergency Relief, Food/Clothing Distribution, People with Disabilities, Recreation & Athletics, Senior Services, United Funds/United Ways, Volunteer Services, Youth Organizations

Application Procedures
Deadlines: None.

Restrictions
Emphasis is on prevention of child abuse in the U.S. and its possessions.

Additional Information
Trust(s): National City Bank

Corporate Officials
Bruce McCrodden: senior vice president, corp. public affairs ED University of Delaware BS. NONPR AFFIL director: Downtown Cleveland Partnership; director: Ohio Chamber of Commerce; director: American Red Cross; director: Center for Families and Children.

Foundation Officials
David A. Daberko: officer B Hudson, OH 1945. ED Denison University BA (1967); Case Western Reserve University MBA (1970). PRIM CORP EMPL chairman, chief executive officer: National City Corp. CORP AFFIL director: Marathon Oil Corp.; director: OMNOVA Solutions Inc. NONPR AFFIL trustee: University Circle Inc.; trustee: University Hospital Health System; trustee: Hawken School; member, trustee: Greater Cleveland Roundtable; co-chairman: Harvest for Hunger Campaign; chairman: Cleveland Tomorrow; member: Financial Services Roundtable; trustee: Case Western Reserve University.

Grants Analysis
Disclosure Period: fiscal year ending June 30, 2004
Total Grants: $17,972,965*
Number of Grants: 1,188 (approx)
Average Grant: $16,044
Highest Grant: $150,000
Lowest Grant: $25
Typical Range: $1,000 to $15,000
***Note:** Giving includes matching gifts and United Way.

Recent Grants
Note: Grants derived from fiscal 2004 Form 990.
Library-Related

10,000	Columbus Metropolitan Library System, Columbus, OH

General

142,857	Cleveland Clinic Foundation, Cleveland, OH
125,000	Cancer Treatment Research Foundation, Arlington Heights, IL
120,187	Columbus Foundation, Columbus, OH
110,000	Allegheny Conference on Community Development, Pittsburgh, PA
62,500	Chicago Botanic Garden, Glencoe, IL
50,000	Athena Foundation, Chicago, IL
50,000	Athena Foundation, Chicago, IL
50,000	Bridges Mentoring Center for Youth Development, Highland Hills, OH
50,000	Citizens Research Council of Michigan, Livonia, MI
50,000	City Year Columbus, Columbus, OH

NATIONAL GRANGE MUTUAL INSURANCE CO.

Company Headquarters
55 West Street
Keene, NH 03431-3348
Web: http://www.msagroup.com

Company Description
Assets: US$442.4 million (2001)
Employees: 900 (2001)
SIC(s): 6331 Fire, Marine & Casualty Insurance, 6351 Surety Insurance.

National Grange Mutual Charitable Trust

Giving Contact
Richard Hyatt, Principal Administrator & Trustee
55 West St.
Keene, NH 03431
Phone: (603)352-4000
Fax: (603)358-1173

Alternate Contact
Phone: 800-225-5646

Description
Founded: 1972
EIN: 237228264
Organization Type: Corporate Foundation
Giving Locations: CA; MD; NH: emphasis on Keene; VA
Grant Types: Award, Capital, Challenge, Employee Matching Gifts, Endowment, General Support, Matching, Project, Research.

Donor Information
Founder: National Grange Mutual Insurance Co.

Financial Summary
Total Giving: $128,973 (2001)
Giving Analysis: Giving for 2001 includes: foundation matching gifts ($6,100); foundation grants to United Way ($69,253).
Assets: $2,355,179 (2001)

Typical Recipients
Arts & Humanities: Arts Associations & Councils, Arts Festivals, Arts & Humanities-General, History & Archaeology, Libraries, Museums/Galleries, Public Broadcasting, Theater

Civic & Public Affairs: Botanical Gardens/Parks, Chambers of Commerce, Clubs, Economic Development, Civic & Public Affairs-General, Housing, Professional & Trade Associations, Public Policy, Safety, Women's Affairs

Education: Arts/Humanities Education, Business Education, Colleges & Universities, Education Funds, Engineering/Technological Education, Education-General, Private Education (Precollege), Secondary Education (Public), Student Aid, Vocational & Technical Education

Environment: Environment-General, Resource Conservation

Health: Arthritis, Cancer, Children's Health/Hospitals, Clinics/Medical Centers, Emergency/Ambulance Services, Health-General, Health Organizations, Heart, Home-Care Services, Hospices, Kidney, Medical Research, Multiple Sclerosis, Nursing Services, Prenatal Health Issues

International: International Development

Religion: Churches, Religious Welfare

Social Services: Animal Protection, Community Service Organizations, Crime Prevention, Domestic Violence, Emergency Relief, Food/Clothing Distribution, Homes, Recreation & Athletics, Scouts, Social Services-General, Special Olympics, Substance Abuse, United Funds/United Ways, YMCA/YWCA/YMHA/YWHA

Application Procedures
Initial Contact: The foundation requests applications be made in writing.
Application Requirements: a description of organization, amount requested, and purpose of funds sought.
Deadlines: None.

Restrictions
No support for educational endeavors. Grants are not made to individuals.

Corporate Officials
Philip D. Koerner: chairman, president, chief executive officer, director B Bridgeport, CT 1946. ED University of New Hampshire (1969). PRIM CORP EMPL chairman, president, chief executive officer: National Grange Mutual Insurance Co. CORP AFFIL chairman, president, chief executive officer: Main Saint America Financial Corp.; director: Guilderland Reins Co. NONPR AFFIL director: Alliance American Insurers.

David L. Royer: vice president, treasurer, chief financial officer, director PRIM CORP EMPL vice president, treasurer, chief financial officer, director: National Grange Mutual Insurance Co.

Foundation Officials
Norman E. Brackett: trustee B 1929. ED Bates College AB (1952). PRIM CORP EMPL senior vice president, chief financial officer: Hannaford Brothers Co.
Cotton Mather Cleveland: trustee PRIM CORP EMPL president: Mather Associates.
Jeanne Eddy: trustee
Charles Albert Farmer: trustee B South Newbury, NH 1930. ED Boston University (1952). PRIM CORP EMPL director: National Grange Mutual Insurance Co.
Susan Hay: manager
Raymond Huizenga: trustee
Richard Hyatt: trustee
Terry S. Jacobs: trustee
Philip D. Koerner: trustee (see above)
Thomas M. Van Berkel: trustee

Grants Analysis
Disclosure Period: calendar year ending 2001
Total Grants: $53,620*
Number of Grants: 29
Average Grant: $1,159*
Highest Grant: $20,000
Typical Range: $100 to $7,000
***Note:** Giving excludes United Way, matching gifts. Average grant figure excludes highest grant.

Recent Grants
Note: Grants derived from 2001 Form 990.
General

62,000	Monadnock United Way, Keene, NH
20,000	Keene State College, Keene, NH
7,000	Center Stage, Baltimore, MD

5,320	Greater Keene Chamber of Commerce, Keene, NH
5,000	American Red Cross National Disaster Relief Fund
4,000	United Way of Northeast Florida, Jacksonville, FL
2,753	United Way Services
2,500	American Cancer Society, Baltimore, MD -- for Relay for Life
2,500	InVEST, Alexandria, VA
2,000	Grand Monadnock Arts Council, Monadnock, NH

NATIONAL MACHINERY CO.

Company Headquarters
Tiffin, OH
Web: http://www.nationalmachinery.com

Company Description
Revenue: US$8.7 million (2001)
Employees: 280 (2003)
SIC(s): 3452 Bolts, Nuts, Rivets & Washers.

National Machinery Foundation, Inc.

Giving Contact
Don B. Bero, Assistant Secretary
161 Greenfield Street
Tiffin, OH 44883
Phone: (419)447-5211
Fax: (419)443-2380

Description
EIN: 346520191
Organization Type: Corporate Foundation
Giving Locations: OH: Seneca County
Grant Types: General Support.

Financial Summary
Total Giving: $248,005 (2003); $634,004 (2002); $915,581 (2001). Note: Contributes through foundation only.
Assets: $12,794,671 (2003); $10,630,161 (2002); $12,989,122 (2001)

Typical Recipients
Arts & Humanities: Arts Festivals, Arts & Humanities-General, History & Archaeology, Libraries, Museums/Galleries, Performing Arts, Public Broadcasting, Theater
Civic & Public Affairs: Botanical Gardens/Parks, Community Foundations, Economic Development, Employment/Job Training, Civic & Public Affairs-General, Housing, Law & Justice, Legal Aid, Municipalities/Towns, Parades/Festivals, Safety, Urban & Community Affairs
Education: Afterschool/Enrichment Programs, Agricultural Education, Business Education, Colleges & Universities, Community & Junior Colleges, Education Funds, Elementary Education (Public), Education-General, Leadership Training, Literacy, Minority Education, Preschool Education, Private Education (Precollege), Public Education (Precollege), Religious Education, School Volunteerism, Science/Mathematics Education, Secondary Education (Private), Secondary Education (Public), Student Aid, Vocational & Technical Education
Environment: Protection, Resource Conservation, Watershed
Health: AIDS/HIV, Cancer, Children's Health/Hospitals, Clinics/Medical Centers, Emergency/Ambulance Services, Health-General, Geriatric Health, Health Organizations, Heart, Hospices, Hospitals, Medical Rehabilitation, Mental Health, Nursing Services, Single-Disease Health Associations
Religion: Religious Welfare
Social Services: Animal Protection, At-Risk Youth, Big Brothers/Big Sisters, Camps, Child Welfare, Community Centers, Community Service Organizations, Crime Prevention, Day Care, Domestic Violence, Emergency Relief, Family Services, Homes, Recreation & Athletics, Refugee Assistance, Scouts, Senior Services, Substance Abuse, United Funds/United Ways, YMCA/YWCA/YMHA/YWHA, Youth Organizations

Application Procedures
Initial Contact: Send a letter of request.
Application Requirements: Specify financial need and purpose.
Deadlines: None.

Restrictions
Distributions are limited to organizations and individuals in the general Seneca County area.

Additional Information
In addition to grant making, the foundation assists needy individuals, operates a scholarship program, and awards citizenship gifts.

Corporate Officials
Larry Baker: vice president employee relations PRIM CORP EMPL vice president employee relations: National Machinery Co.

Foundation Officials
Larry Baker: secretary, treasurer, trustee (see above)
M. Patricia Hillmer: trustee
Donna J. Kin: executive secretary
N. E. Martin: trustee

Grants Analysis
Disclosure Period: calendar year ending 2003
Total Grants: $174,555*
Number of Grants: 74
Average Grant: $1,980*
Highest Grant: $30,000
Lowest Grant: $25
Typical Range: $1,000 to $10,000
*Note: Giving excludes scholarships and gifts to individuals. Average grant figure excludes highest grant.

Recent Grants
Note: Grants derived from 2003 Form 990.
Library-Related

1,000	Tiffin Seneca Public Library, Tiffin, OH

General

30,000	Tiffin Theatre Inc., Tiffin, OH
20,000	Betty Jane Memorial Rehabilitation, Tiffin, OH
20,000	Tiffin University, Tiffin, OH
10,000	Habitat for Humanity Inc., Tiffin, OH
10,000	Tiffin Community YMCA, Tiffin, OH
5,250	Tiffin-Seneca United Way, Tiffin, OH
5,000	Heidelberg College, Tiffin, OH
5,000	Patchworks House Inc., Tiffin, OH
5,000	St. Francis Home Inc., Tiffin, OH
5,000	Teen Center Tiffin/Seneca, Tiffin, OH

NATIONAL MANUFACTURING CO.

Company Headquarters
7 W. Madison St.
Chicago, IL 60602

Company Description
Employees: 1,000
SIC(s): 2400 Lumber & Wood Products, 3400 Fabricated Metal Products.

NMC Foundation

Giving Contact
Joseph L. Bittorf, Vice Chairperson
NMC Foundation
1 1st Avenue
Sterling, IL 61081
Phone: (815)625-1320
Fax: (815)625-1333
E-mail: jlbittorf@natman.com

Description
EIN: 363802369
Organization Type: Corporate Foundation
Giving Locations: headquarters area only.
Grant Types: Matching, Operating Expenses.

Financial Summary
Total Giving: $269,830 (2002); $294,507 (2001)
Giving Analysis: Giving for 2002 includes: foundation matching gifts ($11,050); foundation grants to United Way ($52,250)
Assets: $718,164 (2002); $718,047 (2001)
Gifts Received: $300,000 (2002); $328,150 (2001); $70,000 (2000). Note: National Manufacturing Co. made a contribution in 2002.

Typical Recipients
Arts & Humanities: Music, Public Broadcasting, Visual Arts
Civic & Public Affairs: Botanical Gardens/Parks, Chambers of Commerce, Clubs, Civic & Public Affairs-General, Housing, Legal Aid, Municipalities/Towns, Nonprofit Management, Urban & Community Affairs
Education: Arts/Humanities Education, Colleges & Universities, Community & Junior Colleges, Education Funds, Elementary Education (Public), Education-General, International Studies, Private Education (Precollege), Public Education (Precollege), Science/Mathematics Education, Secondary Education (Private), Secondary Education (Public), Student Aid, Vocational & Technical Education
Health: Alzheimer's Disease, Cancer, Emergency/Ambulance Services, Health Funds, Heart, Hospices, Public Health, Single-Disease Health Associations
Religion: Religious Welfare
Social Services: Animal Protection, Camps, Child Welfare, Community Service Organizations, Crime Prevention, Day Care, Food/Clothing Distribution, Scouts, Shelters/Homelessness, Substance Abuse, United Funds/United Ways, YMCA/YWCA/YMHA/YWHA, Youth Organizations

Application Procedures
Initial Contact: Send an application in writing to the chairperson.
Application Requirements: Include a description of organization, purpose of funds sought, and proof of tax-exempt status.
Deadlines: None.

Restrictions
Foundation does not provide grants for religiouss, political, fraternal, or labor organizations; organizations that discriminate on any basis other than need; sponsorship of teams or others whose purpose is to in turn raise money for another cause; sponsorship of athletic teams; solicitation in the form of mass mailings; or goodwill advertising or sponsorship of publications.

Corporate Officials
Keith W. Benson, III: president, chief executive officer PRIM CORP EMPL president, chief executive officer: National Manufacturing Co.

Keith W. Benson, Jr.: chairman, director PRIM CORP EMPL chairman, director: National Manufacturing Co. CORP AFFIL chairman: National Manufacturing Co.

Charles R. Phillips: vice president finance PRIM CORP EMPL vice president finance: National Manufacturing Co.

Foundation Officials

Peter M. Benson: director CORP AFFIL director: National Manufacturing Co.

Joseph L. Bittorf: chairperson PRIM CORP EMPL vice president engineering: National Manufacturing Co.

John M. Gvozdjak: secretary, treasurer

Timothy B. Sullivan: chairperson CORP AFFIL director: National Manufacturing Co.

Grants Analysis

Disclosure Period: calendar year ending 2002
Total Grants: $206,530*
Number of Grants: 55
Average Grant: $1,049*
Highest Grant: $52,000
Lowest Grant: $250
Typical Range: $500 to $20,000
***Note:** Giving excludes matching gifts and United Way. Average grant figure excludes three highest grants totaling $152,000.

Recent Grants

Note: Grants derived from 2003 Form 990.
General

145,400	Public Charities, Sterling, IL
44,200	Secondary Schools, IL
29,700	Public Charities
18,500	Elementary Schools, IL
9,550	Public/Private Colleges, IL
4,500	Civic Organizations, IL
3,900	Community Health, IL
3,870	Public/Private Universities
3,000	Associated Colleges of Illinois, Chicago, IL
1,500	Secondary Schools, IL

NATIONAL PRESTO INDUSTRIES INC.

Company Headquarters

Eau Claire, WI
Web: http://www.gopresto.com

Company Description

Founded: 1905
Ticker: NPK
Exchange: NYSE
Revenue: US$133.7 million (2002)
Employees: 347 (2003)
SIC(s): 3634 Electric Housewares & Fans, 5064 Electrical Appliances--Television & Radio.

Operating Locations

National Presto Industries, Inc. (DE--Wilmington; MN--Minneapolis; MS--Canton, Jackson; VI; WI--Eau Claire)

Presto Foundation

Giving Contact

Norma Jaenke, Executive Director
Presto Foundation
3925 North Hastings Way
Eau Claire, WI 54703
Phone: (715)839-2119
Fax: (715)839-2122

Description

EIN: 396045769
Organization Type: Corporate Foundation
Giving Locations: WI: Northwestern Wisconsin, especially Eau Claire and Chippewa Falls headquarters and operating communities.
Grant Types: General Support, Scholarship.

Financial Summary

Total Giving: $600,700 (fiscal year ending May 31, 2003); $654,627 (fiscal 2001). Note: Contributes through corporate direct giving program and foundation.
Giving Analysis: Giving for fiscal 2003 includes: foundation grants to United Way ($27,850); foundation scholarships ($227,390); fiscal 2001: foundation grants to United Way ($23,800); foundation scholarships ($183,077); foundation ($447,750)
Assets: $9,659,231 (fiscal 2003); $12,842,018 (fiscal 2001)

Typical Recipients

Arts & Humanities: Arts & Humanities-General, Libraries, Museums/Galleries, Performing Arts, Public Broadcasting
Civic & Public Affairs: Botanical Gardens/Parks, Community Foundations, Employment/Job Training, Civic & Public Affairs-General, Housing, Municipalities/Towns, Philanthropic Organizations
Education: Afterschool/Enrichment Programs, Business Education, Colleges & Universities, Community & Junior Colleges, Education Funds, Engineering/Technological Education, Public Education (Precollege), Science/Mathematics Education, Secondary Education (Private), Secondary Education (Public), Special Education, Student Aid, Vocational & Technical Education
Environment: Environment-General, Wildlife Protection
Health: Cancer, Children's Health/Hospitals, Emergency/Ambulance Services, Health Funds, Heart, Hospitals, Medical Research, Multiple Sclerosis, Outpatient Health Care, Single-Disease Health Associations
Religion: Churches, Jewish Causes, Ministries, Religious Organizations, Religious Welfare, Synagogues/Temples
Social Services: Animal Protection, Camps, Community Centers, Community Service Organizations, Emergency Relief, Food/Clothing Distribution, Homes, People with Disabilities, Recreation & Athletics, Shelters/Homelessness, Social Services-General, Special Olympics, United Funds/United Ways, YMCA/YWCA/YMHA/YWHA, Youth Organizations

Application Procedures

Initial Contact: Send a brief letter.
Application Requirements: Include a description of organization and project, amount requested, proposed budget, and proof of tax-exempt status.
Deadlines: None.
Notes: Additional information may be requested by the foundation.

Restrictions

Company does not make contributions to organizations outside operating areas. Scholarships are for children of employees.

Additional Information

Publications: Annual Report

Corporate Officials

Maryjo Rose Cohen: president, chief executive officer, director B Eau Claire, WI 1952. ED University of Michigan (1973); University of Michigan JD (1976). PRIM CORP EMPL president, chief executive officer, director: National Presto Industries, Inc. CORP AFFIL secretary, treasurer, director: Presto Export Ltd.; secretary, treasurer, director: Presto Manufacturing Co.;

vice president, director: National Pipeline Co.; secretary, treasurer, director: National Defense Corp.; secretary, assistant treasurer, director: National Holding Investment Co.; vice president, secretary, treasurer, director: Jackson Sales & Storage Co.; vice president, director: National Automatic Pipeline Oper Inc.; secretary, treasurer, director: Canton Sales & Storage Co.; secretary, treasurer, director: Century Leasing & Liquidating Inc.

Melvin Samuel Cohen: chairman B Minneapolis, MN January 16, 1918. ED University of Minnesota BS (1939); University of Minnesota JD (1941). PRIM CORP EMPL chairman: National Presto Industries, Inc. ADD CORP EMPL vice president, director: National Automatic Pipeline Oper Inc.; president: National Defense Corp.; president: National Holding International Co.; vice president, director: National Pipeline Co.; president: Canton Sales & Storage Co.; president, director: Jackson Sales & Storage Co.; chairman, president, director: Presto International Ltd.; president, director: Presto Manufacturing Co.; president: Presto Export Ltd. CORP AFFIL president: Presto Export Ltd.; chairman, president: Presto Manufacturing Co.; president: Canton Sales & Storage Co.; president: Century Leasing & Liquidating Inc.

Foundation Officials

Dean Boehne: trustee
Eileen Phillips Cohen: trustee
Maryjo Rose Cohen: vice president, treasurer, trustee (see above)
Melvin Samuel Cohen: chairman, president, trustee (see above)
Geraldine Eaton: secretary, trustee
John Frank: vice president, trustee
Norma Jaenke: executive director
Richard Myhers: trustee
Arthur Petzoad: vice president, trustee

Grants Analysis

Disclosure Period: fiscal year ending May 31, 2003
Total Grants: $345,460*
Number of Grants: 90
Average Grant: $2,537*
Highest Grant: $119,650
Lowest Grant: $50
Typical Range: $500 to $5,000
***Note:** Giving excludes scholarships; United Way. Average grant figure excludes highest grant.

Recent Grants

Note: Grants derived from 2004 Form 990.
General

209,000	Career Development Center, Eau Claire, WI
60,625	University of Wisconsin, Eau Claire, WI
35,000	Paul Bunyan Logging Camp Museum, Eau Claire, WI
11,741	University of Wisconsin, Madison, WI
10,000	College of St. Scholastica, Duluth, MN
10,000	Covenant Chapel, Leawood, KS
10,000	Georgetown University, Washington, DC
10,000	Lee University, Cleveland, TN
10,000	Lee University, Cleveland, TN
10,000	Mississippi State University Controller, MS

NATIONAL STANDARD CO.

Company Headquarters

1618 Terminal Rd.
Niles, MI 49120
Web: http://www.nationalstandard.com

Company Description

Employees: 1,495
SIC(s): 3300 Primary Metal Industries, 3400 Fabricated Metal Products.

National Standard Foundation

Giving Contact
R. D. McMillion, Vice President & Secretary
1618 Terminal Rd.
Niles, MI 49120
Phone: (616)683-8100
Fax: (616)683-2803

Description
EIN: 386089682
Organization Type: Corporate Foundation
Giving Locations: headquarters community.
Grant Types: General Support, Scholarship.

Financial Summary
Total Giving: $32,140 (fiscal year ending January 31, 2001). Note: Fiscal 1997 Giving includes scholarship ($22,000), United Way ($6,500).
Giving Analysis: Giving for fiscal 2001 includes: foundation grants to United Way ($9,940); foundation scholarships ($15,000)
Assets: $2,093 (fiscal 2001)
Gifts Received: $26,700 (fiscal 2001); $35,000 (fiscal 2000); $40,000 (fiscal 1997). Note: Contributions were received from National-Standard Co.

Typical Recipients
Arts & Humanities: Arts Centers, Libraries, Public Broadcasting
Civic & Public Affairs: Clubs, Community Foundations, Civic & Public Affairs-General, Public Policy, Safety, Urban & Community Affairs
Education: Agricultural Education, Business Education, Colleges & Universities, Education-General, Secondary Education (Public)
Health: Cancer, Health-General, Health Organizations, Public Health, Single-Disease Health Associations
Religion: Religious Welfare
Social Services: Community Service Organizations, Crime Prevention, Food/Clothing Distribution, Recreation & Athletics, Shelters/Homelessness, Social Services-General, United Funds/United Ways, Veterans, Volunteer Services, YMCA/YWCA/YMHA/YWHA

Application Procedures
Initial Contact: Send a brief letter of inquiry. with detailed description of how the contribution will be used.
Deadlines: None.

Additional Information
Foundation also provides scholarships for children of employees.

Corporate Officials
W. D. Grafer: vice president financeo, director PRIM CORP EMPL vice president finance: National Standard Co.
John E. Guth, Jr.: chairman, director PRIM CORP EMPL chairman, director: National Standard Co.
Michael B. Savitske: president, chief executive officer, director B Allentown, PA 1941. ED University of Notre Dame BS (1964); University of Notre Dame (1964). PRIM CORP EMPL president, chief executive officer, director: National Standard Co. CORP AFFIL director: Factory Mutual Insurance Co.

Foundation Officials
Michael K. Conn: vice president, secretary PRIM CORP EMPL manager human resources: National Standard Co.
W. D. Grafer: treasurer (see above)
R. D. McMillion: vice president, secretary

G. R. Northcutt: president
Michael B. Savitske: president (see above)
F. K. Welling: treasurer

Grants Analysis
Disclosure Period: fiscal year ending January 31, 2001
Total Grants: $7,200*
Number of Grants: 4
Highest Grant: $4,000
Lowest Grant: $100
*Note: Giving excludes scholarships and United Way.

Recent Grants
Note: Grants derived from 2000 Form 990.
General

5,500	United Way of Greater Niles, Niles, MI
4,440	Stillwater Area United Way, Stillwater, OK
4,000	Lake Michigan College Educational Fund, Benton Harbor, MI
2,000	Greater Niles Community Development Corp., Niles, MI
100	Niles Service League, Niles, MI
100	South Bend Youth Hockey, Inc., South Bend, IN

NEBCO EVANS

Company Headquarters
Greenwich, CT

Company Description
Employees: 400
SIC(s): 3273 Ready-Mixed Concrete.

Abel Foundation

Giving Contact
J. Ross McCown, Vice President
PO Box 80268
Lincoln, NE 68501
Phone: (402)434-1212
Fax: (402)434-1799
E-mail: nebcoinfo@nebcoinc.com
Web: http://www.abelfoundation.org

Description
Founded: 1951
EIN: 476041771
Organization Type: Corporate Foundation
Giving Locations: NE
Grant Types: General Support, Matching, Multiyear/Continuing Support.

Donor Information
Founder: Abel Construction Co.

Financial Summary
Total Giving: $403,127 (2003); $678,940 (2002); $493,790 (2001). Note: Contributes through foundation only.
Giving Analysis: Giving for 2002 includes: foundation grants to United Way ($45,166); 2001: foundation grants to United Way ($45,640); foundation ($448,150)
Assets: $4,473,217 (2003); $2,840,225 (2002); $3,470,601 (2001)
Gifts Received: $985,923 (2003); $205,000 (2002); $1,191,288 (1999). Note: In 2002 and 2003, contributions were received from NEBCO. In 1996, contributions were received from NEBCO ($150,000); and Constructors, Inc. ($19,000). In 1994, contributions were received from NEBCO ($830,921); and Constructors, Inc. ($14,500).

Typical Recipients
Arts & Humanities: Arts Associations & Councils, Arts Centers, Arts Festivals, Arts Funds, Ballet, Arts & Humanities-General, History & Archaeology, Libraries, Literary Arts, Museums/Galleries, Music, Performing Arts, Public Broadcasting, Theater
Civic & Public Affairs: Botanical Gardens/Parks, Community Foundations, Economic Development, Economic Policy, Employment/Job Training, Civic & Public Affairs-General, Housing, Professional & Trade Associations, Urban & Community Affairs, Women's Affairs, Zoos/Aquariums
Education: Afterschool/Enrichment Programs, Agricultural Education, Arts/Humanities Education, Business Education, Colleges & Universities, Economic Education, Education Funds, Elementary Education (Public), Education-General, Health & Physical Education, Leadership Training, Literacy, Preschool Education, Private Education (Precollege), Public Education (Precollege), Science/Mathematics Education, Secondary Education (Public), Student Aid
Environment: Environment-General, Resource Conservation
Health: Children's Health/Hospitals, Clinics/Medical Centers, Emergency/Ambulance Services, Eyes/Blindness, Health-General, Geriatric Health, Health Funds, Health Organizations, Heart, Hospitals, Mental Health, Research/Studies Institutes, Single-Disease Health Associations, Transplant Networks/Donor Banks
Religion: Churches, Religion-General, Religious Organizations, Religious Welfare
Social Services: Animal Protection, At-Risk Youth, Child Abuse, Child Welfare, Community Centers, Community Service Organizations, Counseling, Domestic Violence, Emergency Relief, Family Planning, Family Services, Food/Clothing Distribution, Homes, People with Disabilities, Recreation & Athletics, Scouts, Senior Services, Social Services-General, Substance Abuse, United Funds/United Ways, YMCA/YWCA/YMHA/YWHA, Youth Organizations

Application Procedures
Initial Contact: Send a brief letter of inquiry.
Application Requirements: Include a description of organization, amount requested, purpose of funds sought, recently audited financial statement, and proof of tax-exempt status.
Deadlines: None.

Corporate Officials
James P. Abel: president, director B 1950. PRIM CORP EMPL president, director: NEBCO. CORP AFFIL vice president: Concrete Industries Inc.; director: Constructors Inc.; director: Ameritas Life Insurance Corp.

Foundation Officials
Alice Abel: director
Elizabeth N. Abel: director
James P. Abel: president (see above)
John C. Abel: director CORP AFFIL officer: Constructors Inc.; officer: Kerford Limestone Inc.
Mary C. Abel: director
James Watt Hewitt: vice president, treasurer B Hastings, NE 1932. ED Hastings College (1950-1952); University of Nebraska BS (1954); University of Nebraska JD (1956); University of Nebraska MA (1994). CORP AFFIL community director: Norwest Bank. NONPR AFFIL member: Phi Delta Phi; trustee: University Nebraska Foundation; member: Newcomen Society; member: Nebraska Rose Society; executive vice president, director: Nebraska State Historical Society Foundation; director: Nature Conservancy Nebraska Saint Chapter; member: Nebraska Bar Association; member: Lincoln Rose Society; member: Fed Bar Association; member: Lincoln Bar Association; director: Bryan Memorial Hospital Foundation; member: Business Roundtable; member: Beta Theta Pi; fellow: American Bar Foundation; member: American Rose Society; member: American Bar Associa-

tion. CLUB AFFIL Country Club Lincoln; Nebraska Club.

J. Ross McCown: vice president, secretary B 1946. ED University of Nebraska. PRIM CORP EMPL vice president: NEBCO.

Grants Analysis

Disclosure Period: calendar year ending 2003
Total Grants: $368,850*
Number of Grants: 91
Average Grant: $4,053
Highest Grant: $40,000
Lowest Grant: $50
Typical Range: $1,000 to $10,000
***Note:** Giving excludes United Way.

Recent Grants

Note: Grants derived from 2003 Form 990.
General

40,000	YMCA, Chicago, IL
26,000	First Plymouth, Lincoln, NE
25,000	Cornhusker Place, Lincoln, NE
25,000	First Plymouth, Lincoln, NE
25,000	Lincoln Parks and Recreation Sunken Gardens, Lincoln, NE
23,000	Nebraska Wesleyan University, Lincoln, NE
20,000	Boy Scouts, Irving, TX
16,440	United Way, Lincoln, NE
16,437	United Way, Lincoln, NE
15,000	CEDARS, Lincoln, NE

GEORGE W. NEILSON FOUNDATION

Giving Contact

Suzanne Liapis, Trustee
PO Box 692
Bemidji, MN 56619
Phone: (218)444-4963

Description

Founded: 1962
EIN: 416022186
Organization Type: Private Foundation
Giving Locations: MN: Bemidgi including surrounding area
Grant Types: General Support.

Donor Information

Founder: the late George W. Neilson

Financial Summary

Total Giving: $1,124,752 (2003)
Assets: $24,724,565 (2003)
Gifts Received: $8,695,378 (2000); $15,009 (1999); $240,513 (1998). Note: In 2000, contributions were received from G.W. Nielson Trust for Katherine Cram and Katherine Cram Rev Trust. In 1998 and 1999, contributions were received from Katherine N. Cram. In 1996, contributions were received from Katherine N. Cram.

Typical Recipients

Arts & Humanities: Arts Institutes, Community Arts, History & Archaeology, Libraries, Literary Arts, Museums/Galleries, Music, Theater
Civic & Public Affairs: Community Foundations, Economic Development, Employment/Job Training, Civic & Public Affairs-General, Nonprofit Management, Professional & Trade Associations, Safety, Urban & Community Affairs, Zoos/Aquariums
Education: Agricultural Education, Arts/Humanities Education, Business Education, Colleges & Universities, Education Funds, Gifted & Talented Programs, Minority Education, Public Education (Precollege), Science/Mathematics Education, Secondary Educa-

tion (Public)
Environment: Environment-General
Health: Children's Health/Hospitals, Emergency/ Ambulance Services, Hospices, Hospitals, Medical Rehabilitation, Nursing Services, Public Health
International: International Environmental Issues
Religion: Religious Organizations, Religious Welfare
Science: Scientific Centers & Institutes
Social Services: Animal Protection, Child Welfare, Community Service Organizations, Emergency Relief, Family Planning, Recreation & Athletics, Scouts, Senior Services, United Funds/United Ways, Youth Organizations

Application Procedures

Initial Contact: General outline of proposal.
Deadlines: None.
Notes: Foundation is not accepting applications at this time.

Restrictions

Does not support individuals or provide funds for endowments or fellowship.

Grants Analysis

Disclosure Period: calendar year ending 2003
Total Grants: $1,124,752
Number of Grants: 19
Average Grant: $13,672*
Highest Grant: $550,000
Lowest Grant: $200
Typical Range: $10,000 to $20,000
***Note:** Average grant figure excludes three highest grants ($906,000).

Recent Grants

Note: Grants derived from 2003 Form 990.
General

550,000	North Country Health Services, Bemidji, MN -- for Katharine Neilson cram skilled care facility
256,000	Bemidji State University, Bemidji, MN -- for wetlands ecology chair
100,000	Boys and Girls Club, Bemidji, MN -- for building pledge
50,000	Bemidji Girls Fastpitch, Bemidji, MN -- for restroom facilities
25,000	Paul Bunyan Playhouse, Bemidji, MN -- for building pledge
20,000	Headwaters Science Center, Bemidji, MN -- for roof repairs
18,000	Neilson Spearhead Center, Bemidji, MN -- for road repair
17,500	Headwaters School of Music and Art, Bemidji, MN -- for equipment and repairs
14,750	American Red Cross, Washington, DC -- for equipment and remodeling
13,900	Professional Association of Treatment Homes, Bemidji, MN -- for telephone systems and computers upgrade

NESHOLM FAMILY FOUNDATION

Giving Contact

120 Lakeside Avenue., Suite 340
Seattle, WA 98122
Phone: (206)358-3388

Description

Founded: 1987
EIN: 943055422
Organization Type: Private Foundation
Giving Locations: WA: Seattle
Grant Types: Project.

Donor Information

Founder: the late Elmer J. Nesholm

Financial Summary

Total Giving: $2,841,930 (2003)
Assets: $73,500,677 (2003)

Typical Recipients

Arts & Humanities: Arts Centers, Arts Funds, Arts Outreach, Ballet, Community Arts, Dance, Ethnic & Folk Arts, Historic Preservation, History & Archaeology, Libraries, Museums/Galleries, Music, Opera, Performing Arts, Public Broadcasting, Theater
Civic & Public Affairs: Botanical Gardens/Parks, Civil Rights, Economic Development, Employment/ Job Training, Housing, Municipalities/Towns, Native American Affairs, Public Policy, Urban & Community Affairs, Women's Affairs, Zoos/Aquariums
Education: Afterschool/Enrichment Programs, Arts/ Humanities Education, Colleges & Universities, Education Reform, Environmental Education, Education-General, Leadership Training, Legal Education, Literacy, Private Education (Precollege), Public Education (Precollege), Science/Mathematics Education, Special Education
Health: Adolescent Health Issues, AIDS/HIV, Alzheimer's Disease, Cancer, Children's Health/ Hospitals, Clinics/Medical Centers, Emergency/ Ambulance Services, Geriatric Health, Health Organizations, Home-Care Services, Hospices, Hospitals, Long-Term Care, Mental Health, Nursing Services, Prenatal Health Issues, Preventive Medicine/ Wellness Organizations, Public Health, Respiratory
International: Foreign Arts Organizations, International Affairs, International Organizations
Religion: Religious Organizations, Religious Welfare
Science: Scientific Centers & Institutes
Social Services: At-Risk Youth, Child Welfare, Community Centers, Community Service Organizations, Day Care, Delinquency & Criminal Rehabilitation, Domestic Violence, Emergency Relief, Family Planning, Family Services, Food/Clothing Distribution, Homes, Recreation & Athletics, Refugee Assistance, Senior Services, Sexual Abuse, Shelters/Homelessness, Substance Abuse, Volunteer Services, YMCA/ YWCA/YMHA/YWHA, Youth Organizations

Application Procedures

Initial Contact: Request application guidelines. Foundation accepts the Pacific Northwest Grantmakers Common Application.
Review Process: Foundation meets monthly, excluding July and August, to consider requests.

Additional Information

Publications: Application Guidelines
Trust(s): Bank of America NT & SA (SeaFirst) WA

Foundation Officials

Joseph M. Gaffney: director
Edgar K. Marcuse, MD: director
John F. Nesholm: director
Laurel Nesholm: executive director

Grants Analysis

Disclosure Period: calendar year ending 2003
Total Grants: $2,841,930
Number of Grants: 93
Average Grant: $25,190*
Highest Grant: $200,000
Lowest Grant: $1,000
Typical Range: $10,000 to $50,000
***Note:** Average grant figure excludes four highest grants ($600,000).

Recent Grants

Note: Grants derived from 2003 Form 990.
General

600,000	Seattle Center Foundation, Seattle, WA -- for enhancements to the renovation of McCaw Hall
200,000	Alliance for Education, Seattle, WA -- for middle school initiative
200,000	Seattle Opera, Seattle, WA

150,000	Alliance for Education, Seattle, WA -- for middle school initiative
150,000	Alliance for Education, Seattle, WA -- for middle school initiative
100,000	Alliance for Education, Seattle, WA -- for middle school initiative
100,000	Contemporary Theatre, Seattle, WA -- towards recovery plan
52,079	Children's Hospital Foundation -- for pediatric palliative care training program
50,000	ElderHealth Northwest -- for integrated neighborhood network
50,000	University of Washington, Seattle, WA -- for child health institute

NESTLE PURINA PETCARE CO.

Company Headquarters
Checkerboard Sq.
St. Louis, MO 63164-0001
Web: http://www.purina.com

Company Description
Employees: 22,435
SIC(s): 2047 Dog & Cat Food, 3692 Primary Batteries--Dry & Wet.
Parent Company: Nestle S.A., Avenue Nestle 55, Vevey, Switzerland

Operating Locations
Ralston Purina Co. (CA--Los Angeles, San Diego; CO--Denver; CT; KY--Louisville; MN--Minneapolis; MO--St. Louis; NY; OH--Zanesville; TN--Memphis)

Nonmonetary Support
Type: Cause-related Marketing & Promotion; Donated Equipment; Donated Products; In-kind Services; Loaned Employees; Loaned Executives; Workplace Solicitation

Ralston Purina Trust Fund

Giving Contact
Fred H. Perabo, Secretary
Ralston Purina Co.
Checkerboard Square
St. Louis, MO 63164-0001
Phone: (314)982-3234
Fax: (314)982-2752
Web: http://Purina.com/company/profile/profile_articles.asp?article=367

Alternate Contact
C/O The Northern Trust Co.
50 South La Salle Street
Chicago, IL 60675
Phone: (312)630-6000

Description
EIN: 431209652
Organization Type: Corporate Foundation
Giving Locations: MO: St. Louis headquarters and operating communities.
Grant Types: Capital, Employee Matching Gifts, Endowment, General Support, Project.
Note: Employee matching gift ratio: 1 to 1, up to $1,000 annually.

Financial Summary
Total Giving: $1,864,221 (fiscal year ending August 31, 2002); $1,780,702 (fiscal 2001). Note: Contributes through corporate direct giving program and foundation.

Assets: $15,887,487 (fiscal 2002); $18,968,516 (fiscal 2001)
Gifts Received: $3,750,000 (fiscal 1996); $1,000,000 (fiscal 1994); $1,000,000 (fiscal 1993). Note: Contributions are received from the Ralston Purina Company.

Typical Recipients
Arts & Humanities: Arts Associations & Councils, Arts Centers, Arts Funds, Historic Preservation, History & Archaeology, Libraries, Museums/Galleries, Music, Performing Arts, Public Broadcasting, Theater
Civic & Public Affairs: African American Affairs, Botanical Gardens/Parks, Business/Free Enterprise, Chambers of Commerce, Civil Rights, Clubs, Community Foundations, Economic Development, Employment/Job Training, Civic & Public Affairs-General, Housing, Municipalities/Towns, Nonprofit Management, Parades/Festivals, Professional & Trade Associations, Public Policy, Urban & Community Affairs, Women's Affairs, Zoos/Aquariums
Education: Arts/Humanities Education, Business Education, Colleges & Universities, Community & Junior Colleges, Economic Education, Education Associations, Education Funds, Elementary Education (Private), Education-General, Literacy, Medical Education, Minority Education, Preschool Education, Private Education (Precollege), Public Education (Precollege), Science/Mathematics Education, Secondary Education (Private), Secondary Education (Public), Special Education, Student Aid, Vocational & Technical Education
Environment: Environment-General
Health: Alzheimer's Disease, Cancer, Children's Health/Hospitals, Health Policy/Cost Containment, Health Organizations, Hospices, Hospitals, Medical Research, Nursing Services, Single-Disease Health Associations
International: International Relations
Religion: Jewish Causes, Ministries, Religious Organizations, Religious Welfare, Seminaries, Social/Policy Issues
Science: Scientific Centers & Institutes
Social Services: Animal Protection, At-Risk Youth, Child Welfare, Community Centers, Community Service Organizations, Crime Prevention, Delinquency & Criminal Rehabilitation, Domestic Violence, Emergency Relief, Family Planning, Family Services, Food/Clothing Distribution, Homes, People with Disabilities, Recreation & Athletics, Scouts, Senior Services, Shelters/Homelessness, Substance Abuse, United Funds/United Ways, Volunteer Services, YMCA/YWCA/YMHA/YWHA, Youth Organizations

Application Procedures
Initial Contact: Request guidelines, then send a written proposal.
Application Requirements: Complete applications will include: clear statement of need, timetable of accomplishment, background on organization and staff who would administer grant, plan for post-grant evaluation, proof of 501(c)(3) status, amount requested, detailed program budget, and copy of most recent financial statement.
Deadlines: None.
Evaluative Criteria: Project can be duplicated and has a prevention component.
Decision Notification: Proposals are reviewed quarterly.

Restrictions
The fund does not support individuals; religious or politically partisan causes; projects that require funding outside the United States or its possessions; loans or investment funds; veterans or fraternal organizations, unless they furnish services to the general public; tickets for dinners, benefits, exhibits, conferences, sports events, or other short-term activities; advertisements; or underwriting of deficits or post-event funding.

Additional Information
Publications: Contribution Guidelines

Corporate Officials
W. Patrick McGinnis: chief executive officer B 1947.
PRIM CORP EMPL chief executive officer: Ralston Purina Co.

Foundation Officials
Kevin Berryman: trustee
Susan Denigan: trustee
Fred H. Perabo: secretary board control PRIM CORP EMPL director community affairs: Ralston Purina Co.
James Ryan: trustee

Grants Analysis
Disclosure Period: fiscal year ending August 31, 2002
Total Grants: $940,344*
Number of Grants: 42
Average Grant: $12,246*
Highest Grant: $150,000
Lowest Grant: $2,000
Typical Range: $2,500 to $25,000 and $100,000 to $150,000
*Note: Giving excludes matching gifts and United Way. Average grant figure excludes four highest grants ($475,000).

Recent Grants
Note: Grants derived from 2003 Form 990.
General

175,000	Tony Larussa's Animal Rescue Foundation, Walnut Creek, CA
127,500	United Way of Greater Saint Louis, St. Louis, MO
127,500	United Way of Greater Saint Louis, St. Louis, MO
127,500	United Way of Greater Saint Louis, St. Louis, MO
50,000	Cardinal Ritter College Prep Inc., St. Louis, MO
50,000	Cardinal Ritter College Prep Inc., St. Louis, MO
50,000	Friends of Peabody Elementary School, Cambridge, MA
25,000	Downtown Now, St. Louis, MO
25,000	March of Dimes WalkAmerica, White Plains, NY
25,000	Mathews Dickey Boys Club, St. Louis, MO

ROY R. AND MARIE S. NEUBERGER FOUNDATION

Giving Contact
Gloria Silverman
Roy R. and Marie S. Neuberger Foundation
605 3rd Avenue, 41st Floor
New York, NY 10158
Phone: (212)476-5866

Description
Founded: 1954
EIN: 136066102
Organization Type: Private Foundation
Giving Locations: NY
Grant Types: General Support.

Donor Information
Founder: Roy R. Neuberger, Marie S. Neuberger

Financial Summary
Total Giving: $711,567 (2003); $782,069 (2001)
Assets: $14,504,403 (2003); $15,571,656 (2001)

Gifts Received: $88,575 (1994). Note: In 1991, contributions were received from Roy R. Neuberger.

Typical Recipients

Arts & Humanities: Arts Associations & Councils, Arts Centers, Arts Institutes, Arts Outreach, Dance, Ethnic & Folk Arts, Arts & Humanities-General, Historic Preservation, History & Archaeology, Libraries, Museums/Galleries, Music, Performing Arts, Public Broadcasting

Civic & Public Affairs: African American Affairs, Botanical Gardens/Parks, Ethnic Organizations, Civic & Public Affairs-General, Urban & Community Affairs, Women's Affairs, Zoos/Aquariums

Education: Arts/Humanities Education, Business Education, Colleges & Universities, Education Funds, Education-General, Legal Education, Private Education (Precollege), Science/Mathematics Education, Social Sciences Education

Environment: Resource Conservation, Wildlife Protection

Health: Emergency/Ambulance Services, Health Organizations, Hospitals, Medical Research, Mental Health, Nursing Services, Research/Studies Institutes, Single-Disease Health Associations

Religion: Religion-General, Jewish Causes, Religious Organizations, Synagogues/Temples

Social Services: Community Service Organizations, People with Disabilities, United Funds/United Ways, Youth Organizations

Application Procedures

Initial Contact: Send a brief letter of inquiry describing program or project.

Application Requirements: Include proof of tax-exempt status.

Deadlines: None.

Restrictions

Provides grants for higher education, cultural programs, and fine arts. Does not support individuals.

Foundation Officials

Ann N. Aceves: vice president

James A. Neuberger: vice president

Roy R. Neuberger: president, treasurer, director B Bridgeport, CT July 21, 1903. ED New York University. PRIM CORP EMPL senior partner: Neuberger & Berman. CORP AFFIL chairman: Guardian Mutual Fund. NONPR AFFIL member: Society Securities Analysts; trustee emeritus: Whitney Museum American Art; member: New York Society Security Analysts Institute; member: Society Ethical Culture; member president council: Museum City New York; member collector's committee: National Gallery Art; council friends: Institute Fine Arts; trustee: Metropolitan Museum Art; director coll ctr: Bard College; director: City Center Music Drama New York; member: American Federation Arts. CLUB AFFIL City Athletic Club; Harmonie Club; Century Association.

Roy S. Neuberger: vice president

Grants Analysis

Disclosure Period: calendar year ending 2003

Total Grants: $711,567

Number of Grants: 135

Average Grant: $4,162*

Highest Grant: $100,000

Lowest Grant: $100

Typical Range: $1,000 to $10,000

*Note: Average grant figure excludes two highest grants ($158,000).

Recent Grants

Note: Grants derived from 2003 Form 990.

General

100,000	Museum of Modern Art, New York, NY
58,000	Bank Street College Fund, New York, NY -- for mathematics leadership program
50,000	Metropolitan Museum of Art, New York, NY
50,000	United Jewish Appeal Federation, New York, NY
35,000	Hineni
25,000	Channel 13, New York, NY
25,000	Channel 13, New York, NY
25,000	Mt. Holyoke College, South Hadley, MA -- capital campaign
23,800	Santa Fe Symphony, Santa Fe, NM
20,000	Jewish Life Foundation, Los Altos, CA

NEW JERSEY NATURAL GAS CO.

Company Headquarters

1415 Wyckoff Rd.
Wall, NJ 07719
Web: http://www.njliving.com

Company Description

Employees: 832

SIC(s): 4924 Natural Gas Distribution.

Parent Company: New Jersey Resources Corp., 1415 Wyckoff Rd., Wall, NJ, United States

Nonmonetary Support

Type: Donated Equipment; Loaned Employees

New Jersey Natural Gas Foundation

Giving Contact

Tom Kononowitz, Vice President
PO Box 1464
Wall, NJ 07719
Phone: (732)938-1134
Fax: (732)938-7183
Web: http://www2.njng.com/community/

Alternate Contact

Jim O'Keefe, Community Relations

Description

EIN: 222835065

Organization Type: Corporate Foundation

Former Name: New Jersey Resources Foundation, Inc. (1998).

Giving Locations: NJ: Monmouth County, Ocean County, portions of Morris County company's service area.

Grant Types: General Support, Matching.

Financial Summary

Total Giving: $647,182 (fiscal year ending September 30, 2003); $317,845 (fiscal 2002); $339,281 (fiscal 2001). Note: Contributes through foundation only.

Assets: $732,400 (fiscal 2003); $37,182 (fiscal 2002); $16,585 (fiscal 2001)

Gifts Received: $1,330,932 (fiscal 2003); $317,845 (fiscal 2002); $339,281 (fiscal 2001). Note: Contributions are received from New Jersey Natural Gas Co.

Typical Recipients

Arts & Humanities: Arts Centers, Arts & Humanities-General, Libraries

Civic & Public Affairs: African American Affairs, Botanical Gardens/Parks, Community Foundations, Economic Development, Civic & Public Affairs-General, Philanthropic Organizations, Public Policy, Safety, Urban & Community Affairs, Women's Affairs

Education: Colleges & Universities, Community & Junior Colleges, Education Funds, Education Reform, Education-General, Minority Education, Public Education (Precollege), Secondary Education (Public), Student Aid

Environment: Environment-General

Health: Cancer, Children's Health/Hospitals, Clinics/Medical Centers, Diabetes, Emergency/Ambulance Services, Health-General, Health Organizations, Hospitals, Prenatal Health Issues, Public Health, Single-Disease Health Associations

Religion: Jewish Causes, Religious Welfare, Social/Policy Issues

Social Services: Big Brothers/Big Sisters, Child Welfare, Community Centers, Community Service Organizations, Day Care, Family Services, Food/Clothing Distribution, People with Disabilities, Recreation & Athletics, Scouts, Social Services-General, Substance Abuse, United Funds/United Ways, YMCA/YWCA/YMHA/YWHA, Youth Organizations

Application Procedures

Initial Contact: Send a typewritten letter of inquiry.

Application Requirements: Provide a statement of purpose, amount requested, description of constituency served, and proof of tax-exempt status.

Deadlines: None.

Review Process: Inquiries are reviewed and evaluated weekly; foundation requests additional information as necessary.

Decision Notification: The foundation board meets quarterly to review larger requests; small requests are decided upon within a shorter time frame.

Additional Information

In 1998, Co. changed foundation name because New Jersey Natural Gas is a more recognized name. Foundation priorities did not change.

Corporate Officials

Laurence M. Downes: president, chief executive officer, director, chairman B Hackensack, NJ 1957. ED Iona College BA (1979); Iona College MBA (1981). PRIM CORP EMPL president, chief executive officer, director, chairman: New Jersey Resources Corp. CORP AFFIL president: New Jersey Natural Energy Co.; president, chief executive officer, chairman: New Jersey Natural Gas Co.; president: New Jersey Energy Co. NONPR AFFIL member: Financial Executives Institute; member: National Investor Relations Institute; chairman: American Gas Association.

Glenn C. Lockwood: senior vice president, chief financial officer B 1961. ED Saint Peter's College BS (1983). PRIM CORP EMPL senior vice president, chief financial officer: New Jersey Resources Corp. ADD CORP EMPL chief financial officer, treasurer: New Jersey Energy Co.

Foundation Officials

Laurence M. Downes: trustee (see above)

Oleta J. Harden: secretary ED University of California, Los Angeles JD (1979). PRIM CORP EMPL senior vice president, secretary, general counsel: New Jersey Resources Corp. CORP AFFIL secretary: New Jersey Natural Energy Co.; secretary: NJR Energy Corp.; secretary: Commercial Realty Resources Corp.

Thomas F. Hayes: trustee

Thomas J. Kononowitz: vice president B 1942. PRIM CORP EMPL senior vice president marketing & consumer service: New Jersey Natural Gas Co. CORP AFFIL senior vice president: New Jersey Resources Corp.

Glenn C. Lockwood: treasurer (see above)

Mary Ann Martin: trustee PRIM CORP EMPL vice president consumer & community relations: New Jersey Natural Gas Co.

Grants Analysis

Disclosure Period: fiscal year ending September 30, 2003

Total Grants: $602,157*

Number of Grants: 46

Average Grant: $13,090

Highest Grant: $100,000

Lowest Grant: $25

Typical Range: $100 to $5,000

*Note: Giving excludes matching gifts and United Way.

Recent Grants

Note: Grants derived from fiscal 2001 Form 990.
General

6,650	March of Dimes, Lakewood, NJ -- sponsor

NEW-LAND FOUNDATION

Giving Contact

Renee Schwartz, Secretary, Treasurer, & Director
1114 Avenue of the Americas, 46th Floor
New York, NY 10036-7798
Phone: (212)479-6162
Fax: (212)841-6275

Description

Founded: 1941
EIN: 136086562
Organization Type: General Purpose Foundation
Giving Locations: nationally.
Grant Types: General Support, Operating Expenses, Project, Research.

Donor Information

Founder: The New-Land Foundation was incorporated in 1941 in New York by Joseph Buttinger and Muriel Buttinger.

Financial Summary

Total Giving: $1,824,150 (2002). Note: Amount given figures for 1995-1997 were provided by the foundation.
Assets: $31,017,993 (2002)
Gifts Received: $290,824 (1994); $162,008 (1993); $2,899,992 (1992). Note: Contributions were received from the estate of Joseph Buttinger.

Typical Recipients

Arts & Humanities: Arts Institutes, Arts Outreach, Historic Preservation, Libraries, Museums/Galleries, Music
Civic & Public Affairs: African American Affairs, Asian American Affairs, Botanical Gardens/Parks, Business/Free Enterprise, Civil Rights, Community Foundations, Economic Development, Economic Policy, Civic & Public Affairs-General, Hispanic Affairs, Housing, Law & Justice, Legal Aid, Native American Affairs, Professional & Trade Associations, Public Policy, Urban & Community Affairs, Women's Affairs
Education: Colleges & Universities, Education Associations, Education Funds, Education Reform, Elementary Education (Private), Engineering/ Technological Education, Education-General, Legal Education, Literacy, Medical Education, Minority Education, Science/Mathematics Education, Special Education, Student Aid
Environment: Air/Water Quality, Energy, Forestry, Environment-General, Protection, Research, Resource Conservation, Watershed, Wildlife Protection
Health: Clinics/Medical Centers, Health Policy/Cost Containment, Hospitals, Medical Research, Medical Training, Mental Health, Research/Studies Institutes
International: Foreign Arts Organizations, Health Care/Hospitals, Human Rights, International Development, International Environmental Issues, International Organizations, International Peace & Security Issues, International Relations
Religion: Jewish Causes
Science: Scientific Centers & Institutes
Social Services: Child Welfare, Community Service Organizations, Family Planning, Family Services, Homes, Recreation & Athletics, Senior Services, Social Services-General, Volunteer Services, Youth Organizations

Application Procedures

Initial Contact: Initial contact should be in writing to request guidelines, application form, and proposal format.
Application Requirements: Organizations requesting support from the foundation will need to submit an application form, a proposal abstract, the budget of the organization or project which includes sources and amounts of additional support, a list of the board and executive staff members, a copy of the applicant's tax exempt ruling, a copy of the organization's annual report and/or last audited financial statement, and a one-page letter summarizing the proposal. The letter should state the purpose of the project and anticipated results, the nature and number of clients t he project will serve, and the method of follow-up the applicant will employ to authenticate results.
Deadlines: Deadlines for receipt of proposals are February 1 and August 1.
Review Process: Only notification of the board's positive decisions are sent, approximately two weeks after the semi-annual board meetings.

Restrictions

Grants are not made to individuals. Grants are made to foreign charities only if the charity has a fiscal agent in the United States with tax-exempt status. The foundation does not typically fund programs in the following areas: educational institutions, medicine, religion, and general social programs including homelessness, poverty, domestic violence, drug addiction, or crime rehabilitation. The foundation does not typically award grants for capital campaigns, publications, films, endowment campaigns, building campaigns, or conferences.

Additional Information

Publications: Application Guidelines; Application Form

Foundation Officials

Ann Harvey: director
Joan Harvey: director
Renee Gerstler Schwartz: secretary-treasurer, director B Brooklyn, NY 1933. ED Brooklyn College AB (1953); Columbia University LLB (1955). PRIM CORP EMPL attorney, partner: Kronish, Lieb, Weiner & Hellman LLP. NONPR AFFIL member: Association Bar New York City.

Grants Analysis

Disclosure Period: calendar year ending 2002
Total Grants: $1,824,150
Number of Grants: 122
Average Grant: $14,014*
Highest Grant: $72,500
Lowest Grant: $792
Typical Range: $5,000 to $25,000
*Note: Average grant figure excludes two highest grants ($142,500).

Recent Grants

Note: Grants derived from 2002 Form 990.
General

72,500	Westchester Institute, New York, NY
70,000	Westchester Institute for Training in Psychoanalysis and Psychotherapy, New York, NY
50,000	Yale Child Study Center, New Haven, CT
30,000	Center for Defense Information Inc., Washington, DC
30,000	Center for Reproductive Law and Policy, New York, NY
29,041	Sigmund Freud Museum, London United Kingdom
28,119	Sigmund Freud Museum, London United Kingdom
27,837	Sigmund Freud Museum, London United Kingdom
25,000	Alaska Conservation Foundation, Anchorage, AK
25,000	Aspen Wilderness Workshop, Aspen, CO

NEW YORK FOUNDATION

Giving Contact

Maria Mottola, Executive Director
350 Fifth Avenue, Suite 2901
New York, NY 10118-2996
Phone: (212)594-8009
Web: http://www.nyf.org

Description

Founded: 1909
EIN: 135626345
Organization Type: General Purpose Foundation
Giving Locations: NY: New York metropolitan area
Grant Types: General Support, Project, Seed Money.

Donor Information

Founder: "The New York Foundation was established in 1909 by a gift of $1 million from the late Alfred A. Heinsheimer, bequeathed to him by his brother, Louis A. Heinsheimer." In 1925, the foundation received a $2.4 million bequest from the estate of Lionel J. Salomon, specifically designated for programs for needy youth and the elderly. In 1929, the foundation received an additional $6 million bequest upon the death of Alfred M. Heinsheimer, then the president of the foundation.

Financial Summary

Total Giving: $5,501,470 (2003); $4,987,004 (2002); $5,108,265 (2001)
Assets: $72,845,521 (2003); $67,342,426 (2002); $78,268,578 (2001)

Typical Recipients

Arts & Humanities: Film & Video, Libraries, Theater
Civic & Public Affairs: African American Affairs, Asian American Affairs, Botanical Gardens/Parks, Business/Free Enterprise, Civil Rights, Clubs, Community Foundations, Economic Development, Employment/Job Training, Ethnic Organizations, Gay/ Lesbian Issues, Civic & Public Affairs-General, Hispanic Affairs, Housing, Law & Justice, Legal Aid, Minority Business, Native American Affairs, Nonprofit Management, Philanthropic Organizations, Professional & Trade Associations, Public Policy, Urban & Community Affairs, Women's Affairs, Zoos/ Aquariums
Education: Afterschool/Enrichment Programs, Colleges & Universities, Community & Junior Colleges, Education Funds, Education Reform, Education-General, International Studies, Leadership Training, Minority Education, Public Education (Precollege), Social Sciences Education, Student Aid
Environment: Environment-General
Health: Adolescent Health Issues, AIDS/HIV, Cancer, Geriatric Health, Health Policy/Cost Containment, Health Organizations, Heart, Hospitals, Hospitals (University Affiliated), Mental Health, Nutrition, Outpatient Health Care, Prenatal Health Issues, Preventive Medicine/Wellness Organizations, Public Health, Single-Disease Health Associations
International: Foreign Educational Institutions, Human Rights, International Affairs, International Environmental Issues, International Peace & Security Issues, International Relief Efforts
Religion: Churches, Jewish Causes, Religious Organizations, Religious Welfare
Social Services: Animal Protection, At-Risk Youth, Child Welfare, Community Centers, Community Service Organizations, Counseling, Crime Prevention, Delinquency & Criminal Rehabilitation, Domestic Violence, Emergency Relief, Family Services, Food/ Clothing Distribution, Homes, People with Disabilities, Recreation & Athletics, Refugee Assistance, Se-

nior Services, Sexual Abuse, Shelters/Homelessness, Social Services-General, Substance Abuse, Volunteer Services, Youth Organizations

Application Procedures

Initial Contact: The foundation cannot review suggested projects by telephone and requests that inquiries be made in writing. Send a letter of inquiry.

Application Requirements: The initial letter should include information outlining the project, the organization's budget needs, and the amount requested. If interested, the foundation will request a full proposal following the New York-New Jersey Common Application Form.

Deadlines: Proposals must be received by November 1 for the February trustees' meeting, March 1 for the June meeting, and July 1 for the October meeting. Applicants are advised not to wait until application deadlines to submit a letter of request or to receive help in meeting emergency needs.

Review Process: Applicants generally will receive a response to the initial letter within ten days. All grants are made by the board of trustees, which meets three times a year. Foundation officers generally meet with applicants to evaluate the proposed project.

Restrictions

The foundation does not make grants to individuals and does not support capital campaigns, research studies, films, conferences, international organizations, or publications other than those initiated by the foundation. Grant requests for programs outside New York City will be considered only if they focus on youth, the elderly, or the poor.

Additional Information

After the foundation has dispensed a grant, they offer support to the grant recipient. Services include: training sessions; informal meetings with the foundation staff and board; and opportunities to meet with other organizations being funded.

Publications: Annual Report

Foundation Officials

Thomas I. Acosta: vice chairman
Alan Altschuler: trustee
Sayu Bhojwani: trustee
Margaret Ann Booth: trustee B New York, NY 1946. ED University of Wisconsin BS (1968). PRIM CORP EMPL president: M. Booth & Associates Inc.
Gladys Carrion: trustee
Dana Michelle Davis: trustee
David J. Dobrof: trustee
Dr. Rose Dobrof: secretary B Denver, CO 1924. ED University of Colorado BA (1945); University of Pittsburgh MSW (1948); Columbia University DSW (1976). PRIM NONPR EMPL professor: Hunter College. NONPR AFFIL member: Pi Gamma Mu; co-chairwoman: United States Committee Celebration UN Year of Older Persons; member: Phi Beta Kappa; member: New York Academy Science; executive committee: New York Community Trust Center Policy Aging; member: National Council Aging; fellow: New York Academy Medicine; member: National Association Social Workers; editor-in-chief: Journal Gerontological Social Work; lecturer: Mount Sinai School of Medicine; member: Friends Relatives Institutionalized Aged; member: Gerontological Society; member policy committee: Federal Council Aging; senior fellow: Brookdale Foundation; member: Delta Sigma Rho; member: American Public Welfare Association; member: American Society Aging; member: Academy Humanities Sciences; board member: American Federation Aging Research.
A. Carleton Dukess: chairman, trustee
Madeline Einhorn Glick: treasurer, trustee
Stephen Heyman: trustee
Chung Wha Hong: trustee
Martha Jones: trustee
William M. Kelly: trustee B 1949. ED Villanova University BS (1970-1972). PRIM CORP EMPL executive vice president, director: Blue Tee Corp. CORP

AFFIL executive vice president, director: UTL Holding Inc.
Peter Kwong: trustee
Thomas Mackell, Jr.: trustee
Maria Mottola: executive director
Jason Warwin: trustee

Grants Analysis

Disclosure Period: calendar year ending 2003
Total Grants: $5,501,470
Number of Grants: 307
Average Grant: $17,920
Highest Grant: $50,000
Lowest Grant: $100
Typical Range: $10,000 to $30,000

Recent Grants

Note: Grants derived from 2003 Form 990.
General

50,000	Northwest Bronx Community and Clergy Coalition, New York, NY -- to organize residents of Northwest Bronx through neighborhood affiliates
40,000	Community Resource Exchange, New York, NY -- to provide individual technical assistance to New York foundation grantees
30,000	Community Resource Exchange, New York, NY -- to provide individual technical assistance to New York foundation grantees
25,000	Albanian American Women's Organization, New York, NY -- to strengthen and increase advocacy and organizing work in Albanian-American community
25,000	Albanian American Women's Organization, New York, NY -- to strengthen and increase advocacy and organizing work in Albanian-American community
25,000	Ansob Center for Refugees, New York, NY -- general support for a community-based center
25,000	Ansob Center for Refugees, New York, NY -- general support for a community-based center
25,000	Asian American Legal Defense and Education Fund, New York, NY -- to hire a staff attorney with immigration expertise
25,000	Community Food Resource Center, New York, NY -- for project to increase the low-income people for earning income tax credit
25,000	Council of Pakistan Organization, New York, NY -- for the south Asian rights projects

NEW YORK LIFE INSURANCE CO.

Company Headquarters

New York, NY
Web: http://www.newyorklife.com

Company Description

Revenue: US$27.175 billion (2004)
Profit: US$1.213 billion (2004)
Employees: 12200 (2003)
Fortune Rank: 68, per FORTUNE Magazine's list of 500 Largest U.S. Corporations (2004).
SIC(s): 6311 Life Insurance.

Operating Locations

New York Life Insurance Co. (CT--Greenwich; DE--Wilmington; GA--Marietta; NJ--Fort Lee; TX--Austin, Dallas)

Nonmonetary Support

Volunteer Programs: Provides grants to local grass-roots organizations where employees volunteer.

New York Life Foundation

Giving Contact

Peter J. Bushyeager, President
51 Madison Avenue, Room 604
New York, NY 10010-1655
Phone: (212)576-4902
E-mail: NYLFoundation@newyorklife.com
Web: http://www.newyorklife.com/foundation

Alternate Contact

Phone: (212)576-3865

Description

EIN: 132989476
Organization Type: Corporate Foundation
Giving Locations: CA: San Francisco/San Ramon; FL: Tampa; GA: Atlanta; MN: Minneapolis; NY: New York; OH: Cleveland; TX: Dallas nationally.
Grant Types: Capital, Employee Matching Gifts, General Support, Project, Scholarship.
Note: Employee matching gift ratio: 1 to 1 for higher education.

Financial Summary

Total Giving: $6,005,326 (2002); $9,663,615 (2001). Note: Contributes through foundation only.
Giving Analysis: Giving for 2002 includes: foundation matching gifts ($584,705); foundation grants to United Way ($1,275,050).
Assets: $83,821,407 (2002); $72,615,739 (2001).
Gifts Received: $13,883,460 (2002); $8,655,780 (2001); $4,563,327 (2000). Note: Contributions were received from New York Life Insurance Company.

Typical Recipients

Arts & Humanities: Arts Associations & Councils, Arts Centers, Arts Institutes, Ballet, Community Arts, Historic Preservation, Libraries, Museums/Galleries, Music, Performing Arts, Public Broadcasting, Theater
Civic & Public Affairs: African American Affairs, Asian American Affairs, Botanical Gardens/Parks, Business/Free Enterprise, Civil Rights, Community Foundations, Economic Development, Economic Policy, Employment/Job Training, Civic & Public Affairs-General, Housing, Law & Justice, Legal Aid, Municipalities/Towns, Nonprofit Management, Philanthropic Organizations, Professional & Trade Associations, Public Policy, Urban & Community Affairs, Women's Affairs, Zoos/Aquariums
Education: Afterschool/Enrichment Programs, Arts/Humanities Education, Business Education, Colleges & Universities, Community & Junior Colleges, Education Associations, Education Funds, Education Reform, Education-General, Health & Physical Education, International Studies, Leadership Training, Legal Education, Literacy, Medical Education, Minority Education, Public Education (Precollege), Religious Education, Science/Mathematics Education, Special Education, Student Aid
Environment: Energy, Environment-General, Protection
Health: AIDS/HIV, Clinics/Medical Centers, Emergency/Ambulance Services, Eyes/Blindness, Geriatric Health, Health Organizations, Hospitals, Medical Rehabilitation, Medical Research, Medical Training, Mental Health, Nursing Services, Single-Disease Health Associations, Transplant Networks/Donor Banks
Religion: Religious Organizations
Science: Science Museums, Scientific Organizations
Social Services: Big Brothers/Big Sisters, Camps, Child Welfare, Community Centers, Community Service Organizations, Counseling, Crime Prevention,

Day Care, Domestic Violence, Emergency Relief, Family Services, Food/Clothing Distribution, People with Disabilities, Recreation & Athletics, Scouts, Senior Services, Shelters/Homelessness, Substance Abuse, United Funds/United Ways, Volunteer Services, YMCA/YWCA/YMHA/YWHA, Youth Organizations

Application Procedures

Initial Contact: Send a written proposal, no longer than two pages in length, on the applicant organization's letterhead.

Application Requirements: Include a brief description of the specific program for which support is sought, including objectives, timetable for implementation, population and geographic area served, budget, how the project will be sustained, methods for evaluation and utilization results; proof of tax-exempt status; list of officers and board members; brief a description of organization; latest annual report; recently audited financial statement; current IRS Form 990; current itemized budget and funding sources; and a list of corporate and foundation contributors during the prior 12 months. Supportive material and documentation may be attached.

Deadlines: None.

Review Process: Foundation staff review and research each proposal to determine its eligibility for foundation funding. If the foundation is interested in a particular proposal, the foundation will request interviews with the applicant organization's staff and conduct site visits.

Evaluative Criteria: The foundation gives preference to proposals that include opportunities for New York Life employee volunteer involvement.

Decision Notification: Board meets in March, June, September, and December.

Restrictions

In general, the foundation does not make grants to individuals; government agencies; sectarian or religious organizations; social, professional, athletic, or veterans' organizations; seminars, conferences or trips; endowments, memorials, or capital campaigns; organizations that are members of United Ways already supported by the foundation; fundraising events, telethons, races, or similar activities; goodwill advertising; basic or applied research; or organizations that discriminate on the basis of race, color, creed, gender, or national origin.

Additional Information

The foundation requires periodic reports from all organizations that it supports.

Publications: Foundation Annual Report; Application Guidelines

Corporate Officials

Carol Joan Reuter: vice president, president, chief executive officer B Brooklyn, NY 1941. ED Saint John's University BA (1962). PRIM CORP EMPL vice president: New York Life Insurance Co. NONPR AFFIL member corporate associates: United Way America.

Sy Sternberg: chairman, president, chief executive officer ED City College of New York BA. NONPR AFFIL trustee: Hackley School; vice chairman: Kennedy Center Corporate Fund; trustee: Big Brothers/Big Sisters of New York; chairman: City University of New York Business Leadership Council.

Foundation Officials

Carolyn M. Buscarino: director

Peter J. Bushyeager: president, director, chief executive officer

Michael T. Delahaye: director NONPR AFFIL executive board: Boy Scouts of America.

Theodore J. Kohnen: treasurer

Sy Sternberg: chairman, director (see above)

George J. Trapp: secretary, director

Richard W. Zuccaro: vice president

Grants Analysis

Disclosure Period: calendar year ending 2002

Total Grants: $4,145,571*

Number of Grants: 232

Average Grant: $15,782*

Highest Grant: $500,000

Lowest Grant: $500

Typical Range: $5,000 to $30,000

*Note: Giving excludes matching gifts and United Way. Average grant figure excludes highest grant.

Recent Grants

Note: Grants derived from 2004 Form 990.

General

8,700	American Red Cross, Birmingham, AL
699	Energy East Foundation Inc., San Francisco, CA

NEW YORK MERCANTILE EXCHANGE

Company Headquarters

1 NOR End Ave.
New York, NY 10282
Web: http://www.nymex.com

Company Description

Employees: 375
SIC(s): 6231 Security & Commodity Exchanges.

Nonmonetary Support

Type: Donated Equipment

New York Mercantile Exchange Charitable Foundation

Giving Contact

Madeline Boyd, Chairman Executive Committee
New York Mercantile Exchange Charitable Foundation
Executive Committee
1 North End Avenue
World Financial Center, Room 1440
New York, NY 10282-1101
Phone: (212)299-2517
E-mail: charitablefoundation@nymex.com
Web: http://www.nymex.com/jsp/about/cs_relief_fund.jsp

Description

Founded: 1989
EIN: 133586378
Organization Type: Corporate Foundation
Giving Locations: principally near operating locations and to national organizations.
Grant Types: Emergency, General Support, Project, Research, Scholarship, Seed Money.

Donor Information

Founder: Established in 1989 by the New York Mercantile Exchange.

Financial Summary

Total Giving: $1,709,583 (2003); $3,412,267 (2002); $1,287,536 (2001)

Assets: $932,802 (2003); $2,078,557 (2002); $2,249,701 (2001)

Gifts Received: $960,643 (2003); $3,488,953 (2002); $1,776,956 (2001). Note: In 2003, contributions were received from 2 D Photo Production LLC ($7,000), CBM & Associates International ($10,000), and miscellaneous contributions from individuals ($943,643). In 2000 and 2001, substantial contributions were received from the New York Mercantile Exchange Corp. In 1995, contributions were received from the New York Mercantile Exchange Corp. ($500,000), MBF Clearing Corp. ($11,440), Pioneer Futures ($15,270), Tudor Investment Corp. ($10,000), Richard Schaeffer ($7,000), and Philbro Energy ($5,000); miscellaneous contributions of less than $5,000 each also were received.

Typical Recipients

Arts & Humanities: Arts Associations & Councils, Arts Outreach, Community Arts, Arts & Humanities-General, Libraries, Museums/Galleries, Music, Performing Arts, Public Broadcasting, Theater

Civic & Public Affairs: Asian American Affairs, Botanical Gardens/Parks, Business/Free Enterprise, Community Foundations, Employment/Job Training, Ethnic Organizations, Civic & Public Affairs-General, Hispanic Affairs, Housing, Inner-City Development, Philanthropic Organizations, Professional & Trade Associations, Public Policy, Urban & Community Affairs, Women's Affairs

Education: Afterschool/Enrichment Programs, Colleges & Universities, Education Funds, Education Reform, Elementary Education (Public), Environmental Education, Faculty Development, Education-General, Gifted & Talented Programs, Medical Education, Private Education (Precollege), Public Education (Precollege), Special Education, Student Aid

Environment: Air/Water Quality, Environment-General, Resource Conservation, Wildlife Protection

Health: Adolescent Health Issues, AIDS/HIV, Cancer, Children's Health/Hospitals, Clinics/Medical Centers, Diabetes, Emergency/Ambulance Services, Health-General, Health Funds, Hospices, Hospitals, Hospitals (University Affiliated), Medical Rehabilitation, Multiple Sclerosis, Public Health, Research/Studies Institutes, Single-Disease Health Associations, Trauma Treatment

Religion: Churches, Dioceses, Religion-General, Jewish Causes, Religious Welfare, Synagogues/Temples

Science: Science Museums

Social Services: Big Brothers/Big Sisters, Camps, Child Abuse, Child Welfare, Community Centers, Community Service Organizations, Counseling, Crime Prevention, Day Care, Delinquency & Criminal Rehabilitation, Domestic Violence, Emergency Relief, Family Services, Food/Clothing Distribution, Homes, People with Disabilities, Recreation & Athletics, Senior Services, Shelters/Homelessness, Social Services-General, Substance Abuse, Volunteer Services, YMCA/YWCA/YMHA/YWHA, Youth Organizations

Application Procedures

Initial Contact: Send a brief letter of inquiry.

Application Requirements: Include proof of tax-exempt status.

Deadlines: None.

Restrictions

Does not support individuals.

Corporate Officials

Patrick F. Conroy: vice president, director PRIM CORP EMPL vice president: New York Mercantile Exchange.

Daniel Rappaport: chairman, director PRIM CORP EMPL chairman, director: New York Mercantile Exchange.

R. Patrick Thomson: president, director PRIM CORP EMPL president, director: New York Mercantile Exchange.

Foundation Officials

Neil Citrone: director

Albert Helmig: director

Steven Karvellas: director

Lewis A. Raibley, III: chief financial officer

Daniel Rappaport: president, director (see above)

Gary Rizzi: secretary, director

Richard Schaeffer: director
Mitchell Steinhause: vice president, director
Vincent Viola: chairman, director

Grants Analysis
Disclosure Period: calendar year ending 2003
Total Grants: $1,623,583*
Number of Grants: 240
Average Grant: $6,765
Highest Grant: $100,000
Lowest Grant: $125
Typical Range: $2,000 to $10,000
*Note: Giving excludes scholarships.

Recent Grants
Note: Grants derived from 2003 Form 990.
General

100,000	American Camping Association, New York, NY -- to fund camperships for inner-city children to attend summer camps
50,000	Brooklyn Bureau of Community Service, Brooklyn, NY -- to fund the jets academy program
25,000	Chai Lifeline, New York, NY -- to support summer camp services
25,000	National Italian American Foundation, Washington, DC -- to fund a scholarship
25,000	Tuesday's Children, Manhasset, NY -- to expand programs to enhance the quality of life for children
24,800	Swim Across America, Darien, CT -- to sponsor a swim relay team
20,000	Lower Manhattan Cultural Council, New York, NY -- to sponsor 30th anniversary circle
20,000	Police Athletic League, Freehold, NJ -- to support a game room
17,500	Miracle Foundation, Garden City, NY -- to help with the construction of miracle building
15,000	College of St. Francis Xavier, New York, NY -- to support the corpus of the Lt. Kevin Dowdell FDNY memorial scholarship

New York Stock Exchange Inc.

Company Headquarters
New York, NY
Web: http://www.nyse.com

Company Description
Employees: 1,440
SIC(s): 6231 Security & Commodity Exchanges.

New York Stock Exchange Foundation, Inc.

Giving Contact
Robert T. Zito
11 Wall Street, 6th Floor
New York, NY 10005
Phone: (212)656-5057
Fax: (212)656-5629

Alternate Contact
Phone: (212)656-5290

Description
EIN: 133203195
Organization Type: Corporate Foundation
Giving Locations: DC: Washington; NY: New York

Grant Types: Employee Matching Gifts, General Support.

Financial Summary
Total Giving: $3,454,854 (2002); $2,370,963 (2001). Note: Contributes through foundation only.
Giving Analysis: Giving for 2002 includes: foundation grants to United Way ($100,000); foundation matching gifts ($156,354)
Assets: $19,354,404 (2002); $23,219,248 (2001)
Gifts Received: $3,048,809 (2002); $1,500,000 (2001); $1,500,000 (2000). Note: Contributions were received from New York Stock Exchange, Inc.

Typical Recipients
Arts & Humanities: Arts Associations & Councils, Arts Centers, Arts Funds, Ballet, Community Arts, History & Archaeology, Libraries, Museums/Galleries, Music, Opera, Performing Arts, Public Broadcasting, Theater
Civic & Public Affairs: African American Affairs, Botanical Gardens/Parks, Civil Rights, Economic Development, Economic Policy, Ethnic Organizations, Civic & Public Affairs-General, Law & Justice, Municipalities/Towns, Philanthropic Organizations, Public Policy, Safety, Urban & Community Affairs, Women's Affairs
Education: Afterschool/Enrichment Programs, Business Education, Business-School Partnerships, Colleges & Universities, Economic Education, Education Funds, Education-General, Health & Physical Education, Legal Education, Medical Education, Minority Education, Private Education (Precollege), Public Education (Precollege), Student Aid
Environment: Environment-General
Health: Adolescent Health Issues, Cancer, Clinics/Medical Centers, Hospitals, Hospitals (University Affiliated)
Religion: Religious Organizations, Religious Welfare
Science: Science Museums
Social Services: At-Risk Youth, Camps, Child Welfare, Community Service Organizations, Crime Prevention, Day Care, Emergency Relief, Food/Clothing Distribution, People with Disabilities, Recreation & Athletics, Scouts, Shelters/Homelessness, Social Services-General, United Funds/United Ways, Volunteer Services, YMCA/YWCA/YMHA/YWHA, Youth Organizations

Application Procedures
Initial Contact: Send a brief letter.
Application Requirements: Include a description of the program.
Deadlines: None.

Corporate Officials
John A. Thain: chief executive officer ED Massachusetts Institute of Technology BS (1977); Harvard University MBA (1979). PRIM CORP EMPL chief executive officer: New York Stock Exchange Inc.

Foundation Officials
Carol Bartz: director
William B. Harrison, Jr.: director
Keith R. Helsby: treasurer B Scranton, PA 1944. ED Gettysburg College (1966). PRIM NONPR EMPL senior vice president, chief financial officer: New York Stock Exchange, Inc.
Alan Holzer: controller
Joseph A. Mahoney: director
Sir Deryck C. Maughan: director B Consett, United Kingdom 1947. ED University of London Kings College BA (1969); Stanford University MBA (1978). PRIM CORP EMPL vice chairman: Citigroup Inc. NONPR AFFIL member: Trilateral Commission.
George C. McNamee: chairman, director
Robert M. Murphy: director
Leon Pannetta: 2004
Robert T. Zito: secretary, director

Grants Analysis
Disclosure Period: calendar year ending 2002
Total Grants: $3,198,500*
Number of Grants: 67
Average Grant: $33,054*
Highest Grant: $550,000
Lowest Grant: $1,000
Typical Range: $10,000 to $50,000
*Note: Giving excludes matching gifts and United Way. Average grant figure excludes two highest grants ($1,050,000).

Recent Grants
Note: Grants derived from 2003 Form 990.
Library-Related

25,000	Pierpont Morgan Library, New York, NY -- towards educational causes
15,000	New York Public Library, New York, NY -- towards educational causes

General

550,000	New York University Downtown Hospital, New York, NY -- towards charitable causes
500,000	New York City Public Private Initiatives Inc., New York, NY -- towards charitable causes
150,000	Duke University School of Law, Durham, NC -- towards educational causes
150,000	Vanderbilt University Law School, Nashville, TN -- towards educational causes
125,000	St. Vincent's Hospital Medical Center, New York, NY -- towards charitable causes
125,000	Securities Industry Foundation for Economic Education, New York, NY -- towards educational causes
100,000	Lincoln Center for the Performing Arts, New York, NY -- towards charitable causes
100,000	Metropolitan Museum of Art, New York, NY -- towards charitable causes
100,000	New York Presbyterian Hospital, New York, NY -- towards charitable causes
100,000	United Way of Tri State, New York, NY -- towards charitable causes

New York Times Co.

Company Headquarters
229 W. 43rd Street
New York, NY 10036
Phone: (212)556-1234
Web: http://www.nytco.com

Company Description
Founded: 1896
Ticker: NYT
Exchange: NYSE
Revenue: US$3.227 billion (2003)
Profit: US$302.7 million (2003)
Employees: 12400 (2003)
SIC(s): 2711 Newspapers, 2721 Periodicals, 4832 Radio Broadcasting Stations, 4833 Television Broadcasting Stations.

Operating Locations
New York Times Co. (AL--Florence, Gadsden, Huntsville, Tuscaloosa; CA--Santa Barbara, Santa Rosa; CT--Trumbull; FL--Avon Park, Gainesville, Lake City, Lakeland, Leesburg, Ocala, Palatka, Sarasota, Sebring; IL--Moline; KY--Harlan, Madisonville, Middlesboro; LA--Opelousas, Thibodaux; ME--Madison; MA--Billerica, Boston; MS--Booneville, Corinth; NJ--Carlstadt, Cherry Hill; NC--Hendersonville, Lexington, Wilmington; PA--Avoca; RI--Newport; SC--Spartanburg; TN--Memphis, Tazewell)

New York Times Co. Foundation

Giving Contact

Jack Rosenthal, President
229 W. 43rd Street
10th Floor
New York, NY 10036-3959
Phone: (212)556-1886
Fax: (212)556-4450
Web: http://nytco.com/company/foundation/
index.html

Description

EIN: 136066955
Organization Type: Corporate Foundation
Giving Locations: NY: New York metropolitan area communities served by company affiliates; some internationally; some nationally.
Grant Types: Employee Matching Gifts, General Support, Multiyear/Continuing Support, Scholarship.
Note: Employee matching gift ratio: 1.5 to 1 up to $3,000 annually.

Financial Summary

Total Giving: $6,489,480 (2003); $5,809,233 (2002); $5,859,668 (2001). Note: Contributes through corporate direct giving program and foundation.
Assets: $2,601,808 (2003); $1,854,144 (2002); $2,110,418 (2001)
Gifts Received: $7,425,000 (2003); $7,000,000 (2002); $5,700,000 (2001). Note: Contributions are received from The New York Times Company.

Typical Recipients

Arts & Humanities: Arts Centers, Arts Festivals, Arts Institutes, Arts Outreach, Ballet, Community Arts, Dance, Ethnic & Folk Arts, Film & Video, Historic Preservation, History & Archaeology, Libraries, Literary Arts, Museums/Galleries, Music, Opera, Performing Arts, Public Broadcasting, Theater
Civic & Public Affairs: Botanical Gardens/Parks, Clubs, Economic Development, Employment/Job Training, First Amendment Issues, Civic & Public Affairs-General, Housing, Law & Justice, Municipalities/ Towns, Professional & Trade Associations, Safety, Urban & Community Affairs, Women's Affairs
Education: Arts/Humanities Education, Business Education, Colleges & Universities, Community & Junior Colleges, Engineering/Technological Education, Faculty Development, Journalism/Media Education, Leadership Training, Legal Education, Literacy, Minority Education, Private Education (Precollege), Public Education (Precollege), School Volunteerism, Science/Mathematics Education, Special Education, Student Aid
Environment: Air/Water Quality, Environment-General, Wildlife Protection
Health: Children's Health/Hospitals
International: Foreign Arts Organizations, Foreign Educational Institutions
Religion: Jewish Causes
Science: Science Exhibits & Fairs, Science Museums, Scientific Centers & Institutes
Social Services: Community Service Organizations, Crime Prevention, Delinquency & Criminal Rehabilitation, Food/Clothing Distribution, Homes, Recreation & Athletics, Senior Services, Shelters/ Homelessness, Social Services-General, Substance Abuse, United Funds/United Ways, Volunteer Services, YMCA/YWCA/YMHA/YWHA, Youth Organizations

Application Procedures

Initial Contact: Submit a brief letter. Letters from organizations in New York should be addressed to the foundation president; letters from organizations located outside New York should be addressed to the nearest Times Company business unit.
Application Requirements: Include a description of organization, amount requested, purpose of funds sought, recently audited financial statement, proof of tax-exempt status, list of the board of directors, and other potential sources of support.
Deadlines: December 1 and June 1.
Decision Notification: The board of directors meets at least twice annually, within the first and third quarter of each calendar year, to review the president's recommendations and authorize grants to be disbursed.
Notes: An optional application form is available on the foundation's web site. The foundation discourages elaborate/lengthy proposals.

Restrictions

Does not support individuals; sectarian religious institutions and causes; capital improvements; or health, drug, or alcohol therapy.

Additional Information

The company also administers the New York Times Neediest Cases Fund, which raises about $5 million annually for organizations that respond to urban needs such as hunger and homelessness.
Grantees must submit a post-grant report accounting for expenditures.
Publications: Foundation Annual Report

Corporate Officials

John Fellows Akers: member, director, publisher B Boston, MA 1934. ED Yale University BS (1956). PRIM CORP EMPL consultant: New York Times Co. CORP AFFIL director: Springs Industries Inc.; director: WR Grace & Co.; director: PepsiCo. NONPR AFFIL trustee: California Institute Technology; trustee: Metropolitan Museum Art.
Russell T. Lewis: president, chief executive officer B 1947. PRIM CORP EMPL president, chief operating officer: New York Times Co. CORP AFFIL vice chairman: Affiliated Publications Inc.
Arthur Ochs Sulzberger, Jr.: director, chairman, publisher B Mt. Kisco, NY 1951. ED Tufts University BA (1974); Harvard University Graduate School of Business Administration (1985). PRIM CORP EMPL director, chairman emeritus: New York Times Co. NONPR AFFIL member: Newspaper Association America; director: Times Square Business Improvement District.

Foundation Officials

R. Anthony Benten: assistant treasurer
Rhonda L. Brauer: secretary
Laura J. Corwin: secretary B Cambridge, MA 1945. ED Brown University AB (1966); University of Pennsylvania MA (1967); University of Pennsylvania PhD (1970); Yale University JD (1975). PRIM CORP EMPL vice president, secretary: New York Times Co. ADD CORP EMPL secretary: Golf Digest/Tennis Inc.; secretary: Sarasota Herald-Tribune Co.
Jacqueline H. Dryfoos: chairman, director
Leonard P. Forman: senior vice president
Michael Golden: senior vice president, director
James C. Lessersohn: vice president, treasurer
Ellen R. Marram: director
John M. O'Brien: senior vice president
Randall K. Short: assistant treasurer
Donald M. Stewart: director PRIM NONPR EMPL president, chief executive officer: College Board. CORP AFFIL director: Campbell Soup Co. NONPR AFFIL advisor: Grinnell College; adj lect: John F. Kennedy School Government; president, chief executive officer: Chicago Community Trust.
Solomon Brown Watson, IV: senior vice president, general counsel B Salem, NJ 1944. ED Howard University BA (1966); Harvard University JD (1971). PRIM CORP EMPL senior vice president, general counsel: New York Times Co. ADD CORP EMPL secretary, director: Cruising World Publishings. CORP AFFIL director: Affiliated Publications Inc. NONPR AFFIL member legal aff committee: Newspaper Association America; director: Veterans Advisor Board; member: Massachusetts Bar Association; member: Association Bar New York City; director: Legal Aid Society; member: American Bar Association; director: American Corporate Counsel Association; director: American Arbitration Association; director: Agent Orange Asst Fund.

Grants Analysis

Disclosure Period: calendar year ending 2003
Total Grants: $5,167,020*
Number of Grants: 350 (approx)
Average Grant: $14,763
Highest Grant: $175,000 (approx)
Typical Range: $4,000 to $50,000
*Note: Giving includes matching gifts.

Recent Grants

Note: Grants derived from 2001 Form 990.
General

100,000	American Museum of Natural History, New York, NY -- for biobulletin in hall of biodiversity
50,000	Roundabout Theater, New York, NY -- for arts in education for public schools
50,000	Studio in a School, New York, NY -- for Child Care Centers
45,000	Foreign Policy Association, New York, NY -- for production of world maps and web post for publication
40,000	Argus Community, Bronx, NY -- for recovering substance abuse
40,000	City Parks Foundation, New York, NY -- for Nature Programs
30,000	Brooklyn Botanic Garden, Brooklyn, NY -- for environment and sciences programs for teachers and children
30,000	Center for Court Innovation, New York, NY -- for operating expenses
30,000	Chamber Music Society of Lincoln Center, New York, NY -- for career development for young musicians
30,000	Columbia Business School, New York, NY -- for MBSA Real Estate Program

THE NEW YORKER MAGAZINE

Company Headquarters

4 Broadway
New York, NY 10004
Web: http://www.newyorker.com

Company Description

Employees: 400
SIC(s): 2700 Printing & Publishing.
Parent Company: Advance Magazine Publishers

Nonmonetary Support

Type: Donated Equipment

Giving Contact

David Carey, Publisher
4 Times Square 42nd St. 7th Ave.
New York, NY 10036
Phone: (212)286-5900

Description

Organization Type: Corporate Giving Program
Giving Locations: headquarters area only.
Grant Types: Award, Employee Matching Gifts, General Support, Multiyear/Continuing Support, Scholarship.

Financial Summary

Total Giving: Company does not disclose contributions figures.

Typical Recipients

Arts & Humanities: Arts Appreciation, Arts Associations & Councils, Arts Centers, Arts Festivals, Arts Funds, Arts Institutes, Community Arts, Dance, Ethnic & Folk Arts, Arts & Humanities-General, Historic Preservation, Libraries, Literary Arts, Museums/Galleries, Music, Opera, Performing Arts, Public Broadcasting, Theater, Visual Arts

Civic & Public Affairs: Civil Rights, First Amendment Issues, Civic & Public Affairs-General, Law & Justice, Legal Aid, Women's Affairs, Zoos/Aquariums

Education: Arts/Humanities Education, Colleges & Universities, Education Associations, Education Funds, Elementary Education (Private), Education-General, Journalism/Media Education, Literacy, Medical Education, Minority Education, Preschool Education, Public Education (Precollege), Science/Mathematics Education, Special Education

Health: Emergency/Ambulance Services, Health-General, Geriatric Health, Health Policy/Cost Containment, Health Funds, Health Organizations, Hospices, Hospitals, Medical Rehabilitation, Medical Research, Medical Training, Mental Health, Nursing Services, Nutrition, Public Health, Single-Disease Health Associations

International: Health Care/Hospitals

Science: Observatories & Planetariums, Scientific Centers & Institutes, Scientific Organizations

Social Services: Child Welfare, Community Service Organizations, Domestic Violence, Family Planning, Family Services, Food/Clothing Distribution, People with Disabilities, Refugee Assistance, Senior Services, Shelters/Homelessness, Social Services-General, Substance Abuse, United Funds/United Ways, Volunteer Services, Youth Organizations

Application Procedures

Initial Contact: Send a brief letter of inquiry and a full proposal.

Application Requirements: Include a description of organization, amount requested, purpose of funds sought, and proof of tax-exempt status.

Deadlines: None.

Restrictions

Does not support individuals, religious organizations for sectarian purposes, or political or lobbying groups.

Corporate Officials

Thomas Florio: chairman, president, chief executive officer, director PRIM CORP EMPL chairman, president, chief executive officer, director: New Yorker Magazine.

Grants Analysis

Typical Range: $50 to $1,000

NEWALLIANCE
BANCSHARES INC.

Company Headquarters

195 Church St.
New Haven, CT 06510
Phone: (203)789-2767
Fax: (203)789-2650
Web: http://www.newalliancebank.com

Company Description

Founded: 1838
Ticker: NAL
Former Name: New Haven Savings Bank.
Assets: US$373 million (2002)
Employees: 600 (2002)
SIC(s): 6036 Savings Institutions Except Federal.

NewAlliance Foundation

Giving Contact

Kim A. Healey, Vice President
195 Church St.
New Haven, CT 06510-2009
Phone: (203)784-5057
Web: http://www.nhsb.com/foundation/default.asp

Description

Founded: 1998
Organization Type: Corporate Foundation
Former Name: New Haven Savings Bank Foundation, Inc. (2004).
Grant Types: General Support.

Financial Summary

Total Giving: $490,129 (fiscal year ending March 31, 2003); $426,317 (fiscal 2002); $379,880 (fiscal 2001)
Giving Analysis: Giving for fiscal 2003 includes: foundation matching gifts ($7,880); foundation grants to United Way ($47,250); fiscal 2002: foundation grants to United Way ($93,700) fiscal 2001: foundation grants to United Way ($84,000)
Assets: $8,054,008 (fiscal 2003); $10,039,467 (fiscal 2002); $8,671,739 (fiscal 2001)
Gifts Received: $1,464,439 (fiscal 2002); $2,700,000 (fiscal 2001); $2,200,137 (fiscal 1999). Note: Contributions were received from New Haven Savings Bank.

Typical Recipients

Arts & Humanities: Arts Associations & Councils, Arts Funds, Arts Outreach, Ballet, Community Arts, Arts & Humanities-General, Historic Preservation, Libraries, Museums/Galleries, Music, Theater

Civic & Public Affairs: Community Foundations, Economic Development, Civic & Public Affairs-General, Housing, Municipalities/Towns, Nonprofit Management, Philanthropic Organizations, Urban & Community Affairs

Education: Afterschool/Enrichment Programs, Arts/Humanities Education, Business Education, Colleges & Universities, Education-General, Leadership Training, Literacy, Private Education (Precollege), Public Education (Precollege), School Volunteerism

Health: Cancer, Children's Health/Hospitals, Health Funds, Hospitals, Multiple Sclerosis, Nursing Services, Outpatient Health Care, Single-Disease Health Associations

Social Services: Animal Protection, Big Brothers/Big Sisters, Child Welfare, Community Centers, Community Service Organizations, Counseling, Family Services, Senior Services, Social Services-General, United Funds/United Ways, YMCA/YWCA/YMHA/YWHA, Youth Organizations

Application Procedures

Initial Contact: No specific form required at this time.

Application Requirements: Include certification of nonprofit status, audited financial statements, a description of need and authorization by board of requesting charity.

Deadlines: None.

Foundation Officials

Kenneth P. Kaminsky: president, director
Paul A. McCraven: vice president, secretary, treasurer
Julia McNamara: director
Cornell Scott: chairman, director

Grants Analysis

Disclosure Period: fiscal year ending March 31, 2003
Total Grants: $434,999*
Number of Grants: 66
Average Grant: $5,923*
Highest Grant: $50,000
Lowest Grant: $500
Typical Range: $1,000 to $10,000

***Note:** Giving excludes United Way and matching gifts. Average grant figure excludes highest grant.

Recent Grants

Note: Grants derived from 2002 Form 990.
Library-Related

2,500	Southern Connecticut Library Council, Hamden, CT

General

88,200	United Way Greater New Haven, New Haven, CT
25,000	Central Connecticut Coast YMCA, New Haven, CT
22,500	Neighborhood Housing Services of New Haven Inc., New Haven, CT
20,000	National Arts Stabilization, New Haven, CT
20,000	St. Raphael Foundation, New Haven, CT
15,000	Yale New Haven Hospital, New Haven, CT
10,000	Amistad Academy, New Haven, CT
10,000	Summerbridge New Haven, New Haven, CT
7,500	Learning for Life/Connecticut Yankee Council, Milford, CT
7,500	Southern Connecticut Conference, CT

CHARLOTTE W.
NEWCOMBE FOUNDATION

Giving Contact

Janet A. Fearon, Executive Director
35 Park Place
Princeton, NJ 08542-6918
Phone: (609)924-7022

Description

Founded: 1979
EIN: 232120614
Organization Type: Specialized/Single Purpose Foundation
Giving Locations: nationally.
Grant Types: Endowment, Fellowship, General Support, Matching, Scholarship.

Donor Information

Founder: The Charlotte W. Newcombe Foundation is a private foundation created under the will of Mrs. Newcombe, who died in 1979, and left a fortune in excess of $34 million. In her will, Mrs. Newcombe nominated five trustees, charged them with the creation of a scholarship foundation to bear her name, and funded the foundation with half of her residual estate.

The Charlotte W. Newcombe Foundation was chartered in Pennsylvania in November 1979, and opened its administrative offices in Princeton, NJ, in January 1980.

Financial Summary

Total Giving: $1,777,687 (2002); $1,928,950 (2001)
Giving Analysis: Giving for 2002 includes: foundation fellowships ($733,700) foundation scholarships ($1,037,000)
Assets: $37,675,763 (2002); $45,295,265 (2001)

Typical Recipients

Arts & Humanities: Libraries
Civic & Public Affairs: Community Foundations, Nonprofit Management
Education: Colleges & Universities, Community & Junior Colleges, Continuing Education, Education Funds, Religious Education, Student Aid
Religion: Seminaries

Application Procedures

Initial Contact: Prospective applicant institutions should send a letter or telephone the foundation. For fellowships, applicants should request applications by mid-November from the Woodrow Wilson National Fellowship Foundation, CN 5281, Princeton, NJ 08543-5281, (609)452-7007. Information on the scholarships will be sent to qualifying schools who call or write the foundation. Colleges and universities applying for scholarships for students with disabilities and scholarships for mature women can obtain application materials from June through October.

Deadlines: Deadlines for returning completed applications are November 1 for applying organizations for students with disabilities and mature women scholarships and mid-December for fellowships. No deadlines are listed for the scholarships at Presbyterian colleges.

Review Process: For colleges and universities in the Foundation's Programs, trustees' decisions are announced in May for funding beginning in July. Applicants for fellowships will be notified in April for fellowships that begin in June or September.

Restrictions

The foundation only supports colleges and universities through scholarships and fellowships for undergraduate and graduate students; no aid is available for post-doctoral fellowships. Funding goes to programs that have been developed and continued by the Foundation's trustees. Scholarships are not granted for publicly supported two-year colleges. In the program for mature women, no grants are made to professional schools. A college or university may apply for funding in only one of these two scholarship programs. No grants are given to individuals, community organizations, or for staffing, program development, or building funds. No loans are made.

The foundation does not make grants to individual students. grants to individual students. The foundation primarily supports preselected organizations.

Additional Information

The Foundation funds selected colleges and universities. These institutions handle all administrative details, including selection of recipients and the awarding of fellowships and scholarships. Individuals may not apply directly to the foundation for grants.

The foundation asks applicant colleges/universities to call to determine eligibility.

Publications: Annual Report

Foundation Officials

Robert Merrihew Adams: trustee B Philadelphia, PA 1937. ED Princeton University AB (1959); Oxford University BA (1961); Princeton Theological Seminary BD (1962); Oxford University MA (1965); Cornell University MA (1967); Cornell University PhD (1969). PRIM NONPR EMPL professor philosophy: University of California, Los Angeles. NONPR AFFIL member: Society Christian Ethics; member: Society Christian Philosophers; member: American Philosophical Association; member: American Academy Religion; member: American Association University Professors; member: American Academy of Arts & Sciences.

K. Roald Bergethon: trustee B Tromso, Norway June 08, 1918. ED DePauw University AB (1938); Cornell University MA (1940); Cornell University PhD (1945). NONPR AFFIL member: Phi Theta Pi; member: Sigma Delta Chi; member: Phi Eta Sigma; member: Phi Kappa Phi; president emeritus: Lafayette College; member: Phi Beta Kappa. CLUB AFFIL Cornell Club; Northampton Country Club.

Sallie G. Campbell: associate director

Janet A. Fearon: executive director, trustee

Aaron E. Gast: trustee ED Wheaton College BA (1950); Princeton Theological Seminary MDiv (1953); Edinburgh University PhD (1956). PRIM NONPR EMPL executive director: Philadelphia Presbytery Homes Inc. CORP AFFIL director: Premier Life Insurance Co.; director: Covenant Life Insurance Co. NONPR AFFIL member: Presbytery Philadelphia; member: Union League Philadelphia; vice president:

Philadelphia Presbytery Apartments; director: Presbyterian/University Pennsylvania Medical School; member: American Management Association.

Thomas P. Glassmoyer: trustee B Reading, PA September 04, 1915. ED Ursinus College AB (1936); University of Pennsylvania LLB (1939). PRIM CORP EMPL retired partner: Schnader Harrison Segal & Lewis. CORP AFFIL secretary, director: Lawrence McFadden Co. NONPR AFFIL trustee: Bernard G Segal Foundation; chairman executive committee: Ursinus College; member: Philadelphia Bar Association; fellow: Pennsylvania Bar Foundation; member: Pennsylvania Folklife Society; member: Order Coif; member: Pennsylvania Bar Association; lecturer: New York University Institute Federal Taxation; member: Order Arrow; member: Lawyers Club; member: National Association College & University Attorneys; member: Judge Advocates Association; member: American Bar Association; member: Federation Bar Association. CLUB AFFIL Union League Club; Manorlu Club; Manufacturers Golf Club & Country Club.

Grants Analysis

Disclosure Period: calendar year ending 2002
Total Grants: $6,987*
Number of Grants: 2
Highest Grant: $4,987
Lowest Grant: $2,000
***Note:** Giving excludes fellowship and scholarship.

Recent Grants

Note: Grants derived from 2002 Form 990.
General

733,700	Woodrow Wilson National Fellowship Foundation, Princeton, NJ -- toward the doctoral dissertation fellowships
50,000	Grant to the Charlotte W Newcombe Endowed Scholarship Fund, Princeton, NJ -- toward the Charlotte W. Newcombe Endowed Scholarship Fund
50,000	University of Pennsylvania, Philadelphia, PA -- toward scholarships for students with disabilities
47,500	Temple University, Philadelphia, PA -- funds for scholarships for students with disabilities
45,000	Gallaudet University, Washington, DC -- funds for scholarships for students with disabilities
45,000	New York University, New York, NY -- funds for scholarships for students with disabilities
42,500	Pennsylvania State University, University Park, PA -- toward scholarships for students with disabilities
32,500	Bloomfield College, Bloomfield, NJ -- funds for scholarships for disadvantaged students
32,500	Davis & Elkins College, Elkins, WV -- toward scholarships for disadvantaged students
32,500	Jamestown College, Jamestown, ND -- funds for scholarships

HENRY MAYO NEWHALL FOUNDATION

Giving Contact

Prudence J. Noon, President
96 Fountainhead Ct.
Martinez, CA 94553
Phone: (925)228-9821
E-mail: info@newhallfoundation.org
Web: http://www.newhallfoundation.org/

Description

Founded: 1963
EIN: 946073084

Organization Type: Private Foundation
Giving Locations: CA
Grant Types: General Support.

Donor Information

Founder: the late Alice O'Meara, Newhall Land and Farming Co.

Typical Recipients

Arts & Humanities: Arts Institutes, Historic Preservation, Libraries, Music, Theater
Civic & Public Affairs: Economic Development, Civic & Public Affairs-General, Hispanic Affairs, Rural Affairs, Urban & Community Affairs
Education: Agricultural Education, Arts/Humanities Education, Colleges & Universities, Elementary Education (Private), Elementary Education (Public), Preschool Education, Private Education (Precollege), Public Education (Precollege), Secondary Education (Public), Student Aid
Environment: Environment-General
Health: Children's Health/Hospitals, Clinics/Medical Centers, Emergency/Ambulance Services, Hospitals, Research/Studies Institutes
Religion: Churches, Religious Welfare
Science: Science Museums
Social Services: Child Welfare, Community Service Organizations, Domestic Violence, Family Services, Food/Clothing Distribution, Recreation & Athletics, Shelters/Homelessness, United Funds/United Ways, YMCA/YWCA/YMHA/YWHA, Youth Organizations

Application Procedures

Initial Contact: Send a brief letter of inquiry describing program or project.
Deadlines: None.

Foundation Officials

Mrs. Robert Chesebrough, Jr.: director
Judith McBean Cosper: director
Mary V. Gorman: chief financial officer
David N. Hill: president
Marion Hill: vice president
Anthony Newhall: secretary
David S. Newhall: president
George A. Newhall: director
Jane Newhall: director B 1914. CORP AFFIL director: Newhall Land & Farming Co.
Jon Newhall: director
Roger Newhall: director
Edwin Newhall Woods: director PRIM CORP EMPL director: Newhall Land and Farming.
Prudence J. Noon: president

Grants Analysis

Disclosure Period: calendar year ending 2000
Total Grants: $546,391
Number of Grants: 61
Average Grant: $8,957
Highest Grant: $40,000
Typical Range: $1,000 to $15,000

Recent Grants

Note: Grants derived from 2001 Form 990.
General

40,000	Santa Clarita Child and Family Center Foundation, Santa Clarita, CA -- Growing with Our Community capital campaign
25,000	California Agricultural Leadership Program, Atascadero, CA -- operations
25,000	Partners in Care Foundation, Burbank, CA -- adult day health center
22,500	Piru Elementary School, Piru, CA -- School Art Program
20,000	Boys and Girls Club of Santa Clarita Valley, Santa Clarita, CA -- Project Learn
20,000	Boys and Girls Club of Santa Maria Valley, Santa Maria, CA -- Project Learn
20,000	Santa Maria Valley YMCA, Santa Maria, CA -- financial assistance to families

16,000	Santa Maria Joint Union High School District, Santa Maria, CA -- scholarship program
15,000	Santa Clara Valley Food Pantry, Newhall, CA -- Senior Day and children's daily program
15,000	Santa Maria Valley YMCA, Valencia, CA -- Youth Leadership Program

JEROME A. AND ESTELLE R. NEWMAN ASSISTANCE FUND

Giving Contact
Howard A. Newman, Chairman & Director
925 Westchester Ave., Suite 308
White Plains, NY 10604
Phone: (914)993-0777

Description
Founded: 1954
EIN: 136096241
Organization Type: Private Foundation
Giving Locations: NY
Grant Types: General Support.

Donor Information
Founder: Howard A. Newman and the late Jerome A. Newman

Financial Summary
Total Giving: $467,500 (fiscal year ending June 30, 2003); $428,500 (fiscal 2002); $377,000 (fiscal 2001). Note: Fiscal 1997 Giving includes scholarship ($20,000).
Assets: $8,782,604 (fiscal 2003); $8,824,706 (fiscal 2002); $8,845,545 (fiscal 2001)

Typical Recipients
Arts & Humanities: Arts Festivals, Ballet, Community Arts, Dance, Libraries, Museums/Galleries, Music, Opera, Performing Arts, Public Broadcasting, Theater
Civic & Public Affairs: Civil Rights, Employment/Job Training, Ethnic Organizations, Civic & Public Affairs-General, Housing, Law & Justice, Municipalities/Towns, Philanthropic Organizations, Public Policy, Women's Affairs
Education: Business Education, Colleges & Universities, Legal Education, Private Education (Precollege), Student Aid
Health: Clinics/Medical Centers, Heart, Hospitals, Medical Research, Multiple Sclerosis, Nursing Services, Research/Studies Institutes
International: International Development, Missionary/Religious Activities
Religion: Jewish Causes, Religious Organizations
Science: Scientific Centers & Institutes
Social Services: Animal Protection, Child Welfare, Community Service Organizations, People with Disabilities, Recreation & Athletics, United Funds/United Ways, Youth Organizations

Application Procedures
Initial Contact: The foundation requests applications be made in writing.
Application Requirements: a description of organization and activities.
Deadlines: None.

Foundation Officials
Michael Greenberg: treasurer, director
Robert H. Haines: secretary, director
Andrew H. Levy: director
Patricia Nanon: vice president, director
Howard A. Newman: chairman, director

William C. Newman: president, director B New York, NY 1926. ED City College of New York BBA (1947). PRIM CORP EMPL chairman, chief executive officer: New Plan Realty Trust. NONPR AFFIL trustee: Baruch College Fund; member: National Association Real Estate Investment Trusts. CLUB AFFIL Princeton Club; Boca Rio Country Club; Braeburn Country Club; Aspinal Curzon Club.
Victoria Woolner Samuels: director
William C. Scott: director
Jerry I. Speyer: director

Grants Analysis
Disclosure Period: fiscal year ending June 30, 2003
Total Grants: $467,500
Number of Grants: 19
Average Grant: $12,794*
Highest Grant: $100,000
Lowest Grant: $2,500
Typical Range: $5,000 to $25,000
*****Note:** Average grant figure excludes four highest grants ($250,000).

Recent Grants
Note: Grants derived from fiscal 2003 Form 990.
General

100,000	Jewish Guild for the Blind, New York, NY -- facility renovation
50,000	Trickle Up, New York, NY -- for training equipment
50,000	United Jewish Appeal Federation of Jewish Philanthropies, New York, NY -- program for the aged
50,000	Yard Inc., New York, NY -- for community workshops
40,000	Bennington College, Bennington, VT -- for scholarship fund
25,000	Columbia College, Columbia, SC -- for scholarship fund
25,000	Juilliard School, New York, NY -- for dance program
25,000	New York Shakespeare Festival, New York, NY -- for Estelle R. Newman theater lobby renovation
25,000	Northern Westchester Hospital, Mt. Kisco, NY -- for emergency equipment fund
20,000	American Jewish Committee, New York, NY -- for library upgrade

NEWMAN FAMILY FOUNDATION

Giving Contact
Craig S. Skulsky, Treasurer
5455 Corporate Dr., Suite 300
Troy, MI 48098-2620
Phone: (248)641-8400

Description
Founded: 1992
EIN: 382986180
Organization Type: Private Foundation
Grant Types: General Support.

Financial Summary
Total Giving: $71,875 (2003); $96,433 (2001)
Assets: $1,948,761 (2003); $1,822,410 (2001)

Typical Recipients
Arts & Humanities: Arts Funds, Libraries, Museums/Galleries, Public Broadcasting
Civic & Public Affairs: African American Affairs, Ethnic Organizations, Gay/Lesbian Issues, Civic & Public Affairs-General, Law & Justice
Education: Colleges & Universities, Medical Education, Social Sciences Education, Student Aid

Health: Alzheimer's Disease, Cancer, Emergency/Ambulance Services, Health-General, Health Funds, Health Organizations, Hospitals, Medical Research, Research/Studies Institutes
Religion: Jewish Causes, Religious Welfare, Synagogues/Temples
Social Services: Child Abuse, Community Centers, Food/Clothing Distribution

Application Procedures
Initial Contact: The foundation requests applications be made in writing.
Deadlines: None.

Foundation Officials
Donald L. Newman: vice president
Steven E. Newman: president
Craig S. Skulsky: treasurer

Grants Analysis
Disclosure Period: calendar year ending 2003
Total Grants: $71,875
Number of Grants: 19
Average Grant: $604*
Highest Grant: $61,000
Lowest Grant: $15
Typical Range: $100 to $1,000
*****Note:** Average grant figure excludes highest grant.

Recent Grants
Note: Grants derived from 2003 Form 990.
General

61,000	University of Michigan, Ann Arbor, MI
2,500	Albion College, Albion, MI
2,500	Progressive Film Foundation
2,500	William Beaumont Foundation, Royal Oak, MI
1,000	Hillel Foundation, Washington, DC
1,000	Yad Ezra, Oak Park, MI
500	Ann Foundation, St. Paul, MN
139	B'Nai Brith Foundation of USA, Milwaukee, WI
125	Detroit Public Television, Detroit, MI
100	Andre Bosse Center, Hart, MI

NEWMAN'S OWN INC.

Company Headquarters
Westport, CT
Web: http://www.newmansown.com

Company Description
Revenue: US$100 million (2001)
Employees: 20 (2001)
SIC(s): 5149 Groceries & Related Products Nec.

Newman's Own Foundation

Giving Contact
Joan Williams
Newman's Own Foundation
246 Post Road East
Westport, CT 06880-3615
Phone: (203)222-0136
Fax: (203)227-5630
Web: http://www.newmansown.com/5_good.html

Description
Founded: 1989
EIN: 061247230
Organization Type: Corporate Foundation
Giving Locations: internationally, where Newman's Own is sold; Australia; New Zealand
Grant Types: General Support.

Financial Summary

Total Giving: $416,700 (fiscal year ending August 31, 2003); $220,785 (fiscal 2001). Note: Contributes through corporate direct giving program and foundation.
Giving Analysis: Giving for fiscal 2001 includes: foundation ($220,785)
Assets: $361,041 (fiscal 2003); $718,535 (fiscal 2001)
Gifts Received: $340,595 (fiscal 2003); $299,954 (fiscal 2001); $358,566 (fiscal 2000). Note: The foundation receives contributions from Meadowlea Foods.

Typical Recipients

Arts & Humanities: Community Arts, Libraries, Museums/Galleries, Public Broadcasting, Theater
Civic & Public Affairs: Housing, Public Policy
Education: Literacy, Public Education (Precollege)
Environment: Environment-General
Health: Arthritis, Children's Health/Hospitals, Health Funds, Hospices, Hospitals, Medical Rehabilitation, Single-Disease Health Associations
International: Foreign Arts Organizations, Foreign Educational Institutions, International-General, Health Care/Hospitals, Human Rights, International Development, International Environmental Issues, International Organizations, International Peace & Security Issues, International Relations, International Relief Efforts, Missionary/Religious Activities
Religion: Religious Welfare
Social Services: Camps, Child Abuse, Child Welfare, Community Centers, Community Service Organizations, Delinquency & Criminal Rehabilitation, Domestic Violence, Family Services, Food/Clothing Distribution, Homes, People with Disabilities, Senior Services, Shelters/Homelessness, Youth Organizations

Application Procedures

Initial Contact: Send a detailed written proposal after reviewing guidelines. Grant guidelines are posted on the company's web site in March.
Deadlines: Proposals are accepted between April 1 and July 1.
Review Process: Proposals are acknowledged within 6-8 weeks of receipt.
Notes: Only award recipients are notified. Faxed proposals are not accepted. Any materials submitted are nonreturnable.

Restrictions

Funds may not be used for propaganda purposes or to attempt to influence legislation.

Additional Information

Foundation requires regular reports of the progress of the project for which funds are granted. In addition to application information listed above, grant seekers must furnish specific certificates or other adequate proof that the organization is recognized as a bona fide charity under the laws of the country in which it operates.
Publications: Guidelines Sheet

Corporate Officials

Aaron Edward Hotchner: vice president, treasurer B Saint Louis, MO June 28, 1920. ED Washington University AB (1941). PRIM CORP EMPL vice president, treasurer: Newman's Own Inc. NONPR AFFIL member: PEN; member: Writers Guild America; vice president: Hole in the Wall Gang Camp; member: Missouri Bar Association; member: Authors Guild Foundation; member: Dramatists Guild; member: Authors Guild. CLUB AFFIL Century Club.
Paul L. Newman: president B Cleveland, OH 1925. ED Kenyon College BA (1949); Yale University School of Drama (1951).

Foundation Officials

Jamie K. Gerard: secretary CORP AFFIL secretary: Newmans Own Inc.
Paul L. Newman: president, director (see above)
Joanne Gignilliat Woodward: director B Thomasville, GA 1930. ED Neighborhood Playhouse Dramatic School; Louisiana State University (1947-1949).

Grants Analysis

Disclosure Period: fiscal year ending August 31, 2003
Total Grants: $416,700
Number of Grants: 90
Average Grant: $3,390*
Highest Grant: $115,000
Lowest Grant: $1,800
Typical Range: $2,000 to $5,000
***Note:** Average grant figure excludes highest grant.

Recent Grants

Note: Grants derived from 2004 Form 990.
General

8,000	Aunties & Uncles Co-operative Family, Rydalmere Australia -- caring volunteers for vulnerable children
8,000	Aussie Helpers, Dalby Australia -- help needy
8,000	Autism Victoria, Ashburton Australia -- autism programs
8,000	Baptist Community Service, Unicy, SA Australia -- assist homeless
8,000	Baptist Inner City Ministries, Sydney, NW Australia -- assist homeless
8,000	Big Brothers Big Sisters, Richmond Australia -- mentoring for youth
8,000	Breakaway Camps Inc., Preston Australia -- for youth
8,000	Can Survive, Camberwell Australia -- telephone hopeline
8,000	Children's Leukemia and Cancer Society Inc., Red Hill Australia -- children with leukemia and cancer
8,000	Deaf Society of New South Wales, Parramatta Australia -- programs for deaf people

NEWMIL BANCORP

Company Headquarters

New Milford, CT
Web: http://www.newmil.com

Company Description

Founded: 1987
Ticker: NMIL
Exchange: NASDAQ
Assets: US$661.6 million (2002)
Employees: 183 (2002)
SIC(s): 6036 Savings Institutions Except Federal, 6712 Bank Holding Companies.

New Milford Savings Bank Foundation

Giving Contact

Francis J. Wiatr, President & Chief Executive Officer
19 Main St.
PO Box 600
New Milford, CT 06776-0600
Phone: (860)355-7600

Description

Founded: 1985
EIN: 061140115
Organization Type: Corporate Foundation

Giving Locations: CT: Northwest Connecticut
Grant Types: General Support.

Financial Summary

Total Giving: $134,280 (2003); $83,407 (2001)
Giving Analysis: Giving for 2003 includes: foundation grants to United Way ($7,040)
Assets: $563,035 (2003); $531,630 (2001)
Gifts Received: $50,345 (2003). Note: In 2003, contributions were received from Newmil Bank.

Typical Recipients

Arts & Humanities: Arts Associations & Councils, Arts Centers, Historic Preservation, History & Archaeology, Libraries, Music, Performing Arts, Theater
Civic & Public Affairs: Chambers of Commerce, Clubs, Community Foundations, Economic Development, Employment/Job Training, Civic & Public Affairs-General, Housing, Parades/Festivals, Safety, Urban & Community Affairs, Women's Affairs
Education: Arts/Humanities Education, Colleges & Universities, Education Funds, Private Education (Precollege), Public Education (Precollege), Secondary Education (Public), Student Aid
Environment: Environment-General
Health: Emergency/Ambulance Services, Health Funds, Health Organizations, Home-Care Services, Hospices, Hospitals, Mental Health, Prenatal Health Issues
International: Health Care/Hospitals
Religion: Churches, Jewish Causes, Religious Welfare, Synagogues/Temples
Social Services: Child Welfare, Community Centers, Community Service Organizations, Day Care, Family Services, Food/Clothing Distribution, Homes, Recreation & Athletics, Scouts, Senior Services, Sexual Abuse, Shelters/Homelessness, Social Services-General, United Funds/United Ways, YMCA/YWCA/YMHA/YWHA, Youth Organizations

Application Procedures

Initial Contact: The foundation has no formal grant application procedure or application form.
Deadlines: None.

Corporate Officials

Ian McMahon: chief financial officer, treasurer, director B Limerick, Ireland 1959. ED University of Dublin (1980); University of Dublin (1981). PRIM CORP EMPL chief financial officer, treasurer: NewMil Bancorp. CORP AFFIL treasurer, chief financial officer: Nowalk Bank.
Francis J. Wiatr: president, chief executive officer, director PRIM CORP EMPL president, chief executive officer, director: NewMil Bancorp.

Foundation Officials

Willis H. Barton, Jr.: vice president
Herbert E. Bullock: director
Joseph Carlson, II: director
Kevin L. Dumas: director
Laurie G. Gonthier: director
Paul N. Jaber: director
Robert J. McCarthy: director
Ian McMahon: treasurer (see above)
Betty F. Pacocha: secretary, director
Suzanne L. Powers: director
Anthony M. Rizzo: director
Francis J. Wiatr: president, director (see above)
Mary C. Williams: vice president, director

Grants Analysis

Disclosure Period: calendar year ending 2003
Total Grants: $127,240*
Number of Grants: 177
Average Grant: $495*
Highest Grant: $40,000
Lowest Grant: $50
Typical Range: $100 to $1,000
***Note:** Giving excludes United Way. Average grant figure excludes highest grant.

Recent Grants

Note: Grants derived from 2003 Form 990.
General

40,000	New Milford Hospital, New Milford, CT -- capital campaign
10,000	Children's Center, New Milford, CT
5,000	Regional YMCA of Western Connecticut, New Milford, CT
5,000	Western Connecticut State University, Danbury, CT
4,220	Housatonic/Shepaug United Way, New Milford, CT
4,000	Regional Hospice of Western Connecticut Inc., Danbury, CT
3,000	Waterbury Symphony Orchestra, Waterbury, CT
2,720	United Way of Northern Fairfield County, Danbury, CT
2,500	Charles Ives Center for the Arts Inc., Danbury, CT
2,500	Hord Foundation Inc., Danbury, CT

NIAGARA MOHAWK HOLDINGS INC.

Company Headquarters

300 Erie Boulevard West
Syracuse, NY 13202
Phone: (315)474-1511
Fax: (315)460-1429
Web: http://www.niagramohawk.com

Company Description

Founded: 1998
Ticker: NMK
Exchange: NYSE
Employees: 8,400
SIC(s): 4911 Electric Services, 4925 Gas Production & Distribution Nec, 4931 Electric & Other Services Combined.

Operating Locations

Niagara Mohawk Power Corp. (DC--Washington; NY--Buffalo, Camillus, Cortland, Fulton, Hudson, Manlius, New Hartford, Niagara Falls, Oswego, Pulaski, Syracuse)

Nonmonetary Support

Type: Donated Equipment
Volunteer Programs: Sponsors a volunteer grant program and a community action team.

Niagara Mohawk Foundation

Giving Contact

Carolyn A. May
300 Erie Boulevard
Syracuse, NY 13202
Phone: (315)428-5691
Web: http://www.nationalgridus.com/niagaramohawk/about_us/community.asp

Description

EIN: 223132237
Organization Type: Corporate Giving Program
Giving Locations: NY: Upstate New York service areas.
Grant Types: Capital, Employee Matching Gifts, General Support, Matching, Multiyear/Continuing Support.
Note: Employee matching gift ratio: 1 to 1.

Financial Summary

Total Giving: $1,480,315 (2002); $1,938,438 (2001)
Giving Analysis: Giving for 2002 includes: foundation grants to United Way ($583,090)
Assets: $1,800,001 (2002); $2,915,556 (2001)
Gifts Received: $531,707 (2002); $1,843,037 (2001); $1,517,477 (2000). Note: Contributions were received from Niagara Mohawk Foundation Checking.

Typical Recipients

Arts & Humanities: Arts Associations & Councils, Ethnic & Folk Arts, Arts & Humanities-General, Historic Preservation, History & Archaeology, Libraries, Literary Arts, Museums/Galleries, Music, Opera, Performing Arts, Public Broadcasting, Theater
Civic & Public Affairs: Botanical Gardens/Parks, Economic Development, Employment/Job Training, Civic & Public Affairs-General, Housing, Municipalities/Towns, Native American Affairs, Parades/Festivals, Philanthropic Organizations, Professional & Trade Associations, Rural Affairs, Safety, Urban & Community Affairs, Zoos/Aquariums
Education: Afterschool/Enrichment Programs, Agricultural Education, Business Education, Colleges & Universities, Community & Junior Colleges, Education Funds, Education-General, International Exchange, Leadership Training, Legal Education, Minority Education, Preschool Education, Private Education (Precollege), Science/Mathematics Education, Social Sciences Education
Environment: Environment-General, Protection, Resource Conservation, Wildlife Protection
Health: Cancer, Children's Health/Hospitals, Clinics/Medical Centers, Emergency/Ambulance Services, Health-General, Heart, Hospices, Hospitals, Prenatal Health Issues, Single-Disease Health Associations, Trauma Treatment
International: Foreign Arts Organizations, International Organizations
Religion: Religious Welfare, Social/Policy Issues
Science: Science Museums
Social Services: Camps, Child Welfare, Community Centers, Community Service Organizations, Delinquency & Criminal Rehabilitation, Emergency Relief, Family Services, Food/Clothing Distribution, People with Disabilities, Recreation & Athletics, Scouts, Shelters/Homelessness, Social Services-General, Special Olympics, United Funds/United Ways, YMCA/YWCA/YMHA/YWHA, Youth Organizations

Application Procedures

Initial Contact: See web site for Community Giving Appplication Form and instructions.
Deadlines: None.
Decision Notification: Requests are reviewed quarterly on a case-by-case basis.

Restrictions

The company does not fund: individuals; organizations that discriminate on the basis of race, color, religion, gender, national origin, disability, age, marital status,or veteran status; organizations located outside the geographic boundaries of our service territory, except to fund a specific project that is delivered directly to customer communities; organizations that spend more than 25% of their budget on overhead and fundraising; or political or lobbying organizations.

Corporate Officials

Albert J. Budney, Jr.: president, director B 1948. ED Princeton University BS (1968); Harvard University MBA (1974). PRIM CORP EMPL president: Niagara Mohawk Holdings Inc. CORP AFFIL director: Telergy Inc.; director: Telergy Operating Inc.
William E. Davis: chairman, chief executive officer B Schenevus, NY 1942. ED United States Naval Academy (1964); George Washington University (1971). PRIM CORP EMPL chairman, chief executive officer: Niagara Mohawk Power Corp. CORP AFFIL director: Utilities Mutual Insurance Co.; director: Canadian Ni-

agara Power; director: Opinac Energy. NONPR AFFIL director: Edison Electric Institute; director: Nuclear Energy Institute; director: Center for Clean Air Policy; director: Crouse-Irving Memorial Hospital; director: Association of Edison Illuminating Companies.

Foundation Officials

Susan M. Crossett: secretary
William F. Edwards: trustee
Gary R. Jesmain: president
Gary R. Jesmain: president
Carolyn A. May: director
Steven W. Tasker: treasurer

Grants Analysis

Disclosure Period: calendar year ending 2002
Total Grants: $855,199*
Number of Grants: 165
Average Grant: $5,183
Highest Grant: $67,137
Lowest Grant: $50
Typical Range: $1,000 to $10,000
*Note: Giving excludes United Way and volunteer grants.

Recent Grants

Note: Grants derived from 2003 Form 990.
Library-Related

10,000	Friends of the Central Library, Pleasant Hill, CA

General

201,374	United Way of Central New York, Syracuse, NY
193,236	American Red Cross, Washington, DC
98,141	United Way of Buffalo & Erie County, Buffalo, NY
80,000	Nature Conservancy, Arlington, VA
75,000	Syracuse Symphony, Syracuse, NY
65,997	United Way of Greater Utica, Utica, NY
51,488	United Way of Northeastern New York, Albany, NY
40,000	Genesee Community College, Batavia, NY
40,000	Paul Smiths College, Paul Smiths, NY
35,000	American Heart Association, Dallas, TX

NLI INTERNATIONAL INC.

Company Headquarters

1251 Ave. Of The America
New York, NY 10020

Company Description

SIC(s): 6311 Life Insurance.
Parent Company: Nippon Life Insurance Co., 5-12 Imabashi 3-chome, Chuo-ku, Osaka, Japan

Operating Locations

Nippon Life Insurance Co. of America (NY--New York); NLI Asset Management Corp. (NY--New York); NLI Properties (NY--New York); NLI Properties Central (IL--Chicago); NLI Properties West (CA--Los Angeles); NLI Research Institute (NY--New York); PanAgora Asset Management (MA--Boston)

Giving Contact

Kyoko Yamaguchi, Administrative Coordinator
1251 Avenue of the Americas, Suite 5210
New York, NY 10020
Phone: (212)403-3400
Fax: (212)764-9773

Description

Organization Type: Corporate Giving Program
Giving Locations: headquarters community.
Grant Types: Seed Money.

Typical Recipients

Arts & Humanities: Ethnic & Folk Arts, Arts & Humanities-General, Libraries

Civic & Public Affairs: Asian American Affairs, Botanical Gardens/Parks, Inner-City Development, Public Policy, Urban & Community Affairs

Education: Education Associations, Elementary Education (Public), Education-General, Private Education (Precollege), Special Education

Environment: Environment-General, Resource Conservation

Health: Children's Health/Hospitals, Hospitals

International: International-General, International Relations

Social Services: Community Centers, Community Service Organizations, Social Services-General, United Funds/United Ways

Application Procedures

Initial Contact: Unsolicited requests are not encouraged.

Restrictions

Does not support individuals, religious organizations for sectarian purposes, or political or lobbying groups.

Corporate Officials

Mr. Takeshi Furichi: president, chief executive officer PRIM CORP EMPL president, chief executive officer: NLI International.

EDWARD JOHN NOBLE FOUNDATION, INC.

Giving Contact

E.J. Noble-Smith, President
PO Box 954
383 Main Street, Unit 2
Ridgefield, CT 06877
Phone: (203)438-5690

Description

Founded: 1940
EIN: 061055586
Organization Type: General Purpose Foundation
Giving Locations: GA: Georgia coast; NY: New York metropolitan area
Grant Types: Capital, Challenge, Endowment, General Support, Multiyear/Continuing Support, Operating Expenses, Project, Research.

Donor Information

Founder: The foundation was established in Connecticut in 1940 by the late Edward John Noble. Successful in confectionery manufacturing and commercial broadcasting, Mr. Noble was chairman of the board of Beechnut Lifesavers, and chairman of the finance committee of American Broadcasting Company and Paramount Theaters. He created the American Broadcasting Company from National Broadcasting Company's Blue Network, which he had purchased.

A pilot, Mr. Noble spoke out on the need for federal regulations for private and commercial aviation, and in 1938 President Franklin D. Roosevelt appointed him chairman of the newly created Civil Aeronautics Authority. Following this assignment, he became the first Under Secretary of Commerce. In addition, Mr. Noble's commitment to preserving the St. Lawrence River Valley's natural beauty while increasing commerce led President Dwight D. Eisenhower to appoint him to the board of the St. Lawrence Seaway Commission in 1954.

Financial Summary

Total Giving: $7,920,376 (2003); $6,591,253 (2002); $6,638,855 (2001)

Assets: $144,586,439 (2003); $122,453,270 (2002); $140,885,073 (2001)

Typical Recipients

Arts & Humanities: Arts Associations & Councils, Arts Centers, Arts Festivals, Arts Funds, Arts Institutes, Arts Outreach, Dance, Film & Video, Arts & Humanities-General, Historic Preservation, History & Archaeology, Libraries, Museums/Galleries, Music, Opera, Performing Arts, Public Broadcasting, Theater, Visual Arts

Civic & Public Affairs: Botanical Gardens/Parks, Community Foundations, Economic Development, Civic & Public Affairs-General, Law & Justice, Legal Aid, Nonprofit Management, Philanthropic Organizations, Professional & Trade Associations, Urban & Community Affairs, Zoos/Aquariums

Education: Arts/Humanities Education, Colleges & Universities, Education Associations, Education Reform, Environmental Education, Faculty Development, Health & Physical Education, Medical Education, Minority Education, Private Education (Precollege), School Volunteerism, Science/Mathematics Education, Secondary Education (Public), Special Education, Student Aid

Environment: Forestry, Environment-General, Protection, Resource Conservation, Wildlife Protection

Health: Cancer, Children's Health/Hospitals, Clinics/Medical Centers, Health-General, Health Funds, Health Organizations, Hospitals, Medical Research, Medical Training, Trauma Treatment

International: Foreign Educational Institutions, Health Care/Hospitals, International Affairs, International Environmental Issues, International Relations

Religion: Churches, Religion-General

Science: Science Museums, Scientific Labs, Scientific Organizations

Social Services: At-Risk Youth, Child Welfare, Community Centers, Community Service Organizations, Counseling, Family Planning, Family Services, People with Disabilities, Senior Services, Volunteer Services, YMCA/YWCA/YMHA/YWHA, Youth Organizations

Application Procedures

Initial Contact: Applicants should send a brief letter to the foundation describing the project.

Application Requirements: A brief description and purpose of the organization; a statement of need, project objectives, and duration; qualifications of personnel; program budget; other sources of income, and those being sought; a copy of the most recent 501(c)(3) and 509(a) rulings from the IRS; a recent financial statement; and a list of officers and directors or trustees. If there is a sufficient interest, a formal grant application will be sent.

Deadlines: None, for letter requests. Grant applications must be received the first day of the month preceding the month of a Trustee meeting. The Trustees meet quarterly in January, April, July, and October.

Review Process: All requests are reviewed and answered as soon as possible. If interested, the foundation will request further information as needed and a meeting, if appropriate. Notification of Trustee's decision on grant applications is usually made within 2 weeks.

Notes: The foundation only reviews requests from organizations that are tax-exempt under the 501(c)(3) IRS code.

Restrictions

Grants are not made to individuals, publications, performances, films, or television projects. The foundation does not consider support for buildings or equipment. In medical education and health care, the directors have generally limited grants to hospitals with which the foundation has had long association.

Additional Information

Publications: Annual Report

Foundation Officials

Dr. William G. Conway: director
E. Mary Heffernan: treasurer
Harold B. Johnson: director
Frank Y. Larkin: vice chairman, director B 1917. ED Princeton University (1937). NONPR AFFIL treasurer: Saint Catherine Island Foundation.
June Noble Larkin: chairwoman, director B New York, NY 1922. ED Sarah Lawrence College BA (1944). CORP AFFIL board directors: US Trust Co. Connecticut. NONPR AFFIL committee member: New York Public Library, Library Performing Arts; president: Saint Catherine Island Foundation; member: New York International Festival Arts; trustee: Museum Modern Art; member: National Society Colonial Dames State New York; chairman, trustee: Juilliard School Music; member, board directors: Lincoln Center Performing Arts. CLUB AFFIL Colony Club; Sulgrave Club.
Deborah A. Menton-Nightlinger: executive director, secretary
Daniel L. Moseley: director
E. J. Noble Smith: president, director
Dr. Joseph W. Polisi: director B New York, NY 1947. ED University of Connecticut BA (1969); Tufts University MA (1970); Tufts University MusM (1973); Tufts University MMusArts (1975); Yale University DMA (1980). PRIM NONPR EMPL president: Juilliard School.
Bradford K. Smith: director ED New School for Social Research MA; University of Michigan BA.
David S. Smith, Jr.: director
Jeremy T. Smith: director
Maribeth Smith: director
Malcolm L. Stein: director
Carroll Livingston Wainwright, Jr.: director B New York, NY 1925. ED Yale University AB (1949); Harvard University LLB (1952). PRIM CORP EMPL partner: Milbank, Tweed, Hadley & McCloy. CORP AFFIL trustee: US Trust Co. New York; director: US Trust Co. NONPR AFFIL member government board: New York Community Trust; member: New York State Bar Association; honorary trustee: Cooper Union Advancement Science Art; member: Association Bar New York City; trustee: Boys Club New York; honorary trustee: American Museum Natural History; member: American Bar Association. CLUB AFFIL Maidstone Club; Union Club; Downtown Club.

Grants Analysis

Disclosure Period: calendar year ending 2003
Total Grants: $7,920,376
Number of Grants: 50
Average Grant: $49,065*
Highest Grant: $2,000,000
Lowest Grant: $7,150
Typical Range: $20,000 to $100,000
*Note: Average grant figure excludes four highest grants ($5,663,382).

Recent Grants

Note: Grants derived from 2003 Form 990.

General

2,000,000	Juilliard School, New York, NY -- for the humanities program
2,000,000	Museum of Modern Art, New York, NY -- to support the endowment, renovation and expansion activities
863,382	Wildlife Conservation Society, Bronx, NY -- to support the wildlife survival center
800,000	Saint Catherine's Island Foundation Inc., Midway, GA
400,000	Juilliard School, New York, NY -- for the endowment fund
250,000	Brooklyn Museum of Art, Brooklyn, NY -- for the audience development
233,638	American Museum of Natural History, New York, NY -- for the collections management and transfer
150,000	Jazz at Lincoln Center, New York, NY

66,425   State University of New York at Potsdam, Potsdam, NY -- to support the community performance series

55,909   American Museum of Natural History, New York, NY -- for the research program

SAMUEL ROBERTS NOBLE FOUNDATION

Giving Contact
Michael A. Cawley, President & Trustee
PO Box 2180
2510 Sam Noble Parkway
Ardmore, OK 73401
Phone: (580)223-5810
Fax: (580)221-6212
E-mail: macawley@noble.org
Web: http://www.noble.org

Description
Founded: 1945
EIN: 730606209
Organization Type: General Purpose Foundation
Giving Locations: OK: Southwestern USA.
Grant Types: Capital, Employee Matching Gifts, Endowment, General Support, Matching, Multiyear/Continuing Support, Operating Expenses, Project, Research, Scholarship.

Donor Information
Founder: Lloyd Noble, an Oklahoma oilman who developed the Noble Drilling and Samedan Oil corporations, provided the funding to create the Samuel Roberts Noble Foundation in 1945. The foundation was named for Lloyd Noble's father. Six family members sit on the current board of trustees.

Financial Summary
Total Giving: $9,819,101 (fiscal year ending October 31, 2002); $9,576,032 (fiscal 2001 approx)
Giving Analysis: Giving for fiscal 2002 includes: foundation scholarships ($410,623)
Assets: $923,725,497 (fiscal 2002)
Gifts Received: $142,318 (fiscal 2002); $25,000 (fiscal 2000); $728,991 (fiscal 1996). Note: In fiscal 2002, contributions were received from University of California ($46,886) and NASA ($95,430). In fiscal 1996, the foundation received a gift from Sam Noble. A gift was received in fiscal 1995 from Ray London.

Typical Recipients
Arts & Humanities: Arts Centers, Arts Funds, Arts Institutes, Ethnic & Folk Arts, Historic Preservation, History & Archaeology, Libraries, Museums/Galleries, Music, Performing Arts, Public Broadcasting
Civic & Public Affairs: Botanical Gardens/Parks, Business/Free Enterprise, Chambers of Commerce, Community Foundations, Economic Development, Economic Policy, Civic & Public Affairs-General, Housing, Law & Justice, Legal Aid, Municipalities/Towns, Nonprofit Management, Parades/Festivals, Professional & Trade Associations, Public Policy, Rural Affairs, Safety, Urban & Community Affairs, Zoos/Aquariums
Education: Afterschool/Enrichment Programs, Agricultural Education, Business Education, Colleges & Universities, Continuing Education, Economic Education, Education Associations, Education Funds, Education Reform, Faculty Development, Education-General, Health & Physical Education, Journalism/Media Education, Literacy, Medical Education, Private Education (Precollege), Public Education (Precollege), Science/Mathematics Education, Secondary Education (Public), Social Sciences Education, Special Education, Student Aid, Vocational & Technical Education

Environment: Environment-General, Wildlife Protection
Health: Cancer, Children's Health/Hospitals, Clinics/Medical Centers, Diabetes, Emergency/Ambulance Services, Eyes/Blindness, Health Policy/Cost Containment, Health Organizations, Heart, Hospices, Hospitals, Medical Rehabilitation, Medical Research, Mental Health, Nursing Services, Preventive Medicine/Wellness Organizations, Public Health, Research/Studies Institutes, Single-Disease Health Associations, Transplant Networks/Donor Banks
International: International Affairs, International Organizations, International Peace & Security Issues, Missionary/Religious Activities
Religion: Churches, Religion-General, Ministries, Religious Organizations, Religious Welfare
Science: Science Museums, Scientific Centers & Institutes, Scientific Organizations
Social Services: Animal Protection, At-Risk Youth, Child Abuse, Child Welfare, Community Service Organizations, Day Care, Domestic Violence, Family Planning, Family Services, Food/Clothing Distribution, Homes, People with Disabilities, Recreation & Athletics, Scouts, Senior Services, Shelters/Homelessness, Social Services-General, Substance Abuse, United Funds/United Ways, Volunteer Services, YMCA/YWCA/YMHA/YWHA, Youth Organizations

Application Procedures
Initial Contact: Applicants should send a preliminary letter addressed to Mr. Michael A. Cawley, President, summarizing the project for which a grant is requested.
Application Requirements: The proposal summary for public affairs should not exceed two pages and should contain information about the organization, the project for which the organization is seeking funds, and the specific request. If there is sufficient interest, the foundation will send the applicant a formal grant application. For primary areas of giving, the letter should contain background information about the requesting organization, specific details about the proposed project, and the amount needed. The foundation will then send application forms as needed.
Deadlines: March 1, June 1, September 1, and December 1.
Review Process: Notification of the trustees' decision is usually made within two weeks following the meeting.
Notes: Formal proposals received prior to review of the summary will not be considered.

Restrictions
Grants are not made to individuals. The foundation does not make loans.

Additional Information
Publications: Annual Report; Guidelines; Application Form

Foundation Officials
Ann Noble Brown: trustee
David R. Brown, MD: trustee emeritus
Michael A. Cawley: president B 1947. PRIM NONPR EMPL president, trustee: Samuel Roberts Noble Foundation Inc. CORP AFFIL director: Noble Affiliates Inc.
Vivian Noble DuBose: trustee
Patrick A. Jones: chief financial officer, vice president, treasurer
Edward E. Noble: trustee B Ardmore, OK 1928. ED University of Oklahoma BS Geology (1951).
Maria Noble: trustee
Mary Jane Noble: trustee emeritus
Larry A. Pulliam: executive vice president, secretary B 1948.

Grants Analysis
Disclosure Period: fiscal year ending October 31, 2002
Total Grants: $9,408,478*

Number of Grants: 74
Average Grant: $63,689*
Highest Grant: $2,822,868
Lowest Grant: $4,500
Typical Range: $25,000 to $100,000
*Note: Giving excludes scholarships. Average grant excludes two highest grants ($4,822,868).

Recent Grants
Note: Grants derived from 2002 Form 990.
General

2,822,868   University of Oklahoma Foundation, Norman, OK -- towards genome sequencing project

149,200   Southern Oklahoma Technology Center, Ardmore, OK -- towards classroom renovation and parking lot construction

100,000   Take Two Alternative Education Services of Southern Oklahoma Inc., Ardmore, OK -- towards operating support

50,000   Washington Legal Foundation, Washington, DC -- towards legal education media project

40,000   YMCA of Ardmore, Ardmore, OK

25,000   University of Oklahoma Foundation, Norman, OK -- towards uniforms and equipments

11,552   United Fund of Ardmore Inc., Ardmore, OK -- towards match for employees contribution

10,962   United Fund of Ardmore Inc., Ardmore, OK -- towards match for employees contribution

10,000   Southwestern Diabetic Foundation Inc., Gainesville, TX -- to replace the cafeteria floor and purchase a scissor lift

8,460   Western Oklahoma State College, Altus, OK -- towards summer academy in plant biology

JAMES AND ELISE NOLAN CHARITABLE TRUST

Giving Contact
Judith A. Baker
PO Box 927
Wrangell, AK 99929
Phone: (907)874-2323
Fax: (907)874-7595

Description
Founded: 1992
EIN: 926021559
Organization Type: Private Foundation
Giving Locations: AK: Southeastern Alaska
Grant Types: General Support.

Financial Summary
Total Giving: $426,725 (2001)
Assets: $5,544,574 (2001)

Typical Recipients
Arts & Humanities: Arts Associations & Councils, Ethnic & Folk Arts, Arts & Humanities-General, Historic Preservation, History & Archaeology, Libraries, Museums/Galleries, Music, Public Broadcasting, Theater
Civic & Public Affairs: Chambers of Commerce, Clubs, Civic & Public Affairs-General, Native American Affairs, Parades/Festivals, Urban & Community Affairs
Education: Arts/Humanities Education, Business Education, Colleges & Universities, Literacy, Public Education (Precollege), Student Aid
Environment: Environment-General
Health: Children's Health/Hospitals, Clinics/Medical Centers, Emergency/Ambulance Services, Hospitals,

Medical Research, Public Health, Transplant Networks/Donor Banks
Religion: Churches, Ministries, Religious Organizations, Religious Welfare
Social Services: Camps, Community Service Organizations, Recreation & Athletics, Scouts, Social Services-General, Substance Abuse, Veterans, Youth Organizations

Application Procedures

Initial Contact: Send a brief letter of inquiry.
Application Requirements: Include purpose of funds sought and proof of tax-exempt status.
Deadlines: None. Committee meets to award funds in early October.

Restrictions

Grants are not made to individuals.

Foundation Officials

Maribeth Conway: vice president, trustee
David L. Dobbs: trustee

Grants Analysis

Disclosure Period: calendar year ending 2001
Total Grants: $426,725
Number of Grants: 17
Average Grant: $7,643*
Highest Grant: $304,432
Lowest Grant: $300
Typical Range: $5,000 to $10,000
*Note: Average grant figure excludes highest grant.

Recent Grants

Note: Grants derived from 2001 Form 990.
Library-Related

22,264	Friends of the Library, Wrangelle, AK -- for landscaping and exterior modifications
5,600	Irene Ingle Public Library, Wrangell, AK -- for computer purchases

General

20,000	Seventh Day Adventist Church, Wrangell, AK -- for camp renovation
18,000	St. Philip's Episcopal Church, Wrangell, AK -- for roof repairs
15,000	Wrangell Public Schools, Wrangell, AK -- for Scholarship Program
7,500	Wrangell Public Schools, Wrangell, AK -- for Southeast Alaska Art Festival
1,600	4-H Youth Shooting Program, Wrangell, AK
1,065	Wrangell Little League, Wrangell, AK -- for backstops
1,000	Discovery Southeast, Juneau, AK -- for Nature Studies Program
1,000	Wrangell Public Schools, Wrangell, AK -- for school libraries
500	KSTK Wrangell Radio Group, Wrangell, AK -- for performing arts promotion

NORCLIFFE FOUNDATION

Giving Contact

Dana Pigott, President
999 3rd Ave., Suite 1006
Seattle, WA 98104
Phone: (206)682-4820
E-mail: arline@thenorcliffefoundation.com
Web: http://www.thenorcliffefoundation.com

Description

Founded: 1952
EIN: 916029352
Organization Type: Private Foundation
Giving Locations: Pacific Northwest USA.
Grant Types: Capital, Conference/Seminar, Emer-

gency, Endowment, General Support, Operating Expenses, Project, Seed Money.

Donor Information

Founder: the late Theiline M. McCone

Financial Summary

Total Giving: $4,622,820 (fiscal year ending November 30, 2002)
Giving Analysis: Giving for fiscal 2002 includes: foundation grants to United Way ($85,000)
Assets: $116,059,823 (fiscal 2002)
Gifts Received: $1,639,394 (fiscal 2002); $447,974 (fiscal 2000); $1,949,553 (fiscal 1999). Note: In fiscal 2002, contributions were received from Lee W. Rolfe ($26,000), Ann Wyckoff ($152,964), Mary Pigott ($65,480), Charles Pigott ($1,295,100), and Martha Wyckoff ($99,850). In fiscal 2000, contributions were received from Lee W. Rolfe ($45,000), Judy Pigott Swenson ($24,973), Mary Pigott ($65,250), Theiline P. Scheumann ($312,750). In fiscal 1999, contributions were received from James C. Pigott ($156,157), Ann P. Wyckoff ($1,699,563), and Lee W. Rolfe ($93,833). In fiscal 1999 contributions were received from James C. Pigott ($156,157), Ann P. Wyckoff ($1,699,563) and Lee W. Rlofe ($93.833). In fiscal 1996, contributions were received from James C. Pigott ($125,775), Ann P. Wyckoff ($290,875), T. Evans Wyckoff ($145,973), Lee W. Rolfe ($35,700), Susan Wyckoff Pohl ($7,073), Theiline P. Scheumann ($35,000), Martha W. Byrne ($144,300), Glen and Alison Milliman ($45,380), Charles M. Pigott ($581,714), and Wyco LP ($25,500).

Typical Recipients

Arts & Humanities: Ballet, Historic Preservation, History & Archaeology, Libraries, Museums/Galleries, Music, Opera, Performing Arts, Public Broadcasting, Theater
Civic & Public Affairs: Clubs, Community Foundations, Economic Development, Economic Policy, Civic & Public Affairs-General, Housing, Rural Affairs, Urban & Community Affairs, Women's Affairs, Zoos/Aquariums
Education: Business Education, Colleges & Universities, Legal Education, Private Education (Precollege), Public Education (Precollege), Religious Education, Science/Mathematics Education, Secondary Education (Private), Special Education
Environment: Environment-General, Resource Conservation
Health: AIDS/HIV, Cancer, Children's Health/Hospitals, Clinics/Medical Centers, Emergency/Ambulance Services, Geriatric Health, Health Funds, Hospices, Hospitals, Medical Research, Mental Health, Nursing Services, Research/Studies Institutes, Single-Disease Health Associations
International: Health Care/Hospitals
Religion: Churches, Dioceses, Religion-General, Ministries, Religious Organizations, Religious Welfare
Science: Science Museums, Scientific Centers & Institutes
Social Services: Animal Protection, Child Welfare, Community Centers, Community Service Organizations, Family Services, Food/Clothing Distribution, Refugee Assistance, Senior Services, United Funds/United Ways, YMCA/YWCA/YMHA/YWHA, Youth Organizations

Application Procedures

Initial Contact: Send one copy of a letter proposal.
Application Requirements: Include a list of board members and proof of tax-exempt status.
Deadlines: None.

Restrictions

Areas of funding include capital campaigns, operating budgets, and special projects. Does not support individuals or deficit financing.

Additional Information

Publications: Program Policy Statement; Application Guidelines

Foundation Officials

Lisa Anderson: trustee
Theiline Cramer: trustee
Arline Hefferline: secretary
Mary Ellen Hughes: trustee
Dana Pigott: trustee
James C. Pigott: trustee B Seattle, WA 1936. ED Stanford University BCE (1959); Harvard University Graduate School of Business Administration MBA (1963). PRIM CORP EMPL president: Pigott Enterprises. CORP AFFIL vice chairman: EK Williams & Co.; director: PACCAR; president, director: Norcliffe Co.; director: Northern Life Insurance Co.; director: Americold Corp.; president: Management Reports & Services. NONPR AFFIL chairman, trustee: Seattle University. CLUB AFFIL Bohemian Club; Rainier Club.
Mary P. Pigott: trust
Susan Wyckoff Pohl: trustee
Lee W. Rolfe: trustee
Theiline P. Scheumann: treasurer
Ann Pigott Wyckoff: president

Grants Analysis

Disclosure Period: fiscal year ending November 30, 2002
Total Grants: $4,537,820*
Number of Grants: 183
Average Grant: $20,893*
Highest Grant: $735,359
Lowest Grant: $100
Typical Range: $10,000 to $50,000
*Note: Giving excludes United Way. Average grant figure excludes highest grant.

Recent Grants

Note: Grants derived from fiscal 2002 Form 990.
Library-Related

335,179	Seattle Public Library Foundation, Seattle, WA

General

735,359	Seattle University, Seattle, WA
366,510	Young Men's Christian Association of Seattle, Seattle, WA
335,179	Young Men's Christian Association of Seattle, Seattle, WA
306,400	University Preparatory Academy, Seattle, WA
166,666	Puget Sound Environmental Learning Center, Seattle, WA
151,545	Seattle Center Foundation, Seattle, WA
125,000	Fred Hutchinson Cancer Research Center, Seattle, WA
125,000	Overlake School, Seattle, WA
125,000	St. Luke Parish
113,236	Kindering Center, Belleevue, WA

NORCROSS WILDLIFE FOUNDATION

Giving Contact

Richard Reagan, Grants Administrator
PO Box 269
Wales, MA 01081-0269
Phone: (212)362-4831
Fax: (212)362-4783
Web: http://www.norcrossws.org
Note: Application address.

Alternate Contact

250 West 88th St.
Suite 806
New York, NY 10024

Phone: (212)362-4831
Fax: (212)362-4783
Note: Foundation headquarters.

Description

Founded: 1964
EIN: 132041622
Organization Type: Specialized/Single Purpose Foundation
Giving Locations: nationally.
Grant Types: General Support, Project.

Donor Information

Founder: The foundation was established in 1964 by Arthur D. Norcross and June Norcross Webster, both deceased.

Financial Summary

Total Giving: $1,264,131 (2002); $1,869,461 (2001)
Assets: $58,201,976 (2002); $67,553,653 (2001)
Gifts Received: $40,000 (2002); $102,000 (2001); $28,534 (2000). Note: In 2002, contributions were received from Trout Unlimited. In 2001, contributions were received from James & Diana Young. In 2000, contributions were received from the estate of A. Norcross. In 1997, contributions were received from the estate of A. Norcross and the New England Salmon Association.

Typical Recipients

Arts & Humanities: History & Archaeology, Museums/Galleries
Civic & Public Affairs: Botanical Gardens/Parks, Clubs, Community Foundations, Employment/Job Training, Gay/Lesbian Issues, Civic & Public Affairs-General, Hispanic Affairs, Law & Justice, Municipalities/Towns, Native American Affairs, Nonprofit Management, Public Policy, Rural Affairs, Safety, Urban & Community Affairs, Zoos/Aquariums
Education: Agricultural Education, Arts/Humanities Education, Colleges & Universities, Elementary Education (Private), Environmental Education, Medical Education, Private Education (Precollege), School Volunteerism, Special Education
Environment: Air/Water Quality, Energy, Forestry, Environment-General, Protection, Research, Resource Conservation, Watershed, Wildlife Protection
Health: AIDS/HIV, Children's Health/Hospitals, Clinics/Medical Centers, Emergency/Ambulance Services, Hospitals
International: International Development, International Environmental Issues, International Organizations
Religion: Religion-General, Jewish Causes, Religious Welfare
Science: Science Museums, Scientific Centers & Institutes, Scientific Labs, Scientific Organizations, Scientific Research
Social Services: Camps, Child Welfare, Community Service Organizations, Counseling, Crime Prevention, Family Services, Food/Clothing Distribution, Homes, People with Disabilities, Recreation & Athletics, Youth Organizations

Application Procedures

Initial Contact: Applicants should send a letter requesting application guidelines to Richard Reagan, PO Box 269, Wales, MA 01081.
Application Requirements: Grant requests accepted only for amounts under $10,000. Grant proposals should be on the organization's letterhead, in letter form no longer than two pages (with an optional one-page budget breakdown), describing the organization's work/objectives and containing the request itself, with a specific funding amount. Fourteen copies must be submitted and one copy of the IRS tax determination letter.
Deadlines: None.
Review Process: Only those requests conforming to the foundation's guidelines will be accepted; others will be returned. Decisions are made approximately quarterly. Final notification will be made quarterly.

Notes: Applications will not be accepted without guidelines.

Restrictions

The foundation does not renew earlier grants, match other grantmakers' gifts, or fund research. It does not contribute to general operating budgets, cover salaries, personnel or other overhead items; nor does it make multiyear commitments of funds or contribute to endowments.

Applying organizations should not send annual reports, fancy brochures, abstracts, press releases, newspaper articles, or glowing testimonials. The foundation does not want proposals in impressive but useless binders. It requires that proposals are sent via regular First Class or Priority Mail only. Requests sent by certified or overnight express mail are a waste of money and will be refused/returned automatically. Requests sent via FAX will not be accepted.

Additional Information

The foundation offers programs in environmental education at the 5,000-acre Norcross Wildlife Sanctuary in Monson, MA. Call (413) 267-9654 for more information.
Publications: Application Guidelines

Foundation Officials

Fred C. Anderson: director
Warren Balgooyen: director
Joseph A. Catalano: secretary, director
Albia Dugger: director
Edward Gallagher: director
Arthur D. Norcross, Jr.: director
Karen Outlaw: director NONPR AFFIL controller: Robin Hood Foundation.
Michael Patrick: director
Richard Reagan: president, treasurer, director B 1940.
Chris Stresser: director
Ted Wilson: director

Grants Analysis

Disclosure Period: calendar year ending 2002
Total Grants: $1,264,131
Number of Grants: 251
Average Grant: $5,036
Highest Grant: $55,000
Lowest Grant: $500
Typical Range: $1,000 to $10,000

Recent Grants

Note: Grants derived from 2002 Form 990.
General

55,000	Town of Wales, Wales, MA
25,000	Forest Society of Maine, Bangor, ME -- toward the cost of Big Spencer Mountain acquisition
25,000	Town of Monson, Monson, MA
20,000	New England Forestry Foundation, Groton, MA -- toward the conservation easement stewardship program
15,000	Living Oceans/National Audubon Society, New York, NY -- funds to cover publishing costs of additional Seafood Wallet Cards
13,400	Hornocker Wildlife Institute, Bozeman, MT -- funds for the purchase of Wolverine-tracking field equipment
12,000	Land Trust Alliance, Washington, DC -- funds for specialized computer soft/hardware for LTAnet
10,000	Center for Alaskan Coastal Studies Inc., Homer, AK -- toward materials for facilities repair and improvement
10,000	Connecticut Fund for the Environment, New Haven, CT -- funds to cover publishing cost of public-information brochures
10,000	Coral Reef Alliance, Berkeley, CA -- toward publishing costs of the newsletter

NORD FAMILY FOUNDATION

Giving Contact

Sharon White, Controller
747 Milan Ave.
Amherst, OH 44001
Phone: (440)984-3939
Fax: (440)984-3934
E-mail: info@nordff.org
Web: http://www.nordff.org
Note: toll free (800)745-8946

Description

Founded: 1988
EIN: 341595929
Organization Type: General Purpose Foundation
Giving Locations: CO: Denver; OH: Lorain County area, Boston Cuyahoga County area; SC: Columbia Lorain County area
Grant Types: Challenge, Endowment, General Support, Operating Expenses, Project.

Donor Information

Founder: The Nord Family Foundation, established in late 1988, is the successor to the Nordson Foundation, which was created as a trust by the late Walter G. Nord in 1952, and dissolved in October 1988. Mr. Nord believed that business has a social responsibility to the community from which it draws its human resources. To that end, the Nordson Corporation eventually began to designate five percent of its pre-tax domestic profits as its philanthropic commitment to the communities where it operated. Much of this commitment was fulfilled through annual contributions to the Nordson Foundation. Because of this relationship, the foundation often awarded grants with the corporation's interests in mind and adopted the corporation's geographic giving preferences as its own. By the late 1980s, certain factors had emerged which resulted in a decision to dissolve the Nordson Foundation. IRS divestiture rules required the foundation, by the end of 1989, to phase out its ownership of a substantial number of Nordson Corporation shares bequeathed by Virginia Nord, the widow of Walter Nord. The divestiture resulted in large increases in assets and grant making, and by 1988 the foundation had become one of the ten largest private foundations in Ohio.

However, financial matters were not the only factors that influenced the decision to create a new foundation. If the foundation were to continue on the mission begun by Walter and Virginia Nord, it was felt that the foundation needed to begin nurturing a new generation of trustees. In addition, since the corporation had acquired new leadership, the time had come for it to establish its own direct grant-making program.

The result of these considerations was the creation of the Nord Family Foundation and Nordson Corporation Foundation, two new and separate entities to carry on the philanthropic traditions of Walter and Virginia Nord and the Nordson Corporation.

Financial Summary

Total Giving: $3,177,497 (2002)
Giving Analysis: Giving for 2002 includes: foundation matching gifts ($10,821)
Assets: $68,061,098 (2002)
Gifts Received: $635,844 (2002). Note: In 2002, contributions were received from Evan Nord ($570,844) and Lorain Community Foundation ($65,000).

Typical Recipients

Arts & Humanities: Arts Centers, Arts Festivals, Arts Funds, Arts Institutes, Arts Outreach, Dance, Historic Preservation, History & Archaeology, Libraries, Museums/Galleries, Music, Opera, Performing Arts, Public Broadcasting, Theater, Visual Arts
Civic & Public Affairs: African American Affairs, Bo-

tanical Gardens/Parks, Business/Free Enterprise, Civil Rights, Community Foundations, Economic Development, Economic Policy, Employment/Job Training, Civic & Public Affairs-General, Hispanic Affairs, Housing, Legal Aid, Minority Business, Municipalities/Towns, Native American Affairs, Philanthropic Organizations, Professional & Trade Associations, Public Policy, Rural Affairs, Urban & Community Affairs, Women's Affairs, Zoos/Aquariums

Education: Afterschool/Enrichment Programs, Arts/Humanities Education, Colleges & Universities, Community & Junior Colleges, Education Associations, Education Funds, Education Reform, Education-General, Leadership Training, Minority Education, Private Education (Precollege), Public Education (Precollege), Social Sciences Education, Special Education, Student Aid

Environment: Air/Water Quality, Environment-General, Resource Conservation

Health: Adolescent Health Issues, Alzheimer's Disease, Cancer, Children's Health/Hospitals, Clinics/Medical Centers, Emergency/Ambulance Services, Eyes/Blindness, Health-General, Health Funds, Health Organizations, Mental Health, Nursing Services, Public Health

Religion: Religion-General, Ministries, Religious Welfare

Science: Science Exhibits & Fairs, Science Museums, Scientific Centers & Institutes

Social Services: At-Risk Youth, Big Brothers/Big Sisters, Child Abuse, Child Welfare, Community Centers, Community Service Organizations, Counseling, Crime Prevention, Day Care, Domestic Violence, Family Planning, Family Services, Food/Clothing Distribution, Homes, People with Disabilities, Recreation & Athletics, Senior Services, Sexual Abuse, Shelters/Homelessness, Social Services-General, Substance Abuse, United Funds/United Ways, Volunteer Services, YMCA/YWCA/YMHA/YWHA, Youth Organizations

Application Procedures

Initial Contact: The foundation does not currently use an application form. Only one copy of a proposal is required.

Application Requirements: Proposals should include a cover letter from the organization's chief executive director; one-page abstract of the proposal; detailed description of the project, including background information, statement of objectives, project budget, and plan for evaluating results; and a copy of the organization's IRS tax-exempt status letter. The application should also include a statement of the organization's purpose; list of current board members; and a copy of the organization's most recent financial statements.

Deadlines: Applications are due April 1 for a June decision, August 1 for an October decision, and December 1 for a February decision.

Review Process: Foundation trustees meet at least three times a year to review grant requests. These meetings are usually held in October, February, and June.

Restrictions

Endowment funds, debt reduction, and research projects are not within the foundation's areas of interest. In general, the foundation does not support capital campaigns unless the projects meet specific criteria. General support requests will be considered under certain conditions. The foundation does not fund advertising, tickets for fundraising activities, or individuals.

Additional Information

The staff of the Nord Family Foundation is available to answer questions or discuss problems concerning grant applications. The foundation maintains a library of reference materials and grant-writing tools and will assist potential applicants in the process of applying for a grant.

Publications: Annual Report; Guidelines

Foundation Officials

Randall Barbato: trustee
Samuel Berk: trustee
Pam Ignat: trustee
Emma Newby Mason: trustee B Bowling Green, OH 1937. ED Mercyhurst College BA (1959); Case Western Reserve University JD (1978). PRIM CORP EMPL senior vice president: Lorain National Bank. NONPR AFFIL member: Rotary International.
John Mullaney: executive director
Shannon Nord: trustee

Grants Analysis

Disclosure Period: calendar year ending 2002
Total Grants: $3,166,676*
Number of Grants: 248
Average Grant: $12,769
Highest Grant: $175,000
Lowest Grant: $500
Typical Range: $1,000 to $25,000
Note: Giving excludes matching gifts.

Recent Grants

Note: Grants derived from 2002 Form 990.
General

125,000	Center for Applied Special Technology, Wakefield, MA -- towards universal design for learning at pilot schools
100,000	Center for Leadership in Education, Elyria, OH -- towards strengthening the quality of school restructuring
75,350	Oberlin Early Childhood Center, Oberlin, OH -- towards childcare subsidies
68,000	Nurturing Center, Kalispell, MT -- towards team parenting program
67,000	Lorain County Board of Mental Health, Elyria, OH -- towards integrating mental health and school services
65,000	Oberlin Early Childhood Center, Oberlin, OH -- to integrate creative arts into childhood education
50,364	Amherst Historical Society, Amherst, MA -- for maintenance and repair of property
50,000	Lorain County Access to Higher Education Program Inc., Elyria, OH -- towards access programming in schools
50,000	South Lorain Community Development Corporation, Lorain, OH -- towards affordable home ownership opportunities
50,000	YWCA of Elyria, Elyria, OH -- towards a single resident occupancy for homeless women

NORDSON CORP.

Company Headquarters

28601 Clements Rd.
Westlake, OH 44145
Web: http://www.nordson.com

Company Description

Founded: 1909
Ticker: NDSN
Exchange: NASDAQ
Revenue: US$647.8 million (2002)
Employees: 3483 (2003)
SIC(s): 3569 General Industrial Machinery Nec, 5084 Industrial Machinery & Equipment.

Operating Locations

Nordson Corp. (CA--Sand City; GA--Atlanta, Norcross; OH--Amherst, Elyria; WI--Menomonee, New Richmond)

Nonmonetary Support

Type: Donated Equipment; Donated Products; Loaned Employees
Volunteer Programs: Company operates the Time'n

Talent (T'nT) program, which links employees with volunteer opportunities in the community and generates new community service projects.

Nordson Corp. Foundation

Giving Contact

Constance Haqq, Executive Director
28601 Clemens Road
Westlake, OH 44145-1148
Phone: (440)892-1580
Fax: (440)892-9507
E-mail: kladiner@nordson.com
Web: http://www.nordson.com/corporate/grants.html
Note: Contact for Northeastern Ohio requests.

Alternate Contact

Symone McClain, Community Relations Manager/Atlanta
Nordon Corp.
11475 Lakefield Drive
Duluth, GA 30097
Phone: (770)497-3661
E-mail: smcclain@nordson.com
Note: Contact for Greater Atlanta requests.

Description

Founded: 1952
EIN: 341596194
Organization Type: Corporate Foundation
Giving Locations: GA: Atlanta; MA: Southeastern Massachusetts; OH, headquarters and operating communities; RI, San Diego County
Grant Types: Capital, Employee Matching Gifts, General Support, Project, Research, Scholarship.
Note: Employee matching gift ratio: 1 to 1 up to $5,000 annually per employee or retiree.

Financial Summary

Total Giving: $1,040,540 (fiscal year ending October 31, 2002); $1,519,940 (fiscal 2001). Note: Contributes through corporate direct giving program and foundation.
Giving Analysis: Giving for fiscal 2002 includes: foundation scholarships ($5,000)
Assets: $1,505,043 (fiscal 2002); $2,988,220 (fiscal 2001)
Gifts Received: $800,000 (fiscal 2000); $1,000,000 (fiscal 1997); $1,500,000 (fiscal 1995). Note: Contributions are received from Nordson Corp.

Typical Recipients

Arts & Humanities: Arts Centers, Arts Festivals, Arts Institutes, Arts Outreach, Community Arts, Ethnic & Folk Arts, Arts & Humanities-General, Historic Preservation, History & Archaeology, Libraries, Literary Arts, Museums/Galleries, Music, Opera, Performing Arts, Public Broadcasting, Theater

Civic & Public Affairs: African American Affairs, Botanical Gardens/Parks, Business/Free Enterprise, Civil Rights, Clubs, Community Foundations, Economic Development, Employment/Job Training, Civic & Public Affairs-General, Hispanic Affairs, Housing, Law & Justice, Legal Aid, Municipalities/Towns, Native American Affairs, Nonprofit Management, Professional & Trade Associations, Public Policy, Urban & Community Affairs, Zoos/Aquariums

Education: Afterschool/Enrichment Programs, Arts/Humanities Education, Business Education, Colleges & Universities, Community & Junior Colleges, Education Associations, Education Funds, Education Reform, Elementary Education (Private), Elementary Education (Public), Engineering/Technological Education, Education-General, Gifted & Talented Programs, International Studies, Leadership Training, Literacy, Medical Education, Minority Education, Preschool Education, Private Education (Precollege), Public Education (Precollege), Science/Mathematics

Education, Secondary Education (Private), Secondary Education (Public), Social Sciences Education, Special Education, Student Aid, Vocational & Technical Education

Environment: Environment-General

Health: Clinics/Medical Centers, Emergency/Ambulance Services, Health Funds, Health Organizations, Hospices, Medical Rehabilitation, Medical Research, Mental Health, Nursing Services, Preventive Medicine/Wellness Organizations, Single-Disease Health Associations, Speech & Hearing

International: International Relations

Religion: Churches, Religion-General, Ministries, Religious Welfare

Science: Science Exhibits & Fairs, Science Museums, Scientific Centers & Institutes

Social Services: At-Risk Youth, Big Brothers/Big Sisters, Child Abuse, Child Welfare, Community Centers, Community Service Organizations, Counseling, Crime Prevention, Day Care, Delinquency & Criminal Rehabilitation, Domestic Violence, Family Services, Food/Clothing Distribution, Homes, People with Disabilities, Recreation & Athletics, Scouts, Senior Services, Shelters/Homelessness, Substance Abuse, United Funds/United Ways, Volunteer Services, YMCA/YWCA/YMHA/YWHA, Youth Organizations

Application Procedures

Initial Contact: Write to request application from foundation staff in Westlake, OH, Atlanta, GA, or Monterey, CA, or obtain the application from the foundation's web site.

Application Requirements: Send an original and one copy of the completed application form, a copy of current 501(c)(3) form and a list of organization's officers and trustees, with affiliations.

Deadlines: November 15 for review in January, February 15 for review in April, May 15 for July and August 15 for review in October.

Review Process: The foundation board of trustees reviews written applications at quarterly meetings in January, April, July, and October.

Evaluative Criteria: Geographic location and constituency served; special interest in disadvantaged persons, minorities, the handicapped, and projects which attack root causes of problems.

Decision Notification: Applicants are notified of the trustees' funding decisions in writing.

Notes: The foundation encourages potential applicants to contact a foundation staff member prior to submitting an application to ensure that a grant request falls within the foundation's priorities.

Additional Information

Approximately 5% of pretax profit is budgeted for charitable contributions.

On October 31, 1988, approximately $51 million in foundation assets were transferred to the Nord Family Foundation. The Nordson Foundation (EIN: 34-6539234) was liquidated and transferred $1.5 million to a newly established Nordson Corporation Foundation (EIN: 34-1596194) that continues to support charitable causes located in Nordson Corp. manufacturing cities. manufacturing cities. manufacturing cities. manufacturing cities. manufacturing cities.

Publications: Contributions Report to the Community

Corporate Officials

Christian C. Bernadotte: vice president B 1949. PRIM CORP EMPL vice president: Nordson Corp.

Foundation Officials

Constance T. Haqq: executive director

Grants Analysis

Disclosure Period: fiscal year ending October 31, 2002

Total Grants: $1,035,540

Number of Grants: 136

Average Grant: $5,592*

Highest Grant: $100,000

Lowest Grant: $1,000

Typical Range: $1,000 to $20,000

*Note: Average grant figure excludes four highest grants ($275,000)

Recent Grants

Note: Grants derived from 2003 Form 990.

General

100,000	Center for Leadership in Education, Elyria, OH
100,000	Center for Leadership in Education, Elyria, OH
35,000	Oberlin Foundation of Independent Colleges, Oberlin, OH
25,000	Intel International Science & Engineering Fair, Santa Clara, CA
25,000	Purdue Foundation, West Lafayette, IN
20,000	Case Reserve Western University, Cleveland, OH
20,000	Elyria YMCA, Elyria, OH
19,000	Access Program
15,000	El Centro de Servicios Sociales, Lorain, OH
15,000	Lorain County Urban League, Lorain, OH

NORFOLK SHIPBUILDING & DRYDOCK CORP.

Company Headquarters

750 W. Berkley Ave.
Norfolk, VA 23523

Company Description

Employees: 2,000
SIC(s): 3731 Ship Building & Repairing.

Norfolk Shipbuilding and Drydock Corp. Charitable Trust

Giving Contact

Norfolk Shipbuilding and Drydock Corp. Charitable Trust
Bank of America
PO Box 2100
Norfolk, VA 23501
Phone: (804)788-2067

Description

EIN: 546036745
Organization Type: Corporate Foundation
Giving Locations: headquarters and operating communities.
Grant Types: Capital, General Support, Multiyear/Continuing Support.

Financial Summary

Gifts Received: $58 (1999); $1,453 (1995); $200,144 (1992). Note: In 1992, major contributions were received from Norfolk Shipbuilding & Drydock Corp. ($200,000).

Typical Recipients

Arts & Humanities: Arts Associations & Councils, Arts Centers, Arts Funds, Arts & Humanities-General, Historic Preservation, History & Archaeology, Libraries, Museums/Galleries, Music, Opera, Public Broadcasting

Civic & Public Affairs: African American Affairs, Business/Free Enterprise, Civic & Public Affairs-General, Professional & Trade Associations, Urban & Community Affairs, Zoos/Aquariums

Education: Business Education, Colleges & Universities, Community & Junior Colleges, Economic Education, Education Associations, Education Funds, Medical Education, Minority Education, Private Education (Precollege), Student Aid

Environment: Air/Water Quality, Resource Conservation

Health: Children's Health/Hospitals, Emergency/Ambulance Services, Health-General, Health Organizations, Hospitals

Science: Science Exhibits & Fairs, Scientific Centers & Institutes, Scientific Organizations

Social Services: Child Welfare, Community Service Organizations, Emergency Relief, Social Services-General, United Funds/United Ways

Application Procedures

Initial Contact: Send a brief letter of inquiry.
Deadlines: None.

Additional Information

Trust(s): Bank of America

Corporate Officials

Thomas J. Bradburn: chief executive officer, president chief operating officer, secretary, director PRIM CORP EMPL chief executive officer, president: Norfolk Shipbuilding & Drydock Corp.

William Peavy Fricks: chairman, chief executive officer B Byron, GA 1944. ED Auburn University BS (1966); College of William & Mary MBA (1970). PRIM CORP EMPL chairman, chief executive officer: Newport News Shipbuilding, Inc.

John L. Roper, IV: executive vice president, chief operating officer, secretary, director B Norfolk, VA 1953. ED Hampden-Sydney College (1975). PRIM CORP EMPL executive vice president, chief operating officer, secretary, director: Norfolk Shipbuilding & Drydock Corp. CORP AFFIL secretary, treasurer, director: Marepcon Corp. International; director: John L. Roper Corp.; director: Lonsdale Corp.

John Lonsdale Roper, III: president, chief executive officer, director B Norfolk, VA 1927. ED University of Virginia BSME (1949); Massachusetts Institute of Technology BS (1951). PRIM CORP EMPL president, chief executive officer, director: Norfolk Shipbuilding & Drydock Corp. NONPR AFFIL director, member executive committee: Shipbuilders Council America; member: Society Naval Architects & Marine Engineers; president, director: Marepcon Corp. International; president, director: John L Roper Corp.; director: Flagship Group Ltd; president, director: Londsale Corp.; director: American Bureau Shipping; director: Cruise International.

Grants Analysis

Disclosure Period: calendar year ending 2000

Total Grants: $32,000

Number of Grants: 5

Highest Grant: $10,000

Lowest Grant: $1,000

Recent Grants

Note: Grants derived from 2001 Form 990.

General

10,000	Mariner's Museum, Newport News, VA
10,000	Virginia Opera Association, Norfolk, VA
6,800	Wisconsin Foundation, Madison, WI
2,000	Chrysler Museum, Norfolk, VA
2,000	Virginia Foundation for Independent Colleges, Richmond, VA
1,000	Coastal Conservation Association, Houston, TX
1,000	Virginia College Fund, Richmond, VA

NORMAN FOUNDATION

Giving Contact

June Makela, Program Director
Norman Foundation, Inc.

147 East 48th Street
New York, NY 10017
Phone: (212)230-9830
Fax: (212)230-9849
E-mail: info@normanfdn.org
Web: http://www.normanfdn.org

Description
Founded: 1938
EIN: 131862694
Organization Type: General Purpose Foundation
Giving Locations: nationally.
Grant Types: General Support.

Donor Information
Founder: The Norman Foundation was created in 1935 by the late Aaron E. Norman, and has since been augmented by his children and grandchildren. The original name of the foundation was the Assistance Fund, which in 1943 was changed to the Aaron E. Norman Fund, and then to the current name in 1970. Today, its members and directors include the descendants of Aaron E. Norman and their spouses.

Financial Summary
Total Giving: $1,111,500 (2003); $1,065,050 (2002); $1,115,311 (2001)
Assets: $23,093,633 (2003); $22,484,170 (2002); $23,016,587 (2001)
Gifts Received: $5,000 (1995). Note: Contributions were received from Dorothy Norman.

Typical Recipients
Arts & Humanities: Arts Associations & Councils, Arts Centers, Arts & Humanities-General, Museums/Galleries, Public Broadcasting
Civic & Public Affairs: African American Affairs, Asian American Affairs, Botanical Gardens/Parks, Business/Free Enterprise, Civil Rights, Community Foundations, Economic Development, Economic Policy, Employment/Job Training, First Amendment Issues, Gay/Lesbian Issues, Civic & Public Affairs-General, Hispanic Affairs, Housing, Law & Justice, Legal Aid, Minority Business, Municipalities/Towns, Native American Affairs, Nonprofit Management, Philanthropic Organizations, Professional & Trade Associations, Public Policy, Rural Affairs, Safety, Urban & Community Affairs, Women's Affairs
Education: Colleges & Universities, Education Associations, Education Funds, Education Reform, Education-General, International Studies, Leadership Training, Private Education (Precollege)
Environment: Air/Water Quality, Energy, Environment-General, Protection, Resource Conservation, Wildlife Protection
Health: AIDS/HIV, Children's Health/Hospitals, Health Policy/Cost Containment, Hospices, Medical Research, Mental Health, Public Health
International: Health Care/Hospitals, Human Rights, International Affairs, International Development, International Environmental Issues
Religion: Churches, Religious Welfare, Social/Policy Issues
Social Services: Animal Protection, Child Welfare, Community Service Organizations, Counseling, Crime Prevention, Day Care, Domestic Violence, Emergency Relief, Family Planning, Family Services, Food/Clothing Distribution, People with Disabilities, Recreation & Athletics, Refugee Assistance, Shelters/Homelessness, Social Services-General, Special Olympics, Youth Organizations

Application Procedures
Initial Contact: The foundation has no standard application form. Prospective grantees are encouraged to initiate the process by sending a brief letter of inquiry to the Program Director. The foundation does accept the New York Area Common Application Form. The foundation actively seeks letters of inquiry from new organizations that may lack previous fundraising experience.
Application Requirements: An initial inquiry should

explain the scope and significance of the problem to be addressed; the organization's proposed response and (if appropriate) how this strategy builds upon the organization's past work; the specific, demonstrable effects the project would have if successful; and how the project promotes systemic change and otherwise relates to the foundation's philosophy. If the proposal is deemed promising, the organization would be encouraged to submit a full proposal which should include detailed organization and project budgets, including a breakdown of cur rent and prospective income from foundations and other sources; background on project staff; a descriptive list of board members; a letter of support; and documentation of tax-exempt status.
Deadlines: Deadlines: August 1, 2003 (Civil Rights), December 1, 2003 (Environmental Justice), March 1, 2004, (Economic Justice), and August 2, 2004 (Civil Rights).
Review Process: The foundation acknowledges receipt of proposals by postcard or letter. The committee meets at least three times a year.
Notes: The foundation does not accept applications by e-mail.

Restrictions
The foundation only makes grants to tax-exempt organizations that focus on domestic issues. Grants are never made to individuals, universities or to support conferences, scholarships, research, cultural films, media and arts projects, direct social service delivery programs, capital funding projects, fund-raising drives or other grant-making organizations.

Additional Information
Publications: Annual Report; Grant Guidelines

Foundation Officials
Melissa Bunnen: director, treasurer
Robert L. Bunnen, Jr.: director
Alice Franklin: director, vice president
Andrew D. Franklin: director
Deborah Weil Harrington: director
Honor Lassalle: president
Philip E. Lassalle: director
Abigail Norman: director
Margaret Norman: director, secretary
Rebecca Norman: director
Sarah E. Norman: director
Belinda Bunnen Reusch: director
Diana Lassalle Turner: director
Amanda E. Weil: director, vice president
Sandison E. Weil: director
William S. Weil: director

Grants Analysis
Disclosure Period: calendar year ending 2003
Total Grants: $1,111,500
Number of Grants: 48
Average Grant: $27,788
Highest Grant: $25,000
Lowest Grant: $5,000
Typical Range: $10,000 to $50,000

Recent Grants
Note: Grants derived from 2002 Form 990.
General

25,000	Carolina Alliance for a Fair Employment, Greenville, SC
25,000	Chinese Staff and Workers' Association, New York, NY
25,000	El Puente Community Development Corporation, El Paso, TX
20,000	Angeles Alliance for a New Economy, Los Angeles, CA
20,000	Arkansas Public Policy Panel, Little Rock, AR
20,000	Asian Pacific Environmental Net, Oakland, CA
20,000	Californians for Justice, Oakland, CA
20,000	Chicago Coalition for the Homeless, Chicago, IL
20,000	Citizens Coal Council, Denver, CO
20,000	Environmental Community Action Inc., Atlanta, GA

NORMANDIE FOUNDATION

Giving Contact
Andrew E. Norman, President & Treasurer
147 E. 48th St.
New York, NY 10017
Phone: (212)230-9800

Description
Founded: 1966
EIN: 136213564
Organization Type: Private Foundation
Giving Locations: MA: Barnstable County; NY: Rockland County, New York
Grant Types: General Support.

Donor Information
Founder: Andrew E. Norman, the Aaron E. Norman Fund

Financial Summary
Total Giving: $293,583 (2001)
Giving Analysis: Giving for 2001 includes: foundation grants to United Way ($2,500)
Assets: $6,294,456 (2001)
Gifts Received: $30,102 (2001); $309,068 (1999); $298,500 (1994). Note: In 2001, contributions were received from Margaret Norman ($21,634) and Abigail Norman ($8,468). In 1999, contributions were received from Andrew E. Norman and Margaret Norman.

Typical Recipients
Arts & Humanities: Arts Centers, Community Arts, History & Archaeology, Libraries, Museums/Galleries, Performing Arts, Public Broadcasting
Civic & Public Affairs: African American Affairs, Civil Rights, Civic & Public Affairs-General, Legal Aid, Parades/Festivals, Philanthropic Organizations, Public Policy, Urban & Community Affairs
Education: Arts/Humanities Education, Colleges & Universities, Education Funds, Legal Education, Medical Education, Minority Education
Environment: Air/Water Quality, Environment-General, Resource Conservation
Health: AIDS/HIV, Hospices, Hospitals
International: Foreign Educational Institutions, Human Rights, International Affairs, International Development, International Environmental Issues, International Organizations, International Peace & Security Issues, International Relations, International Relief Efforts
Religion: Religion-General, Religious Welfare, Seminaries
Science: Science Museums, Scientific Centers & Institutes, Scientific Labs, Scientific Research
Social Services: At-Risk Youth, Child Welfare, Community Service Organizations, Emergency Relief, Family Planning, Food/Clothing Distribution, Recreation & Athletics, Social Services-General, Substance Abuse, United Funds/United Ways, Volunteer Services, Youth Organizations

Application Procedures
Initial Contact: Send a brief letter of inquiry.
Application Requirements: Include description of proposals and proof of tax-exempt status.
Deadlines: None.

Foundation Officials
Nancy Norman Lassalle: vice president, secretary
Andrew E. Norman: president, treasurer B New

York, NY 1930. ED Harvard University BA (1951); Harvard University JD (1954).

Grants Analysis

Disclosure Period: calendar year ending 2001
Total Grants: $291,083*
Number of Grants: 62
Average Grant: $2,768*
Highest Grant: $75,000
Lowest Grant: $65
Typical Range: $1,000 to $5,000
***Note:** Giving excludes United Way. Average grant figure excludes two highest grants ($125,000).

Recent Grants

Note: Grants derived from 2001 Form 990.
General

75,000	International Rescue Committee, New York, NY
50,000	Africa Action, Washington, DC
25,250	ACLU Foundation, New York, NY
25,000	Africa Fund, New York, NY
20,000	Vanguard Foundation, San Francisco, CA
16,600	Somerville Haitian Coalition, Somerville, MA
15,000	Vanguard Foundation, San Francisco, CA
10,000	Government Accountability Project, Washington, DC
10,000	International Society for Ecology and Culture, Berkeley, CA
10,000	Neighbor to Neighbor Education Fund, CA

DELLORA A. AND LESTER J. NORRIS FOUNDATION

Giving Contact

Eugene W. Butler, Treasurer
303 E. Main Street
PO Box 4325
St. Charles, IL 60174
Phone: (630)584-2500
Fax: (630)584-1020

Description

Founded: 1979
EIN: 363054939
Organization Type: Family Foundation
Giving Locations: CO; FL; IL: nationally.
Grant Types: General Support.

Donor Information

Founder: The foundation was established in 1979 in Illinois by the late Dellora A. Norris and Lester J. Norris.

Financial Summary

Total Giving: $1,790,000 (2003); $2,022,710 (2002); $2,448,000 (2001)
Giving Analysis: Giving for 2002 includes: foundation grants to United Way ($5,000)
Assets: $34,777,561 (2003); $31,355,733 (2002); $37,464,674 (2001)
Gifts Received: $967,549 (1997); $1,290,066 (1993); $645,033 (1992). Note: Contributions were received from the estate of Lester J. Norris.

Typical Recipients

Arts & Humanities: Arts Centers, Arts Festivals, Ethnic & Folk Arts, Historic Preservation, History & Archaeology, Libraries, Museums/Galleries, Music, Opera
Civic & Public Affairs: Botanical Gardens/Parks, Clubs, Community Foundations, Economic Development, Civic & Public Affairs-General, Municipalities/

Towns, Parades/Festivals, Philanthropic Organizations, Professional & Trade Associations, Urban & Community Affairs, Women's Affairs, Zoos/Aquariums
Education: Business Education, Colleges & Universities, Education Funds, Elementary Education (Private), Education-General, Private Education (Precollege), Public Education (Precollege), Science/Mathematics Education, Secondary Education (Private), Secondary Education (Public), Special Education, Student Aid
Health: AIDS/HIV, Cancer, Children's Health/Hospitals, Clinics/Medical Centers, Diabetes, Health Funds, Health Organizations, Heart, Hospices, Hospitals, Medical Rehabilitation, Medical Research, Mental Health, Public Health, Respiratory, Single-Disease Health Associations
International: International-General
Religion: Churches, Religion-General, Religious Organizations, Religious Welfare
Social Services: Animal Protection, Child Welfare, Community Centers, Counseling, Crime Prevention, Day Care, Emergency Relief, Family Services, Food/Clothing Distribution, People with Disabilities, Recreation & Athletics, Scouts, Senior Services, Shelters/Homelessness, Substance Abuse, United Funds/United Ways, YMCA/YWCA/YMHA/YWHA, Youth Organizations

Application Procedures

Initial Contact: Submit a preliminary letter to the foundation.
Deadlines: None. Applications are accepted throughout the year.

Foundation Officials

Eugene W. Butler: treasurer B 1932. PRIM CORP EMPL chairman: Harris Bank Batavia National Association. CORP AFFIL chairman, president: Harris Bank Saint Charles; director: Cedric Spring Associates.
Joann N. Collins: president
George N. Gaynor: vice president
Pamela Norris: director
Robert C. Norris: chairman
Howard S. Tuthill, III: secretary B Mount Vernon, NY 1947. PRIM CORP EMPL partner: Kelley, Drye & Warren.

Grants Analysis

Disclosure Period: calendar year ending 2002
Total Grants: $2,017,710*
Number of Grants: 105
Average Grant: $19,216
Highest Grant: $150,000
Lowest Grant: $1,000
Typical Range: $10,000 to $40,000
***Note:** Giving excludes United Way.

Recent Grants

Note: Grants derived from 2002 Form 990.

General

150,000	City of Naples-Norris Center at Cambier Park
100,000	International College, Naples, FL
100,000	Northwestern University, Evanston, IL
100,000	Seacrest Country Day School, Naples, FL
75,000	St. Ignatius College Preparatory, Chicago, IL
65,310	YMCA of Collier County, Naples, FL
50,000	Arizona Heart Institute, Phoenix, AZ
50,000	Barrows Neurological Women's Board Foundation, Phoenix, AZ
50,000	Delnor-Community Health Care Foundation, Geneva, IL
50,000	Denver Academy, Denver, CO

KENNETH T. AND EILEEN L. NORRIS FOUNDATION

Giving Contact

Ronald R. Barnes, Executive Director & Trustee
11 Golden Shore, Suite 450
Long Beach, CA 90802
Phone: (562)435-8444
Fax: (562)436-0584
E-mail: savannah@ktn.org
Web: http://www.norrisfoundation.org

Description

Founded: 1963
EIN: 956080374
Organization Type: General Purpose Foundation
Giving Locations: CA: Los Angeles County area
Grant Types: Capital, Endowment, General Support, Matching, Multiyear/Continuing Support, Operating Expenses, Professorship, Project, Research, Scholarship.

Donor Information

Founder: The late Kenneth T. Norris and his late wife, Eileen Norris, established the foundation in 1963. Mr. Norris was the founder, chairman of the board, and president of Norris Industries in Los Angeles. He had a great interest in supporting the Los Angeles area community. His special focus was in academic achievement and research.

Financial Summary

Total Giving: $7,786,550 (fiscal year ending November 30, 2003); $8,275,828 (fiscal 2002); $9,121,291 (fiscal 2001)
Assets: $166,621,210 (fiscal 2003); $157,458,631 (fiscal 2002)
Gifts Received: $139,378 (fiscal 1993); $190,000 (fiscal 1992 approx)

Typical Recipients

Arts & Humanities: Arts Associations & Councils, Arts Centers, Arts Institutes, Community Arts, Film & Video, Libraries, Museums/Galleries, Music, Performing Arts, Public Broadcasting, Theater
Civic & Public Affairs: African American Affairs, Botanical Gardens/Parks, Community Foundations, Employment/Job Training, Civic & Public Affairs-General, Hispanic Affairs, Philanthropic Organizations, Public Policy
Education: Arts/Humanities Education, Colleges & Universities, Elementary Education (Private), Engineering/Technological Education, Education-General, Health & Physical Education, Leadership Training, Literacy, Medical Education, Private Education (Precollege), Public Education (Precollege), Science/Mathematics Education, Secondary Education (Private), Secondary Education (Public), Special Education, Student Aid, Vocational & Technical Education
Health: AIDS/HIV, Alzheimer's Disease, Cancer, Children's Health/Hospitals, Clinics/Medical Centers, Diabetes, Emergency/Ambulance Services, Eyes/Blindness, Health Organizations, Heart, Hospices, Hospitals, Kidney, Medical Rehabilitation, Medical Research, Research/Studies Institutes, Respiratory, Single-Disease Health Associations, Speech & Hearing, Trauma Treatment
International: Health Care/Hospitals, International Relief Efforts
Religion: Dioceses, Religious Welfare
Science: Science Museums, Scientific Centers & Institutes, Scientific Organizations
Social Services: At-Risk Youth, Child Abuse, Child Welfare, Community Service Organizations, Counseling, Crime Prevention, Day Care, Emergency Relief, Family Planning, Family Services, Food/Clothing Distribution, People with Disabilities, Recreation & Athletics, Shelters/Homelessness, Social Services-

General, Substance Abuse, Volunteer Services, YMCA/YWCA/YMHA/YWHA, Youth Organizations

Application Procedures

Initial Contact: Organizations should request the application guidelines.

Application Requirements: A full proposal must include the history and goals of the organization, a project description, the action plan and expected outcomes of the project, a list of other contributors to the project, most recent audited financial statements, proof of 501(c)(3) tax-exempt status, the percentage of revenues coming from federal, state, and local governments, a list of current directors, the foundation's Grant Application form, and any additional information about the project.

Deadlines: Applications accepted from May 1 through June 30 for Medicine grants; February 15 through March 31 for Youth grants; from May 1 though June 30 for Education/Science; and December 1 and January 31 for Community and Cultural grants.

Decision Notification: The foundation responds within four months of the application deadline.

Restrictions

The foundation does not fund political organizations/campaigns, foreign organizations, or individuals.

Additional Information

Due to funding limitations, the trustees prefer to initiate the grants given.

The Norris Foundation provides continuous funding for many organizations, and because of this, few new programs are added to the budget each year.

The foundation provides accounting services and investment advice to nonprofits.

Publications: Annual Report; Grant Qualifications; Guidelines; Application Form

Foundation Officials

Ronald R. Barnes: executive director, trustee
William G. Corey, MD: medical advisor, trustee
Lisa D. Hansen: chairman, trustee
James R. Martin: trustee
Bradley K. Norris: trustee
Harlyne J. Norris: trustee
Kenneth T. Norris, Jr.: trustee emeritus
Kimberley Presley: trustee
Walter J. Zanino: controller, trustee

Grants Analysis

Disclosure Period: fiscal year ending November 30, 2003
Total Grants: $7,786,550
Number of Grants: 306
Average Grant: $15,979*
Highest Grant: $2,145,000
Lowest Grant: $2,000
Typical Range: $5,000 to $25,000
***Note:** Average grant figure excludes three highest grants ($2,945,000).

Recent Grants

Note: Grants derived from fiscal 2003 Form 990.
General

2,145,000	USC / Norris Comprehensive Cancer Center, Los Angeles, CA
400,000	Huntington Library Art Collections and Botanical Gardens, San Marino, CA
400,000	Keck Graduate Institute of Applied Life Science, Claremont, CA
150,000	Children's Hospital of Los Angeles, Los Angeles, CA
140,000	California Institute of Technology, Pasadena, CA
140,000	USC-School of Medicine, Los Angeles, CA
90,000	Saint John's Hospital & Health Center Foundation, Santa Monica, CA
80,000	Las Floristas, San Marino, CA
75,000	Norris Center for the Performing Arts, Rolling Hills Estates, CA
75,000	Norris Center for the Performing Arts, Rolling Hills Estates, CA

NORTH FAMILY TRUST

Giving Contact

Edward T. Hogan, Trustee
North Family Trust
212 Main Street, Suite 4
Wakefield, RI 02879
Phone: (401)782-4488

Description

Founded: 1992
EIN: 056091467
Organization Type: Private Foundation
Giving Locations: RI: Newport County
Grant Types: General Support.

Financial Summary

Total Giving: $142,500 (fiscal year ending June 30, 2001)
Assets: $2,987,589 (fiscal 2001)
Gifts Received: $410,260 (fiscal 1997); $632 (fiscal 1995); $519 (fiscal 1994). Note: In fiscal 1997, contributions were received from the Charles Stuart North Trust (EIN 056076208) which was merged into the North Family Trust on June 28, 1996.

Typical Recipients

Arts & Humanities: Arts & Humanities-General, Libraries, Museums/Galleries, Music
Civic & Public Affairs: Urban & Community Affairs
Education: Colleges & Universities, Elementary Education (Public), Private Education (Precollege), Science/Mathematics Education, Special Education
Health: Cancer, Hospices, Hospitals, Mental Health, Nursing Services
Religion: Religious Welfare
Social Services: Big Brothers/Big Sisters, Community Centers, Community Service Organizations, Domestic Violence, Family Services, Food/Clothing Distribution, Recreation & Athletics, Youth Organizations

Application Procedures

Initial Contact: Send a brief letter of inquiry.
Application Requirements: Include proof of tax-exempt status and specific purpose of funds sought.
Deadlines: Within 30 days from date of advertisement.

Restrictions

Restricted to Newport County, RI.

Foundation Officials

Robert Cummings: trustee
Edward T. Hogan: trustee

Grants Analysis

Disclosure Period: fiscal year ending June 30, 2001
Total Grants: $142,500
Number of Grants: 50
Average Grant: $2,850
Highest Grant: $10,000
Typical Range: $1,000 to $5,000

Recent Grants

Note: Grants derived from fiscal 2001 Form 990.
General

10,000	Rogers High School Science Department, Newport, RI -- science computer facility for high tech
8,000	Visiting Nurse Health Services, Portsmouth, RI -- provide hospice service
5,000	Hospice Care of Rhode Island, Providence, RI -- care for terminally ill
5,000	Lucy's Hearth, Newport, RI -- programs for homeless mothers
5,000	Newport Art Museum, Newport, RI -- funding for program with Boys and Girls Clubs
5,000	Newport Hospital Foundation, Newport, RI -- stress/EKG room in cardiopulmonary department
5,000	Rhode Island Meals on Wheels, Providence, RI -- meals to homebound elderly
5,000	Swanhurst Chorus, Newport, RI -- support performances
5,000	University of Rhode Island, Kingston, RI -- for graduate and undergraduate programs
3,500	Elmhurst Elementary School, Portsmouth, RI -- funding for Marine Programs

NORTH SHORE FOUNDATION

Giving Contact

Toy D. Savage, Jr., Secretary, Treasurer & Director
Bank of America Center, Suite 1420
Norfolk, VA 23510
Phone: (757)640-1414

Description

Founded: 1982
EIN: 521296293
Organization Type: Private Foundation
Giving Locations: VA
Grant Types: General Support.

Donor Information

Founder: Constance S. duPont Darden

Financial Summary

Total Giving: $74,027 (fiscal year ending April 30, 2004); $157,000 (fiscal 2002); $408,500 (fiscal 2001)
Giving Analysis: Giving for fiscal 2001 includes: foundation grants to United Way ($33,500)
Assets: $2,609 (fiscal 2004); $1,164,019 (fiscal 2002); $830 (fiscal 2001)
Gifts Received: $75,000 (fiscal 2004); $1,320,589 (fiscal 2002); $173,561 (fiscal 2001). Note: In fiscal 2004, contributions were received from North Shore Foundation. In fiscal 2000 and 2002, contributions were received from Constance S. duPont Darden.

Typical Recipients

Arts & Humanities: Arts Associations & Councils, Arts Centers, Arts Funds, Arts & Humanities-General, History & Archaeology, Libraries, Museums/Galleries, Music, Opera, Performing Arts, Public Broadcasting
Civic & Public Affairs: Civil Rights, Economic Development, Employment/Job Training, Civic & Public Affairs-General, Housing, Urban & Community Affairs, Zoos/Aquariums
Education: Business Education, Colleges & Universities, Community & Junior Colleges, Education Funds, International Studies, Minority Education, Private Education (Precollege), Student Aid
Environment: Air/Water Quality, Environment-General, Resource Conservation, Watershed, Wildlife Protection
Health: Children's Health/Hospitals, Emergency/Ambulance Services, Health Funds, Medical Research, Mental Health
International: Health Care/Hospitals, Human Rights, International Affairs, International Development, International Organizations, International Relations, International Relief Efforts, Missionary/Religious Activities
Religion: Churches, Dioceses, Ministries, Missionary Activities (Domestic), Religious Organizations,

Religious Welfare
Social Services: Animal Protection, Big Brothers/Big Sisters, Child Welfare, Community Centers, Community Service Organizations, Day Care, Family Planning, Family Services, Homes, Senior Services, United Funds/United Ways, Youth Organizations

Application Procedures

Initial Contact: Send a brief letter of inquiry describing program or project.
Deadlines: None.

Foundation Officials

Joshua P. Darden, Jr.: president, director
Toy D. Savage, Jr.: secretary, treasurer, director B Norfolk, VA 1921. ED University of Virginia BA (1943); University of Virginia LLB (1948). chairman distribution committee: Norfolk Foundation; trustee: Virginia Foundation for Independent Colleges; trustee: East Virginia Medicine School Foundation CORP AFFIL trustee: Chrysler Museum; director: Sentara Health System. NONPR AFFIL trustee deacon: Freemason St Baptist Church; trustee: Virginia Historical Society.

Grants Analysis

Disclosure Period: fiscal year ending April 30, 2004
Total Grants: $74,027
Number of Grants: 6
Highest Grant: $21,000
Lowest Grant: $2,027
Typical Range: $5,000 to $20,000

Recent Grants

Note: Grants derived from fiscal 2004 Form 990.
General
21,000	Virginia Opera, Norfolk, VA	
21,000	Virginia Symphony, Norfolk, VA	
15,000	American Society of Ancient Instruments, Elkins Park, PA	
10,000	Chesapeake Bay Foundation, Annapolis, MD	
5,000	Cantata Chorus, Virginia Beach, VA	
2,027	Chesapeake Bay Foundation, Annapolis, MD	

MARY MOODY NORTHEN FOUNDATION

Giving Contact

Betty Massey, Executive Director
PO Box 1300
Galveston, TX 77553
Phone: (409)765-9770
Fax: (409)762-7055

Description

Founded: 1964
EIN: 751171741
Organization Type: General Purpose Foundation
Giving Locations: TX; VA
Grant Types: General Support.

Donor Information

Founder: The foundation was established in 1964 by the late Mary Moody Northen.

Financial Summary

Total Giving: $547,086 (2002); $501,875 (2001)
Assets: $62,258,551 (2002); $66,631,397 (2001)
Gifts Received: $10,000 (1998); $1,000 (1995)

Typical Recipients

Arts & Humanities: Arts Centers, Arts & Humanities-General, History & Archaeology, Libraries, Museums/Galleries, Music
Civic & Public Affairs: Employment/Job Training,

Civic & Public Affairs-General, Philanthropic Organizations, Urban & Community Affairs
Education: Colleges & Universities, Engineering/Technological Education, Preschool Education, Vocational & Technical Education
Environment: Environment-General, Resource Conservation, Wildlife Protection
Health: Cancer, Mental Health, Single-Disease Health Associations
Religion: Religion-General, Religious Welfare
Science: Science Exhibits & Fairs, Scientific Research
Social Services: Child Abuse

Application Procedures

Initial Contact: Applicants should send a brief letter of inquiry and evidence of the organization's federal tax status, as a preliminary to a formal application.
Application Requirements: The letter should concisely describe the project and its intended purpose. This will serve to initiate a request for a formal application from the foundation if it is within the current scope of its operations and if funds are believed available.
Deadlines: None.
Review Process: Applicants should allow two or three months for the formal application to be processed.

Restrictions

Grants limited to Texas and Virginia.

Additional Information

Publications: Guide to Applications for Grants

Foundation Officials

Robert Lee Moody: secretary, director B 1935. ED University of Houston (1955-1956). PRIM CORP EMPL chairman, president, chief executive officer, director: American National Insurance Co. ADD CORP EMPL chairman, chief executive officer, director: National Western Life Insurance Co. CORP AFFIL director: Mary Moody Northern Inc.; president: Moody Investments; director: Bank Galveston NA; president, director: Moody Bancshares Inc. NONPR AFFIL chairman, director: Transitional Learning Center.
Edward L. Protz: president, director
G. William Rider: vice president, treasurer, director CORP AFFIL director: Bank Galveston NA.

Grants Analysis

Disclosure Period: calendar year ending 2002
Total Grants: $547,086
Number of Grants: 8
Average Grant: $13,155*
Highest Grant: $455,000
Lowest Grant: $2,000
Typical Range: $5,000 to $20,000
***Note:** Average grant figure excludes highest grant.

Recent Grants

Note: Grants derived from 2002 Form 990.
Library-Related
5,000	Rosenberg Library, Galveston, TX	

General
455,000	Center for 20th Century, Galveston, TX -- to operate the moody mansion and museum	
31,875	Wilderness Conservancy, Mountain Lake, VA -- towards corner store exhibition	
24,490	Virginia Polytechnic Institute, Blacksburg, VA	
15,000	Galveston College, Galveston, TX	
11,221	Salvation Army, Galveston, TX	
2,500	Galveston Island Outdoor Musicals, Galveston, TX	
2,000	Southwest Foundations, Dallas, TX	

NORTHWEST NATURAL GAS CO.

Company Headquarters

Portland, OR
Web: http://www.nwnatural.com

Company Description

Founded: 1859
Ticker: NWN
Exchange: NYSE
Assets: US$1.342 billion (2002)
Employees: 1291 (2003)
SIC(s): 4924 Natural Gas Distribution.

Operating Locations

Northwest Natural Gas Co. (OR--Newport)

Nonmonetary Support

Type: Donated Equipment; Donated Products; In-kind Services; Loaned Employees; Loaned Executives

Giving Contact

Marie Krasnow, Administrative Assistant
220 Northwest 2nd Avenue
Portland, OR 97209
Phone: (503)226-4211
Fax: (503)220-2584
E-mail: 6cr@nwnatural.com
Note: Marie Krasnows' extension is 3346

Alternate Contact

Von Summers, Manager of philanthropy
E-mail: von.summers@nwnatural.com

Description

Organization Type: Corporate Giving Program
Giving Locations: headquarters and operating communities.
Grant Types: Capital, Employee Matching Gifts, General Support, Multiyear/Continuing Support, Operating Expenses, Project, Research, Scholarship, Seed Money.
Note: Employee matching gifts support the United Way.

Financial Summary

Total Giving: $875,000 (2005 approx); $850,000 (2004); $825,000 (2003). Note: Contributes through corporate direct giving program only.

Typical Recipients

Arts & Humanities: Arts Appreciation, Arts Associations & Councils, Arts Centers, Arts Festivals, Arts Funds, Arts Institutes, Community Arts, Dance, Ethnic & Folk Arts, Arts & Humanities-General, Historic Preservation, Libraries, Museums/Galleries, Music, Opera, Performing Arts, Public Broadcasting, Theater, Visual Arts
Civic & Public Affairs: Economic Development, Civic & Public Affairs-General, Housing, Professional & Trade Associations, Urban & Community Affairs, Women's Affairs, Zoos/Aquariums
Education: Business Education, Colleges & Universities, Elementary Education (Private), Education-General, Minority Education
Health: Health-General, Health Organizations, Hospices, Hospitals, Medical Rehabilitation, Mental Health, Single-Disease Health Associations
Science: Science Exhibits & Fairs
Social Services: Animal Protection, Child Welfare, Community Centers, Counseling, Day Care, Delinquency & Criminal Rehabilitation, Food/Clothing Distribution, Homes, People with Disabilities, Senior Services, Shelters/Homelessness, Social Services-General, Substance Abuse, United Funds/United Ways, Volunteer Services, Youth Organizations

Application Procedures

Initial Contact: A brief letter of inquiry and a full proposal.
Application Requirements: Description of organization, amount requested, purpose of funds sought, and proof of tax-exempt status.
Deadlines: None.

Restrictions

Does not support individuals, religious organizations for sectarian purposes, or political or lobbying groups. Company will not accept proposals from organizations outside of company service areas.

Additional Information

The company gives to the Oregon Community Foundation, who in turn re-grants to nonprofit organizations.

Corporate Officials

Gregg Kantor: vice president, chief executive officer, chairman PRIM CORP EMPL vice president: Northwest Natural Gas Co.
Richard G. Reiten: president, chief executive officer, chairman PRIM CORP EMPL president, chief executive officer, chairman: Northwest Natural Gas Co.
George E. Richardson, Jr.: chairman contributions PRIM CORP EMPL chairman contributions: Northwest Natural Gas Co.

Giving Program Officials

Von Summers: Manager of Philanthropy

Grants Analysis

Disclosure Period: calendar year ending 2000
Total Grants: $619,900
Typical Range: $500 to $5,000

PETER NORTON FAMILY FOUNDATION

Giving Contact

Anne Etheridge, Executive Director
225 Arizona Ave., Suite 350
Santa Monica, CA 90401
Phone: (310)576-7700
Fax: (310)576-7701

Description

Founded: 1988
EIN: 954195347
Organization Type: Private Foundation
Giving Locations: CA
Grant Types: General Support.

Donor Information

Founder: Peter Norton, Eileen Norton

Financial Summary

Total Giving: $4,595,260 (2003)
Assets: $29,085,259 (2003)
Gifts Received: $13,294,044 (1997). Note: In 1997, contributions were received from Peter Norton.

Typical Recipients

Arts & Humanities: Arts Associations & Councils, Arts Centers, Arts Funds, Arts Institutes, Dance, Ethnic & Folk Arts, Film & Video, Arts & Humanities-General, Historic Preservation, History & Archaeology, Libraries, Museums/Galleries, Music, Performing Arts, Public Broadcasting, Visual Arts
Civic & Public Affairs: African American Affairs, Civil Rights, Gay/Lesbian Issues, Women's Affairs
Education: Arts/Humanities Education, Colleges & Universities, Education-General, Minority Education, Private Education (Precollege)
Environment: Air/Water Quality

Health: AIDS/HIV, Cancer, Clinics/Medical Centers
International: Foreign Arts Organizations
Social Services: Child Welfare, Community Centers, Community Service Organizations, Domestic Violence, Family Planning, Family Services, People with Disabilities, Youth Organizations

Application Procedures

Initial Contact: Submit a brief letter of inquiry.
Application Requirements: Include a description of organization, amount requested, and purpose of funds sought.
Deadlines: None.

Restrictions

Foundation does not accept support individuals or religious organizations for sectarian purposes.

Foundation Officials

Anne Etheridge: secretary, treasurer
Eileen Norton: vice president
Peter Norton: president B 1943. CORP AFFIL director: Symantec Corp.

Grants Analysis

Disclosure Period: calendar year ending 2003
Total Grants: $4,595,260
Number of Grants: 121
Average Grant: $15,344*
Highest Grant: $1,000,000
Lowest Grant: $1,000
Typical Range: $5,000 to $30,000
*Note: Average grant figure excludes four highest grants ($2,800,000).

Recent Grants

Note: Grants derived from 2003 Form 990.
General

1,000,000	Armand Hammer Museum of Art and Culture, Los Angeles, CA -- for capital campaign building fund
1,000,000	Symphony Space Inc., New York, NY -- towards capital fund
500,000	PS 1 Contemporary Art Center, Long Island City, NY
300,000	California Institute of the Arts, Santa Clanta, CA -- for faculty leave initiative
100,000	Ancient Egypt Research Associates Inc., Cambridge, MA
100,000	Armand Hammer Museum of Art and Culture, Los Angeles, CA -- for board gift
100,000	California Institute of the Arts, Santa Clanta, CA -- for annual giving commitment
100,000	Creative Capital Foundation, New York, NY
100,000	Reed College, Portland, OR
100,000	Signature Theatre Company, New York, NY -- for office building expenses

NORTON FOUNDATION

Giving Contact

Lucy Crawford, Executive Director
Norton Foundation
4350 Brownsboro Rd., Suite 133
Louisville, KY 40207
Phone: (502)893-9549
Fax: (502)896-9378
E-mail: nortfound@aol.com
Web: http://www.nortonfoundation.com

Description

Founded: 1958
EIN: 616024040
Organization Type: Private Foundation
Giving Locations: KY

Grant Types: General Support, Operating Expenses.

Donor Information

Founder: Mrs. George W. Norton

Financial Summary

Total Giving: $742,426 (2003); $997,400 (2001)
Giving Analysis: Giving for 2001 includes: foundation grants to United Way ($31,250)
Assets: $17,708,000 (2004 approx); $17,935,497 (2003); $20,233,473 (2001)

Typical Recipients

Arts & Humanities: Arts Centers, Arts Festivals, Arts Funds, Ballet, Community Arts, Ethnic & Folk Arts, Libraries, Museums/Galleries, Music, Opera, Performing Arts, Public Broadcasting, Theater, Visual Arts
Civic & Public Affairs: African American Affairs, Botanical Gardens/Parks, Community Foundations, Economic Development, Civic & Public Affairs-General, Housing, Law & Justice, Legal Aid, Philanthropic Organizations, Urban & Community Affairs, Women's Affairs, Zoos/Aquariums
Education: Colleges & Universities, Economic Education, Education Associations, Education Funds, Education Reform, Elementary Education (Private), Education-General, Private Education (Precollege), Public Education (Precollege), Special Education
Environment: Environment-General, Resource Conservation, Wildlife Protection
Health: Preventive Medicine/Wellness Organizations, Public Health
International: International Peace & Security Issues, Missionary/Religious Activities
Religion: Churches, Religion-General, Ministries, Religious Organizations, Religious Welfare
Science: Scientific Centers & Institutes
Social Services: At-Risk Youth, Child Abuse, Child Welfare, Community Centers, Community Service Organizations, Domestic Violence, Family Planning, Family Services, Food/Clothing Distribution, Homes, People with Disabilities, Shelters/Homelessness, Substance Abuse, United Funds/United Ways, Volunteer Services, Youth Organizations

Application Procedures

Initial Contact: Send a cover letter and full proposal.
Application Requirements: Include a description of organization, amount requested, recently audited financial statement, proof of tax-exempt status (three copies of each).
Deadlines: Quarterly; contact foundation.

Restrictions

Does not support individuals or private foundations. Local charitable needs are given priority.

Foundation Officials

Mr. Richard H. C. Clay: director
Lucy Crawford: executive director
Robert W. Dulaney: vice president
Jane Norton Newton: vice president

Grants Analysis

Disclosure Period: calendar year ending 2003
Total Grants: $742,426
Number of Grants: 40
Average Grant: $16,257*
Highest Grant: $74,668
Lowest Grant: $5,000
Typical Range: $5,000 to $30,000
*Note: Average grant figure excludes two highest grants ($124,668).

Recent Grants

Note: Grants derived from 2003 Form 990.
General

74,668	Waldorf School of Louisville, Louisville, KY
50,000	Kentucky Art and Craft Foundation, Louisville, KY

45,500	Association of Waldorf Schools of North America, Fair Oaks, CA
35,508	Jefferson County Public Schools, Louisville, KY
35,000	Family Place, Louisville, KY
30,000	Louisville Central Community Center, Louisville, KY
28,750	National Institute on Children, Youth & Families Inc., Louisville, KY
25,000	Collaborative for Teaching and Learning, Louisville, KY
25,000	Kentucky Center for the Arts, Louisville, KY
25,000	Prichard Committee for Academic Excellence, Lexington, KY

GERALDI NORTON MEMORIAL CORP.

Giving Contact

Christopher S. Eklund, Treasurer
c/o Hackbarth and Hudson, P.C.
20 N. Wacker Dr., Suite 1520
Chicago, IL 60606

Description

Founded: 1952
EIN: 366069997
Organization Type: Private Foundation
Giving Locations: IL: Chicago metropolitan area
Grant Types: General Support.

Donor Information

Founder: the late Grace Geraldi Norton

Typical Recipients

Arts & Humanities: Arts Centers, Arts Festivals, Arts Institutes, Historic Preservation, History & Archaeology, Libraries, Museums/Galleries, Music, Opera, Performing Arts, Public Broadcasting, Theater
Civic & Public Affairs: Botanical Gardens/Parks, Clubs, Community Foundations, Civic & Public Affairs-General, Law & Justice, Legal Aid, Nonprofit Management, Zoos/Aquariums
Education: Colleges & Universities, Education Funds, Legal Education, Medical Education, Minority Education, Private Education (Precollege), Science/Mathematics Education, Secondary Education (Private), Student Aid
Environment: Forestry, Environment-General, Resource Conservation, Watershed
Health: Alzheimer's Disease, Cancer, Children's Health/Hospitals, Clinics/Medical Centers, Diabetes, Health Organizations, Hospices, Hospitals, Medical Rehabilitation, Medical Research, Mental Health, Prenatal Health Issues, Research/Studies Institutes, Single-Disease Health Associations, Speech & Hearing
International: Health Care/Hospitals
Religion: Religious Welfare
Science: Science Museums
Social Services: Child Welfare, Community Service Organizations, Family Services, People with Disabilities, Recreation & Athletics, Shelters/Homelessness, United Funds/United Ways, Volunteer Services, Youth Organizations

Application Procedures

Initial Contact: Send a brief letter of inquiry describing program.
Application Requirements: purpose of funds sought.
Deadlines: None. Grants usually are awarded in December.

Restrictions

Does not support individuals.

Foundation Officials

Christopher S. Eklund: treasurer
Dariel Ann Eklund: vice president
Peter H. Eklund: member
Sally S. Eklund: secretary
Kathryn E. Wise: secretary

Grants Analysis

Disclosure Period: calendar year ending 2000
Total Grants: $141,800
Number of Grants: 43
Average Grant: $2,424*
Highest Grant: $40,000
Typical Range: $1,000 to $5,000
*Note: Average grant figure excludes highest grant.

Recent Grants

Note: Grants derived from 2001 Form 990.
General

40,000	University of Chicago Arthur L. Herbst Professorship, Chicago, IL
21,000	Music Institute of Chicago, Chicago, IL
15,000	Harvard College Fund, Cambridge, MA
10,000	Juvenile Diabetes Association, New York, NY
10,000	University of Chicago Department of Radiation and Cellular Oncology, Chicago, IL
5,000	Children's Memorial Medical Center, Chicago, IL
5,000	Narsad Research Institute, Great Neck, NY
5,000	Women's Board of Northwestern Memorial Hospital, Chicago, IL
2,500	Art Institute of Chicago, Chicago, IL
2,500	Chicago Historical Society, Chicago, IL

NOVELL

Company Headquarters

Orem, UT
Web: http://www.novell.com

Company Description

Employees: 5,800
SIC(s): 3500 Industrial Machinery & Equipment, 7300 Business Services.

Operating Locations

Novell (UT--Salem)

Nonmonetary Support

Type: Donated Products

Giving Contact

Corporate Giving Program
PO Box 1156
Salem, UT 84653
Phone: (801)861-7000

Alternate Contact

Linda Linfield
1555 North Technology Way
Orem, UT 84097-2399

Description

Organization Type: Corporate Giving Program
Giving Locations: CA: Santa Clara County; UT: Wasatch Front
Grant Types: Award, Multiyear/Continuing Support, Project.

Typical Recipients

Arts & Humanities: Arts Associations & Councils, Arts Centers, Arts Festivals, Arts Outreach, Ballet, Community Arts, Dance, Ethnic & Folk Arts, Arts & Humanities-General, Libraries, Museums/Galleries, Music, Opera, Performing Arts, Theater

Civic & Public Affairs: Business/Free Enterprise, Community Foundations, Civic & Public Affairs-General, Philanthropic Organizations, Professional & Trade Associations
Education: Business Education, Faculty Development, Education-General, Science/Mathematics Education, Vocational & Technical Education
Environment: Wildlife Protection
Health: Arthritis, Cancer, Diabetes, Health-General, Home-Care Services, Nursing Services
Science: Science-General, Observatories & Planetariums, Science Museums, Scientific Centers & Institutes, Scientific Organizations
Social Services: Community Centers, Community Service Organizations, Food/Clothing Distribution, Homes, People with Disabilities, Shelters/Homelessness, Social Services-General, United Funds/United Ways, Volunteer Services

Application Procedures

Initial Contact: Send letter requesting corporate giving guidelines. Deadline for cash grants is July 31. Requests for software donations may be submitted throughout the year.

Restrictions

Does not support individuals, religious organizations for sectarian purposes, political or lobbying groups, organizations that discriminate, conferences, national health organizations, sports or entertainment marketing, fraternal organizations, or organizations outside operating areas.

Additional Information

Publications: Corporate Giving Guidelines

Corporate Officials

Jack L. Messman: president, chief executive officer ED Harvard University MBA; University of Delaware BS. PRIM CORP EMPL president, chief executive officer: Novell.
Dr. Eric Schmidt: chairman ED Princeton University BSEE; University of California at Berkeley MSEE; University of California at Berkeley PhD. PRIM CORP EMPL chairman: Novell.

Grants Analysis

Typical Range: $1,000 to $2,500

NICHOLAS H. NOYES, JR. MEMORIAL FOUNDATION

Giving Contact

Kelly L. Mills, Assistant Secretary
1950 E. Greyhound Pass, 18-356
Carmel, IN 46033-7730
Phone: (317)844-8009
Fax: (317)844-8099
E-mail: admin@noyesfoundation.org
Web: http://www.noyesfoundation.org

Description

Founded: 1951
EIN: 351003699
Organization Type: Family Foundation
Giving Locations: IN: Indianapolis
Grant Types: Capital, Endowment, General Support, Multiyear/Continuing Support, Project, Scholarship.

Donor Information

Founder: Incorporated in 1951 by the late Nicholas H. Noyes and the late Marguerite Lilly Noyes.

Financial Summary

Total Giving: $2,494,000 (2004 approx); $2,726,500 (2003); $3,500,288 (2002)
Giving Analysis: Giving for 2003 includes: founda-

tion grants to United Way ($135,000); 2002: foundation grants to United Way ($100,000)
Assets: $50,000,000 (2004 approx); $58,988,693 (2003); $53,620,480 (2002)
Gifts Received: $6,640 (1996). Note: In 1998, contributions were received from the Nicholas H. Noyes Employees Trust.

Typical Recipients

Arts & Humanities: Arts Associations & Councils, Arts Centers, Ballet, Dance, Historic Preservation, History & Archaeology, Libraries, Museums/Galleries, Music, Opera, Performing Arts, Public Broadcasting, Theater
Civic & Public Affairs: Botanical Gardens/Parks, Community Foundations, Employment/Job Training, Civic & Public Affairs-General, Housing, Urban & Community Affairs, Zoos/Aquariums
Education: Agricultural Education, Arts/Humanities Education, Business Education, Colleges & Universities, Education Associations, Education Funds, Elementary Education (Private), Engineering/Technological Education, International Studies, Leadership Training, Literacy, Medical Education, Minority Education, Private Education (Precollege), Public Education (Precollege), Science/Mathematics Education, Secondary Education (Private), Student Aid, Vocational & Technical Education
Environment: Environment-General, Resource Conservation
Health: Cancer, Children's Health/Hospitals, Clinics/Medical Centers, Diabetes, Emergency/Ambulance Services, Health Funds, Hospitals, Medical Rehabilitation, Medical Research, Nursing Services, Preventive Medicine/Wellness Organizations, Single-Disease Health Associations
International: Foreign Arts Organizations
Religion: Churches, Ministries, Religious Welfare, Seminaries
Social Services: Animal Protection, Big Brothers/Big Sisters, Camps, Child Welfare, Community Centers, Community Service Organizations, Counseling, Day Care, Family Planning, Family Services, Food/Clothing Distribution, Homes, People with Disabilities, Refugee Assistance, Scouts, Shelters/Homelessness, Social Services-General, Special Olympics, Substance Abuse, United Funds/United Ways, YMCA/YWCA/YMHA/YWHA, Youth Organizations

Application Procedures

Initial Contact: The foundation requests applications be made in writing.
Application Requirements: Potential applicants are encouraged to check the foundation's website or call the foundation for current deadlines and guidelines.
Deadlines: February 1 and August 31.
Review Process: Board meets twice a year; proposals received by the deadlines will normally be reviewed in the two months following.

Restrictions

Grants are not made to individuals or for loans. Grants are usually awarded to organizations within Indiana.

Foundation Officials

Mrs. Avery Augustine: director
Nancy Ayres: president, director
Lisa Carrington: director
Kelly L. Mills: assistant secretary
Elizabeth H. Noyes: director
Evan L. Noyes, Jr.: director
Henry S. Noyes: director
Nicholas S. Noyes: vice president, secretary, director
Robert Hugh Reynolds: president, director B Saint Louis, MO 1937. ED Yale University BA (1958); Harvard University JD (1964). PRIM CORP EMPL partner: Barnes & Thornburg. CORP AFFIL vice chairman: Terralex. NONPR AFFIL director: Japan American Society Indiana; board governors: Legacy

Fund; member: International Bar Association; board director: Indianapolis Convention & Visitors Association; board director: Indianapolis Economic Development Corp.; member: Indianapolis Bar Association; fellow: Indianapolis Bar Foundation; member: Indiana Bar Association; fellow: Indiana Bar Foundation; board director: Greater Indianapolis Foreign Trade Zone; board director: Greater Indianapolis Progress Committee; member: Greater Indianapolis Chamber of Commerce; member: American Bar Association; board director: Boy Scouts America Crossroads Council. CLUB AFFIL University Club; Economic Club Indianapolis; Skyline Club.
L. Gene Tanner: treasurer, director B Indianapolis, IN 1932. ED Indiana University BA (1955). PRIM CORP EMPL vice chairman: NatCity Investments. CORP AFFIL director: Biomet Inc.; director: Circle Ventures Inc.

Grants Analysis

Disclosure Period: calendar year ending 2003
Total Grants: $2,591,500*
Number of Grants: 129
Average Grant: $17,532*
Highest Grant: $100,000
Lowest Grant: $2,000
Typical Range: $5,000 to $25,000
*Note: Giving excludes United Way. Average grant figure excludes four highest grants ($400,000).

Recent Grants

Note: Grants derived from 2003 Form 990.
Library-Related
50,000   Indianapolis-Marion County Public Library Foundation Inc., Indianapolis, IN -- for renovation expansion

General
100,000   Goodwill Industries of Central Indiana Inc., Indianapolis, IN -- for Tech West Program
100,000   Independent Colleges of Indiana Foundation, Indianapolis, IN -- to assist annual scholarship
100,000   Indianapolis Museum of Art, Indianapolis, IN -- fund for new vision expansion program
100,000   United Way of Central Indiana, Indianapolis, IN
75,000   Flanner House, Indianapolis, IN -- to support building fund
75,000   International School of Indiana, Indianapolis, IN -- fund for fulfilling the Promise Capital Campaign
75,000   Martin University, Indianapolis, IN -- fund for property acquisition and demolition
75,000   United Negro College Fund Inc., Indianapolis, IN -- fund for annual scholarship
70,000   Riley Children's Foundation, Indianapolis, IN -- to support Riley children's hospital
70,000   Wishard Memorial Foundation/ Indianapolis Health Institute, Indianapolis, IN

NSTAR

Company Headquarters

800 Boylston St.
Boston, MA 02199
Phone: (617)424-2000
Fax: (617)424-2904
Web: http://www.nstaronline.com

Company Description

Founded: 1999
Ticker: NST
Exchange: NYSE
Formed by Merger of: BEC Energy and Commonwealth Energy System (1999).

Assets: US$5.328 billion (2001)
Employees: 3200 (2003)
SIC(s): 4900 Electric, Gas & Sanitary Services, 6500 Real Estate, 6700 Holding & Other Investment Offices.

Operating Locations

Commonwealth Energy Systems (MA--Cambridge); NSTAR Electric (MA--Wareham)

Nonmonetary Support

Type: Donated Equipment; Workplace Solicitation
Note: Co. donates used furniture. Co. donated approximately $20,000 in equipment in 1998.

NSTAR Foundation

Giving Contact

Foundation Administrator
NSTAR Foundation
800 Boylston St.
Boston, MA 02199
Phone: (781)441-8853

Description

EIN: 042754285
Organization Type: Corporate Foundation
Giving Locations: MA: Eastern Massachusetts, Boston
Grant Types: Capital, Challenge, Employee Matching Gifts, General Support, Matching, Project, Seed Money.
Note: Employee matching gift ratio: 1 to 1 to education.

Financial Summary

Total Giving: $0 (2003). Note: Contributes through corporate direct giving program and foundation.
Assets: $0 (2003)
Gifts Received: $1,100,000 (1994); $1,100,000 (1993); $700,000 (1992). Note: Contributions were received from the Boston Edison Co.

Typical Recipients

Arts & Humanities: Arts Institutes, Arts Outreach, Ballet, Dance, Historic Preservation, Libraries, Museums/Galleries, Music, Performing Arts
Civic & Public Affairs: Economic Development, Employment/Job Training, Housing, Law & Justice, Municipalities/Towns, Philanthropic Organizations, Professional & Trade Associations, Safety, Urban & Community Affairs, Zoos/Aquariums
Education: Afterschool/Enrichment Programs, Business-School Partnerships, Colleges & Universities, Education Reform, Elementary Education (Public), Engineering/Technological Education, Leadership Training, Minority Education, Preschool Education, Private Education (Precollege), Religious Education, Science/Mathematics Education, Student Aid
Health: AIDS/HIV, Alzheimer's Disease, Cancer, Clinics/Medical Centers, Emergency/Ambulance Services, Health Organizations, Hospices, Hospitals, Long-Term Care, Nursing Services, Single-Disease Health Associations
Religion: Religious Welfare, Social/Policy Issues
Science: Science Museums
Social Services: Community Centers, Community Service Organizations, Counseling, Emergency Relief, Family Services, Food/Clothing Distribution, People with Disabilities, Recreation & Athletics, Senior Services, Shelters/Homelessness, United Funds/United Ways, Youth Organizations

Application Procedures

Initial Contact: All proposals must be submitted using an Associated Grantmakers of Massachusetts Common Proposal Format; guidelines revised in 1998.
Application Requirements: Include recent annual report, budget for organization and specific project re-

quiring funding, specific amount of funding requested, other funding sources either at hand or anticipated, provision for accountability to project sponsors, and proof of tax-exempt status.

Deadlines: February 15 (for April assessment), July 15 (for September), and October 1 (for December).

Review Process: Company volunteers serve on the Foundation Task Force and review requests, make site visits, and conduct interviews; Task Force makes recommendations to foundation trustees.

Evaluative Criteria: Organization is tax-exempt and serves an Edison community; program has measurable goals and objectives that relate to a foundation concern; realistic strategy for achieving goals; provide company with appropriate recognition; employee volunteer involvement; funding is for a specific project, not general support; positive impact on the community; demonstrated need; non-duplication of services; plans for continued operation; long-term solutions.

Decision Notification: Trustees assess proposals in April, September, and December.

Restrictions

Proposals for same project will not be considered more than once within a one-year period. The foundation does not usually support capital campaigns (building as well as renovation); commitments beyond one year; events such as dinners, conferences, workshops, symposiums, etc.; and programs receiving substantial support from others. The foundation also limits its consideration of contributions to third party organizations, preferring to support direct program grants.

Additional Information

In 1999, Boston Edison's holding company, BEC Energy, and Commonwealth Energy System merged to form NSTAR. Boston Edison is a subsidiary of NSTAR.

Publications: Foundation Annual Report; Guidelines

Corporate Officials

Alison Alden: senior vice president sales, service, human resources PRIM CORP EMPL senior vice president sales, service, human resources: Boston Edison Co. CORP AFFIL senior vice president sales, services, human resources: BEC Energy.

John J. Connolly: director corporate relations PRIM CORP EMPL director corporate relations: Boston Edison Co.

Douglas S. Horan: senior vice president, general counsel, secretary ED Case Western Reserve University BS; Johns Hopkins University MA; Northeastern University JD. PRIM CORP EMPL senior vice president, general counsel, secretary: NSTAR ADD CORP EMPL senior vice president, general counsel: BEC Energy.

James J. Judge: senior vice president corporate service business unit, treasurer ED Babson College. PRIM CORP EMPL senior vice president corporate service business unit, treasurer: Boston Edison Co. ADD CORP EMPL vice president, treasurer: BEC Energy Inc.; treasurer: Boston Energy Technology Group Inc.; treasurer: Harbor Electric Energy Co.; senior vice president, chief financial officer: NSTAR.

Ronald A. Ledgett: senior vice president B 1938. ED Stanford University. PRIM CORP EMPL senior vice president: Boston Edison Co.

Foundation Officials

Douglas S. Horan: trustee (see above)
James J. Judge: trustee (see above)

Grants Analysis

Disclosure Period: calendar year ending 2003
Typical Range: $1,000 to $10,000
Note: No grants awarded in 2003.

Recent Grants

Note: Grants derived from 1996 Form 990.

General

1,743	Associate Grant Making Baystate, Boston, MA -- operating support

THE JOHN NUVEEN CO.

Company Headquarters

Chicago, IL
Web: http://www.nuveen.com

Company Description

Founded: 1992
Ticker: JNC
Exchange: NYSE
Former Name: Nuveen & Co., Inc.
Operating Revenue: US$396.4 million (2002)
Employees: 597 (2002)
SIC(s): 6200 Security & Commodity Brokers.
Parent Company: St. Paul Travelers Companies Inc., 385 Washington Street, St. Paul, MN, United States

Nonmonetary Support

Type: Donated Equipment; Donated Products; In-kind Services

Giving Contact

Janice Thea
333 W. Wacker Dr.
Chicago, IL 60606
Phone: (312)917-7700

Description

Organization Type: Corporate Giving Program
Giving Locations: headquarters and operating communities.
Grant Types: Capital, Employee Matching Gifts, General Support, Matching, Multiyear/Continuing Support, Operating Expenses.

Typical Recipients

Arts & Humanities: Arts Associations & Councils, Arts Centers, Arts Festivals, Arts Institutes, Arts Outreach, Community Arts, Arts & Humanities-General, Libraries, Museums/Galleries, Music, Opera, Public Broadcasting

Civic & Public Affairs: Clubs, Economic Development, Economic Policy, Employment/Job Training, Ethnic Organizations, Housing, Inner-City Development, Minority Business, Philanthropic Organizations, Public Policy, Urban & Community Affairs, Women's Affairs, Zoos/Aquariums

Education: Afterschool/Enrichment Programs, Arts/Humanities Education, Business Education, Colleges & Universities, Community & Junior Colleges, Economic Education, Education Associations, Education Funds, Elementary Education (Private), Faculty Development, Education-General, International Exchange, Journalism/Media Education, Legal Education, Literacy, Preschool Education, Private Education (Precollege), Secondary Education (Private), Secondary Education (Public)

Health: Cancer, Children's Health/Hospitals, Clinics/Medical Centers, Health Policy/Cost Containment, Health Funds, Hospices, Hospitals (University Affiliated), Long-Term Care, Medical Research, Multiple Sclerosis

International: International Affairs
Science: Science Museums

Social Services: At-Risk Youth, Child Welfare, Community Centers, Community Service Organizations, Counseling, Day Care, Delinquency & Criminal Rehabilitation, Domestic Violence, Family Planning, Family Services, Food/Clothing Distribution, Homes, People with Disabilities, Senior Services, Shelters/Homelessness, Social Services-General, Substance Abuse, United Funds/United Ways, Youth Organizations

Application Procedures

Initial Contact: a full proposal
Application Requirements: a description of organization, amount requested, purpose of funds sought, recently audited financial statement, and proof of tax-exempt status

Restrictions

Does not support individuals, religious organizations for sectarian purposes, political or lobbying groups, or organizations outside operating areas.

Additional Information

Publications: Corporate Contributions Guidelines; Application Form

Corporate Officials

John P. Amboian: executive vice president, chief financial officer PRIM CORP EMPL president: John Nuveen Co.

Anthony Taylor Dean: president, chief operating officer B McPherson, KS 1945. ED University of Chicago; Yale University (1967). PRIM CORP EMPL president, chief operating officer: John Nuveen Co.

Timothy R. Schwertfeger: chairman, chief executive officer B Chicago, IL 1949. ED Northwestern University (1971); Georgetown University (1974). PRIM CORP EMPL chairman, chief executive officer: John Nuveen Co.

Grants Analysis

Typical Range: $2,500 to $5,000

OAK GROVE SCHOOL

Giving Contact

Joann Clark-Austin, President
PO Box 150
South China, ME 04358
Phone: (207)622-6339

Alternate Contact

Lucia Whittelsey
163 Silver Street
Waterville, ME 04901
Note: For scholarship requests.

Description

Founded: 1993
EIN: 010211537
Organization Type: Private Foundation
Grant Types: General Support, Scholarship.

Financial Summary

Total Giving: $107,073 (fiscal year ending June 30, 2001)
Giving Analysis: Giving for fiscal 2001 includes: foundation scholarships ($10,000)
Assets: $1,892,997 (fiscal 2001)
Gifts Received: $6,073 (fiscal 2001); $25,028 (fiscal 1998); $5,236 (fiscal 1997). Note: Note: In fiscal 1998, contributions were received from Archie W. Berry Jr. ($20,000).

Typical Recipients

Arts & Humanities: Arts Centers, Film & Video, Libraries, Opera

Education: Arts/Humanities Education, Colleges & Universities, Faculty Development, Education-General, International Studies, Medical Education, Minority Education, Private Education (Precollege), Public Education (Precollege), Science/Mathematics Education, Secondary Education (Private), Secondary Education (Public), Student Aid

Health: Adolescent Health Issues, Hospices, Nursing Services

Religion: Religious Organizations, Religious Welfare

Social Services: Community Service Organizations, Family Planning, Youth Organizations

Application Procedures

Initial Contact: Request application form and guidelines.
Deadlines: January 15.

Additional Information

Publications: Oak Grove Application Form and financial aid forms.

Foundation Officials

Leroy Austin: corporator
Archie Berry: corporator
Margaret Cates: corporator
Paul Cates: corporator
Joann Clark Austin, Esq.: president
Elizabeth Cole: corporator
David Duplessie: corporator
Elizabeth Eldridge: corporator
Richard Guttmacher: vice president
Bernard Huebner: corporator
Gerald Robbins: corporator
Nathaniel Shed: treasurer
Lucia Whittelsey: clerk

Grants Analysis

Disclosure Period: fiscal year ending June 30, 2001
Total Grants: $97,073*
Number of Grants: 31*
Average Grant: $2,894*
Highest Grant: $10,268
Lowest Grant: $500
Typical Range: $1,000 to $7,000
*Note: Giving excludes scholarships. Average grant figure excludes highest grant.

Recent Grants

Note: Grants derived from fiscal 2001 Form 990.
General

10,268	Madison High School, Madison, ME -- TV and video production class
10,000	Meeting School, Rindge, NH -- scholarships
5,240	Lawrence High school, Fairfield, ME
5,171	Mt. View High School, Thorndike, ME
5,000	Community School, Camden, ME -- Passages Program
5,000	Family Planning Association of Maine, Augusta, ME -- teen outreach program
5,000	Friends of Art and Film, Waterville, ME -- Maine International Film Festival
4,387	Erskine Academy, China, ME -- Eleanor Woodman Fund-Nursing Services
4,000	Maine Youth Alliance, Waterville, ME -- cultural arts
3,800	Hospice Volunteers, Waterville, ME -- art therapy in youth grieving

OAK TREE CHARITABLE FOUNDATION

Giving Contact

Sherwood C. Chillingworth, Executive Vice President
285 W. Huntington Dr.
Arcadia, CA 91007
Phone: (626)574-6346

Description

Founded: 1995
EIN: 954506950
Organization Type: Private Foundation
Giving Locations: CA: San Gabriel Valley, Southern California, Los Angeles metropolitan area
Grant Types: General Support.

Donor Information

Founder: Established in 1995 by the Oak Tree Racing Assn.

Financial Summary

Total Giving: $359,842 (fiscal year ending May 31, 2001)
Assets: $5,564,328 (fiscal 2001)
Gifts Received: $4,000,000 (fiscal 1995). Note: In fiscal 1995, contributions were received from the Oak Tree Racing Assn.

Typical Recipients

Arts & Humanities: History & Archaeology, Museums/Galleries, Music
Civic & Public Affairs: Civic & Public Affairs-General, Professional & Trade Associations, Women's Affairs
Education: Agricultural Education, Colleges & Universities, Education-General, School Volunteerism, Student Aid, Vocational & Technical Education
Health: Cancer, Hospitals, Medical Rehabilitation, Medical Research, Single-Disease Health Associations
Religion: Churches, Religious Welfare
Science: Scientific Labs
Social Services: Animal Protection, Big Brothers/Big Sisters, Camps, Child Welfare, Community Service Organizations, Crime Prevention, Recreation & Athletics, Scouts, Substance Abuse

Application Procedures

Initial Contact: Contact foundation for its grant application.
Application Requirements: Include a description of organization, amount requested, purpose of funds sought, recently audited financial statement, and proof of tax-exempt status.
Deadlines: March 31 of each year

Restrictions

Does not support individuals, religious organizations for sectarian purposes, political or lobbying groups, or organizations outside operating areas.

Additional Information

Foundation will support organizations outside its operating area that benefit the thoroughbred horse racing industry.
Publications: Application Form

Foundation Officials

John H. Barr: vice president
Thomas R. Capehart: vice president
Sherwood C. Chillingworth: executive vice president
Clement L. Hirsch: president
William T. Pascoe, III: vice president, treasurer
Mrs. Bernard J. Ridder: vice president
Jack K. Robbins: vice president, secretary

Grants Analysis

Disclosure Period: fiscal year ending May 31, 2001
Total Grants: $359,842*
Number of Grants: 84
Average Grant: $3,372*
Highest Grant: $80,000
Lowest Grant: $100
Typical Range: $200 to $5,000
*Note: Average grant figure excludes highest grant.

Recent Grants

Note: Grants derived from 2001 Form 990.
General

80,000	California Thoroughbred Trainers, Arcadia, CA
68,000	California Thoroughbred Horsemen's Foundation, Arcadia, CA -- health and recreation programs for low-income families
60,000	Edwin J. Gregson Foundation, Arcadia, CA -- stable recreation and staff support
25,000	Grayson-Jockey Club Research Foundation, New York, NY
20,000	Race Track Chaplaincy of America, Belmont, CA -- spiritual and social welfare programs
17,500	California Philharmonic Foundation, Pasadena, CA -- community symphony orchestra
10,500	Race Track Chaplaincy of America, Belmont, CA -- spiritual and social welfare programs
10,000	Church of Our Saviour, El Monte, CA -- food pantry and job training for low income families, capital campaign
10,000	Don MacBeth Memorial Jockey Fund, Beverly Hills, CA -- thoroughbred riders
10,000	Edwin J. Gregson Foundation, Arcadia, CA -- assistance to backstretch employees and families

CHARLES O'BLENESS FOUNDATION

Giving Contact

c/o Huntington National Bank NA
41 S. High St.
Columbus, OH 43215
Phone: (614)480-5453

Description

Founded: 1963
EIN: 316042978
Organization Type: Private Foundation
Giving Locations: OH: Athens County
Grant Types: General Support.

Donor Information

Founder: the late Charles O'Bleness, Charles O'Bleness Foundation No. 1

Financial Summary

Total Giving: $142,713 (fiscal year ending June 30, 2004); $170,402 (fiscal 2002); $163,652 (fiscal 2001)
Assets: $3,256,763 (fiscal 2004); $3,240,781 (fiscal 2002); $3,566,394 (fiscal 2001)

Typical Recipients

Arts & Humanities: Arts Associations & Councils, Arts Centers, Arts Festivals, Historic Preservation, History & Archaeology, Libraries, Museums/Galleries, Performing Arts, Theater
Civic & Public Affairs: Botanical Gardens/Parks, Chambers of Commerce, Economic Development, Civic & Public Affairs-General, Housing, Nonprofit Management, Parades/Festivals, Rural Affairs
Education: Colleges & Universities, International Studies, Medical Education, Secondary Education (Public), Student Aid
Environment: Environment-General
Health: Emergency/Ambulance Services, Hospices, Hospitals, Mental Health, Nursing Services, Prenatal Health Issues
Religion: Churches, Religious Welfare
Social Services: Animal Protection, Child Welfare, Community Service Organizations, Crime Prevention, Recreation & Athletics, Scouts, Social Services-General, United Funds/United Ways, Youth Organizations

Application Procedures

Initial Contact: The foundation has no formal grant application procedure or application form.
Deadlines: October 15.

Additional Information

Trust(s): Huntington National Bank NA

Foundation Officials

John M. Jones: adv
David Vogt: adv

Grants Analysis

Disclosure Period: fiscal year ending June 30, 2004
Total Grants: $142,713
Number of Grants: 10
Average Grant: $8,885*
Highest Grant: $62,750
Lowest Grant: $75
Typical Range: $5,000 to $15,000
*****Note:** Average grant figure excludes highest grant.

Recent Grants

Note: Grants derived from fiscal 2004 Form 990.
General

62,750	O'Bleness Memorial Hospital, Athens, OH -- for imaging equipment
25,000	Ohio University, Athens, OH -- towards cutler scholar program
16,000	Ohio Valley Summer Theater, Athens, OH -- towards summer theater
12,438	Athens High School, Athens, OH -- for PTO library project
10,000	Athens County Habitat for Humanity, Athens, OH -- for park at little red school house
10,000	O'Bleness Memorial Hospital, Athens, OH
5,282	National Alliance for the Mentally Ill, Athens, OH
169	National Child Safety Council, Jackson, MI -- for Athens county safety pup program
75	Athens Invitational Marching Festival, Athens, OH -- towards grand champion sponsor fee

A. LINDSAY AND OLIVE B. O'CONNOR FOUNDATION

Giving Contact

Donald F. Bishop, Jr., President & Executive Director
BSB Bank & Trust
PO Box 1056
Binghamton, NY 13902
Phone: (607)538-9248
Fax: (607)538-1650

Description

Founded: 1965
EIN: 166063485
Organization Type: General Purpose Foundation
Giving Locations: NY: Delaware County and contiguous rural counties in upstate New York
Grant Types: Capital, Endowment, General Support, Project, Scholarship.

Donor Information

Founder: The foundation was established in 1965 by the late Olive B. O'Connor.

Financial Summary

Total Giving: $2,837,605 (2003); $2,938,980 (2002); $2,981,839 (2001)
Giving Analysis: Giving for 2003 includes: foundation scholarships ($10,000); 2002: foundation scholarships ($324,450).
Assets: $68,201,510 (2003); $60,943,536 (2002); $72,766,636 (2001)
Gifts Received: $2,894,720 (1998)

Typical Recipients

Arts & Humanities: Arts Associations & Councils, Arts Centers, Arts Institutes, Historic Preservation, History & Archaeology, Libraries, Literary Arts, Museums/Galleries, Music, Performing Arts, Theater
Civic & Public Affairs: Botanical Gardens/Parks, Community Foundations, Economic Development, Employment/Job Training, Civic & Public Affairs-General, Housing, Inner-City Development, Law & Justice, Municipalities/Towns, Philanthropic Organizations, Professional & Trade Associations, Safety, Urban & Community Affairs, Zoos/Aquariums
Education: Agricultural Education, Colleges & Universities, Community & Junior Colleges, Education Funds, Education Reform, Elementary Education (Private), Engineering/Technological Education, Education-General, Health & Physical Education, Legal Education, Medical Education, Private Education (Precollege), Public Education (Precollege), School Volunteerism, Student Aid
Environment: Forestry, Environment-General, Resource Conservation, Watershed
Health: Emergency/Ambulance Services, Health Funds, Heart, Hospices, Hospitals, Medical Rehabilitation, Single-Disease Health Associations
Religion: Churches, Ministries, Religious Organizations, Religious Welfare
Science: Science Museums
Social Services: Community Centers, Community Service Organizations, Day Care, People with Disabilities, Scouts, Senior Services, Social Services-General, United Funds/United Ways, Youth Organizations

Application Procedures

Initial Contact: Applicants should contact the foundation for an application form. Foundation accepts phone calls Monday through Friday from 9 a.m. to 3 p.m. only.
Application Requirements: In addition to the information required on the application, the foundation requires applicants to provide proof of tax-exempt status under IRS section 501(c)(3) or proof that the applicant is a unit of the government. It is preferred, but not required, to have sketches or drawings submitted on legal size or smaller paper. In almost all cases, a site visit will be arranged after the full application has been filed. Proposals of $5,000 or less are considered on a monthly basis if the proposal meets the following conditions: the organization is located in or directly benefits Delaware County, NY; applicant has not received a grant from the foundation for the same project in the last three years; and applicant is prepared to match funds dollar for dollar.
Deadlines: None, for grant requests of $5,000 or less.

Restrictions

As a general rule, the foundation will not make grants to individuals; for meeting annual operating expenditures or retiring existing debts, and prefers to make grants of a non-recurring nature. Grants are generally restricted to programs that have a direct impact on the quality of life in Delaware County and the seven contiguously surrounding counties in upstate New York (Broome, Chenango, Greene, Otsego, Schoharie, Sullivan, and Ulster).

Additional Information

Publications: Program Policy Statement; Grant Application

Foundation Officials

Donald F. Bishop, II: president, executive director
Robert L. Bishop, II: chairman, member advisory committee
Charlotte Bishop Hill: vchairwoman, mem adv comm
Pamela Hill: executive secretary, treasurer
Suzanne Hill: director
William J. Murphy: director, mem adv comm

Eugene E. Peckham: director, mem adv comm B Stamford, CT 1940. ED Wesleyan University BA (1962); Harvard University JD (1965). PRIM CORP EMPL partner: Hinman, Howard & Kattell. NONPR AFFIL member: New York State Bar Association; adj professor acctg: State University New York Binghamton; member: House of Delaware; treasurer: Joint Legislative Advisory Committee Estates Powers & Trusts Law & Surrogates Court Procedure Act; member: Broome County Bar Association; member: Federal Bar Associations 6th Judicial District; fellow: American College Trust & Estate Counsel; trustee: Binghampton Boys Girls Club.

Grants Analysis

Disclosure Period: calendar year ending 2003
Total Grants: $2,827,605*
Number of Grants: 197
Average Grant: $8,218*
Highest Grant: $1,000,000
Lowest Grant: $155
Typical Range: $1,000 to $20,000
*****Note:** Giving excludes scholarships. Average grant figure excludes two highest grants ($1,225,000).

Recent Grants

Note: Grants derived from 2003 Form 990.
General

1,000,000	O'Connor Hospital, Delhi, NY
249,310	Catskill Revitalization Corporation, Stamford, NY
225,000	Catskill Watershed Partnership Museum, Stamford, NY -- watershed museum
167,000	Town of Kortright, Bloomville, NY -- flood damage mitigation
140,000	Delaware County Department of Public Works, Delhi, NY -- new covered bridge
105,000	Catskill Forest Association, Arkville, NY
100,000	Watershed Agricultural Council for the New York City, Walton, NY -- Stamford town brook research project
99,110	Mary Imogene Bassett Hospital Bassett Health Care, Cooperstown, NY -- partnership for nursing opportunities program
87,000	College Foundation at Delhi, Delhi, NY
84,500	Delaware County Planning Board, Delhi, NY -- data conversion upgrades

KATHRYN O'CONNOR FOUNDATION

Giving Contact

D. H. Braman, Jr., President
1 O'Connor Plz., Suite 1100
Victoria, TX 77901
Phone: (361)578-6271

Description

Founded: 1951
EIN: 746039415
Organization Type: Private Foundation
Giving Locations: TX: Southern Texas, especially Victoria and Refugio counties and the surrounding area
Grant Types: Capital, Emergency, Endowment, General Support, Multiyear/Continuing Support, Operating Expenses, Professorship, Seed Money.

Donor Information

Founder: the late Kathryn S. O'Connor, Tom O'Connor, Jr., Dennis O'Connor

Financial Summary

Total Giving: $333,760 (2003)
Assets: $5,971,771 (2003)
Gifts Received: $1,000 (2003); $16,429 (2000); $87 (1995). Note: In 2000, contributions were received

from Louise S. O'Connor. In 1995, contributions were received from the Texas Sanitation Co. ($65) and Alice Wilson ($22).

Typical Recipients

Arts & Humanities: Arts Associations & Councils, Ethnic & Folk Arts, History & Archaeology, Libraries, Museums/Galleries, Music, Theater

Civic & Public Affairs: Municipalities/Towns, Parades/Festivals

Education: Continuing Education, Elementary Education (Private), Education-General, Literacy, Medical Education, Private Education (Precollege), Public Education (Precollege), Religious Education, Science/Mathematics Education, Secondary Education (Private), Student Aid

Health: Arthritis, Health Organizations, Hospices, Hospitals, Kidney, Prenatal Health Issues

Religion: Churches, Dioceses, Ministries, Religious Organizations, Religious Welfare

Science: Science Museums

Social Services: Child Abuse, Community Service Organizations, Domestic Violence, Family Services, Food/Clothing Distribution, Homes, People with Disabilities, Senior Services, Social Services-General, Substance Abuse, Youth Organizations

Application Procedures

Initial Contact: Send a brief letter of inquiry describing program or project. Include a resume of activities and amount requested.

Deadlines: None.

Restrictions

Generally limited to religious and educational organizations. Does not support individuals.

Foundation Officials

Venable B. Proctor: secretary

Grants Analysis

Disclosure Period: calendar year ending 2003
Total Grants: $333,760
Number of Grants: 19
Average Grant: $8,515*
Highest Grant: $121,500
Lowest Grant: $500
Typical Range: $1,000 to $20,000
*Note: Average grant figure excludes two highest grants ($189,010).

Recent Grants

Note: Grants derived from 2003 Form 990.
General

121,500	St. Joseph High School, Victoria, TX
67,510	St. Dennis Church, Refugio, TX
20,250	Nazareth Academy, Victoria, TX
20,250	Our Lady of Victory School, Victoria, TX
20,250	Trinity Episcopal School, Victoria, TX
10,000	Diocese of Victoria, Victoria, TX -- for presidio labahia operations
10,000	Refugio County Memorial Hospital District, Refugio, TX
9,000	Mid-Coast Family Services, Victoria, TX
7,500	Perpetual Help Home Inc., Victoria, TX
7,500	Victoria Independent School District, Victoria, TX -- for youth program

ROBERT STEWART AND HELEN PFEIFFER ODELL FUND

Giving Contact

Eugene Ranghiasci, Vice President
Wells Fargo Bank
420 Montgomery St., 5th Fl.
San Francisco, CA 94104

Phone: (415)396-3215
Fax: (415)834-0604

Description

Founded: 1967
EIN: 946132116
Organization Type: General Purpose Foundation
Giving Locations: CA: Northern California, with emphasis on San Francisco
Grant Types: General Support.

Donor Information

Founder: Established in 1967 by the late Robert Stewart Odell and the late Helen Pfeiffer Odell.

Financial Summary

Total Giving: $1,852,152 (2003); $2,269,090 (2002); $2,300,000 (2001)
Assets: $40,682,579 (2003); $34,375,952 (2002); $40,000,000 (2001)

Typical Recipients

Arts & Humanities: Arts Festivals, Ethnic & Folk Arts, History & Archaeology, Libraries, Museums/Galleries, Music, Opera, Performing Arts, Theater

Civic & Public Affairs: Botanical Gardens/Parks, Community Foundations, Economic Development, Civic & Public Affairs-General, Housing, Law & Justice, Legal Aid, Parades/Festivals, Philanthropic Organizations, Public Policy, Safety, Urban & Community Affairs, Zoos/Aquariums

Education: Afterschool/Enrichment Programs, Business Education, Colleges & Universities, Economic Education, Education Funds, Elementary Education (Private), Education-General, International Studies, Minority Education, Preschool Education, Private Education (Precollege), Public Education (Precollege), Religious Education, School Volunteerism, Science/Mathematics Education, Secondary Education (Private), Secondary Education (Public), Student Aid

Environment: Environment-General, Protection, Resource Conservation

Health: Children's Health/Hospitals, Clinics/Medical Centers, Eyes/Blindness, Health Organizations, Heart, Hospitals, Medical Rehabilitation, Medical Research, Mental Health, Prenatal Health Issues, Preventive Medicine/Wellness Organizations, Public Health

International: Foreign Educational Institutions, Human Rights, International Affairs, International Environmental Issues, International Organizations, Missionary/Religious Activities

Religion: Churches, Religion-General, Religious Organizations, Religious Welfare, Seminaries

Science: Science Museums, Scientific Centers & Institutes

Social Services: At-Risk Youth, Child Welfare, Community Service Organizations, Day Care, Family Services, Homes, People with Disabilities, Recreation & Athletics, Scouts, Shelters/Homelessness, Social Services-General, United Funds/United Ways, Youth Organizations

Application Procedures

Initial Contact: Organizations should send a letter to the Fund.

Application Requirements: Letters should detail the project for which the grant is sought and a copy of the IRS tax exemption letter showing that the applicant is a public charity.

Deadlines: None. The board meets four or five times per year. The foundation requests that applications be sent early in the calendar year to assure consideration.

Review Process: The trustees make payments between October 15 and December 31 of each year.

Restrictions

The fund only makes grants to public charities. Grants are not made to individuals.

Additional Information

Wells Fargo Bank serves as a corporate trustee to the Fund.
Publications: Guidelines

Foundation Officials

James P. Conn: trustee B 1938. PRIM CORP EMPL president, director: Bay Meadows Catering Inc. CORP AFFIL president: The Tipsters.

Paul B. Fay, Jr.: trustee B 1918. PRIM CORP EMPL president: Fay Improvement Co. CORP AFFIL director: First America Title Insurance Co.; director: Vestaur Securities Inc.; director: First America Finance Corp.

Grants Analysis

Disclosure Period: calendar year ending 2003
Total Grants: $1,852,152
Number of Grants: 71
Average Grant: $25,031*
Highest Grant: $100,000
Lowest Grant: $1,000
Typical Range: $10,000 to $50,000
*Note: Average grant figure excludes highest grant.

Recent Grants

Note: Grants derived from 2003 Form 990.
General

50,000	Anthony Immaculate Conception School, San Francisco, CA
50,000	Bellarmine College Preparatory, San Jose, CA
50,000	Blind Babies Foundation, San Francisco, CA
50,000	Community Foundation Silicon Valley, San Jose, CA
50,000	Dominican Sisters of Mission San Jose, Fremont, CA
50,000	Gonzaga University, Spokane, WA
50,000	Legion of Christ Inc., New York, NY
50,000	Mercy High School College Preparatory School, San Francisco, CA
50,000	Notre Dame High School, Sherman Oaks, CA
50,000	Sacred Heart Saint Dominic Elementary, CA

O'DONNELL FOUNDATION

Giving Contact

Carolyn R. Bacon, Executive Director
100 Crescent Court, Suite 1660
Dallas, TX 75201
Phone: (214)871-5800
Fax: (214)855-8988
Web: http://www.odf.org

Description

Founded: 1957
EIN: 756023326
Organization Type: General Purpose Foundation
Giving Locations: TX
Grant Types: Capital, Endowment, General Support, Research.

Donor Information

Founder: The O'Donnell Foundation was established in Texas in 1957 by Peter O'Donnell Jr., and Mrs. Peter O'Donnell Jr.

Financial Summary

Total Giving: $22,249,368 (fiscal year ending November 30, 2003); $4,163,489 (fiscal 2001). Note: Fiscal 1997 Giving includes stock donation ($5,415,206).
Assets: $140,065,598 (fiscal 2003); $147,567,013 (fiscal 2001)
Gifts Received: $7,850,000 (fiscal 2003); $650,000

(fiscal 2001); $3,282,875 (fiscal 1999). Note: In fiscal 2003, contributions were received from Edith Jones O'Donnell. In fiscal 2001, contributions were received from Edith Jones O'Donnell and Peter O'Donnell, Jr. In fiscal 2000, contributions were received from Edith Jones O'Donnell ($3,376,875) and Peter O'Donnell, Jr. ($435,238).

Typical Recipients

Arts & Humanities: Arts Associations & Councils, Arts Centers, Arts Outreach, Ballet, Community Arts, Ethnic & Folk Arts, Arts & Humanities-General, History & Archaeology, Libraries, Literary Arts, Museums/Galleries, Music, Opera, Public Broadcasting

Civic & Public Affairs: Botanical Gardens/Parks, Business/Free Enterprise, Community Foundations, Economic Development, Economic Policy, Employment/Job Training, Civic & Public Affairs-General, Municipalities/Towns, Philanthropic Organizations, Professional & Trade Associations, Public Policy, Urban & Community Affairs

Education: Afterschool/Enrichment Programs, Business Education, Colleges & Universities, Economic Education, Education Associations, Education Funds, Education Reform, Elementary Education (Private), Elementary Education (Public), Engineering/Technological Education, Faculty Development, Education-General, Literacy, Medical Education, Minority Education, Private Education (Precollege), Public Education (Precollege), Science/Mathematics Education, Secondary Education (Private), Secondary Education (Public), Student Aid

Environment: Forestry

Health: Clinics/Medical Centers, Health Funds, Hospitals (University Affiliated), Medical Research, Respiratory

International: Foreign Arts Organizations

Religion: Churches

Science: Scientific Centers & Institutes, Scientific Organizations, Scientific Research

Social Services: Child Welfare, Counseling, Scouts, YMCA/YWCA/YMHA/YWHA

Application Procedures

Initial Contact: Requests for grants should be made by letter.

Application Requirements: Applicants should submit a brief letter outlining the project and including a timetable, budget, list of funds already pledged to the project, and the specific contribution requested. A list of the organization's governing board and a copy of the IRS determination letter of tax-exempt status for the organization should be attached to the application.

Deadlines: None.

Review Process: The board of directors meets as required.

Restrictions

The foundation prefers to give charitable and educational grants to local institutions. No grants are made to individuals, and the foundation does not award scholarships, fellowships, loans, or prizes.

Foundation Officials

Carolyn R. Bacon: chief executive director PRIM CORP EMPL secretary, treasurer, director: Baker Brokerage.

Duncan Eugene Boeckman: director

Rita C. Clements: vice president NONPR AFFIL vice chairman: University Texas System.

Dr. Philip O'Bryan Montgomery, Jr.: director B Montgomery, AL 1921. ED Southern Methodist University BS (1942); Columbia University MD (1945). PRIM NONPR EMPL professor: Southwestern Medical School. NONPR AFFIL member: Texas Medical Association; member: Tissue Culture Association; member: Society Experimental Biology & Medicine; member: Professional Group Medical Electronic Institute Radio Engineers; trustee: Saint Marks School Texas; member: Pan-American Medical Association; member: International Society Cell Biology; founder:

Optical Society Texas; member: International Federation Medical Electronic; member: Biophysics Society; member: International Academy Pathology; fellow: American Society Clinical Pathologists; member: American Society Experimental Pathology; member: American Society Cell Biology; member: American Association University Professors; member: American Medical Association; member: American Association Cancer Research; member: American Association Pathologists & Bacteriologists; member: American Academy Forensic Sciences; member: American Academy of Arts & Sciences. CLUB AFFIL president, director: Damon Runyon Club.

Edith Jones O'Donnell: secretary, treasurer

Peter O'Donnell, Jr.: president

Grants Analysis

Disclosure Period: fiscal year ending November 30, 2003

Total Grants: $22,249,368

Number of Grants: 23

Average Grant: $75,628*

Highest Grant: $7,012,956

Lowest Grant: $385

Typical Range: $5,000 to $100,000

*****Note:** Average grant excludes four highest grants ($20,812,435).

Recent Grants

Note: Grants derived from fiscal 2002 Form 990.

General

3,615,000	University of Texas Southwestern Medical Center at Dallas, Dallas, TX -- towards research
1,500,000	Southwestern Medical Foundation, Dallas, TX -- towards endowment
1,000,000	Dallas County Community College District Fund Inc., Dallas, TX -- towards endowment
1,000,000	Johns Hopkins University, Baltimore, MD -- towards endowment
794,000	University of Texas at Austin, Austin, TX -- towards education & research
651,976	Advanced Placement Strategies Inc., Dallas, TX -- for education
500,000	Dallas Museum of Art, Dallas, TX -- for acquisition
500,000	Southern Methodist University, Dallas, TX -- towards building fund
403,000	National Center for Educational Accountability, Austin, TX -- towards operations and research
121,403	University of Texas at Austin, Austin, TX -- towards furniture art consulting services books

THE OFFIELD FAMILY FOUNDATION

Giving Contact

Marie Larson, Secretary
400 North Michigan Avenue, Room 407
Chicago, IL 60611
Phone: (312)467-5480
Fax: (312)467-0473

Description

Founded: 1953
EIN: 366066240
Organization Type: Family Foundation
Giving Locations: nationally.
Grant Types: General Support.

Donor Information

Founder: Incorporated in 1940 by Dorothy Wrigley Offield.

Financial Summary

Total Giving: $4,267,535 (fiscal year ending June 30, 2003); $7,089,456 (fiscal 2002)

Giving Analysis: Giving for fiscal 2003 includes: nonmonetary support ($100,035) fiscal 2002: nonmonetary support ($3,131,956)

Assets: $94,025,971 (fiscal 2003); $93,738,656 (fiscal 2002)

Gifts Received: $1,823,344 (fiscal 2003); $3,042,062 (fiscal 2002); $1,623,211 (fiscal 2000). Note: In fiscal 2002 and 2003, contributions were received from Charitable Lead Unitrust FBO James Offield and Charitable Lead Unitrust FBO Paxson Offield and from Offield Charitable Lead Unitrust.

Typical Recipients

Arts & Humanities: Arts Associations & Councils, Arts Centers, Arts Festivals, Film & Video, Arts & Humanities-General, Historic Preservation, History & Archaeology, Libraries, Museums/Galleries, Music, Performing Arts, Public Broadcasting

Civic & Public Affairs: Botanical Gardens/Parks, Business/Free Enterprise, Clubs, Community Foundations, Employment/Job Training, Civic & Public Affairs-General, Inner-City Development, Municipalities/Towns, Professional & Trade Associations, Public Policy, Safety, Urban & Community Affairs, Women's Affairs, Zoos/Aquariums

Education: Arts/Humanities Education, Colleges & Universities, Education Funds, Environmental Education, Education-General, Medical Education, Private Education (Precollege), Public Education (Precollege), Student Aid

Environment: Air/Water Quality, Environment-General, Protection, Research, Resource Conservation, Watershed, Wildlife Protection

Health: Cancer, Children's Health/Hospitals, Clinics/Medical Centers, Emergency/Ambulance Services, Health Funds, Health Organizations, Hospices, Hospitals, Hospitals (University Affiliated), Medical Research, Public Health, Transplant Networks/Donor Banks, Trauma Treatment

International: International Environmental Issues

Religion: Churches, Religious Welfare

Science: Science Museums, Scientific Centers & Institutes

Social Services: Animal Protection, At-Risk Youth, Camps, Child Welfare, Community Service Organizations, Day Care, Domestic Violence, Family Planning, Family Services, Food/Clothing Distribution, Homes, People with Disabilities, Recreation & Athletics, Scouts, Special Olympics, Substance Abuse, United Funds/United Ways, Youth Organizations

Application Procedures

Initial Contact: Applicants should mail a letter of inquiry describing the proposed project, information about the organization, and its future goals.

Deadlines: None.

Review Process: The board makes final decisions on grants at its meeting in June.

Additional Information

Although the Santa Catalina Island Conservancy is a private foundation, the Offield Family Foundation maintains expenditures responsibility.

Foundation Officials

Raymond Hibner Drymalski: treasurer B Chicago, IL 1936. ED Georgetown University BA (1958); University of Michigan JD (1961). PRIM CORP EMPL partner: Bell Boyd & Lloyd. CORP AFFIL director: Northwestern Memorial Corp. NONPR AFFIL member: American Bar Association; director: Northwestern Memorial Hospital. CLUB AFFIL Economic Club.

Marie Larson: secretary

Chase Offield: director

James S. Offield: vice president, director PRIM CORP EMPL president: El Rojo Grande Ranch.

Meighan Offield: director

Paxson H. Offield: president, director B 1951. ED

University of Denver (1975). PRIM CORP EMPL president: Santa Catalina Island Co. ADD CORP EMPL president: SCI.

Grants Analysis

Disclosure Period: fiscal year ending June 30, 2003
Total Grants: $4,266,500*
Number of Grants: 56
Average Grant: $54,009*
Highest Grant: $750,000
Lowest Grant: $500
Typical Range: $10,000 to $100,000
***Note:** Giving excludes stock grants-in-kind. Average grant figure excludes two highest grants ($1,350,000).

Recent Grants

Note: Grants derived from fiscal 2003 Form 990.
Library-Related

10,000	Harbor Springs Library Association, Harbor Springs, MI

General

750,000	Pfleger Institute of Environmental Research, Oceanside, CA
600,000	Little Traverse Conservancy, Harbor Springs, MI
500,000	Northern Michigan Hospital Foundation, Petoskey, MI
300,000	Peregrine Fund, Boise, ID
240,000	Billfish Foundation, Ft. Lauderdale, FL
200,000	Sedona Cultural Park, Sedona, AZ
130,000	Aspen Music Associates, Aspen, CO
100,000	Crooked Tree Arts Council, Petoskey, MI
100,000	Petoskey Harbor Springs Area Community Foundation, Petoskey, MI
100,000	Planned Parenthood Northern Michigan, Petoskey, MI

OG&E ELECTRIC SERVICES

Company Headquarters

Oklahoma City, OK
Web: http://www.oge.com

Company Description

Former Name: Oklahoma Gas & Electric Co.
Employees: 2,765
SIC(s): 1311 Crude Petroleum & Natural Gas, 4911 Electric Services, 4922 Natural Gas Transmission.

Nonmonetary Support

Type: Loaned Employees; Loaned Executives
Note: Nonmonetary support is provided by the company.

Oklahoma Gas & Electric Co. Foundation

Giving Contact

Steven E. Moore, President & Director
PO Box 321
Oklahoma City, OK 73101
Phone: (405)553-3622
Fax: (405)553-3567

Alternate Contact

321 North Harvey
Oklahoma City, OK 73102

Description

Founded: 1957
EIN: 736093572
Organization Type: Corporate Foundation
Giving Locations: OK: headquarters and operating communities.
Grant Types: Capital, Employee Matching Gifts, General Support, Scholarship.

Donor Information

Founder: Oklahoma Gas and Electric Co.

Financial Summary

Total Giving: $795,185 (2002); $926,521 (2001). Note: Contributes through foundation only.
Assets: $1,337,176 (2002); $1,310,413 (2001)
Gifts Received: $800,000 (2002); $1,400,000 (2001); $600,000 (2000). Note: Contributions are received from Oklahoma Gas and Electric Co.

Typical Recipients

Arts & Humanities: Arts Associations & Councils, Arts Funds, Arts Institutes, Ballet, Ethnic & Folk Arts, Arts & Humanities-General, Historic Preservation, History & Archaeology, Libraries, Museums/Galleries, Music, Theater
Civic & Public Affairs: Botanical Gardens/Parks, Business/Free Enterprise, Community Foundations, Economic Development, Civic & Public Affairs-General, Municipalities/Towns, Parades/Festivals, Professional & Trade Associations, Urban & Community Affairs, Zoos/Aquariums
Education: Business Education, Business-School Partnerships, Colleges & Universities, Community & Junior Colleges, Economic Education, Education Funds, Education-General, Medical Education, Private Education (Precollege), Public Education (Precollege), Science/Mathematics Education, Secondary Education (Public), Special Education
Environment: Forestry, Protection, Resource Conservation
Health: Children's Health/Hospitals, Clinics/Medical Centers, Emergency/Ambulance Services, Health-General, Health Funds, Health Organizations, Heart, Hospitals, Medical Research, Public Health, Transplant Networks/Donor Banks
International: International Affairs
Religion: Missionary Activities (Domestic), Religious Welfare
Science: Science Museums
Social Services: Camps, Community Service Organizations, Counseling, Emergency Relief, Family Planning, Family Services, Food/Clothing Distribution, People with Disabilities, Recreation & Athletics, Scouts, Senior Services, Special Olympics, United Funds/United Ways, YMCA/YWCA/YMHA/YWHA, Youth Organizations

Application Procedures

Initial Contact: Send a brief letter.
Application Requirements: Include an outline of the proposed project, amount requested, and proof of 501(c)(3) status.
Deadlines: None.

Restrictions

Does not support fraternal organizations, individuals, political or lobbying groups, or religious organizations for sectarian purposes. Preference given to organizations in service areas.

Foundation Officials

Carla Brockman: secretary, treasurer
Steven Moore: president B Sayre, OK 1946. ED University of Oklahoma BBA (1968); University of Oklahoma JD (1971). PRIM CORP EMPL chairman, president, chief executive officer, director: OGE Energy Corp.
A. M. Strecker: executive vice president, chief operating officer B Seiling, OK 1943. ED Oklahoma State University BSEE (1971). PRIM CORP EMPL executive vice president, chief operating officer: OG&E Electric Services. CORP AFFIL senior vice president: Oklahoma Gas & Electric Co.
J. R. Strecker: vice president, director

Grants Analysis

Disclosure Period: calendar year ending 2002
Total Grants: $728,261*
Number of Grants: 74
Average Grant: $9,841
Highest Grant: $80,000
Lowest Grant: $500
Typical Range: $1,000 to $10,000 and $25,000 to $60,000
***Note:** Giving excludes matching gifts.

Recent Grants

Note: Grants derived from 2003 Form 990.
General

80,000	Oklahoma Christian University of Science and Arts, Oklahoma city, OK
60,000	Allied Arts, Oklahoma City, OK
60,000	National Cowboy and Western Heritage Museum, Oklahoma City, OK
60,000	Oklahoma Centennial Commemoration Fund, Oklahoma City, OK
60,000	Oklahoma State University Foundation, Stillwater, OK
50,000	Oklahoma City University, Oklahoma City, OK
40,000	YMCA, Oklahoma City, OK
30,000	Mission Oklahoma City, Oklahoma City, OK
30,000	Oklahoma City Museum of Art, Oklahoma City, OK
20,000	Oklahoma School of Science and Mathematics, Oklahoma City, OK

OHIO NATIONAL LIFE INSURANCE CO.

Company Headquarters

2720 S. River Rd.
Des Plaines, IL 60018

Company Description

Employees: 600
SIC(s): 6311 Life Insurance, 6321 Accident & Health Insurance.

Nonmonetary Support

Type: Donated Equipment; Workplace Solicitation

Ohio National Foundation

Giving Contact

Anthony G. Esposito, Trustee
Ohio National Life Insurance Co.
One Financial Way
Cincinnati, OH 45242
Phone: (513)794-6493

Description

Founded: 1987
EIN: 311230164
Organization Type: Corporate Foundation
Giving Locations: OH: Cincinnati
Grant Types: Capital, Employee Matching Gifts, General Support, Multiyear/Continuing Support, Research, Scholarship.

Donor Information

Founder: Ohio National Life Insurance Co.

Financial Summary

Total Giving: $609,196 (2002); $592,871 (2001)
Giving Analysis: Giving for 2002 includes: foundation matching gifts ($16,021); foundation grants to

United Way ($137,290); 2001: foundation matching gifts ($20,205); foundation grants to United Way ($142,330) foundation ($430,336)
Assets: $1,221,340 (2002); $2,009,598 (2001)
Gifts Received: $10,961 (2002); $1,002,675 (2001); $143,374 (1996). Note: In 2002, contributions were received from Ohio National Life Insurance Co.

Typical Recipients

Arts & Humanities: Arts Centers, Arts Festivals, Arts Funds, Arts Institutes, Ballet, Film & Video, Arts & Humanities-General, History & Archaeology, Libraries, Museums/Galleries, Music, Opera, Performing Arts, Public Broadcasting, Theater
Civic & Public Affairs: African American Affairs, Botanical Gardens/Parks, Chambers of Commerce, Clubs, Community Foundations, Economic Policy, Employment/Job Training, Ethnic Organizations, Civic & Public Affairs-General, Housing, Inner-City Development, Law & Justice, Municipalities/Towns, Philanthropic Organizations, Public Policy, Safety, Urban & Community Affairs, Women's Affairs, Zoos/Aquariums
Education: Afterschool/Enrichment Programs, Arts/Humanities Education, Business Education, Colleges & Universities, Continuing Education, Economic Education, Education Associations, Education Funds, Education-General, Legal Education, Literacy, Minority Education, Private Education (Precollege), Religious Education, Student Aid
Environment: Environment-General
Health: AIDS/HIV, Alzheimer's Disease, Cancer, Children's Health/Hospitals, Clinics/Medical Centers, Diabetes, Eyes/Blindness, Health-General, Health Policy/Cost Containment, Heart, Home-Care Services, Hospices, Hospitals, Medical Rehabilitation, Medical Research, Multiple Sclerosis, Public Health
Religion: Dioceses, Religion-General, Jewish Causes, Ministries, Religious Organizations, Religious Welfare, Social/Policy Issues
Science: Scientific Research
Social Services: Child Welfare, Community Centers, Family Services, Food/Clothing Distribution, People with Disabilities, Recreation & Athletics, Scouts, Senior Services, Shelters/Homelessness, Special Olympics, Substance Abuse, United Funds/United Ways, YMCA/YWCA/YMHA/YWHA, Youth Organizations

Application Procedures

Initial Contact: Send a brief letter of inquiry.
Application Requirements: Include a description of organization and proof of tax-exempt status.
Deadlines: None.

Restrictions

Does not support individuals, religious organizations for sectarian purposes, or political or lobbying groups.

Corporate Officials

Howard C. Becker: vice president, president, chief executive officer, director PRIM CORP EMPL vice president: Ohio National Life Insurance Co.
Ronald J. Dolan: senior vice president, chief financial officer, director B Cincinnati, OH 1947. ED University of Cincinnati (1969); University of Michigan (1970). PRIM CORP EMPL executive vice president, chief financial officer, director: Ohio National Life Insurance Co.
David B. O'Malley: chairman, president, chief executive officer, director PRIM CORP EMPL chairman, president, chief executive officer, director: Ohio National Life Insurance Co.

Foundation Officials

Howard C. Becker: trustee (see above)
Christopher A. Carlson: trustee
Ronald J. Dolan: trustee (see above)
Anthony G. Esposito: trustee PRIM CORP EMPL senior vice president human resources: Ohio National Life Insurance Co.
Diane Hagenbuch: trustee

David B. O'Maley: trustee (see above)
D. Gates Smith: trustee

Grants Analysis

Disclosure Period: calendar year ending 2002
Total Grants: $455,885*
Number of Grants: 64
Average Grant: $5,805*
Highest Grant: $50,000
Lowest Grant: $145
Typical Range: $1,000 to $10,000
*Note: Giving excludes matching gifts and United Way. Average grant figure excludes two highest grants ($96,000).

Recent Grants

Note: Grants derived from 2003 Form 990.
General
137,290	United Way, Cincinnati, OH -- towards annual campaign
50,000	Cincinnati 2012 Inc., Cincinnati, OH -- towards capital fund
46,000	University of Cincinnati Foundation, Cincinnati, OH -- fund for operations
35,777	National Underground Railroad Freedom Center, Cincinnati, OH -- towards capital fund
24,956	Fine Arts Fund, Cincinnati, OH -- fund for annual campaign
23,280	Children's Hospital Medical Center, Cincinnati, OH -- towards capital fund
22,000	Cincinnati Parks Foundation, Cincinnati, OH -- fund for operations
20,000	Cincinnati Institute of Fine Arts, Cincinnati, OH -- fund for operations
16,000	Sycamore Senior Center, Cincinnati, OH
15,000	John P. March Educational Foundation, Cincinnati, OH -- fund for annual campaign

GEORGE A. OHL, JR. TRUST

Giving Contact

George A. Ohl, Jr. Trust
Care of Wachovia Bank
765 Broad Street
Newark, NJ 07101

Description

Founded: 1947
EIN: 226024900
Organization Type: Private Foundation
Giving Locations: NJ
Grant Types: Capital, General Support, Project, Research, Scholarship, Seed Money.

Donor Information

Founder: the late George A. Ohl, Jr.

Financial Summary

Total Giving: $324,155 (2004)
Assets: $5,408,910 (2004)
Gifts Received: $2,893 (1994)

Typical Recipients

Arts & Humanities: Arts Associations & Councils, Arts Festivals, Arts Funds, Arts Outreach, History & Archaeology, Libraries, Museums/Galleries, Performing Arts, Theater
Civic & Public Affairs: Employment/Job Training, Civic & Public Affairs-General, Housing, Philanthropic Organizations, Urban & Community Affairs, Zoos/Aquariums
Education: Arts/Humanities Education, Colleges & Universities, Education Associations, Education Funds, Education Reform, Engineering/

Technological Education, Education-General, Medical Education, Minority Education, Private Education (Precollege), Public Education (Precollege), Science/Mathematics Education, Secondary Education (Private), Secondary Education (Public), Student Aid, Vocational & Technical Education
Environment: Environment-General
Health: AIDS/HIV, Arthritis, Cancer, Children's Health/Hospitals, Clinics/Medical Centers, Geriatric Health, Health Funds, Health Organizations, Heart, Hospitals, Long-Term Care, Medical Rehabilitation, Mental Health, Outpatient Health Care, Prenatal Health Issues, Public Health, Research/Studies Institutes, Single-Disease Health Associations
International: Health Care/Hospitals
Religion: Jewish Causes, Ministries, Religious Welfare, Social/Policy Issues
Science: Scientific Centers & Institutes
Social Services: At-Risk Youth, Child Abuse, Child Welfare, Community Centers, Community Service Organizations, Crime Prevention, Day Care, Delinquency & Criminal Rehabilitation, Domestic Violence, Family Planning, Family Services, Food/Clothing Distribution, People with Disabilities, Recreation & Athletics, Scouts, Senior Services, Substance Abuse, Veterans, YMCA/YWCA/YMHA/YWHA, Youth Organizations

Application Procedures

Initial Contact: Send a brief letter of inquiry.
Deadlines: October 31.

Additional Information

Publications: Application Guidelines
Trust(s): Wachovia Bank NA NJ

Grants Analysis

Disclosure Period: calendar year ending 2004
Total Grants: $324,155
Number of Grants: 29
Average Grant: $10,684*
Highest Grant: $25,000
Lowest Grant: $3,000
Typical Range: $5,000 to $20,000
*Note: Average grant figure excludes highest grant.

Recent Grants

Note: Grants derived from 2004 Form 990.
General
25,000	Saint Clare's Foundation, Denville, NJ
20,000	Babyland Family Services Inc., Newark, NJ
20,000	Caregivers of Central Ocean County Inc., Beachwood, NJ
20,000	New Jersey Theatre Alliance, Morristown, NJ
20,000	Partnership in Philanthropy, Chatham, NJ
15,000	Community Action Service Center Inc., Princeton, NJ
15,000	Teach For America, Newark, NJ
14,947	Kimball Medical Center Foundation, Lakewood, NJ
12,000	New Jersey Institute of Technology, Newark, NJ
11,108	Coriell Institute for Medical Research, Camden, NJ

THE JOHN R. OISHEI FOUNDATION

Giving Contact

Thomas E. Baker, President
One HSBC Center, Suite 3650
Buffalo, NY 14203-2805
Phone: (716)856-9490
Fax: (716)856-9493
E-mail: glhouck@oisheifdt.org
Web: http://www.oisheifdt.org

Description

Founded: 1941
EIN: 160874319
Organization Type: General Purpose Foundation
Former Name: Julia R. and Estelle L. Foundation (1997).
Giving Locations: NY: Greater Western New York area, Buffalo
Grant Types: Challenge, General Support, Multi-year/Continuing Support, Professorship, Research, Scholarship, Seed Money.

Financial Summary

Total Giving: $11,046,474 (2002)
Giving Analysis: Giving for 2002 includes: foundation grants to United Way ($375,000); foundation scholarships ($660,573); 2001: foundation grants to United Way ($200,000); foundation scholarships ($655,707)
Assets: $204,755,690 (2002); $245,467,978 (2001)
Gifts Received: $983,305 (2002); $871,038 (2001); $640,020 (2000). Note: In 2001 and 2002, contributions were received from Oishei Consolidated Trust.

Typical Recipients

Arts & Humanities: Arts Institutes, Historic Preservation, History & Archaeology, Libraries, Literary Arts, Museums/Galleries, Music, Performing Arts, Public Broadcasting, Theater, Visual Arts
Civic & Public Affairs: Community Foundations, Civic & Public Affairs-General, Law & Justice, Legal Aid, Professional & Trade Associations, Public Policy, Safety, Zoos/Aquariums
Education: Afterschool/Enrichment Programs, Arts/Humanities Education, Colleges & Universities, Education Associations, Education Funds, Education-General, Medical Education, Private Education (Precollege), Secondary Education (Private), Secondary Education (Public), Special Education, Student Aid, Vocational & Technical Education
Health: AIDS/HIV, Alzheimer's Disease, Cancer, Children's Health/Hospitals, Clinics/Medical Centers, Emergency/Ambulance Services, Geriatric Health, Health Funds, Health Organizations, Home-Care Services, Hospices, Hospitals, Hospitals (University Affiliated), Long-Term Care, Medical Research, Mental Health, Research/Studies Institutes, Speech & Hearing
International: Foreign Educational Institutions, Health Care/Hospitals, Human Rights, International Affairs
Religion: Churches, Dioceses, Religious Welfare, Seminaries
Science: Science Museums, Scientific Centers & Institutes
Social Services: Animal Protection, Camps, Child Welfare, Community Service Organizations, Crime Prevention, Emergency Relief, Family Services, Food/Clothing Distribution, People with Disabilities, Recreation & Athletics, Scouts, Senior Services, Shelters/Homelessness, Substance Abuse, United Funds/United Ways, YMCA/YWCA/YMHA/YWHA, Youth Organizations

Application Procedures

Initial Contact: Prospective applicants should send a preliminary letter of inquiry to the foundation. There are no formal application procedures.
Application Requirements: A proposal should contain the following information: a concise statement of the program or project, the amount of funding requested, a brief description of the nature and activities of the applicant, proof of tax-exempt status, and a list of officers and directors of the organization.
Deadlines: None.
Review Process: In most instances, applicants will receive a written response within two months; distributions are made throughout the year.

Restrictions

The foundation reports that its support is limited to the Buffalo, NY, metropolitan area. Additionally, the foundation does not make grants for operating expenses, endowment funds, capital campaigns or collegiate scholarships. Private foundations and individuals are also not eligible for funding.

Additional Information

The foundation has undergone a process of review and change, which has resulted in a major change in giving focus.
Publications: Guidelines

Foundation Officials

Thomas E. Baker: president, director
Christopher T. Dunstan: director
Richard D. Fors: director
Erland E. Kailbourne: director, board chairman B Whiteville, NY 1941. ED State University of New York Alfred AAS (1961). CORP AFFIL director: Chautauqua Airlines. NONPR AFFIL director, member: Rochester Chamber of Commerce; trustee: State University New York; senior chapter president: Robert Morris Associates. CLUB AFFIL Wellsville Country Club; Rochester Country Club; Shriners Club; Masons Club; Elks Club; Genesee Valley Club.
Allan R. Wiegley: treasurer, director

Grants Analysis

Disclosure Period: calendar year ending 2002
Total Grants: $10,010,901*
Number of Grants: 105
Average Grant: $90,494*
Highest Grant: $390,000
Lowest Grant: $5,000
Typical Range: $25,000 to $200,000
*Note: Giving excludes scholarships and United Way. Average grant figure excludes two highest grants ($690,000).

Recent Grants

Note: Grants derived from 2002 Form 990.
General

390,000	Western New York Educational Television Association Inc., Buffalo, NY
300,000	Graycliff Conservancy Inc., Derby, NY
300,000	Western New York Educational Television Association Inc., Buffalo, NY
270,000	Niagara Falls Memorial Medical Center Foundation, Niagara Falls, NY
257,000	University of Buffalo Foundation Inc., Buffalo, NY
257,000	University at Buffalo Foundation Inc., Buffalo, NY
250,000	Boys & Girls Clubs of Buffalo Inc., Buffalo, NY
250,000	Roswell Park Alliance Foundation, Buffalo, NY
250,000	University at Buffalo Foundation Inc., Buffalo, NY
241,000	Hospice Foundation of Western New York Inc., Cheektowaga, NY

OKI AMERICA INC.

Company Headquarters

Hackensack, NJ
Web: http://oki.co.jp

Company Description

Employees: 1,700
SIC(s): 3661 Telephone & Telegraph Apparatus, 3663 Radio & T.V. Communications Equipment, 3674 Semiconductors & Related Devices.
Parent Company: Oki Electric Industry Company Ltd., 7-12 Toranomon 1-chome, Minato-ku, Tokyo, Japan

Operating Locations

Cascade Design Automation (CA--Santa Clara; WA--Bellevue); Oki (CA--Costa Mesa); Oki Advanced Technology (CA--San Jose); Oki America Inc. (CA--San Francisco, Sunnyvale; GA--Atlanta; NJ--Camden, Mount Laurel; NY--New York; OR--Tualatin); OKI Semiconductor Group (CA--Sunnyvale); OKI Telecom Group (GA--Swanee); Okidata Group (NJ--Mount Laurel)

Nonmonetary Support

Type: Donated Products; Workplace Solicitation

Giving Contact

Elva Peelo, HR Asst.
785 North Mary Ave.
Sunnyvale, CA 94085
Phone: (408)720-1900
Fax: (408)720-1918

Description

Organization Type: Corporate Giving Program
Giving Locations: NJ: Bergen County operating locations.
Grant Types: Multiyear/Continuing Support, Scholarship

Financial Summary

Total Giving: Company does not disclose contributions figures.

Typical Recipients

Arts & Humanities: Community Arts
Civic & Public Affairs: Professional & Trade Associations
Education: Education-General, International Exchange
Social Services: Emergency Relief

Application Procedures

Notes: Oki America is currently not accepting proposals at this time. The Co. is currently in the process of corporate-wide reorganization efforts and their definition of local communities, corporate giving policies, and procedure will be significantly altered in the future.

Corporate Officials

Tetsuji Banno: president PRIM CORP EMPL president: Oki America Inc. ADD CORP EMPL chief executive officer: Oki Telecom Inc.

Grants Analysis

Note: A more recent grants list was unavailable.

Recent Grants

Note: Grants derived from 1996 grants list.
Library-RelatedFort Lee Public Library, Ft. Lee, NJ

GeneralJapan Society, New York, NYJapanese Chamber of Commerce, New York, NYMusic from Japan, New York, NYPalisade Chamber Orchestra, Palisade, NJ

OLD DOMINION BOX CO.

Company Headquarters

120 Dillard Rd.
Madison Heights, VA 24572

Company Description

Employees: 600
SIC(s): 2600 Paper & Allied Products, 3500 Industrial Machinery & Equipment.

Operating Locations

Old Dominion Box Co. (VA--Lynchburg)

Old Dominion Box Co. Foundation

Giving Contact
Wayne Lankford, Chairman
PO Box 680
Lynchburg, VA 24505
Phone: (434)929-6701

Description
EIN: 546036792
Organization Type: Corporate Foundation
Giving Locations: VA
Grant Types: General Support.

Financial Summary
Total Giving: $29,300 (fiscal year ending November 30, 2001)
Assets: $565,798 (fiscal 2001)
Gifts Received: $50,000 (fiscal 1996); $250 (fiscal 1994); $100 (fiscal 1992). Note: In fiscal 1994, contributions were received from Old Dominion Box Co. In fiscal 1996, contributions were received from Dillard Investment Corp.

Typical Recipients
Arts & Humanities: Arts Centers, Historic Preservation, Libraries, Music
Civic & Public Affairs: African American Affairs, Clubs, Economic Development, Employment/Job Training, Civic & Public Affairs-General, Legal Aid, Professional & Trade Associations, Safety, Urban & Community Affairs, Women's Affairs
Education: Arts/Humanities Education, Business Education, Colleges & Universities, Community & Junior Colleges, Education Associations, Education Funds, Engineering/Technological Education, Education-General, Private Education (Precollege)
Environment: Forestry
Health: Emergency/Ambulance Services, Health Organizations, Heart, Single-Disease Health Associations
Religion: Churches, Jewish Causes, Religious Welfare, Social/Policy Issues
Social Services: Animal Protection, Community Service Organizations, Counseling, Crime Prevention, Food/Clothing Distribution, Recreation & Athletics, Special Olympics, United Funds/United Ways, YMCA/YWCA/YMHA/YWHA, Youth Organizations

Application Procedures
Initial Contact: Send brief letter describing program.
Deadlines: None.

Corporate Officials
Frank H. Buhler: chairman, chief financial officer B Arlington, VA 1926. ED Miami University (1950). PRIM CORP EMPL chairman: Old Dominion Box Co. CORP AFFIL director: Smithfield Co.; chairman, president: Palmetto Box; director: Piedmont Label Co.; chairman: Halltown Paperboard Co.; president: Little Rock Packaging Co.; chairman: Dacam Corp.; president, director: Dillard Investment Corp. NONPR AFFIL president, director: Old Dominion Box Co. Foundation.
Michael O. Buhler: president, director PRIM CORP EMPL president, director: Old Dominion Box Co.
R. Lewis Francis: vice president, chief financial officer PRIM CORP EMPL vice president, chief financial officer: Old Dominion Box Co.

Foundation Officials
Amy Buhler: secretary, treasurer
Frank H. Buhler: president (see above)
Michael O. Buhler: vice president (see above)
R. Lewis Francis: secretary, treasurer (see above)

Grants Analysis
Disclosure Period: fiscal year ending November 30, 2001

Total Grants: $29,300
Number of Grants: 9
Highest Grant: $20,000
Lowest Grant: $200

Recent Grants
Note: Grants derived from fiscal 2001 Form 990.
General

20,000	Lynchburg College, Lynchburg, VA
5,000	Academy of Music, Lynchburg, VA
1,000	Colonial Williamsburg Foundation, Williamsburg, VA
1,000	New Land Jobs, Lynchburg, VA
1,000	Virginia Foundation for Independent Colleges, Richmond, VA
300	Moneli Volunteer Rescue Squad, Madison Heights, VA
250	Crisis Line of Central Virginia, Lynchburg, VA
250	James River Day School, Lynchburg, VA
200	New Vistas School, Lynchburg, VA
200	Virginia College Fund, Richmond, VA

OLESON FOUNDATION

Giving Contact
Dr. John R. Spencer, Director
6645 N. Long Lake Rd.
Traverse City, MI 49684
Phone: (616)946-9349

Description
Founded: 1959
EIN: 386083080
Organization Type: Private Foundation
Giving Locations: MI: northwestern area of Michigan
Grant Types: General Support.

Donor Information
Founder: Gerald W. Oleson, Frances M. Oleson Foundation

Financial Summary
Total Giving: $737,810 (2001)
Giving Analysis: Giving for 2001 includes: foundation grants to United Way ($5,000)
Assets: $16,397,882 (2001)
Gifts Received: $1,650,100 (1997); $2,385,928 (1994). Note: In 1994, contributions were received from the estate of Frances M. Oleson.

Typical Recipients
Arts & Humanities: Arts Institutes, Historic Preservation, History & Archaeology, Libraries, Museums/Galleries, Opera, Performing Arts
Civic & Public Affairs: Botanical Gardens/Parks, Clubs, Community Foundations, Civic & Public Affairs-General, Housing, Parades/Festivals, Urban & Community Affairs
Education: Agricultural Education, Colleges & Universities, Elementary Education (Public), Education-General, Private Education (Precollege), Public Education (Precollege), School Volunteerism, Special Education
Environment: Environment-General, Resource Conservation, Watershed, Wildlife Protection
Health: Children's Health/Hospitals, Clinics/Medical Centers, Health Organizations, Hospitals, Prenatal Health Issues, Public Health, Transplant Networks/Donor Banks
Religion: Churches, Ministries, Religious Organizations, Religious Welfare
Science: Scientific Centers & Institutes
Social Services: Animal Protection, At-Risk Youth, Big Brothers/Big Sisters, Camps, Child Welfare, Community Service Organizations, Counseling, Crime Prevention, Family Services, Recreation &

Athletics, Scouts, Senior Services, Social Services-General, Special Olympics, United Funds/United Ways, Volunteer Services, Youth Organizations

Application Procedures
Initial Contact: Send a brief letter of inquiry.
Application Requirements: Include a description of organization, amount requested, purpose of funds sought, and proof of tax-exempt status.
Deadlines: None.

Foundation Officials
Julius H. Beers: treasurer
Richard Ford: secretary
Donald W. Oleson: vice president
Gerald W. Oleson: president
John R. Spencer, MD: director

Grants Analysis
Disclosure Period: calendar year ending 2001
Total Grants: $732,810*
Number of Grants: 67
Average Grant: $9,952*
Highest Grant: $76,000
Lowest Grant: $100
Typical Range: $2,500 to $20,000
*Note: Giving excludes United Way. Average grant figure excludes highest grant.

Recent Grants
Note: Grants derived from 2001 Form 990.
General

76,000	Traverse City Area Public Schools, Traverse City, MI
45,000	Grand Traverse Regional Land Conservancy, Traverse City, MI
33,600	Cherryland Humane Society, Traverse City, MI
30,000	Great Lakes Children's Museum, Traverse City, MI
25,000	Charlevoix Area Hospital, Charlevoix, MI
25,000	Grand Traverse County Parks and Recreation Department, Traverse City, MI
25,000	Grand Traverse Heritage Center, Traverse City, MI
25,000	Music House Museum, Acme, MI
25,000	St. Mary's School, Lake Leelanau, MI
20,000	Conversation Resource Alliance, Traverse City, MI

OLIN CORP.

Company Headquarters
Norwalk, CT
Web: http://www.olin.com

Company Description
Founded: 1892
Ticker: OLN
Exchange: NYSE
Revenue: US$1.301 billion (2002)
Employees: 5700 (2003)
SIC(s): 2812 Alkalies & Chlorine, 2819 Industrial Inorganic Chemicals Nec, 2821 Plastics Materials & Resins, 2865 Cyclic Crudes & Intermediates.

Operating Locations
Olin Corp. (AL--McIntosh; AZ--Chandler; CA--San Leandro, Santa Clara; CT--New Haven, Stamford, Stratford, Waterbury; FL--St. Marks, St. Petersburg; GA--Augusta; IL--Marion; LA--Lake Charles; MO--Independence; NJ--West Paterson; NY--Niagara Falls; TN--Charleston; WA--Redmond; WV--South Charleston; WI--Baraboo)

Nonmonetary Support
Volunteer Programs: Supports programs which include employee volunteers. Also awards Volunteer

Recognition grants; organizations where employees volunteer receive grants of $500 to $3,000.
Contact: Carmella Piacentini, Manager Corporate Contributions
Note: Annual competitive award program for long-term significant employee, retiree or family member volunteer affiliation.

Olin Corp. Charitable Trust

Giving Contact
Carmella V. Piacenini, Administrator
501 Merritt 7
PO Box 4500
Norwalk, CT 06856-4500
Phone: (203)750-3301
Fax: (203)750-3065
E-mail: cpiacentini@corp.olin.com
Web: http://www.olin.com/about/charitable.asp

Alternate Contact
Care of Wachovia Bank N.A.
PO Box 3099, NC6732
Winston-Salem, NC 27150-6732
Phone: (336)732-5252

Description
EIN: 436022750
Organization Type: Corporate Foundation
Giving Locations: communities where employees work and live; some support for national organizations.
Grant Types: Award, Capital, Challenge, Conference/Seminar, Department, Emergency, Employee Matching Gifts, Fellowship, General Support, Multiyear/Continuing Support, Project, Research, Scholarship, Seed Money.
Note: Employee matching gift ratio: 1 to 1 for active employees; 0.5 to 1 for retirees.

Financial Summary
Total Giving: $406,884 (2002); $1,086,558 (2001). Note: Contributes through corporate direct giving program and foundation. Giving includes trust.
Giving Analysis: Giving for 2002 includes: foundation scholarships ($2,500); foundation matching gifts ($9,861); foundation grants to United Way ($31,910)
Assets: $64,783 (2002); $515,761 (2001)
Gifts Received: $1,200,000 (2001). Note: In 2001, contributions were received from Orlin Corp.

Typical Recipients
Arts & Humanities: Arts Appreciation, Arts Associations & Councils, Arts Centers, Arts Institutes, Community Arts, Dance, Historic Preservation, Libraries, Museums/Galleries, Music, Opera, Performing Arts, Public Broadcasting, Theater, Visual Arts
Civic & Public Affairs: African American Affairs, Business/Free Enterprise, Chambers of Commerce, Civil Rights, Economic Development, Economic Policy, Employment/Job Training, Civic & Public Affairs-General, Minority Business, Municipalities/Towns, Professional & Trade Associations, Public Policy, Urban & Community Affairs, Zoos/Aquariums
Education: Afterschool/Enrichment Programs, Business Education, Business-School Partnerships, Colleges & Universities, Community & Junior Colleges, Education Associations, Education Funds, Elementary Education (Public), Engineering/Technological Education, Environmental Education, Education-General, Literacy, Medical Education, Minority Education, Private Education (Precollege), Public Education (Precollege), Science/Mathematics Education, Secondary Education (Public), Student Aid, Vocational & Technical Education
Environment: Air/Water Quality, Environment-General, Protection, Resource Conservation, Wildlife Protection

Health: Cancer, Children's Health/Hospitals, Clinics/Medical Centers, Emergency/Ambulance Services, Geriatric Health, Health Funds, Health Organizations, Hospices, Hospitals, Medical Rehabilitation, Mental Health, Nursing Services, Public Health, Single-Disease Health Associations
International: Foreign Educational Institutions, International Affairs, International Development, International Environmental Issues
Religion: Religious Organizations
Science: Science Museums, Scientific Centers & Institutes
Social Services: At-Risk Youth, Community Centers, Community Service Organizations, Emergency Relief, Family Services, Food/Clothing Distribution, Scouts, Senior Services, Shelters/Homelessness, Special Olympics, Substance Abuse, United Funds/United Ways, Volunteer Services, YMCA/YWCA/YMHA/YWHA, Youth Organizations

Application Procedures
Initial Contact: Submit a one- or two-page letter.
Application Requirements: Provide a description of organization, amount requested, purpose of funds sought, recently audited financial statement, and proof of tax-exempt status.
Deadlines: None.
Review Process: The foundation conducts an initial review to determine relation to priorities, areas of interest, and geographic proximity
Decision Notification: Ongoing.

Restrictions
Foundation does not support loans, dinners or special events, fraternal organizations, goodwill advertising, individuals, political or lobbying groups, or religious organizations for sectarian purposes.
Does not provide general support to member agencies of united funds. May consider capital campaign support.

Corporate Officials
Donald Wayne Griffin: chairman, president, chief executive officer, director B Evansville, IN 1937. ED Syracuse University; Indiana University BA (1954-1957); University of Evansville BA (1961). CORP AFFIL director: Rayonier Timberlands LP; director: Riverbend Bancshares Inc.; director: Rayonier Forest Resources Co.; director: Rayonier Inc.; director: AC Nielsen Corp.; director: Illinois State Bank E Alton. NONPR AFFIL director: Southwest Illinois Industry Association; director: Wildlife Management Institute; director: Small Arms Ammunition Manufacturer; director: National Shooting Sports Foundation; life member: Navy League; member: Illinois Chamber of Commerce; director: Leadership Council Southwest Illinois; director: Buffalo Bill Historical Center; director: Chemical Manufacturers Association; member: American Society Metals; member: Association U.S. Army.
Peter C. Kosche: senior vice president corporate affairs PRIM CORP EMPL senior vice president corporate affairs: Olin Corp.
Anthony W. Ruggiero: executive vice president, chief financial officer ED Fordham University BS (1963); Columbia University MBA (1964). PRIM CORP EMPL executive vice president, chief financial officer: Olin Corp.

Foundation Officials
Donald Wayne Griffin: trustee (see above)
Peter C. Kosche: trustee (see above)
Carmella V. Piacentini: administrator

Grants Analysis
Disclosure Period: calendar year ending 2002
Total Grants: $362,613*
Number of Grants: 106
Average Grant: $3,421
Highest Grant: $40,000
Lowest Grant: $100
Typical Range: $1,000 to $5,000

*Note: Giving excludes matching gifts, scholarship, and United Way.

Recent Grants
Note: Grants derived from 2003 Form 990.
General

55,000	National Merit Scholarship Corporation, Charlotte, NC
40,599	Webster University, Charlotte, NC
30,000	Junior Achievement of Southwest Connecticut, Charlotte, NC
20,000	Naugatuck Valley Project, Charlotte, NC
9,808	University of Missouri-Rolla, Charlotte, NC
9,000	Webster University, Charlotte, NC
9,000	YMCA, Charlotte, NC
8,438	Yale-New Haven Hospital, Charlotte, NC
8,000	Boys Scout of America, Charlotte, NC
5,485	Washington County School Board, Charlotte, NC

JOHN M. OLIN FOUNDATION

Giving Contact
James Piereson, Executive Director
330 Madison Avenue, 22nd Floor
New York, NY 10017
Phone: (212)661-2670
Fax: (212)661-5917
E-mail: inquiry@jmof.org
Web: http://www.jmof.org

Description
Founded: 1953
EIN: 376031033
Organization Type: General Purpose Foundation
Giving Locations: internationally; nationally.
Grant Types: Conference/Seminar, Fellowship, General Support, Professorship, Project, Research.

Donor Information
Founder: The John M. Olin Foundation was established in 1953 by the late John Merrill Olin (1892-1982), an inventor, industrialist, conservationist, and philanthropist. "Mr. Olin was committed to the preservation of the principles of political and economic liberty as they have been expressed in American thought, institutions and practice."
In 1994, the foundation received a gift of $94 million from a trust created for John M. Olin's wife, Evelyn. Mrs. Olin died in 1993.

Financial Summary
Total Giving: $11,159,453 (2003); $17,062,603 (2002); $20,486,946 (2001). Note: 1997 Giving includes matching gifts ($7,411).
Assets: $43,073,482 (2003); $60,000,000 (2002 approx); $71,196,916 (2001)
Gifts Received: $50,000 (1996); $94,305,566 (1994); $120,000 (1993). Note: In 1990, the foundation's gift came from the Killgore Trusts. In January 1994, the foundation received $94 million from a trust created for John M. Olin's wife, Evelyn; Mrs. Olin died in 1993.

Typical Recipients
Arts & Humanities: Arts Appreciation, Arts Associations & Councils, Arts Funds, Film & Video, History & Archaeology, Libraries, Literary Arts, Museums/Galleries, Public Broadcasting
Civic & Public Affairs: Business/Free Enterprise, Civil Rights, Community Foundations, Economic Policy, Civic & Public Affairs-General, Law & Justice, Legal Aid, Professional & Trade Associations, Public Policy, Women's Affairs
Education: Arts/Humanities Education, Business

Education, Colleges & Universities, Continuing Education, Economic Education, Education Associations, Education Funds, Education Reform, Faculty Development, Education-General, International Exchange, International Studies, Journalism/Media Education, Legal Education, Social Sciences Education
Environment: Environment-General
Health: Health Policy/Cost Containment, Health Organizations, Single-Disease Health Associations
International: Foreign Educational Institutions, International Affairs, International Peace & Security Issues, International Relations
Religion: Jewish Causes, Social/Policy Issues
Science: Scientific Centers & Institutes
Social Services: Crime Prevention

Application Procedures
Review Process: Foundation will be closing in the next few years.

Restrictions
The foundation normally does not fund administrative overhead costs. In addition, grants will not be considered for endowment or building programs, annual giving programs, direct support for individuals, or programs without significant import for national affairs. Grants will be made only to institutions that provide a responsible fiscal agent and are tax-exempt under section 501(c)(3) of the Internal Revenue Code.

Additional Information
Publications: Annual Report

Foundation Officials
Peter Magnus Flanigan: trustee B New York, NY 1923. ED Princeton University BA (1947). CORP AFFIL director: Per Scholas Inc.; advisor: Warburg Dillon Read LLC.
George Joseph Gillespie, III: president, treasurer B New York, NY 1930. ED Georgetown University AB (1952); Harvard University LLB (1955). PRIM CORP EMPL partner: Cravath, Swaine & Moore. CORP AFFIL director: Washington Post Co. NONPR AFFIL director, chairman emeritus: National Multiple Sclerosis Society; trustee: New York University Medical Center; director: Madison Square Boys Club; secretary, director: Museum Television & Radio; member: Century Association; trustee, treasurer: Cooper-Hewitt National Design Museum. CLUB AFFIL Prouts Neck Country Club; Winged Foot Golf Club; member: Portland Country Club; Double Eagle Club; Falmouth Country Club; American Yacht Club.
Caroline M. Hemphill: director special programs, assistant secretary-treasurer
Charles Field Knight: trustee B Lake Forest, IL January 20, 1936. ED Cornell University BS (1958); Cornell University MBA (1959). CORP AFFIL director: Southwest Bell Corp.; director: Morgan Stanley Dean Witter Co.; director: SBC Communications Inc.; director: Caterpillar Inc.; director: IBM Corp.; director: Anheuser-Busch Companies Inc.; director: Baxter International Inc. NONPR AFFIL member: Sigma Phi Epsilon; director, trustee: Washington University; director: Arts & Education Council. CLUB AFFIL Log Cabin Club; Saint Louis Country Club; Crystal Downs Club; Glen View Golf Club; Chicago Club.
Eugene Flewellyn Williams, Jr.: chairman, trustee B Saint Louis, MO 1923. ED Yale University BA (1945).

Grants Analysis
Disclosure Period: calendar year ending 2003
Total Grants: $11,159,453
Number of Grants: 62
Average Grant: $165,155*
Highest Grant: $1,085,000
Lowest Grant: $1,500
Typical Range: $50,000 to $250,000
*Note: Average grant figure excludes highest grants.

Recent Grants
Note: Grants derived from 2002 Form 990.

General

750,000	Harvard University, Cambridge, MA -- towards law and economics
750,000	Harvard University, Cambridge, MA -- towards law economics and business
717,365	Yale University, New Haven, CT -- towards law and economics
691,945	Harvard University, Cambridge, MA -- towards strategic studies
400,000	Heritage Foundation, Washington, DC -- towards domestic policy studies and fellowship in political economy
400,000	Manhattan Institute for Policy Research, New York, NY -- towards fellowship for an initiative on America and the center for medical process
325,000	New York University, New York, NY -- towards the activities of the programs on education and civil society
305,000	Harvard University, Cambridge, MA -- towards education policy and governance
272,000	University of Rochester, Rochester, NY -- towards doctoral fellowship and program in competitive strategy
251,268	Stanford University, Stanford, CA -- towards program in law and Economics

SPENCER T. AND ANN W. OLIN FOUNDATION

Giving Contact
Warren M. Shapleigh, President
7701 Forsyth Boulevard, Suite 1040
St. Louis, MO 63105
Phone: (314)727-6202
Fax: (314)727-6157

Description
Founded: 1957
EIN: 376044148
Organization Type: General Purpose Foundation
Giving Locations: nationally.
Grant Types: Fellowship, General Support, Project, Research.

Donor Information
Founder: The foundation was established in 1957 by the late Ann W. Olin and Spencer T. Olin, and receives distributions from the S. Truman Olin Jr., Charitable Lead Trust and the Spencer T. Olin Charitable Lead Trust.

Financial Summary
Total Giving: $9,359,500 (2003); $8,578,915 (2002); $8,241,972 (2001)
Giving Analysis: Giving for 2003 includes: foundation grants to United Way ($25,000); 2002: foundation grants to United Way ($25,000); 2001: foundation grants to United Way ($25,000)
Assets: $12,839,553 (2003); $21,940,807 (2002); $32,562,550 (2001)
Gifts Received: $607,503 (2000); $2,276,490 (1998); $12,482,240 (1995). Note: Contributions were received from the Spencer T. Olin Charitable Lead Trust and the S. Truman Olin, Jr., Charitable Lead Trust.

Typical Recipients
Arts & Humanities: Arts Associations & Councils, Arts Centers, Arts Festivals, Arts Funds, Arts & Humanities-General, Historic Preservation, History & Archaeology, Libraries, Museums/Galleries, Music, Opera, Public Broadcasting, Theater
Civic & Public Affairs: African American Affairs, Botanical Gardens/Parks, Business/Free Enterprise, Community Foundations, Economic Development, Employment/Job Training, Civic & Public Affairs-

General, Nonprofit Management, Philanthropic Organizations, Professional & Trade Associations, Public Policy, Urban & Community Affairs, Women's Affairs, Zoos/Aquariums
Education: Afterschool/Enrichment Programs, Arts/Humanities Education, Business Education, Colleges & Universities, Community & Junior Colleges, Continuing Education, Economic Education, Education Associations, Education Funds, Education Reform, Elementary Education (Private), Engineering/Technological Education, Education-General, Gifted & Talented Programs, Leadership Training, Medical Education, Minority Education, Private Education (Precollege), Public Education (Precollege), Science/Mathematics Education, Secondary Education (Private), Special Education, Student Aid, Vocational & Technical Education
Environment: Energy, Environment-General, Protection, Resource Conservation, Wildlife Protection
Health: Alzheimer's Disease, Arthritis, Cancer, Clinics/Medical Centers, Emergency/Ambulance Services, Geriatric Health, Hospices, Hospitals, Medical Research, Nursing Services, Preventive Medicine/Wellness Organizations, Speech & Hearing
International: Foreign Educational Institutions, International Environmental Issues
Religion: Churches, Dioceses, Religious Organizations, Religious Welfare
Science: Science Museums, Scientific Centers & Institutes
Social Services: Animal Protection, Community Service Organizations, Day Care, Emergency Relief, Family Planning, Family Services, Food/Clothing Distribution, People with Disabilities, Recreation & Athletics, Shelters/Homelessness, Social Services-General, United Funds/United Ways, YMCA/YWCA/YMHA/YWHA, Youth Organizations

Application Procedures
Initial Contact: Applicants should send a brief letter to the foundation's president.
Application Requirements: The letter should include a brief description of the program or project for which funding is requested and the need for it; information about the total cost of the program or project; specific amount requested; list of other sources of funding and amount raised or expected to be secured; time frame in which the funds are to be expended; copy of the most recent financial statement with balance sheet and income and expense statement; and a copy of the IRS letter determining tax-exempt status.

Restrictions
The foundation reports that it is only considering proposals from those organizations where there is a history of past support; no new proposals are being accepted because of long term commitments, to which the foundation is attending in stages.
It is the general policy of the foundation not to make grants for endowment funds, deficit financing, or ordinary annual operating expenses; for secondary education, except in special cases and for projects where there is a history of past support; to provide funding for more than three consecutive years; to support projects which are substantially financed by public tax funds; to make grants to individuals or for individual scholarships; to fund conferences, seminars, workshops, travel, or exhibits; or to make grants to national health or welfare organizations, to churches for religious purposes, or to other private foundations or projects requiring expenditure responsibility.

Foundation Officials
Eunice O. Higgins: secretary, trustee
William W. Higgins: board member, trustee
Marquita L. Kunce: assistant treasurer
Rolla Mottaz: board member, trustee
John C. Pritzlaff, Jr.: board member, trustee
Mary O. Pritzlaff: vice president, trustee
Warren M. Shapleigh: president, trustee CORP AFFIL director: Barry-Wehmiller Group Inc.; director:

Midland Container Corp.
Barbara Olin Taylor: board member, trustee
F. Morgan Taylor, Jr.: board member, trustee
J. Lester Willemetz: board member, treasurer

Grants Analysis

Disclosure Period: calendar year ending 2003
Total Grants: $9,334,500*
Number of Grants: 42
Average Grant: $87,750*
Highest Grant: $2,000,000
Lowest Grant: $1,500
Typical Range: $25,000 to $200,000
*Note: Giving excludes United Way. Average grant excludes four highest grants ($6,000,000).

Recent Grants

Note: Grants derived from 2003 Form 990.
General

2,000,000	Smith College, Northampton, MA
2,000,000	Washington University, St. Louis, MO
1,000,000	Choate Rosemary Hall, Wallingford, CT
1,000,000	Hamden Hall Country Day School, Whitneyville, CT
600,000	Ohio Center for Effective Schools, Kent, OH
500,009	Deerfield Academy, Deerfield, MA
500,000	All Kinds of Minds, Chapel Hill, NC
500,000	Boys & Girls Club of Greenwich Inc., Greenwich, CT
327,684	Erie-Huron-Ottawa Educational Service Center, Sandusky, OH
300,000	Robert E. Lee Memorial Association, Stratford, VA

OLIVER MEMORIAL TRUST FOUNDATION

Giving Contact

Charles F. Nelson, Trust Officer and Vice President
c/o Wells Fargo Bank Indiana
112 W. 49th St., 14th Fl.
South Bend, IN 46601
Phone: (219)237-3475
Fax: (219)237-3317

Description

Founded: 1959
EIN: 356013076
Organization Type: Private Foundation
Giving Locations: IN: South Bend
Grant Types: Capital, Endowment, Multiyear/Continuing Support, Project, Seed Money.

Donor Information

Founder: the late C. Frederick Cunningham, Gertrude Oliver Cunningham, the late Walter C. Steenburg, Jane Cunningham Wanner, J. Oliver Cunningham

Financial Summary

Total Giving: $591,835 (2001)
Giving Analysis: Giving for 2001 includes: foundation grants to United Way ($11,000)
Assets: $11,518,224 (2001)
Gifts Received: $20,000 (2001); $20,017 (2000); $20,000 (1999). Note: In 2000, contributions were received from Jane Warriner. In 1999, contributions were received from Mr. and Mrs. J. Oliver Cunningham. In 1993, contributions were received from Jane C. Warriner ($25,000) and J. Oliver Cunningham ($25,000).

Typical Recipients

Arts & Humanities: Arts Associations & Councils, Arts Festivals, Community Arts, Dance, Historic Preservation, History & Archaeology, Libraries, Museums/Galleries, Music, Performing Arts
Civic & Public Affairs: Botanical Gardens/Parks, Civic & Public Affairs-General, Parades/Festivals, Zoos/Aquariums
Education: Business Education, Colleges & Universities, Education Associations, Education Funds, Journalism/Media Education, Medical Education, Minority Education, Religious Education, Student Aid
Health: Children's Health/Hospitals, Hospices, Hospitals, Medical Research
Religion: Churches, Ministries, Religious Organizations, Religious Welfare, Seminaries
Social Services: At-Risk Youth, Big Brothers/Big Sisters, Camps, Child Welfare, Community Service Organizations, People with Disabilities, Shelters/Homelessness, Social Services-General, United Funds/United Ways, YMCA/YWCA/YMHA/YWHA, Youth Organizations

Application Procedures

Initial Contact: Send a brief letter of inquiry.
Application Requirements: Include proof of tax-exempt status, purpose of funds sought, amount requested, what percent of the total cost the request is, and a breakdown of how the money will be spent.
Deadlines: None.

Restrictions

Does not support individuals or organizations outside operating areas.

Additional Information

Trust(s): Wells Fargo Bank NA

Grants Analysis

Disclosure Period: calendar year ending 2001
Total Grants: $580,835*
Number of Grants: 30
Average Grant: $17,595*
Highest Grant: $53,000
Typical Range: $5,000 to $30,000
*Note: Giving excludes United Way. Average grant figure excludes highest grant.

Recent Grants

Note: Grants derived from 2001 Form 990.
General

53,000	Camp Millhouse, South Bend, IN
50,000	Northern Indiana Historical Society, South Bend, IN
50,000	Notre Dame University, Notre Dame, IN
40,634	Northern Indiana Historical Society, South Bend, IN
40,634	Northern Indiana Historical Society, South Bend, IN
40,634	Northern Indiana Historical Society, South Bend, IN
40,634	Northern Indiana Historical Society, South Bend, IN
30,000	Potawatomi Zoological Society, South Bend, IN
25,000	Bethel College, South Bend, IN
25,000	Homeless Center, Notre Dame, IN

GEORGE AND CAROL OLMSTED FOUNDATION

Giving Contact

150 S. Washington Street, Suite 403
Falls Church, VA 22046
Phone: (703)536-3500
E-mail: scholars@olmstedfoundation.org
Web: http://www.olmstedfoundation.org

Description

Founded: 1960
EIN: 546049005
Organization Type: Private Foundation
Giving Locations: DC: Washington metropolitan area
Grant Types: General Support, Scholarship.

Donor Information

Founder: George Olmsted

Financial Summary

Total Giving: $1,636,639 (2003)
Giving Analysis: Giving for 2003 includes: foundation scholarships ($345,739)
Assets: $47,822,532 (2003)
Gifts Received: $7,000,000 (2000); $1,556,222 (1996); $153,067 (1995). Note: In 1996, contributions were received from the estate of Carol Olmsted.

Typical Recipients

Arts & Humanities: Historic Preservation, History & Archaeology, Libraries, Museums/Galleries
Education: Colleges & Universities, International Studies, Secondary Education (Private), Student Aid, Vocational & Technical Education
Social Services: Community Service Organizations, Scouts, Veterans, Youth Organizations

Application Procedures

Initial Contact: Grant requests must be initiated by a member of the board of director and approved by a majority of the members of the board.
Review Process: Board meets in January, April, July, and October.

Restrictions

Does not support individuals (except for Olmsted Scholars).

Additional Information

Provides educational grants for two years of graduate study and other educational experiences in a foreign country to three competitively selected career officers per year.
Publications: Annual Report

Foundation Officials

Rear Adm. Larry R. Marsh: director, president, chief executive officer
Joseph McManus, Esq.: secretary, treasurer
Brig. Gen. Bruce K. Scott: director
Adm. Carlisle Albert H. Trost: director, chairman B Valmeyer, IL 1930. ED Washington University (1948-1949); United States Naval Academy BS (1953); University of Freiberg (1960-1962). CORP AFFIL director: Louisiana Land & Exploration Co.; director: Precision Components Corp.; director: GPU Nuclear Corp.; director: Lockheed Martin Corp.; director: General Public Utility Corp.; director: Bird-Johnson Co.; director: General Dynamics Corp. NONPR AFFIL trustee, member: U.S. Naval Alumni Association; member: U.S. Naval Institute; trustee: U.S. Naval Academy Foundation.

Grants Analysis

Disclosure Period: calendar year ending 2003
Total Grants: $1,290,900*
Number of Grants: 12
Average Grant: $43,433*
Highest Grant: $300,000
Lowest Grant: $20,000
Typical Range: $25,000 to $50,000
*Note: Giving excludes scholarship. Average grant figure excludes three highest grants ($900,000).

Recent Grants

Note: Grants derived from 2003 Form 990.
General

300,000	U.S. Air Force Academy Association of Graduates, U.S. Air Force Academy, CO -- for tri-service academy program
300,000	US Military Academy, West Point, NY -- for tri-service academy program

300,000	US Naval Academy Alumni Association, Annapolis, MD -- for tri-service academy program
150,000	Saint James School, St. James, MD -- for construction of hollow way hall
50,000	National Capital Area Council Boy Scouts of America, Bethesda, MD -- for operation and maintenance of Camp Olmsted
50,000	U.S. Air Force Academy Association of Graduates, U.S. Air Force Academy, CO -- for Air Force ROTC overseas program
25,000	U.S. Air Force Academy Association of Graduates, U.S. Air Force Academy, CO -- for annual assembly
25,000	US Military Academy, West Point, NY -- for foreign affairs conference
25,000	US Military Academy, West Point, NY -- for construction of military heritage center
25,000	US Naval Academy Alumni Association, Annapolis, MD -- for foreign affairs conference

ELIS OLSSON MEMORIAL FOUNDATION

Giving Contact
Thelma Downey, Executive Director
PO Box 151
West Point, VA 23181
Phone: (804)843-9066
Fax: (804)843-9068

Description
Founded: 1966
EIN: 546062436
Organization Type: Family Foundation
Giving Locations: VA
Grant Types: Fellowship, General Support, Professorship.

Donor Information
Founder: Established in 1966 by the late Inga Olsson Nylander and the late Signe Maria Olsson.

Financial Summary
Total Giving: $1,008,000 (2003); $1,220,989 (2001)
Assets: $23,452,719 (2003); $25,752,783 (2001)
Gifts Received: $14,869 (2003); $20,330 (2001); $28,885 (2000). Note: In 1998, 2001, and 2003, contributions were received from The Sture Gordon Olsson Charitable Lead Unitrust.

Typical Recipients
Arts & Humanities: Arts Appreciation, Arts Associations & Councils, Arts Centers, Arts Festivals, Arts Institutes, Historic Preservation, History & Archaeology, Libraries, Literary Arts, Museums/Galleries, Performing Arts, Theater
Civic & Public Affairs: African American Affairs, Employment/Job Training, Civic & Public Affairs-General, Municipalities/Towns, Nonprofit Management, Philanthropic Organizations, Public Policy, Safety, Urban & Community Affairs, Zoos/Aquariums
Education: Agricultural Education, Arts/Humanities Education, Business Education, Colleges & Universities, Community & Junior Colleges, Education Associations, Education Funds, Elementary Education (Private), Engineering/Technological Education, Faculty Development, Education-General, Legal Education, Literacy, Medical Education, Minority Education, Private Education (Precollege), Religious Education, School Volunteerism, Science/Mathematics Education, Secondary Education (Private), Secondary Education (Public), Special Education, Student Aid, Vocational & Technical Education
Environment: Air/Water Quality, Forestry, Environment-General, Resource Conservation, Wildlife Pro-

tection
Health: Alzheimer's Disease, Cancer, Children's Health/Hospitals, Clinics/Medical Centers, Emergency/Ambulance Services, Health-General, Health Funds, Health Organizations, Heart, Home-Care Services, Hospices, Hospitals, Hospitals (University Affiliated), Long-Term Care, Medical Rehabilitation, Medical Research, Public Health, Research/Studies Institutes, Respiratory, Single-Disease Health Associations
International: Missionary/Religious Activities
Religion: Churches, Dioceses, Ministries, Religious Organizations, Religious Welfare, Seminaries
Science: Science Museums, Scientific Centers & Institutes
Social Services: Animal Protection, At-Risk Youth, Camps, Child Welfare, Community Service Organizations, Counseling, Day Care, Emergency Relief, Family Services, Food/Clothing Distribution, Homes, People with Disabilities, Scouts, Senior Services, Shelters/Homelessness, Social Services-General, Volunteer Services, Youth Organizations

Application Procedures
Initial Contact: The foundation requests applications be made in writing.
Application Requirements: Applications should be in written form and a copy of the organization's tax determination letter should be attached to the proposal. The foundation notes that the applicant's charitable purpose should be clearly stated.
Deadlines: None.

Restrictions
Grants are not made on individuals or political groups.

Foundation Officials
Thelma L. Downey: executive director
Shirley C. Olsson: vice president, trustee
Sture Gordon Olsson: chairman, director B Richmond, VA July 01, 1920. ED University of Virginia BS (1942). PRIM CORP EMPL chairman emeritus: Chesapeake Corp. CORP AFFIL director: Citizens & Farmers Bank. CLUB AFFIL West Point Country Club.

Grants Analysis
Disclosure Period: calendar year ending 2003
Total Grants: $1,008,000
Number of Grants: 85
Average Grant: $6,195*
Highest Grant: $200,000
Lowest Grant: $250
Typical Range: $1,000 to $15,000
*Note: Average grant figure excludes three highest grants ($500,000).

Recent Grants
Note: Grants derived from 2003 Form 990.
General

200,000	Diocese of Virginia, Richmond, VA
200,000	University of Virginia School of Engineering & Applied Science, Charlottesville, VA
100,000	National D Day Memorial Foundation, Bedford, VA
50,000	Virginia Historical Society, Richmond, VA
50,000	Virginia Institute of Marine Science, Gloucester Point, VA
25,000	Appomattox Regional Governors School for the Arts & Technology, Petersburg, VA
25,000	Christchurch School, Christchurch, VA
25,000	Foundation for Historic Christ Church, Irvington, VA
25,000	Walkerton Community Fire Association, Walkerton, VA
25,000	West Point Volunteer Fire Dept and Rescue Squad Inc., West Point, VA

ONE VALLEY BANK N.A.

Company Headquarters
7th St. & Avery St.
Parkersburg, WV 26101

Company Description
Employees: 1,600
SIC(s): 6022 State Commercial Banks.
Parent Company: One Valley Bancorp Inc.

One Valley Bank Foundation

Giving Contact
Michael W. Stajduhar, Senior Vice President
BB & T
PO Box 1793
Charleston, WV 25326
Phone: (304)348-7000

Description
EIN: 556017269
Organization Type: Corporate Foundation
Giving Locations: WV
Grant Types: General Support, Scholarship.

Financial Summary
Total Giving: $651,870 (2002); $581,600 (2001)
Giving Analysis: Giving for 2002 includes: foundation scholarships ($2,000); foundation grants to United Way ($93,000); 2001: foundation grants to United Way ($68,500)
Assets: $8,724,820 (2002); $10,728,155 (2001)
Gifts Received: $16,334 (2002); $10,083,253 (2001); $112,631 (2000). Note: Foundation is not required to attach Schedule B.

Typical Recipients
Arts & Humanities: Arts Associations & Councils, Arts Centers, Arts Festivals, Arts Funds, Arts & Humanities-General, History & Archaeology, Libraries, Museums/Galleries, Music, Public Broadcasting, Theater
Civic & Public Affairs: Business/Free Enterprise, Chambers of Commerce, Community Foundations, Economic Development, Employment/Job Training, Civic & Public Affairs-General, Housing, Parades/Festivals, Public Policy, Rural Affairs, Urban & Community Affairs, Women's Affairs
Education: Arts/Humanities Education, Business Education, Colleges & Universities, Economic Education, Education Associations, Education Funds, Education Reform, Elementary Education (Public), Education-General, Legal Education, Literacy, Medical Education, Public Education (Precollege), Science/Mathematics Education, Secondary Education (Public), Special Education, Student Aid
Health: Cancer, Children's Health/Hospitals, Clinics/Medical Centers, Health-General, Health Policy/Cost Containment, Health Funds, Health Organizations, Hospices, Hospitals, Preventive Medicine/Wellness Organizations, Research/Studies Institutes, Single-Disease Health Associations
Religion: Ministries, Religious Welfare
Science: Science Museums
Social Services: At-Risk Youth, Camps, Child Welfare, Community Centers, Community Service Organizations, Domestic Violence, Family Services, Food/Clothing Distribution, Homes, People with Disabilities, Recreation & Athletics, Scouts, Senior Services, Social Services-General, United Funds/United Ways, Volunteer Services, YMCA/YWCA/YMHA/YWHA, Youth Organizations

Application Procedures
Initial Contact: The foundation has no formal grant application procedure or application form.
Deadlines: None.

Restrictions
Does not support individuals. Foundation supports organizations in the state of West Virginia only.

Corporate Officials
Phyllis H. Arnold: president, chief executive officer, director B Parkersburg, WV 1948. ED West Virginia State University (1970); Marshall University (1976). PRIM CORP EMPL president, chief executive officer, director: One Valley Bank NA. NONPR AFFIL trustee: CAMCARE.
Frederick H. Belden, Jr.: executive vice president PRIM CORP EMPL executive vice president: One Valley Bancorp Inc.
Lloyd P. Calvert: senior vice president corporate committee B Charleston, WV 1936. ED Marshall University (1958); Rutgers University (1972). PRIM CORP EMPL senior vice president corporate committee: One Valley Bank NA.
J. Holmes Morrison: chairman, director PRIM CORP EMPL chairman, director: One Valley Bancorp of West Virginia.
Michael W. Stajduhar: senior vice president PRIM CORP EMPL senior vice president: One Valley Bank NA.

Foundation Officials
Phyllis H. Arnold: mem, trustee (see above)
Robert Francis Baronner: director B Hollidaysburg, PA 1926. ED Saint Francis College BS (1950); University of Wisconsin (1958). PRIM CORP EMPL chairman: One Valley Bancorp Inc. ADD CORP EMPL director: One Valley Bnk NA. CLUB AFFIL Rotary Club.
Frederick H. Belden, Jr.: mem, trustee (see above)
Lloyd P. Calvert: member, trustee (see above)
Nelle Ratrie Chilton: member, trustee
J. Holmes Morrison: mem, trustee (see above)
John L. D. Payne: mem, trustee
Brent Robinson: member, trustee
Steven M. Rubin: member, trustee
K. Richard C. Sinclair: mem, trustee
Michael W. Stajduhar: mem (see above)
Edwin H. Welch: member, trustee
Thomas D. Wilkerson: mem, trustee
John Williams: member, trustee

Grants Analysis
Disclosure Period: calendar year ending 2002
Total Grants: $556,870*
Number of Grants: 100
Average Grant: $3,694*
Highest Grant: $74,000
Lowest Grant: $500
Typical Range: $1,000 to $10,000
*Note:** Giving excludes United Way; scholarship. Average grant figure excludes three highest grants.

Recent Grants
Note: Grants derived from 2003 Form 990.
Library-Related
5,000	Rockbridge Regional Library, Lexington, WV

General
83,000	West Virginia Independent Colleges & Universities, Charleston, WV
44,100	United Way of Kanawha Valley, Charleston, WV
30,000	BIDCO, Charleston, WV
25,000	Funds for the Arts, Charleston, WV
20,000	Avampato Discovery Museum Foundation, Charleston, WV
16,000	Covenant House, Charleston, WV
14,000	Charleston Renaissance Corp, Charleston, WV
13,880	CAMC Foundation, Charleston, WV

11,000	RCCR, Charleston, WV
11,000	United Way of Berkeley/Morgan Counties, Martinsburg, WV

ONEIDA SAVINGS BANK

Company Headquarters
182 Main Street
Oneida, NY 13421-0240
Web: http://www.oneidabank.com

Company Description
Founded: 1866
SIC(s): 6036 Savings Institutions Except Federal.
Parent Company: Oneida Financial Corp., 182 Main St., Oneida, NY, United States

Oneida Savings Bank Charitable Foundation

Giving Contact
Eric Stickels
PO Box 240
182 Main Street
Oneida, NY 13421-0240
Phone: (315)363-2000

Description
Founded: 1999
EIN: 161561680
Organization Type: Corporate Foundation
Giving Locations: principally near operating locations and to national organizations.
Grant Types: General Support.

Financial Summary
Total Giving: $53,635 (2001)
Assets: $1,583,190 (2001)
Gifts Received: $801,620 (1998). Note: In 1998, contributions were received from Oneida Financial Corp.

Typical Recipients
Arts & Humanities: Libraries
Civic & Public Affairs: Clubs, Civic & Public Affairs-General, Safety
Education: Student Aid
Social Services: Camps, Family Services, Recreation & Athletics, Senior Services

Application Procedures
Initial Contact: Submit a letter of request.
Deadlines: None.

Foundation Officials
Thomas H. Dixon: director
Michael R. Kallet: president
William Matthews: director
Ann K. Pierz: director
Eric E. Stickels: treasurer, secretary

Grants Analysis
Disclosure Period: calendar year ending 2001
Total Grants: $53,635
Number of Grants: 13
Average Grant: $2,683*
Highest Grant: $21,435
Lowest Grant: $500
Typical Range: $1,000 to $10,000
*Note:** Average grant figure excludes highest grant.

Recent Grants
Note: Grants derived from 2001 Form 990.
Library-Related
10,000	Hamilton Public Library, Hamilton, NY -- building fund

General
21,435	Madison County Chapter of NYSARC
4,000	CAP
4,000	Orchard Hill Club of the Oneida Healthcare Center, Oneida, NY
3,000	Camden Soccer Club
2,500	Madison County Children's Camp
2,200	Oneida Fireman's Benevolent Association Grant, Oneida, NY
2,000	Camden Rotary Club Grant
1,000	Canastota Dollars for Scholars
1,000	Madison Family Outreach
1,000	Mid-York Senior Homes, Inc., Utica, NY

ONTARIO CORP.

Company Headquarters
123 E. Adams St.
Muncie, IN 47305
Web: http://www.muncieontheweb.com

Company Description
Employees: 612
SIC(s): 3700 Transportation Equipment, 3800 Instruments & Related Products.

Nonmonetary Support
Type: Donated Equipment; In-kind Services; Loaned Employees; Loaned Executives; Workplace Solicitation

Ontario Corp. Foundation

Giving Contact
Ruth Kiger
Ontario Corp. Foundation
123 East Adams Street
Muncie, IN 47305
Phone: (765)747-9001
Fax: (765)747-0331

Description
EIN: 310991589
Organization Type: Corporate Foundation
Giving Locations: IN
Grant Types: Award, Capital, Challenge, Employee Matching Gifts, Endowment, General Support, Multiyear/Continuing Support, Operating Expenses, Project, Scholarship, Seed Money.

Financial Summary
Total Giving: $290,133 (fiscal year ending June 30, 2004); $326,839 (fiscal 2003); $142,550 (fiscal 2001)
Giving Analysis: Giving for fiscal 2004 includes: foundation grants to United Way ($14,883); fiscal 2001: foundation grants to United Way ($9,500)
Assets: $172,515 (fiscal 2004); $415,529 (fiscal 2003); $1,138,318 (fiscal 2001)
Gifts Received: $5,000 (fiscal 2003); $85,000 (fiscal 2001); $199,298 (fiscal 1998)

Typical Recipients
Arts & Humanities: Arts Associations & Councils, Arts Centers, Arts Festivals, Arts Funds, Community Arts, Arts & Humanities-General, History & Archaeology, Libraries, Museums/Galleries, Music, Performing Arts, Public Broadcasting, Theater
Civic & Public Affairs: Business/Free Enterprise, Chambers of Commerce, Community Foundations, Economic Development, Economic Policy, Civic & Public Affairs-General, Housing, Professional & Trade Associations, Public Policy, Zoos/Aquariums
Education: Afterschool/Enrichment Programs, Arts/Humanities Education, Business Education, Business-School Partnerships, Colleges & Universities,

Community & Junior Colleges, Economic Education, Education Associations, Education Funds, Engineering/Technological Education, Education-General, Minority Education, Private Education (Precollege), Science/Mathematics Education, Secondary Education (Private), Secondary Education (Public), Vocational & Technical Education

Environment: Environment-General, Resource Conservation

Health: Health-General, Health Organizations, Heart, Hospitals

Religion: Ministries, Religious Organizations, Religious Welfare, Seminaries

Science: Science Exhibits & Fairs

Social Services: At-Risk Youth, Big Brothers/Big Sisters, Family Services, Recreation & Athletics, Scouts, Social Services-General, Special Olympics, United Funds/United Ways, Volunteer Services, YMCA/YWCA/YMHA/YWHA, Youth Organizations

Application Procedures

Initial Contact: The foundation has no formal grant application procedure or application form.
Deadlines: None.

Restrictions

Does not support individuals or political or lobbying groups.

Corporate Officials

John W. Martin: chief financial officer PRIM CORP EMPL chief financial officer: Ontario Corp.

Van P. Smith: chairman B Oneida, NY 1928. ED Colgate University (1950); Georgetown University Law Center (1955). PRIM CORP EMPL chairman: Ontario Corp. CORP AFFIL partner: Village Developers; director: Standard Locknut & Lockwasher; director: Summit Bank Muncie; partner: Smitties Mens Store; chairman: Pyromet Industries; chairman: Sherry Laboratories; chairman: Pyromet Corp.; chairman: Pyromet Enterprises; director: PSI Resources; chairman: Pyromet; director: Ontario Tech; director: PSI Energy; chairman: Ontario Forge Corp.; chairman: Ontario System Corp.; chairman: Ontario Development Corp.; chairman: Ontario Environmental; director: Meridian Mutual Insurance Co.; chairman: Metlab Testing Services; director: Maxon Corp.; chairman: James Laboratories; director: Lilly Industries; director: Duland Toll & Engineering; director: NG Gilbert Corp.; director: Dalton Foundries Inc.; partner: DE Aviation; vice chairman, director: AAA Hoosier Motor Club & Affiliated Companies; chairman: CDS Engineering. NONPR AFFIL member: Theta Chi; director: U.S. Chamber of Commerce; director: Newman Foundation Indiana; member: W. W. Rich Foundation; director: Muncie Symphony Association; director: National Advisory Council Small Business Administration; trustee: Interlochen Center Arts; trustee: La Lumiere School; director: Indiana Labor & Management Council; director: Indiana Manufacturers Association; director: Indiana Commission Higher Education; director: Indiana Economic Develop Council; member: Indiana Bar Association; director: Indiana Chamber of Commerce; director: Governments Fiscal Policy Advisory Council; member: Delta Theta Phi; member: Forging Industry Association; trustee: Colgate University; director: Delta Sigma Pi; director: Business-Industry Political Action Committee; trustee: Catholic University America; member: American Bar Association; member: Beta Gamma Sigma; director: Alliance Metalworking Industry; director: American Automobile Association; trustee: Academy Community Leadership. CLUB AFFIL Rotary International Club; Skyline Club; Knights of Columbus; Meridian Hills Country Club; Elks Club; In Society Chicago Club; Columbia Club.

Mr. Kelly N. Stanley: president, chief executive officer PRIM CORP EMPL president, chief executive officer: Ontario Corp.

Foundation Officials

Jan P. Abbs: secretary
Ronald K. Fauquher: vice president
John W. Martin: treasurer (see above)
Mark C. Smith: president
Van P. Smith: chairman (see above)
Mr. Kelly N. Stanley: vice president (see above)

Grants Analysis

Disclosure Period: fiscal year ending June 30, 2003
Total Grants: $295,005*
Number of Grants: 36
Average Grant: $3,208*
Highest Grant: $50,000
Lowest Grant: $500
Typical Range: $1,000 to $5,000
*****Note:** Giving excludes United Way and miscellaneous grants totaling ($3,825). Average grant figure excludes four highest grants ($192,350).

Recent Grants

Note: Grants derived from fiscal 2004 Form 990.
General

100,000	Ball State Foundation, Muncie, IN
80,000	Ball Memorial Hospital, Muncie, IN
60,000	Pope John Paul II Cultural Center, Washington, DC
14,883	United Way of Delaware County, Muncie, IN
10,000	Cardinal Greenway, Muncie, IN
10,000	Motivate Our Minds, Muncie, IN
8,750	Muncie Boys and Girls Club, Muncie, IN
5,000	Indiana Information Technology Association, Indianapolis, IN
1,000	Delaware Advancement Corporation, Muncie, IN

OPPENSTEIN BROTHERS FOUNDATION

Giving Contact

Sheila K. Rice, Program Officer
PO Box 13095
Kansas City, MO 64199-3095
Phone: (816)234-8671
Fax: (816)234-8690

Description

Founded: 1975
EIN: 436203035
Organization Type: General Purpose Foundation
Giving Locations: MO: Kansas City metropolitan area
Grant Types: Capital, Challenge, Conference/Seminar, Department, Emergency, General Support, Operating Expenses, Project, Seed Money.
Note: Metropolitan Kansas City area only.

Donor Information

Founder: Established in 1975 by the late Michael Oppenstein.

The Oppenstein brothers --Louis, Sam, Harry, and Michael-- moved from Denver, CO, to Kansas City, MO, in 1902. In Kansas City, they opened a jewelry store, which they eventually sold to begin business activities directed toward investments in downtown real estate.

All four brothers were active in community affairs.

Financial Summary

Total Giving: $1,532,700 (fiscal year ending March 31, 2002); $32,109,166 (fiscal 2001)
Assets: $31,353,648 (fiscal 2002)

Typical Recipients

Arts & Humanities: Arts Associations & Councils, Arts Funds, Arts Institutes, Arts Outreach, Ballet, Dance, Libraries, Museums/Galleries, Music, Opera, Performing Arts, Public Broadcasting, Theater

Civic & Public Affairs: Clubs, Community Foundations, Economic Development, Ethnic Organizations, Civic & Public Affairs-General, Hispanic Affairs, Housing, Philanthropic Organizations, Professional & Trade Associations, Safety, Urban & Community Affairs, Women's Affairs, Zoos/Aquariums

Education: Colleges & Universities, Community & Junior Colleges, Economic Education, Education Funds, Education-General, Gifted & Talented Programs, Private Education (Precollege), Public Education (Precollege), Science/Mathematics Education, Special Education, Vocational & Technical Education

Environment: Environment-General

Health: AIDS/HIV, Alzheimer's Disease, Cancer, Children's Health/Hospitals, Clinics/Medical Centers, Emergency/Ambulance Services, Eyes/Blindness, Health Organizations, Heart, Hospices, Hospitals, Medical Rehabilitation, Mental Health, Prenatal Health Issues, Public Health, Single-Disease Health Associations, Transplant Networks/Donor Banks

International: International Relations

Religion: Jewish Causes, Ministries, Religious Organizations, Religious Welfare

Science: Scientific Centers & Institutes

Social Services: At-Risk Youth, Big Brothers/Big Sisters, Camps, Child Abuse, Child Welfare, Community Centers, Community Service Organizations, Counseling, Day Care, Domestic Violence, Family Planning, Family Services, Food/Clothing Distribution, Homes, People with Disabilities, Recreation & Athletics, Scouts, Senior Services, Sexual Abuse, Shelters/Homelessness, Social Services-General, Substance Abuse, United Funds/United Ways, Volunteer Services, YMCA/YWCA/YMHA/YWHA, Youth Organizations

Application Procedures

Initial Contact: The foundation requests applications be made in writing. Guidelines are available upon request.

Application Requirements: Before submitting a proposal to the disbursement committee, current background information must be submitted including: agency name, address, phone number and contact person; agency mission statement and brief history; list of board of directors, the number giving financial support and their aggregate support; number of full and part time staff and volunteers, and the hours they serve; most recent audited financial statement and current statement of income and expenses; budget for the coming year; and a copy of the IRS tax determination letter and agency's EIN. Additional information is needed when submitting a full proposal; refer to guidelines pamphlet for specifics.

Deadlines: Proposals must be submitted three weeks prior to a board meeting.

Review Process: The board generally meets every other month. Decisions are made within two to four months.

Restrictions

The foundation does not give to individuals, medical research, annual campaigns, building funds, scholarships, fellowships, medical equipment, endowment funds, or loans. Grants will be made only to agencies that provide direct services in the Kansas City metropolitan area for religious, charitable, scientific, and educational purposes.

Additional Information

Grants for significant improvements in quality or quantity of services will be favored over grants for deficit financing.

Publications: Informational Brochure (including Application Guidelines)

Foundation Officials

Mary Bloch: member disbursement committee
Laura Kemper Fields: mem disbursement comm
Roger T. Hurwitz: mem disbursement comm

John A. Morgan: chairman disbursement comm
Sheila K. Rice: program officer NONPR AFFIL finance director: YMCA Springfield Missouri.

Grants Analysis

Disclosure Period: fiscal year ending March 31, 2002
Total Grants: $1,532,700*
Number of Grants: 87
Average Grant: $17,617
Typical Range: $1,000 to $400,000
*Note: Grants analysis provided by foundation.

Recent Grants

Note: Grants derived from 2002 Form 990.
Library-Related

200,000	Nelson Gallery Foundation, Kansas City, MO
200,000	Nelson Gallery Foundation, Kansas City, MO

General

60,000	Children's Mercy Hospital, Kansas City, MO
50,000	Guadalupe Center Inc., Kansas City, MO
50,000	Jewish Federation of Greater Kansas City, Overland Park, KS
50,000	Jewish Federation of Greater Kansas City, Overland Park, KS
45,000	Kansas City Friends of Alvin Ailey, Kansas City, MO
30,000	Kansas City Chapter of Young Audiences Inc, Kansas City, MO
30,000	Missouri Repertory Theatre Inc, Kansas City, MO
30,000	Union Station Kansas City Inc, Kansas City, MO
25,000	Central City School Fund, Kansas City, MO
25,000	Charter School Partnership Fund, Kansas City, MO

JOHN M. O'QUINN FOUNDATION

Giving Contact

John M. O'Quinn, President
440 Louisiana
Houston, TX 77002
Phone: (713)236-2659

Description

Founded: 1986
EIN: 760206844
Organization Type: Private Foundation
Giving Locations: TX
Grant Types: General Support.

Donor Information

Founder: John M. O'Quinn

Financial Summary

Total Giving: $4,546,320 (2003)
Assets: $30,954,624 (2003)
Gifts Received: $2,636,843 (2003); $15,000,000 (1995); $8,429,788 (1994). Note: In 1995 and 2003, contributions were received from John M. O'Quinn.

Typical Recipients

Arts & Humanities: Ballet, Libraries, Museums/Galleries, Opera, Public Broadcasting, Theater
Civic & Public Affairs: African American Affairs, Botanical Gardens/Parks, Civil Rights, Clubs, Civic & Public Affairs-General, Housing, Law & Justice, Legal Aid, Municipalities/Towns, Public Policy, Safety, Urban & Community Affairs, Women's Affairs
Education: Agricultural Education, Arts/Humanities Education, Colleges & Universities, Continuing Edu-

cation, Education Funds, Elementary Education (Public), Engineering/Technological Education, Education-General, International Studies, Legal Education, Medical Education, Minority Education, Private Education (Precollege), Public Education (Precollege), School Volunteerism, Secondary Education (Private), Student Aid
Environment: Environment-General, Resource Conservation
Health: AIDS/HIV, Cancer, Children's Health/Hospitals, Clinics/Medical Centers, Diabetes, Health Organizations, Heart, Hospitals, Kidney, Multiple Sclerosis, Prenatal Health Issues, Public Health, Respiratory, Single-Disease Health Associations
International: International Relief Efforts
Religion: Churches, Jewish Causes, Ministries, Religious Welfare
Science: Science Museums
Social Services: Animal Protection, Child Abuse, Child Welfare, Community Centers, Community Service Organizations, Crime Prevention, Domestic Violence, Family Planning, Food/Clothing Distribution, People with Disabilities, Recreation & Athletics, Scouts, Senior Services, Social Services-General, Substance Abuse, Youth Organizations

Application Procedures

Initial Contact: The foundation has no formal grant application procedure or application form.
Deadlines: None.

Foundation Officials

Robert A. Higley: secretary, treasurer
John M. O'Quinn: president B 1941. ED Rice University; University of Houston BS (1965); University of Houston JD (1967). PRIM CORP EMPL partner: O'Quinn, Kerensky & McAninch. NONPR AFFIL director: University Houston Law Alumni Association; trustee: University Houston Law Foundation; member: Texas Bar Association; director: Texas Trial Lawyers Association; director: Houston Trial Lawyers Association; trustee: Regent University; director: American Trial Lawyers Association.

Grants Analysis

Disclosure Period: calendar year ending 2003
Total Grants: $4,546,320
Number of Grants: 20
Average Grant: $51,184*
Highest Grant: $2,625,000
Lowest Grant: $4,000
Typical Range: $20,000 to $100,000
*Note: Average grant figure excludes two highest grants ($3,625,000).

Recent Grants

Note: Grants derived from 2003 Form 990.

General

2,625,000	Children's Assessment Center Foundation, Houston, TX
1,000,000	Texas Heart Institute, Houston, TX
220,000	Houston Area Women's Center, Houston, TX
150,000	MD Anderson Center, Houston, TX
97,800	University of Houston Law Foundation, Houston, TX
80,000	Business Assessment Group, Houston, TX
72,300	South Texas College of Law, Houston, TX
67,000	University of Houston, Houston, TX
50,000	Baylor College of Medicine, Houston, TX
50,000	Houston Athletics Foundation, Houston, TX

ORCHARD FOUNDATION

Giving Contact

M. Gordon Erlich, Trustee
Bingham McCutchen, LLP
PO Box 2587
South Portland, ME 04116
Phone: (207)799-0686
E-mail: orchard@maine.rr.com
Web: http://www.orchardfoundation.org

Description

Founded: 1991
EIN: 046660214
Organization Type: Private Foundation
Giving Locations: NY: New England area.
Grant Types: Award, Capital, General Support, Multiyear/Continuing Support, Operating Expenses, Project, Seed Money.

Financial Summary

Total Giving: $924,202 (2002); $939,027 (2001). Note: Contributes through foundation only.
Assets: $11,366,770 (2002); $13,647,021 (2001)
Gifts Received: $700,000 (2002); $2,981,162 (2001); $1,049,573 (2000). Note: In 2002, contributions were received from Leigh Fibers Holdings, Inc. and Leigh Fibers, Inc.

Typical Recipients

Arts & Humanities: Arts Associations & Councils, Arts Centers, Arts Festivals, Film & Video, Arts & Humanities-General, Historic Preservation, History & Archaeology, Libraries, Museums/Galleries, Music, Public Broadcasting
Civic & Public Affairs: Community Foundations, Economic Development, Economic Policy, Employment/Job Training, Civic & Public Affairs-General, Hispanic Affairs, Native American Affairs, Philanthropic Organizations, Public Policy, Women's Affairs
Education: Arts/Humanities Education, Business Education, Colleges & Universities, Community & Junior Colleges, Education Funds, Engineering/Technological Education, Environmental Education, Education-General, International Studies, Literacy, Medical Education, Minority Education, Private Education (Precollege), Public Education (Precollege), Science/Mathematics Education, Secondary Education (Private), Student Aid, Vocational & Technical Education
Environment: Air/Water Quality, Forestry, Environment-General, Protection, Resource Conservation, Watershed, Wildlife Protection
Health: AIDS/HIV, Alzheimer's Disease, Arthritis, Children's Health/Hospitals, Clinics/Medical Centers, Health Funds, Hospices, Hospitals, Medical Research, Multiple Sclerosis, Nursing Services, Outpatient Health Care, Respiratory
International: Health Care/Hospitals, International Development, International Environmental Issues, International Organizations, International Relief Efforts
Religion: Churches, Dioceses, Religious Organizations, Religious Welfare
Science: Scientific Centers & Institutes, Scientific Research
Social Services: Camps, Child Abuse, Child Welfare, Community Centers, Community Service Organizations, Counseling, Crime Prevention, Delinquency & Criminal Rehabilitation, Domestic Violence, Family Planning, Family Services, People with Disabilities, Senior Services, Shelters/Homelessness, Social Services-General, Youth Organizations

Application Procedures

Initial Contact: See foundation website for application procedures, then send a one-page concept letter via fax or e-mail.
Application Requirements: Concept letters should include a description of organization and its history, project title, goal, means for accomplishing goal, and

anticipated result. Include the total organization budget, total project budget, and amount requested. Ensure that the letter includes a contact name, address, phone number, e-mail address, and organizational website address (if applicable). Do not send material in plastic covers or binders. Videos and cassettes will not be accepted.

Deadlines: Applications must be postmarked by March 1 and September 1.

Notes: If the foundation is interested in a project described in the concept letter, it will request a four-page proposal. Grantees must file progress reports with the foundation.

Restrictions

Grants are not made to individuals, endowments, annual or capital campaigns, museums, religious programs or religion-affiliated organizations, conference participation/travel unrelated to current foundation grant, scholarships, fellowships, equipment needs, film and video projects, building projects, or loans.

Additional Information

The foundation office is staffed by a part-time executive director and is closed for most of June, July and August. The foundation encourages potential applicants to leave messages and reports that all phone or e-mail messages will be answered in time.

Publications: Proposal Guidelines

Corporate Officials

Carl P. Lehner: president, chief executive officer ED Amherst College. PRIM CORP EMPL president, chief executive officer: Leigh Fibers, Inc.

Philip Lehner: chairman B 1924. ED Harvard College. PRIM CORP EMPL chairman: Leigh Fibers, Inc.

Foundation Officials

Carl P. Lehner: trustee (see above)
Philip Lehner: trustee (see above)

Grants Analysis

Disclosure Period: calendar year ending 2002
Total Grants: $924,202
Number of Grants: 103
Average Grant: $8,160*
Highest Grant: $50,000
Lowest Grant: $100
Typical Range: $3,000 to $15,000
***Note:** Average grant does not include two highest grants of $50,000 each.

Recent Grants

Note: Grants derived from 2002 Form 990.
General

50,000	Harvard University, Cambridge, VA -- for capital campaign
50,000	Smith College Alumnae Fund, Northampton, MA -- for 50th reunion year gift
30,000	Massachusetts Institute of Technology, Cambridge, MA -- for Mechanical Engineering Department
30,000	Vermont Public Interest Research Group Education Fund, Montpelier, VT -- Vermont Democracy Project
25,000	Miss, Inc., Stuart, FL -- for operating support
25,000	Well School, Peterborough, NH -- for operating support
25,000	Well School, Peterborough, NH -- for operating support
20,000	Friends of the Earth, Burlington, VT -- for Environmental Enforcement Watchdog Project
20,000	Lahey Clinic Foundation, Burlington, MA -- Institute of Urology
20,000	Zamorano, Washington, DC -- support Escuela Agricola Panamericana Zamorano

ORE-IDA FOODS

Company Headquarters
345 Bobwhite Ct.
Boise, ID 83706

Company Description
Employees: 5,600
SIC(s): 2037 Frozen Fruits & Vegetables, 2038 Frozen Specialties Nec.
Parent Company: H.J. Heinz Co., 600 Grant Street, Pittsburgh, PA, United States

Operating Locations
Ore-Ida Foods (OR; WI)

Nonmonetary Support
Type: Donated Equipment; Donated Products; In-kind Services

H. J. Heinz Co. Foundation

Giving Contact
Tammy Aupperle, Program Directory
PO Box 185
Pittsburgh, PA 15230-9897
Phone: (412)234-5255
E-mail: heinz.foundation@hjheinz.com
Web: http://www.heinz.com/jsp/foundation.jsp

Description
EIN: 300055087
Organization Type: Corporate Foundation
Giving Locations: headquarters and operating communities.
Grant Types: Capital, Conference/Seminar, Employee Matching Gifts, Endowment, General Support, Scholarship.

Financial Summary
Total Giving: $4,971,938 (fiscal year ending April 30, 2004); $575,623 (fiscal 2003); $5,835,996 (fiscal 2002)
Giving Analysis: Giving for fiscal 2004 includes: foundation matching gifts ($600,880); foundation ($4,371,058); fiscal 2003: foundation ($161,152); foundation matching gifts ($414,470); fiscal 2001: foundation grants to United Way ($818,500); foundation matching gifts ($1,164,766)
Assets: $1,515,610 (fiscal 2004); $1,530,801 (fiscal 2003); $1,530,801 (fiscal 2002)
Gifts Received: $6,000,000 (fiscal 2004); $6,000,000 (fiscal 2001); $6,000,000 (fiscal 1998).
Note: In 2001, contributions were received from H.J. Heinz Co.

Typical Recipients
Arts & Humanities: Arts Associations & Councils, Arts Funds, Dance, Arts & Humanities-General, Libraries, Museums/Galleries, Music, Opera, Performing Arts, Public Broadcasting, Theater
Civic & Public Affairs: African American Affairs, Economic Development, Civic & Public Affairs-General, Philanthropic Organizations
Education: Agricultural Education, Arts/Humanities Education, Business Education, Colleges & Universities, Education Funds, Elementary Education (Private), Environmental Education, Education-General, Literacy, Medical Education, Minority Education, Preschool Education, Private Education (Precollege), Public Education (Precollege), Student Aid
Environment: Resource Conservation
Health: Children's Health/Hospitals, Clinics/Medical Centers, Health Funds, Health Organizations, Hospitals, Nutrition
International: Foreign Educational Institutions, International Environmental Issues

Religion: Religious Organizations
Science: Science-General
Social Services: Animal Protection, Child Welfare, Day Care, Family Services, Food/Clothing Distribution, People with Disabilities, Shelters/Homelessness, United Funds/United Ways, Volunteer Services, Youth Organizations

Application Procedures
Initial Contact: Send a brief letter of inquiry.
Application Requirements: Include program information that describes purposes/goals of the organization, plans for current year, and summary of previous year's programs/projects; the specific purpose for funds being requested; how program/project objectives will be accomplished; two whom and where the program will be offered, including populations and/or geographic areas; how the project will be sustained after the grant ends. Policy decisions should include the type of governing structure, including the names of those on the governing board; a brief description of the major decisions over the last year affecting policy, goals, finances, etc. by the governing body. Provide the following financial and tax information: copy of current sources of income and expense (annual budget), copy of project budget related to proposed grant, copy of 501(c)(3) letter; the impact of the proposed program; indicate the extent to which Heinz employees, retirees, or directors are involved with the organization and any volunteer opportunities available within the organization.

Restrictions
Does not support individuals, religious organizations for sectarian purposes, or political or lobbying groups.

Additional Information
Company gives through its parent company's foundation, the Heinz Foundation. Profile reflects Ore-Ida's priorities.
Trust(s): Mellon Bank

Corporate Officials
Richard M. Wamhoff: president, chief executive officer, director PRIM CORP EMPL president, chief executive officer, director: Ore-Ida Foods.

Grants Analysis
Disclosure Period: fiscal year ending April 30, 2004
Total Grants: $4,971,938*
Number of Grants: 544
Average Grant: $7,315*
Highest Grant: $1,000,000
Typical Range: $500 to $5,000 and $10,000 to $50,000
***Note:** Giving includes matching gifts. Average grant excludes highest grant.

Recent Grants
Note: Grants derived from fiscal 2003 Form 990.
General

300,000	American Ireland Fund, Boston, MA -- for scholarship fund - O'Reilly family fund
100,000	American Ireland Fund, Boston, MA -- grant for chair in institute for neuroscience at Trinity college
14,471	H. J. Heinz Company, Pittsburgh, PA

EDWARD B. OSBORN CHARITABLE TRUST

Giving Contact
Gloria M. Osborn, Trustee
c/o US Trust Co. of New York
114 W. 47th St.
New York, NY 10036
Phone: (212)852-1000

Description

Founded: 1961
EIN: 136071296
Organization Type: Private Foundation
Giving Locations: FL; NY
Grant Types: General Support.

Donor Information

Founder: Edward B. Osborn

Financial Summary

Total Giving: $415,600 (fiscal year ending October 31, 2001)
Giving Analysis: Giving for fiscal 2001 includes: foundation grants to United Way ($1,000)
Assets: $7,303,416 (fiscal 2001)
Gifts Received: $1,474 (fiscal 1994)

Typical Recipients

Arts & Humanities: Arts Associations & Councils, Arts Centers, Ballet, Dance, Historic Preservation, Libraries, Museums/Galleries, Music, Opera, Performing Arts, Public Broadcasting, Theater
Civic & Public Affairs: Botanical Gardens/Parks, Employment/Job Training, Civic & Public Affairs-General, Urban & Community Affairs, Women's Affairs, Zoos/Aquariums
Education: Colleges & Universities, Education-General, Private Education (Precollege)
Environment: Air/Water Quality, Environment-General, Resource Conservation
Health: Alzheimer's Disease, Cancer, Clinics/Medical Centers, Diabetes, Heart, Hospices, Hospitals, Medical Research, Nursing Services, Single-Disease Health Associations
International: International Relations
Religion: Churches
Social Services: Community Service Organizations, Family Planning, Food/Clothing Distribution, People with Disabilities, Recreation & Athletics, Substance Abuse, Veterans, Youth Organizations

Application Procedures

Initial Contact: Send a brief letter of inquiry.
Application Requirements: Include a description of organization.
Deadlines: None.

Additional Information

Trust(s): US Trust Co NY

Grants Analysis

Disclosure Period: fiscal year ending October 31, 2001
Total Grants: $411,600*
Number of Grants: 49
Average Grant: $5,904*
Highest Grant: $50,000
Lowest Grant: $300
Typical Range: $1,000 to $10,000
*Note: Giving excludes United Way. Average grant excludes three highest grants ($140,000).

Recent Grants

Note: Grants derived from 2002 Form 990.
Library-Related
5,000	Frick Collection, New York, NY

General
50,000	Fund for Park Avenue, New York, NY
25,000	Boys Club of New York, New York, NY
25,000	Doe Fund, New York, NY
25,000	University of Minnesota, Minneapolis, MN
24,000	Boys Club of New York, New York, NY
15,000	Center of the American Experiment, Minneapolis, MN
15,000	High Peaks Education Foundation
15,000	Minnesota Public Radio, MN
10,000	Alzheimer's Association, Miami, FL
10,000	University of Minnesota, Minneapolis, MN

OSBORNE ENTERPRISES

Company Headquarters

5869 Hackmann Ave., NE
Fridley, MN 55432

Company Description

Employees: 56

Weldon F. Osborne Foundation

Giving Contact

Glenn C. Stophel, Executive Director
Weldon F. Osborne Foundation
1000 Tallan Bldg.
2 Union Square
Chattanooga, TN 37402
Phone: (423)757-0227

Description

EIN: 626026442
Organization Type: Corporate Foundation
Giving Locations: TN, Chattanooga
Grant Types: Capital, Conference/Seminar, General Support, Matching, Multiyear/Continuing Support, Operating Expenses, Scholarship, Seed Money.

Donor Information

Founder: Osborne Enterprises

Financial Summary

Total Giving: $920,693 (fiscal year ending June 30, 2003); $670,208 (fiscal 2002); $1,002,725 (fiscal 2001)
Giving Analysis: Giving for fiscal 2001 includes: foundation scholarships ($5,000); foundation grants to United Way ($15,000); foundation ($982,725)
Assets: $20,883,657 (fiscal 2003); $20,933,336 (fiscal 2002); $22,644,536 (fiscal 2001)
Gifts Received: $20,269,552 (fiscal 1999); $450,211 (fiscal 1997); $40,000 (fiscal 1994). Note: In 2001, contributions were received from the Estate of Eleanor Osborne ($54,154), Osborne Enterprises ($50,000); and East Ridge Development ($70,000).

Typical Recipients

Arts & Humanities: Arts Associations & Councils, Arts Institutes, Arts & Humanities-General, Music, Performing Arts
Civic & Public Affairs: Business/Free Enterprise, Chambers of Commerce, Clubs, Community Foundations, Economic Development, Civic & Public Affairs-General, Inner-City Development, Parades/Festivals, Urban & Community Affairs, Zoos/Aquariums
Education: Afterschool/Enrichment Programs, Business Education, Colleges & Universities, Education Funds, Elementary Education (Private), Education-General, Health & Physical Education, Leadership Training, Literacy, Preschool Education, Private Education (Precollege), Public Education (Precollege), Religious Education, Secondary Education (Private), Secondary Education (Public), Student Aid
Environment: Air/Water Quality, Environment-General, Resource Conservation
Health: Children's Health/Hospitals, Health-General, Health Funds, Hospices, Hospitals, Mental Health
Religion: Bible Study/Translation, Churches, Ministries, Religious Organizations, Religious Welfare, Social/Policy Issues
Social Services: Big Brothers/Big Sisters, Child Abuse, Child Welfare, Community Service Organizations, Counseling, Crime Prevention, Delinquency & Criminal Rehabilitation, Family Services, Food/Clothing Distribution, People with Disabilities, Recreation & Athletics, Scouts, Senior Services, Special Olympics, United Funds/United Ways, Veterans, YMCA/YWCA/YMHA/YWHA, Youth Organizations

Application Procedures

Initial Contact: Send letter requesting application form. Requesting organizations must be tax-exempt under Section 501(c)(3).
Application Requirements: Include name of organization along with contact information; tax-exempt status; purpose of mission; budget amount requested; project start and end dates; and collaborating organizations; brief summary of goals; list of Board of DirectorS or Trustees; and a copy of an IRS tax exempt determination letter.
Deadlines: None.
Review Process: Grants are considered quarterly and may be submitted at any time.

Restrictions

Grants are not made to individuals.

Additional Information

On February 28, 1999, the Osborne Building Corporation was sold to Mr. Robert P. Corker, Jr.
Publications: Application Form

Foundation Officials

Harold S. Wilson: president, executive director

Grants Analysis

Disclosure Period: fiscal year ending June 30, 2003
Total Grants: $908,693*
Number of Grants: 64
Average Grant: $10,624*
Highest Grant: $150,000
Lowest Grant: $500
Typical Range: $1,000 to $25,000
*Note: Giving excludes scholarship and United Way. Average grant figure excludes two highest grants ($250,000).

Recent Grants

Note: Grants derived from fiscal 2004 Form 990.
General
150,000	Public Education Foundation, Chattanooga, TN
150,000	Public Education Foundation, Chattanooga, TN
150,000	Public Education Foundation, Chattanooga, TN
100,000	Chattanooga Christian Community Foundation, Chattanooga, TN
55,440	University of Tennessee Chattanooga's School of Nursing, Chattanooga, TN
50,000	Community Foundation of Greater Chattanooga, Chattanooga, TN
25,000	Chattanooga Christian School, Chattanooga, TN
25,000	Memorial Health Care System Foundation, Medina, NY
25,000	Partnership for Families, Children and Adults, Chattanooga, TN
24,800	TC Thompson Children's Hospital Foundation Inc., Chattanooga, TN

I. A. O'SHAUGHNESSY FOUNDATION

Giving Contact

Timothy P. O'Shaughnessy, President, Director
332 Minnesota Street, Suite W-1271
St. Paul, MN 55101
Phone: (651)222-2323
Fax: (651)222-6368
E-mail: iaoshaughnessyfd@qwest.net
Note: Alternate Phone (651)222-2323

Description

Founded: 1941
EIN: 416011524

Organization Type: Family Foundation
Giving Locations: KS; MN; TX
Grant Types: Capital, Endowment, General Support, Matching, Multiyear/Continuing Support, Project, Seed Money.

Donor Information

Founder: Mrs. I. A. O'Shaughnessy established the O'Shaughnessy Foundation in 1941. In 1960, a bequest of $5 million from the estate of Mrs. I. A. O'Shaughnessy went to the foundation. The Globe Oil and Refining Companies and Lario Oil and Gas were also donors.

Financial Summary

Total Giving: $3,026,674 (2003); $2,725,000 (2001)
Giving Analysis: Giving for 2001 includes: foundation grants to United Way ($10,000)
Assets: $85,806,034 (2003); $83,573,060 (2001)

Typical Recipients

Arts & Humanities: Arts Associations & Councils, Arts Centers, Arts Festivals, Arts Funds, Arts Institutes, Arts Outreach, Ballet, Historic Preservation, History & Archaeology, Libraries, Literary Arts, Museums/Galleries, Music, Opera, Performing Arts, Public Broadcasting, Theater, Visual Arts
Civic & Public Affairs: Botanical Gardens/Parks, Business/Free Enterprise, Chambers of Commerce, Civil Rights, Clubs, Community Foundations, Employment/Job Training, Civic & Public Affairs-General, Hispanic Affairs, Housing, Philanthropic Organizations, Urban & Community Affairs
Education: Arts/Humanities Education, Business Education, Colleges & Universities, Economic Education, Education Associations, Education Funds, Elementary Education (Private), Elementary Education (Public), Engineering/Technological Education, Faculty Development, Education-General, International Exchange, Literacy, Medical Education, Minority Education, Preschool Education, Private Education (Precollege), Public Education (Precollege), Religious Education, Science/Mathematics Education, Secondary Education (Private), Secondary Education (Public), Social Sciences Education, Student Aid
Environment: Environment-General
Health: Alzheimer's Disease, Cancer, Children's Health/Hospitals, Clinics/Medical Centers, Health Funds, Health Organizations, Heart, Hospices, Hospitals, Hospitals (University Affiliated), Medical Rehabilitation, Mental Health, Prenatal Health Issues, Public Health
International: International-General, International Development, International Organizations, Missionary/Religious Activities
Religion: Churches, Religion-General, Jewish Causes, Ministries, Religious Organizations, Religious Welfare, Social/Policy Issues
Science: Science Museums
Social Services: Animal Protection, At-Risk Youth, Child Abuse, Child Welfare, Community Centers, Community Service Organizations, Domestic Violence, Family Services, Food/Clothing Distribution, People with Disabilities, Recreation & Athletics, Senior Services, Shelters/Homelessness, Substance Abuse, United Funds/United Ways, YMCA/YWCA/YMHA/YWHA, Youth Organizations

Application Procedures

Initial Contact: Applicants should send a brief letter of inquiry requesting a grant application form. All grant actions are initiated by the directors or their representatives for the geographical regions in which they reside. Application information received at the foundation office is forwarded to the directors for their review.
Application Requirements: If, after reviewing the grant application form, the directors determine that the application falls within the foundation's areas of interest, they will request additional information and/or a full proposal.
Deadlines: None.

Review Process: The board meets several times each year.
Decision Notification: No notification is sent if a grant request is denied.

Restrictions

The foundation does not make grants to individuals or organizations in foreign countries.

Additional Information

Normally grant actions are initiated by the directors or their representatives and for the areas in which they reside.
Publications: Application Form; Guidelines

Foundation Officials

John Bultena: secretary, treasurer
Carol L. Lyman: vice president, director
Eileen O'Shaughnessy: secretary, director
John F. O'Shaughnessy, Jr.: vice president, director B 1939. PRIM CORP EMPL president, treasurer, director: General Parts & Supply Co.
Mary K. O'Shaughnessy: vice president, director
Michelle O'Shaughnessy Traeger: vice president, director
Kathryn Wysong: vice president, director

Grants Analysis

Disclosure Period: calendar year ending 2003
Total Grants: $3,026,674
Number of Grants: 100
Average Grant: $30,267
Highest Grant: $200,000
Lowest Grant: $5,500
Typical Range: $10,000 to $50,000

Recent Grants

Note: Grants derived from 2002 Form 990.
General

250,000	Midland Memorial Foundation, Midland, TX -- towards the medical office building
250,000	Plan International USA Inc, Warwick, RI -- towards unfunded child survival projects
216,000	Newman University, Wichita, KS -- towards the sports complex
100,000	Charter Fund, Denver, CO -- towards general charitable purposes
100,000	Kent Denver Country Day School, Englewood, CO -- towards competition field project
100,000	Lake Country Montessori School, Minneapolis, MN -- towards educational goals and programs
100,000	Little Sisters of the Poor Holy Family Residence, St. Paul, MN -- towards planning of the residence renovation project
100,000	St Louis University the Center for Liturgy, St. Louis, MO -- as endowment for center for liturgy
100,000	YMCA of Midland Windows of Opportunity, Midland, TX -- towards special project
65,000	Saint Jude Catholic Church, Kapolei, HI -- towards building fund capital campaign

BERNARD OSHER FOUNDATION

Giving Contact

Patricia T. Nagle, Senior Vice President
One Ferry Bldg., Suite 255
San Francisco, CA 94111
Phone: (415)861-5587
Fax: (415)677-5868
E-mail: nagle@osherfoundation.com

Description

Founded: 1977
EIN: 942506257
Organization Type: General Purpose Foundation
Giving Locations: CA: Alameda County, San Francisco County
Grant Types: Fellowship, General Support, Project, Research, Scholarship, Seed Money.

Donor Information

Founder: The foundation was established in 1977 by Bernard Osher. Mr. Osher is a prominent businessman and community leader in the San Francisco Bay Area.

Financial Summary

Total Giving: $21,125,127 (2003); $18,531,762 (2001)
Giving Analysis: Giving for 2003 includes: foundation grants to United Way ($25,000); 2001: foundation grants to United Way ($25,000)
Assets: $79,750,243 (2003); $55,902,955 (2001)
Gifts Received: $48,576,187 (2003); $19,687,500 (1996). Note: In 1996, contributions were received from Bernard Osher.

Typical Recipients

Arts & Humanities: Arts Associations & Councils, Arts Centers, Arts Festivals, Arts Funds, Arts Institutes, Arts Outreach, Ballet, Dance, Ethnic & Folk Arts, Film & Video, Arts & Humanities-General, History & Archaeology, Libraries, Literary Arts, Museums/Galleries, Music, Opera, Performing Arts, Public Broadcasting, Theater
Civic & Public Affairs: Botanical Gardens/Parks, Community Foundations, Civic & Public Affairs-General, Hispanic Affairs, Law & Justice, Legal Aid, Parades/Festivals, Public Policy, Urban & Community Affairs, Zoos/Aquariums
Education: Afterschool/Enrichment Programs, Arts/Humanities Education, Colleges & Universities, Continuing Education, Education Funds, Education-General, International Exchange, International Studies, Journalism/Media Education, Leadership Training, Medical Education, Private Education (Precollege), Science/Mathematics Education, Social Sciences Education, Student Aid, Vocational & Technical Education
Environment: Environment-General, Resource Conservation, Wildlife Protection
Health: AIDS/HIV, Cancer, Diabetes, Health Organizations, Hospitals, Medical Research, Mental Health
International: Foreign Arts Organizations, International Affairs, International Organizations, International Peace & Security Issues, International Relations, Missionary/Religious Activities
Religion: Churches, Religious Organizations, Religious Welfare
Science: Observatories & Planetariums, Science Museums, Scientific Centers & Institutes
Social Services: At-Risk Youth, Child Welfare, Community Centers, Community Service Organizations, Family Planning, Family Services, Food/Clothing Distribution, People with Disabilities, Recreation & Athletics, Shelters/Homelessness, Social Services-General, Substance Abuse, United Funds/United Ways, Youth Organizations

Application Procedures

Initial Contact: Applicants should submit a letter of inquiry.
Application Requirements: Initial letters should include a background of the organization, including qualifications of people involved; a description of the nature and scope of proposed project or program and anticipated results; a preliminary timetable and budget outline; financial statement for most recent completed year of operation; evidence of tax-exempt status; names of appropriate governing authority; and evidence of request approval.
Deadlines: None.

Review Process: If the letter of inquiry falls within the foundation's areas of interest, the board will request a more detailed proposal. All applications will receive a prompt response from the foundation.

Restrictions

Generally, the foundation does not fund requests for capital improvements, normal operating expenses, deficits, or fundraising campaigns. The foundation may not make direct grants to individuals.

Additional Information

Publications: Application Guidelines

Foundation Officials

David Agger: director ED Lehigh University BS. CORP AFFIL chief executive officer: Nexspace LLC; director: Vintara. NONPR AFFIL director: Mount Zion Health Fund; fellow: Wexner Heritage Foundation of New York.

Dr. Frederick Emery Balderston: director B 1923. PRIM CORP EMPL associate dean: University California Graduate School Business Administration. NONPR AFFIL board trustees: American Field Service International Scholarships Inc.; emeritus professor, Haas School of Business: University California at Berkeley.

Phyllis Cook: director NONPR AFFIL director: Jewish Community Federation San Francisco.

Robert Friend: director ED University of California at Berkeley. PRIM CORP EMPL president, chief executive officer, director: Kutler Clothiers Inc. CORP AFFIL president: Howard Properties. NONPR AFFIL president: Friend Family Foundation; chairman: UC San Francisco's Diabetes Center Campaign.

Ron Kaufman: director

Barbro Osher: president NONPR AFFIL consul general: Sweden.

Patricia Tracy-Nagle: senior vice president NONPR AFFIL director: The Barbro Osher Pro Suecia Foundation.

Grants Analysis

Disclosure Period: calendar year ending 2003
Total Grants: $21,100,127*
Number of Grants: 152
Average Grant: $39,588*
Highest Grant: $4,100,000
Lowest Grant: $500
Typical Range: $10,000 to $50,000
*Note: Giving excludes United Way. Average grant figure excludes nine highest grants ($15,439,100).

Recent Grants

Note: Grants derived from 2001 Form 990.
General

4,250,000	UCSF Foundation, San Francisco, CA
2,875,210	Exploratorium, San Francisco, CA
2,750,000	Harvard Medical-Osher Institute, Boston, MA
1,049,168	Golden Gate National Parks Association, San Francisco, CA
610,000	University of Southern Maine, Portland, ME
549,168	Asian Art Museum, San Francisco, CA
500,000	Portland Museum of Art, Portland, ME
3,050,210	KQED, San Francisco, CA
150,000	SF Zoological Society, San Francisco, CA
150,000	UC Berkeley/International House, Berkeley, CA

OSHKOSH B'GOSH INC.

Company Headquarters

Oshkosh, WI
Web: http://www.oshkoshbgosh.com

Company Description

Founded: 1895
Ticker: GOSHA
Exchange: NASDAQ
Revenue: US$437 million (2002)
Employees: 4690 (2003)
SIC(s): 2325 Men's/Boys' Trousers & Slacks, 2326 Men's/Boys' Work Clothing, 2369 Girls'/Children's Outerwear Nec.

Operating Locations

Oshkosh B'Gosh, Inc. (CA--Los Angeles; KY--Albany, Columbia, Liberty; NY--New York; TN--Byrdstown, Celina, Gainesboro, Jamestown, McEwen, White House; TX--Dallas)

Nonmonetary Support

Type: Donated Products
Note: NOT Nonmonetary support is provided in the form of gift certificates.
Contact: Anne Spangler

Oshkosh B'Gosh Foundation Inc.

Giving Contact

David Omachinski, Vice President
PO Box 300
Oshkosh, WI 54902
Phone: (920)232-4140
Fax: (920)231-8621
Web: http://www.oshkoshbgosh.com

Alternate Contact

Michael D. Wachtel, President
OshKosh B'Gosh Foundation, Inc.
112 Otter Avenue
Oshkosh, WI 54901

Description

EIN: 391525020
Organization Type: Corporate Foundation
Giving Locations: operating locations.
Grant Types: Award, Capital, Emergency, General Support, Scholarship.
Note: Scholarships are available for high school graduates in the communities in which Oshkosh B'Gosh, Inc. plants or facilities are located.

Financial Summary

Total Giving: $427,653 (2002); $415,745 (2001). Note: Contributes through foundation only.
Giving Analysis: Giving for 2001 includes: foundation scholarships ($78,750); foundation grants to United Way ($83,777); foundation ($253,218)
Assets: $1,089,090 (2002); $1,159,821 (2001)
Gifts Received: $450,000 (2002); $450,000 (2001); $600,000 (1999). Note: Contributions are received from Oshkosh B'Gosh, Inc.

Typical Recipients

Arts & Humanities: Arts Associations & Councils, Arts Centers, Arts Festivals, Community Arts, Dance, Libraries, Museums/Galleries, Music, Opera, Performing Arts, Public Broadcasting

Civic & Public Affairs: Botanical Gardens/Parks, Business/Free Enterprise, Chambers of Commerce, Community Foundations, Civic & Public Affairs-General, Housing, Parades/Festivals, Philanthropic Organizations, Professional & Trade Associations, Public Policy, Urban & Community Affairs, Zoos/Aquariums

Education: Afterschool/Enrichment Programs, Agricultural Education, Arts/Humanities Education, Business Education, Colleges & Universities, Community & Junior Colleges, Education Funds, Elementary Education (Private), Education-General, Literacy, Medical Education, Minority Education, Private Education (Precollege), Public Education (Precollege), Science/

Mathematics Education, Student Aid, Vocational & Technical Education

Environment: Environment-General, Watershed

Health: Cancer, Children's Health/Hospitals, Clinics/Medical Centers, Diabetes, Emergency/Ambulance Services, Eyes/Blindness, Health Funds, Health Organizations, Heart, Medical Rehabilitation, Mental Health, Respiratory, Single-Disease Health Associations, Speech & Hearing

International: International-General, International Environmental Issues, International Organizations, International Relief Efforts

Religion: Jewish Causes

Science: Science Museums

Social Services: At-Risk Youth, Big Brothers/Big Sisters, Camps, Child Abuse, Child Welfare, Community Service Organizations, Counseling, Day Care, Domestic Violence, Family Services, People with Disabilities, Recreation & Athletics, Scouts, Senior Services, Sexual Abuse, Special Olympics, United Funds/United Ways, YMCA/YWCA/YMHA/YWHA, Youth Organizations

Application Procedures

Initial Contact: Send brief letter.
Application Requirements: Include a description of organization; amount requested and purpose of funds sought; audited financial statement; and proof of tax-exempt status.
Deadlines: None.
Notes: The foundation reports there are no standard application procedures for grants. Scholarship applicants located in Oshkosh B'Gosh operating communities should contact their high school guidance counselor to obtain a formal application and deadline date.

Restrictions

The foundation only supports organizations and provides scholarships to individuals where a corporate office or sewing facility is located.

Corporate Officials

Douglas W. Hyde: chairman, president, chief executive officer B 1950. PRIM CORP EMPL chairman, president, chief executive officer: Oshkosh B'Gosh, Inc.

David L. Omachinski: chief financial officer, treasurer, vice president B Appleton, WI 1952. ED University of Wisconsin BA (1974). PRIM CORP EMPL chief financial officer, treasurer, vice president: Oshkosh B'Gosh Inc. CORP AFFIL director: White Clover Dairy; director: Archorbank SSB; director: Fox Cities Bank. NONPR AFFIL member: Knights of Columbus; member: Rotary International; treasurer: Art Paine Center & Arboretum; member: Financial Executives Institute; member: American Institute CPAs.

Michael D. Wachtel: chief operating officer B 1954. ED University of Wisconsin Pharmacy (1977). PRIM CORP EMPL chief operating officer: Oshkosh B'Gosh, Inc.

Foundation Officials

Michael D. Wachtel: president (see above)

Grants Analysis

Disclosure Period: calendar year ending 2002
Total Grants: $273,116*
Number of Grants: 37
Average Grant: $7,382*
Highest Grant: $60,000
Lowest Grant: $150
Typical Range: $500 to $5,000
*Note: Giving excludes scholarships and United Way.

Recent Grants

Note: Grants derived from 2003 Form 990.
General

57,294	United Way, Oshkosh, WI
53,000	Oskosh YMCA, Oshkosh, WI
47,500	Paine Art Center Arboretum, Oshkosh, WI

16,500	Boys Girls Club of Oshkosh, Oshkosh, WI
13,555	Mercy Medical Center Foundation, Oshkosh, WI
13,409	United Way of Summer County, Gallatin, TN
10,000	Children's Hospital Foundation, Neenah, WI
10,000	Oshkosh Foundation, Oshkosh, WI
6,750	Junior Achievement of Oshkosh, Oshkosh, WI
5,635	American Cancer Society, Appleton, WI

OTTENHEIMER BROTHERS FOUNDATION

Giving Contact
Grainger Williams, Board Member
425 West Capital, Suite 1516
Little Rock, AR 72201
Phone: (501)372-6167

Description
Founded: 1965
EIN: 716059988
Organization Type: Private Foundation
Giving Locations: AR: Pulaski County, Little Rock, North Little Rock
Grant Types: General Support.

Financial Summary
Total Giving: $263,698 (fiscal year ending April 30, 2002); $241,180 (fiscal 2001)
Assets: $5,829,137 (fiscal 2002); $5,834,108 (fiscal 2001)

Typical Recipients
Arts & Humanities: Arts Centers, Historic Preservation, Libraries
Civic & Public Affairs: Botanical Gardens/Parks, Business/Free Enterprise, Chambers of Commerce, Clubs, Economic Development, Civic & Public Affairs-General, Housing, Public Policy, Urban & Community Affairs
Education: Afterschool/Enrichment Programs, Business Education, Colleges & Universities, Literacy, Science/Mathematics Education
Environment: Environment-General
Health: AIDS/HIV, Children's Health/Hospitals, Health Organizations
Religion: Religion-General, Jewish Causes, Religious Organizations, Synagogues/Temples
Science: Science Museums
Social Services: Animal Protection, Camps, Child Welfare, Community Centers, Community Service Organizations, Family Planning, Family Services, Food/Clothing Distribution, People with Disabilities, Recreation & Athletics, Sexual Abuse, Youth Organizations

Application Procedures
Initial Contact: Send a brief letter of inquiry. and a full proposal.
Application Requirements: Include a description of organization, amount requested, purpose of funds sought, recently audited financial statement, and proof of tax-exempt status.
Deadlines: None.

Restrictions
Foundation does not support individuals, religious organizations for sectarian purposes, political or lobbying groups, organizations outside operating areas, or scholarships.

Foundation Officials
Larry Alman: board of directors
Steve Bauman: secretary

Gus Blass, III: board of directors
Noland Blass, Jr.: board director
E. C. Eichenbaum: chairman
Judy Grundfest: board director
Julianne D. Grundfest: board of directors
Edward M. Penick: board director
Louis Rosen: board director
Fred Selz: board director
Sam C. Sowell: board of directors
Sam B. Strauss, Jr.: board director
E. Grainger Williams: board director

Grants Analysis
Disclosure Period: fiscal year ending April 30, 2002
Total Grants: $263,698
Number of Grants: 20
Average Grant: $8,616*
Highest Grant: $100,000
Lowest Grant: $100
Typical Range: $500 to $31,250
*Note: Average grant figure excludes highest grant.

Recent Grants
Note: Grants derived from fiscal 2002 Form 990.
Library-Related

31,250	Central Arkansas Library System, Little Rock, AR

General

100,000	University of Arkansas Medical Sciences, Little Rock, AR
31,250	Arkansas Territorial Restoration, Little Rock, AR
25,000	Arkansas Arts Center, Little Rock, AR
25,000	Greater Little Rock Chamber of Commerce, Little Rock, AR
15,000	Park Positive Atmosphere Reaches Kids
12,500	Little Rock Boys and Girls Club, Little Rock, AR
5,268	B'nai Israel Temple, Evansville, IN
5,000	B'nai Israel Cemetery Foundation
5,000	Planned Parenthood of Arkansas and East Oklahoma, OK
3,000	Rotary Club of Little Rock International Youth Project, Little Rock, AR

THE OVERBROOK FOUNDATION

Giving Contact
M. Sheila McGoldrick, Grants Manager
122 East 42nd Street, Suite 2500
New York, NY 10168-2500
Phone: (212)661-8710
Fax: (212)661-8664
E-mail: contact@overbrookfoundation.org
Web: http://www.overbrook.org

Description
Founded: 1948
EIN: 136088860
Organization Type: Family Foundation
Giving Locations: CT; NY: New York metropolitan area nationally.
Grant Types: General Support, Multiyear/Continuing Support.

Donor Information
Founder: The Overbrook Foundation was incorporated in New York in 1948 by Frank Altschul (d. 1982), the late Helen G. Altschul and their three children. Frank Altschul was the chairman of General American Investors Company, a New York City investment company now chaired by his son, Arthur Altschul.

Financial Summary
Total Giving: $7,084,310 (2003); $7,605,674 (2002)
Assets: $158,988,747 (2003); $133,641,018 (2002)

Gifts Received: $79,938 (2000); $31,308 (1998); $41,216 (1997). Note: In 1998, contributions were received from Emily and Stephen Altschul, Julie, Michael, and Robert Graham, Jr., Margaret Lang, and Isaiah Orozco.

Typical Recipients
Arts & Humanities: Arts Associations & Councils, Arts Centers, Arts Festivals, Arts Institutes, Dance, Film & Video, Arts & Humanities-General, Historic Preservation, History & Archaeology, Libraries, Literary Arts, Museums/Galleries, Music, Opera, Performing Arts, Public Broadcasting, Theater
Civic & Public Affairs: Botanical Gardens/Parks, Business/Free Enterprise, Civil Rights, Community Foundations, Economic Development, Economic Policy, Employment/Job Training, First Amendment Issues, Gay/Lesbian Issues, Civic & Public Affairs-General, Housing, Inner-City Development, Law & Justice, Legal Aid, Nonprofit Management, Philanthropic Organizations, Professional & Trade Associations, Public Policy, Safety, Urban & Community Affairs, Women's Affairs, Zoos/Aquariums
Education: Afterschool/Enrichment Programs, Arts/Humanities Education, Colleges & Universities, Education Associations, Education Funds, Elementary Education (Private), Education-General, International Exchange, Legal Education, Literacy, Minority Education, Private Education (Precollege), Religious Education, Secondary Education (Private), Social Sciences Education, Student Aid
Environment: Energy, Environment-General, Protection, Research, Resource Conservation, Watershed, Wildlife Protection
Health: AIDS/HIV, Emergency/Ambulance Services, Health Policy/Cost Containment, Health Organizations, Hospices, Hospitals, Hospitals (University Affiliated), Medical Research, Mental Health, Nursing Services, Single-Disease Health Associations
International: Foreign Arts Organizations, Foreign Educational Institutions, International-General, Health Care/Hospitals, Human Rights, International Environmental Issues, International Organizations, International Peace & Security Issues, International Relations, International Relief Efforts
Religion: Churches, Jewish Causes, Religious Welfare
Science: Science Museums, Scientific Centers & Institutes
Social Services: Animal Protection, Child Welfare, Community Centers, Community Service Organizations, Counseling, Crime Prevention, Delinquency & Criminal Rehabilitation, Emergency Relief, Family Planning, Family Services, Food/Clothing Distribution, Homes, People with Disabilities, Recreation & Athletics, Senior Services, Shelters/Homelessness, Social Services-General, Substance Abuse, United Funds/United Ways, Volunteer Services, YMCA/YWCA/YMHA/YWHA, Youth Organizations

Application Procedures
Initial Contact: Send a brief letter of inquiry.
Deadlines: None.

Restrictions
No grants are given to individuals.

Foundation Officials
Arthur G. Altschul, Jr.: director
Charles Altschul: director
Serena Altschul: director
Stephen Frank Altschul: vice chairman, treasurer, director B New York, NY 1957. ED Harvard University AB (1979); Massachusetts Institute of Technology PhD (1987). PRIM NONPR EMPL senior investigator: National Library of Medicine.
Stephen A. Foster: president, chief executive officer
Julie Graham: director
Kathryn C. Graham: director
Kathryn G. Graham: director
Robert C. Graham, Jr.: chairman, director
C. Kooijman: director

Frances Labaree: vice chairman, secretary, director
Isaiah Lang: director
Vincent McGee: director

Grants Analysis
Disclosure Period: calendar year ending 2003
Total Grants: $7,084,310
Number of Grants: 330
Average Grant: $21,477
Highest Grant: $200,000
Lowest Grant: $500
Typical Range: $5,000 to $50,000

Recent Grants
Note: Grants derived from 2003 Form 990.
Library-Related
| 70,000 | William A. Farnsworth Library & Art Museum Inc., Rockland, ME -- funding for general operating support |

General
200,000	Barnard College, New York, NY -- toward renovation of auditorium in Altschul Hall
130,000	City Lore Inc., New York, NY -- funding for New York Center of the World
100,000	Columbia University, New York, NY -- funding for three classes of the Overbrook Conservation Fellows Program
100,000	NARAL Pro-Choice America Foundation, Washington, DC -- toward the Choice For America (CFA) initiative
100,000	National Public Radio Inc., Washington, DC -- toward endowment fund for excellence
100,000	People for the American Way Foundation, Washington, DC -- funding for election protection
85,000	Environmental Defense, Boston, MA -- toward sustainable paper production and consumption
85,000	Natural Resources Defense Council Inc., New York, NY -- toward recycling initiative and paper industry reform project
80,000	EcoLogic Enterprise Ventures Inc., Cambridge, MA -- toward Green Loan Fund for Latin America
80,000	Worldwatch Institute, Washington, DC -- funding for worldlwatch project on consumption

OVERLAKE FOUNDATION

Giving Contact
Thomas L. Keller, Vice President & Treasurer
PO Box 2549
Victoria, TX 77902
Phone: (361)573-4383

Description
Founded: 1981
EIN: 751793068
Organization Type: Private Foundation
Giving Locations: TX
Grant Types: General Support.

Donor Information
Founder: Mary Alice Fitzpatrick

Financial Summary
Total Giving: $514,981 (fiscal year ending November 30, 2001)
Assets: $7,793,452 (fiscal 2001)

Typical Recipients
Arts & Humanities: Arts Associations & Councils, Arts & Humanities-General, Historic Preservation, History & Archaeology, Libraries, Literary Arts, Museums/Galleries, Music, Public Broadcasting, Theater
Civic & Public Affairs: Clubs, Community Founda-

tions, Civic & Public Affairs-General, Nonprofit Management, Parades/Festivals, Professional & Trade Associations, Rural Affairs, Safety, Urban & Community Affairs, Women's Affairs, Zoos/Aquariums
Education: Agricultural Education, Arts/Humanities Education, Colleges & Universities, Education Funds, Elementary Education (Public), Engineering/Technological Education, Education-General, Literacy, Medical Education, Private Education (Precollege), Science/Mathematics Education, Secondary Education (Private), Student Aid
Environment: Environment-General
Health: Cancer, Children's Health/Hospitals, Emergency/Ambulance Services, Health Funds, Health Organizations, Hospices, Hospitals, Medical Rehabilitation, Medical Research, Nursing Services, Public Health, Research/Studies Institutes, Single-Disease Health Associations
Religion: Bible Study/Translation, Churches, Religious Organizations, Religious Welfare
Science: Science Museums, Scientific Labs
Social Services: Animal Protection, At-Risk Youth, Camps, Child Welfare, Community Service Organizations, Counseling, Day Care, Domestic Violence, Family Services, Homes, Recreation & Athletics, Senior Services, Sexual Abuse, Shelters/Homelessness, Social Services-General, Substance Abuse, YMCA/YWCA/YMHA/YWHA, Youth Organizations

Application Procedures
Initial Contact: The foundation has no formal grant application procedure or application form.

Foundation Officials
Michael Scott Anderson: director
Steven Craig Anderson: director
Rayford L. Keller: president, assistant treasurer
Thomas L. Keller: vice president, treasurer, assistant secretary
Donald J. Malouf: vice president, secretary

Grants Analysis
Disclosure Period: fiscal year ending November 30, 2001
Total Grants: $514,981
Number of Grants: 56
Average Grant: $5,833*
Highest Grant: $100,000
Lowest Grant: $1,000
Typical Range: $1,000 to $10,000
***Note:** Average grants figure excludes highest two highest grants ($200,000).

Recent Grants
Note: Grants derived from fiscal 2002 Form 990.

General
87,500	Our Lady of Victory Cathedral, Victoria, TX
40,000	Barrow Neurological Foundation, Phoenix, AZ
27,000	Refugio Volunteer Fire Department, Refugio, TX
20,000	Victoria County Senior Citizens Association, Victoria, TX
15,000	Elf Louise, San Antonio, TX
15,000	Mid-Coast Family Services, Victoria, TX
15,000	Perpetual Help Home, Victoria, TX
10,000	American Social Health Association, Research Triangle Park, NC
10,000	Golden Crescent Casa, Inc., Victoria, TX
10,000	Goliad County Fair Association, Goliad, TX

OWEN INDUSTRIES

Company Headquarters
501 Ave. H
Carter Lake, IA 51510

Company Description
Employees: 480
SIC(s): 3441 Fabricated Structural Metal, 6719 Holding Companies Nec.

Operating Locations
Owen Industries (IA--Carter Lake)

Owen Foundation

Giving Contact
Robert E. Owen, President, Trustee
2200 Abbott Dr.
Carter Lake, IA 51510
Phone: (712)347-5500

Description
Founded: 1959
EIN: 476025298
Organization Type: Corporate Foundation
Giving Locations: NE
Grant Types: General Support.

Donor Information
Founder: Paxton & Vierling Steel Co., Missouri Valley Steel Co., Northern Plains Steel Co.

Financial Summary
Total Giving: $73,600 (fiscal year ending November 30, 2001)
Assets: $20,260 (fiscal 2001)
Gifts Received: $54,000 (fiscal 2001); $200,000 (fiscal 2000); $180,000 (fiscal 1998). Note: Contributions were received from Owen Industries, Inc.

Typical Recipients
Arts & Humanities: Arts Appreciation, Arts Associations & Councils, Community Arts, Historic Preservation, History & Archaeology, Libraries, Museums/Galleries, Music, Opera, Performing Arts, Theater
Civic & Public Affairs: Botanical Gardens/Parks, Civic & Public Affairs-General, Women's Affairs, Zoos/Aquariums
Education: Agricultural Education, Colleges & Universities, Private Education (Precollege)
Environment: Resource Conservation
Health: Children's Health/Hospitals, Diabetes, Emergency/Ambulance Services, Health Organizations, Hospitals, Transplant Networks/Donor Banks
Religion: Churches, Ministries, Religious Welfare
Social Services: Animal Protection, Child Welfare, Community Service Organizations, People with Disabilities, Recreation & Athletics, Scouts, United Funds/United Ways, YMCA/YWCA/YMHA/YWHA, Youth Organizations

Application Procedures
Initial Contact: The foundation has no formal grant application procedure or application form.
Deadlines: None.

Corporate Officials
Carl Harrison: vice president finance, chief financial officero B Lawton, IA 1936. ED Morningside College (1961). PRIM CORP EMPL vice president finance, chief financial officer: Owens Industries. CORP AFFIL vice president fin: Northern Plains Steel Co.; vice president fin: Paxton & Vierling Steel Co.; vice president fin: Missouri Valley Steel Co.; vice president fin: Central Plains Steel Co.; vice president fin: Lincoln Steel Co.
Robert E. Owen: chairman, president, chief executive officer B Omaha, NE 1943. ED Iowa State Uni-

versity of Science & Technology (1966). PRIM CORP EMPL chairman, president, chief executive officer: Owen Industries. CORP AFFIL vice president, director: Northern Plains Steel Co.; president: Paxton & Vierling Steel Co.; president, director: Missouri Valley Steel Co.; president, director: Central Plains Steel Co.; president, director: Lincoln Steel Co.

Foundation Officials
Sam R. Brower: secretary, treasurer
Dolores C. Owen: trustee
Richard F. Owen: vice president, trustee
Robert E. Owen: president, trustee (see above)

Grants Analysis
Disclosure Period: fiscal year ending November 30, 2001
Total Grants: $73,600
Number of Grants: 7
Average Grant: $8,100*
Highest Grant: $25,000
Lowest Grant: $500
Typical Range: $1,000 to $15,000
*Note: Average grant figure excludes highest grant.

Recent Grants
Note: Grants derived from fiscal 2001 Form 990.
General

25,000	Boys and Girls Club of Omaha, Omaha, NE
22,600	Knights of AkSarBen Foundation, Omaha, NE
20,000	Bellevue University Foundation, Bellevue, NE
2,500	Boy Scouts of America, Evansville, IN
2,000	Child Saving Institute, Omaha, NE
1,000	University of Nebraska Foundation, Lincoln, NE
500	Council Bluffs YMCA, Council Bluffs, IA

ALVIN AND LUCY OWSLEY FOUNDATION

Giving Contact
Alvin M. Owsley, Jr., Trustee
65 Briar Hollow Ln.
Houston, TX 77027
Phone: (713)622-1352

Description
Founded: 1950
EIN: 756047221
Organization Type: Private Foundation
Giving Locations: TX
Grant Types: Capital, Emergency, General Support, Multiyear/Continuing Support, Operating Expenses, Research, Scholarship, Seed Money.

Donor Information
Founder: the late Alvin M. Owsley, Lucy B. Owsley

Financial Summary
Total Giving: $465,655 (2001)
Giving Analysis: Giving for 2001 includes: foundation scholarships ($500)
Assets: $7,894,548 (2001)
Gifts Received: $500 (2000). Note: In fiscal 2001, contributions were received from Alvin Owsley ($500).

Typical Recipients
Arts & Humanities: Arts Centers, Arts Festivals, Ballet, Community Arts, Dance, Historic Preservation, History & Archaeology, Libraries, Museums/Galleries, Music, Opera, Theater
Civic & Public Affairs: Botanical Gardens/Parks, Clubs, Civic & Public Affairs-General, Municipalities/

Towns, Rural Affairs, Urban & Community Affairs
Education: Arts/Humanities Education, Colleges & Universities, Education-General, Health & Physical Education, Legal Education, Medical Education, Private Education (Precollege), Public Education (Precollege), Secondary Education (Public), Student Aid
Environment: Environment-General, Wildlife Protection
Health: Adolescent Health Issues, AIDS/HIV, Cancer, Children's Health/Hospitals, Clinics/Medical Centers, Diabetes, Eyes/Blindness, Health Policy/Cost Containment, Heart, Hospitals, Medical Research, Mental Health, Multiple Sclerosis, Prenatal Health Issues, Public Health, Single-Disease Health Associations
International: International Environmental Issues
Religion: Churches, Missionary Activities (Domestic), Religious Welfare
Science: Science Museums, Scientific Centers & Institutes, Scientific Research
Social Services: Animal Protection, At-Risk Youth, Child Abuse, Child Welfare, Community Centers, Community Service Organizations, Crime Prevention, Domestic Violence, Family Planning, Family Services, People with Disabilities, Recreation & Athletics, Scouts, Shelters/Homelessness, United Funds/United Ways, Volunteer Services, YMCA/YWCA/YMHA/YWHA, Youth Organizations

Application Procedures
Initial Contact: Send a letter of not more than two pages.
Deadlines: None.
Notes: Enclosures not accepted with initial contact.

Restrictions
Does not support individuals or provide loans. Awards restricted to Texas only.

Foundation Officials
Wendy Garrett: trustee
Alvin Mansfield Owsley, Jr.: trustee B Dallas, TX 1926. ED Princeton University AB (1949); University of Texas JD, LLB (1952). PRIM CORP EMPL chairman, director: Ball Corp. NONPR AFFIL member: Society Mayflower Descendants; member: Texas Bar Association; member: Phi Delta Phi; fellow: Houston Bar Association Foundation; member, board visitors: M D Anderson Cancer Center; member: Houston Bar Association; member: American Bar Association; fellow: American College Trial Lawyers. CLUB AFFIL Tejas Club; Houston Country Club; Leland Country Club.
David Thomas Owsley: trustee B Dallas, TX 1929. ED Harvard University AB (1951); New York University MFA (1964). NONPR AFFIL member acquisition committee: Dallas Mas Art; member advisory council: Institute Asia Studies. CLUB AFFIL Leland Country Club; Ducks Unlimited Club; Knickerbocker Club.

Grants Analysis
Disclosure Period: calendar year ending 2001
Total Grants: $464,155*
Number of Grants: 50
Average Grant: $6,483*
Highest Grant: $100,000
Typical Range: $1,000 to $10,000
*Note: Giving excludes United Way; Scholarship. Average grant figure excludes two highest grants ($140,000).

Recent Grants
Note: Grants derived from 2001 Form 990.
General

100,000	Dallas Museum of Art, Dallas, TX
40,000	Botanical Research Institute of Texas, Ft. Worth, TX
35,500	Baylor College of Medicine, Houston, TX
35,000	Houston Ballet Foundation, Houston, TX
25,000	Boy Scouts of America Sam Houston Area, Houston, TX
10,000	Boys and Girls Country, Hockley, TX
10,000	Boys and Girls Harbor, Inc., Houston, TX
10,000	First Presbyterian Church, Dallas, TX
10,000	Houston Arboretum and Nature Center, Houston, TX
10,000	National Center Policy Analysis, Dallas, TX

OXFORD FOUNDATION

Giving Contact
Philip L. Calhoun
Oxford Foundation
125-D Lancaster Avenue
Strasburg, PA 17579
Phone: (717)687-9335
Fax: (717)687-9336
E-mail: pcalhoun@oxfordfoundation.org
Web: http://www.oxfordfoundation.org

Alternate Contact
Gwen L. Shirey
E-mail: gshirey@oxfordfoundation.org

Description
Founded: 1947
EIN: 236278067
Organization Type: Family Foundation
Giving Locations: PA: nationally
Grant Types: Capital, Endowment, Fellowship, General Support, Multiyear/Continuing Support, Research, Scholarship.

Donor Information
Founder: Established in 1947 by John H. Ware III and Marian S. Ware.

Financial Summary
Total Giving: $4,676,880 (2003); $3,250,230 (2002); $3,010,843 (2001)
Giving Analysis: Giving for 2002 includes: foundation grants to United Way ($4,600); foundation scholarships ($35,857); foundation fellowships ($45,000); foundation matching gifts ($68,907)
Assets: $70,446,826 (2003); $60,406,110 (2002); $62,681,937 (2001)
Gifts Received: $377,750 (2003); $122,498 (2002); $122,498 (2000). Note: In 2002, contributions were received from a distribution from John H. Ware III, Charitable Lead Annuity. In 2003, contributions were received from Marilyn Ware ($255,252) and from the John H. Ware III, Charitable Lead Annuity ($122,498).

Typical Recipients
Arts & Humanities: Dance, Historic Preservation, History & Archaeology, Libraries, Museums/Galleries, Music, Opera, Performing Arts, Public Broadcasting, Theater
Civic & Public Affairs: Botanical Gardens/Parks, Civil Rights, Community Foundations, Economic Policy, Ethnic Organizations, Civic & Public Affairs-General, Law & Justice, Municipalities/Towns, Philanthropic Organizations, Professional & Trade Associations, Public Policy, Rural Affairs, Safety, Urban & Community Affairs, Zoos/Aquariums
Education: Agricultural Education, Arts/Humanities Education, Colleges & Universities, Community & Junior Colleges, Economic Education, Education Funds, Education-General, International Exchange, Medical Education, Minority Education, Private Education (Precollege), Public Education (Precollege), Special Education
Environment: Environment-General, Protection, Resource Conservation, Wildlife Protection
Health: Alzheimer's Disease, Arthritis, Cancer, Children's Health/Hospitals, Clinics/Medical Centers, Diabetes, Emergency/Ambulance Services, Health Organizations, Hospices, Hospitals, Hospitals

(University Affiliated), Medical Research, Mental Health, Nursing Services, Prenatal Health Issues, Public Health, Single-Disease Health Associations
International: Health Care/Hospitals, International Environmental Issues
Religion: Churches, Religion-General, Ministries, Religious Organizations, Religious Welfare, Seminaries
Science: Scientific Centers & Institutes
Social Services: Animal Protection, Big Brothers/Big Sisters, Child Welfare, Community Centers, Community Service Organizations, Counseling, Crime Prevention, Day Care, Domestic Violence, Family Planning, People with Disabilities, Recreation & Athletics, Scouts, Senior Services, Sexual Abuse, Social Services-General, Substance Abuse, YMCA/YWCA/YMHA/YWHA, Youth Organizations

Application Procedures
Initial Contact: Send a brief letter of inquiry., or see foundation website for application procedures.
Application Requirements: Before submitting a complete application, a one-page summary should be submitted. It should include an agency description, history, mission statement, proposed project with budget, other possible funding sources, what the agency wishes to accomplish and how it plans to do so.
Deadlines: None.
Review Process: The initial inquiry will be reviewed within one month of receipt. All inquiries will receive a response; it will consist of a denial with an explanation or a request for a full proposal.

Restrictions
The foundation does not make grants to individuals, for scholarships, or loans.

Additional Information
In 2005, the foundation announced that it will reorganize into four new Ware family foundations: 1675 Foundation, Ferree Foundation, The Woods Charitable Foundation, and the Oxford Area Foundation. Visit the foundation website for further details at www.oxfordfoundation.org.

Foundation Officials
Carol Ware Gates: vice president, treasurer
Marilyn Ware Lewis: vice president, secretary B Philadelphia, PA 1944. ED American University; University of Pennsylvania. PRIM CORP EMPL chairman, director: American Water Works Co. Inc. CORP AFFIL director: Penn Fuel Gas Inc.; PP&L Resources Inc.; director: CIGNA Corp.
Eleanor Ross: assistant secretary, assistant treasurer
John H. Ware, IV: vice president
Marian S. Ware: chairman, president
Paul W. Ware: vice president B Philadelphia, PA 1946. ED Franklin and Marshall College (1972). CORP AFFIL retired chairman: Penn Fuel Gas Inc.; director: York Water Co.; director: America Water Works Co. Inc.; director: Emerald Asset Management Inc.

Grants Analysis
Disclosure Period: calendar year ending 2003
Total Grants: $4,676,880
Number of Grants: 221
Average Grant: $21,162
Highest Grant: $500,000
Lowest Grant: $500
Typical Range: $1,000 to $50,000

Recent Grants
Note: Grants derived from 2003 Form 990.
Library-Related
25,000   Oxford Library, Oxford, PA
General
500,000   Juvenile Diabetes Foundation International, Bala Cynwyd, PA -- for diabetes research

500,000   Lincoln University, Lincoln, PA -- for general operations
500,000   National Constitution Center, Philadelphia, PA -- for bronze statue of a founding father
284,775   Swarthmore College, Swarthmore, PA -- for Parrish hall renovations
200,000   University of Pennsylvania School of Nursing, Philadelphia, PA
100,000   Arthritis Foundation, Philadelphia, PA -- for action plan
100,000   Oxford Borough Office and Public Works Department, Oxford, PA
100,000   Pennsylvania Academy of Music, Lancaster, PA
100,000   Pennsylvania Academy of Music, Lancaster, PA -- for restructuring of administrative work force
75,000   Quecreek Mine Rescue Foundation, Somerset, PA -- for monument for life site

PACIFIC LIFE INSURANCE CO.

Company Headquarters
Newport Beach, CA
Web: http://www.pacificlife.com

Company Description
Revenue: US$4.93 billion (2004)
Profit: US$539.4 million (2004)
Employees: 2500 (2003)
Fortune Rank: 395, per FORTUNE Magazine's list of 500 Largest U.S. Corporations (2004).
SIC(s): 6311 Life Insurance, 6321 Accident & Health Insurance, 6371 Pension, Health & Welfare Funds, 6799 Investors Nec.

Operating Locations
Pacific Mutual Life Insurance Co. (CA--Covina, Fountain Valley, Los Angeles, Newport Beach, Walnut Creek; CT--Farmington; FL--Tampa, West Palm Beach; MA--Framingham; NC--Greensboro; OH--Dayton; OR--Portland; TN--Nashville; TX--Dallas, Houston; UT--Ogden; WA--Kirkland)

Nonmonetary Support
Value: $503,182 (2001)
Type: Donated Equipment; In-kind Services
Volunteer Programs: Company supports employee volunteerism through the Good Guys program, steering volunteers to local community projects.

Pacific Life Foundation

Giving Contact
Robert G. Haskell, President
700 Newport Center Drive
Newport Beach, CA 92660-6397
Phone: (949)219-3787
Web: http://www.pacificlife.com/AboutPacificLife/FoundationorCommunity/index.htm

Description
EIN: 953433806
Organization Type: Corporate Foundation
Giving Locations: AZ: Phoenix; CA: Orange County, and some statewide organizations primarily to organizations in areas with large concentrations of company employees; some funding nationally.
Grant Types: Award, Capital, Employee Matching Gifts, General Support, Multiyear/Continuing Support.
Note: Employee matching gift ratio: 1 to 1 for higher education.

Financial Summary
Total Giving: $2,879,730 (2002); $3,199,414 (2001). Note: Contributes through corporate direct giving program and foundation. 2000 total giving does not include Pacific Life in-kind support; corporate direct giving figure includes Pacific Life direct grants ($200,000) and event support ($132,300).
Giving Analysis: Giving for 2002 includes: foundation grants to United Way ($312,810); 2001: foundation grants to United Way ($308,127); foundation matching gifts ($397,213); nonmonetary support ($503,182); foundation ($2,644,833)
Assets: $30,994,633 (2002); $37,517,609 (2001)
Gifts Received: $74,630 (2002); $49,414 (2001); $7,022,104 (2000). Note: In 2002, contributions were received from Pacific Life Insurance Company.

Typical Recipients
Arts & Humanities: Arts Associations & Councils, Arts Centers, Arts Festivals, Arts Funds, Arts Institutes, Ballet, Dance, Ethnic & Folk Arts, Film & Video, Arts & Humanities-General, Historic Preservation, Libraries, Museums/Galleries, Music, Opera, Performing Arts, Public Broadcasting, Theater
Civic & Public Affairs: Asian American Affairs, Botanical Gardens/Parks, Civil Rights, Clubs, Community Foundations, Economic Development, Economic Policy, Employment/Job Training, Civic & Public Affairs-General, Hispanic Affairs, Housing, Law & Justice, Legal Aid, Municipalities/Towns, Nonprofit Management, Professional & Trade Associations, Public Policy, Safety, Urban & Community Affairs, Women's Affairs, Zoos/Aquariums
Education: Afterschool/Enrichment Programs, Business Education, Business-School Partnerships, Colleges & Universities, Continuing Education, Economic Education, Education Funds, Education Reform, Environmental Education, Education-General, Health & Physical Education, Leadership Training, Medical Education, Minority Education, Private Education (Precollege), Public Education (Precollege), School Volunteerism, Science/Mathematics Education, Secondary Education (Public), Special Education, Student Aid
Environment: Air/Water Quality, Environment-General, Wildlife Protection
Health: AIDS/HIV, Alzheimer's Disease, Cancer, Children's Health/Hospitals, Diabetes, Emergency/Ambulance Services, Eyes/Blindness, Geriatric Health, Health Policy/Cost Containment, Health Funds, Health Organizations, Heart, Hospices, Hospitals, Medical Rehabilitation, Medical Research, Medical Training, Mental Health, Multiple Sclerosis, Nutrition, Prenatal Health Issues, Preventive Medicine/Wellness Organizations, Public Health, Respiratory, Single-Disease Health Associations, Speech & Hearing, Trauma Treatment
International: Health Care/Hospitals, International Environmental Issues, Missionary/Religious Activities
Religion: Religion-General, Jewish Causes, Religious Welfare
Science: Science Museums, Scientific Centers & Institutes, Scientific Research
Social Services: At-Risk Youth, Child Abuse, Child Welfare, Community Service Organizations, Counseling, Day Care, Delinquency & Criminal Rehabilitation, Domestic Violence, Emergency Relief, Family Planning, Family Services, Food/Clothing Distribution, Homes, People with Disabilities, Recreation & Athletics, Refugee Assistance, Senior Services, Shelters/Homelessness, Social Services-General, Substance Abuse, United Funds/United Ways, Veterans, Volunteer Services, YMCA/YWCA/YMHA/YWHA, Youth Organizations

Application Procedures
Initial Contact: The foundation does not have a grant application form.
Application Requirements: Proposals should include a description of the program/project to be fund-

ed, including a needs statement and objectives (1-2 pages); organization's current annual budget (revenues and expenditures) and most recent audited financial statement; budget for project to be funded; list of other agency contributors and levels of support; a list of the agency's board of directors, advisory board members, and staff; proof of tax-exempt status; and a copy of the agency's information brochure, if available.

Deadlines: August 31 (postmark date), for consideration for the following calendar year's budget.

Evaluative Criteria: Applications are evaluated on the type of activity being promoted; population affected; how regional issues are confronted; how progress can be documented; supportiveness of public welfare; need served by proposed activity and duplication of function; and the benefit to or involvement of employees.

Decision Notification: Applicants are notified of funding decisions in mid-December, with payment made before the end of January.

Notes: The foundation does not accept faxed or e-mailed applications, nor does it accept videos.

Restrictions

Foundation does not support individuals; political parties, candidates, or partisan political organizations; veterans and labor organizations, fraternal organizations, athletic clubs, or social clubs; religious organizations for sectarian or denominational purposes, except for programs that are available to anyone; fundraising events; or advertising sponsorship.

Additional Information

Generally prefers to make annual grants. Organizations may reapply annually, but grants typically are made to one organization for no more than three consecutive years.

The foundation reports that each year it selects five to seven areas of special focus (e.g. AIDS, homelessness, Hispanic needs) and makes major grants in that focus area. These grants are usually made later in the calendar year after the foundation has done considerable research. research. research. research.

Publications: Community Involvement Report

Corporate Officials

Marianne Beaz: vice president client service & pension investments PRIM CORP EMPL vice president client service & pension investments: Pacific Mutual Life Insurance Co.

Anthony J. Bonno: senior vice president human resources PRIM CORP EMPL senior vice president human resources: Pacific Mutual Life Insurance Co.

David R. Carmichael: senior vice president, general counsel, director PRIM CORP EMPL senior vice president, general counsel, director: Pacific Mutual Life Insurance Co. CORP AFFIL senior vice president: Pacific Life Insurance Co.; director: PM Group Life Insurance Co.

Marc Scott Franklin: senior vice president strategic planning B Norwalk, CT 1959. ED Claremont McKenna College (1982); University of Chicago (1982). PRIM CORP EMPL senior vice president strategic planning: Pacific Mutual Life Insurance Co.

Robert G. Haskell: senior vice president public affairs B Orange, CA 1952. ED University of Southern California (1974); University of Southern California (1979). PRIM CORP EMPL senior vice president public affairs: Pacific Mutual Life Insurance Co.

Audrey L. Milfs: vice president, corporate secretary, director B 1945. PRIM CORP EMPL vice president, corporate secretary, director: Pacific Mutual Life Insurance Co. CORP AFFIL secretary: Pacific Mutual Distributors.

Michele Myszka: community relations director, public affairs

Glenn Stanley Schafer: president, director B Saint Johns, MI 1949. ED Michigan State University (1971); University of Detroit (1975). PRIM CORP EMPL president, director: Pacific Mutual Life Insurance Co. ADD CORP EMPL chief financial officer:

Pacific Financial Asset Management Corp.; director: Pacific Life & Annuity Co.; president: Pacific Mutual Holding Co. CORP AFFIL director: Pimco Advisor LP. NONPR AFFIL member: Financial Executives Institute; fellow: Life Management Institute; director: Court Appointed Special Advocates; member: American Institute CPAs.

Thomas C. Sutton: chairman, chief executive officer, director B Atlanta, GA 1942. ED University of Toronto BS (1965); Harvard University (1982). PRIM CORP EMPL chairman, chief executive officer, director: Pacific Mutual Life Insurance Co. CORP AFFIL chairman: PM Group Life Insurance Co.; director: Pimco Advisor LP; chairman: Pacific Life Corp.; director: Pacific Mutual Distributors; director: Pacific Finance Asset Management Corp.; director: Edison International; director: Newhall Land & Farming Co. NONPR AFFIL fellow: Society Actuaries; member affiliates advisory board: University California Irvine School Management; member: Pacific Studies Actuarial Club; member: American Academy of Actuaries.

Khanh T. Tran: executive vice president, chief financial officer, director B Saigon, Vietnam 1956. ED Whittier College (1977); University of California (1980). PRIM CORP EMPL senior vice president, chief financial officer, director: Pacific Mutual Life Insurance Co. NONPR AFFIL member: Life Office Management Association; member: Treasury Management Association; member: Finance Executive Institute; member: Finance Officer Group.

Raymond L. Watson: vice chairman PRIM CORP EMPL vice chairman: Irvine Co. CORP AFFIL director: Walt Disney Co.

Foundation Officials

Edward R. Byrd: chief financial officer PRIM CORP EMPL chief financial officer: Pacific Mutual Distributor.

Robert G. Haskell: president, director (see above)

Michael T. McLaughlin: general counsel

Audrey L. Milfs: secretary (see above)

Michele Myszka: vice president, director (see above)

Thomas C. Sutton: chairman, director (see above)

Grants Analysis

Disclosure Period: calendar year ending 2002
Total Grants: $2,566,920*
Number of Grants: 338
Average Grant: $6,729*
Highest Grant: $292,580
Lowest Grant: $500
Typical Range: $2,500 to $10,000 and $10,000 to $100,000
*Note: Giving excludes United Way. Average grant figure excludes highest grant.

Recent Grants

Note: Grants derived from 2003 Form 990.

General

276,422	United Way of Orange County, Irvine, CA
150,000	National Fish and Wildlife Foundation, San Francisco, CA
120,000	Orange County Department of Education Advancement Via Individual Determination Program, San Diego, CA
100,000	South Coast Repertory, Costa Mesa, CA
72,500	Cambodian Family Inc., Santa Ana, CA
65,000	Saddleback Community Outreach, Laguna Hills, CA
60,500	Orange County Coastkeeper, Newport Beach, CA
53,000	NAMI, Santa Ana, CA
50,000	Aquarium of the Pacific, Long Beach, CA
50,000	Assistance League of Newport Mesa, Costa Mesa, CA

PACIFICARE HEALTH SYSTEMS

Company Headquarters
3120 Lake Center Drive
Santa Ana, CA 92704
Phone: (714)825-5200
Fax: (714)825-5045
Web: http://www.phs.com

Company Description
Founded: 1978
Ticker: PHSY
Exchange: NASDAQ
Acquired: FHP International.
Revenue: US$12.276 billion (2004)
Profit: US$303.2 million (2004)
Employees: 7700 (2003)
Fortune Rank: 172, per FORTUNE Magazine's list of 500 Largest U.S. Corporations (2004).

PacifiCare Health System Foundation

Giving Contact
Riva Gebel, Director
3120 Lake Center Dr.
Mail Stop LC01-320
PO Box 25186
Santa Ana, CA 92704
Phone: (714)825-5233
Fax: (714)825-5028
Note: Applications sent via U.S. mail should be addressed to the PO Box; those sent via delivery service should be addressed to the street address.

Description
Founded: 1996
EIN: 330473608
Organization Type: Corporate Foundation
Giving Locations: AZ: within company service areas; CA: within company service area; CO: within company service areas; NV: within company service areas; OK: within company service area; OR: within company service area; TX: within company service areas; WA: within company service areas; Guam: ; within company service areas.
Grant Types: General Support, Project.

Financial Summary
Total Giving: $1,977,148 (2002); $2,246,860 (2001). Note: Contributes through corporate direct giving program and foundation.
Giving Analysis: Giving for 2002 includes: foundation grants to United Way ($50,000)
Assets: $4,197,268 (2002); $2,322,678 (2001)
Gifts Received: $4,393,402 (2002); $1,132,819 (2001); $856,731 (2000). Note: In 2002, contributions were received from PacifiCare Health Plan Administrators ($372,000), Marilyn A. McCullough ($6,000), PacifiCare of California, Inc. ($3,500,000), and other miscellaneous contributions of less than $5,000 ($515,402). In 2001, contributions were received from PacifiCare Health Plan Administrators ($617,375), Marilyn A. McCullough ($6,000), and other miscellaneous contributions of less than $5,000 ($509,444). In fiscal 2000, contributions were received from Terry Hartshorn ($50,000), Pacificare Health Plan Administrators ($100,000), Pacificare of California ($35,013), Pacificare of Asia Pacific ($18,048), Alan Hoops ($119,652), and other miscellaneous contributions less than $5,000 each ($534,018). In fiscal 1999, contributions were received from PacifiCare of California ($5,790,000); PacifiCare Health Plan Administrators ($1,689,195); Alan Hoops ($91,194); Terry Hartshorn ($85,570); and miscellaneous contributions of approximately

$5,000 or less. In fiscal 1996, contributions were received from C. William Wood ($6,200). In fiscal 1995, contributions were received from PacifiCare of California ($1,000,000), PacifiCare Health Systems ($750,000), Terry Hartshorn PacifiCare Health Systems ($750,000), Terry Hartshorn ($131,527), Hal C. Hylton ($20,000), and C. William Wood ($5,000); miscellaneous contributions under $5,000 each, totaling $1,002,843 also were received.

Typical Recipients

Arts & Humanities: Ballet, Libraries, Museums/Galleries, Public Broadcasting, Theater
Civic & Public Affairs: Asian American Affairs, Community Foundations, Economic Development, Employment/Job Training, Civic & Public Affairs-General, Hispanic Affairs, Housing, Municipalities/Towns, Philanthropic Organizations, Women's Affairs, Zoos/Aquariums
Education: Afterschool/Enrichment Programs, Colleges & Universities, Education Associations, Education-General, Leadership Training, Preschool Education, Public Education (Precollege), Science/Mathematics Education, Special Education
Environment: Environment-General, Resource Conservation
Health: Adolescent Health Issues, AIDS/HIV, Alzheimer's Disease, Arthritis, Cancer, Children's Health/Hospitals, Clinics/Medical Centers, Diabetes, Emergency/Ambulance Services, Health-General, Geriatric Health, Health Funds, Health Organizations, Heart, Hospices, Hospitals, Long-Term Care, Medical Rehabilitation, Medical Research, Mental Health, Multiple Sclerosis, Prenatal Health Issues, Preventive Medicine/Wellness Organizations, Public Health, Single-Disease Health Associations
International: Missionary/Religious Activities
Religion: Churches, Ministries, Missionary Activities (Domestic), Religious Organizations, Religious Welfare
Social Services: Animal Protection, At-Risk Youth, Big Brothers/Big Sisters, Camps, Child Abuse, Child Welfare, Community Centers, Community Service Organizations, Counseling, Crime Prevention, Day Care, Domestic Violence, Emergency Relief, Family Services, Food/Clothing Distribution, Homes, People with Disabilities, Recreation & Athletics, Senior Services, Sexual Abuse, Shelters/Homelessness, Social Services-General, Substance Abuse, United Funds/United Ways, Volunteer Services, Youth Organizations

Application Procedures

Initial Contact: Call or write to request guidelines, application form, and checklist; then submit two copies of completed form and application materials.
Application Requirements: Include (in duplicate) the completed application form; checklist form; cover letter signed by either the chief executive officer or appointee of the organization, summarizing the proposed project, problem addressed, and amount requested, along with name and phone number of contact person; a proposal of two to five pages; proof of tax-exempt status; recently audited financial statement; current operating budgets and line item budget for the project; most recent IRS Form 990, signed and dated, including all schedules; list of major funders and amounts; list of board of directors; any other support documents; and a one paragraph summary of any previous support from the PacifiCare Foundation. The two to five page proposal must include background information and qualifications of the applicant organization, including purpose, current programs, and activities; description of the problem or need; description of the proposed project including goals, objective, timeline, staffing and evaluation of the project; geographic area served by the organization; and line item project budget, including an explanation of how the organization will secure future funding.
Deadlines: January 1 or July 1.
Review Process: Proposals reviewed by foundation staff, then forwarded to an Employee Allocation Committee for review; committees make recommendations to foundation board of directors.
Decision Notification: Board meets in June and December, decisions announced in late-June and late-December.

Restrictions

Grants are only considered to nonprofit, tax-exempt organizations serving company market areas, and which have been in existence at least two years. Grants are not considered for the following: arts/cultural programs, professional or technical associations, annual campaigns or fundraising, research, endowments, conferences or seminars, individuals, private foundations, programs which promote religious doctrine, sponsorship of special events, scholarships, challenge grants, matching grants, capital campaigns or multiple year requests.

Additional Information

Organizations may re-apply annually; only one grant may be received per organization per year.
Publications: Annual Report; Application Form and Guidelines

Corporate Officials

Bradford A. Bowlus: executive vice presidento, director PRIM CORP EMPL executive vice president: PacifiCare Health Systems Inc. ADD CORP EMPL principal: PacifiCare California. NONPR AFFIL member: Young Presidents' Organization.
Robert N. Franklin: senior vice president public affairs PRIM CORP EMPL senior vice president public affairs: PacifiCare Health Systems Inc.
Wanda A. Lee: senior vice president corporate human resources PRIM CORP EMPL senior vice president corporate human resources: PacifiCare Health Systems Inc.
Howard G. Phanstiel: president, chief executive officer, director ED Syracuse University BA; Syracuse University MA. ADD CORP EMPL president, chief executive officer, director: PacifiCare Health Systems Inc.

Foundation Officials

Bradford A. Bowlus: president, chief executive officer (see above)
Nick Franklin: senior vice president
James Frey: director
Riva Gebel: director
Terry O'Dell Hartshorn: chairman B 1944. ED University of California, Los Angeles BS (1967); University of California, Los Angeles MS (1979). CORP AFFIL president, chief executive officer: UniHealth America.
Alan R. Hoops: director B 1947. ED University of California, Los Angeles BA (1969); University of Washington MS (1973).
Howard G. Phanstiel: president, chief executive officer (see above)
C. William Wood: president

Grants Analysis

Disclosure Period: calendar year ending 2002
Total Grants: $1,927,148*
Number of Grants: 340
Average Grant: $4,222*
Highest Grant: $300,000
Lowest Grant: $100
Typical Range: $300 to $5,000
*Note: Giving excludes United Way. Average grant figure excludes two highest grants ($500,000).

Recent Grants

Note: Grants derived from 2003 Form 990.
General

500,000	American Heart Association, Dallas, TX
200,000	American Diabetes Association, Alexandria, VA
50,000	Dream Foundation, Santa Barbara, CA
50,000	Health Funders Partnership, Irvine, CA
25,000	Dream Foundation, Santa Barbara, CA
25,000	Dream Foundation, Santa Barbara, CA
25,000	Dream Foundation, Santa Barbara, CA
25,000	Dream Foundation, Santa Barbara, CA
25,000	Goodwill Industries, Los Angeles, CA
25,000	Painted Turtle, Malibu, CA

PACIFICORP

Company Headquarters

Portland, OR
Web: http://www.pacificorp.com

Company Description

Founded: 1910
Ticker: SPI
Exchange: NYSE
Assets: US$10.671 billion (2001)
Employees: 6300 (2001)
SIC(s): 1041 Gold Ores, 1044 Silver Ores, 1094 Uranium, Radium & Vanadium Ores, 4911 Electric Services.

Operating Locations

PacifiCorp (AK--Anchorage, Bethel, Fairbanks; MT--Billings; OR--Hillsboro, Salem, Wilsonville; WA--Vancouver; WV)

Nonmonetary Support

Type: Donated Equipment; Workplace Solicitation
Note: Nonmonetary support is provided by the company.

PacifiCorp Foundation

Giving Contact

Isaac Regenstreif, Executive Director
Pacificorp Foundation
825 NE Multnomah, Suite 2000
Portland, OR 97232-4116
Phone: (503)813-7257
Fax: (503)813-7249
Web: http://www.pacificorpfoundation.org/

Alternate Contact

Phone: (503)813-5908

Description

Founded: 1988
EIN: 943089826
Organization Type: Corporate Foundation
Giving Locations: CA: Northern California; ID; NV; OR; UT; WA; WY
Grant Types: Capital, Emergency, General Support, Multiyear/Continuing Support, Project, Research, Scholarship.

Donor Information

Founder: Pacific Power & Light Co., Utah Power & Light Co., Pacific Telecom, Inc., Pacificorp Financial Services

Financial Summary

Total Giving: $2,361,047 (fiscal year ending March 31, 2003); $2,279,322 (fiscal 2002); $2,538,471 (fiscal 2001). Note: In 2000, the foundation changed from a calendar year to a fiscal year. Giving for 1999 reflects grants made from 01/01/1999 to 12/31/1999; giving for fiscal 2000 includes grants made from 01/01/2000 to 03/31/2000; giving for fiscal 2001 reflects grants made from 04/01/2000 to 03/31/2001.
Giving Analysis: Giving for fiscal 2001 includes: foundation scholarships ($58,750); foundation matching gifts ($142,274); foundation grants to United Way ($354,536); foundation ($1,982,911)
Assets: $30,784,856 (fiscal 2003); $36,366,402 (fiscal 2002); $37,361,708 (fiscal 2001)

Gifts Received: $3,000,000 (fiscal 2003); $63,000 (fiscal 2002); $5,000,000 (fiscal 2000). Note: Contributions are received from Pacific Power & Light Co., Pacific Telecom, Inc. and PacifiCorp Holdings, Inc.

Typical Recipients

Arts & Humanities: Arts Associations & Councils, Arts Festivals, Ballet, Historic Preservation, Libraries, Museums/Galleries, Music, Opera, Performing Arts, Public Broadcasting, Theater

Civic & Public Affairs: African American Affairs, Botanical Gardens/Parks, Community Foundations, Economic Development, Employment/Job Training, Civic & Public Affairs-General, Housing, Law & Justice, Rural Affairs, Urban & Community Affairs, Zoos/Aquariums

Education: Afterschool/Enrichment Programs, Arts/Humanities Education, Business Education, Colleges & Universities, Education Associations, Education Funds, Elementary Education (Public), Education-General, Private Education (Precollege), Public Education (Precollege), Science/Mathematics Education, Student Aid

Environment: Energy, Environment-General, Protection, Resource Conservation, Wildlife Protection

Health: AIDS/HIV, Children's Health/Hospitals, Emergency/Ambulance Services, Health Organizations, Hospitals, Public Health

International: International Organizations

Science: Science Museums

Social Services: At-Risk Youth, Child Welfare, Community Centers, Community Service Organizations, Family Planning, Family Services, Food/Clothing Distribution, People with Disabilities, Recreation & Athletics, Scouts, Shelters/Homelessness, United Funds/United Ways, YMCA/YWCA/YMHA/YWHA, Youth Organizations

Application Procedures

Initial Contact: Send a one-page summary and a proposal of no more than 20 pages (including attachments and application form) to foundation; contact appropriate subsidiary or local manager.

Application Requirements: Complete, submit, and print a copy of application form, which includes contact information and TIN for applicant; information concerning previously received support from the Foundation or Pacificorp subsidiaries; signed acknowledgement by organization's CEO of proposal approval; a description of organization and its particular qualifications for funding activity; and an estimate of people served and their locations. Include a letter of request, no more than one page requesting Foundation assistance. On the one page summary, include project seeking support; importance of project; total project budget; percentage of total operating budget that project budget represents; amount requested; itemized amounts of financial support requested by other donors, or already pledged or contributed by other donors, and indication if it is a matched grant; and the way in which funds would be applied and the resulting benefits. Other information on the project should include, project description and who will benefit; statement of project status (new or continuing) and whether it is demonstration, pilot, or replication; explanation of needs that the project addresses and indication of community support; overall project goals, impact, and specific and measurable objectives; description of how project will be evaluated; description of project staff and qualifications; and indication of collaboration with other organizations doing similar work. Budget information should include, breakdown of items in each category; purpose of funds sought and the application of funds; itemized description of other financial support received or pledged; explanation of project sustainability after funding period is over; and recently audited financial statement. Proof of tax-exempt status is also required.

Deadlines: March 15 for education and research organizations; June 15 for civic and community grants and others not covered in other categories; September 15 for arts and cultural organizations; December 15 for health, welfare, and social service organizations.

Review Process: Requests up to $5,000 are reviewed quarterly by the Foundation Contributions Committee. Largest grants are considered at quarterly foundation board meetings.

Restrictions

Foundation grants are not made to any non-charitable purpose; establishment or support of endowments; operating deficits; individuals; to religious organizations for religious purposes; political organizations, campaigns, or candidates for political office; organizations that discriminate against individuals on the basis of creed, color, sex, age, national origin or veteran status; veterans or fraternal organizations; sponsorship or advertising that directly benefits marketing or sales programs of PacifiCorp or its operating companies; memberships in chambers of commerce, taxpayer associations, and other bodies; capital campaigns; conferences, conventions, and events; and projects outside the six-state region served by PacifiCorp subsidiaries. benefit PacifiCorp or its operating companies.

Additional Information

Direct giving by the company will go only to organizations that are ineligible for grants under foundation guidelines. Subsidiaries and divisions of PacifiCorp that contribute to the PacifiCorp Foundation include Pacific Power, Pacific Telecom, and PacifiCorp Holdings, Inc.

Subsidiaries: Pacific Power, 920 SW 6th Ave., Portland, OR 97204 (503) 464-5000; Pacific Telecom, 805 Broadway, Box 9901, Vancouver, WA 98669, (360) 905-5800; PacifiCorp Holdings, Inc., 825 NE Multnomah, Suite 775, Portland, OR 97232.

PacifiCorp merged with Scottish Power in November 1999. 825 NE Multnomah, Suite 775, Portland, OR 97232.

PacifiCorp merged with Scottish Power in November 1999.

Corporate Officials

John A. Bohling: senior vice president vice president, chief financial officer B Salt Lake City, UT 1943. ED University of Utah BSEE (1968); University of Delaware MBA (1972). PRIM CORP EMPL senior vice president: PacifiCorp.

Richard T. O'Brien: senior executive vice president, chief financial officer ED Chicago State University BA (1976); Portland State University JD (1985). PRIM CORP EMPL senior executive vice president, chief financial officer: PacifiCorp.

Foundation Officials

Ernest Bloch, II: executive director
John A. Bohling: board member (see above)
Pamela Bradford: executive director
Gary Charlestein: secretary, treasurer
Henry Hewitt: director
Tom Imeson: chairman, director PRIM CORP EMPL vice president public affairs & communications: Public Affairs & Communications.
Judi Johansen: director
Jack Kelly: director
William Landels: director
Richard T. O'Brien: member (see above)
Michael Pittman: chairman
Gloria Quirk: assistant secretary
Isaac Regenstreif: executive director
Alan Richardson: executive director
Richard Walje: director

Grants Analysis

Disclosure Period: fiscal year ending March 31, 2003
Total Grants: $1,591,987*
Number of Grants: 244
Average Grant: $6,525
Highest Grant: $100,000

Lowest Grant: $500
Typical Range: $1,000 to $10,000
*Note: Giving excludes United Way.

Recent Grants

Note: Grants derived from 2003 Form 990.

General

185,000	United Way of the Columbia, Portland, OR -- for fall 2002 community giving campaign
100,984	United Way of the Great Salt Lake Area, Salt Lake City, UT -- for annual campaign
100,000	Oregon Department of Education, Salem, OR -- for project optimize
100,000	United Way of Sweetwater County, Rock Springs, WY -- for employee match Bridger power plant
100,000	Utah Humanities Council, Salt Lake City, UT -- for Utah learning initiative-motheread/fatheread program
100,000	Wyoming Department of Family Services, Cheyenne, WY -- for raising readers in Wyoming-early childhood literacy project
55,000	United Way of the Columbia, Portland, OR -- for success by 6 program
55,000	United Way of the Columbia, Portland, OR -- for success by 6 program
55,000	United Way of the Columbia, Portland, OR -- for success by 6 program
55,000	United Way of the Columbia, Portland, OR -- for success by 6 program

DAVID AND LUCILE PACKARD FOUNDATION

Giving Contact

Carol S. Larson, President & Chief Executive Officer
300 Second Street, Suite 200
Los Altos, CA 94022
Phone: (650)948-7658
Fax: (650)948-5793
Web: http://www.packard.org

Description

Founded: 1964
EIN: 942278431
Organization Type: Family Foundation
Giving Locations: CA: Monterey County, San Mateo County, Santa Clara County, Santa Cruz County internationally; nationally.
Grant Types: Award, Capital, Challenge, Conference/Seminar, Emergency, Employee Matching Gifts, Fellowship, General Support, Loan, Matching, Multiyear/Continuing Support, Operating Expenses, Project, Seed Money.

Donor Information

Founder: The David and Lucile Packard Foundation was established in 1964. The foundation's donors are David Packard, the foundation's president, and his late wife, Lucile Salter Packard. The couple's four children, David Woodley Packard, Nancy Ann Packard Burnett, Susan Packard Orr, and Julie Elizabeth Packard, have all served on their parents' foundation. David Packard and William Hewlett founded Hewlett-Packard Company in 1938. The company became a major manufacturer of test and measurement instruments and microcomputers. Mr. Packard also served as United States Secretary of Defense between 1969 and 1971.

Financial Summary

Total Giving: $217,000,000 (2004 approx); $277,891,647 (2003); $198,858,516 (2002)
Giving Analysis: Giving for 2003 includes: foundation grants to United Way ($387,300)
Assets: $5,200,000,000 (2004 approx);

$5,982,468,233 (2003); $4,793,893,254 (2002)
Gifts Received: $1,323,421 (2000); $1,744,006 (1998); $1,744,006 (1997). Note: In 2000, contributions were received from the Estate of David Packard ($807,611) and the David and Lucile S. Packard Trust II ($515,810). In 1997 and 1998, contributions were received from the David and Lucile S. Packard Trust II. The foundation received annual contributions from Hewlett-Packard common stock through 2003.

Typical Recipients

Arts & Humanities: Arts Associations & Councils, Arts Centers, Arts Funds, Ballet, Community Arts, Dance, Ethnic & Folk Arts, Film & Video, Arts & Humanities-General, Historic Preservation, History & Archaeology, Libraries, Literary Arts, Museums/Galleries, Music, Opera, Performing Arts, Public Broadcasting, Theater

Civic & Public Affairs: Botanical Gardens/Parks, Business/Free Enterprise, Civil Rights, Community Foundations, Economic Development, Employment/Job Training, Civic & Public Affairs-General, Housing, Municipalities/Towns, Native American Affairs, Nonprofit Management, Philanthropic Organizations, Professional & Trade Associations, Public Policy, Rural Affairs, Urban & Community Affairs, Women's Affairs, Zoos/Aquariums

Education: Afterschool/Enrichment Programs, Arts/Humanities Education, Business Education, Colleges & Universities, Education Associations, Education Funds, Education Reform, Elementary Education (Private), Engineering/Technological Education, Environmental Education, Faculty Development, Education-General, International Exchange, International Studies, Literacy, Medical Education, Minority Education, Private Education (Precollege), Public Education (Precollege), School Volunteerism, Science/Mathematics Education, Secondary Education (Public), Student Aid, Vocational & Technical Education

Environment: Air/Water Quality, Energy, Forestry, Environment-General, Protection, Resource Conservation, Watershed, Wildlife Protection

Health: Children's Health/Hospitals, Clinics/Medical Centers, Emergency/Ambulance Services, Health-General, Health Policy/Cost Containment, Health Funds, Health Organizations, Heart, Hospitals, Long-Term Care, Medical Research, Nursing Services, Nutrition, Prenatal Health Issues, Preventive Medicine/Wellness Organizations, Public Health, Research/Studies Institutes

International: Foreign Educational Institutions, Health Care/Hospitals, International Development, International Environmental Issues, International Organizations, International Peace & Security Issues, International Relations, International Relief Efforts

Religion: Churches, Religion-General, Jewish Causes, Religious Welfare

Science: Science Museums, Scientific Centers & Institutes, Scientific Organizations, Scientific Research

Social Services: At-Risk Youth, Child Welfare, Community Centers, Community Service Organizations, Counseling, Day Care, Family Planning, Family Services, Food/Clothing Distribution, Homes, People with Disabilities, Recreation & Athletics, Refugee Assistance, Shelters/Homelessness, United Funds/United Ways, YMCA/YWCA/YMHA/YWHA, Youth Organizations

Application Procedures

Initial Contact: See foundation website for program and application information, then submit a brief letter of inquiry in area of interest.

Application Requirements: Letter of inquiry should provide descriptive title for the project and should explain the project's objectives, significance, funding needs, and relationship to the specific grantmaking priorities of the foundation. Proposals should include a cover letter with a description of organization; amount requested; organization's legal name, address and telephone number; and name of contact person. Background information should include history and purpose of organization, as well as the people and groups served. Also include a description of the program and its objectives; evidence of program's need; geographic area to be served; outline of program; and anticipated methods of evaluation. Personnel information should include who will implement the program and their qualifications, as well as names and affiliations of the directors, senior staff and trustees. Financial information should include sources of the organization's funds (both public and private); organization's budget for the years in which the program will take place; detailed project budget showing other sources of support, and the amount requested from the foundation; and the most recent audited financial statement. Attach to proposal a copy of the IRS exemption letter; documentation that the proposal is supported by organization's board of directors; attach other supporting material if necessary.

Deadlines: December 15, March 15, June 15, and September 15 for proposals.

Review Process: The foundation's board meets in March, June, September, and December.

Restrictions

Foundation does not make grants to individuals or to support religious purposes.

Additional Information

The foundation is affiliated with the Monterey Bay Aquarium Research Institute, the Stanford Theater Foundation, and the Packard Humanities Institute. The foundation provides other services such as management assistance and loans for land purchase and low-income housing.

Request a copy of guidelines and a faculty directory for contacts in the specific program areas.

Publications: Annual Report; Program Guidelines; The Future of Children (Quarterly Journal)

Foundation Officials

Nancy Ann Packard Burnett: trustee, vice chairman NONPR AFFIL trustee: Monterey Bay Aquarium.

Robert Joy Glaser, MD: emeritus trustee B Saint Louis, MO September 11, 1918. ED Harvard University SB (1940); Harvard University MD (1943); Rush University Medical College LHO (1973); City University of New York Mount Sinai Medical School DS (1984). NONPR AFFIL life member: Washington University William Greenleaf Eliot Society; member: Western Association Physicians; consulting professor: Stanford University; trustee: Washington University; trustee: Saint Louis University; member: Sigma Xi; editor: Pharos; director: Packard Humanities; director: Pharmagenesis; member: National Institute Allergy Infectious Disease; member: Institute Medicine; member: National Academy Sciences; member: Harvard University Medical School Alumni; member: Central Society Clinical Research; director: DCI; member: Association American Medical Colleges; member: Association American Physicians; member: American Society Clinical Investigation; member: American Society Experimental Pathology; member: American Federation Clinical Research; fellow: American Association Advancement Science; member: American Clinical & Climatological Association; fellow: American Academy of Arts & Sciences; member: Alpha Omega Alpha. CLUB AFFIL Harvard Club; Century Club.

Donald Kennedy: trustee

Carol S. Larson: president, chief executive officer, trustee B MN. ED Stanford University BA (1975); Yale University Law School JD (1978). NONPR AFFIL board member: Grantmakers for Children Youth & Families; board member: Northern California Grantmakers Association.

Franklin M. Orr, Jr.: trustee ED Stanford University BS (1969); University of Minnesota PhD (1976). NONPR AFFIL director: Monterey Bay Aquarium Research Institute.

Susan Packard Orr: chairman, trustee ED New Mexico Tech MS; Stanford University BA (1968); Stanford University MBA (1970); New Mexico Institute Mining and Technology MS (1984). PRIM CORP EMPL chief executive officer president, owner: Technology Resource Assistance Center. CORP AFFIL director: Hewlett-Packard Co.; founder: Telosa. NONPR AFFIL director: Childrens Health Counsel; trustee: Stanford University.

Julie Elizabeth Packard: vice chairman, trustee B 1954. ED University of California, Santa Cruz (1978). NONPR AFFIL director: Monterey Bay Aquarium Research Institute; member: Pew Oceans Commission; director: California Nature Conservancy; executive director, chairman: Monterey Bay Aquarium.

Lewis Emmett Platt: trustee B Johnson City, NY 1941. ED Cornell University BSME (1964); University of Pennsylvania MBA (1966). PRIM CORP EMPL chairman: Boeing Co. NONPR AFFIL chairman: World Trade Organization Task Force Member; board counsel: YMCA United States of America; board of overseers: Wharton School; member: Mid-Peninsula Young Men's Christian Association; member: Science Apparatus Manufacturing Association; co-chairman: Joint Venture Silicon Valley Network Board; director: Cornell University; member: Institute Electrical & Electronics Engineers; member: Computer Systems Policy Project; member: The Business Council; member: Business Roundtable.

William Kane Reilly: trustee B Decatur, IL 1940. ED Yale University BA (1962); Harvard University JD (1965); Columbia University MS (1971). PRIM CORP EMPL president, chief executive officer: Aqua International Partners LP. CORP AFFIL director: Ionics; director: Royal Caribbean International; president, chief executive officer: Aqua International Partners; director: E.I. du Pont de Nemours & Co. NONPR AFFIL trustee: Presidio Trust; chairman: World Wildlife Fund; director: National Geographic Society; trustee: American Academy in Rome; board of advisors: Goldman School of Public Policy at University of California at Berkeley.

Frank H. Roberts: emeritus trustee

Allan Rosenfield, MD: trustee NONPR AFFIL chairman: AmFar Public Policy Committee; chairman: New York Dept. of Health AIDS Advisory Council.

Robert Stephens: trustee

Edwin E. Van Bronkhorst: emeritus trustee

George Vera: vice president, chief financial officer

Colburn S. Wilbur: trustee B Palo Alto, CA 1935. ED Stanford University BA (1956); Stanford University MBA (1960).

Barbara Wright: secretary PRIM CORP EMPL partner: Finch, Montgomery & Wright.

Grants Analysis

Disclosure Period: calendar year ending 2003
Total Grants: $277,504,347*
Number of Grants: 1,422
Average Grant: $195,151
Typical Range: $25,000 to $500,000
*Note: Giving includes fellowships. Giving excludes United Way.

Recent Grants

Note: Grants derived from 2003 Form 990.
General

34,000,000 Lucile Packard Foundation for Children's Health, Palo Alto, CA -- to support children's health initiative

21,500,000 Monterey Bay Aquarium Research Institute, Moss landing, CA -- for operations research projects and capital expenses

9,583,833 Monterey Bay Aquarium Research Institute, Moss Landing, CA -- for operations research projects and capital expenses

8,300,000 Nature Conservancy Inc., Arlington, VA -- support for the operation and restoration of the Ranch

6,500,000 Resources Legacy Fund Foundation, Sacramento, CA -- for a regranting program related to California coastal marine initiative

5,000,000 Board of Trustees of the Land Stanford Jr. University, Stanford, CA -- to support the campaign for undergraduate education

5,000,000 Children's Health Council of the Mid-Peninsula, Palo Alto, CA -- for the endowment campaign

5,000,000 Energy Foundation, San Francisco, CA -- support for the China sustainable energy program

4,383,400 National Fish and Wildlife Foundation, Washington, DC -- support for the purchase of land in fee and salt-making rights for Cargill properties

3,920,205 Oregon State University, Corvallis, OR -- for the partnership for interdisciplinary studies of coastal oceans

WILLIAM S. PALEY FOUNDATION, INC.

Giving Contact
Patrick S. Gallagher, Executive Director
1 East 53rd Street, Suite 1400
New York, NY 10022
Phone: (212)888-2520
Fax: (212)308-7845
E-mail: wspf@asan.com

Description
Founded: 1936
EIN: 136085929
Organization Type: General Purpose Foundation
Giving Locations: NY: New York
Grant Types: Capital, General Support, Multiyear/Continuing Support.

Donor Information
Founder: The foundation was established in 1936 by the late William S. Paley (1901-1990), the founder and former chairman of CBS. He bequeathed more than $40 million to the foundation from his estimated personal fortune of $460 million.

Mr. Paley, a native of Chicago, began his college education at the University of Chicago but earned his bachelors of science degree from the University of Pennsylvania in 1922. He also received honorary PhDs from Ithaca College, University of Southern California, Adelphi University, Bates College, University of Pennsylvania, Brown University, Pratt Institute, Dartmouth College, and Columbia University, where he served as a trustee from 1950 to 1973.

Mr. Paley lived in New York City, home to two of his favorite charities, the Museum of Broadcasting, which he founded in 1976, and the Museum of Modern Art, where he served as chairman from 1972 to 1985. In his will, he left his valuable private art collection to the museum.

Mr. Paley, divorced from his first wife, married Barbara (Babe) Cushing in 1947. Barbara Paley died in 1978. Jeffrey Hearst and Hillary Hearst Byers are his two children from his first marriage to the former Dorothy Hart Hearst. He has two stepchildren by his second marriage, Amanda Ross and Stanley Mortimer, III, and two children, Kate C. Paley and William C. Paley, who currently serve as officers of the foundation.

Financial Summary
Total Giving: $5,158,796 (2003); $3,928,548 (2002)
Assets: $116,734,137 (2003); $106,651,521 (2002)
Gifts Received: $84,276 (1995); $108,691 (1992).
Note: Contributions were received from the estate of William Paley and from the Employees Trust Under Will of Samuel Paley in 1995.

Typical Recipients
Arts & Humanities: Arts Appreciation, Arts Associations & Councils, Arts Centers, Arts Funds, Arts Insti-

tutes, Arts Outreach, Dance, Historic Preservation, History & Archaeology, Libraries, Museums/Galleries, Performing Arts, Public Broadcasting, Theater, Visual Arts

Civic & Public Affairs: Botanical Gardens/Parks, Community Foundations, Ethnic Organizations, Civic & Public Affairs-General, Law & Justice, Legal Aid, Municipalities/Towns, Professional & Trade Associations, Public Policy, Safety, Urban & Community Affairs, Zoos/Aquariums

Education: Arts/Humanities Education, Colleges & Universities, Elementary Education (Public), Education-General, International Exchange, International Studies, Legal Education, Literacy, Medical Education, Private Education (Precollege), Public Education (Precollege), Religious Education, Secondary Education (Private), Secondary Education (Public), Social Sciences Education, Special Education, Student Aid

Environment: Resource Conservation

Health: Alzheimer's Disease, Cancer, Children's Health/Hospitals, Clinics/Medical Centers, Health Organizations, Hospices, Hospitals, Hospitals (University Affiliated), Single-Disease Health Associations

International: Foreign Arts Organizations, Foreign Educational Institutions, International Organizations, International Relations, International Relief Efforts, Missionary/Religious Activities

Religion: Religion-General, Jewish Causes, Religious Organizations, Religious Welfare, Seminaries

Science: Scientific Labs

Social Services: Animal Protection, At-Risk Youth, Child Welfare, Community Centers, Community Service Organizations, Counseling, Delinquency & Criminal Rehabilitation, Emergency Relief, Family Planning, Family Services, Food/Clothing Distribution, People with Disabilities, Refugee Assistance, Scouts, Social Services-General, Substance Abuse, United Funds/United Ways, YMCA/YWCA/YMHA/YWHA, Youth Organizations

Application Procedures
Initial Contact: Proposals should be made in writing.
Application Requirements: The foundation reports that no particular application form is required, but full financial information should be disclosed.
Deadlines: None.

Restrictions
The foundation does not make grants to individuals.

Foundation Officials
Patrick S. Gallagher: executive director
George Joseph Gillespie, III: director B New York, NY 1930. ED Georgetown University AB (1952); Harvard University LLB (1955). PRIM CORP EMPL partner: Cravath, Swaine & Moore. CORP AFFIL director: Washington Post Co. NONPR AFFIL director, chairman emeritus: National Multiple Sclerosis Society; trustee: New York University Medical Center; director: Madison Square Boys Club; secretary, director: Museum Television & Radio; member: Century Association; trustee, treasurer: Cooper-Hewitt National Design Museum. CLUB AFFIL Prouts Neck Country Club; Winged Foot Golf Club; member: Portland Country Club; Double Eagle Club; Falmouth Country Club; American Yacht Club.
Sidney W. Harl: vice president, director
Henry A. Kissinger: chairman, director
Daniel L. Mosley: director, secretary, treasurer
William Cushing Paley: vice president, director B 1948. PRIM CORP EMPL president, vice president, director: VM Development. CORP AFFIL executive vice president, director: Texwipe Co.
Phillip A. Raspe, Jr.: assistant treasurer

Grants Analysis
Disclosure Period: calendar year ending 2003
Total Grants: $5,158,796
Number of Grants: 42
Average Grant: $19,103*
Highest Grant: $2,710,000

Lowest Grant: $500
Typical Range: $10,000 to $25,000
*Note: Average grant excludes three highest grants ($4,413,796).

Recent Grants
Note: Grants derived from 2003 Form 990.
Library-Related
2,500 Katonah Village Library, Katonah, NY
General
2,710,000 Museum of Television and Radio, New York, NY
1,203,000 Museum of Television and Radio, New York, NY
500,000 Museum of Television and Radio, New York, NY
225,000 Greenpark Foundation Inc., New York, NY
100,000 Museum of Modern Art, New York, NY
75,000 Jerusalem Foundation Inc., New York, NY
50,000 Franklin and Eleanor Roosevelt Institute, Hyde Park, NY
30,000 Auburn Theological Seminary, New York, NY
25,000 Jackson Laboratory, Bar Harbor, ME
25,000 Jefferson Scholars Foundation, Charlottesville, VA

PALISADES EDUCATIONAL FOUNDATION

Giving Contact
Gerald J. Dunworth, Treasurer
665 5th Ave., 11th Fl.
New York, NY 10022
Phone: (212)688-5151

Description
Founded: 1949
EIN: 516015053
Organization Type: Private Foundation
Giving Locations: CT: Southern Connecticut; NJ: Northern New Jersey; NY headquarters and operating communities.
Grant Types: Multiyear/Continuing Support, Operating Expenses, Scholarship.

Donor Information
Founder: Prentice-Hall

Financial Summary
Total Giving: $300,000 (2001)
Giving Analysis: Giving for 2001 includes: foundation scholarships ($12,500)
Assets: $5,698,314 (2001)

Typical Recipients
Arts & Humanities: Arts Associations & Councils, Arts Centers, Arts & Humanities-General, Libraries, Music

Civic & Public Affairs: Employment/Job Training, Civic & Public Affairs-General, Native American Affairs

Education: Arts/Humanities Education, Business Education, Colleges & Universities, Community & Junior Colleges, Education Associations, Education Funds, International Studies, Legal Education, Medical Education, Minority Education, Private Education (Precollege), Science/Mathematics Education, Special Education, Student Aid

Health: Cancer, Children's Health/Hospitals, Clinics/Medical Centers, Emergency/Ambulance Services, Hospitals, Medical Research, Prenatal Health Issues, Single-Disease Health Associations

International: Foreign Educational Institutions

Religion: Religious Welfare

Science: Science Museums
Social Services: At-Risk Youth, Camps, Child Welfare, Community Service Organizations, Crime Prevention, Family Services, Homes, People with Disabilities, Recreation & Athletics, Scouts, Senior Services, Shelters/Homelessness, Substance Abuse, Volunteer Services, YMCA/YWCA/YMHA/YWHA, Youth Organizations

Application Procedures
Initial Contact: Send a brief letter of inquiry describing program and projected budget.
Deadlines: None.

Foundation Officials
Frederick W. Anthony: secretary
Ralph F. Anthony: president, director
Gerald J. Dunworth: treasurer, director
Colin Gunn: director
Donald A. Schaefer: vice president, director

Grants Analysis
Disclosure Period: calendar year ending 2001
Total Grants: $287,500*
Number of Grants: 36
Average Grant: $8,455
Highest Grant: $35,000
Typical Range: $1,000 to $20,000
***Note:** Giving excludes scholarships.

Recent Grants
Note: Grants derived from 2001 Form 990.
General

35,000	Colgate University, Hamilton, NY -- for educational fund
35,000	Marist Brothers Cancer Camp, South Orange, NJ
27,000	Englewood Hospital, Englewood, NJ
20,000	University of Bridgeport, Bridgeport, CT -- for annual fund
15,000	Contact We Care, Inc., Westfield, NJ
15,000	Volunteer Center of Bergen County, Hackensack, NJ
12,000	Coalition for the Homeless, Summit, NJ -- for operating expenses
7,500	Gettysburg College, Gettysburg, PA -- for Bob Smith scholarship fund
7,500	Medical Missions for Children, Jersey City, NJ
7,500	National Center for Adoption, Washington, DC

FRANK LOOMIS PALMER FUND

Giving Contact
Marjorie Alexandre Davis, Vice President
Fleet Bank
777 Main St., CTEH 40222B
Hartford, CT 06115
Phone: (860)986-7696
Fax: (860)952-7395
E-mail: marjorie_alexandre_davis@fleet.com

Description
Founded: 1936
EIN: 066026043
Organization Type: General Purpose Foundation
Giving Locations: CT: New London
Grant Types: Award, Capital, Conference/Seminar, General Support, Matching, Multiyear/Continuing Support, Project, Research, Scholarship, Seed Money.

Donor Information
Founder: Established in 1936 by the late Virginia Palmer in memory of her father, Frank Loomis Palmer.

Financial Summary
Total Giving: $1,513,369 (fiscal year ending July 31, 2002); $1,109,736 (fiscal 2001)
Assets: $28,106,239 (fiscal 2002)
Gifts Received: $20,000 (fiscal 1995). Note: In 1995, contributions were received from the Bodenwein Foundation.

Typical Recipients
Arts & Humanities: Arts Centers, Arts Festivals, Arts Institutes, Arts Outreach, Arts & Humanities-General, Historic Preservation, History & Archaeology, Libraries, Museums/Galleries, Music, Opera, Theater
Civic & Public Affairs: Botanical Gardens/Parks, Community Foundations, Economic Development, Employment/Job Training, Ethnic Organizations, Civic & Public Affairs-General, Hispanic Affairs, Housing, Legal Aid, Municipalities/Towns, Parades/Festivals, Professional & Trade Associations, Public Policy, Safety, Urban & Community Affairs, Women's Affairs, Zoos/Aquariums
Education: Afterschool/Enrichment Programs, Arts/Humanities Education, Colleges & Universities, Education Reform, Elementary Education (Private), Elementary Education (Public), Engineering/Technological Education, Education-General, International Studies, Leadership Training, Literacy, Minority Education, Private Education (Precollege), Public Education (Precollege), School Volunteerism, Secondary Education (Private), Secondary Education (Public), Social Sciences Education, Special Education, Student Aid, Vocational & Technical Education
Environment: Environment-General
Health: AIDS/HIV, Children's Health/Hospitals, Emergency/Ambulance Services, Health Organizations, Hospices, Hospitals, Medical Rehabilitation, Mental Health, Nursing Services, Preventive Medicine/Wellness Organizations, Public Health, Single-Disease Health Associations
Religion: Churches, Jewish Causes, Missionary Activities (Domestic), Religious Welfare
Science: Science Museums, Scientific Centers & Institutes, Scientific Organizations
Social Services: At-Risk Youth, Big Brothers/Big Sisters, Child Welfare, Community Centers, Community Service Organizations, Counseling, Domestic Violence, Emergency Relief, Family Planning, Family Services, Food/Clothing Distribution, People with Disabilities, Recreation & Athletics, Scouts, Shelters/Homelessness, Social Services-General, Substance Abuse, United Funds/United Ways, Volunteer Services, YMCA/YWCA/YMHA/YWHA, Youth Organizations

Application Procedures
Initial Contact: Initial contact should be by telephone to request an application and guidelines.
Application Requirements: Proposal should include a completed application form, an audited financial statement for the most recent year or a treasurer's report, and a project budget (for organizations in the formative stages), an IRS tax-exempt letter dated after 1969, and a proposed operating budget for the period of time in which the desired grant will be used. For organizations that are new or unfamiliar to the foundation, a brief organizational background is required. Please see guidelines for additional requirements for churches and municipalities.
Deadlines: Completed applications including all required supporting data for grants must be submitted by May 15 and November 15 of each year. If these dates fall on a Saturday or Sunday, the deadline is not extended. Applications postmarked on the day of the deadline are accepted. Complete applications received after the deadline will be held for the next review period.
Review Process: Grant awards are announced on February 1 and August 1 in "The Day" newspaper. Following the announcement, a letter will be sent to all applicants confirming the approval or denial of their request.
Notes: If awarded, a post grant evaluation is due one year from the date of the grant.

Restrictions
Grants will be limited to activities conducted or organizations located in New London. Special consideration may be given to grantees whose programs offer the possibility of matching grants. Grants are not made to individuals, for endowments, for deficit financing, or for reimbursement for items purchased prior to grant request.

Additional Information
The foundation lists the Fleet Bank as a corporate trustee.
Publications: Informational Brochure (including Application Guidelines)

Foundation Officials
Marjorie Alexandre Davis: contact

Grants Analysis
Disclosure Period: fiscal year ending July 31, 2002
Total Grants: $1,513,369
Number of Grants: 92
Average Grant: $11,948*
Highest Grant: $150,000
Lowest Grant: $600
Typical Range: $5,000 to $25,000
***Note:** Average grant figure excludes three highest grants ($450,000).

Recent Grants
Note: Grants derived from 2002 Form 990.
General

150,000	New London Development Corporation for House of New London, New London, CT
150,000	New London Development Corporation for House of New London, New London, CT
150,000	New London Development Corporation for House of New London, New London, CT
60,000	New London Main Street Corp., New London, CT
60,000	Opportunities Industrialization Center of New London County Inc.
50,000	Garde Arts Center, New London, CT
50,000	Garde Arts Center, New London, CT
50,000	Mitchell College, New London, CT
46,615	Save Ocean Beach Inc., New London, CT
40,000	Leadership Education and Athletics in Partnership, New Haven, CT

PAMIDA INC.

Company Headquarters
Omaha, NE
Web: http://www.pamida.com

Company Description
Revenue: US$300 million (2001)
Employees: 2500 (2001)
SIC(s): 5300 General Merchandise Stores.

Operating Locations
Pamida, Inc. (IL; IA; KS; MI; MO; MT; NE; ND; WI; WY)

Giving Contact
Mary Linley, Secr.
PO Box 3856
Omaha, NE 68103
Phone: (402)339-2400
Fax: (402)596-7330

Description

Organization Type: Corporate Giving Program
Giving Locations: headquarters and operating communities.
Grant Types: Challenge, Conference/Seminar, Emergency, Endowment, General Support.

Typical Recipients

Arts & Humanities: Arts Funds, Arts & Humanities-General, Libraries, Museums/Galleries
Civic & Public Affairs: Botanical Gardens/Parks, Clubs, Community Foundations, Civic & Public Affairs-General, Parades/Festivals, Safety, Urban & Community Affairs
Education: Agricultural Education, Colleges & Universities, Elementary Education (Public), Education-General, Private Education (Precollege), School Volunteerism, Student Aid
Health: Children's Health/Hospitals, Emergency/Ambulance Services, Health-General, Geriatric Health, Health Funds, Hospitals
Social Services: Community Centers, Community Service Organizations, Crime Prevention, Food/Clothing Distribution, People with Disabilities, Recreation & Athletics, Senior Services, Social Services-General, Substance Abuse, Veterans, Youth Organizations

Application Procedures

Initial Contact: Send a brief letter of inquiry.
Application Requirements: Include a description of organization, amount requested, purpose of funds sought, and proof of tax-exempt status.
Deadlines: None.

Restrictions

Does not support individuals, religious organizations for sectarian purposes, political or lobbying groups, or organizations outside operating areas.

Additional Information

The Pamida Foundation was dissolved in 1995. The company continues to support local organizations through a decentralized corporate giving program with individual stores handling requests and administering independent budgets. The focus is on addressing needs at the local level. Pamida's stores in its 15-state operating region handle requests from local organizations. Contact the stores directly. Organizations in Omaha may contact corporate headquarters.

Corporate Officials

Steven S. Fishman: chairman, president, chief executive officer PRIM CORP EMPL chairman, president, chief executive officer: Pamida.

Grants Analysis

Typical Range: $100 to $1,000

THOMAS ANTHONY PAPPAS CHARITABLE FOUNDATION

Giving Contact

John C. Pappas, Executive Director
PO Box 463
Belmont, MA 02478-0004
Phone: (781)862-2802

Description

Founded: 1975
EIN: 510153284
Organization Type: Family Foundation
Giving Locations: MA

Grant Types: Capital, Endowment, Fellowship, Research, Scholarship.

Donor Information

Founder: Incorporated in 1975 by the late Thomas Anthony Pappas.

Financial Summary

Total Giving: $826,670 (2001)
Assets: $20,321,536 (2001)

Typical Recipients

Arts & Humanities: Arts Associations & Councils, Arts Centers, Ballet, Dance, Arts & Humanities-General, Historic Preservation, History & Archaeology, Literary Arts, Museums/Galleries, Music, Performing Arts, Public Broadcasting, Theater
Civic & Public Affairs: Clubs, Community Foundations, Economic Development, Ethnic Organizations, Civic & Public Affairs-General, Law & Justice, Municipalities/Towns, Parades/Festivals, Philanthropic Organizations, Professional & Trade Associations, Public Policy, Urban & Community Affairs, Women's Affairs, Zoos/Aquariums
Education: Arts/Humanities Education, Business Education, Colleges & Universities, Community & Junior Colleges, Education-General, International Studies, Leadership Training, Legal Education, Medical Education, Minority Education, Private Education (Precollege), Science/Mathematics Education, Secondary Education (Private), Special Education, Student Aid
Health: Alzheimer's Disease, Arthritis, Cancer, Children's Health/Hospitals, Clinics/Medical Centers, Eyes/Blindness, Health-General, Health Organizations, Heart, Hospices, Hospitals, Kidney, Long-Term Care, Medical Rehabilitation, Medical Research, Nursing Services, Research/Studies Institutes, Respiratory, Single-Disease Health Associations
International: Foreign Educational Institutions, Health Care/Hospitals, Missionary/Religious Activities
Religion: Churches, Dioceses, Religion-General, Jewish Causes, Religious Organizations, Religious Welfare
Science: Science-General, Scientific Research
Social Services: Animal Protection, Big Brothers/Big Sisters, Camps, Child Welfare, Community Service Organizations, Counseling, Delinquency & Criminal Rehabilitation, Emergency Relief, Family Services, Food/Clothing Distribution, Homes, People with Disabilities, Recreation & Athletics, Scouts, Senior Services, Shelters/Homelessness, Special Olympics, Substance Abuse, YMCA/YWCA/YMHA/YWHA, Youth Organizations

Application Procedures

Initial Contact: The foundation requests applications be made in writing.
Application Requirements: Applications should include the name and address of the organization, telephone number, fax number, e-mail address, and individual to contact; the purpose of the organization; amount requested; the organization's other sources of support; a detailed description of the project and the use of the funds requested; and an IRS current exemption status and a copy of the latest determination letter.
Deadlines: September 30.

Restrictions

The foundation reports no private foundations will be considered without complete expenditure control. Grants are not made to individuals.

Additional Information

Publications: Program Policy Statement; Application Guidelines

Foundation Officials

Helen K. Pappas: director PRIM CORP EMPL clerk, director: Dudley Supermarket Inc.

John C. Pappas: director
Sophia H. Pappas: director
Donald J. Young: director

Grants Analysis

Disclosure Period: calendar year ending 2001
Total Grants: $826,670
Number of Grants: 43
Average Grant: $19,225
Highest Grant: $200,000
Lowest Grant: $1,000
Typical Range: $1,000 to $10,000 and $100,000 to $200,000

Recent Grants

Note: Grants derived from 2002 Form 990.
General

250,000	Perkins College, Watertown, MA -- toward completion of pledge
100,000	Bentley College, Waltham, MA -- assistance for CAP lectureship
100,000	Boston Foundation for Sight, Chestnut Hill, MA -- funding for free eye care
100,000	Harvard Medical School, Boston, MA -- assistance for Zervas professorship
25,000	Francis Ouimet Caddy BCC, Norton, MA -- assistance for caddy scholarship
15,000	West Suburban YMCA, Newton, MA -- funding for capital improvements
10,000	Big Brothers, Boston, MA -- funding for programs
10,000	Boston Ballet, Boston, MA -- funding for programs
10,000	Boston Symphony, Boston, MA -- assistance for opening night
10,000	Plimoth Plantation, Plymouth, MA -- assistance for field trips

PARAMETRIC TECHNOLOGY CORP.

Company Headquarters

140 Kendrick St.
Needham, MA 02494
Web: http://www.ptc.com

Company Description

Founded: 1985
Ticker: PMTC
Exchange: NASDAQ
Operating Revenue: US$742 million (2002)
Employees: 3803 (2002)
SIC(s): 7372 Prepackaged Software.

Nonmonetary Support

Type: Donated Equipment

Giving Contact

Susan Carens-Peterson, Treasury Analyst
100 Crosby Dr.
Bedford, MA 01730
Phone: (617)275-1800
Note: Ext. 2901

Description

Organization Type: Corporate Giving Program
Grant Types: General Support.

Typical Recipients

Arts & Humanities: Arts & Humanities-General, Libraries, Public Broadcasting
Civic & Public Affairs: Employment/Job Training, Civic & Public Affairs-General, Urban & Community Affairs
Education: Education-General, Preschool Education, Private Education (Precollege), Public Education (Precollege)

Health: Health-General, Hospitals
Social Services: Child Welfare

Corporate Officials

Eugene Bullis: chief financial officer PRIM CORP EMPL chief financial officer: Computervision Corp.
Kathleen Cole: president, chief executive officer PRIM CORP EMPL president, chief executive officer: Computervision Corp.
Russell E. Planitzer: chairman B South Orange, NJ 1944. ED United States Naval Academy (1966); Harvard University Graduate School of Business Administration (1974). PRIM CORP EMPL chairman: Computervision Corp. CORP AFFIL director: Voyager Software Corp.; director: Wellfleet Communication; director: Stardent Computer; director: Easel Corp.; director: Intersolv.

SAMUEL P. PARDOE FOUNDATION

Giving Contact

Mary Phillips, Administrator
c/o Grants Management Associates
77 Summer St. 8th Floor
Boston, MA 02110
Phone: (617)426-7172
Fax: (617)426-5441
Web: http://www.grantsmanagement.com

Description

Founded: 1989
EIN: 521660757
Organization Type: Private Foundation
Giving Locations: NH
Grant Types: Capital, General Support, Project.

Donor Information

Founder: Helen P. Pardoe Trust, the late Samuel P. Pardoe

Financial Summary

Total Giving: $522,460 (fiscal year ending June 30, 2004); $594,739 (fiscal 2002)
Assets: $10,785,598 (fiscal 2004); $10,349,633 (fiscal 2002)
Gifts Received: $7,892 (fiscal 1994). Note: In fiscal 1994, contributions were received from Tiffey and Pardoe ($2,566) and Pardoe and Hansen ($5,326).

Typical Recipients

Arts & Humanities: History & Archaeology, Libraries, Museums/Galleries, Music
Civic & Public Affairs: Economic Development, Civic & Public Affairs-General, Housing, Philanthropic Organizations, Women's Affairs
Education: Colleges & Universities, Education Reform, Education-General, Minority Education, Preschool Education, Private Education (Precollege), Secondary Education (Private), Secondary Education (Public), Special Education
Environment: Air/Water Quality, Forestry, Environment-General, Resource Conservation, Wildlife Protection
Health: AIDS/HIV, Cancer, Children's Health/Hospitals, Clinics/Medical Centers, Prenatal Health Issues, Public Health
Religion: Churches, Jewish Causes, Religious Welfare
Science: Scientific Centers & Institutes
Social Services: Child Welfare, Community Service Organizations, Counseling, Family Services, Food/Clothing Distribution, People with Disabilities, Recreation & Athletics, Shelters/Homelessness, Social Services-General, Youth Organizations

Application Procedures

Initial Contact: Request application form and guidelines.
Deadlines: Prior to January 15.

Restrictions

Does not support religious organizations for sectarian purposes, individuals, political or lobbying groups, operating expenses, endowments, scholarships, loans, deficits, special events, fundraising activities, or advertising.

Additional Information

Publications: Application Form; Guidelines

Foundation Officials

Charles E. Pardoe: treasurer
Charles H. Pardoe, II: president
Prescott Bruce Pardoe: vice president
E. Spencer Pardoe Ballou: secretary

Grants Analysis

Disclosure Period: fiscal year ending June 30, 2004
Total Grants: $522,460
Number of Grants: 29
Average Grant: $5,647*
Highest Grant: $220,000
Lowest Grant: $100
Typical Range: $1,000 to $10,000
***Note:** Average grant figure excludes two highest grants ($370,000).

Recent Grants

Note: Grants derived from fiscal 2004 Form 990.
General

220,000	Prescott Conservancy Inc., Boston, MA
150,000	Audubon Society of New Hampshire, Concord, NH
50,200	New Hampshire Geographic Information System Conservation, Boston, MA
15,000	Child and Family Services, Manchester, NH
10,000	New Hampshire Music Festival, Center Harbor, NH
7,500	Girls Incorporated of New Hampshire, Manchester, NH
6,500	Vinalhaven Land Trust, Vinalhaven, ME
5,000	Antioch New England Graduate School, Keene, NH
5,000	Children's Alliance of New Hampshire, Concord, NH
5,000	Ozanam Place Inc., Laconia, NH

PARK BANK

Company Headquarters

1700 W. Bender Rd.
Milwaukee, WI 53209

Company Description

Employees: 164

Park Bank Foundation

Giving Contact

Carolyn A. Torcivia, Secretary
Park Bank Foundation
330 E. Kilbourn Ave.
Milwaukee, WI 53202
Phone: (414)270-3209

Description

Founded: 1980
EIN: 391365837
Organization Type: Corporate Foundation
Giving Locations: WI: Milwaukee metropolitan area
Grant Types: General Support.

Financial Summary

Total Giving: $179,243 (2003); $163,570 (2001)
Assets: $841,149 (2003); $899,012 (2001)
Gifts Received: $150,000 (2003); $150,000 (2001); $149,000 (2000). Note: Contributions were received from Park Bank.

Typical Recipients

Arts & Humanities: Arts Centers, Arts Funds, Arts Institutes, Dance, Historic Preservation, Libraries, Museums/Galleries, Performing Arts, Public Broadcasting, Theater
Civic & Public Affairs: Botanical Gardens/Parks, Clubs, Economic Development, Employment/Job Training, Civic & Public Affairs-General, Hispanic Affairs, Housing, Municipalities/Towns, Parades/Festivals, Public Policy, Safety, Urban & Community Affairs, Women's Affairs
Education: Business Education, Colleges & Universities, Education Funds, Engineering/Technological Education, Education-General, Leadership Training, Medical Education, Private Education (Precollege), Public Education (Precollege), Religious Education, Secondary Education (Private), Student Aid
Environment: Environment-General
Health: Arthritis, Cancer, Children's Health/Hospitals, Clinics/Medical Centers, Emergency/Ambulance Services, Eyes/Blindness, Health Funds, Health Organizations, Heart, Hospitals, Long-Term Care, Medical Training, Nursing Services, Preventive Medicine/Wellness Organizations, Public Health, Research/Studies Institutes, Respiratory, Single-Disease Health Associations, Transplant Networks/Donor Banks
International: Foreign Arts Organizations
Religion: Churches, Religion-General, Jewish Causes, Ministries, Religious Welfare
Social Services: Child Abuse, Child Welfare, Community Centers, Community Service Organizations, Counseling, Domestic Violence, Family Services, Food/Clothing Distribution, People with Disabilities, Recreation & Athletics, Scouts, Senior Services, Social Services-General, United Funds/United Ways, YMCA/YWCA/YMHA/YWHA, Youth Organizations

Application Procedures

Initial Contact: Send letter of inquiry describing the requesting organization; include financials and tax-exempt status.
Application Requirements: a description of organization, amount requested, purpose of funds sought, recently audited financial statement, and proof of tax-exempt status
Deadlines: None. Board meets quarterly, and proposals are only reviewed during those meetings.

Restrictions

Gives only in the greater Milwaukee area.

Additional Information

Company reports that about 30% of contributions support social services; 30%, civic affairs and community development; 20%, health organizations; 12%, arts and humanities; 7%, education; and 1%, conservation and historic preservation.

Corporate Officials

P. Michael Mahoney: chairman, president, chief executive officer, director PRIM CORP EMPL chairman, president, chief executive officer, director: Park Bank. CORP AFFIL president: Bank Managers Corp.
Bob Makowski: chief financial officer PRIM CORP EMPL chief financial officer: Park Bank.

Foundation Officials

Lorraine A. Kelly: vice president, director
Michael J. Kelly: vice president, director
P. Michael Mahoney: president, director (see above)
Carolyn A. Torcivia: secretary
James W. Wright: treasurer, director

Grants Analysis

Disclosure Period: calendar year ending 2003
Total Grants: $153,243*
Number of Grants: 116
Average Grant: $1,321
Highest Grant: $6,000
Lowest Grant: $100
Typical Range: $500 to $3,000
*Note: Giving excludes United Way.

Recent Grants

Note: Grants derived from 2003 Form 990.
General

26,000	United Way of Greater Milwaukee, Milwaukee, WI
6,000	Rogers Memorial Hospital Foundation, Oconomowoc, WI
5,000	Medical College of Wisconsin, Milwaukee, WI
5,000	Medical College of Wisconsin Cancer Center, Milwaukee, WI
5,000	Milwaukee Redevelopment Corporation, Milwaukee, WI
5,000	Parkinson Research Institute, Milwaukee, WI
5,000	United Performing Arts Fund, Milwaukee, WI
5,000	Wisconsin Lutheran College, Milwaukee, WI
3,333	Hart Park Rotary Stage, Wauwatosa, WI
3,000	Nehemiah Project, Milwaukee, WI

PARK FOUNDATION

Giving Contact

Leslie . Myers, Executive Director
PO Box 550
Ithaca, NY 14851
Phone: (607)272-9124
Fax: (607)272-6057

Description

Founded: 1966
EIN: 166071043
Organization Type: Private Foundation
Giving Locations: NY: Central New York
Grant Types: Award, Emergency, Fellowship, General Support, Matching, Multiyear/Continuing Support.

Donor Information

Founder: RHP, Inc.

Financial Summary

Total Giving: $13,892,678 (2003); $23,203,708 (2002); $29,473,930 (2001)
Giving Analysis: Giving for 2002 includes: foundation grants to United Way ($76,200)
Assets: $353,855,433 (2003); $451,536,939 (2002); $546,921,909 (2001)
Gifts Received: $2,852,613 (1999); $1,004,674 (1994). Note: In 1994, contributions were received from Dorothy D. Park.

Typical Recipients

Arts & Humanities: Art History, Arts & Humanities-General, Historic Preservation, Libraries, Museums/Galleries, Music, Public Broadcasting
Civic & Public Affairs: Economic Development, Civic & Public Affairs-General, Safety, Urban & Community Affairs, Zoos/Aquariums
Education: Arts/Humanities Education, Business Education, Colleges & Universities, Community & Junior Colleges, Economic Education, Education Funds, Environmental Education, Faculty Development, Education-General, Journalism/Media Education, Leadership Training, Legal Education, Private Education (Precollege), Religious Education, Science/Mathematics Education, Secondary Education (Public), Special Education, Student Aid
Environment: Air/Water Quality, Forestry, Environment-General, Protection, Research
Health: Cancer, Diabetes, Eyes/Blindness, Heart, Hospices, Hospitals, Medical Rehabilitation, Prenatal Health Issues
International: Foreign Arts Organizations, Missionary/Religious Activities
Religion: Churches, Missionary Activities (Domestic), Religious Welfare, Synagogues/Temples
Science: Science Museums, Scientific Labs, Scientific Research
Social Services: Animal Protection, Big Brothers/Big Sisters, Community Service Organizations, Homes, United Funds/United Ways, YMCA/YWCA/YMHA/YWHA

Application Procedures

Initial Contact: Request grant inquiry form.
Application Requirements: Letters of request should include a description of organization and purpose of funds sought.
Deadlines: None.

Restrictions

Does not support: individuals, religious organizations for sectarian purposes, political or lobbying groups, or for-profit organizations.

Additional Information

Publications: Brochure; Grant Inquiry Form

Foundation Officials

Joanne V. Florino: executive director ED Cornell University MA (1975).
Elizabeth P. Fowler: treasurer
Adelaide P. Gomer: vice president, secretary
Alicia P. Gomer: jr. advisory
Jerome B. Libin: director NONPR AFFIL trustee: Washington Lawyers' Committee.
Dorothy D. Park: president, chairman
Roy H. Park, III: jr. advisory
Roy H. Park, Jr.: vice president NONPR AFFIL president, chairman: Triad Foundation.
Richard G. Robb: director ED Ohio State University BA. NONPR AFFIL trustee: NC State University.

Grants Analysis

Disclosure Period: calendar year ending 2003
Total Grants: $13,892,678
Number of Grants: 281
Average Grant: $47,282*
Highest Grant: $653,627
Lowest Grant: $10
Typical Range: $20,000 to $100,000
*Note: Average grant figure excludes highest grant.

Recent Grants

Note: Grants derived from 2001 Form 990.
General

1,192,263	Cornell University Johnson Graduate School of Management, Ithaca, NY -- Park Leadership Fellows Program
1,192,263	Cornell University Johnson Graduate School of Management, Ithaca, NY -- Park Leadership Fellows Program
750,000	Educational Broadcasting Corporation, New York, NY -- Underwriting for Nature and American Masters
750,000	Educational Broadcasting Corporation, New York, NY -- Underwriting for Nature and American Masters
750,000	WGBH Educational Foundation, Springfield, MA -- Underwrite the series NOVA
750,000	WGBH Educational Foundation, Springfield, MA -- Underwrite the series NOVA
662,393	North Carolina State University, Raleigh, NC -- (Class of 2005) Park Scholarships
563,920	University of North Carolina at Chapel Hill, Chapel Hill, NC -- Park Fellowships in the master's and doctoral program
563,915	University of North Carolina at Chapel Hill, Chapel Hill, NC -- Park Fellowships in the master's and doctoral program
500,000	Educational Broadcasting Corporation, New York, NY -- Support production of three specials

MOSES L. PARSHELSKY FOUNDATION

Giving Contact

Tony B. Berk, Trustee
26 Court St.
Brooklyn, NY 11242
Phone: (718)875-8883

Description

Founded: 1949
EIN: 111848260
Organization Type: Private Foundation
Giving Locations: NY: Brooklyn, Queens
Grant Types: General Support.

Donor Information

Founder: Moses L. Parshelsky

Financial Summary

Total Giving: $268,600 (2001)
Assets: $7,785,198 (2001)

Typical Recipients

Arts & Humanities: Arts Associations & Councils, Arts Institutes, Dance, Libraries, Literary Arts, Museums/Galleries, Music, Performing Arts
Civic & Public Affairs: Botanical Gardens/Parks, Civic & Public Affairs-General, Philanthropic Organizations, Zoos/Aquariums
Education: Colleges & Universities, Faculty Development, Religious Education, Special Education
Health: Cancer, Children's Health/Hospitals, Clinics/Medical Centers, Eyes/Blindness, Geriatric Health, Health Funds, Hospitals, Medical Research, Mental Health, Prenatal Health Issues, Respiratory, Single-Disease Health Associations
Religion: Jewish Causes, Religious Organizations
Social Services: Camps, Community Centers, Community Service Organizations, Family Planning, Family Services, Food/Clothing Distribution, People with Disabilities, Recreation & Athletics, Senior Services, YMCA/YWCA/YMHA/YWHA, Youth Organizations

Application Procedures

Initial Contact: Send a brief letter of inquiry.
Application Requirements: Include a description of organization, amount requested, purpose of funds sought, and proof of tax-exempt status. No phone inquiries.
Deadlines: May 31.

Restrictions

Emphasis is on medical, rehabilitation, and geriatric treatment facilities, and religious, educational, and youth services organizations.

Foundation Officials

Tony B. Berk: trustee
Josephine B. Krinsky: trustee
Robert Daniel Krinsky: trustee B Brooklyn, NY 1937. ED Antioch College BA (1957). PRIM CORP EMPL chairman: Segal (Martin E) Co. NONPR AFFIL member working committee: National Coordinating Comm Multi-employer Pension Plans; chairman, member, director: National Dance Institute; fellow: Conference Actuaries Public Practice; director: Harbor Festival Foundation; member, director: Association Private Pension and Welfare Plans; member: Century Association; member: American Academy of Actuaries; chairman, trustee: Antioch University.

Grants Analysis

Disclosure Period: calendar year ending 2001
Total Grants: $268,600
Number of Grants: 32
Average Grant: $7,051*
Highest Grant: $50,000
Typical Range: $1,000 to $10,000
*Note: Average grant excludes highest grant.

Recent Grants

Note: Grants derived from 2001 Form 990.
Library-Related

4,000	New York Public Library, New York, NY -- to support the Jewish Division of the library
2,500	Brooklyn Public Library, Brooklyn, NY -- for the Ready to Read Educational Program for children

General

50,000	Brookdale Hospital & Medical Center, Brooklyn, NY -- for hospital services
30,000	Metropolitan Jewish Geriatric Foundation, Brooklyn, NY -- for repairs, renovations and capital improvements
20,000	Vacamas Programs for Youth, New York, NY -- to support and maintain Camp Vacuums
16,500	National Jewish Center for Immunology and Respiratory Medicine, Denver, CO -- for young patients with asthma and rheumatism
16,000	Jewish Braille Institute of America, New York, NY -- on behalf of Talking Book Library
9,999	DOROT, Inc., New York, NY -- to feed and befriend the needy elderly
7,500	Lexington School and Center for the Deaf, Jackson Heights, NY -- hearing support for the Elderly
6,500	Helen Keller Services for the Blind, Brooklyn, NY -- for ongoing programs for blind and visually impaired senior citizens
6,000	North Shore Long Island Jewish Health System Foundation, Great Neck, NY -- for Schneider Children's Hospital
5,500	92nd Street YM & YMHA, New York, NY -- for year-end purposes

RALPH M. PARSONS FOUNDATION

Giving Contact

Wendy Hoppe, Executive Director & Secretary
1055 Wilshire Boulevard, Suite 1701
Los Angeles, CA 90017
Phone: (213)482-3185
Fax: (213)482-8878
E-mail: hoppe@rmpf.org
Web: http://www.rmpf.org

Description

Founded: 1961
EIN: 956085895
Organization Type: General Purpose Foundation
Giving Locations: CA: Los Angeles County; some giving nationally
Grant Types: Capital, Challenge, General Support, Project, Scholarship, Seed Money.
Note: The foundation also considers requests for unrestricted funds.

Donor Information

Founder: The foundation was established in 1961 by Ralph M. Parsons (1896-1974). Despite his modest beginnings as the son of a Long Island fisherman, Mr. Parsons established and led one of the world's largest engineering and construction firms, Parsons Cor-

poration. He was a pioneer in missile and space launch facilities and nuclear plants.

In 1961, Mr. Parsons established a modest foundation. Upon his death in 1974, the grant-making organization received a bequest from his estate valued at approximately $154 million. This foundation is managed independently of the Parsons Corporation.

Financial Summary

Total Giving: $14,000,358 (2003); $14,005,012 (2002)
Assets: $337,296,973 (2003); $276,496,721 (2002); $323,000,000 (2001)

Typical Recipients

Arts & Humanities: Arts Centers, Arts Institutes, Arts Outreach, Ballet, Dance, Ethnic & Folk Arts, Historic Preservation, History & Archaeology, Libraries, Museums/Galleries, Music, Opera, Performing Arts, Public Broadcasting, Theater

Civic & Public Affairs: Botanical Gardens/Parks, Civil Rights, Employment/Job Training, Civic & Public Affairs-General, Hispanic Affairs, Housing, Law & Justice, Nonprofit Management, Philanthropic Organizations, Professional & Trade Associations, Public Policy, Safety, Urban & Community Affairs, Zoos/Aquariums

Education: Arts/Humanities Education, Colleges & Universities, Community & Junior Colleges, Economic Education, Education Associations, Education Funds, Education Reform, Elementary Education (Private), Engineering/Technological Education, Faculty Development, Education-General, Health & Physical Education, Legal Education, Literacy, Minority Education, Preschool Education, Private Education (Precollege), Public Education (Precollege), Science/Mathematics Education, Secondary Education (Private), Secondary Education (Public), Special Education, Student Aid, Vocational & Technical Education

Environment: Environment-General

Health: Adolescent Health Issues, AIDS/HIV, Alzheimer's Disease, Cancer, Children's Health/Hospitals, Clinics/Medical Centers, Eyes/Blindness, Geriatric Health, Health Funds, Health Organizations, Heart, Hospitals, Hospitals (University Affiliated), Long-Term Care, Medical Research, Mental Health, Prenatal Health Issues, Preventive Medicine/Wellness Organizations, Speech & Hearing, Trauma Treatment

International: Health Care/Hospitals

Religion: Churches, Jewish Causes, Religious Welfare

Science: Observatories & Planetariums, Science Museums, Scientific Centers & Institutes, Scientific Research

Social Services: At-Risk Youth, Child Abuse, Child Welfare, Community Centers, Community Service Organizations, Counseling, Crime Prevention, Day Care, Delinquency & Criminal Rehabilitation, Domestic Violence, Emergency Relief, Family Planning, Family Services, Food/Clothing Distribution, People with Disabilities, Recreation & Athletics, Refugee Assistance, Scouts, Senior Services, Shelters/Homelessness, Substance Abuse, Volunteer Services, YMCA/YWCA/YMHA/YWHA, Youth Organizations

Application Procedures

Initial Contact: Submit a preliminary letter to the executive director, outlining the nature of the project for which funding is sought, the amount requested, and justification for such a request.
Application Requirements: The preliminary letter should include brief information on the applying organization and proof of tax-exempt status.
Deadlines: None. The staff submits applications to the board of directors five times each year, in alternate months beginning in February. For the sake of fairness, applications are considered in chronological order. Due to the large number of proposals that the foundation receives, applicants should be prepared

for a period of delay leading up to a final decision.
Review Process: The foundation's staff makes an initial screening of the application and a decision is made within three months on whether the applicant is qualified. The foundation does not encourage communications with its directors. If the decision is affirmative, more detailed information may be requested and a date set for a meeting or on-site visit.

Restrictions

The foundation only contributes to tax-exempt, 501(c)(3) organizations that are not classified as private foundations.

The foundation generally does not support fundraising events, dinners, or mass mailings; individuals; conferences, seminars, or workshops; religious or fraternal purposes; tax-supported organizations; endowments; federated fundraising appeals; programs for which substantial support from government or other sources is readily available; or to support candidates for political office, or to influence legislation.

Additional Information

Publications: Annual Report

Foundation Officials

Robert F. Erburu: chairman, director B Ventura, CA 1930. ED University of Southern California BA (1952); Harvard University JD (1955). CORP AFFIL director: Marsh & McLennan Companies Inc. NONPR AFFIL trustee: National Gallery Art; director: Pacific Council on International Policy; life director: Independent Colleges Southern California; member: American Bar Association; chairman board trustee: H.E. Huntington Library Art Gallery.
Joseph G. Hurley: director PRIM CORP EMPL president: Hurley Grassini & Wrinkle.
Edgar R. Jackson: director
Everett Broadstone Laybourne: director B Springfield, OH October 26, 1911. ED Ohio State University BA (1932); Harvard University JD (1935). CORP AFFIL director: Viking Industries; director: McBain Instruments; director: Pacific Energy Corp.; director: CalEnergy Co. Inc.; director: Coldwater Investment Co.; director: Brouse-Whited Packaging Co. NONPR AFFIL chairman: WAIF Inc.; member: World Affairs Council; member: Roscomare Valley Association; member: Selden Society; member: Los Angeles County Bar Association; member: Phi Beta Kappa; member: Big Ten Universities Club Southern California. CLUB AFFIL California Club; Bel-Air Country Club.
Elizabeth H. Lowe: director
James A. Thomas: director B 1935. PRIM CORP EMPL managing partner: Maguire Partners.
Robert E. Tranquada: director
Franklin E. Ulf: director B Pittsburgh, PA 1932. ED Pomona College BA (1953); University of Southern California MBA (1960). CORP AFFIL chairman: Pacific Homes Corp.; chairman: US Trust Co.
Gayle Wilson: director ED Stanford University BS. PRIM NONPR EMPL first lady: State of California. NONPR AFFIL trustee: California Institute Technology; trustee: Center Excellence in Education.

Grants Analysis

Disclosure Period: calendar year ending 2003
Total Grants: $14,000,358*
Number of Grants: 255
Average Grant: $53,151*
Highest Grant: $500,000
Lowest Grant: $500
Typical Range: $10,000 to $100,000
*Note: Giving includes scholarships; matching gifts. Average grant figure excludes highest grant.

Recent Grants

Note: Grants derived from 2003 Form 990.
General

500,000	Friends of the Observatory, Los Angeles, CA
350,000	Pomona College, Claremont, CA

325,000	Keck Graduate Institute of Applied Life Sciences, Claremont, CA
250,000	Claremont University Consortium, Claremont, CA
250,000	Kidspace Museum, Pasadena, CA
250,000	Mary Star of the Sea High School, San Pedro, CA
250,000	VIP Community Mental Health Center, Los Angeles, CA
200,000	California Science Center Foundation, Los Angeles, CA
200,000	Santa Barbara Botanic Garden, Santa Barbara, CA
200,000	Southwest Museum, Los Angeles, CA

ALBERT PARVIN FOUNDATION

Giving Contact
Harvey G. Joffe, Chief Financial Officer & Director
c/o Lewis, Joffee & Co.
10880 Wilshire Boulevard, Suite 520
Los Angeles, CA 90024
Phone: (310)475-5676
Fax: (310)475-5268

Description
Founded: 1960
EIN: 952158989
Organization Type: Private Foundation
Giving Locations: CA
Grant Types: Endowment, General Support.

Donor Information
Founder: Albert O. Parvin

Financial Summary
Total Giving: $381,156 (2001)
Assets: $8,420,821 (2001)
Gifts Received: $50,000 (1997)

Typical Recipients
Arts & Humanities: Arts Centers, Film & Video, Arts & Humanities-General, Libraries, Museums/Galleries, Music, Public Broadcasting, Theater
Civic & Public Affairs: Botanical Gardens/Parks, Clubs, Civic & Public Affairs-General, Housing, Law & Justice, Legal Aid, Parades/Festivals, Philanthropic Organizations, Public Policy, Safety, Urban & Community Affairs, Women's Affairs
Education: Arts/Humanities Education, Colleges & Universities, Education Funds, Education-General, Minority Education, Science/Mathematics Education, Special Education
Health: AIDS/HIV, Alzheimer's Disease, Cancer, Children's Health/Hospitals, Clinics/Medical Centers, Emergency/Ambulance Services, Eyes/Blindness, Geriatric Health, Health Organizations, Heart, Hospices, Hospitals, Long-Term Care, Medical Research, Mental Health, Prenatal Health Issues, Preventive Medicine/Wellness Organizations, Public Health, Research/Studies Institutes
International: Foreign Arts Organizations, Foreign Educational Institutions, International-General, Health Care/Hospitals, International Affairs, International Relief Efforts
Religion: Jewish Causes, Religious Organizations, Religious Welfare, Social/Policy Issues
Science: Science Museums
Social Services: Camps, Child Welfare, Community Service Organizations, Domestic Violence, Family Planning, People with Disabilities, Senior Services, Social Services-General, YMCA/YWCA/YMHA/YWHA, Youth Organizations

Application Procedures
Initial Contact: Send a brief letter of inquiry.
Application Requirements: Include a description of organization and purpose of funds sought.
Deadlines: None.

Foundation Officials
Harvey G. Joffe: cfo, director
Phyllis Parvin: president
Stanley Parvin: director
Mary C. Rudin: director
Bernard Silbert: director
Steven Silbert: director

Grants Analysis
Disclosure Period: calendar year ending 2001
Total Grants: $381,156
Number of Grants: 52
Average Grant: $3,697*
Highest Grant: $90,000
Lowest Grant: $125
Typical Range: $500 to $5,000
*Note: Average grant figure excludes three highest grants ($200,071).

Recent Grants
Note: Grants derived from 2002 Form 990.
General

90,000	UCLA Kennamer Fund, Los Angeles, CA
50,000	City of Hope, Los Angeles, CA
50,000	University of Hawaii, Honolulu, HI
36,000	Heredity Disease Foundation, Santa Monica, CA
30,000	UCLA Foundation/UCLA Medical Center, Los Angeles, CA
25,000	Jewish Free Loan Association, Los Angeles, CA
15,000	One Voice, Charlotte, NC
15,000	Wellness Community, New York, NY
10,000	Fulfillment Fund, Los Angeles, CA
10,000	SO Poverty Law Center

PATRON SAINTS FOUNDATION

Giving Contact
Jacquie Fennessy, Executive Director
Patron Saints Foundation
PO Box 40706
Pasadena, CA 91104-7706
Phone: (626)797-2303

Description
Founded: 1986
EIN: 953484257
Organization Type: Private Foundation
Giving Locations: CA: West San Gabriel Valley area
Grant Types: Capital, General Support.

Financial Summary
Total Giving: $515,342 (fiscal year ending June 30, 2001)
Assets: $10,636,378 (fiscal 2001)
Gifts Received: $875,000 (fiscal 1998). Note: In fiscal 1998, contributions were received from the Rose Trust.

Typical Recipients
Civic & Public Affairs: Hispanic Affairs
Education: Education Associations, Medical Education, Preschool Education, Special Education
Environment: Resource Conservation
Health: AIDS/HIV, Cancer, Children's Health/Hospitals, Clinics/Medical Centers, Emergency/Ambulance Services, Health Organizations, Heart, Hospitals, Medical Research, Mental Health, Nursing Services, Prenatal Health Issues, Preventive Medicine/Wellness Organizations, Public Health, Trauma Treatment
Religion: Religious Organizations, Religious Welfare, Social/Policy Issues
Social Services: Community Service Organizations, Counseling, Day Care, Domestic Violence, Family Services, Homes, People with Disabilities, Recreation & Athletics, Senior Services, Substance Abuse, YMCA/YWCA/YMHA/YWHA

Application Procedures
Initial Contact: Submit grant application form.
Application Requirements: Include completed application form, proof of tax-exempt status, a recent annual report, a recent audited statement, a list of board members including affiliations, a budget for the current year, a current financial statement, and a list of major sources of support.
Deadlines: March 1 and October 1.

Restrictions
Supports health care programs/projects which are not inconsistent with the moral and religious principles of the Patron Saints Foundation.

Additional Information
Publications: Application Guidelines; Application Form

Foundation Officials
Gretchen Berger: director
Michael J. Costello: director PRIM CORP EMPL executive administration: Santa Teresita Hospital.
J. Benjamin Earl: director
Dr. W. Allan Edmiston: president, director PRIM CORP EMPL physician: Pasadena Cardiovasular Consultants.
Jacquie Fennessy: executive director
Lydia Fernandez-Palmer: director
James W. Graunke: secretary, director PRIM CORP EMPL executive director: Scripps Home.
Margaret Landry: adv PRIM CORP EMPL clinical resource specialist: HF System.
James R. Lee: director
Albert Lowe: director
Dr. Robert Nesbitt: director
Victor Petrone: director
Dorothy B. Shea: president, director
Sally Sims: director PRIM CORP EMPL educator: Covina Valley Unified School District.
Debra J. Spiegel: adv PRIM CORP EMPL financial consultant: Kemper Securities Group.
Melinda Thompson: treasurer, director PRIM CORP EMPL enrolled agent: Melinda Thompson & Associates.
Sharon Thralls: director
Melinda Winston: hon director

Grants Analysis
Disclosure Period: fiscal year ending June 30, 2001
Total Grants: $515,342
Number of Grants: 40
Average Grant: $12,884
Highest Grant: $34,000
Typical Range: $5,000 to $15,000

Recent Grants
Note: Grants derived from fiscal 2001 Form 990.
General

34,000	Santa Teresita Hospital Foundation, Pasadena, CA -- medical equipment
26,000	Scripps Home, Altadena, CA -- hospital beds
25,000	Villa Esperanza, Pasadena, CA -- speech therapy
19,320	Community Health Alliance, Pasadena, CA -- clinic services
18,000	Pasadena Unified School District, Pasadena, CA -- Early Childhood Program
17,455	LaVie Counseling Center, Pasadena, CA -- pregnancy prevention
16,500	Sisters of Social Service, Los Angeles, CA -- psychological counseling
15,000	AIDS Service Center, Pasadena, CA -- Family and Pediatrics Program

15,000	American Cancer Society, Pasadena, CA -- patient transportation
15,000	Descanso Gardens, La Canada, CA -- Horticultural Therapist

PATTEE FOUNDATION

Giving Contact
Gordon B. Patee, President & Director
c/o Dennis Mc Curry
State 700 Krystal Building
Chattanooga, TN 37402-2581
Phone: (423)756-6585

Description
Founded: 1989
EIN: 621376116
Organization Type: Private Foundation
Giving Locations: nationally.
Grant Types: General Support.

Financial Summary
Total Giving: $334,000 (fiscal year ending June 30, 2004); $420,000 (fiscal 2002); $396,500 (fiscal 2001)
Giving Analysis: Giving for fiscal 2002 includes: foundation grants to United Way ($20,000)
Assets: $5,201,904 (fiscal 2004); $5,600,487 (fiscal 2002); $7,375,848 (fiscal 2001)
Gifts Received: $2,252,734 (fiscal 1997); $1,360,625 (fiscal 1995)

Typical Recipients
Arts & Humanities: Arts Associations & Councils, Ballet, History & Archaeology, Libraries, Museums/ Galleries, Music
Civic & Public Affairs: Civic & Public Affairs-General, Professional & Trade Associations
Education: Colleges & Universities, Private Education (Precollege), Science/Mathematics Education, Student Aid
Environment: Wildlife Protection
Health: Clinics/Medical Centers, Hospitals, Hospitals (University Affiliated), Medical Research
International: International Environmental Issues
Religion: Churches
Science: Science Museums
Social Services: People with Disabilities

Application Procedures
Initial Contact: Send a brief letter of inquiry.
Deadlines: None.

Foundation Officials
Anne L. Pattee: secretary, director
Dorothy E. Pattee: director
Gordon B. Pattee: president, director

Grants Analysis
Disclosure Period: fiscal year ending June 30, 2004
Total Grants: $334,000
Number of Grants: 16
Average Grant: $13,143*
Highest Grant: $100,000
Lowest Grant: $1,000
Typical Range: $5,000 to $20,000
*Note: Average grant figure excludes two highest grants ($150,000).

Recent Grants
Note: Grants derived from fiscal 2004 Form 990.
General

100,000	World Wildlife Fund, Washington, DC
50,000	Siskin Children's Institute, Chattanooga, TN
40,000	Good Shepherd Episcopal Church, Lookout Mountain, TN
30,000	New York Presbyterian Hospital, New York, NY
25,000	Lewa Wildlife Conservancy, Marshall, VA
25,000	Memorial Hospital of Chattanooga, Chattanooga, TN
20,000	Allied Arts of Chattanooga, Chattanooga, TN
10,000	Lewa Wildlife Conservancy, Marshall, VA
10,000	New York Presbyterian Hospital, New York, NY
10,000	New York Presbyterian Hospital, New York, NY

W. I. PATTERSON CHARITABLE FUND

Giving Contact
Robert B. Shust, Trustee
920 Oliver Bldg.
Pittsburgh, PA 15222
Phone: (412)281-5580

Description
Founded: 1955
EIN: 256028639
Organization Type: Private Foundation
Giving Locations: PA: Allegheny County
Grant Types: Capital, Emergency, General Support, Operating Expenses, Research.

Donor Information
Founder: the late W. I. Patterson

Financial Summary
Total Giving: $249,847 (fiscal year ending July 31, 2004)
Giving Analysis: Giving for fiscal 2004 includes: foundation scholarships ($3,000)
Assets: $4,841,070 (fiscal 2004)

Typical Recipients
Arts & Humanities: Arts Associations & Councils, Historic Preservation, Libraries, Music, Opera, Public Broadcasting
Civic & Public Affairs: Botanical Gardens/Parks, Economic Policy, Employment/Job Training, Philanthropic Organizations, Urban & Community Affairs, Zoos/Aquariums
Education: Afterschool/Enrichment Programs, Colleges & Universities, Education Funds, Legal Education, Minority Education, Special Education
Health: Arthritis, Cancer, Children's Health/ Hospitals, Diabetes, Emergency/Ambulance Services, Eyes/Blindness, Health Funds, Heart, Hospitals, Kidney, Medical Rehabilitation, Medical Research, Nursing Services, Public Health, Single-Disease Health Associations
International: Health Care/Hospitals
Religion: Ministries, Religious Welfare
Science: Scientific Centers & Institutes
Social Services: Big Brothers/Big Sisters, Child Abuse, Child Welfare, Community Service Organizations, Emergency Relief, Family Planning, Family Services, Food/Clothing Distribution, Homes, People with Disabilities, Scouts, Senior Services, Sexual Abuse, Shelters/Homelessness, Special Olympics, Youth Organizations

Application Procedures
Initial Contact: Send brief letter describing program and full proposal.
Application Requirements: Description of organization, purpose of funds sought, proof of tax-exempt status, and list of officers and directors.
Deadlines: June 30.

Restrictions
Does not support individuals.

Foundation Officials
Robert B. Shust: trustee
Robert B. Wolf: trustee

Grants Analysis
Disclosure Period: fiscal year ending July 31, 2004
Total Grants: $246,847*
Number of Grants: 45
Average Grant: $4,475*
Highest Grant: $49,969
Lowest Grant: $1,000
Typical Range: $1,000 to $10,000
*Note: Giving excludes scholarships. Average grant figure excludes highest grant.

Recent Grants
Note: Grants derived from 2004 Form 990.
Library-Related

49,969	Carnegie Library of Pittsburgh, Pittsburgh, PA -- for public library system

General

10,000	Caring Habits, Zelienople, PA -- for character building program for elementary school children
7,500	Pittsburgh Symphony Orchestra, Pittsburgh, PA -- for musical support
7,377	Society for the Preservation of the Duquesne Heights Incline, Pittsburgh, PA -- endowment and expenses for civic and historical programs
6,000	Allegheny Cemetery Historical Association, Pittsburgh, PA -- for the preservation of the cemetery heritage
6,000	Greater Pittsburgh Council Boys Scouts of America, Pittsburgh, PA -- for services to help youth develop skills to be productive citizens and future leaders
6,000	Junior Achievement of Southwest Pennsylvania, Pittsburgh, PA
6,000	Pittsburgh Parks Conservancy, Pittsburgh, PA -- for revitalization of Pittsburgh city parks
5,000	Pittsburgh Vision Services, Pittsburgh, PA -- for general support of programs for the blind
5,000	Pittsburgh Zoo and Aquarium, Pittsburgh, PA -- for educating youth about importance of conserving wildlife and natural resources

HAZEL PATTERSON MEMORIAL TRUST

Giving Contact
William D. Omohundro, Trustee
130 S. Main St.
Buffalo, WY 82834-1846
Phone: (307)684-2207

Description
Founded: 1990
EIN: 742557301
Organization Type: Private Foundation
Giving Locations: WY: Johnson County
Grant Types: General Support.

Donor Information
Founder: Established in 1990 by the late Hazel Patterson.

Financial Summary
Total Giving: $50,000 (fiscal year ending September 30, 2004); $61,501 (fiscal 2001)
Assets: $1,085,149 (fiscal 2004); $1,244,974 (fiscal 2001)

Typical Recipients

Arts & Humanities: Arts Associations & Councils, Arts & Humanities-General, History & Archaeology, Libraries, Museums/Galleries

Civic & Public Affairs: Botanical Gardens/Parks, Clubs, Civic & Public Affairs-General, Public Policy

Education: Agricultural Education, Preschool Education, Student Aid

Environment: Resource Conservation

Health: Clinics/Medical Centers, Emergency/ Ambulance Services, Health Organizations, Hospitals, Prenatal Health Issues, Preventive Medicine/ Wellness Organizations, Research/Studies Institutes

Social Services: Animal Protection, Child Welfare, Community Service Organizations, Day Care, Domestic Violence, Emergency Relief, Food/Clothing Distribution, Recreation & Athletics, Senior Services, Social Services-General, YMCA/YWCA/YMHA/ YWHA, Youth Organizations

Application Procedures

Initial Contact: Request an application from the trust and send a brief letter of inquiry.

Deadlines: Variable deadlines.

Additional Information

Limited to Johnson County, WY.

Foundation Officials

Donald P. Kraen: trustee
William D. Omohundro: trustee
Sandra Todd: trustee

Grants Analysis

Disclosure Period: fiscal year ending September 30, 2004

Total Grants: $50,000
Number of Grants: 15
Average Grant: $3,333
Highest Grant: $10,000
Lowest Grant: $550
Typical Range: $1,000 to $5,000

Recent Grants

Note: Grants derived from fiscal 2004 Form 990.

General

10,000	Johnson County Young Men's Christian Association, Buffalo, WY -- purchase heat lamps and senior trips
9,500	Buffalo Senior Center, Buffalo, WY -- daybreak program, meals on wheels, in-home care program
8,870	Buffalo Children's Center, Buffalo, WY -- towards scholarships and equipment purchases
7,000	Johnson County Health Care, Buffalo, WY -- towards labor and delivery bed
3,500	NW Scottish Rite Childhood Clinic, Buffalo, WY -- towards family assistance
1,800	Johnson - Sheridan Youth Home, Buffalo, WY -- towards furniture purchase
1,700	Mountain Plains Heritage Park, Buffalo, WY -- towards tree watering system
1,500	Child Development Center, Buffalo, WY -- towards scholarships
1,100	Johnson County Arts and Humanities, Buffalo, WY -- Shakespeare in the school program Bob Berky workshops
1,000	Johnson County 4-H Council, Buffalo, WY -- towards scholarships

JOSEPHINE BAY PAUL AND C. MICHAEL PAUL FOUNDATION

Giving Contact

Frederick Bay, Chairman
PO Box 20218
New York, NY 10025
Phone: (212)932-0408

Description

Founded: 1962
EIN: 131991717
Organization Type: Private Foundation
Giving Locations: NY: New York City Nationally, with focus on Northeastern states.
Grant Types: General Support, Multiyear/Continuing Support, Operating Expenses, Project, Seed Money.

Donor Information

Founder: Josephine Bay Paul

Financial Summary

Total Giving: $1,923,078 (2001)
Assets: $50,418,380 (2001)

Typical Recipients

Arts & Humanities: Arts Associations & Councils, Arts Outreach, Libraries, Music, Performing Arts, Theater

Civic & Public Affairs: Botanical Gardens/Parks, Civic & Public Affairs-General, Public Policy, Rural Affairs

Education: Arts/Humanities Education, Colleges & Universities, Education Reform, Environmental Education, Education-General, Leadership Training, Medical Education, Private Education (Precollege), Public Education (Precollege), School Volunteerism, Secondary Education (Public)

Environment: Research

Science: Science Museums

Social Services: Community Service Organizations, Family Planning

Application Procedures

Initial Contact: Send a brief letter of inquiry requesting guidelines.

Application Requirements: Include a description of organization, proof of tax-exempt status, purpose of funds sought, amount requested, and recently audited financial statement.

Deadlines: March 1, September 1, and December 1.

Restrictions

Grants restricted primarily to arts in education, educational restructuring., environmental education, service learning and united support for chamber music ensembles.

Foundation Officials

Frederick Bay: chairman, executive director

Daniel Anthony Demarest: secretary, treasurer B Plainfield, NJ 1924. ED Harvard University BA (1948); Harvard University LLB (1951). NONPR AFFIL member: City Bar Association; member: Phi Beta Kappa. CLUB AFFIL Knickerbocker New York Club.

Hans A. Ege: vice president

Synnova Bay Hayes: president, treasurer

Corrine Steel: director

Grants Analysis

Disclosure Period: calendar year ending 2001
Total Grants: $1,889,850*
Number of Grants: 141
Average Grant: $11,035*
Highest Grant: $400,000
Typical Range: $5,000 to $30,000

*Note: Giving excludes awards to individuals. Average grant figure excludes largest grant.

Recent Grants

Note: Grants derived from 2001 Form 990.

General

400,000	Marine Biological Laboratory, Woods Hole, MA
132,500	Harmony School Education Center, Bloomington, IN
125,000	Lake Champlain Maritime Museum at Basin Harbor, Inc., Vergennes, VT
100,000	Snelling Center for Government, Burlington, VT
100,000	University of Vermont, Burlington, VT -- John Dewey Project
75,000	Lake Champlain Maritime Museum at Basin Harbor, Inc., Vergennes, VT
50,000	Center for Peace Education, Carrboro, NC
50,000	Community School, S. Tamworth, NH
50,000	Education Commission of the States, Denver, CO
35,000	Citizens' Committee for Children of New York, New York, NY

FRANK E. AND SEBA B. PAYNE FOUNDATION

Giving Contact

M. Catherine Ryan, Vice President, Bank of America
Bank of America
231 South LaSalle Street
Chicago, IL 60697
Phone: (312)828-1785
Fax: (312)828-0806

Description

Founded: 1962
EIN: 237435471
Organization Type: Family Foundation
Giving Locations: IL: Chicago; PA: Bethlehem
Grant Types: Capital, General Support, Operating Expenses, Project.

Donor Information

Founder: The Frank E. and Seba B. Payne Foundation was established in 1962 by Seba B. Payne, the widow of Frank E. Payne.

Financial Summary

Total Giving: $5,740,100 (fiscal year ending June 30, 2004); $7,000,000 (fiscal 2003 approx); $7,631,100 (fiscal 2002)

Giving Analysis: Giving for fiscal 2002 includes: foundation scholarships ($73,300)

Assets: $126,660,674 (fiscal 2004); $124,431,458 (fiscal 2002)

Typical Recipients

Arts & Humanities: Arts Associations & Councils, Arts Festivals, Arts & Humanities-General, Historic Preservation, History & Archaeology, Libraries, Literary Arts, Museums/Galleries, Music, Public Broadcasting, Theater

Civic & Public Affairs: Community Foundations, Economic Development, Civic & Public Affairs-General, Law & Justice, Municipalities/Towns, Philanthropic Organizations, Urban & Community Affairs

Education: Afterschool/Enrichment Programs, Arts/ Humanities Education, Colleges & Universities, Education Associations, Education Funds, Environmental Education, Education-General, Literacy, Minority Education, Preschool Education, Private Education (Precollege), Public Education (Precollege), Religious Education, Science/Mathematics Education, Special Education, Student Aid

Environment: Protection, Wildlife Protection
Health: AIDS/HIV, Children's Health/Hospitals, Clinics/Medical Centers, Emergency/Ambulance Services, Eyes/Blindness, Hospitals, Medical Rehabilitation, Nursing Services, Public Health, Single-Disease Health Associations, Speech & Hearing, Transplant Networks/Donor Banks
Religion: Churches, Dioceses, Ministries, Religious Organizations, Religious Welfare
Science: Scientific Centers & Institutes
Social Services: Animal Protection, At-Risk Youth, Big Brothers/Big Sisters, Child Abuse, Child Welfare, Community Centers, Community Service Organizations, Counseling, Crime Prevention, Day Care, Delinquency & Criminal Rehabilitation, Domestic Violence, Emergency Relief, Family Planning, Family Services, Food/Clothing Distribution, Homes, People with Disabilities, Recreation & Athletics, Scouts, Senior Services, Shelters/Homelessness, Social Services-General, Substance Abuse, United Funds/United Ways, Volunteer Services, YMCA/YWCA/YMHA/YWHA, Youth Organizations

Application Procedures

Initial Contact: Requests should be submitted in writing.
Application Requirements: Requests should include the name, address, and a brief history of the organization; a list of its officers and directors; purpose for which funds are requested; evidence of need for the proposed project; most recent financial statements, including sources of funds and information on fund-raising activities and costs; estimate of time and funds required to complete project; and proof of tax-exempt status.
Deadlines: March 15 and October 15.
Review Process: The foundation's board generally meets in the spring and fall.

Restrictions

Grants are not made to individuals. Giving is generally limited to the Bethlehem, PA area.

Additional Information

Bank of America serves as a corporate trustee for the foundation.
Publications: Instructions to Applicants

Foundation Officials

Susan Hurd Cummings: trustee
Priscilla Payne Hurd: co-trustee

Grants Analysis

Disclosure Period: fiscal year ending June 30, 2004
Total Grants: $5,740,100
Number of Grants: 72
Average Grant: $40,582*
Highest Grant: $1,364,950
Lowest Grant: $1,000
Typical Range: $20,000 to $100,000
*Note: Average grant figure excludes three highest grants ($2,939,950).

Recent Grants

Note: Grants derived from fiscal 2004 Form 990.
Library-Related

143,100	Bethlehem Area Public Library, Bethlehem, PA
46,000	Memorial Library of Nazareth and Vicinity, Nazareth, PA
23,500	Riegelsville Public Library, Riegelsville, PA

General

1,364,950	Moravian College, Bethlehem, PA
1,075,000	St. Luke's Hospital & Health Network, Bethlehem, PA
500,000	DeSales University, Center Valley, PA
200,000	Upper Bucks Regional Emergency Services Inc., Revere, PA
130,000	Associated Colleges of Illinois, Chicago, IL

125,000	Lehigh Valley PBS WLTV Lehigh Valley Channel 39, Bethlehem, PA
100,000	American Friends Service Committee, Philadelphia, PA
100,000	American Red Cross, Bethlehem, PA
100,000	Good Shepherd, Allentown, PA
100,000	Hunger Project, New York, NY

AMELIA PEABODY CHARITABLE FUND

Giving Contact

Cheryl Gideon, Administrator
Amelia Peabody Charitable Fund Trust
10 Post Office Square North, Suite 995
Boston, MA 02109
Phone: (617)451-6178

Alternate Contact

Margaret St. Clair, Co-Managing Trustee
1 Hollis Street, Suite 215
Wellesley, MA 02482

Description

Founded: 1942
EIN: 237364949
Organization Type: General Purpose Foundation
Giving Locations: MA: Boston metropolitan area New England.
Grant Types: Capital, Challenge, Endowment, General Support, Matching, Project, Research, Scholarship.

Donor Information

Founder: The Amelia Peabody Charitable Fund was established in Massachusetts. In 1985 the fund absorbed a share of the assets of the Eaton Foundation, also based in Massachusetts.

Financial Summary

Total Giving: $6,908,151 (2003); $7,000,000 (2002 approx); $9,504,600 (2001)
Giving Analysis: Giving for 2003 includes: foundation scholarships ($100,000) 2002: foundation scholarships ($100,000)
Assets: $162,274,258 (2003); $145,657,024 (2002)
Gifts Received: $75,200 (2003); $72,267 (2002); $155,000 (1998). Note: In 2002 and 2003, contributions were received from The Amelia Peabody Annuity Trust.

Typical Recipients

Arts & Humanities: Art History, Arts Centers, Ballet, Arts & Humanities-General, Historic Preservation, History & Archaeology, Libraries, Museums/Galleries, Music, Opera, Performing Arts, Public Broadcasting, Theater
Civic & Public Affairs: Asian American Affairs, Botanical Gardens/Parks, Clubs, Economic Development, Employment/Job Training, Civic & Public Affairs-General, Hispanic Affairs, Housing, Law & Justice, Philanthropic Organizations, Professional & Trade Associations, Public Policy, Urban & Community Affairs, Women's Affairs, Zoos/Aquariums
Education: Afterschool/Enrichment Programs, Arts/Humanities Education, Colleges & Universities, Education Associations, Education Reform, Engineering/Technological Education, Faculty Development, Education-General, International Studies, Leadership Training, Legal Education, Medical Education, Minority Education, Private Education (Precollege), Public Education (Precollege), Religious Education, Science/Mathematics Education, Secondary Education (Private), Special Education, Student Aid, Vocational & Technical Education
Environment: Environment-General, Resource Conservation, Wildlife Protection

Health: Alzheimer's Disease, Arthritis, Cancer, Children's Health/Hospitals, Clinics/Medical Centers, Diabetes, Emergency/Ambulance Services, Eyes/Blindness, Health-General, Geriatric Health, Health Organizations, Heart, Home-Care Services, Hospitals, Long-Term Care, Medical Research, Medical Training, Nursing Services, Prenatal Health Issues, Public Health, Single-Disease Health Associations, Speech & Hearing
International: Health Care/Hospitals
Religion: Churches, Dioceses, Jewish Causes, Religious Welfare, Social/Policy Issues
Science: Science Museums, Scientific Centers & Institutes, Scientific Labs
Social Services: Animal Protection, At-Risk Youth, Big Brothers/Big Sisters, Camps, Child Welfare, Community Centers, Community Service Organizations, Counseling, Day Care, Family Planning, Family Services, Homes, People with Disabilities, Recreation & Athletics, Scouts, Senior Services, Shelters/Homelessness, Social Services-General, Substance Abuse, Volunteer Services, YMCA/YWCA/YMHA/YWHA, Youth Organizations

Application Procedures

Initial Contact: Applicants should request guidelines from the foundation.
Application Requirements: Proposals should be made by letter. The letter should explain the nature of the nonprofit operation, and must include a copy of the IRS exemption letter. Include figures indicating the amount of the budget spent on overhead and the amount for programs, financial statements for the last fiscal year, a copy of the applicant's most recent 990, and a list of directors/trustees. Also, proposals should identify applications pending with other foundations and any commitments confirmed.
Deadlines: There are four filing deadlines during the year. The deadlines for 2004 are January 30, April 27, August 5, and October 29.

Restrictions

Grants are not made to organizations funded principally with tax dollars. Further, the trustees do not fund operating budgets or start-up funds, and funds for salaries are never considered. No funds are granted to religious organizations, nonprofits outside the United States, political action groups, to other grant-making organizations, or to any annual appeal. Grants are not made to individuals. The fund does not give to any state or municipal agency (including any public school, university, or public property) or for the purpose of producing any type of film, theatrical production, publication, exhibit, or conference. The fund does not make loans or give multiyear commitments. multiyear commitments.

Additional Information

The foundation reports that most of its grants are for capital expenses. The foundation does not fund specific areas of interest; rather, decisions are based primarily on the quality and need of a proposal.
Publications: Guidelines

Foundation Officials

Jo Anne Borek: executive director, trustee
Richard A. Leahy: trustee
William A. Lowell: trustee PRIM CORP EMPL vice president: Bath Iron Works Corp. CORP AFFIL vice president: Portland Ship Repair.
J. Elisabeth Rice: trustee
Patricia E. Rice: trustee

Grants Analysis

Disclosure Period: calendar year ending 2003
Total Grants: $6,898,151*
Number of Grants: 176
Average Grant: $36,561*
Highest Grant: $500,000
Lowest Grant: $1,000
Typical Range: $5,000 to $50,000 and $100,000 to $200,000

*Note: Giving excludes schs. Average grant figure excludes highest grant.

Recent Grants

Note: Grants derived from 2002 Form 990.

General

500,018	New England Aquarium, Boston, MA -- for renovations
500,018	Peabody Essex Museum, Salem, MA -- for construction
250,009	Northeastern University, Boston, MA -- for construction
250,009	School of the Museum of Fine Arts, Boston, MA -- for endowment
250,000	Trust for Public Land, Boston, MA -- to purchase Betty's Neck in Lakeville
200,000	Lahey Clinic Foundation, Burlington, MA -- for diagnostic and imaging technology
200,000	Medical Foundation, Inc., Boston, MA -- for research investigators
200,000	Saint Francis House, Boston, MA -- for renovations
150,000	University of Massachusetts Memorial Foundation, Worcester, MA -- for construction of laboratory
147,000	Franciscan Children's Hospital and Rehabilitation, Boston, MA -- for technical infrastructure

AMELIA PEABODY FOUNDATION

Giving Contact

Margaret N. St. Clair, Co-Managing Trustee
One Hollis Street
Wellesley, MA 02482
Phone: (781)237-6468
Fax: (781)237-5014
E-mail: jsmith@ameliapeabody.org
Web: http://www.ameliapeabody.org

Description

Founded: 1985
EIN: 046036558
Organization Type: General Purpose Foundation
Giving Locations: MA
Grant Types: Capital, Challenge, General Support, Matching, Multiyear/Continuing Support, Operating Expenses, Seed Money.

Donor Information

Founder: Established in 1985 by the late Amelia Peabody.

Financial Summary

Total Giving: $6,942,200 (2003); $7,847,790 (2001)
Assets: $167,868,383 (2003); $173,027,835 (2001)
Gifts Received: $9,776 (1992)

Typical Recipients

Arts & Humanities: Ethnic & Folk Arts, Film & Video, Libraries, Museums/Galleries, Opera, Performing Arts
Civic & Public Affairs: African American Affairs, Botanical Gardens/Parks, Clubs, Community Foundations, Economic Development, Employment/Job Training, Civic & Public Affairs-General, Hispanic Affairs, Housing, Law & Justice, Legal Aid, Municipalities/Towns, Public Policy, Urban & Community Affairs, Women's Affairs
Education: Afterschool/Enrichment Programs, Agricultural Education, Colleges & Universities, Continuing Education, Education Associations, Education Reform, Elementary Education (Private), Education-General, Leadership Training, Medical Education, Preschool Education, Private Education (Precollege), Public Education (Precollege), Secondary Education

(Private), Special Education, Student Aid
Environment: Environment-General
Health: Clinics/Medical Centers, Diabetes, Emergency/Ambulance Services, Health Organizations, Hospitals, Medical Research, Public Health, Single-Disease Health Associations
International: Health Care/Hospitals
Religion: Ministries, Religious Organizations, Religious Welfare
Science: Science Museums
Social Services: At-Risk Youth, Big Brothers/Big Sisters, Camps, Child Welfare, Community Centers, Community Service Organizations, Day Care, Family Services, Food/Clothing Distribution, Homes, People with Disabilities, Recreation & Athletics, Shelters/Homelessness, Social Services-General, Substance Abuse, United Funds/United Ways, YMCA/YWCA/YMHA/YWHA, Youth Organizations

Application Procedures

Initial Contact: The foundation requests that an applicant's first contact with the foundation be a completed Grant Proposal Form, available on the foundation's web site. Calls may be made to the foundation's office with procedural questions about the application process itself, but foundation staff does not provide preliminary advice on the appropriateness of proposals.

Application Requirements: Proposals must include seven copies of the completed Grant Proposal Form, a cover summary, organization profile, proposal narrative, board-approved organization budget, project budget, and a listing of funding sources. One copy of the following attachments is also required: proof of tax-exempt status (or, if a fiscal agent is used, a copy of their 501(c)(3) along with a statement from them accepting fiscal responsibility); a current listing of board members including town residences, positions held, and other affiliations; a listing of key staff people, including relevant background information; year-to-date financial statement; and recently audited financial statement, or if none is available, most recent tax filing. These materials should be submitted in hard copy to the foundation's office, and a single e-mail copy of the following components should be sent to jsmith@ameliapeabody.org: cover summary, organization profile, proposal narrative, organization budget, and project budget.

Deadlines: January 30; May 1; August 14; and November 6. Verify current deadlines, as they may vary slightly from year to year.

Restrictions

The foundation does not make grants to support projects outside the state of Massachusetts. Grants are generally not made to individuals or for endowment funds, scholarships, fellowships, loans, performances, film making, conferences, professorships, research, or program-related investments.

Additional Information

Publications: Guidelines Letter

Foundation Officials

Margaret N. St. Clair: co-managing trustee
Bayard D. Waring: co-managing trustee
Philip B. Waring: vice president grant making

Grants Analysis

Disclosure Period: calendar year ending 2003
Total Grants: $6,942,200
Number of Grants: 100
Average Grant: $64,063*
Highest Grant: $600,000
Lowest Grant: $5,000
Typical Range: $10,000 to $100,000
*Note: Average grant figure excludes highest grant.

Recent Grants

Note: Grants derived from 2001 Form 990.

General

750,000	Metro Lacrosse, Boston, MA -- new initiative
750,000	YMCA, Boston, MA -- building new Malden YMCA
600,000	Boston Bar Foundation, Boston, MA -- James D. St. Clair Court Education Project
400,000	Paige Company, Inc/Paige Academy, Roxbury, MA -- renovations at Paige Academy
203,000	Project Adventure, Inc., Atlanta, GA -- Lawrence Youth Program
200,000	Friends of Lynn Community Charter Schools, Inc. -- expansion of school facility and program
170,000	Adelante, Inc, Lawrence, MA -- School Success Program
150,000	Boys and Girls Club of Boston, Boston, MA -- capital campaign
150,000	Citizens School, Boston, MA -- technology initiative
150,000	Old Colony Y, Brockton, MA -- capital campaign

PELL FAMILY FOUNDATION

Giving Contact

Eda Pell, President
100 Smith Ranch Rd., No. 325
San Rafael, CA 94903-1900
Phone: (415)491-0901
Fax: (415)491-1431

Description

Founded: 1991
EIN: 680262734
Organization Type: Private Foundation
Giving Locations: CA
Grant Types: General Support.

Donor Information

Founder: Established in 1991 by Joseph and Eda Pell.

Financial Summary

Total Giving: $406,335 (fiscal year ending September 30, 2004); $489,785 (fiscal 2001)
Assets: $7,969,840 (fiscal 2004); $5,466,414 (fiscal 2001)
Gifts Received: $1,001,965 (fiscal 2004); $1,000,600 (fiscal 2001); $1,000,000 (fiscal 2000).
Note: Contributions were received from Joseph and Eda Pell.

Typical Recipients

Arts & Humanities: Ballet, Film & Video, Libraries, Museums/Galleries, Music
Civic & Public Affairs: Ethnic Organizations, Civic & Public Affairs-General, Women's Affairs
Education: Arts/Humanities Education, Colleges & Universities, Community & Junior Colleges, Education Associations, Education Funds, Preschool Education, Private Education (Precollege), Religious Education, School Volunteerism
Health: Cancer, Emergency/Ambulance Services, Health Funds, Hospitals, Medical Research
International: Foreign Educational Institutions, Missionary/Religious Activities
Religion: Jewish Causes, Missionary Activities (Domestic), Synagogues/Temples
Social Services: Child Welfare, Community Centers, Community Service Organizations, Emergency Relief, Family Services, Food/Clothing Distribution, Senior Services, Social Services-General, Substance Abuse, United Funds/United Ways

Application Procedures

Initial Contact: Send a brief letter of inquiry on organization's letterhead.
Deadlines: None.

Foundation Officials

Eda Pell: president
Joseph Pell: vice president

Grants Analysis

Disclosure Period: fiscal year ending September 30, 2004
Total Grants: $406,335
Number of Grants: 51
Average Grant: $4,611*
Highest Grant: $75,000
Lowest Grant: $50
Typical Range: $1,000 to $10,000
*Note: Average grant figure excludes three highest grants ($185,000).

Recent Grants

Note: Grants derived from fiscal 2004 Form 990.
General

75,000	Brandeis University Summer Institute, Waltham, MA
60,000	Lehrhaus Judaica, Berkeley, CA
50,000	Brandeis University, Waltham, MA
50,000	Jewish Community Federation, San Francisco, CA
26,500	Holocaust Center of Northern California, San Francisco, CA
25,000	Marin General Hospital Foundation, San Rafael, CA
20,000	Marin Jewish Community Center, San Rafael, CA
20,000	University of California Davis Foundation, Davis, CA
13,000	Temple Rodef Sholom, San Rafael, CA
5,500	Fine Arts Museums, San Francisco, CA

PELLA CORP.

Company Headquarters

Pella, IA
Web: http://www.pella.com

Company Description

Revenue: US$922 million (2002)
Employees: 7100 (2003)
SIC(s): 2431 Millwork, 3231 Products of Purchased Glass.

Operating Locations

Pella Corp. (IA--Pella)

Pella Rolscreen Foundation

Giving Contact

Mary Van Zante, Secretary
Pella Rolscreen Foundation
102 Main Street
Pella, IA 50219
Phone: (641)621-6224
E-mail: mavzante@pella.com

Description

EIN: 237043881
Organization Type: Corporate Foundation
Giving Locations: IA: central and western Iowa
Grant Types: Capital, Conference/Seminar, Employee Matching Gifts, Endowment, General Support.
Note: Employee matching gift ratio: 1 to 1.

Financial Summary

Total Giving: $1,710,096 (2003); $1,616,902 (2002); $1,978,350 (2001). Note: Contributes through corporate direct giving program and foundation.
Giving Analysis: Giving for 2001 includes: foundation scholarships (approx $47,000); foundation ($3,286,129)
Assets: $15,118,626 (2003); $12,918,537 (2002); $14,067,517 (2001)
Gifts Received: $1,243,802 (2003); $1,700,000 (2002); $1,046,104 (2001). Note: Contributions are received from Pella Corp.

Typical Recipients

Arts & Humanities: Arts Associations & Councils, Arts Centers, Historic Preservation, History & Archaeology, Libraries, Literary Arts, Museums/Galleries, Music, Opera, Performing Arts, Public Broadcasting, Theater, Visual Arts
Civic & Public Affairs: Botanical Gardens/Parks, Business/Free Enterprise, Chambers of Commerce, Civil Rights, Clubs, Community Foundations, Economic Development, Civic & Public Affairs-General, Housing, Municipalities/Towns, Parades/Festivals, Philanthropic Organizations, Professional & Trade Associations, Safety, Urban & Community Affairs, Zoos/Aquariums
Education: Arts/Humanities Education, Business Education, Colleges & Universities, Community & Junior Colleges, Economic Education, Education Funds, Education Reform, Elementary Education (Private), Engineering/Technological Education, Faculty Development, Education-General, Leadership Training, Preschool Education, Private Education (Precollege), Public Education (Precollege), Science/Mathematics Education, Secondary Education (Private), Secondary Education (Public), Special Education, Student Aid, Vocational & Technical Education
Environment: Forestry, Environment-General
Health: AIDS/HIV, Cancer, Children's Health/Hospitals, Clinics/Medical Centers, Emergency/Ambulance Services, Health Policy/Cost Containment, Health Funds, Hospices, Hospitals, Outpatient Health Care, Transplant Networks/Donor Banks
Religion: Churches, Ministries, Religious Organizations, Religious Welfare
Science: Science Exhibits & Fairs, Scientific Centers & Institutes
Social Services: Camps, Child Abuse, Child Welfare, Community Centers, Community Service Organizations, Crime Prevention, Day Care, Family Services, Food/Clothing Distribution, People with Disabilities, Recreation & Athletics, Scouts, Senior Services, Social Services-General, Substance Abuse, United Funds/United Ways, Volunteer Services, YMCA/YWCA/YMHA/YWHA, Youth Organizations

Application Procedures

Initial Contact: Submit a full proposal.
Application Requirements: Include a description of organization, statement of need, amount requested, purpose of funds sought, project budget, recently audited financial statement, and proof of tax-exempt status.
Deadlines: None; board meets quarterly.

Restrictions

Grants are not made to individuals, except to children of employees under scholarship program. Product donations are not made.

Corporate Officials

Gary M. Christensen: president, chief executive officer B 1943. PRIM CORP EMPL president, chief executive officer: Pella Corp. CORP AFFIL director: Butler Manufacturing Co.
Charles Farver: chairman PRIM CORP EMPL chairman: Pella Corp.
Joan Kuyper Farver: chairman emeritus, director B 1919. ED Grinnell College BA (1941). PRIM CORP EMPL chairman emeritus, director: Pella Corp.

Foundation Officials

Gary M. Christensen: president, director (see above)
Charles Farver: treasurer, director (see above)
Joan Kuyper Farver: director (see above)
M. R. Haught: president, director
Mary Van Zante: secretary

Grants Analysis

Disclosure Period: calendar year ending 2003
Total Grants: $1,036,093*
Number of Grants: 202
Average Grant: $4,180*
Highest Grant: $195,990
Lowest Grant: $100
Typical Range: $500 to $20,000
*Note: Giving excludes matching gifts, scholarship, gifts to individuals, and United Way. Average grant figure excludes highest grant.

Recent Grants

Note: Grants derived from 2003 Form 990.
General

20,000	Iowa College Foundation, Des Moines, IA
20,000	Iowa State University College of Engineering, Ames, IA
20,000	St. Anthony's Regional Hospital, Carroll, IA
18,200	Greater Shenandoah Foundation, Shenandoah, IA
17,000	City of Story City, Story City, IA
15,000	Iowa Games, Ames, IA
15,000	Shenandoah Health Care Foundation, Shenandoah, IA
15,000	Sioux Center Community Foundation, Sioux Center, IA
15,000	Stepping Stones Early Learning Center, Knoxville, IA
10,000	Fairfield City Schools, Fairfield, IA

H.E. AND RUBY PELZ TRUST

Giving Contact

William A. Abney, Co-Trustee
PO Box 1386
Marshall, TX 75671-1386
Phone: (903)938-6611

Description

Founded: 1992
EIN: 746392477
Organization Type: Private Foundation
Former Name: Ruby Pelz Foundation (2002).
Giving Locations: TX
Grant Types: General Support, Operating Expenses.

Financial Summary

Total Giving: $54,378 (2001)
Giving Analysis: Giving for 2001 includes: foundation gifts to individuals ($518)
Assets: $1,197,379 (2001)

Typical Recipients

Arts & Humanities: Arts Associations & Councils, Historic Preservation, Libraries, Museums/Galleries, Music
Civic & Public Affairs: African American Affairs, Civic & Public Affairs-General
Education: Colleges & Universities, Literacy, Private Education (Precollege), Secondary Education (Public), Student Aid
Health: Clinics/Medical Centers, Emergency/

Ambulance Services, Health-General, Health Organizations, Hospices
International: International Organizations
Religion: Religion-General, Religious Welfare
Social Services: Child Welfare, Community Service Organizations, Crime Prevention, Scouts, Youth Organizations

Application Procedures
Initial Contact: Send a brief letter of inquiry.
Deadlines: None.

Additional Information
Trust(s): Bank One NA

Foundation Officials
Cary M. Abney: secretary
Ruben K. Abney: co-trustee
William A. Abney: co-trustee
Martha Key: co-trustee

Grants Analysis
Disclosure Period: calendar year ending 2001
Total Grants: $53,860*
Number of Grants: 26
Average Grant: $2,071
Highest Grant: $5,000
Typical Range: $500 to $5,000
*Note: Giving excludes grants to individuals.

Recent Grants
Note: Grants derived from 2001 Form 990.
Library-Related
500	Marshall Public Library, Marshall, TX -- operations

General
7,270	Drug Shop, The, Marshall, TX -- medical
5,000	Hospice of East Texas, Tyler, TX -- operations
5,000	Michelson Museum of Art, Marshall, TX -- operations
5,000	Society of St. Stephen, Marshall, TX -- operations
5,000	Trinity Day School, Marshall, TX -- operations
3,000	Marshall Symphony Society, Marshall, TX -- operations
2,500	Boys and Girls Club of Harrison County, Marshall, TX -- operations
2,500	Courthouse Centennial Campaign, Marshall, TX -- operations
2,500	Empty Stocking Fund, Marshall, TX -- operations
2,500	Harrison County Foster Children, Marshall, TX -- operations

WILLIAM PENN FOUNDATION

Giving Contact
Barbara Scace, Director, Grants Management
2 Logan Sq., 11th Fl.
100 N. 18th St.
Philadelphia, PA 19103-2757
Phone: (215)988-1830
Fax: (215)988-1823
E-mail: moreinfo@williampennfoundation.org
Web: http://www.wpennfdn.org/

Alternate Contact
Barbara Scace, Manager, Grants Management

Description
Founded: 1945
EIN: 231503488
Organization Type: General Purpose Foundation
Giving Locations: PA: Philadelphia including Bucks,

Camden, Chester, Delaware, Montgomery, and Philadelphia counties
Grant Types: Capital, Challenge, General Support, Loan, Matching, Multiyear/Continuing Support, Operating Expenses, Project.

Donor Information
Founder: The William Penn Foundation was established in 1945 by Otto Haas (1872-1960) and his wife, Phoebe. Mr. Haas immigrated to the United States from Germany at the turn of the century. He helped develop and market an innovative leather tanning process which proved to be highly popular in the United States and later in South America. He built a career based on his expertise in industrial chemicals. His wife, Phoebe Waterman Haas, was born in North Dakota, educated at Vassar, and was an astronomer. In 1945, Otto and Phoebe Haas established the Phoebe Waterman Foundation. Reflecting the founders' postwar concerns, grants were used to fund European relief, provide scholarships for fatherless children, and support medical and educational institutions. When Otto Haas died in 1960, the foundation received the bulk of his estate. Mrs. Haas continued adding funds to the foundation until her death in 1967. In 1970, the name of the foundation was changed to the Haas Community Foundation. In 1974, it was renamed the William Penn Foundation, reflecting its close ties to Philadelphia.

Financial Summary
Total Giving: $57,700,000 (2004 approx); $56,009,358 (2003); $62,676,176 (2002). Note: 1998 Giving includes two special Fiftieth Anniversary Grants totaling $7,639,747.
Giving Analysis: Giving for 2001 includes: foundation matching gifts ($988,745); foundation grants to United Way ($4,692,454)
Assets: $1,101,044,286 (2003); $893,790,597 (2002); $1,047,720,982 (2001)
Gifts Received: $16,647,600 (2003); $15,543,570 (2002); $19,147,000 (1998). Note: In 1998, 2002 and 2003, contributions were received from Otto Haas Charitable Trusts.

Typical Recipients
Arts & Humanities: Arts Associations & Councils, Arts Centers, Arts Festivals, Arts Funds, Arts Institutes, Arts Outreach, Ballet, Community Arts, Dance, Ethnic & Folk Arts, Historic Preservation, History & Archaeology, Libraries, Literary Arts, Museums/Galleries, Music, Opera, Performing Arts, Public Broadcasting, Theater, Visual Arts
Civic & Public Affairs: Botanical Gardens/Parks, Business/Free Enterprise, Civil Rights, Clubs, Community Foundations, Economic Development, Economic Policy, Employment/Job Training, First Amendment Issues, Civic & Public Affairs-General, Hispanic Affairs, Housing, Inner-City Development, Law & Justice, Legal Aid, Nonprofit Management, Professional & Trade Associations, Public Policy, Urban & Community Affairs, Women's Affairs, Zoos/Aquariums
Education: Afterschool/Enrichment Programs, Arts/Humanities Education, Business-School Partnerships, Colleges & Universities, Community & Junior Colleges, Economic Education, Education Associations, Education Funds, Education Reform, Elementary Education (Private), Engineering/Technological Education, Environmental Education, Faculty Development, Education-General, Legal Education, Literacy, Medical Education, Minority Education, Preschool Education, Public Education (Precollege), School Volunteerism, Science/Mathematics Education, Secondary Education (Public), Social Sciences Education
Environment: Air/Water Quality, Environment-General, Protection, Resource Conservation, Watershed, Wildlife Protection
Health: Children's Health/Hospitals, Clinics/Medical Centers, Emergency/Ambulance Services, Geriatric Health, Health Organizations, Nursing Services, Pre-

natal Health Issues, Public Health
Religion: Religious Organizations, Religious Welfare
Science: Science Museums, Scientific Centers & Institutes, Scientific Labs
Social Services: At-Risk Youth, Child Abuse, Child Welfare, Community Centers, Community Service Organizations, Counseling, Crime Prevention, Day Care, Delinquency & Criminal Rehabilitation, Domestic Violence, Family Planning, Family Services, Homes, Recreation & Athletics, Senior Services, Shelters/Homelessness, Social Services-General, United Funds/United Ways, Volunteer Services, YMCA/YWCA/YMHA/YWHA, Youth Organizations

Application Procedures
Initial Contact: Visit foundation website, email moreinfo@wpennfoundation.org, or call to request application guidelines or register for an Information Session (held every few weeks for grantseekers).
Deadlines: None.
Review Process: All proposals are initially reviewed to determine whether they fall within the foundation's geographic areas of interest and current funding priorities. Those meeting these criteria are then subject to further study and investigation. Those not meeting the criteria receive prompt notification. If additional information is required during the further review, which may take several months, applicants will be contacted by a staff member. Applicants receive written notice of a decision within a week after it is made.
Notes: The foundation prefers that proposals not be elaborate or expensively packaged.

Restrictions
Only written requests are accepted. Grants are made only to IRS 501(c)(3) organizations located in the five-county southeast Pennsylvania area and Camden County, New Jersey. Grants are not made to institutions that discriminate on the basis of race, creed, gender, or sexual orientation; scholarships, fellowships, or grants to individuals; debt reduction; sectarian religious activities, political lobbying, or legislative activities; hospital capital projects; profit-making enterprises; non-public schools or charter schools; programs to treat or rehabilitate those with specific physical, medical, or psychological conditions or diagnoses; programs targeted for the elderly; medical research; direct replacement of discontinued government support; private foundations; or national or international programs.

Additional Information
Foundation holds regular information sessions at its offices.
Publications: Annual Report; Grantmaking Priorities and Guidelines

Foundation Officials
Michael Bailin: director
Christine James Brown: director
Joseph A. Dworetzky: director NONPR AFFIL member: American Bar Association; member: American College of Bankruptcy.
Louise M. Foster: chief financial officer ED Saint Joseph's University BA.
David W. Haas: chairman CORP AFFIL director: Rohm and Haas Co.
Duncan A. Haas: director
Frederick R. Haas: vice chairman, secretary NONPR AFFIL vice chairman: Rosenbach Museum & Library.
William D. Haas: director
Gary Hack: director
Robert E. Hanrahan, Jr.: director CLUB AFFIL member: Naval Institute Foundation Leadership Club.
Feather Houstoun: president
Thomas M. McKenna: director ED Columbia University MSW (1961). NONPR AFFIL director, fels certificate program: Nonprofit Management at University Pennsylvania; director: Philadelphia Safe and Sound; director: Foundation for Big Brothers Big Sisters of

American; member: National Advisory Council for Americas Promise.

Judge Anthony J. Scirica: director B Norristown, PA 1940. ED Wesleyan University BA (1962); University of Michigan Law School JD (1965). NONPR AFFIL chief justice: U.S. Supreme Court.

Lise Yasui: director

Grants Analysis

Disclosure Period: calendar year ending 2004
Total Grants: $57,700,000 (approx)
Number of Grants: 215
Average Grant: $268,372
Highest Grant: $5,000,000
Lowest Grant: $1,000
Typical Range: $50,000 to $500,000

Recent Grants

Note: Grants derived from 2003 Form 990.

Library-Related

264,683   Athenaeum of Philadelphia, Philadelphia, PA -- towards documentation and digitization of records

General

2,000,000   Barnes Foundation, Merion, PA -- towards capital and endowment needs

1,100,000   Eastern National, Ft. Washington, PA -- towards development and construction of independent park institute

1,100,000   Philadelphia Youth Network, Philadelphia, PA -- towards youth workforce development program

1,070,910   Nonprofit Finance Fund, New York, NY -- towards dedicated fund and technical assistance to child care providers

990,000   Pennsylvania Horticultural Society, Philadelphia, PA -- to enhance stewardship of cities key transit corridors and parks

750,000   United Way of Southeastern Pennsylvania, Philadelphia, PA -- to increase investment in high quality child care

725,000   Northwest Interfaith Movement Inc., Philadelphia, PA -- towards early child care and education providers

680,000   United Way of Southeastern Pennsylvania, Philadelphia, PA -- to stabilize and revitalize the neighborhoods

605,000   United Way of Southeastern Pennsylvania, Philadelphia, PA -- towards services for children, youth and family

590,558   School District of Philadelphia, Philadelphia, PA -- towards early childhood initiative

J.C. PENNEY COMPANY INC.

Company Headquarters

6501 Legacy Dr.
Plano, TX 75024-3698
Web: http://www.jcpenney.net

Company Description

Founded: 1902
Ticker: JCP
Exchange: NYSE
Revenue: US$25.678 billion (2004)
Profit: US$524 million (2004)
Employees: 250000 (2003)
Fortune Rank: 74, per FORTUNE Magazine's list of 500 Largest U.S. Corporations (2004).
SIC(s): 5311 Department Stores, 5961 Catalog & Mail-Order Houses.

Operating Locations

J.C. Penney Co., Inc. (TX--Dallas, Plano)
Note: Operates 1,752 stores in the USA and Puerto Rico.

Nonmonetary Support

Value: $1,900,000 (2001)
Type: Cause-related Marketing & Promotion; Donated Products; Workplace Solicitation
Note: NOT NOTE: Cause-related marketing and promotion is offered through the JCPenney Afterschool program. Donated products are provided for disaster relief. Workplace solicitation is conducted for the United Way only.
Volunteer Programs: In order to enhance employees' volunteer activities, the company sponsors the James Cash Penney Award for Community Service, which provides grants to organizations for which employees volunteer.
Note: Company provides nonmonetary support through local store managers. In-kind gifts at fair market value.

J.C. Penney Co. Fund

Giving Contact

Robin Caldwell, Executive Director, President
PO Box 10001
Dallas, TX 75301-8101
Phone: (972)431-1341
Fax: (972)431-1355
E-mail: jsiegel@jcpenney.com
Web: http://www.jcpenney.net/company/commrel/index.htm

Description

EIN: 133274961
Organization Type: Corporate Foundation
Giving Locations: headquarters and operating communities.
Grant Types: Emergency, General Support.

Financial Summary

Total Giving: $776,317 (fiscal year ending March 31, 2003); $923,477 (fiscal 2002); $447,174 (fiscal 2001). Note: Contributes through corporate direct giving program and foundation.
Giving Analysis: Giving for fiscal 2002 includes: foundation grants to United Way ($350)
Assets: $4,353,168 (fiscal 2003); $4,953,173 (fiscal 2002); $6,151,179 (fiscal 2001)
Gifts Received: $158,072 (fiscal 2003); $17,706 (fiscal 2002). Note: Contributions are received from J.C. Penney Corp., Inc.

Typical Recipients

Arts & Humanities: Arts Associations & Councils, Dance, Libraries, Museums/Galleries, Music, Opera, Performing Arts, Public Broadcasting, Theater
Civic & Public Affairs: African American Affairs, Business/Free Enterprise, Civil Rights, Community Foundations, Economic Development, Employment/Job Training, Civic & Public Affairs-General, Hispanic Affairs, Housing, Minority Business, Nonprofit Management, Philanthropic Organizations, Public Policy, Safety, Urban & Community Affairs, Women's Affairs, Zoos/Aquariums
Education: Afterschool/Enrichment Programs, Agricultural Education, Business Education, Business-School Partnerships, Colleges & Universities, Community & Junior Colleges, Economic Education, Education Funds, Education Reform, Elementary Education (Private), Elementary Education (Public), Education-General, Leadership Training, Literacy, Minority Education, Preschool Education, Public Education (Precollege), Science/Mathematics Education, Special Education, Student Aid
Environment: Environment-General
Health: Children's Health/Hospitals, Clinics/Medical Centers, Emergency/Ambulance Services, Health Organizations, Hospices, Hospitals, Transplant Networks/Donor Banks
Religion: Religious Welfare
Social Services: Community Service Organizations, Day Care, Emergency Relief, Food/Clothing Distribu-

tion, People with Disabilities, Recreation & Athletics, Shelters/Homelessness, Social Services-General, Substance Abuse, United Funds/United Ways, Veterans, Volunteer Services, Youth Organizations

Application Procedures

Initial Contact: Submit a brief written proposal.
Application Requirements: Include a description and purpose of funds sought for the organization and expected outcomes and program milestones. The company suggests that prospective applicants visit the J.C. Penney web site (www.jcpenney.net), click on Community Relations, then on Contribution Guidelines, and follow the application instructions.
Deadlines: None.
Evaluative Criteria: Prefers organizations that demonstrate efficient management, serve a broad sector of the community, have an identifiable impact on the community, are striving to broaden their base of support, have proven record of success, provide direct services to clients, and national projects that have a multiplier effect by benefiting local organizations across the country.
Decision Notification: Minor grants of $5,000 or less are made throughout the year; major grants follow quarterly meetings of public affairs committee or the management committee.

Restrictions

Does not support individuals, religious or membership organizations (unless activity of benefit to entire community), goodwill advertising, testimonial dinners or other fundraising events, international projects, conferences and seminars, pilot projects, or film and video projects.

Additional Information

Company has operating locations in nearly all 50 states.
Priorities established by company headquarters; budget goals based on resources available. Through "Associate Involvement Fund," JCPenney units make small grants to organizations where employees are actively involved. National grants are fewer and larger and focus on "multiplier" organizations that increase effectiveness of local agencies.
Contributions to individual colleges and universities, hospitals, and community-based organizations are normally made by local units. and community-based organizations are normally made by local units.

Corporate Officials

Marilee J. Cumming: president, women's apparel-keting PRIM CORP EMPL president, women's apparel: J.C. Penney Co. Inc.
Gale Duff-Bloom: president co. communications & marketing PRIM CORP EMPL president co. communications & marketing: J.C. Penney Co. Inc.
Allen I. Questrom: chairman, chief executive officer B Newton, MA 1941. ED Boston University BS (1964). PRIM CORP EMPL chairman, chief executive officer: J.C. Penney Co. CORP AFFIL director: Interpublic Group Companies Inc. NONPR AFFIL member: Business Council; member: National Committee of the Whitney Museum of American Art; trustee: Boston University.

Giving Program Officials

Jeannette Siegel: committee relations, manager

Foundation Officials

W. J. Alcom: treasurer
V. J. Castagna: director
R. B. Cavanaugh: director
G. L. Davis: director
R. K. Hood: secretary
C. R. Lotter: director
F. N. Napoli: assistant treasurer
S. F. Raish: director
M. W. Taxter: director
J. J. Vawnnek: assistant secretary
W. C. Watkins: director

Grants Analysis

Disclosure Period: fiscal year ending March 31, 2003
Total Grants: $923,127*
Number of Grants: 746
Average Grant: $745
Highest Grant: $25,000
Lowest Grant: $25
Typical Range: $125 to $3,000
*Note: Giving excludes United Way.

Recent Grants

Note: Grants derived from 2004 Form 990.
Library-Related

2,000	Rockland Public Library Endowment Association, Rockland, ME -- library program

General

168,298	United Way of Metropolitan Dallas, Dallas, TX
34,180	Distributive Education Clubs of America, Reston, VA -- retail merchandising competitive event
28,750	National Minority Supplier Development Council, New York, NY
25,000	American Red Cross, San Diego, CA -- southern California fires
25,000	American Red Cross, Washington, DC -- disaster relief
25,000	National Organization on Disability, Washington, DC -- emergency preparedness initiative
25,000	University of Florida, Gainesville, FL -- annual sponsorship
25,000	USO World Headquarters, Arlington, VA -- programs and services for service men in remote area
20,000	Conference Board, New York, NY
20,000	United Negro College Fund, Fairfax, VA

WILLIAM N. AND MYRIAM PENNINGTON FOUNDATION

Giving Contact

Kent Green, Controller
William N. and Myriam Pennington Foundation
441 W. Plumb Lane
Reno, NV 89509
Phone: (775)333-9100

Description

Founded: 1989
EIN: 943096845
Organization Type: Private Foundation
Giving Locations: NV
Grant Types: Capital, General Support, Scholarship.

Donor Information

Founder: William N. Pennington

Financial Summary

Total Giving: $583,850 (2001)
Giving Analysis: Giving for 2001 includes: foundation scholarships ($43,000)
Assets: $11,382,755 (2001)
Gifts Received: $631,250 (2000); $2,000,000 (1998); $3,475,000 (1996). Note: In 1998 and 2000, contributions were received from William N. Pennington.

Typical Recipients

Arts & Humanities: Public Broadcasting
Civic & Public Affairs: Civic & Public Affairs-General, Parades/Festivals
Education: Colleges & Universities, Education-

General, Medical Education, Public Education (Precollege), Special Education, Student Aid
Health: Cancer, Emergency/Ambulance Services, Health-General, Health Organizations, Respiratory, Speech & Hearing
Social Services: Community Service Organizations, Family Services, People with Disabilities, Recreation & Athletics, Scouts, Senior Services, YMCA/YWCA/YMHA/YWHA

Application Procedures

Initial Contact: Send a narrative of the project or program.
Application Requirements: Include a description of organization, purpose of funds sought, recently audited financial statement, proof of tax-exempt status, and most recent Form 990.
Deadlines: None.
Review Process: Applications are reviewed only twice each year.

Restrictions

Grants are restricted to education, health, and medical research.

Foundation Officials

Richard P. Banis: treasurer
Donald L. Carano: trustee
John Mackell: trustee
Myriam Pennington: trustee
William N. Pennington: chairman B 1923. CORP AFFIL director: Circus Circus Enterprises.

Grants Analysis

Disclosure Period: calendar year ending 2001
Total Grants: $540,850*
Number of Grants: 25
Average Grant: $12,341*
Highest Grant: $200,000
Lowest Grant: $1,000
Typical Range: $3,000 to $40,000
*Note: Giving excludes scholarships. Average grant figure excludes two highest grants ($300,000).

Recent Grants

Note: Grants derived from 2001 Form 990.
General

200,000	University of Nevada Reno School of Medicine, Reno, NV -- for medical library and educational building
100,000	Rochester General Hospital Foundation, Rochester, NY -- for neurosurgical center
40,000	University of Nevada Reno Foundation, Reno, NV -- for scholarships
30,000	CAP, Reno, NV -- for New York Disaster Relief
25,000	American Academy of Achievement, Malibu, CA
25,000	Assistance League of Reno-Sparks, Reno, NV -- for operation school bell and senior food pantry
20,000	Boys and Girls Club of the Truckee, Reno, NV -- for After School Food Program
20,000	St. Mary's Health Network, Reno, NV -- for Youth Dental Sealant Program
19,300	University of Nevada Reno Department of Speech Pathology and Audiology, Reno, NV -- for equipment purchases
15,000	YMCA of the Sierra, Reno, NV -- for Before and After School Childcare Programs

PEOPLES ENERGY CORP.

Company Headquarters

Chicago, IL
Web: http://www.pecorp.com

Company Description

Founded: 1855
Ticker: PGL
Exchange: NYSE
Assets: US$2.727 billion (2002)
Employees: 2396 (2003)
SIC(s): 4924 Natural Gas Distribution, 6719 Holding Companies Nec.

Operating Locations

Peoples Energy Corp. (IL--Chicago, Waukegan)

Nonmonetary Support

Type: Donated Equipment; In-kind Services; Loaned Employees; Loaned Executives
Volunteer Programs: Company sponsors an employee volunteer program at a local childcare agency and in annual community service projects.

Giving Contact

Richard Turner, Manager, Corporate Contributions
Peoples Energy Corp.
130 E. Randolph Dr.
Chicago, IL 60601
Phone: (312)240-7516
Fax: (312)240-4389

Alternate Contact

Marilyn Randell-Ellis, Corporate Contributions Representative

Description

Organization Type: Corporate Giving Program
Giving Locations: company service area.
Grant Types: Employee Matching Gifts, General Support, Operating Expenses, Project.
Note: Employee matching gift ratio: 2 to 1 for gifts to primary and secondary schools and hospitals; 1 to 1 for gifts to other eligible institutions.

Financial Summary

Total Giving: $1,000,000 (fiscal year ending , 2005 approx); $1,000,000 (fiscal 2004); $1,000,000 (fiscal 2003). Note: Contributes through corporate direct giving program only.
Giving Analysis: Giving for fiscal 2002 includes: corporate direct giving (approx $978,000) fiscal 2001: corporate direct giving (approx $900,000)

Typical Recipients

Arts & Humanities: Arts Associations & Councils, Arts Institutes, Dance, Ethnic & Folk Arts, Historic Preservation, Libraries, Museums/Galleries, Opera, Performing Arts, Public Broadcasting, Theater
Civic & Public Affairs: Civil Rights, Economic Development, Economic Policy, Employment/Job Training, Housing, Law & Justice, Professional & Trade Associations, Urban & Community Affairs, Women's Affairs, Zoos/Aquariums
Education: Colleges & Universities, Community & Junior Colleges, Elementary Education (Private), Literacy, Private Education (Precollege), Public Education (Precollege)
Health: Health Organizations, Hospitals
Science: Observatories & Planetariums
Social Services: Child Welfare, Community Centers, Community Service Organizations, Family Services, Homes, Senior Services, Shelters/Homelessness, United Funds/United Ways, Volunteer Services, Youth Organizations

Application Procedures

Initial Contact: Send letter requesting guidelines and application form, then send written proposal. Company accepts, but does not require, the Chicago Area Grant Application Form.
Application Requirements: Application packet should include: one-page cover letter with organization name, full mailing address, and telephone number of contact person, statement of purpose of the request, and amount requested; brief narrative

summary (one to three pages) describing background and objectives of the program, concise history of organization, description of program, anticipated timelines, expected outcomes, evaluation methodology, the applicant's capacity to manage the planned activity, and discussion of how program fits company's funding interests; operating budget with planned expenses and income sources; project budget with funds raised and sources; recently audited financial statement; list of Chicago-area contributors and amounts given; proof of tax-exempt status; and list of governing board members with affiliations.
Deadlines: None.
Review Process: All requests are reviewed by the contributions staff; this review process sometimes includes a visit to the soliciting agency and an evaluation of audited financial statements; gathered information then is evaluated against the company's overall contribution policies and grants are disbursed to those who qualify.
Evaluative Criteria: Clearly-stated objectives, long-range planning, active participation of board members, and description of funding sources that will help expand agency's support.

Restrictions
Contributions will not be made to individuals; organizations not eligible for tax-deductible support; organizations that discriminate by race, color, creed, or national origin; political organizations or campaigns; organizations whose prime purpose is to influence legislation; religious organizations for purely sectarian purposes; agencies or institutions owned and operated by local, state, or federal governments; trips or tours; or special occasion or goodwill advertising. Services greater Chicago area only.

Additional Information
Requests for specific capital or endowment purposes are generally limited to 0.5% of total amount sought.
Publications: Contribution Guidelines; Application Form

Corporate Officials
Desiree Glapion Rogers: senior vice president B New Orleans, LA 1959. ED Wellesley College BS (1981); Harvard University MBA (1985). PRIM CORP EMPL senior vice president: People's Energy Corp. CORP AFFIL vice president corporate communications: Peoples Gas, Light & Coke Co. NONPR AFFIL director: Smithsonian Institute; director: WTTW Channel 11; director: National Museum Natural History; trustee: Museum Contemporary Art; director: Museum Science & Industry; chairman: Chicago Children's Museum; trustee: Harvard Business School Club Chicago. CLUB AFFIL Economic Club; Wellesley Club.

Giving Program Officials
Richard Turner: manager corporate contributions

PEPCO HOLDINGS INC.

Company Headquarters
701 9th St. NW
Washington, DC 20068
Web: http://www.pepcoholdings.com

Company Description
Founded: 2002
Ticker: POM
Exchange: NYSE
Former Name: Potomac Electric Power Co. (2001);
Acquired: Conectiv (2002).
Revenue: US$7.221 billion (2004)
Profit: US$258.7 million (2004)
Employees: 5719 (2003)
Fortune Rank: 288, per FORTUNE Magazine's list

of 500 Largest U.S. Corporations (2004).
SIC(s): 4911 Electric Services.

Operating Locations
Potomac Electric Power Co. (DC; MD; PA; TX)

Giving Contact
Pamela Holman, Contributions Coordinator
701 9th NW, Suite 1003
Washington, DC 20068
Phone: (202)872-3488
Fax: (202)331-6659

Description
Organization Type: Corporate Giving Program
Giving Locations: DC: Washington company service area of greater Washington DC
Grant Types: Capital, Project.

Financial Summary
Total Giving: $2,000,000 (2005 approx); $2,000,000 (2004); $2,000,000 (2003). Note: Contributes through corporate direct giving program only.

Typical Recipients
Arts & Humanities: Arts Associations & Councils, Arts Centers, Dance, Historic Preservation, Libraries, Museums/Galleries, Music, Opera, Performing Arts, Public Broadcasting, Theater
Civic & Public Affairs: Business/Free Enterprise, Civil Rights, Employment/Job Training, Municipalities/Towns, Urban & Community Affairs, Women's Affairs
Education: Colleges & Universities, Education Associations, Education Funds, Literacy, Minority Education, Public Education (Precollege), Science/Mathematics Education, Student Aid
Environment: Environment-General
Health: Health Organizations, Hospices, Hospitals, Medical Research, Single-Disease Health Associations
International: International Peace & Security Issues
Religion: Churches, Religious Organizations
Social Services: Animal Protection, Child Welfare, Community Service Organizations, Family Services, Food/Clothing Distribution, People with Disabilities, Recreation & Athletics, Senior Services, Shelters/Homelessness, Substance Abuse, United Funds/United Ways, Youth Organizations

Application Procedures
Initial Contact: Submit a written proposal.
Application Requirements: Include a description of organization, including goals, structure, and sources of funding; amount requested, purpose of funds sought; proof of tax-exempt status.
Deadlines: None, but proposal should be submitted well in advance of need.
Review Process: Contributions Committee reviews requests on a case-by-case basis.

Restrictions
Funds only organizations in company's service territory; does not provide operating funds.

Corporate Officials
Dennis Wraase: president, chief executive officer ED George Washington University MS; University of Maryland BS. PRIM CORP EMPL president, chief executive officer: Pepco Holdings Inc. CORP AFFIL director: Southeastern Electric Exchange; director: Association of Edison Illuminating Companies. NONPR AFFIL director: Washington Hospital Center; director: Washington Performing Arts Society; executive board member: National Capital Area Council Boy Scouts of America; member: Federation City Council.

Giving Program Officials
William T. Torgerson: vice president, cfo B Annapolis, MD 1944. ED Princeton University BA (1966); University of Maryland JD (1973). PRIM CORP EMPL senior vice president external affairs, general coun-

sel: Potomac Electric Power Co. CORP AFFIL senior vice president: Constellation Energy Corp.

ANN PEPPERS FOUNDATION

Giving Contact
Jack H. Alexander, Secretary
PO Box 50146
Pasadena, CA 91115-0146
Phone: (626)449-0793

Description
Founded: 1959
EIN: 952114455
Organization Type: Private Foundation
Giving Locations: CA: Los Angeles metropolitan area
Grant Types: General Support, Scholarship.

Donor Information
Founder: the late Ann Peppers

Financial Summary
Total Giving: $500,253 (2001)
Giving Analysis: Giving for 2001 includes: foundation scholarships ($135,000)
Assets: $10,452,956 (2001)

Typical Recipients
Arts & Humanities: Arts Centers, History & Archaeology, Libraries, Museums/Galleries, Music, Public Broadcasting
Civic & Public Affairs: Employment/Job Training, Housing, Law & Justice, Public Policy, Women's Affairs
Education: Afterschool/Enrichment Programs, Arts/Humanities Education, Colleges & Universities, Education Funds, Education Reform, Engineering/Technological Education, Faculty Development, Education-General, Leadership Training, Literacy, Medical Education, Minority Education, Preschool Education, Private Education (Precollege), Public Education (Precollege), Science/Mathematics Education, Social Sciences Education, Special Education, Student Aid, Vocational & Technical Education
Environment: Environment-General
Health: Cancer, Children's Health/Hospitals, Clinics/Medical Centers, Emergency/Ambulance Services, Eyes/Blindness, Health-General, Geriatric Health, Health Organizations, Hospitals, Kidney, Medical Research, Mental Health, Prenatal Health Issues, Public Health, Research/Studies Institutes, Speech & Hearing
International: Health Care/Hospitals
Religion: Churches, Religion-General, Religious Organizations, Religious Welfare, Seminaries, Social/Policy Issues
Social Services: Animal Protection, At-Risk Youth, Child Welfare, Community Centers, Community Service Organizations, Crime Prevention, Domestic Violence, Family Services, Food/Clothing Distribution, Homes, People with Disabilities, Recreation & Athletics, Scouts, Senior Services, Shelters/Homelessness, Social Services-General, Volunteer Services, Youth Organizations

Application Procedures
Initial Contact: Send a full proposal.
Application Requirements: Include a description of organization, amount requested, purpose of funds sought, recently audited financial statement, and proof of tax-exempt status.
Deadlines: None.
Notes: Grants are usually made quarterly.

Restrictions
Does not support individuals or government entities.

Foundation Officials

Jack H. Alexander: secretary
Philip V. Swan: vice president, treasurer
Howard O. Wilson: treasurer

Grants Analysis

Disclosure Period: calendar year ending 2001
Total Grants: $365,253*
Number of Grants: 73
Average Grant: $5,003
Highest Grant: $25,000
Lowest Grant: $1,000
Typical Range: $1,000 to $10,000
*Note: Giving excludes scholarship.

Recent Grants

Note: Grants derived from 2001 Form 990.
Library-Related

5,000	Huntington Library, San Marino, CA -- school tours

General

15,000	California Institute of Technology, Pasadena, CA -- scholarship
10,000	Polytechnic School, Pasadena, CA -- Skills Enrichment Program
8,000	Historical Society of Southern California, Los Angeles, CA -- Pasadena Sketch Book
5,000	Florence Crittenton Center, Los Angeles, CA -- fund residential treatment
5,000	House Ear Institute, Los Angeles, CA -- help family camp
5,000	Los Angeles Area Council Boy Scouts of America, Los Angeles, CA -- teach good character and citizenship
5,000	Mount St. Mary's College, Los Angeles, CA -- scholarship
5,000	Volunteers of America of Los Angeles, Los Angeles, CA -- expansion of drop-in center
4,353	Young and Healthy, Pasadena, CA -- computer work stations
3,500	Pasadena Senior Center, Pasadena, CA -- program endowment fund

PERDUE FARMS

Company Headquarters

517 W. Main St.
Salisbury, MD 21801
Web: http://www.perdue.com

Company Description

Revenue: US$2.7 billion (2001)
Employees: 18,500
SIC(s): 0251 Broiler, Fryer & Roaster Chickens, 2015 Poultry Slaughtering & Processing.

Operating Locations

Perdue Farms (MD--Salisbury)

Arthur W. Perdue Foundation

Giving Contact

Howard L. Millard
Arthur W. Perdue Foundation
PO Box 1537
Salisbury, MD 21802-1537
Phone: (410)543-3217
Fax: (410)543-3908

Description

EIN: 526054332
Organization Type: Corporate Foundation

Giving Locations: AL; CT; DE; IN; KY; MD; NC; SC; TN; VA; WV
Grant Types: General Support.

Financial Summary

Total Giving: $1,093,000 (2003); $1,041,000 (2002); $2,410,000 (2001)
Giving Analysis: Giving for 2001 includes: foundation ($2,410,000)
Assets: $2,541,303 (2003); $3,290,818 (2002); $4,327,871 (2001)
Gifts Received: $260,000 (2002); $6,598,429 (2000). Note: In 2000, contributions were received from Franklin P. Perdue.

Typical Recipients

Arts & Humanities: Libraries
Civic & Public Affairs: Community Foundations, Municipalities/Towns, Philanthropic Organizations
Education: Afterschool/Enrichment Programs, Education Funds, Elementary Education (Public), Literacy, Public Education (Precollege)
Health: Clinics/Medical Centers, Hospices, Hospitals, Trauma Treatment
Religion: Churches
Social Services: Animal Protection, Shelters/Homelessness, Social Services-General

Application Procedures

Initial Contact: Send a brief letter of inquiry.
Application Requirements: Include a description of organization, amount requested, and purpose of funds sought.
Deadlines: None.

Corporate Officials

Francis H. Connolly: director taxes, director PRIM CORP EMPL director taxes: Perdue Farms.
Franklin P. Perdue: chairman executive committee B 1920. ED Salisbury State University. PRIM CORP EMPL chairman executive committee: Perdue Farms.
James Arthur Perdue: chairman, chief executive officer B 1949. ED Wake Forest University BS (1973); Southeastern Massachusetts University MS (1976); University of Washington PhD (1983). PRIM CORP EMPL chairman, chief executive officer: Perdue Farms. CORP AFFIL chairman: Perdue Transportation.
Bob Turley: president, chief operating officer, director PRIM CORP EMPL president, chief operating officer, director: Perdue Farms.

Foundation Officials

Eileen F. Burza: secretary, treasurer
Francis H. Connolly: secretary, treasurer (see above)
Thomas E. Mahn: director
Franklin P. Perdue: president (see above)
James Arthur Perdue: vice president (see above)
Mary H. Perdue: director

Grants Analysis

Disclosure Period: calendar year ending 2003
Total Grants: $1,093,000
Number of Grants: 9
Average Grant: $11,625*
Highest Grant: $1,000,000
Lowest Grant: $1,000
Typical Range: $10,000 to $200,000
*Note: Average grant figure excludes highest grant.

Recent Grants

Note: Grants derived from 2003 Form 990.
General

1,000,000	Community Foundation of the Eastern Shore Phase II, Salisbury, MD -- to support Kresge Challenge grant
75,000	Wor-Wic Community College Foundation, Salisbury, MD
25,000	Wor-Wic Community College Foundation, Salisbury, MD
20,000	Shore Memorial Hospital, Somers Point, NJ -- for radiation therapy
12,500	Christian Shelter Building Fund -- for refrigeration and freezer
10,000	Junior Achievement of the Eastern Shore Inc., Colorado Springs, CO
10,000	Peninsula Regional Medical Center, Salisbury, MD -- for image checker equipment
10,000	Ridge Campaign of North Carolina, Charlotte, NC
4,500	Association of Baltimore Area Grantmakers, Baltimore, MD
1,000	Peninsula Regional Medical Center, Salisbury, MD -- monitoring system for trauma center

PERRY FOUNDATION

Giving Contact

Frances H. Fife, President & Trustee
PO Box 558
Charlottesville, VA 22902
Phone: (434)977-5679

Description

Founded: 1946
EIN: 546036446
Organization Type: Private Foundation
Giving Locations: VA: Charlottesville
Grant Types: General Support.

Donor Information

Founder: the late Hunter Perry, the late Lillian Perry Edwards

Financial Summary

Total Giving: $1,161,674 (2002); $1,197,900 (2001)
Giving Analysis: Giving for 2002 includes: foundation grants to United Way ($55,000)
Assets: $21,336,906 (2002); $25,450,454 (2001)

Typical Recipients

Arts & Humanities: Historic Preservation, History & Archaeology, Libraries, Museums/Galleries, Music, Performing Arts, Public Broadcasting, Theater
Civic & Public Affairs: Botanical Gardens/Parks, Clubs, Employment/Job Training, Civic & Public Affairs-General, Housing, Municipalities/Towns, Public Policy, Urban & Community Affairs
Education: Colleges & Universities, Community & Junior Colleges, Education Funds, Education Reform, Faculty Development, Education-General, Minority Education, Private Education (Precollege), Public Education (Precollege), Science/Mathematics Education, Special Education, Student Aid
Environment: Air/Water Quality, Environment-General, Resource Conservation, Wildlife Protection
Health: Children's Health/Hospitals, Clinics/Medical Centers, Emergency/Ambulance Services, Health Organizations, Heart, Hospices, Hospitals, Mental Health, Prenatal Health Issues
Religion: Churches, Ministries, Religious Welfare
Science: Science Museums
Social Services: Animal Protection, At-Risk Youth, Camps, Community Service Organizations, Emergency Relief, Family Services, Food/Clothing Distribution, People with Disabilities, Recreation & Athletics, Senior Services, Shelters/Homelessness, United Funds/United Ways

Application Procedures

Initial Contact: Send a brief letter of inquiry. or a full proposal.
Application Requirements: Include a description of organization, purpose of funds sought, amount requested, and proof of tax-exempt status.
Deadlines: None.

Restrictions

Grants are not made to individuals.

Foundation Officials

Roberta F. Brownfield: trustee
Susan M. Cabell: trustee
Francis Fife: vice president, trustee
Gary C. McGee: secretary, trustee B Washington, DC 1940. ED College of William & Mary BS (1962); University of Virginia LLB (1965). PRIM CORP EMPL partner: MacQuire, Woods, Battle & Boothe. NONPR AFFIL member: Virginia State Bar; member: Virginia State Bar Association; member: Charlottesville Bar Association; member: Omicron Delta Kappa.
George C. Palmer, II: president, trustee B Columbus, GA 1922. ED University of Virginia (1942). PRIM CORP EMPL chairman: Piedmont Tractor Co. CORP AFFIL director: Dominion Resources Inc.; director: Sovran Financial Corp. NONPR AFFIL director: Atlantic Rural Exposition; trustee: Thomas Jefferson Memorial Foundation.
Suzanne J. Straton: trustee
Wade Tremblay: trustee

Grants Analysis

Disclosure Period: calendar year ending 2002
Total Grants: $1,106,674*
Number of Grants: 32
Average Grant: $28,127*
Highest Grant: $100,000
Lowest Grant: $3,789
Typical Range: $10,000 to $50,000
*Note: Giving excludes United Way. Average grant figure excludes three highest grants ($291,000).

Recent Grants

Note: Grants derived from 2001 Form 990.
General

155,000	United Way, Charlottesville, VA
100,000	Blue Ridge School, Dyke, VA -- wastewater treatment plant
100,000	Charlottesville Albemarle Rescue Squad, Charlottesville, VA
100,000	Paramount Theater, Charlottesville, VA
88,000	Jefferson Area Board for Aging, Charlottesville, VA
75,000	Charlottesville Albemarle SPCA, Charlottesville, VA
67,000	Piedmont Housing Alliance, Charlottesville, VA
54,150	Bridge Ministry, Charlottesville, VA
50,000	Shenandoah Shakespeare, Staunton, VA
45,000	Village School, Charlottesville, VA

PETERLOON FOUNDATION

Giving Contact

Paul George Sittenfeld, Secretary & Trustee
201 E. 5th St.
Cincinnati, OH 45202
Phone: (513)421-5886

Description

Founded: 1958
EIN: 316037801
Organization Type: Private Foundation
Giving Locations: KY: Northern part of state; OH: Cincinnati metropolitan area
Grant Types: Capital, Emergency, General Support, Multiyear/Continuing Support.

Donor Information

Founder: the late John J. Emery

Financial Summary

Total Giving: $75,836 (fiscal year ending December 30, 2001)
Giving Analysis: Giving for fiscal 2001 includes:

foundation grants to United Way ($10,000)
Assets: $6,397,070 (fiscal 2001)

Typical Recipients

Arts & Humanities: Arts Associations & Councils, Arts Centers, Arts Funds, Arts Institutes, Community Arts, Ethnic & Folk Arts, Historic Preservation, History & Archaeology, Libraries, Museums/Galleries, Music, Performing Arts, Public Broadcasting, Theater, Visual Arts
Civic & Public Affairs: Botanical Gardens/Parks, Community Foundations, Economic Development, Civic & Public Affairs-General, Housing, Legal Aid, Safety, Urban & Community Affairs, Zoos/Aquariums
Education: Arts/Humanities Education, Colleges & Universities, Continuing Education, Engineering/Technological Education, Environmental Education, Faculty Development, Education-General, Literacy, Private Education (Precollege), Science/Mathematics Education, Secondary Education (Public), Vocational & Technical Education
Environment: Environment-General
Health: Cancer, Clinics/Medical Centers, Eyes/Blindness, Health Organizations, Heart, Hospices, Long-Term Care, Multiple Sclerosis, Preventive Medicine/Wellness Organizations, Single-Disease Health Associations
International: International Environmental Issues
Religion: Religious Welfare
Science: Science Museums
Social Services: At-Risk Youth, Child Welfare, Community Centers, Community Service Organizations, Day Care, Delinquency & Criminal Rehabilitation, Family Planning, Food/Clothing Distribution, Homes, People with Disabilities, Recreation & Athletics, Scouts, Senior Services, Shelters/Homelessness, Social Services-General, United Funds/United Ways, YMCA/YWCA/YMHA/YWHA, Youth Organizations

Application Procedures

Initial Contact: The foundation has no formal grant application procedure or application form.
Deadlines: None.

Foundation Officials

John L. Campbell: trustee
Ethan Emery: trustee
Irene E. Goodale: trustee
John E. Lanier: trustee
Melissa Emery Lanier: vice president, trustee
Judith M. Mitchell: trustee
Paul George Sittenfeld: secretary, trustee
Lela Emery Steele: president, treasurer, trustee
Elizabeth Steele Hoyt: trustee

Grants Analysis

Disclosure Period: fiscal year ending December 30, 2001
Total Grants: $65,836*
Number of Grants: 24
Average Grant: $2,243*
Highest Grant: $12,000
Typical Range: $1,000 to $5,000
*Note: Giving excludes United Way. Average grant figure excludes highest grant.

Recent Grants

Note: Grants derived from 2001 Form 990.
General

12,000	Fine Arts Fund, Cincinnati, OH -- annual fund
10,000	United Way, Cincinnati, OH -- annual fund
8,000	Salvation Army, Cincinnati, OH -- for emergency fund
5,000	Cincinnati Institute of Fine Arts, Cincinnati, OH -- memorial grant for community art programs
5,000	Drop Inn Center Shelterhouse, Cincinnati, OH -- for Chemical Dependency and Education Programs

5,000	St. Paul Lutheran Village, Cincinnati, OH -- assist with purchasing a bus for physically impaired residents
5,000	Taft Museum, Cincinnati, OH -- for capital campaign
5,000	Wellness Community, Cincinnati, OH -- for Hope Campaign
3,000	Summer Bridge of Cincinnati, Cincinnati, OH -- for special programs for elementary and middle school children
2,500	Children's International Summer Villages, Cincinnati, OH -- support for children's summer programs

EDWARD V. AND JESSIE L. PETERS CHARITABLE TRUST

Giving Contact

Susan K. Betz, Trust Officer
Care of National City Bank
PO Box 318
Oil City, PA 16301
Phone: (814)678-3625

Description

Founded: 1991
EIN: 256358729
Organization Type: Private Foundation
Giving Locations: PA
Grant Types: General Support.

Financial Summary

Total Giving: $275,000 (2003); $42,000 (2001)
Assets: $6,180,185 (2003); $6,346,665 (2001)
Gifts Received: $2,754,182 (2001). Note: In 2001, contributions were received from Jessie L. Peters Trusts.

Typical Recipients

Arts & Humanities: Historic Preservation, History & Archaeology, Libraries, Museums/Galleries, Music
Civic & Public Affairs: Civic & Public Affairs-General, Municipalities/Towns
Education: Education Funds
Health: Cancer, Children's Health/Hospitals, Clinics/Medical Centers, Emergency/Ambulance Services, Hospitals, Nursing Services
Religion: Religious Welfare
Social Services: Community Service Organizations, Emergency Relief, Family Services, People with Disabilities, Scouts, United Funds/United Ways, Volunteer Services, YMCA/YWCA/YMHA/YWHA

Application Procedures

Initial Contact: Send letter stating purpose of funds sought. Enclose proof of tax-exempt status.
Application Requirements: Provide proof of tax-exempt status and purpose of funds sought.
Deadlines: November 1.

Additional Information

Trust(s): Natl City Bank PA

Grants Analysis

Disclosure Period: calendar year ending 2003
Total Grants: $275,000
Number of Grants: 13
Average Grant: $28,846
Highest Grant: $60,000
Lowest Grant: $5,000
Typical Range: $10,000 to $50,000

Recent Grants

Note: Grants derived from 2003 Form 990.
Library-Related

25,000	Franklin Library Association, Franklin, PA

General

60,000	United Way of Venango County, Reno, PA
50,000	DeBence Antique Music World, Franklin, PA
50,000	Franklin YMCA, Franklin, PA
20,000	Borough of Sugarcreek, Franklin, PA
20,000	Clarion University Foundation Inc., Oil City, PA
10,000	City of Oil City, Oil City, PA
10,000	Reno Volunteer Fire Department, Reno, PA
10,000	Salvation Army of Oil City, Oil City, PA
5,000	Oil City Area YMCA, Oil City, PA

CHARLES F. PETERS FOUNDATION

Giving Contact
Joanna M. Mayo, Vice President
c/o National City Bank of PA
20 Stanwix Street
Pittsburgh, PA 15222-4802
Phone: (412)644-8002

Description
Founded: 1965
EIN: 256070765
Organization Type: Private Foundation
Giving Locations: PA: McKeesport
Grant Types: General Support.

Donor Information
Founder: Charles F. Peters

Financial Summary
Total Giving: $141,000 (2003)
Assets: $3,032,640 (2003)
Gifts Received: $2,000 (2003). Note: In 2003, contributions were received from Mr. & Mrs. Ernest Remp.

Typical Recipients
Arts & Humanities: Arts Associations & Councils, History & Archaeology, Libraries, Literary Arts, Music, Theater
Civic & Public Affairs: Clubs, Civic & Public Affairs-General, Urban & Community Affairs
Education: Colleges & Universities, Private Education (Precollege), Student Aid
Health: Health Organizations, Hospitals, Hospitals (University Affiliated)
Religion: Churches, Religious Organizations, Religious Welfare, Synagogues/Temples
Social Services: Community Service Organizations, Food/Clothing Distribution, Homes, Scouts, United Funds/United Ways, YMCA/YWCA/YMHA/YWHA, Youth Organizations

Application Procedures
Initial Contact: a brief letter of inquiry and full proposal
Application Requirements: a description of organization, amount requested, purpose of funds sought, proof of tax-exempt status, and geographic area served
Deadlines: None.

Restrictions
Grants may not exceed $5,000.

Additional Information
Preference is given to churches and public civic causes, and other charitable organizations in and near McKeesport, PA
Trust(s): National City Bank of PA

Foundation Officials
Herman A. Haase: admin
Joanna M. Mayo: director
Robert A. Stone: admin

Grants Analysis
Disclosure Period: calendar year ending 2003
Total Grants: $141,000
Number of Grants: 85
Average Grant: $1,659
Highest Grant: $5,000
Lowest Grant: $500
Typical Range: $1,000 to $3,000

Recent Grants
Note: Grants derived from 2003 Form 990.
Library-Related

5,000	Carnegie Library of McKeesport, McKeesport, PA -- for additional furnishings

General

5,000	Greater Pittsburgh Community Food Bank, Duquesne, PA
5,000	Greater Pittsburgh Council, Boys Scouts of America, Pittsburgh, PA -- for scouting programs in the McKeesport area
5,000	Human Services of Western Pennsylvania, McKeesport, PA -- for mon-yough area
5,000	McKeesport Little Theater, McKeesport, PA -- for repairs and operating expenses
5,000	McKeesport YMCA, McKeesport, PA -- for three initiatives
5,000	Penn State McKeesport, McKeesport, PA -- for endowment scholarship fund
5,000	University of Pittsburgh Medical Center, McKeesport, PA
3,000	Garden Club of McKeesport, McKeesport, PA -- for lighting improvements
3,000	My Rec, McKeesport, PA -- for program support

LEON S. PETERS FOUNDATION

Giving Contact
Alice Peters, President & Chief Financial Officer
4170 S. Fowler
Fresno, CA 93725
Phone: (559)994-0543

Description
Founded: 1959
EIN: 946064669
Organization Type: Private Foundation
Giving Locations: CA: Fresno
Grant Types: Capital, General Support, Operating Expenses, Scholarship.

Donor Information
Founder: the late Leon S. Peters

Financial Summary
Total Giving: $443,000 (fiscal year ending November 30, 2004); $1,361,624 (fiscal 2001). Note: Fiscal 1997 Giving includes United Way ($10,000).
Assets: $16,698,754 (fiscal 2004); $15,128,822 (fiscal 2001).

Typical Recipients
Arts & Humanities: Dance, History & Archaeology, Libraries, Museums/Galleries, Music, Public Broadcasting, Theater
Civic & Public Affairs: Botanical Gardens/Parks, Ethnic Organizations, Civic & Public Affairs-General, Parades/Festivals, Zoos/Aquariums
Education: Colleges & Universities, Community & Junior Colleges, Education Funds, Faculty Develop-

ment, Legal Education, Literacy, Minority Education, Private Education (Precollege), Public Education (Precollege), Secondary Education (Public), Student Aid
Environment: Forestry, Environment-General, Resource Conservation
Health: Cancer, Children's Health/Hospitals, Clinics/Medical Centers, Emergency/Ambulance Services, Health Funds, Heart, Hospices, Hospitals, Mental Health, Public Health, Single-Disease Health Associations
International: International Organizations, International Relief Efforts, Missionary/Religious Activities
Religion: Bible Study/Translation, Churches, Missionary Activities (Domestic), Religious Organizations, Religious Welfare, Seminaries
Science: Science Museums
Social Services: At-Risk Youth, Big Brothers/Big Sisters, Child Abuse, Child Welfare, Community Service Organizations, Emergency Relief, Family Services, Food/Clothing Distribution, Homes, People with Disabilities, Scouts, Shelters/Homelessness, Social Services-General, United Funds/United Ways, YMCA/YWCA/YMHA/YWHA, Youth Organizations

Application Procedures
Initial Contact: Send a brief letter of inquiry.
Deadlines: None.

Restrictions
Does not support individuals.

Foundation Officials
Craig Apregan: director
Alice A. Peters: president, director
Darrell Peters: director
Kenneth Peters: director
Peter P. Peters: vice president, secretary
Ronald Peters: director

Grants Analysis
Disclosure Period: fiscal year ending November 30, 2004
Total Grants: $443,000
Number of Grants: 50
Average Grant: $7,306*
Highest Grant: $85,000
Lowest Grant: $1,000
Typical Range: $1,000 to $10,000
*****Note:** Average grant figure excludes highest grant.

Recent Grants
Note: Grants derived from fiscal 2004 Form 990.

General

85,000	Community Medical Foundation, Fresno, CA -- funds for operation administration and scholarships
30,000	Craig School of Business, Fresno, CA -- funds for academic scholarships
25,000	CSUF Scholarship Fund, Fresno, CA -- funds for academic scholarships
25,000	State Center Community College, Fresno, CA -- funds for academic scholarships
20,000	Fresno Rotary Centennial, Fresno, CA -- funds for operation and administration
15,000	Craycroft Center, Fresno, CA -- funds for operation and administration
15,000	Fresno Philharmonic, Fresno, CA -- funds for operation and administration
15,000	Fresno Rescue Mission, Fresno, CA -- funds for operation and administration
15,000	Poverello House, Fresno, CA -- funds for operation and administration
15,000	San Joaquin River Parkway, Fresno, CA -- funds for operation and administration

R. D. AND LINDA PETERS FOUNDATION

Giving Contact

Richard Hugo, Director
c/o Bank One Wisconsin Trust Co. NA
PO Box 1308
Milwaukee, WI 53201
Phone: (414)765-2800

Description

Founded: 1965
EIN: 396097994
Organization Type: Private Foundation
Giving Locations: WI: Brillion
Grant Types: General Support, Research, Scholarship.

Donor Information

Founder: the late R. D. Peters

Financial Summary

Total Giving: $331,694 (2001)
Giving Analysis: Giving for 2001 includes: foundation ($331,694)
Assets: $6,346,995 (2001)

Typical Recipients

Arts & Humanities: History & Archaeology, Libraries, Museums/Galleries, Theater
Civic & Public Affairs: Botanical Gardens/Parks, Municipalities/Towns, Zoos/Aquariums
Education: Agricultural Education, Colleges & Universities, Environmental Education, Education-General, Medical Education, Public Education (Pre-college), Science/Mathematics Education, Secondary Education (Public), Student Aid
Environment: Forestry, Environment-General, Resource Conservation, Wildlife Protection
Health: Children's Health/Hospitals, Health Organizations
International: International Environmental Issues
Religion: Churches, Religion-General, Religious Organizations, Religious Welfare
Science: Observatories & Planetariums
Social Services: Child Welfare, Community Service Organizations, Homes, People with Disabilities, Senior Services, Social Services-General, YMCA/YWCA/YMHA/YWHA, Youth Organizations

Application Procedures

Initial Contact: Send a brief letter of inquiry.
Application Requirements: Include a description of organization, purpose of funds sought, and amount requested.
Deadlines: None.
Review Process: Board meets quarterly.

Restrictions

Grants are normally restricted to the Brillion area, conservation endeavors, metallurgical research, and projects for youth.

Additional Information

Trust(s): Bank One WI Trust Co NA

Foundation Officials

Richard Hugo: assistant secretary, assistant treasurer
Lowell O. Reese: director
Harold Wolf: director

Grants Analysis

Disclosure Period: calendar year ending 2001
Total Grants: $331,694
Number of Grants: 30
Average Grant: $8,496*
Highest Grant: $85,300
Typical Range: $1,000 to $15,000
*Note: Average grant figure exludes highest grant.

Recent Grants

Note: Grants derived from 2001 Form 990.
Library-Related
5,000   Brillion Public Library, Brillion, WI
General
85,300   Brillion High School, Brillion, WI
55,200   New Hope Center, Chilton, WI
50,000   Medical College of Wisconsin, Milwaukee, WI
25,000   Children's Hospital of Wisconsin, Milwaukee, WI
15,000   Holy Family Catholic Church, South Pasadena, CA
11,000   Trinity Evangelical Lutheran Church, Brillion, WI
10,044   Brillion Public Schools, Brillion, WI
10,000   International Crane Foundation, Baraboo, WI
8,000   Brillion Nature Center, Brillion, WI
6,300   Center for Deaf and Blind Persons, Milwaukee, WI

ELLSWORTH AND CARLA PETERSON CHARITABLE FOUNDATION

Giving Contact

Carla J. Peterson, Trustee
Ellsworth and Carla Peterson Charitable Foundation
55 Utopia Circle
Sturgeon Bay, WI 54235-1542
Phone: (920)743-4093

Description

Founded: 1992
EIN: 396566719
Organization Type: Private Foundation
Giving Locations: WI
Grant Types: General Support.

Donor Information

Founder: the late Ellsworth L. Peterson

Financial Summary

Total Giving: $285,210 (fiscal year ending October 31, 2004); $556,490 (fiscal 2001)
Giving Analysis: Giving for fiscal 2004 includes: foundation scholarships ($1,000); foundation grants to United Way ($11,000); fiscal 2001: foundation scholarships ($1,000); foundation grants to United Way ($10,000)
Assets: $2,644,961 (fiscal 2004); $3,188,441 (fiscal 2001)
Gifts Received: $750 (fiscal 2004); $335,962 (fiscal 1998); $500,360 (fiscal 1997). Note: Contributions were received from Ellsworth L. Peterson Revocable Trust.

Typical Recipients

Arts & Humanities: Arts Centers, Arts Festivals, Ethnic & Folk Arts, Historic Preservation, History & Archaeology, Libraries, Museums/Galleries, Music, Performing Arts, Public Broadcasting, Theater
Civic & Public Affairs: Economic Development, Civic & Public Affairs-General, Housing, Urban & Community Affairs
Education: Arts/Humanities Education, Colleges & Universities, Education-General, Medical Education, Preschool Education
Environment: Environment-General
Health: Cancer, Health Organizations, Hospitals
Religion: Churches, Religious Welfare
Science: Science Museums
Social Services: Animal Protection, Community Centers, Community Service Organizations, Day Care, Family Services, Recreation & Athletics,

Scouts, United Funds/United Ways, Veterans, YMCA/YWCA/YMHA/YWHA

Application Procedures

Initial Contact: Send an outline of the purpose of funds sought.
Deadlines: None.

Restrictions

The foundation does not support religious organizations for sectarian purposes, political or lobbying groups, or organizations outside operating areas.

Foundation Officials

Carla J. Peterson: trustee
Ellsworth Lorin Peterson: trustee B Sturgeon Bay, WI 1924. ED United States Merchant Marine Academy (1946). PRIM CORP EMPL chief executive officer, director: Peterson Builders. CORP AFFIL chairman: Bank Sturgeon Bay. NONPR AFFIL director: Shipbuilders Council America; member: Society Naval Architects & Marine Engineers; member: National Security Industry Association; member: American Society Naval Engineers. CLUB AFFIL Rotary Club.

Grants Analysis

Disclosure Period: fiscal year ending October 31, 2004
Total Grants: $273,210*
Number of Grants: 105
Average Grant: $2,146*
Highest Grant: $50,000
Lowest Grant: $40
Typical Range: $500 to $5,000
*Note: Giving excludes scholarships and United Way. Average grant figure excludes highest grant.

Recent Grants

Note: Grants derived from 2001 Form 990.
Library-Related
8,333   New Northern Door Library Fund, The
General
394,034   YMCA, Lima, OH
25,000   Fairfield Public Gallery
25,000   United States Merchant Marine Academy Foundation, Inc., Kings Point, NY
10,000   Crossroad at Big Creek
10,000   Retreat at Upland Farm, St. Bonifacius, MN
10,000   United Way Door County, Sturgeon Bay, WI
8,000   American Folklore Theater, Fish Creek, WI
5,250   Door Community Auditorium, Fish Creek, WI
5,000   Door County Humane Society, Sturgeon Bay, WI
5,000   Door County Land Trust Inc., Ephraim, WI

FOLKE H. PETERSON CHARITABLE FOUNDATION

Giving Contact

Howard L. Usher, Trust Officer
c/o SunBank South FL
PO Box 14728
Ft. Lauderdale, FL 33302
Phone: (305)765-7477

Description

Founded: 1988
EIN: 656040055
Organization Type: Private Foundation
Grant Types: General Support.

Donor Information

Founder: the late Folke H. Peterson

Financial Summary

Total Giving: $3,272,800 (fiscal year ending November 30, 2003)
Assets: $21,972,128 (fiscal 2003)
Gifts Received: $7,300,451 (fiscal 1994); $1,126,200 (fiscal 1992). Note: In fiscal 1992, contributions were received from the estate of Folke H. Peterson.

Typical Recipients

Arts & Humanities: Libraries, Public Broadcasting
Civic & Public Affairs: Botanical Gardens/Parks, Civic & Public Affairs-General, Zoos/Aquariums
Education: Colleges & Universities
Environment: Environment-General, Resource Conservation, Wildlife Protection
International: International Environmental Issues
Science: Science Museums
Social Services: Animal Protection, Community Service Organizations

Application Procedures

Initial Contact: Send a brief letter of inquiry.
Deadlines: None.

Restrictions

Emphasis is on organizations that provide care and prevent cruelty to animals.

Additional Information

Trust(s): Suntrust Bank South FL

Foundation Officials

Don E. Champion: trustee
Richard K. Kornmeier: trustee
Emily Van Vliet: trustee

Grants Analysis

Disclosure Period: fiscal year ending November 30, 2003
Total Grants: $1,600,800
Number of Grants: 67
Average Grant: $2,394*
Highest Grant: $400,000
Lowest Grant: $500
Typical Range: $1,000 to $5,000
*Note: Average grant figure excludes four highest grants ($1,450,000).

Recent Grants

Note: Grants derived from fiscal 1999 Form 990.

Library-Related
13,000	Broward Public Library Foundation, Ft. Lauderdale, FL

General
400,000	University of Florida, Gainesville, FL
400,000	University of Miami, Miami, FL
400,000	Wildlife Care Center SPCA, Ft. Lauderdale, FL
12,000	Ocean Impact, West Palm Beach, FL
11,500	Beaks
11,000	National Greyhound Adoption, Philadelphia, PA
8,000	Florida Wildlife Care, Inc., FL
8,000	H.A.W.K.E. Inc
7,800	Zoological Society, FL
7,500	WJCT TV Inc., FL

HAL AND CHARLIE PETERSON FOUNDATION

Giving Contact

John Mosty, Secretary-Treasurer
PO Box 293870
Kerrville, TX 78029-3870
Phone: (830)896-2262
Fax: (830)896-2283
E-mail: hcpfn@ktc.com

Description

Founded: 1990
EIN: 741109626
Organization Type: Private Foundation
Giving Locations: TX: Kerr and adjacent counties
Grant Types: General Support.

Donor Information

Founder: Established in 1990 by James Avery Craftsman.

Financial Summary

Total Giving: $2,414,246 (2003)
Giving Analysis: Giving for 2003 includes: foundation grants to United Way ($100)
Assets: $51,680,225 (2003)
Gifts Received: $35,838 (2003); $60,940 (2000); $116,991 (1998). Note: In 2003, contributions were received from John Mosty ($15,025) and Randy Johnson ($17,604). In 1998, a substantial contributor was the F. Galbraith Trust ($104,309).

Typical Recipients

Arts & Humanities: Arts Associations & Councils, Arts Centers, Ballet, Ethnic & Folk Arts, Arts & Humanities-General, Historic Preservation, History & Archaeology, Libraries, Museums/Galleries, Music, Performing Arts
Civic & Public Affairs: Botanical Gardens/Parks, Clubs, Civic & Public Affairs-General, Housing, Inner-City Development, Safety
Education: Agricultural Education, Arts/Humanities Education, Colleges & Universities, Community & Junior Colleges, Education Funds, Education-General, Literacy, Medical Education, Preschool Education, Private Education (Precollege), Public Education (Precollege), Science/Mathematics Education, Student Aid, Vocational & Technical Education
Environment: Environment-General, Resource Conservation
Health: Alzheimer's Disease, Cancer, Clinics/Medical Centers, Emergency/Ambulance Services, Health-General, Hospices, Hospitals, Medical Rehabilitation, Nursing Services, Preventive Medicine/Wellness Organizations
Religion: Churches, Religion-General, Religious Organizations, Religious Welfare
Social Services: Animal Protection, At-Risk Youth, Big Brothers/Big Sisters, Camps, Child Welfare, Community Service Organizations, Counseling, Crime Prevention, Day Care, People with Disabilities, Recreation & Athletics, Scouts, Senior Services, Shelters/Homelessness, Social Services-General, Special Olympics, Substance Abuse, United Funds/United Ways, Volunteer Services, YMCA/YWCA/YMHA/YWHA, Youth Organizations

Application Procedures

Initial Contact: Request application form and guidelines.
Deadlines: None.

Restrictions

Organization must be 501 c(3) to be considered for grants.

Additional Information

Publications: Application Form; Guidelines

Foundation Officials

W. H. Cowden, Jr.: vice president
Charles H. Johnston: director
Nowlin McBryde: director
John Mosty: secretary, treasurer
Scott Parker: president
C. D. Peterson: director
James Stehling: director

Grants Analysis

Disclosure Period: calendar year ending 2003
Total Grants: $2,414,146*
Number of Grants: 52
Average Grant: $46,426
Highest Grant: $199,000
Lowest Grant: $100
Typical Range: $5,000 to $100,000
*Note: Giving excludes United Way.

Recent Grants

Note: Grants derived from 2001 Form 990.

Library-Related
45,000	Medina Community Library, Medina, TX -- to assist with renovations of building for new library

General
250,000	Playhouse 2000, Inc., Kerrville, TX -- assist with renovations and improvements to the Kathleen C. Cailloux City Center
199,600	Schreiner University, Kerrville, TX -- fund various programs
183,800	Notre Dame School, Kerrville, TX -- fund purchase of various gymnasium equipment
135,504	Kerrville Playscape, Inc., Kerrville, TX -- fund installation of playground equipment in the Singing Wind Park
120,000	Schreiner College, Kerrville, TX -- fund street repairs on the college campus
96,708	Ingram Independent School District, Ingram, TX -- fund the purchase and installation of new computer lab equipment
92,925	Kerr County Sheriff's Department, Kerrville, TX -- fund video equipment for the Sheriff's Department
89,038	Holy Cross Lutheran School, Kerrville, TX -- fund playground equipment, copier and van
83,200	Hill Country Community MHMR Center, Kerrville, TX -- fund purchase of vehicles for agency use
80,400	Star Programs, Inc., Ingram, TX -- assist with construction of new Gym Activity Center

LORENE M. PETRIE TRUST

Giving Contact

Michael Pond
c/o Bank of America
715 Peachtree St. NE, GA2-002-08-01
Atlanta, GA 30308
Phone: (404)607-2237

Description

Founded: 1983
EIN: 916256555
Organization Type: Private Foundation
Giving Locations: WA: Kittatas County, Yakima County
Grant Types: General Support.

Donor Information

Founder: the late Lorene Petrie

Financial Summary

Total Giving: $125,000 (fiscal year ending July 31, 2004); $50,000 (fiscal 2001). Note: Fiscal 1997 Giving includes United Way ($26,000).
Assets: $678,346 (fiscal 2004); $866,854 (fiscal 2002); $978,940 (fiscal 2001)

Typical Recipients

Arts & Humanities: Arts Associations & Councils, Community Arts, History & Archaeology, Libraries, Museums/Galleries, Music, Public Broadcasting, Theater
Civic & Public Affairs: Botanical Gardens/Parks, Community Foundations, Municipalities/Towns, Rural Affairs, Urban & Community Affairs, Women's Affairs
Education: Colleges & Universities, Community & Junior Colleges, Education-General, Student Aid, Vocational & Technical Education
Environment: Environment-General
Health: Clinics/Medical Centers, Emergency/Ambulance Services, Health Organizations, Hospitals, Public Health
Social Services: Child Welfare, Food/Clothing Distribution, Recreation & Athletics, YMCA/YWCA/YMHA/YWHA, Youth Organizations

Application Procedures

Initial Contact: Send brief letter describing program.
Deadlines: None.

Additional Information

Trust(s): Bank of America
Trust(s): Bank of America

Grants Analysis

Disclosure Period: fiscal year ending July 31, 2004
Total Grants: $125,000
Number of Grants: 1

Recent Grants

Note: Grants derived from 2004 Form 990.
General

125,000	Gallery One, Ellensburg, WA -- towards building restoration project

JACK PETTEYS MEMORIAL FOUNDATION

Giving Contact

Judy Gunnon
PO Box 324
Brush, CO 80723
Phone: (970)842-5101
Fax: (970)842-5105

Description

Founded: 1943
EIN: 846036239
Organization Type: Private Foundation
Giving Locations: AL; CO: Northeastern Colorado
Grant Types: General Support, Scholarship.

Financial Summary

Total Giving: $407,465 (2001)
Giving Analysis: Giving for 2001 includes: foundation grants to United Way ($1,350); foundation scholarships ($94,100)
Assets: $7,688,720 (2001)

Typical Recipients

Arts & Humanities: Arts Associations & Councils, History & Archaeology, Libraries, Museums/Galleries, Performing Arts, Public Broadcasting
Civic & Public Affairs: Civic & Public Affairs-General, Municipalities/Towns, Parades/Festivals, Safety, Urban & Community Affairs

Education: Agricultural Education, Arts/Humanities Education, Colleges & Universities, Community & Junior Colleges, Public Education (Precollege), Science/Mathematics Education, Student Aid
Health: Children's Health/Hospitals, Clinics/Medical Centers, Emergency/Ambulance Services, Geriatric Health, Health Organizations, Hospitals, Long-Term Care, Medical Rehabilitation, Mental Health
International: Health Care/Hospitals
Religion: Ministries
Social Services: Community Service Organizations, Day Care, Family Services, Food/Clothing Distribution, People with Disabilities, Recreation & Athletics, Scouts, Senior Services, United Funds/United Ways, Youth Organizations

Application Procedures

Initial Contact: Send a brief letter of inquiry.
Deadlines: December 1.

Restrictions

Northeastern Colorado area.

Additional Information

Trust(s): Farmers State Bank

Foundation Officials

Robert Hansen: director
Robert A. Petteys: director
Helen C. Watrous: director

Grants Analysis

Disclosure Period: calendar year ending 2001
Total Grants: $312,015*
Number of Grants: 10
Average Grant: $6,037*
Highest Grant: $131,650
***Note:** Giving excludes scholarships, United Way. Average grant figure excludes two highest grants ($251,650).

Recent Grants

Note: Grants derived from 2001 Form 990.
General

131,650	East Morgan County Hospital, Brush, CO -- equipment
120,000	East Morgan County Hospital Foundation, Brush, CO -- new century challenge
15,000	Eastern County Services for the Developmentally Disabled, Sterling, CO -- materials
12,500	City of Brush, Brush, CO -- boys and girls baseball
10,435	Brush Volunteer Fire Department, Brush, CO -- equipment
7,500	Fort Morgan Heritage Foundation, Ft. Morgan, CO -- remodel and expansion project
7,200	Colorado School of Mines, Golden, CO -- scholarships
4,000	Rocky Mountain Public Broadcasting Services, Denver, CO
2,260	Northeastern Colorado Transportation Authority, Denver, CO -- van
750	United Way of Morgan County, Decatur, AL -- 2001 campaign

PEW CHARITABLE TRUSTS

Giving Contact

Rebecca W. Rimel, President & CEO
One Commerce Sq.
2005 Market St., Suite 1700
Philadelphia, PA 19103
Phone: (215)575-9050
Fax: (215)575-4939
E-mail: info@pewtrusts.com
Web: http://www.pewtrusts.com

Alternate Contact

Phone: (215)419-6000

Description

Founded: 1948
EIN: 236299309
Organization Type: General Purpose Foundation
Giving Locations: PA: Philadelphia internationally; nationally.
Grant Types: Conference/Seminar, Fellowship, General Support, Project, Research.

Donor Information

Founder: The Pew Charitable Trusts is the collective name for the seven individual charitable trusts established by the two sons and two daughters of Joseph N. Pew, the founder of the Sun Oil Company. The first of the trusts, the Pew Memorial Trust, was founded in 1948. Smaller trusts were subsequently established to fund the Pews' personal philanthropic interests. Those included within the Pew Charitable Trusts are the Pew Memorial Trust; J. Howard Pew Freedom Trust; Mabel Pew Myrin Trust; J. N. Pew, Jr., Charitable Trust; Medical Trust; Mary Anderson Trust; and Knollbrook Trust. Because there is overlap in the areas that the seven trusts support, they share a single set of guidelines to establish eligibility for funding. Grant funds are allocated from the individual trusts based on their funding priorities.

John Howard Pew, the second son of Joseph N. Pew, was born in 1882 in Bradford, PA. Following graduation from Grove City College in 1900, and after taking several advanced courses at the Massachusetts Institute of Technology, he joined the Sun Oil Company. He and his brother, Joseph N. Pew Jr., assumed control of the company in 1912 after their father's death. His personal trust, established in 1957, supports organizations and institutions embodying the values of hard work, Christian values, free enterprise, and access to opportunity for all individuals. He also assisted numerous organizations dedicated to improving the quality of life in Philadelphia. J. Howard Pew died in 1971.

Mary Ethel Pew, the third child of Joseph N. Pew, was born in 1884 in Pittsburgh, PA. After graduating from Bryn Mawr College in 1906, she remained in Philadelphia where the Pew family relocated from Pittsburgh. Following her mother's death from cancer, Mary Ethel Pew devoted her resources to the support of cancer research and health care both as a volunteer and a board member for various institutions. She became particularly interested in Philadelphia's Lankenau Hospital and Institute for Cancer Research. She also funded various Philadelphia cultural, educational, and social service organizations. The Medical Trust was established in 1979 through her will.

Joseph N. Pew Jr., the youngest son of Joseph N. Pew, was born in 1886 in Pittsburgh, PA. After graduating with a degree in mechanical engineering from Cornell University in 1908, he worked briefly in the administrative offices of Sun Oil before leaving to learn the business from the ground up as an oilman in Illinois and as a roadlayer in South America. In 1912, upon his father's death, he became a vice president of the company. During his years at Sun, Mr. Pew focused his energies on designing new methods and products for the company. His contributions to educational and charitable institutions reflected his belief in free political expression, equal opportunity, and the free market system. The J. N. Pew, Jr., Charitable Trust was established from his estate following his death in 1963.

Mabel Pew Myrin, the youngest daughter of Joseph N. Pew, was born in 1889 in Pittsburgh, PA. Married in 1919, she and her husband, H. Alarik W. Myrin, moved to Argentina where they managed ranch property and developed mineral resources. After returning to the United States in the 1930s, they dedicated themselves to improving educational methods, aiding the handicapped, and preserving soil fertility. Mrs. Myrin strongly supported both the Waldorf educational method which takes a holistic approach to teaching, and the Camphill movement which applies Waldorf methods to the care and education of the handicapped. She also served as a trustee or board member for many institutions. The Mabel Pew Myrin Trust was established in 1957 to improve the human condition through support to the arts, education, health, and human services. She died in 1972.

Financial Summary

Total Giving: $143,398,000 (2003 approx); $166,330,000 (2002); $230,135,400 (2001)
Assets: $4,000,000,000 (2003 approx); $3,800,000,000 (2002 approx); $4,682,000,000 (2001 approx)

Typical Recipients

Arts & Humanities: Arts Festivals, Arts Funds, Arts Outreach, Dance, Ethnic & Folk Arts, Film & Video, Historic Preservation, History & Archaeology, Libraries, Museums/Galleries, Music, Opera, Performing Arts, Public Broadcasting, Theater, Visual Arts
Civic & Public Affairs: Botanical Gardens/Parks, Business/Free Enterprise, Clubs, Economic Development, Economic Policy, Employment/Job Training, First Amendment Issues, Civic & Public Affairs-General, Housing, Philanthropic Organizations, Professional & Trade Associations, Public Policy, Rural Affairs, Urban & Community Affairs, Women's Affairs, Zoos/Aquariums
Education: Afterschool/Enrichment Programs, Arts/Humanities Education, Colleges & Universities, Continuing Education, Education Associations, Education Reform, Elementary Education (Private), Environmental Education, Faculty Development, Education-General, International Exchange, International Studies, Journalism/Media Education, Leadership Training, Literacy, Medical Education, Minority Education, Private Education (Precollege), Public Education (Precollege), Religious Education, Science/Mathematics Education, Social Sciences Education, Student Aid, Vocational & Technical Education
Environment: Air/Water Quality, Energy, Forestry, Environment-General, Protection, Resource Conservation, Watershed, Wildlife Protection
Health: Adolescent Health Issues, AIDS/HIV, Cancer, Children's Health/Hospitals, Emergency/Ambulance Services, Geriatric Health, Health Policy/Cost Containment, Health Organizations, Home-Care Services, Nutrition, Prenatal Health Issues, Public Health
International: Foreign Arts Organizations, Foreign Educational Institutions, Health Care/Hospitals, Human Rights, International Affairs, International Development, International Environmental Issues, International Organizations, International Peace & Security Issues, International Relations, International Relief Efforts, Missionary/Religious Activities, Trade
Religion: Churches, Religion-General, Jewish Causes, Ministries, Religious Organizations, Religious Welfare, Seminaries, Social/Policy Issues
Science: Science Museums, Scientific Centers & Institutes, Scientific Organizations, Scientific Research
Social Services: Child Welfare, Community Service Organizations, Crime Prevention, Domestic Violence, Family Planning, Family Services, Refugee Assistance, Senior Services, Substance Abuse, United Funds/United Ways, Volunteer Services, Youth Organizations

Application Procedures

Initial Contact: Contact the Trusts for application guidelines, which include a list of program staff members. Send a brief letter of inquiry (preferably fewer than three pages), summarizing the proposal, to the appropriate program staff member.
Application Requirements: The inquiry should summarize the project for which support is sought. This should fit within guidelines for funding. Letters should include a description of the organization, nature of work and a brief history of achievements, especially as they relate to the issue to be addressed;

a statement of the problem to be addressed and an explanation of how it will be addressed; brief description of anticipated achievements or outcomes; description of time frame of proposed activities; estimated costs for the project or activity; and what is being requested from the Trusts. Full proposals are not encouraged without an initial contact with the staff.
Deadlines: None.
Review Process: Letters of inquiry are reviewed by the appropriate program staff and grant seekers will be notified within four to six weeks either by telephone or letter whether a request meets the funding criteria and guidelines of the program. If the request is of interest to the Trusts, the applicant will be asked to submit a full proposal, and an application package will be forwarded for completion. If the proposal is approved for funding, the applicant will be notified by letter within four to six weeks of a board meeting. The board of trustees meets in March, June, September, and December.
Notes: Prospective applicants are encouraged to request a copy of the Trusts' annual program guidelines and procedures pamphlet that provides detailed information on areas of interest to the Trusts, as well as funding restrictions. Examples of work, articles, reports, videos or other material should not be submitted with a letter of inquiry.

Restrictions

In general, the Trusts do not provide funding for capital funds, endowments, debt reduction, general operations, library acquisitions, or individuals.

Additional Information

The Glenmede Trust Company manages the funds and serves as trustee. In 1986, it reorganized the seven Trusts into one division for purposes of grant-making and administration.
Although the Trusts have an interdisciplinary grants fund for proposals that fit within the guidelines of two or more programs, this status is determined by program officers at the Trusts. Applicants should apply to the program that suits their proposal.
The Trusts report that they offer occasional seminars and workshops on how to apply for grants to special programs, as well as communications and strategic planning assistance to selected grantees.
Publications: Annual Report; Application Form; Guidelines

Foundation Officials

Henry B. Bernstein: director finance ED University of Pennsylvania Wharton School BS.
Maureen K. Byrnes: director health human services program ED Le Moyne College BA; University of North Carolina, Chapel Hill MPA. NONPR AFFIL vice president: Association American Universities.
Robert Henderson Campbell: director B Pittsburgh, PA 1937. ED Princeton University BS (1959); Carnegie Mellon University MS (1961); Massachusetts Institute of Technology MA (1978). CORP AFFIL director: Vical Inc.; director: CIGNA Corp.; director: Hershey Foods Corp. NONPR AFFIL member: American Petroleum Institute; director: Rocky Mountain Institute.
Susan Williams Catherwood: director CORP AFFIL director: PECO Energy Co. NONPR AFFIL director: Monell Chemical Senses Center; vice chairman: University Pennsylvania; vice chairman: Executive Service Corps..
Marian A. Godfrey: director civic life initiatives ED Radcliffe College; Yale University School of Drama. NONPR AFFIL chairman: Arts Policy Roundtable of Americans for the Arts; director: Maine College of Art.
Joy A. Horwitz: director legal affairs ED Cornell University BA; University of Pennsylvania JD.
Donald Kimelman: director information initiatives ED Columbia University Graduate School of Journalism; Yale University BA.
Thomas W. Langfitt, MD: director B Clarksburg, WV April 20, 1927. ED Princeton University AB (1949); Johns Hopkins University MD (1953). PRIM CORP

EMPL chairman, president, chief executive officer, director: Glenmede Trust Co. CORP AFFIL president, chief executive officer: Glenmede Trust Co. NONPR AFFIL member: Society Neural Surgeons; member: Society of Neurological Surgeons; member: National Academy Sciences; fellow: Royal College Surgeons; member: American Philosophical Society; member: Institute Medicine. CLUB AFFIL Union League Club.
Arthur E. Pew, III: director NONPR AFFIL member: Bermuda Biological Station for Research.
J. Howard Pew, II: chairman, director
Joseph N. Pew, IV, MD: director
Mary Catharine Pew, MD: director
Robert Anderson Pew: director B Philadelphia, PA 1936. ED Princeton University (1954-1956); Temple University BS (1959); Massachusetts Institute of Technology MS (1970). CORP AFFIL executive committee: Sunoco Inc. NONPR AFFIL trustee: Curtis Institute Music; council of emeritus director: Philadelphia Orchestra; trustee, chairman: Childrens Hospital Philadelphia; honorary member: American Hospital Association; trustee, vice chairman: Bryn Mawr College; member: Aircraft Owners & Pilots Association. CLUB AFFIL Union League Club; Seal Harbor Club; Merion Cricket Club; Northeast Harbor Fleet Club.
Sandy Pew: director
Joshua S. Reichert: director environment program ED Princeton University MS; Princeton University PhD; University of California, Davis BS.
Rebecca Webster Rimel: president, chief executive officer, director ED University of Virginia BS (1973); James Madison University MBA (1983). CORP AFFIL director: Deutsch Banc Flag Investors Funds. NONPR AFFIL vice chairman: Thomas Jefferson Memorial Foundation; member: Virginia State Nurses Association; member: Greater Philadelphia Chamber of Commerce; member: Council Foundations; member: Emergency Department Nurses Association; member: American Public Health Association; member: American Nurses Association; member: American Philosophical Society; member: American Association Neurosurgical Nurses; member: American Academy Nursing.
Susan K. Urahn: director, policy initiatives, education program ED University of Minnesota GA; University of Minnesota PhD.
Robert G. Williams: director

Grants Analysis

Disclosure Period: calendar year ending 2002
Total Grants: $166,330,000*
Number of Grants: 287
Average Grant: $579,547
Highest Grant: $9,920,000
Lowest Grant: $15,000
Typical Range: $250,000 to $1,000,000
***Note:** Grants analysis provided by foundation.

Recent Grants

Note: Grants derived from 2001 Form 990.
General

1,000,000	Energy Foundation, San Francisco, CA
1,000,000	Union of Concerned Scientists, Inc., Washington, DC -- support efforts to increase the nation's commitment to energy efficiency and renewable energy
975,000	Pennsylvania Conservation Center, Harrisburg, PA -- for a statewide environmental organization for Pennsylvania
766,000	Strategies for the Global Environment, Inc., Arlington, VA -- support of the Pew Center
734,000	U.S. Working Group, Washington, DC -- to establish a certification infrastructure in Canada
666,000	Children's Hospital Foundation, Philadelphia, PA -- to support an information system for primary care delivery and outcomes research
633,000	Border WaterWorks, Santa Fe, NM -- help communities along the United State-Mexico border

600,000   Environmental Defense Fund, New York, NY -- for continuation of the Alliance for Environmental Innovation

571,000   Earthjustice Legal Defense Fund, Washington, DC -- continued support of the Ocean Law Project

566,000   Center for Agricultural Partnerships, Inc., Asheville, NC -- help implement practices resulting measurable and long-term benefits for farmers and the environment

THE CARL AND LILY PFORZHEIMER FOUNDATION, INC.

Giving Contact

Carl H. Pforzheimer, III, President, Treasurer, Director
650 Madison Avenue, 23rd Floor
New York, NY 10022
Phone: (212)223-6500
Fax: (212)223-2693

Description

Founded: 1942
EIN: 135624374
Organization Type: General Purpose Foundation
Giving Locations: NY: New York nationally.
Grant Types: General Support.

Donor Information

Founder: The foundation was established in 1942 by Carl H. Pforzheimer. Many members of the family serve as officers or directors of the foundation.

Financial Summary

Total Giving: $4,858,407 (2003); $5,712,338 (2002)
Assets: $28,540,898 (2003); $29,420,945 (2002)

Typical Recipients

Arts & Humanities: Arts Appreciation, Arts Associations & Councils, Arts Centers, Arts Festivals, Arts Funds, Arts Institutes, Arts Outreach, Community Arts, Dance, Film & Video, Historic Preservation, History & Archaeology, Libraries, Literary Arts, Museums/Galleries, Music, Opera, Performing Arts, Public Broadcasting, Theater, Visual Arts
Civic & Public Affairs: Botanical Gardens/Parks, Clubs, Community Foundations, Economic Development, Employment/Job Training, Civic & Public Affairs-General, Law & Justice, Municipalities/Towns, Nonprofit Management, Professional & Trade Associations, Public Policy, Urban & Community Affairs, Zoos/Aquariums
Education: Arts/Humanities Education, Colleges & Universities, Community & Junior Colleges, Continuing Education, Education Associations, Education Funds, Education Reform, Environmental Education, Education-General, Literacy, Minority Education, Preschool Education, Private Education (Precollege), Public Education (Precollege), Secondary Education (Public), Student Aid, Vocational & Technical Education
Environment: Environment-General, Protection, Wildlife Protection
Health: AIDS/HIV, Cancer, Children's Health/Hospitals, Clinics/Medical Centers, Emergency/Ambulance Services, Eyes/Blindness, Health-General, Hospitals, Nursing Services, Preventive Medicine/Wellness Organizations
International: Foreign Arts Organizations, International Affairs, International Development
Religion: Synagogues/Temples
Science: Science Museums, Scientific Centers & Institutes, Scientific Organizations
Social Services: At-Risk Youth, Child Abuse, Child

Welfare, Community Centers, Community Service Organizations, Emergency Relief, Family Services, People with Disabilities, Scouts, Substance Abuse, Volunteer Services, Youth Organizations

Application Procedures

Initial Contact: Send full outline of the project.
Application Requirements: There is no formal application form, but proposals should include financial information.
Deadlines: None.
Review Process: The board meets quarterly in April, June, October, and December. Notification usually occurs following the meeting.

Restrictions

The foundation does not make grants to individuals or for bricks and mortar projects.

Foundation Officials

Edgar D. Aronson: director B New York, NY 1,934. ED Harvard University AB (1956); Harvard University MBA (1962). PRIM CORP EMPL president: EDACO Inc. CORP AFFIL director: Petrogas Ltd.; director: HL Oakes Co. Inc.; director: MidAmerican Energy Holdings Co.; director: CalEnergy Co. Inc.; director: Hertford Inc. NV; director: APL NV. NONPR AFFIL member: Marine Corps Res Officers Association; trustee: South Street Seaport Museum; member: Cruising Association; member: 1st Marine Division Association. CLUB AFFIL Royal York YS; Mensa; New York Yacht Club; Eire Club; Harvard Club; Annabels Club; Bass Harbor Yacht Club.
Edith S. Aronson: director
Nancy P. Aronson: vice president, director
Anthony L. Ferranti: comptroller
George L. K. Frelinghuysen: assistant treasurer, director ED Princeton University (1973); Columbia University (1975).
Mary Kitabjian: assistant secretary
Carl A. Pforzheimer: director
Carl Howard Pforzheimer, III: president, treasurer, director B 1936. ED Harvard University MBA (1963). PRIM CORP EMPL Carl H Pforzheimer & Co. NONPR AFFIL chairman board, director: Visiting Nurse Service New York.
Carol K. Pforzheimer: director
Elizabeth S. Pforzheimer: director
Martin Franklin Richman: secretary B Newark, NJ 1930. ED Saint Lawrence University BA (1950); Harvard University LLB (1953). PRIM CORP EMPL counsel: Kirkpatrick & Lockhart LLP. NONPR AFFIL fellow: New York State Bar Foundation; vice chairman, trustee: Saint Lawrence University; member: New York State Bar Association; director: Friends Law Library Congress; member: New York County Lawyers Association; member: Association Bar New York City; member: Federal Bar Association; member: American Law Institute; member: American Bar Association; fellow: American Bar Foundation.
Thomas Sobol: director

Grants Analysis

Disclosure Period: calendar year ending 2003
Total Grants: $4,858,407
Number of Grants: 45
Average Grant: $50,258*
Highest Grant: $1,247,573
Lowest Grant: $6,000
Typical Range: $25,000 to $100,000
*Note: Average grants figure excludes three highest grants ($2,747,573).

Recent Grants

Note: Grants derived from 2003 Form 990.
Library-Related
1,247,573   New York Public Library, New York, NY
100,000   Wilton Library Association Inc., Wilton, CT
50,000   Library Foundation of Martin County, FL
50,000   Morgan Library, New York, NY

General
1,000,000   Wellesley College, Wellesley, MA
500,000   Radcliffe Institute, Cambridge, MA
307,500   Mount Sinai Medical Center, New York, NY
150,000   Dance Theatre of Harlem, New York, NY
150,000   Woodrow Wilson National Fellowship Foundation, Princeton, NJ
100,000   Lincoln Center Institute, New York, NY
100,000   National Civic League, Denver, CO
100,000   New Alternatives for Children, New York, NY
85,000   Council of Independent Colleges, Washington, DC
83,334   Mystic Seaport, Mystic, CT

PHELPS DODGE CORP.

Company Headquarters

Phoenix, AZ
Web: http://www.phelpsdodge.com

Company Description

Founded: 1834
Ticker: PD
Exchange: NYSE
Acquired: Cyprus Amax (1999).
Revenue: US$7.089 billion (2004)
Profit: US$1.046 billion (2004)
Employees: 13000 (2003)
Fortune Rank: 299, per FORTUNE Magazine's list of 500 Largest U.S. Corporations (2004).
SIC(s): 1021 Copper Ores, 2819 Industrial Inorganic Chemicals Nec, 2895 Carbon Black, 3331 Primary Copper.

Operating Locations

Phelps Dodge Corp. (AZ--Morenci, Phoenix; AR--El Dorado; CA--Irvine; FL--Coral Gables; GA--Atlanta, Trenton; IN--Fort Wayne; KY--Edmonton, Henderson, Hopkinsville; LA--Franklin; NJ--Bayway, Elizabeth; NM--Hurley, Santa Rita, Tyrone; NY--Ossining; NC--Laurinburg; OH--Springfield; TX--El Paso; WV--Moundsville)

Nonmonetary Support

Type: Donated Products; In-kind Services

Phelps Dodge Foundation

Giving Contact

Ann Gibson, Community Affairs
One N. Central Avenue
Phoenix, AZ 85004-4416
Phone: (602)366-8100
Fax: (602)234-8082
E-mail: phx-communityaffairs@phelpsdodge.com
Web: http://www.phelpsdodge.com/index-community.html

Alternate Contact

Grants Administrator
Phelps Dodge Corp.
One N. Central Avenue
Phoenix, AZ 85004-4416
Phone: 800-528-1182
Note: Contact for proposal submission and general questions. Inquiries to the 800 number should be directed to extension 6050.

Description

EIN: 136077350
Organization Type: Corporate Foundation
Giving Locations: communities where company maintains major operating facilities.

Grant Types: Employee Matching Gifts, General Support, Multiyear/Continuing Support, Scholarship. **Note:** Matching gifts, equal to 25% to 30% of annual grants, are made to educational, non-profit voluntary hospitals, family issues, cultural organizations and institutions.

Financial Summary

Total Giving: $1,161,207 (2002); $2,101,793 (2001). Note: Contributes through corporate direct giving program and foundation.
Giving Analysis: Giving for 2002 includes: foundation matching gifts ($828); foundation scholarships ($178,110); foundation grants to United Way ($261,745); foundation ($750,524)
Assets: $15,143,204 (2002); $18,470,532 (2001)
Gifts Received: $500,000 (1995)

Typical Recipients

Arts & Humanities: Arts Associations & Councils, Arts Centers, Arts Funds, Arts Outreach, Ballet, Community Arts, Arts & Humanities-General, History & Archaeology, Libraries, Literary Arts, Museums/Galleries, Music, Opera, Performing Arts, Public Broadcasting, Theater
Civic & Public Affairs: Botanical Gardens/Parks, Business/Free Enterprise, Civil Rights, Community Foundations, Economic Development, Economic Policy, Employment/Job Training, Civic & Public Affairs-General, Hispanic Affairs, Housing, Law & Justice, Professional & Trade Associations, Public Policy, Safety, Urban & Community Affairs, Women's Affairs, Zoos/Aquariums
Education: Arts/Humanities Education, Business Education, Colleges & Universities, Community & Junior Colleges, Economic Education, Education Associations, Education Funds, Engineering/Technological Education, Environmental Education, Education-General, Health & Physical Education, International Exchange, International Studies, Medical Education, Minority Education, Private Education (Precollege), Science/Mathematics Education, Student Aid
Environment: Environment-General
Health: AIDS/HIV, Cancer, Children's Health/Hospitals, Clinics/Medical Centers, Emergency/Ambulance Services, Geriatric Health, Health Funds, Health Organizations, Hospitals, Kidney, Medical Research, Medical Training
International: Foreign Educational Institutions, International-General, Health Care/Hospitals, International Peace & Security Issues, International Relations, International Relief Efforts
Religion: Religious Organizations, Religious Welfare
Science: Science-General, Science Museums, Scientific Centers & Institutes
Social Services: Child Abuse, Child Welfare, Community Service Organizations, Counseling, Day Care, Delinquency & Criminal Rehabilitation, Domestic Violence, Emergency Relief, Family Planning, Family Services, Recreation & Athletics, Scouts, Senior Services, Shelters/Homelessness, Social Services-General, United Funds/United Ways, YMCA/YWCA/YMHA/YWHA, Youth Organizations

Application Procedures

Initial Contact: Send a brief letter on the organization's letterhead and a proposal.
Application Requirements: Include a two-page summary statement of the organization's project or program and current needs, including amount requested, purpose of funds sought, funding period, and key program or deadline dates; program budget outlining all sources of financial support, including amounts committed or pending that may leverage a contributions by Phelps Dodge; audited financial statement for the most recent fiscal year; and proof of tax-exempt status. Requests for more than $5,000 must also include a brief description of how the proposal meets community needs that are not currently being met by other organizations; an explanation of how the organization is qualified to carry out the pro-

posal; an evaluation plan; a project timetable for implementation, communication and evaluation; the organization's operating budget for the past two years, indicating the percentages allocated for program/services; administration; fundraising and general expenses.
Deadlines: None.
Decision Notification: The budget is determined at the annual meeting held in September.

Restrictions

Does not support discriminatory organizations; programs in communities where Phelps Dodge does not operate; individuals; advertising; fraternal, veterans or labor organizations; religious activities, churches, or church sponsored programs limited to church members; political or lobbying groups; foundations that are grant-making entities; auxiliary organizations (unless the auxiliary is the sole fundraising arm of the parent organization); debt-reduction or operation deficit funding; capital campaigns or equipment; or organizations that pose a conflict with the goals, programs, products or employees of Phelps Dodge.

Additional Information

Company matches employee contributions to accredited colleges and universities, including junior colleges; privately financed, nonprofit accredited secondary schools; voluntary hospitals; museums; performing arts organizations; botanical gardens; public broadcasting services; or zoological societies.
Publications: A Tradition of Giving

Corporate Officials

S. David Colton: vice president, general counsel ED Brigham Young University BA; Brigham Young University J. Reuben Clark College of Law JD. PRIM CORP EMPL senior vice president, general counsel: Phelps Dodge Corp. NONPR AFFIL member: American Bar Association; member: Utah State Bar Association.
Ramiro G. Peru: senior vice president, chief financial officer B Morenci, AZ 1956. ED University of Arizona BS (1978). PRIM CORP EMPL senior vice president, chief financial officer: Phelps Dodge Corp.
David L. Pulatie: senior vice president human resources ED Arizona State College BS; Northern Arizona University MA.
Timothy R. Snider: senior vice president ED Northern Arizona University BS. PRIM CORP EMPL senior vice president: Phelps Dodge Corp. ADD CORP EMPL president: Phelps Dodge Mining Co.
Gregory W. Stevens: vice president, treasurer ED Yale University BA. PRIM CORP EMPL vice president, treasurer: Phelps Dodge Corp.
Robert C. Swan: vice president, secretary PRIM CORP EMPL vice president, secretary: Phelps Dodge Corp.
J. Steven Whisler: chairman, president, chief executive officer B 1954. ED Colorado School of Mines MS; University of Colorado BS; University of Denver College of Law JD. PRIM CORP EMPL chairman, president, chief executive officer: Phelps Dodge Corp. CORP AFFIL director: Burlington Northern Santa Fe Corp.; director: Southern Peru Copper Corp. NONPR AFFIL chairman: Copper Development Association; member: Mining Metallurgical Society America; member: American Institute Mining Engineers.

Foundation Officials

Amelia Anderson: assistant treasurer
S. David Colton: director (see above)
Kalidas Madhavpeddi: member
Ramiro G. Peru: director (see above)
David L. Pulatie: president (see above)
Timothy R. Snider: member (see above)
Gregory W. Stevens: treasurer, vice president (see above)
J. Steven Whisler: member (see above)

Grants Analysis

Disclosure Period: calendar year ending 2002
Total Grants: $720,524*
Number of Grants: 118
Average Grant: $6,106
Highest Grant: $154,000
Lowest Grant: $20
Typical Range: $250 to $25,000
*Note: Giving excludes matching gifts; scholarship; United Way.

Recent Grants

Note: Grants derived from 2003 Form 990.
General

209,000	American Red Cross, Phoenix, AZ
50,893	National Merit Scholarship Corporation, Evanston, IL
50,000	Colorado School of Mines, Golden, CO
38,500	Institute of International Education, AZ
30,000	Artshare
30,000	Colorado School of Mines, Golden, CO
25,000	Challenger Learning Center, Alexandria, VA
25,000	Maricopa Community Colleges Foundation
25,000	Phoenix Zoo, Phoenix, AZ
20,000	Aid to Adoption of Special Kids, Phoenix, AZ

DR. AND MRS. ARTHUR WILLIAM PHILLIPS CHARITABLE TRUST

Giving Contact

Bertha Winters, Admin. Assistant
229 Elm St.
PO Box 316
Oil City, PA 16301-0316
Phone: (814)676-2736

Description

Founded: 1978
EIN: 256201015
Organization Type: Private Foundation
Giving Locations: PA: Northwestern Pennsylvania
Grant Types: General Support, Project, Scholarship.

Donor Information

Founder: the late Arthur William Phillips

Financial Summary

Total Giving: $580,028 (fiscal year ending September 30, 2004); $586,375 (fiscal 2002)
Giving Analysis: Giving for fiscal 2001 includes: foundation scholarships ($150,000)
Assets: $13,613,528 (fiscal 2004); $11,857,963 (fiscal 2002)

Typical Recipients

Arts & Humanities: Arts Centers, Historic Preservation, History & Archaeology, Libraries, Museums/Galleries, Music, Theater
Civic & Public Affairs: Botanical Gardens/Parks, Civic & Public Affairs-General, Safety, Urban & Community Affairs
Education: Colleges & Universities, Education Associations, Education Funds, Education-General, Minority Education, Science/Mathematics Education, Secondary Education (Private), Student Aid
Health: Cancer, Children's Health/Hospitals, Emergency/Ambulance Services, Health Organizations, Heart, Hospitals, Nursing Services, Prenatal Health Issues, Single-Disease Health Associations
Religion: Churches, Religious Welfare
Science: Scientific Organizations
Social Services: Camps, Child Welfare, Community

Service Organizations, Domestic Violence, Family Services, People with Disabilities, Recreation & Athletics, Scouts, Senior Services, YMCA/YWCA/YMHA/YWHA, Youth Organizations

Application Procedures

Initial Contact: Requests must be submitted in triplicate. Include a description of organization, annual budget, and proof of tax-exempt status.
Deadlines: None.

Restrictions

Preference is given to organizations having medical or educational purposes.

Foundation Officials

Judge William E. Breene: trustee
Edith Gilmore Letcher: trustee
William J. McFate: trustee

Grants Analysis

Disclosure Period: fiscal year ending September 30, 2004
Total Grants: $580,028
Number of Grants: 27
Average Grant: $13,201*
Highest Grant: $200,000
Lowest Grant: $1,500
Typical Range: $5,000 to $20,000
*Note: Average grant figure excludes two highest grants ($250,000).

Recent Grants

Note: Grants derived from fiscal 2004 Form 990.
General

200,000	Grove City College, Grove City, PA -- to assist with renovations at Carnegie alumni center
50,000	Mercyhurst College, Erie, PA -- to assist with the purchase of scientific equipment for Mercyhurst Analytical and conservation center
33,000	Oil City Area Young Men's Christian Association, Oil City, PA -- for handicap ramp for swimming pool and new van for child care program
25,000	Allegheny Clarion Valley School District, Foxburg, PA -- to assist with purchase of equipment for wellness/fitness center
25,000	Penn State Erie, Behrend College, Erie, PA -- addition to scholarship fund
25,000	Sugar Valley Lodge, Franklin, PA -- to assist with food purchases for residents
25,000	Thiel College, Greenville, PA -- to assist with academic center renovations
25,000	Westminster College, New Wilmington, PA -- to assist with old main renovations
20,000	City of Oil City, Oil City, PA -- for automated systems hardware and software for oil city library
20,000	Keystone Tall Tree Girl Scout Council, Kittanning, PA -- for capital improvements to construct low and high ropes courses at singing hills

L. E. PHILLIPS FAMILY FOUNDATION

Giving Contact

Melvin S. Cohen, President and Director
National Presto Industries
3925 N. Hastings Way
Eau Claire, WI 54703
Phone: (715)839-2139
Fax: (715)839-2148

Description

Founded: 1943
EIN: 396046126
Organization Type: Family Foundation
Giving Locations: WI: Chippewa County, Eau Claire County, Northwestern Wisconsin
Grant Types: Capital, General Support, Operating Expenses, Professorship, Project, Research, Scholarship.

Donor Information

Founder: Lewis E. Phillips established the L. E. Phillips Charities in Wisconsin in 1943. The foundation's name recently was changed to the L. E. Phillips Family Foundation. Mr. Phillips was president and director of the manufacturing business of Ed Phillips and Sons Company. He was head of National Presto Industries, formerly named the National Pressure Cooker Company, for over 25 years. The foundation is administered primarily by members of the Phillips family, including Lewis E. Phillip's son-in-law, Melvin Samuel Cohen, who is the current chairman of National Presto Industries.

Financial Summary

Total Giving: $2,981,850 (fiscal year ending February 28, 2004); $2,707,000 (fiscal 2003 approx); $2,707,000 (fiscal 2002 approx)
Giving Analysis: Giving for fiscal 2004 includes: foundation scholarships ($5,700); foundation grants to United Way ($15,000); fiscal 2001: foundation scholarships ($4,200); foundation grants to United Way ($15,000)
Assets: $68,459,361 (fiscal 2004); $63,000,000 (fiscal 2002 approx); $60,613,751 (fiscal 2001)
Gifts Received: $127,201 (fiscal 1997); $127,201 (fiscal 1996); $599,849 (fiscal 1995). Note: In fiscal 1993-1997, contributions were received from Edith Phillips 1983 Charitable Trust. In fiscal 1995, contributions were received from Boy Scout Camp Trust u/w L. E. Phillips.

Typical Recipients

Arts & Humanities: Arts Associations & Councils, Arts Centers, Arts Institutes, Ballet, Dance, Libraries, Museums/Galleries, Music, Opera, Public Broadcasting, Theater
Civic & Public Affairs: Business/Free Enterprise, Clubs, Community Foundations, Employment/Job Training, Ethnic Organizations, Civic & Public Affairs-General, Law & Justice, Legal Aid, Parades/Festivals, Philanthropic Organizations, Professional & Trade Associations, Public Policy, Safety, Urban & Community Affairs
Education: Arts/Humanities Education, Business Education, Colleges & Universities, Faculty Development, Education-General, Gifted & Talented Programs, Leadership Training, Legal Education, Medical Education, Minority Education, Private Education (Precollege), Public Education (Precollege), Religious Education, Secondary Education (Private), Secondary Education (Public), Student Aid, Vocational & Technical Education
Environment: Resource Conservation, Wildlife Protection
Health: AIDS/HIV, Children's Health/Hospitals, Health-General, Geriatric Health, Health Policy/Cost Containment, Health Organizations, Heart, Hospitals, Hospitals (University Affiliated), Medical Rehabilitation, Medical Research, Public Health, Single-Disease Health Associations
International: Foreign Arts Organizations, International Environmental Issues, International Peace & Security Issues, Missionary/Religious Activities
Religion: Churches, Dioceses, Jewish Causes, Religious Welfare, Social/Policy Issues, Synagogues/Temples
Social Services: Animal Protection, Big Brothers/Big Sisters, Community Centers, Community Service Organizations, Crime Prevention, Day Care, People with Disabilities, Recreation & Athletics, Scouts, Senior Services, Special Olympics, Substance Abuse, United Funds/United Ways, YMCA/YWCA/YMHA/YWHA, Youth Organizations

Application Procedures

Initial Contact: The foundation has no formal application requirements or procedures. Applicants should send a letter of inquiry.
Application Requirements: The letter should describe the organization and project for which funds are sought and include a budget.
Deadlines: The foundation prefers to receive inquiries before the end of the fiscal year in February.

Restrictions

Grants are not made to individuals.

Foundation Officials

James F. Bartl: secretary, director B Saint Paul, MN 1940. ED Saint Thomas University (1962); Marquette University JD (1965). PRIM CORP EMPL secretary: National Presto Industries, Inc. CORP AFFIL assistant secretary: Presto Manufacturing Co. NONPR AFFIL member: American Society of Corporate Secretaries.
Maryjo Rose Cohen: vice president, treasurer, director B Eau Claire, WI 1952. ED University of Michigan (1973); University of Michigan JD (1976). PRIM CORP EMPL president, chief executive officer, director: National Presto Industries, Inc. CORP AFFIL secretary, treasurer, director: Presto Export Ltd.; secretary, treasurer, director: Presto Manufacturing Co.; vice president, director: National Pipeline Co.; secretary, treasurer, director: National Defense Corp.; secretary, assistant treasurer, director: National Holding Investment Co.; vice president, secretary, treasurer, director: Jackson Sales & Storage Co.; vice president, director: National Automatic Pipeline Oper Inc.; secretary, treasurer, director: Canton Sales & Storage Co.; secretary, treasurer, director: Century Leasing & Liquidating Inc.
Patricia Ellenson: assistant secretary-treasurer
Edith Phillips: vice president, director

Grants Analysis

Disclosure Period: fiscal year ending February 28, 2004
Total Grants: $2,961,150*
Number of Grants: 99
Average Grant: $3,022*
Highest Grant: $2,665,000
Lowest Grant: $25
Typical Range: $100 to $5,000
*Note: Giving excludes scholarships and United Way. Average grant figure excludes highest grant.

THE JAY AND ROSE PHILLIPS FAMILY FOUNDATION

Giving Contact

Amy K. Crawford, Executive Director
10 Second Street NE, Suite 200
Minneapolis, MN 55413
Phone: (612)623-1654
Fax: (612)623-1653
E-mail: phillipsfnd@phillipsfnd.org
Web: http://www.phillipsfnd.org

Description

Founded: 1944
EIN: 416019578
Organization Type: Family Foundation
Giving Locations: MN: seven-county metropolitan area of Minneapolis/St. Paul, MN
Grant Types: Capital, General Support, Project, Research, Scholarship, Seed Money.

Donor Information

Founder: The Jay and Rose Phillips Family Foundation was incorporated in 1944, with funds donated by Jay Phillips and members of the Phillips family.

Financial Summary

Total Giving: $10,369,601 (2003); $9,200,329 (2002); $9,529,712 (2001)
Assets: $190,535,204 (2003); $169,864,604 (2002); $194,210,759 (2001)
Gifts Received: $243,024 (1994); $13,208,515 (1993); $1,360,157 (1992)

Typical Recipients

Arts & Humanities: Arts Associations & Councils, Arts Centers, Historic Preservation, Libraries, Museums/Galleries, Music, Public Broadcasting, Theater
Civic & Public Affairs: African American Affairs, Asian American Affairs, Civil Rights, Clubs, Community Foundations, Economic Development, Employment/Job Training, Ethnic Organizations, Civic & Public Affairs-General, Hispanic Affairs, Housing, Law & Justice, Native American Affairs, Philanthropic Organizations, Professional & Trade Associations, Public Policy, Urban & Community Affairs, Women's Affairs, Zoos/Aquariums
Education: Colleges & Universities, Education Associations, Education Funds, Elementary Education (Private), Education-General, International Studies, Legal Education, Medical Education, Minority Education, Private Education (Precollege), Public Education (Precollege), Religious Education, Secondary Education (Private), Social Sciences Education, Student Aid
Environment: Environment-General
Health: AIDS/HIV, Cancer, Children's Health/Hospitals, Clinics/Medical Centers, Health-General, Health Funds, Health Organizations, Heart, Hospices, Hospitals, Long-Term Care, Medical Rehabilitation, Medical Research, Mental Health, Multiple Sclerosis, Prenatal Health Issues, Public Health, Research/Studies Institutes, Single-Disease Health Associations
International: Health Care/Hospitals
Religion: Religion-General, Jewish Causes, Ministries, Religious Organizations, Religious Welfare, Social/Policy Issues, Synagogues/Temples
Science: Science Museums
Social Services: At-Risk Youth, Camps, Child Welfare, Community Centers, Community Service Organizations, Counseling, Crime Prevention, Day Care, Domestic Violence, Emergency Relief, Family Planning, Family Services, Food/Clothing Distribution, Homes, People with Disabilities, Recreation & Athletics, Senior Services, Sexual Abuse, Shelters/Homelessness, Social Services-General, United Funds/United Ways, Volunteer Services, YMCA/YWHA/YMHA/YWHA, Youth Organizations

Application Procedures

Initial Contact: Applicants who are unsure about whether they meet the foundation's funding criteria are encouraged to submit a one-page letter of interest to the foundation. The foundation staff reviews all letters of interest, and the applicant will be notified regarding whether the foundation would like the organization to submit a full proposal.
Application Requirements: Send one unbound copy including information on purpose of funds sought and amount requested; type of request (special program or project, capital, technical assistance, general operating support, etc.); a description of organization including date founded, history, mission, and current and planned programs; objectives and activities for funds sought; evidence of need; how the request addresses the foundation's guidelines and special concerns; population to be served, including geographical area, number of persons to be served, ages income levels, and special needs of individuals served. Provide evidence of the organization's ability to manage the program/project, including qualifica-

tions and experience of the administrative staff responsible for management of your organization and project. Describe the expected outcomes of your program or project in terms of real changes in the lives of your constituents. Describe methods used to measure outcomes. Include description of short and longer-range fundraising costs, and statement of the percentage of annual operating budget expended on direct fundraising costs and lobbying activities, if applicable. Your application must be signed by your executive director and your board chair or his/her designee before it can be considered. All applications must include proof of tax-exempt status, copy of most recent annual report, recently audited financial statement; current year-to-date operating budget; percentage of budget used for fundraising; current donors and list of proposals pending with other funding sources.

If you are requesting funding for a special or capital project, you must submit the following: board approved project budget including projected income and expenses, total amount requested and sources of funds received or committed, list of proposals pending with other funding sources, organizational chart, a list of current board members and officers, and final report or progress report on last grant, if applicable.
Deadlines: None.
Review Process: The foundation will send confirmation of application receipt. The trustees meet approximately every four months and completed applications are reviewed in the order in which they are received. The foundation reports that the review process usually takes about four-to-six months.
Evaluative Criteria: The foundation gives special attention to proposals that reflect the following values: self-sufficiency should be a goal of all efforts to assist people; families should be strengthened as nurturing and financially stable environments for children; the quality of health care should be continually improved for the benefit of all people; quality education is the key to individual success; people with disabilities and the elderly should be able to live as independently as possible; good relations among people of all races and religions should be fostered and discrimination should be actively opposed; and the arts should be supported primarily as a vehicle to address social issues.

Restrictions

The foundation will not make grants to organizations operating for profit, political campaigns or lobbying efforts to influence legislation, endowment campaigns, or individuals. The foundation requests that all initial inquiries from prospective applicants be by mail, not by telephone or by personal visits to the foundation office.

Funding is restricted to the state of Minnesota. Previously funded organizations will be reviewed only after a full report on the previous grant has been received. Grants are awarded only to 501(c)(3) organizations.

Additional Information

The foundation was formerly called Phillips Foundation. be fostered and discrimination should be actively opposed; and the arts should be supported primarily as a vehicle to address social issues. Grants are awarded only to 501(c)(3) organizations. be fostered and discrimination should be actively opposed; and the arts should be supported primarily as a vehicle to address social issues. Grants are awarded only to 501(c)(3) organizations.
Publications: Annual Report; Guidelines

Foundation Officials

Erik P. Bernstein: trustee
Paula P. Bernstein: trustee
William E. Bernstein: trustee PRIM CORP EMPL chief executive officer: Lockheed Information Technology Co.
Amy K. Crawford: executive director
Patricia A. Cummings: executive director

Jack I. Levin: trustee
John P. Levin: trustee
Suzan Levin: trustee
Edward Jay Phillips: trustee
Jeanne Phillips: trustee
Morton B. Phillips: trustee
Pauline Phillips: trustee emeritus
Rose Phillips: trustee

Grants Analysis

Disclosure Period: calendar year ending 2003
Total Grants: $10,369,601
Number of Grants: 383
Average Grant: $24,684*
Highest Grant: $500,000
Lowest Grant: $277
Typical Range: $5,000 to $50,000
*Note: Average grant figure excludes two highest grants ($965,000).

Recent Grants

Note: Grants derived from 2003 Form 990.
General

500,000	Mayo Foundation, Rochester, MN -- fund for Abigail Van Buren Alzheimer's Research project
465,000	Minneapolis Jewish Federation, Minneapolis, MN -- to support Rottenberg Family Assisted Living Residence at Sholom Community Alliance
456,537	Minneapolis Jewish Federation, Minneapolis, MN
287,000	Jewish Family Service of Colorado, Denver, CO -- to assist senior and adult services
250,000	Jewish Community Center of San Francisco, San Francisco, CA -- for capital campaign
250,000	Jewish Family and Children's Services, San Francisco, CA -- fund for Disability project
250,000	Local Initiatives Support Corporation, St. Paul, MN -- grant to fully capitalize the Predevelopment Loan Fund
200,000	Stanford University, Stanford, CA -- fund for undergraduate education
120,000	University of St. Thomas, St. Paul, MN -- to support the Jay Philips Center for Jewish Christian Learning
100,000	Anti-Defamation League of B'nai B'rith, Los Angeles, CA -- to assist in general operations

ELLIS L. PHILLIPS FOUNDATION

Giving Contact

Ellis L. Phillips, III, President
Ellis L. Phillips Foundation
233 Commonwealth Avenue, Suite 2
Boston, MA 02116
Phone: (617)424-7607
Fax: (617)424-6391
E-mail: elpfndtn@gis.net
Web: http://www.ellislphillipsfndn.org

Description

Founded: 1930
EIN: 135677691
Organization Type: Private Foundation
Giving Locations: MA: Boston and surrounding areas Northern New England.
Grant Types: General Support, Seed Money.

Donor Information

Founder: the late Ellis L. Phillips

Financial Summary

Total Giving: $530,640 (fiscal year ending June 30, 2002); $528,195 (fiscal 2001)
Assets: $4,681,344 (fiscal 2002); $6,009,230 (fiscal 2001)
Gifts Received: $50,000 (fiscal 2002)

Typical Recipients

Arts & Humanities: Arts Associations & Councils, Community Arts, Historic Preservation, History & Archaeology, Libraries, Museums/Galleries, Music, Theater, Visual Arts
Civic & Public Affairs: Nonprofit Management, Philanthropic Organizations, Women's Affairs
Education: Arts/Humanities Education, Education Funds, Environmental Education, Education-General, Private Education (Precollege), Science/Mathematics Education
Environment: Forestry, Environment-General, Wildlife Protection
Health: Clinics/Medical Centers
Religion: Churches
Social Services: Camps, Child Welfare, Community Centers, Community Service Organizations, Family Services

Application Procedures

Initial Contact: Send a brief letter of inquiry requesting application guidelines.
Application Requirements: 2-4 page letter describing the organization, history, mission, major accomplishments, problem to be addressed, proposed solution, planned activities, and anticipated outcomes. Also include an abstract summarizing above information, proof of tax-exempt status, itemized project budget, and organization budget. For grants of $7,500 or more, include recently audited financial statement, listing of board of directors with affiliations and titles, and three independent references (optional).
Deadlines: January 1, April 1, and September 1.
Review Process: The board meets in February, May, and October.
Evaluative Criteria: Evaluated on the priority of the project within the Foundation's program interests, the anticipated impact of the project on the public and the organization, the organizational capacity, and the resources requested and current funds available.

Restrictions

Does not support individuals or provide funds for scholarships.

Additional Information

Publications: Annual Report (including Application Guidelines)

Foundation Officials

David Lloyd Brown: director
Cornelia Grumman: director
David L. Grumman: director, mem
Dr. George E. McCully: director
Walter C. Paine: director
Ellis Laurimore Phillips, III: president, director, mem
Ellis Laurimore Phillips, Jr.: vice president, director, mem B New York, NY 1921. ED Princeton University AB (1942); Columbia University LLB (1948); Keuka College LLD (1956).
Cynthia Phillips Prosser: secretary, director
E. Clinton Swift: director
K. Noel P. Zimmermann: secretary, director

Grants Analysis

Disclosure Period: fiscal year ending June 30, 2002
Total Grants: $530,640
Number of Grants: 5
Highest Grant: $467,500
Lowest Grant: $640

Recent Grants

Note: Grants derived from fiscal 2002 Form 990.

General

467,500	Catalog for Philanthropy, Boston, MA -- support experimental project
25,000	Boston Modern Orchestra Project, Boston, MA -- transfer of foundation
25,000	New England Conservatory, Boston, MA -- capital campaign
12,500	Barton Center for Diabetes Education, Oxford, MA -- capital campaign
640	Council on Foundations, Washington, DC -- portion of annual dues

COLUMBUS PHIPPS FOUNDATION

Giving Contact

Paul D. Buchanan, Trustee
PO Box 1145
Clintwood, VA 24228
Phone: (540)926-8152

Description

Founded: 1994
EIN: 546338751
Organization Type: Private Foundation
Giving Locations: VA: Dickenson County
Grant Types: General Support, Scholarship.

Donor Information

Founder: Established in 1994 by Beulah G. Phipps.

Financial Summary

Total Giving: $298,787 (fiscal year ending March 31, 2004); $192,045 (fiscal 2001). Note: Fiscal 1997 Giving includes scholarship ($92,070).
Giving Analysis: Giving for fiscal 2004 includes: foundation scholarships ($227,387); fiscal 2001: foundation scholarships ($130,350)
Assets: $10,290,852 (fiscal 2004); $3,869,886 (fiscal 2001)
Gifts Received: $2,820,583 (fiscal 2004); $2,166 (fiscal 2001); $270,589 (fiscal 1999). Note: In fiscal 1997, fiscal 1999, and fiscal 2004, contributions were received from the estate Beulah G. Phipps.

Typical Recipients

Arts & Humanities: Arts Associations & Councils, Arts Centers, Libraries, Music, Opera, Theater
Civic & Public Affairs: Botanical Gardens/Parks, Municipalities/Towns
Education: Arts/Humanities Education, Colleges & Universities, Community & Junior Colleges, Education-General, Legal Education, Medical Education, Private Education (Precollege), Public Education (Precollege), Student Aid
Science: Science Exhibits & Fairs, Science Museums

Application Procedures

Initial Contact: Request application form.
Deadlines: May 15.

Restrictions

Grants are restricted to cultural activities for residents of Dickenson County, VA and scholarships for graduates of Dickenson County.

Additional Information

Publications: Application Form

Foundation Officials

Carol P. Buchanan: trustee
Betty Jo Dodson: mem
Rita F. Justice: mem

Grants Analysis

Disclosure Period: fiscal year ending March 31, 2004

Total Grants: $71,400*
Number of Grants: 15
Average Grant: $2,786*
Highest Grant: $32,400
Typical Range: $1,000 to $5,000
***Note:** Giving excludes scholarships. Average grant figure excludes highest grant.

Recent Grants

Note: Grants derived from 2004 Form 990.
Library-Related

4,000	Jonnie B. Deel Library -- grant to purchase information display unit, children's mural, bulletin
2,000	Haysi Public Library, Haysi, VA -- grant to purchase encyclopedia, visual aids, and titles for AV collection

General

32,400	Dickenson County School, Clintwood, VA
23,000	University of Virginia's College at Wise, Wise, VA -- towards 1st semester awards
5,000	Baker Center Theater Project
5,000	Pro-Art Association, Wise, VA -- cultural grant for the marionette program
5,000	Science Museum of Virginia, Richmond, VA -- grant for outreach program for elementary schools in Dickenson County
5,000	Town of Clintwood -- for the chase house interior restoration
5,000	University of Virginia's, Wise, VA -- grant for purpose of assisting with the renovation of the old student science
3,000	University of Virginia's College at Wise, Wise, VA -- educational grants for two Dickenson county students to participate in summer study

PHOENIX HOME LIFE MUTUAL INSURANCE CO.

Company Headquarters

Hartford, CT
Web: http://www.phl.com

Company Description

Employees: 3,800
SIC(s): 6311 Life Insurance.

Operating Locations

Phoenix Home Life Mutual Insurance Co. (CT--Enfield, Hartford; MA--Greenfield; NY--Albany)

Nonmonetary Support

Type: Cause-related Marketing & Promotion

Phoenix Foundation

Giving Contact

Jane L. Driscoll, Vice President
Phoenix Foundation
1 American Row
Hartford, CT 06102-5056
Phone: (860)403-5630
Fax: (860)403-5755
E-mail: Tina.Muzzy@phoenixwm.com
Web: http://www.phoenixwm.com

Alternate Contact

Phone: (860)403-7831
Web: http://www.ctphilanthropy.org
Note: Alternate contact information is for grant application requests.

Description

EIN: 061493188
Organization Type: Corporate Foundation

Giving Locations: nationally.
Grant Types: Employee Matching Gifts, General Support.
Note: Employee matching gift ratio: 1 to 1.

Financial Summary

Total Giving: $1,413,393 (2003); $2,164,958 (2002); $2,366,361 (2001). Note: Contributes through corporate direct giving program and foundation. Giving includes matching gifts. 1998 Giving includes corporate direct giving ($300,000); foundation ($800,000).
Assets: $7,554,455 (2003); $7,601,182 (2002); $8,911,779 (2001)
Gifts Received: $705,627 (2003); $17,030 (2002); $98,866 (2001). Note: Contributions are received from PM Holdings.

Typical Recipients

Arts & Humanities: Arts Associations & Councils, Arts Centers, Arts Funds, Dance, Historic Preservation, History & Archaeology, Libraries, Music, Performing Arts, Public Broadcasting
Civic & Public Affairs: African American Affairs, Botanical Gardens/Parks, Civil Rights, Community Foundations, Economic Development, Employment/Job Training, Civic & Public Affairs-General, Hispanic Affairs, Housing, Law & Justice, Legal Aid, Public Policy, Zoos/Aquariums
Education: Afterschool/Enrichment Programs, Business Education, Colleges & Universities, Education Associations, Education Funds, Elementary Education (Public), Education-General, Public Education (Precollege), Student Aid
Environment: Protection
Health: AIDS/HIV, Cancer, Children's Health/Hospitals, Emergency/Ambulance Services, Health-General, Hospices, Hospitals, Prenatal Health Issues, Single-Disease Health Associations
Religion: Churches, Dioceses, Ministries, Religious Welfare
Social Services: Camps, Child Welfare, Community Service Organizations, Counseling, Domestic Violence, Family Services, People with Disabilities, Recreation & Athletics, Shelters/Homelessness, United Funds/United Ways, YMCA/YWCA/YMHA/YWHA, Youth Organizations

Application Procedures

Initial Contact: Send written request for application.
Application Requirements: Include description of agency and its objectives; amount requested and how it will be used; organization budget for upcoming year; description of other support received, including support received from the United Way or any government entities; account of staff size, including qualifications; statement of organization's board's composition and affiliations; copy of most recent annual report; demonstration that organization serves one of the giving areas; description of how organization measures progress towards its goals; and proof of tax-exempt status. Also include a narrative of no more than five pages providing organization information, grant purpose, evaluation process, financial information, and other supporting materials.
Deadlines: September 15.
Decision Notification: Requests are considered during the fourth quarter of each calendar year; company will notify agencies of outcome during early January of the following year. first quarter

Additional Information

Publications: Guidelines; Application form

Foundation Officials

Katherine P. Cody: treasurer
Sheila K. Dubinsky: assistant treasurer
Michele U. Farley: director
Brian A. Giantonio: secretary
Michael E. Haylon: director, chairman
Bonnie J. Malley: director
James D. Wehr: director
Dona D. Young: director

Grants Analysis

Disclosure Period: calendar year ending 2003
Total Grants: $1,227,993*
Number of Grants: 887
Average Grant: $1,384
Highest Grant: $55,000
Lowest Grant: $25
Typical Range: $100 to $15,000
*Note: Giving excludes United Way.

Recent Grants

Note: Grants derived from 2003 Form 990.
General

157,000	United Way of Capital Area, Hartford, CT
55,000	Greater Hartford Arts Council, Hartford, CT
50,000	Hartford Public Schools, Hartford, CT
50,000	Hartford Public Schools, Hartford, CT
50,000	University of Connecticut, Storrs, CT -- toward campaign UCONN
43,500	University of Connecticut, Storrs, CT -- toward the Day of Pride scholarship
40,500	University of Connecticut, Storrs, CT -- toward the Day of Pride scholarship
38,000	Bushnell Memorial Hall, Hartford, CT
30,000	Hartford Hospital, Hartford, CT
30,000	Hartford Hospital, Hartford, CT

TATIANA PIANKOVA FOUNDATION

Giving Contact

Mildred C. Brinn, President, Treasurer & Director
570 Park Avenue
New York, NY 10021
Phone: (212)758-7764

Description

Founded: 1983
EIN: 133142090
Organization Type: Private Foundation
Grant Types: General Support.

Donor Information

Founder: Susan Polachek

Financial Summary

Total Giving: $140,450 (fiscal year ending July 31, 2004); $325,850 (fiscal 2001)
Assets: $3,730,836 (fiscal 2004); $5,220,391 (fiscal 2001)

Typical Recipients

Arts & Humanities: Arts Associations & Councils, Arts Centers, Arts Institutes, Ballet, Community Arts, Dance, Arts & Humanities-General, Historic Preservation, History & Archaeology, Libraries, Literary Arts, Museums/Galleries, Music, Opera, Performing Arts, Theater, Visual Arts
Civic & Public Affairs: Botanical Gardens/Parks, Civic & Public Affairs-General, Urban & Community Affairs, Women's Affairs
Education: Arts/Humanities Education, Colleges & Universities, Education-General, Medical Education, Preschool Education, Private Education (Precollege), Religious Education
Environment: Resource Conservation
Health: Cancer, Health-General, Health Organizations, Hospices, Hospitals, Long-Term Care, Medical Research
International: Foreign Arts Organizations, Foreign Educational Institutions, International Affairs, International Organizations, International Relations
Religion: Churches
Science: Science Museums
Social Services: Child Welfare, Community Service Organizations, Counseling, Family Services, Homes,

People with Disabilities, Recreation & Athletics, Senior Services, Social Services-General, Veterans, Youth Organizations

Application Procedures

Initial Contact: Send a brief letter of inquiry.
Application Requirements: Include an outline of purpose and requirements of the organization.
Deadlines: None.

Restrictions

Primarily supports preselected organizations.

Foundation Officials

Mildred Cunningham Brinn: president, treasurer, director
Peter F. De Gaetano: secretary, director

Grants Analysis

Disclosure Period: fiscal year ending July 31, 2004
Total Grants: $140,450
Number of Grants: 40
Average Grant: $2,288*
Highest Grant: $28,500
Lowest Grant: $150
Typical Range: $1,000 to $5,000
*Note: Average grant figure excludes two highest grants ($53,500).

Recent Grants

Note: Grants derived from 2004 Form 990.
General

28,500	St. Bartholomew's Church, New York, NY
25,000	Skowhegan School of Painting and Sculpture, New York, NY
19,000	Parrish Art Museum, Southampton, NY
8,000	Southampton Fresh Air Home, Southampton, NY
5,500	Museum Trustee Association, Washington, DC
5,000	Metropolitan Opera, New York, NY
5,000	Museum of Modern Art, New York, NY
5,000	Southampton Care Center, Southampton, NY
3,500	American Ireland Fund, New York, NY
3,500	Metropolitan Museum of Art, New York, NY

ALBERT PICK, JR. FUND

Giving Contact

Cleopatra B. Alexander, Executive Director
Albert Pick, Jr. Fund
30 North Michigan Avenue, Suite 1002
Chicago, IL 60602
Phone: (312)236-1192
E-mail: info@albertpickjrfund.org
Web: http://www.albertpickjrfund.org

Description

Founded: 1947
EIN: 366071402
Organization Type: General Purpose Foundation
Giving Locations: IL: Chicago
Grant Types: Capital, General Support, Multiyear/Continuing Support, Project.

Donor Information

Founder: Incorporated in 1947 by the late Albert Pick Jr.

Financial Summary

Total Giving: $1,560,500 (2002)
Assets: $19,779,290 (2002)
Gifts Received: $8,416 (2002); $92,364 (2000); $12,976 (1998). Note: Harris Associates contributed in 2002.

Typical Recipients

Arts & Humanities: Arts Associations & Councils, Arts Festivals, Arts Funds, Arts Institutes, Arts Outreach, Community Arts, Dance, Ethnic & Folk Arts, History & Archaeology, Libraries, Museums/Galleries, Music, Opera, Performing Arts, Public Broadcasting, Theater

Civic & Public Affairs: Asian American Affairs, Botanical Gardens/Parks, Economic Development, Employment/Job Training, Civic & Public Affairs-General, Hispanic Affairs, Housing, Municipalities/Towns, Nonprofit Management, Philanthropic Organizations, Public Policy, Urban & Community Affairs, Zoos/Aquariums

Education: Afterschool/Enrichment Programs, Agricultural Education, Arts/Humanities Education, Business Education, Colleges & Universities, Continuing Education, Education Associations, Education Reform, Education-General, International Studies, Literacy, Minority Education, Preschool Education, Public Education (Precollege), Science/Mathematics Education, Special Education, Student Aid

Environment: Air/Water Quality, Environment-General, Resource Conservation

Health: AIDS/HIV, Children's Health/Hospitals, Clinics/Medical Centers, Emergency/Ambulance Services, Health Organizations, Hospices, Hospitals, Long-Term Care, Medical Training, Prenatal Health Issues, Preventive Medicine/Wellness Organizations, Public Health, Single-Disease Health Associations

International: Foreign Arts Organizations, Human Rights

Religion: Jewish Causes, Religious Organizations, Religious Welfare

Science: Observatories & Planetariums, Science Museums, Scientific Organizations

Social Services: Child Welfare, Community Service Organizations, Day Care, Domestic Violence, Family Planning, Family Services, Food/Clothing Distribution, Homes, People with Disabilities, Scouts, Senior Services, Sexual Abuse, Shelters/Homelessness, Substance Abuse, United Funds/United Ways, YMCA/YWCA/YMHA/YWHA, Youth Organizations

Application Procedures

Initial Contact: A preliminary letter of inquiry is not required prior to submitting an application. Call or write the fund for application form.

Application Requirements: Proposals should be as brief as possible and include the following: a history of the organization, a description of current programs, a description of the proposed project, and the intended use of the funds requested; proof of tax-exempt status from the IRS and a ruling that the organization is publicly supported under section 509(a) of the IRS code; the names, affiliations, and addresses of governing board members, officers, and staff; a current financial statement, preferably audited; the projected annual budgets for the organization and the project; a list of principal sources of income; and a description of the geographic area served.

Deadlines: January 21, April 1, July 1, and October 1. Proposals from cultural organizations should be submitted by the July 1 deadline.

Review Process: The board meets in March or April, June, September, and December.

Restrictions

The fund will not consider proposals from organizations whose fiscal year ends on the same month as the board meeting's review of that request. Grants are not made to individuals., to religious organisation, or for political purposes. The fund does not support hospitals, local chapters of single-disease associations, umbrella organisation, building or endowment funds, deficit financing, long-term projects, advertising, scholarships, fundraising, or fraternal, veterans, labor, or athletic groups. Additionally, the fund does not support student aid or campaigns for reduction of debts.

Additional Information

Publications: Program Policy Statement; Application Guidelines

Foundation Officials

Cleopatra B. Alexander: executive director
Gregory M. Darnieder: secretary
Burton B. Kaplan: treasurer, vice president
Ralph I. Lewy: treasurer B Leiwen, Germany 1931. ED Roosevelt University BS (1953). PRIM CORP EMPL president: Ralph Lewy Ltd. NONPR AFFIL member: American Institute of Certified Public Accountants.
Robert B. Lifton: director, chairman
Albert Pick, III: vice president, director

Grants Analysis

Disclosure Period: calendar year ending 2002
Total Grants: $1,560,500
Number of Grants: 97
Average Grant: $12,878*
Highest Grant: $150,000
Lowest Grant: $150
Typical Range: $1,500 to $15,000
*Note: Average grant figure excludes three highest grants totaling $350,000.

Recent Grants

Note: Grants derived from 2002 Form 990.
Library-Related

10,000	Newberry Library, Chicago, IL -- for educational outreach

General

150,000	Sherwood Conservatory of Music, Chicago, IL -- for youth music education initiative
100,000	Mexican Fine Arts Center Museum, Chicago, IL -- for educational outreach
100,000	Resurrection Project, Chicago, IL -- for Community Development Projects
85,000	DuSable Museum of African American History, Chicago, IL -- for Reflections in Black Exhibition
80,000	YMCA Training Alliance, Chicago, IL -- for Youth Philanthropy Initiative
60,000	Children's First Fund, Chicago, IL -- for expanded vision screening program
50,000	Deborah's Place, Chicago, IL -- for operating
50,000	Gateway Charitable Foundation, Chicago, IL -- for substance abuse prevention
25,000	BUILD, Inc., Beaumont, TX -- for Project Build
25,000	Neighborhood Housing Services, Chicago, IL -- for Solutions to Predatory Lending

MARY PICKFORD FOUNDATION

Giving Contact

Henry Stotsenberg, President
43460 Ridge Park Dr.
Temecula, CA 92590
Phone: 800-333-8128
Web: http://www.marypickford.com/found.html

Description

Founded: 1968
EIN: 956093487
Organization Type: Private Foundation
Giving Locations: CA
Grant Types: Endowment, General Support, Scholarship.

Donor Information

Founder: the late Mary Pickford Rogers

Financial Summary

Total Giving: $523,596 (fiscal year ending May 31, 2003); $831,950 (fiscal 2001). Note: Fiscal 1997 Giving includes scholarship ($170,000), United Way ($1,000).
Giving Analysis: Giving for fiscal 2003 includes: foundation scholarships ($58,900); fiscal 2001: foundation scholarships ($9,000)
Assets: $12,044,482 (fiscal 2003); $14,181,524 (fiscal 2001)
Gifts Received: $1,289,454 (fiscal 2000)

Typical Recipients

Arts & Humanities: Arts Funds, Arts Outreach, Film & Video, Historic Preservation, Libraries, Museums/Galleries, Music, Public Broadcasting, Theater, Visual Arts

Civic & Public Affairs: Clubs, Civic & Public Affairs-General, Philanthropic Organizations, Professional & Trade Associations, Urban & Community Affairs

Education: Arts/Humanities Education, Colleges & Universities, Education Funds, Education-General, Legal Education, Science/Mathematics Education, Student Aid

Health: Children's Health/Hospitals, Clinics/Medical Centers, Emergency/Ambulance Services, Geriatric Health, Health Organizations, Hospitals, Long-Term Care, Medical Research, Prenatal Health Issues, Single-Disease Health Associations

International: Health Care/Hospitals, International Affairs, Missionary/Religious Activities

Religion: Jewish Causes, Religious Welfare

Science: Science Museums

Social Services: Child Welfare, Community Service Organizations, Domestic Violence, Homes, People with Disabilities, Scouts, Senior Services, Shelters/Homelessness, Youth Organizations

Application Procedures

Initial Contact: Send a brief letter of inquiry.
Application Requirements: Include amount requested and purpose of funds sought.
Deadlines: None.

Restrictions

Provides grants to worthy and needy students and charities.

Foundation Officials

Keith Lawrence: chief financial officer, director
Gary E. Shoffner: secretary, director
Henry Stotsenberg: president, director

Grants Analysis

Disclosure Period: fiscal year ending May 31, 2003
Total Grants: $464,696*
Number of Grants: 51
Average Grant: $7,239*
Highest Grant: $60,000
Lowest Grant: $200
Typical Range: $1,000 to $10,000
*Note: Giving excludes scholarships. Average grant figure excludes two highest grants ($110,000).

Recent Grants

Note: Grants derived from 2004 Form 990.
General

60,000	Motion Picture and Television Fund, Woodland Hills, CA
50,000	USC School of Gerontology, Los Angeles, CA
40,000	American Film Institute, Los Angeles, CA
40,000	UCLA School of Theater, Los Angeles, CA
40,000	USC School of Television, Los Angeles, CA
35,000	Mary Pickford Education Foundation, Culver City, CA
30,000	Mary Pickford Education Foundation, Culver City, CA

25,000	Art Center College of Design, Pasadena, CA
25,000	Mary Pickford Education Foundation, Culver City, CA
25,000	Santa Monica City College, Santa Monica, CA

HAROLD WHITWORTH PIERCE CHARITABLE TRUST

Giving Contact
Elizabeth D. Nichols, Grant Administrator
c/o Nichols and Pratt
50 Congress St., Suite 832
Boston, MA 02109
Phone: (617)523-8368
Fax: (617)523-8949
E-mail: piercetrust@nichols-pratt.com

Description
Founded: 1960
EIN: 046019896
Organization Type: Private Foundation
Giving Locations: MA: Boston area
Grant Types: Capital, General Support, Project, Seed Money.

Donor Information
Founder: the late Harold Whitworth Pierce

Financial Summary
Total Giving: $1,376,400 (2002); $1,242,685 (2001)
Giving Analysis: Giving for 2002 includes: foundation grants to United Way ($5,000)
Assets: $23,122,298 (2002); $26,345,200 (2001)

Typical Recipients
Arts & Humanities: Arts Centers, Ballet, Historic Preservation, History & Archaeology, Libraries, Museums/Galleries, Music, Public Broadcasting, Theater
Civic & Public Affairs: Asian American Affairs, Botanical Gardens/Parks, Clubs, Economic Development, Employment/Job Training, Civic & Public Affairs-General, Hispanic Affairs, Municipalities/Towns, Native American Affairs, Nonprofit Management, Urban & Community Affairs, Women's Affairs, Zoos/Aquariums
Education: Arts/Humanities Education, Business-School Partnerships, Colleges & Universities, Education Associations, Education Funds, Education Reform, Engineering/Technological Education, Faculty Development, Education-General, International Studies, Leadership Training, Literacy, Medical Education, Minority Education, Preschool Education, Private Education (Precollege), Science/Mathematics Education, Student Aid, Vocational & Technical Education
Environment: Air/Water Quality, Forestry, Environment-General, Research, Wildlife Protection
Health: Emergency/Ambulance Services, Health Organizations, Hospitals, Medical Research
International: Human Rights, International Environmental Issues
Religion: Churches, Religious Organizations, Religious Welfare, Social/Policy Issues
Science: Science Museums, Scientific Centers & Institutes
Social Services: At-Risk Youth, Camps, Child Welfare, Community Centers, Community Service Organizations, Day Care, Family Planning, Family Services, Food/Clothing Distribution, People with Disabilities, Recreation & Athletics, YMCA/YWCA/YMHA/YWHA, Youth Organizations

Application Procedures
Initial Contact: Send a brief letter of inquiry.
Application Requirements: Include brochure, financial statement, proof of tax-exempt status, how goals will be met, amount requested, and how additional needed money will be raised.
Deadlines: Concept letters due March 1 and September 15. Invited proposals due mid April and mid October.

Restrictions
Trustees are required to give 25% of the trust's yearly net income to Milton Hospital and $5,000 to St. Michael's Church. Remaining funds are awarded to other charities at the discretion of the trustees. Unsolicited medical research proposals are not accepted.

Foundation Officials
James R. Nichols: trustee
Harold I. Pratt: trustee

Grants Analysis
Disclosure Period: calendar year ending 2002
Total Grants: $1,371,400*
Number of Grants: 53
Average Grant: $21,565*
Highest Grant: $250,000
Lowest Grant: $5,000
Typical Range: $10,000 to $50,000
*Note: Giving excludes United Way. Average grant figure excludes highest grant.

Recent Grants
Note: Grants derived from 2001 Form 990.
General

100,000	Massachusetts Audubon Society, Lincoln, MA
75,000	Milton Hospital, Milton, MA
75,000	Milton Medical Center, Milton, MA
75,000	Unitarian Universalist Association, Boston, MA
50,000	Boys and Girls Club for Chelsea, Chelsea, OK
43,665	Woods Hole Research Center, Woods Hole, MA
30,000	Boston Center for the Arts, Boston, MA
30,000	Boston Plan for Excellence, Boston, MA
30,000	Boston Plan for Excellence - Annenberg, Boston, MA
30,000	Medical Foundation, Boston, MA

PINE TREE FOUNDATION

Giving Contact
A. Morris Williams, Jr., Chairman, Treasurer, & Director
120 Righters Mill Rd.
Gladwyne, PA 19035
Phone: (610)649-4601

Description
Founded: 1986
EIN: 222751187
Organization Type: Private Foundation
Giving Locations: PA
Grant Types: General Support.

Donor Information
Founder: A. Morris Williams, Jr., Ruth W. Williams

Financial Summary
Total Giving: $1,445,000 (fiscal year ending July 31, 2002)
Assets: $23,012,047 (fiscal 2002); $20,928,359 (fiscal 2001)
Gifts Received: $648,350 (fiscal 2002); $4,539,755 (fiscal 1997); $750,000 (fiscal 1996). Note: In fiscal 2002, contributions were received from A. Morris & Ruth W. Williams Jr.

Typical Recipients
Arts & Humanities: Ballet, Arts & Humanities-General, Libraries, Music, Performing Arts
Civic & Public Affairs: Economic Development, Civic & Public Affairs-General, Housing, Zoos/Aquariums
Education: Colleges & Universities, Education Funds, Education-General, Literacy, Private Education (Precollege), Religious Education
Environment: Environment-General
Health: Clinics/Medical Centers, Mental Health
International: Foreign Arts Organizations, Health Care/Hospitals, International Relief Efforts
Religion: Religious Welfare
Social Services: Community Service Organizations, Food/Clothing Distribution, Recreation & Athletics, Shelters/Homelessness, Social Services-General

Application Procedures
Initial Contact: Send brief letter describing program. Include a description of organization, amount requested, purpose of funds sought, recently audited financial statement, and proof of tax-exempt status.
Deadlines: None.

Foundation Officials
Susan W. Beltz: director
Joanne W. Markman: director
A. Morris Williams, Jr.: president, director
Ruth W. Williams: secretary, treasurer, director

Grants Analysis
Disclosure Period: fiscal year ending July 31, 2002
Total Grants: $1,445,000
Number of Grants: 22
Average Grant: $65,682
Highest Grant: $300,000
Lowest Grant: $5,000
Typical Range: $20,000 to $100,000

Recent Grants
Note: Grants derived from 2002 Form 990.
Library-Related

50,000	Free Library of Philadelphia, Philadelphia, PA

General

300,000	CARE, Atlanta, GA
200,000	Duke University, Durham, NC
200,000	Habitat for Humanity, Americus, GA
200,000	Philadelphia Orchestra, Philadelphia, PA
100,000	College of Wooster, Wooster, OH
100,000	Philadelphia Scholars Fund, Philadelphia, PA
100,000	Salvation Army, Philadelphia, PA
50,000	Project Forward Leap, Lancaster, PA
25,000	Pennsylvania Ballet, Philadelphia, PA
20,000	Stop ALD Foundation, Houston, TX

PINEYWOODS FOUNDATION

Giving Contact
Bob Bowman, Secretary
515 S. 1st St.
Lufkin, TX 75901
Phone: (936)634-7444

Alternate Contact
PO Box 3659
Lufkin, TX 75903
Phone: (936)634-4415

Description
Founded: 1984
EIN: 751922533

Organization Type: Private Foundation
Giving Locations: TX
Grant Types: Capital, General Support, Project, Seed Money.

Donor Information

Founder: the Southland Foundation

Financial Summary

Total Giving: $158,780 (2003); $162,113 (2001)
Assets: $2,604,818 (2003); $2,923,838 (2001)
Gifts Received: $10,000 (2000); $10,000 (1997); $89,944 (1992). Note: In 1997, contributions were received from Brookshire Brothers. In 2000, contributions were received from from Angelina & Neches River Railroad.

Typical Recipients

Arts & Humanities: Arts Associations & Councils, Community Arts, Arts & Humanities-General, History & Archaeology, Libraries, Museums/Galleries, Theater, Visual Arts
Civic & Public Affairs: African American Affairs, Botanical Gardens/Parks, Chambers of Commerce, Community Foundations, Economic Development, Employment/Job Training, Civic & Public Affairs-General, Housing, Law & Justice, Municipalities/Towns, Professional & Trade Associations, Safety, Urban & Community Affairs, Women's Affairs, Zoos/Aquariums
Education: Colleges & Universities, Education Associations, Education-General, Minority Education, Public Education (Precollege), Student Aid
Environment: Air/Water Quality, Forestry, Environment-General, Resource Conservation
Health: Cancer, Clinics/Medical Centers, Emergency/Ambulance Services, Health Organizations, Home-Care Services, Hospices, Hospitals, Long-Term Care, Public Health
Religion: Religious Welfare
Social Services: Animal Protection, Big Brothers/Big Sisters, Community Centers, Community Service Organizations, Domestic Violence, Family Services, People with Disabilities, Recreation & Athletics, Senior Services, Substance Abuse, United Funds/United Ways, Youth Organizations

Application Procedures

Initial Contact: Send correct name, address, and phone number of applicant. Also provide a brief resume of the operations of the applicant, an explanation of the request evidencing the need, service to be rendered, and how, when, and where members of the public will be benefited.
Deadlines: None.

Restrictions

Preference is for funding purchases or supplies, aiding construction projects, and administrative expenses. Grants are not made to governmental units, state colleges, universities, churches, religious organizations, and general fund drives.

Foundation Officials

John Firth Anderson: chairman B Saginaw, MI 1928. ED Michigan State University BA (1949); University of Illinois MS (1950). PRIM CORP EMPL Presbytery de Cristo. NONPR AFFIL member: Southwest Library Association; member: World Alliance Reformed Churches; member: Arizona Library Association; member: California Library Association; member: Arizona AssociationCounty Librarians; member: Arizona China Council; member: American Library Association. CLUB AFFIL member: Beta Phi Mu.
Bob Bowman: secretary
George Henderson, III: treasurer B Hurtsboro, AL 1932. ED Wayne State University BA (1957); Wayne State University MA (1959); Wayne State University PhD (1965). NONPR AFFIL member: Phi Kappa Phi; professor sociology: University Oklahoma; member: National Association Human Rights Workers; member: Omicron Delta Kappa; member: International Society Law Enforcement Criminal Justice Instituteructors; member: Kappa Alpha Psi; member: Inter-University Seminar Armed Forces Society; member: Delta Tau Kappa; member: Golden Key; member: Association Black Sociologists; member: Association Supervision Curriculum Development; member: American Association University Professors; member: American Sociological Association; member: American Association Higher Education.

Grants Analysis

Disclosure Period: calendar year ending 2003
Total Grants: $158,780
Number of Grants: 20
Average Grant: $4,877*
Highest Grant: $40,000
Lowest Grant: $647
Typical Range: $2,500 to $10,000
*Note: Average grant figure excludes two highest grants ($71,000).

Recent Grants

Note: Grants derived from 2004 Form 990.
Library-Related

6,500	Kurth Memorial Library, Lufkin, TX

General

66,440	George Henderson Jr. Exposition Center, Lufkin, TX
37,500	Chamber of Commerce, Lufkin, TX
15,000	Natural Resource Foundation of Texas, Midland, TX
8,142	Pinecrest Retirement Center, Lufkin, TX
7,500	Texas Forest Service, College Station, TX
5,611	Angelina County Senior Citizens Center, Lufkin, TX
5,000	Angelina Art Alliance, Lufkin, TX
5,000	East Texas Regional Aircraft Association, Diboll, TX
5,000	Sinclair Children's Center, Woodville, TX

PINKERTON FOUNDATION

Giving Contact

Joan Colello, Executive Director & Secretary
Pinkerton Foundation
630 Fifth Ave., Ste. 1755
New York, NY 10111
Phone: (212)332-3385
Fax: (212)332-3399
E-mail: pinkfdn@pinkertonfdn.org
Web: http://www.fdncenter.org/grantmaker/pinkerton

Description

Founded: 1966
EIN: 136206624
Organization Type: General Purpose Foundation
Giving Locations: NY: New York
Grant Types: Employee Matching Gifts, General Support, Project, Seed Money.

Donor Information

Founder: The Pinkerton Foundation was established in 1966 by the late Robert Allan Pinkerton (1904-1967). Mr. Pinkerton served as the chairman and chief executive officer of Pinkerton's Inc. for more than 35 years. He was the great-grandson of Allan Pinkerton, a Scottish immigrant, who had founded in 1850 what would become the oldest and largest security company in the world. The company was sold in 1983, and today there is no connection between the foundation and Pinkerton's Inc.

Financial Summary

Total Giving: $6,481,314 (2003); $6,853,298 (2002); $6,630,610 (2001). Note: 1998 Giving includes Trustee-Designated grants ($175,000).
Giving Analysis: Giving for 2003 includes: foundation matching gifts ($2,496); 2002: foundation matching gifts ($2,416)
Assets: $143,322,866 (2003); $129,794,573 (2002); $141,531,849 (2001)
Gifts Received: $22,356 (2002); $26,000 (2000); $17,100 (1998). Note: Berkshire Hathaway contributed in 2002.

Typical Recipients

Arts & Humanities: Arts Centers, Ballet, Dance, Ethnic & Folk Arts, Arts & Humanities-General, History & Archaeology, Libraries, Literary Arts, Museums/Galleries, Music, Public Broadcasting, Theater
Civic & Public Affairs: Botanical Gardens/Parks, Clubs, Community Foundations, Economic Development, Employment/Job Training, Civic & Public Affairs-General, Hispanic Affairs, Housing, Law & Justice, Legal Aid, Municipalities/Towns, Nonprofit Management, Professional & Trade Associations, Public Policy, Urban & Community Affairs, Women's Affairs, Zoos/Aquariums
Education: Afterschool/Enrichment Programs, Arts/Humanities Education, Business Education, Colleges & Universities, Education Associations, Education Funds, Education Reform, Elementary Education (Private), Elementary Education (Public), Education-General, Leadership Training, Literacy, Minority Education, Preschool Education, Private Education (Precollege), Public Education (Precollege), School Volunteerism, Science/Mathematics Education, Special Education, Student Aid
Environment: Environment-General
Health: AIDS/HIV, Clinics/Medical Centers, Hospitals, Hospitals (University Affiliated), Nursing Services, Outpatient Health Care, Public Health, Research/Studies Institutes
Religion: Religious Organizations, Religious Welfare
Science: Science Exhibits & Fairs, Science Museums, Scientific Centers & Institutes
Social Services: At-Risk Youth, Big Brothers/Big Sisters, Child Welfare, Community Centers, Community Service Organizations, Counseling, Crime Prevention, Day Care, Delinquency & Criminal Rehabilitation, Domestic Violence, Family Planning, Family Services, Food/Clothing Distribution, People with Disabilities, Recreation & Athletics, Sexual Abuse, Social Services-General, Substance Abuse, Volunteer Services, YMCA/YWCA/YMHA/YWHA, Youth Organizations

Application Procedures

Initial Contact: Applicants should write a brief letter of inquiry, not to exceed two pages, prior to a formal proposal or application for a grant.
Application Requirements: The letter should describe the grantee organization, the proposed project and its goals, an estimated budget, IRS 501(c)(3) status, list of other agencies solicited, and the name and qualifications of the person directing the project. For other than direct service projects, the program description should also include the possibilities for practical application of the project's efforts and findings.
Deadlines: None. Letters of inquiry are welcome throughout the year.
Review Process: The board meets in May and December.

Restrictions

Grants are awarded only to nonprofit, public organizations that are tax-exempt under IRS 501(c)(3). The foundation does not make grants to individuals, provide emergency assistance, nor does it support medical research or the direct provision of health care or religious education. It generally does not make grants to support conferences, publications, or media. Proposals for building renovations or other capital projects are not considered unless they are integrally related to the foundation's program objectives or are an outgrowth of one of its grantee's programs.

Additional Information

Publications: Guidelines for Grant Seekers; Biennial Report

Foundation Officials

Joan Colello: secretary, executive director, trustee

Eugene C. Fey: treasurer, trustee

George Joseph Gillespie, III: president, trustee B New York, NY 1930. ED Georgetown University AB (1952); Harvard University LLB (1955). PRIM CORP EMPL partner: Cravath, Swaine & Moore. CORP AFFIL director: Washington Post Co. NONPR AFFIL director, chairman emeritus: National Multiple Sclerosis Society; trustee: New York University Medical Center; director: Madison Square Boys Club; secretary, director: Museum Television & Radio; member: Century Association; trustee, treasurer: Cooper-Hewitt National Design Museum. CLUB AFFIL Prouts Neck Country Club; Winged Foot Golf Club; member: Portland Country Club; Double Eagle Club; Falmouth Country Club; American Yacht Club.

Michael Stewart Joyce: trustee B Cleveland, OH 1942. ED Cleveland State University BA (1967); Walden University PhD (1974). CORP AFFIL director: Blue Cross Blue Shield United Wisconsin. NONPR AFFIL director: United Wisconsin Services Inc.; member: White House Fellowships Eastern Regional Selection Panel; director: United Way Wisconsin; member: Sovereign Military Order Malta; member advisory board: U.S. Information Agency International Cultural & Education Exchange; chairman: Philanthropy Roundtable; member executive committee: President Private Sector Study Cost Control Grace Commission; member: Mont Pelerin Society; member: National Committee Civic Renewal; trustee: Foundation Cultural Review; secretary: Institute Education Affairs; member: Cardinal's Committee Laity Archdiocese New York; member selection committee: Clare Booth Luce Fund. CLUB AFFIL University Milwaukee Club; Milwaukee Club; Union League New York City Club.

Daniel L. Mosley: trustee

Richard M. Smith: trustee B Detroit, MI 1946. ED Albion College BA (1968); Columbia University MS (1970); Albion College LLD (1993). PRIM CORP EMPL president, editor-in-chief, director: Newsweek Inc. NONPR AFFIL director: Magazine Publishers Association; member: Phi Beta Kappa; trustee: Cooper-Hewitt National Design Museum; council: Foreign Relations; member: American Society Magazine Editors; council: Century Association; trustee: Albion College.

Thomas Joseph Sweeney, Jr.: trustee B New York, NY 1923. ED New York University BA (1947); Columbia University JD (1949). PRIM CORP EMPL partner: Decker, Hubbard, Welden & Sweeney. CORP AFFIL chairman inst trustee & investment committee: Morgan Guaranty Trust Co. New York. NONPR AFFIL director: WR Kenan Fund; member: New York State Bar Association.

Grants Analysis

Disclosure Period: calendar year ending 2003
Total Grants: $6,478,818*
Number of Grants: 123
Average Grant: $52,673
Highest Grant: $350,000
Lowest Grant: $90
Typical Range: $25,000 to $100,000
*Note: Giving excludes matching gifts.

Recent Grants

Note: Grants derived from 2003 Form 990.
Library-Related
50,000	New York Public Library, New York, NY

General
350,000	Young Adult Capacity Initiative, New York, NY
266,419	Public /Private Ventures, New York, NY
250,000	Madison Square Boys and Girls Club, New York, NY
200,000	Saint Nicholas Neighborhood Preservation Corporation, Brooklyn, NY
150,000	Friends of the Children, Brooklyn, NY
150,000	Goddard Riverside Community Center, New York, NY
115,000	Friends of Island Academy Inc., New York, NY
100,000	Good Shepherd Services, New York, NY
100,000	Kings County District Attorney's Office, Hanford, CA
100,000	New Settlement Apartments Community Services, Bronx, NY

PIONEER TRUST BANK, N.A.

Company Headquarters

1190 Oak St., SE
Salem, OR 97301

Company Description

Employees: 50
SIC(s): 6000 Depository Institutions.

Operating Locations

Pioneer Trust Bank, NA (OR--Salem)

Pioneer Trust Bank, NA, Foundation

Giving Contact

Pioneer Trust Bank, NA Foundation
PO Box 2305
Salem, OR 97308
Phone: (503)363-3136

Description

EIN: 930881673
Organization Type: Corporate Foundation
Giving Locations: OR: Salem
Grant Types: Challenge, Emergency, General Support, Operating Expenses, Project, Research, Seed Money.

Financial Summary

Total Giving: $53,500 (2001)
Giving Analysis: Giving for 2001 includes: foundation grants to United Way ($3,500)
Assets: $942,762 (2001)
Gifts Received: $91,650 (1992). Note: In 1992, contributions were received from Pioneer Trust Bank Corp.

Typical Recipients

Arts & Humanities: Arts Associations & Councils, Arts Festivals, Arts Outreach, Arts & Humanities-General, Historic Preservation, History & Archaeology, Libraries, Museums/Galleries, Music, Performing Arts, Public Broadcasting, Theater, Visual Arts

Civic & Public Affairs: Clubs, Community Foundations, Civic & Public Affairs-General, Housing, Municipalities/Towns, Urban & Community Affairs, Women's Affairs

Education: Elementary Education (Public), Education-General, Literacy, Private Education (Precollege), Secondary Education (Public), Student Aid

Environment: Environment-General, Resource Conservation

Health: Emergency/Ambulance Services, Eyes/Blindness, Health-General, Health Organizations, Hospices, Hospitals, Medical Research

Religion: Missionary Activities (Domestic), Religious Welfare

Social Services: Animal Protection, Child Welfare, Community Service Organizations, Domestic Violence, Family Services, Food/Clothing Distribution, People with Disabilities, Scouts, Social Services-General, Special Olympics, United Funds/United Ways, YMCA/YWCA/YMHA/YWHA, Youth Organizations

Application Procedures

Initial Contact: Send a brief letter of inquiry.
Application Requirements: Include a description of organization, amount requested, purpose of funds sought, recently audited financial statement, and proof of tax-exempt status.
Deadlines: October 31.

Restrictions

Does not support individuals, political or lobbying groups, or organizations outside operating areas. Generally does not support organizations located outside of Salem, OR and the surrounding area.

Additional Information

Trust(s): Pioneer Trust Bank NA

Corporate Officials

Michael S. Compton: president PRIM CORP EMPL president: Pioneer Trust Bank NA.

Grants Analysis

Disclosure Period: calendar year ending 2001
Total Grants: $50,000*
Number of Grants: 38
Average Grant: $1,316
Highest Grant: $12,500
Typical Range: $500 to $2,000
*Note: Giving excludes United Way.

Recent Grants

Note: Grants derived from 2001 Form 990.
Library-Related
1,150	Salem Public Library Foundation, Salem, OR

General
12,500	Salem Area Habitat for Humanity, Salem, OR
5,000	Salem Riverfront Carousel, Salem, OR
3,500	United Way, Salem, OR
2,000	American Red Cross, Salem, OR
1,100	Assistance League of Salem, Salem, OR
1,100	Young Women's Christian Association, Salem, OR
1,000	Boys and Girls Club of Salem, Salem, OR
1,000	Cascade Area Council for Boy Scouts, Salem, OR
1,000	Family Building Blocks, Salem, OR
1,000	Friends of Deepwood, Salem, OR

MINNIE STEVENS PIPER FOUNDATION

Giving Contact

Carlos Otero, Executive Director & Secretary
GPM South Tower, Suite 200
800 NW Loop 410
San Antonio, TX 78216-5699
Phone: (210)525-8494
Fax: (210)341-6627
E-mail: cotero@mspf.org
Web: http://www.mspf.org

Description

Founded: 1950
EIN: 741292695
Organization Type: General Purpose Foundation
Giving Locations: TX
Grant Types: Loan, Scholarship.

Donor Information

Founder: Incorporated in 1950 by the late Randall G. Piper and the late Minnie Stevens Piper.

Financial Summary

Total Giving: $1,500,000 (2002 approx); $567,640 (2001)
Assets: $25,497,565 (2001)
Gifts Received: $343 (2001); $55,886 (2000); $37,993 (1999). Note: In 2000, contributions were received from William C. & Alta Foster. In 1999, substantial contributions were received from William C. & Alta Foster ($25,632 non-cash) and Denton Engineering Co. ($11,000).

Typical Recipients

Arts & Humanities: Arts Centers, Arts Festivals, Arts Funds, Arts Institutes, Ballet, Community Arts, Ethnic & Folk Arts, Historic Preservation, History & Archaeology, Libraries, Museums/Galleries, Music, Opera, Performing Arts, Public Broadcasting, Theater
Civic & Public Affairs: Hispanic Affairs, Law & Justice, Nonprofit Management, Philanthropic Organizations, Professional & Trade Associations
Education: Arts/Humanities Education, Colleges & Universities, Community & Junior Colleges, Education Funds, Education Reform, Engineering/Technological Education, Faculty Development, Education-General, International Studies, Legal Education, Literacy, Medical Education, Minority Education, Private Education (Precollege), Public Education (Precollege), Religious Education, Science/Mathematics Education, Secondary Education (Private), Secondary Education (Public), Social Sciences Education, Student Aid
Health: Cancer, Eyes/Blindness, Health Organizations, Hospitals, Medical Research, Mental Health, Public Health
International: Health Care/Hospitals
Religion: Churches
Science: Science Exhibits & Fairs, Scientific Centers & Institutes
Social Services: Child Welfare, Community Centers, Community Service Organizations, Crime Prevention, Domestic Violence, Food/Clothing Distribution, People with Disabilities, Substance Abuse, United Funds/United Ways, YMCA/YWCA/YMHA/YWHA, Youth Organizations

Application Procedures

Initial Contact: The foundation has no formal grant application procedure or application form. for grants. Student loan inquiries should contact the foundation for a loan application.
Application Requirements: Written grant proposals should be accompanied by proof of tax-exempt status.
Deadlines: Grant applications should be submitted by February 1 and July 1. Deadlines for scholarships, student loan requests, fellowships and professor awards vary by program.
Review Process: The board meets twice annually.

Restrictions

The Bexar County Scholarship Clearing House program is restricted to students in Bexar County, Texas. The Pipers Scholars Program is restricted to certain counties in Texas. Scholarships awarded by invitation only by nomination process from high school counselor. No grants are made to institutions outside the State of Texas, or to organizations which discriminate on the grounds of race, color, creed, or sex. Grant requests will be considered only from organizations which have qualified for non-profit status by the Internal Revenue Service under the IRS code and applicable regulations. The foundation will not consider grant requests for building fund campaigns or endowments, unless under exceptional circumstances.

Additional Information

The foundation provides grants from income only. Though continuing programs of the foundation require the greater portion of annual distributable income, the remainder is granted in minimal amounts by the board of directors for a variety of purposes, with a focus on projects in the field of higher education, especially those that are student oriented.
Publications: Purpose; Policy; Programs Brochure; Application Guidelines

Foundation Officials

Paul T. Curl: director
Lewis M. Fox: director
Martin R. Harris: treasurer
Carlos Otero: executive director, assistant secretary-treasurer
J. Burleson Smith: director
John H. Wilson, II: president B 1927. ED Colorado School of Mines (1944-1949). PRIM CORP EMPL president, director: Piper Petroleum Co. CORP AFFIL principal: Wilson Exploration Co.

Grants Analysis

Disclosure Period: calendar year ending 2001
Total Grants: $167,500*
Number of Grants: 34
Average Grant: $3,047*
Highest Grant: $35,000
Lowest Grant: $50
Typical Range: $1,000 to $5,000
*Note: Giving excludes scholarships and United Way. Average grant figure excludes two highest grants ($70,000).

Recent Grants

Note: Grants derived from 2001 Form 990.
Library-Related

5,000	San Antonio Public Library Foundation, San Antonio, TX

General

322,640	Piper Professors Program, San Antonio, TX
75,000	Piper Professors Program, San Antonio, TX -- for Superior Teaching Awards
35,000	Cancer Therapy and Research Center, San Antonio, TX
35,000	Southwest Foundation for Biomedical Research, San Antonio, TX
5,000	Baptist Memorial Hospital, San Antonio, TX
5,000	Cancer Therapy and Research Center, San Antonio, TX
5,000	College of St. Thomas More in Texas, Ft. Worth, TX
5,000	James Dick Foundation for Performing Arts Festival, Institute at Round Top, Round Top, TX
5,000	Our Lady of the Lake University, San Antonio, TX
5,000	St. Edward's University, Austin, TX

PITTSBURG & MIDWAY COAL MINING CO.

Company Headquarters

Englewood, CO
Web: http://www.chevron.com

Company Description

Employees: 1,325
SIC(s): 1200 Coal Mining, 1221 Bituminous Coal & Lignite--Surface, 1222 Bituminous Coal--Underground.

Operating Locations

Pittsburg & Midway Coal Mining Co. (AL--Tuscaloosa; NM--Gallup, Raton; WY--Kemmerer)

Giving Contact

Robert Johnson, Manager, Public Affairs
PO Box 6518
Englewood, CO 80155-6518
Phone: (303)930-3600
Fax: (303)930-4189

Description

Organization Type: Corporate Giving Program
Giving Locations: principally near operating locations and to national organizations.
Grant Types: Award, Emergency, General Support, Multiyear/Continuing Support, Scholarship.

Typical Recipients

Arts & Humanities: Arts Appreciation, Arts Associations & Councils, Arts Centers, Arts Festivals, Community Arts, Arts & Humanities-General, Libraries, Museums/Galleries, Music, Public Broadcasting
Civic & Public Affairs: Botanical Gardens/Parks, Chambers of Commerce, Clubs, Civic & Public Affairs-General, Native American Affairs, Parades/Festivals, Professional & Trade Associations, Public Policy, Urban & Community Affairs
Education: Agricultural Education, Colleges & Universities, Community & Junior Colleges, Education Funds, Education Reform, Elementary Education (Public), Engineering/Technological Education, Education-General, Public Education (Precollege), Science/Mathematics Education
Environment: Air/Water Quality, Energy, Environment-General, Resource Conservation, Wildlife Protection
Health: Children's Health/Hospitals, Clinics/Medical Centers, Emergency/Ambulance Services, Eyes/Blindness, Health-General, Hospitals, Medical Rehabilitation, Prenatal Health Issues, Research/Studies Institutes
Science: Science-General, Science Exhibits & Fairs, Scientific Organizations
Social Services: Child Welfare, Community Centers, Community Service Organizations, Crime Prevention, Day Care, Delinquency & Criminal Rehabilitation, Domestic Violence, Emergency Relief, Family Services, Recreation & Athletics, Senior Services, Social Services-General, United Funds/United Ways, Volunteer Services, Youth Organizations

Application Procedures

Initial Contact: Generally, charitable contributions are made upon request/recommendation of mine managers. The company is not soliciting additional requests for contributions.

Restrictions

Does not support group or individual travel expenses.

Additional Information

Contributions typically are aligned with company business interests. As a Chevron subsidiary, all contributions are part of Chervon's total (see separate entry).

Corporate Officials

Barry G. McGrath: chairman, president PRIM CORP EMPL chairman, president: Pittsburg & Midway Coal Mining Co.

Grants Analysis

Typical Range: $10 to $1,000*
*Note: Typical grant size is less than $1,000.

Recent Grants

Note: Grants derived from 1998 Form 990.
General
4-H Clubs, Remmener, NY
Child Development Center, Remmener, NY

Ducks Unlimited, Ft. Collins, CO
Four Corners Science Fair, Gallup, MN
Gallup Lions Club Rodeo, Gallup, NM
Navajo Way, Window Rock, AZ
Rocky Mount Elic Foundation, Remmener, NY
Rocky Mountain Coal Mining Institute, Lakewood, CO
United Way, Gallup, NM

PITTSBURGH CHILD GUIDANCE FOUNDATION

Giving Contact
Dr. Claire A. Walker, Executive Director
425 Sixth Ave., Suite 2460
Pittsburgh, PA 15219
Phone: (412)434-1665
Fax: (412)434-0406
E-mail: pcgf@smartbuilding.org
Web: http://trfn.clpgh.org/pcgf/index.shtml

Description
Founded: 1982
EIN: 250965465
Organization Type: Private Foundation
Giving Locations: PA: Allegheny County
Grant Types: Project, Research.

Financial Summary
Total Giving: $218,864 (2001)
Assets: $5,851,065 (2001)
Gifts Received: $100 (1999); $100 (1997)

Typical Recipients
Arts & Humanities: Arts Centers, Arts Outreach
Civic & Public Affairs: Community Foundations, Nonprofit Management, Philanthropic Organizations, Urban & Community Affairs
Education: Afterschool/Enrichment Programs, Arts/Humanities Education, Education-General, Literacy, Preschool Education, Special Education
Health: Children's Health/Hospitals, Mental Health, Prenatal Health Issues
Religion: Churches, Ministries, Religious Organizations, Social/Policy Issues
Social Services: At-Risk Youth, Big Brothers/Big Sisters, Camps, Child Abuse, Child Welfare, Community Centers, Community Service Organizations, Crime Prevention, Day Care, Family Services, Food/Clothing Distribution, Recreation & Athletics, Scouts, Sexual Abuse, Shelters/Homelessness, Social Services-General, Substance Abuse, YMCA/YWCA/YMHA/YWHA, Youth Organizations

Application Procedures
Initial Contact: Submit a one- to two-page letter of intent.
Application Requirements: Include the project's purpose, beneficiaries, activities, total costs, amount requested, and amounts and sources of other revenue (actual and potential).
Deadlines: Discretionary grants are typically due the first Wednesday in March and September.
Review Process: Foundation staff and trustees will review letters of intent; if a proposal is of interest to the foundation, the applicant will be invited to submit a formal application using the foundation's application form.

Restrictions
The foundation does not fund operating or capital expenses.

Additional Information
In 2003, the Foundation announced its 2003-2008 Area of Emphasis: Helping the community address the losses experienced by children whose parents are incarcerated. All Area of Emphasis Program

Grants will focus on this issue. In addition to the Area of Emphasis Program, the foundation also makes Discretionary Grants, which are made to various organizations for projects that support children's development. As of press time, unsolicited requests were not being accepted for Area of Emphasis grants, and grantmaking was temporarily suspended within the Discretionary Grants program. Contact the foundation or check the foundation's web site for updates on these programs.
Publications: Informational Brochure (including Application Guidelines); Grants List

Foundation Officials
Carmen Anderson: trustee PRIM CORP EMPL executive director: Healthy Start Inc.
Duane T. Ashley: trustee
Randolph W. Brockington: trustee
Jane C. Burger: trustee
Eileen H. Christman: president
Nancy E. Curry: trustee B Brockway, PA 1931. ED Grove City College BA (1952); University of Pittsburgh MEd (1956); University of Pittsburgh PhD (1972). NONPR AFFIL member: National Association Education Young Children; professor emeritus: University Pittsburgh School Social Work; member: American Psychological Association; member: American Associate University Professors; member: American Psychoanalytic Association.
Judith M. Davenport: trustee
Carolyn D. Duronio: secretary
Jesse Fife, Jr.: trustee
David B. Hartmann: trustee
John D. Houston, II: trustee
Claudia L. Hussein: trustee
Kelly J. Keckher: trustee
John G. Lovelace: trustee
W. Thomas McGough, Jr.: secretary
Thelma Lovette Morris: trustee
Evelyn L. Murrin: trustee
Ronald Edward Peters: trustee
Lloyd F. Stamy, Jr.: treasurer
Mary Margaret Stamy: trustee
Claire Walker: executive director
Nancy D. Washington: president
Jeffrey A. Wlahofsky: trustee

Grants Analysis
Disclosure Period: calendar year ending 2001
Total Grants: $218,864
Number of Grants: 11
Average Grant: $19,897
Highest Grant: $40,633
Lowest Grant: $11,500
Typical Range: $10,000 to $25,000

Recent Grants
Note: Grants derived from 2001 Form 990.
General

40,633	Schenley Heights Community Development Program, Pittsburgh, PA -- After-School Program
25,000	Young Men and Women's African Heritage Association, Pittsburgh, PA -- support for adopted and foster children
23,205	YMCA of Pittsburgh Centre Avenue Program Center, Pittsburgh, PA -- After-School Program and summer day camp
22,500	Hosanna House, Wilkinsburg, PA -- children with academic and behavior difficulties
21,000	East Side Community Collaborative, Pittsburgh, PA -- help for young children of substance abusers
19,825	Hazelwood Youth Football and Cheerleading Association, Pittsburgh, PA -- support for athletic teams and mentoring
17,501	North Hills Youth Ministry, Pittsburgh, PA -- academic assistance for children
12,926	Zion Christian Church, Pittsburgh, PA -- After-School and Summer Programs
12,500	East End Cooperative Ministry, Pittsburgh, PA -- children with academic and behavioral difficulty
12,274	Greater Pittsburgh Community Food Bank, Duquesne, PA -- foodbank services, After-School Programs

HARRY PLANKENHORN FOUNDATION

Giving Contact
Fred A. Foulkrod, Treasurer
Harry Plankenhorn Foundation
Care of Covenant United Church of Christ
202 E. Third Street
Williamsport, PA 17701
Phone: (570)326-3308

Description
Founded: 1959
EIN: 246023579
Organization Type: Private Foundation
Giving Locations: PA: Lycoming County
Grant Types: General Support.

Donor Information
Founder: the late Harry Plankenhorn

Financial Summary
Total Giving: $346,806 (2003); $411,426 (2001)
Assets: $7,511,589 (2003); $8,464,548 (2001)
Gifts Received: $100 (2001); $50,100 (2000); $199 (1999). Note: In 1996, contributions were received from Ruth Askey.

Typical Recipients
Arts & Humanities: Libraries
Civic & Public Affairs: Civic & Public Affairs-General, Housing, Law & Justice, Safety, Urban & Community Affairs
Education: Agricultural Education, Preschool Education, Special Education, Student Aid
Health: Cancer, Clinics/Medical Centers, Emergency/Ambulance Services, Health Organizations, Heart, Hospitals, Long-Term Care, Mental Health, Multiple Sclerosis, Preventive Medicine/Wellness Organizations, Respiratory, Single-Disease Health Associations
Religion: Churches, Ministries, Religious Welfare
Social Services: Animal Protection, Camps, Child Welfare, Community Centers, Community Service Organizations, Counseling, Emergency Relief, Family Services, People with Disabilities, Recreation & Athletics, Scouts, Shelters/Homelessness, United Funds/United Ways, YMCA/YWCA/YMHA/YWHA, Youth Organizations

Application Procedures
Initial Contact: Requests may be made orally; however, any request for $5,000 or more must be made in writing and presented to the board of directors at a designated meeting.
Deadlines: None.

Foundation Officials
Barbara Ertel: trustee
Fred A. Foulkrod: treasurer
Charles F. Greevy, III: president
Carl O. Hieber: trustee
W. Herbert Poff, III: trustee
Robert M. Reeder: assistant secretary
Carolyn Seifert: trustee
Abram M. Snyder: vice president
Nancy Stearns: secretary
Eleanor W. Whiting: assistant treasurer

Grants Analysis

Disclosure Period: calendar year ending 2003
Total Grants: $346,806
Number of Grants: 24
Average Grant: $12,687*
Highest Grant: $55,000
Lowest Grant: $1,000
Typical Range: $1,000 to $25,000
*Note: Average grant figure excludes highest grant.

Recent Grants

Note: Grants derived from 2003 Form 990.
General

55,000	American Rescue Workers, Williamsport, PA -- aid for disasters, hardship, relief
45,000	Hope Enterprises, Williamsport, PA -- towards annual contribution
45,000	Shepherd of the Streets, Williamsport, PA
38,500	North Central Sight Services, Williamsport, PA -- annual contributions for operations
22,500	Salvation Army, Williamsport, PA -- contribution for camp fund and operations
15,000	Habitat for Humanity, Williamsport, PA -- towards contribution for home construction
15,000	Sister Vincent Medical Clinic, Williamsport, PA -- towards medical assistance for the needy
10,000	American Red Cross, Williamsport, PA -- aid to Lyco city family disaster fund
10,000	Lycoming County Health Improvement, Williamsport, PA -- funding - first time mothers program
10,000	St. Anthony's Center, Williamsport, PA -- contribution for medical clinic

PLOUGH FOUNDATION

Giving Contact

Rick C. Masson, Jr., Executive Director & Trustee
6410 Poplar Ave., Ste. 710
Memphis, TN 38119
Phone: (901)761-9180
Fax: (901)761-6186
E-mail: mail@plough.org

Description

Founded: 1960
EIN: 237175983
Organization Type: General Purpose Foundation
Giving Locations: TN: primarily in Shelby County and Memphis
Grant Types: Capital, Challenge, Emergency, Endowment, Fellowship, General Support, Multiyear/Continuing Support, Professorship, Project, Research, Scholarship, Seed Money.

Donor Information

Founder: The Plough Foundation was established in 1960, with funds donated by the late Abe Plough. In 1920, Abe Plough bought the St. Joseph Company of Chattanooga, TN, best known as the manufacturer of children's aspirin. He eventually bought twenty-seven companies. A 1971 merger with the Schering pharmaceutical company resulted in the formation of the Schering-Plough Corporation.

Financial Summary

Total Giving: $7,759,487 (2003); $8,211,935 (2002); $10,250,000 (2001)
Assets: $167,702,816 (2003); $145,983,192 (2002); $186,537,000 (2001)
Gifts Received: $191,716 (2003); $137,997 (2002); $800,000 (2000 approx). Note: Contributions were received from Plough family members Patricia R. Burnham, Jocelyn P. Rudner, DD R. Eisenberg, and Diane R. Goldstein.

Typical Recipients

Arts & Humanities: Arts Associations & Councils, Arts Outreach, Ballet, Arts & Humanities-General, History & Archaeology, Libraries, Museums/Galleries, Music, Opera, Performing Arts, Public Broadcasting
Civic & Public Affairs: African American Affairs, Business/Free Enterprise, Chambers of Commerce, Civil Rights, Clubs, Community Foundations, Economic Development, Ethnic Organizations, Civic & Public Affairs-General, Housing, Inner-City Development, Municipalities/Towns, Nonprofit Management, Parades/Festivals, Philanthropic Organizations, Urban & Community Affairs, Women's Affairs, Zoos/Aquariums
Education: Afterschool/Enrichment Programs, Agricultural Education, Arts/Humanities Education, Business Education, Colleges & Universities, Education Reform, Elementary Education (Private), Engineering/Technological Education, Education-General, Leadership Training, Medical Education, Preschool Education, Public Education (Precollege), Social Sciences Education, Student Aid
Environment: Watershed, Wildlife Protection
Health: AIDS/HIV, Alzheimer's Disease, Cancer, Clinics/Medical Centers, Emergency/Ambulance Services, Eyes/Blindness, Health Funds, Hospitals, Mental Health, Outpatient Health Care, Single-Disease Health Associations
International: Missionary/Religious Activities
Religion: Jewish Causes, Ministries, Religious Organizations, Religious Welfare, Synagogues/Temples
Science: Scientific Organizations
Social Services: Big Brothers/Big Sisters, Child Welfare, Community Centers, Community Service Organizations, Crime Prevention, Day Care, Emergency Relief, Family Services, Food/Clothing Distribution, People with Disabilities, Recreation & Athletics, Scouts, Senior Services, Shelters/Homelessness, Social Services-General, Special Olympics, Substance Abuse, United Funds/United Ways, Veterans, Volunteer Services, YMCA/YWCA/YMHA/YWHA, Youth Organizations

Application Procedures

Initial Contact: A brief concept letter (not exceeding three pages) should be sent to the executive director. After review of the concept letter, a full application may be invited.
Application Requirements: Concept letters should include information about the purpose of the request and planned use of funds. Applications should contain a sound and efficient business plan, including such considerations as control of overhead, mergers with similar groups, and other cost-containment activities, realistic budgets, formal long and short term plans and the presence of endowment or reserve funds, evidence of strong leadership capabilities in the board and administrative staff, and evidence of the organization's tax-exempt status from the Internal Revenue Service.
Deadlines: January 10, April 10, July 10, October 10. Concept letters should be sent at least 10 days prior to the deadlines.
Review Process: Upon receipt of the application, some or all of the following steps must be completed by our office: staff review, executive committee review, application review, interview, site visit, and reference check. The process can be expected to take as much as six weeks. Approved applications will be forwarded to the board of trustees for study prior to the quarterly board meeting. The full board must approve any grants to be funded by the foundation.
Notes: Grant applications are considered on a first-come/first-served basis. It is advantageous to submit requests early to allow time for review. Every effort will be made to process all concept letters within two weeks of receipt.

Restrictions

The foundation rarely provides grants outside the Memphis and Shelby County area. The foundation will not consider requests for assistance to address a "crisis management" situation caused by poor initial planning or poor execution of the program. The foundation does not make grants to individuals or fund annual operating budgets.

Additional Information

National Bank of Commerce is listed as the corporate trustee for the foundation. Many grants carry a stipulation that other contributed amounts must be obtained by the organization as matching funds.
Publications: Brochure

Foundation Officials

Patricia R. Burnham: trustee
Eugene J. Callahan, Esq.: trustee PRIM CORP EMPL partner: Wormser Kiely Gale & Jacobs.
Robert A. Compton: trustee
Sharon R. Eisenberg: trustee
Rick C. Masson: executive director, trustee
Larry Papasan: trustee B Etta, MS 1940. ED Northwest Mississippi Junior College (1959-1960); Mississippi State University BScE (1963). CORP AFFIL president, director: Smith & Nephew Richards Inc.; director: First America National Bank Memphis. NONPR AFFIL member: Tennessee Municipal Electric Power Association; member: Tennessee Valley Public Power Association; director: Memphis Boys Club; member advisory board: Memphis State University Fogelman College Business; director: Junior Achievement Memphis; director: LeMoyne-Owen College; director: Goals Memphis; membership chairman: Boy Scouts America; director: Electric Power Research Institute; member: American Management Association; member: American Public Power Association; member: American Gas Association.
Diane Rudner: trustee
Jocelyn P. Rudner: trustee
James Francis Springfield: trustee B Memphis, TN 1929. ED Rhodes College BA (1951); Memphis State University LLB (1960). NONPR AFFIL member: Tennessee Bankers Association; member: Tennessee Bar Association; member: Sigma Nu; member board visitors: Memphis State University Cecil C Humphreys School Law; member: Omicron Delta Kappa; member advisory board: Memphis Alzheimers Association; member: Memphis and Shelby County Bar Association; member: Bank Administration Institute; member: Estate Planning Council Memphis.
Steven Wishnia: trustee

Grants Analysis

Disclosure Period: calendar year ending 2003
Total Grants: $7,759,487
Number of Grants: 54
Average Grant: $113,163*
Highest Grant: $1,000,000
Lowest Grant: $1,000
Typical Range: $50,000 to $200,000
*Note: Average grant figure excludes two highest grants ($1,875,000).

Recent Grants

Note: Grants derived from 2003 Form 990.
General

1,000,000	Temple Israel, Memphis, TN
875,000	WONDERS, Memphis, TN -- for the Memphis International cultural series
500,000	Alzheimer's Day Services of Memphis, Memphis, TN -- toward building renovation
500,000	Junior Achievement of Memphis and the Mid-South Inc., Memphis, TN -- funding for building renovation
500,000	Memphis Tomorrow, Memphis, TN -- toward program development
500,000	WONDERS, Memphis, TN -- for The Memphis International cultural series

431,608 University of Memphis, Memphis, TN -- funding for program development
350,000 Memphis Jewish Federation, Germantown, TN
250,000 Memphis Biotech Foundation, Memphis, TN -- funding for program development
250,000 Memphis Shelby Crime Commission, Memphis, TN -- toward program development

PLYM FOUNDATION

Giving Contact
Donald F. Walter, Vice President & Treasurer
423 Sycamore St., Suite 101
Niles, MI 49120
Phone: (269)684-3248

Description
Founded: 1952
EIN: 386069680
Organization Type: Private Foundation
Giving Locations: MI
Grant Types: Capital, General Support, Research.

Donor Information
Founder: Mrs. Francis J. Plym

Financial Summary
Total Giving: $743,500 (fiscal year ending September 30, 2004); $262,500 (fiscal 2001)
Giving Analysis: Giving for fiscal 2004 includes: foundation grants to United Way ($10,000); fiscal 2001: foundation grants to United Way ($2,500)
Assets: $7,042,519 (fiscal 2004); $6,606,885 (fiscal 2001)
Gifts Received: $2,130,323 (fiscal 1995); $207,774 (fiscal 1994). Note: In fiscal 1995, contributions were received from the estate of Lawrence J. Plym.

Typical Recipients
Arts & Humanities: Libraries, Music, Theater
Civic & Public Affairs: Economic Development, Employment/Job Training, Civic & Public Affairs-General, Inner-City Development, Safety, Urban & Community Affairs
Education: Business Education, Colleges & Universities, Education Funds, Education-General, Private Education (Precollege), Public Education (Precollege), Science/Mathematics Education, Student Aid
Environment: Environment-General, Resource Conservation
Health: Clinics/Medical Centers, Health-General, Hospices, Hospitals, Medical Research, Nursing Services, Prenatal Health Issues
Religion: Churches
Social Services: Community Service Organizations, Emergency Relief, Family Services, Senior Services, Shelters/Homelessness, Social Services-General, United Funds/United Ways, YMCA/YWCA/YMHA/YWHA, Youth Organizations

Application Procedures
Initial Contact: Send a written request.
Application Requirements: Include a description of organization, amount requested, purpose of funds sought, proof of tax-exempt status.
Deadlines: None.

Restrictions
The foundation does not support individuals, political or lobbying groups, or organizations outside operating areas.

Foundation Officials
Sarah P. Campbell: vice president
James F. Keenan: secretary
Andrew J. Plym: vice president

J. Eric Plym: president
Donald F. Walter: vice president, treasurer

Grants Analysis
Disclosure Period: fiscal year ending September 30, 2004
Total Grants: $173,500*
Number of Grants: 11
Average Grant: $8,167*
Highest Grant: $50,000
Lowest Grant: $500
Typical Range: $1,000 to $15,000
*Note: Giving excludes United Way. Average grant figure excludes two highest grants ($100,000).

Recent Grants
Note: Grants derived from fiscal 2004 Form 990.
General
50,000 City of Niles, Niles, MI -- for city improvement
50,000 University of Illinois, Urbana, IL
25,000 Hillsdale College, Spring Arbor, MI
10,000 Lakeland Hospital, Niles, MI
10,000 Logan Center for the Special Person
10,000 United Way of Greater Niles, Niles, MI
6,250 St. Edwards School
6,000 Fernwood, Niles, MI -- to support nature preservation
4,350 St. Joseph Valley React, South Bend, IN
700 Niles Township Fire Department, Niles, MI

PNC FINANCIAL SERVICES GROUP INC.

Company Headquarters
1 PNC Plaza
249 5th Ave.
Pittsburgh, PA 15222-2707
Web: http://www.pnc.com

Company Description
Ticker: PNC
Exchange: NYSE
Revenue: US$6.315 billion (2004)
Profit: US$1.197 billion (2004)
Employees: 23200 (2003)
Fortune Rank: 323, per FORTUNE Magazine's list of 500 Largest U.S. Corporations (2004).

PNC Bank Foundation

Giving Contact
Mia Hallett, Vice President and Manager
PNC Foundation
One PNC Plaza, 29th Floor
249 Fifth Avenue
Pittsburgh, PA 15222
Phone: (412)762-7076
Fax: (412)705-1062
E-mail: foundations@pncbank.com
Web: http://www.pnc.com/aboutus/pncfoundation.html

Alternate Contact
PNC Bank, NA P2-PTPP-10-3
Pittsburgh, PA 15222-2705
Phone: (412)762-8889

Description
Founded: 1970
EIN: 251202255
Organization Type: Corporate Foundation
Former Name: PNC Bank Foundation (2000).
Former Name: PNC Foundation (2004).
Giving Locations: areas served by PNC Bank Corp.

---

and affiliates.
Grant Types: Capital, Employee Matching Gifts, General Support, Multiyear/Continuing Support.
Note: Employee matching gift ratio: 1 to 1 up to $2,500.

Financial Summary
Total Giving: $10,577,013 (2003); $10,547,261 (2002); $11,579,055 (2001). Note: Contributes through foundation only.
Giving Analysis: Giving for 2001 includes: foundation matching gifts ($902,000); foundation program-related investments ($1,991,000); foundation ($10,515,000)
Assets: $10,617,619 (2003); $6,541,242 (2002); $745,925 (2001)
Gifts Received: $14,511,500 (2003); $8,559,680 (1995); $4,896,626 (1994). Note: In 2003, contributions were received from PNC Financial Services Group ($14,500,000), Stephen G. Thieke and Margaret V. Thieke ($1,500), and PFPC ($10,000). Foundation receives contributions from PNC Bank Corp.

Typical Recipients
Arts & Humanities: Arts Associations & Councils, Arts Centers, Arts Festivals, Arts Funds, Ballet, Community Arts, Arts & Humanities-General, Historic Preservation, History & Archaeology, Libraries, Literary Arts, Museums/Galleries, Music, Opera, Performing Arts, Public Broadcasting, Theater
Civic & Public Affairs: African American Affairs, Botanical Gardens/Parks, Business/Free Enterprise, Chambers of Commerce, Clubs, Community Foundations, Economic Development, Economic Policy, Employment/Job Training, Ethnic Organizations, Civic & Public Affairs-General, Housing, Legal Aid, Minority Business, Municipalities/Towns, Parades/Festivals, Philanthropic Organizations, Professional & Trade Associations, Public Policy, Safety, Urban & Community Affairs, Zoos/Aquariums
Education: Afterschool/Enrichment Programs, Arts/Humanities Education, Business Education, Colleges & Universities, Community & Junior Colleges, Education Associations, Education Funds, Faculty Development, Education-General, International Studies, Leadership Training, Literacy, Preschool Education, Private Education (Precollege), Student Aid
Environment: Environment-General, Resource Conservation
Health: Cancer, Children's Health/Hospitals, Clinics/Medical Centers, Health Funds, Health Organizations, Heart, Home-Care Services, Hospices, Hospitals, Long-Term Care, Medical Rehabilitation, Single-Disease Health Associations
International: International Development
Religion: Churches, Jewish Causes, Ministries, Religious Welfare
Science: Science Museums, Scientific Centers & Institutes
Social Services: Child Welfare, Community Centers, Community Service Organizations, Delinquency & Criminal Rehabilitation, Domestic Violence, Emergency Relief, Family Services, Food/Clothing Distribution, People with Disabilities, Recreation & Athletics, Scouts, Senior Services, Shelters/Homelessness, United Funds/United Ways, YMCA/YWCA/YMHA/YWHA, Youth Organizations

Application Procedures
Initial Contact: Send a brief letter or proposal.
Application Requirements: Include organization name, address, e-mail address, and contact; one-page proposal summary with amount requested requested and total cost of project or program; full proposal with, brief description of the organization and its purpose; statement of problem or need to be addressed; geographic area served and population served; recruitment outreach/management structure; statement of expected accomplishments and method of evaluation; project schedule and board-approved budget; track record of working with community organizations and civic leadership; list of staff members

and board members; proof of tax-exempt status; list of recent contributions and amounts; fundraising plan for the project; board-approved organization budget; audited financial statements for the previous year; resumes of key staff members; strategic or long-range plan for the organization; and brochures, pamphlets, or other descriptive material, if available.
Deadlines: None.

Restrictions

Does not support organizations that discriminate by race, color, creed, gender, or national origin; religious organizations, except for non-sectarian activities; loans or grants to individuals; conferences and seminars; or tickets and goodwill ads.

Additional Information

The company changed its name from Pittsburgh National Bank to PNC Bank Corp. and the foundation from Pittsburgh National Bank Foundation to PNC Bank Foundation.

Corporate Officials

James Edward Rohr: chairman, chief executive officer, president, director B Cleveland, OH 1948. ED University of Notre Dame BA (1970); Ohio State University MBA (1972). PRIM CORP EMPL chief executive officer, president, director, chief operating officer: PNC Financial Services Group ADD CORP EMPL director: Blackrock Inc.; director: Midland Loan Service Inc.; president: PNC Bank National Association. CORP AFFIL director: Equitable Resources Inc.; director: Allegheny Technologies Inc.; director: Black-Rock Inc. NONPR AFFIL member advisory board: Salvation Army; director: Shadyside Hospital; vice chairman: Pennsylvania Business Roundtable; director: Greater Pittsburgh Council Boy Scouts America; chairman: National Flag Foundation; member: Bankers Roundtable; member: Allegheny Conference; member: American Bankers Association. CLUB AFFIL director: Duquesne Club.

Foundation Officials

Eva T. Blum: chairman
Joan L. Gulley: director
Joseph C. Guyaux: director
Neil F. Hall: director

Grants Analysis

Disclosure Period: calendar year ending 2003
Total Grants: $8,634,499*
Number of Grants: 661 (approx)
Average Grant: $13,063
Highest Grant: $300,000
Lowest Grant: $100
Typical Range: $1,000 to $25,000
***Note:** Giving excludes United Way.

Recent Grants

Note: Grants derived from 2003 Form 990.

General

431,250	United Way of Southeastern Pennsylvania, Pittsburgh, PA
300,000	Development Training Institute
300,000	University of Pittsburgh, Pittsburgh, PA
294,123	United Way of Southeastern Pennsylvania, Philadelphia, PA
259,934	Metro United Way, Kentucky, IN
240,000	University of Pittsburgh, Pittsburgh, PA
154,405	Penn State University, PA
150,000	Garden State Arts Center Foundation
138,643	Pittsburgh Symphony Society, Pittsburgh, PA
120,000	Inroads Inc.

PNM RESOURCES INC.

Company Headquarters

Alvarado Sq.
Albuquerque, NM 87158-0001
Web: http://www.pnm.com

Company Description

Founded: 1917
Ticker: PNM
Exchange: NYSE
Assets: US$3.027 billion (2002)
Employees: 2637 (2003)
SIC(s): 4900 Electric, Gas & Sanitary Services, 4923 Gas Transmission & Distribution, 4931 Electric & Other Services Combined, 4941 Water Supply.

Operating Locations

Public Service Co. of New Mexico (NM--Albuquerque)

Nonmonetary Support

Type: Donated Equipment; In-kind Services; Loaned Employees; Loaned Executives

PNM Foundation

Giving Contact

Chandra Manning, Senior Community Relations Representative
Alvarado Sq., MS 1110
Albuquerque, NM 87158-2708
Phone: (505)241-2209
Web: http://www.pnmfoundation.org

Description

Founded: 1983
EIN: 850309005
Organization Type: Corporate Foundation
Giving Locations: NM
Grant Types: Award, Employee Matching Gifts, Endowment, General Support, Matching, Multiyear/Continuing Support, Seed Money.
Note: Employee contributions must be at least $25, but not more than $1,000 per calendar year.

Donor Information

Founder: Public Service Co. of New Mexico

Financial Summary

Total Giving: $529,179 (2003); $434,604 (2002); $486,341 (2001)
Giving Analysis: Giving for 2002 includes: foundation matching gifts ($58,929); foundation ($375,675)
Assets: $11,447,626 (2003); $7,818,312 (2002); $11,344,461 (2001)
Gifts Received: $5,000,000 (2001); $30,000 (2000).
Note: In 2000, contributions were received from Public Service Co. of New Mexico.

Typical Recipients

Arts & Humanities: Arts Associations & Councils, Arts Centers, Dance, Ethnic & Folk Arts, Historic Preservation, History & Archaeology, Libraries, Literary Arts, Museums/Galleries, Music, Performing Arts, Public Broadcasting, Theater
Civic & Public Affairs: African American Affairs, Business/Free Enterprise, Community Foundations, Employment/Job Training, Civic & Public Affairs-General, Hispanic Affairs, Housing, Law & Justice, Native American Affairs, Urban & Community Affairs, Women's Affairs, Zoos/Aquariums
Education: Afterschool/Enrichment Programs, Agricultural Education, Arts/Humanities Education, Business Education, Business-School Partnerships, Colleges & Universities, Economic Education, Education Funds, Education Reform, Elementary Education (Private), Elementary Education (Public), Engineering/Technological Education, Faculty Development,

Education-General, Literacy, Minority Education, Preschool Education, Private Education (Precollege), Public Education (Precollege), Science/Mathematics Education, Secondary Education (Private), Secondary Education (Public), Social Sciences Education, Special Education, Student Aid
Environment: Environment-General, Resource Conservation
Health: AIDS/HIV, Cancer, Children's Health/Hospitals, Diabetes, Health Organizations, Hospices, Hospitals, Prenatal Health Issues, Preventive Medicine/Wellness Organizations, Research/Studies Institutes, Respiratory, Speech & Hearing, Transplant Networks/Donor Banks
Religion: Religion-General, Religious Organizations
Science: Observatories & Planetariums, Scientific Research
Social Services: Animal Protection, Big Brothers/Big Sisters, Camps, Community Centers, Community Service Organizations, Counseling, Day Care, Domestic Violence, Emergency Relief, Family Services, Food/Clothing Distribution, People with Disabilities, Recreation & Athletics, Scouts, Shelters/Homelessness, Social Services-General, United Funds/United Ways, YMCA/YWCA/YMHA/YWHA, Youth Organizations

Application Procedures

Initial Contact: Send letter requesting application guidelines and form. The direct giving program has three focus areas: teacher skills, higher education, and K-12 education, including health and human services needs to children in school. Requests for direct contributions are reviewed the first of each month. The minimum grant is $5,000. While there are no deadlines, the foundation board of directors meets three times per year to review and approve proposals for funding.
Application Requirements: Include proof of tax-exempt status, copies of organization's mission and vision statements, list of current board of directors, recently audited financial statement, detailed budget, and amount requested. Also may include a detailed narrative, not more than four pages in length.
Deadlines: January 15; May 15; September 15.
Evaluative Criteria: Decisions are based on proposal merits and outcomes of each specific request.

Restrictions

Grants are not given to or for sectarian or religious organizations, programs, or activities; testimonial dinners, fund-raising events or advertising; payments of loans, interest, taxes, or debt retirement; individuals; endowments; programs or projects that duplicate existing services and/or programs; operational and maintenance expenses (except for seed money or pilot projects); capital projects; or United Way agencies except for comptroller projects not normally funded by United Way gifts.

Additional Information

"The Foundation seeks to fund projects that can be replicated across the state, that are funded jointly with local or other funding sources, and that affect a large number of people. Proposals that involve children, senior citizens, minorities, and low or fixed income families receive special consideration. The Foundation also encourages requests that address the diverse groups within our community." Foundation 2002 Form 990
Publications: Grant Policies; Application Guidelines (including Application Form)

Corporate Officials

Barbara Barsky: vice president, president, chief executive officer PRIM CORP EMPL senior vice president, secretary: Public Service Co. of New Mexico.
Max H. Maerki: senior vice president B Aarau, Switzerland 1940. PRIM CORP EMPL senior vice president, chief financial officer: Public Service Co. of New Mexico. CORP AFFIL director: Sunterra Gas Processing Co.; director: ACE Insurance Co. Bermuda

Ltd.; director: Sunterra Gas Gathering Co. NONPR AFFIL member: American Management Association; member: Financial Executives Institute.

Jeffry Sterba: chairman, president, chief executive officer PRIM CORP EMPL chairman, president, chief executive officer: Public Service Co. of New Mexico.

Foundation Officials

Barbara Barsky: trustee (see above)
Marc Christensen: trustee
Ramon Gonzalez: secretary, treasurer
Sarita Loehr: trustee
Debbie O'Callaghan: trustee
Diane Ogawa: trustee
Pat Ortiz: trustee
Eddie Padilla: vice president
Carol Radosevich: president
Shirley Ragin: trustee

Grants Analysis

Disclosure Period: calendar year ending 2003
Total Grants: $210,560*
Number of Grants: 102
Average Grant: $1,095*
Highest Grant: $100,000
Lowest Grant: $600
Typical Range: $250 to $10,000
*Note: Giving excludes matching gifts. Average grant figure excludes highest grant.

Recent Grants

Note: Grants derived from 2003 Form 990.
Library-Related
5,000	Embudo Valley Library, Dixon, NM

General
100,000	New Mexico State University Foundation Incorporated, Las Cruces, NM
36,000	Southeast New Mexico Community Action Corporation, Carlsbad, NM
16,000	PNM Statewide Mathematics Contest, Albuquerque, NM
15,000	Mimbres Region Arts Council, Silver City, NM
13,000	Animal Humane Association of New Mexico, Albuquerque, NM
10,000	Behavioral Health Research Center, Albuquerque, NM
10,000	Camp Fire, Albuquerque, NM
10,000	Keshet Dance Company, Albuquerque, NM
7,500	Southwestern College, Santa Fe, NM
6,500	New Mexico Experimental Programme to Stimulate Competitive Research, Albuquerque, NM

DOROTHY W. POITRAS CHARITABLE TRUST

Giving Contact

James Poitras, Trustee
198 Highland St.
Holliston, MA 01746
Phone: (508)429-6281

Description

Founded: 1992
EIN: 046638933
Organization Type: Private Foundation
Grant Types: General Support.

Financial Summary

Gifts Received: $35 (fiscal year ending June 30, 1998); $16,636 (fiscal 1992). Note: In fiscal 1992, contributions were received from James W. and Patricia T. Poitras ($76) and the estate of Dorothy W. Poitras ($16,500).

Typical Recipients

Arts & Humanities: Arts Centers, Libraries
Civic & Public Affairs: Botanical Gardens/Parks, Civic & Public Affairs-General, Native American Affairs
Education: Engineering/Technological Education, Student Aid
Environment: Forestry, Environment-General, Research
Health: AIDS/HIV, Cancer, Hospices, Hospitals, Medical Research, Single-Disease Health Associations
Religion: Churches, Ministries, Religious Organizations
Social Services: Child Welfare, Community Service Organizations, Family Services, YMCA/YWCA/YMHA/YWHA, Youth Organizations

Application Procedures

Initial Contact: Send a full proposal.
Application Requirements: Include proof of tax-exempt status.
Deadlines: April 1.

Foundation Officials

Edward Poitras: trustee
James Poitras: trustee
Kay Poitras: trustee
Patricia Poitras: trustee

Grants Analysis

Disclosure Period: fiscal year ending June 30, 2000
Total Grants: $57,500*
Number of Grants: 10
Average Grant: $3,438*
Highest Grant: $20,000
Typical Range: $1,000 to $5,000
*Note: Giving excludes scholarship. Average grant figure excludes two highest grants ($30,000).

Recent Grants

Note: Grants derived from fiscal 2002 Form 990.
General
17,600	St. Alban's Episcopal Church, Cape Elizabeth, ME
12,500	Campus Crusade for Christ, Orlando, FL
12,500	Crossroads Community Foundation, Natick, MA
10,000	Search Ministries, Minneapolis, MN

POLK BROTHERS FOUNDATION, INC.

Giving Contact

Nikki Will Stein, Executive Director
20 West Kinzie Avenue
Suite 1110
Chicago, IL 60610
Phone: (312)527-4684
Fax: (312)527-4681
E-mail: questions@polkbrosfdn.org
Web: http://www.polkbrosfdn.org

Description

Founded: 1957
EIN: 366108293
Organization Type: Family Foundation
Giving Locations: IL: Chicago
Grant Types: Capital, Employee Matching Gifts, General Support, Matching, Multiyear/Continuing Support, Operating Expenses, Project, Research.

Donor Information

Founder: The foundation was established in 1957 by the members of the Polk family, who owned and operated the Polk Bros. chain of retail stores.

Financial Summary

Total Giving: $14,865,107 (fiscal year ending August 31, 2003); $14,705,632 (fiscal 2002)
Giving Analysis: Giving for fiscal 2003 includes: foundation matching gifts ($683,081); fiscal 2002: foundation matching gifts ($796,370)
Assets: $328,870,395 (fiscal 2003); $320,428,705 (fiscal 2002)
Gifts Received: $1,000 (fiscal 1997); $1,040,260 (fiscal 1995); $1,648,899 (fiscal 1994). Note: In fiscal 1994, contributions were received from Sol Polk Trust.

Typical Recipients

Arts & Humanities: Arts Associations & Councils, Arts Centers, Arts Festivals, Arts Funds, Arts Institutes, Arts Outreach, Ballet, Dance, Ethnic & Folk Arts, History & Archaeology, Libraries, Museums/Galleries, Music, Opera, Performing Arts, Public Broadcasting, Theater, Visual Arts
Civic & Public Affairs: African American Affairs, Asian American Affairs, Botanical Gardens/Parks, Clubs, Community Foundations, Economic Development, Economic Policy, Employment/Job Training, Ethnic Organizations, Gay/Lesbian Issues, Civic & Public Affairs-General, Housing, Law & Justice, Legal Aid, Municipalities/Towns, Professional & Trade Associations, Public Policy, Urban & Community Affairs, Women's Affairs, Zoos/Aquariums
Education: Afterschool/Enrichment Programs, Arts/Humanities Education, Business Education, Colleges & Universities, Education Associations, Education Funds, Education Reform, Faculty Development, Education-General, International Studies, Leadership Training, Minority Education, Preschool Education, Private Education (Precollege), Public Education (Precollege), Science/Mathematics Education, Secondary Education (Private), Secondary Education (Public), Student Aid
Health: AIDS/HIV, Children's Health/Hospitals, Clinics/Medical Centers, Health Organizations, Hospitals, Medical Rehabilitation, Mental Health, Nursing Services, Prenatal Health Issues, Public Health
International: Missionary/Religious Activities
Religion: Jewish Causes, Ministries, Religious Welfare
Science: Observatories & Planetariums, Science Museums, Scientific Centers & Institutes
Social Services: Animal Protection, At-Risk Youth, Child Abuse, Child Welfare, Community Centers, Community Service Organizations, Day Care, Delinquency & Criminal Rehabilitation, Family Services, Food/Clothing Distribution, Homes, People with Disabilities, Refugee Assistance, Senior Services, Shelters/Homelessness, Substance Abuse, United Funds/United Ways, YMCA/YWCA/YMHA/YWHA, Youth Organizations

Application Procedures

Initial Contact: Request an application form.
Deadlines: None.
Review Process: Proposals are scheduled for review in the order in which they are received; decisions are made at quarterly board meetings in February, May, August and November. Health proposals are reviewed in the spring and fall only.
Notes: Applicants must have 501(c)(3) status. The Foundation will only award a grant once every twelve months to an organization and will not review more than three consecutive requests from an organization through the Small Grants program. A site visit or interview may be scheduled by a program officer as part of the review process.

Restrictions

Grants are not made to individuals. In addition, funds are not awarded to organizations that devote a substantial portion of their activities to attempting to influence legislation or to participating in campaigns on behalf of candidates for public office; religious institutions seeking support for programs whose participants are restricted by religious affiliation or whose services promote a particular creed; purchase dinner or raffle tickets or advertising in dinner programs; medical, scientific, or academic research; or tax-generating entities (municipalities, school districts, etc.) for services within their normal responsibilities. The foundation will generally not fund more than five percent of an organization's operating budget.

Additional Information
Publications: Application Form; Annual Report

Foundation Officials
Bruce R. Bachmann: director
Sidney Epstein: treasurer B Chicago, IL 1923. ED University of Illinois BS (1943). PRIM CORP EMPL chairman: A. Epstein & Sons International. CORP AFFIL director: Amalgamated Trust & Savings Bank; trustee: Northwestern Mutual Life Insurance Co. NONPR AFFIL member: Tau Beta Pi; life member: University Chicago Hospitals & Clinics; member: Sigma Tau; member: Sigma Xi; member: Phi Kappa Phi; member: Polish-U.S. Economic Council; life trustee: Orchestral Association Chicago; member: Phi Eta Sigma; member, board directors: Lyric Opera Chicago; director: Michael Reese Foundation; member: Chi Epsilon; founder, director: Chicago Youth Center. CLUB AFFIL Standard Club.
Sandra P. Guthman: president, chief executive officer
J. Ira Harris: vice president PRIM CORP EMPL chairman: J. I. Harris & Associates. CORP AFFIL director: Manpower Inc.; vice chairman: Pritzker Organization LLC.
Howard J. Polk: director
Gordon S. Prussian: secretary
Raymond F. Simon: vice president

Grants Analysis
Disclosure Period: fiscal year ending August 31, 2003
Total Grants: $14,182,026*
Number of Grants: 446
Average Grant: $31,798
Highest Grant: $200,000
Lowest Grant: $100
Typical Range: $5,000 to $50,000
*Note: Giving excludes matching gifts.

Recent Grants
Note: Grants derived from 2003 Form 990.
General

400,000	Chicago Music and Dance Theater, Chicago, IL
200,000	Big Shoulders Fund, Chicago, IL
200,000	Millennium Park, Chicago, IL
160,000	Jewish United Fund, Chicago, IL
150,000	Gates High School Redesign Fund, Chicago, IL
150,000	Spertus Institute of Jewish Studies, Chicago, IL
140,000	Chicago Youth Centers, Chicago, IL
100,000	Chicago Public Education Fund, Chicago, IL
100,000	Children's First Fund, Chicago, IL
100,000	College Misericordia, Dallas, PA

WILLIAM B. POLLOCK CO. FOUNDATION

Giving Contact
Jeanette McElheney, Trust Officer
c/o Bank One Trust Co.
106 East Market Street
Warren, OH 44481
Phone: (330)742-6822

Description
Founded: 1952
EIN: 346514078
Organization Type: Private Foundation
Giving Locations: OH: Youngstown
Grant Types: General Support.

Typical Recipients
Arts & Humanities: Arts Institutes, Community Arts, Historic Preservation, History & Archaeology, Libraries, Music
Civic & Public Affairs: Business/Free Enterprise, Chambers of Commerce, Clubs, Community Foundations, Economic Development, Civic & Public Affairs-General, Public Policy, Urban & Community Affairs
Education: Business Education, Colleges & Universities, Education Associations, Education Funds, Education-General, Private Education (Precollege)
Health: Children's Health/Hospitals, Clinics/Medical Centers, Emergency/Ambulance Services, Health Organizations, Home-Care Services, Hospices, Hospitals, Nutrition
Religion: Jewish Causes, Religious Organizations, Religious Welfare
Science: Scientific Centers & Institutes
Social Services: At-Risk Youth, Child Welfare, Community Service Organizations, Family Planning, Food/Clothing Distribution, Homes, People with Disabilities, Recreation & Athletics, Senior Services, Substance Abuse, United Funds/United Ways, YMCA/YWCA/YMHA/YWHA, Youth Organizations

Application Procedures
Initial Contact: The foundation has no formal grant application procedure or application form.
Deadlines: None.

Additional Information
Trust(s): Bank One Trust Co.

Foundation Officials
Franklin Bennett: trustee

Grants Analysis
Disclosure Period: calendar year ending 2000
Total Grants: $55,000*
Number of Grants: 6
Highest Grant: $20,000
Lowest Grant: $5,000
*Note: Giving excludes United Way.

Recent Grants
Note: Grants derived from 2001 Form 990.

General

20,000	Youngstown and Mahoning Valley United Way, Youngstown, OH
15,000	YMCA, Youngstown, OH
10,000	Planned Parenthood, Youngstown, OH
5,000	Butler Institute of American Art, Youngstown, OH
5,000	Mahoning Valley Historical Society, Youngstown, OH
5,000	Ohio Foundation of Independent Colleges, Columbus, OH
5,000	Paisley House, Youngstown, OH
5,000	Youngstown Warren Regional Chamber of Commerce Foundation, Youngstown, OH
2,400	HELP Hotline Crisis Center, Youngstown, OH
800	Youth Leadership Mahoning Valley, Warren, OH

C. NORTHROP POND AND ALETHEA MARDER POND FOUNDATION

Giving Contact
Grace Pond Fisher, Trustee
c/o United Trust Bank
1130 RT 22 East
Bridgewater, NJ 08807
Phone: (908)429-2328

Description
Founded: 1999
EIN: 226727894
Organization Type: Private Foundation
Grant Types: General Support.

Financial Summary
Total Giving: $287,000 (fiscal year ending April 30, 2004); $151,000 (fiscal 2001)
Giving Analysis: Giving for fiscal 2004 includes: foundation grants to United Way ($10,000); fiscal 2001: foundation grants to United Way ($4,000)
Assets: $11,041,690 (fiscal 2004); $2,534,043 (fiscal 2001)

Typical Recipients
Arts & Humanities: Historic Preservation, Libraries, Public Broadcasting
Civic & Public Affairs: Civic & Public Affairs-General
Education: Colleges & Universities, Private Education (Precollege), Public Education (Precollege)
Environment: Environment-General, Resource Conservation
Health: Clinics/Medical Centers, Emergency/Ambulance Services, Hospitals
Religion: Churches
Social Services: Animal Protection, United Funds/United Ways

Additional Information
Trust(s): PNC Bank

Foundation Officials
Grace Pond Fisher: trustee
Charles N. Pond, Jr.: trustee

Grants Analysis
Disclosure Period: fiscal year ending April 30, 2004
Total Grants: $277,000*
Number of Grants: 31
Average Grant: $8,935*
Highest Grant: $20,000
Lowest Grant: $2,000
Typical Range: $5,000 to $10,000
*Note: Giving excludes United Way.

Recent Grants
Note: Grants derived from fiscal 2001 Form 990.
Library-Related

4,000	South Dennis Library Fund, South Dennis, MA

General

15,000	Crescent Avenue Presbyterian Church, Plainfield, NJ
10,000	Muhlenberg Hospital Foundation, Plainfield, NJ
10,000	New Jersey Conservation Foundation, Far Hills, NJ
10,000	Plainfield Foundation, Bridgewater, NJ
10,000	Princeton University, Princeton, NJ
10,000	Salisbury School, Salisbury, CT
10,000	Wardlaw Hartidge School, Edison, NJ
8,000	Orenda Wildlife Trust, West Barnstable, MA
8,000	Plainfield Health Center, Plainfield, NJ
6,000	Liberty Hall, South Dennis, MA

WILLIAM J. AND LIA G. POORVU FOUNDATION

Giving Contact
William J. Poorvu, Trustee
PO Box 380828
Cambridge, MA 02238
Phone: (617)576-1010
Fax: (617)576-1030

Description
Founded: 1978
EIN: 042651199
Organization Type: Private Foundation
Giving Locations: MA
Grant Types: General Support.

Donor Information
Founder: William J. Poorvu

Financial Summary
Total Giving: $659,165 (2001)
Assets: $13,474,456 (2001)
Gifts Received: $1,025,000 (2001); $840,000 (2000); $912,438 (1999). Note: In 2001, contributions were received from William J. Poorvu ($800,000); Lia G. Poorvu ($200,000); and May C. Poorvu ($25,000). In 2000, contributions were received from Lia G. Poorvu ($200,000), May C. Poorvu ($25,000) and William J. Poorvu ($615,000). In 1999, contributions were received from Lia G. Poorvu ($100,000) and William J. Poorvu ($9,500).

Typical Recipients
Arts & Humanities: Arts Outreach, Community Arts, Film & Video, Historic Preservation, History & Archaeology, Libraries, Museums/Galleries, Music, Public Broadcasting, Theater, Visual Arts
Civic & Public Affairs: Business/Free Enterprise, Economic Development, Civic & Public Affairs-General, Law & Justice, Public Policy
Education: Arts/Humanities Education, Business Education, Colleges & Universities, Education-General, Minority Education, Private Education (Precollege), Secondary Education (Public), Student Aid
Health: AIDS/HIV, Health-General, Health Organizations, Hospitals, Medical Research, Mental Health, Public Health, Single-Disease Health Associations
International: Foreign Educational Institutions
Religion: Jewish Causes
Science: Science Museums
Social Services: At-Risk Youth, Child Welfare, Community Service Organizations, Family Planning, Recreation & Athletics, Shelters/Homelessness

Application Procedures
Initial Contact: The foundation has no formal grant application procedure or application form.
Application Requirements: Complete information on the charitable purpose of the request is required.
Deadlines: None.

Restrictions
Does not support individuals.

Foundation Officials
Lia G. Poorvu: trustee
William J. Poorvu: trustee

Grants Analysis
Disclosure Period: calendar year ending 2001
Total Grants: $659,165
Number of Grants: 31
Average Grant: $12,385*
Highest Grant: $200,000
Lowest Grant: $500
Typical Range: $5,000 to $25,000
***Note:** Average grant figure excludes two highest grants ($300,000).

Recent Grants
Note: Grants derived from 2001 Form 990.
Library-Related

5,000	Boston Public Library Foundation, Boston, MA

General

200,000	Wellesley College, Wellesley, MA
100,000	Gardner Museum, Boston, MA
90,000	Yale University, New Haven, CT
75,000	National Public Radio Foundation, Boston, MA
50,000	Harvard Business School, Boston, MA
25,000	Boston Foundation, Boston, MA
25,000	Longy School of Music, Boston, MA
15,000	WGBH, Boston, MA
10,000	American Red Cross, Washington, DC
10,000	Boston Baroque, Boston, MA

JAMES HYDE PORTER TESTAMENTARY TRUST

Giving Contact
c/o SunTrust Bank
PO Box 4248
Macon, GA 31208
Phone: (478)741-2265
Fax: (478)755-5190

Description
Founded: 1949
EIN: 586034882
Organization Type: Private Foundation
Giving Locations: GA: Bibb County, Newton County
Grant Types: Capital, General Support.

Donor Information
Founder: the late James Hyde Porter

Financial Summary
Total Giving: $617,029 (2002); $425,125 (2001)
Assets: $10,450,699 (2002); $12,569,855 (2001)

Typical Recipients
Arts & Humanities: Arts Associations & Councils, Arts Festivals, Arts Institutes, Arts Outreach, Community Arts, Ethnic & Folk Arts, Historic Preservation, History & Archaeology, Libraries, Museums/Galleries, Music, Opera, Theater
Civic & Public Affairs: Clubs, Community Foundations, Civic & Public Affairs-General, Housing
Education: Arts/Humanities Education, Colleges & Universities, Engineering/Technological Education, Education-General, Literacy, Medical Education, Private Education (Precollege), Public Education (Precollege), Secondary Education (Public), Student Aid
Health: AIDS/HIV, Children's Health/Hospitals, Emergency/Ambulance Services, Health-General, Health Organizations, Hospices, Long-Term Care, Medical Research, Public Health, Speech & Hearing
Religion: Churches, Ministries, Religious Welfare
Science: Science Museums
Social Services: Child Welfare, Community Centers, Community Service Organizations, Counseling, Family Services, Food/Clothing Distribution, Homes, People with Disabilities, Recreation & Athletics, Scouts, Shelters/Homelessness, Social Services-General, United Funds/United Ways, YMCA/YWCA/YMHA/YWHA, Youth Organizations

Application Procedures
Initial Contact: Send seven copies of the proposal form, IRS and foundation documentation, and supplemental information.
Deadlines: April 20.

Additional Information
Publications: Application Guidelines
Trust(s): SunTrust Bank Middle GA NA

Foundation Officials
Rev. Lester Ariail: manager
Dr. Rodney M. Browne: mgr
Leland Collins: manager
Dr. W. L. Dobbs: mgr
Jack Ellis: manager
Ben F. Hendricks: mgr
Larry Justice: mgr
Katherine M. Kalish: mgr
Jim Marshall: manager
Don Martin: manager
Davis Morgan: mgr
Tommy Olmstead: manager
Dr. Henry Patton: mgr
Sam Ramsey: manager
Ed S. Sell, Jr.: mgr B Athens, GA 1917. ED University of Georgia BA (1937); University of Georgia JD (1939). PRIM CORP EMPL partner: Sell & Melton PRIM NONPR EMPL county atty: Bibb County. CORP AFFIL county attorney: Bibb County Georgia. NONPR AFFIL member: Shriners; trustee: Wesleyan College; member: Phi Delta Phi; member: Phi Kappa Phi; Masons; member: Phi Beta Kappa; member: Macon Bar Association; member: Macon Circuit Bar Association; member: City Lions; member: Georgia Bar Association; member: American Bar Foundation. CLUB AFFIL City Club; River North Club; 191 Club.
Rev. William Wade: manager

Grants Analysis
Disclosure Period: calendar year ending 2002
Total Grants: $617,029
Number of Grants: 40
Average Grant: $13,659*
Highest Grant: $49,000
Lowest Grant: $500
Typical Range: $5,000 to $30,000
***Note:** Average grant figure excludes two highest grants ($98,000).

Recent Grants
Note: Grants derived from 2001 Form 990.
Library-Related

64,379	Newton County Library, Covington, GA

General

70,000	Concert Association Newton County, Covington, GA
25,000	Macon Rescue Mission, Macon, GA
25,000	Mercer University, Atlanta, GA
25,000	Museum of Arts and Sciences, Macon, GA
25,000	Newton Macon Inc., Macon, GA
25,000	Ronald McDonald House, Macon, GA
25,000	Tubman African American Museum, Macon, GA
25,000	Wesleyan College, Wellesley, MA
20,000	Georgia Trust for Historic Preservation, Atlanta, GA
20,000	Macon Outreach, Macon, GA

PORTSMOUTH GENERAL HOSPITAL FOUNDATION

Giving Contact
Alan Gollihue, Executive Director
360 Crawford Street
Portsmouth, VA 23704
Phone: (757)391-0000
E-mail: office@pghfoundation.org
Web: http://www.pghfoundation.org

Description

Founded: 1987
EIN: 541463392
Organization Type: Private Foundation
Giving Locations: VA
Grant Types: General Support.

Financial Summary

Total Giving: $506,254 (fiscal year ending June 30, 2004); $934,226 (fiscal 2002); $985,834 (fiscal 2001). Note: Fiscal 1997 Giving includes United Way ($360).
Assets: $15,375,600 (fiscal 2004); $14,560,791 (fiscal 2002); $17,365,029 (fiscal 2001)
Gifts Received: $200 (fiscal 2004); $3,893 (fiscal 2002); $6,950 (fiscal 2001)

Typical Recipients

Arts & Humanities: Arts Festivals, Dance, History & Archaeology, Libraries, Museums/Galleries, Music, Theater, Visual Arts
Civic & Public Affairs: Economic Development, Civic & Public Affairs-General, Urban & Community Affairs
Education: Arts/Humanities Education, Colleges & Universities, Community & Junior Colleges, Education Funds, Education-General, Medical Education, Preschool Education, Private Education (Precollege), Public Education (Precollege)
Environment: Air/Water Quality, Environment-General
Health: AIDS/HIV, Cancer, Children's Health/Hospitals, Clinics/Medical Centers, Diabetes, Emergency/Ambulance Services, Geriatric Health, Health Funds, Health Organizations, Heart, Hospices, Hospitals, Medical Research, Nursing Services, Public Health, Single-Disease Health Associations
International: Foreign Arts Organizations
Religion: Churches, Jewish Causes, Religious Welfare
Social Services: At-Risk Youth, Camps, Child Abuse, Child Welfare, Community Service Organizations, Crime Prevention, Day Care, Domestic Violence, Emergency Relief, Family Planning, Family Services, Food/Clothing Distribution, People with Disabilities, Recreation & Athletics, Scouts, Special Olympics, Substance Abuse, Volunteer Services, YMCA/YWCA/YMHA/YWHA, Youth Organizations

Application Procedures

Initial Contact: Send full proposal. Include amount requested and purpose of funds sought.
Deadlines: None.

Foundation Officials

Patrick A. Clifford: program assistant PRIM CORP EMPL chairman, director: Richard D. Irwin.
Alan E. Gollihue: executive director
Leslie Harding: director
Karl S. Morrisette: director
Horace S. Savage, Jr.: chairman
Harry Short: director
Burle U. Stromberg: director
Nancy G. Wren: vice chairman

Grants Analysis

Disclosure Period: fiscal year ending June 30, 2004
Total Grants: $506,254
Number of Grants: 76
Average Grant: $6,661
Highest Grant: $50,000
Lowest Grant: $150
Typical Range: $1,000 to $10,000

Recent Grants

Note: Grants derived from fiscal 2004 Form 990.
General

50,000	Virginia Sports Hall of Fame, Portsmouth, VA
32,000	Child and Family Services, Portsmouth, VA -- for healthy family
30,000	Jewish Family Service, Virginia Beach, VA -- for Pam program
25,000	Elizabeth River Project, Norfolk, VA
25,000	Ports Schools Foundation -- for access program
24,000	Ports Community Health
22,000	Friends of Ports Juvenile Court, Portsmouth, VA -- for casa program
20,000	American Cancer Society, Atlanta, GA
20,000	American Red Cross, Portsmouth, VA -- for health and safety
20,000	Child and Family Services, Portsmouth, VA -- for fast program

HERMAN T. AND PHENIE R. POTT FOUNDATION

Giving Contact

James L. Collins, Executive Director
PO Box 387
St. Louis, MO 63166
Phone: (314)418-2643
Fax: (314)418-2349

Description

Founded: 1963
EIN: 436041541
Organization Type: General Purpose Foundation
Giving Locations: MO: St. Louis
Grant Types: Multiyear/Continuing Support, Operating Expenses, Project.

Donor Information

Founder: Established in 1963.

Financial Summary

Total Giving: $1,249,200 (2001)
Assets: $29,767,444 (2001)
Gifts Received: $596,361 (2000); $397,211 (1999); $578,291 (1998). Note: The foundation received a contribution in 1997 and 2000 from the Phenie R. Pott Charitable Lead Unitrust.

Typical Recipients

Arts & Humanities: Arts Associations & Councils, Historic Preservation, Libraries, Museums/Galleries, Music, Opera
Civic & Public Affairs: Botanical Gardens/Parks, Community Foundations, Economic Development, Employment/Job Training, Civic & Public Affairs-General, Housing, Philanthropic Organizations, Public Policy, Urban & Community Affairs, Zoos/Aquariums
Education: Afterschool/Enrichment Programs, Business Education, Colleges & Universities, Education Funds, Engineering/Technological Education, Education-General, Minority Education, Science/Mathematics Education, Special Education, Student Aid, Vocational & Technical Education
Environment: Environment-General
Health: Alzheimer's Disease, Children's Health/Hospitals, Diabetes, Emergency/Ambulance Services, Eyes/Blindness, Health Organizations, Heart, Hospitals, Medical Rehabilitation, Medical Research, Mental Health, Multiple Sclerosis, Preventive Medicine/Wellness Organizations, Respiratory, Single-Disease Health Associations, Speech & Hearing
Religion: Churches, Ministries, Religious Organizations, Religious Welfare
Social Services: At-Risk Youth, Big Brothers/Big Sisters, Camps, Child Abuse, Child Welfare, Community Service Organizations, Counseling, Day Care, Domestic Violence, Emergency Relief, Family Planning, Family Services, Food/Clothing Distribution, Homes, People with Disabilities, Scouts, Senior Services, Shelters/Homelessness, Special Olympics, Substance Abuse, United Funds/United Ways, YMCA/YWCA/YMHA/YWHA, Youth Organizations

Application Procedures

Initial Contact: Submit a brief letter of inquiry. The foundation requests applications be made in writing.
Application Requirements: proof of tax-exempt status
Deadlines: March 1.

Restrictions

Grants are made only to organizations exempt under section 501(c)(3) of the IRS code. Grants are not made to individuals. Grants are made primarily to organizations in the St. Louis area. Grants are not given to churches, but may be awarded to church special outreach programs. Grants for programs are favored over capital campaigns; no grants are made to endowments.

Foundation Officials

James Collins: executive director, member advisory committee

Grants Analysis

Disclosure Period: calendar year ending 2000
Total Grants: $1,191,000*
Number of Grants: 125
Average Grant: $8,395*
Highest Grant: $150,000
Typical Range: $2,000 to $20,000
***Note:** Giving excludes scholarships and United Way. Average grant figure excludes highest grant.

Recent Grants

Note: Grants derived from 2002 Form 990.
Library-Related

80,000	St Louis Mercantile Library Association, St. Louis, MO

General

150,000	Salvation Army, St. Louis, MO
110,000	Family Resource Center, St. Louis, MO
85,000	Ranken Jordan Home for Convalescent Crippled Children, St. Louis, MO
55,000	Washington University, St. Louis, MO
50,000	Grace Hill Settlement House, St. Louis, MO
45,000	Alliance for the Mentally Ill Inc., St. Louis, MO
35,000	Missouri Colleges Fund, St. Louis, MO
35,000	United Way of Greater St Louis, St. Louis, MO
25,000	Big Brother & Big Sisters of Greater St Louis, St. Louis, MO
25,000	Missouri Girlstown Foundation, Kingdom City, MO

POTTS AND SIBLEY FOUNDATION

Giving Contact

Robert W. Bechtel, Co-Trustee, Manager & Director
PO Box 8907
Midland, TX 79708
Phone: (915)686-7051

Description

Founded: 1967
EIN: 756081070
Organization Type: Private Foundation
Giving Locations: TX
Grant Types: General Support.

Donor Information

Founder: Effie Potts Sibley Irrevocable Trust

Financial Summary

Total Giving: $204,900 (fiscal year ending July 31, 2002); $141,500 (fiscal 2001)

Assets: $4,432,793 (fiscal 2002); $4,154,399 (fiscal 2001)

Typical Recipients

Arts & Humanities: Arts Institutes, Community Arts, History & Archaeology, Libraries, Museums/ Galleries, Music
Civic & Public Affairs: Housing, Municipalities/ Towns, Zoos/Aquariums
Education: Arts/Humanities Education, Colleges & Universities, Community & Junior Colleges, Education Funds, Engineering/Technological Education, Education-General, Private Education (Precollege), Science/Mathematics Education, Social Sciences Education, Vocational & Technical Education
Environment: Environment-General, Research, Resource Conservation, Wildlife Protection
Health: Children's Health/Hospitals, Eyes/Blindness, Hospices, Hospitals, Medical Research, Mental Health, Research/Studies Institutes
International: International Environmental Issues
Religion: Churches, Religious Welfare
Science: Science Museums, Scientific Research
Social Services: People with Disabilities, Scouts

Application Procedures

Initial Contact: Application form required.
Deadlines: None.

Foundation Officials

Robert W. Bechtel: co-trustee, mgr, director
Maurice Randolph Bullock: co-trustee, director B Colorado City, TX August 20, 1913. ED University of Texas LLB (1936). OCCUPATION attorney. NONPR AFFIL member: Texas Trial Lawyers Association; member: West Texas Chamber of Commerce; fellow: Texas Bar Foundation; member executive committee: Texas Law Enforcement Foundation; member: Southwest Legal Foundation; member: Texas Bar Association; member: Permian Basin Petroleum Association; member: Order Coif; member: Pecos County Chamber of Commerce; member: Midland County Bar Association; fellow: American College Trust & Estate Counsel; member: American Judicature Society; member: American Bar Association.
Allen G. McGuire: director, co-trustee
Tom Scott: director
D. J. Sibley: director
Hiram Sibley: chairman

Grants Analysis

Disclosure Period: fiscal year ending July 31, 2002
Total Grants: $204,900
Number of Grants: 28
Average Grant: $6,478*
Highest Grant: $30,000
Lowest Grant: $2,000
Typical Range: $2,000 to $10,000
*Note: Average grant figure excludes highest grant.

Recent Grants

Note: Grants derived from 2002 Form 990.
Library-Related
6,000	Recording Library for the Blind, Midland, TX

General
30,000	Siblley Environmental Learning Center, Midland, TX
25,000	Siblley Environmental Learning Center, Midland, TX
10,000	Big Bend Educational Corporation, Alpine, TX
10,000	Community Children's Clinic, Midland, TX
10,000	Midland Memorial Hospital Foundation, Midland, TX
8,000	Herman Hospital Hyberbaric Studies, Houston, TX
7,500	Permian Basin Petroleum Museum, Midland, TX
7,500	Salvation Army, Midland, TX
7,000	Austin Symphony, Austin, TX
7,000	Chihuahuan Desert Research, Austin, TX

POWELL FAMILY FOUNDATION

Giving Contact

Carrie Hoelscher, Secretary
4350 Shawnee Mission Parkway, Suite 280
Fairway, KS 66205
Phone: (913)236-0003
Fax: (913)262-0058

Description

Founded: 1969
EIN: 237023968
Organization Type: Family Foundation
Giving Locations: MO: Kansas City metropolitan area
Grant Types: Capital, General Support, Operating Expenses, Scholarship.

Donor Information

Founder: The Powell Family Foundation was established in 1969 by George E. Powell, former chairman of the Yellow Freight System of Delaware. The foundation gives preference to projects in the the Kansas City area where Mr. Powell lived. In keeping with Mr. Powell's beliefs, the foundation continues to support organizations that enrich the family, religious values, community involvement, and youth organizations. The foundation gives priority to the funding of Christian Science programs and to activities and programs for youth. The foundation's trustees are members of the Powell family.

Financial Summary

Total Giving: $1,351,000 (2002 approx); $1,532,000 (2001)
Assets: $21,918,928 (2001)

Typical Recipients

Arts & Humanities: Libraries, Literary Arts, Museums/Galleries, Public Broadcasting
Civic & Public Affairs: Botanical Gardens/Parks, Community Foundations, Civic & Public Affairs-General, Law & Justice, Nonprofit Management, Philanthropic Organizations, Public Policy, Safety, Urban & Community Affairs, Women's Affairs, Zoos/ Aquariums
Education: Agricultural Education, Business Education, Colleges & Universities, Education Associations, Education Funds, Faculty Development, Education-General, Minority Education, Private Education (Precollege), Public Education (Precollege), Science/ Mathematics Education, Special Education, Student Aid, Vocational & Technical Education
Environment: Environment-General, Resource Conservation
Health: Cancer
International: International Peace & Security Issues
Religion: Churches, Religious Organizations, Religious Welfare
Social Services: Camps, Child Welfare, Community Centers, Community Service Organizations, Family Planning, Family Services, Food/Clothing Distribution, Recreation & Athletics, Scouts, United Funds/ United Ways, YMCA/YWCA/YMHA/YWHA, Youth Organizations

Application Procedures

Initial Contact: Contact the foundation to obtain guidelines.
Review Process: The trustees meet in November of each year.

Restrictions

Building programs and grants for endowment purposes are rarely considered. The foundation does not fund individuals, organizations involved in the arts, the medical field, or social welfare. No grants are made for projects outside the continental United States.

Organizations must be tax-exempt under section 501(c)(3).

Additional Information

Publications: Guidelines

Foundation Officials

Barbara Powell Allen: secretary
Nicholas K. Powell: vice president PRIM CORP EMPL president: Colt Energy Inc.

Grants Analysis

Disclosure Period: calendar year ending 2001
Total Grants: $137,500*
Number of Grants: 10
Average Grant: $13,750
Highest Grant: $25,000
Lowest Grant: $1,000
Typical Range: $1,000 to $10,000 and $15,000 to $25,000
*Note: Giving excludes grants to the Powell Gardens.

Recent Grants

Note: Grants derived from 2002 Form 990.
General
1,266,000	Powell Gardens, Kingsville, MO
25,000	Kansas City Museum, Kansas City, MO -- for science city
25,000	Pembroke Hill School, Kansas City, MO -- for capital campaign
20,000	Kansas City Public Television, Kansas City, MO -- for capital campaign
15,000	Women's Employment Network, Kansas City, MO
8,000	Kansas City Community Gardens, Kansas City, MO
2,500	Planned Parenthood, Kansas City, MO
1,000	Garden Conservancy, Cold Spring, NY

POWELL FOUNDATION

Giving Contact

Nancy Powell Moore, Foundation Manager
2121 San Felipe, Suite 110
Houston, TX 77019
Phone: (713)523-7557
Fax: (713)523-7553
E-mail: info@powellfoundation.org
Web: http://www.powellfoundation.org

Description

Founded: 1967
EIN: 746104592
Organization Type: Private Foundation
Giving Locations: TX: Harris County, Travis County, Walker County
Grant Types: General Support, Project.

Donor Information

Founder: the late Ben H. Powell, Kitty King Powell

Financial Summary

Total Giving: $694,655 (2001)
Assets: $15,763,614 (2001)

Typical Recipients

Arts & Humanities: Arts Associations & Councils, Arts Festivals, Arts Outreach, Ballet, Arts & Humanities-General, Historic Preservation, History & Archaeology, Libraries, Literary Arts, Museums/Galleries, Music, Opera, Public Broadcasting, Theater, Visual Arts
Civic & Public Affairs: Botanical Gardens/Parks, Community Foundations, Economic Development, Employment/Job Training, Civic & Public Affairs-General, Hispanic Affairs, Housing, Municipalities/ Towns, Professional & Trade Associations, Urban & Community Affairs, Women's Affairs, Zoos/

Aquariums

Education: Afterschool/Enrichment Programs, Arts/ Humanities Education, Business Education, Business-School Partnerships, Colleges & Universities, Education Associations, Education Reform, Elementary Education (Public), Faculty Development, Education-General, International Studies, Legal Education, Literacy, Minority Education, Private Education (Precollege), Public Education (Precollege), Science/ Mathematics Education, Secondary Education (Private), Social Sciences Education, Special Education

Environment: Environment-General, Protection, Resource Conservation

Health: Adolescent Health Issues, AIDS/HIV, Clinics/ Medical Centers, Emergency/Ambulance Services, Eyes/Blindness, Hospitals (University Affiliated), Mental Health, Public Health, Research/Studies Institutes, Single-Disease Health Associations, Speech & Hearing

Religion: Churches, Ministries, Religious Welfare, Seminaries

Science: Science Museums

Social Services: Child Abuse, Child Welfare, Community Centers, Community Service Organizations, Emergency Relief, Family Planning, Family Services, Homes, Scouts, Shelters/Homelessness, Substance Abuse, Volunteer Services, Youth Organizations

Application Procedures

Initial Contact: The foundation requests applications be made in writing.

Application Requirements: Include organization's purpose and a summary of its activities; its budget; a copy of the organization's IRS tax-exempt letter, evidence of its IRS status as a public entity, and a statement that the letter is current and has not been revoked; a list of board members; and a list of past and present funders, including project, date, and amount.

Deadlines: None.

Restrictions

Grants are not made to religious organizations for sectarian purposes, testimonial dinners, fund raising events, advertising, other private foundations, or individuals, or to cover past operating deficits or debt retirement, grants for building requests, or multi-year commitments.

Foundation Officials

Antonia Scott Day: vice president, director, secretary

Marian P. Harrison: director, assistant treasurer

Harvin Moore, IV: director

Nancy Powell Moore: foundation manager, director, president, treasurer

Katherine Osborne: director

Ben H. Powell, V: director, vice president

Kitty King Powell: director

Grants Analysis

Disclosure Period: calendar year ending 2001

Total Grants: $694,655

Number of Grants: 77

Average Grant: $9,021

Highest Grant: $55,000

Lowest Grant: $250

Typical Range: $300 to $25,000

Recent Grants

Note: Grants derived from 2001 Form 990.

Library-Related

10,000	Harris County Public Library, Houston, TX

General

55,000	Child-Centered School Initiative of Greater Houston Area, Houston, TX
55,000	Greater Houston Community Foundation, Houston, TX
30,000	American National Red Cross, Houston, TX
25,000	Communities in Schools Houston, Inc., Houston, TX

25,000	Teach for America, Houston, TX
22,500	KIPP, Inc, Houston, TX
15,000	Gulf Coast Trades Center, New Waverly, TX
15,000	Huntsville Independent School District, Huntsville, TX
14,400	Fifth Ward Enrichment Program, Houston, TX
12,895	Aspiring Youth Foundation, Houston, TX

POWERS FOUNDATION

Giving Contact

C. Cody White, Jr., President & Treasurer
Powers Foundation
PO Box 1607
Shreveport, LA 71165
Phone: (318)429-1525
Fax: (318)429-2070

Description

Founded: 1967
EIN: 756080974
Organization Type: Private Foundation
Giving Locations: LA: Bossier City, Shreveport
Grant Types: General Support.

Donor Information

Founder: the late Gussie N. Power

Financial Summary

Total Giving: $224,500 (fiscal year ending July 31, 2002); $217,000 (fiscal 2001)
Assets: $4,949,005 (fiscal 2002); $4,982,784 (fiscal 2001)
Gifts Received: $50,000 (fiscal 1998)

Typical Recipients

Arts & Humanities: Ballet, History & Archaeology, Libraries, Museums/Galleries, Music

Civic & Public Affairs: Chambers of Commerce, Clubs, Community Foundations, Civic & Public Affairs-General, Urban & Community Affairs

Education: Business Education, Colleges & Universities, Education Funds, Education Reform, Literacy, Private Education (Precollege), Public Education (Precollege), Secondary Education (Public)

Health: Arthritis, Emergency/Ambulance Services, Hospitals (University Affiliated), Medical Research

Religion: Churches, Religious Organizations, Religious Welfare

Science: Science Museums

Social Services: Child Abuse, Child Welfare, Community Service Organizations, Counseling, Food/ Clothing Distribution, Homes, People with Disabilities, Scouts, Senior Services, Substance Abuse, Volunteer Services, YMCA/YWCA/YMHA/YWHA, Youth Organizations

Application Procedures

Initial Contact: Send a brief letter of inquiry.

Application Requirements: Include a description of organization and proof of tax-exempt status.

Deadlines: None.

Foundation Officials

C. Cody White, Jr.: president, treasurer

Sara Margaret White: vice president, secretary

Stephen C. White: vice president

Grants Analysis

Disclosure Period: fiscal year ending July 31, 2002

Total Grants: $224,500

Number of Grants: 27

Average Grant: $4,761*

Highest Grant: $35,000

Lowest Grant: $1,000

Typical Range: $1,000 to $10,000

*Note: Average grant figure excludes four highest grants ($115,000).

Recent Grants

Note: Grants derived from 2002 Form 990.

General

35,000	Volunteers of America, Shreveport, LA
30,000	SCI Port Discovery Center, Shreveport, LA
25,000	Highland Center Foundation, Shreveport, LA
25,000	Youth Choirs, Inc., Shreveport, LA -- civic
15,000	Shreveport Community Renewal, Shreveport, LA -- civic
10,000	Christian Service Program, Shreveport, LA
10,000	Graland Country Day School, Denver, CO
10,000	Louisiana State University Health Sciences Center, Shreveport, LA -- for medical research
10,000	Red Cross, New York, NY
10,000	Shreveport Garden Study Club, Shreveport, LA -- civic

PPG INDUSTRIES INC.

Company Headquarters

One PPG Place
Pittsburgh, PA 15272
Phone: (412)434-3131
Web: http://www.ppg.com

Company Description

Founded: 1883
Ticker: PPG
Exchange: NYSE
Acquired: Porter Paint Co..
Revenue: US$9.513 billion (2004)
Profit: US$683 million (2004)
Employees: 32900 (2003)
Fortune Rank: 236, per FORTUNE Magazine's list of 500 Largest U.S. Corporations (2004).
SIC(s): 2812 Alkalies & Chlorine, 2851 Paints & Allied Products, 2869 Industrial Organic Chemicals Nec, 2891 Adhesives & Sealants.
Parent Company: Courtaulds Coatings Inc., 91-291 Kalaeloa Boulevard, Kapolei, HI, United States
Parent Revenue: US$15,207,700,000 (2001)

Operating Locations

PPG Industries, Inc. (AR--El Dorado; KS--Lenexa; LA--Lake Charles; OH--Cleveland; PA--Pittsburgh; WV--Natrium; WI--Oak Creek)

Porter Paint Foundation, Inc.

Giving Contact

W.R. Niblock, President
Porter Paint Foundation, Inc
419 Village Lake Drive
Louisville, KY 40245
Phone: (502)244-2205

Description

Founded: 1985
EIN: 611094575
Organization Type: Corporate Foundation
Giving Locations: KY
Grant Types: General Support.
Note: Also supports special programs.

Financial Summary

Total Giving: $6,000 (2003)
Assets: $124,778 (2003)

Typical Recipients

Arts & Humanities: Ethnic & Folk Arts, Libraries, Museums/Galleries
Civic & Public Affairs: Business/Free Enterprise, Legal Aid, Municipalities/Towns, Professional & Trade Associations
Education: Business Education, Colleges & Universities, Economic Education, Education Associations, Education Funds, Education-General, Private Education (Precollege), Public Education (Precollege)
Science: Scientific Centers & Institutes
Social Services: Camps, People with Disabilities, Scouts, Shelters/Homelessness, YMCA/YWCA/YMHA/YWHA

Application Procedures

Initial Contact: The foundation requests applications be made in writing.
Application Requirements: Include need and purpose of funds sought.
Deadlines: None.

Restrictions

Does not support individuals, political or lobbying groups, or organizations outside operating areas.

Foundation Officials

Robert E. Champagne: vice president, director
W. Robert Niblock: president, director B Philadelphia, PA 1928. ED Drexel University BS (1951); University of Chicago Graduate School of Business Administration MBA (1956). CORP AFFIL vice president corporate devel, secretary, director: Courtaulds Coatings. NONPR AFFIL director: Junior Achievement Kentuckiana; director: Kentucky Education Foundation. CLUB AFFIL Jefferson Club; Wynn Stay Club.

Grants Analysis

Disclosure Period: calendar year ending 2003
Total Grants: $6,000
Number of Grants: 10
Average Grant: $600
Highest Grant: $2,000
Lowest Grant: $100
Typical Range: $300 to $2,000

Recent Grants

Note: Grants derived from 2003 Form 990.
Library-Related

500	Library Foundation, Louisville, KY
300	Jefferson County Law Library, Louisville, KY

General

2,000	Kentucky Council on Economic Education, Louisville, KY
1,300	Boy Scouts of America, Louisville, KY
650	Young Men's Christian Association Safe Place Services, Louisville, KY
500	Kentucky Engineering Foundation Inc., Frankfort, KY
350	Legal Aid Society, Louisville, KY
200	Custom Quality Services, Louisville, KY
100	Camp Piomingo Young Men's Christian Association of Greater Louisville, Louisville, KY
100	Portland Museum, Louisville, KY

PPG Industries Inc.

Company Headquarters

One PPG Place
Pittsburgh, PA 15272
Phone: (412)434-3131
Web: http://www.ppg.com

Company Description

Founded: 1883
Ticker: PPG
Exchange: NYSE
Acquired: Porter Paint Co..
Revenue: US$9.513 billion (2004)
Profit: US$683 million (2004)
Employees: 32900 (2003)
Fortune Rank: 236, per FORTUNE Magazine's list of 500 Largest U.S. Corporations (2004).
SIC(s): 2812 Alkalies & Chlorine, 2851 Paints & Allied Products, 2869 Industrial Organic Chemicals Nec, 2891 Adhesives & Sealants.

Operating Locations

PPG Industries, Inc. (AR--El Dorado; KS--Lenexa; LA--Lake Charles; OH--Cleveland; PA--Pittsburgh; WV--Natrium; WI--Oak Creek)

Nonmonetary Support

Type: In-kind Services
Volunteer Programs: Sponsors the GIVE Program to recognize employee involvement in volunteerism. Employees may apply for one grant of $250 annually to benefit an eligible non-profit organization for whom they volunteer.
Note: PPG does not coordinate or track its in-kind giving.

PPG Industries Foundation

Giving Contact

Jeffrey R. Gilbert, Executive Director
PPG Industries Foundation
One PPG Pl.
Pittsburgh, PA 15272
Phone: (412)434-2788
Web: http://corporate.ppg.com/PPG/corporate/AboutUs/PPGIndustriesFoundation/default.htm

Description

EIN: 256037790
Organization Type: Corporate Foundation
Giving Locations: PA: Pittsburgh headquarters and operating communities; nationally.
Grant Types: Capital, Department, Emergency, Employee Matching Gifts, General Support, Matching, Multiyear/Continuing Support, Operating Expenses, Project.
Note: Employee matching gift ratio: 1 to 1 up to $10,000 per eligible donor per organization. Minimum for matching is $25 and the maximum is $10,000 for an organization. Limit is $20,000 per year per donor.

Financial Summary

Total Giving: $5,465,850 (2002); $4,958,246 (2001).
Note: Contributes through corporate direct giving program and foundation.
Giving Analysis: Giving for 2001 includes: foundation matching gifts ($1,390,000); foundation ($3,568,246)
Assets: $15,564,720 (2002); $22,975,397 (2001)
Gifts Received: $755,681 (2002); $5,186,912 (2001); $5,000,000 (2000). Note: Foundation receives contributions from PPG Industries.

Typical Recipients

Arts & Humanities: Arts Associations & Councils, Arts Centers, Arts Festivals, Arts Institutes, Arts Outreach, Ballet, Community Arts, Dance, Historic Preservation, History & Archaeology, Libraries, Literary Arts, Museums/Galleries, Music, Opera, Performing Arts, Public Broadcasting, Theater
Civic & Public Affairs: Botanical Gardens/Parks, Business/Free Enterprise, Civil Rights, Community Foundations, Economic Development, Economic Policy, Employment/Job Training, Civic & Public Affairs-General, Housing, Law & Justice, Municipalities/Towns, Professional & Trade Associations, Public Policy, Safety, Urban & Community Affairs, Women's Affairs, Zoos/Aquariums

Education: Business Education, Business-School Partnerships, Colleges & Universities, Community & Junior Colleges, Economic Education, Education Associations, Education Funds, Education Reform, Engineering/Technological Education, Environmental Education, Faculty Development, Education-General, International Studies, Minority Education, Private Education (Precollege), Public Education (Precollege), Science/Mathematics Education, Secondary Education (Private), Secondary Education (Public), Student Aid
Environment: Environment-General
Health: Clinics/Medical Centers, Emergency/Ambulance Services, Eyes/Blindness, Health Policy/Cost Containment, Health Funds, Health Organizations, Hospitals, Long-Term Care, Medical Rehabilitation, Mental Health, Nursing Services, Public Health, Single-Disease Health Associations
International: International Relations
Religion: Churches, Jewish Causes, Religious Organizations, Religious Welfare, Seminaries
Science: Observatories & Planetariums, Science Exhibits & Fairs, Scientific Centers & Institutes, Scientific Organizations, Scientific Research
Social Services: Child Welfare, Community Centers, Community Service Organizations, Day Care, Emergency Relief, Family Services, Food/Clothing Distribution, Homes, People with Disabilities, Scouts, Senior Services, Shelters/Homelessness, Social Services-General, United Funds/United Ways, Volunteer Services, YMCA/YWCA/YMHA/YWHA, Youth Organizations

Application Procedures

Initial Contact: Send a one- to two-page letter to foundation if organizations are located in Pittsburgh area or are national in scope; organizations serving communities where PPG facilities are located should direct inquiries to local PPG agent.
Application Requirements: Include proof of tax-exempt status; organization's mission statement; grant's purpose and objectives; summary of the project; amount requested and rationale; schedule of implementation; description of benefits to be achieved and population served; plans for evaluating and reporting results; recently audited financial statement; financial analysis for the project; person in charge of the project and his or her qualifications; and list of board members and their affiliations.
Deadlines: By September for grants in the following year, though grant requests are accepted year-round.
Review Process: Screening committee reviews appeals quarterly; committee decides on grants of less than $10,000; board reviews grants of more than $10,000.
Evaluative Criteria: Correspondence of applicant's goal to foundation's priorities; available resources; financial need of organization; foundation's past experience with organization; applicant's capability and reputation; funds available from other funders; duplication of work; population served; proposal's clarity and breadth; and practices of other corporate funders. Priority is given to local organizations dedicated to enhancing the welfare of PPG communities.

Restrictions

No grant application for less than $100 will be considered. Foundation does not support operating funds of United Way agencies; political activities or organizations; individuals; endowments; organizations outside the United States or its territories; projects which would directly benefit PPG Industries, Inc.; advertising in benefit publications; sectarian groups for religious purposes; special events; or telephone solicitations.

Additional Information

To ensure sensitivity to local needs in PPG plant communities, the foundation has developed a local agent system. Approximately 40 company managers, most of whom live in PPG plant communities, have been designated as local agents for the foundation.

Once a year agents recommend a budget for contributions in their communities to a screening committee for presentation to the foundation board.

Publications: Foundation Annual Report

Corporate Officials

Raymond W. LeBoeuf: director, chairman, chief executive officer B Chicago, IL 1946. ED Northwestern University BA (1967); University of Illinois MBA (1970). PRIM CORP EMPL director, chairman, chief executive officer: PPG Industries, Inc. CORP AFFIL chairman: Keeler & Long Inc.; director: Praxair Inc. NONPR AFFIL director: Magee-Women's Hospital; trustee: Robert Morris College; member: Financial Executives Institute.

Foundation Officials

Charles E. Bunch: director
Fred Denk: secretary
James C. Diggs: vice president
Jeffrey R. Gilbert: executive director
Susan M. Kreh: treasurer
Raymond W. LeBoeuf: director (see above)
Mary Ann Mackey: foundation accountant
David H. McClain: assistant secretary
Maurice V. Peconi: vice president B New Kensington, PA. ED Duquesne University MBA; Duquesne University BS. PRIM CORP EMPL vice president: PPG Industries Inc. NONPR AFFIL director: Pittsburgh Childrens Museum.
Sue Sloan: senior program officer
Kevin F. Sullivan: vice president B Baltimore, MD. ED Case Western Reserve University; Franklin and Marshall College. PRIM CORP EMPL vice president: PPG Industries Inc. NONPR AFFIL director: Society Plastics Industry.
Donna Lee Walker: vice president

Grants Analysis

Disclosure Period: calendar year ending 2002
Total Grants: $3,632,439*
Number of Grants: 819
Average Grant: $4,435
Highest Grant: $570,000
Lowest Grant: $100
Typical Range: $1,000 to $20,000
*Note: Giving excludes scholarship and matching gifts.

Recent Grants

Note: Grants derived from 2003 Form 990.
General

570,000	Pittsburgh Zoo & Pittsburgh Aquarium, Pittsburgh, PA
525,000	United Way, PA
445,940	National Merit Scholarship Corporation, Pittsburgh, PA
357,900	General Office C F
102,000	American Chemical Society
100,000	University of Pittsburgh, Pittsburgh, PA
80,000	United Way, Los Angeles, CA
70,000	Robert Morris University, PA
60,000	Alleg Conf Community Development, Pittsburgh, PA
55,000	Pittsburgh Public Theatre, Pittsburgh, PA

THE PRAIRIE FOUNDATION

Giving Contact

Benjamin L. Blake, Director
303 W. Wall Avenue, Suite 1901
Midland, TX 79701
Phone: (432)683-1777

Description

Founded: 1957
EIN: 756012458

Organization Type: Private Foundation
Giving Locations: CA: San Francisco metropolitan area; TX: Laredo, Midland, Odessa
Grant Types: General Support.

Donor Information

Founder: David Fasken Special Trust

Financial Summary

Total Giving: $374,000 (2002); $386,000 (2001)
Giving Analysis: Giving for 2002 includes: foundation grants to United Way ($25,000)
Assets: $8,795,331 (2002); $8,429,353 (2001)
Gifts Received: $500,000 (1995); $810,612 (1994).
Note: In 1995, contributions were received from Barbara Fasken.

Typical Recipients

Arts & Humanities: Ballet, Community Arts, Libraries, Music, Opera, Theater
Civic & Public Affairs: Botanical Gardens/Parks, Clubs, Civic & Public Affairs-General, Hispanic Affairs, Housing, Municipalities/Towns, Public Policy, Safety, Urban & Community Affairs, Zoos/Aquariums
Education: Business Education, Colleges & Universities, Education-General, Literacy, Private Education (Precollege)
Environment: Air/Water Quality, Environment-General
Health: AIDS/HIV, Cancer, Children's Health/Hospitals, Emergency/Ambulance Services, Eyes/Blindness, Health Organizations, Hospices, Hospitals, Medical Rehabilitation
Religion: Churches, Religion-General, Religious Organizations, Religious Welfare
Science: Scientific Labs
Social Services: At-Risk Youth, Big Brothers/Big Sisters, Camps, Child Abuse, Child Welfare, Community Service Organizations, Crime Prevention, Domestic Violence, Family Services, Food/Clothing Distribution, Homes, People with Disabilities, Recreation & Athletics, Scouts, Senior Services, Sexual Abuse, Social Services-General, Substance Abuse, United Funds/United Ways, Veterans, Youth Organizations

Application Procedures

Initial Contact: Request proposal summary form and guidelines.
Deadlines: None.

Restrictions

Does not support individuals, religious organizations for sectarian purposes, political or lobbying groups, or organizations outside operating areas.

Additional Information

Publications: Proposal Summary Form; Guidelines

Foundation Officials

Louis A. Bartha: secretary, director
Benjamin L. Blake: director
Norbert J. Dickman: vice president, director
Robert T. Dickson: president, director
Lynda James: secretary

Grants Analysis

Disclosure Period: calendar year ending 2002
Total Grants: $349,000*
Number of Grants: 39
Average Grant: $7,868*
Highest Grant: $50,000
Lowest Grant: $2,500
Typical Range: $2,500 to $15,000
*Note: Giving excludes United Way. Average grant figure excludes highest grant.

Recent Grants

Note: Grants derived from 2001 Form 990.
General

60,000	Boy Scouts of America, Midland, TX
25,000	Thacher School, Ojai, CA
25,000	United Way of Midland, Midland, TX
20,000	Four Winds Westward Ho Camp, Deer Harbor, WA
17,500	Friends of The Veterans, Monterey, CA
15,000	Casa de Amigos, Midland, TX
15,000	Safe Place, Austin, TX
12,500	LULAC Council 12, Laredo, TX
12,500	Congregation of St. John, Laredo, TX
12,500	Laredo Philharmonic Chorale, Laredo, TX

ABRA PRENTICE FOUNDATION

Giving Contact

Harris Trust & Savings Bank
Attn: T-PLIS-111/7W
PO Box 755
Chicago, IL 60690-0755
Phone: (312)461-7551

Description

Founded: 1980
EIN: 363092281
Organization Type: Private Foundation
Giving Locations: IL
Grant Types: Endowment, General Support, Multi-year/Continuing Support, Professorship.

Donor Information

Founder: Abra Prentice Wilkin

Financial Summary

Total Giving: $100,000 (2001)
Assets: $12,885,517 (2001)
Gifts Received: $600,864 (2001); $500,000 (1992).
Note: In 2001, contributions were received from Mrs. Abra P. Wilkin. In 1992, contributions were received from Abra Prentice Wilkin ($500,000).

Typical Recipients

Arts & Humanities: Historic Preservation, Libraries, Public Broadcasting
Education: Colleges & Universities, Medical Education, Private Education (Precollege), Science/Mathematics Education
Environment: Air/Water Quality
Health: Hospitals
Religion: Churches

Application Procedures

Initial Contact: The foundation has no formal grant application procedure or application form.
Deadlines: None.

Restrictions

Grants limited to organizations with 501 (c)(3) exempt status.

Foundation Officials

Robert F. Carr, III: director
Don Harold Reuben: secretary B Chicago, IL 1928. ED Northwestern University BS (1949); Northwestern University JD (1952). PRIM CORP EMPL counsel: Altheimer & Gray. CORP AFFIL director: Heitman Financial. NONPR AFFIL trustee: Northwestern University; member: Phi Eta Sigma; fellow: International Academy Trial Lawyers; member supervisory panel: Fed Defender Program; member: Illinois Bar Association; member: Chicago Bar Association; member: Beta Alpha Psi; member: Beta Gamma Sigma; member: American Law Institute; fellow: American College Trial Lawyers; member: American Judicature Society; fellow: American Bar Foundation; fellow: American Arbitration Association; member: American Bar Association. CLUB AFFIL Tavern Club; Union League Club; Spring Club; Mid-America Club; Order of Coif; Law Club; Chicago Club; Desert Riders Palm

Springs Club; Casino Club.
Jere Scott Senko: director
Abra Prentice Wilkin: president B 1942. ED Northwestern University. CORP AFFIL trustee: Northwestern Memorial Hosp.

Grants Analysis

Disclosure Period: calendar year ending 2001
Total Grants: $100,000
Number of Grants: 4
Highest Grant: $50,000
Lowest Grant: $10,000
Typical Range: $10,000 to $50,000

Recent Grants

Note: Grants derived from 2001 Form 990.
Library-Related
10,000   Newberry Library, Chicago, IL
General
50,000   St. Chrysostom's Church, Chicago, IL
25,000   WTTW Channel 11, Chicago, IL
15,000   Geneva Lake Water Safety Committee, Lake Geneva, WI

T. ROWE PRICE ASSOCIATES

Company Headquarters

PO Box 17630
Baltimore, MD 21297-1302
Phone: 800-225-5132
E-mail: info@troweprice.com
Web: http://www.troweprice.com

Company Description

Founded: 1937
Ticker: TROW
Exchange: NASDAQ
Employees: 2,587
SIC(s): 6282 Investment Advice.

Operating Locations

T. Rowe Price Associates (MD--Baltimore)

Nonmonetary Support

Type: In-kind Services
Note: NOT Value of in-kind giving activities and gifts is not tracked.
Volunteer Programs: The foundation sponsors several volunteer events per year, including: New Song Investment Academy Program, in partnership with a local inner-city school; Habitat for Humanity, employees volunteer on a weekly basis throughout the year to build or renovate a sponsored house; United Way Day of Caring, in conjunction with the corporate United Way campaign; Dollars for Doers, matches employee's volunteer hours with a financial donation; Susan G. Komen Race for the Cure, with over 350 employee participants; Dragon Boat Race, employees practice more than 800 hours to race for a local charity; Holiday Giving Program, with employee donations for the needy; and Red Cross Blood Drive, to encourage participation in blood donation.

T. Rowe Price Associates Foundation

Giving Contact

A. C. Hubbard, Jr., President
100 E. Pratt St., 8th Fl.
Baltimore, MD 21202
Phone: (410)345-3603
Fax: (410)345-2848

Description

EIN: 521231953
Organization Type: Corporate Foundation
Giving Locations: headquarters and operating communities.
Grant Types: Capital, Employee Matching Gifts, General Support, Multiyear/Continuing Support, Project.
Note: Employee matching gift ratio: 1:1.

Financial Summary

Total Giving: $3,170,000 (2002); $3,742,327 (2001).
Note: Contributes through corporate direct giving program and foundation.
Assets: $17,724,000 (2002); $25,226,034 (2001)
Gifts Received: $30,000 (2001); $6,045,925 (2000); $6,040,249 (1999). Note: Contributions are received from T. Rowe Price Group Inc.

Typical Recipients

Arts & Humanities: Arts Festivals, Arts Funds, Arts Institutes, Arts Outreach, Community Arts, Arts & Humanities-General, Historic Preservation, History & Archaeology, Libraries, Museums/Galleries, Music, Opera, Performing Arts, Public Broadcasting, Theater
Civic & Public Affairs: African American Affairs, Botanical Gardens/Parks, Business/Free Enterprise, Community Foundations, Economic Development, Employment/Job Training, Civic & Public Affairs-General, Housing, Inner-City Development, Minority Business, Philanthropic Organizations, Professional & Trade Associations, Public Policy, Safety, Urban & Community Affairs, Zoos/Aquariums
Education: Arts/Humanities Education, Business Education, Colleges & Universities, Continuing Education, Education Funds, Elementary Education (Private), Environmental Education, Education-General, Literacy, Medical Education, Minority Education, Private Education (Precollege), Public Education (Precollege), Religious Education, Secondary Education (Private), Special Education, Student Aid
Environment: Environment-General, Resource Conservation, Watershed
Health: Adolescent Health Issues, Emergency/Ambulance Services, Health Organizations, Heart, Hospitals, Mental Health, Single-Disease Health Associations
Religion: Dioceses, Jewish Causes, Religious Welfare
Science: Science Museums, Scientific Centers & Institutes, Scientific Research
Social Services: Child Abuse, Child Welfare, Community Service Organizations, Family Services, Food/Clothing Distribution, People with Disabilities, Recreation & Athletics, Scouts, Shelters/Homelessness, Social Services-General, United Funds/United Ways, Youth Organizations

Application Procedures

Initial Contact: Send a brief letter or proposal.
Application Requirements: Include a description of the organization, with a brief history; copy of IRS determination letter; latest audited financial report; current operating budget and sources of income; list of organization's board members; annual report; and number of paid and volunteer employees. Information regarding the particular program should include purpose and objectives; needs to be addressed; population served; plan of action and timeframe; qualifications of administrators; total funding required and projected sources; method of evaluation (measurement of success) and amount requested.
Deadlines: None.
Notes: All requests should be in writing.

Restrictions

Company does not support individuals, hospitals, healthcare providers, religious organizations for sectarian purposes, or political or lobbying groups. No support is given to organizations which are not 501(c)(3) public charities, or to United Way/Combined Health Agency organizations (although capital campaigns will be considered).

Foundation Officials

Stephen W. Boesel: vice president, secretary, treasurer, trustee B Niles, OH 1944. ED Baldwin-Wallace College (1968); University of Denver (1969). PRIM CORP EMPL managing director: T.Rowe Price Associates Inc. ADD CORP EMPL vice president: T.Rowe Price New Era Fund Inc.
Ann Allston Boyce: vice president, trustee
Meredith Callanan: trustee CORP AFFIL member corp. advisory board: Johns Hopkins Children's Center.
Albert C. Hubbard, Jr.: president
Mary J. Miller: vice president, trustee PRIM CORP EMPL vice president: T. Rowe Price. CORP AFFIL managing director: T. Rowe Price Associates Inc.
Vernon Reid: trustee NONPR AFFIL director: Baltimore Educational Scholarship Trust; director: Enoch Pratt Free Library.
Christine D. Stein: program director
William F. Wendler, II: vice president, trustee

Grants Analysis

Disclosure Period: calendar year ending 2002
Total Grants: $2,755,000*
Number of Grants: 217*
Average Grant: $12,500
Highest Grant: $100,000
Lowest Grant: $500
Typical Range: $500 to $100,000
*Note: Giving excludes United Way. Number of grants excludes matching gifts. Grants analysis provided by foundation.

Recent Grants

Note: Grants derived from 2003 Form 990.
Library-Related
22,835   Enoch Pratt Free Library, Baltimore, MD
General
275,000   United Way of Central Maryland, Baltimore, MD
269,410   T Rowe Price Program for Charitable Giving, Baltimore, MD
126,144   Baltimore Symphony Orchestra, Baltimore, MD
70,000   Morgan State University Foundation Inc., Baltimore, MD
63,155   Loyola College in Maryland, Baltimore, MD
58,683   Baltimore Zoo, Baltimore, MD
58,050   Maryland Institute College of Art, Baltimore, MD
53,929   St Pauls School, Brooklandville, MD
52,750   Baltimore Educational Scholarship Trust, Baltimore, MD
50,000   Archdiocese or Baltimore Catholic Schools, Baltimore, MD

LOUIS AND HAROLD PRICE FOUNDATION

Giving Contact

Rosemary L. Guidone, Executive Vice President
1371 Hecla Dr., Suite B-1
Louisville, CO 80027
Phone: (303)665-9201
Fax: (303)665-1027
E-mail: grantinquiry@pricefoundation.org
Web: http://www.pricefoundation.org

Description

Founded: 1951
EIN: 136121358
Organization Type: General Purpose Foundation

Giving Locations: CA: Los Angeles including the metropolitan area; NY: New York including the metropolitan area; Israel
Grant Types: Department, General Support, Matching, Multiyear/Continuing Support.

Donor Information
Founder: Established in 1951 by the late Louis Price and Harold Price.

Financial Summary
Total Giving: $3,395,547 (2003); $3,436,833 (2002); $3,359,743 (2001)
Assets: $79,929,446 (2003); $73,528,995 (2002); $82,700,172 (2001)

Typical Recipients
Arts & Humanities: Arts Associations & Councils, Libraries, Museums/Galleries, Music, Performing Arts, Public Broadcasting, Theater
Civic & Public Affairs: Botanical Gardens/Parks, Civil Rights, Community Foundations, Economic Development, Employment/Job Training, Ethnic Organizations, First Amendment Issues, Civic & Public Affairs-General, Housing, Law & Justice, Legal Aid, Municipalities/Towns, Philanthropic Organizations, Public Policy, Urban & Community Affairs, Women's Affairs
Education: Afterschool/Enrichment Programs, Arts/Humanities Education, Business Education, Colleges & Universities, Education Funds, Engineering/Technological Education, Education-General, Gifted & Talented Programs, Preschool Education, Private Education (Precollege), Public Education (Precollege), Religious Education, Social Sciences Education, Student Aid
Environment: Environment-General, Protection, Resource Conservation
Health: AIDS/HIV, Alzheimer's Disease, Arthritis, Cancer, Children's Health/Hospitals, Clinics/Medical Centers, Emergency/Ambulance Services, Eyes/Blindness, Health-General, Health Funds, Health Organizations, Heart, Hospitals, Kidney, Long-Term Care, Medical Rehabilitation, Medical Research, Mental Health, Multiple Sclerosis, Outpatient Health Care, Public Health, Research/Studies Institutes, Single-Disease Health Associations
International: Foreign Educational Institutions, International-General, Health Care/Hospitals, International Development, International Peace & Security Issues, International Relief Efforts, Missionary/Religious Activities
Religion: Churches, Jewish Causes, Religious Organizations, Religious Welfare, Synagogues/Temples
Social Services: Animal Protection, At-Risk Youth, Child Welfare, Community Centers, Community Service Organizations, Counseling, Crime Prevention, Delinquency & Criminal Rehabilitation, Emergency Relief, Family Services, Food/Clothing Distribution, People with Disabilities, Recreation & Athletics, Senior Services, Shelters/Homelessness, Social Services-General, United Funds/United Ways, Youth Organizations

Application Procedures
Initial Contact: Send a brief letter of inquiry. limited to two pages.
Deadlines: None.

Restrictions
The foundation does not give support for building funds, capital campaigns, or endowments; or to large, public charities.

Foundation Officials
George Asch: trustee B 1937. ED Columbia University BA (1959). PRIM CORP EMPL president: Ashton Group Inc. ADD CORP EMPL vice president: Seifert Gray & Co. Inc.
Lisa Beshkov: trustee
Rosemary Guidone: executive vice president, secretary, treasurer, trustee

Linda Vitti Herbst: trustee
Timothy Jones: president, trustee
Pauline Price: chairman, trustee
Bonnie Vitti: trustee

Grants Analysis
Disclosure Period: calendar year ending 2003
Total Grants: $3,395,547
Number of Grants: 211
Average Grant: $14,265*
Highest Grant: $400,000
Lowest Grant: $100
Typical Range: $1,000 to $25,000
*Note: Average grant figure excludes highest grant.

Recent Grants
Note: Grants derived from 2003 Form 990.
General

400,000	Price Institute for Entrepreneurial Studies, New York, NY
225,000	United Jewish Fund of Greater Los Angeles, Los Angeles, CA
200,000	University of California, Los Angeles, CA -- in support of Harold Price center for entrepreneurial studies
150,000	Jules Stein Eye Institute, Los Angeles, CA -- retina research fund
125,000	University of Colorado Entrepreneurship Center for Music, Boulder, CO
100,000	Radiation and Public Health Project, New York, NY -- to support programs like baby teeth study & baby boomer cancer research
100,000	University of Colorado Children's Learning Center, Boulder, CO -- Pauline Price initiatives
100,000	University of Colorado Herbst Program of Humanities, Boulder, CO
75,000	University of California, Berkeley, CA -- commitment and enhanced support for entrepreneurship
75,000	University of Colorado Children's Learning Center, Boulder, CO -- Pauline Price program

LUCIEN B. AND KATHERINE E. PRICE FOUNDATION

Giving Contact
Dr. Edward P. Flanagan, Secretary
PO Box 790
Manchester, CT 06040
Phone: (203)627-2335

Description
Founded: 1922
EIN: 066068868
Organization Type: Private Foundation
Giving Locations: CT; VT
Grant Types: General Support.

Financial Summary
Total Giving: $202,000 (2001)
Assets: $4,787,246 (2001)

Typical Recipients
Arts & Humanities: Libraries
Civic & Public Affairs: Civic & Public Affairs-General, Professional & Trade Associations, Urban & Community Affairs
Education: Colleges & Universities, Education-General, Legal Education, Preschool Education, Private Education (Precollege), Public Education (Precollege), Religious Education, Science/Mathematics Education, Secondary Education (Private), Second-

ary Education (Public), Student Aid
Environment: Wildlife Protection
Health: Cancer, Children's Health/Hospitals, Hospitals, Medical Rehabilitation, Nursing Services
International: Health Care/Hospitals, International Affairs, International Relief Efforts
Religion: Churches, Dioceses, Religion-General, Missionary Activities (Domestic), Religious Organizations, Religious Welfare, Seminaries
Social Services: At-Risk Youth, Camps, Community Service Organizations, Food/Clothing Distribution, Scouts, Social Services-General, Youth Organizations

Application Procedures
Initial Contact: The foundation requests applications be made in writing.
Application Requirements: Include purpose of funds sought.
Deadlines: None.

Foundation Officials
Morgan P. Ames: treasurer
Rev. Colin Bircumshaw: vice president
Rev. Colin Bircumshow: director
Rev. Joseph L. Federal: director
Rev. J. T. Fitzgerald: vice president
Dr. Edward P. Flanagan: secretary
Sheila Flanagan: treasurer
Rev. Francis V. Krukowski: president

Grants Analysis
Disclosure Period: calendar year ending 2001
Total Grants: $202,000
Number of Grants: 32
Average Grant: $3,935*
Highest Grant: $80,000
Lowest Grant: $500
Typical Range: $1,000 to $5,000
*Note: Average grant figure excludes highest grant.

Recent Grants
Note: Grants derived from 2001 Form 990.
Library-Related

8,000	St. James School Library Fund, Baltimore, MD

General

80,000	Diocese of Salt Lake City, Salt Lake City, UT
24,000	St. Francis Hospital and Medical Center, Hartford, CT
12,000	St. James School, Baltimore, MD
10,000	Hesburg CCFM
10,000	Holy Cross Brothers
10,000	St. Joseph Catholic, Macon, GA
4,000	Holy Apostle Seminary
4,000	Holy Family Retreat House
4,000	Mercyknoll, West Hartford, CT
4,000	St. James School, Baltimore, MD

PRIDDY FOUNDATION

Giving Contact
David Wolverton, Trustee
807 8th Street
City National Building, Suite 1010
Wichita Falls, TX 76301
Phone: (940)723-8720
Fax: (940)723-8656
E-mail: info@priddyfdn.org
Web: http://www.priddyfdn.org

Description
Founded: 1963
EIN: 756029882
Organization Type: Private Foundation
Giving Locations: OK: Southern OK; TX: Northern Texas, Wichita Falls

Grant Types: Capital, Emergency, General Support, Matching, Multiyear/Continuing Support, Project.

Donor Information

Founder: Established in 1963 by the late Ashley H. Priddy, Robert T. Priddy, the late Swannanoa H. Priddy, and the late Walter M. Priddy.

Financial Summary

Total Giving: $3,465,078 (2003); $3,600,000 (2002); $3,300,000 (2001 approx)
Assets: $80,158,711 (2003); $80,000,000 (2002); $75,000,000 (2001)
Gifts Received: $9,000,000 (2001); $10,478,443 (1999); $18,741,041 (1997). Note: In fiscal 1997 and 1999, contributions were received from Mr. and Mrs. Robert Priddy.

Typical Recipients

Arts & Humanities: Arts Centers, Ballet, Community Arts, Film & Video, Historic Preservation, Libraries, Museums/Galleries, Music, Opera, Performing Arts, Public Broadcasting
Civic & Public Affairs: Community Foundations, Economic Development, Employment/Job Training, Civic & Public Affairs-General, Housing, Law & Justice, Legal Aid, Nonprofit Management, Parades/Festivals, Urban & Community Affairs
Education: Colleges & Universities, Community & Junior Colleges, Education Associations, Education Funds, Education Reform, Education-General, Leadership Training, Literacy, Medical Education, Private Education (Precollege), Public Education (Precollege), Secondary Education (Private), Student Aid
Environment: Environment-General
Health: Alzheimer's Disease, Children's Health/Hospitals, Clinics/Medical Centers, Emergency/Ambulance Services, Health-General, Health Funds, Health Organizations, Hospices, Hospitals, Medical Rehabilitation, Mental Health, Prenatal Health Issues
International: International Relations
Religion: Churches, Ministries, Religious Organizations, Religious Welfare
Social Services: At-Risk Youth, Big Brothers/Big Sisters, Child Welfare, Community Centers, Community Service Organizations, Counseling, Crime Prevention, Domestic Violence, Emergency Relief, Family Services, Food/Clothing Distribution, People with Disabilities, Scouts, Senior Services, Shelters/Homelessness, Special Olympics, Substance Abuse, United Funds/United Ways, Volunteer Services, YMCA/YWCA/YMHA/YWHA, Youth Organizations

Application Procedures

Initial Contact: Request application from foundation.
Application Requirements: If a project is approved for consideration, a more detailed application is required. Include proof of tax-exempt status as defined under 501 (c)(3) of the IRS code. The applicant must be considered "not a private foundation" within the meaning of Section 509 (a) of the code. In most cases a site visit and application review session will be scheduled.
Deadlines: February 15 and August 15, for preliminary applications and March 15 and September 15 for grant applications.
Review Process: The board of the foundation meets in May and November, applicants will be notified by mail immediately following the board meeting.

Restrictions

Does not support individuals. The foundation does not normally fund annual operating budget on an ongoing basis, research, endowments, lobbying activities, individual scholarships, or specific church denominations or their projects (with exception of the first Presbyterian Church of Wichita Falls and other Presbyterian sponsored organizations).

Additional Information

Publications: Program Policy Statement; Application Form; Guidelines; annual report

Foundation Officials

Rick Boone: trustee
Bill Daniel: trustee
Dr. David Flack: trustee
Ralph Harvey, III: trustee
Phyllis Hiraki: trustee
Berneice R. Leath: secretary, treasurer
Martin Litteken: trustee
Nancy Marks: trustee
Betsy Priddy: adv director
Randy Priddy: adv director
Robert T. Priddy: trustee emeritus
Ruby N. Priddy: advisory trustee
Ken Telg: trustee
Julia Whitmire: trustee
David Wolverton: trustee
David Wolverton: president PRIM NONPR EMPL United Regional Health Care System.

Grants Analysis

Disclosure Period: calendar year ending 2003
Total Grants: $3,465,078
Number of Grants: 80
Average Grant: $31,604*
Highest Grant: $500,000
Lowest Grant: $1,000
Typical Range: $10,000 to $50,000
*Note: Average grant figure excludes two highest grants ($1,000,000).

Recent Grants

Note: Grants derived from 2003 Form 990.
General

500,000	United Regional Health Care Foundation, Wichita Falls, TX -- funding for master facility plan
500,000	Young Men's Christian Association of Wichita Falls, Wichita Falls, TX -- toward capital campaign
200,000	Midwestern State University, Wichita Falls, TX -- toward MSU/WFMAC merger
200,000	Midwestern State University, Wichita Falls, TX -- toward MSU/WFMAC merger
167,159	North Central Texas Community Health Care Center Inc., Wichita Falls, TX -- toward provider and specialty care
124,000	North Central Texas Community Health Care Center Inc., Wichita Falls, TX -- toward expanded dental practice
100,000	Midwestern State University, Wichita Falls, TX -- funding for honors program scholarship
100,000	National Center for Educational Accountability, Austin, TX -- toward best practices study and interactive website
100,000	Wichita Falls Independent School District, Wichita Falls, TX -- toward breakthrough to literacy program
90,000	Camp Summit Inc., Dallas, TX -- toward capital campaign

PRINCIPAL FINANCIAL GROUP

Company Headquarters

Des Moines, IA
Web: http://www.principal.com

Company Description

Founded: 1879
Ticker: PFG
Exchange: NYSE
Revenue: US$8.755 billion (2004)
Profit: US$825.6 million (2004)
Employees: 14976 (2003)
Fortune Rank: 253, per FORTUNE Magazine's list of 500 Largest U.S. Corporations (2004).

SIC(s): 6159 Miscellaneous Business Credit Institutions, 6282 Investment Advice, 6311 Life Insurance, 6321 Accident & Health Insurance.

Operating Locations

Principal Financial Group (IA--Des Moines, Mason City, Waterloo; NE--Grand Island)
Note: Principal Financial Group and subsidiaries operate throughout the USA.

Nonmonetary Support

Type: Donated Equipment
Contact: Steve Thilges, Community Relations Associate
Note: Nonmonetary support is provided by the company to local organizations only. Support in 1997 was valued at $710,145.

Principal Financial Group Foundation, Inc.

Giving Contact

Laura Sauser, Contributions Consultant
711 High Street
Des Moines, IA 50392-0001
Phone: (515)247-5091
Fax: (515)246-5475
Web: http://www.principal.com/about/giving/index.htm

Alternate Contact

Lori Hess

Description

Founded: 1987
EIN: 421312301
Organization Type: Corporate Foundation
Giving Locations: IA: Des Moines occasional nationally and internationally; operating locations.
Grant Types: Capital, Employee Matching Gifts, General Support, Project, Scholarship.
Note: Employee matching gift ratio: 1 to 1 to higher education and United Way.

Financial Summary

Total Giving: $5,896,289 (2002). Note: Contributes through corporate direct giving program and foundation.
Assets: $58,315,597 (2002)
Gifts Received: $70,000,030 (1998); $9,999,963 (1997)

Typical Recipients

Arts & Humanities: Arts Centers, Ballet, Community Arts, Dance, Arts & Humanities-General, History & Archaeology, Libraries, Museums/Galleries, Music, Opera, Performing Arts, Public Broadcasting, Theater
Civic & Public Affairs: Botanical Gardens/Parks, Business/Free Enterprise, Civil Rights, Community Foundations, Economic Development, Employment/Job Training, Civic & Public Affairs-General, Housing, Legal Aid, Municipalities/Towns, Parades/Festivals, Urban & Community Affairs, Women's Affairs, Zoos/Aquariums
Education: Afterschool/Enrichment Programs, Agricultural Education, Business Education, Business-School Partnerships, Colleges & Universities, Community & Junior Colleges, Education Funds, Elementary Education (Public), Faculty Development, Education-General, International Studies, Literacy, Minority Education, Preschool Education, Private Education (Precollege), Public Education (Precollege), Science/Mathematics Education, Student Aid
Environment: Environment-General, Wildlife Protection
Health: AIDS/HIV, Alzheimer's Disease, Cancer, Children's Health/Hospitals, Diabetes, Emergency/Ambulance Services, Health-General, Health Policy/

Cost Containment, Health Funds, Health Organizations, Hospices, Medical Research, Mental Health, Respiratory, Single-Disease Health Associations
International: International Affairs, International Peace & Security Issues, International Relations
Religion: Ministries, Religious Organizations, Religious Welfare
Science: Scientific Centers & Institutes
Social Services: Animal Protection, At-Risk Youth, Big Brothers/Big Sisters, Child Welfare, Community Service Organizations, Day Care, Family Planning, Family Services, Food/Clothing Distribution, People with Disabilities, Recreation & Athletics, Scouts, Senior Services, Shelters/Homelessness, Social Services-General, Special Olympics, Substance Abuse, United Funds/United Ways, Veterans, Volunteer Services, YMCA/YWCA/YMHA/YWHA, Youth Organizations

Application Procedures

Initial Contact: Contact the foundation to receive a form to return with the proposal (or obtain from the foundation's web site), then submit proposal (include ten copies with the original).
Application Requirements: Cover letter outlining amount requested, purpose of funds sought, and anticipated budget; an itemized budget including current and anticipated funds, sources of income, contributions received to date, fundraising expenses, other expected expenses, most recently audited financial statement, and current IRS tax filing; background information on the organization including goals, geographic scope, number of paid employees and total salary expense, and amount of volunteer involvement; other corporations, government agencies or foundations being approached for funding; names and business affiliations of organization's officers and board of directors (including advisory boards or committees relevant to proposal) and frequency of scheduled board meetings; need for the funding and method of program/project evaluation; proof of tax-exempt status; and evaluation of any previous years' funding that has been received from the Foundation.
Deadlines: March 1 for Health & Human Services, June 1 for Education, September 1 for Arts and Culture, and December 1 for Recreation and Tourism.
Decision Notification: Review process generally takes six to ten weeks.
Notes: Original application must be sent along with nine copies for review. One copy of the audited financial statements and annual report need to be submitted with grant proposal.

Restrictions

Does not support athletic, fraternal, social or veterans' organizations; conference, seminar, or festival participation; individuals; endowments or memorials; political or lobbying groups; trade, industry, or professional organizations; sectarian, religious and denominational organizations; fellowships; individual K-12 schools; libraries; goodwill advertising; capital fund drives for hospitals or health care facilities; grantmaking bodies (except for United Way and independent college funds); private foundations; organizations whose activities are mostly international; tax-supported organizations; scholarships, fellowships, or internships through school; or operating expenses of programs receiving United Way support. whose activities are mostly international; social organizations tax-supported organizations; or operating expenses of programs receiving United Way support.

Additional Information

Grant renewals are not automatic, and the foundation expects an annual report from all grant recipients. The foundation was formerly known as the Principal Foundation.
Publications: Guidelines; Social Responsibility Report

Grants Analysis

Disclosure Period: calendar year ending 2002
Total Grants: $5,896,289*
Number of Grants: 1193
Average Grant: $4,942
Highest Grant: $305,270
Lowest Grant: $1
Typical Range: $20,000 to $50,000
*Note: Giving includes matching gifts; United Way.

Recent Grants

Note: Grants derived from 2003 Form 990.
Library-Related

300,000	Public Library of Des Moines Foundation, Des Moines, IA

General

333,365	United Way of Central Iowa, Des Moines, IA
281,105	United Way of Central Iowa, Des Moines, IA
184,828	Science Center of Iowa, Des Moines, IA
135,000	Drake University, Des Moines, IA
80,000	Polk County Housing Trust Fund, Washington, DC
71,732	Greater Des Moines Community Foundation, Des Moines, IA
71,732	Greater Des Moines Community Foundation, Des Moines, IA
70,000	Iowa College Foundation, Des Moines, IA
62,500	Animal Rescue League of Iowa Inc., Des Moines, IA
50,000	Orchard Place, Des Moines, IA

PROCTER & GAMBLE COMPANY, COSMETICS DIV.

Company Headquarters

Hunt Valley, MD
Web: http://www.pg.com

Company Description

Former Name: Noxell Corp.
Revenue: US$43.377 billion (2003)
SIC(s): 2844 Toilet Preparations.
Parent Company: Procter & Gamble Co., Cincinnati, OH, United States

Operating Locations

Procter & Gamble Co. Cosmetics Division (MD--Baltimore, Cockeysville)

Nonmonetary Support

Note: Employee matching gift ratio: 2 to 1.

Procter & Gamble Cosmetics Foundation

Giving Contact

Carroll A. Bodie, Treasurer
11050 York Rd.
Hunt Valley, MD 21030
Phone: (410)527-5703
Fax: (410)316-8025

Description

Founded: 1951
EIN: 526041435
Organization Type: Corporate Foundation
Giving Locations: MD: Baltimore metropolitan area some support to nationally organizations with local chapters; NY: New York City.
Grant Types: Capital, Challenge, Employee Match-

ing Gifts, Endowment, General Support, Research, Scholarship.

Donor Information

Founder: Noxell Corp.

Financial Summary

Total Giving: $341,681 (fiscal year ending June 30, 2003); $471,123 (fiscal 2002); $284,279 (fiscal 2001). Note: Contributes through foundation only.
Giving Analysis: Giving for fiscal 2001 includes: foundation grants to United Way ($8,500); foundation grants ($275,779)
Assets: $1,298,436 (fiscal 2003); $1,501,110 (fiscal 2002); $1,732,760 (fiscal 2001)
Gifts Received: $200,000 (fiscal 2003); $400,000 (fiscal 2002); $210,000 (fiscal 2000). Note: Contributions are received from Noxell Corp.

Typical Recipients

Arts & Humanities: Arts Associations & Councils, Arts Centers, Arts Festivals, Arts Funds, Arts Institutes, Dance, Historic Preservation, Libraries, Museums/Galleries, Music, Opera, Performing Arts, Public Broadcasting, Theater, Visual Arts
Civic & Public Affairs: African American Affairs, Business/Free Enterprise, Chambers of Commerce, Civil Rights, Clubs, Community Foundations, Economic Development, Economic Policy, Employment/Job Training, Ethnic Organizations, Civic & Public Affairs-General, Hispanic Affairs, Housing, Inner-City Development, Law & Justice, Minority Business, Municipalities/Towns, Nonprofit Management, Philanthropic Organizations, Professional & Trade Associations, Safety, Urban & Community Affairs, Women's Affairs, Zoos/Aquariums
Education: Afterschool/Enrichment Programs, Arts/Humanities Education, Business Education, Business-School Partnerships, Colleges & Universities, Community & Junior Colleges, Economic Education, Education Associations, Education Funds, Education Reform, Elementary Education (Private), Elementary Education (Public), Engineering/Technological Education, Education-General, Health & Physical Education, Literacy, Medical Education, Minority Education, Private Education (Precollege), Religious Education, Science/Mathematics Education, Secondary Education (Private), Secondary Education (Public), Student Aid
Environment: Environment-General, Protection, Wildlife Protection
Health: AIDS/HIV, Cancer, Children's Health/Hospitals, Clinics/Medical Centers, Diabetes, Emergency/Ambulance Services, Health Organizations, Heart, Hospitals, Medical Rehabilitation, Mental Health, Nursing Services, Public Health, Respiratory, Single-Disease Health Associations
International: Foreign Arts Organizations, Foreign Educational Institutions, International Affairs, International Relations
Religion: Jewish Causes
Science: Science Museums, Scientific Centers & Institutes, Scientific Research
Social Services: At-Risk Youth, Child Welfare, Community Centers, Community Service Organizations, Crime Prevention, Domestic Violence, Emergency Relief, Family Services, Food/Clothing Distribution, People with Disabilities, Recreation & Athletics, Scouts, Senior Services, Shelters/Homelessness, Social Services-General, Substance Abuse, United Funds/United Ways, Volunteer Services, YMCA/YWCA/YMHA/YWHA, Youth Organizations

Application Procedures

Initial Contact: Send a brief letter of inquiry and a proposal.
Application Requirements: Include a description of organization with background and history, amount requested, purpose of funds sought, other contributors, two most recently audited financial statement, current budget, list of officers and directors, and proof of tax-exempt status.

Deadlines: None.
Review Process: The board meets semiannually, in May and November.

Restrictions

Does not support individuals or political or lobbying groups.

Foundation Officials

Carroll A. Bodie: vice president, secretary, treasurer
Cheryl G. Hudgins: vice president
Marc S. Pritchard: president PRIM CORP EMPL general manager: Proctor & Gamble Co. Cosmetics & Fragrance Division. CORP AFFIL vice president: Procter & Gamble Co.

Grants Analysis

Disclosure Period: fiscal year ending June 30, 2003
Total Grants: $326,479*
Number of Grants: 100
Average Grant: $3,265
Highest Grant: $30,250
Lowest Grant: $25
Typical Range: $1,000 to $10,000
***Note:** Giving excludes scholarship; United Way.

Recent Grants

Note: Grants derived from fiscal 2004 Form 990.
General

45,000	Billie Holiday Vocal Competition Center Stage, Baltimore, MD
33,000	Ruxton Country School, Owings Mills, MD
30,000	Baltimore School for the Arts, Baltimore, MD
30,000	YMCA of Central Maryland, Baltimore, MD
27,500	Independent College Fund of Maryland, Baltimore, MD
22,500	GBMC, Baltimore, MD
20,000	Baltimore & Ohio Railroad Museum Inc., Baltimore, MD
20,000	National Aquarium in Baltimore, Baltimore, MD
15,000	American Cancer Society, Atlanta, GA
15,000	Baltimore Symphony Orchestra, Baltimore, MD

MATTINA R. PROCTOR FOUNDATION

Giving Contact

Alvin S. Hochberg, Trustee
c/o Broude & Hochberg
75 Federal Street, Suite 1310
Boston, MA 02110-1904
Phone: (617)748-5100
Fax: (617)748-5100
E-mail: law@broude.com

Description

Founded: 1991
EIN: 111067014
Organization Type: Private Foundation
Giving Locations: ME; MA
Grant Types: General Support, Research.

Donor Information

Founder: Established in 1991 by Mattina R. Proctor.

Financial Summary

Total Giving: $331,000 (2002); $383,500 (2001)
Assets: $4,946,537 (2002); $6,468,211 (2001)
Gifts Received: $510,670 (2000); $1,514,792 (1998); $500,000 (1996). Note: In 1998, contributions were received from Mattina R. Proctor Revocable Trust.

Typical Recipients

Arts & Humanities: Arts & Humanities-General, Libraries, Music, Opera
Education: Colleges & Universities, Education-General, Health & Physical Education, Private Education (Precollege)
Health: AIDS/HIV, Cancer, Children's Health/Hospitals, Clinics/Medical Centers, Diabetes, Emergency/Ambulance Services, Eyes/Blindness, Health-General, Health Organizations, Heart, Hospitals, Medical Research, Nursing Services
International: International Affairs
Religion: Churches
Science: Science Museums
Social Services: Emergency Relief, Food/Clothing Distribution, Recreation & Athletics, Senior Services, Social Services-General

Application Procedures

Initial Contact: Send a brief letter of inquiry.
Application Requirements: Include a description of organization, purpose of funds sought, and proof of tax-exempt status.
Deadlines: None.

Foundation Officials

Alvin S. Hochberg: trustee
Mattina R. Proctor: trustee

Grants Analysis

Disclosure Period: calendar year ending 2002
Total Grants: $331,000
Number of Grants: 20
Average Grant: $7,579*
Highest Grant: $187,000
Lowest Grant: $1,500
Typical Range: $2,500 to $15,000
***Note:** Average grant figure excludes highest grant.

Recent Grants

Note: Grants derived from 2001 Form 990.
General

60,000	Barbara Bush Children's Hospital Pediatric Lead Poison Screening Project, ME
50,000	Maine Health, ME -- telemedicine
50,000	MGH Pediatric Hematology/Oncology, Boston, MA
30,000	MGH Cancer Center, Boston, MA -- DNA sequencer
25,000	Boston Lyric Opera, Boston, MA
25,000	Joslin Diabetes Center, Boston, MA
25,000	MGH Cancer Center, Boston, MA
25,000	MGH Cancer Center, Boston, MA -- TB Project
20,000	University of New England, Biddeford, ME
17,000	Tatra Foundation -- recording of Shakespeare songs

MORTIMER R. PROCTOR TRUST

Giving Contact

c/o Chittenden Bank
PO Box 820
2 Burlington Sq.
Burlington, VT 05402
Phone: (802)658-4000

Description

Founded: 1978
EIN: 036020099
Organization Type: Private Foundation
Giving Locations: VT: Proctor
Grant Types: Emergency, Operating Expenses, Project.

Financial Summary

Gifts Received: $29 (1995); $48,337 (1994). Note: In 1995, contributions were received from Proctor Hospital Davis Trust Fund.

Typical Recipients

Arts & Humanities: History & Archaeology, Libraries, Music
Civic & Public Affairs: Community Foundations, Civic & Public Affairs-General, Housing, Municipalities/Towns, Safety, Urban & Community Affairs
Education: Business Education, Elementary Education (Private), Elementary Education (Public), International Studies, Private Education (Precollege), Public Education (Precollege), Religious Education, Science/Mathematics Education, Secondary Education (Public)
Religion: Churches, Religious Organizations
Social Services: Child Welfare, Community Service Organizations, Crime Prevention, Emergency Relief, Food/Clothing Distribution, People with Disabilities, Recreation & Athletics, Scouts, Youth Organizations

Application Procedures

Initial Contact: The foundation requests applications be made in writing.
Deadlines: None.

Additional Information

Publications: Annual Report
Trust(s): Chittenden Bank

Grants Analysis

Disclosure Period: calendar year ending 2000
Total Grants: $210,084
Number of Grants: 12
Average Grant: $9,211*
Highest Grant: $108,758
Typical Range: $5,000 to $20,000
***Note:** Average grant figure excludes highest grant.

Recent Grants

Note: Grants derived from 2001 Form 990.
General

85,975	Proctor High School, Proctor, VT -- fund special programs
63,012	Proctor Elementary School, Proctor, VT
24,000	Proctor Volunteer Fire Department, Proctor, VT -- purchase equipment
22,730	Town of Proctor, Proctor, VT -- support mapping, pool, skate rink
10,580	St. Dominic's Church, Proctor, VT -- classroom dividers and handicap bath rooms
9,575	Union Church of Proctor, Proctor, VT
3,000	Proctor Community Concerns Council, Proctor, VT
1,900	Proctor Free Library, Proctor, VT -- purchase books
1,200	Children's Center Union Proctor, Proctor, VT
1,110	RSVP, Proctor, VT -- exercise program

PROGRESS ENERGY INC.

Company Headquarters

410 S. Wilmington St.
Raleigh, NC 27601-1748
Web: http://www.progress-energy.com

Company Description

Founded: 2000
Ticker: PGN
Exchange: NYSE
Former Name: Carolina Power & Light Co.;
Acquired: Florida Progress (2000); Florida Power Corp.;
Also Known As: Progress Energy Carolinas, Inc..

Revenue: US$9.772 billion (2004)
Profit: US$759 million (2004)
Employees: 15300 (2003)
Fortune Rank: 229, per FORTUNE Magazine's list of 500 Largest U.S. Corporations (2004).
SIC(s): 4911 Electric Services.

Operating Locations

Carolina Power & Light Co. (DC--Washington); Carolina Power & Light Co. (SC; TN--Newport)

Nonmonetary Support

Value: $1,010,000 (2000 approx)
Type: Donated Equipment; In-kind Services

Progress Energy Foundation

Giving Contact

Tammy S. Brown, Secretary
Progress Energy
PO Box 1551
Raleigh, NC 27602-1551
Phone: (919)546-4112
Fax: (919)546-4338
Web: http://www.progress-energy.com/community/

Description

EIN: 561720636
Organization Type: Corporate Foundation
Former Name: CP&L Foundation.
Giving Locations: principally near operating locations and to national organizations.
Grant Types: Capital, Conference/Seminar, Department, Employee Matching Gifts, General Support, Matching, Project.

Financial Summary

Total Giving: $9,738,662 (2003); $9,441,876 (2002); $7,340,106 (2001). Note: Contributes through corporate direct giving program and foundation.
Giving Analysis: Giving for 2002 includes: foundation grants to United Way ($37,684)
Assets: $755,173 (2003); $5,436,475 (2002); $8,593,262 (2001)
Gifts Received: $5,000,000 (2003); $5,844,402 (2002); $14,559,252 (2001). Note: In 2002 and 2003, contributions were received from Progress Energy Co. In 2001, contributions were received from Progress Energy Co. ($9,900,000) and Florida Progress Foundation ($4,659,252).

Typical Recipients

Arts & Humanities: Arts Associations & Councils, Arts Centers, Arts Funds, Ballet, Film & Video, Arts & Humanities-General, Historic Preservation, History & Archaeology, Libraries, Museums/Galleries, Music, Performing Arts, Public Broadcasting, Theater
Civic & Public Affairs: African American Affairs, Botanical Gardens/Parks, Business/Free Enterprise, Chambers of Commerce, Community Foundations, Economic Development, Civic & Public Affairs-General, Housing, Law & Justice, Municipalities/Towns, Nonprofit Management, Parades/Festivals, Professional & Trade Associations, Urban & Community Affairs, Zoos/Aquariums
Education: Afterschool/Enrichment Programs, Agricultural Education, Business Education, Business-School Partnerships, Colleges & Universities, Community & Junior Colleges, Education Associations, Education Funds, Engineering/Technological Education, Faculty Development, Education-General, Legal Education, Minority Education, Private Education (Precollege), Public Education (Precollege), School Volunteerism, Science/Mathematics Education, Student Aid
Environment: Air/Water Quality, Energy, Environment-General, Protection, Resource Conservation
Health: Emergency/Ambulance Services, Health

Funds, Health Organizations, Hospitals, Single-Disease Health Associations
Science: Science Museums
Social Services: At-Risk Youth, Child Abuse, Child Welfare, Community Service Organizations, Delinquency & Criminal Rehabilitation, Domestic Violence, Emergency Relief, Family Services, Food/Clothing Distribution, Recreation & Athletics, Scouts, Substance Abuse, United Funds/United Ways, Volunteer Services, YMCA/YWCA/YMHA/YWHA, Youth Organizations

Application Procedures

Initial Contact: Call or write for brochure.
Application Requirements: Complete applications will include a cover letter signed by the president, director, or equivalent official of the institution; proof of tax-exempt status; executive summary of planned activities; narrative section with clear a description of organization and overall strategy of proposed activities; budget for the proposed project; and additional institutional information and financial data.
Deadlines: February 1, May 1, August 1, and November 1.
Review Process: Foundation's board of directors meets in March, June, September, and December to consider and award grants. All applicants will be notified of decisions within 15 days of board meeting.
Notes: Grantees must submit written progress reports.

Restrictions

Does not support individuals, religious organizations for sectarian purposes, or goodwill advertising.

Additional Information

Progress Energy was formed in 2000 when CP&L Energy expanded into Florida and acquired Florida Progress.

Corporate Officials

William Cavanaugh, III: chairman, president, chief executive officer supply B New Orleans, LA 1939. ED Tulane University BSME (1961). PRIM CORP EMPL chairman, president, chief executive officer: Carolina Power & Light Co. NONPR AFFIL board of visitors: University of North Carolina Flagler School of Business; chairman: World Association of Nuclear Operators; member: National Academy of Engineering; director: Research Triangle Foundation.
Glen Harden: executive vice president, chief financial officer B Falfurrias, TX 1951. ED Tulane University (1973); Tulane University (1975). PRIM CORP EMPL executive vice president, chief financial officer: Carolina Power & Light Co.
Robert B. McGehee: executive vice president, general counsel B Vicksburg, MS 1943. ED United States Naval Academy (1966); University of Texas JD (1973). PRIM CORP EMPL president chief operating officer: Progress Energy. NONPR AFFIL board of directors: US Chamber of Commerce; director: World Association of Nuclear Operators; director: Institute of Nuclear Power Operations; vice chairman, director: Nuclear Energy Institute; director: Edison Electric Institute; member: Florida Council of 100; vice chairman: Atomic Energy Committee, American Bar Association; member: Business Roundtable.
William Stanley Orser: executive vice president energy supply B New London, CT 1945. ED United States Naval Academy BS (1966); United States Naval Academy MS (1971). PRIM CORP EMPL group president: Progress Energy. NONPR AFFIL member: National Nuclear Accrediting board; member: Nuclear Energy Institute.

Giving Program Officials

Tammy S. Brown: manager community relations PRIM CORP EMPL manager corp. community relations: Carolina Power & Light Co.

Foundation Officials

Tammy S. Brown: secretary (see above)
William Cavanaugh, III: president, director (see above)
Fred N. Day, IV: vice president, director ED Mars Hill College BS. NONPR AFFIL director: North Carolina Engineering Foundation; chairman: North Carolina Zoological Society.
H. William Habermeyer, Jr.: vice president, director ED George Washington University MS; US Naval Academy BA. CORP AFFIL director: Raymond James Financial. NONPR AFFIL chairman: Tampa Bay Partnership; trustee: University of South Florida; director: Suncoast Boys & Girls Clubs; director: Pinellas Education Foundation; director: Salvador Dali Museum; director: Florida Chamber of Commerce; director: Florida Council on Economic Education; director: Enterprise Florida Inc.; trustee: Eckerd College.
William D. Johnson: vice president, director ED Duke University BA; University of NC JD.
Robert B. McGehee: vice president, director (see above)
William Stanley Orser: vice president, director (see above)
Peter M. Scott, III: treasurer, director ED University of NC MBA; University of NC BS. NONPR AFFIL director: North Carolina Museum of Art Foundation.
Robert M. Williams: assistant secretary

Grants Analysis

Disclosure Period: calendar year ending 2003
Total Grants: $8,870,361*
Number of Grants: 271
Average Grant: $28,841*
Highest Grant: $441,000
Lowest Grant: $862
Typical Range: $10,000 to $50,000
*Note: Giving excludes United Way; scholarship. Average grant figure excludes three highest grants ($1,141,000).

Recent Grants

Note: Grants derived from 2003 Form 990.
General

600,000	Public School Forum of North Carolina, Raleigh, NC
350,000	Carolina Ballet Inc., Raleigh, NC
350,000	Carolina Ballet Inc., Raleigh, NC
300,000	Salvador Dali Museum, NC
250,000	University of Central Florida Inc., Orlando, FL
150,000	Carolina Ballet Inc., Raleigh, NC
150,000	Food Bank of North Carolina, Raleigh, NC
137,596	North Carolina Division of Social Services, Raleigh, NC
137,596	North Carolina Division of Social Services, Raleigh, NC
130,000	Nature Conservancy Inc., Arlington, VA

PROSPECT HILL FOUNDATION

Giving Contact

Laura Callanan, Executive Director & Secretary
Prospect Hill Foundation
99 Park Avenue, Suite 2220
New York, NY 10016-1601
Phone: (212)370-1165
Fax: (212)599-6282
Web: http://www.fdncenter.org/grantmaker/prospecthill

Description

Founded: 1960
EIN: 136075567
Organization Type: Family Foundation

Giving Locations: NY: preference is given to organisation located in the northeastern United States.
Grant Types: Capital, Challenge, Department, General Support, Matching, Project, Scholarship.
Note: The foundation operates an employee matching contributions program.

Donor Information

Founder: The Prospect Hill Foundation was established in 1960. William S. Beinecke, the foundation's donor and president, was chairman of Sperry & Hutchinson Company of New York City. In 1983, the foundation merged with the Frederick W. Beinecke Fund, which was established by his parents, Frederick and Carrie Sperry Beinecke.

Financial Summary

Total Giving: $3,262,177 (fiscal year ending June 30, 2003); $3,753,203 (fiscal 2002); $4,193,283 (fiscal 2001)
Giving Analysis: Giving for fiscal 2003 includes: foundation matching gifts ($129,889); fiscal 2002: foundation matching gifts ($190,157); fiscal 2001: foundation matching gifts (approx $1,191,620)
Assets: $60,591,056 (fiscal 2003); $62,188,663 (fiscal 2002); $72,215,204 (fiscal 2001)
Gifts Received: $84,371 (fiscal 2003); $6,082 (fiscal 1995). Note: Contributions were received from trusts established by Carrie Sperry Beinecke, Frederick W. Beinecke, and William S. Beinecke. In 1989, the foundation changed its fiscal year from a calendar year to one ending June 30.

Typical Recipients

Arts & Humanities: Ballet, Dance, Historic Preservation, History & Archaeology, Libraries, Museums/Galleries, Music, Performing Arts, Theater
Civic & Public Affairs: Botanical Gardens/Parks, Civil Rights, Clubs, Employment/Job Training, Civic & Public Affairs-General, Law & Justice, Native American Affairs, Public Policy, Urban & Community Affairs, Women's Affairs, Zoos/Aquariums
Education: Arts/Humanities Education, Colleges & Universities, Education Associations, Education Reform, Elementary Education (Private), Faculty Development, International Studies, Leadership Training, Legal Education, Minority Education, Private Education (Precollege), Student Aid, Vocational & Technical Education
Environment: Air/Water Quality, Forestry, Environment-General, Protection, Research, Resource Conservation, Watershed, Wildlife Protection
Health: Emergency/Ambulance Services, Health Policy/Cost Containment, Heart, Hospitals, Medical Research, Prenatal Health Issues
International: Foreign Educational Institutions, Health Care/Hospitals, International Environmental Issues, International Peace & Security Issues, International Relations, International Relief Efforts
Religion: Churches, Ministries, Religious Welfare
Science: Science Museums
Social Services: Child Welfare, Community Service Organizations, Delinquency & Criminal Rehabilitation, Family Planning, Social Services-General, Youth Organizations

Application Procedures

Initial Contact: Thorough review of guidelines is strongly suggested prior to contacting foundation. Send two copies of a letter of application, which should be no longer than three pages.
Application Requirements: Letters should summarize the organization's history and goals; project for which funding is sought; contribution of the project to other work in the field or to the organization's own development; the organization's total budget and staff size; project budget; and a list of the organization's board of directors. If the foundation is interested in the proposal, more information will be requested.
Deadlines: None. Grant requests may be submitted anytime. The foundation's directors meet five times a year.

Review Process: All material is reviewed by the executive director and one or more board members. Response generally is provided within four weeks. Whenever possible, applicants will be visited by a representative of the foundation before it acts on a proposal.

Restrictions

Proposals from social services, arts, cultural, and educational institutions are accepted upon invitation only. The foundation does not consider grants for individuals, scholarly research, or sectarian religious activities. It favors project support over general support requests.

Additional Information

The foundation requires a final narrative and financial report from all grantees (Brochure should be requested before letter is submitted.)
Publications: Grants List; Guidelines

Foundation Officials

Robert J. Barletta: treasurer PRIM CORP EMPL treasurer, director: Antaeus Enterprises Inc.
Elizabeth G. Beinecke: vice president, director
John B. Beinecke: president, director PRIM CORP EMPL vice president, secretary, director: Antaeus Enterprises Inc. NONPR AFFIL director: National Audubon Society.
William Sperry Beinecke: chairman, director B New York, NY May 22, 1914. ED Yale University BA (1936); Columbia University LLB (1940). PRIM CORP EMPL co-founder: Casey Beinecke & Chase. CORP AFFIL director: Antaeus Enterprises Inc. NONPR AFFIL chairman emeritus: Hudson River Foundation Science & Environmental Research; honorary trustee: Pingry School; life trustee: Central Park Conservancy; member: Council Foreign Relations; honorary trustee: American Museum Natural History. CLUB AFFIL member: Yale Club; member: Ocean Club; member: Sky Club; member: Gulf Stream Golf Club; member: Little Club; member: Bohemian Club; member: Eastward Ho Country Club; member: Baltusrol Golf Club.
Laura Callanan: executive director, secretary
Frances Beinecke Elston: director
Nettie Foskett: admin
Sarah Beinecke Richardson: director

Grants Analysis

Disclosure Period: fiscal year ending June 30, 2003
Total Grants: $3,132,288*
Number of Grants: 114
Average Grant: $21,913*
Highest Grant: $250,000
Lowest Grant: $5,000
Typical Range: $10,000 to $50,000
*Note: Giving excludes matching gifts. Average grant figure excludes three highest grants ($700,000).

Recent Grants

Note: Grants derived from fiscal 2003 Form 990.
Library-Related

25,000	New York Public Library, New York, NY -- towards the library's preservation program

General

250,000	New York Philharmonic, New York, NY -- to endow the principal associate concertmaster chair
250,000	Yale University, New Haven, CT -- to establish a professorship
200,000	Yale University, New Haven, CT -- towards forestry and environmental studies
75,000	Nature Conservancy, Arlington, VA -- towards purchase of land
50,000	Adirondack Council, Elizabethtown, NY -- towards the forever wild capital campaign
50,000	Fifth Avenue Presbyterian Church, New York, NY -- towards capital campaign
50,000	Heritage Harbor Museum, Providence, RI -- towards planning and design of the museum
50,000	New York Botanical Garden, Bronx, NY -- towards the institute of economic botany
50,000	New York City Ballet, New York, NY
50,000	New York City Ballet, New York, NY -- towards capital campaign

OLIVE HIGGINS PROUTY FOUNDATION

Giving Contact

Stephen A. Bergquist, Vice President
c/o U.S. Trust Co.
PO Box 55122
Boston, MA 02205
Phone: (617)897-3215

Description

Founded: 1952
EIN: 046046475
Organization Type: Private Foundation
Giving Locations: MA: Worcester Eastern part of the state, Worcester
Grant Types: General Support, Operating Expenses.

Donor Information

Founder: Olive Higgins Prouty

Financial Summary

Total Giving: $240,000 (2003); $273,000 (2001)
Assets: $4,155,028 (2003); $4,627,119 (2001)

Typical Recipients

Arts & Humanities: Arts Centers, History & Archaeology, Libraries, Museums/Galleries, Music, Performing Arts, Public Broadcasting
Civic & Public Affairs: Community Foundations, Civic & Public Affairs-General, Law & Justice, Legal Aid, Philanthropic Organizations, Public Policy, Safety, Urban & Community Affairs, Women's Affairs
Education: Agricultural Education, Colleges & Universities, Continuing Education, Education Associations, Engineering/Technological Education, Education-General, Leadership Training, Minority Education, Private Education (Precollege), Secondary Education (Private)
Environment: Environment-General, Resource Conservation, Watershed, Wildlife Protection
Health: Alzheimer's Disease, Children's Health/Hospitals, Clinics/Medical Centers, Diabetes, Health Organizations, Hospices, Hospitals, Medical Research, Mental Health, Public Health, Single-Disease Health Associations
International: International Peace & Security Issues, International Relief Efforts
Science: Scientific Research
Social Services: Community Service Organizations, Domestic Violence, Family Planning, Family Services, Sexual Abuse, Youth Organizations

Application Procedures

Initial Contact: Send a brief letter of inquiry.
Deadlines: September 30.

Additional Information

Publications: Application Guidelines

Foundation Officials

Thomas P. Jalkut: trustee
Hillary Prouty: trustee
Lewis I. Prouty: treasurer
Richard Prouty: trustee
William Mason Smith, III: president

Grants Analysis

Disclosure Period: calendar year ending 2003
Total Grants: $240,000
Number of Grants: 41
Average Grant: $4,750*
Highest Grant: $50,000
Lowest Grant: $1,000
Typical Range: $2,000 to $7,000
*Note: Average grant figure excludes highest grant.

Recent Grants

Note: Grants derived from 2003 Form 990.
Library-Related

12,000	Mattapoisett Library, Mattapoisett, MA

General

50,000	Children's Medical Center, Dayton, OH
13,000	Austen Riggs Center, Stockbridge, MA
12,000	Audubon Washington, Seattle, WA
9,000	World Wildlife Fund, Washington, DC
8,000	Southern Poverty Law Center, Montgomery, AL
7,000	Cambridge Center for Adult Education, Cambridge, MA
6,000	Planned Parenthood Federation, Boston, MA
6,000	Upper Raritan Watershed Association, Gladstone, NJ
6,000	Wellesley College, Wellesley, MA

PROVIDENCE GAS CO.

Company Headquarters

Providence, RI

Company Description

Employees: 539
SIC(s): 4900 Electric, Gas & Sanitary Services.
Parent Company: Providence Energy Corp., 14860 Montfort Dr., Dallas, TX, United States

Operating Locations

Providence Gas Co. (MA--North Attleboro; RI--Providence)

Nonmonetary Support

Type: Donated Equipment; In-kind Services; Loaned Executives; Workplace Solicitation

Giving Contact

Helen Toohey, Director, Community Relations
100 Weybosset St.
Providence, RI 02903
Phone: (401)272-5040
Fax: (401)273-4243

Description

Organization Type: Corporate Giving Program
Grant Types: Capital, Employee Matching Gifts, General Support, Operating Expenses.

Typical Recipients

Arts & Humanities: Arts Appreciation, Arts Associations & Councils, Arts Festivals, Arts & Humanities-General, Libraries, Museums/Galleries, Music, Opera, Performing Arts, Visual Arts
Civic & Public Affairs: Civil Rights, Economic Development, Civic & Public Affairs-General, Housing, Urban & Community Affairs
Education: Colleges & Universities, Community & Junior Colleges, Economic Education, Education-General, Health & Physical Education, Private Education (Precollege), Public Education (Precollege), Science/Mathematics Education
Environment: Environment-General
Health: Health-General
Social Services: Community Service Organizations, Food/Clothing Distribution, Shelters/Homelessness,

Social Services-General, Substance Abuse, United Funds/United Ways, Youth Organizations

Application Procedures

Initial Contact: Send letter of inquiry including a description of organization, amount requested, purpose of funds sought, and proof of tax-exempt status.

Corporate Officials

James H. Dodge: chairman, chief executive officer, president, director B Toledo, OH 1940. ED University of Michigan (1962); University of Michigan (1963). PRIM CORP EMPL chairman, chief executive officer, president, director: Providence Energy Corp.
Gary S. Gillheeney: chief financial officer B Providence, RI 1955. ED American International College (1978); Bryant College (1983). PRIM CORP EMPL chief financial officer: Providence Gas Co. CORP AFFIL treasurer: North Attleboro Gas Co.; treasurer: Providence Energy Corp.; treasurer: Newport America.

PROVIDENCE JOURNAL-BULLETIN CO.

Company Headquarters

75 Fountain St.
Providence, RI 02902
Web: http://www.projo.com

Company Description

SIC(s): 2711 Newspapers, 4833 Television Broadcasting Stations, 4841 Cable & Other Pay Television Services.
Parent Company: Belo Corp., 400 S. Record Street, Dallas, TX, United States

Operating Locations

Providence Journal-Bulletin Co. (MA; RI--Providence)

Nonmonetary Support

Type: Cause-related Marketing & Promotion; Donated Equipment; Donated Products; In-kind Services; Loaned Employees; Loaned Executives; Workplace Solicitation
Note: Annual nonmonetary support is approximately $10,000.

Providence Journal Charitable Foundation

Giving Contact

Mary Ellen Ahern, Community Services and Gift Committee Director
75 Fountain Street
Providence, RI 02902-9985
Phone: (401)277-7597
Fax: (401)277-7529
E-mail: mary_ellen_ahern@projo.com

Alternate Contact

Sandra Radcliffe, Trustee
Providence Journal Charitable Foundation
Phone: (401)277-7291

Description

EIN: 056015372
Organization Type: Corporate Foundation
Giving Locations: RI
Grant Types: Capital, Endowment, General Support, Matching, Multiyear/Continuing Support, Operating Expenses, Project, Research, Scholarship, Seed Money.

Financial Summary

Total Giving: $1,174,800 (2003); $1,452,067 (2001). Note: Contributes through foundation only.
Assets: $13,605,580 (2003); $15,413,724 (2001)
Gifts Received: $350,123 (1994); $3,515,353 (1992)

Typical Recipients

Arts & Humanities: Arts Appreciation, Arts Associations & Councils, Arts Centers, Ballet, Community Arts, Arts & Humanities-General, Historic Preservation, History & Archaeology, Libraries, Museums/Galleries, Music, Performing Arts, Public Broadcasting, Theater
Civic & Public Affairs: African American Affairs, Botanical Gardens/Parks, Business/Free Enterprise, Chambers of Commerce, Community Foundations, Economic Development, Civic & Public Affairs-General, Hispanic Affairs, Housing, Legal Aid, Minority Business, Municipalities/Towns, Parades/Festivals, Professional & Trade Associations, Public Policy, Urban & Community Affairs, Women's Affairs, Zoos/Aquariums
Education: Arts/Humanities Education, Business Education, Colleges & Universities, Education Associations, Education Funds, Elementary Education (Public), Education-General, Literacy, Private Education (Precollege), Public Education (Precollege), Secondary Education (Private), Secondary Education (Public), Special Education, Student Aid
Environment: Environment-General, Protection, Resource Conservation, Watershed
Health: Adolescent Health Issues, AIDS/HIV, Cancer, Emergency/Ambulance Services, Geriatric Health, Health Organizations, Hospices, Hospitals, Long-Term Care, Medical Rehabilitation, Mental Health, Nursing Services, Research/Studies Institutes, Single-Disease Health Associations
International: Health Care/Hospitals, International Affairs
Religion: Churches, Religious Welfare
Social Services: Child Welfare, Community Centers, Community Service Organizations, Domestic Violence, Family Planning, Family Services, Food/Clothing Distribution, People with Disabilities, Recreation & Athletics, Scouts, Senior Services, Sexual Abuse, Shelters/Homelessness, Social Services-General, Substance Abuse, United Funds/United Ways, Volunteer Services, Youth Organizations

Application Procedures

Initial Contact: Submit a written proposal.
Application Requirements: Include a description of organization; project description; amount requested; purpose of funds sought; other sources of funding, and other companies approached; a copy of IRS 501 (c)(3); recent financial statements; list of board of directors.
Deadlines: None; requests are accepted on a quarterly basis.

Foundation Officials

Sandra Radcliffe: trustee
Mark Ryan: trustee
Henry D. Sharpe, Jr.: trustee
Howard Sutton: president, chief executive officer B Irvington, NJ 1950. ED University of Notre Dame (1972); Providence College (1978). PRIM CORP EMPL president, general manager, assistant publisher: The Providence Journal. CORP AFFIL president: Rhode Island Monthly Communication.
John W. Wall: trustee

Grants Analysis

Disclosure Period: calendar year ending 2003
Total Grants: $1,064,800*
Number of Grants: 38
Average Grant: $28,021
Highest Grant: $100,000
Lowest Grant: $5,000
Typical Range: $5,000 to $25,000
*Note: Giving excludes United Way.

Recent Grants

Note: Grants derived from 2003 Form 990.
Library-Related

100,000	Providence Public Library, Providence, RI
15,000	Company of the Redwood Library and Athenaeum, Newport, RI

General

60,000	Nature Conservancy, Arlington, VA
55,000	University of Rhode Island Foundation, Kingston, RI
50,000	Greater Providence Young Men's Christian Association
50,000	Heritage Harbor Corporation, Providence, RI
50,000	Rhode Island Community Food Bank Association, Providence, RI
50,000	Salvation Army & its Components, Baltimore, MD
50,000	Save the Bay Inc., Providence, RI
50,000	United Way of Southeastern New England Inc., Providence, RI
50,000	United Way of Southeastern New England Inc., Providence, RI
30,000	Bryant College of Business Administration, Providence, RI

PROVIDENT COMMUNITY FOUNDATION

Giving Contact

Julie Ganong, The Provident Bank
5 Market Street
Amesbury, MA 01913-2408
Phone: (978)388-0050
E-mail: jganong@theprovidentbank.com
Web: http://www.theprovidentbank.com

Description

Founded: 1997
EIN: 043397455
Organization Type: Private Foundation
Grant Types: General Support.

Financial Summary

Total Giving: $177,187 (2003); $355,961 (2001)
Assets: $2,516,595 (2003); $3,037,429 (2001)
Gifts Received: $2,151,118 (1997)

Typical Recipients

Arts & Humanities: Arts Centers, Libraries, Museums/Galleries
Civic & Public Affairs: Economic Development, Ethnic Organizations, Civic & Public Affairs-General, Philanthropic Organizations, Safety
Education: Afterschool/Enrichment Programs, Education-General, Public Education (Precollege)
Environment: Watershed
Health: Hospitals
Social Services: Community Service Organizations, Counseling, Food/Clothing Distribution, Social Services-General, YMCA/YWCA/YMHA/YWHA, Youth Organizations

Application Procedures

Initial Contact: Send a brief letter of inquiry.
Deadlines: First Tuesday in March, June, September and December.

Foundation Officials

Robert A. Becker: president, director
John J. Cameron: director
Robert A. Gonthier, Jr.: director
Jay E. Gould: director
Lawrence C. Hoyt, Jr.: director
Laurie H. Knapp: director
Richard L. Peeke: director

Raymond E. Pouliot: director
Lorraine E. Sanborn: director
Wayne S. Tatro: director

Grants Analysis

Disclosure Period: calendar year ending 2003
Total Grants: $177,187
Number of Grants: 46
Average Grant: $2,493*
Highest Grant: $65,000
Lowest Grant: $89
Typical Range: $1,000 to $5,000
*Note: Average grant figure excludes highest grant.

Recent Grants

Note: Grants derived from 2003 Form 990.
Library-Related

27,178	Amesbury Public Library, Amesbury, MA

General

65,000	Alliance Charitable Foundation, Waltham, MA
7,200	Amesbury Summer Youth Program, Amesbury, MA
6,000	Northern Essex Elder Transport, Amesbury, MA
6,000	YWCA, Newburyport, MA
5,000	Anna Jaques Hospital, Newburyport, MA
5,000	Firehouse Center for the Arts, Newburyport, MA
5,000	Opportunity Works, Newburyport, MA
3,323	Our Neighbor's Table, Amesbury, MA
3,019	Amesbury Carriage Museum, Amesbury, MA

PRUDENTIAL INSURANCE COMPANY OF AMERICA

Company Headquarters

751 Broad Street
Newark, NJ 07102-3777
Phone: (973)802-6000
Fax: (973)367-6476
Web: http://www.prudential.com

Company Description

Ticker: PRU
Exchange: OTC
Employees: 92,966
SIC(s): 6311 Life Insurance, 6321 Accident & Health Insurance, 6331 Fire, Marine & Casualty Insurance.

Operating Locations

Prudential Insurance Co. of America (AZ--Phoenix, Scottsdale; AR--Little Rock; CA--Fresno, Los Angeles, Pleasanton, Sacramento, Sunnyvale, Westlake Village, Woodland Hills; DC; FL--Deerfield Beach, Fort Lauderdale, Jacksonville, Maitland, Orlando; GA--Atlanta; IL--Chicago, Des Plaines, Downers Grove; LA--Monroe, New Orleans; MA--Boston; MI--Southfield; MS--Greenville; MO--Creve Coeur; NE--Kearney; NJ--Chatham, Holmdel, Iselin, Newark, Pleasantville; NY--New York; NC--Charlotte; OH--Cincinnati, Columbus; OK--Oklahoma City, Tulsa; PA--Fort Washington, Horsham; TN--Memphis, Nashville; TX--Austin, Bellaire, Houston, San Antonio; VA--Richmond; WA--Tri-Cities)

Nonmonetary Support

Type: Donated Equipment; In-kind Services; Loaned Employees; Loaned Executives
Volunteer Programs: Company supports Prudential CARES (Community, Action Renewal Efforts) which provides individual and team building volunteer programs for Prudential employees and retirees at local nonprofits. Also supports Global Volunteer Day.
Contact: Emma Perry, Community Relations Consultant

Note: 1997 employee volunteer hours totaled 76,011. 1997 nonmonetary support: $250,000.

Prudential Foundation

Giving Contact

Lata Reddy, Secretary
213 Washington Street
Newark, NJ 07102
Phone: (973)802-3780
Fax: (973)802-3345
E-mail: community.resources@prudential.com
Web: http://www.prudential.com/community

Alternate Contact

The Prudential Foundation
751 Broad Street, 15th Floor
Newark, NJ 07102-3777

Description

EIN: 222175290
Organization Type: Corporate Foundation
Giving Locations: AZ: Phoenix; CA: Los Angeles; FL: Jacksonville; GA: Atlanta; MN: Minneapolis; NJ: particularly Newark; PA: Philadelphia; TX: Houston headquarters and operating communities; nationally.
Grant Types: Employee Matching Gifts, Fellowship, General Support, Multiyear/Continuing Support, Scholarship.
Note: Employee matching gift ratio: 2 to 1 for the first $100 donated; 1 to 1 for donations of $101 to $5,000. Contact for matching gift information: (800) 554-5846.

Financial Summary

Total Giving: $20,695,459 (2003); $21,062,053 (2002); $37,518,379 (2001). Note: Contributes through corporate direct giving program and foundation.
Assets: $80,741,570 (2003); $83,693,506 (2002); $101,178,198 (2001)
Gifts Received: $20,006,288 (2002); $2,474 (2001). Note: In 2002, contributions were received from Prudential Insurance Co. ($19,991,566) and Newark Fund for Excellence ($14,722).

Typical Recipients

Arts & Humanities: Arts Associations & Councils, Arts Centers, Arts Funds, Arts Institutes, Community Arts, Dance, Historic Preservation, History & Archaeology, Libraries, Museums/Galleries, Music, Opera, Performing Arts, Public Broadcasting
Civic & Public Affairs: African American Affairs, Botanical Gardens/Parks, Business/Free Enterprise, Civil Rights, Community Foundations, Economic Development, Economic Policy, Employment/Job Training, Civic & Public Affairs-General, Hispanic Affairs, Housing, Law & Justice, Legal Aid, Municipalities/Towns, Nonprofit Management, Philanthropic Organizations, Professional & Trade Associations, Public Policy, Safety, Urban & Community Affairs, Women's Affairs
Education: Afterschool/Enrichment Programs, Arts/Humanities Education, Business Education, Colleges & Universities, Community & Junior Colleges, Continuing Education, Economic Education, Education Associations, Education Funds, Education Reform, Elementary Education (Private), Elementary Education (Public), Engineering/Technological Education, Faculty Development, Education-General, Health & Physical Education, Journalism/Media Education, Leadership Training, Legal Education, Literacy, Medical Education, Minority Education, Preschool Education, Private Education (Precollege), Public Education (Precollege), Religious Education, School Volunteerism, Science/Mathematics Education, Secondary Education (Private), Social Sciences Education, Special Education, Student Aid, Vocational & Technical Education
Environment: Environment-General

Health: AIDS/HIV, Children's Health/Hospitals, Clinics/Medical Centers, Emergency/Ambulance Services, Geriatric Health, Health Policy/Cost Containment, Health Organizations, Hospitals, Medical Rehabilitation, Medical Training, Mental Health, Public Health, Research/Studies Institutes

International: Human Rights, International Relations

Religion: Religious Welfare

Social Services: At-Risk Youth, Child Abuse, Child Welfare, Community Centers, Community Service Organizations, Counseling, Crime Prevention, Day Care, Delinquency & Criminal Rehabilitation, Emergency Relief, Family Planning, Family Services, Food/Clothing Distribution, Homes, People with Disabilities, Recreation & Athletics, Scouts, Senior Services, Shelters/Homelessness, Substance Abuse, United Funds/United Ways, Veterans, Volunteer Services, Youth Organizations

Application Procedures

Initial Contact: Download an application form from foundation website, or use the New York Area Common Application Form.

Application Requirements: Include 3-page concept paper (optional); completed application form; proof of tax-exempt status; latest audited financial statement; itemized budget of project; breakdown of current funding sources, including the amount received from each source; and names and qualifications of those conducting the project.

Deadlines: None.

Review Process: Proposals reviewed continuously.

Evaluative Criteria: Emphasizes direct-service, rather than policy-oriented grants. Evaluates organization's ability to direct project; identify specific and measurable short- and long-term objectives; demonstrate that approach is the most effective; develop a complete and realistic budget; ability to continue program after funding ceases; and evaluate outcome of project.

Decision Notification: For grants up to $200,000: decisions made within 30 days of receipt of application; for grants over $200,000: decisions made by Board of Trustees in April, August, and December.

Notes: Foundation requests that no faxed applications or videotapes be sent. Do not phone for application status.

Restrictions

Grants are not made to veterans, labor, religious, political, fraternal, or athletic groups, except when program benefits or provides services to the community at large; individuals; organizations that do not have 501(c)(3) status; general operating support for single-disease health organizations, except local AIDS groups; goodwill advertising; or fundraising events. Foundation generally does not fund capital campaigns, annual fund drives, or endowments.

Additional Information

Every three years foundation staff examines public and nonprofit environments, in order to direct foundation grant-making procedures, and reviews and revises foundation's strategic plan accordingly.

Publications: Prudential Community Resources; Application Form; Guidelines

Corporate Officials

C. Edward Chaplin: senior vice president, treasurer ED Harvard University MS; Rutgers University BS. CORP AFFIL director: MBIA, Inc. NONPR AFFIL director, treasurer: Executive Leadership Council; trustee: Newark School of the Arts.

Robert C. Golden: executive vice president

Jon F. Hanson: director PRIM CORP EMPL chairman: Hampshire Management Co. CORP AFFIL director: Prudential Insurance Co. America; director: Winnebago Industries; director: Pascack Community Bank; director: Consolidated Delivery Logistics; director: HealthSouth Corp.; director: Arrow Electronics Inc..

Anthony Piszel: senior vice president ED Golden

Gate University MBA; Rutgers University BA. NONPR AFFIL member: American Institute of CPAs.

Arthur Frederick Ryan: chairman, president, chief executive officer, director B Brooklyn, NY 1942. ED Providence College BA (1963). PRIM CORP EMPL chairman, chief executive officer, president: The Prudential Insurance Co. of America. CORP AFFIL director: Prudential Financial; director: Prudential Insurance. NONPR AFFIL vice chairman operations division, vice chairman government relations council: American Bankers Association; program manager: CHIPS Same Day Settlement New York Clearing House.

Giving Program Officials

Pindaros Roy Vagelos: trustee B Westfield, NJ 1929. ED University of Pennsylvania AB (1950); Columbia University MD (1954). CORP AFFIL director: Theravance Inc.; chairman, director: Regeneron Pharmaceuticals Inc. NONPR AFFIL director: New Jersey Center Performing Arts; trustee: University Pennsylvania; member: Institute of Medicine, National Academy of Sciences; member: National Academy Sciences; trustee: Danforth Foundation; director: Donald Danforth Plant Science Center; chairman board of visitors: Columbia University Medicine Center; member: American Society Biological Chemists; member: Business Roundtable; member: American Chemical Society; member: American Philosophical Society; member: American Academy of Arts & Sciences.

Foundation Officials

C. Edward Chaplin: treasurer (see above)

Brian Cloonan: assistant comptroller

Robert C. Golden: trustee (see above)

Jean D. Hamilton: trustee CORP AFFIL trustee: First Eagle Variable Funds; director: RenaissanceRe Holdings Ltd.; trustee: First Eagle Funds.

Jon F. Hanson: trustee (see above)

Constance J. Homer: trustee

Gabriella Morris: president

Gabriella Morris: president

Anthony Piszel: comptroller (see above)

Lata N. Reddy: secretary

Arthur Frederick Ryan: trustee (see above)

Ida F. Schmertz: trustee

Dennis Sullivan: assistant comptroller ED Columbia University MBA; New York University BA.

Sharon C. Taylor: chairman, trustee

Pindaros Roy Vagelos: trustee (see above)

Stanley C. Van Ness: trustee B 1934. ED Rutgers University AB (1955); Rutgers University JD (1963). NONPR AFFIL member: Mercer County Bar Association; member: New Jersey State Bar Association; director: Education Law Center; trustee: Jersey Short Hospital.

Grants Analysis

Disclosure Period: calendar year ending 2003

Total Grants: $10,358,700*

Number of Grants: 38

Average Grant: $117,803*

Highest Grant: $6,000,000

Lowest Grant: $2,500

Typical Range: $250 to $50,000 and $100,000 to $350,000

*Note: Giving excludes matching gifts, scholarship, and United Way. Average grant figure excludes highest grant.

Recent Grants

Note: Grants derived from 2003 Form 990.

General

500,000	Sesame Workshop, New York, NY
450,000	United Way of Essex and West Hudson, Newark, NJ -- toward support of childhood development programs
335,000	Alvin Ailey Dance Foundation, New York, NY -- toward endowment support for ongoing dance residencies
335,000	New American Schools, Alexandria, VA -- toward support of leadership development programs in school districts
330,000	Drew University, Madison, NJ -- for providing financial assistance to minority students
330,000	Rutgers University Foundation, New Brunswick, NJ
300,000	Youthbuild USA Inc., Somerville, MA -- toward support and creation of affiliates of YouthBuild
250,000	National Black Child Development Institute Inc., Washington, DC
200,000	La Casa De Don Pedro, Newark, NJ
135,000	Enterprise Center, Philadelphia, PA -- toward development of an entrepreneurship curriculum for students

PRUDENTIAL SECURITIES INC.

Company Headquarters

199 Water Street
New York, NY 10292
Web: http://www.prufn.com

Company Description

Former Name: Prudential-Bache Securities.
Employees: 17,000
SIC(s): 6211 Security Brokers & Dealers.
Parent Company: Prudential Insurance Company of America, 751 Broad Street, Newark, NJ, United States

Operating Locations

Prudential Securities Inc. (IL--Chicago; MA--Boston; NJ--Newark; NY--New York)

Nonmonetary Support

Type: In-kind Services

Prudential Securities Foundation

Giving Contact

Elizabeth A. Longley, Vice President
213 Washington St., 8th Fl.
Newark, NJ 07102
Phone: (212)214-7471
Fax: (212)214-5541
E-mail: liz_longley@prusec.com

Description

EIN: 136193023
Organization Type: Corporate Foundation
Giving Locations: NY
Grant Types: Award, General Support, Scholarship.

Financial Summary

Total Giving: $958,451 (fiscal year ending January 31, 2003); $883,325 (fiscal 2001). Note: Contributes through foundation only.

Giving Analysis: Giving for fiscal 2003 includes: foundation scholarships ($26,875); fiscal 2001: foundation ($883,325).

Assets: $131,529 (fiscal 2003); $11,465 (fiscal 2001)

Gifts Received: $1,050,000 (fiscal 2003); $803,819 (fiscal 2001); $902,895 (fiscal 2000). Note: In fiscal 2001, contributions were received from Prudential Securities. In fiscal 2001, contributions were received from Prudential Securities ($800,000) and other donors.

Typical Recipients

Arts & Humanities: Arts Associations & Councils, Arts Centers, Arts Institutes, Ballet, Ethnic & Folk Arts, Arts & Humanities-General, History & Archaeology, Libraries, Museums/Galleries, Music, Opera, Performing Arts, Public Broadcasting, Theater

Civic & Public Affairs: African American Affairs, Botanical Gardens/Parks, Business/Free Enterprise, Civil Rights, Community Foundations, Economic Development, Employment/Job Training, Civic & Public Affairs-General, Housing, Law & Justice, Municipalities/Towns, Philanthropic Organizations, Professional & Trade Associations, Public Policy, Safety, Urban & Community Affairs, Women's Affairs, Zoos/Aquariums

Education: Afterschool/Enrichment Programs, Arts/Humanities Education, Business Education, Colleges & Universities, Economic Education, Education Associations, Education Funds, Education Reform, Education-General, Literacy, Minority Education, Public Education (Precollege), School Volunteerism, Secondary Education (Private), Student Aid

Environment: Environment-General

Health: Arthritis, Cancer, Children's Health/Hospitals, Emergency/Ambulance Services, Health Organizations, Heart, Hospitals, Hospitals (University Affiliated), Medical Research, Mental Health, Outpatient Health Care, Single-Disease Health Associations, Transplant Networks/Donor Banks

International: International Peace & Security Issues, Missionary/Religious Activities

Religion: Churches, Jewish Causes, Religious Organizations, Religious Welfare, Synagogues/Temples

Science: Science Museums

Social Services: Big Brothers/Big Sisters, Community Service Organizations, Crime Prevention, Emergency Relief, Food/Clothing Distribution, People with Disabilities, Recreation & Athletics, Refugee Assistance, Scouts, Senior Services, Shelters/Homelessness, Social Services-General, Substance Abuse, United Funds/United Ways, Volunteer Services, YMCA/YWCA/YMHA/YWHA, Youth Organizations

Application Procedures

Initial Contact: Send a written proposal.
Deadlines: None.

Restrictions

Limited to New York, with a focus on education.

Corporate Officials

Elizabeth A. Longley: 1st vice presidenteo PRIM CORP EMPL 1st vice president: Prudential Securities Inc.

Leland B. Paton: president capital marketings, director, member executive committee B Worcester, MA 1943. PRIM CORP EMPL president capital marketings, director, member executive committee: Prudential Securities Inc. CORP AFFIL director: Prudential Securities Group Inc. NONPR AFFIL member: Securities Industry Association; member: Securities Industry Institute; member: New York Stock Exchange Inc.; director: Riverdale Country School; member: American Marketing Association; director: Chicago Board Options Exchange; exchange officer: America Stock Exchange Inc. CLUB AFFIL Mid-Ocean Club; Long Cove Club; Bond Club; Harvard Club; Apawanis Club.

Hardwick Simmons: chairman, chief executive officer B Baltimore, MD 1940. ED Harvard University BA (1962); Harvard University MBA (1966). PRIM CORP EMPL chairman, chief executive officer: Prudential Securities Inc. CORP AFFIL president, chief executive officer, director: Prudential Securities Group Inc.; chief executive officer, director: Prudential Capital & Investment Services; president: First Financial Fund Inc. NONPR AFFIL director: Chicago Board Options Exchange. CLUB AFFIL Bond Club.

Foundation Officials

Gary J. Gunning: vice president
William Horan: vice president
Elizabeth A. Longley: vice president corporate affairs (see above)
Mary P. O'Malley: president, director
Paul Waldman: vice president

Grants Analysis

Disclosure Period: fiscal year ending January 31, 2003
Total Grants: $931,576*
Number of Grants: 49
Average Grant: $12,463*
Highest Grant: $333,334
Lowest Grant: $500
Typical Range: $1,000 to $15,000
*Note: Giving excludes scholarship. Average grant figure excludes highest grant.

Recent Grants

Note: Grants derived from 2003 Form 990.
Library-Related

10,000	New York Public Library, New York, NY -- for participation in the corporate partners program

General

333,334	South Street Seaport Museum, New York, NY -- towards Schermerhorn row renovation project
150,000	Metropolitan Museum of Arts, New York, NY -- for participation in the corporate patron program
50,000	Jazz at Lincoln Center, New York, NY -- towards awards gala and benefit concert
35,000	New York City Partnership Foundation, New York, NY
30,000	City Parks Foundation, New York, NY
29,725	Memorial Sloan Kettering Cancer Center, New York, NY -- to support the Evelyn H Lauder breast center
25,000	NYC2012 Inc., New York, NY -- grant to bring the Olympic games
25,000	Wall Street Rising, New York, NY -- to fund Wall Street rising's art downtown festival
21,875	Citizens' Scholarship Foundation of America, St. Peter, MN
20,000	Carnegie Hall Society Inc., New York, NY

PUBLIC SERVICE ELECTRIC & GAS CO.

Company Headquarters

80 Park Plaza
Newark, NJ 07102
Web: http://www.pseg.com

Company Description

SIC(s): 4931 Electric & Other Services Combined.
Parent Company: Public Service Enterprise Group Inc., 80 Park Plaza, Newark, NJ, United States

Operating Locations

Public Service Electric & Gas Co. (NJ--Camden, Elizabeth, Jersey City, New Brunswick, Paramus, Paterson, Ridgewood, Trenton)

Nonmonetary Support

Type: Donated Equipment; In-kind Services
Volunteer Programs: Company supports Dollars for Doers and Recognizing Excellence programs.
Contact: Marion C. O'Neill, Manager, Corp. Contributions

Public Service Electric & Gas Foundation

Giving Contact

Maria B. Pinho, Jr., President
PSEG Foundation
80 Park Plaza, Mail Code T-10
Newark, NJ 07101
Phone: (973)430-5763
Fax: (973)297-1480
E-mail: maria.pinho@pseg.com
Web: http://www.pseg.com/community

Description

EIN: 223125880
Organization Type: Corporate Foundation
Former Name: Public Service Electric & Gas Foundation.
Giving Locations: nationally for education grants; primarily in service area.
Grant Types: Challenge, Employee Matching Gifts, General Support, Multiyear/Continuing Support, Project, Scholarship, Seed Money.

Financial Summary

Total Giving: $3,462,625 (2003); $3,617,126 (2002); $1,333,700 (2001). Note: Contributes through corporate direct giving program and foundation.
Giving Analysis: Giving for 2002 includes: foundation scholarships ($15,000); foundation grants to United Way ($488,000); foundation gifts to individuals ($716,000); 2001: foundation ($1,333,700); corporate direct giving ($2,045,176)
Assets: $3,058,878 (2003); $6,453,651 (2002); $9,603,814 (2001)
Gifts Received: $320,689 (2002); $10,000,000 (1999). Note: Contributions are received from Public Service Electric & Gas Co.

Typical Recipients

Arts & Humanities: Arts Centers, Arts Funds, Historic Preservation, Libraries, Museums/Galleries, Performing Arts, Public Broadcasting, Theater

Civic & Public Affairs: African American Affairs, Community Foundations, Economic Development, Employment/Job Training, Gay/Lesbian Issues, Housing, Law & Justice, Professional & Trade Associations, Public Policy, Safety, Urban & Community Affairs, Women's Affairs

Education: Business Education, Colleges & Universities, Community & Junior Colleges, Education Funds, Elementary Education (Private), Engineering/Technological Education, Leadership Training, Minority Education, Private Education (Precollege), Public Education (Precollege), Science/Mathematics Education, Secondary Education (Private)

Environment: Environment-General

Health: Cancer, Emergency/Ambulance Services, Health Funds, Hospitals, Hospitals (University Affiliated)

Science: Science Exhibits & Fairs, Science Museums, Scientific Centers & Institutes

Social Services: Child Welfare, Community Service Organizations, Counseling, Day Care, Delinquency & Criminal Rehabilitation, Emergency Relief, Food/Clothing Distribution, People with Disabilities, Recreation & Athletics, Senior Services, Social Services-General, Substance Abuse, United Funds/United Ways, Veterans, YMCA/YWCA/YMHA/YWHA, Youth Organizations

Application Procedures

Initial Contact: Send a full proposal.
Application Requirements: Include general statement indicating purpose or mission of organization; names and affiliations of officers and board members; purpose and objectives of program; total cost of program; proof of tax-exempt status; audited financial statements for the last fiscal year; other support sources that have been approached, and level of sup-

port; indication as to whether organization receives United Way funds.

Deadlines: None.

Notes: Requests for funding of local initiatives should be sent to the local PSE&G office. Organization with statewide or Newark-based programs should direct application to the foundation.

Restrictions

Does not support individuals; organizations that are not tax-exempt; organizations outside company's service territory; religious organizations; political causes, candidates, organizations, or campaigns; organizations which discriminate on the basis of race, sex, or religion; lobbying organizations; athletic, labor, or fraternal groups; organizations that address single health issues; or endowments.

Additional Information

Publications: Corporate Responsibility Report

Corporate Officials

E. James Ferland: chairman, president, chief executive officersibility B Boston, MA March 19, 1943. ED Harvard University; University of Maine BSME (1964); University of New Haven MBA (1979). PRIM CORP EMPL chairman, president, chief executive officer, director: Public Service Enterprise Group Inc. CORP AFFIL director: Public Service Resources Corp.; chairman, chief executive officer, director: Public Service Electric & Gas Co.; chairman, chief executive officer, director: PSEG Energy Technologies Inc.; director: PSEG Global Inc.; director: Hartford Steam Boiler Inspection & Insurance Co.; director: HSB Group Inc.; director: First Fidelity Bancorp; director: Foster Wheeler Corp.; chairman, chief executive officer: Enterprise Diversified Holdings Inc. NONPR AFFIL member: Edison Electric Institute; director: Nuclear Energy Institute; director: Association of Edison Illuminating Companies; director: Committee for Economic Development; member: American Gas Association.

Thomas M. O'Flynn: executive vice president, chief financial officer ED Northwestern University BA (1982); University of Chicago MBA (1986). PRIM CORP EMPL executive vice president, chief financial officer: Public Service Enterprise Group Inc.

William J. Walsh, Jr.: director corporate responsibility PRIM CORP EMPL director corporate responsibility: Public Service Enterprise Group Inc.

Foundation Officials

Edward J. Biggins, Jr.: secretary
Patrick M. Burke: assistant secretary
Frank Cassidy: trustee
Frederick D. DeSanti: trustee
Robert J. Dougherty, Jr.: trustee
James T. Foran: general counsel
Ralph Izzo: trustee
Mark G. Kahrer: assistant treasurer
Alfred C. Koeppe: trustee ED Rutgers University BA; Seton Hall University JD. PRIM CORP EMPL president, chief executive officer: Bell Atlantic New Jersey. CORP AFFIL director: Digital Solutions Inc.
Thomas M. O'Flynn: trustee (see above)
Morton A. Plawner: vice president, treasurer
Patricia A. Rado: trustee
Ardeshir Rostami: assistant treasurer
R. Edwin Selover: trustee
William J. Walsh, Jr.: president (see above)

Grants Analysis

Disclosure Period: calendar year ending 2003
Total Grants: $3,462,625
Number of Grants: 20*
Average Grant: $32,250*
Highest Grant: $500,000
Lowest Grant: $5,000*
Typical Range: $1,000 to $10,000
*Note: Number of grants and lowest grant figure exclude various one-time gifts to beneficiaries

($2,349,875). Average grant figure excludes highest grant.

Recent Grants

Note: Grants derived from 2003 Form 990.
General

500,000	Liberty Science Center, Jersey City, NJ
500,000	Liberty Science Center, Jersey City, NJ
200,000	American Red Cross/Metro New Jersey Chapter, Fairfield, NJ
160,000	Robert Wood Johnson University Hospital, New Brunswick, NJ
100,000	Community Agencies Corporation of New Jersey, Holmdel, NJ
95,000	Robert Wood Johnson University Foundation, New Brunswick, NJ
82,000	Habitat for Humanity, Newark, NJ
75,000	National Football Foundation, Morristown, NJ
67,000	University of Medicine & Dentistry of New Jersey, New Brunswick, NJ
60,000	Hackensack University Medical Center Foundation, Hackensack, NJ

PUBLIC WELFARE FOUNDATION

Giving Contact

Larry Kressley, Executive Director
1200 U Street NW
Washington, DC 20009
Phone: (202)965-1800
Fax: (202)265-8851
E-mail: reviewcommittee@publicwelfare.org
Web: http://www.publicwelfare.org

Description

Founded: 1947
EIN: 540597601
Organization Type: General Purpose Foundation
Giving Locations: nationally.
Grant Types: General Support, Matching, Operating Expenses, Project, Seed Money.

Donor Information

Founder: The Public Welfare Foundation was founded in 1947 by Charles Edward Marsh, an Ohio newspaperman. Mr. Marsh believed that newspapers were semi-public utilities which contributed to the improvement of society. This philosophy, coupled with a strong humanitarian instinct, inspired him to use the income from some of the newspapers he owned to establish a foundation.

Financial Summary

Total Giving: $18,000,000 (fiscal year ending October 31, 2005 approx); $17,992,990 (fiscal 2003); $18,897,950 (fiscal 2002)
Assets: $412,834,102 (fiscal 2003); $370,135,448 (fiscal 2002); $410,715,283 (fiscal 2001)

Typical Recipients

Arts & Humanities: Arts Institutes, Ballet, Historic Preservation, History & Archaeology, Libraries, Music, Theater
Civic & Public Affairs: African American Affairs, Asian American Affairs, Botanical Gardens/Parks, Business/Free Enterprise, Civil Rights, Economic Development, Economic Policy, Employment/Job Training, Gay/Lesbian Issues, Civic & Public Affairs-General, Hispanic Affairs, Housing, Inner-City Development, Law & Justice, Legal Aid, Native American Affairs, Nonprofit Management, Philanthropic Organizations, Public Policy, Rural Affairs, Safety, Urban & Community Affairs, Women's Affairs, Zoos/Aquariums
Education: Afterschool/Enrichment Programs, Col-

leges & Universities, Education Funds, Education Reform, Environmental Education, Faculty Development, Education-General, Legal Education, Minority Education, Private Education (Precollege), Student Aid
Environment: Air/Water Quality, Environment-General, Protection, Resource Conservation, Wildlife Protection
Health: Adolescent Health Issues, AIDS/HIV, Children's Health/Hospitals, Clinics/Medical Centers, Emergency/Ambulance Services, Health-General, Geriatric Health, Health Policy/Cost Containment, Health Organizations, Home-Care Services, Hospitals, Hospitals (University Affiliated), Medical Research, Mental Health, Nursing Services, Nutrition, Prenatal Health Issues, Public Health
International: Health Care/Hospitals, Human Rights, International Development, International Environmental Issues, International Organizations, International Peace & Security Issues, International Relief Efforts
Religion: Churches, Ministries, Religious Welfare
Science: Science Museums
Social Services: Child Welfare, Community Centers, Community Service Organizations, Counseling, Crime Prevention, Delinquency & Criminal Rehabilitation, Domestic Violence, Family Planning, Family Services, Food/Clothing Distribution, Homes, People with Disabilities, Refugee Assistance, Senior Services, Shelters/Homelessness, Social Services-General, Veterans, Youth Organizations

Application Procedures

Initial Contact: Applicants should call for application guidelines and then send a letter of inquiry, including a cover letter, to the foundation. If the foundation is interested, a proposal will be requested.

Application Requirements: A two page letter of inquiry should describe the work to be conducted. The letter should be accompanied by a cover sheet, which includes: the name and address of the organization, contact person, telephone and fax numbers, one paragraph summarizing the organization's purpose and activities, one paragraph summarizing the proposal, the relationship of the proposal to the organization's mission statement, total annual organizational budget and fiscal year, total project budget, dollar amount requested, and time period the grant will cover (with beginning and ending dates), tax exempt status and amount committed from other funding sources. The narrative should include the purpose of the request, problem being addressed, demographics served, and how you will address the need or concern, and how your work promotes systemic change. Also include a one-page budget showing all funding and expenses for organization or project to be funded. See submission guidelines for funding renewal guidelines.

Deadlines: None. The screening committee reviews applications on a daily basis.

Review Process: The foundation requests that all materials be written in English and addressed to the Review Committee. Applicants should not request preliminary meetings until a letter of inquiry has been submitted. Within one month of receiving the request, the foundation will notify the applicant whether the request has been accepted for consideration. If accepted, a proposal will be requested at that time. It generally takes an additional two to three months for the foundation to notify the applicant if it has approved the proposal. Funds should be sought for the following operating year in most cases. Decisions are made by the board of directors which meets regularly during the year.

Notes: Applicants should review the foundation's annual report and guidelines before applying to increase their chances of receiving support.

Restrictions

The foundation generally does not fund conferences, endowments, foreign study, graduate work, individuals, publications, research projects, scholarships, seminars, government projects, and workshops.

Additional Information

Each year a good portion of the grantees are first-time recipients.
Publications: Annual Report; Application Guidelines (Spanish Translation Available)

Foundation Officials

Laura Callanan: director
Peter Benjamin Edelman: director B Minneapolis, MN 1938. ED Harvard University AB (1958); Harvard University LLB (1961). NONPR AFFIL president: New Israel Fund; member: Washington lawyers Committee Civil Rights Under Law; director: National Youth Law Center; co-director: Joint Degree in Law & Public Policy, Harvard; director: Juvenile Law Center; Chapin Hall Center Children; professor law: Georgetown University; director: Center Law Social Policy; director: Americans for Peace Now; director: Center Community Change.
Thomas Ehrlich: director
Juliet Villarreal Garcia: director
Antoinette M. Haskell: director emeritus B 1918.
Robert H. Haskell: vice chairman B 1940. PRIM CORP EMPL executive vice president, director: Martinsville Bulletin Inc. CORP AFFIL senior vice president: Pacific Life Insurance Co. NONPR AFFIL first vice chairman, executive committee: Public Affairs Council.
Brent L. Henry: director B Philadelphia, PA 1947. ED Princeton University BA (1969); Yale University JD (1973); Yale University MS (1973). PRIM CORP EMPL vice president: Green Door Inc. ADD CORP EMPL adj professor: Howard University School Business Administration; secretary: Medlantic Enterprise Inc.; vice president, general counsel: Medlantic Healthcare Group. CORP AFFIL vice president, general counsel: MedStar Healthcare Group. NONPR AFFIL member: National Bar Association; trustee: Princeton University; member: District of Columbia Bar Association; member: American Bar Association; director: Bazelon Center for Mental Health Law.
Larry Kressley: executive director B Allentown, PA 1949. ED Goddard College; Antioch College MD (1976). NONPR AFFIL project director: Rural America; member, director: Washington Regional Association Grantmakers; member: National Network Grantmakers; trustee: Goddard College; director: National Committee for Responsive Philanthropy; member committee inclusiveness: Council Foundations.
Myrtis H. Powell: director PRIM NONPR EMPL vice president: Miami University. NONPR AFFIL grants review committee: Greater Cincinnati Foundation.
Thomas J. Scanlon: chairman
Thomas W. Scoville: director
Jerome W. D. Stokes: director
C. Elizabeth Warner: secretary, treasurer

Grants Analysis

Disclosure Period: fiscal year ending October 31, 2003
Total Grants: $17,992,990
Number of Grants: 527
Average Grant: $34,142
Highest Grant: $250,000
Lowest Grant: $5,000
Typical Range: $10,000 to $50,000

Recent Grants

Note: Grants derived from 2003 Form 990.
General

250,000	Natural Resources Defense Council, New York, NY -- support for the climate center
150,000	South Africa Development Fund, Boston, MA
125,000	Center for Community Change, Washington, DC
100,000	Friends of the Earth, Washington, DC
100,000	Legal Aid Bureau, Baltimore, MD

90,000	Community Catalyst, Boston, MA
75,000	Alliance for Justice, Washington, DC
75,000	Center on Fathers Families and Public Policy (CFFPP), Madison, WI
75,000	Chicago Coalition for the Homeless (CCH), Chicago, IL
75,000	Chicago Coalition for the Homeless (CCH), Chicago, IL

PUBLIX SUPERMARKETS

Company Headquarters

1936 George Jenkins Boulevard
Lakeland, FL 33815
Web: http://www.publix.com

Company Description

Founded: 1921
Ticker: PUSH
Exchange: OTC
Revenue: US$18.686 billion (2004)
Profit: US$819.4 million (2004)
Employees: 125000 (2003)
Fortune Rank: 117, per FORTUNE Magazine's list of 500 Largest U.S. Corporations (2004).
SIC(s): 5411 Grocery Stores.

Operating Locations

Publix Supermarkets (FL--Lakeland)

Publix Supermarkets Charities

Giving Contact

Carol Barnett, Chairperson
PO Box 407
Lakeland, FL 33815
Phone: (863)686-8754
Web: http://www.publix.com/about/CommunityInvolvement.do

Description

Founded: 1967
EIN: 596194119
Organization Type: Corporate Foundation
Giving Locations: AL; FL; GA; SC
Grant Types: Capital, Challenge, Employee Matching Gifts, General Support, Multiyear/Continuing Support, Operating Expenses, Project, Scholarship.

Donor Information

Founder: The foundation was established in 1967 by George W. Jenkins.

Financial Summary

Total Giving: $22,667,969 (2003); $18,482,224 (2002); $24,002,437 (2001)
Giving Analysis: Giving for 2002 includes: foundation grants to United Way ($6,710,600)
Assets: $460,422,346 (2003); $404,166,673 (2002); $460,932,750 (2001)
Gifts Received: $43,660 (1999); $2,850,350 (1997); $50,257,597 (1996). Note: In 1996, contributions were received from Florida Combined Life Insurance Co., the estate of Mr. George Jenkins, and various donors.

Typical Recipients

Arts & Humanities: Arts Associations & Councils, Arts Centers, Arts Festivals, Community Arts, Libraries, Museums/Galleries, Performing Arts, Public Broadcasting, Theater
Civic & Public Affairs: African American Affairs, Business/Free Enterprise, Chambers of Commerce, Community Foundations, Economic Policy, Gay/Lesbian Issues, Civic & Public Affairs-General, Hous-

ing, Municipalities/Towns, Public Policy, Rural Affairs, Zoos/Aquariums
Education: Agricultural Education, Colleges & Universities, Community & Junior Colleges, Economic Education, Education Funds, Education Reform, Education-General, Minority Education, Private Education (Precollege), Public Education (Precollege), Secondary Education (Private), Student Aid
Environment: Environment-General, Wildlife Protection
Health: Cancer, Clinics/Medical Centers, Emergency/Ambulance Services, Geriatric Health, Hospices, Hospitals, Single-Disease Health Associations, Transplant Networks/Donor Banks
International: Foreign Arts Organizations, International Affairs
Religion: Churches, Ministries, Religious Organizations, Religious Welfare
Science: Observatories & Planetariums, Science Museums, Scientific Centers & Institutes
Social Services: At-Risk Youth, Camps, Child Welfare, Community Service Organizations, Emergency Relief, Family Planning, Family Services, Food/Clothing Distribution, Homes, People with Disabilities, Scouts, Shelters/Homelessness, Substance Abuse, United Funds/United Ways, YMCA/YWCA/YMHA/YWHA, Youth Organizations

Application Procedures

Initial Contact: The foundation requests applications be made in writing.
Application Requirements: Applicants should include the purpose of the request, a copy of 501(c)(3) determination letter from IRS, and the latest financial statement of the organization.
Deadlines: None.

Restrictions

Grants are not made to individuals.

Corporate Officials

John A. Attaway, Jr.: general counsel B 1959.
Carol J. Barnett: director NONPR AFFIL member: Southern Regional Task Force on Child Care.
Tina P. Johnson: senior vice president, director B 1959. ED University of South Florida BA (1980). PRIM CORP EMPL treasurer, director: Publix Super Markets Inc. NONPR AFFIL member: University of South Florida Alumni Association.

Foundation Officials

Carol J. Barnett: chairman, chief executive officer (see above)
Hoyt R. Barnett: vice president, director B Raleigh, NC 1943. ED Florida Southern College BS (1965). PRIM CORP EMPL executive vice president, director: Publix Supermarkets Inc. NONPR AFFIL member: Central Florida Transportation Initiative. CLUB AFFIL president: Lone Pine Golf Club Inc.
Tina P. Johnson: treasurer (see above)

Grants Analysis

Disclosure Period: calendar year ending 2003
Total Grants: $14,507,500*
Number of Grants: 3,400 (approx)
Average Grant: $4,267
Highest Grant: $100,000
Lowest Grant: $25
Typical Range: $1,000 to $5,000
*****Note:** Giving excludes United Way.

Recent Grants

Note: Grants derived from 2003 Form 990.
General

1,474,800	United Way of Central Florida, Highland, FL
1,263,200	United Way of Atlanta Metro, Atlanta, GA
1,139,600	United Way of Tampa Bay, Tampa, FL
859,200	United Way, Ft. Lauderdale, FL
628,700	United Way, Miami, FL
625,900	United Way, Orlando, FL
553,300	United Way, FL

350,400 United Way, Ft. Myers, FL
296,900 United Way of Northeast Florida, Jacksonville, FL
237,700 United Way, Charlotte, NC

PULITZER INC.

Company Headquarters
900 N. Tucker Blvd.
St. Louis, MO 63101
Web: http://www.pulitzer.net

Company Description
Founded: 1878
Ticker: PTZ
Exchange: NYSE
Former Name: Pulitzer Publishing Co..
Revenue: US$416 million (2002)
Employees: 3800 (2003)
SIC(s): 2711 Newspapers.

Operating Locations
Pulitzer, Inc. (AZ--Phoenix, Tucson; IN--Fort Wayne; KY--Louisville; MO--St. Louis; NE--Omaha; NM--Albuquerque; NC--Winston-Salem; SC--Greenville)

Nonmonetary Support
Type: Cause-related Marketing & Promotion; Donated Products; In-kind Services
Contact: Tracy Rouch, Promotions Mgr.

Pulitzer Foundation

Giving Contact
Alan G. Silverglat, Secretary & Treasurer
Pulitzer Foundation
900 North Tucker Boulevard
St. Louis, MO 63101
Phone: (314)340-8440
Fax: (314)340-3133

Description
EIN: 436052854
Organization Type: Corporate Foundation
Giving Locations: MO: St. Louis metropolitan area
Grant Types: Capital, Endowment, General Support, Project, Scholarship.

Financial Summary
Total Giving: $418,100 (2002); $506,850 (2001).
Note: Contributes through foundation only.
Giving Analysis: Giving for 2001 includes: foundation grants to United Way ($220,000); foundation ($286,850)
Assets: $644,704 (2002); $705,784 (2001)
Gifts Received: $391,350 (2002); $375,850 (2001); $397,350 (2000). Note: In 2002, contributions were received from Pulitzer Inc. ($30,000) and St. Louis Post-Dispatch LLC ($361,350). In 2001, contributions were received from St. Louis Post-Dispatch LLC ($345,850) and Pulitzer Inc. ($30,000). In 1999, contributions were received from Pulitzer Broadcasting Co.($92,000); WESH Television, Inc. ($34,000); KCCI Television Inc ($10,000); Pulitzer Inc ($261,029); WDSU Television ($16,000) and Star Publishing ($12,000).

Typical Recipients
Arts & Humanities: Arts Appreciation, Arts Associations & Councils, Arts Centers, Arts Festivals, Arts Funds, Arts Institutes, Dance, Ethnic & Folk Arts, Arts & Humanities-General, Historic Preservation, History & Archaeology, Libraries, Museums/Galleries, Music, Opera, Performing Arts, Public Broadcasting, Theater, Visual Arts
Civic & Public Affairs: African American Affairs,

Asian American Affairs, Botanical Gardens/Parks, Business/Free Enterprise, Civil Rights, Clubs, Community Foundations, Economic Development, Employment/Job Training, First Amendment Issues, Civic & Public Affairs-General, Law & Justice, Philanthropic Organizations, Professional & Trade Associations, Public Policy, Urban & Community Affairs, Women's Affairs, Zoos/Aquariums
Education: Arts/Humanities Education, Business Education, Colleges & Universities, Education Funds, Education-General, International Exchange, Journalism/Media Education, Legal Education, Medical Education, Minority Education, Private Education (Precollege), Public Education (Precollege), Science/Mathematics Education, Secondary Education (Private), Special Education, Student Aid, Vocational & Technical Education
Environment: Environment-General, Resource Conservation
Health: AIDS/HIV, Cancer, Children's Health/Hospitals, Emergency/Ambulance Services, Home-Care Services, Hospices, Hospitals, Long-Term Care, Mental Health, Multiple Sclerosis, Preventive Medicine/Wellness Organizations, Respiratory, Single-Disease Health Associations
International: International-General, Human Rights, International Organizations, International Relations
Religion: Churches, Dioceses, Jewish Causes, Religious Organizations, Religious Welfare
Science: Scientific Centers & Institutes
Social Services: Child Welfare, Community Centers, Community Service Organizations, Emergency Relief, Family Planning, Family Services, Food/Clothing Distribution, Homes, People with Disabilities, Recreation & Athletics, Scouts, Senior Services, Shelters/Homelessness, United Funds/United Ways, YMCA/YWCA/YMHA/YWHA, Youth Organizations

Application Procedures
Initial Contact: Send a brief letter or proposal.
Application Requirements: Include a description of organization, amount requested, purpose of funds sought, recently audited financial statement, proof of tax-exempt status.
Deadlines: None.
Review Process: Foundation board meets every other month.

Restrictions
Applications from individuals are not accepted.

Corporate Officials
Cole C. Campbell: editorvpr B Roanoke, VA. ED University of North Carolina BA. PRIM CORP EMPL editor: Saint Louis Post Dispatch. NONPR AFFIL journalism advisory board: Norfolk State University.
Ronald H. Ridgway: senior vice president B 1938. ED Ohio State University. PRIM CORP EMPL senior vice president: Pulitzer Publishing Co. CORP AFFIL vice president: Star Publishing Co.; treasurer: WESH Television Inc.; vice president finance: KETV Television Inc.; senior vice president fin, director: Saint Louis Post Dispatch.

Foundation Officials
Cole C. Campbell: director (see above)
Terrance C.Z. Egger: director ED Augustana College. PRIM CORP EMPL vice president: Pulitzer Publishing Co.
Ronald H. Ridgway: secretary, treasurer, director (see above)
Alan G. Silverglat: secretary, treasurer, director
Robert C. Woodworth: president, director

Grants Analysis
Disclosure Period: calendar year ending 2002
Total Grants: $293,000*
Number of Grants: 29
Average Grant: $10,103
Highest Grant: $50,000
Lowest Grant: $250

Typical Range: $250 to $25,000
*Note: Giving excludes United Way.

Recent Grants
Note: Grants derived from 2003 Form 990.
General
25,000 Saint Louis Art Museum, St. Louis, MO -- towards membership
15,000 Saint Louis Symphony Orchestra, St. Louis, MO
11,190 American Press Institute, Reston, VA
5,000 National Society of Newspaper Columnists, San Francisco, CA
2,500 Committee to Protect Journalists, New York, NY
2,500 Media Law Resource Centers, New York, NY
1,000 Center of Contemporary Art, St. Louis, MO
1,000 Saint Patrick Center, St. Louis, MO
1,000 Three-Legged Race, Minneapolis, MN
500 Maine Coast Heritage Trust, Topsham, ME

NINA MASON PULLIAM CHARITABLE TRUST

Giving Contact
Mary Price, Director of Grants
135 N. Pennsylvania Street, Suite 1200
Indianapolis, IN 46204-1956
Phone: (317)231-6075
Fax: (317)231-9208
E-mail: hivey@nmpct.org
Web: http://www.ninapulliamtrust.org/html

Alternate Contact
2201 E. Camelback Rd., Suite 600B
Phoenix, AZ 85016
Phone: (602)955-3000
Fax: (602)955-8029
Note: Alternate address is for Arizona organizations.

Description
Founded: 1997
EIN: 356644088
Organization Type: Private Foundation
Giving Locations: AZ: Phoenix metro area; IN: Indianapolis metro area
Grant Types: General Support.

Financial Summary
Total Giving: $13,000,000 (2004 approx); $11,901,931 (2003); $15,643,576 (2002)
Giving Analysis: Giving for 2001 includes: foundation grants to United Way ($145,000)
Assets: $341,196,980 (2003); $295,408,743 (2002); $367,393,493 (2001)
Gifts Received: $109,401 (1999); $38,128,196 (1998); $363,806,664 (1997). Note: In 1998 and 1999, contributions were received from Nina Mason Pulliam estate.

Typical Recipients
Arts & Humanities: Arts Centers, Libraries, Museums/Galleries, Theater
Civic & Public Affairs: Botanical Gardens/Parks, Community Foundations, Economic Development, Civic & Public Affairs-General, Housing, Public Policy, Women's Affairs, Zoos/Aquariums
Education: Colleges & Universities, Education Funds, Engineering/Technological Education, Health & Physical Education, Medical Education, Minority Education
Environment: Protection, Wildlife Protection
Health: Cancer, Children's Health/Hospitals, Clinics/Medical Centers, Eyes/Blindness, Geriatric Health,

Health Funds, Hospitals, Mental Health, Nursing Services, Single-Disease Health Associations
Religion: Dioceses, Ministries
Science: Scientific Centers & Institutes
Social Services: Animal Protection, At-Risk Youth, Big Brothers/Big Sisters, Camps, Child Abuse, Child Welfare, Community Centers, Community Service Organizations, Domestic Violence, Emergency Relief, Family Services, Food/Clothing Distribution, People with Disabilities, Recreation & Athletics, Senior Services, Shelters/Homelessness, Substance Abuse, United Funds/United Ways, Veterans, YMCA/YWCA/YMHA/YWHA, Youth Organizations

Application Procedures

Initial Contact: Send a brief letter of inquiry.
Application Requirements: Preliminary proposal letter should include a description of organization, description of need, time frame, budget, and description of target population. Submit six copies of preliminary letter, preliminary application form, and board of directors listing. Submit one copy of proof of tax-exempt status and annual report.
Deadlines: January 14, May 13, and September 13 for preliminary applications. These vary slightly year to year so check the website for verification of deadline dates.
Decision Notification: Preliminary application notification is in 3 months and final funding notification is in 6 months after preliminary deadline.

Foundation Officials

Harriet M. Ivey: president, chief executive officer
Robert L. Lowry: chief financial officer
Frank Eli Russell: trustee B Kokomo, IN December 06, 1920. ED Evansville College AB (1942); Indiana University JD (1951). PRIM CORP EMPL chairman: Central Newspapers, Inc. CORP AFFIL director: Muncie Newspapers Inc.; director: Phoenix Newspapers Inc.; chairman retirement committee: Hoosier State Press; director: Indianapolis Newspapers Inc.; president, director: Bradley Paper Co.; president, director: Central Newsprint. NONPR AFFIL member: Sigma Alpha Epsilon; member: Tax Executives Institute; member: Salvation Army; member: Shriners; member: Order Coif; member: Phi Delta Phi; member, director: Newspaper Advertising Bureau; director: Nina Mason Pulliam Charitable Trust; member: Masons; member: Midwest Pension Conference; member: Indianapolis Bar Association; member, director: Institute Newspaper Contrs & Financial Offs; director, vice president: Indiana Association Credit Management; member: Indiana Bar Association; member: Indiana Association Colleges; member: Indiana Association CPA's; director: Eiteljorg Museum; member: Free Accepted Masons; member: Ancient Accepted Scottish Rite; director: Central Newspapers Foundation; member: American Bar Association; member: American Institute CPAs. CLUB AFFIL Meridian Hills Country Club; Skyline Club; Columbia Club; Indianapolis Athletic Club.
Nancy M. Russell: trustee
Carol P. Schatt: trustee

Grants Analysis

Disclosure Period: calendar year ending 2003
Total Grants: $11,901,931*
Number of Grants: 195
Average Grant: $61,036
Highest Grant: $1,000,000
Typical Range: $10000 to $150,000
*Note: Giving includes United Way.

Recent Grants

Note: Grants derived from 2003 Form 990.
Library-Related
250,000	Indianapolis Marion County Public Library Foundation, Indianapolis, IN -- towards Indianapolis special collection room

General
500,000	Heard Museum, Phoenix, AZ -- towards reinstallation of Native Peoples of the Southwest galleries
250,000	Grand Canyon National Park Foundation, Flagstaff, AZ -- to create and maintain trail system
249,761	Ivy Tech Foundation Inc., Indianapolis, IN -- towards support for Nina Mason Pulliam Legacy Scholars program
237,549	Maricopa County Community Colleges District Foundation, Tempe, AZ -- towards support for Nina Mason Pulliam Legacy Scholars program
224,000	International Center of Indianapolis Inc., Indianapolis, IN -- towards expanding the Bridges to the World program
218,827	Arizona State University Foundation, Tempe, AZ -- towards support for Nina Mason Pulliam Legacy Scholars program
200,000	Raphael Health Center Inc., Indianapolis, IN -- towards expanding health care facility
175,000	Community Services of Arizona Inc., Chandler, AZ -- to purchase and equip modular day care building
175,000	Wishard Memorial Foundation, Indianapolis, IN -- towards coordinating care under a geriatric team
153,684	Indiana University Foundation, Bloomington, IN -- towards support for Nina Mason Pulliam Legacy Scholars program

PUTERBAUGH FOUNDATION

Giving Contact

Norris J. Welker, Managing Trustee
PO Box 1206
McAlester, OK 74502-1206
Phone: (918)426-1591

Description

Founded: 1949
EIN: 736092193
Organization Type: Private Foundation
Giving Locations: OK
Grant Types: Capital, Endowment, General Support, Matching, Professorship, Project, Research, Scholarship.

Donor Information

Founder: the late Jay Garfield Puterbaugh, the late Leela Oliver Puterbaugh

Financial Summary

Total Giving: $394,914 (2001). Note: 1997 Giving includes United Way ($35,200).
Giving Analysis: Giving for 2001 includes: foundation scholarships ($11,000); foundation grants to United Way ($50,000)
Assets: $8,866,936 (2001)

Typical Recipients

Arts & Humanities: Arts Associations & Councils, Arts Institutes, History & Archaeology, Libraries, Literary Arts, Public Broadcasting
Civic & Public Affairs: Botanical Gardens/Parks, Chambers of Commerce, Clubs, Economic Development, Civic & Public Affairs-General, Inner-City Development, Law & Justice, Legal Aid, Municipalities/Towns, Safety, Urban & Community Affairs
Education: Colleges & Universities, Economic Education, Elementary Education (Public), Education-General, Literacy, Medical Education, Preschool Education, Public Education (Precollege), Student Aid, Vocational & Technical Education

Environment: Environment-General
Health: Cancer, Children's Health/Hospitals, Clinics/Medical Centers, Emergency/Ambulance Services, Health Organizations, Hospices, Hospitals, Medical Research, Nursing Services, Speech & Hearing
Religion: Religious Welfare
Science: Scientific Centers & Institutes, Scientific Organizations
Social Services: At-Risk Youth, Child Welfare, Community Service Organizations, Crime Prevention, Family Planning, Family Services, Homes, People with Disabilities, Shelters/Homelessness, Substance Abuse, United Funds/United Ways, Youth Organizations

Application Procedures

Initial Contact: Send a full proposal.
Application Requirements: Describe the organization and program or project; include specific purpose of funds sought, other sources of support, and proof of tax-exempt status.
Decision Notification: Budget commitments are completed approximately one year in advance.

Restrictions

Does not support individuals.

Additional Information

Preference is given to local charities which provide broad public benefit.
Publications: Financial Statement

Foundation Officials

Frank G. Edwards: trustee
Don C. Phelps: mng trustee
Steven W. Taylor: trustee
Norris J. Welker: trustee

Grants Analysis

Disclosure Period: calendar year ending 2001
Total Grants: $333,914*
Number of Grants: 22
Average Grant: $9,496*
Highest Grant: $125,000
Typical Range: $1,000 to $50,000
*Note: Giving excludes United Way and scholarship. Average grant figure excludes highest grant.

Recent Grants

Note: Grants derived from 2001 Form 990.

General
125,000	Boys and Girls Club of McAlester, McAlester, OK -- program support, building project
50,928	McAlester Public Schools, McAlester, OK -- television program and program support
50,000	McAlester United Way, Inc., McAlester, OK -- program support
50,000	Oklahoma Medical Research Foundation, Oklahoma City, OK -- medical research funding
23,500	Eastern Oklahoma State College, Wilburton, OK -- Nursing Program support
15,000	American Red Cross, Pittsburg County Chapter, McAlester, OK -- program support
15,000	McAlester Chamber Foundation, McAlester, OK -- Industrial Development Program support
13,970	Youth Emergency Shelter, Inc., McAlester, OK -- facility upgrading project
8,500	McAlester Rotary Foundation, McAlester, OK -- Rotary Park
5,250	CASA of Pittsburg County, McAlester, OK -- program support

PUTNAM FOUNDATION

Giving Contact
David F. Putnam, Trustee
150 Congress St.
Keene, NH 03431-0323
Phone: (603)352-2448
Fax: (603)355-1185

Description
Founded: 1952
EIN: 026011388
Organization Type: Private Foundation
Giving Locations: NH
Grant Types: Capital, General Support.

Donor Information
Founder: David F. Putnam

Financial Summary
Total Giving: $531,178 (fiscal year ending October 31, 2001)
Giving Analysis: Giving for fiscal 2001 includes: foundation scholarships ($1,000)
Assets: $8,107,228 (fiscal 2001)
Gifts Received: $9,987 (fiscal 2001); $59,925 (fiscal 2000); $59,928 (fiscal 1998). Note: In 1998, contributions received were in the form of Markem Class C stock.

Typical Recipients
Arts & Humanities: Arts Associations & Councils, Arts Institutes, Community Arts, Dance, Ethnic & Folk Arts, Historic Preservation, History & Archaeology, Libraries, Museums/Galleries, Music, Opera, Public Broadcasting, Theater
Civic & Public Affairs: Botanical Gardens/Parks, Business/Free Enterprise, Community Foundations, Civic & Public Affairs-General, Hispanic Affairs, Housing, Municipalities/Towns, Parades/Festivals, Philanthropic Organizations, Professional & Trade Associations, Urban & Community Affairs, Women's Affairs
Education: Arts/Humanities Education, Colleges & Universities, Education Funds, Engineering/Technological Education, Faculty Development, Education-General, International Studies, Leadership Training, Minority Education, Private Education (Precollege), Science/Mathematics Education, Secondary Education (Public), Social Sciences Education, Student Aid
Environment: Air/Water Quality, Forestry, Environment-General, Resource Conservation
Health: Clinics/Medical Centers, Emergency/Ambulance Services, Health Organizations, Hospices, Hospitals
International: International Relations, Missionary/Religious Activities
Religion: Churches, Religion-General
Science: Science Museums
Social Services: Community Service Organizations, Food/Clothing Distribution, Recreation & Athletics, Scouts, Social Services-General, United Funds/United Ways, YMCA/YWCA/YMHA/YWHA, Youth Organizations

Application Procedures
Initial Contact: Send a brief letter of inquiry.
Application Requirements: Include purpose of funds sought and provide relevant facts and information.
Deadlines: None.

Restrictions
Awards are limited to historical preservation, cultural enhancement, and ecological maintenance.

Foundation Officials
Rosamond P. Delori: trustee, secretary
David F. Putnam: trustee

James A. Putnam: trustee PRIM CORP EMPL president: Markem Corp.
Rosamond Putnam: trustee

Grants Analysis
Disclosure Period: fiscal year ending October 31, 2001
Total Grants: $530,178*
Number of Grants: 74
Average Grant: $7,165
Highest Grant: $33,333
Lowest Grant: $250
Typical Range: $1,000 to $10,000
*Note: Giving excludes scholarships.

Recent Grants
Note: Grants derived from 2002 Form 990.
General

50,000	Dublin School, Dublin, NH -- for capital campaign fund
50,000	Home Healthcare Hospice and Community Services, Nashua, NH -- to create new Eldercare Center for region
25,000	Colonial Theater Group, Keene, NH -- to support operations
25,000	Harns Center for Conservation Education, Hancock, NH -- to support building renovation project
25,000	Monadnock United Way, Keene, NH -- in support of 2001-2002 campaign
25,000	New Hampshire Center for Public Policy Studies, Chichester, NH -- to hire deputy to assist the director
20,000	Curner Gallery of Art, Manchester, NH -- to support technology base initiative
20,000	Keene State College, Keene, NH -- to support art department fellowship
13,970	Monadnock Area Psychotherapy and Spirituality Services, Keene, NH -- to help install local area network
12,000	New England College, Henniker, NH -- to support the Putnam International scholarship

QUAKER CHEMICAL CORP.

Company Headquarters
1 Quaker Park
901 Hector St.
Conshohocken, PA 19428-0809
Web: http://www.quakerchem.com

Company Description
Founded: 1918
Ticker: KWR
Exchange: NYSE
Revenue: US$274.5 million (2002)
Employees: 1141 (2003)
SIC(s): 2821 Plastics Materials & Resins, 2841 Soap & Other Detergents, 2842 Polishes & Sanitation Goods, 2899 Chemical Preparations Nec.

Operating Locations
Quaker Chemical Corp. (CA--Fontana, Placentia, Pomona, South El Monte; GA--Savannah; MI--Detroit; OK--Sapulpa; PA--Conshohocken, Philadelphia; TX--Conroe, Fort Worth)

Nonmonetary Support
Type: Loaned Employees; Loaned Executives

Quaker Chemical Foundation

Giving Contact
Shirley Widdoes, Secretary
Quaker Chemical Foundation
Elm and Lee Streets
Conshohocken, PA 19428
Phone: (610)832-4301
Fax: (610)832-4282

Description
EIN: 236245803
Organization Type: Corporate Foundation
Giving Locations: headquarters and operating communities.
Grant Types: Employee Matching Gifts, General Support, Scholarship.
Note: Employee matching gift ratio: 1 to 1 for education, health and welfare, cultural organisation, and civic and community affairs, up to $1,000 annually.

Financial Summary
Total Giving: $234,754 (fiscal year ending June 31, 2002); $274,977 (fiscal 2001). Note: Contributes through foundation only.
Giving Analysis: Giving for fiscal 2001 includes: foundation scholarships ($39,771); foundation matching gifts ($60,403); foundation ($174,803)
Assets: $346,799 (fiscal 2002); $477,145 (fiscal 2001)
Gifts Received: $125,000 (fiscal 2002); $83,000 (fiscal 2001); $307,000 (fiscal 2000). Note: Contributions were received from the Quaker Chemical Corporation.

Typical Recipients
Arts & Humanities: Arts Associations & Councils, Arts Centers, Arts Festivals, Arts Funds, Arts Institutes, Arts Outreach, Ballet, Community Arts, Dance, Arts & Humanities-Beneral, Historic Preservation, History & Archaeology, Libraries, Museums/Galleries, Music, Opera, Performing Arts
Civic & Public Affairs: Botanical Gardens/Parks, Business/Free Enterprise, Economic Development, Employment/Job Training, Civic & Public Affairs-General, Housing, Nonprofit Management, Urban & Community Affairs, Women's Affairs, Zoos/Aquariums
Education: Arts/Humanities Education, Colleges & Universities, Community & Junior Colleges, Engineering/Technological Education, Environmental Education, Education-General, International Exchange, Literacy, Private Education (Precollege), Special Education, Student Aid, Vocational & Technical Education
Environment: Environment-General
Health: Eyes/Blindness, Health Funds, Health Organizations, Heart, Home-Care Services, Hospices, Hospitals, Medical Research, Nursing Services, Nutrition, Single-Disease Health Associations
International: Health Care/Hospitals, International Affairs, International Organizations, International Relations
Religion: Religious Welfare
Science: Science Exhibits & Fairs, Science Museums, Scientific Centers & Institutes
Social Services: At-Risk Youth, Child Welfare, Community Service Organizations, Counseling, Crime Prevention, Family Services, Food/Clothing Distribution, Homes, People with Disabilities, Recreation & Athletics, Scouts, Senior Services, Sexual Abuse, Social Services-General, Substance Abuse, United Funds/United Ways, Volunteer Services, Youth Organizations

Application Procedures
Initial Contact: Request guidelines, then send written grant application.
Application Requirements: Grant applications must

include: project description with a pro-forma budget; annual operating budget and audited financial statements; list of funding sources, including past major contributors with amounts, recent applications with results, and anticipated future funding sources; list of board members and officers.
Deadlines: April 30.

Restrictions

Distributions limited to tax-exempt organizations in geographic locations where the corporation has operations in the United States.
Generally does not support brick and mortar projects.

Additional Information

Publications: Guidelines

Corporate Officials

Ronald James Naples: president, chief executive officer, director B Passaic, NJ 1945. ED United States Military Academy BS (1967); Tufts University Fletcher School of Law & Diplomacy MA (1972); Harvard University MBA (1974). PRIM CORP EMPL president, chief executive officer, director: Quaker Chemical Corp. CORP AFFIL director: Advanta Corp. NONPR AFFIL member: President Commission White House Fellows; director: University Arts; member: Harvard Business School Alumni Association; director: Philadelphia Museum Art; vice chairman, director: Free Library Philadelphia Federation; vice chairman: Greater Philadelphia First Corp.; director: Foreign Policy Research Institute; director: Childrens Hospital Philadelphia; member advisory board: Fletcher School Law & Diplomacy; member: Association Grads U.S. Military Academy. CLUB AFFIL Pyramid Club; Racquet Club; Harvard Business School Philadelphia Club.

Foundation Officials

Katherine N. Coughenour: trustee
Edwin J. Delattre: trustee CORP AFFIL director: Quaker Chemical Corp.
Alan J. Keyser: trustee
Kathleen Lasota: secretary
Karl Henry Spaeth: chairman, trustee B Philadelphia, PA 1929. ED Haverford College AB (1951); Oxford University (1955); Harvard University JD (1958). PRIM CORP EMPL vice president, secretary: Quaker Chemical Corp. CORP AFFIL secretary: SB Decking Inc. CLUB AFFIL Philadelphia Cricket Club; Philadelphia Club.
Jane Williams: trustee

Grants Analysis

Disclosure Period: fiscal year ending June 31, 2002
Total Grants: $169,557*
Number of Grants: 117
Average Grant: $1,449
Highest Grant: $5,000
Lowest Grant: $150
Typical Range: $500 to $3,500
*Note: Giving excludes matching gifts and scholarship.

Recent Grants

Note: Grants derived from 2002 Form 990.
Library-Related

2,500	William Jeanes Memorial Library, Lafayette Hill, PA
2,000	Conshohocken Free Library, Conshohocken, PA

General

3,500	Opera Company of Philadelphia, Philadelphia, PA
3,500	Young Audiences of Eastern Pennsylvania, Philadelphia, PA
3,000	Cabrini College, Radnor, PA
3,000	Philadelphia Museum of Art, Philadelphia, PA
3,000	Philadelphia Orchestra, Philadelphia, PA
2,500	Academy of Natural Sciences, Philadelphia, PA
2,500	Bach Festival of Philadelphia, Philadelphia, PA
2,500	Bryn Mawr College, Bryn Mawr, PA
2,500	Colonial Meals on Wheels, Conshohocken, PA
2,500	Colonial Neighborhood Council, Conshohocken, PA

QUANEX CORP.

Company Headquarters

1900 W. Loop S, Ste. 1500
Houston, TX 77027
Web: http://www.quanex.com

Company Description

Founded: 1927
Ticker: NX
Exchange: NYSE
Revenue: US$994.4 million (2002)
Employees: 3153 (2003)
SIC(s): 3312 Blast Furnaces & Steel Mills, 3317 Steel Pipe & Tubes, 3341 Secondary Nonferrous Metals, 3365 Aluminum Foundries.

Operating Locations

Quanex Corp. (AR--Fort Smith; IL--Chatsworth, Lincolnshire; IA--Davenport; MI--Jackson; MS--New Albany; TX--Houston; UT--Park City; WI--Rice Lake)

Nonmonetary Support

Type: Donated Equipment; Donated Products

Quanex Foundation

Giving Contact

Sandy Hatcher, Director Corporate Communications
1900 West Loop S., Suite 1500
Houston, TX 77027
Phone: (713)961-4600

Description

Founded: 1951
EIN: 366065490
Organization Type: Corporate Foundation
Giving Locations: AR; IL; IN; IA; MI; MN; TX; WI
Grant Types: General Support, Scholarship.

Donor Information

Founder: La Salle Steel Co.

Financial Summary

Total Giving: $357,086 (2002); $240,483 (2001)
Giving Analysis: Giving for 2001 includes: foundation scholarships ($22,410); foundation grants to United Way ($49,073); foundation ($169,000)
Assets: $5,366,925 (2002); $6,276,162 (2001)
Gifts Received: $500,000 (1999); $500,000 (1996); $200,000 (1995)

Typical Recipients

Arts & Humanities: Arts Centers, Arts Festivals, Arts Funds, Arts Institutes, Arts Outreach, Libraries, Museums/Galleries, Music, Opera, Performing Arts, Public Broadcasting, Theater
Civic & Public Affairs: Botanical Gardens/Parks, Chambers of Commerce, Clubs, Community Foundations, Economic Development, Civic & Public Affairs-General, Housing, Law & Justice, Municipalities/Towns, Parades/Festivals, Philanthropic Organizations, Professional & Trade Associations, Rural Affairs, Safety, Urban & Community Affairs
Education: Afterschool/Enrichment Programs, Agricultural Education, Business Education, Colleges & Universities, Community & Junior Colleges, Education Funds, Elementary Education (Private), Engineering/Technological Education, Education-General, Literacy, Minority Education, Preschool Education, Private Education (Precollege), Public Education (Precollege), Secondary Education (Private), Secondary Education (Public), Student Aid, Vocational & Technical Education
Environment: Resource Conservation
Health: AIDS/HIV, Cancer, Children's Health/Hospitals, Clinics/Medical Centers, Diabetes, Emergency/Ambulance Services, Eyes/Blindness, Health Organizations, Heart, Hospices, Hospitals, Kidney, Medical Research, Nutrition, Public Health, Research/Studies Institutes, Single-Disease Health Associations, Speech & Hearing
Religion: Ministries, Religious Welfare, Social/Policy Issues
Science: Science Museums
Social Services: Animal Protection, Big Brothers/Big Sisters, Community Service Organizations, Crime Prevention, Domestic Violence, Emergency Relief, Family Services, People with Disabilities, Recreation & Athletics, Scouts, Senior Services, Shelters/Homelessness, Special Olympics, United Funds/United Ways, YMCA/YWCA/YMHA/YWHA, Youth Organizations

Application Procedures

Initial Contact: The foundation has no formal grant application procedure or application form. Submit a full proposal in any format.
Deadlines: October 31.

Restrictions

Does not support individuals, religious organizations for sectarian purposes, political or lobbying groups, or organizations outside operating areas.

Corporate Officials

Paul J. Giddens: vice president human resources PRIM CORP EMPL vice president human resources: Quanex Corp.
Raymond A. Jean: chairman, president, chief executive officer, director ED University of Chicago MBA; University of Maine BS. PRIM CORP EMPL president, chief executive officer, director: Quanex Corp.
Terry M. Murphy: vice president finance, chief financial officer B Syracuse, NY 1948. ED University of Wisconsin BS (1970); Marquette University MBA (1974); Seton Hall University JD (1980). PRIM CORP EMPL vice president finance, chief financial officer: Quanex Corp. NONPR AFFIL member: American Bar Association; member: American Institute of CPA's.
Vernon E. Oechsle: chairman, director PRIM CORP EMPL chairman, director: Quanex Corp.

Foundation Officials

Paul J. Giddens: director, president (see above)
Terry M. Murphy: vice president, director (see above)

Grants Analysis

Disclosure Period: calendar year ending 2002
Total Grants: $266,173*
Number of Grants: 185
Average Grant: $3,131
Highest Grant: $7,500
Lowest Grant: $200
Typical Range: $100 to $5,000
*Note: Giving excludes scholarship and United Way.

Recent Grants

Note: Grants derived from 2003 Form 990.
Library-Related

2,000	Forrest Library, Forrest, IL

General

24,295	United Way of Jackson County, Jackson, MI
24,126	United Way of Fort Smith, Ft. Smith, AR
23,877	United Way of Jackson County, Jackson, MI
23,520	National Merit Scholarship Corporation, Chicago, IL

21,926	United way of Quad Cities Inc., Davenport, IA
20,000	Figge Arts Center, Davenport, IA
15,612	United Way of Texas Gulf Coast, TX
15,000	University of Saint Thomas, Houston, TX
10,438	United Way of Rice Lake, Rice Lake, WI
10,000	Barbara Bush Foundation for Family Literacy, Houston, TX

QUINCY NEWSPAPERS

Company Headquarters
Quincy, IL
Web: http://www.whig.com

Company Description
Employees: 400
SIC(s): 2700 Printing & Publishing, 4800 Communications.

Operating Locations
Quincy Newspapers (IL--Quincy)

Oakley-Lindsay Foundation of Quincy Newspapers and Its Subsidiaries

Giving Contact
Thomas A. Oakley, Community Relations Director
1130 S. 5th St.
Quincy, IL 62301
Phone: (217)223-5100

Description
EIN: 237025198
Organization Type: Corporate Foundation
Giving Locations: IL
Grant Types: General Support, Scholarship.

Financial Summary
Total Giving: $249,275 (2003); $237,575 (2002); $155,095 (2001)
Assets: $277,083 (2003); $510,455 (2002); $733,911 (2001)
Gifts Received: $500 (2002); $213,334 (2000); $178,508 (1998). Note: In 2000, contributions were received from Quincy Broadcasting Co. ($92,582), Quincy Newspapers, Inc. ($51,606), WSJV Television, Inc. ($11,239), KTTC Television ($11,200), WVVA Television, Inc. ($11,620), KTIV Television ($16,347), WREX Television, Inc. ($9,503), and the New Jersey Herald ($9,237). In 1998, contributions were received from Quincy Broadcasting Co. ($67,351), Quincy Newspapers, INC. ($6,124), WSJV Television, INC. ($9,001), KTTC Television ($10,247), WVVA Television, INC. ($13,222), KTIV Television ($8,265), and the New Jersey Herald ($8,265).

Typical Recipients
Arts & Humanities: Arts Associations & Councils, Arts Centers, Arts Funds, Community Arts, Arts & Humanities-General, Historic Preservation, History & Archaeology, Libraries, Literary Arts, Museums/Galleries, Music, Opera, Public Broadcasting, Theater
Civic & Public Affairs: Business/Free Enterprise, Chambers of Commerce, Clubs, Community Foundations, Economic Development, Civic & Public Affairs-General, Housing, Native American Affairs, Philanthropic Organizations, Professional & Trade Associations, Urban & Community Affairs
Education: Afterschool/Enrichment Programs, Arts/

Humanities Education, Colleges & Universities, Community & Junior Colleges, Education Funds, Education-General, Journalism/Media Education, Literacy, Private Education (Precollege), Secondary Education (Private), Student Aid, Vocational & Technical Education
Environment: Environment-General, Watershed
Health: Alzheimer's Disease, Arthritis, Cancer, Children's Health/Hospitals, Emergency/Ambulance Services, Hospitals, Research/Studies Institutes
Religion: Churches, Religious Welfare
Science: Science Museums
Social Services: Camps, Community Centers, Community Service Organizations, Day Care, Emergency Relief, Family Services, Food/Clothing Distribution, Homes, Recreation & Athletics, Senior Services, Social Services-General, Special Olympics, United Funds/United Ways, Volunteer Services, YMCA/YWCA/YMHA/YWHA, Youth Organizations

Application Procedures
Initial Contact: The foundation has no formal grant application procedure or application form.
Deadlines: None.

Corporate Officials
David Graff: chief financial officer, controllerdirector PRIM CORP EMPL chief financial officer, controller: Quincy Newspapers.
Peter Anthony Oakley: committee relations director PRIM CORP EMPL committee relations director: Quincy Newspapers.
Thomas A. Oakley: president, chief executive officer, publisher, editor PRIM CORP EMPL president, chief executive officer, publisher, editor: Quincy Newspapers.

Foundation Officials
Joseph Bonansinga: director
John Chadwick: director
James W. Collins: director
Joseph I. Conover: director
James L. Deschepper: director
Leo T. Henning: director
Leo T. Henning: director
Laurin Jorstad: director
F. M. Lindsay, Jr.: director
Martin M. Lindsay: director
Lucy Lindsay Smith: director
Larry R. Manne: director
Robert E. Miller: director
Allen M. Oakley: director
David R. Oakley: director
Donald M. Oakley: director
Peter Anthony Oakley: secretary (see above)
Ralph M. Oakley: director
Thomas A. Oakley: president, treasurer (see above)
Susan Oakley Day: director
Larry C. Roe: director
R. Kent Roeder: director
Charles Roth: director
Scott T. Ruff: director
Kevin J. Sargent: director
Bruce R. Tomlinson: director
Jerome P. Watson: director
Charles E. Webb: director
Dennis Williams: director

Grants Analysis
Disclosure Period: calendar year ending 2003
Total Grants: $225,475*
Number of Grants: 60
Average Grant: $3,144*
Highest Grant: $40,000
Lowest Grant: $50
Typical Range: $1,000 to $5,000
*Note: Giving excludes scholarships and United Way. Average grant figure excludes highest grant.

Recent Grants
Note: Grants derived from 2003 Form 990.

General

40,000	Blessing Foundation, Quincy, IL -- toward the cancer center
30,000	Madison Fireworks Fund Inc., Madison, WI
26,000	Knowledge Network, Springfield, IL -- toward support of infrastructure
22,900	YWCA, Quincy, IL -- for a therapeutic spa
20,200	United Way of Adams County, Quincy, IL
10,000	Adams County Chapter- American Red Cross, Quincy, IL
10,000	Good News of Christmas, Quincy, IL -- toward support of indigent families
5,500	Friends of Indian Mounds Pool, Quincy, IL
4,250	Symphony of Trees, Quincy, IL
4,000	Da Wiebring Wgem Arc Gol, Quincy, IL

QUIVEY-BAY STATE FOUNDATION

Giving Contact
Ted Cannon, Secretary & Treasurer
1515 E. 20th St.
Scottsbluff, NE 69361
Phone: (308)635-1135
Fax: (308)635-3701

Description
Founded: 1948
EIN: 476024159
Organization Type: Private Foundation
Giving Locations: NE: Western Nebraska
Grant Types: General Support, Scholarship.

Donor Information
Founder: M. S. Oulvey, Mrs. M. S. Quivey

Financial Summary
Total Giving: $209,200 (fiscal year ending January 31, 2004); $250,850 (fiscal 2002); $252,040 (fiscal 2001)
Assets: $4,336,559 (fiscal 2004); $4,925,010 (fiscal 2002); $5,407,759 (fiscal 2001)
Gifts Received: $100 (fiscal 1999)

Typical Recipients
Arts & Humanities: Arts Centers, Historic Preservation, History & Archaeology, Libraries, Music
Civic & Public Affairs: Clubs, Economic Development, Civic & Public Affairs-General, Professional & Trade Associations, Rural Affairs, Urban & Community Affairs, Zoos/Aquariums
Education: Colleges & Universities, Community & Junior Colleges, Education Funds, Engineering/Technological Education, Education-General, Public Education (Precollege), Religious Education, Student Aid
Environment: Environment-General
Health: Cancer, Children's Health/Hospitals, Clinics/Medical Centers, Emergency/Ambulance Services, Health Funds, Health Organizations, Kidney, Long-Term Care, Outpatient Health Care, Prenatal Health Issues, Respiratory
International: Health Care/Hospitals
Religion: Churches, Jewish Causes, Ministries, Religious Organizations, Religious Welfare
Science: Science Museums
Social Services: Animal Protection, Camps, Child Welfare, Community Centers, Community Service Organizations, Day Care, Delinquency & Criminal Rehabilitation, Homes, People with Disabilities, Recreation & Athletics, Scouts, Social Services-General, United Funds/United Ways, Volunteer Services, YMCA/YWCA/YMHA/YWHA, Youth Organizations

Application Procedures

Initial Contact: Send a brief letter of inquiry.
Application Requirements: Include a description of organization and purpose of funds sought.
Deadlines: None.

Restrictions

Does not support individuals or provide funds for endowments.

Foundation Officials

Ted Cannon: secretary, treasurer

Grants Analysis

Disclosure Period: fiscal year ending January 31, 2004
Total Grants: $209,200
Number of Grants: 45
Average Grant: $4,186*
Highest Grant: $25,000
Lowest Grant: $150
Typical Range: $1,000 to $10,000
*Note: Average grant figure excludes highest grant.

Recent Grants

Note: Grants derived from 2004 Form 990.
Library-Related
10,000	Friends of the Mitchell Library, Hillsdale, MI

General
25,000	YMCA, Lincoln, NE
20,500	Nebraska Independent College Foundation, Omaha, NE
20,500	Western Nebraska Community College Foundation, Scottsbluff, NE
12,000	Boy Scouts of America, Omaha, NE
11,500	Regional West Medical Center Foundation, Scottsbluff, NE
10,000	Campfire Inc.
10,000	Campus House Inc., Kearney, NE
10,000	Panhandle Humane Society, Scottsbluff, NE
7,500	Guiding Star Girls Scout Council, Ogallala, NE

R&B MACHINE TOOL CO.

Company Headquarters

118 E. Michigan Ave.
Saline, MI 48176
Web: http://www.rbmachine.com

Company Description

Employees: 275
SIC(s): 3500 Industrial Machinery & Equipment.

Operating Locations

R&B Machine Tool Co. (MI--Saline)

Edward F. Redies Foundation

Giving Contact

118 E. Michigan Ave.
Saline, MI 48176
Phone: (734)429-0154

Description

Founded: 1981
EIN: 382391326
Organization Type: Corporate Foundation
Giving Locations: MI
Grant Types: Capital, Project, Scholarship.

Donor Information

Founder: R & B Machine Tool Co.

Financial Summary

Total Giving: $304,700 (2002); $316,100 (2001). Note: In 1996 Giving includes scholarship ($5,000), United Way (8,000).
Assets: $4,135,352 (2002); $5,544,512 (2001)
Gifts Received: $50,000 (1998); $100,000 (1995); $200,000 (1994). Note: In 1995 and 1998, contributions were received from the R & B Machine Tool Co.

Typical Recipients

Arts & Humanities: Historic Preservation, Libraries, Museums/Galleries, Theater
Civic & Public Affairs: Botanical Gardens/Parks, Chambers of Commerce, Civic & Public Affairs-General, Municipalities/Towns, Safety
Education: Business Education, Colleges & Universities, Community & Junior Colleges, Education Funds, Engineering/Technological Education, Education-General, Private Education (Precollege), Public Education (Precollege), Science/Mathematics Education, Secondary Education (Private), Secondary Education (Public), Special Education, Student Aid
Environment: Environment-General
Health: Children's Health/Hospitals, Clinics/Medical Centers, Emergency/Ambulance Services, Health Organizations, Hospices, Hospitals, Kidney, Long-Term Care, Medical Rehabilitation, Nursing Services, Preventive Medicine/Wellness Organizations, Public Health
Religion: Churches, Religious Organizations, Religious Welfare
Science: Science Museums
Social Services: At-Risk Youth, Big Brothers/Big Sisters, Camps, Child Welfare, Community Service Organizations, Emergency Relief, Family Services, Food/Clothing Distribution, Homes, People with Disabilities, Recreation & Athletics, Senior Services, Social Services-General, Special Olympics, Substance Abuse, United Funds/United Ways, Youth Organizations

Application Procedures

Initial Contact: Send a brief cover letter, signed by an authorized individual of the organization.
Application Requirements: Clearly state the purpose of funds sought, amount requested, and the time period in which funds will be used. Also include proof of tax-exempt status and detailed financial data, including total estimated price, proposed method of financing, other sources of funding, and expected completion date.
Deadlines: March 31.

Restrictions

The foundation considers applications for grants from well-established, tax exempt organizations seeking funds for capital improvements, equipment purchases, or other special needs of a tangible asset nature.

Foundation Officials

Karen Redies: treasurer, secretary

Grants Analysis

Disclosure Period: calendar year ending 2002
Total Grants: $264,700*
Number of Grants: 30
Average Grant: $5,882*
Highest Grant: $50,000
Lowest Grant: $1,000
Typical Range: $1,000 to $10,000
*Note: Giving excludes scholarship. Average grant figure excludes two highest grants ($100,000).

Recent Grants

Note: Grants derived from 2003 Form 990.
Library-Related
3,000	Saline Public Library, Saline, MI

General
50,000	City of Saline Recreation Parks Fund, Saline, MI
50,000	Father Gabriel Richard High School, Ann Arbor, MI -- building fund
20,000	Boysville of Michigan, Clinton, MI
20,000	Washtenaw Christian Academy, Saline, MI
15,000	Houghton Memorial Scholarship Saline Area Schools, Saline, MI
10,000	Jack Crabtree Scholarship, Saline, MI
7,000	Father Gabriel Richard High School, Ann Arbor, MI -- scholarship fund
5,000	American Red Cross, Ann Arbor, MI
5,000	Ann Arbor Hospice, Ann Arbor, MI
5,000	Eastern Michigan University, Ypsilanti, MI

SIDNEY AND ESTHER RABB CHARITABLE FOUNDATION

Giving Contact

Carol R. Goldberg, Trustee
c/o Avcar Group Ltd.
225 Franklin St., Suite 2700
Boston, MA 02110-2804
Phone: (617)695-1946

Description

Founded: 1952
EIN: 046039595
Organization Type: Private Foundation
Giving Locations: FL; MA: emphasis on Boston Northeast.
Grant Types: General Support.

Donor Information

Founder: the late Sidney R. Rabb

Financial Summary

Total Giving: $394,550 (2001)
Assets: $7,642,249 (2001)

Typical Recipients

Arts & Humanities: History & Archaeology, Libraries, Museums/Galleries, Music, Public Broadcasting
Civic & Public Affairs: Parades/Festivals, Women's Affairs
Education: Arts/Humanities Education, Colleges & Universities, Environmental Education, Faculty Development, Education-General, Public Education (Precollege), Science/Mathematics Education, Social Sciences Education
Health: Children's Health/Hospitals, Health Organizations, Hospices, Hospitals, Medical Rehabilitation, Medical Research
Religion: Jewish Causes, Synagogues/Temples
Science: Science Museums
Social Services: Day Care, Family Planning, Food/Clothing Distribution, Scouts, Senior Services, Sexual Abuse

Application Procedures

Initial Contact: Send a brief letter of inquiry describing program or project.
Deadlines: None.

Foundation Officials

Helene R. Cahners-Kaplan: trustee
Avram J. Goldberg: trustee
Carol Rabb Goldberg: trustee B Newton, MA 1931. ED Tufts University BA (1955); Harvard University Graduate School of Business Administration (1969). PRIM CORP EMPL president: AVCAR Group. CLUB AFFIL Commercial Merchants Boston Club.
Deborah B. Goldberg: trustee
Joshua R. Goldberg: trustee

Grants Analysis

Disclosure Period: calendar year ending 2001
Total Grants: $394,550
Number of Grants: 27
Average Grant: $8,040*
Highest Grant: $185,500
Lowest Grant: $1,000
Typical Range: $1,000 to $20,000
*Note:** Average grant figure excludes highest grant.

Recent Grants

Note: Grants derived from 2001 Form 990.

Library-Related

8,000	Boston Public Library Foundation, Boston, MA

General

185,500	Combined Jewish Philanthropies, Boston, MA
25,000	Planned Parenthood League of Massachusetts, Boston, MA
20,000	Boston Latin School Foundation, Boston, MA
20,000	WGBH Education Foundation, Boston, MA
17,500	Make A Wish Foundation of Metro New York, Inc., New York, NY
15,500	University of Massachusetts Center Foundation, Amherst, MA
15,000	Boston Symphony Orchestra, Boston, MA
11,250	Putney School, Putney, VT
8,000	Brookline Senior Center, Brookline, MA
7,500	Park School

SIDNEY R. RABB CHARITABLE TRUST

Giving Contact

Carol R. Goldbert, Trustee
225 Franklin Street, Suite 2700
Boston, MA 02110-2804
Phone: (617)695-1946

Description

Founded: 1952
EIN: 222754563
Organization Type: Private Foundation
Giving Locations: MA
Grant Types: Capital.

Donor Information

Founder: Esther V. Rabb

Financial Summary

Total Giving: $734,025 (fiscal year ending August 31, 2001)
Assets: $16,637,916 (fiscal 2001)

Typical Recipients

Arts & Humanities: Community Arts, Libraries, Museums/Galleries, Music, Public Broadcasting, Theater
Civic & Public Affairs: Botanical Gardens/Parks, Community Foundations, Civic & Public Affairs-General, Nonprofit Management, Philanthropic Organizations
Education: Arts/Humanities Education, Colleges & Universities, Elementary Education (Public), Education-General, Leadership Training, Legal Education, Medical Education, Private Education (Precollege), Public Education (Precollege), Secondary Education (Private), Social Sciences Education
Health: Children's Health/Hospitals, Clinics/Medical Centers, Hospices, Hospitals, Medical Rehabilitation, Medical Research, Mental Health
Religion: Jewish Causes, Religious Organizations, Synagogues/Temples

Social Services: Big Brothers/Big Sisters, Child Welfare, Family Planning, Senior Services, Sexual Abuse, United Funds/United Ways, Youth Organizations

Application Procedures

Initial Contact: There is no set form for application.
Application Requirements: At a minimum, proposals should include a concise statement of the purpose of funds sought, current year's operating budget, recently audited financial statement, a list of board members, proof of tax-exempt status, and resumes of all key staff personnel. If the grant is sought for a specific program, the staff and budget for that program must be described.
Deadlines: None.

Restrictions

Does not support individuals.

Additional Information

Trust(s): Bingham Dana LLP Palmer and Dodge LLP

Foundation Officials

Nancy L. Cahners: trustee
Helene R. Cahners-Kaplan: trustee
M. Gordon Ehrlich, Esq.: trustee B Springfield, MA 1930. ED Yale University BS (1951); Harvard University LLB (1954). PRIM CORP EMPL partner: Bingham, Dana & Gould. NONPR AFFIL chairman, member: Boston Tax Forum; member: Massachusetts Bar Association; chairman, member: Boston Estate Planning & Business Council; member: American Law Institute; trustee: Beth Israel Hospital; member: American Bar Association.
Carol Rabb Goldberg: trustee B Newton, MA 1931. ED Tufts University BA (1955); Harvard University Graduate School of Business Administration (1969). PRIM CORP EMPL president: AVCAR Group. CLUB AFFIL Commercial Merchants Boston Club.
Arthur B. Page: trustee

Grants Analysis

Disclosure Period: fiscal year ending August 31, 2001
Total Grants: $734,025
Number of Grants: 27
Average Grant: $15,232*
Highest Grant: $338,000
Lowest Grant: $2,000
Typical Range: $5,000 to $30,000
*Note:** Average grant figure excludes highest grant.

Recent Grants

Note: Grants derived from 2001 Form 990.

Library-Related

17,000	Boston Public Library Foundation, Boston, MA

General

338,000	Combined Jewish Philanthropies, Boston, MA
43,000	Avalon Elementary School
37,500	Boston Jewish Community Women's Fund, Boston, MA
35,000	Boston Symphony Orchestra, Boston, MA
35,000	Landmark School, Boston, MA
26,500	Beth Israel Deaconess Medical Center, Boston, MA
25,000	Brandeis University, Waltham, MA -- Women's Studies Program
25,000	Hebrew College, Brookline, MA
25,000	Naples Botanical Garden, Naples, FL
18,000	Berkshire Hills Music Academy, Inc., South Hadley, MA

ED RACHAL FOUNDATION

Giving Contact

Paul D. Altheide, Chief Executive Officer and Secretary
500 N. Shoreline, Suite 1002
Corpus Christi, TX 78471
Phone: (361)881-9040
Fax: (361)881-9885
E-mail: info@edrachal.org
Web: http://www.edrachal.org

Description

Founded: 1965
EIN: 741116595
Organization Type: Private Foundation
Giving Locations: TX
Grant Types: General Support, Scholarship.

Financial Summary

Total Giving: $1,301,378 (fiscal year ending August 31, 2004); $501,633 (fiscal 2001)
Assets: $39,643,937 (fiscal 2004); $41,022,239 (fiscal 2001)

Typical Recipients

Arts & Humanities: Historic Preservation, Libraries, Museums/Galleries, Music, Public Broadcasting
Civic & Public Affairs: Community Foundations, Civic & Public Affairs-General, Law & Justice, Parades/Festivals, Safety
Education: Agricultural Education, Colleges & Universities, Education Funds, Engineering/Technological Education, Environmental Education, Education-General, International Studies, Preschool Education, Private Education (Precollege), Public Education (Precollege), Science/Mathematics Education, Secondary Education (Public), Social Sciences Education, Student Aid
Environment: Air/Water Quality, Environment-General, Resource Conservation, Wildlife Protection
Health: Cancer, Emergency/Ambulance Services, Hospitals, Medical Research, Public Health, Single-Disease Health Associations, Trauma Treatment
Religion: Churches, Religious Welfare
Social Services: Animal Protection, Big Brothers/Big Sisters, Camps, Child Welfare, Community Service Organizations, Crime Prevention, Delinquency & Criminal Rehabilitation, Emergency Relief, Family Planning, Family Services, Recreation & Athletics, Scouts, Shelters/Homelessness, Social Services-General, Substance Abuse, Volunteer Services, YMCA/YWCA/YMHA/YWHA, Youth Organizations

Application Procedures

Initial Contact: Send a brief letter of inquiry describing program or project.
Deadlines: None.

Foundation Officials

Paul D. Altheide: secretary, chief executive officer
Richard Schendel: treasurer
Robert L. Walker: vice chairman
John D. White: chairman

Grants Analysis

Disclosure Period: fiscal year ending August 31, 2004
Total Grants: $1,301,378
Number of Grants: 72
Average Grant: $13,234*
Highest Grant: $250,000
Lowest Grant: $500
Typical Range: $5,000 to $30,000
*Note:** Average grant figure excludes two highest grants ($375,000).

Recent Grants

Note: Grants derived from 2004 Form 990.

General

250,000	Texas Agricultural & Mechanical University Press, College Station, TX -- for series in nautical archaeology
125,000	Texas Agricultural & Mechanical Foundation, College Station, TX
100,000	Texas Agricultural & Mechanical Foundation, College Station, TX -- for professorship/chair for chemical synthesis
75,000	South Texas Children's Home Inc., Beeville, TX -- for cottage renovation
50,000	Cliff Maus Village Trust, Corpus Christi, TX -- for exterior critical repair
50,000	Institute of Nautical Archaeology, College Station, TX -- for the conservation of Denbigh project
50,000	Service of the Emergency Aid Resource Center for the Homeless Inc., Houston, TX -- for tiny treasures program
50,000	Texas Agricultural & Mechanical Foundation, College Station, TX -- for corps of cadets academic learning center
50,000	Texas Agricultural & Mechanical Foundation, College Station, TX -- for Jones Forest education center
35,000	Del Mar College Foundation Inc., Corpus Christi, TX -- for 18-wheel truck for truck driving school

RAHR MALTING CO.

Company Headquarters

301 4th Ave. S, Ste. 567
Minneapolis, MN 55415
Web: http://www.rahr.com

Company Description

Employees: 100
SIC(s): 2000 Food & Kindred Products, 2083 Malt.

Operating Locations

Rahr Malting Co. (MN--Shakopee)

Rahr Foundation

Giving Contact

Frederick W. Rahr, President & Director
Rahr Foundation
567 Grain Exchange
PO Box 15186
Minneapolis, MN 55415-0186
Phone: (612)332-5161
Fax: (612)332-6841

Description

Founded: 1942
EIN: 396046046
Organization Type: Corporate Foundation
Giving Locations: MN: Minneapolis metropolitan area; WI: Manitowoc
Grant Types: General Support.

Donor Information

Founder: Rahr Malting Co.

Financial Summary

Total Giving: $265,435 (2003); $271,685 (2002); $275,125 (2001)
Assets: $4,898,486 (2003); $4,487,512 (2002); $6,062,903 (2001)

Typical Recipients

Arts & Humanities: Arts Centers, Arts Institutes, Arts Outreach, Community Arts, Ethnic & Folk Arts, Historic Preservation, History & Archaeology, Libraries, Music, Opera, Public Broadcasting, Theater

Civic & Public Affairs: Botanical Gardens/Parks, Clubs, Community Foundations, Civic & Public Affairs-General, Municipalities/Towns, Public Policy, Urban & Community Affairs, Zoos/Aquariums
Education: Afterschool/Enrichment Programs, Agricultural Education, Arts/Humanities Education, Business Education, Colleges & Universities, Education Funds, Engineering/Technological Education, Education-General, Leadership Training, Medical Education, Minority Education, Private Education (Precollege), Religious Education, Student Aid, Vocational & Technical Education
Environment: Air/Water Quality, Environment-General, Protection, Resource Conservation, Watershed, Wildlife Protection
Health: Arthritis, Children's Health/Hospitals, Clinics/Medical Centers, Emergency/Ambulance Services, Health Organizations, Hospitals, Medical Rehabilitation, Medical Research
International: International Environmental Issues
Religion: Religious Welfare
Science: Science Museums
Social Services: Animal Protection, Community Service Organizations, Domestic Violence, Emergency Relief, Family Planning, Family Services, People with Disabilities, Recreation & Athletics, Scouts, Senior Services, Shelters/Homelessness, Special Olympics, United Funds/United Ways, YMCA/YWCA/YMHA/YWHA, Youth Organizations

Application Procedures

Initial Contact: Request application form.
Deadlines: March 15.

Restrictions

Does not support individuals, religious organizations for sectarian purposes, political or lobbying groups, or organizations outside operating areas.

Additional Information

Provides scholarships to children of employees of Rahr Malting Co. and its affiliates.

Corporate Officials

John F. Alsip, III: president, chief executive officer, director B 1937. PRIM CORP EMPL president, chief executive officer, director: Rahr Malting Co.
T. C. Haffenreffer, Jr.: vice chairman, director PRIM CORP EMPL vice chairman, director: Rahr Malting Co.
Jim Olson: chief financial officer, controller, vice president financial PRIM CORP EMPL chief financial officer, controller, vice president financial: Rahr Malting Co.
Guido R. Rahr, Jr.: chairman, director B Milwaukee, WI 1928. ED Dartmouth College (1951). PRIM CORP EMPL chairman, director: Rahr Malting Co. CORP AFFIL director: Manitowoc Co.

Foundation Officials

George D. Gackle: treasurer, director B Kulm, ND 1925. ED University of North Dakota (1949). PRIM CORP EMPL director: Rahr Malting Co. CORP AFFIL vice president, director: Lakeside Machine Shop.
Jack D. Gage: director
Mary Gresham: secretary, director
Frederick W. Rahr: president, director
Guido R. Rahr, Jr.: vice president, director (see above)

Grants Analysis

Disclosure Period: calendar year ending 2003
Total Grants: $264,435*
Number of Grants: 68
Average Grant: $3,889
Highest Grant: $25,500
Lowest Grant: $100
Typical Range: $1,000 to $5,000
*Note: Giving excludes scholarships.

Recent Grants

Note: Grants derived from 2003 Form 990.

General

25,500	Minnesota Private College Fund, MN
25,000	University of Minnesota-College of Agriculture, St. Paul, MN -- toward the Rahr foundation graduate endowment
21,000	Rahr Foundation Scholarship Fund
10,000	Ducks Unlimited -- for the Minnesota shallow lakes program
10,000	Nature Conservancy
10,000	Shakopee Area Catholic Education Center, Shakopee, MN
8,500	Minnesota Opera, St. Paul, MN
7,100	Courage Center, Golden Valley, MN
7,000	Guthrie Theater Foundation, Minneapolis, MN
7,000	Woodland Dunes Nature Center, Manitowoc, WI

M. E. RAKER FOUNDATION

Giving Contact

John E. Hogan, President
6207 Constitution Drive.
Ft. Wayne, IN 46804
Phone: (219)436-2182
Fax: (219)432-3146

Description

Founded: 1984
EIN: 311040474
Organization Type: Private Foundation
Giving Locations: IN
Grant Types: General Support, Scholarship.

Donor Information

Founder: the late M. E. Raker

Financial Summary

Total Giving: $540,445 (fiscal year ending June 30, 2002); $510,670 (fiscal 2001)
Giving Analysis: Giving for fiscal 2001 includes: foundation scholarships ($31,500)
Assets: $9,703,243 (fiscal 2002); $11,513,080 (fiscal 2001)

Typical Recipients

Arts & Humanities: Arts Appreciation, Arts & Humanities-General, History & Archaeology, Libraries, Museums/Galleries, Public Broadcasting, Theater
Civic & Public Affairs: Botanical Gardens/Parks, Chambers of Commerce, Employment/Job Training, Civic & Public Affairs-General, Housing, Rural Affairs, Urban & Community Affairs, Zoos/Aquariums
Education: Agricultural Education, Business Education, Colleges & Universities, Elementary Education (Private), Elementary Education (Public), Education-General, Health & Physical Education, Private Education (Precollege), Religious Education, Science/Mathematics Education, Secondary Education (Private), Special Education, Student Aid
Environment: Environment-General, Resource Conservation
Health: AIDS/HIV, Cancer, Children's Health/Hospitals, Clinics/Medical Centers, Emergency/Ambulance Services, Eyes/Blindness, Health Organizations, Hospitals, Mental Health
Religion: Churches, Ministries, Religious Organizations, Religious Welfare
Science: Scientific Centers & Institutes
Social Services: Big Brothers/Big Sisters, Child Welfare, Community Service Organizations, Day Care, Food/Clothing Distribution, People with Disabilities, Recreation & Athletics, Scouts, Senior Services, Sexual Abuse, Shelters/Homelessness, Substance Abuse, YMCA/YWCA/YMHA/YWHA, Youth Organizations

Application Procedures

Initial Contact: Grant application form.s will be furnished upon request.
Deadlines: None.

Restrictions

Does not support individuals or make grants in furtherance of the arts.

Additional Information

Publications: Application Form; Guidelines

Foundation Officials

John E. Hogan: president
John N. Pichon: director
Stephen J. Williams: director

Grants Analysis

Disclosure Period: fiscal year ending June 30, 2002
Total Grants: $508,945*
Number of Grants: 60
Average Grant: $8,482
Highest Grant: $25,000
Lowest Grant: $1,000
Typical Range: $1,000 to $20,000
*Note: Giving excludes scholarships.

Recent Grants

Note: Grants derived from fiscal 2002 Form 990.
General

25,000	Friends of Matea Park, Grabil, IN -- for Metea County Park Nature Center
25,000	Junior Achievement, Ft. Wayne, IN -- for Development of Exchange City Program
20,000	Anthony Wayne Services, Ft. Wayne, IN -- for Home Pointe Program
20,000	Fort Wayne Public Television, Ft. Wayne, IN -- for building and system upgrade
20,000	Fort Wayne Public Television, Ft. Wayne, IN -- for building and system upgrade
15,600	Learning and Development Center, Ft. Wayne, IN -- for Preschool Program
15,000	Benoit Academy, Ft. Wayne, IN -- for new roof
15,000	Boys and Girls Club of Fort Wayne, Ft. Wayne, IN -- for program expenses
15,000	Salvation Army, Ft. Wayne, IN -- for elevator
15,000	YMCA of Greater Fort Wayne, Ft. Wayne, IN -- for Jorgenson YMC

RALPH'S GROCERY CO.

Company Headquarters

Compton, CA
Web: http://www.ralphs.com

Company Description

Employees: 15,000
SIC(s): 5411 Grocery Stores.

Operating Locations

Ralph's Grocery Co. (CA--Compton)

Nonmonetary Support

Type: Donated Equipment; In-kind Services

Ralph's-Food 4 Less Foundation

Giving Contact

Jan Golleher, Executive Director
PO Box 54143
Los Angeles, CA 90054
Phone: (310)884-6250
Fax: (310)884-2590

Web: http://ralphs.com/ corpnewsinfo_charitablegiving_art5.htm

Alternate Contact

1100 West Artesia Boulevard
Compton, CA 90220
Note: Alternate address is for grant application pickup.

Description

Founded: 1992
EIN: 330492352
Organization Type: Corporate Foundation
Giving Locations: CA: southern California
Grant Types: General Support, Project, Scholarship.

Donor Information

Founder: Food 4 Less Supermarkets, Ron Burkle, Ralph Grocery Co.

Financial Summary

Total Giving: $1,784,751 (2001)
Assets: $2,988,650 (2001)
Gifts Received: $1,530,344 (2001); $3,691,534 (2000); $3,613,729 (1998). Note: In 1998, contributions were received from Western Union Financial Services ($200,000); Anheuser-Busch, Inc. ($124,293); Ralphs Grocery Co. ($40,000); and numerous other donors who contributed less than $40,000 each. In 1995, contributions were received from Anheuser-Busch ($154,000), Ralphs Grocery Co. ($855,000), Western Union ($400,000), Miller Brewing Co. ($63,335), and Coors Brewing ($95,500); numerous other donors contributed less than $50,000 each.

Typical Recipients

Arts & Humanities: Arts Centers, Arts Festivals, Arts Institutes, Ethnic & Folk Arts, Film & Video, Historic Preservation, History & Archaeology, Libraries, Museums/Galleries, Music, Performing Arts, Theater
Civic & Public Affairs: African American Affairs, Asian American Affairs, Botanical Gardens/Parks, Clubs, Economic Development, Employment/Job Training, Ethnic Organizations, Civic & Public Affairs-General, Hispanic Affairs, Housing, Inner-City Development, Law & Justice, Legal Aid, Municipalities/Towns, Public Policy, Safety, Urban & Community Affairs
Education: Afterschool/Enrichment Programs, Business Education, Colleges & Universities, Education Funds, Education Reform, Education-General, International Studies, Literacy, Medical Education, Minority Education, Private Education (Precollege), Public Education (Precollege), Religious Education, Science/Mathematics Education, Secondary Education (Public), Special Education, Student Aid
Environment: Environment-General, Protection
Health: AIDS/HIV, Cancer, Children's Health/Hospitals, Clinics/Medical Centers, Diabetes, Emergency/Ambulance Services, Eyes/Blindness, Health Organizations, Heart, Hospitals, Mental Health, Multiple Sclerosis, Prenatal Health Issues, Single-Disease Health Associations
International: Foreign Educational Institutions, Human Rights
Religion: Churches, Religion-General, Jewish Causes, Missionary Activities (Domestic), Religious Organizations, Religious Welfare
Science: Science Museums
Social Services: Animal Protection, At-Risk Youth, Big Brothers/Big Sisters, Camps, Child Abuse, Child Welfare, Community Service Organizations, Crime Prevention, Domestic Violence, Emergency Relief, Family Planning, Food/Clothing Distribution, Homes, People with Disabilities, Recreation & Athletics, Scouts, Senior Services, Social Services-General, Substance Abuse, United Funds/United Ways, Veterans, YMCA/YWCA/YMHA/YWHA, Youth Organizations

Application Procedures

Initial Contact: Send letter of request.
Application Requirements: Include a thorough outline of the program, including the amount requested, how funds will be used and whom they will serve, budget, funding sources, proof of tax-exempt status, and supporting materials.
Deadlines: None.
Review Process: Foundation is administered by the community religious department of the Ralphs Grocery Company under the direction of a Board of Trustees and an executive director. Proposals are reviewed by the executive director; a grants committee appointed by the board gives final approval of allocations.

Restrictions

Grants are not made to individuals, memorial campaigns, political activities, endowment campaigns, or to fund programs that are discriminatory.

Corporate Officials

Ron Burkle: chairman, chief executive officer PRIM CORP EMPL chairman: Ralph's Grocery Co.
Sam Duncan: president, chief executive officer PRIM CORP EMPL president: Ralph's Grocery Co.

Foundation Officials

Ron Burkle: chairman (see above)
Sam Duncan: president (see above)

Grants Analysis

Disclosure Period: calendar year ending 2001
Total Grants: $1,726,201*
Number of Grants: 332
Average Grant: $5,199
Highest Grant: $235,432
Lowest Grant: $500
Typical Range: $500 to $25,000
*Note: Giving excludes scholarship.

Recent Grants

Note: Grants derived from 2004 Form 990.
General

100,000	Susan G. Komen Breast Cancer Foundation, Costa Mesa, CA
50,000	American Red Cross, Washington, DC
33,250	Los Angeles Urban League, Los Angeles, CA
21,250	Reviving Baseball in Inner Cities, Los Angeles, CA
20,000	Susan G. Komen Breast Cancer Foundation, Las Vegas, NV
20,000	Susan G Komen Breast Cancer Foundation, Las Vegas, NV
17,970	City of Hope, Los Angeles, CA
15,000	Citizenship Education Fund, Chicago, IL
15,000	City of Riverside Park and Recreation Department, Riverside, CA
15,000	Long Beach Veterans Day Parade Committee, Long Beach, CA

RASKOB FOUNDATION FOR CATHOLIC ACTIVITIES, INC.

Giving Contact

Frederick J. Perella, Jr., Executive Vice President
PO Box 4019
Wilmington, DE 19807
Phone: (302)655-4440
Fax: (302)655-3223
Web: http://www.rfca.org

Description

Founded: 1945
EIN: 510070060
Organization Type: Family Foundation
Giving Locations: internationally; nationally.
Grant Types: Challenge, Conference/Seminar, Emergency, General Support, Loan, Matching, Multi-year/Continuing Support, Operating Expenses, Project, Seed Money.

Donor Information

Founder: The Raskob Foundation for Catholic Activities was established in 1945 by John J. Raskob and his wife, Helena S. Raskob. Mr. Raskob (d. 1950) was vice president of DuPont, chairman of the board of General Motors, and one of the builders of the Empire State Building. The foundation that he established is unusual in that it is a membership corporation, with the membership made up primarily of Raskob family members. There are over 90 members.

Financial Summary

Total Giving: $4,844,331 (2003)
Assets: $137,195,991 (2003)
Gifts Received: $20,000 (1997)

Typical Recipients

Arts & Humanities: Historic Preservation
Civic & Public Affairs: Business/Free Enterprise, Community Foundations, Employment/Job Training, Ethnic Organizations, Civic & Public Affairs-General, Hispanic Affairs, Housing, Law & Justice, Legal Aid, Native American Affairs, Philanthropic Organizations, Safety, Urban & Community Affairs
Education: Colleges & Universities, Community & Junior Colleges, Education Funds, Elementary Education (Private), Faculty Development, Education-General, Leadership Training, Medical Education, Minority Education, Private Education (Precollege), Religious Education, Secondary Education (Private), Secondary Education (Public), Special Education, Student Aid, Vocational & Technical Education
Health: Adolescent Health Issues, AIDS/HIV, Children's Health/Hospitals, Clinics/Medical Centers, Health Funds, Health Organizations, Hospices, Hospitals, Medical Rehabilitation, Mental Health, Nursing Services, Preventive Medicine/Wellness Organizations, Public Health
International: Foreign Educational Institutions, International-General, Health Care/Hospitals, International Development, International Environmental Issues, International Organizations, International Peace & Security Issues, International Relief Efforts, Missionary/Religious Activities
Religion: Bible Study/Translation, Churches, Dioceses, Religion-General, Ministries, Missionary Activities (Domestic), Religious Organizations, Religious Welfare, Social/Policy Issues
Science: Science-General
Social Services: At-Risk Youth, Child Welfare, Community Centers, Community Service Organizations, Counseling, Day Care, Delinquency & Criminal Rehabilitation, Domestic Violence, Emergency Relief, Family Planning, Family Services, Food/Clothing Distribution, Homes, People with Disabilities, Recreation & Athletics, Refugee Assistance, Senior Services, Shelters/Homelessness, Social Services-General, Substance Abuse, Volunteer Services, Youth Organizations

Application Procedures

Initial Contact: The foundation should be contacted by letter or fax to determine eligibility and to obtain an application form and guidelines.
Application Requirements: A full application requires a completed original application form; narrative summary of the proposal (not to exceed five pages); detailed budget of the proposed project; copy of the latest annual auditor's report or financial statement, listing actual income, assets, and expenditures; and a letter from the Ordinary of the Diocese (where the project will take place) commenting on the proposed project. Religious orders not under the jurisdiction of an Ordinary must send a letter to the local Ordinary from the Provincial, Abbot, Mother Superior, etc., informing him about the application. A copy of the letter must be submitted to the foundation.
Deadlines: Applications for the springboard of trustees meeting must be received between December 8 and February 8. Applications for the fall meeting must be received between June 8 and August 8. Applicants are urged to submit applications as early as possible during these time periods.
Review Process: The board of trustees meets twice a year, in the spring and fall. Applications are considered on their merits. Need and the good to be accomplished are prime considerations. It is the board's policy to stretch its funds to help as many different Catholic activities as it can. Most grants are, therefore, under $15,000.

Restrictions

The foundation only accepts applications from Roman Catholic tax-exempt organizations listed in the *Official Catholic Directory* published by P.J. Kenedy & Sons, New York. The foundation does not accept applications for debt reduction, scholarly research leading to a degree, continuing subsidies, or for after-the-fact funding. It makes no grants to individuals or for tuition. It does not consider applications for scholarships, fellowships, or endowments. As a general rule, capital campaigns and construction projects have a low priority. The Foundation does not generally make contributions to the same organization on a continuing or regular basis.

Additional Information

The foundation has a particular interest in projects in which self-help and local support are demonstrated.
Publications: Biennial Report; Application Form; Guidelines

Foundation Officials

Ann R. Borden: trustee
Helen R. Doordan: president, trustee
Sister Patricia Geuting: trustee
Thomas Geuting, III: secretary, trustee
Patrick W. McGrory: trustee
Frederick J. Perella, Jr.: executive vice president
Anthony W. Raskob, Jr.: first vice president, trustee
B. Russell Raskob: treasurer, trustee
Christopher R. Raskob: second vice president, trustee
Richard G. Raskob: trustee
Timothy T. Raskob: assistant treasurer, trustee
William F. Raskob, III: chairman, trustee
Edward H. Robinson: trustee
Lucia I. Robinson: trustee
Margaret Y. Robinson: trustee
Theresa G. Robinson: second assistant treasurer, trustee

Grants Analysis

Disclosure Period: calendar year ending 2003
Total Grants: $4,844,331
Number of Grants: 426
Average Grant: $11,372
Highest Grant: $548,250
Lowest Grant: $250
Typical Range: $1,000 to $25,000

Recent Grants

Note: Grants derived from 2003 Form 990.
General

548,250	Pacific Institute for Community Organization, Oakland, CA -- to implement the Skipper initiative
260,000	National Catholic Community Foundation, Annapolis, MD
150,000	Life Directions USA, Wyandotte, MI -- to implement complete development based restructuring
100,000	New Haven Sponsoring Committee Elm City Congregations Organized, New Haven, CT -- towards financing for the Nehemiah Housing program
75,000	Sisters of St. Francis of Assisi, Baltimore, MD -- towards renovation of former Motherhouse of congregation's frail and elderly Sisters
50,000	Instituto Fe y Vida, Stockton, CA
50,000	RENEW International, Plainfield, NJ -- towards development of faith sharing materials
45,000	Sisters of Mercy, West Hartford, CT -- to underwrite meeting expenses of a coordinating committee of religious women ministering in Africa
40,000	Archdiocese of Santa Fe, Albuquerque, NM -- to underwrite salary, rentals etc., to organize and conduct special events for young adults
40,000	Diocese of Gallup, Gallup, NM -- towards renovation of Catholic Indian center building

MILTON M. RATNER FOUNDATION

Giving Contact

Therese M. Thorn, Treasurer
PO Box 250628
Franklin, MI 48025
Phone: (414)765-2017

Description

Founded: 1968
EIN: 386160330
Organization Type: Private Foundation
Giving Locations: GA; MI
Grant Types: Capital, Endowment, General Support, Project, Research, Scholarship.

Donor Information

Founder: Milton M. Ratner Trust

Financial Summary

Total Giving: $407,300 (fiscal year ending August 31, 2004); $569,700 (fiscal 2001)
Giving Analysis: Giving for fiscal 2004 includes: foundation grants to United Way ($30,000); fiscal 2001: foundation grants to United Way ($50,000)
Assets: $8,384,691 (fiscal 2004); $9,450,329 (fiscal 2001)

Typical Recipients

Arts & Humanities: Arts Associations & Councils, History & Archaeology, Libraries, Music, Theater
Civic & Public Affairs: Civic & Public Affairs-General, Municipalities/Towns, Urban & Community Affairs
Education: Colleges & Universities, Continuing Education, Education Funds, Engineering/Technological Education, Education-General, Legal Education, Literacy, Medical Education, Private Education (Precollege), Public Education (Precollege), Religious Education, Science/Mathematics Education, Secondary Education (Public), Student Aid, Vocational & Technical Education
Health: Alzheimer's Disease, Children's Health/Hospitals, Clinics/Medical Centers, Diabetes, Emergency/Ambulance Services, Health Funds, Health Organizations, Heart, Hospices, Hospitals, Medical Research, Single-Disease Health Associations
Religion: Churches, Jewish Causes, Ministries, Religious Organizations, Religious Welfare, Synagogues/Temples
Social Services: Animal Protection, At-Risk Youth, Child Welfare, Community Service Organizations,

Delinquency & Criminal Rehabilitation, Family Services, People with Disabilities, Recreation & Athletics, Scouts, United Funds/United Ways, Volunteer Services, Youth Organizations

Application Procedures

Initial Contact: Send a brief letter of inquiry.
Application Requirements: Include proof of tax-exempt status, an outline of the proposed budget, and program objectives.
Deadlines: August 31.

Restrictions

Does not support individuals.

Foundation Officials

Charles R. McDonald: vice president, trustee
Mary Jo Ratner Rosson: president, trustee
Therese M. Thorn: treasurer

Grants Analysis

Disclosure Period: fiscal year ending August 31, 2004
Total Grants: $377,300*
Number of Grants: 48
Average Grant: $7,860
Highest Grant: $20,000
Lowest Grant: $1,000
Typical Range: $5,000 to $15,000
*Note: Giving excludes United Way.

Recent Grants

Note: Grants derived from 2004 Form 990.
General

20,000	Calhoun Gordon Arts Council, Calhoun, GA -- Ratner theatre building fund
20,000	Friends of the Gem Theatre Inc., Calhoun, GA -- capital campaign
20,000	Gordon Hospital Foundation, Calhoun, GA -- capital campaign
15,000	United Way Community Services, Detroit, MI
15,000	United Way Gordon County, Calhoun, GA
10,000	Alfred University, Alfred, NY -- for scholarship endowment fund
10,000	Alzheimer's Disease and Related Disorders Association Inc., Chicago, IL -- for research support
10,000	Alzheimer's Disease and Related Disorders Association Inc., Dalton, GA
10,000	Appalachian Technical College, Jasper, GA -- for scholarship endowment fund
10,000	Bucknell University, Lewisburg, PA -- Mike Andrew's memorial scholarship

A. C. RATSHESKY FOUNDATION

Giving Contact

Michealle Larkins, Program Officer
c/o GMA
77 Summer Street, 8th Fl.
Boston, MA 02110-1006
Phone: (617)426-7080
Fax: (617)426-7087
E-mail: ratsheskyfoundation@grantsmanagement.com
Web: http://www.grantsmanagement.com/ratshesky.html
Note: Ms. Larkins' telephone extension is 302.

Description

Founded: 1916
EIN: 046017426
Organization Type: Private Foundation
Giving Locations: MA: Boston and contiguous communities

Grant Types: Capital, Emergency, General Support, Operating Expenses, Project.

Donor Information

Founder: the late A. C. Ratshesky and family

Financial Summary

Total Giving: $233,600 (2001)
Assets: $8,077,012 (2001)
Gifts Received: $34,794 (1995); $7,000 (1994); $87,410 (1992). Note: In 1995, contributions were received from the estate of Hetty Kaffenburgh.

Typical Recipients

Arts & Humanities: Arts Associations & Councils, Arts Centers, Arts Outreach, Community Arts, Dance, Ethnic & Folk Arts, History & Archaeology, Libraries, Museums/Galleries, Music, Opera, Performing Arts, Theater
Civic & Public Affairs: Asian American Affairs, Civil Rights, Economic Development, Employment/Job Training, Ethnic Organizations, Civic & Public Affairs-General, Hispanic Affairs, Housing, Law & Justice, Municipalities/Towns, Parades/Festivals, Philanthropic Organizations, Public Policy, Safety, Urban & Community Affairs, Women's Affairs
Education: Afterschool/Enrichment Programs, Arts/Humanities Education, Business Education, Education Reform, Elementary Education (Private), Education-General, Literacy, Minority Education, Preschool Education, Private Education (Precollege), School Volunteerism, Science/Mathematics Education, Secondary Education (Private), Secondary Education (Public)
Health: Clinics/Medical Centers, Public Health
Religion: Religion-General, Jewish Causes, Religious Welfare
Science: Science Museums
Social Services: Big Brothers/Big Sisters, Camps, Child Welfare, Community Service Organizations, Counseling, Day Care, Domestic Violence, Family Planning, Family Services, Refugee Assistance, Senior Services, Shelters/Homelessness, Social Services-General, Substance Abuse, Volunteer Services, Youth Organizations

Application Procedures

Initial Contact: Submit a full proposal.
Application Requirements: The foundation accepts the Common Proposal Format available at http://www.agmconnect.org.
Deadlines: March 1, for evaluation at a May/June board meeting; September 1, for a November meeting; and December 1, for a February/March meeting. All applications for summer programs are due in March.
Notes: The foundation does not accept proposals submitted in folders, binders, or report covers.

Restrictions

Does not support individuals; national organizations; capital campaigns, endowments, or fundraising activities; conferences; web sites; research; municipal, state, or federal agencies; religious instruction or worship services; health programs; or public schools, including pilot and charter schools.

Additional Information

Publications: Annual Report; Application Guidelines

Foundation Officials

Michealle Larkins: program officer
Roberta Morse Levy: secretary
Edith Morse Millender: assistant secretary
Alan Morse: vice president
Alan R. Morse, Jr.: trustee
Cecily Morse: director
Eric Robert Morse: president
John Morse, Jr.: treasurer
Timothy Morse: assistant treasurer
Rebecca Morse Steinfield: trustee

Linda G. Ortwein: trustee
Laurie Morse Sprague: assistant treasurer

Grants Analysis

Disclosure Period: calendar year ending 2001
Total Grants: $233,600
Number of Grants: 51
Average Grant: $4,580
Highest Grant: $15,000
Typical Range: $3,000 to $10,000

Recent Grants

Note: Grants derived from 2001 Form 990.
General

15,000	Management Consulting Services Management Consulting Services, Boston, MA
8,000	Summerbridge Cambridge, Cambridge, MA
7,500	Casa Myrna Vasquez, Boston, MA
7,000	Casa Esperanza, Roxbury, MA
6,000	Cambodian Community of Massachusetts, Chelsea, MA
6,000	Greater Boston Youth Symphony Orchestras (GBYSO), Boston, MA
5,000	Algebra Project, Boston, MA
5,000	Arts in Progress, Boston, MA
5,000	Associated Grantmakers, Boston, MA
5,000	Brookline Library Foundation, Brookline, MA

RAY FOUNDATION

Giving Contact

James C. Ray, President & Director
2241 Park Place Suite A-1
Minden, NV 89423
Phone: (775)782-8337

Description

Founded: 1962
EIN: 810288819
Organization Type: Private Foundation
Giving Locations: NV; NM; ND; WA
Grant Types: Capital, Emergency, General Support, Multiyear/Continuing Support, Operating Expenses, Project, Research, Scholarship, Seed Money.

Donor Information

Founder: James C. Ray, the late Joan L. Ray

Financial Summary

Total Giving: $200,000 (fiscal year ending June 30, 2002 approx); $3,892,859 (fiscal 2001)
Giving Analysis: Giving for fiscal 2001 includes: foundation scholarships ($50,000)
Assets: $13,718,219 (fiscal 2001)
Gifts Received: $1,770,000 (fiscal 1995). Note: In fiscal 1995, contributions were received from James C. Ray.

Typical Recipients

Arts & Humanities: Arts Centers, Historic Preservation, History & Archaeology, Libraries, Museums/Galleries, Music, Performing Arts, Theater
Civic & Public Affairs: Housing, Philanthropic Organizations, Professional & Trade Associations, Safety, Urban & Community Affairs
Education: Colleges & Universities, Community & Junior Colleges, Journalism/Media Education, Leadership Training, Private Education (Precollege), Public Education (Precollege), Science/Mathematics Education, Special Education, Student Aid
Environment: Air/Water Quality, Resource Conservation
Health: Clinics/Medical Centers, Hospices, Long-Term Care, Medical Rehabilitation, Mental Health
Religion: Religious Welfare

Science: Science Museums, Scientific Centers & Institutes
Social Services: At-Risk Youth, Child Welfare, Community Service Organizations, Family Services, Recreation & Athletics, Substance Abuse, Youth Organizations

Application Procedures

Initial Contact: Send brief letter of inquiry, not exceeding two pages, summarizing the grant request. Include the exact name of applicant, address, telephone number, date of application, a description of organization, proof of tax-exempt status, purpose of funds sought, budget for the project, amount requested and sources of other funding, plans for cooperation with other institutions or organizations, if any, and signatures and titles of project director and chief administrative officer.
Deadlines: None.
Review Process: Applications are considered as they are received.

Restrictions

Emphasis is on programs that address the problem of substance abuse and preventative projects involving children. Does not support individuals.

Additional Information

Publications: Application Guidelines

Foundation Officials

Mary Cornwall: secretary, treasurer
John S. Darrell: director
Jeffrey L. Hesson: director
Carrie Landvater: secretary, treasurer
James C. Ray: president
June M. Ray: director
Jeffrey J. Tempas: director

Grants Analysis

Disclosure Period: fiscal year ending June 30, 2001
Total Grants: $3,842,859*
Number of Grants: 6
Average Grant: $69,818*
Highest Grant: $3,073,950
Typical Range: $20,000 to $100,000
*Note: Giving excludes scholarship. Average grant figure excludes two highest grants ($3,423,950).

Recent Grants

Note: Grants derived from fiscal 2002 Form 990.

General

3,073,950	University of North Dakota Center of Innovation, Grand Forks, ND -- for UND-COIF endowment
350,000	University of North Dakota Center of Innovation, Grand Forks, ND -- for entrepreneurship chair and School of Business
250,000	Museum of Flight, Seattle, WA -- NASA Aeronautics Education Lab
60,625	EAA Aviation Foundation, Oshkosh, WI -- for lodge on lower level
50,000	Bosque School, Albuquerque, NM -- for the Center for Performing Arts
50,000	University of North Dakota Aerospace Foundation, Grand Forks, ND -- for Graduate Capstone Project
50,000	University of North Dakota Foundation, Grand Forks, ND -- for Donald Smith Aerospace Scholarship
5,000	Family Support Council, Minden, NV -- for Safe House Project
3,284	Albuquerque Little Theatre, Albuquerque, NM -- for eclipse night

RAYMOND CORP.

Company Headquarters

South Canal St.
PO Box 130
Greene, NY 13778-0130
Phone: (607)656-2311
Web: http://www.raymondcorp.com

Company Description

Founded: 1928
Revenue: US$430 million (2001)
Employees: 2,900
SIC(s): 3500 Industrial Machinery & Equipment.

Operating Locations

Raymond Corp. (NY--Binghamton; VI--St. Thomas)

Raymond Foundation

Giving Contact

Theresa Brant, Assistant Executive Secretary
Raymond Foundation
PO Box 1273E
Greene, NY 13778
Phone: (607)656-8897

Description

Founded: 1964
EIN: 166047847
Organization Type: Corporate Foundation
Giving Locations: CA: limited to areas of company operations; NY: limited to areas of company operations
Grant Types: Capital, Matching, Project.

Donor Information

Founder: the late George G. Raymond

Financial Summary

Total Giving: $417,108 (2003); $231,352 (2002); $237,625 (2001)
Assets: $5,616,661 (2003); $5,192,791 (2002); $5,835,628 (2001)
Gifts Received: $75,000 (2003); $146,592 (2002); $50,000 (2001). Note: Contributions are received from Raymond Corp.

Typical Recipients

Arts & Humanities: Art History, Arts Associations & Councils, Historic Preservation, History & Archaeology, Libraries, Music, Performing Arts, Public Broadcasting
Civic & Public Affairs: Business/Free Enterprise, Chambers of Commerce, Clubs, Employment/Job Training, Civic & Public Affairs-General, Housing, Municipalities/Towns, Parades/Festivals, Public Policy, Rural Affairs, Safety, Urban & Community Affairs, Zoos/Aquariums
Education: Business Education, Colleges & Universities, Community & Junior Colleges, Education Associations, Education Funds, Engineering/Technological Education, Education-General, Literacy, Preschool Education, Private Education (Precollege), Public Education (Precollege), Secondary Education (Private), Student Aid
Health: Cancer, Children's Health/Hospitals, Clinics/Medical Centers, Emergency/Ambulance Services, Eyes/Blindness, Health Funds, Health Organizations, Heart, Hospices, Hospitals, Kidney, Preventive Medicine/Wellness Organizations, Respiratory, Single-Disease Health Associations
International: Missionary/Religious Activities
Religion: Religious Welfare
Science: Science Museums, Scientific Centers & Institutes
Social Services: Animal Protection, Big Brothers/Big Sisters, Child Welfare, Community Service Organizations, Day Care, Emergency Relief, Food/Clothing

Distribution, People with Disabilities, Recreation & Athletics, Scouts, Senior Services, Special Olympics, Substance Abuse, United Funds/United Ways, Veterans, Volunteer Services, YMCA/YWCA/YMHA/YWHA, Youth Organizations

Application Procedures

Initial Contact: Send a brief letter of inquiry.
Application Requirements: detailed request, other sources of funding, proof of tax-exempt status, annual budget, annual report, and projet budget.
Deadlines: None.

Additional Information

Publications: Application Guidelines

Corporate Officials

James J. Malvaso: president, chief executive officer, director PRIM CORP EMPL president, chief executive officer, director: Raymond Corp.

Foundation Officials

Theresa Brant: assistant executive secretary
Patrick J. McManus: treasurer
Richard Najarian: trustee
George G. Raymond, III: executive secretary
John Riley: trustee

Grants Analysis

Disclosure Period: calendar year ending 2003
Total Grants: $389,592*
Number of Grants: 49
Average Grant: $1,762*
Highest Grant: $305,000
Lowest Grant: $25
Typical Range: $1,000 to $5,000
*Note: Giving excludes scholarships and United Way. Average grant figure excludes highest grant.

Recent Grants

Note: Grants derived from 2003 Form 990.

General

305,000	Alfred University-Raymond Family School of Business
20,000	Lourdes Hospital Foundation, Binghamton, NY
7,500	Lowes Charitable and Educational Foundation
5,500	American Heart Association, Dallas, TX
5,000	Cornell University, Ithaca, NY
5,000	Lemoyne University, Syracuse, NY
5,000	Lemoyne University, Syracuse, NY
5,000	Lourdes Hospital Auxiliary, Binghamton, NY
5,000	Nazareth College -- for the scholarship fund raising project
5,000	Utica College of Syracuse University, Utica, NY -- for tuition scholarship

RAYONIER INC.

Company Headquarters

Jacksonville, FL
Web: http://www.rayonier.com

Company Description

Founded: 1926
Ticker: RYN
Exchange: NYSE
Former Name: ITT Rayonier.
Revenue: US$1.117 billion (2002)
Employees: 2200 (2003)
SIC(s): 2411 Logging, 2421 Sawmills & Planing Mills--General, 2611 Pulp Mills, 3087 Custom Compound of Purchased Resins.

Operating Locations
Rayonier Inc. (CT--Hartford, Stamford, Trumbull; MA--Boston; NJ--Midland Park, Paramus, Secaucus; WA--Hoquiam)

Nonmonetary Support
Type: In-kind Services

Rayonier Foundation

Giving Contact
Jay A. Fredericksen, Vice President
50 North Laura Street, Suite 1900
Jacksonville, FL 32202
Phone: (904)357-9100

Description
Founded: 1952
EIN: 136064462
Organization Type: Corporate Foundation
Giving Locations: headquarters area only.
Grant Types: Employee Matching Gifts, General Support, Scholarship.

Donor Information
Founder: ITT Rayonier, Inc.

Financial Summary
Total Giving: $851,215 (2002); $551,789 (2001)
Assets: $4,311,554 (2002); $4,719,913 (2001)
Gifts Received: $979,250 (2002); $412,750 (2001); $1,040,700 (2000). Note: Contributions received from Rayonier, Inc.

Typical Recipients
Arts & Humanities: Arts Associations & Councils, Arts Centers, Historic Preservation, History & Archaeology, Libraries, Museums/Galleries, Music, Performing Arts, Public Broadcasting
Civic & Public Affairs: African American Affairs, Business/Free Enterprise, Chambers of Commerce, Clubs, Economic Development, Economic Policy, Employment/Job Training, Civic & Public Affairs-General, Municipalities/Towns, Philanthropic Organizations, Professional & Trade Associations, Safety, Urban & Community Affairs, Zoos/Aquariums
Education: Agricultural Education, Arts/Humanities Education, Business Education, Colleges & Universities, Community & Junior Colleges, Economic Education, Education Associations, Education Funds, Elementary Education (Public), Engineering/Technological Education, Environmental Education, Education-General, International Studies, Legal Education, Literacy, Minority Education, Preschool Education, Private Education (Precollege), Public Education (Precollege), Science/Mathematics Education, Secondary Education (Public), Special Education, Student Aid, Vocational & Technical Education
Environment: Forestry, Environment-General, Resource Conservation
Health: Children's Health/Hospitals, Hospices, Hospitals, Mental Health
Religion: Religious Welfare
Science: Science Museums
Social Services: Camps, Child Abuse, Child Welfare, Community Centers, Community Service Organizations, Counseling, Day Care, Delinquency & Criminal Rehabilitation, Domestic Violence, Emergency Relief, Food/Clothing Distribution, People with Disabilities, Recreation & Athletics, Scouts, Senior Services, Shelters/Homelessness, Substance Abuse, United Funds/United Ways, Volunteer Services, YMCA/YWCA/YMHA/YWHA, Youth Organizations

Application Procedures
Initial Contact: Send a a brief letter of inquiry.
Application Requirements: Include a description of organization and program, amount requested, and proof of tax-exempt status.

Deadlines: November 15 for scholarships.
Decision Notification: Board meets in February; notification one month after meeting.
Notes: Application forms are available for scholarship programs from the foundation.

Additional Information
Foundation awards scholarships to outstanding black students residing within and graduating from a high school within Wayne County, GA, or Nassau County, FL. Also awards scholarships to outstanding students (without regard to race) residing within and graduating from a high school within Wayne, GA, Nassau, FL, and Mason, Clallam, and Grays Harbor, WA. Scholarship decisions are made locally. Contact foundation for more information and applications. Company reports that it is no longer affiliated with ITT Corp.

Corporate Officials
William S. Berry: executive vice president forest resources & wood products B Placerville, CA 1941. ED University of California at Berkeley BS (1964); University of Michigan MS (1965). PRIM CORP EMPL executive vice president forest resources & wood products: Rayonier Inc. CORP AFFIL president, director: Rayonier New Zealand.
Wallace L. Nutter: president, chief executive officer, director B Astoria, OR 1944. ED University of Washington BA (1967); Harvard University Graduate School of Business Administration (1987). PRIM CORP EMPL president, chief executive officer, director: Rayonier Inc. CORP AFFIL director: Rayonier Forest Resources Co. NONPR AFFIL member board governments: National Council Paper Industry Air & Stream Improvement.

Foundation Officials
MacDonald Auguste: treasurer B 1948. ED City University of New York BA (1969-1976); Pace University MBA (1979). CORP AFFIL treasurer: Rayonier Timberlands LP.
William S. Berry: director (see above)
John Beckman Canning: secretary B Chicago, IL 1943. ED Princeton University AB (1965); Columbia University LLB (1968). PRIM CORP EMPL corporate secretary, associate general counsel: Rayonier Inc. CORP AFFIL vice president, director: Beckman Bros. NONPR AFFIL member: Columbia University Law School Alumni Association; director: Stamford Symphony Orchestra; member: American Society of Corporate Secretaries; member: American Bar Association.
Jay A. Fredericksen: vice president, director CORP AFFIL vice president corp. relations: Rayonier Inc.
Wallace L. Nutter: director (see above)
Wendy Pugnetti: assistant secretary

Grants Analysis
Disclosure Period: calendar year ending 2002
Total Grants: $529,775*
Number of Grants: 174
Average Grant: $3,045
Highest Grant: $10,000
Lowest Grant: $250
Typical Range: $100 to $5,000
*Note: Giving excludes scholarship, matching gifts, and United Way.

Recent Grants
Note: Grants derived from 2003 Form 990.
General

375,000	Directors CAP University of Oklahoma, Norman, OK
56,000	United Way of South Georgia, Waycross, GA
39,700	United Way Northeast Florida, Nassau City, FL
37,973	United Way Northeast Florida, Jacksonville, FL
11,169	United Way of Kings County, Seattle, WA
10,000	Altamaha Technical College, Jesup, GA
10,000	Emory University, Atlanta, GA
10,000	University of California, Berkeley, CA
10,000	Wellesley College, Wellesley, MA
8,000	University of Miami, Coral Gables, FL

RBC CENTURA

Company Headquarters
1910 Wesleyan Blvd.
Rocky Mount, NC 27804
Web: http://www.centura.com

Company Description
Employees: 2,100
SIC(s): 6700 Holding & Other Investment Offices.
Parent Company: RBC Financial Group, P.O. Box 1, Royal Bank Plaza, Toronto, ON, Canada

Centura First Savings Foundation of Rutherford County

Giving Contact
Juanita Newton
PO Box 388
Forest City, NC 28043
Phone: (828)236-8814

Description
Founded: 1993
EIN: 561832201
Organization Type: Corporate Foundation
Giving Locations: NC: Rutherford County
Grant Types: General Support.

Financial Summary
Total Giving: $75,000 (2003). Note: 1997 Giving includes United Way ($6,000).
Giving Analysis: Giving for 2003 includes: foundation grants to United Way ($5,000)
Assets: $1,555,256 (2003)

Typical Recipients
Arts & Humanities: History & Archaeology, Libraries, Museums/Galleries, Music
Civic & Public Affairs: Business/Free Enterprise, Employment/Job Training, Civic & Public Affairs-General, Housing
Health: Cancer, Emergency/Ambulance Services, Hospices, Mental Health
Religion: Ministries, Religious Organizations, Religious Welfare
Social Services: Animal Protection, At-Risk Youth, Camps, Community Centers, Community Service Organizations, Crime Prevention, Domestic Violence, Emergency Relief, Family Planning, Family Services, Recreation & Athletics, Scouts, Social Services-General, Special Olympics, United Funds/United Ways, Youth Organizations

Application Procedures
Initial Contact: Request application form.
Deadlines: None.

Restrictions
Preference is made to organizations and individuals in Rutherford County.

Additional Information
Trust(s): Centura Bank

Corporate Officials
Steven Goldstein: chief financial officer, president PRIM CORP EMPL chief financial officer: Centura Bank.

Frank Pattillo: vice chairman PRIM CORP EMPL vice chairman: Centura Bank.

Cecil W. Sewell, Jr.: chairman, president B Morehead City, NC 1946. ED University of North Carolina (1969); Rollins College (1971). PRIM CORP EMPL chairman, president: Centura Bank.

Grants Analysis

Disclosure Period: calendar year ending 2003
Total Grants: $70,000*
Number of Grants: 37
Average Grant: $1,892
Highest Grant: $6,500
Lowest Grant: $500
Typical Range: $1,000 to $5,000
***Note:** Giving excludes United Way.

Recent Grants

Note: Grants derived from 2003 Form 990.
General

6,500	Pilot Club of Rutherford, Forest City, NC -- for FBO kidsenses
6,000	Hospice, Nashville, TN -- for building fund
5,000	American Red Cross, Washington, DC -- for house fire victims
5,000	Rutherford County Community Center -- for workshops for children
5,000	Rutherford County Yokefellow Center, Spindale, NC -- for crisis assistance
5,000	South Mountain Christian Camp, Bostic, NC -- for scholarships
5,000	Symphony of Rutherford County, Forest City, NC
5,000	United Way of Rutherford County, Murfreesboro, TN -- for week of caring supplies
3,000	Family Resources, Pittsburgh, PA -- for domestic violence
2,000	Rutherford County Farm Museum, Forest City, NC

CHARLES L. READ FOUNDATION

Giving Contact

Rodger K. Herrigel, Secretary
374 Millburn Ave.
Millburn, NJ 07041
Phone: (201)379-5850

Description

Founded: 1954
EIN: 226053510
Organization Type: Private Foundation
Giving Locations: CO; MA; NJ; NY; VA
Grant Types: General Support.

Donor Information

Founder: Charles L. Read

Financial Summary

Total Giving: $170,750 (2001)
Assets: $3,681,615 (2001)

Typical Recipients

Arts & Humanities: Dance, Ethnic & Folk Arts, Historic Preservation, History & Archaeology, Libraries, Museums/Galleries, Music, Performing Arts, Theater
Civic & Public Affairs: Clubs, Employment/Job Training, Civic & Public Affairs-General, Housing, Professional & Trade Associations, Rural Affairs, Safety, Women's Affairs
Education: Colleges & Universities, Continuing Education, Education Funds, Education-General, Legal Education, Private Education (Precollege), Public Education (Precollege), Religious Education, School Volunteerism, Student Aid

Environment: Environment-General, Protection, Resource Conservation, Watershed
Health: Arthritis, Cancer, Children's Health/Hospitals, Emergency/Ambulance Services, Eyes/Blindness, Geriatric Health, Health Organizations, Hospices, Hospitals, Long-Term Care, Medical Research, Mental Health, Public Health, Respiratory, Speech & Hearing
International: Foreign Educational Institutions, Missionary/Religious Activities
Religion: Churches, Jewish Causes, Religious Organizations, Religious Welfare
Science: Scientific Centers & Institutes
Social Services: Camps, Child Welfare, Community Centers, Community Service Organizations, Counseling, Day Care, Homes, People with Disabilities, Recreation & Athletics, Shelters/Homelessness, United Funds/United Ways, Veterans, YMCA/YWCA/YMHA/YWHA, Youth Organizations

Application Procedures

Initial Contact: Send a brief letter of inquiry.
Application Requirements: purpose of funds sought, recently audited financial statement, and proof of tax-exempt status.
Deadlines: None.

Foundation Officials

Richard Eisenberg: vice president
Saul Eisenberg: treasurer
Fred Herrigel, III: president
Rodger K. Herrigel: secretary

Grants Analysis

Disclosure Period: calendar year ending 2001
Total Grants: $170,750
Number of Grants: 76
Average Grant: $1,905*
Highest Grant: $26,000
Lowest Grant: $500
Typical Range: $1,000 to $5,000
***Note:** Average grant figure excludes highest grant.

Recent Grants

Note: Grants derived from 2001 Form 990.
Library-Related

10,000	Louise Adelia Read Memorial Library, Hancock, NY

General

26,000	Trust & Agency Fund Hancock Central School, Hancock, NY
8,000	Tanglewood, Lenox, MA
5,000	Drew University, Madison, NJ
5,000	Fairview Lake and Watershed Conservation Foundation, Stillwater, NJ
5,000	Southside Hospital, Bayshore, NY
5,000	Summit Foundation, Breckenridge, CO
4,000	Morristown Memorial Hospital, Morristown, NJ
4,000	Overlook Hospital Foundation, Summit, NJ
3,000	Barrington Stage Company, Great Barrington, MA
3,000	Carriage House, Breckenridge, CO

READER'S DIGEST ASSOCIATION INC.

Company Headquarters

Pleasantville, NY
Web: http://www.readersdigest.com

Company Description

Ticker: RDA
Exchange: OTC
Revenue: US$2.368 billion (2002)
Employees: 4700 (2003)
SIC(s): 2721 Periodicals.

Operating Locations

Reader's Digest Association, Inc. (CT--Ridgefield; GA--Pinola, Stone Mountain; NY--Brewster)

Nonmonetary Support

Volunteer Programs: Reader's Digest employees, employee spouses, and retirees can receive grants for nonprofit groups where they actively volunteer. The company operates a Double-Match Gift Program where employees and retirees may give up to $10,000 per year to charities of their choice.

Reader's Digest Foundation

Giving Contact

Claudia L. Edwards, Executive Director
1 Reader's Digest Rd.
Pleasantville, NY 10570
Phone: (914)244-5370
Fax: (914)244-7642
E-mail: carolyn.malile@readersdigest.com
Web: http://www.rd.com

Description

EIN: 136120380
Organization Type: Corporate Foundation
Giving Locations: nationally.
Grant Types: Employee Matching Gifts, General Support, Multiyear/Continuing Support, Scholarship.

Financial Summary

Total Giving: $2,515,922 (fiscal year ending June 30, 2002); $3,221,938 (fiscal 2001). Note: Contributes through corporate direct giving program and foundation.
Giving Analysis: Giving for fiscal 2002 includes: foundation program-related investments ($57,750); foundation scholarships ($129,300); foundation matching gifts ($844,150).
Assets: $16,548,401 (fiscal 2002); $21,098,720 (fiscal 2001)
Gifts Received: $23,346 (fiscal 2001); $17,254 (fiscal 1997); $13,334 (fiscal 1996). Note: In fiscal 2001, contributions were received from DeWitt Wallace-Lila Wallace Preferred Stock Trust. 1997, contributions were received from DeWitt Wallace-Lila Acheson Wallace.

Typical Recipients

Arts & Humanities: Arts Centers, Ballet, Libraries, Museums/Galleries, Performing Arts, Theater
Civic & Public Affairs: Community Foundations, Ethnic Organizations, Civic & Public Affairs-General, Hispanic Affairs, Municipalities/Towns, Philanthropic Organizations, Professional & Trade Associations
Education: Afterschool/Enrichment Programs, Business Education, Colleges & Universities, Education Associations, Education Funds, Education Reform, Engineering/Technological Education, Education-General, Journalism/Media Education, Literacy, Minority Education, Private Education (Precollege), Public Education (Precollege), Science/Mathematics Education, Secondary Education (Private), Special Education, Student Aid
Health: Cancer, Children's Health/Hospitals, Clinics/Medical Centers, Diabetes, Health Funds, Heart, Medical Research, Mental Health, Single-Disease Health Associations
Religion: Religion-General, Jewish Causes, Religious Organizations, Religious Welfare, Social/Policy Issues
Science: Science Museums
Social Services: Animal Protection, Child Welfare, Community Service Organizations, Emergency Relief, People with Disabilities, Recreation & Athletics, Scouts, Senior Services, United Funds/United Ways, Volunteer Services, Youth Organizations

Application Procedures

Initial Contact: Send a brief letter.

Application Requirements: Include a description of project and the sponsoring organization; description of need, target group, and timetable; explanation of why funding would solve a problem and meet a need; the degree to which the program can generate long-term funding; a demonstration of how funding would have a direct impact on a social need; a description of community, public and private sector involvement (if applicable); a description of measurable outcomes and timetables; audited financial statements for the current year; current itemized budget for project and organization; total project cost, other funding sources, and total requested from foundation; and evidence of tax-exempt status and latest IRS Form 990. Form 990.

Deadlines: April 1, August 1, and December 1, to be considered in the following month.

Review Process: If initial letter meets foundation guidelines, full proposals (due by the dates listed above) will be requested.

Restrictions

The foundation does not support individuals or religious, veterans', fraternal, political, environmental, or cultural organizations. Grants are not made for dinners, audiovisual productions, legislative or lobbying purposes, or to organizations that are not tax-exempt. The foundation generally does not support capital or endowment campaigns, medical research, health-related activities, international charities, local chapters of national organizations, conferences, publications, or annual operating costs. Funding is generally for the company's immediate geographical area. Some programs give nationally.

Additional Information

The foundation prefers to support direct service projects rather than grants for general support or to intermediary funding agencies.

Funding is usually made on a one-time basis, and exceptions are generally limited to a maximum of three consecutive years.

The foundation seeks to support those organizations that demonstrate responsible management and that provide timely reports to the directors of the foundation on the disposition of funds and program results. results. results.

Publications: Reader's Digest Foundation Annual Report

Corporate Officials

Jack A. Smith: senior vice president PRIM CORP EMPL senior vice president: The Reader's Digest Association, Inc.

Foundation Officials

Claudia L. Edwards: executive director
Francoise Hanonik: director
William H. Magill: treasurer
Gary S. Rich: director
Thomas O. Ryder: chairman
Mary Terry: secretary

Grants Analysis

Disclosure Period: fiscal year ending June 30, 2002
Total Grants: $1,484,722*
Number of Grants: 39
Average Grant: $16,971*
Highest Grant: $556,809
Lowest Grant: $1,000
Typical Range: $5,000 to $20,000
*Note: Giving excludes matching gifts; scholarships; volunteer program-related investments. Average grant figure excludes two highest grants ($856,809).

Recent Grants

Note: Grants derived from fiscal 2003 Form 990.

Library-Related
417,906	Nixon Library, Yorba Linda, CA -- to support expenses
250,000	Nixon Library, Yorba Linda, CA -- towards partners for peace program

General
301,000	Boys and Girls Clubs of America, Atlanta, GA -- towards the youth of the year program
250,000	United Way of Westchester and Putnam, White Plains, NY
150,000	Girl Scouts of United States, Atlanta, GA
124,100	College Scholarship Program -- towards scholarship programs
111,111	Laird Center Marshfield Clinic, Marshfield, WI
110,000	United Way International, Washington, DC -- towards European flood relief
100,000	Eisenhower Foundation, Abilene, KS -- towards Eisenhower library
100,000	Northern Westchester Hospital Foundation, Mt. Kisco, NY
75,000	Educators for Social Responsibility, Cambridge, MA
35,000	United Negro College Fund, Fairfax, VA -- towards scholarship programs

RED DEVIL

Company Headquarters

2400 Vauxhall Rd.
Union, NJ 07083
Web: http://www.reddevil.com

Company Description

Employees: 350
SIC(s): 2800 Chemicals & Allied Products, 3400 Fabricated Metal Products.

Red Devil Foundation

Giving Contact

Jane T. Lee, Chairman & Director
Red Devil Foundation
2400 Vauxhall Road
Union, NJ 07083-5035
Phone: (908)688-6900
Note: Contact for information on grant program.

Alternate Contact

Human Resources Department
Red Devil Inc.
Note: Contact for information on scholarship program.

Description

EIN: 226063889
Organization Type: Corporate Foundation
Giving Locations: NJ
Grant Types: General Support, Scholarship.

Financial Summary

Total Giving: $3,907 (fiscal year ending November 30, 2003); $17,137 (fiscal 2001)
Giving Analysis: Giving for fiscal 2003 includes: foundation scholarships ($600); fiscal 2001: foundation scholarships ($3,050)
Assets: $13,712 (fiscal 2003); $43,579 (fiscal 2001)
Gifts Received: $18,750 (fiscal 2000); $36,250 (fiscal 1999); $18,750 (fiscal 1998). Note: Contributions were received from Red Devil Inc.

Typical Recipients

Arts & Humanities: Arts Associations & Councils, Arts & Humanities-General, Historic Preservation, History & Archaeology, Museums/Galleries, Music, Opera, Performing Arts, Theater
Civic & Public Affairs: Clubs, Civic & Public Affairs-General, Parades/Festivals, Professional & Trade Associations, Public Policy, Urban & Community Affairs, Zoos/Aquariums
Education: Afterschool/Enrichment Programs, Arts/Humanities Education, Business Education, Colleges & Universities, Medical Education, Private Education (Precollege), School Volunteerism, Student Aid
Environment: Environment-General, Resource Conservation
Health: Cancer, Children's Health/Hospitals, Clinics/Medical Centers, Emergency/Ambulance Services, Health Organizations, Hospitals, Hospitals (University Affiliated), Medical Rehabilitation, Medical Research, Single-Disease Health Associations
International: International Environmental Issues
Religion: Churches, Dioceses
Science: Science Museums
Social Services: Animal Protection, Child Welfare, Community Service Organizations, Crime Prevention, People with Disabilities, Recreation & Athletics, Scouts, Social Services-General, Youth Organizations

Application Procedures

Initial Contact: Request application form for scholarships; for grants, send a brief letter of inquiry detailing request.
Deadlines: For scholarships; April 1, for grants None.

Restrictions

Does not support individuals, political or lobbying groups, or organizations outside operating areas.

Additional Information

Provides scholarships to children of employees.
Publications: Scholarship Application

Corporate Officials

Jane T. Lee: chairman, director, director B Morristown, NJ 1954. ED Fairleigh Dickinson University; Randolph-Macon College (1976). PRIM CORP EMPL chairman, director: Red Devil. NONPR AFFIL chairman: Hunterdon Hall Farm; member: National Association Manufacturer; director: Hand Tools Institute; member: American Cutlery Mfr Association; member: American Hardware Manufacturer Association.
D. R. MacPherson: president, chief executive officer, director PRIM CORP EMPL president, chief executive officer, director: Red Devil.

Foundation Officials

Jane T. Lee: trustee (see above)
Mary Lee: trustee
Mary Lee Subourne: trustee

Grants Analysis

Disclosure Period: fiscal year ending November 30, 2003
Total Grants: $3,307*
Number of Grants: 8
Average Grant: $209*
Highest Grant: $1,842
Lowest Grant: $25
Typical Range: $100 to $500
*Note: Giving excludes scholarships. Average grant figure excludes highest grant.

Recent Grants

Note: Grants derived from fiscal 2003 Form 990.

General
1,842	Paper Mill Playhouse, Millburn, NJ -- towards patron support
1,000	Somerset Medical Center, Somerville, NJ
600	Drew University, Madison, NJ -- towards scholarship
150	Arc of Hunterdon County, Flemington, NJ

100	Long Island Lutheran Middle and High School, Brookville, NY -- in memory of A. Eugene Anderson
75	American Museum of Natural History, New York, NY -- towards member support
65	New Jersey State Association of Letter Carriers, Hackensack, NJ -- towards muscular dystrophy fund
50	Kids Corporation II, Newark, NJ -- towards mountain classroom
25	Union Emergency Services, Union, NJ -- towards emergency care services, ambulances

RED WING SHOE COMPANY INC.

Company Headquarters

314 Main St., Ste. 2
Red Wing, MN 55066
Web: http://www.redwingshoe.com

Company Description

Employees: 1200 (2003)
SIC(s): 3143 Men's Footwear Except Athletic.

Red Wing Shoe Co. Foundation

Giving Contact

Stacy Crownhart, Secretary
Red Wing Shoe Co. Foundation
314 Main Street
Red Wing, MN 55066-2300
Phone: (651)388-8211
Fax: (651)385-1760

Description

EIN: 416020177
Organization Type: Corporate Foundation
Giving Locations: KY: Danville; MN: Minneapolis, Red Wing, St. Paul; MO: Potosi
Grant Types: Award, Capital, General Support.

Financial Summary

Total Giving: $726,184 (2002); $799,803 (2001). Note: Contributes through foundation only.
Assets: $374,163 (2002); $815,950 (2001)
Gifts Received: $400,000 (2002); $700,000 (2001); $215,000 (2000). Note: Contributions are received from the Red Wing Shoe Co.

Typical Recipients

Arts & Humanities: Arts Associations & Councils, Arts Centers, Arts Institutes, Film & Video, Arts & Humanities-General, Historic Preservation, History & Archaeology, Libraries, Museums/Galleries, Music, Performing Arts, Public Broadcasting, Theater
Civic & Public Affairs: Botanical Gardens/Parks, Business/Free Enterprise, Chambers of Commerce, Clubs, Community Foundations, Economic Development, Civic & Public Affairs-General, Housing, Law & Justice, Municipalities/Towns, Nonprofit Management, Philanthropic Organizations, Public Policy, Safety, Urban & Community Affairs, Women's Affairs, Zoos/Aquariums
Education: Afterschool/Enrichment Programs, Arts/Humanities Education, Business Education, Colleges & Universities, Economic Education, Education Associations, Education Funds, Education Reform, Environmental Education, Faculty Development, Education-General, Public Education (Precollege), Science/Mathematics Education, Secondary Education (Public), Social Sciences Education, Special Education, Student Aid

Environment: Air/Water Quality, Environment-General, Resource Conservation, Wildlife Protection
Health: Cancer, Children's Health/Hospitals, Clinics/Medical Centers, Emergency/Ambulance Services, Health Organizations, Hospices, Medical Rehabilitation, Preventive Medicine/Wellness Organizations, Single-Disease Health Associations
International: International Development, International Environmental Issues, International Organizations
Religion: Churches, Religion-General, Religious Welfare
Science: Science Museums, Scientific Centers & Institutes
Social Services: Child Welfare, Community Centers, Community Service Organizations, Crime Prevention, Emergency Relief, Family Services, Food/Clothing Distribution, People with Disabilities, Recreation & Athletics, Scouts, Social Services-General, Special Olympics, Substance Abuse, United Funds/United Ways, YMCA/YWCA/YMHA/YWHA, Youth Organizations

Application Procedures

Initial Contact: Send a brief letter.
Application Requirements: Include description of activities or projects, and a copy of tax exemption certificate.
Deadlines: None.

Restrictions

Grants are not made to individuals.

Foundation Officials

Suzanne Blue: director
Stacy Brownhart: director
Silas B. Foot, III: director
William J. Sweasy: chief executive officer B 1953. PRIM CORP EMPL chairman: Red Wing Hotel Co.

Grants Analysis

Disclosure Period: calendar year ending 2002
Total Grants: $671,184*
Number of Grants: 29
Average Grant: $4,340*
Highest Grant: $333,334
Lowest Grant: $500
Typical Range: $1,000 to $10,000
*Note: Giving excludes United Way. Average grant figure excludes three highest grants ($558,334).

Recent Grants

Note: Grants derived from 2003 Form 990.

General

333,334	YMCA Capital Campaign, Minneapolis, MN -- towards capital campaign
125,000	Ind School District 256, Red Wing, MN -- towards environmental education
100,000	Ind School District, Red Wing, MN -- towards environmental education
40,000	Sheldon Theatre, Minneapolis, MN -- as general fund
25,000	United Way of Red Wing, Red Wing, MN -- as general fund
15,000	Heart of Kentucky United Way, Lexington, KY -- as general fund
15,000	Heart of Kentucky United Way, Lexington, KY -- as general fund
10,500	YMCA Century Club, Minneapolis, MN -- towards sponsorship
10,000	Guthrie on the River, Minneapolis, MN -- towards capital campaign
5,000	Lake City, Salt Lake City, UT -- towards environmental education

NELL J. REDFIELD FOUNDATION

Giving Contact

Gerald C. Smith, Director
PO Box 61
Reno, NV 89501
Phone: (702)323-1373
Fax: (702)323-4476

Description

Founded: 1982
EIN: 237399910
Organization Type: Private Foundation
Giving Locations: NV: Reno
Grant Types: Capital, General Support, Scholarship.

Donor Information

Founder: the late Nell J. Redfield

Financial Summary

Total Giving: $1,497,547 (2003); $1,305,946 (2001)
Assets: $34,240,348 (2003); $30,365,747 (2001)
Gifts Received: $2,400,000 (2003); $3,174,519 (2001); $3,280,000 (1999). Note: In 1998, 1999, 2001, and 2003, contributions were received from the Nell J. Redfield Trust.

Typical Recipients

Arts & Humanities: Arts Outreach, Libraries, Museums/Galleries, Music, Public Broadcasting, Theater
Education: Afterschool/Enrichment Programs, Arts/Humanities Education, Business Education, Colleges & Universities, Community & Junior Colleges, Education Funds, Elementary Education (Public), Education-General, Literacy, Private Education (Precollege), Public Education (Precollege), Science/Mathematics Education, Student Aid
Health: Adolescent Health Issues, Children's Health/Hospitals, Diabetes, Health-General, Health Funds, Hospices, Hospitals, Medical Research, Public Health, Single-Disease Health Associations, Speech & Hearing
Religion: Religious Organizations, Religious Welfare
Social Services: Animal Protection, At-Risk Youth, Child Welfare, Community Service Organizations, Crime Prevention, Domestic Violence, Family Planning, Family Services, Food/Clothing Distribution, Homes, People with Disabilities, Recreation & Athletics, Scouts, Senior Services, Shelters/Homelessness, Substance Abuse, United Funds/United Ways, YMCA/YWCA/YMHA/YWHA, Youth Organizations

Application Procedures

Initial Contact: Send letter requesting application form.
Deadlines: June 1. Applications accepted beginning January 15.

Restrictions

Grants are limited to advancement of healthcare, medical research, care of handicapped children and the aged, education, and religion.

Additional Information

Trust(s): Farmers & Merchants Trust Co

Foundation Officials

Iris G. Brewerton: director
Betty Alyce Jones: director
Helen Jeane Jones: director
Gerald C. Smith: manager, director
Kenneth G. Walker: director

Grants Analysis

Disclosure Period: calendar year ending 2003
Total Grants: $1,497,547
Number of Grants: 40
Average Grant: $14,930*

Highest Grant: $500,000
Lowest Grant: $1,000
Typical Range: $5,000 to $25,000
*Note: Average grant figure excludes five highest grants ($974,999).

Recent Grants

Note: Grants derived from 2003 Form 990.
Library-Related

40,833	Washoe County Library Foundation, Reno, NV -- fund the young people's library	

General

500,000	University of Nevada, Reno Foundation, Reno, NV -- to fund the Nell J. Redfield campus building
166,666	Nevada Museum of Art, Reno, NV -- for construction of the Redfield exploration center
125,000	Truckee Meadows Community College, Reno, NV -- to fund the renovation of keystone theatre
100,000	Saint Mary's Foundation, Reno, NV -- for Sun Valley clinic expansion program
83,333	Boys and Girls Club of Truckee Meadows, Reno, NV -- for matching campaign related to Reynolds
50,000	University of Nevada, Reno Foundation, Reno, NV -- scholarships for the college of engineering
36,526	Sage Ridge School, Reno, NV -- to fund student scholarships for year 2003
30,000	Special Recreation Services Inc., Reno, NV -- tuition for campers
25,000	Reno Chamber Orchestra, Reno, NV -- production costs for 2003-2004 season concert

REED FOUNDATION (NY)

Giving Contact

Jane Gregory-Rubin, Secretary & Director
444 Madison Ave., Suite 2901
New York, NY 10022-6903
Phone: (212)688-2170

Description

Founded: 1949
EIN: 131990017
Organization Type: General Purpose Foundation
Giving Locations: NY: emphasis on New York broad geographic distribution.
Grant Types: General Support, Project.

Donor Information

Founder: the late Samuel Rubin

Financial Summary

Total Giving: $1,208,026 (2003); $1,241,456 (2001)
Assets: $13,156,888 (2003); $14,676,266 (2001)

Typical Recipients

Arts & Humanities: Arts Associations & Councils, Arts Centers, Arts Festivals, Arts Funds, Arts Outreach, Community Arts, Ethnic & Folk Arts, Film & Video, Arts & Humanities-General, Historic Preservation, History & Archaeology, Libraries, Literary Arts, Museums/Galleries, Music, Opera, Performing Arts, Public Broadcasting, Theater
Civic & Public Affairs: Asian American Affairs, Civil Rights, Community Foundations, Employment/Job Training, Civic & Public Affairs-General, Legal Aid, Nonprofit Management, Philanthropic Organizations, Professional & Trade Associations, Public Policy, Urban & Community Affairs
Education: Arts/Humanities Education, Colleges & Universities, Education-General, International Exchange, International Studies, Legal Education, Med-

ical Education, Private Education (Precollege), Religious Education
Health: Heart, Medical Research, Research/Studies Institutes
International: Foreign Arts Organizations, Foreign Educational Institutions, Human Rights, International Relations
Science: Scientific Centers & Institutes
Social Services: Community Service Organizations, Recreation & Athletics

Application Procedures

Initial Contact: Send a brief letter of inquiry.
Deadlines: None.

Restrictions

Grants are not made to individuals.

Foundation Officials

Jane Gregory Rubin: secretary, director B Richmond, VA 1944. ED Vassar College BA (1965); Columbia University JD (1975); New York University LLM (1984). PRIM CORP EMPL director: InterAmericas. NONPR AFFIL advisory board: Vermont Studio Center; vice chairman, director: Volunteer Lawyers Arts; member: Union Internationale des Avocats; member: Copyright Society USA; member professional advisory council: Lincoln Center Performing Arts; member: Association Bar New York City; board governors: John Carter Brown Library; member: American Arbitration Association; member: American Bar Association.
Lara R. Rubin: director
Maia A. Rubin: treasurer
Peter L. Rubin: director
Reed Rubin: president, director

Grants Analysis

Disclosure Period: calendar year ending 2003
Total Grants: $1,208,026
Number of Grants: 77
Average Grant: $9,174*
Highest Grant: $280,000
Lowest Grant: $75
Typical Range: $1,000 to $20,000
*Note: Average grant figure excludes two highest grants ($520,000).

Recent Grants

Note: Grants derived from 2003 Form 990.
General

280,000	New York Foundation for the Arts, New York, NY
240,000	Research Institute for the Study of Man, New York, NY
56,600	El Museo del Barrio, New York, NY
55,800	New York City Opera, New York, NY
37,500	Smithsonian Institution, Washington, DC
30,000	New York University, New York, NY -- for educational purposes
26,067	Caribbean Contemporary Arts, Port of Spain Trinidad and Tobago -- for educational purposes
25,000	Hebrew Union College - Jewish Institute of Religion, Cincinnati, OH
25,000	Yale University, New Haven, CT
24,480	Cuban Artists Fund, New York, NY

REEVES FOUNDATION (OH)

Giving Contact

Don A. Ulrich, Executive Director
PO Box 441
Dover, OH 44622-0441
Phone: (330)364-4660

Description

Founded: 1966
EIN: 346575477
Organization Type: General Purpose Foundation
Giving Locations: OH: Tuscarawas County
Grant Types: Capital, Project, Scholarship.

Donor Information

Founder: Established in 1966 by the late Margaret J. Reeves, the late Helen F. Reeves, and the late Samuel J. Reeves.

Financial Summary

Total Giving: $742,745 (2001)
Assets: $23,622,428 (2001)

Typical Recipients

Arts & Humanities: Arts Centers, Historic Preservation, History & Archaeology, Libraries, Museums/Galleries, Music, Public Broadcasting, Theater
Civic & Public Affairs: Botanical Gardens/Parks, Civic & Public Affairs-General, Municipalities/Towns, Parades/Festivals, Rural Affairs, Safety, Urban & Community Affairs
Education: Agricultural Education, Arts/Humanities Education, Colleges & Universities, Education Funds, Elementary Education (Private), Elementary Education (Public), Education-General, Private Education (Precollege), Public Education (Precollege), Science/Mathematics Education, Secondary Education (Private), Secondary Education (Public), Student Aid
Environment: Environment-General, Resource Conservation
Health: Alzheimer's Disease, Cancer, Children's Health/Hospitals, Clinics/Medical Centers, Emergency/Ambulance Services, Hospices, Hospitals, Public Health
Religion: Churches, Religious Welfare
Social Services: Animal Protection, Big Brothers/Big Sisters, Community Centers, Community Service Organizations, Counseling, Crime Prevention, Emergency Relief, People with Disabilities, Recreation & Athletics, Scouts, Senior Services, Shelters/Homelessness, United Funds/United Ways, Volunteer Services, YMCA/YWCA/YMHA/YWHA, Youth Organizations

Application Procedures

Initial Contact: Applications should be in writing.
Application Requirements: Include a concise outline of the amount requested and purpose of funds sought.
Deadlines: None.
Review Process: The board meets bimonthly.

Restrictions

The foundation reports grants are made for charitable and educational purposes, with emphasis on capital expenditures rather than operating budgets. No grants are made to individuals, or for annual campaigns, seed money, emergency funds, deficit financing, land acquisition, renovation projects, endowment funds, fellowships, special projects, publications, conferences, or loans.

Foundation Officials

W. E. Lieser: secretary, treasurer, trustee
Thomas V. Patton: trustee
Ronald L. Pissocra: trustee
Margaret H. Reeves: president, trustee
Thomas R. Scheffer: vice president, trustee
Don A. Ulrich: executive director
Jeffrey T. Wagner: trustee
W. E. Zimmerman: executive vice president, trustee

Grants Analysis

Disclosure Period: calendar year ending 2001
Total Grants: $742,745
Number of Grants: 28
Average Grant: $26,527
Highest Grant: $151,465

Lowest Grant: $1,259
Typical Range: $10,000 to $40,000

Recent Grants

Note: Grants derived from 2002 Form 990.
General

250,000	Tuscarawas County University Foundation, New Philadelphia, OH -- 2002 grant for the science and technology center building
250,000	Union Hospital, Union, NJ -- for 2002 addition project towards Boulevard South
125,000	Tuscarawas County University Foundation, New Philadelphia, OH -- for one half 2003 grant payment towards the science and technology building
125,000	Union Hospital, Union, NJ -- for one half 2003 grant towards Boulevard South addition project
115,000	Twin City Hospital, Dennison, OH -- towards purchase of new patient hospital beds
50,000	Central Catholic High School, Toledo, OH -- for science curriculum renovation project
50,000	Personal and Family Counseling Services, New Philadelphia, OH -- for grant payments two and three of three pledge commitment of $25,000 each
45,000	Dover Historical society, Dover, OH -- for general operations fund for 2003
45,000	Tuscarawas County Council for Churches, New Philadelphia, OH -- for general fund campaign for 2003 and emergency assistance request
39,000	Society for Equal Access Independent Living Center Inc., Caldwell, OH -- for handicap accessible van

REGENSTEIN FOUNDATION

Giving Contact

Susan Regenstein Frank, Chairman
8600 West Bryn Mawr Avenue, Suite 560N
Chicago, IL 60631
Phone: (773)693-6464
Fax: (773)693-2480

Alternate Contact

Robert H. Mecca

Description

Founded: 1950
EIN: 363152531
Organization Type: General Purpose Foundation
Giving Locations: IL: Chicago metropolitan area
Grant Types: Capital, Endowment, General Support, Loan, Multiyear/Continuing Support, Operating Expenses, Project.

Donor Information

Founder: The foundation was established in 1950, with the late Joseph Regenstein and Helen Regenstein as donors.

Financial Summary

Total Giving: $2,780,000 (2003); $4,370,000 (2002); $52,500,000 (2001)
Assets: $7,484,513 (2003); $65,880,925 (2002); $72,000,000 (2001)

Typical Recipients

Arts & Humanities: Arts Institutes, Historic Preservation, History & Archaeology, Libraries, Museums/Galleries, Music, Opera, Public Broadcasting, Theater

Civic & Public Affairs: Botanical Gardens/Parks, Clubs, Law & Justice, Nonprofit Management, Philanthropic Organizations, Professional & Trade Associations, Public Policy, Zoos/Aquariums
Education: Colleges & Universities, Education-General, Medical Education, Preschool Education, Private Education (Precollege)
Health: Clinics/Medical Centers, Health-General, Health Organizations, Heart, Hospitals, Medical Rehabilitation, Mental Health, Nursing Services, Prenatal Health Issues, Single-Disease Health Associations, Transplant Networks/Donor Banks
Religion: Jewish Causes, Religious Organizations, Religious Welfare, Synagogues/Temples
Science: Science Museums
Social Services: Animal Protection, Child Welfare, Community Service Organizations, Crime Prevention, Delinquency & Criminal Rehabilitation, Family Planning, Family Services, Food/Clothing Distribution, Homes, People with Disabilities, Scouts, Senior Services, Sexual Abuse, United Funds/United Ways, Volunteer Services, Youth Organizations

Application Procedures

Initial Contact: Proposals should be made in writing.
Application Requirements: Applicants should send a cover letter summarizing request, one copy of full proposal, and supplementary materials including total need for project and source of other funding (if any), copy of IRS tax-exempt letter, and a copy of the most recent audited annual report.
Deadlines: March 31 and September 30.
Notes: Applications should be signed by the Chief Executive Officer of organization.

Restrictions

The foundation reports that most grants are made on the initiative of the foundation's trustees; only a very small percentage of applicants can expect to obtain funds. Because long-range pledges often make income unavailable for substantial periods of time, it is suggested that applicants needing immediate help apply to individuals or businesses in a position to make immediate grants. The foundation does not make grants to individuals. The foundation does not conduct personal interviews with an applicant except upon the foundation's initiative.

Additional Information

Publications: General Information Letter

Foundation Officials

Anita Bury: assistant secretary
Joan Gorsuch: secretary
Betty Regenstein Hartman: vice president, director
Robert A. Mecca: vice president, director, treasurer B 1951.
Joseph Regenstein, Jr.: president, director B Chicago, IL 1923. ED Brown University (1945). PRIM CORP EMPL chairman: Arvey Corp.
Thomas A. Staszak: contr, assistant treasurer

Grants Analysis

Disclosure Period: calendar year ending 2003
Total Grants: $2,780,000
Number of Grants: 33
Average Grant: $25,161*
Highest Grant: $1,000,000
Lowest Grant: $1,000
Typical Range: $5,000 to $50,000
*Note: Average grant figure excludes two highest grants ($2,000,000).

Recent Grants

Note: Grants derived from 2001 Form 990.
General

2,000,000	Lincoln Park Zoological Society, Chicago, IL -- for research and modify large mammal exhibit
1,000,000	Chicago Botanic Garden, Glencoe, IL -- for construction
750,000	Chicago Zoological Society, Brookfield, IL -- for construction and development of Wolf Woods
500,000	Lincoln Park Zoological Society, Chicago, IL -- for demolition and rebuilding of the Great Ape House
35,000	Health Care Foundation, Steamboat Springs, CO -- for the purchase of orthopedic equipment
20,000	Walnut Street Theater, Philadelphia, PA -- for Touring Outreach Programs and Camp Walnut
12,000	Wyndcroft School, Pottstown, PA -- for renovation of art room
10,000	Child, Inc., Wilmington, DE -- for Battered Women's Shelter Program
10,000	Children and Families First, Wilmington, DE -- for 2002 friends campaign
10,000	Epilepsy Foundation of Eastern Pennsylvania, Philadelphia, PA -- for women and children's educational programs

REGIS CORP.

Company Headquarters

7201 Metro Blvd.
Edina, MN 55439

Company Description

Ticker: RGIS
Exchange: AMEX
Employees: 31,000 (1999)
SIC(s): 7231 Beauty Shops.

Operating Locations

Regis Corp. (MN--Eden Prairie, Minneapolis)

Regis Foundation

Giving Contact

Myron Kunin, President
7201 Metro Boulevard
Minneapolis, MN 55439-2103
Phone: (952)947-7777
Fax: (952)947-7900
Web: http://www.regiscorp.com/corporate/communityInvolve.html

Description

Founded: 1981
EIN: 411410790
Organization Type: Corporate Foundation
Giving Locations: MN: Minneapolis and surrounding area
Grant Types: Capital, General Support, Scholarship.
Note: Scholarship program is administered by the Minneapolis Board of Education.

Financial Summary

Total Giving: $1,552,964 (fiscal year ending June 30, 2003); $1,741,857 (fiscal 2002); $1,330,615 (fiscal 2001). Note: Contributes through foundation only.
Assets: $1,866,692 (fiscal 2003); $250,125 (fiscal 2002); $150,055 (fiscal 2001)
Gifts Received: $3,170,361 (fiscal 2003); $1,901,386 (fiscal 2002); $1,334,327 (fiscal 2001). Note: Foundation receives contributions from Regis Corp.

Typical Recipients

Arts & Humanities: Arts Associations & Councils, Arts Centers, Arts Institutes, Arts & Humanities-General, Libraries, Museums/Galleries, Music, Opera, Public Broadcasting, Theater
Civic & Public Affairs: Community Foundations, Ethnic Organizations, Civic & Public Affairs-General,

Housing, Law & Justice, Philanthropic Organizations, Urban & Community Affairs
Education: Business Education, Colleges & Universities, Education Associations, Education Funds, Education-General, Public Education (Precollege), Social Sciences Education, Student Aid
Health: Cancer, Medical Research
Religion: Jewish Causes, Religious Organizations, Synagogues/Temples
Social Services: Child Welfare, Community Service Organizations, Emergency Relief, People with Disabilities, United Funds/United Ways, YMCA/YWCA/YMHA/YWHA, Youth Organizations

Application Procedures

Initial Contact: Submit a brief letter of inquiry.
Application Requirements: Include a description of organization, amount requested, and purpose of funds sought.
Deadlines: None.
Notes: Applications for scholarships are available at Minneapolis public high schools.

Corporate Officials

Myron Kunin: chairman, director B Minneapolis, MN 1928. ED University of Minnesota BA (1949). PRIM CORP EMPL chairman, director: Regis Corp. CORP AFFIL ltd. partner: Rosepointe Housing; director: Supercuts Inc.; president: Regis Collection Inc.; chairman, principal stockholder: Curtis Squire Inc.; president: Red River Broadcasting Corp.

Foundation Officials

Paul Finkelstein: director
Bert M. Gross: secretary B 1929. PRIM CORP EMPL senior vice president, general council, secretary: Regis Corporation. CORP AFFIL legal counsel: Phillips Gross & Aaron Pennsylvania.
David B. Kunin: vice president
Myron Kunin: president (see above)
Randy Pearce: director

Grants Analysis

Disclosure Period: fiscal year ending June 30, 2003
Total Grants: $1,356,964*
Number of Grants: 16
Average Grant: $28,761*
Highest Grant: $800,000
Lowest Grant: $1,000
Typical Range: $5,000 to $80,000
***Note:** Giving excludes scholarship; United Way. Average grant figure excludes two highest grants ($954,300).

Recent Grants

Note: Grants derived from fiscal 2004 Form 990.
Library-Related
3,000	Minneapolis Central Library, Minneapolis, MN

General
975,000	Minneapolis Jewish Federation, Minnetonka, MN
140,000	Minneapolis Public Schools, Minneapolis, MN
110,000	University of Minnesota Foundation, Minneapolis, MN -- towards holocaust studies
81,500	Walker Art Center, Minneapolis, MN -- towards Regis dialogues
76,750	Guthrie Theater, Minneapolis, MN
62,000	Minnesota Public Radio, St. Paul, MN
60,000	Saint Cloud State University, St. Cloud, MN
56,000	United Way of Minneapolis Area, Minneapolis, MN
54,500	Minneapolis Institute of Arts, Minneapolis, MN
25,000	Students in Free Enterprise The Jack Shewmaker Center, Springfield, MD

REICHHOLD CHEMICALS INC.

Company Headquarters

PO Box 13582
Research Triangle Park, NC 27709
Phone: (919)990-7500
Fax: (919)990-7711
Web: http://www.reichhold.com

Company Description

Founded: 1929
Employees: 3,500
SIC(s): 2821 Plastics Materials & Resins.

Operating Locations

DIC Americas (NJ--Fort Lee); DIC Digital Supply Corp. (NJ--Teaneck); DIC Trading (U.S.A.) (NJ--Fort Lee); Dynaric (NJ--Teaneck); Earthrise Farms (CA--Glendale); Earthrise Trading Co. (CA--Petaluma); Film Division (NJ--Clark); General Printing Ink (IL--Northlake); Kohl & Madden Printing Ink Corp. Division (NJ--Fort Lee); KVK (U.S.A.) (NJ--New Brunswick); Polychrome Corp. Division (NJ--Fort Lee); Premier Polymers (TX--Alvin); Product Design Center (OH--Westerville); RBH Dispersions (NJ--Bound Brook); Reichhold Chemicals (NY--Buffalo); NC--Durham); Spencer Kellogg (NY--Buffalo); Sun Chemical Corp. (NJ--Fort Lee); Sun Chemical Corp. of Michigan (MI--Muskegon); Sun Chemical General Printing (IL--Northlake); Sun Chemical Pigments Division (OH--Cincinnati); Surface Technologies (NC--Durham); US Ink Corp. (NJ--Carlstadt)

Giving Contact

PO Box 13582
Research Triangle Park, NC 27709
Phone: (919)990-7500

Description

Organization Type: Corporate Giving Program
Giving Locations: headquarters area only.
Grant Types: Capital, Employee Matching Gifts.

Typical Recipients

Arts & Humanities: Arts Funds, Libraries, Museums/Galleries, Music, Performing Arts
Education: Business Education, Colleges & Universities, Economic Education, Public Education (Precollege)
Health: Health Organizations, Hospitals, Single-Disease Health Associations
Social Services: Community Service Organizations, United Funds/United Ways, Youth Organizations

Application Procedures

Initial Contact: Send letter of inquiry including a description of organization, need addressed, and amount requested. Plants can be contacted directly. Other subsidiaries of Dai Nippon administer independent programs.

Corporate Officials

Phillip D. Ashkettle: president, chief executive officer, director PRIM CORP EMPL president, chief executive officer, director: Reichhold Chemicals.
William Eberle: controller PRIM CORP EMPL controller: Reichhold Chemicals.

REIDLER FOUNDATION

Giving Contact

Diana L. James, Secretary & Treasurer
c/o Fleet Bank, Trust Dept.
101 W. Broad St., Box 518
Hazleton, PA 18201

Phone: (570)454-7654

Description

Founded: 1944
EIN: 246022888
Organization Type: Private Foundation
Giving Locations: PA: Ashland, Hazleton
Grant Types: General Support.

Donor Information

Founder: John W. Reidler

Financial Summary

Total Giving: $485,000 (fiscal year ending October 31, 2001). Note: Fiscal 1997 Giving includes scholarship ($26,500); United Way ($5,000).
Giving Analysis: Giving for fiscal 2001 includes: foundation grants to United Way ($5,000); foundation scholarships ($14,500)
Assets: $9,119,636 (fiscal 2001)
Gifts Received: $31,458 (fiscal 2001); $30,984 (fiscal 2000); $35,950 (fiscal 1998). Note: In fiscal 1998, 2000, and 2001, contributions were received from Dr. Howard D. and Mrs. Ann B. Fegan.

Typical Recipients

Arts & Humanities: Arts Associations & Councils, Arts Centers, Arts & Humanities-General, History & Archaeology, Libraries, Music, Public Broadcasting
Civic & Public Affairs: Community Foundations, Economic Development, Employment/Job Training, Civic & Public Affairs-General, Native American Affairs, Zoos/Aquariums
Education: Arts/Humanities Education, Colleges & Universities, Education Funds, Medical Education, Private Education (Precollege), Science/Mathematics Education, Secondary Education (Private), Student Aid
Environment: Air/Water Quality, Environment-General, Resource Conservation, Wildlife Protection
Health: AIDS/HIV, Cancer, Children's Health/Hospitals, Clinics/Medical Centers, Emergency/Ambulance Services, Health-General, Hospices, Hospitals, Multiple Sclerosis, Nursing Services
International: International Development, International Peace & Security Issues
Religion: Churches, Dioceses, Ministries, Religious Welfare
Social Services: Animal Protection, Child Welfare, Community Centers, Community Service Organizations, Delinquency & Criminal Rehabilitation, Family Planning, Family Services, Food/Clothing Distribution, Homes, People with Disabilities, Senior Services, United Funds/United Ways, YMCA/YWCA/YMHA/YWHA, Youth Organizations

Application Procedures

Initial Contact: Send a brief letter of inquiry describing program or project, and letter from supervising provincial.
Deadlines: None.

Restrictions

Does not support individuals.

Foundation Officials

Ann B. Fegan: president
Howard D. Fegan: trustee
John H. Fegan: trustee
Eugene C. Fish, Esq.: trustee B 1910. ED University of Pennsylvania Wharton School (1931); University of Pennsylvania School of Law (1934). PRIM CORP EMPL chairman, secretary, director: Eastern Foundry Co. CORP AFFIL chairman: Peerless Industries Inc.
Robert K. Gicking: vice president B Hazleton, PA 1931. ED Lafayette College (1952). PRIM CORP EMPL president, director: Hazleton National Bank. CORP AFFIL president: First Valley Corp.
Diana L. James: secretary, treasurer
Carl J. Reidler: trustee
Paul G. Reidler: president emeritus

Grants Analysis

Disclosure Period: fiscal year ending October 31, 2001
Total Grants: $465,500*
Number of Grants: 69
Average Grant: $6,206*
Highest Grant: $43,500
Lowest Grant: $500
Typical Range: $1,000 to $10,000
***Note:** Giving excludes scholarships; United Way. Average grant figure excludes highest grant.

Recent Grants

Note: Grants derived from 2002 Form 990.
Library-Related

37,000	Bethlehem Area Public Library, Bethlehem, PA -- projects
22,500	Bethlehem Area Public Library, Bethlehem, PA -- endowment fund
20,000	Hazelton Area Public Library, Hazelton, PA -- endowment fund
10,000	Hazelton Area Public Library, Hazelton, PA -- book fund

General

42,500	Schuykill Area Community Foundation, Ashland, PA -- charitable trust
30,000	AIDS Outreach, Allentown, PA -- operations
23,500	WVIA Public Television and Radio, Pittston, PA -- operations
20,000	Appalachian Mountain Club, Boston, MA -- Mountain Club's 125th Anniversary capital campaign
20,000	Planned Parenthood of Northeast Pennsylvania, Trexlertown, PA -- Marti King-Pringle Legacy Fund
10,000	Grace Episcopal Church, Allentown, PA
10,000	Grace Episcopal Church, Allentown, PA -- Grace Montessori School
10,000	Trinity Evangelical Lutheran Church, Hazleton, PA -- endowment fund
10,000	Wildlands Conservancy, Emmaus, PA -- operating support
10,000	WVIA Public Television and Radio, Pittston, PA -- endowment fund

REILLY INDUSTRIES INC.

Company Headquarters

1500 S. Tibbs Ave.
Indianapolis, IN 46241
Web: http://www.deet.com

Company Description

Employees: 50 (2003)
SIC(s): 2812 Alkalies & Chlorine, 2821 Plastics Materials & Resins, 2822 Synthetic Rubber, 2865 Cyclic Crudes & Intermediates.

Operating Locations

Reilly Industries, Inc. (NC--Greensboro)

Reilly Foundation

Giving Contact

300 North Meridian Street, Suite 1500
Indianapolis, IN 46204-1763
Phone: (317)248-6464
Fax: (317)248-6472

Description

Founded: 1962
EIN: 352061750
Organization Type: Corporate Foundation
Giving Locations: company operating locations, mainly Indianapolis, IN.

Grant Types: Employee Matching Gifts, General Support, Scholarship.

Donor Information

Founder: Reilly Industries

Financial Summary

Total Giving: $280,400 (2002); $331,370 (2001). Note: Contributes through foundation only.
Giving Analysis: Giving for 2002 includes: foundation matching gifts ($12,050); foundation grants to United Way ($51,400); 2001: foundation matching gifts ($7,870); foundation grants to United Way ($63,250); foundation ($260,250)
Assets: $809,025 (2002); $1,088,857 (2001)
Gifts Received: $200,000 (2000); $300,000 (1999); $600,000 (1998). Note: Contributions were received from Reilly Industries.

Typical Recipients

Arts & Humanities: Arts Appreciation, Arts Associations & Councils, Arts Centers, Arts Outreach, Ballet, Arts & Humanities-General, Historic Preservation, History & Archaeology, Libraries, Museums/Galleries, Music, Opera, Performing Arts, Theater
Civic & Public Affairs: African American Affairs, Civic & Public Affairs-General, Housing, Law & Justice, Public Policy, Safety, Urban & Community Affairs, Zoos/Aquariums
Education: Afterschool/Enrichment Programs, Business Education, Colleges & Universities, Community & Junior Colleges, Economic Education, Education Associations, Education Funds, Elementary Education (Private), Elementary Education (Public), Engineering/Technological Education, Education-General, Health & Physical Education, Leadership Training, Minority Education, Private Education (Precollege), Public Education (Precollege), Social Sciences Education, Student Aid, Vocational & Technical Education
Environment: Air/Water Quality, Environment-General, Resource Conservation
Health: Cancer, Children's Health/Hospitals, Clinics/Medical Centers, Health Organizations, Hospitals, Long-Term Care, Medical Rehabilitation, Medical Research, Public Health, Transplant Networks/Donor Banks
International: Foreign Arts Organizations, International-General, International Organizations
Religion: Religion-General, Ministries, Religious Organizations, Religious Welfare, Seminaries
Science: Scientific Centers & Institutes
Social Services: At-Risk Youth, Big Brothers/Big Sisters, Camps, Child Abuse, Child Welfare, Community Centers, Community Service Organizations, Counseling, Day Care, Domestic Violence, Family Planning, Family Services, Food/Clothing Distribution, Homes, People with Disabilities, Recreation & Athletics, Scouts, Senior Services, Shelters/Homelessness, Social Services-General, Special Olympics, United Funds/United Ways, Volunteer Services, YMCA/YWCA/YMHA/YWHA, Youth Organizations

Application Procedures

Initial Contact: Write a letter of intent.
Application Requirements: For grant requests: a description of organization and project, amount requested, and purpose of funds sought. For scholarship requests: tuition receipts and grade reports.
Deadlines: None.
Review Process: Trustees review requests at quarterly meetings.

Restrictions

Scholarship awards are limited to children of qualified employees.

Corporate Officials

Robert D. McNeeley: president, director, director B 1944. ED Purdue University BS (1967). PRIM CORP EMPL president, director: Reilly Industries, Inc.

CORP AFFIL polytechnical: Solar Aluminum Technology Services.
Thomas E. Reilly, Jr.: chairman, chief executive officer, director B 1939. ED Stanford University BA (1961); Harvard University Graduate School of Business Administration MBA (1963). PRIM CORP EMPL chairman, chief executive officer, director: Reilly Industries, Inc. CORP AFFIL director: Lilly Industries Inc.; director: Bank One Corp. NONPR AFFIL director: Methodist Hospital of Indiana.

Foundation Officials

Heather Murphy: trustee
Elizabeth C. Reilly: trustee
Michael Rodman: trustee
Kevin Wilhelm: trustee

Grants Analysis

Disclosure Period: calendar year ending 2002
Total Grants: $216,950*
Number of Grants: 48
Average Grant: $4,520
Highest Grant: $21,000
Lowest Grant: $500
Typical Range: $1,000 to $10,000
***Note:** Giving excludes matching gifts and United Way.

Recent Grants

Note: Grants derived from 2003 Form 990.
General

50,000	United Way Central Indiana, Indianapolis, IN
21,500	Ruth Lilly Health Education Center, Indianapolis, IN
21,000	Butler University, Indianapolis, IN
19,000	Associated Colleges, IN
17,000	Indianapolis Zoo, Indianapolis, IN
16,500	Indianapolis Public Schools, Indianapolis, IN
15,000	East 10th United Methodist
14,000	Junior Achievement, Indianapolis, IN
12,500	Indianapolis Symphony Orchestra, Indianapolis, IN
11,000	Earlham College, Richmond, IN

REINBERGER FOUNDATION

Giving Contact

Robert N. Reinberger, Co-Director
27600 Chagrin Boulevard, Suite 1200
Cleveland, OH 44122
Phone: (216)292-2790
Fax: (216)292-4466

Description

Founded: 1968
EIN: 346574879
Organization Type: Family Foundation
Giving Locations: OH: Cleveland, Columbus
Grant Types: Capital, Challenge, Endowment, General Support.

Donor Information

Founder: The Reinberger Foundation was established in 1968 by Clarence T. Reinberger, a Cleveland businessman who developed the Automotive Parts Company and later became the chairman of Genuine Parts. Following Mr. Reinberger's death in 1968, the foundation received half of its current assets. The remainder of its assets were acquired following the death of Mr. Reinberger's wife, Louise Reinberger. The Reinbergers had no children; the foundation is directed by two of Mr. Reinberger's nephews.

Financial Summary
Total Giving: $3,458,321 (2003); $3,679,056 (2002)
Assets: $74,352,236 (2003); $62,794,945 (2002)

Typical Recipients
Arts & Humanities: Arts Associations & Councils, Arts Centers, Arts Festivals, Arts Institutes, Ballet, Arts & Humanities-General, Historic Preservation, History & Archaeology, Libraries, Literary Arts, Museums/Galleries, Music, Opera, Performing Arts, Public Broadcasting, Theater, Visual Arts
Civic & Public Affairs: Botanical Gardens/Parks, Clubs, Community Foundations, Economic Development, Employment/Job Training, Civic & Public Affairs-General, Housing, Law & Justice, Nonprofit Management, Philanthropic Organizations, Professional & Trade Associations, Rural Affairs, Urban & Community Affairs, Zoos/Aquariums
Education: Afterschool/Enrichment Programs, Arts/Humanities Education, Colleges & Universities, Education Funds, Engineering/Technological Education, Education-General, Leadership Training, Legal Education, Literacy, Medical Education, Private Education (Precollege), Public Education (Precollege), Science/Mathematics Education
Environment: Environment-General
Health: Alzheimer's Disease, Cancer, Children's Health/Hospitals, Clinics/Medical Centers, Health-General, Health Funds, Health Organizations, Hospitals, Hospitals (University Affiliated), Long-Term Care, Medical Rehabilitation, Medical Research, Preventive Medicine/Wellness Organizations, Public Health, Speech & Hearing
Religion: Churches, Jewish Causes, Ministries, Religious Welfare
Science: Science Exhibits & Fairs, Science Museums, Scientific Centers & Institutes
Social Services: Animal Protection, At-Risk Youth, Big Brothers/Big Sisters, Camps, Child Welfare, Community Centers, Community Service Organizations, Family Planning, Family Services, Food/Clothing Distribution, People with Disabilities, Recreation & Athletics, Senior Services, Sexual Abuse, Social Services-General, YMCA/YWCA/YMHA/YWHA, Youth Organizations

Application Procedures
Initial Contact: There are no application forms or guidelines. Applicants should submit one copy of a full proposal.
Application Requirements: Written applications should include a clear statement of purpose and a copy of the organization's exemption letter from the IRS. The foundation will request further information on proposals of interest.
Deadlines: None.
Review Process: The board of directors meets in November, February, May and August. The review process takes about six months. The board acknowledges the receipt of an application and may require an interview.

Restrictions
Grants are not made to individuals.

Foundation Officials
Sara R. Dyer: trustee
Karen R. Hooser: trustee
Richard Heer Oman: secretary, trustee B Columbus, OH 1926. ED Ohio State University BA (1948); Ohio State University JD (1951). PRIM CORP EMPL counsel: Vorys, Sater, Seymour & Pease. NONPR AFFIL member: Ohio State Bar Association; fellow: Ohio State Bar Foundation; member: Columbus Bar Association; member: American Bar Association; member: American College Trust & Estate Counsel. CLUB AFFIL Nantucket Yacht Club; Rocky Fort Hunt & Country Club; Columbus Club; Kit Kat Club.
Robert N. Reinberger: co-director, trustee
William C. Reinberger: co-director, trustee

Grants Analysis
Disclosure Period: calendar year ending 2003
Total Grants: $3,458,321
Number of Grants: 74
Average Grant: $46,734
Highest Grant: $285,714
Lowest Grant: $1,000
Typical Range: $10,000 to $100,000

Recent Grants
Note: Grants derived from 2003 Form 990.
General

285,714	Cleveland Clinic Foundation, Cleveland, OH
250,000	Case Western Reserve University, Cleveland, OH
208,333	Great Lakes Science Center, Cleveland, OH
110,000	Berea Children's Home and Family Services, Cleveland, OH
109,000	Church of the Saviour, Cleveland, OH
100,000	Cleveland Metroparks Zoological Society, Cleveland, OH
100,000	Cleveland Museum of Natural History, Cleveland, OH
100,000	Columbus Academy, Columbus, OH
100,000	Heritage Day Health Centers, Columbus, OH
100,000	Lawrence School, Cleveland, OH

RELIABLE LIFE INSURANCE CO.

Company Headquarters
231 W. Lockwood Ave.
Webster Groves, MO 63119
Web: http://www.unitrin.com/lhi.htm

Company Description
Employees: 1,250
SIC(s): 6311 Life Insurance, 6321 Accident & Health Insurance.

Operating Locations
Reliable Life Insurance Co. (AR--El Dorado, Jonesboro, Little Rock, Texarkana; TX--Austin, Beaumont, Corpus Christi, Dallas, Fort Worth, Harlingen, Houston, Lubbock, McAllen, Midland, San Antonio, Tyler, Waco)

Nonmonetary Support
Type: Loaned Employees; Workplace Solicitation

Reliable Life Insurance Co. Foundation

Giving Contact
Anne Skelton, Trustee
231 W. Lockwood Ave.
St. Louis, MO 63119-2327
Phone: (314)968-6743

Description
EIN: 431735442
Organization Type: Corporate Foundation
Giving Locations: MO; WI: states where company does business.
Grant Types: Emergency, General Support, Multiyear/Continuing Support, Scholarship.

Financial Summary
Total Giving: $14,066 (2001)
Gifts Received: $250 (1998). Note: In 1998, contributions were received from A. Riley, Virginia Broleman, Garden Club, and The Reliance Life Insurance Company.

Typical Recipients
Arts & Humanities: Arts Appreciation, Arts Centers, Arts & Humanities-General, Libraries, Museums/Galleries, Music, Theater
Civic & Public Affairs: African American Affairs, Botanical Gardens/Parks, Community Foundations, Employment/Job Training, Civic & Public Affairs-General, Housing, Inner-City Development, Philanthropic Organizations, Zoos/Aquariums
Education: Afterschool/Enrichment Programs, Arts/Humanities Education, Business Education, Colleges & Universities, Education Funds, Education-General, Special Education
Health: Adolescent Health Issues, Alzheimer's Disease, Arthritis, Cancer, Children's Health/Hospitals, Health-General, Heart, Speech & Hearing
Religion: Religion-General, Missionary Activities (Domestic), Religious Welfare
Science: Science Museums
Social Services: At-Risk Youth, Child Welfare, Community Centers, Community Service Organizations, Day Care, Emergency Relief, Family Services, Food/Clothing Distribution, Homes, People with Disabilities, Scouts, Social Services-General, Special Olympics, United Funds/United Ways, YMCA/YWCA/YMHA/YWHA, Youth Organizations

Application Procedures
Initial Contact: Send a brief letter of inquiry and a full proposal. Include a description of organization, amount requested, purpose of funds sought, recently audited financial statement, and proof of tax-exempt status.
Deadlines: None.

Restrictions
Does not support individuals, religious organizations for sectarian purposes, political or lobbying groups, or organizations outside operating areas.

Corporate Officials
David Chomeau: chairman, president, chief operating officer, director B Saint Louis, MO 1937. ED Carleton College (1958). PRIM CORP EMPL chairman, president, chief operating officer, director: Reliable Life Insurance Co.
Stuart Chomeau: vice chairman, director PRIM CORP EMPL vice chairman, director: Reliable Life Insurance Co.
Lewis Baker Shepley: executive vice president, chief financial officer, director B Saint Louis, MO 1939. ED Yale University (1962); Yale University (1965). PRIM CORP EMPL executive vice president, chief financial officer, director: Reliable Life Insurance Co.

Foundation Officials
David D. Chomeau: trustee
Gregory P. LaVigne: trustee
James F. Seidler: trustee
Anne Skelton: trustee

Grants Analysis
Disclosure Period: calendar year ending 2000
Total Grants: $100,000
Number of Grants: 1

Recent Grants
Note: Grants derived from 2001 Form 990.
General

9,000	Missouri College Fund, Jefferson City, MO
3,000	Hope Center Salvation Army, St. Louis, MO
1,000	Friends of Father Dickson Cemetery, St. Louis, MO
500	Children's Home Society, St. Louis, MO
500	KidzLink, St. Louis, MO

66   Tatman Foundation, Ephraim, WI -- for
      University of California Marine Science
      Department

RESCO INC.

Company Headquarters
Honolulu, HI

Company Description
Employees: 300
SIC(s): 5000 Wholesale Trade--Durable Goods.

Locations Foundation

Giving Contact
Board of Directors
Locations Foundation
3465 Waialae Avenue, 4th Floor
Honolulu, HI 96816-2660
Phone: (808)735-4200

Description
Founded: 1988
EIN: 990267351
Organization Type: Corporate Foundation
Giving Locations: HI: Honolulu
Grant Types: General Support.

Donor Information
Founder: Resco, Inc.

Financial Summary
Total Giving: $16,342 (2003). Note: 1997 Giving includes United Way ($2,500).
Giving Analysis: Giving for 2003 includes: foundation grants to United Way ($2,000)
Assets: $215,327 (2003)
Gifts Received: $25,580 (2003); $18,760 (2000); $14,074 (1999). Note: In 2003, contributions were received from William Chee.

Typical Recipients
Arts & Humanities: Arts & Humanities-General, Libraries, Music, Performing Arts, Public Broadcasting, Theater
Civic & Public Affairs: Asian American Affairs, Botanical Gardens/Parks, Clubs, Civic & Public Affairs-General, Public Policy, Urban & Community Affairs, Women's Affairs
Education: Colleges & Universities, Education-General, Preschool Education, Private Education (Precollege), School Volunteerism, Science/Mathematics Education, Secondary Education (Private), Secondary Education (Public)
Health: Arthritis, Cancer, Children's Health/Hospitals, Diabetes, Health Organizations, Heart, Hospices, Hospitals, Medical Rehabilitation, Mental Health, Prenatal Health Issues, Public Health, Respiratory, Single-Disease Health Associations
Religion: Religious Organizations, Religious Welfare
Social Services: At-Risk Youth, Big Brothers/Big Sisters, Child Welfare, Community Centers, Community Service Organizations, Crime Prevention, Emergency Relief, Family Services, Food/Clothing Distribution, Recreation & Athletics, Scouts, Social Services-General, Special Olympics, Substance Abuse, United Funds/United Ways, YMCA/YWCA/YMHA/YWHA, Youth Organizations

Application Procedures
Initial Contact: The foundation has no formal grant application procedure or application form.
Deadlines: None.

Restrictions
Grants are not made to individuals.

Corporate Officials
William Chee: chairman, president, director PRIM CORP EMPL chairman, president, director: Resco Products.

Grants Analysis
Disclosure Period: calendar year ending 2003
Total Grants: $14,342*
Number of Grants: 11
Average Grant: $1,059*
Highest Grant: $3,750
Lowest Grant: $500
Typical Range: $500 to $2,000
*****Note:** Giving excludes United Way. Average grant figure excludes highest grant.

Recent Grants
Note: Grants derived from 2003 Form 990.
General

3,750	Adopt a Teacher, Aiea, HI
2,500	Adult Friends for Youth, Honolulu, HI
2,000	Aloha United Way, Honolulu, HI
2,000	American Cancer Society, Atlanta, GA
1,050	Angel Tree, Merrifield, VA
1,000	Big Brothers Big Sisters, Philadelphia, PA
952	Women in Need, New York, NY
800	Ronald McDonald Charities, Honolulu, HI
790	Make a Difference Day
500	Asia Pacific Exchange

RESEARCH CORP.

Giving Contact
Daniel Gasch, Chief Financial Officer
4703 E. Camp Lowell Dr., Suite 201
Tucson, AZ 85712
Phone: (520)571-1111
Fax: (520)571-1119
E-mail: awards@rescorp.org
Web: http://www.rescorp.org

Description
Founded: 1912
EIN: 131963407
Organization Type: Specialized/Single Purpose Foundation
Giving Locations: nationally; Canada
Grant Types: Award.

Donor Information
Founder: The Research Corporation was founded in 1912, with the late Frederick Gardner Cottrell as a donor. Dr. Cottrell, a noted scientist, inventor, and philanthropist, established the foundation for the advancement of science and technology with the assistance of the Secretary of the Smithsonian Institution, Charles Doolittle Walcott. The Research Corporation, which was one of the first U.S. foundations, was the only one wholly devoted to science.
Dr. Cottrell, born in Oakland, CA, in 1877, received a bachelor's degree from the University of California in 1896. He taught high school chemistry, before pursuing advanced degrees from the University of Berlin in 1901 and the University of Leipzig in 1902. Dr. Cottrell then returned to America to teach at the University of California.
While an instructor at the University of California, he invented the Cottrell Electrical Precipitator. The device, which is still in use today, became the primary means for controlling industrial air pollution and the basis for his fortune.
In 1912, after taking a job with the U.S. Bureau of Mines, he established the Research Corporation with the patent rights from his invention. Dr. Cottrell believed that science should be the principal beneficiary for his invention and wanted the foundation to develop it and use any monies from it to provide means for scientific investigation and research by contributing funds to the Smithsonian Institution and other institutions. For the foundation's board, he recruited men prominent in academe and industry, including Dr. Walcott, as the foundation's co-founder.
Over the past eighty years, the Research Corporation has contributed well over $125 million to research projects proposed by young academic scientists, twenty-three of whom have won Nobel Prizes. A number of other prominent academic inventors have followed Dr. Cottrell's example and have contributed inventions to the corporation for the furthering of academic science.
Dr. Cottrell married Jessie Mae Fulton in 1904. Dr. Cottrell died in 1948, leaving no immediate survivors.

Financial Summary
Total Giving: $5,621,643 (2003); $8,411,094 (2002); $6,162,071 (2001)
Assets: $154,107,995 (2003); $131,961,562 (2002); $147,729,096 (2001)
Gifts Received: $167,000 (2001); $198,053 (2000); $438,138 (1998). Note: In 2001, contributions were received from M.J. Murdock Charitable Trust ($40,000), Camille & Henry Dreyfus Foundation ($73,000), and Welch Foundation ($54,000). In 2000, contributions were received from the MJ Murdock Charitable Trust ($170,553) and the Camille and Henry Dreyfus Foundation ($27,500).

Typical Recipients
Arts & Humanities: Ballet, Arts & Humanities-General, Libraries, Museums/Galleries, Music, Public Broadcasting, Theater
Civic & Public Affairs: Business/Free Enterprise, Hispanic Affairs, Nonprofit Management, Public Policy
Education: Afterschool/Enrichment Programs, Agricultural Education, Arts/Humanities Education, Business Education, Colleges & Universities, Economic Education, Faculty Development, Education-General, Journalism/Media Education, Medical Education, Science/Mathematics Education, Secondary Education (Public)
Health: Diabetes, Health-General
International: Foreign Educational Institutions
Religion: Religious Welfare
Science: Scientific Organizations, Scientific Research
Social Services: Child Welfare, Recreation & Athletics, Senior Services, Special Olympics, Substance Abuse, YMCA/YWCA/YMHA/YWHA, Youth Organizations

Application Procedures
Initial Contact: See foundation website for application guidelines.
Application Requirements: Applicants should read the complete guidelines at the foundation website, then submit the electronic application request form found at the end of the guidelines.
Deadlines: There are target dates for specific programs at the foundation, such as the Cottrell College Science Awards and Cottrell Scholars Awards. Contact the foundation for specific deadlines.
Review Process: After internal evaluation, formal applications will be invited from those inquiries that are of further interest.

Restrictions
The foundation does not make awards to individuals or businesses. Cottrell College Science Awards encourage research with undergraduates and are open to faculty in non-PhD granting departments of astronomy, chemistry, and physics. Cottrell Scholars Awards are for young university faculty members in their third year of a tenure track position who wish to excel at both research and teaching.
Research Innovation Awards are for research university faculty in chemistry, physics, and astronomy who propose original, innovative research and teaching program; they are open to faculty whose first tenure-track position began in the current or preceding cal-

endar year. Research Opportunity Awards target tenured science faculty at graduate institutions aimed at re-establishing research programs. It is restricted to PhD granting departments of astronomy, chemistry, and physics, and the first step is a nomination by the department chair. Guidelines for specific programs are available from the foundation website.

Occasionally, proposals may be considered for novel research projects that are unlikely to receive support from more traditional sources. Requests for funding that might be obtained from other more appropriate sources, to supplement already substantial funding or to simply extend mature projects, are not encouraged.

Additional Information

Publications: Annual Report (including Application Guidelines); Application Form; Program Brochures; Occasional Reports on Research and Education in the Physical Sciences; Newsletter

Foundation Officials

Herbert S. Adler: director ED University of Pennsylvania. PRIM CORP EMPL principal: Halcyon/Slifka Management Co. NONPR AFFIL member: American Friends English Heritage; member: American Friends Winchester Cathedral.

Stuart Jessup Bigelow Crampton: director B New York, NY 1936. ED Williams College BA (1958); Oxford University Worcester College BA (1960); Harvard University PhD (1964); Oxford University Worcester College MA (1965). PRIM NONPR EMPL professor: Williams College. CORP AFFIL consult: Sherman Fairchild Scientific Equipment Program Westat Inc. NONPR AFFIL member: Sigma Phi; member: Sigma Xi; member board assessment physics labs: National Institute Standards & Technology; member: American Association Physics Teachers; fellow: American Physics Society.

Michael P. Doyle, PhD: vice president, secretary ED Iowa State University PhD; University of Saint Thomas.

Robert Michael Gavin, Jr.: director B Coatesville, PA 1940. ED Saint John's University BA (1962); Iowa State University PhD (1966). ADD CORP EMPL president: Cranbrook Educational Community. CORP AFFIL director: Fortis Money Fund Inc.; director: Research Corp.; director: Fortis Income Portfolios Inc.; director: Fortis Funds Research Corp.; director: Fortis Growth Fund Inc.; director: Fortis Financial Group Inc.

Dr. James M. Gentile: president OCCUPATION dean natural sciences: Hope College.

Robert Holland, Jr.: director B 1940. ED City University of New York Bernard M. Baruch College MBA; Union College BSME. CORP AFFIL director: UNC Ventures Inc.; director: TruMark Manufacturing Co.; director: AC Nielsen Corp.; director: Olin Corp.; director: Mutual Life Insurance Co. New York; director: Frontier Corp.; director: Middlesex Mutual Insurance Co. NONPR AFFIL director: Lincoln Center Theater; chairman, trustee: Spelman College; director: Harlem Junior Tennis Program; trustee: Atlanta University Center.

Suzanne Denbo Jaffe: treasurer B Washington, DC 1943. PRIM CORP EMPL managing director: Hamilton Co. CORP AFFIL director: Olin Corp.; director: Creative Biomolecules Axel Johnson Inc.; director: Crossroads Capital LP. NONPR AFFIL trustee: University Pennsylvania; member: Women's Forum; trustee: Pennsylvania Women; director: National Postal Forum; member New York women business committee: Oversees Education Fund International; member: International Womens Forum; board governors, vice president: Jewish Community Relations Council; member: Finance Womens Association; director: Fordham University; member advisory committee: Childrens Aid Society; business advisory board: Columbia University Graduate School Business; president: American Jewish Committee. CLUB AFFIL Economic Club; Harmonie Club.

Joan Selverstone Valentine: director

Geoffrey King Walters: director B Baton Rouge, LA 1931. ED Rice University BA (1953); Duke University PhD (1956). PRIM NONPR EMPL professor: Rice University. NONPR AFFIL fellow: American Physics Society.

Laurel Lynn Wilkening: director B Richland, WA 1944. ED Reed College BA (1966); University of California, San Diego PhD (1970). PRIM NONPR EMPL chancellor: University of California, Irvine. CORP AFFIL director: Research Corp.; director: Seagate Technology Inc. NONPR AFFIL trustee: Reed College; trustee: UCAR; member: Phi Beta Kappa; director: Planetary Society; member: American Association Advancement Science; member: American Geophysical Union.

Grants Analysis

Disclosure Period: calendar year ending 2003
Total Grants: $5,621,643
Number of Grants: 297
Average Grant: $18,928
Highest Grant: $75,000
Typical Range: $5,000 to $40,000

Recent Grants

Note: Grants derived from 2001 Form 990.
General

75,000	Arizona State University, Tempe, AZ -- study of oxidative processes in duplex DNA
75,000	Boston University, Boston, MA -- search for the origin of mass and a b-Quark trigger for the DO experiment
75,000	California Institute of Technology, Pasadena, CA -- study on enantioselective organocatalysis
75,000	Case Western Reserve University, Cleveland, OH -- to conduct a probe on the evolution of galaxy clusters
75,000	Clemson University, Clemson, SC -- experimental study on synthesis and fabrication of novel fluoropolymers for photonic applications
75,000	Columbia University, New York, NY -- research in C-H bond activation in a complex chemical assembly
75,000	Dartmouth College, Hanover, NH -- study on stellar ages and cosmology
75,000	Louisiana State University, Baton Rouge, LA -- research on molecular architecture of functionalized organic materials using novel fluro-organic mesophases
75,000	Southern Illinois University, Carbondale, IL -- for research in nanoscale electron transfer
75,000	Suny at Stony Brook, Stony Brook, NY -- research on physical chemistry

RETIREMENT RESEARCH FOUNDATION

Giving Contact

Marilyn Hennessy, President
Retirement Research Foundation
8765 West Higgins Road, Suite 430
Chicago, IL 60631-4170
Phone: (773)714-8080
Fax: (773)714-8089
E-mail: info@rrf.org
Web: http://www.rrf.org

Description

Founded: 1950
EIN: 362429540
Organization Type: General Purpose Foundation
Giving Locations: FL: direct service projects; IL: Chicago metropolitan area

Grant Types: General Support, Matching, Multiyear/ Continuing Support, Project, Research, Seed Money.

Donor Information

Founder: "The Retirement Research Foundation was established by John D. MacArthur, a Chicago resident and businessman, in 1950. Upon Mr. MacArthur's death in 1978, the foundation was the recipient of major assets and began active grant making in 1979. MacArthur also established the John D. and Catherine T. MacArthur Foundation. However, each foundation is separate and totally independent of the other."

Financial Summary

Total Giving: $6,977,572 (2003); $9,482,842 (2002)
Giving Analysis: Giving for 2003 includes: foundation matching gifts ($175,955); 2002: foundation matching gifts ($172,694)
Assets: $160,020,177 (2003); $141,301,871 (2002)

Typical Recipients

Arts & Humanities: Film & Video, Libraries, Public Broadcasting

Civic & Public Affairs: Asian American Affairs, Civil Rights, Community Foundations, Economic Development, Employment/Job Training, Civic & Public Affairs-General, Hispanic Affairs, Housing, Law & Justice, Legal Aid, Nonprofit Management, Professional & Trade Associations, Public Policy, Rural Affairs, Safety, Urban & Community Affairs, Women's Affairs

Education: Arts/Humanities Education, Colleges & Universities, Community & Junior Colleges, Continuing Education, Economic Education, Education Associations, Education-General, Health & Physical Education, Literacy, Medical Education, Private Education (Precollege), School Volunteerism, Secondary Education (Private), Social Sciences Education

Environment: Resource Conservation

Health: Alzheimer's Disease, Cancer, Children's Health/Hospitals, Clinics/Medical Centers, Diabetes, Emergency/Ambulance Services, Eyes/Blindness, Health-General, Geriatric Health, Health Policy/Cost Containment, Health Funds, Health Organizations, Heart, Home-Care Services, Hospices, Hospitals, Long-Term Care, Medical Research, Mental Health, Nursing Services, Preventive Medicine/Wellness Organizations, Public Health, Single-Disease Health Associations, Speech & Hearing, Transplant Networks/Donor Banks

Religion: Churches, Dioceses, Jewish Causes, Religious Organizations, Religious Welfare, Seminaries

Social Services: Big Brothers/Big Sisters, Community Centers, Community Service Organizations, Counseling, Crime Prevention, Day Care, Family Planning, Family Services, Food/Clothing Distribution, Homes, People with Disabilities, Refugee Assistance, Senior Services, Shelters/Homelessness, Volunteer Services, YMCA/YWCA/YMHA/YWHA

Application Procedures

Initial Contact: The foundation does not have a standard application form. Applications must be submitted in writing. Contact the foundation for guidelines.

Application Requirements: Applications should include a two- to three-page summary of the project, its significance, and its cost. In addition, proposals should address specific project objectives and give a description of the methods. A timetable and line item budget, including other sources of funds and a budget justification, should be included. If relevant, plans for continued support should be described. Curricula vitae, not to exceed eight pages, should be included for project directors and key staff. Information on the applicant organization should include its history, accomplishments, audited financial reports, annual reports, and specific qualifications for the proposed project. Include a plan for the dissemination of project results, as appropriate. A copy of the applicant's tax-exempt status under Section 501(c)(3), and of classification as "not a private foundation" under Section

509(a) of the Internal Revenue Code, must be included. All applications must be signed by the chief executive officer of the applicant organization and submitted in triplicate.

Research proposals should describe the experimental design, procedures to be used to accomplish the objectives, sequence of the investigation, kinds of data to be obtained, and the means by which data will be analyzed and interpreted.

Model projects and service proposals should describe the project design, target group, change to be effected, resources and method of delivery, sequence of activities planned to meet project objectives, and methods and criteria to be used to evaluate the outcome of the project.

Education and training proposals should describe the target group; educational needs to be met; content, methods, sequence, and location of educational experiences; and the methods and criteria which will be used to evaluate the educational program.

Deadlines: Deadlines for receipt of applications are February 1, May 1, and August 1.

Review Process: Decisions are usually made four months after the deadline dates.

Restrictions

The foundation does not provide support for construction or renovation of facilities; general operating expenses of established organizations; endowment or developmental campaigns; scholarships; loans; grants to individuals; projects outside the United States; dissertation research; production of films or videos; computer equipment; or conferences, publications, and travel, unless they are components of foundation-funded projects. Generally, support of projects beyond a three-year period will not be provided.

Additional Information

The foundation is particularly interested in innovative projects that develop and/or demonstrate new approaches to the problems of older adults and have the potential for regional or national impact. Consideration of service or service development projects that do not have this potential are limited geographically to Illinois, Indiana, Iowa, Kentucky, Michigan, Missouri, Wisconsin, and Florida.

Publications: Program Guidelines; Application Procedures; Two-Year Report; 10-Year Retrospective Report; Accessible Faith: A Technical Guide for Accessibility in Houses of Worship

Foundation Officials

William J. Gentle: trustee, treasurer
Marilyn Hennessy: president B 1936.
Webster H. Hurley: trustee
Edward J. Kelly: chairman, trustee
Sharon F. Markham: associate vice president
Nathaniel P. McParland, MD: trustee
Marvin Meyerson: trustee CORP AFFIL director: Bankers Life Insurance Co. New York.
Bart T. Murphy: trustee
John F. Santos, PhD: trustee
Sister Stella Louise Slomka: trustee B November 13, 1920. NONPR AFFIL president, director: Saint Mary Nazareth Hospital.
Ruth Ann Watkins: secretary, trustee

Grants Analysis

Disclosure Period: calendar year ending 2003
Total Grants: $6,801,617*
Number of Grants: 231
Average Grant: $29,444
Highest Grant: $165,664
Lowest Grant: $1,000
Typical Range: $5,000 to $50,000
***Note:** Giving excludes matching gifts.

Recent Grants

Note: Grants derived from 2003 Form 990.

General

213,321	Florida International University, Miami, FL
204,543	Wendell Johnson Speech and Hearing Clinic, Iowa City, IA
200,000	National Council on the Aging Inc., Washington, DC
196,000	Interfaith Refugee & Immigration Ministries, Chicago, IL
174,988	Counseling Center of Lake View, Chicago, IL
152,673	Florida Agricultural and Mechanical University, Tallahassee, FL
150,000	Health & Disability Advocates, Chicago, IL
150,000	Will Feed Community Organization, Chicago, IL
149,579	University of Kentucky, Lexington, KY
135,280	University of Illinois, Urbana, IL

ALLENE REUSS MEMORIAL TRUST

Giving Contact

Richard Pershan, Co-Trustee
LeBoeuf, Lamb, Greene & Mac Rae, LLP
Attn: Mr. Richard Pershan, Esq. Trustee
125 West 55th Street
New York, NY 10019-5389
Phone: (212)635-1518

Description

Founded: 1996
EIN: 137086745
Organization Type: Private Foundation
Giving Locations: NY: New York and surrounding area
Grant Types: General Support.

Financial Summary

Total Giving: $542,375 (2003); $652,003 (2001)
Assets: $15,130,514 (2003); $13,907,326 (2001)
Gifts Received: $46,691 (2001); $5,138,913 (1996).
Note: In 2001, contributions were received from the Estate of Henry Reuss.

Typical Recipients

Arts & Humanities: Libraries
Civic & Public Affairs: Civic & Public Affairs-General
Education: Colleges & Universities, Preschool Education
Health: Clinics/Medical Centers, Eyes/Blindness
Religion: Jewish Causes
Social Services: Community Service Organizations, Day Care, People with Disabilities

Application Procedures

Application Requirements: Send a brief letter of inquiry.
Deadlines: None.

Additional Information

Trust(s): Bank of NY

Foundation Officials

Richard Pershan, Esq.: co-trustee

Grants Analysis

Disclosure Period: calendar year ending 2003
Total Grants: $542,375
Number of Grants: 17
Average Grant: $23,146*
Highest Grant: $83,333
Lowest Grant: $5,000
Typical Range: $10,000 to $50,000
***Note:** Average grant figure excludes three highest grants ($218,333).

Recent Grants

Note: Grants derived from 2001 Form 990.
Library-Related

90,000	New York Public Library, New York, NY

General

105,000	Hunter College, New York, NY
60,000	Yale University, New Haven, CT
51,142	Baruch College, New York, NY -- for computer center
50,861	Recording for the Blind and Dyslexic, Princeton, NJ
50,000	Lighthouse, Philadelphia, PA
50,000	Orbis, New York, NY
50,000	Saint Vincent's Catholic Medical Center
40,000	Visions, New York, NY
37,000	Joan and Sanford Weill Medical College, New York, NY
25,000	New York Community Trust, New York, NY

CHARLES H. REVSON FOUNDATION

Giving Contact

Lisa E. Goldberg, President
Charles H. Revson Foundation
55 East 59th Street, 23rd Floor
New York, NY 10022
Phone: (212)935-3340
Fax: (212)688-0633
E-mail: info@revsonfoundation.org
Web: http://www.revsonfoundation.org

Description

Founded: 1956
EIN: 136126105
Organization Type: General Purpose Foundation
Giving Locations: NY: New York
Grant Types: Fellowship, General Support, Project, Research, Scholarship, Seed Money.

Donor Information

Founder: Charles H. Revson was born in Boston in 1906, was brought up in Manchester, NH, and went to New York City as a young man. In 1932, he founded Revlon, Inc., which he subsequently built into a major international corporation. In 1956, he established the Charles H. Revson Foundation, through which he donated more than $10 million during his lifetime. The majority of these gifts went to organizations serving the Jewish community, medical institutions, and schools and universities, particularly in New York, his adopted city. On his death in 1975, Charles Revson endowed the foundation from his estate. He gave the board of directors unusual freedom to innovate, leaving them the discretion to chart the foundation's course. In 1978, with its first full-time staff and formal grantmaking procedures, the foundation began to make special project grants.

Financial Summary

Total Giving: $6,576,433 (2003); $10,882,036 (2002)
Assets: $157,167,206 (2003); $138,989,104 (2002)

Typical Recipients

Arts & Humanities: Arts Funds, Arts Institutes, Arts Outreach, Ballet, Dance, Ethnic & Folk Arts, Film & Video, Arts & Humanities-General, Historic Preservation, Libraries, Literary Arts, Museums/Galleries, Public Broadcasting, Theater
Civic & Public Affairs: African American Affairs, Business/Free Enterprise, Community Foundations, Economic Development, Economic Policy, Employment/Job Training, Ethnic Organizations, Civic & Public Affairs-General, Housing, Inner-City Development, Law & Justice, Legal Aid, Nonprofit Manage-

ment, Philanthropic Organizations, Professional & Trade Associations, Public Policy, Urban & Community Affairs, Women's Affairs

Education: Arts/Humanities Education, Colleges & Universities, Education Associations, Education Reform, Elementary Education (Private), Education-General, Legal Education, Medical Education, Preschool Education, Public Education (Precollege), Science/Mathematics Education, Social Sciences Education, Student Aid

Environment: Environment-General

Health: AIDS/HIV, Cancer, Clinics/Medical Centers, Medical Research

International: Foreign Arts Organizations, Foreign Educational Institutions, International-General, Human Rights, International Affairs, International Development, International Environmental Issues, International Organizations, International Peace & Security Issues, Missionary/Religious Activities

Religion: Jewish Causes, Religious Welfare, Seminaries, Social/Policy Issues, Synagogues/Temples

Social Services: Child Welfare, Community Service Organizations, Emergency Relief, Food/Clothing Distribution, Refugee Assistance, Shelters/Homelessness, Youth Organizations

Application Procedures

Initial Contact: Applicants should send a letter by regular mail to the foundation.

Application Requirements: The letter should include a description of the proposed project and the purpose and activities of the applicant organization. It also should include background information on the project, objectives of the project, and methods to be used in accomplishing them; qualifications and responsibilities of the principal staff members; current and projected budgets; latest audited financial statement; amount, duration, and specific purposes of requested grant; plans for evaluation and future funding; other sources of support; tax-exempt status and classification; financial statements; and a list of the board of directors with their affiliations.

Deadlines: None.

Review Process: Proposals are reviewed by the foundation staff and acted on by the board of directors at regular meetings. The evaluation of grant applications is ongoing throughout the year.

Restrictions

Support is not given for local health appeals, individuals, building or endowment campaigns, matching gifts, grass-roots organizations, direct service, or routine budgetary support. No loans are made.

Additional Information

Publications: Report (biennially); Guidelines; Religious Liberty in a Post-9/11 World; Telecommunications and World Jewish Renewal; The Changing Nature of American Philanthropy

Foundation Officials

Red Burns: director

Eli N. Evans: president emeritus B 1936.

Henry Louis Gates, Jr.: director

Lisa E. Goldberg: president, director

Philip Leder: director, chairman B Washington, DC 1934. ED Harvard University AB (1956); Harvard University MD (1960). PRIM NONPR EMPL professor genetics: Harvard University, School of Medicine. CORP AFFIL director: Monsanto Co.; director: Genome Therapeutic Corp. NONPR AFFIL member: Institute Medicine; member: National Academy Sciences; senior investigator: Howard Hughes Medical Institute; professor genetics: Harvard University Medical School.

Dr. Ruth Mandel: director PRIM CORP EMPL president: Boca Beauty Franchise Inc.

Martha Louise Minow: director ED University of Michigan AB (1975); Harvard University EdM (1976); Yale University JD (1979). PRIM NONPR EMPL professor: Harvard University. NONPR AFFIL trustee emeritus: Judge Baker Children's Center; member:

Law Society Association; executive co-director: Harvard Children's Studies; director: Judge David L. Bazelon Center Mental Health Law; director: Covenant Foundation.

Louis Perlmutter: director

Charles H. Revson, Jr.: secretary, treasurer

Robert Singer Rifkind: director B New York, NY 1936. ED Yale University BA (1958); Harvard University JD (1961). PRIM CORP EMPL partner: Cravath, Swaine & Moore. NONPR AFFIL fellow: New York State Bar Foundation; member: Phi Beta Kappa; board governors, chairman: Jewish Theological Seminary; member: Association Bar New York City; member: Council Foreign Relations; president, director: American Jewish Committee; member: American Law Institute; fellow: American College Trial Lawyers; member: American Bar Association; member: American Bar Foundation.

Harold Tanner: president B New York, NY 1932. ED Cornell University BS (1952); Harvard University MBA (1956). PRIM CORP EMPL president: Tanner & Co. CORP AFFIL director: TIG Holdings Inc. NONPR AFFIL member: Council Foreign Relations; co-founder: Volunteer Urban Consult Group; chairman: Classroom Inc.; chairman board trustee: Cornell University; chairman: American Jewish Committee. CLUB AFFIL Century Country Club; Harmonie Club.

Grants Analysis

Disclosure Period: calendar year ending 2003
Total Grants: $6,576,433*
Number of Grants: 54
Average Grant: $116,536*
Highest Grant: $400,000
Lowest Grant: $1,000
Typical Range: $20,000 to $200,000
*Note: Giving includes fellowship. Average grant figure excludes highest grant.

Recent Grants

Note: Grants derived from 2003 Form 990.

Library-Related

37,500	Library of America, New York, NY -- to support distribution of Reporting Civil Rights American Journalism 1941-1973

General

400,000	Tel Aviv University Environmental Simulation Laboratory, Tel Aviv Israel -- to set up computerized environmental simulation laboratory
365,500	Teachers College Columbia University, New York, NY -- to provide support and training to all new K-8 teachers
351,900	New York University School of Law, New York, NY -- to enable law students to work in public interest law organization
350,000	Jerusalem Institute for Israel Studies, Jerusalem Israel -- towards continued support of the Jerusalem Institute for Israel Studies
350,000	Jewish Media Fund, New York, NY -- towards development of Jewish Heritage Video Collections
300,000	Children's Defense Fund, Washington, DC -- towards public education activities and its Communication Department
300,000	Citizens Union Foundation, New York, NY -- to expand a website for people interested in public policy
300,000	Columbia University, New York, NY
250,000	Center on Budget and Policy Priorities, Washington, DC -- towards monitoring and public education activities related to the federal budget
250,000	Sesame Workshop, New York, NY -- to support production of new sesame street

REXAM INC.

Company Headquarters

4201 Congress St., Ste. 340
Charlotte, NC 28209
Web: http://www.rexam.com

Company Description

Employees: 3,200
SIC(s): 3081 Unsupported Plastics Film & Sheet, 6719 Holding Companies Nec.
Parent Company: Rexam PLC, 4 Millbank, London, United Kingdom

Operating Locations

McCorquodale ColorCard (MD--Whiteford); MiTek Industries (MO--Chesterfield); Mitek Industries (MO--St. Louis); Otis Specialty Papers (ME--Jay); Rexam Cartons (NC--Pineville); Rexam Closures (IN--Evansville, Princeton); Rexam Containers-US (IL--Flora; MO--Union); Rexam Custom (NC--Matthews; SC--Spartanburg); Rexam DSI (MA--South Hadley); Rexam Extrusions (WI--Oshkosh); Rexam Flexible Packaging (NC--Greensboro); Rexam Graphics (MA--South Hadley; OR--Portland); Rexam Medical Packaging (IL--Mundelein; MA--Ashland; MN--Lakeville; NJ--Mount Holly); Rexam Mulox U.S.A. (GA--Baxley, Macon); Rexam Performance Products (SC--Lancaster); Rexam Plastics Group (NC--Charlotte); Rexam Print Packaging Group (NC--Charlotte); Rexam Release (IL--Bedford Park, Chicago, Oak Brook)

Rexam Foundation

Giving Contact

Frank Brown, President
4201 Congress St., Ste. 340
Charlotte, NC 28209
Phone: (704)551-1500
Fax: (704)551-1572

Description

EIN: 136165669
Organization Type: Corporate Foundation
Giving Locations: operating communities.
Grant Types: Capital, Challenge, Employee Matching Gifts, Endowment, General Support, Scholarship.

Financial Summary

Total Giving: $28,618 (2004). Note: 1997 Giving includes matching gifts ($18,510), scholarship ($14,500).
Assets: $1,350 (2004)
Gifts Received: $29,018 (2004); $67,787 (1999); $69,464 (1997). Note: Contributions were received from Rexam Inc.

Typical Recipients

Arts & Humanities: Arts Associations & Councils, Libraries, Music, Performing Arts
Civic & Public Affairs: Chambers of Commerce
Education: Business-School Partnerships, Colleges & Universities, Community & Junior Colleges, Private Education (Precollege), Student Aid
Health: Health Organizations, Hospices, Single-Disease Health Associations
International: International Environmental Issues
Science: Science Museums
Social Services: Child Welfare, United Funds/United Ways, YMCA/YWCA/YMHA/YWHA, Youth Organizations

Application Procedures

Initial Contact: The foundation requests applications be made in writing.
Deadlines: None.

Corporate Officials
Frank C. Brown: president PRIM CORP EMPL president: Rexam.

Foundation Officials
Frank C. Brown: president (see above)

Grants Analysis
Disclosure Period: calendar year ending 2004
Total Grants: $28,618*
Note: Grants list unavailable for 2004.

Recent Grants
Note: Grants derived from 1997 Form 990.
General

10,000	Johnson C. Smith University, Charlotte, NC
5,500	YMCA
5,000	Arts and Science Council
5,000	Discovery Place, Charlotte, NC
5,000	Queens College, Charlotte, NC
4,913	United Way Central Carolinas, Charlotte, NC
500	World Wildlife Fund, Washington, DC

CHRISTOPHER REYNOLDS FOUNDATION

Giving Contact
Andrea Panaritis, Executive Director, Secretary, & Treasurer
267 5th Avenue, Suite 1001
New York, NY 10016
Phone: (212)532-1606
Fax: (212)532-1403
E-mail: inquiries@creynolds.org
Web: http://www.creynolds.org

Description
Founded: 1952
EIN: 136129401
Organization Type: General Purpose Foundation
Giving Locations: MI; NY; OH; U.S. organizations working in Indochina; Cambodia; Lao People's Democratic Republic; Vietnam
Grant Types: Conference/Seminar, General Support, Multiyear/Continuing Support, Project, Research.

Donor Information
Founder: Incorporated in 1952 by the late Libby Holman Reynolds.

Financial Summary
Total Giving: $1,722,153 (fiscal year ending January 31, 2002); $2,233,012 (fiscal 2001)
Assets: $32,251,925 (fiscal 2002); $35,680,927 (fiscal 2001)
Gifts Received: $3,084 (fiscal 1997); $331,944 (fiscal 1996)

Typical Recipients
Arts & Humanities: Arts & Humanities-General, Libraries, Literary Arts
Civic & Public Affairs: African American Affairs, Asian American Affairs, Civil Rights, Community Foundations, Economic Development, Economic Policy, Employment/Job Training, Ethnic Organizations, Civic & Public Affairs-General, Hispanic Affairs, Law & Justice, Native American Affairs, Nonprofit Management, Professional & Trade Associations, Public Policy, Urban & Community Affairs
Education: Afterschool/Enrichment Programs, Colleges & Universities, Education Reform, Education-General, Health & Physical Education, International Exchange, International Studies, Medical Education, Minority Education, Private Education (Precollege), Student Aid
Environment: Environment-General, Protection, Wildlife Protection
Health: Clinics/Medical Centers, Health Organizations, Mental Health, Public Health, Speech & Hearing
International: Foreign Arts Organizations, Foreign Educational Institutions, International-General, Health Care/Hospitals, Human Rights, International Affairs, International Development, International Environmental Issues, International Organizations, International Peace & Security Issues, International Relations, International Relief Efforts, Missionary/Religious Activities
Religion: Churches, Religion-General, Religious Organizations, Religious Welfare
Science: Science-General
Social Services: Community Service Organizations, Refugee Assistance, Social Services-General, Veterans, Youth Organizations

Application Procedures
Initial Contact: The foundation does not use a formal grant application form.
Application Requirements: Proposals should include specific objectives, detailed estimated budgets, qualifications of the organizations and individuals involved, and proof of tax-exempt status from the IRS. Six copies of the proposal are required.
Deadlines: Contact the foundation by phone, fax, or e-mail for dates.
Review Process: Meetings are generally held in January, May, and September.

Restrictions
The foundation does not make grants for building funds, medical research, educational or religious institutions (except in relation to research on subjects that fall within the scope of the foundation's current interests), or general operating or overhead expenses (except for newly organized entities whose objectives fall within the areas of the foundation's current interests).

Additional Information
Publications: Multi-Year Report (including Application Guidelines)

Foundation Officials
Dr. John R. Boettiger: director
Jack Clareman: treasurer
Suzanne Derrer: director
Dr. Michael Kahn: president, director
Andrea Panaritis: executive director, secretary
Robert Vitarelli: program officer

Grants Analysis
Disclosure Period: fiscal year ending January 31, 2002
Total Grants: $1,722,153
Number of Grants: 79
Average Grant: $18,874*
Highest Grant: $250,000
Lowest Grant: $250
Typical Range: $10,000 to $40,000
Note: Average grant figure excludes highest grant.

Recent Grants
Note: Grants derived from 2002 Form 990.
General

250,000	New World Foundation, New York, NY
140,000	Center for National Policy, Washington, DC
75,000	Washington Office of Latin America, Washington, DC
70,000	Center for International Policy Inc., Washington, DC
70,000	World Policy Institute, New York, NY
60,000	Medical Education Co-operation With Cuba (MEDICC), Atlanta, GA
55,000	Latin American Working Group - CIP, Washington, DC
50,000	Lexington Institute, Arlington, VA
50,000	National Security Archive Fund Inc., Washington, DC
50,000	Oxfam America, Boston, MA

DONALD W. REYNOLDS FOUNDATION

Giving Contact
Karina K. Mayer, Program Associate
1701 Village Center Circle
Las Vegas, NV 89134
Phone: (702)804-6000
Fax: (702)804-6099
E-mail: generalquestions@dwrf.org
Web: http://www.dwreynolds.org

Description
Founded: 1954
EIN: 716053383
Organization Type: General Purpose Foundation
Giving Locations: AR; NV; OK: nationally for aging and cardiovascular research programs.
Grant Types: Capital, Challenge, Employee Matching Gifts, General Support.

Donor Information
Founder: Established in 1954 by Donald W. Reynolds, who signed over all his stock and assets to the foundation in 1977 and who generously endowed it through his estate upon his death in 1993. Mr. Reynolds owned Donrey Media Group which includes more than 50 daily newspapers, radio and television stations, and billboard and cable operations.
Mr. Reynolds graduated from the University of Missouri School of Journalism in 1927. He purchased his first newspaper in 1940 in Oklahoma. He lived in Las Vegas, NV. Mr. Reynolds is survived by three children and was married three times. His children are not involved with the foundation.
The original incorporators and members of the first governing board are Clifford A. Jones; Carol Delander; Louis Wiener, Jr.; and Herbert M. Jones, all from Las Vegas, NV.

Financial Summary
Total Giving: $53,083,397 (2003); $30,031,522 (2002); $105,189,603 (2001)
Giving Analysis: Giving for 2002 includes: foundation grants to United Way ($29,000); foundation matching gifts ($107,620); 2001: foundation matching gifts ($209,124); foundation grants to United Way ($513,895).
Assets: $1,176,968,796 (2003); $1,311,709,405 (2002); $1,177,625,162 (2001)
Gifts Received: $803,824,000 (1994); $802,000,000 (1993)

Typical Recipients
Arts & Humanities: Arts Associations & Councils, Arts Centers, Ballet, Community Arts, Dance, Arts & Humanities-General, Historic Preservation, Libraries, Museums/Galleries, Music, Performing Arts, Public Broadcasting, Theater
Civic & Public Affairs: Business/Free Enterprise, Clubs, Economic Development, First Amendment Issues, Civic & Public Affairs-General, Hispanic Affairs, Housing, Legal Aid, Municipalities/Towns, Parades/Festivals, Professional & Trade Associations, Urban & Community Affairs, Women's Affairs
Education: Agricultural Education, Business Education, Colleges & Universities, Community & Junior Colleges, Education Associations, Education Funds, Elementary Education (Public), Engineering/Technological Education, Education-General, Journalism/Media Education, Legal Education, Literacy, Medical Education, Preschool Education, Private Ed-

ucation (Precollege), Public Education (Precollege), Secondary Education (Private), Social Sciences Education, Student Aid

Environment: Environment-General, Wildlife Protection

Health: AIDS/HIV, Cancer, Children's Health/ Hospitals, Clinics/Medical Centers, Diabetes, Emergency/Ambulance Services, Geriatric Health, Health Funds, Health Organizations, Heart, Hospices, Hospitals, Hospitals (University Affiliated), Medical Research, Single-Disease Health Associations

Religion: Bible Study/Translation, Churches, Religion-General, Religious Welfare

Science: Scientific Research

Social Services: At-Risk Youth, Big Brothers/Big Sisters, Child Welfare, Community Centers, Community Service Organizations, Counseling, Family Services, Food/Clothing Distribution, Homes, People with Disabilities, Recreation & Athletics, Scouts, Senior Services, Shelters/Homelessness, Substance Abuse, United Funds/United Ways, Volunteer Services, YMCA/YWCA/YMHA/YWHA, Youth Organizations

Application Procedures

Initial Contact: A thorough review of the foundation's guidelines is strongly recommended to determine eligibility.

Grants provided through the Aging & Quality of Life and Cardiovascular Clinical Research programs are available through a request for proposals process initiated by the foundation.

The Capital Grants program is extremely competitive and applicants must adhere to a strict set of guidelines, which may be obtained by contacting the foundation or consulting the foundation's web page.

The Community Services Centers grant program also has a very specific set of guidelines, which can be obtained from the foundation or its web site.

Planning and Technical Assistance grants are restricted to organizations that meet the eligibility standards of the Capital Grants program. If eligibility requirements are met, a prospective applicant may obtain a Planning Grant application form and guidelines by contacting the foundation or consulting its web site.

Notes: The grant program is extremely competitive. A successful application must demonstrate that the project is responsive to a well-documented need; is provided in an efficient manner that minimizes administrative costs; is thoroughly planned; will benefit the applicant organization and its clients and community; is driven by effective volunteer and staff leadership; is financially viable and, once the project is complete, financially secure for the foreseeable future; is appropriate for the program(s) to be housed in the proposed facility; is cost-effective; and increases the capacity, effectiveness, efficiency, quality and/or success of the applicant and program. Proposals submitted via fax or electronic mail will not be accepted. An applicant wishing to know when their proposal arrived should send it "return receipt requested" or contact their carrier to confirm delivery; the foundation's small staff cannot track the numerous applications.

Restrictions

Refer to foundation guidelines for complete eligibility requirements. eligible if the program is governed by an independent board, is separately incorporated and tax-exempt in its own right, and provides services to a diverse population without regard to religious preference. The foundation will not serve as a substitute funding source for civic or governmental projects normally provided by local, state, or federal tax dollars, bonds, or user fees.

The foundation will not consider the following: grants to individuals; proposals for site acquisition, endowments, or debt retirement; proposals for program support or annual fund-raising appeals; and renovation and capital equipment projects with total costs of less than $500,000.

Additional Information

The trustees reserve the right to amend the program at any time.

Publications: Annual Report; Guidelines

Foundation Officials

Steven L. Anderson: president ED University of Arkansas BA (1976). NONPR AFFIL member: Dean's Circle, University of Arkansas; member, professional advisory panel: University Arkansas School of Architecture.

Keith G. Boman, MD: trustee B Boulder City, NV June 01, 1949. ED University of California, Santa Barbara BA (1971); George Washington School of Medicine MD (1975). PRIM CORP EMPL partner: Cardiovascular Consultants NV. NONPR AFFIL trustee: Nevada Ballet; member: Sigma Chi Alumni Association; advisory council: Make-A-Wish Foundation of Southern Nevada; member: George Washington University Alumni Association; director: Las Vegas Philharmonic; member: American Medical Association; member: Clark County Medical Association; member: American Heart Association; member: Alpha Omega Alpha; member: American College of Cardiology.

Barbara H. Hanna: trustee

Courtney E. Latta: senior program officer

Neal R. Pendergraft: trustee

Donald E. Pray: trustee B Tulsa, OK 1932. ED University of Tulsa BS (1955); University of Oklahoma LLB (1963). PRIM CORP EMPL counsel: Jackman, Pray, Walker. NONPR AFFIL member: American Bar Association; fellow: American Bar Foundation. CLUB AFFIL president: Summit Club.

John V. Schlereth: trustee PRIM CORP EMPL owner: Four Points Hotel ITT Sheridan.

Robert E. Slater: trustee

Fred W. Smith: chairman, trustee B Arkoma, OK 1934. ED Arizona Polytechnic College. PRIM CORP EMPL president, chief executive officer: Donrey Media Group ADD CORP EMPL vice president: Scores Inc.

Jonathan Smith, OD: trustee

Wes Smith: trustee

Barbara Smith Campbell: trustee ED University of Nevada, Reno BA. NONPR AFFIL director: Reno-Sparks Chamber of Commerce; director: United Way of the Sierras; director: Nevada Women Fund; chairman: Nevada Tax Commission; member: Nevada Taxpayers Association; director: KNPB Public Television.

Debby Smith Magness: trustee

Joel R. Stubblefield: trustee PRIM NONPR EMPL president: Westark Community College. NONPR AFFIL president: University Arkansas-Fort Smith.

Grants Analysis

Disclosure Period: calendar year ending 2003
Total Grants: $53,083,397
Number of Grants: 186
Average Grant: $124,988*
Highest Grant: $9,065,984
Lowest Grant: $200
Typical Range: $25,000 to $200,000
*Note: Average grant figures excludes eight highest grants ($30,835,465).

Recent Grants

Note: Grants derived from 2003 Form 990.
Library-Related
710,239   Choctaw County Library Inc., Hugo, OK
General
9,065,984   Stanford University, Stanford, CA
7,535,155   University of Oklahoma, Norman, OK
5,510,401   Arkansas Children's Hospital, Little Rock, AR
5,236,041   Fayetteville Boys & Girls Club, Fayetteville, AR
5,000,000   Mount Vernon Ladies Association of the Union, Mt. Vernon, VA
4,792,150   Tulsa Boys Home, Tulsa, OK

4,409,271   Southern Arkansas University, Magnolia, AR
3,761,758   University of Arkansas for Medical Sciences (UAMS), Little Rock, AR
3,681,757   United Way of Southeast Arkansas, Pine Bluff, AR
3,597,723   University of Texas Southwestern Medical Center at Dallas, Dallas, TX

EDGAR & FRANCIS REYNOLDS FOUNDATION

Giving Contact

Fred Glade, Trustee
PO Box 1492
Grand Island, NE 68802
Phone: (308)384-0957
E-mail: lbbst@kdsi.net

Description

Founded: 1977
EIN: 470589941
Organization Type: Private Foundation
Giving Locations: NE: Central Nebraska, Grand Island
Grant Types: Capital, Research, Scholarship.

Donor Information

Founder: the late Edgar Reynolds

Financial Summary

Total Giving: $376,857 (2001)
Giving Analysis: Giving for 2001 includes: foundation grants to United Way ($1,000)
Assets: $8,723,640 (2001)
Gifts Received: $1,910,989 (1998)

Typical Recipients

Arts & Humanities: Arts Associations & Councils, History & Archaeology, Libraries, Museums/Galleries

Civic & Public Affairs: Botanical Gardens/Parks, Chambers of Commerce, Community Foundations, Housing, Municipalities/Towns, Philanthropic Organizations, Safety, Zoos/Aquariums

Education: Agricultural Education, Business Education, Colleges & Universities, Community & Junior Colleges, Education Funds, Education-General, Public Education (Precollege)

Environment: Air/Water Quality, Environment-General, Wildlife Protection

Health: Clinics/Medical Centers, Hospitals

Religion: Religious Welfare

Social Services: Animal Protection, At-Risk Youth, Big Brothers/Big Sisters, Child Welfare, Crime Prevention, Emergency Relief, Food/Clothing Distribution, People with Disabilities, Recreation & Athletics, United Funds/United Ways, Veterans, YMCA/YWCA/YMHA/YWHA, Youth Organizations

Application Procedures

Initial Contact: Request an application form.
Application Requirements: Provide full details on proposed project and need.
Deadlines: None.

Restrictions

Does not support religious organizations for sectarian purposes, political or lobbying groups, or organizations outside operating areas.

Additional Information

Publications: Application Guidelines

Foundation Officials

John R. Brownell: secretary PRIM CORP EMPL attorney: Lauritsen, Brownell, Brostrom, Stehlik & Thayer.

Grants Analysis

Disclosure Period: calendar year ending 2001
Total Grants: $375,857*
Number of Grants: 17
Average Grant: $9,500*
Highest Grant: $142,857
Lowest Grant: $900
Typical Range: $1,000 to $25,000
*Note: Giving excludes United Way. Average grant excludes three highest grants ($242,857).

Recent Grants

Note: Grants derived from 2001 Form 990.
General

142,857	Fonner Park Event Center, Grand Island, NE -- program support
50,000	Central Community College, Grand Island, NE -- program support
50,000	YMCA, Grand Island, NE -- program support
25,000	Crane Meadows Nature Center, Grand Island, NE -- program support
25,000	Hall County Historical Society, Grand Island, NE -- program support
25,000	YWCA, Grand Island, NE
20,000	Crisis Center, Grand Island, NE -- program support
12,500	Nebraska Independent College Foundation, Omaha, NE -- program support
7,500	Grand Island Youth Baseball, Inc., Grand Island, NE -- program support
6,100	American Red Cross, Grand Island, NE -- program support

RICHARD S. REYNOLDS FOUNDATION

Giving Contact

Victoria Pitrelli, Executive Director
1403 Pemberton Road, Suite 102
Richmond, VA 23233
Phone: (804)740-7350
Fax: (804)740-7807

Description

Founded: 1965
EIN: 546037003
Organization Type: General Purpose Foundation
Giving Locations: VA: Central Virginia, particularly Richmond
Grant Types: Capital, Challenge, Emergency, Endowment, General Support, Matching, Multiyear/Continuing Support, Operating Expenses, Professorship, Project, Research, Scholarship.

Donor Information

Founder: The foundation was established in 1965 by the late Julia L. Reynolds.

Financial Summary

Total Giving: $1,600,000 (fiscal year ending June 30, 2003 approx); $1,847,300 (fiscal 2002); $1,456,780 (fiscal 2001)
Giving Analysis: Giving for fiscal 2001 includes: foundation fellowships ($45,000) foundation scholarships ($126,070)
Assets: $34,807,856 (fiscal 2002); $39,562,412 (fiscal 2001)
Gifts Received: $43,013 (fiscal 2002); $38,526 (fiscal 2001); $47,800 (fiscal 2000 approx). Note: In 2002 contributions were received from David P. Reynolds Irrevocable Trust and Reynolds Foundation Trustee.

Typical Recipients

Arts & Humanities: Arts Associations & Councils, Arts Outreach, Ballet, Dance, Ethnic & Folk Arts, Historic Preservation, History & Archaeology, Libraries, Museums/Galleries, Music, Opera, Performing Arts, Theater
Civic & Public Affairs: Botanical Gardens/Parks, Business/Free Enterprise, Community Foundations, Economic Policy, Employment/Job Training, Civic & Public Affairs-General, Housing, Nonprofit Management, Professional & Trade Associations, Urban & Community Affairs, Zoos/Aquariums
Education: Afterschool/Enrichment Programs, Business Education, Colleges & Universities, Education Associations, Education Funds, Engineering/Technological Education, Environmental Education, Faculty Development, Education-General, Leadership Training, Literacy, Medical Education, Private Education (Precollege), Public Education (Precollege), Science/Mathematics Education, Secondary Education (Private), Special Education, Student Aid
Environment: Air/Water Quality, Environment-General
Health: Cancer, Children's Health/Hospitals, Clinics/Medical Centers, Emergency/Ambulance Services, Health Funds, Heart, Hospitals, Medical Rehabilitation, Medical Research, Mental Health, Multiple Sclerosis, Respiratory, Transplant Networks/Donor Banks
International: Foreign Arts Organizations, Human Rights, International Organizations
Religion: Churches, Jewish Causes, Religious Organizations, Religious Welfare, Seminaries
Science: Science Museums
Social Services: Animal Protection, At-Risk Youth, Child Welfare, Community Service Organizations, Emergency Relief, Family Services, Food/Clothing Distribution, Homes, People with Disabilities, Recreation & Athletics, Scouts, Senior Services, Shelters/Homelessness, Special Olympics, YMCA/YWCA/YMHA/YWHA, Youth Organizations

Application Procedures

Initial Contact: Applicants should send a brief letter with a description of the organization's primary focus and an outline of the proposal.
Application Requirements: Proposals should include verification of applicant's tax-exempt status by the IRS and a current budget or recent set of financial statements.
Deadlines: October 31 and April 30.
Review Process: The board meets in November and May each year.
Notes: Grants are typically made prior to the fiscal year end in June.

Restrictions

The organization must be a public charity or qualified organization (educational, literary, scientific, or religious) described in Section 170(C) of the Internal Revenue Code.

Foundation Officials

Glenn R. Martin: vice president, director
David Parham Reynolds: president, director B Bristol, TN June 16, 1915. ED Princeton University. PRIM CORP EMPL chairman emeritus, director: Reynolds Metals Co. NONPR AFFIL member: Primary Aluminum Institute; trustee emeritus: University Richmond; trustee emeritus: Lawrenceville School; member: Aluminum Association; honorary member: American Institute Architects.
Richard Samuel Reynolds, III: secretary, director B New York, NY 1934. ED Princeton University BA (1956). PRIM CORP EMPL managing director: Reynolds Trusts. NONPR AFFIL vice president: Missionary Emergency Fund.
William Gray Reynolds, Jr.: treasurer, director B New York, NY 1939. ED University of Pennsylvania BA (1962); University of Virginia JD (1965). PRIM CORP EMPL vice president government relations &

public affairs: Reynolds Metals Co. CORP AFFIL director: Wachovia Corp.

Grants Analysis

Disclosure Period: fiscal year ending June 30, 2002
Total Grants: $1,752,200*
Number of Grants: 54
Average Grant: $27,430*
Highest Grant: $200,000
Lowest Grant: $1,000
Typical Range: $7,000 to $50,000
*Note: Giving excludes scholarships. Average grant figure excludes two highest grants ($325,821).

Recent Grants

Note: Grants derived from fiscal 2002 Form 990.
General

200,000	Virginia Historical Society, Richmond, VA -- Reynolds Center for Virginia Business History
125,821	Collegiate School, Richmond, VA -- Lower School renovation
100,000	Mount Vernon Ladies Association of the Union, Mt. Vernon, VA -- annual giving
100,000	St. Catherine's School, Richmond, VA -- Athletic Program Fund
60,000	Boys and Girls Clubs, Richmond, VA -- annual giving
50,534	Virginia Historical Society, Richmond, VA -- story of Virginia exhibit
50,000	Edmonson County Board of Education -- Youth Service Center
50,000	Hand Workshop Art Center, Richmond, VA -- artist in residence studio
50,000	Jamestown-Yorktown Foundation, Williamsburg, VA -- African artifacts acquisition
50,000	Jewish Community Center, Richmond, VA -- capital campaign

R.J. REYNOLDS TOBACCO

Company Headquarters

401 N. Main Street
Winston-Salem, NC 27101
Phone: (336)741-5000
Fax: (336)741-4238
Web: http://www.rjrt.com

Company Description

Ticker: RJR
Exchange: OTC
Acquired: Nabisco Group Holdings (2000).
Revenue: US$5.267 billion (2003)
Profit: (US$3.446 billion) (2003)
Employees: 7,900
SIC(s): 2024 Ice Cream & Frozen Desserts, 2035 Pickles, Sauces & Salad Dressings, 2038 Frozen Specialties Nec, 2043 Cereal Breakfast Foods.

Operating Locations

RJR Nabisco Inc. (CA--San Leandro; NJ--East Hanover; NY--Bronx, New York; NC--Winston-Salem; PR--Guaynabo; WI--Wrightstown)
Note: Operates throughout the USA.

R. J. Reynolds Foundation

Giving Contact

Stephen R. Strawsburg, President
PO Box Box 2959
Winston-Salem, NC 27102-2959
Phone: (336)741-5315

Description

Founded: 1996
EIN: 581681920
Organization Type: Corporate Foundation
Former Name: R. J. Reynolds Tobacco Company Foundation.
Giving Locations: NC
Grant Types: General Support.

Financial Summary

Total Giving: $2,622,260 (2003)
Giving Analysis: Giving for 2003 includes: foundation scholarships ($244,451); foundation grants to United Way ($550,000) foundation matching gifts ($886,309).
Assets: $44,286,035 (2003)
Gifts Received: $4,700,000 (2003). Note: In 2003, contributions were received from R. J. Reynolds Tobacco Comapny.

Typical Recipients

Arts & Humanities: Arts Associations & Councils, Arts Centers, Libraries, Music
Civic & Public Affairs: Civic & Public Affairs-General, Hispanic Affairs, Housing, Professional & Trade Associations, Safety
Education: Agricultural Education, Arts/Humanities Education, Business Education, Colleges & Universities, Education-General, Private Education (Precollege), Public Education (Precollege), Secondary Education (Public), Student Aid
Health: Hospices
International: Foreign Educational Institutions
Religion: Religious Welfare
Science: Science-General
Social Services: Child Welfare, Community Service Organizations, Day Care, Family Services, People with Disabilities, Substance Abuse, United Funds/United Ways, Volunteer Services, YMCA/YWCA/YMHA/YWHA, Youth Organizations

Foundation Officials

Dan Fawley: assistant treasurer
Jackson W. Henson: director, secretary
Michael O. Johnson: director, assistant secretary
Lynn L. Lane: director, treasurer
Tommy J. Payne: director, vice president
Janet Quintal: assistant treasurer
Andrew J. Schindler: director, chairman
Frank Skinner: director, vice president
Vivian L. Turner: chairman

Grants Analysis

Disclosure Period: calendar year ending 2003
Total Grants: $2,622,660*
Number of Grants: 79
Average Grant: $22,282
Highest Grant: $884,634
Typical Range: $2,000 to $30,000
*****Note:** Giving includes matching gifts, scholarships, United Way.

Recent Grants

Note: Grants derived from 2000 Form 990.
Library-Related

5,000	Forsyth County Public Library, Winston-Salem, NC -- establish bilingual mini-libraries

General

625,000	United Way of Forsyth County, Winston-Salem, NC -- annual campaign
125,000	Arts Council, Inc., Winston-Salem, NC -- annual campaign
100,000	North Carolina Partnership for Children, Raleigh, NC -- smart start projects
100,000	Reynolda House, Inc., Winston-Salem, NC -- capital campaign
94,000	Winston Salem Forsyth County Schools, Winston-Salem, NC -- expand AVID Program
90,000	Yadkin County School System, Yadkinville, NC -- support After-School Program
62,000	North Carolina Tobacco Foundation, Raleigh, NC -- operating expenses
43,000	University of Kentucky, Lexington, KY -- operating expense
41,667	YMCA of Greater Winston-Salem, Winston-Salem, NC -- capital campaign
40,500	National Merit Scholarship Corporation, Evanston, IL -- four year scholarships

RGK FOUNDATION

Giving Contact

Gregory A. Kozmetsky, President, Chairman, Treasurer
1301 West 25th Street
Suite 300
Austin, TX 78705-4236
Phone: (512)474-9298
Fax: (512)474-7281
E-mail: jhampton@rgkfoundation.org
Web: http://www.rgkfoundation.org

Description

Founded: 1966
EIN: 746077587
Organization Type: Family Foundation
Giving Locations: nationally.
Grant Types: Challenge, Conference/Seminar, General Support, Multiyear/Continuing Support, Project, Research.

Donor Information

Founder: The RGK Foundation was established in 1966 by Dr. George Kozmetsky and his wife, Ronya Kozmetsky. Dr. Kozmetsky currently sits on the board of several corporations including Teledyne, Inc., which he co-founded in 1960.

Dr. Kozmetsky, a son of Russian immigrants, was born in Seattle, WA, in 1917. He taught at Harvard University and Carnegie-Mellon University before he started his business career in Los Angeles with Hughes Aircraft Company (1952-54), then Litton Company (1954-59). He left Teledyne in 1966 when he took the position of dean of the college and graduate school of business at the University of Texas at Austin. He stayed there for sixteen years until 1982 when he went on to head the school's Institute for Constructive Capitalism.

Currently, Dr. Kozmetsky serves on the RGK Foundation as its donor and trustee. His wife, Ronya, and his two children, Gregory Allen Kozmetsky and Nadya Anne Kozmetsky Scott, also serve on the foundation.

Financial Summary

Total Giving: $2,428,894 (2004 approx); $1,199,255 (2003); $3,693,276 (2002)
Assets: $117,633,980 (2003); $103,516,130 (2001)
Gifts Received: $8,002,313 (2000); $1,000 (1998); $16,500,000 (1997). Note: The majority of yearly donations come in the form of stock from George and Ronya Kozmetsky.

Typical Recipients

Arts & Humanities: Arts Outreach, Film & Video, Libraries, Museums/Galleries, Music, Opera, Public Broadcasting
Civic & Public Affairs: Business/Free Enterprise, Clubs, Economic Development, Employment/Job Training, Civic & Public Affairs-General, Hispanic Affairs, Housing, Legal Aid, Public Policy, Urban & Community Affairs, Women's Affairs
Education: Afterschool/Enrichment Programs, Arts/Humanities Education, Business Education, Colleges & Universities, Continuing Education, Education Reform, Elementary Education (Public), Engineering/Technological Education, Environmental Education, Faculty Development, Education-General, International Studies, Leadership Training, Legal Education, Literacy, Medical Education, Minority Education, Preschool Education, Private Education (Precollege), Public Education (Precollege), Science/Mathematics Education, Secondary Education (Public), Social Sciences Education, Special Education, Student Aid, Vocational & Technical Education
Environment: Environment-General, Resource Conservation
Health: Arthritis, Cancer, Children's Health/Hospitals, Clinics/Medical Centers, Diabetes, Eyes/Blindness, Geriatric Health, Health Policy/Cost Containment, Health Organizations, Heart, Hospices, Hospitals, Hospitals (University Affiliated), Kidney, Medical Research, Mental Health, Nursing Services, Prenatal Health Issues, Public Health, Research/Studies Institutes, Respiratory, Single-Disease Health Associations, Speech & Hearing, Transplant Networks/Donor Banks
International: Foreign Educational Institutions, Health Care/Hospitals, International Development
Religion: Religion-General, Jewish Causes, Religious Welfare
Science: Science-General, Scientific Centers & Institutes
Social Services: At-Risk Youth, Child Abuse, Child Welfare, Community Centers, Community Service Organizations, Crime Prevention, Day Care, Domestic Violence, Family Services, People with Disabilities, Scouts, Senior Services, Shelters/Homelessness, Social Services-General, Substance Abuse, Youth Organizations

Application Procedures

Initial Contact: Applicants should call or write the foundation to request an application form.
Application Requirements: The following information must accompany one unbound copy of the grant proposal: completed RGK application form; current annual report, if applicable; a brief background of the organization; a description of the proposed project; a concise statement of the necessity for the project; an explanation of the use of the funds; the amount requested, a detailed project budget; other potential sources of funding; current financial statements, including current annual operating budget; most recently filed IRS Form 990; list of board of directors; and proof of charitable status.
Deadlines: None.
Review Process: Grant proposals are reviewed on an ongoing basis. Upon receipt of a completed application, applicants are asked to allow three months for proposal review.

Restrictions

The foundation does not fund individuals, organizations limited by race or religion, organizations that are not tax-exempt, facilities or equipment, or for indirect costs.

Additional Information

Medical grant requests should follow NIH guidelines, but only one copy of proposal is required.
The foundation requires grantees to provide interim and final grant reports.
Publications: Informational Brochure (including Application Guidelines); Application Form

Foundation Officials

Patricia Ann Hayes: trustee B Binghamton, NY 1944. ED College of Saint Rose BA (1968); Georgetown University PhD (1974). PRIM NONPR EMPL president: Saint Edwards University. NONPR AFFIL president: Saint Edward's University Inc.; executive vice president, chief operating officer: Seton Healthcare Network; director: KLRU-Public Television.
Charles Edwin Hurwitz: trustee B Kilgore, TX 1940. ED University of Oklahoma BA (1962). PRIM CORP EMPL chairman, chief executive officer, president: MAXXAM Group Inc. ADD CORP EMPL chairman,

chief executive officer, president: MAXXAM Group Holdings Inc. CORP AFFIL director: Kaiser Aluminum Corp.; director: KLU; vice chairman, director: Kaiser Aluminum & Chemical Corp.

Cynthia Kozmetsky: trustee, treasurer, vice president, secretary

Gregory Allen Kozmetsky: president, chairman, trustee B 1946. ED University of Texas, Austin (1968-1972). PRIM CORP EMPL president: KMS Ventures Inc.

Ronya Kozmetsky: don, trustee B 1927. PRIM CORP EMPL vice president: KMS Ventures Inc.

Michael E. Patrick: director CORP AFFIL director: Cooper Energy Services; director: Cooper Turbo Compressor; director: Cooper Cameron Valves; director: BJ Services Co.; director: Cooper Cameron Corp.

Nadya Ann Kozmetsky Scott: vice president, trustee

Grants Analysis

Disclosure Period: calendar year ending 2003
Total Grants: $1,199,255
Number of Grants: 58
Average Grant: $16,654*
Highest Grant: $250,000
Lowest Grant: $1,500
Typical Range: $5,000 to $30,000
*Note: Average grant figure excludes highest grant.

Recent Grants

Note: Grants derived from 2001 Form 990.
General

1,000,000	University of Texas at Austin, Austin, TX -- support the establishment of the RGK Center for Philanthropy and Community Service
304,390	SafePlace, Austin, TX -- support to construct an on-site school for children
254,000	University of Texas Medical Branch at Galveston, Galveston, TX -- for Web-Based Nursing Distance Education Program
200,000	Children's Hospital Foundation of Austin, Austin, TX -- to establish permanent endowment fund for Child Life Program
165,000	Health Sciences Foundation of the Medical University of South Carolina, Charleston, SC -- support Scleroderma research
163,437	Detroit Public Schools, Detroit, MI -- support for "Project Read"
150,000	Project Grad, Los Angeles, CA -- for residential math institute
145,000	James Dick Foundation, Round Top, TX -- for Festival Institute
142,372	Texas Fragile Families Initiative, Austin, TX -- for Tandem Prenatal and Parenting Program
125,000	Austin Public Education Foundation, Austin, TX -- for Principles of Learning Initiative

RHEINSTROM HILL COMMUNITY FOUNDATION

Giving Contact

Richard Koskey, President
502 Union St.
Hudson, NY 12534
Phone: (518)828-1565

Description

Founded: 1987
EIN: 141683989
Organization Type: Private Foundation

Giving Locations: NY: Columbia County
Grant Types: Project.

Financial Summary

Total Giving: $278,510 (fiscal year ending 1, 2002); $319,750 (fiscal 2001)
Giving Analysis: Giving for fiscal 2002 includes: foundation grants to United Way ($2,500)
Assets: $1,411,327 (fiscal 2002); $1,739,503 (fiscal 2001)
Gifts Received: $141,500 (fiscal 2002). Note: In fiscal 2002, contributions were received from Irene and Carroll Rheinstrom Trust.

Typical Recipients

Arts & Humanities: Historic Preservation, Libraries, Music
Civic & Public Affairs: Clubs, Civic & Public Affairs-General, Housing, Safety
Education: Community & Junior Colleges, Elementary Education (Private), Literacy, Private Education (Precollege), Student Aid
Health: Emergency/Ambulance Services, Hospitals
Religion: Churches
Social Services: People with Disabilities, United Funds/United Ways

Application Procedures

Initial Contact: The foundation reports no specific application guidelines. Send a brief letter of inquiry, including statement of purpose, amount requested, and proof of tax-exempt status.
Deadlines: None.

Restrictions

Grants are generally limited to applicants in Columbia County, NY.

Foundation Officials

Ed Herrington: vice president
Jean Howe Lossi: secretary
Richard P. Koskey: secretary
Carmi Rapport: vice president
Carrol Rheinstrom: president
Majorie Rheinstrom: vice president

Grants Analysis

Total Grants: $276,010*
Number of Grants: 28
Average Grant: $4,847*
Highest Grant: $100,000
Lowest Grant: $250
Typical Range: $2,000 to $25,000
*Note: Giving excludes United Way. Average grant figure excludes two highest grants ($150,000).

Recent Grants

Note: Grants derived from fiscal 2002 Form 990.
Library-Related

2,500	Hillsdale Public Library, Hillsdale, NY

General

100,000	Taconic Hills Central Schools, Taconic, NY -- aquatic center funding
50,000	Hawthorne Valley School, Ghent, NY -- campus construction
25,000	Town of Ancram, Ancram, NY
23,000	Community Rescue Squad, Hudson, NY -- squad upgrades
10,000	Columbia Green Community College, Columbia Green, NY
10,000	Hudson Boys and Girls Club, Hudson, NY
10,000	Town of Copake, Copake, NY
6,000	Northeast Millerton Library, Millerton, NY
5,000	Camphill Village USA, Copake, NY
5,000	Irondale Cemetery Association, Irondale, NY -- operational repairs and losses

ALBERT W. RICE CHARITABLE FOUNDATION

Giving Contact

Stephen Fritch
Albert W. Rice Charitable Foundation
c/o Fleet Asset Management Grantmaking
PO Box 6768
Providence, RI 02940
Phone: (401)276-7248
Web: http://www.fleet.com

Description

Founded: 1959
EIN: 046028085
Organization Type: Private Foundation
Giving Locations: MA: Worcester
Grant Types: Capital, General Support, Project.

Donor Information

Founder: the late Albert W. Rice

Financial Summary

Total Giving: $268,500 (2004)
Giving Analysis: Giving for 2004 includes: foundation grants to United Way ($6,000)
Assets: $6,387,538 (2004)

Typical Recipients

Arts & Humanities: Arts Associations & Councils, Arts Centers, Arts Festivals, Arts Funds, Community Arts, Ethnic & Folk Arts, Historic Preservation, History & Archaeology, Libraries, Museums/Galleries, Music, Performing Arts, Public Broadcasting, Theater
Civic & Public Affairs: Clubs, Community Foundations, Economic Development, Civic & Public Affairs-General, Hispanic Affairs, Municipalities/Towns, Rural Affairs, Urban & Community Affairs
Education: Arts/Humanities Education, Business Education, Colleges & Universities, Community & Junior Colleges, Education Associations, Education Reform, Engineering/Technological Education, Faculty Development, Preschool Education, Private Education (Precollege), Secondary Education (Private)
Environment: Environment-General, Resource Conservation, Wildlife Protection
Health: Cancer, Clinics/Medical Centers, Emergency/Ambulance Services, Health Funds, Health Organizations, Home-Care Services, Hospices, Medical Research, Public Health
International: Foreign Arts Organizations
Religion: Churches
Science: Scientific Centers & Institutes, Scientific Labs, Scientific Research
Social Services: Child Welfare, Community Service Organizations, Family Services, Food/Clothing Distribution, Substance Abuse, United Funds/United Ways, YMCA/YWCA/YMHA/YWHA, Youth Organizations

Application Procedures

Initial Contact: Send a brief letter of inquiry, or call to request guidelines.
Application Requirements: Include a description of program or project.
Deadlines: April and October of each year.

Restrictions

Does not support individuals, religious organizations for sectarian purposes, political or lobbying groups, or organizations outside operating areas.

Additional Information

Supports local education, family service, and preventive health care.
Trust(s): Fleet Natl Bank MA

Grants Analysis

Disclosure Period: calendar year ending 2004
Total Grants: $262,500*
Number of Grants: 15
Average Grant: $15,893*
Highest Grant: $40,000
Typical Range: $5,000 to $25,000
***Note:** Giving excludes United Way. Average grant figure excludes highest grant.

Recent Grants

Note: Grants derived from 2000 Form 990.

General

25,000	EcoTarium, Worcester, MA
15,000	Children's Friend Society, Worcester, MA
7,500	American Cancer Society, Worcester, MA
7,500	Great Brook Valley Health Center, Worcester, MA
7,500	Worcester Dynamy, Worcester, MA
5,000	Family Services of Central Massachusetts, Worcester, MA
5,000	Junior Achievement of Central Massachusetts, Worcester, MA
5,000	United Way of Central Massachusetts, Worcester, MA
5,000	VNA of Worcester Home Health Systems, Inc., Worcester, MA
5,000	Worcester Academy, Worcester, MA

RICE FOUNDATION

Giving Contact

Peter Nolan, President
8600 Gross Point Road
Skokie, IL 60077-2151
Phone: (847)581-9999

Description

Founded: 1947
EIN: 366043160
Organization Type: General Purpose Foundation
Giving Locations: IL: Chicago
Grant Types: General Support.

Donor Information

Founder: The Rice Foundation was established in 1947 by the late Daniel F. Rice.

Financial Summary

Total Giving: $3,245,655 (2003); $3,951,800 (2002)
Giving Analysis: Giving for 2003 includes: foundation grants to United Way ($1,000)
Assets: $92,567,769 (2003); $87,565,552 (2002)
Gifts Received: $200 (2002); $4,800 (1993); $300 (1992). Note: Foundation was not required to file Schedule B with its 2002 return.

Typical Recipients

Arts & Humanities: Arts Associations & Councils, Arts Festivals, Arts Funds, Arts Institutes, Ballet, Historic Preservation, History & Archaeology, Libraries, Literary Arts, Museums/Galleries, Music, Opera, Performing Arts, Public Broadcasting, Theater
Civic & Public Affairs: Botanical Gardens/Parks, Community Foundations, Economic Development, Employment/Job Training, Ethnic Organizations, Civic & Public Affairs-General, Housing, Law & Justice, Legal Aid, Philanthropic Organizations, Public Policy, Safety, Urban & Community Affairs, Women's Affairs, Zoos/Aquariums
Education: Arts/Humanities Education, Colleges & Universities, Community & Junior Colleges, Education Associations, Education Funds, Elementary Education (Public), Environmental Education, Education-General, International Studies, Medical Education, Private Education (Precollege), Public Education (Precollege), School Volunteerism, Science/

Mathematics Education, Secondary Education (Private), Special Education, Student Aid
Environment: Environment-General, Protection, Resource Conservation, Wildlife Protection
Health: Arthritis, Cancer, Children's Health/Hospitals, Clinics/Medical Centers, Health-General, Geriatric Health, Health Organizations, Home-Care Services, Hospitals, Hospitals (University Affiliated), Long-Term Care, Medical Rehabilitation, Mental Health, Prenatal Health Issues, Public Health, Respiratory, Single-Disease Health Associations
International: Foreign Educational Institutions
Religion: Religion-General, Ministries, Religious Organizations, Religious Welfare
Science: Observatories & Planetariums, Science Museums
Social Services: Big Brothers/Big Sisters, Camps, Child Abuse, Child Welfare, Community Centers, Community Service Organizations, Crime Prevention, Family Services, Homes, People with Disabilities, Recreation & Athletics, Senior Services, Shelters/Homelessness, Social Services-General, Substance Abuse, United Funds/United Ways, Volunteer Services, Youth Organizations

Application Procedures

Initial Contact: Applications should be submitted in writing.
Application Requirements: Applications should include a statement describing the applicant organization and its activities, the amount and purpose of the grant requested, and proof of IRS tax-exempt status.
Deadlines: None.

Restrictions

Grants are not made to individuals.

Foundation Officials

Marilynn Bruder Alsdorf: director ED Northwestern University (1946).
John D. Gray: director
Cori Nolan: vice president, secretary, director
Peter G. Nolan: president, director
Robin Nolan: vice president, director
Sieglinde Schneider: secretary, director
Richard T. Schroeder: treasurer, director
David P. Winchester: director

Grants Analysis

Disclosure Period: calendar year ending 2003
Total Grants: $3,244,655*
Number of Grants: 140
Average Grant: $12,642*
Highest Grant: $1,000,000
Lowest Grant: $100
Typical Range: $1,000 to $25,000
***Note:** Giving excludes United Way. Average grant figure excludes two highest grants ($1,500,000).

Recent Grants

Note: Grants derived from 2003 Form 990.

General

1,000,000	Maryville Academy, Des Plaines, IL
500,000	Evanston Northwestern Healthcare, Evanston, IL
300,000	Mercy Home for Boys & Girls, Chicago, IL
250,000	Advocate Lutheran General Children's Hospital, Park Ridge, IL
125,000	Lincoln Park Zoo, Chicago, IL
80,000	Mobile C.A.R.E. Foundation, Chicago, IL
80,000	Rush University Medical Center, Chicago, IL
50,000	Chicago Botanic Garden, Chicago, IL
50,000	Lincoln Park Zoo, Chicago, IL
50,000	Wetlands Initiative, Chicago, IL

RICH FOUNDATION

Giving Contact

Anne Berg, Grant Consultant
11 Piedmont Center, Suite 204
Atlanta, GA 30305
Phone: (404)262-2499
Fax: (404)266-2123

Description

Founded: 1942
EIN: 586038037
Organization Type: General Purpose Foundation
Giving Locations: GA: Atlanta metropolitan area
Grant Types: Capital, Endowment, General Support.

Donor Information

Founder: The foundation was established in 1942 in Georgia by the officers of Rich's, Inc., a chain of department stores based in Atlanta, and was funded by profits of Rich's, Inc. until 1976.

Financial Summary

Total Giving: $1,907,500 (fiscal year ending January 31, 2004)
Giving Analysis: Giving for fiscal 2004 includes: foundation grants to United Way ($100,000)
Assets: $45,734,828 (fiscal 2004)

Typical Recipients

Arts & Humanities: Arts Centers, Arts Institutes, Arts Outreach, Ballet, Dance, Arts & Humanities-General, History & Archaeology, Libraries, Museums/Galleries, Music, Opera, Performing Arts, Public Broadcasting, Theater
Civic & Public Affairs: Botanical Gardens/Parks, Clubs, Community Foundations, Employment/Job Training, Civic & Public Affairs-General, Housing, Inner-City Development, Law & Justice, Legal Aid, Philanthropic Organizations, Women's Affairs, Zoos/Aquariums
Education: Arts/Humanities Education, Colleges & Universities, Economic Education, Education Associations, Education Funds, Education Reform, Education-General, International Studies, Literacy, Medical Education, Minority Education, Preschool Education, Private Education (Precollege), Science/Mathematics Education, Special Education
Environment: Environment-General, Resource Conservation
Health: Cancer, Children's Health/Hospitals, Emergency/Ambulance Services, Eyes/Blindness, Health-General, Health Organizations, Heart, Hospices, Hospitals, Medical Research, Mental Health, Multiple Sclerosis, Nursing Services, Prenatal Health Issues, Preventive Medicine/Wellness Organizations, Single-Disease Health Associations
International: Health Care/Hospitals
Religion: Jewish Causes, Ministries, Religious Organizations, Religious Welfare, Synagogues/Temples
Science: Science Museums
Social Services: Animal Protection, Big Brothers/Big Sisters, Camps, Child Abuse, Child Welfare, Community Centers, Community Service Organizations, Counseling, Domestic Violence, Family Services, Food/Clothing Distribution, Homes, People with Disabilities, Scouts, Senior Services, Shelters/Homelessness, Social Services-General, United Funds/United Ways, Volunteer Services, YMCA/YWCA/YMHA/YWHA, Youth Organizations

Application Procedures

Initial Contact: Applicants should submit a preliminary letter to the foundation requesting an official grant application.
Application Requirements: The letter should include an autobiographical sketch of the organization, estimate of project expenses, and lists of other sources of funding.
Deadlines: The quarterly deadlines for submitting

proposals are December 15, March 15, June 15, and September 15.

Review Process: Trustees meet quarterly to review grant proposals.

Notes: Application must include a completed official application form for proposal to be considered.

Restrictions

The foundation does not support individuals, conferences and seminars, accumulated debt or loans, religious purposes, special events such as fundraising dinners and sporting events, legislative or lobbying efforts, political or fraternal organizations. Organizations must be non-sectarian in services to be eligible.

Additional Information

Publications: Application Form; Application Guidelines

Foundation Officials

Thomas J. Asher: vice president, secretary
David S. Baker: trustee B Jacksonville, FL 1937. ED University of Pennsylvania BS (1958); Harvard University LLB (1961). NONPR AFFIL member: Georgia Bar Association; trustee, chairman: Howard School; fellow: American Bar Foundation; member: American Law Institute; member: American Bar Association. CLUB AFFIL Standard Club; Ashford Club.
Anne P. Berg: grant consultant
Joel Goldberg: president
Margaret S. Weiller: treasurer, trustee

Grants Analysis

Disclosure Period: fiscal year ending January 31, 2004
Total Grants: $1,807,500*
Number of Grants: 85
Average Grant: $21,265
Highest Grant: $150,000
Lowest Grant: $2,500
Typical Range: $5,000 to $50,000
*Note: Giving excludes United Way.

Recent Grants

Note: Grants derived from 2003 Form 990.
General

150,000	Howard School, Atlanta, GA
125,000	Atlanta Cardiovascular Research Institute, Atlanta, GA
125,000	Atlanta College of Art, Atlanta, GA
125,000	High Museum of Art, Atlanta, GA
100,000	Boy Scouts, Atlanta Area, Atlanta, GA
100,000	Girl Scout Council, Atlanta, GA
100,000	The Temple
100,000	United Way of Atlanta
100,000	Woodruff Arts Center, Atlanta, GA
75,000	St. Joseph Mercy Foundation, Atlanta, GA

RICH FOUNDATION INC.

Giving Contact

Robert N. Rich, President
1 Landmark Sq.
Stamford, CT 06901
Phone: (203)359-2900

Description

Founded: 1984
EIN: 222544173
Organization Type: Private Foundation
Giving Locations: CT: Stamford primarily in lower Stamford
Grant Types: General Support.

Donor Information

Founder: F.D. Rich Co., Inc., members of the Rich family

Financial Summary

Total Giving: $52,600 (fiscal year ending June 30, 2001)
Giving Analysis: Giving for fiscal 2001 includes: foundation grants to United Way ($10,000)
Assets: $844,876 (fiscal 2001)
Gifts Received: $39,000 (fiscal 2001); $30,000 (fiscal 1998); $15,000 (fiscal 1996). Note: In fiscal 19986, contributions were received from F. D. Rich Company.

Typical Recipients

Arts & Humanities: Arts Centers, Arts Festivals, Libraries, Museums/Galleries, Music, Opera, Public Broadcasting
Civic & Public Affairs: Economic Development, Civic & Public Affairs-General, Housing, Urban & Community Affairs
Education: Colleges & Universities, Education-General
Environment: Environment-General
Health: Hospitals, Medical Research
Religion: Religion-General, Jewish Causes, Religious Welfare
Social Services: Child Welfare, Community Service Organizations, People with Disabilities, United Funds/United Ways, YMCA/YWCA/YMHA/YWHA, Youth Organizations

Application Procedures

Initial Contact: Contact the foundation by phone to request an application form. Applicants are urged to consult with the foundation staff in the development of their proposals.
Decision Notification: Board meets in September for budgets commencing October 1 and ending September 30 of the following calendar year and in March for supplementary budget requests.

Restrictions

Grants are made only to selected, qualified non-profit organizations. Foundation does not make contributions to organizations whose purpose involves the solicitation of propaganda or to organizations that attempt to influence legislation, the outcome of public elections, or voter registration drives.

Foundation Officials

Colleen Graham: secretary
Frank D. Rich, Jr.: president PRIM CORP EMPL chairman, director: F.D. Rich Co.
Robert N. Rich: vice president PRIM CORP EMPL president, director: F.D. Rich Co.
Thomas L. Rich: vice president

Grants Analysis

Disclosure Period: fiscal year ending June 30, 2001
Total Grants: $42,600*
Number of Grants: 26
Average Grant: $1,638
Highest Grant: $5,000
Lowest Grant: $200
Typical Range: $1,000 to $5,000
*Note: Giving excludes United Way.

Recent Grants

Note: Grants derived from fiscal 2001 Form 990.
Library-Related

1,000	Ferguson Library Foundation, Stamford, CT

General

10,000	United Way, Stamford, CT
5,500	Stamford Symphony, Stamford, CT
5,000	St. Luke's Life Works, Stamford, CT
5,000	Stamford Center for Arts, Stamford, CT
5,000	Stamford Center for Arts, Stamford, CT
3,250	Stamford Downtown Special Services, Stamford, CT
3,000	Kids in Crisis, Cos Cob, CT
1,800	Boys and Girls Club of Stamford, Stamford, CT
1,400	Stamford Education, Stamford, CT
1,000	Castle Cares Inc., Stamford, CT

RICH PRODUCTS CORP.

Company Headquarters

1150 Niagara St.
Buffalo, NY 14213
Web: http://www.richs.com

Company Description

Revenue: US$1.58 billion (2002)
Employees: 6500 (2003)
SIC(s): 2037 Frozen Fruits & Vegetables, 2038 Frozen Specialties Nec, 2053 Frozen Bakery Products Except Bread.

Operating Locations

Rich Products Corp. (CA--Escalon; GA--St. Simons Island; NJ--Vineland; OH--Dayton, Hilliard; TN--Gallatin)

Rich Family Foundation

Giving Contact

David A. Rich, Executive Director
Rich Family Foundation
1150 Niagara Street
PO Box 245
Buffalo, NY 14240-0245
Phone: (716)878-8363
Fax: (716)878-8775

Description

Founded: 1961
EIN: 166026199
Organization Type: Corporate Foundation
Giving Locations: NY: Buffalo
Grant Types: General Support.

Donor Information

Founder: Rich Products Corporation

Financial Summary

Total Giving: $569,948 (2002); $935,138 (2001). Note: Contributes through foundation only.
Assets: $3,752,226 (2002); $3,679,720 (2001)
Gifts Received: $720,000 (2002); $1,417,764 (2001); $660,000 (2000). Note: In 2000 and 2002, contributions were received from Rich Products Corporation. In 1997, contributions were received from Rich Products Corporation and Robert E. Rich.

Typical Recipients

Arts & Humanities: Arts Associations & Councils, Arts Centers, Arts Institutes, Historic Preservation, History & Archaeology, Libraries, Museums/Galleries, Music, Performing Arts, Public Broadcasting, Theater
Civic & Public Affairs: Botanical Gardens/Parks, Business/Free Enterprise, Clubs, Community Foundations, Economic Development, Civic & Public Affairs-General, Professional & Trade Associations, Safety, Urban & Community Affairs, Zoos/Aquariums
Education: Arts/Humanities Education, Business Education, Colleges & Universities, Continuing Education, Economic Education, Education Funds, Elementary Education (Private), Education-General, Leadership Training, Legal Education, Literacy, Private Education (Precollege), Religious Education, Special Education, Student Aid
Environment: Wildlife Protection
Health: Alzheimer's Disease, Cancer, Children's Health/Hospitals, Clinics/Medical Centers, Diabetes, Emergency/Ambulance Services, Health-General, Health Funds, Health Organizations, Heart, Hospi-

tals, Medical Rehabilitation, Medical Research, Multiple Sclerosis, Prenatal Health Issues, Public Health, Single-Disease Health Associations
International: Missionary/Religious Activities
Religion: Churches, Dioceses, Religion-General, Jewish Causes, Ministries, Religious Organizations, Religious Welfare, Social/Policy Issues
Science: Science Museums
Social Services: Animal Protection, Child Welfare, Community Centers, Community Service Organizations, Counseling, Family Services, Food/Clothing Distribution, People with Disabilities, Recreation & Athletics, Special Olympics, Substance Abuse, United Funds/United Ways, Youth Organizations

Application Procedures
Initial Contact: Send formal letter of request.
Deadlines: None.

Corporate Officials
Robert E. Rich, Jr.: president, director B Buffalo, NY 1941. ED University of Rochester MBA; Williams College (1963). PRIM CORP EMPL president, director: Rich Products Corp. ADD CORP EMPL president: BR Guest Ltd.; president: Bison Baseball Inc.; president: Palm Beach National Golf Country Club; president: Wichita Baseball Inc. CORP AFFIL vice chairman: Casa Di Bertacchi Corp. NONPR AFFIL vice chairman, director: Buffalo Sabres Hockey Club.

Foundation Officials
Robert E. Rich, Jr.: secretary (see above)

Grants Analysis
Disclosure Period: calendar year ending 2002
Total Grants: $527,973*
Number of Grants: 162
Average Grant: $2,519*
Highest Grant: $75,000
Lowest Grant: $50
Typical Range: $100 to $5,000
*Note: Giving excludes United Way and scholarships. Average grant figure excludes two highest grants ($125,000).

Recent Grants
Note: Grants derived from 2003 Form 990.
General

75,000	Students in Free Enterprise, Springfield, MO
25,000	Buffalo Fine Arts Academy, Buffalo, NY
25,000	Buffalo Philharmonic Orchestra, Buffalo, NY
25,000	National Restaurant Association Educational Foundation, Chicago, IL
25,000	Shea's Performing Arts Center, Buffalo, NY
10,000	Baptist Health Systems of South Florida Foundation Inc., Miami, FL
10,000	Hunter's Hope Foundation, Orchard Park, NY
10,000	NRA Foundation Inc, Fairfax, VA
7,500	United Way of Buffalo and Erie County, Buffalo, NY
7,500	United Way of Buffalo and Erie County, Buffalo, NY

C. E. RICHARDSON BENEVOLENT FOUNDATION

Giving Contact
Betty S. King, Secretary
PO Box 1120
Pulaski, VA 24301
Phone: (540)980-6628

Description
Founded: 1979
EIN: 510227549
Organization Type: Private Foundation
Giving Locations: VA: limited to 30 miles north and south of Interstate 81 from Lexington to Abingdon, VA
Grant Types: General Support, Scholarship.

Financial Summary
Total Giving: $161,723 (fiscal year ending May 31, 2004); $200,000 (fiscal 2001)
Giving Analysis: Giving for fiscal 2004 includes: foundation scholarships ($20,000)
Assets: $4,298,686 (fiscal 2004); $4,634,867 (fiscal 2001)

Typical Recipients
Arts & Humanities: Arts Centers, Historic Preservation, History & Archaeology, Libraries, Museums/Galleries, Theater
Civic & Public Affairs: Botanical Gardens/Parks, Civic & Public Affairs-General, Municipalities/Towns, Safety, Women's Affairs
Education: Agricultural Education, Arts/Humanities Education, Colleges & Universities, Community & Junior Colleges, Education Funds, Education-General, Medical Education, Private Education (Precollege), Religious Education, Science/Mathematics Education, Secondary Education (Public), Student Aid
Health: Cancer, Children's Health/Hospitals, Clinics/Medical Centers, Emergency/Ambulance Services, Health Funds, Hospices, Preventive Medicine/Wellness Organizations
Religion: Churches, Religious Welfare
Social Services: Animal Protection, Big Brothers/Big Sisters, Community Service Organizations, Emergency Relief, Family Services, Food/Clothing Distribution, People with Disabilities, Recreation & Athletics, Scouts, Senior Services, Special Olympics, United Funds/United Ways, YMCA/YWCA/YMHA/YWHA, Youth Organizations

Application Procedures
Initial Contact: Application form required.
Deadlines: September 15.

Restrictions
Does not support individuals.

Additional Information
Publications: Application Guidelines

Foundation Officials
Betty S. King: secretary
James D. Miller: trustee
Annie S. Muire: trustee
James C. Turk: trustee B Roanoke, VA 1923. ED Roanoke College AB (1949); Washington & Lee University LLB (1952). PRIM CORP EMPL chief judge: U.S. District Court. CORP AFFIL director: 1st & Merchants National Bank Rafford. NONPR AFFIL trustee: Rafford Community Hospital; member: Virginia Senate; member: Phi Beta Kappa; member: Omnicron Delta Kappa; member: Order Coif.

Grants Analysis
Disclosure Period: fiscal year ending May 31, 2004
Total Grants: $141,723*
Number of Grants: 40
Average Grant: $3,543
Highest Grant: $10,000
Lowest Grant: $850
Typical Range: $1,000 to $5,000
*Note: Giving excludes scholarships.

Recent Grants
Note: Grants derived from 2004 Form 990.
General

10,000	Emory and Henry College, Emory, VA -- to fund site plans for new student housing
10,000	Radford University Foundation Inc., Radford, VA -- for student scholarship assistance
8,000	Lynchburg College, Lynchburg, VA -- to complete renovation of a field laboratory at the Claytor Nature Center
7,500	Carroll Wellness Center, Hillsville, VA -- financial assistance for memberships, equipment purchases and activities
6,000	Hensel Eckman YMCA, Pulaski, VA -- to supply family and youth membership scholarships, to purchase two computers and for programs
5,500	Virginia Foundation of Independent Colleges, Richmond, VA -- for strengthening library services at the fifteen member colleges
5,000	Fine Arts Center for the New River Valley Inc., Pulaski, VA
5,000	Free Clinic of Pulaski County Inc., Pulaski, VA -- to provide prescription medicines and supplies and dental services for clinic patients
5,000	Friends of the Pulaski Theatre Inc., Pulaski, VA -- to bring programming into the area in 2004
5,000	Friends of Randolph Park Inc., Pulaski, VA -- to purchase a new and safer base covering for the children's playground

SID W. RICHARDSON FOUNDATION

Giving Contact
Valleau Wilkie, Jr., Executive Vice President
309 Main Street
Ft. Worth, TX 76102
Phone: (817)336-0494
Fax: (817)332-2176
E-mail: cjohns@sidrichardson.org
Web: http://www.sidrichardson.org

Description
Founded: 1947
EIN: 756015828
Organization Type: General Purpose Foundation
Giving Locations: TX: Ft. Worth some giving in other areas of Texas
Grant Types: Capital, Challenge, General Support, Operating Expenses, Project, Research.

Donor Information
Founder: The foundation was established in 1947 by the late Sid W. Richardson (d. 1959) to support organizations and programs serving the people of Texas. The purpose of the foundation, as stated in the charter, is "to support any benevolent, charitable, educational, or missionary undertaking."
In 1962, the foundation acquired substantial assets from the late Mr. Richardson's estate. In 1965, income from the assets became available, and the foundation began its major grant-making program. Sid Richardson was a life-long resident of Texas, with interests in oil, cattle, and land. He also collected western art, which is on permanent exhibit in the foundation-supported Sid Richardson Collection of Western Art. "Although his interests reached beyond Texas and his personal contacts were world-wide, he retained his immediate concern for the people of his home state. For this reason, he provided in the Foundation's charter that all grants be awarded to recipients within the state of Texas."

Financial Summary
Total Giving: $8,909,750 (2003); $11,000,000 (2002 approx); $34,798,143 (2001)
Giving Analysis: Giving for 2003 includes: founda-

tion grants to United Way ($75,000)
Assets: $338,085,978 (2003); $230,000,000 (2002 approx); $257,816,716 (2001)

Typical Recipients

Arts & Humanities: Arts Associations & Councils, Arts Centers, Ballet, Ethnic & Folk Arts, Libraries, Literary Arts, Museums/Galleries, Music, Opera, Performing Arts, Public Broadcasting, Theater
Civic & Public Affairs: Botanical Gardens/Parks, Chambers of Commerce, Community Foundations, Economic Development, Employment/Job Training, Civic & Public Affairs-General, Housing, Law & Justice, Public Policy, Rural Affairs, Urban & Community Affairs, Women's Affairs
Education: Afterschool/Enrichment Programs, Arts/Humanities Education, Business Education, Colleges & Universities, Education Associations, Education Funds, Elementary Education (Private), Engineering/Technological Education, Environmental Education, Faculty Development, Education-General, Health & Physical Education, Leadership Training, Literacy, Medical Education, Preschool Education, Private Education (Precollege), Public Education (Precollege), School Volunteerism, Science/Mathematics Education, Secondary Education (Public), Social Sciences Education, Student Aid
Environment: Environment-General, Research, Wildlife Protection
Health: Cancer, Children's Health/Hospitals, Clinics/Medical Centers, Diabetes, Emergency/Ambulance Services, Eyes/Blindness, Health-General, Health Policy/Cost Containment, Health Organizations, Heart, Hospitals, Hospitals (University Affiliated), Medical Research, Nursing Services, Outpatient Health Care, Prenatal Health Issues, Public Health, Research/Studies Institutes
Religion: Churches, Ministries, Religious Organizations, Religious Welfare
Science: Science Museums, Scientific Centers & Institutes, Scientific Research
Social Services: At-Risk Youth, Child Welfare, Community Centers, Community Service Organizations, Crime Prevention, Day Care, Family Planning, Family Services, Food/Clothing Distribution, Homes, People with Disabilities, Recreation & Athletics, Scouts, Senior Services, Social Services-General, Substance Abuse, United Funds/United Ways, Volunteer Services, YMCA/YWCA/YMHA/YWHA, Youth Organizations

Application Procedures

Initial Contact: Applicants should send a preliminary letter briefly describing the project or program prior to filing a formal application. If the project falls within foundation guidelines, a formal proposal will be accepted.
Application Requirements: The foundation will supply a grant application form requesting information regarding the nature of the organization, objectives, activities, personnel, need to be met, and the project that meets this need. Applicants may submit any additional information and a supplementary proposal in narrative form, to clarify and explain the application. A copy of the organization's 501(c)(3) letter should also be included, where applicable.
Deadlines: Applications must be received by January 15.
Review Process: Foundation staff may conduct a site visit after a formal application has been accepted. Board decisions on all requests are reported by mail.

Restrictions

Grants are not made to individuals. Grants are limited to programs and projects in Texas. Organizations must be classified as tax-exempt under Section 501(c)(3) of the Internal Revenue Code, and as other than a private foundation, Section 509(a). Alternatively, an organization may qualify if it is classified under Section 170(c)(1) and the contribution is to be used exclusively for public purposes.

Additional Information

Grantees receive a letter of agreement outlining the terms and conditions of the grant. The Sid Richardson Foundation is related to the Bass Foundation (Ft. Worth).
Publications: Annual Report (including Guidelines)

Foundation Officials

Edward Perry Bass: vice president, director B Fort Worth, TX 1945. ED Yale University (1968). PRIM CORP EMPL owner: Fine Line Inc.
Lee M. Bass: vice president, director
Nancy Lee Bass: vice president, director
Perry Richardson Bass: president, director B Wichita Falls, TX November 11, 1914. ED Yale University BS (1937). PRIM CORP EMPL president, director: Perry R. Bass Inc. CORP AFFIL chairman, chief executive officer, director: Sid Richardson Carbon & Gas Co.; chairman: Bass Enterprises Production Co. NONPR AFFIL member ad hoc committee: Texas Energy Natural Resources Advisory Committee; member executive committee: Texas Mid-Continent Oil & Gas Association; member advisory committee board visitors: Maryland Anderson Hospital & Tumor Institute; member: Independent Petroleum Association America; member: American Association Petroleum Geologists; member executive committee: American Petroleum Institute; member: All-American Wildcatters. CLUB AFFIL Royal Ocean Racing Club; Petroleum Club; River Crest Country Club; Fort Worth Club; New York Yacht Club; president: City Club Fort Worth Inc.; Fort Worth Boat Club.
Sid Richardson Bass: vice president, director B Fort Worth, TX 1943. ED Yale University (1965); Stanford University MBA (1968). PRIM CORP EMPL Sid R. Bass Inc. CORP AFFIL president: Bass Enterprises Production Co.; vice president: Sid Richardson Carbon & Gas Co.
M. E. Chappell: treasurer, director B 1916. PRIM CORP EMPL vice president, director: Mel Wheeler Inc.
Jo Helen Rosacker: secretary, associate director

Grants Analysis

Disclosure Period: calendar year ending 2003
Total Grants: $8,834,750*
Number of Grants: 128
Average Grant: $66,415*
Highest Grant: $400,000
Lowest Grant: $2,500
Typical Range: $25,000 to $150,000
*Note: Giving excludes United Way. Average grant figure excludes highest grant.

Recent Grants

Note: Grants derived from 2001 Form 990.
Library-Related
175,000   Fort Worth Public Library Foundation, Ft. Worth, TX -- Provide office space for Library Foundation in new facility
General
24,000,000 MPA Foundation, Ft. Worth, TX -- Support construction of the new Modern Art Museum
500,000   Amon Carter Museum of Western Art, Ft. Worth, TX -- Support Amon Carter Museum in the expansion of the facility
500,000   Fort Worth Symphony Orchestra Association, Ft. Worth, TX -- Support for the last half of the 00-01 season and the first half of the 01-02 season
400,000   Harris Hospital - Methodist, Ft. Worth, TX -- Assist in the construction of the Neurointernventional Radiology Suite
360,000   Performing Arts Fort Worth, Inc., Ft. Worth, TX -- Support completion of the rehearsal facilities
300,000   Fort Worth Country Day School Faculty Bonus Trust, Ft. Worth, TX -- General support for 5/01 through 4/02

259,200   Fort Worth Education and Research Foundation for Pain Management, Ft. Worth, TX -- Assist in expenses relating to the closing of the institute
250,000   Boys and Girls Club of Greater Ft Worth, Ft Worth, TX -- Support establishment of the new Polytechnic Heights Club
250,000   Van Cliburn Foundation, Ft. Worth, TX -- Support the Eleventh Piano Competition
210,000   University of Texas at Austin Marine Science Institute, Austin, TX -- Support Marine Fisheries Research project

ANN S. RICHARDSON FUND

Giving Contact

Stephen Bois, Trust Officer
c/o J.P. Morgan Chase Bank
1211 Avenue of the Americas, 34th Fl.
New York, NY 10036
Phone: (212)789-4073

Description

Founded: 1965
EIN: 136192516
Organization Type: Private Foundation
Giving Locations: CT; NY
Grant Types: General Support.

Donor Information

Founder: the late Anne S. Richardson

Financial Summary

Total Giving: $655,000 (fiscal year ending July 31, 2004); $1,086,498 (fiscal 2001)
Assets: $12,719,859 (fiscal 2004); $13,734,294 (fiscal 2001)
Gifts Received: $20,000 (fiscal 1998)

Typical Recipients

Arts & Humanities: Arts Associations & Councils, Historic Preservation, History & Archaeology, Libraries, Museums/Galleries, Music, Opera, Performing Arts, Public Broadcasting
Civic & Public Affairs: Botanical Gardens/Parks, Clubs, Economic Development, Housing, Public Policy, Women's Affairs
Education: Arts/Humanities Education, Colleges & Universities, Education-General, Literacy, Minority Education, Private Education (Precollege), Student Aid
Environment: Environment-General, Resource Conservation
Health: Cancer, Children's Health/Hospitals, Clinics/Medical Centers, Health Organizations, Heart, Hospices, Hospitals, Long-Term Care, Medical Research, Single-Disease Health Associations
International: International Affairs, International Organizations
Religion: Churches, Religious Organizations, Religious Welfare
Science: Science Museums, Scientific Centers & Institutes
Social Services: Child Welfare, Community Centers, Community Service Organizations, Counseling, Domestic Violence, Family Planning, Family Services, Food/Clothing Distribution, Scouts, Senior Services, Substance Abuse, United Funds/United Ways, Volunteer Services, Youth Organizations

Application Procedures

Initial Contact: Send a brief letter of inquiry.
Deadlines: None.

Restrictions

Does not support individuals or provide endowment funds, scholarships, or loans.

Additional Information
Trust(s): J.P. Morgan Chase Bank

Grants Analysis
Disclosure Period: fiscal year ending July 31, 2004
Total Grants: $655,000
Number of Grants: 31
Average Grant: $21,129
Highest Grant: $65,000
Typical Range: $5,000 to $40,000

Recent Grants
Note: Grants derived from 2000 Form 990.
General

10,000	American Heart Association
10,000	Boys Club of New York, New York, NY
10,000	Boys Scouts, Westchester, NY
10,000	Garden and Conservation Trust, New York, NY
10,000	Memorial Sloan-Kettering, New York, NY
10,000	Morningside House Nursing, Bronx, NY
10,000	New York Hospital, New York, NY
10,000	New York Landmarks Conservancy, New York, NY
10,000	Norwalk Hospital Development Fund, Norwalk, CT
10,000	Prep for Prep, New York, NY

RIDER-POOL FOUNDATION

Giving Contact
c/o PNC Bank NA
1600 Market Street, 4th Floor
Philadelphia, PA 19103
Phone: (215)585-3997

Description
Founded: 1957
EIN: 236207356
Organization Type: Private Foundation
Giving Locations: PA: Allentown
Grant Types: Capital, Emergency, Endowment, Fellowship, General Support, Project, Research.

Donor Information
Founder: Dorothy Rider-Pool

Financial Summary
Total Giving: $392,772 (2003)
Assets: $9,742,343 (2003)
Gifts Received: $20,000 (2000)

Typical Recipients
Arts & Humanities: Arts Centers, Ballet, History & Archaeology, Libraries, Museums/Galleries, Music, Performing Arts, Theater
Civic & Public Affairs: Community Foundations, Economic Development, Civic & Public Affairs-General, Hispanic Affairs, Municipalities/Towns, Professional & Trade Associations, Urban & Community Affairs
Education: Arts/Humanities Education, Business Education, Business-School Partnerships, Colleges & Universities, Community & Junior Colleges, Education Funds, Environmental Education, Faculty Development, Education-General, Private Education (Precollege), Public Education (Precollege), Secondary Education (Private), Special Education, Student Aid
Environment: Environment-General, Resource Conservation, Wildlife Protection
Health: Health Organizations, Public Health
Religion: Churches, Religious Welfare
Science: Scientific Centers & Institutes
Social Services: Animal Protection, Child Welfare, Community Service Organizations, Counseling, Crime Prevention, Food/Clothing Distribution, People with Disabilities, Recreation & Athletics, Scouts, Se-

nior Services, United Funds/United Ways, YMCA/YWCA/YMHA/YWHA, Youth Organizations

Application Procedures
Initial Contact: The foundation requests applications be made in writing.
Deadlines: None.

Additional Information
Trust(s): PNC Bank NA

Foundation Officials
Edward J. Donley: trustee
Leon Conrad Holt, Jr.: treasurer B Reading, PA 1925. ED Lehigh University BS (1948); University of Pennsylvania JD (1951). CORP AFFIL director: VF Corp.; director: Air Products & Chemicals. NONPR AFFIL member: Tunkhannock Creek Association; member advisory board: University Pennsylvania Institute Law & Economics; trustee: Pool (Dorothy Rider) Health Care Trust; director: Pennsylvanians Modern Courts; director: Pocono Lake Preserve; member: New York City Bar Association; member: Pennsylvania Society; member executive committee: Machinery & Allied Products Institute; director: Nature Conservancy Pennsylvania Chapter; trustee: Committee for Economic Development; director: Lehigh County United Fund; member: American Bar Association; member: Allentown Chamber of Commerce; member: Alpha Tau Omega; trustee: Allentown Art Museum. CLUB AFFIL Lehigh Country Club.
John P. Jones, III: trustee

Grants Analysis
Disclosure Period: calendar year ending 2003
Total Grants: $392,772
Number of Grants: 52
Average Grant: $5,480*
Highest Grant: $68,772
Lowest Grant: $500
Typical Range: $1,000 to $10,000
*Note: Average grant figure excludes two highest grants ($118,772).

Recent Grants
Note: Grants derived from 2003 Form 990.
General

68,772	Dorothy Rider Pool Health Care Charitable Trust, Allentown, PA
50,000	Allentown School District Community Counsel, Allentown, PA
25,000	Community Action Committee of the Lehigh Valley, Bethlehem, PA
20,000	Allentown Art Museum, Allentown, PA
15,000	Lehigh University, Bethlehem, PA
12,500	Illick's Mill Partnership for Environmental Education, Bethlehem, PA
10,000	Bach Choir of Bethlehem, Bethlehem, PA
10,000	Cedar Crest College, Allentown, PA
10,000	Congregations United for Neighborhood Action, Allentown, PA
10,000	Touch Stone Theatre, Bethlehem, PA

RIEDMAN FOUNDATION

Giving Contact
John R. Riedman, Principal Manager
45 East Avenue
Rochester, NY 14604
Phone: (716)232-4424

Description
Founded: 1980
EIN: 222279168
Organization Type: Private Foundation
Giving Locations: NH; NY; ND
Grant Types: General Support, Research.

Donor Information
Founder: Frank J. Riedman, Jr., John R. Riedman, Riedman Corp.

Financial Summary
Total Giving: $634,400 (2001)
Giving Analysis: Giving for 2001 includes: foundation grants to United Way ($6,000)
Assets: $11,068,106 (2001)
Gifts Received: $370,000 (2000); $300,251 (1999); $225,623 (1996). Note: In 2000, contributions were received from John R. Riedman ($220,000) and the Riedman Corp. ($211,623).In 1996, contributions were received from John R. Riedman ($14,000) and the Riedman Corp. ($150,000).

Typical Recipients
Arts & Humanities: Arts Associations & Councils, Libraries, Museums/Galleries, Music, Public Broadcasting
Civic & Public Affairs: Chambers of Commerce, Economic Development, Civic & Public Affairs-General, Housing, Municipalities/Towns, Zoos/Aquariums
Education: Colleges & Universities, Community & Junior Colleges, Private Education (Precollege), Science/Mathematics Education
Health: Cancer, Children's Health/Hospitals, Clinics/Medical Centers, Emergency/Ambulance Services, Health Organizations, Hospitals, Medical Rehabilitation, Single-Disease Health Associations
International: Foreign Arts Organizations
Science: Science Museums, Scientific Centers & Institutes
Social Services: Child Welfare, Community Service Organizations, Emergency Relief, Homes, Scouts, United Funds/United Ways, YMCA/YWCA/YMHA/YWHA

Application Procedures
Initial Contact: The foundation has no formal grant application procedure or application form.
Deadlines: None.

Foundation Officials
John R. Riedman: manager

Grants Analysis
Disclosure Period: calendar year ending 2001
Total Grants: $628,400*
Number of Grants: 46
Average Grant: $6,270*
Highest Grant: $250,000
Typical Range: $500 to $10,000
*Note: Giving excludes United Way. Average grant figure excludes two highest grants ($340,000).

Recent Grants
Note: Grants derived from 2001 Form 990.
Library-Related

25,000	Rundel Library Foundation, Rochester, NY

General

250,000	Rochester Museum and Science Center, Rochester, NY
90,000	County of Monroe, Rochester, NY
50,000	Trinity Medical Center Foundation, Minot, ND
25,000	St. John Fisher College, Rochester, NY
25,000	WXXI, Rochester, NY
10,000	Alfred University, Alfred, NY
10,000	Chamber of Commerce, Rochester, NY
10,000	Housing Opportunities, Rochester, NY
10,000	Rochester Museum and Science Center, Rochester, NY
10,000	Society for the Protection of Children, Concord, NH

RIEKE CORP.

Company Headquarters
Auburn, IN
Web: http://www.riekepackaging.com

Company Description
Revenue: US$62.1 million (2001)
Employees: 350
SIC(s): 3000 Rubber & Miscellaneous Plastics Products, 3053 Gaskets, Packing & Sealing Devices, 3400 Fabricated Metal Products, 3412 Metal Barrels, Drums & Pails.
Parent Company: TriMas Corp.

Rieke Corp. Foundation

Giving Contact
Donald E. Kelley, Trustee
500 W. 7th St.
Auburn, IN 46706
Phone: (260)461-6470
Fax: (260)925-0023

Description
EIN: 510158651
Organization Type: Corporate Foundation
Giving Locations: IN; NY; TX
Grant Types: Emergency, General Support.

Financial Summary
Total Giving: $68,500 (fiscal year ending September 30, 2001)
Assets: $1,162,806 (fiscal 2001)
Gifts Received: $20,000 (fiscal 2001); $20,000 (fiscal 2000); $20,000 (fiscal 1999)

Typical Recipients
Arts & Humanities: Arts Associations & Councils, Historic Preservation, History & Archaeology, Libraries, Museums/Galleries, Music
Civic & Public Affairs: Chambers of Commerce, Community Foundations, Economic Development, Housing, Municipalities/Towns, Urban & Community Affairs
Education: Business Education, Colleges & Universities, Public Education (Precollege), Special Education
Health: Cancer, Geriatric Health, Health Organizations, Hospitals
Religion: Ministries
Science: Science Exhibits & Fairs
Social Services: Animal Protection, Big Brothers/Big Sisters, Child Welfare, Community Service Organizations, Food/Clothing Distribution, People with Disabilities, Recreation & Athletics, Senior Services, Shelters/Homelessness, Substance Abuse, United Funds/United Ways, YMCA/YWCA/YMHA/YWHA, Youth Organizations

Application Procedures
Initial Contact: Submit either a written or personal request.
Deadlines: August 31.

Additional Information
Trust(s): Wells Fargo Bank IN NA

Corporate Officials
Lynn A. Brooks: president, chief executive officer PRIM CORP EMPL president, chief executive officer: Rieke Corp.
Phillip Keating: chairman PRIM CORP EMPL chairman: Rieke Corp.
Dave Worthington: chief financial officer PRIM CORP EMPL chief financial officer: Rieke Corp.

Foundation Officials
Donald E. Kelley: trustee
Glenn T. Rieke: trustee
Mahlon E. Rieke: trustee

Grants Analysis
Disclosure Period: fiscal year ending September 30, 2001
Total Grants: $68,500
Number of Grants: 14
Average Grant: $2,607*
Highest Grant: $20,000
Typical Range: $1,000 to $5,000
*Note: Average grant figure excludes two highest grants ($32,000).

Recent Grants
Note: Grants derived from fiscal 2001 Form 990.
Library-Related

7,000	Eckhart Public Library, Eckhart, IN

General

20,000	City of Auburn, Auburn, NY
12,000	DeKalb Council On Aging, IN
12,000	DeKalb Council On Aging, IN
5,000	Auburn Cord Duesenberg Museum, Auburn, IN
5,000	DeKalb County YMCA, IN
3,000	Children First Center, IN
3,000	DeKalb Central School, IN
3,000	Filling Station Youth Center
2,500	DeKalb County Habitat for Humanity, Auburn, IN
2,500	DeKalb Humane Society, DeKalb, IN

MABEL LOUISE RILEY FOUNDATION

Giving Contact
Nancy A. Saunders, Administrative Manager
77 Summer St., 8th Flr.
Boston, MA 02110
Phone: (617)399-1850
Fax: (617)399-1851
E-mail: rileyfoundation@kl.com

Description
Founded: 1972
EIN: 046278857
Organization Type: General Purpose Foundation
Giving Locations: MA: Boston
Grant Types: Capital, Challenge, Endowment, General Support, Multiyear/Continuing Support, Project, Seed Money.

Donor Information
Founder: Mabel Louise Riley, the only child of Agnes Winslow Riley and Charles E. Riley, was born in Boston in 1883. Her father was president of H & B American Machine Company in Pawtucket, RI. Described as "generous and concerned for the needs of others," she supported numerous charities throughout her lifetime. Miss Riley died in 1971, and with her death provided for the charitable organizations she had supported. A portion of her wealth went to friends, families, and charities. The remainder was used to establish the Mabel Louise Riley Charitable Trust, now known as the Mabel Louise Riley Foundation, which became active in May 1972.

Financial Summary
Total Giving: $1,981,577 (2003); $1,971,578 (2002)
Assets: $53,699,136 (2003); $45,283,911 (2002)
Gifts Received: $100,000 (2002). Note: In 2002, contributions were received from The Annie E. Casey Foundation.

Typical Recipients
Arts & Humanities: Arts Associations & Councils, Arts Centers, Arts Funds, Ballet, Community Arts, Dance, Ethnic & Folk Arts, Film & Video, Arts & Humanities-General, Historic Preservation, History & Archaeology, Libraries, Museums/Galleries, Music, Performing Arts, Theater, Visual Arts
Civic & Public Affairs: African American Affairs, Asian American Affairs, Botanical Gardens/Parks, Business/Free Enterprise, Civil Rights, Clubs, Community Foundations, Economic Development, Employment/Job Training, Civic & Public Affairs-General, Hispanic Affairs, Housing, Municipalities/Towns, Nonprofit Management, Philanthropic Organizations, Professional & Trade Associations, Public Policy, Safety, Urban & Community Affairs, Women's Affairs, Zoos/Aquariums
Education: Agricultural Education, Arts/Humanities Education, Business Education, Colleges & Universities, Elementary Education (Private), Environmental Education, Faculty Development, Education-General, Leadership Training, Legal Education, Literacy, Medical Education, Minority Education, Preschool Education, Private Education (Precollege), Public Education (Precollege), Religious Education, Science/Mathematics Education, Social Sciences Education, Special Education
Environment: Environment-General, Resource Conservation, Wildlife Protection
Health: Clinics/Medical Centers, Diabetes, Emergency/Ambulance Services, Health Policy/Cost Containment, Health Organizations, Hospitals, Long-Term Care, Mental Health, Prenatal Health Issues
International: Human Rights
Religion: Churches, Religious Organizations, Religious Welfare, Seminaries
Social Services: At-Risk Youth, Big Brothers/Big Sisters, Camps, Child Welfare, Community Centers, Community Service Organizations, Counseling, Crime Prevention, Day Care, Family Planning, Family Services, Food/Clothing Distribution, People with Disabilities, Recreation & Athletics, Refugee Assistance, Scouts, Shelters/Homelessness, Social Services-General, Substance Abuse, United Funds/United Ways, Veterans, Volunteer Services, YMCA/YWCA/YMHA/YWHA, Youth Organizations

Application Procedures
Initial Contact: Applicants are required to submit a brief summary of their proposal (not more than 2 pages) before submitting a formal grant request. The Foundation will notify the applicant if a grant request will be reviewed by the foundation. If the filing of a grant request is authorized, it must be made using the Common Proposal Format of Associated Grantmakers in Boston, Massachusetts.

Application Requirements: All proposals must include a brief history of the organization, its goals, achievements, indication of whom it serves, and what services it performs; list of board members and resumes and qualifications of involved staff; organization's current and anticipated operating budgets, recent audited financial statement, and complete copy of the most recent IRS 990 form; and a current copy of the IRS tax exemption letter that additionally indicates the organization's status as a public charity. The proposal should also provide a brief description of the reason for which the grant is required, including goals, specific objectives, explanation of the project's compatibility with other programs implemented by the organization, description of special events or approaches planned, and a timetable of these activities. Also required are the project's budget, indication of other potential sources of support, future means of support, summary of expected benefits of the project, and the proposed method of evaluation of these benefits.

Deadlines: Grant meetings of the foundation are scheduled for March, June, September, and December. A formal grant request will not be acted upon unless filed at least 30 days before the first day of the

month in which the grant meeting occurs.
Review Process: Applicants are welcome to contact the program staff before submitting proposals. The trustees may make field visits to interesting programs and will hold meetings with those organizations selected for funding.

Restrictions

Grants generally are not made to charitable organizations outside Massachusetts, toward deficits or regular operating budgets, as the sole source of support, for activities supported by the general public, to units of government, or to individuals or organizations on behalf of individuals. Grants are not made to support personal needs, travel, research, publications, loans, scholarships, national organizations, campaigns, or sectarian religious purposes.

Additional Information

Applicants who have been invited to submit a formal proposal and whose request was subsequently turned down, must wait a full year prior to reapplication. Organizations that have received grants should wait two full years before reapplication.
Publications: Annual Report; Guidelines; Application Form

Foundation Officials

Andrew C. Bailey, Esq.: trustee B Waltham, MA 1921. ED Amherst College AB (1944); Cornell University LLB (1948). PRIM CORP EMPL attorney: Powers & Hall. CORP AFFIL clerk, director: Warwick Mills Holding Co. Inc.
Douglas Danner: trustee B Philadelphia, PA 1924. ED Harvard University AB (1946); Boston University JD (1949). PRIM CORP EMPL attorney: Powers & Hall.
Robert W. Holmes, Jr.: trustee B Fall River, MA 1944. ED Harvard University BA (1967); Boston University JD (1970). PRIM CORP EMPL attorney: Powers & Hall. CORP AFFIL clerk, director: MacDonald Mott Inc.; vice president, clerk, director: Powers & Hall Prof Corp.

Grants Analysis

Disclosure Period: calendar year ending 2003
Total Grants: $1,981,577
Number of Grants: 39
Average Grant: $48,068*
Highest Grant: $155,000
Lowest Grant: $2,000
Typical Range: $10,000 to $100,000
***Note:** Average grant figure excludes highest grant.

Recent Grants

Note: Grants derived from 2002 Form 990.

General
265,672	Family Nurturing Center Inc., Dorchester, MA
250,000	Massachusetts Golf Association, Norton, MA
200,000	Italian Home, Jamaica Plain, MA
150,000	Big Brothers of Massachusetts Bay, Boston, MA
100,000	Federated Dorchester Neighborhood Houses, Inc., Dorchester, MA
75,000	Year Up, Boston, MA
75,000	YMCA of Greater Boston, Boston, MA
70,000	Food Project, Lincoln, MA
50,000	Boston Neighborhood Network, Boston, MA
50,000	Casa Nueva Vida Inc.

FANNIE E. RIPPEL FOUNDATION

Giving Contact

Barbara Vanderkolk Gardner, President & Chief Executive Officer
180 Mt. Airy Road, Suite 200
Basking Ridge, NJ 07920-2021
Phone: (908)766-0404
Fax: (908)766-0527
E-mail: rippel@attglobal.net
Web: http://www.fdncenter.org/grantmaker/rippel

Description

Founded: 1953
EIN: 221559427
Organization Type: Specialized/Single Purpose Foundation
Giving Locations: nationally; Middle Atlantic Seaboard.
Grant Types: Capital, Conference/Seminar, General Support, Matching, Project, Research.

Donor Information

Founder: Julius S. Rippel, the foundation's donor, was born in Newark, NJ, and resided in the area until his death in 1950. Mr. Rippel was an orphan who began working at an early age. He became wealthy as a young man and was widely respected in his community as a banker and an investor. In his will, he provided for the establishment of the Fannie E. Rippel Foundation in memory of his wife. The foundation was established in 1953.

Financial Summary

Total Giving: $4,018,960 (fiscal year ending April 30, 2004); $5,228,220 (fiscal 2003); $5,228,220 (fiscal 2002)
Assets: $73,572,613 (fiscal 2004); $67,426,027 (fiscal 2003); $81,457,958 (fiscal 2002)

Typical Recipients

Arts & Humanities: Public Broadcasting
Civic & Public Affairs: Women's Affairs
Education: Colleges & Universities, Engineering/Technological Education, Education-General, Health & Physical Education, Medical Education, Student Aid
Health: Cancer, Children's Health/Hospitals, Clinics/Medical Centers, Diabetes, Emergency/Ambulance Services, Eyes/Blindness, Health-General, Geriatric Health, Health Organizations, Heart, Hospitals, Hospitals (University Affiliated), Medical Rehabilitation, Medical Research, Public Health, Research/Studies Institutes
International: Health Care/Hospitals
Religion: Jewish Causes, Religious Welfare
Science: Scientific Labs
Social Services: Emergency Relief, YMCA/YWCA/YMHA/YWHA

Application Procedures

Initial Contact: The foundation does not use standard application forms. A detailed letter of inquiry may be sent to the foundation office.
Application Requirements: Details of the project, project's cost, indication that the proposed project is approved by the institution, and the signature of a senior executive in the institution. The applicant organization will be notified if additional information is required.
Deadlines: None.
Review Process: Fund requests are read initially by the foundation staff. If the proposal falls within the foundation's giving range, it is reviewed further by the board of trustees.

Restrictions

Grants are not made to individuals and rarely to challenge campaigns. Operating budgets are not supported. Proposals should not be submitted until one has been requested by the foundation. An initial letter of inquiry is strongly preferred.

Additional Information

Publications: Annual Report

Foundation Officials

Bruce N. Bensley: trustee, member
S. Jervis Brinton, Jr.: trustee emeritus B Ardmore, PA 1923. ED Williams College BA (1948); New York University MBA (1953); Rutgers University Stonier Graduate School of Banking (1959). PRIM CORP EMPL president: Brinton Eaton Associates. CORP AFFIL director: Peerless Tube Co.
John D. Campbell: trustee, member
Barbara Vanderkolk Gardner: president, chief executive officer
Laura K. Landy: trustee, member
Edward W. Probert: chairman, trustee, member CORP AFFIL board advisorys: Whitehead Institute Biomedical Research. NONPR AFFIL co chairman: Jersey Battered Womens Service; governing board solicitor capital campaign: Morristown Membership Hospital. CLUB AFFIL Somerset Hills Country Club; Mountain Lake Club; Royal Dormach Golf Club; Morristown Club; Morristown Field Club.
Nancy L. Ryan: secretary
Albert L. Strunk, MD: trustee, member CORP AFFIL treasurer: Women's Health Care Specialists.
Irene B. Weber: treasurer

Grants Analysis

Disclosure Period: fiscal year ending April 30, 2004
Total Grants: $4,018,960
Number of Grants: 17
Average Grant: $204,310*
Highest Grant: $750,000
Lowest Grant: $50,000
Typical Range: $100,000 to $350,000
***Note:** Average grant figure excludes highest grant.

Recent Grants

Note: Grants derived from fiscal 2003 Form 990.

General
400,000	Children's Hospital Corporation, Boston, MA -- toward purchase of equipment
360,680	Hamot Medical Center, Erie, PA -- toward purchase of hardware and software and ancillary expenses
350,000	Fred Hutchinson Cancer Research Center, Seattle, WA
300,000	Scripps Research Institute, La Jolla, CA
300,000	Trustees of the University of Pennsylvania, Philadelphia, PA -- toward establishment of a center for research on women's health
250,000	Atlantic Health System Inc., Florham Park, NJ -- toward establishment of a breast center
250,000	Atlantic Health System Inc., Florham Park, NJ -- toward construction of heart hospital
250,000	St Luke's Roosevelt Hospital Center, New York, NY -- toward creation of new outpatient facilities
200,000	Children's Hospital of Philadelphia, Philadelphia, PA -- toward development of a Neuro-Cardiac research program
200,000	Englewood Hospital and Medical Center, Englewood, NJ -- toward purchase of equipment

GEORGE AND MARY RITTER CHARITABLE TRUST

Giving Contact
Imogene S. Meyer, Trust Officer
c/o Key Trust Co. Ohio NA
PO Box 10099
Toledo, OH 43699-0099
Phone: (419)259-4968

Description
Founded: 1982
EIN: 346781636
Organization Type: Private Foundation
Giving Locations: OH: Toledo
Grant Types: General Support, Operating Expenses, Scholarship.

Donor Information
Founder: the late George W. Ritter

Financial Summary
Gifts Received: $885,858 (fiscal year ending November 30, 2000). Note: In 2000, contributions were received from George W. Ritter Trusts.

Typical Recipients
Arts & Humanities: Libraries, Museums/Galleries
Civic & Public Affairs: Clubs, Civic & Public Affairs-General, Law & Justice
Education: Colleges & Universities, Education-General, Student Aid
Health: Children's Health/Hospitals, Hospitals, Hospitals (University Affiliated)
Religion: Churches, Religious Organizations, Religious Welfare, Synagogues/Temples
Social Services: Community Service Organizations, Scouts, YMCA/YWCA/YMHA/YWHA, Youth Organizations

Application Procedures
Initial Contact: Request application form.
Deadlines: None.

Additional Information
Publications: Application Form
Trust(s): Key Trust Company

Foundation Officials
Larry Firestine: adv
Edgar A. Gibson: adv
James D. Harvey: adv

Grants Analysis
Disclosure Period: fiscal year ending November 30, 2000
Total Grants: $533,645*
Number of Grants: 25
Average Grant: $21,345
Highest Grant: $80,044
Typical Range: $10,000 to $40,000
*Note: Giving excludes Scholarships.

Recent Grants
Note: Grants derived from fiscal 2002 Form 990.
Library-Related
47,116	Ritter Library, Vermillion, OH

General
86,385	Baldwin Wallace College, Berea, OH
70,674	Promedica, Toledo, OH
61,890	Toledo Museum of Art, Toledo, OH
54,714	St. Vincent Hospital, Toledo, OH
48,494	Shriners Hospital, Atlanta, GA
24,836	Ohio State Bar Foundation, Columbus, OH
24,836	Toledo Rotary Club Foundation, Toledo, OH
24,836	YWCA, Toledo, OH
24,756	YMCA, Toledo, OH
24,120	Flower Hospital, Sylvania, OH

JOHN A. AND DELIA T. ROBERT CHARITABLE TRUST 2

Giving Contact
S. Collins-Compere, Trust Officer
Regions Bank
PO Box 10247
Birmingham, AL 35202
Phone: (205)326-7224

Description
Founded: 1995
EIN: 636193757
Organization Type: Private Foundation
Giving Locations: AL: Birmingham
Grant Types: General Support.

Financial Summary
Total Giving: $52,204 (fiscal year ending March 31, 2003); $63,315 (fiscal 2001)
Assets: $936,454 (fiscal 2003); $1,188,064 (fiscal 2001)

Typical Recipients
Arts & Humanities: Libraries
Civic & Public Affairs: Civic & Public Affairs-General
Education: Afterschool/Enrichment Programs, Arts/Humanities Education, Education Funds, Education-General, Public Education (Precollege), Student Aid
Health: Eyes/Blindness, Health Organizations, Hospitals, Public Health
Religion: Churches, Religious Welfare
Social Services: Child Abuse, Community Service Organizations, People with Disabilities, Shelters/Homelessness

Application Procedures
Initial Contact: Send a letter describing project. Include a list of other sources of funding, proof of tax-exempt status, current financial data, and amount requested.
Application Requirements: Include a list of other sources of funding, proof of tax-exempt status, current financial data, and amount requested.
Deadlines: None.

Restrictions
Political gifts are excluded per REGS IRC SEC 501 (c)(3) and 170(c)(2).

Additional Information
Grants are awarded for religious, science, literary, as education purposes.
Trust(s): Regions Bank

Foundation Officials
Arlene S. Henley: co-trustee

Grants Analysis
Disclosure Period: fiscal year ending March 31, 2003
Total Grants: $52,204
Number of Grants: 9
Average Grant: $4,651*
Highest Grant: $15,000
Lowest Grant: $2,000
Typical Range: $2,500 to $7,500
*Note: Average grant figure excludes highest grant.

Recent Grants
Note: Grants derived from 2003 Form 990.

Library-Related
5,000	Birmingham Public Library, Birmingham, AL

General
15,000	Lakeshore Foundation, Birmingham, AL
12,000	Spring Valley School Foundation, Spring Valley, WI
7,500	Alabama Lions Sight Conservation, Birmingham, AL
3,000	Eastlake United Methodist Church, Birmingham, AL
3,000	Oak Hill Memorial Association, Birmingham, AL
2,500	Girls Incorporated of Central, Birmingham, AL
2,204	Cornerstone Schools of Alabama, North Birmingham, AL
2,000	First Light, Inc., Birmingham, AL

DORA ROBERTS FOUNDATION

Giving Contact
Rick Piersall, Senior Vice President, Bank One
PO Box 2050
Ft. Worth, TX 76113
Phone: (817)884-4442
Fax: (817)884-4294

Description
Founded: 1948
EIN: 756013899
Organization Type: General Purpose Foundation
Giving Locations: TX: Big Spring
Grant Types: Capital, General Support, Project.

Donor Information
Founder: Established in 1948 by the late Dora Roberts.

Financial Summary
Total Giving: $1,677,829 (fiscal year ending June 30, 2002); $2,522,454 (fiscal 2001)
Assets: $38,600,762 (fiscal 2002); $40,798,084 (fiscal 2001)
Gifts Received: $5,000 (fiscal 1994); $5,000 (fiscal 1993)

Typical Recipients
Arts & Humanities: Historic Preservation, History & Archaeology, Libraries, Museums/Galleries, Music
Civic & Public Affairs: Chambers of Commerce, Clubs, Employment/Job Training, Civic & Public Affairs-General, Hispanic Affairs, Housing, Municipalities/Towns, Safety, Urban & Community Affairs
Education: Agricultural Education, Business Education, Colleges & Universities, Community & Junior Colleges, Education Funds, Engineering/Technological Education, Education-General, Medical Education, Private Education (Precollege), Public Education (Precollege), Secondary Education (Public), Student Aid
Health: Cancer, Heart, Hospices, Hospitals, Medical Rehabilitation
Religion: Churches, Religious Welfare
Social Services: Animal Protection, At-Risk Youth, Child Welfare, Community Centers, Community Service Organizations, Crime Prevention, Delinquency & Criminal Rehabilitation, Family Services, Food/Clothing Distribution, Homes, Recreation & Athletics, Scouts, Senior Services, Sexual Abuse, Social Services-General, YMCA/YWCA/YMHA/YWHA, Youth Organizations

Application Procedures
Initial Contact: The foundation requests applications be made in writing.

Application Requirements: Proposals should include the purpose and amount of the request, a brief narrative history of the organization's purpose and work, budgetary information pertaining to the requested grant, a list of trustees or directors and principal staff, and a copy of an IRS exemption letter.
Deadlines: Proposals must be received by September 30.
Review Process: The board meets annually in November or December. Decisions are generally made by the end of December.

Restrictions
Grants are not made to individuals or outside the state of Texas.

Additional Information
Bank One, Texas, N.A. serves as a corporate trustee for the foundation.

Foundation Officials
Lisa Canter: board member
Roger Canter: board member
Hon. Judge Bob Moore: board mem
Sue Garrett Partee: board mem
Rick Piersall: sr vice president
J. P. Taylor: board mem PRIM CORP EMPL president, director: First National Bank.
R. H. Weaver: board mem CORP AFFIL director: First National Bank.

Grants Analysis
Disclosure Period: fiscal year ending June 30, 2002
Total Grants: $1,677,829
Number of Grants: 35
Average Grant: $43,024*
Highest Grant: $215,000
Lowest Grant: $3,000
Typical Range: $10,000 to $100,000
*Note: Average grant figure excludes highest grant.

Recent Grants
Note: Grants derived from fiscal 2002 Form 990.
General
215,000	Salvation Army
180,000	Howard College, Big Spring, TX
150,000	Big Spring Humane Society, Big Spring, TX
100,000	Lone Star SPCA, Midland, TX
78,000	First United Methodist Church
72,000	Senior Citizens Center
70,000	Howard County Council on Aging
68,000	Crossroads Tennis
67,939	Dora Roberts Rehab Center, Big Spring, TX
50,000	Heritage Museum

ROBERTSHAW CHARITABLE FOUNDATION

Giving Contact
Deborah L. Bridge, Manager
116 N. Main Street
Greensburg, PA 15601
Phone: (724)832-7576

Description
Founded: 1990
EIN: 251622184
Organization Type: Private Foundation
Giving Locations: PA: Western Pennsylvania with emphasis on Westmoreland County
Grant Types: General Support.

Donor Information
Founder: Established in 1990 by John A. Robertshaw, Jr.

Financial Summary
Total Giving: $65,400 (fiscal year ending June 30, 2004); $101,146 (fiscal 2001)
Assets: $1,285,005 (fiscal 2004); $1,506,276 (fiscal 2001)
Gifts Received: $82,600 (fiscal 1997); $30,000 (fiscal 1995); $10,000 (fiscal 1994). Note: In fiscal 1997, contributions were received from John A. Robertshaw, Jr.

Typical Recipients
Arts & Humanities: Arts Festivals, Ballet, Historic Preservation, Libraries, Museums/Galleries, Music, Public Broadcasting, Theater
Civic & Public Affairs: Botanical Gardens/Parks, Community Foundations, Economic Development, Housing, Municipalities/Towns
Education: Arts/Humanities Education, Colleges & Universities, Education-General, Gifted & Talented Programs, International Studies, Private Education (Precollege), Science/Mathematics Education, Secondary Education (Private), Student Aid
Environment: Environment-General, Resource Conservation
Health: Children's Health/Hospitals, Emergency/Ambulance Services, Hospitals, Preventive Medicine/Wellness Organizations
Religion: Religion-General, Religious Organizations, Religious Welfare
Social Services: Animal Protection, At-Risk Youth, Community Service Organizations, Emergency Relief, Food/Clothing Distribution, Homes, People with Disabilities, Recreation & Athletics, Scouts, Social Services-General, Special Olympics, Youth Organizations

Application Procedures
Initial Contact: Send a brief letter of inquiry.
Application Requirements: Include a description of organization.
Deadlines: Semi-annually.

Foundation Officials
Natalie R. Kelley: director
Lisa Robertshaw Moeller: director
Anne B. Robertshaw: director
John A. Robertshaw, III: director
John A. Robertshaw, Jr.: chairman
Marc B. Robertshaw: director

Grants Analysis
Disclosure Period: fiscal year ending June 30, 2004
Total Grants: $65,400
Number of Grants: 32
Average Grant: $2,044
Highest Grant: $4,000
Lowest Grant: $1,000
Typical Range: $1,000 to $4,000

Recent Grants
Note: Grants derived from fiscal 2004 Form 990.
General
4,000	Westmoreland Suzuki School of Music, Greensburg, PA -- towards purchase of new copier
3,500	American Red Cross, Greensburg, PA -- towards the disaster portion of service delivery plan & training disaster volunteers and purchasing disaster supplies
3,400	Make-A-Wish Foundation, Pittsburgh, PA -- towards local wish in Westmoreland County
3,000	Homes Build Hope, Greensburg, PA -- towards roof and air conditioning improvements for the welcome home shelter
3,000	Kiski School, Saltsburg, PA -- towards placing a campus virtual tour on school website
3,000	Pilot Dogs Inc., Columbus, OH -- towards scholarship to train a dog for a blind individual
3,000	St. Emma's Retreat House, Greensburg, PA -- towards parking lot expansion
3,000	Westmoreland Symphony Orchestra, Greensburg, PA -- towards Westmoreland youth concerts
2,500	Special Olympics, Greensburg, PA -- towards athletes sports fund
2,000	Laurel Ballet Performing Company, Greensburg, PA -- towards the purchase of a Harlequin studio floor

ROBINSON-BROADHURST FOUNDATION

Giving Contact
Charles K. McKenzie, Executive Director & President
101 Main St.
PO Box 160
Stamford, NY 12167-0160
Phone: (607)652-2508

Description
Founded: 1984
EIN: 222558699
Organization Type: Private Foundation
Giving Locations: CT: Stamford; MA: Winchendon; NY: Worcester
Grant Types: Capital, General Support, Project, Scholarship.

Donor Information
Founder: the late Anna Broadhurst, the late R. Avery Robinsn

Financial Summary
Total Giving: $1,882,878 (fiscal year ending April 30, 2004); $1,805,751 (fiscal 2001)
Giving Analysis: Giving for fiscal 2004 includes: foundation scholarships ($28,000); fiscal 2001: foundation scholarships ($28,000)
Assets: $49,721,814 (fiscal 2004); $48,692,761 (fiscal 2001)
Gifts Received: $7,319,909 (fiscal 2000); $742,692 (fiscal 1997); $484 (fiscal 1996). Note: In fiscal 2000, contributions were received from the estate of Winnie M. Robinson.

Typical Recipients
Arts & Humanities: Arts Associations & Councils, Arts Centers, History & Archaeology, Libraries, Museums/Galleries, Music, Public Broadcasting
Civic & Public Affairs: Botanical Gardens/Parks, Community Foundations, Economic Development, Civic & Public Affairs-General, Housing, Municipalities/Towns, Public Policy, Safety, Urban & Community Affairs
Education: Arts/Humanities Education, Community & Junior Colleges, Education-General, Private Education (Precollege), Public Education (Precollege), Science/Mathematics Education, Secondary Education (Public), Student Aid
Health: Clinics/Medical Centers, Emergency/Ambulance Services, Health Funds, Health Organizations, Hospices, Public Health
Religion: Churches, Ministries, Religious Organizations, Religious Welfare
Social Services: Camps, Child Welfare, Community Centers, Day Care, Family Planning, Recreation & Athletics, Scouts, Senior Services, Social Services-General, Youth Organizations

Application Procedures

Initial Contact: Request application form.
Deadlines: December 31.

Foundation Officials

Ralph Beisler: secretary, trustee
Ernest P. Fletcher, Jr.: treasurer, trustee
William H. Lister: trustee
Charles K. McKenzie: executive director, president
Martin A. Parks: vice president, trustee

Grants Analysis

Disclosure Period: fiscal year ending April 30, 2004
Total Grants: $1,854,878*
Number of Grants: 88
Average Grant: $16,181*
Highest Grant: $174,000
Lowest Grant: $500
Typical Range: $5,000 to $30,000
*Note: Giving excludes scholarships. Average grant figure excludes three highest grants ($479,471).

Recent Grants

Note: Grants derived from fiscal 2003 Form 990.
General

174,000	Town of Winchendon, Winchendon, MA -- for educational programs
155,471	Wendell P. Clark Memorial Association, Winchendon, MA -- for capital improvement
150,000	Wendell P. Clark Memorial Association, Winchendon, MA -- for programs
88,860	Town of Winchendon, Winchendon, MA -- for facility improvements-HVAC
80,000	Town of Winchendon, Winchendon, MA -- for highway repairs
75,000	Town of Stamford, Hobart, NY -- for road equipment
61,780	Town of Harpersfield, Harpersfield, NY -- for equipment acquisition
60,000	Town of Worcester, East Worcester, NY -- for equipment
55,000	Stamford Central School, Stamford, NY -- for EDP equipment update
50,000	Village of Stamford, Stamford, NY -- for fire department equipment acquisition

DONALD AND SYLVIA ROBINSON FAMILY FOUNDATION

Giving Contact

Donald Robinson, President
Donald and Sylvia Robinson Family Foundation
6507 Wilkins Ave.
Pittsburgh, PA 15217
Phone: (412)661-1200

Description

EIN: 237062017
Organization Type: Private Foundation
Giving Locations: PA: Pittsburgh including metropolitan area
Grant Types: Emergency, General Support.

Donor Information

Founder: Donald and Sylvia Robinson

Financial Summary

Total Giving: $143,561 (fiscal year ending October 31, 2004); $267,885 (fiscal 2001)
Assets: $3,232,247 (fiscal 2004); $3,464,316 (fiscal 2001)
Gifts Received: $198,096 (fiscal 2000); $303,775 (fiscal 1999); $349,863 (fiscal 1998). Note: In fiscal

1998 and 2000, contributions were received from Donald and Sylvia Robinson.

Typical Recipients

Arts & Humanities: Arts Associations & Councils, Arts Centers, Arts Funds, Film & Video, Arts & Humanities-General, Historic Preservation, History & Archaeology, Libraries, Museums/Galleries, Music, Performing Arts, Public Broadcasting, Theater, Visual Arts
Civic & Public Affairs: Botanical Gardens/Parks, Economic Development, Ethnic Organizations, Civic & Public Affairs-General, Professional & Trade Associations, Urban & Community Affairs, Women's Affairs
Education: Colleges & Universities, Education-General, Journalism/Media Education, Minority Education, Private Education (Precollege), Student Aid
Environment: Environment-General, Research, Resource Conservation, Watershed
Health: AIDS/HIV, Cancer, Children's Health/Hospitals, Eyes/Blindness, Hospices, Hospitals, Preventive Medicine/Wellness Organizations
International: International Peace & Security Issues, Missionary/Religious Activities
Religion: Churches, Jewish Causes, Religious Organizations, Religious Welfare, Synagogues/Temples
Science: Science Museums, Scientific Centers & Institutes
Social Services: Community Service Organizations, Delinquency & Criminal Rehabilitation, Family Services, Sexual Abuse, Shelters/Homelessness, United Funds/United Ways

Application Procedures

Initial Contact: Send a brief letter of inquiry. Include a description of organization, amount requested, purpose of funds sought, recently audited financial statement, and proof of tax-exempt status.
Application Requirements: Include a description of organization, amount requested, purpose of funds sought, and proof of tax-exempt status.
Deadlines: None.

Restrictions

Grants are not made to individuals.

Foundation Officials

Carol Robinson: trustee
Donald Robinson: trustee
Stephen Robinson: trustee
Sylvia Robinson: trustee

Grants Analysis

Disclosure Period: fiscal year ending October 31, 2004
Total Grants: $143,561
Number of Grants: 173
Average Grant: $830
Highest Grant: $7,500
Lowest Grant: $100
Typical Range: $100 to $1,000

Recent Grants

Note: Grants derived from 2004 Form 990.
Library-Related

5,000	Carnegie Library of Pittsburgh, Pittsburgh, PA

General

7,500	Carnegie Institute, Pittsburgh, PA
6,000	Jewish Federation of South Palm Beach County, Boca Raton, FL
5,000	Medill School of Journalism, Evanston, IL
5,000	Southern Alleghenies Museum of Art, Loretto, PA
5,000	University of Pittsburgh Cancer Institute, Pittsburgh, PA
5,000	Western Pennsylvania Conservancy, Pittsburgh, PA
4,000	Delaware Museum of Natural History, Wilmington, DE

3,000	American Orchid Society, Delray Beach, FL
3,000	Phipps Conservatory & Botanical Gardens, Pittsburgh, PA

MAURICE R. ROBINSON FUND

Giving Contact

Marian I. Steffens, Secretary
c/o Chase Bank
1211 Sixth Ave., 34th Fl.
New York, NY 10036
Phone: (212)789-4073

Description

Founded: 1960
EIN: 136161094
Organization Type: Private Foundation
Giving Locations: NY: nationally.
Grant Types: General Support.

Donor Information

Founder: Maurice R. Robinson, Florence L. Robinson

Financial Summary

Gifts Received: $49,980 (fiscal year ending June 30, 1993); $40,000 (fiscal 1992). Note: In fiscal 1993, contributions were received from Scholastic, Inc. ($48,980) and Scott Newman Foundation ($1,000).

Typical Recipients

Arts & Humanities: Arts Associations & Councils, Arts Centers, Arts Festivals, Arts Funds, Arts Institutes, Arts Outreach, Community Arts, Dance, Arts & Humanities-General, History & Archaeology, Libraries, Literary Arts, Museums/Galleries, Music
Civic & Public Affairs: Civil Rights, Economic Development, Employment/Job Training, Civic & Public Affairs-General, Professional & Trade Associations, Public Policy
Education: Arts/Humanities Education, Colleges & Universities, Education Funds, Education Reform, Elementary Education (Public), Faculty Development, Journalism/Media Education, Leadership Training, Private Education (Precollege), Public Education (Precollege), Secondary Education (Private), Social Sciences Education, Special Education, Student Aid
Environment: Environment-General
Health: Hospitals
International: International Affairs
Religion: Churches, Ministries, Religious Organizations
Science: Observatories & Planetariums
Social Services: Child Welfare, Community Service Organizations, Delinquency & Criminal Rehabilitation, Family Services, Social Services-General

Application Procedures

Initial Contact: Send a brief letter of inquiry.
Application Requirements: a description of organization, purpose of funds sought, and proof of tax-exempt status.
Deadlines: None.

Restrictions

Preference is given to educational institutions for youth and colleges offering majors in communications, broadcasting, and journalism.

Foundation Officials

Katherine Carsky: vice president
Claudia Cohl: vice president B Detroit, MI 1939. ED Wayne State University BA (1961). PRIM CORP EMPL vice president, founding editor: Home Office Co. CORP AFFIL vice president, pub director: Pro-

fessional Publishing Group.
Ernest B. Fleishman: first vice president PRIM CORP EMPL senior vice president ed & corporate relations: Scholastic.
John Quinn: treasurer
Marian I. Steffens: secretary
Barbara D. Sullivan, Esq.: president

Grants Analysis
Disclosure Period: fiscal year ending June 30, 2000
Typical Range: $5,000 to $25,000
Note: No grants list available for 2000.

Recent Grants
Note: Grants derived from fiscal 2001 Form 990.
General

450,000	Alliance for Young Arts, New York, NY
20,000	Constitutional Rights Foundation, Los Angeles, CA
20,000	Seton Hall Prep, New York, NY
10,000	Harlem RBI, New York, NY
10,000	NCTE
10,000	See Forever, Washington, DC
10,000	Trinity College, Washington, DC
10,000	Very Special Arts
5,000	Alaska Sea Life Project
5,000	Catamount Arts, St. Johnsbury, VT

ROCKEFELLER BROTHERS FUND, INC.

Giving Contact
Benjamin R. Shute, Jr., Secretary
437 Madison Avenue, 37th Floor
New York, NY 10022-7001
Phone: (212)812-4200
Fax: (212)812-4299
E-mail: info@rbf.org
Web: http://www.rbf.org
Note: The Fund also has an office in Pocantico Hills, NY.

Description
Founded: 1940
EIN: 131760106
Organization Type: Family Foundation
Formed by Merger of: Rockefeller Brothers Fund and Charles E. Culpeper Foundation (1999).
Giving Locations: NY: New York internationally; nationally.
Grant Types: Capital, Challenge, Conference/Seminar, Fellowship, General Support, Matching, Multiyear/Continuing Support, Operating Expenses, Project, Seed Money.

Donor Information
Founder: The Rockefeller family's fortune stems from John Davison Rockefeller (1839-1937), founder of the Standard Oil Trust and the first billionaire in history. His five grandsons, Nelson Rockefeller, John Rockefeller, Laurance S. Rockefeller, Winthrop Rockefeller, and David Rockefeller, and his granddaughter, Abby Rockefeller Mauze, established the Rockefeller Brothers Fund in 1940. A substantial gift from their father, John D. Rockefeller Jr., in 1951, and a bequest from his estate in 1960, constitute the fund's basic endowment. The fund is also affiliated with the Asian Cultural Council in New York.

Financial Summary
Total Giving: $20,288,000 (2003 approx); $22,950,390 (2002); $25,657,906 (2001)
Assets: $622,583,676 (2002); $684,464,383 (2001)
Gifts Received: $293,544 (2002); $282,934 (2001); $654,901 (2000). Note: The fund occasionally receives gifts from various Rockefeller family members.

Typical Recipients
Arts & Humanities: Arts Associations & Councils, Arts Institutes, Dance, Arts & Humanities-General, Historic Preservation, Libraries, Museums/Galleries, Music, Opera, Public Broadcasting, Theater
Civic & Public Affairs: Asian American Affairs, Botanical Gardens/Parks, Clubs, Community Foundations, Economic Development, Civic & Public Affairs-General, Housing, Law & Justice, Nonprofit Management, Philanthropic Organizations, Professional & Trade Associations, Public Policy, Rural Affairs, Urban & Community Affairs
Education: Arts/Humanities Education, Colleges & Universities, Education Associations, Education Reform, Elementary Education (Public), Environmental Education, Faculty Development, Education-General, International Exchange, International Studies, Literacy, Minority Education, Preschool Education, Public Education (Precollege), Science/Mathematics Education, Social Sciences Education, Vocational & Technical Education
Environment: Air/Water Quality, Energy, Forestry, Environment-General, Protection, Research, Resource Conservation, Watershed, Wildlife Protection
Health: Speech & Hearing
International: Foreign Arts Organizations, Foreign Educational Institutions, International-General, Health Care/Hospitals, International Affairs, International Development, International Environmental Issues, International Organizations, International Peace & Security Issues, International Relations, International Relief Efforts, Trade
Social Services: Child Welfare, Community Service Organizations, Day Care, Family Services, Social Services-General, Volunteer Services

Application Procedures
Initial Contact: Letters of inquiry (no more than two to three pages in length) should be addressed to the fund's secretary.
Application Requirements: Letters of inquiry should include a description of organization and project for which funding is sought, how it relates to the fund's program, information on principal staff members involved with the proposal, synopsis of the budget, and the amount requested.
Full proposals, when requested, should include a complete a description of organization or project, background and research leading to the development of the proposal, methods by which the project will be carried out, qualifications and experience of the project's or organization's principal staff members, list of board members and advisors, detailed budget, copy of the organization's IRS determination letter of tax-exempt status, and a copy of the organization's most recent financial statement (preferably audited).
Deadlines: None, except for the Charles E. Culpeper Scholarships in Medical Science, for which deadlines are posted on the foundation's web site.
Review Process: If a project is taken up for grant consideration, the staff will ask for additional information, including a full proposal, and, usually, an interview. Proposals from former grantees will be considered only after earlier grants have been evaluated and the grantees have submitted the necessary reports of expenditures of those grants. Grants are awarded by the trustees, who meet regularly throughout the year.

Restrictions
The fund does not support building projects or land acquisition. Neither, as a general rule, does the fund make grants to individuals nor does it support research, graduate study, or the writing of books or dissertations by individuals. There are three exceptions. The Rockefeller Brothers Fund Fellowships, under the education program, are awarded to individuals selected from colleges that, because of their particular support of minority students, have been invited by the fund to participate in the fellowship program. Second, through the Program for Asian Projects, the fund

supports projects that exemplify both the spirit of the Ramon Magsaysay Awards and the program concerns of the fund; these grants are available only to Ramon Magsaysay Awardees, including individuals, and to the Ramon Magsaysay Award Foundation. Third, the Charles E. Culpeper Scholarships in Medical Science are designed to support the career development of academic physicians.
The Fund has certain geographic restrictions based on program area. The Sustainable Resource Use and Global Security programs focus on North America and East and Southeast Asia; the Sustainable Resource Use program also includes the Russian Far East and the Global Security program also includes Central and Eastern Europe and Southern Africa. The Nonprofit Sector program places an emphasis on the United States, as well as East and Southeast Asia. The Arts and Culture, Health, and Education programs provide grants only in the United States.

Additional Information
The Fund for Asian Projects supports projects in Asia related to the interests of the Ramon Magsaysay Award Foundation and of the Magsaysay awardees. Grants from this fund are made by the trustees of the Rockefeller Brothers Fund with recommendations from a board of advisors made up of Magsaysay Awardees and officers of the Ramon Magsaysay Award Foundation.
The Fund's Pocantico Conference Center provides a setting where nonprofit organizations and public-sector institutions can bring together people of diverse backgrounds and perspectives to engage critical issues related to the fund's philanthropic program, leading to new levels of understanding and creative resolution of problems.
In July 1999, the Charles E. Culpeper Foundation of Stamford, Connecticut, merged with the Rockefeller Brothers Fund to form the Rockefeller Brothers Fund, Inc.
Publications: Annual Report; Guidelines; Grants Listing; Occasional Papers; Press Releases

Foundation Officials
David Jacobus Callard: trustee B Boston, MA 1938. ED Princeton University AB (1959); Union Theological Seminary (1964-1965); New York University JD (1969). PRIM CORP EMPL president: Wand Partners Inc. CORP AFFIL general partner: Wand Investments LP. NONPR AFFIL trustee: Panorama Trust; board directors: Union Theological Seminary; director: Episcopal Charities Diocese New York. CLUB AFFIL Knickerbocker Club; Elkridge Club.
Richard M. Chasin: trustee B Brooklyn, NY 1936. ED Yale University BA (1956); Harvard University MD (1960). NONPR AFFIL member: Phi Beta Kappa; senior associate: Public Conversations Project; associate professor clin psychiatry: Harvard University Medical School; del: International Physicians Prevention Nuclear War; member: American Psychiatric Association; fellow: American Society for Psychodrama and Group Therapy; member: American Academy Child & Adolescent Psychiatry; member: American Family Therapy Academy.
Jessica P. Einhorn: trustee ED Barnard College MS; Barnard College BA; Princeton University PhD. NONPR AFFIL dean, Nitze school of Advanced international studie: Johns Hopkins University; director: Pitney Bowes Inc..
Neva R. Goodwin: vice chairman, trustee B New York, NY 1944. ED Harvard College BA (1966); Harvard University Kennedy School of Government MPA (1982); Boston University PhD (1987); Boston University PhD (1987). NONPR AFFIL chairman, program committee: Winrock International Institute Agricultural Development; founding trustee: World Game Institute; co-director: Tufts University Global Development & Environment Institute; member, advisory council: College Atlantic; fellow: Human Development and Capability Association; director: Coalition for Environmentally Responsible Economy.
Stephen B. Heintz: president ED Yale University BA.

NONPR AFFIL board of governors: Partnership for Public Service.

Priscilla Lewis: program officer, peace and security ED Oberlin College BA; Yale University MA. NONPR AFFIL director: American Forum for Global Education.

William Henry Luers: advisory trustee B Springfield, IL 1929. ED Columbia University MA; Hamilton College BA (1951); Northwestern University (1951-1952); Columbia University MA (1957). PRIM NONPR EMPL president: Metropolitan Museum of Art. CORP AFFIL director: Wickes Inc.; director: Wickes Lumber Co.; director: Scudder New Europe Fund; director: Story First Corp.; director: Scudder Equities & Security Funds; director: Scudder Global/International Funds; director: Brazil Fund; director: IDEX Corp. NONPR AFFIL advisory council: Trust Mutual Understanding; president, chief executive officer: UN Association of the US; member: Council Foreign Relations; director: Institute East-West Studies; fellow: American Academy of Arts & Sciences; trustee, advisory council: Appeal Conscience Foundation. CLUB AFFIL board directors: Economic Club New York.

William F. McCalpin: executive vice president, chief operating officer NONPR AFFIL vice president, trustee: Asian Cultural Council; director: Solar Development Foundation.

James E. Moltz: trustee B Williamsport, PA 1932. ED Williams College BS (1954); University of Pennsylvania Wharton School MBA (1956). CORP AFFIL vice chairman: ISI. NONPR AFFIL member financial committee: Williams College; chairman: Woods Hole Oceanographic Institute; trustee: Sterling Francine Clark Art Institute; member: Financial Analysts Federation; member: Society Security Analysts; trustee: Darien Library. CLUB AFFIL Windsor Club; director: Wee Burn Country Club; Rockefeller Center Club; Union League Club.

James E. Moltz: trustee B Williamsport, PA 1932. ED Williams College BS (1954); University of Pennsylvania Wharton School MBA (1956). PRIM CORP EMPL chief investment officer: Deutsche Bank Securities Inc. CORP AFFIL vice chairman: ISI. NONPR AFFIL member financial committee: Williams College; chairman: Woods Hole Oceanographic Institute; trustee: Sterling Francine Clark Art Institute; member: Financial Analysts Federation; member: Society Security Analysts; trustee: Darien Library. CLUB AFFIL Windsor Club; director: Wee Burn Country Club; Rockefeller Center Club; Union League Club.

John Morning: trustee B Cleveland, OH 1932. ED Pratt Institute BFA (1955). PRIM CORP EMPL president: John Morning Design. NONPR AFFIL member, board director: New York Landmarks Conservancy; chairman: Vivian Beaumont Theater; member education committee: Museum Modern Art; vice chairman: New York City Cultural Affairs Advisory Committee; director: Association Government Boards, Colleges & Universities; trustee: City University New York; member: American Academy Dramatic Arts; member: American Institute Graphic Arts.

Ruth Rawlings Mott: trustee B El Paso, TX 1901. ED Pratt Institute BFA (1955). NONPR AFFIL member, board director: New York Landmarks Conservancy; chairman: Vivian Beaumont Theater; member education committee: Museum Modern Art; vice chairman: New York City Cultural Affairs Advisory Committee; director: Association Government Boards, Colleges & Universities; trustee: City University New York; member: American Academy Dramatic Arts; member: American Institute Graphic Arts.

Abby Milton Rockefeller O'Neill: advisory trustee B Oyster Bay, NY 1928. NONPR AFFIL trustee: Asian Cultural Council.

Robert B. Oxnam: trustee NONPR AFFIL president emeritus: Asia Society.

Richard D. Parsons: advisory trustee ED Union University JD; University of Hawaii BA. CORP AFFIL director: Estee Lauder; president, chief executive officer: Time Warner Inc.; director: Citigroup. NONPR AFFIL director: Howard University; director: Museum

of Modern Art; chairman: Apollo Theatre Foundation; director: Colonial Williamsburg Foundation.

David Rockefeller, Sr.: advisory trustee B New York, NY June 12, 1915. ED Harvard University BS (1936); University of Chicago PhD (1940). CORP AFFIL chairman: Rockefeller Center Properties Trust Inc.; stockholder: Greenrock Corp. NONPR AFFIL honorary chairman: International House; life trustee: University Chicago; director: Council Foreign Relations; member: International Executive Service Corps; honorary chairman: American Society; director, honorary chairman: Center Inter-American Relations. CLUB AFFIL University Club; New York Yacht Club; River Club; Harvard Club; The Links Club; Century Club.

David Rockefeller, Jr.: trustee B New York, NY 1941. ED Harvard University AB (1963); Harvard University JD (1966). PRIM CORP EMPL vice chairman: Rockefeller Family & Associates. NONPR AFFIL member: Council on Foreign Relations; vice chairman: National Park Foundation; director: Asian Cultural Council.

Richard Gilder Rockefeller: advisory trustee B 1949. ED Harvard University (1971); Harvard University EdM (1973); Harvard University MD (1979). PRIM CORP EMPL physician: Clinical Faculty.

Steven Clark Rockefeller: chairman, trustee B 1936. ED Princeton University AB (1958); Union Theological Seminary MDiv (1963); Columbia University PhD (1973). NONPR AFFIL director: Asian Cultural Council.

Benjamin R. Shute, Jr.: secretary ED Harvard University MA; Harvard University BA (1959). NONPR AFFIL trustee: Trinity School; trustee: William Caspar Graustein Membership Fund; board of advisors: New York Law School National Center on Philanthropy and the Law; chairman, governing council: Rockefeller Archive Center; trustee: The Interchurch Center; director: National Council of Nonprofit Associations; director: Independent Sector. CLUB AFFIL Cosmopolitan Club.

Edmond D. Villani: trustee B 1947. ED Georgetown University BA (1968); University of Pennsylvania PhD (1973). PRIM CORP EMPL president: Scudder Kemper Investments. NONPR AFFIL chairman board of directors: Georgetown University.

Boris A. Wessely: treasurer ED San Diego State University BA. NONPR AFFIL advisory board: Investment Management Institute; finance committee: Trust for Civil Society in Central & Eastern Europe.

Frank G. Wisner: trustee ED Princeton University BA. NONPR AFFIL director: Refugees' International; director: U.S. Bangladesh Council; director: Business Council on International Understanding; director: Institute for the Study of Diplomacy; director: American University of Beirut; director: American University of Cairo; vice chairman: American International Group; director: American School of Tangiers.

Tadataka Yamada, MD: trustee B Tokyo, Japan 1945. ED Stanford University BA; New York University School Medicine MD (1971). PRIM NONPR EMPL councillor: Association American Physicians. CORP AFFIL director: diaDexus Inc.; director, executive director, chairman research & development: GlaxoSmithKline. NONPR AFFIL councillor: Association of American Physicians; member: Institute of Medicine; member, past president: American Gastroenterological Association; member: American Society Clinical Investigation; member: American Academy of Arts & Sciences; master: American College Physicians.

Grants Analysis

Disclosure Period: calendar year ending 2002
Total Grants: $22,950,390*
Number of Grants: 500 (approx)
Average Grant: $45,901
Highest Grant: $500,000
Typical Range: $20,000 to $100,000
***Note:** Giving includes scholarships.

Recent Grants

Note: Grants derived from 2001 Form 990.
Library-Related
250,000	Pierpont Morgan Library, New York, NY -- for endowment

General
500,000	Demos-A Network for Ideas and Actions, LTD, New York, NY -- for operating support
500,000	Museum of Modern Art, New York, NY -- for an endowment in the name of Charles E. Culpeper
400,000	Solar Development Foundation, Arlington, VA
300,000	Colonial Williamsburg Foundation, Williamsburg, VA -- for an endowment
300,000	Demos-A Network for Ideas and Actions, LTD, New York, NY
250,000	Forest Stewardship Council, Oaxaca, OX Mexico
250,000	Philanthropic Research, Inc., Williamsburg, VA -- to support its GuideStar web site
225,000	Cornerstone Theater Company, Los Angeles, CA -- for endowment
200,000	Asian Cultural Council, New York, NY -- to the organization's unrestricted grants program in 2001
200,000	Ecotrust Canada, Vancouver, BC Canada -- to its efforts to create a conservation economy along the British Columbia coast

WINTHROP ROCKEFELLER FOUNDATION

Giving Contact

Dr. Sybil J. Hampton, President
308 East Eighth Street
Little Rock, AR 72202-3999
Phone: (501)376-6854
Fax: (501)374-4797
E-mail: webfeedback@wrfoundation.org
Web: http://www.wrockefellerfoundation.org

Description

Founded: 1973
EIN: 710285871
Organization Type: General Purpose Foundation
Giving Locations: AR
Grant Types: General Support, Seed Money.
Note: Foundation also provides grants for organizational development.

Donor Information

Founder: The Winthrop Rockefeller Foundation is a successor to the Rockwin Fund, which was established by Winthrop Rockefeller to support his charitable interests during his lifetime. Upon his death in 1973, Mr. Rockefeller bequeathed money to a charitable trust to be used for innovative purposes, and a foundation was established shortly thereafter.

Winthrop Rockefeller was governor of Arkansas from 1966 to 1970 and a grandson of John D. Rockefeller. He was Arkansas's first Republican governor since the Reconstruction, as well as a successful cattle rancher and businessman. He was dedicated to improving educational and economic opportunities in Arkansas, and to improving relations among races.

Financial Summary

Total Giving: $6,376,015 (2003); $8,711,335 (2002)
Giving Analysis: Giving for 2002 includes: foundation scholarships ($35,000)
Assets: $134,196,832 (2003); $118,599,874 (2002)
Gifts Received: $2,520,125 (2003); $2,073,625 (2002); $690,000 (2000). Note: Contributions were

received from a trust established under the will of Winthrop Rockefeller.

Typical Recipients

Arts & Humanities: Arts Associations & Councils, Arts Centers, Arts Funds, Dance, Film & Video, Historic Preservation, History & Archaeology, Libraries, Museums/Galleries, Music, Performing Arts, Public Broadcasting, Theater

Civic & Public Affairs: African American Affairs, Business/Free Enterprise, Clubs, Community Foundations, Economic Development, Economic Policy, Employment/Job Training, Civic & Public Affairs-General, Housing, Law & Justice, Legal Aid, Minority Business, Municipalities/Towns, Nonprofit Management, Philanthropic Organizations, Professional & Trade Associations, Public Policy, Rural Affairs, Urban & Community Affairs, Women's Affairs

Education: Agricultural Education, Arts/Humanities Education, Business Education, Colleges & Universities, Community & Junior Colleges, Education Associations, Education Funds, Education Reform, Elementary Education (Private), Engineering/Technological Education, Faculty Development, Education-General, International Studies, Legal Education, Literacy, Medical Education, Minority Education, Preschool Education, Public Education (Precollege), School Volunteerism, Science/Mathematics Education, Secondary Education (Private), Special Education, Student Aid, Vocational & Technical Education

Environment: Environment-General, Protection, Resource Conservation

Health: AIDS/HIV

International: Health Care/Hospitals

Religion: Ministries, Religious Welfare

Science: Science Museums, Scientific Centers & Institutes, Scientific Organizations

Social Services: At-Risk Youth, Camps, Child Welfare, Community Centers, Community Service Organizations, Family Services, Food/Clothing Distribution, People with Disabilities, Scouts, Senior Services, United Funds/United Ways, Volunteer Services, YMCA/YWCA/YMHA/YWHA, Youth Organizations

Application Procedures

Initial Contact: See foundation website for application details, then send a two- to three-page concept paper plus information form.
Deadlines: None.

Restrictions

The foundation generally does not fund capital expenditures, endowments, scholarships, fellowships, annual or general fund drives, projects with an impact outside of Arkansas, most types of research, travel, individuals, projects completed prior to application, project deficits, or normal operating costs. The foundation only funds organizations operating in Arkansas.

Additional Information

Grantee must use funds in accordance with proposal. The foundation may withhold payments if it is not satisfied with a grantee's performance.
The foundation, in cooperation with the Shorebank Corporation of Chicago, has invested several million dollars in the Southern Development Bancorporation to provide financial and technical assistance through affiliated ventures addressing rural economic development.
Publications: Annual Report; Guidelines

Foundation Officials

Ivye L. Allen: director
Kay Kelley Arnold: director
Overtis Hicks Brantley: director
Ralph D. Christy: director
Mark C. Doramus: director
Greg Hartz: director
J. Michael Jones: director

Al Lopez: director
Bob J. Nash: director
Daniel V. Rainey: director
Winthrop Paul Rockefeller: vchairman, director B New York, NY 1948. ED Texas Christian University (1974). PRIM CORP EMPL chief executive officer: Winrock Farms. CORP AFFIL director: Arrow Automotive Industries; director, stockholder: Searock Inc.
Mary Sanchez: director
Ruby Takanishi: director
Lori Villarosa: director

Grants Analysis

Disclosure Period: calendar year ending 2003
Total Grants: $6,376,015
Number of Grants: 67
Average Grant: $66,423*
Highest Grant: $804,568
Lowest Grant: $6,400
Typical Range: $25,000 to $100,000
Note: Average grant figure excludes three highest grants ($2,124,959).

Recent Grants

Note: Grants derived from 2003 Form 990.
Library-Related
171,537   Central Arkansas Library System, Little Rock, AR -- toward development of on-line Encyclopedia of Arkansas History and Culture
General
804,568   Yale University, New Haven, CT -- funding to strengthen and expand the School of the 21st Century model to schools
725,751   University of Arkansas Foundation, Little Rock, AR -- funding to support implementation of a project
594,640   Japanese American National Museum, Los Angeles, CA -- support for implementation of exhibit
316,924   University of Arkansas Foundation, Fayetteville, AR -- toward production of video documentary
218,996   Helping Individuals Receive Employment Inc. (H.I.R.E.), Little Rock, AR -- funding to support and document outcomes of workforce initiatives for disabled people
205,510   Capital Resource Corporation, Little Rock, AR -- toward policy options for creation and growth of knowledge-based industry
200,000   Enterprise Corporation for the Delta, Jackson, MS -- funding for group's expansion efforts
172,900   Arkansas Arts Center Foundation, Little Rock, AR
156,250   Arkansas Science and Technology Authority, Little Rock, AR -- toward project to build policy infrastructure for entrepreneurial growth
154,250   Arkansas Museum of Discovery, Little Rock, AR -- funding for planning and youth programs

DAVID ROCKEFELLER FUND

Giving Contact

Marnie Pillsbury, Executive Director
30 Rockefeller Plz., Rm. 5600
New York, NY 10112
Phone: (212)649-5600

Description

Founded: 1989
EIN: 133533359
Organization Type: Private Foundation

Giving Locations: ME: Seal Harbor; NY: Pocantico
Grant Types: General Support.

Donor Information

Founder: Established in 1989 by David Rockefeller, Jr.

Financial Summary

Total Giving: $659,100 (2002); $2,931,457 (2001)
Giving Analysis: Giving for 2002 includes: foundation matching gifts ($250)
Assets: $7,316,060 (2002); $7,980,949 (2001)
Gifts Received: $558,982 (2002); $1,215,000 (2000); $742,786 (1998). Note: In 1998, 2000, and 2002, contributions were received from David Rockefeller.

Typical Recipients

Arts & Humanities: Arts Associations & Councils, Ethnic & Folk Arts, Arts & Humanities-General, Historic Preservation, History & Archaeology, Libraries, Museums/Galleries, Music, Public Broadcasting, Theater

Civic & Public Affairs: Botanical Gardens/Parks, Economic Development, Civic & Public Affairs-General, Housing, Law & Justice, Municipalities/Towns, Parades/Festivals, Philanthropic Organizations, Safety, Urban & Community Affairs, Women's Affairs

Education: Arts/Humanities Education, Colleges & Universities, Education-General, Leadership Training, Private Education (Precollege), Public Education (Precollege), Science/Mathematics Education

Environment: Air/Water Quality, Environment-General, Resource Conservation

Health: Children's Health/Hospitals, Clinics/Medical Centers, Hospitals, Nursing Services, Prenatal Health Issues, Public Health

Religion: Churches, Missionary Activities (Domestic), Religious Welfare

Science: Science Museums, Scientific Labs

Social Services: Child Welfare, Community Service Organizations, Counseling, Day Care, Delinquency & Criminal Rehabilitation, Family Planning, Family Services, Food/Clothing Distribution, Homes, Recreation & Athletics, Scouts, United Funds/United Ways, YMCA/YWCA/YMHA/YWHA, Youth Organizations

Application Procedures

Initial Contact: The foundation has no formal grant application procedure or application form.
Deadlines: None.
Decision Notification: The Fund does not notify organizations requesting grants of its decision unless a grant is awarded.

Restrictions

Does not support individuals or organizations outside operating areas. Foundation only supports tax-exempt organizations which are located in and contribute to Seal Harbor, Maine, and the Counties of Westchester and Columbia in New York.

Foundation Officials

Colin G. Cambell: director
Christopher J. Kennan: director
Marnie S. Pillsbury: executive director
Richard E. Salomon: secretary, treasurer, director

Grants Analysis

Disclosure Period: calendar year ending 2002
Total Grants: $658,850*
Number of Grants: 125
Average Grant: $5,271
Highest Grant: $30,000
Lowest Grant: $500
Typical Range: $1,000 to $10,000
Note: Giving excludes matching gifts.

Recent Grants

Note: Grants derived from 2001 Form 990.

General

2,212,657	Stone Barns Restoration Corporation, New York, NY
50,000	College of the Atlantic, Bar Harbor, ME
25,000	Cases, New York, NY
25,000	Historic Hudson Valley, Tarrytown, NY
25,000	Lower Manhattan Cultural Council, Manhattan, NY
25,000	Northwest Atlantic Marine Alliance, Saco, ME
25,000	Osborne Association, New York, NY
25,000	Women's Prison Association and Home, Inc., New York, NY
20,000	Conservation International, Washington, DC
20,000	Correctional Association of New York, New York, NY

ROCKWELL AUTOMATION INC.

Company Headquarters

777 E. Wisconsin Avenue, Suite 1400
Milwaukee, WI 53202
Web: http://www.rockwellautomation.com

Company Description

Ticker: ROK
Exchange: NYSE
Former Name: Rockwell International Corp..
Revenue: US$4.516 billion (2004)
Profit: US$414.9 million (2004)
Employees: 21500 (2003)
Fortune Rank: 429, per FORTUNE Magazine's list of 500 Largest U.S. Corporations (2004).
SIC(s): 3465 Automotive Stampings, 3493 Steel Springs Except Wire, 3555 Printing Trades Machinery, 3679 Electronic Components Nec.

Operating Locations

Rockwell International Corp. (CA--Costa Mesa, Downey, Hayward, Newbury Park, Pleasanton, Seal Beach; CO--Fort Carson; FL--Melbourne; GA--Tucker; IL--Decorra; IA--Cedar Rapids, Fairfield; KY--Florence, Frankfort, Hopkinsville; LA--Shreveport; MA--Westford; MI--Brighton, Southfield; MO--St. Ann; NE--Bellevue; NJ--Lebanon; NC--Maxton; OH--Heath; OK--McAlester, Oklahoma City; PA--Pittsburgh; SC--York; TN--Gordonsville, Morristown; TX--El Paso, Houston; VA--Arlington, Vienna; WA--Kirkland, Renton; WI--Oshkosh)

Nonmonetary Support

Type: Cause-related Marketing & Promotion; Donated Equipment; Donated Products; In-kind Services; Loaned Employees
Note: Company provides nonmonetary support.

Rockwell International Corp. Trust

Giving Contact

Christine G. Rodriguez
1201 South Second Street
Milwaukee, WI 53204
Phone: (414)212-5258
Web: http://www.rockwellautomation.com/about_us/citizenship.html

Description

EIN: 251072431
Organization Type: Corporate Foundation
Giving Locations: headquarters and operating communities; nationally to education.
Grant Types: Capital, Employee Matching Gifts, General Support, Multiyear/Continuing Support, Scholarship.
Note: Employee matching gift ratio: 1 to 1 to accredited colleges and accredited public and private elementary and high schools. Company will match gifts of more than $25 to a maximum of $10,000 per employee annually.

Financial Summary

Total Giving: $3,546,577 (fiscal year ending September 30, 2003); $3,231,256 (fiscal 2002); $5,560,644 (fiscal 2001). Note: Contributes through corporate direct giving program and foundation.
Giving Analysis: Giving for fiscal 2001 includes: foundation scholarships ($78,774); foundation matching gifts ($602,220); foundation grants to United Way ($1,178,500); foundation ($4,382,144)
Assets: $3,459,799 (fiscal 2003); $6,879,853 (fiscal 2002); $15,386,346 (fiscal 2001)
Gifts Received: $10,000,000 (fiscal 2000); $10,000,000 (fiscal 1999); $8,500,000 (fiscal 1994). Note: Contributions received from Rockwell International Corporation.

Typical Recipients

Arts & Humanities: Arts Associations & Councils, Arts Centers, Arts Festivals, Arts Funds, Arts Institutes, Community Arts, Dance, Arts & Humanities-General, Historic Preservation, History & Archaeology, Libraries, Museums/Galleries, Music, Opera, Performing Arts, Public Broadcasting, Theater
Civic & Public Affairs: African American Affairs, Asian American Affairs, Business/Free Enterprise, Chambers of Commerce, Civil Rights, Community Foundations, Economic Development, Economic Policy, Employment/Job Training, Civic & Public Affairs-General, Hispanic Affairs, Housing, Law & Justice, Legal Aid, Minority Business, Municipalities/Towns, Nonprofit Management, Professional & Trade Associations, Public Policy, Safety, Urban & Community Affairs, Women's Affairs, Zoos/Aquariums
Education: Afterschool/Enrichment Programs, Business Education, Colleges & Universities, Community & Junior Colleges, Continuing Education, Economic Education, Education Associations, Education Funds, Education Reform, Engineering/Technological Education, Faculty Development, Education-General, Gifted & Talented Programs, International Studies, Literacy, Medical Education, Minority Education, Private Education (Precollege), Public Education (Precollege), Science/Mathematics Education, Special Education, Student Aid, Vocational & Technical Education
Environment: Environment-General, Protection, Resource Conservation
Health: Cancer, Children's Health/Hospitals, Emergency/Ambulance Services, Health Policy/Cost Containment, Health Funds, Health Organizations, Hospices, Hospitals, Medical Rehabilitation, Mental Health, Public Health, Single-Disease Health Associations
International: Health Care/Hospitals, International Affairs, International Peace & Security Issues, International Relations
Religion: Bible Study/Translation, Churches, Religious Welfare
Science: Science-General, Science Exhibits & Fairs, Science Museums, Scientific Centers & Institutes, Scientific Organizations
Social Services: Big Brothers/Big Sisters, Child Welfare, Community Centers, Community Service Organizations, Counseling, Delinquency & Criminal Rehabilitation, Domestic Violence, Emergency Relief, Family Services, People with Disabilities, Recreation & Athletics, Scouts, Shelters/Homelessness, Substance Abuse, United Funds/United Ways, Volunteer Services, YMCA/YWCA/YMHA/YWHA, Youth Organizations

Application Procedures

Initial Contact: Send a brief letter or proposal.
Application Requirements: Information should include a description of organization, amount requested, purpose of funds sought, recently audited financial statement, proof of tax-exempt status, list of other funding sources, and any other pertinent information.
Deadlines: None.
Decision Notification: Within 90 days of receipt of proposal.
Notes: Organizations providing services in communities with Rockwell facilities should contact the local Community Affairs administrator to start a grant request. "The Rockwell International Corporation Trust has identified two distinct funding priorities, and special consideration will be given to proposals that integrate these issues: 1) Education and youth development, with emphasis in math, science, and engineering; and 2) Culture and the arts, with emphasis on youth educational programs." Rockwell International Corporation Trust Guidelines. Trust also gives to health, social services, and civic organizations and gives special consideration to organizations where employees volunteer. The majority of giving to these organizations is through United Way.

Restrictions

Does not support individuals, fraternal organizations, religious organizations for sectarian purposes, general endowments, deficit reduction, federated campaigns, organizations or projects outside the US, non tax-exempt organizations, or private foundations.

Corporate Officials

W. Michael Barnes: senior vice president finance & planning, chief financial officer B 1938. ED Texas A&M University MA; Texas A&M University BA; Texas A&M University PhD (1968). PRIM CORP EMPL senior vice president finance & planning, chief financial officer: Rockwell International Corp. NONPR AFFIL member: Council Financial Executives.
Donald Ray Beall: director, executive committee B Beaumont, CA 1938. ED University of California, Los Angeles; San Jose State University BS (1960); University of Pittsburgh MBA (1961). PRIM CORP EMPL chairman, executive committee: Rockwell Collins, Inc. ADD CORP EMPL president: Collins International Service Corp. CORP AFFIL chairman: Procter & Gamble Co.; chairman: Times Mirror Co.; director: Conexant Systems Inc.; director: Meritor Automotive Inc.; director: BP Amoco Corp. NONPR AFFIL fellow: American Institute Aeronautics & Astronautics; fellow: Society Manufacturing Engineers.
William Joseph Calise, Jr.: senior vice president, secretary, general counsel B New York, NY 1938. ED Bucknell University BA (1960); Columbia University JD (1963); Columbia University MBA (1963). PRIM CORP EMPL senior vice president, secretary, general counsel: Rockwell Automation, Inc.. NONPR AFFIL member: Association Bar New York City. CLUB AFFIL Rockefeller Center Club; Duquesne Club.
Donald H. Davis, Jr.: president, chief executive officer, chairman B 1939. ED Texas A&M University BSME (1962); Texas A&M University MBA (1963). PRIM CORP EMPL president, chief executive officer, chairman: Rockwell International Corp. CORP AFFIL director: Ingram Micro Inc.
Joseph H. Garrett, Jr.: vice president government & international operations PRIM CORP EMPL vice president government & international operations: Rockwell International Corp.

Foundation Officials

W. Michael Barnes: member trust committee (see above)
Donald Ray Beall: president (see above)
John A. Coleman: assistant secretary
Donald H. Davis, Jr.: chairman trust committee (see above)

Grants Analysis

Disclosure Period: fiscal year ending September 30, 2003
Total Grants: $2,324,600*

Number of Grants: 137
Average Grant: $16,968
Highest Grant: $200,000
Lowest Grant: $1,000
Typical Range: $1,000 to $25,000 and $50,000 to $300,000
***Note:** Giving excludes matching gifts, scholarships, and United Way.

Recent Grants
Note: Grants derived from fiscal 2003 Form 990.
Library-Related
| 25,000 | Milwaukee Public Library Foundation, Milwaukee, WI |

General
414,162	United Way of Greater Milwaukee Inc., Milwaukee, WI
230,000	United Way of the Upper Valley, Lebanon, NH
200,000	Clemson University Foundation, Clemson, SC
200,000	Museum of Science and Industry, Chicago, IL
166,000	Texas A&M University Foundation, College Station, TX
135,000	United Performing Arts Fund, Milwaukee, WI
100,000	Lynde and Harry Bradley Technology Academy, Milwaukee, WI
100,000	UCLA Foundation Charitable Fund, Los Angeles, CA
60,000	Boys & Girls Club of Greater Milwaukee Inc., Milwaukee, WI
60,000	Milwaukee County Historical Society, Milwaukee, WI

ROCKWELL FUND, INC.

Giving Contact
R. Terry Bell, President
Rockwell Fund, Inc.
1330 Post Oak Boulevard, Suite 1825
Houston, TX 77056
Phone: (713)629-9022
Fax: (713)629-7702
Web: http://www.rockfund.org

Description
Founded: 1931
EIN: 746040258
Organization Type: General Purpose Foundation
Giving Locations: TX: Houston limited giving outside of the Houston area
Grant Types: Capital, Endowment, Fellowship, General Support, Matching, Scholarship.
Note: The fund also provides equipment and technical support.

Donor Information
Founder: Established in 1931 by members of the James M. Rockwell family, Rockwell Brothers & Company, and the Rockwell Lumber Company.

Financial Summary
Total Giving: $4,718,653 (2003); $5,019,675 (2002); $5,755,860 (2001)
Giving Analysis: Giving for 2002 includes: foundation grants to United Way ($55,000) 2001: foundation scholarships ($87,500)
Assets: $114,424,446 (2003); $102,177,274 (2002); $117,251,750 (2001)
Gifts Received: $1,000 (2002). Note: In 2002, contributions were received from Foundation Properties, Inc.

Typical Recipients
Arts & Humanities: Arts Associations & Councils, Arts Institutes, Arts Outreach, Ballet, Dance, Historic Preservation, History & Archaeology, Libraries, Museums/Galleries, Music, Opera, Performing Arts, Public Broadcasting, Theater
Civic & Public Affairs: African American Affairs, Botanical Gardens/Parks, Community Foundations, Economic Development, Employment/Job Training, Hispanic Affairs, Housing, Legal Aid, Urban & Community Affairs, Women's Affairs, Zoos/Aquariums
Education: Agricultural Education, Arts/Humanities Education, Business Education, Colleges & Universities, Community & Junior Colleges, Education Associations, Education Reform, Elementary Education (Private), Engineering/Technological Education, Environmental Education, Faculty Development, Education-General, Health & Physical Education, Legal Education, Literacy, Medical Education, Preschool Education, Private Education (Precollege), Religious Education, School Volunteerism, Science/Mathematics Education, Secondary Education (Private), Special Education, Student Aid
Environment: Environment-General, Resource Conservation
Health: Adolescent Health Issues, AIDS/HIV, Cancer, Children's Health/Hospitals, Clinics/Medical Centers, Emergency/Ambulance Services, Eyes/Blindness, Health Organizations, Heart, Hospices, Hospitals, Medical Rehabilitation, Medical Research, Mental Health, Nursing Services, Prenatal Health Issues, Public Health, Single-Disease Health Associations, Speech & Hearing, Transplant Networks/Donor Banks
Religion: Churches, Ministries, Religious Organizations, Religious Welfare
Science: Science Exhibits & Fairs, Science Museums
Social Services: Animal Protection, At-Risk Youth, Big Brothers/Big Sisters, Camps, Child Abuse, Child Welfare, Community Centers, Community Service Organizations, Counseling, Day Care, Delinquency & Criminal Rehabilitation, Emergency Relief, Family Planning, Family Services, Food/Clothing Distribution, Homes, People with Disabilities, Recreation & Athletics, Scouts, Senior Services, Shelters/Homelessness, Substance Abuse, United Funds/United Ways, Volunteer Services, YMCA/YWCA/YMHA/YWHA, Youth Organizations

Application Procedures
Initial Contact: Applicants should contact the fund to request a copy of its application form and guidelines.
Application Requirements: One unbound copy of the proposal should be submitted and should include the following: a one-page cover letter written on the organization's letterhead, and signed by the president or chairman of the board; grant application form; copy of IRS determination letter; financial statement of past fiscal year, audited, if available; complete copy of IRS 990 tax return most recently submitted; list of current officers and board members; copies of either a small general information brochure or a one-page general information fact sheet--not to be substituted with an annual report; and a proposal narrative limited to no more than five pages. This needs to be concise and to the point, and should consist of the following: the organization's mission statement and a brief history; a discussion on the use of the proposed grant; specific amount requested; and the projected timetable for the use of the grant. If the funds are for a project, the total cost of the project should be given as well as the total raised and pledged so far, and the project budget including income and expenses. Graphs, floor plans, photographs, maps or diagrams are included in the five page limit. After reviewing the proposal, if additional materials are needed, the staff will then make a request.
Deadlines: February 1, May 1, August 1, and November 1.
Review Process: The staff reviews proposals to determine whether they fall within the Fund's current areas of interest and funding priorities. Written notification is sent within three weeks after a quarterly meeting (generally held in January, April, July, and October) to advise applicants of the decisions of the trustees.
Notes: Omission of any required information, as outlined in the guideline and application form, or receipt after deadline date, will result in delay of consideration or rejection of the application.

Restrictions
The Fund does not make grants or loans to individuals, for trips, dinners, or special events, or for medical research. The Fund does not participate in feasibility studies or fundraising benefits, nor does it respond to mass appeal solicitations.

Additional Information
Publications: Application Form; Guidelines; Annual Report

Foundation Officials
R. Terry Bell: president, trustee B 1945. PRIM CORP EMPL partner: Caolo & Bell.
Bennie Green: treasurer, trustee
Mary Jo Loyd: corp secretary, trustee
Helen N. Sterling: trustee emerita B 1906.

Grants Analysis
Disclosure Period: calendar year ending 2003
Total Grants: $4,718,653*
Number of Grants: 168
Average Grant: $28,087
Highest Grant: $117,134
Lowest Grant: $399
Typical Range: $10,000 to $50,000
***Note:** Giving includes scholarships.

Recent Grants
Note: Grants derived from 2002 Form 990.
General
125,000	South Texas College of Law, Houston, TX -- expansion of general civic to include pro bono legal assistance services
100,000	Project Grad, Houston, TX -- operating support
100,000	Southern Methodist University, Dallas, TX -- endowment
100,000	University of Texas Health Science Center Houston, Houston, TX -- endowed chair
100,000	William Marsh Rice University, Houston, TX -- postdoctoral fellowship endowment
96,734	St. Agnes Academy, Houston, TX -- purchase of two Collins Bus Corporation
85,000	Texas Tech University Foundation, Lubbock, TX -- endowed professorship
80,000	Brookwood Community, Brookshire, TX -- Continuing Care Facility Program
80,000	Teach for America, Houston, TX -- operating support
75,000	Seniors Place, Inc., Houston, TX -- operating support

FRED M. RODDY FOUNDATION

Giving Contact
Augusta Haydock
c/o Fleet National Bank
100 Federal St.
Boston, MA 02110
Phone: (617)434-4644

Alternate Contact
Phone: (401)278-8700

Description
Founded: 1969
EIN: 056037528

Organization Type: Private Foundation
Giving Locations: RI: nationally.
Grant Types: General Support.

Donor Information

Founder: the late Fred M. Roddy

Financial Summary

Total Giving: $683,499 (2004)
Giving Analysis: Giving for 2004 includes: foundation scholarships ($104,500)
Assets: $15,750,014 (2004)

Typical Recipients

Arts & Humanities: Libraries
Civic & Public Affairs: Civic & Public Affairs-General, Hispanic Affairs, Housing, Urban & Community Affairs
Education: Afterschool/Enrichment Programs, Colleges & Universities, Elementary Education (Private), Education-General, Medical Education, Minority Education, Private Education (Precollege), Secondary Education (Private), Student Aid
Health: AIDS/HIV, Cancer, Children's Health/Hospitals, Clinics/Medical Centers, Emergency/Ambulance Services, Health Organizations, Heart, Hospitals, Long-Term Care, Medical Research, Nursing Services, Prenatal Health Issues
Religion: Religious Organizations, Religious Welfare
Social Services: At-Risk Youth, Big Brothers/Big Sisters, Camps, Family Services, Food/Clothing Distribution, People with Disabilities, Senior Services, YMCA/YWCA/YMHA/YWHA, Youth Organizations

Application Procedures

Initial Contact: Send a written proposal and an annual report.
Deadlines: None.

Additional Information

Trust(s): Fleet National Bank NA

Foundation Officials

Shawn P. Buckless: clerk
Mrs. Lee Kintzel: co-trustee
Richard B. Lafleur: treasurer
David I. McIntyre: director

Grants Analysis

Disclosure Period: calendar year ending 2004
Total Grants: $578,999*
Number of Grants: 27
Average Grant: $17,462*
Highest Grant: $125,000
Typical Range: $10,000 to $30,000
***Note:** Giving excludes scholarships. Average grant figure excludes highest grant.

Recent Grants

Note: Grants derived from 2000 Form 990.

General

50,000	Lifespan, Rochester, NY
50,000	Progreso Latino, Central Falls, RI
50,000	University of Tennessee, Knoxville, TN
50,000	University of Tennessee, Knoxville, TN
40,000	Brown University, Providence, RI
40,000	Providence College, Providence, RI
32,243	Bradley Hospital Foundation, Providence, RI
30,200	Camp Twin Lakes, Atlanta, GA
29,000	Family Service, Providence, RI
25,000	University of Tennessee, Knoxville, TN

ROGERS FAMILY FOUNDATION

Giving Contact

Irving E. Rogers, III, Trustee
PO Box 100
Lawrence, MA 01842
Phone: (978)946-2000

Description

Founded: 1957
EIN: 046063152
Organization Type: Private Foundation
Giving Locations: MA: the greater Merrimack Valley, MA area
Grant Types: General Support.

Donor Information

Founder: Irving E. Rogers, Eagle-Tribune Publishing Co., Martha B. Rogers

Financial Summary

Gifts Received: $665,354 (2000); $250,705 (1996); $238,632 (1995). Note: In 2000, contributions were received from Andover Publishing Co. ($38,000), Eagle-Tribune Publishing Co. ($500,000), Eagle-Tribune Realty Trust ($100,000), Rogers Investment Corp ($9,000), Consolidated Press Inc. ($15,000) and Derry Publishing Co. ($3,354). In 1996, contributions were received from Andover Publishing Co. ($23,000), Eagle-Tribune Publishing Co. ($197,250), Eagle-Tribune Realty Trust ($10,000), Rogers Investment Corp ($3,400), and Derry Publishing Co. ($17,055).

Typical Recipients

Arts & Humanities: Arts Festivals, Community Arts, Ethnic & Folk Arts, Historic Preservation, History & Archaeology, Libraries, Museums/Galleries, Music, Theater
Civic & Public Affairs: Community Foundations, Civic & Public Affairs-General, Housing, Parades/Festivals, Urban & Community Affairs
Education: Business Education, Colleges & Universities, Community & Junior Colleges, Education-General, Legal Education, Minority Education, Private Education (Precollege), Secondary Education (Private), Student Aid
Environment: Watershed
Health: Clinics/Medical Centers, Emergency/Ambulance Services, Home-Care Services, Hospitals, Medical Rehabilitation, Medical Research, Respiratory
Religion: Churches, Religion-General, Ministries, Religious Organizations, Religious Welfare, Synagogues/Temples
Science: Science Museums
Social Services: Big Brothers/Big Sisters, Child Welfare, Community Centers, Community Service Organizations, Day Care, Family Services, Homes, People with Disabilities, Recreation & Athletics, Senior Services, Shelters/Homelessness, United Funds/United Ways, YMCA/YWCA/YMHA/YWHA, Youth Organizations

Application Procedures

Initial Contact: The foundation has no formal grant application procedure or application form. Submit a brief outline of the proposed project and budget.
Deadlines: None.

Restrictions

Does not support individuals.

Foundation Officials

Irving E. Rogers, III: trustee
Irving E. Rogers, Jr.: trustee PRIM CORP EMPL president, publisher, treasurer, general manager: Eagle-Tribune Publishing Co.
Jacqueline H. Rogers: trustee

Stephen Hitchcock Rogers: trustee B Flushing, NY 1930. ED Princeton University BA (1952); Columbia University MA (1956); Harvard University MDA (1962).

Grants Analysis

Disclosure Period: calendar year ending 2000
Total Grants: $905,887*
Number of Grants: 72
Average Grant: $6,421*
Highest Grant: $450,000
Typical Range: $1,000 to $10,000
***Note:** Giving excludes United Way. Average grant amount excludes highest grant.

Recent Grants

Note: Grants derived from 2001 Form 990.

General

340,000	Merrimack College, North Andover, MA
65,700	Free Christian Church, Andover, MA
50,000	Free Christian Church, Andover, MA
50,000	Holy Family Hospital, Methuen, MA
50,000	UNH Foundation, Inc., Durham, NH
45,000	Merrimack Valley United Way, Lawrence, MA
25,000	Andover School of Montessori, Andover, MA
25,000	Family Service, Lawrence, MA
25,000	Free Christian Church, Andover, MA
25,000	Holy Family Hospital, Methuen, MA

RUSSELL HILL ROGERS FUND FOR THE ARTS

Giving Contact

Jean Winchell, Managing Trustee
4040 Broadway, Suite 605
San Antonio, TX 78209
Phone: (210)826-8781

Description

Founded: 1986
EIN: 742403914
Organization Type: Private Foundation
Giving Locations: TX: Bexar County
Grant Types: General Support.

Financial Summary

Total Giving: $836,860 (2001)
Assets: $14,672,580 (2001)

Typical Recipients

Arts & Humanities: Arts Centers, Ballet, Community Arts, Dance, Ethnic & Folk Arts, Arts & Humanities-General, Libraries, Museums/Galleries, Music, Opera, Performing Arts, Public Broadcasting, Theater
Education: Arts/Humanities Education
International: Foreign Arts Organizations
Religion: Jewish Causes
Social Services: Community Centers

Application Procedures

Initial Contact: The foundation has no formal grant application procedure or application form.
Deadlines: None.

Restrictions

Grants are not made to individuals.

Additional Information

Supports creative and performing arts in the San Antonio metropolitan area.
Trust(s): Bank of America, N.A.

Foundation Officials

Frank P. Christian: mng trustee
Barbara S. Condos: mng trustee

Robert R. Linde: mng trustee
Allan G. Paterson, Jr.: mng trustee
Jean Rogers Winchell: mng trustee

Grants Analysis

Disclosure Period: calendar year ending 2001
Total Grants: $836,860
Number of Grants: 24
Average Grant: $23,619*
Highest Grant: $170,000
Typical Range: $15,000 to $50,000
*Note: Average grant figure excludes two highest grants ($270,000).

Recent Grants

Note: Grants derived from 2001 Form 990.
Library-Related
170,000	San Antonio Public Library Foundation, San Antonio, TX -- promotion of the arts

General
100,000	McNay Art Museum, San Antonio, TX -- promotion of the arts
85,000	Arts San Antonio, San Antonio, TX -- promotion of the arts
85,000	Lyric Opera of San Antonio, San Antonio, TX -- promotion of the arts
83,500	San Antonio Symphony, San Antonio, TX -- promotion of the arts
81,235	San Pedro Playhouse, San Antonio, TX -- promotion of the arts
45,000	KLRN - Public Television, San Antonio, TX -- promotion of the arts
25,000	San Antonio Chamber Music Society, San Antonio, TX -- promotion of the arts
20,000	Firelight Players, San Antonio, TX -- promotion of the arts
20,000	Tuesday Musical Club - Artist Series, San Antonio, TX -- promotion of the arts
15,000	Cactus Pear Music Festival, San Antonio, TX -- promotion of the arts

ROGOW BIRKEN FOUNDATION

Giving Contact

Gary Greenberg, President
c/o Birken Mfg.
3 Old Windsor Rd.
Bloomfield, CT 06002
Phone: (860)242-2211
Fax: (860)242-2749

Description

Founded: 1981
EIN: 061051591
Organization Type: Private Foundation
Giving Locations: NY: New York
Grant Types: General Support.

Donor Information

Founder: Louis B. Rogow

Financial Summary

Total Giving: $433,291 (2003)
Giving Analysis: Giving for 2003 includes: foundation grants to United Way ($2,500); foundation scholarships ($148,291).
Assets: $8,449,199 (2003)
Gifts Received: $355,345 (2003); $1,540,554 (1994); $8,807,407 (1993). Note: In fiscal 2003, contributions were received from Helen Rogow Trust. In fiscal 1994, contributions were received from the estate of Louis B. Rogow.

Typical Recipients

Arts & Humanities: Libraries, Opera
Civic & Public Affairs: Civic & Public Affairs-

General
Education: Colleges & Universities, Education-General, Legal Education, Private Education (Precollege), Student Aid
Health: Arthritis, Cancer, Children's Health/Hospitals, Clinics/Medical Centers, Medical Research
International: Health Care/Hospitals, Missionary/Religious Activities
Religion: Jewish Causes, Religious Welfare
Social Services: Youth Organizations

Application Procedures

Initial Contact: The foundation requests applications be made in writing.
Deadlines: None.

Foundation Officials

Paul Bourdeau: secretary
Gary Greenberg: vice president
Sidney Greenberg: president
Bruce Rogow: executive vice president

Grants Analysis

Disclosure Period: calendar year ending 2003
Total Grants: $282,500*
Number of Grants: 67
Average Grant: $3,371*
Highest Grant: $60,000
Lowest Grant: $100
Typical Range: $1,000 to $5,000
*Note: Giving excludes scholarships; United Way. Average grant figure excludes highest grant.

Recent Grants

Note: Grants derived from 2003 Form 990.
Library-Related
25,000	Transylvania City Library Foundation

General
60,000	Federation
25,000	Nova Southeastern University Law Center, Ft. Lauderdale, FL
20,000	Community Children's Medical Center
20,000	Nova University Law School, Ft. Lauderdale, FL
15,000	Syracuse University, Syracuse, NY -- for scholarship
15,000	Syracuse University, Syracuse, NY -- for scholarship
13,680	Brownard and May School -- for scholarship
9,945	Yeshiva University, New York, NY -- for scholarship
9,000	College of Charleston, Charleston, SC -- for scholarship

FELIX AND ELIZABETH ROHATYN FOUNDATION

Giving Contact

Felix G. Rohatyn, President & Director
c/o Lazard, Freres & Co.
30 Rockefeller Plaza
New York, NY 10020
Phone: (212)750-0666

Description

Founded: 1968
EIN: 237015644
Organization Type: Private Foundation
Giving Locations: DC; NY: New York metropolitan area; TX; WY
Grant Types: Emergency, General Support, Multiyear/Continuing Support.

Donor Information

Founder: Felix G. Rohatyn

Financial Summary

Total Giving: $2,447,221 (2001)
Assets: $8,403,323 (2001)
Gifts Received: $1,000,000 (2001); $2,000,000 (2000); $2,000,000 (1999). Note: In 2001, contributions were received from Felix G. Rohatyn ($1,000,000). In 2000, contributions were received from Elizabeth F. Rohatyn. In 1999, contributions were received from Felix G. Rohatyn ($700,000) and Elizabeth F. Rohatyn ($1,300,000). In 1998, contributions were received from Felix G. Rohatyn ($967,112) and Elizabeth F. Rohatyn ($510,000).

Typical Recipients

Arts & Humanities: Arts Associations & Councils, Arts Centers, Arts Funds, Arts Outreach, Ballet, Community Arts, Dance, Historic Preservation, History & Archaeology, Libraries, Literary Arts, Museums/Galleries, Music, Opera, Public Broadcasting, Theater, Visual Arts
Civic & Public Affairs: Botanical Gardens/Parks, Civic & Public Affairs-General, Municipalities/Towns, Public Policy, Urban & Community Affairs, Women's Affairs
Education: Colleges & Universities, Continuing Education, Education Funds, Education Reform, Elementary Education (Private), Faculty Development, Education-General, International Exchange, Literacy, Medical Education, Minority Education, Private Education (Precollege), Public Education (Precollege), Secondary Education (Private), Special Education, Student Aid
Environment: Environment-General, Resource Conservation
Health: Cancer, Emergency/Ambulance Services, Eyes/Blindness, Hospitals, Medical Research, Single-Disease Health Associations, Transplant Networks/Donor Banks
International: Foreign Arts Organizations, Health Care/Hospitals, Human Rights, International Organizations, International Relations, International Relief Efforts, Missionary/Religious Activities
Religion: Churches, Jewish Causes, Religious Organizations, Religious Welfare
Science: Scientific Centers & Institutes
Social Services: Big Brothers/Big Sisters, Child Welfare, Community Centers, Community Service Organizations, Family Services, People with Disabilities, Senior Services, Shelters/Homelessness, Youth Organizations

Application Procedures

Initial Contact: Send a brief letter of inquiry.
Application Requirements: a description of organization.
Deadlines: None.

Foundation Officials

Vivien Stiles Duffy: executive director
Melvin L. Heinemen: secretary, treasurer, director
Elizabeth Rohatyn: vice president, director
Felix George Rohatyn: president, director B Vienna, Austria 1928. ED Middlebury College BS (1948). PRIM CORP EMPL partner: Lazard Freres & Co. CORP AFFIL director: General Instrument; director: Pfizer Inc.
Nicholas Rohatyn: secretary, treasurer, director

Grants Analysis

Disclosure Period: calendar year ending 2001
Total Grants: $2,447,221
Number of Grants: 132
Average Grant: $7,033*
Highest Grant: $700,000
Typical Range: $1,000 to $10,000
*Note: Average grant figure excludes five highest grants ($1,518,884).

Recent Grants

Note: Grants derived from 2001 Form 990.

Library-Related

100,000	New York Public Library, New York, NY
75,000	New York Public Library, New York, NY

General

700,000	Carnegie Hall Society, New York, NY
443,884	Teaching Matters, New York, NY
200,000	Memorial Sloan-Kettering Cancer Center, New York, NY
85,834	Lenox Hill Neighborhood House, New York, NY
50,000	Center for Strategic and International Studies, Washington, DC
50,000	Drawing Center, New York, NY
50,000	Nature Conservancy of Wyoming, Lander, WY
50,000	Progressive Policy Institute, Washington, DC
50,000	University of Texas at Dallas, Dallas, TX
40,000	American Jewish Historical Society, New York, NY

ROLLINS-LUETKEMEYER FOUNDATION

Giving Contact

Robert F. Wilson, Treasurer & Foundation Manager
105 W. Chesapeake Avenue
Suite 109
Towson, MD 21204-4710
Phone: (410)296-2948
Fax: (410)337-2682

Description

Founded: 1961
EIN: 526041536
Organization Type: Private Foundation
Giving Locations: MD: Baltimore metropolitan area
Grant Types: General Support.

Donor Information

Founder: the late Mary S. Rollins

Financial Summary

Total Giving: $3,098,182 (2001)
Assets: $62,125,046 (2001)
Gifts Received: $65,381 (2001); $180,097 (2000); $12,577,633 (1998). Note: In 2001 and 2000, contributions were received fromv John A. Luetkemeyer, Jr. In 1998, contributions were received from John A. Luetremeyer, Sr.($5,287,225); John A. Luetkemeyer, Jr. Charitable remainder trust ($4,284,440); estate of Anne A. Luetkemeyer ($3,005,968).

Typical Recipients

Arts & Humanities: Arts Centers, Arts Institutes, Community Arts, Arts & Humanities-General, History & Archaeology, Libraries, Museums/Galleries, Music, Theater
Civic & Public Affairs: Botanical Gardens/Parks, Community Foundations, Civic & Public Affairs-General, Housing, Law & Justice, Parades/Festivals, Safety, Urban & Community Affairs
Education: Colleges & Universities, Education Funds, Environmental Education, Education-General, Private Education (Precollege), Public Education (Precollege), Religious Education, Student Aid
Environment: Environment-General, Resource Conservation
Health: Clinics/Medical Centers, Emergency/Ambulance Services, Hospitals, Medical Research, Mental Health, Multiple Sclerosis, Preventive Medicine/Wellness Organizations
Religion: Churches, Jewish Causes, Seminaries
Science: Scientific Centers & Institutes
Social Services: Child Abuse, Community Service Organizations, Family Services, Food/Clothing Distribution, Homes, People with Disabilities, Recreation &

Athletics, Scouts, Special Olympics, United Funds/United Ways

Application Procedures

Initial Contact: Send a brief letter of inquiry.
Application Requirements: Include a description of organization, amount requested, purpose of funds sought, and proof of tax-exempt status.
Deadlines: None.

Restrictions

Does not support individuals.

Foundation Officials

Richard E. Levine: secretary
Anne A. Luetkemeyer: secretary, director
John A. Luetkemeyer, Jr.: president
Anne L. Stone: vice president
James D. Stone: director
Robert F. Wilson: treasurer

Grants Analysis

Disclosure Period: calendar year ending 2001
Total Grants: $3,098,182
Number of Grants: 35
Average Grant: $56,912*
Highest Grant: $1,163,182
Lowest Grant: $3,500
Typical Range: $10,000 to $100,000
*Note: Average grant figure excludes highest grant.

Recent Grants

Note: Grants derived from 2001 Form 990.
General

1,163,182	McDonogh School, Owings Mills, MD
550,000	Lawrenceville School, Lawrenceville, NJ
260,000	Williams College, Hanover, NH
100,000	Garrison Forest School, Owings Mills, MD
75,000	Ladew Topiary Gardens, Monkton, MD
60,000	Maryland Historical Society, Baltimore, MD
51,000	Irvine Nature Center, Baltimore, MD
50,000	Baltimore Chesapeake Bay Outward Bound Program, Baltimore, MD
50,000	Baltimore Museum of Art, Baltimore, MD
50,000	Brown Memorial Woodbrook Presbyterian Church, Baltimore, MD

ROSAMARY FOUNDATION

Giving Contact

Richard W. Freeman, Jr., Chairman
PO Box 13218
New Orleans, LA 70185-3218
Phone: (504)895-1984
Fax: (504)895-1988
Web: http://www.rosamary.org

Description

Founded: 1939
EIN: 726024696
Organization Type: Family Foundation
Giving Locations: LA: New Orleans
Grant Types: Capital, Challenge, Endowment, General Support, Matching, Multiyear/Continuing Support, Operating Expenses, Project, Seed Money.

Donor Information

Founder: The RosaMary Foundation was established in 1939, with funds donated by members of the Alfred Bird Freeman family. Alfred Bird Freeman (1881-1957) was chairman of the Louisiana Coca-Cola Bottling Company. The foundation was named after Mr. Freeman's daughters, Mrs. Rosa Keller and Mrs. Mary Ella Wisdom.

Financial Summary

Total Giving: $2,145,200 (2004); $2,512,859 (2002); $2,486,092 (2001)
Giving Analysis: Giving for 2004 includes: foundation grants to United Way ($250,000)
Assets: $39,171,233 (2002); $54,860,341 (2001)
Gifts Received: $4,475 (2002); $37,719 (1998)

Typical Recipients

Arts & Humanities: Arts Associations & Councils, Arts Centers, Arts Festivals, Arts Outreach, Ballet, Arts & Humanities-General, Historic Preservation, Libraries, Museums/Galleries, Music, Opera, Performing Arts, Public Broadcasting, Theater
Civic & Public Affairs: African American Affairs, Botanical Gardens/Parks, Community Foundations, Economic Development, Civic & Public Affairs-General, Housing, Philanthropic Organizations, Professional & Trade Associations, Public Policy, Safety, Urban & Community Affairs, Zoos/Aquariums
Education: Afterschool/Enrichment Programs, Arts/Humanities Education, Business Education, Colleges & Universities, Economic Education, Education Reform, Education-General, International Studies, Literacy, Minority Education, Private Education (Precollege), Public Education (Precollege), Science/Mathematics Education, Secondary Education (Private), Student Aid
Environment: Air/Water Quality, Environment-General
Health: AIDS/HIV, Clinics/Medical Centers, Eyes/Blindness, Health Organizations, Hospitals, Medical Research, Research/Studies Institutes, Transplant Networks/Donor Banks
International: Foreign Educational Institutions
Religion: Churches, Dioceses, Religion-General, Religious Organizations, Religious Welfare, Social/Policy Issues
Social Services: Animal Protection, At-Risk Youth, Big Brothers/Big Sisters, Camps, Child Welfare, Community Service Organizations, Crime Prevention, Day Care, Emergency Relief, Family Planning, Homes, People with Disabilities, Recreation & Athletics, Scouts, Shelters/Homelessness, Social Services-General, Special Olympics, United Funds/United Ways, YMCA/YWCA/YMHA/YWHA, Youth Organizations

Application Procedures

Initial Contact: Applicants should request an application form and guidelines, or download the necessary documents from the foundation's web site.
Application Requirements: Proposals should include a proposal narrative, including background on the organization, a description of the program for which funding is sought, and plans for program evaluation; completed Proposal Summary Sheet and a Status Certification Form (available from the foundation). The following attachments are required: financial information for the overall organization, including the organization's current and prior year operating budget and recently audited financial statement; financial information for the project/program (if applicable), including a project/program budget, list of staff members involved with their percentage of time to be spent on project, list of names and amounts requested of other funding sources, specific uses of the requested grant, and in-kind support; list of the organization's board of directors and their principal affiliations; criteria for board selection; one-paragraph resumes of key organizational staff including key project/program staff; name, address and telephone number of a person familiar with the organization, excluding a board member or employee; IRS determination letter indicating 501(c)(3) and 509(a) tax exempt status; most recent annual report, if available; and agency affiliation with federated funds or public agencies.
Deadlines: Deadlines for submitting proposals are February 1 and September 1. Applicants are encouraged to submit proposals early to receive appropriate

consideration.

Review Process: The trustees meet twice a year, in the spring and in the fall to make funding decisions.
Notes: Interviews are conducted only at the initiation of the foundation. Videotapes are not accepted.

Restrictions

Organizations must be tax-exempt under IRS Code Section 501(c)(3) or be a governmental agency. Grants are not made to individuals. The foundation does not purchase tickets or participate in fundraising events such as galas.

Additional Information

Publications: Guidelines

Foundation Officials

Adelaide Wisdom Benjamin: trustee B New Orleans, LA 1932. ED Hollins College (1950-1952); Newcomb College BA (1954); Tulane University JD (1956). NONPR AFFIL advisory board: Tulane Summer Lyric Theatre; instructor: Tulane University extension; trustee: Southeast Louisiana Girl Scouts Council; trustee: Newcomb Childrens Center; director: Public Radio WWNO; trustee: New Orleans Museum Art Fellows Forum; director: National Symphony Orchestra Washington; member: New Orleans Bar Association; trustee: Loyola University; member: Louisiana Bar Association; trustee: Louisiana Museum Foundation Board; member: American Bar Association; member: League Women Voters. CLUB AFFIL life member: Thomas Wolfe Society; member: Quarante Club; member: Sybarites Club; member: Le Debut des Jeunes Filles; member: New Orleans Town Gardeners Club; member: Junior League New Orleans; member: American Symphony Orchestra League; member: Debutante Club.
Andrew Benjamin: trustee
Caroline Loughlin: trustee
Toni Myers: admin
Betty Wisdom: trustee
Carlos Zervigon: trustee
Mary K. Zervigon: trustee

Grants Analysis

Disclosure Period: calendar year ending 2004
Total Grants: $1,895,200*
Number of Grants: 44
Average Grant: $18,933*
Highest Grant: $600,000
Lowest Grant: $1,200
Typical Range: $5,000 to $40,000
*Note: Giving excludes United Way. Average grant figure excludes two highest grants ($1,100,000).

Recent Grants

Note: Grants derived from 2002 Form 990.
General

500,000	New Orleans Museum of Art, New Orleans, LA -- for the Sydney and Walda Besthoff Sculpture Garden
400,000	Greater New Orleans Educational Television Foundation, New Orleans, LA -- for New Orleans Teleplex
50,000	Greater New Orleans Foundation, New Orleans, LA -- operating support
50,000	Louisiana Children's Museum, New Orleans, LA -- for Zoom Zone Exhibit
45,000	Neighborhood Housing Services, New Orleans, LA -- for children's arts and cultural center
35,000	Louisiana Philharmonic Orchestra, New Orleans, LA -- support for 2002 season
30,000	Resources for Human Development, Philadelphia, PA -- for New Orleans Womanspace
26,000	New Orleans Museum of Art, New Orleans, LA -- for Educational Program for 2002-2003
25,000	Archbishop's Community Appeal, New Orleans, LA -- annual support

25,000	Greater New Orleans Foundation, New Orleans, LA -- for operating support

BILLY ROSE FOUNDATION

Giving Contact

Terri C. Mangino, Executive Director
805 Third Ave., 23rd Floor
New York, NY 10022
Phone: (212)407-7745
Fax: (212)407-7799

Description

Founded: 1958
EIN: 136165466
Organization Type: General Purpose Foundation
Giving Locations: NY: New York
Grant Types: General Support, Project.

Donor Information

Founder: Incorporated in 1958 by Billy Rose (d. 1966), whose interests included theatrical production, songwriting, the stock market, real estate investments, and art collecting. His activities in the stock market accounted for much of the fortune. His will provided for a bequest of more than $10 million to the foundation.

Financial Summary

Total Giving: $1,000,000 (2002 approx); $1,014,000 (2001)
Assets: $13,231,942 (2001)
Gifts Received: $5,000 (1993)

Typical Recipients

Arts & Humanities: Arts Associations & Councils, Arts Centers, Arts Festivals, Arts Funds, Arts Institutes, Arts Outreach, Ballet, Dance, Ethnic & Folk Arts, Film & Video, Arts & Humanities-General, Historic Preservation, Libraries, Literary Arts, Museums/ Galleries, Music, Opera, Performing Arts, Public Broadcasting, Theater, Visual Arts
Civic & Public Affairs: Botanical Gardens/Parks, Civic & Public Affairs-General, Philanthropic Organizations, Public Policy
Education: Arts/Humanities Education, Business Education, Colleges & Universities, Education Associations, Education Reform, Education-General, Legal Education, Private Education (Precollege), Student Aid
Environment: Environment-General
Health: Cancer, Clinics/Medical Centers, Health Organizations, Hospitals, Medical Rehabilitation, Medical Research, Nursing Services, Single-Disease Health Associations, Transplant Networks/Donor Banks
International: Foreign Arts Organizations, Foreign Educational Institutions, Missionary/Religious Activities
Religion: Churches, Religion-General, Jewish Causes, Religious Organizations, Religious Welfare
Social Services: Community Centers, Community Service Organizations, Family Planning, Family Services, People with Disabilities, YMCA/YWCA/YMHA/ YWHA, Youth Organizations

Application Procedures

Initial Contact: Applications should be submitted in letter form.
Application Requirements: The letter should summarize the need for support and include the amount of the request. A copy of the IRS determination letter of tax-exempt status and any recent publicity articles also should be included.
Deadlines: None.

Restrictions

Grants are made only to organizations described in section 170(c) of the IRS code of 1954/1986: (501(c)3 designations only), and not to individuals.

Foundation Officials

James R. Cherry: chairman, treasurer, director
James R. Cherry, Jr.: vice president, assistant treasurer, director B New York, NY 1938. ED Harvard University (1959); New York University School of Law JD (1962). PRIM CORP EMPL associate general counsel: Philip Morris Management Corp. NONPR AFFIL member: American Bar Association.
Terri C. Mangino: executive director, assistant secretary
Edward J. Walsh, Jr.: secretary
John Wohlstetter: vice president, director

Grants Analysis

Disclosure Period: calendar year ending 2001
Total Grants: $1,014,000
Number of Grants: 74
Average Grant: $9,438*
Highest Grant: $325,000
Lowest Grant: $1,000
Typical Range: $2,500 to $25,000
*Note: Average grant figure excludes highest grant.

Recent Grants

Note: Grants derived from 2002 Form 990.
Library-Related

10,000	Queens Borough Public Library, Jamaica, NY
1,000	Queens Library Foundation, Jamaica, NY

General

325,000	American Friends of the Israel Museum, New York, NY
25,000	American Theatre Wing Inc., New York, NY
25,000	National Foundation for Facial Reconstruction, New York, NY
25,000	National Symphony Orchestra, Washington, DC
25,000	Skin Cancer Foundation, New York, NY
25,000	Washington Bach Consort, Washington, DC
20,000	Clarisse B. Kampel Foundation
20,000	Convent of the Sacred Heart, New York, NY
20,000	Fordham University, Bronx, NY
20,000	New York University Center Music Therapy for Children, New York, NY

ROSENBERG FOUNDATION

Giving Contact

Linda Moll, Grants & Office Manager
47 Kearny Street, Suite 804
San Francisco, CA 94108
Phone: (415)421-6105
Fax: (415)421-0141
E-mail: rosenfdn@rosenbergfdn.org
Web: http://www.rosenbergfdn.org/

Description

Founded: 1935
EIN: 941186182
Organization Type: General Purpose Foundation
Giving Locations: CA: grantss are made outside California to operate productions in California and to national organizations
Grant Types: General Support, Project.

Donor Information

Founder: Established in 1936 with a bequest from Max L. Rosenberg, a native Californian and head of Rosenberg Brothers and Co., a San Francisco dried fruit firm. In 1969, the foundation received an additional bequest from the estate of Mrs. Charlotte S. Mack, one of the foundation's early directors.

Financial Summary

Total Giving: $3,191,077 (2003); $3,347,465 (2002)
Assets: $59,837,084 (2003); $53,819,061 (2002)
Gifts Received: $297 (2002); $4,898 (1998); $44,000 (1997). Note: The foundation is not required to file schedule B with its return for 2002.

Typical Recipients

Arts & Humanities: Libraries, Music
Civic & Public Affairs: African American Affairs, Asian American Affairs, Business/Free Enterprise, Civil Rights, Community Foundations, Economic Development, Economic Policy, Employment/Job Training, First Amendment Issues, Civic & Public Affairs-General, Hispanic Affairs, Housing, Law & Justice, Legal Aid, Nonprofit Management, Philanthropic Organizations, Professional & Trade Associations, Public Policy, Rural Affairs, Urban & Community Affairs, Women's Affairs
Education: Colleges & Universities, Economic Education, Education-General, International Studies, Minority Education, Social Sciences Education
Environment: Environment-General
Health: Health Policy/Cost Containment, Health Funds
International: Human Rights, International Development, International Relief Efforts
Religion: Religious Welfare
Social Services: Child Welfare, Community Service Organizations, Day Care, Emergency Relief, Family Services, Refugee Assistance, Senior Services, Social Services-General, United Funds/United Ways, Youth Organizations

Application Procedures

Initial Contact: Letters of inquiry describing the proposed project, the applying organization, and anticipated budget should be sent to the foundation. If the proposed project falls within the foundation's program priorities, a formal application will be requested.
Application Requirements: A formal application should include a narrative proposal indicating the problem to be addressed; the plan of the project and its activities and goals; names and qualifications of the staff; the lasting significance of the project; anticipated goals and proposed evaluation of the project; plan for disseminating results of the project; future plans for the project; an itemized budget indicating project cost; grant amount requested; other sources of support; length of time for which support is requested and estimated future budgets; and materials describing the organization such as history, experience, a copy o f IRS form indicating tax-exempt status, list of board members, and indication of the organization's status on affirmative action in reference to gender and minority groups.
Deadlines: None.
Review Process: After a formal application has been received by the foundation, a visit and interview will be arranged. There is generally a two or three month waiting period before the foundation reviews an application.

Restrictions

The Foundation's policies preclude grants to continue or expand projects started with funds from other sources. Grants are not given for scholarships, endowments, capital purposes, operating purposes, or matching gifts. Grants are not made to individuals, for fund-raising events, for construction or acquisition of property, for direct service programs, or for the operating expenses of ongoing programs. The Foundation makes grants to purchase equipment, produce films, or publish materials only when such grants are a necessary part of a larger project supported by the Foundation. The Foundation recommends applicants review grants listed on the website to get a sense of projects that receive funding.

Additional Information

Approved grants are paid in installments. Organizations receiving support are required to provide the foundation with periodic progress reports and itemized expenditure lists. The foundation expects unexpended funds to be returned.
Publications: Guidelines; Annual Report

Foundation Officials

Phyllis Cook: director NONPR AFFIL director: Jewish Community Federation San Francisco.
James M. Edgar: director B New York, NY 1936. ED Cornell University BA (1959); Cornell University MBA (1960). PRIM CORP EMPL senior partner: Edgar, Dunn & Co. CORP AFFIL director: Associated Oregon Industries Service Corp. NONPR AFFIL member: San Francisco Planning and Urban Research Board; director: Tau Beta Pi; director: San Francisco Chamber of Commerce; director: California Society Certified Public Accountants; director: Harding Lawson Association Group; director: American Institute of Certified Public Accountants; member: Bay Area Council; director: Active San Francisco Mayor's Financial Advisory Committee. CLUB AFFIL Pacific-Union Club.
Robert E. Friedman: director
Bill Ong Hing: director
Herma Hill Kay: director B Orangeburg, SC 1934. ED Southern Methodist University BA (1956); University of Chicago JD (1959). PRIM NONPR EMPL dean, professor: University of California, Berkeley. NONPR AFFIL director: Equal Rights Advocates California; member: Order Coif; member: California Bar Association; member: California Women Lawyers; member: Association American Law Schools; member: Bar U.S. Supreme Court; member: American Academy of Arts & Sciences; member council: American Law Institute.
Leslie L. Luttgens: director
Shauna I. Marshall: vice chairman, director
Albert F. Moreno: chairman, director ED University of San Diego BA (1966); University of California at Berkeley JD (1970). PRIM CORP EMPL senior vice president, general counsel, secretary: Levi Strauss & Co. CORP AFFIL director: New Century Energies Inc.
Kirke P. Wilson: president, secretary

Grants Analysis

Disclosure Period: calendar year ending 2003
Total Grants: $3,191,077
Number of Grants: 59
Average Grant: $54,086
Highest Grant: $191,000
Lowest Grant: $1,000
Typical Range: $10,000 to $75,000

Recent Grants

Note: Grants derived from 2003 Form 990.
General

191,000	Legal Aid Society Employment Law Center, San Francisco, CA -- language rights project
163,606	National Center for Youth Law, Oakland, CA -- child support enforcement project
140,000	Farm Worker Justice Fund, Washington, DC -- guest worker project
130,000	Strategic Actions for a Just Economy, Los Angeles, CA -- welfare to work banking project
125,000	Western Center on Law and Poverty Inc, Los Angeles, CA -- welfare to work policies
115,000	National Immigrant Law Center, Los Angeles, CA -- immigrant employment rights project
106,250	Asian Law Caucus, San Francisco, CA -- garment worker advocacy and reform project
100,000	Center on Policy Initiatives, San Diego, CA -- living wage standards and accountable development project
93,750	Chinese for Affirmative Action, San Francisco, CA -- language rights initiative
93,750	Korean Immigrant Workers Advocates of Southern California, Los Angeles, CA -- market workers justice campaign

LOUISE AND CLAUDE ROSENBERG, JR. FAMILY FOUNDATION

Giving Contact

Claude N. Rosenberg, Jr., Secretary
c/o Hughes Bookkeeping Service
1459 18th St., Suite 167
San Francisco, CA 94107
Phone: (415)824-1288

Description

Founded: 1986
EIN: 943031132
Organization Type: Private Foundation
Giving Locations: CA: San Francisco
Grant Types: Fellowship, General Support, Research.

Donor Information

Founder: Claude N. Rosenberg, Jr., chairman of New Tithing Group, and Louise J. Rosenberg

Financial Summary

Total Giving: $1,868,000 (fiscal year ending October 31, 2002)
Giving Analysis: Giving for fiscal 2002 includes: foundation scholarships ($500,000)
Assets: $30,568,809 (fiscal 2002)
Gifts Received: $1,352,260 (fiscal 1995); $1,780,227 (fiscal 1994); $1,200,050 (fiscal 1993). Note: In fiscal 1994, contributions were received from Claude and Louise Rosenberg, Jr. ($1,548,408) and the estate of Claude Rosenberg, Sr. ($231,819).

Typical Recipients

Arts & Humanities: Arts Appreciation, Arts Centers, Arts Festivals, Arts Outreach, Ballet, Dance, Ethnic & Folk Arts, Arts & Humanities-General, Libraries, Literary Arts, Museums/Galleries, Music, Opera, Performing Arts, Public Broadcasting, Theater, Visual Arts
Civic & Public Affairs: Botanical Gardens/Parks, Community Foundations, Economic Development, Civic & Public Affairs-General, Municipalities/Towns, Parades/Festivals, Philanthropic Organizations, Public Policy, Urban & Community Affairs, Women's Affairs, Zoos/Aquariums
Education: Afterschool/Enrichment Programs, Arts/Humanities Education, Business Education, Colleges & Universities, Continuing Education, Education Funds, Education Reform, Elementary Education (Public), Education-General, Leadership Training, Literacy, Private Education (Precollege), Public Education (Precollege), Religious Education, School Volunteerism, Science/Mathematics Education, Secondary Education (Private), Secondary Education (Public), Student Aid
Environment: Air/Water Quality, Environment-General, Resource Conservation, Wildlife Protection
Health: Cancer, Clinics/Medical Centers, Diabetes, Eyes/Blindness, Geriatric Health, Health Organizations, Hospitals, Medical Rehabilitation, Medical Research, Multiple Sclerosis, Research/Studies Institutes, Single-Disease Health Associations
International: Foreign Educational Institutions, Human Rights, International Affairs, International Issues, International Peace & Security Issues, International Relations, Missionary/Religious Activities
Religion: Churches, Jewish Causes, Synagogues/

Temples
Social Services: Camps, Child Welfare, Community Centers, Community Service Organizations, Crime Prevention, Family Services, Food/Clothing Distribution, People with Disabilities, Recreation & Athletics, United Funds/United Ways, Volunteer Services, Youth Organizations

Application Procedures

Initial Contact: The foundation has no formal grant application procedure or application form.
Deadlines: None.

Restrictions

Charities must qualify under the provisions of IRS Code Section 501(C) (3)

Foundation Officials

John P. Levin, Jr.: director
Claude Newman Rosenberg, Jr.: secretary B San Francisco, CA 1928. ED Stanford University BA (1950); Stanford University MBA (1952). CORP AFFIL lecturer, member advisor counc: Grad Sch Business. NONPR AFFIL chairman advisory council: Stanford University School Business; trustee: University High School San Francisco; director: San Francisco Ballet Association; president: Stanford University Graduate School Business Alumni Association; director: Jewish Welfare Federation; director: Presbyterian Childrens Cancer Research Center; director: Jewish Community Center; member: Financial Analysts San Francisco; director: International Hospitality Center. CLUB AFFIL Concordia-Argonaut Club; Family Club; California Tennis Club.
Louise J. Rosenberg: president

Grants Analysis

Disclosure Period: fiscal year ending October 31, 2002
Total Grants: $1,368,000*
Number of Grants: 15
Average Grant: $97,714*
Highest Grant: $500,000
Lowest Grant: $500
Typical Range: $2,500 to $10,000 and $25,000 to $46,000
*Note: Giving excludes fellowships. Average grants figure excludes highest grants.

Recent Grants

Note: Grants derived from 2002 Form 990.

General

500,000	Stanford University, Stanford, CA -- for the Center for Social Innovation Fund
500,000	Stanford University Graduate School of Business, Stanford, CA -- The Rosenberg Facility Scholar Fund
166,000	Harvard Graduate School of Education, Cambridge, MA -- for Origins of Human Creativity Project
100,000	Leadership High School, San Francisco, CA
60,000	California Trout, San Francisco, CA
46,250	Ruth Asawa Fund, San Francisco, CA -- for Aikos Projects in the Schools
40,000	Leadership Public Schools, San Francisco, CA
40,000	Omega Boys Club, San Francisco, CA
30,000	St. John's Educational Thresholds Center, San Francisco, CA
28,000	Philanthropic Ventures Foundation, Oakland, CA -- for High School Newspaper Support Program

HAROLD C. AND MARJORIE Q. ROSENBERRY TUSCARAWAS COUNTY FOUNDATION

Giving Contact

Larry Gibbs, Trust Officer
c/o Belmont National Bank
PO Box 249
St. Clairsville, OH 43950
Phone: (740)695-3323

Description

Founded: 1994
EIN: 341772635
Organization Type: Private Foundation
Giving Locations: OH: Tuscarawas County
Grant Types: General Support.

Financial Summary

Total Giving: $362,647 (2001)
Assets: $7,371,757 (2001)
Gifts Received: $6,026,133 (1994)

Typical Recipients

Arts & Humanities: Community Arts, Historic Preservation, History & Archaeology, Libraries, Museums/Galleries, Music, Theater
Civic & Public Affairs: Botanical Gardens/Parks, Clubs, Civic & Public Affairs-General, Parades/Festivals, Rural Affairs, Safety, Urban & Community Affairs
Education: Arts/Humanities Education, Colleges & Universities, Education-General, Public Education (Precollege), School Volunteerism, Science/Mathematics Education, Secondary Education (Private), Secondary Education (Public)
Environment: Resource Conservation
Health: Children's Health/Hospitals, Emergency/Ambulance Services, Hospitals
Religion: Churches, Religious Welfare
Science: Observatories & Planetariums
Social Services: Big Brothers/Big Sisters, Community Centers, Community Service Organizations, Counseling, People with Disabilities, Recreation & Athletics, Senior Services, Social Services-General, Substance Abuse, United Funds/United Ways, YMCA/YWCA/YMHA/YWHA, Youth Organizations

Application Procedures

Initial Contact: Request application from the selection committee.
Deadlines: None.

Additional Information

Trust(s): Belmont National Bank

Foundation Officials

Larry Gibbs: trustee

Grants Analysis

Disclosure Period: calendar year ending 2001
Total Grants: $362,647
Number of Grants: 32
Average Grant: $11,333
Highest Grant: $35,255
Lowest Grant: $999
Typical Range: $5,000 to $20,000

Recent Grants

Note: Grants derived from 2002 Form 990.
General

28,106	Kent State University Tuscarawas Campus, New Philadelphia, OH -- for equipment
26,500	Dover City Schools, Dover, OH -- for Dover Carter Stadium Project
20,878	Indian Valley School Middle School, Tuscarawas, OH -- for renovation to auditorium
20,006	Claymont City Schools, Uhrichsville, OH -- replacement of elementary computer lab
20,000	City of New Philadelphia New Philadelphia Fire Department, New Philadelphia, OH -- for Waterworks Lighting Project
20,000	Dover City Schools, Dover, OH -- to purchase transportation van
18,450	Tuscarawas County Council for Churches, New Philadelphia, OH -- to upgrade existing computers
17,524	Tuscarawas Valley High School, Zoarville, OH -- to purchase 10 laptop computers
17,000	New Philadelphia Schools, New Philadelphia, OH -- to purchase 16 station computer lab
16,710	Personal and Family Counseling Services, New Philadelphia, OH -- for construction

IDA AND WILLIAM ROSENTHAL FOUNDATION

Giving Contact

Catherine C. Brawer, President & Director
67A E. 77th St.
New York, NY 10021-4335
Phone: (212)737-1011

Description

Founded: 1953
EIN: 136141274
Organization Type: Private Foundation
Giving Locations: NY: New York metropolitan area; Dominican Republic: ; support for projects in the Dominican Republic through national organizations.
Grant Types: Project, Scholarship, Seed Money.

Donor Information

Founder: the late Ida Rosenthal, the late William Rosenthal

Typical Recipients

Arts & Humanities: Arts Associations & Councils, Arts Centers, Arts Institutes, Dance, Historic Preservation, History & Archaeology, Libraries, Museums/Galleries, Music, Public Broadcasting, Theater
Civic & Public Affairs: Botanical Gardens/Parks, Civil Rights, Ethnic Organizations, Hispanic Affairs, Legal Aid, Public Policy, Women's Affairs
Education: Afterschool/Enrichment Programs, Arts/Humanities Education, Colleges & Universities, Education Funds, Minority Education, Preschool Education, Private Education (Precollege), Secondary Education (Public), Student Aid
Health: Hospitals
Social Services: Day Care, Scouts

Application Procedures

Initial Contact: Send a brief letter of proposal with an a full proposal.
Application Requirements: Include a brief narrative history of the organization, including the scope of its current activities and the kind and size of the audience served; and explanation of how the proposed project meets the objectives of the organization; a list of board members; a list of government, corporate, and foundation support received over the past five years; recently audited financial statement; proof of tax-exempt status; the name, title, and resume of the person who will direct the project; and itemized budget showing how the rest of the project will be funded;

and an agreement to provide the foundation with a self-evaluation of the project within three months of completion. completion.

Deadlines: None.

Restrictions

Does not support individuals or provide loans. The foundation no longer accepts applications from social service agencies.

Additional Information

Publications: Application Procedures

Foundation Officials

Catherine Coleman Brawer: president, director B New York, NY 1943. ED Sarah Lawrence College (1964); New York University (1966). CORP AFFIL director: Maidenform Inc.

Robert A. Brawer: vice president, director

Abraham Pascal Kanner: vice president B New York, NY 1911. ED New York University (1931); Harvard University (1933). PRIM CORP EMPL vice president, treasurer: Maidenform.

Steven N. Masket: assistant secretary

Ann Brownell Sloane: assistant treasurer

Grants Analysis

Disclosure Period: fiscal year ending August 31, 1999

Total Grants: $68,358*

Number of Grants: 15

Average Grant: $4,557

Highest Grant: $11,550

Typical Range: $1,000 to $10,000

*Note: Giving excludes scholarships.

Recent Grants

Note: Grants derived from 2002 Form 990.

General

15,000	Independent Curators International, New York, NY -- Walk Ways
15,000	Institute of Find Arts, New York University, New York, NY -- for the Ida and William Rosenthal Foundation Fellowship for one or more outstanding first-year students
15,000	University of Chicago, Chicago, IL -- Ida and William Rosenthal Scholarship
10,000	Sarah Lawrence College, Bronxville, NY -- Theater Outreach Program
6,400	Community School 211, Bronx, NY -- Choral Music Program
6,000	Boy Scouts of America - Northern New Jersey Chapter, Verona, NJ -- Camp Lewis
5,000	Park McCullough House Association, North Bennington, VT -- expand educational outreach program
5,000	Plimoth Plantation, Plymouth, MA -- support interns
3,200	Music Conservatory of Westchester, White Plains, NY -- partial scholarships for four female minority students with need
2,500	Children's Discovery Museum, Bloomington, IL -- Family Fun Program

LOIS AND RICHARD ROSENTHAL FOUNDATION

Giving Contact

Richard Rosenthal, Officer
1507 Dana Ave.
Cincinnati, OH 45207
Phone: (513)531-2222

Description

Founded: 1987
EIN: 311203666

Organization Type: Private Foundation
Giving Locations: OH: Cincinnati
Grant Types: General Support.

Financial Summary

Total Giving: $153,150 (2001)
Assets: $5,536,204 (2001)
Gifts Received: $4,097,898 (2000). Note: In 2000, contributions were received from Richard Rosenthal.

Typical Recipients

Arts & Humanities: Arts Centers, Arts Funds, Ballet, Libraries, Museums/Galleries, Performing Arts, Theater

Civic & Public Affairs: Botanical Gardens/Parks

International: International Relations

Religion: Religious Organizations

Social Services: Family Planning, Food/Clothing Distribution

Application Procedures

Initial Contact: Send a brief letter of inquiry.

Application Requirements: Include purpose of funds sought, budget, and date funds are needed.

Deadlines: None.

Foundation Officials

Jennie D. Berliant: trustee

Mark H. Berliantt: trustee

Toni Birckhead: trustee

David S. Rosenthal: trustee

Lois R. Rosenthal: trustee

Richard H. Rosenthal: trustee

Grants Analysis

Disclosure Period: calendar year ending 2001

Total Grants: $153,150

Number of Grants: 12

Average Grant: $12,763

Highest Grant: $50,000

Lowest Grant: $350

Typical Range: $1,000 to $30,000

Recent Grants

Note: Grants derived from 2001 Form 990.

Library-Related

15,000	Mercantile Library, Cincinnati, OH

General

50,000	Freestore and Food Bank, Cincinnati, OH
30,000	Cincinnati Playhouse in the Park, Cincinnati, OH
30,000	Cincinnati Playhouse in the Park, Cincinnati, OH
12,500	Contemporary Arts Center, Cincinnati, OH
10,000	Cincinnati Ballet, Cincinnati, OH
2,000	Contemporary Arts Center, Cincinnati, OH
2,000	Contemporary Arts Center, Cincinnati, OH
1,000	Cincinnati Parks Foundation, Cincinnati, OH
350	Cincinnati Ballet, Cincinnati, OH
250	PPSONK, Cincinnati, OH

ROSS FOUNDATION

Giving Contact

Hal Ross, Vice President
105 S. Broadway, Suite 740
Wichita, KS 67202-2009
Phone: (316)264-4981
Fax: (316)264-4981

Description

Founded: 1961
EIN: 486125814
Organization Type: Private Foundation

Giving Locations: CA; CT; FL; KS; NE; OH
Grant Types: Emergency, Endowment, General Support, Research, Scholarship.

Donor Information

Founder: the late G. Murray Ross

Financial Summary

Total Giving: $264,960 (2001)
Giving Analysis: Giving for 2001 includes: foundation scholarships ($100,000)
Assets: $5,915,076 (2001)
Gifts Received: $1,168,584 (1997)

Typical Recipients

Arts & Humanities: Arts Associations & Councils, Arts Centers, Ballet, Community Arts, Arts & Humanities-General, Historic Preservation, History & Archaeology, Libraries, Museums/Galleries, Music

Civic & Public Affairs: Civic & Public Affairs-General, Law & Justice, Parades/Festivals, Zoos/Aquariums

Education: Colleges & Universities, Education Associations, Education-General, Public Education (Precollege), Religious Education

Environment: Environment-General

Health: Cancer, Clinics/Medical Centers

Religion: Churches, Religion-General, Religious Organizations, Religious Welfare

Social Services: Animal Protection, Big Brothers/Big Sisters, Child Welfare, Community Service Organizations, People with Disabilities, Youth Organizations

Application Procedures

Initial Contact: send a brief letter of inquiry

Application Requirements: a description of organization, amount requested, purpose of funds sought, proof of tax-exempt status

Deadlines: None.

Restrictions

Does not support individuals, political or lobbying groups, organizations outside operating areas

Additional Information

The foundation has no formal grant application procedure or application form.

Foundation Officials

Norman W. Jeter: president

Hal Ross: vice president

Susan Ross Sheets: secretary, treasurer

Grants Analysis

Disclosure Period: calendar year ending 2001

Total Grants: $164,960*

Number of Grants: 30

Average Grant: $2,999*

Highest Grant: $75,000

Typical Range: $1,000 to $5,000

*Note: Giving excludes scholarships. Average grant excludes highest grant.

Recent Grants

Note: Grants derived from 2001 Form 990.

Library-Related

5,000	Hays Public Library Trust, Hays, KS

General

100,000	Ottawa University, Ottawa, KS
75,000	Kansas State University Endowment Association, Manhattan, KS
10,000	Communities in School, Fernandina, FL
10,000	New Leash on Life, A, Bethel, CT
8,955	Oxford-Sumner County Historical Museum
5,000	Big Brothers and Big Sisters, LaGrange, KY
5,000	Chase County Courthouse, Imperial, NE
5,000	First Presbyterian Church, Hays, KS
5,000	Kansas State Historical Society, Topeka, KS
5,000	Victory in the Valley, Wichita, KS

WILL ROSS MEMORIAL FOUNDATION

Giving Contact
Mary Ann W. LaBahn, Vice President & Treasurer
PO Box 17814
Milwaukee, WI 53217
Phone: (414)765-2800

Description
Founded: 1963
EIN: 396044673
Organization Type: Private Foundation
Giving Locations: WI: Milwaukee metropolitan area
Grant Types: Capital, General Support, Project.

Financial Summary
Total Giving: 1997 Giving includes United Way ($75,000).
Gifts Received: $42,588 (1997). Note: In 1997, contributions were received from the estate of Pearl L. Baldwin.

Typical Recipients
Arts & Humanities: Arts Centers, Arts Funds, Arts Institutes, Community Arts, Dance, Libraries, Literary Arts, Museums/Galleries, Music, Opera, Performing Arts, Theater
Civic & Public Affairs: Botanical Gardens/Parks, Economic Development, Employment/Job Training, Civic & Public Affairs-General, Hispanic Affairs, Housing, Municipalities/Towns, Urban & Community Affairs, Zoos/Aquariums
Education: Arts/Humanities Education, Colleges & Universities, Continuing Education, Health & Physical Education, Literacy, Medical Education, Minority Education, Private Education (Precollege), Public Education (Precollege), Student Aid
Environment: Environment-General, Resource Conservation
Health: AIDS/HIV, Alzheimer's Disease, Cancer, Children's Health/Hospitals, Clinics/Medical Centers, Eyes/Blindness, Geriatric Health, Health Organizations, Hospitals, Medical Rehabilitation, Mental Health, Nursing Services, Public Health, Respiratory, Transplant Networks/Donor Banks
Science: Scientific Centers & Institutes
Social Services: At-Risk Youth, Child Welfare, Community Centers, Community Service Organizations, Family Planning, Food/Clothing Distribution, Homes, People with Disabilities, Shelters/Homelessness, United Funds/United Ways, Veterans, Youth Organizations

Application Procedures
Initial Contact: The foundation has no formal grant application procedure or application form. Send Send a brief letter of inquiry and a full proposal. include amount requested, purpose of funds sought, a description of organization, recently audited financial statement, and pts.
Deadlines: December.
Notes: Applications are considered at quarterly meetings.

Restrictions
Does not support individuals, religious organizations for sectarian purposes, political or lobbying groups, or organizations outside operating areas.

Foundation Officials
John D. Bryson, Jr.: president
David Lucas Kinnamon: secretary, director B Madison, WI 1941. ED University of Wisconsin BA (1963); University of Wisconsin JD (1966). PRIM CORP EMPL partner: Quarles & Brady. CORP AFFIL member: Wisconsin Acad Scis Arts & Letters; member: Phi Beta Kappa; member: Phi Beta Phi; member: Estate Counsel Forum; member: Order Coif. NONPR AFFIL director: Riveredge Nature Center; member: WI Bar Association; trustee: Nature Conservancy Wisconsin Chapter; director: Park People Milwaukee County; director: Ice Park & Trail Foundation; member: Milwaukee Bar Association; fellow: American College Trust & Estate Counsel; member: American Bar Association. CLUB AFFIL University Club.
Mary Ann LaBahn: vice president, treasurer

Grants Analysis
Disclosure Period: calendar year ending 2000
Total Grants: $245,500*
Number of Grants: 42
Average Grant: $5,845
Highest Grant: $28,000
Typical Range: $1,000 to $10,000
*Note: Giving excludes United Way.

Recent Grants
Note: Grants derived from 2001 Form 990.
General

75,000	United Way of Greater Milwaukee, Milwaukee, WI
70,000	UPAF, Milwaukee, WI
34,000	Milwaukee Art Museum, Milwaukee, WI
25,000	Medical College of Wisconsin Cancer Center, Milwaukee, WI
15,000	Planned Parenthood, Milwaukee, WI
10,000	Blood Center Research Foundation, Milwaukee, WI
9,000	Milwaukee Public Museum, Milwaukee, WI
6,000	Harambee Community School, Milwaukee, WI
6,000	Milwaukee Institute of Art and Design, Milwaukee, WI
5,500	Riveredge Nature Center, Newburg, WI

ROSS PRODUCTS DIVISION, ABBOTT LABORATORIES

Company Headquarters
625 Cleveland Ave.
Columbus, OH 43215

Company Description
Former Name: Ross Laboratories.
Employees: 500
SIC(s): 2000 Food & Kindred Products, 2023 Dry, Condensed & Evaporated Dairy Products.

Nonmonetary Support
Type: Donated Equipment; Donated Products

Giving Contact
Contributions Committee
625 Cleveland Ave.
Columbus, OH 43215
Phone: (614)624-7677
Note: ALT: (800)986-8510

Description
Organization Type: Corporate Giving Program
Giving Locations: headquarters and operating communities.
Grant Types: General Support, Multiyear/Continuing Support, Operating Expenses, Project, Research, Scholarship.

Financial Summary
Total Giving: Company does not disclose contributions figures.

Typical Recipients
Arts & Humanities: Arts Associations & Councils, Ballet, Community Arts, Arts & Humanities-General, Libraries, Museums/Galleries, Opera, Theater
Civic & Public Affairs: Chambers of Commerce, Civil Rights, Civic & Public Affairs-General, Inner-City Development, Philanthropic Organizations, Urban & Community Affairs, Zoos/Aquariums
Education: Colleges & Universities, Education Associations, Education Funds, Education-General
Health: AIDS/HIV, Alzheimer's Disease, Cancer, Children's Health/Hospitals, Health-General, Health Organizations, Hospitals, Hospitals (University Affiliated), Medical Research, Nutrition, Prenatal Health Issues
Science: Science-General
Social Services: Camps, Child Welfare, Community Centers, Community Service Organizations, Domestic Violence, Emergency Relief, Family Services, Food/Clothing Distribution, Homes, Senior Services, Shelters/Homelessness, Social Services-General, United Funds/United Ways, Youth Organizations

Application Procedures
Initial Contact: Send a brief letter of inquiry.
Application Requirements: a description of organization, amount requested, purpose of funds sought, and proof of tax-exempt status.

Restrictions
Does not support individuals and religious organizations for sectarian purposes.

Corporate Officials
Joyce Amundson: president, chief executive officer Ross Products Division PRIM CORP EMPL president, chief executive officer Ross Products Division: Abbott Laboratories.

Grants Analysis
Typical Range: $50 to $1,000

ROSSI FAMILY FOUNDATION

Giving Contact
L. Jay Rossi, President
18 Ohlone
Portola Valley, CA 94028
Phone: (650)851-4327

Description
Founded: 1990
EIN: 943106122
Organization Type: Private Foundation
Grant Types: General Support.

Donor Information
Founder: Established in 1990 by L. Jay Rossi, the foundation's president, and Marjorie Nye Rossi, the foundation's vice president, secretary, and treasurer.

Financial Summary
Total Giving: $158,801 (fiscal year ending June 30, 2001)
Assets: $1,949,621 (fiscal 2001)
Gifts Received: $232,519 (fiscal 2001); $18,982 (fiscal 1996); $30,392 (fiscal 1995). Note: In fiscal 1996 and 2000, contributions were received from Mr. and Mrs. L. Jay Rossi.

Typical Recipients
Arts & Humanities: Arts Associations & Councils, Theater
Civic & Public Affairs: Employment/Job Training, Civic & Public Affairs-General, Hispanic Affairs
Education: Arts/Humanities Education, Colleges & Universities, Faculty Development, Education-General, Private Education (Precollege), Religious Education, Science/Mathematics Education, Special

Education, Student Aid
Environment: Environment-General, Resource Conservation
Health: Arthritis, Children's Health/Hospitals, Health Organizations, Medical Research, Single-Disease Health Associations
Science: Scientific Centers & Institutes
Social Services: Animal Protection, At-Risk Youth, Child Welfare, Community Centers, Domestic Violence, Family Planning, Food/Clothing Distribution, Senior Services, Shelters/Homelessness, Social Services-General, Youth Organizations

Application Procedures
Initial Contact: Send a brief letter of inquiry.
Application Requirements: a brief description of project.
Deadlines: None.

Foundation Officials
Craig Hall Rossi: trustee
Safford Jay Rossi: trustee
Janeen Rossi: director
L. Jay Rossi: president
Marjorie Nye Rossi: vice president, secretary, treasurer
Merilee Rossi: director
Merilee Rossi Buckley: trustee
Janeen Rossi Kouzi: trustee
Lizabeth Rossi Schuetz: trustee

Grants Analysis
Disclosure Period: fiscal year ending June 30, 2001
Total Grants: $158,801
Number of Grants: 14
Average Grant: $2,627*
Highest Grant: $114,651
Typical Range: $1,000 to $5,000
*Note: Average grant figure excludes highest grant.

Recent Grants
Note: Grants derived from fiscal 2002 Form 990.
General

50,000	OICW, Menlo Park, CA -- for two contributions
11,500	Stanford University, Stanford, CA -- grants for golf and basketball
10,000	Loaves and Fishes, Sacramento, CA -- for charity's Women's Empowerment Program
10,000	Marin County Bicycle Coalition, San Anselmo, CA -- for the Safe Route Program
6,300	Environmental Volunteers, Palo Alto, CA -- to underwrite the 30th anniversary party of the charity
6,000	School Environment Education Docents, Novato, CA -- to the Habitat Project
5,000	National Alliance for Excellence, Matawan, NJ -- for a middle school library
5,000	Resource Area for Teachers, San Jose, CA -- for operating capital for the charity
5,000	Yosemite Fund, San Francisco, CA -- annual campaign
3,000	School of the Pacific, Berkeley, CA -- annual campaign

JUDITH ROTHSCHILD FOUNDATION

Giving Contact
Elizabeth Slater, Vice President, Grant Program
1110 Park Ave.
New York, NY 10128
Phone: (212)831-4114
Fax: (212)831-6222
Web: http://fdncenter.org/grantmaker/rothschild

Description
Founded: 1993
EIN: 133736320
Organization Type: Private Foundation
Giving Locations: NY: New York
Grant Types: General Support.

Donor Information
Founder: Established in 1993 by the late Judith Rothschild.

Financial Summary
Total Giving: $270,000 (2003); $250,000 (2002 approx); $8,027,058 (2001)
Assets: $28,099,647 (2001)
Gifts Received: $248,200 (2001); $345,400 (1999); $40,456,223 (1994). Note: In 2001, contributions were received from Boris Kerdimun ($107,700), Elaine Lustig Cohen ($6,900) and Varvara Rodchenko ($133,600). In 1994, contributions were received from the estate of Judith Rothschild.

Typical Recipients
Arts & Humanities: Arts Associations & Councils, Arts Centers, Arts Funds, Arts Outreach, Ethnic & Folk Arts, Arts & Humanities-General, Historic Preservation, Literary Arts, Museums/Galleries, Visual Arts
Civic & Public Affairs: Civic & Public Affairs-General
Education: Arts/Humanities Education, Colleges & Universities
Health: Cancer
International: Foreign Arts Organizations, Foreign Educational Institutions
Social Services: Community Service Organizations.

Application Procedures
Initial Contact: Request application guidelines.
Deadlines: Applications are accepted between April 15 and September 15.

Additional Information
Publications: Application Guidelines

Foundation Officials
Harvey S. Shipley Miller: trustee

Grants Analysis
Disclosure Period: calendar year ending 2003
Total Grants: $270,000
Number of Grants: 22
Average Grant: $12,272
Highest Grant: $30,000
Lowest Grant: $5,000
Typical Range: $5,000 to $20,000

Recent Grants
Note: Grants derived from 2001 Form 990.
General

6,500,000	American Swedish Heritage Museum
1,056,000	Philadelphia Museum of Art, Philadelphia, PA -- artwork
75,775	Philadelphia Museum of Art, Philadelphia, PA -- Women's Committee
25,000	Addison Gallery of American Art, Andover, MA
25,000	Albright Knox Art Gallery, Buffalo, NY
20,000	El Paso Museum of Art, El Paso, TX
17,950	Museum of Modern Art, New York, NY
16,100	Museum of American Folk Art, New York, NY
15,912	American Museum in Britain United Kingdom
15,400	Phillips Collection, Washington, DC

ROUSE CO.

Company Headquarters
10400 Little Patuxent Parkway
Columbia, MD 21044
Web: http://www.therousecompany.com

Company Description
Founded: 1939
Ticker: RSE
Exchange: NYSE
Operating Revenue: US$1.221 billion (2002)
Employees: 3169 (2003)
SIC(s): 1531 Operative Builders, 6512 Nonresidential Building Operators.

Operating Locations
Rouse Co. (AR--Fayetteville; CA--Santa Monica; CO--Colorado Springs, Denver; DC--Washington; FL--Jacksonville, Miami, Tallahassee; GA--Atlanta, Augusta, Decatur; IA--Ames, Keokuk, Marshalltown, Muscatine, West Burlington; KY--Louisville; LA--Gretna, New Orleans, Shreveport; MD--Baltimore, Easton, Glen Burnie, Parkville; MA--Springfield; MI--Taylor; MN--Minnetonka; MO--St. Louis; NJ--Burlington, Cherry Hill, Paramus, Voorhees, Woodbridge; NY--New York, Staten Island; OH--Dayton; PA--Exton, Greensburg, Philadelphia, Plymouth Meeting; TX--Austin, Galveston, Houston, San Antonio; WA--Seattle; WI--Milwaukee)

Nonmonetary Support
Value: $50,000 (1999); $50,000 (1998)
Type: Donated Equipment; In-kind Services; Loaned Employees
Volunteer Programs: The company encourages its employees to volunteer time to nonprofit groups and organizations through its Volunteer Contributions Program. Through this program, the company provides grants of up to $1,000 to nonprofit organizations at which the Rouse employees volunteer. Volunteer grants are awarded in the fields of health, education, human services, arts and humanities, community affairs, museums, conservation and preservation.

Rouse Co. Foundation

Giving Contact
Margaret P. Mauro, Executive Director
Rouse Co. Foundation
10275 Little Patuxent Pkwy.
Columbia, MD 21044
Phone: (410)992-6000
Fax: (410)992-6363
Web: http://therousecompany.com/whoweare/community/index.html

Description
Founded: 1967
EIN: 526056273
Organization Type: Corporate Foundation
Giving Locations: MD: Central Maryland
Grant Types: Capital, Challenge, Department, Employee Matching Gifts, Endowment, General Support, Matching, Multiyear/Continuing Support, Operating Expenses, Project, Scholarship, Seed Money.
Note: The company matches employee gifts to accredited colleges and universities, elementary, middle and high schools, both public and private.

Donor Information
Founder: Rouse Co.

Financial Summary
Total Giving: $1,342,601 (2003); $1,263,406 (2002); $1,312,756 (2001). Note: Contributes through corporate direct giving program and foundation.
Assets: $6,853,141 (2003); $7,093,215 (2002); $4,031,326 (2001)

Gifts Received: $3,993,924 (2002); $1,000,000 (2001); $925,000 (2000). Note: Contributions are received from The Hughes Corp.

Typical Recipients

Arts & Humanities: Arts Associations & Councils, Arts Centers, Arts Festivals, Arts Funds, Arts Institutes, Arts Outreach, Community Arts, Dance, Ethnic & Folk Arts, Film & Video, Arts & Humanities-General, Historic Preservation, History & Archaeology, Libraries, Literary Arts, Museums/Galleries, Music, Opera, Performing Arts, Public Broadcasting, Theater, Visual Arts

Civic & Public Affairs: Botanical Gardens/Parks, Community Foundations, Economic Development, Employment/Job Training, Ethnic Organizations, Civic & Public Affairs-General, Housing, Public Policy, Urban & Community Affairs, Zoos/Aquariums

Education: Arts/Humanities Education, Business Education, Colleges & Universities, Community & Junior Colleges, Education Funds, Education Reform, Education-General, Legal Education, Minority Education, Public Education (Precollege), Social Sciences Education, Special Education, Student Aid

Environment: Environment-General, Research, Resource Conservation

Health: Cancer, Clinics/Medical Centers, Hospices, Hospitals, Hospitals (University Affiliated), Prenatal Health Issues, Preventive Medicine/Wellness Organizations, Single-Disease Health Associations

International: International Relations

Religion: Ministries, Religious Welfare

Science: Scientific Centers & Institutes

Social Services: Big Brothers/Big Sisters, Camps, Child Welfare, Community Centers, Community Service Organizations, Crime Prevention, Domestic Violence, Family Services, Food/Clothing Distribution, Homes, People with Disabilities, Recreation & Athletics, Scouts, Senior Services, Sexual Abuse, Shelters/Homelessness, Substance Abuse, United Funds/United Ways, Volunteer Services, YMCA/YWCA/YMHA/YWHA, Youth Organizations

Application Procedures

Initial Contact: Make a preliminary inquiry by telephone or in writing.

Application Requirements: If foundation feels that the request for funding falls within foundation guidelines, a written request may be submitted. Include amount requested and intended use; a description of organization, its history and activities; the name(s) and qualifications of the person(s) who will administer the grant; a copy of the most recent tax-exemption ruling statement from the IRS. If the request is for a specific project or program, provide goals and objectives for project or program; population to be served; schedule for implementation; and method of evaluating its effectiveness. Requests for $2,500 or more should also include a list of the organization's board of directors and officers, a copy of the most recent audited financial statement, and an organizational or project budget for the current year showing expenses and income by source.

Deadlines: None.

Restrictions

Does not support religious programs, endowments, individuals, or political advocacy. Organizations must be tax-exempt under 501(c)(3) or 509(a). Grants are primarily provided to organizations located in the Central Maryland area.

Additional Information

Publications: Informational Brochure (including Application Guidelines)

Corporate Officials

Anthony W. Deering: chairman, chief executive officer chief financial officer B 1945. ED Drexel University BS (1969); University of Pennsylvania MBA (1971). PRIM CORP EMPL chairman, chief executive officer: Rouse Co. CORP AFFIL president: Village Cross Keys Inc.; president: White Marsh Mall Inc.; president: Rouse-Tampa Inc.; treasurer: Salem Mall Inc.; president: Rouse-Oakwood Shopping Center; chief financial officer: Rouse Philadelphia Inc.; president: Rouse-Milwaukee Inc.; president: Rouse Missouri Holding Co.; chief financial officer: Rouse Management Service Corp.; chairman: Rouse Marshalltown Center; senior vice president: Rouse Co. Saint Louis Inc.; senior vice president: Rouse Co. Texas Inc.; president: Rouse Co. Oregon Inc.; officer: Rouse Co. Owings Mills Inc.; chief financial officer: Rouse Co. Ohio Inc.; treasurer: Rouse Co. Massachusetts Inc.; president: Rouse Co. Michigan Inc.; president: Rouse Co. Florida Inc.; president: Rouse Co. Illinois Inc.; director: Plymouth Meeting Mall Inc.; president: Rouse Co. Colorado Inc.; senior vice president: North Star Mall Inc.; president: Paramus Park Inc.; senior vice president: Hanendale Mall Inc.; president: Louisville Shopping Center; chairman: Exton Square Inc.; treasurer: Governor's Square Inc.; president: Columbia Mall Inc.; chief financial officer: Columbia Management Inc.; chief financial officer: Charlottetown Inc.

Jeffrey H. Donahue: senior vice president, chief financial officer ED University of Pennsylvania MBA; Cornell University (1966). PRIM CORP EMPL senior vice president, chief financial officer: Rouse Co. CORP AFFIL vice president: Village Cross Keys Inc.; chief financial officer: Woodbridge Center Inc.; chief financial officer: Rouse-Tampa Inc.; treasurer: Salem Mall Inc.; chairman: Rouse Marshalltown Center; treasurer: Rouse Philadelphia Inc.; chief financial officer: Rouse Hotel Management Inc.; chief financial officer: Rouse Management Service Corp.; chief financial officer: Rouse Co. New Jersey Inc.; trustee: Rouse Co. Owings Mills Inc.; trustee: North Star Mall Inc.; vice president: Rouse Co. Massachusetts Inc.; chief financial officer: Exton Square Inc.; vice president: Governor's Square Inc.; vice president: Charlottetown Inc.

Foundation Officials

Pat Dayton: vice president, treasurer, trustee

Anthony W. Deering: chairman, president, trustee (see above)

Margaret Mauro: executive director, secretary, trustee

Douglas A. McGregor: trustee B 1942. ED Rutgers University BA (1963); Case Western Reserve University JD (1967). PRIM CORP EMPL executive vice president development & Cope: The Rouse Co. CORP AFFIL president: Rouse-Teachers Properties Inc.; executive vice president: Woodbridge Center Inc.; executive vice president: North Star Mall Inc.; executive vice president: Rouse Co. Owings Mills Inc.

Al Scavo: trustee

Grants Analysis

Disclosure Period: calendar year ending 2003
Total Grants: $1,182,601*
Number of Grants: 273
Average Grant: $4,332
Highest Grant: $100,000
Lowest Grant: $100
Typical Range: $250 to $10,000
*Note: Giving excludes United Way.

Recent Grants

Note: Grants derived from 2003 Form 990.
General

100,000	New Song Community Learning Center, Baltimore, MD
100,000	United Way of Central Maryland, Baltimore, MD
80,000	Peabody Institute, Baltimore, MD
75,000	Hippodrome Foundation Inc., Baltimore, MD
60,000	United Way of Central Maryland, Baltimore, MD
50,000	Howard Community College Educational Foundation Inc., Columbia, MD
42,857	Howard County General Hospital, Columbia, MD
40,000	Baltimore Zoo, Baltimore, MD
40,000	Enterprise Foundation, Columbia, MD
30,000	Walters Art Museum, Baltimore, MD

MAY MITCHELL ROYAL FOUNDATION

Giving Contact

Richard O. Hartley, Chairman, Grants Committee
11735 Quail Village Way
Naples, FL 34119-8802
Phone: (941)598-4148
Fax: (941)514-1834

Alternate Contact

PO Box 75000, MC 3302
Detroit, MI 48275-3302
Phone: (517)839-2285

Description

Founded: 1981
EIN: 382387140
Organization Type: Private Foundation
Giving Locations: FL; HI; MI
Grant Types: General Support, Research, Scholarship.

Donor Information

Founder: May Mitchell Royal Trust Foundation

Financial Summary

Total Giving: $149,179 (fiscal year ending September 30, 2001)
Giving Analysis: Giving for fiscal 2001 includes: foundation scholarships ($10,000)
Assets: $2,797,842 (fiscal 2001)

Typical Recipients

Arts & Humanities: Libraries, Public Broadcasting
Civic & Public Affairs: Clubs
Education: Colleges & Universities, Medical Education, Student Aid
Health: Cancer, Children's Health/Hospitals, Clinics/Medical Centers, Diabetes, Emergency/Ambulance Services, Eyes/Blindness, Health Organizations, Heart, Hospices, Hospitals, Medical Research, Mental Health, Public Health, Single-Disease Health Associations, Transplant Networks/Donor Banks
Religion: Churches
Social Services: Child Welfare, Community Service Organizations, Domestic Violence, Family Services, People with Disabilities, Substance Abuse, Veterans, Youth Organizations

Application Procedures

Initial Contact: Send a brief letter of inquiry.
Application Requirements: Include proof of tax-exempt status, financial information, and a list of officers and trustees.
Deadlines: May 30.

Restrictions

Preference is given to research and treatment of cancer, vision and heart diseases, hospital equipment, and nurse training.

Additional Information

Trust(s): Comerica Bank

Foundation Officials

Tyrone W. Gillespie: grant comm
Richard O. Hartley: chairman grant comm
Susan J. Hartley: grant committee
Michael Kennerly: grant committee
Ruth C. Lishman: grant comm

Grants Analysis

Disclosure Period: fiscal year ending September 30, 2001
Total Grants: $139,179*
Number of Grants: 14
Average Grant: $7,363*
Highest Grant: $25,823
Lowest Grant: $2,000
Typical Range: $2,500 to $15,000
*Note: Giving excludes scholarships. Average grant figure excludes two highest grants ($50,823).

Recent Grants

Note: Grants derived from fiscal 2002 Form 990.
General

24,500	Mid-Michigan Medical Center, Midland, MI -- to purchase imaging system
23,661	St. Joseph Mercy Hospital, Pontiac, MI -- to purchase cardiac monitors
17,191	Shriners Hospitals for Children, Honolulu, HI -- to purchase sterile processing system
15,250	Leader Dogs for the Blind, Rochester, MI -- purchase surgical laser for Veterinary Dept.
15,000	Kresge Eye Institute, Detroit, MI -- eye diseases research
10,000	Hawaii Lions Foundation, Honolulu, HI -- for corneal transplant program
10,000	Saginaw Valley State University, University Center, MI -- for nursing scholarships
5,000	Hospice of Chippewa, Chippewa, MI -- for hospice program
5,000	Hospice of Kona, Kona, HI -- support hospice program
3,000	Children's Cancer Center, Tampa, FL -- for financial assistance

ROYAL & SUNALLIANCE USA INC.

Company Headquarters

9300 Arrowpoint Blvd.
Charlotte, NC 28273-8135
Web: http://www.royalsunalliance-usa.com

Company Description

Founded: 1978
Former Name: Royal Insurance Co. of America;
Acquired: Orion Capital Companies (1999).
Revenue: US$3.051 billion (2002)
Employees: 5,700 (2002)
SIC(s): 6331 Fire, Marine & Casualty Insurance, 6719 Holding Companies Nec.
Parent Company: Royal & SunAlliance Insurance Group PLC, 30 Berkeley Sq., London, United Kingdom

Operating Locations

American & Foreign Insurance Co. (NC--Charlotte); Commerical Marketing Systems (NC--Charlotte); Globe Indemnity Co. (NC--Charlotte); Milbank Insurance Co. (SD--Milbank); Newark Insurance Co. (NC--Charlotte); Phoenix Assurance of New York (NY--New York); Royal Indemnity Co. (NC--Charlotte); Royal Life Insurance Co. of America (NY--New York; NC--Charlotte); Royal & SunAlliance U.S.A., Inc. (KS; ME; MD; MA; NH; NJ; NY; NC--Charlotte; PA; TX; UT; VA); Safeguard Insurance Co. (NC--Charlotte); Sun Alliance U.S.A. (NY--New York); Sun Insurance Co. of New York (NY--New York)

Nonmonetary Support

Type: Cause-related Marketing & Promotion; Donated Equipment; In-kind Services
Volunteer Programs: Company actively encourages employee volunteerism, including an Education

Week. Special consideration is given to requests for funding if an employee is involved in the organization in a meaningful voluntary capacity.

Royal & SunAlliance Insurance Foundation, Inc.

Giving Contact

Fred E. Dabney, II, Executive Director & Vice President
Royal & SunAlliance Insurance Foundation
9300 Arrowpoint Blvd.
Charlotte, NC 28201-1000
Phone: (704)522-2056
Fax: (704)522-2055

Description

Founded: 1989
EIN: 561658178
Organization Type: Corporate Foundation
Giving Locations: areas where producers, employees, and customers reside.
Grant Types: Employee Matching Gifts, General Support, Multiyear/Continuing Support.
Note: Employee matching gift ratio: 1 to 1 up to $1,000 for gifts to higher education only.

Donor Information

Founder: Established in 1989 by Royal Insurance.

Financial Summary

Total Giving: $412,120 (2003); $684,090 (2002); $1,039,630 (2001). Note: Contributes through corporate direct giving program and foundation.
Giving Analysis: Giving for 2001 includes: foundation matching gifts ($32,287); foundation grants to United Way ($174,560); foundation ($832,783)
Assets: $1,057,048 (2003); $1,286,130 (2002); $896,543 (2001)
Gifts Received: $300,000 (2003); $1,300,000 (2002); $1,365,000 (2001). Note: In 2003 and 2002, contributions were received from Royal Group Inc. In 2001, contributions were received from Royal Group Inc., Security Insurance Co. of Hartford, and Royal Indemnity Co.

Typical Recipients

Arts & Humanities: Arts Appreciation, Arts Associations & Councils, Arts Centers, Community Arts, Dance, Ethnic & Folk Arts, Arts & Humanities-General, Historic Preservation, Libraries, Museums/Galleries, Music, Opera, Performing Arts, Public Broadcasting, Theater, Visual Arts
Civic & Public Affairs: African American Affairs, Business/Free Enterprise, Civil Rights, Economic Development, Civic & Public Affairs-General, Housing, Philanthropic Organizations, Public Policy, Safety
Education: Business Education, Colleges & Universities, Community & Junior Colleges, Continuing Education, Education Funds, Education Reform, Elementary Education (Private), Education-General, Literacy, Minority Education, Preschool Education, Private Education (Precollege), Public Education (Precollege), Science/Mathematics Education, Special Education, Student Aid
Environment: Environment-General
Health: Adolescent Health Issues, AIDS/HIV, Cancer, Children's Health/Hospitals, Emergency/Ambulance Services, Health-General, Geriatric Health, Health Funds, Health Organizations, Heart, Home-Care Services, Hospices, Hospitals, Mental Health, Public Health, Single-Disease Health Associations
Religion: Ministries, Religious Welfare
Science: Science Museums
Social Services: Child Abuse, Child Welfare, Community Centers, Community Service Organizations, Counseling, Crime Prevention, Emergency Relief,

Family Services, Homes, People with Disabilities, Recreation & Athletics, Refugee Assistance, Senior Services, Shelters/Homelessness, Social Services-General, Special Olympics, Substance Abuse, United Funds/United Ways, Volunteer Services, YMCA/YWCA/YMHA/YWHA, Youth Organizations

Application Procedures

Initial Contact: Write for application form, then submit written proposal.
Application Requirements: Include completed application; what makes Royal & SunAlliance an appropriate donor; list of current board of directors; schedule of board meetings; budgetary information; sources of income, with amounts; proof of IRS tax-exemption; and current financial statement.
Deadlines: None.
Evaluative Criteria: Priority is given to education, health, and human service organizations, and to geographic areas where the largest numbers of the company's producers, customers, and employees reside; also favors requests from organizations when an employee is involved in a meaningful voluntary capacity.

Restrictions

Does not support individuals, religious organizations for sectarian purposes, political or lobbying groups, organizations outside operating areas, fraternal organizations, medical research, veterans' organizations, broadcast fundraising, or endowments. With few exceptions, does not support operating funds of United Way member agencies nor other Foundations which support various organizations.

No funding may be secured through telephone solicitation or direct mail marketing. Contributions also will not be made to an organization solely because a company officer or employee is involved in fundraising efforts. fundraising efforts.

Additional Information

Royal & Sun Alliance was created in 1996 with the merger of two of Britain's biggest insurance companies, Royal Insurance and Sun Alliance.

The majority of contributions stay within the state of North Carolina and are decided upon at corporate headquarters. Field offices across the United States have autonomy to make smaller discretionary donations. At the headquarters, the board of directors meets quarterly to vote on all expenditures of over $2,500.

Capital funding requests are presented for consideration once per year at the annual meeting of the board of directors. Priority is given to industry-related projects.
Publications: Application Guidelines; Brochure

Corporate Officials

Fred E. Dabney, II: vice president corporate communications B Harrisburg, IL 1937. ED Southern Illinois University BA (1958). NONPR AFFIL member: Public Relations Society America; chairman: University Radio Foundation; member: Institute Business Home Safety; member: International Association of Business Communicators.
Wendy T. Harrigan: information technology executive
Elizabeth McLaughlin: chairman
Joyce W. Wheeler: vice president, corporate secretary B Durham, NC 1951. ED Albright College (1973); University of Houston (1980). CORP AFFIL corporate secretary: Royal Surplus Lines Insurance Co.; corporate secretary: Safeguard Insurance Co.; section: Royal Group Inc.

Foundation Officials

Sean A. Beatty: treasurer, director
Fred E. Dabney, II: executive director, vice president (see above)
David M. Davenport: director
Alan T. Dickson: director
Wendy T. Harrigan: director (see above)
Roderick P. Hoover, Jr.: director

Laura S. Lawrence: director
Elizabeth McLaughlin: president, director (see above)
Stephen M. Mulready: director
Linda Y. Pettigrew: secretary
Jack Reddy: director
Joyce W. Wheeler: director (see above)

Grants Analysis

Disclosure Period: calendar year ending 2003
Total Grants: $412,120*
Number of Grants: 94 (approx)
Average Grant: $4,384
Typical Range: $1,000 to $20,000
*Note: No grants list available for 2002 or 2003.

Recent Grants

Note: Grants derived from 2001 Form 990.
General

125,000	American Red Cross, Charlotte, NC -- Budget-Convention
100,000	Spencer Education Foundation, Inc. -- Broderick/Tighe
50,000	American Red Cross, Charlotte, NC -- Unbudgeted-9-11 Disaster Relief Fund
50,000	Charlotte Symphony Orchestra, Charlotte, NC -- Budget Pops in Park-McLaughlin
50,000	New York Fire 9-11 Disaster Relief Fund, Washington, DC -- Unbudgeted-9-11 Disaster Relief Fund
42,600	United Way Central Carolinas, Charlotte, NC -- Budget
42,500	United Way Central Carolinas, Charlotte, NC -- Budget
42,500	United Way Central Carolinas, Charlotte, NC -- Budget
42,500	United Way Central Carolinas, Charlotte, NC -- Budget
40,000	Arts and Science Council, Charlotte, NC -- Budget-Dabney

CELE H. AND WILLIAM B. RUBIN FAMILY FUND

Giving Contact

Ellen R. Gordon, President
32 Monadnock Road
Wellesley Hills, MA 02481-1338
Phone: (781)235-4751
Fax: (781)235-4692

Description

Founded: 1943
EIN: 116026235
Organization Type: Family Foundation
Giving Locations: nationally.
Grant Types: General Support.

Donor Information

Founder: Incorporated in 1943 by members of the Joseph Rubin family, the Sweets Co. of America, Inc., Joseph Rubin and Sons, Inc., Tootsie Roll Industries, Inc., and others.

Financial Summary

Total Giving: $3,034,458 (2002)
Giving Analysis: Giving for 2002 includes: foundation grants to United Way ($6,000)
Assets: $48,014,090 (2002)
Gifts Received: $1,050,000 (2002); $1,100,000 (2000); $1,000,000 (1998). Note: In 2002, contributions were received from Tootsie Roll Industries, Inc.

Typical Recipients

Arts & Humanities: Arts Funds, Ballet, Historic Preservation, History & Archaeology, Libraries, Museums/

Galleries, Music, Performing Arts
Civic & Public Affairs: Botanical Gardens/Parks, Economic Development, Civic & Public Affairs-General, Hispanic Affairs, Housing, Law & Justice, Municipalities/Towns, Philanthropic Organizations, Public Policy, Urban & Community Affairs, Women's Affairs, Zoos/Aquariums
Education: Business Education, Colleges & Universities, Community & Junior Colleges, Continuing Education, Education Funds, Engineering/Technological Education, Education-General, Legal Education, Medical Education, Preschool Education, Private Education (Precollege), Public Education (Precollege), Secondary Education (Private)
Environment: Air/Water Quality, Environment-General, Research, Resource Conservation, Wildlife Protection
Health: Alzheimer's Disease, Arthritis, Cancer, Clinics/Medical Centers, Diabetes, Health Organizations, Heart, Hospices, Hospitals, Kidney, Medical Rehabilitation, Medical Research, Multiple Sclerosis, Prenatal Health Issues, Public Health, Research/Studies Institutes, Single-Disease Health Associations
International: Health Care/Hospitals, Human Rights, International Affairs, International Relief Efforts, Missionary/Religious Activities
Religion: Jewish Causes, Religious Organizations, Religious Welfare
Science: Observatories & Planetariums, Science Museums, Scientific Centers & Institutes
Social Services: At-Risk Youth, Child Welfare, Community Service Organizations, Delinquency & Criminal Rehabilitation, Family Services, Food/Clothing Distribution, Homes, People with Disabilities, Recreation & Athletics, Refugee Assistance, Shelters/Homelessness, Social Services-General, United Funds/United Ways, YMCA/YWCA/YMHA/YWHA, Youth Organizations

Application Procedures

Initial Contact: The foundation has no formal grant application procedure or application form.
Deadlines: None.

Foundation Officials

Ellen Rubin Gordon: president, director B New York, NY 1931. ED Vassar College (1948-1950); Brandeis University BA (1965); Harvard University (1968). PRIM CORP EMPL president, chief operating officer, director: Tootsie Roll Industries. CORP AFFIL director: Bestfoods; vice president, director: HDI Investment Corp. NONPR AFFIL member advisory council: Stanford University Graduate School Business; member council division biological science: University Chicago Pritzker School Medicine; member: Radcliffe College Partner; member advisory council: Northwestern University Kellogg Graduate School Management; active: Presidents Export Council; trustee, member: Northwestern University Associates; member, board fellows: Harvard University Medical School; member, director: National Confectioners Association; member university resources & overseers committee: Harvard University.
Melvin Jay Gordon: vice president, director B Boston, MA November 26, 1919. ED Harvard University BA (1941); Harvard University MBA (1943). PRIM CORP EMPL chairman, chief executive officer, director: Tootsie Roll Industries. CORP AFFIL president, director: HDI Investment Corp.

Grants Analysis

Disclosure Period: calendar year ending 2002
Total Grants: $3,028,458*
Number of Grants: 86
Average Grant: $10,284*
Highest Grant: $2,144,000
Lowest Grant: $100
Typical Range: $100 to $5,000 and $10,000 to $80,000
*Note: Giving excludes United Way. Average grant figure excludes highest grant.

Recent Grants

Note: Grants derived from 2002 Form 990.
Library-Related

76,500	Wellesley Free Library, Wellesley, MA

General

2,144,000	Fleet Charitable Gift Fund, Boston, MA
500,000	Harvard University Medical School, Boston, MA
77,000	Combined Jewish Philanthropies of Greater Boston, Boston, MA
32,500	Kellogg Graduate School of Management, Evanston, IL
31,000	Meadowbrook School, Weston, MA
26,000	Juvenile Diabetes Foundation, Chicago, IL
15,000	Food Allergy Institute, New York, NY
15,000	Radcliffe Institute for Advanced Studied, Cambridge, MA
10,000	University of Chicago, Chicago, IL
7,500	Harvard Business School, Boston, MA

SAMUEL RUBIN FOUNDATION

Giving Contact

Lauranne Jones, Grants Administrator
Samuel Rubin Foundation, Inc.
777 United Nations Plaza
New York, NY 10017
Phone: (212)697-8945
Fax: (212)682-0886
E-mail: info@samuelrubinfoundation.org
Web: http://www.samuelrubinfoundation.org

Description

Founded: 1949
EIN: 136164671
Organization Type: General Purpose Foundation
Giving Locations: internationally; nationally.
Grant Types: General Support, Project.

Donor Information

Founder: Incorporated in New York in 1949 from funds donated by the late Samuel Rubin, the founder of Faberge. He was also a founder of the New York University Bellevue Medical Center and the American Symphony Orchestra.

Financial Summary

Total Giving: $946,349 (fiscal year ending June 30, 2002)
Assets: $11,883,273 (fiscal 2002)
Gifts Received: $660 (fiscal 1994); $30,000 (fiscal 1993)

Typical Recipients

Arts & Humanities: Arts Associations & Councils, Arts Centers, Arts Funds, Community Arts, Film & Video, Arts & Humanities-General, History & Archaeology, Libraries, Literary Arts, Museums/Galleries, Music, Performing Arts, Public Broadcasting, Theater
Civic & Public Affairs: Asian American Affairs, Botanical Gardens/Parks, Business/Free Enterprise, Civil Rights, Community Foundations, Economic Development, Economic Policy, Employment/Job Training, Civic & Public Affairs-General, Housing, Law & Justice, Legal Aid, Nonprofit Management, Parades/Festivals, Philanthropic Organizations, Public Policy, Safety, Urban & Community Affairs, Women's Affairs
Education: Arts/Humanities Education, Colleges & Universities, Community & Junior Colleges, Education Associations, Education Funds, Education Reform, Education-General, Health & Physical Education, International Studies, Legal Education, Public Education (Precollege), Science/Mathematics Education, Social Sciences Education
Environment: Air/Water Quality, Environment-

General
Health: Health-General, Hospitals, Medical Research
International: Foreign Educational Institutions, International-General, Health Care/Hospitals, Human Rights, International Affairs, International Development, International Environmental Issues, International Organizations, International Peace & Security Issues, International Relations, International Relief Efforts, Missionary/Religious Activities
Religion: Churches, Religion-General, Jewish Causes, Religious Welfare
Science: Scientific Centers & Institutes
Social Services: Child Welfare, Community Service Organizations, Crime Prevention, Domestic Violence, Family Services, Food/Clothing Distribution, Homes, Shelters/Homelessness, Veterans, YMCA/YWCA/YMHA/YWHA, Youth Organizations

Application Procedures

Initial Contact: The foundation has no formal application procedures. Applicants should submit a proposal in writing.
Application Requirements: A proposal must describe in detail the organization and the project. Include a budget and tax-exempt status letter.
Deadlines: The first Friday in January, September, and May.
Review Process: The board of directors meets three times a year. However, limited funds and recurring commitments restrict the board's grantmaking ability.

Restrictions

The foundation does not award grants for building funds, scholarships, endowments, or to individuals. At its February 2003 meeting, the board of directors of the foundation decided that, as a consequence of the economic downturn, it would not be awarding new grants for the remainder of the fiscal year. In addition, applications for the next fiscal year, beginning July 1, 2003, will be accepted only from those eligible organisation that have been previous recipients of support from the foundation; previous support, however, does not guarantee future support.

Additional Information

Applications sent by facsimile transmission or e-mail will not be given consideration.
Publications: Program Policy Statement

Foundation Officials

Charles L. Mandelstam: secretary B Brookline, MA 1927. ED Harvard College BA (1949); Yale College LLB (1952). PRIM CORP EMPL partner: Dornbush, Mensch, Mandelstam & Silverman New York City. NONPR AFFIL member: Phi Beta Kappa; member, director: Societe d'Exploitation Agricole Rhodienne; member: Association Bar New York City; counselor: North Salem New York Open Land Foundation.
Cora Weiss: president B New York, NY 1934. ED University of Wisconsin BA (1956); Hunter College (1956-1958). NONPR AFFIL director: Peace Action; director: US-NIS Women's Consortium; vice president: International Peace Bureau; director: Downtown Community TV; director: Interlegal USA.
Daniel Weiss: director
Judy Weiss: vice president
Peter Weiss: treasurer B Vienna, Austria 1925. ED Saint John's College AB (1949); Yale University JD (1952). CORP AFFIL counsel: The Chanel Co. Ltd. NONPR AFFIL co-president: International Association Lawyers Against Nuclear Arms; chairman: Lawyers Committee Nuclear Policy; vice president: Center Constitutional Rights.
Tamara Weiss: director

Grants Analysis

Disclosure Period: fiscal year ending June 30, 2002
Total Grants: $946,349
Number of Grants: 74
Average Grant: $9,672*
Highest Grant: $150,000

Lowest Grant: $1,000
Typical Range: $1,000 to $15,000
*Note: Average grant figure excludes two highest grants ($250,000).

Recent Grants

Note: Grants derived from fiscal 2002 Form 990.
Library-Related
5,000   Meiklejohn Civil Liberties Library, Berkeley, CA
General
150,000   Transitional Institute
100,000   PEF Israel Endowment Fund, New York, NY
40,000   Americans for Peace Now, Washington, DC
40,000   Lawyers Committee on Nuclear Policy, New York, NY
37,000   A.J. Muste Memorial Institute, New York, NY
34,000   Africa Fund, New York, NY
30,000   Global Kids, New York, NY
25,000   Downtown Community Television Center, New York, NY
22,500   Hampshire College, Amherst, MA
20,000   Peaceworkers, San Francisco, CA

HELENA RUBINSTEIN FOUNDATION

Giving Contact

Diane Moss, President & Chief Executive Officer
477 Madison Avenue, 7th Floor
New York, NY 10022-5802
Phone: (212)750-7310
Fax: (212)750-9798
Web: http://www.fdncenter.org/grantmaker/rubinstein

Description

Founded: 1953
EIN: 136102666
Organization Type: General Purpose Foundation
Giving Locations: NY: New York
Grant Types: Fellowship, General Support, Operating Expenses, Project, Research, Scholarship.

Donor Information

Founder: Established in 1953 by businesswoman Helena Rubinstein, who was born in Poland in 1871. At the age of twenty she began her cosmetics business with one product, a face cream. Her cosmetics empire expanded to London in 1902, to Paris in 1906, and to New York in 1912. During her lifetime she accumulated significant collections of African sculptures, modern paintings and sculptures, Oriental and Oceanic art, and Egyptian antiques. The foundation was a major beneficiary of her legacy when she died in 1965.

Financial Summary

Total Giving: $2,354,781 (fiscal year ending May 31, 2004); $1,967,232 (fiscal 2003); $2,604,958 (fiscal 2002)
Assets: $34,455,105 (fiscal 2002); $40,474,526 (fiscal 2001)

Typical Recipients

Arts & Humanities: Arts Associations & Councils, Arts Centers, Arts Festivals, Arts Funds, Arts Institutes, Arts Outreach, Ballet, Dance, Libraries, Museums/Galleries, Music, Opera, Performing Arts, Public Broadcasting, Theater, Visual Arts
Civic & Public Affairs: Economic Development, Employment/Job Training, Ethnic Organizations, Housing, Law & Justice, Municipalities/Towns, Professional & Trade Associations, Public Policy, Urban &

Community Affairs, Women's Affairs
Education: Afterschool/Enrichment Programs, Arts/Humanities Education, Colleges & Universities, Education Reform, Faculty Development, Education-General, Gifted & Talented Programs, Health & Physical Education, Legal Education, Literacy, Medical Education, Minority Education, Preschool Education, Public Education (Precollege), Science/Mathematics Education, Social Sciences Education, Special Education, Student Aid, Vocational & Technical Education
Environment: Air/Water Quality, Resource Conservation
Health: AIDS/HIV, Alzheimer's Disease, Cancer, Children's Health/Hospitals, Clinics/Medical Centers, Eyes/Blindness, Geriatric Health, Health Funds, Health Organizations, Hospitals, Medical Rehabilitation, Medical Research, Medical Training, Nursing Services, Prenatal Health Issues, Preventive Medicine/Wellness Organizations, Public Health, Single-Disease Health Associations
International: Foreign Arts Organizations, Health Care/Hospitals, Human Rights, International Affairs, International Peace & Security Issues, International Relief Efforts
Religion: Jewish Causes, Seminaries
Science: Science Museums, Scientific Centers & Institutes
Social Services: At-Risk Youth, Big Brothers/Big Sisters, Child Welfare, Community Centers, Community Service Organizations, Counseling, Day Care, Family Planning, Family Services, Recreation & Athletics, Senior Services, Shelters/Homelessness, Substance Abuse, United Funds/United Ways, YMCA/YWCA/YMHA/YWHA, Youth Organizations

Application Procedures

Initial Contact: The foundation does not publish an application form, but the New York Common Application Form may be used. Organizations seeking funding should submit a brief letter rather than make telephone inquiries.
Application Requirements: Letters of inquiry should include an outline of project; goals; budget; amount requested; other funding sources; a description of the organization and its current budget.
Deadlines: None.
Review Process: Every proposal and inquiry is acknowledged by letter. Additional information may be requested if the proposal is of interest to the foundation. A meeting or site visit may be arranged by the foundation. Proposals are acted upon by the board of directors, which meets semi-annually, in May and November. Grants are not renewed automatically, but are considered on the basis of evaluation of reports, site visits, priorities, and the availability of funds.

Restrictions

Grants are made only to tax-exempt non-profit organizations. Generally, they are for a one-year period. Scholarship and fellowship grants are made directly to institutions. General operating grants are made, but the foundation prefers to support specific projects or programs. The foundation does not support individuals or film or video projects. Grants are rarely made to support endowments or capital campaigns. The foundation does not make loans, or provide emergency funds. Grants are typically restricted to organizations in New York City.

Additional Information

Grantees are expected to submit interim reports within six to eight months after receipt of a grant award. A final report is also recommended at the end of the grant period.
Publications: Biennial report

Foundation Officials

Deborah DeCotis: director
Robert S. Friedman: secretary, treasurer
Diane Moss: president, chief executive officer

Louis E. Slesin: director
Suzanne Slesin: director

Grants Analysis

Disclosure Period: fiscal year ending May 31, 2004
Total Grants: $2,354,781
Number of Grants: 128
Average Grant: $18,397
Highest Grant: $150,000
Lowest Grant: $100
Typical Range: $10,000 to $25,000

Recent Grants

Note: Grants derived from 2002 Form 990.
Library-Related

150,000	New York Public Library, New York, NY -- provides renovation
50,000	Libraries for the Future, New York, NY -- provides initiative to help public libraries

General

150,000	Thirteen/WNET, New York, NY -- offers sponsorship of children's educational television programming
150,000	United Jewish Appeal - Federation of Jewish Philanthropies of New York, New York, NY -- provides support of federation agencies
100,000	Whitney Museum of American Art, New York, NY -- for Helena Rubinstein education chair endowment
50,000	Goddard Riverside Community Center, New York, NY -- provides college-counseling program
50,000	Museum of Modern Art, New York, NY -- provides stipend support
50,000	New York Foundation for the Arts, New York, NY -- assists with exhibition of the works of painting fellows
40,000	Kress Vision Program, New York, NY -- offers eye exams and follow-up care
35,000	Columbia University, School of General Studies, New York, NY -- provides scholarships for women
35,000	Women's Housing and Economic Development Corporation, Bronx, NY -- provides job training and support services
30,000	Children's Health Fund, New York, NY -- provides mobile pediatric program and asthma education

RUDIN FOUNDATION

Giving Contact

Susan H. Rapaport, Administrator
345 Park Ave.
New York, NY 10154
Phone: (212)407-2400

Description

Founded: 1960
EIN: 136113064
Organization Type: Private Foundation
Giving Locations: NY: New York
Grant Types: General Support.

Donor Information

Founder: Jack Rudin, Lewis Rudin

Financial Summary

Gifts Received: $1,425,900 (2000); $1,970,300 (1999); $916,200 (1996). Note: In 2000, major contributions were received from 945 Fifth Ave. ($102,000), Rudin Estates Co. ($115,600) and 415 Madison ($1,180,400); 12 other donors made contributions of $34,800 or less each. In 1994, major contributions were received from 945 Fifth Ave. ($102,000), 80 Pine ($341,600), 415 Madison ($62,800), Rudin Estates Co. ($54,000), and Rudin

Management Co. ($46,000); 16 other donors made contributions of $33,700 or less each.

Typical Recipients

Arts & Humanities: Arts Associations & Councils, Arts Funds, Dance, Film & Video, Libraries, Museums/Galleries, Music, Performing Arts, Theater
Civic & Public Affairs: African American Affairs, Botanical Gardens/Parks, Business/Free Enterprise, Economic Development, Civic & Public Affairs-General, Law & Justice, Municipalities/Towns, Parades/Festivals, Philanthropic Organizations, Public Policy, Safety, Urban & Community Affairs, Women's Affairs, Zoos/Aquariums
Education: Arts/Humanities Education, Business Education, Colleges & Universities, Elementary Education (Private), Faculty Development, Education-General, Literacy, Minority Education, Private Education (Precollege), Public Education (Precollege), Science/Mathematics Education, Secondary Education (Public), Social Sciences Education
Health: Clinics/Medical Centers, Geriatric Health, Health Organizations, Hospitals, Long-Term Care, Medical Research, Respiratory, Single-Disease Health Associations, Speech & Hearing
International: International Environmental Issues, International Organizations
Religion: Churches, Dioceses, Jewish Causes, Religious Organizations, Religious Welfare, Seminaries, Synagogues/Temples
Social Services: Big Brothers/Big Sisters, Child Welfare, Community Centers, Community Service Organizations, Crime Prevention, Delinquency & Criminal Rehabilitation, Family Services, Food/Clothing Distribution, Recreation & Athletics, Senior Services, Shelters/Homelessness, Substance Abuse, United Funds/United Ways, Volunteer Services, Youth Organizations

Application Procedures

Initial Contact: Send a brief letter of inquiry.
Application Requirements: Include a description of organization and proof of tax-exempt status.
Deadlines: None.

Foundation Officials

Beth Rudin DeWoody: president, director
David B. Levy: treasurer, director
John Lewin: vice president, director
John Leland Sills: director B New York, NY 1942. ED Rensselaer Polytechnic Institute BS (1964); Rensselaer Polytechnic Institute MS (1965); Fordham University JD (1969); New York University LLM (1974). CORP AFFIL director: Park Place Productions Inc. NONPR AFFIL member: New York State Bar Association; director: Westchester Lyric Festival; member: Association Bar of City of New York; member: American Bar Association. CLUB AFFIL member: New York Road Runners Club.
Richard C. Snider: secretary, director
Jeffrey Steinman: executive vice president, director

Grants Analysis

Disclosure Period: calendar year ending 2000
Total Grants: $1,264,416
Number of Grants: 186
Average Grant: $5,754*
Highest Grant: $200,000
Typical Range: $1,000 to $10,000
*Note: Average grant figure excludes highest grant.

Recent Grants

Note: Grants derived from 2001 Form 990.
General

100,000	United Jewish Appeal, New York, NY
55,000	Armory High School Sports Foundation, New York, NY
46,250	Cathedral Church of St. John the Divine, New York, NY
42,000	Central Synagogue, New York, NY
42,000	Westside Community Garden, Inc., New York, NY

30,000	Jewish Theological Seminary of America, New York, NY
29,004	New York City Police Foundation, New York, NY
25,000	Carnegie Hall Corporation, New York, NY
25,000	Congregation Rodeph Sholom, New York, NY
25,000	FDNY Fire Safety Education Fund, New York, NY

SAMUEL AND MAY RUDIN FOUNDATION

Giving Contact

Susan H. Rapaport, Administrator
c/o Rudin
345 Park Avenue
New York, NY 10154
Phone: (212)407-2400

Description

Founded: 1976
EIN: 132906946
Organization Type: Private Foundation
Giving Locations: NY: New York
Grant Types: General Support.

Donor Information

Founder: the late Samuel Rudin

Financial Summary

Total Giving: $0 (fiscal year ending June 30, 2004)
Assets: $94 (fiscal 2004)
Gifts Received: $4,000,000 (fiscal 1997); $3,188,199 (fiscal 1996); $5,940,608 (fiscal 1995). Note: In fiscal 1996, contributions were received from the trust of Samuel Rudin.

Typical Recipients

Arts & Humanities: Arts Associations & Councils, Arts Centers, Arts Festivals, Dance, Historic Preservation, History & Archaeology, Libraries, Museums/Galleries, Music, Public Broadcasting, Theater, Visual Arts
Civic & Public Affairs: Botanical Gardens/Parks, Employment/Job Training
Education: Arts/Humanities Education, Colleges & Universities, Legal Education, Medical Education, Minority Education, Religious Education, Social Sciences Education, Student Aid
Environment: Environment-General, Resource Conservation
Health: AIDS/HIV, Cancer, Children's Health/Hospitals, Emergency/Ambulance Services, Eyes/Blindness, Health Organizations, Heart, Hospitals, Long-Term Care, Mental Health, Transplant Networks/Donor Banks
International: Health Care/Hospitals, Missionary/Religious Activities
Religion: Jewish Causes
Science: Science Exhibits & Fairs, Science Museums
Social Services: At-Risk Youth, Child Welfare, Community Service Organizations, People with Disabilities, Recreation & Athletics, Scouts, Substance Abuse

Application Procedures

Initial Contact: Send a brief letter of inquiry.
Application Requirements: brochure describing organization's purpose and activities and proof of tax-exempt status.
Deadlines: None.

Restrictions

Preference is given to museums and educational institutions.

Additional Information

The foundation's 2001 990 indicates that it is liquidating its assets and giving away its funds.

Foundation Officials

Madeleine Rudin Johnson: vice president, director
Jack Rudin: chairman, director B 1924. PRIM CORP EMPL chairman, director: Rudin Management Co. Inc. CORP AFFIL partner: 345 Park Co.; partner: Whitehall Co.
Katherine L. Rudin: vice president, director

Grants Analysis

Disclosure Period: fiscal year ending June 30, 2004
Total Grants: $0*
Note: No grants awarded in 2004.

Recent Grants

Note: Grants derived from fiscal 1996 Form 990.
General

500,000	United Jewish Appeal, New York, NY -- Operation Exodus
215,000	Memorial Sloan-Kettering Cancer Center, New York, NY -- Roberta C. Rudin Leukemia Research Fund
150,000	Columbia University Harlem Hospital Center, New York, NY -- Incarnation Children's Center Medical Staff
75,000	New York University, New York, NY -- Rudin Merit Scholarship Program
60,000	St. Vincent's Hospital and Medical Center, New York, NY -- supportive care program for AIDS patients
50,000	Children's Storefront, New York, NY
50,000	Conservancy for Historic Battery Park, New York, NY -- summer concert series
50,000	Cornell University Medical College New York Hospital, New York, NY -- optic nerve regeneration for glaucoma
50,000	Margaret M. Dyson Vision Research Institute, Cornell University Medical College, New York, NY -- research on optic nerve and glaucoma
50,000	Medical Development for Israel, Children's Medical Center, New York, NY

FRAN AND WARREN RUPP FOUNDATION

Giving Contact

Nicholas R. Gesouras
Keybank National Association
42 North Main Street
42 North Main Street
Mansfield, OH 44902
Phone: (419)525-7665

Description

Founded: 1977
EIN: 341230690
Organization Type: Private Foundation
Giving Locations: OH: Mansfield
Grant Types: General Support, Matching, Operating Expenses, Scholarship.

Donor Information

Founder: Fran Rupp, Warren Rupp

Financial Summary

Total Giving: $1,219,135 (2002). Note: In 1996 Giving includes scholarship ($78,500).
Giving Analysis: Giving for 2002 includes: foundation matching gifts ($10,000); foundation scholarships ($15,000)
Assets: $16,297,090 (2002)
Gifts Received: $36,000 (2002); $36,000 (2000);

$36,000 (1999). Note: Contributors in 2002 were John W. Rupp Charitable Lead Trust, Sheron A. Rupp Charitable Lead Trust, and Suzanne R. Hartung Charitable Lead Trust.

Typical Recipients

Arts & Humanities: Arts Associations & Councils, Arts Funds, Community Arts, Film & Video, History & Archaeology, Libraries, Museums/Galleries, Music, Public Broadcasting, Theater
Civic & Public Affairs: Civic & Public Affairs-General, Housing, Safety, Urban & Community Affairs
Education: Arts/Humanities Education, Colleges & Universities, Environmental Education, Education-General, Minority Education, Private Education (Precollege), Science/Mathematics Education, Student Aid, Vocational & Technical Education
Environment: Environment-General, Resource Conservation, Sanitary Systems, Wildlife Protection
Health: Children's Health/Hospitals, Clinics/Medical Centers, Eyes/Blindness, Health-General, Hospitals, Kidney, Medical Rehabilitation, Medical Research, Mental Health, Nursing Services, Public Health, Research/Studies Institutes
Religion: Religious Organizations, Religious Welfare
Science: Science-General, Scientific Centers & Institutes
Social Services: Animal Protection, Big Brothers/Big Sisters, Camps, Child Welfare, Community Service Organizations, Crime Prevention, Domestic Violence, Family Planning, Family Services, People with Disabilities, Recreation & Athletics, Scouts, Shelters/Homelessness, Social Services-General, Volunteer Services, YMCA/YWCA/YMHA/YWHA, Youth Organizations

Application Procedures

Initial Contact: Send a brief letter of inquiry. Applicants will be provided with appropriate forms for submitting proposals.
Deadlines: None.

Additional Information

Publications: Application Form

Foundation Officials

Frances R. Christian: chairman
Miles W. Christian: trustee
Suzanne R. Hartung: vice president
Sheron Adeline Rupp: vice president B Mansfield, OH 1943. ED Denison University BA (1965); University of Massachusetts MFA (1982). NONPR AFFIL guest artist, lecturer: Springfield Museum Fine Arts; guest artist, lecturer: University Massachusetts; guest artist, lecturer: Portland School Art; guest artist, lecturer: Massachusetts College Art; guest artist, lecturer: New York University; guest artist, lecturer: Deerfield Academy; guest artist, lecturer: Hartford School Art; guest artist, lecturer: Bard College; guest artist, lecturer: Boston Musical School.
Donald E. Smith: president
Timothy S. Smith: secretary, treasurer

Grants Analysis

Disclosure Period: calendar year ending 2002
Total Grants: $1,194,135*
Number of Grants: 33
Average Grant: $18,004*
Highest Grant: $600,000
Lowest Grant: $1,500
Typical Range: $5,000 to $50,000
Note: Giving excludes scholarships; matching gifts. Average grants figure excludes highest grants.

Recent Grants

Note: Grants derived from 2002 Form 990.
General

600,000	Medcentral Health System, Mansfield, OH -- for capital improvements
80,000	Ashland University, Ashland, OH -- renovation of Kettering Science Center
66,667	Johnny Appleseed Heritage Center, Mansfield, OH -- support amphitheater construction
50,000	Richland County Foundation, Mansfield, OH -- for construction of park pavilion and City of Mansfield
46,115	Richland County Habitat for Humanity, Mansfield, OH -- for Shelby building project
45,255	Richland Performing Arts Association, Mansfield, OH -- for installation of hydraulic tandem stage lift
40,000	Mansfield Police Athletic League, Mansfield, OH -- for bleachers and OCIE Hill Community Center
33,333	Mohican School in the Out-of-Doors, Butler, OH -- for phase III construction of adult facility
30,000	Community Action for Capable Youth, Mansfield, OH -- Informed Teens Program
25,000	Mansfield Humane Society, Mansfield, OH -- for building project

TOM RUSSELL CHARITABLE FOUNDATION

Giving Contact

Thomas A. Hearn, Vice President & Director
2 Transam Plaza, Suite 200
Oakbrook Terrace, IL 60181
Phone: (630)916-0123
Fax: (630)916-0567

Description

Founded: 1960
EIN: 366082517
Organization Type: Private Foundation
Giving Locations: IL: Chicago metropolitan area
Grant Types: General Support.

Donor Information

Founder: the late Thomas C. Russell, Wrap-On Co., Inc., Huron and Orleans Building Corp.

Financial Summary

Total Giving: $660,000 (fiscal year ending August 31, 2004). Note: Fiscal 1996 Giving includes United Way ($4,000).
Giving Analysis: Giving for fiscal 2004 includes: foundation grants to United Way ($5,000)
Assets: $14,240,791 (fiscal 2004)

Typical Recipients

Arts & Humanities: Historic Preservation, Libraries, Public Broadcasting
Civic & Public Affairs: Employment/Job Training, Civic & Public Affairs-General, Housing, Legal Aid, Parades/Festivals, Philanthropic Organizations, Zoos/Aquariums
Education: Arts/Humanities Education, Colleges & Universities, Education Reform, Education-General, Private Education (Precollege), Secondary Education (Private), Student Aid
Environment: Environment-General
Health: Cancer, Hospitals, Hospitals (University Affiliated), Medical Rehabilitation, Medical Research, Single-Disease Health Associations
International: International Organizations, International Relief Efforts
Religion: Churches, Religious Organizations, Religious Welfare
Science: Scientific Centers & Institutes, Scientific Organizations
Social Services: At-Risk Youth, Child Welfare, Com-

munity Centers, Community Service Organizations, Food/Clothing Distribution, People with Disabilities, Recreation & Athletics, Scouts, Senior Services, Shelters/Homelessness, YMCA/YWCA/YMHA/YWHA, Youth Organizations

Application Procedures

Initial Contact: The foundation has no formal grant application procedure or application form.
Application Requirements: Request should include descriptive material about the organization and the most current financial data.
Deadlines: None.

Additional Information

Publications: Application Guidelines

Foundation Officials

J. Kirby Aiken: director
John L. Bishop: treasurer, director
Thomas A. Hearn: president, director
David S. Lindquist: vice president, director
J. Tod Meserow: secretary, director
Frank S. Scarlati, Jr.: assistant secretary, director

Grants Analysis

Disclosure Period: fiscal year ending August 31, 2004
Total Grants: $655,000*
Number of Grants: 70
Average Grant: $8,015*
Highest Grant: $60,000
Lowest Grant: $5,000
Typical Range: $5,000 to $20,000
*Note: Giving excludes United Way. Average grant figure excludes two highest grant ($110,000).

Recent Grants

Note: Grants derived from 2004 Form 990.
General

60,000	Alice Lloyd College, Pippa Passes, KY
50,000	Northwestern University, Chicago, IL
25,000	Donka Inc., Wheaton, IL
25,000	Inter Faith Food Shuttle, Raleigh, NC
20,000	Cumberland College, Williamsburg, KY
20,000	St. Jude House, Crown Point, IN
15,000	Beacon Therapeutic School Inc., Chicago, IL
15,000	Central Oklahoma Community Action Agency, Norman, OK
15,000	Emporia Rescue mission, Emporia, KS
10,000	Capital Area Soccer League, Raleigh, NC

JOSEPHINE S. RUSSELL CHARITABLE TRUST

Giving Contact

Lee Crooks, Trust Officer
c/o PNC Bank NA
PO Box 1198
Cincinnati, OH 45201
Phone: (513)651-8377

Description

Founded: 1976
EIN: 316195446
Organization Type: Private Foundation
Giving Locations: OH: Cincinnati metropolitan area
Grant Types: Capital, General Support, Project, Seed Money.

Donor Information

Founder: the late Josephine Schell Russell

Financial Summary

Total Giving: $417,104 (fiscal year ending June 30, 2004); $820,050 (fiscal 2001)

Giving Analysis: Giving for fiscal 2004 includes: foundation scholarships ($15,000); foundation grants to United Way ($20,000); fiscal 2001: foundation grants to United Way ($7,500); foundation scholarships ($10,000)
Assets: $11,437,873 (fiscal 2004); $13,240,951 (fiscal 2001)

Typical Recipients

Arts & Humanities: Arts Centers, Arts Institutes, Ballet, Community Arts, Arts & Humanities-General, Historic Preservation, Libraries, Literary Arts, Museums/Galleries, Music, Opera, Performing Arts, Public Broadcasting, Theater
Civic & Public Affairs: African American Affairs, Botanical Gardens/Parks, Clubs, Community Foundations, Economic Development, Employment/Job Training, Civic & Public Affairs-General, Housing, Legal Aid, Native American Affairs, Parades/Festivals, Urban & Community Affairs, Women's Affairs, Zoos/Aquariums
Education: Afterschool/Enrichment Programs, Arts/Humanities Education, Colleges & Universities, Continuing Education, Elementary Education (Private), Education-General, Literacy, Private Education (Precollege), Public Education (Precollege), Science/Mathematics Education, Secondary Education (Private), Special Education, Student Aid
Environment: Environment-General, Resource Conservation
Health: Adolescent Health Issues, Cancer, Children's Health/Hospitals, Health Organizations, Home-Care Services, Hospices, Long-Term Care, Mental Health, Prenatal Health Issues, Preventive Medicine/Wellness Organizations, Public Health, Respiratory, Single-Disease Health Associations, Speech & Hearing
Religion: Churches, Jewish Causes, Ministries, Religious Welfare, Social/Policy Issues
Social Services: Big Brothers/Big Sisters, Child Welfare, Community Centers, Community Service Organizations, Day Care, Delinquency & Criminal Rehabilitation, Domestic Violence, Family Services, Food/Clothing Distribution, People with Disabilities, Scouts, Senior Services, Shelters/Homelessness, Substance Abuse, United Funds/United Ways, Volunteer Services, YMCA/YWCA/YMHA/YWHA, Youth Organizations

Application Procedures

Initial Contact: Submit seven copies of proposal.
Application Requirements: Include name, address, telephone number, and founding date of organization; names and titles of trustees, officers, and key executives or employees; a description of organization and its current activities; geographic area and population served; purpose of funds sought and community benefits expected; amount requested and expected budget; plan for permanent financial support of project, if applicable; listing of any other area organizations with similar purpose or services; listing of other sources solicited for funding; budget and most recent financial information; and proof of tax-exempt status.
Deadlines: One month prior to scheduled meeting on third Friday of January and July.

Additional Information

Publications: Informational Brochure (including Application Guidelines)
Trust(s): PNC Bank OH NA

Grants Analysis

Disclosure Period: fiscal year ending June 30, 2004
Total Grants: $382,104*
Number of Grants: 27
Average Grant: $14,152
Highest Grant: $50,000
Lowest Grant: $5,000
Typical Range: $5,000 to $25,000
*Note: Giving excludes United Way and scholarships.

Recent Grants

Note: Grants derived from fiscal 2004 Form 990.
General

50,000	Zoological Society of Cincinnati, Cincinnati, OH -- to support animal hospital
30,000	Cincinnati Art Museum, Cincinnati, OH -- to support Cincinnati wing capital campaign
30,000	Lincoln Heights Health Care, Cincinnati, OH
30,000	Mercy Health System of Southwest Ohio, Cincinnati, OH -- for emergency department redesign and renovation
25,000	Art Academy of Cincinnati, Cincinnati, OH
25,000	Bayley Place, Cincinnati, OH -- to build new wellness center
20,000	Stepping Stones Center, Cincinnati, OH -- for preschool services
20,000	United Way and Community Chest, Cincinnati, OH
15,000	Lighthouse Youth Services, Cincinnati, OH -- to support youth crisis center capital expenses
13,419	Brighton Center, Newport, KY -- to support bright days renovation project

RUSSELL FAMILY FOUNDATION

Giving Contact

Stephanie Anderson, Grants Manager
PO Box 2567
Gig Harbor, WA 98335
Phone: (253)851-0460

Description

Founded: 1995
EIN: 911663336
Organization Type: Private Foundation
Giving Locations: WA: Tacoma and Pierce County
Grant Types: General Support.

Financial Summary

Total Giving: $4,542,500 (2003); $4,458,239 (2002)
Giving Analysis: Giving for 2002 includes: foundation grants to United Way ($10,000)
Assets: $118,061,698 (2003); $99,348,092 (2002)
Gifts Received: $12,500 (2003); $124,326 (2002); $792,859 (1999). Note: In 1996 and 1999, contributions were received from were received from D. Michael Sullivan ($599,980) and Human Solidarity ($40,000). contributions were received from D. Michael Sullivan.

Typical Recipients

Arts & Humanities: Arts Associations & Councils, Arts Institutes, History & Archaeology, Libraries, Museums/Galleries, Public Broadcasting
Civic & Public Affairs: Community Foundations, Ethnic Organizations, Civic & Public Affairs-General, Housing, Nonprofit Management, Philanthropic Organizations, Public Policy, Urban & Community Affairs
Education: Colleges & Universities, Community & Junior Colleges, Education Reform, Environmental Education, Education-General, Gifted & Talented Programs, Leadership Training, Literacy, Private Education (Precollege), Secondary Education (Private)
Environment: Air/Water Quality, Environment-General, Protection, Resource Conservation, Watershed
Health: Clinics/Medical Centers, Health-General, Health Organizations, Mental Health
International: Foreign Arts Organizations, International Affairs
Religion: Churches, Religious Welfare
Social Services: Community Service Organizations,

Scouts, Social Services-General, United Funds/ United Ways, Youth Organizations

Application Procedures
Initial Contact: Submit a one-page letter of inquiry.
Application Requirements: Include organization's mission and project description.
Deadlines: Feb. 2 and July 12.
Evaluative Criteria: Foundation grantmaking focuses on environmental sustainability, focused locally on Puget Sound, environmental education and green business practices; Jane's Fund focused locally on grassroots leadership in Tacoma and Pierce County, and the George F. Russell Jr. Fund focused globally on peace and security issues in Eastern Europe, Russia and Asia Pacific.

Additional Information
Publications: Application Form; Guidelines

Foundation Officials
Sarah R. Cavanaugh: secretary, director
Dion R. Rurik: director
Eric A. Russell: director
George F. Russell, Jr.: vice president, director
Jane T. Russell: president, treasurer, director
Richard Russell: director

Grants Analysis
Disclosure Period: calendar year ending 2003
Total Grants: $4,542,500
Number of Grants: 173
Average Grant: $24,084*
Highest Grant: $400,000
Lowest Grant: $25
Typical Range: $5,000 to $50,000
*Note: Average grant figure excludes highest grant.

Recent Grants
Note: Grants derived from 2001 Form 990.
Library-Related

50,000	Pierce County Library-Foundation, Tacoma, WA -- funding towards kids bookmobile

General

332,500	Tacoma Art Museum, Tacoma, WA
200,000	Chapel Hill Presbyterian Church, Gig Harbor, WA
200,000	East West Institute, New York, NY -- funding towards general support
200,000	East West Institute, New York, NY
150,000	Leland Stanford Junior University, Stanford, CA
140,000	Friends of the Cedar River Watershed, Seattle, WA
125,000	City of Tacoma, Tacoma, WA -- conducting feasibility study for aquarium/marine science center
100,000	Bellarmine Preparatory School, Tacoma, WA -- renovation of math & science building
100,000	East West Institute, New York, NY -- funding towards general support
100,000	First Place, Seattle, WA -- funding towards summer school program

JOSEPHINE G. RUSSELL TRUST

Giving Contact
Clifford E. Elias, Managing Trustee
70 East St.
Methuen, MA 01844
Phone: (978)687-0501

Description
Founded: 1934
EIN: 042136910

Organization Type: Private Foundation
Giving Locations: MA: Lawrence including surrounding communities
Grant Types: Capital, Emergency, General Support, Project, Scholarship.

Donor Information
Founder: the late Josephine G. Russell

Financial Summary
Total Giving: 1997 Giving includes United Way ($5,000).

Typical Recipients
Arts & Humanities: Arts Centers, History & Archaeology, Libraries, Museums/Galleries
Civic & Public Affairs: Asian American Affairs, Chambers of Commerce, Community Foundations, Civic & Public Affairs-General, Hispanic Affairs, Housing, Legal Aid, Municipalities/Towns, Urban & Community Affairs
Education: Business Education, Colleges & Universities, Community & Junior Colleges, Education-General, Private Education (Precollege), Public Education (Precollege), School Volunteerism, Secondary Education (Private)
Health: Children's Health/Hospitals, Clinics/Medical Centers, Home-Care Services, Hospitals, Medical Research, Nursing Services, Trauma Treatment
International: International Organizations
Religion: Churches, Jewish Causes, Religious Welfare
Social Services: At-Risk Youth, Big Brothers/Big Sisters, Child Welfare, Community Centers, Community Service Organizations, Family Services, Food/Clothing Distribution, People with Disabilities, Recreation & Athletics, Scouts, Shelters/Homelessness, United Funds/United Ways, YMCA/YWCA/YMHA/YWHA, Youth Organizations

Application Procedures
Initial Contact: Request application guidelines.
Deadlines: January 31.

Restrictions
Grants are awarded for the care, healing, and nursing of the sick and injured, the relief and aid of the poor, the training and education of the young, and for social services in the city of Lawrence. Does not support individuals.

Additional Information
Publications: Application Guidelines

Foundation Officials
Archer L. Bolton, Jr.: trustee
Clifford E. Elias, Esq.: managing trustee
Eileen M. Khoury: trustee
Rev. Joachim Lally: trustee
Marsha E. Rich: trustee

Grants Analysis
Disclosure Period: calendar year ending 2000
Total Grants: $357,235
Number of Grants: 38
Average Grant: $9,400
Highest Grant: $40,000
Typical Range: $5,000 to $20,000

Recent Grants
Note: Grants derived from 2001 Form 990.
General

50,000	Lawrence General Hospital, Lawrence, MA
40,000	Holy Family Hospital
25,000	Central Catholic High School
20,000	Merrimack College, North Andover, MA
15,000	Lawrence Youth Center, Lawrence, MA
14,500	Lazarus House, Lawrence, MA
14,175	Lawrence Boys & Girls Club, Lawrence, MA
12,000	Seton Asian Community Center

10,000	Lawrence Public Schools, Lawrence, MA
10,000	Neighbors In Need, Seattle, WA

DAVID CLAUDE RYAN FOUNDATION

Giving Contact
Jerome D. Ryan, President
PO Box 6409
San Diego, CA 92166
Phone: (619)497-1171

Description
Founded: 1959
EIN: 956051140
Organization Type: Private Foundation
Giving Locations: CA: statewide, San Diego
Grant Types: Multiyear/Continuing Support.

Donor Information
Founder: Jerome D. Ryan, Gladys B. Ryan

Financial Summary
Total Giving: $42,050 (2001)
Assets: $2,818,542 (2001)
Gifts Received: $20,000 (2001); $30,000 (2000); $50,568 (1999). Note: In 2001, contributions were received from Jerome D. Ryan ($10,000) and Anne E. Ryan ($10,000). In 2000, contributions were received from Jerome D. Ryan. In 1999, contributions were received from Anne E. Ryan ($40,600) and Jerome D. Ryan ($9,968).

Typical Recipients
Arts & Humanities: Libraries, Museums/Galleries, Public Broadcasting
Civic & Public Affairs: Civic & Public Affairs-General, Legal Aid, Zoos/Aquariums
Education: Colleges & Universities, Education-General, Medical Education, Minority Education, Private Education (Precollege), Special Education
Health: Children's Health/Hospitals, Emergency/Ambulance Services, Eyes/Blindness, Hospices, Single-Disease Health Associations
International: Health Care/Hospitals, International Organizations, International Relief Efforts, Missionary/Religious Activities
Religion: Bible Study/Translation, Churches, Religion-General, Ministries, Missionary Activities (Domestic), Religious Organizations, Religious Welfare
Science: Science-General, Science Museums
Social Services: At-Risk Youth, Camps, Child Welfare, Community Service Organizations, Domestic Violence, Family Services, Food/Clothing Distribution, People with Disabilities, Recreation & Athletics, Scouts, Special Olympics, United Funds/United Ways, YMCA/YWCA/YMHA/YWHA, Youth Organizations

Application Procedures
Initial Contact: Send a brief letter of inquiry.
Application Requirements: Include the organization's charitable activities and proof of tax-exempt status.
Deadlines: None.

Restrictions
Does not support individuals.

Foundation Officials
Gladys B. Ryan: vice president, secretary, treasurer
Jerome D. Ryan: president
Stephen M. Ryan: vice president, secretary, treasurer

Grants Analysis
Disclosure Period: calendar year ending 2001
Total Grants: $42,050

Number of Grants: 33
Average Grant: $1,274
Highest Grant: $4,000
Lowest Grant: $100
Typical Range: $1,000 to $5,000

Recent Grants

Note: Grants derived from 2001 Form 990.
General

4,000	San Diego Aerospace Museum, San Diego, CA
3,500	World Vision International, Monrovia, CA
3,300	Pacific Legal Foundation, Sacramento, CA
3,000	Peninsula YMCA, San Mateo, CA
2,800	San Diego Rescue Mission, San Diego, CA
2,100	Capital Ministries, Santa Ana, CA
2,000	Children's Hospital
2,000	Community Campership Council, San Diego, CA
2,000	Coral Ridge Ministries, Ft. Lauderdale, FL
2,000	Salvation Army, Port Huron, MI

S.G. FOUNDATION

Giving Contact

Richard Kieding, Director & President
PO Box 444
Buellton, CA 93427
Phone: (805)688-0088
Fax: (805)686-1250
E-mail: sgfound@utech.net

Description

Founded: 1984
EIN: 330048410
Organization Type: Private Foundation
Giving Locations: CA; CO; CT; HI; IL; OR; WA; WI
Grant Types: Endowment, Fellowship.

Donor Information

Founder: F. Javier Alverdo

Financial Summary

Total Giving: $702,834 (2003); $875,421 (2001)
Giving Analysis: Giving for 2001 includes: foundation fellowships ($60,000)
Assets: $13,354,354 (2003); $10,386,999 (2001)
Gifts Received: $2,658,077 (2003). Note: In 2003, contributions were received from Refugio Ranches ($2,618,077) and Northwest Medical Teams ($40,000).

Typical Recipients

Arts & Humanities: Libraries
Civic & Public Affairs: Community Foundations, Economic Development, Employment/Job Training, Civic & Public Affairs-General, Legal Aid, Public Policy
Education: Agricultural Education, Colleges & Universities, International Exchange, Leadership Training, Literacy, Medical Education, Minority Education, Private Education (Precollege), Science/Mathematics Education
Health: Emergency/Ambulance Services, Health-General, Health Funds
International: Health Care/Hospitals, International Affairs, International Development, International Relief Efforts
Religion: Churches, Ministries, Missionary Activities (Domestic), Religious Organizations, Religious Welfare
Social Services: Animal Protection, Camps, Community Service Organizations, Crime Prevention, Day Care, Domestic Violence, Emergency Relief, Family Services, Food/Clothing Distribution, People with Disabilities, Sexual Abuse, Shelters/Homelessness, Social Services-General, Substance Abuse, YMCA/YWCA/YMHA/YWHA, Youth Organizations

Application Procedures

Initial Contact: Send a brief letter of inquiry.
Application Requirements: Include a description of organization and program or project.
Deadlines: None.

Foundation Officials

John Donati: director
Russell Fraser: director
Lynn R. Gildred: secretary
Stuart C. Gildred, Jr.: director
Richard Kieding: president
Joseph Lambert: treasurer
William Sauer: vice president
Dessie Schmidt: assistant secretary

Grants Analysis

Disclosure Period: calendar year ending 2003
Total Grants: $702,834
Number of Grants: 31
Average Grant: $20,094*
Highest Grant: $100,000
Lowest Grant: $500
Typical Range: $10,000 to $50,000
***Note:** Average grant figure excludes highest grant.

Recent Grants

Note: Grants derived from 2003 Form 990.
General

100,000	Amigos de Honduras, Seattle, WA -- for emergency relief hurricane
85,000	International Foundation, Washington, DC -- for Westmont bethel hospital
53,500	Mercy Ships, Garden Valley, TX -- towards staff, education project
50,000	Focus on the Family, Colorado Springs, CO -- towards alliance defense fund
50,000	World Relief, Baltimore, MD -- towards Nicaraguan agricultural expansion
45,623	Food for the Hungry, Scottsdale, AZ -- to support housing project-Romania
40,000	Opportunity International, San Jose, CA -- towards Latin America standardizing project
27,321	Young Life of Santa Ynez Valley, Solvang, CA
27,300	Direct Relief International, Santa Barbara, CA -- for Manos de Ayuda clinic in Mexico
25,000	Santa Ynez Valley Hospital Foundation, Solvang, CA -- towards endowment fund

S&T BANCORP INC.

Company Headquarters

43 S. 9th St.
Indiana, PA 15701
Web: http://www.stbank.com/

Company Description

Founded: 1902
Ticker: STBA
Exchange: NASDAQ
Assets: US$2.332 billion (2001)
Employees: 767 (2003)
SIC(s): 6022 State Commercial Banks, 6712 Bank Holding Companies.

Operating Locations

S&T Bancorp (PA--Indiana)

S&T Bancorp Charitable Foundation

Giving Contact

James C. Miller, President
Main Office
PO Box 190
Indiana, PA 15701-0190
Phone: (724)465-1443

Description

Founded: 1993
EIN: 251716950
Organization Type: Corporate Foundation
Giving Locations: headquarters and operating communities.
Grant Types: Capital, General Support, Scholarship.

Financial Summary

Total Giving: $369,890 (2002); $346,275 (2001)
Giving Analysis: Giving for 2001 includes: foundation grants to United Way ($41,000); foundation ($305,275)
Assets: $42,352 (2002); $180,099 (2001)
Gifts Received: $263,925 (2002); $60,350 (2001); $72,900 (2000). Note: Contributions are received from S&T Bank.

Typical Recipients

Arts & Humanities: Arts Associations & Councils, Arts Festivals, Arts Institutes, Ballet, Community Arts, Historic Preservation, History & Archaeology, Libraries, Museums/Galleries, Music, Opera, Theater
Civic & Public Affairs: Botanical Gardens/Parks, Business/Free Enterprise, Clubs, Community Foundations, Economic Development, Employment/Job Training, Civic & Public Affairs-General, Municipalities/Towns, Parades/Festivals, Professional & Trade Associations, Safety, Urban & Community Affairs
Education: Agricultural Education, Business Education, Colleges & Universities, Community & Junior Colleges, Education Funds, Education Reform, Education-General, Preschool Education, Private Education (Precollege), Public Education (Precollege), Student Aid, Vocational & Technical Education
Health: Cancer, Children's Health/Hospitals, Clinics/Medical Centers, Diabetes, Emergency/Ambulance Services, Health Funds, Health Organizations, Heart, Hospices, Hospitals, Multiple Sclerosis, Nursing Services, Preventive Medicine/Wellness Organizations, Public Health, Single-Disease Health Associations, Transplant Networks/Donor Banks
International: Foreign Educational Institutions
Religion: Churches, Religious Welfare
Science: Scientific Centers & Institutes
Social Services: Animal Protection, Big Brothers/Big Sisters, Child Welfare, Community Centers, Community Service Organizations, Emergency Relief, Family Services, Homes, People with Disabilities, Recreation & Athletics, Scouts, Senior Services, Special Olympics, United Funds/United Ways, Veterans, YMCA/YWCA/YMHA/YWHA, Youth Organizations

Application Procedures

Initial Contact: Submit a written application.
Application Requirements: Include amount requested and purpose of funds sought.
Deadlines: None.
Review Process: The contributions committee meets monthly.

Restrictions

Does not support organizations outside bank's marketing area.

Additional Information

Trust(s): S&T Bank

Corporate Officials

Robert D. Duggan: chairman, chief executive officer chief financial officer PRIM CORP EMPL chairman, chief executive officer: S&T Bancorp.
James C. Miller: president, director PRIM CORP EMPL president, director: S&T Bancorp.
Robert E. Rout: senior vice president, chief financial officer PRIM CORP EMPL senior vice president, chief financial officer: S&T Bancorp.

Foundation Officials

Robert D. Duggan: chairman (see above)
Edward C. Hauck: vice president
H. William Klumpp: treasurer
James C. Miller: president (see above)

Grants Analysis

Disclosure Period: calendar year ending 2002
Total Grants: $318,390*
Number of Grants: 84
Average Grant: $2,631*
Highest Grant: $100,000
Lowest Grant: $160
Typical Range: $1,000 to $5,000
*Note: Giving excludes scholarship and United Way. Average grant figure excludes highest grant.

Recent Grants

Note: Grants derived from 2003 Form 990.
Library-Related

7,500	Plum Borough Community Library, Plum, PA
5,000	New Bethlehem Library, New Bethlehem, PA
5,000	Plum Borough Community Library, Plum, PA
2,500	Summerville Public Library, Summerville, MA

General

100,000	Indiana Healthcare Foundation, Indiana, PA
28,000	United Way of Indiana County, Indiana, PA
25,000	Punxsutawney Area Hospital, Punxsutawney, PA
20,000	Clarion Hospital Foundation, Clarion, PA
12,000	Dubois Area United Way, Dubois, PA
10,000	Dubois Area Catholic School, Dubois, PA
10,000	United Valley Soccer Association, New Bethlehem, PA
6,000	Brookville Area United Fund, Brookville, PA
6,000	Jefferson County Area Agency on Aging, Brookville, PA
5,000	Clarion University Foundation, Clarion, PA

FRANKLIN I. SAEMANN FOUNDATION

Giving Contact

Amy C. Kilgus-Chamley
PO Box 105
Morrison, IL 61270
Phone: (219)267-8141

Description

Founded: 1983
EIN: 626171002
Organization Type: Private Foundation
Giving Locations: IA
Grant Types: General Support.

Donor Information

Founder: Franklin I. Saemann

Financial Summary

Total Giving: $557,500 (fiscal year ending June 30, 2002)
Assets: $9,649,232 (fiscal 2002)
Gifts Received: $1,494,527 (fiscal 1999); $1,249,837 (fiscal 1997); $6,443,962 (fiscal 1996). Note: In fiscal 1999, contributions were received from Irene Saemann Estate.

Typical Recipients

Arts & Humanities: Community Arts, Arts & Humanities-General, History & Archaeology, Libraries, Literary Arts, Public Broadcasting
Civic & Public Affairs: Botanical Gardens/Parks, Community Foundations, Municipalities/Towns, Urban & Community Affairs
Education: Colleges & Universities, Education-General, Literacy, Minority Education
Health: Cancer, Hospices, Hospitals, Prenatal Health Issues, Single-Disease Health Associations
Religion: Bible Study/Translation, Churches, Religious Welfare
Social Services: Big Brothers/Big Sisters, Child Welfare, Community Service Organizations, Domestic Violence, Family Planning, People with Disabilities, Senior Services, Shelters/Homelessness, United Funds/United Ways, YMCA/YWCA/YMHA/YWHA, Youth Organizations

Application Procedures

Initial Contact: Send a brief letter of inquiry.
Application Requirements: Include brief description, current budget, amount requeted, financial statement from previous year, IRS determination letter, and current list of board of directors.
Deadlines: April 1

Foundation Officials

Amy C. Kilgus: trustee
Joann A. Kilgus: trustee
Thomas E. List: trustee
June Waller: trustee
Katherine A. Waller: trustee

Grants Analysis

Disclosure Period: fiscal year ending June 30, 2002
Total Grants: $557,500
Number of Grants: 33
Average Grant: $5,241*
Highest Grant: $295,000
Typical Range: $1,000 to $10,000
*Note: Average grant figure excludes two highest grants.

Recent Grants

Note: Grants derived from fiscal 2002 Form 990.

General

295,000	Wartburg College, Waverly, IA -- further education
100,000	Carthage College, Kenosha, WI -- further higher education
22,500	Cardinal Center, Warsaw, IN -- for services for disabled persons
15,000	Wartburg Seminary, Waverly, IA -- to further education
10,500	Charleston Public Library, Charleston, WV -- further education
10,000	Arts and Cultural Alliance, Newport, RI -- to promote art and culture
10,000	Heartline Pregnancy Center, Warsaw, IN -- services for pregnant women
10,000	Kosciusko Community Senior Service, Warsaw, IN -- to promote senior services
10,000	Kosciusko Community YMCA, Warsaw, IN -- youth activities
10,000	United Way Kosciusko County, Warsaw, IN -- community services

SAFECO CORP.

Company Headquarters

Seattle, WA
Web: http://www.safeco.com

Company Description

Founded: 1923
Ticker: SAFC
Exchange: NASDAQ
Revenue: US$7.335 billion (2004)
Profit: US$562.4 million (2004)
Employees: 11200 (2003)
Fortune Rank: 285, per FORTUNE Magazine's list of 500 Largest U.S. Corporations (2004).
SIC(s): 6159 Miscellaneous Business Credit Institutions, 6211 Security Brokers & Dealers, 6311 Life Insurance, 6719 Holding Companies Nec.

Operating Locations

SAFECO Corp. (CA--Fountain Valley, Glendale, San Ramon; CO--Denver; GA--Stone Mountain; IL--Hoffman Estates; MO--St. Louis; OH--Cincinnati; TN--Nashville; TX--Plano; VA--Midlothian)

Nonmonetary Support

Volunteer Programs: Company has a Volunteer Awards Program through which over 11,000 employees nationwide can participate.

Giving Contact

Christopher Wiggins, Community Relations
SAFECO Corp.
SAFECO Plaza
Seattle, WA 98185
Phone: (206)545-5299
Fax: (206)545-5730
E-mail: roslin@safeco.com
Web: http://www.safeco.com/safeco/about/giving/giving.asp

Alternate Contact

E-mail: hocr@safeco.com
Note: For Seattle-area grant seekers.

Description

Organization Type: Corporate Giving Program
Giving Locations: headquarters and operating communities in the United States.
Grant Types: Conference/Seminar, Employee Matching Gifts, General Support.
Note: Company matches employee gifts to local organisation and the United Way.

Financial Summary

Total Giving: $4,000,000 (2002 approx); $4,100,000 (2001 approx). Note: Contributes through corporate direct giving program only.

Typical Recipients

Arts & Humanities: Arts Funds, Community Arts, Dance, Historic Preservation, Libraries, Museums/Galleries, Opera, Performing Arts, Public Broadcasting, Visual Arts
Civic & Public Affairs: Economic Development, Employment/Job Training, Housing, Nonprofit Management, Public Policy, Safety, Urban & Community Affairs, Zoos/Aquariums
Education: Arts/Humanities Education, Business Education, Colleges & Universities, Continuing Education, Economic Education, Education Associations, Elementary Education (Private), Literacy, Minority Education, Private Education (Precollege), Public Education (Precollege)
Environment: Environment-General
Health: Health Policy/Cost Containment, Health Organizations, Mental Health, Nutrition, Public Health, Single-Disease Health Associations
Social Services: Community Service Organizations, Day Care, Delinquency & Criminal Rehabilitation,

Emergency Relief, People with Disabilities, Senior Services, Shelters/Homelessness, Substance Abuse, United Funds/United Ways, Volunteer Services, Youth Organizations

Application Procedures

Initial Contact: Call or write for application and guidelines, then call before submitting a formal proposal.

Application Requirements: A formal proposal should be four pages of less, plus attachments. Include cover letter; completed application form; how project meets guidelines and criteria; organization's mission statement and purpose, history of accomplishments, governance, area and population served, and role of volunteers (if a collaboration, describe lead agency and relation to others); needs statement, acknowledging existing similar projects, and how proposed project differs, and any efforts to work cooperatively; proposal, including how needs will be addressed, projected goals, objectives, timeline, anticipated impact, population to benefit, how work will be monitored and success evaluated, potential and actual sources of current support, and plan for future support; the following attachments: proof of tax-exempt status, list of board members with affiliations, key organizational staff with titles and functions, IRS Form 990, most recent audited financial statement, one-page summary of actual income and expenses for the past two years, listing of funding sources and amounts for those years, organization's operating budget, detailed project budget, letters from collaborating agencies (if appropriate).

Deadlines: None.

Review Process: All requests are evaluated, either at home office or branch office.

Evaluative Criteria: Program's capability and soundness of financial management and fiscal policies; competency and policy-making authority of board of directors; demonstration that program does not represent unnecessary duplication of services; program is designed to promote self-sufficiency, focuses on prevention rather treatment of problems; can sustain itself beyond company funding; and the organization promotes collaboration between other organizations and individuals.

Decision Notification: Grant requests are reviewed on a quarterly basis.

Notes: Application should be sent to nearest company office.

Restrictions

As a general rule, SAFECO does not make contributions to individuals; projects or programs operating outside the United States; national programs; endowment funds; religious, fraternal, or political groups or projects; general fundraising events; goodwill advertising; loans or investments; film or video production; operating deficits or debt retirement; health education, research, or prevention; amateur arts; amateur sports teams or athletic scholarships; conferences; research; or fraternal, professional, or membership organizations.

Additional Information

Company was founded in 1923 as a property and casualty insurance company. Today, they've added life and health insurance; real estate management and investments and commercial credit and asset management to their list of operations.

Company sets aside approximately two percent of pre-tax income annually for contributions programs.

Company will consider requests from communities where significant numbers of SAFECO employees live and work.

Contributions are given for one year with no implied renewals.

Company may require recipients to provide an audited financial statement at year's end and periodic reports on the project.

Publications: Boomerang Giving: Flight Instruction Manual (guidelines); Application Form

Grants Analysis

Disclosure Period: calendar year ending 2001
Total Grants: $4,100,000
Number of Grants: 600 (approx)
Average Grant: $6,833 (approx)
Highest Grant: $500,000
Lowest Grant: $25
Typical Range: $10,000 to $15,000* and $1,000 to $2,000*

*Note: First grant range represents grants made by the home office; second grant range represents grants made by field offices.

SAGE FOUNDATION

Giving Contact

Melissa Sage Fadim, Chairman, President & Treasurer
PO Box 1919
Brighton, MI 48116
Phone: (810)227-7660

Description

Founded: 1954
EIN: 386041518
Organization Type: Family Foundation
Giving Locations: nationally.
Grant Types: Capital, Endowment, General Support, Matching, Multiyear/Continuing Support.

Donor Information

Founder: Established in 1954 by the late Charles F. Sage (d. 1961) and his wife, the late Effa L. Sage. After Mr. Sage's death, the foundation received stock in Tecumseh Products Company, valued at more than $7 million.

Financial Summary

Total Giving: $2,337,700 (2003); $2,614,522 (2002); $2,636,467 (2001)
Assets: $54,994,795 (2003); $47,598,120 (2002); $57,127,616 (2001)

Typical Recipients

Arts & Humanities: Arts Associations & Councils, Arts Centers, Arts Festivals, Arts Funds, Arts Institutes, Film & Video, Arts & Humanities-General, Libraries, Museums/Galleries, Music, Opera, Performing Arts, Public Broadcasting, Theater

Civic & Public Affairs: Asian American Affairs, Botanical Gardens/Parks, Clubs, Community Foundations, Economic Development, Civic & Public Affairs-General, Hispanic Affairs, Municipalities/Towns, Nonprofit Management, Parades/Festivals, Philanthropic Organizations, Public Policy, Safety, Urban & Community Affairs, Zoos/Aquariums

Education: Agricultural Education, Arts/Humanities Education, Colleges & Universities, Education-General, International Studies, Legal Education, Minority Education, Preschool Education, Private Education (Precollege), Public Education (Precollege), Science/Mathematics Education, Secondary Education (Private), Secondary Education (Public), Special Education, Student Aid

Health: AIDS/HIV, Alzheimer's Disease, Arthritis, Cancer, Children's Health/Hospitals, Clinics/Medical Centers, Emergency/Ambulance Services, Eyes/Blindness, Geriatric Health, Health Funds, Health Organizations, Heart, Hospices, Hospitals, Hospitals (University Affiliated), Long-Term Care, Medical Rehabilitation, Medical Research, Mental Health, Public Health, Single-Disease Health Associations

International: Foreign Arts Organizations, Health Care/Hospitals, Human Rights, Missionary/Religious Activities

Religion: Churches, Dioceses, Religion-General, Ministries, Religious Organizations, Religious Welfare

Science: Science-General, Science Museums
Social Services: Child Welfare, Community Service Organizations, Counseling, Crime Prevention, Domestic Violence, Family Services, Homes, People with Disabilities, Recreation & Athletics, Shelters/Homelessness, Substance Abuse, Youth Organizations

Application Procedures

Initial Contact: Initial contact should be in writing.
Application Requirements: Applicants should include the amount of funds needed, intended outcome of the project or program, plans to reach the objective, plans to evaluate the results, photocopy of the organization's tax-exempt determination letter, and the name of the individual responsible for administering the program. General information that would aid the board of trustees in making a decision should be included.
Deadlines: None.

Restrictions

The foundation has no grant-making restrictions as to geographic area, charitable fields, or types of institutions.

Foundation Officials

John J. Ayaub: vice president, secretary, trustee
Melissa Sage Booth Fadim: chairwoman, president, treasurer, trustee
Ann Sage Price: trustee
James E. Van Doren: trustee

Grants Analysis

Disclosure Period: calendar year ending 2003
Total Grants: $2,337,700
Number of Grants: 114
Average Grant: $20,506
Highest Grant: $250,000
Lowest Grant: $1,000
Typical Range: $5,000 to $50,000

Recent Grants

Note: Grants derived from 2003 Form 990.
General

250,000	Orchestral Association/Chicago Symphony Orchestra, Chicago, IL
150,000	Orchestral Association/Chicago Symphony Orchestra, Chicago, IL
125,000	Chicago Classical Recording Foundation, Chicago, IL
125,000	Music Institute of Chicago, Winnetka, IL
100,000	Ravinia Festival, Highland Park, IL
75,000	Ravinia Festival, Highland Park, IL
75,000	Rush-Presbyterian-St. Luke's Medical Center, Chicago, IL
50,000	Big Shoulders Fund, Chicago, IL
50,000	Bixby Community Health Foundation, Adrian, MI
50,000	Illinois Philharmonic Orchestra, Park Forest, IL

LOUIS P. SAIA FOUNDATION

Giving Contact

Louis P. Saia, Trustee
Louis P. Saia Foundation
1405 Bayou Black Drive
Houma, LA 70360-7453
Phone: (985)876-0660

Description

Founded: 1987
EIN: 721086475
Organization Type: Private Foundation
Giving Locations: LA: Harahan, Houma, Lockport,

New Orleans, Schriever; OH: Steubenville; TN: Memphis
Grant Types: General Support, Research.

Financial Summary

Total Giving: $60,850 (2003)
Assets: $1,071,429 (2003)

Typical Recipients

Arts & Humanities: Arts & Humanities-General
Education: Arts/Humanities Education, Education Funds, Private Education (Precollege), Student Aid
Health: Children's Health/Hospitals, Hospitals
Religion: Churches, Dioceses, Religion-General, Religious Organizations, Religious Welfare
Social Services: Child Abuse, Child Welfare, Food/Clothing Distribution, People with Disabilities, Substance Abuse

Application Procedures

Initial Contact: Apply verbally or in writing.
Deadlines: None.

Foundation Officials

Ann M. Saia: trustee
Louis P. Saia: trustee
Lyndon Saia: trustee

Grants Analysis

Disclosure Period: calendar year ending 2003
Total Grants: $60,850
Number of Grants: 24
Average Grant: $2,124*
Highest Grant: $12,000
Lowest Grant: $25
Typical Range: $1,000 to $5,000
*Note: Average grant figure excludes highest grant.

Recent Grants

Note: Grants derived from 2003 Form 990.
General

12,000	St. Francis de Sales Cathedral, Houma, LA -- for insurance premium
7,000	Sacred Heart of Jesus Church, New Orleans, LA
5,000	Bayou Area Children's Foundation, Houma, LA
5,000	Cabrini High School, New Orleans, LA
5,000	Terrebonne Children's Advocacy, Houma, LA
4,500	Mary's Helpers Inc., Marrero, LA -- for purchase of a crucifix
4,000	St. Vincent de Paul Store, Houma, LA
3,000	St. Jude's Children's Hospital, Memphis, TN
3,000	Sisters of St. Joseph of Media, New Orleans, LA
1,500	Christian Brothers Foundation, New Orleans, LA

SAINT CROIX FOUNDATION

Giving Contact

Jeffrey T. Peterson, Assistant Secretary
c/o US Bank NA
101 E. Fifth St.
St. Paul, MN 55101
Phone: (651)466-8735

Description

Founded: 1950
EIN: 416011826
Organization Type: Private Foundation
Giving Locations: MN; WI
Grant Types: Capital, Emergency, General Support, Operating Expenses.

Donor Information

Founder: Ianthe B. Hardenbergh, I. Hardenbergh Charitable Annuity Trust, Gabrielle Hardenbergh

Financial Summary

Total Giving: $816,184 (2003); $596,200 (2001)
Giving Analysis: Giving for 2003 includes: foundation grants to United Way ($5,000); 2001: foundation grants to United Way ($37,000)
Assets: $9,734,387 (2003); $10,762,101 (2001)
Gifts Received: $170,000 (2003); $421,526 (2001); $472,500 (2000). Note: In 2003, contributions were received from Hardenbergh Charitable Annuity Trust. In 2001, contributions were received from Hardenbergh Charitable Annuity Trust ($249,000), and Gabrielle Hardenbergh ($2,775,000). In 2000, contributions were received from I. Hardenbergh Charitable Annuity Trust ($170,000) and Cabrielle Hardenbergh ($302,500). In 1999, contributions were received from I. Hardenbergh Charitable Annuity Trust ($320,000) and Cabrielle Hardenbergh ($4,089). In 1998, contributions were received from Hardenbergh Charitable Annuity Trust ($170,000) and Cabrielle Hardenbergh ($149,926).

Typical Recipients

Arts & Humanities: Arts Centers, Arts Funds, Community Arts, Historic Preservation, History & Archaeology, Museums/Galleries, Music, Opera, Performing Arts, Theater
Civic & Public Affairs: Economic Development, Civic & Public Affairs-General, Housing, Urban & Community Affairs
Education: Colleges & Universities, Education Funds, Private Education (Precollege), Public Education (Precollege)
Health: Cancer, Children's Health/Hospitals, Clinics/Medical Centers, Emergency/Ambulance Services, Health-General, Health Organizations, Heart, Hospitals, Medical Rehabilitation, Prenatal Health Issues, Public Health
International: Health Care/Hospitals
Religion: Churches, Religious Organizations, Religious Welfare
Science: Science Museums
Social Services: Camps, Child Welfare, Community Service Organizations, Day Care, Family Services, People with Disabilities, Scouts, United Funds/United Ways, Volunteer Services, YMCA/YWCA/YMHA/YWHA, Youth Organizations

Application Procedures

Initial Contact: The foundation requests applications be made in writing. Provide complete information so that request may be evaluated.
Deadlines: None.

Restrictions

Grants are made only to organizations located in the Stillwater/St. Paul area in Minnesota. Grants are made to charitable institutions of learning, hospitals, sanitariums, and churches and religious organizations to aid and assist needy and oppressed persons.

Foundation Officials

Edgerton Bronson: treasurer
Robert S. Davis: president, director B Stillwater, MN 1914. ED University of Minnesota (1934). PRIM CORP EMPL director: H M Smyth Co. CORP AFFIL director: Heartland Technology. CLUB AFFIL Elks Club.
Quentin O. Heimerman: vice president
Jeffrey T. Peterson: secretary, director
Raymond A. Reister: director B Sioux City, IA 1929. ED Harvard University AB (1952); Harvard University LLB (1955). NONPR AFFIL member: Minneapolis Bar Association; vice president: Minneapolis Historical Society; member: American College Trust & Estate Counsel; member: Hennipin County Bar Association; member: American Bar Association. CLUB AFFIL Minneapolis Club; Harvard Club.

Grants Analysis

Disclosure Period: calendar year ending 2003
Total Grants: $811,184*
Number of Grants: 95
Average Grant: $6,643*
Highest Grant: $100,000
Lowest Grant: $1,000
Typical Range: $1,000 to $10,000
*Note: Giving excludes United Way. Average grant figure excludes three highest grants ($200,000).

Recent Grants

Note: Grants derived from 2001 Form 990.
General

100,000	Croixdale Residence and Apartments, Bayport, MN -- capital campaign
32,000	United Way of St. Paul Area, St. Paul, MN
30,000	Children's Home Society of Minnesota, St. Paul, MN -- capital campaign
30,000	Presbyterian Homes, St. Paul, MN -- Arden Hills Apartments
21,000	Indianhead Council BSA, St. Paul, MN
20,000	Children's Health Care Foundation, Roseville, MN -- Midwest Children's Resource Center
20,000	Family Means of St. Croix, St. Paul, MN
19,000	HOPE Adoption and Family Services, St. Paul, MN -- capital campaign
16,000	Girl Scout Council of St. Croix Valley, St. Croix, MN
16,000	Minnesota Private College Fund, Minneapolis, MN

SAINT FRANCIS BANK

Company Headquarters

Milwaukee, WI

Company Description

Employees: 247
SIC(s): 6035 Federal Savings Institutions.
Parent Company: St. Francis Capital Corp., 13400 Bishops Lane, Ste. 350, Brookfield, WI, United States

Operating Locations

Saint Francis Bank (WI--Brookfield)

St. Francis Bank Foundation

Giving Contact

Mary D. Patzlaff, Secretary
13400 Bishops Ln., Suite 350
Brookfield, WI 53005-6203
Phone: (262)787-8719

Description

Founded: 1984
EIN: 391535393
Organization Type: Corporate Foundation
Giving Locations: WI: Milwaukee
Grant Types: General Support.

Financial Summary

Total Giving: $149,335 (fiscal year ending September 30, 2003); $174,435 (fiscal 2002); $173,031 (fiscal 2001)
Assets: $721,052 (fiscal 2003); $709,449 (fiscal 2002); $750,361 (fiscal 2001)
Gifts Received: $500 (fiscal 2003). Note: In fiscal 1991, contributions were received from St. Francis Bank, F.S.B. ($30,300) and others ($2,500).

Typical Recipients

Arts & Humanities: Arts Centers, Arts Festivals, Ballet, Historic Preservation, History & Archaeology, Libraries, Museums/Galleries, Music, Performing Arts

Civic & Public Affairs: Botanical Gardens/Parks, Economic Development, Civic & Public Affairs-General, Hispanic Affairs, Housing, Municipalities/Towns, Urban & Community Affairs, Women's Affairs, Zoos/Aquariums

Education: Business-School Partnerships, Colleges & Universities, Education-General, Literacy, Private Education (Precollege), Student Aid, Vocational & Technical Education

Health: AIDS/HIV, Alzheimer's Disease, Children's Health/Hospitals, Clinics/Medical Centers, Health Funds, Health Organizations, Heart, Public Health

Religion: Jewish Causes, Religious Welfare

Science: Science Museums

Social Services: Big Brothers/Big Sisters, Child Welfare, Community Centers, Community Service Organizations, Food/Clothing Distribution, Social Services-General, United Funds/United Ways, YMCA/YWCA/YMHA/YWHA, Youth Organizations

Application Procedures

Initial Contact: Send a brief letter of inquiry.

Application Requirements: Include amount requested and purpose of funds sought.

Deadlines: None.

Corporate Officials

Thomas R. Perz: president, chief executive officer PRIM CORP EMPL president, chief executive officer: St Francis Bank.

John C. Schlosser: chairman, director B Englewood, NJ 1928. ED Pace University (1953). PRIM CORP EMPL chairman, director: St Francis Bank ADD CORP EMPL chairman: Saint Francis Capital Corp.

John Sorenson: chief financial officer PRIM CORP EMPL chief financial officer: St Francis Bank.

Foundation Officials

Richard W. Double: director

William F. Double: director

David J. Drury: director

Rudolph T. Hoppe: director

Willaim Hotz: vice president

Brian T. Kaye: secretary PRIM CORP EMPL executive vice president: St Francis Bank.

Gerald A. Kiefer, Esq.: director

Edward W. Mentzer: director

Thomas R. Perz: vice president, director (see above)

Jeffrey A. Reigle: director

Robert V. Rice: director

John C. Schlosser: president, director (see above)

Anthony O. Schmidt: director

Bruce R. Sherman: treasurer

Julia H. Taylor: director

Edward O. Templeton: director CORP AFFIL director: Saint Francis Capital Corp.

Marianne T. Zapall: secretary

Grants Analysis

Disclosure Period: fiscal year ending September 30, 2003

Total Grants: $107,087*

Number of Grants: 13

Average Grant: $5,189*

Highest Grant: $25,000

Lowest Grant: $100

Typical Range: $100 to $15,000

*Note: Giving excludes matching gifts, scholarships, and United Way. Average grant excludes two highest grants ($100,000).

Recent Grants

Note: Grants derived from fiscal 2003 Form 990.

General

26,000	United Way , Alexandria, VA
25,000	Sharon Lynne Wilson Center, Brookfield, WI
25,000	Zoological Society of Milwaukee County, Milwaukee, WI
16,667	My Home Your Home Inc.

12,000	Bay View Community Center, Milwaukee, WI
5,500	Children's Hospital Foundation, Oakland, CA
5,000	Community Memorial Foundation, Hinsdale, IL
5,000	J. Kyle Brard Leadership Foundation
5,000	Literacy Services of Wisconsin, Milwaukee, WI
5,000	Ronald McDonald House, Oak Brook, IL

ST. GILES FOUNDATION

Giving Contact

Richard T. Arkwright, President
420 Lexington Avenue, Suite 2329
New York, NY 10170
Phone: (212)338-9001

Description

Founded: 1979

EIN: 111630806

Organization Type: General Purpose Foundation

Giving Locations: NY

Grant Types: General Support, Research, Scholarship.

Donor Information

Founder: Established by the James Tisdale Trust, Jesse Ridley, the late Louis W. Arnold, and the late Marvin Leavens.

Financial Summary

Total Giving: $842,837 (fiscal year ending March 31, 2002); $648,677 (fiscal 2001)

Giving Analysis: Giving for fiscal 2001 includes: foundation scholarships ($50,000)

Assets: $26,660,901 (fiscal 2002); $27,995,630 (fiscal 2001)

Gifts Received: $27,236 (fiscal 2001); $10,180 (fiscal 2000); $55,701 (fiscal 1999). Note: In fiscal 2002, contributions were received from the estate of Daisy Oliver Berry. Contributions were received from the Estate of Ann B. Hallet.

Typical Recipients

Arts & Humanities: Historic Preservation

Education: Colleges & Universities, Faculty Development, Medical Education, Special Education, Student Aid

Health: AIDS/HIV, Cancer, Children's Health/Hospitals, Clinics/Medical Centers, Health-General, Hospitals, Medical Rehabilitation, Medical Research, Mental Health, Prenatal Health Issues

Religion: Religious Organizations, Religious Welfare

Science: Scientific Labs

Social Services: Community Service Organizations, Day Care, Emergency Relief, Family Services, People with Disabilities

Application Procedures

Initial Contact: The foundation requests applicants submit a detailed written request for funding.

Deadlines: None.

Restrictions

The foundation reports that although it does not impose restrictions on giving, it does have a primary interest in children's orthopedics.

Foundation Officials

Richard T. Arkwright: president PRIM CORP EMPL executive vice president: Seifert Gray & Co. Inc. NONPR AFFIL president, director: Brooklyn Society for Prevention.

John J. Bennett, Jr.: secretary

Edward Ridley Finch, Jr.: general counsel, trustee B Westhampton Beach, NY August 31, 1919. ED

Princeton University AB (1941); New York University JD (1947). NONPR AFFIL president, director: Saint Nicholas Society New York; trustee: Whittell Trust College; treasurer: Jessie Ridley Foundation; member: Pennsylvania Bar Association; member faculty advisory committee department politics: Princeton University; president, director: New York Institute Special Education; member: New York State Bar Association; life trustee: Metropolitan Museum Art; director: National Space Society; member: International Institute Space Law; member: Judge Advocates Association; member: International Astronautical Academy; member: International Bar Association; member: Florida Bar Association; member: Inter-American Bar Association; member: Federal Bar Association; president: Finch Trusts; member: American Law Institute; member: Association Bar New York City; sr member: American Institute Aeronautics & Astronautics; member: American Judicature Society; member: American Bar Association; fellow: American Bar Foundation; treasurer: Adams Memorial Fund; panelist: American Arbitration Association. CLUB AFFIL University Washington Club; Westhampton Country Club; Union League Club; University New York Club; Princeton Club; Union Club; Bathing Corp. Southampton Club; Long Island Club.

John H. Livingston: vice president

Robert Battin Mackay: trustee B Brooklyn, NY 1945. ED Boston University BS (1968); Harvard University MEd (1972); Boston University PhD (1980). PRIM NONPR EMPL director: Society for the Preservation of Long Island Antiquities. NONPR AFFIL member advisory committee: New York State Historic Maritime Areas; trustee: Theodore Roosevelt Association; member: New York State County Parks; member: New York State Heritage Areas; trustee: Homsland Foundation; chairman: New York State Board Historical Preservation. CLUB AFFIL New York Yacht Club.

Samuel H. Owens: treasurer

Grants Analysis

Disclosure Period: fiscal year ending March 31, 2002

Total Grants: $792,837*

Number of Grants: 9

Highest Grant: $400,000

Lowest Grant: $15,000

*Note: Giving excludes scholarships.

Recent Grants

Note: Grants derived from 2002 Form 990.

General

400,000	Hospital for Special Surgery, New York, NY -- St. Giles Chair in Pediatric Genetic Research
265,000	Rockefeller University, New York, NY -- research for childhood leukemia
182,837	Cold Spring Harbor Laboratory Association, Cold Spring Harbor, NY -- for research study
135,000	Brigham and Women's Hospital, Harvard Medical School, Boston, MA -- for research extension study of the Role of Ca2 Sensing Receptor in Bone Disease
125,000	New York Presbyterian Hospital, New York, NY -- reconstruction program
50,000	September 11th Fund, New York, NY -- help needy families and children
35,000	Pediatric Orthopedic Society of North America, Rosemont, IL -- for the Memorial Award
25,000	Cumberland College, Williamsburg, KY -- Scholarship Assistance Program
25,000	St. Hilda's and St. Hugh's School, New York, NY -- for scholarship assistance program to aid disabled and financially needy students
17,500	Interfaith Neighbors, Inc., New York, NY -- Peace of Mind Project

ST. PAUL TRAVELERS COMPANIES INC.

Company Headquarters
385 Washington Street
St. Paul, MN 55102
Phone: (651)310-7911
Fax: (651)310-3386
Web: http://www.stpaultravelers.com

Company Description
Ticker: STA
Exchange: NYSE
Former Name: St. Paul Companies, Inc..
Revenue: US$22.934 billion (2004)
Profit: US$955 million (2004)
Employees: 9700 (2003)
Fortune Rank: 85, per FORTUNE Magazine's list of 500 Largest U.S. Corporations (2004).
SIC(s): 6331 Fire, Marine & Casualty Insurance.

Operating Locations
Saint Paul Companies Inc. (CO; CT; DE; FL; ID; IL; IN; KS; MA; MN; MT; NJ; NY; ND; OH; OR; TX; WA; WI)

Subsidiary Companies
IL: The John Nuveen Co., Chicago

Nonmonetary Support
Type: Donated Equipment; Loaned Employees; Workplace Solicitation
Volunteer Programs: Company-sponsored volunteer projects have included: Junior Achievement, Metro Paint-A-Thon, Voluntary Action Center, Wilson Hi-Rise, Retiree Volunteer Program, Special Olympics, Habitat for Humanity, and school pairing projects.
Contact: Ron McKinley, Vice President
Phone: (651)310-2623
Note: The company also provides printing services to nonprofits.

St. Paul Travelers Foundation

Giving Contact
Mary Pickard, President & Executive Director
St. Paul Companies, Inc. Foundation
385 Washington Street
St. Paul, MN 55102-1396
Phone: (651)310-7911
Fax: (651)310-2327
Web: http://www.stpaultravelers.com/about/community/index.html

Description
Organization Type: Corporate Foundation
Giving Locations: MD: Baltimore area; MN: Minneapolis, St. Paul; select areas where company has large business presence; United Kingdom
Grant Types: Capital, Employee Matching Gifts, Endowment, Fellowship, General Support, Matching, Multiyear/Continuing Support, Project, Scholarship.
Note: Employee matching gift ratio: 1 to 1; 2 to 1 to organisation with 50 hours of employee volunteer time.

Financial Summary
Total Giving: $8,356,419 (2002); $12,000,348 (2001). Note: Contributes through corporate direct giving program and foundation.
Assets: $231,540 (2002)
Gifts Received: $8,625,605 (2002); $9,503,359 (2000); $7,786,709 (1999). Note: Contributions are received from The St. Paul Companies, Inc.

Typical Recipients
Arts & Humanities: Arts Associations & Councils, Arts Centers, Arts Funds, Arts Institutes, Arts Outreach, Community Arts, Dance, Ethnic & Folk Arts, Arts & Humanities-General, History & Archaeology, Libraries, Literary Arts, Museums/Galleries, Music, Performing Arts, Public Broadcasting, Theater
Civic & Public Affairs: African American Affairs, Asian American Affairs, Business/Free Enterprise, Chambers of Commerce, Clubs, Economic Development, Employment/Job Training, Civic & Public Affairs-General, Hispanic Affairs, Housing, Municipalities/Towns, Native American Affairs, Nonprofit Management, Philanthropic Organizations, Professional & Trade Associations, Urban & Community Affairs, Women's Affairs, Zoos/Aquariums
Education: Arts/Humanities Education, Business Education, Colleges & Universities, Community & Junior Colleges, Education Reform, Faculty Development, Education-General, International Studies, Leadership Training, Literacy, Minority Education, Private Education (Precollege), Public Education (Precollege), Social Sciences Education, Student Aid
Environment: Environment-General
Health: Adolescent Health Issues, AIDS/HIV, Cancer, Clinics/Medical Centers
International: International-General, International Affairs
Religion: Religious Welfare
Science: Science Museums, Scientific Centers & Institutes
Social Services: At-Risk Youth, Child Welfare, Community Centers, Community Service Organizations, Day Care, Emergency Relief, Family Services, Recreation & Athletics, Scouts, Senior Services, United Funds/United Ways, Volunteer Services, YMCA/YWCA/YMHA/YWHA, Youth Organizations

Application Procedures
Initial Contact: Submit a one- to two-page letter to the foundation describing the request.
Application Requirements: Include the organization's mission; purpose of funds sought; amount requested; and time span for funding.
Deadlines: None.
Review Process: Staff committee conducts initial review and prepares research report for executive management.
Evaluative Criteria: Preference is given organizations that demonstrate a commitment to their communities by ensuring that their governing bodies include representatives from the community and collaborative efforts and initiatives that fit more than one of the Foundation's priority funding areas. National organizations may be considered for specific initiatives that fall within the Foundation's focus areas; such requests are more likely to receive funding if they support or leverage the potential of other Foundation grantees.
Decision Notification: Foundation staff responds by phone within two weeks of receiving letter of inquiry to indicate whether or not a full proposal is advised.
Notes: If you have received Foundation funding in the past, you may contact the foundation directly to obtain application materials without going through the letter of inquiry phase.

Restrictions
Does not fund sectarian religious organizations unless the funds will be used in the direct interest of the entire community; veterans' or fraternal organizations; political or lobbying organizations; benefits, fundraisers, walk-a-thons, telethons, galas, or other revenue-generating events; advertising; scholarships to individuals; health or disease-specific organizations; health care or other emergency assistance to individuals; hospitals or other health services generally supported by third-party reimbursement mechanisms; replacement of government funding; start-up, capital, or operations of public or charter schools; human services such as counseling, chemical abuse, or family programs; environmental programs; special events, except when the event is a key strategy in a continuum of efforts to achieve community goals in the foundation's priority areas; organizations that discriminate on the basis of race, gender, religion, culture, age, physical disability, sexual orientation, or veteran status; or nonacademic job placement programs.

Additional Information
The company also provides some grants through The St. Paul Companies Maryland Foundation.
Corporate contributions currently average about 2% of pretax operating earnings averaged over a three-year period.
Regional offices have separate giving programs.
St. Paul Companies completed its merger with USF&G Corp. in April 1998. USF&G and St. Paul had combined revenues of $9.6 billion in 1997.
Publications: Community Affairs Distribution Report; Grant Application; Partners in Giving - St. Paul's Matching Gift Program Brochure; Guidelines; Application Information

Corporate Officials
Andy Bessette: executive vice president, chief administrative officer
Jay Fishman: chairman, chief executive officer CORP AFFIL director: Nuveen Investments Inc.; director: Xilinx Inc.; director: Cognex Corp.; director: Neurotech Development.
John A. MacColl: vice chairman, general counsel
Mary Pickard: vice president committee affairs PRIM CORP EMPL vice president committee affairs: St. Paul Companies Inc. NONPR AFFIL director: Citizen's League; member: Conference Board.

Giving Program Officials
Deb Anderson: manager

Foundation Officials
Andy Bessette: director, vice chairman (see above)
Jay Fishman: director, chairman (see above)
Christopher Gerst: assistant corporate secretary
John A. MacColl: director (see above)
Michael Newman: vice president CORP AFFIL chief financial officer: Blackstone Crystal Holdings Capital Partners.
Mary Pickard: director, president (see above)
Kurt Schwarzkopf: corporate secretary

Grants Analysis
Disclosure Period: calendar year ending 2002
Total Grants: $6,066,180*
Number of Grants: 168
Average Grant: $26,529
Highest Grant: $200,000
Lowest Grant: $50
Typical Range: $50 to $1,500 and $5,000 to $100,000
***Note:** Giving excludes matching gifts; scholarship; United Way.

Recent Grants
Note: Grants derived from 2002 Form 990.
General

450,000	Greater Twin Cities United Way, Minneapolis, MN -- operating support
250,000	Manhattan College, Riverdale, NY -- scholarships
200,000	Children's Theater Company, Minneapolis, MN -- capital support
200,000	Hamline University, St. Paul, MN -- support for the Center for Excellence in Urban Teaching
200,000	Minnesota Private College Fund, St. Paul, MN -- Urban Education Scholarship Program
200,000	Project for Pride in Living, Inc., Minneapolis, MN -- capital support
150,000	Family Housing Fund, Minneapolis, MN -- Public Education initiative

140,000	Local Initiatives Support Corporation, New York, NY -- operating support
100,000	Hmong American Partnership, St. Paul, MN -- capital support
100,000	Minnesota Minority Education Partnership, Minneapolis, MN -- operating support

LUCY PANNILL SALE FOUNDATION

Giving Contact
Joseph R. Cobbe, President & Director
231 East Church Street, 5th Floor
Martinsville, VA 24112
Phone: (276)632-9871

Description
Founded: 1995
EIN: 541726783
Organization Type: Private Foundation
Giving Locations: VA
Grant Types: Endowment, General Support, Operating Expenses, Scholarship.

Financial Summary
Total Giving: $507,997 (fiscal year ending May 31, 2001)
Giving Analysis: Giving for fiscal 2001 includes: foundation gifts to individuals ($2,000); foundation grants to United Way ($20,000); foundation scholarships ($84,429)
Assets: $2,798,778 (fiscal 2001)
Gifts Received: $22,000 (fiscal 2000); $1,075,000 (fiscal 1997). Note: In fiscal 2000, contributions were received from Lucy Pannill Sale ($22,000). In fiscal 1997, contributions were received from UMI Alumni Agency and William Lechter Pannill Scholarship Foundation.

Typical Recipients
Arts & Humanities: Arts Associations & Councils, Historic Preservation, History & Archaeology, Libraries
Civic & Public Affairs: Chambers of Commerce, Community Foundations, Civic & Public Affairs-General, Urban & Community Affairs
Education: Colleges & Universities, Community & Junior Colleges, Private Education (Precollege), Public Education (Precollege), Student Aid
Health: Children's Health/Hospitals, Clinics/Medical Centers, Emergency/Ambulance Services, Health-General
Religion: Churches, Religion-General, Religious Welfare
Social Services: Domestic Violence, Family Services, Recreation & Athletics, Scouts, United Funds/United Ways, YMCA/YWCA/YMHA/YWHA

Application Procedures
Initial Contact: Send a brief letter of inquiry.
Application Requirements: Include amount requested and purpose of funds sought.
Deadlines: None.
Decision Notification: Applicants will be notified of the foundation's decision within two months.

Foundation Officials
Joseph R. Cobbe: president, director
John B. La Faye: director
Lucy P. Sale: director

Grants Analysis
Disclosure Period: fiscal year ending May 31, 2001
Total Grants: $401,568*
Number of Grants: 41
Average Grant: $8,063*

Highest Grant: $71,000
Lowest Grant: $500
Typical Range: $5,000 to $10,000
*Note: Giving excludes gifts to individuals; scholarship; United Way. Average grant figure excludes highest grant.

Recent Grants
Note: Grants derived from 2002 Form 990.
Library-Related

| 20,000 | Blue Ridge Regional Library, Martinsville, VA |

General

71,000	Martinsville County Chamber of Commerce, Martinsville, VA
67,429	Virginia Military Institute, Lexington, VA
26,000	Martinsville Red Wave AAU, Martinsville, VA
25,000	Carlisle School, Martinsville, VA
25,000	Episcopal Church Maintenance Fund, Martinsville, CA
25,000	Mission Center, Martinsville, VA
22,000	Piedmont Community Service, Martinsville, VA
20,000	United Way of Martinsville and Henry County, Martinsville, VA
15,000	Martinsville Youth Football, Martinsville, VA
15,000	Piedmont Arts Association, Martinsville, VA

RICHARD SALTONSTALL CHARITABLE FOUNDATION

Giving Contact
Dudley Willis, Trustee
50 Congress Street, Rm. 800
Boston, MA 02109
Phone: (617)227-8660
Fax: (617)227-4470

Description
Founded: 1964
EIN: 046078934
Organization Type: Private Foundation
Giving Locations: MA
Grant Types: General Support, Research.

Financial Summary
Total Giving: $1,153,775 (2002)
Giving Analysis: Giving for 2002 includes: foundation grants to United Way ($230,000)
Assets: $20,765,581 (2002)

Typical Recipients
Arts & Humanities: Dance, History & Archaeology, Libraries, Museums/Galleries, Music, Public Broadcasting
Civic & Public Affairs: Botanical Gardens/Parks, Clubs, Civic & Public Affairs-General, Native American Affairs, Rural Affairs, Women's Affairs, Zoos/Aquariums
Education: Agricultural Education, Health & Physical Education, Leadership Training, Medical Education, Minority Education, Private Education (Precollege), Special Education
Environment: Air/Water Quality, Environment-General, Protection, Resource Conservation, Watershed
Health: Alzheimer's Disease, Children's Health/Hospitals, Clinics/Medical Centers, Eyes/Blindness, Hospices, Hospitals
Science: Science Museums
Social Services: Counseling, Day Care, Family Services, People with Disabilities, Substance Abuse, United Funds/United Ways, Youth Organizations

Application Procedures
Initial Contact: The foundation has no formal grant application procedure or application form.
Deadlines: None.

Foundation Officials
Robert Ashton Lawrence: trustee B Boston, MA 1926. ED Yale University (1947). PRIM CORP EMPL partner: Saltonstall Co. CORP AFFIL director: State Street Growth Fund Inc.; director: State Street Investment Trust; director: State Street Exchange Fund; director: Metropolitan Series Fund; director: New York Times Co.; director: Metropolitan Life Portfolios; director: Metropolitan Life State Street Mutual Funds; director: Fifty Associates; executive vice president: FMR Corp.
Emily S. Lewis: trustee
Dudley H. Willis: trustee
Sally S. Willis: trustee

Grants Analysis
Disclosure Period: calendar year ending 2002
Total Grants: $923,775*
Number of Grants: 34*
Average Grant: $27,169*
Highest Grant: $175,000
Lowest Grant: $2,000
Typical Range: $5,000 to $50,000
*Note: Giving excludes United Way.

Recent Grants
Note: Grants derived from 2002 Form 990.
General

175,000	United Way of Massachusetts Bay, Boston, MA
150,000	Brigham and Women's Hospital, Boston, MA
100,000	New England Aquarium, Boston, MA
75,000	Charles River School, Dover, MA
60,000	Harvard University School of Public Health, Cambridge, MA
55,000	United Way of Massachusetts Bay, Boston, MA
50,000	Boston Symphony Orchestra, Boston, MA
50,000	Museum of Fine Arts, Boston, MA
46,775	Massachusetts Historical Society, Boston, MA
40,000	New England Medical Center, Boston, MA

EARL C. SAMS FOUNDATION

Giving Contact
Bruce Sams Hawn, President
101 N. Shoreline Blvd., Suite 602
Corpus Christi, TX 78401
Phone: (361)888-6485
Fax: (361)884-4241

Description
Founded: 1946
EIN: 741463151
Organization Type: General Purpose Foundation
Giving Locations: TX: Southern Texas
Grant Types: General Support, Matching, Project.

Donor Information
Founder: Incorporated in 1946 by the late Earl C. Sams.

Financial Summary
Total Giving: $1,194,700 (2001)
Assets: $28,260,350 (2001)

Typical Recipients

Arts & Humanities: Arts Centers, Ballet, Museums/Galleries, Music, Performing Arts, Public Broadcasting, Theater

Civic & Public Affairs: Asian American Affairs, Botanical Gardens/Parks, Community Foundations, Employment/Job Training, Civic & Public Affairs-General, Housing, Municipalities/Towns, Philanthropic Organizations, Public Policy, Rural Affairs, Women's Affairs, Zoos/Aquariums

Education: Colleges & Universities, Elementary Education (Public), Engineering/Technological Education, Environmental Education, Faculty Development, Education-General, Literacy, Medical Education, Private Education (Precollege), Public Education (Precollege), School Volunteerism, Science/Mathematics Education, Student Aid

Environment: Air/Water Quality, Environment-General, Protection, Resource Conservation, Wildlife Protection

Health: AIDS/HIV, Alzheimer's Disease, Arthritis, Cancer, Children's Health/Hospitals, Diabetes, Emergency/Ambulance Services, Health-General, Heart, Kidney, Medical Rehabilitation, Medical Research, Mental Health

International: International Relations

Religion: Churches, Ministries, Religious Welfare, Social/Policy Issues

Science: Science Museums, Scientific Research

Social Services: Animal Protection, At-Risk Youth, Child Abuse, Child Welfare, Community Service Organizations, Counseling, Crime Prevention, Emergency Relief, Family Planning, Family Services, Food/Clothing Distribution, People with Disabilities, Recreation & Athletics, Scouts, Shelters/Homelessness, Social Services-General, Substance Abuse, United Funds/United Ways, Volunteer Services, YMCA/YWCA/YMHA/YWHA, Youth Organizations

Application Procedures

Initial Contact: The foundation requests written proposals with documentation to support request and adequate information for the board of directors to evaluate the proposal.

Deadlines: None. The foundation requests that proposals are submitted one month prior to board meetings to be considered at that meeting.

Review Process: The board meets quarterly.

Restrictions

Grants are made solely to tax-exempt 501(c)(3) organizations. The foundation does not make grants to individuals.

Foundation Officials

Bruce Sams Hawn: president, chief executive officer, director
Nancy Hawn: director
Ed Jensen: assistant treasurer
Susan Ohnmacht: secretary
Susan Hawn Yuras: chairman, vice president, director

Grants Analysis

Disclosure Period: calendar year ending 2001
Total Grants: $1,194,700
Number of Grants: 60
Average Grant: $19,912
Highest Grant: $155,000
Lowest Grant: $1,000
Typical Range: $1,000 to $25,000

Recent Grants

Note: Grants derived from 2001 Form 990.
General
155,000	Texas State Aquarium, Corpus Christi, TX -- toward the construction of Dolphin Bay Exhibit
100,000	Making Main Street Happen, Inc., Houston, TX -- redevelopment of Main Street Houston
100,000	St. James Episcopal School, Houston, TX -- toward capital campaign
100,000	South Texas Public Broadcasting, Corpus Christi, TX -- toward the cost for conversion to DTV
77,500	Valley Zoological Society, Brownsville, TX -- White Rhino Moat Project
50,000	Palmer Drug Abuse Program, Corpus Christi, TX -- operating budget
40,000	Corpus Christi Metro Ministries, Corpus Christi, TX -- toward the support of the Rainbow House and Rustic House
30,000	Charity League, Corpus Christi, TX -- toward Charity League's 2000 Charity
30,000	Del Mar College Foundation, Corpus Christi, TX -- toward the construction of the Center for Early Learning
25,000	Art Center of Corpus Christi, Corpus Christi, TX -- toward renovation and expansion of existing facility

FAN FOX AND LESLIE R. SAMUELS FOUNDATION

Giving Contact

Joseph C. Mitchell, President and Director
350 Fifth Avenue, Suite 4301
New York, NY 10118
Phone: (212)239-3030
Fax: (212)239-3039
E-mail: info@samuels.org
Web: http://www.samuels.org

Description

Founded: 1981
EIN: 133124818
Organization Type: General Purpose Foundation
Giving Locations: NY: New York metropolitan area
Grant Types: General Support, Multiyear/Continuing Support, Project, Scholarship, Seed Money.

Donor Information

Founder: Established in Utah in 1959 by the late Mr. Leslie R. Samuels and Mrs. Leslie R. Samuels. The Foundation was originally called the Samuels-Auerbach Foundation and was reincorporated in New York in 1981.

Financial Summary

Total Giving: $8,809,070 (fiscal year ending July 31, 2003); $10,046,033 (fiscal 2001)
Giving Analysis: Giving for fiscal 2003 includes: foundation scholarships ($50,000); fiscal 2001: foundation scholarships ($202,750)
Assets: $169,414,252 (fiscal 2003); $222,235,661 (fiscal 2001)
Gifts Received: $180,934 (fiscal 2000); $711,701 (fiscal 1998); $29,771 (fiscal 1993). Note: In fiscal 1998 and 2000, contributions were received from the trusts of Fannie Fox Samuels and Leslie R. Samuels.

Typical Recipients

Arts & Humanities: Arts Associations & Councils, Arts Centers, Arts Festivals, Arts Funds, Arts Outreach, Ballet, Dance, Libraries, Music, Opera, Performing Arts, Theater

Civic & Public Affairs: Ethnic Organizations, Law & Justice, Public Policy, Urban & Community Affairs

Education: Arts/Humanities Education, Colleges & Universities, Education Funds, Education-General, Medical Education, Private Education (Precollege)

Health: Adolescent Health Issues, AIDS/HIV, Alzheimer's Disease, Cancer, Children's Health/Hospitals, Clinics/Medical Centers, Diabetes, Geriatric Health, Health Policy/Cost Containment, Health Funds, Health Organizations, Heart, Home-Care Services, Hospices, Hospitals, Hospitals (University Affiliated), Long-Term Care, Medical Rehabilitation, Medical Research, Mental Health, Nursing Services, Prenatal Health Issues, Public Health, Research/Studies Institutes, Respiratory

Religion: Jewish Causes

Science: Scientific Research

Social Services: Community Service Organizations, Delinquency & Criminal Rehabilitation, Family Services, People with Disabilities, Senior Services, Shelters/Homelessness, Substance Abuse

Application Procedures

Initial Contact: Letters of inquiry should be directed to the foundation's program officer. There are no application forms.

Application Requirements: Include a copy of 501(c)(3) letter, board of directors list, project budget, most recent financial statement, and current contributors list. Letters should briefly summarize the proposal and state the amount requested. Costly presentations are discouraged.

Deadlines: None.

Review Process: All letters are acknowledged within two months. If a proposal is of interest, an appointment will be arranged to discuss details before it is presented to the board, which meets in January, April, July, and October.

Restrictions

All funding is restricted to the five boroughs of New York City. The foundation reports that it no longer supports community service organizations, education, or media. It also does not support individuals. The foundation has a small budget for arts-in-education programming. No grants are made for operating expenses, building funds, or fund-raising campaigns.

Additional Information

Publications: Biennial Report

Foundation Officials

Morton J. Bernstein: director B 1917.
Marvin A. Kaufman: chairman, director B 1932.
Robert Marx: director, vice president
Joseph C. Mitchell: president, director
Carlos Dupre Moseley: director B Laurens, SC September 21, 1914. ED Duke University BA (1935); Philadelphia Conservatory of Music (1941-1944). NONPR AFFIL member: Phi Eta Sigma; member: Pi Kappa Lambda; member: Mu Phi Epsilon; member: Phi Beta Kappa; life trustee: Converse College; member: Metropolitan Opera Association; member: Century Association. CLUB AFFIL Piedmont Club.
Joseph W. Polisi: director
Jacqueline Taylor: director
Michael L. Ziegler: director

Grants Analysis

Disclosure Period: fiscal year ending July 31, 2003
Total Grants: $8,759,070*
Number of Grants: 227
Average Grant: $36,545*
Highest Grant: $500,000
Lowest Grant: $500
Typical Range: $15,000 to $50,000
*Note: Giving excludes scholarships. Average grant figure excludes highest grant.

Recent Grants

Note: Grants derived from 2003 Form 990.
Library-Related
50,000	New York Public Library, New York, NY -- fund for Theatre Film and Tape Archive

General
500,000	Carnegie Hall Society Inc., New York, NY
350,000	New York City Opera, New York, NY
300,000	Philharmonic - Symphony Society of New York Inc., New York, NY -- fund for Satur-

	day Matinee Concert and Rush Hour Concerts
250,000	Brooklyn Academy of Music Inc., Brooklyn, NY
250,000	Brooklyn Academy of Music Inc., Brooklyn, NY
250,000	Metropolitan Opera Association Inc., New York, NY -- fund for the production of Hector Berlioz's "Benvenuto Cellini"
250,000	New York City Ballet, New York, NY -- grant for commissioning and the performance of new works
200,000	Lincoln Center for the Performing Arts Inc., New York, NY -- fund for "Live From Lincoln Center"
200,000	Lincoln Center for the Performing Arts Inc., New York, NY -- to assist "Live from Lincoln Center"
150,000	Chamber Music Society of Lincoln Center Inc., New York, NY

GEORGE H. SANDY FOUNDATION

Giving Contact
Chester R. MacPhee, Jr., Trustee
PO Box 591717
San Francisco, CA 94159-1717
Phone: (415)765-2122

Description
Founded: 1960
EIN: 946054473
Organization Type: Private Foundation
Giving Locations: CA: San Francisco Bay area
Grant Types: Capital, Emergency, Multiyear/Continuing Support, Operating Expenses, Project, Scholarship.

Donor Information
Founder: the late George H. Sandy

Financial Summary
Total Giving: $1,222,000 (2001)
Giving Analysis: Giving for 2001 includes: foundation scholarships ($110,000)
Assets: $20,121,630 (2001)

Typical Recipients
Arts & Humanities: Libraries, Museums/Galleries
Civic & Public Affairs: Employment/Job Training, Civic & Public Affairs-General, Hispanic Affairs, Philanthropic Organizations, Urban & Community Affairs, Women's Affairs
Education: Afterschool/Enrichment Programs, Business-School Partnerships, Colleges & Universities, Elementary Education (Private), Elementary Education (Public), Education-General, Leadership Training, Legal Education, Literacy, Medical Education, Preschool Education, Private Education (Precollege), School Volunteerism, Science/Mathematics Education, Secondary Education (Public), Special Education, Student Aid
Environment: Wildlife Protection
Health: AIDS/HIV, Cancer, Children's Health/Hospitals, Emergency/Ambulance Services, Health Organizations, Heart, Home-Care Services, Hospitals, Long-Term Care, Medical Research, Mental Health, Prenatal Health Issues, Single-Disease Health Associations, Speech & Hearing, Trauma Treatment
International: Health Care/Hospitals, International Organizations, Missionary/Religious Activities
Religion: Churches, Jewish Causes, Religious Organizations, Religious Welfare
Social Services: Animal Protection, Big Brothers/Big Sisters, Camps, Child Abuse, Child Welfare, Community Service Organizations, Counseling, Day Care, Domestic Violence, Family Services, Food/Clothing Distribution, Homes, People with Disabilities, Recreation & Athletics, Shelters/Homelessness, Substance Abuse, Veterans, Volunteer Services, Youth Organizations

Application Procedures
Initial Contact: Send a brief letter of inquiry describing program or project.
Deadlines: None.

Restrictions
Contributions are made primarily to support local activities benefiting the handicapped and infirm.

Additional Information
Trust(s): Union Bank CA

Foundation Officials
Thomas J. Feeney, Esq.: trustee
Chester R. MacPhee, Jr.: trustee

Grants Analysis
Disclosure Period: calendar year ending 2001
Total Grants: $1,012,000*
Number of Grants: 75
Average Grant: $13,493
Highest Grant: $35,000
Typical Range: $10,000 to $20,000
*Note: Giving excludes scholarships.

Recent Grants
Note: Grants derived from 2001 Form 990.
General

35,000	San Francisco Society for the Prevention of Cruelty to Animals, San Francisco, CA -- Hearing Dog Program
30,000	Books Aloud, San Jose, CA -- to support their Books Aloud Program
30,000	Eastside College Preparatory School, East Palo Alto, CA -- for Shoot for the Starts and tuition free co-educational private school education
30,000	Environmental Travel Companions, San Francisco, CA -- provides first hand environmental education and wilderness experiences to handicapped, disabled and needy persons
30,000	RCH, Inc., San Francisco, CA -- for After School and Day Camp Program
30,000	Volunteer Auxiliary of the Youth Guidance Center, San Francisco, CA -- for assistance for abandoned, neglected, abused and troubled children
25,000	Halleck Creek Riding Club for the Handicapped Children, Inverness, CA -- recreational and therapeutic activities for handicapped and disabled children
25,000	Jean Weingarten Peninsula Oral School for the Deaf, San Francisco, CA -- to support the expansion of their Parent and Infant Toddler Program
25,000	Laguna Honda Hospital Volunteers, San Francisco, CA -- to support volunteer efforts
25,000	Larkin Street Youth Center, San Francisco, CA -- for the Lark Inn Program

SANDY HILL FOUNDATION

Giving Contact
Frank E. Walsh, Jr., Chairman
330 South St.
PO Box 1975
Morristown, NJ 07962-1975
Phone: (973)540-9020

Description
Founded: 1987
EIN: 222668774
Organization Type: Private Foundation
Giving Locations: NJ
Grant Types: Capital, General Support, Multiyear/Continuing Support, Operating Expenses, Scholarship.

Donor Information
Founder: Frank E. Walsh, Jr.

Financial Summary
Total Giving: $1,842,352 (2001)
Giving Analysis: Giving for 2001 includes: foundation grants to United Way ($50,000)
Assets: $35,711,035 (2001)
Gifts Received: $2,089,644 (2000); $88,750 (1999); $6,651,784 (1996). Note: In 2000, contributions were received from Frank E. Walsh.

Typical Recipients
Arts & Humanities: Arts Funds, History & Archaeology, Libraries, Performing Arts
Civic & Public Affairs: Community Foundations, Employment/Job Training, Civic & Public Affairs-General, Parades/Festivals, Philanthropic Organizations, Public Policy, Safety, Urban & Community Affairs
Education: Arts/Humanities Education, Colleges & Universities, Education Associations, Education Funds, Education Reform, Legal Education, Private Education (Precollege), Secondary Education (Private), Student Aid
Health: AIDS/HIV, Alzheimer's Disease, Cancer, Clinics/Medical Centers, Health Organizations, Hospices, Hospitals, Medical Research, Single-Disease Health Associations
International: International Relief Efforts
Religion: Churches, Dioceses, Religious Organizations, Religious Welfare, Seminaries, Social/Policy Issues
Social Services: At-Risk Youth, Child Welfare, Community Service Organizations, Domestic Violence, Emergency Relief, Food/Clothing Distribution, Homes, People with Disabilities, Recreation & Athletics, Senior Services, Shelters/Homelessness, United Funds/United Ways, Youth Organizations

Application Procedures
Initial Contact: The foundation has no formal grant application procedure or application form.
Deadlines: None.

Foundation Officials
Meghan Walsh Cioffi: vice president
Robert F. Cioffi: vice president
Frank E. Walsh, III: vice president
Frank E. Walsh, Jr.: chairman B 1941. PRIM CORP EMPL executive vice president: Wesray Capital Corp. CORP AFFIL director: WJAR TV.
Jeffrey R. Walsh: secretary, treasurer
Joseph Walsh: president
Karen R. Walsh: vice president
Mary D. Walsh: vice president

Grants Analysis
Disclosure Period: calendar year ending 2001
Total Grants: $1,792,353*
Number of Grants: 136
Average Grant: $11,972*
Highest Grant: $200,000
Typical Range: $5,000 to $20,000
*Note: Giving excludes United Way. Average grant figure excludes highest grant. .

Recent Grants
Note: Grants derived from 2001 Form 990.
General

200,000	Diocese of Paterson, Clifton, NJ
100,000	Catholic Charities USA, Washington, DC

100,000	Covenant House, Newark, NJ
100,000	Seton Hall Preparatory School, West Orange, NJ
100,000	Seton Hall University, South Orange, NJ
90,000	University of Vermont, Burlington, VT
30,000	Children's Center, Cedar Knolls, NJ
25,000	Boys and Girls Club of Newark, Newark, NJ
25,000	Community Foodbank of New Jersey, Hillside, NJ
25,000	Corpus Christi Church, Chatham, NJ

SAPIRSTEIN-STONE-WEISS FOUNDATION

Giving Contact
Gary Weiss, Vice President & Secretary
One American Road
Cleveland, OH 44144
Phone: (216)252-7300
Fax: (216)252-6777

Description
Founded: 1952
EIN: 346548007
Organization Type: Family Foundation
Giving Locations: Eastern USA.
Grant Types: General Support.

Donor Information
Founder: Incorporated in 1952 by the late Jacob Sapirstein.

Financial Summary
Total Giving: $1,884,918 (fiscal year ending May 31, 2003); $2,125,832 (fiscal 2002); $2,157,426 (fiscal 2001)
Assets: $19,174,022 (fiscal 2003); $21,630,413 (fiscal 2002); $25,277,107 (fiscal 2001)

Typical Recipients
Arts & Humanities: Libraries, Museums/Galleries
Civic & Public Affairs: Business/Free Enterprise, Civil Rights, Economic Development, Ethnic Organizations, Civic & Public Affairs-General, Philanthropic Organizations
Education: Colleges & Universities, Education Funds, Elementary Education (Private), Education-General, International Exchange, Literacy, Minority Education, Private Education (Precollege), Religious Education, Secondary Education (Private), Secondary Education (Public), Special Education
Environment: Environment-General
Health: Clinics/Medical Centers, Health Organizations, Hospitals, Long-Term Care, Preventive Medicine/Wellness Organizations
International: Foreign Arts Organizations, Foreign Educational Institutions, International-General, International Development, International Relations, Missionary/Religious Activities
Religion: Churches, Jewish Causes, Religious Organizations, Seminaries, Synagogues/Temples
Social Services: Camps, Child Welfare, Community Centers, Community Service Organizations, Family Services, Homes, People with Disabilities, Senior Services, United Funds/United Ways, Veterans, Youth Organizations

Application Procedures
Initial Contact: The foundation requests applications be made in writing.
Deadlines: January 15.

Restrictions
The foundation does not make grants or scholarships to individuals.

Foundation Officials
Gary M. Lippe: trustee B 1945. ED Ohio State University (1968). PRIM CORP EMPL vice president, corporate purchasing: American Greetings Corp. CORP AFFIL president: Quality Greeting Card Distribution Co.
Steven Tatar: trustee
Elie Weiss: trustee
Gary Weiss: vice president, secretary, trustee
Jeffrey Weiss: trustee PRIM CORP EMPL senior vice president product development: American Greetings Corp.
Judith Weiss: trustee
Morry Weiss: president, trustee B Czech Republic May 19, 1940. ED Wayne State University; Case Western Reserve University BS (1963). PRIM CORP EMPL chairman: American Greetings Corp. CORP AFFIL director: Artistic Greetings Inc.; director: National City Bank Corp..
Zev Weiss: treasurer, trustee

Grants Analysis
Disclosure Period: fiscal year ending May 31, 2003
Total Grants: $1,884,918
Number of Grants: 71
Average Grant: $6,672*
Highest Grant: $781,899
Lowest Grant: $100
Typical Range: $1,000 to $10,000
*Note: Average grant figure excludes two highest grants ($1,424,583).

Recent Grants
Note: Grants derived from 2003 Form 990.
Library-Related

| 5,500 | Jewish Outreach Center, Dallas, TX |

General

781,899	Fuchs Mizrachi School, Cleveland, OH
642,684	Jewish Community Federation, Cleveland, OH
50,000	American Jewish Joint Distribution Committee, New York, NY
50,000	Young Israel for Camp Stone, Cleveland, OH
40,000	AMIT Women, New York, NY
37,700	Hebrew Academy of Cleveland, Cleveland Heights, OH
31,915	Yeshiva University, New York, NY
25,000	Solomon Schechter Day School, Shaker Heights, OH
25,000	Union of Orthodox Jewish Congregations, New York, NY
20,000	Menorah Park Center for Senior Living, Beachwood, OH

SARA LEE CORP.

Company Headquarters
Chicago, IL
Web: http://www.saralee.com

Company Description
Founded: 1939
Ticker: SLE
Exchange: NYSE
Revenue: US$19.566 billion (2004)
Profit: US$1.272 billion (2004)
Employees: 145800 (2003)
Fortune Rank: 114, per FORTUNE Magazine's list of 500 Largest U.S. Corporations (2004).
SIC(s): 2011 Meat Packing Plants, 2013 Sausages & Other Prepared Meats, 2032 Canned Specialties, 2038 Frozen Specialties Nec.

Operating Locations
Sara Lee Corp. (AL--Athens, Florence, Montgomery, Scottsboro; AZ--Glendale; AR--Clarksville, Little Rock; CA--Hayward, Los Angeles, Modesto, San Diego, San Francisco; CT--Stamford; DE--Dover; FL--Miami, Pinellas Park; GA--Atlanta, Calhoun, Cartersville, Eastman, Fitzgerald, Midway, Milledgeville, Newnan, Wrightsville; IL--Bensenville, Champaign, Chicago, Elk Grove Village; IN--Dubois, Indianapolis; IA--Des Moines, New Hampton, Storm Lake; KS--Lenexa; KY--Alexandria; MI--Detroit, Grand Rapids, Livonia, Traverse City; MN--Minneapolis; MS--Jackson, Olive Branch, West Point; MO--Kansas City, St. Joseph, St. Louis; NV--Henderson; NJ--Secaucus; NM--Las Cruces; NY--New York, Rochester; NC--Asheboro, Asheville, Cary, Charlotte, Dunn, Eden, Forest City, High Point, Kernersville, Laurel Hill, Lumberton, Maxton, Morganton, Mount Airy, Rockingham, Rural Hill, Sanford, Tarboro, Weaverville, Winston-Salem, Yadkinville; OH--Cincinnati, Columbus, Valley View; PA--Douglassville, Philadelphia, Pittsburgh; SC--Barnwell, Charleston, Columbia, Conway, Florence, Greenville, Hartsville, Marion; TN--LaVergne, Martin, Memphis, Mountain City, Nashville; TX--Dallas; VA--Galax, Gretna, Hillsville, Rocky Mount, Salem; WA--Algona, Tacoma; WI--Milwaukee, New London)

Subsidiary Companies
NC: Sara Lee Hosiery Inc., Winston-Salem

Nonmonetary Support
Value: $19,000,000 (2000 approx); $23,420,000 (1999)
Type: Donated Products
Note: NOT The estimated value for fiscal 1999 is at cost.
Volunteer Programs: Company maintains a 15 to 20 person "Employee Volunteerism Committee," which is responsible for organizing approximately eight programs per year. Also sponsors a "Board Placement Program," through which company executives in the Chicago area are recruited to serve on nonprofit boards. These organizations also may be eligible for a $1,000 grant.
Contact: Robin Tryloff, Executive Director
Note: Various division-level personnel are responsible for nonmonetary distributions.

Sara Lee Foundation

Giving Contact
Ms. Robin Tryloff, President, Executive Director
3 First National Plaza
46th Floor
Chicago, IL 60602-4261
Phone: (312)558-8426
Fax: (312)419-3192
E-mail: saralee@eaymatch.com
Web: http://www.saraleefoundation.org

Alternate Contact
Matching Grant Program
PO Box 8258
Princeton, NJ 08543-8258
Phone: 877-756-2824
Fax: (609)799-8019

Description
EIN: 363150460
Organization Type: Corporate Foundation
Giving Locations: IL: Chicago metropolitan area principally near operating locations and to national organizations.
Grant Types: Award, Capital, Employee Matching Gifts, General Support, Operating Expenses, Project.
Note: Employee matching gift ratio: 2 to 1 up to $1,000 per employee annually. Employee matching gift ratio: 1 to 1 up to $10,000.

Financial Summary
Total Giving: $5,605,879 (fiscal year ending June 30, 2002); $6,939,421 (fiscal 2001)
Assets: $13,655,699 (fiscal 2002); $10,800,325 (fis-

cal 2001)
Gifts Received: $9,279,401 (fiscal 2002); $568,842 (fiscal 2001); $501,854 (fiscal 2000). Note: Contributions are received from Sara Lee Corp.

Typical Recipients

Arts & Humanities: Arts Associations & Councils, Arts Centers, Arts Festivals, Arts Funds, Arts Institutes, Ballet, Community Arts, Dance, Ethnic & Folk Arts, Film & Video, Arts & Humanities-General, Historic Preservation, History & Archaeology, Libraries, Museums/Galleries, Music, Opera, Performing Arts, Public Broadcasting, Theater, Visual Arts

Civic & Public Affairs: African American Affairs, Asian American Affairs, Business/Free Enterprise, Civil Rights, Economic Development, Employment/Job Training, Civic & Public Affairs-General, Hispanic Affairs, Housing, Law & Justice, Legal Aid, Nonprofit Management, Philanthropic Organizations, Professional & Trade Associations, Public Policy, Urban & Community Affairs, Women's Affairs, Zoos/Aquariums

Education: Arts/Humanities Education, Business Education, Colleges & Universities, Education Associations, International Exchange, International Studies, Legal Education, Literacy, Minority Education, Private Education (Precollege), Student Aid

Health: AIDS/HIV, Cancer, Children's Health/Hospitals, Health Organizations, Hospitals, Nutrition, Prenatal Health Issues, Public Health, Research/Studies Institutes

International: Foreign Educational Institutions, Human Rights, International Peace & Security Issues, International Relations, International Relief Efforts

Religion: Jewish Causes, Religious Organizations, Religious Welfare

Science: Observatories & Planetariums, Science Museums

Social Services: Child Welfare, Community Centers, Community Service Organizations, Counseling, Day Care, Domestic Violence, Family Planning, Family Services, Food/Clothing Distribution, Homes, People with Disabilities, Refugee Assistance, Scouts, Senior Services, Shelters/Homelessness, Social Services-General, Substance Abuse, United Funds/United Ways, Volunteer Services, YMCA/YWCA/YMHA/YWHA, Youth Organizations

Application Procedures

Initial Contact: Send a brief letter, or call requesting annual contributions report and application; to apply to divisions, call local division for information.

Application Requirements: Along with your completed application form, submit audit for most recently completed fiscal year (or an IRS Form 990 with a financial statement, for organizations with expenses of less than $150,000 that have not had an audit); current fiscal year operating budget, including anticipated revenues and expenses; list of current members of the board of directors with their titles and affiliations; list of key administrative and program/artistic staff, including a one-paragraph biography for each key staff member; proof of tax-exempt status; list of confirmed grants of $1,000 or more from private and public sources for the most recent fiscal year, including donor name and specific amounts; most recent annual report, or other descriptive information if an annual report is not produced; if project support is requested, submit a current and projected budget for the year for which funds are being requested with anticipated income and expenses; for cultural requests, attach reviews and/or samples of artistic work from the previous 18 months (include no more than six reviews/samples). Include two complete sets of all requested materials.

Deadlines: No later than first working day of March or September for consideration at quarterly meetings held after those months.

Review Process: Acknowledgment of receipt is sent to applicant. If proposal meets guidelines, it is placed on foundation agenda. If proposal does not meet guidelines, it is declined. Foundation staff reviews approved proposals and schedules meetings and site visits, if needed. Foundation discusses applicants at quarterly board meetings and approves or rejects requests.

Evaluative Criteria: Proposals are evaluated based on relevance to the foundation's priorities; unique contribution of the applicant; the ability of the project to reach underserved communities, populations, or audiences; innovation; leadership; effectiveness; feasibility and perceived need for services or the project; community support and involvement; sound management; and employee involvement.

Decision Notification: Applications are acknowledged upon receipt and organizations are notified by letter of the foundation's decision after quarterly meetings.

Notes: Proposals must be submitted on the foundation's application form.

Restrictions

The following are not eligible for grants: capital and endowment campaigns; individuals; organizations with a limited constituency, such as fraternal or veterans groups; organizations that limit services to members of one religious group or seek to propagate a particular belief or creed; governmental or quasi-governmental organizations; political organizations or groups promoting one ideological view; elementary or secondary schools, either public or private; single-disease health organizations or hospitals concentrating their research or treatment in one area of human disease; tickets to dinners and other events; goodwill advertising in yearbooks or dinner or event programs; or national or international organizations with limited relationship to local Sara Lee operations.

Additional Information

Company has operating locations in nearly all 50 states. Sara Lee's contributions program is decentralized. About two-fifths of total contributions are made by the foundation, which is the main philanthropic vehicle for the Chicago corporate office. The remainder is distributed by divisions, which administer their own programs including nonmonetary giving and volunteer services.

Organizations should not submit a contribution application more than once in any 12-month period. Grants are not automatically renewed, and recipients desiring renewed support should submit a request approximately two months prior to the anniversary of their grant(s). A renewal request should include the organization's most recent audited financial statement, current year's operating budget, updated board of directors list, and summary of how the previous year's grant was used. An application form is not necessary for grant renewal requests.

Sara Lee maintains a policy that annual cash and product contributions shall represent at least 2% of domestic pretax income.

At the corporate and division levels, company forms active partnerships with particularly effective local organizations and encourages employee involvement.

Corporate Officials

Paul A. Allaire: director
Frans H.J.J. Andriessen: director
Duane L. Burnham: director
Charles W. Coker: director
James S. Crown: director
Willie D. Davis: director
Vernon E. Jordan, Jr.: director
James L. Ketelsen: director
Joan D. Manley: director
C. Steven McMillan: president, chief executive officer PRIM CORP EMPL president, chief executive officer: Sara Lee Corp.
Cary D. McMillan: executive vice president, chief financial officer, chief administrative officer PRIM CORP EMPL executive vice president, chief financial officer, chief administrative officer: Sara Lee Corp.
Frank L. Meysman: director

Rozanne L. Ridgway: director
Richard L. Thomas: director
Robin Tryloff: executive director community relations PRIM CORP EMPL director community relations: Sara Lee Corp.
Hans B. Van Liemt: director
John D. Zeglis: director

Foundation Officials

Julie B. A. Brooks: grants coordinator
James K. Hahn: assistant secretary
R. Henry Kleeman: assistant secretary
Mary T. Malloy: secretary
Ted McDougal: director
C. Steven McMillan: director (see above)
Ho Yan J. Ng: supervisor administration and budget
Roderick A. Palmore: vice president, secretary
Cassandra M. Pulley: director
Robert J. Rizzo: senior coordinator
Timothy M. Russell: manager community initiatives program
Judy E. Schaefer: assistant vice president
Patrick M. Sheahan: deputy director, assistant vice president
Robin Tryloff: president, executive director, director (see above)
James A. Wabich: assistant secretary
J. Randall White: director
Elynor Alberta Williams: director B Baton Rouge, LA 1946. ED Spelman College BS (1966); Cornell University Graduate School of Business Administration MS (1973). PRIM CORP EMPL president, managing director: Chestnut, Pearson & Assoc.. NONPR AFFIL member: National Association Female Executives; member: Public Relations Society America; member: International Association of Business Communicators.
Cheryl L. Yuen: consultant - cultural program

Grants Analysis

Disclosure Period: fiscal year ending June 30, 2002
Total Grants: $3,897,388*
Number of Grants: 179
Average Grant: $20,491*
Highest Grant: $250,000
Lowest Grant: $282
Typical Range: $2,500 to $25,000
***Note:** Giving excludes matching gifts, scholarship, and United Way. Average grant figure excludes highest grant.

Recent Grants

Note: Grants derived from fiscal 2003 Form 990.

General

365,000	United Way, Chicago, IL
350,000	Art Institute of Chicago, Chicago, IL
250,000	Orchestral Association, Chicago, IL
200,000	Music and Dance Theater Chicago, Chicago, IL
200,000	Steppenwolf Theatre Company, Chicago, IL
196,140	National Merit Scholarship Corporation, Evanston, IL
125,000	Hubbard Street Dance Chicago, Chicago, IL
100,000	Chicago Shakespeare Theater, Chicago, IL
100,000	Joffrey Ballet of Chicago Inc., Chicago, IL
100,000	Lookingglass Theatre Company, Chicago, IL

NEWELL B. SARGENT FOUNDATION

Giving Contact

Charles W. Smith, Trustee
PO Box 50581
Casper, WY 82605

Phone: (307)577-0724

Description

Founded: 1984
EIN: 830271536
Organization Type: Private Foundation
Giving Locations: WY: emphasis on Worland
Grant Types: General Support, Scholarship.

Donor Information

Founder: Newell B. Sargent

Financial Summary

Total Giving: $952,778 (fiscal year ending October 31, 2004)
Assets: $20,974,533 (fiscal 2004)
Gifts Received: $251,170 (fiscal 2004); $200,000 (fiscal 2000); $200,000 (fiscal 1999). Note: In fiscal 2004, contributions were received from Newell Sargent and Vera Sargent Trusts. In fiscal 1998 and 2000, contributions were received from Newell B. Sargent.

Typical Recipients

Arts & Humanities: Arts Festivals, Community Arts, Dance, History & Archaeology, Libraries, Museums/Galleries, Music, Theater
Civic & Public Affairs: Business/Free Enterprise, Chambers of Commerce, Clubs, Community Foundations, Economic Development, Employment/Job Training, Civic & Public Affairs-General, Law & Justice, Municipalities/Towns, Parades/Festivals, Public Policy, Safety, Urban & Community Affairs, Women's Affairs
Education: Colleges & Universities, Community & Junior Colleges, Elementary Education (Public), Education-General, Literacy, Medical Education, Minority Education, Private Education (Precollege), Public Education (Precollege), Secondary Education (Public), Student Aid
Environment: Environment-General, Resource Conservation
Health: Alzheimer's Disease, Cancer, Children's Health/Hospitals, Emergency/Ambulance Services, Eyes/Blindness, Health Organizations, Heart, Hospitals, Respiratory, Speech & Hearing
International: International-General
Religion: Churches, Ministries, Religious Organizations, Religious Welfare
Social Services: Animal Protection, Child Welfare, Community Service Organizations, Counseling, Crime Prevention, Emergency Relief, Food/Clothing Distribution, Homes, People with Disabilities, Scouts, Senior Services, Shelters/Homelessness, Veterans, Youth Organizations

Application Procedures

Initial Contact: The foundation has no formal grant application procedure or application form. Send a brief letter of inquiry.
Deadlines: None.

Foundation Officials

Charles W. Smith: trustee

Grants Analysis

Disclosure Period: fiscal year ending October 31, 2004
Total Grants: $952,778
Number of Grants: 12
Average Grant: $4,864*
Highest Grant: $899,278
Lowest Grant: $500
Typical Range: $1,000 to $5,000
*Note: Average grant figure excludes highest grant.

Recent Grants

Note: Grants derived from 2004 Form 990.
General

899,278	Wyoming Community Foundation Washakie Museum, Laramie, WY	
30,000	New Hope Property, Worland, WY -- for cemetery fund	
12,500	New Hope Humane Society, Worland, WY	
5,000	West Side Elementary School, Worland, WY	
1,000	Central Wyoming Rescue Mission, Casper, WY	
1,000	Montana Rescue, Billings, MT	
1,000	Mother Seton House, Casper, WY	
1,000	Northwest Community Action Programs, Casper, WY	
500	Washakie County Ministerial Association, Worland, WY	
500	Worland Senior Citizens, Worland, WY	

SARKEYS FOUNDATION

Giving Contact

Susan C. Frantz, Program Officer
530 East Main Street
Norman, OK 73071
Phone: (405)364-3703
Fax: (405)364-8191
E-mail: cheri@sarkeys.org
Web: http://www.sarkeys.org

Description

Founded: 1962
EIN: 730736496
Organization Type: Private Foundation
Giving Locations: OK
Grant Types: Capital, Endowment, General Support, Matching, Multiyear/Continuing Support, Project.

Donor Information

Founder: Established in 1962 by S. J. Sarkeys.

Financial Summary

Total Giving: $3,436,498 (fiscal year ending November 30, 2003); $3,848,147 (fiscal 2002); $2,876,899 (fiscal 2001)
Assets: $88,595,024 (fiscal 2003); $82,423,726 (fiscal 2002); $93,131,312 (fiscal 2001)

Typical Recipients

Arts & Humanities: Art History, Arts Associations & Councils, Arts Centers, Arts Festivals, Arts Funds, Arts Institutes, Ballet, Dance, Arts & Humanities-General, Historic Preservation, History & Archaeology, Libraries, Museums/Galleries, Music, Opera, Performing Arts, Theater
Civic & Public Affairs: Asian American Affairs, Botanical Gardens/Parks, Community Foundations, Economic Development, Employment/Job Training, Civic & Public Affairs-General, Hispanic Affairs, Housing, Legal Aid, Municipalities/Towns, Native American Affairs, Nonprofit Management, Philanthropic Organizations, Urban & Community Affairs, Zoos/Aquariums
Education: Afterschool/Enrichment Programs, Agricultural Education, Arts/Humanities Education, Colleges & Universities, Community & Junior Colleges, Education Funds, Education Reform, Engineering/Technological Education, Education-General, Leadership Training, Legal Education, Literacy, Medical Education, Private Education (Precollege), Public Education (Precollege), Religious Education, Science/Mathematics Education, Special Education, Student Aid
Environment: Environment-General, Research, Resource Conservation
Health: AIDS/HIV, Alzheimer's Disease, Cancer, Children's Health/Hospitals, Clinics/Medical Centers, Diabetes, Emergency/Ambulance Services, Eyes/Blindness, Health Organizations, Hospices, Hospitals, Medical Rehabilitation, Medical Research, Mental Health, Prenatal Health Issues, Public Health, Single-Disease Health Associations, Speech & Hearing
International: International Relations
Religion: Churches, Ministries, Religious Organizations, Religious Welfare
Science: Science Museums, Scientific Centers & Institutes, Scientific Labs, Scientific Research
Social Services: Animal Protection, At-Risk Youth, Big Brothers/Big Sisters, Camps, Child Abuse, Child Welfare, Community Centers, Community Service Organizations, Counseling, Day Care, Domestic Violence, Family Planning, Family Services, Food/Clothing Distribution, Homes, People with Disabilities, Scouts, Senior Services, Sexual Abuse, Shelters/Homelessness, Social Services-General, Special Olympics, Substance Abuse, YMCA/YWCA/YMHA/YWHA, Youth Organizations

Application Procedures

Initial Contact: Contact the foundation for an application form or obtain the form from the foundation's web site.
Application Requirements: The application form should be single-spaced, unbound, stapled, and printed on only one side of white, 8 1/2- by 11-inch paper. Along with the completed application form, the foundation requires the following attachments: a cover letter; a description of organization (one- to two-pages in length); a three- to four-page description of the project that describes the problem or need, how the project will solve or alleviate the problem, how the project relates to or helps fulfill the organization's mission, the organization's qualifications to address the problem or need (if the problem or need is external), anticipated outcomes of the project, the mechanisms in place to evaluate the success or failure of the project, project time frame, and how ongoing or future needs will be funded after the grant ends; a line-item budget for each year of the project; a list of secured funds and pledges for this project; a list of all outstanding requests and their amounts for this project; a list of other potential sources of funding, if any, for this project; a list of current board members which includes their names and professions; a list of current staff members and their position titles; a complete copy of the IRS tax-exempt determination letter stating that the organization is not a private foundation and that it has IRS Code section 501(c)(3) status; and a copy of the organization's most recent audit.
Deadlines: Proposals are accepted from December 15 through February 1 for inclusion on the foundation's April agenda, and from June 1 through August 1 for inclusion on the October agenda.
Review Process: The trustees meet in April, and October to consider proposals. Organizations whose applications are accepted for inclusion on the agenda for the April or October meetings will be notified.
Notes: The foundation does not accept faxed or e-mailed proposals. Organizations are limited to one application per calendar year or twelve-month period.

Restrictions

The foundation normally does not fund local programs appropriately financed within the community, direct mail solicitations and annual campaigns, out-of-state institutions, hospitals, operating expenses, purchase of vehicles, grants to individuals, responsibility for permanent financing of a program, for-profit organizations or programs, start-up funding for new organizations, feasibility studies, grants which trigger expenditure responsibility by the Sarkeys Foundation, direct support to government agencies, individual public or private elementary or secondary schools (unless they are serving the needs of a special population which are not being met elsewhere), or religious institutions and their subsidiaries. E-mailed proposals. E-mailed proposals.

Additional Information

Close adherence to the guidelines will maximize the opportunity for a successful proposal.
Publications: Guidelines Brochure

Foundation Officials

Teresa B. Adwan: trustee
Richard A. Bell: trustee, vice president PRIM CORP EMPL attorney: Richardd A. Bell.
Cheri D. Cartwright: executive director, assistant secretary-treasurer
Susan C. Frantz: program officer
Fred Gipson: trustee
Kim Henry: trustee
Dan Little: trustee PRIM CORP EMPL president: Fayette Enterprises Inc.
Joseph W. Morris: trustee PRIM CORP EMPL partner: Gable & Gotwals.
Robert S. Rizley: trustee
Dr. Paul F. Sharp: trustee B Kirksville, MO January 19, 1918. ED Phillips University AB (1939); University of Minnesota PhD (1947). NONPR AFFIL president emeritus: University Oklahoma; distinguished professor history: University Science and Arts Oklahoma; member: Phi Kappa Phi; member: Pi Gamma Nu; member: Phi Beta Kappa; member: Phi Delta Kappa; member: Phi Alpha Theta.
Ann M. Way: senior program officer
Terry W. West: president, trustee

Grants Analysis

Disclosure Period: fiscal year ending November 30, 2003
Total Grants: $3,436,498
Number of Grants: 68
Average Grant: $43,336*
Highest Grant: $533,000
Lowest Grant: $100
Typical Range: $10,000 to $75,000
*Note: Average grant figure excludes highest grant.

Recent Grants

Note: Grants derived from fiscal 2003 Form 990.

Library-Related

25,000	Choctaw Library Guild, Choctaw, OK -- towards construction of a lower level sun deck

General

533,000	University of Oklahoma Foundation, Norman, OK -- towards construction of the law library
200,000	Oklahoma Arts Institute, Oklahoma City, OK -- towards endowment for summer institute scholarships
200,000	Oklahoma School of Science and Mathematics Foundation, Oklahoma City, OK -- towards the construction and naming of the dormitory addition
150,000	Assistance League of Norman, Norman, OK -- towards capital campaign for construction of a new headquarters and operation school bell facility
100,000	Norman Community Foundation, Norman, OK -- towards operating endowment
100,000	Norman Firehouse Art Center, Norman, OK -- towards phase one of the capital campaign
100,000	Oklahoma Medical Research Foundation, Oklahoma City, OK -- towards the Sarkeys chair in Alzheimer's research
100,000	Special Care, Oklahoma City, OK -- towards construction of a new facility
80,000	Center for Children and Families Inc., Norman, OK -- as emergency operating expenses
70,000	Seminole State College Educational Foundation Inc., Seminole, OK -- towards the renovation and expansion of the S.J. Sarkeys dormitory

SASCO FOUNDATION

Giving Contact

Uwe Linder, Vice President & Trust Officer
JP Morgan Chase Bank
1211 Avenue of the Americas, 34th Fl.
New York, NY 10036-8890
Phone: (212)789-4159

Description

Founded: 1951
EIN: 136046567
Organization Type: Private Foundation
Giving Locations: CT; ME; NY
Grant Types: General Support.

Donor Information

Founder: the late Leila E. Riegel, Katherine R. Emory

Financial Summary

Total Giving: $273,500 (2001)
Assets: $6,482,312 (2001)

Typical Recipients

Arts & Humanities: Historic Preservation, History & Archaeology, Libraries, Music, Public Broadcasting
Civic & Public Affairs: Botanical Gardens/Parks, Community Foundations, Civic & Public Affairs-General, Native American Affairs, Nonprofit Management, Philanthropic Organizations, Public Policy, Urban & Community Affairs, Women's Affairs, Zoos/Aquariums
Education: Afterschool/Enrichment Programs, Colleges & Universities, Private Education (Precollege), Secondary Education (Private)
Environment: Air/Water Quality, Forestry, Environment-General, Resource Conservation, Wildlife Protection
Health: Alzheimer's Disease, Cancer, Clinics/Medical Centers, Emergency/Ambulance Services, Hospitals, Medical Research, Nursing Services, Transplant Networks/Donor Banks
International: Health Care/Hospitals, International Relief Efforts
Religion: Churches, Religious Organizations, Religious Welfare
Science: Science Museums
Social Services: Animal Protection, Child Welfare, Community Service Organizations, Delinquency & Criminal Rehabilitation, Family Planning, Family Services, Food/Clothing Distribution, Scouts, Shelters/Homelessness, United Funds/United Ways, Volunteer Services, YMCA/YWCA/YMHA/YWHA, Youth Organizations

Application Procedures

Initial Contact: Send cover letter and full proposal.
Application Requirements: Include goals and purpose of funds sought.
Deadlines: November 30.

Additional Information

Trust(s): JPMorgan Chase Bank

Foundation Officials

Lucy E. Ambach: trustee
Benjamin Emory: trustee
Katherine Emory Stookey: trustee

Grants Analysis

Disclosure Period: calendar year ending 2001
Total Grants: $273,500
Number of Grants: 40
Average Grant: $6,838
Highest Grant: $25,000
Lowest Grant: $1,000
Typical Range: $1,000 to $15,000

Recent Grants

Note: Grants derived from 2001 Form 990.

General

25,000	Children's Aid Society, New York, NY
15,000	Family Care International, New York, NY
15,000	Landmark Volunteers, Sheffield, MA
12,500	Central Park Conservancy, New York, NY
12,500	Land Trust Alliance, Washington, DC
10,000	Blue Hill Heritage Trust, Blue Hill, ME
10,000	Chapin School, New York, NY
10,000	Connecticut Fund for the Environment, New Haven, CT
10,000	Maine Coast Heritage Trust, Brunswick, ME
10,000	Maine Coast Heritage Trust, Brunswick, ME

HELEN M. SAUNDERS CHARITABLE FOUNDATION TRUST

Giving Contact

Coleman H. Casey, Attorney
c/o Shipman and Goodwin LLP
1 American Row
Hartford, CT 06103-2819
Phone: (860)251-5000

Description

Founded: 1985
EIN: 066284362
Organization Type: Private Foundation
Giving Locations: CA: emphasis on Hartford
Grant Types: Endowment, General Support.

Financial Summary

Total Giving: $265,625 (fiscal year ending June 30, 2001). Note: Fiscal 1997 Giving includes United Way ($1,250).
Giving Analysis: Giving for fiscal 2001 includes: foundation grants to United Way ($3,000)
Assets: $5,864,667 (fiscal 2001)

Typical Recipients

Arts & Humanities: Arts Associations & Councils, Arts Centers, Arts & Humanities-General, Libraries, Literary Arts, Music, Opera, Performing Arts, Public Broadcasting
Civic & Public Affairs: Botanical Gardens/Parks, Employment/Job Training, Civic & Public Affairs-General
Education: Arts/Humanities Education, Colleges & Universities, Education Associations, Education Funds, Faculty Development, Literacy, Private Education (Precollege), Public Education (Precollege), Student Aid
Health: Hospitals, Nursing Services
International: Foreign Arts Organizations
Religion: Churches, Ministries, Religious Organizations, Religious Welfare
Social Services: Camps, Child Welfare, People with Disabilities, United Funds/United Ways, YMCA/YWCA/YMHA/YWHA

Application Procedures

Initial Contact: Request guidelines.
Deadlines: None.

Restrictions

Does not support individuals. Supports only organizations with tax-exempt documentation.

Additional Information

Publications: Grant Request Guidelines

Foundation Officials

Coleman H. Casey: trustee

Grants Analysis

Disclosure Period: fiscal year ending June 30, 2001
Total Grants: $262,625*
Number of Grants: 41
Average Grant: $6,405*
Highest Grant: $30,000
Lowest Grant: $150
Typical Range: $100 to $10,000
*Note: Giving excludes UNW.

Recent Grants

Note: Grants derived from fiscal 2001 Form 990.
Library-Related

30,000	Wadsworth Athenaeum, Hartford, CT -- Michael Sweerts exhibition
20,000	Wadsworth Athenaeum, Hartford, CT -- Sol LeWitt Cube Show
15,000	Wadsworth Athenaeum, Hartford, CT -- Gauguin exhibit

General

20,000	Hartford Symphony Orchestra, Hartford, CT
20,000	Lasell College, Hartford, CT
17,500	Lasell College, Hartford, CT
15,000	Greater Hartford Arts Council, Hartford, CT -- United Arts campaign
14,000	Hartford Symphony Orchestra, Hartford, CT -- Capriccio
13,500	Loomis Chaffee School, Hartford, CT
10,000	Asylum Hill Congregational Church, Hartford, CT -- music series
10,000	Cedar Hill Cemetery Association, Hartford, CT
10,000	CONCORA, New Britain, CT -- support Great Sacred Music of the Mystics
10,000	Connecticut Public Television and Radio, Hartford, CT -- Partners for a Digital Connecticut

SAW ISLAND FOUNDATION

Giving Contact

R. Bruce Mosbacher, President
524 Moore Rd., Suite A
Woodside, CA 94062
Phone: (650)851-9990

Description

Founded: 1974
EIN: 237454106
Organization Type: Private Foundation
Former Name: Emil Mosbacher, Jr. Foundation.
Giving Locations: CT; NY
Grant Types: General Support.

Donor Information

Founder: Emil Mosbacher, Jr., Emil Mosbacher III, John D. Mosbacher, R. Bruce Mosbacher

Financial Summary

Total Giving: $501,000 (fiscal year ending November 30, 2004); $672,500 (fiscal 2001)
Giving Analysis: Giving for fiscal 2004 includes: foundation grants to United Way ($1,000); fiscal 2001: foundation grants to United Way ($1,000)
Assets: $14,891,548 (fiscal 2004); $14,324,527 (fiscal 2001)
Gifts Received: $640,713 (fiscal 2004); $1,794,000 (fiscal 2001); $114,037 (fiscal 1995). Note: In fiscal 2001 and 2004, contributions were received from The Emil Mosbacher Jr. Charitable Annuity Trust. In fiscal 1995, contributions were received from Emil Mosbacher, Jr.

Typical Recipients

Arts & Humanities: Arts & Humanities-General, History & Archaeology, Libraries, Museums/Galleries, Opera, Public Broadcasting, Theater
Civic & Public Affairs: Botanical Gardens/Parks, Civil Rights, Community Foundations, Civic & Public Affairs-General, Hispanic Affairs, Philanthropic Organizations, Public Policy
Education: Colleges & Universities, Faculty Development, International Exchange, Legal Education, Medical Education, Private Education (Precollege), Public Education (Precollege), Science/Mathematics Education, Student Aid
Health: AIDS/HIV, Cancer, Children's Health/Hospitals, Clinics/Medical Centers, Health Funds, Health Organizations, Heart, Hospices, Hospitals, Medical Rehabilitation, Medical Research, Single-Disease Health Associations
International: Foreign Educational Institutions, Health Care/Hospitals, Human Rights, International Organizations, International Peace & Security Issues
Religion: Churches, Religious Welfare
Science: Science Museums
Social Services: Animal Protection, Community Service Organizations, Family Services, People with Disabilities, Recreation & Athletics, Scouts, Substance Abuse, United Funds/United Ways, YMCA/YWCA/YMHA/YWHA, Youth Organizations

Application Procedures

Initial Contact: Send brief letter.
Application Requirements: Describe program and include any pertinent information.
Deadlines: None.

Restrictions

Does not support individuals.

Foundation Officials

Nancy J. Ditz: secretary, treasurer
Patricia R. Mosbacher: vice president
R. Bruce Mosbacher: president

Grants Analysis

Disclosure Period: fiscal year ending November 30, 2004
Total Grants: $500,000*
Number of Grants: 40
Average Grant: $7,432*
Highest Grant: $100,000
Lowest Grant: $100
Typical Range: $1,000 to $10,000
*Note: Giving excludes United Way. Average grant figure excludes three highest grants ($225,000).

Recent Grants

Note: Grants derived from fiscal 2004 Form 990.
General

100,000	Lucile Packard Foundation for Children, Palo Alto, CA -- support of pediatric research programs fellowship grants
75,000	Regents of university of California, San Francisco, CA -- to support the research efforts of the general clinical research center
50,000	Stanford University, Stanford, CA -- provision of scholarship educational, financial aid
40,000	Hospital for Special Surgery, New York, NY -- support of orthopedic research programs
25,000	Dartmouth College, Hanover, NH -- provision of scholarship educational, financial aid
25,000	Regents of University of California, San Francisco, CA -- to support the research efforts of the general clinical research center
20,000	Memorial Sloan Kettering Cancer Center, New York, NY -- support for head and neck research programs
20,000	Menlo School, Atherton, CA -- provision of scholarship educational, financial aid
20,000	Ragazzi, San Meteo, CA -- provision of scholarship educational, financial aid
20,000	San Francisco First Tee, San Francisco, CA -- support for community outreach programs for youth

SAWYER CHARITABLE FOUNDATION

Giving Contact

Carol S. Parks, Manager & Trustee
200 Newbury Street, 4th Fl.
Boston, MA 02116-2504
Phone: (617)262-6920

Description

Founded: 1957
EIN: 046088774
Organization Type: Private Foundation
Giving Locations: greater New England area.
Grant Types: Endowment, General Support.

Donor Information

Founder: Frank Sawyer, William Sawyer, The Brattle Co. Corp., St. Botolph Holding Co., First Franklin Parking Corp.

Financial Summary

Total Giving: $357,025 (2004). Note: 1997 Giving includes United Way ($5,000).
Giving Analysis: Giving for 2004 includes: foundation grants to United Way ($5,000)
Assets: $4,677,720 (2004)
Gifts Received: $36,827 (1998); $341,000 (1997); $1,000 (1995). Note: In 1998, contributions were received from the Estate of Beryl Mills.

Typical Recipients

Arts & Humanities: Arts Centers, Historic Preservation, Libraries, Museums/Galleries, Performing Arts
Civic & Public Affairs: African American Affairs, Clubs, Employment/Job Training, Civic & Public Affairs-General, Public Policy, Urban & Community Affairs, Women's Affairs
Education: Colleges & Universities, Community & Junior Colleges, Education-General, Legal Education, Private Education (Precollege), Secondary Education (Public), Special Education
Environment: Air/Water Quality
Health: AIDS/HIV, Cancer, Children's Health/Hospitals, Clinics/Medical Centers, Emergency/Ambulance Services, Health Organizations, Hospices, Hospitals, Medical Research, Respiratory, Single-Disease Health Associations, Transplant Networks/Donor Banks, Trauma Treatment
International: Health Care/Hospitals, International Relief Efforts
Religion: Churches, Dioceses, Jewish Causes, Religious Organizations, Religious Welfare, Synagogues/Temples
Science: Science Museums
Social Services: Animal Protection, Camps, Child Welfare, Community Service Organizations, Family Services, Homes, People with Disabilities, Scouts, Senior Services, Shelters/Homelessness, Social Services-General, Substance Abuse, United Funds/United Ways, Veterans, Youth Organizations

Application Procedures

Initial Contact: Send cover letter and full proposal.
Application Requirements: Includes purpose of funds sought and proof of tax-exempt status.
Deadlines: October 15.

Restrictions

Does not support individuals or provide funds for administrative expenses, payroll, or building projects.

Foundation Officials

Carol S. Parks: mgr, trustee
Mary S. Quinn: mgr

Grants Analysis

Disclosure Period: calendar year ending 2004
Total Grants: $352,025*
Number of Grants: 91
Average Grant: $2,832*
Highest Grant: $50,000
Lowest Grant: $150
Typical Range: $1,000 to $5,000
*Note: Giving excludes United Way. Average grant figure excludes two highest grants ($100,000).

Recent Grants

Note: Grants derived from 2004 Form 990.
Library-Related
50,000	Suffolk University - Mildred F. Sawyer Library, Boston, MA

General
50,000	Rosie's Place, Boston, MA
25,000	Carroll Center for the Blind, Newton, MA
25,000	Newton Country Day School of the Sacred Heart, Newton, MA
15,000	Pine Street Inn, Boston, MA
15,000	Salvation Army, Alexandria, VA
11,000	Shriner's Burns Institute, Cincinnati, OH
10,000	Little Sisters of the Poor, Totowa, NJ
10,000	Massachusetts Eye and Ear Infirmary, Boston, MA
10,000	Massachusetts Society for Prevention of Cruelty to Animals, Boston, MA

SBC COMMUNICATIONS INC.

Company Headquarters

175 E. Houston
San Antonio, TX 78205-2233
Web: http://www.sbc.com

Company Description

Founded: 1983
Ticker: SBC
Exchange: NYSE
Former Name: Ameritech.
Revenue: US$41.098 billion (2004)
Profit: US$5.887 billion (2004)
Employees: 175400 (2003)
Fortune Rank: 33, per FORTUNE Magazine's list of 500 Largest U.S. Corporations (2004).

SBC Foundation

Giving Contact

Laura P. Sanford, President
130 Travis Street, Suite 3-H-6
San Antonio, TX 78205
Phone: 800-591-9663
Fax: (210)351-2259
Web: http://www.sbc.com/gen/corporate-citizenship?pid=2501

Alternate Contact

Ben Voris, Corporate Manager
Phone: (210)351-5154

Description

EIN: 431353948
Organization Type: Corporate Foundation

Former Name: Southwestern Bell Foundation.
Formed by Merger of: PacTel Foundation (1998).
Giving Locations: AR; CA; CT; DC: Washington; IL; IN; KS; MI; MO; NV; NY; OH; OK; TX; VA; WI nationally.
Grant Types: Capital, Challenge, Employee Matching Gifts, Endowment, General Support, Matching, Multiyear/Continuing Support, Project.
Note: Employee matching gift ratio: 1 to 1 to higher education and cultural institutions.

Financial Summary

Total Giving: $45,607,108 (2003); $95,800,000 (2002 approx); $69,111,239 (2001). Note: Contributes through corporate direct giving program and foundation.
Giving Analysis: Giving for 2001 includes: corporate direct giving (approx $30,300,000); foundation (approx $68,900,000)
Assets: $267,376,836 (2003); $703,000,000 (2002 approx); $536,184,004 (2001)
Gifts Received: $209,112,587 (2001); $29,915,650 (2000); $33,100,000 (1999). Note: Contributions were received from SBC Communications Inc. and its subsidiaries.

Typical Recipients

Arts & Humanities: Arts Appreciation, Arts Associations & Councils, Arts Centers, Arts Festivals, Arts Funds, Arts Institutes, Arts Outreach, Community Arts, Dance, Ethnic & Folk Arts, Historic Preservation, History & Archaeology, Libraries, Museums/Galleries, Music, Opera, Performing Arts, Public Broadcasting, Theater
Civic & Public Affairs: African American Affairs, Botanical Gardens/Parks, Business/Free Enterprise, Clubs, Community Foundations, Economic Development, Employment/Job Training, Ethnic Organizations, Civic & Public Affairs-General, Hispanic Affairs, Inner-City Development, Law & Justice, Minority Business, Municipalities/Towns, Nonprofit Management, Parades/Festivals, Public Policy, Urban & Community Affairs, Women's Affairs, Zoos/Aquariums
Education: Afterschool/Enrichment Programs, Arts/Humanities Education, Business Education, Colleges & Universities, Community & Junior Colleges, Education Associations, Education Funds, Education Reform, Engineering/Technological Education, Faculty Development, Education-General, Leadership Training, Literacy, Medical Education, Minority Education, Public Education (Precollege), School Volunteerism, Science/Mathematics Education, Special Education, Student Aid, Vocational & Technical Education
Environment: Research
Health: AIDS/HIV, Alzheimer's Disease, Cancer, Children's Health/Hospitals, Emergency/Ambulance Services, Health-General, Health Organizations, Hospitals, Medical Research, Mental Health, Public Health
International: Foreign Arts Organizations, Foreign Educational Institutions
Religion: Churches, Dioceses, Jewish Causes, Ministries, Religious Welfare
Science: Science Museums, Scientific Centers & Institutes
Social Services: Child Welfare, Community Centers, Community Service Organizations, Emergency Relief, Family Services, People with Disabilities, Scouts, Senior Services, Shelters/Homelessness, Social Services-General, Special Olympics, United Funds/United Ways, Volunteer Services, YMCA/YWCA/YMHA/YWHA, Youth Organizations

Application Procedures

Initial Contact: Obtain a grant application from the foundation. Completed applications should be prefaced with a brief cover letter; grant requests of a local or statewide nature should be sent to local subsidiary or division; requests of a regional or national nature should be addressed directly to the Foundation.
Application Requirements: Include proof of tax-

exempt status; description of how project fits with foundation's priorities; total project budget and amount requested; brief statement of history and accomplishments; statement of current objectives, including problem being addressed, program budget and amount sought; linkage of project's goals to the foundation's priorities; timetable for implementation and description of expected results; details of fundraising plans, including sources, amounts, and commitments; plans for sustaining activities after conclusion of foundation support; annual report or budget for organization, showing all income sources and expenditures; list of board members; list of accrediting agencies; one-page evaluation component detailing how project success will be measured; line-item budget for project.
Deadlines: None.
Review Process: All requests will be evaluated within four to six weeks after receipt; requesting organization may be contacted for additional information.
Evaluative Criteria: The foundation prefers to fund organizations in operating areas, project-specific proposals within areas of interest, projects that directly impact human needs and have the potential to be self-sustaining and adaptable to other settings, projects that stimulate partnerships among community organizations, and projects with well-defined goals, a clear picture of the need addressed, and specific tracking and evaluation procedures. Organizations seeking support should demonstrate clearly stated objectives, long-range planning, active participation of the governing board, strategies and plans to move from dependency on any one source of support, sound financial principles and practices, and close monitoring of programs.
Notes: Organizations are asked not to submit a proposal more than once in a 12-month period.

Restrictions

Foundation does not support private foundations or organizations without tax-exempt status; organizations that practice discrimination by race, color, creed, gender, sexual orientation, age, or national origin; hospital operating funds or capital funds; operating expenses for organizations supported by the United Way; individuals; political activities or organizations; religious organizations for sectarian purposes; fraternal, veteran, or labor groups when serving only their memberships; disease specific organizations; individual K-12 schools or districts, local school systems or school-system foundations; sports programs or events; cause-related marketing; donation of products or services; or special occasion goodwill advertising and ticket or dinner purchases.

Additional Information

Foundation states a preference for organizations that operate in corporate operating locations and in communities where a significant number of employees live; project-oriented proposals rather than requests for grants to underwrite operating or capital budgets; projects that promote citizen participation and volunteerism; projects that generate public awareness and offer opportunities to leverage contributions; projects that address human needs and whose services are provided directly rather than through intermediary organizations; and projects that develop leadership skills.

SBC Communications is in the process of purchasing Ameritech Corp.

In 1998, the company acquired Pacific Telesis (PacTel) and that company's foundation. The PacTel Foundation was merged into the SBC Foundation.
Publications: Contributions Guidelines

Corporate Officials

Gloria Delgado: vice president, SBC Pioneers ED Trinity University BA. NONPR AFFIL chairman: Nonprofit Benefits Association of Texas; chairman: Nonprofit Resource Center of Texas.
James D. Ellis: senior vice president, general counsel B 1943. ED University of Iowa BBA (1965); Uni-

versity of Missouri JD (1968). PRIM CORP EMPL senior executive vice president, general counsel: SBC Communications Inc. ADD CORP EMPL secretary: Southwestern Bell Telephone Co.

Karen E. Jennings: executive vice president CORP AFFIL director: Cullen/Frost Bankers Inc. NONPR AFFIL director: Washington University.

Edward E. Whitacre, Jr.: chairman, director, chief executive officer B Ennis, TX 1941. ED Texas Technology University BS (1964). PRIM CORP EMPL chairman, director, chief executive officer: SBC Communications Inc. CORP AFFIL director: Burlington Northern Santa Fe Corp.; director: Anheuser-Busch Companies Inc. NONPR AFFIL trustee: Southwest Research Institute; board regents: Texas Technology University & Health Science; member: Learning National Advisory Board; member executive board national council & southern: Boy Scouts America.

Foundation Officials
William Daley: chairman
James D. Ellis: director (see above)
Karen E. Jennings: director (see above)
Harold E. Rainbolt: vice president, secretary B Norman, OK 1929. ED University of Oklahoma (1951); University of Oklahoma (1957). PRIM CORP EMPL chairman: BancFirst Corp.
Laura P. Sanford: president ED University of San Francisco BS. NONPR AFFIL director: Bexar County Arts and Culture Fund; director: Los Compadres de San Antonio Missions National Historic Park.
Randall Stephenson: director
Mike Viola: vice president, treasurer
Rayford Wilkins, Jr.: director

Grants Analysis
Disclosure Period: calendar year ending 2003
Total Grants: $31,116,498*
Number of Grants: 1,468
Average Grant: $19,192*
Highest Grant: $1,000,000
Lowest Grant: $2,000
Typical Range: $5,000 to $50,000
*Note: Giving excludes matching gifts; United Way; scholarships. Average grant figure excludes three highest grants ($3,000,000).

Recent Grants
Note: Grants derived from 2003 Form 990.
General
1,000,000	Cancer Therapy and Research Foundation of South Texas, San Antonio, TX
1,000,000	Historical Centre Foundation, San Antonio, TX
1,000,000	Performing Arts Center of Los Angeles County, Los Angeles, CA
1,000,000	Texas Tech University Foundation, Lubbock, TX
793,573	United Way of the Bay Area, San Francisco, CA
552,257	United Way of Metropolitan Chicago, Chicago, IL
514,000	United Way of Greater Los Angeles, Los Angeles, CA
500,000	Centro Alameda Inc., San Antonio, TX
500,000	NPower, Seattle, WA
500,000	Zoological Society of San Diego, San Diego, CA

SCAIFE FAMILY FOUNDATION

Giving Contact
Barbara M. Sloan, President
777 S. Flagler Dr.
West Tower, Suite 903
West Palm Beach, FL 33401
Web: http://www.scaifefamily.org

Description
Founded: 1983
EIN: 251427015
Organization Type: Family Foundation
Giving Locations: PA: Pittsburgh
Grant Types: Capital, Conference/Seminar, Department, General Support, Operating Expenses, Project, Scholarship.

Donor Information
Founder: Established in 1983 by the late Sarah Mellon Scaife (d. 1965) by the conditions of a trust she provided for her grandchildren. She was the sister of Richard King Mellon, daughter of Richard B. Mellon, and granddaughter of Judge Thomas Mellon, who founded the family's banking and investment fortune.

Financial Summary
Total Giving: $3,500,159 (2003); $3,982,000 (2002)
Assets: $81,989,324 (2003); $75,293,495 (2002)
Gifts Received: Contributions were received from the trust for the grandchildren of Sarah Mellon Scaife.

Typical Recipients
Arts & Humanities: Film & Video, Historic Preservation, Libraries, Museums/Galleries, Opera, Public Broadcasting
Civic & Public Affairs: Botanical Gardens/Parks, Business/Free Enterprise, Civil Rights, Clubs, Economic Development, Economic Policy, Employment/Job Training, Civic & Public Affairs-General, Housing, Inner-City Development, Law & Justice, Legal Aid, Municipalities/Towns, Parades/Festivals, Philanthropic Organizations, Public Policy, Safety, Urban & Community Affairs, Women's Affairs, Zoos/Aquariums
Education: Arts/Humanities Education, Business Education, Colleges & Universities, Community & Junior Colleges, Economic Education, Education Associations, Education Funds, Education Reform, Elementary Education (Public), Environmental Education, Education-General, Leadership Training, Literacy, Medical Education, Minority Education, Private Education (Precollege), Public Education (Precollege), Science/Mathematics Education, Social Sciences Education, Special Education, Student Aid
Environment: Environment-General, Resource Conservation, Wildlife Protection
Health: Cancer, Children's Health/Hospitals, Clinics/Medical Centers, Eyes/Blindness, Health Funds, Health Organizations, Hospices, Hospitals, Kidney, Medical Rehabilitation, Medical Research, Mental Health, Nursing Services, Prenatal Health Issues, Public Health, Single-Disease Health Associations, Speech & Hearing
International: Health Care/Hospitals, International Affairs
Religion: Churches, Ministries, Missionary Activities (Domestic), Religious Organizations, Religious Welfare, Social/Policy Issues
Science: Scientific Centers & Institutes
Social Services: Animal Protection, At-Risk Youth, Big Brothers/Big Sisters, Child Abuse, Child Welfare, Community Centers, Community Service Organizations, Counseling, Day Care, Delinquency & Criminal Rehabilitation, Domestic Violence, Family Planning, Family Services, Food/Clothing Distribution, People with Disabilities, Recreation & Athletics, Senior Services, Shelters/Homelessness, Social Services-General, Substance Abuse, United Funds/United Ways, Volunteer Services, Youth Organizations

Application Procedures
Initial Contact: Initial inquiries to the foundation should be in letter form signed by the organization's president, or authorized representative, and have the approval of the organization's board of directors.
Application Requirements: The letter should include a concise description of the specific program for which funds are requested. Additional information must include a budget for the program and for the organization, the latest audited financial statement, annual report, list of the board of directors, and a copy of the organization's current IRS tax exemption ruling under section 501(c)(3). Additional information may be requested if needed for further evaluation.
Deadlines: None. The foundation normally considers grants at quarterly meetings.
Review Process: The foundation indicates that requests will be acted upon as expeditiously as possible.

Restrictions
The foundation does not make loans and will not consider grants to individuals.

Additional Information
Publications: Annual Report

Foundation Officials
Beth H. Genter: vice president, trustee
Jennie K. Scaife: chairman, trustee
Barbara Sloan: president, secretary, treasurer, trustee
Mary Walton: vice president, trustee

Grants Analysis
Disclosure Period: calendar year ending 2003
Total Grants: $3,500,159
Number of Grants: 65
Average Grant: $42,971*
Highest Grant: $750,000
Lowest Grant: $1,000
Typical Range: $20,000 to $100,000
*Note: Average grant figure excludes highest grant.

Recent Grants
Note: Grants derived from 2003 Form 990.
General
750,000	University of Pittsburgh, Pittsburgh, PA
200,000	Safe Harbor Animal Rescue and Clinic, Jupiter, FL
150,000	Susan G. Komen Foundation, Dallas, TX
121,000	New York University, New York, NY
105,000	All Creatures Sanctuary Inc., Palm Beach Gardens, FL
100,000	Children of Alcoholics Foundation, New York, NY
100,000	National Foundation for Teaching Entrepreneurship, New York, NY
100,000	Norton Museum of Art, West Palm Beach, FL
100,000	Palm Beach Zoo at Dreher Park, West Palm Beach, FL
100,000	Puppies Behind Bars Inc., New York, NY

L. P. SCHENCK CHARITABLE FOUNDATION

Giving Contact
Claudia Latorre, Vice President & Trust Officer
L. P. Schenck Charitable Foundation
c/o PNC Bank NA
41 Oak St.
Ridgewood, NJ 07450
Phone: (201)493-2152

Description
Founded: 1960
EIN: 226040581
Organization Type: Private Foundation
Giving Locations: NJ
Grant Types: General Support, Project.

Donor Information
Founder: the late Lillian Pitkin Schenck

Financial Summary

Total Giving: $475,200 (fiscal year ending August 31, 2004); $544,400 (fiscal 2001)
Assets: $10,541,418 (fiscal 2004); $11,061,676 (fiscal 2001)
Gifts Received: $850 (fiscal 1996)

Typical Recipients

Arts & Humanities: Arts Associations & Councils, Arts Centers, Arts Outreach, Community Arts, Libraries, Museums/Galleries, Music, Performing Arts, Theater
Civic & Public Affairs: Ethnic Organizations, Civic & Public Affairs-General, Urban & Community Affairs
Education: Public Education (Precollege), Science/Mathematics Education
Environment: Environment-General
Health: Cancer, Emergency/Ambulance Services, Geriatric Health, Health Organizations, Hospitals, Mental Health, Single-Disease Health Associations
Religion: Churches, Religious Organizations, Religious Welfare
Social Services: At-Risk Youth, Child Welfare, Community Centers, Community Service Organizations, Day Care, Domestic Violence, Family Planning, Family Services, Food/Clothing Distribution, Homes, People with Disabilities, Scouts, Senior Services, Shelters/Homelessness, Substance Abuse, Volunteer Services, YMCA/YWCA/YMHA/YWHA, Youth Organizations

Application Procedures

Initial Contact: Send a brief letter of inquiry. and a full proposal.
Application Requirements: Include a description of organization, amount requested, purpose of funds sought, recently audited financial statement, and proof of tax-exempt status. Also include previous year's annual report.
Deadlines: August 1.

Restrictions

Does not support individuals, religious organizations for sectarian purposes, political or lobbying groups, or organizations outside operating areas.

Additional Information

Trust(s): PNC Bank NA

Grants Analysis

Disclosure Period: fiscal year ending August 31, 2004
Total Grants: $475,200
Number of Grants: 59
Average Grant: $7,021*
Highest Grant: $68,000
Lowest Grant: $1,000
Typical Range: $1,000 to $15,000
*Note: Average grant figure excludes highest grant.

Recent Grants

Note: Grants derived from 2004 Form 990.
General

68,000	Bergen Family Center Inc., Hackensack, NJ
42,000	Vantage Health System, Englewood, NJ
30,000	Englewood Hospital and Medical Center, Englewood, NJ
30,000	YMCA of Bergen County, Glen Rock, NJ
29,000	Volunteer Center of Bergen County, Hackensack, NJ
22,000	Van Ost Institute for Family Living, Englewood, NJ
19,000	Friendship House, Hackensack, NJ
8,000	St. Paul's Community Development Corporation, Paterson, NJ
8,000	Shelter our Sisters, Hackensack, NJ
8,000	Southeast Senior Center for Independent Living, Englewood, NJ

KARLA SCHERER FOUNDATION

Giving Contact

Karla Scherer, Chairman, Chief Executive Officer, & Trustee
737 North Michigan Ave., Suite 2330
Chicago, IL 60611
Phone: (312)943-9191
Fax: (312)943-9271
Web: http://comnet.org/kschererf

Description

Founded: 1990
EIN: 382877392
Organization Type: Private Foundation
Giving Locations: internationally.
Grant Types: General Support, Scholarship.

Donor Information

Founder: Established in 1990 by Karla Scherer.

Financial Summary

Total Giving: $292,425 (2003); $182,155 (2001)
Giving Analysis: Giving for 2001 includes: foundation scholarships ($122,000)
Assets: $5,847,587 (2003); $5,710,738 (2001)
Gifts Received: $1,000 (2000); $5,000 (1992). Note: In fiscal 1992, contributions were received from the Leon and Toby Cooperman Foundation.

Typical Recipients

Arts & Humanities: Arts Centers, Arts Festivals, Arts Funds, Arts Institutes, History & Archaeology, Libraries, Museums/Galleries, Music, Public Broadcasting, Theater
Civic & Public Affairs: Business/Free Enterprise, Civil Rights, Economic Policy, Civic & Public Affairs-General, Urban & Community Affairs, Women's Affairs
Education: Arts/Humanities Education, Business Education, Colleges & Universities, Economic Education, Education Associations, Engineering/Technological Education, Education-General, International Studies, Legal Education, Preschool Education, Private Education (Precollege), Student Aid, Vocational & Technical Education
Environment: Environment-General, Resource Conservation
Health: Cancer, Children's Health/Hospitals, Clinics/Medical Centers, Health Organizations, Hospitals, Medical Research, Mental Health, Prenatal Health Issues
International: Foreign Arts Organizations, Foreign Educational Institutions, Health Care/Hospitals
Religion: Churches, Religious Welfare
Social Services: Animal Protection, Camps, Child Welfare, Community Centers, Family Planning, People with Disabilities, Social Services-General, Veterans, Youth Organizations

Application Procedures

Initial Contact: Write to request a scholarship application form.
Application Requirements: Describe the particular area(s) of academic interest and a detailed description of career plans. Include a self-addressed, stamped envelope.
Deadlines: March 1 is the deadline for written requests for application forms.
Review Process: If the application form request letter meets the foundation's requirements, an application package will be sent to the applicant.

Restrictions

Scholarship applicants must be women accepted to the Master of Arts program at the University of Chicago.

Additional Information

Beginning in the 2004-2005 school year, scholarships will only be provided to women participating in the Master of Arts program at the University of Chicago.

Foundation Officials

Karla Scherer: chairman, chief executive officer, trustee B Detroit, MI 1937. ED University of Michigan BA (1957). NONPR AFFIL member: Women's Economic Club Detroit; member: Women's Forum Michigan; member visitors committee: Fordham University Graduate School Business Administration; director: Economic Club Detroit; trustee: Eton Academy. CLUB AFFIL Grosse Pointe Club; Renaissance Club; Detroit Country Club; Detroit Athletic Club; Detroit Club.

Grants Analysis

Disclosure Period: calendar year ending 2003
Total Grants: $292,425
Number of Grants: 28
Average Grant: $2,378*
Highest Grant: $228,230
Lowest Grant: $25
Typical Range: $500 to $3,000
*Note: Average grant figure excludes highest grant.

Recent Grants

Note: Grants derived from 2003 Form 990.
General

228,230	Chicago Humanities Festival, Chicago, IL -- for thinking ahead campaign
10,285	Chicago Symphony Orchestra, Chicago, IL
10,010	Cradle, Evanston, IL
10,000	Planned Parenthood Chicago Area, Chicago, IL
10,000	University of Chicago, Chicago, IL -- for humanities visiting committee fund
5,000	Music of the Baroque, Chicago, IL
4,820	Art Institute of Chicago, Chicago, IL
1,500	Chicago Architecture Foundation, Chicago, IL
1,500	Museum of Contemporary Art, Chicago, IL
1,400	Field Museum, Chicago, IL

SCHERING-PLOUGH CORP.

Company Headquarters

2000 Galloping Hill Rd.
Kenilworth, NJ 07033-0530
Web: http://www.sch-plough.com

Company Description

Ticker: SGP
Exchange: OTC
Formed by Merger of: Plough Inc. (1971).
Revenue: US$8.272 billion (2004)
Profit: (US$947 million) (2004)
Employees: 29800 (2001)
Fortune Rank: 264, per FORTUNE Magazine's list of 500 Largest U.S. Corporations (2004).
SIC(s): 2833 Medicinals & Botanicals, 2834 Pharmaceutical Preparations, 2836 Biological Products Except Diagnostic, 2844 Toilet Preparations, 3842 Surgical Appliances & Supplies, 3851 Ophthalmic Goods, 6719 Holding Companies Nec.
Parent Company: Schering AG, Mullerstr. 178, Berlin, Germany

Operating Locations

Schering-Plough Corp. (AR--Little Rock; CA--La Mirada, Palo Alto, San Leandro; DE--Millsboro; FL--Pembroke Pines; GA--Chamblee, Chatsworth; IL--Alsip, Chicago, Des Plaines, Niles; IN--Terre Haute; LA--Baton Rouge; MO--Kansas City; NE--Elkhorn,

Omaha; NJ--Bloomfield, Carteret, Creamridge, Kenilworth, Liberty Corner, Madison, Maplewood, Union; PR--Hato Rey, Las Piedras, Manati; TN--Cleveland; TX--Irving)

Nonmonetary Support

Type: Donated Equipment; Donated Products; In-kind Services

Volunteer Programs: Provides small grants through its Dollar for Volunteer program most used by employees and their families, American Red Cross, health-care services to low-income working people, and university schools of pharmacy.

Contact: Joseph Starkey, Director, Community Affairs

Schering-Plough Foundation

Giving Contact

Christine Fahey, Assistant Secretary
Schering-Plough Foundation
2000 Galloping Hill Road
Kenilworth, NJ 07033
Phone: (908)298-7232
Fax: (908)298-7349
Web: http://www.sch-plough.com

Alternate Contact

Andrew Hageman, Secretary
Schering-Plough Foundation
Phone: (973)822-7000
Note: For direct contributions.

Description

EIN: 221711047
Organization Type: Corporate Foundation
Giving Locations: principally near operating locations and to national organizations.
Grant Types: Capital, Employee Matching Gifts, Endowment, Fellowship, General Support, Multiyear/Continuing Support, Professorship, Research, Scholarship, Seed Money.
Note: Employee matching gift ratio: 1 to 1 for secondary and higher education, hospitals and hospices.

Financial Summary

Total Giving: $2,530,641 (2003); $2,083,312 (2002); $2,451,174 (2001). Note: Contributes through corporate direct giving program and foundation.
Giving Analysis: Giving for 2002 includes: foundation matching gifts ($432,275); 2001: foundation matching gifts ($234,404); foundation ($2,216,770)
Assets: $11,932,791 (2003); $13,154,449 (2002); $15,859,026 (2001)
Gifts Received: $1,500,000 (2000); $1,500,000 (1997); $1,500,000 (1996). Note: Contributions were received from Schering-Plough Corp.

Typical Recipients

Arts & Humanities: Arts Associations & Councils, Arts Centers, Arts Festivals, Arts Funds, Community Arts, Dance, Ethnic & Folk Arts, Arts & Humanities-General, Historic Preservation, History & Archaeology, Libraries, Museums/Galleries, Music, Performing Arts, Public Broadcasting, Theater
Civic & Public Affairs: Civil Rights, Community Foundations, Economic Development, Economic Policy, Ethnic Organizations, Civic & Public Affairs-General, Hispanic Affairs, Housing, Legal Aid, Nonprofit Management, Philanthropic Organizations, Professional & Trade Associations, Public Policy, Urban & Community Affairs, Zoos/Aquariums
Education: Afterschool/Enrichment Programs, Arts/Humanities Education, Business Education, Colleges & Universities, Education Associations, Education Funds, Engineering/Technological Education, Faculty Development, Education-General, Health & Physical Education, Legal Education, Literacy, Medical Ed-

ucation, Minority Education, Preschool Education, Private Education (Precollege), Public Education (Precollege), Science/Mathematics Education, Special Education, Student Aid, Vocational & Technical Education
Health: Alzheimer's Disease, Cancer, Children's Health/Hospitals, Clinics/Medical Centers, Emergency/Ambulance Services, Health-General, Geriatric Health, Health Policy/Cost Containment, Health Funds, Health Organizations, Hospices, Hospitals, Hospitals (University Affiliated), Long-Term Care, Medical Rehabilitation, Medical Research, Medical Training, Mental Health, Public Health, Research/Studies Institutes, Single-Disease Health Associations, Transplant Networks/Donor Banks
International: Health Care/Hospitals, International Affairs, International Peace & Security Issues, International Relations
Religion: Churches, Religious Welfare
Science: Scientific Centers & Institutes, Scientific Labs, Scientific Organizations, Scientific Research
Social Services: Child Welfare, Community Centers, Community Service Organizations, Domestic Violence, Family Services, Food/Clothing Distribution, People with Disabilities, Shelters/Homelessness, Substance Abuse, United Funds/United Ways, YMCA/YWCA/YMHA/YWHA, Youth Organizations

Application Procedures

Initial Contact: Submit a written proposal. Application forms are available by request and from the foundation's web site.
Application Requirements: Include specific purpose of funds sought, background information on requesting organization, major programs and services rendered, proof of tax-exempt status, latest audited financial statements, program budget (if application relates to specific activity); supporting material (including annual report) is desirable.
Deadlines: July 1 for foundation only.
Decision Notification: Requests are reviewed continually; board meets annually in the fall.
Notes: Requests that do not include the information above will be returned to applicants.

Restrictions

Grants are not made to individuals.

Additional Information

Occasionally makes product donations, primarily to assist efforts of U.S. organizations working in developing countries. Surplus equipment is made available to organizations in operating communities.
Foundation historically pays grants for annual support in the fourth quarter of the year.

Corporate Officials

Andrew F. Hageman: manager, corporate philanthropy PRIM CORP EMPL manager corporate philanthropy: Schering-Plough Corp.
Fred Hassan: chairman, chief executive officer, president, director B 1945. ED Harvard University MBA; Imperial College of Science and Technology BS. PRIM CORP EMPL chairman, chief executive officer: Schering-Plough Corp. CORP AFFIL director: Avon Products Inc. NONPR AFFIL chairman: Health-Care Institute New Jersey.
E. Kevin Moore: vice president, treasurer ED University of North Carolina BA; University of South Carolina MBA. PRIM CORP EMPL vice president, treasurer: Schering-Plough Corp.

Foundation Officials

Robert Bertolini: board of trustees
C. Ron Cheeley: board of trustees
Joseph C. Conners: trustee
Christine Fahey: assistant secretary
Andrew F. Hageman: secretary (see above)
E. Kevin Moore: treasurer (see above)
Thomas Sabatino: board of trustees
Joseph P. Starkey: president
Nina M. Wells: president

Jack L. Wyszomierski: trustee, member B 1955. ED Carnegie Mellon University BS (1977); Carnegie Mellon University MS (1978). PRIM CORP EMPL executive vice president, chief financial officer: Schering-Plough Corp. CORP AFFIL director: Exelixis Inc.; executive vice president, chief financial officer: VWR International Inc..

Grants Analysis

Disclosure Period: calendar year ending 2003
Total Grants: $1,926,818*
Number of Grants: 64
Average Grant: $27,410*
Highest Grant: $200,000
Lowest Grant: $7,000
Typical Range: $10,000 to $50,000
*Note: Giving excludes matching gifts. Average grant figure excludes highest grant.

Recent Grants

Note: Grants derived from 2003 Form 990.
General

200,000	Saint Barnabas Health Care, Livingston, NJ
100,000	Trinitas Hospital, Elizabeth, NJ
75,750	Tufts University-School of Medicine, Medford, MA
66,160	National Merit Scholarship Corporation, Evanston, IL
60,000	Pharmaceutical Research and Manufacturers of America Foundation, Washington, DC
50,000	American Chemical Society, Washington, DC
50,000	Brown University-Leadership Alliance, Providence, RI
50,000	Caucus Educational Corporation, Bloomfield, NJ
50,000	Columbia University - Department of Ophthalmology, New York, NY
50,000	Hollings Cancer Center at the Medical University of South Carolina, Charleston, SC

SCHERMAN FOUNDATION

Giving Contact

Sandra Silverman, President & Executive Director
16 East 52nd Street, Suite 601
New York, NY 10022-5306
Phone: (212)832-3086
Fax: (212)838-0154
E-mail: info@scherman.org
Web: http://www.scherman.org

Description

Founded: 1943
EIN: 136098464
Organization Type: General Purpose Foundation
Giving Locations: NY: New York emphasis on metropolitan New York City for the arts and social welfare
Grant Types: General Support, Multiyear/Continuing Support.

Donor Information

Founder: Established in 1941 by members of the Scherman family, including the late Harry Scherman (d. 1969), one of the founders of the Book-of-the-Month Club. During his lifetime, Mr. Scherman served as a director of the National Bureau of Economic Research and as a trustee of the Mannes College of Music.

Financial Summary

Total Giving: $5,062,700 (2003); $5,224,700 (2002); $6,110,200 (2001)
Assets: $76,375,382 (2003); $68,569,280 (2002); $87,473,557 (2001)

Typical Recipients

Arts & Humanities: Arts Centers, Arts Funds, Arts Institutes, Ballet, Dance, Libraries, Literary Arts, Museums/Galleries, Music, Opera, Performing Arts, Public Broadcasting, Theater, Visual Arts

Civic & Public Affairs: African American Affairs, Asian American Affairs, Botanical Gardens/Parks, Civil Rights, Economic Development, Economic Policy, Employment/Job Training, Ethnic Organizations, Civic & Public Affairs-General, Hispanic Affairs, Housing, Law & Justice, Legal Aid, Municipalities/Towns, Professional & Trade Associations, Public Policy, Safety, Urban & Community Affairs, Women's Affairs, Zoos/Aquariums

Education: Arts/Humanities Education, Colleges & Universities, Education Associations, Education Funds, Education Reform, Education-General, International Studies, Minority Education, School Volunteerism, Special Education

Environment: Air/Water Quality, Environment-General, Protection, Resource Conservation

Health: Adolescent Health Issues, AIDS/HIV, Health Policy/Cost Containment, Health Organizations, Outpatient Health Care, Prenatal Health Issues

International: Health Care/Hospitals, Human Rights, International Development, International Environmental Issues, International Organizations, International Peace & Security Issues, International Relations, International Relief Efforts, Missionary/Religious Activities

Religion: Jewish Causes, Religious Welfare, Social/Policy Issues

Science: Science Museums, Scientific Centers & Institutes, Scientific Organizations

Social Services: At-Risk Youth, Child Welfare, Community Centers, Community Service Organizations, Counseling, Crime Prevention, Delinquency & Criminal Rehabilitation, Domestic Violence, Family Planning, Family Services, Food/Clothing Distribution, Refugee Assistance, Senior Services, Shelters/Homelessness, Social Services-General, Volunteer Services, Youth Organizations

Application Procedures

Initial Contact: Applicants should submit a brief letter to the president outlining the purpose for which funds are sought.

Application Requirements: Include a budget; program description; recent audited financial statement; present sources of support; evidence of tax-exempt status; and list of the board of directors and key personnel.

Deadlines: None.

Review Process: Applications that fall within the scope of interests of the foundation will be asked to provide additional information. The board meets four times a year; dates of the meetings are not fixed.

Decision Notification: Applicants are notified within six weeks if a proposal has been declined or is under consideration.

Notes: The foundation does not accept proposals via fax or over the Internet.

Restrictions

The foundation generally does not fund individuals, colleges, universities, or professional schools; conferences, symposia, capital campaigns, specific film, video or art productions; or medical, science or engineering research. In the fields of arts and social welfare, priorities are in New York City only. No grants are made for medical, science, or engineering research.

Additional Information

Grants are made only to 501 (c) (3) organizations.
Publications: Annual Report; Statement of Policy and Procedures

Foundation Officials

Susanna Bergtold: secretary, director
Hillary Brown: director

David R. Jones: director
Gordon N. Litwin: director
John J. O'Neil, Esq.: director
Mitchell C. Pratt: treasurer, program officer
Axel G. Rosin: director, chairman emeritus
Katharine S. Rosin: secretary, director
Anthony M. Schulte: director
Sandra Silverman: president, executive director
Karen R. Sollins: chairman, director
Marcia T. Thompson: director
John Wroclawski: director

Grants Analysis

Disclosure Period: calendar year ending 2003
Total Grants: $5,062,700
Number of Grants: 141
Average Grant: $35,906
Highest Grant: $100,000
Lowest Grant: $1,000
Typical Range: $10,000 to $50,000

Recent Grants

Note: Grants derived from 2003 Form 990.
Library-Related

180,000	New York Public Library, New York, NY

General

105,000	Legal Aid Society, New York, NY
100,000	UJA - Federation of New York, New York, NY
80,000	Engender Health, New York, NY
80,000	Planned Parenthood of New York City, New York, NY
75,000	NAACP Legal Defense and Educational Fund, New York, NY
75,000	National Environmental Trust, Washington, DC -- toward a global warming public education campaign
75,000	Partnership Project, Washington, DC
70,000	Religious Coalition for Reproductive Choice Education Fund, Washington, DC
65,000	American Civil Liberties Union Foundation, New York, NY
65,000	Green Peace Fund / Ozone Action, Washington, DC

FRANCES SCHERMER CHARITABLE TRUST

Giving Contact

Steve Volk, Vice President & Trust Officer
Frances Schermer Charitable Trust
Care of City National Bank
PO Box 1141
Beverly Hills, CA 90210
Phone: (310)888-6324
Fax: (310)888-6288

Description

Founded: 1980
EIN: 956685749
Organization Type: Private Foundation
Giving Locations: CA; OH; PA
Grant Types: General Support.

Donor Information

Founder: the late Charles I. Schermer, Frances Schermer

Financial Summary

Total Giving: $110,752 (fiscal year ending June 30, 2002); $106,554 (fiscal 2001)
Giving Analysis: Giving for fiscal 2002 includes: foundation grants to United Way ($2,500) fiscal 2001: foundation grants to United Way ($2,500)
Assets: $2,114,984 (fiscal 2002); $2,308,382 (fiscal 2001)

Typical Recipients

Arts & Humanities: Arts Associations & Councils, Arts Institutes, Libraries, Music, Public Broadcasting, Theater

Civic & Public Affairs: Business/Free Enterprise, Clubs, Community Foundations, Ethnic Organizations, Civic & Public Affairs-General, Urban & Community Affairs

Education: Colleges & Universities, Education-General, Minority Education, Private Education (Pre-college), Religious Education, Secondary Education (Private)

Health: AIDS/HIV, Cancer, Children's Health/Hospitals, Clinics/Medical Centers, Emergency/Ambulance Services, Eyes/Blindness, Health Organizations, Hospices, Kidney, Long-Term Care, Multiple Sclerosis

International: International-General, Missionary/Religious Activities

Religion: Churches, Jewish Causes, Ministries, Religious Organizations, Religious Welfare, Synagogues/Temples

Social Services: Camps, Child Welfare, Community Centers, Community Service Organizations, Counseling, Domestic Violence, Food/Clothing Distribution, People with Disabilities, Scouts, Senior Services, Shelters/Homelessness, United Funds/United Ways, YMCA/YWCA/YMHA/YWHA, Youth Organizations

Application Procedures

Initial Contact: Send a brief letter of inquiry.
Deadlines: None.

Additional Information

Trust(s): City National Bank

Foundation Officials

Saul Friedman: co-trustee
James L. Pazol: co-trustee
Bruce Sherman: co-trustee

Grants Analysis

Disclosure Period: fiscal year ending June 30, 2002
Total Grants: $108,252*
Number of Grants: 45
Average Grant: $2,406
Highest Grant: $10,000
Lowest Grant: $250
Typical Range: $500 to $10,000
*Note:** Giving excludes United Way.

Recent Grants

Note: Grants derived from fiscal 2002 Form 990.

General

10,000	Mahoning Lodge 339, Youngstown, OH
10,000	Youngstown Area Jewish Federation, Youngstown, OH
10,000	Youngstown State University, Youngstown, OH
10,000	Zionist Organization of America, Southfield, MI
6,250	Los Angeles Jewish Federation Foundation, Los Angeles, CA
5,000	HELP Hotline Crisis Center, Youngstown, OH
5,000	United Jewish Communities, Youngstown, OH
5,000	Youngstown Area Jewish Federation, Youngstown, OH
5,000	Youngstown Foundation, Boardman, OH
5,000	Youngstown Foundation for Jewish Federation, Youngstown, OH

S. H. AND HELEN R. SCHEUER FAMILY FOUNDATION INC.

Giving Contact
Linda Ehrlich, Administrative Director
350 Fifth Avenue, Suite 1413
New York, NY 10118
Phone: (212)947-9009
Fax: (212)947-9770
E-mail: linda@61associates.com

Description
Founded: 1943
EIN: 136062661
Organization Type: Family Foundation
Giving Locations: NY: New York metropolitan area; Israel
Grant Types: General Support, Scholarship.

Donor Information
Founder: Established in New York in 1943 by the late S. H. Scheuer, a New York investor and philanthropist, and his late wife, Helen R. Scheuer, with other family members. Mr. Scheuer was interested in subsidized housing for the elderly.

Financial Summary
Total Giving: $1,248,840 (fiscal year ending November 30, 2002); $1,616,995 (fiscal 2001)
Assets: $12,346,887 (fiscal 2002); $12,886,102 (fiscal 2001)
Gifts Received: $113,000 (fiscal 2002); $452,000 (fiscal 2001); $452,000 (fiscal 2000). Note: In fiscal 2001 and 2002, contributions were received from the Helen R. Scheuer Trust 3. In fiscal 2000, contributions were received from the trusts of Helen R. and S. H. Scheuer.

Typical Recipients
Arts & Humanities: Arts Associations & Councils, Arts Centers, Arts Funds, Arts Institutes, Dance, Arts & Humanities-General, History & Archaeology, Museums/Galleries, Music, Opera, Performing Arts, Theater, Visual Arts
Civic & Public Affairs: Botanical Gardens/Parks, Business/Free Enterprise, Chambers of Commerce, Community Foundations, Economic Development, Ethnic Organizations, Civic & Public Affairs-General, Housing, Law & Justice, Legal Aid, Philanthropic Organizations, Public Policy, Urban & Community Affairs, Women's Affairs
Education: Arts/Humanities Education, Colleges & Universities, Education Associations, Education Funds, Education Reform, Engineering/Technological Education, Environmental Education, Faculty Development, Education-General, Gifted & Talented Programs, International Studies, Legal Education, Literacy, Medical Education, Preschool Education, Private Education (Precollege), Religious Education, Social Sciences Education, Special Education, Student Aid
Environment: Air/Water Quality, Environment-General, Protection
Health: Clinics/Medical Centers, Emergency/Ambulance Services, Geriatric Health, Hospitals, Mental Health, Nursing Services
International: Foreign Arts Organizations, Foreign Educational Institutions, Health Care/Hospitals, International Environmental Issues, International Peace & Security Issues, International Relations, International Relief Efforts, Missionary/Religious Activities
Religion: Jewish Causes, Ministries, Missionary Activities (Domestic), Religious Organizations, Religious Welfare, Seminaries, Synagogues/Temples
Science: Scientific Centers & Institutes
Social Services: Camps, Child Welfare, Community Centers, Community Service Organizations, Counseling, Day Care, Domestic Violence, Emergency Relief, Family Planning, Family Services, People with Disabilities, Recreation & Athletics, Refugee Assistance, Senior Services, United Funds/United Ways, YMCA/YWCA/YMHA/YWHA, Youth Organizations

Application Procedures
Initial Contact: Applicants should send a brief letter proposal of one to three pages.
Application Requirements: The proposal should contain the following: proof of IRS tax-exempt status; a short history of the organization and its purpose; a description of the project goal and qualifications of the staff involved; the amount of funding requested; and anticipated long- and short-term advantages of the project affecting the foundation, as well as all others who stand to benefit.
Deadlines: None.

Restrictions
Foundation primarily supports preselected organizations, but does review unsolicited requests as well.

Foundation Officials
Linda Ehrlich: administrative director
Elizabeth H. Scheuer: secretary
Laura L. Scheuer: vice president
Richard Jonas Scheuer: president B Long Lake, NY 1917. ED Harvard University (1939); New York University MA (1971). NONPR AFFIL chairman board governors: Hebrew Union College.
Sidney J. Silberman, Esq.: treasurer

Grants Analysis
Disclosure Period: fiscal year ending November 30, 2002
Total Grants: $1,248,840
Number of Grants: 167
Average Grant: $7,478
Highest Grant: $114,716
Lowest Grant: $1,000
Typical Range: $2,000 to $15,000

Recent Grants
Note: Grants derived from fiscal 2002 Form 990.
General

60,000	Cambridge College, Cambridge, MA
50,000	Emelin Theatre for the Performing Arts, Mamaroneck, NY
50,000	Jewish Board of Family & Children's Services Inc., New York, NY
50,000	New Israel Fund, Washington, DC
50,000	Sarah Lawrence College, Bronxville, NY
50,000	Swarthmore College, Swarthmore, PA
49,500	City Parks Foundation, New York, NY
40,000	Purchase College Association SUNY College at Purchase, Purchase, NY
30,000	Institute for the Advancement of Education in Jaffa, Brooklyn, NY
25,000	Hampshire College, Amherst, MA

SARAH I. SCHIEFFELIN RESIDUARY TRUST

Giving Contact
Grace Allen, Trust Officer
c/o The Bank of New York
1290 6th Avenue
New York, NY 10020
Phone: (212)635-1520

Description
Founded: 1976
EIN: 136724459
Organization Type: Private Foundation
Giving Locations: NY: New York
Grant Types: Multiyear/Continuing Support.

Donor Information
Founder: the late Sarah I. Schieffelin

Financial Summary
Total Giving: $614,319 (fiscal year ending March 31, 2004); $683,711 (fiscal 2001)
Assets: $13,489,047 (fiscal 2004); $14,692,378 (fiscal 2001)

Typical Recipients
Arts & Humanities: Arts Centers, Historic Preservation, History & Archaeology, Libraries, Museums/Galleries, Music, Opera, Performing Arts
Civic & Public Affairs: Botanical Gardens/Parks, Civic & Public Affairs-General, Zoos/Aquariums
Education: Colleges & Universities, Education Reform, Private Education (Precollege)
Environment: Environment-General, Resource Conservation, Wildlife Protection
Health: Cancer, Children's Health/Hospitals, Emergency/Ambulance Services, Heart, Hospitals
Religion: Churches
Science: Science Museums
Social Services: Animal Protection, At-Risk Youth, Child Welfare, Community Service Organizations, People with Disabilities, Shelters/Homelessness

Application Procedures
Initial Contact: Send a brief letter of inquiry.
Deadlines: March 31.

Additional Information
Trust(s): Bank of NY

Foundation Officials
Thomas B. Fenlon, Esq.: trustee B Long Branch, NJ November 12, 1904. ED Georgetown University AB (1925); Columbia University LLB (1928). PRIM CORP EMPL partner: Emmet, Marvin & Martin. NONPR AFFIL trustee: Saint Catherines Church; director: Traphagen School Fashion; member: New York State Bar Association; member: American Bar Association; member: New York City Bar Association.

Grants Analysis
Disclosure Period: fiscal year ending March 31, 2004
Total Grants: $614,319
Number of Grants: 41
Average Grant: $10,070*
Highest Grant: $61,432
Lowest Grant: $4,959
Typical Range: $5,000 to $20,000
***Note:** Average grant figure excludes four highest grants ($241,728).

Recent Grants
Note: Grants derived from 2001 Form 990.
Library-Related

25,000	New York Public Library, New York, NY

General

38,500	National Audubon Society, New York, NY
38,500	National Wildlife Federation, New York, NY
38,500	St. Mary's Church, Manhasset, MA
38,500	St. Thomas Church, New York, NY
30,000	American Red Cross, New York, NY
25,000	Covenant House, New York, NY
15,000	Community Service Society, New York, NY
10,000	Calvary Fund
10,000	Central Park Conservancy, New York, NY
10,000	Lincoln Center for the Performing Arts, New York, NY

DOROTHY SCHIFF FOUNDATION

Giving Contact
Adele Hall-Sweet, President
53 E. 66th St.
New York, NY 10021
Phone: (212)789-5042

Description
Founded: 1951
EIN: 136018311
Organization Type: Private Foundation
Giving Locations: MA; NY
Grant Types: Emergency, General Support, Research, Scholarship.

Donor Information
Founder: the late Dorothy Schiff, New York Post Corp.

Financial Summary
Total Giving: $4,998,000 (2003); $840,000 (2001)
Giving Analysis: Giving for 2004 includes: foundation scholarships ($30,000); 2001: foundation scholarships ($25,000)
Assets: $6,017,548 (2003); $12,304,777 (2001)
Gifts Received: $49,500 (1993)

Typical Recipients
Arts & Humanities: Arts Associations & Councils, History & Archaeology, Libraries, Museums/Galleries, Public Broadcasting
Civic & Public Affairs: Clubs, Economic Development, Employment/Job Training, Civic & Public Affairs-General, Law & Justice, Municipalities/Towns, Professional & Trade Associations, Public Policy, Urban & Community Affairs
Education: Arts/Humanities Education, Colleges & Universities, Education Funds, Education Reform, Engineering/Technological Education, Medical Education, Minority Education, Private Education (Precollege), Public Education (Precollege), School Volunteerism, Science/Mathematics Education, Secondary Education (Private), Social Sciences Education, Special Education, Student Aid
Environment: Environment-General, Resource Conservation
Health: AIDS/HIV, Cancer, Hospitals, Medical Research, Nursing Services, Prenatal Health Issues, Single-Disease Health Associations
International: Health Care/Hospitals, Human Rights
Religion: Jewish Causes
Science: Scientific Centers & Institutes, Scientific Labs
Social Services: At-Risk Youth, Child Welfare, Community Centers, Community Service Organizations, Crime Prevention, Family Planning, Family Services, People with Disabilities, Refugee Assistance, Shelters/Homelessness, Social Services-General, Youth Organizations

Application Procedures
Initial Contact: Send a brief letter of inquiry describing program or project.
Deadlines: None.

Additional Information
Trust(s): JP Morgan Chase Bank

Foundation Officials
Mortimer W. Hall: treasurer
Sara Ann Kramarsky: secretary
Adele Hall Sweet: president

Grants Analysis
Disclosure Period: calendar year ending 2003
Total Grants: $4,968,000*
Number of Grants: 47
Average Grant: $60,349*

Highest Grant: $1,500,000
Lowest Grant: $5,000
Typical Range: $25,000 to $100,000
***Note:** Giving excludes scholarships. Average grant figure excludes four highest grants ($2,373,000).

Recent Grants
Note: Grants derived from 2003 Form 990.
General
1,500,000	New York University Endowment, New York, NY -- for the Dorothy Schiff professorship in Genomics
500,000	Channel 13, New York, NY -- for news and public affairs programming
323,000	Cornell University School of Veterinary Medicine, Ithaca, NY
300,000	Robin Hood, New York, NY -- for a library in New York City public school named for Dorothy Schiff
250,000	Henry Street Settlement House, New York, NY
150,000	Boys and Girls Harbor Inc., New York, NY
100,000	Coker College, Hartsville, SC
100,000	Global Kids, New York, NY
100,000	Lenox Hill Hospital, New York, NY
100,000	Planned Parenthood of New York City, New York, NY

EDWARD G. SCHLIEDER EDUCATIONAL FOUNDATION

Giving Contact
Pierre F. Lapeyre, Assistant Secretary
Hibernia National Bank
313 Carondelet St., 1st Fl.
New Orleans, LA 70130
Phone: (504)533-5535
Fax: (504)533-3669

Description
Founded: 1945
EIN: 720408974
Organization Type: Specialized/Single Purpose Foundation
Giving Locations: LA: limited to educational institutions in Louisiana
Grant Types: Capital, Endowment, Operating Expenses, Research.

Donor Information
Founder: Incorporated in 1945 by the late Edward G. Schlieder.

Financial Summary
Total Giving: $417,773 (2001)
Assets: $41,639,221 (2001)

Typical Recipients
Arts & Humanities: Arts & Humanities-General, Libraries
Education: Business Education, Colleges & Universities, Elementary Education (Private), Engineering/Technological Education, Environmental Education, Faculty Development, Education-General, Medical Education, Preschool Education, Private Education (Precollege), Public Education (Precollege), Religious Education, Science/Mathematics Education, Secondary Education (Private), Secondary Education (Public)
Environment: Wildlife Protection
Health: Cancer, Children's Health/Hospitals, Health Policy/Cost Containment, Health Organizations, Hospitals (University Affiliated), Medical Research, Nutrition
Religion: Religion-General, Religious Welfare, Seminaries
Social Services: Recreation & Athletics

Application Procedures
Initial Contact: The foundation requests applications be made in writing, outlining the proposal.
Deadlines: None.

Restrictions
The foundation reports grants are made only to educational institutions within the state of Louisiana.

Foundation Officials
Pierre S. Lapeyre: executive consult, assistant secretary
Donald J. Nalty: chairman, director B 1932. PRIM CORP EMPL vice president: Hibernia National Bank. CORP AFFIL vice president: Controlled Business Inc.
Elizabeth S. Nalty: president, director
Jill Nalty: treasurer, director
John M. Ward: director, secretary
Thomas D. Westfeldt: director, vice president B 1951. ED Louisiana State University (1975). PRIM CORP EMPL president: Westfeldt Brothers.

Grants Analysis
Disclosure Period: calendar year ending 2001
Total Grants: $417,773
Number of Grants: 3
Average Grant: $139,258
Highest Grant: $333,000
Lowest Grant: $25,000
Typical Range: $25,000 to $150,000

Recent Grants
Note: Grants derived from 2001 Form 990.
General
333,000	Tulane University, New Orleans, LA -- for Westfeldt Practice Competition Complex
59,773	Louisiana State University Health Science Center Foundation, New Orleans, LA -- surgical chairs and lights
25,000	Jesuit High School, New Orleans, LA -- for capital and facilities Maintenance Program

ALBERT G. AND OLIVE H. SCHLINK FOUNDATION

Giving Contact
Robert A. Wiedemann, President & Secretary
49 Benedict Ave., Suite C
Norwalk, OH 44857
Phone: (419)668-8211

Description
Founded: 1966
EIN: 346574722
Organization Type: Private Foundation
Giving Locations: AL; CA; MI; NC; OH
Grant Types: Capital, Emergency, General Support, Research, Scholarship.

Donor Information
Founder: the late Albert G. Schlink, the late Olive H. Schlink

Financial Summary
Total Giving: $512,259 (2004); $618,767 (2001)
Assets: $13,804,843 (2004); $14,353,030 (2001)

Typical Recipients
Arts & Humanities: History & Archaeology, Libraries
Civic & Public Affairs: Clubs, Community Foundations, Civic & Public Affairs-General

Education: Colleges & Universities, Education-General, Medical Education, Private Education (Pre-college), Student Aid
Health: Cancer, Clinics/Medical Centers, Diabetes, Eyes/Blindness, Health-General, Geriatric Health, Health Organizations, Hospices, Hospitals, Long-Term Care, Medical Rehabilitation, Medical Research, Nursing Services, Research/Studies Institutes, Respiratory, Single-Disease Health Associations
Religion: Churches, Religion-General, Religious Welfare
Science: Science Museums
Social Services: Animal Protection, Community Service Organizations, Food/Clothing Distribution, People with Disabilities, Recreation & Athletics, Scouts, Senior Services, Shelters/Homelessness

Application Procedures

Initial Contact: Send a a brief letter of inquiry.
Application Requirements: Include a description of organization, amount requested, purpose of funds sought, proof of tax-exempt status.
Deadlines: None.

Restrictions

Does not support individuals. Grants to religious organizations are favored, as are grants for the indigent aged and the handicapped, especially the visually handicapped.

Additional Information

Grants to religious organisation are favored as are grants to assist programs for the aged, especially the indigent aged and for the handicapped, especially the visually handicapped, so long as such programs to not duplicate existing or governmental programs.
Publications: Application Guidelines

Foundation Officials

John D. Allton: treasurer
Curtis J. Koch: vice president
Dorothy E. Wiedemann: trustee
Robert A. Wiedemann: president

Grants Analysis

Disclosure Period: calendar year ending 2004
Total Grants: $512,259
Number of Grants: 21
Average Grant: $15,329*
Highest Grant: $121,000
Lowest Grant: $4,000
Typical Range: $5,000 to $30,000
*Note:** Average grant figure excludes two highest grants ($221,000).

Recent Grants

Note: Grants derived from 2004 Form 990.
General

121,000	Little Sisters of the Poor, Cleveland, OH -- for Mary and Joseph home
100,000	Little Sisters of the Poor, Oregon, OH -- for sacred hearts home
40,000	Community Foundation of Greater Lorain County, Lorain, OH -- fund for Huron County
33,989	Saint Francis Health Care Center, Green Springs, OH
30,000	Bowling Green State University College of Health and Human Services, Bowling Green, OH -- for three scholarship endowment fund
25,000	Salk Institute, La Jolla, CA
25,000	Sight Center, Toledo, OH
20,000	Diabetes Camping Association, Laceys Spring, AL
20,000	Firelands Catholic Education Development Office Inc., Norwalk, OH
19,539	Stein Hospice, Sandusky, OH

SCHLUMBERGER LTD.

Company Headquarters
153 E. 53rd St., 57th Fl.
New York, NY 10022-4624
Web: http://www.slb.com

Company Description
Founded: 1972
Ticker: SLB
Exchange: NYSE
Revenue: US$13.612 billion (2002)
Employees: 77000 (2003)
SIC(s): 1300 Oil & Gas Extraction, 3500 Industrial Machinery & Equipment, 3600 Electronic & Other Electrical Equipment, 3800 Instruments & Related Products.

Operating Locations
Anadrill (TX--Sugar Land); Dowell Schlumber Inc. (TX--Houston); Geco Geophysical Company, Inc. (TX--Houston); Schlumberger CAD/CAM Div. (MI--Ann Arbor); Schlumberger Industries-Electricity Management (GA--Norcross); Schlumberger Ltd. (CA--Mountain View, Oxnard, San Jose; CT--Bridgeport; GA--Norcross; MI--Ann Arbor; NY--Elmsford; OR--Medford; PA--Archbold; TX--Dallas, Houston); Schlumberger Well Services (TX--Houston)
Note: Operates internationally.

Schlumberger Foundation

Giving Contact
Arthur W. Alexander, Executive Director
Schlumberger Foundation
153 E. 53 Street, 57th Floor
New York, NY 10022
Phone: (212)350-9400
Fax: (212)350-9440
Web: http://www.slb.com/seed/

Description
EIN: 237033142
Organization Type: Corporate Foundation
Giving Locations: NY: New York nationally to education.
Grant Types: Capital, Fellowship, General Support, Professorship, Project, Research, Scholarship.

Financial Summary
Total Giving: $83,000 (2003); $325,000 (2002); $1,464,404 (2001). Note: Contributes through foundation only.
Giving Analysis: Giving for 2001 includes: foundation fellowships ($105,000); foundation scholarships ($213,267); foundation ($541,137); foundation gifts to individuals ($605,000)
Assets: $25,830,631 (2003); $21,166,980 (2002); $26,268,715 (2001)

Typical Recipients
Arts & Humanities: Arts Centers, Ballet, Dance, Ethnic & Folk Arts, Historic Preservation, Libraries, Literary Arts, Museums/Galleries, Music, Opera, Performing Arts, Public Broadcasting, Theater
Civic & Public Affairs: Botanical Gardens/Parks, Economic Development, Economic Policy, Civic & Public Affairs-General, Legal Aid, Minority Business, Nonprofit Management, Professional & Trade Associations, Women's Affairs
Education: Arts/Humanities Education, Business Education, Colleges & Universities, Economic Education, Education Associations, Education Reform, Engineering/Technological Education, Faculty Development, Education-General, International Studies, Medical Education, Minority Education, Private Education (Precollege), Public Education (Precollege),

Science/Mathematics Education, Social Sciences Education, Special Education, Student Aid
Environment: Environment-General, Resource Conservation, Wildlife Protection
Health: Alzheimer's Disease, Cancer, Children's Health/Hospitals, Eyes/Blindness, Hospices, Hospitals, Medical Research, Single-Disease Health Associations
International: Foreign Educational Institutions, International Relations
Religion: Churches, Religious Organizations
Science: Science Museums, Scientific Centers & Institutes
Social Services: Child Welfare, Community Service Organizations, Day Care, Family Planning, Family Services, Food/Clothing Distribution, People with Disabilities, Shelters/Homelessness, Social Services-General, Substance Abuse, Youth Organizations

Application Procedures
Initial Contact: Send a brief letter or proposal.
Application Requirements: Include a description of organization, amount requested, purpose of funds sought, recently audited financial statement, time period covered, and proof of tax-exempt status.
Deadlines: None.

Restrictions
Grants are generally limited to colleges and universities emphasizing engineering and natural sciences, and cultural institutions.

Additional Information
According to Schlumberger Ltd., it has three headquarters: Paris, France; The Hague, Netherlands; and New York, NY.

Corporate Officials
Dugald Euan Baird: chairman, president, chief executive officer B Aberdeen, United Kingdom 1937. ED Aberdeen University (1955); Cambridge University BA (1960); Trinity College (1957-1960); Aberdeen University LLD (1995); Dundee University LLD (1998). PRIM CORP EMPL chairman, president, chief executive officer: Schlumberger Ltd. CORP AFFIL director: Paribas. NONPR AFFIL trustee: Carnegie Institute of Washington; trustee: The Haven Management Trust.
Arthur Lindenauer: executive vice president, chief financial officer B New York, NY 1937. ED Dartmouth College BA (1958); Dartmouth College Amos Tuck Graduate School of Business Administration MBA (1959). PRIM CORP EMPL executive vice president, chief financial officer: Schlumberger Ltd. ADD CORP EMPL president: Schlumberger Technology Corp.; president: Schlumberger Electricities. NONPR AFFIL member: American Institute CPAs.

Foundation Officials
Jamal Ainul: vice president, treasurer
Michael Benjamin: vice president, controller
Stephanie Cox: vice president, secretary
Maarten Scholten: chairman, president

Grants Analysis
Disclosure Period: calendar year ending 2003
Total Grants: $83,000
Number of Grants: 5
Average Grant: $16,600
Highest Grant: $35,000
Lowest Grant: $3,000
Typical Range: $1,000 to $10,000 and $20,000 to $50,000

Recent Grants
Note: Grants derived from 2003 Form 990.
General

35,000	Louisiana Engineering Advancement Program, New Orleans, LA
25,000	American Geological Institute, Alexandria, VA

13,000	American University of Beirut, Beirut Lebanon
7,000	New York University Center for French Civilization and Culture, New York, NY
3,000	Oklahoma Engineering Foundation, Oklahoma City, OK

JACOB G. SCHMIDLAPP TRUST NO. 1

Giving Contact
Lawra J. Baumann, Foundation Officer
Care of Fifth Third Bank
Department 00864
Cincinnati, OH 45263
Phone: (513)579-6034
Fax: (513)744-6997

Description
Founded: 1927
EIN: 316019680
Organization Type: General Purpose Foundation
Giving Locations: OH: Cincinnati metropolitan area
Grant Types: Capital, Challenge, General Support, Seed Money.

Donor Information
Founder: Established in 1927 by Jacob Godfrey Schmidlapp (1849-1919), a successful Cincinnati banker and industrialist. Mr. Schmidlapp was also a deeply committed philanthropist. In addition to establishing the Jacob G. Schmidlapp Trust, he funded the Emma Louise Schmidlapp wing of the Cincinnati Art Museum in memory of his daughter; the Rudolph Oscar Schmidlapp Fund to maintain the Cincinnati Art Museum, in memory of an infant son; and the Emilie Balke Schmidlapp dormitory at the Cincinnati College of Music, in memory of his wife. He also created the Charlotte Schmidlapp Fund in memory of another daughter killed in an automobile accident.

Unusual for its time, this fund has been providing no-interest education loans and counseling to women from the Cincinnati area since 1908. Mr. Schmidlapp funded his charitable trusts in 1908 and played an active role in deciding what each should support. He believed that experiments in grant making should be encouraged. Even if unsuccessful, the knowledge gained from one's mistakes would ensure overall progress.

Financial Summary
Total Giving: $3,703,667 (fiscal year ending September 30, 2003); $4,659,769 (fiscal 2002); $3,215,499 (fiscal 2001)
Giving Analysis: Giving for fiscal 2002 includes: foundation grants to United Way ($50,000); fiscal 2001: foundation grants to United Way ($25,000)
Assets: $53,887,993 (fiscal 2003); $48,323,796 (fiscal 2002); $63,103,712 (fiscal 2001)

Typical Recipients
Arts & Humanities: Arts Associations & Councils, Arts Centers, Arts Funds, Arts Institutes, Arts & Humanities-General, Historic Preservation, Libraries, Museums/Galleries, Music, Opera, Public Broadcasting, Theater
Civic & Public Affairs: African American Affairs, Botanical Gardens/Parks, Business/Free Enterprise, Clubs, Community Foundations, Economic Development, Employment/Job Training, Civic & Public Affairs-General, Housing, Municipalities/Towns, Philanthropic Organizations, Urban & Community Affairs, Women's Affairs, Zoos/Aquariums
Education: Afterschool/Enrichment Programs, Arts/Humanities Education, Colleges & Universities, Community & Junior Colleges, Economic Education, Education Funds, Education Reform, Environmental Edu-

cation, Faculty Development, Education-General, Medical Education, Minority Education, Preschool Education, Private Education (Precollege), Public Education (Precollege), Religious Education, Science/Mathematics Education, Secondary Education (Private), Secondary Education (Public), Special Education, Student Aid
Health: Adolescent Health Issues, Arthritis, Cancer, Children's Health/Hospitals, Clinics/Medical Centers, Diabetes, Emergency/Ambulance Services, Geriatric Health, Health Funds, Health Organizations, Heart, Hospices, Hospitals, Long-Term Care, Medical Rehabilitation, Mental Health, Multiple Sclerosis, Nursing Services, Prenatal Health Issues, Preventive Medicine/Wellness Organizations, Public Health, Single-Disease Health Associations, Speech & Hearing, Trauma Treatment
Religion: Churches, Dioceses, Jewish Causes, Ministries, Missionary Activities (Domestic), Religious Organizations, Religious Welfare, Seminaries
Science: Science Museums, Scientific Centers & Institutes
Social Services: At-Risk Youth, Child Welfare, Community Centers, Community Service Organizations, Counseling, Day Care, Domestic Violence, Emergency Relief, Family Planning, Family Services, Food/Clothing Distribution, Homes, People with Disabilities, Recreation & Athletics, Scouts, Senior Services, Shelters/Homelessness, Substance Abuse, United Funds/United Ways, Volunteer Services, YMCA/YWCA/YMHA/YWHA, Youth Organizations

Application Procedures
Initial Contact: A short letter should be sent to the foundation officer describing a proposal before submitting a completed application. The trust does not have an application form; it does provide detailed information on the desired format of a written application upon request.
Application Requirements: Formal applications should include name, address, and telephone number of the organization; date established; national affiliations, if any; purposes and activities of the organization and services provided; purpose and amount of requested grant; budget; list of other sources of funding; plans for permanent funding if project is a continuing one; latest balance sheet and annual operating statement, including percentages of budget received from United Way and from federal, state, or other sources; percentage of costs paid by program recipients; and date of the most recent prior application to a foundation administered by the Fifth Third Bank. A document must also be provided stating that if a grant is received, a report will be made within one month of completion of the project detailing how the funds were spent. Additional material, such as pamphlets or supporting letters, should not be included.
Deadlines: February 10, May 10, August 10, and November 10.
Review Process: The committee meets quarterly. All grants are reviewed by the Charitable Foundations Screening Committee which forwards recommendations to the trust committee of the board of directors of the Fifth Third Bank. All grants must be approved by the trust committee.

Restrictions
The trust does not make grants for operating expenses, sectarian religious or political purposes, for scholarships, or to other foundations or individuals.

Additional Information
Organizations receiving grants from any of the trusts are generally not eligible for additional grants during the following three years. Recipients must be a tax-exempt organization.
Publications: Guidelines
Trust(s): Fifth Third Bank

Grants Analysis
Disclosure Period: fiscal year ending September 30, 2003
Total Grants: $3,703,667
Number of Grants: 55
Average Grant: $60,447*
Highest Grant: $250,000
Lowest Grant: $5,000
Typical Range: $25,000 to $100,000
*Note: Average grant figure excludes two highest grants ($500,000).

Recent Grants
Note: Grants derived from fiscal 2003 Form 990.
General

250,000	Arthritis Foundation, Cincinnati, OH -- project support
250,000	Cincinnati Arts School Inc., Cincinnati, OH
166,666	Dan Beard council Boy Scouts of America, Cincinnati, OH
150,000	Greater Cleveland YMCA, Cleveland, OH
137,500	Toledo Museum of Art, Toledo, OH
125,000	Bellarmine University, Louisville, KY
125,000	Catholic Diocese of Toledo, Toledo, OH -- endowment
125,000	University of Dayton, Dayton, OH
100,000	Children's Scholarship Fund of Greater Cincinnati, Oxford, OH
100,000	College of Mount Saint Joseph, Cincinnati, OH

JACOB G. SCHMIDLAPP TRUST NO. 2

Giving Contact
Heida Jark, Trust Officer
c/o Fifth Third Bank
38 Fountain Sq. Plz., Department 00864
Cincinnati, OH 45263
Phone: (513)534-4397

Description
Founded: 1916
EIN: 316020109
Organization Type: Private Foundation
Giving Locations: OH: Cincinnati metropolitan area
Grant Types: Capital, General Support.

Donor Information
Founder: the late Jacob G. Schmidlapp

Financial Summary
Total Giving: $316,667 (fiscal year ending September 30, 2003)
Assets: $3,341,194 (fiscal 2003)
Gifts Received: $474,638 (fiscal 1992)

Typical Recipients
Arts & Humanities: Ballet, Historic Preservation, History & Archaeology, Libraries, Museums/Galleries, Performing Arts, Public Broadcasting
Civic & Public Affairs: Clubs, Community Foundations, Economic Development, Employment/Job Training, Nonprofit Management, Urban & Community Affairs
Education: Colleges & Universities, Education Funds, Elementary Education (Private), Environmental Education, Education-General, Literacy, Private Education (Precollege), Science/Mathematics Education, Secondary Education (Private)
Environment: Environment-General
Health: Arthritis, Cancer, Clinics/Medical Centers, Hospitals
Religion: Dioceses, Religious Welfare
Science: Scientific Centers & Institutes
Social Services: Community Centers, Community

Service Organizations, Counseling, Day Care, United Funds/United Ways, Youth Organizations

Application Procedures
Initial Contact: Request application guidelines.
Deadlines: February 1, May 1, August 1, and November 1.

Restrictions
Does not support individuals, religious organizations for sectarian purposes, or political or lobbying groups.

Additional Information
Publications: Annual Report; Application Guidelines
Trust(s): Fifth Third Bank

Grants Analysis
Disclosure Period: fiscal year ending September 30, 2003
Total Grants: $316,667
Number of Grants: 2
Highest Grant: $250,000
Lowest Grant: $66,667

Recent Grants
Note: Grants derived from fiscal 2003 Form 990.
General

250,000	Arthritis Foundation, Cincinnati, OH
66,667	Bowling Green State University, Bowling Green, OH

KILIAN J. AND CAROLINE F. SCHMITT FOUNDATION

Giving Contact
Gary J. Lindsay, Secretary & Treasurer
care of HSBC Bank U.S.A.
One HSBC Plaza
Rochester, NY 14604-2407
Phone: (716)264-0030

Description
Founded: 1991
EIN: 223087449
Organization Type: Private Foundation
Giving Locations: NY: Rochester
Grant Types: General Support.

Donor Information
Founder: the late Killian J. Schmitt, the late Caroline F. Schmitt

Financial Summary
Total Giving: $357,500 (fiscal year ending February 28, 2004)
Assets: $9,976,585 (fiscal 2004)

Typical Recipients
Arts & Humanities: Libraries, Museums/Galleries, Public Broadcasting
Civic & Public Affairs: Clubs, Economic Development, Employment/Job Training, Civic & Public Affairs-General, Zoos/Aquariums
Education: Arts/Humanities Education, Colleges & Universities, Engineering/Technological Education, Faculty Development, Medical Education, Private Education (Precollege), Religious Education, Science/Mathematics Education, Special Education, Student Aid, Vocational & Technical Education
Environment: Resource Conservation
Health: Alzheimer's Disease, Cancer, Children's Health/Hospitals, Emergency/Ambulance Services, Health-General, Home-Care Services, Hospices, Kidney, Long-Term Care, Medical Rehabilitation, Multiple Sclerosis, Public Health, Speech & Hearing
International: Health Care/Hospitals, International Organizations

Religion: Churches, Dioceses, Religious Welfare
Science: Scientific Centers & Institutes
Social Services: Camps, Child Welfare, Community Service Organizations, Domestic Violence, Food/Clothing Distribution, People with Disabilities, Senior Services, Shelters/Homelessness, Social Services-General

Application Procedures
Initial Contact: Request application form.
Deadlines: None.

Restrictions
Emphasis is on higher education and medical research.

Additional Information
Publications: Application Form

Foundation Officials
James R. Dray: director
Leon Fella: director
Robert H. Fella: president
Alfred Hallenbeck: director
Gary J. Lindsay: secretary, treasurer
Michael Charles Walker, Sr.: vice president B Rochester, NY 1940. ED University of Colorado BA (1962); Columbia Pacific University MBA (1982); Columbia Pacific University DBA (1984). CORP AFFIL president, chief executive officer: Presbyterian Residence Center Corp. NONPR AFFIL member professional advisory committee: Self Help Hard Hearing; member business advisory board: State University New York; member: New York Saint Board Professional Medicine Conduct; member: Rotary; member: New York Association Homes & Services Aging; member: New York Saint Bankers Association; chairman: Monroe County Bond Services Comm; chairman, director: Genesee Region Home Care Association; vice president, director: Kilian & Caroline Schmitt Foundation; member: American Marketing Association; member: American Association Homes Aging. CLUB AFFIL Ridgemont Country Club.

Grants Analysis
Disclosure Period: fiscal year ending February 28, 2004
Total Grants: $357,500
Number of Grants: 26
Average Grant: $8,438*
Highest Grant: $105,000
Lowest Grant: $1,000
Typical Range: $1,000 to $10,000
*Note: Average grant figure excludes two highest grants ($155,000).

Recent Grants
Note: Grants derived from fiscal 2004 Form 990.
General

125,000	University of Rochester, Rochester, NY -- for medical school research
105,000	Rochester Institute of Technology, Rochester, NY
50,000	Nazareth College of Rochester, Rochester, NY
21,000	Rochester Rotary Charitable Trust Inc., Rochester, NY -- for sunshine camp improvements
10,000	Hope Hall, Rochester, NY -- capital campaign for renovation projects
5,000	National Multiple Sclerosis Society, Rochester, NY -- for reach the stars campaign
5,000	Wilson Commencement Park, Rochester, NY -- for education program
4,000	Rochester Institute of Technology, Rochester, NY
3,500	WXXI Public Broadcasting, Rochester, NY
2,500	Mercy Center for the Aging, Rochester, NY

SCHMOKER FAMILY FOUNDATION

Giving Contact
Catherine S. Schmoker, President
6616 Biscayne Blvd.
Edina, MN 55436-1704
Phone: (612)336-3126

Description
Founded: 1987
EIN: 363493282
Organization Type: Private Foundation
Giving Locations: MN
Grant Types: General Support, Operating Expenses.

Financial Summary
Total Giving: $197,500 (2003); $186,500 (2001)
Giving Analysis: Giving for 2003 includes: foundation grants to United Way ($10,000) 2001: foundation grants to United Way ($10,000)
Assets: $2,711,610 (2003); $2,808,337 (2001)
Gifts Received: $42,626 (2001). Note: In 2001, contributions were received from NBC Foundation ($40,880) and Catherine Stuart Schmoker ($1,746).

Typical Recipients
Arts & Humanities: Libraries, Music, Performing Arts, Theater
Civic & Public Affairs: Civic & Public Affairs-General, Women's Affairs
Education: Colleges & Universities, Education Funds, Education-General, Private Education (Precollege), Public Education (Precollege)
Health: Hospices
Religion: Seminaries
Social Services: Social Services-General, United Funds/United Ways

Application Procedures
Initial Contact: The foundation reports no specific application guidelines. Send a brief letter of inquiry, including statement of purpose, amount requested, and proof of tax-exempt status.
Application Requirements: Include a description of organization, purpose of funds sought, and amount requested. The organization should also furnish an opinion to the effect that: 1) the organization has been certified by the IRS and is in fact acting as an organization described in Section 501(c)(3) of the Internal Revenue Code to which contributions are deductible under Section 170(c)(2)(b) of the Code, and furnish the organization's tax identification number; and 2) that the organization is either a) one which comes within the definition contained in paragraphs 1, 2, or 3 of Section 509(a) of the Internal Revenue Code, or b) that if the organization is a "private foundation" as described in Section 509(a) that it is also an "operating foundation" as defined in Section 4942(j)(3) of the Internal Revenue Code.
Deadlines: None.
Decision Notification: Notice of approval, rejection, or requests for additional information are usually sent within two months of application.

Foundation Officials
Lisa S. Hesdorffer: vice president, director
Catherine S. Hunnewell: vice president, director, assistant secretary
Catherine M. Schmoker: president, director
Richard C. Schmoker: treasurer, director
William C. Schmoker: secretary, director

Grants Analysis
Disclosure Period: calendar year ending 2003
Total Grants: $187,500*
Number of Grants: 14
Average Grant: $3,708*
Highest Grant: $105,500

Lowest Grant: $500
Typical Range: $1,000 to $5,000
*Note: Giving excludes United Way. Average grant figure excludes two highest grants ($143,000).

Recent Grants

Note: Grants derived from 2003 Form 990.
Library-Related

3,000	Library Foundation of Hennepin County, Minnetonka, MN

General

105,500	University of Nebraska Foundation, Lincoln, NE
37,500	Jeremiah Program, Minneapolis, MN
10,000	Children's Theatre Company, Minneapolis, MN -- towards theatre education
10,000	Greater Twin Cities United Way, Minneapolis, MN
8,000	Blake Schools, Edina, MN
5,000	Delta Gamma Foundation, Columbus, OH
3,000	Ordway Center for the Performing Arts, St. Paul, MN
3,000	VocalEssence, Minneapolis, MN
3,000	Voyageur Outward Bound, Minneapolis, MN

DR. LOUIS A. AND ANNE B. SCHNEIDER FOUNDATION

Giving Contact

Denise Andorfer, Trustee
National City Bank
PO Box 110
Ft. Wayne, IN 46802
Phone: (260)461-6218

Description

Founded: 1987
EIN: 311193706
Organization Type: Private Foundation
Giving Locations: IN: Ft. Wayne; NY: New York
Grant Types: General Support.

Financial Summary

Total Giving: $145,000 (fiscal year ending November 30, 2004); $20,136 (fiscal 2001)
Assets: $12,429,473 (fiscal 2004); $374,157 (fiscal 2001)
Gifts Received: $11,662,038 (fiscal 2004). Note: In fiscal 2004, contributions were received from Schneider Trusts.

Typical Recipients

Arts & Humanities: Arts Funds, Libraries, Opera, Public Broadcasting, Theater
Civic & Public Affairs: Ethnic Organizations
Education: Colleges & Universities, Education-General, Medical Education
International: Foreign Arts Organizations
Religion: Religious Welfare, Seminaries, Synagogues/Temples
Science: Scientific Centers & Institutes, Scientific Research
Social Services: Food/Clothing Distribution

Application Procedures

Initial Contact: Send a brief letter of inquiry.
Application Requirements: Include purpose of funds sought, amount requested, and proof of tax-exempt status.
Deadlines: None.

Grants Analysis

Disclosure Period: fiscal year ending November 30, 2004

Total Grants: $145,000
Number of Grants: 9
Average Grant: $16,111*
Highest Grant: $25,000
Lowest Grant: $5,000
Typical Range: $5,000 to $25,000
*Note: Average grant figure excludes highest grant.

Recent Grants

Note: Grants derived from fiscal 2004 Form 990.
Library-Related

25,000	Allen County Public Library Foundation, Ft. Wayne, IN

General

25,000	Fort Wayne Jewish Federation, Ft. Wayne, IN
25,000	Metropolitan Opera of New York, New York, NY
25,000	Teachers College Columbia University, New York, NY
10,000	Congregation B'nai Jacob, Ft. Wayne, IN
10,000	Jewish Theological Seminary, New York, NY
10,000	New York University School of Medicine, New York, NY
10,000	Temple Achduth Vesholom, Ft. Wayne, IN
5,000	National Foundation for Jewish Culture, New York, NY

SCHOENLEBER FOUNDATION

Giving Contact

Peter C. Haensel, President & Director
111 E. Wisconsin Ave., Suite 1800
Milwaukee, WI 53202
Phone: (414)276-3400

Description

Founded: 1965
EIN: 391049364
Organization Type: Private Foundation
Giving Locations: WI: Milwaukee metropolitan area
Grant Types: General Support, Scholarship.

Donor Information

Founder: the late Marie and Louise Schoenleber

Financial Summary

Total Giving: $390,000 (2003)
Assets: $7,740,390 (2003)
Gifts Received: $500 (1992). Note: In 1992, contributions were received from Arnold Investment Counsel.

Typical Recipients

Arts & Humanities: Arts Associations & Councils, Arts Institutes, Community Arts, Historic Preservation, History & Archaeology, Libraries, Museums/Galleries, Music, Theater
Civic & Public Affairs: Botanical Gardens/Parks, Business/Free Enterprise, Community Foundations, Employment/Job Training, Ethnic Organizations, Civic & Public Affairs-General, Hispanic Affairs, Housing, Law & Justice, Public Policy, Urban & Community Affairs, Zoos/Aquariums
Education: Arts/Humanities Education, Business Education, Colleges & Universities, Education Funds, Engineering/Technological Education, Education-General, Literacy, Medical Education, Private Education (Precollege), Public Education (Precollege), Student Aid
Environment: Environment-General, Resource Conservation
Health: Children's Health/Hospitals, Hospitals, Long-Term Care, Medical Rehabilitation, Medical Re-

---

search, Single-Disease Health Associations
International: International Affairs
Religion: Churches, Religious Welfare
Social Services: Community Centers, Community Service Organizations, Counseling, Family Planning, Family Services, People with Disabilities, Recreation & Athletics, Shelters/Homelessness, YMCA/YWCA/YMHA/YWHA, Youth Organizations

Application Procedures

Initial Contact: Request application form.
Deadlines: August 30.

Additional Information

Publications: Application Form

Foundation Officials

Frank W. Bastian: secretary, director
Peter C. Haensel: president, director
Walter Schorrak: director

Grants Analysis

Disclosure Period: calendar year ending 2003
Total Grants: $390,000
Number of Grants: 26
Average Grant: $15,000*
Highest Grant: $50,000
Lowest Grant: $2,500
Typical Range: $5,000 to $25,000
*Note: Average grant figure excludes highest grant.

Recent Grants

Note: Grants derived from 2003 Form 990.
Library-Related

50,000	Milwaukee Public Library Foundation, Milwaukee, WI

General

35,000	University of Wisconsin Foundation, Madison, WI
25,000	University of Wisconsin Milwaukee Foundation, Milwaukee, WI
20,000	Lake Park Friends, Milwaukee, WI
20,000	Milwaukee School of Engineering, Milwaukee, WI
20,000	Milwaukee Symphony Orchestra, Milwaukee, WI
20,000	University of Wisconsin Milwaukee Foundation, Milwaukee, WI
15,000	Leopold Nature Center, Monona, WI
15,000	Little Traverse Conservancy, Harbor Springs, MI
15,000	Marquette University, Milwaukee, WI

DR. SCHOLL FOUNDATION

Giving Contact

Pamela Scholl, President
1033 Skokie Boulevard, Suite 230
Northbrook, IL 60062
Phone: (847)559-7430
Web: http://www.drschollfoundation.com

Description

Founded: 1947
EIN: 366068724
Organization Type: General Purpose Foundation
Giving Locations: IL
Grant Types: General Support, Project.

Donor Information

Founder: The Dr. Scholl Foundation (formerly William M. Scholl Foundation) was created in 1947 by Dr. William M. Scholl. "At 18, he enrolled in Illinois Medical College, now Loyola University, and was awarded his M.D. degree in 1904. That same year, he established Scholl, Inc., a manufacturer of orthopedic devices and footwear. He died in 1968 leaving Scholl, Inc., and the foundation in the hands of his nephews. The foundation received the bulk of his estate, and Scholl, Inc., was sold in 1979."

Financial Summary

Total Giving: $3,011,119 (2003); $3,214,723 (2002)
Giving Analysis: Giving for 2003 includes: foundation scholarships ($725,000); 2002: foundation scholarships ($695,000)
Assets: $150,081,568 (2003); $137,019,562 (2002)

Typical Recipients

Arts & Humanities: Arts Festivals, Arts Institutes, Ballet, History & Archaeology, Libraries, Museums/ Galleries, Music, Opera, Public Broadcasting
Civic & Public Affairs: Botanical Gardens/Parks, Clubs, Economic Development, Employment/Job Training, Civic & Public Affairs-General, Housing, Law & Justice, Legal Aid, Native American Affairs, Professional & Trade Associations, Public Policy, Zoos/Aquariums
Education: Arts/Humanities Education, Colleges & Universities, Education Associations, Education Funds, Education Reform, Elementary Education (Private), Engineering/Technological Education, Faculty Development, Education-General, Legal Education, Medical Education, Minority Education, Private Education (Precollege), Science/Mathematics Education, Secondary Education (Private), Special Education, Student Aid
Environment: Environment-General, Resource Conservation
Health: Cancer, Children's Health/Hospitals, Clinics/ Medical Centers, Eyes/Blindness, Health-General, Health Funds, Health Organizations, Heart, Hospices, Hospitals, Hospitals (University Affiliated), Medical Research, Prenatal Health Issues, Research/Studies Institutes, Single-Disease Health Associations
International: Foreign Arts Organizations, Foreign Educational Institutions, International-General, Health Care/Hospitals, International Affairs, International Organizations, International Peace & Security Issues, International Relief Efforts, Missionary/ Religious Activities
Religion: Churches, Religious Organizations, Religious Welfare
Science: Science Museums, Scientific Organizations
Social Services: Animal Protection, Child Welfare, Community Centers, Community Service Organizations, Crime Prevention, Emergency Relief, Family Services, Food/Clothing Distribution, Homes, People with Disabilities, Recreation & Athletics, Scouts, Senior Services, Shelters/Homelessness, Substance Abuse, Volunteer Services, YMCA/YWCA/YMHA/ YWHA, Youth Organizations

Application Procedures

Initial Contact: Applicants should obtain a copy of the foundation's standard application form and guidelines. The form is required along with one copy of a full proposal.
Application Requirements: Include a complete description of the specific project or program; a detailed budget for the project or program; a list of personnel assigned to the project or program and their qualifications; financial statements for the latest fiscal year, audited or unaudited; a list of officers and directors; a copy of Internal Revenue Service determination that applicant is an exempt organization under Section 501 (c)(3) of the Internal Revenue Code, except for religious organizations under blanket exemption; a legible federal employer identification number (FEIN) (the name of the applying organization must be identical with that of the exemption letter-proposals without a valid letter will be returned); affidavit forms must be returned for non-U.S. applicants who do not have a 501 (c)(3) determination letter; and the original signed application (no alterations and no copies).
Deadlines: Applications must be received by March

1 and November 1 to be considered.
Review Process: Applications are acknowledged. The foundation notifies applicants of its decisions in November, and distribution of grants occurs in December.

Restrictions

"In general, the Foundation does not consider the following for funding: organizations not eligible for tax-deductible support; political organizations or campaigns, or groups whose prime purpose is to influence legislation; foundations that are themselves grant-making bodies; public education; grants to individuals; general endowment grants; unrestricted purpose grants; general support grants; grants for the reduction of an operating deficit or to liquidate a debt; testimonial dinners and similar benefit programs involving purchases of tables, tickets, or advertisements; or installment grants, but the Foundation gives consideration to subsequent applications pertaining to the same project." Written requests only.

Additional Information

Applicants must present their request in the form of a special project or program designed to achieve a desirable result. All grantees are asked to sign an agreement that requires a full report to be filed at the conclusion of the project, including a statement of the results achieved by the grant. Only one application per organization will be considered annually.
Publications: Application Form; Program Guidelines

Foundation Officials

Mary Ann Hynes: director
John A. Nitschke: treasurer, director
Richard B. Patterson: director
David L. Royalty: director
Daniel Scholl: director
Jack E. Scholl: secretary, director
Jeanne M. Scholl: director
Michael W. Scholl: director
Pamela Scholl: president, director, chairperson
Susan Scholl: director
Douglas C. Witherspoon: director

Grants Analysis

Disclosure Period: calendar year ending 2003
Total Grants: $2,286,119*
Number of Grants: 139
Average Grant: $16,647
Highest Grant: $125,000
Lowest Grant: $1,000
Typical Range: $5,000 to $30,000
*Note: Giving excludes scholarships.

Recent Grants

Note: Grants derived from 2003 Form 990.
Library-Related

10,000	Chicago Public Library Foundation, Chicago, IL -- to provide after school homework help and guidance for children

General

600,000	Big Shoulders Fund, Chicago, IL -- for scholarship program
250,000	Dr. William M. Scholl College of Podiatric Medicine, North Chicago, IL -- for scholarship program and feet first project
171,000	Cambridge Foundation, Cambridge United Kingdom -- for professorship at Cambridge center for brain repair
125,000	Hospice Care, Douglas United Kingdom -- for the establishment of the William M. school
50,000	Boulder Parks and Recreation Foundation, Chicago, IL
50,000	Evanston Northwestern Healthcare, Evanston, IL -- for cardiac electrophysiology laboratory and nursing development program
50,000	Mayo Foundation, Rochester, MN -- for medical research
50,000	Metropolitan Family Services, Chicago, IL -- to support high risk families and children's
50,000	St. George's Church Organ Appeal United Kingdom -- for purchase of new organ
50,000	University of Notre Dame, Notre Dame, IN -- for scholarship program

SCHOOLER FAMILY FOUNDATION (OHIO)

Giving Contact

S. Dean Schooler, President, Treasurer
PO Box 1300
Coshocton, OH 43812
Phone: (303)449-0918

Description

Founded: 1987
EIN: 311157433
Organization Type: Private Foundation
Giving Locations: OH: Coshocton County
Grant Types: Capital, Conference/Seminar, Endowment, General Support, Project, Research, Seed Money.

Donor Information

Founder: Seward D. Schooler, Edith Schooler

Financial Summary

Total Giving: $146,992 (2003); $364,752 (2001)
Giving Analysis: Giving for 2003 includes: foundation scholarships ($20,000); 2001: foundation matching gifts ($9,503); foundation scholarships ($10,000)
Assets: $6,292,673 (2003); $6,866,795 (2001)
Gifts Received: $693,297 (1996); $4,069,000 (1993). Note: In 1996, contributions were received from Seward D. Schooler Sr.

Typical Recipients

Arts & Humanities: Film & Video, Historic Preservation, Libraries, Museums/Galleries, Music, Performing Arts, Public Broadcasting
Civic & Public Affairs: Botanical Gardens/Parks, Community Foundations, Economic Development, Civic & Public Affairs-General, Housing, Nonprofit Management, Philanthropic Organizations, Professional & Trade Associations, Urban & Community Affairs
Education: Arts/Humanities Education, Business Education, Colleges & Universities, Education Funds, Education-General, Literacy, Preschool Education, Private Education (Precollege), Religious Education, Science/Mathematics Education, Secondary Education (Public), Special Education, Student Aid
Health: Cancer, Children's Health/Hospitals, Clinics/ Medical Centers, Emergency/Ambulance Services, Health Organizations, Hospices, Hospitals, Transplant Networks/Donor Banks
International: Foreign Educational Institutions
Religion: Churches
Social Services: Animal Protection, Big Brothers/Big Sisters, Community Service Organizations, Domestic Violence, People with Disabilities, Recreation & Athletics, Scouts, Youth Organizations

Application Procedures

Initial Contact: Send a brief letter of inquiry requesting guidelines.
Application Requirements: Include a description of organization, amount requested, purpose of funds sought, recently audited financial statement, and proof of tax-exempt status.
Deadlines: None.

Restrictions

Grants are not made to individuals.

Additional Information

Publications: Application Guidelines

Foundation Officials

C. Fenning Pierce: secretary
David R. Schooler: vice president
Heather L. Schooler: trustee
S. Dean Schooler: president, treasurer

Grants Analysis

Disclosure Period: calendar year ending 2003
Total Grants: $126,992*
Number of Grants: 15
Average Grant: $5,499*
Highest Grant: $50,000
Lowest Grant: $94
Typical Range: $1,000 to $10,000
*Note: Giving excludes scholarships. Average grant figure excludes highest grant.

Recent Grants

Note: Grants derived from 2003 Form 990.
General

50,000	Coshocton County Memorial Hospital, Coshocton, OH -- for extended care facility
20,000	Echoing Hills Village, Warsaw, OH -- for new electric beds program
15,000	Habitat for Humanity of Coshocton County, Coshocton, OH -- for site acquisition and home construction
13,000	Coshocton Foundation, Coshocton, OH
10,650	Coshocton Foundation, Coshocton, OH
10,000	Citizens for Humane Action, Westerville, OH -- for organizational development
10,000	Ohio Foundation of Independent Colleges, Columbus, OH -- for 2002-2003 Ohio scholars program
10,000	Ohio Foundation of Independent Colleges, Columbus, OH -- for 2003-2004 Ohio scholars program
6,000	Friends of the Animal Shelter, Coshocton, OH -- organizational development and fundraising
1,128	Boys and Girls Clubs of Columbus, Columbus, OH -- for athletic event admission

SCHOONMAKER J-SEWKLY VALLEY HOSPITAL TRUST

Giving Contact

Laurie Moritz, Trust Officer
c/o Mellon Bank NA
PO Box 185
Pittsburgh, PA 15230
Phone: (412)234-0023

Description

EIN: 256016020
Organization Type: Private Foundation
Giving Locations: PA: Pittsburgh
Grant Types: General Support.

Financial Summary

Total Giving: $367,500 (fiscal year ending September 30, 2003); $402,500 (fiscal 2001)
Giving Analysis: Giving for fiscal 2003 includes: foundation grants to United Way ($50,000); fiscal 2001: foundation grants to United Way ($57,500)
Assets: $7,742,477 (fiscal 2003); $7,804,093 (fiscal 2001)

Typical Recipients

Arts & Humanities: Historic Preservation, History & Archaeology, Libraries, Museums/Galleries, Music
Civic & Public Affairs: Botanical Gardens/Parks,

Chambers of Commerce, Civic & Public Affairs-General, Urban & Community Affairs, Women's Affairs
Education: Colleges & Universities, Education Associations, Education Funds, Legal Education, Medical Education, Private Education (Precollege), Religious Education, Student Aid
Environment: Environment-General
Health: AIDS/HIV, Emergency/Ambulance Services, Health Funds, Health Organizations, Hospitals
Religion: Churches, Religion-General, Seminaries
Science: Scientific Centers & Institutes
Social Services: At-Risk Youth, Community Service Organizations, Emergency Relief, Family Services, Scouts, Shelters/Homelessness, United Funds/United Ways, Youth Organizations

Application Procedures

Initial Contact: Send letter requesting application form.
Deadlines: None.

Additional Information

Publications: Application Form
Trust(s): Mellon Bank NA

Grants Analysis

Disclosure Period: fiscal year ending September 30, 2003
Total Grants: $317,500*
Number of Grants: 21
Average Grant: $9,306*
Highest Grant: $50,000
Lowest Grant: $3,500
Typical Range: $5,000 to $20,000
*Note: Giving excludes United Way. Average grant figure excludes three highest grants ($150,000).

Recent Grants

Note: Grants derived from fiscal 2004 Form 990.
General

50,000	Princeton University, Princeton, NJ
50,000	St. Stephen's Church, Sewickley, PA
50,000	United Way of Allegheny County, Pittsburgh, PA
20,000	Princeton Alumni Association of Western Pennsylvania, Pittsburgh, PA
17,500	Pittsburgh Symphony, Pittsburgh, PA
15,000	Carnegie Museums of Pittsburgh, Pittsburgh, PA
15,000	Sewickley Academy, Sewickley, PA
15,000	Shadyside Hospital Foundation, Pittsburgh, PA
11,500	American Red Cross, Pittsburgh, PA
10,000	Ellis School, Pittsburgh, PA

SCHUMANN FUND FOR NEW JERSEY

Giving Contact

Barbara Reisman, Executive Director
Schumann Fund for New Jersey
21 Van Vleck Street
Montclair, NJ 07042
Phone: (973)509-9883
Fax: (973)509-1149
E-mail: breisman@worldnet.att.net
Web: http://fdncenter.org/grantmaker/schumann/index.html

Description

Founded: 1988
EIN: 521556076
Organization Type: General Purpose Foundation
Giving Locations: NJ: Essex County
Grant Types: Conference/Seminar, General Support, Multiyear/Continuing Support, Project, Seed Money.

Donor Information

Founder: Established in 1988 by the Florence and John Schumann Foundation.

Financial Summary

Total Giving: $1,732,050 (2003); $2,019,615 (2001)
Giving Analysis: Giving for 2001 includes: foundation grants to United Way ($12,500)
Assets: $30,611,088 (2003); $34,671,553 (2001)

Typical Recipients

Arts & Humanities: Historic Preservation, Libraries, Music, Public Broadcasting
Civic & Public Affairs: Botanical Gardens/Parks, Clubs, Community Foundations, Economic Development, Civic & Public Affairs-General, Hispanic Affairs, Housing, Legal Aid, Nonprofit Management, Public Policy, Urban & Community Affairs, Women's Affairs
Education: Afterschool/Enrichment Programs, Colleges & Universities, Education Associations, Education Funds, Education Reform, Elementary Education (Private), Elementary Education (Public), Environmental Education, Faculty Development, Education-General, Leadership Training, Literacy, Minority Education, Preschool Education, Private Education (Precollege), Public Education (Precollege), School Volunteerism, Social Sciences Education, Special Education, Student Aid
Environment: Air/Water Quality, Forestry, Environment-General, Protection, Resource Conservation, Watershed
Health: AIDS/HIV, Diabetes, Health Organizations, Mental Health, Prenatal Health Issues, Public Health, Single-Disease Health Associations
Religion: Churches, Dioceses, Religious Welfare
Social Services: At-Risk Youth, Child Abuse, Child Welfare, Community Service Organizations, Counseling, Day Care, Emergency Relief, Family Planning, Family Services, Scouts, Shelters/Homelessness, Social Services-General, Volunteer Services, YMCA/YWCA/YMHA/YWHA, Youth Organizations

Application Procedures

Initial Contact: Submit a written request. The New York/New Jersey common application form. may be used if applicants so choose.
Application Requirements: Include a description of the organization's objectives, activities, and leadership; amount requested; purpose of funds sought; and plans for its accomplishment. Proposal should be accompanied by a copy of organization's recently audited financial statement, an expense budget identifying all sources of income, project's time frame and future funding plans, list of the board of directors, and a copy of organization's IRS tax-exempt determination letter.
Deadlines: January 15, April 15, July 15, or October 15.
Review Process: The board meets four times a year in March, June, September, and December. The foundation indicates that action on proposals may be reserved for a later quarter, but it will reply promptly to requests.

Restrictions

In general, the fund does not accept applications for capital campaigns, annual giving, endowment, direct support of individuals, or local programs in counties other than Essex. Projects in the arts, healthcare, and housing development are generally beyond the foundation's scope.

Additional Information

Publications: Annual Report

Foundation Officials

Aubin Z. Ames: trustee
Leonard S. Coleman, Jr.: trustee B Montclair, NJ 1949. ED Harvard University MPA; Princeton University BA. PRIM CORP EMPL president, treasurer: Na-

tional League of Professional Baseball Clubs. CORP AFFIL director: Omnicom Group Inc.; director: Owens Corning; director: H.J. Heinz Co.; director: New Jersey Resources Corp.; director: Beneficial Corp.; director: Cendant Corp.; director: Avis Group Holdings Inc.; director: Avis Rent-A-Car Inc.

Christopher J. Daggett: chairman PRIM CORP EMPL William E Simon & Sons.

Andrew Christian Halvorsen: treasurer, trustee B Englewood, NJ 1946. ED Brown University AB (1968); University of Pennsylvania MBA (1972). PRIM CORP EMPL chief financial officer, director: Beneficial Corp. CORP AFFIL chief financial officer: Beneficial Arizona Inc.

George R. Harris: trustee
John Noonan: trustee
Alan Rosenthal: trustee

Grants Analysis

Disclosure Period: calendar year ending 2003
Total Grants: $1,732,050
Number of Grants: 92
Average Grant: $18,827
Highest Grant: $100,000
Lowest Grant: $1,500
Typical Range: $10,000 to $50,000

Recent Grants

Note: Grants derived from 2001 Form 990.
General

73,265	Montclair State University, Upper Montclair, NJ -- for Leadership Institute for Early Childhood Education
50,000	Chad School Foundation, Newark, NJ -- for operations
50,000	ISLES, Trenton, NJ -- for Healthy City Initiative
50,000	New Jersey Community Loan Fund, Trenton, NJ -- for Lighthouse Project implementation
50,000	New Jersey Community Loan Fund, Trenton, NJ -- for Newark Lighthouse Initiative
50,000	Tri-State Transportation Campaign, New York, NY -- for operating support for work in New Jersey
47,500	St. Columbia Neighborhood Club, Newark, NJ -- operating support
40,000	Association for Children of New Jersey, Newark, NJ -- for Early Learning Initiative
40,000	North Ward Center, Newark, NJ -- for operating support
40,000	Unified Vailsburg Services Organization, Newark, NJ -- for operating support

VICTOR E. AND CAROLINE E. SCHUTTE FOUNDATION

Giving Contact

David P. Ross, Senior Vice President & Trust Officer
Bank of America, N.A.
1200 Main St., 14th Fl.
Kansas City, MO 64105
Phone: (816)979-7481

Description

Founded: 1994
EIN: 431661684
Organization Type: Private Foundation
Giving Locations: KS: Kansas City
Grant Types: General Support.

Financial Summary

Total Giving: $646,500 (2003)
Assets: $14,389,151 (2003)

Gifts Received: $56,721 (1998); $2,461,056 (1995); $9,253,700 (1994). Note: In 1998, contributions were received from the estate of Caroline Schutte.

Typical Recipients

Arts & Humanities: Libraries, Museums/Galleries, Theater
Education: Business Education, Colleges & Universities, Private Education (Precollege), Special Education
Health: Cancer, Children's Health/Hospitals, Clinics/Medical Centers, Health-General, Home-Care Services, Hospitals, Kidney, Single-Disease Health Associations
Religion: Churches, Synagogues/Temples
Social Services: Family Services, Recreation & Athletics, Scouts, Senior Services, Youth Organizations

Application Procedures

Initial Contact: Send a letter of no more than three pages.
Application Requirements: Include appropriate attachments.
Deadlines: None.

Additional Information

Trust(s): Bank of America, NA

Grants Analysis

Disclosure Period: calendar year ending 2003
Total Grants: $646,500
Number of Grants: 19
Average Grant: $27,583*
Highest Grant: $150,000
Lowest Grant: $10,000
Typical Range: $10,000 to $50,000
*Note: Average grant figures excludes highest grant.

Recent Grants

Note: Grants derived from 2001 Form 990.
Library-Related

25,000	Harry S. Truman Library Institute, Independence, MO -- capital campaign

General

250,000	Truman Medical Center, Kansas City, MO -- endowment chair in women's health
150,000	Nelson Atkins Museum of Art, Kansas City, MO -- capital campaign
62,500	St. Luke's Hospital Foundation, Kansas City, MO -- Paul G. Koontz Chair
56,000	Heartland Presbyterian Center, Parkville, MD -- renovations
50,000	Leukemia and Lymphoma Society Mid-America Chapter, Shawnee Mission, KS -- support outreach campaign
30,000	Boy Scouts of America of America Council, Kansas City, MO -- roofing and fencing at Scout Reservation
30,000	Rockhurst High School, Kansas City, MO -- library challenge
15,000	Unity Temple on the Plaza, Kansas City, MO -- Skinner Organ
10,000	ALS Association, Prairie Village, KS -- annual auction
10,000	Avila College, Kansas City, MO -- lighting endowment fund

CHARLES SCHWAB CORP.

Company Headquarters

101 Montgomery St.
San Francisco, CA 94104
Web: http://www.schwab.com

Company Description

Ticker: SCH
Exchange: OTC

Acquired: U.S. Trust Corp. (2000).
Revenue: US$4.705 billion (2004)
Profit: US$286 million (2004)
Employees: 16300 (2003)
Fortune Rank: 411, per FORTUNE Magazine's list of 500 Largest U.S. Corporations (2004).

Nonmonetary Support

Type: Donated Equipment
Volunteer Programs: The company has a formal employee volunteer program and sponsors various volunteer programs during the year throughout the U.S., including Habitat for Humanity and Christmas in April.
Note: Foundation provides nonmonetary support. Application procedure is the same as for printing. In-kind services are for printing only.

Charles Schwab Corp. Foundation

Giving Contact

Elinore Robey, Senior Manager, Community Investor Services
Charles Schwab Corp. Foundation
101 Montgomery St., 28th Floor
MS-SF120KNY-28-353
San Francisco, CA 94104
Phone: 877-408-5438
Fax: (415)636-3262
E-mail: CIS@schwab.com
Web: http://www.aboutschwab.com/sstory/communityservices.html

Description

EIN: 943192615
Organization Type: Corporate Foundation
Giving Locations: CA: San Francisco communities where there are Schwab branch offices.
Grant Types: Capital, Conference/Seminar, Emergency, Employee Matching Gifts, General Support, Multiyear/Continuing Support, Project.
Note: Employee matching gift ratio: 2 to 1 up to $5,000.

Financial Summary

Total Giving: $3,700,000 (fiscal year ending June 31, 2004 approx); $3,700,000 (fiscal 2003 approx); $4,011,636 (fiscal 2002). Note: Contributes through corporate direct giving program and foundation.
Assets: $4,553,969 (fiscal 2002); $4,435,358 (fiscal 2001)
Gifts Received: $4,948,056 (fiscal 2002); $5,148,764 (fiscal 2001); $2,611,365 (fiscal 2000). Note: In 2002, contributions were received from Charles Schwab & Co., Inc.

Typical Recipients

Arts & Humanities: Arts Associations & Councils, Arts Centers, Arts Festivals, Arts Outreach, Ballet, Community Arts, Dance, Ethnic & Folk Arts, Historic Preservation, Libraries, Museums/Galleries, Music, Opera, Performing Arts, Public Broadcasting
Civic & Public Affairs: African American Affairs, Asian American Affairs, Botanical Gardens/Parks, Business/Free Enterprise, Civil Rights, Clubs, Community Foundations, Economic Development, Employment/Job Training, Gay/Lesbian Issues, Civic & Public Affairs-General, Hispanic Affairs, Housing, Law & Justice, Nonprofit Management, Philanthropic Organizations, Professional & Trade Associations, Public Policy, Urban & Community Affairs, Women's Affairs, Zoos/Aquariums
Education: Afterschool/Enrichment Programs, Arts/Humanities Education, Business Education, Colleges & Universities, Economic Education, Education Funds, Education Reform, Elementary Education (Public), Faculty Development, Education-General, Leadership Training, Literacy, Medical Education, Mi-

nority Education, Preschool Education, Private Education (Precollege), Public Education (Precollege), School Volunteerism, Science/Mathematics Education, Secondary Education (Private), Secondary Education (Public), Social Sciences Education, Special Education, Student Aid, Vocational & Technical Education

Environment: Environment-General, Protection, Resource Conservation, Wildlife Protection

Health: AIDS/HIV, Arthritis, Cancer, Children's Health/Hospitals, Clinics/Medical Centers, Diabetes, Emergency/Ambulance Services, Health-General, Health Organizations, Heart, Home-Care Services, Hospices, Kidney, Medical Research, Mental Health, Multiple Sclerosis, Nursing Services, Prenatal Health Issues, Single-Disease Health Associations, Transplant Networks/Donor Banks

International: Health Care/Hospitals, International Environmental Issues, International Organizations, International Relief Efforts

Religion: Religion-General, Jewish Causes, Ministries, Religious Welfare

Science: Science Museums, Scientific Centers & Institutes

Social Services: Animal Protection, At-Risk Youth, Big Brothers/Big Sisters, Child Welfare, Community Service Organizations, Day Care, Domestic Violence, Emergency Relief, Family Planning, Family Services, Food/Clothing Distribution, People with Disabilities, Recreation & Athletics, Senior Services, Shelters/Homelessness, Social Services-General, Substance Abuse, United Funds/United Ways, Volunteer Services, YMCA/YWCA/YMHA/YWHA, Youth Organizations

Application Procedures
Initial Contact: Call or write for guidelines, then submit a formal proposal.
Application Requirements: Include mission statement, program objectives, amount requested and how funds will be used, population served, plan for evaluation, names of any Schwab employee volunteers, and name of nearest Schwab branch. Attachments should include list of board of director; list of foundation and corporate funders, most recent annual report or Form 990, proof of tax-exempt status, current operating and program budgets, and list of board of directors or trustees.
Deadlines: None.
Decision Notification: Applicants will receive a written response within 60 days of receipt.
Notes: Schwab employees personally involved with a nonprofit organization applying for funding are encouraged to attach a letter of endorsement to the organization's grant proposal.

Restrictions
Foundation does not fund: advertising; athletic or sporting activities, teams or students associations; business development activities; cause-related marketing projects; conferences or seminars; fraternal or exclusive membership organizations; fundraising events; individuals; organizations that engage in discriminatory practices; organizations without current nonprofit 501(c)(3) status; political or lobbying organizations; private foundations; publications, films, videos, or television programs; religious or sectarian organizations; sponsorships or promotional events; or group travel. The foundation does not provide capital, challenge, or seed funding and rarely funds institutions of higher learning, hospitals, or single-disease associations (although such organizations may be funded through employee matching gifts).

Additional Information
The Charles Schwab Corporation Foundation was created in December 1993.
Publications: Program Guidelines

Corporate Officials
David Steven Pottruck: president, co-chief executive officer, director B 1948. ED University of Pennsyl-

vania BA (1970); University of Pennsylvania MBA (1972). PRIM CORP EMPL president, co-chief executive officer, director: Charles Schwab & Co., Inc. CORP AFFIL president, chief operating officer: Charles Schwab Corp.; director: Charles Schwab Corp.; director: Preview Travel Inc.; director: Intel Corp.; director: McKesson Corp.; director: Decibel Instruments Inc. NONPR AFFIL trustee: University Pennsylvania.
Charles R. Schwab: chairman, co-chief executive officer, director B Sacramento, CA 1937. ED Stanford University MBA (1959); Stanford University MBA (1961). PRIM CORP EMPL chairman, co-chief executive officer, director: Charles Schwab & Co., Inc. CORP AFFIL director: Siebel Systems, Inc.; director: TransAmerica Corp.; director: The Gap Inc.; chairman: Schwab Holding Inc.

Foundation Officials
Charles R. Schwab: chairman (see above)

Grants Analysis
Disclosure Period: fiscal year ending June 31, 2002
Total Grants: $4,011,636*
Number of Grants: 2,482
Average Grant: $1,616
Highest Grant: $146,649
Lowest Grant: $13
Typical Range: $1,000 to $5,000
***Note:** Giving includes United Way; matching gifts.

Recent Grants
Note: Grants derived from 2003 Form 990.
General
191,250	Boys and Girls Clubs of America, Atlanta, GA
125,000	Stanford University, Stanford, CA
20,000	Oakland Zoo, Oakland, CA
20,000	Youth Empowering Systems, Sepastopol, CA
15,000	Boys and Girls Clubs of America, Atlanta, GA
13,672	American Red Cross, Washington, DC
10,109	AIDS Walk of San Francisco, San Francisco, CA
10,000	International Medical Corps, Los Angeles, CA
10,000	San Francisco Opera Association, San Francisco, CA
9,267	American Red Cross, Washington, DC

SCHWAB-ROSENHOUSE MEMORIAL FOUNDATION

Giving Contact
Stanley Blaine
PO Box 4004
Concord, CA 94524
Phone: (609)683-2364

Description
Founded: 1998
EIN: 686136241
Organization Type: Private Foundation
Giving Locations: CA: Sacramento including surrounding counties
Grant Types: Scholarship.

Financial Summary
Total Giving: $522,141 (2003); $871,500 (2001)
Giving Analysis: Giving for 2003 includes: foundation scholarships ($509,641); 2001: foundation scholarships ($859,000)
Assets: $8,459,608 (2003); $10,196,929 (2001)
Gifts Received: $750,000 (1998). Note: In 1998, contributions were received from Rosenhouse Family Trust.

Typical Recipients
Arts & Humanities: Libraries
Education: Colleges & Universities, Student Aid

Application Procedures
Initial Contact: Request application form.
Deadlines: February 1.

Foundation Officials
Sandra Felderstein: distribution trustee
Candice Fields: Distribution trustee
Iving Herman, PhD: Distribution trustee
Dr. Marvin Kamras: distribution trustee
John Lewis: Distribution trustee
Charles Nadler, PhD: Distribution trustee
Linda Van Rees: financial trustee
Joel Zimmerman: distribution trustee

Grants Analysis
Disclosure Period: calendar year ending 2001
Total Grants: $12,500*
Number of Grants: 1
***Note:** Giving excludes scholarships.

Recent Grants
Note: Grants derived from 2003 Form 990.
General
12,500	Sacramento Public Library Foundation, Sacramento, CA -- for scholarship resource center

ARNOLD A. SCHWARTZ FOUNDATION

Giving Contact
Steven A. Kunzman, Vice President
15 Mountain Boulevard
Warren, NJ 07059-5611
Phone: (908)757-7800

Description
Founded: 1953
EIN: 226034152
Organization Type: Private Foundation
Giving Locations: NJ: central New Jersey
Grant Types: General Support.

Donor Information
Founder: the late Arnold A. Schwartz

Financial Summary
Total Giving: $219,500 (fiscal year ending November 30, 2003); $421,200 (fiscal 2001)
Assets: $4,062,193 (fiscal 2003); $5,831,457 (fiscal 2001)

Typical Recipients
Arts & Humanities: History & Archaeology, Libraries
Civic & Public Affairs: Clubs, Employment/Job Training, Civic & Public Affairs-General, Housing
Education: Arts/Humanities Education, Colleges & Universities, Gifted & Talented Programs, Private Education (Precollege), Public Education (Precollege), Special Education, Student Aid
Environment: Wildlife Protection
Health: Alzheimer's Disease, Cancer, Children's Health/Hospitals, Clinics/Medical Centers, Emergency/Ambulance Services, Eyes/Blindness, Health Funds, Health Organizations, Heart, Hospitals, Mental Health, Multiple Sclerosis, Outpatient Health Care, Prenatal Health Issues, Public Health, Single-Disease Health Associations
Religion: Jewish Causes, Religious Organizations, Religious Welfare
Social Services: At-Risk Youth, Camps, Child Welfare, Community Service Organizations, Counseling, Day Care, Family Services, Food/Clothing Distribu-

tion, People with Disabilities, Recreation & Athletics, Senior Services, Shelters/Homelessness, Substance Abuse, United Funds/United Ways, Volunteer Services, YMCA/YWCA/YMHA/YWHA, Youth Organizations

Application Procedures
Initial Contact: Send a brief letter of inquiry. stating the purpose of the contribution.
Deadlines: September 30.

Restrictions
Does not support individuals or provide funds for endowments.

Foundation Officials
Victor DiLeo: trustee
Louis Harding: secretary
Edward D. Kunzman: president
Steven Kunzman: vice president
David Lackland: trustee
Robert Shapiro: trustee B Plainfield, NJ 1942. ED University of California, Los Angeles BS (1965); Loyola University JD (1968). NONPR AFFIL member: National Association Criminal Defense Lawyers; member: Trial Lawyers Public Justice; member: California Attys Criminal Justice; member: Century City Bar Association.
Kenneth W. Turnbull: treasurer CORP AFFIL president, chief executive officer: United National Bank.

Grants Analysis
Disclosure Period: fiscal year ending November 30, 2003
Total Grants: $219,500
Number of Grants: 67
Average Grant: $3,276
Highest Grant: $15,000
Lowest Grant: $500
Typical Range: $1,000 to $5,000

Recent Grants
Note: Grants derived from fiscal 2003 Form 990.
Library-Related
10,000	Arnold Schwartz Memorial Library, Dunellen, NJ

General
15,000	Muhlenberg Foundation, Plainfield, NJ
10,000	Deborah Hospital Foundation, Browns Mills, NJ
10,000	McAuley School, Watchung, NJ
10,000	Wardlaw Hartridge School, Edison, NJ
7,500	FISH Hospitality Program, Dunellen, NJ
7,500	Fish Inc.
7,500	John F. Kennedy Medical Foundation, Edison, NJ
5,000	YMCA, Plainfield, NJ
5,000	YWCA, Plainfield, NJ

ARNOLD AND MARIE SCHWARTZ FUND FOR EDUCATION AND HEALTH RESEARCH

Giving Contact
Marie D. Schwartz, President
465 Park Ave.
New York, NY 10022

Description
Founded: 1971
EIN: 237115019
Organization Type: Private Foundation
Giving Locations: NY: New York
Grant Types: General Support.

Donor Information
Founder: Arnold Schwartz Charitable Trust.

Financial Summary
Total Giving: $245,220 (fiscal year ending March 31, 2004); $478,492 (fiscal 2002); $719,380 (fiscal 2001)
Assets: $5,781,297 (fiscal 2004); $5,743,214 (fiscal 2002); $2,387,442 (fiscal 2001)

Typical Recipients
Arts & Humanities: Arts Associations & Councils, Arts Festivals, Arts Institutes, Ballet, Dance, Ethnic & Folk Arts, Historic Preservation, History & Archaeology, Libraries, Museums/Galleries, Music, Opera, Performing Arts, Public Broadcasting
Civic & Public Affairs: Botanical Gardens/Parks, Clubs, Civic & Public Affairs-General, Housing, Law & Justice, Minority Business, Parades/Festivals, Professional & Trade Associations, Public Policy, Safety, Women's Affairs, Zoos/Aquariums
Education: Arts/Humanities Education, Colleges & Universities, Education Reform, Health & Physical Education, Medical Education
Environment: Air/Water Quality, Environment-General, Wildlife Protection
Health: Cancer, Emergency/Ambulance Services, Health Organizations, Hospitals, Hospitals (University Affiliated), Medical Research, Single-Disease Health Associations
International: Foreign Educational Institutions, Human Rights, Missionary/Religious Activities
Religion: Bible Study/Translation, Churches, Jewish Causes, Ministries, Religious Organizations, Religious Welfare, Synagogues/Temples
Social Services: Child Welfare, Community Service Organizations, Crime Prevention, Family Services, Recreation & Athletics, Youth Organizations

Application Procedures
Initial Contact: Send a brief letter of inquiry describing program or project.
Deadlines: None.

Foundation Officials
Sylvia Kassel: director
Ruth Kerstein: secretary, director
Nellie Jane McDonald: director
Marie D. Schwartz: trustee

Grants Analysis
Disclosure Period: fiscal year ending March 31, 2004
Total Grants: $245,220
Number of Grants: 31
Average Grant: $6,507*
Highest Grant: $50,000
Lowest Grant: $70
Typical Range: $1,000 to $10,000
*Note: Average grant figure excludes highest grant.

Recent Grants
Note: Grants derived from 2004 Form 990.
General
50,000	Parkinson's Disease Foundation, New York, NY
35,050	Police Athletic League, New York, NY
26,000	New York Botanical Gardens, Bronx, NY
25,500	Department of State Diplomatic Reception Room, Washington, DC
17,500	Church of the Transfiguration, New York, NY
10,000	Arnold and Marie Schwartz College of Pharmacy, Brooklyn, NY
10,000	Friends of High Line, New York, NY
10,000	International Faresh of Friendship
10,000	National Symphony Orchestra, Washington, DC
10,000	St. Andrew's Episcopal Church, Albany, NY

SCOTT FETZER CO.

Company Headquarters
865 Bassett Rd.
Westlake, OH 44145
Web: http://www.berkshirehathaway.com

Company Description
Employees: 14,000
SIC(s): 3400 Fabricated Metal Products, 3600 Electronic & Other Electrical Equipment.
Parent Company: Berkshire Hathaway Inc., 1440 Kiewit Plaza, Omaha, NE, United States

Operating Locations
Scott Fetzer Co. (OH--Westlake)

Scott & Fetzer Foundation

Giving Contact
Edie DeSantis, Executive Secretary
28800 Clemens Rd.
Westlake, OH 44145
Phone: (440)892-3000

Description
Founded: 1967
EIN: 346596076
Organization Type: Corporate Foundation
Giving Locations: OH
Grant Types: General Support.

Donor Information
Founder: the Scott Fetzer Co.

Financial Summary
Total Giving: $186,289 (2003); $141,807 (2002); $138,050 (2001)
Assets: $392,313 (2003); $388,190 (2002); $398,137 (2001)
Gifts Received: $186,595 (2003); $127,094 (2002); $140,915 (2001). Note: Contributions are received from the Scott Fetzer Co.

Typical Recipients
Arts & Humanities: Arts Associations & Councils, Arts Centers, Ballet, Community Arts, History & Archaeology, Libraries, Music, Opera, Performing Arts, Public Broadcasting, Theater
Civic & Public Affairs: Business/Free Enterprise, Clubs, First Amendment Issues, Civic & Public Affairs-General, Legal Aid, Municipalities/Towns, Parades/Festivals, Safety, Urban & Community Affairs, Zoos/Aquariums
Education: Afterschool/Enrichment Programs, Business Education, Colleges & Universities, Community & Junior Colleges, Economic Education, Education Associations, Education Funds, Elementary Education (Private), Elementary Education (Public), Education-General, Literacy, Private Education (Precollege), Public Education (Precollege), Secondary Education (Private), Secondary Education (Public), Student Aid
Environment: Watershed
Health: Arthritis, Cancer, Children's Health/Hospitals, Health Funds, Health Organizations, Heart, Hospices, Hospitals, Medical Research, Multiple Sclerosis, Prenatal Health Issues, Public Health, Single-Disease Health Associations
International: Foreign Arts Organizations, Foreign Educational Institutions, International Organizations
Religion: Religious Welfare, Social/Policy Issues
Science: Science Exhibits & Fairs, Science Museums
Social Services: Camps, Child Welfare, Community Service Organizations, Food/Clothing Distribution, Homes, People with Disabilities, Recreation & Athlet-

ics, Senior Services, Special Olympics, United Funds/United Ways, Volunteer Services, Youth Organizations

Application Procedures

Initial Contact: The foundation requests applications be made in writing. Federal identification number is required.
Deadlines: None.

Restrictions

Grants are not made to individuals.

Corporate Officials

Ralph Edward Schey: chairman, chief executive officer, director B Cleveland, OH 1924. ED Ohio University (1948); Harvard University BusAdmin (1950). PRIM CORP EMPL chairman, chief executive officer, director: Scott Fetzer Co. CORP AFFIL director: Hauserman Co.
Kenneth J. Semelsberger: president, chief executive officer, chief operating officer, director B Marsteller, PA 1936. ED Ohio State University BBA (1970); Cleveland State University MBA (1972). PRIM CORP EMPL president, chief executive officer, chief operating officer, director: Scott Fetzer Co. CORP AFFIL production manager: Holan Corp.; president: Stahl Division Scott & Fetzer Co.; Sales & Contracts manager: Barth Cleve McNeil Corp.
William W. T. Stephans: chief financial officer PRIM CORP EMPL chief financial officer: Scott Fetzer Co.

Foundation Officials

John W. Gretta: assistant treasurer
Timothy S. Guster: vice president, secretary
Patricia M. Scanlon: secretary
Ralph Edward Schey: chairman (see above)
Kenneth J. Semelsberger: president (see above)
William W. T. Stephans: vice president, treasurer (see above)

Grants Analysis

Disclosure Period: calendar year ending 2003
Total Grants: $130,339*
Number of Grants: 54
Average Grant: $1,515*
Highest Grant: $50,000
Lowest Grant: $25
Typical Range: $500 to $2,500
***Note:** Giving excludes United Way. Average grant figure excludes highest grant.

Recent Grants

Note: Grants derived from 2003 Form 990.

Library-Related
10,000	American Library Association, Chicago, IL
1,500	Catholic Library Association

General
50,000	Cleveland Food Bank, Cleveland, OH
20,000	Direct Selling Education Foundation, Washington, DC
12,500	United Way, Cleveland, OH
12,500	United Way, Cleveland, OH
12,500	United Way, Cleveland, OH
11,250	United Way, Cleveland, OH
5,000	Cleveland Opera, Cleveland, OH
5,000	Cleveland State University Foundation, Cleveland, OH
5,000	Komen Race for the Cure, Cleveland, OH
5,000	Southwest Community Health Foundation, Middleburg Heights, OH

VIRGINIA STEELE SCOTT FOUNDATION

Giving Contact

Maria O. Grant, President & Director
1151 Oxford Rd.
San Marino, CA 91108
Phone: (626)405-2152

Description

Founded: 1974
EIN: 237365076
Organization Type: Private Foundation
Giving Locations: CA: Pasadena/Los Angeles
Grant Types: General Support.

Donor Information

Founder: the late Virginia Steele Scott, Grace C. Scott

Financial Summary

Total Giving: $1,249,000 (fiscal year ending June 30, 2004); $268,000 (fiscal 2002); $275,000 (fiscal 2001)
Assets: $10,147,541 (fiscal 2004); $9,741,773 (fiscal 2002); $10,053,308 (fiscal 2001)
Gifts Received: In 1991, contributions were received from the Grace C. Scott Trust.

Typical Recipients

Arts & Humanities: Arts Associations & Councils, Arts Centers, Arts Institutes, Community Arts, Arts & Humanities-General, Libraries, Museums/Galleries, Music, Performing Arts, Theater
Civic & Public Affairs: Botanical Gardens/Parks
Education: Arts/Humanities Education
International: Foreign Arts Organizations
Social Services: Community Centers

Application Procedures

Initial Contact: Send a one-page letter of inquiry.
Application Requirements: Include five copies of the following: one-page statement of organization's mission and specific need for financial support; one-page financial summary of the most recent fiscal year; and most recent IRS letter proving non-profit status.
Deadlines: September 30.

Restrictions

Grants are limited to visual and performing arts in Pasadena and Los Angeles.

Foundation Officials

Margaret R. Galbraith: director
Maria O. Grant: president, director
Paul Johnson Karlstrom: secretary, director B Seattle, WA 1941. ED Stanford University BA (1964); University of California, Los Angeles MA (1969); University of California, Los Angeles PhD (1973). NONPR AFFIL member adv board: Jacob Lawrence Catalogue Raisonni Project; director: Southwest Art History Council; West coast reg director: Huntington Library; member editorial board: California Historical Society; member adv board: Humanities West; director: Bay Area Video Coalition.
Jack Pettker: director
Henry J. Tanner: vice president, treasurer, director
Robert Rodgers Wark: president emeritus B Edmonton, AB Canada 1924. ED University of Alberta BA (1944); University of Alberta MA (1946); Harvard University MA (1949); Harvard University PhD (1952). NONPR AFFIL member: College Art Association America.

Grants Analysis

Disclosure Period: fiscal year ending June 30, 2004
Total Grants: $1,249,000
Number of Grants: 14
Average Grant: $6,167*

Highest Grant: $1,000,000
Lowest Grant: $2,500
Typical Range: $2,500 to $10,000
***Note:** Average grant figure excludes two highest grants ($1,175,000).

Recent Grants

Note: Grants derived from fiscal 2004 Form 990.
Library-Related
1,000,000	Huntington Library, San Marino, CA
175,000	Huntington Library, San Marino, CA
27,500	Huntington Library, San Marino, CA

General
5,000	Armory Center for Arts, Pasadena, CA
5,000	Art Center College of Design, Pasadena, CA
5,000	Pacific Asia Museum, Pasadena, CA
5,000	Pasadena Conservatory of Music, Pasadena, CA
5,000	Pasadena Symphony, Pasadena, CA
5,000	Southwest Chamber Music, Pasadena, CA
4,000	Pasadena Playhouse, Pasadena, CA

WILLIAM E. SCOTT FOUNDATION

Giving Contact

Robert W. Decker, President, Treasurer & Director
801 Cherry Street, Suite 2000
Ft. Worth, TX 76102-3708
Phone: (817)336-2400

Description

Founded: 1960
EIN: 756024661
Organization Type: Private Foundation
Giving Locations: LA; NM; OK; TX: emphasis on the Fort Worth-Tarrant County area
Grant Types: Capital, General Support, Project.

Donor Information

Founder: the late William E. Scott

Financial Summary

Total Giving: $561,550 (fiscal year ending May 31, 2004); $394,751 (fiscal 2002); $857,200 (fiscal 2001)
Giving Analysis: Giving for fiscal 2001 includes: foundation grants to United Way ($25,000)
Assets: $18,354,165 (fiscal 2004); $17,053,058 (fiscal 2002); $18,563,962 (fiscal 2001)

Typical Recipients

Arts & Humanities: Arts Associations & Councils, Arts Centers, Arts Festivals, Arts Funds, Ballet, Community Arts, Dance, Historic Preservation, History & Archaeology, Libraries, Museums/Galleries, Music, Opera, Performing Arts, Public Broadcasting, Theater
Civic & Public Affairs: Clubs, Community Foundations, Civic & Public Affairs-General, Housing, Nonprofit Management, Professional & Trade Associations, Safety, Urban & Community Affairs, Women's Affairs, Zoos/Aquariums
Education: Afterschool/Enrichment Programs, Arts/Humanities Education, Colleges & Universities, Community & Junior Colleges, Education Funds, Education Reform, Education-General, Medical Education, Private Education (Precollege), Public Education (Precollege), Special Education
Health: AIDS/HIV, Children's Health/Hospitals, Clinics/Medical Centers, Emergency/Ambulance Services, Health Organizations, Medical Research, Prenatal Health Issues, Research/Studies Institutes, Respiratory, Single-Disease Health Associations
International: Foreign Arts Organizations, Missionary/Religious Activities

Religion: Churches, Ministries, Religious Welfare, Social/Policy Issues
Science: Science Museums
Social Services: Big Brothers/Big Sisters, Child Welfare, Community Centers, Community Service Organizations, Crime Prevention, Delinquency & Criminal Rehabilitation, Domestic Violence, Family Planning, Homes, People with Disabilities, Recreation & Athletics, Scouts, Substance Abuse, United Funds/United Ways, Volunteer Services, YMCA/YWCA/YMHA/YWHA, Youth Organizations

Application Procedures

Initial Contact: The foundation requests applications be made in writing.
Deadlines: None.

Additional Information

Publications: Application Guidelines

Foundation Officials

Robert W. Decker: president, treasurer, director
Raymond B. Kelly, III: vice president, secretary, director

Grants Analysis

Disclosure Period: fiscal year ending May 31, 2004
Total Grants: $561,550
Number of Grants: 41
Average Grant: $9,271*
Highest Grant: $100,000
Lowest Grant: $50
Typical Range: $1,000 to $15,000
*Note: Average grant figure excludes two highest grants ($200,000).

Recent Grants

Note: Grants derived from 2004 Form 990.
Library-Related

15,000	Fort Worth Public Library Foundation, Ft. Worth, TX

General

100,000	Cook Children's Medical Center, Ft. Worth, TX
100,000	Michigan Press Association Foundation, Ft. Worth, TX
25,000	Child Study Center, Ft. Worth, TX
25,000	College for All Texans Foundation, Austin, TX
25,000	Dr. May Owen Memorial Foundation, Ft. Worth, TX
25,000	James and Dorothy Doss Heritage and Culture Center, Ft. Worth, TX
25,000	Tarrant County Academy of Medicine, Ft. Worth, TX
20,000	Fort Worth Opera, Ft. Worth, TX
20,000	Fort Worth Symphony, Ft. Worth, TX

WILLIAM H., JOHN G., AND EMMA SCOTT FOUNDATION

Giving Contact

Hugh K. Leary, Executive Director & Treasurer
c/o Davenport & Co. LLC
901 E. Cary St.
Richmond, VA 23285
Phone: (804)780-2000

Description

Founded: 1956
EIN: 540648772
Organization Type: Private Foundation
Giving Locations: VA: Commonwealth
Grant Types: Capital, General Support, Scholarship.

Donor Information

Founder: the late John G. Scott, Emma Scott Taylor

Financial Summary

Total Giving: $460,000 (fiscal year ending September 30, 2004); $435,000 (fiscal 2001)
Giving Analysis: Giving for fiscal 2001 includes: foundation grants to United Way ($23,000)
Assets: $10,445,118 (fiscal 2004); $10,554,105 (fiscal 2001)

Typical Recipients

Arts & Humanities: Arts Associations & Councils, Arts Centers, Ballet, History & Archaeology, Libraries, Literary Arts, Museums/Galleries, Music, Public Broadcasting
Civic & Public Affairs: Botanical Gardens/Parks, Clubs, Civic & Public Affairs-General, Housing, Rural Affairs, Urban & Community Affairs
Education: Colleges & Universities, Education Funds, Education-General, Private Education (Precollege), Public Education (Precollege), Religious Education, Science/Mathematics Education, Student Aid
Environment: Environment-General
Health: Children's Health/Hospitals, Clinics/Medical Centers, Emergency/Ambulance Services
Religion: Churches, Dioceses, Ministries, Religious Organizations, Religious Welfare, Seminaries
Science: Science Museums
Social Services: At-Risk Youth, Child Abuse, Child Welfare, Community Service Organizations, Day Care, Food/Clothing Distribution, Homes, People with Disabilities, Scouts, Senior Services, Shelters/Homelessness, YMCA/YWCA/YMHA/YWHA, Youth Organizations

Application Procedures

Initial Contact: Send a letter stating financial need.
Deadlines: None.

Foundation Officials

William Hill Brown, III: trustee
Susanne B. Crump: trustee
Charles M. Guthridge: trustee
Hugh K. Leary: executive director, treasurer
Edwin Palmer Munson: secretary B Richmond, VA 1935. ED University of Virginia (1957); University of Richmond (1980). PRIM CORP EMPL vice president, legal counsel: Computer Co.
Robert Fillmore Norfleet, Jr.: president B Richmond, VA 1940. ED Washington & Lee University BA (1962); Rutgers University (1972). PRIM CORP EMPL executive vice president, senior credit officer: Crestar Bank Corp.
C. Cotesworth Pinckney: vice president
E. Bryson Powell: trustee

Grants Analysis

Disclosure Period: fiscal year ending September 30, 2004
Total Grants: $460,000
Number of Grants: 20
Average Grant: $20,000*
Highest Grant: $50,000
Lowest Grant: $10,000
Typical Range: $10,000 to $40,000
*Note: Average grant figure excludes two highest grants ($100,000).

Recent Grants

Note: Grants derived from fiscal 2004 Form 990.
General

50,000	St. Catherine's School, Richmond, VA
50,000	St. Christopher's School, Richmond, VA
33,500	Commonwealth Catholic Charities, Richmond, VA
25,000	Christchurch School, Christchurch, VA -- fund for building renovation
25,000	Goodwill Industries, Richmond, VA -- fund for building renovation
25,000	Healing Place, Richmond, VA
25,000	Memorial Child Guidance Clinic, Richmond, VA -- fund for building renovation
25,000	New Life for Youth, Beaverdam, VA -- fund to upgrade water system
25,000	St. John's Church Foundation, Richmond, VA -- ADA accessibility
25,000	William Byrd Community House, Richmond, VA -- fund to purchase vehicle

SCOULAR CO.

Company Headquarters

2027 Dodge St.
Omaha, NE 68102

Company Description

Employees: 240
SIC(s): 4200 Trucking & Warehousing, 4221 Farm Product Warehousing & Storage, 5100 Wholesale Trade--Nondurable Goods.

Operating Locations

Scoular Co. (AZ; CA; CO; FL; IL; KS; MN; MO; NE--Omaha; NY; OH; SC)

Scoular Foundation

Giving Contact

Marshall E. Faith, Chairman
2027 Dodge St., Suite 300
Omaha, NE 68102
Phone: (402)342-3500
Fax: (402)342-4493

Description

EIN: 363323189
Organization Type: Corporate Foundation
Giving Locations: headquarters and operating communities.
Grant Types: General Support.

Financial Summary

Total Giving: $203,059 (2003)
Giving Analysis: Giving for 2003 includes: foundation grants to United Way ($4,300)
Assets: $5,615 (2003)
Gifts Received: $208,125 (2003); $110,300 (2000); $99,050 (1999). Note: Contributions were received from The Scoular Co.

Typical Recipients

Arts & Humanities: Arts Associations & Councils, Arts Funds, Arts Outreach, Arts & Humanities-General, History & Archaeology, Libraries, Museums/Galleries, Music, Opera, Performing Arts, Theater
Civic & Public Affairs: Chambers of Commerce, Employment/Job Training, Civic & Public Affairs-General, Housing, Rural Affairs, Urban & Community Affairs, Zoos/Aquariums
Education: Business Education, Colleges & Universities, Education Funds, Faculty Development, Education-General, Minority Education, Student Aid
Health: Alzheimer's Disease, Cancer, Children's Health/Hospitals, Diabetes, Emergency/Ambulance Services, Heart, Hospices, Hospitals, Medical Rehabilitation, Respiratory
Religion: Churches, Ministries, Missionary Activities (Domestic), Religious Organizations, Religious Welfare, Social/Policy Issues
Social Services: At-Risk Youth, Big Brothers/Big Sisters, Camps, Child Welfare, Community Service Organizations, Day Care, Family Services, Food/Clothing Distribution, Homes, People with Disabilities, Recreation & Athletics, Scouts, Social Services-General, United Funds/United Ways, Veterans, YMCA/YWCA/YMHA/YWHA, Youth Organizations

Application Procedures

Initial Contact: Submit a brief letter of inquiry.
Application Requirements: Include a description of organization, amount requested, purpose of funds sought, and proof of tax-exempt status.
Deadlines: None.

Restrictions

Does not support individuals, political or lobbying groups, or organizations outside operating areas.

Corporate Officials

Marshall E. Faith: chairman, director PRIM CORP EMPL chairman, director: Scoular Co.
Duane A. Fischer: president, chief executive officer, director PRIM CORP EMPL president, chief executive officer, director: Scoular Co.
Timothy J. Regan: chief financial officer B Atchison, KS 1956. ED Kansas State University BS (1978). PRIM CORP EMPL chief financial officer: Scoular Co. NONPR AFFIL member: Elks; member: Knights of Columbus; director: Catholic Charities.

Foundation Officials

Marshall E. Faith: trustee (see above)

Grants Analysis

Disclosure Period: calendar year ending 2003
Total Grants: $198,769*
Number of Grants: 69
Average Grant: $2,881
Highest Grant: $25,000
Lowest Grant: $25
Typical Range: $1,000 to $5,000
*Note: Giving excludes United Way.

Recent Grants

Note: Grants derived from 2003 Form 990.
General

25,000	Steifel Theater, Salina, KS
20,000	Bethphage Foundation, Omaha, NE
20,000	Heritage Joslyn Foundation, Omaha, NE
10,000	Creighton University, Omaha, NE
10,000	Quality Living Inc., Omaha, NE
8,333	Knights of Aksarben Foundation, Omaha, NE
7,100	Salvation Army, Omaha, NE
5,750	University of Nebraska Foundation, Lincoln, NE
5,000	Children's Scholarship Fund of Omaha, Omaha, NE
5,000	First Presbyterian Church, Salina, KS

E.W. Scripps Co.

Company Headquarters

Cincinnati, OH
Web: http://www.scripps.com

Company Description

Founded: 1878
Ticker: SSP
Exchange: NYSE
Revenue: US$1.535 billion (2002)
Employees: 7800 (2003)
SIC(s): 2711 Newspapers.

Operating Locations

E.W. Scripps Co. (AL--Birmingham; AZ--Phoenix; CA--Los Angeles, Redding, San Luis Obispo, South Gate, Thousand Oaks, Tulare, Watsonville; CO--Denver, Longmont; DC; FL--Destin, Jupiter, Naples, Palm Beach, Stuart, Tampa; GA--Rome; IN--Evansville; MD--Baltimore; MI--Detroit; MO--Kansas City; NM--Albuquerque; OH--Cincinnati, Cleveland; OK--Tulsa; SC; TN--Knoxville, Memphis; TX--El Paso; VA; WV)

Nonmonetary Support

Type: Donated Equipment; Donated Products; In-kind Services; Loaned Employees; Loaned Executives
Note: NOT NOT Scripps newspapers and broadcast stations across the United States determine their level of involvement in the community. Contact local Scripps executive.

Scripps Howard Foundation

Giving Contact

Judith G. Clabes, President & CEO
Scripps Howard Foundation
312 Walnut Street
PO Box 5380
Cincinnati, OH 45201-5380
Phone: (513)977-3000
Fax: (513)977-3800
E-mail: cottingham@scripps.com
Web: http://www.scripps.com/foundation

Alternate Contact

Judith G. Clabes, President & Chief Executive Officer
Scripps Howard Foundation
Phone: (513)977-3048
E-mail: clabes@scripps.com
Note: Receives Greater Cincinnati Fund, Community Fund, and Journalism Fund proposals.

Description

EIN: 316025114
Organization Type: Corporate Foundation
Giving Locations: OH: operating locations, Cincinnati metropolitan area nationally, with emphasis on operating locations; particularly Greater Cincinnati, OH.
Grant Types: Award, Capital, Conference/Seminar, Employee Matching Gifts, Endowment, Fellowship, General Support, Operating Expenses, Project, Research, Scholarship, Seed Money.
Note: Scholarships are awarded to students preparing for careers in print and electronic journalism. Matches gifts to educational institutions.

Financial Summary

Total Giving: $5,248,980 (2003); $9,246,690 (2002); $6,817,871 (2001)
Giving Analysis: Giving for 2001 includes: foundation matching gifts ($165,000); foundation scholarships ($984,342); foundation ($5,565,185)
Assets: $71,112,934 (2003); $63,673,805 (2002); $79,188,870 (2001)
Gifts Received: $2,072,075 (2003); $3,384,752 (2002); $5,353,518 (2001). Note: In 2003, contributions were received from Lamb & Barnosky, LLP ($61,230), Beaton Family Trust ($39,698), E.W. Scripps Co. ($102,727), Esward W. Scripps, Jr. ($90,000), Margaret Scripps ($5,000), Robert P. Scripps ($1,375,000), William H. Scripps ($50,000), Jack R. Howard Trust ($36,227), Cindy S. Leising ($271,675), Kenneth W. Lowe ($5,000), and miscellaneous contributions less than $5,000 per person ($35,518). In 2002, contributions were received from E.W. Scripps Co. ($102,393), Edward W. Scripps ($90,000), Robert P. Scripps ($1,333,400), Jack R. Howard Trust ($1,653,832), Cindy S. Leising ($125,000), Kenneth W. Lowe ($5,000), Ruth A. May ($25,000), and miscellaneous contributions less than $5,000 per person ($50,127). In 2001, contributions were received from E.W. Scripps Co. ($96,619); Edward W. Scripps, Jr. ($85,000); Robert P. Scripps ($1,508,400); William H. Scripps ($50,000); Mary Kay Blake ($5,000); Annie Lou Hanna ($19,204); Jack R. Howard Trust ($3,355,711); Cindy S. Leising ($125,000); Lawrence A. Leser ($13,240); Ruth A. May ($25,000); and miscellaneous contributions of less than $5,000 per person ($70,345).

Typical Recipients

Arts & Humanities: Arts Centers, Arts Festivals, Arts Funds, Arts Institutes, Ballet, Community Arts, Arts & Humanities-General, History & Archaeology, Libraries, Literary Arts, Museums/Galleries, Music, Performing Arts, Public Broadcasting, Theater
Civic & Public Affairs: African American Affairs, Botanical Gardens/Parks, Business/Free Enterprise, Chambers of Commerce, Clubs, Community Foundations, Economic Development, Employment/Job Training, First Amendment Issues, Civic & Public Affairs-General, Housing, Law & Justice, Minority Business, Municipalities/Towns, Nonprofit Management, Professional & Trade Associations, Public Policy, Urban & Community Affairs, Women's Affairs, Zoos/Aquariums
Education: Arts/Humanities Education, Business Education, Colleges & Universities, Economic Education, Education Funds, Elementary Education (Public), Engineering/Technological Education, Environmental Education, Faculty Development, Journalism/Media Education, Legal Education, Literacy, Minority Education, Preschool Education, Private Education (Precollege), Religious Education, Science/Mathematics Education, Secondary Education (Public), Special Education, Student Aid, Vocational & Technical Education
Environment: Environment-General
Health: Children's Health/Hospitals, Emergency/Ambulance Services, Geriatric Health, Health Organizations, Prenatal Health Issues, Preventive Medicine/Wellness Organizations
International: Foreign Arts Organizations, International-General, Human Rights, International Affairs, International Relations
Religion: Dioceses, Religion-General, Religious Welfare
Science: Science Museums
Social Services: Big Brothers/Big Sisters, Child Welfare, Community Centers, Community Service Organizations, Food/Clothing Distribution, People with Disabilities, Recreation & Athletics, Scouts, Substance Abuse, United Funds/United Ways, YMCA/YWCA/YMHA/YWHA, Youth Organizations

Application Procedures

Initial Contact: Send a full written proposal.
Application Requirements: For Greater Cincinnati Fund or Community Fund requests, include a description of organization, recently audited financial statement, a description of the program for which support is requested including rationale, a detailed projected budget, schedule of implementation, methods of evaluating and reporting results, and qualification of program manager; description of other sources of funding; a copy of the IRC Section 501(c)(3) determination letter; recent financial statement; and names and affiliations of members of the organization's Board of Directors or other governing body.

For Journalism Fund requests, submit an appropriate request in writing.
Deadlines: None.
Review Process: Decisions are based on written proposals; personal interviews are discouraged.
Evaluative Criteria: For scholarships: good scholastic standing, interest in journalism and evidence of work in this field, letters of recommendation from faculty or employer, financial need, willingness of student to pay part of educational expenses, U.S. citizenship. For Greater Cincinnati Fund and Community Fund grants: programs which impact communities where company operates, are measurable with stated goals and objectives, demonstrate effectiveness and innovation, can serve as models, and can be eventually self-supporting.
Decision Notification: Proposals will be reviewed and applicants notified within 90 days after receipt of all required information.

Restrictions

Contributions for capital needs, including renovation, equipment and construction, are not encouraged except in special circumstances; specific projects and programs are preferred over general operating funds. In general, only one contribution per year will be made to any single organization, including support for fund-raising events. Multi-year contributions are discouraged. The foundation normally does not provide support to organizations that receive United Way or Fine Arts or other general campaign funds that are already supported by the foundation.

The foundation does not make contributions to individuals; religious organizations unless they are engaged in a significant program benefiting the entire community; political causes or candidates; anti-business organizations; courtesy advertising; organizations that discriminate on the basis of race, creed, religion, gender or national origin; private foundations; organizations not qualifying as IRS Section 501(c)(3) organizations; or veterans', fraternal, or labor groups. Fund-raising events such as walks, runs, golf outings, or neighborhood-special events, except for those in which an employee is personally participating. The foundation does not support disease-related events or events strictly related to research, nor does it purchase tables for public or private K-12 schools, school districts, or their foundations.

Additional Information

Capital requests are not encouraged; specific programs or projects are favored over operating support. The Scripps Howard Foundation was incorporated in 1962, as a charitable nonprofit organization.
Publications: Scripps Howard Foundation Progress Report; Guidelines for Scholarships; Special Journalism Grants and Awards

Corporate Officials

William Robert Burleigh: chairman, chief executive officer, director B Evansville, IN 1935. ED Marquette University BA (1957). PRIM CORP EMPL chairman: E.W. Scripps Co. CORP AFFIL director: Ohio National Financial Services; director: Xtek Inc.; director: Evansville Courier Co. Inc.

Colleen Christner Conant: branch manager B Oklahoma City, OK 1947. ED Oklahoma City University MusB (1970). PRIM CORP EMPL branch manager: EW Scripps Co. CORP AFFIL chief executive officer: Boulder Publishing Inc.

Alan M. Horton: senior vice president newspapers ED Yale University (1965). PRIM CORP EMPL senior vice president newspapers: E.W. Scripps Co.

Kenneth W. Lowe: president, chief executive officer, director B April 07, 1950. PRIM CORP EMPL president, chief executive officer, director: E.W. Scripps Co.

J. Robert Routt: vice president, controller B 1954. ED University of Kentucky BS. PRIM CORP EMPL vice president, controller: E.W. Scripps Co.

Charles Edward Scripps: chairman executive committee, director B San Diego, CA January 27, 1920. ED College of William & Mary (1938-1940); Pomona College (1940-1941). PRIM CORP EMPL chairman executive committee, director: E.W. Scripps Co. CORP AFFIL director: Scripps Howard Broadcasting Co.; director: Evansville Courier Co. Inc. NONPR AFFIL trustee: Edward W. Scripps Trust; member: Theta Delta Chi; trustee: Freedoms Foundation; member national board advisors: Salvation Army; member: CAP.

Paul K. Scripps: director ED Claremont Men's College BA.

Foundation Officials

Drew Berry: trustee
William Robert Burleigh: member (see above)
Judy G. Clabes: president, chief executive officer, member B Henderson, KY 1945. ED University of Kentucky BA (1967); Indiana State University MPA

(1984).
Deborah Cooper: administrator assistant
Peter Copeland: trustee
Patty Cottingham: executive director, secretary
Clyde Gray: trustee
Pamela (Howard) Gumprecht: trustee ED Sarah Lawrence College (1963). CLUB AFFIL Cosmopolitan Club.
Julia Scripps Heidt: trustee
Pamela Howard: trustee
John F. Lansing: trustee
Angus McEachran: trustee
Susan Packard: trustee
J. Robert Routt: trustee (see above)
Charles Edward Scripps: member (see above)
Edward W. Scripps, Jr.: trustee
Edward Wyllis Scripps, II: member B San Diego, CA 1929. ED Pomona College.
Maggie Scripps: trustee
Paul K. Scripps: trustee (see above)
E. John Wolfzom: trustee, treasurer

Grants Analysis

Disclosure Period: calendar year ending 2003
Total Grants: $4,458,384*
Number of Grants: 374
Average Grant: $10,641*
Highest Grant: $250,000
Lowest Grant: $25
Typical Range: $1,000 to $10,000
*Note: Giving excludes matching gifts and scholarships. Average grant figure excludes two highest grants ($500,000).

Recent Grants

Note: Grants derived from 2003 Form 990.
General

271,675	University of Colorado Foundation Inc., Boulder, CO -- for Ted Scripps fellowships
250,000	Hampton University, Hampton, VA
250,000	Marquette University, Milwaukee, WI
125,000	Columbia University, New York, NY
115,000	United Way, Cincinnati, OH -- annual fund drive
100,782	National Merit Scholarship Corporation, Evanston, IL -- for national merit scholarship program
100,000	National Underground Railroad Freedom Center, Cincinnati, OH -- capital campaign
100,000	Northern Kentucky University Foundation, Highland Heights, KY
100,000	Ohio University Foundation, Athens, OH
100,000	Ohio University Foundation, Athens, OH -- for Scripps Howard visiting professional chair

SCURLOCK FOUNDATION

Giving Contact

Julia McIlheran
700 Louisiana, Suite 3920
Houston, TX 77002
Phone: (713)236-1500
Fax: (713)222-2419

Description

Founded: 1954
EIN: 741488953
Organization Type: Private Foundation
Giving Locations: TX
Grant Types: Award, Emergency, General Support, Multiyear/Continuing Support.

Donor Information

Founder: Established in 1954 by the late E. C. Scurlock, the late D. E. Farnsworth, the late W. C. Scurlock, I. S. Blanton, and Scurlock Oil Co.

Financial Summary

Total Giving: $1,101,773 (2002)
Giving Analysis: Giving for 2002 includes: foundation grants to United Way ($10,000)
Assets: $15,883,069 (2002)
Gifts Received: $6,327 (2000); $6,500 (1999); $6,040 (1998). Note: In 2000, contributions were received from Scurlock Oil Company.

Typical Recipients

Arts & Humanities: Arts Associations & Councils, Arts Festivals, Arts Institutes, Arts Outreach, Ballet, Dance, Arts & Humanities-General, Historic Preservation, History & Archaeology, Libraries, Literary Arts, Museums/Galleries, Music, Opera, Performing Arts, Theater, Visual Arts

Civic & Public Affairs: Botanical Gardens/Parks, Clubs, Community Foundations, Civic & Public Affairs-General, Professional & Trade Associations, Urban & Community Affairs, Women's Affairs, Zoos/Aquariums

Education: Afterschool/Enrichment Programs, Arts/Humanities Education, Business Education, Business-School Partnerships, Colleges & Universities, Continuing Education, Education Associations, Education Reform, Engineering/Technological Education, Education-General, Health & Physical Education, Literacy, Medical Education, Private Education (Precollege), Religious Education, Secondary Education (Private), Secondary Education (Public), Social Sciences Education, Special Education, Student Aid

Environment: Environment-General, Research, Resource Conservation, Wildlife Protection

Health: Cancer, Children's Health/Hospitals, Clinics/Medical Centers, Diabetes, Eyes/Blindness, Health-General, Geriatric Health, Health Organizations, Hospices, Hospitals, Hospitals (University Affiliated), Medical Research, Mental Health, Multiple Sclerosis, Public Health, Single-Disease Health Associations, Speech & Hearing

International: Foreign Arts Organizations, International Affairs

Religion: Bible Study/Translation, Churches, Religion-General, Jewish Causes, Ministries, Missionary Activities (Domestic), Religious Organizations, Religious Welfare

Science: Science Museums

Social Services: Animal Protection, Camps, Child Welfare, Community Centers, Community Service Organizations, Crime Prevention, Day Care, Delinquency & Criminal Rehabilitation, Emergency Relief, Family Services, Homes, People with Disabilities, Recreation & Athletics, Scouts, Senior Services, Shelters/Homelessness, United Funds/United Ways, Volunteer Services, YMCA/YWCA/YMHA/YWHA, Youth Organizations

Application Procedures

Initial Contact: Send a request on the organization's letterhead.
Application Requirements: Provide a description of organization, purpose of funds sought, and proof of tax-exempt status.
Deadlines: None.

Restrictions

The foundation does not support individuals or provide loans.

Foundation Officials

Eddy S. Blanton: vice president, director
Jack S. Blanton, Jr.: vice president, director B Houston, TX 1953. ED University of Texas (1975). PRIM CORP EMPL chairman: Nicklos Drilling Co.
Laura L. Blanton: president, director
Kenneth Fisher: secretary, treasurer, director B Ta-

coma, WA 1944. ED University of Oregon BS (1968); University of Oregon BFA (1969); University of Oregon MFA (1971). OCCUPATION sculptor. NONPR AFFIL member: Portland Art Association.
Elizabeth B. Wareing: president

Grants Analysis

Disclosure Period: calendar year ending 2002
Total Grants: $1,091,773*
Number of Grants: 145
Average Grant: $5,845*
Highest Grant: $250,000
Lowest Grant: $100
Typical Range: $1,000 to $10,000
*Note: Giving excludes United Way. Average grant excludes highest grant.

Recent Grants

Note: Grants derived from 2002 Form 990.
General

250,000	Methodist Hospital Foundation, Houston, TX
165,000	Lon Morris College, Jacksonville, TX
63,900	Museum of Fine Arts, Houston, TX
51,000	Texas Children's Hospital, Houston, TX
50,660	Episcopal High School, Bellaire, TX
50,000	A Campaign for River Oaks
33,000	College of Biblical Studies, Houston, TX
30,000	Star of Hope, Houston, TX
21,000	Rice University Graduate School of Business, Houston, TX
20,360	Neuhaus Education Center, Bellaire, TX

SEABURY FOUNDATION

Giving Contact

Tom Iskalis
c/o Northern Trust Co.
50 S. LaSalle Street
Chicago, IL 60675
Phone: (312)630-6000

Description

Founded: 1947
EIN: 366027398
Organization Type: Family Foundation
Giving Locations: IL: Chicago metropolitan area
Grant Types: General Support, Project, Scholarship.

Donor Information

Founder: Established in 1947 by the late Charles Ward Seabury and the late Louise Lovett Seabury.

Financial Summary

Total Giving: $1,696,737 (2002); $2,438,490 (2001)
Giving Analysis: Giving for 2002 includes: foundation scholarships ($127,787)
Assets: $21,908,151 (2002); $27,928,499 (2001)

Typical Recipients

Arts & Humanities: Arts Associations & Councils, Arts Centers, Arts Outreach, Dance, Ethnic & Folk Arts, Film & Video, Historic Preservation, History & Archaeology, Libraries, Museums/Galleries, Music, Opera, Performing Arts, Public Broadcasting, Theater
Civic & Public Affairs: Asian American Affairs, Botanical Gardens/Parks, Business/Free Enterprise, Clubs, Community Foundations, Economic Development, Employment/Job Training, Civic & Public Affairs-General, Hispanic Affairs, Housing, Inner-City Development, Native American Affairs, Public Policy, Safety, Urban & Community Affairs, Women's Affairs, Zoos/Aquariums
Education: Afterschool/Enrichment Programs, Arts/Humanities Education, Colleges & Universities, Education Funds, Education Reform, Education-General, Health & Physical Education, International Studies,

Literacy, Minority Education, Preschool Education, Private Education (Precollege), Public Education (Precollege), Religious Education, Secondary Education (Public), Social Sciences Education, Special Education, Student Aid, Vocational & Technical Education
Environment: Forestry, Environment-General, Protection, Resource Conservation, Watershed, Wildlife Protection
Health: Adolescent Health Issues, Cancer, Children's Health/Hospitals, Clinics/Medical Centers, Emergency/Ambulance Services, Health Funds, Hospices, Hospitals, Medical Rehabilitation, Medical Research, Mental Health, Nursing Services, Prenatal Health Issues, Public Health, Single-Disease Health Associations
International: Foreign Arts Organizations, Foreign Educational Institutions, International Development, Missionary/Religious Activities
Religion: Religion-General, Ministries, Religious Welfare, Seminaries
Science: Science Museums, Scientific Research
Social Services: At-Risk Youth, Child Welfare, Community Centers, Community Service Organizations, Day Care, Delinquency & Criminal Rehabilitation, Domestic Violence, Emergency Relief, Family Planning, Family Services, Food/Clothing Distribution, Homes, People with Disabilities, Scouts, Social Services-General, United Funds/United Ways, Volunteer Services, YMCA/YWCA/YMHA/YWHA, Youth Organizations

Application Procedures

Initial Contact: The foundation has no formal policy for accepting applications.
Deadlines: None..
Notes: The foundation prefers first-time requests for special projects funds, though requests for operating funds will occasionally be considered.
The foundation has developed a schedule of qualified charitable organizations in various fields generally restricted to greater the Chicago area to which contributions are made on a somewhat annual basis, based upon need.

Restrictions

Unsolicited applications are accepted from the Chicago metropolitan area only. The foundation does not make loans, nor does it fund benefits, capital campaigns, or individuals.

Additional Information

Trust(s): Northern Trust Co.

Foundation Officials

D. William Boone: trustee
Robert S. Boone: trustee
Robert D. Fisk: trustee
Seabury J. Hibben: trustee
Louise Fisk Morris: trustee B 1942. PRIM CORP EMPL chairman: Pinnacle Oil Co.
Charlene Brown Seabury: executive secretary, trustee
David D. Seabury: trustee

Grants Analysis

Disclosure Period: calendar year ending 2002
Total Grants: $1,568,950*
Number of Grants: 107
Average Grant: $14,663
Highest Grant: $50,000
Lowest Grant: $200
Typical Range: $5,000 to $30,000
*Note: Giving excludes scholarship.

Recent Grants

Note: Grants derived from 2002 Form 990.
General

50,000	Berea College, Berea, KY -- for building/ renovation of Sustainability and Environmental Studies House

50,000	Good News Partners, Chicago, IL -- toward partial salary for chief operating officer and property manager
50,000	Hope Network West Michigan, Grand Rapids, MI -- for substance abuse education /group work
50,000	Howard Area Community Center, Chicago, IL -- for summer camp 2002
45,000	Family Matters, Chicago, IL -- toward teen men program
40,000	Family Matters, Chicago, IL -- to increase financial capacity
40,000	Target Hope, Chicago, IL -- for purchase of a 56 seat motor coach
35,000	Homebase Youth Services, Phoenix, AZ -- toward salary for quarter time MD in clinic and six interns, continuation of therapist position
35,000	Homeboyz Interactive Inc., Milwaukee, WI -- for Chicago training academy in Rogers Park
35,000	Liberty Wildlife, Scottsdale, AZ -- for triage/treatment & orphan care - new medical center

GEORGE AND EFFIE SEAY MEMORIAL TRUST

Giving Contact

Elizabeth D. Seaman, Consultant
c/o Bank of America
PO Box 26903
Richmond, VA 23261
Phone: (804)788-2963

Description

Founded: 1957
EIN: 546030604
Organization Type: Private Foundation
Giving Locations: VA
Grant Types: Capital, General Support, Operating Expenses, Project.

Donor Information

Founder: the late George J. Seay, the late Effie L. Seay

Financial Summary

Total Giving: $179,500 (fiscal year ending June 30, 2004); $386,505 (fiscal 2001)
Assets: $3,853,698 (fiscal 2004); $3,516,512 (fiscal 2001)
Gifts Received: $4,298 (fiscal 1997)

Typical Recipients

Arts & Humanities: Arts Associations & Councils, Arts Institutes, Arts Outreach, History & Archaeology, Libraries, Museums/Galleries, Music, Opera, Performing Arts, Theater
Civic & Public Affairs: Employment/Job Training, Civic & Public Affairs-General, Housing, Legal Aid, Urban & Community Affairs
Education: Afterschool/Enrichment Programs, Agricultural Education, Colleges & Universities, Education-General, Literacy, Medical Education, Private Education (Precollege), Special Education, Vocational & Technical Education
Environment: Environment-General, Resource Conservation
Health: Cancer, Children's Health/Hospitals, Clinics/Medical Centers, Health Organizations, Heart, Hospices
Religion: Churches, Ministries, Religious Organizations, Religious Welfare
Social Services: Animal Protection, Camps, Child Welfare, Community Centers, Community Service Organizations, Day Care, Emergency Relief, Family

Planning, Family Services, Food/Clothing Distribution, People with Disabilities, Scouts, Senior Services, Shelters/Homelessness, United Funds/United Ways, Volunteer Services, Youth Organizations

Application Procedures

Initial Contact: Request application guidelines.
Application Requirements: Include a description of project; budget; amount of matching funds, plans for procurement of additional funds; recently audited financial statement; qualifications of project personnel; list of trustees and directors; proof of tax-exempt status.
Deadlines: May 1 and November 1.

Restrictions

The foundation does not support individuals, religious organizations for sectarian purposes, annual fund appeals, or scholarship.

Additional Information

Publications: Informational Brochure (including Application Guidelines)
Trust(s): Bank of America NA

Foundation Officials

Elizabeth D. Seaman: consult

Grants Analysis

Disclosure Period: fiscal year ending June 30, 2004
Total Grants: $179,500
Number of Grants: 16
Average Grant: $11,219
Highest Grant: $15,000
Lowest Grant: $7,500
Typical Range: $10,000 to $15,000

Recent Grants

Note: Grants derived from fiscal 2004 Form 990.
General

15,000	Friends Association for Children, Richmond, VA
15,000	Richmond Symphony, Richmond, VA -- symphonic music appreciation
15,000	Virginia Mentoring Partnership, Richmond, VA -- training programs
15,000	William Byrd Community House, Richmond, VA
12,000	ART 180, Richmond, VA -- education in art
10,000	Benedictine Sisters of Virginia, Bristow, VA
10,000	Richmond Community Action Program, Richmond, VA
10,000	Richmond Court Appointed Special Advocates, Richmond, VA -- abused and neglected children advocates
10,000	Virginia Symphony, Norfolk, VA -- symphonic music appreciation
10,000	Wellspring Foundation, Fairfax, VA -- services for mentally retarded

SEBASTIAN FOUNDATION

Giving Contact

David S. Sebastian, Executive Director
3333 Evergreen Dr. NE, Suite 110
Grand Rapids, MI 49525
Phone: (616)361-1996

Description

Founded: 1980
EIN: 382340219
Organization Type: Private Foundation
Giving Locations: MI: Kent County, Grand Rapids
Grant Types: General Support.

Donor Information

Founder: Audrey M. Sebastian, James R. Sebastian

Financial Summary

Total Giving: $1,240,750 (fiscal year ending August 31, 2004); $1,348,800 (fiscal 2001)
Giving Analysis: Giving for fiscal 2001 includes: foundation grants to United Way ($180,000)
Assets: $23,271,404 (fiscal 2004); $23,366,398 (fiscal 2001)
Gifts Received: $4,000,000 (fiscal 1995). Note: In fiscal 1995, contributions were received from James R. Sebastian.

Typical Recipients

Arts & Humanities: Arts Associations & Councils, Arts Institutes, Community Arts, History & Archaeology, Libraries, Museums/Galleries, Music, Opera
Civic & Public Affairs: African American Affairs, Botanical Gardens/Parks, Clubs, Economic Development, Civic & Public Affairs-General, Housing, Legal Aid, Native American Affairs, Nonprofit Management, Philanthropic Organizations, Women's Affairs, Zoos/Aquariums
Education: Afterschool/Enrichment Programs, Arts/Humanities Education, Business Education, Colleges & Universities, Education Funds, Medical Education, Minority Education, Private Education (Precollege), Public Education (Precollege), Secondary Education (Private), Secondary Education (Public)
Environment: Resource Conservation
Health: Emergency/Ambulance Services, Health-General, Geriatric Health, Health Organizations, Home-Care Services, Hospices, Nursing Services, Public Health, Single-Disease Health Associations
International: International Affairs, International Relations
Religion: Churches, Ministries, Religious Organizations, Religious Welfare
Social Services: At-Risk Youth, Camps, Child Welfare, Community Centers, Community Service Organizations, Family Planning, Family Services, Food/Clothing Distribution, Homes, People with Disabilities, Scouts, Senior Services, United Funds/United Ways, Volunteer Services, YMCA/YWCA/YMHA/YWHA, Youth Organizations

Application Procedures

Initial Contact: Send a brief letter of inquiry.
Application Requirements: Include purpose of funds sought, budget, balance sheet, officers and directors, other contributors, and proof of tax-exempt status.
Deadlines: None.

Restrictions

Does not support individuals.

Foundation Officials

Audrey M. Sebastian: trustee
David S. Sebastian: executive director
John O. Sebastian: trustee

Grants Analysis

Disclosure Period: fiscal year ending August 31, 2004
Total Grants: $1,240,750
Number of Grants: 57
Average Grant: $16,681*
Highest Grant: $150,000
Lowest Grant: $300
Typical Range: $10,000 to $30,000
*Note: Average grant figure excludes three highest grants ($340,000).

Recent Grants

Note: Grants derived from 2004 Form 990.
General

150,000	Heart of West Michigan United Way, Grand Rapids, MI
100,000	Kent County Michigan, Grand Rapids, MI -- towards health care for indigent
90,000	First United Methodist Church, Grand Rapids, MI
65,000	Grand Rapids Art Museum, Grand Rapids, MI
55,000	Second Harvest Gleaners, Grand Rapids, MI
50,000	Albion College, Albion, MI
50,000	Camp Blodgett, Grand Rapids, MI
50,000	Grand Rapids Children's Museum, Grand Rapids, MI
50,000	Grand Valley University Foundation, Grand Rapids, MI
40,000	Baxter Community Center, Grand Rapids, MI

SECURITY BENEFIT LIFE INSURANCE CO.

Company Headquarters

Topeka, KS
Web: http://www.securitybenefit.com

Company Description

Employees: 600
SIC(s): 6153 Short-Term Business Credit, 6311 Life Insurance, 6321 Accident & Health Insurance.

Operating Locations

Security Benefit Life Insurance Co. (KS--Topeka)

Nonmonetary Support

Type: Donated Equipment; In-kind Services

Security Benefit Life Insurance Co. Charitable Trust

Giving Contact

Howard Fricke, Trustee
One Security Benefit Place
Topeka, KS 66636-0001
Phone: (785)438-3000

Description

Founded: 1976
EIN: 486211612
Organization Type: Corporate Foundation
Giving Locations: KS: Topeka some giving in other areas of Kansas
Grant Types: General Support, Matching.

Financial Summary

Total Giving: $533,336 (2002); $564,378 (2001). Note: Contributes through foundation only.
Giving Analysis: Giving for 2002 includes: foundation grants to United Way ($72,320); 2001: foundation scholarships ($100); foundation grants to United Way ($73,020); foundation ($491,258)
Assets: $826,967 (2002); $1,562,483 (2001)
Gifts Received: $1,500,000 (1999); $333,840 (1998); $367,500 (1996). Note: Contributions were received from Security Benefit Life Industry Co.

Typical Recipients

Arts & Humanities: Arts Associations & Councils, Arts Centers, Ballet, Dance, Historic Preservation, History & Archaeology, Libraries, Museums/Galleries, Music, Performing Arts, Public Broadcasting, Theater
Civic & Public Affairs: African American Affairs, Chambers of Commerce, Clubs, Community Foundations, Employment/Job Training, Civic & Public Af-

fairs-General, Hispanic Affairs, Housing, Legal Aid, Municipalities/Towns, Parades/Festivals, Philanthropic Organizations, Professional & Trade Associations, Public Policy, Urban & Community Affairs, Women's Affairs, Zoos/Aquariums

Education: Afterschool/Enrichment Programs, Business Education, Colleges & Universities, Economic Education, Education Associations, Education Funds, Education Reform, Elementary Education (Private), Environmental Education, Faculty Development, Education-General, Medical Education, Minority Education, Private Education (Precollege), Public Education (Precollege), Religious Education, Secondary Education (Private), Secondary Education (Public), Student Aid, Vocational & Technical Education

Environment: Resource Conservation

Health: Cancer, Children's Health/Hospitals, Diabetes, Emergency/Ambulance Services, Health Funds, Health Organizations, Heart, Hospices, Mental Health, Prenatal Health Issues, Single-Disease Health Associations, Transplant Networks/Donor Banks

Religion: Churches, Religious Organizations, Religious Welfare

Science: Scientific Research

Social Services: Animal Protection, Big Brothers/Big Sisters, Child Abuse, Child Welfare, Community Centers, Community Service Organizations, Family Planning, Family Services, Food/Clothing Distribution, People with Disabilities, Recreation & Athletics, Scouts, Senior Services, Shelters/Homelessness, Social Services-General, United Funds/United Ways, Volunteer Services, YMCA/YWCA/YMHA/YWHA, Youth Organizations

Application Procedures

Initial Contact: Send a brief letter.
Deadlines: None.

Additional Information

The trust lists Security Benefit Trust Company as a corporate trustee.

Corporate Officials

Howard R. Fricke: chairman B 1936. PRIM CORP EMPL chairman: Security Benefit Life Insurance Co. CORP AFFIL president: Security Distributor Inc. Co. LLC; president: Security Management; president, director: Security Benefit Group Inc.; director: Oneok Inc.; director: Payless Shoe Source Inc.

Foundation Officials

John Dicus: trustee
Howard R. Fricke: trustee (see above)
Kirs Robbins: trustee

Grants Analysis

Disclosure Period: calendar year ending 2002
Total Grants: $461,016*
Number of Grants: 304
Average Grant: $1,517
Highest Grant: $35,000
Lowest Grant: $25
Typical Range: $300 to $3,000
*Note: Giving excludes United Way.

Recent Grants

Note: Grants derived from 2003 Form 990.
General

75,000	United Way of Greater Topeka, Topeka, KS
35,000	Salvation Army, Topeka, KS
25,000	Brown Foundation, Topeka, KS
20,000	Let's Help Inc., Topeka, KS
20,000	Let's Help Inc., Topeka, KS
20,000	Topeka Performing Arts Center, Topeka, KS
20,000	Washburn Endowment Association, Topeka, KS
20,000	YWCA, Topeka, KS
15,000	Topeka Performing Arts Center, Topeka, KS
12,000	Stormont-Vail Foundation, Topeka, KS

SECURITY LIFE OF DENVER INSURANCE CO.

Company Headquarters

1331 17th St., Ste. 808
Denver, CO 80202
Web: http://www.ing-securitylife.com

Company Description

Employees: 650
SIC(s): 6311 Life Insurance.

Operating Locations

Security Life of Denver Insurance Co. (CA; CO--Denver; FL; GA; KS; MA; TX)

Nonmonetary Support

Type: Donated Equipment; Workplace Solicitation

Giving Contact

Nancy Montgomery
Security Life of Denver
Security Life Center
1290 Broadway
Denver, CO 80203
Phone: (303)860-1290

Description

Organization Type: Corporate Giving Program
Giving Locations: CO: emphasis on Denver states where there is an agent.
Grant Types: Capital, Employee Matching Gifts, General Support, Multiyear/Continuing Support, Operating Expenses, Project.

Financial Summary

Total Giving: $260,000 (2001). Note: Contributes through corporate direct giving program only.

Typical Recipients

Arts & Humanities: Arts Associations & Councils, Arts Outreach, Ballet, Arts & Humanities-General, Historic Preservation, History & Archaeology, Libraries, Museums/Galleries, Music, Opera, Public Broadcasting

Civic & Public Affairs: Botanical Gardens/Parks, Chambers of Commerce, Urban & Community Affairs, Zoos/Aquariums

Education: Afterschool/Enrichment Programs, Arts/Humanities Education, Business Education, Elementary Education (Private), Elementary Education (Public), Education-General, Literacy

Health: AIDS/HIV, Cancer, Eyes/Blindness, Health-General, Single-Disease Health Associations

Religion: Jewish Causes

Social Services: At-Risk Youth, Domestic Violence, Emergency Relief, Food/Clothing Distribution, People with Disabilities, Recreation & Athletics, Senior Services, Social Services-General, United Funds/United Ways, Youth Organizations

Application Procedures

Initial Contact: Send a brief letter of inquiry.
Application Requirements: Include a description of organization, amount requested, purpose of funds sought, and time frame within which contribution is needed.

Restrictions

Does not support political or lobbying groups or religious organizations for sectarian purposes.

Corporate Officials

Stephen Christopher: president, chief operating officer, chief executive officer PRIM CORP EMPL president, chief operating officer: Security Life Denver Insurance Co. CORP AFFIL director: First Ing Life Insurance of New York. NONPR AFFIL director: Professional Examination Service.

Grants Analysis

Total Grants: $325,000
Typical Range: $1,000 to $5,000
Note: A more recent grants list was unavailable.

Recent Grants

Note: Grants derived from 1996 grants list.
*Library-Related*Denver Public Library, Denver, CO
*General*Bayaud Industries, Denver, COCommunity Resources, Denver, CODenver Public Schools, Denver, COFood Bank of the Rockies, Denver, COMetro State College, Denver, COOneday Foundation, Denver, COSafe House of Denver, Denver, COVolunteers for Outdoor Colorado, Denver, COColorado Symphony Orchestra, Denver, CO

SEDGWICK INC.

Company Headquarters

Memphis, TN
Web: http://www.sedgwick.com

Company Description

Former Name: Sedgwick James Inc.
Employees: 360
SIC(s): 6411 Insurance Agents, Brokers & Service.
Parent Company: Sedgwick Group Inc., 153 N. Saluda Dr., No. H, Marietta, SC, United States

Operating Locations

Sedgwick, Inc. (TN--Memphis); Sedgwick Noble Lowndes (TN--Memphis)

Giving Contact

Jean Swolenski, Matching Gifts Program
1000 Ridgeway Loop Rd.
Memphis, TN 38120
Phone: (901)684-3797

Description

Organization Type: Corporate Giving Program
Giving Locations: TN: principally near operating locations and to national organizations.
Grant Types: Employee Matching Gifts.

Typical Recipients

Arts & Humanities: Arts Appreciation, Arts Associations & Councils, Arts Centers, Arts Festivals, Arts Funds, Arts Institutes, Community Arts, Dance, Ethnic & Folk Arts, Historic Preservation, Libraries, Literary Arts, Museums/Galleries, Music, Opera, Performing Arts, Public Broadcasting, Theater, Visual Arts

Civic & Public Affairs: Safety, Zoos/Aquariums

Education: Agricultural Education, Arts/Humanities Education, Business Education, Colleges & Universities, Community & Junior Colleges, Continuing Education, Economic Education, Education Associations, Education Funds, Elementary Education (Private), Engineering/Technological Education, Faculty Development, Health & Physical Education, International Exchange, International Studies, Journalism/Media Education, Legal Education, Literacy, Medical Education, Minority Education, Preschool Education, Private Education (Precollege), Public Education (Precollege), Science/Mathematics Education, Social Sciences Education, Special Education, Student Aid

Environment: Environment-General

Science: Observatories & Planetariums, Scientific

Organizations
Social Services: Social Services-General

Application Procedures

Initial Contact: Send brief letter of inquiry.
Application Requirements: Include a description of organization, amount requested, purpose of funds sought, recently audited financial statements, and proof of tax-exempt status.
Deadlines: December 15, all requests after the deadline will be considered the following year.

Restrictions

Does not support individuals, religious organizations for sectarian purposes (however programs sponsored by a religious organization may be eligible), fraternal organizations, veteran's organizations, unions, or political or lobbying groups.

Additional Information

As a member of the Per Cent Club in the U.K., Sedgwick contributes a minimum of 0.5% of its U.K. pretax profit to community initiatives through single donations or contributions phased over several years.

Corporate Officials

Ronald J. Kutella: president vice president, chief financial officer, director PRIM CORP EMPL president: Sedgwick.
Quill O'Healy: chairman, chief executive officer, director PRIM CORP EMPL chairman, chief executive officer, director: Sedgwick.
James B. Wiertelak: senior vice president, chief financial officer, director PRIM CORP EMPL senior vice president, chief financial officer, director: Sedgwick.

SEHERR-THOSS FOUNDATION

Giving Contact

Dennis Bernat, Trust Officer
c/o Bessemer Trust Co. NA
630 5th Ave.
New York, NY 10111
Phone: (212)708-9216

Description

Founded: 1990
EIN: 136959146
Organization Type: Private Foundation
Grant Types: General Support.

Donor Information

Founder: Sonia Seherr-Thoss

Financial Summary

Total Giving: $140,780 (2003)
Assets: $3,982,787 (2003)
Gifts Received: $1,000,000 (1992)

Typical Recipients

Arts & Humanities: History & Archaeology, Libraries
Civic & Public Affairs: Civic & Public Affairs-General
Education: Education Associations, Public Education (Precollege), Secondary Education (Public)
Health: Hospitals
Religion: Churches, Religious Organizations, Religious Welfare
Science: Scientific Centers & Institutes
Social Services: Social Services-General

Application Procedures

Initial Contact: Send a written request.
Deadlines: None.

Restrictions

Grants are not made to individuals.

Additional Information

Trust(s): Bessemer Trust Co NA

Foundation Officials

Bruce C. Farrell: member
Deborah C. Foord: member
Henry W. Seherr-Thoss: vice president
Sonia P. Seherr-Thoss: president
Clayton B. Spencer: director

Grants Analysis

Disclosure Period: calendar year ending 2003
Total Grants: $140,780
Number of Grants: 6
Highest Grant: $55,000
Lowest Grant: $4,000

Recent Grants

Note: Grants derived from 2003 Form 990.
General

55,000	Charlotte Hungerford Hospital, Torrington, CT -- for upgrading of hospital's emergency department
45,000	Our Lady of Grace Church, Bantam, CT -- for repairs and improvement of church property
15,000	Wisdom House, Litchfield, CT -- for repair of roadways
13,780	Trinity Church, Litchfield, CT -- for restoring the stained glass altar window
8,000	Saint Paul's Church, Bantam, CT -- for repairing of the steeple
4,000	Litchfield Cemetery Association, Litchfield, CT -- for tree planting program

SEIDMAN FAMILY FOUNDATION

Giving Contact

Robin Volock
Seidman Family Foundation
8316 Calle Petirrojo NW
Albuquerque, NM 87120
Phone: (505)898-4977

Description

Founded: 1950
EIN: 136098204
Organization Type: Private Foundation
Giving Locations: nationally.
Grant Types: Capital, Endowment, General Support, Multiyear/Continuing Support, Research.

Donor Information

Founder: the late Frank E. Seidman, the late Esther I. Seidman

Financial Summary

Total Giving: $232,355 (2003); $227,725 (2001)
Giving Analysis: Giving for 2001 includes: foundation grants to United Way ($4,000)
Assets: $3,624,176 (2003); $4,196,289 (2001)
Gifts Received: $5,000 (1992). Note: In fiscal 1992, contributions were received from American Institute of Certified Public Accountants.

Typical Recipients

Arts & Humanities: Arts Associations & Councils, Arts Funds, Arts Outreach, Ballet, Community Arts, Dance, Arts & Humanities-General, Historic Preservation, History & Archaeology, Libraries, Museums/Galleries, Performing Arts, Public Broadcasting, Theater
Civic & Public Affairs: Botanical Gardens/Parks, Community Foundations, Gay/Lesbian Issues, Civic & Public Affairs-General, Housing, Native American Affairs, Public Policy, Urban & Community Affairs, Women's Affairs, Zoos/Aquariums
Education: Agricultural Education, Arts/Humanities Education, Business Education, Colleges & Universities, Elementary Education (Public), Education-General, Journalism/Media Education, Leadership Training, Legal Education, Literacy, Preschool Education, Private Education (Precollege), Public Education (Precollege), School Volunteerism, Science/Mathematics Education, Secondary Education (Private), Special Education, Student Aid
Environment: Air/Water Quality, Environment-General, Resource Conservation, Watershed
Health: AIDS/HIV, Emergency/Ambulance Services, Heart, Hospitals, Medical Rehabilitation, Nursing Services
International: Health Care/Hospitals, International Relief Efforts
Religion: Churches, Religious Welfare
Science: Scientific Centers & Institutes
Social Services: Big Brothers/Big Sisters, Child Welfare, Community Service Organizations, Counseling, Domestic Violence, Family Planning, Family Services, Food/Clothing Distribution, People with Disabilities, Recreation & Athletics, Substance Abuse, United Funds/United Ways, Youth Organizations

Application Procedures

Initial Contact: The foundation has no formal grant application procedure or application form.
Deadlines: None.

Foundation Officials

Margaret Ann Cole: trustee
D. Thomas Seidman: chairman
Jane R. Seidman: vice chairman
Lewis William Seidman: trustee B Grand Rapids, MI 1921. ED Dartmouth College AB (1943); Harvard University LLB (1948); University of Michigan MBA (1949). NONPR AFFIL member: DC Bar Association. CLUB AFFIL University Club; Nantucket Yacht Club; Chevy Chase Club; Crystal Downs Club.
Nancy Caroline Seidman: treasurer
Sarah B. Seidman: trustee
Sarah L. Seidman: secretary
Tracy H. Seidman: trustee

Grants Analysis

Disclosure Period: calendar year ending 2003
Total Grants: $232,355*
Number of Grants: 85
Average Grant: $2,632
Highest Grant: $50,000
Lowest Grant: $110
Typical Range: $500 to $5,000
*Note: Giving excludes United Way.

Recent Grants

Note: Grants derived from 2003 Form 990.
General

25,000	Corcoran Gallery of Art, Washington, DC
20,000	American Council for Capital Formation Center for Policy Research, Washington, DC
10,000	Gerald R. Ford Foundation, Grand Rapids, MI -- for birthday celebration
10,000	Nantucket Cottage Hospital, Nantucket, MA
10,000	UMass Dartmouth College, Dartmouth, MA
7,500	New Mexico Water Dialogue, Santa Fe, NM
5,000	American Theatre of Actors, New York, NY
5,000	Harvard College, Cambridge, MA
5,000	Harvard Law School, Cambridge, MA
5,000	University of San Diego, San Diego, CA -- for real estate institute

WILLIAM G. SELBY AND MARIE SELBY FOUNDATION

Giving Contact
Debra M. Jacobs, President, Chief Executive Officer
1800 Second Street, Suite 750
Sarasota, FL 34236
Phone: (941)957-0442
Fax: (941)957-3135
Web: http://www.selbyfdn.org

Alternate Contact
Debra Jacobs
PO Box 267
Sarasota, FL 34230

Description
Founded: 1955
EIN: 596121242
Organization Type: General Purpose Foundation
Giving Locations: FL: Sarasota Manatee, Charlotte, DeSoto Florida counties
Grant Types: Capital, Challenge, General Support, Scholarship.

Donor Information
Founder: Established in 1955 by the late William G. Selby (d. 1956) and his wife, Marie Selby. Mr. Selby, who was a co-founder of the Selby Oil Company in Ohio. In addition, he was a large stockholder in Texaco, and owned extensive mineral interests in the Colorado Rocky Mountain region. The foundation is affiliated with the Beattie, Sarasota County, Paddock, and Posey Foundations, all of First Union Bank.

Financial Summary
Total Giving: $3,373,962 (fiscal year ending May 31, 2003); $3,706,228 (fiscal 2001)
Giving Analysis: Giving for fiscal 2003 includes: foundation scholarships ($399,300)
Assets: $65,096,162 (fiscal 2003); $78,520,483 (fiscal 2001)
Gifts Received: $2,245,267 (fiscal 1993)

Typical Recipients
Arts & Humanities: Arts Associations & Councils, Arts Centers, Ballet, Film & Video, Historic Preservation, History & Archaeology, Libraries, Museums/Galleries, Music, Opera, Performing Arts, Public Broadcasting, Theater, Visual Arts
Civic & Public Affairs: Botanical Gardens/Parks, Business/Free Enterprise, Community Foundations, Economic Policy, Employment/Job Training, Civic & Public Affairs-General, Hispanic Affairs, Housing, Inner-City Development, Law & Justice, Legal Aid, Municipalities/Towns, Public Policy, Urban & Community Affairs, Women's Affairs, Zoos/Aquariums
Education: Afterschool/Enrichment Programs, Agricultural Education, Arts/Humanities Education, Business Education, Colleges & Universities, Community & Junior Colleges, Economic Education, Education Associations, Education Funds, Engineering/Technological Education, Education-General, Literacy, Minority Education, Preschool Education, Public Education (Precollege), School Volunteerism, Science/Mathematics Education, Secondary Education (Private), Secondary Education (Public), Student Aid, Vocational & Technical Education
Environment: Air/Water Quality, Resource Conservation
Health: AIDS/HIV, Cancer, Children's Health/Hospitals, Emergency/Ambulance Services, Hospices, Hospitals, Medical Research, Mental Health, Nursing Services, Prenatal Health Issues, Research/Studies Institutes, Single-Disease Health Associations
Religion: Dioceses, Ministries, Religious Welfare
Science: Science Museums, Scientific Centers & Institutes, Scientific Labs
Social Services: Animal Protection, At-Risk Youth, Big Brothers/Big Sisters, Camps, Child Abuse, Child Welfare, Community Centers, Community Service Organizations, Counseling, Day Care, Domestic Violence, Emergency Relief, Family Planning, Family Services, Food/Clothing Distribution, People with Disabilities, Recreation & Athletics, Senior Services, Substance Abuse, United Funds/United Ways, Volunteer Services, YMCA/YWCA/YMHA/YWHA, Youth Organizations

Application Procedures
Initial Contact: Applicants should contact the administrative agent for a copy of their application procedures.
Application Requirements: Along with the completed application, supporting information may be submitted to describe the organization and the project.
Deadlines: February 1 and August 1.
Review Process: The grants committee reviews proposals and notifies applicants of their decisions within five months of the deadline. The trustees evaluate applications on the basis of the proposed project's value to society, soundness of sponsoring organization, sources of other financial support, and assurance of future maintenance of the project without an undesirable financial burden to the sponsoring organization or taxpayer.
Decision Notification: Applicants will be notified in writing of the acceptance or rejection of their request within the time frame outlined on the Foundation Matrix.

Restrictions
No grants are given to individuals, or for endowment funds, operating budgets, continuing support, annual campaigns, deficit financing, seed money, or emergency funds. It also does not support special projects, research, graduate study, publications, travel, surveys, seminars, workshops, conferences, loans, fund raising, or program advertising. The foundation does not give to organizations outside of Sarasota and adjoining counties, to other foundations, or to the United Way. It prefers not to support projects that are normally financed by public tax funds. The foundation usually does not make grants payable in installments in future years.

Additional Information
First Union Bank serves as corporate trustee for the foundation.
In order to be eligible for a Selby scholarship, a student must be a bona fide resident of Sarasota or Manatee counties before attending college, and must attend a participating Florida college or university. A minimum grade point average of 3.0 is required. Students seeking a scholarship should write to the Florida college or university in which he or she has an interest. The foundation reports that scholarships are also available for Sarasota County residents who choose to attend colleges outside the State of Florida. These students should apply directly to the Foundation office by March 1 for the upcoming academic year.
Publications: Guidelines; Application Form

Foundation Officials
John B. Davidson: member admin committee B 1931. ED Duke University; University of Colorado. PRIM CORP EMPL president: Davidson Drugs Inc.
Debra M. Jacobs: president, secretary, chief executive officer NONPR AFFIL vice president: Ringling School Art & Design.
Doug Mrstik: vice chairman
Charles E. Stottlemyer: chairman, mem admin comm CORP AFFIL director: FCCI Mutual Insurance Co.; director: Florida Employers Insurance Service Corp.

Grants Analysis
Disclosure Period: fiscal year ending May 31, 2003
Total Grants: $2,974,662*
Number of Grants: 40
Average Grant: $49,683*
Highest Grant: $766,777
Lowest Grant: $10,000
Typical Range: $25,000 to $100,000
***Note:** Giving excludes scholarships. Average grant figure excludes two highest grants ($1,086,700).

Recent Grants
Note: Grants derived from 2003 Form 990.
Library-Related

20,000	Friends of the Fruitville Public Library, Sarasota, FL

General

766,777	Sarasota Family YMCA Inc., Sarasota, FL
320,000	John and Mable Ringling Museum of Art Foundation Inc., Sarasota, FL
160,000	School Board of Sarasota County, Sarasota, FL
158,740	Florida Studio Theatre Inc., Sarasota, FL
150,000	Southeastern Guide Dogs Inc., Palmetto, FL
125,000	Manatee Community College Foundation Inc., Bradenton, FL
125,000	Sarasota Memorial Health Care System, Sarasota, FL
100,500	Education Foundation of Sarasota County Inc., Sarasota, FL
100,000	Bon Secours Venice Healthcare, Venice, FL
80,719	Sarasota Opera Association Inc., Sarasota, FL

SELF FAMILY FOUNDATION

Giving Contact
Mamie W. Nicholson, Program Officer
PO Box 1017
Greenwood, SC 29648-1017
Phone: (864)941-4036
Fax: (864)941-4091
E-mail: info@selffoundation.org
Web: http://www.selffoundation.org

Description
Founded: 1942
EIN: 570400594
Organization Type: Family Foundation
Giving Locations: SC: emphasis on Greenwood area
Grant Types: Capital, Challenge, Conference/Seminar, Endowment, General Support, Project, Research, Scholarship.

Donor Information
Founder: Founded in 1942 by the late James C. Self. Mr. Self was the founder of Greenwood Mills in Greenwood, SC. The original purpose of the foundation was to construct a hospital for Greenwood County. This mission was realized on November 1, 1951. At the time of the hospital's dedication, Mr. Self remarked that it was "a debt of gratitude to the community that has been good to me."

Financial Summary
Total Giving: $1,359,849 (2003); $11,498,322 (2001)
Giving Analysis: Giving for 2003 includes: foundation grants to United Way ($35,000)
Assets: $35,701,322 (2003); $38,883,095 (2001)

Typical Recipients

Arts & Humanities: Arts Associations & Councils, Historic Preservation, History & Archaeology, Libraries, Museums/Galleries, Opera, Performing Arts, Public Broadcasting, Theater

Civic & Public Affairs: Clubs, Community Foundations, Economic Development, Civic & Public Affairs-General, Housing, Municipalities/Towns, Nonprofit Management, Philanthropic Organizations, Professional & Trade Associations, Safety, Zoos/Aquariums

Education: Afterschool/Enrichment Programs, Arts/Humanities Education, Business Education, Business-School Partnerships, Colleges & Universities, Continuing Education, Education Funds, Education Reform, Elementary Education (Private), Elementary Education (Public), Faculty Development, Education-General, Leadership Training, Literacy, Medical Education, Preschool Education, Private Education (Precollege), Public Education (Precollege), Science/Mathematics Education, Social Sciences Education, Special Education, Student Aid, Vocational & Technical Education

Environment: Environment-General

Health: Adolescent Health Issues, Alzheimer's Disease, Cancer, Children's Health/Hospitals, Clinics/Medical Centers, Eyes/Blindness, Heart, Home-Care Services, Hospices, Hospitals, Medical Research, Research/Studies Institutes

Religion: Ministries, Religious Welfare

Science: Scientific Centers & Institutes

Social Services: At-Risk Youth, Child Abuse, Child Welfare, Community Centers, Community Service Organizations, Day Care, Domestic Violence, Family Planning, Family Services, Food/Clothing Distribution, People with Disabilities, Recreation & Athletics, Senior Services, Sexual Abuse, Special Olympics, United Funds/United Ways, YMCA/YWCA/YMHA/YWHA, Youth Organizations

Application Procedures

Initial Contact: Contact the foundation program officer by phone or submit a letter of inquiry prior to submitting a full proposal.

Application Requirements: If a proposal is requested by the foundation, it should include description of objectives and activities, organization leadership, purpose of funds sought, an implementation plan (using existing community assets, both human and financial), and how results will be measured. Applicants also must include a copy of IRS tax-exempt determination letter and recently audited financial statement, including a budget identifying income sources and expenses.

Deadlines: Proposals must be received by February 15, May 15, August 15, or November 15.

Review Process: Trustees meet the third week of March, June, September, and December. Late applications are held for consideration at the next meeting.

Restrictions

Grants are made from income only and for periods not to exceed three years. Grants are not made to individuals. The foundation does not provide loans, recurring grants, or operational support. Applicants must have the financial potential to sustain the project on a continuing basis after foundation funding.

Additional Information

Publications: Annual Report

Foundation Officials

William B. Allin: treasurer

George W. Ballentine, Jr.: trustee B 1954. ED Clemson University (1975). PRIM CORP EMPL vice president: George Ballentine Ford Inc.

David L. Bell: trustee

Virginia S. Brennan: trustee, chairman CORP AFFIL director: Greenwood Mills Inc.

R. Boykin Curry, Jr.: trustee emeritus CORP AFFIL director: United Savings Bank.

Gwen Dickenson: administrative assistant

John Murphy: trustee

Mamie W. Nicholson: program officer

James Cuthbert Self, III: trustee PRIM CORP EMPL vice president: Greenwood Mills Inc.

Dr. Sally E. Self: secretary, trustee

William Matthews Self: vice chairman, trustee B 1948. PRIM CORP EMPL president, chief executive officer, director: Greenwood Mills Inc. ADD CORP EMPL director: Greenwood Development Corp.; chairman: Greenwood Holding Corp.; president, chief executive officer, director: Lindale Manufacturing Co.

Paul E. Welder: trustee B Kansas City, MO 1943. ED University of Virginia (1965). PRIM CORP EMPL executive vice president financial, director: Greenwood Mills Inc. CORP AFFIL director: Jeantex SACA; director: Tejidos Argentinos SA; director: Crescent-Greenwood.

Frank J. Wideman, III: president

Grants Analysis

Disclosure Period: calendar year ending 2003

Total Grants: $1,324,849*

Number of Grants: 45

Average Grant: $14,258*

Highest Grant: $325,000

Lowest Grant: $1,000

Typical Range: $5,000 to $25,000

*Note: Giving excludes United Way. Average grant figure excludes three highest grants ($726,000).

Recent Grants

Note: Grants derived from 2001 Form 990.

General

10,000,000	Upper Savannah Council of Governments, Greenwood, SC -- establish the Upper Savannah Sudden and Severe Economic Dislocation Loan Fund
325,000	Greenwood Genetic Center, Greenwood, SC -- unrestricted grant in memory of Jim Sell
90,000	Arts Council of Greenwood, Greenwood, SC -- Cultural Center Feasibility Study
85,000	American Legion Post 20, Greenwood, SC -- Restoration of American Legion Building
75,000	Partnership for a Greenwood County, Greenwood, SC -- support of workforce development in Greenwood County
64,450	South Carolina Aquarium, Charleston, SC -- support the education leadership program for South Carolina Teachers
63,322	Greenwood Community Children's Center, Greenwood, SC -- Healthy Beginnings Programs
56,000	Lander Foundation, Greenwood, SC -- additional funding for Montessori Education program
51,200	Greenwood Genetic Center, Greenwood, SC -- configuring additional research and diagnostic laboratories and acquiring gene and chromosome analytic instruments
50,200	Lander Foundation, Greenwood, SC -- pre-kindergarten through graduate studies professional education at Lander University

SEMMES FOUNDATION

Giving Contact

Thomas R. Semmes, President & Director
800 Navarro, Suite 210
San Antonio, TX 78205
Phone: (210)225-0887

Description

Founded: 1952

EIN: 746062264

Organization Type: Private Foundation

Giving Locations: TX: San Antonio

Grant Types: Capital, Conference/Seminar, Emergency, General Support, Multiyear/Continuing Support, Operating Expenses, Professorship, Project, Research, Seed Money.

Donor Information

Founder: the late Douglas R. Semmes

Financial Summary

Total Giving: $823,830 (2003)

Giving Analysis: Giving for 2003 includes: foundation grants to United Way ($30,000); foundation scholarships ($99,000)

Assets: $19,585,047 (2003)

Gifts Received: $45,738 (2003); $45,738 (2000); $45,738 (1999). Note: In 1999, 2000, and 2003, contributions were received from the Julia Yates Semmes.

Typical Recipients

Arts & Humanities: Arts Centers, Arts Festivals, Ethnic & Folk Arts, Libraries, Museums/Galleries, Music, Public Broadcasting

Civic & Public Affairs: Community Foundations, Employment/Job Training, Nonprofit Management, Philanthropic Organizations, Professional & Trade Associations

Education: Colleges & Universities, Education Funds, Literacy, Private Education (Precollege), Public Education (Precollege), Science/Mathematics Education, Student Aid

Health: Cancer, Children's Health/Hospitals, Heart, Hospices, Nutrition

International: International Affairs

Religion: Churches, Religious Welfare, Social/Policy Issues

Science: Science Museums, Scientific Centers & Institutes

Social Services: Animal Protection, Child Abuse, Child Welfare, Community Service Organizations, Day Care, Family Planning, Family Services, People with Disabilities, United Funds/United Ways, YMCA/YWCA/YMHA/YWHA, Youth Organizations

Application Procedures

Initial Contact: Send a concise written proposal with proof of tax-exempt status.

Deadlines: None.

Restrictions

Does not support individuals or provide loans.

Foundation Officials

Carol Duffell: secretary, treasurer

Lucian L. Morrison, Jr.: director CORP AFFIL director: Group Maintenance America.

D. R. Semmes, Jr.: director

Patricia A. Semmes: director

Thomas R. Semmes: president, director

Grants Analysis

Disclosure Period: calendar year ending 2003

Total Grants: $694,830*

Number of Grants: 20

Average Grant: $11,585*

Highest Grant: $200,000

Lowest Grant: $500

Typical Range: $5,000 to $25,000

*Note: Giving excludes United Way, scholarships. Average grant figure excludes three highest grants ($497,888).

Recent Grants

Note: Grants derived from 2003 Form 990.

Library-Related

197,888	San Antonio Public Library Foundation, San Antonio, TX -- new branch library grant

General

200,000	McNay Art Museum, San Antonio, TX -- endowment fund
100,000	San Antonio Academy, San Antonio, TX -- for faculty salary endowment
99,000	Trinity University, San Antonio, TX -- Semmes foundation science scholarship fund
30,000	United Way of San Antonio and Bexar County, San Antonio, TX
25,000	Alamo Heights School Foundation, San Antonio, TX
25,000	McNay Art Museum, San Antonio, TX -- for internship program
13,360	University of Texas at Austin, Austin, TX
13,334	McNay Art Museum, San Antonio, TX -- towards library support
10,100	McNay Art Museum, San Antonio, TX

LOUISE TAFT SEMPLE FOUNDATION

Giving Contact
Eileen M. Heyob
425 Walnut Street, Suite 1800
Cincinnati, OH 45202
Phone: (513)381-2838
Fax: (513)381-0205

Description
Founded: 1941
EIN: 310653526
Organization Type: Family Foundation
Giving Locations: OH: Hamilton County, Cincinnati
Grant Types: Capital, Challenge, Endowment, General Support, Project.

Donor Information
Founder: Incorporated in 1941 by the late Louise Taft Semple.

Financial Summary
Total Giving: $1,095,191 (2002)
Giving Analysis: Giving for 2002 includes: foundation scholarships ($25,000); foundation grants to United Way ($72,000).
Assets: $18,138,194 (2002)

Typical Recipients
Arts & Humanities: Arts Associations & Councils, Arts Centers, Arts Funds, Arts Outreach, Ballet, Ethnic & Folk Arts, Arts & Humanities-General, Historic Preservation, History & Archaeology, Libraries, Museums/Galleries, Music, Opera, Performing Arts, Public Broadcasting, Theater
Civic & Public Affairs: African American Affairs, Botanical Gardens/Parks, Clubs, Community Foundations, Economic Development, Employment/Job Training, Civic & Public Affairs-General, Housing, Inner-City Development, Legal Aid, Municipalities/Towns, Parades/Festivals, Public Policy, Urban & Community Affairs, Women's Affairs, Zoos/Aquariums
Education: Afterschool/Enrichment Programs, Arts/Humanities Education, Colleges & Universities, Education Funds, Elementary Education (Private), Engineering/Technological Education, Faculty Development, Education-General, Legal Education, Preschool Education, Private Education (Precollege), Public Education (Precollege), Science/Mathematics Education, Secondary Education (Private), Secondary Education (Public), Special Education, Student Aid
Environment: Environment-General, Protection, Resource Conservation
Health: AIDS/HIV, Children's Health/Hospitals, Medical Rehabilitation, Preventive Medicine/Wellness Or-

ganizations, Speech & Hearing
International: International Affairs, International Relations
Religion: Religion-General, Religious Organizations, Religious Welfare
Social Services: Camps, Child Welfare, Community Centers, Community Service Organizations, Family Services, Food/Clothing Distribution, Homes, People with Disabilities, Recreation & Athletics, Scouts, Senior Services, Substance Abuse, United Funds/United Ways, YMCA/YWCA/YMHA/YWHA, Youth Organizations

Application Procedures
Initial Contact: Initial contact may be a letter outlining purpose of proposal, other financial support, and amount requested. The foundation does not have a specific application form.
Application Requirements: Full proposals should include the name, address, and telephone number of the applying organization, as shown on the IRS tax-exempt letter; the purpose and activities of the organization; the geographic areas served by the organization; the names of the officers, board of directors or trustees, executive director, and secretary; the amount of the grant requested with a budget for the project and the purpose for which it will be used; any other sources contacted for support, with the amounts requested from each; and the organization's latest balance sheet and annual operating statement.
Deadlines: The foundation's board of trustees meets the first Mondays of April, July, October, and December. Applications should be submitted accordingly.
Review Process: The foundation's board of trustees considers grant proposals and makes funding decisions.

Restrictions
The foundation does not support individuals, general purposes, research, or loans.

Foundation Officials
James Ralph Bridgeland, Jr.: secretary, trustee B Cleveland, OH 1929. ED University of Akron BA (1951); Harvard University MA (1955); Harvard University JD (1957). CORP AFFIL director: SHV North America Inc.; director, member executive committee: Star Banc Cincinnati; director: Seinau-Fisher Studios Inc.; director, member executive committee: Firstar Bank NA; director: David J. Joseph Co.; director: Robert A. Cline Co.; director: Art Stamping Inc. NONPR AFFIL member: Ohio Bar Association; instructor: University Cincinnati; trustee: Jobs Cincinnati Graduates; trustee: Harvard University Alumni Association; trustee: Hillside Trust; president, trustee: Cincinnati Symphony Orchestra; trustee: Cincinnati Institute Fine Arts; trustee: Cincinnati Opera; member: Cincinnati Bar Association; member: American Bar Association; member: Association Library Scholars Critics; member: American Arbitration Association. CLUB AFFIL mem: Queen City Club; mem: Harvard Club; mem: Cincinnati Literacy Club; mem: Commonwealth Club.
William De Witt: trustee
Anne T. Lawrence: trustee
John T. Lawrence, Jr.: treasurer, trustee CORP AFFIL director: America Annuity Group Inc.
Dudley S. Taft: chairman, trustee PRIM CORP EMPL president, chief executive officer: Taft Broadcasting Co. CORP AFFIL director: Tribune Co.; director: Union Central Life Insurance Co.; director: Fifth Third Bank; director: CINergy Corp.; director: Fifth Third Bancorp. CLUB AFFIL treasurer, director: Queen City Club.
Mrs. Robert A. Taft, II: trustee
John Tytus: trustee

Grants Analysis
Disclosure Period: calendar year ending 2002
Total Grants: $998,191*
Number of Grants: 35
Average Grant: $22,006*

Highest Grant: $250,000
Lowest Grant: $2,000
Typical Range: $5,000 to $50,000
***Note:** Giving excludes United Way; scholarships. Average grant figure excludes highest grant.

Recent Grants
Note: Grants derived from 2002 Form 990.
General

250,000	Taft Museum, Cincinnati, OH
78,000	Fine Arts Fund, Cincinnati, OH
72,000	United Way, Cincinnati, OH
71,429	Cincinnati Country Day School, Cincinnati, OH
71,429	Seven Hills School, Cincinnati, OH
50,000	Contemporary Arts Center, Cincinnati, OH
50,000	National Underground Railroad Freedom Center, Cincinnati, OH
50,000	TAFT School
33,333	WCET Channel, Cincinnati, OH
25,000	Children's Scholarship Fund, Oxford, OH

SEMPRA ENERGY

Company Headquarters
101 Ash Street
San Diego, CA 92101-3017
Phone: (619)696-2000
Fax: (619)696-4463
Web: http://www.sempra.com

Company Description
Ticker: SRE
Exchange: NYSE
Former Name: San Diego Gas & Electric;
Formed by Merger of: Pacific Enterprises and Enova (2001);
Former Name: Southern California Gas Co. (2001).
Revenue: US$9.611 billion (2004)
Profit: US$895 million (2004)
Employees: 12807 (2003)
Fortune Rank: 235, per FORTUNE Magazine's list of 500 Largest U.S. Corporations (2004).
SIC(s): 1521 Single-Family Housing Construction, 4923 Gas Transmission & Distribution, 4931 Electric & Other Services Combined, 6552 Subdividers & Developers Nec, 6719 Holding Companies Nec.

Operating Locations
Sempra Energy (CA--Carlsbad, Chula Vista, Coronado, Encino, Irvine, San Diego, San Onofre, Santa Ana)

Nonmonetary Support
Type: Cause-related Marketing & Promotion; Donated Equipment; In-kind Services; Workplace Solicitation
Volunteer Programs: The company promotes employee volunteerism through Team San Diego Gas & Electric, a group of nearly 1,200 employees and family members who volunteer in hands-on community service projects.

Giving Contact
Molly Cartmill, Director Corporate Community Relations
Sempra Energy
101 Ash St.
San Diego, CA 92101-3017
Phone: (619)696-4297
Fax: (619)696-1868
E-mail: community@sempra.com
Web: http://www.sempra.com/community

Alternate Contact
Phone: 877-SEMPRA-9
Note: Toll free number.

Description

Organization Type: Corporate Giving Program
Giving Locations: CA: Southern California
Grant Types: Conference/Seminar, Emergency, Employee Matching Gifts, Project.

Financial Summary

Total Giving: $10,000,000 (2004 approx); $10,000,000 (2003); $7,980,000 (2002 approx). Note: Contributes through corporate direct giving program only. Giving includes corporate direct giving; memberships; local economic development. 1996 Giving includes nonmonetary support.
Assets: $15,156,000,000 (2001)

Typical Recipients

Arts & Humanities: Arts Centers, Arts Festivals, Arts Funds, Arts Institutes, Community Arts, Dance, Ethnic & Folk Arts, Historic Preservation, Libraries, Museums/Galleries, Music, Opera, Performing Arts, Theater, Visual Arts
Civic & Public Affairs: Economic Development, Employment/Job Training, Legal Aid, Professional & Trade Associations, Safety, Zoos/Aquariums
Education: Arts/Humanities Education, Business Education, Colleges & Universities, Economic Education, Education Funds, Elementary Education (Private), Engineering/Technological Education, Health & Physical Education, Literacy, Medical Education, Minority Education, Preschool Education, Science/Mathematics Education
Environment: Environment-General
Health: Geriatric Health, Health Organizations, Hospices, Hospitals, Medical Research, Mental Health, Single-Disease Health Associations
Science: Observatories & Planetariums, Science Exhibits & Fairs, Scientific Organizations
Social Services: Child Welfare, Community Centers, Community Service Organizations, Counseling, Day Care, Delinquency & Criminal Rehabilitation, Emergency Relief, Family Services, Food/Clothing Distribution, People with Disabilities, Recreation & Athletics, Senior Services, Shelters/Homelessness, Substance Abuse, United Funds/United Ways, Volunteer Services, Youth Organizations

Application Procedures

Initial Contact: See website for Community Partnership Request Form, then submit a written request.
Application Requirements: Include name of organization, contact person and title, address, phone and fax number; a description of organization, including purpose, size and audience served; description of program or project, with target audience: ethnicity, number of people, age, etc.; amount requested; geographic area served; description of need, including relevant research; budget for the project, including personnel, operating and direct costs; list of other contributors and funding levels; method of evaluation; current budget for organization, including revenue sources and reserve or contingency funds; description of volunteer support; list of board members, advisory board, and staff; proof of tax-exempt status; description of how SDG&E's participation will be highlighted; and tax I.D. number.
Deadlines: None.
Evaluative Criteria: Project is in one of company's focus areas; builds alliances between businesses, nonprofits, schools and media; delivers specific benefits or services to community; provides company with leadership opportunity; demonstrates commitment to measuring results; use financial, labor, and volunteer resources wisely; reach ethnically diverse communities. The company prefers to make direct contributions, rather than to other grant-making organizations; to fund programs that reach consumers or businesses with direct benefits; and to fund single-year efforts as opposed to multi-year commitments.
Decision Notification: Applicants are notified on a monthly basis.

Restrictions

The company generally does not provide funds for general operating expenses; travel expenses; loans or loan guarantees; debt reduction or past operating deficits; liquidating an organization; reducing or donating the cost of any gas or electric service that other customers must pay for (except for customers who are helped through our winter assistance program); building funds or capital campaigns.
No grants are made to individuals; private foundations or endowment funds; grantmaking organizations; discriminatory organizations; sectarian religious activities or political activities.
No grants are made to individuals; private foundations or endowment funds; grantmaking organizations; discriminatory organizations; sectarian religious activities or political activities.

Additional Information

The company provides for corporate and regional contributions. Corporate contributions dollars exist to support community-wide organizations and activities that benefit citizens throughout the markets where they do business. Regional contributions dollars exist to support organizations and activities that benefit citizens living within certain geographic areas of the community.
The company supports the Employee Contributions Club, which funds local community projects, and a holiday food drive.
Publications: Community Partnership Request Form; Annual Review

Corporate Officials

Molly Cartmill: chairman, president, director PRIM CORP EMPL chairman, president: Sempra Energy. NONPR AFFIL director: San Diego Workforce Partnership Inc..
Donald E. Felsinger: president, chief operating officer, director B Safford, AZ 1947. ED Stanford University MBA; University of Arizona BS (1972). PRIM CORP EMPL president, chief operating officer, director: Sempra Energy.

Giving Program Officials

Molly Cartmill: director corporate contributions (see above)

Grants Analysis

Typical Range: $1,000 to $50,000

SENECA FOODS CORP.

Company Headquarters

1162 Pittsford Victor Rd.
Pittsford, NY 14534

Company Description

Employees: 1,336
SIC(s): 2000 Food & Kindred Products, 2300 Apparel & Other Textile Products, 4500 Transportation by Air.

Operating Locations

Seneca Foods Corp. (MN--Rochester; NY--Marion, Pittsford)

Seneca Foods Foundation

Giving Contact

Kraig H. Kayser, President, Chief Executive Officer, Director
3736 S. Main St.
Marion, NY 14505
Phone: (315)926-8100

Description

Founded: 1989
EIN: 222996324
Organization Type: Corporate Foundation
Giving Locations: headquarters and operating communities.
Grant Types: General Support.

Financial Summary

Total Giving: $102,257 (fiscal year ending March 31, 2004); $177,953 (fiscal 2001). Note: Fiscal 1997 Giving includes United Way ($8,825).
Giving Analysis: Giving for fiscal 2004 includes: foundation grants to United Way ($9,500); fiscal 2001: foundation grants to United Way ($11,500)
Assets: $4,021,837 (fiscal 2004); $3,132,580 (fiscal 2001)
Gifts Received: $17,340 (fiscal 2004); $24,699 (fiscal 2001); $13,500 (fiscal 1997). Note: Contributions were received from Seneca Foods Corp.

Typical Recipients

Arts & Humanities: Arts Associations & Councils, Arts & Humanities-General, Libraries, Museums/Galleries, Music, Performing Arts, Public Broadcasting
Civic & Public Affairs: Botanical Gardens/Parks, Chambers of Commerce, Clubs, Economic Policy, Civic & Public Affairs-General, Housing, Minority Business, Parades/Festivals, Professional & Trade Associations, Safety, Urban & Community Affairs, Zoos/Aquariums
Education: Agricultural Education, Business Education, Colleges & Universities, Community & Junior Colleges, Environmental Education, Education-General, Private Education (Precollege), Public Education (Precollege), Science/Mathematics Education, Secondary Education (Private), Student Aid, Vocational & Technical Education
Environment: Research, Wildlife Protection
Health: Alzheimer's Disease, Cancer, Children's Health/Hospitals, Diabetes, Emergency/Ambulance Services, Health-General, Health Organizations, Heart, Hospices, Hospitals, Medical Rehabilitation, Multiple Sclerosis, Prenatal Health Issues
International: International Environmental Issues
Religion: Churches, Jewish Causes, Religious Welfare
Science: Science-General
Social Services: Big Brothers/Big Sisters, Camps, Child Welfare, Community Service Organizations, Delinquency & Criminal Rehabilitation, Emergency Relief, Family Services, People with Disabilities, Recreation & Athletics, Scouts, Social Services-General, Special Olympics, Substance Abuse, United Funds/United Ways, Veterans, YMCA/YWCA/YMHA/YWHA, Youth Organizations

Application Procedures

Initial Contact: The foundation has no formal grant application procedure or application form.
Deadlines: None.

Corporate Officials

Kraig H. Kayser: president, chief executive officer, director PRIM CORP EMPL president, chief executive officer, director: Seneca Foods Corp.
Arthur S. Wolcott: chairman, director B Corning, NY 1926. ED Cornell University (1949). PRIM CORP EMPL chairman, director: Seneca Foods Corp. CORP AFFIL director: Moog.

Foundation Officials

Kraig H. Kayser: president, chief executive officer, director (see above)
Philip G. Paras: treasurer, assistant secretary
Susan W. Stuart: director
Jeffrey L. Van Riper: secretary B Ithaca, NY 1956. ED Morrisville College (1976); Clarkson University (1978). PRIM CORP EMPL secretary, controller: Seneca Foods Corp. NONPR AFFIL member: Insti-

tute of Management Accountants.
Arthur S. Wolcott: chairman, director (see above)

Grants Analysis

Disclosure Period: fiscal year ending March 31, 2001
Total Grants: $92,757*
Number of Grants: 83
Average Grant: $826*
Highest Grant: $25,000
Typical Range: $100 to $2,000
***Note:** Giving excludes United Way. Average grant figure excludes highest grant.

Recent Grants

Note: Grants derived from 2000 Form 990.
General

33,916	NY Agriculture Research, NY
33,500	Rochester Institute of Technology, Rochester, NY
25,000	Cornell University, Ithaca, NY
20,000	City of Glencoe Parks
20,000	University of Wisconsin, Madison, WI
16,000	Midwest Food Processing Association
15,000	Harley School, Rochester, NY
12,400	FFA
10,900	United Way Funds
10,000	Clasp Homes, Westport, CT

SENTRY INSURANCE, A MUTUAL CO.

Company Headquarters

Stevens Point, WI
Web: http://www.sentry-insurance.com

Company Description

Employees: 4,314
SIC(s): 6311 Life Insurance.

Operating Locations

Sentry Insurance, A Mutual Co. (WI--Stevens Point)

Nonmonetary Support

Note: Undisclosed amounts of nonmonetary support are given by the company.

Sentry Insurance Foundation Inc.

Giving Contact

Margie Coker-Nelson, Executive Director, Vice President
1800 N Point Drive
Stevens Point, WI 54481
Phone: (715)346-6000
Fax: (715)346-6405

Description

EIN: 391037370
Organization Type: Corporate Foundation
Giving Locations: nationally; areas with large employee populations.
Grant Types: Employee Matching Gifts, General Support, Scholarship.

Financial Summary

Total Giving: $686,034 (2002); $957,244 (2001). Note: Contributes through foundation only.
Giving Analysis: Giving for 2001 includes: foundation scholarships ($124,767); foundation grants to United Way ($129,250); foundation matching gifts ($281,156); foundation ($422,071)
Assets: $293,996 (2002); $379,221 (2001)
Gifts Received: $628,165 (2002); $499,875 (1999);

$670,750 (1998). Note: Contributions are received from Sentry Insurance, A Mutual Co.

Typical Recipients

Arts & Humanities: Arts Associations & Councils, Arts Festivals, Community Arts, History & Archaeology, Libraries, Music, Public Broadcasting, Theater
Civic & Public Affairs: Business/Free Enterprise, Chambers of Commerce, Clubs, Community Foundations, Employment/Job Training, Civic & Public Affairs-General, Housing, Public Policy, Urban & Community Affairs
Education: Afterschool/Enrichment Programs, Business Education, Colleges & Universities, Community & Junior Colleges, Economic Education, Education Associations, Education Funds, Elementary Education (Private), Engineering/Technological Education, Education-General, Gifted & Talented Programs, Legal Education, Medical Education, Minority Education, Private Education (Precollege), Public Education (Precollege), Religious Education, Science/Mathematics Education, Secondary Education (Private), Secondary Education (Public), Student Aid, Vocational & Technical Education
Environment: Environment-General, Wildlife Protection
Health: Cancer, Health Organizations, Heart, Hospitals, Medical Research, Public Health
International: Health Care/Hospitals
Religion: Religion-General, Religious Organizations, Religious Welfare, Seminaries
Social Services: Animal Protection, At-Risk Youth, Camps, Community Service Organizations, Delinquency & Criminal Rehabilitation, Domestic Violence, Emergency Relief, Family Services, People with Disabilities, Recreation & Athletics, Scouts, Social Services-General, Special Olympics, Substance Abuse, United Funds/United Ways, Veterans, Volunteer Services, YMCA/YWCA/YMHA/YWHA, Youth Organizations

Application Procedures

Initial Contact: Send letter of request.
Application Requirements: Include description of program and amount of contribution sought.
Deadlines: None.

Corporate Officials

Gregory C. Mox: vice president human resources PRIM CORP EMPL vice president human resources: Sentry Insurance, A Mutual Co.
Dale R. Schuh: president, chief executive officer, chairman ED Lawrence University. PRIM CORP EMPL president, chief executive officer, chairman: Sentry Insurance, A Mutual Co. CORP AFFIL chairman: Sentry Life Insurance Co.

Foundation Officials

Gregory C. Mox: president, chairman, director (see above)
William M. O'Reilly: secretary

Grants Analysis

Disclosure Period: calendar year ending 2002
Total Grants: $176,320*
Number of Grants: 33
Average Grant: $3,760*
Highest Grant: $56,000
Lowest Grant: $200
Typical Range: $100 to $15,000
***Note:** Giving excludes matching gifts, scholarships, and United Way. Average grant figure excludes highest grant.

Recent Grants

Note: Grants derived from 2003 Form 990.
General

60,000	St. Paul Lutheran School, Stevens Point, WI
60,000	Stevens Point Area Catholic School, Stevens Point, WI

20,732	University of Wisconsin, Stevens Point, WI
12,282	Operation Bootstrap, Stevens Point, WI
9,600	Trinity Lutheran School, Wausau, WI
7,710	University of Wisconsin, Madison, WI
7,187	Salvation Army, Stevens Point, WI
6,728	Ripon College, Ripon, WI
6,600	Milwaukee School of Engineering, Milwaukee, WI
6,375	Marquette University, Milwaukee, WI

SETON CO.

Company Headquarters

Morristown, PA

Company Description

Former Name: Seton Leather Co.
Employees: 1,400
SIC(s): 3111 Leather Tanning & Finishing.

Seton Co. Foundation

Giving Contact

Gail Kurz
Seton Co. Foundation
c/o Seton Co.
101 Eisenhower Parkway
Roseland, NJ 07068
Phone: (973)226-4551

Description

EIN: 226029254
Organization Type: Corporate Foundation
Giving Locations: FL; MA; MI; NJ; NY; PA
Grant Types: General Support.

Financial Summary

Total Giving: $171,890 (2003); $80,085 (2001)
Giving Analysis: Giving for 2001 includes: foundation grants to United Way ($2,250)
Assets: $985,045 (2003); $1,276,913 (2001)
Gifts Received: $112,165 (2001); $250,000 (1997); $250,000 (1996). Note: In 2001, contributions were received from Seton Co. ($100,000); Sadelco USA Corp. ($11,275); and anonymous donors. In 1997, contributions were received from Seton Co.

Typical Recipients

Arts & Humanities: Ballet, Libraries, Museums/Galleries, Music, Opera, Performing Arts, Public Broadcasting, Theater
Civic & Public Affairs: Chambers of Commerce, Clubs, Economic Development, Ethnic Organizations, Civic & Public Affairs-General, Housing, Parades/Festivals, Safety, Women's Affairs
Education: Colleges & Universities, Community & Junior Colleges, Education Funds, Education Reform, Engineering/Technological Education, Education-General, Legal Education, Literacy, Medical Education, Private Education (Precollege), Science/Mathematics Education, Secondary Education (Private), Student Aid
Environment: Air/Water Quality, Resource Conservation
Health: AIDS/HIV, Cancer, Clinics/Medical Centers, Health Organizations, Hospices, Hospitals, Medical Rehabilitation, Mental Health, Multiple Sclerosis, Prenatal Health Issues, Preventive Medicine/Wellness Organizations
International: Health Care/Hospitals, International Peace & Security Issues
Religion: Churches, Jewish Causes, Ministries, Religious Welfare, Social/Policy Issues
Science: Scientific Labs
Social Services: Animal Protection, At-Risk Youth,

Child Welfare, Community Centers, Community Service Organizations, Family Planning, Recreation & Athletics, Scouts, Special Olympics, United Funds/United Ways, Volunteer Services, YMCA/YWCA/YMHA/YWHA, Youth Organizations

Application Procedures
Initial Contact: Send a brief letter of inquiry.
Application Requirements: Include a description of organization, amount requested, and statement of program.
Deadlines: None.

Corporate Officials
Philip K. Kaltenbacher: chairman, president, chief executive officer, director B Orange, NJ 1937. ED Yale University (1959); Yale University (1963). PRIM CORP EMPL chairman, president, chief executive officer, director: Seton Co. CORP AFFIL chairman, chief executive officer: Selco Trucking Co.; chairman, chief executive officer: Wilmington Leather Coatings; chairman, chief executive officer: Norwood Industries.

Foundation Officials
Robert DeMajistre: trustee
Philip K. Kaltenbacher: trustee (see above)

Grants Analysis
Disclosure Period: calendar year ending 2003
Total Grants: $171,890
Number of Grants: 66
Average Grant: $2,605
Highest Grant: $25,000
Lowest Grant: $25
Typical Range: $100 to $3,000

Recent Grants
Note: Grants derived from 2003 Form 990.
General

25,000	Martha's Vineyard Hospital, Oak Bluffs, MA
25,000	Saxton Volunteer Fire Company, Saxton, PA
20,400	BMW Charity Pro-Am, Spartanburg, SC
15,000	Animal Rescue Coalition, Sarasota, FL
10,000	Cathedral School, New York, NY
10,000	Ringling Museum of Art, Sarasota, FL
5,200	Jewish Federation of Palm Beach County, West Palm Beach, FL
5,000	Asolo Theatre Company, Sarasota, FL
4,365	Congregation B'nai Jeshurun, Short Hills, NJ
2,500	Boy Scouts of America, Detroit, MI

SETZER FOUNDATION

Giving Contact
Hardie C. Setzer, Trustee
2555 3rd St., Suite 200
Sacramento, CA 95818
Phone: (916)422-2555

Description
Founded: 1965
EIN: 946115578
Organization Type: Private Foundation
Giving Locations: CA
Grant Types: General Support.

Donor Information
Founder: members of the Setzer family

Financial Summary
Total Giving: $516,329 (fiscal year ending March 31, 2003); $904,496 (fiscal 2001). Note: Fiscal 1997 Giving includes scholarship ($400), United Way ($3,200).

Assets: $7,221,412 (fiscal 2003); $10,135,778 (fiscal 2001)
Gifts Received: $1,814 (fiscal 1997)

Typical Recipients
Arts & Humanities: Ballet, Community Arts, Arts & Humanities-General, History & Archaeology, Libraries, Museums/Galleries, Music, Opera, Performing Arts, Public Broadcasting, Theater
Civic & Public Affairs: Community Foundations, Economic Development, Civic & Public Affairs-General, Legal Aid, Nonprofit Management, Public Policy, Safety, Urban & Community Affairs, Zoos/Aquariums
Education: Business Education, Colleges & Universities, Environmental Education, Education-General, Legal Education, Private Education (Precollege), Secondary Education (Private)
Environment: Forestry, Environment-General, Wildlife Protection
Health: Arthritis, Cancer, Children's Health/Hospitals, Clinics/Medical Centers, Diabetes, Emergency/Ambulance Services, Health Organizations, Heart, Hospitals, Kidney, Medical Research, Multiple Sclerosis, Prenatal Health Issues, Single-Disease Health Associations, Speech & Hearing, Transplant Networks/Donor Banks
International: International Environmental Issues
Religion: Religious Welfare
Science: Science Museums, Scientific Centers & Institutes
Social Services: Animal Protection, At-Risk Youth, Child Welfare, Community Service Organizations, Emergency Relief, Family Services, Food/Clothing Distribution, People with Disabilities, Recreation & Athletics, Scouts, Senior Services, United Funds/United Ways, YMCA/YWCA/YMHA/YWHA, Youth Organizations

Application Procedures
Initial Contact: The foundation has no formal grant application procedure or application form.
Deadlines: None.

Foundation Officials
G. Cal Setzer: trustee
Hardie C. Setzer: trustee
Mark Setzer: trustee

Grants Analysis
Disclosure Period: fiscal year ending March 31, 2003
Total Grants: $516,329*
Number of Grants: 327
Average Grant: $817*
Highest Grant: $250,000
Lowest Grant: $10
Typical Range: $100 to $2,000
*Note: Average grant figure excludes highest grant.

Recent Grants
Note: Grants derived from 2003 Form 990.
General

250,000	McClellen Aviation Museum Foundation, North Highlands, CA
15,000	California Musical Theatre, Sacramento, CA
13,000	Sacramento Zoological Society, Sacramento, CA
10,000	Children's Receiving Home, Sacramento, CA
10,000	Sacramento Regional Foundation, Sacramento, CA
8,000	Crocker Art Museum, Sacramento, CA
5,000	Boy Scouts of America, Sacramento, CA
5,000	Dobbins/Oregon House Improvement Foundation, Oregon House, CA
5,000	KVIE, Sacramento, CA
5,000	National Kidney Foundation, Sacramento, CA

SEVEN SPRINGS FOUNDATION

Giving Contact
Martha D. Lyddon, President
11801 Dorothy Anne Way
Cupertino, CA 95014
Phone: (408)252-2728

Description
Founded: 1979
EIN: 942570260
Organization Type: Private Foundation
Giving Locations: CA
Grant Types: General Support, Project.

Financial Summary
Total Giving: $183,300 (2003); $240,106 (2001)
Assets: $3,780,163 (2003); $4,813,971 (2001)
Gifts Received: $1,803 (1995); $262,291 (1994); $4,137 (1993). Note: In 1995, contributions were received from Dorothy S. Lyddon.

Typical Recipients
Arts & Humanities: Arts Associations & Councils, Ethnic & Folk Arts, Film & Video, History & Archaeology, Libraries, Literary Arts, Museums/Galleries, Public Broadcasting
Civic & Public Affairs: Botanical Gardens/Parks, Economic Policy, Employment/Job Training, Civic & Public Affairs-General, Law & Justice, Public Policy, Urban & Community Affairs, Women's Affairs, Zoos/Aquariums
Education: Colleges & Universities, Environmental Education, Faculty Development, Medical Education, Private Education (Precollege), Religious Education, Social Sciences Education
Environment: Air/Water Quality, Forestry, Environment-General, Protection, Research, Resource Conservation, Wildlife Protection
Health: Mental Health, Nursing Services, Public Health
International: Human Rights, International Affairs, International Development, International Environmental Issues, International Organizations, International Peace & Security Issues, International Relations
Religion: Religion-General, Religious Organizations, Religious Welfare
Science: Scientific Centers & Institutes, Scientific Research
Social Services: At-Risk Youth, Child Welfare, Community Service Organizations, Counseling, Domestic Violence, Family Planning, Food/Clothing Distribution, United Funds/United Ways, YMCA/YWCA/YMHA/YWHA, Youth Organizations

Application Procedures
Initial Contact: The foundation has no formal grant application procedure or application form.
Deadlines: None.

Foundation Officials
Grant Lyddon: vice president
John Knight Lyddon: secretary
Martha D. Lyddon: president

Grants Analysis
Disclosure Period: calendar year ending 2003
Total Grants: $183,300
Number of Grants: 41
Average Grant: $4,471
Highest Grant: $20,000
Lowest Grant: $500
Typical Range: $1,000 to $10,000

Recent Grants
Note: Grants derived from 2003 Form 990.

General

20,000	Institute of Noetic Sciences, Sausalito, CA
20,000	Planetary Coral Reef Foundation, Santa Fe, NM
15,000	Colorado College Development Office, Colorado Springs, CO
10,000	Earth Island Institute, San Francisco, CA
10,000	Resource Renewal Institute, San Francisco, CA
10,000	Southern Utah Wilderness Foundation, Salt Lake City, UT
8,300	Rainforest Action Network, San Francisco, CA
5,000	Silicon Valley Toxics Coalition, San Jose, CA
5,000	Women's Institute for Leadership Development for Human Rights, San Francisco, CA
5,000	Youth for Environment Sanity Earthsave Foundation, Santa Cruz, CA

ADAM AND MARIA SARAH SEYBERT INSTITUTION FOR POOR BOYS AND GIRLS

Giving Contact
Judith L. Bardes, Executive Directory
PO Box 8228
Philadelphia, PA 19101-8228
Phone: (215)828-8145

Description
Founded: 1914
EIN: 236260105
Organization Type: Private Foundation
Giving Locations: PA: Philadelphia
Grant Types: Emergency, General Support, Research, Scholarship, Seed Money.

Donor Information
Founder: the late Henry Seybert

Financial Summary
Total Giving: $259,100 (2003). Note: In 1996 Giving includes scholarship ($2,500).
Assets: $6,257,048 (2003)

Typical Recipients
Arts & Humanities: Arts Outreach, Arts & Humanities-General, Libraries, Theater, Visual Arts
Civic & Public Affairs: Botanical Gardens/Parks, Community Foundations, Economic Development, Employment/Job Training, Civic & Public Affairs-General, Hispanic Affairs, Housing, Urban & Community Affairs, Women's Affairs
Education: Afterschool/Enrichment Programs, Arts/Humanities Education, Colleges & Universities, Education Funds, Education Reform, Elementary Education (Private), Elementary Education (Public), Engineering/Technological Education, Literacy, Preschool Education, Private Education (Precollege), School Volunteerism, Science/Mathematics Education, Secondary Education (Public), Student Aid
Health: AIDS/HIV, Children's Health/Hospitals, Clinics/Medical Centers, Health Funds, Health Organizations, Hospitals, Prenatal Health Issues, Public Health
Religion: Churches, Dioceses, Religious Organizations, Religious Welfare
Science: Scientific Centers & Institutes
Social Services: Camps, Child Abuse, Child Welfare, Community Centers, Community Service Organizations, Counseling, Day Care, Domestic Violence, Family Planning, Family Services, Food/Clothing Distribution, Homes, Sexual Abuse, YMCA/YWCA/YMHA/YWHA, Youth Organizations

Application Procedures
Initial Contact: Request application guidelines.
Deadlines: January 2, April 1, and October 1.

Restrictions
Does not support individuals.

Additional Information
Publications: Application Guidelines; Annual Report

Foundation Officials
Judith L. Bardes: executive director
William C. Bullitt: president, trustee
Susan C. Day, MD: vice president, trustee
Graham Stanley Finney: trustee B Greenwich, CT 1930. ED Washington & Lee University (1948-1949); Yale University BA (1952); Harvard University MPA (1954). PRIM CORP EMPL senior partner: Conservation Co. NONPR AFFIL director: Replication & Program Systems; member: Union Benevolent Association; member: 21st Century League. CLUB AFFIL mem: Yale Club.
Rev. David I. Hagan: trustee

Grants Analysis
Disclosure Period: calendar year ending 2003
Total Grants: $259,100
Number of Grants: 35
Average Grant: $7,403*
Highest Grant: $15,000
Lowest Grant: $3,000
Typical Range: $1,000 to $10,000
*Note: Average grant figure excludes highest grant.

Recent Grants
Note: Grants derived from 2003 Form 990.
General

15,000	FD Educational Fund, Philadelphia, PA -- for North Star outreach, after-school program
7,000	Southwest Community Enrichment Center, Philadelphia, PA -- for teen enrichment program
5,000	CHOICE, Philadelphia, PA -- towards youth education program
5,000	Clay Studio, Philadelphia, PA -- ceramic art classes for teens at Philadelphia youth study center
5,000	Community Women's Education Project, Philadelphia, PA -- community women's education project kids -to qualify for accreditation
5,000	Literacy Action Project, Philadelphia, PA -- replacement books for 100 book challenge at Kearny elementary school
5,000	Maternity Care Coalition of Greater Philadelphia, Philadelphia, PA -- for specialty teen advocate in Germantown area
5,000	Philabundance, Philadelphia, PA -- towards project ABC
5,000	Philadelphia Student Union, Philadelphia, PA
5,000	Philadelphia Training Program, Philadelphia, PA

SHAPIRO FAMILY CHARITABLE FOUNDATION

Giving Contact
Ralph J. Shapiro, Chairman
9401 Wilshire Blvd., Ste. 1201
Beverly Hills, CA 90212
Phone: (310)550-0960
Fax: (310)205-3879

Description
Founded: 1983
EIN: 953887151
Organization Type: Private Foundation
Former Name: Hanover Foundation.
Giving Locations: CA
Grant Types: General Support.

Donor Information
Founder: Ralph J. Shapiro, Shirley Shapiro, Kihi Foundation, Knoll International Holdings, Inc.

Financial Summary
Total Giving: $1,425,875 (fiscal year ending January 31, 2004); $1,284,550 (fiscal 2002); $396,395 (fiscal 2001)
Giving Analysis: Giving for fiscal 2004 includes: foundation grants to United Way ($1,205,000); fiscal 2002: foundation grants to United Way ($950,000); fiscal 2001: foundation grants to United Way ($176,000)
Assets: $4,529,463 (fiscal 2004); $3,619,917 (fiscal 2002); $3,976,092 (fiscal 2001)
Gifts Received: $1,025,650 (fiscal 2004); $818,408 (fiscal 2002); $405,838 (fiscal 2001). Note: In fiscal 2004, contributions were received from Raps Industries ($520,650), B.D. & F.K. Fischer ($5,000) and SDI Industries ($500,000). In fiscal 2001, contributions were received from Ralph & Shirley Shapiro ($485,351), Alison D. Shaprio ($87,295), Pete Kameron Living Trust ($150,000), and Raps Industries ($95,762). In fiscal 2001, contributions were received from Earl W. Kavanau ($5,000) and Ralph J. and Shirley Shapiro ($400,838). In fiscal 2000, contributions were received from Flavia Kavanau ($10,000) and Ralph J. and Shirley Shapiro ($195,380). In fiscal 1999, contributions were received from Earl W. Kavanau ($4,000), Lawrence N. Field ($55,000), and Ralph J. and Shirley Shapiro ($53,433). In fiscal 1997, contributions were received from Earl Kavanau ($7,200) and Ralph J. and Shirley Shapiro ($234,150).

Typical Recipients
Arts & Humanities: Arts & Humanities-General, Libraries, Literary Arts, Museums/Galleries, Music, Opera, Public Broadcasting
Civic & Public Affairs: Botanical Gardens/Parks, Civil Rights, Community Foundations, Economic Development, Civic & Public Affairs-General, Housing, Law & Justice, Legal Aid, Public Policy, Urban & Community Affairs
Education: Colleges & Universities, Education Funds, Education Reform, Legal Education, Medical Education, Minority Education, Private Education (Precollege), Student Aid
Environment: Environment-General, Resource Conservation
Health: Alzheimer's Disease, Cancer, Children's Health/Hospitals, Clinics/Medical Centers, Health-General, Heart, Hospitals (University Affiliated), Mental Health, Trauma Treatment
International: Foreign Arts Organizations, Health Care/Hospitals, International Organizations, Missionary/Religious Activities
Religion: Jewish Causes, Religious Welfare
Social Services: Child Welfare, Community Service Organizations, Family Planning, People with Disabilities, Recreation & Athletics, Special Olympics, United Funds/United Ways, Volunteer Services, YMCA/YWCA/YMHA/YWHA, Youth Organizations

Application Procedures
Initial Contact: The foundation has no formal grant application procedure or application form.
Deadlines: None.

Foundation Officials
Floyd P. Cook, Jr.: chief financial officer
Ava Coyne: secretary
Alison D. Shapiro: vice president
Peter W. Shapiro: vice president
Ralph J. Shapiro: chairman
Shirley Shapiro: president

Grants Analysis
Disclosure Period: fiscal year ending January 31, 2004
Total Grants: $220,875*
Number of Grants: 105
Average Grant: $1,491*
Highest Grant: $65,800
Lowest Grant: $50
Typical Range: $500 to $5,000
*Note: Giving excludes United Way. Average grant figure excludes highest grant.

Recent Grants
Note: Grants derived from 2004 Form 990.
General

1,205,000	United Way, Los Angeles, CA
65,800	United Cerebral Palsy, Chatsworth, CA
25,000	Administrative Office of the Courts, San Francisco, CA
15,100	University of California - Los Angeles Foundation, Los Angeles, CA
11,000	United Friends of Children, Culver City, CA
6,000	Sun Valley Writers' Conference, Ketchum, ID
5,000	First African Methodist Episcopal Assistance Corporation, Los Angeles, CA
5,000	Michigan Law School, Ann Arbor, MI
3,000	Community Partners, Sherman Oaks, CA
3,000	Los Angeles World Affairs Council, Los Angeles, CA

CHARLES MORTON SHARE TRUST

Giving Contact
Mike Carroll
c/o Heritage Trust Co.
PO Box 21708
Oklahoma City, OK 73156
Phone: (405)848-8899

Description
Founded: 1959
EIN: 736090984
Organization Type: Private Foundation
Giving Locations: OK
Grant Types: General Support, Scholarship.

Donor Information
Founder: the late Charles Morton Share

Financial Summary
Total Giving: $253,408 (fiscal year ending June 30, 2004); $102,174 (fiscal 2001)
Assets: $10,866,985 (fiscal 2004); $10,145,493 (fiscal 2001)

Typical Recipients
Arts & Humanities: Arts Associations & Councils, Arts Institutes, Arts & Humanities-General, History & Archaeology, Libraries, Museums/Galleries, Music, Performing Arts, Theater
Civic & Public Affairs: Clubs, Community Foundations, Civic & Public Affairs-General, Municipalities/Towns, Parades/Festivals, Professional & Trade Associations, Safety, Urban & Community Affairs
Education: Colleges & Universities, Education Funds, Education Reform, Literacy, Medical Educa-

tion, Public Education (Precollege), Science/Mathematics Education, Secondary Education (Public)
Environment: Air/Water Quality
Health: Clinics/Medical Centers, Diabetes, Eyes/Blindness, Hospitals, Medical Research
Religion: Religious Welfare
Science: Science Museums
Social Services: Community Service Organizations, Crime Prevention, Delinquency & Criminal Rehabilitation, Family Services, People with Disabilities, Recreation & Athletics, Scouts, Veterans, Youth Organizations

Application Procedures
Initial Contact: The foundation has no formal grant application procedure or application form. Send enough information to identify the organization and the nature of the request.
Deadlines: None.

Restrictions
Does not support individuals.

Additional Information
Trust(s): Heritage Trust Company

Foundation Officials
Donald Benson: trustee
J. R. Holder: trustee
Johnny C. Jones: trustee
Darrell Kline: trustee

Grants Analysis
Disclosure Period: fiscal year ending June 30, 2004
Total Grants: $253,408
Number of Grants: 12
Average Grant: $6,934*
Highest Grant: $100,000
Lowest Grant: $50
Typical Range: $5,000 to $10,000
*Note: Average grant figure excludes three highest grants ($191,000).

Recent Grants
Note: Grants derived from fiscal 2004 Form 990.
General

100,000	City of Alva, Alva, OK -- towards library
50,000	Nescatonga Arts And Humanity
41,000	Alva Public School, Alva, OK
14,858	Alva Mural Society, Alva, OK
10,000	Northwest Family Services
10,000	Northwestern Oklahoma State University, Alva, OK -- towards concert series
7,500	City of Alva, Alva, OK
5,000	Heartland Best, Alva, OK
5,000	Northwestern Oklahoma State University, Alva, OK -- towards Oklahoma army national
5,000	Waynoka Fire Department, Waynoka, OK

SHARON STEEL CORP.

Company Headquarters
Farrell, PA

Company Description
Employees: 3,000
SIC(s): 1200 Coal Mining, 3300 Primary Metal Industries, 3400 Fabricated Metal Products, 5000 Wholesale Trade--Durable Goods.
Parent Company: Sharon Specialty Steel Inc.

Operating Locations
Sharon Steel Corp. (PA--Farrell)

Sharon Steel Foundation

Giving Contact
Hume R. Steyer, Esq.
c/o Seward and Kissel
1 Battery Park Plaza
New York, NY 10004

Description
Founded: 1953
EIN: 256063133
Organization Type: Corporate Foundation
Giving Locations: PA
Grant Types: General Support.

Donor Information
Founder: Sharon Steel Corp.

Financial Summary
Total Giving: $238,272 (2003)
Assets: $4,523,932 (2003)

Typical Recipients
Arts & Humanities: Arts Institutes, Community Arts, Libraries, Music, Opera, Performing Arts, Public Broadcasting, Theater
Civic & Public Affairs: Botanical Gardens/Parks, Business/Free Enterprise, Chambers of Commerce, Clubs, Economic Development, Civic & Public Affairs-General, Housing, Municipalities/Towns, Professional & Trade Associations
Education: Afterschool/Enrichment Programs, Business Education, Colleges & Universities, Continuing Education, Education-General, Minority Education, Preschool Education, Private Education (Precollege), Science/Mathematics Education, Student Aid
Environment: Air/Water Quality, Protection
Health: Children's Health/Hospitals, Geriatric Health, Health Funds, Hospitals, Medical Research, Prenatal Health Issues, Preventive Medicine/Wellness Organizations, Single-Disease Health Associations
Religion: Churches, Religious Organizations, Religious Welfare
Social Services: Camps, Child Welfare, Community Service Organizations, Counseling, Family Services, People with Disabilities, Recreation & Athletics, Scouts, Special Olympics, United Funds/United Ways, YMCA/YWCA/YMHA/YWHA, Youth Organizations

Application Procedures
Initial Contact: Send a brief letter of inquiry. Include a description of organization, amount requested, purpose of funds sought, recently audited financial statement, and proof of tax-exempt status.
Deadlines: None.

Additional Information
The company remained in Chapter 11 bankruptcy as of July 1995. Charitable contributions were severely curtailed.

Foundation Officials
Christian L. Oberbeck: trustee
Malvin Gustav Sandler: trustee B Pittsburgh, PA 1946. ED Bucknell University BS (1967); Duquesne University JD (1972). PRIM CORP EMPL senior vice president, general counsel, secretary: Sharon Steel Corp. CORP AFFIL member: Pennsylvania Bar Association; member: Coalition Empl through Exports; member: America Bar Association; member: America Trial Lawyers Association. NONPR AFFIL member: Delta Theta Phi.
Hume R. Steyer: trustee

Grants Analysis
Disclosure Period: calendar year ending 2003
Total Grants: $89,100*
Number of Grants: 17
Average Grant: $4,944*
Highest Grant: $10,000

Lowest Grant: $700
Typical Range: $1,000 to $5,000
*Note: Giving excludes scholarships; United Way. Average grant figure excludes highest grant.

Recent Grants

Note: Grants derived from 2003 Form 990.
General

40,172	Pennsylvania State University, Sharon, PA -- for scholarships
25,000	Phillips Exeter Academy, Exeter, NH -- for scholarships
22,000	Hotchkiss School, Lakeville, CT -- for scholarships
20,000	Brown University, Providence, RI -- for scholarships
20,000	Brunswick School, Greenwich, CT
20,000	United Way of Mercer County, Sharon, PA
15,000	Westminster College, New Wilmington, PA -- for scholarships
10,000	Pennsylvania State University, Sharon, PA
10,000	Tuxedo Park School, Tuxedo Park, NY
8,000	Westminster College, New Wilmington, PA

EVELYN SHARP FOUNDATION

Giving Contact

Paul Cronson, Secretary & Trustee
c/o Peter Sharp & Co.
545 Madison Ave.
New York, NY 10022
Phone: (212)977-1300

Description

Founded: 1952
EIN: 136119532
Organization Type: Private Foundation
Giving Locations: NY
Grant Types: General Support.

Donor Information

Founder: Evelyn Sharp

Financial Summary

Total Giving: $569,178 (fiscal year ending June 30, 2003)
Assets: $9,643,485 (fiscal 2003)
Gifts Received: $75,652 (fiscal 2003). Note: In fiscal 2003, contributions were received from Mary Cronson.

Typical Recipients

Arts & Humanities: Arts Associations & Councils, Arts Centers, Arts Funds, Arts Institutes, Arts Outreach, Ballet, Dance, Ethnic & Folk Arts, Arts & Humanities-General, Libraries, Museums/Galleries, Music, Opera, Performing Arts, Public Broadcasting, Theater
Civic & Public Affairs: Botanical Gardens/Parks, Employment/Job Training, Civic & Public Affairs-General, Parades/Festivals, Public Policy, Urban & Community Affairs, Women's Affairs
Education: Arts/Humanities Education, Colleges & Universities, Education-General, Private Education (Precollege)
Health: Heart, Hospitals, Medical Research, Prenatal Health Issues
International: Foreign Arts Organizations, International Organizations, International Relations
Religion: Jewish Causes, Religious Organizations, Religious Welfare
Science: Science Museums
Social Services: Child Welfare, Community Service

Organizations, Family Planning, Family Services, People with Disabilities, Social Services-General, Youth Organizations

Application Procedures

Initial Contact: Send a brief letter of inquiry.
Deadlines: None.

Foundation Officials

Mary Cronson: president, trustee
Paul Cronson: secretary, trustee
Barry Tobias: treasurer, trustee
Claus Virch: trustee

Grants Analysis

Disclosure Period: fiscal year ending June 30, 2003
Total Grants: $569,178
Number of Grants: 110
Average Grant: $4,763*
Highest Grant: $50,000
Lowest Grant: $50
Typical Range: $1,000 to $5,000
*Note: Average grant figure excludes highest grant.

Recent Grants

Note: Grants derived from fiscal 2003 Form 990.
General

50,000	Solomon Guggenheim Foundation, New York, NY
30,000	New York City Ballet, New York, NY
30,000	New York City Opera, New York, NY
25,000	Julliard School, New York, NY
25,000	Julliard School, New York, NY
25,000	Symphony Space, New York, NY
20,000	Planned Parenthood, New York, NY
20,000	School of American Ballet, New York, NY
16,750	Marilyn Home Foundation, New York, NY
15,000	Brooklyn Academy of Music, Brooklyn, NY

SHATZ, SCHWARTZ & FENTIN P.C.

Company Headquarters

1441 Main St., No. 1100
Springfield, MA 01103

Company Description

SIC(s): 8100 Legal Services.

Shatz, Schwartz & Fentin Charitable Foundation

Giving Contact

Steven J. Schwartz, Trustee
1441 Main St., Suite 1100
Springfield, MA 01103
Phone: (413)737-1131
Fax: (413)736-0375

Description

EIN: 042712836
Organization Type: Corporate Foundation
Giving Locations: headquarters area only.
Grant Types: General Support.

Donor Information

Founder: Gary S. Fentin, Timothy P. Mulhern, Steven J. Schwartz, Stephen A. Shatz, James B. Sheils

Financial Summary

Total Giving: $53,210 (fiscal year ending August 31, 2004); $52,492 (fiscal 2002); $82,642 (fiscal 2001)

Giving Analysis: Giving for fiscal 2002 includes: foundation grants to United Way ($5,000); fiscal 2001: foundation grants to United Way ($5,000)
Assets: $9,911 (fiscal 2004); $7,497 (fiscal 2002); $38,892 (fiscal 2001)
Gifts Received: $55,370 (fiscal 2004); $21,383 (fiscal 2002); $120,994 (fiscal 2001). Note: In fiscal 2004, contributions were received from Stephen A. Shatz ($7,581), Steven J. Schwartz ($7,581), Gary S. Fentin ($6,674), Timothy P. Mulhern ($6,674), James B. Sheils ($8,544), and Steven Weiss ($5,984). In fiscal 2001, contributions were received from Ellen W. Freyman and Steven Weiss. In fiscal 1995, contributions were received from Stephen A. Shatz ($3,250), Steven J. Schwartz ($3,250), Gary S. Fentin ($3,000), Timothy P. Mulhern ($1,750), James B. Sheils ($1,100), and Ann I. Weber ($1,000).

Typical Recipients

Arts & Humanities: Arts Associations & Councils, Libraries, Music, Public Broadcasting
Civic & Public Affairs: Clubs, Civic & Public Affairs-General, Housing, Law & Justice, Legal Aid, Parades/Festivals, Urban & Community Affairs
Education: Afterschool/Enrichment Programs, Arts/Humanities Education, Business Education, Community & Junior Colleges, Education-General, Private Education (Precollege), Public Education (Precollege), School Volunteerism, Secondary Education (Public), Student Aid
Environment: Environment-General
Health: AIDS/HIV, Alzheimer's Disease, Cancer, Children's Health/Hospitals, Clinics/Medical Centers, Emergency/Ambulance Services, Health Organizations, Heart, Hospices, Research/Studies Institutes, Respiratory, Single-Disease Health Associations
Religion: Jewish Causes, Synagogues/Temples
Social Services: Child Welfare, Community Centers, Community Service Organizations, Day Care, Family Services, Food/Clothing Distribution, People with Disabilities, Recreation & Athletics, Scouts, Senior Services, United Funds/United Ways, YMCA/YWCA/YMHA/YWHA, Youth Organizations

Application Procedures

Initial Contact: The foundation has no formal grant application procedure or application form.
Deadlines: None.

Corporate Officials

Gary S. Fentin: senior partner PRIM CORP EMPL senior partner: Shatz Schwartz & Fentin PC.
Timothy P. Mulhern: partner PRIM CORP EMPL partner: Shatz Schwartz & Fentin PC.
Steven J. Schwartz: senior partner PRIM CORP EMPL senior partner: Shatz Schwartz & Fentin PC.
Stephen A. Shatz: counsel PRIM CORP EMPL counsel: Shatz Schwartz & Fentin PC.
James Bernard Sheils: partner, vice president B New Rochelle, NY 1950. ED Holy Cross College AB (1972); Boston College JD (1975). PRIM CORP EMPL partner, vice president: Shatz Schwartz & Fentin PC. NONPR AFFIL member: Massachusetts Bar Association; member: Smaller Business Association; member: Hampden County Bar Association; member: American Bar Association; member: Association Commercial Financial Attorney.
A. I. Weber: partner PRIM CORP EMPL partner: Shatz Schwartz & Fentin PC.

Foundation Officials

Gary S. Fentin: trustee (see above)
Timothy P. Mulhern: trustee (see above)
Steven J. Schwartz: trustee (see above)
Stephen A. Shatz: trustee (see above)
James Bernard Sheils: trustee (see above)

Grants Analysis

Disclosure Period: fiscal year ending August 31, 2004
Total Grants: $48,210*
Number of Grants: 53

Average Grant: $446*
Highest Grant: $25,000
Lowest Grant: $25
Typical Range: $100 to $1,000
***Note:** Giving excludes United Way. Average grant figure excludes highest grant.

Recent Grants

Note: Grants derived from 2004 Form 990.
General

25,000	Children's Study Home, Springfield, MA -- to enhance educational program
5,000	United Way of Pioneer Valley, Springfield, MA
5,000	YMCA, Springfield, MA -- to serve human needs
3,000	Goodwill Industries, Springfield, MA -- support/train people in need
2,500	YWCA, Springfield, MA -- towards services to women
2,000	Dunbar Community Center, Springfield, MA -- to assist people from welfare to work
1,000	Pioneer Valley Free Health Services, Springfield, MA -- to provide health services to uninsured
1,000	Western Massachusetts Legal Services, Springfield, MA -- towards fund free legal assistance to needy
600	Community Music School, Springfield, MA -- to support education in music
500	Springfield Symphony Orchestra, Springfield, MA

ARCH W. SHAW FOUNDATION

Giving Contact
William W. Shaw, Trustee
HC 3 Box 60B
Birch Tree, MO 65438
Phone: (417)764-3701
Fax: (417)764-3706

Description
Founded: 1949
EIN: 366055262
Organization Type: Private Foundation
Giving Locations: IL; MA; MO
Grant Types: General Support.

Donor Information
Founder: the late Arch W. Shaw

Financial Summary
Total Giving: $720,000 (2004); $525,000 (2001)
Giving Analysis: Giving for 2004 includes: foundation scholarships ($55,000)
Assets: $16,085,911 (2004); $11,458,670 (2001)

Typical Recipients
Arts & Humanities: Historic Preservation, History & Archaeology, Libraries, Museums/Galleries, Music, Theater
Civic & Public Affairs: Botanical Gardens/Parks, Clubs, Civic & Public Affairs-General, Law & Justice, Professional & Trade Associations, Women's Affairs, Zoos/Aquariums
Education: Arts/Humanities Education, Colleges & Universities, Environmental Education, Education-General, Medical Education, Private Education (Pre-college), Science/Mathematics Education, Secondary Education (Private), Student Aid
Environment: Environment-General, Resource Conservation
Health: Alzheimer's Disease, Cancer, Children's Health/Hospitals, Clinics/Medical Centers, Diabetes,

Emergency/Ambulance Services, Eyes/Blindness, Health Funds, Hospices, Hospitals, Medical Rehabilitation, Medical Research, Outpatient Health Care, Prenatal Health Issues
International: International Relief Efforts
Religion: Religious Organizations, Religious Welfare
Social Services: Child Welfare, Community Centers, Community Service Organizations, Emergency Relief, Family Services, Food/Clothing Distribution, People with Disabilities, Substance Abuse, United Funds/United Ways, Youth Organizations

Application Procedures
Initial Contact: Send a brief letter of inquiry.
Application Requirements: Describe purpose of funds sought.
Deadlines: None.

Restrictions
Does not support individuals or private foundations.

Foundation Officials
Arch W. Shaw, II: trustee
Bruce P. Shaw: trustee
Roger D. Shaw, Jr.: trustee
William W. Shaw: trustee

Grants Analysis
Disclosure Period: calendar year ending 2004
Total Grants: $665,000*
Number of Grants: 86
Average Grant: $7,733
Highest Grant: $50,000
Lowest Grant: $1,000
Typical Range: $1,000 to $10,000
***Note:** Giving excludes scholarship.

Recent Grants
Note: Grants derived from 2004 Form 990.
General

50,000	Advocate Charter Foundation
30,000	Americares, New Canaan, CT
30,000	Bowdoin College, Brunswick, ME
25,000	Ozarks Medical Center Foundation, West Plains, MO
20,000	American Red Cross, Kansas City, MO
20,000	Children's Service Society, Racine, WI
20,000	Hyslop Foundation
20,000	St. Marks School
20,000	South Norfolk Association for Retarded Children
20,000	Southwest Missouri State University, West Plains, MO -- for scholarship fund

SHAW'S SUPERMARKETS INC.

Company Headquarters
East Bridgewater, MA
Web: http://www.shaws.com

Company Description
Revenue: US$4.4 billion (2001)
Employees: 30682 (2003)
SIC(s): 5411 Grocery Stores.
Parent Company: J. Sainsbury PLC, 33 Holborn, London, United Kingdom

Operating Locations
Shaw's Supermarkets, Inc. (CT; ME--Portland; MA; NH; NJ--East Bridgewater)

Nonmonetary Support
Type: Donated Products

Shaw's Supermarkets Charitable Foundation

Giving Contact
PO Box 6768
Providence, RI 02940-6768
Web: http://www.shaws.com/Public/about_us/community_commitment.cfm

Alternate Contact
Fleet National Bank, Trustee
Two Portland Square
Portland, ME 04104

Description
Founded: 1959
EIN: 016008389
Organization Type: Corporate Foundation
Giving Locations: ME; MA; NH; RI; VT: headquarters and operating communities.
Grant Types: Capital, Challenge, General Support, Scholarship.

Donor Information
Founder: Brockton Public Market, Inc. & George C. Shaw Co., & Subsidiaries

Financial Summary
Total Giving: $659,500 (fiscal year ending July 31, 2003); $508,500 (fiscal 2002); $922,000 (fiscal 2001). Note: Contributes through corporate direct giving program and foundation.
Giving Analysis: Giving for fiscal 2001 includes: foundation ($208,500); foundation grants to United Way ($300,000)
Assets: $1,327,775 (fiscal 2003); $1,414,044 (fiscal 2002); $922,768 (fiscal 2001)
Gifts Received: $530,000 (fiscal 2003); $940,000 (fiscal 2002); $750,000 (fiscal 2001). Note: Contributions are received from Shaw's Supermarkets.

Typical Recipients
Arts & Humanities: Arts Appreciation, Arts Associations & Councils, Arts Funds, Arts Outreach, Historic Preservation, History & Archaeology, Libraries, Museums/Galleries, Music, Public Broadcasting, Theater
Civic & Public Affairs: Business/Free Enterprise, Community Foundations, Economic Development, Civic & Public Affairs-General, Municipalities/Towns, Safety, Urban & Community Affairs, Zoos/Aquariums
Education: Arts/Humanities Education, Colleges & Universities, Education Funds, Environmental Education, Secondary Education (Public)
Environment: Environment-General
Health: Children's Health/Hospitals, Clinics/Medical Centers, Emergency/Ambulance Services, Eyes/Blindness, Geriatric Health, Health Funds, Health Organizations, Hospices, Hospitals, Nursing Services, Public Health, Single-Disease Health Associations
Science: Science Museums
Social Services: Animal Protection, Child Welfare, Community Service Organizations, Day Care, Domestic Violence, Food/Clothing Distribution, Recreation & Athletics, Scouts, Senior Services, Shelters/Homelessness, United Funds/United Ways, YMCA/YWCA/YMHA/YWHA, Youth Organizations

Application Procedures
Initial Contact: For regional requests in Maine, New Hampshire, Vermont and the Greater Boston area of Massachusetts, contact: Regional Vice President, Northern Region Office, Shaw's Supermarkets, Inc., P.O. Box 3566 Portland, ME 04104 For requests in Connecticut, Rhode Island and all other parts of Massachusetts, contact: Regional Vice President, Southern Region Office, Shaw's Supermarkets, Inc., P.O. Box 300 South Easton, MA 02375. For corporate funding, contact: Senior Vice President, Operations Shaw's Supermarkets, Inc., 140 Laurel St., East

Bridgewater, MA 02333.
Application Requirements: Include proof of 501(c)(3) status and full description of event or cause with request.

Additional Information
Trust(s): Fleet National Bank

Corporate Officials
David Brimner: chairman vice president administration, treasurer, director PRIM CORP EMPL chairman: Shaw's Supermarkets, Inc.
Ross McLaren: chief executive officer PRIM CORP EMPL chief executive officer: Shaw's Supermarkets, Inc.
Scott W. Ramsay: executive vice president administration, treasurer, director PRIM CORP EMPL executive vice president administration, treasurer, director: Shaw's Supermarkets, Inc. ADD CORP EMPL treasurer: Shaw Equipment Corp.

Grants Analysis
Disclosure Period: fiscal year ending July 31, 2003
Total Grants: $277,500*
Number of Grants: 34
Average Grant: $5,984*
Highest Grant: $80,000
Lowest Grant: $1,000
Typical Range: $2,500 to $10,000
*Note: Giving excludes scholarship; United Way. Average grant figure excludes highest grant.

Recent Grants
Note: Grants derived from 2003 Form 990.
Library-Related

2,500	Mattapoisett Library, Mattapoisett, MA

General

380,000	United Ways of New England, Boston, MA
80,000	Old Colony YMCA's Central Division, Brockton, MA
25,000	Dimock Community Health Center, Roxbury, MA
25,000	Dimock Community Health Center, Roxbury, MA
20,000	Maine Medical Center, Portland, ME
10,000	Good Shepherd Food Bank, Auburn, ME
10,000	Maine Discovery Museum, Bangor, ME
10,000	Old Dartmouth Historical Society, New Bedford, MA
10,000	South Shore Health and Education Foundation, South Weymouth, MA
6,000	Boys & Girls Club of Taunton, Taunton, MA

SHEAFFER PEN CORP.

Company Headquarters
Fort Madison, IA
Web: http://www.bicpen.com

Company Description
Former Name: Sheaffer Inc.
Revenue: US$69.5 million (2001)
Employees: 450 (2001)
SIC(s): 3951 Pens & Mechanical Pencils.

Operating Locations
Gefinor U.S.A. (NY--New York); Sheaffer Pen Corp. (IA--Fort Madison); Sheaffer Pen Crownmark (RI--Lincoln)

Nonmonetary Support
Type: Donated Products; Workplace Solicitation

Giving Contact
Michele Beach, Admin. Asst.
301 Ave. H
Ft. Madison, IA 52627
Phone: (319)372-3300
Fax: (319)376-3148
E-mail: michele.beach@brcworld.com

Description
Organization Type: Corporate Giving Program
Grant Types: Capital, General Support.

Typical Recipients
Arts & Humanities: Arts Associations & Councils, Arts Centers, Community Arts, Dance, Historic Preservation, Libraries, Museums/Galleries, Music, Performing Arts, Theater
Civic & Public Affairs: Employment/Job Training
Education: Colleges & Universities
Health: Health Policy/Cost Containment, Health Organizations, Hospitals, Mental Health, Single-Disease Health Associations
Social Services: Child Welfare, Community Centers, Community Service Organizations, Family Services, People with Disabilities, Substance Abuse, United Funds/United Ways, Youth Organizations

Application Procedures
Initial Contact: For large grants, write letter one year in advance. For smaller contributions, send a letter any time and include the same information.
Application Requirements: Include a description of organization, amount and purpose of funds sought, a recently audited financial statement, and proof of tax-exempt status.

Corporate Officials
Keith Bloomquist: controller, chief operating officer, director PRIM CORP EMPL controller: Sheaffer Pen Corp.
Owen Jones: chief executive officer, chief operating officer, director PRIM CORP EMPL chief executive officer, chief operating officer, director: Sheaffer Pen Corp.

EDNA M. SHEARY TRUST FOR CHARITY

Giving Contact
Martha M. Heil, Senior Trust Specialist
c/o Mellon Bank NA
PO Box 185
Pittsburgh, PA 15230-9897
Phone: (717)221-3037

Description
Founded: 1991
EIN: 251695940
Organization Type: Private Foundation
Giving Locations: PA
Grant Types: General Support.

Donor Information
Founder: Established in 1991 by the late Edna M. Sheary.

Financial Summary
Total Giving: $288,790 (fiscal year ending May 31, 2004); $397,983 (fiscal 2001)
Assets: $729,613 (fiscal 2004); $1,672,338 (fiscal 2001)

Typical Recipients
Arts & Humanities: History & Archaeology, Libraries, Museums/Galleries, Music, Public Broadcasting
Civic & Public Affairs: Business/Free Enterprise,

Civic & Public Affairs-General, Legal Aid, Public Policy, Safety, Urban & Community Affairs, Women's Affairs
Education: Colleges & Universities, Education-General, Private Education (Precollege), Public Education (Precollege), School Volunteerism, Secondary Education (Public)
Environment: Resource Conservation
Health: Cancer, Emergency/Ambulance Services, Health Organizations, Home-Care Services, Hospitals, Long-Term Care, Research/Studies Institutes
Religion: Churches, Religion-General, Ministries, Religious Organizations, Religious Welfare, Seminaries
Social Services: Camps, Community Centers, Community Service Organizations, Day Care, Family Services, People with Disabilities, Recreation & Athletics, Scouts, Youth Organizations

Application Procedures
Initial Contact: Request application form.
Deadlines: April 1.

Additional Information
Publications: Application Form
Trust(s): Mellon Bank NA

Grants Analysis
Disclosure Period: fiscal year ending May 31, 2004
Total Grants: $288,790
Number of Grants: 12
Average Grant: $8,072*
Highest Grant: $200,000
Typical Range: $5,000 to $10,000
*Note: Average grant excludes three highest grants ($300,000).

Recent Grants
Note: Grants derived from 2000 Form 990.
Library-Related

50,000	Public Library Union County
40,000	Kaufman County Library, Kaufman, TX

General

200,000	Christ Lutheran Church, Abbotsford, WI
50,000	Hemlock Girl Scout Council, Harrisburg, PA
50,000	Susquehanna University, Selinsgrove, PA
30,000	Mifflinburg Buggy Museum
22,250	Albright Life Learning, Reading, PA
20,000	Evangelical Community Hospital, Lewisburg, PA
12,716	Slifer House Museum
9,088	Messiah Evangelical Lutheran Church, Fairview Park, OH
8,947	Noah's Ark Day Care Center
6,525	Concern, Bartlesville, OK

RALPH C. SHELDON FOUNDATION INC.

Giving Contact
Miles L. Lasser, Executive Director, Secretary & Assistant Treasurer
7 E. 3rd St.
Jamestown, NY 14701
Phone: (716)664-9890
Fax: (716)483-6116

Description
Founded: 1948
EIN: 166030502
Organization Type: Private Foundation
Giving Locations: NY: Southern Chautauqua County
Grant Types: Capital, Emergency, General Support.

Donor Information

Founder: Julia S. Livengood, Isabel M. Sheldon

Financial Summary

Total Giving: $1,995,703 (fiscal year ending May 31, 2004); $1,680,312 (fiscal 2002); $1,477,190 (fiscal 2001)

Giving Analysis: Giving for fiscal 2004 includes: foundation grants to United Way ($98,500); fiscal 2002: foundation grants to United Way ($88,500); fiscal 2001: foundation grants to United Way ($83,000)

Assets: $9,959,478 (fiscal 2004); $9,441,899 (fiscal 2002); $10,152,667 (fiscal 2001)

Gifts Received: $1,394,775 (fiscal 2004); $1,737,326 (fiscal 2002); $1,380,143 (fiscal 2001). Note: Contributions were received from the Ralph C. Sheldon Trust.

Typical Recipients

Arts & Humanities: Arts Associations & Councils, Arts Centers, Arts Funds, Arts Institutes, Community Arts, Arts & Humanities-General, History & Archaeology, Libraries, Museums/Galleries, Music, Performing Arts, Theater

Civic & Public Affairs: Community Foundations, Economic Development, Employment/Job Training, Hispanic Affairs, Housing, Inner-City Development, Law & Justice, Urban & Community Affairs, Zoos/Aquariums

Education: Colleges & Universities, Community & Junior Colleges, Continuing Education, Environmental Education, Education-General, Literacy, Private Education (Precollege), Public Education (Precollege), Special Education, Student Aid

Environment: Environment-General, Resource Conservation, Wildlife Protection

Health: Cancer, Heart, Hospices, Hospitals, Medical Training, Nursing Services

Social Services: Big Brothers/Big Sisters, Camps, Child Welfare, Community Service Organizations, Crime Prevention, Day Care, Family Services, Food/Clothing Distribution, People with Disabilities, Recreation & Athletics, Scouts, Senior Services, United Funds/United Ways, YMCA/YWCA/YMHA/YWHA, Youth Organizations

Application Procedures

Initial Contact: Send a brief letter of inquiry.

Application Requirements: Include a description of organization, amount requested, purpose of funds sought, how project benefits Southern Chantauqua County, recently audited financial statement, and proof of tax-exempt status.

Deadlines: None.

Restrictions

Does not support individuals, religious organizations for sectarian purposes, political or lobbying groups, or organizations outside operating areas. Only supports organizations in Southern Chautauqua County.

Additional Information

Publications: Application Form

Foundation Officials

Mark I. Hampton: vice president
Miles L. Lasser: executive director, secretary
J. Elizabeth Sheldon: president
Peter B. Sullivan: director
Barclay O. Wellman: treasurer

Grants Analysis

Disclosure Period: fiscal year ending May 31, 2004
Total Grants: $1,897,203*
Number of Grants: 93
Average Grant: $9,519*
Highest Grant: $500,000
Lowest Grant: $100
Typical Range: $1,000 to $20,000
***Note:** Giving excludes United Way. Average grant figure excludes four highest grants ($1,050,000).

Recent Grants

Note: Grants derived from 2004 Form 990.
Library-Related

80,000	James Prendergast Library Association, Jamestown, NY -- new auto library system

General

500,000	Woman's Christian Association Hospital, Jamestown, NY
300,000	Jamestown Boys and Girls Club, Jamestown, NY -- for swimming pool project
150,000	Jamestown Center City Development Corporation, Jamestown, NY -- for Jamestown Ice Arena
100,000	Roger Tory Peterson Institute, Jamestown, NY
93,000	United Way of Southern Chautauqua County, Jamestown, NY
50,000	Chautauqua Striders, Jamestown, NY
50,000	Jamestown Audubon Society, Jamestown, NY -- for nature center renovation
50,000	Robert H Jackson Center Inc., Jamestown, NY -- for center renovations
45,000	Chautauqua Institution, Chautauqua, NY

SHELL OIL CO.

Company Headquarters

One Shell Plaza
Houston, TX 77002
Web: http://www.shellus.com

Company Description

Acquired: Pennzoil-Quaker State Co. (2002).
Revenue: US$26.943 billion (2001)
SIC(s): 1311 Crude Petroleum & Natural Gas, 2819 Industrial Inorganic Chemicals Nec, 2822 Synthetic Rubber, 2879 Agricultural Chemicals Nec.
Parent Company: Royal Dutch/Shell Group of Cos., Carel Van Bylandtlaan 16, The Hague, Netherlands

Operating Locations

Billiton Metals, Inc. (NY--New York); Criterion Catalyst Co. L.P. (TX--Houston); LL&E Petroleum Marketing (LA--New Orleans); Shell Chemical Co. (TX--Houston); Shell Development Co. (TX--Houston); Shell Oil Co. (CA--Bishop, Concord, Elk Grove, Livermore, Los Angeles, Madera, Martinez, Moreno Valley, Riverside, San Bruno, San Jose, Van Nuys, Willows; CT--Bridgeport; DC--Washington; FL--Bradenton, Fort Lauderdale, Holly Hill, Melbourne, Miami, New Port Richey, North Port, Ocala, Tampa; GA--Atlanta, Nashville; HI--Honolulu, Kahului; IL--Arlington Heights, Berwyn, Chatham, Effingham, Harristown, Mount Auburn, Sibley, Skokie; IN--Hammond; KY--Louisville; LA--Gibson, Golden Meadow, Kenner, Metairie, Norco, Plaquemine; MD--Rockville; MA--Fall River, West Boylston, Westwood, Worcester; MI--Farmington Hills, Grand Haven, Jackson, South Boardman, Spring Lake; MN--Minneapolis; MS--Collins, Columbus, Jackson, Pelahatchie; MO--St. Louis; NV--Reno; NJ--Swearen; NY--Jamaica, New York; OH--Cincinnati, Columbus, Dayton, Lima, Sunbury, Tipp City, Westerville, Willoughby; PA--Pittsburgh; SC--Spartanburg; TN--Knoxville; TX--Baytown, Deer Park, Douglassville, Houston, Mount Pleasant, Pharr, Seminole, Sugar Land; VA--Reston); Shell Pipe Line Corp. (TX--Houston); Tejas Gas Corp. (TX--Houston)
Note: Operates internationally.

Nonmonetary Support

Type: Loaned Employees; Loaned Executives
Volunteer Programs: Company sponsors "Shell Employees and Retirees Volunteerism Effort" (SERVE), through which company employees and retirees have participated in housing rehabilitation projects, educational television solicitations, school clothing drives, and picnics for mentally handicapped children. Employees also serve on the boards of various organizations and loaned executives work with United Way campaigns.
Note: Contact the Manager of Corporate Relations for nonmonetary support information.

Shell Oil Co. Foundation

Giving Contact

Betty Lynn McHam, vice president
Shell Oil Co. Foundation
One Shell Plaza
PO Box 2099
Houston, TX 77252
Phone: (713)241-4480
Fax: (713)241-3329
E-mail: SOCFoundation@shellus.com
Web: http://www.countonshell.com/community/involvement/shell_foundation.html

Description

Founded: 1953
EIN: 136066583
Organization Type: Corporate Foundation
Giving Locations: nationally, with emphasis on communities where Shell employees are located.
Grant Types: Capital, Department, Emergency, Employee Matching Gifts, Fellowship, General Support, Operating Expenses, Project, Research.
Note: Employee matching gift ratio: 2 to 1 up to $500; 1 to 1 up to $5,000 per employee annually, for higher education only.

Donor Information

Founder: Shell Oil Co. & other participating companies.

Financial Summary

Total Giving: $16,661,106 (2003); $23,000,000 (2002 approx); $24,039,664 (2001). Note: Contributes through corporate direct giving program and foundation.

Assets: $43,293,010 (2003); $66,393,687 (2001)

Gifts Received: $140,000 (2003); $11,028,000 (2001); $1,290,897 (2000). Note: In 2003, contributions were received from miscellaneous Shell Companies. In 2001, Shell Co. Foundation received contributions from miscellaneous Shell Companies ($11,003,000); Ron Leftwich ($25,000).

Typical Recipients

Arts & Humanities: Arts Centers, Arts Festivals, Arts Outreach, Ballet, Dance, Historic Preservation, History & Archaeology, Libraries, Museums/Galleries, Music, Opera, Performing Arts, Theater

Civic & Public Affairs: African American Affairs, Botanical Gardens/Parks, Business/Free Enterprise, Civil Rights, Clubs, Community Foundations, Economic Development, Economic Policy, Employment/Job Training, Civic & Public Affairs-General, Hispanic Affairs, Housing, Law & Justice, Parades/Festivals, Philanthropic Organizations, Public Policy, Rural Affairs, Safety, Urban & Community Affairs, Women's Affairs, Zoos/Aquariums

Education: Business Education, Colleges & Universities, Economic Education, Education Associations, Education Funds, Education Reform, Elementary Education (Private), Engineering/Technological Education, Faculty Development, Education-General, Health & Physical Education, International Studies, Journalism/Media Education, Legal Education, Medical Education, Minority Education, Private Education (Precollege), Public Education (Precollege), Science/Mathematics Education, Secondary Education (Private), Secondary Education (Public), Student Aid

Environment: Energy, Environment-General, Resource Conservation, Wildlife Protection

Health: Children's Health/Hospitals, Clinics/Medical Centers, Eyes/Blindness, Health Funds, Health Organizations, Heart, Hospices, Hospitals, Hospitals (University Affiliated), Medical Rehabilitation, Medical Research, Mental Health, Single-Disease Health Associations

International: International Organizations, International Peace & Security Issues, International Relations

Religion: Ministries, Religious Welfare

Science: Science Exhibits & Fairs, Science Museums, Scientific Centers & Institutes, Scientific Organizations

Social Services: Child Welfare, Community Centers, Community Service Organizations, Delinquency & Criminal Rehabilitation, Emergency Relief, Family Services, Food/Clothing Distribution, People with Disabilities, Recreation & Athletics, Scouts, Senior Services, Shelters/Homelessness, Substance Abuse, United Funds/United Ways, Volunteer Services, Youth Organizations

Application Procedures

Initial Contact: Send a brief letter and full proposal to the National Merit Scholarship Corporation.

Application Requirements: Include a description of structure, purpose, history, and programs of organization; summary of need for support and proposed use; detailed financial data on organization (independent audit, budget, sources of income, breakdown of expenditures by program, administration, and fund raising); copies of forms 501(c)(3), 509(a), and Form 990; list of donors, and their level of support.

Deadlines: August 15 before the year the organization or project needs funding.

Restrictions

Foundation does not fund organizations outside the United States; educational capital campaigns; endowments; endowed chairs at colleges and universities; or hospital operating expenses; fundraising events; or individuals. The foundation does not provide in-kind donations or product contributions.

Additional Information

Companies participating in the Shell Oil Co. Foundation include Shell Oil Co.; Shell Offshore, Inc.; Shell Pipe Line Corp.; Shell Western E&P, Inc.; Pecten Chemicals, Inc.; Pecten International Co.; and Pecten Middle East Services Co.

Shell Oil also contributes internationally through the Shell Foundation; see www.shellfoundation.org for details.

Publications: Foundation Annual Report

Corporate Officials

Michael Howard Grasley: senior vice president B Barberton, OH 1937. ED University of Kentucky MS; Ohio University (1958); University of Florida PhD (1963). PRIM CORP EMPL senior vice president: Shell Oil Co. NONPR AFFIL director: Chemical Manufacturers Association; member: Society Chemical Industry.

Foundation Officials

T. T. Coles: director
G. M. Cowan: director
R. J. Decyk: director
L. L. Eisenhans: director, president
T. J. Garland: secretary
V. M. Hanafin: director
S. B. Hopkins: vice president
W. G. Hougland: assistant secretary
G. R. Hulinger: treasurer
M. F. Keeth: director
C. A. Lamboley: director
A. M. Nolte: assistant treasurer
A. Y. Noojin: director
R. M. Restucci: director

Grants Analysis

Disclosure Period: calendar year ending 2003
Total Grants: $8,251,328*
Number of Grants: 378
Average Grant: $21,829
Highest Grant: $590,000
Lowest Grant: $500
Typical Range: $1,000 to $35,000
*Note: Giving excludes matching gifts, scholarships, and United Way.

Recent Grants

Note: Grants derived from 2003 Form 990.
General

3,464,758	United Way of the Texas Gulf Coast, Houston, TX
2,600,000	United Way of the Texas Gulf Coast, Houston, TX
1,908,332	Rice University, Houston, TX
1,205,125	Texas Southern University Foundation, Houston, TX
911,900	Awty International School, Houston, TX
785,600	United Way of the Texas Gulf Coast, Houston, TX
599,595	St Charles Parish Public Schools, Luling, LA
590,000	Rice University, Houston, TX
446,869	Educational Testing Service, Princeton, NJ
430,640	National Merit Scholarship Corporation, Chicago, IL

SHELTER MUTUAL INSURANCE CO.

Company Headquarters

1817 W. Broadway
Columbia, MO 65203
Web: http://www.shelterinsurance.com

Company Description

Assets: US$752 million (2001)
Employees: 1600 (2001)
SIC(s): 6311 Life Insurance, 6321 Accident & Health Insurance.

Operating Locations

Shelter Mutual Insurance Co. (MO--Columbia)

Shelter Insurance Foundation

Giving Contact

Raymond E. Jones, Secretary & Director
1817 West Broadway
Columbia, MO 65218
Phone: (573)214-4290
Fax: (573)446-5727

Description

Founded: 1981
EIN: 431224155
Organization Type: Corporate Foundation
Giving Locations: AK; CO; IL; IN; IA; KS; KY; LA; MS; MO, Columbia; NE; OK; TN
Grant Types: General Support, Research, Scholarship.

Financial Summary

Total Giving: $634,483 (fiscal year ending June 30, 2003); $774,633 (fiscal 2002); $623,787 (fiscal 2001). Note: Contributes through corporate direct giving program and foundation.
Giving Analysis: Giving for fiscal 2001 includes:

foundation ($168,087); foundation scholarships ($455,000)
Assets: $5,229,667 (fiscal 2003); $5,543,795 (fiscal 2002); $6,447,804 (fiscal 2001)
Gifts Received: $109,575 (fiscal 2003); $166,461 (fiscal 2002); $134,803 (fiscal 2001). Note: In fiscal 2003, contributions were received from individuals or businesses of less than $5,000 each ($109,575). Contributions are received from Shelter Life Insurance Co., Shelter Mutual Insurance Co., the Buffalo News, and Sidlee W. Leeper.

Typical Recipients

Arts & Humanities: Arts Associations & Councils, History & Archaeology, Libraries, Music
Civic & Public Affairs: Clubs, Employment/Job Training, Civic & Public Affairs-General, Housing, Minority Business, Parades/Festivals, Public Policy, Safety, Urban & Community Affairs, Women's Affairs
Education: Arts/Humanities Education, Business Education, Colleges & Universities, Education Associations, Education Funds, Elementary Education (Private), Education-General, Gifted & Talented Programs, Legal Education, Medical Education, Private Education (Precollege), Public Education (Precollege), Religious Education, Secondary Education (Public), Special Education, Student Aid
Health: AIDS/HIV, Alzheimer's Disease, Cancer, Children's Health/Hospitals, Heart, Hospitals, Kidney, Medical Research, Preventive Medicine/Wellness Organizations, Single-Disease Health Associations
Religion: Churches, Religious Welfare
Social Services: Animal Protection, Big Brothers/Big Sisters, Child Abuse, Child Welfare, Community Service Organizations, Crime Prevention, Food/Clothing Distribution, People with Disabilities, Recreation & Athletics, Scouts, Senior Services, Special Olympics, United Funds/United Ways, Veterans, Volunteer Services, Youth Organizations

Application Procedures

Initial Contact: Send a preliminary letter to the foundation.
Application Requirements: Include a brief description of the request.
Deadlines: None.
Notes: Corporate grants are made only through scholarships by a local Shelter Insurance agent for local high schools in that area.

Corporate Officials

Max J. Dills: director PRIM CORP EMPL director: Shelter Mutual Insurance Co.
Robert J. Feller: vice president B Cairo, IL 1941. ED Western Illinois University (1964). PRIM CORP EMPL vice president: Shelter Mutual Insurance Co.
Raymond E. Jones: executive vice president, secretary B Chillocothe, MO 1941. ED Missouri State University (1962). PRIM CORP EMPL executive vice president, secretary: Shelter Mutual Insurance Co. CORP AFFIL secretary: Daniel Boone Underwriters LLC.
Gustav J. Lehr: chairman, director B 1930. PRIM CORP EMPL chairman, director: Shelter Mutual Insurance Co. CORP AFFIL chairman: Daniel Boone Underwriters LLC; chairman, director: Shelter General Insurance Co.
David C. Mattson: director PRIM CORP EMPL director: Shelter Mutual Insurance Co.

Foundation Officials

Robert T. Cox: director PRIM CORP EMPL executive: Ace Manufacturing & Parts Co. CORP AFFIL director: Shelter Financial Services.
J. Donald Duello: president, treasurer, director B 1943. ED University of Missouri, Columbia (1961-1965). PRIM CORP EMPL vice president finance: Shelter Financial Services. CORP AFFIL vice president: Shelter General Insurance Co.
Jerry French: director
Raymond E. Jones: secretary, director (see above)
Gustav J. Lehr: vice president, director (see above)

John W. Lenox: director CORP AFFIL president: Shelter Financial Services; president: Shelter General Insurance Co.

Don A. McCubbin: director

Rick L. Means: director

Joe Moseley: director

James A. Offutt: director B Mexico, MO 1934. ED University of Missouri. PRIM CORP EMPL executive vice president, director, chairman: Shelter Mutual Insurance Co. CORP AFFIL director: Shelter Financial Services; vice president: Shelter General Insurance Co.

Daniel Scotten: director

Grants Analysis

Disclosure Period: fiscal year ending June 30, 2003

Total Grants: $106,483*

Number of Grants: 56

Average Grant: $1,901

Highest Grant: $10,000

Lowest Grant: $100

Typical Range: $1,000 to $5,000

*Note: Giving excludes scholarships.

Recent Grants

Note: Grants derived from fiscal 2004 Form 990.

General

387,419	Agent Scholarship Awards
379,500	Agent Scholarship Awards -- for various high school seniors
75,000	Scholarship Program -- for children of agents and employees
14,132	Columbia College, Columbia, MO
10,705	University of Missouri, Columbia, MO
10,000	Audrey J. Walton Stadium, Warrensburg, MO
10,000	University of Missouri, Columbia, MO
9,906	Central Missouri State University, Warrensburg, MO
9,905	Stephens College, Columbia, MO
9,000	Stephens College, Columbia, MO

SHENANDOAH LIFE INSURANCE CO.

Company Headquarters

2301 Brambleton Ave., SW
Roanoke, VA 24015
Web: http://www.shenlife.com

Company Description

Assets: US$1.951 billion (2002)

Employees: 300 (2002)

SIC(s): 6311 Life Insurance.

Operating Locations

Shenandoah Life Insurance Co. (VA--Roanoke)

Nonmonetary Support

Type: Donated Equipment; In-kind Services; Loaned Employees; Loaned Executives; Workplace Solicitation

Giving Contact

Betty Lafon, Administrative Assistant to the President
PO Box 12847
2301 Bramboeton Ave.
Roanoke, VA 24029
Phone: (540)985-4400
Fax: (540)857-5914

Description

Organization Type: Corporate Giving Program

Giving Locations: VA

Grant Types: Capital, Emergency, Employee Matching Gifts, General Support, Operating Expenses, Project, Scholarship.

Financial Summary

Total Giving: Figures do not include public relations donations.

Typical Recipients

Arts & Humanities: Arts Appreciation, Arts Associations & Councils, Arts Centers, Dance, Ethnic & Folk Arts, Historic Preservation, Libraries, Literary Arts, Museums/Galleries, Music, Opera, Performing Arts, Public Broadcasting, Theater, Visual Arts

Civic & Public Affairs: Civil Rights, Economic Development, Economic Policy, Employment/Job Training, Professional & Trade Associations, Safety, Urban & Community Affairs, Zoos/Aquariums

Education: Business Education, Colleges & Universities, Community & Junior Colleges, Economic Education, Education Associations, Education Funds, Faculty Development, Health & Physical Education, Medical Education, Minority Education, Special Education, Student Aid

Environment: Environment-General

Health: Emergency/Ambulance Services, Health Policy/Cost Containment, Health Funds, Health Organizations, Medical Research, Medical Training, Mental Health, Single-Disease Health Associations

Science: Observatories & Planetariums, Science Exhibits & Fairs

Social Services: Community Service Organizations, Counseling, Emergency Relief, Food/Clothing Distribution, Recreation & Athletics, Shelters/Homelessness, United Funds/United Ways, Youth Organizations

Application Procedures

Initial Contact: Send full proposal.

Application Requirements: Include a description of organization, amount requested, the purpose of funds sought, and proof of tax-exempt status. All requests must be in writing.

Deadlines: None.

Restrictions

Does not support individuals, religious organizations for sectarian purposes, entertainment groups, war veterans organizations, advertising, athletic events such as golf or tennis tournaments, fund-raising endeavors of United Way agencies, or political or lobbying groups.

Additional Information

Publications: Contributions Policy

Corporate Officials

Robert W. Clark: president, chief executive officer, director B Brattleboro, VT 1946. ED University of Connecticut (1968); University of Hartford (1973). PRIM CORP EMPL president, chief executive officer, director: Shenandoah Life Insurance Co.

Warner Norris Dalhouse: director B Roanoke, VA 1934. ED University of Virginia BS (1956). PRIM CORP EMPL director: Shenandoah Life Insurance Co. CORP AFFIL chairman, chief executive officer: First United Nations National Bank Virginia; director: Carilion Health Systems. NONPR AFFIL member: University Virginia; member: Virginia Governor Economic Advisory Council; president: Roanoke Public Library Foundation; member: Partnership for Urban Virginia.

Edward J. Machado: senior vice president, chief financial officer PRIM CORP EMPL senior vice president, chief financial officer: Shenandoah Life Insurance Co.

Grants Analysis

Note: Company reports that grant size varies.

SHENANDOAH TELECOMMUNICATIONS CO.

Company Headquarters

124 S. Main St.
Edinburg, VA 22824
Web: http://www.shentel.com

Company Description

Founded: 1902

Ticker: SHEN

Exchange: NASDAQ

Revenue: US$93 million (2002)

Employees: 268 (2002)

SIC(s): 4813 Telephone Communications Except Radiotelephone, 4841 Cable & Other Pay Television Services.

ShenTel Foundation

Giving Contact

Christopher E. French, President
ShenTel Foundation
PO Box 459
Edinburg, VA 22824
Phone: (540)984-4141

Description

Founded: 1990

EIN: 541549765

Organization Type: Corporate Foundation

Grant Types: General Support.

Donor Information

Founder: Shenandoah Telecommunications Co.

Financial Summary

Total Giving: $70,970 (2003)

Assets: $1,628,115 (2003)

Typical Recipients

Arts & Humanities: Libraries, Music, Public Broadcasting

Civic & Public Affairs: Community Foundations, Employment/Job Training, Civic & Public Affairs-General, Parades/Festivals, Safety

Education: Agricultural Education, Community & Junior Colleges, Education-General, Literacy, Private Education (Precollege), Public Education (Precollege), Student Aid

Health: Cancer, Emergency/Ambulance Services, Heart, Hospitals, Prenatal Health Issues

Religion: Religious Welfare

Social Services: Community Service Organizations, Counseling, Food/Clothing Distribution, Scouts, Shelters/Homelessness

Application Procedures

Initial Contact: Request application form.

Application Requirements: With completed application, include the latest annual report, a list of board members, and a current detailed budget.

Deadlines: None.

Restrictions

Limited to organizations within the service area of Shenandoah Telecommunications Company and its subsidiaries.

Corporate Officials

Noel M. Borden: vice chairman, director PRIM CORP EMPL vice chairman, director: Shenandoah Telecommunications Co.

Christopher E. French: president, director PRIM CORP EMPL president, director: Shenandoah Telecommunications Co.

Warren B. French, Jr.: chairman, director PRIM CORP EMPL chairman, director: Shenandoah Telecommunications Co.

Lawrence F. Paxton: vice president financial PRIM CORP EMPL vice president financial: Shenandoah Telecommunications Co.

Foundation Officials

Noel M. Borden: director (see above)
Dick D. Bowman: treasurer
Ken L. Burch: director
Christopher E. French: president (see above)
Grover M. Holler, Jr.: director
Harold Morrison, Jr.: director CORP AFFIL director: Shenandoah Telecommunications Co.
Zane Neff: director CORP AFFIL director: Shenandoah Telecommunications Co.
Lawrence F. Paxton: secretary (see above)
James E. Zerkel, II: director CORP AFFIL director: Shenandoah Telecommunications Co.

Grants Analysis

Disclosure Period: calendar year ending 2003
Total Grants: $70,970
Number of Grants: 65*
Average Grant: $1,092
Highest Grant: $6,750
Typical Range: $100 to $2,500
***Note:** Number of grants is approximate.

Recent Grants

Note: Grants derived from 2003 Form 990.
Library-Related
2,500	Shenandoah County Library, Edinburg, VA

General
6,750	WVPT Public Television, Harrisonburg, VA
2,500	American Cancer Society
2,500	Boy Scouts of America
1,500	Shenandoah Valley Music Festival, Edinburg, VA
1,250	Shenandoah Area Girl Scouts, Edinburg, VA

HAROLD AND HELEN SHEPHERD FOUNDATION

Giving Contact

H. H. Hayner, Trustee
PO Box 1757
Walla Walla, WA 99362-0348
Phone: (509)527-3500

Description

Founded: 1996
EIN: 911708510
Organization Type: Private Foundation
Grant Types: General Support, Scholarship.

Financial Summary

Total Giving: $241,110 (2003); $293,100 (2001)
Giving Analysis: Giving for 2003 includes: foundation scholarships ($25,000) 2001: foundation scholarships ($71,000)
Assets: $4,922,567 (2003); $5,626,259 (2001)
Gifts Received: $92,278 (1998); $4,913,983 (1996).
Note: In 1998, contributions were received from the Helen Shepherd Foundation ($80,682), Charles Schwab & Co. ($11,500), and Baker Boyer National Bank ($96).

Typical Recipients

Arts & Humanities: History & Archaeology, Libraries, Museums/Galleries, Music
Civic & Public Affairs: Botanical Gardens/Parks, Chambers of Commerce, Civic & Public Affairs-

General, Municipalities/Towns, Professional & Trade Associations
Education: Colleges & Universities, Community & Junior Colleges, Education-General, Medical Education, Public Education (Precollege), Student Aid
Health: Hospices, Public Health
Religion: Churches, Ministries
Social Services: Recreation & Athletics, Senior Services

Application Procedures

Initial Contact: Send a brief letter of inquiry.
Deadlines: November 1.

Foundation Officials

Herman Henry Hayner: trustee B Fairfield, WA September 25, 1916. ED Washington State University BA (1938); University of Oregon JD (1946). NONPR AFFIL member: Walla Walla County Bar Association; member: Washington State Bar Association; fellow: American College Trust & Estate Counsel; member: Walla Walla Chamber of Commerce; fellow: American Bar Association. CLUB AFFIL Walla Walla Country Club; Rotary Club.
Gary Houser: trustee

Grants Analysis

Disclosure Period: calendar year ending 2003
Total Grants: $216,110*
Number of Grants: 15
Average Grant: $9,008*
Highest Grant: $90,000
Lowest Grant: $1,000
Typical Range: $5,000 to $20,000
***Note:** Giving excludes scholarship. Average grant figure excludes highest grant.

Recent Grants

Note: Grants derived from 2003 Form 990.
General
90,000	Walla Walla Community College, Walla Walla, WA
29,210	Pomeroy School District, Pomeroy, WA -- towards numerous educational projects
25,000	Washington State University, Pullman, WA -- towards scholarship
20,000	Pomeroy Babe Ruth, Pomeroy, WA
20,000	Washington State University, Pullman, WA -- towards athletics
12,000	Washington State University, Pullman, WA -- towards WSU library
10,900	City of Dayton, Dayton, WA -- for swimming pool support
8,000	Garfield County Historical Association, Pomeroy, WA
5,000	Pomeroy Spinners Club, Pomeroy, WA
5,000	Walla Walla Symphony Society, Walla Walla, WA

MARGARET E. SHERMAN TRUST

Giving Contact

Linwood M. Erskine, Jr., Trustee
Margaret E. Sherman Trust
30 Highland Street
Worcester, MA 01609-2704
Phone: (508)753-7100

Description

Founded: 1987
EIN: 046047750
Organization Type: Private Foundation
Giving Locations: MA: primarily Worcester County
Grant Types: General Support.

Financial Summary

Total Giving: $70,000 (2003); $91,000 (2001)
Assets: $1,595,543 (2003); $1,956,103 (2001)

Typical Recipients

Arts & Humanities: Historic Preservation, History & Archaeology, Libraries, Museums/Galleries, Music
Civic & Public Affairs: Botanical Gardens/Parks
Education: Colleges & Universities, Medical Education, Science/Mathematics Education, Special Education
Environment: Watershed
Health: Medical Research
Religion: Churches
Science: Scientific Centers & Institutes
Social Services: Recreation & Athletics

Application Procedures

Initial Contact: The foundation reports no specific application guidelines. Send a brief letter of inquiry, including statement of purpose, amount requested, and proof of tax-exempt status.
Deadlines: None.

Restrictions

The foundation restricts its funding to historical, educational, and medical organizations in Massachusetts.

Foundation Officials

Linwood M. Erskine, Jr.: trustee

Grants Analysis

Disclosure Period: calendar year ending 2003
Total Grants: $70,000
Number of Grants: 20
Average Grant: $3,500
Highest Grant: $10,000
Lowest Grant: $2,000
Typical Range: $2,000 to $10,000

Recent Grants

Note: Grants derived from 2003 Form 990.
Library-Related
10,000	American Antiquarian Society, Worcester, MA
10,000	Northboro Historical Society, Northboro, MA
3,000	Northboro Public Library, Northboro, MA

General
10,000	Worcester Historical Museum, Worcester, MA
5,000	Masonic Learning Center, Worcester, MA
3,000	Old Sturbridge Village, Sturbridge, MA
3,000	Trinity Church, Northboro, MA
3,000	United Church, Winchester, NH
3,000	West Boylston Congregational Church, West Boylston, MA
3,000	Worcester County Horticultural Society, Boylston, MA

SHERWIN-WILLIAMS CO.

Company Headquarters

Cleveland, OH
Web: http://www.sherwinwilliams.com

Company Description

Founded: 1866
Ticker: SHW
Exchange: NYSE
Revenue: US$6.113 billion (2004)
Profit: US$393.3 million (2004)
Employees: 25777 (2003)
Fortune Rank: 331, per FORTUNE Magazine's list of 500 Largest U.S. Corporations (2004).
SIC(s): 2816 Inorganic Pigments, 2819 Industrial In-

organic Chemicals Nec, 2851 Paints & Allied Products, 2869 Industrial Organic Chemicals Nec.

Operating Locations
Sherwin-Williams Co. (CA--Anaheim, Emeryville, Hayward, Oakland; FL--Winter Haven; GA--Buford, La Grange, Morrow; IL--Effingham, Elk Grove Village; IN--Greencastle; KS--Coffeyville; MD--Baltimore, Crisfield, Hunt Valley; MI--Holland; NV--Reno, Sparks; NJ--Newark; OH--Bedford Heights, Columbus, Deshler; PA--York; PR--San Juan; TX--Garland, Waco)

Sherwin-Williams Foundation

Giving Contact
Barbara Gadosik, Director, Corporate Contributions
Sherwin-Williams Co.
101 Prospect Avenue NW
Cleveland, OH 44115
Phone: (216)566-2000
Fax: (216)566-3266

Description
EIN: 346555476
Organization Type: Corporate Foundation
Giving Locations: headquarters and operating communities, primarily Cleveland.
Grant Types: Capital, Employee Matching Gifts, General Support.

Financial Summary
Total Giving: $990,455 (2002); $1,015,720 (2001). Note: Contributes through foundation only.
Giving Analysis: Giving for 2001 includes: foundation matching gifts ($177,476)
Assets: $13,466,292 (2002); $14,727,501 (2001)
Gifts Received: $1,000,000 (2000); $12,000 (1999); $660,000 (1996). Note: Contributions were received from Sherwin-Williams Co.

Typical Recipients
Arts & Humanities: Arts Centers, Arts Institutes, Ballet, Arts & Humanities-General, Historic Preservation, History & Archaeology, Libraries, Museums/Galleries, Music, Opera, Performing Arts, Public Broadcasting, Theater
Civic & Public Affairs: Botanical Gardens/Parks, Business/Free Enterprise, Community Foundations, Economic Development, Economic Policy, Employment/Job Training, Ethnic Organizations, Civic & Public Affairs-General, Housing, Law & Justice, Legal Aid, Minority Business, Municipalities/Towns, Parades/Festivals, Philanthropic Organizations, Professional & Trade Associations, Public Policy, Safety, Urban & Community Affairs
Education: Afterschool/Enrichment Programs, Agricultural Education, Business Education, Business-School Partnerships, Colleges & Universities, Economic Education, Education Funds, Engineering/Technological Education, Education-General, Medical Education, Minority Education, Preschool Education, Private Education (Precollege), Science/Mathematics Education, Secondary Education (Private), Student Aid, Vocational & Technical Education
Environment: Environment-General, Protection
Health: Cancer, Children's Health/Hospitals, Diabetes, Emergency/Ambulance Services, Health Funds, Heart, Hospices, Hospitals, Hospitals (University Affiliated), Long-Term Care, Medical Rehabilitation, Multiple Sclerosis, Preventive Medicine/Wellness Organizations, Public Health, Respiratory, Single-Disease Health Associations
International: Health Care/Hospitals
Religion: Churches, Dioceses, Religion-General, Jewish Causes, Ministries, Religious Organizations, Religious Welfare
Science: Science Museums, Scientific Centers & In-

stitutes
Social Services: Big Brothers/Big Sisters, Camps, Child Welfare, Community Centers, Community Service Organizations, Crime Prevention, Domestic Violence, Family Services, People with Disabilities, Recreation & Athletics, Scouts, Senior Services, Shelters/Homelessness, Social Services-General, United Funds/United Ways, Volunteer Services, YMCA/YWCA/YMHA/YWHA, Youth Organizations

Application Procedures
Initial Contact: Send a written proposal.
Application Requirements: Include a description of organization, including its structure, purpose, and history; list of officers and directors; detailed description of current programs and activities; amount requested; purpose of funds sought; description of project, including community needs to be addressed, program objectives, activities to be undertaken, timetable, fully defined project budget, and sources of committed and pending support; current operating budget with income and expenditures; current list of donors and amounts received; recent annual report; most recently audited financial statement; annual report; and proof of tax-exempt status.
Deadlines: None.

Restrictions
Foundation does not support endowments, individuals, research, religious or political organizations, dinners or special events, fraternal organizations, goodwill advertising, member agencies of united funds, sports programs, or elementary and secondary education. Only organizations serving company operating areas receive support.

Corporate Officials
Thomas Allen Commes: president, chief operating officer, director B Aurora, IL 1942. ED Saint Thomas College BA (1964). PRIM CORP EMPL president, chief operating officer, director: Sherwin-Williams Co. CORP AFFIL director: Centerior Energy Corp.; officer: KeyCorp.
Thomas E. Hopkins: vice president human resources ED Malone College (1978); Cleveland State University (1982). PRIM CORP EMPL vice president human resources: Sherwin-Williams Co. NONPR AFFIL member: Students Free Enterprise.

Foundation Officials
C. M. Connor: president, trustee
Barbara Gadosik: director corporate contributions PRIM CORP EMPL director corporate contributions: Sherwin-Williams Co.
S. P. Hennessy: secretary, treasurer, trustee
Thomas E. Hopkins: assistant secretary, trustee (see above)

Grants Analysis
Disclosure Period: calendar year ending 2002
Total Grants: $563,960*
Number of Grants: 96
Average Grant: $4,463*
Highest Grant: $140,000
Lowest Grant: $200
Typical Range: $1,000 to $10,000
*Note: Giving excludes matching gifts; scholarships; and United Way. Average grant figure excludes highest grant.

Recent Grants
Note: Grants derived from 2003 Form 990.
General

182,000	United Way Services Inc., Cleveland, OH
37,500	Cleveland Tomorrow Inc., Cleveland, OH
28,000	Musical Arts Association, Cleveland, OH
25,000	Painting Contractors Education Partnership Trust, Fairfax, VA
25,000	Students in Free Enterprise, Springfield, OH
20,000	Cleveland Scholarship Programs Inc., Cleveland, OH

10,600	United Way Crusade of Mercy, Chicago, IL
10,000	Catholic Diocese of Cleveland Foundation, Cleveland, OH
10,000	Great Lakes Museum, Cleveland, OH
10,000	Keep America Beautiful, Stamford, CT

BARBARA INGALLS SHOOK FOUNDATION

Giving Contact
Barbara Ingalls-Shook, Chairman & Treasurer
206 Hart Fell Crescent
Birmingham, AL 35223-2905
Phone: (205)970-0060

Description
Founded: 1980
EIN: 630792812
Organization Type: Private Foundation
Giving Locations: AL; CO
Grant Types: General Support, Research.

Donor Information
Founder: Robert I. Ingalls Testamentary Trust II

Financial Summary
Total Giving: $320,255 (fiscal year ending August 31, 2001)
Assets: $7,068,820 (fiscal 2001)
Gifts Received: In 1990, contributions were received from Robert Ingalls Testamentary Trust.

Typical Recipients
Arts & Humanities: Arts Centers, Arts Festivals, Ballet, Dance, Film & Video, History & Archaeology, Libraries, Museums/Galleries, Music, Theater
Civic & Public Affairs: Botanical Gardens/Parks, Clubs, Community Foundations, Civic & Public Affairs-General, Native American Affairs, Philanthropic Organizations, Public Policy, Urban & Community Affairs, Zoos/Aquariums
Education: Arts/Humanities Education, Colleges & Universities, Education Reform, Medical Education, Private Education (Precollege), Special Education
Environment: Environment-General, Wildlife Protection
Health: Alzheimer's Disease, Cancer, Children's Health/Hospitals, Clinics/Medical Centers, Eyes/Blindness, Health-General, Health Funds, Heart, Hospitals, Medical Rehabilitation, Medical Research, Mental Health, Public Health, Research/Studies Institutes
International: Health Care/Hospitals, International Environmental Issues, International Organizations, International Peace & Security Issues
Religion: Churches, Ministries, Missionary Activities (Domestic), Religious Organizations, Religious Welfare
Science: Science Museums, Scientific Centers & Institutes
Social Services: Animal Protection, At-Risk Youth, Child Welfare, Community Service Organizations, Counseling, People with Disabilities, Scouts, Senior Services, Shelters/Homelessness, Substance Abuse, United Funds/United Ways, YMCA/YWCA/YMHA/YWHA, Youth Organizations

Application Procedures
Initial Contact: Send a brief letter of inquiry including proof of tax-exempt status.
Deadlines: None.
Review Process: Decisions usually are made within six months.

Restrictions
The majority of grants are made for medical purposes.

Additional Information

Publications: Application Form

Foundation Officials

Joseph E. Gibbs: trustee
Adele Shook Merck: trustee
Barbara Ingalls Shook: chairman, treasurer
Elesabeth Ridgely Shook: trustee
Robert P. Shook: president, secretary
Lem C. Stabler, Jr.: trustee
William Bew White, Jr.: trustee

Grants Analysis

Disclosure Period: fiscal year ending August 31, 2001
Total Grants: $320,255
Number of Grants: 59
Average Grant: $3,042*
Highest Grant: $143,800
Lowest Grant: $100
Typical Range: $1,000 to $5,000
*Note: Average grant figure excludes highest grant.

Recent Grants

Note: Grants derived from 2002 Form 990.
General

115,000	St. Vincent's Foundation Centennial Lodge Fund
25,000	24 Hours of Aspen Foundation
25,000	International Auto-Immune Disease Research Foundation
10,000	Alexis De Tocqueville Society
10,000	Aspen Valley Medical Foundation, Aspen, CO
10,000	Mayo Clinic Foundation, Rochester, NY
6,780	Sloan-Kettering Cancer Center, New York, NY
6,000	Better Basics, Birmingham, AL
5,365	Cathedral Church of the Advent, Birmingham, AL
5,200	University of Virginia, Charlottesville, VA

SHORE FUND

Giving Contact

Laurie Moritz, Trust Officer
c/o Mellon Bank
PO Box 185
Pittsburgh, PA 15230-0185
Phone: (412)234-0023

Description

Founded: 1982
EIN: 256220659
Organization Type: Private Foundation
Giving Locations: FL; MD; MO; PA
Grant Types: General Support, Operating Expenses, Research.

Donor Information

Founder: Benjamin R. Fisher, Fisher Charitable Trusts I and II

Financial Summary

Total Giving: $148,250 (2003); $83,500 (2001)
Assets: $4,319,522 (2003)
Gifts Received: $1,750 (2001); $25,000 (1998); $192,982 (1996). Note: In fiscal 1996, contributions were received from the Benjamin Fisher and Lillian Shore Fund.

Typical Recipients

Arts & Humanities: History & Archaeology, Libraries, Literary Arts, Museums/Galleries, Music, Theater
Civic & Public Affairs: Botanical Gardens/Parks, Business/Free Enterprise, Community Foundations, Economic Development, Civic & Public Affairs-

General, Housing, Legal Aid, Parades/Festivals, Philanthropic Organizations, Urban & Community Affairs
Education: Arts/Humanities Education, Colleges & Universities, Education Funds, Education-General, International Studies, Literacy, Private Education (Precollege), Public Education (Precollege), Religious Education, Science/Mathematics Education, Secondary Education (Private), Secondary Education (Public), Student Aid
Environment: Environment-General, Resource Conservation
Health: Cancer, Children's Health/Hospitals, Clinics/Medical Centers, Emergency/Ambulance Services, Health Organizations, Hospices, Hospitals, Kidney, Medical Rehabilitation, Medical Research, Mental Health, Nursing Services, Public Health, Trauma Treatment
International: Foreign Arts Organizations, Health Care/Hospitals, International Affairs
Religion: Churches, Jewish Causes, Ministries, Religious Welfare, Seminaries
Science: Scientific Centers & Institutes, Scientific Labs
Social Services: Animal Protection, Big Brothers/Big Sisters, Child Welfare, Community Service Organizations, Counseling, Delinquency & Criminal Rehabilitation, Emergency Relief, Family Planning, Family Services, Food/Clothing Distribution, People with Disabilities, Senior Services, Shelters/Homelessness, Special Olympics, Substance Abuse, United Funds/United Ways, Volunteer Services, YMCA/YWCA/YMHA/YWHA, Youth Organizations

Application Procedures

Initial Contact: Request application guidelines and deadline information.

Additional Information

Trust(s): Mellon Bank

Grants Analysis

Disclosure Period: calendar year ending 2003
Total Grants: $148,250
Number of Grants: 22
Average Grant: $4,679*
Highest Grant: $50,000
Lowest Grant: $1,000
Typical Range: $1,000 to $10,000
*Note: Average grant figure excludes highest grant.

Recent Grants

Note: Grants derived from 2001 Form 990.
General

25,000	Hammond-Harwood House Association, Annapolis, MD
15,000	Western Pennsylvania Humane Society, Pittsburgh, PA
10,000	University of Pittsburgh, Pittsburgh, PA
5,000	Carriage House Children's Center, Pittsburgh, PA
5,000	Mary Institute and St. Louis Country Day School, St. Louis, MO
5,000	Race for the Cure, Pittsburgh, PA
5,000	Trinity By-The-Cove Episcopal Church, Naples, FL
3,500	Conservancy of Southwest Florida, Naples, FL
2,500	Calvary Fund of the Women Center and Shelter, Pittsburgh, PA
2,500	Carol R. Brown Fund, Pittsburgh, PA

HUGH I. SHOTT, JR. FOUNDATION

Giving Contact

Richard W. Wilkinson, President
c/o First Century Bank of Bluefield

500 Federal Street
PO Box 1559
Bluefield, WV 24701
Phone: (304)325-8181
Fax: (304)325-3727

Description

Founded: 1985
EIN: 550650833
Organization Type: General Purpose Foundation
Giving Locations: VA: Southwest Virginia; WV: Southern West Virginia
Grant Types: Capital, Challenge, General Support, Professorship.

Donor Information

Founder: Established in 1985 by the late Hugh I. Shott Jr..

Financial Summary

Total Giving: $1,840,830 (2001)
Assets: $37,309,229 (2001)

Typical Recipients

Arts & Humanities: Arts Appreciation, Arts Associations & Councils, Arts Funds, Community Arts, Film & Video, Arts & Humanities-General, Historic Preservation, History & Archaeology, Libraries, Museums/Galleries, Performing Arts
Civic & Public Affairs: Botanical Gardens/Parks, Business/Free Enterprise, Clubs, Community Foundations, Economic Development, Civic & Public Affairs-General, Housing, Municipalities/Towns, Philanthropic Organizations, Safety, Urban & Community Affairs, Women's Affairs
Education: Business Education, Colleges & Universities, Community & Junior Colleges, Continuing Education, Education Associations, Faculty Development, Journalism/Media Education, Private Education (Precollege), Public Education (Precollege), Religious Education, Science/Mathematics Education, Secondary Education (Public)
Environment: Environment-General, Sanitary Systems
Health: Clinics/Medical Centers, Emergency/Ambulance Services, Hospices, Hospitals, Public Health
Religion: Ministries, Religious Organizations, Religious Welfare
Science: Scientific Centers & Institutes
Social Services: Community Centers, Community Service Organizations, Crime Prevention, Emergency Relief, Family Planning, Food/Clothing Distribution, Homes, People with Disabilities, Recreation & Athletics, Scouts, Senior Services, Shelters/Homelessness, United Funds/United Ways, Volunteer Services, Youth Organizations

Application Procedures

Initial Contact: Write foundation for application form, then submit full proposal.
Application Requirements: Completed application form must be accompanied by a grant proposal briefly describing project, detailed project budget, qualifications of personnel, financial statements for latest fiscal year, list of principal officers and directors, and a copy of IRS tax-exempt letter.
Deadlines: None.
Review Process: The board meets bimonthly.

Restrictions

The foundation's grantmaking is restricted to southwest Virginia and southern West Virginia.

Additional Information

Publications: Application Form

Foundation Officials

Byron K. Satterfield: treasurer PRIM CORP EMPL executive vice president, trust officer, director: First Century Bank NA.
Scott Shott: vice president B Bluefield, WV 1926. ED

West Virginia University (1950); Washington & Lee University JD (1951). PRIM CORP EMPL secretary, director: Paper Supply Co. CORP AFFIL director: First Century Bank NA; director: Mountaineer Resources Inc.; director: Cumberland Care Center Inc.
Richard W. Wilkinson: president B Welch, WV 1932. ED University of Virginia (1955-1962); University of Virginia JD (1962). PRIM CORP EMPL president, chief executive officer, director: First Century Bank NA. CORP AFFIL president, director: Pocahontas Bankshares.

Grants Analysis
Disclosure Period: calendar year ending 2001
Total Grants: $1,840,830
Number of Grants: 30
Average Grant: $61,361
Highest Grant: $250,000
Lowest Grant: $3,750
Typical Range: $15,000 to $100,000

Recent Grants
Note: Grants derived from 2001 Form 990.
Library-Related
50,000	Craft Memorial Library, Bluefield, WV

General
250,000	City of Bluefield, Bluefield, WV
225,000	Boy Scouts of America- Buckskin Council, Bluefield, WV
170,000	McDowell County Economic Development Authority, McDowell, WV
111,000	East River Soccer Association, Bluefield, WV
105,370	City of Bluefield, Bluefield, WV
100,000	McDowell County Board of Education, McDowell, WV
100,000	Mercer County Board of Education, Princeton, WV
100,000	Tazewell County Board of Education, Bluefield, VA
68,210	Lecture Series, Bluefield, WV
50,000	American Red Cross, Bluefield, WV

SHUBERT FOUNDATION

Giving Contact
Vicki Reiss, Executive Director
234 W. 44th St.
New York, NY 10036
Phone: (212)944-3777
Fax: (212)944-3767
Web: http://www.shubertfoundation.org

Description
Founded: 1945
EIN: 136106961
Organization Type: Specialized/Single Purpose Foundation
Giving Locations: nationally.
Grant Types: General Support, Operating Expenses.

Donor Information
Founder: Established in 1945 as the Sam S. Shubert Foundation by Lee Shubert and Jacob J. Shubert, in memory of their brother. The name was changed to the Shubert Foundation in 1971. The brothers contributed annually to the foundation. The foundation's funds were increased significantly by funds received from the estate of Lee Shubert in 1970 and from the estate of Jacob J. Shubert in 1972. The foundation is the sole shareholder of the Shubert Organization, which owns and operates the Shubert theaters.

Financial Summary
Total Giving: $13,514,500 (fiscal year ending May 31, 2003); $12,562,000 (fiscal 2001)
Assets: $249,240,752 (fiscal 2003); $251,889,489

(fiscal 2001)
Gifts Received: $145,162 (fiscal 2003); $188,797 (fiscal 2001); $291,499 (fiscal 2000). Note: In 1999, 2000, 2001, and 2003, contributions were received from the trust of Lee Shubert. In 1995, contributions were received from the trust of Lee Shubert and the estate of Karina Adair.

Typical Recipients
Arts & Humanities: Arts Associations & Councils, Arts Festivals, Arts Funds, Arts Institutes, Ballet, Dance, Arts & Humanities-General, Libraries, Museums/Galleries, Music, Opera, Performing Arts, Theater, Visual Arts
Civic & Public Affairs: Municipalities/Towns, Philanthropic Organizations
Education: Afterschool/Enrichment Programs, Arts/Humanities Education, Colleges & Universities
Health: Clinics/Medical Centers, Hospitals (University Affiliated)
International: Foreign Arts Organizations
Religion: Jewish Causes

Application Procedures
Initial Contact: All requests must be submitted on the foundation's application form.
Application Requirements: Include a copy of letter of tax-exempt determination, and audited financial statements for the most recent fiscal year. The audited financial statement should include a comparative statement to the prior year.
Deadlines: Applications must be received no later than December 1 to qualify for a grant.
Review Process: All grants are announced and disbursed in late May.

Restrictions
The foundation does not provide funds for audience development, direct subsidies to reduced-price admissions, or performing groups whose principal purpose is to bring theatrical productions to specialized audiences. Support is generally not provided for "bricks and mortar" projects.

Additional Information
The foundation maintains an archive for the preservation of performing arts history.
Publications: Annual Report; Guidelines; Application Form

Foundation Officials
John Werner Kluge: director B Chemnitz, Germany 1914. ED Columbia University BA (1937). PRIM CORP EMPL president, chairman board, executive vice president: Benale Holdings Corp. ADD CORP EMPL chairman board, president: Metromedia Co.; chairman, director: Metromedia International Group Inc.; chairman, president, director: Metromedia Hotels New York Inc.; chairman, director: Morven Farms; chairman, treasurer, president: Silver City Sales Co.; chairman, treasurer: Tri-Suburban Broadcasting Corp. CORP AFFIL chairman, treasurer: Tri-Suburban Broadcasting Corp.; director: Waldorf Astoria Corp.; chairman, president, director: Radisson Empire Hotel; chairman, treasurer, president: Silver City Sales Co.; director: Occidental Petroleum Corp.; shareholder: Muze Inc.; director: National Bank Maryland; member advisory council: Manufacturers Hanover Trust Co.; member: Marriott-Hot Shoppes Inc.; director: Kluge Finkelstein & Co.; chairman, director: JWK Properties Inc.; chairman, treasurer: Kluge & Co.; general partner: Jost Hotels LLC; director: Just One Break Inc.; director: Jimbo's Jumbos Inc.; director: Chock Full O Nuts Corp.; director: Conair Inc.; director: Belding Hemingway Co. Inc. NONPR AFFIL member: Washington Board Trade; member: Washington Food Brokers Association; vice president, board directors: United Cerebal Palsy Research & Education Foundation Inc.; member: National Sugar Brokers Association; board governors: New York College Osteopathic Medicine; member: National Association Radio & Television Broadcasters; member:

National Food Brokers Association; trustee: Miliken University Strang Clinic; member: Grocery Manufacturer Reps Washington; member: Grocery Wheels Washington; member: Advertising Council New York City; director: Brand Names Foundation; member: Advertising Club Washington. CLUB AFFIL University New York Club; University District of Columbia Club; Metropolitan New York Club; Olympic Club; Figure Skating Club; Marco Polo Club; Columbia Associates; Army-Navy Country Club; Broadcasters Club.
Vicki Reiss: executive director
Gerald Schoenfeld: chairman, director B 1924. ED University of Illinois BS (1947); New York University LLB (1949). PRIM CORP EMPL chairman, director: Shubert Organization Inc. ADD CORP EMPL chairman, director: Shubert Ticketing Services Division. NONPR AFFIL first vice president, director: League American Theatres.
Lee J. Seidler: treasurer, director B Newark, NJ 1935. ED Columbia College BA (1956); Columbia University MS (1957); Columbia University PhD (1965). PRIM CORP EMPL manager director emeritus: Bear Stearns & Co. Inc. CORP AFFIL director: Shubert Organization; director: Synthetic Indiana Inc.; director: Players International.
Philip J. Smith: director
Michael Ira Sovern: director, president B New York, NY 1931. ED Columbia University AB (1953); Columbia University LLB (1955). PRIM NONPR EMPL chancellor Kent professor: Columbia University School Law. CORP AFFIL director: Warner-Lambert Co.; director: Sequa Corp.; director: Shubert Organization; director: Kollsman Systems Management Division; director: Parke-Davis Division; director: Kollsman Military Systems Division; director: Kollsman Avionics Division; director: Kollsman Instrument Division; director: Consumer Health Products Division; director: Greater New York Insurance Group; director: AT&T Corp.; director: Chase Manhattan Bank NA; director: America Chicle Division. NONPR AFFIL member: New Jersey Board Mediation Panel Arbitration; director: WNET-TV/Channel 13; trustee: Kaiser Family Foundation; member: National Academy Arbitrators; member: Freedom Forum Newseum Inc.; chairman: Japan Society; chairman national advisory council: Freedom Forum Media Studies Center; member: Association Bar New York City; member: Council Foreign Relations; member: American Law Institute; director: Asian Cultural Council; member: American Arbitration Association; member: American Bar Association; chairman: American Academy Rome; fellow: American Academy of Arts & Sciences.
Stuart Subotnick: director
Irving M. Wall: director

Grants Analysis
Disclosure Period: fiscal year ending May 31, 2003
Total Grants: $13,514,500
Number of Grants: 342
Average Grant: $39,516
Highest Grant: $240,000
Typical Range: $15,000 to $75,000

Recent Grants
Note: Grants derived from 2003 Form 990.
General
275,000	Vivian Beaumont Theater Inc., New York, NY
240,000	Chicago Theatre Group Inc., Chicago, IL
240,000	South Coast Repertory Inc., Costa Mesa, CA
220,000	Washington Drama Society Inc., Washington, DC
210,000	Manhattan Theatre Club Inc., New York, NY
210,000	New York Shakespeare Festival, New York, NY
210,000	Roundabout Theatre Company, New York, NY
175,000	Ballet Theatre Foundation Inc., New York, NY

175,000   Center Theatre Group of Los Angeles, Los Angeles, CA
170,000   Actors Fund of America, New York, NY

SIEBERT LUTHERAN FOUNDATION

Giving Contact
Ronald D. Jones, President
2600 North Mayfair Road, Suite 390
Wauwatosa, WI 53226-1392
Phone: (414)257-2656
Fax: (414)257-1387
E-mail: contactus@Siebertfoundation.org
Web: http://www.SiebertFoundation.org

Description
Founded: 1952
EIN: 396050046
Organization Type: General Purpose Foundation
Giving Locations: WI
Grant Types: Capital, Conference/Seminar, General Support, Matching, Multiyear/Continuing Support, Operating Expenses, Project, Scholarship, Seed Money.

Donor Information
Founder: Established in 1952 by Albert F. Siebert (1879-1960), founder of Milwaukee Electric Tool Company. Mr. Siebert "elected to give his entire interest in his company to religious causes, using the Siebert Lutheran Foundation to accomplish this gift."
Born on October 18, 1879, in Dayton, OH, the son of a Lutheran minister, Albert F. Siebert pursued a sales career with National Cash Register, later accepting a position as sales manager of the A. H. Peterson Manufacturing Company in Milwaukee, WI. In 1924, he founded the Milwaukee Electric Tool Company, leading it to expansion and profitability. During the Depression, the company underwent financial difficulties. Mr. Siebert, a religious man, vowed that if his company survived he would give his entire interest in the company to the church. The company prospered beyond his expectations, and the foundation materialized as a result of his vow. Before Mr. Siebert's death, he was able to witness the initial impact of the foundation on the Lutheran community. In 1976, the foundation sold its interest in Milwaukee Electric Tool Corporation to Amstar Corporation.

Financial Summary
Total Giving: $3,787,100 (2003); $5,115,426 (2002); $5,000,000 (2001 approx)
Assets: $89,574,674 (2003); $76,685,343 (2002); $95,868,070 (2001)
Gifts Received: $56,200 (2000); $57,100 (1996); $44,000 (1995 approx). Note: In 2000, contributions were received from Siebert Real Estate Trust.

Typical Recipients
Arts & Humanities: Music
Civic & Public Affairs: Civic & Public Affairs-General, Women's Affairs
Education: Colleges & Universities, Continuing Education, Education Associations, Education Funds, Elementary Education (Private), Faculty Development, Education-General, Leadership Training, Minority Education, Preschool Education, Private Education (Precollege), Religious Education, Secondary Education (Private), Secondary Education (Public), Student Aid
Environment: Forestry
Health: Adolescent Health Issues, AIDS/HIV, Cancer, Clinics/Medical Centers, Geriatric Health, Hospitals, Long-Term Care, Nursing Services, Public Health
International: Missionary/Religious Activities

Religion: Churches, Religion-General, Ministries, Missionary Activities (Domestic), Religious Organizations, Religious Welfare, Seminaries
Social Services: Child Welfare, Community Service Organizations, Counseling, Day Care, Emergency Relief, Family Services, Food/Clothing Distribution, People with Disabilities, Refugee Assistance, Senior Services, Social Services-General, Youth Organizations

Application Procedures
Initial Contact: The foundation suggests that applicants request detailed instructions prior to submission of a grant proposal. A personal meeting, telephone interview, or a written outline of the project is recommended before submitting a full proposal.
Application Requirements: Grant proposals must follow a dictated format and be numbered according to a four-part outline. Part one must include the full legal name of the organization or congregation, with address and telephone number; name of chief executive officer or pastor with title, business address, and telephone number; name of individual preparing the proposal, with title, business address, and telephone number; amount of funds needed; and a brief description or outline of project/program. Part two must include responses to questions outlined in the proposal instructions. Part three must be attached with the following information: a copy of IRS tax-exempt determination letter, current financial statement or audited report, program or project budget, and a copy of the minutes of the organization's governing body or the congregation's church council authorizing the grant proposal. Part four is for any attachments or other information which support the grant proposal, such as printed materials, charts, graphs, photographs, or illustrations. One copy of each will suffice. Mail the completed proposal in a large flat envelope. It should be accompanied by a brief letter describing the project/program and the amount requested.
Deadlines: Proposals must be postmarked by March 1, June 1, September 1, and December 1. The board of directors schedules its meetings during the month following each deadline. If the deadline falls on a holiday or weekend, the closing date for grant proposals will be the last working day prior to the holiday or weekend.
Review Process: The foundation requires that applicants follow set guidelines when submitting grant proposals. A brief transmittal letter must accompany each proposal. This letter should be typewritten on the organization's or church's letterhead and be signed by the chief executive officer or pastor. It is not necessary to include letters of recommendation or testimonials from other sources. Photographs and exhibits should be kept to a minimum. Prior to submitting proposals, authorization should be received from the applicant's governing body or from the church board or council. Grant proposals should be brief and concise. Applicants will be notified of approval or rejection of their requests. If approved, grantees may be required to sign and return a grant agreement form prior to the distribution of funds.

Restrictions
Grants occasionally are made to provide seed money or start-up costs for a project. Grants generally are given for a one-year period. Recipients must be tax-exempt and must operate within the United States. Grants are not approved for other grant-making foundations, endowment funds, undergraduate and graduate fellowships and scholarships, or trusts. Grants generally are not given to churches for capital or operating expenses. Grants are made for Lutheran churches and organizations.

Additional Information
Publications: Application Guidelines; Policy Guidelines

Foundation Officials
Richard C. Barkow: director B 1938. ED Valparaiso University (1960). PRIM CORP EMPL president: Barker Aug G Manufacturing Co.
Chris Michael Bauer: vice chairman, director B Milwaukee, WI 1948. ED University of Wisconsin BBA (1969-1970); Marquette University MBA (1976). ADD CORP EMPL president: Firstar Bank NA. NONPR AFFIL first vice president: Milwaukee World Festival Inc.; secretary, treasurer: Saint Luke's Medical Center Inc.
Ned W. Bechthold: chairman, director B 1936. PRIM CORP EMPL president: Zenith Tech Inc. CORP AFFIL director: Northeast Asphalt Inc.; president: Payne & Dolan Inc.
Frederick H. Groth: director CLUB AFFIL treasurer: Blue Mound Country Club.
Knute Jacobson: director
Ronald D. Jones: president, director
Raymond J. Perry: director
W. David Romoser: assistant treasurer, director
Julie Van Cleave: director
John C. Zimdars, Jr.: treasurer, director

Grants Analysis
Disclosure Period: calendar year ending 2003
Total Grants: $3,787,100
Number of Grants: 315
Average Grant: $10,787*
Highest Grant: $400,000
Lowest Grant: $500
Typical Range: $5,000 to $20,000
*Note: Average grant figure excludes highest grant.

Recent Grants
Note: Grants derived from 2003 Form 990.
General
250,000	Time of Grace Ministry, Milwaukee, WI -- for an evangelism program
215,000	Garden Homes Lutheran Church, Milwaukee, WI -- for renovation of school
200,000	Concordia University, Milwaukee, WI
200,000	Next Door Foundation Inc., Milwaukee, WI -- for support of family programs
200,000	Wisconsin Lutheran College, Wauwatosa, WI
125,000	Evangelical Lutheran Church in America, Milwaukee, WI -- toward youth ministry programs
125,000	Finlandia University, Hancock, MI
100,000	Living Word Lutheran High School, Slinger, WI
100,000	Lutheran High School Association of Greater Milwaukee, Milwaukee, WI
100,000	PAVE, Milwaukee, WI -- toward support to low-income children to continue their education

SIERRA HEALTH FOUNDATION

Giving Contact
Len McCandliss, President & Chief Executive Officer
1321 Garden Highway
Sacramento, CA 95833
Phone: (916)922-4755
Fax: (916)922-4024
E-mail: info@sierrahealth.org
Web: http://www.sierrahealth.org/

Description
Founded: 1984
EIN: 680050036
Organization Type: Specialized/Single Purpose Foundation
Giving Locations: CA: 26 counties in Northern California

Grant Types: Capital, Challenge, Conference/Seminar, Employee Matching Gifts, General Support, Matching, Multiyear/Continuing Support, Seed Money.

Donor Information

Founder: The perpetual funding base for Sierra Health Foundation's philanthropic efforts was provided by Foundation Health Plan and Foundation Health Corporation, formerly known as Americare Health Corporation. Sierra Health Foundation was incorporated in 1984, in conjunction with the conversion of Foundation Health Plan (FHP) from nonprofit to for-profit status.

Financial Summary

Total Giving: $1,975,502 (2003); $2,066,392 (2001)
Giving Analysis: Giving for 2003 includes: foundation grants to United Way ($10,000); foundation matching gifts ($105,690)
Assets: $137,031,490 (2003); $156,278,280 (2001)

Typical Recipients

Arts & Humanities: Community Arts, Libraries, Music, Public Broadcasting
Civic & Public Affairs: African American Affairs, Asian American Affairs, Clubs, Community Foundations, Economic Policy, Municipalities/Towns, Nonprofit Management, Public Policy, Rural Affairs, Urban & Community Affairs, Women's Affairs
Education: Elementary Education (Public), Education-General, Health & Physical Education, Leadership Training, Legal Education, Medical Education, Public Education (Precollege), School Volunteerism
Environment: Air/Water Quality
Health: Adolescent Health Issues, AIDS/HIV, Cancer, Children's Health/Hospitals, Clinics/Medical Centers, Emergency/Ambulance Services, Eyes/Blindness, Health-General, Geriatric Health, Health Policy/Cost Containment, Health Organizations, Heart, Hospices, Hospitals, Long-Term Care, Medical Rehabilitation, Medical Research, Medical Training, Mental Health, Nursing Services, Outpatient Health Care, Prenatal Health Issues, Public Health, Research/Studies Institutes, Respiratory, Single-Disease Health Associations, Trauma Treatment
International: Health Care/Hospitals
Religion: Religion-General, Religious Welfare
Social Services: At-Risk Youth, Child Abuse, Child Welfare, Community Service Organizations, Crime Prevention, Domestic Violence, Emergency Relief, Family Planning, Family Services, People with Disabilities, Scouts, Senior Services, Shelters/Homelessness, Substance Abuse, Youth Organizations

Application Procedures

Initial Contact: Periodic funding opportunities will be posted on the website.
Notes: Contact for mini-grants is Ms. Dorothy Meehan, Vice President.

Restrictions

The foundation does not support individuals, endowments, lobbying efforts, or projects that benefit only the members of a private or religious group. General fund drives and annual appeals are not supported. The foundation will not generally support recreation programs, operating budgets, deficits, clinical research, major equipment purchases, or conferences.

Additional Information

Besides making grants, the foundation also provides program development and technical assistance.
Publications: Grants List; Newsletter; Application Guidelines Application Form; Informational Brochure; Fact Sheet

Foundation Officials

Steve Barrow: program officer
Byron Demorest, MD: director
George Deubel: director

J. Rodney Eason: chairman, director
Manuel A. Esteban, PhD: director B Barcelona, Spain 1940. ED University of Calgary BA (1969); University of Calgary MA (1970); University of California, Santa Barbara PhD (1976). PRIM CORP EMPL president, professor: California State University, Chico.
Wendy Everett: director
Albert R. Jonsen: director B San Francisco, CA 1931. ED Gonzaga University BA (1955); Gonzaga University MA (1956); University of Santa Clara (1963); Yale University PhD (1967). PRIM NONPR EMPL professor of medical ethics: University of Washington, School of Medicine. NONPR AFFIL member: Society Health & Human Values; chairman department medical history & ethics: University Washington Medicine School; member: National Rifle Association; member: Society Christian Ethics; member: Institute Medicine NAS; fellow: Institute Social Ethics & Life Science; member: American Society Law & Medicine; member: Commission AIDS Research.
Father Leo McAllister: secretary, director
Len McCandliss: president, director
Dorothy A. Meehan: vice president B 1953. ED University of Washington (1975); University of Cincinnati (1978-1981).
Leah Morris, RN: program officer managed care and health grants
Robert E. Petersen: director B Los Angeles, CA 1926. PRIM CORP EMPL founder, chairman board emeritus: Petersen Publishing Co. ADD CORP EMPL owner: Petersen Aviation Inc.; owner, chairman board: Petersen Properties. NONPR AFFIL founder: Petersen Automotive Museum; director: Thalians; director: Boys Club America. CLUB AFFIL Southern California Safari Club; Chevaliers du Tastevin Club; Conferie de la Chaine des Rotisseurs Club; Balboa Bay Yacht Club; Catalina Island Yacht Club.
James Schubert, MD: director
Sandra R. Smoley, RN: director PRIM NONPR EMPL secretary: California Department Health & Welfare.
Steve Vorous: chief financial officer

Grants Analysis

Disclosure Period: calendar year ending 2003
Total Grants: $1,859,812*
Number of Grants: 44
Average Grant: $32,376*
Highest Grant: $200,000
Lowest Grant: $5,000
Typical Range: $10,000 to $50,000
*Note: Giving excludes United Way; matching gifts. Average grant figure excludes two highest grants ($300,000).

Recent Grants

Note: Grants derived from 2001 Form 990.
General

72,900	Effort, Inc., Sacramento, CA -- to support medically-monitored residential detoxication services for low-income and medically uninsured abusers
70,000	Butte County, Oroville, CA -- to provide access to health, social employment, crime prevention, elder and child care
25,000	Safety Center, Inc, Sacramento, CA -- to provide health education to school age children in underserved communities
15,000	Community Services Planning Council, Inc , Sacramento, CA -- to promote health and human services
10,000	American Red Cross, Sacramento Sierra Chapter, Sacramento, CA -- to support disaster relief services in memory of Mr. Frank Cotta
10,000	California Coalition for Children's Safety and Health, Sacramento, CA
10,000	California HICAP Association, Oakland, CA -- to provide improved Medicare information
10,000	Dental Health Foundation, Oakland, CA -- support public education on the topic of flouride
10,000	El Dorado Women's Center, Placerville, CA -- to remodel two bathrooms in the emergency domestic violence shelter
10,000	Grantmakers in Health, Washington, DC -- to support organization's issue dialogue on oral health

SIERRA PACIFIC INDUSTRIES

Company Headquarters

Redding, CA
Web: http://www.sierrapacificind.com

Company Description

Revenue: US$1.425 billion (2002)
Employees: 3900 (2003)
SIC(s): 2421 Sawmills & Planing Mills--General, 2431 Millwork.

Sierra Pacific Foundation

Giving Contact

Stephanie Donham
PO Box 496028
Redding, CA 96049-6028
Phone: (530)378-8000
Fax: (530)378-8109
E-mail: foundation@spi-ind.com
Web: http://www.sierrapacificind.com/Company/SPFoundation.htm

Description

Founded: 1978
EIN: 942574178
Organization Type: Corporate Foundation
Giving Locations: headquarters and operating communities.
Grant Types: General Support, Scholarship.

Donor Information

Founder: Established and funded in 1979 by R. H. "Curly" Emmerson and Sierra Pacific Industries.

Financial Summary

Total Giving: $496,729 (fiscal year ending June 30, 2002); $325,375 (fiscal 2001). Note: Contributes through foundation only.
Giving Analysis: Giving for fiscal 2003 includes: foundation scholarships ($367,125); fiscal 2002: foundation scholarships ($260,507); fiscal 2001: foundation scholarships ($325,375).
Assets: $345,795 (fiscal 2002)
Gifts Received: $375,250 (fiscal 2002); $550,250 (fiscal 2000); $200 (fiscal 1998). Note: In fiscal 2002, contributions were received from Sierra Pacific Industries. In fiscal 1996, contributions were received from Sierra Pacific Industries ($500,000) and the Memorial for Ida. C. Emmerson ($22,812). In fiscal 2000, contributions Sierra Pacific Industries.

Typical Recipients

Arts & Humanities: Arts Associations & Councils, Arts Centers, Arts Festivals, Arts & Humanities-General, Libraries, Museums/Galleries, Music, Opera, Public Broadcasting
Civic & Public Affairs: Botanical Gardens/Parks, Business/Free Enterprise, Chambers of Commerce, Clubs, Civic & Public Affairs-General, Housing, Parades/Festivals, Rural Affairs, Safety, Urban & Community Affairs, Women's Affairs
Education: Agricultural Education, Business Education, Colleges & Universities, Elementary Education

(Public), Engineering/Technological Education, Education-General, Minority Education, Private Education (Precollege), Public Education (Precollege), Secondary Education (Public), Student Aid, Vocational & Technical Education
Environment: Forestry, Environment-General, Resource Conservation, Wildlife Protection
Health: Cancer, Emergency/Ambulance Services, Health Organizations, Heart, Hospices, Hospitals, Medical Research, Nutrition, Single-Disease Health Associations, Transplant Networks/Donor Banks
International: International Relief Efforts
Religion: Churches, Religious Organizations, Religious Welfare
Science: Observatories & Planetariums, Science Museums
Social Services: Child Welfare, Community Centers, Community Service Organizations, Crime Prevention, Food/Clothing Distribution, Recreation & Athletics, Scouts, Senior Services, Shelters/Homelessness, Social Services-General, Volunteer Services, YMCA/YWCA/YMHA/YWHA, Youth Organizations

Application Procedures
Initial Contact: Obtain a contribution request form from nearest Sierra Pacific office or by calling (530) 378-8000.
Deadlines: March 31.

Restrictions
Scholarships are restricted to dependent children of Sierra Pacific employees. Foundation primarily funds preselected organizations.

Corporate Officials
A. A. Emmerson: president B 1929. PRIM CORP EMPL president: Sierra Pacific Industries.
George Emmerson: vice president B 1956. ED Oregon State University (1978). PRIM CORP EMPL vice president: Sierra Pacific Industries.

Foundation Officials
Carolyn Emmerson Dietz: chairman, president B 1959.
George Emmerson: director (see above)

Grants Analysis
Disclosure Period: fiscal year ending June 30, 2002
Total Grants: $236,222*
Number of Grants: 266
Average Grant: $888
Highest Grant: $25,000
Lowest Grant: $25
Typical Range: $100 to $2,000
*Note: Giving excludes scholarships.

Recent Grants
Note: Grants derived from fiscal 2004 Form 990.
General

12,000	Northern California SAF, Grass Valley, CA
6,003	Plumas-Sierra Junior Livestock Sale, Quincy, CA
5,089	Tehama Junior Livestock Auction, Red Bluff, CA
5,000	Sacramento River Discovery Center, Sacramento, CA
2,975	Calaveras County Junior Livestock Auction, Angels Camp, CA
2,728	El Dorado City Fair Junior Livestock Auction, Placerville, CA
2,682	Redwood Acres Junior Livestock Auction, Eureka, CA
2,500	American Cancer Society Valentine Fantasy, New York, NY
2,500	American Cancer Society Valentine Fantasy, New York, NY
2,500	Department of Forestry, Sacramento, CA

SIERRA PACIFIC RESOURCES

Company Headquarters
Reno, NV
Web: http://www.sierrapacificresources.com

Company Description
Founded: 1984
Ticker: SRP
Exchange: NYSE
Revenue: US$2.991 billion (2002)
Employees: 3150 (2003)
SIC(s): 4924 Natural Gas Distribution, 4931 Electric & Other Services Combined, 6719 Holding Companies Nec.

Operating Locations
Sierra Pacific Resources (NV--Reno)

Nonmonetary Support
Type: In-kind Services
Volunteer Programs: Company employees are active in the community, participating in the Day of Caring, blood drives, and events such as the Special Olympics and the March of Dimes WalkAmerica.

Sierra Pacific Resources Charitable Foundation

Giving Contact
Karen Foster, Secretary, Treasurer
PO Box 30150
Reno, NV 89520
Phone: (702)579-1589
E-mail: kfoster@sppc.com
Web: http://www.sierrapacific.com/comenv/comrel/foundation/

Description
Founded: 1988
EIN: 880244735
Organization Type: Corporate Foundation
Giving Locations: CA: Northeastern California; NV: Northern Nevada headquarters and operating communities.
Grant Types: Employee Matching Gifts, General Support, Project.
Note: Employee matching gift ratio: 1 to 1 for donations to Special Assistance Fund for Energy (SAFE).

Donor Information
Founder: Sierra Pacific Resources

Financial Summary
Total Giving: $380,351 (2003); $278,185 (2002); $327,750 (2001). Note: Contributes through corporate direct giving program and foundation.
Assets: $198,439 (2003); $17,101 (2002); $265,939 (2001)
Gifts Received: $532,000 (2003); $80,000 (2002); $320,000 (2001). Note: Contributions are received from Sierra Pacific Resources.

Typical Recipients
Arts & Humanities: Arts Associations & Councils, Arts Centers, Arts Funds, Community Arts, Ethnic & Folk Arts, Arts & Humanities-General, Libraries, Museums/Galleries, Music, Opera, Performing Arts, Public Broadcasting, Theater
Civic & Public Affairs: African American Affairs, Botanical Gardens/Parks, Business/Free Enterprise, Clubs, Community Foundations, Economic Development, Employment/Job Training, Civic & Public Affairs-General, Hispanic Affairs, Housing, Municipalities/Towns, Native American Affairs, Parades/Festivals, Professional & Trade Associations, Rural

Affairs, Safety, Urban & Community Affairs, Women's Affairs
Education: Agricultural Education, Business Education, Colleges & Universities, Community & Junior Colleges, Education Funds, Education Reform, Elementary Education (Public), Engineering/Technological Education, Education-General, Legal Education, Literacy, Preschool Education, Public Education (Precollege), Religious Education, Science/Mathematics Education
Environment: Forestry, Environment-General, Research, Resource Conservation, Watershed, Wildlife Protection
Health: AIDS/HIV, Alzheimer's Disease, Cancer, Children's Health/Hospitals, Diabetes, Emergency/Ambulance Services, Heart, Hospitals, Mental Health, Public Health, Respiratory, Single-Disease Health Associations
Religion: Religion-General, Religious Welfare, Social/Policy Issues
Science: Science Museums, Scientific Research
Social Services: Animal Protection, Big Brothers/Big Sisters, Camps, Child Welfare, Community Centers, Community Service Organizations, Crime Prevention, Delinquency & Criminal Rehabilitation, Family Planning, Family Services, Food/Clothing Distribution, People with Disabilities, Recreation & Athletics, Scouts, Senior Services, Social Services-General, United Funds/United Ways, YMCA/YWCA/YMHA/YWHA, Youth Organizations

Application Procedures
Initial Contact: Submit a brief letter of inquiry.
Deadlines: None.

Restrictions
The foundation does not make grants to individuals, athletic or sporting events/teams, and does not fund religious organizations. Grants are limited to areas of service. The organization will provide limited employee time to nonprofit organizations if the circumstances require.

Additional Information
Publications: Annual Report

Corporate Officials
William E. Peterson: general counsel, chief financial officer, treasurer B 1943. ED College of the Holy Cross; North Carolina State University BA; University of South Carolina. PRIM CORP EMPL secretary: Sierra Energy Co. ADD CORP EMPL general counsel: Sierra Pacific Power Co. CORP AFFIL senior vice president, general counsel, corp. secretary: Sierra Pacific Resources.
Mark A. Ruelle: senior vice president, chief financial officer, treasurer ED University of North Dakota BA; University of North Dakota MBA. PRIM CORP EMPL senior vice president, chief financial officer, treasurer: Sierra Pacific Resources. CORP AFFIL chief financial officer: Sierra Pacific Power Co. NONPR AFFIL member: National Association Business Economists; member: Planning Forum; member strategic planning committee: Edison Electric Institute; member: American Gas Association.

Foundation Officials
Gary Aldax: director
Jeff Ceccarelli: chairman
Karen C. Foster: secretary, treasurer
Lisa Harris: administrator
Greg Lambert: director
Don Sims: director
Sandy Walsh: director

Grants Analysis
Disclosure Period: calendar year ending 2003
Total Grants: $330,351*
Number of Grants: 132
Average Grant: $1,734*
Highest Grant: $55,000
Lowest Grant: $50

Typical Range: $500 to $5,000
*Note: Giving excludes United Way. Average grant figure excludes two highest grants ($105,000).

Recent Grants

Note: Grants derived from 2003 Form 990.
General

55,000	United Way of Southern Nevada, Las Vegas, NV
50,000	University of Nevada Reno Foundation, Reno, NV
25,000	United Way of Northern Nevada, Reno, NV
15,000	Desert Research Institute, NV
15,000	Nevada Museum of Art, Reno, NV
12,500	United Way of Northern Nevada, Reno, NV
12,500	United Way of Northern Nevada, Reno, NV
10,000	Boy Scouts of America, Las Vegas, NV
10,000	Desert Research Institute, NV
10,000	Education Collaborative of Washoe County, Reno, NV

SILVERMAN FAMILY FOUNDATION

Giving Contact

Michael D. Silverman, Trustee
600 Washington Avenue
Carlstadt, NJ 07072
Phone: (201)842-6200

Description

Founded: 1979
EIN: 226067078
Organization Type: Private Foundation
Former Name: Jaydor Foundation.
Giving Locations: NJ
Grant Types: Award, Capital, Endowment, General Support, Multiyear/Continuing Support, Scholarship.

Financial Summary

Total Giving: $58,582 (fiscal year ending August 31, 2004); $40,763 (fiscal 2002)
Giving Analysis: Giving for fiscal 2002 includes: foundation grants to United Way ($250)
Assets: $134 (fiscal 2004); $5,733 (fiscal 2002)
Gifts Received: $56,500 (fiscal 2004); $34,000 (fiscal 2002); $45,000 (fiscal 2000). Note: In 2002 and fiscal 2004, contributions were received from Silverman Holding Corp. In fiscal 1996, 1997, and 2000, contributions were received from the Jay Dor Corp.

Typical Recipients

Arts & Humanities: Community Arts, Arts & Humanities-General, Libraries, Museums/Galleries, Music, Performing Arts, Theater
Civic & Public Affairs: African American Affairs, Chambers of Commerce, Ethnic Organizations, Civic & Public Affairs-General, Philanthropic Organizations, Professional & Trade Associations, Urban & Community Affairs
Education: Education Funds, Education-General, Minority Education, Private Education (Precollege), Student Aid
Environment: Environment-General, Research
Health: Cancer, Children's Health/Hospitals, Clinics/Medical Centers, Diabetes, Emergency/Ambulance Services, Health-General, Health Funds, Heart, Hospices, Hospitals, Medical Rehabilitation, Mental Health, Multiple Sclerosis, Single-Disease Health Associations
International: Foreign Educational Institutions, International Peace & Security Issues, International Relief Efforts, Missionary/Religious Activities
Religion: Churches, Dioceses, Religion-General, Jewish Causes, Social/Policy Issues, Synagogues/Temples
Science: Science-General
Social Services: Recreation & Athletics, Scouts, Social Services-General, Special Olympics, United Funds/United Ways, Veterans, YMCA/YWCA/YMHA/YWHA, Youth Organizations

Application Procedures

Initial Contact: Send a brief letter of inquiry and a full proposal.
Application Requirements: Include a description of organization, amount requested, purpose of funds sought, and proof of tax-exempt status.
Deadlines: None.

Restrictions

Grants are not made to individuals.

Corporate Officials

Louis Healey: chief financial officer, director PRIM CORP EMPL chief financial officer: Jaydor Corp.
Barry S. Silverman: chairman, director PRIM CORP EMPL chairman, director: Jaydor Corp.
Michael David Silverman: president, chief executive officer, director B Newark, NJ 1946. ED Yale University BA (1968). PRIM CORP EMPL president, chief executive officer, director: Jaydor Corp. CORP AFFIL member: Heublein Distributor Advisor Council. NONPR AFFIL member: Wine and Spirit Wholesalers of America; member: Wine and Spirit Wholesalers Association; member: Seagram Family Association.

Foundation Officials

Barry S. Silverman: trustee (see above)
Jeffrey Silverman: trustee
Michael David Silverman: trustee (see above)

Grants Analysis

Disclosure Period: fiscal year ending August 31, 2004
Total Grants: $58,582
Number of Grants: 20
Average Grant: $715*
Highest Grant: $45,000
Lowest Grant: $20
Typical Range: $100 to $1,000
*Note: Average grant figure excludes highest grant.

Recent Grants

Note: Grants derived from 2004 Form 990.

General

45,000	United Jewish Communities of Metrowest New Jersey, Whippany, NJ
5,000	Givat Haviva Educational Foundation, New York, NY
3,000	Ray Tye Medical Aid Foundation, Braintree, MA
1,825	Temple B'nai Abraham, Livingston, NJ
500	Juvenile Diabetes Research Foundation, Bala Cynwyd, PA
250	National Multiple Sclerosis Society, Paramus, NJ
250	Ray Tye Medical Aid Foundation, Braintree, MA
150	Emmanuel Cancer Foundation, Scotch Plains, NJ
120	Temple Emanu-El, Westfield, NJ
100	American Society for Yad Vashem, Milwaukee, WI

MELVIN AND BREN SIMON CHARITABLE FOUNDATION NUMBER ONE

Giving Contact

Deborah Simon
PO Box 7033
Indianapolis, IN 46207-7033
Phone: (317)636-1600

Description

Founded: 1998
EIN: 352049367
Organization Type: Private Foundation
Grant Types: General Support.

Financial Summary

Total Giving: $2,684,185 (fiscal year ending June 30, 2003); $1,439,007 (fiscal 2001)
Giving Analysis: Giving for fiscal 2003 includes: foundation grants to United Way ($12,500) fiscal 2001: foundation grants to United Way ($5,000)
Assets: $2,248,952 (fiscal 2003); $3,917,281 (fiscal 2001)
Gifts Received: $1,605,420 (fiscal 2003); $3,062,875 (fiscal 2001); $3,609,375 (fiscal 1998). Note: In fiscal 2001 and 2003, contributions were received from Melvin Simon & Associates, Inc. In fiscal 1998, contributions were received from Melvin and Bren Simon.

Typical Recipients

Arts & Humanities: Museums/Galleries, Music
Civic & Public Affairs: Ethnic Organizations, Civic & Public Affairs-General, Professional & Trade Associations
Education: Arts/Humanities Education, Education-General, Private Education (Precollege), Religious Education
Health: Children's Health/Hospitals
Religion: Jewish Causes
Social Services: Animal Protection, Community Service Organizations, Shelters/Homelessness

Application Procedures

Initial Contact: The foundation requests applications be made in writing.
Application Requirements: Include a description of organization, amount requested, and purpose of funds sought.

Foundation Officials

Bren Simons: trustee
Melvin J. Simons: trustee

Grants Analysis

Disclosure Period: fiscal year ending June 30, 2003
Total Grants: $2,671,685*
Number of Grants: 108
Average Grant: $13,022*
Highest Grant: $200,000
Lowest Grant: $200
Typical Range: $10,000 to $20,000
*Note: Giving excludes United Way. Average grant figure excludes nine highest grants ($1,382,500).

Recent Grants

Note: Grants derived from fiscal 2003 Form 990.
General

200,000	Beth-El Zedeck, Indianapolis, IN -- towards rabbinic chair endowment
171,875	Jewish Federation of Greater Indianapolis, Indianapolis, IN
171,875	Jewish Federation of Greater Indianapolis, Indianapolis, IN
171,875	Jewish Federation of Greater Indianapolis, Indianapolis, IN

171,875	Jewish Federation of Greater Indianapolis, Indianapolis, IN
159,338	New Hope Charities, West Palm Beach, FL -- campo Nuevo esperanza
143,964	New Hope Charities, West Palm Beach, FL -- for girl's vocational school
100,000	Americans for Gun Safety, San Francisco, CA
100,000	University of Judaism, Bel Air, CA
33,471	New Hope Charities, West Palm Beach, FL

SIDNEY, MILTON, AND LEOMA SIMON FOUNDATION

Giving Contact
Joseph C. Warner, Trustee
Sidney, Milton, and Leoma Simon Foundation
101 Plaza Real South, Suite 405
Boca Raton, FL 33432
Phone: (561)391-3482

Description
Founded: 1964
EIN: 656282105
Organization Type: Private Foundation
Grant Types: General Support, Research.

Donor Information
Founder: the late Milton Simon

Financial Summary
Total Giving: $641,000 (fiscal year ending May 31, 2004); $648,000 (fiscal 2001)
Assets: $16,696,728 (fiscal 2004); $16,328,864 (fiscal 2001)

Typical Recipients
Arts & Humanities: Libraries, Performing Arts, Public Broadcasting, Theater
Civic & Public Affairs: Ethnic Organizations, Civic & Public Affairs-General, Zoos/Aquariums
Education: Arts/Humanities Education, Business Education, Legal Education, Private Education (Precollege), Public Education (Precollege)
Environment: Environment-General, Wildlife Protection
Health: Alzheimer's Disease, Arthritis, Cancer, Clinics/Medical Centers, Diabetes, Eyes/Blindness, Geriatric Health, Health Organizations, Hospitals, Medical Research, Prenatal Health Issues, Research/Studies Institutes, Respiratory, Single-Disease Health Associations, Speech & Hearing
International: Health Care/Hospitals, International Peace & Security Issues, International Relations
Religion: Jewish Causes, Synagogues/Temples
Social Services: Camps, Child Welfare, Crime Prevention, People with Disabilities, Recreation & Athletics, Special Olympics, Youth Organizations

Application Procedures
Initial Contact: Send a brief letter of inquiry.
Application Requirements: Describe program or project.
Deadlines: None.

Foundation Officials
Burt Bergenfield: trustee
Joseph C. Warner: trustee
Meryll Warner: trustee

Grants Analysis
Disclosure Period: fiscal year ending May 31, 2004
Total Grants: $641,000
Number of Grants: 66

Average Grant: $9,712
Highest Grant: $14,000
Lowest Grant: $4,000
Typical Range: $5,000 to $14,000

Recent Grants
Note: Grants derived from 2004 Form 990.
General

14,000	American Foundation for the Blind, New York, NY
14,000	American Jewish Joint Distribution Committee, New York, NY
14,000	National Jewish Medical Research Center, Denver, CO
12,000	Alzheimer's Disease and Related Disorders Association Inc., Chicago, IL
12,000	Arthritis Foundation, Atlanta, GA
12,000	Columbia Presbyterian Medical Center, New York, NY
12,000	Fidelco Guide Dog Foundation, Bloomfield, CT
12,000	Foundation Fighting Blindness, Owings Mills, MD
12,000	Hole in the Wall Gang Camp Fund Inc., New Haven, CT
12,000	Wildlife Conservation Society, Bronx, NY

WILLIAM E. SIMON FOUNDATION

Giving Contact
William E. Simon, Jr., Co-Chairman
310 South Street, PO Box 1913
Morristown, NJ 07962-1913
Phone: (973)898-0290
Fax: (973)898-4733
Web: http://www.wesimonfoundation.org

Alternate Contact
J. Peter Simon, Co-Chairman

Description
Founded: 1967
EIN: 136217788
Organization Type: Family Foundation
Former Name: William E. and Carol G. Simon Foundation.
Giving Locations: nationally, with emphasis in New York Metro, Los Angeles, and the San Francisco Bar metropolitan areas.
Grant Types: Employee Matching Gifts, Endowment, General Support, Matching, Multiyear/Continuing Support.

Donor Information
Founder: Established in the mid 1980s by William E. Simon, former secretary of the treasury under former Presidents Richard Nixon and Gerald Ford.
Mr. Simon was born in 1927 in Paterson, NJ, went to Newark Academy, then Lafayette College where he graduated in 1951 with a bachelor's degree in government and law. He went right to work on Wall Street, specializing in government securities and municipal bonds. He rose to become a senior partner in Salomon Brothers, a large investment firm where his annual salary is estimated to have been between $2 million and $3 million in 1971 and 1972.
He left Wall Street in 1972 when he was appointed as the deputy secretary of the treasury under George Schultz. One year later, Mr. Simon was named the administrator of the Federal Energy Office where, as the "energy czar," he coordinated the country's energy policy during the energy crisis. He left that post to become the secretary of the treasury in 1974 where he served until 1977, when he left government service.
Before he began his government service, Mr. Simon had placed in a blind trust his assets which had declined about 60% in value. Once back in private life, Mr. Simon began to rebuild his personal wealth by establishing his own network of consultancies and corporate relationships. He combined his economic expertise with his recent government service to negotiate financial opportunities with the largest companies in the country. He joined a dozen or so blue-chip corporate and philanthropic boards including Xerox Corporation and the John M. Olin Foundation. In 1981, Mr. Simon and Ray Chambers founded Wesray Corporation, an investment and banking firm that specialized in leveraged buyouts. The company became one of the largest private companies in the country with sales of $1.8 billion in 1983. Today, Mr. Simon directs his own company, William E. Simon and Sons, located in Morristown, NJ. His personal fortune was estimated to be approximately $300 million in 1991.
Mr. Simon's accomplishments reflect a personal philosophy of hard work and a belief in the free enterprise system. His associates have described him as a nonstop worker who can regularly put in 18-hour days. He authored two books, including "A Time for Truth," an account of his Washington, DC, experiences and conservative economics, which was a bestseller for 30 weeks. He donated the proceeds to his alma mater, Lafayette College in Easton, PA. He has served on or is currently serving on the boards of more than 60 charitable organizations. He has received more than 50 awards, and he is a member of more than 20 clubs across the country.
He married Carol Girard in 1950. The couple had seven children: William E. Simon, Jr., John P. Simon, Mary Beth Simon Streep, Carol Leigh Simon Porges, Aimee Simon Bloom, Julie Ann Simon, and Johanna Katrina Simon. The eight members of the family serve as officers or directors of the William E. Simon Foundation.

Financial Summary
Total Giving: $6,797,142 (2003); $7,314,602 (2002)
Giving Analysis: Giving for 2002 includes: foundation grants to United Way ($10,334)
Assets: $27,203,738 (2003); $22,011,197 (2002)
Gifts Received: $9,401,655 (2003); $16,323,151 (2002); $2,957,015 (2000). Note: In 2002, contributions were received from the estate of William E. Simon. In 2000, contributions were received from William E. Simon.

Typical Recipients
Arts & Humanities: Arts Associations & Councils, Arts Centers, Arts Funds, Dance, Arts & Humanities-General, Historic Preservation, History & Archaeology, Libraries, Museums/Galleries, Music, Performing Arts
Civic & Public Affairs: African American Affairs, Botanical Gardens/Parks, Business/Free Enterprise, Civil Rights, Clubs, Community Foundations, First Amendment Issues, Civic & Public Affairs-General, Housing, Law & Justice, Municipalities/Towns, Nonprofit Management, Philanthropic Organizations, Professional & Trade Associations, Public Policy, Safety, Urban & Community Affairs, Women's Affairs, Zoos/Aquariums
Education: Afterschool/Enrichment Programs, Arts/Humanities Education, Business Education, Colleges & Universities, Community & Junior Colleges, Education Associations, Education Funds, Education Reform, Elementary Education (Private), Elementary Education (Public), Education-General, Gifted & Talented Programs, Leadership Training, Legal Education, Minority Education, Private Education (Precollege), Public Education (Precollege), Religious Education, Science/Mathematics Education, Secondary Education (Private), Secondary Education (Public), Special Education, Student Aid
Environment: Air/Water Quality, Environment-General, Protection, Resource Conservation
Health: Cancer, Clinics/Medical Centers, Health-General, Health Funds, Health Organizations, Hospices, Hospitals, Medical Rehabilitation, Medical Re-

search, Multiple Sclerosis, Nursing Services, Public Health, Research/Studies Institutes, Single-Disease Health Associations, Transplant Networks/Donor Banks

International: Foreign Arts Organizations, International Affairs, International Organizations, International Peace & Security Issues, International Relations, International Relief Efforts, Missionary/Religious Activities

Religion: Bible Study/Translation, Churches, Dioceses, Religion-General, Ministries, Missionary Activities (Domestic), Religious Organizations, Religious Welfare, Seminaries, Social/Policy Issues

Science: Scientific Centers & Institutes, Scientific Research

Social Services: Animal Protection, At-Risk Youth, Big Brothers/Big Sisters, Child Welfare, Community Centers, Community Service Organizations, Day Care, Delinquency & Criminal Rehabilitation, Family Planning, Family Services, Food/Clothing Distribution, Homes, People with Disabilities, Recreation & Athletics, Shelters/Homelessness, Social Services-General, Substance Abuse, United Funds/United Ways, Veterans, YMCA/YWCA/YMHA/YWHA, Youth Organizations

Application Procedures

Initial Contact: Request copy of guidelines and application procedures in writing or by telephone, or download them from the foundation's web site.
Deadlines: None.

Restrictions

The foundation does not make grants to individuals or for programs outside the US.

Additional Information

Publications: Guidelines; application form.

Foundation Officials

Aimee Simon Bloom: vice president, treasurer, director
Charles F. Festo: assistant secretary
Daniel Mosley: director
Julie Simon Munro: director
Michael Oliveri: assistant treasurer
James Piereson, PhD: director B Grand Rapids, MI 1946. ED Michigan State University BA (1968); Michigan State University PhD (1973). NONPR AFFIL member: Philadelphia Society; member advisory committee: University Rochester Simon Graduate School Business Administration; director: DonorsTrust; member: American Historical Association. CLUB AFFIL Union League Club.
Leigh Simon Porges: vice president, secretary, director
J. Peter Simon: co-chairman, director B 1927. PRIM CORP EMPL executive director, director: William E. Simon & Sons.
William Edward Simon, Jr.: co-chairman, director B 1951. PRIM CORP EMPL executive director: William E Simon & Sons.
Johanna K. Simon-Morris: director
Mary B. Simon Streep: director

Grants Analysis

Disclosure Period: calendar year ending 2003
Total Grants: $6,797,142
Number of Grants: 350
Average Grant: $15,330*
Highest Grant: $800,000
Lowest Grant: $25
Typical Range: $1,000 to $25,000
***Note:** Average grant figure excludes three highest grants ($1,477,566).

Recent Grants

Note: Grants derived from 2003 Form 990.
General

800,000	Morristown Memorial Health Foundation, Morristown, NJ
375,000	Princeton Academy of the Sacred Heart, Princeton, NJ
302,566	Cynthia L. and William E. Simon Junior Foundation, New Jersey, NJ
250,000	John M. Templeton Foundation, Radnor, PA
250,000	Prison Fellowship Ministries, Reston, VA
200,000	Newark Academy, Livingston, NJ
150,000	Angelicum University Fund, New York, NY
150,000	Children's Scholarship Fund, New York, NY
125,000	Southern California Children's Scholarship Fund, Long Beach, CA
100,000	Church of Saint Vincent Ferrer, New York, NY

SIMPSON INVESTMENT CO.

Company Headquarters

1301 5th Ave., Ste. 2800
Seattle, WA 98101
Web: http://www.simpson.com

Company Description

Employees: 83
SIC(s): 6719 Holding Companies Nec.

Operating Locations

Simpson Investment Co. (MI--Plainwell, Vicksburg; OR--Eugene, Portland, West Linn; WA--Shelton, Tacoma)
Note: Operates in various cities and towns in the above states.

Nonmonetary Support

Value: $20,707 (1998)
Volunteer Programs: The company sponsors a United Way "Day of Caring" program where employees volunteer their time to help a designated United Way organization.
Note: Donated products include paper.

Matlock Foundation

Giving Contact

Beverly J. Holland, Public Affairs Manager
917 E. 11th St.
Tacoma, WA 98421
Phone: (253)779-6400
Fax: (253)280-9000
E-mail: bhollan@simpson.com
Web: http://www.simpson.com

Description

EIN: 916029303
Organization Type: Corporate Giving Program
Giving Locations: CA: Del Norte County, Humboldt County; OR: Lincoln County, Tillamook County; WA: Grays Harbor County, King County, Mason County, Pierce County, Thurston County
Grant Types: Capital, Employee Matching Gifts, General Support.
Note: Employee matching gift ratio: 1 to 1.

Financial Summary

Total Giving: $900,000 (2002 approx); $818,354 (2001). Note: Contributes through corporate direct giving program and foundation.
Giving Analysis: Giving for 2002 includes: corporate direct giving (approx $285,000); foundation (approx $615,000); 2001: foundation grants to United Way ($79,497); corporate direct giving ($95,768); foundation ($643,089).
Gifts Received: $633,179 (2000); $595,056 (1998);

$574,975 (1997). Note: Contributions were received from Simpson Investment Company, Simpson Paper Company, Simpson Timber Company, and Pacific Western Extruded Plastics Company.

Typical Recipients

Arts & Humanities: Arts Associations & Councils, Arts Institutes, Arts & Humanities-General, Historic Preservation, History & Archaeology, Libraries, Museums/Galleries, Music, Opera, Performing Arts, Theater

Civic & Public Affairs: African American Affairs, Botanical Gardens/Parks, Community Foundations, Economic Development, Economic Policy, Civic & Public Affairs-General, Municipalities/Towns, Professional & Trade Associations, Safety, Urban & Community Affairs, Zoos/Aquariums

Education: Agricultural Education, Business Education, Colleges & Universities, Community & Junior Colleges, Continuing Education, Economic Education, Education Funds, Education Reform, Elementary Education (Private), Engineering/Technological Education, Environmental Education, Education-General, Private Education (Precollege), Public Education (Precollege), School Volunteerism, Science/Mathematics Education, Student Aid

Environment: Forestry, Environment-General, Resource Conservation, Watershed, Wildlife Protection

Health: Arthritis, Children's Health/Hospitals, Clinics/Medical Centers, Emergency/Ambulance Services, Geriatric Health, Health Organizations, Hospices, Hospitals, Nursing Services, Transplant Networks/Donor Banks, Trauma Treatment

International: International Relief Efforts

Religion: Churches, Dioceses, Religion-General, Ministries, Religious Welfare

Science: Science Exhibits & Fairs, Science Museums, Scientific Centers & Institutes

Social Services: At-Risk Youth, Big Brothers/Big Sisters, Child Abuse, Child Welfare, Community Centers, Community Service Organizations, Family Services, Food/Clothing Distribution, Recreation & Athletics, Scouts, Senior Services, Sexual Abuse, Shelters/Homelessness, Social Services-General, Substance Abuse, United Funds/United Ways, Volunteer Services, YMCA/YWCA/YMHA/YWHA, Youth Organizations

Application Procedures

Initial Contact: Letter or telephone call requesting grant application.
Application Requirements: Completed application form; list of other donors, including names and amounts; list of board of directors; operating budget of organization for previous year and current year-to-date; and project/program budget.
Deadlines: April 15th and September 15th for requests of greater than $1,000.
Evaluative Criteria: The degree of support from Simpson employees; amount of enthusiasm in the community for the organization or drive; relative size and importance of company operations in the community and balance among Simpson communities; total amount being raised in the overall campaign, compared with the request being made of Simpson; needs of organization or program for which funding is requested; amount of previous Simpson contributions to the organization; amount committed by other companies, foundations, and/or governments (projects should demonstrate broad-based community support); and proximity of the requesting organization to the company operations or headquarters. When possible, contributions will support organizations of interest to or recommended by Simpson employees. The Fund prefers to make capital contributions or provide one-time "seed money" for programs.
Decision Notification: Grant applications are reviewed throughout the year.

Restrictions

Does not support individuals or provide funds for endowments or loans.

Additional Information

Foundation is sponsored by Simpson Investment Company and its subsidiaries, which include Simpson Paper Company, Simpson Timber Company, and Pacific Western Extruded Plastics Company. Matlock Foundation does not make grants, but allocates money to the Simpson Fund for giving. The Matlock Foundation filed its final tax return as of January 1, 2001, with a corporate giving program managed by the Simpson Fund taking its place.
Publications: Application Form

Corporate Officials

Beverly J. Holland: public affairs manager
Colin Moseley: chairman, chief executive officer B 1960. ED Northwestern University MBA (1988). PRIM CORP EMPL chairman, chief executive officer: Simpson Investment Co.
William Garrard Reed, Jr.: director B 1939. ED Duke University; Harvard University Graduate School of Business Administration MBA (1969). PRIM CORP EMPL director: Simpson Investment Co. CORP AFFIL director: PACCAR Inc.; director: SAFECO Corp.; director: Microsoft Corp.

Foundation Officials

Colin Moseley: director (see above)

Grants Analysis

Disclosure Period: calendar year ending 2001
Total Grants: $818,354*
Number of Grants: 294
Average Grant: $2,500
Highest Grant: $50,000
Lowest Grant: $125
Typical Range: $500 to $5,000
*Note: Grants analysis provided by the company.

Recent Grants

Note: Grants derived from 2000 Form 990.
General

52,500	YMCA Seattle, Seattle, WA
36,478	United Way Mason County, Shelton, WA
35,000	Redwood Discovery Museum, Arcata, CA
34,464	United Way King County, Seattle, WA
22,000	Forest Foundation, Auburn, CA
21,500	United Funds of Humboldt County, Eureka, CA
20,000	Senior Services for South Sound, Olympia, WA
18,808	United Way of Pierce County, Tacoma, WA
15,000	Safeplace Rape Relief, Olympia, WA
14,468	Humboldt Senior Citizens Council, Eureka, CA

Typical Recipients

Arts & Humanities: Libraries
Civic & Public Affairs: Civic & Public Affairs-General, Safety, Urban & Community Affairs
Health: Clinics/Medical Centers, Hospices, Public Health
Social Services: Child Welfare, Emergency Relief, Homes, Shelters/Homelessness, Youth Organizations

Application Procedures

Initial Contact: Contact foundation to request guidelines and the Request for Funding form.
Application Requirements: Submit completed Request for Funding form, including a description of organization, proof of tax-exempt status, amount requested, project or program budget, and contact person.
Deadlines: March 31.

Foundation Officials

Howard S. Kaylor: trustee
Omer T. Kaylor: contact person
Horace D. Kefauver: trustee
Stuart L. Mullendore: trustee

Grants Analysis

Disclosure Period: calendar year ending 2001
Total Grants: $76,100
Number of Grants: 5
Highest Grant: $22,700
Lowest Grant: $9,500
Typical Range: $12,500 to $18,900

Recent Grants

Note: Grants derived from 2002 Form 990.
Library-Related

5,971	Reach, Inc., Hagerstown, MD -- electric pallet jack

General

15,000	American Red Cross -- capital building project
10,612	Southeastern Washington County Health and Community Services Corporation, Washington, DC -- building repairs
8,500	Maugansville Goodwill Volunteer Fire Company, Inc. -- upgrade breathing equipment
7,500	Wells House, Inc. -- capital project
5,000	Children in Need, Inc. -- supplies and personal needs
4,591	First Hose Company of Boonsboro, Boonsboro, MD -- extraction equipment

Financial Summary

Total Giving: $985,000 (2001)
Assets: $3,664,791 (2001)
Gifts Received: $387,000 (1998); $483,000 (1997); $1,455,000 (1996). Note: In 1998, contributions were received from L. J. Skaggs Foundation Trust ($370,000), and M. C. Skaggs ($17,000). In 1997, contributions were received from the L. J. Skaggs Fdn. Trust ($450,000) and M. C. Skaggs ($33,000).

Typical Recipients

Arts & Humanities: Arts Associations & Councils, Arts Centers, Arts Festivals, Dance, Ethnic & Folk Arts, Historic Preservation, History & Archaeology, Libraries, Museums/Galleries, Music, Opera, Performing Arts, Theater
Civic & Public Affairs: Botanical Gardens/Parks, Civic & Public Affairs-General, Public Policy, Rural Affairs, Zoos/Aquariums
Education: Arts/Humanities Education, Colleges & Universities, Environmental Education, Education-General, International Studies, Private Education (Precollege), Religious Education
Environment: Environment-General, Resource Conservation, Wildlife Protection
Health: AIDS/HIV, Diabetes
International: Foreign Arts Organizations, Foreign Educational Institutions, International-General, Health Care/Hospitals, International Development, International Environmental Issues, International Organizations, Missionary/Religious Activities
Religion: Churches, Missionary Activities (Domestic), Religious Welfare

Application Procedures

Initial Contact: Applicants should submit a brief letter of inquiry.
Application Requirements: a description of organization, amount requested, purpose of funds sought income and expenses information, and the expertise of key personnel.
Deadlines: June 1.

Restrictions

The foundation will not fund individuals, capital or annual fund drives, residence home programs, halfway houses, sectarian religious organizations, or budget deficits.

Additional Information

Publications: Annual Report

Foundation Officials

Donald D. Crawford, Jr.: treasurer, director B Long Beach, CA 1936.
Jane C. Davis: vice president, director
Georgia Fulstone: vice president, director
Philip M. Jelley: secretary, director
Joseph W. Martin, Jr.: treasurer, director
Michael M.K. Sebree: assistant secretary, director
Mary C. Skaggs: president, director

Grants Analysis

Disclosure Period: calendar year ending 2001
Total Grants: $985,000
Number of Grants: 64
Average Grant: $11,855*
Highest Grant: $125,000
Lowest Grant: $1,000
Typical Range: $5,000 to $20,000
*Note: Average grant figure excludes two highest grants ($250,000).

Recent Grants

Note: Grants derived from 2002 Form 990.
General

125,000	Historic Mount Vernon, Mt. Vernon, VA
125,000	National Trust, London United Kingdom
75,000	San Francisco Opera, San Francisco, CA
50,000	Santa Fe Opera, Santa Fe, NM

ALBERT E. AND NAOMI B. SINNISEN FOUNDATION

Giving Contact

Howard S. Kaylor
Albert E. and Naomi B. Sinnisen Foundation
c/o Ferris Baker Watts
113 South Potomac Street
Hagerstown, MD 21740
Phone: (301)733-7111

Description

Founded: 1987
EIN: 526321486
Organization Type: Private Foundation
Giving Locations: MD
Grant Types: General Support.

Financial Summary

Total Giving: $76,100 (2001)
Assets: $1,405,788 (2001)

L. J. SKAGGS AND MARY C. SKAGGS FOUNDATION

Giving Contact

Philip M. Jelley, Secretary & Director
1221 Broadway, 21st Floor
Oakland, CA 94612-1837
Phone: (510)451-3300
Fax: (510)451-1527

Description

Founded: 1967
EIN: 946174113
Organization Type: General Purpose Foundation
Giving Locations: CA: theater grants limited to Northern California nationally.
Grant Types: General Support, Project, Research.

Donor Information

Founder: the late L. J. Skaggs, Mary C. Skaggs

40,000	Colonial Williamsburg Foundation, Williamsburg, VA
40,000	National Trust for Historic Preservation, Washington, DC
25,000	English Heritage, London United Kingdom
25,000	Grace Cathedral, San Francisco, CA
25,000	Merola Opera Program, San Francisco, CA
25,000	Oregon Shakespeare Festival, Ashland, OR

SKILLMAN FOUNDATION

Giving Contact

Carol Goss, President, Chief Executive Officer
600 Renaissance Center, Suite 1700
Detroit, MI 48243
Phone: (313)393-1185
Fax: (313)393-1187
E-mail: mailbox@skillman.org
Web: http://www.skillman.org

Description

Founded: 1960
EIN: 381675780
Organization Type: Specialized/Single Purpose Foundation
Giving Locations: MI: Wayne, Oakland, and Macomb Counties, Detroit
Grant Types: Capital, Conference/Seminar, Employee Matching Gifts, General Support, Multiyear/Continuing Support, Operating Expenses, Project, Scholarship, Seed Money.

Donor Information

Founder: The Skillman Foundation is a private foundation incorporated in Detroit, MI, in 1960 by Rose P. Skillman, who was the widow of Robert Skillman (d. 1945), an early and longtime officer and director of 3M Corporation. During their lifetimes, the Skillmans' philanthropic interests focused on providing assistance and care for children and young people, especially the disadvantaged living in Southeastern Michigan.

The foundation operated as a conduit for Rose Skillman's philanthropic giving until her death in 1983, at which time her assets were distributed to the foundation.

Financial Summary

Total Giving: $18,401,301 (2003); $19,480,722 (2002); $24,494,656 (2001)
Giving Analysis: Giving for 2003 includes: foundation grants to United Way ($525,000); 2002: foundation grants to United Way ($525,000)
Assets: $485,637,894 (2003); $417,920,060 (2002); $503,499,412 (2001)

Typical Recipients

Arts & Humanities: Arts Associations & Councils, Arts Centers, Arts Funds, Arts Institutes, Ethnic & Folk Arts, History & Archaeology, Libraries, Literary Arts, Museums/Galleries, Music, Opera, Performing Arts, Public Broadcasting, Theater
Civic & Public Affairs: African American Affairs, Asian American Affairs, Community Foundations, Economic Development, Employment/Job Training, Civic & Public Affairs-General, Hispanic Affairs, Housing, Law & Justice, Municipalities/Towns, Native American Affairs, Nonprofit Management, Parades/Festivals, Philanthropic Organizations, Professional & Trade Associations, Public Policy, Urban & Community Affairs, Zoos/Aquariums
Education: Afterschool/Enrichment Programs, Agricultural Education, Arts/Humanities Education, Colleges & Universities, Education Associations, Education Funds, Education Reform, Elementary Education (Public), Engineering/Technological Education, Education-General, Literacy, Medical Education, Minority Education, Preschool Education, Private Education (Precollege), Public Education (Precollege), Science/Mathematics Education, Secondary Education (Public), Social Sciences Education, Student Aid, Vocational & Technical Education
Health: Adolescent Health Issues, AIDS/HIV, Children's Health/Hospitals, Health Policy/Cost Containment, Health Organizations, Hospitals, Medical Research, Mental Health, Nursing Services, Prenatal Health Issues, Preventive Medicine/Wellness Organizations, Public Health, Research/Studies Institutes, Respiratory, Trauma Treatment
International: Health Care/Hospitals, International Relief Efforts
Religion: Jewish Causes, Religious Organizations, Religious Welfare, Social/Policy Issues
Science: Scientific Centers & Institutes
Social Services: At-Risk Youth, Big Brothers/Big Sisters, Child Abuse, Child Welfare, Community Service Organizations, Counseling, Crime Prevention, Day Care, Delinquency & Criminal Rehabilitation, Domestic Violence, Emergency Relief, Family Planning, Family Services, Food/Clothing Distribution, Homes, People with Disabilities, Recreation & Athletics, Scouts, Senior Services, Sexual Abuse, Shelters/Homelessness, Social Services-General, Substance Abuse, United Funds/United Ways, Volunteer Services, YMCA/YWCA/YMHA/YWHA, Youth Organizations

Application Procedures

Initial Contact: Contact the foundation or check its web site to obtain guidelines and a Letter of Intent Cover Sheet. After reviewing guidelines and eligibility criteria, submit a letter of intent.
Application Requirements: Letters of intent should be accompanied by the completed cover sheet form and should provide estimated project costs and revenues; a brief description of the purpose, objectives, and general methodology of the project; proof of tax-exempt status; recently audited financial statement; a recent annual report or brochure describing the organization; and, if available, a current strategic plan. and problems it addresses; goal of the project, including measurable objectives and results to be achieved; project plan describing project history and past accomplishments, target population, number of people served, timeline, and a list of specific activities; a description of organization, including history, mission, board, staff and current clients and description of services; revenue plan, including other sources of funding; evaluation plan, including method of evaluation, any additional questions, information sources and analysis, who will conduct the evaluation; plan for continued support of the project following the conclusion of the foundation's funding; total project budget, audited financial statement; and current annual report. audited financial statement; and current annual report.
Deadlines: None.
Review Process: During the review process, a staff member will be assigned to help develop the proposal. The program staff member will prepare a recommendation to present to the foundation's program group, which will decide whether or not the project falls within the foundation's goals. If the program group invites the applicant to submit a complete grant application, the assigned staff member will continue to assist the applicant with the full grant application process. The foundation's trustees review grant applications five times each year, generally in February, April, June, September, and November. The review process takes three months and the foundation will notify the organization in writing when their application has been received and when a decision has been made.
Evaluative Criteria: The proposed program must include a method for evaluating its effectiveness, the organization must intend to continue the program after the grant period has ended; and the grant request should be for a minimum of $10,000.
Notes: The foundation asks that applications are not faxed. The foundation will usually only make grants for one year and for no more than 25 percent of an organization's general operations cost.

Restrictions

Grants are made in Wayne, Oakland, and Macomb counties, Michigan only. The foundation reports that it does not make grants that may jeopardize an organization's public charity status because the amount requested is too large in relation to the past level of public support; to new organizations or to organizations that had IRS qualifying public revenues of less than $100,000 for the preceding year; research, or deficit funding; for generic fund-raising requests; loans; individuals; or to organizations that discriminate against people because of age, race, creed, gender, religion, disability, sexual orientation, or ethnicity. Only organizations that are tax-exempt under IRC Section 501(c)(3) and can provide a copy of a financial audit conducted by an independent certified public accountant may apply for funding. Organizations classified as a private foundation under IRC Section 509(a) are not eligible.

Additional Information

The foundation asks all prospective applicants to review its Grantmaking Policies and Procedures before submitting a proposal. The foundation discourages contact with any trustee regarding specific applications.

One month after notification of grant approval, the foundation meets with nonprofits to discuss reporting requirements. The foundation requires organizations to submit period reports and information about the program, including a signed copy of award letter, six-month progress and expenditure report, final evaluation and expenditure reports, etc.

About one-half of the foundation's grants are initiated by the foundation through collaborative projects aimed at priority goals within the foundation's program areas.
Publications: Annual Report; Newsletter; Grantmaking Policies and Procedures

Foundation Officials

Dr. Lillian Bauder: chairman, trustee B 1939. ED Douglass College (1961); University of Michigan (1973). PRIM CORP EMPL vice president corporate affairs: Masco Corp. CORP AFFIL director: DTE Energy Co.; director: Comerica Bank; director: Detroit Edison Co. NONPR AFFIL director: Michigan Council for Arts & Cultural Affairs.
William McNulty Brodhead: trustee B Cleveland, OH 1941. ED Wayne State University BA (1965); University of Michigan JD (1967). PRIM CORP EMPL partner: Plunkett & Cooney PC. NONPR AFFIL trustee: Michigan Children; co-chairman: Wayne County Youth; chairman: Covenant House Michigan; chairman: Focus: Hope.
Richard Connell: vice president, treasurer, chief information officer
Walter E. Douglas: trustee B 1933. PRIM CORP EMPL president, director: Avis Ford Inc. CORP AFFIL president: DHT Transportation Inc. NONPR AFFIL director: Detroit Symphony Orchestra.
Stephen E. Ewing: vice chairman, trustee B 1944. ED DePauw University BA (1965); Michigan State University MBA (1971); Harvard University Graduate School of Business Administration MBA (1982). PRIM CORP EMPL president, chief executive officer, director: Michigan Consolidated Gas Co. ADD CORP EMPL branch manager: Michigan Consolidated Gas Co. Grand Rapids; president: MCN Energy Group Inc.; president: Michcon Pipeline Co. CORP AFFIL director: Michcon Gathering Co.; president, chief executive officer: DTE Energy Co. NONPR AFFIL member: National Petroleum Council.
Edsel B. Ford, II: trustee B 1949. ED Babson University BA (1972). PRIM CORP EMPL vice president, director: Ford Motor Co. CORP AFFIL director: Ford

Motor Co. NONPR AFFIL director: Henry Ford Health System; vice chairman, national advisory board: Salvation Army; director: Detroit Metropolitan Wayne County Airport Commission; director: Federal Reserve Bank of Chicago; director: CATCH; director: Detroit 300.

Carol Goss: president, chief executive officer ED University of Michigan BA; University of Michigan MSW. NONPR AFFIL member: Grantmakers for Children, Youth and Families; member: Women & Philanthropy; member: Association of Black Foundation Executivies.

Amyre Makupson: trustee B Detroit, MI September 30, 1947. ED Fisk University BA (1970); American University MA (1972). NONPR AFFIL director: Providence Hospital Foundation; director: Sickle Cell Association; director: March of Dimes; director: Alzheimer's Association; director: Covenant House Michigan.

Robert S. Taubman: trustee CORP AFFIL chairman, president, chief executive officer, director: Taubman Co. LLC; director: Comerica Bank; director: Sotheby's Holdings Inc. NONPR AFFIL director: Real Estate Roundtable; trustee: Urban Land Institute.

Jane R. Thomas: trustee

Grants Analysis

Disclosure Period: calendar year ending 2003
Total Grants: $17,876,301*
Number of Grants: 126
Average Grant: $132,690*
Highest Grant: $1,290,000
Lowest Grant: $80
Typical Range: $50,000 to $300,000
*Note: Giving excludes United Way. Average grant figure excludes highest grant.

Recent Grants

Note: Grants derived from 2002 Form 990.
General

1,197,000	Youth Sports and Recreation Commission, Detroit, MI -- continue support for general operations and mini-grants program
950,000	Youth Sports and Recreation Commission, Detroit, MI -- continue support for work alternative for youth project's summer programming
500,000	Free Press Charities Inc., Detroit, MI -- provide matching funds for donations generated by the Detroit Free Press's Summer Dreams wish book program
500,000	Local Initiatives Support Corporation, New York, NY -- build capacity of community development corporations to develop affordable housing & other neighborhood assets for children & families in Detroit
461,000	Eastern Michigan University, Ypsilanti, MI -- support the Comer schools and families initiative in its final year ensuring sustainable support for the Comer model
450,000	Southeastern Michigan Health Association, Detroit, MI -- intensify campaign to get all pediatricians in Detroit & Wayne County to input immunization information on the centralized immunization registry
441,000	Comer Schools and Families Initiative School District of the City of Detroit, Detroit, MI -- transition the Comer schools and families initiative to a sustainable project to facilitate educational reform and improve student achievement
431,000	Community Health and Social Services Inc., Detroit, MI -- support the La Vida partnership in Southwest Detroit to prevent domestic violence against Latino women
400,000	School District of the City of Detroit, Detroit, MI -- implement the Malcolm Baldrige approach for school improvement and performance excellence program within Detroit public schools district
381,000	Third Judicial Circuit Court of Michigan Family Intervention, Detroit, MI -- develop 2 family visitation centers providing safe, nurturing places for non-custodial parents to visit their children & to learn new parenting skills

LILLIAN M. SLATER TRUST

Giving Contact

Donald W. Krauter, Trustee
14 Birch Lane
Scotia, NY 12302
Phone: (518)399-1869

Description

Founded: 1997
EIN: 146179935
Organization Type: Private Foundation
Giving Locations: NY: Capital district area
Grant Types: General Support.

Financial Summary

Total Giving: $92,121 (2001)
Assets: $2,302,009 (2001)

Typical Recipients

Arts & Humanities: Libraries, Museums/Galleries, Music
Civic & Public Affairs: Civic & Public Affairs-General
Religion: Churches, Ministries
Social Services: Homes, Senior Services, Social Services-General, YMCA/YWCA/YMHA/YWHA

Application Procedures

Initial Contact: Submit a brief letter of inquiry.
Application Requirements: Include purpose of funds sought, amount requested, and a description of organization.
Deadlines: September 1.

Restrictions

Applicant must be a 501(c)(3) organization, preferably in the capital district area of New York.

Foundation Officials

Donald W. Krauter: trustee
William W. Price: trustee
Frances M. Summerville: trustee

Grants Analysis

Disclosure Period: calendar year ending 2001
Total Grants: $92,121
Number of Grants: 11
Average Grant: $8,375
Highest Grant: $25,000
Lowest Grant: $1,000
Typical Range: $2,500 to $20,000

Recent Grants

Note: Grants derived from 2001 Form 990.
Library-Related

25,000	Green Mountain College, Poultney, VT -- fund to establish a chaplaincy program

General

20,000	First United Methodist Church, Schenectady, NY -- for current expense budget
10,121	First United Methodist Church, Schenectady, NY -- for advertising campaign
10,000	Annie Schaffer Senior Citizens Center, Schenectady, NY -- for new air conditioning unit
10,000	Getting the Word Out, Lake Clear, NY -- towards publishing Adirondacks explorer news publication
5,000	Bethesda House, Schenectady, NY -- to fund a chief staff position
2,500	Home Furnishings Program, Schenectady, NY -- for new larger door at warehouse
2,500	Schenectady Inner City Ministry, Schenectady, NY -- for Crisis Network Program
2,500	YMCA of Parkside, NY -- for Summer Program
2,000	Schenectady Symphony Orchestra, Schenectady, NY -- for mentoring concert with students
1,000	World Awareness Children's Museum, Glens Falls, NY -- for the 2002 Genie Challenge Fund

SLEMP FOUNDATION

Giving Contact

Patricia L. Durbin, Trust Officer
US Bank NA
PO Box 5208 M.L. CN-OH-W5EB
Cincinnati, OH 45201
Phone: (513)762-8878

Description

Founded: 1943
EIN: 316025080
Organization Type: Private Foundation
Giving Locations: VA: Lee County, Wise County
Grant Types: Endowment, General Support, Multiyear/Continuing Support, Operating Expenses, Project, Scholarship.

Donor Information

Founder: Founded in 1943 under the will of the late C. Bascom Slemp, a former U.S. Congressman from Virginia.

Financial Summary

Total Giving: $905,110 (fiscal year ending June 30, 2003); $1,096,665 (fiscal 2001). Note: Giving includes scholarships ($284,000) fiscal 1998; ($277,000) fiscal 1997.
Giving Analysis: Giving for fiscal 2003 includes: foundation scholarships ($270,000); fiscal 2001: foundation scholarships ($318,000)
Assets: $18,998,209 (fiscal 2003); $22,113,065 (fiscal 2001)
Gifts Received: $1,000 (fiscal 2001); $1,300 (fiscal 1997); $2,300 (fiscal 1996). Note: In fiscal 2001, contributions were received from David & Cathy Kinsler. In fiscal 1996, contributions were received from Katherine MacMillan, $300; Tammy and Tommy Baker, $500; and $1,500 from Wolfe & Farmer. In fiscal 1997, contributions were received from David A. and Kathy G. Kinsler, $1,000; and Katherine MacMillan, $300.

Typical Recipients

Arts & Humanities: Arts Associations & Councils, Arts Centers, Arts Outreach, Community Arts, Arts & Humanities-General, History & Archaeology, Libraries, Museums/Galleries, Music, Performing Arts, Theater
Civic & Public Affairs: Botanical Gardens/Parks, Clubs, Civic & Public Affairs-General, Municipalities/Towns, Safety
Education: Afterschool/Enrichment Programs, Agricultural Education, Arts/Humanities Education, Colleges & Universities, Community & Junior Colleges, Education Associations, Education Funds, Elementary Education (Public), Education-General, Literacy, Preschool Education, Private Education (Precollege), Public Education (Precollege), Science/Mathematics Education, Secondary Education (Private), Secondary Education (Public), Special Education, Student

Aid

Environment: Air/Water Quality, Environment-General

Health: Cancer, Children's Health/Hospitals, Clinics/Medical Centers, Emergency/Ambulance Services, Hospices

Religion: Churches, Religious Welfare, Seminaries

Social Services: Camps, Child Abuse, Child Welfare, Community Centers, Community Service Organizations, People with Disabilities, Recreation & Athletics, Scouts, Senior Services, Youth Organizations

Application Procedures

Initial Contact: The foundation has no formal grant application procedure or application form.

Application Requirements: The application should include name address and telephone number of organization; any national organization affiliation; date organization was established; a copy of IRS Service letter; organization's purpose and activities; services provided; target audience and how many served per year; names of officers and governing board; copy of the most recent balance sheet and annual operating statement; percentage of budget received from United Appeal, federal or state funding, and/or other sources; percentage of costs of organization paid for by recipients; purpose of grant and how it would benefit residents of Lee and Wise Counties, VA; and budget for specific project, if applicable. project, if applicable.

Deadlines: None. Student applications due before October 15.

Review Process: The trustees meet usually in April, July, and November to review grant applications.

Additional Information

The Foundation provides scholarships to individuals for higher education (for residents or descendants of Lee or Wise Counties, Virginia).

Publications: Application Form

Trust(s): US Bank NA

Foundation Officials

Mary Virginia Edmonds: trustee
Pamela S. Edmonds: trustee
John A. Reid: trustee
Melissa Smith Sircy: trustee
James C. Smith: trustee
Nancey E. Smith: trustee

Grants Analysis

Disclosure Period: fiscal year ending June 30, 2003
Total Grants: $635,110*
Number of Grants: 18
Average Grant: $8,444*
Highest Grant: $299,716
Lowest Grant: $100
Typical Range: $1,000 to $15,000
***Note:** Giving excludes scholarships. Average grant figure excludes two highest grants ($500,000).

Recent Grants

Note: Grants derived from fiscal 2003 Form 990.
Library-Related
600	Wise County Friends of the Library, Wise, VA -- funding for author's dinner

General
299,716	University of Virginia College, Wise, VA -- funding for construction of student center
200,284	University of Virginia College, Wise, VA -- funding for construction of student center
25,000	University of Virginia College, Wise, VA -- toward radio station operating expenses
25,000	University of Virginia College, Wise, VA -- funding for construction of student center
20,000	Pro-Art Association, Wise, VA -- funding for concert series
10,000	Hospice Support Services, Appalachia, VA -- funding for operating expenses
10,000	Virginia State Parks Foundation, Richmond, VA -- toward annual expenses

10,000	Virginia State Parks Foundation, Richmond, VA -- toward annual expenses
6,500	Lee County Public Schools, Jonesville, VA -- funding for orchestra performances
6,000	Lee & Wise Co 4-H Club, Jonesville, VA -- funding for organization's programs

ROY W. SLUSHER CHARITABLE FOUNDATION

Giving Contact
Jerry Redfern, Foundation Manager
PO Box 3357
Springfield, MO 65808-3357
Phone: (417)882-9090

Description
Founded: 1988
EIN: 436339151
Organization Type: Private Foundation
Giving Locations: MO
Grant Types: General Support.

Financial Summary
Total Giving: $180,960 (fiscal year ending February 28, 2004); $188,223 (fiscal 2001)
Assets: $6,610,689 (fiscal 2004); $3,543,321 (fiscal 2001)

Typical Recipients
Arts & Humanities: Libraries, Performing Arts, Public Broadcasting

Education: Colleges & Universities, Community & Junior Colleges, Elementary Education (Public), Student Aid, Vocational & Technical Education

Health: Cancer, Children's Health/Hospitals, Clinics/Medical Centers, Diabetes, Heart, Hospitals, Single-Disease Health Associations

International: Foreign Arts Organizations, International Relief Efforts, Missionary/Religious Activities

Religion: Churches, Religion-General, Religious Organizations, Religious Welfare

Social Services: At-Risk Youth, Camps, Community Centers, Community Service Organizations, Counseling, Domestic Violence, Emergency Relief, Family Services, People with Disabilities, Recreation & Athletics, Social Services-General, Youth Organizations

Application Procedures
Initial Contact: Request a proposal summary sheet and application guidelines from the foundation.
Deadlines: None.
Decision Notification: Board meets in March and September.

Restrictions
Does not support individuals, religious organizations for sectarian purposes, political or lobbying groups, and organizations outside operating areas.

Additional Information
Publications: Application Guidelines; Proposal Summary Sheet
Trust(s): U.S. Bank

Foundation Officials
Charles A. Fuller, Jr.: fdn mgr

Grants Analysis
Disclosure Period: fiscal year ending February 28, 2004
Total Grants: $180,960
Number of Grants: 36
Average Grant: $5,027
Highest Grant: $16,960

Lowest Grant: $1,000
Typical Range: $1,000 to $10,000

Recent Grants
Note: Grants derived from fiscal 2004 Form 990.
General
16,960	Ozark Technical Community College, Springfield, MO
15,000	College of Ozarks, Pt. Lookout, MO -- towards scholarships
11,000	Springfield Victory Mission, Springfield, MO
10,500	Bethal Mission Church, Kolar Gold Fields, KA India
10,000	Bradleyville R-1 School District, Bradleyville, MO
9,500	Convoy of Hope, Springfield, MO -- to feed the hungry
8,500	Salvation Army, Branson, MO
8,000	Christian Athletes, Springfield, MO
8,000	Lake Country Boys & Girls Club, Forsyth, MO -- aid in building new Boys and Girls Club
7,000	Sloan - Kettering Memorial, New York, NY -- towards cancer

SMART FAMILY FOUNDATION

Giving Contact
Raymond L. Smart, President
74 Pin Oak Lane
Wilton, CT 06897-1329
Phone: (203)834-0400
Fax: (203)834-0412

Description
Founded: 1951
EIN: 061232323
Organization Type: Family Foundation
Giving Locations: nationally.
Grant Types: General Support, Project, Research.

Donor Information
Founder: Established in 1951 by the Smart family.

Financial Summary
Total Giving: $6,800,001 (2003); $7,175,603 (2002); $7,100,001 (2001)
Assets: $175,867,638 (2003); $151,606,496 (2002); $168,327,786 (2001)

Typical Recipients
Arts & Humanities: Arts Associations & Councils, Arts Centers, Arts Festivals, Arts Institutes, Ballet, Film & Video, History & Archaeology, Libraries, Literary Arts, Museums/Galleries, Music, Opera, Performing Arts, Public Broadcasting, Theater, Visual Arts

Civic & Public Affairs: Asian American Affairs, Botanical Gardens/Parks, Civil Rights, Community Foundations, Civic & Public Affairs-General, Law & Justice, Municipalities/Towns, Professional & Trade Associations, Public Policy, Urban & Community Affairs

Education: Afterschool/Enrichment Programs, Arts/Humanities Education, Business Education, Colleges & Universities, Continuing Education, Education Funds, Education Reform, Elementary Education (Private), Environmental Education, Faculty Development, Education-General, International Studies, Leadership Training, Legal Education, Medical Education, Private Education (Precollege), Public Education (Precollege), Science/Mathematics Education, Social Sciences Education

Environment: Environment-General, Protection, Resource Conservation

Health: Clinics/Medical Centers, Eyes/Blindness,

Geriatric Health, Health Organizations, Hospitals, Hospitals (University Affiliated), Medical Research, Mental Health, Research/Studies Institutes, Single-Disease Health Associations

International: Foreign Educational Institutions, Health Care/Hospitals, Human Rights, International Environmental Issues, International Peace & Security Issues

Religion: Religion-General, Jewish Causes

Science: Science Museums, Scientific Centers & Institutes, Scientific Organizations

Social Services: Animal Protection, At-Risk Youth, Child Welfare, Community Service Organizations, Crime Prevention, Family Planning, Family Services, People with Disabilities, Recreation & Athletics, Senior Services, Social Services-General, Substance Abuse, YMCA/YWCA/YMHA/YWHA, Youth Organizations

Application Procedures

Initial Contact: An informal letter outlining the project.

Application Requirements: The letter should include the purpose for which aid is sought, resources needed, personnel involved, and a description of the methods to be used in completing the project.

Deadlines: None.

Restrictions

The Foundation does not give grants to individuals or for-profit businesses.

Foundation Officials

Ellen Oswald: director, member
Mary Smart: secretary

Grants Analysis

Disclosure Period: calendar year ending 2003
Total Grants: $6,800,001
Number of Grants: 88
Average Grant: $61,638*
Highest Grant: $750,122
Lowest Grant: $5,000
Typical Range: $20,000 to $100,000
*Note: Average grant figure excludes two highest grants ($1,499,102).

Recent Grants

Note: Grants derived from 2002 Form 990.

Library-Related
75,000	Stanford University Libraries, Stanford, CA -- towards funding present operating expenses

General
1,011,500	University of Chicago, Chicago, IL -- towards funding present operating expenses
902,003	Amistad Academy, New Haven, CT -- towards funding present operating expenses
600,000	Calgary Academy, Bar Harbor, ME -- towards funding present operating expenses
350,000	Smart Museum of Art, Chicago, IL -- towards funding present operating expenses
310,000	Save San Francisco Bay Association, San Francisco, CA -- towards funding present operating expenses
200,000	Conservation International, Washington, DC -- towards funding present operating expenses
200,000	New Jersey Performing Arts Center, Newark, NJ -- towards funding present operating expenses
189,310	Harvard Law School, Cambridge, MA -- towards funding present operating expenses
155,160	Center for Jewish History, New York, NY -- towards funding present operating expenses

125,000	New York-New Jersey Trail Conference, Mahwah, NJ -- towards funding present operating expenses

CLARA BLACKFORD SMITH AND W. AUBREY SMITH CHARITABLE FOUNDATION

Giving Contact

Linda Hunt, Board Member
Bank of America
330 W. Main St.
Denison, TX 75020
Phone: (903)465-2131

Description

Founded: 1985
EIN: 756314114
Organization Type: General Purpose Foundation
Giving Locations: TX: primarily Grayson County
Grant Types: Capital, General Support, Project, Scholarship, Seed Money.

Donor Information

Founder: Established in 1985 by the late Clara Blackford Smith for religious, charitable, educational, scientific and literary purposes.

Financial Summary

Total Giving: $502,798 (fiscal year ending June 30, 2002)
Giving Analysis: Giving for fiscal 2002 includes: foundation matching gifts ($3,000); foundation grants to United Way ($20,000); foundation scholarships ($40,000)
Assets: $17,726,551 (fiscal 2002)

Typical Recipients

Arts & Humanities: Historic Preservation, History & Archaeology, Libraries, Museums/Galleries, Music, Performing Arts, Theater

Civic & Public Affairs: Botanical Gardens/Parks, Community Foundations, Economic Development, Civic & Public Affairs-General, Housing, Inner-City Development, Municipalities/Towns, Safety, Urban & Community Affairs

Education: Afterschool/Enrichment Programs, Arts/Humanities Education, Colleges & Universities, Community & Junior Colleges, Education Funds, Elementary Education (Public), Engineering/Technological Education, Education-General, Literacy, Medical Education, Private Education (Precollege), Public Education (Precollege), Special Education, Student Aid

Environment: Environment-General

Health: Cancer, Children's Health/Hospitals, Clinics/Medical Centers, Diabetes, Emergency/Ambulance Services, Geriatric Health, Health Funds, Health Organizations, Heart, Hospices, Hospitals, Medical Rehabilitation, Medical Research, Nursing Services, Public Health

Religion: Churches

Social Services: At-Risk Youth, Big Brothers/Big Sisters, Camps, Child Welfare, Community Service Organizations, Crime Prevention, Day Care, Domestic Violence, Food/Clothing Distribution, People with Disabilities, Recreation & Athletics, Scouts, Senior Services, Shelters/Homelessness, Substance Abuse, United Funds/United Ways, Youth Organizations

Application Procedures

Initial Contact: Request application from foundation. Applicants submit eight copies of grant application.

Application Requirements: An application with a brief description of organization; program or project

to be considered, including purpose, desired impact, timetable and criteria for evaluation; amount requested; budget information, including prior, current and projected budgets; other sources of funding; copy of IRS determination letter; and a list of trustees or directors.

Deadlines: March 31, June 30, September 30 and December 31.

Review Process: The board meets quarterly to review applicants. The foundation may request a more detailed proposal, additional information or a visit from a representative from the organization, after reviewing application.

Notes: Recipients are requested to provide the foundation with a brief report concerning the results or benefits derived from the grant.

Restrictions

The foundation does not make grants to individuals, provide loans or deficit financing, or ordinarily make general support grants for ongoing operating expenses.

Additional Information

The foundation is administered by Bank of America of Texas, N.A.

Publications: Grant Application Information Sheet

Foundation Officials

King Campbell: chairman
Jerry Culpepper: advisor, director
Wayne E. Delaney: director, advisor
Linda Hunt: board member
Jack Lilley: director
H. W. Totten, Jr.: director

Grants Analysis

Disclosure Period: fiscal year ending June 30, 2002
Total Grants: $765,236*
Number of Grants: 58
Average Grant: $10,794*
Highest Grant: $150,000
Lowest Grant: $400
Typical Range: $5,000 to $25,000
*Note: Giving excludes scholarships; matching gifts, United Way. Average grant figure excludes highest grant.

Recent Grants

Note: Grants derived from fiscal 2002 Form 990.

Library-Related
15,000	Denison Public Library, Denison, TX

General
150,000	Texoma Healthcare System, Denison, TX
70,000	University of Texas-MD Anderson Cancer Center, Denison, TX
50,000	Denison ISD School, Denison, TX -- toward resurface of track and runways
50,000	Grayson County Shelter, Denison, TX
33,688	Grayson Co. Frontier Village, Denison, TX -- funding for construction of historical research center
32,815	Denison Education Foundation, Denison, TX
25,000	Austin College, Sherman, TX -- toward scholarships for pre-medical students
25,000	Southwestern Diabetic Foundation, Galesville, TX
22,250	North Texas Civic Chorus Inc., Denison, TX -- toward the library and orchestra project
20,000	Denison Independent School District Education Foundation, Denison, TX

ARLENE H. SMITH CHARITABLE FOUNDATION

Giving Contact
Timothy M. Hunter, Treasurer
1533 E. 12th St.
Erie, PA 16511
Phone: (814)459-4495

Description
Founded: 1982
EIN: 251515142
Organization Type: Private Foundation
Giving Locations: PA: Corry
Grant Types: General Support.

Donor Information
Founder: the late Arlene H. Smith

Financial Summary
Total Giving: $229,339 (2003); $260,736 (2001)
Assets: $4,404,841 (2003); $4,537,087 (2001)

Typical Recipients
Arts & Humanities: Libraries
Civic & Public Affairs: Clubs, Community Foundations, Civic & Public Affairs-General, Professional & Trade Associations, Safety
Education: Colleges & Universities, Education-General
Health: Cancer, Children's Health/Hospitals, Clinics/Medical Centers, Emergency/Ambulance Services, Hospices, Hospitals
Religion: Religious Welfare
Social Services: At-Risk Youth, Community Service Organizations, Counseling, Crime Prevention, Food/Clothing Distribution, Recreation & Athletics, Scouts, Shelters/Homelessness, Social Services-General, United Funds/United Ways, YMCA/YWCA/YMHA/YWHA, Youth Organizations

Application Procedures
Initial Contact: Applications should include two copies of the request for funding provided by the foundation, proof of tax-exempt status, list of board members, recently audited financial statement, program and agency budgets, and the most recent annual report.
Deadlines: None.

Restrictions
Grants are not made to individuals.

Additional Information
Publications: Request for Funding Form; Procedures

Foundation Officials
John E. Britton, Esq.: assistant secretary, director
James D. Cullen, Esq.: secretary, director
Timothy M. Hunter: treasurer
Stephen J. Mahoney: president, director
Frank K. Smith: vice president, director

Grants Analysis
Disclosure Period: calendar year ending 2003
Total Grants: $229,339*
Number of Grants: 16
Average Grant: $11,024*
Highest Grant: $40,000
Lowest Grant: $2,000
Typical Range: $1,000 to $20,000
*Note: Average grant figure excludes two highest grants ($75,000).

Recent Grants
Note: Grants derived from 2003 Form 990.

Library-Related
13,500	Corry Public Library, Corry, PA

General
40,000	YMCA, Corry, PA
35,000	Corry Community Foundation, Erie, PA
25,000	Perseus House Inc., Erie, PA
24,000	American Cancer Society, Corry, PA
22,500	Corry Higher Education Council, Corry, PA
14,000	Counseling Services Center Inc., Corry, PA
11,500	Carpenters for Christ Inc., Corry, PA
10,189	Corry Concerned for Youth, Corry, PA
7,000	Association for Counselor Education and Supervision, Erie, PA

JOHN SMITH CHARITIES

Giving Contact
Bill Bridges, Administrator
Bank of America
PO Box 608
Greenville, SC 29608
Fax: (864)271-5930

Description
Founded: 1985
EIN: 570806327
Organization Type: Family Foundation
Giving Locations: SC: Upstate South Carolina
Grant Types: Capital, Emergency, Endowment, General Support, Scholarship.

Donor Information
Founder: Established in 1985 by the late John I. Smith.

Financial Summary
Total Giving: $441,000 (fiscal year ending July 31, 2001)
Assets: $26,319,700 (fiscal 2001)
Gifts Received: $127,221 (fiscal 2001). Note: In fiscal 2001, contributions were received from the estate of Mamie Sullivan.

Typical Recipients
Arts & Humanities: Arts Festivals, History & Archaeology, Libraries, Museums/Galleries, Music, Performing Arts, Public Broadcasting, Theater
Civic & Public Affairs: African American Affairs, Chambers of Commerce, Clubs, Community Foundations, Economic Development, Civic & Public Affairs-General, Housing, Municipalities/Towns, Parades/Festivals, Philanthropic Organizations, Public Policy, Urban & Community Affairs, Women's Affairs
Education: Arts/Humanities Education, Colleges & Universities, Education Associations, Education Reform, Education-General, Literacy, Medical Education, Preschool Education, Private Education (Precollege), Religious Education, Secondary Education (Public), Special Education
Environment: Environment-General
Health: Cancer, Clinics/Medical Centers, Emergency/Ambulance Services, Health Organizations, Hospitals, Hospitals (University Affiliated), Long-Term Care, Mental Health, Single-Disease Health Associations
International: International Peace & Security Issues
Religion: Churches, Religion-General, Ministries, Religious Organizations, Religious Welfare, Seminaries
Social Services: At-Risk Youth, Camps, Child Abuse, Child Welfare, Community Service Organizations, Counseling, Day Care, Emergency Relief, Family Planning, Food/Clothing Distribution, Homes, People with Disabilities, Scouts, Senior Services, Shelters/Homelessness, Social Services-General,

United Funds/United Ways, YMCA/YWCA/YMHA/YWHA, Youth Organizations

Application Procedures
Initial Contact: Applicants should submit a brief letter.
Application Requirements: Letters should include the purpose and requirements of the applicant's program, as well as other necessary information.
Deadlines: October 1, January 1, and July 1.
Review Process: The board meets three times per year to consider grant applications, in January, July, and October.

Additional Information
NationsBank Trust is the agent of the foundation.

Foundation Officials
Wilbur Y. Bridgers: president
Jefferson V. Smith, III: director, secretary
W. Thomas Smith: vice president, treasurer

Grants Analysis
Disclosure Period: fiscal year ending July 31, 2001
Total Grants: $441,000
Number of Grants: 31
Average Grant: $11,414*
Highest Grant: $50,000
Typical Range: $5,000 to $20,000
*Note: Average grant figure excludes two highest grants ($100,000).

Recent Grants
Note: Grants derived from 2002 Form 990.
Library-Related
100,000	Greenville Library Capital Fund, Greenville, SC
10,000	Spartanburg County Public Library, Spartanburg, SC

General
303,000	Davidson College, Davidson, NC
150,000	South Carolina First Steps, SC
132,500	Miracle Hill Ministries, Spartanburg, SC
100,000	Community Foundation of Greater Greenville, Greenville, SC
100,000	United Way of Greenville County, Greenville, SC
80,000	Furman University, Greenville, SC
80,000	Presbyterian College, Newberry, SC
72,500	Urban League of the Upstate, Greenville, SC
70,000	Rosewood, Greenville, SC
50,000	Hollins Cancer Center, Charleston, SC

A.O. SMITH CORP.

Company Headquarters
Milwaukee, WI
Web: http://www.aosmith.com

Company Description
Founded: 1889
Ticker: AOS
Exchange: NYSE
Revenue: US$1.469 billion (2002)
Employees: 17000 (2003)
SIC(s): 3089 Plastics Products Nec, 3443 Fabricated Plate Work--Boiler Shops, 3523 Farm Machinery & Equipment, 3714 Motor Vehicle Parts & Accessories.

Operating Locations
A.O. Smith Corp. (AR--Little Rock; CA--Irvine; FL--Williston; IL--Chicago, Granite City; KS--Wichita; KY--Bowling Green, Mount Sterling; MD--Belcamp; MI--Farmington Hills; NC--Mebane; OH--Bellevue, Upper Sandusky; SC--McBee; TN--Milan; TX--El Paso; WA--Seattle; WI--Milwaukee)

A.O. Smith Foundation, Inc.

Giving Contact
Edward J. O'Connor, Secretary
PO Box 245001
Milwaukee, WI 53224-9501
Phone: (414)359-4100
Fax: (414)359-4064

Description
Founded: 1955
EIN: 396076724
Organization Type: Corporate Foundation
Giving Locations: communities where company has manufacturing facilities.
Grant Types: Capital, Employee Matching Gifts, General Support, Operating Expenses, Project, Scholarship.

Financial Summary
Total Giving: $1,158,547 (2001). Note: Contributes through corporate direct giving program and foundation.
Giving Analysis: Giving for 2001 includes: foundation matching gifts ($29,107); foundation scholarships ($84,740); foundation grants to United Way ($231,700)
Assets: $7,777,565 (2001)

Typical Recipients
Arts & Humanities: Arts Funds, Dance, Historic Preservation, Libraries, Museums/Galleries, Music, Performing Arts
Civic & Public Affairs: Business/Free Enterprise, Civil Rights, Economic Development, Nonprofit Management, Safety, Urban & Community Affairs
Education: Business Education, Colleges & Universities, Community & Junior Colleges, Economic Education, Education Funds, Engineering/Technological Education, Literacy, Medical Education, Minority Education, Student Aid
Environment: Environment-General
Health: Emergency/Ambulance Services, Hospitals, Medical Rehabilitation, Mental Health, Public Health
Social Services: Child Welfare, Community Centers, Community Service Organizations, Family Services, Homes, People with Disabilities, Recreation & Athletics, Senior Services, Shelters/Homelessness, Substance Abuse, United Funds/United Ways, Youth Organizations

Application Procedures
Initial Contact: Send a letter or proposal on the organization's letterhead.
Application Requirements: Include name, location, and a description of organization; proof of tax-exempt status; geographic area served; explanation of activity for which support is sought; amount requested; description of benefits to be achieved and who will receive them; budget, including other sources of income; and plans for reporting results.
Deadlines: By October 30 to be considered for following year's budget; requests are reviewed in the order that they are received.
Review Process: The foundation is governed by a four-member board, including the company's vice president of human resources & public affairs.
Decision Notification: The board meets annually in June, with special meetings held periodically when necessary.
Notes: Also forward any printed materials describing your organization that may lend support to the application.

Restrictions
The foundation does not make contributions to politically active organizations seeking to influence legislation, nor does it fund individuals.

Additional Information
A.O. Smith Corp. employees are encouraged to take an active part in civic affairs.

Corporate Officials
John J. Kita: vice president, treasurer, controller, director PRIM CORP EMPL vice president, treasurer, controller: A.O. Smith Corp.
Robert Joseph O'Toole: chairman, president, chief executive officer, director B Chicago, IL 1941. ED Loyola University BS (1961). PRIM CORP EMPL chairman, president, chief executive officer, director: A.O. Smith Corp. CORP AFFIL director: Protection Mutual Insurance Co.; director: Smith Fiberglass Products Inc.; director: FM Global Insurance; director: Firstar Bank NA; director: Firstar Corp.; director: Briggs & Stratton Corp.

Foundation Officials
John J. Kita: treasurer (see above)
Edward J. O'Connor: secretary, director B Saint Louis, MO. ED Saint Louis University (1962). PRIM CORP EMPL vice president human resources & public affairs: A.O. Smith Corp.
Robert Joseph O'Toole: director (see above)
Arthur O. Smith: president B 1930. CORP AFFIL director: AO Smith Corp.; chairman, chief executive officer: Smith Investment Co.; director: Central Studies Distributing Service Inc.

Grants Analysis
Disclosure Period: calendar year ending 2001
Total Grants: $813,000*
Number of Grants: 152
Average Grant: $5,026*
Highest Grant: $54,000
Lowest Grant: $250
Typical Range: $1,000 to $10,000
*Note: Giving excludes United Way, matching gifts, and scholarships. Average grant figure excludes highest grant.

RICHARD AND SUSAN SMITH FAMILY FOUNDATION

Giving Contact
Susan F. Smith, Trustee
1280 Boylston St., Suite 100
Chestnut Hill, MA 02467-1719
Phone: (617)278-5220

Description
Founded: 1970
EIN: 237090011
Organization Type: Private Foundation
Giving Locations: MA: Boston metropolitan area
Grant Types: Capital, Fellowship, General Support, Project.

Donor Information
Founder: the late Marian Smith, and Richard A. Smith

Financial Summary
Total Giving: $3,137,560 (fiscal year ending April 30, 2003); $2,093,750 (fiscal 2002); $1,189,750 (fiscal 2001)
Giving Analysis: Giving for fiscal 2003 includes: foundation grants to United Way ($62,500); fiscal 2002: foundation grants to United Way ($50,000); fiscal 2001: foundation grants to United Way ($10,000)
Assets: $114,656,596 (fiscal 2003); $93,598,816 (fiscal 2002); $91,050,784 (fiscal 2001)
Gifts Received: $41,869 (fiscal 2003); $30,903 (fiscal 2002); $75,234,795 (fiscal 2001). Note: In fiscal

2001, contributions were received from Richard A. & Susan F. Smith ($75,205,039) and ADR Charitable Foundation and Trust ($29,756). In fiscal 2000, contributions were received from Robert A. Smith ($73,740), Brian and Debra Knez ($73,740), John and Amy Berylson ($73,740), Richard A. and Susan F. Smith ($1,027,946), and ADR Charitable Foundation and Trust ($23,461). In fiscal 1996, contributions received from Richard A. Smith 1976 Charitable Trust ($575,000), Marian Smith DRA 1976 Charitable Trust ($315,000), and ADR Charitable Foundation and Trust ($15,358).

Typical Recipients
Arts & Humanities: Arts Institutes, Arts & Humanities-General, Libraries, Museums/Galleries, Music, Performing Arts, Public Broadcasting
Civic & Public Affairs: Ethnic Organizations, Civic & Public Affairs-General, Law & Justice, Parades/Festivals, Philanthropic Organizations, Safety, Zoos/Aquariums
Education: Arts/Humanities Education, Business Education, Colleges & Universities, Education Funds, Education-General, Legal Education, Preschool Education, Private Education (Precollege), Public Education (Precollege), Religious Education, Secondary Education (Private), Social Sciences Education, Student Aid
Environment: Environment-General
Health: Cancer, Children's Health/Hospitals, Clinics/Medical Centers, Diabetes, Eyes/Blindness, Health-General, Health Funds, Health Organizations, Hospices, Hospitals, Hospitals (University Affiliated), Medical Rehabilitation, Medical Research, Prenatal Health Issues, Preventive Medicine/Wellness Organizations, Single-Disease Health Associations, Speech & Hearing
Religion: Jewish Causes, Synagogues/Temples
Social Services: Camps, Child Welfare, Community Service Organizations, Family Services, Food/Clothing Distribution, Recreation & Athletics, United Funds/United Ways, Youth Organizations

Application Procedures
Initial Contact: Send a brief letter of inquiry and full proposal.
Application Requirements: Include a description of organization, purpose of funds sought, amount requested, recently audited financial statement, and proof of tax-exempt status.
Deadlines: None.

Additional Information
Publications: Application Guidelines

Foundation Officials
Amy S. Berylson: trustee
John G. Berylson: trustee
David Ford: executive director
Brian J. Knez: trustee B 1957. ED Arizona State University (1979); Boston College (1984). PRIM CORP EMPL president, co-chief executive officer, director: Harcourt General, Inc. ADD CORP EMPL chief executive officer: Harcourt Inc.; president, chief executive officer, director: Harcourt Brace & Co.
Debra S. Knez: trustee
Robert A. Smith: trustee B 1959. ED Harvard University AB (1981); Harvard University MBA (1987). PRIM CORP EMPL co-chief executive officer, director, president: Harcourt General, Inc. ADD CORP EMPL co-chief executive officer: Harcourt Inc. CORP AFFIL chairman, chief executive officer group vice president: Neiman Marcus Group Inc.
Susan F. Smith: trustee
Dana A. Weiss: trustee

Grants Analysis
Disclosure Period: fiscal year ending April 30, 2003
Total Grants: $3,075,060*
Number of Grants: 49
Average Grant: $54,689*
Highest Grant: $450,000

Lowest Grant: $250
Typical Range: $25,000 to $100,000
***Note:** Giving excludes United Way. Average grant figure excludes highest grant.

Recent Grants

Note: Grants derived from fiscal 2003 Form 990.
Library-Related

25,000	Boston Public Library, Boston, MA -- towards education

General

450,000	Combined Jewish Philanthropies, Boston, MA -- towards social services
295,000	Boys and Girls Clubs of Boston, Boston, MA
238,000	Steppingstone Foundation, Boston, MA
237,500	Facing History and Ourselves, Brookline, MA -- towards education
200,000	Bell, Chestnut Hill, MA
200,000	Year Up, Boston, MA
170,000	Children's Hospital Trust, Boston, MA -- towards health
153,260	Brown University, Providence, RI -- towards education
150,000	Children's Hospital, Boston, MA -- towards health
150,000	Israel in Crisis -- towards social services

KELVIN AND ELEANOR SMITH FOUNDATION

Giving Contact

Carol W. Zett, Grants Manager
30195 Chagrin Blvd., Suite 275
Cleveland, OH 44124
Phone: (216)591-9111

Description

Founded: 1955
EIN: 346555349
Organization Type: General Purpose Foundation
Giving Locations: OH: Cleveland metropolitan area
Grant Types: General Support, Operating Expenses, Project.

Donor Information

Founder: Established in 1955 by the late Kelvin Smith.

Financial Summary

Total Giving: $5,836,959 (fiscal year ending October 31, 2003); $4,927,775 (fiscal 2002)
Assets: $141,261,711 (fiscal 2003); $121,197,802 (fiscal 2002)
Gifts Received: $1,774,216 (fiscal 2000); $36,917,437 (fiscal 1999); $2,098 (fiscal 1992). Note: Contributions were received from the Estate of Eleanor A. Smith.

Typical Recipients

Arts & Humanities: Arts Associations & Councils, Arts Centers, Arts Funds, Arts Institutes, Arts Outreach, Arts & Humanities-General, Historic Preservation, History & Archaeology, Libraries, Museums/Galleries, Music, Opera, Performing Arts, Public Broadcasting, Theater, Visual Arts
Civic & Public Affairs: Botanical Gardens/Parks, Clubs, Employment/Job Training, Civic & Public Affairs-General, Municipalities/Towns, Nonprofit Management, Philanthropic Organizations, Professional & Trade Associations, Public Policy, Urban & Community Affairs, Zoos/Aquariums
Education: Arts/Humanities Education, Business Education, Colleges & Universities, Economic Education, Education Reform, Education-General, Literacy, Medical Education, Private Education (Precollege), Public Education (Precollege), Science/

Mathematics Education, Secondary Education (Public), Special Education, Student Aid
Environment: Forestry, Environment-General, Protection, Resource Conservation
Health: Cancer, Children's Health/Hospitals, Clinics/Medical Centers, Eyes/Blindness, Health Funds, Health Organizations, Hospices, Hospitals, Hospitals (University Affiliated), Medical Rehabilitation, Mental Health, Nursing Services, Prenatal Health Issues, Preventive Medicine/Wellness Organizations, Speech & Hearing
International: International Affairs
Religion: Ministries, Religious Organizations, Religious Welfare
Science: Science Museums, Scientific Centers & Institutes, Scientific Research
Social Services: Animal Protection, Camps, Child Welfare, Community Service Organizations, Day Care, Family Planning, Family Services, Food/Clothing Distribution, People with Disabilities, Recreation & Athletics, Senior Services, Shelters/Homelessness, Substance Abuse, Youth Organizations

Application Procedures

Initial Contact: The foundation has no formal application form. An initial written application should be submitted.
Application Requirements: Each grant request should include a two-page cover letter that outlines the reason for the request or the specific project to be funded, and the amount of funds being requested. This letter should by signed by the Executive Director and the Board President.
The proposal should also include: background information of your organization such as history, mission, types of programs offered, and clients served; the number of full-time and part-time staff positions; a description of your project or needs to be addressed, including specific goals and ways to meet them, project budget and timeline, key personnel involved, anticipated outcome or impact, method of evaluation, and plans for the continuation of your project or program. Include information on how foundation funds will be used; other foundation, government, and public support; and your plan for follow-up funding; a copy of your organization's line item expense budget and most recent audited financial statement; and a list of current board members, most recent annual report, and a copy of the IRS letter confirming your Internal Revenue Code 501(c)(3) status.
Deadlines: None.
Review Process: Each request will be acknowledged upon receipt, and a written notification of the board's decision will be sent after each meeting.
Notes: A site visit may be necessary prior to consideration of proposal.

Restrictions

The foundation does not fund endowments, individuals or political subdivisions, nor do they make loans. The foundation does not respond to mass mailings for annual appeals.

Additional Information

Publications: Application Guidelines

Foundation Officials

Charles L. Bolton: trustee
Michael D. Eppig, MD: trustee
Andrew Lawrie Fabens, III: secretary B Washington, DC 1942. ED Yale University AB (1964); University of Chicago JD (1967). PRIM CORP EMPL partner: Thompson Hine & Flory. NONPR AFFIL member: Cleveland Bar Association; member: Ohio Bar Association; trustee: Bascom Little Fund; fellow: American College Trust & Estate Counsel; trustee: American McGregor Home. CLUB AFFIL member: Rawfand Club; member: Union Club; member: Cleveland Skating Club; member: Novel Club.
William G. LaPlace: treasurer
Ellen S. Mavec: president

Lucia S. Nash: co-chairman
William G. O'Neill, Jr.: trustee
Cara S. Stirn: co-chairman, trustee

Grants Analysis

Disclosure Period: fiscal year ending October 31, 2003
Total Grants: $5,836,959
Number of Grants: 62
Average Grant: $56,559*
Highest Grant: $1,000,000
Lowest Grant: $1,500
Typical Range: $10,000 to $100,000
***Note:** Average grant figure excludes three highest grants ($2,500,000).

Recent Grants

Note: Grants derived from 2003 Form 990.
General

1,000,000	Cleveland Botanical Garden, Cleveland, OH
1,000,000	Cleveland Museum of Art, Cleveland, OH
500,000	Laurel School, Cleveland, OH -- fund for capital campaign
500,000	Musical Arts Association, Cleveland, OH -- fund for capital campaign
450,000	Cleveland Foodbank Inc., Cleveland, OH
400,000	Hathaway Brown School, Shaker Heights, OH -- for capital campaign
375,000	Nature Conservancy, Dublin, OH
150,000	Cleveland Museum of Art, Cleveland, OH
150,000	Musical Arts Association, Cleveland, OH -- fund for blossom initiative
150,000	Trinity Commons Foundation, Cleveland, OH -- fund for capital campaign

RALPH L. SMITH FOUNDATION

Giving Contact

David P. Ross, Senior Vice President
c/o Bank of America
PO Box 419119
Kansas City, MO 64141
Phone: (816)979-7481

Description

Founded: 1952
EIN: 446008508
Organization Type: Private Foundation
Giving Locations: AZ; CA; MO; OR
Grant Types: General Support.

Donor Information

Founder: the late Harriet T. Smith, the late Ralph L. Smith

Financial Summary

Total Giving: $1,260,375 (2003); $1,133,050 (2001)
Assets: $21,158,213 (2003); $22,884,609 (2001)

Typical Recipients

Arts & Humanities: Ethnic & Folk Arts, Libraries, Museums/Galleries, Music, Public Broadcasting, Theater
Civic & Public Affairs: Botanical Gardens/Parks, Community Foundations, Economic Development, Gay/Lesbian Issues, Civic & Public Affairs-General, Hispanic Affairs, Housing, Legal Aid, Municipalities/Towns, Native American Affairs, Nonprofit Management, Public Policy, Rural Affairs, Women's Affairs
Education: Arts/Humanities Education, Colleges & Universities, Education Funds, Faculty Development, Education-General, Leadership Training, Private Education (Precollege), Public Education (Precollege), Science/Mathematics Education
Environment: Resource Conservation

Health: AIDS/HIV, Cancer, Children's Health/Hospitals, Medical Rehabilitation, Medical Research, Public Health, Single-Disease Health Associations
International: Foreign Educational Institutions, Health Care/Hospitals
Religion: Churches
Science: Scientific Organizations
Social Services: Big Brothers/Big Sisters, Community Service Organizations, Crime Prevention, Domestic Violence, Family Planning, Family Services, Food/Clothing Distribution, Shelters/Homelessness, Social Services-General, Substance Abuse, Youth Organizations

Application Procedures

Initial Contact: Send a brief letter of no more than three pages with appropriate attachments after initial phone call.
Deadlines: None.

Additional Information

Trust(s): Bank of America NA

Foundation Officials

Harriet S. Denison: trustee
E. M. Douthat, III: director
Neil T. Douthat: director
Paul N. Douthat: trustee
Neil T. Smith: trustee
Ralph L. Smith, Jr.: director

Grants Analysis

Disclosure Period: calendar year ending 2003
Total Grants: $1,260,375
Number of Grants: 155
Average Grant: $8,131
Highest Grant: $42,500
Lowest Grant: $1,000
Typical Range: $1,000 to $15,000

Recent Grants

Note: Grants derived from 2003 Form 990.
General

62,000	Tucson Botanical Gardens, Tucson, AZ
42,500	Amyotrophic Lateral Sclerosis Association of Georgia, Atlanta, GA
40,000	Flora Foundation, Kailua Kona, HI
35,000	Arizona Aerospace Foundation Inc., Tucson, AZ -- to support Challenger education center
35,000	KUAT - The University of Arizona, Tucson, AZ -- underwrite Nova for 2004
22,000	Mano a Mano, Salem, OR
20,000	Barstow School, Kansas City, MO
20,000	Orme School, Mayer, AZ
10,000	Children's Healthcare of Atlanta, Atlanta, GA -- to support the festival of trees
10,000	Druid Hills Presbyterian Church, Atlanta, GA

WILLIAM R. AND SARA BABB SMITH FOUNDATION

Giving Contact

James T. Chafin, III, Secretary & Treasurer
PO Box 2000
McDonough, GA 30253
Phone: (770)957-4466

Description

Founded: 1995
EIN: 586306403
Organization Type: Private Foundation
Giving Locations: GA: Henry County
Grant Types: General Support, Scholarship.

Financial Summary

Total Giving: $75,000 (2003)
Giving Analysis: Giving for 2003 includes: foundation scholarships ($17,000)
Assets: $1,605,135 (2003)
Gifts Received: $2,522 (1995); $480,963 (1994).
Note: In 1994, contributions were received from William and Sara Smith.

Typical Recipients

Arts & Humanities: Libraries
Civic & Public Affairs: Civic & Public Affairs-General, Municipalities/Towns
Education: Elementary Education (Public), Education-General, Leadership Training, Public Education (Precollege), Secondary Education (Private), Secondary Education (Public), Student Aid, Vocational & Technical Education
Social Services: Child Welfare, Community Service Organizations, Family Services, Scouts, Senior Services, YMCA/YWCA/YMHA/YWHA, Youth Organizations

Application Procedures

Initial Contact: Send a brief letter of inquiry.
Application Requirements: Include purpose of funds sought.
Deadlines: None.

Restrictions

Emphasis is on social and educational needs.

Foundation Officials

Hans Broder: president
James T. Chafin, III: secretary, treasurer
Nancy R. Smith: vice president
William R. Smith: chairman
Roy W. Swann: trustee

Grants Analysis

Disclosure Period: calendar year ending 2003
Total Grants: $58,000*
Number of Grants: 8
Average Grant: $6,143*
Highest Grant: $15,000
Lowest Grant: $1,000
Typical Range: $1,000 to $10,000
*Note: Giving excludes scholarship. Average grant figure excludes highest grant.

Recent Grants

Note: Grants derived from 2003 Form 990.

General

15,000	A Friend's House, McDonough, GA
15,000	Joseph Sams School, Fayetteville, GA -- for scholarships to Henry county children
13,500	Henry County Department of Family & Children's Services -- funds for the assistance of senior citizens and childcare
12,500	Henry County Public Schools, McDonough, GA -- grants for special educational projects
8,000	Senior Citizens Center -- for support of pavilion construction project
5,000	Girl Scouts of Pine Valley Council, Griffin, GA -- for support of camp Cecil Jackson
2,000	Henry County High School Foundation Inc. -- scholarship for vocational training
2,000	Youth Leadership Henry -- support of the youth leadership training
1,000	Henry County Genealogical Society, Kewanee, IL -- for payment of property insurance
1,000	Henry County YMCA, New Castle, IN -- for financial needs scholarships for summer camp

STANLEY SMITH HORTICULTURAL TRUST

Giving Contact

William L. Culberson
PO Box 51759
Durham, NC 27717
Phone: (415)391-0292

Description

Founded: 1970
EIN: 946209165
Organization Type: Private Foundation
Giving Locations: nationally.
Grant Types: Capital, General Support, Operating Expenses, Project, Research.

Donor Information

Founder: May Smith

Financial Summary

Total Giving: $712,831 (2003); $796,974 (2001)
Assets: $15,413,144 (2003); $17,931,211 (2001)

Typical Recipients

Arts & Humanities: Arts Outreach, History & Archaeology, Libraries, Museums/Galleries
Civic & Public Affairs: Botanical Gardens/Parks, Clubs, Community Foundations, Economic Development, Civic & Public Affairs-General, Women's Affairs, Zoos/Aquariums
Education: Agricultural Education, Arts/Humanities Education, Colleges & Universities, Economic Education, Education Funds, Environmental Education, Education-General
Environment: Environment-General, Research, Resource Conservation
Health: Hospitals
International: Foreign Arts Organizations, Health Care/Hospitals, International Environmental Issues, International Organizations, Trade
Science: Scientific Centers & Institutes, Scientific Organizations
Social Services: Recreation & Athletics

Application Procedures

Initial Contact: Send cover letter and full proposal.
Application Requirements: Include purpose of funds sought, proof of tax-exempt status, and a copy of most recent Form 990 PF.
Deadlines: Applications are accepted from April 15 through September 1.

Restrictions

Project must be horticultural in nature with significant educational bias. Does not support individuals.

Foundation Officials

John P. Collins, Jr.: trustee
R. M. Collins: trustee
James Ronald Gibbs: trustee
N. D. Matheny: trustee

Grants Analysis

Disclosure Period: calendar year ending 2003
Total Grants: $712,831
Number of Grants: 49
Average Grant: $14,546
Highest Grant: $51,943
Lowest Grant: $2,500
Typical Range: $5,000 to $30,000

Recent Grants

Note: Grants derived from 2003 Form 990.
General

51,943	Missouri Botanical Garden Board of Trustees, St. Louis, MO -- for Flora of China, Orchid checklist
20,000	Cabrillo College Foundation, Aptos, CA -- for improvements to the Salvia garden

20,000	Holden Arboretum, Kirtland, OH -- for BG-BASE initiative in Latin America
20,000	International Dendrological Research Institute, Wellesley, MA -- for dendrological atlas project
20,000	Minnesota Landscape Arboretum Foundation, Chanhassen, MN -- for Rhododendron garden
20,000	Organization for Tropical Studies Inc., Durham, NC -- for research fellowship at Wilson garden
20,000	Ruth Bancroft Garden Inc., Walnut Creek, CA -- towards the salary of assistant garden director
20,000	Santa Barbara Botanic Garden Inc., Santa Barbara, CA -- as partial salary for head gardener, Ojai valley botanic garden
20,000	Tohono Chul Park Inc., Tucson, AZ -- for design and construction of desert living courtyard
20,000	University of Minnesota, St. Paul, MN -- towards development of sterile/dwarf woody-plant cultivars for department of horticultural science

M. W. SMITH, JR. FOUNDATION

Giving Contact
Kenneth E. Niemeyer
c/o AmSouth Bank NA
PO Drawer 1628
Mobile, AL 36633
Phone: (251)342-0402

Description
Founded: 1960
EIN: 636018078
Organization Type: Private Foundation
Giving Locations: AL: Southwest Alabama
Grant Types: Capital, Emergency, Endowment, General Support, Multiyear/Continuing Support, Operating Expenses, Project, Research, Scholarship, Seed Money.

Donor Information
Founder: the late M. W. Smith, Jr.

Financial Summary
Total Giving: $111,900 (fiscal year ending June 30, 2004); $100,565 (fiscal 2002); $142,754 (fiscal 2001)
Assets: $2,576,208 (fiscal 2004); $2,430,547 (fiscal 2002); $2,644,334 (fiscal 2001)

Typical Recipients
Arts & Humanities: Arts Associations & Councils, Community Arts, Dance, Historic Preservation, History & Archaeology, Libraries, Museums/Galleries
Civic & Public Affairs: Botanical Gardens/Parks, Community Foundations, Civic & Public Affairs-General, Municipalities/Towns, Urban & Community Affairs, Zoos/Aquariums
Education: Private Education (Precollege), Science/Mathematics Education
Environment: Forestry, Environment-General, Resource Conservation, Wildlife Protection
Health: Children's Health/Hospitals, Health-General, Mental Health
Religion: Churches, Religious Welfare
Science: Science Exhibits & Fairs
Social Services: Child Welfare, Community Service Organizations, People with Disabilities, Shelters/Homelessness, United Funds/United Ways, Youth Organizations

Application Procedures
Initial Contact: Send brief letter describing program.
Deadlines: None.

Restrictions
Does not support individuals.

Additional Information
Trust(s): Am South Bank

Foundation Officials
Joeseph Baker, Jr.: committee member
Louis M. Finlay, Jr.: comm mem
John Martin: comm mem
Maida S. Pearson: chairman
Mary M. Riser: secretary

Grants Analysis
Disclosure Period: fiscal year ending June 30, 2004
Total Grants: $111,900
Number of Grants: 15
Average Grant: $5,338*
Highest Grant: $25,000
Lowest Grant: $500
Typical Range: $2,000 to $9,000
*Note: Average grant figure excludes two highest grants ($42,500).

Recent Grants
Note: Grants derived from fiscal 2004 Form 990.
Library-Related

5,000	Mobile Public Library, Mobile, AL

General

25,000	Canton Bend United Methodist Church, Camden, AL
17,500	Ramer United Methodist Church, Ramer, AL
12,405	Wilmer Hall, Mobile, AL
11,595	Bayside Academy, Daphne, AL
10,000	Canton Bend Cemetery Foundation, Camden, AL
9,000	St. Stephens Historical Commission, St. Stephens, AL
5,000	Foundation for New Media, Hoboken, NJ
5,000	Mary's Shelter, Santa Ana, CA
3,500	Ala-Tom Resource Conservation, Grove Hill, AL

ETHEL SERGEANT CLARK SMITH MEMORIAL FUND

Giving Contact
Diane Stables
c/o Wachovia Bank
P.O. Box 7558
Philadelphia, PA 19101
Phone: (215)985-7917
Fax: (215)985-3922

Description
Founded: 1977
EIN: 236648857
Organization Type: Private Foundation
Giving Locations: PA: Delaware County
Grant Types: Capital, Emergency, General Support, Multiyear/Continuing Support, Operating Expenses, Project, Research, Scholarship, Seed Money.

Donor Information
Founder: the late Ethel Sergeant Clark Smith

Financial Summary
Total Giving: $620,000 (fiscal year ending May 31, 2004); $726,000 (fiscal 2002); $938,299 (fiscal 2001)
Assets: $14,122,097 (fiscal 2004); $14,730,023 (fiscal 2002); $17,532,231 (fiscal 2001)

Typical Recipients
Arts & Humanities: Arts Centers, Community Arts, Dance, Historic Preservation, Libraries, Museums/Galleries, Music
Civic & Public Affairs: Botanical Gardens/Parks, Economic Development, Employment/Job Training, Civic & Public Affairs-General, Housing, Law & Justice, Legal Aid, Safety, Urban & Community Affairs, Women's Affairs, Zoos/Aquariums
Education: Colleges & Universities, Education-General, Literacy, Private Education (Precollege), Public Education (Precollege), Science/Mathematics Education, Special Education, Vocational & Technical Education
Environment: Environment-General, Protection
Health: Clinics/Medical Centers, Health Organizations, Hospitals, Prenatal Health Issues, Public Health, Speech & Hearing
Religion: Churches, Dioceses, Ministries, Religious Organizations, Religious Welfare
Social Services: At-Risk Youth, Child Welfare, Community Centers, Community Service Organizations, Crime Prevention, Domestic Violence, People with Disabilities, Recreation & Athletics, Scouts, United Funds/United Ways, Volunteer Services, YMCA/YWCA/YMHA/YWHA, Youth Organizations

Application Procedures
Initial Contact: Send cover letter and full proposal.
Application Requirements: Include a description of organization, amount requested, purpose of funds sought, recently audited financial statement, and proof of tax-exempt status.
Deadlines: March 1 and September 1 for completed proposals.

Restrictions
Does not support individuals or provide loans.

Additional Information
Publications: Multi-Year Report (including Application Guidelines)
Trust(s): Wachovia Bank NA

Grants Analysis
Disclosure Period: fiscal year ending May 31, 2004
Total Grants: $620,000
Number of Grants: 53
Average Grant: $11,698
Highest Grant: $50,000
Lowest Grant: $2,000
Typical Range: $5,000 to $20,000

Recent Grants
Note: Grants derived from 2000 Form 990.
Library-Related

25,000	Sleighton School, Media, PA -- refurbishing library and purchase appliances

General

40,000	Cheyney University, Cheyney, PA -- renovations
25,000	Chespenn Health Services -- immunization program
25,000	CityTeam Ministries, San Jose, CA -- improvements for third floor
25,000	Delaware County Legal Assistance, DE
25,000	Delaware County Legal Assistance, DE
25,000	Domestic Abuse Project of Delaware County, Media, PA
25,000	Eastern College, St. Davids, PA -- renovations to accommodate Templeton honors college
25,000	Maternity Care Coalition, Philadelphia, PA
25,000	Riddle Memorial Hospital, Media, PA -- education expansion
25,000	Wayne Art Center -- expand facilities and renovation of the Masonic Hall

MAY AND STANLEY SMITH TRUST

Giving Contact
N. D. Matheny, Trustee
720 Market Street, Suite 250
San Francisco, CA 94102-2500
Phone: (415)391-0292

Description
EIN: 946435244
Organization Type: Private Foundation
Giving Locations: CA
Grant Types: General Support, Scholarship.

Donor Information
Founder: May Smith

Financial Summary
Total Giving: $405,000 (2003); $458,000 (2001)
Giving Analysis: Giving for 2003 includes: foundation scholarships ($80,000); 2001: foundation scholarships ($55,000)
Assets: $8,142,746 (2003); $9,497,455 (2001)

Typical Recipients
Arts & Humanities: Arts Outreach, Dance, Ethnic & Folk Arts, Arts & Humanities-General, Libraries, Music, Performing Arts, Theater, Visual Arts
Civic & Public Affairs: Employment/Job Training, Housing, Law & Justice, Parades/Festivals, Urban & Community Affairs
Education: Arts/Humanities Education, Business Education, Education Associations, Elementary Education (Private), Education-General, Literacy, Minority Education, Preschool Education, Private Education (Precollege), Science/Mathematics Education, Special Education, Student Aid
Health: AIDS/HIV, Arthritis, Cancer, Children's Health/Hospitals, Eyes/Blindness, Health Funds, Health Organizations, Home-Care Services, Hospitals, Long-Term Care, Medical Research, Mental Health, Public Health, Single-Disease Health Associations, Speech & Hearing
International: Foreign Educational Institutions, Health Care/Hospitals, Human Rights, International Organizations, Missionary/Religious Activities
Religion: Jewish Causes, Missionary Activities (Domestic), Religious Organizations, Religious Welfare
Social Services: Animal Protection, Big Brothers/Big Sisters, Camps, Child Abuse, Child Welfare, Community Centers, Community Service Organizations, Counseling, Delinquency & Criminal Rehabilitation, Domestic Violence, Family Services, Food/Clothing Distribution, Homes, People with Disabilities, Recreation & Athletics, Senior Services, Sexual Abuse, Social Services-General, YMCA/YWCA/YMHA/YWHA, Youth Organizations

Application Procedures
Initial Contact: Send a brief letter of inquiry.
Application Requirements: Describe program or project, proof of tax-exempt status and copy of Form 990 PF.
Deadlines: Applications are accepted from April 15 through September 30.

Restrictions
Awards grants to organizations that provide care and/or housing for disadvantaged children, the blind, and the aged.

Foundation Officials
John P. Collins, Jr.: trustee
James Ronald Gibbs: trustee
N. D. Matheny: trustee

Grants Analysis
Disclosure Period: calendar year ending 2003
Total Grants: $325,000*

Number of Grants: 82
Average Grant: $3,963
Highest Grant: $6,000
Lowest Grant: $500
Typical Range: $1,000 to $5,000
***Note:** Giving excludes scholarships.

Recent Grants
Note: Grants derived from 2003 Form 990.
General

6,000	Baulines Craft Guild, San Rafael, CA
6,000	Camping Unlimited for Retarded Children Inc., El Sobrante, CA -- for integrated summer day camp
6,000	Children of the Night, Van Nuys, CA -- on-site school for child victims of prostitution
6,000	Dream Foundation, Santa Barbara, CA -- funding six final wishes for terminally ill adults
6,000	East Bay Waldorf School Association Inc., El Sobrante, CA -- for tuition assistance
6,000	Juma Ventures, San Francisco, CA -- associate intern employment training program
6,000	Lincoln Center for the Performing Arts Inc., New York, NY -- arts education program for children with disabilities
6,000	Our Lady of Grace School, Castro Valley, CA -- for tuition assistance
6,000	Painted Turtle Gang Camp Foundation, Malibu, CA -- operational support for year round camp
6,000	Saint Paul's School, Oakland, CA -- for tuition assistance

SMOOT CHARITABLE FOUNDATION

Giving Contact
Thomas J. Kennedy, Vice President
PO Box 2567
Salina, KS 67402-2567
Phone: (785)825-4674
Fax: (785)825-5936

Description
Founded: 1976
EIN: 480851141
Organization Type: Private Foundation
Giving Locations: KS: Saline County
Grant Types: General Support.

Financial Summary
Total Giving: $578,447 (fiscal year ending June 30, 2004); $594,771 (fiscal 2002); $631,317 (fiscal 2001). Note: Fiscal 1997 Giving includes United Way ($31,000).
Giving Analysis: Giving for fiscal 2004 includes: foundation grants to United Way ($54,000); fiscal 2002: foundation grants to United Way ($45,000); fiscal 2001: foundation grants to United Way ($45,000)
Assets: $12,456,660 (fiscal 2004); $12,037,051 (fiscal 2002); $13,569,193 (fiscal 2001)

Typical Recipients
Arts & Humanities: Arts Centers, Arts Institutes, Community Arts, Libraries, Museums/Galleries, Music, Theater
Civic & Public Affairs: Community Foundations, Employment/Job Training, Civic & Public Affairs-General, Housing, Municipalities/Towns
Education: Colleges & Universities, Education-General, Private Education (Precollege), Science/Mathematics Education, Secondary Education (Private)
Health: Health Funds

Religion: Churches, Religious Welfare
Social Services: Big Brothers/Big Sisters, Child Abuse, Child Welfare, Community Centers, Community Service Organizations, Counseling, Day Care, Domestic Violence, Emergency Relief, Food/Clothing Distribution, People with Disabilities, Recreation & Athletics, Scouts, Substance Abuse, United Funds/United Ways, YMCA/YWCA/YMHA/YWHA, Youth Organizations

Application Procedures
Initial Contact: Send a brief letter of inquiry describing program or project.
Application Requirements: Include purpose of funds sought and proof of tax-exempt status.
Deadlines: None.

Foundation Officials
Janice L. Doherty: secretary
Thomas J. Kennedy: vice president
Dr. Robert W. Weber: president
George W. Yarnevich: vice president

Grants Analysis
Disclosure Period: fiscal year ending June 30, 2004
Total Grants: $524,447*
Number of Grants: 32
Average Grant: $4,833*
Highest Grant: $289,447
Lowest Grant: $1,000
Typical Range: $1,000 to $10,000
***Note:** Giving excludes United Way. Average grant figure excludes two highest grants ($379,447).

Recent Grants
Note: Grants derived from fiscal 2004 Form 990.
General

289,447	Salina Family YMCA, Salina, KS
90,000	Kansas Wesleyan University, Salina, KS
54,000	Salina Area United Way, Salina, KS
30,000	YWCA, Salina, KS
20,000	Greater Salina Community Foundation, Salina, KS
15,000	Salina Art Center, Salina, KS
15,000	SP Manor Capital Campaign, Salina, KS
10,000	Salina Regional Health Center Foundation, Salina, KS
5,000	Girl Scouts of Central Kansas Inc., Salina, KS
5,000	Occupational Center of Central Kansas Inc., Salina, KS

FRANK LITZ SMOOT CHARITABLE TRUST

Giving Contact
Diana S. Coulthard, Trustee
c/o First Community Bank
PO Box 950
Bluefield, WV 24701-0950
Phone: (304)325-7151

Description
Founded: 1992
EIN: 550717997
Organization Type: Private Foundation
Grant Types: General Support.

Financial Summary
Total Giving: $37,500 (2003)
Giving Analysis: Giving for 2003 includes: foundation scholarships ($10,000)
Assets: $967,849 (2003)
Gifts Received: $300 (1994); $95,721 (1993)

Typical Recipients
Arts & Humanities: Arts Festivals, Arts Outreach, Historic Preservation, History & Archaeology, Li-

braries, Museums/Galleries

Civic & Public Affairs: Chambers of Commerce, Clubs, Economic Development, Civic & Public Affairs-General, Municipalities/Towns, Safety, Urban & Community Affairs

Education: Colleges & Universities, Community & Junior Colleges, Elementary Education (Public), Engineering/Technological Education, Education-General, Gifted & Talented Programs, Secondary Education (Public), Student Aid

Health: Hospitals

Religion: Bible Study/Translation, Churches, Religious Welfare

Science: Science Museums, Scientific Centers & Institutes

Social Services: Camps, Community Service Organizations, United Funds/United Ways

Application Procedures

Initial Contact: Submit a written request.
Application Requirements: Outline the organization's programs and purpose of funds sought.
Deadlines: None.

Restrictions

Limited to southern WV and southwestern VA.

Additional Information

Trust(s): First Community Bank

Foundation Officials

Diana S. Coulthard: trustee

Grants Analysis

Disclosure Period: calendar year ending 2003
Total Grants: $27,500*
Number of Grants: 14
Average Grant: $1,964
Highest Grant: $5,000
Lowest Grant: $500
Typical Range: $500 to $5,000
***Note:** Giving excludes scholarship.

Recent Grants

Note: Grants derived from 2003 Form 990.

General

5,000	Bluefield College, Bluefield, VA
5,000	Festival of the Arts, Richlands, VA
5,000	Tazewell Community Hospital, Tazewell, VA
4,000	Bluefield Union Mission, Bluefield, WV
1,500	Bluefield High School, Bluefield, WV
1,500	Christ Episcopal Church, Bluefield, WV
1,000	Bluefield State College, Bluefield, WV
1,000	Greater Bluefield Chamber of Commerce, Bluefield, WV
1,000	Historic Crab Orchard Museum, Tazewell, VA
500	Bluefield Historical Society, Bluefield, WV

MARION C. SMYTH TRUST

Giving Contact

T. William Bigelow, Jr., Trustee
1001 Elm Street
Manchester, NH 03101
Phone: (603)623-3420

Description

Founded: 1946
EIN: 026005793
Organization Type: Private Foundation
Giving Locations: NH: Greater Manchester limited statewide giving
Grant Types: General Support, Multiyear/Continuing Support, Scholarship.

Donor Information

Founder: the late Marion C. Smyth

Financial Summary

Total Giving: $286,698 (2003)
Giving Analysis: Giving for 2003 includes: foundation scholarships ($22,700)
Assets: $5,480,312 (2003)

Typical Recipients

Arts & Humanities: Arts Institutes, Community Arts, Libraries, Museums/Galleries, Music, Opera, Public Broadcasting, Theater
Civic & Public Affairs: Civic & Public Affairs-General
Education: Arts/Humanities Education, Colleges & Universities, Private Education (Precollege), Student Aid
Religion: Churches

Application Procedures

Initial Contact: Send a brief letter of inquiry and a full proposal.
Application Requirements: Include a description of organization, amount requested, purpose of funds sought, recently audited financial statement, proof of tax-exempt status.
Deadlines: None.
Notes: Scholarship applicants should request an application form.

Restrictions

The foundation does not support political or lobbying groups or organizations outside operating areas.

Additional Information

Provides scholarships to college students who major in music. Also supports organizations for music purposes.

Grants Analysis

Disclosure Period: calendar year ending 2003
Total Grants: $263,998*
Number of Grants: 33
Average Grant: $8,000
Highest Grant: $20,000
Lowest Grant: $500
Typical Range: $1,000 to $10,000
***Note:** Giving excludes scholarships.

Recent Grants

Note: Grants derived from 2003 Form 990.

General

34,000	University of New Hampshire, Durham, NH
20,000	University of New Hampshire, Durham, NH
18,000	Berklee College of Music, Boston, MA
13,500	New Hampshire Symphony Orchestra, Manchester, NH
12,000	University of New Hampshire, Durham, NH
11,000	Plymouth State College, Plymouth, NH
10,000	New Hampshire Philharmonic, Manchester, NH
10,000	New Hampshire Public TV, Durham, NH
10,000	Palace Theater Trust, Manchester, NH
7,500	Manchester Choral Society, Manchester, NH

HARRY E. AND FLORENCE W. SNAYBERGER MEMORIAL FOUNDATION

Giving Contact

E. Lori Smith, Relationship Banking Specialist
c/o M & T Bank
1 S. Center St.
Pottsville, PA 17901
Phone: (570)622-4200

Alternate Contact

1 M & T Plaza, 8th Fl.
Buffalo, NY 14203
Phone: (716)842-5506

Description

Founded: 1976
EIN: 232056361
Organization Type: Private Foundation
Giving Locations: PA: Schuylkill County
Grant Types: General Support, Scholarship.

Donor Information

Founder: the late Harry E. Snayberger

Financial Summary

Total Giving: $146,231 (fiscal year ending March 31, 2004); $241,985 (fiscal 2002)
Giving Analysis: Giving for fiscal 2004 includes: foundation scholarships ($124,731); fiscal 2002: foundation scholarships ($149,310)
Assets: $4,361,142 (fiscal 2004); $4,500,186 (fiscal 2002)

Typical Recipients

Arts & Humanities: Arts Associations & Councils, Arts & Humanities-General, Libraries, Music, Theater
Civic & Public Affairs: Business/Free Enterprise
Education: Agricultural Education, Colleges & Universities, Public Education (Precollege), Special Education, Vocational & Technical Education
International: Foreign Educational Institutions
Religion: Churches, Religious Welfare
Social Services: Child Welfare, Day Care, Family Services, People with Disabilities, Recreation & Athletics, Scouts, Special Olympics, YMCA/YWCA/YMHA/YWHA, Youth Organizations

Application Procedures

Initial Contact: Send letter requesting application form.
Deadlines: February 26.

Restrictions

Does not fund political or lobbying groups or organizations outside operating areas.

Additional Information

Provides scholarships to individuals for higher education. Trust(s): M & T Bank
Trust(s): M & T Bank

Grants Analysis

Disclosure Period: fiscal year ending March 31, 2004
Total Grants: $21,500*
Number of Grants: 53
Average Grant: $406
Highest Grant: $1,800
Lowest Grant: $200
Typical Range: $200 to $1,000
***Note:** Giving excludes scholarships.

Recent Grants

Note: Grants derived from 2004 Form 990.

Library-Related

500	Frackville Free Public Library, Frackville, PA
500	Minersville Public Library, Minersville, PA
500	Orwigsburg Area Free Public Library, Orwigsburg, PA
500	Port Carbon Public Library, Port Carbon, PA
500	Pottsville Free Public Library, Pottsville, PA

General

2,500	Hawk Mountain Council, Boy Scouts of America, Pottsville Pike, PA
1,800	Girl Scouts - Penn's Woods Council, Wilkes-Barre, PA
1,000	Make - A - Wish Foundation, Phoenix, AZ
1,000	Saint Joseph Center for Special Learning, St. Pottsville, PA
500	Special Olympics, PA

SNEE-REINHARDT CHARITABLE FOUNDATION

Giving Contact
Virginia Davis
c/o PNC Advisors
2 PNC Plaza, 33rd Floor
Pittsburgh, PA 15222-2705
Phone: (412)762-3748

Description
Founded: 1987
EIN: 256292908
Organization Type: Private Foundation
Giving Locations: PA
Grant Types: General Support.

Donor Information
Founder: Katherine E. Snee

Financial Summary
Total Giving: $875,003 (2003); $831,298 (2001)
Assets: $21,348,473 (2003); $21,761,406 (2001)
Gifts Received: $100,271 (2003); $11,381,781 (2001); $100 (2000). Note: In 2001 and 2003, contributions were received from Katherine E. Snee estate and trusts ($10,506,117) and Tim Heasley Trust ($875,664). In 1995, contributions were received from D. Osiol Crut.

Typical Recipients
Arts & Humanities: Arts Centers, Community Arts, Ethnic & Folk Arts, Arts & Humanities-General, History & Archaeology, Libraries, Literary Arts, Museums/Galleries, Music, Public Broadcasting, Theater
Civic & Public Affairs: Botanical Gardens/Parks, Economic Development, Employment/Job Training, Civic & Public Affairs-General, Housing, Municipalities/Towns, Philanthropic Organizations, Safety, Urban & Community Affairs, Women's Affairs, Zoos/Aquariums
Education: Business Education, Colleges & Universities, Education Funds, Environmental Education, Education-General, Literacy, Medical Education, Private Education (Precollege), Public Education (Precollege), Religious Education, Science/Mathematics Education, Special Education
Environment: Environment-General, Resource Conservation
Health: Alzheimer's Disease, Children's Health/Hospitals, Emergency/Ambulance Services, Geriatric Health, Health Organizations, Hospitals, Kidney, Medical Rehabilitation, Medical Research, Nursing Services, Prenatal Health Issues, Single-Disease Health Associations

Religion: Churches, Dioceses, Ministries, Religious Organizations, Religious Welfare
Science: Scientific Centers & Institutes
Social Services: Child Welfare, Community Service Organizations, Crime Prevention, Family Services, Homes, People with Disabilities, Scouts, Senior Services, Shelters/Homelessness, Special Olympics, United Funds/United Ways, Volunteer Services, YMCA/YWCA/YMHA/YWHA, Youth Organizations

Application Procedures
Initial Contact: Send a brief letter of inquiry.
Deadlines: None.

Additional Information
Trust(s): PNC Bank NA

Grants Analysis
Disclosure Period: calendar year ending 2003
Total Grants: $875,003
Number of Grants: 57
Average Grant: $12,074*
Highest Grant: $123,000
Lowest Grant: $1,578
Typical Range: $5,000 to $25,000
*Note: Average grant figure excludes three highest grants ($223,000).

Recent Grants
Note: Grants derived from 2003 Form 990.
General

123,000	University of Pittsburgh Center Institute, Pittsburgh, PA
50,000	Buzz Project, Bridgeville, PA
50,000	University of Pittsburgh Medical Center Rehabilitation Institute, Pittsburgh, PA
38,196	Center in the Woods Inc., California, PA
25,500	Hope Network, Pittsburgh, PA
25,000	Greater Pittsburgh Literacy Council, Pittsburgh, PA
25,000	National Aviary in Pittsburgh, Pittsburgh, PA
25,000	Province of St. Augustine, Pittsburgh, PA
25,000	St. Anne's Catholic Church, Webster Springs, PA
25,000	Wings for Children Inc., Pittsburgh, PA

JOHN BEN SNOW FOUNDATION

Giving Contact
Jonathan L. Snow, Vice President & Treasurer
50 Presidential Plaza
Syracuse, NY 13202
Phone: (315)471-5256

Description
Founded: 1948
EIN: 136112704
Organization Type: Private Foundation
Giving Locations: NY: Central NY, Oswego County
Grant Types: Capital, General Support, Matching, Project, Scholarship.

Donor Information
Founder: the late John Ben Snow

Financial Summary
Total Giving: $191,100 (2003); $287,550 (2001)
Assets: $6,635,264 (2003); $7,006,249 (2001)

Typical Recipients
Arts & Humanities: Arts Associations & Councils, Arts Institutes, Historic Preservation, History & Archaeology, Libraries, Literary Arts, Museums/Galleries, Music, Opera, Performing Arts, Public Broadcasting, Theater

Civic & Public Affairs: Botanical Gardens/Parks, Community Foundations, Employment/Job Training, Civic & Public Affairs-General, Nonprofit Management, Philanthropic Organizations
Education: Arts/Humanities Education, Colleges & Universities, Engineering/Technological Education, Education-General, Journalism/Media Education, Legal Education, Literacy, Minority Education, Private Education (Precollege), Public Education (Precollege), Social Sciences Education, Special Education, Student Aid
Environment: Resource Conservation
Health: Children's Health/Hospitals, Clinics/Medical Centers, Health Organizations, Hospitals, Public Health, Speech & Hearing
Religion: Churches, Religious Organizations
Social Services: Animal Protection, Camps, Child Welfare, Community Service Organizations, Day Care, Food/Clothing Distribution, People with Disabilities, YMCA/YWCA/YMHA/YWHA, Youth Organizations

Application Procedures
Initial Contact: Send a a brief letter of inquiry on organization letterhead.
Application Requirements: Include a brief background of the organization, a description of the proposed project, and amount requested.
Deadlines: April 1, for grant application forms.
Review Process: If the letter of inquiry meets the foundation's guidelines, a grant application form will be sent to the applicant.
Decision Notification: Final funding decisions are made in writing by July 1.

Restrictions
Does not support individuals, endowments, operating budgets, tax-supported or for-profit groups, contingency funding, or religious organizations.

Additional Information
Publications: Annual Report (including Application Guidelines)

Foundation Officials
Valerie A. Macfie: board member
Allen R. Malcolm: board member
Bruce L. Malcolm: board member
Emelie Melton-Williams: secretary
David H. Snow: president
Jonathan L. Snow: vice president, treasurer

Grants Analysis
Disclosure Period: calendar year ending 2003
Total Grants: $191,100
Number of Grants: 18
Average Grant: $10,617
Highest Grant: $30,000
Lowest Grant: $150
Typical Range: $5,000 to $15,000

Recent Grants
Note: Grants derived from 2003 Form 990.
General

30,000	Maxwell School, Syracuse, NY
25,000	Clarkson University, Potsdam, NY
21,950	Pulaski Academy and Central School, Pulaski, NY
15,000	Camp Good Days and Special Times, Mendon, NY
15,000	Student Conservation Association Inc., Charlestown, NH
12,000	School Press Institute, Syracuse, NY
10,000	Food Bank of Central New York, East Syracuse, NY
10,000	Pompey Historical Society, Manlius, NY
10,000	Seneca Cayuga ARC, Waterloo, NY
9,000	Cayuga County Home for Children, Auburn, NY

JOHN BEN SNOW MEMORIAL TRUST

Giving Contact
Jonathan Snow, Trustee
Jefferson Tower
50 Presidential Plaza, Suite 106
Syracuse, NY 13202

Description
Founded: 1974
EIN: 136633814
Organization Type: General Purpose Foundation
Giving Locations: NY: Eastern USA.
Grant Types: Capital, Challenge, Matching, Seed Money.

Donor Information
Founder: Incorporated in 1948 by the late John Ben Snow, who was born and raised in Pulaski, NY, a small village north of Syracuse. He graduated from New York University in 1904 and began employment at the Woolworth organization. A man of vision, he was attracted to mass-market sales and introduced innovative retailing techniques. He rose rapidly through the ranks of Woolworth from stock boy to corporate director, initially in New York, and finally in Great Britain, where he accumulated a small fortune through hard work, saving, and wise investments. After retiring from Woolworth's in 1939, Mr. Snow devoted the remainder of his life to building the Speidel chain of newspapers and publishing the "Western Horseman." He was fond of animals, especially horses, and enjoyed racing, fox hunting, polo, and range riding. Throughout his life, John Ben Snow shared his wealth with relatives, friends, business associates, and fellow Pulaskians. He gave generously and freely to those persons and causes he cherished. He preferred to invest in people, especially the young, by making financial assistance available. He also believed in improving the quality of life in Pulaski and its environs.

Financial Summary
Total Giving: $1,401,500 (2001)
Assets: $27,192,340 (2001)

Typical Recipients
Arts & Humanities: Arts Associations & Councils, Arts Centers, Arts Institutes, Arts Outreach, Ballet, Ethnic & Folk Arts, Film & Video, Arts & Humanities-General, Historic Preservation, History & Archaeology, Libraries, Museums/Galleries, Music, Opera, Performing Arts, Public Broadcasting, Theater
Civic & Public Affairs: Botanical Gardens/Parks, Community Foundations, Economic Development, Employment/Job Training, Civic & Public Affairs-General, Housing, Law & Justice, Municipalities/Towns, Native American Affairs, Philanthropic Organizations, Professional & Trade Associations, Safety, Urban & Community Affairs, Women's Affairs, Zoos/Aquariums
Education: Agricultural Education, Arts/Humanities Education, Business Education, Colleges & Universities, Community & Junior Colleges, Economic Education, Education Funds, Environmental Education, Faculty Development, Education-General, Journalism/Media Education, Legal Education, Literacy, Medical Education, Minority Education, Private Education (Precollege), Public Education (Precollege), Science/Mathematics Education, Secondary Education (Private), Social Sciences Education, Student Aid
Environment: Air/Water Quality, Environment-General, Protection, Resource Conservation
Health: Alzheimer's Disease, Cancer, Children's Health/Hospitals, Clinics/Medical Centers, Geriatric Health, Health Funds, Health Organizations, Hospices, Hospitals, Medical Research
International: Foreign Educational Institutions, Human Rights, International Environmental Issues
Religion: Churches, Ministries, Religious Welfare
Science: Science-General, Science Museums, Scientific Centers & Institutes, Scientific Organizations
Social Services: Animal Protection, At-Risk Youth, Child Welfare, Community Service Organizations, Day Care, Delinquency & Criminal Rehabilitation, Family Planning, Food/Clothing Distribution, People with Disabilities, Recreation & Athletics, Scouts, Senior Services, Shelters/Homelessness, Social Services-General, YMCA/YWCA/YMHA/YWHA, Youth Organizations

Application Procedures
Initial Contact: An initial letter of inquiry should be sent to the trust.
Application Requirements: Letters of inquiry should include the legal name and official address of the organization; a brief summary of the project; the name and address of the person responsible for the dispersal of the grant; a copy of the organization's IRS exemption letter; and a copy of the most recent audited financial statement.
Deadlines: Proposal deadline is April 15.
Review Process: The trustees will request more information and a complete application, as necessary. The trustees meet once a year, usually in June. The present trustees prefer to give challenge and matching grants, pilot programs, and seed funding.

Restrictions
The trust does not make grants to individuals, government agencies, endowment funds, religious organizations, or unspecified projects. They generally do not contribute to tax-supported institutions.

Additional Information
Publications: Annual Report; Application Form; Guidelines
Trust(s): Bank of New York

Foundation Officials
Allen R. Malcolm: trustee
Rollan D. Melton: trustee
Ann M. Scanlon: program director
Jonathan L. Snow: trustee

Grants Analysis
Disclosure Period: calendar year ending 2001
Total Grants: $1,401,500
Number of Grants: 79
Average Grant: $17,741
Highest Grant: $100,000
Typical Range: $5,000 to $40,000

Recent Grants
Note: Grants derived from 2002 Form 990.

Library-Related
15,000	Washoe Library Foundation
10,000	Tompkins County Public Library, Ithaca, NY

General
50,000	Central Valley Center for the Arts Inc., Modesto, CA
50,000	Pulaski Academy and Central School, Pulaski, NY
50,000	Syracuse University, Syracuse, NY
50,000	Washington College, Chestertown, MD
45,000	Saint Mary's Health Network, Reno, NV
42,500	Colonial Williamsburg Foundation, Williamsburg, VA
40,000	Independent College Fund of New York, Albany, NY
30,000	Frost Valley YMCA, Claryville, NY
30,000	Papermill Playhouse, Millburn, NJ
30,000	Saint Mary's Health Network, Reno, NV

HARRISON C. AND MARGARET A. SNYDER CHARITABLE TRUST

Giving Contact
Marie Boyles, Trust Officer
c/o M & T Trust Co.
One M & T Plaza, 8th Fl.
Buffalo, NY 14203
Phone: (716)842-5680

Description
Founded: 1996
EIN: 256436588
Organization Type: Private Foundation
Giving Locations: PA: Blair County
Grant Types: General Support.

Financial Summary
Total Giving: $61,555 (2003); $74,999 (2001)
Assets: $1,359,485 (2003); $1,418,438 (2001)
Gifts Received: $15,710 (1996); $1,115,547 (1995)

Typical Recipients
Arts & Humanities: Libraries
Civic & Public Affairs: African American Affairs, Civic & Public Affairs-General
Education: Business Education, Public Education (Precollege)
Health: Children's Health/Hospitals, Emergency/Ambulance Services
Religion: Churches, Religious Organizations, Religious Welfare
Social Services: Animal Protection, Big Brothers/Big Sisters, Food/Clothing Distribution, Social Services-General, Volunteer Services, YMCA/YWCA/YMHA/YWHA

Application Procedures
Initial Contact: Send a brief letter of inquiry.
Application Requirements: purpose of funds sought and proof of tax-exempt status.
Deadlines: November 1.

Restrictions
Limited to organizations in Blair County, PA.

Additional Information
Trust(s): M & T Trust Co.

Foundation Officials
William R. Collins, Jr.: trustee
Daniel J. Ratchford: trustee

Grants Analysis
Disclosure Period: calendar year ending 2003
Total Grants: $61,555
Number of Grants: 24
Average Grant: $2,565
Highest Grant: $8,000
Lowest Grant: $1,000
Typical Range: $1,000 to $5,000

Recent Grants
Note: Grants derived from 2003 Form 990.

Library-Related
4,500	Altoona Public Library, Altoona, PA
2,500	Hollidaysburg Library, Hollidaysburg, PA

General
8,600	Altoona Food Bank, Altoona, PA
5,000	Bishop Guilfoyle, Altoona, PA
5,000	Hollidaysburg Area SD Foundation, Duncansville, PA
4,000	New Day Inc., Altoona, PA
3,000	Big Brothers/ Big Sisters, Altoona, PA
2,500	Phoenix Volunteer Fire Co, Hollidaysburg, PA
2,500	Rescue Mission
2,500	Salvation Army, Altoona, PA

FROST AND MARGARET SNYDER FOUNDATION

Giving Contact
Mollie Determan, Assistant Vice President & Trust Officer
c/o KeyBank
1101 Pacific Ave., 3rd Fl.
Tacoma, WA 98402
Phone: (253)305-7208

Description
Founded: 1957
EIN: 916030549
Organization Type: Private Foundation
Giving Locations: WA
Grant Types: General Support.

Donor Information
Founder: the late Frost Snyder and the late Margaret Snyder

Financial Summary
Total Giving: $558,100 (2003)
Assets: $12,264,917 (2003)

Typical Recipients
Arts & Humanities: Arts & Humanities-General, Public Broadcasting
Civic & Public Affairs: Civic & Public Affairs-General, Law & Justice
Education: Colleges & Universities, Medical Education, Private Education (Precollege), Public Education (Precollege), Religious Education, Secondary Education (Private), Secondary Education (Public), Student Aid
Health: Health Organizations, Hospices, Hospitals, Medical Research, Public Health
International: International Peace & Security Issues
Religion: Churches, Dioceses, Ministries, Religious Organizations, Religious Welfare
Social Services: Community Centers, Community Service Organizations

Application Procedures
Initial Contact: Send a brief letter of inquiry.
Application Requirements: Include a description of organization, amount requested, and purpose of funds.
Deadlines: September 1.

Restrictions
Limited to Catholic organizations. Does not support individuals.

Additional Information
Trust(s): KeyBank NA

Grants Analysis
Disclosure Period: calendar year ending 2003
Total Grants: $558,100
Number of Grants: 15
Average Grant: $32,007*
Highest Grant: $100,000
Lowest Grant: $5,000
Typical Range: $10,000 to $50,000
*Note: Average grant figure excludes highest grant.

Recent Grants
Note: Grants derived from 2001 Form 990.
General

100,000	Archdiocese of Seattle, Seattle, WA
75,000	St. Nicholas Parish, Los Altos, CA
70,000	John F. Kennedy High School, Denver, CO
60,000	Bellarmine High School
60,000	Central Catholic High School
50,000	CVO
50,000	O'Dea High School, Seattle, WA
50,000	Seattle University, Seattle, WA
40,000	St. Martin's College
35,000	Gonzaga University, Spokane, WA

HAROLD B. AND DOROTHY A. SNYDER FOUNDATION

Giving Contact
Audrey Snyder, Executive Director & Trustee
PO Box 671
Moorestown, NJ 08057
Phone: (610)799-8312

Description
Founded: 1971
EIN: 222316043
Organization Type: Private Foundation
Giving Locations: NJ: Union County
Grant Types: General Support, Loan, Multiyear/Continuing Support, Operating Expenses, Project, Seed Money.

Donor Information
Founder: the late Harold B. Snyder, Sr.

Financial Summary
Total Giving: $375,533 (fiscal year ending September 30, 2004); $417,365 (fiscal 2001)
Giving Analysis: Giving for fiscal 2004 includes: foundation scholarships ($23,419); fiscal 2001: foundation scholarships ($13,821)
Assets: $13,520,604 (fiscal 2004); $14,439,037 (fiscal 2001)
Gifts Received: $4,550 (fiscal 2001); $950 (fiscal 2000); $1,629 (fiscal 1998). Note: In fiscal 1996, contributions were received from E. Allison ($425), A. Cortese ($545), D. Demarco ($100), F. Donlon ($100), M. Flowers ($180), J. Hoell ($1,500), T. Jones ($50), G. Karch ($100), J. Leynoe ($250), R. Nalbone ($500), A. Snyder ($1,000), N. Wu ($500), and A. Sarnese ($200).

Typical Recipients
Arts & Humanities: History & Archaeology, Libraries
Civic & Public Affairs: Community Foundations, Employment/Job Training, Civic & Public Affairs-General, Housing, Nonprofit Management, Philanthropic Organizations, Professional & Trade Associations, Urban & Community Affairs, Women's Affairs
Education: Business Education, Colleges & Universities, Engineering/Technological Education, Literacy, Medical Education, Preschool Education, Private Education (Precollege), Religious Education, Science/Mathematics Education, Special Education, Student Aid, Vocational & Technical Education
Health: Cancer, Children's Health/Hospitals, Clinics/Medical Centers, Health-General, Health Organizations, Hospitals, Long-Term Care, Nursing Services, Prenatal Health Issues, Public Health, Single-Disease Health Associations
Religion: Churches, Religious Organizations, Religious Welfare, Seminaries
Social Services: Community Service Organizations, Counseling, Crime Prevention, Day Care, Domestic Violence, Family Services, Homes, People with Disabilities, Shelters/Homelessness, YMCA/YWCA/YMHA/YWHA, Youth Organizations

Application Procedures
Initial Contact: Submit 5 copies of a proposal, not more than 4 pages long.
Application Requirements: Include a description of organization, amount requested, purpose of funds sought, recently audited financial statement, and proof of tax-exempt status.
Deadlines: None.

Additional Information
Provides scholarships to residents of New Jersey entering the Presbyterian ministry, nursing, and the building construction industry.

Foundation Officials
Ethelyn Allison: trustee
Melvin Cook: trustee
Arline Snyder Cortese: trustee
Lillian Palumbo, PhD: trustee
Audrey Snyder: executive director, trustee
Phyllis Johnson Snyder: trustee
Joseph A. Vallene, III: trustee
James V. Whittenburg: trustee

Grants Analysis
Disclosure Period: fiscal year ending September 30, 2004
Total Grants: $352,114*
Number of Grants: 6
Highest Grant: $194,978
Lowest Grant: $500
Typical Range: $5,000 to $50,000
*Note: Giving excludes scholarships.

Recent Grants
Note: Grants derived from fiscal 2004 Form 990.
General

194,978	First Presbyterian of Elizabeth, Elizabeth, NJ
100,000	Kendell Presbyterian Church, Kendell Park, NJ
5,000	University of Medicine and Dentistry of New Jersey, Newark, NJ
2,500	Seton Hall University, South Orange, NJ
2,000	Rutgers, Newark, NJ
2,000	Rutgers, Newark, NJ
2,000	Steven Institute, Hoboken, NJ
1,500	Bloomfield College, Bloomfield, NJ
1,500	Eastern Nazarene College, Quincy, MA
1,500	Eastern Nazarene College, Quincy, MA

WILLIAM I. AND PATRICIA S. SNYDER FOUNDATION

Giving Contact
K. Sidney Neuman, Secretary
Grant Bldg., 3rd Fl.
Pittsburgh, PA 15219
Phone: (412)338-1108

Description
Founded: 1996
EIN: 251773015
Organization Type: Private Foundation
Giving Locations: PA: Pittsburgh
Grant Types: General Support.

Financial Summary
Total Giving: $243,700 (fiscal year ending August 31, 2004); $322,500 (fiscal 2002)
Assets: $1,546,269 (fiscal 2004); $1,710,455 (fiscal 2002)
Gifts Received: $175,679 (fiscal 1996). Note: In fiscal 1996, contributions were received from W.I. Snyder Corp.

Typical Recipients
Arts & Humanities: Arts Associations & Councils
Education: Private Education (Precollege)
Health: Children's Health/Hospitals, Hospitals
Religion: Jewish Causes
Social Services: People with Disabilities, Shelters/Homelessness

Application Procedures

Initial Contact: Submit detailed proposal with budget.
Deadlines: No deadline.

Restrictions

Foundation does not support political or lobbying groups.

Foundation Officials

K. Sidney Newman: secretary
Patricia S. Snyder: vice president
William I. Snyder: president

Grants Analysis

Disclosure Period: fiscal year ending August 31, 2004
Total Grants: $243,700
Number of Grants: 10
Average Grant: $4,689*
Highest Grant: $201,500
Lowest Grant: $250
Typical Range: $1,000 to $10,000
*Note: Average grant figure excludes highest grant.

Recent Grants

Note: Grants derived from 2004 Form 990.
General

201,500	Sewickley Valley Hospital Foundation, Sewickley, PA
10,000	Portersville Christian School, Portersville, PA
10,000	Tree of Life Congregation, Pittsburgh, PA
8,500	Bayith Lepleito - Girls Town Jerusalem, Brooklyn, NY -- for foster child and summer camp program
5,000	Carnegie Institute, Pittsburgh, PA -- for art appreciation
5,000	Children's Museum of Pittsburgh, Pittsburgh, PA
2,000	Greensboro Jewish Federation, Greensboro, NC
1,200	Children's Hospital of Pittsburgh Foundation, Pittsburgh, PA -- to purchase books by Pearl Simmons
250	Beth Samuel Jewish Center, Ambridge, PA
250	Beth Samuel Jewish Center, Ambridge, PA

SOLOW FOUNDATION

Giving Contact

Sheldon H. Solow, President
9 W. 57th St.
New York, NY 10019-2601
Phone: (212)751-1100

Description

Founded: 1978
EIN: 132950685
Organization Type: Private Foundation
Giving Locations: NY: New York
Grant Types: General Support.

Donor Information

Founder: Sheldon H. Solow

Financial Summary

Total Giving: $309,170 (fiscal year ending October 31, 2003)
Assets: $8,866,922 (fiscal 2003)
Gifts Received: $3,000,024 (fiscal 1994). Note: In fiscal 1994, contributions were received from Sheldon Solow.

Typical Recipients

Arts & Humanities: Arts Associations & Councils, Arts Centers, Arts Funds, Community Arts, Ethnic & Folk Arts, Libraries, Museums/Galleries, Music, Performing Arts, Theater
Civic & Public Affairs: African American Affairs, Botanical Gardens/Parks, Economic Development, Civic & Public Affairs-General, Housing, Law & Justice, Municipalities/Towns, Philanthropic Organizations, Professional & Trade Associations, Public Policy, Urban & Community Affairs
Education: Arts/Humanities Education, Colleges & Universities, Education Associations, Education Reform, Elementary Education (Private), Education-General, Legal Education, Medical Education, Public Education (Precollege), Religious Education, Social Sciences Education, Special Education, Student Aid
Environment: Air/Water Quality
Health: Clinics/Medical Centers, Heart, Hospitals, Multiple Sclerosis, Nursing Services, Research/Studies Institutes, Single-Disease Health Associations
International: Foreign Arts Organizations, Human Rights, International Development, International Organizations, Missionary/Religious Activities
Religion: Churches, Jewish Causes
Social Services: Animal Protection, Child Welfare, Community Service Organizations, Recreation & Athletics, Scouts, Social Services-General, Substance Abuse, United Funds/United Ways, Youth Organizations

Application Procedures

Initial Contact: The foundation has no formal grant application procedure or application form.
Deadlines: None.

Foundation Officials

Leonard Lazarus: secretary
Sheldon Henry Solow: don, president B 1926. PRIM CORP EMPL member: Solow Building Co. LLC ADD CORP EMPL president: Solow Management Corp.; president: Solow Realty Development Co.
Rosalie S. Wolff: vice president

Grants Analysis

Disclosure Period: fiscal year ending October 31, 2003
Total Grants: $309,170
Number of Grants: 11
Average Grant: $20,917*
Highest Grant: $100,000
Lowest Grant: $6,000
Typical Range: $10,000 to $40,000
*Note: Average grant figure excludes highest grant.

Recent Grants

Note: Grants derived from 2003 Form 990.

General

100,000	Solow Art and Architecture Foundation, New York, NY
45,000	Solow Art and Architecture Foundation, New York, NY
40,000	Solow Art and Architecture Foundation, New York, NY
38,670	Metropolitan Museum of Art, New York, NY
25,000	Partnership for Public Service, Washington, DC
23,000	Solow Art and Architecture Foundation, New York, NY
10,000	American Alternative Foundation
9,500	Lincoln Center Real Estate and Construction Council, New York, NY
6,000	National Jewish Medical and Research Center, Denver, CO
6,000	New York University, New York, NY

SONOCO PRODUCTS CO.

Company Headquarters

Hartsville, SC
Web: http://www.sonoco.com

Company Description

Founded: 1899
Ticker: SON
Exchange: NYSE
Revenue: US$2.812 billion (2002)
Employees: 15200 (2003)
SIC(s): 2421 Sawmills & Planing Mills--General, 2499 Wood Products Nec, 2631 Paperboard Mills, 2679 Converted Paper Products Nec.

Operating Locations

Sonoco Products Co. (GA--Marietta; NC--Statesville; PR; SC--Hartsville)
Note: Operates 165 branch or manufacturing facilities in the U.S., 25 in Canada, and 78 in other foreign countries.

Nonmonetary Support

Type: Donated Equipment; Donated Products

Sonoco Foundation

Giving Contact

Joyce Beasley, Manager, Community Affairs
One North 2nd Street, Mail Stop A09
Hartsville, SC 29550
Phone: (843)383-7000
Fax: (843)383-7008
E-mail: joyce.beasley@sonoco.com
Web: http://www.sonoco.com/sonoco_foundation.htm

Description

EIN: 570752950
Organization Type: Corporate Foundation
Giving Locations: SC: counties in which employees reside.
Grant Types: Award, Emergency, Employee Matching Gifts, Endowment, General Support, Matching, Multiyear/Continuing Support, Project, Research, Scholarship.
Note: Employee matching gift ratio: 1 to 1 for higher education.

Financial Summary

Total Giving: $1,872,074 (2003); $2,071,165 (2002); $2,029,206 (2001). Note: Contributes through corporate direct giving program and foundation. Giving includes foundation.
Assets: $52,177 (2003); $14,251 (2002); $416 (2001). Note: The asset amount for 2000 is a negative number.
Gifts Received: $1,910,000 (2003); $2,085,000 (2002); $2,030,000 (2001). Note: Contributions received from Sonoco Products Co.

Typical Recipients

Arts & Humanities: Arts Associations & Councils, Arts Centers, Arts Festivals, Arts Funds, Arts Institutes, Community Arts, Dance, Arts & Humanities-General, Historic Preservation, History & Archaeology, Libraries, Museums/Galleries, Music, Opera, Performing Arts, Public Broadcasting, Theater
Civic & Public Affairs: African American Affairs, Botanical Gardens/Parks, Business/Free Enterprise, Chambers of Commerce, Clubs, Community Foundations, Economic Development, Civic & Public Affairs-General, Hispanic Affairs, Housing, Inner-City Development, Municipalities/Towns, Parades/Festivals, Professional & Trade Associations, Public Policy, Safety, Urban & Community Affairs, Women's Affairs, Zoos/Aquariums
Education: Afterschool/Enrichment Programs, Arts/

Humanities Education, Business Education, Business-School Partnerships, Colleges & Universities, Community & Junior Colleges, Economic Education, Education Associations, Education Funds, Education Reform, Elementary Education (Private), Elementary Education (Public), Engineering/Technological Education, Environmental Education, Faculty Development, Education-General, Health & Physical Education, Minority Education, Preschool Education, Private Education (Precollege), Public Education (Precollege), Science/Mathematics Education, Secondary Education (Public), Student Aid, Vocational & Technical Education

Environment: Forestry, Environment-General, Resource Conservation

Health: Cancer, Children's Health/Hospitals, Emergency/Ambulance Services, Eyes/Blindness, Health-General, Health Organizations, Heart, Hospitals, Medical Rehabilitation, Medical Research, Mental Health, Multiple Sclerosis, Research/Studies Institutes, Single-Disease Health Associations

Science: Science Exhibits & Fairs, Scientific Centers & Institutes

Social Services: Animal Protection, Camps, Child Welfare, Community Centers, Community Service Organizations, Domestic Violence, Emergency Relief, Family Services, Homes, People with Disabilities, Recreation & Athletics, Scouts, Shelters/Homelessness, Social Services-General, Special Olympics, Substance Abuse, United Funds/United Ways, Volunteer Services, YMCA/YWCA/YMHA/YWHA, Youth Organizations

Application Procedures

Initial Contact: Request application guidelines, then send an application letter (no more than 3 pages) with explanation of charitable purposes.

Application Requirements: Include name, address, telephone number and IRS tax-exempt classification of organization; summary of the purpose of funds, and evidence of need; amount of money requested and its proposed use.

Deadlines: None.

Review Process: Foundation reviews applications quarterly.

Restrictions

Foundation supports selected activities in the form of one-time or, on occasion, multi-year grants. One time grants receive the strongest consideration.

Requests for grants for the following are ineligible: projects in areas where the company has no operations; individuals; private foundations; courtesy advertising, testimonial dinners; loans or investments, pledges longer than five years; automatic renewal of grants; lobbying for political purposes; projects which are sensitive, controversial or harmful, or which pose a potential conflict of interest to the company; organizations that discriminate in any way and are inconsistent with national equal opportunity policies.

The foundation generally does not contribute to the following: intermediary funding agencies that channel monies to donee organizations, except the United Way; projects that consist simply of fund-raising events; grants to cover operating deficits; memorials; national organizations where local or regional chapters are supported; endowments; fraternal, social, labor or veterans' organizations; memberships; conferences, workshops, or seminars; "brick and mortar" building grants.

Foundation prefers not to be the only funding source for a project. Awards will be made to qualified charities only.

Corporate Officials

Peter C. Browning: chief executive officer, president, director B Boston, MA 1941. ED Colgate University BA (1963); University of Chicago MBA (1976). PRIM CORP EMPL chief executive officer, president, director: Sonoco Products Co. CORP AFFIL director: Phoenix Home Life Mutual Insurance Co.; director: Wachovia Corp.; director: Lowe's Co. Inc.; director:

Nucor Corp. NONPR AFFIL member council: Chicago Graduate School; member board visitors: McCall School Business/Queens College. CLUB AFFIL member: DeBordieu Country Club; member: Quail Hollow Country Club.

Charles Westfield Coker: vice president B Florence, SC 1933. ED Princeton University BA (1955); Harvard University MBA (1957). PRIM CORP EMPL vice president: Sonoco Products Co. ADD CORP EMPL president: Sonoco Puerto Rico Inc. CORP AFFIL director: Sara Lee Corp.; director: Springs Industries Inc.; director: Carolina Power & Light Co.; director: NCNB Corp.; director: BankAmerica Corp. NONPR AFFIL director: Hollings Cancer Center; member: Palmetto Business Forum. CLUB AFFIL Rotary Club.

Harris E. DeLoach, Jr.: president, chief executive officer B Columbia, SC 1944. ED University of South Carolina BBA (1966); University of South Carolina JD (1969). PRIM CORP EMPL president, chief executive officer: Sonoco Products Co. CORP AFFIL director: Sebro Plastics Inc. NONPR AFFIL member: Rotary International; member: South Carolina Bar Association; member: Darlington County Bar Association; member: Hartsville Chamber of Commerce; member: 4th Jud. Cir. Association South Carolina; member: American Bar Association.

Harry J. Moran: executive vice president B Pasadena, CA 1932. ED Loyola University (1954). PRIM CORP EMPL executive vice president: Sonoco Products Co. CORP AFFIL president, director: Sonoco Containers Canada; director: Sonoco France; director: Sonoca Latin America; director: Engraph Corp.; director: Keating Corp.; chairman: CMB-Sonoco Europe.

Foundation Officials

Charles Westfield Coker: trustee (see above)
Charles J. Hupfer: trustee B 1946. ED University of North Carolina, Charlotte MS; University of North Carolina BS (1968). PRIM CORP EMPL vice president, secretary, chief financial officer: Sonoco Products Co. ADD CORP EMPL treasurer: Speciality Packaging Group Inc.

Grants Analysis

Disclosure Period: calendar year ending 2003
Total Grants: $1,959,074*
Number of Grants: 232
Average Grant: $6,316*
Highest Grant: $500,000
Lowest Grant: $25
Typical Range: $100 to $25,000
*Note: Giving excludes United Way. Average grant figure excludes highest grant.

Recent Grants

Note: Grants derived from 2003 Form 990.
General

500,000	Coker College, Hartsville, SC
250,000	Thomas Hart Academy, Hartsville, SC
200,000	University of South Carolina Educational Foundation, Columbia, SC
100,000	Coker College, Hartsville, SC
100,000	Coker College, Hartsville, SC
70,482	Hartsville United Way, Hartsville, SC
60,000	Pee Dee Area Council-Boy Scouts of America, Florence, SC
50,000	Black Creek Arts Council, Hartsville, SC
30,000	Communities in Schools for Darlington County, Hartsville, SC
27,000	Black Creek Arts Council, Hartsville, SC

SORDONI FOUNDATION

Giving Contact

William B. Sardoni, President and Treasurer
45 Owen St.
Forty Fort, PA 18704-4305

Phone: (570)283-1211
Fax: (570)288-3663

Description

Founded: 1946
EIN: 246017505
Organization Type: Private Foundation
Giving Locations: PA: Northeastern Pennsylvania
Grant Types: Capital, Endowment, General Support, Multiyear/Continuing Support, Project, Seed Money.

Donor Information

Founder: the late Andrew J. Sordoni, Sr., the late Andrew J. Sordoni, Jr., Andrew J. Sordoni III, the late Mrs. Andrew J. Sordoni, Sr., the late Mrs. Andrew J. Sordoni, Jr., Mrs. Andrew J. Sordoni III

Financial Summary

Total Giving: $447,966 (2003); $774,205 (2001)
Giving Analysis: Giving for 2003 includes: foundation grants to United Way ($200,000); 2001: foundation grants to United Way ($16,670)
Assets: $12,819,257 (2003); $13,007,949 (2001)
Gifts Received: $100 (2001); $2,325 (2000); $70,063 (1998). Note: In 1996, contributions were received from Andrew J. Sordoni, III ($25,000), William B. Sordoni ($4,800), and Sordoni Construction Co. (20,000).

Typical Recipients

Arts & Humanities: Arts Associations & Councils, Arts Festivals, Community Arts, Libraries, Museums/Galleries, Music, Public Broadcasting, Theater
Civic & Public Affairs: Botanical Gardens/Parks, Economic Development, Civic & Public Affairs-General, Municipalities/Towns, Public Policy, Urban & Community Affairs
Education: Arts/Humanities Education, Colleges & Universities, Community & Junior Colleges, Education Funds, Private Education (Precollege), Vocational & Technical Education
Environment: Environment-General, Research, Resource Conservation, Wildlife Protection
Health: Cancer, Emergency/Ambulance Services, Health Organizations, Hospices, Hospitals, Medical Rehabilitation, Medical Research, Nursing Services
Religion: Religion-General, Jewish Causes, Religious Organizations, Religious Welfare, Seminaries
Science: Scientific Organizations
Social Services: Camps, Child Welfare, Community Centers, Community Service Organizations, Domestic Violence, Family Services, People with Disabilities, Scouts, Senior Services, United Funds/United Ways, YMCA/YWCA/YMHA/YWHA, Youth Organizations

Application Procedures

Initial Contact: Send a brief letter of inquiry describing program or project.
Deadlines: None.

Restrictions

Does not support individuals or provide scholarships.

Foundation Officials

Richard Allan: director
A. William Kelly: director
John J. Menapace: director
Patrick J. Solano: director
Andrew John Sordoni, III: chairman, secretary B Pratt, KS 1943. ED University of Notre Dame (1961-1964); King's College BA (1967). PRIM CORP EMPL chairman, director: Sordoni Construction Services ADD CORP EMPL chairman executive committee: United Pennsylvania Bank. CORP AFFIL chairman: Mercom; chairman: Public Service Enterprises Pennsylvania; director: Harsco Corp. NONPR AFFIL director: Valley Medical Center Geisinger WY; director: WVIA; director: Pennsylvanians Effective Government; director: Pennsylvania Chamber Business & Industry; member: Pennsylvania Jazz Society; member: New Jersey Jazz Society. CLUB AFFIL Sons De-

sert New York Club; Westmoreland Country Club; Friars Club.

Margaret Sordoni: director
Susan F. Sordoni: director
William B. Sordoni: president, treasurer B 1944. ED University of Notre Dame; Wilkes College. PRIM CORP EMPL president, treasurer: Sordoni Construction Services. CORP AFFIL president: Sordoni Enterprises; vice chairman, president: Whiteman Tower; director: Mercom; vice chairman: Commonwealth Telephone Co.; president: Evergreen Capital Corp.

Grants Analysis

Disclosure Period: calendar year ending 2003
Total Grants: $247,966*
Number of Grants: 31
Average Grant: $4,849*
Highest Grant: $102,500
Lowest Grant: $250
Typical Range: $1,000 to $10,000
***Note:** Giving excludes United Way. Average grant figure excludes highest grant.

Recent Grants

Note: Grants derived from 2003 Form 990.
General

200,000	United Way of Wyoming Valley, Wilkes-Barre, PA
102,500	College Misericordia, Dallas, PA
60,000	University of Scranton, Scranton, PA
20,000	Moses Taylor Hospital, Scranton, PA
10,000	WVIA, Pittston, PA
6,666	Northeast Regional Cancer Institute, Scranton, PA
6,255	Wyoming Seminary, Kingston, PA
5,295	King's College, Wilkes-Barre, PA
5,000	Hawk Mount Sanctuary Association, Kempton, PA
2,500	Northeast Pennsylvania Philharmonic, Avoca, PA

SOUND SHORE FOUNDATION

Giving Contact

T. Gibbs Kane, Jr., Trustee
350 Stuyvesant Ave.
Rye, NY 10580
Phone: (203)629-1980

Description

Founded: 1987
EIN: 222777141
Organization Type: Private Foundation
Giving Locations: NY
Grant Types: General Support.

Financial Summary

Total Giving: $63,100 (2003); $68,100 (2001)
Assets: $1,027,869 (2003); $1,115,098 (2001)
Gifts Received: $1,254 (2001)

Typical Recipients

Arts & Humanities: Libraries
Education: Minority Education, Private Education (Precollege)
Health: Health Organizations, Hospitals, Multiple Sclerosis
Religion: Churches
Social Services: Animal Protection, Social Services-General

Application Procedures

Initial Contact: The foundation reports no specific application guidelines. Send a brief letter of inquiry, including statement of purpose, amount requested, and proof of tax-exempt status.
Deadlines: None.

Grants Analysis

Disclosure Period: calendar year ending 2003
Total Grants: $63,100
Number of Grants: 20
Average Grant: $2,795*
Highest Grant: $10,000
Lowest Grant: $450
Typical Range: $1,000 to $5,000
***Note:** Average grant figure excludes highest grant.

Recent Grants

Note: Grants derived from 2001 Form 990.
Library-Related

2,000	Rye Free Reading Room, Rye, NY

General

4,250	National Multiple Sclerosis, New York, NY
4,000	Immaculate Conception Church, New York, NY
1,000	International Etchells Class, New York, NY
1,000	Port Chester Carver Center, Port Chester, NY
1,000	Prep for Prep, New York, NY
850	Foundation for United Hospital, Port Chester, NY
250	ASPCA, New York, NY

SOUTH BEND TRIBUNE CORP.

Company Headquarters

225 N. Colfax Ave.
South Bend, IN 46626

Company Description

Employees: 270
SIC(s): 2711 Newspapers.
Parent Company: Schurz Communications, 223 W. Colfax Ave., South Bend, IN, United States

Operating Locations

South Bend Tribune Corp. (IN--South Bend)

Schurz Communications Foundation

Giving Contact

Todd F. Schurz, President
225 West Colfax Avenue
South Bend, IN 46624
Phone: (574)287-1001
Fax: (574)236-1765

Description

Founded: 1940
EIN: 356024357
Organization Type: Corporate Foundation
Giving Locations: IN: South Bend and surrounding area
Grant Types: General Support.

Donor Information

Founder: South Bend Tribune and WSBT

Financial Summary

Total Giving: $152,600 (2002); $153,700 (2001)
Giving Analysis: Giving for 2002 includes: foundation grants to United Way ($57,000); 2001: foundation grants to United Way ($56,750); foundation ($96,950)
Assets: $694,619 (2002); $894,910 (2001)
Gifts Received: $39,000 (2002); $153,565 (2001); $147,891 (2000). Note: Contributions were received from South Bend Tribune and WSBT.

Typical Recipients

Arts & Humanities: Arts Centers, Arts Festivals, Historic Preservation, History & Archaeology, Libraries, Museums/Galleries, Music, Performing Arts, Public Broadcasting
Civic & Public Affairs: African American Affairs, Botanical Gardens/Parks, Community Foundations, Economic Development, Civic & Public Affairs-General, Municipalities/Towns, Parades/Festivals, Urban & Community Affairs, Zoos/Aquariums
Education: Business Education, Colleges & Universities, Education Funds, Private Education (Precollege)
Health: Hospices, Speech & Hearing
Religion: Religious Organizations, Religious Welfare
Social Services: Child Welfare, Community Service Organizations, Shelters/Homelessness, United Funds/United Ways, YMCA/YWCA/YMHA/YWHA, Youth Organizations

Application Procedures

Initial Contact: The foundation has no formal grant application procedure or application form.
Deadlines: None.

Restrictions

Gives only to organizations located in the South Bend, Indiana area.

Corporate Officials

Mark Hocker: controller, editor, director PRIM CORP EMPL controller: South Bend Tribune Corp.
Todd F. Schurz: president, publisher, editor, director PRIM CORP EMPL president, publisher, editor, director: South Bend Tribune Corp.

Foundation Officials

James D. Freeman: secretary
David C. Ray: vice president
James Montgomery Schurz: treasurer B South Bend, IN 1933. ED Stanford University (1956). PRIM CORP EMPL senator vice president newspapers, director: Schurz Communs.
Todd F. Schurz: president (see above)

Grants Analysis

Disclosure Period: calendar year ending 2002
Total Grants: $95,600*
Number of Grants: 12
Average Grant: $4,560*
Highest Grant: $25,000
Lowest Grant: $650
Typical Range: $1,000 to $10,000
***Note:** Giving excludes United Way. Average grant figure excludes two highest grants ($50,000).

Recent Grants

Note: Grants derived from 2003 Form 990.

General

39,000	United Way of St. Joseph County/ South Bend Tribune, South Bend, IN
31,450	United Way of St. Joseph County/ WSBT, South Bend, IN
25,000	YWCA, South Bend, IN
20,000	Community Foundation of Joseph County, South Bend, IN
10,000	Holy Cross College, South Bend, IN
5,950	Center for Hospice and Pallative Care Inc., South Bend, IN
3,400	South Bend Symphony, South Bend, IN
1,350	Hearing & Speech Center of St. Joseph County, South Bend, IN
1,000	South Bend Regional Museum of Art, South Bend, IN
1,000	United Way of Greater Niles, Niles, MI

SOUTH PLAINS FOUNDATION

Giving Contact
Robert P. Anderson, Director
511 Avenue K
Lubbock, TX 79408
Phone: (806)792-9009

Description
Founded: 1989
EIN: 752294100
Organization Type: Private Foundation
Giving Locations: TX: West Texas
Grant Types: Fellowship, General Support, Project, Research, Scholarship, Seed Money.

Financial Summary
Total Giving: $127,621 (fiscal year ending June 30, 2004); $171,618 (fiscal 2001)
Giving Analysis: Giving for fiscal 2001 includes: foundation scholarships ($7,500)
Assets: $4,490,363 (fiscal 2004); $4,651,009 (fiscal 2001)
Gifts Received: $19,096 (fiscal 1997). Note: In fiscal 1990, contributions were received from the estate of Mildred Jones ($4,250) and miscellaneous donors ($191).

Typical Recipients
Arts & Humanities: Arts Centers, History & Archaeology, Libraries, Museums/Galleries, Music, Performing Arts, Public Broadcasting
Civic & Public Affairs: Chambers of Commerce, Employment/Job Training, Civic & Public Affairs-General, Nonprofit Management, Philanthropic Organizations, Women's Affairs
Education: Arts/Humanities Education, Colleges & Universities, Engineering/Technological Education, Education-General, Health & Physical Education, Literacy, Medical Education, Preschool Education, Public Education (Precollege), Student Aid
Health: Alzheimer's Disease, Emergency/Ambulance Services, Eyes/Blindness, Health-General, Health Organizations, Hospices, Hospitals, Kidney, Medical Rehabilitation, Medical Research, Mental Health, Public Health
Science: Science Museums
Social Services: Animal Protection, Family Services, Food/Clothing Distribution, People with Disabilities, Scouts, Social Services-General, Special Olympics, Substance Abuse, Volunteer Services, Youth Organizations

Application Procedures
Initial Contact: The foundation has no standard application form for either the research grant program or the small grants program; however, proposals should be a maximum of five pages and include the title of the study or project; name of the sponsoring institution; principal investigator or coordinator, with curriculum vitae attached for research grants; and abstract of the proposed study or project, not to exceed 100 words. Additionally, research grant proposals should include a statement of purpose, objectives, and goals of the study; review of relevant background research; procedures to be followed and populations being studied; procedures to be followed in analyzing results; expected outcomes; and an outline of the proposed budget.
Deadlines: None.

Restrictions
The specific focus of proposals must be concerned with one of the following areas; basic research in an area of health care, clinical investigations related to the rehabilitation of people with chronic illnesses, applied research problems focused on the treatment of people with behavioral, mental, or physical problems, or research problems of a generic nature which have some applicability to human services.

Additional Information
Awards research grants to individuals for medical and/or behavioral science research focused on some aspect of health care or human services.
Publications: Proposal Guidelines

Foundation Officials
Robert P. Anderson, PhD: director
Bill Armstrong: president, director PRIM CORP EMPL vice president: McKesson Corp.
Max L. Ince: secretary, treasurer
William Miller: vice president, director
Jim S. Moore, PhD: director
Sandy Ogletree: director

Grants Analysis
Disclosure Period: fiscal year ending June 30, 2004
Total Grants: $127,621
Number of Grants: 18
Average Grant: $5,154*
Highest Grant: $40,000
Lowest Grant: $350
Typical Range: $1,000 to $10,000
***Note:** Average grant figure excludes highest grant.

Recent Grants
Note: Grants derived from fiscal 2004 Form 990.
General

40,000	Texas Tech University Health Sciences Center, Amarillo, TX -- for medical research
13,915	Lubbock Area Coalition, Lubbock, TX
12,000	Youth Corps, Dallas, TX
10,656	South Plains Food Bank, Lubbock, TX
10,000	Kidney Foundation
10,000	Volunteer Center of Lubbock, Lubbock, TX
7,500	Special Olympics, Austin, TX
5,000	Lubbock Symphony Orchestra, Lubbock, TX
4,000	Lubbock Area Foundation, Lubbock, TX
3,000	Lubbock Regional Art Center, Lubbock, TX

SOUTH WAITE FOUNDATION

Giving Contact
Richard B. Carnahan, Custodian
c/o KeyBank NA
127 Public Sq., MC OH-01-27-1709
Cleveland, OH 44114-1306
Phone: (216)828-9770

Description
Founded: 1953
EIN: 346526411
Organization Type: Private Foundation
Giving Locations: OH: Cleveland
Grant Types: Capital, General Support, Multiyear/Continuing Support, Operating Expenses.

Donor Information
Founder: the late Francis M. Sherwin, Margaret H. Sherwin

Financial Summary
Total Giving: $124,500 (2003)
Giving Analysis: Giving for 2003 includes: foundation scholarships ($1,000); foundation grants to United Way ($4,000)
Assets: $2,582,925 (2003)

Typical Recipients
Arts & Humanities: Arts Associations & Councils, Historic Preservation, History & Archaeology, Libraries, Museums/Galleries, Music, Public Broadcasting
Civic & Public Affairs: Botanical Gardens/Parks, Civic & Public Affairs-General, Municipalities/Towns, Parades/Festivals
Education: Colleges & Universities, Community & Junior Colleges, Health & Physical Education, Minority Education, Private Education (Precollege), Student Aid
Environment: Environment-General, Resource Conservation, Watershed, Wildlife Protection
Health: Cancer, Clinics/Medical Centers, Health Organizations, Hospitals, Medical Rehabilitation, Medical Research, Public Health, Speech & Hearing
International: International-General, International Environmental Issues, International Organizations
Science: Science Museums, Scientific Centers & Institutes, Scientific Labs
Social Services: Child Welfare, Community Service Organizations, Delinquency & Criminal Rehabilitation, Family Planning, People with Disabilities, Substance Abuse, United Funds/United Ways, YMCA/YWCA/YMHA/YWHA, Youth Organizations

Application Procedures
Initial Contact: The foundation has no formal grant application procedure or application form.
Deadlines: None.

Restrictions
The trustees normally only make grants to organizations with which they are thoroughly familiar, and they maintain a close working relationship with these selected charities.

Additional Information
Trust(s): KeyBank NA

Foundation Officials
Brian Sherwin: president
Dennis Sherwin: mem
Peter Sherwin: mem

Grants Analysis
Disclosure Period: calendar year ending 2003
Total Grants: $119,500*
Number of Grants: 23
Average Grant: $5,196*
Highest Grant: $10,000
Lowest Grant: $1,000
Typical Range: $1,000 to $10,000
***Note:** Giving excludes scholarships and United Way. Average grant figure excludes highest grant.

Recent Grants
Note: Grants derived from 2001 Form 990.
General

12,000	United Way Services, Cleveland, OH -- for operations
10,000	Cleveland Clinic Foundation, Cleveland, OH -- for prostate cancer research
10,000	Jackson Laboratory, Bar Harbor, ME -- FMS endowment
10,000	Lake Metro Park Systems, Kirtland, OH -- for Wildlife Center expansion in memory of Margaret Halle Sherwin
10,000	Nature Conservancy, Dublin, OH -- Ohio chapter unrestricted
10,000	Recovery Resources, Cleveland, OH -- for operations
10,000	Willoughby Fine Arts Association, Mentor, OH -- for operations
8,000	Chagrin River Watershed Partnership, Willoughby, OH -- for computer projection equipment
8,000	William J. and Dorothy K. O'Neill Foundation, Pepper Pike, OH -- for NY Police and Fire Widow's and Children's Fund

7,000   Laurel School, Shaker Heights, OH -- for Joan Crile Foster Memorial

SOUTHWAYS FOUNDATION

Giving Contact
Jon K. Crow, Vice President & Treasurer
c/o Sargent Management Co.
901 Marquette Ave., Suite 2630
Minneapolis, MN 55402
Phone: (612)596-3260
Fax: (612)338-2084
E-mail: southways@smcinv.com
Web: http://www.southwaysfoundation.org/

Description
Founded: 1950
EIN: 416018502
Organization Type: Private Foundation
Giving Locations: CT; MN; NY; VA
Grant Types: Capital, Endowment, General Support, Matching, Multiyear/Continuing Support, Project, Research.

Donor Information
Founder: the late John S. Pillsbury and family

Financial Summary
Total Giving: $838,391 (2003); $1,193,629 (2001)
Giving Analysis: Giving for 2003 includes: foundation grants to United Way ($54,000); foundation matching gifts ($97,462); 2001: foundation grants to United Way ($60,000); foundation matching gifts ($89,834).
Assets: $9,893,170 (2003); $11,284,604 (2001)
Gifts Received: $203,997 (1994); $13,360 (1993); $1,620,012 (1992). Note: In 1994, contributions were received from Stanley R. Resor ($200,000), Sarah P. Kletter ($1,000), and Marian S. Pillsbury ($1,455); six other donors made contributions of $845 or less each.

Typical Recipients
Arts & Humanities: Arts Associations & Councils, Arts Centers, Arts Institutes, Community Arts, History & Archaeology, Libraries, Music, Opera, Performing Arts, Public Broadcasting, Theater
Civic & Public Affairs: Botanical Gardens/Parks, Public Policy, Urban & Community Affairs, Zoos/Aquariums
Education: Colleges & Universities, Education Funds, Legal Education, Literacy, Private Education (Precollege), Student Aid, Vocational & Technical Education
Environment: Air/Water Quality, Environment-General
Health: Single-Disease Health Associations
Religion: Churches, Religious Organizations
Social Services: Animal Protection, Child Welfare, Community Centers, Community Service Organizations, Crime Prevention, Family Planning, Family Services, Recreation & Athletics, United Funds/United Ways, YMCA/YWCA/YMHA/YWHA, Youth Organizations

Application Procedures
Initial Contact: The foundation has no formal grant application procedure or application form.
Deadlines: None.

Foundation Officials
Jon K. Crow: vice president
Katharine P. Jose: president, trustee
Lucy C. Mitchell: assistant treasurer, trustee
George Sturgis Pillsbury, Jr.: trustee B Crystal Bay, MN 1921. ED Yale University AB (1943). PRIM CORP EMPL chairman: Sargent Manufacturing Co. CLUB AFFIL River Club; Seminole Golf Club; Minne-

apolis Club; Minnetonka Yacht Club; Everglades Club; Minneapolis Athletic Club; Bath & Tennis Club.
John S. Pillsbury, III: trustee
Eleanor C. Winston: secretary, trustee

Grants Analysis
Disclosure Period: calendar year ending 2003
Total Grants: $686,929*
Number of Grants: 132
Average Grant: $5,204
Highest Grant: $50,000
Lowest Grant: $104
Typical Range: $1,000 to $10,000
*Note: Giving excludes matching gifts and United Way.

Recent Grants
Note: Grants derived from 2001 Form 990.
General

100,000	Westminster Presbyterian Church, Minneapolis, MN
50,000	Blake School, Hopkins, MN
50,000	Guthrie Theater, Minneapolis, MN
50,000	Minnesota Historical Society, St. Paul, MN
50,000	Minnesota Historical Society, St. Paul, MN
40,000	Guthrie Theater, Minneapolis, MN
40,000	Rockefeller University, New York, NY
35,000	United Way of Minneapolis Area, Minneapolis, MN
25,000	Pillsbury Neighborhood Services, Minneapolis, MN
25,000	United Way of Minneapolis Area, Minneapolis, MN

SOUTHWEST NEWS HERALD

Company Headquarters
6225 S. Kedzie Ave.
Chicago, IL 60629

Operating Locations
Herald News (IL--Joliet)

Herald Newspapers Foundation, Inc.

Giving Contact
Bruce Sagan, President
Herald Newspapers Foundation, Inc.
815 W. Van Buren, Suite 550
Chicago, IL 60607
Phone: (312)666-7776

Description
EIN: 237193553
Organization Type: Corporate Foundation
Giving Locations: IL: Chicago
Grant Types: General Support.

Financial Summary
Gifts Received: $50,000 (fiscal year ending August 31, 1999); $50,000 (fiscal 1998); $53,500 (fiscal 1997). Note: In fiscal 1999, contributions were received from Paul Sagan ($25,000) and Alex Sagan ($25,000). In fiscal 1998, contributions were received from Paul Sagan and Alex Sagan. In fiscal 1997, contributions were received from Bruce Sagan.

Typical Recipients
Arts & Humanities: Arts Associations & Councils, Arts Centers, Arts Institutes, Ballet, Dance, Arts & Humanities-General, Historic Preservation, History & Ar-

chaeology, Libraries, Literary Arts, Museums/Galleries, Music, Performing Arts, Public Broadcasting, Theater, Visual Arts
Civic & Public Affairs: Botanical Gardens/Parks, Business/Free Enterprise, Civil Rights, Community Foundations, Civic & Public Affairs-General, Housing, Public Policy, Urban & Community Affairs, Women's Affairs
Education: Arts/Humanities Education, Colleges & Universities, Education Reform, Education-General, Private Education (Precollege), Religious Education, Secondary Education (Private)
Environment: Resource Conservation
Health: AIDS/HIV, Cancer, Eyes/Blindness, Medical Rehabilitation, Medical Research
International: Foreign Arts Organizations, Missionary/Religious Activities
Religion: Jewish Causes
Science: Science Museums, Scientific Centers & Institutes
Social Services: Community Service Organizations, Family Planning, People with Disabilities, Youth Organizations

Application Procedures
Initial Contact: The foundation has no formal grant application procedure or application form.
Deadlines: None.

Corporate Officials
Richard Orlikoff: vice president PRIM CORP EMPL vice president: Herald News.
Bruce Sagan: president PRIM CORP EMPL president: Herald News Paper Inc.

Foundation Officials
Richard Orlikoff: secretary (see above)
Bruce Sagan: president (see above)

Grants Analysis
Disclosure Period: fiscal year ending August 31, 2000
Total Grants: $65,705
Number of Grants: 43
Average Grant: $1,267*
Highest Grant: $12,500
Typical Range: $500 to $5,000
*Note: Average grant figure excludes highest grant.

Recent Grants
Note: Grants derived from 2002 Form 990.

Library-Related

5,000	Chicago Public Library Foundation, Chicago, IL

General

5,000	Dana Farber Cancer Institute, Boston, MA
5,000	Foundation Fighting Blindness, Hunt Valley, MD
5,000	University of Chicago, Chicago, IL
4,700	Steppenwolf Theater Company, Chicago, IL
4,120	Rush Presbyterian-St. Luke's Medical Center, Chicago, IL
3,000	Joffrey Ballet Center Concert Group Inc., Chicago, IL
2,500	Columbia Land Conservancy, Chatham, NY
2,500	Koussevitsky Music Foundation, Inc., New York, NY
2,000	Planned Parenthood Chicago, Chicago, IL
1,750	Near South Planning Board, Chicago, IL

SOUTHWESTERN ELECTRIC POWER CO.

Company Headquarters
428 Travis St.
Shreveport, LA 71156
Web: http://www.aep.com

Company Description
Revenue: US$1.084 billion (2002)
Employees: 1,372 (2002)
SIC(s): 4900 Electric, Gas & Sanitary Services.
Parent Company: American Electric Power, 1 Riverside Plaza, Columbus, OH, United States

Operating Locations
Southwestern Electric Power Co. (AR--Fayetteville, Texarkana; LA--Shreveport; TX--Longview)

Nonmonetary Support
Type: Donated Equipment; Loaned Employees

Giving Contact
John Hubbard, Community Service Manager
428 Travis St.
Shreveport, LA 71101
Phone: (318)222-2141
Fax: (318)673-3135

Description
Organization Type: Corporate Giving Program
Giving Locations: headquarters and operating communities.
Grant Types: Capital, General Support, Seed Money.

Typical Recipients
Arts & Humanities: Arts Associations & Councils, Arts Festivals, Community Arts, Historic Preservation, Libraries, Public Broadcasting, Theater
Civic & Public Affairs: Chambers of Commerce, Clubs, Community Foundations, Economic Development, Parades/Festivals, Urban & Community Affairs
Education: Colleges & Universities, Community & Junior Colleges, Education-General, Health & Physical Education, Science/Mathematics Education
Health: Cancer, Children's Health/Hospitals, Clinics/Medical Centers, Health-General, Heart, Hospitals, Medical Research
Social Services: Community Centers, Community Service Organizations, Emergency Relief, Family Services, Recreation & Athletics, Social Services-General, United Funds/United Ways, Youth Organizations

Application Procedures
Initial Contact: Send a brief letter of inquiry.
Application Requirements: a description of organization, amount requested, and purpose of funds sought.

Restrictions
Does not support individuals, religious organizations for sectarian purposes, or political or lobbying groups.

Corporate Officials
E. R. Brooks: chairman, chief executive officer, chief financial officer PRIM CORP EMPL chairman: Southwestern Electric Power Co.
Michael H. Madison: president, chief executive officer, chief financial officer B Tulsa, OK 1948. ED University of Oklahoma (1971). PRIM CORP EMPL president, chief executive officer, chief financial officer: Southwestern Electric Power Co.

Grants Analysis
Note: Typical grant size is less than $1,000.

SOVEREIGN BANK

Company Headquarters
Wyomissing, PA
Web: http://www.sovereignbank.com

Company Description
Employees: 4,100
SIC(s): 6035 Federal Savings Institutions.
Parent Company: Sovereign Bancorp, 1500 Market St., Philadelphia, PA, United States

Operating Locations
Sovereign Bank (DE--New Castle; NJ--Bergen, Essex, Morris Plains, Somerset; PA--Berks, Bucks, Delaware, Lancaster, Lehigh Valley, Mercer, Middlesex, Montgomery, Northampton, Union City)

Nonmonetary Support
Type: Cause-related Marketing & Promotion; Donated Equipment; Donated Products; In-kind Services; Workplace Solicitation

Sovereign Bank Foundation

Giving Contact
Joseph E. Schupp, Foundation Manager
Sovereign Bank Foundation
1130 Berkshire Boulevard
Wyomissing, PA 19610
Phone: (610)378-6190

Alternate Contact
Phone: (610)320-8400

Description
EIN: 232548113
Organization Type: Corporate Foundation
Giving Locations: NJ: Mercer County bank or service areas.
Grant Types: Capital, General Support, Multiyear/Continuing Support.

Financial Summary
Total Giving: $2,335,923 (2002); $1,250,804 (2001)
Giving Analysis: Giving for 2001 includes: foundation matching gifts ($4,340); foundation ($1,246,464).
Gifts Received: $2,335,938 (2002); $1,250,804 (2001); $338,778 (2000). Note: The foundation receives contributions from Sovereign Bank.

Typical Recipients
Arts & Humanities: Arts Festivals, Arts Outreach, Community Arts, Historic Preservation, Libraries, Museums/Galleries, Music, Opera, Performing Arts, Public Broadcasting
Civic & Public Affairs: African American Affairs, Asian American Affairs, Business/Free Enterprise, Civil Rights, Community Foundations, Economic Development, Employment/Job Training, Ethnic Organizations, Gay/Lesbian Issues, Civic & Public Affairs-General, Hispanic Affairs, Housing, Inner-City Development, Law & Justice, Municipalities/Towns, Native American Affairs, Nonprofit Management, Parades/Festivals, Philanthropic Organizations, Professional & Trade Associations, Public Policy, Urban & Community Affairs, Women's Affairs
Education: Afterschool/Enrichment Programs, Arts/Humanities Education, Business Education, Colleges & Universities, Community & Junior Colleges, Education Funds, Education-General, Literacy, Minority Education, Secondary Education (Public), Student Aid
Environment: Environment-General
Health: AIDS/HIV, Children's Health/Hospitals, Clinics/Medical Centers, Health-General, Heart, Hospitals, Multiple Sclerosis, Public Health, Single-Disease Health Associations

Religion: Churches, Religious Welfare, Social/Policy Issues
Social Services: Camps, Child Welfare, Community Centers, Community Service Organizations, Crime Prevention, Day Care, Domestic Violence, Emergency Relief, Family Planning, Family Services, Food/Clothing Distribution, Homes, People with Disabilities, Recreation & Athletics, Scouts, Senior Services, Sexual Abuse, Shelters/Homelessness, Social Services-General, Substance Abuse, United Funds/United Ways, Volunteer Services, YMCA/YWCA/YMHA/YWHA, Youth Organizations

Application Procedures
Initial Contact: Send a full proposal.
Application Requirements: Include a description of organization, needs of the project, population served, and a listing of the directors of the organization.
Deadlines: None.

Restrictions
Does not support individuals, religious organizations for sectarian purposes, political or lobbying groups, organizations outside operating areas, organizations that are not tax-exempt/nonprofit, or beauty scholarship pageants.

Additional Information
Publications: Guidelines Brochure

Corporate Officials
Richard E. Mohn: chairman, director, chairman PRIM CORP EMPL chairman, director: Sovereign Bank. CORP AFFIL chairman: Cloister Spring Water Co.
Jay S. Sidhu: president, chief executive officer, chairman PRIM CORP EMPL president, chief executive officer, chairman: Sovereign Bank.

Foundation Officials
Brenda Campbell: treasurer
John Hamill: director
Thomas Kennedy: vice president
John V. Killen: president, director
John Merva: secretary
Richard E. Mohn: director (see above)
Joseph E. Schupp: vice president
Jay S. Sidhu: director (see above)

Grants Analysis
Disclosure Period: calendar year ending 2002
Total Grants: $2,157,413*
Number of Grants: 495
Average Grant: $4,358
Highest Grant: $40,000
Lowest Grant: $500
Typical Range: $500 to $10,000
*****Note:** Giving excludes matching gifts and United Way.

Recent Grants
Note: Grants derived from 2003 Form 990.
Library-Related

10,000	Ester Community Library, Reading, PA
10,000	New Library Building Campaign

General

2,00,000	United Way of New England, Boston, MA
70,000	United Way of Berks County, Reading, PA
50,000	March of Dimes, Cranbury, NJ
50,000	Second Miles -- Camp Hill
45,000	Caron Foundation, Wernersville, PA
33,000	Monmouth Housing Alliance, Eatontown, NJ
30,000	Governor Mifflin Soccer Club, Shillington, PA
30,000	New Jersey Citizens Action, Hackensack, NJ
25,000	ARC of Essex County, Livingston, NJ
25,000	Housing and Community Development Network of New Jersey, Trenton, NJ

ELIOT SPALDING FOUNDATION

Giving Contact
Peter T. Gianas, Secretary
4400 E. Broadway, Suite 800
Tucson, AZ 85711
Phone: (520)795-6630
Fax: (520)327-1922

Description
Founded: 1954
EIN: 866050507
Organization Type: Private Foundation
Giving Locations: AZ: Tucson
Grant Types: General Support.

Financial Summary
Total Giving: $165,000 (2003); $135,000 (2001)
Giving Analysis: Giving for 2003 includes: foundation grants to United Way ($78,725); 2001: foundation grants to United Way ($94,000)
Assets: $3,438,200 (2003); $3,740,795 (2001)
Gifts Received: $191,118 (1995); $23,731 (1994).
Note: In 1995, contributions were received from the Ponomaref estate and the Link Trust.

Typical Recipients
Arts & Humanities: Historic Preservation, Libraries, Museums/Galleries
Civic & Public Affairs: Botanical Gardens/Parks, Civic & Public Affairs-General, Housing
Education: Colleges & Universities, Community & Junior Colleges, Student Aid
Environment: Resource Conservation
Health: Alzheimer's Disease, Clinics/Medical Centers, Emergency/Ambulance Services
Religion: Churches, Religious Welfare
Social Services: Animal Protection, Child Welfare, Community Service Organizations, Day Care, Food/Clothing Distribution, People with Disabilities, Recreation & Athletics, Social Services-General, United Funds/United Ways, YMCA/YWCA/YMHA/YWHA, Youth Organizations

Application Procedures
Initial Contact: Submit a typewritten request.
Application Requirements: Include purpose of funds sought and proof of tax-exempt status.
Deadlines: November 1.

Foundation Officials
Peter T. Gianas: executive director
Samuel P. Goddard, Jr.: director
Clayton E. Niles: director
Clayton N. Niles: president
James M. Sakrison: director

Grants Analysis
Disclosure Period: calendar year ending 2003
Total Grants: $86,275*
Number of Grants: 18
Average Grant: $4,487*
Highest Grant: $10,000
Lowest Grant: $500
Typical Range: $1,000 to $5,000
*Note: Giving excludes United Way. Average grant figure excludes highest grant.

Recent Grants
Note: Grants derived from 2001 Form 990.
Library-Related
3,000	Libraries LTD, Tucson, AZ

General
74,000	United Way of Greater Tucson, Tucson, AZ
20,000	United Way of Greater Tucson, Tucson, AZ
7,500	Angel Charity For Children, Tucson, AZ
6,000	Boys/Girls Club of Tucson, Tucson, AZ
5,000	Dollars for Scholars, Tucson, AZ
5,000	Tucson Community Food Bank, Tucson, AZ
3,000	New Horizons, Goldthwaite, TX
3,000	Southern Arizona Child Advocacy Center, Tucson, AZ
3,000	Youth Own Their Own, Tucson, AZ
2,500	Children to Children, Tucson, AZ

SPANG & CO.

Company Headquarters
100 Brugh Ave.
Butler, PA 16001

Company Description
Employees: 1,200
SIC(s): 3200 Stone, Clay & Glass Products, 3600 Electronic & Other Electrical Equipment.

Operating Locations
Spang & Co. (PA--Butler)

Spang & Co. Charitable Trust

Giving Contact
K. R. McKnight, Contact
PO Box 11422
Pittsburgh, PA 15230-0422
Phone: (412)963-9363

Description
EIN: 256020192
Organization Type: Corporate Foundation
Giving Locations: PA
Grant Types: General Support.

Donor Information
Founder: Spang & Co.

Financial Summary
Total Giving: $285,150 (2002); $215,250 (2001)
Giving Analysis: Giving for 2002 includes: foundation ($285,150)
Assets: $7,874,411 (2002); $9,857,009 (2001)
Gifts Received: $2,703 (2001); $9,864 (2000); $7,879,830 (1999). Note: In 2000, contributions were received from employees. In 1999, contributions were received from Spang employees ($9,263) and the estate of F.E. Rath, Sr. ($7,870,567). In 1998, contributions were received from Spang & Co. employees.

Typical Recipients
Arts & Humanities: Ballet, Historic Preservation, History & Archaeology, Libraries, Museums/Galleries, Music, Opera, Public Broadcasting, Theater
Civic & Public Affairs: Botanical Gardens/Parks, Business/Free Enterprise, Chambers of Commerce, Community Foundations, Economic Development, Economic Policy, Civic & Public Affairs-General, Parades/Festivals, Philanthropic Organizations, Professional & Trade Associations, Safety, Zoos/Aquariums
Education: Colleges & Universities, Medical Education, Private Education (Precollege), Special Education
Health: Cancer, Children's Health/Hospitals, Clinics/Medical Centers, Eyes/Blindness, Health Funds, Heart, Hospitals, Hospitals (University Affiliated), Kidney, Medical Research, Nursing Services, Single-Disease Health Associations
Science: Scientific Centers & Institutes
Social Services: Animal Protection, Camps, Child Welfare, Community Service Organizations, Crime Prevention, Delinquency & Criminal Rehabilitation, Domestic Violence, Food/Clothing Distribution, People with Disabilities, Recreation & Athletics, Scouts, Social Services-General, United Funds/United Ways, Volunteer Services, YMCA/YWCA/YMHA/YWHA, Youth Organizations

Application Procedures
Initial Contact: Send a brief letter of inquiry.
Application Requirements: Include name, location, a description of organization, amount requested, and proof of tax-exempt status.
Deadlines: Ninety days before the end of the calendar quarter.

Corporate Officials
Frank E. Rath, Jr.: chairman, president, chief executive officer, director B 1946. ED Carnegie Mellon University BS (1968). PRIM CORP EMPL chairman, president, chief executive officer, director: Spang & Co.

Foundation Officials
D. F. Rath: trustee
Frank E. Rath, Jr.: trustee (see above)
R. A. Rath, Jr.: trustee

Grants Analysis
Disclosure Period: calendar year ending 2002
Total Grants: $285,150
Number of Grants: 45
Average Grant: $4,208*
Highest Grant: $100,000
Lowest Grant: $100
Typical Range: $500 to $10,000
*Note: Average grant figure excludes highest grant.

Recent Grants
Note: Grants derived from 2003 Form 990.
Library-Related
5,000	Butler Area Public Library, Butler, PA

General
50,000	Shadyside Hospital Foundation, Pittsburgh, PA
25,000	Johns Hopkins Fund for Research, Baltimore, MD
22,000	Phipps Conservatory, Pittsburgh, PA
10,000	Allegheny Heart Institute, Pittsburgh, PA
10,000	Booneville Development Corporation, Booneville, AR
10,000	Carnegie Mellon University, Pittsburgh, PA
10,000	Pittsburgh Symphony Society, Pittsburgh, PA
5,000	Boy Scouts Of America Moraine Trails Council, Butler, PA
5,000	Children's Hospital of Pittsburgh, Pittsburgh, PA
5,000	Pittsburgh Zoo, Pittsburgh, PA

SPARTAN STORES INC.

Company Headquarters
850 76th St. SW
Grand Rapids, MI 49518-8700
Web: http://www.spartanstores.com

Company Description
Founded: 1917
Ticker: SPTN
Exchange: NASDAQ
Former Name: Seaway Food Town, Inc. (2000).
Revenue: US$3.256 billion (2003)
Profit: (US$122.3 million) (2003)
Employees: 6900 (2003)
SIC(s): 5141 Groceries--General Line, 5411 Grocery Stores, 5912 Drug Stores & Proprietary Stores.

Operating Locations

Food Town Supermarkets (OH--Maumee, Toledo)
Note: Company operates 24 Food Town Supermarkets, 20 Food Town Plus Supermarkets, and 22 discount drug stores under the name of "Pharm."

Nonmonetary Support

Type: Cause-related Marketing & Promotion; Donated Products; In-kind Services; Workplace Solicitation

Giving Contact

Terry Blanding, Community Affairs Specialist
PO Box 8700
Grand Rapids, MI 49518
Phone: (616)878-2000
E-mail: terry_blanding@spartansstores.com

Alternate Contact

Mary DeChow, Director of Government Relations
Phone: (616)878-2469

Description

Organization Type: Corporate Giving Program
Giving Locations: MI: Southeastern Michigan; OH: Northwest Ohio headquarters area only.
Grant Types: General Support, Multiyear/Continuing Support.

Financial Summary

Total Giving: Contributes through corporate direct giving program only.

Typical Recipients

Arts & Humanities: Arts Appreciation, Arts Associations & Councils, Arts Centers, Arts Festivals, Community Arts, Ethnic & Folk Arts, Libraries, Museums/Galleries, Opera, Performing Arts, Public Broadcasting, Theater, Visual Arts
Civic & Public Affairs: Philanthropic Organizations, Zoos/Aquariums
Education: Colleges & Universities, Elementary Education (Private), Literacy
Health: Geriatric Health, Health Organizations, Hospitals, Nutrition
Religion: Churches, Synagogues/Temples
Science: Science Exhibits & Fairs
Social Services: Child Welfare, Community Centers, Community Service Organizations, Domestic Violence, Food/Clothing Distribution, Recreation & Athletics, Shelters/Homelessness, Substance Abuse, Youth Organizations

Application Procedures

Initial Contact: Submit a brief letter of inquiry and full proposal.
Application Requirements: Include a description of organization, amount requested, purpose of funds sought, and proof of tax-exempt status.
Deadlines: One month in advance of date that funds are needed.

Restrictions

Does not support individuals, political or lobbying groups, or organizations outside operating areas.

Additional Information

Seaway Food Town, Inc., was acquired by Spartan Stores, Inc., in August 2000. The company, now called Food Town Supermarkets, operates as a subsidiary of Spartan Stores, Inc.

Giving Program Officials

Pat Nowak: PRIM CORP EMPL director public relations & community affairs: Food Town Supermarkets.

Grants Analysis

Typical Range: $2,500 to $5,000

VICTOR E. SPEAS FOUNDATION

Giving Contact

David P. Ross, Senior Vice President
Bank of America
PO Box 419119
Kansas City, MO 64141-6119
Phone: (816)979-7481
Fax: (816)979-7916

Alternate Contact

Phone: 800-213-0245

Description

Founded: 1947
EIN: 446008340
Organization Type: Family Foundation
Giving Locations: MO: Kansas City metropolitan area
Grant Types: Capital, Challenge, General Support, Project, Seed Money.

Donor Information

Founder: Established as a trust in 1947 by the late Victor E. Speas, chairman of Speas Company. Both Mr. Speas and the Speas Company, a vinegar and apple products manufacturing firm, contributed to the foundation.

Financial Summary

Total Giving: $1,939,428 (2003); $1,970,135 (2001)
Assets: $31,904,551 (2003); $35,009,966 (2001)

Typical Recipients

Arts & Humanities: Arts Centers, Historic Preservation, Libraries, Museums/Galleries, Theater
Civic & Public Affairs: Business/Free Enterprise, Community Foundations, Economic Development, Economic Policy, Employment/Job Training, Civic & Public Affairs-General, Hispanic Affairs, Housing, Municipalities/Towns, Nonprofit Management, Philanthropic Organizations, Urban & Community Affairs, Women's Affairs
Education: Afterschool/Enrichment Programs, Business Education, Colleges & Universities, Continuing Education, Education Associations, Education-General, Health & Physical Education, Medical Education, Minority Education, Preschool Education, Private Education (Precollege), Science/Mathematics Education, Secondary Education (Public)
Health: AIDS/HIV, Cancer, Children's Health/Hospitals, Clinics/Medical Centers, Emergency/Ambulance Services, Geriatric Health, Health Policy/Cost Containment, Health Funds, Health Organizations, Heart, Home-Care Services, Hospices, Hospitals, Kidney, Medical Rehabilitation, Mental Health, Nursing Services, Nutrition, Public Health, Research/Studies Institutes, Single-Disease Health Associations, Speech & Hearing, Trauma Treatment
Religion: Jewish Causes, Ministries, Religious Welfare
Social Services: Animal Protection, At-Risk Youth, Child Welfare, Community Centers, Community Service Organizations, Counseling, Family Services, Homes, People with Disabilities, Senior Services, Sexual Abuse, Shelters/Homelessness, Substance Abuse, United Funds/United Ways, Volunteer Services, Youth Organizations

Application Procedures

Initial Contact: An initial phone call is suggested. There are no formal application forms.
Application Requirements: Initial applications should be no more than three pages and should include the appropriate attachments. Eligible grantees will be asked to submit one copy of a full proposal. Interviews may be requested if the foundation is interested in a submitted proposal.
Deadlines: None.

Review Process: The board meets bimonthly. Notification, if funding will be provided, normally takes about two months.

Restrictions

Funding is restricted to improving the quality of health care in the Kansas City area. Grants are not made for endowment campaigns.

Additional Information

The Victor E. Speas Foundation and the John W. and Effie E. Speas Memorial Trust are affiliated.
Trust(s): Bank of America

Foundation Officials

David P. Ross: bank rep, contact PRIM CORP EMPL senior vice president: NationsBank Corp.

Grants Analysis

Disclosure Period: calendar year ending 2003
Total Grants: $1,939,428
Number of Grants: 46
Average Grant: $38,098*
Highest Grant: $225,000
Lowest Grant: $150
Typical Range: $10,000 to $50,000
*Note: Average grant figure excludes highest grant.

Recent Grants

Note: Grants derived from 2001 Form 990.
General

200,000	Community Resource Network, Kansas City, MO -- operating support
150,000	Support Kansas City, Inc., Kansas City, MO -- start-up costs
147,000	Oznam, Kansas City, MO -- support of capital project
113,540	Healthy Kansas City, Kansas City, MO -- operating expenses and E-Health Project
79,000	Campfire Boys and Girls Heartland Council, Kansas City, MO -- Project AIM
75,000	Niles Home for Children, Kansas City, MO -- software and technology upgrades
75,000	Synergy Services, Kansas City, MO -- upgrading technology
73,550	Northland Therapeutic Riding Center, Kearney, MO -- support of start-up of program and web fees and annual audit
69,292	Amethyst Place, Kansas City, MO -- housing program for drug and alcohol recovery patients
67,000	Mattie Rhodes Center, Kansas City, MO -- capital campaign

JOHN W. AND EFFIE E. SPEAS MEMORIAL TRUST

Giving Contact

David P. Ross, Senior Vice President
Bank of America
PO Box 419119
Kansas City, MO 64105
Phone: (816)979-7481
Fax: (816)979-7916

Description

Founded: 1947
EIN: 446008249
Organization Type: Family Foundation
Giving Locations: KS: Johnson County, Wyandotte County; MO: Cass County, Clay County, Jackson County, Platte County
Grant Types: Capital, Challenge, General Support, Operating Expenses, Project, Research, Seed Money.

Donor Information

Founder: Established in 1947 by the Speas family, including the late Effie E. Speas and the late Victor E. Speas.

Financial Summary

Total Giving: $2,113,603 (2003); $2,576,368 (2001)
Assets: $29,908,399 (2003); $34,860,469 (2001)
Gifts Received: $100,000 (1998). Note: In 1998, contributions were received from Victor Speas Foundation.

Typical Recipients

Arts & Humanities: Libraries, Public Broadcasting
Civic & Public Affairs: Business/Free Enterprise, Community Foundations, Economic Development, Employment/Job Training, Civic & Public Affairs-General, Municipalities/Towns, Nonprofit Management, Urban & Community Affairs
Education: Colleges & Universities, Community & Junior Colleges, Environmental Education, Education-General, Health & Physical Education, Medical Education, Religious Education, Science/Mathematics Education
Health: Alzheimer's Disease, Cancer, Children's Health/Hospitals, Clinics/Medical Centers, Emergency/Ambulance Services, Eyes/Blindness, Geriatric Health, Health Policy/Cost Containment, Health Organizations, Heart, Home-Care Services, Hospices, Hospitals, Hospitals (University Affiliated), Kidney, Long-Term Care, Medical Rehabilitation, Medical Research, Medical Training, Mental Health, Multiple Sclerosis, Nursing Services, Nutrition, Prenatal Health Issues, Preventive Medicine/Wellness Organizations, Public Health, Single-Disease Health Associations, Speech & Hearing, Transplant Networks/Donor Banks
Religion: Jewish Causes, Religious Welfare
Social Services: At-Risk Youth, Child Abuse, Child Welfare, Community Centers, Community Service Organizations, Crime Prevention, Family Services, People with Disabilities, Recreation & Athletics, Senior Services, Shelters/Homelessness, Special Olympics, Substance Abuse, United Funds/United Ways, Volunteer Services, Youth Organizations

Application Procedures

Initial Contact: A preliminary phone call is requested. If interested, the trust will request a complete project proposal.
Application Requirements: Applications should be in the form of a three-page letter with the appropriate attachments.
Deadlines: None.
Review Process: The board meets twice a month. Notification follows about two months after receipt of proposal.

Restrictions

The trust does not fund individuals or endowments. Funding is restricted to metropolitan Kansas City.

Additional Information

Bank of America serves as the corporate trustee. The John W. and Effie E. Speas Memorial Trust and the Victor E. Speas Foundation are affiliated.

Foundation Officials

David P. Ross: bank rep, contact PRIM CORP EMPL senior vice president: NationsBank Corp.

Grants Analysis

Disclosure Period: calendar year ending 2003
Total Grants: $2,113,603
Number of Grants: 35
Average Grant: $60,389
Highest Grant: $262,000
Lowest Grant: $2,000
Typical Range: $20,000 to $100,000

Recent Grants

Note: Grants derived from 2001 Form 990.
General

224,000	Community Resource Network, Kansas City, MO -- support of infrastructure requirements
165,062	Rockhurst University, Kansas City, MO -- communication sciences
155,000	Truman Medical Center Foundation, Kansas City, MO -- Kansas City Care Network
139,000	Seton Center, Inc., Kansas City, MO -- Kansas City Community Care Project
105,000	Research Health Foundation, Kansas City, MO -- software purchase
100,000	Kansas University Endowment Association, Kansas City, KS -- construction of new center
100,000	Missouri 4-H Foundation, Columbia, MO -- Aim Urban Program
100,000	Park University, Parkville, MO -- expanded health care program
100,000	Support Kansas City, Inc., Kansas City, MO -- start-up costs
100,000	Swope Parkway Health Center, Kansas City, MO -- support of continuity campaign

SPECIALTY MANUFACTURING CO.

Company Headquarters

5858 Centerville Road
St. Paul, MN 55127
Web: http://www.specialtymfgco.com

Company Description

Employees: 140

Boss Foundation

Giving Contact

Dan McKeown, Treasurer
Boss Foundation
5858 Centerville Rd.
St. Paul, MN 55127-6804
Phone: (651)653-0599

Description

EIN: 416038452
Organization Type: Corporate Foundation
Giving Locations: MN
Grant Types: General Support.

Financial Summary

Total Giving: $184,000 (fiscal year ending June 30, 2004); $208,427 (fiscal 2003); $203,360 (fiscal 2001)
Assets: $4,990,133 (fiscal 2004); $4,330,736 (fiscal 2003); $4,505,801 (fiscal 2001)
Gifts Received: $30,000 (fiscal 2004); $30,000 (fiscal 2003); $25,000 (fiscal 2001). Note: In fiscal 2001, 2002, and 2003, contributions were received from Specialty Manufacturing Co. In fiscal 1999 and fiscal 2000, contributions were received from Specialty Manufacturing Co. ($25,000) and William Boss Trust A ($76,164).

Typical Recipients

Arts & Humanities: Arts Associations & Councils, Arts Centers, Arts Festivals, Arts Funds, Arts Institutes, Community Arts, Arts & Humanities-General, Historic Preservation, History & Archaeology, Libraries, Literary Arts, Museums/Galleries, Music, Opera, Public Broadcasting, Theater, Visual Arts
Civic & Public Affairs: Botanical Gardens/Parks,

Clubs, Community Foundations, Native American Affairs, Zoos/Aquariums
Education: Agricultural Education, Arts/Humanities Education, Colleges & Universities, Education Funds, Faculty Development
Health: Emergency/Ambulance Services, Mental Health
Religion: Churches
Science: Science Museums
Social Services: Child Welfare, Community Service Organizations, Family Services, Special Olympics, Substance Abuse

Application Procedures

Initial Contact: Request application guidelines.
Application Requirements: Include a one-page letter stating amount requested, purpose of funds sought, proof of tax-exempt status, and any other support documents.
Deadlines: Proposals received by September 1 will be considered at the annual meeting.

Restrictions

Preference given to organizations furthering or engaged in the performing and fine arts.

Additional Information

Publications: Application Guidelines

Corporate Officials

Bruce A. Lawin: president, chief executive officer B Long Prairie, MN 1934. ED Saint Cloud State College (1958). PRIM CORP EMPL president, chief executive officer: Specialty Manufacturing Co. CORP AFFIL president, director: Sandy Manufacturing Co.; president, director: TMichigan Plastics.
Mark Nosbush: chief financial officer PRIM CORP EMPL chief financial officer: Specialty Manufacturing Co.

Foundation Officials

W. Andrew Boss: president, director
Dan McKeown: treasurer
Heidi McKeown: vice president, secretary, director
Nancy B. Sandberg: chairman, director PRIM CORP EMPL chairman: The Specialty Manufacturing Co.

Grants Analysis

Disclosure Period: fiscal year ending June 30, 2004
Total Grants: $184,000
Number of Grants: 42
Average Grant: $4,381
Highest Grant: $15,000
Lowest Grant: $1,000
Typical Range: $1,000 to $5,000

Recent Grants

Note: Grants derived from fiscal 2004 Form 990.
Library-Related

5,000	Friends of the St. Paul Public Library, St. Paul, MN

General

15,000	St. Paul Rotary Foundation, Roseville, MN
5,000	Children's Home Society of Minnesota, St. Paul, MN
5,000	Children's Theatre Company, Minneapolis, MN
5,000	Como Zoological Society, St. Paul, MN
5,000	COMPAS, St. Paul, MN
5,000	East Side Arts Council, St. Paul, MN
5,000	Grand Excursion, St. Paul, MN
5,000	Hand in Hand, St. Paul, MN
5,000	Joan Mondale Gallery Endowment
5,000	Metropolitan State University Foundation, St. Paul, MN

ROY M. SPEER FOUNDATION

Giving Contact
Richard W. Baker, Trustee
2535 Success Dr.
Odessa, FL 33556
Phone: (727)372-8808

Description
Founded: 1986
EIN: 592785945
Organization Type: Private Foundation
Grant Types: Endowment, General Support, Research.

Financial Summary
Total Giving: $711,300 (fiscal year ending June 30, 2004); $860,300 (fiscal 2001)
Assets: $15,504,672 (fiscal 2004); $18,089,902 (fiscal 2001)

Typical Recipients
Arts & Humanities: Libraries
Civic & Public Affairs: Civic & Public Affairs-General, Zoos/Aquariums
Education: Colleges & Universities, Medical Education, Private Education (Precollege), Religious Education
Health: Cancer, Hospitals, Hospitals (University Affiliated), Single-Disease Health Associations
Religion: Churches, Religion-General, Jewish Causes, Missionary Activities (Domestic), Religious Organizations, Religious Welfare, Synagogues/Temples
Social Services: Emergency Relief, Scouts, Senior Services

Application Procedures
Initial Contact: Foundation requests a written narrative. Include purpose of funds sought.
Deadlines: None.

Foundation Officials
Richard W. Baker: trustee

Grants Analysis
Disclosure Period: fiscal year ending June 30, 2004
Total Grants: $711,300
Number of Grants: 6
Highest Grant: $585,000
Lowest Grant: $10,300
Typical Range: $25,000 to $30,000
Note: Average grant figure excludes two highest grants ($421,300).

Recent Grants
Note: Grants derived from fiscal 2004 Form 990.
General

585,000	Practical Christianity Foundation, Odessa, FL
36,000	First Baptist Church, Elfers, FL
30,000	Memorial Sloan-Kettering Cancer Center, New York, NY
25,000	University of Florida College of Medicine, Gainesville, FL
25,000	University of Florida - Shands Health Care, Gainesville, FL
10,300	Stetson University, DeLand, FL

SPERANDIO FAMILY FOUNDATION

Giving Contact
Jacqueline Sperandio, Vice President
Bessemer Trust Co., Tax Dept.

630 Fifth Ave., 34th Fl.
New York, NY 10111
Phone: (212)708-9216

Description
Founded: 1998
EIN: 161490918
Organization Type: Private Foundation
Grant Types: General Support.

Financial Summary
Total Giving: $85,073 (fiscal year ending August 31, 2003); $56,868 (fiscal 2001)
Giving Analysis: Giving for fiscal 2001 includes: foundation grants to United Way ($11,000)
Assets: $1,783,911 (fiscal 2003); $1,977,427 (fiscal 2001)
Gifts Received: $1,445,040 (fiscal 2001); $525,100 (fiscal 1996). Note: In fiscal 2001, contributions were received from Robert and Jacqueline Sperandio.

Typical Recipients
Arts & Humanities: Libraries, Museums/Galleries, Public Broadcasting
Civic & Public Affairs: Clubs, Civic & Public Affairs-General, Women's Affairs
Education: Colleges & Universities, Education-General, Religious Education, Secondary Education (Private)
Health: Adolescent Health Issues, Alzheimer's Disease, Cancer, Children's Health/Hospitals, Emergency/Ambulance Services, Health-General, Nursing Services, Public Health, Respiratory
International: Foreign Arts Organizations
Religion: Churches
Social Services: At-Risk Youth, Big Brothers/Big Sisters, Domestic Violence, People with Disabilities, United Funds/United Ways, Volunteer Services, YMCA/YWCA/YMHA/YWHA

Application Procedures
Initial Contact: Send a brief letter of inquiry.
Application Requirements: Include purpose of funds sought.
Deadlines: None.

Restrictions
Funds organizations benefiting children and women.

Foundation Officials
Elizabeth F. Sperandio: trustee
Jacqueline Sperandio: vice president
Mark C. Sperandio: trustee
Robert B. Sperandio: president, secretary

Grants Analysis
Disclosure Period: fiscal year ending August 31, 2003
Total Grants: $85,073*
Typical Range: $1,000 to $5,000
*Note: Grant list incomplete for 2003.

Recent Grants
Note: Grants derived from 2003 Form 990.
Library-Related

5,500	Sno - Isle Regional Library, Marysville, WA
2,500	Friends of the Everett Public Library, Everett, WA

General

3,600	Stratford Festival of Canada, Stratford, ON Canada
3,000	Roswell Park Alliance Foundation, Buffalo, NY
2,000	Ontario ARC, Canandaigua, NY
1,500	Big Brothers/Big Sisters, Rochester, NY
1,000	Aquinas Institute, Rochester, NY
1,000	Cocoon House, Everett, WA
1,000	Women's Foundation of Genesee Valley, Rochester, NY
1,000	WXXI, Rochester, NY

BELLA SPEWACK ARTICLE 5TH TRUST

Giving Contact
Arthur Elias, Contact
Bank of New York
One Wall St., 28th Fl.
New York, NY 10286
Phone: (212)635-1520

Alternate Contact
98 Riverside Drive
New York, NY 10024

Description
Founded: 1992
EIN: 133669246
Organization Type: Private Foundation
Giving Locations: NY
Grant Types: General Support.

Financial Summary
Total Giving: $60,000 (fiscal year ending June 30, 2004); $95,000 (fiscal 2001)
Assets: $1,408,899 (fiscal 2004); $1,744,522 (fiscal 2001)
Gifts Received: $67,544 (fiscal 2004). Note: In fiscal 2004, contributions were received from the estate of Bella Spewac.

Typical Recipients
Arts & Humanities: Arts Funds, Libraries, Music, Performing Arts, Theater
Civic & Public Affairs: Civil Rights, Civic & Public Affairs-General
Education: Colleges & Universities, Preschool Education
Health: Emergency/Ambulance Services, Single-Disease Health Associations
International: Health Care/Hospitals, Missionary/Religious Activities
Religion: Jewish Causes, Religious Welfare
Social Services: Child Welfare, Shelters/Homelessness

Application Procedures
Initial Contact: Send a brief letter of inquiry.
Deadlines: None.

Additional Information
Trust(s): Bank NY

Foundation Officials
Arthur Elias: trustee
Lois Elias: trustee

Grants Analysis
Disclosure Period: fiscal year ending June 30, 2004
Total Grants: $60,000
Number of Grants: 9
Average Grant: $1,000*
Highest Grant: $52,000
Lowest Grant: $500
Typical Range: $500 to $3,000
*Note: Average grant figure excludes highest grant.

Recent Grants
Note: Grants derived from fiscal 2001 Form 990.
Library-Related

2,000	Columbia University Rare Book and Manuscript Library, New York, NY
1,000	New York Public Library, New York, NY

General

60,000	Dramatists Guild Fund, New York, NY
10,000	Friends of Israel Sport Center for the Disabled, New York, NY
3,000	Actors Fund of America, New York, NY
3,000	Interfaith Assembly of Homeless and Housing, New York, NY

3,000	United Jewish Appeal Federation, New York, NY
2,500	Children's Defense Fund, Washington, DC
2,000	Salvation Army, Abilene, TX
1,500	Dorot, New York, NY
1,500	National Council of Jewish Women, New York, NY
1,500	New York Civil Liberties Union, New York, NY

ALEXANDER C. AND TILLIE S. SPEYER FOUNDATION

Giving Contact
Alexander C. Speyer, Jr., Trustee
1202 Benedum Trees Bldg.
Pittsburgh, PA 15222
Phone: (412)281-7225

Description
Founded: 1962
EIN: 256051650
Organization Type: Private Foundation
Giving Locations: DC; MD; MA; NY; PA; VA; WY
Grant Types: General Support.

Donor Information
Founder: members of the Speyer family

Financial Summary
Total Giving: $262,362 (2003); $320,696 (2001).
Note: 1997 Giving includes United Way ($10,000).
Giving Analysis: Giving for 2003 includes: foundation grants to United Way ($16,000); 2001: foundation grants to United Way ($17,000)
Assets: $6,408,199 (2003); $5,869,718 (2001)
Gifts Received: $124,625 (1999); $200,028 (1996).
Note: In 1999, contributions were received from A.C. Speyer, Jr. ($54,000) and Darthea Speyer ($70,625). In 1996, contributions were received from Alexander C. Speyer, Jr. ($101,313) and Darthea Speyer ($98,715).

Typical Recipients
Arts & Humanities: Arts Associations & Councils, Arts Centers, Arts Festivals, Arts Institutes, Community Arts, Ethnic & Folk Arts, Arts & Humanities-General, Libraries, Literary Arts, Museums/Galleries, Music, Public Broadcasting, Visual Arts
Civic & Public Affairs: Botanical Gardens/Parks, Civil Rights, Community Foundations, Civic & Public Affairs-General, Nonprofit Management
Education: Arts/Humanities Education, Colleges & Universities, Education Funds, Education Reform, Education-General, International Exchange, Preschool Education, Private Education (Precollege), Public Education (Precollege), Science/Mathematics Education, Secondary Education (Private)
Environment: Air/Water Quality, Environment-General, Resource Conservation
Health: Cancer, Emergency/Ambulance Services, Eyes/Blindness, Hospitals, Public Health
International: Health Care/Hospitals, International Relations, Missionary/Religious Activities
Religion: Churches, Jewish Causes, Religious Organizations, Religious Welfare, Seminaries, Synagogues/Temples
Science: Scientific Centers & Institutes
Social Services: Community Service Organizations, Crime Prevention, Delinquency & Criminal Rehabilitation, Family Planning, Food/Clothing Distribution, Homes, People with Disabilities, United Funds/United Ways

Application Procedures
Initial Contact: The foundation has no formal grant application procedure or application form.
Deadlines: None.

Foundation Officials
Darthea Speyer: trustee

Grants Analysis
Disclosure Period: calendar year ending 2003
Total Grants: $246,362*
Number of Grants: 78
Average Grant: $2,831*
Highest Grant: $28,398
Lowest Grant: $50
Typical Range: $1,000 to $5,000
*Note: Giving excludes United Way. Average grant figure excludes highest grant.

Recent Grants
Note: Grants derived from 2001 Form 990.
General

23,125	Carnegie Museum of Art, Pittsburgh, PA
22,000	Carnegie Mellon University, Pittsburgh, PA
20,000	Western Pennsylvania Conservancy, Mill Run, PA
18,000	New York Studio School of Drawing and Painting, New York, NY
17,000	United Way of Southwestern Pennsylvania, Pittsburgh, PA
15,806	Rodef Shalom Congregation, Pittsburgh, PA
15,000	New York Times Neediest Cases, New York, NY
15,000	United Jewish Federation, Pittsburgh, PA
13,000	Byrd Hoffman Foundation, New York, NY
11,500	Sidwell Friends School, Washington, DC

SETH SPRAGUE EDUCATIONAL AND CHARITABLE FOUNDATION

Giving Contact
Linda R. Franciscovich, Managing Director
U.S. Trust Co.
114 W. 47th Street
New York, NY 10036
Phone: (212)852-1000
Fax: (212)852-3377

Alternate Contact
Phone: (212)852-3629

Description
Founded: 1939
EIN: 136071886
Organization Type: General Purpose Foundation
Giving Locations: MA; NY: nationally.
Grant Types: General Support, Operating Expenses, Project, Research, Seed Money.

Donor Information
Founder: Established in 1939 by Seth Sprague, the Sprague Educational and Charitable Foundation is administered by its trustees and the United States Trust Company of New York. All of the trustees were either associates of Mr. Sprague or familiar with his philanthropic pursuits.
Seth Sprague was a graduate of Norwich Academy and a lifetime employee of F. H. Foster and Company, a Boston cotton processing corporation of which he eventually became president. Mr. Sprague died in 1941.

Financial Summary
Total Giving: $2,500,000 (2003); $2,390,571 (2002); $3,280,000 (2001);
Assets: $58,147,019 (2003); $54,663,473 (2002); $63,403,075 (2001)

Typical Recipients
Arts & Humanities: Arts Associations & Councils, Arts Centers, Arts Funds, Arts Institutes, Ballet, Dance, Ethnic & Folk Arts, Arts & Humanities-General, Historic Preservation, History & Archaeology, Libraries, Literary Arts, Museums/Galleries, Music, Opera, Performing Arts, Public Broadcasting, Theater
Civic & Public Affairs: Botanical Gardens/Parks, Business/Free Enterprise, Clubs, Community Foundations, Economic Development, Employment/Job Training, Ethnic Organizations, Civic & Public Affairs-General, Law & Justice, Parades/Festivals, Philanthropic Organizations, Professional & Trade Associations, Public Policy, Urban & Community Affairs, Women's Affairs, Zoos/Aquariums
Education: Arts/Humanities Education, Colleges & Universities, Community & Junior Colleges, Education Associations, Education Funds, Education-General, International Studies, Journalism/Media Education, Legal Education, Medical Education, Minority Education, Private Education (Precollege), Public Education (Precollege), Religious Education, Social Sciences Education, Special Education, Student Aid, Vocational & Technical Education
Environment: Air/Water Quality, Environment-General, Resource Conservation
Health: AIDS/HIV, Arthritis, Cancer, Children's Health/Hospitals, Clinics/Medical Centers, Emergency/Ambulance Services, Health-General, Geriatric Health, Health Funds, Health Organizations, Hospices, Hospitals, Medical Rehabilitation, Medical Research, Medical Training, Mental Health, Nursing Services, Single-Disease Health Associations
International: International Relations
Religion: Churches, Religious Welfare, Seminaries, Social/Policy Issues
Science: Science Museums, Scientific Centers & Institutes, Scientific Labs
Social Services: Animal Protection, At-Risk Youth, Big Brothers/Big Sisters, Camps, Child Welfare, Community Centers, Community Service Organizations, Counseling, Crime Prevention, Delinquency & Criminal Rehabilitation, Domestic Violence, Emergency Relief, Family Planning, Family Services, People with Disabilities, Recreation & Athletics, Senior Services, Shelters/Homelessness, Substance Abuse, Volunteer Services, Youth Organizations

Application Procedures
Initial Contact: Initial contact should be a written request.
Application Requirements: Applications should include a summary (two pages), budget, audited financial statement, and an IRS determination letter.
Deadlines: April 15.
Review Process: The board of directors meets in March, June, September and November.

Restrictions
The foundation does not give grants for research or capital expenditures. In addition, the foundation does not make grants to individuals or to organizations located outside the United States.

Additional Information
Publications: Guidelines
Trust(s): US Trust Co. of New York

Foundation Officials
Patricia Dunnington: trustee
Arline Ripley Greenleaf: trustee
Jacqueline DeNeuflize Simpkins: trustee CLUB AFFIL Chilton Club; Colony Club.

Grants Analysis

Disclosure Period: calendar year ending 2003
Total Grants: $2,500,000
Number of Grants: 290
Average Grant: $8,621
Highest Grant: $50,000
Lowest Grant: $500
Typical Range: $1,000 to $10,000

Recent Grants

Note: Grants derived from 2002 Form 990.
Library-Related
2,500,000 Sturgis Library, Barnstable, MA
2,500,000 Sturgis Library, Barnstable, MA
General
5,000,000 New York Hospital Cornell Medical Center Fund Inc., New York, NY
4,500,000 Woodberry Forest School, Woodberry Forest, VA
4,500,000 Woodberry Forest School, Woodberry Forest, VA
4,500,000 Woodberry Forest School, Woodberry Forest, VA
3,500,000 Battery Conservancy Inc., New York, NY
3,500,000 Memorial Sloan-Kettering, New York, NY
3,000,000 Conservancy for Historic Battery Park Inc., New York, NY
3,000,000 Riley School Inc., Glen Cove, ME
2,600,000 Montpelier Foundation, Montpelier Station, VA
2,500,000 Alfred University, Alfred, NY

SPRINGS FOUNDATION, INC.

Giving Contact

Angela McRae, Executive Director
1826 Second Baxter Crossing
Ft. Mill, SC 29708
Phone: (803)548-2002
Fax: (803)548-1797

Description

Founded: 1968
EIN: 570426344
Organization Type: Private Foundation
Former Name: Spring/Close Foundation.
Giving Locations: NC; SC: Chester Township, Fort Mill Township, Lancaster County
Grant Types: Capital, Conference/Seminar, General Support, Loan, Professorship, Seed Money.

Donor Information

Founder: Established in 1968 by members of the Springs and Close families.

Financial Summary

Total Giving: $2,363,006 (2003); $3,321,348 (2002 approx); $1,129,274 (2001)
Giving Analysis: Giving for 2003 includes: foundation grants to United Way ($50,000); foundation scholarships ($200,496); 2001: foundation scholarships ($1,900)
Assets: $42,884,019 (2003); $3,000,000 (2002 approx); $14,286,512 (2001)
Gifts Received: $1,500 (2003); $432,053 (1998); $2,126,350 (1997). Note: In 1998, contributions were received from Patricia Close ($255,123), Leroy S. Close ($101,113), and Frances A. Close ($75,067). In 1997, the foundation received 7 donations from individuals, including a $2,025,050 gift from Anne S. Close.

Typical Recipients

Arts & Humanities: Art History, Arts Associations & Councils, Film & Video, Historic Preservation, History & Archaeology, Libraries, Museums/Galleries, Performing Arts, Public Broadcasting, Theater
Civic & Public Affairs: Economic Development, Civic & Public Affairs-General, Housing, Law & Justice, Nonprofit Management, Philanthropic Organizations, Public Policy, Safety, Urban & Community Affairs
Education: Arts/Humanities Education, Business Education, Business-School Partnerships, Colleges & Universities, Community & Junior Colleges, Education Associations, Elementary Education (Private), Elementary Education (Public), Environmental Education, Education-General, Legal Education, Minority Education, Preschool Education, Private Education (Precollege), Public Education (Precollege), Science/Mathematics Education, Vocational & Technical Education
Environment: Environment-General, Resource Conservation
Health: AIDS/HIV, Alzheimer's Disease, Clinics/Medical Centers, Diabetes, Emergency/Ambulance Services, Health-General, Hospices, Hospitals, Mental Health, Prenatal Health Issues
Religion: Churches, Ministries
Science: Scientific Centers & Institutes, Scientific Organizations
Social Services: Animal Protection, At-Risk Youth, Child Welfare, Community Centers, Community Service Organizations, Day Care, Emergency Relief, Food/Clothing Distribution, People with Disabilities, Recreation & Athletics, Scouts, Social Services-General, Substance Abuse, United Funds/United Ways, Youth Organizations

Application Procedures

Initial Contact: Send cover letter and full proposal.
Application Requirements: Include a description of organization, amount requested, purpose of funds sought, recently audited financial statement, and proof of tax-exempt status.
Deadlines: March 15 and November 1.
Review Process: The board meets twice per year. The fall meeting is held on the Wednesday prior to Thanksgiving.

Additional Information

The foundation was formerly known as the Close Foundation.
Publications: Annual Report

Foundation Officials

Crandall C. Bowles: director
James Bradley: director CORP AFFIL director: Springs Co.
Charles Alan Bundy: director B Cheraw, SC 1930. ED Wofford College BA (1951). NONPR AFFIL member: Lancaster County Chamber of Commerce; director: Springs Memorial Hospital. CLUB AFFIL Rotary Club.
Anne Springs Close: chairman, president, director CORP AFFIL director: Springs Co. Investment Division; director: Square Records; director: Springs Co.; director: America Insurance Agency; director: Catawba Insurance Agency.
Derick Springsteen Close: director CORP AFFIL director: Springs Co. Investment Division; director, international sales: Springs Industries Inc.; director: Springs Co.; director: Catawba Insurance Agency; director: South E Huffman Corp.; director: America Insurance Agency.
Elliott Springs Close: director CORP AFFIL director: Springs Co.; director: Springs Co. Investment Division; director: Kanawha Insurance Co. Inc.; director: America Insurance Agency; director: Catawba Insurance Agency.
Frances A. Close: director
Hugh William Close, Jr.: president, director
Katherine Anne Close, MD: director
Leroy Springs Close: director B 1950. PRIM CORP EMPL president, chief executive officer: Sandlapper Fabrics. CORP AFFIL director: Springs Co. Investment Division; director: Springs Industries Inc.; director: Springs Co.; director: America Insurance Agency;

director: Catawba Insurance Agency.
Dehler Hart: director
Robert Holcombe, Jr.: director
Angela McCrae: executive director
William G. Taylor: director

Grants Analysis

Disclosure Period: calendar year ending 2003
Total Grants: $2,112,510*
Number of Grants: 79
Average Grant: $20,353*
Highest Grant: $525,000
Lowest Grant: $500
Typical Range: $5,000 to $40,000
***Note:** Giving excludes scholarships; United Way. Average grant figure excludes highest grant.

Recent Grants

Note: Grants derived from 2003 Form 990.
General
75,000 Keystone -- towards building expansion
50,000 Saluda Center, Saluda, SC -- for new facilities
50,000 SC Center for Grassroots & Nonprofit Leadership, Clemson, SC

SPRINGS FOUNDATION, INC.

Giving Contact

Angela McCrae, Jr., Executive Director
1826 Second Baxter Crossing
Ft. Mill, SC 29708
Phone: (803)548-2002
Fax: (803)548-1797

Description

Founded: 1942
EIN: 570426344
Organization Type: General Purpose Foundation
Giving Locations: SC: Chester Township, Fort Mill Township, Lancaster County
Grant Types: Capital, Challenge, General Support, Matching, Operating Expenses, Seed Money.

Donor Information

Founder: Colonel Elliott White Springs (1896-1959) was the founder of Springs Industries, one of the largest textile manufacturers in the United States. He established the foundation, formerly called the Elliott White Springs Foundation, in 1942. His wife, Frances Ley Springs, continued her husband's philanthropic interests through her work at the foundation. "Her estate provided the means for expanded philanthropic work over a wider geographic area. Those funds began what is now called the Close Foundation."

Financial Summary

Total Giving: $1,472,090 (2001)
Assets: $35,488,538 (2001)
Gifts Received: $700 (2000); $750 (1998); $1,200 (1997). Note: In 1997 and 2000, contributions were received from members of the Close family and Dehler Hart.

Typical Recipients

Arts & Humanities: Arts Associations & Councils, Community Arts, Libraries, Music, Theater
Civic & Public Affairs: Botanical Gardens/Parks, Clubs, Economic Development, Employment/Job Training, Civic & Public Affairs-General, Housing, Law & Justice, Municipalities/Towns, Safety, Urban & Community Affairs
Education: Arts/Humanities Education, Business-School Partnerships, Colleges & Universities, Education Funds, Education Reform, Elementary Education (Public), Medical Education, Public Education (Pre-

college), Secondary Education (Public), Student Aid
Environment: Environment-General
Health: AIDS/HIV, Cancer, Clinics/Medical Centers, Emergency/Ambulance Services, Health Organizations, Hospices, Hospitals, Mental Health, Nutrition, Prenatal Health Issues
Religion: Churches, Religion-General, Ministries, Religious Organizations, Religious Welfare
Science: Science-General
Social Services: Animal Protection, Camps, Child Welfare, Community Service Organizations, Counseling, Crime Prevention, Delinquency & Criminal Rehabilitation, Emergency Relief, Family Services, Recreation & Athletics, Scouts, Senior Services, Social Services-General, Substance Abuse, United Funds/United Ways, YMCA/YWCA/YMHA/YWHA, Youth Organizations

Application Procedures

Initial Contact: Initial contact should be in the form of a brief letter.
Application Requirements: Letters should provide a brief statement of need; a copy of tax-exempt letter should accompany initial proposal.
Deadlines: Proposals are due by March 1 and November 1.
Review Process: The president researches the proposal for merit, eligibility, and priority status. Recommendations are then presented to the board for approval. The board meets in April and November.

Restrictions

Grants are not made to individuals.

Additional Information

The Spring Foundation manages an interest-free student loan program which is available to students who reside in or whose parents work in Lancaster County, Chester Township or Fort Mill Township in South Carolina and who plan to attend a four-year accredited college in South Carolina. The Springs Foundation is also affiliated with the Close Foundation located in Lancaster, SC.
Publications: Annual Report; Guidelines; Application Form

Foundation Officials

Crandall C. Bowles: director
Charles Alan Bundy: director B Cheraw, SC 1930. ED Wofford College BA (1951). NONPR AFFIL member: Lancaster County Chamber of Commerce; director: Springs Memorial Hospital. CLUB AFFIL Rotary Club.
Anne Springs Close: donor, chairwoman, director CORP AFFIL director: Springs Co. Investment Division; director: Square Records; director: Springs Co.; director: America Insurance Agency; director: Catawba Insurance Agency.
Derick Springsteen Close: director CORP AFFIL director: Springs Co. Investment Division; director, international sales: Springs Industries Inc.; director: Springs Co.; director: Catawba Insurance Agency; director: South E Huffman Corp.; director: America Insurance Agency.
Elliott Springs Close: director CORP AFFIL director: Springs Co.; director: Springs Co. Investment Division; director: Kanawha Insurance Co. Inc.; director: America Insurance Agency; director: Catawba Insurance Agency.
Hugh William Close, Jr.: president, director
Katherine Anne Close, MD: director
Leroy Springs Close: director B 1950. PRIM CORP EMPL president, chief executive officer: Sandlapper Fabrics. CORP AFFIL director: Springs Co. Investment Division; director: Springs Industries Inc.; director: Springs Co.; director: America Insurance Agency; director: Catawba Insurance Agency.
Pat Close: director
Dehler Hart: director
James H. Hodges: secretary, treasurer, director PRIM CORP EMPL secretary, general counsel: Springs Co. NONPR AFFIL member: Phi Beta

Kappa.
Robert L. Holcombe, Jr.: director
William G. Taylor: director B 1956. ED Washington & Lee University BA (1978); Wake Forest University MBA (1980). PRIM CORP EMPL president, treasurer, director: Springs Co. CORP AFFIL director: Kanawha Insurance Co. Inc.; chairman: Springland Inc.

Grants Analysis

Disclosure Period: calendar year ending 2001
Total Grants: $1,047,262*
Number of Grants: 60
Average Grant: $8,852*
Highest Grant: $525,000
Lowest Grant: $1,000
Typical Range: $1,000 to $25,000
*Note: Giving excludes United Way and scholarship. Average grant excludes highest grant.

Recent Grants

Note: Grants derived from 2002 Form 990.
General

525,000	Joint Recreation Commission for Lancaster County, Lancaster, SC -- for operating support
125,000	Chester County YMCA, Chester, SC -- for indoor pool
114,500	United Way Fund of Lancaster, Lancaster, SC
100,000	Joint Recreation Commission for Lancaster County, Lancaster, SC -- for swimming pool
58,900	Chester County Hospital, Chester, SC
52,000	Chester County Emergency Medical Services, Chester, SC
50,000	Tree Tops Community Camp, Lancaster, SC
45,000	King of Kings Ministries, Lancaster, SC -- for Joshua House renovations
33,000	Christian Services of Lancaster County, Lancaster, SC -- for Adopt a Child
29,752	Lancaster County School District, Lancaster, SC

SPX CORP.

Company Headquarters

13515 Ballantyne Corporate Pl.
Charlotte, NC 28277
Web: http://www.spx.com

Company Description

Ticker: SPW
Exchange: NYSE
Former Name: Sealed Power Corp.
Revenue: US$5.795 billion (2004)
Profit: (US$17.1 million) (2004)
Employees: 22200 (2003)
Fortune Rank: 345, per FORTUNE Magazine's list of 500 Largest U.S. Corporations (2004).
SIC(s): 3423 Hand & Edge Tools Nec, 3429 Hardware Nec, 3491 Industrial Valves, 3544 Special Dies, Tools, Jigs & Fixtures.

Operating Locations

SPX Corp. (GA; IL--Des Plaines; IN--Auburn, Rochester; MI--Alma, Dowagiac, Jackson, Muskegon, St. Johns, Warren, Whitehall, Zeeland; MS; OH--Montpelier; PA)

SPX Foundation

Giving Contact

Tina Betlejewski, President
700 Terrace Point Drive
Muskegon, MI 49443-3301

Phone: (231)724-5121
Fax: (231)724-5720

Description

Founded: 1984
EIN: 386058308
Organization Type: Corporate Foundation
Giving Locations: primarily in plant communities.
Grant Types: Capital, Employee Matching Gifts, General Support.

Donor Information

Founder: SPX Corp.

Financial Summary

Total Giving: $978,117 (2002); $512,815 (2001)
Giving Analysis: Giving for 2001 includes: foundation grants to United Way ($32,148); foundation matching gifts ($312,783)
Assets: $977,603 (2002); $1,560,588 (2001)
Gifts Received: $373,800 (2002); $2,191,250 (2001); $781,632 (1994). Note: In 2002, contributions were received from O-Z Gedney Company Inc. In 2001, contributions were received from SPX Corp. ($300,000) and EGS Electrical Group ($1,891,250). In 1994, contributions of $780,332 were received from SPX Corp., and $1,300 received from First Chicago.

Typical Recipients

Arts & Humanities: Arts Associations & Councils, Arts Centers, Arts Festivals, Arts & Humanities-General, Libraries, Museums/Galleries, Music, Opera, Performing Arts, Public Broadcasting, Theater
Civic & Public Affairs: Botanical Gardens/Parks, Business/Free Enterprise, Chambers of Commerce, Clubs, Community Foundations, Economic Development, Economic Policy, Civic & Public Affairs-General, Housing, Municipalities/Towns, Nonprofit Management, Parades/Festivals, Professional & Trade Associations, Safety, Urban & Community Affairs, Women's Affairs
Education: Afterschool/Enrichment Programs, Arts/Humanities Education, Business Education, Colleges & Universities, Community & Junior Colleges, Education Funds, Engineering/Technological Education, Education-General, Minority Education, Private Education (Precollege), Public Education (Precollege), Science/Mathematics Education
Environment: Environment-General
Health: Cancer, Children's Health/Hospitals, Diabetes, Emergency/Ambulance Services, Eyes/Blindness, Health-General, Health Organizations, Heart, Hospitals, Multiple Sclerosis, Single-Disease Health Associations
Religion: Churches, Religion-General, Ministries, Religious Organizations, Religious Welfare, Seminaries
Science: Scientific Centers & Institutes, Scientific Organizations
Social Services: Animal Protection, Child Abuse, Child Welfare, Community Service Organizations, Crime Prevention, Emergency Relief, Family Planning, Family Services, Food/Clothing Distribution, People with Disabilities, Recreation & Athletics, Scouts, Social Services-General, Special Olympics, Substance Abuse, United Funds/United Ways, Volunteer Services, YMCA/YWCA/YMHA/YWHA, Youth Organizations

Application Procedures

Initial Contact: Send a letter of inquiry.
Application Requirements: Include a description of organization, amount requested, purpose of funds sought, and proof of tax-exempt status.
Deadlines: None.

Corporate Officials

John B. Blystone: chairman, president, chief executive officer, director B Erie, PA 1953. ED University of Pittsburgh BS (1975). PRIM CORP EMPL chairman, president, chief executive officer, director: SPX Corp. CORP AFFIL director: Worthington Indiana Inc.

Patrick J. O'Leary: vice president finance, treasurer, chief financial officer PRIM CORP EMPL vice president finance, treasurer, chief financial officer: SPX Corp.

Foundation Officials

John B. Blystone: trustee (see above)
Robert B. Foreman: vice president, trustee
Christopher J. Kearney: trustee ED DePaul University; Notre Dame College. PRIM CORP EMPL vice president, secretary, general counsel: SPX Corp.
Patrick J. O'Leary: secretary, treasurer, trustee (see above)

Grants Analysis

Disclosure Period: calendar year ending 2002
Total Grants: $342,000*
Number of Grants: 12
Average Grant: $22,000*
Highest Grant: $100,000
Lowest Grant: $2,500
Typical Range: $20,000 to $50,000
*Note: Giving excludes matching gifts; United Way. Average grant figure excludes highest grant.

Recent Grants

Note: Grants derived from 2003 Form 990.
General

100,000	Advantage Carolina, Charlotte, NC
89,320	Champions for Education, Charlotte, NC
36,245	United Way, Charlotte, NC
33,333	Charlotte Country Day School, Charlotte, NC
32,000	Family Center, Bristol, CT
25,000	Arts and Science Council, Charlotte, NC
25,000	Charlotte Symphony, Charlotte, NC
25,000	Grand Valley State University, Allendale, MI
20,000	Charlotte Regional Partnership, Charlotte, NC
20,000	Levine Museum, Charlotte, NC

SQUARE D CO.

Company Headquarters

Palatine, IL
Web: http://www.squared.com

Company Description

Revenue: US$1.2 billion (2001)
Employees: 17000 (2001)
SIC(s): 3497 Metal Foil & Leaf, 3499 Fabricated Metal Products Nec, 3612 Transformers Except Electronic, 3613 Switchgear & Switchboard Apparatus.
Parent Company: Schneider S.A., 43-45 Blvd. Franklin-Roosevelt, Rueil-Malmaison, France

Operating Locations

Electrical Distribution Business (TN--Smyrna); Schneider Automation (MA--North Andover); Square D Automation Products (WI--Milwaukee); Square D Co. (AL--Clayton, Leeds; CA--Bakersfield, Costa Mesa; FL--Clearwater; GA--Atlanta, Norcross; IL--Niles, Palatine, Schiller Park; IN--Huntington, Peru; IA--Cedar Rapids; KY--Florence, Lexington; MO--Columbia; NE--Lincoln; NJ--Secaucus; NC--Asheville, Knightdale, Monroe, Raleigh; OH--Middletown, Oxford; PA--Harrisburg; SC--Columbia, Seneca; TN--Memphis, Nashville, Smyrna; TX--Bedford, Dallas, Fort Worth, Mesquite; WA--Mercer Island; WI--Milwaukee, Oshkosh); Square D Co.-Assembly Operations (FL--Clearwater); Square D Co.-Central Distribution Center (TN--Memphis); Square D Co.-Control Products (NC--Knightdale); Square D Co.-Pacifico (CA--San Ysidro); Square D Co.-Transformer Business Division (WI--Milwaukee);

Square D Middletown Plant (OH--Middletown); Square D Oxford Plant (OH--Oxford); Square D Seneca Plant (SC--Seneca)

Nonmonetary Support

Type: Donated Equipment
Contact: Tammy Sittinger, Foundation Coordinator

Square D Foundation

Giving Contact

Harry Wilson, Secretary
Square D Foundation
1415 South Roselle Road
Palatine, IL 60067
Phone: (847)397-2600
Fax: (847)397-2804

Description

EIN: 366054195
Organization Type: Corporate Foundation
Giving Locations: manufacturing facility communities.
Grant Types: Capital, Employee Matching Gifts, Operating Expenses, Project.

Financial Summary

Total Giving: $1,542,609 (2003); $1,974,732 (2002); $1,946,280 (2001). Note: Contributes through foundation only.
Giving Analysis: Giving for 2001 includes: foundation grants to United Way ($334,868); foundation matching gifts ($340,927); foundation ($1,270,485)
Assets: $112,579 (2003); $149,883 (2002); $122,098 (2001)
Gifts Received: $1,566,714 (2003); $1,956,994 (2002); $2,108,060 (2001). Note: Foundation receives contributions from the Square D Company.

Typical Recipients

Arts & Humanities: Arts Associations & Councils, Arts Centers, Arts Festivals, Arts Funds, Arts Institutes, Dance, Libraries, Museums/Galleries, Music, Opera, Public Broadcasting, Theater
Civic & Public Affairs: Botanical Gardens/Parks, Business/Free Enterprise, Civic & Public Affairs-General, Legal Aid, Minority Business, Parades/Festivals, Philanthropic Organizations, Rural Affairs, Safety, Urban & Community Affairs
Education: Agricultural Education, Arts/Humanities Education, Business Education, Colleges & Universities, Community & Junior Colleges, Economic Education, Education Funds, Elementary Education (Public), Engineering/Technological Education, Education-General, Minority Education, Public Education (Precollege), Student Aid, Vocational & Technical Education
Health: Cancer, Children's Health/Hospitals, Clinics/Medical Centers, Emergency/Ambulance Services, Health Funds, Hospitals, Long-Term Care, Medical Research, Mental Health, Single-Disease Health Associations
Religion: Religion-General
Science: Science-General, Science Museums
Social Services: At-Risk Youth, Child Welfare, Community Centers, Community Service Organizations, Emergency Relief, Family Services, Food/Clothing Distribution, Homes, People with Disabilities, Recreation & Athletics, Scouts, Senior Services, Shelters/Homelessness, United Funds/United Ways, YMCA/YWCA/YMHA/YWHA, Youth Organizations

Application Procedures

Initial Contact: Submit a written request.
Application Requirements: Include a short cover letter or proposal describing the organization, the need for funds, and plans for use of the funds; amount requested and evaluation plans; an operating budget for the current year, showing breakdown of expenses and sources of income; a list of the board's

members; a list of corporate and foundation contributors in the last year; proof of tax-exempt status; and any additional information pertinent to the proposal.
Deadlines: Submit proposals to local Square D facilities/plants between June and August for funding during the next calendar year.
Evaluative Criteria: The organization must provide a general public service and be supported by the public. Grant should be for non-controversial purposes. Effective management, adequate budgetary controls, and proof of an annual audit are required.
Decision Notification: Contributions budget is established in the fourth quarter for the following year.

Restrictions

Does not make contributions to religious organizations (except where support is used for nondenominational social service); political groups and organizations; labor unions and organizations; organizations making requests by telephone; organizations listed by the U.S. Attorney General as subversive or front organizations; or individuals.
Since foundation supports United Way in corporate communities, donations normally are not made to organizations receiving support through United Way.

Corporate Officials

Walter W. Kurczewski: vice president, secretary, general counsel B 1943. ED University of Illinois AB (1965); University of Michigan JD (1968). PRIM CORP EMPL vice president, secretary, general counsel: Square D Co.
Frank P. Sullivan: vice president sales & marketing B 1953. ED Harvard University BA (1974); University of Chicago MBA (1980). PRIM CORP EMPL vice president sales & marketing: Square D Co.

Foundation Officials

D. Buchanan: vice president, director
M. F. Cox: vice president, director
C. Curtis: vice president, director
R. P. Fiorani: vice president, director
P. Gann: vice president
A. Huntington: vice president, director
H. Japlon: president, director
Walter W. Kurczewski: president, director (see above)
Dick O'Shanna: treasurer, vice president, director
C. Richardson: vice president
Tammy Sittinger: coord
Frank P. Sullivan: vice president, director (see above)
James R. White: secretary, director
Jo Ellyn Willis: vice president, director
H. Wilson: secretary, treasurer

Grants Analysis

Disclosure Period: calendar year ending 2003
Total Grants: $1,524,609*
Number of Grants: 265 (approx)
Average Grant: $5,753
Highest Grant: $135,000 (approx)
Typical Range: $1,000 to $6,000
*Note: A more recent grants list was unavailable.

Recent Grants

Note: Grants derived from 2001 Form 990.
General

112,875	National Merit Scholarship Corporation, Evanston, IL
100,000	NESC
75,000	Independent Electrical Contractors Foundation (IEC), Alexandria, VA
75,000	Independent Electrical Contractors Foundation (IEC), Alexandria, VA
54,332	United Way Triangle Area, Raleigh, NC
51,649	United Way of Asheville and Buncombe County, Asheville, NC
50,000	Clemson University Foundation, Clemson, SC
40,000	Children's Harbor, Birmingham, AL
40,000	Iowa State University, Ames, IA

40,000   University of Chicago, Chicago, IL

DONALD B. AND DOROTHY L. STABLER FOUNDATION

Giving Contact
William J. King, Chairman
M & T Investment Group
213 Market St.
Harrisburg, PA 17101
Phone: (717)255-2045

Description
Founded: 1966
EIN: 236422944
Organization Type: Private Foundation
Giving Locations: PA
Grant Types: Capital, Endowment, General Support, Multiyear/Continuing Support, Operating Expenses, Professorship, Scholarship.

Donor Information
Founder: Stabler Companies

Financial Summary
Total Giving: $751,967 (2003); $673,000 (2001)
Giving Analysis: Giving for 2003 includes: foundation grants to United Way ($20,000); 2001: foundation grants to United Way ($20,000)
Assets: $15,422,799 (2003); $14,739,655 (2001)
Gifts Received: $402,250 (2003); $102,085 (2001); $51,500 (2000). Note: In 2003, contributions were received from Dorothy L. Stabler. In 2001, contributions were received from Work Area Protection Corp., Eastern Industries, Inc., Protection Service, Inc., Stabler Development Co. and Miscellaneous. In 2000, contributions were received from Work Area Protection Corp ($25,000) and Eastern Industries ($25,000), and miscellaneous support of $1,500. In 1999, contributions were received from Work AWork Area Protection Corprea Protection Corp ($303,000), Center Valley Club, Inc. ($21,000), Elco-Hausman Construction Corp ($3,000), Eastern Industries, Inc. ($539,000), Precision Solar Control ($65,000), Protection Services ($102,000), Stabler Development Company ($22,000), and miscellaneous support (less than $5,000).

Typical Recipients
Arts & Humanities: Libraries, Music, Performing Arts, Public Broadcasting
Civic & Public Affairs: Clubs, Civic & Public Affairs-General, Housing
Education: Colleges & Universities, Community & Junior Colleges, Education Funds, Education Reform, Faculty Development, Legal Education, Medical Education, Private Education (Precollege), Public Education (Precollege), Student Aid
Health: Alzheimer's Disease, Clinics/Medical Centers, Emergency/Ambulance Services, Heart, Hospices, Hospitals, Medical Research, Mental Health, Prenatal Health Issues, Public Health
Religion: Churches, Dioceses, Religious Organizations, Religious Welfare
Social Services: Child Welfare, Community Service Organizations, Family Services, Food/Clothing Distribution, People with Disabilities, Scouts, Senior Services, Substance Abuse, United Funds/United Ways, Volunteer Services, YMCA/YWCA/YMHA/YWHA, Youth Organizations

Application Procedures
Initial Contact: Send a brief letter of inquiry.
Application Requirements: Describe program or project, and include purpose of funds sought and re-

cently audited financial statement.
Deadlines: None.

Foundation Officials
Cyril C. Dunmire, Jr.: director PRIM CORP EMPL chairman, president, chief executive officer, treasurer: Stabler Companies.
William Joseph King: chairman B Philadelphia, PA 1929. ED University of Pennsylvania Wharton School (1954); LaSalle University MBA (1979). PRIM CORP EMPL chairman, chief executive officer: Dauphin Deposit Bank & Trust Co. CORP AFFIL director: Hempt Brothers; director: Millers Mutual Insurance Co.
David H. Schaper: director
Richard Anson Zimmerman: director B Lebanon, PA 1932. ED Pennsylvania State University BA (1952); Lebanon Valley College LLD (1992). PRIM CORP EMPL retired chairman: Hershey Foods Corp. CORP AFFIL director: Lance Inc.; director: Westvaco Corp.; director: Eastman Kodak Co.; director: Hershey Trust Co. NONPR AFFIL trustee: Pennsylvania State University; trustee: Un Theological Seminary; director: Grocery Manufacturer America. CLUB AFFIL Carlton Club; Hershey Country Club.

Grants Analysis
Disclosure Period: calendar year ending 2003
Total Grants: $731,967*
Number of Grants: 60
Average Grant: $9,410*
Highest Grant: $55,000
Lowest Grant: $500
Typical Range: $5,000 to $15,000
*Note: Giving excludes United Way. Average grant figure excludes four highest grants ($205,000).

Recent Grants
Note: Grants derived from 2001 Form 990.
Library-Related
10,000	Frederickson Library, Camp Hill, PA

General
60,000	Catholic Diocese of Allentown, Allentown, PA
50,000	Lehigh University, Bethlehem, PA -- Stabler Foundation fund
50,000	Lehigh University, Bethlehem, PA -- renovation of Stabler Arena
50,000	Pinnacle Health Foundation, Harrisburg, PA
50,000	Wilson College, Chambersburg, PA -- Curran Scholarship Program
45,000	Catholic Diocese of Harrisburg, Harrisburg, PA
35,000	Harrisburg Area YMCA, Harrisburg, PA
35,000	Johns Hopkins University Disease Research Center, Baltimore, MD -- rheumatic disease research
25,000	Goodwill Industries of Central Pennsylvania, Harrisburg, PA
20,000	United Way of the Capital Region, Harrisburg, PA

STACKNER FAMILY FOUNDATION

Giving Contact
John Treiber, Executive Director
PO Box 597
Hartland, WI 53029
Phone: (414)277-5000

Description
Founded: 1966
EIN: 396097597
Organization Type: Private Foundation
Giving Locations: WI: greater Milwaukee area
Grant Types: Capital, General Support, Multiyear/

Continuing Support, Operating Expenses, Project, Research, Seed Money.

Donor Information
Founder: the late John S. Stackner, the late Irene M. Stackner

Financial Summary
Total Giving: $711,755 (fiscal year ending August 31, 2004); $797,425 (fiscal 2001)
Giving Analysis: Giving for fiscal 2004 includes: foundation grants to United Way ($5,000)
Assets: $14,627,045 (fiscal 2004); $15,665,391 (fiscal 2001)

Typical Recipients
Arts & Humanities: Arts Centers, Museums/Galleries
Civic & Public Affairs: Clubs, Economic Development, Civic & Public Affairs-General, Hispanic Affairs, Housing, Parades/Festivals, Women's Affairs
Education: Colleges & Universities, Education Funds, Elementary Education (Private), Education-General, Health & Physical Education, Medical Education, Private Education (Precollege), Religious Education, Science/Mathematics Education, Special Education, Student Aid
Health: Cancer, Children's Health/Hospitals, Health Funds, Health Organizations, Heart, Hospitals, Long-Term Care, Medical Research, Public Health, Single-Disease Health Associations
Religion: Religion-General, Religious Welfare
Science: Science Museums
Social Services: Big Brothers/Big Sisters, Child Welfare, Community Centers, Community Service Organizations, Family Services, People with Disabilities, Recreation & Athletics, Scouts, Social Services-General, United Funds/United Ways, YMCA/YWCA/YMHA/YWHA, Youth Organizations

Application Procedures
Initial Contact: Send a letter of application.
Application Requirements: Include description of program, brochures or other descriptive materials, budget information, amount requested, purpose of funds sought, and recently audited financial statement.
Deadlines: Prior to quarterly meetings in January, April, July, and October.

Restrictions
Does not support individuals or provide scholarships or loans.

Foundation Officials
Patrick William Cotter: assistant secretary
David Lee MacGregor: assistant secretary, director B Cedar Rapids, IA 1932. ED University of Wisconsin BBA (1954); University of Wisconsin LLB (1956). PRIM CORP EMPL partner: Quarles & Brady. NONPR AFFIL member: National Association Estate Planning Councs; member: WI Bar Association; member: Milwaukee Bar Association; member: American Bar Association; fellow: American College Trust & Estate Counsel.
Paul J. Tilleman: treasurer, director
John A. Treiber: vice president, secretary, executive director
Patricia S. Treiber: president, director

Grants Analysis
Disclosure Period: fiscal year ending August 31, 2004
Total Grants: $706,755*
Number of Grants: 152
Average Grant: $4,650
Highest Grant: $25,000
Lowest Grant: $188
Typical Range: $1,000 to $10,000
*Note: Giving excludes United Way.

Recent Grants

Note: Grants derived from 2004 Form 990.
General

25,000	Grand Avenue Club, Milwaukee, WI
25,000	Oconomowoc Memorial Hospital Foundation, Oconomowoc, WI
25,000	Town and Country YMCA, Oconomowoc, WI
25,000	YWCA Waukesha County, Waukesha, WI
20,000	Community Memorial Foundation, Menomonee Falls, WI
20,000	Wheaton College, Wheaton, IL
15,000	Women's Center, Waukesha, WI
10,000	Aurora Family Service, Milwaukee, WI
10,000	Milwaukee Center for Independence, Milwaukee, WI
10,000	Youth Arts Center, Milwaukee, WI

STACKPOLE-HALL FOUNDATION

Giving Contact

William C. Conrad, Executive Secretary
44 South St. Marys Street
St. Marys, PA 15857
Phone: (814)834-1845
Fax: (814)834-1869

Description

Founded: 1951
EIN: 256006650
Organization Type: Family Foundation
Giving Locations: PA: Elk County
Grant Types: Capital, General Support, Project, Seed Money.

Donor Information

Founder: Established as a trust in Pennsylvania in 1951 by the late L. G. Hall, J. H. Stackpole, Mrs. Adelaide Stackpole, and by Harrison C. Stackpole. James Hall Stackpole (1902-1964), son of Harrison C. Stackpole and the former Sallie Hall, was chairman of Stackpole Carbon Company. A portion of the foundation's funds are restricted by the donors through specific bequests to designated religious and educational organizations.

Financial Summary

Total Giving: $850,000 (2002 approx); $980,963 (2001)
Assets: $24,595,464 (2001)

Typical Recipients

Arts & Humanities: Arts Associations & Councils, Ethnic & Folk Arts, Historic Preservation, History & Archaeology, Libraries, Museums/Galleries, Music
Civic & Public Affairs: Botanical Gardens/Parks, Community Foundations, Economic Development, Employment/Job Training, Civic & Public Affairs-General, Housing, Inner-City Development, Municipalities/Towns, Nonprofit Management, Parades/Festivals, Philanthropic Organizations, Professional & Trade Associations, Safety, Urban & Community Affairs
Education: Arts/Humanities Education, Colleges & Universities, Community & Junior Colleges, Education Associations, Education Funds, Education-General, Medical Education, Minority Education, Preschool Education, Private Education (Precollege), Public Education (Precollege), Religious Education, Science/Mathematics Education, Secondary Education (Private), Social Sciences Education, Vocational & Technical Education
Environment: Forestry, Environment-General, Resource Conservation, Watershed
Health: Children's Health/Hospitals, Clinics/Medical Centers, Emergency/Ambulance Services, Health-General, Health Funds, Hospices, Hospitals, Mental Health, Nursing Services, Public Health, Speech & Hearing
Religion: Churches, Dioceses, Religion-General, Jewish Causes, Religious Organizations, Religious Welfare
Social Services: At-Risk Youth, Child Abuse, Child Welfare, Community Centers, Community Service Organizations, Family Planning, Food/Clothing Distribution, Homes, People with Disabilities, Recreation & Athletics, Scouts, Senior Services, Shelters/Homelessness, Substance Abuse, United Funds/United Ways, Volunteer Services, YMCA/YWCA/YMHA/YWHA, Youth Organizations

Application Procedures

Initial Contact: Applicants should telephone the foundation before submitting a request. After initial inquiry, a brief letter may be sent. If the board is interested in a project, it will request a more complete proposal.
Application Requirements: Applicants should include a brief background of the organization; any previous support from the foundation within the last ten years; a detailed description of the project for which the grant is being sought; an explanation of who will be responsible for carrying out project goals, with a definition of their qualifications; most recent audited financial statements; project budget, including sources of support and a statement identifying the specific amount being requested; and a list of current officers, directors, and administrative staff. Applicants should also include two copies of the IRS determination letter indicating tax-exempt status.
Deadlines: None.
Review Process: The board meets in February, May, August, and November.

Restrictions

No grants are made to individuals. Requests for operating grants or endowment grants are generally accorded low priority.

Additional Information

The Foundation Trustees have established a policy designating the area of geographic priority to be Elk County, PA, and the communities in which the donors, the donors' families, and the trustees reside.
Publications: Annual Report; Guidelines

Foundation Officials

William C. Conrad: executive secretary
Douglas R. Dobson: trustee, vice chairman PRIM CORP EMPL vice chairman, director: Stackpole Corp.
Helen Hall Drew: trustee
Lyle G. Hall: chairman, trustee B 1929. ED Yale University (1948-1951); Harvard University (1969); Boston University BS (1975); Episcopal Divinity School MA (1978). PRIM CORP EMPL chairman: Stackpole Corp.
Megan Hall: trustee PRIM CORP EMPL secretary: Pittsburgh Hearing, Speech & Deafness Service.
J. M. Hamlin Johnson: trustee B Ridgeway, PA 1925. ED Grove City College BS (1949); Pennsylvania State University (1969). CORP AFFIL director: Stackpole Corp.; partner: J & B Co.; director: Hamlin Bank & Trust Co. NONPR AFFIL director: Saint Marys Regional Medical Center; director: United Fund Saint Mary; member: National Association Accountants; director: ELCAM Vocational Rehabilitation Center; director: Home Health Services; director: Community Nurses Elk Cameron Counties. CLUB AFFIL Bavarian Hills Club.
Alexander Sheble-Hall: trustee
Harrison Clinton Stackpole: honorary trustee B Ridgeway, PA 1914. ED Yale University.
R. Dauer Stackpole: trustee CORP AFFIL director: Stackpole Corp.
Sara-Jane Stackpole: trustee
Scott Stackpole: trustee

Grants Analysis

Disclosure Period: calendar year ending 2001
Total Grants: $980,963
Number of Grants: 92
Average Grant: $15,809
Highest Grant: $50,000
Typical Range: $5,000 to $25,000

Recent Grants

Note: Grants derived from 2002 Form 990.
Library-Related

13,000	Wilcox Public Library, Wilcox, PA -- funding for computer lab
10,000	Johnsonburg Public Library, Johnsonburg, PA -- assistance for library renovations
2,500	Elk County Community Foundation, St. Mary's, PA -- toward St. Mary's library fund

General

50,000	Elk County Community Foundation, St. Mary's, PA -- toward operating funds
48,371	Grace Episcopal Church, Ridgway, PA -- toward initial grant distribution
39,768	Grace Episcopal Church, Ridgway, PA -- toward final grant distribution
37,209	Episcopal Diocese of North West Pennsylvania, Erie, PA -- toward initial grant distribution
30,592	Episcopal Diocese of North West Pennsylvania, Erie, PA -- toward final grant distribution
30,333	Bradford Educational Foundation, Bradford, PA -- toward classroom technology and faculty training
29,120	City of St. Mary's, St. Mary's, PA -- for summer jobs program/Stackpole-Hall share
26,400	St. Mary's Area School District, St. Mary's, PA -- funding for building for partial hospitalization program
25,000	Crystal Fire Department, St. Mary's, PA -- assistance for rescue truck
25,000	Fox Township Hospital Equipment Program, Kersey, PA -- funding for building to house hospital equipment

JAMES L. STAMPS FOUNDATION

Giving Contact

Delores J. Boutault, Manager
2000 E. Fourth Street, Suite 230
Santa Ana, CA 92705-3814
Phone: (714)568-9740
Fax: (714)568-9754

Description

Founded: 1963
EIN: 956086125
Organization Type: General Purpose Foundation
Giving Locations: CA: Pacific coast states and Arizona
Grant Types: Capital, Emergency, Matching, Operating Expenses, Project.

Donor Information

Founder: Incorporated in 1963 by the late James L. Stamps.

Financial Summary

Total Giving: $1,397,400 (2002); $1,109,996 (2001)
Giving Analysis: Giving for 2002 includes: foundation scholarships ($335,000)
Assets: $28,532,630 (2002); $28,518,292 (2001)

Typical Recipients

Arts & Humanities: Film & Video, Libraries
Civic & Public Affairs: Economic Development, Employment/Job Training, Civic & Public Affairs-General, Hispanic Affairs, Housing, Municipalities/Towns, Public Policy
Education: Colleges & Universities, Education-General, Legal Education, Private Education (Precollege), Religious Education, Science/Mathematics Education, Secondary Education (Private), Student Aid
Health: Clinics/Medical Centers, Emergency/Ambulance Services, Public Health
International: Foreign Educational Institutions, International Affairs, International Development, International Organizations, Missionary/Religious Activities
Religion: Bible Study/Translation, Churches, Religion-General, Ministries, Missionary Activities (Domestic), Religious Organizations, Religious Welfare, Seminaries, Social/Policy Issues
Science: Scientific Labs
Social Services: Camps, Community Service Organizations, Food/Clothing Distribution, Homes, Senior Services, Shelters/Homelessness, YMHA/YWCA/YMHA/YWHA, Youth Organizations

Application Procedures

Initial Contact: The foundation requests applications be made in writing.
Application Requirements: The foundation requests a brief inquiry that includes a copy of the organization's IRS tax-exempt letter 501(c)(3), a brief summary of the project, the amount requested, and a copy of the prior fiscal year's financial statement. The organization may be asked to develop a more detailed proposal.

Although the foundation does not require a specific form for full proposals, it suggests that an organization include the following information: a clear description of the project, what it may be expected to achieve, and its importance; a detailed expense budget, showing how the requested funds would be spent during what time periods and how the major elements of expense were estimated (if applicable); information concerning the organization and its responsible officers who intend to carry out the project, including a brief description of organization, the names and affiliations of the directors or trustees, the name(s) and qualifications of the person(s) who would administer the grant, and an audited balance sheet and income statement for the previous fiscal year; a copy of the most recent tax-exempt ruling from the IRS, along with a statement as to any revisions which may be pending or a statement that there has been no change and none is pending; an endorsement by the administrative head if the proposal is from a department or individual of the organization (if possible, it should comment upon the relative priority of the request compared with other needs which the organization may ask the foundation to support); and a letter of support from authorities and/or organizations in the applicant's field.
Deadlines: The board meets bimonthly, and proposals should be submitted to the foundation at least one month prior to the board meeting at which consideration of the proposal is desired.
Review Process: The foundation will send written notice to applicants concerning all board decisions to approve or deny grant proposals, usually within 10 working days following the board meeting involved. Each proposal will be accepted or rejected in writing only.
Notes: Organizations wishing material returned in the event of rejection should so state in the proposal. The foundation prohibits personal interviews with trustees collectively or individually, either before or after filing a proposal.

Restrictions

The foundation primarily supports Evangelical Protestant-based organizations in the Pacific Coast States. The foundation ordinarily does not make grants in installments for future years; favor projects that are normally financed by public tax funds; favor trustee membership in organizations in which grants are made; make grants for endowments, contingency, or deficit funding, conferences, seminars, workshops, travel purposes, or exhibits the publication of books or magazines, producing films, or for public or educational radio or television purposes. No grants are made to individuals, for scholarships or fellowships.

Additional Information

Publications: Application Guidelines

Foundation Officials

Delores J. Boutault: manager
E. C. Boutault: president, trustee
Richard S. Kredel: secretary, treasurer, trustee
Willis R. Leach: trustee treasurer: Leach Grain Milling Co.
Thomas P. Lynch: chairman, trustee
Richard Salyer: vice president

Grants Analysis

Disclosure Period: calendar year ending 2002
Total Grants: $1,062,400*
Number of Grants: 47
Average Grant: $22,604
Highest Grant: $150,000
Lowest Grant: $1,000
Typical Range: $10,000 to $40,000
*Note: Giving excludes scholarships.

Recent Grants

Note: Grants derived from 2002 Form 990.
General

150,000	Hope International University, Fullerton, CA -- construction of Student Center
100,000	Azusa Pacific University, Azusa, CA -- library
100,000	California Baptist University, Riverside, CA -- for University Center Program
100,000	Westmont College, Santa Barbara, CA -- computer equipment
50,000	Forest Home Christian Conference Center, Forest Falls, CA -- electrical power lines
50,000	Hume Lake Christian Camps, Fresno, CA -- chapel construction
50,000	Hume Lake Christian Camps, Fresno, CA -- Joshua Project 2002
50,000	Vanguard University, Costa Mesa, CA -- Graduate Programs
26,000	Church Resource Ministries, Anaheim, CA
25,150	Youthbuilders, San Juan Capistrano, CA -- computer equipment

STANDARD STEEL

Company Headquarters

500 North Walnut Street
Burnham, PA 17009
Web: http://www.standardsteel.com

Company Description

Former Name: Freedom Forge Corp. (2002)
Chap. 11 Reorg. Bankruptcy (2001);
Former Name: American Welding & Manufacturing Co..
SIC(s): 3300 Primary Metal Industries.

Operating Locations

Freedom Forge Corp. (PA--Latrobe)

Freedom Forge Corp. Foundation

Giving Contact

Thomas J. McGuigan, Vice President, Human Resources & Administration
500 North Walnut Street
Burnham, PA 17009
Phone: (717)248-4911

Description

EIN: 346516721
Organization Type: Corporate Foundation
Giving Locations: OH
Grant Types: General Support, Scholarship.

Financial Summary

Total Giving: $49,172 (2004)
Giving Analysis: Giving for 2004 includes: foundation grants to United Way ($17,000); foundation scholarships ($17,500)
Assets: $1,308,687 (2004)

Typical Recipients

Arts & Humanities: Arts Associations & Councils, History & Archaeology, Libraries, Museums/Galleries, Music, Performing Arts, Public Broadcasting
Civic & Public Affairs: Clubs, Economic Development, Economic Policy, Civic & Public Affairs-General, Municipalities/Towns, Professional & Trade Associations, Public Policy, Urban & Community Affairs
Education: Agricultural Education, Business Education, Colleges & Universities, Education Funds, Engineering/Technological Education, Education-General, Private Education (Precollege)
Environment: Environment-General, Resource Conservation, Wildlife Protection
Health: Cancer, Children's Health/Hospitals, Hospices, Hospitals, Kidney, Medical Research, Multiple Sclerosis, Prenatal Health Issues, Single-Disease Health Associations
Religion: Religious Welfare
Science: Science Exhibits & Fairs, Scientific Organizations
Social Services: Animal Protection, Community Service Organizations, Delinquency & Criminal Rehabilitation, Food/Clothing Distribution, People with Disabilities, Recreation & Athletics, Scouts, Special Olympics, Substance Abuse, United Funds/United Ways, YMCA/YWCA/YMHA/YWHA, Youth Organizations

Application Procedures

Initial Contact: The foundation requests applications be made in writing. Include a description of organization, amount requested, purpose of funds sought, recently audited financial statement, and proof of tax-exempt status.
Deadlines: None.

Additional Information

Trust(s): Kish Bank Asset Mgmt

Corporate Officials

Herbert C. Graves: chairman, chief operating officer, director PRIM CORP EMPL chairman: Freedom Forge Corp.
Mr. Dana L. Patterson: chief financial officer PRIM CORP EMPL chief financial officer: Freedom Forge Corp.
James A. Spendiff: president, chief operating officer, director B Troy, NY 1943. ED University of Pennsylvania (1965). PRIM CORP EMPL president, chief operating officer, director: Freedom Forge Corp. ADD CORP EMPL director, president: FFC Holding Inc.; director, president: Freedom Forge Holdings Inc.

Grants Analysis

Disclosure Period: calendar year ending 2004
Total Grants: $14,672*
Number of Grants: 6
Average Grant: $2,445
Highest Grant: $5,000
Lowest Grant: $232
Typical Range: $1,500 to $5,000
***Note:** Giving excludes United Way and scholarships.

Recent Grants

Note: Grants derived from 2001 Form 990.

Library-Related

5,000	Mifflin County Library, Lewistown, PA	
1,000	Mifflin County Library, Lewistown, PA	

General

30,000	Juniata Valley YMCA, Juniata Valley, PA
10,000	Lewistown Hospital, Lewistown, PA
5,000	Belleville Minnonite School, Belleville, PA
5,000	Burnham Fire Company -- for seminar
3,500	Nittany Valley Symphony, State College, PA
2,500	American Museum of Fly Fishing, Manchester, VT -- to revitalize county
2,500	Bryn Mawr College, Bryn Mawr, PA
2,500	Pennsylvania State University, Philadelphia, PA
2,500	Pennsylvania State University, Philadelphia, PA
2,500	Pennsylvania State University, Philadelphia, PA

STANLEY WORKS

Company Headquarters

New Britain, CT
Web: http://www.stanleyworks.com

Company Description

Founded: 1843
Ticker: SWK
Exchange: NYSE
Revenue: US$2.624 billion (2001)
Employees: 13500 (2003)
SIC(s): 2542 Partitions & Fixtures Except Wood, 3315 Steel Wire & Related Products, 3429 Hardware Nec, 3442 Metal Doors, Sash & Trim.

Operating Locations

The Stanley Works (AZ--Phoenix; CA--Chatsworth, Costa Mesa, Monrovia, San Dimas, Visalia; CT--Clinton, Farmington; FL--Orlando; GA--Atlanta, Covington; IN--Shelbyville; KS--Lenexa; MA--Worcester; MI--Birmingham, Novi; MN--Two Harbors; MS--Tupelo; MO--St. Louis; NH--Claremont; NC--Charlotte, Sanford; OH--Cleveland, Columbus, Georgetown, Sabina, Washington Court House; OR; PA--Allentown, Royersford, York; RI--East Greenwich; TN--Pulaski, Shelbyville; TX--Carrollton, Dallas; VT--Pittsfield, Shaftsbury; VA--Richmond, Winchester)

Nonmonetary Support

Type: Donated Products; Workplace Solicitation
Note: Nonmonetary support is approximately $150,000 annually.

Giving Contact

Tim Perra, Communications Manager for Human Resources
1000 Stanley Drive
New Britain, CT 06053
Phone: (860)225-5111
E-mail: tperra@stanleyworks.com
Web: http://www.stanleyworks.com/a_responsibility.asp

Description

Organization Type: Corporate Giving Program
Giving Locations: operating location communities.
Grant Types: Capital, Challenge, Employee Matching Gifts, General Support, Operating Expenses, Seed Money.
Note: Employee matching gift ratio: 1 to 1.

Financial Summary

Total Giving: $1,500,000 (2001 approx). Note: Contributes through corporate direct giving program only.

Typical Recipients

Arts & Humanities: Arts Associations & Councils, Community Arts, Dance, Arts & Humanities-General, Libraries, Museums/Galleries, Music, Opera, Performing Arts, Public Broadcasting, Theater
Civic & Public Affairs: African American Affairs, Business/Free Enterprise, Community Foundations, Economic Policy, Employment/Job Training, Civic & Public Affairs-General, Housing, Urban & Community Affairs
Education: Business Education, Colleges & Universities, Economic Education, Elementary Education (Private), Elementary Education (Public), Engineering/Technological Education, Literacy, Minority Education, Public Education (Precollege), Science/Mathematics Education
Environment: Environment-General, Resource Conservation
Health: Cancer, Children's Health/Hospitals, Emergency/Ambulance Services, Hospitals, Medical Research
International: International Development
Religion: Churches, Religious Welfare
Science: Science Exhibits & Fairs
Social Services: Community Service Organizations, Family Services, Homes, People with Disabilities, Shelters/Homelessness, Substance Abuse, United Funds/United Ways, Youth Organizations

Application Procedures

Initial Contact: Send a brief letter or proposal.
Application Requirements: Include a description of organization and how it will affect Stanley employees, amount requested, purpose of funds sought, recently audited financial statement, proof of 501(c)(3) tax-exempt status, identification of company employees involved with organization.
Deadlines: Contact foundation for current deadlines.
Review Process: Reviews grant request three times a year.
Evaluative Criteria: Involvement of company personnel with organization; organization's qualifications to provide services; company's feeling of responsibility to organization or community; operate in a Stanley community; endorsement of local company management; organization's service population.

Restrictions

No funds will be given outside communities where Stanley has operations.
Company does not fund national organizations, operating funds, research projects, athletic programs, health research organizations, endowment funds, organizations which are not tax-exempt, private foundations, or individuals.

Additional Information

In 1999, the company announced that new giving program guidelines were being prepared for the 2000 grant cycle.
Publications: Guidelines Sheet; Annual Report; grants List

Corporate Officials

Herschel Herndon: director, Global Communication

Grants Analysis

Typical Range: $1,000 to $5,000

STANS FOUNDATION

Giving Contact

Steven H. Stans, President
PO Box 1018
Arcadia, CA 91007
Phone: (626)446-8285

Description

Founded: 1945
EIN: 366008663
Organization Type: Private Foundation
Giving Locations: CA
Grant Types: Capital, Conference/Seminar, General Support, Multiyear/Continuing Support, Research.

Donor Information

Founder: Maurice H. Stans, the late Kathleen C. Stans

Financial Summary

Total Giving: $97,024 (2003); $339,238 (2001)
Giving Analysis: Giving for 2003 includes: foundation grants to United Way ($2,000)
Assets: $4,247,890 (2003); $3,499,258 (2001)
Gifts Received: $53,000 (1995)

Typical Recipients

Arts & Humanities: Historic Preservation, History & Archaeology, Libraries, Museums/Galleries, Music, Performing Arts, Public Broadcasting
Civic & Public Affairs: Botanical Gardens/Parks, Civil Rights, Clubs, Civic & Public Affairs-General, Housing, Legal Aid, Parades/Festivals, Public Policy, Urban & Community Affairs
Education: Colleges & Universities, Education Funds, Education Reform, Engineering/Technological Education, Education-General, International Studies, Journalism/Media Education, Private Education (Precollege)
Environment: Watershed, Wildlife Protection
Health: Clinics/Medical Centers, Eyes/Blindness, Hospices, Hospitals, Medical Research, Mental Health, Research/Studies Institutes, Single-Disease Health Associations
International: International Affairs, International Environmental Issues, International Peace & Security Issues
Religion: Churches, Jewish Causes, Ministries, Religious Organizations, Religious Welfare, Social/Policy Issues
Science: Science Museums, Scientific Centers & Institutes
Social Services: Animal Protection, Child Welfare, Community Service Organizations, Scouts, United Funds/United Ways, Youth Organizations

Application Procedures

Initial Contact: Send a brief letter of inquiry.
Deadlines: None.

Foundation Officials

Walter E. Helmick: vice president, assistant treasurer
Steven H. Stans: president
Theodore M. Stans: executive vice president, treasurer

Grants Analysis

Disclosure Period: calendar year ending 2003
Total Grants: $95,024*
Number of Grants: 33
Average Grant: $2,880
Highest Grant: $10,000
Lowest Grant: $300
Typical Range: $1,000 to $5,000
***Note:** Giving excludes United Way.

Recent Grants

Note: Grants derived from 2003 Form 990.

General

17,242	Florida Gulf Coast University Foundation, Ft. Myers, FL
10,000	Sisters of Providence, IN
10,000	University of California Regents, CA
10,000	Young Artists International, Los Angeles, CA
7,500	University of Central Florida Foundation, Orlando, FL
5,182	Florida Gulf Coast University Foundation, Ft. Myers, FL
5,000	Father Wasson's Orphans Inc., Prescott, AZ
5,000	US Sportsman Alliance Foundation
2,500	Ducks Unlimited, Memphis, TN
2,000	Northwestern University, Evanston, IL

STARDUST FOUNDATION

Giving Contact

Gerald Bisgrove, Chief Executive Officer/Chairman
6730 North Scottsdale Road, Suite 230
Scottsdale, AZ 85253
Phone: (480)607-5800
Fax: (480)607-5801
E-mail: lkilgas@stardustco.com

Description

Founded: 1993
EIN: 860735230
Organization Type: Private Foundation
Giving Locations: AZ
Grant Types: General Support.

Donor Information

Founder: The foundation was established in 1993.

Financial Summary

Total Giving: $2,143,780 (2003); $6,066,207 (2002); $662,561 (2001)
Giving Analysis: Giving for 2003 includes: foundation grants to United Way ($50,000); 2002: foundation grants to United Way ($3,027)
Assets: $25,848,100 (2003); $17,892,651 (2002); $25,374,894 (2001)
Gifts Received: $7,250,100 (2003); $2,000,000 (2001); $1,000,000 (2000). Note: In 2003, contributions were received from Gerald Bisgrove. In 2000 and 2001, contributions were received from Stardust Holdings, Inc. In 1998, contributions were received from Gerald Bisgrove and Bisgrove Financial Management.

Typical Recipients

Arts & Humanities: Arts & Humanities-General, Museums/Galleries, Music, Theater
Civic & Public Affairs: Chambers of Commerce, Clubs, Community Foundations, Employment/Job Training, Civic & Public Affairs-General, Housing, Legal Aid, Municipalities/Towns, Native American Affairs, Nonprofit Management, Parades/Festivals, Public Policy, Safety, Urban & Community Affairs, Women's Affairs, Zoos/Aquariums
Education: Afterschool/Enrichment Programs, Colleges & Universities, Economic Education, Education Funds, Education Reform, Elementary Education (Public), Education-General, Leadership Training, Private Education (Precollege), Secondary Education (Private), Special Education, Student Aid
Environment: Wildlife Protection
Health: AIDS/HIV, Cancer, Children's Health/ Hospitals, Health Organizations, Heart, Hospices, Kidney, Medical Rehabilitation, Medical Research, Public Health, Research/Studies Institutes
International: International Relief Efforts
Religion: Churches, Dioceses, Religion-General, Ministries, Religious Organizations, Religious Welfare

Science: Scientific Centers & Institutes
Social Services: Animal Protection, At-Risk Youth, Child Abuse, Child Welfare, Community Centers, Community Service Organizations, Delinquency & Criminal Rehabilitation, Domestic Violence, Family Planning, Family Services, Food/Clothing Distribution, Homes, Recreation & Athletics, Shelters/ Homelessness, Social Services-General, Special Olympics, Substance Abuse, United Funds/United Ways, Veterans, Volunteer Services, YMCA/YWCA/ YMHA/YWHA, Youth Organizations

Application Procedures

Initial Contact: Applicants should send a brief letter of inquiry.
Application Requirements: Included name and address of contact person to whom any requests for further information may be directed.
Deadlines: September 30.

Restrictions

Grants are given by invitation only.

Additional Information

Publications: Application Form

Foundation Officials

Debra Bisgrove: secretary, vice president, director
Gerald Bisgrove: president, director

Grants Analysis

Disclosure Period: calendar year ending 2003
Total Grants: $2,093,780*
Number of Grants: 59
Average Grant: $25,755*
Highest Grant: $600,000
Lowest Grant: $25
Typical Range: $5,000 to $50,000
*Note: Giving excludes United Way. Average grant figure excludes highest grant.

Recent Grants

Note: Grants derived from 2003 Form 990.

General

600,000	Magdalen College, Warner, NH
250,000	Stardust Center, Tempe, AZ
125,000	Arizona Quest for Kids, Phoenix, AZ
100,000	Barrow Neurological Institute, Phoenix, AZ
100,000	Desert Mission Food Bank, Phoenix, AZ
100,000	Phoenix Day, Phoenix, AZ
100,000	Salvation Army, Phoenix, AZ
100,000	Stardust Neighborhood Foundation, Scottsdale, AZ
96,000	Arizona Family Housing Fund, Scottsdale, AZ
65,000	Young Life, Phoenix, AZ

NELDA C. AND H. J. LUTCHER STARK FOUNDATION

Giving Contact

Sherrie Sheppard, Grants Administrator
601 W. Green Avenue
PO Box 909
Orange, TX 77631-0909
Phone: (409)883-3513
Fax: (409)883-3530
E-mail: stark@starkfoundation.org
Web: http://www.starkfoundation.org

Description

Founded: 1961
EIN: 746047440
Organization Type: General Purpose Foundation

Giving Locations: LA: Southwest Louisiana; TX: Southeast Texas
Grant Types: General Support, Project, Scholarship.

Donor Information

Founder: Established in 1961 by H. J. Lutcher Stark and his wife, Nelda Childers Stark. Mr. Stark's business included the Lutcher & Moore Lumber Company, the First National Bank of Orange, and Vinton Petroleum. After Mr. Stark's death in 1965, the foundation received the Stark's sizeable art collection, including American Western art of the nineteenth and twentieth centuries, Native American artifacts, and a selection of decorative arts including a collection of Steuben glass. The entire collection is now housed in the Stark Museum of Art, owned and operated by the foundation. The art museum is part of a civic and cultural center in downtown Orange, TX, that also includes the W. H. Stark House, the Frances Ann Lutcher Theater for the Performing Arts, a church, and a park. The W. H. Stark House, a restored Victorian mansion built in 1894, is open to the public for tours. The foundation built the Frances Ann Lutcher Theater for the Performing Arts for the City of Orange, TX, as the major forum for the performing arts in Orange County. In 1986, the foundation assumed responsibility for the facility's operating expenses.

Financial Summary

Total Giving: $1,527,000 (2002); $5,125,484 (2001)
Giving Analysis: Giving for 2002 includes: foundation matching gifts ($23,939); foundation grants to United Way ($25,680); foundation scholarships ($50,750); 2001: foundation matching gifts ($5,000); foundation grants to United Way ($100,000); foundation scholarships ($418,400)
Assets: $167,709,225 (2002); $179,182,452 (2001)
Gifts Received: $11,103,290 (2002); $1,110,016 (1999); $1,250,000 (1998). Note: The foundation receives gifts from Nelda C. Stark, chairman, donor, and trustee of the foundation.

Typical Recipients

Arts & Humanities: Arts Associations & Councils, Historic Preservation, History & Archaeology, Libraries, Museums/Galleries, Music, Opera, Public Broadcasting
Civic & Public Affairs: African American Affairs, Botanical Gardens/Parks, Community Foundations, Civic & Public Affairs-General, Municipalities/Towns, Safety, Urban & Community Affairs
Education: Arts/Humanities Education, Business Education, Colleges & Universities, Education Funds, Engineering/Technological Education, Environmental Education, Education-General, Literacy, Private Education (Precollege), Social Sciences Education, Student Aid
Environment: Environment-General, Wildlife Protection
Health: Cancer, Children's Health/Hospitals, Diabetes, Eyes/Blindness, Hospices, Single-Disease Health Associations, Transplant Networks/Donor Banks
Religion: Churches, Missionary Activities (Domestic), Religious Organizations, Religious Welfare
Social Services: At-Risk Youth, Camps, Emergency Relief, Family Services, Homes, People with Disabilities, Scouts, Senior Services, Social Services-General, Special Olympics, Substance Abuse, United Funds/United Ways, Veterans, Youth Organizations

Application Procedures

Initial Contact: Send five copies of a letter of proposal.
Application Requirements: The letter should include a brief description of the project signed by president or chief executive officer; brief history, description, programs, and mission of the organization; timeline (beginning and ending dates); amount requested; list of other funding sources and amounts; and proof of tax-exempt status under IRS Section

501(c)(3).

Deadlines: January 1, May 1, and September 1.
Review Process: If the Grant Committee determines the project to be within the scope of Foundation interests and funding, the organization will be requested to furnish further information. The foundation board usually meets monthly.

Restrictions

No grants are made to individuals, or for endowment, continuing support, or operating budgets. Grants for scholarships are made through the Texas Interscholastic League Foundation.

Additional Information

In 2001, the foundation changed its fiscal year to end on December 31.
Publications: Annual Report

Foundation Officials

Eunice R. Benckenstein: vice chairman, trustee B 1911.
Walter G. Riedel, III: secretary, treasurer
Nelda Childers Stark: chairman B Orange, TX 1909. ED Denton College.

Grants Analysis

Disclosure Period: calendar year ending 2002
Total Grants: $1,435,631*
Number of Grants: 24
Average Grant: $25,686*
Highest Grant: $844,842
Lowest Grant: $500
Typical Range: $10,000 to $50,000
***Note:** Giving excludes scholarships, United Way, and matching gifts. Average grant figure excludes highest grant.

Recent Grants

Note: Grants derived from 2002 Form 990.

Library-Related
31,500	Orange Public Library, Orange, TX -- toward purchase of reference materials

General
844,842	West Orange-Cove CISD, Orange, TX -- toward technology infrastructure upgrade and teacher training
135,000	Little Cypress-Mauriceville CISD, Orange, TX -- assist the Lexia reading software program
100,249	Vidor High School-English Department, Vidor, TX -- funding for English writing lab
55,000	Orange Christian Services, Orange, TX -- purchase of special purpose truck and replacement of the roof
50,000	Jason Alliance of Southeast Texas, Beaumont, TX -- funding for curriculum and training materials
40,000	Julie Rogers "Gift of Life" Program, Beaumont, TX -- funding for mammography and prostate screening for the disadvantaged
25,680	United Way of Orange Co, Orange, TX
25,500	KVLU Public Radio, Beaumont, TX -- to underwrite local broadcast of international network
24,610	American Red Cross, Orange, TX -- toward purchase of automated external defibrillators and equipment
23,939	City of West Orange-Police Department, West Orange, TX -- grant for records system/computer

STARR FOUNDATION

Giving Contact

Florence A. Davis, President
70 Pine Street, 14th Fl.
New York, NY 10270
Phone: (212)770-5202
Fax: (212)425-6261
E-mail: grants@starrfoundation.org
Web: http://fdncenter.org/grantmaker/starr/

Description

Founded: 1955
EIN: 136151545
Organization Type: General Purpose Foundation
Giving Locations: NY: New York, metropolitan area internationally; nationally; nationally; internationally.
Grant Types: Capital, Emergency, Endowment, General Support, Multiyear/Continuing Support, Professorship, Project, Scholarship.

Donor Information

Founder: Established in New York in 1955 by Cornelius Vander Starr (1892-1968). Mr. Starr attended the University of California, and passed the California Bar exam at age 21. After serving in World War I, he resided in China and established the Asia Life and American Asiatic Life Insurance Companies. By the 1930s, his insurance activities and investments in real estate and automobiles extended throughout the Far East. After World War II, he renamed the companies the American Life Insurance Company. At the time of his death, his operations expanded to a group of 100 insurance companies in about 130 countries. Since the 1970s, the foundation has received considerable donations of stock from the corporate directors of American International Group.

Financial Summary

Total Giving: $188,856,235 (2003); $209,301,410 (2002); $219,755,392 (2001)
Giving Analysis: Giving for 2003 includes: foundation scholarships ($7,311,666); 2002: foundation scholarships ($5,654,369)
Assets: $3,577,378,889 (2003); $3,322,102,520 (2002); $4,813,709,640 (2001)
Gifts Received: $89,531 (2002); $881,289 (2001); $10,785 (2000). Note: In 2000, 2001, and 2002, contributions were received from the Marion Hughes Trust. In 1997, contributions were received from the Marion Hughes Trust and Kwie Ding Wang.

Typical Recipients

Arts & Humanities: Arts Associations & Councils, Arts Centers, Arts Festivals, Arts Funds, Arts Institutes, Dance, Ethnic & Folk Arts, Historic Preservation, History & Archaeology, Libraries, Museums/Galleries, Music, Opera, Performing Arts, Public Broadcasting, Theater
Civic & Public Affairs: Botanical Gardens/Parks, Chambers of Commerce, Civil Rights, Economic Development, Economic Policy, Employment/Job Training, Ethnic Organizations, Civic & Public Affairs-General, Law & Justice, Nonprofit Management, Philanthropic Organizations, Public Policy, Rural Affairs, Urban & Community Affairs, Women's Affairs, Zoos/Aquariums
Education: Afterschool/Enrichment Programs, Arts/Humanities Education, Business Education, Colleges & Universities, Economic Education, Education Associations, Education Funds, Education Reform, Engineering/Technological Education, Health & Physical Education, International Exchange, International Studies, Journalism/Media Education, Legal Education, Medical Education, Minority Education, Private Education (Precollege), Public Education (Precollege), Religious Education, Science/Mathematics Education, Special Education, Student Aid
Environment: Environment-General
Health: AIDS/HIV, Cancer, Children's Health/

Hospitals, Emergency/Ambulance Services, Eyes/Blindness, Health-General, Geriatric Health, Health Policy/Cost Containment, Health Organizations, Heart, Hospices, Hospitals, Kidney, Long-Term Care, Medical Research, Medical Training, Nursing Services, Public Health, Single-Disease Health Associations, Transplant Networks/Donor Banks
International: Foreign Arts Organizations, Foreign Educational Institutions, International-General, Health Care/Hospitals, International Affairs, International Development, International Environmental Issues, International Organizations, International Peace & Security Issues, International Relations, International Relief Efforts, Trade
Religion: Churches, Jewish Causes, Religious Welfare
Science: Science Museums, Scientific Centers & Institutes, Scientific Labs
Social Services: At-Risk Youth, Camps, Child Welfare, Community Centers, Community Service Organizations, Counseling, Crime Prevention, Emergency Relief, Family Planning, Family Services, Food/Clothing Distribution, People with Disabilities, Recreation & Athletics, Refugee Assistance, Senior Services, Shelters/Homelessness, Social Services-General, Substance Abuse, YMCA/YWCA/YMHA/YWHA, Youth Organizations

Application Procedures

Initial Contact: Applications should be submitted in writing. There are no formal application forms.
Application Requirements: Proposals should include a cover letter defining the organization and setting forth the terms of the proposal; project budget; recently audited financial statement; list of other major financial supporters (current and pending); list of the organization's board members and their affiliations; proof of tax-exempt status; and details of overall administrative expenses. Supplementary materials may be included, but the foundation prefers not to receive videotapes.
Deadlines: None.

Restrictions

Grants to individuals are limited to scholarships provided through the foundation's scholarship programs. The foundation will not generally fund organizations that spend more than 25% of their annual expenses on administration and fundraising. Overseas organizations without U.S. tax-exempt status are rarely supported.

Additional Information

The foundation operates four scholarship programs: the Starr Foundation Scholarship Program for "American International" Children (U.S.), the Starr Foundation Scholarship Program for "American International" Children (overseas), the Brewster Starr Scholarship Program, and the Lower Manhattan Starr Scholarship Program.
Publications: Annual Report

Foundation Officials

Florence A. Davis: president, director NONPR AFFIL trustee: Practicing Law Institute; national development committee: Wellesley College; trustee: New York University School of Law; fellow: Foreign Policy Association; director: Institute for Judicial Administration.
Maurice Raymond Greenberg: chairman, director B New York, NY 1925. ED University of Miami BA (1948); New York University School of Law JD (1950). PRIM CORP EMPL chairman, chief executive officer, president: American International Group Inc. CORP AFFIL director: Starr International Co.; director: Transatlantic Holdings Inc.; president, chief executive officer, director: C V Starr & Co.; director: International Lease Finance Corp. NONPR AFFIL chairman: U.S.-China Business Council; founding chairman: United States Philippine Business Committee; president advisory committee: Trade Policy & Negotiations; member: New York State Bar Associa-

tion; member: Police Athletic League; vchmn: Council Foreign Relations; chairman board governors: New York Hospital; president advisory committee: Center Strategic & International Studies; chairman: Asia Society; member: Business Roundtable. CLUB AFFIL Sky Club; India House Club; Lotos Club; Harmonie Club; City Athletic Club; Georgetown Club.

Ta Chun Hsu: director B 1925. CORP AFFIL director: Chinese America Bank. NONPR AFFIL director: Smith-Kettlewell Eye Research Institute.

Sir Edwin Alfred Grenville Manton: director B Earls Colne, United Kingdom January 22, 1909. ED University of London (1925-1927); New York Institute of Sociology (1933-1935). PRIM CORP EMPL senior advisor, director: American International Group Inc. CORP AFFIL director: American International Life Assurance New York; director: Birmingham Fire & Insurance Co. Pennsylvania. CLUB AFFIL member: Old Shastonians Club.

E. E. Matthews: director

John Joseph Roberts: director B Montreal, QC Canada 1922. ED Princeton University BA (1945). PRIM CORP EMPL chairman, chief executive officer, director: American International Underwriters Inc. ADD CORP EMPL vice chairman, director: American International Group Inc. CORP AFFIL senior vice president: CV Starr & Co. Inc.; director: Starr Tech Risks Agency; director: American International Marine Agency New York Inc.; director: Petroleum & Resources Corp.; director: Adams Express Co.; chairman emeritus: America International Group. NONPR AFFIL trustee: The Juillard School; trustee: Washington College.

H. I. Smith: treasurer, director

Ernest Edward Stemple: director B New York, NY 1916. ED Manhattan College AB (1938); Fordham University LLB (1946); New York University LLM (1949); New York University DJS (1951). PRIM CORP EMPL senior, advisor: American International Group Inc. ADD CORP EMPL president, director: Starr International Co. Inc. NONPR AFFIL member: American Bar Association.

Gladys R. Thomas: vice president, secretary ED Bryn Mawr College BA. CLUB AFFIL member, governor: India House Club.

E. S. Tse: director

Grants Analysis

Disclosure Period: calendar year ending 2003
Total Grants: $181,544,569*
Number of Grants: 764
Average Grant: $205,170*
Highest Grant: $25,000,000
Lowest Grant: $1,000
Typical Range: $50,000 to $500,000
*Note: Giving excludes scholarships. Average grant figure excludes highest grants.

Recent Grants

Note: Grants derived from 2001 Form 990.
Library-Related

500,000	George Bush Presidential Library Foundation, College Station, TX -- for endowment or program support
500,000	Manhattan College, Riverdale, NY -- for library and endowment
500,000	New York Public Library, New York, NY -- for South Court Programs

General

25,000,000	American Museum of Natural History, New York, NY -- endowment of the genomics institute
25,000,000	Rockefeller University, New York, NY -- for endowment of clinical research facilities
25,000,000	Weill Medical College of Cornell University, New York, NY -- for construction of new outpatient facility
10,000,000	Weill Medical College of Cornell University, New York, NY -- for Genetic Medicine Program

8,000,000	New York Police and Fire Widows and Children Benefit Fund, New York, NY -- response to September 11
5,000,000	International Trachoma Initiative, Inc., New York, NY
3,000,000	Metropolitan Museum of Art, New York, NY -- for Early Chinese Empire The First Millennium, Han Through Tang
2,500,000	Hospital for Special Surgery, New York, NY -- Discovery to Recovery Research Campaign
2,500,000	Museum of Modern Art, New York, NY -- for MOMA Builds
2,500,000	United Negro College Fund, Fairfax, VA -- for technology enhancement capital campaign

STATE FARM MUTUAL AUTOMOBILE INSURANCE CO.

Company Headquarters

Bloomington, IL
Web: http://www.statefarm.com

Company Description

SIC(s): 6331 Fire, Marine & Casualty Insurance.
Parent Company: State Farm Insurance Cos., 1 State Farm Plaza, Bloomington, IL, United States

Operating Locations

State Farm Mutual Automobile Insurance Co. (AL; AZ; CA; CO; GA; IL--Bloomington; IN; LA; MI; MN; MO; NE; NY; OH; OK; OR; TN; TX; VA)

Nonmonetary Support

Type: Donated Equipment; Donated Products; In-kind Services
Volunteer Programs: Company-sponsored volunteer programs include loaned executives for United Way campaigns, Junior Achievement advisors, and Red Cross Blood drives. Interested employees complete a questionnaire, then receive a newsletter of volunteer activities. Employees participate in activities on their own initiative.
Note: The company provides nonmonetary support.

State Farm Companies Foundation

Giving Contact

Mindy Laub
State Farm Companies Foundation
One State Farm Plaza
Bloomington, IL 61710-0001
Phone: (309)766-5309
Fax: (309)766-2314
Web: http://www.statefarm.com/foundati/foundati.htm

Description

Founded: 1963
EIN: 366110423
Organization Type: Corporate Foundation
Giving Locations: near major offices.
Grant Types: Capital, Employee Matching Gifts, Endowment, Fellowship, Matching, Multiyear/Continuing Support, Scholarship.
Note: Employee matching gift ratio: 1 to 1 up to $1,000 per contribution. Matching and employee matching gifts are for four-year colleges and universities only.

Financial Summary

Total Giving: $17,650,329 (2003); $21,758,492 (2002); $12,878,268 (2001). Note: Contributes through corporate direct giving program and foundation.
Assets: $13,984,071 (2003); $31,378,017 (2002); $52,285,140 (2001)
Gifts Received: $56,000,026 (1998); $4,750,000 (1993); $3,000,000 (1992). Note: Foundation received contributions from State Farm Life Insurance Co. and State Farm Mutual Automobile Insurance Co.

Typical Recipients

Arts & Humanities: Arts Associations & Councils, Ethnic & Folk Arts, History & Archaeology, Libraries, Museums/Galleries, Public Broadcasting, Theater
Civic & Public Affairs: African American Affairs, Community Foundations, Economic Policy, Employment/Job Training, Civic & Public Affairs-General, Hispanic Affairs, Law & Justice, Native American Affairs, Professional & Trade Associations, Public Policy, Safety, Urban & Community Affairs, Women's Affairs, Zoos/Aquariums
Education: Afterschool/Enrichment Programs, Arts/Humanities Education, Business Education, Business-School Partnerships, Colleges & Universities, Community & Junior Colleges, Economic Education, Education Associations, Education Funds, Education Reform, Faculty Development, Education-General, International Studies, Leadership Training, Medical Education, Minority Education, Private Education (Precollege), Public Education (Precollege), Science/Mathematics Education, Student Aid, Vocational & Technical Education
Health: Cancer, Children's Health/Hospitals, Clinics/Medical Centers, Hospitals, Medical Rehabilitation, Public Health
International: Foreign Educational Institutions
Religion: Religious Organizations, Religious Welfare
Science: Science Museums
Social Services: Child Welfare, Community Service Organizations, Day Care, Family Services, Substance Abuse, United Funds/United Ways, YMCA/YWCA/YMHA/YWHA, Youth Organizations

Application Procedures

Initial Contact: Send a written proposal.
Application Requirements: Include description and purpose of the project; amount requested; project action plan and time frame; expected results; total cost and budget; sources and levels of expected funding; annual report; recently audited financial statement; copies of IRS 501(c)(3) and 509(a)1, 2, or 3 rulings; and fund-raising campaign time frame.
Deadlines: Submission deadlines for Foundation Scholarship Program, December 31 each year; Fellowship Program, February 15 each year; Doctoral Program, March 31 each year; Matching Gift and Good Neighbor Programs are ongoing.

Restrictions

Does not support seminars or conferences, or individuals (other than for scholarships). To qualify for the Foundation Scholarship Program, parents and legal guardians must be a State Farm Company employee, agent or retiree; Fellowship Program, must be a majoring in a business related field and be a U.S. citizen, at time of application, must be current full-time college junior or senior, with minimum GPA of 3.6 on a 4.0 scale; Doctoral Program, must be U.S. citizen; Matching Gift Program, must be four-year or above degree, granting U.S. accredited college or university; and Good Neighbor Grant Program, must volunteer at least 40 hours a year to a qualified nonprofit organization, public or private school, or government municipality.

Additional Information

Scholarship, fellowship, doctoral program, matching gifts, and Good Neighbor Program grants have spe-

cific forms and/or applications for submission.
Publications: Foundation Contributions Report

Corporate Officials

Edward Barry Rust, Jr.: chairman, president, chief executive officer, director B Chicago, IL 1950. ED Southern Methodist University JD; Lawrence University (1968-1969); Illinois Wesleyan University BS (1972); Southern Methodist University JD (1975); Southern Methodist University MBA (1975). PRIM CORP EMPL chairman, president, chief executive officer, director: State Farm Mutual Automobile Insurance Co. CORP AFFIL chief executive officer, president: State Farm Life Insurance Co.; chief executive officer, president: State Farm Investment Management Corp.; chief executive officer, president: State Farm Life & Annuity Co.; chief executive officer, president: State Farm International Services Inc.; chief executive officer, president: State Farm General Insurance Co.; chief executive officer, president: State Farm Insurance Companies; chief executive officer, president: State Farm Fire & Casualty Co.; director: Helmerich & Payne Inc.; director: McGraw-Hill Companies Inc.; director: Caterpillar Inc. NONPR AFFIL member: Texas State Bar Association; member business advisory council: University Illinois College Commerce & Business Administration; director: National Center for Educational Accountability; trustee: Illinois Wesleyan University; member, trustee: Insurance Institute America; chairman emeritus: Illinois Business Roundtable; trustee: The Conference Board; member: Illinois Bar Association; co-chairman: Business Roundtable; co-chairman: Business Coalition for Excellence in Education; chairman: Business Higher Education Forum; member: American Institute Property & Liability Underwriters; director: Achieve Inc.; member: American Bar Association.
Laura P. Sullivan: vice president, secretary, counsel B Des Moines, IA 1947. ED Cornell University BA (1971); Drake University JD (1972). PRIM CORP EMPL vice president, secretary, counsel: State Farm Mutual Automobile Insurance Co. CORP AFFIL secretary: State Farm Lloyds Inc.; vice president, secretary, counsel: State Farm Life & Accident Assurance Co.; vice president, secretary, counsel: State Farm Life Insurance Co.; secretary, vice president, counsel, director: State Farm General Insurance Co.; assistant treasurer, director: State Farm Indemnity Co.; vice president, secretary, counsel: State Farm Annuity & Life Insurance Co.; secretary, vice president, counsel: State Farm Fire & Casualty Co. NONPR AFFIL member: American Bar Association; member: American Corporate Counsel Association.
Vincent Joseph Trosino, Sr.: vice chairman, chief operating officer, director B Upland, PA 1940. ED Villanova University (1962); Illinois State University (1973). PRIM CORP EMPL executive vice president, vice chairman, chief operating officer, director: State Farm Mutual Automobile Insurance Co. CORP AFFIL director: Vulcan Materials Co.; vice chairman, member, executive committee: State Farm Mutual Insurance Co.; director: State Farm Life & Annuity Co.; vice chairman, member executive committee, director: State Farm Life Insurance Co.; director: State Farm Investment Management Corp.; director: State Farm Life & Accident Assurance Co.; director: State Farm International Services Inc.; member executive committee director: State Farm Fire & Casualty Co.; director: State Farm General Insurance Co. NONPR AFFIL director: National Italian American Foundation.

Foundation Officials

Willie Brown: vice president ED Illinois State University BA. NONPR AFFIL president: Illinois Wesleyan Associates.
Peggy Echols: vice president NONPR AFFIL director: Kids Voting USA.
Dr. W. H. Knight, Jr.: director ED Columbia University JD; University of North Carolina BA. NONPR AFFIL member: National Bar Association; dean, professor of law: University of Washington School of Law; member: American Bar Association.

Mindy Laub: assistant secretary
Lori Manning: assistant secretary
Dr. Susan Phillips: director ED Agnes Scott College BA (1967); Louisiana State University MS (1971); Louisiana State University PhD (1973). CORP AFFIL director: State Farm Mutal Automobile Insurance; director: Chicago Board Options Exchange; director: Kroger Co. NONPR AFFIL dean, professor of finance: George Washington University School of Business; director: National Futures Association.
Edward Barry Rust, Jr.: chairman (see above)
Laura P. Sullivan: vice president, secretary (see above)
Michael Tipsord: treasurer ED Illinois Wesleyan University BA; University of Illinois JD. NONPR AFFIL member: Illinois State Bar Association; trustee: Illinois Wesleyan University; member: American Bar Association.
Vincent Joseph Trosino, Sr.: assistant secretary (see above)

Grants Analysis

Disclosure Period: calendar year ending 2003
Total Grants: $11,812,853*
Number of Grants: 311
Average Grant: $23,137*
Highest Grant: $2,663,628
Lowest Grant: $500
Typical Range: $2,000 to $50,000
*Note: Giving excludes matching gifts, scholarships, fellowships, doctoral awards, gifts to individuals, and United Way. Average grant figure excludes two highest grants ($4,663,628).

Recent Grants

Note: Grants derived from 2003 Form 990.
Library-Related

200,000	Abraham Lincoln Presidential Library Foundation, Springfield, IL	

General

2,000,000	Illinois State University - College of Business, Normal, IL	
1,683,076	National Merit Scholarship Corporation, Evanston, TX	
625,000	Youth Service America, Washington, DC	
413,000	Illinois State University, Bloomington, IL	
350,000	National Association for the Advancement of Colored People, Baltimore, MD	
316,200	National Board for Professional Teaching Standards, Southfield, MI	
300,000	Learning Space, Issaquah, WA	
289,656	United Way of McLean County, Bloomington, IL	
250,000	Academy for Educational Development Inc., New York, NY	
250,000	Heartland Community College, Normal, IL	

STATE STREET CORP.

Company Headquarters

225 Franklin Street
Boston, MA 02110
Web: http://www.statestreet.com

Company Description

Founded: 1792
Ticker: STT
Exchange: NYSE
Revenue: US$5.861 billion (2004)
Profit: US$798 million (2004)
Employees: 19850 (2003)
Fortune Rank: 341, per FORTUNE Magazine's list of 500 Largest U.S. Corporations (2004).

Nonmonetary Support

Type: Cause-related Marketing & Promotion; Donated Equipment; In-kind Services; Loaned Employees;

Loaned Executives
Volunteer Programs: State Street Global Outreach is a company-wide volunteer program that encourages employee participation in company-sponsored programs, pairs employees who are interested in volunteer opportunities with non-profit organizations with missions that are of interest to the employees, and offers each employee one work day a year for volunteer efforts.

State Street Foundation

Giving Contact

George A. Bowman, Jr., Vice President, Community Affairs
State Street Boston Corp.
225 Franklin Street
Boston, MA 02110-2804
Phone: (617)664-3381
Fax: (617)451-6315
E-mail: gabowman@statestreet.com

Alternate Contact

PO Box 351
Boston, MA 02101
Phone: (617)664-4331

Description

EIN: 046401847
Organization Type: Corporate Foundation
Giving Locations: MA: Boston including the metro area
Grant Types: Capital, Challenge, Employee Matching Gifts, General Support, Project.

Financial Summary

Total Giving: $12,304,157 (2003); $11,567,240 (2002); $9,734,549 (2001). Note: Contributes through foundation only.
Giving Analysis: Giving for 2001 includes: foundation ($7,343,852)
Assets: $4,191,269 (2003); $2,645,096 (2002); $1,971,682 (2001)
Gifts Received: $14,434,000 (2003); $12,781,000 (2002); $11,084,326 (2001). Note: Contributions are received from State Street Bank & Trust and Boston Financial Data Services.

Typical Recipients

Arts & Humanities: Arts Associations & Councils, Arts Centers, Arts Institutes, Arts Outreach, Ballet, Community Arts, Dance, Ethnic & Folk Arts, Arts & Humanities-General, Historic Preservation, History & Archaeology, Libraries, Museums/Galleries, Music, Opera, Performing Arts, Theater
Civic & Public Affairs: African American Affairs, Asian American Affairs, Botanical Gardens/Parks, Business/Free Enterprise, Civil Rights, Clubs, Community Foundations, Economic Development, Economic Policy, Employment/Job Training, Ethnic Organizations, Civic & Public Affairs-General, Hispanic Affairs, Housing, Inner-City Development, Law & Justice, Minority Business, Municipalities/Towns, Nonprofit Management, Public Policy, Safety, Urban & Community Affairs, Women's Affairs, Zoos/Aquariums
Education: Afterschool/Enrichment Programs, Arts/Humanities Education, Business Education, Business-School Partnerships, Colleges & Universities, Continuing Education, Economic Education, Education Associations, Education Funds, Education Reform, Elementary Education (Private), Elementary Education (Public), Engineering/Technological Education, Faculty Development, Education-General, Leadership Training, Literacy, Medical Education, Minority Education, Preschool Education, Private Education (Precollege), Public Education (Precollege), School Volunteerism, Science/Mathematics Education, Secondary Education (Public), Social Sciences Education, Student Aid, Vocational & Technical Edu-

cation

Health: Adolescent Health Issues, AIDS/HIV, Cancer, Children's Health/Hospitals, Clinics/Medical Centers, Diabetes, Eyes/Blindness, Geriatric Health, Health Policy/Cost Containment, Health Funds, Health Organizations, Hospitals, Medical Rehabilitation, Mental Health, Public Health

International: Health Care/Hospitals, International Affairs, International Organizations, International Relief Efforts

Religion: Jewish Causes, Religious Organizations, Religious Welfare

Science: Science Museums

Social Services: Animal Protection, At-Risk Youth, Big Brothers/Big Sisters, Child Abuse, Child Welfare, Community Centers, Community Service Organizations, Counseling, Delinquency & Criminal Rehabilitation, Domestic Violence, Emergency Relief, Family Services, Food/Clothing Distribution, Homes, People with Disabilities, Recreation & Athletics, Refugee Assistance, Scouts, Shelters/Homelessness, Social Services-General, United Funds/United Ways, Veterans, YMCA/YWCA/YMHA/YWHA, Youth Organizations

Application Procedures

Initial Contact: Call or write for guidelines, then send full proposal.

Application Requirements: Include an executive summary (two-page maximum) on organization's letterhead, including: statement of project's principal objective; expected measurable outcome; total project budget, including dollar amount requested and any other anticipated sources of funding; description of population to be affected; project's timetable; name and telephone number of directors, and primary contact person. The proposal (six-page maximum) should include: profile of organization and mission statement; description of the project to be funded; project's purpose; project's history and measures of success; services to be provided; cost to users of the services; profile of the population to be served; primary short-and long-term objectives; description of how the stated objectives will be achieved and the results quantified; plan for sustaining project after funding has ended. The following attachments should also be included: a copy of the organization's 501(c)(3) determination letter; a detailed projected budget for the current fiscal year (including a list of courses and amounts of support--in hand and expected--and, if applicable, the fundraising strategy for obtaining additional funds); a project and operating budget, if the request is for a project; a list of the board of directors and key officers, including business affiliations; resume of the program director and any staff members that are essential to the success of the project; audited financial statements (or IRS Forms 990) for the most recent two years; sources of corporate and foundation support for the most recent two years; and any other supporting material that would help in proposal evaluation.

Deadlines: None.

Review Process: Proposals are reviewed quarterly, in March, June, September, and December.

Decision Notification: Funding decisions are communicated by letter within about 90 days of receipt.

Notes: Also accepts the Associated Grantmakers of Massachusetts grant application form. Organizations may submit a funding request during a calendar year in which they are not receiving payments from a prior grant awarded.

Restrictions

The foundation does not support scholarships or fellowships; research projects; emergency cash flow, deficit spending, debt liquidation; seed money or start-up programs; trips, tours, or transportation expenses; or films or videos.

Foundation seldom makes multiyear grants, or for general operating support.

Additional Information

Publications: Guidelines
Trust(s): State Street Bank & Trust

Corporate Officials

George A. Bowman, Jr.: vice president community affairs PRIM CORP EMPL vice president community affairs: State Street Bank & Trust Co.

David Anthony Spina: chairman, chief executive officer B New York, NY 1942. ED College of the Holy Cross BS (1964); Harvard University MBA (1972). PRIM CORP EMPL chairman, chief executive officer: State Street Bank & Trust Co. CORP AFFIL chairman emeritus: Massachusetts Housing Investment Corp. CLUB AFFIL member: Commercial Club of Boston.

Foundation Officials

George A. Bowman, Jr.: foundation manager, vice president (see above)
Lilo Navales de Garne: foundation officer
Judith Mullen: vice president
Jennifer Waldner: assistant vice president

Grants Analysis

Disclosure Period: calendar year ending 2003
Total Grants: $10,264,156*
Number of Grants: 1,668
Average Grant: $5,957*
Highest Grant: $333,333
Lowest Grant: $25
Typical Range: $3,000 to $25,000
*Note: Giving excludes United Way. Average grant figure excludes highest grant.

Recent Grants

Note: Grants derived from 2003 Form 990.
Library-Related

100,000	Boston Public Library Foundation, Boston, MA

General

500,000	United Way, Alexandria, VA
500,000	United Way, Fitchburg, MA
500,000	United Way of Massachusetts Bay, Boston, MA
300,000	Urban League of Eastern Massachusetts, Roxbury, MA
200,000	Planning Office of Urban Affairs
200,000	United Way Millennium Fund, Fitchburg, MA
183,778	Community Technology Centers, WA
150,000	Boston Medical Center, Boston, MA
150,000	Brandeis University, Waltham, MA
125,000	Boston Housing Partnership Inc., Boston, MA

STATLER FOUNDATION

Giving Contact

Edward M. Flynn, Chairman
107 Delaware Avenue, Suite 680
Buffalo, NY 14202
Phone: (716)852-1104
Fax: (716)852-3968

Description

Founded: 1934
EIN: 131889077
Organization Type: Specialized/Single Purpose Foundation
Giving Locations: NY: internationally; nationally.
Grant Types: Capital, Professorship, Scholarship.

Donor Information

Founder: The death of Ellsworth Milton Statler in 1928 marked the end of an era in the hotel industry and the passing of one of the most creative and resourceful hoteliers to have practiced the profession. It is also significant because Statler's will provided for

the creation of the Statler Foundation "(to support) research work for the benefit of the (hotel) industry... training and making more proficient the workers in the hotels, for the benefit of the industry as a whole."

To fund his posthumous endeavor, Statler transferred to the newly-created Foundation 10,000 shares of Statler Company stock, then valued at some $10 a share. Since its creation in 1934, the Foundation's endowment has grown to $28.5 million dollars, while also spinning off millions of dollars in grants to numerous educational institutions in furtherance of Statler's objectives.

For nearly 40 years, Statler's widow, Alice Seidler Statler, served as chairman of the trustees of the Statler Foundation. It was appropriate that Mrs. Statler, who served for many years as Statler's personal secretary and who remained his business confidate, should oversee the early work and development of the Foundation. On Mrs. Statler's death in 1969, the chairmanship of the Foundation passed successively to Ward B. Arbury, Peter J. Crotty, Robert Koren, and Arthur Musarra.

Financial Summary

Total Giving: $702,953 (2003); $2,000,000 (2002 approx); $1,632,164 (2001)
Assets: $32,223,335 (2003); $34,124,284 (2001)

Typical Recipients

Civic & Public Affairs: Civic & Public Affairs-General, Professional & Trade Associations

Education: Arts/Humanities Education, Business Education, Colleges & Universities, Community & Junior Colleges, Continuing Education, Faculty Development, Education-General, International Studies, Minority Education, Private Education (Precollege), Science/Mathematics Education, Student Aid, Vocational & Technical Education

Health: Children's Health/Hospitals, Eyes/Blindness, Hospitals

International: Foreign Educational Institutions, International-General, International Affairs, International Development

Religion: Churches, Religious Welfare

Social Services: Camps, Community Centers, Community Service Organizations, Food/Clothing Distribution, People with Disabilities, Social Services-General, YMCA/YWCA/YMHA/YWHA, Youth Organizations

Application Procedures

Initial Contact: A letter of inquiry requesting application form.

Application Requirements: Along with the completed application, submit 13 copies of the following information: name, address and phone number; paragraph of history; copy of IRS tax-exempt letter; other sources of funding; list of board officers; purpose of organization; number of people served; most recent financial audit; purpose of project and description of need; amount requested; other sources that have been approached for funding; total cost of project; time period; EEO policy and affirmative action statement; other organizations assisting with project; and future support. Application must be signed by the chief executive of organization.

Deadlines: None.

Review Process: The foundation reviews and processes all requests for support by August or September.

Restrictions

The foundation makes grants for education and training in the hospitality field (hotels, motels, and food service) only.

Foundation Officials

Robert B. Bennett: trustee B Fitchburg, MA 1941. ED Babson College BSBA (1963); University of Massachusetts MBA (1966); Harvard University (1980-1981). PRIM CORP EMPL chairman, president, chief executive officer: ONBAN Corp. CORP AFFIL member: Retail Finance Services Group NA; chairman: Health Care Data System Inc.; chairman: Crouse Irving Memorial Properties Inc.; director: Fays Inc.; director: Cirrus System Inc.; member: Association Bank Holding Companies; chairman: CIMH Enterprises Inc. NONPR AFFIL trustee: Syracuse Stage; trustee: Syracuse Symphony Orchestra; director: Senior Olympics; member: National Retail Banking Planners Association; director: Onondaga County Industries Development Corp.; director: Metropolitan Development Association; trustee: Illinois College; director: Crouse Irving Memorial Hospital; director: Greater Syracuse Chamber of Commerce; director: Community Bank Association New York State; member: Financial Executives Institute; executive council: Boy Scouts America Onondaga Region; trustee: Citizens Foundation; member: Bank Administration Institute; member: American Bankers Association.

Marguerite Collesano: trustee
William J. Cunningham, Jr.: trustee
Joseph DiNardo: trustee PRIM CORP EMPL president: Dinardo Dinardo & Lukasik PC.
Peter J. Fiorella, Jr.: trustee
Edward M. Flynn: trustee
Ernestine R. Green: chairwoman, trustee
Arthur F. Musarra: trustee
Carlo M. Perfetto: trustee
Arthur V. Sabia: trustee
Herbert Siegel: chairman
Peter Vinolus: vice chairman, trustee

Grants Analysis

Disclosure Period: calendar year ending 2003
Total Grants: $702,953*
Number of Grants: 28
Average Grant: $18,741*
Highest Grant: $196,812
Lowest Grant: $1,000
Typical Range: $5,000 to $50,000
*Note: Average grant figure excludes highest grant.

Recent Grants

Note: Grants derived from 2002 Form 990.
General

254,000	Niagara University, Niagara Falls, NY -- to assist in the renovation of St. Vincent's Hall
100,000	Blind Association of Western New York, New York, NY -- to assist the National Statler Center for Careers in Hospitality Service
100,000	Culinary Institute of America, Hyde Park, NY -- to assist the Statler Digital Video Library
50,000	Florida International University, Miami, FL -- fund for Ellsworth M. Statler Professorship

JOHN STAUFFER CHARITABLE TRUST

Giving Contact

Mr. H. Jess Senecal, Trustee
301 North Lake Avenue, 10th Floor
Pasadena, CA 91101-4108
Phone: (626)793-9400
Fax: (626)793-5900

Description

Founded: 1974
EIN: 237434707
Organization Type: Specialized/Single Purpose Foundation
Giving Locations: CA
Grant Types: Endowment, Fellowship, General Support, Professorship, Project, Research, Scholarship.
Note: The foundation also provides funding for building and equipment.

Donor Information

Founder: Established in 1974 under the will of the late John Stauffer, an officer and director of the Stauffer Chemical Company who was particularly interested in educational concerns and hospitals.

Financial Summary

Total Giving: $3,000,000 (fiscal year ending May 31, 2004); $2,800,000 (fiscal 2003); $4,000,000 (fiscal 2001). Note: Figure for 1997 was provided by the foundation.
Assets: $44,395,101 (fiscal 2004); $42,316,855 (fiscal 2003); $59,971,355 (fiscal 2001). Note: Figures for 1997 and 1998 provided by the foundation.

Typical Recipients

Arts & Humanities: Libraries
Education: Colleges & Universities, Engineering/Technological Education, Legal Education, Science/Mathematics Education, Student Aid
Health: Cancer, Children's Health/Hospitals, Clinics/Medical Centers, Emergency/Ambulance Services, Eyes/Blindness, Health Organizations, Heart, Hospitals, Medical Rehabilitation, Medical Research, Mental Health, Outpatient Health Care, Public Health
International: Health Care/Hospitals
Religion: Churches, Religious Welfare
Science: Scientific Research
Social Services: Child Welfare, Community Service Organizations, Delinquency & Criminal Rehabilitation, Family Planning, Family Services, Food/Clothing Distribution, People with Disabilities, Scouts, Senior Services, Substance Abuse, YMCA/YWCA/YMHA/YWHA, Youth Organizations

Application Procedures

Initial Contact: Send a letter stating purpose of funds sought, and amount requested, and include proof of tax-exempt status. The foundation maintains precise application guidelines; organizations are encouraged to request a copy of the guidelines before submitting a proposal.
Application Requirements: Proposals should include the amount requested; an explanation of the need for the subject of the grant; the goals; the manner in which John Stauffer's name will be memorialized; full financial information, including a detailed budget for the project to be assisted by the grant; and a statement of whether other sources of funding are being sought, and if so, which other sources are providing funding.
All applications must be executed by an officer of the grantee institution. Applications signed by a division or department head must be approved and countersigned by the head of the organization or institution, or by an officer thereof. Applicants should submit the latest IRS tax-exempt determination letter, stating that the grantee is not a private foundation, as well as the latest audited balance sheet and statement of income and expenditures. In addition, the trust would like to see a tax-exempt letter from the State of California. Letters of support from authorities and/or organizations in the applicant's field are encouraged.
All proposals and letters should be submitted in three copies, one for each of the trustees.
Deadlines: None. The board meets quarterly and accepts applications any time.
Review Process: If the proposal needs amplification or clarification, the trust will request the needed information in writing. Applicants are notified in writing whether or not the grant is being given. Decisions are made within six to nine months. Proposals will not be returned, and may be peer-reviewed.
Notes: Those receiving grants are required to send a report on the use of the funds to the trust, including a certification that the funds have been used for the purpose for which the grant was made. The trust reserves the right to call for a reasonable audit of the use of grant funds conducted by its representatives at its own expense. If grants were used for purposes

other than that for which the grant was made, the total amount of the grant must be returned.

Restrictions

Grants are not made to organizations which, in turn, distribute them to others at their own discretion. Grants are not made to individuals, to influence legislation or elections, to discriminatory groups, for sectarian religious activities, for loans or operating expenses, deficit financing, or general fund drives or annual appeals.

Additional Information

Those denied a grant may submit a new application in the future, but should not request reinstatement of a prior request which has been denied. The trust prefers to participate with other donors when making grants.
Recipients may be required to provide matching funds. Also, large grants may be distributed over a period of two or more years.
Publications: Policy Guidelines

Foundation Officials

Carl M. Franklin: chairman
H. Jess Senecal: co-trustee
Michael S. Whalen: co-trustee ED California State University BA (1976); University of California at Berkeley JD (1979). NONPR AFFIL member: Order Coif; fellow: Phi Beta Kappa; member: Los Angeles County Bar Association; fellow: Center Creative Photography; director: Constitutional Rights Foundation; member: Beta Gamma Sigma.

Grants Analysis

Disclosure Period: fiscal year ending May 31, 2004
Total Grants: $3,000,000
Number of Grants: 4
Highest Grant: $1,250,000
Lowest Grant: $500,000

Recent Grants

Note: Grants derived from 2003 Form 990.
General

1,250,000	USC Loker Hydrocarbon Research, Los Angeles, CA
750,000	Children's Hospital of Los Angeles, Los Angeles, CA
750,000	University of Redlands, Redlands, CA
500,000	Claremont Graduate University, Claremont, CA

STAUNTON FARM FOUNDATION

Giving Contact

Joni Schwager, Executive Director
650 Smithfield St., Suite 210
Pittsburgh, PA 15222
Phone: (412)281-8020
Fax: (412)232-3115
E-mail: jschwager@stauntonfarm.org
Web: http://www.stauntonfarm.org

Description

Founded: 1937
EIN: 250965573
Organization Type: Specialized/Single Purpose Foundation
Giving Locations: PA: Southwestern Pennsylvania
Grant Types: Award, General Support, Matching, Multiyear/Continuing Support.

Donor Information

Founder: Established in Pennsylvania in 1937 with funds donated by Mrs. Matilda S. McCready (born Matilda Staunton Craig). Mrs. McCready's original wish was that funds from the foundation would be used to erect a home for the mentally ill. However, her estate lacked the necessary funds for such an undertaking.

Mrs. McCready realized her original intentions may not always be practical and stated, "In the event that advances in medical sciences or in social conditions render carrying on of the home...impractical, the directors of Staunton Farm may, with the consent of Orphan's Court of Allegheny County, PA, change its character so as to suit the needs of the times, keeping always in view the effort to alleviate the conditions of the sick and unfortunate."

Financial Summary
Total Giving: $1,852,394 (2001)
Assets: $44,504,580 (2001)

Typical Recipients
Arts & Humanities: Libraries
Civic & Public Affairs: African American Affairs, Botanical Gardens/Parks, Community Foundations, Employment/Job Training, Gay/Lesbian Issues, Civic & Public Affairs-General, Nonprofit Management, Professional & Trade Associations, Urban & Community Affairs, Women's Affairs
Education: Afterschool/Enrichment Programs, Colleges & Universities, Education Funds, Education Reform, Elementary Education (Public), Education-General, Gifted & Talented Programs, Literacy, Medical Education, Preschool Education, Private Education (Precollege), Public Education (Precollege), Special Education
Health: AIDS/HIV, Alzheimer's Disease, Children's Health/Hospitals, Clinics/Medical Centers, Eyes/Blindness, Health-General, Health Funds, Health Organizations, Hospices, Hospitals, Medical Rehabilitation, Mental Health, Public Health, Single-Disease Health Associations
Religion: Churches, Jewish Causes, Ministries, Religious Organizations, Religious Welfare
Social Services: Child Abuse, Child Welfare, Community Centers, Community Service Organizations, Counseling, Crime Prevention, Day Care, Delinquency & Criminal Rehabilitation, Domestic Violence, Emergency Relief, Family Planning, Family Services, Food/Clothing Distribution, Homes, People with Disabilities, Recreation & Athletics, Scouts, Senior Services, Sexual Abuse, Shelters/Homelessness, Social Services-General, Substance Abuse, United Funds/United Ways, YMCA/YWCA/YMHA/YWHA, Youth Organizations

Application Procedures
Initial Contact: A letter of inquiry should be sent describing the organization and proposed project. After initial review, prospective grantees may be asked to make a formal application using the Grantmakers of Western Pennsylvania Common Application Form for consideration by the Foundation's Project Committee.
Deadlines: Formal applications are generally due February 11, August 4, and November 3. Prospective grantees should plan accordingly.

Restrictions
The foundation does not usually contribute to general operating support, endowment funds, building campaigns, conferences, or grants to individuals. Exceptions have been made in situations where the conduct of the project is directly dependent upon altered or new facilities.

Additional Information
The foundation reports that current selection criteria favors those requests that focus on providing direct patient care in the mental health field.
Publications: Guidelines; Application; Brochure; Grants List; History

Foundation Officials

Grants Analysis
Disclosure Period: calendar year ending 2001
Total Grants: $1,852,394*
Number of Grants: 56
Average Grant: $30,600*
Highest Grant: $100,000
Lowest Grant: $500
Typical Range: $10,000 to $50,000
*Note: Average grant figure excludes two highest grants ($200,000).

Recent Grants
Note: Grants derived from 2001 Form 990.

General
100,000	Holy Family Institute, Pittsburgh, PA
100,000	Pittsburgh Council on Public Education, Pittsburgh, PA
90,115	Neighborhood Academy, Pittsburgh, PA
83,000	Foundation for California University of Pennsylvania, California, PA
65,000	Allegheny Department of Human Services, Pittsburgh, PA
65,000	Family Resources, Pittsburgh, PA
63,000	NAMI of Southwestern Pennsylvania, Pittsburgh, PA
55,825	Allegheny General Hospital Singer Research Institute, Pittsburgh, PA
55,000	YWCA of Greater Pittsburgh, Pittsburgh, PA
53,677	Bethlehem Haven, Pittsburgh, PA

KENT D. AND MARY L. STEADLEY MEMORIAL TRUST

Giving Contact
Lareta Garnier, Trust Officer
c/o Bank of America
Springfield, MO 65801
Phone: (417)227-6237

Description
Founded: 1970
EIN: 436120866
Organization Type: Private Foundation
Giving Locations: MO: Carthage
Grant Types: Capital, General Support.

Financial Summary
Total Giving: $813,800 (2003); $926,950 (2001)
Assets: $19,669,614 (2003); $20,173,304 (2001)

Typical Recipients
Arts & Humanities: Arts Associations & Councils, Arts Centers, Historic Preservation, Libraries, Museums/Galleries
Civic & Public Affairs: Civic & Public Affairs-General, Municipalities/Towns, Urban & Community Affairs
Education: Education Funds, Elementary Education (Private), Elementary Education (Public), Private Education (Precollege), Public Education (Precollege), Science/Mathematics Education
Health: Clinics/Medical Centers, Heart, Medical Rehabilitation
Religion: Ministries, Religious Welfare
Social Services: Animal Protection, Domestic Violence, Recreation & Athletics, Scouts, Senior Services, Substance Abuse, YMCA/YWCA/YMHA/YWHA

Application Procedures
Initial Contact: Contact the trustee to request an application form.
Deadlines: None.

Restrictions
Limited to organizations in or near Carthage, Missouri that are not beneficiaries of local or national campaigns.

Additional Information
Publications: Application Form
Trust(s): Bank of America

Grants Analysis
Disclosure Period: calendar year ending 2003
Total Grants: $813,800
Number of Grants: 11
Average Grant: $21,663*
Highest Grant: $290,500
Lowest Grant: $3,300
Typical Range: $5,000 to $50,000
*Note: Average grant figure excludes three highest grants ($640,500).

Recent Grants
Note: Grants derived from 2001 Form 990.
General
281,500	Carthage R-9 School, Carthage, MO -- construction and educational programs
150,000	City of Carthage, Carthage, MO -- Fair Acres sports complex
100,000	McCune Brooks Hospital, Carthage, MO -- capital budget items
56,250	Magic Moments Riding Therapy -- capital improvements
56,250	Main Street Carthage, Carthage, MO -- Carthage VIP Town Days Program

50,000	Boy Scouts of America, Joplin, MI -- multipurpose building
50,000	Community Clinic Carthage, Carthage, MO -- start up expenses
50,000	Innovative Industries, Inc., Carthage, MO -- building renovation
50,000	Ozark Area Girl Scout Council, Joplin, MO -- new lodge at Camp Mintahama
30,000	Main Street Carthage, Carthage, MO -- gazebo construction

STEARNS FOUNDATION

Giving Contact
Roger R. Stearns, Secretary
PO Box 50
Hutchinson, MN 55350-0050
Phone: (320)587-2137
Fax: (320)587-7646

Description
Founded: 1989
EIN: 411609446
Organization Type: Private Foundation
Giving Locations: MN: Hutchinson
Grant Types: General Support.

Financial Summary
Total Giving: $29,420 (fiscal year ending March 31, 2004); $27,761 (fiscal 2001)
Assets: $299,081 (fiscal 2004); $171,163 (fiscal 2001)
Gifts Received: $23,682 (fiscal 2001); $18,173 (fiscal 2000); $45,855 (fiscal 1999). Note: In fiscal 2001, contributions were received from Stearnswood, Inc. ($23,432) and Robert H. Stearns ($250). In fiscal 2000, contributions were received from Stearnswood, Inc. In fiscal 1999, contributions were received from Robert H. Stearns ($250) and Stearnswood, Inc.($45,605).

Typical Recipients
Arts & Humanities: Libraries, Music
Civic & Public Affairs: Community Foundations, Civic & Public Affairs-General, Parades/Festivals, Safety
Education: Colleges & Universities, Economic Education, Education Funds, Elementary Education (Public), Education-General, Public Education (Precollege), Student Aid
Health: Cancer, Health Organizations, Hospices, Hospitals, Long-Term Care, Medical Rehabilitation
Social Services: At-Risk Youth, Community Service Organizations, Crime Prevention, Domestic Violence, Food/Clothing Distribution, Recreation & Athletics, Youth Organizations

Application Procedures
Initial Contact: Submit a written application.
Application Requirements: Specify the purpose of funds sought and the benefit.
Deadlines: None.

Foundation Officials
Mary A. Anderson: vice president
Roger R. Stearns: president, secretary

Grants Analysis
Disclosure Period: fiscal year ending March 31, 2004
Total Grants: $29,420
Number of Grants: 50
Average Grant: $588
Highest Grant: $5,300
Lowest Grant: $30
Typical Range: $100 to $1,500

Recent Grants
Note: Grants derived from 2001 Form 990.
General

6,700	Hutchinson Youth Hockey Association, Hutchinson, MN -- support arena expansion
4,680	Hutchinson Area Foundation for Health Care, Hutchinson, MN -- support to purchase equipment at hospital and nursing home
2,000	McLeod County Food Shelf, Glencoe, MN -- support for area food shelf
1,500	City of Hutchinson, Hutchinson, MN -- support for fire prevention week activities
1,400	Dollars for Scholars, Hutchinson, MN -- scholarships
1,093	American Cancer Society, Minneapolis, MN -- support for research
1,000	Courage Center, Golden Valley, MN -- support for rehabilitation center
759	Hutchinson Public Schools 423, Hutchinson, MN -- support for school children
750	Hutchinson Jaycee Water Carnival, Hutchinson, MN -- support annual community celebration
520	University of Minnesota, Minneapolis, MN -- support for athletic programs

ARTEMAS W. STEARNS TRUST

Giving Contact
Clifford E. Elias, Trustee
70 East St.
Methuen, MA 01844
Phone: (978)687-0501
Fax: (978)688-7689

Description
Founded: 1896
EIN: 042137061
Organization Type: Private Foundation
Giving Locations: MA: Lawrence including surrounding area
Grant Types: Capital, Emergency, General Support, Project, Scholarship.

Donor Information
Founder: the late Artemas W. Stearns

Financial Summary
Total Giving: $150,900 (2003)
Assets: $4,794,001 (2003)

Typical Recipients
Arts & Humanities: History & Archaeology, Libraries
Civic & Public Affairs: Chambers of Commerce, Community Foundations, Civic & Public Affairs-General, Hispanic Affairs, Housing, Municipalities/Towns, Women's Affairs
Education: Colleges & Universities, Education-General, Preschool Education, Private Education (Precollege), Public Education (Precollege), Religious Education, Science/Mathematics Education, Secondary Education (Private)
Health: Children's Health/Hospitals, Clinics/Medical Centers, Health Organizations, Home-Care Services, Hospitals, Nursing Services
International: International Affairs
Religion: Churches, Jewish Causes, Religious Welfare
Social Services: Big Brothers/Big Sisters, Child Welfare, Community Centers, Community Service Organizations, Counseling, Crime Prevention, Family Services, Food/Clothing Distribution, People with Disabilities, Recreation & Athletics, Scouts, Senior Services, Shelters/Homelessness, Social Services-

General, United Funds/United Ways, YMCA/YWCA/YMHA/YWHA, Youth Organizations

Application Procedures
Initial Contact: Request application guidelines.
Deadlines: January 31.

Restrictions
Grants are awarded to non-profit and charitable homes, nursing homes, convalescent homes, retirement homes, sanitaria, homes for the aged, hospitals, and other organizations that provide care for indigent aged people and for the relief of the deserving poor of the city of Lawrence. Grants are not made to individuals.

Additional Information
Publications: Application Guidelines

Foundation Officials
Clifford E. Elias, Esq.: trustee
Eileen M. Khoury: trustee
Marsha E. Rich: trustee

Grants Analysis
Disclosure Period: calendar year ending 2003
Total Grants: $150,900
Number of Grants: 25
Average Grant: $4,388*
Highest Grant: $25,000
Lowest Grant: $500
Typical Range: $1,000 to $5,000
*Note: Average grant figure excludes two highest grants ($50,000).

Recent Grants
Note: Grants derived from 2003 Form 990.
General

25,000	Holy Family Hospital, Methuen, MA
25,000	Lawrence General Hospital, Lawrence, MA
12,000	Lawrence Boys and Girls Club, Lawrence, MA
10,000	Adelante Inc., Lawrence, MA
10,000	Si Se Puede Inc., North Andover, MA
7,500	YWCA of Greater Lawrence, Lawrence, MA
7,000	Neighbors in Need, Lawrence, MA
5,000	Big Brother/Big sister, Lawrence, MA
5,000	Bread and Roses, Lawrence, MA
5,000	Central Catholic High School, Lawrence, MA

BERTHA STEBENS CHARITABLE FOUNDATION

Giving Contact
Bertha Stebens Charitable Foundation
119 Second Street NW
Mason City, IA 50401-3198
Phone: (641)423-1913

Description
Founded: 1987
EIN: 421280907
Organization Type: Private Foundation
Giving Locations: IA: Cerro Gordo County, Mason City
Grant Types: General Support.

Financial Summary
Total Giving: $102,600 (fiscal year ending July 31, 2004); $84,731 (fiscal 2001)
Assets: $1,903,350 (fiscal 2004); $1,808,501 (fiscal 2001)

Typical Recipients

Arts & Humanities: Arts Festivals, Arts Funds, Museums/Galleries, Music, Public Broadcasting, Theater

Civic & Public Affairs: Community Foundations, Municipalities/Towns, Rural Affairs

Education: Preschool Education, Private Education (Precollege), Student Aid

Health: Clinics/Medical Centers, Hospices, Hospitals

Religion: Religious Welfare

Social Services: Community Centers, Emergency Relief, People with Disabilities, Scouts, YMCA/YWCA/YMHA/YWHA

Application Procedures

Initial Contact: Submit a written request.

Application Requirements: Include name, address, and a description of organization; proof of tax-exempt status; tax ID number; current financial statements; list of officers and directors; contact person; amount requested; purpose of funds sought; and date funds are needed.

Deadlines: May 31.

Restrictions

The foundation only funds 501(c)(3) charities located in Cerro Gordo County, IA.

Foundation Officials

Harold R. Winston, Sr.: director

Grants Analysis

Disclosure Period: fiscal year ending July 31, 2004
Total Grants: $102,600
Number of Grants: 46
Average Grant: $2,230
Highest Grant: $10,000
Lowest Grant: $500
Typical Range: $1,000 to $5,000

Recent Grants

Note: Grants derived from 2001 Form 990.
General

25,000	Mason City Foundation, Mason City, IA -- for construction of music man square
5,000	KCMR Radio, Mason City, IA -- for new copy machine
5,000	Mason City Family YMCA, Mason City, IA -- for construction of new building
4,000	North Iowa Area Community College, Mason City, IA -- for 2 art theater scholarships
3,500	Charles H. MacNider Museum -- for puppet performances/workshops
3,000	Mason City Choral Music Guild, Mason City, IA -- for robes and costumes
3,000	Stevens Children's Theater -- for building improvements
2,500	Good Shepherd Health Center, Inc. -- for Telephone Reassurance Program
2,500	Nora Springs Rock Falls Community School, Nora Springs, IA -- for scholarships
2,000	American Red Cross -- for health and safety information resources and disaster services

STEELCASE INC.

Company Headquarters

Grand Rapids, MI
Web: http://www.steelcase.com

Company Description

Founded: 1912
Ticker: SCS
Exchange: NYSE
Revenue: US$2.586 billion (2002)

Profit: US$1 million (2002)
Employees: 14200 (2003)
SIC(s): 2521 Wood Office Furniture, 2522 Office Furniture Except Wood, 2531 Public Building & Related Furniture, 3577 Computer Peripheral Equipment Nec.

Operating Locations

Steelcase Inc. (AL--Athens; CA--Tustin; MI--Grand Rapids, Kentwood; NC--Asheville, Fletcher, High Point)

Nonmonetary Support

Type: Donated Products; In-kind Services
Contact: Howard Sutton, Vice President of Corporate Relations
Note: The company provides nonmonetary support.

Steelcase Foundation

Giving Contact

Susan K. Broman, Executive Director
Steelcase Foundation
PO Box 1967
Grand Rapids, MI 49501
Phone: (616)653-0364
Fax: (616)475-2200
E-mail: sbroman@steelcase.com

Alternate Contact

Phone: (616)246-9860

Description

EIN: 386050470
Organization Type: Corporate Foundation
Giving Locations: principally near operating locations and to national organizations.
Grant Types: Capital, Employee Matching Gifts, General Support, Matching, Project, Scholarship, Seed Money.
Note: Employee matching gift ratio: 1 to 1 for gifts to educational institutions.

Financial Summary

Total Giving: $7,062,096 (fiscal year ending November 30, 2002); $6,697,121 (fiscal 2001). Note: Contributes through corporate direct giving program and foundation.
Assets: $104,743,934 (fiscal 2002); $117,903,929 (fiscal 2001)
Gifts Received: $3,824,790 (fiscal 2002); $5,305,200 (fiscal 2001); $5,321,800 (fiscal 2000). Note: Contributions are received from Steelcase, Inc.

Typical Recipients

Arts & Humanities: Arts Associations & Councils, Arts Centers, Arts Funds, Arts Institutes, Ballet, Dance, Ethnic & Folk Arts, Arts & Humanities-General, Historic Preservation, History & Archaeology, Libraries, Literary Arts, Museums/Galleries, Music, Opera, Performing Arts, Public Broadcasting, Theater

Civic & Public Affairs: African American Affairs, Botanical Gardens/Parks, Business/Free Enterprise, Chambers of Commerce, Clubs, Community Foundations, Economic Development, Employment/Job Training, Civic & Public Affairs-General, Hispanic Affairs, Housing, Inner-City Development, Municipalities/Towns, Native American Affairs, Public Policy, Urban & Community Affairs, Women's Affairs, Zoos/Aquariums

Education: Afterschool/Enrichment Programs, Agricultural Education, Arts/Humanities Education, Business Education, Colleges & Universities, Community & Junior Colleges, Economic Education, Education Associations, Education Funds, Elementary Education (Private), Environmental Education, Education-General, Leadership Training, Literacy, Medical Education, Preschool Education, Private Education (Precollege), Public Education (Precollege), Religious

Education, Special Education, Student Aid
Environment: Protection, Resource Conservation
Health: AIDS/HIV, Arthritis, Cancer, Children's Health/Hospitals, Clinics/Medical Centers, Emergency/Ambulance Services, Eyes/Blindness, Health-General, Geriatric Health, Health Policy/Cost Containment, Health Organizations, Hospices, Kidney, Medical Rehabilitation, Mental Health, Nutrition, Prenatal Health Issues, Public Health, Respiratory, Single-Disease Health Associations
International: International-General
Religion: Churches, Ministries, Religious Organizations, Religious Welfare
Social Services: Animal Protection, Camps, Child Abuse, Child Welfare, Community Centers, Community Service Organizations, Counseling, Delinquency & Criminal Rehabilitation, Domestic Violence, Emergency Relief, Family Planning, Family Services, Food/Clothing Distribution, Homes, People with Disabilities, Recreation & Athletics, Scouts, Senior Services, Shelters/Homelessness, Substance Abuse, United Funds/United Ways, Volunteer Services, YMCA/YWCA/YMHA/YWHA, Youth Organizations

Application Procedures

Initial Contact: Send letter requesting application.
Application Requirements: Letter should be on organizational letterhead, signed by the chief executive, and include: description of organization and project, copy of IRS 501(c)(3) nonprofit certification. Additional information required with application are: financial statements, including current budget showing expenses and revenues and principal sources and amount requesteds of ongoing annual support; project budget for which funds are sought; brief narrative description of project, including indication of need; descriptive literature, if available, explaining organization and its services; if program is part of a larger organization, letter of support from management must accompany application; description of how the success of this project will be determined; names, business affiliation and address of board of directors; any other helpful material; include cover letter briefly recapping the proposal; do not submit applications in binders or folders; brief narrative of the history of the organization; and must be signed by CEO or president of the Board.
Deadlines: Contact foundation for the next deadline.

Restrictions

The foundation does not make grants to individuals, organizations that have received a foundation grant in the last 12 months, fraternal organizations, political or lobbying groups, for conferences or seminars, or for dinners or special events.

Donations to religiously-affiliated programs are made only when the objectives benefit the entire community. Programs with substantial religious overtones of a sectarian nature are not considered.

Foundation does not support groups that discriminate against people because of race, sex, disability, or national origin.

Foundation does not support groups that discriminate against people because of race, sex, disability, or national origin.

Additional Information

The foundation and company endeavor to support organizations in which company employees are board members, volunteers, or clients, or where employees are part of the benefiting community.

The foundation prefers to participate with others in providing financial support for a project and occasionally will structure its grants to encourage broad support by others.

Old Kent Bank and Trust Company serves as a corporate trustee for the foundation.

Foundation requires reports from recipients detailing financial accounting of grant expenditures and accomplishments.

Publications: Annual Report
Trust(s): Fifth Third Bank

Corporate Officials

James P. Hackett: president, chief executive officer B April 22, 1955. ED University of Michigan BA (1977). PRIM CORP EMPL president, chief executive officer: Steelcase Inc.

Peter M. Wege, II: director PRIM CORP EMPL president: Greylock Inc. CORP AFFIL director: Steelcase Inc.

Foundation Officials

Susan K. Broman: executive director, trustee
James P. Hackett: trustee (see above)
Earl Holton: trustee
David Dyer Hunting, Jr.: trustee B Grand Rapids, MI 1926. ED University of Michigan (1948).
Frank Henry Merlotti: trustee B Herrin, IL 1926.
Robert Cunningham Pew, II: trustee B Syracuse, NY 1923. ED Wesleyan University BA. PRIM CORP EMPL chairman emeritus: Steelcase Inc. CORP AFFIL director: Old Kent Financial Corp.; director: Foremost Corp. America. NONPR AFFIL director: Michigan Strategic Fund; director: National Organization Disability; director: Grand Rapids Employers Association; board control: Grand Valley State College; member: Governments Commission Jobs & Economic Development; director: Grand Rapids Chamber of Commerce; director: Economic Development Corp. Grand Rapids; member: Chi Psi. CLUB AFFIL University Club; Lost Tree Club; Peninsular Club; Kent Country Club.
Howard Sutton: trustee B Chicago, IL 1936. ED Michigan State University BA (1958). NONPR AFFIL member: Association of National Advertisers Inc.; member: Business & Professional Advertisers Association; member: American Advertising Federation; member: American Marketing Association.
Peter M. Wege, II: vice president (see above)
Kate Pew Wolters: chairperson

Grants Analysis

Disclosure Period: fiscal year ending November 30, 2002
Total Grants: $6,058,996*
Number of Grants: 394
Average Grant: $15,378
Highest Grant: $523,500
Lowest Grant: $25
Typical Range: $50 to $50,000 and $100,000 to $500,000
***Note:** Giving excludes matching gifts; scholarship; United Way.

Recent Grants

Note: Grants derived from fiscal 2003 Form 990.

General

704,000	Heart of West Michigan United Way, Grand Rapids, MI
625,000	Grand Rapids Art Museum, Grand Rapids, MI
310,000	Child and Family Resource Council, Grand Rapids, MI
300,000	American Red Cross, Grand Rapids, MI
213,640	Calvin College, Grand Rapids, MI
182,716	Grand Valley State University, Allendale, MI
158,363	Grand Rapids Symphony, Grand Rapids, MI
130,000	Orange County United Way, Irvine, CA
125,000	St. John's Home, Grand Rapids, MI
125,000	South End Community Outreach, Grand Rapids, MI

STEELE-REESE FOUNDATION

Giving Contact

William T. Buice, III, Co-Trustee
32 Washington Square West
New York, NY 10011
Phone: (212)557-7700
Fax: (212)286-8513
Note: Contact for general inquiries.

Alternate Contact

Charles U. Buice
1 Main St., Apt. 6F
Brooklyn, NY 11201
Note: Contact for Idaho and Montana.

Description

Founded: 1955
EIN: 136034763
Organization Type: General Purpose Foundation
Giving Locations: GA: Northern Georgia; ID; KY: Appalachian region of the state; MT; NC: Appalachian region of the state; TN: Appalachian region of the state; WA
Grant Types: Endowment, General Support, Scholarship.

Donor Information

Founder: Established in 1955 by Eleanor Steele Reese, whose father Charles Steele was a partner of J.P. Morgan. Eleanor Steele was born in New York City in 1893. After pursuing a career as an opera singer and recitalist in Europe and the United States for two decades, she moved to the western United States. She met and married Emmet P. Reese in 1941. At the time of their marriage, he and Eleanor bought and operated a small working ranch near Shoup, ID. In the mid-1950s, they moved to a large ranch in Salmon, ID, which they operated until a few years before her death in 1977. Emmet P. Reese died in 1982. The original trustees of the foundation were Sidney W. Davidson and J.P. Morgan & Co., Inc. Davidson and J.P. Morgan & Co., Inc.

Financial Summary

Total Giving: $1,733,496 (fiscal year ending August 31, 2003); $2,469,000 (fiscal 2001)
Assets: $40,753,822 (fiscal 2003); $44,990,348 (fiscal 2001)

Typical Recipients

Arts & Humanities: Arts Associations & Councils, Arts Outreach, Community Arts, Ethnic & Folk Arts, Arts & Humanities-General, Historic Preservation, History & Archaeology, Libraries, Literary Arts, Museums/Galleries, Opera, Public Broadcasting, Theater
Civic & Public Affairs: Civil Rights, Clubs, Community Foundations, Economic Development, Employment/Job Training, Civic & Public Affairs-General, Housing, Legal Aid, Municipalities/Towns, Philanthropic Organizations, Public Policy, Rural Affairs, Safety, Urban & Community Affairs, Women's Affairs
Education: Arts/Humanities Education, Colleges & Universities, Community & Junior Colleges, Continuing Education, Education Associations, Education Reform, Elementary Education (Private), Education-General, Literacy, Private Education (Precollege), Public Education (Precollege), Science/Mathematics Education, Special Education, Student Aid
Environment: Environment-General, Resource Conservation, Wildlife Protection
Health: AIDS/HIV, Alzheimer's Disease, Clinics/Medical Centers, Emergency/Ambulance Services, Health-General, Heart, Hospices, Hospitals, Long-Term Care, Medical Rehabilitation, Nursing Services, Public Health, Single-Disease Health Associations, Transplant Networks/Donor Banks
International: International Peace & Security Issues, Missionary/Religious Activities

Religion: Churches, Religious Welfare
Science: Science Museums, Scientific Centers & Institutes
Social Services: Animal Protection, Child Abuse, Child Welfare, Community Centers, Community Service Organizations, Counseling, Crime Prevention, Delinquency & Criminal Rehabilitation, Domestic Violence, Family Planning, Family Services, Food/Clothing Distribution, Homes, People with Disabilities, Senior Services, Shelters/Homelessness, Social Services-General, Substance Abuse, United Funds/United Ways, Volunteer Services, Youth Organizations

Application Procedures

Initial Contact: Applicants should review the foundation's policy and criteria, available upon request, in detail. If a proposal seems warranted, applicants should write a succinct factual letter of no more than a page in length. Any brief printed material that is pertinent to an application should also be included. High school seniors in Lemhi and Custer Counties, ID, may apply for undergraduate scholarships through their schools. Personal and telephone inquiries are discouraged.
Application Requirements: A copy of IRS letter of determination with application.
Deadlines: March 1.
Review Process: Decisions on grants are made once a year in June and are paid in August or September.

Restrictions

The foundation prefers not to fund emergencies; community chests or similar drives; conferences and workshops; efforts to influence school boards and other elections; planning, research, experimental or untested projects; endowments for small organizations; recreational facilities; athletic or academic competitions or related travel; computers or other technology for schools; religious or political organizations. The foundation will not make grants to individuals or to non tax-exempt organizations.

Additional Information

Morgan Guaranty Trust Company of New York serves as the corporate trustee for the foundation.
Publications: Annual Report (includes Detailed Grant Application Information)

Foundation Officials

William T. Buice, III: co-trustee ED Duke University (1964). NONPR AFFIL chairman: Asheville School.

Grants Analysis

Disclosure Period: fiscal year ending August 31, 2003
Total Grants: $1,733,496
Number of Grants: 74
Average Grant: $23,426
Highest Grant: $125,000
Lowest Grant: $5,000
Typical Range: $10,000 to $50,000

Recent Grants

Note: Grants derived from 2001 Form 990.
Library-Related

28,000	Eastern Idaho Library Network Consortium, Soda Springs, ID

General

80,000	Metropolitan Opera, New York, NY
65,000	Ashton Memorial, Inc., Ashton, ID
55,000	Mountain Association for Community Economic Development, Berea, KY
50,000	Appalachia Service Project, Johnson City, TN
50,000	Appalshop, Inc., Whitesburg, KY
50,000	Community Foundation of Western North Carolina, Inc., Asheville, NC
50,000	Eagle Rock Art Guild, Idaho Falls, ID
50,000	Homemaker Services of Idaho, Inc., Idaho Falls, ID

50,000	Interfaith of Bell County, Inc., Pineville, KY
50,000	Intermountain Planned Parenthood, Billings, MT

ALBERT STEIGER MEMORIAL FUND

Giving Contact
Albert E. Steiger, Jr., President
PO Box 392
Springfield, MA 01102-0392
Phone: (413)732-8875

Description
Founded: 1953
EIN: 046051750
Organization Type: Private Foundation
Giving Locations: MA: Hampden County
Grant Types: Capital, General Support, Project.

Donor Information
Founder: Ralph A. Steiger, Chauncey A. Steiger, Albert Steiger, Inc.

Financial Summary
Total Giving: $84,000 (2003); $162,000 (2001)
Assets: $979,338 (2003); $1,088,759 (2001)

Typical Recipients
Arts & Humanities: Arts Associations & Councils, Arts Funds, History & Archaeology, Libraries, Museums/Galleries, Music, Performing Arts, Public Broadcasting, Theater
Civic & Public Affairs: Botanical Gardens/Parks, Business/Free Enterprise, Community Foundations, Civic & Public Affairs-General
Education: Arts/Humanities Education, Colleges & Universities, Education Funds, Public Education (Precollege), School Volunteerism, Student Aid
Health: Health Funds, Health Organizations, Hospitals, Nursing Services, Prenatal Health Issues
International: Foreign Arts Organizations
Science: Science Museums
Social Services: Community Centers, Community Service Organizations, Homes, Scouts, Social Services-General, United Funds/United Ways, YMCA/YWCA/YMHA/YWHA, Youth Organizations

Application Procedures
Initial Contact: Send brief letter describing program.
Deadlines: None.

Restrictions
Does not support individuals. Limited to charitable purposes in or around Hampden County, MA.

Foundation Officials
Richard Sherman Milstein: clerk B Westfield, MA 1926. ED Harvard University BA (1948); Boston University JD (1952). PRIM CORP EMPL partner: Ely & King. CORP AFFIL consulting director: Massachusetts Continuing Legal Education. NONPR AFFIL vice chairman: Westfield Academy; life member, trustee: WGBY Public Television Springfield; trustee: Visting Nurses Western MA; member: Springfield Library Museum Association; trustee, general council: Springfield Symphony Orchestra; life fellow: Massachusetts Bar Foundation; trustee: Applewood at Amherst; trustee: Baystate Hospital; member: American Law Institute; life member: American Bar Foundation; fellow: American College Trust & Estate Counsel.
Albert E. Steiger, III: director
Albert E. Steiger, Jr.: president
Allen Steiger: treasurer
Philip C. Steiger, II: director
Ralph A. Steiger, II: director

Grants Analysis
Disclosure Period: calendar year ending 2003
Total Grants: $84,000
Number of Grants: 8
Average Grant: $8,714*
Highest Grant: $23,000
Lowest Grant: $3,000
Typical Range: $5,000 to $15,000
*Note: Average grant figure excludes highest grant.

Recent Grants
Note: Grants derived from 2003 Form 990.
General

23,000	WGBY-TV Channel 57, Springfield, MA
15,000	Baystate Health Systems Capital, Springfield, MA
15,000	Greater Springfield YMCA, Springfield, MA
15,000	Greater Springfield YWCA, Springfield, MA
5,000	Friends of Grandmothers' Garden
5,000	Loomis House, Northfield, MN
3,000	Springfield Museums, Springfield, MA
3,000	Springfield Symphony Orchestra, Springfield, MA

BERT L. AND PATRICIA S. STEIGLEDER CHARITABLE TRUST

Giving Contact
Henry J. Loos, Trustee
c/o Quarles & Brady
411 E. Wisconsin Ave., Suite 2040
Milwaukee, WI 53202-4497
Phone: (414)765-5047

Description
Founded: 1992
EIN: 396541246
Organization Type: Private Foundation
Giving Locations: WI: Milwaukee
Grant Types: General Support.

Donor Information
Founder: the late Bert S. Steigleder

Financial Summary
Total Giving: $461,000 (fiscal year ending June 30, 2004); $582,166 (fiscal 2001)
Giving Analysis: Giving for fiscal 2004 includes: foundation grants to United Way ($25,000) fiscal 2001: foundation grants to United Way ($10,000)
Assets: $10,089,104 (fiscal 2004); $11,044,879 (fiscal 2001)
Gifts Received: $131,273 (fiscal 1995); $2,109,900 (fiscal 1994). Note: In fiscal 1995, contributions were received from the estate of Bert S. Steigleder.

Typical Recipients
Arts & Humanities: Arts Funds, Arts Institutes, Ballet, Historic Preservation, Libraries, Museums/Galleries, Music, Opera, Performing Arts, Theater
Civic & Public Affairs: Community Foundations, Employment/Job Training, Civic & Public Affairs-General, Public Policy
Education: Business Education, Colleges & Universities, Environmental Education, Health & Physical Education, Legal Education, Medical Education, Private Education (Precollege), Public Education (Precollege)
Environment: Environment-General, Resource Conservation
Health: Cancer, Children's Health/Hospitals, Clinics/Medical Centers, Mental Health, Transplant Networks/Donor Banks

Religion: Religious Organizations, Religious Welfare
Social Services: Community Service Organizations, Domestic Violence, Family Planning, Senior Services, YMCA/YWCA/YMHA/YWHA, Youth Organizations

Application Procedures
Initial Contact: Send a brief letter of inquiry.
Application Requirements: proof of tax-exempt status.
Deadlines: None.

Restrictions
Grants are generally made to organizations that are cultural, artistic, educational, or health care related.

Additional Information
Trust(s): U.S. Bank

Foundation Officials
Henry J. Loos: trustee B 1940. ED Colgate University BA (1962); Harvard University LLB (1965). PRIM CORP EMPL secretary: Charter Manufacturing Co. CORP AFFIL director: Wisconsin Paper Products Co.; director: Young Radiator Co.; secretary: Olsten Milwaukee Inc. NONPR AFFIL member: Milwaukee Bar Association; member: Wisconsin Bar Association; member: American Bar Association; member: Florida Bar Association.

Grants Analysis
Disclosure Period: fiscal year ending June 30, 2004
Total Grants: $436,000*
Number of Grants: 30
Average Grant: $13,310*
Highest Grant: $50,000
Lowest Grant: $2,500
Typical Range: $5,000 to $25,000
*Note: Giving excludes United Way. Average grant figure excludes highest grant.

Recent Grants
Note: Grants derived from fiscal 2004 Form 990.
General

50,000	Marquette University, Milwaukee, WI -- capital campaign
35,000	Nature Conservancy of Wisconsin, Madison, WI
25,000	Greater Milwaukee Foundation, Milwaukee, WI -- for Mequon park project
25,000	Medical College of Wisconsin, Milwaukee, WI -- addition to Steigleder cancer research fund
25,000	United Performing Arts Fund, Milwaukee, WI
25,000	University School of Milwaukee, Milwaukee, WI -- capital campaign and upper school science addition
20,000	Milwaukee Symphony Orchestra, Milwaukee, WI
20,000	Schlitz Audubon Nature Center, Milwaukee, WI -- addition to raptor building
16,000	United Performing Arts Fund, Milwaukee, WI
15,000	Nature Conservancy of Wisconsin, Madison, WI

B. A. AND ELINOR W. STEINHAGEN BENEVOLENT TRUST

Giving Contact
Hibernia National Bank
PO Box 3928
Beaumont, TX 77704
Phone: (409)880-1415
E-mail: imoncla@hibernia.com

Description

Founded: 1939
EIN: 746039544
Organization Type: Private Foundation
Giving Locations: TX: Jefferson County
Grant Types: Capital, Endowment, General Support, Project, Research, Seed Money.

Donor Information

Founder: the late B. A. Steinhagen, the late Elinor W. Steinhagen

Financial Summary

Total Giving: $398,314 (fiscal year ending August 31, 2003); $354,184 (fiscal 2001). Note: Fiscal 1997 Giving includes United Way ($15,000).
Giving Analysis: Giving for fiscal 2003 includes: foundation grants to United Way ($40,000); fiscal 2001: foundation grants to United Way ($30,000)
Assets: $6,210,712 (fiscal 2003); $6,685,697 (fiscal 2001)

Typical Recipients

Arts & Humanities: Arts Associations & Councils, Arts Centers, Arts Institutes, Community Arts, Historic Preservation, History & Archaeology, Libraries, Museums/Galleries, Music, Public Broadcasting, Theater
Civic & Public Affairs: Botanical Gardens/Parks, Community Foundations, Civic & Public Affairs-General, Hispanic Affairs, Housing, Legal Aid, Minority Business, Urban & Community Affairs
Education: Business Education, Education Reform, Elementary Education (Private), Elementary Education (Public), Education-General, Preschool Education, Private Education (Precollege), Public Education (Precollege), Science/Mathematics Education, Vocational & Technical Education
Environment: Wildlife Protection
Health: Cancer, Clinics/Medical Centers, Geriatric Health, Health Organizations, Hospitals, Medical Rehabilitation, Medical Research, Mental Health, Nutrition, Single-Disease Health Associations
Religion: Churches, Ministries, Religious Welfare
Science: Science Museums
Social Services: At-Risk Youth, Child Welfare, Community Service Organizations, Day Care, Family Services, Food/Clothing Distribution, People with Disabilities, Senior Services, Sexual Abuse, Shelters/Homelessness, Social Services-General, Substance Abuse, United Funds/United Ways, YMCA/YWCA/YMHA/YWHA, Youth Organizations

Application Procedures

Initial Contact: Application form required.
Deadlines: May 31.

Restrictions

Foundation does not fund individuals, religious organizations for sectarian purposes, political or lobbying groups, or organizations outside operating areas.

Additional Information

Publications: Application Guidelines
Trust(s): Hibernia National Bank TX

Grants Analysis

Disclosure Period: fiscal year ending August 31, 2003
Total Grants: $358,314*
Number of Grants: 15
Average Grant: $18,451*
Highest Grant: $100,000
Lowest Grant: $2,000
Typical Range: $10,000 to $25,000
*Note: Giving excludes United Way. Average grant figure excludes highest grant.

Recent Grants

Note: Grants derived from 2003 Form 990.

General

100,000	Schlesinger Healthcare Centers, Beaumont, TX -- for emergency roof repair
40,000	United Way of Beaumont, Beaumont, TX
35,000	Southeast Texas Arts Council, Beaumont, TX
25,000	Boys' Haven of America Inc., Beaumont, TX -- towards the funding for the Steinhagen cottage
25,000	Lamar Institute of Technology, Beaumont, TX -- for digital X-ray equipment
25,000	Memorial Hermann Hospital, Beaumont, TX
21,076	Art Museum of Southeast Texas, Beaumont, TX -- for a/c equipment
20,000	Art Studio Inc., Beaumont, TX -- for facility expansion and upgrade
15,000	Family Services of Southeast Texas, Beaumont, TX -- for healthy families parenting outreach and counseling
15,000	Symphony of Southeast Texas, Beaumont, TX -- to provide complimentary tickets to its master series concerts

JAMES HALE STEINMAN FOUNDATION

Giving Contact

M. Steven Weaver, Secretary Scholarship Committee
8 W. King St.
PO Box 128
Lancaster, PA 17608-0128
Phone: (717)291-8607

Description

Founded: 1952
EIN: 236266377
Organization Type: Private Foundation
Giving Locations: PA: Lancaster
Grant Types: Capital, General Support, Scholarship.

Donor Information

Founder: the late James Hale Steinman, the late Louise Steinman von Hess, Lancaster Newspapers, Inc.

Financial Summary

Total Giving: $1,257,014 (2003); $1,455,374 (2001)
Giving Analysis: Giving for 2003 includes: foundation grants to United Way ($65,000); foundation scholarships ($76,500); 2001: foundation scholarships ($60,000); foundation grants to United Way ($60,000)
Assets: $28,289,965 (2003); $27,083,446 (2001)
Gifts Received: $1,000,000 (2003); $1,000,000 (2001); $1,000,000 (2000). Note: In 2003, contributions were received from Lancaster Newspapers ($800,000) and Intelligencer Printing Co. ($200,000). In 1999 and 2000, contributions were received from Lancaster Newspapers ($680,000), Intelligencer Printing Co. ($320,000). In 1998, contributions were received from Lancaster Newspapers, Inc. ($480,000) and Intelligence Printing Co. ($320,000). In 1996, contributions were received from Lancaster Newspapers ($360,000), Intelligencer Printing Co. ($320,000), and Delmarva Broadcasting Co. ($120,000).

Typical Recipients

Arts & Humanities: Arts Associations & Councils, Arts Festivals, Community Arts, Arts & Humanities-General, Historic Preservation, History & Archaeology, Libraries, Museums/Galleries, Music, Opera, Theater
Civic & Public Affairs: Botanical Gardens/Parks, Economic Development, Ethnic Organizations, Civic & Public Affairs-General, Municipalities/Towns, Parades/Festivals, Philanthropic Organizations, Public Policy, Urban & Community Affairs
Education: Afterschool/Enrichment Programs, Arts/Humanities Education, Business Education, Colleges & Universities, Education Associations, Education-General, Private Education (Precollege), Secondary Education (Private), Student Aid
Environment: Resource Conservation
Health: Cancer, Clinics/Medical Centers, Emergency/Ambulance Services, Eyes/Blindness, Heart, Hospices, Hospitals, Medical Research, Multiple Sclerosis, Single-Disease Health Associations
Religion: Churches, Religious Organizations, Religious Welfare, Seminaries
Social Services: Community Service Organizations, Family Planning, People with Disabilities, Recreation & Athletics, Scouts, Social Services-General, United Funds/United Ways, YMCA/YWCA/YMHA/YWHA, Youth Organizations

Application Procedures

Initial Contact: Scholarship application form available for employees' children. Others seeking grants should send a letter of inquiry describing their organization.
Deadlines: February 28 for scholarships.

Additional Information

Scholarships are awarded to newspaper carriers and children of employees.
Publications: Application Form

Foundation Officials

Dennis A. Getz: secretary PRIM CORP EMPL vice president, controller: Lancaster Newspapers.
Caroline S. Nunan: chairman CORP AFFIL director: Intelligencer Printing Co.; director: Lancaster Newspapers Inc.
Willis Weidman Shenk: treasurer B Manheim, PA 1915. PRIM CORP EMPL chairman, director: Lancaster Newspapers Inc. CORP AFFIL chairman, director: Intelligencer Printing Co.; chairman: Steinman Coal Corp.; chairman: Commonwealth Mailing Service; chairman: Delmarva Broadcasting Co. Inc. NONPR AFFIL member: National Association Accts; member: Pennsylvania Institute CPA's. CLUB AFFIL Lancaster Country Club.
Beverly R. Steinman: vchairman CORP AFFIL director: Intelligencer Printing Co.; director: Lancaster Newspapers Inc.

Grants Analysis

Disclosure Period: calendar year ending 2003
Total Grants: $1,115,514*
Number of Grants: 64
Average Grant: $9,911*
Highest Grant: $491,139
Lowest Grant: $500
Typical Range: $1,000 to $20,000
*Note: Giving excludes United Way; scholarships. Average grant figure excludes highest grant.

Recent Grants

Note: Grants derived from 2001 Form 990.
General

408,016	Conestoga House Foundation, Conestoga, PA
75,000	Boys & Girls Club of Lancaster, Inc., Lancaster, PA
75,000	Marion DuPont Scott Equine Medical Center
75,000	Pennsylvania Academy of Music, Lancaster, PA
62,107	Conestoga House Foundation, Conestoga, PA
60,000	James Hale Stein Foundation Scholarships, Lancaster, PA
60,000	United Way of Lancaster County, Lancaster, PA
50,000	Boys & Girls Club of Lancaster, Inc., Lancaster, PA

50,000 Lancaster General Hospital, Lancaster, PA

50,000 Lititz Moravian Church

JOHN FREDERICK STEINMAN FOUNDATION

Giving Contact

M. Steven Weaner, Secretary, Fellowship Program
PO Box 128
Lancaster, PA 17608-0128
Phone: (717)291-8607

Description

Founded: 1952
EIN: 236266378
Organization Type: Private Foundation
Giving Locations: PA: emphasis on the Lancaster area
Grant Types: Capital, Fellowship, General Support.

Donor Information

Founder: the late John Frederick Steinman, the late Shirley W. Steinman, Lancaster Newspapers

Financial Summary

Total Giving: $1,265,578 (2003); $1,514,250 (2001)
Giving Analysis: Giving for 2003 includes: foundation fellowships ($59,703); foundation grants to United Way ($65,000); 2001: foundation scholarships ($58,000); foundation grants to United Way ($60,000)
Assets: $26,830,491 (2003); $27,856,450 (2001)
Gifts Received: $160,000 (1992)

Typical Recipients

Arts & Humanities: Arts Appreciation, Arts Associations & Councils, Arts Festivals, Community Arts, Arts & Humanities-General, Historic Preservation, History & Archaeology, Libraries, Literary Arts, Museums/Galleries, Music, Opera, Theater
Civic & Public Affairs: African American Affairs, Botanical Gardens/Parks, Community Foundations, Economic Development, Employment/Job Training, Ethnic Organizations, Civic & Public Affairs-General, Housing, Legal Aid, Municipalities/Towns, Parades/Festivals, Public Policy, Urban & Community Affairs
Education: Arts/Humanities Education, Business Education, Colleges & Universities, Community & Junior Colleges, Education-General, Literacy, Private Education (Precollege), Religious Education, Secondary Education (Private), Vocational & Technical Education
Environment: Air/Water Quality, Resource Conservation
Health: Cancer, Children's Health/Hospitals, Clinics/Medical Centers, Emergency/Ambulance Services, Eyes/Blindness, Health-General, Heart, Hospices, Hospitals, Medical Research, Mental Health, Nursing Services, Public Health, Single-Disease Health Associations
Religion: Churches, Religion-General, Religious Organizations, Religious Welfare, Seminaries
Social Services: At-Risk Youth, Community Service Organizations, Day Care, Family Planning, Family Services, People with Disabilities, Recreation & Athletics, Scouts, Sexual Abuse, Shelters/Homelessness, Substance Abuse, United Funds/United Ways, YMCA/YWCA/YMHA/YWHA, Youth Organizations

Application Procedures

Initial Contact: Application for fellowship program available upon request. For other grants, send a letter of inquiry.
Deadlines: February 1.

Restrictions

Fellowships restricted to graduate programs in mental health.

Additional Information

Provides fellowships for graduate study in mental health.
Publications: Application Form

Foundation Officials

Dennis A. Getz: secretary PRIM CORP EMPL vice president, controller: Lancaster Newspapers.
Henry Pildner, Jr.: trustee CORP AFFIL director: Intelligencer Printing Co.
Willis Weidman Shenk: treasurer B Manheim, PA 1915. PRIM CORP EMPL chairman, director: Lancaster Newspapers Inc. CORP AFFIL chairman, director: Intelligencer Printing Co.; chairman: Steinman Coal Corp.; chairman: Commonwealth Mailing Service; chairman: Delmarva Broadcasting Co. Inc. NONPR AFFIL member: National Association Accts; member: Pennsylvania Institute CPA's. CLUB AFFIL Lancaster Country Club.
Pamela M. Thye: chairman CORP AFFIL director: Intelligencer Printing Co.

Grants Analysis

Disclosure Period: calendar year ending 2003
Total Grants: $1,140,875*
Number of Grants: 107
Average Grant: $8,413*
Highest Grant: $132,500
Lowest Grant: $500
Typical Range: $5,000 to $10,000
***Note:** Giving excludes fellowships; United Way. Average grant figure excludes two highest grants ($257,500).

Recent Grants

Note: Grants derived from 2001 Form 990.
General
125,000 Boys Club and Girls Club of Lancaster, Inc., Lancaster, PA
125,000 Linden Hall School for Girls, Lititz, PA
125,000 Pennsylvania Academy of Music, Lancaster, PA
100,000 Elizabethtown College, Elizabethtown, PA
100,000 Lancaster General Hospital, Lancaster, PA
60,000 United Way of Lancaster County, Lancaster, PA
58,000 JFSF Fellowships
50,000 Arbor Place, Lancaster, PA
50,000 Harrisburg Area Community College, Harrisburg, PA
50,000 Lititz Moravian Church

STEMMONS FOUNDATION

Giving Contact

Ann C. Carlisle, Secretary, Treasurer & Manager
PO Box 143127
Irving, TX 75014-3127
Phone: (972)650-9162

Description

Founded: 1963
EIN: 756039966
Organization Type: Private Foundation
Giving Locations: TX: Dallas
Grant Types: General Support, Scholarship.

Financial Summary

Total Giving: $933,100 (2003)
Assets: $8,225,964 (2003)
Gifts Received: $307,129 (2003). Note: In 2003,

contributions were received from the estate of John M. Stemmons.

Typical Recipients

Arts & Humanities: Arts Outreach, Community Arts, Dance, Arts & Humanities-General, Historic Preservation, Libraries, Music, Opera, Public Broadcasting, Theater
Civic & Public Affairs: Botanical Gardens/Parks, Employment/Job Training, Civic & Public Affairs-General, Public Policy, Urban & Community Affairs, Women's Affairs, Zoos/Aquariums
Education: Arts/Humanities Education, Colleges & Universities, Education Funds, Elementary Education (Public), Education-General, Medical Education, Minority Education, Private Education (Precollege), Public Education (Precollege), Religious Education
Environment: Wildlife Protection
Health: AIDS/HIV, Alzheimer's Disease, Children's Health/Hospitals, Emergency/Ambulance Services, Health-General, Health Organizations, Hospitals, Kidney, Long-Term Care, Medical Research, Mental Health, Nursing Services, Prenatal Health Issues, Public Health, Single-Disease Health Associations, Speech & Hearing
International: Human Rights, International Environmental Issues
Religion: Churches, Religion-General, Ministries, Religious Organizations, Religious Welfare
Social Services: Animal Protection, Child Welfare, Community Centers, Community Service Organizations, Family Planning, Family Services, Food/Clothing Distribution, Homes, People with Disabilities, Scouts, Social Services-General, United Funds/United Ways, YMCA/YWCA/YMHA/YWHA, Youth Organizations

Application Procedures

Initial Contact: Send a brief letter of inquiry describing program or project.
Application Requirements: Include a description of organization and purpose of funds sought.
Deadlines: None.

Foundation Officials

Ann C. Carlisle: secretary, vice president
Allison S. Simon: president
Heinz K. Simon: vice president
Jean H. Stemmons: vice president

Grants Analysis

Disclosure Period: calendar year ending 2003
Total Grants: $933,100
Number of Grants: 53
Average Grant: $10,662*
Highest Grant: $200,000*
Lowest Grant: $2,500
Typical Range: $5,000 to $20,000
***Note:** Average grant figure excludes three highest grants ($400,000).

Recent Grants

Note: Grants derived from 2001 Form 990.
General
25,000 United Way of Metropolitan Dallas, Dallas, TX
20,000 Goodwill Industries of Dallas, Inc., Dallas, TX
20,000 Southwestern Medical Foundation, Dallas, TX
15,000 Brain Research and Treatment Center, Dallas, TX
12,500 Dallas Opera, Dallas, TX
10,000 American Red Cross Dallas Area Chapter, Dallas, TX
10,000 American Red Cross Dallas Area Chapter, Dallas, TX
10,000 Children's Medical Center at Dallas, Dallas, TX
10,000 Dallas Symphony Orchestra, Dallas, TX
10,000 Episcopal School of Dallas, Dallas, TX

STERLING-TURNER FOUNDATION

Giving Contact

Eyvonne Moser, Executive Director
815 Walker Street, Suite 1543
Houston, TX 77002-5724
Phone: (713)237-1117
Fax: (713)223-4638
E-mail: patricia@sterlingturnerfoundation.org
Web: http://www.sterlingturnerfoundation.org

Description

Founded: 1956
EIN: 741460482
Organization Type: General Purpose Foundation
Former Name: Turner Charitable Foundation (1998).
Giving Locations: TX
Grant Types: Capital, Challenge, Department, Emergency, Endowment, Fellowship, General Support, Matching, Operating Expenses, Project, Research, Scholarship, Seed Money.

Donor Information

Founder: Incorporated in 1956 by the late Isla Carroll Turner and the late P. E. Turner.

Financial Summary

Total Giving: $2,619,500 (2003); $2,497,000 (2002)
Assets: $41,655,293 (2003); $37,375,886 (2002)

Typical Recipients

Arts & Humanities: Arts Associations & Councils, Ballet, Dance, Arts & Humanities-General, Historic Preservation, Libraries, Literary Arts, Museums/Galleries, Music, Opera, Performing Arts, Public Broadcasting, Theater
Civic & Public Affairs: Botanical Gardens/Parks, Clubs, Economic Development, Civic & Public Affairs-General, Hispanic Affairs, Law & Justice, Legal Aid, Philanthropic Organizations, Safety, Urban & Community Affairs, Women's Affairs, Zoos/Aquariums
Education: Afterschool/Enrichment Programs, Agricultural Education, Arts/Humanities Education, Colleges & Universities, Education Funds, Elementary Education (Private), Elementary Education (Public), Environmental Education, Faculty Development, Education-General, Literacy, Medical Education, Preschool Education, Private Education (Precollege), Public Education (Precollege), Religious Education, Science/Mathematics Education, Secondary Education (Private), Social Sciences Education, Special Education, Student Aid
Environment: Environment-General, Resource Conservation
Health: AIDS/HIV, Cancer, Children's Health/Hospitals, Clinics/Medical Centers, Emergency/Ambulance Services, Eyes/Blindness, Health Funds, Health Organizations, Heart, Hospices, Hospitals, Medical Research, Mental Health, Nursing Services, Research/Studies Institutes, Single-Disease Health Associations, Speech & Hearing
International: Missionary/Religious Activities
Religion: Churches, Dioceses, Religion-General, Ministries, Religious Organizations, Religious Welfare, Social/Policy Issues
Science: Science Museums, Scientific Centers & Institutes
Social Services: At-Risk Youth, Big Brothers/Big Sisters, Child Abuse, Child Welfare, Community Centers, Community Service Organizations, Day Care, Delinquency & Criminal Rehabilitation, Emergency Relief, Family Planning, Family Services, Food/Clothing Distribution, Homes, People with Disabilities, Recreation & Athletics, Scouts, Shelters/Homelessness, Social Services-General, Special Olympics, Substance Abuse, Volunteer Services, YMCA/YWCA/YMHA/YWHA, Youth Organizations

Application Procedures

Initial Contact: The foundation requests applications be made in writing.
Application Requirements: The application must include a copy of IRS code section 501(c)(3) exemption letter.
Deadlines: March 1 by 5:00pm.
Review Process: The board meets on the first Tuesday in April.

Restrictions

The foundation makes grants only to exempt charities in the state of Texas. Grants are not made to individuals.

Additional Information

Publications: Guidelines; Application Form

Foundation Officials

Thomas Eugene Berry: assistant secretary, trustee B San Antonio, TX 1923. ED Southwestern University BBA (1944); University of Texas BBA (1949); University of Texas LLB (1951). OCCUPATION attorney. CORP AFFIL vice president: Goodrich Operating Co. Inc. NONPR AFFIL trustee: Turner Charitable Foundation; trustee: Isla Carroll Turner Friendship Trust; member: Texas Academy Probate & Trust Lawyers; member: State Bar Texas; board director: Student Aid Foundation; member: NG Association Texas; member: Phi Delta Phi; trustee: Hope Center Youth & Family Services; member: Houston Bar Association; trustee: R.H. and E.F. Goodrich Foundation; trustee, board director: Hermann Eye Fund; member: Delta Kappa Epsilon; trustee: MB Flake Home Old Ladies; fellow: American College Tax Counsel; fellow: American College Trust & Estate Counsel; member: American Bar Association.
Carroll R. Goodman: assistant secretary, trustee
Chaille W. Hawkins: assistant secretary, trustee
Christiana R. McConn: secretary, trustee
Eyvonne Moser: executive director
Isla C. Reckling: treasurer, trustee
James S. Reckling: assistant secretary, trustee
John B. Reckling: assistant secretary, trustee
Stephen M. Reckling: assistant secretary, trustee
T. R. Reckling, IV: assistant secretary, trustee
T. R. Reckling, III: president, trustee
Thomas K. Reckling: assistant secretary, trustee B 1961. OCCUPATION Texas Capital Securities Inc.
Bert F. Winston, III: assistant secretary, trustee
Bert F. Winston, Jr.: vice president, trustee
Mrs. Blake W. Winston: assistant secretary, trustee
L. David Winston: assistant secretary, trustee

Grants Analysis

Disclosure Period: calendar year ending 2003
Total Grants: $2,619,500
Number of Grants: 70
Average Grant: $28,228*
Highest Grant: $400,000
Lowest Grant: $2,000
Typical Range: $5,000 to $50,000
*Note: Average grant figure excludes two highest grants ($700,000).

Recent Grants

Note: Grants derived from 2003 Form 990.
General

400,000	Saint Joseph Hospital Foundation, Houston, TX
300,000	Brookwood Community, Brookshire, TX
200,000	Saint Thomas High School, Houston, TX
180,000	University of Texas MD Anderson Cancer Center, Houston, TX
105,000	Kinkaid School, Houston, TX
100,000	Episcopal High School, Bellaire, TX
100,000	Hunt Volunteer Fire Department, Hunt, TX
100,000	Ingram Tom Moore H S, Ingram, TX
90,000	Schreiner University, Kerrville, TX
65,000	Trinity Episcopal Church, Houston, TX

ABBOT AND DOROTHY H. STEVENS FOUNDATION

Giving Contact

Elizabeth A. Beland, Administrator
PO Box 111
North Andover, MA 01845
Phone: (978)688-7211
Fax: (978)686-1620

Description

Founded: 1953
EIN: 046107991
Organization Type: General Purpose Foundation
Giving Locations: MA: preference given to Merrimack Valley Area and greater Lawrence Area
Grant Types: Capital, Emergency, Endowment, General Support, Matching.

Donor Information

Founder: Established in 1953 by the late Abbot Stevens.

Financial Summary

Total Giving: $1,150,950 (2001)
Assets: $23,997,510 (2001)

Typical Recipients

Arts & Humanities: Arts Centers, Arts Outreach, Ballet, Dance, Ethnic & Folk Arts, Film & Video, Arts & Humanities-General, Historic Preservation, History & Archaeology, Libraries, Museums/Galleries, Music, Opera, Performing Arts, Public Broadcasting, Theater
Civic & Public Affairs: Community Foundations, Civic & Public Affairs-General, Hispanic Affairs, Housing, Municipalities/Towns, Native American Affairs, Philanthropic Organizations, Safety, Urban & Community Affairs, Zoos/Aquariums
Education: Afterschool/Enrichment Programs, Arts/Humanities Education, Business Education, Colleges & Universities, Community & Junior Colleges, Education Funds, Education Reform, Elementary Education (Private), Education-General, Leadership Training, Literacy, Minority Education, Private Education (Precollege), Public Education (Precollege), Secondary Education (Private), Social Sciences Education, Special Education
Environment: Environment-General, Resource Conservation, Watershed, Wildlife Protection
Health: Cancer, Children's Health/Hospitals, Clinics/Medical Centers, Emergency/Ambulance Services, Health-General, Health Funds, Health Organizations, Home-Care Services, Hospitals, Medical Research, Mental Health, Nursing Services, Trauma Treatment
International: Missionary/Religious Activities
Religion: Churches, Dioceses, Religious Organizations
Science: Science Museums
Social Services: At-Risk Youth, Community Centers, Community Service Organizations, Delinquency & Criminal Rehabilitation, Family Services, Food/Clothing Distribution, Homes, People with Disabilities, Recreation & Athletics, Senior Services, Shelters/Homelessness, Social Services-General, Substance Abuse, United Funds/United Ways, Veterans, YMCA/YWCA/YMHA/YWHA, Youth Organizations

Application Procedures

Initial Contact: Submit a written proposal. The foundation accepts the Associated Grantmakers of Massachusetts Common Proposal Format.
Application Requirements: The body of the proposal should be no more than five pages plus appendices. Also include a one-page cover letter summarizing the proposal and with a request for a specific grant amount. A proposal must include proof of tax-exempt status; proof of incorporation in Massachusetts; names of officers, directors or trustees of the organization; recently audited financial statement; in-

stitutional income and expense budget for the current fiscal year; detailed program budget for which support is requested; starting and completion dates of proposed program and planned cash flow; and current status of fundraising, including other sources being solicited for funds. Provide name, address and telephone number of contact person. address, and telephone number of whom you wish contacted.

Deadlines: None.

Review Process: The trustees meet monthly (except for July and August) to review applications.

Notes: Applications will be considered for experimental and demonstration projects, program expansion, evaluation, renovation, new construction programs, capital funding, and to 501(c)(3) organizations for the benefit of another awaiting its own tax-exempt status.

Restrictions

No grants will be made to individuals, state or federal agencies, national organizations, or annual campaigns. The trustees will not normally consider more than one application from an agency in the same calendar year, except for summer youth programs. The foundation funds only Massachusetts charitable organizations, with preference given to Merrimack Valley area and the Greater Lawrence area.

Additional Information

The foundation reports an affiliation with the Nathaniel and Elizabeth P. Stevens Foundation, also located in Massachusetts.

Publications: Program Policy Statement; Applications Guidelines

Foundation Officials

Elizabeth A. Beland: administrator

Phebe S. Miner: trustee CORP AFFIL officer: Ames Textile Corp.

Christopher W. Rogers: trustee

Samuel S. Rogers: mng trustee

Grants Analysis

Disclosure Period: calendar year ending 2001
Total Grants: $1,135,950*
Number of Grants: 99
Average Grant: $11,474
Highest Grant: $100,000
Lowest Grant: $100
Typical Range: $1,000 to $25,000
***Note:** Giving excludes United Way.

Recent Grants

Note: Grants derived from 2002 Form 990.

General

100,000	American Textile History Museum, Lowell, MA
100,000	Ayer Mill Clock Tower Restoration Fund, Boston, MA
50,000	Lawrence Family Development & Education Fund, Lawrence, MA
50,000	Merrimack College, North Andover, MA
50,000	Presentation of Mary Academy, Methuen, MA
25,000	Essex County Community Foundation, Topsfield, MA
25,000	Governor Dummer Academy, Waltham, MA
25,000	Grand Lowell Community Foundation, Grand Rapids, MI
25,000	Mental Health Resources Plus, Atlanta, GA
25,000	Tabor Academy, Marion, MA

NATHANIEL AND ELIZABETH P. STEVENS FOUNDATION

Giving Contact

Elizabeth A. Beland, Administrator
PO Box 111
North Andover, MA 01845
Phone: (978)688-7211

Description

Founded: 1943
EIN: 042236996
Organization Type: Private Foundation
Giving Locations: MA: emphasis on the greater Lawrence area
Grant Types: Capital, Challenge, Emergency, Endowment, General Support, Matching, Operating Expenses, Project, Seed Money.

Donor Information

Founder: the late Nathaniel Stevens

Financial Summary

Total Giving: $650,180 (2003). Note: 1997 Giving includes United Way ($12,800).
Giving Analysis: Giving for 2003 includes: foundation grants to United Way ($16,200)
Assets: $16,713,738 (2003)

Typical Recipients

Arts & Humanities: Arts Centers, Ethnic & Folk Arts, Historic Preservation, History & Archaeology, Libraries, Museums/Galleries, Music, Opera, Theater
Civic & Public Affairs: Asian American Affairs, Economic Development, Civic & Public Affairs-General, Hispanic Affairs, Housing, Native American Affairs, Philanthropic Organizations, Safety, Urban & Community Affairs, Women's Affairs, Zoos/Aquariums
Education: Afterschool/Enrichment Programs, Colleges & Universities, Community & Junior Colleges, Education Reform, Faculty Development, Education-General, Leadership Training, Private Education (Precollege), Public Education (Precollege), School Volunteerism, Science/Mathematics Education, Secondary Education (Private), Secondary Education (Public)
Environment: Air/Water Quality, Environment-General, Watershed
Health: Adolescent Health Issues, Cancer, Children's Health/Hospitals, Clinics/Medical Centers, Emergency/Ambulance Services, Health Organizations, Hospitals, Medical Rehabilitation, Mental Health
Religion: Churches, Jewish Causes, Religious Organizations, Religious Welfare
Science: Science Museums
Social Services: At-Risk Youth, Child Welfare, Community Centers, Community Service Organizations, Counseling, Day Care, Family Planning, Family Services, Food/Clothing Distribution, Homes, People with Disabilities, Recreation & Athletics, Senior Services, Shelters/Homelessness, Social Services-General, United Funds/United Ways, YMCA/YWCA/YMHA/YWHA, Youth Organizations

Application Procedures

Initial Contact: Request application guidelines.
Deadlines: None.

Restrictions

Does not support individuals.

Additional Information

Publications: Application Guidelines

Foundation Officials

Joshua L. Miner, IV: trustee
Phebe S. Miner: trustee CORP AFFIL officer: Ames

Textile Corp.
Samuel S. Rogers: trustee

Grants Analysis

Disclosure Period: calendar year ending 2003
Total Grants: $633,980*
Number of Grants: 122
Average Grant: $5,197
Highest Grant: $27,000
Lowest Grant: $250
Typical Range: $1,000 to $10,000
***Note:** Giving excludes United Way.

Recent Grants

Note: Grants derived from 2001 Form 990.

General

150,000	Merrimack Valley YMCA, Lawrence, MA
50,000	Essex County Community Foundation, Peabody, MA
50,000	Governor Dummer Academy, South Byfield, MA
25,000	Bread and Roses, Inc., Norwalk, CT
25,000	Lowell Catholic High School, Lowell, MA
25,000	Outward Bound - USA, Garrison, NY
20,000	Merrimack River Watershed Council, Lawrence, MA
16,000	Bread and Roses, Inc., Norwalk, CT
15,000	CLASS, Indianapolis, IN
15,000	Essex Art Center, Essex, MA

STEWARDSHIP FOUNDATION

Giving Contact

Dr. Cary A. Paine, Executive Director
Stewardship Foundation
PO Box 1278
Tacoma, WA 98401-1278
Phone: (253)620-1340
Fax: (253)572-2721
E-mail: info@stewardshipfdn.org
Web: http://www.stewardshipfdn.org

Description

Founded: 1962
EIN: 916020515
Organization Type: General Purpose Foundation
Giving Locations: nationally.
Grant Types: General Support, Project, Research.

Donor Information

Founder: Established in 1962 by Charles Davis Weyerhaeuser, a son of the Frederick Edward Weyerhaeuser (1872-1945), former president of Weyerhaeuser Timber Company.

Financial Summary

Total Giving: $5,611,933 (2003); $6,925,980 (2002); $7,400,000 (2001 approx)
Assets: $115,944,286 (2003); $115,058,278 (2002); $111,000,000 (2001)
Gifts Received: $14,586,654 (2000); $50,000 (1995); $500 (1994)

Typical Recipients

Arts & Humanities: Public Broadcasting, Theater
Civic & Public Affairs: Civil Rights, Economic Development, Employment/Job Training, Civic & Public Affairs-General, Law & Justice, Legal Aid, Professional & Trade Associations, Public Policy, Rural Affairs, Urban & Community Affairs
Education: Colleges & Universities, Education-General, International Exchange, Leadership Training, Minority Education, Private Education (Precollege), Public Education (Precollege), Religious Education, Student Aid
Environment: Environment-General

Health: Children's Health/Hospitals, Emergency/Ambulance Services, Eyes/Blindness, Medical Research, Mental Health, Prenatal Health Issues, Public Health

International: Foreign Educational Institutions, Health Care/Hospitals, Human Rights, International Affairs, International Development, International Environmental Issues, International Organizations, International Peace & Security Issues, International Relations, International Relief Efforts, Missionary/Religious Activities

Religion: Bible Study/Translation, Churches, Religion-General, Ministries, Missionary Activities (Domestic), Religious Organizations, Religious Welfare, Seminaries, Social/Policy Issues

Science: Scientific Centers & Institutes, Scientific Research

Social Services: Camps, Child Welfare, Community Centers, Community Service Organizations, Crime Prevention, Delinquency & Criminal Rehabilitation, Domestic Violence, Emergency Relief, Family Planning, Family Services, Food/Clothing Distribution, People with Disabilities, Refugee Assistance, Shelters/Homelessness, Social Services-General, Substance Abuse, Youth Organizations

Application Procedures

Initial Contact: Potential applicants should send a brief letter to the foundation.

Application Requirements: Letters should include a description of the proposed project along with the organization's budget and sources of revenue. If a program falls within foundation interests, an application form will be sent.

Deadlines: None.

Review Process: Directors meet quarterly. An organization making a request will usually receive a response from the foundation within 30 days from the time of the request.

Restrictions

Grants are almost exclusively given to evangelical Christian institutions.

Grants are not made for the following purposes: seed funding for start-up organizations; scholarships or fellowships to individuals; endowments; debt retirement; media time and program production; or for propagandizing or influencing elections or legislation. Grants are not made to churches, but only to parachurch organizations, as well as to a few local, secular, community-based organizations. Grants are primarily made in support of operating expenses rather than for capital projects. Grants are not made to agencies that serve only their own community except for those local agencies serving the citizens of the greater Tacoma/Seattle/Puget Sound area; the foundation will, however, consider local programs that have national or international significance. Grants are not made to organizations where, because of location or other reasons, the cost of evaluation is out of proportion to the size of the anticipated grant. Grants are generally limited to 10% of total operating or capital budgets and 25% of total funding. Grants are generally for one year's duration; multiple-year requests are considered only when subject to annual review by the distribution committee.

Foundation Officials

Carl T. Fynboe: board member
Donald W. Mowat: board member
Annette Thayer Black Weyerhaeuser: board member
Dr. William Toycen Weyerhaeuser: chairman B Tacoma, WA 1943. ED Stanford University (1966); Fuller Graduate School of Psychology PhD (1975). PRIM CORP EMPL owner, chairman: Yelm Telephone Co. CORP AFFIL director: Columbia Banking System Inc.; director: Potlatch Corp.

Grants Analysis

Disclosure Period: calendar year ending 2003
Total Grants: $5,611,933

Number of Grants: 172
Average Grant: $28,109*
Highest Grant: $500,000
Lowest Grant: $5,000
Typical Range: $5,000 to $50,000
***Note:** Average grant figure excludes two highest grants ($833,333).

Recent Grants

Note: Grants derived from 2002 Form 990.

General

500,000	Wycliffe Bible Translators, Huntington Beach, CA -- funding for relocation of organization
250,000	Project Mercy, Ft. Wayne, IN -- toward daycare and worship center construction
250,000	Young Life, Colorado Springs, CO -- funding for wildhorse canyon camp
225,000	Presbytery of North Puget Sound, Everett, WA -- funding for establishment of ecumenical center
200,000	Discovery Institute, Seattle, WA -- funding for the wedge initiative
150,000	Interdev, Seattle, WA -- funding for breakthrough strategy
132,000	Young Life, Colorado Springs, CO -- funding for urban ministry in Northwest
128,000	CRISTA Ministries, Seattle, WA -- toward leadership development
100,000	CRISTA Ministries, Seattle, WA -- funding for general operations
100,000	Opportunity International, Oak Brook, IL -- toward Philippines transformational banking initiative

DONNELL B. AND ELIZABETH DEE SHAW STEWART EDUCATIONAL FOUNDATION

Giving Contact

Mary L. Barker, Trustee
c/o Wells Fargo Bank
PO Box 9936
Ogden, UT 84409
Phone: (801)626-9531

Description

Founded: 1977
EIN: 876179880
Organization Type: Private Foundation
Giving Locations: UT: Ogden
Grant Types: Capital, General Support, Scholarship.

Donor Information

Founder: Elizabeth D. S. Stewart

Financial Summary

Total Giving: $850,390 (2003); $8,496,180 (2002)
Giving Analysis: Giving for 2003 includes: foundation grants to United Way ($75,000)
Assets: $77,532,055 (2003); $63,129,795 (2002)
Gifts Received: $11,107 (2000); $1,078,987 (1996); $300,452 (1995). Note: In 2000, contributions were received from Elizabeth Stewart Estate.

Typical Recipients

Arts & Humanities: Arts Centers, Ballet, Dance, Historic Preservation, Libraries, Museums/Galleries, Music, Opera, Performing Arts, Public Broadcasting, Theater

Civic & Public Affairs: Botanical Gardens/Parks, Clubs, Community Foundations, Employment/Job Training, Civic & Public Affairs-General, Municipalities/Towns, Philanthropic Organizations, Public Policy, Rural Affairs, Safety, Urban & Community Affairs

Education: Arts/Humanities Education, Colleges & Universities, Education Funds, Elementary Education (Private), Education-General, Private Education (Precollege), Public Education (Precollege), Secondary Education (Private), Vocational & Technical Education

Environment: Environment-General, Resource Conservation, Wildlife Protection

Health: Arthritis, Children's Health/Hospitals, Emergency/Ambulance Services, Eyes/Blindness, Health Funds, Health Organizations, Heart, Hospices, Hospitals, Single-Disease Health Associations

International: International Relief Efforts

Religion: Churches, Missionary Activities (Domestic), Religious Welfare

Science: Science Museums, Scientific Centers & Institutes

Social Services: Camps, Child Welfare, Community Centers, Community Service Organizations, Counseling, Crime Prevention, Emergency Relief, Family Services, People with Disabilities, Scouts, Substance Abuse, United Funds/United Ways, Veterans, Volunteer Services, Youth Organizations

Application Procedures

Initial Contact: Send a brief letter of inquiry.
Deadlines: September 30 is suggested deadline.

Additional Information

Trust(s): Wells Fargo Bank

Foundation Officials

Mary L. Barker: trustee
Orville Rex Child: trustee
Dean W. Hurst: co-vice chairman
Kristen Hurst-Hyde: director
Jack D. Lampros: chairman
Jamie Shenefelt: director
C. William Stromberg: co-vice chairman
Richard Stromberg: director

Grants Analysis

Disclosure Period: calendar year ending 2003
Total Grants: $575,390*
Number of Grants: 21
Average Grant: $15,610*
Highest Grant: $263,200
Lowest Grant: $500
Typical Range: $5,000 to $30,000
***Note:** Giving excludes United Way. Average grant figure excludes highest grant.

Recent Grants

Note: Grants derived from 2003 Form 990.

General

263,200	Weber State University, Ogden, UT -- for the exempt purposes
81,000	Ogden Symphony Ballet Foundation, Ogden, UT -- for the exempt purposes
75,000	United Way Of Northern Utah, Ogden, UT -- for the exempt purposes
50,000	Brigham Young University, Rexburg, ID -- for the exempt purposes
30,000	South High Alumni Association, Salt Lake City, UT -- for the exempt purposes
25,000	American Red Cross of Northern Utah, Ogden, UT -- for the exempt purposes
25,000	University of Florida, Gainesville, FL -- for the exempt purposes
20,000	Egyptian Theatre Foundation, Ogden, UT -- for the exempt purposes
20,000	Rotary Club of Ogden Foundation, Ogden, UT -- for the exempt purposes
11,200	Davis School District Foundation, Farmington, UT -- for the exempt purposes

GLEN AND DOROTHY STILLWELL CHARITABLE TRUST

Giving Contact
John F. Bradley, Trustee
301 N. Lake Ave., 10th Fl.
Pasadena, CA 91101-4108
Phone: (626)793-9400

Description
Founded: 1981
EIN: 956751888
Organization Type: Private Foundation
Giving Locations: CA: Orange County; TN: Davidson, Williamson
Grant Types: General Support.

Donor Information
Founder: Glen Stillwell, Dorothy Stillwell

Financial Summary
Total Giving: $104,830 (fiscal year ending November 30, 2004); $121,500 (fiscal 2001)
Assets: $1,985,517 (fiscal 2004); $2,255,783 (fiscal 2001)

Typical Recipients
Arts & Humanities: Libraries, Performing Arts
Civic & Public Affairs: Employment/Job Training, Housing
Education: Afterschool/Enrichment Programs, Special Education
Health: Children's Health/Hospitals, Eyes/Blindness, Mental Health, Outpatient Health Care, Single-Disease Health Associations
Religion: Churches, Religious Welfare
Social Services: At-Risk Youth, Big Brothers/Big Sisters, Child Abuse, Child Welfare, Community Service Organizations, Day Care, Delinquency & Criminal Rehabilitation, Domestic Violence, Family Services, Food/Clothing Distribution, Homes, People with Disabilities, Senior Services, Sexual Abuse, Shelters/Homelessness, Substance Abuse, Veterans, YMCA/YWCA/YMHA/YWHA, Youth Organizations

Application Procedures
Initial Contact: Submit a letter of inquiry and full proposal.
Application Requirements: Include objectives to be achieved, the manner in which the name of the trust will be recognized, detailed budget, a description of organization, amount requested, purpose of funds sought, recently audited financial statement, proof of tax-exempt status, and proof of non-private foundation status.
Deadlines: None.

Restrictions
Emphasis is on grants to organizations which provide assistance to the needy, infirm, educationally handicapped, drug and alcohol dependent, blind, hearing impaired, abused, and other disadvantaged persons.

Additional Information
The foundation reports that 95% of contributions are allocated to Health and Human Services and 5% to Education for the blind and handicapped.
Publications: Application Guidelines

Foundation Officials
John F. Bradley: trustee
Timothy J. Gosney: trustee
H. Jess Senecal: trustee

Grants Analysis
Disclosure Period: fiscal year ending November 30, 2004

Total Grants: $104,830
Number of Grants: 12
Average Grant: $8,736
Highest Grant: $12,000
Lowest Grant: $1,000
Typical Range: $5,000 to $10,000

Recent Grants
Note: Grants derived from fiscal 2004 Form 990.
General

12,000	Big Brothers/Big Sisters, Tustin, CA -- mentoring program for children of incarcerated parents
12,000	Orangewood Children's Foundation, Garden Grove, CA -- counseling, housing and support for Orange County's emancipated foster children in an apartment under appropriate supervision
10,000	Casa Youth Shelter, Los Alamitos, CA -- operating costs for youth shelter due to increased insurance costs and cuts in government funding
10,000	John Henry Foundation, Santa Ana, CA -- life skills classes for adult suffering from mental illness
10,000	Nashville Child Advocacy Center, Nashville, TN -- special emergency needs fund for center dealing with abused children
10,000	OC Interfaith Shelter, Costa Mesa, CA -- transitional shelter for 12 to 14 homeless families
10,000	Operation Stand Down Nashville, Nashville, TN -- program for drug and alcohol free transitional living for military veteran women
10,000	St. Marks Presbyterian Church, Newport Beach, CA -- part-time administrative assistant and computer system for Newport community counseling center
5,000	Friendship Shelter, Laguna Beach, CA -- challenge gift for new donors to cover operating costs of emergency shelter
5,000	Project Dignity, Garden Grove, CA -- for program assisting homeless children and their families living in motels

STOCKER FOUNDATION

Giving Contact
Patricia O'Brien, Executive Director
559 Broadway Avenue, 2nd Floor
Lorain, OH 44052-1744
Phone: (440)246-5719
E-mail: contact@stockerfoundation.org
Web: http://www.stockerfoundation.org

Description
Founded: 1979
EIN: 341293603
Organization Type: Private Foundation
Giving Locations: AZ: Southern Arizona; NM: Dona Ana County; OH: Lorain County
Grant Types: Capital, Emergency, Endowment, General Support, Multiyear/Continuing Support, Operating Expenses, Project, Research, Scholarship, Seed Money.

Donor Information
Founder: Beth K. Stocker

Financial Summary
Total Giving: $606,345 (2003); $2,481,330 (2001). Note: Fiscal 1997 Giving includes scholarship ($107,275).
Giving Analysis: Giving for 2001 includes: foundation grants to United Way ($15,000)
Assets: $45,824,840 (2003); $35,474,642 (2001)
Gifts Received: $3,000,000 (2003); $1,615,903

(2001); $1,307,542 (2000). Note: In 2003, contributions were received from Beth K. Stocker. In fiscal 1996, 1998 and 2001, contributions were received from Beth K. Stocker.

Typical Recipients
Arts & Humanities: Arts Associations & Councils, Arts Outreach, Dance, History & Archaeology, Libraries, Museums/Galleries, Music, Opera, Performing Arts, Public Broadcasting, Theater, Visual Arts
Civic & Public Affairs: African American Affairs, Botanical Gardens/Parks, Community Foundations, Economic Development, Employment/Job Training, Hispanic Affairs, Housing, Legal Aid, Native American Affairs, Philanthropic Organizations, Public Policy, Urban & Community Affairs, Zoos/Aquariums
Education: Afterschool/Enrichment Programs, Agricultural Education, Arts/Humanities Education, Business Education, Colleges & Universities, Community & Junior Colleges, Education Funds, Education Reform, Engineering/Technological Education, Environmental Education, Education-General, Leadership Training, Legal Education, Literacy, Private Education (Precollege), Public Education (Precollege), School Volunteerism, Student Aid, Vocational & Technical Education
Environment: Environment-General, Resource Conservation
Health: AIDS/HIV, Alzheimer's Disease, Arthritis, Cancer, Children's Health/Hospitals, Clinics/Medical Centers, Emergency/Ambulance Services, Health Organizations, Hospices, Long-Term Care, Medical Rehabilitation, Medical Research, Medical Training, Mental Health, Nursing Services, Prenatal Health Issues, Preventive Medicine/Wellness Organizations, Single-Disease Health Associations
Religion: Jewish Causes, Ministries, Religious Welfare
Social Services: At-Risk Youth, Big Brothers/Big Sisters, Child Abuse, Child Welfare, Community Centers, Community Service Organizations, Counseling, Crime Prevention, Day Care, Domestic Violence, Emergency Relief, Family Planning, Family Services, Food/Clothing Distribution, People with Disabilities, Scouts, Senior Services, Sexual Abuse, Shelters/Homelessness, Substance Abuse, United Funds/United Ways, Volunteer Services, YMCA/YWCA/YMHA/YWHA, Youth Organizations

Application Procedures
Initial Contact: Call or write the foundation requesting application guidelines before submitting a proposal.
Deadlines: January 15, May 15, and September 1.

Restrictions
Emphasis is on innovative, short-term youth development, public education, aid to the handicapped and disadvantaged, cultural programs, women's issues, and programs that have the promise of a solution. Does not provide loans or support individuals, religious organizations for sectarian purposes, political or lobbying groups, public school services required by law, deficit financing, or annual campaigns.

Additional Information
Publications: Application Guidelines

Foundation Officials
Mary Ann Dobras: trustee
Benjamin P. Norton: trustee
Sara Jane Norton: trustee
Beth K. Stocker: president
Anne Woodling: trustee
Nancy Elizabeth Woodling: trustee

Grants Analysis
Disclosure Period: calendar year ending 2003
Total Grants: $606,345
Number of Grants: 58
Average Grant: $9,760*
Highest Grant: $50,000

Lowest Grant: $150
Typical Range: $1,000 to $15,000
*Note: Average grant figure excludes highest grant.

Recent Grants

Note: Grants derived from 2003 Form 990.
General

100,000	Community Foundation of Greater Lorain County, Lorain, OH -- as a nonprofit management fund, a capacity-building initiative
50,000	Lorain County Rape Crisis, Lorain, OH -- toward the implementation of the Child Advocacy Center-one child, one place, one time project
40,000	Girl Scouts of Erie Shores, Lorain, OH -- towards capital request to support the renovation of camp Timberlane
25,000	El Rio Community Health Center, Tucson, AZ -- to support extending community-based health care to medically underserved children and youth in Pima County
25,000	First Step Clinic, Las Cruces, NM -- to support the construction of a permanent First Step Clinic
20,000	New Beginnings for Women & Children, Tucson, AZ -- to support the youth advantage program
18,400	Cuyahoga Community College Foundation, Cleveland, OH -- toward the establishment of a Reggio Emilia inspired preschool classroom
18,000	Girl Scouts of Chaparral Council Inc., Albuquerque, NM -- to implement the studio 2B outreach program
16,000	Mesilla Valley Court Appointed Special Advocates Inc., Las Cruces, NM -- toward the education program for CASA volunteers
15,000	Center for Leadership in Education, Elyria, OH -- to operationalize a long-range strategic plan

STOCKMAN FAMILY FOUNDATION TRUST

Giving Contact

Harvey S. Stockman
1041 Matador SE
Albuquerque, NM 87123
Phone: (505)881-3953

Description

Founded: 1991
EIN: 856104630
Organization Type: Private Foundation
Giving Locations: DC: Washington; NJ; NM; NY
Grant Types: General Support.

Donor Information

Founder: Established in 1991 by Hervey S. and Sarah H. Stockman.

Financial Summary

Total Giving: $875,500 (fiscal year ending November 30, 2004); $844,215 (fiscal 2001)
Assets: $19,467,477 (fiscal 2004); $17,393,210 (fiscal 2001)
Gifts Received: $300,000 (fiscal 2004); $300,000 (fiscal 2001); $290,000 (fiscal 2000). Note: In fiscal 2004, 2001, 2000, 1998, and 1995, contributions were received from Hervey S. and Sarah H. Stockman.

Typical Recipients

Arts & Humanities: Arts Centers, Arts Institutes, Ethnic & Folk Arts, Arts & Humanities-General, His-

toric Preservation, History & Archaeology, Libraries, Museums/Galleries, Performing Arts, Visual Arts
Civic & Public Affairs: Community Foundations, Hispanic Affairs
Education: Arts/Humanities Education, Colleges & Universities, Environmental Education, Private Education (Precollege)
International: Foreign Arts Organizations, Foreign Educational Institutions
Science: Science Museums

Application Procedures

Initial Contact: Send a brief letter of inquiry.
Application Requirements: Include proof of tax-exempt status under IRS Section 501(c)(3).
Deadlines: None.

Additional Information

Trust(s): Banker's Trust Co.

Foundation Officials

Karl W. Gustafson: treasurer
Hervey S. Stockman, Jr.: vice president
Hervey S. Stockman: president
Sarah A. Stockman: chairman, secretary

Grants Analysis

Disclosure Period: fiscal year ending November 30, 2004
Total Grants: $875,500
Number of Grants: 19
Average Grant: $37,088*
Highest Grant: $150,000
Lowest Grant: $5,000
Typical Range: $10,000 to $50,000
*Note: Average grant figure excludes two highest grants ($245,000).

Recent Grants

Note: Grants derived from fiscal 2004 Form 990.
General

150,000	Walters Art Gallery, Baltimore, MD -- to support the position of senior conservator of manuscripts and rare books
95,000	University of New Mexico, Albuquerque, NM -- towards support for a museum conservator and conservation technician
77,000	Wheelwright Museum of the American Indian, Santa Fe, NM -- towards fund for conservation of Navajo & Pueble collections, educational programs, internships & provide conservation lab & storage necessities
75,000	New Mexico State University, Las Cruces, NM -- towards support of a Pre-Graduate studies program in art conservation
66,600	Evergreen House, Johns Hopkins University, Baltimore, MD -- to complete phase III of the Japanese Arts Collection Project
65,000	University College London, London United Kingdom -- towards conservation of metal material in the Sir Flanders Petrie Palestinian Collection
50,000	Baltimore Museum of Art, Baltimore, MD -- to support endowed chair for the museum's senior conservator
50,000	University of Buffalo, Buffalo, NY -- to support the completion of the bronze casting and installation of Carl Rumsey's Olympic sports Bas-Reliefs
40,000	Fine Arts Museum of San Francisco, San Francisco, CA -- towards conservation of oil paintings
40,000	Williamstown Art Conservation Center, Williamstown, MA -- to support the position of advanced intern in paintings conservation

STODDARD CHARITABLE TRUST

Giving Contact

Warner S. Fletcher, Chairman
370 Main Street, 12th Floor
Worcester, MA 01608
Phone: (508)798-8621
Fax: (508)791-6454
E-mail: wfletcher@ftwlaw.com

Description

Founded: 1939
EIN: 046023791
Organization Type: Family Foundation
Giving Locations: MA: Worcester
Grant Types: General Support.

Donor Information

Founder: Established in 1939 by the late Harry G. Stoddard (d. 1969), chairman of Wyman Gordon Company and of the Worcester Telegram and Gazette. He was president of the Worcester Community Chest and a director of the Worcester YMCA and the Worcester Boys Club.

Financial Summary

Total Giving: $3,210,500 (2003); $3,283,500 (2002); $4,774,500 (2001)
Giving Analysis: Giving for 2003 includes: foundation grants to United Way ($120,000); 2002: foundation grants to United Way ($120,000)
Assets: $73,075,332 (2003); $63,164,853 (2002); $75,741,687 (2001)
Gifts Received: $616,969 (2001); $8,040,140 (2000); $5,726,102 (1999). Note: In 2001, contributions were received from Stephen B. Loring ($615,094) and the Estate of Helen E. Stoddard ($1,875).

Typical Recipients

Arts & Humanities: Arts Appreciation, Arts Centers, Arts Funds, Ethnic & Folk Arts, Film & Video, Historic Preservation, History & Archaeology, Libraries, Museums/Galleries, Music, Performing Arts, Public Broadcasting, Theater
Civic & Public Affairs: Botanical Gardens/Parks, Business/Free Enterprise, Clubs, Community Foundations, Economic Development, Employment/Job Training, Civic & Public Affairs-General, Hispanic Affairs, Housing, Legal Aid, Municipalities/Towns, Native American Affairs, Parades/Festivals, Professional & Trade Associations, Urban & Community Affairs
Education: Afterschool/Enrichment Programs, Agricultural Education, Arts/Humanities Education, Business Education, Business-School Partnerships, Colleges & Universities, Community & Junior Colleges, Education Associations, Education Funds, Education Reform, Elementary Education (Private), Engineering/Technological Education, Education-General, Literacy, Medical Education, Private Education (Precollege), Science/Mathematics Education, Secondary Education (Private), Special Education, Student Aid, Vocational & Technical Education
Environment: Environment-General, Resource Conservation, Wildlife Protection
Health: Cancer, Children's Health/Hospitals, Clinics/Medical Centers, Diabetes, Health-General, Health Funds, Health Organizations, Home-Care Services, Hospices, Hospitals (University Affiliated), Medical Rehabilitation, Medical Research, Mental Health, Nursing Services, Preventive Medicine/Wellness Organizations, Public Health
Religion: Churches, Jewish Causes, Ministries, Religious Welfare
Science: Science Museums, Scientific Centers & Institutes, Scientific Research
Social Services: At-Risk Youth, Big Brothers/Big Sisters, Child Abuse, Child Welfare, Community Centers, Community Service Organizations, Counseling,

Day Care, Emergency Relief, Family Planning, Family Services, Food/Clothing Distribution, Homes, People with Disabilities, Scouts, Senior Services, Sexual Abuse, Shelters/Homelessness, Substance Abuse, United Funds/United Ways, YMCA/YWCA/YMHA/YWHA, Youth Organizations

Application Procedures

Initial Contact: Apply in writing.
Application Requirements: Four copies of a proposal must be submitted. Proposal should include a description of organization and its total budget, amount needed, projected budget, and proof of tax-exempt status.
Deadlines: None.
Review Process: The trust acknowledges receipt of applications. An interview may be required. The decision-making process takes about three months.

Restrictions

The trust does not make grants to individuals and rarely makes grants to organizations outside Worcester, MA.

Foundation Officials

Allen W. Fletcher: trustee B 1948. PRIM CORP EMPL chairman, treasurer: Worcester Publishing Inc. CORP AFFIL chairman, treasurer: Worcester Business Journal; chairman, treasurer: Worcester Magazine; chairman, treasurer: Hartford Business Journal.
Warner S. Fletcher: chairman, trustee B Worcester, MA 1945. ED Williams College BA (1967); Boston University JD (1973). PRIM CORP EMPL treasurer: Fletcher, Tilton & Whipple PC. CORP AFFIL director: Wyman-Gordon Co.
Judith S. King: trustee, treasurer CORP AFFIL director: Wyman-Gordon Co.
Valerie S. Loring: secretary, trustee

Grants Analysis

Disclosure Period: calendar year ending 2003
Total Grants: $3,090,500*
Number of Grants: 65
Average Grant: $37,151*
Highest Grant: $400,000
Lowest Grant: $2,000
Typical Range: $10,000 to $50,000
*Note: Giving excludes United Way. Average grant figure excludes two highest grants ($750,000).

Recent Grants

Note: Grants derived from 2003 Form 990.
Library-Related

100,000	American Antiquarian Society, Worcester, MA -- towards building addition and renovation

General

400,000	Worcester Historical Museum, Worcester, MA -- leadership challenge grant
350,000	Bancroft School, Worcester, MA -- towards schools initiative
150,000	American Red Cross, Worcester, MA -- towards construction of new headquarters building
150,000	UMass Memorial Health Care, Worcester, MA -- towards construction of ambulatory surgery center
150,000	Y O U INC., Worcester, MA -- improvement of cottage hill academy
120,000	United Way of Central Massachusetts, Worcester, MA -- challenge grant
100,000	Anna Maria College, Paxton, MA -- towards Miriam hall renovation project
100,000	Bridge of Central Massachusetts, Worcester, MA
100,000	Broad Meadow Brook Conservation Center and Wildlife Sanctuary, Worcester, MA -- towards acquisition of property
100,000	Central Massachusetts Symphony Orchestra, Worcester, MA -- towards capital campaign

STONE FOUNDATION

Giving Contact

Gerald C. Shea, Secretary & Treasurer
Stone Foundation, Inc.
c/o HHG Foundation Services
PO Box 4004
Darien, CT 06820
Phone: (203)348-1500

Description

Founded: 1964
EIN: 237148468
Organization Type: Private Foundation
Giving Locations: CT: Eastern seaboard.
Grant Types: Capital, Endowment, General Support.

Donor Information

Founder: the late Marion H. Stone, the late Charles Lynn Stone

Financial Summary

Total Giving: $556,020 (2003); $766,000 (2001)
Assets: $15,705,062 (2003); $15,871,396 (2001)

Typical Recipients

Arts & Humanities: Arts Outreach, Libraries, Museums/Galleries, Music
Civic & Public Affairs: Community Foundations, Economic Development, Legal Aid, Nonprofit Management, Philanthropic Organizations, Zoos/Aquariums
Education: Arts/Humanities Education, Colleges & Universities, Faculty Development, Education-General, Medical Education, Private Education (Precollege), Science/Mathematics Education, Secondary Education (Private)
Health: Cancer, Children's Health/Hospitals, Clinics/Medical Centers, Hospitals, Nursing Services
Religion: Religious Welfare
Science: Science Museums, Scientific Labs
Social Services: Camps, Family Planning, Family Services, Social Services-General, Substance Abuse

Application Procedures

Initial Contact: a brief letter of inquiry
Application Requirements: Outline of the proposed project, a statement of its significance, proposed budget

Restrictions

Preference is given to established educational institutions or research organizations. Does not support individuals.

Additional Information

Grants are usually considered at the fall meeting.
Publications: Application Guidelines

Foundation Officials

Dr. Charles Lynn Stone, Jr.: president, trustee
Edward Eldredge Stone: vice president, trustee

Grants Analysis

Disclosure Period: calendar year ending 2003
Total Grants: $556,020
Number of Grants: 14
Average Grant: $39,716
Highest Grant: $100,000
Lowest Grant: $12,500
Typical Range: $25,000 to $50,000

Recent Grants

Note: Grants derived from 2003 Form 990.
General

100,000	Columbia School of Nursing, New York, NY
83,500	Bank Street School, New York, NY
70,000	Fairfield Country Day School, Fairfield, CT
50,000	Huntington Hospital, Huntington, NY
25,000	CASA, New York, NY
25,000	Cold Spring Harbor Laboratory, Cold Spring Harbor, NY
25,000	Family & Children's Agency, Norwalk, CT
25,000	Frontier Nursing Services, Lexington, KY
21,270	Hastings College, Hastings, NE
12,500	Fairfield County Community Foundation, Stamford, CT

FRANCE STONE FOUNDATION

Giving Contact

Joseph S. Heyman, President & Trustee
608 Madison Ave., Ste. 1000
Toledo, OH 43604
Phone: (419)252-6230

Description

Founded: 1952
EIN: 346523033
Organization Type: Private Foundation
Giving Locations: IN; MI; OH
Grant Types: Capital, General Support, Multiyear/Continuing Support, Research, Scholarship.

Donor Information

Founder: the late George A. France, the France Stone Co., and subsidiaries

Financial Summary

Total Giving: $562,560 (2003); $536,100 (2001)
Giving Analysis: Giving for 2001 includes: foundation grants to United Way ($5,000)
Assets: $11,900,016 (2003); $13,177,532 (2001)

Typical Recipients

Arts & Humanities: Ballet, Community Arts, History & Archaeology, Libraries, Museums/Galleries, Music, Opera, Public Broadcasting
Civic & Public Affairs: Botanical Gardens/Parks, Business/Free Enterprise, Clubs, Civic & Public Affairs-General
Education: Business Education, Colleges & Universities, Education Funds, Legal Education, Literacy, Medical Education, Minority Education, Private Education (Precollege)
Health: Children's Health/Hospitals, Clinics/Medical Centers, Emergency/Ambulance Services, Eyes/Blindness, Health Organizations, Heart, Hospices, Hospitals, Multiple Sclerosis, Preventive Medicine/Wellness Organizations, Respiratory, Single-Disease Health Associations
Religion: Churches, Religious Welfare
Social Services: Animal Protection, Camps, Child Welfare, Community Centers, Community Service Organizations, Food/Clothing Distribution, Homes, People with Disabilities, Scouts, Social Services-General, United Funds/United Ways, YMCA/YWCA/YMHA/YWHA, Youth Organizations

Application Procedures

Initial Contact: Send cover letter and full proposal.
Application Requirements: Include purpose of funds sought.
Deadlines: None.

Restrictions

Generally limited to medical, educational, and religious organizations. Does not support individuals.

Foundation Officials

Andrew E. Anderson: secretary, treasurer, trustee
Joseph S. Heyman: president, trustee
Ollie J. Risner: vice president, trustee

Grants Analysis

Disclosure Period: calendar year ending 2003
Total Grants: $562,560
Number of Grants: 33
Average Grant: $15,393*
Highest Grant: $70,000
Lowest Grant: $1,000
Typical Range: $5,000 to $20,000
*Note: Average grant figure excludes highest grant.

Recent Grants

Note: Grants derived from 2003 Form 990.
General

70,000	Hospice Foundation, Toledo, OH
64,260	Toledo Museum of Art, Toledo, OH
51,000	Boy Scouts of America, Toledo, OH
50,000	Salvation Army, Toledo, OH
40,000	Sunshine Children's Home, Toledo, OH
30,000	Cherry Street Mission, Toledo, OH
30,000	Toledo Society for the Blind, Toledo, OH
30,000	Toledo Symphony Association, Toledo, OH
25,000	Toledo Humane Society, Toledo, OH
20,000	Read for Literacy, Toledo, OH

H. CHASE STONE TRUST

Giving Contact

Janice M. Eder, Trust Officer
c/o Bank One Colorado Springs NA
30 E. Pikes Peak
Colorado Springs, CO 80942
Phone: (719)471-5074

Description

EIN: 846066113
Organization Type: Private Foundation
Giving Locations: CO: El Paso County
Grant Types: General Support.

Financial Summary

Total Giving: $156,000 (2003); $103,000 (2001)
Giving Analysis: Giving for 2003 includes: foundation grants to United Way ($20,000)
Assets: $3,625,390 (2003); $3,655,564 (2001)
Gifts Received: $10,000 (1996). Note: In 1996, contributions were received from the Luther McCauley Charitable Trust.

Typical Recipients

Arts & Humanities: Arts Associations & Councils, Arts Centers, Arts Outreach, Dance, History & Archaeology, Libraries, Museums/Galleries, Music, Opera, Performing Arts, Public Broadcasting, Theater
Civic & Public Affairs: Community Foundations, Economic Development, Civic & Public Affairs-General, Housing, Municipalities/Towns, Parades/Festivals, Safety, Urban & Community Affairs, Women's Affairs, Zoos/Aquariums
Education: Arts/Humanities Education, Business Education, Colleges & Universities, Faculty Development, Education-General, Literacy, Preschool Education, Private Education (Precollege), Public Education (Precollege), Science/Mathematics Education, Student Aid
Environment: Environment-General
Health: Alzheimer's Disease, Cancer, Children's Health/Hospitals, Clinics/Medical Centers, Emergency/Ambulance Services, Health Organizations, Hospices, Medical Research, Mental Health, Preventive Medicine/Wellness Organizations, Research/Studies Institutes, Single-Disease Health Associations
Religion: Ministries, Religious Welfare
Science: Scientific Organizations
Social Services: At-Risk Youth, Child Abuse, Community Centers, Community Service Organizations, Domestic Violence, Family Planning, Family Services, Food/Clothing Distribution, People with Disabilities, Recreation & Athletics, Scouts, Senior Services, Special Olympics, Substance Abuse, United Funds/United Ways, YMCA/YWCA/YMHA/YWHA, Youth Organizations

Application Procedures

Initial Contact: Send a written narrative letter.
Application Requirements: Include amount requested, purpose of funds sought, and who will benefit from the grant.
Deadlines: April 30 and October 31.

Restrictions

Does not support individuals.

Additional Information

Trust(s): Bank One Trust Co.

Grants Analysis

Disclosure Period: calendar year ending 2003
Total Grants: $136,000*
Number of Grants: 16
Average Grant: $6,067*
Highest Grant: $45,000
Lowest Grant: $1,000
Typical Range: $1,000 to $10,000
*Note: Giving excludes United Way. Average grant figure excludes highest grant.

Recent Grants

Note: Grants derived from 2001 Form 990.
Library-Related

20,000	Pikes Peak Library, Colorado Springs, CO

General

20,000	World Arena, Colorado Springs, CO
12,000	University of Colorado, Colorado Springs, CO -- Theatreworks
10,000	Colorado Springs Fine Arts Center, Colorado Springs, CO
10,000	Pikes Peak Historical Street Railway, Colorado Springs, CO
10,000	Short Line to Cripple Creek, Colorado Springs, CO
8,000	Children's Literacy Center, Colorado Springs, CO
6,000	Rocky Mountain PBS, Pueblo, CO
5,000	Colorado Springs Children's Chorale, Colorado Springs, CO
2,000	Rock Ledge Ranch Living History, Colorado Springs, CO

STONECUTTER MILLS CORP.

Company Headquarters

300 Dallas St.
Spindale, NC 28160
Web: http://www.stonecuttermills.com

Company Description

Employees: 1,150
SIC(s): 2221 Broadwoven Fabric Mills--Manmade, 2261 Finishing Plants--Cotton, 2262 Finishing Plants--Manmade, 2269 Finishing Plants Nec.

Operating Locations

Stonecutter Mills Corp. (NC--Spindale)

Stonecutter Foundation

Giving Contact

Terri Barringer
Dallas Street

PO Box 157
Spindale, NC 28160
Phone: (828)286-2341

Description

EIN: 566044820
Organization Type: Corporate Foundation
Giving Locations: NC
Grant Types: General Support, Scholarship.

Financial Summary

Total Giving: $504,825 (fiscal year ending March 31, 2003); $503,175 (fiscal 2001). Note: Contributes through foundation only.
Giving Analysis: Giving for fiscal 2003 includes: foundation grants to United Way ($100); foundation scholarships ($62,533); fiscal 2001: foundation grants to United Way ($5,500); foundation ($497,675).
Assets: $7,143,723 (fiscal 2003); $9,448,650 (fiscal 2001)
Gifts Received: $300 (fiscal 1999); $72,420 (fiscal 1993); $39,700 (fiscal 1992). Note: In fiscal 1999, contributions were received from Peter S. Hagerman.

Typical Recipients

Arts & Humanities: Arts Associations & Councils, Libraries, Museums/Galleries, Public Broadcasting
Civic & Public Affairs: Business/Free Enterprise, Civil Rights, Community Foundations, Economic Policy, Employment/Job Training, Civic & Public Affairs-General, Housing, Law & Justice, Legal Aid, Municipalities/Towns, Public Policy, Safety, Urban & Community Affairs
Education: Agricultural Education, Arts/Humanities Education, Colleges & Universities, Community & Junior Colleges, Education Associations, Education Funds, Education Reform, Elementary Education (Private), Elementary Education (Public), Engineering/Technological Education, Education-General, Leadership Training, Private Education (Precollege), Public Education (Precollege), Religious Education, Science/Mathematics Education, Secondary Education (Public)
Environment: Environment-General, Resource Conservation, Wildlife Protection
Health: Hospices, Hospitals, Medical Research, Preventive Medicine/Wellness Organizations
International: Missionary/Religious Activities
Religion: Churches, Dioceses, Ministries, Religious Organizations
Science: Science Museums, Scientific Centers & Institutes
Social Services: Child Welfare, Community Service Organizations, Counseling, Crime Prevention, Domestic Violence, Emergency Relief, Family Services, Homes, Recreation & Athletics, Scouts, Senior Services, Social Services-General, United Funds/United Ways, Youth Organizations

Application Procedures

Initial Contact: Request an application form.
Deadlines: None.

Restrictions

Loans are restricted to residents of local area and require proof of acceptance at an institute of higher learning, financial need, and student records.

Additional Information

Publications: Application Form

Corporate Officials

James R. Cowan: chairman, president, chief executive officer, director B 1945. ED University of North Carolina BS (1967); Indiana University MS (1973). PRIM CORP EMPL chairman, president, chief executive officer, director: Stonecutter Mills Corp. CORP AFFIL chairman: Mitchell Co.

Foundation Officials

D. Daniel Briscoe: director
James R. Cowan: vice president, director (see

above)
Z. E. Dobbins, Jr.: president, director
Dillard Morrow: director
James M. Perry: vice president, director
James T. Strickland: director
Mark L. Summey: director
K. S. Tanner, Jr.: director CORP AFFIL director: Stonecutter Mills Corp.
Thomas P. Walker: secretary, director

Grants Analysis

Disclosure Period: fiscal year ending March 31, 2003
Total Grants: $442,192*
Number of Grants: 44
Average Grant: $6,214*
Highest Grant: $175,000
Lowest Grant: $100
Typical Range: $1,000 to $10,000
*Note: Giving excludes United Way and scholarship. Average grant figure excludes highest grant.

Recent Grants

Note: Grants derived from 2004 Form 990.
Library-Related

1,000	Spindale Public Library, Spindale, NC

General

37,500	Isothermal Community College Foundation Inc., Spindale, NC
17,150	Isothermal Community College Foundation Inc., Spindale, NC
15,000	Alexander Baptist Church, Forest City, NC
13,200	Carolina Educational Opportunity Fund, Winston-Salem, NC
12,500	Isothermal Community College Foundation Inc., Spindale, NC
10,000	Asheville School, Asheville, NC
10,000	Isothermal Community College Foundation Inc., Spindale, NC
10,000	Isothermal Community College Foundation Inc., Spindale, NC
10,000	Isothermal Community College Foundation Inc., Spindale, NC
10,000	Isothermal Planning and Development Commission, Rutherfordton, NC

STORA ENSO

Company Headquarters

231 1st Ave. N.
Wisconsin Rapids, WI 54495-8050
Web: http://www.storaenso.com/na

Company Description

Former Name: Consolidated Papers, Inc. (2000).
Revenue: US$2.338 billion (2001)
Employees: 7,500 (2001)
SIC(s): 2611 Pulp Mills, 2621 Paper Mills, 2631 Paperboard Mills, 2653 Corrugated & Solid Fiber Boxes.
Parent Company: Stora Enso Oyj, Kanavaranta 1, Helsinki, Finland

Operating Locations

Consolidated Papers, Inc. (IL--Chicago; NY--New York; WI--Adams, Biron, Stevens Point, Whiting)

Mead Witter Foundation, Inc.

Giving Contact

Susan Feith, President
Mead Witter Foundation
PO Box 39
Wisconsin Rapids, WI 54495-0039

Phone: (715)424-3004
Fax: (715)424-1314

Description

Founded: 1951
EIN: 396040071
Organization Type: Corporate Foundation
Giving Locations: WI: headquarters and operating communities
Grant Types: Capital, Employee Matching Gifts, Endowment, General Support, Project, Scholarship.
Note: Employee matching gift ratio: 1 to 1 for gifts to higher education, social service organisation, and the arts.

Donor Information

Founder: Consolidated Papers and George W. Mead I

Financial Summary

Total Giving: $3,310,303 (2003); $2,505,521 (2002); $2,866,922 (2001)
Assets: $67,889,302 (2003); $5,715,931 (2002); $68,711,278 (2001)
Gifts Received: $800,100 (2001); $48,000 (2000); $525,000 (1999). Note: In 2000, contributions were received from Sally Hands. In 1998, contributions were received from Consolidated Papers, Inc. ($680,000), Ruth Barker ($25,000), and Sally Hands (24,000). In 2001, George W. Mead II.

Typical Recipients

Arts & Humanities: Arts Associations & Councils, Arts Festivals, Arts Institutes, Ballet, Community Arts, Arts & Humanities-General, Historic Preservation, History & Archaeology, Libraries, Museums/Galleries, Music, Opera, Performing Arts, Public Broadcasting, Theater, Visual Arts
Civic & Public Affairs: Botanical Gardens/Parks, Clubs, Community Foundations, Economic Development, Employment/Job Training, Civic & Public Affairs-General, Housing, Inner-City Development, Law & Justice, Municipalities/Towns, Philanthropic Organizations, Professional & Trade Associations, Public Policy, Safety, Zoos/Aquariums
Education: Afterschool/Enrichment Programs, Agricultural Education, Arts/Humanities Education, Business Education, Colleges & Universities, Continuing Education, Economic Education, Education Associations, Education Funds, Engineering/Technological Education, Environmental Education, Education-General, Gifted & Talented Programs, Literacy, Medical Education, Minority Education, Private Education (Precollege), Public Education (Precollege), Science/Mathematics Education, Secondary Education (Private), Secondary Education (Public), Student Aid, Vocational & Technical Education
Environment: Air/Water Quality, Environment-General, Resource Conservation, Wildlife Protection
Health: AIDS/HIV, Emergency/Ambulance Services, Eyes/Blindness, Health Funds, Health Organizations, Hospices, Hospitals, Medical Rehabilitation, Preventive Medicine/Wellness Organizations, Trauma Treatment
International: International Environmental Issues, International Relations
Religion: Religious Welfare
Science: Science-General, Science Museums, Scientific Centers & Institutes
Social Services: Animal Protection, At-Risk Youth, Big Brothers/Big Sisters, Camps, Child Welfare, Community Service Organizations, Crime Prevention, Day Care, Domestic Violence, Family Planning, Family Services, Food/Clothing Distribution, People with Disabilities, Recreation & Athletics, Scouts, Senior Services, Shelters/Homelessness, Social Services-General, United Funds/United Ways, YMCA/YWCA/YMHA/YWHA, Youth Organizations

Application Procedures

Initial Contact: Send a brief letter of inquiry.
Application Requirements: Information should in-

clude a description of organization, amount requested, a statement of how the request will be used, budgetary and financial documentation, and a copy of the applicant organization's IRS letter of determination indicating that the applicant is an organization to which contributions are deductible under IRS Code Section 170.
Deadlines: March 1 for consideration at June board meeting; September 1 for meeting during late November or early December.

Restrictions

There are no restrictions or limitations on grants. However, educational institutions and charities geographically close to corporate installations of Consolidated Papers, Inc. have been favored in the past. Grants are made directly to organizations furnishing the charitable service or function. Educational institutions are favored.

Corporate Officials

Gorton M. Evans, Jr.: president, chief executive officer, director B 1938. ED Michigan State University BS (1960). PRIM CORP EMPL president, chief executive officer, director: Consolidated Papers, Inc. ADD CORP EMPL president: Inter Lake Wisconsin Inc.; president: Inter Lake Papers Inc.
George Wilson Mead, II: chairman, director B Milwaukee, WI 1927. ED Yale University BS (1950); Institute of Paper Chemistry MS (1952). PRIM CORP EMPL chairman, director: Consolidated Papers, Inc. CORP AFFIL director: Newaygo Timber Co. Ltd.; director: Snap-On Tools Inc.; chairman, director: Consolidated Water Power Co. NONPR AFFIL director, president: Consolidated Civic Foundation; trustee: Institute Paper Chemistry; director: American Forest & Paper Association; member: American Paper Institute.

Foundation Officials

Helen B. Ambuel: director
Susan A. Feith: president
Emily B. McKay: director
George Wilson Mead, II: chairman, treasurer (see above)

Grants Analysis

Disclosure Period: calendar year ending 2003
Total Grants: $3,004,314*
Number of Grants: 46
Average Grant: $7,954*
Highest Grant: $1,800,000
Lowest Grant: $25
Typical Range: $5,000 to $10,000
*Note: Giving excludes scholarships; United Way. Average grant figure excludes two highest grants ($2,654,322).

Recent Grants

Note: Grants derived from 2003 Form 990.
General

1,800,000	Fidelity Charitable Gift Fund, Boston, MA
854,322	Wisconsin Rapids Family Center Inc., Wisconsin Rapids, WI
82,000	International Crane Foundation, Baraboo, WI
72,250	National Merit Scholarship Corporation, Evanston, IL -- towards scholarship
41,105	Wisconsin Rapids SkBers, Wisconsin Rapids, WI
31,600	Beloit College, Beloit, WI
31,500	Lawrence University, Appleton, WI -- towards scholarship
30,175	Adult Day Care of South Wood County Inc., Wisconsin rapids, WI
26,950	Milwaukee School of Engineering, Milwaukee, WI -- towards scholarship
25,700	Girl Scouts of Woodland Council, Wisconsin Rapids, WI

STORAGE TECHNOLOGY CORP.

Company Headquarters
Louisville, CO
Web: http://www.stortek.com

Company Description
Ticker: STK
Exchange: OTC
Employees: 8,300
SIC(s): 3577 Computer Peripheral Equipment Nec.

Operating Locations
Storage Technology Corp. (CO--Longmont, Louisville; FL--Palm Bay; IL--Crestwood; PR--Mayaguez, Ponce; TX--El Paso)

Nonmonetary Support
Type: Donated Equipment; In-kind Services
Volunteer Programs: Employees actively volunteer for a variety of corporate-sponsored activities, including Meals on Wheels, Boy Scouts, community hospitals, food banks, high schools and elementary schools, 4-H clubs, and wildlife and rescue groups. The company initiated the Volunteers in Partnership with the Community (VIP.COM) program in 1998. The program not only encourages employees to volunteer commitments, but also generates additional funds from the company for nonprofit organizations to which employees dedicate time.

StorageTek Foundation

Giving Contact
Amy Redfern, Manager, Community Relations
One StorageTek Drive
Louisville, CO 80028-4305
Phone: (303)661-8256
Fax: (303)673-8876
Web: http://www.storagetek.com/home/about/foundation/

Description
EIN: 841168359
Organization Type: Corporate Foundation
Giving Locations: headquarters area only.
Grant Types: Employee Matching Gifts, General Support, Scholarship.
Note: Employee matching gift ratio: .5 to 1 for gifts to higher education and the United Way.

Financial Summary
Total Giving: $387,899 (2002); $469,587 (2001).
Note: Contributes through corporate direct giving program and foundation.
Assets: $239,935 (2002); $225,172 (2001)
Gifts Received: $402,500 (2002); $740,000 (2001); $590,091 (2000). Note: Contributions were received from Storage Technology Corp.

Typical Recipients
Arts & Humanities: Arts Appreciation, Arts Associations & Councils, Arts Centers, Dance, Arts & Humanities-General, Libraries, Museums/Galleries, Music, Performing Arts, Public Broadcasting, Theater
Civic & Public Affairs: Business/Free Enterprise, Civil Rights, Clubs, Community Foundations, Economic Policy, Civic & Public Affairs-General, Housing, Native American Affairs, Parades/Festivals, Professional & Trade Associations, Public Policy, Urban & Community Affairs, Women's Affairs
Education: Arts/Humanities Education, Business Education, Colleges & Universities, Continuing Education, Economic Education, Education Associations, Education Funds, Education Reform, Engineering/Technological Education, Faculty Development, Education-General, Leadership Training, Literacy, Minor-

ity Education, Preschool Education, Private Education (Precollege), Public Education (Precollege), Science/Mathematics Education, Secondary Education (Private), Secondary Education (Public), Special Education, Student Aid
Health: Arthritis, Cancer, Children's Health/Hospitals, Clinics/Medical Centers, Emergency/Ambulance Services, Health-General, Health Funds, Health Organizations, Heart, Hospices, Hospitals, Medical Rehabilitation, Mental Health, Multiple Sclerosis, Nutrition, Public Health, Single-Disease Health Associations, Transplant Networks/Donor Banks
Religion: Jewish Causes
Science: Science Museums
Social Services: At-Risk Youth, Big Brothers/Big Sisters, Child Welfare, Community Service Organizations, Domestic Violence, Emergency Relief, Family Services, Food/Clothing Distribution, Homes, People with Disabilities, Recreation & Athletics, Scouts, Shelters/Homelessness, Social Services-General, Special Olympics, Substance Abuse, United Funds/United Ways, Volunteer Services, YMCA/YWCA/YMHA/YWHA, Youth Organizations

Application Procedures
Initial Contact: Send a written proposal.
Application Requirements: Include a description and background of organization, project description and purpose, objectives of organization and project, amount requested and purpose of funds sought, unique aspects of project, project budget, funding sources and amounts, list of board members and officers with affiliations, current and/or proposed income and expense budget, recently audited financial statement, and proof of tax-exempt status.
Deadlines: December31.
Evaluative Criteria: The foundation may request additional information and a site visit.
Decision Notification: Evaluation generally takes 2 to 3 months.

Restrictions
The company does not support individuals, religious organizations for sectarian purposes, political or lobbying groups, fraternal organizations, general operating budgets receiving more than 40% of budget from United Way, or trips or tours.

Corporate Officials
Mark McGregor: vice president, treasurer, chief executive officer, director ED Texas A&M University BA (1964). PRIM CORP EMPL vice president, treasurer: Storage Technology Corp.
David E. Weiss: chairman, president, chief executive officer, director B 1944. ED University of Colorado BA (1967); University of Colorado MBA (1989); University of Colorado MA (1989). PRIM CORP EMPL chairman, president, chief executive officer, director: Storage Technology Corp.

Foundation Officials
Michael Klatman: president PRIM CORP EMPL vice president corporate communications: Storage Technology Corp.
Mark McGregor: vice president, treasurer (see above)

Grants Analysis
Disclosure Period: calendar year ending 2002
Total Grants: $264,999*
Number of Grants: 48
Average Grant: $5,521
Highest Grant: $40,000
Lowest Grant: $100
Typical Range: $1,000 to $20,000
*Note: Giving excludes matching gifts, scholarship, and United Way.

Recent Grants
Note: Grants derived from 2003 Form 990.

General

40,000	University of Minnesota Solar Vehicle Project, Minneapolis, MN
35,697	Foothills United Way, Boulder, CO
30,248	Foothills United Way, Boulder, CO
25,000	World T E A M Sports, Charlotte, NC
24,542	Foothills United Way, Boulder, CO
21,000	Xcel Energy Parade of Lights, Denver, CO
20,000	Foundation for Boulder Valley, Boulder, CO
20,000	Student Leadership Institute, Ft. Collins, CO
15,000	Peak Arts Association, Boulder, CO
10,000	Arapahoe House, Thornton, CO

CHARLES H. STOUT FOUNDATION

Giving Contact
Richard M. Stout, President
940 Matley Lane, Suite 3
Reno, NV 89502
Phone: (775)322-4321

Description
Founded: 1982
EIN: 942797249
Organization Type: Private Foundation
Giving Locations: AK: Silvan Springs; CA: Borrego Springs, DelMar; NV: Reno; NY: New York
Grant Types: Endowment, General Support, Scholarship.

Financial Summary
Total Giving: $340,000 (fiscal year ending June 30, 2004); $363,000 (fiscal 2002); $306,890 (fiscal 2001)
Giving Analysis: Giving for fiscal 2004 includes: foundation scholarships ($46,000); fiscal 2001: foundation scholarships ($48,000)
Assets: $7,626,452 (fiscal 2004); $7,256,589 (fiscal 2002); $7,878,061 (fiscal 2001)

Typical Recipients
Arts & Humanities: Arts Associations & Councils, Arts Centers, Arts Festivals, Ethnic & Folk Arts, Arts & Humanities-General, History & Archaeology, Libraries, Museums/Galleries, Music, Opera, Performing Arts, Public Broadcasting, Theater
Civic & Public Affairs: Civic & Public Affairs-General, Housing, Law & Justice, Safety, Women's Affairs
Education: Business Education, Colleges & Universities, Community & Junior Colleges, Faculty Development, Education-General, Journalism/Media Education, Legal Education, Preschool Education, Private Education (Precollege), Student Aid
Environment: Research, Wildlife Protection
Health: Alzheimer's Disease, Emergency/Ambulance Services, Health Organizations, Hospitals, Public Health
International: Health Care/Hospitals
Religion: Religious Welfare, Social/Policy Issues
Science: Science Museums
Social Services: Animal Protection, At-Risk Youth, Child Welfare, Community Service Organizations, Domestic Violence, Family Services, Food/Clothing Distribution, Homes, People with Disabilities, Recreation & Athletics, Scouts, Senior Services, Social Services-General, Substance Abuse, YMCA/YWCA/YMHA/YWHA, Youth Organizations

Application Procedures
Initial Contact: Request application form and procedures.
Application Requirements: Include proof of tax-exempt status.

Deadlines: June 15.
Decision Notification: All applicants will be notified by mail shortly after the annual meeting of Trustees. If an applicant has been denied, it will not be held over for future reconsideration; a new application must be submitted.

Restrictions

Grants are not made to individuals.

Additional Information

Publications: Application Form; Procedures

Foundation Officials

Anne E. McDonald: trustee
Douglas B. McDonald: secretary
Richard M. Stout: president, trustee
Martha Stout Gilweit: trustee, vice president

Grants Analysis

Disclosure Period: fiscal year ending June 30, 2004
Total Grants: $294,000*
Number of Grants: 38
Average Grant: $7,737
Highest Grant: $20,000
Lowest Grant: $1,000
Typical Range: $3,000 to $15,000
*Note: Giving excludes scholarships.

Recent Grants

Note: Grants derived from fiscal 2004 Form 990.
General

20,000	Barnard College, New York, NY -- for scholarship
20,000	Desert Home Care, Borrego Springs, CA
20,000	Lifestyles Inc., Fayetteville, AR
20,000	Mama's Kitchen, San Diego, CA
20,000	Textile Museum, Washington, DC -- funds for computer hardware
15,000	Artwatch International Inc., New York, NY
15,000	Food Bank of Northern Nevada Inc., Sparks, NV
15,000	Nevada Women's Fund, Reno, NV
15,000	Sky Mountain Life School, Escondido, CA
15,000	YMCA of the Sierra, Reno, NV -- funds for underwrite renovations

STRAKE FOUNDATION

Giving Contact

George W. Strake, Jr., President, Treasurer & Director
712 Main Street, Suite 3300
Houston, TX 77002-3291
Phone: (713)216-2400
Fax: (713)216-2401
E-mail: foundation@strake.org

Alternate Contact

Paul L. Robison, executive director

Description

Founded: 1952
EIN: 760041524
Organization Type: General Purpose Foundation
Giving Locations: TX: nationally.
Grant Types: Capital, Emergency, Endowment, General Support, Multiyear/Continuing Support, Project, Research, Scholarship.

Donor Information

Founder: Mr. Strake was an oilman and philanthropist who left the bulk of his estate to the foundation when he died in 1969. Strake Foundation is the successor to Strake Charities Foundation, created in 1952, by a trust instrument executed by its grantors, George W. Strake Sr., and his wife, Susan K. Strake. On January 1, 1983, Strake Foundation, a charitable trust, was dissolved, and all assets of the trust were distributed to the newly-created Strake Foundation, a Texas non-profit corporation.

Mr. Strake, who discovered the Conroe Oil Field in Montgomery County, Texas, was an active civic leader and served on the boards of numerous social service, youth, and Catholic religious organizations. The foundation is supported by Mr. Strake's endowment as well as by funds from the estate of Mrs. Strake, who died in 1975, and by gifts from the founder's children, George W. Strake, Jr. and Georganna S. Parsley, who serve as officers and trustees of the foundation. Susan S. Dilworth, also a donor and daughter of the founder, died in 1988.

Financial Summary

Total Giving: $1,775,700 (2003); $1,938,950 (2002); $2,454,750 (2001)
Giving Analysis: Giving for 2003 includes: foundation scholarships ($14,500); 2002: foundation scholarships ($9,500); foundation grants to United Way ($10,000)
Assets: $47,930,941 (2003); $42,439,208 (2002); $53,121,964 (2001)

Typical Recipients

Arts & Humanities: Ethnic & Folk Arts, Historic Preservation, History & Archaeology, Libraries, Museums/Galleries, Music, Public Broadcasting, Theater
Civic & Public Affairs: Botanical Gardens/Parks, Business/Free Enterprise, Clubs, Economic Development, Economic Policy, Civic & Public Affairs-General, Hispanic Affairs, Housing, Minority Business, Parades/Festivals, Professional & Trade Associations, Public Policy, Rural Affairs, Urban & Community Affairs, Women's Affairs, Zoos/Aquariums
Education: Arts/Humanities Education, Business Education, Colleges & Universities, Education Associations, Education Funds, Education Reform, Engineering/Technological Education, Education-General, Literacy, Medical Education, Minority Education, Preschool Education, Private Education (Precollege), Public Education (Precollege), Religious Education, Science/Mathematics Education, Secondary Education (Private), Secondary Education (Public), Special Education, Student Aid
Environment: Environment-General
Health: Cancer, Children's Health/Hospitals, Clinics/Medical Centers, Health Policy/Cost Containment, Health Organizations, Heart, Hospices, Hospitals, Medical Rehabilitation, Medical Research, Mental Health, Prenatal Health Issues, Public Health, Single-Disease Health Associations, Speech & Hearing, Transplant Networks/Donor Banks
International: International Peace & Security Issues, International Relations
Religion: Churches, Dioceses, Religion-General, Jewish Causes, Ministries, Religious Organizations, Religious Welfare, Social/Policy Issues
Science: Science Museums, Scientific Organizations
Social Services: At-Risk Youth, Child Welfare, Community Centers, Community Service Organizations, Family Services, Homes, People with Disabilities, Recreation & Athletics, Scouts, Shelters/Homelessness, Social Services-General, Substance Abuse, United Funds/United Ways, Volunteer Services, YMCA/YWCA/YMHA/YWHA, Youth Organizations

Application Procedures

Initial Contact: Contact foundation for formal application guidelines and form.
Application Requirements: Completed Application Cover Sheet, one-page description of need, copy of IRS tax exemption letter. If additional information is needed, the foundation will request it.
Deadlines: April 1 and October 1.
Review Process: The board meets in May and November. Final notification is given 45 days after a board meeting.

Restrictions

The foundation does not make grants to individuals, elementary schools, or international projects, for deficit financing, consulting services, technical assistance, or loans. No grants are made to federal or state-supported institutions of higher learning.

Additional Information

The foundation requests that applications not be bound and that no extraneous materials, including videos, accompany applications.
Publications: Annual Report; Guidelines; Application Form

Foundation Officials

Colleen D. Stroup: director

Grants Analysis

Disclosure Period: calendar year ending 2003
Total Grants: $1,761,200*
Number of Grants: 325
Average Grant: $5,419
Highest Grant: $50,000
Lowest Grant: $500
Typical Range: $1,000 to $10,000
*Note: Giving excludes scholarships.

Recent Grants

Note: Grants derived from 2002 Form 990.
Library-Related

10,000	George Bush Presidential Library Foundation, College Station, TX -- endowment education programs

General

50,000	Christus St. Joseph Hospital Foundation, Houston, TX -- campaign for St. Joseph Hospital
50,000	San Jose Clinic, Houston, TX -- four year pledge
50,000	University of St. Thomas, Houston, TX -- Center for Thomistic Studies and Department of Philosophy
35,000	St. John Neumann Catholic Church, Austin, TX -- Vocation Institute for Youth Program
35,000	St. Michael Catholic School, Houston, TX -- for annual fund drive
30,000	St. Mary's Catholic Center Diocese of Austin, College Station, TX -- capital campaign
30,000	University of Notre Dame, Notre Dame, IN -- Center for Ethics and Culture
25,000	Boy Scouts of America Sam Houston Area Council, Houston, TX -- Friends of Scouting Program
25,000	Casa de Esperanza De Los Ninos, Houston, TX -- Intake and Assessment Center
25,000	Holy Rosary Church, Houston, TX -- capital campaign

J. WILLIAM AND MARY HELEN STRAKER CHARITABLE FOUNDATION

Giving Contact

Susan Straker-Henderson, President & Treasurer
925 Military Road
Zanesville, OH 43701-1538
Phone: (740)453-2220

Description

Founded: 1994
EIN: 311396841
Organization Type: Private Foundation

Giving Locations: OH: Muskingum County
Grant Types: Capital, General Support, Matching, Multiyear/Continuing Support.

Donor Information

Founder: Established in 1994 by J. William and Mary H. Straker.

Financial Summary

Total Giving: $27,000 (2001)
Assets: $2,570,670 (2001)
Gifts Received: $2,190,371 (1994). Note: In 1994, contributions were received from J. William and Mary H. Straker.

Typical Recipients

Arts & Humanities: History & Archaeology, Libraries, Museums/Galleries
Civic & Public Affairs: Clubs, Civic & Public Affairs-General, Housing, Urban & Community Affairs
Education: Colleges & Universities, Education-General, Literacy, Minority Education, Private Education (Precollege), Public Education (Precollege)
Environment: Environment-General, Wildlife Protection
Health: AIDS/HIV, Long-Term Care, Single-Disease Health Associations, Transplant Networks/Donor Banks
Religion: Religious Welfare
Social Services: Animal Protection, At-Risk Youth, Big Brothers/Big Sisters, People with Disabilities, Scouts, United Funds/United Ways

Application Procedures

Initial Contact: The foundation has no formal grant application procedure or application form. Submit a brief letter of inquiry.
Application Requirements: Include a description of organization, amount requested, purpose of funds sought, recently audited financial statement, proof of tax-exempt status.
Deadlines: None.

Restrictions

Does not fund individuals, religious organizations for sectarian purposes, political or lobbying groups, or organizations outside operating areas.

Foundation Officials

John W. Straker, Jr.: secretary
Susan Straker Henderson: president, treasurer

Grants Analysis

Disclosure Period: calendar year ending 2001
Total Grants: $27,000
Number of Grants: 7
Average Grant: $3,857
Highest Grant: $15,000
Lowest Grant: $500
Typical Range: $1,000 to $10,000

Recent Grants

Note: Grants derived from 2001 Form 990.
General

15,000	Muskingum City Board of Mental Retardation, Zanesville, OH
5,000	West Muskingum Academic Fund, Zanesville, OH
3,500	Muskingum Area Technical College, Zanesville, OH
1,000	Beningham Museum
1,000	Granville Schools Foundation, Granville, OH
1,000	Zanesville City School Foundation, Zanesville, OH
500	Mary Washington College, Fredericksburg, VA

STRANAHAN FOUNDATION

Giving Contact

Pamela G. Roberts, Program Officer
4159 Holland-Sylvania Road, Suite 206
Toledo, OH 43623
Phone: (419)882-5575
Fax: (419)882-2072
E-mail: proberts@stranahanfoundation.org
Web: http://www.stranahanfoundation.org

Description

Founded: 1944
EIN: 346514375
Organization Type: Family Foundation
Giving Locations: OH: Northwest Ohio
Grant Types: Capital, Challenge, General Support, Matching.

Donor Information

Founder: Established as a family trust in Ohio in 1944 by Robert A. Stranahan, former president and chairman of the Champion Spark Plug Company, and his brother, Frank Stranahan. Robert A. Stranahan Jr., and Duane Stranahan have since contributed substantially to the foundation. Members of the Stranahan family still serve on the board of trustees.

Financial Summary

Total Giving: $2,979,575 (2003); $3,983,000 (2002); $5,200,000 (2001)
Giving Analysis: Giving for 2003 includes: foundation grants to United Way ($150,000)
Assets: $84,336,424 (2003); $70,000,000 (2002 approx)

Typical Recipients

Arts & Humanities: Arts Associations & Councils, Arts Centers, Community Arts, Dance, Historic Preservation, History & Archaeology, Libraries, Museums/Galleries, Music, Opera, Performing Arts, Public Broadcasting, Theater
Civic & Public Affairs: Botanical Gardens/Parks, Civil Rights, Clubs, Community Foundations, Economic Development, Economic Policy, Civic & Public Affairs-General, Hispanic Affairs, Housing, Law & Justice, Nonprofit Management, Philanthropic Organizations, Professional & Trade Associations, Public Policy, Urban & Community Affairs, Zoos/Aquariums
Education: Arts/Humanities Education, Business Education, Colleges & Universities, Community & Junior Colleges, Economic Education, Education Associations, Education Funds, Education Reform, Education-General, Literacy, Medical Education, Private Education (Precollege), Religious Education, Secondary Education (Private), Secondary Education (Public), Student Aid
Environment: Environment-General, Resource Conservation, Wildlife Protection
Health: AIDS/HIV, Alzheimer's Disease, Children's Health/Hospitals, Clinics/Medical Centers, Emergency/Ambulance Services, Eyes/Blindness, Health-General, Geriatric Health, Hospices, Hospitals, Medical Rehabilitation, Mental Health, Preventive Medicine/Wellness Organizations, Respiratory
International: International Environmental Issues
Religion: Ministries, Missionary Activities (Domestic), Religious Organizations, Religious Welfare
Science: Scientific Centers & Institutes
Social Services: Animal Protection, Camps, Child Welfare, Community Service Organizations, Crime Prevention, Day Care, Delinquency & Criminal Rehabilitation, Family Planning, Family Services, Food/Clothing Distribution, Homes, People with Disabilities, Recreation & Athletics, Scouts, Senior Services, Social Services-General, United Funds/United Ways, Volunteer Services, YMCA/YWCA/YMHA/YWHA, Youth Organizations

Application Procedures

Initial Contact: The foundation requests an initial letter of inquiry, not more than two pages in length, which summarizes the project.
Application Requirements: The summary should describe the organization and its history and the proposed project--what is planned and how it will be accomplished--with an approximate budget. Supporting documents should include the organization's mission statement, a copy of current tax exemption letter, and the name of the organization's contact person, with telephone and fax numbers. The foundation will invite applicants to submit further materials.
Deadlines: March 1, July 1 and November 1.
Review Process: Applicants will be notified of the board's decision within two weeks after meetings.

Restrictions

The foundation only funds 501(c)(3) organizations. No grants are made for religious groups; personal businesses; deficit financing; computer projects; film, television or radio productions; international projects; endowment funds; government projects; or individuals.

Additional Information

The foundations grantmaking is guided by the following values: Self-sufficiency, in which our goal is to help people become independent and responsible citizens. Respect for oneself, others, community, and for the environment. Freedom, of thought, speech, religion, and economic choices within a just and democratic society, and Courage, to embrace change and, if necessary, to take the initiative to bring about positive change. These fundamental values are best instilled at a young age within a closely-knit environment. Many of our grants, therefore, are directed towards younger age groups and to smaller, carefully monitored program efforts.

The foundation will not support organizations that discriminate in their leadership, staffing, or service provision on the basis of age, gender, race, ethnicity, sexual orientation, disabilities, national origin, political affiliation or religious beliefs.

Foundation Officials

Diana Foster: trustee
Gerald W. Miller: trustee B Columbus, OH 1941. PRIM CORP EMPL president: Typographic Printing Co.
Frances Parry: trustee
Duane Stranahan, Jr.: trustee PRIM CORP EMPL director: Champion Spark Plug Co.
Mark Stranahan: trustee
Stephen Stranahan: trustee B 1934. PRIM CORP EMPL treasurer: Home Ranch Co. Inc. CORP AFFIL Entelco Corp.
Charles G. Yeager: trustee

Grants Analysis

Disclosure Period: calendar year ending 2003
Total Grants: $2,829,575*
Number of Grants: 65
Average Grant: $34,915*
Highest Grant: $595,000
Lowest Grant: $1,000
Typical Range: $10,000 to $50,000
*Note: Giving excludes United Way. Average grant figure excludes highest grant.

Recent Grants

Note: Grants derived from 2001 Form 990.
Library-Related

37,000	Way Public Library Foundation, Perrysburg, OH -- operating

General

500,000	Public Broadcasting Foundation of Northwest Ohio, Toledo, OH -- operating
400,000	Toledo Museum of Art, Toledo, OH -- operating

364,196	Toledo Community Foundation, Toledo, OH -- operating
327,000	Northwest Ohio Scholarship Fund, Inc., Toledo, OH -- operating
316,000	David Lawrence Center and Foundation, Naples, FL -- operating
300,000	United Way, Toledo, OH -- operating
281,500	Toledo Metropolitan Mission, Toledo, OH -- operating
250,000	Montana Community Foundation, Helena, MT -- operating
250,000	Toledo Symphony, Toledo, OH -- operating
213,903	Hillsdale College, Hillsdale, MI -- operating

STRATFORD FOUNDATION

Giving Contact
Peter A. Wilson, Trustee
Care of Testa, Hurwitz & Thibeault
125 High Street
Boston, MA 02110
Phone: (617)248-7000
Fax: (617)248-7100

Description
Founded: 1983
EIN: 222524023
Organization Type: Family Foundation
Giving Locations: MA: Boston
Grant Types: General Support.

Donor Information
Founder: Established in 1983 by Kenneth H. Olsen, founder and former president of Digital Equipment Corporation, who donated $80 million in Digital stock. Digital produces digital computers, circuit modules, and memory electronic systems and components.

Financial Summary
Total Giving: $8,227,327 (2003); $7,525,787 (2002); $9,010,091 (2001)
Giving Analysis: Giving for 2003 includes: foundation grants to United Way ($100,000); 2002: foundation grants to United Way ($105,000)
Assets: $37,883,390 (2003); $39,097,594 (2002); $58,482,880 (2001)

Typical Recipients
Arts & Humanities: Arts Associations & Councils, Arts Outreach, Film & Video, Historic Preservation, History & Archaeology, Libraries, Museums/Galleries, Music, Public Broadcasting, Theater
Civic & Public Affairs: Business/Free Enterprise, Clubs, Community Foundations, Economic Development, Employment/Job Training, Civic & Public Affairs-General, Housing, Law & Justice, Municipalities/Towns, Native American Affairs, Philanthropic Organizations, Rural Affairs, Urban & Community Affairs, Zoos/Aquariums
Education: Colleges & Universities, Education Associations, Education Funds, Elementary Education (Private), Engineering/Technological Education, Environmental Education, Faculty Development, Education-General, Leadership Training, Minority Education, Preschool Education, Private Education (Precollege), Religious Education, Science/Mathematics Education, Secondary Education (Private), Student Aid
Environment: Environment-General, Protection, Resource Conservation, Wildlife Protection
Health: Cancer, Children's Health/Hospitals, Diabetes, Emergency/Ambulance Services, Health Funds, Health Organizations, Heart, Hospitals, Medical Research, Single-Disease Health Associations
International: Foreign Educational Institutions, International-General, Human Rights, International Organizations, International Relief Efforts, Missionary/Religious Activities
Religion: Bible Study/Translation, Churches, Religion-General, Ministries, Missionary Activities (Domestic), Religious Organizations, Religious Welfare, Seminaries, Social/Policy Issues
Science: Science Museums, Scientific Centers & Institutes
Social Services: At-Risk Youth, Big Brothers/Big Sisters, Camps, Child Abuse, Child Welfare, Community Centers, Community Service Organizations, Family Services, Food/Clothing Distribution, Homes, People with Disabilities, Recreation & Athletics, Shelters/Homelessness, Substance Abuse, United Funds/United Ways, YMCA/YWCA/YMHA/YWHA, Youth Organizations

Application Procedures
Initial Contact: Contact the foundation for an application.
Deadlines: None.

Restrictions
No grants are made to individuals or to political organizations.

Additional Information
Publications: Application Form

Foundation Officials
Ava-Lisa Memmen: trustee
Eeva-Liisa Aulikki Olsen: trustee
Kenneth Harry Olsen: don, trustee B Bridgeport, CT 1926. ED Massachusetts Institute of Technology BSEE (1950); Massachusetts Institute of Technology MS (1952). CORP AFFIL director: Polaroid Corp.; chairman: Advanced Modular Solutions Inc. NONPR AFFIL director: Corporate MIT.
Peter A. Wilson: trustee PRIM CORP EMPL senior vice president: Shawmut Bank Boston. NONPR AFFIL treasurer, director MA division: American Cancer Society.

Grants Analysis
Disclosure Period: calendar year ending 2003
Total Grants: $8,127,327*
Number of Grants: 100
Average Grant: $68,896*
Highest Grant: $875,525
Lowest Grant: $2,000
Typical Range: $25,000 to $100,000
*Note: Giving excludes United Way. Average grant figure excludes two highest grants ($1,375,525).

Recent Grants
Note: Grants derived from 2003 Form 990.

Library-Related
| 250,000 | Concord Library, Springville, NY |

General
875,525	Gordon College, Wenham, MA
500,000	Nature Conservancy, Boston, MA
333,000	Food Project, Lincoln, MA
325,000	Central Indiana Community Foundation, Indianapolis, IN
300,000	Assumption College, Worcester, MA
292,000	Indianapolis Foundation, Indianapolis, IN
265,000	Nature Conservancy, Brunswick, ME
250,000	Council for Christian Colleges & Universities, Washington, DC
250,000	First Presbyterian Church of Hollywood, Hollywood, CA
240,000	Christian Camps & Conferences Inc., Boston, MA

STRAUSS FOUNDATION

Giving Contact
Reginald Middleton, Vice President
First Union National Bank
123 Broad Street, 16th Floor
Philadelphia, PA 19109-1199
Phone: (215)670-4226
Fax: (215)670-4236

Description
Founded: 1951
EIN: 236219939
Organization Type: Family Foundation
Giving Locations: CA: Los Angeles; FL: Palm Beach; PA; Israel
Grant Types: General Support, Research.

Donor Information
Founder: Established in 1951 by Maurice L. Strauss.

Financial Summary
Gifts Received: $902,226 (1992)

Typical Recipients
Arts & Humanities: Arts Associations & Councils, Arts Institutes, Ballet, Dance, Ethnic & Folk Arts, Film & Video, History & Archaeology, Libraries, Museums/Galleries, Music, Opera, Performing Arts, Public Broadcasting, Theater
Civic & Public Affairs: Botanical Gardens/Parks, Community Foundations, Civic & Public Affairs-General, Philanthropic Organizations, Urban & Community Affairs, Zoos/Aquariums
Education: Arts/Humanities Education, Colleges & Universities, Education Funds, Education-General, Leadership Training, Medical Education, Minority Education, Private Education (Precollege)
Environment: Air/Water Quality, Environment-General, Resource Conservation, Watershed, Wildlife Protection
Health: AIDS/HIV, Alzheimer's Disease, Cancer, Clinics/Medical Centers, Diabetes, Eyes/Blindness, Health-General, Health Policy/Cost Containment, Health Organizations, Heart, Hospitals, Medical Research, Public Health, Single-Disease Health Associations, Transplant Networks/Donor Banks, Trauma Treatment
International: Health Care/Hospitals, Human Rights, International Affairs
Religion: Jewish Causes, Synagogues/Temples
Science: Science Museums
Social Services: At-Risk Youth, Big Brothers/Big Sisters, Camps, Child Welfare, Community Service Organizations, Emergency Relief, People with Disabilities, Recreation & Athletics, Shelters/Homelessness, Social Services-General, Substance Abuse, Youth Organizations

Application Procedures
Initial Contact: The foundation reports that unsolicited applications are generally not encouraged. The foundation requests applications be made in writing.
Deadlines: None.

Restrictions
The foundation reports grants are made only to public charities. Grants are not made to individuals.

Additional Information
Trust(s): First Union National Bank

Foundation Officials
Henry A. Gladstone: trustee
Scott Rosen Isdaner: trustee B 1952. PRIM CORP EMPL president: V I P Inc.
Sandra S. Krause: trustee
Reginald Middleton: vice president
Benjamin Strauss: trustee CORP AFFIL director: Pep Boys - Manny Moe & Jack.

Robert Perry Strauss: trustee B 1941. PRIM CORP EMPL president: Noven Pharmaceuticals Inc. NONPR AFFIL director: Enterprise Florida Innovation Partners.

Grants Analysis

Disclosure Period: calendar year ending 2000
Total Grants: $1,607,325
Number of Grants: 297
Average Grant: $5,409
Highest Grant: $90,000
Typical Range: $1,000 to $10,000

Recent Grants

Note: Grants derived from 2002 Form 990.
General

75,000	Federation Allied Jewish Appeal, Philadelphia, PA
50,000	Jewish Federation of Palm Beach County, West Palm Beach, FL
50,000	National Museum of American Jewish History, Philadelphia, PA
35,000	Congregation Bet Ha'am, South Portland, ME
35,000	Rags for Riches, Los Angeles, CA
30,000	Duke University, Durham, NC
30,000	Philadelphia Zoo, Philadelphia, PA
25,000	Ballet Florida, West Palm Beach, FL
25,000	Camp Max Straus Foundation, Los Angeles, CA
25,000	Campbell Hall School, North Hollywood, CA

MARGARET DORRANCE STRAWBRIDGE FOUNDATION OF PENNSYLVANIA II

Giving Contact

Diana S. Wister, President
2011 Renaissance Blvd., Suite 102
King of Prussia, PA 19406
Phone: (610)272-0800

Description

Founded: 1985
EIN: 232371943
Organization Type: Private Foundation
Giving Locations: FL; PA: Eastern USA.
Grant Types: General Support, Multiyear/Continuing Support, Operating Expenses, Research.

Donor Information

Founder: Margaret Dorrance Strawbridge Foundation

Financial Summary

Total Giving: $536,600 (2003)
Assets: $18,970,501 (2003)
Gifts Received: $6,151,609 (1998); $9,000,000 (1997); $254,217 (1995). Note: In 1998, contributions were received from Diane S. Norris Trust. In 1997, contributions were received from Diana S. Wister.

Typical Recipients

Arts & Humanities: Arts Associations & Councils, Arts Centers, Community Arts, Historic Preservation, History & Archaeology, Libraries, Museums/Galleries, Music, Performing Arts, Public Broadcasting
Civic & Public Affairs: Botanical Gardens/Parks, Clubs, Community Foundations, Civic & Public Affairs-General, Professional & Trade Associations, Public Policy, Safety, Urban & Community Affairs, Zoos/Aquariums
Education: Agricultural Education, Arts/Humanities

Education, Colleges & Universities, Education-General, Private Education (Precollege), Religious Education, Student Aid
Environment: Air/Water Quality, Environment-General, Resource Conservation, Wildlife Protection
Health: Cancer, Children's Health/Hospitals, Emergency/Ambulance Services, Hospices, Hospitals, Medical Rehabilitation, Medical Research, Prenatal Health Issues, Public Health, Single-Disease Health Associations
International: Foreign Educational Institutions, International Environmental Issues
Religion: Churches, Ministries, Religious Welfare
Science: Scientific Centers & Institutes, Scientific Labs, Scientific Research
Social Services: Animal Protection, Camps, Child Welfare, Community Service Organizations, Delinquency & Criminal Rehabilitation, Family Planning, People with Disabilities, Recreation & Athletics, Senior Services, Substance Abuse

Application Procedures

Initial Contact: The foundation has no formal grant application procedure or application form.
Deadlines: None.

Restrictions

Does not support individuals or provide loans.

Foundation Officials

Diana S. Wister: president, director B 1939.

Grants Analysis

Disclosure Period: calendar year ending 2003
Total Grants: $536,600
Number of Grants: 75
Average Grant: $7,155
Highest Grant: $25,000
Lowest Grant: $500
Typical Range: $1,000 to $10,000

Recent Grants

Note: Grants derived from 2003 Form 990.
General

40,000	Campus Crusade for Christ International, Orlando, FL -- for ministry support
30,000	Caron Foundation, Wernersville, PA -- assistance for families impacted by addiction
25,000	Hanley Hazelden Foundation, West Palm Beach, FL -- for campus expansion
25,000	Kieve Affective Education Inc., Nobleboro, ME -- for campus renewal project
20,000	Scripture Union, Valley Forge, PA -- for Christian ministry
20,000	Winterthur's - Collector Circle, Winterthur, DE -- for garden restoration
15,000	Mount Desert Island Hospital, Bar Harbor, ME -- for hospital support
15,000	Pennsylvania Horticultural Society, Philadelphia, PA -- for related expenses in Philadelphia flower show
15,000	South Florida Center for Theological Studies, Miami, FL -- for school support
12,000	Bryn Mawr Hospital, Bryn Mawr, PA -- for hospital support

HATTIE M. STRONG FOUNDATION

Giving Contact

Judith B. Cyphers, Secretary & Director of Grants
1620 Eye Street N.W., Suite 700
Washington, DC 20006
Phone: (202)331-1619
Fax: (202)466-2894
E-mail: hmsf@hmstrongfoundation.org
Web: http://www.hmstrongfoundation.org

Description

Founded: 1928
EIN: 530237223
Organization Type: Specialized/Single Purpose Foundation
Giving Locations: DC: Washington metropolitan area for community education grant program nationally for student loan program.
Grant Types: General Support, Loan, Professorship, Project, Research, Seed Money.

Donor Information

Founder: Incorporated in 1928 by the late Hattie M. Strong.

Financial Summary

Total Giving: $875,295 (fiscal year ending August 31, 2002); $815,800 (fiscal 2001)
Giving Analysis: Giving for fiscal 2002 includes: foundation gifts to individuals ($501,000); fiscal 2001: foundation gifts to individuals ($518,810)
Assets: $30,315,090 (fiscal 2002); $31,928,267 (fiscal 2001)
Gifts Received: $1,465 (fiscal 2002); $1,880 (fiscal 2001); $1,105 (fiscal 1999). Note: Gifts for fiscal 1999 and 2001 were from miscellaneous donors, all under $500.

Typical Recipients

Arts & Humanities: Arts Outreach, Arts & Humanities-General, History & Archaeology, Museums/Galleries, Music
Civic & Public Affairs: Economic Development, Employment/Job Training, Civic & Public Affairs-General, Hispanic Affairs, Nonprofit Management, Professional & Trade Associations, Urban & Community Affairs, Women's Affairs
Education: Afterschool/Enrichment Programs, Arts/Humanities Education, Colleges & Universities, Community & Junior Colleges, Continuing Education, Education Funds, Education Reform, Elementary Education (Public), Engineering/Technological Education, Environmental Education, Faculty Development, Education-General, Health & Physical Education, International Studies, Leadership Training, Literacy, Minority Education, Preschool Education, Private Education (Precollege), Public Education (Precollege), School Volunteerism, Science/Mathematics Education, Special Education, Student Aid, Vocational & Technical Education
Environment: Resource Conservation
Health: Heart, Medical Rehabilitation, Prenatal Health Issues, Research/Studies Institutes
Religion: Ministries
Science: Scientific Centers & Institutes
Social Services: Child Welfare, Community Service Organizations, Day Care, Family Services, Food/Clothing Distribution, Social Services-General, YMCA/YWCA/YMHA/YWHA, Youth Organizations

Application Procedures

Initial Contact: For the loan program, students should send an initial letter to the foundation. For the grant program, organizations interested in submitting a proposal should first contact the foundation and request written materials explaining proposal procedures and requirements.
Application Requirements: For the loan program, initial letters should provide a brief personal history and identification of the educational institution attended, the subjects studied, the date studies are expected to be completed, and the amount of funds needed (maximum loan amount is $3,000). If the student qualifies for consideration, application forms are then sent out to be completed and returned to the foundation. For the grant program, organizations should follow the foundation's proposal procedures and requirements as directed.
Deadlines: Students should apply between January 1 and March 31 for loans covering the academic year beginning the following September. Deadlines for

grant proposals are January 15, April 15, July 15, and October 15 to be considered for March, June, September, and December, respectively.

Review Process: Loan applicants are normally notified of the foundation's decision in early July. After a full review of grant proposals by foundation staff, including personal interviews if necessary, proposals are presented to the board for action. Applicants are notified in writing of the board's decision.

Restrictions

For the loan program, foreign students temporarily in the United States do not qualify. For the grant program, the foundation generally does not support building or endowment funds, requests for equipment, research, conferences or seminars, projects designed to educate the general public, or programs of national or international scope. The foundation does not make grants to individuals or provide scholarships.

Additional Information

Publications: Annual Report; Application Form; Application Guidelines

Foundation Officials

Barbara B. Cantrell: director
Judith B. Cyphers: secretary, director grants, office
Thelma L. Eichman: director
Mary D. Janney: director
John Marmaduke Lynham, Jr.: director B Washington, DC 1952. ED Trinity College BS (1975); University of Maryland MBA (1979); George Washington University JD (1983). CORP AFFIL partner: Ross Marsh & Foster; director: JMW Settlements Inc. NONPR AFFIL member: District of Columbia Estate Planning Council; Order of Barristers; member: District of Columbia Bar Association. CLUB AFFIL Metropolitan Club; Chevy Chase Club; Lawyers Club of Washington.
Richard S. T. Marsh: director
Vincent Emory Reed: director emeritus B Saint Louis, MO 1928. ED West Virginia State College BS (1952); Howard University MA (1965); University of Pennsylvania Wharton School (1969); West Virginia State College HLD (1977). PRIM NONPR EMPL assistant secretary elementary & secondary education: U.S. Department of Education. CORP AFFIL director: Home Federal Savings & Loan Association. NONPR AFFIL volunteer: Southeast Youth Football Association; director: Washington YMCA; volunteer: Southeast Boys Club; member: National Education Association; member: Phi Delta Kappa; member: National Association School Security Officers; member: National Association Secondary School Principals; member: NAACP; staff member: District of Columbia Public Schools; member: Kappa Alpha Psi; member: District of Columbia Parent Teacher Association; member: District of Columbia PTA Washington Schools; director: District of Columbia Goodwill Industries; member: American Association School Administrations; member: American Society Business Officals; director: 12 Neediest Kids. CLUB AFFIL Kiwanis Club; Pigskin Club.
Sigrid S. Reynolds: director
Carol Levitt Schwartz: director B Greenville, MS 1944. ED University of Texas BS (1965). NONPR AFFIL director: Washington Hebrew Congregation; director: Whitman Walker Clinic; trustee: John F. Kennedy Center Community Friends Board; vice president advisory board: American Automobile Association; member at large: Council District of Columbia. CLUB AFFIL Cosmos Club.
Bente Strong: director
Henry Strong: chairman, president, officer B Rochester, NY 1923. ED Williams College AB (1949). NONPR AFFIL director: National Symphony Orchestra Association; director: Pomfret School; director: National Capital Chapter ARC; director: M. M. Post Foundation District of Columbia; director: Mount Vernon College; honorary trustee: John F. Kennedy Center Performing Arts. CLUB AFFIL Metro Club; Chevy Chase Club; Gibson Island Club.
Henry L. Strong: vice president, officer
Robin C. Tanner: treasurer, director loans, office

Grants Analysis

Disclosure Period: fiscal year ending August 31, 2002
Total Grants: $363,295*
Number of Grants: 170
Average Grant: $2,137
Highest Grant: $10,000
Lowest Grant: $4,000
Typical Range: $1,000 to $10,000
*Note: Giving excludes scholarship; student loans to individuals.

Recent Grants

Note: Grants derived from 2002 Form 990.
General

10,000	Chesapeake Bay Foundation, Annapolis, MD -- endowment
10,000	District of Columbia Central Kitchen, Washington, DC -- Hire Ground Program
10,000	Homeless Children's Tutorial Project, Inc., Washington, DC -- case management initiative
10,000	Mary's Center for Maternal and Child Care, Washington, DC -- Multi-Cultural Family Literacy Program
10,000	Multicultural Career Intern Program, Washington, DC -- Building Renovations Training Program
10,000	See Forever Foundation, Washington, DC -- tutoring program
10,000	Seed Foundation, Inc., Washington, DC -- academic program
10,000	Teach for America, Washington, DC -- recruitment training
10,000	Washington Jesuit Academy, Washington, DC -- Reading/Language Arts Program
9,000	Full Potential Foundation, Washington, DC -- After-School Tutoring Program

CHARLES J. STROSACKER FOUNDATION

Giving Contact

Marian L. Cimbalki, Assistant Secretary
PO Box 471
Midland, MI 48640-0471
Phone: (989)832-0066

Description

Founded: 1957
EIN: 386062787
Organization Type: General Purpose Foundation
Giving Locations: MI: Midland some statewide funding
Grant Types: Endowment, General Support, Matching, Multiyear/Continuing Support.

Donor Information

Founder: Established in 1957 by the late Charles J. Strosacker (1882-1963), one of the pioneers of the Dow Chemical Company.

Financial Summary

Total Giving: $2,405,776 (2003); $2,681,518 (2001)
Giving Analysis: Giving for 2003 includes: foundation grants to United Way ($148,750); 2001: foundation grants to United Way ($131,900)
Assets: $55,826,811 (2003); $47,897,123 (2001)

Typical Recipients

Arts & Humanities: Arts Centers, Arts & Humanities-General, History & Archaeology, Libraries, Museums/ Galleries, Music, Performing Arts, Public Broadcasting, Theater, Visual Arts
Civic & Public Affairs: Botanical Gardens/Parks, Business/Free Enterprise, Chambers of Commerce, Community Foundations, Economic Development, Economic Policy, Employment/Job Training, Civic & Public Affairs-General, Housing, Inner-City Development, Municipalities/Towns, Native American Affairs, Nonprofit Management, Parades/Festivals, Philanthropic Organizations, Professional & Trade Associations, Safety, Urban & Community Affairs, Women's Affairs, Zoos/Aquariums
Education: Afterschool/Enrichment Programs, Agricultural Education, Business Education, Colleges & Universities, Community & Junior Colleges, Continuing Education, Education Funds, Elementary Education (Public), Engineering/Technological Education, Education-General, Legal Education, Literacy, Medical Education, Minority Education, Preschool Education, Private Education (Precollege), Public Education (Precollege), Science/Mathematics Education, Secondary Education (Public), Student Aid
Environment: Air/Water Quality, Environment-General, Resource Conservation
Health: AIDS/HIV, Clinics/Medical Centers, Emergency/Ambulance Services, Geriatric Health, Health Policy/Cost Containment, Health Organizations, Hospices, Hospitals, Mental Health, Nursing Services, Public Health, Transplant Networks/Donor Banks
Religion: Churches, Religious Welfare
Science: Scientific Centers & Institutes, Scientific Research
Social Services: At-Risk Youth, Big Brothers/Big Sisters, Camps, Child Welfare, Community Centers, Community Service Organizations, Crime Prevention, Domestic Violence, Emergency Relief, Family Planning, Family Services, Food/Clothing Distribution, Homes, People with Disabilities, Recreation & Athletics, Scouts, Senior Services, Substance Abuse, United Funds/United Ways, Volunteer Services, YMCA/YWCA/YMHA/YWHA, Youth Organizations

Application Procedures

Initial Contact: Applications should be made by letter. All correspondence must be in writing, unless the foundation initiates a personal interview.
Application Requirements: The proposal should describe the purpose of the project, amount requested, timetable for funding and completion of the project, a list of other major income sources, and a list of major expenditures. The proposal should also include copies of the IRS letter granting tax-exempt status to the applicant, and the organization's latest financial statements.
Deadlines: Requests should be received by September of the year preceding the time payment is desired.

Restrictions

The foundation does not make grants to individuals.

Additional Information

Publications: Annual Report (including Application Guidelines)

Foundation Officials

Bobbie N. Arnold: executive vice president, trustee
David J. Arnold: chairman, trustee
Kimberlee K. Arnold: associate trustee
John N. Bartos: trustee
James L. Borin: trustee
Lawrence E. Burks: assistant treasurer, trustee B 1934. PRIM CORP EMPL president: Chemical Bank & Trust Co. NONPR AFFIL chairman board: Saginaw-Midland Municipal Water Corp.
Marian L. Cimbalik: assistant secretary, trustee
Carolyn Thrune Durand: trustee
Richard A. Hazelton: president, chief executive officer, trustee
John Samuel Ludington: trustee B Detroit, MI 1928. ED Albion College BS (1951); Saginaw Valley State College JD (1977). PRIM CORP EMPL chairman emeritus, director: Dow Corning Corp. CORP AFFIL

director: Comerica Bank Midland. NONPR AFFIL trustee: Midland Community Center.
Hon. Donna T. Morris: secretary, trustee OCCUPATION Probate Judge.
Richard M. Reynolds: finance vice president, treasurer, trustee
Charles J. Thrune: trustee
Charlie C. Thrune: trustee
Eugene C. Yehle: trustee

Grants Analysis

Disclosure Period: calendar year ending 2003
Total Grants: $2,257,026*
Number of Grants: 109
Average Grant: $20,707
Highest Grant: $150,000
Lowest Grant: $250
Typical Range: $5,000 to $50,000
*Note: Giving excludes United Way.

Recent Grants

Note: Grants derived from 2003 Form 990.
General

375,000	Kalamazoo College, Kalamazoo, MI -- towards reading room
300,000	Midland Area Community Foundation, Midland, MI -- towards entranceway and corridor improvement
160,000	MidMichigan Medical Center, Midland, MI -- towards Gamma Knife funding
150,000	Midland County Educational Service Agency, Midland, MI -- towards fiber optic telecommunications network
150,000	Midland Soccer Club, Midland, MI -- for expanding and renovating parking and fielding
125,000	Albion College, Albion, MI -- towards W C Ferguson administrative building
125,000	Albion College, Albion, MI -- towards W C Ferguson administrative building
125,000	Creative Spirit Center Inc., Midland, MI -- towards land and building purchase and renovation
125,000	Kalamazoo College, Kalamazoo, MI
100,000	Great Lakes Center for Youth Development, Bay City, MI -- for restoring Pere Marquette RR depot

G. B. STUART CHARITABLE FOUNDATION

Giving Contact

Karen E. Faircloth, Secretary & Treasurer
3 S. Hanover St.
Carlisle, PA 17013
Phone: (717)243-3737

Description

Founded: 1977
EIN: 232042245
Organization Type: Private Foundation
Giving Locations: PA: Cumberland County
Grant Types: General Support.

Donor Information

Founder: the late George B. Stuart

Financial Summary

Total Giving: $827,450 (2003). Note: 1997 Giving includes United Way ($1,000).
Giving Analysis: Giving for 2003 includes: foundation grants to United Way ($16,200)
Assets: $16,391,340 (2003)
Gifts Received: $4,118 (2003); $137,352 (2000).
Note: In 2003, contributions were received from the

estate of Blanche E. Stuart. In 1997, contributions were received from Henry L. Stewart.

Typical Recipients

Arts & Humanities: Historic Preservation, History & Archaeology, Libraries
Civic & Public Affairs: Employment/Job Training, Civic & Public Affairs-General, Housing, Law & Justice, Municipalities/Towns, Safety
Education: Colleges & Universities, Community & Junior Colleges, Legal Education, Public Education (Precollege), Science/Mathematics Education
Health: Arthritis, Cancer, Children's Health/Hospitals, Diabetes, Eyes/Blindness, Health Organizations, Heart, Hospitals, Multiple Sclerosis, Prenatal Health Issues, Single-Disease Health Associations
Religion: Bible Study/Translation, Churches, Religion-General, Religious Organizations, Religious Welfare
Social Services: Emergency Relief, Food/Clothing Distribution, Social Services-General, United Funds/United Ways

Application Procedures

Initial Contact: Make a telephone inquiry about the feasibility of the request. Letters of inquiry are also accepted.
Application Requirements: Include a description of organization; amount requested; purpose of funds sought; proof of tax-exempt status
Deadlines: July 1.

Restrictions

Grants are not made to individuals.

Additional Information

Trust(s): Mellon Bank NA, Financial Trust

Foundation Officials

Alison Brockmeyer: director
Barbara E. Falconer: president
Keith D. Falconer: director
Victoria J. Macauley: vice president

Grants Analysis

Disclosure Period: calendar year ending 2003
Total Grants: $811,250*
Number of Grants: 29
Average Grant: $19,856*
Highest Grant: $100,000
Lowest Grant: $200
Typical Range: $10,000 to $30,000
*Note: Giving excludes United Way. Average grant figure excludes three highest grants ($295,000).

Recent Grants

Note: Grants derived from 2003 Form 990.
General

100,000	First Presbyterian Church, Carlisle, PA -- for religious activities
100,000	Military Heritage Foundation, Carlisle, PA -- to provide funding for public service activities
95,000	Cumberland County Bar Foundation, Carlisle, PA -- to provide funding for public service activities
75,000	Dickinson Township, Mt. Holly Springs, PA -- for public purposes
55,000	Cumberland-Goodwill Fire and Rescue, Carlisle, PA -- for purchase of ambulance
52,500	Cumberland County Historical Society, Carlisle, PA -- to provide funding for public service activities
50,000	Borough of Carlisle, Carlisle, PA -- for public purposes
50,000	Dickinson College, Carlisle, PA -- for educational purposes
35,000	Carlisle Area School District, Carlisle, PA -- for educational activities
33,000	Carlisle Area Opportunities Industrialization Center Inc., Carlisle, PA -- to provide funding for public service activities

ELBRIDGE AND EVELYN STUART FOUNDATION

Giving Contact

Anne Myers
c/o Bank One Trust Co. NA
1 Bank One Plaza MS IL1-0486
70 W. Madison
Chicago, IL 60670
Phone: (414)765-2017

Description

Founded: 1961
EIN: 956014019
Organization Type: Private Foundation
Giving Locations: CA
Grant Types: General Support.

Financial Summary

Total Giving: $580,000 (2003); $740,000 (2001)
Assets: $11,536,908 (2003); $13,636,455 (2001)

Typical Recipients

Arts & Humanities: Arts Associations & Councils, Historic Preservation, History & Archaeology, Libraries, Museums/Galleries, Music, Public Broadcasting, Visual Arts
Civic & Public Affairs: Community Foundations, Civic & Public Affairs-General, Nonprofit Management, Philanthropic Organizations
Education: Agricultural Education, Arts/Humanities Education, Business Education, Colleges & Universities, Continuing Education, Education Funds, Elementary Education (Private), Education-General, Private Education (Precollege), Religious Education, Science/Mathematics Education, Social Sciences Education, Special Education, Student Aid
Environment: Environment-General, Resource Conservation, Wildlife Protection
Health: Hospitals, Medical Research
International: Foreign Arts Organizations, Health Care/Hospitals, International Environmental Issues, International Organizations
Religion: Churches, Jewish Causes, Religious Organizations, Religious Welfare
Social Services: Social Services-General, Youth Organizations

Application Procedures

Initial Contact: Send a brief letter of inquiry describing program or project.
Application Requirements: Include a description of organization, purpose of funds sought, and proof of tax-exempt status.
Deadlines: None.

Additional Information

Trust(s): Bank One Trust Co. NA

Grants Analysis

Disclosure Period: calendar year ending 2003
Total Grants: $580,000
Number of Grants: 52
Average Grant: $7,451*
Highest Grant: $200,000
Lowest Grant: $500
Typical Range: $1,000 to $20,000
*Note: Average grant figure excludes highest grant.

Recent Grants

Note: Grants derived from 2003 Form 990.
General

200,000	Teton Science School, Kelly, WY
50,000	All Saints Episcopal Day School
50,000	Stanford University, Stanford, CA
45,000	J. Paul Getty Trust, Los Angeles, CA
25,000	River School, Napa, CA
20,000	Neighborhood Youth Association, Venice, CA
20,000	Winrock International, Little Rock, AR

14,000	New Visions Foundation, Los Angeles, CA
11,000	Princeton University, Princeton, NJ
10,000	Medical Investigation of Neurodevelopmental Disorders Institute, Sacramento, CA

ESTATE OF JOSEPH L. STUBBLEFIELD

Giving Contact

H. H. Hayner, Trustee
249 W. Alder St.
PO Box 1757
Walla Walla, WA 99362
Phone: (509)527-3500

Description

Founded: 1902
EIN: 916031350
Organization Type: Private Foundation
Giving Locations: OR; WA
Grant Types: General Support, Scholarship.

Donor Information

Founder: the late Joseph L. Stubblefield

Financial Summary

Total Giving: $243,864 (2003); $410,640 (2001)
Giving Analysis: Giving for 2003 includes: foundation scholarships ($3,400); foundation grants to United Way ($10,000); 2001: foundation scholarships ($525); foundation grants to United Way ($10,000).
Assets: $5,682,378 (2003); $6,631,414 (2001)
Gifts Received: $2,400 (2001); $173,450 (1996); $10,000 (1995). Note: In 1996, contributions were received from Frank Wilson Trust and Mike Murr.

Typical Recipients

Arts & Humanities: Arts Associations & Councils, Arts Centers, Arts & Humanities-General, History & Archaeology, Libraries, Music
Civic & Public Affairs: Business/Free Enterprise, Chambers of Commerce, Civic & Public Affairs-General, Parades/Festivals, Urban & Community Affairs
Education: Afterschool/Enrichment Programs, Business Education, Colleges & Universities, Community & Junior Colleges, Education Funds, Education-General, Literacy, Private Education (Precollege), Public Education (Precollege), Science/Mathematics Education, Secondary Education (Private), Student Aid
Environment: Environment-General
Health: Cancer, Hospices, Multiple Sclerosis
Religion: Churches, Religious Welfare
Social Services: Child Welfare, Community Service Organizations, Counseling, Crime Prevention, Family Planning, Homes, People with Disabilities, Recreation & Athletics, Scouts, United Funds/United Ways, YMCA/YWCA/YMHA/YWHA, Youth Organizations

Application Procedures

Initial Contact: Send a brief letter of inquiry.
Application Requirements: Include recently audited financial statement and purpose of funds sought.
Deadlines: None; but reasonable time should be allowed for review.

Restrictions

Provides grants to indigent widows.

Foundation Officials

Herman Henry Hayner: trustee B Fairfield, WA September 25, 1916. ED Washington State University BA (1938); University of Oregon JD (1946). NONPR AFFIL member: Walla Walla County Bar Association;

member: Washington State Bar Association; fellow: American College Trust & Estate Counsel; member: Walla Walla Chamber of Commerce; fellow: American Bar Association. CLUB AFFIL Walla Walla Country Club; Rotary Club.
James K. Hayner: trustee

Grants Analysis

Disclosure Period: calendar year ending 2003
Total Grants: $230,464*
Number of Grants: 53
Average Grant: $3,029*
Highest Grant: $40,000
Lowest Grant: $44
Typical Range: $1,000 to $5,000
***Note:** Giving excludes United Way; scholarships. Average grant figure excludes two highest grants ($76,000).

Recent Grants

Note: Grants derived from 2003 Form 990.
General

40,000	Whitman College, Walla Walla, WA
36,000	Washington State University Foundation, Pullman, WA
23,000	Walla Walla Public School, Walla Walla, WA
15,000	Children's Home Society, Walla Walla, WA
11,200	Walla Walla Community College Foundation, Walla Walla, WA
10,000	Community Center for Youth, Walla Walla, WA
10,000	United Way, Walla Walla, WA
10,000	Walla Walla College, Walla Walla, WA
10,000	YMCA, Walla Walla, WA
8,000	First Presbyterian Church, Walla Walla, WA

MORRIS STULSAFT FOUNDATION

Giving Contact

Joseph W. Valentine, Executive Director
100 Bush Street, Suite 825
San Francisco, CA 94104-2521
Phone: (415)986-7117
Fax: (415)986-2521
E-mail: stulsaft@aol.com
Web: http://www.stulsaft.org

Description

Founded: 1953
EIN: 946064379
Organization Type: Specialized/Single Purpose Foundation
Giving Locations: CA: Alameda County, Contra Costa County, Marin County, San Francisco County, San Mateo County, Santa Clara County
Grant Types: Capital, General Support, Project.

Donor Information

Founder: Established in California in 1953 by the Morris Stulsaft Testamentary Trust to aid San Francisco organizations for needy and deserving children, without regard to race, creed, or age.

Financial Summary

Total Giving: $1,342,717 (fiscal year ending June 30, 2003); $1,585,400 (fiscal 2002); $1,200,100 (fiscal 2001)
Assets: $48,708 (fiscal 2002); $117,091 (fiscal 2001). Note: Asset figure for 1996 is for the Morris Stulsaft Testamentary Trust which periodically distributes a percentage of its net income to the foundation.
Gifts Received: $1,115,016 (fiscal 2002); $682,322

(fiscal 1999); $1,089,785 (fiscal 1998). Note: The foundation receives contributions from the Morris Stulsaft Testamentary Trust.

Typical Recipients

Arts & Humanities: Arts Appreciation, Arts Outreach, Dance, History & Archaeology, Libraries, Museums/Galleries, Music, Opera, Performing Arts, Public Broadcasting, Visual Arts
Civic & Public Affairs: Asian American Affairs, Botanical Gardens/Parks, Community Foundations, Economic Development, Employment/Job Training, Civic & Public Affairs-General, Hispanic Affairs, Housing, Law & Justice, Nonprofit Management, Urban & Community Affairs, Women's Affairs, Zoos/Aquariums
Education: Afterschool/Enrichment Programs, Arts/Humanities Education, Business Education, Colleges & Universities, Education Associations, Education Funds, Education Reform, Elementary Education (Private), Elementary Education (Public), Faculty Development, Education-General, Gifted & Talented Programs, Journalism/Media Education, Leadership Training, Legal Education, Literacy, Medical Education, Minority Education, Preschool Education, Private Education (Precollege), Public Education (Precollege), School Volunteerism, Science/Mathematics Education, Secondary Education (Private), Special Education, Student Aid, Vocational & Technical Education
Environment: Resource Conservation, Wildlife Protection
Health: Adolescent Health Issues, AIDS/HIV, Cancer, Children's Health/Hospitals, Clinics/Medical Centers, Diabetes, Emergency/Ambulance Services, Eyes/Blindness, Heart, Hospitals, Medical Rehabilitation, Medical Research, Mental Health, Nursing Services, Prenatal Health Issues, Preventive Medicine/Wellness Organizations, Public Health, Research/Studies Institutes, Single-Disease Health Associations, Speech & Hearing, Trauma Treatment
International: Foreign Educational Institutions, International Development, International Environmental Issues, International Relief Efforts, Missionary/Religious Activities
Religion: Dioceses, Jewish Causes, Ministries, Religious Welfare
Science: Science Museums, Scientific Centers & Institutes
Social Services: At-Risk Youth, Big Brothers/Big Sisters, Camps, Child Abuse, Child Welfare, Community Centers, Community Service Organizations, Counseling, Crime Prevention, Day Care, Delinquency & Criminal Rehabilitation, Domestic Violence, Family Planning, Family Services, Food/Clothing Distribution, Homes, People with Disabilities, Recreation & Athletics, Refugee Assistance, Senior Services, Sexual Abuse, Shelters/Homelessness, Social Services-General, Substance Abuse, United Funds/United Ways, Volunteer Services, YMCA/YWCA/YMHA/YWHA, Youth Organizations

Application Procedures

Initial Contact: The foundation provides an application form, which must be used.
Application Requirements: Along with the "Application for Grant" form, additional narrative information may be provided, along with descriptive attachments. In addition, the following items must be provided for each grant request: revenue and expense budget for the proposed program; current agency total revenue and expense budget; evaluation report on this program, if available; most recent agency audit or financial statements; most recent IRS Form 990, with attachments; current list of officers and directors, showing occupations and affiliations. For first time applicants, the following items must also be submitted: IRS letter of tax exemption under Section 501(c)(3), IRS letter classifying the organization as "not a private foundation" under Section 509(a), California Franchise Tax Board letter of exemption under Section 23701(d), and articles of incorporation.

Deadlines: None.

Review Process: The board meets in January, March, May, July, September, and November. If interested, the board of directors may require a representative from the applying organization to provide a presentation (of not more than half an hour) to a committee of the board. All applications are acknowledged. Notice of approval or rejection, or requests for more information, are usually made within six months.

Restrictions

No grants are made to individuals or for emergency funds, endowments, deficit funding, or sectarian purposes. Only one request per organization in a twelve-month period will be reviewed.

Additional Information

Publications: Biennial Report; Application Guidelines

Foundation Officials

Roy L. Bouque: director
Adele Corvin: president
Dana Corvin: director
Dorothy S. Corvin: director
Joan Nelson Dills: administrator
Raymond Marks: secretary, treasurer B 1922.
Edward A. Miller: director PRIM CORP EMPL partner, treasurer: Flinn Gray & Herterich.
Susan Mora: assistant administration
Isadore Pivnick: vice president, director
Joseph Valentine: director

Grants Analysis

Disclosure Period: fiscal year ending June 30, 2003
Total Grants: $1,342,717
Number of Grants: 147
Average Grant: $9,134
Highest Grant: $50,000
Lowest Grant: $1,063
Typical Range: $5,000 to $20,000

Recent Grants

Note: Grants derived from fiscal 2002 Form 990.
Library-Related

10,000	Oakland Public Library Foundation, Oakland, CA -- funds for the after school program providing assistance to children and teens

General

100,000	Peninsula Jewish Community Service, Belmont, CA -- funds for capital campaign to accommodate additional childcare, arts programs, etc
30,000	East Oakland Youth Development Center, Oakland, CA -- funds to improve the Art Studio to increase class size in after school program
25,000	Alameda Boys & Girls Club, Alameda, CA -- funds for the construction of a tech center, classroom and library
25,000	Arriba Juntos, San Francisco, CA -- funds for the expansion of a recreational facility for at risk youth
25,000	Homesafe, San Jose, CA -- funds for the capital campaign to build transitional housing for battered women and children
25,000	Japanese Community Youth Council, San Francisco, CA -- funds to provide quality childcare services to low income families
25,000	Quality Child Care Initiative, San Francisco, CA -- toward a collaborative effort to increase the availability and quality of child care among low-income families
25,000	Samaritan House, San Mateo, CA -- funds for the free clinic capital campaign serving the uninsured working poor
25,000	San Francisco State University Foundation / Mission High School, San Francis-

co, CA -- funds for the science workshop for students

23,500	First Place Fund For Youth, Oakland, CA -- toward preparation of foster youth for emancipation and supporting them after discharge

NORMAN J. STUPP FOUNDATION

Giving Contact

Cindy Lewis, Trust Officer
c/o Commerce Bank
8000 Forsyth Blvd.
Clayton, MO 63105
Phone: (314)746-7322

Description

Founded: 1952
EIN: 436027433
Organization Type: Private Foundation
Giving Locations: MO: St. Louis
Grant Types: Capital, Endowment, General Support, Operating Expenses, Project, Research, Scholarship.

Donor Information

Founder: the late Norman J. Stupp

Financial Summary

Total Giving: $851,333 (fiscal year ending June 30, 2004); $1,004,667 (fiscal 2002); $1,103,917 (fiscal 2001)
Assets: $19,141,844 (fiscal 2004); $18,540,637 (fiscal 2002); $21,755,161 (fiscal 2001)

Typical Recipients

Arts & Humanities: Arts Centers, Arts Outreach, Historic Preservation, History & Archaeology, Libraries, Museums/Galleries, Music, Opera, Public Broadcasting, Theater
Civic & Public Affairs: African American Affairs, Botanical Gardens/Parks, Civic & Public Affairs-General, Municipalities/Towns, Public Policy, Zoos/Aquariums
Education: Colleges & Universities, Community & Junior Colleges, Education-General, Literacy, Medical Education, Private Education (Precollege), Science/Mathematics Education, Special Education, Vocational & Technical Education
Environment: Environment-General
Health: AIDS/HIV, Alzheimer's Disease, Cancer, Children's Health/Hospitals, Emergency/Ambulance Services, Eyes/Blindness, Health Organizations, Hospitals, Hospitals (University Affiliated), Medical Research
Religion: Religious Welfare
Science: Science Museums, Scientific Centers & Institutes
Social Services: At-Risk Youth, Big Brothers/Big Sisters, Camps, Child Welfare, Community Service Organizations, Domestic Violence, Family Services, Food/Clothing Distribution, People with Disabilities, Substance Abuse, United Funds/United Ways, YMCA/YWCA/YMHA/YWHA, Youth Organizations

Application Procedures

Initial Contact: The foundation has no formal grant application procedure or application form.
Deadlines: March 1 and September 1.

Additional Information

Trust(s): Commerce Trust Co.

Grants Analysis

Disclosure Period: fiscal year ending June 30, 2004
Total Grants: $851,333

Number of Grants: 64
Average Grant: $13,302
Highest Grant: $62,500
Lowest Grant: $1,000
Typical Range: $5,000 to $20,000

Recent Grants

Note: Grants derived from fiscal 2004 Form 990.
General

62,500	Saint Louis Symphony Orchestra, St. Louis, MO
50,000	Missouri Botanical Garden Board of Trustees, St. Louis, MO
50,000	St. Louis University, St. Louis, MO
50,000	St. Louis University Eye Institute, St. Louis, MO
50,000	St. Louis University High School, St. Louis, MO
33,333	Trailnet Inc., St. Louis, MO
25,000	City Academy Inc., St. Louis, MO
25,000	Missouri Botanical Garden Board of Trustees, St. Louis, MO
25,000	Ranken - Jordan Home for Convalescent Crippled Children, St. Louis, MO
20,000	Fontbonne University, St. Louis, MO

ROY AND CHRISTINE STURGIS CHARITABLE AND EDUCATIONAL TRUST (AR)

Giving Contact

Barry Findley, Trustee
PO Box 7599
Little Rock, AR 72217
Phone: (501)664-8525

Description

Founded: 1979
EIN: 710495345
Organization Type: Private Foundation
Giving Locations: AR
Grant Types: General Support.

Donor Information

Founder: the late Roy Sturgis, Christine Sturgis

Financial Summary

Total Giving: $601,360 (2003); $598,244 (2001)
Assets: $13,743,908 (2003); $14,903,063 (2001)

Typical Recipients

Arts & Humanities: Arts Centers, Historic Preservation, Libraries, Museums/Galleries, Performing Arts, Public Broadcasting, Theater
Civic & Public Affairs: Safety
Education: Arts/Humanities Education, Colleges & Universities, Education-General, Preschool Education, Private Education (Precollege), Public Education (Precollege), Secondary Education (Private), Secondary Education (Public), Vocational & Technical Education
Health: Arthritis, Children's Health/Hospitals, Home-Care Services, Hospices, Hospitals
International: Missionary/Religious Activities
Religion: Churches, Dioceses, Religious Organizations, Religious Welfare
Science: Science Museums
Social Services: Animal Protection, Child Welfare, Community Service Organizations, Recreation & Athletics, Youth Organizations

Application Procedures

Initial Contact: Send a brief letter of inquiry.
Application Requirements: Include proof of tax-exempt status, most recent Form 990, and purpose

of funds sought.
Deadlines: None.

Restrictions
Gives in Arkansas only.

Foundation Officials
Barry B. Findley: trustee
Katie Speer: trustee

Grants Analysis
Disclosure Period: calendar year ending 2003
Total Grants: $601,360
Number of Grants: 22
Average Grant: $20,068*
Highest Grant: $100,000
Lowest Grant: $694
Typical Range: $5,000 to $30,000
*Note: Average grant figure excludes two highest grants ($200,000).

Recent Grants
Note: Grants derived from 2001 Form 990.
General

50,000	Ouachita Baptist University, Arkadelphia, AR
40,000	Francois Baptist Church
35,000	Christ the King Church, Little Rock, AR
35,000	Cornerstone Family Church
35,000	First Baptist Church, Malvern, AR
35,000	Immaculate Conception Church, Little Rock, AR
25,000	Arkansas Easter Seal Society, Little Rock, AR
25,000	Bethal AME Church
24,000	University of Arkansas Fayetteville, Fayetteville, AR
22,000	University of Arkansas Little Rock, Little Rock, AR

ROY AND CHRISTINE STURGIS CHARITABLE AND EDUCATIONAL TRUST (TX)

Giving Contact
Daniel J. Kelly, Trust Officer
Bank of America NA
PO Box 830241
Dallas, TX 75283-0241
Phone: (214)209-2422
Fax: (214)209-1997

Description
Founded: 1981
EIN: 756331832
Organization Type: General Purpose Foundation
Giving Locations: AR; TX: Dallas County
Grant Types: Capital, Challenge, Endowment, General Support, Operating Expenses, Project, Research, Scholarship.

Donor Information
Founder: Established in 1981 by the estate of Christine Sturgis. There is a Roy and Christine Sturgis Charitable and Educational Trust in Arkansas, as well as a Roy and Christine Sturgis Foundation, also in Arkansas.

Financial Summary
Total Giving: $2,590,000 (fiscal year ending September 30, 2003); $2,735,000 (fiscal 2001)
Giving Analysis: Giving for fiscal 2003 includes: foundation scholarships ($125,000)
Assets: $45,014,222 (fiscal 2003); $51,992,162 (fiscal 2001)

Typical Recipients
Arts & Humanities: Arts Associations & Councils, Arts Centers, Arts Outreach, Ballet, Dance, Ethnic & Folk Arts, Arts & Humanities-General, Historic Preservation, History & Archaeology, Libraries, Literary Arts, Museums/Galleries, Music, Opera, Performing Arts, Public Broadcasting, Theater
Civic & Public Affairs: African American Affairs, Botanical Gardens/Parks, Clubs, Economic Development, Civic & Public Affairs-General, Hispanic Affairs, Housing, Legal Aid, Municipalities/Towns, Nonprofit Management, Public Policy, Urban & Community Affairs, Women's Affairs, Zoos/Aquariums
Education: Afterschool/Enrichment Programs, Agricultural Education, Arts/Humanities Education, Business Education, Colleges & Universities, Community & Junior Colleges, Education Funds, Education Reform, Elementary Education (Public), Education-General, Gifted & Talented Programs, Legal Education, Literacy, Medical Education, Private Education (Precollege), Public Education (Precollege), Science/Mathematics Education, Secondary Education (Private), Secondary Education (Public), Special Education, Student Aid
Environment: Environment-General
Health: Adolescent Health Issues, Alzheimer's Disease, Cancer, Children's Health/Hospitals, Clinics/Medical Centers, Diabetes, Eyes/Blindness, Health-General, Health Organizations, Heart, Hospices, Hospitals, Hospitals (University Affiliated), Kidney, Long-Term Care, Nursing Services, Single-Disease Health Associations, Transplant Networks/Donor Banks
International: International Development
Religion: Churches, Ministries, Missionary Activities (Domestic), Religious Organizations, Religious Welfare
Science: Science Museums
Social Services: At-Risk Youth, Camps, Child Welfare, Community Centers, Community Service Organizations, Domestic Violence, Family Services, Food/Clothing Distribution, People with Disabilities, Recreation & Athletics, Scouts, Senior Services, Shelters/Homelessness, Social Services-General, Substance Abuse, United Funds/United Ways, Volunteer Services, YMCA/YWCA/YMHA/YWHA, Youth Organizations

Application Procedures
Initial Contact: Potential applicants must request an application form by mail.
Application Requirements: Application form should be filled out completely, with attachments to answer the questions on the form. The original and one copy of the complete application should be sent. Information that should be included with application is a copy of IRS 501(c)(3) letter; brief history of organization, its purpose and the people it serves; a one page budget outline; list of board members, with addresses and phone numbers; postcard that came with application; and the previous year's audited financial statement. The trust does not accept videos, cassettes, or books.
Deadlines: Proposals must be postmarked by December 31.
Review Process: Grant decision meetings are held in late April.
Decision Notification: Applicants will be notified by mail by May 31 of acceptance or declination of the grant request.
Notes: Personal interviews are not permitted; visits to the applicant organization will be conducted at the discretion of the trustee after application is received. Grant recipients must wait one year after final grant payment to reapply for funds.

Restrictions
The trust does not fund individuals, scholarships or tuition for individuals, seminars, loans, or political organizations. Grants are only made to charitable organizations in Arkansas and Texas.

Additional Information
Trustees consider grant requests which do not exceed $200,000. Funding for amounts above $200,000 will be considered on very limited basis. Charitable organizations which received a one payment grant must skip a year before applying for a new grant. Organizations which receive multiyear support cannot apply again while receiving payments and must skip a year from the date last payment is received.
The foundation designates 65% of funds for the state of Arkansas and 35% for the state of Texas, mostly for organizations in Dallas County.
Publications: Guidelines; Application Form
Trust(s): Bank of America NA trustee

Grants Analysis
Disclosure Period: fiscal year ending September 30, 2003
Total Grants: $2,465,000*
Number of Grants: 51
Average Grant: $48,333
Highest Grant: $250,000
Lowest Grant: $10,000
Typical Range: $20,000 to $100,000
*Note: Giving excludes scholarships.

Recent Grants
Note: Grants derived from fiscal 2001 Form 990.
General

500,000	University of Arkansas, Fayetteville, AR
200,000	Henderson State University, Arkadelphia, AR -- new Honors College Hall
100,000	Arkansas Cancer Research Foundation, Little Rock, AR -- Community Cancer Control Program
100,000	Arkansas Governor's Mansion Renovation, Little Rock, AR
100,000	Hendrix College, Conway, AR
100,000	Junior League of Little Rock, Inc., Little Rock, AR -- purchase and renovate historic building in downtown
100,000	Little Rock Boys & Girls Club, Little Rock, AR
100,000	Ouachita Baptist University, Arkadelphia, AR
100,000	Tomberlin Community Development Center, Little Rock, AR -- to purchase and install pre-fabricated building
75,000	Baylor University, Waco, TX -- Sturgis Endowed Scholarship Fund

SUBARU OF AMERICA INC.

Company Headquarters
2235 Terrace 70 W.
Cherry Hill, NJ 08002
Web: http://www.subaru.com

Company Description
Employees: 668
SIC(s): 5012 Automobiles & Other Motor Vehicles.
Parent Company: Fuji Heavy Industries Ltd., Subaru Bldg., 7-2 Nishi-Shinjuku 1-chome, Shinjuku-ku, Tokyo, Japan

Operating Locations
Fuji Heavy Industries U.S.A. (NJ--Cherry Hill); Robin America (IL--Wood Dale); Schuman Carriage Co. (HI--Honolulu); Subaru of America (IL--Des Plaines; MD--Savage; NJ--Cherry Hill, Moorestown); Subaru of America Central Region (CO--Aurora); Subaru of America Southeast Region (FL--West Palm Beach; GA--Austell); Subaru of America Western (OR--Portland); Subaru of America Western Region (CA--

Irvine); Subaru Credit Corp. (NJ--Cherry Hill); Subaru Distributor Corp. (NY--Orangeburg); Subaru Financial Services (NJ--Cherry Hill); Subaru-Isuzu Automotive (IN--Lafayette); Subaru Leasing Corp. (NJ--Cherry Hill); Subaru Mid-America (IL--Addison); Subaru of New England (MA--Norwood); Subaru Northwest Region (OR--Portland); Subaru Research & Design (CA--Garden Grove); Subaru Southwest Region (TX--San Antonio)

Subaru of America Foundation, Inc.

Giving Contact
Sandra Capell, Administrator
Subaru of America Foundation
PO Box 6000
Cherry Hill, NJ 08034-6000
Phone: (856)488-8500
Fax: (856)488-3274

Description
EIN: 222531774
Organization Type: Corporate Foundation
Former Name: Subaru of America Foundation (2004).
Giving Locations: CO: Aurora; GA: Austell; IL: Addison; NJ: Cherry Hill primary focus is around the company's Cherry Hill headquarters location, Moorestown; OR: Portland
Grant Types: Employee Matching Gifts, General Support, Project.

Financial Summary
Total Giving: $288,123 (2003); $256,993 (2002); $236,389 (2001). Note: Figures for foundation only and do not include company direct giving.
Giving Analysis: Giving for 2001 includes: foundation grants to United Way ($16,000); foundation matching gifts ($22,439); foundation scholarships ($30,575).
Assets: $1,842,215 (2003); $1,625,234 (2002); $1,725,758 (2001)
Gifts Received: $300,000 (2003); $300,000 (2002); $300,000 (2001). Note: Contributions were received from Subaru of America.

Typical Recipients
Arts & Humanities: Arts Associations & Councils, Arts Centers, Arts Outreach, Ballet, Dance, Film & Video, History & Archaeology, Libraries, Museums/Galleries, Music, Theater
Civic & Public Affairs: Asian American Affairs, Botanical Gardens/Parks, Civic & Public Affairs-General, Law & Justice, Nonprofit Management, Safety, Urban & Community Affairs
Education: Afterschool/Enrichment Programs, Business Education, Colleges & Universities, Education Funds, Education Reform, Elementary Education (Public), Faculty Development, Education-General, International Exchange, Literacy, Minority Education, Preschool Education, Private Education (Precollege), Public Education (Precollege), Science/Mathematics Education, Secondary Education (Private), Special Education, Student Aid
Environment: Resource Conservation, Wildlife Protection
Health: AIDS/HIV, Alzheimer's Disease, Cancer, Children's Health/Hospitals, Diabetes, Emergency/Ambulance Services, Heart, Hospices, Hospitals, Medical Rehabilitation, Multiple Sclerosis, Nursing Services, Single-Disease Health Associations, Trauma Treatment
International: Health Care/Hospitals, International Affairs
Religion: Religious Organizations, Religious Welfare
Science: Science Museums
Social Services: Animal Protection, At-Risk Youth, Big Brothers/Big Sisters, Child Abuse, Child Welfare,

Community Service Organizations, Counseling, Crime Prevention, Day Care, Domestic Violence, Family Planning, Family Services, Food/Clothing Distribution, Homes, People with Disabilities, Shelters/Homelessness, Substance Abuse, United Funds/United Ways, Veterans, Volunteer Services, YMCA/YWCA/YMHA/YWHA, Youth Organizations

Application Procedures
Initial Contact: Send a brief letter of inquiry with a 10, self-addressed unstamped envelope to the foundation to receive a copy of "Policies and Guidelines."

Restrictions
Because foundation prefers to fund grass-roots organizations, it will not consider grants to organizations that have fund balances in excess of two years of current operating budget.

Grants are limited to organizations that are tax-exempt under Section 501(c)(3). Organizations that the foundation trustees prefer not to fund include, but are not limited to, the following: individuals; veterans, fraternal, and/or labor organizations; government agencies; direct support of churches, religious groups, or sectarian groups; social, membership, or other groups that serve the special interests of their constituency; advertising in charitable publications; sponsorship of special events or athletic activities; capital campaigns; political organizations, campaigns, or candidates running for public office; organizations that benefit individuals or groups outside the U.S.; and organizations which, in policy or practice, discriminate against a person or group on the basis of age, political affiliation, race, national origin, ethnicity, gender, religious belief, disability, or sexual orientation.

Foundation does not donate vehicles.

Additional Information
As a general rule, national organizations are not eligible for foundation funds. However, small grants may be considered to organizations that impact foundation or corporate goals. Decisions will be at the sole discretion of the foundation staff, contributions committee, and trustees.

Eligibility for employee matching gifts includes nonprofit institutions/organizations located in the United States that are recognized by the Internal Revenue Service as tax-exempt under Section 501(c)(3), excluding religious, political, or fraternal organizations.

Recipients of grants are expected to submit a written evaluation or report concerning the impact of their project in the community.

Only proposals received in response to a RFP are accepted. The foundation does not accept unsolicited funding requests. Only one proposal per organization will be considered within any 12-month period. The foundation makes no multiyear grants, although it may consider to renew support of a project. However, all funding requests must be submitted annually in response to a RFP.

Publications: Policies and; Guidelines; Requests for Proposals (Rfps)

Corporate Officials
Thomas J. Doll: vice president, chief financial officer, director PRIM CORP EMPL vice president, chief financial officer: Subaru Am.
Yasuo Fujiki: chairman, chief executive officer, director PRIM CORP EMPL chairman, chief executive officer, director: Subaru Am.
George T. Muller: president, chief operating officer, director B Philadelphia, PA 1949. ED Duke University (1971); Philadelphia College (1972). PRIM CORP EMPL president, chief operating officer, director: Subaru Am. NONPR AFFIL member: Financial Executives Institute; member: National Investor Relations Institute; member: American Institute of CPA's.

Foundation Officials
Mamoru Aida: trustee
Thomas J. Doll: trustee (see above)

Sheila Gallucci-David: trustee
Scott Mogren: trustee
Takao Saito: president, trustee
Joseph T. Scharff: secretary, treasurer, trustee B 1944. ED LaSalle College BA (1969). PRIM CORP EMPL treasurer: Subaru American Inc. ADD CORP EMPL treasurer: Subaru Acceptance Corp.; trustee: Subaru Leasing Corp.

Grants Analysis
Disclosure Period: calendar year ending 2003
Total Grants: $150,925*
Number of Grants: 23
Average Grant: $6,562
Highest Grant: $18,000
Lowest Grant: $250
Typical Range: $1,000 to $10,000
*Note: Giving excludes United Way, scholarships, and matching gifts.

Recent Grants
Note: Grants derived from 2003 Form 990.
General

39,345	Scholarship Foundation, Cherry Hill, NJ -- scholarship program
18,000	Camden Children's Garden, Camden, NJ -- supports grow lab programs, which support math and science
15,000	Walt Whitman Cultural Arts Center, Camden, NJ -- support first year of the Storefronts projects
12,000	University of Medicine and Dentistry of New Jersey Foundation, Stratford, NJ -- support teacher training on bullying in schools
10,000	Apple Farms Art & Music Center, Elmer, NJ -- support community outreach programs
10,000	Garden State Discovery Museum, Cherry Hill, NJ -- support center for learning program to increase teacher training program
10,000	Perkins Center for the Arts, Moorestown, NJ -- community arts initiative
10,000	United Way of Camden County, Camden, NJ -- annual contribution on behalf of 450 HQ employees
8,625	University of Pennsylvania Museum, Philadelphia, PA -- support international classroom program
6,000	Big City Mountaineers, Castro Valley, CA -- scholarship for at risk urban youth

ALGERNON SYDNEY SULLIVAN FOUNDATION

Giving Contact
Allen E. Strand, President
520 College Hill Dr.
Oxford, MS 38655
Phone: (662)236-6335

Description
Founded: 1930
EIN: 136084596
Organization Type: Private Foundation
Giving Locations: Southeast USA.
Grant Types: General Support, Scholarship.

Donor Information
Founder: the late Mrs. Algernon Sydney Sullivan, the late George Hammond Sullivan, the late Zilph P. Devereaux

Financial Summary
Total Giving: $856,200 (2003); $1,093,000 (2001)
Assets: $17,292,414 (2003); $20,271,064 (2001)

Gifts Received: $1,466 (1994); $32,876 (1993); $25,000 (1992). Note: In 1993, contributions were received from the estate of Vera H. Armstrong.

Typical Recipients

Arts & Humanities: Libraries
Civic & Public Affairs: Urban & Community Affairs
Education: Colleges & Universities, Elementary Education (Private), Private Education (Precollege)
Environment: Air/Water Quality
Health: Cancer, Emergency/Ambulance Services, Hospitals, Nursing Services, Respiratory
Religion: Religious Welfare
Social Services: Child Welfare, Community Service Organizations, People with Disabilities

Application Procedures

Initial Contact: Send a brief letter of inquiry describing program or project.
Deadlines: None.

Restrictions

Does not support individuals.

Additional Information

Provides scholarships and student aid to colleges in the southeastern United States.

Foundation Officials

William E. Bardusch, Jr.: trustee
William D. Bruen, Jr.: trustee
Allan E. Strand: president
Darla J. Wilkinson: trustee
Gray Williams, Jr.: trustee

Grants Analysis

Disclosure Period: calendar year ending 2003
Total Grants: $856,200
Number of Grants: 32
Average Grant: $26,756
Highest Grant: $40,000
Lowest Grant: $200
Typical Range: $20,000 to $40,000

Recent Grants

Note: Grants derived from 2001 Form 990.
General

50,000	Warren Wilson College, Swannanoa, NC
47,000	Lincoln Memorial University, Harrogate, TN
45,000	Lees-McRae College, Banner Elk, NC
44,000	Cumberland College, Williamsburg, KY
37,000	Alice Lloyd College, Pippa Passes, KY
37,000	Bluefield College, Bluefield, VA
37,000	Brenau College, Gainesville, GA
37,000	Campbell University, Buies Creek, NC
37,000	Coker College, Hartsville, SC
37,000	Converse College, Spartanburg, SC

SULZBERGER FOUNDATION

Giving Contact

Marian S. Heiskell, President
229 West 43rd Street, Suite 1031
New York, NY 10036
Phone: (212)556-1755
Fax: (212)556-1434

Description

Founded: 1956
EIN: 136083166
Organization Type: General Purpose Foundation
Giving Locations: nationally; internationally.
Grant Types: Capital, Conference/Seminar, Emergency, Endowment, Fellowship, General Support, Operating Expenses, Professorship, Project, Scholarship, Seed Money.

Donor Information

Founder: Incorporated in 1956 by the late Arthur Hays Sulzberger and the late Iphigene Ochs Sulzberger.

Financial Summary

Total Giving: $2,328,770 (2003); $2,563,708 (2001). Note: 1995 Giving includes scholarships ($76,000).
Giving Analysis: Giving for 2003 includes: foundation grants to United Way ($50,000); 2001: foundation grants to United Way ($50,000)
Assets: $49,290,275 (2003); $48,476,548 (2001)
Gifts Received: $2,000 (2001); $37,205 (1999); $20,092 (1998). Note: The foundation is not required to file Schedule B along with its return for 2001.

Typical Recipients

Arts & Humanities: Arts Associations & Councils, Arts Funds, Ethnic & Folk Arts, Arts & Humanities-General, Historic Preservation, History & Archaeology, Libraries, Literary Arts, Museums/Galleries, Music, Opera, Performing Arts, Public Broadcasting, Theater, Visual Arts
Civic & Public Affairs: Botanical Gardens/Parks, Clubs, Community Foundations, Economic Development, Employment/Job Training, Civic & Public Affairs-General, Housing, Municipalities/Towns, Philanthropic Organizations, Professional & Trade Associations, Public Policy, Safety, Urban & Community Affairs, Zoos/Aquariums
Education: Afterschool/Enrichment Programs, Arts/Humanities Education, Colleges & Universities, Continuing Education, Education Funds, Education Reform, Elementary Education (Private), Faculty Development, Education-General, International Studies, Journalism/Media Education, Leadership Training, Legal Education, Medical Education, Minority Education, Private Education (Precollege), Public Education (Precollege), School Volunteerism, Secondary Education (Private), Student Aid
Environment: Air/Water Quality, Forestry, Environment-General, Resource Conservation, Wildlife Protection
Health: AIDS/HIV, Cancer, Clinics/Medical Centers, Health Organizations, Hospitals, Kidney, Medical Research, Mental Health, Public Health, Single-Disease Health Associations
International: Foreign Arts Organizations, Foreign Educational Institutions, Health Care/Hospitals, International Affairs, International Environmental Issues, International Organizations, International Peace & Security Issues
Religion: Jewish Causes, Religious Organizations, Religious Welfare, Synagogues/Temples
Science: Science Museums, Scientific Organizations
Social Services: At-Risk Youth, Child Welfare, Community Service Organizations, Crime Prevention, Family Planning, Family Services, Food/Clothing Distribution, People with Disabilities, Recreation & Athletics, Sexual Abuse, Shelters/Homelessness, Social Services-General, Substance Abuse, United Funds/United Ways, Volunteer Services, Youth Organizations

Application Procedures

Initial Contact: The foundation has no formal grant application procedure or application form.
Deadlines: None. Written responses to requests are usually received within six to eight weeks.

Restrictions

The foundation makes grants only to public charities described in IRS section 501(c)(3). No grants are made to individuals, or for matching gifts or loans.

Additional Information

Publications: Annual Report

Foundation Officials

Marian Sulzberger Heiskell: president, director B New York, NY 1918. NONPR AFFIL chairman: Council Environment New York City; director: National Audubon Society.
Frederick T. Mason: assistant secretary, assistant treasurer
Arthur Ochs Sulzberger, Sr.: vice president, secretary B New York, NY 1926. ED Columbia University BA (1951); Dartmouth College LLD (1964); Bard College LLD (1967). CORP AFFIL chairman: WQXR-FM; director: Times Printing Co.; chairman: WQEW-AM; chairman: Lakeland Ledger Publishing; chairman: Ledger; president, director: Gadsden Times Inc.; chairman: Interstate Broadcasting Co.; director: Affiliated Publishers Inc.; chairman, director: Chattanooga Times Co. NONPR AFFIL chairman, trustee: Metropolitan Museum Art; member: Sons American Revolution; trustee emeritus: Columbia University. CLUB AFFIL Metro Club; Overseas Press Club; Explorers Club.
Judith P. Sulzberger, MD: vice president, director PRIM NONPR EMPL attending physician: Columbia College, Physicians & Surgeons Genome Center. CORP AFFIL director: New York Times Co.

Grants Analysis

Disclosure Period: calendar year ending 2003
Total Grants: $2,278,770*
Number of Grants: 186
Average Grant: $12,251
Highest Grant: $255,000
Lowest Grant: $100
Typical Range: $5,000 to $20,000
***Note:** Giving excludes United Way.

Recent Grants

Note: Grants derived from 2001 Form 990.
General

265,758	College of Physicians and Surgeons, New York, NY
152,500	Council on the Environment of New York City, New York, NY
150,000	Jewish Campus Life Fund, New York, NY
102,000	Rainforest Alliance, New York, NY
101,000	Columbia College, New York, NY
100,000	Fresh Air Fund, New York, NY
100,000	Loomis Chaffee School, Windsor, CT
100,000	National Park Foundation, Washington, DC
50,000	Allied Arts Fund of Greater Chattanooga, Chattanooga, TN
50,000	Partnership for After School Education, New York, NY

SUMITOMO MITSUI BANKING CORP.

Company Headquarters

3-2 Marunouchi 1-Chome
Chiyoda-ku
Tokyo 100-0005, Japan
Web: http://www.smbc.co.jp/global

Company Description

Assets: US$911.136 billion (2002)
Employees: 24650 (2002)
SIC(s): 6081 Foreign Banks--Branches & Agencies.

Operating Locations

Sumitomo Bank, New York Branch (NY--New York)

SMBC Global Foundation, Inc.

Giving Contact

Naoyuki Kawamoto, President
SMBC Global Foundation

277 Park Avenue
New York, NY 10172
Phone: (212)224-4031

Description
Founded: 1995
EIN: 133766226
Organization Type: Corporate Foundation
Giving Locations: internationally, with emphasis on Asian countries; People's Republic of China; Malaysia; Singapore; Thailand; Vietnam
Grant Types: General Support, Scholarship.

Financial Summary
Total Giving: $649,394 (2002)
Giving Analysis: Giving for 2002 includes: foundation scholarships ($165,194)
Assets: $14,207,552 (2002)
Gifts Received: $10,000 (2002); $3,125,897 (1998); $10,139,057 (1994). Note: In 2002, contributions were received from Moody's Corp. In 1998, contributions were received from Sumitomo Bank.

Typical Recipients
Arts & Humanities: Libraries, Museums/Galleries, Theater
Civic & Public Affairs: Asian American Affairs, Civic & Public Affairs-General, Public Policy
Education: Business Education, Colleges & Universities, Community & Junior Colleges, Education Associations, Education Funds, Education Reform, Education-General, International Studies, Minority Education, Public Education (Precollege), School Volunteerism, Student Aid
Health: Children's Health/Hospitals
International: Foreign Educational Institutions, Health Care/Hospitals, International Affairs, International Organizations
Social Services: At-Risk Youth, Child Welfare, Community Centers, Community Service Organizations, Domestic Violence, Social Services-General, Substance Abuse, YMCA/YWCA/YMHA/YWHA

Application Procedures
Initial Contact: For direct contributions, the company has no formal application procedures and generally preselects recipients. For scholarship program, request application guidelines. Foundation may ask applicants to submit complete biographical records and supporting materials, including a report on academic and professional careers; a detailed statement of academic plans; a statement of plans and commitments after completion of academic program; letters of reference; lists of extracurricular activities; and any other information as may be requested by the selections committee. Applicant may also be required to demonstrate financial need for grant funds. grant funds.

Restrictions
Recipients must be enrolled at an educational institution approved by the foundation or at which the foundation has established a scholarship grant program. The Foundation does not make grants to individuals.

Additional Information
In 1995, scholarships were provided for attendance at Thammasat University, Bangkok, Thailand; Chulalongkorn University, Bangkok, Thailand; Indonesia University, Jakarta, Indonesia; Airlangga University, Surabaya, Indonesia; Gadjah Mada University, Yogakarta, Indonesia; Padjadjaran University, Bandung, Indonesia; Peking University, Beijing, China; Zhongshan University, Quangdong, China; Peoples University of China, Beijing, China; University of International Business and Economics, Beijing, China; Beijing Foreign Studies University, Beijing, China; and Tsinghua University, Beijing, China.

Corporate Officials
Jane Hutta: general counsel, assistant treasurer, staff attorney PRIM CORP EMPL general counsel, assistant treasurer, staff attorney: Sumitomo Bank.
Ryuzo Kodama: director, head Americas Division PRIM CORP EMPL director, head Americas Division: Sumitomo Bank.
Natsuo Okada: president PRIM CORP EMPL president: Sumitomo Bank Securities. CORP AFFIL president: Sumitomo Bank Capital Markets.
Robert A. Rabbino, Jr.: joint general manager PRIM CORP EMPL joint general manager: Sumitomo Bank.
D. Scarborough Smith, III: joint general manager PRIM CORP EMPL joint general manager: Sumitomo Bank.
Nancy Z. Smith: vice president PRIM CORP EMPL vice president: Sumitomo Bank.

Foundation Officials
Shuntaro Higashi: director
Jane Hutta: secretary (see above)
Hiroshi Ine: treasurer
Naoyuki Kawamoto: president, director
Kenneth Pulick: assistant treasurer
Robert A. Rabbino, Jr.: director (see above)
D. Scarborough Smith, III: director (see above)

Grants Analysis
Disclosure Period: calendar year ending 2002
Total Grants: $642,450*
Number of Grants: 15
Average Grant: $13,073*
Highest Grant: $272,500
Lowest Grant: $2,000
Typical Range: $5,000 to $25,000
*Note: Giving excludes scholarships. Average grant figure excludes two highest grants ($472,500).

Recent Grants
Note: Grants derived from 2002 Form 990.

General
272,500	Manhattan Theatre Club, New York, NY -- funds for supporting of a non-profit theatrical company
200,000	NAFSA Association of International Education, Washington, DC -- funds towards support of scholarship programs of a non-profit organization
30,000	American Enterprise Institute for Public Policy Research, Washington, DC -- funds towards support of public policy research
25,000	New York Cares, New York, NY -- funds for support of a non-profit community service organization
25,000	New York University Stern School of Business, New York, NY -- funding to support of development programs for high schools at NYU
16,000	Kingsborough Community College, Brooklyn, NY -- funds towards support of the Edward R. Murrow high school
13,750	Fredrick Douglass Academy, New York, NY -- funds towards support of trip program for a public high school
11,000	Japanese Educational Institute of New York, Greenwich, CT -- funding towards support of non-profit educational institute
10,000	Children's Aid Society, New York, NY -- funds for helping children and their families affected by the world trade center tragedy
10,000	Foreign Policy Association, New York, NY -- funds towards supporting world affairs education to the general public

SOLON E. SUMMERFIELD FOUNDATION, INC.

Giving Contact
William W. Prager, Jr., President
1270 Avenue of the Americas, Suite 2114
New York, NY 10020-1801
Phone: (212)218-7640

Description
Founded: 1939
EIN: 131797260
Organization Type: General Purpose Foundation
Giving Locations: NY: New York nationally; Northeast USA.
Grant Types: Endowment, General Support, Scholarship.

Donor Information
Founder: Established in 1939 by the late Solon E. Summerfield (1877-1947).

Financial Summary
Total Giving: $2,476,056 (2003); $3,106,607 (2001)
Assets: $58,109,091 (2003); $62,719,577 (2001)

Typical Recipients
Arts & Humanities: Libraries, Music, Public Broadcasting
Civic & Public Affairs: Ethnic Organizations, Civic & Public Affairs-General, Law & Justice, Legal Aid, Native American Affairs, Philanthropic Organizations
Education: Arts/Humanities Education, Colleges & Universities, Community & Junior Colleges, Education Funds, Engineering/Technological Education, Education-General, Legal Education, Medical Education, Minority Education, Student Aid
Health: Clinics/Medical Centers, Emergency/Ambulance Services, Eyes/Blindness, Health Organizations, Hospitals, Long-Term Care, Medical Research, Mental Health, Nursing Services, Research/Studies Institutes
Religion: Churches, Jewish Causes, Religious Welfare
Social Services: Camps, Child Abuse, Child Welfare, Community Centers, Community Service Organizations, Domestic Violence, Food/Clothing Distribution, People with Disabilities, Scouts, Shelters/Homelessness, Youth Organizations

Application Procedures
Initial Contact: Send initial letter of inquiry.
Application Requirements: Provide general information about the proposed project and the applicant.
Deadlines: None.

Restrictions
The foundation only makes contributions to organized tax exempt charitable organizations.

Additional Information
Approximately 80% of the foundation's giving goes to pre-selected charities. Generally the foundation makes smaller contributions to new proposals.

Foundation Officials
William W. Prager, Jr.: vice president PRIM CORP EMPL member: Kalb, Voorhis & Co.
Clarence R. Treeger: president, trustee B 1903. ED Columbia University LLB; University of Pennsylvania Wharton School BS. PRIM CORP EMPL partner: Spiro Felstiner Prager & Fruger.
Thomas C. Treeger: treasurer, secretary

Grants Analysis
Disclosure Period: calendar year ending 2003
Total Grants: $2,476,056
Number of Grants: 125
Average Grant: $11,600*
Highest Grant: $549,277

Lowest Grant: $500
Typical Range: $5,000 to $30,000
***Note:** Average grant figure excludes two highest grants ($1,049,277).

Recent Grants

Note: Grants derived from 2001 Form 990.
General

750,000	Kansas University, Lawrence, KS
615,803	Kansas University Endowment Association, Lawrence, KS
75,000	American Foundation for the Blind, New York, NY
75,000	Boys Scouts of America
75,000	Endowment Fund of Phi Kappa Psi, Indianapolis, IN
75,000	Father Flanagan's Boys Home, Boys Town, NE
75,000	Federation of Jewish Philanthropies, New York, NY
75,000	Hebrew Free Loan Society, New York, NY
75,000	Jewish Guild for Blind
75,000	New York Society for Prevention of Cruelty to Children, New York, NY

SUMMERLEE FOUNDATION

Giving Contact

John W. Crain, Program Director, History
5956 Sherry Lane, Suite 610
Dallas, TX 75225-8025
Phone: (214)363-9000
Fax: (214)363-1941
E-mail: info@summerlee.org
Web: http://www.summerlee.org

Alternate Contact

Melanie Lambert, Program Director, Animals
Phone: 800-256-7515
Fax: (719)266-5459

Description

Founded: 1988
EIN: 752252355
Organization Type: Private Foundation
Giving Locations: AZ; CO; LA; MS; MT; NV; NM; ND; OK; OR; SD; TX; WA; WY
Grant Types: General Support.

Donor Information

Founder: Established by the late Annie Lee Roberts.

Financial Summary

Total Giving: $1,418,338 (fiscal year ending June 30, 2002)
Assets: $47,832,395 (fiscal 2002)
Gifts Received: $518 (fiscal 2002); $323,923 (fiscal 1995); $19,743,354 (fiscal 1994). Note: In fiscal 1995, contributions were received from the estate of Annie Lee Roberts.

Typical Recipients

Arts & Humanities: Arts Associations & Councils, Ethnic & Folk Arts, Historic Preservation, History & Archaeology, Libraries, Literary Arts, Museums/Galleries, Performing Arts, Public Broadcasting, Visual Arts
Civic & Public Affairs: Botanical Gardens/Parks, Community Foundations, Civic & Public Affairs-General, Municipalities/Towns, Native American Affairs, Urban & Community Affairs, Zoos/Aquariums
Education: Arts/Humanities Education, Colleges & Universities, Engineering/Technological Education, Education-General, Private Education (Precollege), Social Sciences Education
Environment: Environment-General, Resource Conservation, Wildlife Protection

Health: Health Organizations
International: International Environmental Issues, International Relations
Religion: Religious Organizations
Science: Science Exhibits & Fairs, Science Museums
Social Services: Animal Protection, Community Service Organizations, Shelters/Homelessness, Veterans

Application Procedures

Initial Contact: The foundation encourages prospective applicants to contact the appropriate program officer by phone prior to submitting a written proposal.
Application Requirements: Proposals should include a brief project summary letter (no more than two pages) signed by the organization's chief executive officer describing the proposed project, the need it fulfills, and project timeline. In addition, the application must include a project budget, including specific line items (if the request is part of a larger effort involving more than one funding source, show how the committed funds are to be applied); a brief summary of the organization, its mission, officers and board members, and any key personnel related to the project; a copy of the organization's latest annual financial statement and/or copy of the most recently filed IRS Form 990; and proof of tax-exempt status from the IRS.
Deadlines: The 1st business day of January, May, July, and September.

Restrictions

No grants are made for religious purposes or to individuals. Geographic restrictions may apply to animal program requests; applicants to this program are encouraged to contact the foundation as the geographic restrictions frequently change. Grant requests related to the preservation of historic structures must be no greater than $50,000 and may only be used to preserve a house or building on the National Register of Historic Places.

Additional Information

Publications: Application Guidelines

Foundation Officials

John W. Crain: program director, vice president B Amarillo, TX 1944. ED University of Texas BA (1966); Southwestern Texas University MA (1970); Harvard University (1975); University of California (1979). NONPR AFFIL vice president, director: History Summerlee Foundation; member: Texas State Historical Association; director: Dallas County Historical Foundation.
Lynn Cuny: director
David D. Jackson: president
Melanie Roberts-Lambert: program director, secretary
Ronnie Curtis Tyler: director B Temple, TX 1941. ED Abilene Christian College BSE (1964); Texas Christian University MA (1966); Texas Christian University PhD (1968); Austin College DHL (1986). PRIM CORP EMPL history professor: University TX. NONPR AFFIL member: Texas Institute Letters; director: Texas State History Association; secretary, member: Philosophical Society Texas; member: American Antiquarian Society; member: Phi Beta Kappa.

Grants Analysis

Disclosure Period: fiscal year ending June 30, 2002
Total Grants: $1,418,338
Number of Grants: 116
Average Grant: $12,227
Highest Grant: $150,000
Typical Range: $2,500 to $25,000

Recent Grants

Note: Grants derived from fiscal 2002 Form 990.

General

102,401	Medicine Mounds Preserve Fund Communities Foundation of Texas, Quanah, TX
65,000	San Augustine County Historical Foundation, San Augustine, TX
32,000	SNAP, Spokane, WA
30,000	St. Joseph's Indian School, Chamberlain, SD
25,000	Amarillo Museum of Art, Amarillo, TX
25,000	National Trust for Historic Preservation, Washington, DC
25,000	Panhandle-Plains Historical Museum, Canyon, TX
25,000	Sabine County Historical Foundation, Hemphill, TX
25,000	San Augustine County Historical Foundation, San Augustine, TX
20,000	City of Gainsville, Gainesville, FL

SUNDERLAND FOUNDATION

Giving Contact

James P. Sunderland, Secretary & Trustee
PO Box 25900
Overland Park, KS 66225
Phone: (913)451-8900
Fax: (913)319-6191
E-mail: sunderlandfoundation@ashgrove.com
Web: http://www.sunderlandfoundation.org

Description

Founded: 1945
EIN: 446011082
Organization Type: General Purpose Foundation
Giving Locations: AR; KS; MO; NE
Grant Types: Capital, Emergency, Endowment, General Support, Operating Expenses, Scholarship, Seed Money.

Donor Information

Founder: Incorporated in 1945 by the late Lester T. Sunderland.

Financial Summary

Total Giving: $3,699,500 (2003); $3,836,600 (2002); $2,809,500 (2001)
Giving Analysis: Giving for 2003 includes: foundation scholarships ($5,000) 2001: foundation scholarships ($5,000)
Assets: $81,354,094 (2003); $74,562,216 (2002); $76,512,513 (2001)
Gifts Received: $9,735,000 (1999); $9,360,000 (1997). Note: In 1997 and 1999, the foundation received a gift of Vinton Corp. securities from the Paul Sunderland Trust.

Typical Recipients

Arts & Humanities: Arts Associations & Councils, Arts Centers, Arts Festivals, Arts Institutes, Arts Outreach, Ballet, Community Arts, Arts & Humanities-General, Historic Preservation, History & Archaeology, Libraries, Museums/Galleries, Music, Opera, Performing Arts, Public Broadcasting, Theater
Civic & Public Affairs: Botanical Gardens/Parks, Community Foundations, Economic Policy, Employment/Job Training, Civic & Public Affairs-General, Hispanic Affairs, Housing, Law & Justice, Legal Aid, Municipalities/Towns, Parades/Festivals, Philanthropic Organizations, Professional & Trade Associations, Public Policy, Rural Affairs, Urban & Community Affairs, Zoos/Aquariums
Education: Agricultural Education, Arts/Humanities Education, Business Education, Colleges & Universities, Community & Junior Colleges, Education Associations, Education Funds, Education-General, Pri-

vate Education (Precollege), Public Education (Precollege), Secondary Education (Private), Secondary Education (Public), Special Education, Student Aid

Environment: Forestry, Protection, Resource Conservation

Health: Alzheimer's Disease, Cancer, Children's Health/Hospitals, Clinics/Medical Centers, Eyes/Blindness, Health Funds, Health Organizations, Hospitals, Mental Health, Nursing Services, Research/Studies Institutes, Transplant Networks/Donor Banks

Religion: Churches, Ministries, Religious Organizations, Religious Welfare

Science: Science Museums, Scientific Centers & Institutes, Scientific Research

Social Services: Animal Protection, Big Brothers/Big Sisters, Camps, Child Abuse, Child Welfare, Community Centers, Community Service Organizations, Counseling, Domestic Violence, Emergency Relief, Family Planning, Family Services, Food/Clothing Distribution, Homes, People with Disabilities, Recreation & Athletics, Scouts, Senior Services, Shelters/Homelessness, Social Services-General, United Funds/United Ways, YMCA/YWCA/YMHA/YWHA, Youth Organizations

Application Procedures

Initial Contact: The foundation requests applications be made in writing. The applicant must also make an appointment with Mr. James Sunderland.

Deadlines: None.

Restrictions

The foundation does not support individuals or provide loans.

Foundation Officials

Charles T. Sunderland: vice president, trustee B 1956. ED Trinity University (1974-1978). PRIM CORP EMPL vice president corporate administration, director: Ash Grove Cement Co. ADD CORP EMPL secretary: Ash Grove Aggregates Inc. CORP AFFIL secretary: Century Ready-Mix Inc.; vice president, director: Vinton Corp.; president: Cedar Creek Properties Inc.; vice president, director: Century Concrete Inc.

James P. Sunderland: secretary, trustee B Springfield, MO 1928. ED Washington & Lee University BS (1950); Washington University LLB (1952). PRIM CORP EMPL chairman, director: Ash Grove Cement Co. CORP AFFIL chairman: Vinton Corp.; director: Ash Grove Aggregates Inc.; director: Boatmens First National Bank Kansas City. NONPR AFFIL director: Greater Kansas City Community Foundation.

Kenton W. Sunderland: president, trustee B Kansas City, MO 1958. ED Trinity University (1980). PRIM CORP EMPL secretary, vice president, director: Ash Grove Cement Co.

Robert Sunderland: vice president, trustee B Omaha, NE 1921. ED Washington University BS (1947). PRIM CORP EMPL vice president, treasurer: Vinton Corp. CORP AFFIL hon chairman: Ash Grove Cement Co. CLUB AFFIL Rotary International Club.

W. Sunderland: trustee

Grants Analysis

Disclosure Period: calendar year ending 2003
Total Grants: $3,694,500*
Number of Grants: 95
Average Grant: $38,889
Highest Grant: $250,000
Lowest Grant: $5,000
Typical Range: $15,000 to $50,000
*Note: Giving excludes scholarships.

Recent Grants

Note: Grants derived from 2003 Form 990.

General

250,000	Kaw Valley Habitat for Humanity, Kansas City, KS -- funding for construction project
200,000	Liberty Memorial Association, Kansas City, MO -- funding for restoration project
200,000	Nelson Gallery Foundation, Kansas City, MO -- funding for expansion project
200,000	University of Missouri, Kansas City, MO -- funding for construction project
100,000	Kansas State University Foundation, Manhattan, KS
100,000	Omaha Performing Arts Society, Omaha, NE
100,000	University of Kansas Endowment Association, Lawrence, KS -- funding for capital campaign
75,000	Children's Mercy Hospital, Kansas City, KS -- toward donation
75,000	Greater Kansas City Community Foundation, Kansas City, MO -- toward deposit
70,000	Boy Scouts of America, Kansas City, MO

SUNNEN FOUNDATION

Giving Contact

Kurt J. Kallaus, President
7910 Manchester Avenue
St. Louis, MO 63143
Phone: (314)781-2100
Fax: (314)781-1533
Web: http://www.sunnen.com

Description

Founded: 1953
EIN: 436029156
Organization Type: General Purpose Foundation
Giving Locations: MO: St. Louis metropolitan area & statewide
Grant Types: Award, Capital, Endowment, Matching.

Donor Information

Founder: Established in Missouri in 1953 by Joseph Sunnen, founder of Sunnen Products Company, a manufacturer of high precision tools and gauges. Mr. Sunnen devoted his life and resources to create a public awareness of uncontrolled population growth. He was a pioneer in advancing the proposition that birth control is one answer to the poverty which afflicts mankind.

Financial Summary

Total Giving: $568,600 (2002); $814,950 (2001 approx)
Giving Analysis: Giving for 2002 includes: foundation grants to United Way ($15,000)
Assets: $11,501,072 (2002); $13,230,000 (2001)
Gifts Received: $60,000 (2002)

Typical Recipients

Arts & Humanities: Arts Centers, Historic Preservation, History & Archaeology, Libraries, Museums/Galleries, Music

Civic & Public Affairs: Botanical Gardens/Parks, Clubs, Community Foundations, Economic Policy, First Amendment Issues, Civic & Public Affairs-General, Housing, Public Policy, Safety, Urban & Community Affairs, Women's Affairs, Zoos/Aquariums

Education: Business Education, Colleges & Universities, Continuing Education, Economic Education, Education Associations, Education-General, Medical Education, Private Education (Precollege), Public Education (Precollege), Special Education, Vocational & Technical Education

Environment: Wildlife Protection

Health: Cancer, Children's Health/Hospitals, Clinics/Medical Centers, Emergency/Ambulance Services, Health Policy/Cost Containment, Health Organizations, Single-Disease Health Associations, Speech & Hearing, Transplant Networks/Donor Banks

International: Health Care/Hospitals, International Environmental Issues

Religion: Churches, Religion-General, Ministries, Missionary Activities (Domestic), Religious Organizations, Religious Welfare, Social/Policy Issues

Social Services: Animal Protection, At-Risk Youth, Camps, Child Welfare, Community Centers, Community Service Organizations, Crime Prevention, Day Care, Delinquency & Criminal Rehabilitation, Domestic Violence, Emergency Relief, Family Planning, Family Services, Food/Clothing Distribution, People with Disabilities, Scouts, Senior Services, Shelters/Homelessness, Social Services-General, Special Olympics, Substance Abuse, United Funds/United Ways, YMCA/YWCA/YMHA/YWHA, Youth Organizations

Application Procedures

Initial Contact: Applicants should contact the foundation in writing to request guidelines.

Application Requirements: Formal proposal should not exceed ten pages in length (plus addendum) and should include: project name, name of director, address and telephone number; amount requested; statement of problem or assessment of need; goals of the project and how they will be achieved; qualifications of the organization to carry out the project; how the project will be evaluated; project budget showing type and amount of expenses and revenues, including all sources; plans for future support or funding; other donors solicited for this project and status of those requests. Addendum should include: brief organizational history; IRS letter of determination indicating 501(c)(3) status; organization's most recent audited financial statement, management report and annual report, if available; list of current board of directors. Seven copies of the proposal should be submitted; the foundation does not accept proposals in notebooks, binders, or plastic folders.

Deadlines: August 1.

Review Process: The board meets twice a year, in October and December.

Restrictions

With the exception of specific projects related to its areas of main concern, grants are not made to general operating costs, scholarships, research projects, travel or personal grants, religious bodies, educational institutions, environmental organizations, hospitals or medical charities, or the arts.

Additional Information

Grantees are required to submit a complete evaluation and financial report at the conclusion of the grant period.

Publications: Guidelines

Foundation Officials

Susan S. Brasel: director
Ruth A. Cardinale: secretary B 1961. PRIM CORP EMPL secretary: Sunnen Products Co. CORP AFFIL secretary: Sunquad Corp. Inc.
Kurt J. Kallaus: president
Helen S. Sly: director

Grants Analysis

Disclosure Period: calendar year ending 2002
Total Grants: $553,600*
Number of Grants: 28
Average Grant: $19,771
Highest Grant: $50,250
Lowest Grant: $250
Typical Range: $1,000 to $50,000
*Note: Giving excludes excludes United Way.

Recent Grants

Note: Grants derived from 2002 Form 990.

General

90,000	YMCA - of the Ozarks
55,000	Planned Parenthood - St. Louis Region, St. Louis, MO
50,000	Missouri Historical Society, St. Louis, MO
50,000	Museum of Transportation, Brookline, MA

35,000	Missouri Religious Coalition for Rep Choice, MO
33,000	Court-Appointed Special Advocates, St. Louis, MO
30,000	Planned Parenthood Connecticut, New Haven, CT
27,500	Planned Parenthood Alabama, AL
25,000	Missouri NARAL Foundation, MO
25,000	Washington County Community Center

SUNTRUST BANK ATLANTA

Company Headquarters
Atlanta, GA
Web: http://www.suntrust.com

Company Description
Former Name: Trust Co. Bank.
Revenue: US$7.822 billion (2004)
Profit: US$1.572 billion (2004)
Employees: 2,850
Fortune Rank: 273, per FORTUNE Magazine's list of 500 Largest U.S. Corporations (2004).
SIC(s): 6022 State Commercial Banks.
Parent Company: SunTrust Banks Inc., 303 Peachtree Street NE, Atlanta, GA, United States

Nonmonetary Support
Type: Donated Equipment; Loaned Employees; Loaned Executives; Workplace Solicitation
Contact: Ed Bishop, Vice President
Note: Company provides nonmonetary support.

SunTrust Bank Atlanta Foundation

Giving Contact
Raymond B. King, Group Vice President
Sun Trust Bank, Atlanta
Community Affairs Foundations Program
PO Box 4418, Mail Code 041
Atlanta, GA 30302
Phone: (404)588-8246
Fax: (404)230-5550
Web: http://www.suntrustatlantafoundation.org/

Description
EIN: 586026063
Organization Type: Corporate Foundation
Giving Locations: GA: Atlanta metropolitan area
Grant Types: Capital, Employee Matching Gifts, General Support, Operating Expenses, Project, Research, Seed Money.

Financial Summary
Total Giving: $2,523,436 (2003); $2,920,875 (2002).
Note: Contributes through corporate direct giving program and foundation.
Giving Analysis: Giving for 2002 includes: foundation grants to United Way ($979,699)
Assets: $14,033,558 (2003); $14,515,276 (2002)
Gifts Received: $123,000 (2003); $120,000 (2002); $220,000 (2000). Note: In 2002 a contribution was received from Suntrust Bank.

Typical Recipients
Arts & Humanities: Arts Appreciation, Arts Associations & Councils, Arts Centers, Arts Festivals, Arts Funds, Ballet, Community Arts, Dance, Ethnic & Folk Arts, Historic Preservation, History & Archaeology, Libraries, Museums/Galleries, Music, Opera, Performing Arts, Public Broadcasting, Theater
Civic & Public Affairs: Botanical Gardens/Parks, Business/Free Enterprise, Chambers of Commerce,

Civil Rights, Community Foundations, Economic Development, Economic Policy, Employment/Job Training, Civic & Public Affairs-General, Housing, Law & Justice, Legal Aid, Municipalities/Towns, Nonprofit Management, Philanthropic Organizations, Public Policy, Safety, Urban & Community Affairs, Women's Affairs, Zoos/Aquariums
Education: Arts/Humanities Education, Business Education, Colleges & Universities, Economic Education, Education Funds, Engineering/Technological Education, Education-General, International Exchange, International Studies, Legal Education, Medical Education, Minority Education, Private Education (Precollege), Public Education (Precollege), Religious Education, Science/Mathematics Education, Secondary Education (Private), Special Education, Student Aid, Vocational & Technical Education
Environment: Environment-General, Resource Conservation
Health: Alzheimer's Disease, Children's Health/ Hospitals, Clinics/Medical Centers, Emergency/ Ambulance Services, Geriatric Health, Health Organizations, Hospices, Hospitals, Medical Rehabilitation, Medical Training, Mental Health, Nursing Services, Public Health, Single-Disease Health Associations, Trauma Treatment
International: International Affairs
Religion: Churches, Religion-General, Jewish Causes, Religious Welfare
Science: Scientific Centers & Institutes
Social Services: Camps, Child Welfare, Community Centers, Community Service Organizations, Counseling, Delinquency & Criminal Rehabilitation, Domestic Violence, Emergency Relief, Family Services, Food/Clothing Distribution, Homes, People with Disabilities, Recreation & Athletics, Scouts, Senior Services, Shelters/Homelessness, Social Services-General, Substance Abuse, United Funds/United Ways, Youth Organizations

Application Procedures
Initial Contact: Request guidelines and Fact Sheet from the foundation. A grant application form can be downloaded from the foundation Web site.
Application Requirements: Submit the completed Fact Sheet for grant consideration. Include the following supporting materials: IRS determination letter, list of board of directors and their affiliations, relevant financial material, and case statement or other concise supporting material.
Deadlines: November 30, March 31, or August 31.
Review Process: Applications are summarized and presented quarterly to the distribution committee.
Evaluative Criteria: Emphasis on metropolitan Atlanta, community benefit, project/community coordination and support, timeliness and precedence, organization management and governance, grant multiplier effect, human value and self-help emphasis, and financial management.
Decision Notification: Notification made by letter following meetings held in January, May, and October.

Restrictions
Foundation does not make loans or grants for general operating support, maintenance, or debt service. Does not support political organizations, churches, or individuals.

Additional Information
Community benefit and return on investment are primary considerations in distribution decisions. The committee expects periodic program reports from recipients.
Publications: Application Guidelines
Trust(s): Suntrust Bank

Corporate Officials
Robert R. Long: chairman B 1937. ED Auburn University (1959); Harvard University (1967). PRIM CORP EMPL chairman: SunTrust Bank Atlanta ADD

CORP EMPL director: SunTrust Service Corp.; chairman: SunTrust Bank Georgia Inc.

Foundation Officials
John W. Clay, Jr.: member
Raymond B. King: secretary
Scott Wilfong: member

Grants Analysis
Disclosure Period: calendar year ending 2003
Total Grants: $694,374*
Number of Grants: 141
Average Grant: $4,925
Highest Grant: $40,000
Lowest Grant: $30
Typical Range: $200 to $50,000 and $50,000 to $400,000
***Note:** Giving excludes matching gifts and United Way.

Recent Grants
Note: Grants derived from 2003 Form 990.
General

450,000	United Way of Metropolitan Atlanta, Atlanta, GA
450,000	United Way of Metropolitan Atlanta, Atlanta, GA
91,883	Robert W. Woodruff Arts Center, Atlanta, GA
75,000	United Way of Metropolitan Atlanta, Atlanta, GA
40,000	Rabun Gap Nacoochee School, Rabun Gap, GA
35,000	Atlanta Habitat for Humanity, Atlanta, GA
33,000	Robert W. Woodruff Arts Center, Atlanta, GA
32,000	United Way of the Coastal Empire, Savannah, GA
29,000	Atlanta Falcons Youth Foundation, Flowery Branch, GA
25,000	Augusta Metro Chamber of Commerce, Augusta, GA

SUNTRUST BANKS INC.

Company Headquarters
303 Peachtree Street NE
Atlanta, GA 30308
Web: http://www.suntrust.com

Company Description
Founded: 1985
Ticker: STI
Exchange: NYSE
Formed by Merger of: Crestar Finance Corp. & SunTrust Banks (1998).
Revenue: US$7.071 billion (2003)
Employees: 27578 (2003)

Nonmonetary Support
Contact: James Warrick, Executive Vice President
Note: Co. provides an unspecified amount of nonmonetary support in the form of donated property or land which is no longer used by banks.

Suntrust Foundation - Agency

Giving Contact
Brenda L. Skidmore, President
SunTrust Mid-Atlantic Foundation
919 East Main Street
Richmond, VA 23219
Phone: (804)782-7907
Fax: (804)782-5191

Description

EIN: 237336418
Organization Type: Corporate Foundation
Former Name: Crestar Foundation.
Giving Locations: DC: Washington; MD; VA headquarters and operating communities.
Grant Types: Employee Matching Gifts, General Support, Scholarship.
Note: Employee matching gift ratio: 1 to 1. Company will match any employee's contributions of $25 or more up to an aggregate of $3,000 annually, for eligible educational institutions and cultural organizations.

Financial Summary

Total Giving: $4,030,166 (2003); $4,090,010 (2002); $3,901,502 (2001). Note: Contributes through corporate direct giving program and foundation.
Giving Analysis: Giving for 2002 includes: foundation (approx $4,000,000); 2001: foundation grants to United Way ($524,900); foundation ($3,376,602)
Assets: $5,774,562 (2003); $5,991,889 (2002); $6,561,137 (2001)
Gifts Received: $3,745,834 (2003); $3,412,125 (2002); $4,000,000 (2001). Note: Contributions were received from SunTrust Bank (formerly Crestar) Bank.

Typical Recipients

Arts & Humanities: Arts Associations & Councils, Arts Centers, Arts Festivals, Arts Funds, Arts Outreach, Ballet, Community Arts, Ethnic & Folk Arts, Historic Preservation, History & Archaeology, Libraries, Museums/Galleries, Music, Opera, Performing Arts, Public Broadcasting, Theater
Civic & Public Affairs: Botanical Gardens/Parks, Business/Free Enterprise, Chambers of Commerce, Community Foundations, Economic Development, Economic Policy, Employment/Job Training, Civic & Public Affairs-General, Housing, Minority Business, Nonprofit Management, Parades/Festivals, Philanthropic Organizations, Public Policy, Urban & Community Affairs, Women's Affairs, Zoos/Aquariums
Education: Arts/Humanities Education, Business Education, Colleges & Universities, Community & Junior Colleges, Economic Education, Education Funds, Engineering/Technological Education, Environmental Education, Faculty Development, Literacy, Medical Education, Minority Education, Private Education (Precollege), Public Education (Precollege), Secondary Education (Public), Special Education
Environment: Air/Water Quality, Environment-General, Resource Conservation
Health: AIDS/HIV, Cancer, Children's Health/Hospitals, Clinics/Medical Centers, Emergency/Ambulance Services, Eyes/Blindness, Health Policy/Cost Containment, Health Funds, Health Organizations, Heart, Hospices, Hospitals, Mental Health, Multiple Sclerosis, Single-Disease Health Associations, Speech & Hearing, Transplant Networks/Donor Banks
International: Health Care/Hospitals, International Peace & Security Issues, International Relations
Religion: Dioceses, Religious Organizations, Religious Welfare, Social/Policy Issues
Science: Science Exhibits & Fairs, Science Museums, Scientific Centers & Institutes, Scientific Research
Social Services: Animal Protection, At-Risk Youth, Child Welfare, Community Service Organizations, Domestic Violence, Emergency Relief, Family Services, Food/Clothing Distribution, People with Disabilities, Recreation & Athletics, Scouts, Senior Services, Shelters/Homelessness, Social Services-General, United Funds/United Ways, YMCA/YWCA/YMHA/YWHA, Youth Organizations

Application Procedures

Initial Contact: Send a written application.
Application Requirements: Include support information regarding purpose of the organization and ex-

pected benefits of program.
Deadlines: Applications for large grants should be made on or before October for consideration in the following calendar year.
Review Process: President of foundation or local SunTrust facility makes recommendations to contributions committee, which meets in July and December.
Evaluative Criteria: Request conforms to priority areas, corporate presence in geographic area served by organization, program or activity improves economy and quality of life in community, evidence of good management and active involvement of community leaders, and direct or indirect benefits to corporation or its employees.
Notes: Grants are made primarily to Virginia communities.

Restrictions

No grants are made to political or religious organizations.

Foundation Officials

Jane A. Markins: secretary, treasurer
Brenda L. Skidmore: president

Grants Analysis

Disclosure Period: calendar year ending 2003
Total Grants: $3,541,747*
Number of Grants: 773
Average Grant: $4,582
Highest Grant: $50,000
Lowest Grant: $25
Typical Range: $1,000 to $10,000
*Note: Giving excludes matching gifts; United Way.

Recent Grants

Note: Grants derived from 2003 Form 990.
General

85,000	United Way Services, Richmond, VA
60,000	United Way of the National Capital Area, Washington, DC
55,000	Virginia Foundation for Independent Colleges, Richmond, VA
50,000	American Red Cross, Richmond, VA
50,000	College of William and Mary, Williamsburg, VA
50,000	District of Columbia Board of Trade, Washington, DC
50,000	Hampton University, Hampton, VA
50,000	United Way of Central Maryland, Baltimore, MD
40,000	Business Consortium for the Arts, Norfolk, VA
40,000	United Way Services, Richmond, VA

SUNTRUST BANKS OF FLORIDA

Company Headquarters

281 N. Market Blvd.
Webster, FL 33597

Company Description

Former Name: SunBank N.A..
Employees: 7,900
SIC(s): 6022 State Commercial Banks, 6712 Bank Holding Companies.
Parent Company: SunTrust Banks Inc., 303 Peachtree Street NE, Atlanta, GA, United States

Operating Locations

SunTrust Banks of Florida (FL--Brooksville, Cape Coral, Daytona Beach, Fort Lauderdale, Jacksonville, Miami, Naples, Ocala, Panama City, Pensacola, Plant City, Port Charlotte, Sebring, Tallahassee, Tampa, Vero Beach, Zephyrhills)

SunTrust Banks Foundation

Giving Contact

David Hanson
PO Box 3838
Orlando, FL 32802

Description

EIN: 596877429
Organization Type: Corporate Foundation
Giving Locations: FL
Grant Types: Capital, Endowment, Fellowship, Loan, Multiyear/Continuing Support, Project.

Financial Summary

Total Giving: $350,000 (2002); $232,167 (2001). Note: Contributes through foundation only.
Assets: $9,414,731 (2002); $10,878,367 (2001)
Gifts Received: $344,730 (2002); $400,000 (2001); $717,976 (2000). Note: Contributions were received from Suntrust Banks, Inc.

Typical Recipients

Arts & Humanities: Historic Preservation, History & Archaeology, Libraries, Museums/Galleries
Civic & Public Affairs: Chambers of Commerce, Professional & Trade Associations, Rural Affairs, Urban & Community Affairs, Zoos/Aquariums
Education: Arts/Humanities Education, Colleges & Universities, Community & Junior Colleges, Education Funds, Education-General, Literacy, Minority Education, Special Education, Student Aid
Environment: Protection
Health: Cancer, Clinics/Medical Centers, Health Funds, Hospices, Hospitals, Research/Studies Institutes
International: Foreign Arts Organizations
Science: Scientific Centers & Institutes
Social Services: Child Welfare, Family Services, People with Disabilities, Senior Services, Substance Abuse, Youth Organizations

Application Procedures

Initial Contact: Send a brief letter.
Application Requirements: Include relevant information and proof of tax-exempt status.
Deadlines: None.

Restrictions

Foundation gives specifically to scientific, literary, and educational institutions.

Additional Information

SunBank N.A. is corporate trustee for the foundation.

Grants Analysis

Disclosure Period: calendar year ending 2003
Total Grants: $350,000
Number of Grants: 12
Average Grant: $8,333*
Highest Grant: $200,000
Lowest Grant: $2,500
Typical Range: $5,000 to $10,000
*Note: Average grant figure excludes two highest grants ($250,000).

Recent Grants

Note: Grants derived from 2003 Form 990.
General

200,000	Rollins College, Winter Park, FL
50,000	Florida Agricultural, Orlando, FL
50,000	Trust for Public Land, Tallahassee, FL
20,000	Greenwood School, Putney, VT
20,000	Jackson Memorial Foundation, Miami, FL
12,500	Boys and Girls of Nassau County, NY
10,000	Marion County Senior Services, Flippin, AR
10,000	Polk Community College Foundation, Winter Haven, FL

HARRY AND THELMA SURRENA MEMORIAL FUND

Giving Contact

Clair Robinson
PO Box 27
Buffalo, WY 82834
Phone: (307)684-5574

Description

Founded: 1973
EIN: 237435554
Organization Type: Private Foundation
Giving Locations: WY
Grant Types: General Support.

Financial Summary

Total Giving: $210,000 (fiscal year ending October 31, 2004); $245,000 (fiscal 2002)
Assets: $4,872,535 (fiscal 2004); $4,694,105 (fiscal 2002)

Typical Recipients

Arts & Humanities: Libraries, Museums/Galleries
Civic & Public Affairs: Civic & Public Affairs-General
Education: Colleges & Universities, Education Funds
Health: Hospitals
Religion: Churches, Religious Welfare
Social Services: Child Welfare, Community Service Organizations, Day Care, People with Disabilities, Senior Services, United Funds/United Ways, YMCA/YWCA/YMHA/YWHA, Youth Organizations

Application Procedures

Initial Contact: Send written application.
Deadlines: None.
Review Process: Application approvals or rejections are usually determined in October.

Foundation Officials

Ralph C. Robinson: trustee

Grants Analysis

Disclosure Period: fiscal year ending October 31, 2004
Total Grants: $210,000
Number of Grants: 17
Average Grant: $12,353
Highest Grant: $30,000
Lowest Grant: $3,000
Typical Range: $5,000 to $25,000

Recent Grants

Note: Grants derived from 2004 Form 990.

Library-Related
5,000	Johnston County Library, Buffalo, WY

General
30,000	Buffalo Children's Center, Buffalo, WY
29,000	Children's Center, Sheridan, WY
25,000	Genesis Foundation, Sheridan, WY
25,000	YMCA, Sheridan, WY
25,000	YMCA-Johnston County, Buffalo, WY
15,000	Sheridan College Foundation, Sheridan, WY
10,000	Buffalo Senior Center, Buffalo, WY
10,000	Sheridan Senior Center, Sheridan, WY
10,000	Story Community Church, Story, WY

SUSQUEHANNA-PFALTZGRAFF CO.

Company Headquarters

York, PA
Web: http://www.pfaltzgraff.com

Company Description

Employees: 25 (2003)
SIC(s): 3262 Vitreous China Table & Kitchenware, 3269 Pottery Products Nec, 4832 Radio Broadcasting Stations.

Operating Locations

Susquehanna-Pfaltzgraff Co. (PA--York)

Nonmonetary Support

Type: Donated Equipment; Donated Products; In-kind Services; Loaned Employees; Loaned Executives; Workplace Solicitation
Volunteer Programs: The company provides employee volunteer opportunities with the United Way, Junior Achievement, Boy Scouts, Adopt-A-House, blood drives, walk-a-thons, and a variety of other charities and fundraising events.

Susquehanna-Pfaltzgraff Foundation

Giving Contact

John L. Finlayson, Vice President, Finance & Administration
140 East Market Street
PO Box 2026
York, PA 17405
Phone: (717)848-5500
Fax: (717)771-1440

Description

Founded: 1966
EIN: 236420008
Organization Type: Corporate Foundation
Giving Locations: headquarters and operating communities.
Grant Types: Capital, Challenge, Emergency, Endowment, General Support, Multiyear/Continuing Support, Operating Expenses, Project.

Donor Information

Founder: Susquehanna Radio Corp., the Pfaltzgraff Co.

Financial Summary

Total Giving: $587,218 (2002); $535,068 (2001). Note: Contributes through foundation only.
Giving Analysis: Giving for 2001 includes: foundation grants to United Way ($76,150); foundation ($458,918)
Assets: $1,562,456 (2002); $1,551,138 (2001)
Gifts Received: $725,000 (2002); $400,000 (2001); $450,000 (2000). Note: In 2002, contributions were received from Pfaltzgraff Co. ($125,000), York Cable Television, Inc. ($300,000), Radio San Francisco, Inc. ($44,000), KNBR, Inc. ($43,000), KPLX Limited Partnership ($31,000), KRBE Limited Partnership ($56,000), Susquehanna Radio Corp. ($61,000), Radio Indianapolis, Inc. ($25,000), Indianapolis Radio License Co. ($8,000), Radio Cincinnati, Inc. ($12,000), and Susquehanna Kansas City Partnership ($20,000). In 2001, contributions were received from Pfaltzgraff Co.; York Cable Television, Inc.; Radio San Francisco, Inc.; KNBR, Inc.; KPLX Broadcasting LLP; KRBE Broadcasting LLP; Susquehanna Radio Corp.; Radio Indianapolis, Inc.; Indianapolis Radio License Co.; Radio Cincinnati, Inc.; and Susquehanna Kansas City Partnership. Contributions received prior to 2001 were received from Pfaltzgraff

Co., Cable TV of York, Radio San Francisco, KNBR, KLIF Co., Radio Metroplex, KRBE Co., Susquehanna Radio Corp., Radio Indianapolis, and Indianapolis Radio License Co., Radio Cincinnati.

Typical Recipients

Arts & Humanities: Arts Associations & Councils, Arts Institutes, Community Arts, Dance, Arts & Humanities-General, Historic Preservation, History & Archaeology, Libraries, Museums/Galleries, Music, Opera, Performing Arts, Public Broadcasting, Theater
Civic & Public Affairs: Botanical Gardens/Parks, Chambers of Commerce, Community Foundations, Economic Development, Civic & Public Affairs-General, Housing, Nonprofit Management, Urban & Community Affairs
Education: Agricultural Education, Arts/Humanities Education, Colleges & Universities, Education Associations, Education Funds, Elementary Education (Private), Education-General, Health & Physical Education, Minority Education, Preschool Education, Private Education (Precollege), Public Education (Precollege), Secondary Education (Private), Student Aid, Vocational & Technical Education
Environment: Environment-General, Resource Conservation, Wildlife Protection
Health: Cancer, Children's Health/Hospitals, Eyes/Blindness, Health-General, Hospitals, Medical Rehabilitation, Public Health, Single-Disease Health Associations
International: International Organizations
Religion: Churches, Religious Welfare, Seminaries
Science: Science-General, Science Museums
Social Services: Animal Protection, Camps, Child Welfare, Community Service Organizations, Counseling, Emergency Relief, Homes, People with Disabilities, Recreation & Athletics, Scouts, Social Services-General, United Funds/United Ways, YMCA/YWCA/YMHA/YWHA, Youth Organizations

Application Procedures

Initial Contact: Send a brief letter of inquiry.
Application Requirements: Outline need for funds sought.
Deadlines: None.

Corporate Officials

Louis J. Appell, Jr.: president, chief executive officer B 1924. ED Harvard University (1947). PRIM CORP EMPL president: Susquehanna-Pfaltzgraff Co. ADD CORP EMPL treasurer, director: Casco Cabel Television Bth Maine; vice president, director: Casco Cable Televising Inc.; president: Flemington Companies Inc.; vice president, director: LAB Cincinnati Inc.; president, treasurer, director: Nassau Radio Corp.; president: Penn York Advertising Inc.; president, treasurer, director: Radio Akron Inc.; president treasurer, director: WARM Broadcasting Co. Inc. CORP AFFIL chairman: Susquehanna Radio Corp.; director: York Bank Trust Co.; chairman: Susquehanna Media Co.; chairman: SBC Cable Co.; chief executive officer: Susquehanna Broadcasting Co. Inc.; chairman: Pfaltzgraff Outlet Co.; chairman: Radio Metroplex Inc.; chairman: KRBE Co.; chairman: Pfaltzgraff Co.
John L. Finlayson: vice president finance & administration PRIM CORP EMPL vice president finance & administration: Susquehanna-Pfaltzgraff Co. CORP AFFIL vice president: Susquehanna Media Co.; vice president: Susquehanna Radio Corp.; vice president: Susquehanna Cable Co.; vice president: Pfaltzgraff Outlet Co.; vice president: SBC Cable Co.; vice president: Pfaltzgraff Co.
Mike Sibol: director PRIM CORP EMPL director: Susquehanna-Pfaltzgraff Co.
William H. Simpson: president, chief executive officer B Ithaca, NY 1941. ED United States Air Force Academy (1963); Harvard University (1966). PRIM CORP EMPL president, chief executive officer: Pfaltzgraff Co. CORP AFFIL president: Pfaltzgraff

Outlet Co.; vice president manufacturing: Susque-hanna Pfalzgraff Co.

Foundation Officials

Louis J. Appell, Jr.: president (see above)
William H. Simpson: secretary (see above)

Grants Analysis

Disclosure Period: calendar year ending 2002
Total Grants: $511,468*
Number of Grants: 41
Average Grant: $7,787*
Highest Grant: $200,000
Lowest Grant: $250
Typical Range: $1,000 to $15,000
*Note: Giving excludes United Way. Average grant figure excludes highest grant.

Recent Grants

Note: Grants derived from 2003 Form 990.
Library-Related

20,000	Martin Library, York, PA
15,000	Southern York County Library, Shrewsbury, PA
10,000	Kaltreider Benfer Library, Red Lion, PA
6,000	Hanover Public Library, Hanover, PA
6,000	Mason Dixon Public Library, Stewartstown, PA
5,000	Library of American Broadcasting, College Park, MD

General

125,000	York Adams Boy Scout Campaign, York, PA
100,000	York College of Pennsylvania, York, PA
75,000	United Way of York County, York, PA
34,000	York County Heritage Trust, York, PA
25,000	York Foundation Honoring David Kennedy, York, PA
25,000	York Habitat for Humanity Inc., York, PA
20,000	Penn State University, University Park, PA -- building fund
15,000	Margaret E. Moul Home, York, PA
12,000	Historic York Inc., York, PA
12,000	York County Chapter of the American Red Cross, York, PA

DR. W. C. SWANSON FAMILY FOUNDATION, INC.

Giving Contact

Cindy Purcell, Director
2955 Harrison Boulevard, Suite 201
Ogden, UT 84403
Phone: (801)392-0360
Fax: (801)392-0429

Description

Founded: 1978
EIN: 942478549
Organization Type: Family Foundation
Giving Locations: UT: primarily Northern Utah and Weber County; grants from the rest of Utah are next in priority, then regional requests, and lastly national and international
Grant Types: General Support, Matching, Professorship, Research, Scholarship.

Donor Information

Founder: Established in 1978 by the late Dr. W. C. Swanson with the help of his family, Beryl, Annabel, and Chuck. Lew Costley was appointed trustee and is now an advisory committee member and CFO.

Financial Summary

Assets: $28,511 (2003)

Typical Recipients

Arts & Humanities: Arts Centers, Ballet, Dance, Film & Video, Historic Preservation, History & Archaeology, Libraries, Museums/Galleries, Music, Opera, Performing Arts, Public Broadcasting, Theater
Civic & Public Affairs: Clubs, Civic & Public Affairs-General, Housing, Municipalities/Towns, Philanthropic Organizations, Public Policy, Safety, Urban & Community Affairs
Education: Afterschool/Enrichment Programs, Colleges & Universities, Elementary Education (Private), Education-General, Medical Education, Private Education (Precollege), Public Education (Precollege), Secondary Education (Private), Special Education, Student Aid, Vocational & Technical Education
Environment: Environment-General
Health: Cancer, Children's Health/Hospitals, Emergency/Ambulance Services, Health-General, Health Organizations, Heart, Hospices, Hospitals, Medical Rehabilitation, Public Health, Trauma Treatment
International: Health Care/Hospitals, International Organizations, International Relief Efforts
Religion: Churches, Religious Organizations, Religious Welfare, Social/Policy Issues
Science: Science Museums, Scientific Centers & Institutes
Social Services: Animal Protection, Big Brothers/Big Sisters, Child Abuse, Child Welfare, Community Centers, Community Service Organizations, Crime Prevention, Domestic Violence, Emergency Relief, Family Services, People with Disabilities, Recreation & Athletics, Scouts, Senior Services, Sexual Abuse, Social Services-General, Special Olympics, Substance Abuse, United Funds/United Ways, YMCA/YWCA/YMHA/YWHA, Youth Organizations

Application Procedures

Initial Contact: Contact the foundation for application form and guidelines.
Application Requirements: A copy of requesting organization's IRS 501(c)(3) tax-exemption letter, as well as a copy of the organization's annual report and financial statement with the completed application form and proposal narrative.
Deadlines: The end of the quarter prior to the quarter grant request is considered.
Review Process: Board meetings are held quarterly.

Restrictions

Does not provide grants to individuals. No support is given for salaries and administrative costs; very limited amounts are given for bricks and mortar.

Additional Information

The foundation supports collaboration with other agencies.
Publications: Application Form (including Guidelines); Grant Agreement Newsletter

Foundation Officials

Lew Costley: trustee B 1925. PRIM CORP EMPL secretary: A/Y Car Sales Inc.
Annabel Hofer: director
Cindy Purcell: director
W. Charles Swanson: chief financial officer

Grants Analysis

Disclosure Period: calendar year ending 2003
Typical Range: $1,000 to $25,000
Note: No grants made in 2003.

Recent Grants

Note: Grants derived from 2001 Form 990.
General

15,000	United Way of Northern Utah, Ogden, UT
1,000	National Cancer Center of Mongolia, Bayanzurkh Mongolia

SWIFT CHARITABLE TRUST

Giving Contact

Bryan M. Swift, President
1248 Research Dr.
St. Louis, MO 63122
Phone: (314)991-4300
Fax: (314)991-3080
E-mail: swiftinc@intec.net

Description

Founded: 1952
EIN: 436020812
Organization Type: Private Foundation
Former Name: John S. Swift Co. Inc. Charitable Trust.
Giving Locations: IL; MO
Grant Types: Challenge, Endowment, General Support.

Donor Information

Founder: John S. Swift Co., Inc.

Financial Summary

Total Giving: $99,625 (2003)
Giving Analysis: Giving for 2003 includes: foundation grants to United Way ($250)
Assets: $2,007,030 (2003)
Gifts Received: $110 (1999). Note: In 1990, contributions were received from John S. Swift Co.

Typical Recipients

Arts & Humanities: Arts Centers, Arts Institutes, History & Archaeology, Libraries, Museums/Galleries, Public Broadcasting, Visual Arts
Civic & Public Affairs: Botanical Gardens/Parks, Clubs, Urban & Community Affairs, Zoos/Aquariums
Education: Colleges & Universities, Medical Education, Private Education (Precollege), Public Education (Precollege), Science/Mathematics Education, Student Aid
Environment: Forestry, Environment-General, Resource Conservation, Wildlife Protection
Health: Arthritis, Cancer, Children's Health/Hospitals, Hospitals, Medical Research, Multiple Sclerosis
Religion: Bible Study/Translation, Churches, Religious Welfare
Social Services: Animal Protection, Community Service Organizations, People with Disabilities, Scouts, Social Services-General, Substance Abuse, United Funds/United Ways, YMCA/YWCA/YMHA/YWHA, Youth Organizations

Application Procedures

Initial Contact: Send a brief letter of inquiry.
Deadlines: None.

Additional Information

Trust(s): A.G. Edwards Trust Co.

Corporate Officials

Bryan M. Swift: president PRIM CORP EMPL president: Swift Print Communs.

Foundation Officials

Bryan M. Swift: co-trustee (see above)
Hampden M. Swift: co-trustee

Grants Analysis

Disclosure Period: calendar year ending 2003
Total Grants: $99,375*
Number of Grants: 80
Average Grant: $1,131*
Highest Grant: $10,000
Lowest Grant: $100
Typical Range: $250 to $2,000
*Note: Giving excludes United Way. Average grant figure excludes highest grant.

Recent Grants

Note: Grants derived from 2003 Form 990.
General

10,000	St. Louis Zoo Friends Association, St. Louis, MO
7,500	Lake Forest Academy, Lake Forest, IL
5,000	Cardinal Glennon Children's Hospital, St. Louis, MO
3,500	Trinity College, Palos Heights, IL
2,500	Association of Retarded Children, St. Louis, MO
2,500	Missouri Botanical Garden, St. Louis, MO
2,500	Montini High School, Lombard, IL
2,500	Multiple Sclerosis Society, St. Louis, MO
2,500	Shedd Aquarium, Chicago, IL
2,500	Trust for Public Land, San Francisco, CA

THE SWIG FOUNDATION

Giving Contact

Kent Swig, Trustee
220 Montgomery Street
San Francisco, CA 94104
Phone: (415)291-1100
Fax: (415)291-8373

Description

Founded: 1957
EIN: 946065205
Organization Type: Family Foundation
Giving Locations: CA; NY
Grant Types: Award, Multiyear/Continuing Support.

Donor Information

Founder: Established in 1957 by the late Benjamin H. Swig and members of the Swig family.

Financial Summary

Total Giving: $1,048,722 (2001)
Assets: $20,481,159 (2001)

Typical Recipients

Arts & Humanities: Arts Associations & Councils, Arts Centers, Arts Funds, Arts Institutes, Ballet, Community Arts, Dance, Historic Preservation, History & Archaeology, Libraries, Museums/Galleries, Music, Opera, Performing Arts, Public Broadcasting, Theater

Civic & Public Affairs: Botanical Gardens/Parks, Business/Free Enterprise, Clubs, Community Foundations, Ethnic Organizations, Civic & Public Affairs-General, Housing, Municipalities/Towns, Parades/Festivals, Philanthropic Organizations, Public Policy, Safety, Urban & Community Affairs, Women's Affairs, Zoos/Aquariums

Education: Arts/Humanities Education, Business Education, Colleges & Universities, Education Associations, Education Funds, Environmental Education, Faculty Development, Education-General, Preschool Education, Private Education (Precollege), Public Education (Precollege), Religious Education, School Volunteerism, Science/Mathematics Education, Social Sciences Education, Student Aid

Environment: Air/Water Quality, Energy, Environment-General, Protection

Health: AIDS/HIV, Cancer, Children's Health/Hospitals, Clinics/Medical Centers, Geriatric Health, Health Funds, Health Organizations, Heart, Hospitals, Hospitals (University Affiliated), Medical Research, Single-Disease Health Associations

International: Foreign Arts Organizations, Foreign Educational Institutions, Human Rights, International Affairs, International Environmental Issues, International Organizations, International Peace & Security Issues, Missionary/Religious Activities

Religion: Churches, Religion-General, Jewish Causes, Religious Organizations, Religious Welfare, Synagogues/Temples

Science: Science Museums, Scientific Organizations

Social Services: Child Abuse, Child Welfare, Community Centers, Community Service Organizations, Domestic Violence, Emergency Relief, Family Services, Food/Clothing Distribution, Homes, Recreation & Athletics, Substance Abuse, United Funds/United Ways, YMCA/YWCA/YMHA/YWHA, Youth Organizations

Application Procedures

Initial Contact: Contact the foundation for application guidelines.
Deadlines: None.

Restrictions

The foundation makes grants only to organizations exempt under section 501(c)(3). The foundation does not make grants to individuals. The foundation does not support conferences, seminars, or workshops.

Additional Information

Publications: Guidelines

Foundation Officials

Richard S. Dinner: trustee B 1921. PRIM CORP EMPL vice president, director: Swig Co.
Pam L. Peterson: secretary
Kent Swig: trustee CORP AFFIL shareholder: Brown Harris Stevens Residential.
Richard L. Swig: trustee B Boston, MA 1925. ED University of San Francisco. PRIM CORP EMPL general partner: SIC Hotel Co. CORP AFFIL chairman: AIR Missouri Corporate; general partner: Fairmont Hotel San Francisco.
Robert Swig: trustee PRIM CORP EMPL vice president, director: Swig Weiler & Dinner Development Co.
Steven L. Swig: trustee PRIM CORP EMPL secretary: Swig Co.

Grants Analysis

Disclosure Period: calendar year ending 2001
Total Grants: $1,046,222*
Number of Grants: 375
Average Grant: $2,790
Highest Grant: $50,000
Typical Range: $500 to $20,000
*Note: Giving excludes United Way.

Recent Grants

Note: Grants derived from 2002 Form 990.
Library-Related

10,000	Library Foundation of Los Angeles, Los Angeles, CA
10,000	San Mateo Public Library, San Mateo, CA

General

50,000	Horace Mann School / Israel Bond, Riverdale, NY
33,000	Marin Academy, San Rafael, CA
33,000	Marin Academy, San Rafael, CA
25,000	American Jewish Committee National Relations, San Francisco, CA
25,000	Urban School of San Francisco, San Francisco, CA
20,000	KQED, San Francisco, CA
20,000	Scleroderma Research Foundation, Santa Barbara, CA
20,000	Sun Valley Ballet School, Ketchum, ID
19,426	Central Synagogue, New York, NY
15,750	Drew College Prep, San Francisco, CA

CARL S. SWISHER FOUNDATION

Giving Contact

Kenneth G. Anderson, President & Trustee
1301 Riverplace Boulevard, Suite 2640
Jacksonville, FL 32207
Phone: (904)399-8000
Fax: (904)346-3078

Description

Founded: 1949
EIN: 590998262
Organization Type: Private Foundation
Giving Locations: FL: Jacksonville
Grant Types: Capital, General Support, Project, Scholarship.

Donor Information

Founder: the late Carl S. Swisher

Financial Summary

Total Giving: $286,000 (2004); $339,050 (2001)
Assets: $6,988,174 (2004); $7,510,148 (2001)

Typical Recipients

Arts & Humanities: Arts Associations & Councils, Historic Preservation, History & Archaeology, Libraries, Museums/Galleries, Music, Public Broadcasting

Civic & Public Affairs: Civic & Public Affairs-General, Law & Justice, Legal Aid, Urban & Community Affairs, Zoos/Aquariums

Education: Arts/Humanities Education, Business Education, Colleges & Universities, Education Funds, Engineering/Technological Education, Legal Education, Literacy, Medical Education, Minority Education, Private Education (Precollege), Religious Education, Special Education, Student Aid

Health: Children's Health/Hospitals, Clinics/Medical Centers, Diabetes, Emergency/Ambulance Services, Hospices, Hospitals, Medical Rehabilitation, Medical Research, Research/Studies Institutes, Single-Disease Health Associations

Religion: Churches, Religion-General, Jewish Causes, Missionary Activities (Domestic), Religious Organizations, Religious Welfare

Science: Science Museums

Social Services: Animal Protection, Big Brothers/Big Sisters, Child Welfare, Community Service Organizations, Family Services, Food/Clothing Distribution, Homes, Senior Services, Shelters/Homelessness, United Funds/United Ways, YMCA/YWCA/YMHA/YWHA, Youth Organizations

Application Procedures

Initial Contact: Send a brief letter of inquiry.
Application Requirements: Include the applicant's name, address, employer identification number, and contact person; purpose of funds sought; amount requested; how grant will advance charitable purposes; proof of tax-exempt status; confirmation of current 501(c)(3) status; and balance sheet and income statement.
Deadlines: None.
Review Process: Board meets quarterly.

Restrictions

Does not support individuals.

Foundation Officials

Kenneth G. Anderson: president, trustee
Carolyn H. Charbonnet: secretary, trustee
John H. Lindsey: vice president, trustee
James P. Stevens: treasurer, trustee

Grants Analysis

Disclosure Period: calendar year ending 2004
Total Grants: $286,000
Number of Grants: 54
Average Grant: $4,453*
Highest Grant: $50,000
Lowest Grant: $1,000
Typical Range: $1,000 to $5,000
*Note: Average grant figure excludes highest grant.

Recent Grants

Note: Grants derived from 2001 Form 990.

Library-Related

5,000	Jacksonville Public Library, Jacksonville, FL

General

60,000	Jacksonville University, Jacksonville, FL
50,000	University of Florida, Gainesville, FL
10,500	Diabetes Foundation, Jacksonville, FL
10,000	Children's Home Society of Florida, Jacksonville, FL
10,000	Downtown Ecumenical Services Council, Jacksonville, FL
10,000	Hubbard House, Jacksonville, FL
10,000	IM Sulzbacher Center for the Homeless, Jacksonville, FL
10,000	Museum of Science and History, Jacksonville, FL
10,000	Taylor Residences, Jacksonville, FL
8,000	Trinity Rescue Mission, Jacksonville, FL

F. W. SYMMES FOUNDATION

Giving Contact
Sara Gerald-Huggins, Trust Officer
c/o Wachovia Bank, Trust Dept.
PO Box 969
Greenville, SC 29602

Description
Founded: 1954
EIN: 576017472
Organization Type: Private Foundation
Giving Locations: SC: Greenville
Grant Types: Capital, General Support, Project.

Donor Information
Founder: the late F.W. Symmes

Financial Summary
Total Giving: $603,500 (fiscal year ending March 31, 2004); $833,500 (fiscal 2002); $744,000 (fiscal 2001)
Assets: $14,125,218 (fiscal 2004); $14,805,030 (fiscal 2002); $15,885,753 (fiscal 2001)

Typical Recipients
Arts & Humanities: Arts Associations & Councils, Arts Centers, Arts Outreach, Historic Preservation, History & Archaeology, Libraries, Museums/Galleries, Performing Arts, Theater
Civic & Public Affairs: Civic & Public Affairs-General, Housing, Municipalities/Towns, Urban & Community Affairs, Zoos/Aquariums
Education: Arts/Humanities Education, Colleges & Universities, Education Funds, Education Reform, Literacy, Religious Education, Science/Mathematics Education, Special Education, Student Aid
Environment: Environment-General
Health: Cancer, Clinics/Medical Centers, Emergency/Ambulance Services, Health Organizations, Hospitals, Medical Rehabilitation, Speech & Hearing
Religion: Churches, Ministries, Religious Welfare
Science: Scientific Centers & Institutes
Social Services: Child Welfare, Community Service Organizations, Food/Clothing Distribution, Homes, People with Disabilities, Scouts, Shelters/Homelessness, YMCA/YWCA/YMHA/YWHA

Application Procedures
Initial Contact: Send a brief letter of inquiry describing program or project. Include purpose of funds sought and proof of tax-exempt status.
Deadlines: None.

Restrictions
Does not support individuals.

Additional Information
Publications: Application Guidelines; Informational Brochure
Trust(s): Wachovia Bank NA

Foundation Officials
Eleanor Welling: trustee
F. McKinnon Wilkinson: trustee

Grants Analysis
Disclosure Period: fiscal year ending March 31, 2004
Total Grants: $603,500
Number of Grants: 14
Average Grant: $23,045*
Highest Grant: $150,000
Lowest Grant: $500
Typical Range: $10,000 to $50,000
***Note:** Average grant figure excludes three highest grants ($350,000).

Recent Grants
Note: Grants derived from 2000 Form 990.
General

100,000	Greenville County Museum of Art, Greenville, SC
100,000	Greenville Literacy Association, Greenville, SC
100,000	South Carolina Governor's School of the Arts and Humanities -- fourth installment
50,000	Center for Developmental Services
50,000	Greater Greenville YMCA, Greenville, SC -- second installment of grant
50,000	Miracle Hill Ministries, Greenville, SC
50,000	Safe Harbor, West Chester, PA
42,000	Hidden Treasures Christian School
25,000	Governor's School for Science and Math -- second of three installments
25,000	Hollings Cancer Center, Charleston, SC

TACONIC FOUNDATION

Giving Contact
Hildy Simmons, Managing Director
J.P. Morgan & Co. Inc.
60 Wall St., 46th Fl.
New York, NY 10005
Phone: (212)789-5777
Fax: (212)648-5082

Alternate Contact
Andrew Lane, Assistant Program Officer
Phone: (212)648-3246

Description
Founded: 1958
EIN: 131873668
Organization Type: Specialized/Single Purpose Foundation
Giving Locations: NY: New York nationally.
Grant Types: General Support, Operating Expenses, Project.

Donor Information
Founder: Established in 1958 by the late Mr. Stephen R. Currier and Mrs. Audrey Currier, the former Audrey Mellon Bruce. She was the daughter of Ailsa Mellon, who was the sister of Paul Mellon and the daughter of Andrew Mellon. Mr. and Mrs. Currier, who were lost in the Caribbean on an airplane flight in 1967, left a fund having a current market value of approximately $15 million to carry on their charitable activities.

Typical Recipients
Arts & Humanities: Arts Outreach, Libraries, Literary Arts
Civic & Public Affairs: African American Affairs, Asian American Affairs, Botanical Gardens/Parks, Civil Rights, Economic Development, Employment/Job Training, Civic & Public Affairs-General, Housing, Law & Justice, Minority Business, Nonprofit Management, Philanthropic Organizations, Public Policy, Urban & Community Affairs
Education: Afterschool/Enrichment Programs, Arts/Humanities Education, Colleges & Universities, Education Associations, Education Funds, Education Reform, Education-General, Leadership Training, Literacy, Minority Education, Private Education (Precollege), School Volunteerism
Environment: Resource Conservation
Health: Children's Health/Hospitals
International: Health Care/Hospitals, Human Rights, International Relations
Religion: Churches, Religious Welfare
Social Services: Child Welfare, Community Service Organizations, Counseling, Family Planning, Family Services, Shelters/Homelessness, Youth Organizations

Application Procedures
Application Requirements: Primary goals of organization, most recent annual report, brief history of organization, list of directors or trustees, most recent financial audit, current operating budget, list of foundation and corporate support with amount for most recent and current fiscal year, copy 501(c)3 letter, latest IRS Form 990 (including salary information), description of project including primary purpose, population to be served, anticipated duration, and current budget. Indicate whether organisation has an endowment.
Review Process: Proposals are reviewed three times each year. Final notification comes within two to three months.

Restrictions
Grants are not given for higher education, the elderly, international programs, art and cultural programs, mass media, crime and justice, health, medicine, mental health, ecology and the environment, individual economic development projects, or local community programs outside New York City. The foundation does not make grants to individuals, scholarships, fellowships, or to building or endowment funds. It rarely makes grants for research or loans.

Additional Information
The foundation accepts the New York/New Jersey Common Application Form.
Publications: application guidelines

Foundation Officials
L. F. Boker Doyle: trustee B New York, NY 1931. ED Yale University BA (1953); New York University (1963). PRIM CORP EMPL consultant: Fiduciary Trust Co. International. NONPR AFFIL trustee, secretary: American Museum Natural History; treasurer: Frick Collection.
Alan J. Dworsky: trustee
Jane Lee Eddy: trustee NONPR AFFIL chairman, trustee: Corporate for Youth Energy Corps; president, trustee: Smokey House Project.
Hon. Bill Green: trustee NONPR AFFIL deputy chairman: New York City Housing Development Corp.
Melvin Mister: trustee
John Gerald Simon: trustee B New York, NY 1928. ED Harvard University AB (1950); Yale University LLB (1953). PRIM NONPR EMPL professor: Yale University, Law School. NONPR AFFIL trustee: Open Society Institute; member: Phi Beta Kappa; vice chairman: Cooperative Assistance Fund; member graduate board: Harvard Crimson.

Grants Analysis
Disclosure Period: calendar year ending 2000
Total Grants: $825,000
Number of Grants: 48
Average Grant: $17,188

Highest Grant: $30,000
Lowest Grant: $2,500
Typical Range: $10,000 to $25,000

TANNER COS. (RUTHERFORDTON, NC)

Company Headquarters
Rutherfordton, NC

Company Description
Employees: 800
SIC(s): 2331 Women's/Misses' Blouses & Shirts, 2335 Women's/Misses' Dresses.

Operating Locations
Tanner Companies (NC--Rutherfordton)

Tanner Foundation

Giving Contact
George E. Clayton, III, Treasurer
Tanner Foundation
Rock Road
Rutherfordton, NC 28139
Phone: (828)287-4205
Fax: (828)286-2072

Description
EIN: 510151695
Organization Type: Corporate Foundation
Giving Locations: NC: approximately 75% of grants are made in Rutherford County and surrounding counties
Grant Types: Capital, General Support, Research, Scholarship.

Financial Summary
Total Giving: $392,202 (2002); $392,202 (2001)
Giving Analysis: Giving for 2002 includes: foundation grants to United Way ($49,221); foundation matching gifts ($83,500); 2001: foundation grants to United Way ($49,221); foundation matching gifts ($83,550)
Assets: $106,394 (2001)
Gifts Received: $353,758 (2002); $353,758 (2001); $292,935 (2000). Note: In 2002 a contribution was made by Tanner Companies Limited Partnership.

Typical Recipients
Arts & Humanities: Arts Associations & Councils, Libraries, Museums/Galleries, Music, Public Broadcasting, Theater
Civic & Public Affairs: Chambers of Commerce, Clubs, Community Foundations, Economic Development, Employment/Job Training, Civic & Public Affairs-General, Housing, Professional & Trade Associations, Urban & Community Affairs
Education: Arts/Humanities Education, Colleges & Universities, Community & Junior Colleges, Economic Education, Education Funds, Elementary Education (Private), Elementary Education (Public), Education-General, Minority Education, Private Education (Precollege), Public Education (Precollege), Secondary Education (Public), Special Education
Health: Cancer, Emergency/Ambulance Services, Eyes/Blindness, Health-General, Health Organizations, Heart, Hospices, Hospitals, Prenatal Health Issues, Single-Disease Health Associations
International: Health Care/Hospitals
Religion: Churches, Religious Organizations, Religious Welfare
Social Services: Child Welfare, Emergency Relief, Food/Clothing Distribution, People with Disabilities, Recreation & Athletics, Scouts, Special Olympics, United Funds/United Ways, Youth Organizations

Application Procedures
Initial Contact: Send a full proposal.
Application Requirements: Include a description of the project and proposed budget, amount requested, federal employer identification number, and proof of tax-exempt status.
Deadlines: December 1 for consideration in the following year.

Restrictions
Preference is given to health care, education, and social services.

Corporate Officials
Chapman Johnston: president, chief executive officer PRIM CORP EMPL president, chief executive officer: Tanner Companies.
James T. Tanner: chairman B 1929. ED University of North Carolina (1950). PRIM CORP EMPL chairman: Tanner Companies.

Foundation Officials
Trip Clayton: director PRIM CORP EMPL chief financial officer: Tanner Companies.
Chapman Johnston: vice president (see above)
James T. Tanner: president (see above)
Michael S. Tanner: secretary
Pell Tanner: director

Grants Analysis
Disclosure Period: calendar year ending 2001
Total Grants: $392,202*
Number of Grants: 43
Average Grant: $7,739*
Highest Grant: $67,181
Lowest Grant: $500
Typical Range: $1,000 to $40,000
*Note: Average grant figure excludes highest grant.

Recent Grants
Note: Grants derived from 2001 Form 990.
Library-Related

2,494	UNC - Chapel Hill Friends of the Library, Chapel Hill, NC

General

67,161	American Red Cross National Disaster Relief Fund, Washington, DC
44,875	Kid's Senses, Inc.
40,399	United Way, Mansfield, OH
30,000	North Carolina Public Television Foundation, Research Triangle Park, NC -- Billy Graham
25,000	Spartanburg Mobile Meals, Spartanburg, NC
24,500	Legacy Award
20,000	Lynnwood Foundation, Charlotte, NC
19,081	Community Foundation of Western North Carolina, Asheville, NC
'16,102	United Way September 11th Fund, New York, NY
16,000	Spartanburg County Foundation, Spartanburg, SC

S. MARK TAPER FOUNDATION

Giving Contact
Raymond F. Reisler, Executive Director
12011 San Vicente Boulevard, Suite 400
Los Angeles, CA 90049-4986
Phone: (310)476-5413
Fax: (310)471-4993

Description
Founded: 1989
EIN: 954245076
Organization Type: Private Foundation
Giving Locations: CA
Grant Types: General Support.

Donor Information
Founder: Established in 1989 by the late S. Mark Taper.

Financial Summary
Total Giving: $5,471,004 (2003); $6,061,337 (2002); $6,747,720 (2001)
Assets: $122,436,951 (2003); $110,468,509 (2002); $126,356,043 (2001)
Gifts Received: $94,700,000 (1995); $450,000 (1992). Note: In 1995, contributions were received from the Mark Taper 1969 Trust No. 1.

Typical Recipients
Arts & Humanities: Arts Associations & Councils, Ballet, Dance, Film & Video, History & Archaeology, Libraries, Museums/Galleries, Music, Performing Arts, Public Broadcasting, Theater
Civic & Public Affairs: Asian American Affairs, Civil Rights, Community Foundations, Economic Development, Employment/Job Training, Ethnic Organizations, Civic & Public Affairs-General, Hispanic Affairs, Housing, Law & Justice, Legal Aid, Nonprofit Management, Urban & Community Affairs, Women's Affairs
Education: Afterschool/Enrichment Programs, Arts/Humanities Education, Colleges & Universities, Continuing Education, Education Funds, Education-General, Legal Education, Literacy, Private Education (Precollege), Public Education (Precollege), Social Sciences Education
Environment: Environment-General, Watershed
Health: AIDS/HIV, Alzheimer's Disease, Children's Health/Hospitals, Clinics/Medical Centers, Eyes/Blindness, Health Policy/Cost Containment, Health Funds, Health Organizations, Home-Care Services, Hospices, Medical Rehabilitation, Mental Health, Prenatal Health Issues, Preventive Medicine/Wellness Organizations, Public Health, Single-Disease Health Associations, Speech & Hearing, Transplant Networks/Donor Banks
Religion: Jewish Causes, Religious Organizations, Religious Welfare
Science: Science Museums
Social Services: At-Risk Youth, Camps, Child Abuse, Child Welfare, Community Centers, Community Service Organizations, Counseling, Crime Prevention, Day Care, Domestic Violence, Family Services, Food/Clothing Distribution, Homes, People with Disabilities, Senior Services, Sexual Abuse, Shelters/Homelessness, Social Services-General, Substance Abuse, Youth Organizations

Application Procedures
Initial Contact: Send a brief letter of inquiry.
Application Requirements: Include a description of organization, amount requested, purpose of funds sought, recently audited financial statement, and proof of tax-exempt status.
Deadlines: Applications are accepted from September 1 through February 28.

Restrictions
Does not award grants to individuals.

Foundation Officials
Janice Anne Lazarof: president, director
Cynthia Taper Bolker: vice president
Deborah Taper Ringel: treasurer
Amelia Taper Stabler: secretary

Grants Analysis
Disclosure Period: calendar year ending 2003
Total Grants: $5,471,004
Number of Grants: 68
Average Grant: $58,085*
Highest Grant: $795,500
Lowest Grant: $1,000
Typical Range: $25,000 to $100,000

*Note: Average grant figure excludes three highest grants ($1,695,500).

Recent Grants

Note: Grants derived from 2003 Form 990.
General

795,500	Hadassah Women's Zionist Organization of America Inc., New York, NY
600,000	VIP Community Mental Health Center, Los Angeles, CA
300,000	Los Angeles Community Design Center, Los Angeles, CA
250,000	EL Centro del Pueblo, Los Angeles, CA
250,000	High Tech High, Beverly Hills, CA
250,000	Kidspace Children's Museum, Pasadena, CA
250,000	Valley Community Clinic, North Hollywood, CA
235,000	National Institute of Transplantation, Los Angeles, CA
200,000	Vista Del Mar Child and Family Services, Los Angeles, CA
175,000	California Literacy, Pasadena, CA

TARGET CORP.

Company Headquarters

1000 Nicollet Mall
Minneapolis, MN 55403
Web: http://www.target.com

Company Description

Ticker: TGT
Exchange: NYSE
Former Name: Dayton Hudson.
Revenue: US$49.934 billion (2004)
Profit: US$3.198 billion (2004)
Employees: 192000 (2003)
Fortune Rank: 27, per FORTUNE Magazine's list of 500 Largest U.S. Corporations (2004).

Nonmonetary Support

Type: Cause-related Marketing & Promotion; In-kind Services
Volunteer Programs: Each division of the company has its own volunteer program. Company-wide, Target Corp. jointly sponsors "Day of Giving" in the spring/summer.
Note: Nonmonetary support is provided by local operating divisions. Nonmonetary Support Contact: General Managers at local stores. Nonmonetary support is valued at more than $5,000,000 annually.

Target Foundation

Giving Contact

Community Relations
Target Stores
1000 Nicollet Mall, TPS3080
Minneapolis, MN 55403
Phone: (612)696-6098
Fax: (612)696-5088
E-mail: bridget.mcginnis@target.com
Web: http://www.target.com/target_group/community/community_main.jhtml

Alternate Contact

Target Foundation
33 South Sixth Street, CC-28Y
Minneapolis, MN 55402
E-mail: guidelines@target.com
Web: http://www.targetfoundation.org
Note: Address for application submissions.

Description

Founded: 1918
EIN: 416017088

Organization Type: Corporate Foundation
Former Name: Dayton Hudson Corporate.
Giving Locations: headquarters and operating communities.
Grant Types: Capital, General Support, Project, Scholarship.

Donor Information

Founder: Dayton Hudson Corp. and operating divisions

Financial Summary

Total Giving: $5,100,000 (fiscal year ending January 31, 2003); $87,200,000 (fiscal 2002 approx); $85,800,000 (fiscal 2001 approx). Note: Contributes through corporate direct giving program and foundation.
Giving Analysis: Giving for fiscal 2003 includes: foundation grants to United Way ($1,225,000); fiscal 2001: foundation (approx $9,500,000); corporate direct giving (approx $76,300,000)
Assets: $15,047,417 (fiscal 2003); $16,882,628 (fiscal 2002); $25,628,038 (fiscal 2001). Note: Assets exist as a reserve fund.
Gifts Received: $8,600,000 (fiscal 2003); $2,222,267 (fiscal 2002); $397,750 (fiscal 2001). Note: Contributions were received from Target Corp.

Typical Recipients

Arts & Humanities: Arts Appreciation, Arts Associations & Councils, Arts Centers, Arts Funds, Arts Institutes, Arts Outreach, Community Arts, Dance, Ethnic & Folk Arts, Film & Video, Arts & Humanities-General, History & Archaeology, Libraries, Literary Arts, Museums/Galleries, Music, Opera, Performing Arts, Public Broadcasting, Theater, Visual Arts
Civic & Public Affairs: African American Affairs, Botanical Gardens/Parks, Business/Free Enterprise, Civil Rights, Clubs, Community Foundations, Economic Development, Employment/Job Training, Civic & Public Affairs-General, Hispanic Affairs, Housing, Legal Aid, Minority Business, Municipalities/Towns, Native American Affairs, Nonprofit Management, Professional & Trade Associations, Public Policy, Urban & Community Affairs, Women's Affairs
Education: Arts/Humanities Education, Colleges & Universities, Education Funds, Education Reform, Engineering/Technological Education, International Exchange, Literacy, Private Education (Precollege), Public Education (Precollege), School Volunteerism, Special Education, Student Aid
Health: AIDS/HIV, Children's Health/Hospitals, Health Organizations, Research/Studies Institutes
International: Trade
Religion: Churches, Dioceses, Religious Welfare
Science: Science Museums
Social Services: At-Risk Youth, Child Welfare, Community Centers, Community Service Organizations, Domestic Violence, Emergency Relief, Family Planning, Family Services, Food/Clothing Distribution, People with Disabilities, Refugee Assistance, Shelters/Homelessness, Social Services-General, United Funds/United Ways, YMCA/YWCA/YMHA/YWHA, Youth Organizations

Application Procedures

Initial Contact: Minnesota organizations that fit the foundation's guidelines should contact the foundation to obtain a copy of the foundation's application form and guidelines. Organizations located elsewhere should obtain guidelines and application from the Target, Mervyn's, or Marshall Field's store in their community. Guidelines may also be obtained on each company's web site.
Application Requirements: For proposals to the foundation: Provide a completed application form; amount requested and purpose of funds sought; organization's history and mission statement; list of the board of directors, including names, titles, and affiliations; proof of tax-exempt status; current annual operating budget, with income and expenses; project or program budget detailing expenses and anticipated

sources of income; current list of business and foundation donors including amounts; a copy of the organization's most recent audited financial statement. received. received. received.
Deadlines: None for the foundation, although preferred submission times are February through November. The foundation does not typically make grants in December and January. For corporate contributions, operating divisions may have deadlines. Most stores do not review applications during the fourth quarter of the year due to the holiday shopping season and fiscal year end.
Review Process: Reviews are conducted by foundation staff or staff of operating divisions.
Evaluative Criteria: Whether group is focused within key areas of interest for foundation or operating divisions, and whether they can realistically accomplish their objective.
Decision Notification: Usually within 90 days of receipt of proposal.

Restrictions

The foundation does not make grants to individuals; religious organizations for sectarian purposes; national ceremonies, memorials, conferences, fundraising dinners, testimonials, or similar events; health, recreation, therapeutic programs, living subsidies, or care of disabled persons. Corporate contributions programs have similar restrictions.

Additional Information

Target Corporation's philanthropic contributions policy calls for the company to donate 5% of its federal taxable income annually to charitable organizations. Target operates retail stores including Marshall Field's, Mervyn's, and Target; each chain manages its own corporate contributions program in communities where they have a presence.

The Target Stores contributions program has two program areas: Arts and Family Violence Prevention. The Arts program area focuses on affordable cultural experiences for the entire family such as art exhibits, classes, performances, and programs that bring arts to schools or that take school children to the arts. Family Violence Prevention grants typically support parenting education, family counseling, support groups, and abuse shelters.

Marshall Field's focuses contributions on three areas: Child Abuse Prevention, Youth Self-Sufficiency, and Education Through the Arts. Under the Child Abuse Prevention program, the company supports prevention and intervention programs, mentoring programs for parents and caregivers, crisis nurseries, home-visit programs for at-risk families, and awareness programs. The Youth Self-Sufficiency focus area supports programs that help youth gain employment and leadership skills through job-readiness and life skills programs, mentoring programs, and organizations that education youth of career opportunities and the importance of community service. The Education Through the Arts program funds programs that improve educational outcomes for K-12 students while encouraging youth involvement in the arts.

Mervyn's concentrates its giving on the Arts and Education. The Arts program supports arts programs that give children and families affordable access to the arts, with preference given to programs that reflect community diversity. Typical recipients include school touring programs, family matinees, children's visual arts programs, theater and dance performances, programs bringing artists into the classroom, and live musical performances. Mervyn's Education program provides direct support to schools and funds community-based nonprofit organizations aimed at enhancing the educational development of children. Examples of programs in which the company is interested are school partnerships, leadership development, after-school programs, homework assistance programs, mentoring, and tutoring.

The Target Foundation manages contributions in the Minneapolis/Saint Paul metropolitan area and a small

program of national giving. The foundation focuses its giving on Arts and Social Action. Arts organizations that promote visibility and accessibility at a community level are supported. The Social Action focus area funds programs that provide the basic needs of at-risk populations by providing food, shelter, and clothing.
Publications: Summary of Community Involvement; Grant Application Guidelines

Corporate Officials

Linda L. Ahlers: president, Target Stores PRIM CORP EMPL president: Marshall Field's.
Timothy R. Baer: senior vice president, secretary
Bart Butzer: executive vice president, Target Stores
James Thomas Hale: executive vice president, general counsel, secretary B Minneapolis, MN 1940. ED Dartmouth College BA (1962); University of Minnesota LLB (1965). PRIM CORP EMPL senior vice president, general counsel, secretary: Dayton Hudson Corp. CORP AFFIL director: Tennant Co. NONPR AFFIL member: Order Coif; member: Phi Beta Kappa; director: Minnesota Continuing Legal Education; member executive committee: Fund Legal Aid Society; member: Hennepin County Bar Association.
Diane L. Neal: president, Mervyns B 1957.
Gregg W. Steinhafel: president, Target Stores ED Carroll College BBA; Northwestern University MBA. CORP AFFIL director: The Toro Co..
Gerald L. Storch: vice chairman B 1957. ED Harvard University MBA; Harvard University JD; Harvard University BA. PRIM CORP EMPL senior vice president strategic business: Dayton Hudson Corp. CORP AFFIL director: Sprint Corp.
Robert J. Ulrich: chairman, chief executive officer, director B Minneapolis, MN April 24, 1943. ED University of Minnesota (1967); Stanford University Executive Management Program (1978). PRIM CORP EMPL chairman, chief executive officer, director: Target Corp. CORP AFFIL director: Yum!Brands Inc..
Laysha L. Ward: vice president, community relations

Foundation Officials

Linda L. Ahlers: trustee (see above)
Timothy R. Baer: secretary (see above)
Bart Butzer: executive vice president (see above)
Gail J. Dorn: trustee, vice president PRIM CORP EMPL vice president communications: Dayton Hudson Corp.
Stephen C. Kowalke: vice president, treasurer PRIM CORP EMPL vice president, treasurer: Dayton Hudson Corp.
Diane L. Neal: president, trustee (see above)
Gregg W. Steinhafel: president, trustee (see above)
Gerald L. Storch: trustee (see above)
Robert J. Ulrich: chairman, trustee (see above)
Laysha L. Ward: vice president, trustee (see above)

Grants Analysis

Disclosure Period: fiscal year ending January 31, 2003
Total Grants: $3,875,000*
Number of Grants: 158
Average Grant: $24,682
Highest Grant: $200,000
Lowest Grant: $5,000
Typical Range: $10,000 to $50,000
***Note:** Giving excludes United Way.

Recent Grants

Note: Grants derived from 2004 Form 990.
General

1,261,548	Minneapolis Institute of Arts, Minneapolis, MN
500,000	Guthrie Theater, Minneapolis, MN
456,948	Greater Twin Cities United Way, Minneapolis, MN
350,000	Walker Art Center, Minneapolis, MN
250,000	Catholic Charities Archdiocese of St. Paul, Minneapolis, MN
250,000	Minnesota Orchestral Association, Minneapolis, MN
200,000	Bridge for Runaway Youth, Minneapolis, MN
200,000	People Serving People Inc., Minneapolis, MN
200,000	Sabathani Community Center, Minneapolis, MN
200,000	Second Harvest Heartland, St. Paul, MN

TAUBE FAMILY FOUNDATION

Giving Contact

Thaddeus Taube, Chairman & President
1050 Ralston Ave.
Belmont, CA 94002
Phone: (650)592-3960

Description

Founded: 1980
EIN: 942702180
Organization Type: Private Foundation
Giving Locations: nationally.
Grant Types: General Support.

Donor Information

Founder: members of the Taube family

Financial Summary

Total Giving: $1,169,786 (fiscal year ending November 30, 2003); $971,904 (fiscal 2001)
Giving Analysis: Giving for fiscal 2003 includes: foundation grants to United Way ($250,000); fiscal 2001: foundation grants to United Way ($250,000)
Assets: $19,576,434 (fiscal 2003); $18,562,056 (fiscal 2001)
Gifts Received: $1,920,068 (fiscal 2003); $4,170,862 (fiscal 2001); $3,139,095 (fiscal 2000). Note: In fiscal 1996 and 2003, contributions were received from the Taube Family Trust.

Typical Recipients

Arts & Humanities: Ballet, Libraries, Museums/Galleries, Music, Opera, Public Broadcasting
Civic & Public Affairs: Botanical Gardens/Parks, Business/Free Enterprise, Clubs, Community Foundations, Economic Development, Economic Policy, Civic & Public Affairs-General, Legal Aid, Minority Business, Municipalities/Towns, Public Policy, Safety, Urban & Community Affairs, Zoos/Aquariums
Education: Business-School Partnerships, Colleges & Universities, Education Associations, Education Funds, Education-General, Private Education (Precollege), Religious Education, School Volunteerism, Secondary Education (Private), Social Sciences Education, Student Aid
Health: Arthritis, Cancer, Children's Health/Hospitals, Geriatric Health, Hospices, Hospitals, Hospitals (University Affiliated), Long-Term Care, Medical Research, Multiple Sclerosis, Single-Disease Health Associations
International: Foreign Educational Institutions, International Organizations, International Peace & Security Issues, Missionary/Religious Activities
Religion: Churches, Religion-General, Jewish Causes, Religious Organizations, Religious Welfare
Social Services: Community Centers, Community Service Organizations, Family Services, People with Disabilities, Recreation & Athletics, Scouts, United Funds/United Ways, Volunteer Services, YMCA/YWCA/YMHA/YWHA, Youth Organizations

Application Procedures

Initial Contact: Send a brief letter of inquiry.
Application Requirements: Include purpose of funds sought and amount requested.
Deadlines: None.

Restrictions

Grants are not made to individuals.

Foundation Officials

Beverly Hong: secretary
Thaddeus N. Taube: chairman, president B 1931. ED Stanford University BS (1954); Stanford University MS (1957). PRIM CORP EMPL chairman, director: Woodmont Companies.

Grants Analysis

Disclosure Period: fiscal year ending November 30, 2003
Total Grants: $919,786*
Number of Grants: 66
Average Grant: $8,122*
Highest Grant: $200,000
Lowest Grant: $150
Typical Range: $1,000 to $10,000
***Note:** Giving excludes United Way. Average grant figure excludes two highest grants ($400,000).

Recent Grants

Note: Grants derived from fiscal 2003 Form 990.
General

316,666	University of California San Francisco Foundation, San Francisco, CA
250,000	United Way of the Bay Area, San Francisco, CA
200,000	Hoover Institute, Stanford, CA
200,000	Stanford University Tennis Center, Stanford, CA
50,000	Friends of Recreation & Parks
45,000	Stanford Center for Economic Policy Research, Stanford, CA
30,000	San Francisco Opera Association, San Francisco, CA
15,000	Congregation Beth Am, Los Altos Hills, CA
11,800	Zoofest 2003
10,000	Youth Tennis Advantage, Oakland, CA

A. ALFRED TAUBMAN FOUNDATION

Giving Contact

Fred Henshaw
PO Box 200
200 E. Long Lake Rd.
Bloomfield Hills, MI 48303-0200
Phone: (248)258-6800
Fax: (248)258-7476
E-mail: fhenshaw@taubman.com
Web: http://www.taubman.com

Description

Founded: 1979
EIN: 382219625
Organization Type: Private Foundation
Giving Locations: MI: emphasis on Detroit
Grant Types: Operating Expenses, Research.

Donor Information

Founder: A. Alfred Taubman

Financial Summary

Gifts Received: $6,227,688 (fiscal year ending July 31, 2000); $1,153,705 (fiscal 1999); $1,121,105 (fiscal 1996). Note: In fiscal 1999 and 2000, contributions were received from A. Alfred Taubman Restated Revocable Trust. In fiscal 1996, contributions were received from A. Alfred Taubman.

Typical Recipients

Arts & Humanities: Arts Festivals, Ethnic & Folk Arts, Historic Preservation, History & Archaeology, Libraries, Museums/Galleries

Civic & Public Affairs: African American Affairs, Botanical Gardens/Parks, Chambers of Commerce, Economic Development, Employment/Job Training, Ethnic Organizations, Civic & Public Affairs-General, Hispanic Affairs, Law & Justice, Legal Aid, Municipalities/Towns, Nonprofit Management, Philanthropic Organizations, Professional & Trade Associations, Public Policy, Urban & Community Affairs, Women's Affairs

Education: Colleges & Universities, Education Associations, Engineering/Technological Education, Education-General, Medical Education, Minority Education, Private Education (Precollege), Public Education (Precollege), Student Aid

Environment: Environment-General, Resource Conservation, Wildlife Protection

Health: AIDS/HIV, Alzheimer's Disease, Arthritis, Cancer, Clinics/Medical Centers, Diabetes, Emergency/Ambulance Services, Health Organizations, Heart, Hospices, Hospitals, Kidney, Long-Term Care, Medical Research, Public Health, Single-Disease Health Associations, Transplant Networks/Donor Banks

International: Foreign Arts Organizations, Foreign Educational Institutions, Health Care/Hospitals, International Environmental Issues, International Organizations, International Relations, Missionary/Religious Activities

Religion: Bible Study/Translation, Churches, Jewish Causes, Religious Organizations, Religious Welfare, Social/Policy Issues, Synagogues/Temples

Science: Science Exhibits & Fairs, Scientific Centers & Institutes

Social Services: At-Risk Youth, Camps, Child Welfare, Community Service Organizations, Crime Prevention, Delinquency & Criminal Rehabilitation, Domestic Violence, Family Planning, Family Services, Homes, People with Disabilities, Recreation & Athletics, Scouts, Senior Services, Substance Abuse, United Funds/United Ways, Volunteer Services, YMCA/YWCA/YMHA/YWHA, Youth Organizations

Application Procedures

Initial Contact: Send a a brief letter of inquiry describing program or project.
Application Requirements: Include a description of organization, a brief explanation of what applicant expects to receive from the foundation and why, and a list of previous contributors.
Deadlines: None.

Foundation Officials

Gayle T. Kalisman: president
Jeffrey H. Miro: secretary PRIM CORP EMPL secretary: Sothebys Holdings. CORP AFFIL director: Taubman Co.; director: Woodward & Lothrop Inc.
Gerald R. Poissant: assistant treasurer
A. Alfred Taubman: chairman, treasurer, trustee B Pontiac, MI 1925. ED Lawrence Technological University; University of Michigan (1945-1948); Lawrence Institute of Technology (1948-1949). PRIM CORP EMPL chairman: Taubman Co. CORP AFFIL chairman: Sothebys Holdings; chairman: Taubman Centers; director: Detroit Renaissance Inc.; director: Live Entertainment Canada. NONPR AFFIL chairman: University Pennsylvania Wharton Real Estate Center; trustee: Urban Land Institute; prin benefactor: A Alfred Taubman Medicine Library University Michigan; active: State Michigan Gaming Commission; prin benefactor: A Alfred Taubman Health Care Center; nat board: Smithsonian Associates; chairman emeritus: Smithsonian Institute American Art; chairman: Program American Instns University Michigan; chairman: Michigan Partnership New Education; director: National Realty Commission; director: Friends Art Preservation Embassies; trustee: Harper-Grace Hospital; trustee: Center Creative Studies; president: Arts Community Detroit; chairman: Brown Universitys Public Policy American Instns Program.
Judith M. Taubman: trustee
Robert S. Taubman: trustee B Detroit, MI 1953. PRIM CORP EMPL president, chief executive officer,

director: Taubman Co. CORP AFFIL director: Woodward & Lothrop; director: Washington John Wanamaker Department Store; director: Sotheby's International Realty Corp.; director: Taubman Investment Co. Inc.; director: Mfrs National Bank Detroit; director: A&W Restaurants. NONPR AFFIL trustee: Sinai Hospital; member: Urban Land Institute; member: International Council Shopping Centers; member, board governors: Cranbrook School. CLUB AFFIL Economic Club Detroit.
William S. Taubman: trustee CORP AFFIL director: A&W Restaurants.

Grants Analysis

Disclosure Period: fiscal year ending July 31, 2000
Total Grants: $6,203,505*
Number of Grants: 92
Average Grant: $1,129*
Highest Grant: $1,100,000
Typical Range: $500 to $2,000
*Note: Giving excludes United Way. Average grant figure excludes two highest grants ($6,101,900).

Recent Grants

Note: Grants derived from 2002 Form 990.
General

1,000,000	Jewish Federation of Metropolitan Detroit, Detroit, MI
18,000	United Way, Detroit, MI
5,500	American Jewish Committee, New York, NY
3,000	Jewish Federal of Palm Beach County, West Palm Beach, FL
2,750	Friends of the Israel Defense Forces, New York, NY
2,000	Yeshiva Beth Yehudah, Brooklyn, NY
1,500	Detroit Institute for Children, Detroit, MI
1,000	American Friends of Turkey, Washington, DC
1,000	Breast Cancer Research Foundation, New York, NY
1,000	Detroit Renaissance Foundation, Detroit, MI

ARTHUR C. AND LEE ANNE TAUCK FOUNDATION

Giving Contact

Kendra St. John, Associate Director
PO Box 5020
Norwalk, CT 06855-1445
Phone: (866)828-2536
Fax: (203)286-1340
E-mail: info@tauckfoundation.org
Web: http://www.tauckfoundation.org

Description

Founded: 1994
EIN: 061396951
Organization Type: Private Foundation
Giving Locations: PA
Grant Types: General Support.

Donor Information

Founder: Established in 1994 by Arthur C. Tauck.

Financial Summary

Total Giving: $899,715 (2003)
Giving Analysis: Giving for 2003 includes: foundation grants to United Way ($5,000)
Assets: $15,697,054 (2003)
Gifts Received: $3,797,128 (1994). Note: In 1994, contributions were received from Arthur C. Tauck.

Typical Recipients

Arts & Humanities: Arts & Humanities-General, Libraries, Music, Performing Arts, Public Broadcasting
Civic & Public Affairs: Clubs, Civic & Public Affairs-General, Housing, Parades/Festivals, Professional & Trade Associations
Education: Business Education, Colleges & Universities, Education-General, Private Education (Precollege), Public Education (Precollege)
Environment: Air/Water Quality, Environment-General, Resource Conservation, Wildlife Protection
Health: Emergency/Ambulance Services, Health Organizations, Hospices, Hospitals
International: International Relief Efforts
Science: Scientific Centers & Institutes
Social Services: Camps, Child Welfare, Community Service Organizations, Emergency Relief, Recreation & Athletics, Social Services-General, United Funds/United Ways, YMCA/YWCA/YMHA/YWHA, Youth Organizations

Application Procedures

Initial Contact: The foundation has no formal grant application procedure or application form.
Deadlines: None.

Foundation Officials

Arthur C. Tauck, Jr.: trustee

Grants Analysis

Disclosure Period: calendar year ending 2003
Total Grants: $894,715*
Number of Grants: 116
Average Grant: $4,778*
Highest Grant: $250,000
Lowest Grant: $50
Typical Range: $1,000 to $10,000
*Note: Giving excludes United Way. Average grant figure excludes two highest grants ($350,000).

Recent Grants

Note: Grants derived from 2001 Form 990.
General

300,000	Lehigh University, Bethlehem, PA
57,000	A Better Chance, Westport, MA
25,000	Alaska Raptor Rehabilitation Center, Sitka, AK
25,000	Save America's Treasures, Washington, DC
20,000	Aspira, CT
20,000	Institute of Certified Travel Agents, Wellesley, MA
20,000	Music and Arts Center for Humanity, Bridgeport, CT
15,000	Norwalk Hospital Foundation, Norwalk, CT
12,000	Friends of Green Chimneys, Brewster, NY
10,000	I Have A Dream, Norwalk, CT

TCF NATIONAL BANK MINNESOTA

Company Headquarters

Minneapolis, MN
Web: http://www.tcfbank.com

Company Description

Former Name: TCF Banking & Savings FSB.
SIC(s): 6035 Federal Savings Institutions.
Parent Company: TCF Financial Corp., 200 Lake St. E., Mail Code EX0-03-A, Wayzata, MN, United States

Operating Locations

TCF National Bank Minnesota (MN, Minneapolis)

Nonmonetary Support

Value: $120,000 (2004 approx); $120,000 (2003 approx); $120,000 (2002 approx)
Type: Donated Products; Loaned Employees; Loaned Executives
Volunteer Programs: The company encourages employee volunteerism through local divisions, including programs such as March of Dimes, paint-a-thons, and home-repair days.

TCF Foundation

Giving Contact

Kelly Sack, Corporate Affairs Officer
TCF Foundation
200 Lake Street East (EXO-02-C)
Wayzata, MN 55391-1693
Phone: (952)745-2757
Fax: (952)745-2775
E-mail: ksack@tcfbank.com
Web: http://www.tcfexpress.com/cu_found.htmrequest

Alternate Contact

Contributions Committee
Great Lakes Bancorp
401 East Liberty
Ann Arbor, MI 48104-2298

Description

EIN: 411659826
Organization Type: Corporate Foundation
Giving Locations: MN: headquarters and operating communities
Grant Types: Employee Matching Gifts, General Support, Multiyear/Continuing Support, Project, Scholarship.
Note: Employee matching gift ratio: 1 to 1 for most charitable 501(c)(3) organizations.

Financial Summary

Total Giving: $1,664,000 (2004 approx); $1,849,000 (2003 approx); $1,819,792 (2002)
Giving Analysis: Giving for 2002 includes: foundation scholarships ($67,314)
Assets: $36,995 (2002)
Gifts Received: $1,798,999 (2002); $25 (2000); $1,002,624 (1998). Note: In 2002 contributions were made by TCF National Bank, William A. Cooper, and Friends of Ascension.

Typical Recipients

Arts & Humanities: Arts Associations & Councils, Arts Centers, Arts Funds, Arts Institutes, Arts & Humanities-General, Libraries, Museums/Galleries, Music, Opera, Performing Arts, Public Broadcasting, Theater
Civic & Public Affairs: African American Affairs, Asian American Affairs, Business/Free Enterprise, Chambers of Commerce, Economic Development, Employment/Job Training, Civic & Public Affairs-General, Hispanic Affairs, Housing, Law & Justice, Municipalities/Towns, Nonprofit Management, Professional & Trade Associations, Safety, Urban & Community Affairs, Women's Affairs
Education: Business Education, Business-School Partnerships, Colleges & Universities, Community & Junior Colleges, Education Associations, Education Funds, Elementary Education (Private), Faculty Development, Education-General, Private Education (Precollege), Public Education (Precollege), Science/Mathematics Education, Secondary Education (Public), Student Aid, Vocational & Technical Education
Health: Children's Health/Hospitals, Clinics/Medical Centers, Health-General, Health Funds, Health Organizations, Heart, Hospitals, Kidney, Medical Rehabilitation, Mental Health, Prenatal Health Issues, Public Health, Single-Disease Health Associations, Transplant Networks/Donor Banks
International: International Organizations

Religion: Ministries, Religious Organizations, Religious Welfare
Science: Observatories & Planetariums, Science Museums
Social Services: At-Risk Youth, Child Welfare, Community Centers, Community Service Organizations, Domestic Violence, Family Services, Food/Clothing Distribution, People with Disabilities, Recreation & Athletics, Scouts, Senior Services, Shelters/Homelessness, Social Services-General, Substance Abuse, United Funds/United Ways, Volunteer Services, YMCA/YWCA/YMHA/YWHA, Youth Organizations

Application Procedures

Initial Contact: Send a written grant request in letter form.
Application Requirements: Include a description of organization; list of board members, including information on people who will manage project; audited financial statements, current budget, and next year's budget; mission statement and summary of long-range plans; purpose of contribution requested and relationship to plans; list of major contributors and amounts given; how project relates to foundation's interests and guidelines; methods of evaluating program's effectiveness; company employee involvement; sources of income, current and planned; copy of IRS 501(c)(3) tax-exemption determination letter.
Deadlines: None.
Evaluative Criteria: Charitable grants are made (with few exceptions) only to tax-exempt 501(c)(3) organizations; special consideration is given to those institutions supported by the employees of TCF Financial Corporation or its subsidiaries through their personal contributions of time and/or money.
Decision Notification: Most funding decisions will require at least sixty days for review.
Notes: In Minnesota, all requesters are required to use the Minnesota Common Grant application form. Grant requests may be directed to offices in Michigan, Illinois, Wisconsin, or Minnesota.

Restrictions

The foundation does not make grants to individuals, political parties or candidates, lobbying groups, individual churches or sectarian activities, advertising or subsidizing publications, or social events of otherwise qualified organizations.
Support will be given only to organizations that are able to provide evidence of 501(C)(3) tax-exempt status.
Foundation does not award multi-year grants.
Grants are only made to organizations located in areas where TCF has a bank office. Grants are made to United Way campaigns in communities where TCF has well-established offices.

Additional Information

TCF Bank Minnesota, FSB, was formerly named TCF Bank Savings, FSB.
Publications: Community Affairs Report; Grant Request Guidelines

Corporate Officials

William Allen Cooper: chairman, director counsel, secretary B Detroit, MI 1943. ED Wayne State University BS (1967). PRIM CORP EMPL chairman, director: TCF Bank Minnesota FSB. CORP AFFIL principal: TCF finance Insurance Agency; chairman, director: TCF Financial Corp. NONPR AFFIL member: American Institute CPAs.
Gregory J. Pulles: vice chairman, general counsel, secretary B 1948. ED University of Minnesota BS (1970); University of Minnesota JD (1973). PRIM CORP EMPL vice chairman, general counsel, secretary: TCF Financial Corp. CORP AFFIL executive vice president, secretary: TCF Bank Minnesota FSB; secretary, director: TCF Mortgage Corp.

Giving Program Officials

Kelly Sack: community affairs officer

Foundation Officials

William Allen Cooper: chairman, director (see above)
Mark Jeter: director
Jason E. Korstange: president
Gregory J. Pulles: secretary, director (see above)

Grants Analysis

Disclosure Period: calendar year ending 2002
Total Grants: $1,752,478*
Number of Grants: 152
Average Grant: $11,318*
Highest Grant: $100,000
Lowest Grant: $1,000
Typical Range: $1,500 to $15,000
*Note: Average grant figure excludes highest grant.

Recent Grants

Note: Grants derived from 2003 Form 990.
General

100,000	Ascension Academy, Wayzata, MN
100,000	Ascension Academy, Wayzata, MN
100,000	Friends of Ascension, Plymouth, MN
50,000	Courage Center, Minneapolis, MN -- funds for renovation of courage residence
40,000	Goodwill Industries Inc., St. Paul, MN
40,000	Home Ownership Center, St. Paul, MN
31,146	Patrick Henry High School, Minneapolis, MN
30,000	Minnesota Children's Museum, St. Paul, MN
30,000	Washtenaw Housing Alliance, Ann Arbor, MI
28,500	Scholarship America, St. Peter, MN

TEAGLE FOUNDATION

Giving Contact

Megan Bray, Office Assistant
10 Rockefeller Plaza, Room 920
New York, NY 10020-1903
Phone: (212)373-1972
E-mail: mbray@teaglefoundation.org
Web: http://www.teaglefoundation.org

Description

Founded: 1944
EIN: 131773645
Organization Type: General Purpose Foundation
Giving Locations: nationally; Canada
Grant Types: Employee Matching Gifts, General Support, Project.
Note: Foundation also makes strategic grants.

Donor Information

Founder: Established in 1944 by the late Walter C. Teagle, former president and chairman of the Standard Oil Company (New Jersey), now Exxon Corporation. The foundation's assets also come from bequests from Mr. Teagle's wife, Rowena Lee Teagle, and their son, Walter C. Teagle Jr.

Financial Summary

Total Giving: $8,108,904 (fiscal year ending May 31, 2003); $13,461,243 (fiscal 2002); $11,076,219 (fiscal 2001)
Giving Analysis: Giving for fiscal 2001 includes: foundation grants to United Way ($10,000); foundation matching gifts ($83,489); foundation scholarships ($1,143,750)
Assets: $127,381,513 (fiscal 2003); $148,935,627 (fiscal 2002); $184,000,000 (fiscal 2001 approx)

Typical Recipients

Arts & Humanities: Arts Festivals, Arts Outreach, Ballet, Dance, Arts & Humanities-General, Libraries, Music, Opera, Performing Arts, Theater
Civic & Public Affairs: Civic & Public Affairs-

General

Education: Arts/Humanities Education, Business Education, Colleges & Universities, Community & Junior Colleges, Education Associations, Education Funds, Education Reform, Engineering/Technological Education, Environmental Education, Faculty Development, Leadership Training, Medical Education, Minority Education, Private Education (Precollege), Religious Education, Science/Mathematics Education, Student Aid

Health: Emergency/Ambulance Services, Home-Care Services, Hospitals, Hospitals (University Affiliated)

International: Missionary/Religious Activities

Religion: Churches, Religion-General, Jewish Causes, Ministries, Religious Organizations, Religious Welfare, Seminaries

Social Services: Community Service Organizations, United Funds/United Ways, Youth Organizations

Application Procedures

Initial Contact: Review the website for current funding opportunities.

Notes: Supplemental materials for proposals should be kept to a minimum and videotapes or letters of endorsement should be avoided altogether. Grant-seekers should allow ample time when requesting funds.

Restrictions

The foundation does not support unrestricted grants for scholarships, fellowships or their functional equivalent; grants for buildings, renovation or equipment; college-based programs for pre-college youth, including partnerships with public school systems; large, complex technological systems, infrastructure development or computer hardware; grants for activities which take place outside the United States; or research or doctoral universities or public institutions of any kind.

Additional Information

Publications: Annual Report; Guidelines

Foundation Officials

John Steele Chalsty: chairman B Port Elizabeth, Republic of South Africa 1933. ED University of the Witwatersrand BSc (1952); University of the Witwatersrand MSc (1954); Harvard University MBA (1957); Harvard University Graduate School of Business Administration MSc (1957). PRIM CORP EMPL senior advisor: Credit Suisse First Boston. CORP AFFIL director: Occidental Petroleum Corp.; director: Equitable Co. Inc.; director: IBP Inc. NONPR AFFIL chairman: New York City Economic Development Corp.; trustee: Saint Barnabas Medical Center; vice president, director: Lincoln Center Theater; director: American Ballet Theater; trustee: Columbia University. CLUB AFFIL Short Hills Club; The Links Club; New York City University Club; Harvard Club.

Kenneth P. Cohen: director

Walter Robert Connor: president B Worcester, MA 1934. ED Hamilton College BA (1956); Princeton University PhD (1961). NONPR AFFIL member: Century Association; member: Phi Beta Kappa; member: American Philosophical Society; member advisory board: Athens College; fellow: American Academy of Arts & Sciences; member: American Philosophical Association. CLUB AFFIL Princeton Club.

Sol Gittleman: director

Donna Heiland, PhD: vice president programs

William Chester Jordan: director OCCUPATION professor of history: Princeton University.

Roland M. Machold: director

Mary Patterson McPherson: director

Richard L. Morrill: director

Helena Rosenwasser: assistant treasurer, controller

Anne M. Tatlock: director B White Plains, NY 1939. ED Vassar College BA (1961); New York University MA Economics (1968). CORP AFFIL director: Merck & Co. Inc.; chairman, chief executive officer, director: Fiduciary Trust Company International; director: For-

tune Brands Inc. NONPR AFFIL chairman nominating committee, trustee: American Ballet Theater; trustee: Vassar College.

Anne M. Tatlock: director B White Plains, NY 1939. ED Vassar College BA (1961); New York University MA Economics (1968). PRIM CORP EMPL chairman, chief executive officer: Fiduciary Trust Co. International. CORP AFFIL director: Fortune Brands Inc.; director: Merck & Co. Inc.; chairman, chief executive officer, director: Fiduciary Trust Company International. NONPR AFFIL trustee: Mayo Foundation; trustee: Vassar College; chairman nominating committee, trustee: American Ballet Theater.

Walter C. Teagle, III: director

Eli Weinberg: treasurer, secretary

Stephen H. Weiss: director

Pauline Yu: director

Grants Analysis

Disclosure Period: fiscal year ending May 31, 2003
Total Grants: $7,906,227*
Number of Grants: 80
Average Grant: $98,828
Highest Grant: $250,000
Typical Range: $25,000 to $200,000
*Note: Giving excludes matching gifts, scholarships, and United Way.

Recent Grants

Note: Grants derived from 2003 Form 990.
General

250,000	HealthCare Chaplaincy, New York, NY
205,000	Marygrove College, Detroit, MI -- towards institutional advancement
203,000	Union Theological Seminary, New York, NY
202,000	Independent College Enterprise, Buckhannon, WV
190,000	General Theological Seminary of the Episcopal Church, New York, NY
170,400	Cedar Crest College, Allentown, PA
170,000	Keuka College, Keuka Park, NY -- towards institutional advancement
160,000	Aquinas College, Grand Rapids, MI
144,000	Lenoir-Rhyne College, Hickory, NC
142,000	Eastern Cluster o Lutheran Seminaries, Ocean City, NJ

A. TEICHERT & SONS

Company Headquarters

3500 American River Dr.
Sacramento, CA 95864
Web: http://www.teichert.com

Company Description

Revenue: US$2.108 billion (2002)
Employees: 2100 (2002)
SIC(s): 1771 Concrete Work, 3200 Stone, Clay & Glass Products, 3273 Ready-Mixed Concrete.

Operating Locations

A. Teichert & Sons (CA--Sacramento)

Teichert Foundation

Giving Contact

Frederick A. Teichert, Executive Director
Teichert Foundation
3500 American River Dr.
Sacramento, CA 95864-5802
Phone: (916)484-3011
E-mail: info@teichertfoundation.org
Web: http://www.teichertfoundation.org

Description

Founded: 1990
EIN: 680212355
Organization Type: Corporate Foundation
Giving Locations: headquarters and operating communities.
Grant Types: General Support.

Financial Summary

Total Giving: $553,799 (fiscal year ending March 31, 2004); $430,920 (fiscal 2003); $457,858 (fiscal 2002)
Giving Analysis: Giving for fiscal 2002 includes: foundation grants to United Way ($2,618)
Assets: $6,447,708 (fiscal 2004); $5,226,446 (fiscal 2003); $5,014,416 (fiscal 2002)
Gifts Received: $1,013,560 (fiscal 2004); $1,009,542 (fiscal 2003); $1,012,068 (fiscal 2002).
Note: In fiscal 2003 and 2004, contributions were received from Teichert Inc.

Typical Recipients

Arts & Humanities: Arts Associations & Councils, Ballet, Film & Video, Libraries, Museums/Galleries, Music, Opera, Public Broadcasting, Theater

Civic & Public Affairs: African American Affairs, Business/Free Enterprise, Chambers of Commerce, Clubs, Community Foundations, Economic Development, Employment/Job Training, Civic & Public Affairs-General, Housing, Law & Justice, Legal Aid, Nonprofit Management, Parades/Festivals, Philanthropic Organizations, Public Policy, Safety, Urban & Community Affairs, Zoos/Aquariums

Education: Afterschool/Enrichment Programs, Business Education, Colleges & Universities, Education Funds, Elementary Education (Public), Education-General, Literacy, Private Education (Precollege), Science/Mathematics Education

Environment: Air/Water Quality, Forestry, Environment-General, Resource Conservation

Health: Cancer, Children's Health/Hospitals, Clinics/Medical Centers, Emergency/Ambulance Services, Heart, Mental Health, Multiple Sclerosis, Prenatal Health Issues, Public Health

International: International Relief Efforts, Missionary/Religious Activities

Religion: Religious Welfare

Science: Science-General, Science Museums, Scientific Centers & Institutes

Social Services: Animal Protection, At-Risk Youth, Child Abuse, Child Welfare, Community Service Organizations, Delinquency & Criminal Rehabilitation, Emergency Relief, Family Planning, Family Services, Food/Clothing Distribution, People with Disabilities, Recreation & Athletics, Scouts, Shelters/Homelessness, Special Olympics, Substance Abuse, United Funds/United Ways, Volunteer Services, YMCA/YWCA/YMHA/YWHA, Youth Organizations

Application Procedures

Initial Contact: Application form required.
Application Requirements: Include a description of organization, amount requested, purpose of funds sought, recently audited financial statement, proof of tax-exempt status, and roster of Board of Directors or Advisory Board.
Deadlines: February 28 and August 29.

Restrictions

The foundation does not support individuals, religious organizations for sectarian purposes, political or lobbying groups, or organizations outside operating areas.

Additional Information

Publications: Application Form

Corporate Officials

Norman E. Eilert: senior vice president, chief financial officer PRIM CORP EMPL senior vice president, chief financial officer: A Teichert & Sons.

Louis V. Riggs: chairman, president, chief executive

officer PRIM CORP EMPL chairman, president, chief executive officer: A Teichert & Sons.

John B. Sandman: executive vice president, chief operating officer PRIM CORP EMPL executive vice president, chief operating officer: A Teichert & Sons.

Foundation Officials

Norman E. Eilert: chief financial officer (see above)
Thomas J. Hammer: director B Birmingham, AL 1932. ED University of California at Berkeley (1955); University of California at Berkeley (1960). PRIM CORP EMPL president, chief executive officer, director: Shasta Linen Supply.
Anne S. Haslam: secretary
Judson T. Riggs: director
Frederick A. Teichert: executive director, director
Melita M. Teichert: director

Grants Analysis

Disclosure Period: fiscal year ending March 31, 2004
Total Grants: $553,799
Number of Grants: 85
Average Grant: $3,617*
Highest Grant: $250,000
Lowest Grant: $75
Typical Range: $1,000 to $5,000
*Note: Average grant figure excludes highest grant.

Recent Grants

Note: Grants derived from 2004 Form 990.
General

250,000	Boys and Girls Clubs of Greater Sacramento, Sacramento, CA
10,135	KVIE, Sacramento, CA
10,000	American Red Cross, Sacramento, CA
10,000	California State University, Sacramento, CA
10,000	Children's Receiving Home of Sacramento, Sacramento, CA
10,000	Rebuilding Together, Sacramento, CA
10,000	Sacramento Philharmonic Orchestra, Sacramento, CA
7,700	Cache Creek Conservancy, Woodland, CA
7,500	Black Oak Mine Unified School District, Georgetown, CA
7,500	Parent Resource Center, Modesto, CA

T. L. L. TEMPLE FOUNDATION

Giving Contact

Millard F. Zeagler, Assistant Executive Director
109 Temple Boulevard, Suite 300
Lufkin, TX 75901
Phone: (936)639-5197
Fax: (936)639-5199

Description

Founded: 1962
EIN: 756037406
Organization Type: General Purpose Foundation
Giving Locations: TX: East Texas Pine Timber Belt area
Grant Types: Capital, General Support, Project, Scholarship.

Donor Information

Founder: In 1894, Thomas Lewis Latane Temple started a sawmill and began acquiring timberland in eastern Texas. Arthur Temple, one of his sons, eventually served as president of Temple Industries. He was later succeeded by his son, Arthur Temple, Jr. By 1973, the Temples owned 50% of Temple Industries stock. That same year, they merged their company into Time, Inc., and in return, the Temple family received 15% of Time stock, worth over $60 million. In 1984, Time spun off Temple-Inland, a holding company of which Arthur Temple, Jr., is chairman.

The T. L. L. Temple Foundation was established in 1962 with donations from the late Georgia T. Munz and the late Katherine S. Temple.

Financial Summary

Total Giving: $14,379,836 (fiscal year ending November 30, 2003); $15,014,915 (fiscal 2001)
Giving Analysis: Giving for fiscal 2003 includes: foundation grants to United Way ($35,000); foundation matching gifts ($49,730); foundation scholarships ($156,668); fiscal 2001: foundation scholarships ($55,300); foundation matching gifts ($60,550); foundation grants to United Way ($65,000)
Assets: $296,817,872 (fiscal 2003); $319,332,383 (fiscal 2001)
Gifts Received: $100,000 (fiscal 1994); $100,000 (fiscal 1993). Note: Contributions were received from the estate of Katherine S. Temple.

Typical Recipients

Arts & Humanities: Arts Associations & Councils, Historic Preservation, History & Archaeology, Libraries, Museums/Galleries, Music, Opera, Performing Arts, Theater
Civic & Public Affairs: Chambers of Commerce, Clubs, Employment/Job Training, Civic & Public Affairs-General, Housing, Municipalities/Towns, Native American Affairs, Parades/Festivals, Public Policy, Safety, Urban & Community Affairs, Women's Affairs, Zoos/Aquariums
Education: Agricultural Education, Arts/Humanities Education, Business Education, Colleges & Universities, Continuing Education, Elementary Education (Private), Elementary Education (Public), Engineering/Technological Education, Environmental Education, Faculty Development, Education-General, Medical Education, Minority Education, Preschool Education, Private Education (Precollege), Public Education (Precollege), Science/Mathematics Education, Special Education, Student Aid, Vocational & Technical Education
Environment: Environment-General, Resource Conservation, Wildlife Protection
Health: Alzheimer's Disease, Cancer, Children's Health/Hospitals, Clinics/Medical Centers, Emergency/Ambulance Services, Eyes/Blindness, Health Organizations, Heart, Hospices, Hospitals, Hospitals (University Affiliated), Kidney, Medical Rehabilitation, Medical Research, Mental Health, Prenatal Health Issues, Research/Studies Institutes, Single-Disease Health Associations, Transplant Networks/Donor Banks
International: International Affairs, International Relief Efforts
Religion: Churches, Ministries, Religious Organizations, Religious Welfare, Synagogues/Temples
Science: Science Museums, Scientific Centers & Institutes
Social Services: Animal Protection, Camps, Community Centers, Community Service Organizations, Counseling, Crime Prevention, Day Care, Delinquency & Criminal Rehabilitation, Domestic Violence, Family Planning, Family Services, Food/Clothing Distribution, People with Disabilities, Recreation & Athletics, Scouts, Senior Services, Shelters/Homelessness, Social Services-General, Special Olympics, Substance Abuse, United Funds/United Ways, Veterans, Volunteer Services, YMCA/YWCA/YMHA/YWHA, Youth Organizations

Application Procedures

Initial Contact: Prospective applicants should send a written request to the foundation.
Application Requirements: Applicants should provide the name, address, phone number, charter, articles of incorporation; a copy of constitution and by-laws; copy of exemption letter signed by an authorized office of the organization; names and addresses of officers and directors; a copy of the latest Form 990-PF including Schedule A (if applicable); a copy of the most recent annual audit with independent auditor's report; a detailed copy of the operating budget for the current fiscal year; a brief, but factual resume of the operations of the applicant; and an explanation of the request, with evidence of need.
Deadlines: None.
Review Process: The foundation board meets as case load demands.

Restrictions

The foundation gives only to governmental units, exempt under the Internal Revenue Code, or to nonprofit, charitable organizations having exempt status under Section 501(c)(3) of the Internal Revenue Code evidencing that it is such an organization and is not classified as a "Private Foundation."

No grants are made to churches, religious organizations, or other entities for the propagation of religious faith and/or practices. Grants are also not made to individuals for scholarships, research, or other purposes.

Foundation Officials

Ward R. Burke: trustee
A. Wayne Corley: executive director
Arthur Temple, Jr.: chairman, trustee B Texarkana, AR 1920. ED Williams College; University of Texas (1937-1938). PRIM CORP EMPL director: Contractor's Supplies INC. CORP AFFIL director: Texarkana National Bankshares; director: Temple-Inland Properties Inc.; executive vice president, director: Temple-White Co.; director, chairman emeritus: Temple-Inland Inc.; director: Temple-Eastex Inc.; director: Temple-Inland Financial Services Inc.; director: Lumbermans Investment Corp.; director: Sunbelt Insurance Co.; director: Lufkin Block. NONPR AFFIL director: Saint Michael Hospital Foundation; director: Southern Forest Products Association; director: National Park Foundation; director: Lumberman Merchants Association; director: National Forest Products Association; member: Delta Kappa Epsilon; president, director: John E. Gray Institute; trustee: American Forest Products Association. CLUB AFFIL Crown Colony Country Club.
W. Temple Webber, Jr.: trustee
M. F. Zeagler: assistant executive director

Grants Analysis

Disclosure Period: fiscal year ending November 30, 2003
Total Grants: $14,138,438*
Number of Grants: 91
Average Grant: $65,455*
Highest Grant: $2,637,479
Lowest Grant: $1,000
Typical Range: $25,000 to $125,000
*Note: Giving excludes United Way, scholarships, and matching gifts. Average grant excludes six highest grants ($8,574,760).

Recent Grants

Note: Grants derived from fiscal 2001 Form 990.
Library-Related

464,460	Kurth Memorial Library, Lufkin, TX -- construct new library facility
154,261	Temple Memorial Library and Archives, Diboll, TX -- for archives budget
117,520	Temple Memorial Library and Archives, Diboll, TX -- for budget deficit
55,467	J.R. Huffman Public Library, Hemphill, TX -- for furnishings
25,000	Tyler County Public Library, Woodville, TX -- expansion project

General

3,337,248	Memorial Medical Center of East Texas, Lufkin, TX -- for equipment, software and therapeutic pool
2,500,000	Alzheimer's Disease and Related Disorders Association, Chicago, IL -- Temple Discovery Awards

2,244,138	Stephen F. Austin State University, Nacogdoches, TX -- for the College of Forestry and ecosystem studies
1,423,598	Methodist Retirement Communities, Lufkin, TX -- expansion of the Arbor Facility
500,000	St. Stephen's Episcopal School, Austin, TX -- for renovations, housing facilities and dorms
268,000	St. Cyprian's Episcopal School, Lufkin, TX -- scholarship assistance
250,000	Texas Children's Hospital, Houston, TX -- building for children's capital campaign
246,484	Buckner Baptist Benevolence, Beaumont, TX -- for Buckner Family Place
183,167	Memorial Medical Center of East Texas, Lufkin, TX -- to renovate the share van
150,840	Nacogdoches Treatment Center for Handicapped Children and Adults, Nacogdoches, TX -- for budget deficit

TEMPLE-INLAND INC.

Company Headquarters
303 S. Temple Dr.
Drawer N
Diboll, TX 75941
Web: http://www.templeinland.com

Company Description
Founded: 1983
Ticker: TIN
Exchange: NYSE
Revenue: US$4.767 billion (2004)
Profit: US$165 million (2004)
Employees: 18000 (2003)
Fortune Rank: 405, per FORTUNE Magazine's list of 500 Largest U.S. Corporations (2004).

Temple-Inland Foundation

Giving Contact
M. Richard Warner, Vice President
Temple-Inland Foundation
1300 South Mopac
Austin, TX 78749
Phone: (512)434-8485
Web: http://www.templeinland.com

Description
EIN: 751977109
Organization Type: Corporate Foundation
Giving Locations: headquarters and operating communities.
Grant Types: Employee Matching Gifts, General Support, Scholarship.
Note: The foundation matches contributions to charitable organizations made by employees and retirees (employees may contribute a minimum of $25 up to $3,000); Employee matching gift ratio: 3 to 1 for each dollar on the first $1,000, Employee matching gift ratio: 2 to 1 on the second $1,000, and Employee matching gift ratio: 1 to 1 on the third $1,000.

Financial Summary
Total Giving: $5,309,168 (fiscal year ending June 30, 2003); $4,292,223 (fiscal 2002); $4,154,852 (fiscal 2001)
Giving Analysis: Giving for fiscal 2001 includes: foundation grants to United Way ($388,841); foundation scholarships ($1,138,250); foundation ($2,627,761)
Assets: $3,095,244 (fiscal 2003); $582,585 (fiscal 2002); $400,000 (fiscal 2001)
Gifts Received: $709,225 (fiscal 2003); $4,220,000 (fiscal 2002); $3,812,000 (fiscal 2001). Note: In fiscal

2003, contributions were received from Temple-Inland Forest Products Corp.

Typical Recipients
Arts & Humanities: Arts Associations & Councils, Arts Centers, Ethnic & Folk Arts, Arts & Humanities-General, Libraries, Museums/Galleries, Performing Arts, Theater
Civic & Public Affairs: African American Affairs, Clubs, Community Foundations, Employment/Job Training, Civic & Public Affairs-General, Housing, Law & Justice, Municipalities/Towns, Public Policy, Safety, Urban & Community Affairs, Zoos/Aquariums
Education: Business Education, Colleges & Universities, Education Associations, Education Funds, Education Reform, Elementary Education (Private), Engineering/Technological Education, Education-General, Gifted & Talented Programs, Literacy, Preschool Education, Private Education (Precollege), Public Education (Precollege), Religious Education, Secondary Education (Private), Secondary Education (Public), Vocational & Technical Education
Environment: Forestry, Environment-General, Resource Conservation, Wildlife Protection
Health: Cancer, Children's Health/Hospitals, Clinics/Medical Centers, Health Funds, Health Organizations, Hospices, Hospitals, Medical Research, Prenatal Health Issues, Research/Studies Institutes, Single-Disease Health Associations
Religion: Religious Organizations, Religious Welfare, Seminaries
Science: Science Museums
Social Services: Camps, Child Abuse, Child Welfare, Community Service Organizations, Crime Prevention, Emergency Relief, Family Services, Food/Clothing Distribution, People with Disabilities, Recreation & Athletics, Shelters/Homelessness, Substance Abuse, United Funds/United Ways, Volunteer Services, YMCA/YWCA/YMHA/YWHA, Youth Organizations

Application Procedures
Initial Contact: Request application form, then send a written request.
Application Requirements: Submit a completed application form, a description of organization; amount requested; purpose of funds sought; recently audited financial statements; proof of tax-exempt status.
Deadlines: None.

Restrictions
Does not provide support to individuals; fraternal or veterans organizations; political or lobbying groups; or religious organizations.

Additional Information
Inland Container, a subsidiary, also maintains a foundation.
Publications: Application Form

Foundation Officials
Kenneth M. Jastrow, II: director B 1947. ED University of Texas BA (1970); University of Texas MBA (1971). PRIM CORP EMPL president, chief operating officer: Temple-Inland Inc. ADD CORP EMPL chairman, president: Lumbermans Investment Corp. CORP AFFIL chairman, chief executive officer: Temple-Inland Financial Services Inc.; chairman, chief executive officergroup vice president financial services: Temple-Inland Mortgage Corp.; chairman: Knutson Mortgage Corp.; chairman: Guaranty Federal Bank FSB; director: Inland Paperboard Packaging; chairman: Capitol Mortgage Bankers Inc.
Arthur Temple, III: director B Texarkana, AR April 08, 1920. ED University of Texas, Austin (1937-1938). PRIM CORP EMPL chairman, chief executive officer: Exeter Investment Co. ADD CORP EMPL treasurer: Demcp Manufacturing Co. CORP AFFIL chairman, director: First Bank & Trust East Texas; director: Guaranty Federal Bank FSB; director: Contractors Supplies Inc.

Grants Analysis
Disclosure Period: fiscal year ending June 30, 2003
Total Grants: $3,513,820*
Number of Grants: 1,369
Average Grant: $2,566
Highest Grant: $116,723
Lowest Grant: $25
Typical Range: $75 to $11,000
*Note: Giving excludes scholarship; gifts to individuals; United Way.

Recent Grants
Note: Grants derived from fiscal 2004 Form 990.
Library-Related

36,550	T L L Temple Memorial Library, Diboll, TX
10,075	Monroe County Public Library, Monroeville, IN

General

222,000	United Way of Rome and Floyd Inc., Rome, GA
130,684	United Way Capital Area, Austin, TX
104,585	United Way of Washington Area, Bogalusa, LA
85,075	Boys and Girls Clubs of Deep East Texas, Nacogdoches, TX
78,554	United Way of Metropolitan Dallas, Dallas, TX
75,045	American Cancer Society (ACS), Lufkin, TX
70,000	Orange County United Way, Orange, TX
61,750	Model High School, Rome, GA
55,000	Birmingham-Southern College, Birmingham, AL
46,000	United Way of South Texas, McAllen, TX

HERBERT A. TEMPLETON FOUNDATION

Giving Contact
Ruth B. Richmond, President
1717 SW Park Avenue
Portland, OR 97201
Phone: (503)223-0036

Description
Founded: 1955
EIN: 930505586
Organization Type: Private Foundation
Giving Locations: OR
Grant Types: General Support, Operating Expenses, Project, Seed Money.

Donor Information
Founder: the late Herbert A. Templeton, members of the Templeton family

Financial Summary
Total Giving: $396,595 (2003); $521,350 (2001)
Assets: $15,941,627 (2003); $15,469,460 (2001)
Gifts Received: $301,481 (1999); $36,814 (1995); $2,734,074 (1994). Note: In 1999, contributions were received from the estate of Mr. Bryson. In 1994, contributions were received from Hall R. Templeton.

Typical Recipients
Arts & Humanities: Arts Associations & Councils, Arts Centers, Arts Outreach, Ballet, Community Arts, Ethnic & Folk Arts, Arts & Humanities-General, Historic Preservation, Libraries, Museums/Galleries, Music, Opera, Performing Arts, Theater
Civic & Public Affairs: Civil Rights, Civic & Public Affairs-General, Housing, Legal Aid, Urban & Community Affairs, Women's Affairs
Education: Afterschool/Enrichment Programs, Arts/Humanities Education, Colleges & Universities, Education Funds, Education-General, Minority Education, Private Education (Precollege), Public Educa-

tion (Precollege), Science/Mathematics Education, Student Aid

Environment: Environment-General, Resource Conservation

Religion: Religious Organizations, Religious Welfare, Seminaries

Science: Science Museums

Social Services: At-Risk Youth, Camps, Child Welfare, Community Centers, Community Service Organizations, Counseling, Day Care, Domestic Violence, Family Planning, Family Services, Shelters/Homelessness, Substance Abuse, United Funds/United Ways, Volunteer Services, YMCA/YWCA/YMHA/YWHA, Youth Organizations

Application Procedures

Initial Contact: The foundation has no formal grant application procedure or application form. Send a written proposal.

Application Requirements: Include a description of organization; a description of the project for which funding is requested; potential significance to the community; anticipated costs; project budget; sources of actual or potential support; amount requested; proof of tax-exempt status, financial statements, a list of board of directors; and the name, address and telephone number of a contact person. The proposal should be covered by a one-page transmittal letter which summarizes the grant request.

Deadlines: March 15 and September 15.

Restrictions

Does not support individuals, discriminatory organizations, or capital projects. The foundation does not provide loans. The foundation prefers not to fund programs for the elderly, fellowships, medical services, scientific research and technology, parochial education, program related investment, or endowment funds.

Additional Information

Publications: Program Policy Statement (including Application Guidelines)

Foundation Officials

Jane T. Bryson: vice president, trustee

John E. Bryson: member B New York, NY 1943. ED Stanford University BA (1965); Freie University Berlin (1965-1966); Yale University Law School JD (1969). PRIM CORP EMPL chairman, chief executive officer: Edison International. CORP AFFIL director: The Walt Disney Co.; trustee: Western Asset Funds; director: Pacific America Income Shares Inc.; chairman, chief executive officer: Southern California Edison Co.; chairman: Edison Mission Energy; director: Mission Group Inc.; director: Boeing Co. NONPR AFFIL member: Phi Beta Kappa; member: Stanford University Alumni Association; member: District of Columbia Bar Association; member: Oregon Bar Association; member: California Water Rights Law Review Committee; trustee: Claremont University Center; member: California Bar Association; member: California Pollution Control Financing Authority.

Susan Bryson Nadel: member

Terrence Russell Pancoast: secretary, treasurer, trustee B Everett, WA 1942. ED Whitman College AB (1965); Harvard University LLB (1968). PRIM CORP EMPL partner: Stoel Rives Boley Fraser & Wyse. NONPR AFFIL member, board overseers: Whitman College; member: World Affairs Council; director (Portland OR): Planned Parenthood Association; director: Oregon Art Institute; member: Oregon Bar Association; member: American Bar Association.

Henry R. Richmond: assistant scr, trustee, member

Ruth B. Richmond: president, trustee, member

Robert Templeton: member

Loren L. Wyss: trustee

Grants Analysis

Disclosure Period: calendar year ending 2003

Total Grants: $396,595

Number of Grants: 70

Average Grant: $5,666

Highest Grant: $10,000

Lowest Grant: $1,500

Typical Range: $1,000 to $10,000

Recent Grants

Note: Grants derived from 2001 Form 990.

General

20,000	Self-Enhancement Incorporated, Portland, OR
20,000	YMCA Mid-Willamette Valley
15,000	Children's Museum, Boston, MA
15,000	Ethos Inc.
15,000	Outside In, Portland, OR
15,000	Portland Baroque Orchestra, Portland, OR
12,000	Home Youth and Resource Center
10,000	Albina Ministerial Alliance, Portland, OR
10,000	Boys and Girls Aid Society of Oregon, Portland, OR
10,000	CASA for Children, Inc., Portland, OR

TENSION ENVELOPE CORP.

Company Headquarters

819 E. 19th St.
Kansas City, MO 64108
Web: http://www.treco.com

Company Description

Employees: 400 (2003)
SIC(s): 2677 Envelopes.

Operating Locations

Tension Envelope Corp. (CA--Santa Fe Springs; IA--Des Moines; KS--Marysville; MN--Minneapolis; MO--Kansas City; NJ--Hackensack; NC--Winston-Salem; TN--Memphis).
Note: Includes plant locations.

Tension Envelope Foundation

Giving Contact

Eliot S. Berkley, Secretary
819 East 19th Street, 3rd Floor
Kansas City, MO 64108
Phone: (816)471-3800
Fax: (816)283-1498

Description

Founded: 1954
EIN: 446012554
Organization Type: Corporate Foundation
Giving Locations: MO
Grant Types: General Support.

Donor Information

Founder: Tension Envelope Corp.

Financial Summary

Total Giving: $321,170 (fiscal year ending November 30, 2002); $266,410 (fiscal 2001). Note: Contributes through foundation only.

Giving Analysis: Giving for fiscal 2001 includes: foundation scholarships ($15,000); foundation grants to United Way ($70,450); foundation ($180,960)

Assets: $3,081,959 (fiscal 2002); $3,547,307 (fiscal 2001)

Gifts Received: $120,000 (fiscal 1998); $295,500 (fiscal 1997); $267,000 (fiscal 1996). Note: In 1997, contributions were received from Tension Envelope Corp.

Typical Recipients

Arts & Humanities: Arts Associations & Councils, Arts Centers, Arts Funds, Arts Institutes, Ballet, Community Arts, Dance, Historic Preservation, Libraries, Museums/Galleries, Music, Public Broadcasting, Theater

Civic & Public Affairs: Botanical Gardens/Parks, Business/Free Enterprise, Community Foundations, Economic Development, Ethnic Organizations, Civic & Public Affairs-General, Housing, Legal Aid, Native American Affairs, Professional & Trade Associations, Urban & Community Affairs, Women's Affairs, Zoos/Aquariums

Education: Afterschool/Enrichment Programs, Arts/Humanities Education, Business Education, Business-School Partnerships, Colleges & Universities, Community & Junior Colleges, Continuing Education, Economic Education, Education Funds, Education Reform, Environmental Education, Education-General, International Studies, Literacy, Minority Education, Private Education (Precollege), Public Education (Precollege), Special Education, Student Aid, Vocational & Technical Education

Environment: Environment-General

Health: AIDS/HIV, Children's Health/Hospitals, Clinics/Medical Centers, Health Organizations, Hospices, Hospitals, Mental Health, Public Health, Transplant Networks/Donor Banks

International: Foreign Arts Organizations, International Affairs, International Organizations, International Relations, International Relief Efforts, Missionary/Religious Activities

Religion: Churches, Jewish Causes, Religious Organizations, Religious Welfare, Social/Policy Issues, Synagogues/Temples

Social Services: Child Welfare, Community Centers, Community Service Organizations, Crime Prevention, Day Care, Domestic Violence, Family Planning, Family Services, People with Disabilities, Recreation & Athletics, Senior Services, Sexual Abuse, Shelters/Homelessness, Social Services-General, Substance Abuse, United Funds/United Ways, Volunteer Services, YMCA/YWCA/YMHA/YWHA, Youth Organizations

Application Procedures

Initial Contact: Send a brief letter of request.

Application Requirements: Include a description of organization activities, amount of support requested, purpose of funds sought, a copy of tax-exempt certificate, and a copy of the budget.

Deadlines: None.

Decision Notification: Foundation reviews requests as received and will notify applicants.

Restrictions

Grants are not made to individuals.

Corporate Officials

Eugene Bertram Berkley: chairman, director B Kansas City, MO 1923. ED Duke University BA (1948); Harvard University Graduate School of Business Administration MBA (1950). PRIM CORP EMPL chairman, director: Tension Envelope Corp. CORP AFFIL director: Tension Envelope Corp. New York; director: Reference Press. NONPR AFFIL director: National Youth Information Network; director: Travelfest; director: National Minority Supplier Development Council Inc.; advisory board: National Parks & Conservation Association; director: Institute Entrepreneurial Leadership Inc.; advisory board: National History Museum; member: Flexographic Technology Association; Business Roundtable Apartment Social Service; member: Envelope Manufacturer Association America. CLUB AFFIL Oakwood Country Club; Homestead Country Club.

Richard L. Berkley: treasurer, secretary, director B 1931. PRIM CORP EMPL treasurer, secretary, director: Tension Envelope Corp.

William S. Berkley: president, chief executive officer, director B Kansas City, MO 1956. ED Colorado

College BA (1974-1978); Dartmouth College Amos Tuck Graduate School of Business Administration (1979-1981). PRIM CORP EMPL president, chief executive officer, director: Tension Envelope Corp. CORP AFFIL director: Reference Press.

Walter L. Hiersteiner: vice chairman B Des Moines, IA 1918. ED University of Iowa BA (1939); Harvard University LLB (1942). PRIM CORP EMPL vice chairman: Tension Envelope Corp.

Foundation Officials

Eliot S. Berkley: secretary
Eugene Bertram Berkley: treasurer (see above)
Richard L. Berkley: president (see above)
William S. Berkley: director (see above)
Walter L. Hiersteiner: vice president (see above)
Abraham E. Margolin: director B Saint Joseph, MO October 16, 1907. ED Washington University JD; Washington University LLD. PRIM CORP EMPL attorney: Gage & Tucker. CORP AFFIL director: UMB Mortgage Co.; director: Tension Envelope Corp. NONPR AFFIL member: United States Supreme Court Historical Society; member: World Jewish Congress; member board governors: Research Mental Health Foundation; life member: Truman Medicine Center; member: Metropolitan Kansas City Bar ASN; member: Missouri Bar Association; life member: Menorah Medical Center; member: Heritage Foundation; director, vice president: Jewish Federation Greater Kansas City; member board governors: Hebrew Academy Kansas City; member board governors: City Trust Kansas City; member: Fed Bar Association; member: Cato Institute; member: ATLA; president council, fellow: Brandeis University; governor: American Royal Association; member advisory board: Anti-Defamation League B'nai B'rith; member national executive council: American Joint Distribution Committee; member: American Judicature Society; member: American Jewish Congress; member: American Bar Association; member national executive council: American Jewish Committee. CLUB AFFIL Oakwood Country Club; Kansas City Club.

Grants Analysis

Disclosure Period: fiscal year ending November 30, 2002
Total Grants: $235,720*
Number of Grants: 116
Average Grant: $1,385*
Highest Grant: $76,500
Lowest Grant: $200
Typical Range: $250 to $5,000
*Note: Giving excludes scholarships and United Way. Average grant figure excludes highest grant.

Recent Grants

Note: Grants derived from fiscal 2003 Form 990.

Library-Related
5,000	Kansas City Public Library, Kansas City, MO
2,500	Johnson County Library Foundation, Shawnee Mission, KS

General
70,000	Jewish Federation of Greater Kansas City, Overland Park, KS
55,000	Heart of America United Way, Kansas City, MO
10,000	Jewish Federation of Greater Kansas City, Overland Park, KS
10,000	New Reform Temple, Kansas City, MO
10,000	Village Shalom, Overland Park, KS
6,000	Greater Twin Cities United Way, Minneapolis, MN
6,000	United Way of Central Iowa, Des Moines, IA
5,000	Bank Street College, New York, NY
5,000	Metropolitan Community Colleges, Kansas City, MO
5,000	Pembroke Hill, Kansas City, MO

TERUMO MEDICAL CORP.

Company Headquarters
Somerset, NJ

Company Description
Employees: 500
SIC(s): 3841 Surgical & Medical Instruments, 5122 Drugs, Proprietaries & Sundries.
Parent Company: Terumo Corp., 44-1 2-chome Hatagaya, Shibuya-ku, Tokyo, Japan

Operating Locations
Terumo Medical Corp. (NJ--Somerset); Terumo Medical Factory (MD--Elkton); Terumo Medical-Miami (FL--Miami)

Nonmonetary Support
Type: Donated Products; In-kind Services; Loaned Executives

Giving Contact
Joseph Cupini, Manager, General Affairs
950 Elkton Blvd.
Elkton, MD 21921
Phone: 800-283-7866
Fax: (410)392-7218
E-mail: joe.cupini@terumomedical.com
Web: http://www.terumomedical.com

Description
Organization Type: Corporate Giving Program
Giving Locations: headquarters area only.
Grant Types: Capital, General Support.

Typical Recipients
Arts & Humanities: Libraries, Public Broadcasting
Civic & Public Affairs: Economic Development, Civic & Public Affairs-General, Professional & Trade Associations, Urban & Community Affairs
Education: Business Education, Colleges & Universities, Community & Junior Colleges, Elementary Education (Private), Education-General
Health: Health-General, Hospitals
Social Services: Community Service Organizations, Family Planning, Substance Abuse, Youth Organizations

Corporate Officials
Ronald DeVore: chairman, president, chief executive officer PRIM CORP EMPL chairman, president, chief executive officer: Terumo Med Corp.

TETLEY U.S.A. INC.

Company Headquarters
100 Commerce Dr.
Shelton, CT 06484
Web: http://www.tetley.com

Company Description
Founded: 1995
Former Name: Tetley, Inc.
Employees: 1,000
SIC(s): 2095 Roasted Coffee, 2099 Food Preparations Nec.
Parent Company: Tetley Group Ltd., 325 Oldfield Lane North, Greenford, United Kingdom

Operating Locations
Bustelo Coffee Roasting Co. (NY--Bronx); Southern Tea Co. (GA--Marietta); Tetley U.S.A., Inc. (CT--Shelton; FL; GA; MO; NY; PA)

Nonmonetary Support
Type: Loaned Employees

Giving Contact
Contributions Coordinator
PO Box 856
Shelton, CT 06484-0856
Phone: (203)929-9200
Fax: (203)925-0512
Web: http://www.tetleyusa.com

Description
Organization Type: Corporate Giving Program
Giving Locations: primarily headquarters and operating communities; limited support nationally.
Grant Types: Employee Matching Gifts, General Support, Multiyear/Continuing Support.

Typical Recipients
Arts & Humanities: Arts Centers, Community Arts, Dance, Historic Preservation, Libraries, Museums/Galleries, Music, Performing Arts, Public Broadcasting
Civic & Public Affairs: Economic Development, Safety
Education: Colleges & Universities
Health: Hospitals, Medical Research, Mental Health, Single-Disease Health Associations
Social Services: Community Centers, Community Service Organizations, Domestic Violence, Senior Services, Substance Abuse, United Funds/United Ways, Youth Organizations

Application Procedures
Initial Contact: Send a brief letter of inquiry in spring or fall.
Application Requirements: Include a description of organization, amount and purpose of funds sought, and proof of tax-exempt status.

Restrictions
Program does not support political or religious groups; groups which receive contributions from United Way offices to which the company has made a contribution; or groups that do not qualify as exempt under section 501(c)(3) of the Internal Revenue Code, unless there is an overriding community interest involved.

Corporate Officials
Leon Allen: chairman, chief financial officer PRIM CORP EMPL chairman: Tetley USA, Inc.
Charles McCarthy: president, chief executive officer PRIM CORP EMPL president, chief executive officer: Tetley USA, Inc.
John Petrizzo: vice president, chief financial officer PRIM CORP EMPL vice president, chief financial officer: Tetley U.S.A.

Grants Analysis
Typical Range: $100 to $5,000

JAMES H. AND ALICE TEUBERT CHARITABLE TRUST

Giving Contact
Jimelle Bowen, Executive Director
PO Box 2131
Huntington, WV 25722
Phone: (304)525-6337

Description
Founded: 1987
EIN: 556101813
Organization Type: Private Foundation
Giving Locations: WV: Cabell County, Wayne County
Grant Types: General Support.

Financial Summary

Total Giving: $1,172,403 (fiscal year ending September 30, 2004); $1,203,805 (fiscal 2001)
Assets: $19,363,821 (fiscal 2004); $20,598,072 (fiscal 2001)
Gifts Received: $13,414,860 (fiscal 1994)

Typical Recipients

Arts & Humanities: Libraries, Theater
Civic & Public Affairs: Civic & Public Affairs-General
Education: Colleges & Universities, Education Funds, Education-General, Public Education (Precollege), Special Education
Health: Diabetes, Eyes/Blindness, Health Organizations, Hospitals
International: Health Care/Hospitals
Religion: Religious Welfare
Science: Scientific Research
Social Services: People with Disabilities, Recreation & Athletics, Special Olympics, YMCA/YWCA/YMHA/YWHA, Youth Organizations

Application Procedures

Initial Contact: Send letter requesting application form.
Application Requirements: Include a description of organization, amount requested, purpose of funds sought, recently audited financial statement, and proof of tax-exempt status.
Deadlines: March1 for April Awards, October1 for November Awards. Board meets in April and October.

Restrictions

Limited to organizations which provide aid to the blind.

Foundation Officials

Dr. Michael A. Fiery: mem
David H. Lunsford: mem
Grant McGuire: chairman
Michael Nuce: member
Dr. Matthew A. Rohrbach: mem

Grants Analysis

Disclosure Period: fiscal year ending September 30, 2004
Total Grants: $1,172,403
Number of Grants: 12
Average Grant: $12,003*
Highest Grant: $852,373
Lowest Grant: $100
Typical Range: $5,000 to $20,000
***Note:** Average grant figure excludes two highest grants ($1,052,373).

Recent Grants

Note: Grants derived from fiscal 2004 Form 990.
General

852,373	Cabell - Wayne Association of the Blind, Huntington, WV -- aid to the blind
200,000	American Foundation for the Blind, New York, NY -- aid to the blind
30,000	West Virginia University Foundation, Morgantown, WV -- aid to the blind
22,408	West Virginia Schools for the Blind, Romney, WV -- aid to the blind
18,000	Faith in Action, Huntington, WV -- aid to the blind
16,435	YMCA, Huntington, NY -- aid to the blind
13,500	Theater by the Blind, New York, NY -- aid to the blind
13,207	Ebenezer Medical Outreach Inc., Huntington, WV -- aid to the blind
5,000	Little League, Barboursville, WV -- aid to the blind
3,000	Wayne County Board of Education, Wayne, WV -- aid to the blind

TEXAS INSTRUMENTS INC.

Company Headquarters

Dallas, TX
Web: http://www.ti.com

Company Description

Founded: 1938
Ticker: TXN
Exchange: NYSE
Revenue: US$12.58 billion (2004)
Profit: US$1.861 billion (2004)
Employees: 34154 (2003)
Fortune Rank: 166, per FORTUNE Magazine's list of 500 Largest U.S. Corporations (2004).
SIC(s): 3399 Primary Metal Products Nec, 3571 Electronic Computers, 3575 Computer Terminals, 3674 Semiconductors & Related Devices.

Operating Locations

Texas Instruments Inc. (AL--Huntsville; AZ--Phoenix; CA--Irvine, Redwood City, San Diego, San Jose, Woodland Hills; CO--Englewood; FL--Clearwater, Maitland, Shalimar; GA--Atlanta; IL--Arlington Heights, Chicago, Schaumburg; IN--Carmel; KS--Shawnee Mission; KY--Versailles; MD--Columbia; MA--Attleboro; MI--Central Lake, Novi; MN--Eden Prairie; MO--St. Louis; NY--East Syracuse, Fishkill, Melville, New York; NC--Apex, Charlotte, Raleigh, Shelby; OH--Beavercreek, Cincinnati, Cleveland, Dayton; TN--Johnson City; TX--Austin, Houston, Lubbock, McKinney, Midland, Plano, Stafford, Temple; VA--Arlington, Falls Church; WA--Bellevue; WI--Waukesha)

Nonmonetary Support

Type: Donated Equipment; Loaned Employees; Loaned Executives
Note: Nonmonetary support is provided under company's direct giving program. The company sponsors equipment cost sharing of $1.2 million with Texas colleges

Texas Instruments Foundation

Giving Contact

Ann Pomykal, Director of Corporate and Foundation Giving
Texas Instruments Foundation
PO Box 660199, M/S 8656
Dallas, TX 75266-0199
Phone: (214)480-3221
Fax: (214)480-6820
Web: http://www.ti.com/corp/docs/company/citizen/index.shtml

Description

EIN: 756038519
Organization Type: Corporate Foundation
Giving Locations: TX: emphasis on Texas-based organizations, Dallas nationally.
Grant Types: Capital, Challenge, Employee Matching Gifts, General Support, Operating Expenses, Research, Scholarship.
Note: Employee matching gift ratio: 1 to 1.

Financial Summary

Total Giving: $6,874,157 (2003); $7,212,571 (2002); $6,799,585 (2001). Note: Contributes through corporate direct giving program and foundation.
Assets: $26,096,383 (2003); $21,172,046 (2002); $23,764,464 (2001)
Gifts Received: $8,000,000 (2003); $8,000,000 (2001); $7,500,000 (2000). Note: The foundation receives contributions from Texas Instruments Inc.

Typical Recipients

Arts & Humanities: Arts Centers, Arts Funds, Dance, Arts & Humanities-General, History & Archaeology, Libraries, Museums/Galleries, Music, Opera, Performing Arts, Public Broadcasting, Theater
Civic & Public Affairs: African American Affairs, Botanical Gardens/Parks, Community Foundations, Economic Development, Economic Policy, Employment/Job Training, Civic & Public Affairs-General, Hispanic Affairs, Minority Business, Nonprofit Management, Women's Affairs, Zoos/Aquariums
Education: Afterschool/Enrichment Programs, Business Education, Colleges & Universities, Community & Junior Colleges, Economic Education, Education Associations, Education Funds, Education Reform, Elementary Education (Private), Elementary Education (Public), Engineering/Technological Education, Faculty Development, Education-General, Health & Physical Education, Literacy, Medical Education, Minority Education, Preschool Education, Private Education (Precollege), Public Education (Precollege), Science/Mathematics Education, Secondary Education (Public), Social Sciences Education, Special Education, Student Aid
Environment: Environment-General
Health: AIDS/HIV, Children's Health/Hospitals, Clinics/Medical Centers, Hospitals, Hospitals (University Affiliated), Medical Research, Nursing Services, Research/Studies Institutes
International: Foreign Educational Institutions
Religion: Ministries, Religious Welfare
Science: Science Museums, Scientific Centers & Institutes
Social Services: Child Abuse, Child Welfare, Community Centers, Community Service Organizations, Counseling, Day Care, Family Services, People with Disabilities, Scouts, Shelters/Homelessness, Substance Abuse, United Funds/United Ways, Volunteer Services, YMCA/YWCA/YMHA/YWHA, Youth Organizations

Application Procedures

Initial Contact: Send a brief proposal of not more than two pages.
Application Requirements: Include a a description of organization, population served, amount requested, purpose of funds sought, how the proposal matches funding interests of the foundation, and proof of tax-exempt status.
Deadlines: None.
Decision Notification: Foundation board meets four times a year: March, June, September, December; applicants will be notified of grant decision within three weeks of meeting. The company contributions board reviews and makes decisions as requests are received.

Restrictions

Foundation does not support individuals, political activities, sectarian or denominational religious organizations, veterans organizations, fraternal or labor organizations, courtesy advertising, benefit entertainment/sponsorships, tax-supported institutions, or donation of Texas Instruments products.

Corporate Officials

Thomas James Engibous: chairman, chief executive officer B Saint Louis, MO 1953. ED Purdue University BSEE (1975); Purdue University MSEE (1976). PRIM CORP EMPL chairman: Texas Instruments Inc. NONPR AFFIL member visitors committee: Purdue University Engineering; trustee: Southern Methodist University; member: Dallas Citizens Council; member: Institute Electrical & Electronics Engineers; member: Business Roundtable; director: Catalyst; member: Business Council.
Richard Templeton: president, chief executive officer B 1958. PRIM CORP EMPL president, chief executive officer: Texas Instruments Inc.

Foundation Officials

Thomas James Engibous: director (see above)
Steve Leven: director
Kun Lin: director
Kevin P. March: treasurer, director
Ann Minnis: grants administrator, director
Liston Michael Rice, Jr.: president, director B Dallas, TX 1927. ED University of Texas (1948-1949).
Phil Ritter: director
Shaunna Sowell: director
Cynthia Stewart: secretary
Jack E. Swindle: chairman, director
Bart Thomas: director
Cynthia Trochu: secretary
Tem West: vice president, director

Grants Analysis

Disclosure Period: calendar year ending 2003
Total Grants: $4,211,392*
Number of Grants: 43
Average Grant: $76,462*
Highest Grant: $1,000,000
Lowest Grant: $1,000
Typical Range: $5,000 to $200,000
***Note:** Giving excludes matching gifts, scholarship, and United Way. Average grant figure excludes highest grant.

Recent Grants

Note: Grants derived from 2003 Form 990.
General

1,300,000	United Way of Metropolitan Dallas, Dallas, TX
1,000,000	University of Texas at Dallas-TETC, Richardson, TX
367,000	Dallas Independent School District-Advanced Placement Program, Dallas, TX
350,000	Southern Methodist University-School of Engineering, Dallas, TX
250,000	University of Texas at El Paso, El Paso, TX
200,000	Children's Medical Center, Dallas, TX
200,000	Dallas Center for the Performing Arts, Dallas, TX
200,000	Dallas Independent School District-3rd Grade Reading Program, Dallas, TX
184,033	Southern Methodist University-TI Institute for Reading Research, Dallas, TX
160,912	Head Start of Greater Dallas-Junkins Center, Dallas, TX

TEXTRON INC.

Company Headquarters

40 Westminster St.
Providence, RI 02903
Web: http://www.textron.com

Company Description

Founded: 1923
Ticker: TXT
Exchange: NYSE
Revenue: US$10.312 billion (2004)
Profit: US$365 million (2004)
Employees: 43000 (2003)
Fortune Rank: 216, per FORTUNE Magazine's list of 500 Largest U.S. Corporations (2004).

Textron Charitable Trust

Giving Contact

Cate M. Roberts, Director, Community Affairs
Textron Inc.
40 Westminster Street
Providence, RI 02903
Phone: (401)457-2430

Web: http://www.textron.com/profile/community.html

Alternate Contact

Anthony Limjuco
National Merit Scholarship Corp.
1560 Sherman Avenue
Suite 200
Evanston, IL 60201
Phone: (847)866-5118

Description

EIN: 256115832
Organization Type: Corporate Foundation
Giving Locations: headquarters and operating communities.
Grant Types: Capital, Employee Matching Gifts, General Support, Scholarship.
Note: Employee matching gift ratio: 2 to 1, up to $7,500 annually, to eligible secondary schools, colleges and universities; arts and cultural organizations; hospital; and environmental, conservation and wildlife groups.

Financial Summary

Total Giving: $3,275,401 (2002); $3,121,045 (2001).
Note: Company gives through charitable trust only.
Giving Analysis: Giving for 2001 includes: foundation scholarships ($418,447); foundation matching gifts ($991,986); foundation grants to United Way ($1,009,479); foundation ($3,665,961)
Assets: $11,409,750 (2002); $13,907,706 (2001)
Gifts Received: $9,130,440 (2000); $5,815,388 (1999); $2,000,000 (1997). Note: Contributions received from Textron Corporation.

Typical Recipients

Arts & Humanities: Arts Appreciation, Arts Associations & Councils, Arts Centers, Arts Funds, Arts Institutes, Arts Outreach, Ballet, Community Arts, Dance, Ethnic & Folk Arts, Historic Preservation, Libraries, Museums/Galleries, Music, Opera, Performing Arts, Public Broadcasting, Theater, Visual Arts
Civic & Public Affairs: Botanical Gardens/Parks, Business/Free Enterprise, Chambers of Commerce, Civil Rights, Community Foundations, Economic Development, Economic Policy, Employment/Job Training, Civic & Public Affairs-General, Housing, Law & Justice, Legal Aid, Municipalities/Towns, Nonprofit Management, Parades/Festivals, Philanthropic Organizations, Professional & Trade Associations, Public Policy, Safety, Urban & Community Affairs, Women's Affairs, Zoos/Aquariums
Education: Arts/Humanities Education, Business Education, Colleges & Universities, Community & Junior Colleges, Economic Education, Education Associations, Education Funds, Education Reform, Engineering/Technological Education, Education-General, International Studies, Legal Education, Literacy, Medical Education, Minority Education, Private Education (Precollege), Public Education (Precollege), Science/Mathematics Education, Social Sciences Education, Student Aid, Vocational & Technical Education
Environment: Air/Water Quality, Environment-General, Resource Conservation, Watershed
Health: Cancer, Children's Health/Hospitals, Emergency/Ambulance Services, Health Policy/Cost Containment, Health Organizations, Hospices, Hospitals, Medical Rehabilitation, Prenatal Health Issues, Single-Disease Health Associations
International: Foreign Educational Institutions, Human Rights, International Affairs, International Organizations, International Peace & Security Issues, International Relations
Religion: Missionary Activities (Domestic), Religious Welfare
Science: Science Exhibits & Fairs, Scientific Centers & Institutes
Social Services: Child Welfare, Community Centers, Community Service Organizations, Counseling, Emergency Relief, Family Planning, Food/Clothing Distribution, Homes, People with Disabilities, Recreation & Athletics, Refugee Assistance, Scouts, Senior Services, Shelters/Homelessness, Social Services-General, Special Olympics, Substance Abuse, United Funds/United Ways, Volunteer Services, Youth Organizations

Application Procedures

Initial Contact: Request an application form or obtain one from the company's web site.
Application Requirements: Submit the completed Textron Grant Application Form with proof of tax-exempt status; list of board members, including affiliations, background, town of residence, and number of times board meets; and financial information, including total organizational budget, most recent independent audit or account review, year-to-date financial statement for current year, and other sources of funding with dollar amounts and whether each source is committed, pending, or anticipated. For capital or project support requests, include a project or capital budget for fiscal year(s).
Deadlines: None.
Evaluative Criteria: Proposals will be evaluated on consistency with focus and mission of Textron's contributions program; purpose and impact of proposed request; and involvement of Textron employees.
Decision Notification: Funding decisions are generally communicated with six to eight weeks.

Restrictions

Does not support organizations without 501(c)(3) status; individuals; political, fraternal, or veterans organizations; religious institutions for sectarian activities; or organizations that discriminate based on race, creed, gender, ethnicity, sexual orientation, disability, or age.

Additional Information

Grant recipients are required to complete a post-grant application form and adhere to terms of the grant. A fiscal and program summary must be submitted upon completion of the project.
Rhode Island Hospital Trust National Bank serves as a corporate trustee of the trust.

Corporate Officials

John D. Butler: executive vice president, chief human resources officer ED Michigan State University. PRIM CORP EMPL executive vice president, chief human resources officer: Textron Inc.

Grants Analysis

Disclosure Period: calendar year ending 2002
Total Grants: $2,181,033*
Number of Grants: 641 (approx)
Average Grant: $3,403
Highest Grant: $225,000
Lowest Grant: $50
Typical Range: $100 to $500 and $1,000 to $60,000
***Note:** Giving excludes matching gifts, scholarships, and United Way.

Recent Grants

Note: Grants derived from 2003 Form 990.
Library-Related

83,333	Providence Public Library, Providence, RI
15,000	Providence Public Library, Providence, RI

General

225,000	Textron Chamber Commerce Academy, Providence, RI
181,379	BHTI Employees Humanity Fund, Ft. Worth, TX
110,000	United Way of Southeaster New England, Providence, RI
109,533	Providence College, Providence, RI
100,000	Duke University, Durham, NC
100,000	Heritage Harbor Museum, Providence, RI
100,000	New York Community Trust, New York, NY

91,750	Community Foundation of the National Capital Region, Washington, DC
75,000	University of Rhode Island, Kingston, RI
60,000	City Year Rhode Island, Providence, RI

W. B. AND CANDACE THOMAN FOUNDATION

Giving Contact

Benjamin O. Schwendener, Jr., President & Secretary
222 N. Washington Sq., Suite 400
Lansing, MI 48933-1800
Phone: (517)377-0710
Fax: (517)484-8286
E-mail: kfl@honigmam.com

Description

Founded: 1968
EIN: 237029842
Organization Type: Private Foundation
Giving Locations: MI: Clinton County, Eaton County, Ingham County
Grant Types: Project, Scholarship, Seed Money.

Donor Information

Founder: the late W. B. Thoman, the late Candace Thoman

Financial Summary

Total Giving: $95,000 (2003)
Assets: $2,709,425 (2003)
Gifts Received: $37,715 (1999); $37,715 (1996); $39,215 (1995). Note: In 1996, contributions were received from the W. B. Thoman Residuary Charitable Lead Trust.

Typical Recipients

Arts & Humanities: Community Arts, Dance, Libraries, Music, Opera, Performing Arts, Theater
Civic & Public Affairs: African American Affairs, Legal Aid
Education: Afterschool/Enrichment Programs, Colleges & Universities, Education Funds, Education-General, Gifted & Talented Programs, International Studies, Literacy, Public Education (Precollege), Special Education
Health: Single-Disease Health Associations
International: International Relief Efforts
Social Services: Child Welfare, Community Service Organizations, Family Services, Youth Organizations

Application Procedures

Initial Contact: Send a brief letter of inquiry.
Application Requirements: Proposals should include a description of the project and its goals and purposes, the total budget for the project, sources of funding, reasons why the project needs to be undertaken, whether professional outside consultants or fundraisers are to be hired and the fees involved, current balance sheet and income statement, a copy of most recent 990, proof of tax-exempt status, and a verification signed by the chief executive officer that he or she has personally examined all of the information in the grant request.
Deadlines: None.

Restrictions

Contributions are made for the education and benefit of young people who are orphans or from very poor families. No support for political organizations, churches, or religious organizations or programs.

Additional Information

Awards grants to organizations that provide education and benefits to young people who are orphans or from very poor families.
Publications: Application Guidelines

Foundation Officials

Richard Earl Chapin: trustee B Danville, IL 1925. ED Wabash College AB (1948); University of Illinois MS (1949); University of Illinois PhD (1954). PRIM CORP EMPL director, libs emeritus, professor emeritus: Michigan State University. NONPR AFFIL member: Association Research Libraries; member: Michigan Library Association; member: ALA. CLUB AFFIL mem: Phi Kappa Phi; mem: Sigma Chi; mem: Blue Key Club.
Louis E. Legg: vice president
James L. Reutter: treasurer
Benjamin O. Schwendener, Jr.: president, secretary
Dorothy Silk: trustee

Grants Analysis

Disclosure Period: calendar year ending 2003
Total Grants: $95,000
Number of Grants: 5
Highest Grant: $39,000
Lowest Grant: $1,000
Typical Range: $5,000 to $20,000

Recent Grants

Note: Grants derived from 2001 Form 990.
General

39,000	Literacy Volunteers of America - Capital Area Literacy Coalition, Lansing, MI -- funding for Succeed Program
28,000	Ingham Intermediate School District, Mason, MI -- funding for gifted and talented program
28,000	Ingham Intermediate School District, Mason, MI -- funding for gifted and talented program
24,000	Ingham County Family Court, Lansing, MI -- funding for summer Tutor Liaison Enrichment Program
22,000	Michigan State University, Lansing, MI -- Gifted and Talented Program
20,500	Michigan State University, Lansing, MI -- Gifted and Talented Program
5,000	Boarshead Theater, Lansing, MI -- funding for playwriting, acting workshops for students
4,000	Happendance, Okemos, MI -- Outreach Education Program
500	Tri-County Planning Commission, Lansing, MI -- Water Festival grant

JOAN AND LEE THOMAS FOUNDATION

Giving Contact

Lee B. Thomas, Director
2602 Grassland Dr.
Louisville, KY 40299-2524
Phone: (502)495-1958

Description

Founded: 1990
EIN: 611166955
Organization Type: Private Foundation
Giving Locations: KY
Grant Types: General Support.

Donor Information

Founder: Established in 1990 by Lee B. Thomas, Jr.

Financial Summary

Total Giving: $959,000 (fiscal year ending June 30, 2002); $909,500 (fiscal 2001)
Assets: $19,815,655 (fiscal 2002); $18,842,166 (fiscal 2001)
Gifts Received: $600,000 (fiscal 2002); $600,000 (fiscal 2001); $400,000 (fiscal 2000). Note: In fiscal 1996 and 2002, contributions were received from Lee B. and Joan E. Thomas.

Typical Recipients

Arts & Humanities: Arts Centers, Libraries, Museums/Galleries, Music, Public Broadcasting
Civic & Public Affairs: African American Affairs, Community Foundations, Economic Policy, First Amendment Issues, Civic & Public Affairs-General, Housing, Law & Justice, Legal Aid, Philanthropic Organizations, Public Policy, Rural Affairs, Urban & Community Affairs, Women's Affairs
Education: Colleges & Universities, Education Funds, Elementary Education (Private), Education-General, Literacy, Preschool Education, Private Education (Precollege), Student Aid
Health: Children's Health/Hospitals, Medical Rehabilitation, Nursing Services
International: International Development, International Environmental Issues, International Peace & Security Issues, International Relations
Religion: Religious Organizations, Religious Welfare, Social/Policy Issues
Social Services: At-Risk Youth, Child Welfare, Community Centers, Community Service Organizations, Family Services, Food/Clothing Distribution, Homes, Scouts, Senior Services, United Funds/United Ways, Youth Organizations

Application Procedures

Initial Contact: The foundation has no formal grant application procedure or application form.
Deadlines: None.

Additional Information

Gifts to charitable organizations in the City of Louisville or for the betterment of the city will be given priority.

Foundation Officials

Glenn E. Thomas: director
Dr. Joan E. Thomas: director
Lee B. Thomas: director

Grants Analysis

Disclosure Period: fiscal year ending June 30, 2002
Total Grants: $959,000
Number of Grants: 24
Average Grant: $22,809*
Highest Grant: $210,000
Lowest Grant: $2,000
Typical Range: $10,000 to $30,000
*Note: Average grant excludes three highest grants ($480,000).

Recent Grants

Note: Grants derived from fiscal 2002 Form 990.

Library-Related

15,000	Louisville Free Public Library Fund, Louisville, KY

General

210,000	Home of Innocents, Louisville, KY
170,000	Center for Women and Families, Louisville, KY
100,000	FCNL Education Fund, Washington, DC
70,000	Bellarmine College, Louisville, KY
50,000	Girl Scouts of Kentuckiana, Inc., Louisville, KY
40,000	Lincoln Foundation, Louisville, KY
40,000	World Resources Institute, Washington, DC
30,000	Neighborhood House, Louisville, KY
30,000	Peace Education Program, Louisville, KY
25,000	Brooklawn, Louisville, KY

THOMAS INDUSTRIES

Company Headquarters
4360 Brownboro Rd., Ste. 300
Louisville, KY 40207
Web: http://www.thomasind.com

Company Description
Founded: 1928
Ticker: TII
Exchange: NYSE
Revenue: US$184.4 million (2001)
Employees: 1070 (2001)
SIC(s): 3563 Air & Gas Compressors, 3645 Residential Lighting Fixtures, 3646 Commercial Lighting Fixtures.

Operating Locations
Thomas Industries (KY--Louisville)

Thomas Foundation

Giving Contact
Phillip J. Stuecker, Vice President & Chief Financial Officer
4360 Brownsboro Rd., Suite 300
Louisville, KY 40207
Phone: (502)893-4600
Fax: (502)895-6618

Description
EIN: 396075230
Organization Type: Corporate Foundation
Giving Locations: IL; KY: Louisville; NY
Grant Types: Capital, Emergency, General Support.

Financial Summary
Total Giving: $37,850 (2003); $42,673 (2001)
Giving Analysis: Giving for 2003 includes: foundation grants to United Way ($1,500); 2001: foundation ($1,113).
Assets: $16,397 (2003); $11,831 (2001)
Gifts Received: $45,000 (2003); $50,000 (2001); $40,000 (2000). Note: In 2001 and 2003, contributions were received from Thomas Industries, Inc. ($50,000).

Typical Recipients
Arts & Humanities: Arts Associations & Councils, Arts Funds, History & Archaeology, Libraries, Museums/Galleries, Music, Performing Arts
Civic & Public Affairs: African American Affairs, Botanical Gardens/Parks, Business/Free Enterprise, Clubs, Community Foundations, Economic Development, Civic & Public Affairs-General, Housing, Professional & Trade Associations, Urban & Community Affairs
Education: Business Education, Colleges & Universities, Community & Junior Colleges, Economic Education, Education Associations, Education Funds, Education-General, Literacy, Public Education (Precollege), Secondary Education (Private), Special Education
Health: Arthritis, Cancer, Children's Health/Hospitals, Emergency/Ambulance Services, Health Funds, Heart, Hospices, Hospitals, Medical Rehabilitation, Multiple Sclerosis, Nursing Services, Prenatal Health Issues, Single-Disease Health Associations
Religion: Jewish Causes, Religious Organizations, Religious Welfare
Science: Scientific Centers & Institutes
Social Services: Camps, Child Welfare, Community Service Organizations, Crime Prevention, Emergency Relief, Family Services, Food/Clothing Distribution, Homes, People with Disabilities, Scouts, Senior Services, Shelters/Homelessness, Special Olympics, United Funds/United Ways, Volunteer Services, YMCA/YWCA/YMHA/YWHA, Youth Organizations

Application Procedures
Initial Contact: Submit a brief letter of inquiry.
Deadlines: October 1.

Corporate Officials
Timothy Charles Brown: chairman, president, chief executive officer, director B Louisville, KY 1950. ED Eastern Kentucky University BBA (1972); University of Louisville MBA (1985). PRIM CORP EMPL chairman, president, chief executive officer, director: Thomas Industries. NONPR AFFIL member: Kentucky Society CPA's; state director: National Association Manufacturer; member: American Institute of CPA's.
Phillip James Stuecker: vice president, chief financial officer, secretary B Louisville, KY 1951. ED University of Louisville (1974); University of Louisville (1987). PRIM CORP EMPL vice president, chief financial officer, secretary: Thomas Industries. NONPR AFFIL member: American Institute CPA's; member: Financial Executives Institute.

Foundation Officials
Timothy Charles Brown: president, chief executive officer (see above)
Phillip James Stuecker: vice president, chief financial officer, secretary (see above)
Roger Whitton: controller
Ronald D. Wiseman: treasurer

Grants Analysis
Disclosure Period: calendar year ending 2003
Total Grants: $36,350*
Number of Grants: 31
Average Grant: $1,173
Highest Grant: $5,000
Lowest Grant: $300
Typical Range: $500 to $3,000
*Note: Giving excludes United Way.

Recent Grants
Note: Grants derived from 2003 Form 990.
General

5,000	Greater Louisville Economic Development, Louisville, KY
5,000	University of Wisconsin Sheboygan Foundation, Sheboygan, WI
4,700	Lincoln Heritage Council Boy Scouts of America, Louisville, KY
3,000	Citizens of Louisville Organized and United Together, Louisville, KY
2,500	University of Louisville Foundation, Louisville, KY
1,500	Metro United Way, Louisville, KY
1,000	Home of the Innocents, Louisville, KY
1,000	Kentucky Council on Economic Education, Louisville, KY
1,000	Louisville Urban League, Louisville, KY
1,000	Sacred Heart Village, Louisville, KY

THOMASTON F.S.B.

Company Headquarters
206 N. Church St.
Thomaston, GA 30286

Thomaston Savings Bank Foundation

Giving Contact
James R. Nicol, Secretary
203 Main St.
Thomaston, CT 06787-0907
Phone: (860)283-4373

Description
Founded: 1997
EIN: 061483909
Organization Type: Corporate Foundation
Giving Locations: CT: Bethlehem, Harwinton, Litchfield, Morris, Plymouth, Thomaston, Watertown, Woodbury
Grant Types: General Support.

Financial Summary
Total Giving: $197,390 (2003)
Assets: $4,105,355 (2003)
Gifts Received: $506,048 (2000). Note: In 2000, contributions were received from Thomaston Savings Bank.

Typical Recipients
Arts & Humanities: Libraries, Opera
Civic & Public Affairs: Civic & Public Affairs-General, Housing, Professional & Trade Associations, Safety
Education: Afterschool/Enrichment Programs, Arts/Humanities Education, Elementary Education (Public), Preschool Education, Private Education (Precollege), Public Education (Precollege), Secondary Education (Private), Secondary Education (Public)
Religion: Churches, Religion-General, Religious Organizations
Social Services: Community Service Organizations, Domestic Violence, Food/Clothing Distribution, Recreation & Athletics, Special Olympics, Substance Abuse, Volunteer Services

Application Procedures
Initial Contact: Submit written proposal.
Application Requirements: Include page budget, and a copy of the IRS determination letter.
Deadlines: None.

Foundation Officials
Walter Barber: trustee
Paul Broomhead: trustee
David Carlson: treasurer
Peter Dahlin: president, trustee
Francis Kaminski: chairman, trustee
James Kaniewski: trustee
David Merchant: trustee
James Nicol: secretary
Roger Perreault: trustee
George Seabourne: trustee

Grants Analysis
Disclosure Period: calendar year ending 2003
Total Grants: $197,390
Number of Grants: 96
Average Grant: $1,956*
Highest Grant: $11,610
Lowest Grant: $500
Typical Range: $500 to $3,000
*Note: Average grant figure excludes highest grant.

Recent Grants
Note: Grants derived from 2003 Form 990.
Library-Related

3,000	Watertown Library Association, Watertown, CT
2,500	Thomaston Public Library, Thomaston, CT
General	
11,610	Thomaston Volunteer Fire Department, Thomaston, CT
7,500	Morris Volunteer Fire Department, Morris, CT
7,400	Watertown Fire Department, Watertown, CT
5,395	Bethlehem Fireman's Association Inc., Bethlehem, CT
5,185	Harwinton Westside Volunteer Fire Company Inc., Harwinton, CT
5,000	Bunker Hill Congregational Church, Waterbury, CT

5,000	Thomaston Opera House, Thomaston, CT
3,795	St. Mary School
3,750	Thomaston Volunteer Fire Department Explorer 245, Thomaston, CT
3,583	Swift Middle School Library Media Center, Oakville, CT

THOMASVILLE FURNITURE INDUSTRIES INC.

Company Headquarters
Thomasville, NC
Web: http://www.thomasville.com

Company Description
Employees: 7,000
SIC(s): 2511 Wood Household Furniture, 2512 Upholstered Household Furniture, 2514 Metal Household Furniture.
Parent Company: Armstrong World Industries Inc., Lancaster, PA, United States

Operating Locations
Thomasville Furniture Industries Inc. (MS--Fayette; NC--Statesville, Thomasville; TN--Johnson City; VA--Brookneal, Carysbrook)

Nonmonetary Support
Type: Donated Equipment; Donated Products; Loaned Employees; Loaned Executives
Volunteer Programs: Thomasville employees volunteer in Communities in Schools and Chamber programs and in local school systems and YMCA's.

Thomasville Furniture Industries Foundation

Giving Contact
Vickie Holder, General Manager
PO Box 339
Thomasville, NC 27360
Phone: (336)472-4000
Fax: (336)472-4085
E-mail: vholder@thomasville.com

Description
Founded: 1960
EIN: 566047870
Organization Type: Corporate Foundation
Giving Locations: NC
Grant Types: Award, Endowment, General Support.

Donor Information
Founder: Thomasville Furniture Industries, Inc.

Financial Summary
Total Giving: $300,932 (2002); $367,423 (2001). Note: Contributes through corporate direct giving program and foundation.
Giving Analysis: Giving for 2002 includes: foundation scholarships ($72,450); foundation grants to United Way ($234,937); 2001: foundation ($51,190); foundation scholarships ($70,050); foundation grants to United Way ($246,183)
Assets: $3,645,483 (2002); $4,483,081 (2001)
Gifts Received: $2,257 (1997). Note: Gifts received in 1997 include those from a Thomasville employee.

Typical Recipients
Arts & Humanities: Arts Associations & Councils, Arts Festivals, Community Arts, Libraries, Museums/Galleries, Music, Performing Arts, Theater

Civic & Public Affairs: Economic Development, Civic & Public Affairs-General, Housing, Legal Aid, Urban & Community Affairs
Education: Arts/Humanities Education, Colleges & Universities, Community & Junior Colleges, Education Funds, Elementary Education (Private), Elementary Education (Public), Environmental Education, Education-General, International Studies, Literacy, Minority Education, Private Education (Precollege), Public Education (Precollege), Science/Mathematics Education, Secondary Education (Public), Student Aid, Vocational & Technical Education
Health: Emergency/Ambulance Services, Hospitals, Medical Research, Preventive Medicine/Wellness Organizations
Religion: Religious Welfare
Science: Scientific Centers & Institutes
Social Services: Animal Protection, Child Welfare, Community Centers, Community Service Organizations, Crime Prevention, Family Services, Recreation & Athletics, United Funds/United Ways, YMCA/YWCA/YMHA/YWHA, Youth Organizations

Application Procedures
Initial Contact: Send a letter of request.
Deadlines: None.

Restrictions
Does not support individuals, religious organizations for sectarian purposes, political or lobbying groups, or organizations outside operating areas. Scholarships are only provided to children of employees.

Additional Information
Trust(s): Wachovia Bank, NA

Corporate Officials
Ronald G. Berrier: vice president, treasurer, assistant secretary B Winston-Salem, NC 1943. ED High Point College (1965). PRIM CORP EMPL vice president, treasurer, assistant secretary: Thomasville Furniture Industries Inc.
D. Paul Dascoli: chief financial officer, vice president B Providence, RI 1960. ED Providence College (1982). PRIM CORP EMPL chief financial officer, vice president: Thomasville Furniture Industries Inc.
Christian J. Pfaff: president, chief executive officer PRIM CORP EMPL chairman, president, chief executive officer, director: Thomasville Furniture Industries Inc.

Foundation Officials
Vickie Holder: general manager, administrator operations

Grants Analysis
Disclosure Period: calendar year ending 2002
Total Grants: $300,932*
Number of Grants: 126
Average Grant: $2,388
Highest Grant: $25,000
Typical Range: $500 to $5,000
*Note: Giving includes scholarships; United Way.

Recent Grants
Note: Grants derived from 2003 Form 990.
General

51,644	United Way of Davidson County, Lexington, NC
50,000	United Way of Davidson County, Lexington, NC
50,000	YMCA for Capi, Chicago, IL
10,506	United Way of Davidson County, Lexington, NC
10,000	United Way of Catawba County, Hickory, NC
10,000	United Way of Forsyth County, Winston-Salem, NC
10,000	United Way of Iredell County, Statesville, NC
9,279	United Way of Davidson County, Lexington, NC
8,055	United Way of Davidson County, Lexington, NC
7,108	United Way of Davidson County, Lexington, NC

THOMPSON CHARITABLE FOUNDATION

Giving Contact
Monica Luke, Foundation Manager
4823 Old Kingston Pike
PO Box 10516
Knoxville, TN 37939-0516
Phone: (865)588-0491

Description
Founded: 1987
EIN: 581754763
Organization Type: General Purpose Foundation
Giving Locations: KY: Bell County, Clay County, Laurel County, Leslie County; TN: Anderson County, Blount County, Knox County, Scott County; VA: Buchanan County, Tazewell County
Grant Types: Capital, Department, General Support, Scholarship.

Donor Information
Founder: Established in 1987 by the estate of B. Ray Thompson Sr.

Financial Summary
Total Giving: $3,010,514 (fiscal year ending June 30, 2003); $2,029,473 (fiscal 2001)
Giving Analysis: Giving for fiscal 2001 includes: foundation scholarships ($50,000)
Assets: $39,451,395 (fiscal 2003); $46,344,119 (fiscal 2001)
Gifts Received: $894,818 (fiscal 1997); $2,784,717 (fiscal 1994); $4,353,795 (fiscal 1993)

Typical Recipients
Arts & Humanities: Arts Funds, Arts Institutes, Dance, Film & Video, Arts & Humanities-General, Libraries, Museums/Galleries, Music, Theater
Civic & Public Affairs: Botanical Gardens/Parks, Community Foundations, Employment/Job Training, Civic & Public Affairs-General, Housing, Law & Justice, Philanthropic Organizations, Safety, Urban & Community Affairs, Women's Affairs
Education: Business Education, Colleges & Universities, Community & Junior Colleges, Education Funds, Elementary Education (Public), Education-General, Legal Education, Literacy, Preschool Education, Private Education (Precollege), Public Education (Precollege), Religious Education, Special Education
Environment: Air/Water Quality, Watershed
Health: AIDS/HIV, Cancer, Children's Health/Hospitals, Clinics/Medical Centers, Health-General, Geriatric Health, Health Funds, Health Organizations, Hospices, Hospitals, Medical Rehabilitation, Mental Health, Nursing Services, Prenatal Health Issues, Preventive Medicine/Wellness Organizations, Public Health, Single-Disease Health Associations
Religion: Religion-General, Ministries, Missionary Activities (Domestic), Religious Organizations, Religious Welfare
Social Services: Camps, Child Abuse, Child Welfare, Community Centers, Community Service Organizations, Crime Prevention, Day Care, Delinquency & Criminal Rehabilitation, Domestic Violence, Emergency Relief, Family Planning, Family Services, Food/Clothing Distribution, Homes, People with Disabilities, Recreation & Athletics, Scouts, Shelters/Homelessness, Social Services-General, Volunteer Services, YMCA/YWCA/YMHA/YWHA, Youth Organizations

Application Procedures

Initial Contact: There are no specific application guidelines. Send a letter no longer than two pages describing the project.

Application Requirements: Include a description of the organization, a list of the directors and staff, project's annual budget; IRS tax exemption ruling, estimated project budget, and tentative line items.

Deadlines: March 31, June 30, September 30, and December 31.

Restrictions

The foundation does not support endowments or operating deficits.

Foundation Officials

Carl Ensor, Jr.: director CORP AFFIL director: Bank East Tennessee.

Greg Erickson: director

Monica Luke: manager

Sylvia M. Thompson: director

Merle D. Wolfe: president, director PRIM CORP EMPL president, director: Sun Coal Co. CORP AFFIL director: Jewell Resources Corp.; principal: Jewell Smokeless Coal Corp.

Lindsay Young: director

Grants Analysis

Disclosure Period: fiscal year ending June 30, 2003

Total Grants: $3,010,514

Number of Grants: 55

Average Grant: $44,914*

Highest Grant: $375,000

Lowest Grant: $750

Typical Range: $20,000 to $75,000

*Note: Average grant figure excludes two highest grants ($675,000).

Recent Grants

Note: Grants derived from fiscal 2003 Form 990.

Library-Related

50,000	Blount County Public Library, Maryville, TN -- for library construction

General

375,000	YMCA, Knoxville, TN
300,000	Anderson County Health Department, Knoxville, TN
300,000	Appalachian School of Law, Grundy, VA
220,000	Helen Ross McNabb Center, Knoxville, TN
200,000	Boys and Girls Club of Knoxville, Knoxville, TN
200,000	Tennessee Theatre, Knoxville, TN
150,000	Knoxville Botanical Gardens, Knoxville, TN -- to assist in land purchase
150,000	Southwest Virginia Community College, Richlands, VA -- for building purchase
100,000	Buchanan County Water Public Service Authority, Big Stone Gap, VA -- to assist in water supply
100,000	Maryville College, Maryville, TN -- fund for capital improvement

J. WALTER THOMPSON CO.

Company Headquarters

New York, NY

Web: http://www.jwtworld.com

Company Description

Assets: US$4 billion (2001)

Employees: 9200 (2001)

SIC(s): 7311 Advertising Agencies.

Parent Company: WPP Group PLC, 27 Farm St., London, United Kingdom

Operating Locations

Anspach Grossman Enterprise (NY--New York); Carl Byoir & Associates (NY--New York); CommonHealth U.S.A. (NJ--Parsippany); Einson Freeman (NJ--Paramus); Hill & Knowlton (NY--New York); HLS Corp. (NJ--Little Falls); J. Walter Thompson Co. (AZ--Scottsdale; CA--Los Angeles, San Diego, San Francisco; DC--Washington; FL--Coral Gables; GA--Atlanta; IL--Chicago; MI--Detroit; MO--St. Ann; NJ--Cherry Hill; NY--Fairport, New York; OH--Cincinnati, Columbus; TX--Dallas; UT--Salt Lake City); Mendoza, Dillon & Associates (CA--Newport Beach); MRB Group (NY--New York); Ogilvy & Mather Worldwide (NY--New York); Pace Advertising (NY--New York); RTCdirect (DC--Washington); SBG Enterprises (CA--San Francisco); Simmons (NY--New York); Thomas G. Ferguson Associates (NJ--Parsippany); Timmons & Co. (DC--Washington); Walker Group/CNI Inc. (NY--New York); Winona Research (AZ--Phoenix); WPP Group U.S.A. (NY--New York)

Nonmonetary Support

Type: In-kind Services; Loaned Employees; Loaned Executives; Workplace Solicitation

Note: The company also provides nonmonetary support in the form of creative work/services.

J. Walter Thompson Co. Fund

Giving Contact

Donald Gammon, Secretary

466 Lexington Avenue

New York, NY 10017

Phone: (212)210-7000

Fax: (212)210-6852

Description

EIN: 136020644

Organization Type: Corporate Foundation

Giving Locations: nationally.

Grant Types: Employee Matching Gifts, General Support.

Note: Employee matching gift ratio: 1 to 1 to higher education, up to $2,500 annually.

Financial Summary

Total Giving: $49,707 (fiscal year ending November 30, 2002); $94,324 (fiscal 2001). Note: Contributes through corporate direct giving program and foundation.

Giving Analysis: Giving for fiscal 2002 includes: foundation scholarships ($6,720); foundation matching gifts ($37,987); fiscal 2001: foundation ($94,324)

Assets: $749,421 (fiscal 2002); $636,722 (fiscal 2001)

Gifts Received: $200,000 (fiscal 2002); $200,000 (fiscal 1996); $200,000 (fiscal 1994). Note: Contributions were received from J. Walter Thompson.

Typical Recipients

Arts & Humanities: Arts Centers, Arts Festivals, Arts Funds, Ballet, Dance, Arts & Humanities-General, Historic Preservation, Libraries, Museums/Galleries, Music, Opera, Performing Arts, Theater

Civic & Public Affairs: African American Affairs, Botanical Gardens/Parks, Business/Free Enterprise, Economic Development, Civic & Public Affairs-General, Municipalities/Towns, Professional & Trade Associations, Public Policy, Safety, Women's Affairs

Education: Arts/Humanities Education, Business Education, Colleges & Universities, Education Funds, Education Reform, Engineering/Technological Education, Faculty Development, Education-General, International Exchange, Leadership Training, Medical Education, Minority Education, Private Education (Precollege), Public Education (Precollege), Social Sciences Education, Special Education, Student Aid

Environment: Environment-General, Resource Conservation

Health: Cancer, Clinics/Medical Centers, Diabetes, Health-General, Heart, Hospitals, Medical Rehabilitation, Medical Research, Single-Disease Health Associations, Speech & Hearing

International: Foreign Arts Organizations, International Organizations, International Relations, Trade

Religion: Jewish Causes, Religious Organizations

Science: Science Museums, Scientific Research

Social Services: At-Risk Youth, Community Centers, Community Service Organizations, Crime Prevention, Family Services, Food/Clothing Distribution, Recreation & Athletics, Scouts, Social Services-General, Substance Abuse, United Funds/United Ways, Youth Organizations

Application Procedures

Initial Contact: Submit a brief letter of inquiry.

Application Requirements: Include proof of tax-exempt status.

Deadlines: None.

Restrictions

Does not support individuals, religious organizations for sectarian purposes, or political or lobbying groups.

Corporate Officials

Christopher Jones: chief executive officer, director PRIM CORP EMPL chief executive officer: J. Walter Thompson Co.

Peter A. Schweitzer: president B Chicago, IL 1939. ED University of Michigan BA (1961); Western Michigan University MBA (1967). PRIM CORP EMPL president: J. Walter Thompson Co. NONPR AFFIL member: American Association Advertising Agencies.

Lewis J. Trencher: chief operating officer, director B 1952. ED New York Law School JD; New York University MBA; New York University BS. PRIM CORP EMPL chief operating officer, director: J. Walter Thompson Co.

Foundation Officials

Donald A. Gammon: secretary, director

Donna Matteo: treasurer

Susan Mirsky: vice president, director B New York, NY 1939. ED Smith College BA (1961); New York University (1961-1962). NONPR AFFIL member: New York Human Research Planners; member: New York Personnel Management Association; advisory member: Boys Harbor; member directors committee: Mount Sinai Medical Center New York.

Peter A. Schweitzer: vice president, director (see above)

Lewis J. Trencher: chairman, director (see above)

Grants Analysis

Disclosure Period: fiscal year ending November 30, 2002

Total Grants: $5,000*

Number of Grants: 1

Highest Grant: $5,000

*Note: Giving excludes matching gifts; scholarship.

Recent Grants

Note: Grants derived from fiscal 2003 Form 990.

General

5,220	National Merit Scholarship Corporation, Evanston, IL
5,000	AAAA Foundation, Randallstown, MD

THOMAS THOMPSON TRUST

Giving Contact

William B. Tyler, Trustee

1 Financial Center, Suite 29

Boston, MA 02111

Phone: (617)951-1145

Description
Founded: 1869
EIN: 030179429
Organization Type: Private Foundation
Giving Locations: NY: Rhinebeck including surrounding area; VT: Brattleboro including surrounding area
Grant Types: Capital, Emergency, General Support, Matching, Project.

Donor Information
Founder: the late Thomas Thompson

Financial Summary
Total Giving: $606,810 (fiscal year ending May 31, 2004); $866,345 (fiscal 2001)
Giving Analysis: Giving for fiscal 2004 includes: foundation grants to United Way ($40,000)
Assets: $15,680,575 (fiscal 2004); $17,726,342 (fiscal 2001)
Gifts Received: $500 (fiscal 1999)

Typical Recipients
Arts & Humanities: Arts Centers, Community Arts, Historic Preservation, History & Archaeology, Libraries, Museums/Galleries, Music, Performing Arts, Public Broadcasting
Civic & Public Affairs: Clubs, Community Foundations, Civic & Public Affairs-General, Housing, Municipalities/Towns, Safety, Urban & Community Affairs
Education: Arts/Humanities Education, Colleges & Universities, Education-General, International Exchange, Private Education (Precollege), Secondary Education (Public), Student Aid
Environment: Environment-General, Resource Conservation
Health: AIDS/HIV, Health Funds, Health Organizations, Hospitals, Long-Term Care, Mental Health, Nursing Services, Research/Studies Institutes
International: Foreign Educational Institutions
Religion: Religious Organizations, Religious Welfare
Social Services: At-Risk Youth, Camps, Child Welfare, Community Centers, Community Service Organizations, Counseling, Day Care, Domestic Violence, Family Planning, Homes, Recreation & Athletics, Senior Services, Shelters/Homelessness, United Funds/United Ways, Youth Organizations

Application Procedures
Initial Contact: Call foundation.
Application Requirements: Include a description of organization, amount requested, purpose of funds sought, recently audited financial statement, proof of tax-exempt status.
Deadlines: None.

Restrictions
Foundation does not support organizations that have been in operation for less than three consecutive years.

Foundation Officials
Daniel W. Fawcett: trustee
Albert M. Fortier, Jr.: trustee
William B. Tyler: trustee

Grants Analysis
Disclosure Period: fiscal year ending May 31, 2004
Total Grants: $566,810*
Number of Grants: 36
Average Grant: $9,318*
Highest Grant: $150,000
Lowest Grant: $1,435
Typical Range: $2,500 to $20,000
*Note: Giving excludes United Way. Average grant figure excludes two highest grants ($250,000).

Recent Grants
Note: Grants derived from 2001 Form 990.

Library-Related
14,200	Brooks Memorial Library, Brattleboro, VT -- for Collection Improvement Program

General
100,000	NOH Foundation, Inc.
75,000	South Vermont Health Services Corporation, VT -- for 2nd installment of Diabetes Education Program
50,000	Bard College, Annandale-on-Hudson, NY -- for scholarship endowment
50,000	Marlboro College, Marlboro, VT -- for construction of new lecture hall
50,000	Marlboro College, Marlboro, VT
30,000	Brattleboro Mutual Aid Association, Brattleboro, VT -- for kitchen renovations
30,000	Louis August Jonas Foundation, Inc -- for Camp Rising Sun renovations
25,000	Rhinebeck Aerodrome Museum, Rhinebeck, NY -- for renovations
24,500	Rhinebeck Performing Arts Center, Rhinebeck, NY -- for RUST Program and Daytop Volunteers
20,295	Baptist Home, Abilene, TX -- for van

ANNA W. THORNTON AND ALEXANDER P. THORNTON CHARITABLE TRUST

Giving Contact
Robert Lansford
Care of Bank One Trust Co. NA
PO Box 2050
Ft. Worth, TX 76113-2050
Phone: (817)884-4151

Description
Founded: 1997
EIN: 756496915
Organization Type: Private Foundation
Grant Types: General Support.

Financial Summary
Total Giving: $106,000 (fiscal year ending September 30, 2004); $134,000 (fiscal 2001)
Assets: $2,259,153 (fiscal 2004); $2,393,233 (fiscal 2001)

Typical Recipients
Arts & Humanities: History & Archaeology, Libraries
Civic & Public Affairs: Clubs, Hispanic Affairs, Philanthropic Organizations
Education: Afterschool/Enrichment Programs, Education-General, Student Aid
Health: Eyes/Blindness, Health Funds, Research/Studies Institutes
International: International Relief Efforts
Religion: Churches, Religious Organizations, Religious Welfare
Science: Science Museums
Social Services: At-Risk Youth, Family Services, Homes, People with Disabilities, Social Services-General, Substance Abuse, YMCA/YWCA/YMHA/YWHA, Youth Organizations

Restrictions
The trust gives priority to organizations providing women's and children's services in Tarrant County.

Additional Information
Trust(s): Bank One Trust Co. NA

Grants Analysis
Disclosure Period: fiscal year ending September 30, 2004
Total Grants: $106,000

Number of Grants: 19
Average Grant: $5,889
Highest Grant: $10,800
Lowest Grant: $1,000
Typical Range: $1,000 to $10,000

Recent Grants
Note: Grants derived from fiscal 2004 Form 990.
General
10,800	Southwestern Diabetic Foundation, Gainesville, TX
10,000	Boys and Girls Club of Arlington, Arlington, TX
10,000	Happy Hill Farm Children Home Inc., Granbury, TX
10,000	Score a Goal in the Classroom, Ft. Worth, TX
10,000	YMCA Camp Carter, Ft. Worth, TX
8,000	Cenikor Foundation Inc., Ft. Worth, TX
7,500	Helping Other People Excel Farm Inc., Ft. Worth, TX
5,000	Bobby Bragan Youth Foundation, Ft. Worth, TX
5,000	Junior Achievement, Ft. Worth, TX
5,000	Philanthropy Inc., Dallas, TX

THORNTON FOUNDATION

Giving Contact
Charles B. Thornton, Jr., President
523 W. 6th St., Suite 636
Los Angeles, CA 90014
Phone: (213)629-3867
Fax; (213)629-9201

Description
Founded: 1958
EIN: 956037178
Organization Type: Private Foundation
Giving Locations: CA; MA
Grant Types: General Support, Operating Expenses, Research.

Donor Information
Founder: the late Charles B. Thornton, Flora I. Thornton

Financial Summary
Total Giving: $1,184,000 (2003); $925,500 (2001)
Assets: $25,675,887 (2003); $24,981,068 (2001)
Gifts Received: $4,000 (2003); $29,000 (2001); $7,800 (2000). Note: In 1996, 2000, and 2001 contributions were received from Charles B. Thornton, Jr. In 1999, contributions were received from Charles B. Thorton ($6,000), and W. Laney Thompson ($5,000).

Typical Recipients
Arts & Humanities: Arts Centers, Historic Preservation, Libraries, Museums/Galleries, Music, Public Broadcasting
Civic & Public Affairs: Economic Development, Civic & Public Affairs-General, Municipalities/Towns, Urban & Community Affairs
Education: Afterschool/Enrichment Programs, Arts/Humanities Education, Business Education, Colleges & Universities, Education Reform, Education-General, Legal Education, Minority Education, Preschool Education, Private Education (Precollege), Public Education (Precollege), Science/Mathematics Education, Secondary Education (Private)
Environment: Wildlife Protection
Health: AIDS/HIV, Cancer, Children's Health/Hospitals, Clinics/Medical Centers, Emergency/Ambulance Services, Hospitals, Hospitals (University Affiliated), Medical Research, Research/Studies Institutes, Single-Disease Health Associations, Speech & Hearing
International: International Affairs, International En-

vironmental Issues, International Peace & Security Issues, International Relief Efforts
Religion: Churches, Religion-General, Religious Organizations, Religious Welfare
Science: Science Museums, Scientific Centers & Institutes
Social Services: Community Centers, Day Care, People with Disabilities, Recreation & Athletics, Scouts, Youth Organizations

Application Procedures
Initial Contact: Send a brief letter of inquiry.
Application Requirements: Include a description of the program or project.
Deadlines: None.

Foundation Officials
Terry D. Chapin: secretary
Charles B. Thornton, Jr.: president
William Laney Thornton: vice president

Grants Analysis
Disclosure Period: calendar year ending 2003
Total Grants: $1,184,000
Number of Grants: 70
Average Grant: $7,970*
Highest Grant: $200,000
Typical Range: $1,000 to $10,000
*Note: Average grant figure excludes three highest grants ($402,000).

Recent Grants
Note: Grants derived from 2001 Form 990.
General

170,000	Greenbelt Alliance, San Francisco, CA
100,000	Harvard Westlake School, North Hollywood, CA
100,000	McLean Hospital, Belmont, MA
100,000	Stanford University, Stanford, CA
50,000	Harvard Business School, Boston, MA
50,000	Johns Hopkins Brady Center
40,000	Huntington, San Marino, CA
35,000	Diversity Alliance
25,000	California Pacific Medical Center, San Francisco, CA
25,000	Cate School, Carpinteria, CA

FLORA L. THORNTON FOUNDATION

Giving Contact
Edward A. Landry, Trustee
1 Wilshire Blvd., Suite 2000
Los Angeles, CA 90017-3321
Phone: (213)629-7657
Fax: (213)624-1376

Description
Founded: 1983
EIN: 953855595
Organization Type: Private Foundation
Grant Types: General Support.

Donor Information
Founder: Flora L. Thornton

Financial Summary
Total Giving: $1,684,375 (fiscal year ending November 30, 2004); $1,401,050 (fiscal 2001)
Giving Analysis: Giving for fiscal 2004 includes: foundation grants to United Way ($20,000); fiscal 2001: foundation grants to United Way ($10,000)
Assets: $2,578,386 (fiscal 2004); $3,986,169 (fiscal 2001)
Gifts Received: $166,643 (fiscal 2004); $3,426,745 (fiscal 1998); $1,206,491 (fiscal 1996). Note: In fiscal 1996 and 2004, contributions were received from Flora L. Thornton.

Typical Recipients
Arts & Humanities: Arts Institutes, Ethnic & Folk Arts, Arts & Humanities-General, Historic Preservation, History & Archaeology, Libraries, Museums/Galleries, Music, Opera, Public Broadcasting, Theater
Civic & Public Affairs: Community Foundations, Employment/Job Training, Civic & Public Affairs-General, Municipalities/Towns, Parades/Festivals, Public Policy, Urban & Community Affairs, Zoos/Aquariums
Education: Arts/Humanities Education, Colleges & Universities, Education Funds, Education Reform, Literacy, Medical Education, Private Education (Precollege), Public Education (Precollege), Secondary Education (Private), Secondary Education (Public), Student Aid
Environment: Environment-General
Health: Arthritis, Cancer, Children's Health/Hospitals, Emergency/Ambulance Services, Hospitals, Kidney, Medical Research, Multiple Sclerosis, Outpatient Health Care, Prenatal Health Issues
International: International Affairs
Religion: Churches, Jewish Causes, Religious Organizations
Science: Science Museums, Scientific Centers & Institutes
Social Services: Child Welfare, Community Service Organizations, Food/Clothing Distribution, People with Disabilities, Scouts, Shelters/Homelessness, United Funds/United Ways, Volunteer Services, YMCA/YWCA/YMHA/YWHA, Youth Organizations

Application Procedures
Initial Contact: Send a brief letter of inquiry describing program or project.
Deadlines: None.

Foundation Officials
Glen P. McDaniel: trustee
Flora L. Thornton: trustee
William Laney Thornton: trustee

Grants Analysis
Disclosure Period: fiscal year ending November 30, 2004
Total Grants: $1,664,375*
Number of Grants: 56
Average Grant: $18,785*
Highest Grant: $400,000
Lowest Grant: $1,000
Typical Range: $5,000 to $40,000
*Note: Giving excludes United Way. Average grant figure excludes two highest grants ($650,000).

Recent Grants
Note: Grants derived from fiscal 2004 Form 990.

General

400,000	Pepperdine University, Malibu, CA
250,000	Los Angeles Philharmonic Association, Los Angeles, CA
75,000	EngenderHealth, New York, NY
75,000	National Multiple Sclerosis Society, New York, NY
60,000	International Ecotourism Society, Washington, DC
55,000	Los Angeles County High School for the Arts Foundation, Los Angeles, CA
50,000	Keck Graduate Institute, Claremont, CA
50,000	Population Media Center, Shelburne, VT
50,000	Rare
50,000	St. Matthew's Parish

TIMKEN FOUNDATION OF CANTON

Giving Contact
Nancy Knudsen, Secretary & Treasurer
200 Market Ave, North, Suite 210
Canton, OH 44702-1437
Phone: (330)452-1144
Fax: (330)452-2306
E-mail: dickesd@timkenfoundation.org

Description
Founded: 1934
EIN: 346520254
Organization Type: Family Foundation
Giving Locations: OH: internationally; nationally; operating locations.
Grant Types: Capital, Challenge, General Support, Operating Expenses, Scholarship.

Financial Summary
Total Giving: $8,479,332 (fiscal year ending September 30, 2003); $4,537,943 (fiscal 2002)
Assets: $147,058,428 (fiscal 2003); $152,855,083 (fiscal 2002)

Typical Recipients
Arts & Humanities: Arts Centers, Arts Institutes, Historic Preservation, History & Archaeology, Libraries, Museums/Galleries, Music, Opera, Theater
Civic & Public Affairs: African American Affairs, Botanical Gardens/Parks, Business/Free Enterprise, Chambers of Commerce, Clubs, Community Foundations, Economic Development, Employment/Job Training, Ethnic Organizations, Civic & Public Affairs-General, Housing, Minority Business, Municipalities/Towns, Parades/Festivals, Philanthropic Organizations, Professional & Trade Associations, Urban & Community Affairs, Zoos/Aquariums
Education: Afterschool/Enrichment Programs, Business Education, Colleges & Universities, Community & Junior Colleges, Education Associations, Education Funds, Education Reform, Engineering/Technological Education, Education-General, Medical Education, Minority Education, Preschool Education, Private Education (Precollege), Public Education (Precollege), Science/Mathematics Education, Special Education, Student Aid
Environment: Air/Water Quality, Environment-General, Resource Conservation
Health: Cancer, Clinics/Medical Centers, Emergency/Ambulance Services, Geriatric Health, Health Funds, Heart, Hospices, Hospitals, Nursing Services, Outpatient Health Care, Preventive Medicine/Wellness Organizations
International: Foreign Arts Organizations, Foreign Educational Institutions, International-General, Health Care/Hospitals, International Development, International Organizations, International Peace & Security Issues, International Relief Efforts, Missionary/Religious Activities
Religion: Churches, Ministries, Religious Organizations, Religious Welfare
Social Services: Animal Protection, At-Risk Youth, Camps, Child Welfare, Community Centers, Community Service Organizations, Crime Prevention, Day Care, Domestic Violence, Emergency Relief, Family Services, Food/Clothing Distribution, People with Disabilities, Recreation & Athletics, Scouts, Senior Services, Shelters/Homelessness, Social Services-General, Substance Abuse, United Funds/United Ways, YMCA/YWCA/YMHA/YWHA, Youth Organizations

Application Procedures
Initial Contact: Grant requests should be in writing.
Application Requirements: No specific form of application is required; however, the application must include proof of tax-exempt status under Internal Revenue Code 501(c)(3).

Deadlines: None.
Notes: Makes only capital grants. Does not make grants for operating funds.

Restrictions

The foundation only funds organizations located in areas where the Timken Company has manufacturing facilities.

Additional Information

The foundation is funded by members of the Timken family, who also operate the Timken Co. The company is not directly connected to the foundation.

Foundation Officials

Don D. Dickes: secretary, treasurer, trustee
Nancy Knudsen: secretary, treasurer
W. R. Timken, Jr.: vice president, trustee
Ward J. Timken: president, trustee

Grants Analysis

Disclosure Period: fiscal year ending September 30, 2003
Total Grants: $8,479,332
Number of Grants: 71
Average Grant: $90,137*
Highest Grant: $800,000
Lowest Grant: $5,000
Typical Range: $25,000 to $150,000
*Note: Average grant excludes three highest grants ($2,350,000).

Recent Grants

Note: Grants derived from fiscal 2003 Form 990.
Library-Related

750,000	National First Ladies Library, Canton, OH -- renovate national bank building
50,000	East Lincoln Betterment, Denver, NC -- help build new library
40,000	Alta Vista Town of Staunton River Memorial Library, Alta Vista, VA -- additional space to accommodate all programs

General

800,000	University of Texas MD Anderson Cancer Center, Houston, TX -- bush endowment for innovative Cancer research
500,000	Canton Student Loan Foundation, Canton, OH -- to increase the depleting funds
500,000	Stark Community Foundation, Canton, OH -- renovate CNB building first ladies education and research center
400,000	Walsh University, North Canton, OH
375,000	Stark State College Foundation, Canton, OH -- construct information technical building
339,000	North Canton Medical Foundation, North Canton, OH -- new telephone system
333,000	Wilberforce University, Wilberforce, OH
238,900	Domestic Violence project, Canton, OH -- emergency support to domestic violence victims
200,000	YMCA Central Stark County, Canton, OH -- new lake community center
191,666	Stark Education Partnership, Canton, OH

TINKER FOUNDATION

Giving Contact

Renate Rennie, President & Director
55 East 59th Street, 21st Fl.
New York, NY 10022
Phone: (212)421-6858
Fax: (212)223-3326
E-mail: tinker@tinker.org
Web: http://fdncenter.org/grantmaker/tinker

Description

Founded: 1959
EIN: 510175449
Organization Type: Specialized/Single Purpose Foundation
Giving Locations: internationally; nationally.
Grant Types: Conference/Seminar, General Support, Matching, Multiyear/Continuing Support, Project, Research, Seed Money.

Donor Information

Founder: Established in 1959 by Edward Larocque Tinker (1881-1968), a real estate investor in New York City. After his death in 1968, his estate was bequeathed to the foundation. He originally set up the foundation in memory of his wife, father, and grandfather. "His lifelong devotion to the Iberian tradition in the Old and New Worlds gave definition to the foundation's overall purpose."

Financial Summary

Total Giving: $2,846,650 (2003); $2,741,690 (2002); $3,430,445 (2001)
Assets: $74,043,113 (2003); $65,515,177 (2002); $74,589,872 (2001)

Typical Recipients

Arts & Humanities: Libraries, Public Broadcasting
Civic & Public Affairs: Botanical Gardens/Parks, Business/Free Enterprise, Civil Rights, Economic Development, Economic Policy, Ethnic Organizations, Civic & Public Affairs-General, Hispanic Affairs, Law & Justice, Nonprofit Management, Philanthropic Organizations, Public Policy, Safety, Urban & Community Affairs
Education: Business Education, Colleges & Universities, Economic Education, Education Funds, Environmental Education, International Exchange, International Studies, Legal Education, Minority Education, Science/Mathematics Education, Social Sciences Education
Environment: Air/Water Quality, Forestry, Environment-General, Protection, Research, Resource Conservation, Wildlife Protection
International: Foreign Arts Organizations, Foreign Educational Institutions, International-General, Health Care/Hospitals, Human Rights, International Affairs, International Development, International Environmental Issues, International Organizations, International Peace & Security Issues, International Relations, Missionary/Religious Activities, Trade
Science: Scientific Centers & Institutes
Social Services: Emergency Relief, Family Planning

Application Procedures

Initial Contact: Guidelines and forms for institutional grants are also available on the foundation's web site or by contacting the foundation. Field research grant application materials are available upon request. Telephone and e-mail inquiries are welcome.
Application Requirements: The proposal for an institutional grant should include a completed Proposal Cover Sheet; single-page description of the project including objectives, target audience, methodology, and plan for dissemination of results; full proposal providing more detail on the project's objectives and theoretical, practical and/or policy-related significance; a plan of work describing the activities to be undertaken, and any factors which could delay the plan or change the amount of time required to complete the project or alter the proposed budget; anticipated results; a plan for disseminating the results; description of plan to evaluate short -term and long-term impact of project; contact information for three individuals familiar with the proposed topic, but not directly involved with the project; an itemized project budget; an itemized budget for those expenses for which Tinker Foundation funding is sought; copy of IRS tax-exempt letter; copy of the organization's latest Federal/State Form 990 (U.S. organizations only); latest financial statement; qualifications of the project direc-

tor and personnel, with curricula vitae attached; list of staff and directors; and historical overview of the applying institution. Two copies of the complete proposal, without binders, should be submitted.
Deadlines: Applications are considered semi-annually; March 1 for the summer meeting, September 1 for the winter meeting, and October 1 for field research grants.
Review Process: The board meets in June and December to review grant proposals.

Restrictions

The foundation will not consider institutional grant requests for annual fund raising appeals for such organizations as the Community Chest or United Way; individual research; funding related to health or medical issues; production costs for film, television or radio projects; funding for arts and humanities projects, including art museum collections and exhibits; endowments; construction or major equipment purchases; and general operating support.

Additional Information

The Foundation also has a field research grant competition open to recognized Centers or Institutes of Latin America or Iberian Studies with graduate doctoral programs at accredited United States universities. Contact Foundation for applications instructions. All applications must be submitted in English.
Publications: Annual Report; Application Guidelines

Corporate Officials

John A. Luke, Jr.: chairman, president, chief executive officer, director B New York, NY 1948. ED Lawrence University BA (1971); University of Pennsylvania Wharton School MBA (1979). PRIM CORP EMPL chairman, president, chief executive officer, director: Westvaco Corp. CORP AFFIL director: FM Global Insurance; director: Timken Co.; director: Arkwright Mutual Insurance Co.; director: Bank New York Co. Inc.; director: Arkwright Insurance Co. NONPR AFFIL board governors: NCASI; director: United Negro College Fund; trustee: Lawrence University; member: Council Foreign Relations; trustee: Institute Paper Science Technology; director: American Society; director: Council Americas; chairman: American Forest Foundation; member executive committee, director: American Forest & Paper Association. CLUB AFFIL University Club; Commonwealth Club; The Links Club.

Foundation Officials

William R. Chaney: director B Satanta, KS 1932. ED University of Kansas BA (1953). PRIM CORP EMPL chairman, chief executive officer: Tiffany & Co. CORP AFFIL director: Fifth Avenue Association; director: FAO Schwartz; director: Bank New York Co. Inc. NONPR AFFIL member: Lambda Chi Alpha. CLUB AFFIL Advertising Sales Executives Club.
Sally Grooms Cowal: director
John A. Luke, Jr.: treasurer (see above)
Charles McC. Mathias: director
Charles McCurdy Mathias, Jr.: director B Frederick, MD 1922. ED Haverford College BA (1944); Yale University (1943-1944); University of Maryland LLB (1949). PRIM CORP EMPL chairman: First American Bankshares. NONPR AFFIL visiting professor: Johns Hopkins University.
Kenneth Maxwell: director
Martha Twitchell Muse: chairman B Dallas, TX 1926. ED Barnard College BA (1948); Columbia University MA (1955); Georgetown University DHL (1981). CORP AFFIL director: Bank New York Co. Inc.; director: Bank New York Audit & Examining Center; director: Bank New York Comm Reinvestment Accounting Center; director pension committee: ASARCO Inc. NONPR AFFIL vice chairman board directors: Spanish Institute; member: Woodrow Wilson Center International Scholars; director: New York Stock Exchange Inc.; member advisory council: Lusa-American Development Foundation; member: National Society Colonial Dames; member: Hugue-

not Society; member: International Executive Service Corps; member, board visitors: Georgetown University Edmund A Walsh School Foreign Service; trustee emeritus: Columbia University; director: Council Americas; member, board directors: American Portuguese Society; member, board directors: American Society Inc.; member, board directors: American Foundation; member, board directors: American Council Germany. CLUB AFFIL Colony Club; Metro Club.

Richard de J. Osborne: secretary, director
Renate Rennie: president
Susan L. Segal: director
Alan Stoga: director

Grants Analysis

Disclosure Period: calendar year ending 2003
Total Grants: $2,846,650
Number of Grants: 65*
Average Grant: $42,848*
Highest Grant: $150,000
Lowest Grant: $3,150
Typical Range: $20,000 to $60,000
*Note: Number of grants and average grant exclude miscellaneous smaller grants totaling $61,500.

Recent Grants

Note: Grants derived from 2003 Form 990.
General

150,000	Centro de Estudios Cientificos, Valdivia Chile -- towards the laboratory of Glaciology
90,000	Instituto Centroamencano de Administracion, Alajuela Costa Rica -- towards the market intelligence center
80,000	Council on Foreign Relations, New York, NY -- for the forum of Americas
80,000	Vera Institute of Justice Inc., New York, NY -- towards Chilean prosecution service
76,000	Florida International University Foundation Inc., Miami, FL -- towards Mexican forest policy
70,000	Americas Society Inc., New York, NY -- towards administration
70,000	National Public Radio Inc., Washington, DC -- towards social reporting series
68,000	Fundacion Naturaleza para el Futuro, Buenos Aires Argentina -- towards protecting landscapes
65,000	Brookings Institution, Washington, DC -- towards safety nets and social contract
65,000	Fundacion Instituto de Empresa, Madrid Spain -- towards labour market

TISCORNIA FOUNDATION

Giving Contact

Laurianne T. Davis, President
1010 Main St., Suite A
St. Joseph, MI 49085
Phone: (269)983-4711
Fax: (616)983-6959

Description

Founded: 1942
EIN: 381777343
Organization Type: Private Foundation
Giving Locations: MI
Grant Types: Capital, Emergency, General Support, Multiyear/Continuing Support, Scholarship, Seed Money.

Donor Information

Founder: the late James W. Tiscornia, the late Waldo V. Tiscornia, Auto Specialties Manufacturing Co., Lambert Brake Corp.

Financial Summary

Total Giving: $311,322 (2003). Note: In 1996, Giving includes scholarship ($46,500).
Giving Analysis: Giving for 2003 includes: foundation grants to United Way ($16,500); foundation scholarships ($186,822)
Assets: $3,757,918 (2003)

Typical Recipients

Arts & Humanities: Arts Associations & Councils, Arts Centers, Arts & Humanities-General, History & Archaeology, Libraries, Literary Arts, Museums/Galleries, Music
Civic & Public Affairs: Economic Policy, Civic & Public Affairs-General, Housing, Municipalities/Towns, Parades/Festivals, Urban & Community Affairs
Education: Business Education, Colleges & Universities, Education Funds, Education-General, Literacy, Minority Education, Student Aid
Environment: Environment-General
Health: AIDS/HIV, Cancer, Children's Health/Hospitals, Clinics/Medical Centers, Diabetes, Emergency/Ambulance Services, Health Funds, Health Organizations, Hospices, Prenatal Health Issues, Public Health
Religion: Churches, Ministries, Religious Welfare
Social Services: Camps, Child Welfare, Community Centers, Community Service Organizations, Counseling, Family Planning, Family Services, Food/Clothing Distribution, Recreation & Athletics, Scouts, Shelters/Homelessness, Social Services-General, United Funds/United Ways, Veterans, Volunteer Services, YMCA/YWCA/YMHA/YWHA, Youth Organizations

Application Procedures

Initial Contact: Send a brief letter of inquiry.
Application Requirements: outline of programs and purpose of funds sought.
Deadlines: April 1 for scholarships; October 1 for general grants.

Restrictions

Does not support individuals (except for employee-related scholarships).

Additional Information

Provides scholarships to Northern Berrien County high school students.

Foundation Officials

Laurianne T. Davis: president, executive director
Henry H. Tippett: treasurer
Bernice Tiscornia: vice president
James Tiscornia: vice president

Grants Analysis

Disclosure Period: calendar year ending 2003
Total Grants: $124,500*
Number of Grants: 20
Average Grant: $2,605*
Highest Grant: $75,000
Typical Range: $1,000 to $5,000
*Note: Giving excludes scholarships; United Way. Average grant figure excludes highest grant.

Recent Grants

Note: Grants derived from 2001 Form 990.
Library-Related

25,000	M. Preston Palenske Library, Joseph, MI -- community welfare

General

75,000	Lakeland Health Foundation, Joseph, MI -- community welfare
33,250	Cornerstone Alliance, Benton Harbor, MI -- community welfare
21,000	Salvation Army, Benton Harbor, MI -- community welfare
20,000	United Way, Benton Harbor, MI -- community welfare
16,000	Planned Parenthood Association of Southwestern Michigan, Benton Harbor, MI -- community welfare
15,000	Michigan Colleges Foundation, Inc., Southfield, MI -- education
15,000	Samaritan Counseling Center -- community services
7,500	Twin Cities Area Literacy Council, Benton Harbor, MI -- education
7,000	Southwestern Michigan Symphony, St. Joseph, MI -- community welfare
6,000	WCA, St. Joseph, MI -- community welfare

C. W. TITUS FOUNDATION

Giving Contact

Timothy T. Reynolds, Trustee
950 Philtower Bldg.
Tulsa, OK 74103
Phone: (918)582-8095

Description

Founded: 1968
EIN: 237016981
Organization Type: Private Foundation
Giving Locations: MO; OK
Grant Types: General Support, Project, Research.

Financial Summary

Total Giving: $1,041,761 (2003)
Assets: $19,871,048 (2003)

Typical Recipients

Arts & Humanities: Arts Centers, Ballet, Dance, Historic Preservation, History & Archaeology, Libraries, Museums/Galleries, Music, Opera, Performing Arts, Public Broadcasting
Civic & Public Affairs: Economic Development, Civic & Public Affairs-General, Professional & Trade Associations, Public Policy, Urban & Community Affairs, Zoos/Aquariums
Education: Arts/Humanities Education, Colleges & Universities, Education-General, International Studies, Preschool Education, Private Education (Precollege), Public Education (Precollege), Secondary Education (Public)
Health: Alzheimer's Disease, Cancer, Children's Health/Hospitals, Clinics/Medical Centers, Diabetes, Emergency/Ambulance Services, Health Organizations, Heart, Hospices, Hospitals, Medical Research, Prenatal Health Issues, Respiratory, Single-Disease Health Associations, Speech & Hearing
Religion: Religious Welfare
Social Services: Animal Protection, Community Service Organizations, Crime Prevention, Domestic Violence, Family Planning, Family Services, Food/Clothing Distribution, Homes, People with Disabilities, Scouts, Senior Services, Sexual Abuse, Substance Abuse, United Funds/United Ways, Volunteer Services, YMCA/YWCA/YMHA/YWHA, Youth Organizations

Application Procedures

Initial Contact: The foundation has no formal grant application procedure or application form.
Deadlines: None.

Foundation Officials

Timothy T. Reynolds: trustee

Grants Analysis

Disclosure Period: calendar year ending 2003
Total Grants: $1,041,761
Number of Grants: 60
Average Grant: $6,755*

Highest Grant: $500,000
Lowest Grant: $1,000
Typical Range: $1,000 to $10,000
***Note:** Average grant figure excludes two highest grants ($650,000).

Recent Grants

Note: Grants derived from 2001 Form 990.
Library-Related

80,000	Webb City Library, Webb City, MO -- for children's library

General

200,000	Ozark Public Television, Springfield, MO -- for digital master control
50,000	Development Center of the Ozarks, Springfield, MO -- for budgeted operations
50,000	Kitchen, Springfield, MO -- for budgeted operations
50,000	St. John Medical Center Foundation, Tulsa, OK -- for restorative care unit
20,000	Children's Mercy Hospital, Kansas City, MO -- cancer center
15,000	University Child Care Center, Springfield, MO -- for budgeted operations
10,000	Community Clinic of Joplin, Joplin, MO -- for budgeted operations
10,000	Ronald McDonald House, Tulsa, OK -- for budgeted operations
10,000	Southwest Missouri Chapter of Alzheimer's, Springfield, MO -- for budgeted operations
10,000	Thomas Gilcrease Museum Association, Tulsa, OK -- for budgeted operations

TJX COMPANIES INC.

Company Headquarters

Framingham, MA
Web: http://www.tjx.com

Company Description

Founded: 1962
Ticker: TJX
Exchange: NYSE
Revenue: US$14.913 billion (2004)
Profit: US$664.1 million (2004)
Employees: 105000 (2003)
Fortune Rank: 141, per FORTUNE Magazine's list of 500 Largest U.S. Corporations (2004).
SIC(s): 5699 Miscellaneous Apparel & Accessory Stores.

Operating Locations

TJX Companies, Inc. (DC; FL--Miami, Tampa; GA--Forest Park; MA--Framingham, Mansfield, Natick, Stoughton; NY--New York)

Nonmonetary Support

Range: $150,000 - $500,000
Type: Cause-related Marketing & Promotion; Donated Equipment; Donated Products; In-kind Services; Workplace Solicitation

TJX Foundation, Inc.

Giving Contact

Christine Strickland, Foundation Manager
770 Cochituate Road, Route J5S
Framingham, MA 01701
Phone: (508)390-3199
Fax: (508)390-2091
E-mail: christy_strickland@tjx.com
Web: http://www.tjmaxx.com

Alternate Contact

Phone: (508)380-2300

Description

EIN: 042399760
Organization Type: Corporate Foundation
Giving Locations: MA: Boston principally near operating locations and to national organizations.
Grant Types: Award, Capital, Challenge, Endowment, General Support, Operating Expenses, Project, Scholarship.

Financial Summary

Total Giving: $4,070,943 (fiscal year ending January 31, 2003); $3,571,468 (fiscal 2002); $2,675,456 (fiscal 2001). Note: Contributes through corporate direct giving program and foundation.
Giving Analysis: Giving for fiscal 2001 includes: foundation grants to United Way ($48,700); foundation ($2,626,756)
Assets: $7,457,469 (fiscal 2003); $11,364,985 (fiscal 2002); $14,450,988 (fiscal 2001)
Gifts Received: $137,398 (fiscal 2003); $17,261,354 (fiscal 1999); $17,261,354 (fiscal 1998). Note: Contributions received from TJX Companies, Inc.

Typical Recipients

Arts & Humanities: Arts Associations & Councils, Arts Centers, Arts Funds, Arts Institutes, Community Arts, Dance, Arts & Humanities-General, Historic Preservation, History & Archaeology, Libraries, Museums/Galleries, Performing Arts, Public Broadcasting, Theater
Civic & Public Affairs: African American Affairs, Asian American Affairs, Business/Free Enterprise, Civil Rights, Community Foundations, Employment/Job Training, Ethnic Organizations, Civic & Public Affairs-General, Hispanic Affairs, Housing, Law & Justice, Municipalities/Towns, Philanthropic Organizations, Public Policy, Urban & Community Affairs, Women's Affairs
Education: Afterschool/Enrichment Programs, Arts/Humanities Education, Business Education, Colleges & Universities, Education Associations, Education Funds, Elementary Education (Private), Faculty Development, Education-General, Legal Education, Medical Education, Minority Education, Private Education (Precollege), Public Education (Precollege), Religious Education, Secondary Education (Private), Special Education, Student Aid
Health: AIDS/HIV, Cancer, Children's Health/Hospitals, Clinics/Medical Centers, Diabetes, Emergency/Ambulance Services, Health-General, Health Organizations, Heart, Hospices, Hospitals, Medical Rehabilitation, Medical Research, Mental Health, Nursing Services, Prenatal Health Issues, Public Health, Single-Disease Health Associations
International: Human Rights, International Relief Efforts
Religion: Jewish Causes, Ministries, Religious Welfare
Science: Scientific Centers & Institutes
Social Services: Big Brothers/Big Sisters, Camps, Child Abuse, Child Welfare, Community Centers, Community Service Organizations, Counseling, Crime Prevention, Day Care, Domestic Violence, Emergency Relief, Family Services, Food/Clothing Distribution, Homes, People with Disabilities, Recreation & Athletics, Refugee Assistance, Scouts, Shelters/Homelessness, Social Services-General, Special Olympics, Substance Abuse, United Funds/United Ways, Volunteer Services, YMCA/YWCA/YMHA/YWHA, Youth Organizations

Application Procedures

Initial Contact: Submit requests in writing.
Application Requirements: In three to five pages, include a description of the organization, its purpose, and the year the organization was founded (no more than 2 paragraphs); objective of grant and its target group; a detailed description of the program's (not the organization's) target audience (including age range, number of people, ethnic backgrounds, etc.); evidence of need for such program and organization's

experience with similar problems; method of evaluation; and outline of alternative plan if all necessary funds are not raised. Supporting materials that must be included with the proposal are: program budget and amount requested; proof of tax-exempt status; current audited financial report and statement of functional expenses; current operating budget; list of board of directors, and a list of contributors and amounts received in last fiscal year.
Deadlines: None. For consideration at a specific committee meeting, proposals should be submitted four weeks prior to the meeting (applicants may call to inquire about the cut-off date). Time-sensitive corporate contributions requests must be submitted at least three months prior to the date that funds are needed.
Review Process: The TJX Foundation Allocation Committee considers grant proposals and corporate contributions requests.
Evaluative Criteria: Program within targeted areas of interest.
Decision Notification: Committee meets approximate every other month to consider proposals; decisions are made within 60 to 90 days of receiving proposal.
Notes: Contributions will conform to the following guidelines: education, to programs that benefit children of preschool age through college; social services, to families and children, including the family unit, single-parent families, domestic violence, and physically impaired; health, to organizations providing health care to underserved populations, including prenatal, immunizations and health screenings, preventative care, and alternatives to hospitalization; civic, to programs that improve race relations, community development, and housing; and art/culture, to bring art to new audiences, and encourage people to express themselves through art.

Restrictions

TJX generally will not support individuals, political groups, religious organizations for sectarian purposes, public policy research projects or advocacy, conferences/seminars, publications, international organizations, travel, cash reserves, environmental issues, unrestricted grants, seed money, education loans, fellowships, endowments, capital/renovation campaigns, salary requests, programs in operation for less than 12 months, training money, films or photography, new construction, conventions, consultant fees, other giving organizations, offenders, ex-offenders, scholarly research, endowed scholarships, corrections, daycare, federated drives, legal aid, information and referral, long-term care, multi service, recreation, consumer education, family planning, health planning, occupational safety, public health education, business development, community organizing, consumer education protection, leadership development, tenant rights, voter education, transportation, housing expense reduction, architecture/design, arts service organization, dance, historic preservation, and visual arts. Our charitable contributions will be directed toward those priority or targeted markets in which The TJX Companies, Inc.'s stores, home office and distribution centers are located. Since the Company Headquarters is in the greater Boston area, a larger proportion of the Company's contributions will focus on organizations that favor the Greater Boston and Metro West communities.

Additional Information

TJX Foundation had been known as the Zayre Foundation until fiscal year 1989.
The TJX Companies, Inc. consists of four operating divisions: The Marmaxx Group (T.J. Maxx and Marshalls), Winners, HomeGoods and T.K. Maxx (in Europe).

Corporate Officials

Bernard Cammarata: chairman, chief executive officer B Brooklyn, NY 1940. PRIM CORP EMPL chairman: TJX Companies, Inc.

Donald G. Campbell: executive vice president, chief financial officer B 1951. PRIM CORP EMPL executive vice president, chief financial officer: TJX Companies, Inc.

Edmond J. English: president, chief executive officer PRIM CORP EMPL president, chief executive officer: TJX Companies Inc.

Sherry Lang: vice president & director investor relations PRIM CORP EMPL vice president & director investor relations: TJX Companies, Inc.

Richard G. Lesser: executive vice president, chief operating officer, director B Boston, MA 1935. ED Northeastern University BS. PRIM CORP EMPL executive vice president, chief operating officer, director: TJX Companies, Inc. CORP AFFIL president, chief executive officer: Marshall's Inc.; director: Reebok International Ltd.; president, director: Marmaxx Group.

Virginia Nelson: corporate communications manager PRIM CORP EMPL corporate communications manager: TJX Companies, Inc.

Foundation Officials

Donald G. Campbell: treasurer, director (see above)
Edmond J. English: president, director, chairman (see above)
Nancy Hendrickson: assistant secretary, assistant clerk, assistant treasurer
Ann McCauley: assistant secretary, assistant clerk
Jay Meltzer: secretary, clerk
Mary Reynolds: vice president
Michael Skirvin: vice president

Grants Analysis

Disclosure Period: fiscal year ending January 31, 2003
Total Grants: $3,994,943*
Number of Grants: 690
Average Grant: $5,790
Highest Grant: $125,000
Lowest Grant: $175
Typical Range: $500 to $10,000
*Note: Giving excludes scholarship; United Way.

Recent Grants

Note: Grants derived from 2004 Form 990.
General

227,520	Save the Children, Westport, CT
125,000	Family Violence Prevention Fund, San Francisco, CA
50,000	American Red Cross of Massachusetts, Boston, MA
40,000	American Cancer Society, Greensburg, PA
40,000	United Way of Tri-County, Framingham, MA
30,000	Catholic Schools Foundation, Boston, MA
25,000	Anti-Defamation League, Boston, MA
25,000	Beth Israel Deaconess Medical Center, Boston, MA
25,000	Boston Metropolitan Council for Educational Opportunity, Boston, MA
25,000	Brandeis University, Waltham, MA

TMC INVESTMENT CO.

Company Headquarters

Pittsburgh, PA
Web: http://www.tippins.com

Company Description

Parent Company: Tippins Inc., 435 Butler St., Pittsburgh, PA, United States

Tippins Foundation

Giving Contact

George W. Tippins, Trustee
Three Gateway Center, 13 East
Pittsburgh, PA 15222
Phone: (412)391-0300
Fax: (412)782-7210

Description

EIN: 256282382
Organization Type: Corporate Foundation
Giving Locations: PA
Grant Types: General Support.

Financial Summary

Total Giving: $571,840 (2002); $511,840 (2001). Note: Contributes through foundation only.
Assets: $1,085,585 (2002); $1,740,864 (2001)
Gifts Received: $250,000 (2002); $250,000 (2001); $1,985,229 (2000). Note: Contributions are received from TMC Investment Co.

Typical Recipients

Arts & Humanities: Arts Associations & Councils, Arts Centers, Ballet, Film & Video, Arts & Humanities-General, Historic Preservation, History & Archaeology, Libraries, Museums/Galleries, Music, Opera, Public Broadcasting, Theater
Civic & Public Affairs: Botanical Gardens/Parks, Business/Free Enterprise, Community Foundations, Economic Development, Employment/Job Training, Civic & Public Affairs-General, Law & Justice, Municipalities/Towns, Philanthropic Organizations, Public Policy, Safety, Urban & Community Affairs, Women's Affairs, Zoos/Aquariums
Education: Afterschool/Enrichment Programs, Business Education, Colleges & Universities, Economic Education, Education Associations, Education Funds, Elementary Education (Private), Engineering/Technological Education, Education-General, Minority Education, Private Education (Precollege), Special Education
Environment: Air/Water Quality, Environment-General, Watershed
Health: Alzheimer's Disease, Arthritis, Cancer, Children's Health/Hospitals, Clinics/Medical Centers, Diabetes, Emergency/Ambulance Services, Health-General, Health Funds, Health Organizations, Heart, Hospices, Hospitals, Kidney, Medical Rehabilitation, Medical Research, Public Health, Respiratory, Single-Disease Health Associations
International: International Relief Efforts
Religion: Churches, Ministries, Religious Welfare
Social Services: Animal Protection, Big Brothers/Big Sisters, Child Welfare, Community Service Organizations, Counseling, Delinquency & Criminal Rehabilitation, Domestic Violence, Emergency Relief, Family Services, Food/Clothing Distribution, People with Disabilities, Recreation & Athletics, Scouts, Senior Services, Shelters/Homelessness, Social Services-General, United Funds/United Ways, YMCA/YWCA/YMHA/YWHA, Youth Organizations

Application Procedures

Initial Contact: Send a written request.
Application Requirements: Include a description of organization, purpose of funds sought, amount requested, proof of tax-exempt status.
Deadlines: None.

Foundation Officials

George R. Knapp: executive director, trustee
Charles J. Queenan, Jr.: trustee PRIM CORP EMPL senior counsel: Kirkpatrick & Lockhart. CORP AFFIL director: Crane Co.; director: Allegheny Teledyne Inc.; director: Babcock Lumber Co. NONPR AFFIL director: Allegheny-Singer Research Institute.
Carolyn H. Tippins: trustee
George W. Tippins: trustee
John H. Tippins: trustee

Grants Analysis

Disclosure Period: calendar year ending 2002
Total Grants: $571,840
Number of Grants: 62
Average Grant: $7,735*
Highest Grant: $100,000
Lowest Grant: $500
Typical Range: $500 to $20,000
*Note: Average grant figure excludes highest grant.

Recent Grants

Note: Grants derived from 2003 Form 990.
General

50,000	Alzheimer's Association, Chicago, IL
50,000	Genetics and Aging Unit MGH, Charlestown, MA
50,000	University of Pittsburgh Panther Labworks, Pittsburgh, PA
35,000	Institute for Entrepreneurial Excellence, Pittsburgh, PA
25,000	Alzheimer's Disease Residential Center-UPMC, Pittsburgh, PA
20,000	Salvation Army, Pittsburgh, PA
10,400	Carnegie Museums of Pittsburgh, Pittsburgh, PA
10,000	American Heart Association, Pittsburgh, PA
10,000	Brother's Brother Foundation, Pittsburgh, PA
10,000	Catalyst Connection, Pittsburgh, PA

RANDALL L. TOBIAS FOUNDATION

Giving Contact

Suzanne Hazelett, Executive Director
500 E. 96th Street, Suite 110
Indianapolis, IN 46240
Phone: (317)433-5505
Fax: (317)433-5504
E-mail: snh@rltfound.org
Web: http://www.rltfound.org

Description

Founded: 1995
EIN: 351938355
Organization Type: Private Foundation
Grant Types: General Support, Scholarship.

Donor Information

Founder: Foundation was established in 1994 by Randall L. Tobias.

Financial Summary

Total Giving: $1,196,504 (2001)
Giving Analysis: Giving for 2001 includes: foundation gifts to individuals ($165,000); foundation grants to United Way ($250,000)
Assets: $9,138,439 (2001)
Gifts Received: $60,965 (2001); $1,031,754 (1999); $7,503,130 (1998). Note: In 1996, 1998, 1999, and 2001, contributions were received from Randall L. Tobias.

Typical Recipients

Arts & Humanities: Arts Outreach, Historic Preservation, History & Archaeology, Libraries, Museums/Galleries, Music, Public Broadcasting, Theater
Civic & Public Affairs: Botanical Gardens/Parks, Civic & Public Affairs-General, Public Policy, Safety
Education: Business Education, Colleges & Universities, Education Reform, Elementary Education (Public), Education-General, Literacy, Secondary Education (Public)
Religion: Churches
Social Services: Day Care, Recreation & Athletics, United Funds/United Ways, Youth Organizations

Application Procedures

Initial Contact: Request application guidelines, then send full proposal.

Application Requirements: Completed applications will include a cover sheet with date of application, amount requested, name of organization, contact person and information, EIN, and signature of responsible officer of the organization. A proposal narrative of two to five pages should include purpose of funds sought; what needs will be met by the project and who it will serve; why organization is the appropriate group to meet these needs; plan for continuing project after foundation funding ceases; other funders involved; and expected outcomes. Also attach annual report, most recent financial statement, proposed budget, list of board of directors, and proof of tax-exempt status.

Deadlines: March 1 and September 1.

Decision Notification: Grant awards are announced in the second and fourth quarters. Applicants will be contacted by mail within four weeks of the grant selection process.

Restrictions

Does not support endowment campaigns; fundraising events; federal, state, or local governmental bodies, or political candidates; individuals; or other private foundations.

Additional Information

Provides scholarships to residents of IN who need financial assistance to enable them to attend undergraduate institutions in the U.S.

Publications: Application Guidelines

Foundation Officials

Susie Hazelett: executive director

Randall L. Tobias: president, treasurer B Lafayette, IN 1942. ED Indiana University BS (1964). CORP AFFIL director: Phillips Petroleum Co.; director: Knight-Ridder Inc.; director: Northwest Publications Inc.; director: Kimberly-Clark Corp. NONPR AFFIL director: Indianapolis Symphony Orchestra; member: Theta Chi; board governors: Indianapolis Museum Art; director: Indiana University Foundation; member: Indianapolis Corp. Community Council; vice chairman: Colonial Williamsburg Foundation; trustee: Duke University; member: Business Council; member: Amwell Valley Conservancy. CLUB AFFIL University Club; Woodstock Club; Economic Club Indianapolis; Meridian Hills Country Club; Athletic Club; Columbia Club.

Todd C. Tobias: vice president

Paige N. Tobias-Button: vice president, secretary

Grants Analysis

Disclosure Period: calendar year ending 2001
Total Grants: $781,504*
Number of Grants: 40
Average Grant: $6,191*
Highest Grant: $177,000
Lowest Grant: $15
Typical Range: $1,000 to $10,000
*Note: Giving excludes scholarships, grants to individuals, and United Way. Average grant figure excludes three highest grants

Recent Grants

Note: Grants derived from 2002 Form 990.
General

250,000	United Way Central Indiana, Indianapolis, IN
50,000	Governor's Residence Commission, Indianapolis, IN
40,000	Oaks Academy, Indianapolis, IN
25,000	Indiana University Foundation, Bloomington, IN
15,000	North Central High School, Indianapolis, IN
10,000	Children's Museum, Indianapolis, IN
8,169	Indianapolis Civic Theater, Indianapolis, IN
5,430	Indianapolis Museum of Art, Indianapolis, IN
5,000	Bernards Township Police Department, Basking Ridge, NJ -- 9/11/2001 support
5,000	Crown Hill Foundation, Indianapolis, IN

A.M. TODD CO.

Company Headquarters

1717 Douglas Ave.
Kalamazoo, MI 49007
Phone: (616)343-2603

Company Description

Revenue: US$ (2001)
Employees: 100 (2001)
SIC(s): 2000 Food & Kindred Products, 2800 Chemicals & Allied Products.

Operating Locations

A.M. Todd Co. (MI--Kalamazoo)

A.M. Todd Co. Foundation

Giving Contact

Chris Czopek, Trust Officer
c/o Fifth Third Bank
136 East Michigan Avenue
PO Box 4019
Kalamazoo, MI 49007
Phone: (616)337-6768
Fax: (616)337-6651

Description

EIN: 386055829
Organization Type: Corporate Foundation
Giving Locations: MI: Kalamazoo County
Grant Types: General Support.

Financial Summary

Total Giving: $62,150 (2003)
Giving Analysis: Giving for 2003 includes: foundation grants to United Way ($22,000)
Assets: $369,672 (2003)
Gifts Received: $99,000 (2003); $100,000 (2000); $100,000 (1999). Note: In 2003, contributions were received from A.M. Todd Co. ($75,000) and Zink & Triest Co. ($24,000).

Typical Recipients

Arts & Humanities: Arts Associations & Councils, Arts Festivals, Arts Funds, Arts Institutes, Community Arts, Arts & Humanities-General, Historic Preservation, History & Archaeology, Libraries, Museums/Galleries, Music, Performing Arts, Public Broadcasting

Civic & Public Affairs: Botanical Gardens/Parks, Business/Free Enterprise, Clubs, Economic Development, Civic & Public Affairs-General, Housing, Municipalities/Towns, Parades/Festivals, Urban & Community Affairs, Zoos/Aquariums

Education: Agricultural Education, Business Education, Colleges & Universities, Community & Junior Colleges, Education Associations, Education Reform, Education-General, Science/Mathematics Education, Special Education, Student Aid, Vocational & Technical Education

Environment: Environment-General, Resource Conservation

Health: Cancer, Clinics/Medical Centers, Diabetes, Emergency/Ambulance Services, Health Organizations, Hospices, Prenatal Health Issues, Public Health

International: Foreign Arts Organizations
Religion: Churches, Ministries, Religious Welfare
Science: Scientific Centers & Institutes
Social Services: Big Brothers/Big Sisters, Camps, Child Welfare, Community Service Organizations, Family Planning, Family Services, Food/Clothing Distribution, People with Disabilities, Scouts, Senior Services, Substance Abuse, United Funds/United Ways, YMCA/YWCA/YMHA/YWHA, Youth Organizations

Application Procedures

Initial Contact: Send a brief letter of inquiry. Include proof of tax-exempt status.
Deadlines: None.

Restrictions

Does not support individuals, religious organizations for sectarian purposes, political or lobbying groups, or organizations outside operating areas.

Additional Information

Education support is primarily provided directly by A.M. Todd Co., not the foundation.
Trust(s): Fifth Third Bank

Corporate Officials

Thomas F. Rose: vice president, chief financial officer, chief executive officer PRIM CORP EMPL vice president, chief financial officer: AM Todd Co.

A. J. Todd, III: chairman, president, chief executive officer PRIM CORP EMPL chairman, president, chief executive officer: AM Todd Co.

Foundation Officials

Ian D. Blair: trustee PRIM CORP EMPL vice president trading: AM Todd Co.

A. J. Todd, III: trustee (see above)

Grants Analysis

Disclosure Period: calendar year ending 2003
Total Grants: $40,150*
Number of Grants: 27
Average Grant: $1,150*
Highest Grant: $10,000
Lowest Grant: $100
Typical Range: $500 to $3,000
*Note: Giving excludes United Way. Average grant figure excludes highest grant.

Recent Grants

Note: Grants derived from 2001 Form 990.
General

21,500	Kalamazoo Foundation, Kalamazoo, MI
19,250	Greater Kalamazoo United Way, Kalamazoo, MI
10,000	Lakeside Treatment and Learning Center, Kalamazoo, MI
6,500	Ministry With Community, Kalamazoo, MI
5,000	Boys and Girls Clubs, Kalamazoo, MI
5,000	Kalamazoo Neighborhood Housing Services, Kalamazoo, MI
5,000	Parks Foundation of Kalamazoo County, Kalamazoo, MI
3,000	Heritage Community of Kalamazoo, Kalamazoo, MI
1,500	Junior Achievement of Kalamazoo, Kalamazoo, MI
1,250	Kalamazoo Symphony, Kalamazoo, MI

TOLEDO BLADE CO.

Company Headquarters

541 N. Superior St.
Toledo, OH 43604
Web: http://www.toledoblank.com

Company Description

Employees: 600
SIC(s): 2711 Newspapers.
Parent Company: Block Communications Inc., 541 N. Superior St., Toledo, OH, United States

Nonmonetary Support

Volunteer Programs: Company actively promotes employee volunteerism through participation in the United Way, Read for Literacy, and in activities with the Sherman School, its adopted school.

Blade Foundation

Giving Contact

William Block, Jr., President
Blade Foundation
541 N. Superior Street
Toledo, OH 43604
Phone: (419)245-6210

Description

EIN: 346559843
Organization Type: Corporate Foundation
Giving Locations: OH: Toledo
Grant Types: General Support, Scholarship.

Financial Summary

Total Giving: $169,400 (2003); $204,922 (2002); $272,939 (2001)
Assets: $8,611 (2003); $53,381 (2002); $256,103 (2001)
Gifts Received: $125,000 (2003); $275,000 (2001); $275,000 (2000). Note: In 2000 and 2001, contributions were received from Block Communications. In 1999, contributions were received from Blade Communications.

Typical Recipients

Arts & Humanities: Arts Associations & Councils, Arts Centers, Arts Festivals, Ballet, Community Arts, Historic Preservation, History & Archaeology, Libraries, Literary Arts, Museums/Galleries, Music, Opera, Performing Arts, Public Broadcasting, Theater
Civic & Public Affairs: African American Affairs, Botanical Gardens/Parks, Business/Free Enterprise, Clubs, Economic Development, Employment/Job Training, Ethnic Organizations, First Amendment Issues, Civic & Public Affairs-General, Housing, Law & Justice, Municipalities/Towns, Parades/Festivals, Professional & Trade Associations, Public Policy, Urban & Community Affairs, Women's Affairs, Zoos/Aquariums
Education: Business Education, Colleges & Universities, Community & Junior Colleges, Education Funds, Education Reform, Education-General, Literacy, Medical Education, Minority Education, Private Education (Precollege), Public Education (Precollege), Student Aid
Environment: Resource Conservation
Health: Alzheimer's Disease, Arthritis, Children's Health/Hospitals, Clinics/Medical Centers, Emergency/Ambulance Services, Health Organizations, Hospices, Multiple Sclerosis, Preventive Medicine/Wellness Organizations, Respiratory, Single-Disease Health Associations
International: International Affairs, International Relief Efforts
Religion: Jewish Causes, Ministries, Religious Organizations, Religious Welfare
Science: Science Museums
Social Services: Child Welfare, Community Centers, Community Service Organizations, Emergency Relief, Family Planning, Food/Clothing Distribution, People with Disabilities, Recreation & Athletics, Scouts, Senior Services, United Funds/United Ways, Volunteer Services, YMCA/YWCA/YMHA/YWHA, Youth Organizations

Application Procedures

Initial Contact: Send a proposal in letter format.
Application Requirements: Include a description of organization, amount requested, purpose of funds sought, and proof of tax-exempt status. For scholarships include employee's name and date of employment; SAT score, with date and location where taken; college or university to be attended; expected degree and graduation date.
Deadlines: None for grants; March 1 for scholarships.

Restrictions

Does not support: individuals, religious organizations for sectarian purposes, political or lobbying groups, or organizations outside operating areas. Scholarships are limited to children or legal dependents of full-time employees of the Toledo Blade with at least three years of employment. Children of officers and directors are not eligible.

Corporate Officials

Allan James Block: directorpbl, editor-in-chief, european corresp B Toledo, OH 1954. ED University of Pennsylvania (1977). PRIM CORP EMPL director: Toledo Blade Co. CORP AFFIL director: PG Publishing Co.; president: Blade Broadcasting Co.; director: C-SPAN. NONPR AFFIL trustee: Medical College Ohio. CLUB AFFIL Pennsylvania Club; Toledo Club; Metropolitan Club.
John Robinson Block: co-publisher, editor-in-chief, european corresp B Toledo, OH 1954. ED Yale University BA (1977). PRIM CORP EMPL co-publisher, editor-in-chief, european corresp: Toledo Blade Co. CORP AFFIL vice president, director: PG Publishing Co.; co-publ: Pittsburgh Post-Gazette; executive vice president, director: Blade Communication; co-publ, director: Monterey Peninsula Herald. NONPR AFFIL member: American Society Newspaper Editors; member: Society Professional Journalists. CLUB AFFIL mem: Belmont Country Club; mem: Yale Club.
William Block: chairman, director B New York, NY September 20, 1915. ED Yale University AB (1936). PRIM CORP EMPL chairman, director: Toledo Blade Co. CORP AFFIL co-publ: Pittsburgh Post-Gazette; chairman board: PG Publishing Co. NONPR AFFIL director: Maumee Valley Historical Society; member: Society Professional Journalists; member: International Press Institute; director: Historical Society Western Pennsylvania; director: Inland Press Association; director: Gateway Music; member: American Newspaper Publishers Association; member: American Society Newspaper Editors; trustee emeritus: American Assembly; sponsor: Allegheny Conference Community Development.
William Block, Jr.: president, director B New Haven, CT 1944. ED Trinity College BA (1967); Washington & Lee University JD (1972). PRIM CORP EMPL president, director: Toledo Blade Co. CORP AFFIL president, director: Pittsburgh Post-Gazette-Sun-Telegraph. NONPR AFFIL director: Toledo Symphony; director: United Way Toledo; director: Toledo Museum Art; member: Old Newsboys Goodfellow Association; president: Read for Literacy; member, director: Ohio Newspaper Association. CLUB AFFIL Toledo Club; Toledo Press Club.

Foundation Officials

Gary J. Blair: treasurer, trustee
Allan James Block: vice president, trustee (see above)
John Robinson Block: vice president, trustee (see above)
William Block, Jr.: president, trustee (see above)
William Block: vice president, trustee (see above)
Fritz Byers: assistant secretary
Sandra J. Chavez: secretary, trustee
Lanetta Goings: vice president, trustee

Grants Analysis

Disclosure Period: calendar year ending 2003
Total Grants: $96,900*
Number of Grants: 57
Average Grant: $1,373*
Highest Grant: $20,000
Lowest Grant: $200
Typical Range: $100 to $3,000
***Note:** Giving excludes scholarships and United Way. Average grant figure excludes highest grant.

Recent Grants

Note: Grants derived from 2003 Form 990.
Library-Related

20,000	Toledo-Lucas City Public Library, Toledo, OH

General

62,000	United Way of Greater Toledo, Toledo, OH
10,000	Toledo Museum of Art, Toledo, OH
10,000	Toledo Symphony, Toledo, OH
10,000	Toledo Zoo, Toledo, OH
7,500	Lourdes College, Sylvania, OH
5,000	Jewish Federation of Greater Toledo, Sylvania, OH
5,000	Toledo Public Schools Foundation, Toledo, OH
2,500	St. Ursula Academy, Toledo, OH
2,000	Public Broadcasting Foundation of North West Ohio, Toledo, OH
1,750	Arts Commission of Greater Toledo, Toledo, OH

THE TOMS FOUNDATION

Giving Contact

Ronald L. Grimm, Trustee
PO Box 2466
Knoxville, TN 37901
Phone: (865)544-3000

Description

Founded: 1954
EIN: 626037668
Organization Type: Private Foundation
Giving Locations: TN: Eastern Tennessee
Grant Types: Project.

Donor Information

Founder: the late W. P. Toms

Financial Summary

Total Giving: $4,000 (fiscal year ending June 30, 2004); $24,000 (fiscal 2001)
Assets: $4,212,086 (fiscal 2004); $4,169,082 (fiscal 2002)

Typical Recipients

Arts & Humanities: Arts Associations & Councils, Community Arts, Arts & Humanities-General, History & Archaeology, Libraries, Museums/Galleries, Opera
Civic & Public Affairs: Civic & Public Affairs-General, Housing, Zoos/Aquariums
Education: Colleges & Universities, Education-General, Legal Education, Private Education (Precollege)
Environment: Environment-General
Health: Clinics/Medical Centers, Health Organizations, Medical Research, Single-Disease Health Associations
Religion: Religious Organizations, Religious Welfare
Social Services: Community Service Organizations, Family Services, Food/Clothing Distribution, Scouts, United Funds/United Ways, Youth Organizations

Application Procedures

Initial Contact: a brief letter of inquiry followed by proposal. Submit proposal preferably in June.

Application Requirements: Include a description of organization, amount requested, purpose of funds sought, and proof of tax-exempt status.
Deadlines: June 30. Board meets in September. Decisions are made one month after annual meeting.

Restrictions

Does not support individuals or endowments.

Additional Information

Publications: Annual Report

Foundation Officials

Janet L. Grimm: trustee
R. Brett Grimm: trustee
Ronald L. Grimm: chairman
Thomas R. Ramsey: secretary
Dorothy B. Wilson: vice chairman

Grants Analysis

Disclosure Period: fiscal year ending June 30, 2004
Total Grants: $4,000
Number of Grants: 1

Recent Grants

Note: Grants derived from fiscal 2004 Form 990.
General
4,000   University of Tennessee, Knoxville, TN

TONYA MEMORIAL FOUNDATION

Giving Contact

Maurice H. Martin, President
c/o SunTrust Bank NA
PO Box 1638
736 Market St.
Chattanooga, TN 37402
Phone: (423)756-6600
Fax: (423)757-3691

Alternate Contact

Whitney Durand
1000 Volunteer Bldg.
Chattanooga, TN 37402
Note: Contact for application information.

Description

Founded: 1949
EIN: 626042269
Organization Type: Private Foundation
Giving Locations: TN: Chattanooga
Grant Types: Capital, Multiyear/Continuing Support.

Donor Information

Founder: the late Burkett Miller

Financial Summary

Total Giving: $75,000 (2003); $44,653 (2001)
Assets: $3,768,795 (2003); $4,263,807 (2001)
Gifts Received: $6,972,356 (1994). Note: In 1994, contributions were received from the Willie D. Miller Annuity Trust.

Typical Recipients

Arts & Humanities: Arts Associations & Councils, Libraries, Museums/Galleries, Performing Arts, Public Broadcasting, Theater
Civic & Public Affairs: Botanical Gardens/Parks, Business/Free Enterprise, Community Foundations, Economic Development, Civic & Public Affairs-General, Legal Aid, Municipalities/Towns, Urban & Community Affairs, Zoos/Aquariums
Education: Colleges & Universities, Private Education (Precollege), Public Education (Precollege)
Environment: Environment-General, Resource Conservation

Social Services: Community Centers, Community Service Organizations, Homes, Substance Abuse, United Funds/United Ways, Youth Organizations

Application Procedures

Initial Contact: Submit a letter of no more than three pages describing the project.
Application Requirements: Include a description of organization, most recent Form 990, list of board members, budget for current fiscal year, and proof of tax-exempt status. Send one copy to each of the trustees.
Deadlines: January 10, April 10, July 10, and October 10.
Decision Notification: Applicants will be notified of the foundation's decision following regular meetings held quarterly.

Restrictions

New donors generally restricted to capital projects in Chattanooga, TN.

Foundation Officials

H. Whitney Durand: treasurer, trustee
James R. Hedges, III: chairman, trustee
Maurice H. Martin: president, trustee

Grants Analysis

Disclosure Period: calendar year ending 2003
Total Grants: $75,000
Number of Grants: 3
Highest Grant: $25,000
Lowest Grant: $25,000

Recent Grants

Note: Grants derived from 2003 Form 990.
General
25,000   Cumberland Trail Conference, Crossville, TN -- for construction of Cumberland Trail
25,000   Southeast Tennessee Legal Services, Chattanooga, TN
25,000   WTCI - Channel 45, Chattanooga, TN

TORO CO.

Company Headquarters

8111 Lyndale Ave., S
Bloomington, MN 55420
Web: http://www.toro.com

Company Description

Founded: 1914
Ticker: TTC
Exchange: NYSE
Revenue: US$1.399 billion (2002)
Employees: 5367 (2003)
SIC(s): 3523 Farm Machinery & Equipment, 3524 Lawn & Garden Equipment.

Nonmonetary Support

Value: $100,000 (2002)
Type: Donated Equipment; Donated Products; In-kind Services
Volunteer Programs: The company launched an employee volunteer program in 2003.
Contact: Ellen Watson
Administrator

Toro Foundation

Giving Contact

Stacy Bogart, President
Toro Foundation
8111 Lyndale Avenue South
Bloomington, MN 55420-1196

Phone: (952)887-8911
Fax: (952)887-7291
E-mail: stacy.bogart@toro.com

Description

Founded: 1989
EIN: 363593618
Organization Type: Corporate Foundation
Giving Locations: headquarters and operating communities.
Grant Types: Employee Matching Gifts, General Support.

Financial Summary

Total Giving: $1,291,000 (2002); $380,556 (2001)
Giving Analysis: Giving for 2001 includes: foundation ($380,556)
Assets: $838,379 (2002); $1,007,362 (2001)
Gifts Received: $405,000 (2001); $200,000 (2000); $900,000 (1999). Note: Foundation receives contributions from the Toro Co.

Typical Recipients

Arts & Humanities: Arts Associations & Councils, Arts Institutes, Arts & Humanities-General, History & Archaeology, Literary Arts, Museums/Galleries, Music, Public Broadcasting, Theater
Civic & Public Affairs: Botanical Gardens/Parks, Clubs, Community Foundations, Civic & Public Affairs-General, Housing, Legal Aid, Nonprofit Management, Parades/Festivals, Rural Affairs, Safety, Urban & Community Affairs
Education: Afterschool/Enrichment Programs, Arts/Humanities Education, Business Education, Colleges & Universities, Community & Junior Colleges, Education Funds, Education Reform, Elementary Education (Private), Elementary Education (Public), Environmental Education, Education-General, Private Education (Precollege), Public Education (Precollege), Religious Education, Secondary Education (Private), Secondary Education (Public), Student Aid
Environment: Environment-General, Watershed
Health: AIDS/HIV, Cancer, Diabetes, Emergency/Ambulance Services, Health-General, Heart, Hospitals, Public Health
International: Foreign Educational Institutions, International Environmental Issues, International Organizations
Social Services: Big Brothers/Big Sisters, Child Welfare, Community Service Organizations, Emergency Relief, Food/Clothing Distribution, People with Disabilities, Recreation & Athletics, Scouts, Social Services-General, Substance Abuse, United Funds/United Ways, YMCA/YWCA/YMHA/YWHA, Youth Organizations

Application Procedures

Initial Contact: Send a brief letter of inquiry.
Application Requirements: Include a description of organization, evidence that the people proposing a project are able to carry it to completion, planned method for evaluating the proposed program, a specific budget for the project, operating budget, major donor list, and proof of tax-exempt status.
Deadlines: None.
Review Process: Board meets quarterly.
Notes: The foundation requests that all initial inquiries by made by mail, not by telephone or by personal visits.

Restrictions

Does not support individuals, religious organizations for sectarian purposes, political or lobbying groups, or organizations outside operating areas.

Corporate Officials

Kendrick B. Melrose: chairman, co-president, chief executive officer, director B Orlando, FL 1940. ED Princeton University BS (1962); University of Chicago MBA (1967). PRIM CORP EMPL chairman, co-president, chief executive officer, director: Toro Co.

Foundation Officials

Kendrick B. Melrose: director (see above)
Karen Meyer: director

Grants Analysis

Disclosure Period: calendar year ending 2002
Total Grants: $158,521*
Number of Grants: 100
Average Grant: $2,641 (approx)
Highest Grant: $15,000
Lowest Grant: $300
Typical Range: $100 to $25,000
*Note: Grants analysis provided by foundation. Giving excludes matching gifts, scholarships, and United Way.

Recent Grants

Note: Grants derived from 2003 Form 990.
General

56,136	United Way Minneapolis, Minneapolis, MN -- towards gift first payment
52,000	United Way Minneapolis, Minneapolis, MN -- towards pledge payment
52,000	United Way Minneapolis, Minneapolis, MN -- towards pledge payment
47,864	United Way Minneapolis, Minneapolis, MN -- towards second pledge payment
25,000	United Way of Inland Valleys, Riverside, CA -- towards corporate pledge
15,000	Minnesota Landscape Arboretum Foundation, Chanhassen, MN -- towards Big Bugs exhibition
14,000	Guthrie Theater, Minneapolis, MN -- towards rush line support
12,000	BARC Center, Windom, MN -- for operating grant
11,000	Michigan State University Libraries TGIF System, East Lansing, MI -- towards TGIF grant
10,000	Tomah Fire Department, Tomah, WI -- towards operating grant for breathing apparatus

HARRY A. AND MARGARET D. TOWSLEY FOUNDATION

Giving Contact

Lynn T. White, President
140 Ashman Street, P.O. Box 349
Midland, MI 48640
Phone: (989)837-1100
Fax: (989)837-3240

Description

Founded: 1959
EIN: 386091798
Organization Type: General Purpose Foundation
Giving Locations: MI: especially Ann Arbor and Washtenaw County
Grant Types: Emergency, General Support, Multiyear/Continuing Support, Operating Expenses, Project, Research.

Donor Information

Founder: Established in 1959 in Michigan by Margaret Dow Towsley, who donated a gift of Dow Chemical Company common stock.

Financial Summary

Total Giving: $3,229,283 (2003); $3,150,929 (2001).
Note: 1996 figure includes $34,564 in matching grants.
Giving Analysis: Giving for 2003 includes: foundation matching gifts ($54,750)

Assets: $66,198,486 (2003); $61,394,334 (2001)
Gifts Received: $718,729 (1997); $252,457 (1994)

Typical Recipients

Arts & Humanities: Arts Associations & Councils, Arts Centers, Arts Festivals, Arts Funds, Arts Institutes, Arts & Humanities-General, History & Archaeology, Libraries, Museums/Galleries, Music, Opera, Theater
Civic & Public Affairs: Clubs, Community Foundations, Economic Development, Ethnic Organizations, Civic & Public Affairs-General, Housing, Law & Justice, Nonprofit Management, Parades/Festivals, Philanthropic Organizations, Public Policy, Rural Affairs, Urban & Community Affairs, Women's Affairs
Education: Agricultural Education, Arts/Humanities Education, Colleges & Universities, Community & Junior Colleges, Education Funds, Education Reform, Faculty Development, Education-General, Health & Physical Education, Medical Education, Minority Education, Preschool Education, Private Education (Precollege), Public Education (Precollege), Science/Mathematics Education, Social Sciences Education, Student Aid
Environment: Environment-General, Protection, Resource Conservation, Watershed, Wildlife Protection
Health: Adolescent Health Issues, AIDS/HIV, Alzheimer's Disease, Cancer, Children's Health/Hospitals, Clinics/Medical Centers, Emergency/Ambulance Services, Health-General, Geriatric Health, Health Organizations, Hospices, Hospitals, Kidney, Medical Rehabilitation, Medical Research, Nursing Services, Public Health, Respiratory, Single-Disease Health Associations, Transplant Networks/Donor Banks
International: Health Care/Hospitals
Religion: Churches, Religious Organizations, Religious Welfare
Science: Science Exhibits & Fairs, Science Museums
Social Services: Animal Protection, Big Brothers/Big Sisters, Child Abuse, Child Welfare, Community Centers, Community Service Organizations, Family Planning, Family Services, Food/Clothing Distribution, People with Disabilities, Recreation & Athletics, Scouts, Senior Services, Shelters/Homelessness, Substance Abuse, United Funds/United Ways, Volunteer Services, YMCA/YWCA/YMHA/YWHA, Youth Organizations

Application Procedures

Initial Contact: Prospective applicants should submit a letter and proposal to the foundation. The foundation does not provide application form. for requests. Elaborate presentations are discouraged.
Application Requirements: Applicants should submit a copy of the tax-exempt letter from the IRS; letter establishing that the applicant is not a private foundation; amount requested, need, and intended use; and organization's latest financial statements with an operating budget and other funding sources.
Deadlines: Applications should be submitted between January 1 and March 31 of each year. Send two copies of proposals.
Review Process: Final notification to applicants usually is made during the third quarter of the year.

Restrictions

The foundation does not make direct grants to individuals, provide loan funds, grants to students for scholarships, or grants for travel and conferences. The foundation does not typically provide funds for books, publications, films, tapes, audio-visual or other communication media.

Additional Information

The trustees do not conduct personal interviews with applicants except upon the foundation's initiative. Additional information is frequently requested by the foundation after the application is received.
Publications: Annual Report; Application Guidelines

Foundation Officials

C. Wendell Dunbar: treasurer, trustee
David Winston Inglish: trustee
Jennifer Poteat-Flores: trustee
John E. Riecker: secretary
Margaret Ann Riecker: chairman, trustee NONPR AFFIL advisory cabinet: Council of Michigan Foundations.
Steven Riecker: trustee
Judith D. Rumelhart: vice president, trustee
Margaret E. Thompson, MD: trustee
Lynn T. White: president, trustee

Grants Analysis

Disclosure Period: calendar year ending 2003
Total Grants: $3,174,533*
Number of Grants: 36
Average Grant: $74,986*
Highest Grant: $300,000
Typical Range: $25,000 to $100,000
*Note: Giving excludes matching gifts. Average grant figure excludes three highest grants ($700,000).

Recent Grants

Note: Grants derived from 2003 Form 990.
General

300,000	United Methodist Retirement, Durham, NC
200,000	Case Western Reserve, Cleveland, OH
200,000	Kalamazoo College, Kalamazoo, MI
150,000	Hope College, Holland, MI
125,000	Culver Education Foundation, Culver, IN
100,000	Henry Ford Museum, Dearborn, MI
100,000	Interlochen Center for Arts, Interlochen, MI
100,000	Planned Parenthood, Ann Arbor, MI
60,000	Friends of Con Foster Museum, Traverse City, MI
50,000	Ann Arbor Teen Center Neutral Zone, Ann Arbor, MI

TOZER FOUNDATION

Giving Contact

Tom Simonet, President
Tozer Foundation
101 East 5th Street
St. Paul, MN 55101
Phone: (651)466-8444
Note: Contact for grants only.

Description

Founded: 1946
EIN: 416011518
Organization Type: General Purpose Foundation
Giving Locations: MN: Kanabec County for scholarship program, Pine County for scholarship program, Washington County for scholarship program
Grant Types: General Support, Scholarship.

Financial Summary

Total Giving: $1,811,427 (fiscal year ending October 31, 2002); $1,571,820 (fiscal 2001)
Giving Analysis: Giving for fiscal 2002 includes: foundation grants to United Way ($14,000); foundation scholarships ($1,267,500); fiscal 2001: foundation scholarships ($1,261,750)
Assets: $25,725,649 (fiscal 2002); $29,492,909 (fiscal 2001)
Gifts Received: $213 (fiscal 2001). Note: In fiscal 2001, contributions were received from the Anna Scotten Estate.

Typical Recipients

Arts & Humanities: Arts Centers, Arts Funds, History & Archaeology, Libraries, Music, Opera, Public Broadcasting
Civic & Public Affairs: Business/Free Enterprise,

Municipalities/Towns, Nonprofit Management, Parades/Festivals, Professional & Trade Associations, Public Policy, Urban & Community Affairs
Education: Business Education, Business-School Partnerships, Colleges & Universities, Economic Education, Engineering/Technological Education, Education-General, Minority Education, Public Education (Precollege), Science/Mathematics Education, Secondary Education (Public), Student Aid
Health: Clinics/Medical Centers, Hospitals, Medical Rehabilitation
International: International Relations
Religion: Religious Organizations, Religious Welfare
Science: Science Museums
Social Services: Child Welfare, Community Service Organizations, Family Services, Recreation & Athletics, Scouts, Social Services-General, United Funds/United Ways, Volunteer Services, YMCA/YWCA/YMHA/YWHA, Youth Organizations

Application Procedures

Initial Contact: The foundation requests applications be made in writing. Applications for scholarships may be received through high school guidance counselors.
Application Requirements: Grant applications must outline the nature of the request. Applicant must be a resident.
Deadlines: None.
Review Process: The board meets periodically throughout the year. The board considers scholarship requests at their annual meeting in May. Decisions are made immediately after the meeting.

Foundation Officials

Robert S. Davis: chairman B Stillwater, MN 1914. ED University of Minnesota (1934). PRIM CORP EMPL director: H M Smyth Co. CORP AFFIL director: Heartland Technology. CLUB AFFIL Elks Club.
James Richard Oppenheimer: director B Saint Paul, MN 1921. ED Dartmouth College BA (1942); Yale University JD (1948). PRIM CORP EMPL officer counsel: Oppenheimer, Wolff & Donnelly. NONPR AFFIL member: Ramsey County Bar Association; member: Saint Paul Chamber of Commerce; trustee: Charles K Blandin Residuary Trust; member: Minnesota Bar Association; member: American Bar Association. CLUB AFFIL White Bear Yacht Club; Rotary Club.
John Thomas Simonet: vice president B Stillwater, MN 1926. ED University of Minnesota BBA (1948); University of Minnesota LLB (1951). CORP AFFIL board director: Mairs & Power Growth Fund; board director: Mairs & Power Income Fund; director: Mairs & Power Funds Inc.; director: Donovan Companies; director: First Trust Co.; director: Carondelet Life Care Corp.
John F. Thoreen: director

Grants Analysis

Disclosure Period: fiscal year ending October 31, 2002
Total Grants: $529,927*
Number of Grants: 54
Average Grant: $4,067*
Highest Grant: $188,450
Lowest Grant: $500
Typical Range: $1,000 to $19,000
*Note: Giving excludes scholarships and United Way. Average grant figure excludes two highest grants totaling $318,450.

Recent Grants

Note: Grants derived from 2002 Form 990.
Library-Related
9,000   Friends of the St. Paul Public Library, St. Paul, MN
General
188,450   University of Minnesota Twin Cities, Twin Cities, MN -- scholarship
130,000   Greater Twin Cities United Way, Minneapolis, MN

57,200   University of Wisconsin-Madison, Madison, WI -- scholarship
54,000   Gustavus Adolphus College, St. Peter, MN -- scholarship
54,000   University of Minnesota Duluth, Duluth, MN -- scholarship
49,700   St. Thomas University, St. Paul, MN -- scholarship
45,600   College of St. Benedict, St. Joseph, MN -- scholarship
43,200   Northwestern College, Roseville, MN -- scholarship
39,150   St. Olaf College, Northfield, MN -- scholarship
36,700   College of St. Scholastica, Duluth, MN -- scholarship

TRACTOR & EQUIPMENT CO.

Company Headquarters
Birmingham, AL

Company Description
Employees: 190
SIC(s): 5000 Wholesale Trade--Durable Goods.

Tractor & Equipment Co. Foundation

Giving Contact
Lloyd Adams, Secretary & Treasurer
Tractor & Equipment Co. Foundation
5336 Airport Hwy.
Birmingham, AL 35212
Phone: (205)591-2131
Fax: (205)591-8321

Description
Founded: 1977
EIN: 630718825
Organization Type: Corporate Foundation
Giving Locations: AL
Grant Types: General Support, Scholarship.

Donor Information
Founder: Tractor & Equipment Co.

Financial Summary
Total Giving: $98,715 (2002)
Giving Analysis: Giving for 2002 includes: foundation grants to United Way ($10,800); foundation ($39,400); foundation scholarships ($48,515).
Assets: $139,841 (2002)
Gifts Received: $125,000 (2002); $75,000 (2000); $101,500 (1999). Note: In 2002, contributions were received from Tractor & Equipment Co.

Typical Recipients
Arts & Humanities: History & Archaeology, Libraries
Civic & Public Affairs: Botanical Gardens/Parks, Economic Development, Civic & Public Affairs-General, Professional & Trade Associations
Education: Colleges & Universities, Community & Junior Colleges, Education Funds, Elementary Education (Public), Education-General, Legal Education, Private Education (Precollege), Public Education (Precollege), Secondary Education (Public), Student Aid
Environment: Forestry, Resource Conservation
Health: Cancer, Heart, Hospitals, Mental Health, Multiple Sclerosis, Single-Disease Health Associations
International: Foreign Arts Organizations
Religion: Churches, Ministries, Religious Organiza-

tions, Religious Welfare, Social/Policy Issues
Social Services: Animal Protection, Camps, Child Welfare, Community Service Organizations, Recreation & Athletics, Scouts, United Funds/United Ways, Youth Organizations

Application Procedures
Initial Contact: Application form required for scholarships. No application procedure has been outlined for grants to nonprofit organizations.
Deadlines: March 1.
Notes: Scholarship applications should be addressed to: Mr. J.W. Waitzman, Jr., Tractor & Equipment Company, PO Box 12326 Birmingham, AL 35202.

Restrictions
Scholarships are restricted to children whose parents are employed by Tractor & Equipment Company and who have been accepted at or made application to an accredited institution of higher learning.

Additional Information
Provides scholarships to children of employees.

Corporate Officials
James W. Waitzman, Jr.: chairman, president, chief executive officer PRIM CORP EMPL chairman, president, chief executive officer: Tractor & Equipment Co.

Foundation Officials
Lloyd Adams: secretary, treasurer
J. C. Durden: vice president, director
K. H. Horton: director
J. O. Stracener: director
James W. Waitzman, Jr.: president, director (see above)
Benny F. Winford: secretary, treasurer, director

Grants Analysis
Disclosure Period: calendar year ending 2002
Total Grants: $39,400*
Number of Grants: 15
Average Grant: $1,367*
Highest Grant: $20,266
Typical Range: $1,000 to $5,000
*Note: Giving excludes scholarships and United Way. Average grant figure excludes highest grant.

Recent Grants
Note: Grants derived from 2002 Form 990.

Library-Related
5,000   Mountain Brook Library Foundation, Mountain Brook, AL

General
20,266   Wofford College, Spartanburg, SC -- scholarship
9,000   Stamford University, Birmingham, AL -- scholarship
8,000   University of Central Alabama, Tuscaloosa, AL
5,050   Oklahoma State University, Okmulgee, OK -- scholarship
5,000   St. Francis Xavier, Birmingham, AL
5,000   Vulcan Park Foundation, Birmingham, AL
4,358   Auburn University Foundation, Auburn University, AL -- scholarship
4,000   University of Alabama, Tuscaloosa, AL -- scholarship
3,400   Greater Alabama Council of the Boy Scouts of America, Birmingham, AL
3,000   Stamford University, Birmingham, AL -- scholarship

J. EDWIN TREAKLE FOUNDATION

Giving Contact

John Warren Cooke, President
PO Box 1157
Gloucester, VA 23061
Phone: (804)693-0881

Description

Founded: 1963
EIN: 546051620
Organization Type: Private Foundation
Giving Locations: VA
Grant Types: Capital, General Support, Multiyear/Continuing Support, Research, Scholarship.

Donor Information

Founder: the late J. Edwin Treakle

Financial Summary

Total Giving: $365,000 (fiscal year ending April 30, 2002); $375,000 (fiscal 2001)
Giving Analysis: Giving for fiscal 2002 includes: foundation scholarships ($3,300)
Assets: $7,273,959 (fiscal 2002); $8,275,790 (fiscal 2001)
Gifts Received: $100,000 (fiscal 1992). Note: In 1992, contributions were received from the estate of James B. Martin.

Typical Recipients

Arts & Humanities: Historic Preservation, History & Archaeology, Libraries, Museums/Galleries, Music
Civic & Public Affairs: Housing, Safety, Urban & Community Affairs
Education: Arts/Humanities Education, Colleges & Universities, Community & Junior Colleges, Education Funds, Faculty Development, Education-General, Gifted & Talented Programs, Literacy, Private Education (Precollege), Public Education (Precollege), Science/Mathematics Education, Secondary Education (Public), Student Aid
Environment: Environment-General, Resource Conservation, Wildlife Protection
Health: Cancer, Clinics/Medical Centers, Emergency/Ambulance Services, Medical Research, Nursing Services, Prenatal Health Issues, Single-Disease Health Associations
Religion: Churches, Religious Welfare
Science: Scientific Centers & Institutes
Social Services: Animal Protection, Community Centers, Community Service Organizations, Emergency Relief, Food/Clothing Distribution, Scouts, Social Services-General, Volunteer Services, Youth Organizations

Application Procedures

Initial Contact: Request an application form from foundation.
Deadlines: Applications are accepted between January 1 and April 30.

Restrictions

Preference is given to local and educational organizations. Does not support individuals.

Additional Information

Publications: Application Form

Foundation Officials

John Warren Cooke: president, mgr
Harry E. Dunn: vice president
Cynthia B. Horsley: grants admin
Nancy Powell: administrative assistant

Grants Analysis

Disclosure Period: fiscal year ending April 30, 2002
Total Grants: $361,700*
Number of Grants: 62

Average Grant: $5,834
Highest Grant: $24,000
Lowest Grant: $300
Typical Range: $1,000 to $10,000
*Note: Giving excludes scholarships.

Recent Grants

Note: Grants derived from fiscal 2002 Form 990.
Library-Related

20,000	Friends of Mathews Memorial Library, Mathews, VA -- to purchase books, equipment and furnish new wing
20,000	Gloucester Library Endowment Foundation, White Marsh, VA -- to purchase books, equipment and bookmobile

General

38,000	Gloucester Volunteer Fire and Rescue Squad, Inc., Gloucester, VA -- to purchase equipment
19,000	Abingdon Volunteer Fire Company, Inc., Bena, VA -- to purchase firefighting and training equipment
19,000	Abingdon Volunteer Rescue Squad, Gloucester Point, VA -- to purchase equipment and training
19,000	Mathews Volunteer Fire Department, Inc., Mathews, VA -- to build new fire station at Gwynn's Island
19,000	Mathews Volunteer Rescue Squad, Mathews, VA -- to purchase replacement ambulance
15,000	Gloucester-Mathews Free Clinic, Hayes, VA -- to purchase medication for indigent patients
11,000	Mathews Hich School Crew, Mathews, VA -- use for equipment, expenses, maintenance of equipment
10,500	Gloucester Housing Partnership, Hayes, VA -- for training program to teach building trade to low income people
10,500	Hands Across Mathews, Mathews, VA -- to purchase two mobile home soft elderly
10,000	Animal Care Society, Mathews, VA -- for spay and neuter program and animal aid

EDITH L. TREES CHARITABLE TRUST

Giving Contact

M. Bradley Dean, Trust Officer
PNC Bank NA
620 Liberty Ave.
P2-PTPP-33-5
Pittsburgh, PA 15222
Phone: (412)762-4133

Description

Founded: 1976
EIN: 256026443
Organization Type: Specialized/Single Purpose Foundation
Giving Locations: PA: Pittsburgh
Grant Types: Capital, Department, Endowment, General Support.

Donor Information

Founder: Established in 1976 with funds from the Edith L. Trees Trust. The late Edith Lehm Trees married the late Joe Clifton Trees in January 1929. Joe Trees, an oil and gas businessman, worked for the Benedum Trees Oil Company in western Pennsylvania and served as a trustee for the University of Pittsburgh.

Financial Summary

Total Giving: $2,914,948 (2003)
Assets: $65,282,846 (2003)

Gifts Received: $1,817,510 (2003); $1,907,255 (2000); $1,723,710 (1998). Note: Contributions were received from Edith L. Trees Trust.

Typical Recipients

Arts & Humanities: Arts Centers, Arts Outreach, Arts & Humanities-General, Libraries, Music, Performing Arts, Theater
Civic & Public Affairs: Botanical Gardens/Parks, Community Foundations, Employment/Job Training, Civic & Public Affairs-General, Housing, Municipalities/Towns, Philanthropic Organizations, Public Policy, Urban & Community Affairs
Education: Afterschool/Enrichment Programs, Colleges & Universities, Education-General, Gifted & Talented Programs, Preschool Education, Private Education (Precollege), Public Education (Precollege), Science/Mathematics Education, Special Education, Vocational & Technical Education
Environment: Environment-General
Health: Children's Health/Hospitals, Clinics/Medical Centers, Eyes/Blindness, Health-General, Health Policy/Cost Containment, Health Organizations, Hospitals (University Affiliated), Medical Rehabilitation, Mental Health, Public Health, Single-Disease Health Associations
Religion: Religion-General
Social Services: Camps, Child Welfare, Community Service Organizations, Homes, People with Disabilities, Recreation & Athletics, Scouts, Senior Services, Social Services-General, YMCA/YWCA/YMHA/YWHA, Youth Organizations

Application Procedures

Initial Contact: Organizations should submit a written application.
Application Requirements: The application should detail services provided by the organization for the care and benefit of mentally retarded persons; financial statements for the previous three years; and a copy of IRS exemption letter; and a list of trustees and officers including their connections with the community and with mentally retarded persons.
Deadlines: October 1.

Restrictions

The trust gives only to organizations "for the benefit of mentally-retarded children, or to corporations, associations or agencies organized and operated for that purpose." The trust does not provide grants to individuals.

Additional Information

Trust(s): PNC Bank

Foundation Officials

J. Murray Eagan: trustee, contact
James M. Ferguson, III: trustee

Grants Analysis

Disclosure Period: calendar year ending 2003
Total Grants: $2,914,948
Number of Grants: 77
Average Grant: $37,856
Highest Grant: $230,000
Lowest Grant: $2,390
Typical Range: $20,000 to $50,000

Recent Grants

Note: Grants derived from 2000 Form 990.
General

300,000	Children's Hospital of Pittsburgh Down Syndrome Center of Western Pennsylvania, Pittsburgh, PA -- addition to endowment fund to support patient care, educational services and research of the Down Syndrome Center
275,000	Verland Foundation, Pittsburgh, PA -- to support continuing program of debt reduction and to add to the endowment fund

260,000	ARC Allegheny Foundation, Pittsburgh, PA -- furnish temporary relief and respite care through camping programs
200,000	Allegheny Valley School, Coraopolis, PA -- special campaign for renovations and upgrades of facilities in Western Pennsylvania
140,000	McGuire Memorial Home Foundation, New Brighton, PA -- for closing costs and renovations for another community residence
136,250	Sharp Visions, Pittsburgh, PA -- support camp and extended school year program
130,000	Clelian Heights School for Exceptional Children, Greensburg, PA -- to acquire a tractor and to support an endowment fund
126,742	St. Anthony School Programs, Pittsburgh, PA -- to acquire two vans for use in inclusive education and employment programs
125,000	Early Learning Institute, Pittsburgh, PA -- for endowment fund
100,000	United Cerebral Palsy, Pittsburgh, PA -- to support capital campaign

HARRY C. TREXLER TRUST

Giving Contact
Thomas H. Christman, Executive Director
33 South 7th Street, Suite 205
Allentown, PA 18101
Phone: (610)434-9645
Fax: (610)437-5721

Description
Founded: 1934
EIN: 231162215
Organization Type: General Purpose Foundation
Giving Locations: PA: Lehigh County
Grant Types: Capital, General Support, Operating Expenses, Scholarship.

Donor Information
Founder: Established in 1934, with Harry C. Trexler and Mary M. Trexler as donors. Mr. Trexler was president of Trexler Lumber Company (Allentown, PA) and chairman of Lehigh Portland Cement Company and Bell Telephone Company of Pennsylvania. He was a trustee of Allentown State Hospital, Sacred Heart Hospital (Allentown), St. Luke's Hospital, Lehigh University, Franklin and Marshall College, and Muhlenberg College.
The Trexler will stipulated that one-half of the trust's income be distributed to charitable organizations that serve the benefit of humanity in Lehigh County, one-fourth be paid to the City of Allentown for parks, and one-fourth be added to the foundation's investment assets.

Financial Summary
Total Giving: $5,018,000 (fiscal year ending March 31, 2004); $4,957,350 (fiscal 2003); $4,924,674 (fiscal 2001)
Giving Analysis: Giving for fiscal 2004 includes: foundation scholarships ($100,000); fiscal 2003: foundation scholarships ($185,000); fiscal 2001: foundation scholarships ($60,000)
Assets: $109,129,394 (fiscal 2004); $89,247,335 (fiscal 2003); $119,632,864 (fiscal 2001)
Gifts Received: $87,100 (fiscal 2004); $5,881 (fiscal 1992). Note: In fiscal 2004, contributions were received from PPL Corp.

Typical Recipients
Arts & Humanities: Arts Associations & Councils, Arts Centers, Arts Festivals, Arts Institutes, Arts Outreach, Dance, Historic Preservation, History & Archaeology, Libraries, Museums/Galleries, Music, Opera, Performing Arts, Public Broadcasting, Theater
Civic & Public Affairs: Botanical Gardens/Parks, Economic Development, Civic & Public Affairs-General, Hispanic Affairs, Housing, Inner-City Development, Municipalities/Towns, Safety, Urban & Community Affairs, Women's Affairs
Education: Afterschool/Enrichment Programs, Arts/Humanities Education, Business Education, Colleges & Universities, Community & Junior Colleges, Economic Education, Education Funds, Elementary Education (Private), Education-General, Literacy, Minority Education, Private Education (Precollege), Science/Mathematics Education, Secondary Education (Private), Special Education, Student Aid, Vocational & Technical Education
Environment: Environment-General, Resource Conservation, Wildlife Protection
Health: Children's Health/Hospitals, Clinics/Medical Centers, Emergency/Ambulance Services, Eyes/Blindness, Home-Care Services, Hospitals, Long-Term Care, Medical Rehabilitation, Nursing Services, Transplant Networks/Donor Banks
Religion: Churches, Dioceses, Religion-General, Jewish Causes, Ministries, Religious Welfare
Science: Scientific Centers & Institutes
Social Services: Camps, Child Welfare, Community Centers, Community Service Organizations, Crime Prevention, Emergency Relief, Family Services, People with Disabilities, Recreation & Athletics, Scouts, Senior Services, Shelters/Homelessness, Social Services-General, Volunteer Services, YMCA/YWCA/YMHA/YWHA, Youth Organizations

Application Procedures
Initial Contact: Grant requests should be in letter form.
Application Requirements: Letters should state the purpose of funds sought, the amount requested, and the anticipated public benefit. Proposals also should include a copy of the organization's articles of incorporation and by-laws, proof of IRS nonprofit status, most recent financial statements, an operating budget, a list of other sources of project support, current list of board of directors, federal tax return, and detailed program descriptions with current client statistics. Also answer the following questions: Is your organization registered with the Pennsylvania Bureau of Charitable Organizations? Do you pay money or receive money from any other organizations? Are you controlled by, related to, connected with, or sponsored by another organization? Do you serve clientele from counties other than Lehigh?
Deadlines: Applications must be received prior to December 1 for funding consideration.
Review Process: Trustees meet on the third Tuesday of every month. In these meetings the trustees familiarize themselves with an organization's stated purposes and structure. They also subjectively compare organizations seeking funds, preferring to fund the organization demonstrating a more compelling benefit to the local community.
Notes: Potential grantees are encouraged to meet with the foundation staff prior to submission of a request.

Restrictions
The Foundation does not support organizations outside Lehigh County, PA, individuals, nor private foundations.

Additional Information
The foundation reports that it also offers proposal writing assistance.
Publications: Guidelines

Foundation Officials
Dexter Farrington Baker: trustee B Worcester, MA 1927. ED Lehigh University BS (1950); Lehigh University MBA (1957). CORP AFFIL director: AMP Inc. NONPR AFFIL member: National Association Manufacturers; member: Theta Chi; trustee: Harry C. and Mary M. Trexler Foundation; board associates: Muhlenberg College; member: AICHE; member: American Management Association.
Thomas H. Christman: executive director
Father Daniel George Gambet: trustee ED Niagara University AB (1954); Catholic University America MA (1957); University of Pennsylvania PhD (1963). PRIM NONPR EMPL Allentown College of St. Francis de Sales. CORP AFFIL director: Pennsylvania Power & Light Co. NONPR AFFIL member: Pennsylvania Association Colleges Universities; member board trustee: Valley Youth House; director: Moravian Academy; director: Lehigh Valley Association Independent College; director: Lehigh Valley Community Federated; director: Ben Franklin Manufacturers Resource Center; director: Association Governing Board University & College; chairman: Center Agile Pennsylvania Education; director: Allentown Lehigh County Chamber of Commerce; president: Allentown College of Saint Francis de Sales.
Malcolm J. Gross: trustee
Kathryn A. Stephanoff: chairwoman B Milton, MA 1929. ED Boston University BS (1945); Rutgers University MLS (1969); Allentown College PhD (1982). PRIM CORP EMPL library director: Allentown Public Library. CORP AFFIL advisor: Meridian Bank. NONPR AFFIL director: Lehigh Valley Hospital Board; member: Pennsylvania Library Association; director: Industrial Development Corporation; member: Lehigh County Industrial Authority; member: American Library Association; chairman: Downtown Improvement District Authority. CLUB AFFIL executive board: Women's Club.
Robert C. Wood: trustee

Grants Analysis
Disclosure Period: fiscal year ending March 31, 2004
Total Grants: $4,918,000*
Number of Grants: 111
Average Grant: $27,413*
Highest Grant: $1,465,000
Lowest Grant: $500
Typical Range: $10,000 to $50,000
*Note: Giving excludes scholarships. Average grant figure excludes two highest grants ($1,930,000).

Recent Grants
Note: Grants derived from 2004 Form 990.
Library-Related

75,000	Allentown Public Library, Allentown, PA -- for community outreach celebrating Trexler birthday
65,000	Allentown Public Library, Allentown, PA -- for books, computers, software for students
50,000	Southern Lehigh Public Library, Coopersburg, PA -- for new building

General

1,465,000	City of Allentown, Allentown, PA -- for improving, maintaining and extending parks
465,000	Lehigh Valley Hospital, Allentown, PA -- towards services for adult ambulatory patients
150,000	DeSales University, Center Valley, PA -- for new science center
150,000	Muhlenberg College, Allentown, PA -- for expansion of the Arts Center
150,000	Sacred Heart Hospital, Allentown, PA -- for building improvements
133,380	Allentown School District, Allentown, PA
100,000	Allentown Art Museum, Allentown, PA
100,000	Cedar Crest College, Allentown, PA -- towards scholarships for nursing and elementary education majors
75,000	Lehigh County Historical Society, Allentown, PA -- for the celebration of General Trexler's life and legacy
75,000	Lehigh Valley Public Telecommunications Corporation, Bethlehem, PA -- for

documentary on the life and legacy of General Trexler

TRI-COUNTY TELEPHONE FOUNDATION

Giving Contact
Dennis Wallace, General Manager
PO Box 91
Belhaven, NC 27810-0091
Phone: (252)964-4211

Description
Founded: 1994
EIN: 561742130
Organization Type: Private Foundation
Grant Types: General Support, Scholarship.

Financial Summary
Total Giving: $7,800 (fiscal year ending September 30, 2004); $23,245 (fiscal 2001)
Giving Analysis: Giving for fiscal 2004 includes: foundation scholarships ($7,000); fiscal 2001: foundation scholarships ($5,000)
Assets: $1,393,640 (fiscal 2004); $1,353,543 (fiscal 2001)
Gifts Received: $100 (fiscal 2000)

Typical Recipients
Arts & Humanities: Libraries
Civic & Public Affairs: Clubs, Civic & Public Affairs-General, Rural Affairs, Safety, Urban & Community Affairs
Education: Colleges & Universities, Community & Junior Colleges
Health: Emergency/Ambulance Services, Health Organizations
Social Services: Child Welfare, People with Disabilities, Scouts, Volunteer Services, Youth Organizations

Application Procedures
Initial Contact: The foundation has no formal grant application procedure or application form.
Deadlines: None.

Restrictions
Contributions must benefit the local service area.

Foundation Officials
Edwin M. Baldree: president
Jack Arliss Mason: 2nd vice president
Gary Respess: director
Cecil O. Smith: director
Clarence E. Tetterton: secretary, treasurer
Charlie F. Wallace: 1st vice president
Dennis Wallace: general manager
Frank Waters: director

Grants Analysis
Disclosure Period: fiscal year ending September 30, 2004
Total Grants: $800*
Number of Grants: 1
*Note: Giving excludes scholarships.

Recent Grants
Note: Grants derived from fiscal 2004 Form 990.
General
800   Foundation for Rural Services, Arlington, VA

TRIBUNE CO.

Company Headquarters
435 N. Michigan Avenue
Chicago, IL 60611
Phone: (312)222-9100
Fax: (312)222-1573
Web: http://www.tribune.com

Company Description
Founded: 1847
Ticker: TRB
Exchange: NYSE
Acquired: Times Mirror (2000).
Revenue: US$5.726 billion (2004)
Profit: US$555.5 million (2004)
Employees: 23800 (2003)
Fortune Rank: 348, per FORTUNE Magazine's list of 500 Largest U.S. Corporations (2004).

Nonmonetary Support
Type: Donated Equipment; Donated Products; In-kind Services

Times Mirror Foundation

Giving Contact
Kim McCleary La France, Manager Corporate CTB
Times Mirror Foundation
202 W. First St.
Los Angeles, CA 90053
Phone: (213)237-3005
Fax: (213)237-2116

Description
EIN: 956079651
Organization Type: Corporate Foundation
Giving Locations: CA: nonprofits located in Southern CA headquarters and operating communities.
Grant Types: Capital, Employee Matching Gifts, General Support, Multiyear/Continuing Support, Project, Scholarship.
Note: Employee matching gift ratio: 1 to 1. Company will match gifts made by employees and retirees with a minimum contribution of $25 and a maximum of $10,000 annually. The company grants scholarships to children of Times Mirror employees.

Financial Summary
Total Giving: $3,725,008 (2002); $7,821,126 (2001). Note: Contributes through corporate direct giving program and foundation. 1995 Giving includes foundation.
Assets: $84,655 (2002); $357,922 (2001)
Gifts Received: $3,603,042 (2002); $3,868,023 (2001); $10,650,955 (2000). Note: In 2002, contributions were received from Tribune Company. In 2000, contributions were received from The Times Mirror Co.

Typical Recipients
Arts & Humanities: Arts Associations & Councils, Arts Centers, Arts Funds, Arts Institutes, Ballet, Dance, Ethnic & Folk Arts, Film & Video, Arts & Humanities-General, Historic Preservation, History & Archaeology, Libraries, Literary Arts, Museums/Galleries, Music, Opera, Performing Arts, Public Broadcasting, Theater
Civic & Public Affairs: African American Affairs, Asian American Affairs, Botanical Gardens/Parks, Chambers of Commerce, Civil Rights, Community Foundations, Economic Development, Economic Policy, Employment/Job Training, First Amendment Issues, Civic & Public Affairs-General, Hispanic Affairs, Housing, Legal Aid, Minority Business, Municipalities/Towns, Native American Affairs, Nonprofit Management, Parades/Festivals, Philanthropic Or-

ganizations, Professional & Trade Associations, Public Policy, Urban & Community Affairs, Women's Affairs, Zoos/Aquariums
Education: Afterschool/Enrichment Programs, Arts/Humanities Education, Business Education, Business-School Partnerships, Colleges & Universities, Education Funds, Education Reform, Engineering/Technological Education, Environmental Education, Faculty Development, Education-General, International Studies, Journalism/Media Education, Literacy, Minority Education, Private Education (Precollege), Public Education (Precollege), Social Sciences Education, Student Aid, Vocational & Technical Education
Environment: Environment-General
Health: Cancer, Children's Health/Hospitals, Diabetes, Emergency/Ambulance Services, Eyes/Blindness, Health-General, Medical Research, Respiratory
International: Foreign Arts Organizations, International Affairs, International Organizations, International Relations
Religion: Bible Study/Translation, Dioceses
Science: Science Museums, Scientific Centers & Institutes
Social Services: Big Brothers/Big Sisters, Camps, Child Welfare, Community Centers, Community Service Organizations, Counseling, Domestic Violence, Family Services, Food/Clothing Distribution, Homes, People with Disabilities, Recreation & Athletics, Scouts, Senior Services, Social Services-General, Substance Abuse, United Funds/United Ways, Volunteer Services, YMCA/YWCA/YMHA/YWHA, Youth Organizations

Application Procedures
Initial Contact: Call for guidelines and a grant summary form, which must accompany a full proposal.
Application Requirements: Include a description of organization, its purpose, programs, and project to be considered; statement of the problem the project will address; qualifications of personnel; program goals; methodology; evaluation procedures; proof of tax-exempt status; list of current supporting organizations and amount of support; and organizational budget for current and upcoming fiscal years.
Deadlines: May 1 and November 1; board meets in June and December.
Notes: Organizations in areas served by Times Mirror subsidiaries with significant employee presence should submit requests to subsidiary directly.

Restrictions
Company and foundation do not provide grants for religious, political or fraternal purposes, to veteran or labor groups, for events, or to individuals.
Repeat grant requests will not be considered within a one-year time period.

Additional Information
Grant requests to the Times Mirror Co. are considered as they are received. Company's grants are generally smaller than the foundation's and may include support for fund-raising events. Application criteria and eligibility are similar to those for the foundation.
The foundation makes grants to nonprofit organizations in regions where Times Mirror operating companies are located, a listing of which is located on their website.
Times Mirror also gives through 26 operating units, including the Los Angeles Times, CA; Newsday, Long Island, NY; and The Baltimore Sun Newspaper, MD.
Publications: Contributions Annual Report

Corporate Officials
Kathryn M. Downing: executive vice presidents ED Lewis & Clark College; Stanford University. PRIM CORP EMPL executive vice president: The Times Mirror Co. PRIM NONPR EMPL president, chief executive officer: Los Angeles Times ADD CORP EMPL

president: Mosby Inc.; president, chief executive officer: Mosby Matthew Bender. NONPR AFFIL member: American Association Publishers; director: Friends Law Library Congress.

Bonnie Guiton Hill: vice president B Springfield, IL 1941. ED Mills College BA (1974); California State University, Hayward MS (1975); University of California at Berkeley EdD (1985). CORP AFFIL director: NASouth Dakota Regulation Inc.; director: Niagara Mohawk Power Corp.; director: Hershey Foods Corp.; director: Louisiana-Pacific Corp.; director: AK Steel Corp.; director: Crestar Financial Corp. NONPR AFFIL director: Joint Center Political Economic Studies; director: National Urban League.

Steven J. Schoch: vice president, treasurer B Saint Louis, MO 1958. ED Tufts University (1981); Dartmouth College (1986). ADD CORP EMPL president, chief executive officer: Times Mirror Resource Management Co.

Giving Program Officials

Stephen Charles Meier: vice chairman B Los Angeles, CA 1950. ED Occidental College (1972); Harvard University MBA (1977).

Foundation Officials

Kathryn M. Downing: vice chairman (see above)
Bonnie Guiton Hill: president, chief executive officer (see above)
Steven J. Schoch: treasurer, chief financial officer (see above)
Mark Hinckley Willes: chairman B Salt Lake City, UT 1941. ED Columbia University AB (1963); Columbia University PhD (1967). CORP AFFIL director: Ryder System Inc.; director: Talbots Inc.; director: Black & Decker Corp.; publisher: Los Angeles Times.
Donald Franklin Wright: director B Saint Paul, MN 1934. ED University of Minnesota BME (1957); University of Minnesota MBA (1958). CORP AFFIL chairman: Times Mirror Magazines Inc.; president, chief executive officer: Los Angeles Times. NONPR AFFIL vice chairman: Los Angeles Area Council Boy Scouts America; University Minnesota Alumni Association; director: Associates California Institute Technology; honorary member: Claremont University Graduate School; member: American Newspaper Publishers Association. CLUB AFFIL City Bunker Hill Club.

Grants Analysis

Disclosure Period: calendar year ending 2002
Total Grants: $3,110,008*
Number of Grants: 71
Average Grant: $37,286*
Highest Grant: $500,000
Typical Range: $5,000 to $30,000
*Note: Giving excludes United Way. Average grant figure excludes highest grant.

Recent Grants

Note: Grants derived from 2003 Form 990.
General

500,000	United Way of Greater Los Angeles, Los Angeles, CA
250,000	California Science Center Foundation, Los Angeles, CA
200,000	National Aquarium in Baltimore Inc., Baltimore, MD
200,000	Orange County Performing Arts Center, Costa Mesa, CA
176,000	Friends of the School Volunteer Program of Los Angeles, Los Angeles, CA
120,000	Baltimore Community Foundation, Baltimore, MD
100,000	Camp Courant, Hartford, CT
100,000	Children's Hospital Los Angeles, Los Angeles, CA
75,000	Food Share Inc., Oxnard, CA
70,000	United Way of Orange County, Montgomery, NY

TRIMIX FOUNDATION

Giving Contact

Gail S. Mixer, President
c/o A. Max Kohlenberg, Edwards and Angell
545 S. Main St.
Providence, RI 02903
Phone: (401)274-9200

Description

Founded: 1997
EIN: 050494244
Organization Type: Private Foundation
Giving Locations: MA: Boston, Dalton; NY: Cedarhurst, Schenectady, White Plains; RI: Greenwich, Providence, Warwick
Grant Types: General Support.

Financial Summary

Total Giving: $148,687 (2004); $479,430 (2001)
Assets: $5,055,752 (2004); $4,273,645 (2001)
Gifts Received: $400,000 (2004); $400,000 (2001); $400,000 (2000). Note: Contributions were received from David P. Mixer.

Typical Recipients

Arts & Humanities: Arts Festivals, Arts & Humanities-General, Libraries
Civic & Public Affairs: Civil Rights, Philanthropic Organizations
Education: Business Education, Colleges & Universities, Elementary Education (Private), Elementary Education (Public), Private Education (Precollege), Secondary Education (Public)
Environment: Environment-General
Health: Cancer, Health Organizations, Hospitals
Religion: Churches
Social Services: Recreation & Athletics, Scouts, Special Olympics, Youth Organizations

Application Procedures

Initial Contact: Submit a written request on your organization's letterhead.
Application Requirements: Provide information regarding charitable status and purpose of funds sought.
Deadlines: None.

Foundation Officials

Deborah Kazlauskas: secretary
David P. Mixer: treasurer
Gail S. Mixer: president

Grants Analysis

Disclosure Period: calendar year ending 2004
Total Grants: $148,687
Number of Grants: 41
Average Grant: $3,092*
Highest Grant: $25,000
Lowest Grant: $10
Typical Range: $1,000 to $5,000
*Note: Average grant figure excludes highest grant.

Recent Grants

Note: Grants derived from 2001 Form 990.
Library-Related

500	East Greenwich Free Library, East Greenwich, CT

General

250,000	Berkshire Taconic Community Foundation, Great Barrington, MA
97,000	East Greenwich Public Schools, East Greenwich, RI
70,000	Mother Caroline Academy, Dorchester, MA
10,000	Community Recreation Association, Dalton, MA
10,000	The Providence Community Health Centers, Providence, RI
10,000	Tomorrow Fund, Providence, RI
6,175	Save the Bay, Providence, RI

5,000	The Rhode Island Foundation, Providence, RI
2,871	Citizens Memorial School, Woonsocket, RI
2,500	First Baptist Church, Greenwich, RI

WILLIAM D. TRIPPE TRUST

Giving Contact

Glenn T. York, Jr., President
P.O. Box 246
Cedartown, GA 30125
Phone: (334)690-1411

Description

Founded: 1995
EIN: 586301950
Organization Type: Private Foundation
Grant Types: General Support.

Financial Summary

Total Giving: $406,302 (2003); $561,493 (2001)
Assets: $8,778,383 (2003); $8,990,260 (2001)
Gifts Received: $1,957 (2000); $16,500 (1997); $250,000 (1996). Note: In 1996 and 1997, contributions were received from the estate of William D. Trippe.

Typical Recipients

Civic & Public Affairs: Community Foundations, Municipalities/Towns, Public Policy, Urban & Community Affairs
Education: Education-General
Social Services: Youth Organizations

Application Procedures

Initial Contact: Send a brief letter of inquiry.
Deadlines: None.

Restrictions

Limited to Polk County, GA.

Foundation Officials

James J. Carter, Jr.: director
Lloyd H. Gray, Jr.: director
George E. Mundy: director
Pauline Pledger: secretary
Jane C. Wyatt: director
Glen T. York: president
Michael H. York, Sr.: director

Grants Analysis

Disclosure Period: calendar year ending 2003
Total Grants: $406,302
Number of Grants: 4
Highest Grant: $250,000
Lowest Grant: $9,657

Recent Grants

Note: Grants derived from 2003 Form 990.
General

250,000	City of Cedartown, Cedartown, GA -- towards new facility for boys & girls club
100,000	City of Cedartown, Cedartown, GA -- towards rebeautification project
46,645	City of Cedartown, Cedartown, GA -- towards veteran's memorial park
9,657	Polk School District, Cedartown, GA -- for playground equipment

THE TRULL FOUNDATION

Giving Contact
E. Gail Purvis, Executive Director
404 Fourth Street
Palacios, TX 77465
Phone: (361)972-5241
Fax: (361)972-1109
E-mail: info@trullfoundation.org
Web: http://www.trullfoundation.org

Description
Founded: 1948
EIN: 237423943
Organization Type: Family Foundation
Giving Locations: TX: nationally, although Texas is given preference.
Grant Types: Conference/Seminar, Emergency, General Support, Multiyear/Continuing Support, Operating Expenses, Project, Scholarship.

Donor Information
Founder: Established in 1948 by B. W. Trull and Florence M. Trull for religious, charitable, and educational purposes. Trustees were Robert B. Trull, Harry H. Sisson, and Ralph P. Newsom. By the terms of its indenture, the original foundation expired in 1973. In 1967, the Trull family (Florence M. Trull and her four children) established a new foundation to receive the assets of the old foundation and to run until its assets were expended. The Trull family's fortune stems from farming, land management, and investments.

Financial Summary
Total Giving: $1,007,045 (2002); $1,174,630 (2001)
Assets: $21,646,633 (2002); $25,111,815 (2001)
Gifts Received: $10,000 (1994)

Typical Recipients
Arts & Humanities: Arts Associations & Councils, Arts Festivals, Ethnic & Folk Arts, Film & Video, Historic Preservation, History & Archaeology, Libraries, Museums/Galleries, Music, Opera, Performing Arts, Public Broadcasting, Theater, Visual Arts
Civic & Public Affairs: African American Affairs, Botanical Gardens/Parks, Civil Rights, Clubs, Community Foundations, Economic Development, Employment/Job Training, Civic & Public Affairs-General, Hispanic Affairs, Housing, Law & Justice, Legal Aid, Municipalities/Towns, Nonprofit Management, Public Policy, Rural Affairs, Safety, Urban & Community Affairs, Women's Affairs
Education: Afterschool/Enrichment Programs, Arts/Humanities Education, Colleges & Universities, Community & Junior Colleges, Education Reform, Education-General, Leadership Training, Literacy, Medical Education, Minority Education, Preschool Education, Private Education (Precollege), Public Education (Precollege), Religious Education, Science/Mathematics Education, Secondary Education (Private), Secondary Education (Public), Special Education, Student Aid, Vocational & Technical Education
Environment: Environment-General, Protection, Resource Conservation, Watershed
Health: AIDS/HIV, Cancer, Children's Health/Hospitals, Clinics/Medical Centers, Health-General, Health Policy/Cost Containment, Health Funds, Health Organizations, Medical Rehabilitation, Medical Research, Mental Health, Nutrition, Preventive Medicine/Wellness Organizations, Public Health, Transplant Networks/Donor Banks
International: Foreign Arts Organizations, International-General, Health Care/Hospitals, International Development, International Environmental Issues, International Peace & Security Issues, International Relations, International Relief Efforts, Missionary/Religious Activities
Religion: Bible Study/Translation, Churches, Ministries, Missionary Activities (Domestic), Religious Organizations, Religious Welfare, Seminaries, Social/

Policy Issues
Science: Observatories & Planetariums, Scientific Research
Social Services: At-Risk Youth, Camps, Child Welfare, Community Centers, Community Service Organizations, Counseling, Day Care, Delinquency & Criminal Rehabilitation, Domestic Violence, Emergency Relief, Family Planning, Family Services, Food/Clothing Distribution, Homes, Refugee Assistance, Senior Services, Shelters/Homelessness, Substance Abuse, United Funds/United Ways, Volunteer Services, YMCA/YWCA/YMHA/YWHA, Youth Organizations

Application Procedures
Initial Contact: Current guidelines and grant information available at foundation website. Applicants may also contact foundation in order to receive the proposal fact sheet and grant proposal guidelines.
Application Requirements: Applicants should submit an original and three copies of a full proposal, including: cover letter (2 pages or less), the proposal fact sheet, current agency operating budget (one page), sources of income, project budget (one page), IRS information, and up to five pages of additional information.
Deadlines: None.
Review Process: The Contributions Committee meets throughout the year and will respond to proposal within three months.
Notes: The foundation does not accept faxed proposals. Unexpended funds must be returned to the foundation.

Restrictions
The foundation reports that it usually will not make long term commitments; make grants for buildings, endowments, or research; repeat grants in the same project longer than three years; fund operational expenses except during initial years; or make grants to individuals.

Additional Information
The foundation supports established organizations to develop new programs, assists in proposal writing to work in coordination with other foundations, and conducts seminars/workshops.
The foundation expects periodic progress reports during the funding period.
Publications: Annual Report; Guidelines; Application Form; Proposal Fact Sheet

Foundation Officials
Garland M. Brooking: founder
Gladys Trull Brooking: founder
Colleen Claybourn: secretary, treasurer, trustee, member contributions committee B Gary, IN 1934. NONPR AFFIL director: Presbyterian Historical Society Southwest; member: Sigma Tau Nu; director: Palacios Area Hististorical Association; director: Matagorda County Hististorical Society; director: Matagorda County Historical Commission, Bay City Texas.
Cara Herlin: advisory trustee
Jean Trull Herlin: founder, trustee emeritus
J. Fred Huitt: vice chairman board trustees, member investment committee
Rose C. Lancaster: trustee, member contributions committee
Sarah Olfers: advisory trustee
B. B. Shiflett: founder NONPR AFFIL secretary, executive director: Ralph M Parsons Foundation.
Laura Trull Shiflett: founder
R. Scott Trull: trustee
Robert B. Trull: founder, trustee emeritus PRIM CORP EMPL officer: City State Bank of Palacios. CORP AFFIL director: Northwest Bank Texas Bay City.

Grants Analysis
Disclosure Period: calendar year ending 2002
Total Grants: $1,007,045

Number of Grants: 255
Average Grant: $3,949
Highest Grant: $20,000
Lowest Grant: $250
Typical Range: $1,000 to $5,000

Recent Grants
Note: Grants derived from 2002 Form 990.
General

20,000	Friends of Elder Citizens Inc., Palacios, TX
13,000	A D Players, Houston, TX
12,000	Midfield Community Church, Midfield, TX
10,000	Boys & Girls Club of El Campo, El Campo, TX
10,000	Church World Service, Elkhart, IN
10,000	El Buen Pastor Early Childhood Development Center, Austin, TX
10,000	Friends of Big Bend National Park, Big Bend National Park, TX
10,000	Matagorda County Museum Association, Bay City, TX
10,000	Planned Parenthood Federation of America, New York, NY
10,000	Su Casa De Esperanza Inc., Pharr, TX

TRUMBULL COUNTY SCHOLARSHIP FOUNDATION

Giving Contact
Michael Craig, Chairman
c/o Second National Bank
260 Niles Cortland Rd. NE
Warren, OH 44484
Phone: (330)394-3773

Description
Founded: 1987
EIN: 346545694
Organization Type: Private Foundation
Giving Locations: OH; PA
Grant Types: General Support.

Financial Summary
Total Giving: $9,750 (2003); $8,000 (2001)
Giving Analysis: Giving for 2001 includes: foundation scholarships ($8,000)
Assets: $124,924 (2003); $126,270 (2001)

Typical Recipients
Arts & Humanities: Libraries
Education: Colleges & Universities, Education Reform, Faculty Development, Science/Mathematics Education, Student Aid

Application Procedures
Initial Contact: Contact the foundation to request an application form.
Deadlines: Application deadline is in the spring.

Restrictions
Accepts applications for educational/scholarship purposes only.

Additional Information
Trust(s): Second National Bank of Warren

Grants Analysis
Disclosure Period: calendar year ending 2003
Total Grants: $9,750*
Number of Grants: 11
Average Grant: $886
Highest Grant: $2,000
Lowest Grant: $250
Typical Range: $500 to $1,000
*Note: Giving includes scholarships.

Recent Grants

Note: Grants derived from 2001 Form 990.

Library-Related

1,000	Pittsburgh Technology Institute, Oakdale, PA

General

1,500	Kent State University, Kent, OH
1,000	Ohio State University, Columbus, OH
500	Capital University, Columbus, OH
500	Gannon University, Erie, PA
500	Grove City College, Grove City, PA
500	John Carroll University Institute for Educational Renewal, University Heights, OH
500	Messiah College, Grantham, PA
500	Mount Union College, Alliance, OH
500	Penn State University, University Park, PA
500	Walsh University, Canton, OH

TRUST FOR MUTUAL UNDERSTANDING

Giving Contact

Richard S. Lanier, Trustee
30 Rockefeller Plaza
Room 5600
New York, NY 10112
Phone: (212)632-3405
Fax: (212)632-3409
E-mail: tmu@tmuny.org
Web: http://www.tmuny.org

Description

Founded: 1984
EIN: 133212724
Organization Type: General Purpose Foundation
Giving Locations: nationally; Czech Republic; Hungary; Poland; Russia; Slovakia
Grant Types: Conference/Seminar, Project, Research.
Note: The trust also provides grants for professional exchanges and international travel.

Financial Summary

Total Giving: $3,454,190 (2003); $4,191,481 (2002); $3,912,365 (2001)
Assets: $55,085,435 (2003); $64,089,842 (2001)
Gifts Received: $7,585 (1999); $100,028 (1998); $25,000,000 (1992). Note: In 1999 and 1998, contributions were received from individual donors.

Typical Recipients

Arts & Humanities: Arts Associations & Councils, Arts Centers, Arts Funds, Arts Institutes, Arts Outreach, Dance, Film & Video, Arts & Humanities-General, Historic Preservation, History & Archaeology, Libraries, Museums/Galleries, Music, Performing Arts, Theater, Visual Arts
Civic & Public Affairs: Asian American Affairs, Botanical Gardens/Parks, Civil Rights, Community Foundations, Ethnic Organizations, Civic & Public Affairs-General, Philanthropic Organizations, Public Policy, Urban & Community Affairs
Education: Arts/Humanities Education, Colleges & Universities, Continuing Education, Faculty Development, Education-General, International Exchange, International Studies, Journalism/Media Education, Legal Education, Medical Education, Student Aid
Environment: Energy, Environment-General, Protection, Resource Conservation, Wildlife Protection
Health: AIDS/HIV, Health-General
International: Foreign Arts Organizations, Foreign Educational Institutions, Health Care/Hospitals, Human Rights, International Affairs, International Development, International Environmental Issues, International Organizations, International Peace & Security Issues, International Relations

Religion: Jewish Causes
Science: Scientific Centers & Institutes, Scientific Research
Social Services: Food/Clothing Distribution, Social Services-General, YMCA/YWCA/YMHA/YWHA

Application Procedures

Initial Contact: Applicants are requested to submit an initial letter of inquiry, approximately three months in advance of the deadline for submitting a proposal. Letters of inquiry should include a summary of the project, list of principal institutional participants, amount requested, and a project schedule. If an activity is eligible for review, more detailed information will be requested prior to the formal consideration of a final proposal.
Application Requirements: While the initial inquiry may be made by an individual or Institution in the United States, Russia, or Eastern and Central Europe, the final proposal must be submitted by an American nonprofit involved in the implementation of the project, as the Trust does not make grants directly to organizations in the region. If an activity is eligible for Trust support, an application form requesting more detailed information will be provided to be completed and returned by the American institutional partner.
Deadlines: Proposal deadlines are February 1 for review in June and August 1 for review in December.
Review Process: Grant awards are announced immediately after each meeting.

Restrictions

Although the trust supports institutional activities which foster the exchange of individuals as participants in projects, it does not make grants directly to individuals or to organizations for activities in which only a single participant is involved. The trust does not support one-person exhibitions; solo performance tours; fellowships; retroactive funding; multiyear commitments; inter-regional exchanges; operating expenses; capital campaigns; construction costs; salaries; honoraria; youth and undergraduate exchanges; literature and publication projects; library and equipment purchases; film, media, and mass communications; activities pertaining to nuclear weapons and arms control; or programs concentrating on economic development, public health, and agriculture.

Additional Information

Publications: Application Guidelines; Grants List

Foundation Officials

Richard S. Lanier: director B 1943. ED Tulane University BA (1965); New York University MA (1967). PRIM NONPR EMPL president: Council of Asian Culture.
Elizabeth J. McCormack: trustee ED Manhattanville College BA (1944); Fordham University PhD (1966). PRIM CORP EMPL associate: Rockefeller Family & Associates. CORP AFFIL director: United Health-Care Corp.; trustee: Alliance Capital Management; supervisory director: Arrow Ventures NV. NONPR AFFIL overseer, manager: Memorial Sloan-Kettering Cancer Center; trustee emeritus: Swarthmore College; trustee: The Juilliard School; member: Century Association; member: Council Foreign Relations; member: American Academy of Arts & Sciences; trustee: American Academy Rome.
Donal Clare O'Brien, Jr.: trustee B New York, NY 1934. ED Williams College BA (1956); University of Virginia LLB (1959). PRIM CORP EMPL partner: Milbank, Tweed, Hadley & McCloy. NONPR AFFIL trustee: Wendell Gilley Museum; trustee: Winthrop Rockefeller Charitable Trust; trustee: Trust Mutual Understanding; trustee: Waterfowl Research Foundation; chairman: Quebec Labrador Foundation; member council: Rockefeller University; trustee: North American Wildlife Foundation; trustee: JDR 3rd Fund; chairman: National Audubon Society; member: Council Environmental Quality; board directors: Greenacre Foundation; trustee: American Bird Conser-

vancy; chairman board directors: Atlantic Salmon Federation. CLUB AFFIL mem: Century Association Anglers Club.

Grants Analysis

Disclosure Period: calendar year ending 2003
Total Grants: $3,454,190
Number of Grants: 122
Average Grant: $25,021*
Highest Grant: $436,600
Lowest Grant: $1,600
Typical Range: $10,000 to $50,000
*Note: Average grant figure excludes highest grant.

Recent Grants

Note: Grants derived from 2001 Form 990.

General

95,000	Dance Theater Workshop, New York, NY
75,000	American Russian Young Artists Orchestra, New York, NY
55,000	CEC International Partners, New York, NY
50,000	American Repertory Theater, Cambridge, MA
50,000	CEC International Partners, New York, NY
50,000	Mangol-American Cultural Association, North Brunswick, NJ
50,000	Tamarind Institute, Albuquerque, NM
50,000	Theater Communications Group, Inc., New York, NY
46,000	ISAR, Washington, DC
45,325	Foundation for a Civil Society, New York, NY

TRUST FUNDS

Giving Contact

James T. Healy, President
100 Broadway, 3rd Fl.
San Francisco, CA 94111
Phone: (415)434-3323

Description

Founded: 1934
EIN: 946062952
Organization Type: Private Foundation
Giving Locations: CA: San Francisco including the Bay area
Grant Types: Emergency, General Support, Scholarship, Seed Money.

Donor Information

Founder: Bartley P. Oliver

Financial Summary

Total Giving: $288,700 (2003); $243,795 (2001)
Assets: $8,558,219 (2003); $6,490,684 (2001)
Gifts Received: $209,800 (2003); $5,000 (2001); $20 (2000). Note: In 2001 and 2003, contributions were received from Alfreda Cullinan (deceased).

Typical Recipients

Arts & Humanities: Libraries, Museums/Galleries, Music, Opera
Civic & Public Affairs: Employment/Job Training, Housing, Nonprofit Management, Public Policy, Rural Affairs, Urban & Community Affairs, Women's Affairs
Education: Afterschool/Enrichment Programs, Arts/Humanities Education, Colleges & Universities, Elementary Education (Private), Elementary Education (Public), Faculty Development, Education-General, Literacy, Minority Education, Private Education (Precollege), Religious Education, Science/Mathematics Education, Secondary Education (Private), Secondary Education (Public), Student Aid
Health: Children's Health/Hospitals, Clinics/Medical Centers, Emergency/Ambulance Services, Geriatric

Health, Hospitals, Long-Term Care, Mental Health, Prenatal Health Issues, Research/Studies Institutes
International: Foreign Educational Institutions, Health Care/Hospitals, International Peace & Security Issues, Missionary/Religious Activities
Religion: Churches, Dioceses, Religion-General, Ministries, Missionary Activities (Domestic), Religious Organizations, Religious Welfare, Seminaries, Social/Policy Issues
Social Services: Community Service Organizations, Day Care, Family Planning, Family Services, Food/Clothing Distribution, Scouts, Senior Services, Shelters/Homelessness, Social Services-General, Youth Organizations

Application Procedures
Initial Contact: Send a brief letter of inquiry. Application form for Catholic schools requesting equipment grants.
Deadlines: None.

Restrictions
Preference given to Catholic charities and organizations in San Francisco area, though grants having national or global significance are considered.

Additional Information
Publications: Application Guidelines

Foundation Officials
James T. Healy: president
Thomas J. Kelley: director
Thomas F. Kubasak: chief financial officer
Joan C. O'Rourke: secretary

Grants Analysis
Disclosure Period: calendar year ending 2003
Total Grants: $288,700
Number of Grants: 51
Average Grant: $5,661
Highest Grant: $15,000
Lowest Grant: $200
Typical Range: $1,000 to $10,000

Recent Grants
Note: Grants derived from 2001 Form 990.
General

15,000	Juan Diego Society, San Jose, CA -- for pro-life services
10,200	Holy Spirit School, San Jose, CA -- for reading tables and chairs
10,000	Americans United for Life, Chicago, IL -- for Pro-Life Public Interest Law and Education
10,000	Boy Scouts San Francisco Bay Area Council, San Leardro, CA
10,000	Catholic Social Services, Sacramento, CA -- for Homeless Adult Education Program
10,000	First Resort, Oakland, CA -- for Pro Life Crisis Pregnancy Program
10,000	Sacred Heart Elementary School, San Francisco, CA -- for phonics books, computer hardware and software
10,000	St. Elizabeth High School, Oakland, CA -- for new lockers
8,000	St. Gabriel School, San Francisco, CA -- for renovation of front entry
7,500	CYO San Francisco Boys and Girls Home, San Rafael, CA -- for pregnancy prevention girls' home

TSUMURA INTERNATIONAL INC.

Company Headquarters
Secaucus, NJ

Company Description
Former Name: FMG Tsumura.
Employees: 600
SIC(s): 5122 Drugs, Proprietaries & Sundries.
Parent Company: Tsumura & Co., 12-7 Nibancho, Chiyoda-ku, Tokyo, Japan

Giving Contact
Hideo Anzai, Director
910 Sylvan Ave., Ste. 100
Englewood Cliffs, NJ 07632
Phone: (201)816-6000
Fax: (201)816-8477

Description
Organization Type: Corporate Giving Program
Giving Locations: headquarters and operating communities.
Grant Types: Employee Matching Gifts, General Support, Operating Expenses, Scholarship.

Typical Recipients
Arts & Humanities: Arts Festivals, Libraries, Public Broadcasting
Civic & Public Affairs: Economic Development, Philanthropic Organizations, Zoos/Aquariums
Health: Geriatric Health, Health Organizations, Hospitals
Social Services: Child Welfare, Community Centers, People with Disabilities, Senior Services, Shelters/Homelessness, Youth Organizations

Restrictions
Does not support requests not supported by someone within the company, dinners or special events, individuals, political or lobbying groups, or religious organizations for sectarian purposes.

Corporate Officials
Dennis Newnham: president, chief executive officer PRIM CORP EMPL president, chief executive officer: Tsumura International Inc.
Monty Tsumura: chairman PRIM CORP EMPL chairman: Tsumura International Inc.

Grants Analysis
Typical Range: $10 to $250

MICHAEL TUCH FOUNDATION

Giving Contact
Martha Tuck-Rozett, President
122 E. 42nd Street, Suite 1622
New York, NY 10168
Phone: (212)986-9082

Description
Founded: 1946
EIN: 136002848
Organization Type: Private Foundation
Giving Locations: NY: New York
Grant Types: Fellowship, General Support, Project, Scholarship.

Donor Information
Founder: the late Michael Tuch

Financial Summary
Total Giving: $363,550 (2003); $458,550 (2001)
Assets: $6,870,125 (2003); $8,025,386 (2001)
Gifts Received: $53,673 (2003); $56,023 (2001); $52,726 (2000). Note: Contributions were received from the Michael Tuch Trust.

Typical Recipients
Arts & Humanities: Arts Centers, Arts Festivals, Arts Outreach, Community Arts, Dance, Libraries, Museums/Galleries, Music, Opera, Performing Arts, Public Broadcasting, Theater
Civic & Public Affairs: Botanical Gardens/Parks, Urban & Community Affairs, Zoos/Aquariums
Education: Arts/Humanities Education, Colleges & Universities, Education Reform, Education-General, Minority Education, Religious Education, School Volunteerism, Special Education, Vocational & Technical Education
Environment: Air/Water Quality, Environment-General, Resource Conservation, Wildlife Protection
Health: AIDS/HIV, Children's Health/Hospitals, Mental Health
International: Foreign Educational Institutions, International Relief Efforts
Religion: Jewish Causes, Religious Organizations, Religious Welfare
Science: Science Museums
Social Services: Big Brothers/Big Sisters, Child Welfare, Community Centers, Community Service Organizations, Day Care, Food/Clothing Distribution, People with Disabilities, Recreation & Athletics, Shelters/Homelessness, Substance Abuse, United Funds/United Ways, YMCA/YWCA/YMHA/YWHA, Youth Organizations

Application Procedures
Initial Contact: Send cover letter and full proposal.
Application Requirements: Include a description of organization, amount requested, purpose of funds sought, recently audited financial statement, and proof of tax-exempt status.
Deadlines: None.

Restrictions
Does not support individuals.

Foundation Officials
Martha Rozett: president
Daniel H. Tuck: director
Jonathan S. Tuck: secretary, treasurer

Grants Analysis
Disclosure Period: calendar year ending 2003
Total Grants: $363,550
Number of Grants: 74
Average Grant: $4,295*
Highest Grant: $50,000
Lowest Grant: $1,000
Typical Range: $1,000 to $6,000
*****Note:** Average grant figure excludes highest grant.

Recent Grants
Note: Grants derived from 2001 Form 990.

Library-Related

6,000	Brooklyn Public Library, Brooklyn, NY

General

55,000	Pearl Theatre Company, Inc., New York, NY
11,000	Brooklyn Academy of Music, New York, NY
10,000	Roundabout Theatre Company, New York, NY
9,000	Learning Leaders, Inc., New York, NY
8,500	Jean Cocteau Repertory Theatre, New York, NY
7,500	City Harvest, New York, NY
7,500	Irish Repertory Theatre, New York, NY
7,500	National Choral Council, New York, NY
7,500	National Dance Institute, New York, NY
7,500	Wildlife Conservation Society, Bronx, NY

ROSE E. TUCKER
CHARITABLE TRUST

Giving Contact

Terrence R. Pancoast, Trustee
900 Southwest Fifth Avenue, 26th Floor
Portland, OR 97204
Phone: (503)224-3380
Fax: (503)220-2480
E-mail: tuckertrust@stoel.com

Description

Founded: 1976
EIN: 936119091
Organization Type: General Purpose Foundation
Giving Locations: OR: Portland metropolitan area; some statewide giving
Grant Types: Capital, Challenge, Conference/Seminar, Endowment, General Support, Multiyear/Continuing Support, Operating Expenses, Research.

Donor Information

Founder: Established in 1976 by the late Rose E. Tucker and the Max and Rose Tucker Foundation.

Financial Summary

Total Giving: $1,023,700 (fiscal year ending June 30, 2002); $1,240,750 (fiscal 2001)
Assets: $20,250,449 (fiscal 2002); $23,122,810 (fiscal 2001)

Typical Recipients

Arts & Humanities: Arts Associations & Councils, Arts Festivals, Arts Funds, Arts Institutes, Ballet, Dance, Film & Video, Arts & Humanities-General, Historic Preservation, History & Archaeology, Libraries, Museums/Galleries, Music, Opera, Performing Arts, Public Broadcasting, Theater
Civic & Public Affairs: Botanical Gardens/Parks, Civil Rights, Clubs, Economic Development, Employment/Job Training, Civic & Public Affairs-General, Housing, Law & Justice, Legal Aid, Native American Affairs, Parades/Festivals, Public Policy, Urban & Community Affairs, Zoos/Aquariums
Education: Afterschool/Enrichment Programs, Arts/Humanities Education, Business Education, Colleges & Universities, Community & Junior Colleges, Continuing Education, Education Funds, Elementary Education (Private), Environmental Education, Faculty Development, Education-General, Health & Physical Education, Legal Education, Minority Education, Preschool Education, Private Education (Precollege), Public Education (Precollege), Science/Mathematics Education, Special Education, Student Aid
Environment: Air/Water Quality, Energy, Forestry, Environment-General, Protection, Resource Conservation, Watershed, Wildlife Protection
Health: Alzheimer's Disease, Clinics/Medical Centers, Emergency/Ambulance Services, Health-General, Health Funds, Health Organizations, Hospitals, Medical Rehabilitation, Mental Health, Prenatal Health Issues, Public Health, Single-Disease Health Associations, Speech & Hearing
International: Foreign Educational Institutions, International Affairs, International Environmental Issues
Religion: Jewish Causes, Religious Organizations, Religious Welfare
Science: Science Museums
Social Services: Animal Protection, At-Risk Youth, Camps, Child Abuse, Child Welfare, Community Centers, Community Service Organizations, Counseling, Crime Prevention, Day Care, Family Planning, Family Services, Food/Clothing Distribution, People with Disabilities, Scouts, Senior Services, Substance Abuse, United Funds/United Ways, YMCA/YWCA/YMHA/YWHA, Youth Organizations

Application Procedures

Initial Contact: The trust has no formal grant application procedure or application form. Foundation does require that an application be in writing.
Application Requirements: Send two copies of basic information about the applicant; list of trustees or directors; description of the project for which the funding is requested, including significance to the community; budget; sources of actual or potential support; future funding; and date funds are required. Include one copy of IRS tax exempt letter under Section 501 (c)(3), verification of private foundation status, current financial statements, and a copy of a brochure or other literature describing the applicant's purpose and activities.
Deadlines: None.
Review Process: Payments are normally made within two weeks after the grants are awarded.

Restrictions

The trust does not make grants to individuals, program-related loans or investments, organizations which unfairly discriminate, organizations classified as "private foundations" under Sec. 509(a) of the Internal Revenue Code, conduit organizations, or efforts to carry on propaganda or to influence legislation. No grants are made for fellowships or debt reduction.

Additional Information

The Trust encourages the submission of progress reports indicating how the grant was used and what results were accomplished.
Publications: Application Guidelines; Annual Report

Foundation Officials

Milo E. Ormseth: trustee B Wolf Point, MT 1932. ED Saint Olaf College BA (1954); Harvard University LLB (1959). PRIM CORP EMPL partner: Stoel Rives Boley Jones & Grey. CORP AFFIL secretary, director: Allen Forest Products Co.; secretary, treasurer, director: America River Lumber Co. Inc.
Thomas B. Stoel: trustee

Grants Analysis

Disclosure Period: fiscal year ending June 30, 2002
Total Grants: $1,023,700
Number of Grants: 194
Average Grant: $5,277
Highest Grant: $52,500
Lowest Grant: $1,000
Typical Range: $1,000 to $10,000

Recent Grants

Note: Grants derived from fiscal 2002 Form 990.
Library-Related
7,500	Dexter Library, Dexter, OR

General
52,500	Tucker-Maxon Oral School, Portland, OR -- provides audiology and vision services
40,000	Lewis & Clark College, Portland, OR
40,000	Oregon Symphony, Portland, OR
35,000	Willamette University, Salem, OR
25,000	American Land Institute, Portland, OR
25,000	Campaign for Equal Justice, Portland, OR
25,000	Linfield College, McMinnville, OR
22,000	Natural Resources Defense Council, San Francisco, CA
20,000	Oregon Children's Foundation, Portland, OR -- offers "Start Making a Reader Today" program
20,000	Portland Center Stage, Portland, OR

TUCKER FOUNDATION

Giving Contact

M. Hayne Hamilton, President
Tucker Foundation
600 Krystal Bldg.
Chattanooga, TN 37402

Phone: (423)756-1202

Description

Founded: 1996
EIN: 621603398
Organization Type: Private Foundation
Giving Locations: GA: Atlanta; TN: Hamilton & Bradley Counties, Chattanooga
Grant Types: General Support.

Financial Summary

Total Giving: $1,186,063 (2003); $1,297,336 (2001)
Giving Analysis: Giving for 2003 includes: foundation grants to United Way ($10,000); 2001: foundation grants to United Way ($15,000)
Assets: $23,545,812 (2003); $22,246,539 (2001)

Typical Recipients

Arts & Humanities: Arts & Humanities-General, History & Archaeology, Libraries, Performing Arts
Civic & Public Affairs: Community Foundations, Economic Development, Civic & Public Affairs-General
Education: Colleges & Universities, Community & Junior Colleges, Education-General, Private Education (Precollege), Secondary Education (Private)
Environment: Environment-General, Resource Conservation
Health: Cancer
Religion: Missionary Activities (Domestic)
Social Services: Family Services, Scouts

Application Procedures

Initial Contact: The foundation reports that it does not have a formal application procedure. Submit a brief letter of inquiry.
Deadlines: None.

Additional Information

Although the foundation focuses its grantmaking on Atlanta, GA and Hamilton and Bradley Counties, TN, giving is not exclusive to these locations.

Foundation Officials

Lavina J. Cherry: trustee
Andrew G. Cope: trustee
Pamela K. Cuzzort: treasurer
M. Hayne Hamilton: president
S. K. Johnston, Jr.: trustee

Grants Analysis

Disclosure Period: calendar year ending 2003
Total Grants: $1,176,063*
Number of Grants: 75
Average Grant: $8,749*
Highest Grant: $199,900
Lowest Grant: $84
Typical Range: $5,000 to $10,000
***Note:** Giving excludes United Way. Average grant figure excludes four highest grants ($554,900).

Recent Grants

Note: Grants derived from 2003 Form 990.
General
199,900	Community Foundation of Chattanooga, Chattanooga, TN
130,000	CCE Charitable Foundation, Atlanta, GA
125,000	Wyoming Community Foundation, Laramie, WY
100,000	Tri-State Exhibition Center, Cleveland, TN
50,000	Colorado Springs School, Colorado Springs, CO
50,000	Girls Preparatory School, Chattanooga, TN
50,000	Nature Conservancy, Arlington, VA
50,000	Vanderbilt - Ingram Cancer Center, Nashville, TN
26,000	Chattanooga State Technical Community College, Chattanooga, TN
25,000	Bachman Academy, McDonald, TN

TUPANCY-HARRIS FOUNDATION OF 1986

Giving Contact
Robert N. Karelitz, Vice President
c/o Fiduciary Trust Co.
PO Box 55806
Boston, MA 02205
Phone: (617)482-5270
Fax: (617)482-2078

Description
Founded: 1986
EIN: 046547989
Organization Type: Private Foundation
Giving Locations: MA: Nantucket
Grant Types: General Support.

Donor Information
Founder: the late Oswald A. Tupancy

Financial Summary
Total Giving: $1,421,844 (2003); $2,284,939 (2001)
Assets: $24,858,984 (2003); $28,992,626 (2001)
Gifts Received: $1,510 (1994); $27,309 (1993); $372 (1992)

Typical Recipients
Arts & Humanities: Arts Associations & Councils, Ethnic & Folk Arts, Historic Preservation, History & Archaeology, Libraries, Museums/Galleries, Music, Public Broadcasting, Theater
Civic & Public Affairs: Civic & Public Affairs-General, Native American Affairs, Urban & Community Affairs, Zoos/Aquariums
Education: Colleges & Universities, Community & Junior Colleges, Education-General, Public Education (Precollege)
Environment: Environment-General, Resource Conservation
Health: AIDS/HIV, Clinics/Medical Centers, Hospices, Hospitals, Prenatal Health Issues, Single-Disease Health Associations, Trauma Treatment
Religion: Churches, Religion-General, Religious Organizations
Science: Scientific Centers & Institutes
Social Services: Animal Protection, Big Brothers/Big Sisters, Camps, Child Welfare, Community Service Organizations, Delinquency & Criminal Rehabilitation, Family Services, Recreation & Athletics, Social Services-General, Substance Abuse, Youth Organizations

Application Procedures
Initial Contact: Send a brief letter of inquiry describing program or project.
Application Requirements: Include description of organization.
Deadlines: None.

Restrictions
Does not support individuals; religious organizations for sectarian purposes; political or lobbying groups; or organizations outside operating areas.

Additional Information
Trust(s): Fiduciary Trust Co.

Grants Analysis
Disclosure Period: calendar year ending 2003
Total Grants: $1,421,844
Number of Grants: 29
Average Grant: $19,688*
Highest Grant: $659,991
Lowest Grant: $1,000
Typical Range: $10,000 to $50,000
*Note: Average grant figure excludes three highest grants ($909,991).

Recent Grants
Note: Grants derived from 2001 Form 990.
Library-Related
150,000	Nantucket Athenaeum, Nantucket, MA

General
352,376	Nantucket Conservation Foundation, Nantucket, MA
290,583	Nantucket Historical Association, Nantucket, MA
250,000	Museum of Afro-American History, Boston, MA
250,000	Nantucket Ice Company, Inc., Nantucket, MA
155,000	Nantucket Boys and Girls Club, Nantucket, MA
150,000	Nantucket Community Service Inc., Nantucket, MA
115,331	Sherburne Commons, Nantucket, MA
105,000	Nantucket Cottage Hospital, Nantucket, MA
100,000	Nantucket Maria Mitchell Association, Nantucket, MA
65,000	Strong Wings Inc., Nantucket, MA

COURTNEY S. TURNER CHARITABLE TRUST

Giving Contact
David P. Ross, Sr., Trust Officer
Bank of America
1200 Main St., 14th Fl.
Kansas City, MO 64105
Phone: (816)979-7481
Fax: (816)691-7916

Description
Founded: 1986
EIN: 436316904
Organization Type: General Purpose Foundation
Giving Locations: MO: Atchison, Kansas City metropolitan area
Grant Types: Capital, Matching, Project, Seed Money.

Donor Information
Founder: Established in 1986 by Courtney S. Turner.

Financial Summary
Total Giving: $1,912,907 (2001)
Assets: $34,149,209 (2001)

Typical Recipients
Arts & Humanities: Arts Associations & Councils, Arts Institutes, Dance, Arts & Humanities-General, History & Archaeology, Libraries, Museums/Galleries, Music, Opera, Performing Arts, Public Broadcasting, Theater
Civic & Public Affairs: Botanical Gardens/Parks, Business/Free Enterprise, Community Foundations, Employment/Job Training, Civic & Public Affairs-General, Hispanic Affairs, Housing, Law & Justice, Legal Aid, Minority Business, Parades/Festivals, Zoos/Aquariums
Education: Arts/Humanities Education, Business Education, Colleges & Universities, Elementary Education (Private), Environmental Education, Education-General, Leadership Training, Preschool Education, Private Education (Precollege), Student Aid
Environment: Resource Conservation
Health: Children's Health/Hospitals, Clinics/Medical Centers, Health-General, Heart, Hospitals, Hospitals (University Affiliated), Multiple Sclerosis, Nursing Services, Public Health
Religion: Jewish Causes, Religious Welfare
Science: Science Museums
Social Services: At-Risk Youth, Camps, Child Welfare, Community Centers, Community Service Organizations, Counseling, Day Care, Domestic Violence, Family Services, People with Disabilities, Recreation & Athletics, Scouts, Senior Services, Sexual Abuse, Social Services-General, Substance Abuse, YMCA/YWCA/YMHA/YWHA, Youth Organizations

Application Procedures
Initial Contact: Contact David Ross directly by phone before submitting applications.
Application Requirements: Submit a letter no longer than three pages with the appropriate attachments.
Deadlines: None.

Foundation Officials
David P. Ross: trust officer PRIM CORP EMPL senior vice president: NationsBank Corp.
Daniel C. Weary: trustee B Junction City, KS 1927. ED Harvard University AB (1949); Harvard University Law School LLB (1952). PRIM CORP EMPL partner: Blackwell, Sanders, Matheny, Weary & Lombardi LLP. CORP AFFIL secretary, director: Progressive Manufacturing Co.

Grants Analysis
Disclosure Period: calendar year ending 2001
Total Grants: $1,912,907
Number of Grants: 48
Average Grant: $39,852
Highest Grant: $353,000
Lowest Grant: $1,500
Typical Range: $15,000 to $60,000

Recent Grants
Note: Grants derived from 2001 Form 990.
Library-Related
20,000	Missouri Development Finance Board, Jefferson City, MO -- classroom for democracy campaign support

General
353,000	Benedictine College, Atchison, KS -- renovation projects
200,000	Nelson Atkins Museum of Art, Kansas City, MO -- capital campaign
137,845	Atchison Community Information Network, Atchison, KS -- network's startup costs
130,000	Mid-America Heart Institute, Kansas City, MO -- cardiovascular research center expansion
100,000	KCPT/Channel 19, Kansas City, MO -- campaign for digital system
57,200	De LaSalle Education Center, Kansas City, MO -- computer technology
50,000	Donnelly College, Kansas City, KS -- support "building bridges of opportunity"
50,000	Friends of the Zoo, Kansas City, MO -- consultation costs
50,000	Gardner Institute, Kansas City, KS -- technology support
50,000	Heart of America Family Services, Kansas City, KS -- secure space for Dame La Mano

TURRELL FUND

Giving Contact
Curtland E. Fields, Executive Director
21 Van Vleck Street
Montclair, NJ 07042-2358
Phone: (973)783-9358
Fax: (973)783-9283
E-mail: turrell@turrellfund.org
Web: http://www.fdncenter.org/grantmaker/turrell

Description
Founded: 1935
EIN: 221551936

Organization Type: Specialized/Single Purpose Foundation

Giving Locations: NJ: Union County; VT, Essex County

Grant Types: Capital, Challenge, General Support, Project, Scholarship, Seed Money.

Donor Information

Founder: Established in 1935 by Herbert Turrell and Margaret Turrell. Mr. Turrell was associated with Parke, Davis and Co. and American Home Products. The foundation has some of its assets in the latter company. Since its inception, the Turrell Fund has aided children and youth, a major interest of the Turrells during their lifetimes. Although the foundation originally was empowered to make grants to organizations in New York, New Jersey, and Vermont, the trustees have phased out giving in New York.

Financial Summary

Total Giving: $7,002,903 (2003); $6,704,426 (2002); $7,373,276 (2001)

Giving Analysis: Giving for 2003 includes: foundation grants to United Way ($20,000); 2002: foundation grants to United Way ($2,500)

Assets: $127,477,689 (2003); $111,091,079 (2002); $132,067,520 (2001)

Typical Recipients

Arts & Humanities: Arts Outreach, History & Archaeology, Libraries, Museums/Galleries, Music, Performing Arts

Civic & Public Affairs: African American Affairs, Business/Free Enterprise, Economic Development, Employment/Job Training, Civic & Public Affairs-General, Hispanic Affairs, Housing, Urban & Community Affairs

Education: Afterschool/Enrichment Programs, Arts/Humanities Education, Business Education, Colleges & Universities, Education Associations, Education Funds, Education Reform, Elementary Education (Private), Education-General, Literacy, Medical Education, Minority Education, Preschool Education, Private Education (Precollege), Public Education (Precollege), School Volunteerism, Science/Mathematics Education, Secondary Education (Private), Secondary Education (Public), Special Education, Student Aid

Environment: Resource Conservation

Health: Adolescent Health Issues, AIDS/HIV, Children's Health/Hospitals, Clinics/Medical Centers, Hospitals, Medical Rehabilitation, Preventive Medicine/Wellness Organizations, Research/Studies Institutes

International: International Organizations, International Relief Efforts

Religion: Dioceses, Religion-General, Ministries, Religious Organizations, Religious Welfare

Social Services: At-Risk Youth, Child Abuse, Child Welfare, Community Centers, Community Service Organizations, Counseling, Day Care, Domestic Violence, Family Planning, Family Services, Food/Clothing Distribution, People with Disabilities, Recreation & Athletics, Scouts, Social Services-General, Substance Abuse, United Funds/United Ways, Volunteer Services, YMCA/YWCA/YMHA/YWHA, Youth Organizations

Application Procedures

Initial Contact: Call or write to receive fund's request form.

Application Requirements: The proposal should include the following: completed request form; one copy of the full proposal (no more than seven pages); a copy of the IRS determination letter; a statement confirming tax-exempt status on organization's letterhead and signed by an official; a recent audited financial statement or 990 Form; project or capital budget; budget for the organization; and list of the organization's board of trustees.

Deadlines: Grant requests are accepted between August 1 and September 1, and between January 1 and February 1.

Review Process: Proposals are screened by the board of trustees. Notice of the board's decision is sent out in mid-December and in mid-June.

Evaluative Criteria: Evidence of the need of the services to be provided; organizational resources (staff, facilities, finances) to meet the need; evidence of local support; plans for the organization's evaluation of the project.

Notes: Progress reports and a final accounting of the use of funds is required of all grant recipients.

Restrictions

The fund does not encourage requests for support of cultural activities, and will not fund advocacy, endowment funds, grants to individuals, and most hospital and health care services.

Grants and scholarships are given to residents of New Jersey and Vermont on a priority basis by outside selection committee.

The fund will not accept proposals which are faxed or e-mailed.

Additional Information

Publications: Annual Report

Foundation Officials

Robert L. Aldrich: trustee

Elizabeth W. Christie: trustee

Ann G. Dinse: trustee

Curtland E. Fields: executive director, trustee

William S. Gannon: trustee

Robert H. Grasmere: president, trustee PRIM NONPR EMPL mayor: Maplewood, New Jersey.

Frank Joseph Hoenemeyer: trustee CORP AFFIL director: American International Group.

Julia A. Miller: trustee

S. Larry Prendergast: trustee, chairman

Dr. E. Belvin Williams: secretary, trustee ED Columbia University MS; Columbia University PhD; Columbia University MA; University of Denver.

Sonyia Woloshyn: treasurer

Grants Analysis

Disclosure Period: calendar year ending 2003

Total Grants: $6,982,903*

Number of Grants: 317

Average Grant: $19,493*

Highest Grant: $300,000

Lowest Grant: $780

Typical Range: $5,000 to $50,000

*Note: Giving excludes United Way. Average grant figure excludes three highest grants ($860,000).

Recent Grants

Note: Grants derived from 2003 Form 990.

General

505,000	Chad School Foundation, Newark, NJ -- financial aid and operating support
300,000	North Ward Center Inc., Newark, NJ -- capital support for a middle school facility
260,000	Saint Vincent Academy, Newark, NJ -- financial aid and capital support
150,000	Saint Benedict's Preparatory School, Newark, NJ
140,000	New Jersey Symphony Orchestra, Newark, NJ -- youth program and youth orchestra
127,420	Newark Renaissance House Inc., Newark, NJ -- capital support for new kitchen
100,000	Children's Aid and Family Services, Paramus, NJ
100,000	Learning Community Charter School, Jersey City, NJ
100,000	New Jersey Performing Arts Center, Newark, NJ -- summer youth programs
100,000	YMCA, Dingmans Ferry, PA -- capital support for dinning and program center

TYNDALE HOUSE FOUNDATION

Giving Contact

Mary K. Yehling, Executive Director
351 Executive Drive
Carol Stream, IL 60188
Phone: (630)790-9532
Fax: (630)790-2446

Description

Founded: 1964

EIN: 362555516

Organization Type: Private Foundation

Giving Locations: CO; IL; MI; PA; WA: nationally.

Grant Types: General Support.

Donor Information

Founder: Kenneth N. Taylor, Howard A. Elkind, ENB Charitable Trust

Financial Summary

Total Giving: $2,549,000 (2002); $869,000 (2001)

Giving Analysis: Giving for 2001 includes: foundation ($869,000)

Assets: $88,030,869 (2002); $95,675,799 (2001)

Gifts Received: $1,079,769 (2002); $96,464,443 (2001); $717,808 (2000). Note: In 2002, contributions were received from the Kenneth Taylor Charitable Trust. In 2001, contributions were received from Kenneth and Margaret Taylor ($95,524,158) and the Kenneth Taylor Charitable Trust ($890,285). In 2000, contributions were received from Kenneth Taylor Charitable Trust. In 1999, contributions were received from Kenneth Taylor Charitable Trust ($711,927), Howard Eklind ($93,000), and Three Sons Acres ($35,000).

Typical Recipients

Arts & Humanities: Music, Public Broadcasting

Civic & Public Affairs: African American Affairs, Asian American Affairs, Clubs, Civic & Public Affairs-General, Inner-City Development, Legal Aid, Native American Affairs, Urban & Community Affairs, Women's Affairs

Education: Arts/Humanities Education, Colleges & Universities, Education-General, Religious Education

Health: AIDS/HIV, Transplant Networks/Donor Banks

International: Foreign Arts Organizations, Foreign Educational Institutions, Health Care/Hospitals, International Affairs, International Organizations, International Peace & Security Issues, International Relations, International Relief Efforts, Missionary/Religious Activities

Religion: Bible Study/Translation, Churches, Religion-General, Ministries, Missionary Activities (Domestic), Religious Organizations, Religious Welfare, Seminaries

Social Services: Camps, Community Centers, Family Services, Food/Clothing Distribution, Social Services-General, Youth Organizations

Application Procedures

Initial Contact: Send a brief letter or call the foundation to request a copy of its application guidelines.

Deadlines: December 1.

Restrictions

Limited to Christian literature work.

Foundation Officials

Edward Elliott: director

Edwin L. Frizen, Jr.: director B Chicago, IL 1925. PRIM NONPR EMPL executive director: Interdenominational Foreign Mission Association ADD NONPR EMPL member missions committee: World Evang Fellowship; treasurer editorial com: Evang Missions Information Service.

David M. Howard: director

Doug C. McConnell: president
Ted Noble: director
Robert Reekie: director
Kenneth Nathaniel Taylor: director B Portland, OR May 08, 1917. ED Wheaton College BA (1938); Dallas Theological Seminary (1940-1943); Northern Baptist Theological Seminary ThM (1944). PRIM CORP EMPL chairman, director: Tyndale House Publs. NONPR AFFIL director: Tyndale House Foundation; member: Wheaton College Scholastics Honor Society; trustee: Living Bible Foundation; trustee: Fuller Theological Seminary; member advisory board: International Bible Reading Association.
Margaret W. Taylor: secretary CORP AFFIL director: Tyndale House Publs.
Mark Douglas Taylor: vice president, treasurer B Geneva, IL 1951. ED Duke University BA (1973). PRIM CORP EMPL president, chief executive officer, director: Tyndale House Publs. NONPR AFFIL trustee: Taylor University; member: Wheaton Liquor Control Comm; member: International Bible Society.
Peter W. Taylor: director
Mary Kleine Yehling: executive director

Grants Analysis

Disclosure Period: calendar year ending 2002
Total Grants: $2,549,000
Number of Grants: 112
Average Grant: $15,411*
Highest Grant: $250,000
Lowest Grant: $1,000
Typical Range: $5,000 to $25,000
***Note:** Average grant figure excludes five highest grants ($900,000).

Recent Grants

Note: Grants derived from 2001 Form 990.
General

250,000	International Bible Society, Colorado Springs, CO -- Let There Be Light
200,000	Wycliff Bible Translators, Santa Ana, CA -- the Seed Company
36,000	Pioneers, Orlando, FL -- Bridge to the World
25,000	Western Seminary, Holland, MI -- Viva Network
20,000	Compassion International, Inc., Colorado Springs, CO -- bibles for children
19,000	SIM -- Bible Society of Nigeria
18,000	Interserve USA, Upper Darby, PA -- Bangladesh Tee Bible
17,500	Interserve USA, Upper Darby, PA -- Bangladesh Tee Bible
16,000	Map International, Brunswick, GA -- HIV/AIDS
15,000	Latin American Mission, Miami, FL -- reprint books for ministry use

TYSON FOODS INC.

Company Headquarters

Springdale, AR
Web: http://www.tyson.com

Company Description

Founded: 1935
Ticker: TSN
Exchange: NYSE
Acquired: IBP Fresh Meats, Inc. (2001).
Revenue: US$26.441 billion (2004)
Profit: US$403 million (2004)
Employees: 120000 (2003)
Fortune Rank: 72, per FORTUNE Magazine's list of 500 Largest U.S. Corporations (2004).
SIC(s): 0251 Broiler, Fryer & Roaster Chickens, 2048 Prepared Feeds Nec, 5144 Poultry & Poultry Products.

Operating Locations

Tyson Foods Inc. (AL--Ashland, Blountsville, Heflin, Oxford, Snead; AK--Dutch Harbor, Kodiak Island; AR--Bentonville, Berryville, Bloomer, Clarksville, Fayetteville, Fort Smith, Grannis, Green Forest, Pine Bluff, Russellville, Scranton, Van Buren; CA--Modesto; GA--Buena Vista, Cumming, Vienna; IL--Chicago; IN--Portland; MN--Duluth; MS--Cleveland, Jackson, Vicksburg; MO--Monett, Neosho, Sedalia; NC--Creswell, Monroe, Wilkesboro; OK--Broken Bow, Holdenville, Stilwell; PA--New Holland; TN--Shelbyville, Union City; TX--Carthage, Glen Allen, Harrisonburg, Seguin, Temperanceville; WA--Tacoma)

Zemsky Family Trust

Giving Contact

Sam Zemsky, Manager
6420 SE Harbor Circle
Stuart, FL 34996-1958
Phone: (407)225-1602

Alternate Contact

Shirley Zemsky
Phone: (716)566-2990
Fax: (786)826-5138

Description

Founded: 1987
EIN: 112867625
Organization Type: Corporate Foundation
Giving Locations: NY: Buffalo
Grant Types: General Support.

Donor Information

Founder: Zemco Industries

Financial Summary

Total Giving: $372,170 (2001). Note: Contributes through foundation only.
Assets: $3,150,851 (2001)
Gifts Received: $1,000,000 (2001); $2,013,000 (2000); $150,000 (1998). Note: In 2001, contributions were received from Sam Zemsky. In 2000, contributions were received from Zemco Industries and Sam Zemsky.

Typical Recipients

Arts & Humanities: Arts Associations & Councils, Arts Centers, Arts Festivals, Arts Institutes, Ballet, Dance, Arts & Humanities-General, Historic Preservation, History & Archaeology, Libraries, Museums/Galleries, Music, Performing Arts, Public Broadcasting, Theater
Civic & Public Affairs: Botanical Gardens/Parks, Civil Rights, Community Foundations, Employment/Job Training, Ethnic Organizations, Civic & Public Affairs-General, Law & Justice, Municipalities/Towns, Parades/Festivals, Philanthropic Organizations, Urban & Community Affairs, Zoos/Aquariums
Education: Afterschool/Enrichment Programs, Arts/Humanities Education, Business Education, Colleges & Universities, Education Funds, Education-General, Private Education (Precollege), Religious Education, Secondary Education (Private), Student Aid
Environment: Air/Water Quality, Protection, Wildlife Protection
Health: Alzheimer's Disease, Arthritis, Cancer, Children's Health/Hospitals, Diabetes, Geriatric Health, Health Funds, Health Organizations, Heart, Hospices, Hospitals, Medical Research, Mental Health, Multiple Sclerosis, Prenatal Health Issues, Public Health, Research/Studies Institutes, Respiratory, Single-Disease Health Associations, Speech & Hearing
International: Foreign Arts Organizations, Missionary/Religious Activities
Religion: Churches, Jewish Causes, Religious Welfare, Synagogues/Temples

Science: Science Museums
Social Services: Animal Protection, Camps, Child Abuse, Child Welfare, Community Centers, Community Service Organizations, Domestic Violence, Emergency Relief, Family Planning, Family Services, Food/Clothing Distribution, People with Disabilities, Recreation & Athletics, Scouts, Senior Services, Social Services-General, Special Olympics, Substance Abuse, United Funds/United Ways, YMCA/YWCA/YMHA/YWHA

Application Procedures

Initial Contact: An application form is not required. Send a brief letter of inquiry.
Application Requirements: Include purpose of funds sought and proof of tax-exempt status.
Deadlines: None.
Notes: Foundation does not have a formal application form.

Corporate Officials

Howard Zemsky: president B 1959. ED Michigan State University (1981). PRIM CORP EMPL president: Zemco Industries Inc. Delaware.
Sam Zemsky: chairman, director B 1926. PRIM CORP EMPL chairman, director: Zemco Industries Inc. Delaware.

Foundation Officials

Howard Zemsky: trustee (see above)
Sam Zemsky: trustee (see above)
Shirley Zemsky: trustee

Grants Analysis

Disclosure Period: calendar year ending 2001
Total Grants: $372,170
Number of Grants: 39
Average Grant: $6,478*
Highest Grant: $126,000
Lowest Grant: $200
Typical Range: $500 to $7,500
***Note:** Average grant figure excludes highest grant.

Recent Grants

Note: Grants derived from 2003 Form 990.
Library-Related

1,000	Library Foundation of Buffalo, Buffalo, NY

General

25,000	Martin Memorial Foundation, Stuart, FL
25,000	Temple Beth Ha Sholom, Buffalo, NY
25,000	Tourette Syndrome Association Incorporated, New York, NY
20,000	Chautauqua Institution, Chautauqua, NY
20,000	Roswell Park Cancer Institute, Buffalo, NY
15,000	Albright Knox Art Gallery, Buffalo, NY
15,000	Albright Knox Art Gallery, Buffalo, NY
10,000	National Conference for Community and Justice, New York, NY
10,000	South Area Solomon Schechter Day School, Stoughton, MA
10,000	UB Foundation, Buffalo, NY

UAL CORP.

Company Headquarters

1200 E. Algonquin Rd.
Elk Grove Village, IL 60007
Web: http://www.united.com

Company Description

Ticker: UAL
Exchange: NYSE
Revenue: US$16.391 billion (2004)
Profit: (US$1.721 billion) (2004)
Employees: 10200 (2001)
Fortune Rank: 129, per FORTUNE Magazine's list of 500 Largest U.S. Corporations (2004).

Nonmonetary Support

Volunteer Programs: Co. sponsors employee volunteer programs such as: Believers Program-an educational mentoring and tutoring program; Habitat for Humanity; Take Your Community to Work Day; and AIDS walks.

Through its United We Care Program, co. also awards grants to organizations where employees volunteer.

Note: 1997 nonmonetary support valued at $2,200,000. Co. provides nonmonetary support through air transportation.

United Airlines Foundation

Giving Contact

Sarah M. Lee, Assistant Secretary
United Airlines Foundation
PO Box 66100
Chicago, IL 60666
Phone: (847)700-5714
Fax: (847)700-7345
E-mail: uafoundation@UAL.com
Web: http://www.united.com/page/article/ 0,,1367,00.html

Description

Founded: 1952
EIN: 366109873
Organization Type: Corporate Foundation
Giving Locations: internationally; focusing on cities in which the company maintains its largest operations.
Grant Types: Department, Employee Matching Gifts, General Support, Multiyear/Continuing Support, Project.

Donor Information

Founder: Formed in 1952 to support the United Way and few smaller programs.

Financial Summary

Total Giving: $739,346 (2003); $1,836,200 (2001). Note: Contributes through corporate direct giving program and foundation.
Giving Analysis: Giving for 2001 includes: foundation grants to United Way ($862,750)
Assets: $3,428,160 (2003); $5,227,810 (2001)
Gifts Received: $155,056 (2003); $2,700,000 (2001); $3,001,756 (2000). Note: Contributions were received from United Air Lines, Inc.

Typical Recipients

Arts & Humanities: Arts Associations & Councils, Arts Funds, Arts Institutes, Ballet, Dance, Ethnic & Folk Arts, Historic Preservation, Libraries, Museums/ Galleries, Music, Opera, Theater
Civic & Public Affairs: African American Affairs, Botanical Gardens/Parks, Business/Free Enterprise, Civil Rights, Clubs, Community Foundations, Economic Development, Employment/Job Training, Ethnic Organizations, Civic & Public Affairs-General, Hispanic Affairs, Housing, Native American Affairs, Safety, Urban & Community Affairs, Women's Affairs, Zoos/Aquariums
Education: Afterschool/Enrichment Programs, Arts/ Humanities Education, Business Education, Business-School Partnerships, Colleges & Universities, Education Funds, Education Reform, Education-General, Literacy, Minority Education, Private Education (Precollege), Public Education (Precollege), School Volunteerism, Science/Mathematics Education, Student Aid
Environment: Environment-General, Resource Conservation
Health: Alzheimer's Disease, Cancer, Children's Health/Hospitals, Clinics/Medical Centers, Health-General, Heart, Hospices, Hospitals, Medical Re-

search, Single-Disease Health Associations
International: International-General, International Development, International Environmental Issues, International Relief Efforts
Religion: Dioceses, Ministries, Religious Organizations, Religious Welfare, Seminaries
Science: Observatories & Planetariums, Science Exhibits & Fairs, Science Museums, Scientific Centers & Institutes
Social Services: Animal Protection, Big Brothers/Big Sisters, Child Abuse, Child Welfare, Community Centers, Community Service Organizations, Crime Prevention, Delinquency & Criminal Rehabilitation, Emergency Relief, Family Services, Food/Clothing Distribution, People with Disabilities, Recreation & Athletics, Scouts, Senior Services, Shelters/ Homelessness, Social Services-General, United Funds/United Ways, Volunteer Services, YMCA/ YWCA/YMHA/YWHA, Youth Organizations

Application Procedures

Initial Contact: Submit a brief proposal on organization letterhead.
Application Requirements: Include a one-page executive summary; project summary; date and duration of project; location of activity; target beneficiaries; number of people served; financial, human, and transportation resources requested; intended use of funds, tickets or volunteers; benefits to the community; how program fits company's philanthropic strategy; ability to attract other donors due to company's participation; background and programs; copy of IRS tax-exempt letter; list of board of directors; contributors; annual report; previous and current year budget; and other supporting documents.
Deadlines: Sixty days prior to quarterly meetings in March, June, September, and December.
Review Process: Foundation and corporate contributions committee review proposals and conduct thorough evaluations of selected programs to be reviewed by the board of directors at meetings in the spring and fall.
Evaluative Criteria: Innovative or unusual approach to meeting stated objectives; ability of program to attract or stimulate the support of others; capacity to deal with fundamental issues of critical importance; potential for improvement of society through replication or institutional change.
Decision Notification: Allow at least 90 days prior to any publication and/or event deadlines for review and response; foundation will send a written response stating that the proposal has been accepted, declined, or is pending further consideration.
Notes: Do not send videotapes to the foundation. Supporting documentation will not be returned.

Restrictions

The United Airlines Foundation does not provide in-kind gifts or funding in the following areas: capital or building grants, development campaigns, individuals, political or fraternal organizations, United Way funded agencies, individual public or private schools, or churches. Grants made in funds only to qualifying non-profit tax exempt organizations and generally restricted to communities served by UAL corporation and subsidiaries.

Additional Information

United Airlines supports Habitat for Humanity and Ronald McDonald House Charities through soliciting foreign coins from international customers on their return flights.
Publications: Foundation and Corporate Giving Guidelines

Corporate Officials

John D. Kiker: vice president corporate communications PRIM CORP EMPL vice president corporate communications: United Airlines Inc.
Francesca M. Maher: senior vice president, general counsel, secretary B Chicago, IL 1957. ED Loyola University BA; Loyola University JD. PRIM CORP

EMPL senior vice president, general counsel, secretary: UAL Corp. CORP AFFIL secretary: United Vacations Inc.; senior vice president, general counsel, secretary: United Airlines Inc.; secretary: United Aviation Fuels Corp. Del; secretary: Mileage Plus Inc. NONPR AFFIL director: United Center Community Economic Development Fund; director: YMCA Metropolitan Chicago; member: American Bar Association.
Eileen M. Younglove: contributions manager PRIM CORP EMPL contributions manager: United Airlines Inc.

Foundation Officials

Graham D. Atkinson: director
Frederic F. Brace: treasurer, director
Marian M. Durkin: director
Sara A. Fields: director
Sarah M. Lee: assistant secretary
Peter D. McDonald: vice president, director
Rosemary Moore: president, director
John H. Walker: director

Grants Analysis

Disclosure Period: calendar year ending 2003
Total Grants: $739,346
Number of Grants: 61
Average Grant: $5,953*
Highest Grant: $100,000
Lowest Grant: $1,000
Typical Range: $1,000 to $10,000
*Note: Average grant figure excludes four highest grants ($400,000).

Recent Grants

Note: Grants derived from 2003 Form 990.

General

100,000	Boys and Girls Club, Chicago, IL
100,000	Conservation International, Chicago, IL
100,000	Museum of Science and Industry, Chicago, IL
100,000	United Believers, Chicago, IL
50,000	Big Shoulders Fund, Chicago, IL
33,447	Merit National Achievement, Evanston, IL
30,900	YMCA of Metropolitan Chicago, Chicago, IL -- united we care grant program
25,000	American Red Cross, Washington, DC
25,000	International Breast Cancer Research, Madison, WI
25,000	John G. Shedd Aquarium, Chicago, IL -- United We Care grant program

UBS PAINEWEBBER INC.

Company Headquarters

1285 Avenue of the Americas
New York, NY 10019
Phone: (212)713-2000
Fax: (212)713-4889
Web: http://www.painewebber.com

Company Description

Formed by Merger of: UBS AG and PaineWebber (2000).

Nonmonetary Support

Volunteer Programs: The company sponsors a national volunteer initiative through which employees can access volunteer opportunities at local and national nonprofit organizations via the PaineWebber's Intranet system.

Paine Webber Foundation

Giving Contact

Alicia Bowman, Foundation Contact
UBS Inc.
51 West 52nd Street
23rd Floor
New York, NY 10019
Phone: (201)352-4324

Alternate Contact

Debra Lynne, Corporate Contributions
Paine Webber
1285 Avenue of the Americas, 14th Floor
New York, NY 10019

Description

Founded: 1879
EIN: 046032804
Organization Type: Corporate Foundation
Giving Locations: NY: New York
Grant Types: General Support, Research.

Donor Information

Founder: PaineWebber

Financial Summary

Total Giving: $3,343,917 (2003); $2,275,263 (2002); $4,150,000 (2001). Note: Contributes through corporate direct giving program and foundation.
Assets: $36,500,531 (2003); $38,109,201 (2002); $41,471,867 (2001)
Gifts Received: $425,597 (2003); $2,056,250 (1999); $2,053,828 (1998)

Typical Recipients

Arts & Humanities: Arts Associations & Councils, Arts Centers, Film & Video, Libraries, Museums/ Galleries, Music, Public Broadcasting, Theater
Civic & Public Affairs: Botanical Gardens/Parks, Clubs, Community Foundations, Employment/Job Training, Civic & Public Affairs-General, Housing, Municipalities/Towns, Public Policy, Women's Affairs, Zoos/Aquariums
Education: Business Education, Colleges & Universities, Education Associations, Education Funds, Education Reform, Education-General, Health & Physical Education, Legal Education, Minority Education, Private Education (Precollege), Religious Education, Student Aid
Environment: Environment-General, Protection
Health: AIDS/HIV, Arthritis, Cancer, Children's Health/Hospitals, Diabetes, Emergency/Ambulance Services, Health Funds, Health Organizations, Hospices, Hospitals, Medical Research, Nursing Services, Public Health, Single-Disease Health Associations, Transplant Networks/Donor Banks
International: Foreign Educational Institutions, Health Care/Hospitals, International Development, International Relief Efforts
Religion: Churches, Dioceses, Jewish Causes, Ministries, Religious Organizations, Religious Welfare
Social Services: Animal Protection, At-Risk Youth, Child Abuse, Child Welfare, Community Service Organizations, Counseling, Day Care, Family Services, Food/Clothing Distribution, People with Disabilities, Recreation & Athletics, Senior Services, Shelters/Homelessness, Social Services-General, Special Olympics, Substance Abuse, United Funds/United Ways, YMCA/YWCA/YMHA/YWHA, Youth Organizations

Application Procedures

Initial Contact: For foundation grant requests, submit a brief typewritten letter of inquiry on organization's letterhead. For corporate contributions requests, submit a proposal.
Application Requirements: Foundation requests should include a description of organization, amount requested, and proof of tax-exempt status. Corporate contributions requests should include a description of organization, including the audience and community served by the organization; an outline of the request and a statement explaining how it accomplishes the organization's goals; a description of the organization's anticipated outcomes and benefits resulting from the grant; a certified copy of the organization's audited financial statements for the most recent fiscal year; proof of tax-exempt status; list of board of directors and affiliations; list of major contributors for most recent fiscal year; and most recent annual report.
Deadlines: December 1, for requests submitted to the foundation. None, for proposals submitted to the company.
Review Process: Corporate contributions requests take up to 90 days for review.

Restrictions

The company does not fund mass-mail appeals, political or lobbying groups, or fraternal groups. Organizations must have tax-exempt 501(c)(3) status.

Corporate Officials

Regina A. Dolan: chief financial officer, vice president B 1955. PRIM CORP EMPL chief financial officer, senior vice president: PaineWebber Group Inc. ADD CORP EMPL chief financial officer: Paine Webber Inc.
Joseph J. Grano, Jr.: chairman, chief executive officer B Hartford, CT 1948. PRIM CORP EMPL chairman, chief executive officer: PaineWebber Group Inc. CORP AFFIL president: PaineWebber Inc.

Foundation Officials

Mike Davis: trustee
Regina A. Dolan: trustee (see above)
Matthew Levitan: trustee
Bob Silver: trustee
Mark Sutton: trustee

Grants Analysis

Disclosure Period: calendar year ending 2003
Total Grants: $3,228,333*
Number of Grants: 326
Average Grant: $9,903
Highest Grant: $100,000
Lowest Grant: $500
Typical Range: $25,000 to $100,000
*Note: Giving excludes United Way.

Recent Grants

Note: Grants derived from 2003 Form 990.
General

100,000	CUNY 2003, Cambridge, MA
73,800	City Meals of Wheels, New York, NY
69,500	MS Society, Universal City, CA
62,000	CHOC Foundation for Children, Orange, CA
49,500	New York Special Olympics, New York, NY
42,000	Portland Art Museum, Portland, OR
40,500	City Harvest, New York, NY
38,000	DOVE Foundation, Grand Rapids, MI
35,000	California Community Foundation, Los Angeles, CA
34,200	Child Help USA, Scottsdale, AZ

UEBERROTH FAMILY FOUNDATION

Giving Contact

Virginia Ueberroth, President
PO Box 100
Laguna Beach, CA 92652
Phone: (949)720-9646

Description

Founded: 1984
EIN: 330078919
Organization Type: Private Foundation
Giving Locations: CA
Grant Types: General Support.

Donor Information

Founder: Washington Speakers Bureau

Financial Summary

Gifts Received: $252,000 (fiscal year ending November 30, 2000); $155,640 (fiscal 1999); $141,000 (fiscal 1998). Note: In fiscal 2000, contributions were received from Washington Speakers Bureau ($72,000), William Thompson ($125,000), Autry Foundation ($25,000), Peter and Virginia Ueberroth ($10,000), and Deutsche Bank ($20,000). In fiscal 1997, contributions were received from the Ueberroth Family Trust ($2,293,908) and Washington Speakers Bureau ($172,000). In fiscal 1998, contributions were received from the Washington Speakers Bureau ($131,000); Young Presidents Organization ($5,000); and Time, Inc. ($5,000). In fiscal 1999, contributions were received from Washington Speakers Bureau ($130,000), Bill Budge ($640), Int'l Assn of Conference Ctrs ($10,000), and Provident Mutual ($15,000).

Typical Recipients

Arts & Humanities: Arts Festivals, Arts Institutes, Ballet, Arts & Humanities-General, History & Archaeology, Libraries, Museums/Galleries, Music, Performing Arts, Public Broadcasting
Civic & Public Affairs: African American Affairs, Botanical Gardens/Parks, Chambers of Commerce, Clubs, Community Foundations, Economic Development, Employment/Job Training, Civic & Public Affairs-General, Housing, Public Policy, Rural Affairs, Urban & Community Affairs, Women's Affairs, Zoos/Aquariums
Education: Arts/Humanities Education, Business Education, Colleges & Universities, Education Associations, Education Reform, Education-General, International Exchange, Literacy, Medical Education, Minority Education, Preschool Education, Private Education (Precollege), Public Education (Precollege), School Volunteerism, Science/Mathematics Education, Student Aid
Health: AIDS/HIV, Cancer, Children's Health/Hospitals, Clinics/Medical Centers, Emergency/Ambulance Services, Hospitals, Medical Research, Single-Disease Health Associations
International: Health Care/Hospitals, International Relations, International Relief Efforts
Religion: Churches, Jewish Causes, Religious Welfare
Science: Science Museums, Scientific Centers & Institutes
Social Services: Animal Protection, At-Risk Youth, Big Brothers/Big Sisters, Child Abuse, Child Welfare, Community Service Organizations, Domestic Violence, Family Planning, Family Services, Food/Clothing Distribution, People with Disabilities, Recreation & Athletics, Scouts, Social Services-General, Substance Abuse, United Funds/United Ways, Volunteer Services, YMCA/YWCA/YMHA/YWHA, Youth Organizations

Application Procedures

Initial Contact: Request application form.
Deadlines: None.

Restrictions

Preference is given to CA youth charities.

Additional Information

Publications: Application Form

Foundation Officials
Joseph Ueberroth: treas
Virginia Ueberroth: president
Vicki Ueberroth Booth: secretary

Grants Analysis
Disclosure Period: fiscal year ending November 30, 2000
Total Grants: $486,911*
Number of Grants: 87
Average Grant: $4,389*
Highest Grant: $109,500
Typical Range: $1,000 to $10,000
*Note: Giving excludes United Way. Average grant figure excludes highest grant.

Recent Grants
Note: Grants derived from fiscal 2002 Form 990.
General

121,500	ARCS Foundation, Corona Del Mar, CA
42,980	Laguna Beach Boys and Girls Club, Laguna Beach, CA
40,000	Sage Hill School, Newport Beach, CA
31,000	University of Southern California, Los Angeles, CA
30,000	Ocean Institute, Dana Point, CA
30,000	Orangewood, Garden Grove, CA
22,000	Saint Joseph Ballet, Santa Ana, CA
20,000	Autry Foundation, Los Angeles, CA
19,000	Hoag Hospital Foundation, Newport Beach, CA
16,000	Alpha Chi Omega Foundation, Indianapolis, IN

ABER D. UNGER FOUNDATION

Giving Contact
John A. Feinblatt, President
22 Hunt Cup Circle
Owings Mills, MD 21117
Phone: (410)581-9575

Description
Founded: 1960
EIN: 526034758
Organization Type: Private Foundation
Giving Locations: MD
Grant Types: General Support.

Financial Summary
Total Giving: $177,050 (fiscal year ending February 28, 2004); $245,250 (fiscal 2001)
Assets: $4,143,223 (fiscal 2004); $4,455,529 (fiscal 2001)

Typical Recipients
Arts & Humanities: Arts Centers, Arts Institutes, Community Arts, Libraries, Museums/Galleries, Music, Theater
Civic & Public Affairs: Employment/Job Training, Civic & Public Affairs-General, Housing, Inner-City Development, Municipalities/Towns, Philanthropic Organizations, Professional & Trade Associations, Public Policy, Urban & Community Affairs, Zoos/ Aquariums
Education: Arts/Humanities Education, Colleges & Universities, Education Funds, Education Reform, Education-General, Health & Physical Education, Literacy, Medical Education, Private Education (Precollege), Student Aid
Environment: Environment-General, Resource Conservation
Health: AIDS/HIV, Arthritis, Health Organizations, Hospitals, Mental Health, Preventive Medicine/ Wellness Organizations, Public Health
International: Health Care/Hospitals, Human Rights,

International Development
Religion: Churches, Religious Organizations, Religious Welfare
Social Services: Child Welfare, Community Centers, Community Service Organizations, Crime Prevention, Domestic Violence, Family Planning, Family Services, Food/Clothing Distribution, People with Disabilities, Sexual Abuse, Shelters/Homelessness, Social Services-General, United Funds/United Ways, Volunteer Services

Application Procedures
Initial Contact: The foundation requests applications be made in writing. Include a description of organization, purpose of funds sought, value of project to community, and budget.
Deadlines: None.

Restrictions
Emphasis is on music, medical research, and service and social welfare.

Foundation Officials
John A. Feinblatt: president
Paul C. Wolman, III: director

Grants Analysis
Disclosure Period: fiscal year ending February 28, 2004
Total Grants: $177,050
Number of Grants: 22
Average Grant: $6,050*
Highest Grant: $50,000
Lowest Grant: $250
Typical Range: $1,000 to $10,000
*Note: Average grant figure excludes highest grant.

Recent Grants
Note: Grants derived from fiscal 2004 Form 990.
General

50,000	LAMBDA, New York, NY
20,000	Fund for Educational Excellence, Baltimore, MD
10,000	Fund for the City of New York, New York, NY
10,000	Maryland Business Roundtable, Baltimore, MD
10,000	Peconic Land Trust, Southampton, NY
10,000	Social Work Community Outreach Service, Baltimore, MD
10,000	University of Maryland - Shock Trauma Center, Baltimore, MD
10,000	Volunteer Central - Baltimore Volunteers Unlimited, Baltimore, MD
8,000	INNterim Housing Corporation, Baltimore, MD
7,500	Learning Independence Through Computers, Baltimore, MD

UNILEVER UNITED STATES INC.

Company Headquarters
390 Park Ave.
New York, NY 10022
Web: http://www.unilever.com

Company Description
Founded: 1978
Parent Company: Unilever N.V., Weena 455, Rotterdam, Netherlands

Nonmonetary Support
Type: Cause-related Marketing & Promotion; Donated Equipment; Donated Products

Unilever United States Foundation

Giving Contact
Deirdre Gann
Care of UNUS Tax Department
700 Sylvan Avenue
Englewood Cliffs, NJ 07632
Phone: (201)567-8000

Description
Founded: 1952
EIN: 136122117
Organization Type: Corporate Foundation
Giving Locations: headquarters and operating communities.
Grant Types: Emergency, Employee Matching Gifts, General Support.

Donor Information
Founder: Lever Brothers Co., Van Den Bergh Foods Co, Unilever United States, Inc.

Financial Summary
Total Giving: $4,865,382 (2003); $4,894,000 (2002 approx); $5,775,994 (2001). Note: Contributes through foundation only. 1995 Giving includes United Way ($325,400).
Assets: $1,983,563 (2003); $12,192,310 (2001)
Gifts Received: $438,301 (2003); $17,069,266 (2001); $4,905,900 (2000). Note: In 1995, the foundation received contributions from the sale of 20,500 shares of Colgate Palmolive Co. stock. In 1999, the foundation received $3,343,576 in Colgate Stock, the Unilever Corp. contributed $368,000, and Chesebrough Pond Foundation contributed $5,949.

Typical Recipients
Arts & Humanities: Arts Associations & Councils, Arts Centers, Arts Institutes, Dance, Ethnic & Folk Arts, Historic Preservation, Libraries, Museums/ Galleries, Music, Opera, Performing Arts, Public Broadcasting, Theater
Civic & Public Affairs: African American Affairs, Botanical Gardens/Parks, Business/Free Enterprise, Civil Rights, Economic Development, Economic Policy, Employment/Job Training, Civic & Public Affairs-General, Housing, Law & Justice, Municipalities/ Towns, Nonprofit Management, Philanthropic Organizations, Professional & Trade Associations, Public Policy, Safety, Urban & Community Affairs, Zoos/ Aquariums
Education: Agricultural Education, Business Education, Business-School Partnerships, Colleges & Universities, Community & Junior Colleges, Economic Education, Education Associations, Elementary Education (Private), Engineering/Technological Education, Environmental Education, Education-General, Gifted & Talented Programs, International Studies, Literacy, Medical Education, Minority Education, Private Education (Precollege), Public Education (Precollege), Science/Mathematics Education, Student Aid
Environment: Environment-General, Resource Conservation
Health: Cancer, Children's Health/Hospitals, Clinics/ Medical Centers, Diabetes, Emergency/Ambulance Services, Health Organizations, Heart, Hospitals, Medical Research, Prenatal Health Issues, Respiratory, Single-Disease Health Associations, Trauma Treatment
International: Foreign Educational Institutions, Health Care/Hospitals, Human Rights, International Affairs, International Relations, International Relief Efforts
Religion: Jewish Causes, Religious Welfare, Seminaries
Science: Science Museums, Scientific Organizations
Social Services: Community Centers, Community Service Organizations, Day Care, Family Services,

Food/Clothing Distribution, People with Disabilities, Recreation & Athletics, Senior Services, Shelters/Homelessness, Social Services-General, Special Olympics, Substance Abuse, United Funds/United Ways, Volunteer Services, YMCA/YWCA/YMHA/YWHA, Youth Organizations

Application Procedures

Initial Contact: Submit a letter or proposal on organization's letterhead and signed by its chief executive officer.
Application Requirements: Include the grant's purpose, background information on the organization, the most recent annual report, a copy of the current operating budget, and proof of tax-exempt status.
Deadlines: None; budget is determined annually in February.
Evaluative Criteria: Makes contributions to organizations with clearly defined, achievable goals that have demonstrated their effectiveness and fiscal responsibility.

Restrictions

The foundation does not award grants to individuals, goodwill advertising, fundraising events and testimonial dinners, sectarian religious organizations, labor organizations, political parties or their activities, capital fund campaigns, or veterans groups for fraternal/social purposes.

Foundation Officials

Alan C. Jope: director
Lisa G. Kohn: assistant secretary
Fiona C. Laird: director
Paul McMahon: treasurer
John W. Rice: president, director
Ronald M. Soiefer: secretary, director
David J. Strickland: assistant secretary
Paul W. Wood: vice president, director
C. Perry Yeatman: director

Grants Analysis

Disclosure Period: calendar year ending 2003
Total Grants: $4,330,382*
Number of Grants: 600
Average Grant: $4,725*
Highest Grant: $1,500,000
Lowest Grant: $25
Typical Range: $1,000 to $5,000
*Note: Giving excludes matching gifts. Average grant figure excludes highest grant.

Recent Grants

Note: Grants derived from 2001 Form 990.
General

1,500,000	September 11 Fund, New York, NY
1,000,000	Citizens Scholarship Foundation of America, St. Peter, MN
670,000	National Park Foundation, New York, NY
142,357	National Merit Scholarship Corporation, Evanston, IL
119,700	Jackie Robinson Foundation, New York, NY
100,000	Unilever United States, Englewood Cliffs, NJ
91,000	International Food Information Council, Washington, DC
65,000	United Way Crusade of Mercy, Chicago, IL
61,000	Children's First Fund, Chicago, IL
60,000	Patterson Habitat for Humanity, Paterson, NJ

UNION PACIFIC CORP.

Company Headquarters

1416 Dodge Street, Room 1230
Omaha, NE 68179

Phone: (402)271-5777
Fax: (402)271-6408
Web: http://www.up.com

Company Description

Founded: 1969
Ticker: UNP
Exchange: NYSE
Revenue: US$12.215 billion (2004)
Profit: US$604 million (2004)
Employees: 47000 (2003)
Fortune Rank: 174, per FORTUNE Magazine's list of 500 Largest U.S. Corporations (2004).
SIC(s): 1081 Metal Mining Services, 1311 Crude Petroleum & Natural Gas, 1382 Oil & Gas Exploration Services, 6719 Holding Companies Nec.

Operating Locations

Union Pacific Corp. (AR; CA; CO; ID; KS; LA; MO; NE--Omaha; OK; OR; PA--Bethlehem; TX--Fort Worth; WA)

Union Pacific Foundation

Giving Contact

Darlynn Herweg, Director
1400 Douglas Street
Omaha, NE 68179
Phone: (402)271-5000
Fax: (402)271-5477
Web: http://www.up.com/found/

Description

EIN: 136406825
Organization Type: Corporate Foundation
Giving Locations: AR; CA; CO; DE; DC: Washington; FL; GA; ID; IL; IN; IA; KS; LA; MD; MI; MN; MS; MT; NE; NV; NJ; NM; NY; NC; OH; OK; OR; PA; TN; TX; UT; VA; WA; WI
Grant Types: Award, Capital, Challenge, Employee Matching Gifts, General Support, Multiyear/Continuing Support, Project.
Note: Employee matching gift ratio: 2 to 1 for educational institutions; 1 to 1 for cultural institutions.

Financial Summary

Total Giving: $7,265,359 (2003); $6,887,000 (2002); $5,542,000 (2001). Note: Contributes through corporate direct giving program and foundation. 1996 Giving includes foundation United Way.
Giving Analysis: Giving for 2002 includes: foundation grants to United Way ($1,593,500); foundation ($5,293,500)
Assets: $1,151,115 (2003); $899,651 (2002); $244,358 (2001)
Gifts Received: $7,601,400 (2003); $7,642,101 (2002); $4,651,351 (2001). Note: Contributions are received from Union Pacific Corporation and affiliated Companies.

Typical Recipients

Arts & Humanities: Arts Associations & Councils, Arts Funds, Arts Institutes, Arts Outreach, Ballet, Dance, Historic Preservation, History & Archaeology, Libraries, Museums/Galleries, Music, Opera, Performing Arts, Public Broadcasting, Theater
Civic & Public Affairs: Botanical Gardens/Parks, Business/Free Enterprise, Community Foundations, Economic Development, Civic & Public Affairs-General, Law & Justice, Municipalities/Towns, Professional & Trade Associations, Public Policy, Safety, Urban & Community Affairs, Zoos/Aquariums
Education: Afterschool/Enrichment Programs, Agricultural Education, Arts/Humanities Education, Business Education, Colleges & Universities, Community & Junior Colleges, Economic Education, Education Associations, Education Funds, Engineering/Technological Education, Environmental Education,

Faculty Development, Education-General, Legal Education, Literacy, Minority Education, Religious Education, Science/Mathematics Education, Secondary Education (Public), Social Sciences Education, Special Education, Student Aid
Environment: Air/Water Quality, Environment-General, Research, Resource Conservation, Wildlife Protection
Health: Alzheimer's Disease, Cancer, Children's Health/Hospitals, Clinics/Medical Centers, Emergency/Ambulance Services, Health Funds, Health Organizations, Heart, Hospices, Hospitals, Long-Term Care, Medical Rehabilitation, Medical Research, Mental Health, Prenatal Health Issues, Public Health
Religion: Religious Organizations, Religious Welfare
Science: Science Museums, Scientific Centers & Institutes, Scientific Organizations
Social Services: Child Welfare, Community Centers, Community Service Organizations, Day Care, Domestic Violence, Family Services, Food/Clothing Distribution, Homes, People with Disabilities, Recreation & Athletics, Scouts, Senior Services, Shelters/Homelessness, Social Services-General, Substance Abuse, United Funds/United Ways, YMCA/YWCA/YMHA/YWHA, Youth Organizations

Application Procedures

Initial Contact: Write to request application form.
Application Requirements: Include description of the organization and purpose of funds sought.
Deadlines: August 15 for complete proposal, for consideration in the following year.
Review Process: If initial letter indicates organization's request complies with foundation guidelines, a formal grant request form is sent to the organization to be completed and returned with supplementary data, including recently audited financial statements, 501(c)(3) determination letter, and description of financial support from other businesses.
Evaluative Criteria: Leadership such that financial support will be used to optimum effect, significant public support of activities, non-duplication of activities of other organizations supported by foundation, corporate presence in community served by organization, evidence of other corporate support.
Decision Notification: Board meets annually in January.

Restrictions

Does not support organizations that are not eligible for tax-exempt status under Section 501(c)(3) of the IRS Code; specialized national health or welfare organizations other than through United Way; political organizations; organizations engaged in influencing legislation; religious organizations that are sectarian or denominational in purpose; veterans organizations, labor groups, social clubs, or fraternal organizations; individuals; dinners or special events; goodwill advertising; or grant-making organizations, except allied arts funds and independent college associations.
Only reviews requests for support of capital projects from organizations funded by United Way.

Additional Information

Publications: Application Form

Corporate Officials

Darlynn Herweg: director PRIM CORP EMPL director: Union Pacific Corp.

Foundation Officials

R. K. Davidson: chairman, trustee
I. J. Evans: trustee
A. C. Getz: assistant controller
B. R. Gutschewski: vice president taxes
D. F. Herweg: assistant secretary
Darlynn Herweg: assistant secretary (see above)
J. J. Koraleski: vice president finance, trustee
S. A. Oiness: treasurer
J. B. Phillips: assistant treasurer
R. J. Putz: controller

R. W. Turner: president, trustee
C. W. von Bernuth: general counsel, secretary, trustee
T. E. Whitaker: assistant secretary

Grants Analysis

Disclosure Period: calendar year ending 2003
Total Grants: $6,037,859*
Number of Grants: 394
Average Grant: $15,325
Highest Grant: $279,333
Lowest Grant: $200
Typical Range: $1,000 to $30,000 and $123,000 to $196,000
***Note:** Giving excludes United Way.

Recent Grants

Note: Grants derived from 2003 Form 990.
General

279,333	Education Partnerships, Fairfield, CT
279,333	Education Partnerships, Fairfield, CT
279,333	Education Partnerships, Fairfield, CT
279,333	Education Partnerships, Fairfield, CT
260,000	United Way of the Midlands, Omaha, NE
206,333	Education Partnerships, Fairfield, CT
206,333	Education Partnerships, Fairfield, CT
206,333	Education Partnerships, Fairfield, CT
206,333	Education Partnerships, Fairfield, CT
206,333	Education Partnerships, Fairfield, CT

UNITED ARMENIAN CHARITIES

Giving Contact

Haig Dadourian, President
168 Canal St., Suite 600
New York, NY 10013
Phone: (212)334-0990

Description

Founded: 1951
EIN: 136125023
Organization Type: Private Foundation
Grant Types: General Support.

Donor Information

Founder: Dadour Dadourian

Financial Summary

Total Giving: $189,478 (2003)
Assets: $4,756,932 (2003)
Gifts Received: $62,000 (1996); $10,000 (1993)

Typical Recipients

Arts & Humanities: Public Broadcasting
Civic & Public Affairs: Clubs, Community Foundations, Ethnic Organizations, Civic & Public Affairs-General, Women's Affairs
Education: Colleges & Universities, Minority Education, Private Education (Precollege), Secondary Education (Private)
Health: Cancer, Children's Health/Hospitals, Health-General, Hospices, Hospitals, Hospitals (University Affiliated), Long-Term Care, Single-Disease Health Associations
International: Foreign Educational Institutions, Health Care/Hospitals, International Relief Efforts, Missionary/Religious Activities
Religion: Churches, Dioceses, Religion-General, Missionary Activities (Domestic), Religious Organizations, Religious Welfare, Seminaries
Science: Scientific Research
Social Services: Food/Clothing Distribution, People with Disabilities, Special Olympics

Application Procedures

Initial Contact: The foundation has no formal grant application procedure or application form.
Deadlines: None.

Additional Information

Foundation gives grants primarily for Armenian religious support. The organization also gives support for Armenian education and social services.

Foundation Officials

Alexander Dadourian: vice president
Haig Dadourian: president
Peter Dadourian: treasurer

Grants Analysis

Disclosure Period: calendar year ending 2003
Total Grants: $189,478
Number of Grants: 26
Average Grant: $3,654*
Highest Grant: $98,125
Lowest Grant: $125
Typical Range: $1,000 to $5,000
***Note:** Average grant figure excludes highest grant.

Recent Grants

Note: Grants derived from 2001 Form 990.
General

103,750	Columbia University, New York, NY
103,750	Diocese of the Armenian Church, New York, NY
75,000	Armenian Church Endowment Fund
15,000	Columbia University, New York, NY
6,000	Fund for Armenian Relief, New York, NY
5,000	Interfaith Committee of Remembrance, New York, NY
5,000	Millennium Armenian Children's Vaccine Fund
5,000	St. Nerses Seminary
4,858	Armenian Assembly of the Holy Martyrs, New York, NY
3,500	St. Gregory Armenian Church, New York, NY

UNITED PARAMOUNT NETWORK

Company Headquarters

11800 Wilshire Blvd.
Los Angeles, CA 90025
Web: http://www.upn.com

Company Description

Revenue: US$215 million (2001)
Employees: 80 (2001)
Parent Company: Viacom Inc., 1515 Broadway, New York, NY, United States

WPWR-TV Channel 50 Foundation

Giving Contact

Laura Sampson, Program Officer
2151 N. Elston Avenue
Chicago, IL 60614-3999
Phone: (773)292-5016
Fax: (773)276-6477
E-mail: mail@wpwr50fund.org

Description

Founded: 1992
EIN: 363805338
Organization Type: Corporate Foundation
Giving Locations: IL: Chicago including metropolitan area; IN: Northwest part of the state
Grant Types: General Support, Research.

Financial Summary

Total Giving: $3,948,723 (fiscal year ending February 28, 2002)
Assets: $95,978,425 (fiscal 2002)
Gifts Received: $2,160,250 (fiscal 2002); $7,769,479 (fiscal 2000); $22,029,420 (fiscal 1997).
Note: In fiscal 2000 and 2002, contributions were received from Fred Eychaner. In fiscal 1997, contributions were received from Newsweb Corp. ($8,503,228) and Fred Eychaner ($13,526,192).

Typical Recipients

Arts & Humanities: Arts Associations & Councils, Arts Centers, Arts Institutes, Ballet, Dance, Film & Video, Arts & Humanities-General, Historic Preservation, Libraries, Museums/Galleries, Music, Public Broadcasting, Theater
Civic & Public Affairs: Botanical Gardens/Parks, Employment/Job Training, Gay/Lesbian Issues, Civic & Public Affairs-General, Housing, Law & Justice, Legal Aid, Public Policy, Safety, Urban & Community Affairs, Women's Affairs
Education: Arts/Humanities Education, Colleges & Universities, Education Funds, International Exchange, Journalism/Media Education, Leadership Training, Public Education (Precollege), Vocational & Technical Education
Environment: Air/Water Quality, Environment-General, Protection, Resource Conservation
Health: AIDS/HIV, Cancer, Health Policy/Cost Containment
International: International Organizations
Social Services: Community Service Organizations, People with Disabilities, Refugee Assistance, Shelters/Homelessness, United Funds/United Ways, Youth Organizations

Application Procedures

Initial Contact: Submit two-page letter of intent.
Application Requirements: Include 3 to 5 page proposal describing agency and need for support, audited financial statements, current year budget, list of directors, any relevant publications, annual report, projected income and budget for timeframe of support, current fiscal statement, copy of most recently submitted Form 990, and a copy of IRS determination letter of 501(c)(3) status. Foundation accepts Chicago area grant application form.
Deadlines: April 1 for arts and arts education; August 1 for advocacy and architecture and preservation; November 15 for domestic violence intervention/prevention.
Decision Notification: Grants are made within six months of deadline.
Notes: First time grants average $2,500.

Restrictions

Limited to arts, arts education, advocacy, domestic violence organizations, and architecture and preservation. Foundation does not provide grants to individuals, scholarships, underwriting or tables for special events, public schools, special projects or productions, religious or fraternal purposes, or political campaigns.

Foundation Officials

Barbara Eychaner: director
Fred Eychaner: president
Charles Gross: assistant secretary
Don Hilliker: secretary
Marcia Lipetz: executive director

Grants Analysis

Disclosure Period: fiscal year ending February 28, 2002
Total Grants: $3,908,723*
Number of Grants: 264
Average Grant: $14,806
Highest Grant: $300,000

Lowest Grant: $2,500
Typical Range: $2,500 to $50,000
***Note:** Giving excludes United Way.

Recent Grants

Note: Grants derived from fiscal 2004 Form 990.
Library-Related

1,750,000	William J Clinton Presidential Fund, Little Rock, AR
50,000	Stinson Memorial Library, Anna, IL -- restoration project

General

785,000	Landmarks Preservation Council of Illinois, Chicago, IL
500,000	Joffrey Ballet of Chicago, Chicago, IL
457,481	Joffrey Ballet of Chicago, Chicago, IL
150,000	AIDS Foundation of Chicago, Chicago, IL
120,000	WYIN Channel 56, Merrillville, IN
100,000	Dance Africa, Chicago, IL
100,000	Medill Innocence Project, Evanston, IL
80,004	Research Foundation of State University of New York, Syracuse, NY
63,919	Landmarks Preservation Council of Illinois, Chicago, IL
60,000	Medill South African Reporting Program, Evanston, IL

UNITED PARCEL SERVICE OF AMERICA INC.

Company Headquarters

Atlanta, GA
Phone: (404)828-6130
Web: http://www.ups.com

Company Description

Ticker: UPS
Exchange: OTC
Revenue: US$36.582 billion (2004)
Profit: US$3.333 billion (2004)
Employees: 355000 (2003)
Fortune Rank: 42, per FORTUNE Magazine's list of 500 Largest U.S. Corporations (2004).
SIC(s): 4212 Local Trucking Without Storage, 6719 Holding Companies Nec.

Operating Locations

United Parcel Service of America Inc. (AL--Montgomery; AK--Dillingham; AR--Conway; CA--Anaheim; FL--Fort Pierce, Jacksonville, Miami, Naples; GA--Rome; HI--Honolulu; IL--Joliet, Milan; IN--Crawfordsville, Indianapolis; IA--Cedar Rapids, Davenport, Ottumwa, West Burlington; KS--Lenexa; KY--Louisville; MD--Cumberland, Hagerstown; MN--Albert Lea, Duluth, Minneapolis, St. Paul, Virginia, Winona; MO--Earth City, Joplin; NE--Omaha; NH--Manchester; NJ--Pine Brook; NY--Cortland, East Syracuse, Elmsford, Hastings-on-Hudson, Latham; NC--Charlotte, Jamestown; ND--Dickinson; OH--Cincinnati, Columbus, Hamilton; OK--McAlester, Oklahoma City, Shawnee, Woodward; PA--Pittsburgh; TN--Lawrenceburg, Russellville; TX--Arlington, Dallas, Mesquite, Vernon, Waco; VA--Cedar Bluff, Exmore; WA--Bremerton, Port Angeles; WV--Fairmont, Huntington, South Charleston; WI--Rhinelander, Sheboygan, Watertown, Wausau; WY--Gillette)
Note: Headquarters is in Atlanta, Georgia. Operates both nationally and internationally.

Nonmonetary Support

Type: Loaned Executives; Workplace Solicitation
Volunteer Programs: The UPS Neighbor to Neighbor program matches employees and their family members interested in volunteer opportunities with community service projects based upon their interests, skills, and schedules. UPS volunteers also nom-

inate organizations for grants through the region/ district grant program.
Note: Workplace solicitation is for the United Way only.

UPS Foundation

Giving Contact

Ms. Evern Cooper, Executive Director
UPS Foundation
55 Glenlake Pkwy. NE
Atlanta, GA 30328
Phone: (404)828-6374
Fax: (404)828-7435
Web: http://www.community.ups.com

Description

EIN: 136099176
Organization Type: Corporate Foundation
Giving Locations: nationally.
Grant Types: Employee Matching Gifts, Fellowship, General Support, Multiyear/Continuing Support, Professorship, Project, Research, Scholarship.
Note: Employee matching gift ratio: 1 to 1 for gifts to educational and cultural organisation. Scholarships are provided only for children of employees.

Financial Summary

Total Giving: $36,846,869 (2003); $38,410,665 (2002); $27,199,317 (2001)
Assets: $31,624,594 (2003); $44,597,966 (2002); $65,762,535 (2001)
Gifts Received: $18,054,524 (2003); $16,536,673 (2002); $28,648,806 (1999). Note: Contributions are received from UPS of America, Inc.

Typical Recipients

Arts & Humanities: Arts Associations & Councils, Arts Centers, Arts Festivals, Arts Funds, Ballet, Historic Preservation, History & Archaeology, Literary Arts, Museums/Galleries, Music, Public Broadcasting
Civic & Public Affairs: African American Affairs, Botanical Gardens/Parks, Business/Free Enterprise, Chambers of Commerce, Clubs, Community Foundations, Economic Development, Employment/Job Training, Civic & Public Affairs-General, Hispanic Affairs, Housing, Nonprofit Management, Philanthropic Organizations, Professional & Trade Associations, Public Policy, Rural Affairs, Safety, Urban & Community Affairs, Women's Affairs, Zoos/Aquariums
Education: Afterschool/Enrichment Programs, Business Education, Business-School Partnerships, Colleges & Universities, Community & Junior Colleges, Continuing Education, Economic Education, Education Associations, Education Funds, Education Reform, Elementary Education (Public), Engineering/Technological Education, Faculty Development, Education-General, International Studies, Leadership Training, Literacy, Medical Education, Minority Education, Private Education (Precollege), Public Education (Precollege), Science/Mathematics Education, Special Education, Student Aid, Vocational & Technical Education
Health: AIDS/HIV, Long-Term Care, Medical Rehabilitation, Nursing Services, Single-Disease Health Associations, Trauma Treatment
International: Health Care/Hospitals, Human Rights, International Affairs, International Peace & Security Issues
Religion: Churches, Religion-General, Ministries, Religious Welfare, Social/Policy Issues
Science: Science Museums, Scientific Centers & Institutes, Scientific Organizations
Social Services: At-Risk Youth, Big Brothers/Big Sisters, Child Abuse, Child Welfare, Community Centers, Community Service Organizations, Counseling, Day Care, Domestic Violence, Emergency Relief, Family Planning, Family Services, Food/Clothing Distribution, People with Disabilities, Scouts, Senior Services, Shelters/Homelessness, Social Services-

General, Special Olympics, United Funds/United Ways, Volunteer Services, YMCA/YWCA/YMHA/YWHA, Youth Organizations

Application Procedures

Initial Contact: Send a written proposal, proof of tax exempt status and reflect on specific project.
Application Requirements: Include the description and mission of organization and project; needs addressed by program; goals and objectives; how objectives will be achieved and evaluated; total cost; amount requested; sources of future support; alternate funding sources and dollar amounts; current budget; audited financial statement; annual report; and proof of tax-exempt status.
Deadlines: September 1.
Review Process: Preliminary review by executive director and appropriate grant committees; final review by board of trustees.
Evaluative Criteria: Impact on number of people served and quality of service.

Restrictions

Does not support individuals, religious organizations, or theological functions for sectarian purposes.
Rarely supports capital campaigns, endowments or operating expenses. UPS partnered with 15 other corporations to help the Orphan Foundation of America Project which is a national leadership and scholarship program for foster youth. Focus is on human and educational services on a national scope.

Additional Information

Publications: Annual Report; Guidelines

Foundation Officials

Evern Cooper: president ED Michigan State University BA. NONPR AFFIL director: Points of Light Foundation; chairman: Women Looking Ahead; chairman: Northwest Georgia Girl Scouts Council; chairman: Atlanta Partners for Education; director: Close Up Foundation.
Scott Scott Davis: treasurer, trustee
Michael L. Eskew: trustee ED Purdue University BS. CORP AFFIL director: 3M. NONPR AFFIL trustee: Annie E. Casey Foundation; chairman: US-China Business Council.
Jim A. Kelly: trustee ED Western New England College BS; Western New England College MS. CORP AFFIL chief financial officer, treasurer: Smith & Wesson Holding; director: United Parcel Service; director: HMS Holdings Corp.; director: Northeast Bancorp/ME; director: Dana Corp.; director: Hewitt Associates Inc.; director: Avista Corp.; director: BellSouth Corp.
Joe Pyne: trustee
Lea Soupata: chairman, trustee NONPR AFFIL fellowship: Academy of Human Resources; trustee: Annie E. Casey Foundation.
Rick Warlick: program director
Thomas H. Weidemeyer: secretary, trustee B Brooklyn, NY 1947. ED California State University BA; Western State University JD. PRIM CORP EMPL senior vice president, director: United Parcel Service of America Inc. CORP AFFIL director: NRG Energy Inc.; director: Waste Management Inc.; director: Goodyear Tire & Rubber.

Grants Analysis

Disclosure Period: calendar year ending 2003
Total Grants: $25,282,496*
Number of Grants: 2,454
Average Grant: $10,303
Highest Grant: $465,000
Lowest Grant: $50
Typical Range: $200 to $5,000 and $15,000 to $300,000
***Note:** Giving excludes matching gifts, scholarship and United Way.

Recent Grants

Note: Grants derived from 2003 Form 990.

General

9,244,076	United Way of America, Alexandria, VA
395,000	United Way of Metropolitan Atlanta Inc., North East Atlanta, GA
375,000	Atlanta Fulton County Zoo Inc., Atlanta, GA
350,000	National Black Child Development Institute Inc., Washington, DC
334,000	East Lake Community Foundation Inc., Atlanta, GA
300,000	100 Black Men of America Inc., Atlanta, GA
300,000	Georgia Partnership for Excellence in Education Inc., Atlanta, GA
300,000	Georgia Tech Foundation Inc., Atlanta, GA
300,000	University of Louisville Foundation Inc., Louisville, KY
250,000	American Foundation for the Blind, New York, NY

U.S. BANCORP PIPER JAFFRAY

Company Headquarters

222 S. Ninth Street
Minneapolis, MN 55402
Web: http://www.piperjaffray.com

Company Description

Former Name: Piper Jaffray & Hopwood; Piper Jaffray Companies, Inc. (1999).
Employees: 3,182
SIC(s): 6211 Security Brokers & Dealers, 6719 Holding Companies Nec.
Parent Company: U.S. Bancorp, 800 Nicollet Mall, Minneapolis, MN, United States

Operating Locations

Piper Jaffray Companies Inc. (AZ--Green Valley, Phoenix, Scottsdale, Sun City; CA--Los Angeles, Menlo Park, Sacramento, San Francisco; CO--Boulder, Colorado Springs, Denver, Durango; ID--Idaho Falls, Pocatello, Twin Falls; IA--Ames, Davenport, Des Moines, Mason City, Sioux City, Spencer, Storm Lake, Waterloo; KS--Lawrence; ME--Omaha; MN--Albert Lea, Austin, Bloomington, Brainerd, Duluth, Grand Rapids, Mankato, New Ulm, Rochester, St. Cloud, St. Paul, Two Harbors, Wayzata; MO--Kansas City, St. Louis; MT--Billings, Bozeman, Great Falls, Missoula; NE--Lincoln; NJ--Hoboken; ND--Fargo, Grand Forks; OR--Portland; SD--Brookings, Mitchell, Pierre, Sioux Falls; UT--Provo, Salt Lake City; WA--Aberdeen, Everett, Kennewick, Seattle, Spokane, Walla Walla, Wenatchee; WI--Appleton, Eau Claire, La Crosse, Madison, Milwaukee, Wausau; WY--Gillette, Sheridan)

Nonmonetary Support

Type: Donated Equipment; In-kind Services
Contact: Brenda Cich, Administrative Assistant
E-mail: bcich@pjc.com
Note: 1997 nonmonetary support $15,000. Company provides nonmonetary support. In-kind services are in the form of printing or meeting services; support should be requested by an employee.

U.S. Bancorp Piper Jaffray Foundation

Giving Contact

Marina Lyon, Director, Public Affairs
222 S. Ninth St.
Minneapolis, MN 55402

Phone: (612)342-5501
Fax: (612)342-6085
Web: http://www.piperjaffray.com/about/community_involve.html

Alternate Contact

Phone: (612)342-6000

Description

Founded: 1993
EIN: 411734808
Organization Type: Corporate Foundation
Former Name: Piper Jaffray (2000).
Formed by Merger of: OS Inc. (2002).
Formed by Merger of: U.S. Bancorp and Firstar (2002).
Giving Locations: MN: Twin Cities area headquarters.
Grant Types: Capital, Employee Matching Gifts, Endowment, General Support, Operating Expenses.
Note: Employee matching gift ratio: 1 to 1 to accredited educational institutions and nonprofit organisation, with a minimum of $25 and maximum of $1,000 annually.

Donor Information

Founder: Established in 1993 by Piper Jaffray Companies

Financial Summary

Total Giving: $3,888,000 (2004 approx). Note: In 2003, 2002, and 2001, no grants were awarded. 1998 giving reflects four additional grants made from October 1 to December 31, 1998. Contributes through corporate direct giving program and foundation.
Assets: $1,610,553 (2001). Note: 1998 asset figure reflects change of accounting period from September 30 to December 31.
Gifts Received: $541,309 (2000); $641,675 (1999); $181,018 (1998). Note: Contributions are received from Piper Jaffray Cos.

Typical Recipients

Arts & Humanities: Arts Centers, Arts Festivals, Arts Institutes, Film & Video, Arts & Humanities-General, Libraries, Museums/Galleries, Music, Opera, Performing Arts, Public Broadcasting, Theater
Civic & Public Affairs: African American Affairs, Business/Free Enterprise, Chambers of Commerce, Community Foundations, Economic Development, Employment/Job Training, Civic & Public Affairs-General, Housing, Municipalities/Towns, Native American Affairs, Nonprofit Management, Public Policy, Urban & Community Affairs, Women's Affairs, Zoos/Aquariums
Education: Arts/Humanities Education, Business Education, Colleges & Universities, Community & Junior Colleges, Economic Education, Education Funds, Education Reform, Elementary Education (Private), Education-General, Gifted & Talented Programs, Leadership Training, Minority Education, Private Education (Precollege), Public Education (Precollege), Student Aid, Vocational & Technical Education
Environment: Forestry, Environment-General, Resource Conservation
Health: Cancer, Children's Health/Hospitals, Emergency/Ambulance Services, Hospitals, Long-Term Care, Medical Rehabilitation, Multiple Sclerosis, Public Health
International: Health Care/Hospitals
Religion: Churches, Dioceses, Jewish Causes, Ministries, Religious Organizations, Religious Welfare, Social/Policy Issues
Science: Science Museums
Social Services: At-Risk Youth, Big Brothers/Big Sisters, Child Welfare, Community Centers, Community Service Organizations, Domestic Violence, Emergency Relief, Family Planning, Family Services, Food/Clothing Distribution, People with Disabilities, Recreation & Athletics, Scouts, Shelters/Homelessness, Social Services-General, United

Funds/United Ways, Volunteer Services, YMCA/YWCA/YMHA/YWHA, Youth Organizations

Application Procedures

Initial Contact: Organizations in the Minneapolis/St. Paul metropolitan area may request general operating support by completing an application form from the Foundation; organizations in the Twin Cities area requesting capital support should submit a proposal and supporting material to the foundation; organizations outside the Twin Cities area requesting capital support should submit a proposal to the nearest branch office.
Application Requirements: Both operating and capital support requests should include a cover letter with a summary and amount requested; recent annual report; current operating budget; list of major supporters; recent audited financial statement; copy of IRS 501(c)(3) determination letter; current list of officers, board members and key staff; and a list of contributions received (for capital requests only).
Deadlines: October 31 or May 31, for general operating support; April 30 for capital requests.
Review Process: Organizations are notified within three weeks of application receipt whether or not their applications will be reviewed.
Applications scheduled for review by the Foundation board are assigned a reviewer to discuss the application with a representative from the applying organization. After information is gathered and analyzed, the Foundation board meets and makes a decision.
Evaluative Criteria: In evaluating requests, the committee considers the petitioning organization's: organizational effectiveness, including helping individuals or improving the civic or cultural life of the community; evaluating and maintaining a set value of outcomes; qualified staff members; financial stability and operating efficiency, including fund-raising ability; ongoing support; responsible governing body, including evidence of long-range plans, a good reputation, active and sensitive board members; and Piper Jaffray employee involvement; capital requests are also considered based on how important project is to community.
Decision Notification: Requests are considered during meetings held in February, May, and September.

Restrictions

Foundation will not support the following: programs expansion; specific program costs; event sponsorships; ticket purchases at fundraising events; travel; expenses associated with team competition; basic and applied research.
Also not funded are: health or disease-specific organizations; individuals; newly formed nonprofit organizations; religious organizations for religious purposes; political, veteran, service or fraternal organizations; public or private K-12 schools; public or private higher education institutions; emergency memberships; or 501(c)(4) or (6) organizations.
The Minnesota Common Grant Application Form is not accepted.
Support for higher education is provided through the U.S. Bancorp Community and Higher Education Matching Gift Program.

Additional Information

In 1999, the foundation began the Youth Employment Strategies (YES) initiative. This two-year initiative will provide for effective employment training programs for disadvantaged youth and young adults.
The foundation reports that in 2000 more than 50% of charitable giving will be distributed by the U.S. Bancorp Piper Jaffray Foundation. Remainder of funds are distributed through branch offices and through corporate giving programs.
Publications: Community Involvement Report; Community Affairs Annual Report; Application Form and; Community Support Guidelines

Corporate Officials

Marina Lyon: director public affairs PRIM CORP EMPL president: Pohlad Family Foundation.

Foundation Officials

Charlie Gits: director
Paul Grangaard: director
William Henderson: director
Douglas Heske: director
Rebecca Kurtzahn: secretary
Gregory T. McNellis: director
Tad Piper: president
Craig Shaver, III: president
Greg Sundberg: director
Eric Wilson: director
Robert Wolter: director

Grants Analysis

Disclosure Period: calendar year ending 2000
Total Grants: $1,674,865*
Number of Grants: 162
Average Grant: $10,339
Highest Grant: $80,000
Typical Range: $1,000 to $15,000
*Note: Giving excludes United Way.

Recent Grants

Note: Grants derived from 2000 Form 990.
Library-Related

10,000	Friends of the St. Paul Public Library, St. Paul, MN

General

70,000	Tree Trust, St. Louis Park, MN
70,000	YouthBiz, Inc., Denver, CO
50,000	Sonoma County People for Economic Opportunity, Santa Rosa, CA
40,000	Juma Ventures, San Francisco, CA
40,000	Minnesota Conservation Corps, St. Paul, MN
40,000	People Serving People Inc., Minneapolis, MN
30,000	Milwaukee Community Service Corp, Milwaukee, WI
30,000	Montana Conservation Corps, Inc., Bozeman, MT
30,000	Operation Fresh Start, Bakersfield, CA
30,000	United Way, St. Paul, MN

UNITED STATES-JAPAN FOUNDATION

Giving Contact

George R. Packard, President
145 East 32nd Street, 12th Floor
New York, NY 10016
Phone: (212)481-8753
Fax: (212)481-8762
E-mail: info@us-jf.org
Web: http://www.us-jf.org

Alternate Contact

Reinanzaka Building 1F, 1-14-2
Akasaka
Minato-Ku
Tokyo 107-0052, Japan
E-mail: jdu05456@nifty.ne.jp
Note: Alt. Phone: 03-3586-0541; Alt. Fax: 03-3586-1128;

Description

Founded: 1980
EIN: 133054425
Organization Type: General Purpose Foundation
Giving Locations: nationally; Japan
Grant Types: Fellowship, Project.
Note: The foundation also supports policy studies and teacher training.

Donor Information

Founder: Incorporated in 1980 under the laws of New York as a private American philanthropic organization dedicated to the promotion of greater mutual knowledge between the people of Japan and the United States. It was founded with a grant from the Japan Shipbuilding Industry Foundation so that the mutual interests of the two societies would be more clearly recognized and better appreciated.

Financial Summary

Total Giving: $2,123,008 (2003); $4,770,126 (2001)
Assets: $80,502,801 (2003); $86,979,675 (2001)

Typical Recipients

Arts & Humanities: History & Archaeology, Libraries, Museums/Galleries, Public Broadcasting
Civic & Public Affairs: Employment/Job Training, Ethnic Organizations, Civic & Public Affairs-General, Public Policy
Education: Colleges & Universities, Environmental Education, Faculty Development, Education-General, International Exchange, International Studies, Journalism/Media Education, Public Education (Precollege), Secondary Education (Public), Social Sciences Education
International: Foreign Arts Organizations, Foreign Educational Institutions, International-General, International Affairs, International Development, International Environmental Issues, International Peace & Security Issues, International Relations, Trade
Science: Scientific Centers & Institutes
Social Services: Child Welfare

Application Procedures

Initial Contact: Applicants should submit a proposal letter of 3-4 pages. Initial letter should include: brief description of proposed project and its objectives, any necessary background information on the project and applicant, and a brief budget estimate. Proposal letters will be reviewed by foundation staff and a response will be sent promptly. Full proposals will not be reviewed an will not be returned to the applicant.
Deadlines: Proposals are accepted on a rolling basis. Decisions are made in April and October.
Review Process: The foundation will notify the grant seeker if the proposed project is not of interest. If the foundation is interested, it will request a detailed proposal.
Notes: The prospective grantee should demonstrate how the project will contribute to increased knowledge and understanding of Japan in the U.S. and the U.S. in Japan, within the context of Asia. Multilateral projects will be considered. The foundation does not accept email proposals.

Restrictions

Individuals applying on their own behalf for independent study, research, travel, or participation in meetings are not eligible.

Additional Information

The foundation is governed by a board of trustees made up of representatives from the United States and Japan. The foundation's headquarters are in New York City, with a liaison office in Tokyo.
Publications: Annual Report; Guidelines; Newsletter (quarterly)

Foundation Officials

Thomas Alva Bartlett: chairman B Salem, OR 1930. ED Stanford University AB (1951); Oxford University MA (1953); Stanford University PhD (1959).
John Brademas: trustee B Mishawaka, IN 1927. ED Harvard University BA (1949); Oxford University DPhil (1954). PRIM NONPR EMPL president emeritus: New York University. CORP AFFIL director: Texaco Inc.; director: RCA/NBC; director: Scholastic Inc.; director: NYNEX Corp.; director: Oxford University Press; director: Loews Corp. NONPR AFFIL member, board advisors: Woodrow Wilson Center International Scholars; member central committee: World Council Churches; trustee: University Notre Dame; member: Study National Needs Biomedical & Behavioral Research; board advisors: Trilateral Commission; trustee: Spelman College; senator: Phi Beta Kappa; member: Smithsonian Institute National Board; director: Alexander S. Onassis Public Benefit Foundation; director: New York Stock Exchange Inc.; president emeritus: New York University; member: National Advisory Council Public Service; member: National Committee Student Financial Assistance; chairman advisory committee: National Advisory Committee Fighting Back; member board visitors department : Massachusetts Institute Technology; member: National Academy Sciences; chairman board director: Federal Reserve Bank New York; member board overseers: Harvard University; board advisors: Emory University Carter Center; director: Council Aid Education; board advisors: Dumbarton Oaks Research Library; director: Center National Policy; trustee: Committee for Economic Development; director: Carnegie Endowment National Commission American & New World; director: Berlitz International Inc.; director: Carnegie Commission Science Technology & Government; director: Aspen Institute; director: Athens College (Greece); member: American Legion; director: American Council Arts; member, board directors: American Council Education; director: Academy Educational Development; fellow: American Academy of Arts & Sciences. CLUB AFFIL Ahepa Club; Masons Club.
Gerald L. Curtis: trustee CORP AFFIL director: Bank of Tokyo-Mitsubishi.
Robin Chandler Tippett Duke: trustee B Baltimore, MD 1923. CORP AFFIL director: River Bank America; director: American Home Products Corp.; director: International Flavors & Fragrances Inc. NONPR AFFIL director: East River Bank; member: World Affairs Council; member: Council Foreign Relations; member: American Academy of Arts & Sciences. CLUB AFFIL River Club; Colony Club; Metropolitan Washington Club.
William Frenzel: trustee B 1943. ED University of Minnesota BBA (1966). PRIM CORP EMPL president, director: Rezults.
Shinji Fukukawa: trustee
Minoru Inouye: vchairman, trustee PRIM CORP EMPL president: Kanematsu U.S.A.
Thomas Stephen Johnson: trustee B Racine, WI 1940. ED Trinity College AB (1962); Harvard University MBA (1964). PRIM CORP EMPL chairman, president, chief executive officer: GP Financial Corp. ADD CORP EMPL president, director: Manufacturers Hanover Trust Co.; chairman, chief executive officer: GreenPoint Financial Corp.; chairman, chief executive officer: GreenPoint Bank. CORP AFFIL director: Allegheny Corp.; director: RR Donnelley & Sons Co. NONPR AFFIL trustee: United Way New York; director: WNET-TV/Channel 13; trustee: United States Japan Foundation; director: Online Resources & Communications; trustee: Trinity College; director: Institute International Education; treasurer, director: Cancer Research Institute; member: Council Foreign Relations; trustee: Asia Society.
Christine Manapat: assistant secretary, treasurer
Moriyuki Motono: trustee
Dr. George R. Packard: trustee B Philadelphia, PA 1932. ED Princeton University AB (1954); Tufts University Fletcher School of Law & Diplomacy PhD (1963). PRIM NONPR EMPL vice president: International University of Japan. NONPR AFFIL member: Japan Society New York; member: Phi Beta Kappa; member: Council Foreign Relations; member: Association Asian Studies; director: Atlantic Council. CLUB AFFIL Metropolitan Club.
Yusuke Saraya: trustee, board secretary
Yohei Sasakawa: trustee
Susan Shirk: trustee
Sumiko Takahara: trustee
Jiro Ushio: vchairman board trustee

Grants Analysis
Disclosure Period: calendar year ending 2003
Total Grants: $2,123,008
Number of Grants: 46
Average Grant: $46,152
Highest Grant: $160,000
Lowest Grant: $2,500
Typical Range: $20,000 to $100,000

Recent Grants
Note: Grants derived from 2001 Form 990.
Library-Related

142,500	Library of Congress, Washington, DC -- for Library's Fall 2001 Exhibition of Japanese Art and Literature

General

253,850	Japan Forum, Tokyo Japan -- to develop a multimedia curriculum based on the real lives of seven Japanese students
206,385	Columbia University East Asian Institute, New York, NY -- for a project to explore the areas of policy coordination and cooperation between the US and Japan towards Indonesia
146,250	University of Tennessee at Chattanooga, Chattanooga, TN -- for Japan Studies Project for high school teachers
143,715	University of Maryland Foundation, Inc., College Park, MD -- for the Japan and US study and exchange that links four elementary schools in the US
142,500	Laurasian Institution, Paris, KY -- for Japan Studies Program
140,838	Japan Forum, Tokyo Japan -- to develop a multimedia curriculum based on the real lives of seven Japanese students
122,016	University of Pennsylvania, Philadelphia, PA -- to support teacher-training program in Japan studies for pre-college educators
111,864	University of Oregon Department of History, Eugene, OR -- to develop a system of performance standards and assessment instruments for use in K-12 level Japanese language instruction in the US
109,924	Aichi University of Education, Kariya City Japan -- to assist Japanese teachers increase awareness about the United States in their teaching methods
109,917	Hokkaido University of Education, Sapporo Japan -- for the American Study Program

U.S. STEEL CORP.

Company Headquarters
600 Grant St.
Pittsburgh, PA 15219-2800
Web: http://www.ussteel.com

Company Description
Ticker: X
Exchange: NYSE
Spun Off From: USX Corp (2001); Marathon Oil (2001).
Revenue: US$14.108 billion (2004)
Profit: US$1.091 billion (2004)
Employees: 21,078 (2001)
Fortune Rank: 149, per FORTUNE Magazine's list of 500 Largest U.S. Corporations (2004).

U.S. Steel Foundation

Giving Contact
Susan Kapusta, General Manager
U.S. Steel Foundation

600 Grant Street, Rm. 685
Pittsburgh, PA 15219-2800
Phone: (412)433-5237
Fax: (412)433-6847
Web: http://www.ussteel.com/corp/ussfoundation/ussfound.htm

Alternate Contact
Phone: (412)433-5093

Description
EIN: 136093185
Organization Type: Corporate Foundation
Former Name: USX Foundation (2001).
Giving Locations: nationally, with emphasis on communities where U.S. Steel Corp. operates.
Grant Types: Capital, Employee Matching Gifts, Fellowship, General Support, Matching, Multiyear/Continuing Support, Operating Expenses, Scholarship.
Note: Matching grants awarded for education only.

Financial Summary
Total Giving: $2,411,727 (fiscal year ending November 30, 2003); $3,688,497 (fiscal 2002); $5,916,734 (fiscal 2001). Note: Contributes through foundation only.
Giving Analysis: Giving for fiscal 2001 includes: foundation fellowships ($16,000); foundation scholarships ($895,004); foundation matching gifts ($1,246,619); foundation grants to United Way ($1,619,500); foundation ($2,139,611).
Assets: $4,718,093 (fiscal 2003); $6,929,439 (fiscal 2002); $10,511,365 (fiscal 2001)
Gifts Received: $17,443,943 (fiscal 2001); $6,612,341 (fiscal 2000); $3,513,840 (fiscal 1999). Note: Contributions were received from USX Corp. and its subsidiaries.

Typical Recipients
Arts & Humanities: Arts Associations & Councils, Arts Centers, Arts Festivals, Arts Funds, Ballet, Dance, Historic Preservation, History & Archaeology, Libraries, Museums/Galleries, Music, Opera, Performing Arts, Public Broadcasting, Theater
Civic & Public Affairs: African American Affairs, Asian American Affairs, Business/Free Enterprise, Community Foundations, Economic Policy, Employment/Job Training, Civic & Public Affairs-General, Law & Justice, Minority Business, Professional & Trade Associations, Public Policy, Urban & Community Affairs, Zoos/Aquariums
Education: Afterschool/Enrichment Programs, Arts/Humanities Education, Business Education, Colleges & Universities, Community & Junior Colleges, Economic Education, Education Associations, Education Funds, Education Reform, Elementary Education (Public), Engineering/Technological Education, Environmental Education, Education-General, Leadership Training, Legal Education, Minority Education, Public Education (Precollege), Science/Mathematics Education, Special Education, Student Aid, Vocational & Technical Education
Environment: Air/Water Quality, Environment-General
Health: Children's Health/Hospitals, Health Funds, Health Organizations, Kidney, Medical Rehabilitation, Mental Health, Single-Disease Health Associations, Trauma Treatment
Religion: Churches, Ministries, Religious Organizations, Religious Welfare, Seminaries
Science: Science Museums, Scientific Centers & Institutes, Scientific Organizations, Scientific Research
Social Services: At-Risk Youth, Community Centers, Community Service Organizations, Day Care, Delinquency & Criminal Rehabilitation, Domestic Violence, Family Services, Homes, People with Disabilities, Scouts, Senior Services, Social Services-General, Substance Abuse, United Funds/United Ways, YMCA/YWCA/YMHA/YWHA, Youth Organizations

Application Procedures
Initial Contact: Send a concise letter or executive summary.
Application Requirements: Include a description of project and its goals; brief history or profile of the organization; organization's mission and need, and projected outcomes; a copy of the organization's Internal Revenue Service certification of tax-exempt status under Section 501(c)(3) of Internal Revenue Code; campaign goal or total cost of specific capital need for capital requests; operating budget for the period for which funding is requested for operating requests; and its most recent audited financial report; a statement of sources of committed funds and the amount of support from each contributor; a statement of sources of anticipated support (prospective contributors that have been, or will be, approached for support and the amounts requested); a copy of the most recently audited financial statement; a list of the organization's chief executives and members of the Board of Directors/Trustees, with affiliations; the signature of an authorized executive of the tax-exempt organization; a signed statement of approval by the chief executive of the parent organization if the application originates in a subdivision of such entity; and a signed statement of approval by the corporate relations or development officer of a college or university if the request originates in a department or subdivision.
Deadlines: January 15 for public, cultural, and scientific requests; April 15 for aid to education; July 15 for health and human services requests.
Review Process: Foundation trustees meet in April, July, and October.
Notes: Organizations in the Pittsburgh area may use the Common Grant Application format of the Grantmakers of Western Pennsylvania. Requests for personal interviews and site visits are accommodated as foundation staff schedules permit. Organizations seeking ongoing support must submit a full proposal each year.

Restrictions
The foundation does not support individuals for personal needs or scholarships (aside from the scholarship program for children of employees); religious organizations for religious purposes; organizations whose programs operate outside of the United States; organizations that are not classified as 501(c)(3) tax-exempt; hospitals; nursing homes; other grantmaking foundations; preschool through 12th grade education; individual research projects; economic development; conferences, seminars, or symposia; travel expenses; sponsorship of fundraising or special events; publication of papers, books, magazines, films, videotapes, or audio-visual materials; or operating needs of organizations supported by the United Way. accordance with the above application deadlines.

Additional Information
"In October 2001, the shareholders of USX Corporation approved a restructuring plan to separate the business units into two publicly-traded companies, United States Steel Corporation and Marathon Oil Corporation, effective December 31, 2001. On that date, the USX Foundation was renamed the United States Steel Foundation to... serve the philanthropic interests of United States Steel Corporation.
"A new foundation, the Marathon Oil Company Foundation, has been formed to serve the philanthropic interests of Marathon Oil Corporation." USX Foundation 2001 Annual Report
Publications: Foundation Annual Report

Corporate Officials
Gary Allen Glynn: president, chief executive officer B Springfield, VT 1946. ED University of Vermont BS (1968); University of Pennsylvania MBA (1970). PRIM CORP EMPL president: USX and Carnegie Pension Fund. NONPR AFFIL chairman finance committee: General Services Board Alcoholic Anony-

mous; member: New York Society Security Analysts; member: Financial Executives Institute; member: Association Investment Management & Research. CLUB AFFIL Tuxedo Club; Metro Club; Metro Opera Association; Drones Club; Economic Club New York.

Gretchen R. Haggerty: vice president, treasurer B 1955. ED Case Western Reserve University BS; Duquesne University JD. PRIM CORP EMPL executive vice president, treasurer, chief executive officer: USX Corp. ADD CORP EMPL vice president accounting and finance: United States Steel Group.

Robert M. Hernandez: vice chairman, chief financial officer, director B Pittsburgh, PA 1944. ED University of Pittsburgh AB (1966); University of Pennsylvania Wharton School MBA (1968). PRIM CORP EMPL vice chairman, chief financial officer, director: USX Corp. ADD CORP EMPL chairman: RTI International Metals Inc. CORP AFFIL director: America Casualty Excess Ltd.

Dan D. Sandman: senior vice president human resources, secretary, general counsel B 1949. ED Ohio State University BA (1970); Ohio State University JD (1973). PRIM CORP EMPL senior vice president, chief administrative officer, secretary, general counsel: USX Corp.

Thomas J. Usher: chairman, chief executive officer B Reading, PA 1942. ED University of Pittsburgh BS (1964); University of Pittsburgh MS (1965); University of Pittsburgh PhD (1971). PRIM CORP EMPL chairman, chief executive officer: USX Corp. CORP AFFIL director: PP&G Industries Inc.; director: Transtar Inc.; director: PNC Bank Corp. NONPR AFFIL chairman: United States-Korea Business Council; trustee: University Pittsburgh; member: Dinamo Ovia; chairman: U.S.-Japan Business Council; member: America Iron Steel Engineers; member, chairman: America Iron Steel Institute. CLUB AFFIL Rolling Rock Club; Laurel Valley Golf Club; Oakmont Country Club; Double Eagle Club; Duquesne Club; Burning Tree Club.

Foundation Officials

Albert G. Adkins: assistant comptroller
M. Sharon Cassidy: assistant secretary B Latrobe, PA 1946. ED Wheeling Jesuit University BS (1968); University of Pittsburgh JD (1974). PRIM CORP EMPL general counsel: United States Steel & Carnegie Pension Fund. NONPR AFFIL member: American Bar Association; advisory: Pension Benefit Guaranty Capital.
Roy G. Dorrance: trustee
Patricia P. Funaro: program manager
Gary Allen Glynn: vice president, investment (see above)
David C. Greiner: assistant treasurer
Edward F. Guna: vice president, treasurer
John A. Hammerschmidt: assistant secretary
Marilyn A. Harris: trustee
Robert M. Hernandez: chief financial officer (see above)
Jerry Howard: trustee
Susan M. Kapusta: trustee
Bruce E. Lammel: assistant secretary
David H. Lohr: trustee
Craig D. Mallick: general manager
John T. Mills: trustee
Dan D. Sandman: trustee (see above)
Larry G. Schultz: vice president, comptroller
John P. Surma, Jr.: trustee
Thomas J. Usher: chairman board trustees (see above)
Gary W. Walsh: tax counsel
Gregory A. Zovko: assistant comptroller

Grants Analysis

Disclosure Period: fiscal year ending November 30, 2003
Total Grants: $770,500*
Number of Grants: 80
Average Grant: $6,589*
Highest Grant: $250,000
Lowest Grant: $1,000
Typical Range: $1,000 to $25,000

*Note: Giving excludes matching gifts, scholarships, fellowships, individuals, and United Way. Average grant figure excludes highest grant.

Recent Grants

Note: Grants derived from fiscal 2003 Form 990.
General

245,000	United Way of Allegheny County, Pittsburgh, PA
200,000	Carnegie Mellon University, Pittsburgh, PA
125,000	Braddock's Field Historical Society, Braddock, PA
125,000	Braddock's Field Historical Society, Braddock, PA
105,000	United Way of Allegheny County, Pittsburgh, PA
87,500	Lake Area United Way, Griffith, IN
87,500	Lake Area United Way, Griffith, IN
80,000	Geneva College, Beaver Falls, PA
50,000	Pittsburgh Public Theater, Pittsburgh, PA
50,000	Shadyside Hospital Foundation, Pittsburgh, PA

UNITED STATES SUGAR CORP.

Company Headquarters

111 Ponce De Leon Ave.
Clewiston, FL 33440
Web: http://www.ussugar.com

Company Description

Employees: 2,700
SIC(s): 0133 Sugarcane & Sugar Beets, 0161 Vegetables & Melons.

Operating Locations

United States Sugar Corp. (FL--Clewiston, South Bay)

United States Sugar Corp. Charitable Trust

Giving Contact

Robert E. Coker, Co-Trustee
111 Ponce De Leon Avenue
Clewiston, FL 33440
Phone: (863)983-8121
Fax: (863)983-9827
Web: http://www.ussugar.com/aboutus/aboutus_frame.html

Description

Founded: 1952
EIN: 596142825
Organization Type: Corporate Foundation
Giving Locations: headquarters and operating communities.
Grant Types: Capital, Emergency, Fellowship, General Support, Professorship, Project.

Financial Summary

Total Giving: $348,700 (fiscal year ending October 31, 2004); $398,600 (fiscal 2003); $260,500 (fiscal 2002). Note: Contributes through corporate direct giving program and foundation.
Assets: $1,090,145 (fiscal 2004); $1,397,277 (fiscal 2003); $1,719,768 (fiscal 2002)
Gifts Received: $500,000 (fiscal 1998); $250,000 (fiscal 1997)

Typical Recipients

Arts & Humanities: Arts Associations & Councils, Arts Outreach, History & Archaeology, Libraries, Museums/Galleries, Performing Arts, Public Broadcasting
Civic & Public Affairs: African American Affairs, Botanical Gardens/Parks, Business/Free Enterprise, Chambers of Commerce, Civil Rights, Clubs, Community Foundations, Economic Development, Economic Policy, Civic & Public Affairs-General, Housing, Law & Justice, Legal Aid, Municipalities/Towns, Nonprofit Management, Philanthropic Organizations, Professional & Trade Associations, Public Policy, Rural Affairs, Safety, Urban & Community Affairs, Women's Affairs
Education: Afterschool/Enrichment Programs, Agricultural Education, Arts/Humanities Education, Business Education, Colleges & Universities, Community & Junior Colleges, Economic Education, Education Associations, Education Funds, Education Reform, Elementary Education (Private), Elementary Education (Public), Environmental Education, Education-General, Literacy, Preschool Education, Private Education (Precollege), Public Education (Precollege), Science/Mathematics Education, Secondary Education (Private), Secondary Education (Public), Special Education, Student Aid
Environment: Environment-General, Protection, Resource Conservation
Health: Alzheimer's Disease, Cancer, Children's Health/Hospitals, Clinics/Medical Centers, Diabetes, Emergency/Ambulance Services, Eyes/Blindness, Health Organizations, Heart, Hospices, Hospitals, Medical Rehabilitation, Mental Health, Public Health, Single-Disease Health Associations
International: International Relations
Religion: Churches, Jewish Causes, Religious Welfare
Science: Science Exhibits & Fairs, Science Museums, Scientific Centers & Institutes, Scientific Organizations
Social Services: Big Brothers/Big Sisters, Camps, Child Welfare, Community Centers, Community Service Organizations, Day Care, Emergency Relief, Family Services, People with Disabilities, Recreation & Athletics, Scouts, Shelters/Homelessness, Social Services-General, Substance Abuse, United Funds/United Ways, Volunteer Services, YMCA/YWCA/YMHA/YWHA, Youth Organizations

Application Procedures

Initial Contact: Send a full proposal.
Application Requirements: Include a description of organization; amount requested and purpose of funds sought; recently audited financial statement; and proof of tax-exempt status.
Deadlines: None; trustees meet four times a year.

Additional Information

United States Sugar Corp. reports that its direct giving applies only to organizations located near company's headquarters.

Corporate Officials

J. Nelson Fairbanks: president, chief executive officer, director B 1936. PRIM CORP EMPL president, chief executive officer, director: United States Sugar Corp. CORP AFFIL director: Florida East Coast Industries Inc.; president, director: US Corrulite Corp.

Foundation Officials

Robert H. Buker, Jr.: co-trustee
Robert E. Coker: co-trustee
Malcolm S. Wade, Jr.: co-trustee

Grants Analysis

Disclosure Period: fiscal year ending October 31, 2004
Total Grants: $348,700
Number of Grants: 79
Average Grant: $4,414
Highest Grant: $25,000
Lowest Grant: $500
Typical Range: $1,000 to $5,000

Recent Grants

Note: Grants derived from 2003 Form 990.
Library-Related

3,000	Harlem Community Public Library, Clewiston, FL
2,500	Friends of the LeRoy Collins Leon County Public Library, Tallahassee, FL -- towards support of 2003 author event

General

50,000	City of South Bay, South Bay, FL
50,000	City of South Bay, South Bay, FL
25,000	Glades Day School, Belle Glade, FL
20,000	Clewiston Chamber of Commerce, Clewiston, FL -- towards support of agriculture farm tours
20,000	Clewiston Museum Inc., Clewiston, FL -- towards expansion and renovation of building
15,000	Foundation for Henry County Public Schools, Labelle, FL -- towards CHS athletic program
13,700	Hendry Regional Medical Center, Clewiston, FL -- for life pak-12 biphasic defibrillator monitor
10,000	City of South Bay, South Bay, FL -- towards equipment for property maintenance
10,000	Foundation for Henry County Public Schools, Labelle, FL -- towards LHS athletic program
10,000	Salvation Army, Tampa, FL

UNITED STATES TRUST COMPANY OF NEW YORK

Company Headquarters

New York, NY
Web: http://www.ustrust.com

Company Description

Employees: 2,250
SIC(s): 6022 State Commercial Banks, 6036 Savings Institutions Except Federal, 6282 Investment Advice, 6289 Security & Commodity Services Nec.
Parent Company: U.S. Trust Corp., 114 W. 47th Street, New York, NY, United States
Parent Revenue: US$4,705,000,000 (2004)

Operating Locations

United States Trust Co. of New York (CA--Los Angeles; FL--West Palm Beach; MA--Boston; NY--New York)

Nonmonetary Support

Type: Donated Equipment; In-kind Services
Contact: Maureen Nuget, Vice President

U.S. Trust Corp. Foundation

Giving Contact

Carol A. Strickland, Chairman, Corporate Contributions Committee
U.S. Trust Corp. Foundation
114 West 47th Street
New York, NY 10036-1532
Phone: (212)852-1400
Fax: (212)852-1341
E-mail: foundation@ustrust.com

Description

EIN: 136072081
Organization Type: Corporate Foundation
Giving Locations: CA: Palo Alto, San Francisco; CT:

Essex, Greenwich, Stamford, West Hartford; DE: Wilmington; DC: Washington; FL: Boca Raton, Naples, Palm Beach, Vero Beach; MN: Minneapolis, St. Paul; NJ: Jersey City, Morristown, Princeton; NY: Garden City, New York; NC: Charlotte, Greensboro, Raleigh; OR: Portland; PA: Wayne; TX: Dallas, Houston; VA: McLean; WA: Tacoma
Grant Types: Capital, General Support, Project.
Note: Employee matching gift ratio: 1 to 1 up to $2,000 annually to eligible educational institutions.

Financial Summary

Total Giving: $500,000 (2003); $509,655 (2002); $392,500 (2001). Note: Contributes through foundation only.
Giving Analysis: Giving for 2001 includes: foundation ($392,500)
Assets: $2,645 (2003); $3,478 (2002)
Gifts Received: $491,446 (2003); $520,605 (2002); $600,000 (2000). Note: Contributions are received in the form of various matching gifts.

Typical Recipients

Arts & Humanities: Arts Associations & Councils, Arts Centers, Arts Funds, Arts Outreach, Ballet, Community Arts, Dance, Arts & Humanities-General, Historic Preservation, Libraries, Museums/Galleries, Music, Opera, Performing Arts, Public Broadcasting, Theater, Visual Arts
Civic & Public Affairs: Botanical Gardens/Parks, Business/Free Enterprise, Community Foundations, Economic Development, Employment/Job Training, Civic & Public Affairs-General, Housing, Legal Aid, Minority Business, Nonprofit Management, Philanthropic Organizations, Public Policy, Rural Affairs, Urban & Community Affairs, Women's Affairs, Zoos/Aquariums
Education: Arts/Humanities Education, Business Education, Colleges & Universities, Education Funds, Elementary Education (Public), Engineering/Technological Education, Education-General, International Exchange, International Studies, Literacy, Minority Education, Preschool Education, Private Education (Precollege), Public Education (Precollege), Secondary Education (Private), Special Education, Student Aid, Vocational & Technical Education
Environment: Environment-General
Health: AIDS/HIV, Cancer, Children's Health/Hospitals, Clinics/Medical Centers, Geriatric Health, Health Policy/Cost Containment, Health Funds, Health Organizations, Hospitals, Long-Term Care, Medical Rehabilitation, Nursing Services, Nutrition
Religion: Jewish Causes, Religious Welfare, Seminaries
Science: Science Museums
Social Services: Child Welfare, Community Centers, Community Service Organizations, Delinquency & Criminal Rehabilitation, Emergency Relief, Family Services, Food/Clothing Distribution, Homes, People with Disabilities, Recreation & Athletics, Senior Services, Shelters/Homelessness, Substance Abuse, United Funds/United Ways, Volunteer Services, YMCA/YWCA/YMHA/YWHA, Youth Organizations

Application Procedures

Initial Contact: Request guidelines, then send a written proposal.
Application Requirements: Include a concise description of organization including legal name, history, purpose, activities; purpose for which the grant is requested; amount requested and list of other sources of financial support, including foundations, corporations, and government grants; copy of IRS determination letter indicating 501(c)(3) tax-exempt status; copy of organization's most recently audited financial statement and Form 990; primary goals including a statement of service area and population to which the program is primarily directed; list of officers and board members and their affiliations; budget for current year including sources of projected income and breakdown of actual income versus expense year to date; and description of how the program will

be evaluated, including procedures and criteria.
Deadlines: Grant requests are grouped by program area and scheduled for review by the Corporate Contributions Committee during either the first half or second half of the year; all culture and arts grant proposals received by April 1 in any calendar year will be assured consideration for Foundation funding in the first half of the year; civic and community proposals received by September 1 will be assured funding consideration in the second half of the year.
Review Process: Grant proposals are reviewed by the Corporate Contributions Committee.
Evaluative Criteria: Preference is given to organizations which demonstrate: ability to solve problems and provide direct services; innovativeness of programs; broad-based community support; involvement of U.S. Trust employees; reliance on private support, as opposed to tax-supported organizations; self-sufficiency of participants; large number of constituents served; efficiency and effective administration of funds and programs; ability to become self-sufficient rather than dependent on yearly renewals of support; long-term solutions versus short-term remedies; stimulate broader participation and multiply the impact of the funds provided by attracting other contributors; non-discriminatory practices; support being sought by an organization throughout the community and to the prospects for obtaining this support.
Decision Notification: Organizations applying for a grant receive an acknowledgement of their proposal within two weeks of receipt; grants are disbursed before June 30 or December 31 each year.
Notes: Program will accept the New York Area Common application form. Proposals will not be considered by the Committee until all requested information is received. Proposals that remain incomplete two months after receipt has been acknowledged will be discarded.

Restrictions

The company does not make grants to individuals for educational or any other purpose; religious, veterans, fraternal or labor organizations unless engaged in a significant project benefiting the entire community; organizations, projects or programs outside the United States; political organizations, political candidates, or in support of political activity; organizations requesting support for courtesy advertising, festival participation, telethons, marathons, races, benefits or events, fund-raising dinners, sponsorship of publications or athletic teams; or national associations and member agencies of the United Way and other organizations supported by an umbrella organization.

Additional Information

The foundation selects primarily Manhattan community grants in the area of housing. For job training initiatives, candidates are chosen from the five boroughs of New York City and Nassau County, Long Island.
Trust(s): US Trust Co. of NY Charitable Foundation

Corporate Officials

Martha L. Dinerstein: managing director, head marketing & corporate communications PRIM CORP EMPL managing director, head marketing & corporate communications: United States Trust Co. of New York. NONPR AFFIL member: New York Junior League; director: Women's Economic Roundtable; member: Advertising Women New York; member: Financial Women's Association.
John L. Kirby: chief administrative officer, executive vice president PRIM CORP EMPL chief administrative officer, executive vice president: U.S. Trust Corp.
Jeffrey Stuart Maurer: president, chief operating officer, director B New York, NY 1947. ED Alfred University BA (1969); New York University MBA (1975); Saint John's University JD (1976). PRIM CORP EMPL president, chief operating officer, director: United States Trust Corp. New York.
H. Marshall Schwarz: chairman, chief executive officer B New York, NY 1936. ED Harvard University BA

(1958); Harvard University MBA (1961). PRIM CORP EMPL chairman, chief executive officer: United States Trust Co. of New York. CORP AFFIL director: Bowne & Co. Inc.; director: Atlantic Mutual Companies. NONPR AFFIL trustee: Milton Academy; director: United Way New York City; trustee: Columbia University Teachers College; chairman: American Red Cross Greater New York City.

Frederick B. Taylor: vice chairman, chief investment officer B Albany, NY 1941. ED Wesleyan University BA (1963); University of Pennsylvania Wharton School MBA (1965). PRIM CORP EMPL vice chairman, chief investment officer: United States Trust Co. of New York. CORP AFFIL vice chairman, chief investment officer: US Trust Corp.

Foundation Officials

Carol A. Strickland: chairman corporate contributions committee B Cold Spring, NY 1949. ED Skidmore College BA (1972); New York University (1978). PRIM CORP EMPL corp. secretary, managing directory: United States Trust Co. of New York. CORP AFFIL corporate secretary, senior vice president: US Trust Corp. NONPR AFFIL member: American Society of Corporate Secretaries.

Grants Analysis

Disclosure Period: calendar year ending 2003
Total Grants: $487,500*
Number of Grants: 33
Average Grant: $11,583
Highest Grant: $75,000
Lowest Grant: $5,000
Typical Range: $10,000 to $20,000
***Note:** Giving excludes United Way.

Recent Grants

Note: Grants derived from 2003 Form 990.
Library-Related

15,000	New York Public Library, New York, NY

General

75,000	Central Park Conservancy, New York, NY
30,000	Metropolitan Museum of Art, New York, NY
25,000	Saint Vincent Catholic Medical Centers, New York, NY
20,000	I Have a Dream Foundation, New York, NY
20,000	Lincoln Center for the Performing Arts Inc., New York, NY
20,000	Thompson Orphanage and Training institution, New York, NY
15,000	Figure Skating in Harlem (FSH), New York, NY
15,000	Julia Dyckman Andrus Memorial, Yonkers, NY
15,000	Learning Leaders Inc., New York, NY
15,000	New York Landmarks Conservancy, New York, NY

UNITRODE CORP.

Company Headquarters

Merrimack, NH
Web: http://www.texasinstrument.com

Company Description

Employees: 500
SIC(s): 3674 Semiconductors & Related Devices.
Parent Company: Texas Instruments Inc., Dallas, TX, United States

Operating Locations

Unitrode Corp. (CA--San Jose; NH--Merrimack; NC--Cary)

Nonmonetary Support

Type: Cause-related Marketing & Promotion; Donated Equipment; In-kind Services; Loaned Employees; Loaned Executives

Giving Contact

7 Continental Blvd.
Merrimack, NH 03054
Phone: (603)429-8770

Description

Organization Type: Corporate Giving Program
Giving Locations: headquarters and operating communities.
Grant Types: Award, Capital, Challenge, Conference/Seminar, Emergency, General Support, Operating Expenses, Project, Scholarship.

Typical Recipients

Arts & Humanities: Art History, Arts Associations & Councils, Arts Centers, Arts Festivals, Arts Outreach, Community Arts, Libraries, Museums/Galleries, Music, Opera, Performing Arts, Public Broadcasting, Theater, Visual Arts
Civic & Public Affairs: Business/Free Enterprise, Chambers of Commerce, Community Foundations, Economic Development, Civic & Public Affairs-General, Housing, Municipalities/Towns, Nonprofit Management, Parades/Festivals, Professional & Trade Associations
Education: Afterschool/Enrichment Programs, Arts/Humanities Education, Business Education, Business-School Partnerships, Colleges & Universities, Education Funds, Elementary Education (Private), Environmental Education, Gifted & Talented Programs, Literacy, Private Education (Precollege), Public Education (Precollege), School Volunteerism, Science/Mathematics Education, Secondary Education (Private), Secondary Education (Public), Vocational & Technical Education
Environment: Energy
Health: Adolescent Health Issues, Arthritis, Children's Health/Hospitals, Clinics/Medical Centers, Emergency/Ambulance Services, Home-Care Services, Hospices, Hospitals, Preventive Medicine/Wellness Organizations, Public Health
Religion: Religious Welfare
Science: Science-General, Science Exhibits & Fairs, Science Museums, Scientific Organizations
Social Services: At-Risk Youth, Big Brothers/Big Sisters, Camps, Child Abuse, Community Centers, Community Service Organizations, Crime Prevention, Domestic Violence, Emergency Relief, Food/Clothing Distribution, People with Disabilities, Recreation & Athletics, Scouts, Senior Services, Sexual Abuse, Shelters/Homelessness, Special Olympics, United Funds/United Ways, Veterans, Volunteer Services, YMCA/YWCA/YMHA/YWHA, Youth Organizations

Application Procedures

Initial Contact: Send a brief letter of inquiry.
Application Requirements: a description of organization, amount requested, purpose of funds sought, and proof of tax-exempt status.
Deadlines: None.

Restrictions

Does not support individuals, religious organizations for sectarian purposes, or political or lobbying groups.

Corporate Officials

Robert L. Gable: chairman, director chief financial officer B Baltimore, MD 1930. ED University of Maryland (1952); University of Maryland School of Business Administration (1953). PRIM CORP EMPL chairman, director: Unitrode Corp. CORP AFFIL director: Symbolics Inc.; chairman: New Hampshire Savings Bank Corp.; chairman: Rockingham County Trust Co.; director: Financial Concepts; director: H K Webster Co.; director: Apollo Computer. NONPR

AFFIL vice chairman: Outward Bound.
Robert Richardson: president, chief executive officer, director PRIM CORP EMPL president, chief executive officer, director: Unitrode Corp.
Cosmo S. Trapani: executive vice president, chief financial officer ED Boston College (1961). PRIM CORP EMPL executive vice president, chief financial officer: Unitrode Corp. NONPR AFFIL member: American Institute CPA's.

Grants Analysis

Total Grants: $30,000 (approx)
Typical Range: $50 to $1,000

Recent Grants

Note: Grants derived from 1998 Form 990.
*General*Daniel Webster College, Nashua, NH*Home, Health and Hospice, Nashua, NH*Keystone Hall, Nashua, NH*Merrimack High School, Merrimack, NH*Museum of Science, Boston, MA*Salvation Army, Manchester, NH*Songahegan Health Care Foundation, Songahegan, NH*United Way, Nashua, NH*Up Reach Riding Center, Goffstown, NH*Habitat for Humanity, Durham, NC*

UNIVERSAL STUDIOS

Company Headquarters

100 Universal City Plaza
Universal City, CA 91608-1002
Web: http://www.universalstudios.com

Company Description

Employees: 15,000
SIC(s): 2396 Automotive & Apparel Trimmings, 2731 Book Publishing, 2741 Miscellaneous Publishing, 7812 Motion Picture & Video Production.
Parent Company: Vivendi Universal Entertainment, 100 Universal City Plaza, Universal City, CA, United States
Parent Revenue: US$51,125,000,000 (2001)

Operating Locations

Geffen Records (CA--Los Angeles); G.P. Putnam Sons (NY--New York); GRP Records (NY--New York); MCA Records (CA--Universal City); MCA/Universal Merchandising (CA--Universal City); Merchandising Corp. of America (CA--Universal City); October Films (NY--New York); Spencer Gifts (NJ--Egg Harbor Township); UNI Distribution Corp. (CA--Universal City); Universal Amphitheatre (CA--Universal City); Universal Film Exchanges, Inc. (NY--New York); Universal Studios (CA--Anaheim, Glendale; FL--Orlando; MI--Grand Rapids; PA--Pittsburgh); Universal Studios Development Co. (CA--Universal City); Universal Studios Distributing Co. (NY--New York); Universal Studios Enterprises (CA--Universal City); Universal Studios Hollywood (CA--Universal City); Universal Studios Home Entertainment Group (CA--Universal City); Universal Studios Manufacturing (IL--Pinckneyville; NY--Gloversville); Universal Studios Music Entertainment Group (CA--Universal City); Universal Studios New Ventures (CA--Universal City); Universal Studios Publishing Group (CA--Universal City); Universal Studios Recreation Services Group (CA--Universal City); Universal Studios Television Ltd. (CA--Universal City); Universal Studios TV (CA--Universal City); Universal Studios Videodisc (CA--Universal City); Winterland Productions (CA--San Francisco); Womp's Restaurant Bar & Grill (CA--Universal City); Yosemite Concession Services Co. (CA--Yosemite National Park)

Nonmonetary Support

Type: Donated Equipment; Donated Products; In-kind Services; Loaned Employees
Volunteer Programs: The company holds a compa-

ny-wide annual Volunteer Day during which employees volunteer to work in food banks, build houses with Habitat for Humanity, beautify schools and parks, and provide books to school libraries. In addition, the company sponsors Education is Universal, through which employee volunteers tutor children in schools, provide students with job shadowing opportunities, and hold career days to introduce students to careers within the entertainment industry.

Contact: Nancy Nemecek, Manager, Public Affairs Universal Studios

Note: Company provides nonmonetary support.

Universal Studios Foundation

Giving Contact

Helene Giambone, Foundation Contact
Universal Studios Foundation
100 Universal City Plaza
Universal City, CA 91608
Phone: (818)777-1208
Web: http://www.universalstudios.com/homepage/html/about_us/

Description

Founded: 1956
EIN: 136096061
Organization Type: Corporate Foundation
Giving Locations: CA: Los Angeles
Grant Types: Capital, General Support, Multiyear/Continuing Support, Project.

Donor Information

Founder: MCA Inc.

Financial Summary

Total Giving: $587,475 (fiscal year ending June 31, 2003); $875,000 (fiscal 2002 approx); $877,870 (fiscal 2001). Note: Contributes through foundation only.
Giving Analysis: Giving for fiscal 2001 includes: foundation ($877,870)
Assets: $14,047,666 (fiscal 2003); $14,002,583 (fiscal 2002); $13,897,052 (fiscal 2001)
Gifts Received: $103,110 (fiscal 2003); $97,054 (fiscal 2000); $38,511 (fiscal 1999). Note: Contributions were received from Universal Studios and its subsidiaries.

Typical Recipients

Arts & Humanities: Arts Associations & Councils, Arts Centers, Arts Funds, Arts Institutes, Ballet, Dance, Film & Video, Arts & Humanities-General, Historic Preservation, History & Archaeology, Libraries, Literary Arts, Museums/Galleries, Music, Performing Arts, Public Broadcasting, Theater
Civic & Public Affairs: African American Affairs, Botanical Gardens/Parks, Business/Free Enterprise, Civil Rights, Community Foundations, Economic Development, Employment/Job Training, Civic & Public Affairs-General, Housing, Law & Justice, Philanthropic Organizations, Professional & Trade Associations, Public Policy, Urban & Community Affairs, Women's Affairs, Zoos/Aquariums
Education: Arts/Humanities Education, Business Education, Colleges & Universities, Community & Junior Colleges, Education Associations, Education Funds, Education Reform, Education-General, International Studies, Legal Education, Literacy, Medical Education, Minority Education, Special Education, Student Aid
Environment: Environment-General, Resource Conservation
Health: Alzheimer's Disease, Cancer, Children's Health/Hospitals, Clinics/Medical Centers, Diabetes, Emergency/Ambulance Services, Eyes/Blindness, Health-General, Health Funds, Health Organizations, Hospitals, Medical Research, Mental Health, Multiple Sclerosis, Public Health, Research/Studies Institutes,

Single-Disease Health Associations
Religion: Jewish Causes
Science: Science Museums, Scientific Centers & Institutes
Social Services: Animal Protection, Big Brothers/Big Sisters, Child Welfare, Community Centers, Community Service Organizations, Counseling, Delinquency & Criminal Rehabilitation, Emergency Relief, Family Planning, Family Services, Food/Clothing Distribution, People with Disabilities, Recreation & Athletics, Scouts, Senior Services, Social Services-General, Substance Abuse, United Funds/United Ways, Veterans, Volunteer Services, YMCA/YWCA/YMHA/YWHA, Youth Organizations

Application Procedures

Initial Contact: Send a letter or preliminary proposal of not more than three pages.
Application Requirements: Include a description of organization of organization; purpose and qualification for which support is sought; attach copy of 501(c)(3) not-for-profit IRS determination letter.
Deadlines: None.
Notes: If the foundation is interested in pursuing the possibility of working with the organization, it may request the following information: a statement of objectives, activities, accomplishments, and geographic scope; a list of the names and business or professional affiliations of the organization's officers and board of directors or trustees, the number of board meetings held in the previous year, and whether or not board members are compensated; number and total compensation of paid employees and the number of volunteer workers; a current itemized budget based on total anticipated funds (fund-raising costs should be shown); a list of sources of current income, including the amount received from each source, listing the corporations, foundations, and government agencies that are current sources of major funding; current audited financial statements; a detailed description of the specific program for which support is requested, including an explanation of what the grant is expected to accomplish, how the program will be carried out, and the method or procedure that will be used to evaluate the effectiveness of the program; and a signed statement that the organization will furnish periodic reports indicating the use of any funds provided by the foundation.

Restrictions

Does not support individuals; film, television, or video projects; group trips; private foundations; political campaigns; ad journals; or fund-raising dinners or events.

Additional Information

Publications: Application Guidelines

Corporate Officials

Ronald Meyer: president, chief operating officer, director B 1945. PRIM CORP EMPL president, chief operating officer, director: Universal Studios.

Foundation Officials

Lynn A. Calpeter: executive vice president
Richard Cotton: executive vice president
Todd R. Davis: vice president
Susan N. Fleishman: senior vice president, director
Sharon S. Garcia: assistant secretary
H. Stephen Gordon: vice president
Andrea R. Hartman: assistant secretary
Patricia E. Hutton: executive vice president
Ronald Meyer: president, director (see above)
David H. Meyers: vice president, assistant controller
Elizabeth A. Newell: assistant secretary
Anne B. Nielsen: assistant secretary
Brian J. O'Leary, Jr.: vice president
Marc Palotay: vice president
Mark Pinkerton: vice president, treasurer
Karen Randall: executive vice president, secretary, director
Terry A. Reagan: vice president

Susan E. Weiner: assistant secretary
Mark A. Wooster: assistant secretary

Grants Analysis

Disclosure Period: fiscal year ending June 31, 2003
Total Grants: $587,475
Number of Grants: 26
Average Grant: $16,115*
Highest Grant: $100,000
Lowest Grant: $2,000
Typical Range: $5,000 to $25,000
***Note:** Average grant figure excludes two highest grants ($200,000).

Recent Grants

Note: Grants derived from 2003 Form 990.
General

100,000	Motion Picture and Television, White Plains, NY
100,000	St. Joseph's Medical Center Foundation, Brainerd, MN
50,000	Fulfillment Fund, Los Angeles, CA
50,000	Greater Los Angeles Zoo, Los Angeles, CA
30,000	Facing History and Ourselves, Brookline, MA
25,000	Assistance League of Southern California, Hollywood, CA
25,000	First Book, Washington, DC
25,000	New York University Tish School of Arts, New York, NY
20,000	Chrysalis, Minneapolis, MN
20,000	Help Group, Sherman Oaks, CA

UNOCAL CORP.

Company Headquarters

El Segundo, CA
Web: http://www.unocal.com

Company Description

Founded: 1890
Ticker: UCL
Exchange: NYSE
Revenue: US$8.217 billion (2004)
Profit: US$1.208 billion (2004)
Employees: 6700 (2003)
Fortune Rank: 268, per FORTUNE Magazine's list of 500 Largest U.S. Corporations (2004).
SIC(s): 1311 Crude Petroleum & Natural Gas, 1321 Natural Gas Liquids, 2911 Petroleum Refining, 2992 Lubricating Oils & Greases.

Operating Locations

Unocal Corp. (AL--Saraland; AK--Anchorage, Kenai, Ketchikan; CA--El Segundo; HI--Hilo, Honolulu; LA--Starks; NM--Bloomfield, Cuba; OH--Columbus, Wadsworth; OR--Myrtle Point, Port Orford, Portland; TX--Andrews, Freeport, Snyder, Sugar Land; WA--Spokane; WI--Milwaukee; WY--Lander)

Unocal Foundation

Giving Contact

Laurie Regelbrugge, Manager
Unocal Foundation
1150 Connecticut Ave. NW, Suite 1025
Washington, DC 20036
Phone: (202)267-2782

Description

EIN: 956071812
Organization Type: Corporate Foundation
Giving Locations: nationally, with preference given to locations with Unocal corporate facilities.
Grant Types: Challenge, Department, Employee

Matching Gifts, Fellowship, General Support, Professorship, Project, Research, Scholarship.

Note: Employee matching gift ratio: 1 to 1 for education, up to $5,000 per employee annually.

Financial Summary

Total Giving: $3,293,051 (fiscal year ending January 31, 2003); $6,200,000 (fiscal 2001)

Giving Analysis: Giving for fiscal 2001 includes: foundation grants to United Way ($330,810); foundation ($630,805); corporate direct giving (approx $5,240,000)

Assets: $5,447,252 (fiscal 2003); $2,143,443 (fiscal 2001)

Gifts Received: $636,146 (fiscal 2001); $1,000,000 (fiscal 2000); $1,000,000 (fiscal 1999). Note: Contributions were received from Unocal Corp.

Typical Recipients

Arts & Humanities: Arts Centers, Arts Funds, Arts Institutes, Community Arts, Dance, Arts & Humanities-General, Historic Preservation, Libraries, Museums/Galleries, Music, Opera, Performing Arts, Theater

Civic & Public Affairs: African American Affairs, Botanical Gardens/Parks, Business/Free Enterprise, Civil Rights, Clubs, Community Foundations, Economic Development, Economic Policy, Employment/Job Training, Civic & Public Affairs-General, Hispanic Affairs, Housing, Inner-City Development, Law & Justice, Legal Aid, Minority Business, Municipalities/Towns, Nonprofit Management, Parades/Festivals, Philanthropic Organizations, Professional & Trade Associations, Public Policy, Rural Affairs, Safety, Urban & Community Affairs, Women's Affairs

Education: Agricultural Education, Arts/Humanities Education, Business Education, Colleges & Universities, Community & Junior Colleges, Continuing Education, Economic Education, Education Associations, Education Funds, Education Reform, Engineering/Technological Education, Faculty Development, Education-General, International Exchange, International Studies, Leadership Training, Legal Education, Medical Education, Minority Education, Private Education (Precollege), Public Education (Precollege), Science/Mathematics Education, Secondary Education (Private), Secondary Education (Public), Social Sciences Education, Student Aid

Environment: Energy, Forestry, Environment-General, Protection, Resource Conservation, Wildlife Protection

Health: AIDS/HIV, Arthritis, Cancer, Children's Health/Hospitals, Clinics/Medical Centers, Diabetes, Emergency/Ambulance Services, Health Organizations, Hospices, Hospitals, Medical Rehabilitation, Medical Research, Medical Training, Mental Health, Single-Disease Health Associations

International: Foreign Educational Institutions, International-General, International Affairs, International Organizations, International Relations

Religion: Religion-General, Religious Welfare

Science: Science Exhibits & Fairs, Science Museums, Scientific Centers & Institutes, Scientific Organizations

Social Services: At-Risk Youth, Big Brothers/Big Sisters, Camps, Child Abuse, Child Welfare, Community Service Organizations, Crime Prevention, Family Services, Food/Clothing Distribution, Homes, People with Disabilities, Recreation & Athletics, Scouts, Shelters/Homelessness, Social Services-General, Special Olympics, Substance Abuse, United Funds/United Ways, Volunteer Services, YMCA/YWCA/YMHA/YWHA, Youth Organizations

Application Procedures

Initial Contact: Request guidelines, then submit a brief letter of request.

Application Requirements: Include background of organization, including its goals and objectives; necessity/purpose of grant; amount budgeted for project; most recent audited financial statement and annual report; current year's budget; evaluative criteria;

other organizations solicited and amounts received, pledged, or anticipated; copy of IRS determination letter; copy of most recent IRS Form 990.

Deadlines: Contact foundation for deadlines, as they vary by program.

Restrictions

Foundation does not support grants to individuals; elementary or secondary education; political or lobbying groups; veterans, fraternal, sectarian, social, religious, athletic, choral, band, or similar groups; courtesy advertising; conferences, films, or contests; supplemental operating support for organizations eligible for united funds; governmental agencies or departments; or trade, business, or professional associations; most capital campaigns or endowments. Grants are not renewed automatically; a request for support must be submitted each year.

Corporate Officials

Darrell D. Chessum: treasurer, chairman, director PRIM CORP EMPL treasurer: Unocal Corp. CORP AFFIL treasurer: Poco Graphite Inc.

Michael Thacher: general manager public relations & communications PRIM CORP EMPL general manager public relations & communications: Unocal Corp.

Charles R. Williamson: chief executive officer, chairman, director ED University of Texas PhD (1978). PRIM CORP EMPL chief executive officer, chairman, director: Unocal Corp.

Foundation Officials

Joe D. Cecil: trustee
Darrell D. Chessum: treasurer (see above)
Kari H. Endries: assistant secretary
Daniel A. Franchi: assistant treasurer
Stephen W. Green: trustee
Stephen L. Hayes: vice president
Gregory F. Huger: president, trustee
Roberta E. Kass: secretary
Christine Lelaurin: trustee
M. L. Luli Heras-De Leon: trustee
Brian W. G. Marcotte: trustee
Carl D. Mcaulay: vice president, trustee
Chaiyasuta Siriporn: trustee
George A. Walker: chairman, trustee
Richard L. Walton: assistant treasurer

Grants Analysis

Disclosure Period: fiscal year ending January 31, 2003

Total Grants: $1,838,911*
Number of Grants: 107
Average Grant: $17,186
Highest Grant: $200,000
Lowest Grant: $100
Typical Range: $1,000 to $30,000
*Note: Giving excludes scholarship; matching gifts and United Way.

Recent Grants

Note: Grants derived from 2003 Form 990.
General

200,000	Habitat for Humanity, Anchorage, AK
187,773	JK Group WPG, Bedford, TX
150,000	Pact Institute, Washington, DC
125,000	International Youth Foundation, Baltimore, MD
125,000	University of North Carolina, Chapel Hill, NC
124,650	Citizens Scholarship Foundation, Marblehead, MA
100,000	Nature Conservancy, Arlington, VA
100,000	University of North Carolina, Chapel Hill, NC
90,000	United Way of Calgary, Calgary, AB Canada
75,000	Nature Conservancy, Anchorage, AK

HAROLD AND GRACE UPJOHN FOUNDATION

Giving Contact

Floyd L. Parks, Secretary & Treasurer
136 E. Michigan Ave., 9th Fl., Suite B
Kalamazoo, MI 49007
Phone: (269)344-2818

Description

Founded: 1958
EIN: 386052963
Organization Type: Private Foundation
Giving Locations: MI
Grant Types: Capital, General Support, Project, Seed Money.

Donor Information

Founder: the late Grace G. Upjohn

Financial Summary

Total Giving: $627,112 (fiscal year ending October 31, 2004); $669,000 (fiscal 2001)

Giving Analysis: Giving for fiscal 2004 includes: foundation grants to United Way ($35,000); fiscal 2001: foundation grants to United Way ($75,000)

Assets: $12,417,989 (fiscal 2004); $12,237,916 (fiscal 2001)

Gifts Received: In fiscal 1991, contributions were received from Mary U. Meader.

Typical Recipients

Arts & Humanities: Arts Associations & Councils, Arts Centers, Arts Institutes, Arts Outreach, Dance, Ethnic & Folk Arts, Historic Preservation, History & Archaeology, Libraries, Museums/Galleries, Music, Performing Arts, Theater, Visual Arts

Civic & Public Affairs: African American Affairs, Botanical Gardens/Parks, Business/Free Enterprise, Community Foundations, Economic Development, Employment/Job Training, Civic & Public Affairs-General, Housing, Municipalities/Towns, Nonprofit Management, Parades/Festivals, Philanthropic Organizations, Public Policy, Safety, Urban & Community Affairs, Women's Affairs, Zoos/Aquariums

Education: Arts/Humanities Education, Colleges & Universities, Community & Junior Colleges, Education Associations, Education Funds, Education Reform, Education-General, Gifted & Talented Programs, Minority Education, Private Education (Precollege), Public Education (Precollege), Science/Mathematics Education, Secondary Education (Private)

Environment: Environment-General, Resource Conservation

Health: AIDS/HIV, Children's Health/Hospitals, Clinics/Medical Centers, Emergency/Ambulance Services, Hospitals, Nursing Services, Preventive Medicine/Wellness Organizations, Speech & Hearing

International: International Development

Religion: Churches, Jewish Causes, Ministries, Religious Organizations, Religious Welfare

Social Services: At-Risk Youth, Big Brothers/Big Sisters, Camps, Child Welfare, Community Service Organizations, Counseling, Emergency Relief, Family Planning, Family Services, Food/Clothing Distribution, Homes, People with Disabilities, Recreation & Athletics, Scouts, Senior Services, Substance Abuse, United Funds/United Ways, Volunteer Services, YMCA/YWCA/YMHA/YWHA, Youth Organizations

Application Procedures

Initial Contact: Contact foundation for application form.

Application Requirements: Return completed application form and cover letter signed by an authorized officer of the organization. Also include a list of board members, including occupations, proof of tax-exempt status, a one page budget, and recently au-

dited financial statement.
Deadlines: None.

Restrictions

Does not support individuals.

Additional Information

Publications: Annual Report; Application Form; Guidelines

Foundation Officials

Janet J. Deal-Koestner: president
Mary U. Meader: trustee
Florence U. Orosz: trustee
Jon L. Stryker: trustee

Grants Analysis

Disclosure Period: fiscal year ending October 31, 2004
Total Grants: $592,112*
Number of Grants: 35
Average Grant: $15,944*
Highest Grant: $50,000
Lowest Grant: $1,000
Typical Range: $5,000 to $25,000
***Note:** Giving excludes United Way. Average grant figure excludes highest grant.

Recent Grants

Note: Grants derived from 2004 Form 990.
General

50,000	City of Kalamazoo, Kalamazoo, MI
35,000	Greater Kalamazoo United Way, Kalamazoo, MI
35,000	Junior League of Kalamazoo, Kalamazoo, MI
30,000	Constance Brown Hearing & Speech Center, Kalamazoo, MI
30,000	Kalamazoo Valley Community College, Kalamazoo, MI
30,000	Western Michigan University Foundation, Kalamazoo, MI
29,575	Kalamazoo Community Foundation, Kalamazoo, MI
25,000	Housing Resources Inc., Kalamazoo, MI
25,000	Kalamazoo Child Guidance Clinic, Kalamazoo, MI
25,000	Kalamazoo College, Kalamazoo, MI

LUCY AND ELEANOR S. UPTON CHARITABLE FOUNDATION

Giving Contact

Francis X. O'Brien, Trustee
c/o Carpenter, Bennett & Morrissey
3 Gateway Center
100 Mulberry Street
Newark, NJ 07102-4079
Phone: (973)622-7711

Description

Founded: 1965
EIN: 226074947
Organization Type: Private Foundation
Giving Locations: NJ
Grant Types: Fellowship, General Support, Research.

Donor Information

Founder: the late Eleanor S. Upton

Financial Summary

Total Giving: $242,500 (2003); $179,500 (2001)
Assets: $7,214,827 (2003); $7,631,648 (2001)

Typical Recipients

Arts & Humanities: Community Arts, History & Archaeology, Libraries, Museums/Galleries, Music
Civic & Public Affairs: Urban & Community Affairs
Education: Arts/Humanities Education, Colleges & Universities, Education Funds, Education-General, Private Education (Precollege)
Health: Cancer, Children's Health/Hospitals, Hospitals, Medical Research
Religion: Religious Organizations, Religious Welfare
Science: Science Museums, Scientific Centers & Institutes
Social Services: Child Welfare, Community Service Organizations, Shelters/Homelessness, Youth Organizations

Application Procedures

Initial Contact: The foundation has no formal grant application procedure or application form.
Deadlines: None.

Foundation Officials

William B. Cater: trustee
Francis X. O'Brien: trustee

Grants Analysis

Disclosure Period: calendar year ending 2003
Total Grants: $242,500
Number of Grants: 19
Average Grant: $10,417*
Highest Grant: $55,000
Lowest Grant: $5,000
Typical Range: $5,000 to $20,000
***Note:** Average grant figure excludes highest grant.

Recent Grants

Note: Grants derived from 2003 Form 990.
General

55,000	New Jersey Symphony Orchestra, Newark, NJ
30,000	St. Philip's Academy, Newark, NJ
25,000	Memorial Sloan - Kettering Cancer Center, New York, NY
20,000	Isaiah House, East Orange, NJ
10,000	Chad School, Newark, NJ
10,000	New Jersey Scholars Educators Excellence Dedication Success, Newark, NJ
10,000	Newark Museum, Newark, NY
10,000	Newark Museum, Newark, NY -- for science center
10,000	Rutgers University Foundation, New Brunswick, NJ -- for Thomas A. Edison papers
10,000	St. Benedict's Preparatory School, Newark, NJ

FREDERICK S. UPTON FOUNDATION

Giving Contact

Stephen E. Upton, Trustee
100 Ridgeway
St. Joseph, MI 49085
Phone: (616)982-1905
Fax: (616)982-0323
E-mail: supton@qtm.net

Description

Founded: 1954
EIN: 366013317
Organization Type: Family Foundation
Giving Locations: IL; IN; MA; MI: Southwest Michigan; OH; PA; SC; WI
Grant Types: Challenge, Endowment, Project.
Note: The foundation also provides technical assistance and support for special events.

Donor Information

Founder: Established in 1954 by Frederick S. Upton, who, in 1911, co-founded the Upton Machine Company, the predecessor of the Whirlpool appliance company.

Financial Summary

Total Giving: $1,748,667 (2001)
Assets: $37,534,273 (2001)
Gifts Received: $145 (2001)

Typical Recipients

Arts & Humanities: Arts Associations & Councils, Arts Centers, Arts Festivals, Arts Funds, Arts Institutes, Arts Outreach, Ballet, Dance, Arts & Humanities-General, Historic Preservation, History & Archaeology, Libraries, Literary Arts, Museums/Galleries, Music, Performing Arts, Visual Arts
Civic & Public Affairs: Civic & Public Affairs-General, Housing, Philanthropic Organizations, Safety, Urban & Community Affairs, Women's Affairs, Zoos/Aquariums
Education: Afterschool/Enrichment Programs, Agricultural Education, Arts/Humanities Education, Business Education, Colleges & Universities, Education Funds, Environmental Education, Education-General, Literacy, Minority Education, Preschool Education, Private Education (Precollege), Public Education (Precollege), Religious Education, School Volunteerism, Science/Mathematics Education, Student Aid
Environment: Environment-General, Resource Conservation
Health: AIDS/HIV, Children's Health/Hospitals, Geriatric Health, Health Organizations, Hospitals, Public Health
International: Foreign Arts Organizations, International Organizations
Religion: Churches, Ministries, Religious Organizations, Religious Welfare, Synagogues/Temples
Social Services: Animal Protection, At-Risk Youth, Child Welfare, Community Centers, Community Service Organizations, Counseling, Domestic Violence, Family Planning, Family Services, Food/Clothing Distribution, People with Disabilities, Recreation & Athletics, Senior Services, Shelters/Homelessness, United Funds/United Ways, Volunteer Services, YMCA/YWCA/YMHA/YWHA, Youth Organizations

Application Procedures

Initial Contact: Applicants should submit a letter of inquiry to the foundation and request an application form.
Deadlines: None.
Review Process: The board of trustees usually meets four times annually and applications are considered at that time.

Additional Information

Publications: Application Form

Foundation Officials

Priscilla U. Byrns: trustee
David F. Upton: trustee
Dr. Stephen E. Upton, LHD: chairman board trustees B Benton Harbor, MI 1924. ED University of Michigan (1949). PRIM CORP EMPL senior vice president: Whirlpool Corp. NONPR AFFIL director: Gilmore Music Festival; member: Rotary International.
Sylvia Upton Wood: secretary, trustee NONPR AFFIL director: Camden Military Academy.

Grants Analysis

Disclosure Period: calendar year ending 2001
Total Grants: $1,647,492*
Number of Grants: 282
Average Grant: $5,842
Highest Grant: $100,000
Lowest Grant: $95

Typical Range: $5,000 to $100000
*Note: Giving excludes United Way.

Recent Grants

Note: Grants derived from 2001 Form 990.
General

100,000	Lake Michigan Catholic Schools, MI -- faith and vision for the future campaign
55,000	Salvation Army, Benton Harbor, MI -- Turning Point Program
50,000	American Institute of Medical Preventics, Cleveland, OH -- clinical study on chelation therapy
50,000	Berrien County Intermediate School District, Berrien Springs, MI -- Arts Education Program
50,000	Cornerstone Alliance, Benton Harbor, MI -- strategic plan
50,000	Ele's Place, Lansing, MI -- marketing and promotion of new website
50,000	Lakeland Health Foundation, Benton Harbor, MI -- M. Beckley Upton Women's Center
50,000	Olivet College, Olivet, MI -- athletic and recreational facility
50,000	Olivet College, Olivet, MI -- Instrumental Music Program
45,000	Fort Miami Heritage Society, St. Joseph, MI -- employees

Us Bank

Company Headquarters

1420 Fifth Ave.
Seattle, WA 98101
Web: http://www.usbank.com

Company Description

Employees: 2,300
SIC(s): 6035 Federal Savings Institutions.
Parent Company: U.S. Bancorp, 800 Nicollet Mall, Minneapolis, MN, United States

Operating Locations

US Bank, Washington (WA--Seattle)

Nonmonetary Support

Type: Donated Equipment; In-kind Services; Workplace Solicitation
Note: Workplace solicitation is for United Way only.

Giving Contact

Mary Moore, Vice President & Manager, Community Relations
1420 5th Avenue, Suite 800
PO Box 720 PD-WA-T8CR
Seattle, WA 98111-0720
Phone: 800-872-2657
Fax: (206)340-8554
E-mail: mary.moore@usbank.com
Web: http://www.usbank.com/comm_relations/charit_giving.cfm

Description

Organization Type: Corporate Giving Program
Giving Locations: WA
Grant Types: Capital, Employee Matching Gifts, General Support, Matching, Project, Scholarship.

Financial Summary

Total Giving: $19,000,000 (2004 approx); $2,000,000 (2002 approx); $2,000,000 (2001). Note: Contributes through corporate direct giving program only.

Typical Recipients

Arts & Humanities: Arts Associations & Councils, Arts Centers, Arts Festivals, Arts Funds, Arts Out-

reach, Ballet, Community Arts, Dance, Ethnic & Folk Arts, Arts & Humanities-General, Historic Preservation, Libraries, Museums/Galleries, Music, Opera, Performing Arts, Theater, Visual Arts
Civic & Public Affairs: African American Affairs, Asian American Affairs, Business/Free Enterprise, Chambers of Commerce, Civil Rights, Economic Development, Employment/Job Training, Ethnic Organizations, Gay/Lesbian Issues, Civic & Public Affairs-General, Hispanic Affairs, Housing, Inner-City Development, Native American Affairs, Professional & Trade Associations, Public Policy, Urban & Community Affairs, Women's Affairs, Zoos/Aquariums
Education: Afterschool/Enrichment Programs, Business Education, Business-School Partnerships, Colleges & Universities, Economic Education, Education Reform, Education-General, Literacy, Minority Education, Preschool Education, Special Education
Health: Adolescent Health Issues, AIDS/HIV, Cancer, Children's Health/Hospitals, Health-General, Hospices, Mental Health, Prenatal Health Issues
Science: Science Museums
Social Services: At-Risk Youth, Camps, Child Welfare, Community Centers, Community Service Organizations, Counseling, Day Care, Domestic Violence, Emergency Relief, Family Services, Food/Clothing Distribution, Homes, People with Disabilities, Refugee Assistance, Senior Services, Sexual Abuse, Shelters/Homelessness, Social Services-General, Substance Abuse, United Funds/United Ways, Volunteer Services, YMCA/YWCA/YMHA/YWHA, Youth Organizations

Application Procedures

Initial Contact: Call local branch or corporate headquarters for information.

Restrictions

Company does not make grants to individuals, religious organizations for sectarian purposes, political or lobbying groups, travel expenses, or organizations outside operating areas. Grants are not made to organizations that are not tax-exempt for endowment campaigns; deficit reduction; fundraising events or sponsorships; medically oriented charities; academic medical, or scientific research; organizations receiving United Way funds; individuals K-12 schools; "pass through" organizations or other foundations; or merchant associations chamber memberships, chamber programs, or 501 (c) (4) or (6) organizations.

Additional Information

In 1997, First Bank System acquired U.S. Bancorp of Portland, OR. The merged company is called U.S. Bancorp.

Corporate Officials

Yvonne Blumenthal: vice president & manager, community investment PRIM CORP EMPL vice president & manager, community investment: US Bank, Washington.
Ken Kirkpatrick: president
Mary Moore: vice president & manager community relations PRIM CORP EMPL vice president & manager community relations: US Bank, Washington.

Grants Analysis

Disclosure Period: calendar year ending 1999
Total Grants: $2,400,000 (approx)*
Number of Grants: 285
Average Grant: $8,421
Highest Grant: $247,000
Typical Range: $5,000 to $10,000
*Note: Grants Analysis provided by foundation.

Usg Corp.

Company Headquarters

125 S. Franklin
Chicago, IL 60680-4678
Web: http://www.usg.com

Company Description

Founded: 1902
Ticker: USG
Exchange: NYSE
Revenue: US$4.509 billion (2004)
Profit: US$312 million (2004)
Employees: 13900 (2003)
Fortune Rank: 433, per FORTUNE Magazine's list of 500 Largest U.S. Corporations (2004).
SIC(s): 2621 Paper Mills, 2891 Adhesives & Sealants, 3275 Gypsum Products, 3296 Mineral Wool.

Operating Locations

USG Corp. (AL--Birmingham; CA--Fremont, La Mirada, Plaster City, South Gate, Torrance; FL--Jacksonville; GA--Atlanta; IL--Chicago; IN--East Chicago, Wabash; IA--Fort Dodge, Sperry; LA--New Orleans; MD--Baltimore; MA--Boston; MN--Cloquet, Red Wing; MS--Greenville; MO--North Kansas City; NV--Empire; NJ--Clark, Port Reading; NY--Oakfield; OH--Gypsum, Tipp City, Westlake; OK--Southard; TX--Galena Park, Sweetwater; UT--Sigurd; VA--Norfolk; WA--Tacoma; WI--Walworth)

USG Foundation

Giving Contact

Peter K. Maitland, President
USG Foundation
PO Box 6721
Chicago, IL 60680-6721
Phone: (312)606-4297
Fax: (312)606-5316
Web: http://www.usg.com/USG_Profile/6_5_2_social_respon.asp

Alternate Contact

Margaret Clark, Assistant Secretary
USG Foundation

Description

EIN: 362984045
Organization Type: Corporate Foundation
Giving Locations: IL: nationally, with emphasis on corporate operating locations
Grant Types: Capital, Employee Matching Gifts, General Support, Scholarship.
Note: Employee matching gift ratio: 0.5 to 1.

Financial Summary

Total Giving: $677,481 (2003); $520,063 (2002); $766,591 (2001)
Assets: $1,911,789 (2003); $2,066,829 (2002); $2,065,571 (2001)
Gifts Received: $506,778 (2003); $500,000 (2002); $1,002,797 (2001). Note: In 2002 and 2003, contributions were received from USG Corp. In 2001, contributions were received from USA Corp. Prior to 2001, contributions were received from USG Corp. and the Chicago Tourism Fund.

Typical Recipients

Arts & Humanities: Arts Associations & Councils, Arts Funds, Arts Institutes, Arts & Humanities-General, Historic Preservation, History & Archaeology, Libraries, Museums/Galleries, Music, Opera, Performing Arts, Public Broadcasting, Theater
Civic & Public Affairs: African American Affairs, Botanical Gardens/Parks, Business/Free Enterprise, Chambers of Commerce, Civil Rights, Community Foundations, Economic Development, Employment/Job Training, Civic & Public Affairs-General, Hispanic

Affairs, Housing, Law & Justice, Legal Aid, Public Policy, Safety, Urban & Community Affairs, Women's Affairs, Zoos/Aquariums

Education: Afterschool/Enrichment Programs, Business Education, Colleges & Universities, Economic Education, Education Associations, Education Funds, Education-General, Health & Physical Education, International Studies, Minority Education, Public Education (Precollege), Special Education, Student Aid

Environment: Environment-General, Resource Conservation

Health: AIDS/HIV, Cancer, Children's Health/Hospitals, Clinics/Medical Centers, Diabetes, Eyes/Blindness, Health Organizations, Heart, Hospices, Hospitals, Long-Term Care, Medical Research, Medical Training, Mental Health, Public Health, Single-Disease Health Associations

International: International Organizations, International Relations, Missionary/Religious Activities

Religion: Churches, Jewish Causes, Ministries, Religious Welfare, Social/Policy Issues

Science: Science Museums

Social Services: At-Risk Youth, Camps, Child Welfare, Community Centers, Community Service Organizations, Crime Prevention, Delinquency & Criminal Rehabilitation, Emergency Relief, Family Services, Food/Clothing Distribution, People with Disabilities, Recreation & Athletics, Scouts, Social Services-General, Substance Abuse, United Funds/United Ways, Volunteer Services, YMCA/YWCA/YMHA/YWHA, Youth Organizations

Application Procedures

Initial Contact: Send a full proposal.

Application Requirements: Cover letter should include statement of need or problem; summary of background of the need or problem; specific reasons why the USG Foundation would be interested in the proposal; amount requested and how it will be used. Proposal should be accompanied by a copy of IRS determination letter and most recent financial statements; list of board members; a statement of the program's purpose, and qualifications of organization to obtain objectives; a detailed description of any proposed special project; goals and an itemized plan to achieve goals; supporting literature.

Deadlines: None.

Review Process: Foundation staff reviews all written proposals.

Evaluative Criteria: Evaluation of how the proposed program can effectively respond to societal needs, relevance in daily life, impact upon business and the future, and how grant will fit into the total contributions program.

Decision Notification: Board meets quarterly; responds within two months.

Notes: The foundation gives preference to relevant programs in which employees actively participate.

Restrictions

The foundation does not contribute to organizations without IRS tax-exempt 501(c)(3) status; sectarian organizations having an exclusively religious nature; individuals; political parties, offices, or candidates; fraternal or veterans organizations; primary or secondary schools; organizations that cannot provide adequate accounting records or procedures; or courtesy advertising. In general, organizations already receiving funds through united campaigns will not be considered for additional support.

Additional Information

Publications: Giving Guidelines

Corporate Officials

Richard Harrison Fleming: executive vice president, chief financial officer B Milwaukee, WI 1947. ED University of the Pacific BA (1969); Dartmouth College MBA (1971). PRIM CORP EMPL chief financial officer, senior vice president: USG Corp. ADD CORP EMPL president, treasurer, director: USG Foreign In-

vestments Ltd.; vice president, treasurer, director: USG Interiors Inc. CORP AFFIL director: Family Care Services Metropolitan Chicago. NONPR AFFIL director: Child Welfare League of America.

Foundation Officials

M. A. Clark: assistant secretary

B. J. Cook: vice president

Richard Harrison Fleming: executive vice president, chief financial officer (see above)

Marcia S. Kaminsky: vice president

Peter K. Maitland: president, director B Joliet, IL 1941. PRIM CORP EMPL vice president: USG Corp.

J. S. Metcalf: vice president

J. P. Rodewald: vice president

Grants Analysis

Disclosure Period: calendar year ending 2003

Total Grants: $511,973*

Number of Grants: 51

Average Grant: $8,739*

Highest Grant: $75,000

Lowest Grant: $1,000

Typical Range: $1,000 to $10,000

*Note: Giving excludes matching gifts, scholarship, and United Way. Average grant figure excludes highest grant.

Recent Grants

Note: Grants derived from 2003 Form 990.

General

75,000	Child Welfare of America, Washington, DC
47,920	National Merit Scholarship Corporation (NMSC), Evanston, IL
40,000	Youth Development Foundation of Skills
35,000	Elmhurst College, Elmhurst, IL
30,508	United Way/Crusade of Mercy (UWCM), Chicago, IL
30,000	Lakefront SRO Corporation, Chicago, IL
30,000	Robert Crown Center for Health Education, Hinsdale, IL
20,000	American Red Cross, Washington, DC
20,000	Chicago United Inc., Chicago, IL
20,000	Naperville Performing Arts Association, Naperville, IL

USIBELLI COAL MINE INC.

Company Headquarters

100 River Rd.
Healy, AK 99743

Company Description

Employees: 125

SIC(s): 1221 Bituminous Coal & Lignite--Surface.

Operating Locations

Usibelli Coal Mine, Inc. (AK--Fairbanks, Healy)

Usibelli Foundation

Giving Contact

Becki Phipps, Executive Director
PO Box 1000
Healy, AK 99743
Phone: (907)452-2625
E-mail: info@usibelli.com
Web: http://www.usibelli.com/foundation.html
Note: Ext. 229

Description

Founded: 1991

EIN: 943152617

Organization Type: Corporate Foundation

Giving Locations: AK: Fairbanks, Healy

Grant Types: General Support.

Donor Information

Founder: Usibelli Coal Mine

Financial Summary

Total Giving: $96,900 (2003)

Giving Analysis: Giving for 2003 includes: foundation grants to United Way ($10,625)

Assets: $2,185,409 (2003)

Gifts Received: $268,347 (2000); $3,165 (1999); $5,193 (1997)

Typical Recipients

Arts & Humanities: Arts Festivals, Film & Video, Libraries, Museums/Galleries, Music, Theater

Civic & Public Affairs: Clubs, Civic & Public Affairs-General, Parades/Festivals, Public Policy

Education: Business Education, Colleges & Universities, Education-General, Literacy, Private Education (Precollege), Public Education (Precollege), Science/Mathematics Education, Secondary Education (Public)

Health: Cancer, Children's Health/Hospitals, Health-General, Hospices, Prenatal Health Issues, Public Health, Respiratory

Religion: Churches, Religious Welfare

Social Services: Big Brothers/Big Sisters, Child Welfare, Community Service Organizations, Counseling, Family Services, Homes, People with Disabilities, Recreation & Athletics, Scouts, Senior Services, Social Services-General, United Funds/United Ways, Youth Organizations

Application Procedures

Initial Contact: Send a brief letter of inquiry.

Application Requirements: Include a description of organization, amount requested, purpose of funds sought, recently audited financial statement, and proof of tax-exempt status.

Deadlines: None.

Restrictions

The foundation does not make grants to individuals or for travel purposes.

Corporate Officials

Rick Hundrup: vice president finance, chief financial officerc PRIM CORP EMPL vice president finance, chief financial officer: Usibelli Coal Mine.

Joseph E. Usibelli, Sr.: chairman B Suntrana, AK 1938. ED Stanford University; University of Alaska. PRIM CORP EMPL chairman: Usibelli Coal Mine. NONPR AFFIL trustee: National Coal Council; trustee: University AK Foundation; trustee: Alaska Energy Task Force.

Joseph E. Usibelli, Jr.: president, chief executive officer, director B 1958. ED University of Alaska (1980). PRIM CORP EMPL president, chief executive officer, director: Usibelli Coal Mine.

Foundation Officials

R. Marc Langland: director

A. Kirk Lanterman: secretary, treasurer PRIM CORP EMPL secretary, treasurer: Usibelli Coal Mine.

Joseph E. Usibelli, Jr.: president (see above)

Joseph E. Usibelli, Sr.: chairman (see above)

Rosalie A. Whyel: vice president

Grants Analysis

Disclosure Period: calendar year ending 2003

Total Grants: $86,275*

Number of Grants: 74

Average Grant: $1,166

Highest Grant: $10,000

Lowest Grant: $250

Typical Range: $500 to $3,000

*Note: Giving excludes United Way.

Recent Grants

Note: Grants derived from 2001 Form 990.

General

17,191	United Way, Fairbanks, AK
10,250	Catholic Schools of Alaska, Fairbanks, AK
10,000	Festival Fairbanks, Fairbanks, AK
10,000	Midnight Sun Boy Scouts, Fairbanks, AK
7,000	Alaska Native Heritage Museum, Anchorage, AK
5,200	Denali Borough School District, Healy, AK
5,100	Tri-Valley Fire Department, Healy, AK
5,000	Fairbanks Symphony, Fairbanks, AK
5,000	Kids in Motion, Healy, AK
3,500	Healy Community Playground, Healy, AK

UTICA NATIONAL INSURANCE GROUP

Company Headquarters

180 Genesee St.
New Hartford, NY 13413

Company Description

Employees: 1,450
SIC(s): 6300 Insurance Carriers, 6400 Insurance Agents, Brokers & Service.
Parent Company: Utica Mutual Insurance Co., 10237 Southard Dr., Beltsville, MD, United States

Operating Locations

Utica National Insurance Group (NY--Utica)

Utica National Foundation

Giving Contact

R. Dicks, Treasurer
PO Box 530
Utica, NY 13503
Phone: (315)734-2205

Description

Founded: 1987
EIN: 161313450
Organization Type: Corporate Foundation
Giving Locations: NY: Utica and surrounding area; OH
Grant Types: Emergency, Employee Matching Gifts, General Support, Multiyear/Continuing Support.

Donor Information

Founder: Utica Mutual Insurance

Financial Summary

Total Giving: $241,233 (2003); $284,405 (2001)
Giving Analysis: Giving for 2001 includes: foundation scholarships ($6,500); foundation grants to United Way ($153,230)
Assets: $4,512,647 (2003); $4,767,563 (2001)
Gifts Received: $2,383 (2003); $2,803 (2001); $2,911 (2000). Note: Contributions were received from Utica Mutual Insurance Co.

Typical Recipients

Arts & Humanities: Arts Associations & Councils, Arts Festivals, Arts Funds, Historic Preservation, Libraries, Museums/Galleries, Music, Performing Arts, Public Broadcasting
Civic & Public Affairs: African American Affairs, Civil Rights, Economic Development, Civic & Public Affairs-General, Housing, Legal Aid, Municipalities/Towns, Parades/Festivals, Safety, Urban & Community Affairs
Education: Afterschool/Enrichment Programs, Community & Junior Colleges, Education Funds, Education-General, Preschool Education, Science/Mathematics Education, Student Aid
Health: AIDS/HIV, Children's Health/Hospitals, Clinics/Medical Centers, Emergency/Ambulance Services, Eyes/Blindness, Health-General, Health Organizations, Heart, Home-Care Services, Hospices, Hospitals, Long-Term Care, Medical Research, Mental Health, Public Health, Single-Disease Health Associations
Religion: Churches, Religious Welfare
Science: Science Museums
Social Services: At-Risk Youth, Child Welfare, Community Centers, Community Service Organizations, Crime Prevention, Emergency Relief, Family Services, Food/Clothing Distribution, Homes, People with Disabilities, Recreation & Athletics, Scouts, Senior Services, Shelters/Homelessness, Social Services-General, Special Olympics, United Funds/United Ways, YMCA/YWCA/YMHA/YWHA, Youth Organizations

Application Procedures

Initial Contact: Request application form.
Deadlines: The first 15 days of each calendar quarter.

Restrictions

Limited to the greater Utica area.

Corporate Officials

W. Craig Heston: chairman, chief executive officer, director chief financial officer, treasurer, director B Philadelphia, PA 1935. ED Temple University. PRIM CORP EMPL chairman, chief executive officer, director: Utica National Corp. Group. CORP AFFIL chairman, president, chief executive officer: Utica National Insurance Co. Texas; chairman, chief executive officer: Utica National Life Insurance Co.; director: Security Mutual Life Insurance Co.; chairman, president, chief executive officer: Utica National Insurance Co. DE; director: Marine Midland Bank NA; chairman, chief executive officer: Republic-Franklin Insurance Co.; chairman, chief executive officer: Graphic Arts Mutual Insurance Co.
John R. Zapisek: senior vice president financial, chief financial officer, treasurer, director B Waterville, NY 1938. ED Syracuse University Utica College (1962). PRIM CORP EMPL senior vice president financial, chief financial officer, treasurer, director: Utica Mutual Insurance Co. CORP AFFIL trustee: Savings Bank Utica; director: WEBCO; director: Graphic Arts Mutual Insurance Co.; director: Republic Franklin Insurance Co.

Foundation Officials

C. William Bachman: director
Alfred E. Calligaris: director
Cynthia L. Casale: assistant treasurer
Jerry J. Hartman: director
W. Craig Heston: director (see above)
Herbert P. Ladds, Jr.: director
Nicolas O. Matt: director
Anthony C. Paolozzi: treasurer
J. Douglas Robinson: president, director
Linda E. Romano: director
George P. Wardley: secretary
John R. Zapisek: director (see above)

Grants Analysis

Disclosure Period: calendar year ending 2003
Total Grants: $149,983*
Number of Grants: 21
Average Grant: $7,142
Highest Grant: $10,000
Lowest Grant: $500
Typical Range: $1,000 to $10,000
*Note: Giving excludes United Way, scholarship.

Recent Grants

Note: Grants derived from 2003 Form 990.

Library-Related

8,500	Utica Public Library, Utica, NY -- toward community technology center

General

100,000	Stanley Performing Arts Center, Utica, NY -- funding for expansion project
75,750	United Way of the Greater Utica Area Inc., Utica, NY -- funding for corporate
52,500	Utica Fire Department, Utica, NY -- toward travel IR Hazmat chemical identifier
25,250	United Way of the Mohawk Valley, Utica, NY -- toward contribution payment
10,000	Presbyterian Homes Foundation Inc., New Hartford, NY -- funding for elder spa/wellness center construction project
10,000	United Cerebral Palsy, Utica, NY -- funding for play area
7,000	Kuyahoora Volunteer Ambulance Corporations, Poland, NY -- toward purchase of two stretchers
6,025	LutheranCare Ministries Network Inc., Clinton, NY -- toward seniors multi-media computer center
5,549	Herkimer County Historical Society, Herkimer, NY -- funding for Minolta microfilm reader/printer
5,019	Learning Disability Association of the Mohawk Valley, Utica, NY -- toward textbooks for conference

VALE-ASCHE FOUNDATION

Giving Contact

Mrs. Vale Asche-Russell, President
2001 Kirby Dr., Suite 1010
Houston, TX 77019-6081
Phone: (713)520-7334

Description

Founded: 1956
EIN: 516015320
Organization Type: Private Foundation
Giving Locations: TX: Houston
Grant Types: General Support, Operating Expenses, Project, Research.

Donor Information

Founder: the late Ruby Vale, the late Fred B. Asche

Financial Summary

Total Giving: $437,500 (fiscal year ending November 30, 2001)
Assets: $13,378,530 (fiscal 2001)

Typical Recipients

Arts & Humanities: Arts Outreach, Ballet, Libraries, Museums/Galleries, Opera, Performing Arts, Theater, Visual Arts
Civic & Public Affairs: Botanical Gardens/Parks, Clubs, Economic Development, Employment/Job Training, Hispanic Affairs, Housing, Urban & Community Affairs, Women's Affairs, Zoos/Aquariums
Education: Colleges & Universities, Faculty Development, Education-General, Literacy, Medical Education, Private Education (Precollege), Secondary Education (Private), Social Sciences Education, Special Education
Environment: Forestry, Environment-General
Health: Adolescent Health Issues, AIDS/HIV, Alzheimer's Disease, Cancer, Children's Health/Hospitals, Clinics/Medical Centers, Emergency/Ambulance Services, Eyes/Blindness, Health Organizations (University Affiliated), Hospices, Medical Research, Mental Health, Single-Disease Health Associations, Speech & Hearing, Transplant Networks/Donor Banks

Religion: Churches, Ministries, Religious Organizations, Religious Welfare

Social Services: Animal Protection, At-Risk Youth, Child Abuse, Child Welfare, Community Service Organizations, Counseling, Family Planning, Food/Clothing Distribution, People with Disabilities, Scouts, Senior Services, Shelters/Homelessness, Substance Abuse, Volunteer Services, Youth Organizations

Application Procedures

Initial Contact: The foundation has no formal grant application procedure or application form.
Deadlines: August 31.

Restrictions

Does not support political or lobbying groups or individuals.

Foundation Officials

Asche Ackerman: vice president
Mrs. Vale Asche Russell: president
William E. Blummer: secretary, treasurer
Anna B. Leonard: 2nd vice president
Anna Tippitt: vice president

Grants Analysis

Disclosure Period: fiscal year ending November 30, 2001
Total Grants: $437,500
Number of Grants: 14
Average Grant: $17,042*
Highest Grant: $133,000
Lowest Grant: $5,000
Typical Range: $10,000 to $30,000
*Note: Average grant figure excludes two highest grants ($233,000).

Recent Grants

Note: Grants derived from fiscal 2002 Form 990.
General

500,000	University of Texas M.D. Anderson Cancer Center, Houston, TX -- Bettyanne Asche Murray Fund for research in gynecologic medial oncology
50,000	Northwest Assistance Ministries, Houston, TX -- help enlarge and continue the Meals on Wheels program
35,000	Child Advocates, Houston, TX -- support volunteer training program
25,000	Breath of Life, Houston, TX -- provide clinical and support services of uninsured children
25,000	Gathering Place, Houston, TX -- construction of new home facility
23,200	Children's Assessment Center, Houston, TX -- remodel areas and upgrade equipment
15,000	Junior League of Houston, Houston, TX -- charity ball 2003
15,000	Literacy Advance of Houston, Houston, TX -- provide teaching material, workshop materials for volunteer tutoring program
10,000	AIDS Foundation Houston, Houston, TX -- support of the children of homeless mothers
10,000	Casa De Esperanza, Houston, TX -- Residential Shelter Program

RUBY R. VALE FOUNDATION

Giving Contact

R. Menkiewicz, Trust Officer
c/o PNC Bank
222 Delaware Ave.
Wilmington, DE 19899

Phone: (302)429-1256
Fax: (302)429-5558

Description

Founded: 1960
EIN: 516018883
Organization Type: Private Foundation
Giving Locations: East Coast.
Grant Types: General Support.

Donor Information

Founder: the late Ruby R. Vale

Financial Summary

Total Giving: $127,000 (2003)
Assets: $2,509,602 (2003)

Typical Recipients

Arts & Humanities: Libraries, Museums/Galleries, Visual Arts
Education: Arts/Humanities Education, Colleges & Universities, Legal Education, Private Education (Precollege)
Health: Cancer, Children's Health/Hospitals, Clinics/Medical Centers, Diabetes, Multiple Sclerosis
Social Services: Child Welfare, Community Service Organizations, Day Care, Family Services, Senior Services

Application Procedures

Initial Contact: The foundation has no formal grant application procedure or application form.
Deadlines: September 1.

Additional Information

Trust(s): PNC Bank DE

Grants Analysis

Disclosure Period: calendar year ending 2003
Total Grants: $127,000
Number of Grants: 5
Highest Grant: $75,000
Lowest Grant: $5,000

Recent Grants

Note: Grants derived from 2001 Form 990.
General

100,000	Widener University School of Law, Wilmington, DE
50,000	Winterthur Museum, Winterthur, DE

LAWSON VALENTINE FOUNDATION

Giving Contact

Valentine Doyle, Trustee
1000 Farmington Avenue
West Hartford, CT 06107
Phone: (860)570-0728

Description

Founded: 1989
EIN: 136920044
Organization Type: Private Foundation
Giving Locations: nationally.
Grant Types: General Support.

Donor Information

Founder: Established in 1989 by Alice P. Doyle.

Financial Summary

Total Giving: $1,052,700 (2002)
Assets: $14,069,432 (2002)
Gifts Received: $3,000 (1999); $3,864,001 (1996).
Note: In 1999, contributions were received from Merlin Foundation. In 1996, contributions were received from the Alice P. Doyle Charitable Remainder Annuity Trust.

Typical Recipients

Arts & Humanities: Arts Associations & Councils, Dance, History & Archaeology, Libraries, Museums/Galleries, Music, Opera, Performing Arts, Public Broadcasting, Theater, Visual Arts
Civic & Public Affairs: Botanical Gardens/Parks, Civil Rights, Community Foundations, Civic & Public Affairs-General, Housing, Municipalities/Towns, Professional & Trade Associations, Public Policy, Rural Affairs, Urban & Community Affairs, Women's Affairs
Education: Arts/Humanities Education, Colleges & Universities, Education-General, Literacy, Minority Education, Private Education (Precollege), Secondary Education (Public), Social Sciences Education, Student Aid
Environment: Air/Water Quality, Forestry, Environment-General, Research, Resource Conservation, Watershed
Health: AIDS/HIV, Cancer, Health Organizations, Long-Term Care, Medical Research, Public Health
International: Health Care/Hospitals, Human Rights, International Development, International Environmental Issues, International Organizations, International Peace & Security Issues, International Relations, International Relief Efforts
Religion: Churches, Jewish Causes, Religious Organizations, Religious Welfare, Seminaries
Social Services: Child Welfare, Community Service Organizations, Delinquency & Criminal Rehabilitation, Domestic Violence, Family Services, Food/Clothing Distribution, Senior Services, Social Services-General, Volunteer Services

Application Procedures

Initial Contact: Send a brief letter of inquiry and a full proposal.
Deadlines: None.

Foundation Officials

Allen Doyle: trustee
Valentine Doyle: trustee
Diana Miller: trustee
Lucy Miller: trustee
Paul E. Vawter: trustee
William D. Zabel: trustee B Omaha, NE 1936. ED Princeton University AB (1958); Harvard University LLB (1961). PRIM CORP EMPL partner: Schulte Roth & Zabel LLP. NONPR AFFIL member: Samuel Wazman Cancer Research Foundation; member: Winston Foundation World Peace; advisory board: Project Death America; member: Volunteer Lawyers Arts; member: Picower Medicine Institute; chairman: Princeton University Planned Giving; member: Ottinger Foundation; member: Phi Beta Kappa; member: New York City Bar Association; member: New York State Bar Association; president: Merlin Foundation; trustee: New School Social; director, member: Lawyers Committee Human Rights; member: Lymphoma Foundation; legal counselor: International Confederation Art Dealers; member: Human Rights Watch; fellow: International Academy Estate & Trust Counsel; member: Estate Planning Council; member: Florida Bar Association; member: David H Cogan Foundation; member: Doctors World; director: Brandeis University Tauber Institute; member: American Law Institute; fellow: Brandeis University; member: American Comm Weizmann Institute Science; member: American Friends Israel Museum; member: American Bar Association; fellow: American College Trust & Estate Counsel. CLUB AFFIL Harmonie Club.

Grants Analysis

Disclosure Period: calendar year ending 2002
Total Grants: $1,052,700
Number of Grants: 63
Average Grant: $16,710
Highest Grant: $101,000
Lowest Grant: $1,000
Typical Range: $2,500 to $40,000

Recent Grants

Note: Grants derived from 2002 Form 990.
General

101,000	New World Foundation, New York, NY
65,000	New England Organic Farming Association of New York, South Butler, NY
53,000	Communities United for People, Portland, OR
50,000	Native Seeds Search, Tucson, AZ
50,000	New England Small Farm Institute, Belchertown, MA
45,000	Rights Action, Washington, DC
42,500	Lawyers Committee for Human Rights, New York, NY
40,000	Hartford Food System, Hartford, CT
40,000	Military Toxics Project, Lewiston, ME
37,000	Tides Center, San Francisco, CA

VALLEY FOUNDATION

Giving Contact

Ervie L. Smith, Executive Director
16450 Los Gatos Boulevard, Suite 210
Los Gatos, CA 95032-5594
Phone: (408)358-4545
Fax: (408)358-4548
E-mail: admin@valley.org
Web: http://www.valley.org

Description

Founded: 1984
EIN: 941584547
Organization Type: General Purpose Foundation
Giving Locations: CA: Santa Clara County
Grant Types: Capital, General Support, Matching.

Financial Summary

Total Giving: $3,155,635 (fiscal year ending September 30, 2004); $2,701,500 (fiscal 2003); $2,818,997 (fiscal 2002)
Assets: $55,312,624 (fiscal 2003); $49,628,176 (fiscal 2002); $55,340,387 (fiscal 2001)

Typical Recipients

Arts & Humanities: Arts Associations & Councils, Arts Centers, Arts Funds, Arts Outreach, Ballet, Dance, Film & Video, Historic Preservation, History & Archaeology, Libraries, Museums/Galleries, Music, Opera, Performing Arts, Public Broadcasting, Theater
Civic & Public Affairs: Asian American Affairs, Botanical Gardens/Parks, Clubs, Community Foundations, Employment/Job Training, Civic & Public Affairs-General, Housing, Philanthropic Organizations, Public Policy, Safety, Urban & Community Affairs
Education: Afterschool/Enrichment Programs, Arts/Humanities Education, Business Education, Colleges & Universities, Community & Junior Colleges, Economic Education, Education Associations, Education Funds, Elementary Education (Public), Faculty Development, Literacy, Medical Education, Minority Education, Private Education (Precollege), Public Education (Precollege), School Volunteerism, Science/Mathematics Education, Secondary Education (Private), Secondary Education (Public), Special Education
Environment: Resource Conservation
Health: Adolescent Health Issues, AIDS/HIV, Alzheimer's Disease, Cancer, Children's Health/Hospitals, Clinics/Medical Centers, Diabetes, Emergency/Ambulance Services, Health-General, Geriatric Health, Health Funds, Health Organizations, Heart, Hospices, Medical Rehabilitation, Medical Research, Mental Health, Multiple Sclerosis, Nutrition, Prenatal Health Issues, Preventive Medicine/Wellness Organizations, Public Health, Single-Disease Health Associations
International: International Relief Efforts
Religion: Ministries, Religious Welfare
Science: Science Museums
Social Services: Animal Protection, At-Risk Youth, Big Brothers/Big Sisters, Camps, Child Abuse, Child Welfare, Community Centers, Community Service Organizations, Counseling, Day Care, Domestic Violence, Emergency Relief, Family Services, Food/Clothing Distribution, Homes, People with Disabilities, Recreation & Athletics, Scouts, Senior Services, Shelters/Homelessness, Social Services-General, Substance Abuse, Volunteer Services, YMCA/YWCA/YMHA/YWHA, Youth Organizations

Application Procedures

Initial Contact: Applicants should send a preliminary letter of one or two pages in length. If the foundation is interested, it will invite a full proposal.
Application Requirements: The preliminary letter should describe the general background and purpose of the sponsoring organization; individuals to be involved in the project; the needs to be addressed; the goals and anticipated results of the project; and the amount requested from the foundation. A full proposal should include a general background and purpose of organization; constituents served; names and affiliations of directors and trustees; copy of IRS tax-exempt letter; prior year's financial statement; total budget and sources of organization's funding; project objective and description; evidence of need and value of project; geographic area to be served; outline of project; anticipated evaluation methods; personnel involved and their qualifications; and detailed project budget, other sources of funding, and amount requested.
Deadlines: Applicants should send the preliminary letter one month prior to submitting a full proposal. Proposal deadlines are November 1 for February meeting; February 1 for May meeting; June 1 for September meeting; and August 1 for December meeting.
Review Process: Staff reviews proposals before submitting them to the board. Review often includes a site visit. The Board of Trustees decides on proposals at quarterly meetings.

Restrictions

Applications for grants are accepted only from qualified tax-exempt charitable organizations. Applications will not be accepted for the benefit of individuals or religious purposes. No disbursements may be made which would fund: contractual allowances between insurance companies and health care providers; program losses which accrue to health care providers; or subsidize deductible and coinsurance arrangements under medical and hospital care policies.

Additional Information

The foundation encourages turnover in grants and, therefore, prefers not to fund multiple year requests. Organizations must wait one full year after receiving funding before submitting an another grant.
The foundation prefers to avoid grants which provide more than one-half of an organization's total budget in any twelve- month period.
Publications: Guidelines; Application Forms; Annual Report

Foundation Officials

Phillip R. Boyce: chairman B 1944. PRIM CORP EMPL chairman: Pacific Trust Co. CORP AFFIL Comerica California Inc. NONPR AFFIL director: Physicians Clinical Lab.
Herbert Kain, MD: director
Edgar G. LaVeque, MD: director
Armon Mills: treasurer
Joseph Parisi: director
Ralph Ross: vchairman
Michael Rubenstein: director
Richard Sieve, MD: secretary
Ervie L. Smith: executive director

Grants Analysis

Disclosure Period: fiscal year ending September 30, 2004
Total Grants: $3,155,635
Number of Grants: 75
Average Grant: $37,939*
Highest Grant: $348,165
Lowest Grant: $10,000
Typical Range: $20,000 to $80,000
*Note: Average grant figure excludes highest grant.

Recent Grants

Note: Grants derived from fiscal 2003 Form 990.
General

325,000	Community Foundation Silicon Valley, San Jose, CA
150,000	Los Gatos High School, Los Gatos, CA
100,000	KTEH San Jose Public Television, San Jose, CA
100,000	Los Gatos High School, Los Gatos, CA
100,000	Los Gatos High School, Los Gatos, CA
100,000	Los Gatos High School, Los Gatos, CA
100,000	National Hispanic University, San Jose, CA
100,000	Silicon Valley Children's Fund, San Jose, CA
100,000	Via Rehabilitation Services Inc., Santa Clara, CA
88,000	California Institute for Medical Research, San Jose, CA

WAYNE AND GLADYS VALLEY FOUNDATION

Giving Contact

Michael D. Dresler, Executive Director
Wayne & Gladys Valley Foundation
1939 Harrison Street, Suite 510
Oakland, CA 94612-3532
Phone: (510)466-6060
Fax: (510)466-6067

Description

Founded: 1977
EIN: 953203014
Organization Type: General Purpose Foundation
Giving Locations: CA: nationally, Alameda and Contra Costa county, Contra Costa County, East Bay area, Santa Clara County
Grant Types: Capital, General Support, Matching, Research, Scholarship.

Donor Information

Founder: Established in 1977 by Mr. F. Wayne Valley and Mrs. Gladys Valley. After Mr. Valley's death in 1986, the foundation received substantial funds from his estate and will continue to receive funds over a period of years.
Mr. Valley was the founder and major owner of Citation Builders, headquartered in San Leandro, CA, which became one of the largest single-family homebuilders in California. Besides Citation, Mr. Valley's other business activities included part-ownership of the Oakland Raiders of the National Football League. Mrs. Valley continues to serve as the chairwoman of the foundation.

Financial Summary

Total Giving: $23,459,902 (fiscal year ending September 30, 2003); $15,487,139 (fiscal 2002); $15,712,982 (fiscal 2001)
Giving Analysis: Giving for fiscal 2003 includes: foundation scholarships ($415,000); fiscal 2002: foundation matching gifts ($30,000); foundation scholarships ($588,375); fiscal 2001: foundation scholarships ($630,000)
Assets: $591,480,838 (fiscal 2003); $548,512,301

(fiscal 2002); $588,367,987 (fiscal 2001)
Gifts Received: $12,245,138 (fiscal 2003); $200,972,736 (fiscal 2002); $16,965,701 (fiscal 2001). Note: In 2003, contributions were received from Francis Wayne Valley Trust. In 2002, contributions were received from Gladys Valley Revocable Trust and Francis Wayne Valley Trust.

Typical Recipients

Arts & Humanities: Ballet, Ethnic & Folk Arts, Libraries, Museums/Galleries, Performing Arts, Public Broadcasting, Theater
Civic & Public Affairs: Community Foundations, Economic Policy, Employment/Job Training, Parades/Festivals, Philanthropic Organizations, Professional & Trade Associations, Urban & Community Affairs, Women's Affairs, Zoos/Aquariums
Education: Afterschool/Enrichment Programs, Arts/Humanities Education, Business Education, Colleges & Universities, Community & Junior Colleges, Continuing Education, Economic Education, Education Associations, Education Funds, Education Reform, Elementary Education (Private), Elementary Education (Public), Engineering/Technological Education, Education-General, Legal Education, Literacy, Medical Education, Preschool Education, Private Education (Precollege), Public Education (Precollege), Religious Education, School Volunteerism, Science/Mathematics Education, Secondary Education (Private), Special Education, Student Aid
Environment: Environment-General, Resource Conservation, Wildlife Protection
Health: AIDS/HIV, Alzheimer's Disease, Cancer, Children's Health/Hospitals, Eyes/Blindness, Health Funds, Health Organizations, Heart, Hospices, Hospitals, Medical Research, Mental Health, Prenatal Health Issues, Research/Studies Institutes, Single-Disease Health Associations, Speech & Hearing, Trauma Treatment
Religion: Churches, Dioceses, Religion-General, Jewish Causes, Religious Organizations, Religious Welfare, Seminaries
Science: Observatories & Planetariums, Scientific Centers & Institutes, Scientific Research
Social Services: Animal Protection, Camps, Child Welfare, Community Centers, Community Service Organizations, Day Care, Domestic Violence, Family Services, Food/Clothing Distribution, Homes, People with Disabilities, Recreation & Athletics, Scouts, Senior Services, Sexual Abuse, Shelters/Homelessness, Special Olympics, Volunteer Services, YMCA/YWCA/YMHA/YWHA, Youth Organizations

Application Procedures

Initial Contact: Applicants should submit a two- to three-page summary letter.
Application Requirements: The letter should include the following: goal and purpose of the project; description and brief history of the sponsoring organization; research references, if any, that show the need of the project or the efficacy of the subject method; project time frame; amount requested from the foundation; total project cost, and other funding sources; brief biographies of project administrators; and milestones by which progress or success will be measured. Other materials that should be attached to the summary letter include: income and expense budget for the project and the latest annual financial statement of the sponsoring organization; list of the board of directors of the sponsoring organization; a copy of the IRS tax-exempt determination letter; and a letter from the chief officer of the sponsoring organization stating that tax-exempt status has not been revoked or modified.
Deadlines: None.
Review Process: The board of directors meets quarterly, and the foundation promises a quick preliminary response. If the board is interested, additional information or a site visit may be requested. Personal communication with foundation directors by representatives of the applicant organization is not encouraged.

Restrictions

In general, the foundation will not provide funding to any of the following: individuals; organizations for profit or profit-making enterprises of nonprofit groups; veterans, fraternal, labor, service club, military, or similar organizations whose principal activity is for the benefit of members; lobbying, propaganda, or other attempts to influence legislation or other partisan political activities; fund-raising events, dinners, or similar affairs, or for advertising; no grants are offered outside the United States; or for private operating foundations.

Additional Information

Publications: Informational Brochure; Application Guidelines

Foundation Officials

Robert C. Brown: director
Stephen M. Chandler: president, director
Michael D. Dresler: executive director
Richard M. Kingsland: chief financial officer, secretary, vice president
John P. Stock: director PRIM CORP EMPL chief executive officer: Saylor Hill Co.
Tamara A. Valley: chairman
Carolyn A. Worth: assistant vice president

Grants Analysis

Disclosure Period: fiscal year ending September 30, 2003
Total Grants: $23,044,902*
Number of Grants: 108
Average Grant: $126,275*
Highest Grant: $4,286,000
Lowest Grant: $7,500
Typical Range: $40,000 to $200,000
*Note: Giving excludes scholarships. Average grant figure excludes three highest grants ($9,786,000).

Recent Grants

Note: Grants derived from fiscal 2009 Form 990.
Library-Related
569,000	Library Foundation of Milton-Freewater, Milton-Freewater, OR -- for the construction of a new library
324,000	Library Foundation of Milton-Freewater, Milton-Freewater, OR -- for the construction of a new library

General
3,500,000	University of California Davis School of Veterinary Medicine, Davis, CA -- for renovations and construction, clinical facilities and an addition to the center for companion animal health
2,000,000	Stanford Law School, Stanford, CA
1,428,574	University of California, San Francisco (UCSF), San Francisco, CA -- for construction of phase I of the new campus at Mission Bay in San Francisco
1,250,000	Salk Institute, San Diego, CA -- for renovation and equipment costs for the cell biology initiative
1,000,000	Alameda County Health Care Foundation, Oakland, CA -- for the purchase of equipment for the trauma center
1,000,000	San Domenico School, San Anselmo, CA -- for the construction of an Athletic center
734,000	Roman catholic Diocese of Oakland, Oakland, CA -- for the 'schools in need program'
500,000	Oakland Zoo, Oakland, CA -- for renovation of the children's Zoo
500,000	Pacific Vascular Research Institute, San Francisco, CA -- budget support for the new pacific vascular research laboratory
475,000	Regents of the University of California, San Francisco, CA -- for research project

on angiogenesis as a treatment for coronary heart disease

VALMONT INDUSTRIES INC.

Company Headquarters

Omaha, NE
Web: http://www.valmont.com

Company Description

Ticker: VALM
Exchange: AMEX
Employees: 5074 (2003)
SIC(s): 3523 Farm Machinery & Equipment, 3612 Transformers Except Electronic, 3648 Lighting Equipment Nec.

Operating Locations

Valmont Industries, Inc. (CO--Fort Collins; IL--Danville; IN--Elkhart; NE--Omaha; OK--Tulsa; TX--Brenham, El Paso; UT--Salt Lake City)

Valmont Foundation

Giving Contact

Robert B. Daugherty, Director
One Valmont Plaza
Omaha, NE 68154-5215
Phone: (402)963-1000
Fax: (402)963-1095

Alternate Contact

Terry McClain, Director
Valmont Foundation

Description

Founded: 1976
EIN: 362895245
Organization Type: Corporate Foundation
Giving Locations: NE: limited giving nationally.
Grant Types: Capital, General Support.

Donor Information

Founder: Valmont Industries, Inc.

Financial Summary

Total Giving: $709,750 (fiscal year ending February 28, 2004); $741,674 (fiscal 2003); $737,977 (fiscal 2002). Note: Contributes through foundation only.
Assets: $61,523 (fiscal 2004); $71,128 (fiscal 2003); $62,585 (fiscal 2002)
Gifts Received: $700,005 (fiscal 2004); $750,005 (fiscal 2003); $748,561 (fiscal 2002). Note: Contributions are received from Valmont Industries.

Typical Recipients

Arts & Humanities: Arts Associations & Councils, Arts Funds, Arts Institutes, Ballet, Ethnic & Folk Arts, Arts & Humanities-General, History & Archaeology, Libraries, Museums/Galleries, Music, Opera, Performing Arts, Public Broadcasting, Theater
Civic & Public Affairs: Botanical Gardens/Parks, Business/Free Enterprise, Chambers of Commerce, Clubs, Community Foundations, Economic Development, Ethnic Organizations, Civic & Public Affairs-General, Law & Justice, Minority Business, Parades/Festivals, Philanthropic Organizations, Professional & Trade Associations, Rural Affairs, Safety, Urban & Community Affairs, Women's Affairs, Zoos/Aquariums
Education: Afterschool/Enrichment Programs, Agricultural Education, Business Education, Colleges & Universities, Community & Junior Colleges, Economic Education, Education Associations, Education Funds, Engineering/Technological Education, Facul-

ty Development, Education-General, Literacy, Minority Education, Private Education (Precollege), Public Education (Precollege), Religious Education, Student Aid

Environment: Forestry, Environment-General, Resource Conservation, Wildlife Protection

Health: AIDS/HIV, Arthritis, Children's Health/Hospitals, Diabetes, Emergency/Ambulance Services, Eyes/Blindness, Heart, Hospitals, Kidney, Medical Rehabilitation, Multiple Sclerosis, Nutrition, Single-Disease Health Associations

International: International-General

Religion: Religious Organizations, Religious Welfare, Social/Policy Issues

Science: Science Exhibits & Fairs

Social Services: At-Risk Youth, Child Welfare, Community Service Organizations, Crime Prevention, Domestic Violence, Emergency Relief, Family Services, People with Disabilities, Recreation & Athletics, Scouts, Senior Services, Shelters/Homelessness, Social Services-General, Special Olympics, Substance Abuse, United Funds/United Ways, YMCA/YWCA/YMHA/YWHA, Youth Organizations

Application Procedures

Initial Contact: Send a written letter of solicitation.

Application Requirements: Include statement of organization's objectives; description of proposed use of contribution; Valmont employee involvement, if any; evidence of tax-exempt status defined under section 501(c)(3) of the Internal Revenue Code; list of officers and directors; and other significant donors.

Deadlines: None.

Notes: Please do not phone or fax requests.

Restrictions

The foundation does not make contributions to individuals; organizations with a limited constituency, such as clubs or fraternal and social organizations; support for any type of travel or tours for individuals or groups; or for-profit organizations.

Valmont will generally not consider contributions for organizations in communities where Valmont does not have an operational presence; multi-year funding for a program or project beyond three years; underwriting or sponsorship of specific radio or television programming; emergency operating support for an organization; or athletic events. underwriting or sponsorship of specific radio or television programming; emergency operating support for an organization; or athletic events.

Additional Information

Publications: Guidelines

Corporate Officials

Mogens C. Bay: chairman, chief executive officer chief financial officer B 1953. PRIM CORP EMPL chairman, chief executive officer: Valmont Industries, Inc. CORP AFFIL director: Peter Kiewit Sons Inc.; director: ConAgra Inc. NONPR AFFIL director: Nebraska Health Systems.

Robert B. Daugherty: director B 1922. PRIM CORP EMPL director: Valmont Industries, Inc. NONPR AFFIL trustee: Hastings College Foundation.

Terry James McClain: senior vice president, chief financial officer B Osmond, NE 1948. ED Wayne State University BS (1970); University of South Dakota MBA (1971). PRIM CORP EMPL senior vice president, chief financial officer: Valmont Industries, Inc. NONPR AFFIL member: Financial Executives Institute.

Foundation Officials

Thomas P. Egan, Jr.: officer B 1948. ED Creighton University BSBA (1971); Creighton University JD (1973). PRIM CORP EMPL vice president, corporate counsel, secretary: Valmont Industries, Inc. CORP AFFIL secretary: Microflect Co. Inc.

Terry James McClain: director (see above)

Brian C. Stanley: officer B 1942. PRIM CORP EMPL vice president, controller: Valmont Industries, Inc.

Grants Analysis

Disclosure Period: fiscal year ending February 28, 2004

Total Grants: $561,200*
Number of Grants: 68
Average Grant: $6,884*
Highest Grant: $100,000
Lowest Grant: $125
Typical Range: $1,000 to $10,000

*Note: Giving excludes United Way. Average grant figure excludes highest grant.

Recent Grants

Note: Grants derived from fiscal 2004 Form 990.

General

126,050	United Way of the Midlands and Community Health Agencies Nebraska, Omaha, NE
100,000	Donors Trust, Alexandria, VA
75,000	Omaha Performing Arts Society, Omaha, NE
43,000	Omaha Symphony Association, Omaha, NE
41,600	Knights of Ak-Sar-Ben Foundation, Omaha, NE
27,950	Omaha's Henry Doorly Zoo, Omaha, NE
22,500	Fremont United Way, Fremont, MI
20,000	Zoofari 2003, Louisville, KY
16,050	Greater Omaha Chamber of Commerce, Omaha, NE
15,000	Fremont Area Community Foundation Inc., Fremont, NE

VAN AMERINGEN FOUNDATION, INC.

Giving Contact

Henry P. van Ameringen, President
509 Madison Avenue
New York, NY 10022-5501
Phone: (212)758-6221
Fax: (212)688-2105
Web: http://www.vanamfound.org

Description

Founded: 1950
EIN: 136125699
Organization Type: Specialized/Single Purpose Foundation
Giving Locations: Northeastern USA.
Grant Types: General Support, Multiyear/Continuing Support, Project, Research, Seed Money.

Financial Summary

Total Giving: $4,187,627 (2004); $3,273,048 (2003); $2,624,661 (2002)
Assets: $87,531,557 (2004); $79,367,204 (2003); $79,809,860 (2002)
Gifts Received: $806,682 (2003); $1,266,489 (2000); $319,654 (1999). Note: In 2000, contributions were received from the Estate of Hedwig van Ameringen. In 1999, contributions were received from the Estate of Hedwign van Ameringen ($169,654) and the Arnold L. van Ameringen Trust ($150,000).

Typical Recipients

Arts & Humanities: Arts Associations & Councils, Arts Outreach, Libraries, Museums/Galleries, Public Broadcasting, Visual Arts

Civic & Public Affairs: Civil Rights, Economic Development, Employment/Job Training, Ethnic Organizations, Civic & Public Affairs-General, Hispanic Affairs, Housing, Law & Justice, Legal Aid, Municipalities/Towns, Public Policy, Urban & Community Affairs, Women's Affairs

Education: Afterschool/Enrichment Programs, Colleges & Universities, Education Associations, Educa-

tion Reform, Elementary Education (Public), Faculty Development, Education-General, Leadership Training, Medical Education, Preschool Education, Religious Education, School Volunteerism, Science/Mathematics Education, Special Education, Student Aid

Environment: Energy

Health: AIDS/HIV, Cancer, Children's Health/Hospitals, Clinics/Medical Centers, Emergency/Ambulance Services, Health-General, Geriatric Health, Health Organizations, Hospices, Hospitals, Hospitals (University Affiliated), Long-Term Care, Medical Rehabilitation, Medical Research, Mental Health, Prenatal Health Issues, Preventive Medicine/Wellness Organizations, Single-Disease Health Associations

International: Health Care/Hospitals, International Affairs, International Organizations

Religion: Churches, Jewish Causes, Religious Welfare

Social Services: At-Risk Youth, Camps, Child Welfare, Community Centers, Community Service Organizations, Counseling, Crime Prevention, Day Care, Delinquency & Criminal Rehabilitation, Domestic Violence, Family Services, Homes, People with Disabilities, Refugee Assistance, Senior Services, Shelters/Homelessness, Social Services-General, Substance Abuse, Veterans, Volunteer Services, Youth Organizations

Application Procedures

Initial Contact: Send a brief letter of inquiry.
Application Requirements: Board meets in March, June and November.
Deadlines: None.

Restrictions

The foundation does not fund any programs for mental retardation, physical disabilities, or drug and alcohol problems. No grants are given to individuals, for capital or endowment funds, for annual fund-raising drives, or in support of international organizations or activities. Grants are made only to charitable organizations that are tax-exempt under section 501(c)(3) of the IRS code. Primarily supports preselected organizations.

Additional Information

Short-term funding is favored over long-range commitments, although occasional multi-year grants are approved.

Publications: Annual Report

Foundation Officials

Christina K. Baiocchi: director
Claire M. Fagin: director
T. Eric Galloway: director
Alexandra Herzan: director
Kenneth A. Kind: director
Patricia Kind: director
Valerie Kind-Rubin: director
Andrew Kindfuller: director
Laura K. McKenna: director
George Rowe, Jr.: vice president, secretary, director
Clarence J. Sundram: director
Henry P. van Ameringen: president, director, treasurer B 1931. CORP AFFIL director: International Flavors & Fragrances Inc.

Grants Analysis

Disclosure Period: calendar year ending 2003
Total Grants: $3,273,048
Number of Grants: 82
Average Grant: $39,915
Highest Grant: $150,000
Lowest Grant: $3,000
Typical Range: $10,000 to $50,000

Recent Grants

Note: Grants derived from 2003 Form 990.
General

150,000	Fountain House, New York, NY

116,817	Central Montgomery Mental Health Center, Norristown, PA
100,000	Goddard Riverside Community Center, New York, NY
100,000	International Center for Clubhouse Development, New York, NY
100,000	National All Research on Schizophrenia and Depression, Great Neck, NY
100,000	Ramapo Anchorage Camp, Rhinebeck, NY
100,000	Schuyler Center for Analysis and Advocacy, Albany, NY
87,471	Center for Preventive Psychiatry
80,000	Care for the Homeless, New York, NY
76,000	CareLink Community Support Services, Broomall, PA

JAY AND BETTY VAN ANDEL FOUNDATION

Giving Contact

Jay Van Andel, President
2905 Lucerne SE, Suite 230
Grand Rapids, MI 49546
Phone: (616)942-3267

Description

Founded: 1963
EIN: 237066716
Organization Type: General Purpose Foundation
Giving Locations: MI
Grant Types: Capital, Challenge, Endowment, General Support, Project, Scholarship.

Donor Information

Founder: Established in 1963 by Jay Van Andel and his wife, Betty (Hoekstra) Van Andel. Mr. Van Andel, the co-chairman of Amway International, founded the corporation in 1959 with his high school friend Richard DeVos. The company, which in 1960 had sales of $500,000 and started in the basement of the Van Andel's home in Ada, MI, is today one of the world's largest direct sales organizations with recent sales of $2 billion. Mr. Van Andel's fortune was estimated in 1991 at $3 billion by *Fortune* magazine.

Financial Summary

Total Giving: $15,465,971 (2003); $15,082,631 (2001)
Giving Analysis: Giving for 2003 includes: foundation grants to United Way ($25,000)
Assets: $141,842,825 (2003); $106,597,084 (2001)
Gifts Received: $26,677,938 (2003); $1,226,940 (2001); $29,660,000 (1998). Note: In 2003, contributions were received from Jay Van Andel ($77,938) and Amway Corp. ($26,600,000). In 2001, contributions were received from Richard M. Devos ($1,200,000) and Jay Van Andel ($26,940). In 1998, contributions were received from the Jay Van Andel Trust ($25,660,000) and Amway Corp. ($4,000,000).

Typical Recipients

Arts & Humanities: Arts Centers, Ballet, Libraries, Museums/Galleries, Music, Opera
Civic & Public Affairs: Botanical Gardens/Parks, Business/Free Enterprise, Chambers of Commerce, Economic Development, Economic Policy, Civic & Public Affairs-General, Housing, Parades/Festivals, Public Policy, Urban & Community Affairs, Zoos/Aquariums
Education: Colleges & Universities, Education-General, Private Education (Precollege), Religious Education, Secondary Education (Private), Student Aid
Environment: Research
Health: Alzheimer's Disease, Children's Health/Hospitals, Clinics/Medical Centers, Health-General,
Health Organizations, Hospices, Hospitals, Long-Term Care, Medical Research, Public Health, Research/Studies Institutes
International: International Relief Efforts, Missionary/Religious Activities, Trade
Religion: Bible Study/Translation, Churches, Ministries, Missionary Activities (Domestic), Religious Organizations, Religious Welfare, Seminaries, Social/Policy Issues
Science: Scientific Research
Social Services: Child Welfare, Community Centers, Community Service Organizations, Family Services, People with Disabilities, Scouts, United Funds/United Ways, YMCA/YWCA/YMHA/YWHA, Youth Organizations

Application Procedures

Initial Contact: Applicants should submit a letter of request to the foundation office.
Application Requirements: The letter should contain a brief description of the purpose for which funds are requested and a letter of reference.
Deadlines: None.

Restrictions

The foundation does not give to individuals.

Foundation Officials

Allan Engle: secretary
Kim S. Mitchell: assistant secretary
James J. Rosloniec: treasurer, trustee ED Central Michigan University (1968). PRIM CORP EMPL president, treasurer, director: Amway Properties Corp. ADD CORP EMPL treasurer: Amway Management Co.; president: Amway Capital Group; president: Amway Mutual Fund Inc.; treasurer: Amway Real Estate Corp.
David Van Andel: vice president, trustee PRIM CORP EMPL senior vice president: Amway Corp.
Jay Van Andel: president, trustee B Grand Rapids, MI 1924. ED Yale University (1943-1944); Pratt Junior College (1945); Calvin College (1942-1946). PRIM CORP EMPL senior chairman, co-founder, director: Amway Corp. ADD CORP EMPL chairman, director: Amway International Inc.; chairman, director: Amway Global Inc.; chairman: Amway Properties Corp.; chairman: Merchandising Productions Inc.
Casey Wondergem: contact PRIM CORP EMPL senior public affairs counsel: Amway Corp.

Grants Analysis

Disclosure Period: calendar year ending 2003
Total Grants: $15,440,971*
Number of Grants: 130
Average Grant: $28,716*
Highest Grant: $11,736,571
Lowest Grant: $100
Typical Range: $5,000 to $50,000
*Note: Giving excludes United Way. Average grant figure excludes highest grant.

Recent Grants

Note: Grants derived from 2001 Form 990.
General

10,500,000	Van Andel Institute, Grand Rapids, MI -- for operating
1,256,181	Van Andel Institute, Grand Rapids, MI -- for debt service
900,000	Heritage Foundation, Washington, DC
315,000	Opera Grand Rapids, Grand Rapids, MI
278,000	Ada Christian School, Ada, MI
260,000	Grand Rapids Christian School Association, Grand Rapids, MI
250,000	Grand Action Foundation, Grand Rapids, MI
200,000	Grand Valley State University, Allendale, MI
150,000	Pine Rest Christian Hospital, Grand Rapids, MI
90,000	La Grave Avenue Christian Reformed Church, Grand Rapids, MI

VAN BUREN FOUNDATION

Giving Contact

John O. Manning, Treasurer
c/o Community First Bank
Keosauqua, IA 52565
Phone: (319)293-3794
Fax: (319)293-6151

Description

Founded: 1959
EIN: 426062589
Organization Type: Private Foundation
Giving Locations: IA: Van Buren County
Grant Types: Capital, General Support, Project, Scholarship.

Donor Information

Founder: the late Ralph S. Roberts

Financial Summary

Total Giving: $317,116 (2003); $217,935 (2002 approx); $92,764 (2001)
Giving Analysis: Giving for 2003 includes: foundation scholarships ($23,848); 2001: foundation scholarships ($6,049)
Assets: $6,090,257 (2003); $5,757,643 (2001)
Gifts Received: $8,106 (2000); $7,000 (1999); $300 (1995). Note: In 1995, contributions were received from Farmers State Bank.

Typical Recipients

Arts & Humanities: Historic Preservation, History & Archaeology, Libraries, Music
Civic & Public Affairs: Botanical Gardens/Parks, Clubs, Economic Development, Civic & Public Affairs-General, Inner-City Development, Minority Business, Municipalities/Towns, Parades/Festivals, Public Policy, Rural Affairs, Safety, Urban & Community Affairs
Education: Agricultural Education, Arts/Humanities Education, Elementary Education (Private), Education-General, Literacy, Preschool Education, Private Education (Precollege), Public Education (Precollege), Science/Mathematics Education, Secondary Education (Private), Secondary Education (Public), Vocational & Technical Education
Environment: Environment-General, Resource Conservation
Health: Emergency/Ambulance Services, Health Organizations, Hospices, Hospitals
Religion: Churches, Religious Welfare
Social Services: Crime Prevention, Emergency Relief, Recreation & Athletics, Scouts, Senior Services, Shelters/Homelessness

Application Procedures

Initial Contact: Application forms for grants and scholarships available from foundation or high school counselors in Van Buren County.
Review Process: Proposals are reviewed two times per year.
Evaluative Criteria: Foundation gives preference to requests from organizations which benefit Van Buren County, IA.

Restrictions

No funds shall be awarded to any individual or organization wherein pecuniary profits may be obtained. Grant must not be the sole or complete funds vested in any project.

Additional Information

Educational loans are made to healthcare and medical students from Van Buren county, IA. Educational grants are memorials or awards given to students meeting certain requirements.

Foundation Officials

Jon Finney: vice chairman, secretary
Sandy McLain: vice president

Arthur P. Ovrom: chairman
Rex Strait: director

Grants Analysis
Disclosure Period: calendar year ending 2003
Total Grants: $293,268*
Number of Grants: 27
Average Grant: $3,587*
Highest Grant: $200,000
Lowest Grant: $410
Typical Range: $1,000 to $5,000
*Note: Giving excludes scholarships. Average grant figure excludes highest grant.

Recent Grants
Note: Grants derived from 2001 Form 990.
Library-Related
4,125	Keosauqua Public Library, Keosauqua, IA -- computerize circulation system
1,689	Southeastern Library Services, Davenport, IA -- software upgrade for county libraries
595	Birmingham Public Library, Birmingham, IA -- Ralph Shott Memorial

General
30,000	City of Keosauqua, Keosauqua, IA -- villages of Van Buren budget
11,000	Harmony Community School, Farmington, IA -- music sound system
7,000	City of Cantril, Cantril, IA -- park improvement
5,500	City of Farmington, Farmington, IA -- radio's for EMS
5,500	Van Buren County Conservation, Keosauqua, IA -- Greef Building roof
5,000	Van Buren County Conservation, Keosauqua, IA -- Fox River Project
3,823	Oak Grove Church, Douds, IA -- church restoration
2,000	Lick Creek Township, Birmingham, IA -- roof for Country School
2,000	Milton Heritage Association, Milton, IA -- stained glass window repair
2,000	Van Buren County Red Cross, Keosauqua, IA -- swimming lessons

ELSIE PROCTER VAN BUREN FOUNDATION

Giving Contact
Colin S. Marshall, Trustee
c/o Bingham McCutchen LLC
150 Federal Street
Boston, MA 02110
Phone: (617)951-8576

Description
Founded: 1994
EIN: 043251802
Organization Type: Private Foundation
Grant Types: General Support.

Financial Summary
Total Giving: $206,000 (2003); $244,900 (2001).
Note: In 1998, contributions were received from Elsie F. Van Buren.
Assets: $4,702,752 (2003); $3,989,287 (2001)
Gifts Received: $2,393,485 (1998); $1,233,414 (1994)

Typical Recipients
Arts & Humanities: Libraries, Performing Arts, Public Broadcasting, Theater
Civic & Public Affairs: Community Foundations, Civic & Public Affairs-General, Law & Justice, Nonprofit Management, Women's Affairs
Education: Continuing Education, Environmental

Education, Education-General
Environment: Resource Conservation
Health: Emergency/Ambulance Services
International: International-General, Health Care/Hospitals, Human Rights, International Development, International Peace & Security Issues, International Relief Efforts
Religion: Churches, Religious Organizations
Science: Science-General, Scientific Organizations
Social Services: Family Services, Social Services-General, Youth Organizations

Application Procedures
Initial Contact: The foundation has no formal grant application procedure or application form. Send a brief letter of inquiry.
Deadlines: None.

Foundation Officials
Collin S. Marshall, Esq.: trustee
Elsie Proctor Van Buren: trustee

Grants Analysis
Disclosure Period: calendar year ending 2003
Total Grants: $206,000
Number of Grants: 66
Average Grant: $3,131*
Highest Grant: $25,000
Lowest Grant: $500
Typical Range: $1,000 to $5,000
*Note: Average grant figure excludes highest grant.

Recent Grants
Note: Grants derived from 2003 Form 990.
General
25,000	Harris Center for Conservation Education, Hancock, NH
10,000	American Friends Service Committee, Cambridge, MA
10,000	Conservation Law Foundation, Boston, MA
10,000	Doctors Without Borders USA, New York, NY
10,000	International Rescue Committee, New York, NY
10,000	Nature Conservatory, Concord, NH
10,000	Oxfam America, Boston, MA
10,000	Peterborough Players, Peterborough, NH
10,000	Settlement College Readiness Program, New York, NY
10,000	Union of Concerned Scientists, Cambridge, MA

DEWITT VAN EVERA FOUNDATION

Giving Contact
Margaretta Forrester, Advisor
431 D North Pole Dr.
St. Louis, MO 63105
Phone: (314)862-0067
Fax: (314)862-0649

Description
Founded: 1959
EIN: 876117907
Organization Type: Private Foundation
Giving Locations: U.S.
Grant Types: Capital, Endowment, General Support, Operating Expenses, Scholarship.

Donor Information
Founder: the late Dewitt Van Evera, the late Caroline Irene Van Evera

Financial Summary
Total Giving: $180,000 (2003); $240,500 (2001)
Giving Analysis: Giving for 2003 includes: founda-

tion scholarships ($5,000) 2001: foundation scholarships ($5,000)
Assets: $3,118,614 (2003); $3,515,471 (2001)

Typical Recipients
Arts & Humanities: Arts Centers, Libraries, Public Broadcasting, Theater
Civic & Public Affairs: Civic & Public Affairs-General, Nonprofit Management
Education: Afterschool/Enrichment Programs, Colleges & Universities, Education Associations, Engineering/Technological Education, Minority Education, Private Education (Precollege), Science/Mathematics Education, Secondary Education (Private), Secondary Education (Public), Student Aid
Health: Emergency/Ambulance Services
International: Foreign Educational Institutions
Social Services: Community Service Organizations

Application Procedures
Initial Contact: Send a brief letter of inquiry describing program.
Deadlines: None.
Review Process: Board meets in February and September.

Restrictions
Does not support individuals.

Additional Information
Trust(s): US Bank NA

Foundation Officials
Margaretta Forrester: co-trustee
Colette Lafond: advisory board

Grants Analysis
Disclosure Period: calendar year ending 2003
Total Grants: $175,000*
Number of Grants: 14
Average Grant: $10,000*
Highest Grant: $45,000
Lowest Grant: $5,000
Typical Range: $5,000 to $20,000
*Note: Giving excludes scholarship. Average grant figure excludes highest grant.

Recent Grants
Note: Grants derived from 2001 Form 990.
General
45,000	Northland College, Ashland, WI
35,000	St. Johns Preparatory School, Collegeville, NM
25,000	People Serving People Inc., Minneapolis, MN -- capital campaign
25,000	St. Louis School Choice Partnership Fund, St. Louis, MO -- Today and Tomorrow Educational Foundation
15,000	Center of Contemporary Arts, University City, MO
15,000	College of St. Benedict, St. Joseph, MN
10,000	Blackburn College, Carlinville, IL -- program campaign
10,000	College Summit, Washington, DC
10,000	Logos High School, St. Louis, MO -- capital
10,000	Logos High School, St. Louis, MO -- operating

VAN HOUTEN MEMORIAL FUND (EDWARD W. AND STELLA C.)

Giving Contact
Susan Head, Trust Associate
Wachovia National Bank

190 River Rd., NJ3132
Summit, NJ 07901
Phone: (908)598-3577
Fax: (908)598-3583

Description

Founded: 1979
EIN: 226311438
Organization Type: General Purpose Foundation
Giving Locations: NJ: Bergen County, Passaic County; NY; PA: children's programs are funded statewide
Grant Types: Capital, Project, Seed Money.

Donor Information

Founder: Established in 1979 by the late Stella C. Van Houten.

Financial Summary

Total Giving: $825,090 (fiscal year ending November 30, 2004)
Assets: $20,463,300 (fiscal 2004)

Typical Recipients

Arts & Humanities: Libraries
Civic & Public Affairs: Philanthropic Organizations, Urban & Community Affairs
Education: Colleges & Universities, Medical Education, Private Education (Precollege), Special Education
Health: Cancer, Children's Health/Hospitals, Clinics/Medical Centers, Geriatric Health, Health Funds, Hospitals, Hospitals (University Affiliated), Medical Rehabilitation, Medical Research, Mental Health, Multiple Sclerosis, Prenatal Health Issues, Respiratory, Single-Disease Health Associations
Religion: Churches, Religious Welfare
Social Services: Camps, Child Welfare, Day Care, Family Planning, Homes, Scouts, Social Services-General, YMCA/YWCA/YMHA/YWHA, Youth Organizations

Application Procedures

Initial Contact: The fund requests application be made in writing.
Application Requirements: Proof of 501(c)(3) status.
Deadlines: Proposals should be received 2-3 weeks prior to February 1 for review in March; May 1 for review in June; August 1 for review in September; and November 1 for review in December.
Notes: Request grant proposal format from foundation.

Restrictions

The fund does not make grants to fund-raising events including dinners, benefits, and athletic events, or for general operating needs, endowments or loans. It also does not generally make grants outside of New Jersey, although exceptions are made for applicants in New York.

Additional Information

Publications: Application Guidelines
Trust(s): Wachovia Bank, NA

Foundation Officials

Susan Head: trust associate

Grants Analysis

Disclosure Period: fiscal year ending November 30, 2004
Total Grants: $825,090
Number of Grants: 26
Average Grant: $26,045*
Highest Grant: $100,000
Lowest Grant: $10,000
Typical Range: $10,000 to $50,000
*Note: Average grant figure excludes two highest grants ($200,000).

Recent Grants

Note: Grants derived from fiscal 2004 Form 990.
General

100,000	St. Joseph's Wayne Hospital Foundation, Wayne, NJ
100,000	Valley Hospital Foundation, Palmer, AK
50,000	Eva's Village, Paterson, NJ
50,000	Ridgewood YMCA and the YWCA of Bergen County, Ridgewood, NJ
50,000	Rollins College, Winter Park, FL
50,000	Trinitas Health Foundation, Elizabeth, NJ
48,000	Newark Community Health Centers Inc., Newark, NJ
40,000	Deborah Hospital Foundation, Browns Mills, NJ
37,400	Arnold P. Gold Foundation, Englewood Cliffs, NJ
33,333	St. Joseph's Hospital and Medical Center Foundation, Phoenix, AZ

VAN WERT COUNTY FOUNDATION

Giving Contact

Larry L. Wendel, Executive Secretary
138 E. Main St.
Van Wert, OH 45891
Phone: (419)238-1743
Fax: (419)238-3374
E-mail: vwcf@bright.net

Description

Founded: 1925
EIN: 340907558
Organization Type: Private Foundation
Giving Locations: OH: Paulding County, Van Wert County
Grant Types: General Support, Scholarship.

Donor Information

Founder: the late Charles F. Wassenberg, Gaylord Saltzgaber, the late John D. Ault, Kernan Wright, the late Richard L. Klein, the late Hazel Gleason, the late Constance Eirich

Financial Summary

Total Giving: $823,635 (2003); $1,034,937 (2001)
Giving Analysis: Giving for 2003 includes: foundation scholarships ($293,525); 2001: foundation scholarships ($379,828)
Assets: $33,167,076 (2003); $29,144,954 (2001)
Gifts Received: $1,233,915 (2003); $717,956 (2001); $11,185,487 (2000). Note: In 2001, contributions were received from the Jared Rice ($5,000), Robert & Lucille Muntzinger ($10,000), Van Wert City Schools ($14,750), East Tennessee Foundation ($1,051,596), Charles R. Johnson Estate ($86,398), Roger McMichael ($6,000), Mary Bebout ($5,000), Sumner J. Walters Family trust ($7,500), Isaac Van Wert Post 178 ($7,617), and various contributions of less than $5,000 each also were received ($36,168). In 2001, contributions were received from the Leslie Endowment Funds ($474,194), Men's Garden Club of Van Wert ($7,645), Richard & Francis Pollock Memorial Fund ($222,350), and Kerns & Margaret White Trust Fund ($3,991). In 1999, contributions were received from Gaylord & Elizabeth Saltzgaber Music FD ($189,597), Ruth E. Cottingham Trust Estate ($34,916), Ralph and Arline Wegesin Memorial FD ($10,000), Frank W. Leslie Memorial Fund ($6,415). In 1996, contributions were received from Douglas E. Koch Memorial Funds ($4,300), the Oscar J. Scaer Memorial Fund ($89,000), the Kerns & Margaret Wright Trust Fund ($3,932),the Smith Memorial Fund ($10,000), the Knittle Irrevocable Music Trust ($20,000), the Dr. Keith Gordon Memorial Scholarship Fund ($5,720), the M. Scott and I. Doepker Memorial Fund ($165,149), and the Harry W. and Viola Clay Memorial Fund ($713,642); various contributions of less than $2,000 each also were received.

Typical Recipients

Arts & Humanities: Arts Centers, Arts Institutes, Historic Preservation, History & Archaeology, Libraries, Museums/Galleries, Music, Performing Arts, Theater
Civic & Public Affairs: Botanical Gardens/Parks, Clubs, Civic & Public Affairs-General, Housing, Municipalities/Towns, Parades/Festivals, Safety
Education: Afterschool/Enrichment Programs, Agricultural Education, Arts/Humanities Education, Business Education, Education-General, Leadership Training, Private Education (Precollege), Public Education (Precollege), Vocational & Technical Education
Environment: Air/Water Quality, Environment-General, Resource Conservation
Health: Home-Care Services, Hospitals, Mental Health, Nursing Services
Religion: Churches, Religious Welfare
Social Services: Animal Protection, Child Welfare, Community Service Organizations, Crime Prevention, Day Care, Delinquency & Criminal Rehabilitation, Domestic Violence, Emergency Relief, Family Planning, People with Disabilities, Recreation & Athletics, Senior Services, Social Services-General, United Funds/United Ways, YMCA/YWCA/YMHA/YWHA, Youth Organizations

Application Procedures

Initial Contact: Request application forms and guidelines for scholarship program and grants program.
Application Requirements: Grant proposals should include a description of organization and what will be accomplished, population to be served by project, documented line item budget, proof of tax-exempt status, and other organizational information.
Deadlines: June 3 for scholarship programs; May 15 and November 15 for other grants.

Restrictions

Does not provide loans, support religious activities, or support individuals except for scholarships.

Additional Information

Provides scholarships to residents of Van Wert or Paulding County, OH.
Publications: Application Guidelines; Application Form

Foundation Officials

D. L. Brumback, Jr.: trustee
Michael T. Cross: trustee PRIM CORP EMPL president: First Federal Savings & Loan Association.
William S. Derry: trustee
Clair Dudgeon: trustee
Bruce C. Kennedy: trustee
Watson Ley: trustee
Francis W. Purmort, III: director
Paul W. Purmort, Jr.: trustee
C. Allan Runser: trustee
Donald C. Sutton: trustee
Gerald D. Thatcher: trustee
Roger K. Thompson: trustee ED Rensselaer Polytechnic Institute (1951). PRIM CORP EMPL president: Kennedy Manufacturing Co.
Larry L. Wendel: executive secretary
Robert C. Young: trustee
Michael R. Zedaker: trustee

Grants Analysis

Disclosure Period: calendar year ending 2003
Total Grants: $530,110*
Number of Grants: 97
Average Grant: $5,465
Highest Grant: $61,436
Lowest Grant: $10
Typical Range: $1,000 to $10,000
*Note: Giving excludes scholarships.

Recent Grants

Note: Grants derived from 2001 Form 990.

General

63,000	Vantage Vocational School, Van Wert, OH -- support for Electronic Department
61,630	YMCA, Van Wert, OH -- for building improvements
57,900	YWCA, Van Wert, OH -- for building improvements
55,700	Van Wert City School, Van Wert, OH -- for Music Department
49,147	Wassenburg Art Center, Van Wert, OH
34,757	Wassenburg Art Center, Van Wert, OH -- for staff salaries and payroll taxes
25,000	Marsh Foundation, Van Wert, OH -- for renovations
25,000	Van Wert Community Concerts, Van Wert, OH
15,000	Crestview Schools, Convoy, OH -- for Music Department
15,000	Lima Symphony Orchestra, Lima, OH -- for concert in City of Van Wert

ROBERT C. VANCE CHARITABLE FOUNDATION

Giving Contact

Herbert E. Carlson, Jr., Chairman & President
21 Winesap Rd.
Kensington, CT 06037
Phone: (203)828-6037

Description

Founded: 1960
EIN: 066050188
Organization Type: Private Foundation
Giving Locations: CT: New Britain
Grant Types: General Support.

Donor Information

Founder: the late Robert C. Vance

Financial Summary

Total Giving: $452,284 (fiscal year ending January 31, 2002); $460,000 (fiscal 2001)
Giving Analysis: Giving for fiscal 2002 includes: foundation grants to United Way ($73,000)
Assets: $9,092,336 (fiscal 2002); $9,857,478 (fiscal 2001)

Typical Recipients

Arts & Humanities: Community Arts, Libraries, Museums/Galleries, Music
Civic & Public Affairs: Community Foundations, Employment/Job Training, Civic & Public Affairs-General, Urban & Community Affairs
Education: Colleges & Universities, Education-General, Literacy, Private Education (Precollege), Special Education
Health: Cancer, Hospices, Hospitals, Medical Research, Mental Health
Religion: Religious Organizations, Religious Welfare
Social Services: Child Welfare, Community Centers, Community Service Organizations, Family Planning, Family Services, People with Disabilities, United Funds/United Ways, YMCA/YWCA/YMHA/YWHA, Youth Organizations

Application Procedures

Initial Contact: Send brief letter describing program. Must conform to united community service format.
Deadlines: None.

Restrictions

Does not support individuals.

Additional Information

Trust(s): Fleet National Bank
Publications: Application Guidelines
Trust(s): Shawmut Bank NA

Foundation Officials

Rita H. Beaulieu: treasurer, director
Cheryl C. Carlson: secretary, director
Herbert E. Carlson, Sr.: treasurer, trustee
Herbert E. Carlson, Jr.: chairman, president, director
Robert E. Dragon, MD: director

Grants Analysis

Disclosure Period: fiscal year ending January 31, 2002
Total Grants: $379,284*
Number of Grants: 11
Average Grant: $8,809*
Highest Grant: $200,000
Lowest Grant: $1,000
Typical Range: $2,500 to $30,000
***Note:** Giving excludes United Way. Average grant figure excludes two highest grants totaling $300,000.

Recent Grants

Note: Grants derived from 2002 Form 990.

Library-Related

1,500	Berlin-Peck Memorial Library, Berlin, CT -- purchase large print books and audio taped books

General

200,000	Central Connecticut State University Foundation, New Britain, CT -- for Vance Distinguished Professorship
100,000	Klingberg Family Centers, New Britain, CT -- capital campaign
80,000	New Britain Museum of American Art, New Britain, CT -- capital campaign
73,000	United Way of the Capital Area, Baton Rouge, LA -- annual support
30,000	Central Connecticut State University Foundation, New Britain, CT -- for Vance Distinguished Lecture
6,784	Central Connecticut State University Foundation, New Britain, CT -- for Vance Distinguished Lecture
5,000	Mooreland Hill School, New Britain, CT -- annual support
2,500	Connecticut Choral Artists, New Britain, CT -- support of 2001-2002 season
2,500	Music Series, New Britain, CT -- support of 2002 season
1,000	Literacy Volunteers of America, New Britain, CT -- program funding

VANGUARD GROUP

Company Headquarters

P.O. Box 2600
Valley Forge, PA 19482
Web: http://www.vanguard.com

Company Description

Assets: US$36 billion (2002)
Employees: 10000 (2003)
SIC(s): 6726 Investment Offices Nec.

Operating Locations

Vanguard Group (PA--Valley Forge)

Vanguard Group Foundation

Giving Contact

Tami Wise, Manager
Vanguard Group Foundation
PO Box 2600 (V38)
Valley Forge, PA 19482-2600
Phone: (610)669-6331

Alternate Contact

100 Vanguard Boulevard
Malvern, PA 19355
Phone: (610)669-1000

Description

Founded: 1994
EIN: 232699769
Organization Type: Corporate Foundation
Giving Locations: PA: Delaware Valley
Grant Types: General Support, Operating Expenses, Scholarship

Financial Summary

Total Giving: $2,450,803 (2002); $2,994,351 (2001)
Giving Analysis: Giving for 2001 includes: foundation ($1,357,351); foundation grants to United Way ($1,637,000)
Assets: $4,728,210 (2002); $3,843,843 (2001)
Gifts Received: $3,502,685 (2002); $3,005,178 (2001); $3,007,326 (2000). Note: Contributions were received from various Vanguard Group companies.

Typical Recipients

Arts & Humanities: Arts Associations & Councils, Ballet, Arts & Humanities-General, Historic Preservation, History & Archaeology, Libraries, Museums/Galleries, Music, Performing Arts, Public Broadcasting, Theater
Civic & Public Affairs: Botanical Gardens/Parks, Economic Development, Employment/Job Training, Civic & Public Affairs-General, Housing, Municipalities/Towns, Safety, Urban & Community Affairs, Women's Affairs, Zoos/Aquariums
Education: Afterschool/Enrichment Programs, Arts/Humanities Education, Business Education, Colleges & Universities, Community & Junior Colleges, Economic Education, Education Funds, Elementary Education (Private), Education-General, International Studies, Literacy, Private Education (Precollege), Public Education (Precollege), Science/Mathematics Education, Student Aid
Environment: Environment-General, Protection, Resource Conservation
Health: Cancer, Emergency/Ambulance Services, Health-General, Health Funds, Heart, Hospitals, Medical Rehabilitation, Mental Health, Nursing Services, Public Health
International: International Affairs
Religion: Seminaries
Science: Science Museums, Scientific Centers & Institutes
Social Services: Big Brothers/Big Sisters, Child Welfare, Community Service Organizations, Emergency Relief, Family Services, Food/Clothing Distribution, Homes, People with Disabilities, Recreation & Athletics, Senior Services, United Funds/United Ways, Volunteer Services, YMCA/YWCA/YMHA/YWHA, Youth Organizations

Application Procedures

Initial Contact: Send letter requesting guidelines and "Summary of Grant Request" form.
Application Requirements: Proposals should include the completed Summary of Grant Request form, which requests a description of organization, including goals, history, past projects, staffing, and population served; amount requested; detailed statement on how the foundation's funding will be used and how much will be used for administrative ex-

penses; and a program timetable. Attachments that must accompany the application form are: an audited financial statement for the organization's most recently completed fiscal year and the current year's operating budget; proof of tax-exempt status and a statement from an officer of the organization confirming that the exemption letter is valid; most recent annual report or other materials describing the organization's accomplishments; list of current contributors; list of the organization's board of directors and executive staff, including affiliations; and, if possible, a list of Vanguard employees who serve the organization or its board.

Deadlines: None.

Review Process: Requests are reviewed quarterly.

Evaluative Criteria: The foundation gives preference to requests from organizations or programs that are located in the Delaware Valley; address a well-defined and important need or concern; develop and implement long-term solutions; do not duplicate existing efforts; possess 501(c)(3) status; maintain costs at minimum levels necessary to provide high quality services; and combine the support provided by Vanguard with funds received from other contributors.

Decision Notification: Applicants will be notified about the status of proposal within four to six weeks of receipt. The foundation director will notify applicants in writing regarding the board's final funding decision.

Corporate Officials

John C. Bogle: senior chairmano PRIM CORP EMPL senior chairman: Vanguard Group.

John Joseph Brennan: director, president B Boston, MA 1954. ED Dartmouth College AB (1976); Harvard University MBA (1980). PRIM CORP EMPL director, president: Vanguard Group Inc. CORP AFFIL director: ICI Mutual Insurance Co. NONPR AFFIL member: Financial Executives Institute; government, executive vice president, member: Mutual Fund Education Alliance.

Ralph K. Packard: director, chief financial officer PRIM CORP EMPL director, chief financial officer: Vanguard Group.

Foundation Officials

John C. Bogle: chairman (see above)
John Joseph Brennan: president (see above)
Tim Buckley: director
F. William McNabb: director
Ralph K. Packard: treasurer (see above)
Pauline C. Sealvino: secretary
Tami Wise: foundation manager

Grants Analysis

Disclosure Period: calendar year ending 2002
Total Grants: $1,171,803*
Number of Grants: 538
Average Grant: $2,178
Highest Grant: $63,600
Lowest Grant: $25
Typical Range: $50 to $5,000
*Note: Giving excludes United Way.

Recent Grants

Note: Grants derived from 2003 Form 990.
Library-Related

30,210	Free Library of Philadelphia, Philadelphia, PA
5,500	Helen Kate Furness Free Library, Wallingford, PA
5,000	Athenaeum of Philadelphia, Philadelphia, PA

General

1,550,000	United Way of Southeastern Pennsylvania, Philadelphia, PA
130,000	Valley of the Sun United Way, Phoenix, AZ
87,500	United Way of the Central Carolinas, Charlotte, NC
57,875	Franklin Institute, Philadelphia, PA
40,000	N Power, Philadelphia, PA

27,500	Greater Philadelphia Urban Affairs, Philadelphia, PA
25,000	Nature Conservancy, Conshohocken, PA
25,000	Philadelphia High School Academies Inc., Philadelphia, PA
25,000	Phoenixville YMCA, Phoenixeville, PA
20,000	Village of Arts and Humanities, Philadelphia, PA

VANN FAMILY FOUNDATION

Giving Contact

Sherry S. Connolly, Secretary, Treasurer & Director
11008 Carnoustie Lane
Ft. Wayne, IN 46814
Phone: (216)625-6011

Description

Founded: 1997
EIN: 352008538
Organization Type: Private Foundation
Giving Locations: IN; NC; OH
Grant Types: General Support.

Financial Summary

Total Giving: $120,300 (2003); $138,280 (2001)
Assets: $3,696,173 (2003); $4,047,354 (2001)
Gifts Received: $289,557 (2001); $490,842 (2000); $973,086 (1999). Note: In 2001, 2000, and 1999, contributions were received from James M. Vann. In 1997, contributions were received from Mr. and Mrs. James M. Vann.

Typical Recipients

Arts & Humanities: Arts Associations & Councils, Libraries, Museums/Galleries, Music, Performing Arts
Civic & Public Affairs: Civic & Public Affairs-General, Public Policy
Education: Colleges & Universities, Education Funds, Student Aid
Health: Cancer, Health Funds, Hospices, Medical Rehabilitation, Public Health
Religion: Churches, Religious Welfare
Social Services: Food/Clothing Distribution, Recreation & Athletics, Scouts, Shelters/Homelessness, YMCA/YWCA/YMHA/YWHA

Application Procedures

Initial Contact: Send written request detailing program.
Application Requirements: Include proof of tax-exempt status, list of other contributors, and program revenue and costs.
Deadlines: None.

Foundation Officials

Sherry S. Connolly: secretary, treasurer, director
James M. Vann: chairman, director
Marjorie Lee Vann: president, director

Grants Analysis

Disclosure Period: calendar year ending 2003
Total Grants: $120,300
Number of Grants: 27
Average Grant: $3,204*
Highest Grant: $37,000
Lowest Grant: $100
Typical Range: $500 to $5,000
*Note: Average grant figure excludes highest grant.

Recent Grants

Note: Grants derived from 2003 Form 990.
General

37,000	Aldersgate United Methodist Church, Ft. Wayne, IN
30,000	Jorgensen Family YMCA, Ft. Wayne, IN

15,000	Mayo Foundation, Rochester, MN -- for department of dermatology
5,000	Davidson College, Davidson, NC
5,000	Indiana-Purdue Foundation of Fort Wayne, Ft. Wayne, IN
3,000	YMCA of Fort Wayne, Ft. Wayne, IN
2,500	Long Center, Lafayette, IN
2,500	Vera Bradley Foundation for Breast Cancer, Ft. Wayne, IN
2,000	Fort Wayne Philharmonic, Ft. Wayne, IN
2,000	Interfaith Hospitality Network, Ft. Wayne, IN

RACHAEL AND BEN VAUGHAN FOUNDATION

Giving Contact

Ben F. Vaughan, III, President & Trustee
PO Box 2233
Austin, TX 78768-2233
Phone: (512)477-4726
E-mail: RBVF@aol.com

Description

Founded: 1952
EIN: 746040479
Organization Type: Private Foundation
Giving Locations: TX: South and Central Texas
Grant Types: Capital, Endowment, General Support, Multiyear/Continuing Support, Operating Expenses, Professorship, Project, Research.

Donor Information

Founder: the late Ben F. Vaughan, Jr., the late Rachael Vaughan

Financial Summary

Total Giving: $216,734 (fiscal year ending November 30, 2002)
Assets: $4,502,547 (fiscal 2002)
Gifts Received: $5,903 (fiscal 2000); $19,306 (fiscal 1999); $36,727 (fiscal 1997). Note: In fiscal 1999 contributions were received from, Ben F. Vaughan III ($5,903), Daphne Vaughan ($5,903), and Ben F. Vaughan IV ($5,903).

Typical Recipients

Arts & Humanities: History & Archaeology, Libraries, Museums/Galleries, Performing Arts, Public Broadcasting, Theater
Civic & Public Affairs: Economic Development, Civic & Public Affairs-General, Hispanic Affairs, Housing, Law & Justice, Legal Aid, Native American Affairs, Public Policy, Safety, Urban & Community Affairs, Women's Affairs, Zoos/Aquariums
Education: Arts/Humanities Education, Colleges & Universities, Education Reform, Environmental Education, Faculty Development, Education-General, Literacy, Private Education (Precollege), Religious Education, Science/Mathematics Education, Secondary Education (Public)
Environment: Air/Water Quality, Environment-General, Resource Conservation, Wildlife Protection
Health: AIDS/HIV, Cancer, Children's Health/Hospitals, Clinics/Medical Centers, Health Organizations, Long-Term Care, Research/Studies Institutes
International: Health Care/Hospitals, Human Rights, International Affairs, International Environmental Issues, International Organizations, International Peace & Security Issues, Missionary/Religious Activities
Religion: Churches, Religion-General, Ministries, Religious Organizations, Religious Welfare
Social Services: At-Risk Youth, Child Abuse, Child Welfare, Community Service Organizations, Domestic Violence, Emergency Relief, Family Planning, Family Services, Food/Clothing Distribution, People

with Disabilities, Refugee Assistance, Scouts, Senior Services, Sexual Abuse, Shelters/Homelessness, Substance Abuse, United Funds/United Ways, Veterans, Volunteer Services, YMCA/YWCA/YMHA/YWHA, Youth Organizations

Application Procedures
Initial Contact: Send a brief letter or email to request application.
Application Requirements: Application should include a cover letter, a two- to four-page proposal requesting a specific amount of money, proof of tax-exempt status, Form 990, and detailed budgetary information.
Deadlines: June 1.

Restrictions
Does not provide support to individuals, loans, or grants to non-public charitable organizations.

Additional Information
The foundation's charitable interests are educational, cultural, religious, health care, welfare, youth, women, literacy, and environment organizations.
Publications: Application Guidelines

Foundation Officials
Ben F. Vaughan, IV: vice president, trustee
Ben F. Vaughan, III: president, trustee
Daphne duPont Vaughan: secretary, treasurer, trustee
Genevieve Vaughan: vice president, trustee
William R. Ward, Jr.: assistant secretary, treasurer

Grants Analysis
Disclosure Period: fiscal year ending November 30, 2002
Total Grants: $216,734
Number of Grants: 60
Average Grant: $3,612
Highest Grant: $10,000
Lowest Grant: $500
Typical Range: $1,000 to $5,000

Recent Grants
Note: Grants derived from fiscal 2002 Form 990.

General
10,000	San Marcos River Foundation, San Marcos, TX -- funding for environmental protection
10,000	Share Foundation Building a New El Salvador Today, San Francisco, CA -- funding for agriculture and rural development
10,000	University of Texas Marine Science Institute, Austin, TX
7,500	Any Baby Can of Austin, Austin, TX
7,500	Center for the Studies of Ancient Territories -- toward publication of Metaponto Research
7,500	Girl Scout Tip of Texas Council, Amarillo, TX -- funding for development of new camp facility
7,500	Katapultz, Inc., Austin, TX -- for funding to support technology to disadvantaged
7,500	St. Edwards University, Inc., Austin, TX -- funding for camp scholarships
7,000	Oficina Legal Del Pueblo Unido, Austin, TX -- funding to create clearinghouse for human rights issues
5,334	New Radio and Performing Arts, New York, NY -- funding for radio programs for women

VAUGHAN FURNITURE CO.

Company Headquarters
100 N. Railroad Ave.
Galax, VA 24333

Company Description
Employees: 1,400
SIC(s): 2500 Furniture & Fixtures.

Operating Locations
Vaughan Furniture Co. (VA--Galax)

Vaughan Foundation

Giving Contact
John B. Vaughan, President
1 Railroad Ave.
Galax, VA 24333
Phone: (276)236-6111

Description
EIN: 541295313
Organization Type: Corporate Foundation
Giving Locations: VA
Grant Types: General Support.

Donor Information
Founder: Vaughan Furniture Co.

Financial Summary
Total Giving: $16,532 (fiscal year ending September 30, 2004); $45,590 (fiscal 2001)
Giving Analysis: Giving for fiscal 2004 includes: foundation grants to United Way ($8,482); fiscal 2001: foundation grants to United Way ($15,270)
Assets: $466,638 (fiscal 2004); $411,968 (fiscal 2001)
Gifts Received: $25,000 (fiscal 2004); $50,000 (fiscal 2001); $50,000 (fiscal 2000). Note: Contributions were received from Vaughan Furniture Co.

Typical Recipients
Arts & Humanities: Arts Associations & Councils, Libraries
Civic & Public Affairs: Community Foundations, Civic & Public Affairs-General, Safety
Education: Arts/Humanities Education, Colleges & Universities, Community & Junior Colleges, Education Funds, Education Reform, Elementary Education (Public), Education-General, Secondary Education (Public), Special Education
Health: Alzheimer's Disease, Arthritis, Cancer, Clinics/Medical Centers, Emergency/Ambulance Services, Eyes/Blindness, Health-General, Health Funds, Heart, Multiple Sclerosis, Prenatal Health Issues, Public Health, Respiratory, Single-Disease Health Associations
Religion: Churches, Religious Welfare
Social Services: Camps, Child Welfare, Community Service Organizations, Recreation & Athletics, Scouts, Special Olympics, Substance Abuse, United Funds/United Ways, Volunteer Services

Application Procedures
Initial Contact: The foundation requests applications be made in writing.
Application Requirements: Include proof of tax-exempt status, purpose of funds sought, and a description of organization's charitable purpose.
Deadlines: None.

Restrictions
Grants are not made to individuals.

Corporate Officials
John B. Vaughan: chairman, chief executive officer PRIM CORP EMPL chairman, chief executive officer: Vaughan Furniture Co.
William B. Vaughan: president PRIM CORP EMPL president: Vaughan Furniture Co.

Foundation Officials
Raymond L. Hall, Jr.: secretary, director PRIM CORP EMPL treasurer: Vaughan Furniture Co.
William B. Vaughan: executive vice president, director (see above)

Grants Analysis
Disclosure Period: fiscal year ending September 30, 2004
Total Grants: $8,050*
Number of Grants: 6
Highest Grant: $5,000
Lowest Grant: $50
Typical Range: $500 to $1,000
*Note: Giving excludes United Way.

Recent Grants
Note: Grants derived from fiscal 2004 Form 990.
General
5,130	Twin County United Way, Galax, VA
5,000	Galax Volunteer Fire Department, Galax, VA
1,815	United Way of Patrick County, Stuart, VA
1,537	Johnson City Area United Way, Johnson City, TN
1,000	Arthritis Foundation, Atlanta, GA
1,000	TCR Healthcare Foundation, Galax, VA
500	ACCT III, Galax, VA
500	Patrick County Community Foundation, Stuart, VA
50	Baptist Medical Clinic of Galax, Galax, VA

JIM M. VAUGHN FOUNDATION

Giving Contact
Dr. James M. Vaughn, Jr., Director
830 S. Beckham
Tyler, TX 75701
Phone: (903)597-7652

Description
Founded: 1952
EIN: 756008953
Organization Type: Private Foundation
Giving Locations: TX: Tyler
Grant Types: General Support, Research.

Donor Information
Founder: the late Edgar H. Vaughn, Lillie Mae Vaughn

Financial Summary
Total Giving: $294,430 (2003)
Giving Analysis: Giving for 2003 includes: foundation grants to United Way ($10,000)
Assets: $8,737,346 (2003)
Gifts Received: $308,473 (1994)

Typical Recipients
Arts & Humanities: History & Archaeology, Libraries, Museums/Galleries, Music, Public Broadcasting, Theater
Civic & Public Affairs: Clubs, Economic Development, Employment/Job Training, Civic & Public Affairs-General, Urban & Community Affairs, Women's Affairs
Education: Arts/Humanities Education, Business Education, Colleges & Universities, Community & Junior Colleges, Elementary Education (Private), Edu-

cation-General, Legal Education, Literacy, Medical Education, Minority Education, Private Education (Precollege), Public Education (Precollege), Secondary Education (Private), Student Aid

Health: Alzheimer's Disease, Cancer, Clinics/Medical Centers, Emergency/Ambulance Services, Eyes/Blindness, Health Organizations, Hospices, Hospitals, Hospitals (University Affiliated), Medical Research, Mental Health, Preventive Medicine/Wellness Organizations, Speech & Hearing, Transplant Networks/Donor Banks

International: Health Care/Hospitals, International Organizations, Missionary/Religious Activities

Religion: Churches, Religious Organizations, Religious Welfare, Seminaries, Synagogues/Temples

Science: Science Museums, Scientific Centers & Institutes

Social Services: Child Welfare, Community Service Organizations, Counseling, Day Care, Delinquency & Criminal Rehabilitation, Domestic Violence, Family Planning, Family Services, Food/Clothing Distribution, People with Disabilities, Recreation & Athletics, Scouts, Senior Services, United Funds/United Ways, YMCA/YWCA/YMHA/YWHA, Youth Organizations

Application Procedures

Initial Contact: Send a brief letter of inquiry.
Application Requirements: Include a description of organization, amount requested, purpose of funds sought, proof of tax-exempt status.

Restrictions

Does not support individuals.

Additional Information

Trust(s): JP Morgan Chase Bank

Foundation Officials

Dr. James M. Vaughn: director
James M. Vaughn, Jr.: director

Grants Analysis

Disclosure Period: calendar year ending 2003
Total Grants: $284,430*
Number of Grants: 79
Average Grant: $3,600
Highest Grant: $18,650
Lowest Grant: $25
Typical Range: $1,000 to $5,000
*Note: Giving excludes United Way.

Recent Grants

Note: Grants derived from 2001 Form 990.
General

150,000	Texas College, Tyler, TX
50,000	University of Texas at Tyler Foundation, Tyler, TX
25,000	East Texas Crisis Center, Tyler, TX
25,000	Stewart Regional Blood Bank, Tyler, TX
18,600	University of Texas Tyler, Tyler, TX
13,000	Tyler Junior College, Tyler, TX
12,000	East Texas Medical Center Foundation, Tyler, TX
12,000	University of Texas Medical Branch, Galveston, TX
11,000	Parent Services Center, Inc., Tyler, TX
10,200	PATH, Tyler, TX

JAMES M. VAUGHN, JR. FOUNDATION FUND

Giving Contact

James M. Vaughn, Jr., President
2235 Brentwood
Houston, TX 77019

Description

Founded: 1971
EIN: 237166546
Organization Type: Private Foundation
Grant Types: Fellowship, Research.

Financial Summary

Total Giving: $32,000 (2003)
Assets: $1,593,137 (2003)
Gifts Received: $700 (1997)

Typical Recipients

Arts & Humanities: Arts Centers, Libraries, Museums/Galleries, Theater
Civic & Public Affairs: Civic & Public Affairs-General
Education: Arts/Humanities Education, Colleges & Universities
Health: Mental Health
Religion: Churches, Synagogues/Temples

Application Procedures

Initial Contact: Send resume and cover letter.
Deadlines: None.

Restrictions

Grants are awarded for research in mathematics.

Foundation Officials

James M. Vaughn, Jr.: president
Salle Vaughn: vice president
Jan Werner: secretary, treasurer

Grants Analysis

Disclosure Period: calendar year ending 2003
Total Grants: $32,000
Number of Grants: 6
Average Grant: $5,333
Highest Grant: $11,000
Lowest Grant: $1,000

Recent Grants

Note: Grants derived from 2003 Form 990.
Library-Related

3,500	Pierpont Morgan Library, New York, NY

General

11,000	Metropolitan Museum of Art, New York, NY
10,000	Museum of Fine Arts, Houston, TX
5,000	Studio Museum, New York, NY
1,500	Shepherd School of Music, Houston, TX
1,000	Moore School of Music, Houston, TX

VERIZON COMMUNICATIONS INC.

Company Headquarters

1095 Avenue of the Americas
New York, NY 10036
Web: http://www.verizon.com

Company Description

Founded: 1983
Ticker: VZ
Exchange: NYSE
Formed by Merger of: Bell Atlantic and GTE (2000).
Revenue: US$71.563 billion (2004)
Profit: US$7.83 billion (2004)
Employees: 203065 (2003)
Fortune Rank: 14, per FORTUNE Magazine's list of 500 Largest U.S. Corporations (2004).
Parent Company: Vodafone Group PLC, The Courtyard, 2-4 London Rd., Newbury, United Kingdom

Nonmonetary Support

Type: Donated Equipment
Volunteer Programs: The Verizon Incentive Pro-

gram recognizes employees' contribution of time and talent to nonprofit organizations where they live and work. Under the program, employees apply for a grant for the qualified organization where they volunteered at least 50 hours in a 12 month period. The foundation rewards them with a $500 check for presentation to the designated organization. Employees may request VIP grants on behalf of two separate organizations in a 12 month period for a total of $1,000. The Verizon Team Incentive Program rewards teams of ten or more eligible employees to collectively raise funds for nonprofit organizations across the country through organized pledge-a-thons, such as walk-a-thons or bike-a-thons. Under the program, the foundation matches funds collected by each team up to $25,000 per team to qualified nonprofit organizations.

Verizon Foundation

Giving Contact

Patrick R. Gaston, President
1095 Avenue of the Americas
New York, NY 10036
Phone: (212)395-2295
Fax: (212)398-0951
E-mail: verizon.foundation@verizon.com
Web: http://foundation.verizon.com
Note: The foundation only accepts grant applications online. All correspondence should be done via e-mail. Please see the foundation's web site for details.

Description

Founded: 2000
EIN: 133319048
Organization Type: Corporate Foundation
Giving Locations: operating locations.
Grant Types: Award, Capital, Emergency, Employee Matching Gifts, Fellowship, General Support, Matching, Multiyear/Continuing Support, Scholarship.
Note: Employee matching gift ratio: 1 to 1 up to $23,750 across all giving categories for current employees; up to $15,250 for eligible retirees, only to education organizations.

Donor Information

Founder: Verizon Communications Inc.

Financial Summary

Total Giving: $57,806,517 (2003); $60,511,488 (2002); $77,137,397 (2001). Note: Contributes through corporate direct giving program and foundation. Giving includes foundation only. Giving figures prior to 2000 are for the GTE Foundation.
Giving Analysis: Giving for 2001 includes: foundation scholarships ($1,348,080); foundation grants to United Way ($7,403,845).
Assets: $359,861,621 (2003); $124,675,114 (2002); $80,235,431 (2001). Note: Asset figures before 2000 are for the GTE Foundation.
Gifts Received: $299,046,536 (2003); $150,052,044 (2002); $53,914,344 (2001)

Typical Recipients

Arts & Humanities: Arts Associations & Councils, Arts Centers, Dance, History & Archaeology, Libraries, Literary Arts, Museums/Galleries, Music, Opera, Performing Arts, Public Broadcasting, Theater, Visual Arts
Civic & Public Affairs: African American Affairs, Asian American Affairs, Civil Rights, Community Foundations, Economic Development, Employment/Job Training, Civic & Public Affairs-General, Hispanic Affairs, Law & Justice, Legal Aid, Minority Business, Nonprofit Management, Philanthropic Organizations, Professional & Trade Associations, Public Policy, Urban & Community Affairs, Women's Affairs, Zoos/Aquariums
Education: Afterschool/Enrichment Programs, Business Education, Business-School Partnerships, Col-

leges & Universities, Community & Junior Colleges, Continuing Education, Economic Education, Education Associations, Education Funds, Education Reform, Engineering/Technological Education, Environmental Education, Faculty Development, Education-General, Gifted & Talented Programs, International Studies, Literacy, Minority Education, Private Education (Precollege), Public Education (Precollege), Science/Mathematics Education, Student Aid, Vocational & Technical Education

Environment: Air/Water Quality, Environment-General

Health: Cancer, Emergency/Ambulance Services, Geriatric Health, Health Policy/Cost Containment, Hospitals, Multiple Sclerosis, Transplant Networks/Donor Banks

International: Foreign Educational Institutions, Human Rights

Religion: Seminaries

Science: Science-General, Science Museums, Scientific Centers & Institutes

Social Services: At-Risk Youth, Child Welfare, Community Centers, Community Service Organizations, Counseling, Domestic Violence, Emergency Relief, Family Services, People with Disabilities, Recreation & Athletics, Scouts, Senior Services, Shelters/Homelessness, Substance Abuse, United Funds/United Ways, Volunteer Services, YMCA/YWCA/YMHA/YWHA, Youth Organizations

Application Procedures

Initial Contact: Submit applications online. Average grant figure excludes highest grant.

Application Requirements: Include organization name and address; mission statement; detailed objectives of the project, background, and budget; additional sources of funding; evaluation process; population served; and evidence of 501(c)(3) tax-exempt status.

Deadlines: None.

Review Process: Any proposals submitted online receive a notification of receipt from your local community relations manager within 72 hours of their submission.

Evaluative Criteria: To be eligible for consideration organizations must focus on technology applications and programs in one or more of the following areas: Literacy; Digital Divide; Workforce Development; Employee Volunteerism; Community Technology Development.

Notes: The foundation only accepts electronic proposals through its Apply Online process. See the foundation's web site for details.

Restrictions

Foundation does not support individuals; religious organizations, unless the particular program will benefit a large portion of a community and does not duplicate the work of other agencies in the community; organizations whose primary purpose is to influence legislation; organizations which discriminate on the basis of race, color, sex, sexual orientation, age, religion, national or ethnic origin, pro-life or pro-choice advocacy, or physical disability; organizations which do not have a Section 501(c)(3) public charity status; endowments or capital campaigns; film, music, television, video and media production projects or broadcast program underwriting; research studies, unless related to projects already supported by Verizon; sports sponsorships; performing arts tours; association memberships; or organizations which have received a grant from the Verizon, Bell Atlantic or GTE or the NYNEX Foundations in the last three consecutive years -- you may reapply after a one year hiatus.

Additional Information

The Verizon Foundation was formed in July 2000 after the merger of GTE and Bell Atlantic formed Verizon COIs Inc.

Corporate Officials

Lawrence T. Babbio, Jr.: vice chairman, president ED Stevens Institute of Technology BE (1966); New York University MBA (1970). PRIM CORP EMPL vice chairman, president: Verizon Communications Inc. CORP AFFIL director: Grupo Iusacell SA de CV; director: Aramark Corp. NONPR AFFIL chairman, trustee: Stevens Institute of Technology.

Mary Beth Bardin: executive vice president public affairs & communications ED Ohio University BA (1977). PRIM CORP EMPL executive vice president public affairs & communications: Verizon CommunicationS Inc.

Ivan G. Seidenberg: chairman, chief executive officer, director B New York, NY December 12, 1946. ED City University of New York BA (1972); Pace University MBA (1980). PRIM CORP EMPL president, chief executive officer, director: Verizon Communications Inc. CORP AFFIL director: Honeywell International Inc.; director: Wyeth Inc. NONPR AFFIL director: New York Presbyterian Hospital; member: Rockland Business Council; director: Museum of Television and Radio.

Thomas J. Tauke: executive vice president ED Loras College BA (1972); University of Iowa JD (1974). CORP AFFIL chairman: Home Technology Systems Inc. NONPR AFFIL chairman, board of regents: Loras College; director: US Telecom Association; director: Jobs for America's Graduates; director: Business Industry Political Action Committee.

Foundation Officials

Gale A. Cirigliano: director eSolutions & technology programs

Patrick Gaston: president

Katherine J. Harless: director ED University of Texas BS. CORP AFFIL director: Toro Co..

Michael W. Morrell: vice president, controller

Neil D. Olson: vice president, treasurer

Ivan G. Seidenberg: chairman, director (see above)

Susan A. Sullivan: director strategic planning

Thomas J. Tauke: vice chairman, secretary, director (see above)

Doreen A. Toben: director

Grants Analysis

Disclosure Period: calendar year ending 2003

Total Grants: $57,806,517*

Number of Grants: 17,000 (approx)

Average Grant: $3,165*

Highest Grant: $4,000,000

Lowest Grant: $100

Typical Range: $1,000 to $5,000

***Note:** Giving includes United Way and scholarship. Average grant figure excludes highest grant.

Recent Grants

Note: Grants derived from 2003 Form 990.

General

1,150,025	Pioneers Foundation, Denver, CO
823,921	National Center for Family Literacy Inc., Louisville, KY
503,875	Laubach Literacy International, Syracuse, NY
500,000	Alvin Ailey Dance Foundation Inc., New York, NY
500,000	Philadelphia Youth Tennis Inc., Manayunk, PA
500,000	Ser De Puerto Rico, San Juan Puerto Rico
387,360	Manhattan College, Riverdale, NY
295,000	Reading is Fundamental Inc., Washington, DC
262,000	Aspira Association Inc., Washington, DC
200,000	Greater Bay Area Supporting Organization

VERMILION HEALTHCARE FOUNDATION

Giving Contact

Valeria Saikley
702 N. Logan
Danville, IL 61832
Phone: (217)431-7021

Description

EIN: 371225688

Organization Type: Private Foundation

Giving Locations: IL: Danville

Grant Types: General Support.

Financial Summary

Total Giving: $539,527 (fiscal year ending September 30, 2004); $1,006,230 (fiscal 2001)

Assets: $10,287,826 (fiscal 2004); $10,691,799 (fiscal 2001)

Typical Recipients

Arts & Humanities: Libraries, Museums/Galleries, Music, Theater

Civic & Public Affairs: Inner-City Development, Legal Aid, Municipalities/Towns

Education: Arts/Humanities Education, Community & Junior Colleges, Elementary Education (Private), Education-General, Medical Education, Public Education (Precollege), Science/Mathematics Education, Student Aid

Health: Cancer, Children's Health/Hospitals, Clinics/Medical Centers, Health-General, Hospitals, Long-Term Care, Mental Health, Nursing Services, Transplant Networks/Donor Banks

Religion: Religious Welfare

Social Services: Big Brothers/Big Sisters, Child Welfare, Community Centers, Community Service Organizations, Family Services, Scouts, Senior Services, Sexual Abuse, Social Services-General, United Funds/United Ways, YMCA/YWCA/YMHA/YWHA, Youth Organizations

Application Procedures

Initial Contact: Organizations seeking grants should first call and discuss in general terms the proposed project.

Deadlines: March 15, June 15, September 15, and December 15.

Restrictions

Grants are not usually made for routine operating needs or annual giving.

Additional Information

Publications: Application Guidelines

Foundation Officials

Mary Michael Bateman: chairman

Thomas Bott: director

H. Michael Finkle: director

Robert Kesler: director

Bruce Meachum: director

Judd Peck: vice chairman

Rebecca Schlecht: director

W. John Shane: director

Grants Analysis

Disclosure Period: fiscal year ending September 30, 2004

Total Grants: $539,527

Number of Grants: 15

Average Grant: $15,452*

Highest Grant: $238,652

Lowest Grant: $1,200

Typical Range: $5,000 to $30,000

***Note:** Average grant figure excludes two highest grants ($338,652).

Recent Grants

Note: Grants derived from fiscal 2004 Form 990.
General

238,652	Provena United Samaritans Medical Center, Danville, IL -- for quarterly distributions
100,000	Boys and Girls Club, Danville, IL
75,000	Laura Lee Fellowship House, Danville, IL
30,000	Provena United Samaritans Medical Center, Danville, IL -- for EKG data integration system
25,000	Crosspoint Human Services, Danville, IL -- for special needs parenting classes
25,000	Danville Area Community College, Danville, IL -- for radiologic technology program
20,000	Provena United Samaritans Medical Center, Danville, IL -- for EKG data integration system
10,000	Downtown Danville Inc., Danville, IL -- for renaissance initiative
9,361	Family YMCA, Danville, IL -- for backflow preventer alarm system
8,918	Illinois Community Action Program, Danville, IL -- for playground equipment

MILES HODSDON VERNON FOUNDATION

Giving Contact

Robert C. Thomson, Jr., President, Treasurer & Director
c/o Chadbourne, O'Neill, Thomson, Whalen and Fitzgerald
PO Box 701
Sleepy Hollow, NY 10591-0701
Phone: (914)923-8499

Description

Founded: 1953
EIN: 136076836
Organization Type: Private Foundation
Giving Locations: NY: nationally.
Grant Types: General Support, Research, Scholarship.

Donor Information

Founder: the late Miles Hodsdon Vernon, Martha Hodsdon Kinney, and Louise Hodsdon

Financial Summary

Total Giving: $384,500 (2003)
Giving Analysis: Giving for 2003 includes: foundation scholarships ($65,500).
Assets: $8,664,272 (2003)
Gifts Received: $62,416 (1995); $165,000 (1992).
Note: In 1995, contributions were received from the Miles Hodsdon Vernon Trust.

Typical Recipients

Arts & Humanities: History & Archaeology, Libraries, Music, Public Broadcasting
Education: Colleges & Universities, Education Funds, Faculty Development, Education-General, Medical Education, Private Education (Precollege), Public Education (Precollege), Science/Mathematics Education, Secondary Education (Public), Student Aid
Health: Cancer, Children's Health/Hospitals, Clinics/Medical Centers, Diabetes, Emergency/Ambulance Services, Health Organizations, Hospitals, Long-Term Care, Medical Research, Mental Health, Nursing Services, Single-Disease Health Associations, Trauma Treatment
International: Health Care/Hospitals
Religion: Churches, Religious Welfare, Seminaries
Social Services: Camps, Child Welfare, Community Centers, Community Service Organizations, Day Care, Family Services, Food/Clothing Distribution, Homes, People with Disabilities, Senior Services, Shelters/Homelessness, YMCA/YWCA/YMHA/YWHA, Youth Organizations

Application Procedures

Initial Contact: Send cover letter and full proposal. Include purpose of funds sought, amount requested, total funds needed for project, source of other funds to be used or sought, proof of tax-exempt status, and certification that such status has not been revoked. There are no deadlines.

Foundation Officials

Dennis M. Fitzgerald: vice president, secretary, director
Michele C. Fitzgerald: director
Linda T. Murray: assistant secretary, director
Eloise T. Schundler: assistant secretary, director
Robert C. Thomson, Jr.: president, treasurer, director

Grants Analysis

Disclosure Period: calendar year ending 2003
Total Grants: $319,000*
Number of Grants: 20
Average Grant: $13,105*
Highest Grant: $70,000
Lowest Grant: $1,000
Typical Range: $5,000 to $30,000
*Note: Giving excludes scholarship. Average grant figure excludes highest grant.

Recent Grants

Note: Grants derived from 2001 Form 990.
General

75,000	Camp Speers Eljabar Y.M.C.A., Dingman's Ferry, PA -- cabin construction and rehabilitation
67,000	Wolfeboro Area Children's Center Inc. -- scholarship aid and supplies for youth programs
50,000	Aquinas High School -- scholarship aid, educational supplies
35,000	Family Y.M.C.A. of the Tarrytowns -- educational supplies and scholarship aid
30,000	Presbyterian Church of Westfield, Westfield, NJ -- Agape Soup Kitchen and Youth Programs
20,000	St. Paul's Episcopal Church, El Centro, CA -- Youth and Sunday School Programs
15,000	Warm the Children, Inc., Gloversville, NY -- winter clothes for needy children
10,000	Church of St. John the Baptist, New York, NY -- programs for feeding needy and homeless
10,000	Hamilton College, Clinton, NY -- scholarship aid
10,000	Haverford College, Haverford, PA -- scholarship aid

G. UNGER VETLESEN FOUNDATION

Giving Contact

George Rowe, Jr., President & Director
One Rockefeller Plaza
Suite 301
New York, NY 10020-2002
Phone: (212)586-0700
Fax: (212)245-1863
E-mail: info@monellvetlesen.org
Web: http://www.monellvetlesen.org

Description

Founded: 1955
EIN: 131982695
Organization Type: General Purpose Foundation
Giving Locations: MA; NY: nationally.
Grant Types: General Support.

Donor Information

Founder: Established in 1955 by the late George Unger Vetlesen.

Financial Summary

Total Giving: $3,862,500 (2003); $4,768,000 (2002); $4,730,000 (2001)
Assets: $85,363,954 (2003); $75,832,427 (2002); $86,579,908 (2001)

Typical Recipients

Arts & Humanities: Libraries, Museums/Galleries
Civic & Public Affairs: Clubs, Community Foundations, Ethnic Organizations, Civic & Public Affairs-General, Nonprofit Management, Philanthropic Organizations, Professional & Trade Associations, Public Policy, Zoos/Aquariums
Education: Colleges & Universities, Education Funds, Environmental Education, Education-General, International Studies, Leadership Training, Medical Education, School Volunteerism, Science/Mathematics Education, Special Education, Student Aid, Vocational & Technical Education
Environment: Air/Water Quality, Energy, Forestry, Environment-General, Protection, Research, Resource Conservation, Wildlife Protection
Health: Medical Research
International: Foreign Arts Organizations, Foreign Educational Institutions, International Environmental Issues, International Organizations, International Peace & Security Issues, International Relations
Religion: Churches
Science: Observatories & Planetariums, Science Museums, Scientific Centers & Institutes, Scientific Labs, Scientific Organizations, Scientific Research
Social Services: Recreation & Athletics, Volunteer Services

Application Procedures

Initial Contact: Applicants should submit a simple letter, stating your request.
Deadlines: None.

Foundation Officials

Gary Beauchamp: director
Eugene P. Grisanti: director B Buffalo, NY 1929. ED College of the Holy Cross AB (1951); Boston University LLB (1953); Harvard University LLM (1954).
Ambrose K. Monell: director
Maurizio J. Morello: secretary, assistant treasurer
George Rowe, Jr.: president, director B Ossining, NY 1922. ED Yale University AB (1943); Columbia University LLB (1948). PRIM CORP EMPL partner: Fulton, Duncombe & Rowe. CORP AFFIL director: International Flavors & Fragrances Inc.

Grants Analysis

Disclosure Period: calendar year ending 2003
Total Grants: $3,862,500
Number of Grants: 24
Average Grant: $76,786*
Highest Grant: $750,000
Lowest Grant: $2,500
Typical Range: $25,000 to $150,000
*Note: Average grant figure excludes three highest grants ($2,250,000).

Recent Grants

Note: Grants derived from 2003 Form 990.
General

750,000	Lamont-Doherty Earth Observatory (LDEO), New York, NY
750,000	Scripps Institution of Oceanography, La Jolla, CA -- for global change program

750,000	Woods Hole Oceanographic Institution, Woods Hole, MA
350,000	Marine Biological Laboratory, Woods Hole, MA -- funds for comparative molecular biology & evolution center, marine resources center & veterinary services at the marine resources center
125,000	Oregon State University, Corvallis, OR
125,000	University of Miami, Coral Gables, FL -- for climate studies
100,000	Bermuda Biological Station for Research Inc. (BBSR)
100,000	Massachusetts Institute Of Technology (MIT), Cambridge, MA -- funds for joint program on the science & policy of global change
100,000	Scenic Hudson Inc., Poughkeepsie, NY -- for reclaiming Westchester waterfronts program
100,000	University of Rhode Island, Kingston, RI -- for school of oceanography

VICKSBURG FOUNDATION

Giving Contact
William Oswalt, President
PO Box 177
Vicksburg, MI 49097
Phone: (269)649-9020
Fax: (269)649-0948

Description
Founded: 1943
EIN: 386065237
Organization Type: Private Foundation
Giving Locations: MI: with emphasis on Vicksburg or S.E. Kalamazoo County
Grant Types: Award, Capital, Emergency, Employee Matching Gifts, General Support, Operating Expenses, Project.

Financial Summary
Total Giving: $176,986 (2003); $238,194 (2001)
Giving Analysis: Giving for 2003 includes: foundation grants to United Way ($10,000); foundation scholarships ($27,575)
Assets: $3,833,805 (2003); $4,729,962 (2001)
Gifts Received: $199,593 (2003); $36,243 (2000); $46,671 (1998). Note: In 1995, 2000, and 2003, contributions were received from the Stanley J. Herman Charitable Unitrust.

Typical Recipients
Arts & Humanities: Arts Funds, Arts Institutes, History & Archaeology, Libraries, Museums/Galleries
Civic & Public Affairs: Clubs, Community Foundations, Civic & Public Affairs-General, Law & Justice, Municipalities/Towns, Safety, Urban & Community Affairs
Education: Agricultural Education, Arts/Humanities Education, Business Education, Colleges & Universities, Education Funds, Education Reform, Elementary Education (Public), Education-General, Private Education (Precollege), Public Education (Precollege), Student Aid
Health: Emergency/Ambulance Services, Hospices, Nursing Services
International: Foreign Arts Organizations
Religion: Churches
Social Services: Camps, Community Centers, Community Service Organizations, Crime Prevention, Delinquency & Criminal Rehabilitation, Family Services, People with Disabilities, Recreation & Athletics, Scouts, Senior Services, United Funds/United Ways, YMCA/YWCA/YMHA/YWHA, Youth Organizations

Application Procedures
Initial Contact: Send a brief letter of inquiry describing program. Include a description of organization, amount requested, and proof of tax-exempt status.
Deadlines: None.

Restrictions
Priority is given to organizations which contribute to the betterment of life in the Vicksburg or southeast Kalamazoo County areas.

Additional Information
Trust(s): National City Bank of MI/IL

Foundation Officials
Dr. Lloyd E. Appell: vice president
Danna M. Downing: director
Warren Lawrence: secretary
William Oswalt: president, treasurer

Grants Analysis
Disclosure Period: calendar year ending 2003
Total Grants: $139,411*
Number of Grants: 18
Average Grant: $7,745
Highest Grant: $26,000
Lowest Grant: $900
Typical Range: $1,000 to $10,000
*Note: Giving excludes United Way; scholarships.

Recent Grants
Note: Grants derived from 2003 Form 990.
Library-Related

9,606	Vicksburg District Library, Vicksburg, MI

General

27,575	Vicksburg Community Schools and Foundation, Vicksburg, MI -- towards scholarship
26,000	Vicksburg Community Schools Outdoor Recreation Center, Vicksburg, MI
20,000	Vicksburg Community Schools, Vicksburg, MI -- towards tennis court
17,000	Village of Schoolcraft, Schoolcraft, MI
16,040	Vicksburg Community Schools, Vicksburg, MI -- for equipment
12,000	Kalamazoo Foundation, Kalamazoo, MI -- towards scholarship
10,000	United Way, Vicksburg, MI
9,855	Sunset Lake Elementary School, Vicksburg, MI
5,000	United Soccer Foundation, Kalamazoo, MI -- funds for recreation

VICTORIA FOUNDATION

Giving Contact
Catherine M. McFarland, Secretary & Executive Officer
Victoria Foundation, Inc.
946 Bloomfield Avenue, 2nd Floor
Glen Ridge, NJ 07028
Phone: (973)748-5300
Fax: (973)748-0016
E-mail: info@victoriafoundation.org
Web: http://www.victoriafoundation.org

Description
Founded: 1924
EIN: 221554541
Organization Type: General Purpose Foundation
Giving Locations: NJ: Newark
Grant Types: Capital, Challenge, Emergency, Fellowship, General Support, Loan, Matching, Multiyear/Continuing Support, Operating Expenses, Project, Research, Scholarship, Seed Money.

Donor Information
Founder: Established in 1924 by Hendon Chubb in honor of his mother, Victoria Eddis Chubb.

Financial Summary
Total Giving: $8,601,368 (2003); $8,827,840 (2002); $9,576,200 (2001)
Giving Analysis: Giving for 2003 includes: foundation grants to United Way ($150,000) 2002: foundation grants to United Way ($150,000)
Assets: $200,245,418 (2003); $171,022,683 (2002); $205,149,337 (2001)

Typical Recipients
Arts & Humanities: Historic Preservation, History & Archaeology, Libraries, Museums/Galleries, Music, Performing Arts
Civic & Public Affairs: African American Affairs, Clubs, Economic Development, Employment/Job Training, Civic & Public Affairs-General, Hispanic Affairs, Housing, Nonprofit Management, Urban & Community Affairs, Women's Affairs
Education: Afterschool/Enrichment Programs, Arts/Humanities Education, Colleges & Universities, Community & Junior Colleges, Education Associations, Education Funds, Education Reform, Elementary Education (Private), Elementary Education (Public), Engineering/Technological Education, Environmental Education, Education-General, Gifted & Talented Programs, Leadership Training, Literacy, Medical Education, Minority Education, Private Education (Precollege), Public Education (Precollege), Science/Mathematics Education, Secondary Education (Private), Special Education, Student Aid
Environment: Air/Water Quality, Environment-General, Protection, Resource Conservation
Health: AIDS/HIV, Children's Health/Hospitals, Clinics/Medical Centers, Health-General, Mental Health, Research/Studies Institutes
Religion: Religious Welfare, Seminaries
Science: Science Museums
Social Services: Child Welfare, Community Centers, Community Service Organizations, Day Care, Emergency Relief, Family Planning, Family Services, Food/Clothing Distribution, People with Disabilities, Scouts, Shelters/Homelessness, Substance Abuse, United Funds/United Ways, YMCA/YWCA/YMHA/YWHA, Youth Organizations

Application Procedures
Initial Contact: Applicants should contact the foundation for complete guidelines before submitting a proposal. For land acquisition grants, applicants should submit a one-page letter of inquiry. Foundation staff will invite a full proposal for land acquisition grants after reviewing letters of inquiry.
Application Requirements: Letter of inquiry for land acquisition grants should include a summary of project, estimated total cost, amount requested, maps of property and of the surrounding area, with time of closing.
Proposals for other grants should include a one-page cover sheet, which includes organization information, contact person and telephone, mission, services offered, population served, summary of request (one or two sentences) and amount sought; one-page project summary; operating budget for organization, with itemized projected budget and sources of revenue for fiscal year; one-page project budget, with itemized expenses and names and sources of revenue; narrative describing project and plans for coming year (five pages or less), including purpose of organization, need or problem to be addressed, program objectives, how project will be implemented, time table, project staff and project highlights and accomplishments of the past year (if it's a continuous project); evaluation statement describing how the effectiveness of project will be assessed; report of most recent foundation grant, if applicable (if final report has already been submitted, do not resubmit); list of project staff; list of board of directors and their affiliations; re-

cent annual report; audited financial statement; and a copy of most recent IRS tax-exempt letter.

Deadlines: February 1 for a decision in June, August 1 for a decision in December; proposals from schools are due by March 1 for funding in the beginning of September; None, for land acquisition grants.

Review Process: Proposals are reviewed by trustee committees that make recommendations to the full board for decision. If a proposal falls within foundation guidelines and foundation priorities permit consideration of the grant request, additional information about the organization or project may be requested. As part of the evaluation process, staff members may make site visits to speak directly with project staff and/or board members and to see the organization's work first-hand.

Notes: The foundation also accepts the New York/New Jersey Area Common Application Form, but applicants must use the foundation's cover sheet as described above.

Proposals that are incomplete or are received after the deadline are not considered. Do not send proposals by fax or e-mail.

Restrictions

No grants are made to individuals, either as individuals or through a sponsoring organization.

Additional Information

Organisation may submit proposals only once a year. Applicants are encouraged to call or write the foundation for a copy of their application package. Grantees must submit detailed periodic reports.

Publications: Annual Report; Grant Guidelines; Application form

Foundation Officials

Charles M. Chapin, III: trustee ED Princeton University (1958).

Percy Chubb, III: president, trustee B New York, NY 1934. ED Yale University BA (1956). PRIM CORP EMPL director: Chubb Corp. CORP AFFIL director: Federal Insurance Co.; director: Chubb Colonial Life Insurance Co.; vice chairman, director: Chubb & Son Inc.; vice chairman, director: Bellemead Development Corp. NONPR AFFIL trustee: Mystic Seaport Museum; director: New Jersey Center Performing Arts.

Sally Chubb: trustee NONPR AFFIL chairwoman board: Matheny School & Hospital.

Robert Curvin, PhD: trustee

Charles E. Hance: trustee

Catherine M. McFarland: executive off, secretary CORP AFFIL director: Broad National Bancorporation.

Gordon A. Millspaugh, Jr.: assistant treasurer, trustee B 1934. ED Princeton University AB (1956); Harvard University LLB (1959). PRIM CORP EMPL partner: Herold & Haines.

Franklin E. Parker, IV: trustee

John F. Parker: trustee

Margaret H. Parker: vice president, trustee

Helen Frye Parr: trustee

Sara Chubb Sauvayre: trustee

Kevin Shanley: treasurer, trustee B New York, NY 1942. ED University of Pennsylvania (1964); Harvard University Graduate School of Business Administration (1976). PRIM CORP EMPL president, chief executive officer: Alliance Companies. CORP AFFIL chief executive officer: Memorial Investment Corp.; director: Bellemead Development Corp.; chief executive officer: Integrated Health Products. NONPR AFFIL chairman, director: Newark Museum Association.

Nina Mitchell Wells: trustee

Dr. A. Zachary Yamba: trustee PRIM NONPR EMPL president: Essex Community College.

Grants Analysis

Disclosure Period: calendar year ending 2003
Total Grants: $8,451,368*
Number of Grants: 112

Average Grant: $57,399*
Highest Grant: $725,424
Lowest Grant: $300
Typical Range: $25,000 to $100,000
*****Note:** Giving excludes United Way. Average grant figure excludes four highest grants ($2,252,272).

Recent Grants

Note: Grants derived from 2003 Form 990.
General

725,424	New Jersey Conservation Foundation, Far Hills, NJ -- to assist in environment/land acquisition fund
525,000	New Community Corporation, Newark, NJ -- for general urban programs/rebuilding of distressed neighborhoods
501,086	New Jersey Performing Arts Center, Newark, NJ -- to support general urban programs
500,762	Newark Museum Association, Newark, NJ -- in support of education grant/academic enrichment
399,576	New Jersey Conservation Foundation, Far Hills, NJ -- to assist in environment/land acquisition fund
325,000	New Jersey Performing Arts Center, Newark, NJ -- fund for education/academic enrichment
300,000	Bank Street College of Education, New York, NY -- for education grants/Newark Public Schools
300,000	Children's Literacy Initiative, Philadelphia, PA -- to assist in education/Newark Public Schools
225,000	Chad School Foundation, Newark, NJ -- fund for education/elementary schools
200,000	St. Benedict's Preparatory School, Newark, NJ -- to support education grant/secondary school

VIRGINIA ENVIRONMENTAL ENDOWMENT

Giving Contact

Gerald P. McCarthy, Executive Director
PO Box 790
Richmond, VA 23218
Phone: (804)644-5000
Fax: (804)644-0603
E-mail: info@vee.org
Web: http://www.vee.org

Alternate Contact

Three James Center
1051 East Cary Street, Suite 1400
Richmond, VA 23219

Description

Founded: 1977
EIN: 541041973
Organization Type: Specialized/Single Purpose Foundation
Giving Locations: DC; KY; MD; OH
Grant Types: Challenge, General Support, Matching, Project, Research.

Financial Summary

Total Giving: $1,689,318 (fiscal year ending March 31, 2001)
Giving Analysis: Giving for fiscal 2001 includes: foundation matching gifts ($1,664,080)
Assets: $17,372,200 (fiscal 2001)
Gifts Received: $50,000 (fiscal 1992). Note: In fiscal 1992, the endowment received settlement funds from IR International, Inc., and from Hauni Richmond, Inc.

Typical Recipients

Arts & Humanities: Historic Preservation, History & Archaeology, Libraries

Civic & Public Affairs: Botanical Gardens/Parks, Economic Development, Civic & Public Affairs-General, Housing, Municipalities/Towns, Nonprofit Management, Public Policy, Rural Affairs, Urban & Community Affairs, Zoos/Aquariums

Education: Business Education, Colleges & Universities, Economic Education, Education Reform, Elementary Education (Private), Elementary Education (Public), Engineering/Technological Education, Environmental Education, Faculty Development, Science/Mathematics Education

Environment: Air/Water Quality, Energy, Environment-General, Protection, Resource Conservation, Watershed, Wildlife Protection

Religion: Religious Welfare

Science: Science Museums, Scientific Labs, Scientific Research

Social Services: Family Services

Application Procedures

Initial Contact: Applicants should request guidelines; special eligibility guidelines for the Virginia Mini-Grant Program should be noted.

Application Requirements: Two copies of a full proposal must be sent. Each proposal should include the following: a cover letter identifying the applicant, project title, grant request, matching funds in equal amounts, project schedule, and whether the proposal is being submitted to the Virginia Program, the Virginia Mini-Grant Program, or the Kanawha and Ohio River Valleys Program. Letter should be signed by the organization's chief executive officer or board chairman. Include a project description, limited to five pages, clearly stating the need for the project, goals and objectives, and how they will be achieved, and relevance to other work being done in the field; a description of organization, names and qualifications of key project staff, a list of the members of the governing board, the current operating budget, and a copy of the current tax-exempt ruling from the Internal Revenue Service, if applicable; a line-item budget for the proposed project, showing total project cost, the amount and proposed allocation of grant funds requested from the Endowment, and all sources and amounts of matching funds (committed and anticipated); the project schedule, with specific beginning and ending dates for requested grant support; a detailed plan for evaluating and disseminating project results; and plans for continuing project activities and raising financial support beyond the grant period. Proposals should indicate a thorough assessment of related activities in the target community, identify partnerships for collaboration, and include one or two letters of support.

Deadlines: For the Virginia Program and Virginia Mini-Grant Program: March 15, August 1, and December 1; for the Kanawha and Ohio River Valleys Program: March 15 only. When the date falls on a weekend or holiday, the following business day will be the deadline. Complete proposals must be received by the deadlines; late proposals will not be accepted.

Review Process: The Endowment does not review or comment on preliminary proposals. The board of directors meets three times a year.

Notes: The Endowment has a strict policy on receipt of complete proposals by deadlines. Without exception, late proposals will not be accepted. Proposals may not be submitted by facsimile; please do not include videotapes with grant proposals.

Restrictions

Grants are made to nonprofit, tax-exempt organizations and governmental agencies. Typically, matching funds are required and challenge grants may be offered. Grant funds are not provided for overhead, indirect costs, building renovation or construction, endowments, lawsuits or individuals. Proposals outside of geographic limitations are not reviewed.

Special eligibility guidelines apply to the Virginia Minigrant Program.

Applicants are asked not to apply to the Endowment more than once a year.

Additional Information

Grantees are required to submit periodic progress reports and lists of expenditures as well as final evaluation reports. Approved grants are paid in installments pending receipt of reports.

Local projects should demonstrate potential to serve as models for other communities and include specific plans for dissemination. Education projects must include a teacher-training element. Partnerships among nonprofits, government agencies, and the private sector are encouraged.

Publications: Annual Report

Foundation Officials

Dixon M. Butler: president, director
Paul U. Elbling: director, treasurer
Robert Freeman: director
A. Linwood Holton, Jr.: director B Big Stone Gap, VA 1923. ED Washington & Lee University BA (1944); Harvard University LLB (1949); Virginia State College LLD (1971); Virginia Union University LLD (1972); Washington & Lee University LLD (1972); College of William & Mary LLD (1973). PRIM CORP EMPL partner: Mezzulo & McCandlish. CORP AFFIL director: Interstate Railroad Co. NONPR AFFIL member: Virginia Bar Association; member: Virginia State Bar; member: Roanoke Bar Association; chairman: University Virginia Burket Miller Center Public Affairs; member: District of Columbia Bar Association; member: Omicron Delta Kappa; member: American Bar Association.
Patricia Kluge: vice president, director
Gerald Patrick McCarthy: executive director, secretary B New York, NY 1943. ED Manhattan College BEE (1965); University of Washington MS (1967). NONPR AFFIL member advisory board: Virginia Department Games Fisheries; member: Virginia Water Center Advisory Board; member: Virginia Conservation & Recreation Foundation; board directors: National Conference Christians & Jews; member: Richmond First; member: Conservation Leadership Project; visiting professor environmental studies: Duke University. CLUB AFFIL 2300 Club; Bull & Bear Club.
Alson H. Smith, Jr.: sr vice president, director PRIM CORP EMPL officer: Jefferson Bankshares Inc.

Grants Analysis

Disclosure Period: fiscal year ending March 31, 2001
Total Grants: $1,689,318*
Number of Grants: 38
Average Grant: $28,384*
Highest Grant: $639,092
Lowest Grant: $300
Typical Range: $1,000 to $5,000 and $10,000 to $30,000
*Note: Giving includes matching gifts. Average grant excludes highest grant.

Recent Grants

Note: Grants derived from 2001 Form 990.
Library-Related
1,000	Foundation Center, New York, NY -- for the Philanthropic Center

General
105,399	University of Virginia, Charlottesville, VA -- for creating environmentally wired kids through the use of wireless technology
65,000	American Farmland Trust, Culpepper, VA -- for Virginia Rural Lands Program
61,554	Virginia Polytechnic Institute, Blacksburg, VA -- expanding the soil factors of the Virginia phosphorus index

60,000	Kentucky Waterways Alliance, Munfordville, KY -- for watershed
50,000	Department of Environmental Quality, Richmond, VA -- for Virginia Classroom Grants Program
47,650	League of Conservation Voters, Washington, DC -- testing the viability of a natural resources funding campaign
45,000	Alliance for the Chesapeake Bay, Baltimore, MD -- for builders for the bay
40,000	University of Virginia Institute for Environmental Negotiation, Charlottesville, VA -- for the Virginia Environmental Conflict Resolution Project
30,000	University of Charleston, Charleston, WV -- for Kanawha River Project
23,000	Friends of Chesterfield's Riverfront, Chesterfield, VA -- for exemplary environmental community pilot study

VIYU FOUNDATION

Giving Contact

William Dann, Trustee
591 Main Street
East Aurora, NY 14052-1753
Phone: (716)655-3830

Description

Founded: 1991
EIN: 043064835
Organization Type: Private Foundation
Giving Locations: NY: Western New York state
Grant Types: General Support.

Donor Information

Founder: Established in 1991 by Mr. and Mrs. William Dann.

Financial Summary

Total Giving: $73,000 (fiscal year ending July 31, 2004); $96,000 (fiscal 2001)
Giving Analysis: Giving for fiscal 2004 includes: foundation grants to United Way ($7,000); fiscal 2001: foundation grants to United Way ($7,000)
Assets: $1,516,081 (fiscal 2004); $1,614,554 (fiscal 2001)
Gifts Received: $185,280 (fiscal 1999); $257,725 (fiscal 1997); $124,500 (fiscal 1995). Note: In fiscal 1995 and fiscal 1999, contributions were received from Marion Dann.

Typical Recipients

Arts & Humanities: Historic Preservation, History & Archaeology, Libraries, Music
Civic & Public Affairs: Botanical Gardens/Parks
Education: Private Education (Precollege), Special Education, Student Aid
Environment: Environment-General, Protection
Health: Hospices, Hospitals, Medical Rehabilitation, Medical Research, Public Health, Single-Disease Health Associations
Religion: Religious Welfare, Seminaries
Science: Science Museums
Social Services: Animal Protection, Camps, Family Services, Food/Clothing Distribution, People with Disabilities, United Funds/United Ways

Application Procedures

Initial Contact: Send a brief letter of inquiry.
Deadlines: None.

Foundation Officials

Jesse Dann: trustee
Marion Dann: trustee
William Dann: trustee
William R. Dann, Jr.: trustee
E. W. Dann Stevens: trustee ED Harvard College AB

(1948); Cornell University JD (1951). PRIM CORP EMPL of counsel: Hiscock & Barclay.

Grants Analysis

Disclosure Period: fiscal year ending July 31, 2004
Total Grants: $66,000*
Number of Grants: 17
Average Grant: $3,500*
Highest Grant: $10,000
Lowest Grant: $1,000
Typical Range: $1,000 to $5,000
*Note: Giving excludes United Way. Average grant figure excludes highest grant.

Recent Grants

Note: Grants derived from 2001 Form 990.
Library-Related
1,000	Buffalo 7 Erie County Public Library, Buffalo, NY

General
10,000	Salvation Army, Buffalo, NY
7,000	United Way Buffalo and Erie County, Buffalo, NY
5,000	Beaver Meadow Audubon Society, Buffalo, NY,
5,000	Blind Association of Western New York, Buffalo, NY
5,000	Buffalo Museum of Science, Buffalo, NY
5,000	Buffalo Philharmonic Orchestra Society, Buffalo, NY
5,000	Buffalo Seminary, Buffalo, NY
5,000	Effective Parenting, Buffalo, NY
5,000	Food Bank of Western New York, Buffalo, NY
5,000	Hospice of Buffalo, Buffalo, NY

VODAFONE GROUP PLC

Company Headquarters

The Courtyard
2-4 London Rd.
Newbury RG14 1JX, United Kingdom
Web: http://www.vodafone.com

Company Description

Founded: 1982
Ticker: VOD
Exchange: NYSE
Revenue: US$L34.77 billion (2001)
Employees: 60109 (2003)
SIC(s): 4813 Telephone Communications Except Radiotelephone, 4899 Communications Services Nec.

Nonmonetary Support

Volunteer Programs: Company actively promotes and encourages volunteerism, both through its grantmaking and internal policies.

Vodaphone-US Foundation

Giving Contact

2999 Oak Rd., 9th Floor
Walnut Creek, CA 94597
Phone: (925)210-3870

Description

Founded: 1993
EIN: 680315367
Organization Type: Corporate Foundation
Formed by Merger of: Vodafone Group (1999).
Former Name: Airtouch Communications Foundation (2000).
Giving Locations: AZ; CA, San Francisco, Walnut Creek; CO; DC: Washington; GA: Atlanta; ID; IA; MI;

MN; NE; NM; ND; OH; OR; TX: Dallas; UT; WA; WY areas where company provides cellular and paging operations.
Grant Types: General Support, Project.

Financial Summary

Total Giving: $1,119,375 (2002); $1,341,500 (2001). Note: Fiscal 1996 Giving includes scholarship ($16,000); United Way ($255,000).
Assets: $24,004,151 (2002); $29,042,041 (2001)
Gifts Received: $19,300 (2000); $33,567 (1999); $1,181,240 (1996). Note: In 2000, contributions were received from Vodafone Group plc/Air Touch. In 1996, contributions were received from Airtouch Communications, Inc. and Airtouch Cellular.

Typical Recipients

Arts & Humanities: Arts Associations & Councils, Arts Centers, Arts Festivals, Arts Funds, Ballet, Ethnic & Folk Arts, Arts & Humanities-General, History & Archaeology, Libraries, Museums/Galleries, Music, Opera, Performing Arts, Theater
Civic & Public Affairs: Asian American Affairs, Business/Free Enterprise, Community Foundations, Economic Development, Employment/Job Training, Civic & Public Affairs-General, Housing, Legal Aid, Nonprofit Management, Professional & Trade Associations, Public Policy, Women's Affairs, Zoos/Aquariums
Education: Afterschool/Enrichment Programs, Arts/Humanities Education, Business Education, Colleges & Universities, Continuing Education, Economic Education, Education Funds, Elementary Education (Public), Education-General, International Studies, Literacy, Minority Education, Public Education (Precollege), Science/Mathematics Education, Student Aid
Environment: Air/Water Quality, Environment-General, Resource Conservation
Health: AIDS/HIV, Cancer, Children's Health/Hospitals, Emergency/Ambulance Services, Eyes/Blindness, Public Health, Research/Studies Institutes
International: International Relations, International Relief Efforts
Religion: Religious Welfare
Science: Science Museums, Scientific Centers & Institutes
Social Services: Child Abuse, Child Welfare, Community Service Organizations, Counseling, Emergency Relief, Family Planning, Family Services, Food/Clothing Distribution, Recreation & Athletics, Scouts, Social Services-General, United Funds/United Ways, Volunteer Services, YMCA/YWCA/YMHA/YWHA, Youth Organizations

Application Procedures

Initial Contact: Send a letter requesting detailed guidelines.
Application Requirements: The letter should include background information about the organization and its mission, population served, and its unique role in the community; a description of the program for which funding is requested, including evidence of need, project budget, and how success will be measured; how the organization/program fits the guidelines of foundation; a description of how program/project results will be reported to the foundation; list of the board of directors and their affiliations; and current operating budget, including pending and/or committed sources of income. Copies of the organization's most recent tax return, audited financial statements, and IRS 501(c)(3) determination letter should be provided. affiliations.
Deadlines: None.
Evaluative Criteria: Preference is given to organizations that: seek and achieve excellence in their leadership, client service, operations and results; have an open and cooperative relationship with other community groups in order to most effectively solve problems and avoid duplication of effort and resources; seek funding for projects that are central to their missions; can show how their programs and projects achieve

their intended results; are committed to sustaining the positive results of their work.
Decision Notification: The foundation will review and respond to proposals within 4 to 6 weeks.

Restrictions

The foundation generally does not make grants to support capital or endowment campaigns, fundraising events or goodwill advertising (including benefits), sports activities, cause-related marketing, memberships, emergency appeal or re-granting organizations. The foundation does not provide any Vodafone Communications products or services, nor does it support individuals; political organizations; religious organizations seeking grants for sectarian purposes; fraternal, veteran or labor groups; individual K-12 schools or school districts; or medical clinics or medical research. In addition, the foundation will not support organizations that practice unlawful discrimination in the provision of services.

Additional Information

Priority areas are: "Safe Communities," which includes support of efforts that promote neighborhood security through citizen involvement and that enhance the personal safety of the most vulnerable members of society, and "Transitional Assistance," which includes support of programs and projects that forge connections between people and give them the tools to become contributing and productive members of society.
In 1999, Vodafone Group acquired AirTouch Communications. The company is now known as Vodafone AirTouch Plc.
In 1999, Vodaphone Group acquired AirTouch Communications. The company is now known as Vodaphone AirTouch Plc.
Publications: Guidelines; Foundation Application Procedures; Foundation Grants Report

Foundation Officials

Patricia Anglin: secretary, director
M. Hickey: director
William Keever: director
Terry Kramer: director
Jack Lester: treasurer
Arun Sarin: director PRIM CORP EMPL chief executive USA/Asia Pacific: Vodafone Airtouch PLC. CORP AFFIL director: Cisco Systems Inc.

Grants Analysis

Disclosure Period: calendar year ending 2002
Total Grants: $1,119,375
Number of Grants: 90
Average Grant: $9,768*
Highest Grant: $250,000
Lowest Grant: $375
Typical Range: $1,500 to $25,000
*Note: Average grant figure excludes highest grant.

Recent Grants

Note: Grants derived from 2003 Form 990.
Library-Related

10,000	Laura Bush Foundation for Americas Libraries, Washington, DC -- towards general operating support
10,000	Walnut Creek Library Foundation, Walnut Creek, GA -- towards the Ygnacio Valley library improvement project

General

250,000	American Red Cross, Bay Area Chapter, San Francisco, CA -- towards the disaster relief fund for September 11 2001
100,000	San Francisco Symphony, San Francisco, CA -- towards the youth orchestra and instrument training program
100,000	Yosemite Foundation, San Francisco, CA -- towards the Yosemite Falls Campaign
56,000	Northern California Grantmakers, San Francisco, CA -- towards the Arts loan fund and Emergency loan fund
25,000	California Voter Foundation, Davis, CA -- towards general operating support
25,000	Family Service Agency of San Mateo County, San Mateo, CA -- towards general operating support
25,000	San Francisco Ballet, San Francisco, CA -- towards the Dance in Schools and Communities project
25,000	San Francisco Bay Area Council Boy Scouts of America, San Leandro, CA -- towards capital campaign
25,000	San Francisco Opera Association, San Francisco, CA -- towards the Adler Residency program
20,000	Chabot Space & Science Center, Oakland, CA -- towards general operating support

VOGEL FOUNDATION

Giving Contact

David L. Vogel, President
PO Box 7696
Madison, WI 53707-7696
Phone: (608)241-5454

Description

Founded: 1989
EIN: 391639595
Organization Type: Private Foundation
Giving Locations: FL: Lakeland; WI: Madison
Grant Types: Capital, General Support, Scholarship.

Financial Summary

Total Giving: $26,750 (2003); $35,650 (2001)
Giving Analysis: Giving for 2004 includes: foundation scholarships ($2,000)
Assets: $571,520 (2003); $604,069 (2001)
Gifts Received: $250 (1996); $2,663 (1994); $25,000 (1992). Note: In 1992, contributions were received from Vogel Bros. Building Co.

Typical Recipients

Arts & Humanities: Libraries, Museums/Galleries, Public Broadcasting
Civic & Public Affairs: Economic Development, Civic & Public Affairs-General, Housing, Parades/Festivals, Safety, Urban & Community Affairs, Zoos/Aquariums
Education: Business Education, Colleges & Universities, Engineering/Technological Education, Education-General, Preschool Education, Private Education (Precollege), Science/Mathematics Education, Social Sciences Education, Student Aid
Health: Clinics/Medical Centers, Health Funds, Hospices, Prenatal Health Issues
Religion: Churches, Ministries, Religious Welfare
Social Services: Animal Protection, Camps, Community Centers, Family Services, Homes, People with Disabilities, United Funds/United Ways, YMCA/YWCA/YMHA/YWHA, Youth Organizations

Application Procedures

Initial Contact: The foundation has no formal grant application procedure or application form.
Application Requirements: Applications should include a full description of the project, proof of tax-exempt status, a project budget and a current organizational budget, and anticipated sources of support.
Deadlines: None.
Notes: The foundation generally provides grants in the areas of education, health, and human services.

Restrictions

Grants are not awarded to individuals or for operating expenses.

Foundation Officials

Daniel C. Vogel: vice president
David L. Vogel: president
Peter C. Vogel: secretary

Grants Analysis

Disclosure Period: calendar year ending 2003
Total Grants: $24,750*
Number of Grants: 22
Average Grant: $560*
Highest Grant: $13,000
Lowest Grant: $100
Typical Range: $250 to $1,500
*Note: Giving excludes scholarship. Average grant figure excludes highest grant.

Recent Grants

Note: Grants derived from 2003 Form 990.
General

13,000	Madison Urban Ministry, Madison, WI -- school supplies for needy families
1,500	Salvation Army, Lakeland, FL -- assistance for those in need
1,500	Salvation Army, Madison, WI -- assistance for those in need
1,000	Independent Living Inc., Madison, WI -- for care of elderly
1,000	Oakwood Foundation -- care for elderly
1,000	University of Florida Foundation, Gainesville, FL -- towards scholarship
1,000	University of Wisconsin, Madison, WI -- towards scholarship
750	Lakeland Family YMCA, Lakeland, FL -- towards youth and family center
600	Habitat for Humanity of Dane County Inc., Madison, WI -- funds for affordable housing
600	Habitat for Humanity of Lakeland Inc., Lakeland, FL -- funds for affordable housing

LAURA B. VOGLER FOUNDATION

Giving Contact

Lawrence L. D'Amato, President & Director
PO Box 610508
Bayside, NY 11361-0508
Phone: (718)423-3000

Description

Founded: 1959
EIN: 116022241
Organization Type: Private Foundation
Giving Locations: NY: New York City and Long Island
Grant Types: General Support, Scholarship.

Donor Information

Founder: the late Laura B. Vogler, the late John J. Vogler

Financial Summary

Total Giving: $172,500 (fiscal year ending October 31, 2004); $213,400 (fiscal 2001)
Giving Analysis: Giving for fiscal 2001 includes: foundation grants to United Way ($25,000)
Assets: $4,302,577 (fiscal 2004); $4,655,110 (fiscal 2001)

Typical Recipients

Arts & Humanities: Arts Associations & Councils, Arts Outreach, History & Archaeology, Libraries, Museums/Galleries, Theater
Civic & Public Affairs: Business/Free Enterprise, Employment/Job Training, Civic & Public Affairs-General, Housing, Legal Aid, Nonprofit Management,

Professional & Trade Associations, Urban & Community Affairs, Women's Affairs
Education: Afterschool/Enrichment Programs, Arts/Humanities Education, Business Education, Education-General, Literacy, Private Education (Precollege), Public Education (Precollege), School Volunteerism, Secondary Education (Public), Special Education, Student Aid
Environment: Resource Conservation
Health: AIDS/HIV, Alzheimer's Disease, Cancer, Children's Health/Hospitals, Clinics/Medical Centers, Emergency/Ambulance Services, Eyes/Blindness, Geriatric Health, Health Policy/Cost Containment, Health Organizations, Home-Care Services, Hospitals, Long-Term Care, Mental Health, Nursing Services, Outpatient Health Care, Prenatal Health Issues, Preventive Medicine/Wellness Organizations, Public Health
International: Foreign Educational Institutions
Religion: Ministries, Religious Welfare
Science: Science Museums, Scientific Centers & Institutes
Social Services: At-Risk Youth, Big Brothers/Big Sisters, Camps, Child Abuse, Child Welfare, Community Centers, Community Service Organizations, Crime Prevention, Day Care, Delinquency & Criminal Rehabilitation, Domestic Violence, Family Planning, Family Services, Food/Clothing Distribution, Homes, People with Disabilities, Recreation & Athletics, Scouts, Senior Services, Shelters/Homelessness, Social Services-General, Substance Abuse, YMCA/YWCA/YMHA/YWHA, Youth Organizations

Application Procedures

Initial Contact: Request application, guidelines, and deadlines.
Deadlines: January1, April1, July1, and October1.

Restrictions

Limits grants to organizations concerned with health, well being, and education of children, the disadvantaged and the elderly.

Foundation Officials

Lawrence L. D'Amato: president, director
Lorraine Diamond: secretary
Max Kupferberg: director PRIM CORP EMPL president, chief executive officer, treasurer: Kepco.
I. Jerry Lasurdo: director
Rev. Stephen S. Schwander: director
Robert T. Waldbauer: director
Karen M. Yost: director

Grants Analysis

Disclosure Period: fiscal year ending October 31, 2004
Total Grants: $172,500
Number of Grants: 59
Average Grant: $2,924
Highest Grant: $5,000
Lowest Grant: $2,000
Typical Range: $2,000 to $5,000

Recent Grants

Note: Grants derived from 2004 Form 990.
General

5,000	Active Retirement Community Inc., South Setauket, NY
3,500	Andrew Glover Youth Program Inc., New York, NY -- a court advocacy program
3,500	Books for Kids Foundation, New York, NY -- a literacy program
3,500	Brooklyn Children's Museum Corporation, Brooklyn, NY -- museum team, an after-school program
3,500	Child Abuse Prevention Services Inc., Roslyn, NY -- the set up and speak out middle school bully prevention program
3,500	Citizens Advice Bureau Inc., Bronx, NY -- summer day camp services
3,500	Citykids Foundation Inc., New York, NY -- the bridge building program

3,500	East Harlem Block Nursery Inc., New York, NY -- an after school program
3,500	Facing History and Ourselves National Foundation Inc., New York, NY -- for professional development opportunities to educate on long island
3,500	Grand Street Settlement Inc., New York, NY -- for the American elders program

HENRY VOGT MACHINE CO.

Company Headquarters

1000 W. Ormsby Ave.
Louisville, KY 40210

Company Description

Employees: 20
SIC(s): 3400 Fabricated Metal Products, 3500 Industrial Machinery & Equipment.

Operating Locations

Henry Vogt Machine Co. (KY--Louisville)

Henry Vogt Foundation

Giving Contact

Henry V. Henser, Jr.
1000 West Ormsby
Louisville, KY 40201
Phone: (502)635-3232

Description

Founded: 1958
EIN: 237416717
Organization Type: Corporate Foundation
Giving Locations: KY: Louisville
Grant Types: Capital, General Support, Multiyear/Continuing Support.

Donor Information

Founder: Henry Vogt Machine Co.

Financial Summary

Total Giving: $172,600 (fiscal year ending June 30, 2004); $172,600 (fiscal 2001)
Giving Analysis: Giving for fiscal 2004 includes: foundation grants to United Way ($8,500); fiscal 2001: foundation grants to United Way ($8,500)
Assets: $2,699,518 (fiscal 2004); $3,089,426 (fiscal 2001)
Gifts Received: In 1989, contributions were received from Henry Vogt Machine Co.

Typical Recipients

Arts & Humanities: Arts Funds, Historic Preservation, Museums/Galleries, Public Broadcasting
Civic & Public Affairs: African American Affairs, Economic Development, Employment/Job Training, Civic & Public Affairs-General, Zoos/Aquariums
Education: Afterschool/Enrichment Programs, Business Education, Colleges & Universities, Economic Education, Education Funds, Elementary Education (Public), Education-General, Private Education (Precollege), Public Education (Precollege), Vocational & Technical Education
Environment: Resource Conservation
Health: Health Funds, Hospitals, Mental Health
Religion: Churches
Science: Science Museums
Social Services: Camps, Child Welfare, Community Centers, Community Service Organizations, Family Services, Homes, People with Disabilities, Scouts, Senior Services, United Funds/United Ways, Youth Organizations

Application Procedures

Initial Contact: Send a brief letter of inquiry.
Application Requirements: Include a description of organization, amount requested, and purpose of funds sought.

Restrictions

Does not make grants to individuals.

Corporate Officials

Henry V. Heuser: chairman, director B Louisville, KY June 14, 1914. ED Purdue University (1936). PRIM CORP EMPL chairman, director: Henry Vogt Machine Co. CORP AFFIL director: Enterprises Inc.

Foundation Officials

Margaret S. Culver: secretary, treasurer
Henry V. Heuser, Jr.: president, director
Henry V. Heuser: director (see above)
Leland D. Schlegel, Jr.: vice president, director

Grants Analysis

Disclosure Period: fiscal year ending June 30, 2004
Total Grants: $164,100*
Number of Grants: 20
Average Grant: $6,795*
Highest Grant: $35,000
Lowest Grant: $100
Typical Range: $1,000 to $10,000
***Note:** Giving excludes United Way. Average grant figure excludes highest grant.

Recent Grants

Note: Grants derived from fiscal 2004 Form 990.
General

35,000	Old Walnut Street Capital Camp, Louisville, KY
10,000	American Community Center, Louisville, KY
10,000	Bellarmine University, Louisville, KY
10,000	Cabbage Patch Settlement House, Louisville, KY
10,000	Goodwill Industries, Louisville, KY
10,000	Home of the Innocents, Louisville, KY
10,000	Jewish Hospital Foundation, Louisville, KY
10,000	Kentucky Colleges and Universities, Louisville, KY
10,000	Louisville Zoo Foundation, Louisville, KY
10,000	Neighborhood House, Louisville, KY

FREDERICK A. VOLLBRECHT FOUNDATION

Giving Contact

Kenneth J. Klebba, President & Treasurer
31700 Telegraph Rd., Suite 220
Beverly Hills, MI 48025
Phone: (248)646-0627
Fax: (248)646-0338
E-mail: kklebba@collinsburi.com

Description

Founded: 1959
EIN: 386056173
Organization Type: Private Foundation
Giving Locations: MI
Grant Types: General Support, Research, Scholarship.

Donor Information

Founder: the late Frederick A. Vollbrecht

Financial Summary

Total Giving: $201,850 (2004); $179,740 (2001)
Giving Analysis: Giving for 2001 includes: foundation scholarships ($8,000)
Assets: $2,180,829 (2004); $2,703,286 (2001)

Typical Recipients

Arts & Humanities: Libraries, Music, Theater
Civic & Public Affairs: Business/Free Enterprise, Clubs, Economic Development, Civic & Public Affairs-General, Public Policy, Urban & Community Affairs
Education: Agricultural Education, Business Education, Colleges & Universities, Community & Junior Colleges, Education-General, Literacy, Private Education (Precollege), Special Education, Student Aid
Health: Cancer, Children's Health/Hospitals, Diabetes, Emergency/Ambulance Services, Health Organizations, Heart, Hospices, Hospitals, Kidney, Medical Research, Respiratory, Single-Disease Health Associations, Speech & Hearing
Religion: Religious Welfare
Social Services: At-Risk Youth, Camps, Child Welfare, Community Service Organizations, Family Services, Food/Clothing Distribution, People with Disabilities, Recreation & Athletics, Scouts, United Funds/United Ways, Youth Organizations

Application Procedures

Initial Contact: The foundation requests applications be made in writing.
Deadlines: None.

Additional Information

Publications: Annual Report

Foundation Officials

Kenneth J. Klebba: president, treasurer
Richard E. Mida: vice president, secretary

Grants Analysis

Disclosure Period: calendar year ending 2004
Total Grants: $201,850
Number of Grants: 22
Average Grant: $9,175
Highest Grant: $20,000
Lowest Grant: $800
Typical Range: $1,000 to $5,000

Recent Grants

Note: Grants derived from 2004 Form 990.
General

15,000	American Diabetes Association, Bingham Farms, MI -- for Camp Midicha
3,000	American Diabetes Association, Bingham Farms, MI
3,000	North Oakland SCAMP Funding Corporation, Clarkston, MI -- for camperships
3,000	Old Newsboys' Goodfellow Fund, Detroit, MI
2,000	Lighthouse North, Clarkston, MI
2,000	Stagecrafters, Royal Oak, MI
1,000	American Diabetes Association, Bingham Farms, MI -- for Walk research

VPI FOUNDATION

Giving Contact

Carol Grover, President
VPI Foundation
221 Phillip Ct.
Kohler, WI 53044
Phone: (920)458-4664

Description

Founded: 1993
EIN: 391768404
Organization Type: Private Foundation

Giving Locations: WI, Sheboygan
Grant Types: General Support.

Financial Summary

Total Giving: $43,650 (fiscal year ending September 30, 2004); $77,400 (fiscal 2002 approx); $98,125 (fiscal 2001)
Giving Analysis: Giving for fiscal 2003 includes: foundation grants to United Way ($14,500) fiscal 2001: foundation grants to United Way ($16,250)
Assets: $215,811 (fiscal 2004); $225,698 (fiscal 2002 approx); $386,864 (fiscal 2001)
Gifts Received: $75,000 (fiscal 2001); $120,000 (fiscal 2000). Note: Contributions were received from VPI, LLC.

Typical Recipients

Arts & Humanities: Libraries, Theater
Civic & Public Affairs: Civic & Public Affairs-General
Education: Business Education, Colleges & Universities, Education Funds, Student Aid
Health: Emergency/Ambulance Services
Social Services: At-Risk Youth, United Funds/United Ways, YMCA/YWCA/YMHA/YWHA, Youth Organizations

Application Procedures

Initial Contact: The foundation has no formal grant application procedure or application form. Any application format is acceptable.
Application Requirements: Include a description of organization, amount requested, purpose of funds sought, recently audited financial statement, and proof of tax-exempt status.
Deadlines: None.

Restrictions

Restricted to charitable activities in the area of VPI, LLC and sister locations in Wisconsin, Maryland, and Delaware.

Foundation Officials

Richard L. Blamey: secretary, treasurer, director
John Crawford: vice president, director
Carol Grover: president, director
R. Bruce Grover: vice president, director
Karen Grover Scott: director
Robert H. Leverenz: director
P. Gregory Mickelson: director
Deborah Wente: director

Grants Analysis

Disclosure Period: fiscal year ending September 30, 2004
Total Grants: $29,150*
Number of Grants: 22
Average Grant: $960*
Highest Grant: $9,000
Lowest Grant: $150
Typical Range: $300 to $3,000
***Note:** Giving excludes United Way. Average grant figure excludes highest grant.

Recent Grants

Note: Grants derived from fiscal 2001 Form 990.
Library-Related

4,000	Manitowoc Public Library, Manitowoc, WI

General

10,000	Citizens Scholarship Fund, St. Peter, MN
7,500	United Way Sheboygan, Sheboygan, WI
6,000	Sheboygan Blue Line Association, Sheboygan, WI
5,000	Above and Beyond, Sheboygan, WI -- Hands On Children's Museum
5,000	Above and Beyond, Sheboygan, WI
5,000	Boys and Girls Club, Sheboygan, WI
5,000	JMKAC (John Michael Kohler Arts Center), Sheboygan, WI
5,000	Lakeland College, Sheboygan, WI
5,000	Manitowoc YMCA, Manitowoc, WI

5,000   Sheboygan Theater Company, Sheboygan, WI

JOHN T. VUCUREVICH FOUNDATION

Giving Contact

John T. Vucurevich, Advisory Board
c/o Wells Fargo Bank SD NA
PO Box 1040
Rapid City, SD 57709
Phone: (605)394-3821

Description

Founded: 1989
EIN: 460359829
Organization Type: Private Foundation
Giving Locations: IA; MT; SD: Rapid City; VA
Grant Types: General Support.

Donor Information

Founder: Established in 1989 by John T. Vucurevich.

Financial Summary

Total Giving: $283,950 (2003); $351,415 (2001)
Giving Analysis: Giving for 2003 includes: foundation grants to United Way ($18,500); 2001: foundation grants to United Way ($8,000)
Assets: $8,204,553 (2003); $9,115,516 (2001)
Gifts Received: $100,000 (2000); $1,779,548 (1997); $103,750 (1995). Note: In 1995 and 2000, contributions were received from John T. Vucurevich.

Typical Recipients

Arts & Humanities: Arts Funds, History & Archaeology, Libraries, Museums/Galleries, Music, Opera, Performing Arts, Theater
Civic & Public Affairs: Clubs, Community Foundations, Civic & Public Affairs-General, Housing, Minority Business, Rural Affairs, Urban & Community Affairs, Women's Affairs
Education: Colleges & Universities, Engineering/Technological Education, Education-General, Journalism/Media Education, Medical Education, Private Education (Precollege), School Volunteerism, Secondary Education (Private)
Environment: Wildlife Protection
Health: Children's Health/Hospitals, Hospices, Hospitals
Religion: Churches, Religion-General, Religious Organizations, Religious Welfare
Social Services: At-Risk Youth, Big Brothers/Big Sisters, Child Welfare, Community Service Organizations, Crime Prevention, Domestic Violence, Family Services, Food/Clothing Distribution, People with Disabilities, Recreation & Athletics, Scouts, Sexual Abuse, Substance Abuse, United Funds/United Ways, YMCA/YWCA/YMHA/YWHA, Youth Organizations

Application Procedures

Initial Contact: Send a brief letter of inquiry.
Application Requirements: Include a description of organization, purpose of funds sought, and proof of tax-exempt status.
Deadlines: March 1, June 1, September 1, and December 1.
Evaluative Criteria: Priority given to organizations in the immediate area.
Decision Notification: Within three months after deadline.

Additional Information

Trust(s): Wells Fargo Bank SD NA

Foundation Officials

Dale E. Clement: adv board
Renee Parker: advisory board
Alex Vucurevich: adv board
Thomas J. Vucurevich: adv board

Grants Analysis

Disclosure Period: calendar year ending 2003
Total Grants: $265,450*
Number of Grants: 26
Average Grant: $8,508*
Highest Grant: $52,750
Lowest Grant: $200
Typical Range: $2,000 to $15,000
*Note: Giving excludes United Way. Average grant figures excludes highest grant.

Recent Grants

Note: Grants derived from 2001 Form 990.
General

55,000	Emmanuel Episcopal Church, Rapid City, SD
22,000	Working Against Violence, Inc, Rapid City, SD
21,600	Lutheran Social Services, Rapid City, IA
20,000	CASA Program 7th Circuit Court, Rapid City, SD
20,000	Rapid City YMCA, Rapid City, SD
15,000	Historic Homestake Opera House Society, Lead, SD
15,000	Society of St. Andrew, Big Island, VA
13,200	Youth and Family Services, Rapid City, SD
12,500	Billings Depot, Inc., Billings, MT
11,500	Black Hills Regional Food Bank, Inc., Rapid City, SD

VULCAN MATERIALS CO.

Company Headquarters

2101 Pinson Valley Parkway
Birmingham, AL 35217
Web: http://www.vulcanmaterials.com

Company Description

Founded: 1956
Ticker: VMC
Exchange: NYSE
Acquired: CalMat Co. (1999).
Revenue: US$2.545 billion (2002)
Employees: 8838 (2003)
SIC(s): 1422 Crushed & Broken Limestone, 1423 Crushed & Broken Granite, 2812 Alkalies & Chlorine, 2865 Cyclic Crudes & Intermediates.

Operating Locations

Vulcan Materials Co. (AL--Birmingham, Calera, Childersburg, Gadsden, Helena, Huntsville, Lacon, Madison, Russellville, Scottsboro, Trinity, Tuscumbia; GA--Columbus, Dalton, Fairmount, Grayson, La Grange, Lithia Springs, Lithonia, Newnan, Rabun Gap, Red Oak, Stockbridge, Villa Rica; IL--Crystal Lake, Decatur, Fairbury, Joliet, Lemont, McCook, Momence, Pontiac; IN--Francesville, Lafayette, Monon, South Bend; IA--Cedar Rapids, Garrison, Mentour, Robbins; KY--Brandenburg, Elizabethtown, Fort Knox, Lexington; LA--Geismar; MI; NC--Boone, Charlotte, East Forsyth, Elkin, Enka, Gold Hill, Hendersonville, Morganton, North Wilkesboro, Rockingham, Winston-Salem; SC--Blacksburg, Gray Court, Greenville, Lyman, Pacolet; TN--Athens, Bristol, Clarksville, Cleveland, Dayton, Franklin, Holladay, Kingsport, Knox County, Knoxville, Maryville, Morristown, Nashville, Parsons, Savannah, Sevierville, South Pittsburg, Tazewell; TX--Abilene, Boyd, Bridgeport, Brownwood, Knippa, San Antonio, Uvalde; VA--Danville, Manassas, Occoquan, Richmond, South Boston, Warrenton; WI--Milwaukee, Oconomowoc, Oshkosh, Racine, Sussex)

Nonmonetary Support

Type: Donated Equipment; Donated Products; Inkind Services; Loaned Employees; Loaned Executives; Workplace Solicitation
Note: Nonmonetary support is provided by the company.

Vulcan Materials Co. Foundation

Giving Contact

Mary Russom, Manager Community Programs
Vulcan Materials Co.
PO Box 385014
Birmingham, AL 35253-5014
Phone: (205)298-3229
Fax: (205)298-2960
Web: http://www.vulcanmaterials.com

Description

EIN: 630971859
Organization Type: Corporate Foundation
Giving Locations: states in which company has operations.
Grant Types: Capital, Department, Emergency, Employee Matching Gifts, Endowment, Fellowship, General Support, Multiyear/Continuing Support, Project, Research, Scholarship, Seed Money.
Note: Employee matching gift ratio: 1 to 1 for hospitals and cultural organizations; 2 to 1 to educational institutions. Annual limit of $10,000 per employee.

Financial Summary

Total Giving: $2,760,400 (fiscal year ending November 30, 2003 approx); $2,510,018 (fiscal 2002); $2,770,519 (fiscal 2001). Note: Contributes through corporate direct giving program and foundation.
Assets: $2,986,455 (fiscal 2002); $4,423,500 (fiscal 2001)
Gifts Received: $544,981 (fiscal 2001); $65,610 (fiscal 2000); $118,245 (fiscal 1999). Note: Contributions are received from Vulcan Materials Company.

Typical Recipients

Arts & Humanities: Arts Associations & Councils, Arts Centers, Arts Festivals, Arts Funds, Arts Institutes, Ballet, Community Arts, Dance, Ethnic & Folk Arts, Historic Preservation, History & Archaeology, Libraries, Literary Arts, Museums/Galleries, Music, Opera, Performing Arts, Public Broadcasting, Theater, Visual Arts
Civic & Public Affairs: African American Affairs, Botanical Gardens/Parks, Business/Free Enterprise, Civil Rights, Clubs, Economic Development, Economic Policy, Civic & Public Affairs-General, Minority Business, Municipalities/Towns, Philanthropic Organizations, Public Policy, Urban & Community Affairs, Zoos/Aquariums
Education: Arts/Humanities Education, Business Education, Colleges & Universities, Economic Education, Education Funds, Education Reform, Elementary Education (Private), Engineering/Technological Education, Education-General, Literacy, Minority Education, Public Education (Precollege), Science/Mathematics Education, Secondary Education (Public), Special Education, Student Aid
Environment: Environment-General, Protection, Resource Conservation, Sanitary Systems, Wildlife Protection
Health: Cancer, Children's Health/Hospitals, Clinics/Medical Centers, Emergency/Ambulance Services, Health-General, Health Organizations, Mental Health
International: International Organizations
Religion: Jewish Causes, Ministries, Religious Welfare
Science: Science Exhibits & Fairs, Science Muse-

ums, Scientific Research

Social Services: Animal Protection, Child Welfare, Community Centers, Community Service Organizations, Counseling, Delinquency & Criminal Rehabilitation, Emergency Relief, Family Services, Food/Clothing Distribution, People with Disabilities, Recreation & Athletics, Scouts, Senior Services, Shelters/Homelessness, Social Services-General, Substance Abuse, United Funds/United Ways, YMCA/YWCA/YMHA/YWHA, Youth Organizations

Application Procedures

Initial Contact: Send a one or two-page letter.
Application Requirements: Include a description of organization, amount requested, purpose of funds sought, time lines for the funding and implementation of the project; and method for evaluating success of the project, including how the organization will audit its performance. Attach proof of tax-exempt status, the current year's budget, recently audited financial statement, and a list of directors and executive staff.
Deadlines: None; applications acted upon throughout the year.
Review Process: Proposals are reviewed by secretary/treasurer of foundation; if proposal meets guidelines, it is usually referred to appropriate division office for recommendation by local contributions committee; if proposal is appropriate for decision in headquarters office in Birmingham, AL, it is approved or rejected by secretary/treasurer, president, or full board of trustees, depending on amount of request.
Evaluative Criteria: Relative benefit to community; type of project; financial soundness; organizational efficiency.
Decision Notification: Varies, depending on disposition of the proposal.
Notes: Organizations serving the Birmingham, Alabama area should submit requests to the secretary of the Vulcan Materials Company Foundation. Requests from organizations located outside Birmingham should be mailed to the Division Charitable Contributions Officer in their geographical area. Prospective applicants who have questions regarding the appropriate point of contact in their area may submit questions via e-mail: giving@vmcmail.com.

Restrictions

No grants are awarded to groups with discriminatory practices. The foundation does not fund individuals; organizations outside the United states; telephone or mass-mail appeals; political organizations; testimonial dinners; sectarian religious activities; organizations which have discriminatory practices; or athletic, labor, fraternal and veterans associations. The foundation generally only considers requests from organizations located in communities where Vulcan has operations, offices, or employees.

Giving Program Officials

Mary S. Russom: secretary, treasurer PRIM CORP EMPL administrator committee affairs: Vulcan Materials Co.

Foundation Officials

John A. Heilala: trustee B Detroit, MI 1940. ED Pennsylvania State University (1962); Washington University (1965). PRIM CORP EMPL president: Vulcan Materials Co., Chloralkali Unit.
Donald M. James: chairman B 1949. ED University of Alabama BS (1971); University of Alabama MBA (1973); University of Virginia JD (1977). PRIM CORP EMPL chairman, chief executive officer, director: Vulcan Materials Co.
Mary S. Russom: secretary, treasurer (see above)

Grants Analysis

Disclosure Period: fiscal year ending November 30, 2002
Total Grants: $2,510,018
Number of Grants: 735
Average Grant: $3,314

Recent Grants

Note: Grants derived from fiscal 2003 Form 990.
General

150,000	United Way of Central Alabama, Birmingham, AL
95,400	Samford University, Birmingham, AL
88,000	United Way of Central Alabama, Birmingham, AL
60,000	Children's Health System, Birmingham, AL
50,000	Sloss Furnaces Foundation, Birmingham, AL
50,000	University of Alabama at Birmingham, Birmingham, AL
48,000	United Way of the Plains, Birmingham, AL
44,500	Wildlife Habitat Council, Birmingham, AL
42,000	United Way of Central Alabama, Birmingham, AL
40,000	Birmingham Southern College, Birmingham, AL

CRYSTELLE WAGGONER CHARITABLE TRUST

Giving Contact

Darlene Mann, Senior Vice President & Trust Officer
c/o Bank of America
PO Box 1317
Ft. Worth, TX 76101
Phone: (817)390-6114

Description

Founded: 1982
EIN: 751881219
Organization Type: Private Foundation
Giving Locations: TX: Decatur, Fort Worth some statewide giving
Grant Types: Capital, Emergency, Endowment, General Support, Multiyear/Continuing Support, Operating Expenses, Professorship, Project, Research, Scholarship, Seed Money.

Donor Information

Founder: the late Crystelle Waggoner

Financial Summary

Total Giving: $861,378 (fiscal year ending June 30, 2004); $424,550 (fiscal 2001)
Assets: $14,417,285 (fiscal 2004); $11,220,880 (fiscal 2001)

Typical Recipients

Arts & Humanities: Arts Associations & Councils, Arts Festivals, Arts Funds, Arts Outreach, Ballet, Film & Video, Arts & Humanities-General, Historic Preservation, History & Archaeology, Libraries, Museums/Galleries, Music, Opera, Performing Arts, Theater
Civic & Public Affairs: Clubs, Employment/Job Training, Civic & Public Affairs-General, Hispanic Affairs, Parades/Festivals, Urban & Community Affairs, Women's Affairs
Education: Afterschool/Enrichment Programs, Colleges & Universities, Community & Junior Colleges, Leadership Training, Minority Education, Preschool Education, Private Education (Precollege), Science/Mathematics Education, Special Education, Student Aid
Environment: Environment-General, Resource Conservation
Health: Alzheimer's Disease, Cancer, Children's Health/Hospitals, Clinics/Medical Centers, Emergency/Ambulance Services, Eyes/Blindness, Health Funds, Health Organizations, Heart, Hospitals, Medical Research, Mental Health, Nursing Services, Prenatal Health Issues, Public Health, Research/Studies Institutes, Single-Disease Health Associations,

Speech & Hearing
Religion: Churches, Ministries, Social/Policy Issues
Social Services: Big Brothers/Big Sisters, Child Welfare, Community Service Organizations, Day Care, Domestic Violence, Family Planning, Family Services, Food/Clothing Distribution, Homes, People with Disabilities, Recreation & Athletics, Scouts, Senior Services, Shelters/Homelessness, Substance Abuse, United Funds/United Ways, YMCA/YWCA/YMHA/YWHA, Youth Organizations

Application Procedures

Initial Contact: Send a brief letter of inquiry.
Application Requirements: a description of organization, amount requested, and proof of tax-exempt status.
Deadlines: June 30 and December 31.

Restrictions

Restricted to TX organizations in existence before January 24, 1982.

Additional Information

Publications: Annual Report (including Application Guidelines)
Trust(s): Bank of America

Grants Analysis

Disclosure Period: fiscal year ending June 30, 2004
Total Grants: $861,378
Number of Grants: 70
Average Grant: $9,726*
Highest Grant: $100,000
Lowest Grant: $500
Typical Range: $5,000 to $20,000
***Note:** Average grant figure excludes three highest grants ($200,000).

Recent Grants

Note: Grants derived from fiscal 2004 Form 990.
Library-Related

25,000	Fort Worth Public Library Foundation, Ft. Worth, TX -- funding for new integrated library system gala sponsorship

General

100,000	Cattle Raisers Museum, Ft. Worth, TX
50,000	Baylor All Saints Medical Center, Ft. Worth, TX -- donor recognition wall for the liver, pancreas and cell transplant program
50,000	Harris Methodist Health Foundation, Ft. Worth, TX -- to support Harris Methodist heart center
40,000	Texas Ballet Theater, Ft. Worth, TX -- for underwriting of nutcracker 2004-2005 season
26,000	All Church Home for Children, Ft. Worth, TX
25,000	Boys and Girls Clubs of Greater Fort Worth, Ft. Worth, TX -- funding opportunities for panther golf tournament, boxing at the ballroom and educational enhancement program
25,000	Fort Worth Opera, Ft. Worth, TX -- to support main stage productions children's opera theater young artist studio and opera ball gala sponsorship
25,000	Historic Fort Worth Inc., Ft. Worth, TX -- for restorations
25,000	Van Cliburn Foundation, Ft. Worth, TX

WAHLERT FOUNDATION

Giving Contact

Robert H. Wahlert, President
PO Box 61477
Ft. Myers, FL 33906-1477

Phone: (239)590-0683
E-mail: Bob16307@aol.com

Description

Founded: 1948
EIN: 426051124
Organization Type: Private Foundation
Giving Locations: IA: Dubuque and surrounding tri-state area
Grant Types: General Support, Scholarship.

Donor Information

Founder: Dubuque Packing Co., FDL Foods, Inc., the late H. W. Wahlert, and officers of the foundation

Financial Summary

Total Giving: $214,258 (fiscal year ending November 30, 2003); $282,550 (fiscal 2002). Note: Giving includes United Way ($500).
Assets: $5,522,633 (fiscal 2003); $5,584,081 (fiscal 2002)
Gifts Received: $8,305 (fiscal 2002); $2,250 (fiscal 2000); $2,200 (fiscal 1998). Note: In fiscal 1997 and 2002, contributions were received from Honkamp Krueger & Co.

Typical Recipients

Arts & Humanities: Historic Preservation, History & Archaeology, Libraries, Museums/Galleries, Music, Opera
Civic & Public Affairs: Community Foundations, Economic Development, Employment/Job Training, Civic & Public Affairs-General, Housing, Urban & Community Affairs
Education: Business Education, Colleges & Universities, Community & Junior Colleges, Education Funds, Public Education (Precollege), Religious Education, Secondary Education (Private), Secondary Education (Public), Student Aid
Health: Alzheimer's Disease, Cancer, Children's Health/Hospitals, Clinics/Medical Centers, Health Funds, Health Organizations, Hospices, Hospitals, Hospitals (University Affiliated), Mental Health, Nursing Services, Research/Studies Institutes
International: Missionary/Religious Activities
Religion: Churches, Dioceses, Religion-General, Ministries, Missionary Activities (Domestic), Religious Organizations, Religious Welfare, Seminaries
Social Services: Camps, Community Centers, Community Service Organizations, Family Services, Food/Clothing Distribution, Scouts, Senior Services, Shelters/Homelessness, Social Services-General, Special Olympics, Substance Abuse, United Funds/United Ways, Youth Organizations

Application Procedures

Initial Contact: Submit 1 page letter.
Deadlines: August 15.

Foundation Officials

Kathy Chameli: director
Alfred E. Hughes: secretary
Marni Peck: director
Amy Principi: director
Alan Wahlert: director
Celeste Wahlert: director
David Wahlert: director
Donna Wahlert: director
James Wahlert: director
Mark Wahlert: director
Nancy Wahlert: director
R. C. Wahlert, II: director
Robert H. Wahlert: president, manager B Dubuque, IA 1939. ED University of Iowa BS (1963). PRIM CORP EMPL chairman, president, chief executive officer: FDL Foods/Dubuque Packing Co. CORP AFFIL director: Rigid-Pak Corp.; director: Key City Bank & Trust Co.; director: Edelcar Corp.; director: Hawkeye Banks. NONPR AFFIL president, treasurer, director: Wahlert Foundation. CLUB AFFIL Dubuque Country Club.
Susan Wahlert: director

Grants Analysis

Disclosure Period: fiscal year ending November 30, 2003
Total Grants: $214,258
Number of Grants: 37
Average Grant: $4,563*
Highest Grant: $50,000
Lowest Grant: $1,000
Typical Range: $1,000 to $10,000
*Note: Average grant figure excludes highest grant.

Recent Grants

Note: Grants derived from fiscal 2003 Form 990.
General

50,000	Wahlert High School, Dubuque, IA
20,000	Catholic Charities, Alexandria, VA
15,000	Camp Albrecht Acres, Sherrill, IA
10,000	Dubuque Rescue, Dubuque, IA
10,000	Stonehill Care Center, Dubuque, IA
7,500	Mission Honduras, Chicago, IL
6,000	Alzheimer's Association, Chicago, IL
6,000	Hispanic Ministry of Dubuque, Dubuque, IA
6,000	St. Stephen's Food Bank, Dubuque, IA
6,000	Salvation Army, Alexandria, VA

WILLARD AND PAT WALKER CHARITABLE FOUNDATION

Giving Contact

Tommy Karr
Arvest Trust Company NA
PO Box 5000
Springdale, AR 72765
Phone: (479)756-7031

Description

Founded: 1990
EIN: 716139778
Organization Type: Private Foundation
Giving Locations: AR
Grant Types: General Support, Scholarship.

Donor Information

Founder: Established in 1990 by Willard Walker and Pat Walker.

Financial Summary

Total Giving: $10,822,154 (2003); $6,358,665 (2002)
Assets: $34,145,775 (2003); $42,229,629 (2002)
Gifts Received: $5,562,500 (1994); $891 (1993). Note: In 1994, contributions were received from Willard and Pat Walker.

Typical Recipients

Arts & Humanities: Arts Centers, Libraries, Museums/Galleries, Theater
Civic & Public Affairs: Clubs, Civic & Public Affairs-General, Philanthropic Organizations
Education: Colleges & Universities, Community & Junior Colleges, Economic Education, Education Associations, Faculty Development, Education-General, Literacy, Medical Education, Private Education (Precollege), Public Education (Precollege), Secondary Education (Private), Student Aid
Health: Cancer, Children's Health/Hospitals, Clinics/Medical Centers, Eyes/Blindness, Mental Health, Single-Disease Health Associations
Religion: Churches, Religious Organizations, Religious Welfare
Social Services: Camps, Child Welfare, Community Service Organizations, Day Care, Emergency Relief, Family Services, People with Disabilities, Recreation & Athletics, Senior Services, Social Services-General, Youth Organizations

Application Procedures

Initial Contact: Send a brief letter of inquiry.
Application Requirements: A grant request, not exceeding four pages in length, should include the nature of the request, amount of funds requested, a copy of the IRS determination letter, and taxpayer identification number.
Deadlines: None.
Review Process: The trustees meet three to four times a year and consider requests at the meeting following receipt. Requests received just prior to a scheduled meeting may be delayed until the following meeting. Requests will be considered only once during any twelve-month period.
Notes: Do not send audio or video tapes unless requested.

Foundation Officials

Patricia B. Walker: trustee
Willard J. Walker: trustee

Grants Analysis

Disclosure Period: calendar year ending 2003
Total Grants: $10,822,154*
Number of Grants: 36
Average Grant: $60,769*
Highest Grant: $3,262,635
Lowest Grant: $5,000
Typical Range: $25,000 to $200,000
*Note: Giving includes scholarships. Average grant figure excludes five highest grants ($8,938,328).

Recent Grants

Note: Grants derived from 2003 Form 990.
Library-Related

500,000	Fayetteville Public Library, Fayetteville, AR

General

325,000,	University of Arkansa for Medical Sciences, Little Rock, AR
250,000	Camp Aldersgate, Little Rock, AR
250,000	Fayetteville Boys and Girls Club, Fayetteville, AR
125,000	NBA Lenoir Retirement, Columbia, MO
120,000	Jones Center for Families, Springdale, AR
100,000	Fayetteville High School, Fayetteville, AR
100,000	Fellowship of Christian Athletes, Fayetteville, AR
100,000	Ozark Guidance Center, Springdale, AR
50,000	Bost Foundation Fort Smith, AR
30,000	Kidcare, Springdale, AR

WALKER FOUNDATION

Giving Contact

John S. Jenkins, Director
2829 Lakeland Dr., Suite 1600
Jackson, MS 39232
Phone: (601)939-3003
Fax: (601)939-4433

Description

Founded: 1972
EIN: 237279902
Organization Type: Private Foundation
Giving Locations: MS
Grant Types: General Support, Project, Scholarship.

Donor Information

Founder: the late W. E. Walker, Jr., W. E. Walker Stores

Financial Summary

Total Giving: $560,000 (2003)
Assets: $9,296,426 (2003)
Gifts Received: $462,500 (2003); $393,338 (1999); $935,515 (1998). Note: In 2003, contributions were received from Gloria Walker. In 1994, contributions were received from Gloria M. Walker ($523,438), Alex Langford ($350), and miscellaneous ($800).

Typical Recipients

Arts & Humanities: Arts Associations & Councils, Arts Institutes, Dance, Historic Preservation, History & Archaeology, Libraries, Museums/Galleries, Music, Opera, Performing Arts, Theater
Civic & Public Affairs: African American Affairs, Economic Development, Civic & Public Affairs-General, Housing, Nonprofit Management, Urban & Community Affairs, Zoos/Aquariums
Education: Business Education, Colleges & Universities, Continuing Education, Elementary Education (Private), Engineering/Technological Education, Education-General, Private Education (Precollege), Religious Education, Secondary Education (Private), Special Education, Student Aid
Environment: Wildlife Protection
Health: AIDS/HIV, Arthritis, Cancer, Children's Health/Hospitals, Eyes/Blindness, Health Organizations, Heart, Hospices, Hospitals, Kidney, Medical Research, Research/Studies Institutes, Single-Disease Health Associations, Transplant Networks/Donor Banks
International: Foreign Arts Organizations, Health Care/Hospitals, Missionary/Religious Activities
Religion: Churches, Ministries, Religious Organizations, Religious Welfare, Seminaries
Social Services: Animal Protection, Child Welfare, Community Service Organizations, Crime Prevention, Family Services, People with Disabilities, Recreation & Athletics, Scouts, Special Olympics, United Funds/United Ways, Youth Organizations

Application Procedures

Initial Contact: The foundation has no formal grant application procedure or application form.
Deadlines: None.

Foundation Officials

Leigh B. Allen, III: secretary PRIM CORP EMPL secretary: Walker Lands, Inc.
James M. Daughdrill, III: president
John S. Jenkins: director
W. E. Walker, III: trustee
O. B. Walton, III: assistant secretary B 1954. ED Vanderbilt University BA (1976); Harvard University Graduate School of Business Administration MBA (1978). PRIM CORP EMPL chief financial officer: Walker Lands Inc.

Grants Analysis

Disclosure Period: calendar year ending 2003
Total Grants: $12,000*
Number of Grants: 3
Highest Grant: $548,000
Lowest Grant: $2,000
*Note: Giving excludes grant to Walker Education Foundation ($548,000).

Recent Grants

Note: Grants derived from 2001 Form 990.
General

205,000	McCallie School, Chattanooga, TN
30,000	Mississippi Museum of Art, Jackson, MS
25,000	Ducks Unlimited, Lafayette, LA
25,000	Scripps Research Institute, La Jolla, CA
25,000	Young Life Jackson, Jackson, MS
22,150	St. Andrews Episcopal School, Amarillo, TX
19,500	Boy Scouts of America, Dubuque, IA
15,000	Mississippi Symphony Orchestra, Jackson, MS
10,000	Belhaven College, Jackson, MS
10,000	Home Place

THE WALLACE FOUNDATION

Giving Contact

M. Christine DeVita, President
2 Park Avenue, 23rd Floor
New York, NY 10016
Phone: (212)251-9700
Fax: (212)679-6990
E-mail: wrdf@wallacefunds.org
Web: http://www.wallacefoundation.org

Description

Founded: 1965
EIN: 136183757
Organization Type: General Purpose Foundation
Formed by Merger of: DeWitt Wallace-Reader's Digest Fund (2003).
Formed by Merger of: Lila Wallace-Reader's Digest Fund (2003).
Giving Locations: nationally.
Grant Types: General Support, Multiyear/Continuing Support.

Donor Information

Founder: The fund was established in 1965 by DeWitt Wallace (1889-1981). Mr. Wallace was born in St. Paul, MN. His father was president of Macalester College, where Mr. Wallace studied for two years before transferring to the University of California at Berkeley. In 1922, Mr. Wallace and his wife, Lila Acheson Wallace, founded Reader's Digest with $5,000 in borrowed money. Upon his retirement in 1972, Reader's Digest was the world's most widely read magazine. "He was particularly interested in young people and education, and that continues to be reflected in the Fund's current grant program."

Financial Summary

Total Giving: $49,239,673 (2003); $16,485,441 (2002); $32,339,927 (2001)
Assets: $1,255,301,439 (2003); $645,736,319 (2002); $737,601,779 (2001)
Gifts Received: $176,199 (2003); $6,038 (1996); $375,430 (1993). Note: In 2003, contributions were received from DeWitt Wallace Trust ($21,626) and Lisa Acheson Wallace Trust ($154,573).

Typical Recipients

Arts & Humanities: Arts & Humanities-General, Libraries, Literary Arts, Music
Civic & Public Affairs: African American Affairs, Botanical Gardens/Parks, Business/Free Enterprise, Civil Rights, Clubs, Community Foundations, Employment/Job Training, Civic & Public Affairs-General, Hispanic Affairs, Municipalities/Towns, Nonprofit Management, Parades/Festivals, Professional & Trade Associations, Public Policy, Urban & Community Affairs, Women's Affairs
Education: Afterschool/Enrichment Programs, Agricultural Education, Arts/Humanities Education, Business Education, Business-School Partnerships, Colleges & Universities, Community & Junior Colleges, Continuing Education, Education Associations, Education Funds, Education Reform, Faculty Development, Education-General, International Studies, Journalism/Media Education, Literacy, Minority Education, Preschool Education, Private Education (Precollege), Public Education (Precollege), School Volunteerism, Science/Mathematics Education, Secondary Education (Public), Social Sciences Education, Special Education, Student Aid, Vocational & Technical Education
Environment: Resource Conservation
Health: Clinics/Medical Centers, Hospitals, Medical

Research, Research/Studies Institutes
International: International Peace & Security Issues, International Relations
Religion: Jewish Causes, Religious Organizations
Science: Scientific Centers & Institutes, Scientific Organizations
Social Services: At-Risk Youth, Big Brothers/Big Sisters, Camps, Child Welfare, Community Service Organizations, Crime Prevention, Family Services, Homes, People with Disabilities, Recreation & Athletics, Scouts, United Funds/United Ways, YMCA/YWCA/YMHA/YWHA, Youth Organizations

Application Procedures

Initial Contact: Send a brief letter of inquiry (no more than two pages). The fund requests that video tapes not be sent. The fund does not accept email proposals.
Application Requirements: The initial letter should describe the organization, proposed project and its goal, and include an estimated budget of the project and the portion of the budget requiring funding. The Fund will acknowledge receipt of letters. If the request falls within fund interests, a formal proposal with detailed information will be requested within four weeks.
Deadlines: None.
Review Process: The board meets four times a year to consider proposals. Proposals will be reviewed for the potential contribution to the field, the organization's ability to produce and sustain the proposed projects, plans for documenting both process and results, and the financial stability of the organization.

Restrictions

Unsolicited proposals are rarely funded. Areas currently outside giving guidelines include religious and fraternal organizations; international programs; conferences; historical restoration; health, medical, or social service programs; environmental or conservation programs; capital campaigns, emergency funds, or deficit financing; private foundations; or individuals.

Additional Information

The fund has become more national and less local in its grant making. Generally, the fund does not make grants under $100,000 or grants for long-term annual support of an organization. Multiyear funding will be considered relative to specific needs and the potential of a particular project. Resources are allocated to organizations the foundation has invited to apply, and unsolicited requests are rarely funded.
Publications: Annual Report; Application Guidelines

Foundation Officials

Gordon M. Ambach: director
W. Don Cornwell: director
M. Christine DeVita: president, director ED Queens College BA (1977); Fordham University (1980). CORP AFFIL director: Readers Digest Association Inc.
George Vincent Grune: chairman, director B White Plains, NY 1929. ED Duke University BA (1952); University of Florida (1955-1956). CORP AFFIL director: Travel Holiday; director: Chase Manhattan Corp.; director: Federated Department Stores Inc.; director: Avon Products Inc.; director: Bestfoods. NONPR AFFIL mng director: Metropolitan Opera Association; national leaders fellow: YMCA; member: Institute France Academy des Beaux-Arts; trustee: Metropolitan Museum Art; chairman: Boys & Girls Clubs America. CLUB AFFIL Sky Club; Union League Club; Ponte Vedra Inn Club; Sawgrass Club; Augusta National Golf Club; Blind Brook Country Club.
Susan J. Kropf: director
Peter C. Marzio: director
Robert D. Nagel: director investments
Laraine S. Rothenberg: director B Brooklyn, NY 1947. ED University of Pennsylvania BA (1967); Columbia University JD (1971). PRIM CORP EMPL attorney: McDermott, Will & Emery. NONPR AFFIL member: Association Bar New York City; member:

New York State Bar Association.
Joseph Shenker: director
Walter Vincent Shipley: mem, director B Newark, NJ 1935. ED Williams College (1954-1956); New York University BS (1961); Harvard University Graduate School of Business Administration (1976). PRIM CORP EMPL chairman, chief executive officer: Chase Manhattan Corp. ADD CORP EMPL chairman: Chase Bank of Texas; director: Chase Equity Holding Inc. CORP AFFIL director: Verizon Communications Inc.; director: ExxonMobil Corp.; director: NYNEX Corp.; director: Champion International Corp. NONPR AFFIL director: United Way; director: United Way Tri-State; director: New York Clearing House Association; president: Goodwill Industries Greater New York; director: Lincoln Center Performing Arts; director: Conference Board; member: Council Foreign Relations; member: Business Council; member: Business Roundtable; director: Alice Tully Hall; director: Avery Fisher Hall. CLUB AFFIL The Links Club; Augusta National Golf Club; Baltusrol Golf Club.
Cecil Jesse Silas: director B Miami, FL 1932. ED Georgia Institute of Technology BS (1954). CORP AFFIL director: Milliken & Co.; director: Readers Digest Association Inc.; director: Ascent Entertainment; director: Halliburton Co. NONPR AFFIL trustee: Frank Phillips Foundation; member: U.S. Chamber of Commerce; director: Oklahoma Foundation Excellence; member: Phi Delta Theta; director: Ethics Resource Center; trustee: Georgia Technology Foundation; director: Boys & Girls Clubs America; member: American Petroleum Institute; parton council: Atlantic Council U.S. CLUB AFFIL 25 Year Club.
Bruce Trachtenberg: director commun
Valleau Wilkie, Jr.: executive vice president, executive director

Grants Analysis
Disclosure Period: calendar year ending 2003
Total Grants: $49,239,673
Number of Grants: 114
Average Grant: $391,502*
Highest Grant: $5,000,000
Lowest Grant: $1,230
Typical Range: $50,000 to $500,000
*Note: Average grant figure excludes highest grant.

Recent Grants
Note: Grants derived from 2002 Form 990.
General
1,625,000 Education Development Center Inc., Newton, MA -- to plan & coordinate ongoing technical assistance to the 12 lead districts, to coordinate activities across sites
1,581,000 John F. Kennedy School of Government at Harvard University, Cambridge, MA -- toward a leadership program for superintendents that addresses the multiplicity of skills to successfully manage educational systems
1,338,000 Providence School Department, Providence, RI
1,250,000 Community Foundation for Southeastern Michigan, Detroit, MI -- to improve the educational & social performance of children to southeast Michigan by increasing the involvement of parents
1,125,000 Community Foundation for Greater New Haven, New Haven, CT -- to improve learning for children & families in three neighborhoods to greater New Haven & the surrounding region by building the capacity of families
1,109,224 Hubert H. Humphrey Institute for Public Affairs, Minneapolis, MN -- to improve educational achievement for Hmong children and their families by creating a culture of learning on the west side of St. Paul
1,102,000 St. Louis Public Schools, St. Louis, MO

1,100,000 United Way of Massachusetts Bay, Boston, MA -- to energize and support black and Latino parents' active involvement in achieving academic success for their children
1,000,000 Jefferson County Public Schools, Louisville, KY
901,000 Southern Regional Education Board, Atlanta, GA -- to identify partner universities who will support its efforts to redesign education leadership preparation and build local capacity

GEORGE R. WALLACE FOUNDATION

Giving Contact
Nancy Keller-Go, Clerk
George R. Wallace Foundation
Care of Goodwin, Proctor LLP
1 Exchange Pl.
Boston, MA 02109
Phone: (617)570-1735

Description
Founded: 1963
EIN: 046130518
Organization Type: Private Foundation
Giving Locations: MA
Grant Types: Capital, Endowment, General Support.

Donor Information
Founder: the late George R. Wallace

Financial Summary
Total Giving: $417,000 (2003)
Assets: $8,029,191 (2003)

Typical Recipients
Arts & Humanities: Arts Associations & Councils, Dance, Historic Preservation, History & Archaeology, Libraries, Museums/Galleries, Music, Performing Arts, Public Broadcasting
Civic & Public Affairs: Clubs, Community Foundations, Civic & Public Affairs-General, Housing, Urban & Community Affairs
Education: Business Education, Colleges & Universities, Community & Junior Colleges, Engineering/Technological Education, Environmental Education, Education-General, International Exchange, Minority Education, Private Education (Precollege), Public Education (Precollege), Religious Education, Science/Mathematics Education, Student Aid
Environment: Environment-General, Resource Conservation
Health: Hospices, Hospitals
Religion: Churches, Religion-General, Religious Organizations
Science: Observatories & Planetariums
Social Services: Child Welfare, Community Service Organizations, Domestic Violence, Family Planning, Recreation & Athletics, Senior Services, United Funds/United Ways, YMCA/YWCA/YMHA/YWHA, Youth Organizations

Application Procedures
Initial Contact: Send a written request.
Application Requirements: Proposals should contain a concise statement of the purpose of funds sought, the current year's operating budget, recently audited financial statement, a list of board members, resumes of all key staff people, proof of tax-exempt status, and most recent Form 990.
Deadlines: None.

Restrictions
Does not support individuals.

Foundation Officials
John Grado, Jr.: trustee
George R. Wallace, III: chairman, trustee

Grants Analysis
Disclosure Period: calendar year ending 2003
Total Grants: $417,000
Number of Grants: 19
Average Grant: $21,947
Highest Grant: $60,000
Lowest Grant: $5,000
Typical Range: $5,000 to $50,000

Recent Grants
Note: Grants derived from 2001 Form 990.
Library-Related
25,000   Tuck Library, Concord, NH
General
100,000   Chewonki Foundation, Wiscasset, ME
50,000   Applewild School, Fitchburg, MA
50,000   Babson College, Babson Park, MA
22,695   Our Lady of the Angels, Worcester, MA
20,000   Fitchburg Historical Society, Fitchburg, MA
15,000   United Negro College Fund, Fairfax, VA
10,000   Fitchburg Senior Center, Fitchburg, MA
10,000   Lunenburg United Parish, Lunenburg, MA
10,000   Mother Caroline Academy, Dorchester, MA
10,000   Mother Caroline Academy, Dorchester, MA

WALLACE GENETIC FOUNDATION

Giving Contact
Pat Lee, Co-Executive Director
4900 Massachusetts Avenue, Northwest, Suite 220
Washington, DC 20016
Phone: (202)966-2932
Fax: (202)966-3370
E-mail: president@wallacegenetic.org
Web: http://www.wallacegenetic.org

Alternate Contact
Carolyn Sand, Co-Executive Director

Description
Founded: 1959
EIN: 136162575
Organization Type: Family Foundation
Giving Locations: internationally; nationally.
Grant Types: Challenge, General Support, Matching, Project, Seed Money.

Donor Information
Founder: Incorporated in 1959 in New York by the late Henry A. Wallace.

Financial Summary
Total Giving: $3,920,653 (2003); $3,896,970 (2002); $4,000,000 (2001). Note: In 1996, the foundation divided its resources, providing for three separate foundations. Reduced giving in 1996 and 1997 reflects this change.
Assets: $87,716,704 (2003); $77,014,820 (2002); $79,000,000 (2001).
Gifts Received: $1,000,453 (2003); $728,000 (1994); $665,000 (1993). Note: In 2003, contributions were received from Jean Douglas.

Typical Recipients
Arts & Humanities: Historic Preservation, History & Archaeology, Libraries, Museums/Galleries, Public Broadcasting, Theater
Civic & Public Affairs: Botanical Gardens/Parks,

Economic Development, Economic Policy, Civic & Public Affairs-General, Native American Affairs, Philanthropic Organizations, Professional & Trade Associations, Public Policy, Rural Affairs, Safety, Urban & Community Affairs, Women's Affairs
Education: Agricultural Education, Colleges & Universities, Education Funds, Education Reform, Engineering/Technological Education, Environmental Education, Education-General, Health & Physical Education, International Studies, Medical Education, Private Education (Precollege), Public Education (Precollege), Science/Mathematics Education, Student Aid
Environment: Air/Water Quality, Energy, Forestry, Environment-General, Protection, Research, Resource Conservation, Watershed, Wildlife Protection
Health: Cancer, Children's Health/Hospitals, Clinics/Medical Centers, Health-General, Health Policy/Cost Containment, Health Organizations, Heart, Hospitals, Hospitals (University Affiliated), Medical Research, Nursing Services, Nutrition, Public Health, Respiratory, Single-Disease Health Associations
International: Foreign Educational Institutions, Health Care/Hospitals, Human Rights, International Affairs, International Development, International Environmental Issues, International Organizations, International Peace & Security Issues, International Relations
Religion: Churches, Religious Welfare
Science: Science Museums, Scientific Centers & Institutes, Scientific Labs, Scientific Organizations, Scientific Research
Social Services: Animal Protection, Community Service Organizations, Family Planning, Food/Clothing Distribution, Youth Organizations

Application Procedures

Initial Contact: Applicants should send a letter describing applicant's activities. If the activities are of interest to the foundation, an application form will be sent to the applicant.
Application Requirements: Applicant should send letter to the Foundation describing applicant's activities and the proposed project. Include amount requested, anticipated duration of the project, other sources of support, secured and requested; certification of 501(c)(3) status, and list of board members. If the activities are of interest, the Foundation will send its application form.
Deadlines: Nov. 1.

Restrictions

Grants are not made to individuals or endowments.

Additional Information

In 1996, the foundation divided its resources providing for three separate foundations.
Publications: Informative Brochure

Foundation Officials

Ann D. Cornell: vice president, secretary, director
David Douglas: vice president, director
Jean Wallace Douglas: president, director NONPR AFFIL vice president: America Beautiful Fund.
Pat Lee: co-executive director
Joan D. Murray: vice president, treasurer, director
Carolyn Sand: co-executive director

Grants Analysis

Disclosure Period: calendar year ending 2003
Total Grants: $3,920,653
Number of Grants: 80
Average Grant: $36,970*
Highest Grant: $1,000,000
Lowest Grant: $5,000
Typical Range: $10,000 to $50,000
*Note: Average grant figure excludes highest grant.

Recent Grants

Note: Grants derived from 2003 Form 990.
General
1,000,000 Conservation Fund, Arlington, VA

200,000	Conservation Fund, Arlington, VA
200,000	Duke University, Durham, NC
100,000	Dakota Wesleyan University, Mitchell, SD
81,000	Persephone Productions, Arlington, VA
75,000	Children's Health Environmental Coalition CHEC, Princeton, NJ
75,000	Maret School, Washington, DC
60,000	Seed Savers Exchange, Decorah, IA
55,000	Audubon Naturalist Society, Chevy Chase, MD
50,000	Accokeek Foundation, Accokeek, MD

DOROTHY WAGNER WALLIS TRUST

Giving Contact

Frederick Singley Koontz, Trustee
7 St. Paul Street, Suite 1400
Baltimore, MD 21202-1626
Phone: (410)347-8770
E-mail: fkoontz@wtplaw.com

Description

Founded: 1994
EIN: 526605828
Organization Type: Private Foundation
Giving Locations: MD: Baltimore
Grant Types: General Support.

Financial Summary

Total Giving: $294,854 (2003); $375,900 (2001)
Assets: $6,281,752 (2003); $8,336,311 (2001)

Typical Recipients

Arts & Humanities: Historic Preservation, History & Archaeology, Libraries, Museums/Galleries
Civic & Public Affairs: Civic & Public Affairs-General, Housing, Law & Justice, Legal Aid
Education: Colleges & Universities, Education-General, Private Education (Precollege)
Health: Children's Health/Hospitals, Clinics/Medical Centers, Hospitals (University Affiliated), Long-Term Care
Religion: Churches, Religious Welfare
Social Services: Animal Protection, Community Service Organizations, People with Disabilities, Senior Services, Social Services-General, Substance Abuse

Application Procedures

Initial Contact: The foundation requests applications be made in writing.
Application Requirements: Include a description of organization, purpose of funds sought, charitable activities, and any other pertinent information.
Deadlines: None.

Foundation Officials

Frederick Singley Koontz: trustee

Grants Analysis

Disclosure Period: calendar year ending 2003
Total Grants: $294,854
Number of Grants: 14
Average Grant: $8,739*
Highest Grant: $140,000
Lowest Grant: $5,000
Typical Range: $5,000 to $10,000
*Note: Average grant figure excludes two highest grants ($190,000).

Recent Grants

Note: Grants derived from 2001 Form 990.
General
140,000	Walters Art Gallery, Baltimore, MD
50,000	Baltimore Museum of Art, Baltimore, MD
37,500	Maryland Historical Society, Baltimore, MD
30,000	Historic Hampton, Inc., Baltimore, MD

25,000	Harvard University, Cambridge, MA
25,000	Johns Hopkins University, Baltimore, MD
20,000	Woman's Industrial Exchange of Baltimore, Baltimore, MD
11,400	AIM, Baltimore, MD
10,000	Preservation Society, Baltimore, MD
5,000	Legal Aid Bureau, Baltimore, MD

BLANCHE WALSH CHARITY TRUST

Giving Contact

Robert F. Murphy, Jr., Trustee
174 Central St., Suite 311
Lowell, MA 01852
Phone: (978)454-5655

Description

Founded: 1973
EIN: 046311841
Organization Type: Private Foundation
Giving Locations: New England.
Grant Types: Capital, General Support, Operating Expenses, Scholarship, Seed Money.

Financial Summary

Total Giving: $188,400 (2003); $147,800 (2002); $180,885 (2001)
Giving Analysis: Giving for 2003 includes: foundation scholarships ($29,000); 2002: foundation scholarships ($35,000)
Assets: $5,367,099 (2003); $4,262,247 (2002); $5,274,873 (2001)

Typical Recipients

Arts & Humanities: Libraries
Civic & Public Affairs: Asian American Affairs, Employment/Job Training, Civic & Public Affairs-General, Hispanic Affairs, Housing
Education: Afterschool/Enrichment Programs, Arts/Humanities Education, Colleges & Universities, Continuing Education, Elementary Education (Private), Elementary Education (Public), International Studies, Literacy, Minority Education, Preschool Education, Private Education (Precollege), School Volunteerism, Science/Mathematics Education, Secondary Education (Private), Social Sciences Education, Special Education, Student Aid, Vocational & Technical Education
Health: AIDS/HIV, Cancer, Clinics/Medical Centers, Diabetes, Geriatric Health, Health Organizations, Home-Care Services, Hospices, Hospitals, Long-Term Care, Mental Health, Nutrition, Prenatal Health Issues, Public Health
International: Missionary/Religious Activities
Religion: Churches, Religion-General, Jewish Causes, Ministries, Religious Organizations, Religious Welfare
Social Services: At-Risk Youth, Camps, Child Welfare, Community Service Organizations, Day Care, Domestic Violence, Family Services, Food/Clothing Distribution, People with Disabilities, Recreation & Athletics, Senior Services, Shelters/Homelessness, Social Services-General, Volunteer Services, Youth Organizations

Application Procedures

Initial Contact: Applicants should contact the trust, in writing, to obtain grant application forms.
Deadlines: October 1 for application form request. December 1 for completed application to the trustees.

Restrictions

Limited to Roman Catholic charities.

Additional Information

Publications: Application Guidelines

Foundation Officials

John C. Donohoe: trustee
John E. Leggat, Esq.: trustee
Robert F. Murphy, Jr.: trustee

Grants Analysis

Disclosure Period: calendar year ending 2003
Total Grants: $159,400*
Number of Grants: 58
Average Grant: $2,748
Highest Grant: $5,000
Lowest Grant: $1,000
Typical Range: $1,000 to $5,000
***Note:** Giving excludes scholarships.

Recent Grants

Note: Grants derived from 2001 Form 990.
General

10,000	Academy of Notre Dame, Tyngsborough, MA -- renovate gym
5,000	Merrimack Valley Catholic Charities, Lowell, MA -- food pantry
5,000	St. Michael School, Lowell, MA -- religious books and bible
4,000	Redemptorist Center, Denver, CO -- AIDS/HIV infected children's program
4,000	St. Christopher's Inn, Garrison, NY -- expansion for homeless people
4,000	St. Francis De Sales School, Philadelphia, PA -- after-school childcare
3,500	Central Catholic, Lawrence, MA -- scholarships
3,500	Marie Esther Health Center, Marlborough, MA -- update nursing
3,500	Presentation of Mary Academy, Methuen, MA -- scholarships
3,150	Immaculate Conception School, Lowell, MA -- lab kits for science course

WALSH FOUNDATION

Giving Contact

G. Malcolm Louden, Sr., Secretary & Treasurer
500 W. 7th St., Suite 1007
Ft. Worth, TX 76102
Phone: (817)335-3741

Description

Founded: 1956
EIN: 756021726
Organization Type: Private Foundation
Giving Locations: TX: Ft. Worth
Grant Types: General Support, Multiyear/Continuing Support, Operating Expenses, Project.

Donor Information

Founder: Mary D. Walsh, F. Howard Walsh, Sr.

Financial Summary

Total Giving: $353,400 (2003)
Giving Analysis: Giving for 2003 includes: foundation grants to United Way ($5,000)
Assets: $4,818,388 (2003)
Gifts Received: $251,131 (2003); $505,902 (2000); $110,516 (1999). Note: In 1998, Holland Fleming Walsh ($10,381), F. Howard Walsh, II ($36,594.17), Parker Otwel Roe ($53,359.13), Catherine Lauren Walsh ($69,176.91), Karen Lindsey Walsh ($69,176.91), George Howard Porter, William Frederic Bonnell, Jr. ($20,180), Ellen King Walsh ($20,180), Michael Clinton Porter ($20,180), Allison Karen Walsh ($10,899), Laura Elisabeth Walsh ($10,899), Jonathan Richard Bonnell ($10,626), Tara Winston Walsh ($10,626), Mary Erin Walsh Char. Trust ($9,799), and Mary Erin Walsh '83 Char. Trust ($9,082). In 1996, contributions were received from Amy S. Walsh ($21,622), George Howard Porter ($11,931), William F. Bonnell, Jr., Ellen K. Walsh, and

Michael C. Porter ($11,545 each), Allison K. Walsh and Laura E. Bonnell ($10,899 each), Jonathan R. Bonnell and Tara W. Walsh ($31,481 each), Holland F. Walsh ($21,926), F. Howard Walsh III ($20,858), Parker O. Roe ($19,995), Catherine L. Walsh and Karen L. Walsh ($19,285 each), and the Mary Erin Walsh Charitable Trusts ($18,861).

Typical Recipients

Arts & Humanities: Arts Associations & Councils, Arts Centers, Arts Funds, Arts Institutes, Ballet, Community Arts, Dance, Historic Preservation, History & Archaeology, Libraries, Museums/Galleries, Music, Opera, Performing Arts, Public Broadcasting, Theater
Civic & Public Affairs: Botanical Gardens/Parks, Clubs, Economic Development, Civic & Public Affairs-General, Housing, Parades/Festivals, Rural Affairs, Urban & Community Affairs, Women's Affairs, Zoos/Aquariums
Education: Colleges & Universities, Education Funds, Minority Education, Private Education (Precollege), Secondary Education (Public)
Health: AIDS/HIV, Alzheimer's Disease, Arthritis, Cancer, Children's Health/Hospitals, Health Organizations, Heart, Hospitals, Medical Research, Mental Health, Research/Studies Institutes
International: Foreign Arts Organizations
Religion: Churches, Religious Organizations, Religious Welfare
Science: Science Museums
Social Services: Big Brothers/Big Sisters, Child Welfare, Community Centers, Community Service Organizations, Counseling, Crime Prevention, Domestic Violence, Food/Clothing Distribution, People with Disabilities, Recreation & Athletics, Scouts, United Funds/United Ways, Youth Organizations

Application Procedures

Initial Contact: Send a brief letter of inquiry outlining intended use of funds.
Deadlines: None.

Restrictions

Emphasis is on education, health, performing arts, and general welfare.

Foundation Officials

F. Howard Walsh, Jr.: assistant secretary, assistant treasurer B 1941. ED Texas Christian University BA (1963). PRIM CORP EMPL president, director: F Howard Walsh Jr Oper Co. ADD CORP EMPL owner: Walsh Oil Co.
Mary D. Fleming Walsh: president B Whitewright, TX October 29, 1913. ED Southern Methodist University BA (1934). CORP AFFIL partner: Walsh Co. NONPR AFFIL honorary director: Van Cliburn International Piano Competition; life member: YWCA; member: Texas League Composers; member: Texas Boys Club Auxilliary; member: Texas Christian University Fine Arts Foundation Guild; guarantor: Texas Boys Choir; charter member: Lloyd Shaw Foundation; member: Tarrant County Auxiliary Edna Gladney Home; guarantor: Scholar Cantorum; member: Rae Reimers Bible Study; member: Round Table International; member: National Association Cowbelles; member: Opera Guild; member: Jewel Charity Ball; member: Friends Texas Boys Choir; member: Goodwill Industries Auxiliary; guarantor: Fort Worth Theatre; guarantor: Fort Worth Opera Association; member: Fort Worth Pan Hellenic; member: Fort Worth Childrens Hospital; member: Fort Worth Ballet Association; member: Fort Worth Boys Club; guarantor, member: Fort Worth Art Council; guarantor, member: Fort Worth Ballet; member: Fort Worth Art Association; member: Childrens Hospital Women's Board; member: Colorado Springs Fine Arts Center; member: Child Study Center; member: Chi Omega Carousel; member: Chi Omega Mothers; member: Chi Omega; member: American Guild Organists; member: Big Brothers Tarrant County; member: American Automobile Association; co-founder: American Field

Service Fort Worth; member: American Association University Women. CLUB AFFIL Women's Club; Texas Christian University Women's Club; Ridglea Country Club; Shady Oaks Country Club; Garden of Gods Club; Colonial Country Club; Colorado Springs Country Club.

Grants Analysis

Disclosure Period: calendar year ending 2003
Total Grants: $348,400*
Number of Grants: 23
Average Grant: $8,495*
Highest Grant: $68,500
Lowest Grant: $1,000
Typical Range: $5,000 to $10,000
***Note:** Giving excludes United Way. Average grant excludes three highest grants ($178,500).

Recent Grants

Note: Grants derived from 2003 Form 990.
General

68,500	Texas Christian University, Ft. Worth, TX
60,000	Dorothy Shaw Bell Choir, Ft. Worth, TX
50,000	Littlest Wiseman, Ft. Worth, TX
33,000	Fort Worth Zoo, Ft. Worth, TX
29,000	Fort Worth Country Day School, Ft. Worth, TX
10,000	Edna Gladney Fund, Ft. Worth, TX
10,000	Fort Worth Ballet, Ft. Worth, TX
10,000	Fort Worth Zoo, Ft. Worth, TX
10,000	Longhorn Boy Scouts, Ft. Worth, TX
10,000	Ronald McDonald Foundation, Ft. Worth, TX

MAMIE MCFADDIN WARD HERITAGE FOUNDATION

Giving Contact

c/o Hibernia National Bank
PO Box 3928
Beaumont, TX 77704-3928
Phone: (409)880-1426
Fax: (409)880-1437

Description

Founded: 1976
EIN: 746260525
Organization Type: Family Foundation
Giving Locations: TX: Jefferson County
Grant Types: Capital, Emergency, Seed Money.

Donor Information

Founder: Established in 1976 by the late Mamie McFaddin Ward.

Financial Summary

Total Giving: $1,560,634 (2001)
Assets: $33,188,671 (2001)

Typical Recipients

Arts & Humanities: Arts Associations & Councils, Arts Outreach, Ballet, Historic Preservation, History & Archaeology, Libraries, Museums/Galleries, Music, Theater
Civic & Public Affairs: Community Foundations, Inner-City Development, Philanthropic Organizations
Education: Colleges & Universities, Elementary Education (Private), Legal Education, Private Education (Precollege), Religious Education, Secondary Education (Private), Secondary Education (Public)
Health: Cancer, Children's Health/Hospitals, Clinics/Medical Centers, Emergency/Ambulance Services, Geriatric Health, Long-Term Care, Medical Rehabilitation, Medical Research, Mental Health, Nutrition
Religion: Bible Study/Translation, Religious Welfare
Science: Science Museums
Social Services: At-Risk Youth, Community Service

Organizations, Counseling, Family Services, Food/ Clothing Distribution, Homes, Scouts, Senior Services, Social Services-General, Substance Abuse, YMCA/YWCA/YMHA/YWHA, Youth Organizations

Application Procedures

Initial Contact: Applicants should contact the foundation to request an application form.

Application Requirements: Nine copies of the form should be submitted, along with a budget for the requested project, the current year operating budget for the organization, the organization's most recent financial audit, and the IRS determination letter of tax exempt status under Section 501(c)(3).

Deadlines: August 31.

Review Process: Applicants will be notified of the decision concerning their requests, usually in November.

Notes: Recipients are required to make a report to the trustee as to the utilization or status of awarded funds immediately upon the completion of the project or purpose for which the funds are requested, or annually if not otherwise disbursed. No applications will be considered prior to receipt of reports for previously awarded grants.

Restrictions

There is a general policy against the funding of positions, salaries, or other continuing operational expenses that would subject the organization to becoming dependent upon continued foundation support. No funds are provided for student loans, scholarships or fellowships for individual students, grants for endowment funds, annual fund raisers, or annual operating budgets. Grants are not made to individuals.

Additional Information

Hibernia National Bank is the foundation's corporate trustee.

Foundation Officials

Eugene H. B. McFaddin: trustee
James L. C. McFaddin, Jr.: trustee
Jean Moncla: vice president, trust officer
Ida M. Pyle: trustee
Rosine M. Wilson: trustee

Grants Analysis

Disclosure Period: calendar year ending 2001
Total Grants: $935,747*
Number of Grants: 16
Average Grant: $18,039*
Highest Grant: $665,168
Lowest Grant: $2,300
Typical Range: $2,000 to $45,000
*Note: Giving excludes matching gifts. Average grant figure excludes highest grant.

Recent Grants

Note: Grants derived from 2001 Form 990.
General

726,826	McFaddin Ward House, Beaumont, TX -- roof project, expand visitor's center
50,000	Beaumont Community Players, Beaumont, TX -- new facility
25,000	Texas Energy Museum, Beaumont, TX
20,280	JC Council of Alcohol & Drug Abuse, Beaumont, TX -- purchase van
20,000	All Saints Episcopal School, Beaumont, TX -- funding 3 new play areas
20,000	Jefferson Theater Preservation Society, Beaumont, TX -- building renovation
20,000	UBI Caritas, Beaumont, TX -- building renovation
10,000	Boy Scouts of America, Beaumont, TX -- 250 new tents, cots and mattresses
10,000	BUILD, Inc, Beaumont, TX -- restoration of the Hotel Beaumont
10,000	National Alliance for the Mentally Ill, Beaumont, TX -- training and education of family education

ANNA EMORY WARFIELD MEMORIAL FUND

Giving Contact

Braxton Mitchell, Jr., President
P.O. Box 674
Riderwood, MD 21139
Phone: (410)453-0345

Description

Founded: 1928
EIN: 520785672
Organization Type: Private Foundation
Giving Locations: MD: Baltimore metropolitan area
Grant Types: General Support.

Donor Information

Founder: the late S. Davies Warfield

Financial Summary

Total Giving: $295,740 (2003)
Giving Analysis: Giving for 2003 includes: foundation gifts to individuals ($240,740)
Assets: $5,712,557 (2003)
Gifts Received: $1,500 (1992)

Typical Recipients

Arts & Humanities: Libraries
Civic & Public Affairs: Civic & Public Affairs-General, Nonprofit Management, Philanthropic Organizations
Health: Hospitals
Religion: Religious Welfare
Social Services: Child Welfare, Day Care, Family Services, Homes, Senior Services

Application Procedures

Initial Contact: Send brief letter.
Application Requirements: Include purpose and personal and financial data.
Deadlines: None.

Additional Information

Provides grants to individuals to alleviate poverty and human distress.
Publications: Application Guidelines

Foundation Officials

Mrs. W. Page Dame, Jr.: trustee
Edward K. Dunn, Jr.: treasurer, trustee B Baltimore, MD 1935. ED Princeton University AB (1958); Harvard University MBA (1960). PRIM CORP EMPL chief executive officer, director: Mercantile Mortgage. CORP AFFIL vice chairman, president, director: Mercantile Safe Deposit Trust Co.; director: Aegon USA Inc. NONPR AFFIL chairman, director: Baltimore Community Foundation.
Louis W. Hargrave: vice president, trustee PRIM CORP EMPL vice president: NationsBank Corp.
Mrs. Thomas H. Maddux: trustee
Braxton D. Mitchell: vice president, trustee
Charles B. Reeves, Jr.: president, trustee B Baltimore, MD 1923. ED Princeton University BA (1947); University of Virginia LLB (1951). PRIM CORP EMPL partner: Venable Baetjer & Howard. NONPR AFFIL president: J. L. Kernan Hospital; member: Maryland Bar Association; member: American Bar Association; member: American Judicature Society.
Mrs. Barry Strudwick: trustee
Mrs. Lewis C. Strudwick: trustee
Mrs. Guy Warfield: trustee

Grants Analysis

Disclosure Period: calendar year ending 2003
Total Grants: $55,000*
Number of Grants: 2
Highest Grant: $50,000
Lowest Grant: $5,000
*Note: Giving excludes grants to individuals.

Recent Grants

Note: Grants derived from 2001 Form 990.
General

26,645	Family and Children Services
25,000	Commission on Aging, Greenwich, CT
25,000	Keswick Multi-Care Center, Baltimore, MD
25,000	St. Ann Adult Day Care, St. Francis, WI
750	Foundation Center, Washington, DC

THE ANDY WARHOL FOUNDATION FOR THE VISUAL ARTS

Giving Contact

Pamela Clapp, Program Director
65 Bleecker St., 7th Fl.
New York, NY 10012
Phone: (212)387-7555
Fax: (212)387-7560
E-mail: info@warholfoundation.org
Web: http://www.warholfoundation.org

Alternate Contact

Tim Hunt, Curator
Note: For inquiries about art works.

Description

Founded: 1987
EIN: 133410749
Organization Type: Specialized/Single Purpose Foundation
Giving Locations: nationally.
Grant Types: Fellowship, General Support, Matching, Operating Expenses, Project.

Donor Information

Founder: Established in 1987, shortly after the death of pop artist Andy Warhol. Warhol was the artist who immortalized Marilyn Monroe, Jackie Kennedy Onassis, Campbell's soup cans, and other pop icons with his unique style of drawing and printmaking. He is often credited with starting a unique genre of art, called pop art, in the 1960s. Warhol died on February 22, 1987 from complications of surgery. The foundation was endowed with Warhol's investments, art works, and other personal belongings, such as furniture and jewelry. Much of Warhol's personal belongings were sold at auctions to create a permanent endowment for the foundation.

Financial Summary

Total Giving: $4,607,175 (fiscal year ending April 30, 2003); $4,938,404 (fiscal 2002); $8,972,102 (fiscal 2001)
Giving Analysis: Giving for fiscal 2003 includes: foundation fellowships ($25,000); fiscal 2002: foundation scholarships ($75,000) foundation matching gifts ($125,000)
Assets: $207,063,491 (fiscal 2003); $184,498,490 (fiscal 2002); $169,345,457 (fiscal 2001)
Gifts Received: $513,973 (fiscal 1996); $1,524,155 (fiscal 1995); $2,701,590 (fiscal 1994). Note: Contributions were received from the estate of Andy Warhol.

Typical Recipients

Arts & Humanities: Arts Appreciation, Arts Associations & Councils, Arts Centers, Arts Festivals, Arts Funds, Arts Institutes, Arts Outreach, Community Arts, Dance, Ethnic & Folk Arts, Film & Video, Arts & Humanities-General, Historic Preservation, History & Archaeology, Libraries, Literary Arts, Museums/ Galleries, Performing Arts, Public Broadcasting, Visual Arts
Civic & Public Affairs: Asian American Affairs, Civil

Rights, Employment/Job Training, First Amendment Issues, Civic & Public Affairs-General, Nonprofit Management, Women's Affairs
Education: Arts/Humanities Education, Colleges & Universities, Health & Physical Education, Minority Education, Private Education (Precollege)
Environment: Protection, Resource Conservation
Health: AIDS/HIV
International: Foreign Arts Organizations, International-General
Religion: Churches, Missionary Activities (Domestic)

Application Procedures

Initial Contact: Proposals should be submitted in the form of a two- to three-page letter and include proof of tax-exempt status.
Application Requirements: Letters should a detailed proposal, including objectives, timetables and budget.
Deadlines: March 1 and September 1.
Review Process: Grant notifications are mailed on July 1 and January 1.
Notes: The foundation will contact the organization if additional information is needed.

Restrictions

The foundation generally makes grants on a one-time basis. The foundation does not support individual artists or filmmakers. Applicant organizations must be tax-exempt under section 501(c)(3) of the IRS Code.

Additional Information

Organizations that have previously received funding from the foundation should contact the foundation before applying again.
In 1996, the foundation reported that it had discontinued its educational program area.
Publications: Guidelines

Foundation Officials

Patricia Cruz: director
Vishakha N. Desai: director
Sherri Geldin: director
Richard Gluckman: director
Werner Kramarsky: director
Barbara Kruger: director
Ann R. Leven: director
Kathleen C. Maurer: treasurer, chief financial officer, director
Elizabeth Murray: director
Ann Philbin: director
Robert Storr: director
M. Antoinette Thomas: secretary, director
Joel Wachs: president, director
John Warhola: vice president, director
John Waters: director
Robert G. Wilmers: director

Grants Analysis

Disclosure Period: fiscal year ending April 30, 2003
Total Grants: $4,582,175*
Number of Grants: 106
Average Grant: $39,830*
Highest Grant: $400,000
Lowest Grant: $2,500
Typical Range: $20,000 to $50,000
*Note: Giving excludes fellowships. Average grant figure excludes highest grant.

Recent Grants

Note: Grants derived from fiscal 2003 Form 990.
General

400,000	Creative Capital Foundation, New York, NY
250,000	Andy Warhol Museum, New York, NY -- general support and support for catalogue
113,500	Real Art Ways, New York, NY
110,500	Exit Art, New York, NY
110,429	Space One Eleven, New York, NY
105,000	National Coalition Against Censorship, New York, NY -- arts advocacy initiative

102,748	Dieu Donne Papermill, New York, NY
100,000	Creative Time Inc., New York, NY
99,000	Self-Help Graphics, New York, NY
90,600	Kansas City Artists Coalition, New York, NY

ALBERT AND BESSIE WARNER FUND

Giving Contact

c/o Funding Exchange
666 Broadway, Ste. 500
New York, NY 10012
Phone: (516)725-0145

Description

Founded: 1955
EIN: 136095213
Organization Type: Private Foundation
Giving Locations: NY: New York primarily in the Northeast.
Grant Types: General Support.

Financial Summary

Total Giving: $207,000 (2003); $386,870 (2001)
Assets: $5,933,491 (2003); $5,659,560 (2001)

Typical Recipients

Arts & Humanities: Arts Centers, Arts Funds, Arts Institutes, Dance, Film & Video, Libraries, Museums/Galleries, Music, Public Broadcasting, Theater
Civic & Public Affairs: Botanical Gardens/Parks, Civil Rights, Community Foundations, Civic & Public Affairs-General, Housing, Legal Aid, Nonprofit Management, Philanthropic Organizations, Public Policy, Urban & Community Affairs
Education: Colleges & Universities, Education-General, Legal Education
Environment: Air/Water Quality, Environment-General, Resource Conservation
Health: Children's Health/Hospitals, Hospices, Hospitals, Mental Health
Religion: Jewish Causes, Religious Organizations, Religious Welfare
Social Services: Child Welfare, Community Service Organizations, Crime Prevention, Delinquency & Criminal Rehabilitation, Family Planning, Homes, Recreation & Athletics, Shelters/Homelessness, Social Services-General, Youth Organizations

Application Procedures

Initial Contact: Send a brief letter of inquiry describing program or project.
Deadlines: None.

Foundation Officials

John Steel: trustee
Kitty Steel: trustee
Lewis M. Steel: trustee
Ruth M. Steel: trustee

Grants Analysis

Disclosure Period: calendar year ending 2003
Total Grants: $207,000
Number of Grants: 25
Average Grant: $4,458*
Highest Grant: $100,000
Lowest Grant: $1,000
Typical Range: $1,000 to $10,000
*Note: Average grant figure excludes highest grant.

Recent Grants

Note: Grants derived from 2003 Form 990.
General

100,000	Institute for Policy Studies, Washington, DC
25,000	Telluride Foundation, Telluride, CO
15,000	Link Media

10,000	Fordham University Graduate School, New York, NY
10,000	Institute for Public Affairs
10,000	Parrish Art Museum, Southampton, NY
9,000	Hunter School Parent Teacher Association
5,000	Southampton Hospital, Southampton, NY
3,500	Mid Pennsylvania Legal Services, Gettysburg, PA
2,500	East End Hospice, Westhampton Beach, NY

RILEY J. AND LILLIAN N. WARREN AND BEATRICE W. BLANDING FOUNDATION

Giving Contact

Henry L. Hulbert, Managing Trustee
6 Ford Ave.
Oneonta, NY 13820
Phone: (607)432-6720

Description

Founded: 1972
EIN: 237203341
Organization Type: Private Foundation
Giving Locations: NY: Oneonta
Grant Types: General Support, Scholarship.

Donor Information

Founder: Beatrice W. Blanding

Financial Summary

Total Giving: $971,165 (2003); $1,092,142 (2002); $940,850 (2001)
Giving Analysis: Giving for 2003 includes: foundation grants to United Way ($3,000); foundation scholarships ($5,000); 2002: foundation grants to United Way ($3,000)
Assets: $21,062,376 (2003); $17,930,309 (2002)
Gifts Received: $1,289,434 (2002); $900,000 (2001); $498,259 (2000). Note: In 1995, 2001, and 2002, contributions were received from the estate of Beatrice W. Blanding.

Typical Recipients

Arts & Humanities: History & Archaeology, Libraries, Music, Opera
Civic & Public Affairs: Community Foundations, Employment/Job Training, Civic & Public Affairs-General, Housing, Municipalities/Towns, Urban & Community Affairs
Education: Colleges & Universities, Literacy, Private Education (Precollege), Religious Education
Health: Children's Health/Hospitals, Hospices, Hospitals
Religion: Churches, Religious Organizations, Religious Welfare, Synagogues/Temples
Social Services: Community Service Organizations, Emergency Relief, Family Services, People with Disabilities, Recreation & Athletics, Social Services-General, United Funds/United Ways, Volunteer Services, Youth Organizations

Application Procedures

Initial Contact: Send a brief letter of inquiry.
Application Requirements: Include a description of the program or project.
Deadlines: November 1.

Restrictions

Primary geographic area is around Oneonta, NY.

Foundation Officials

Robert A. Harlem: trustee
Henry L. Hulbert: mng trustee
Maureen P. Hulbert: trustee

Grants Analysis

Disclosure Period: calendar year ending 2003
Total Grants: $963,165*
Number of Grants: 34
Average Grant: $13,661*
Highest Grant: $300,000
Lowest Grant: $1,665
Typical Range: $5,000 to $30,000
*****Note:** Giving excludes United Way; scholarships. Average grant figure excludes two highest grants ($526,000).

Recent Grants

Note: Grants derived from 2001 Form 990.
General

300,000	Hartwick College, Onconta, NY
125,000	St. Mary's School, Oneonta, NY -- for parochial school
81,350	A.O. Fox Memorial Hospital Foundation, Oneonta, NY
80,000	St. Mary's School, Oneonta, NY -- for annual operations
50,000	City of Oneonta, Oneonta, NY -- for parks systems
49,000	Oneonta Boys and Girls Club, Oneonta, NY -- for annual operations
40,000	Catskill Symphony Orchestra, Oneonta, NY
30,000	Temple Beth El, Oneonta, NY -- for building project
25,000	Siena College, Loudonville, NY -- for annual operations
20,000	Catskill Area Hospice, Oneonta, NY -- for operations

WASHINGTON FORREST FOUNDATION

Giving Contact

Deborah G. Lucckese, Vice President
2300 S. 9th St.
Arlington, VA 22204
Phone: (703)920-2200

Description

Founded: 1968
EIN: 237002944
Organization Type: Private Foundation
Giving Locations: VA: Northern Virginia
Grant Types: Capital, Emergency, General Support, Multiyear/Continuing Support, Operating Expenses, Scholarship, Seed Money.

Donor Information

Founder: the late Benjamin M. Smith

Financial Summary

Total Giving: $333,199 (fiscal year ending June 30, 2004); $614,226 (fiscal 2002); $510,115 (fiscal 2001)
Giving Analysis: Giving for fiscal 2001 includes: foundation grants to United Way ($10,000)
Assets: $14,185,677 (fiscal 2004); $17,630,675 (fiscal 2002); $12,954,863 (fiscal 2001)
Gifts Received: $457,000 (fiscal 1992). Note: In 1992, contributions were received from the Virginia Smith Charitable Foundation.

Typical Recipients

Arts & Humanities: Arts Associations & Councils, Arts Centers, Arts Outreach, Community Arts, Dance, Ethnic & Folk Arts, Libraries, Music, Opera, Performing Arts, Public Broadcasting, Theater

Civic & Public Affairs: Community Foundations, Economic Development, Civic & Public Affairs-General, Housing, Philanthropic Organizations, Professional & Trade Associations, Public Policy, Urban & Community Affairs, Women's Affairs
Education: Afterschool/Enrichment Programs, Colleges & Universities, Education Funds, Elementary Education (Public), Education-General, Health & Physical Education, Literacy, Medical Education, Minority Education, Private Education (Precollege), Public Education (Precollege), Religious Education, Secondary Education (Public), Student Aid
Health: AIDS/HIV, Arthritis, Cancer, Children's Health/Hospitals, Clinics/Medical Centers, Emergency/Ambulance Services, Health Organizations, Home-Care Services, Hospices, Mental Health, Research/Studies Institutes, Respiratory
Religion: Churches, Religious Organizations, Religious Welfare
Social Services: Camps, Child Abuse, Child Welfare, Community Service Organizations, Counseling, Delinquency & Criminal Rehabilitation, Domestic Violence, Family Planning, Family Services, Food/Clothing Distribution, Recreation & Athletics, Scouts, Shelters/Homelessness, Substance Abuse, United Funds/United Ways, Volunteer Services, YMCA/YWCA/YMHA/YWHA, Youth Organizations

Application Procedures

Initial Contact: Request application form.
Deadlines: None.
Review Process: Applications are considered by the foundation board of directors four times annually.

Restrictions

Limited to Northern Virginia.

Additional Information

Publications: Program Policy Statement

Foundation Officials

Leslie S. Ariail: secretary
Allison A. Erdle: trustee
Benjamin C. Gravett: trustee
Deborah G. Lucckese: vice president
David D. Peete, Jr.: trustee
Margaret S. Peete: president
Benjamin M. Smith, Jr.: treasurer

Grants Analysis

Disclosure Period: fiscal year ending June 30, 2004
Total Grants: $333,199
Number of Grants: 88
Average Grant: $3,786
Highest Grant: $20,000
Lowest Grant: $500
Typical Range: $1,000 to $5,000

Recent Grants

Note: Grants derived from fiscal 2004 Form 990.
General

20,000	Greenbrier Learning Center, Arlington, VA
15,500	Alexandria Neighborhood Health Services Inc., Alexandria, VA -- to support the Arlandria health center for women and children
10,500	Trinity Episcopal Church - Children's Center, Arlington, VA -- to support school maintenance
10,000	Annandale Christian Community for Action, Annandale, VA
10,000	Arlington Community Temporary Shelter, Arlington, VA
8,700	Drew Model Elementary School, Arlington, VA -- field trips, dance class, photography project, and miscellaneous activity fund for kindergarten and/or Montessori classes
8,000	Carpenter's Shelter, Alexandria, VA -- to support child and family services program

7,500	Northern Virginia Area Health Education Center, Alexandria, VA
7,500	Virginia College Fund, Richmond, VA
7,500	Virginia Foundation for Independent Colleges, Richmond, VA -- Virginia scholars fund

DENNIS R. AND PHYLLIS WASHINGTON FOUNDATION

Giving Contact

Russ Ritter, President
PO Box 16630
Missoula, MT 59808-6630
Phone: (406)523-1300
Fax: (406)523-1339
E-mail: lpaulson@washcorp.com

Description

Founded: 1988
EIN: 363606913
Organization Type: Private Foundation
Giving Locations: MT
Grant Types: General Support.

Donor Information

Founder: Montana Rail Link, Montana Resources, Washington Contractors, Envirocon Modern Machinery Co., Western Transport

Financial Summary

Total Giving: $877,888 (2003); $682,899 (2001)
Giving Analysis: Giving for 2003 includes: foundation grants to United Way ($19,000); foundation scholarships ($352,500); 2001: foundation grants to United Way ($17,000); foundation scholarships ($94,000)
Assets: $13,332,602 (2003); $13,780,535 (2001)
Gifts Received: $983,900 (2003); $1,464,400 (2001); $465,999 (2000). Note: In 2001 and 2003, contributions were received from the following: Dennis and Phyliss, Modern Machinery Company, Montana Rail Link, Norsk Pacific

Typical Recipients

Arts & Humanities: Arts Appreciation, Arts & Humanities-General, History & Archaeology, Music, Theater
Civic & Public Affairs: Clubs, Employment/Job Training, Civic & Public Affairs-General, Housing, Women's Affairs, Zoos/Aquariums
Education: Business Education, Colleges & Universities, Engineering/Technological Education, Environmental Education, Private Education (Precollege), Public Education (Precollege), Science/Mathematics Education, Special Education, Student Aid
Health: Cancer, Children's Health/Hospitals, Diabetes, Emergency/Ambulance Services, Health Organizations, Hospitals, Prenatal Health Issues
International: Foreign Arts Organizations
Religion: Bible Study/Translation, Churches, Ministries, Religious Welfare
Science: Science Exhibits & Fairs
Social Services: At-Risk Youth, Camps, Child Welfare, Community Centers, Community Service Organizations, Crime Prevention, Delinquency & Criminal Rehabilitation, Food/Clothing Distribution, Homes, People with Disabilities, Recreation & Athletics, Scouts, Sexual Abuse, Shelters/Homelessness, Special Olympics, United Funds/United Ways, YMCA/YWCA/YMHA/YWHA, Youth Organizations

Application Procedures

Initial Contact: Request an application form.
Deadlines: None.

Review Process: Contribution committee meets quarterly.

Restrictions

Emphasis is on youth and education in areas where the Washington companies operate.

Foundation Officials

William Brodsky: director
Frank Gardner: director
Brian Sheridan: director
Phyllis Washington: chairman

Grants Analysis

Disclosure Period: calendar year ending 2003
Total Grants: $506,388*
Number of Grants: 40
Average Grant: $10,420*
Highest Grant: $100,000
Lowest Grant: $388
Typical Range: $5,000 to $20,000
*Note: Giving excludes United Way; scholarships. Average grant figure excludes highest grant.

Recent Grants

Note: Grants derived from 2001 Form 990.

General

60,000	Young Life -- Young Life Sculptures
52,000	Crystal Cathedral Ministries, Garden Grove, FL
52,000	Southwest Community Church, Palm Desert, CA -- national community services
50,000	Carroll College, Milwaukee, WI -- build Nelson Stadium
50,000	Carroll College, Milwaukee, WI -- build Nelson Stadium
50,000	Horatio Alger Association, Washington, DC -- 54th annual awards banquet
37,500	YMCA, Missoula, MT -- build Washington Center
33,333	Kidsports, Kalispell, MT -- improvements for the youth complex
33,333	Missoula Mavericks Legion Baseball, Missoula, MT -- equipment and uniforms
25,000	Habitat for Humanity, Missoula, MT -- construction materials

WASHINGTON GROUP INTERNATIONAL INC.

Company Headquarters

720 Park Blvd.
Boise, ID 83712
Web: http://www.wgint.com

Company Description

Founded: 2000
Ticker: WGII
Exchange: NASDAQ
Former Name: Morrison Knudsen (2000);
Acquired: Raytheon (2000).
Operating Revenue: US$3.661 billion (2002)
Profit: US$559.9 million (2002)
Employees: 26000 (2003)

Nonmonetary Support

Type: Donated Equipment; In-kind Services; Loaned Employees; Loaned Executives
Contact: Brenda Barnard, Coordinator

Washington Group Foundation, Inc.

Giving Contact

Marlene Puckett, Administrator, Director, Secretary
Washington Group Foundation
One Morrison Knudsen Plaza
PO Box 73
Boise, ID 83729
Phone: (208)386-5201

Description

EIN: 826005410
Organization Type: Corporate Foundation
Giving Locations: ID: nationally; operating locations.
Grant Types: Employee Matching Gifts.
Note: Employee matching gift ratio: .5 to 1 up to $1,000 annually for educational institutions.

Financial Summary

Total Giving: $212,785 (2003); $309,104 (2002); $346,524 (2001). Note: Contributes through foundation only.
Assets: $5,950,392 (2003); $5,269,267 (2002); $6,250,308 (2001)
Gifts Received: $8,157 (2002); $84,013 (2001); $2,300 (1998). Note: In 2002, contributions were received from WGI Holdings England.

Typical Recipients

Arts & Humanities: Arts Centers, Arts Festivals, Arts Funds, Ballet, Community Arts, Dance, Ethnic & Folk Arts, Arts & Humanities-General, History & Archaeology, Libraries, Museums/Galleries, Music, Opera, Performing Arts, Public Broadcasting, Theater
Civic & Public Affairs: African American Affairs, Business/Free Enterprise, Civil Rights, Community Foundations, Economic Development, Employment/Job Training, Civic & Public Affairs-General, Hispanic Affairs, Housing, Legal Aid, Native American Affairs, Parades/Festivals, Philanthropic Organizations, Professional & Trade Associations, Public Policy, Safety, Urban & Community Affairs, Women's Affairs, Zoos/Aquariums
Education: Arts/Humanities Education, Business Education, Colleges & Universities, Education Associations, Education Funds, Education Reform, Elementary Education (Public), Engineering/Technological Education, Education-General, Minority Education, Private Education (Precollege), Public Education (Precollege), Religious Education, Secondary Education (Private), Student Aid, Vocational & Technical Education
Environment: Environment-General, Resource Conservation, Wildlife Protection
Health: Alzheimer's Disease, Cancer, Children's Health/Hospitals, Clinics/Medical Centers, Diabetes, Emergency/Ambulance Services, Health-General, Health Organizations, Hospices, Hospitals, Long-Term Care, Medical Rehabilitation, Medical Research, Multiple Sclerosis, Public Health, Respiratory, Single-Disease Health Associations
International: Foreign Educational Institutions, International Relations, International Relief Efforts
Religion: Jewish Causes, Religious Organizations, Religious Welfare, Seminaries
Science: Science Museums
Social Services: Animal Protection, At-Risk Youth, Child Welfare, Community Centers, Community Service Organizations, Day Care, Domestic Violence, Family Services, Food/Clothing Distribution, People with Disabilities, Recreation & Athletics, Scouts, Senior Services, Sexual Abuse, Shelters/Homelessness, Social Services-General, United Funds/United Ways, Veterans, YMCA/YWCA/YMHA/YWHA, Youth Organizations

Application Procedures

Initial Contact: Individuals send a written request for a foundation questionnaire. Do not take applications for organizations.
Application Requirements: Completed applications will include activities of the applying organization, specific amount requested, outline of how grant would be used, proof of 501(c)(3) status, and prescribed financial statement and completed questionnaire.
Deadlines: None.
Review Process: Proposals reviewed at regular board meetings.
Evaluative Criteria: Individuals and families requesting aid should reside in the city where the company has a presence, and should be classified as needy. Organizations must have 501(c)(3) status. The importance of the organization to employees, participation of employees in organization, the impact gift will have; and the history of giving to the organization by the foundation and employees, are all taken into consideration.

Restrictions

The foundation is unable to provide grants for business purposes, education such as tuition, legal fees, income taxes, etc.
They are unable to duplicate any services that may be available within the community, and may suggest to applicants other services for which they are qualified.

Additional Information

When approved, limited assistance is distributed as a one-time gift, for which payments are made to service providers or vendors, not given directly to the applicant.

Foundation Officials

Anthony Ferruccio: director
Stephen G. Hanks: president B 1951. ED Brigham Young University BS (1974); University of Utah MBA (1975); University of Idaho JD (1978). PRIM CORP EMPL executive vice president, chief legal officer: Morrison-Knudsen Corp. CORP AFFIL officer: Morrison Knudsen Corp. Delaware Corp.; secretary: Morrison Knudsen Corp. Ohio Corp.; secretary: American Piping Boiler Co.
Betty Hurd: director
James McCallum: director
Matt Reece: treasurer
Dennis Wellen: director
Dawn Yantek: director

Grants Analysis

Disclosure Period: calendar year ending 2002
Total Grants: $56,006*
Number of Grants: 172
Average Grant: $240*
Highest Grant: $15,000
Lowest Grant: $12
Typical Range: $50 to $5,000
*Note: Giving excludes gifts to individuals. Average grant figure excludes highest grant.

Recent Grants

Note: Grants derived from 2002 Form 990.
General

15,000	University of Idaho, Moscow, ID
5,000	Boys and Girls Clubs, Atlanta, GA
3,000	Idaho Black History Museum, Boise, ID
2,500	Idaho Shakespeare Festival, Boise, ID
2,000	Boise Public Schools, Boise, ID
1,500	Boise Public Schools Foundation, Boise, ID
500	El-Ada, Boise, ID
500	Joining together to Stop Sexual Abuse, Cleveland, OH
500	Lakewood Christian Service Center, Lakewood, OH
300	Joint School District 2, Meridian, ID

WASHINGTON MUTUAL INC.

Company Headquarters
1201 3rd Avenue, Suite 1500
Seattle, WA 98101
Phone: (206)461-2000
Fax: (206)554-4807
Web: http://www.wamu.com

Company Description
Founded: 1889
Ticker: WM
Exchange: NYSE
Acquired: Bank United Corp. (2001); Dime Savings Bank of New York, FSB (2001).
Revenue: US$15.962 billion (2004)
Profit: US$2.878 billion (2004)
Employees: 63720 (2003)
Fortune Rank: 131, per FORTUNE Magazine's list of 500 Largest U.S. Corporations (2004).
SIC(s): 6036 Savings Institutions Except Federal.

Operating Locations
Washington Mutual, Inc. (OR--Medford, Salem; UT--Brigham City, Logan, Ogden, Provo, Roy, St. George, West Jordan; WA--Aberdeen, Seattle)

Nonmonetary Support
Value: $2,313,945 (2000 approx)
Type: Donated Equipment; In-kind Services
Volunteer Programs: Employees who work 20 hours or more per week are eligible to receive up to four hours of paid time off each month to do volunteer work through the company's Volunteer Release Time program.
Contact: Lois Harless, Program Manager
Note: Company provides nonmonetary support.

Washington Mutual Foundation

Giving Contact
Washington Mutual Community Relations
999 Third Ave., FIS 2913
Seattle, WA 98104
Phone: (206)490-3249
Web: http://www.wamu.com

Alternate Contact
Phone: 800-258-0543

Description
EIN: 911070920
Organization Type: Corporate Foundation
Former Name: Washington Mutual Bank Foundation.
Giving Locations: AZ; CA; CO; FL; ID; IL; MA; NV; NY; OR; TX; UT; WA: company operating areas.
Grant Types: Capital, Employee Matching Gifts, General Support, Multiyear/Continuing Support, Operating Expenses, Project.
Note: Employee matching gift ratio: 1 to 1, up to $10,000 annually per employee.

Financial Summary
Total Giving: $8,696,151 (2003); $18,797,655 (2002); $16,712,476 (2001). Note: Contributes through corporate direct giving program and foundation.
Assets: $545,126 (2003); $6,911,019 (2002); $25,792,633 (2001)
Gifts Received: $2,437,749 (2003); $150,000 (2002); $41,255,080 (2001). Note: Contributions are received from Washington Mutual Bank.

Typical Recipients
Arts & Humanities: Arts Associations & Councils, Arts Centers, Ballet, Community Arts, Ethnic & Folk Arts, Libraries, Museums/Galleries, Music, Performing Arts, Public Broadcasting, Theater
Civic & Public Affairs: Asian American Affairs, Business/Free Enterprise, Community Foundations, Economic Development, Employment/Job Training, Civic & Public Affairs-General, Hispanic Affairs, Housing, Minority Business, Native American Affairs, Philanthropic Organizations, Public Policy, Urban & Community Affairs, Women's Affairs
Education: Afterschool/Enrichment Programs, Agricultural Education, Arts/Humanities Education, Business Education, Business-School Partnerships, Colleges & Universities, Community & Junior Colleges, Economic Education, Education Associations, Education Funds, Education Reform, Elementary Education (Public), Faculty Development, Education-General, Leadership Training, Literacy, Minority Education, Preschool Education, Private Education (Precollege), Public Education (Precollege), Science/Mathematics Education, Special Education
Environment: Environment-General, Resource Conservation
Health: AIDS/HIV, Cancer, Children's Health/Hospitals, Clinics/Medical Centers, Emergency/Ambulance Services, Geriatric Health, Long-Term Care, Mental Health, Public Health
Religion: Religious Welfare
Science: Scientific Centers & Institutes
Social Services: Camps, Child Welfare, Community Centers, Community Service Organizations, Day Care, Domestic Violence, Family Services, Food/Clothing Distribution, Scouts, Senior Services, United Funds/United Ways, Volunteer Services, YMCA/YWCA/YMHA/YWHA, Youth Organizations

Application Procedures
Initial Contact: Contact the foundation or community relations by letter or phone to request current guidelines and application form.
Application Requirements: Submit a full grant proposal (not to exceed four pages). The proposal should include information about the applicant organization, including organization's name and address; chief executive's name and title; contact person's name, title, phone number, and fax number; counties the organization serves; age, ethnicity, gender, and income demographics of population served by the program, and percentage of people served who are below 80% of median income; names and affiliations of board members; list of Washington Mutual employees who are involved with the organization, and how they support the organization; and proof of tax-exempt status. For school-based programs, include percentage of students eligible for the federal free or reduced lunch program.

A proposal should also include specifics about the funding request, including amount requested; time frame in which funds will be used; the program or project for which you are seeking support and how it relates to your organizational mission; specific program or project goals, objectives, timelines, and anticipated impact; methods for monitoring progress and evaluating success; how the program or project will be funded after the grant period has ended; and letters of agreement or other documentation from any collaborating agencies.

Applicants should include a section on the organization's finances, including total operating budget for the current fiscal year; the organization's sources of revenue for the current and previous fiscal years (with sources and amounts); other sources being solicited for project funding; research; and a detailed budget of the project for which funds are sought, if applicable.
Deadlines: None.
Evaluative Criteria: Preference is given to organizations seeking partial rather than exclusive funding from the foundation. The foundation favors organizations, with emphasis on affordable housing, and K-12

public education. A limited number of civic betterment projects are also considered.
Decision Notification: Applicants are generally notified within 60 days.
Notes: Proposals should be sent to the Washington Mutual community relations department serving your area. National grants and those from the states of Washington, Oregon, Idaho, and Illinois should be submitted to the Seattle community relations office listed at the beginning of this entry. Arizona, California, Nevada, Utah, and Colorado requests should be submitted to: Washington Mutual Community Relations, 350 S. Grant Avenue, Los Angeles, CA 90071 (phone 213-217-4088). Florida, Georgia, and South Carolina proposals should be submitted to: Washington Mutual Community Relations, 200 S. Pine Island Road, Suite 206, Plantation, FL 33321 (phone 954-370-0460). New York, New Jersey, Massachusetts, and Pennsylvania proposals should be submitted to: Washington Mutual Community Relations, 589 Fifth Avenue, New York, NY 10017 (phone 212-326-6127). Requests for Texas should be submitted to: Washington Mutual Community Relations, 3200 SW Freeway, Suite 1330, Houston, TX 77027.

Restrictions
Does not support individuals; organizations without tax-exempt status; organizations which discriminate based on race, religion, creed, age, sex, sexual orientation, national origin, or any reason; religious organizations, unless the project to be funded falls within the foundation's guidelines and is for non-religious purposes; or organizations seeking funds for programs or projects outside of Washington Mutual service areas.

Additional Information
Publications: Foundation Annual Report

Corporate Officials
Craig J. Chapman: chief mortgage div.e services CORP AFFIL director: Cagle's Inc..
Daryl David: executive vice president, human resources ED University of Saint Thomas MBA; Whitworth College BA. NONPR AFFIL director: Center for Effective Organizations.
Brad Bradley Davis: executive vice president, chief marketing officer ED LLB. NONPR AFFIL director: Seattle Art Museum; director: Woodland Park Zoo; chairman: Retail Advertising and Marketing Association.
Craig Davis: president, home loans CORP AFFIL director: Ellie Mae Inc. NONPR AFFIL director: Seattle World Trade Center.
Cheryl Di Re: senior vice president, community relations
Bill Ehrlich: executive vice president, corporate relations ED Washington State University BA.
Steve Freimuth: senior vice president, corporate services
Kerry Kent Killinger: chairman, president, chief executive officer, director B Des Moines, IA 1949. ED University of Iowa BBA (1970); University of Iowa MBA (1971). PRIM CORP EMPL chairman, president, chief executive officer, director: Washington Mutual Inc. CORP AFFIL director: SAFECO Corp. NONPR AFFIL member: Society Financial Analysts; director: Washington Roundtable; director: Seattle Repertory Theatre; member: Seattle Chamber of Commerce; trustee: Seattle Foundation; member: Alliance for Education; fellow: Life Management Institute. CLUB AFFIL Rotary Club.
Marc Kittner: chief legal counsel CORP AFFIL vice president, general counsel: Holland America Line.
Robert H. Miles: senior vice president, controller ED University of Utah MA; University of Utah BA. NONPR AFFIL member: Utah Association of CPA's; member: Washington Society of CPA's; member: Tax Executives Institute; member: Financial Executives International; member: Financial Managers Society; member: American Society of CPA's.
Tim Otani: vice president community relations de-

partment NONPR AFFIL member: Washington State Housing Finance Commission.

J. Benson Porter: senior vice president ED Seattle University JD; Whitman College BA. NONPR AFFIL member: Public Affairs Council; director: Seattle Public Library Foundation; director: Enterprise Foundation.

Foundation Officials

Thomas W. Casey: vice president
Craig J. Chapman: director (see above)
Fay L. Chapman: board of directors
Daryl David: director (see above)
Brad Bradley Davis: director (see above)
Craig Davis: vice president (see above)
Cheryl Di Re: secretary (see above)
Bill Ehrlich: director (see above)
Robert Flowers: director ED University of Washington BA; University of Washington MA. NONPR AFFIL president: African American Heritage Foundation; director: KCTS Television.
Steve Freimuth: director (see above)
Kerry Kent Killinger: president (see above)
Marc Kittner: director (see above)
Robert H. Miles: treasurer (see above)
Deanna W. Oppenheimer: group president NONPR AFFIL chairman, executive committee: University of Puget Sound.
J. Benson Porter: director (see above)

Grants Analysis

Disclosure Period: calendar year ending 2003
Total Grants: $3,214,888*
Number of Grants: 62 (approx)
Average Grant: $35,748*
Highest Grant: $600,000
Lowest Grant: $150
Typical Range: $5,000 to $115,000 and $250,000 to $500,000
***Note:** Giving excludes matching gifts and United Way. Average grant figure excludes two highest grants ($1,070,00).

Recent Grants

Note: Grants derived from 2003 Form 990.
General

1,013,534	United Way, WA
879,951	United Way, CA
600,000	National Board for Professional Teaching Standards, Seattle, WA
470,000	New Teacher Project, Seattle, WA
355,868	United Way, FL
250,000	Achieve Inc., Seattle, WA
250,000	Performing Arts Center for Los Angeles County, Seattle, WA
195,845	United Way, TX
110,528	United Way, IL
110,015	United Way, OR

WASSERSTEIN PERELLA FOUNDATION

Giving Contact

Edward Golden, Trust Officer
c/o Deutsche Bank Trust Co.
PO Box 1297, 21 East
Church Street Station
New York, NY 10008
Phone: (212)454-8602

Alternate Contact

280 Park Ave.
New York, NY 10017

Description

Founded: 1989
EIN: 136916786

Organization Type: Private Foundation
Giving Locations: CA; IL; NY; TX
Grant Types: General Support.

Financial Summary

Total Giving: $777,000 (2001)
Assets: $40,735 (2004); $40,814 (2003); $36,037 (2001)
Gifts Received: $810,000 (2001); $685,060 (2000); $669,000 (1999). Note: In 1999, 2000 and 2001, contributions were received from the Wasserstein Perella Group. In 1995, contributions were received from the Wasserstein Perella Group ($136,000) and Chase NYC ($100,000).

Typical Recipients

Arts & Humanities: Arts Associations & Councils, Arts Festivals, Arts Funds, Ballet, Dance, Film & Video, Libraries, Museums/Galleries, Music, Opera, Performing Arts, Theater
Civic & Public Affairs: African American Affairs, Botanical Gardens/Parks, Civic & Public Affairs-General, Minority Business, Public Policy, Urban & Community Affairs
Education: Business Education, Colleges & Universities, Education-General, Private Education (Precollege)
Environment: Environment-General
Health: Alzheimer's Disease, Children's Health/Hospitals, Geriatric Health, Hospitals, Single-Disease Health Associations
International: International Organizations, International Relief Efforts, Trade
Religion: Jewish Causes, Religious Organizations
Social Services: Child Welfare, Recreation & Athletics

Application Procedures

Initial Contact: Send a brief letter of inquiry.
Deadlines: None.

Additional Information

Trust(s): Deutsche Bank Trust Co.

Grants Analysis

Disclosure Period: calendar year ending 2001
Typical Range: $1,000 to $12,500 and $25,000 to $40,000
Note: No grants awarded in 2004.

Recent Grants

Note: Grants derived from 2001 Form 990.
Library-Related

100,000	New York Public Library, New York, NY

General

40,000	Ravinia Festival Association, Highland Park, IL
30,000	Kent Waldrep National Paralysis Foundation, Dallas, TX
27,500	Arts Connection, New York, NY
27,500	Arts Connection, New York, NY
25,000	American Council on Germany, New York, NY
25,000	Chicago Urban League, Chicago, IL
25,000	Leo Baeck Institute, New York, NY
25,000	Metropolitan Museum of Art, New York, NY
24,500	Chicago Symphony Orchestra, Chicago, IL
20,000	Michael J Fox Foundation

WATERHOUSE FAMILY FOUNDATION

Giving Contact

Lawrence M. Waterhouse, Jr., President
c/o L.M. Waterhouse & Co.

128 Todd Lane
Briarcliff Manor, NY 10510
Phone: (914)762-3232

Description

Founded: 1996
EIN: 133914707
Organization Type: Private Foundation
Grant Types: General Support, Operating Expenses.

Financial Summary

Total Giving: $614,377 (2003); $968,625 (2001)
Assets: $257,115 (2003); $1,281,046 (2001)
Gifts Received: $100,000 (2001); $580,000 (2000). Note: In 2001, contributions were received from Patrick Waterhouse ($50,000) and Kevin Waterhouse ($50,000). In 2000, contributions were received from Lawrence M. Waterhouse.

Typical Recipients

Arts & Humanities: Libraries, Museums/Galleries, Theater
Education: Education-General, Preschool Education, Private Education (Precollege), Secondary Education (Private), Student Aid
Health: Cancer, Clinics/Medical Centers, Medical Research
Religion: Churches
Social Services: Recreation & Athletics, Social Services-General, YMCA/YWCA/YMHA/YWHA

Foundation Officials

Christine A. Waterhouse: director
Jennifer A. Waterhouse: director
Kevin C. Waterhouse: director
Lawrence M. Waterhouse, III: director
Lawrence M. Waterhouse, Jr.: president
Patrick R. Waterhouse: director

Grants Analysis

Disclosure Period: calendar year ending 2003
Total Grants: $614,377
Number of Grants: 25
Average Grant: $9,290*
Highest Grant: $200,000
Lowest Grant: $303
Typical Range: $1,000 to $15,000
***Note:** Average grant figure excludes three highest grants ($410,000).

Recent Grants

Note: Grants derived from 2001 Form 990.
Library-Related

3,000	Bolton Free Library, Bolton Landing, NY

General

450,000	National Theater Workshop of the Handicapped, New York, NY
100,000	Bishop Loughlin High School, New York, NY
100,000	St. Peter's Catholic Church, Chicago, IL
100,000	Villanova College, Villanova, PA
50,000	Morse Foundation
50,000	Westchester Medical Center, Westchester, MA
35,000	Open Door Ossining, Ossining, NY
25,000	Cystic Fibrosis, Cincinnati, OH
10,000	Taft School, Watertown, CT
10,000	Woodlot Christian Preschool

THOMAS J. WATSON FOUNDATION

Giving Contact

Beverly Larson, Executive Director
Thomas J. Watson Foundation
293 South Main Street
Providence, RI 02903

Phone: (401)274-1952
Fax: (401)274-1954
E-mail: tjw@watsonfellowship.org
Web: http://www.WatsonFellowship.org

Description

Founded: 1961
EIN: 136038151
Organization Type: Specialized/Single Purpose Foundation
Giving Locations: nationally.
Grant Types: Fellowship, General Support.

Donor Information

Founder: Founded in 1961 by Mrs. Thomas J. Watson, in honor of her husband who died in 1956. In 1914, Mr. Watson became president of a company that manufactured office machines. Ten years later, the company was renamed International Business Machines Corporation (IBM). Thomas Watson served as the company's president for almost forty years and was succeeded by his son, Thomas J. Watson, Jr. No family members are currently associated with IBM. Both Thomas Watson Jr. and his brother, Arthur K. Watson, have donated additional funds to the foundation.

Financial Summary

Total Giving: $2,261,934 (fiscal year ending May 31, 2003); $2,150,819 (fiscal 2002); $2,362,543 (fiscal 2001). Note: 1997 Giving includes fellowships ($945,565); scholarships ($40,711).
Giving Analysis: Giving for fiscal 2001 includes: foundation scholarships ($72,037) foundation fellowships ($1,384,503)
Assets: $64,129,172 (fiscal 2003); $68,719,830 (fiscal 2002); $72,353,604 (fiscal 2001)
Gifts Received: $20,000 (fiscal 2003); $1,500 (fiscal 1994); $616 (fiscal 1993). Note: In 2003, contributions were received from John D. and Catherine T. MacArthur Foundation ($10,000) and the Rockefeller Foundation ($10,000). Contributions were received from the Arthur K. Watson Trust in New York City.

Typical Recipients

Arts & Humanities: Arts & Humanities-General, History & Archaeology, Libraries, Literary Arts, Museums/Galleries, Music, Performing Arts
Civic & Public Affairs: Botanical Gardens/Parks, Civic & Public Affairs-General, Philanthropic Organizations, Urban & Community Affairs
Education: Colleges & Universities, Education Associations, Education Funds, Elementary Education (Private), Engineering/Technological Education, Environmental Education, Faculty Development, Education-General, Private Education (Precollege), Public Education (Precollege), Secondary Education (Private), Social Sciences Education, Student Aid, Vocational & Technical Education
Environment: Air/Water Quality, Environment-General, Protection, Resource Conservation, Wildlife Protection
Health: AIDS/HIV, Children's Health/Hospitals
International: Foreign Arts Organizations, Foreign Educational Institutions
Religion: Churches, Religious Organizations, Religious Welfare
Social Services: Community Service Organizations, YMCA/YWCA/YMHA/YWHA

Application Procedures

Deadlines: Fellowship nominations must be received by the 1st Tuesday in November; nominees' completed applications must arrive by the 1st Tuesday in November.
Review Process: Awards will be announced by the third Monday in March.
Notes: Nominations for the Thomas J. Watson Fellowship are open to all graduating seniors of participating colleges and universities. Contact foundation for list of institutions.

Additional Information

J.P. Morgan Chase Bank is listed as corporate trustee of the foundation.
Publications: Fellowship Program Brochure
Trust(s): J.P. Morgan Chase Bank

Foundation Officials

Elizabeth B. Buckner: member advisory board
Walker G. Buckner, Jr.: member advisory board
John N. Irwin, III: mem adv board B 1954. ED Princeton University (1976). PRIM CORP EMPL vice president, managing director: Hillside Industries Inc. CORP AFFIL vice president, managing director, director: Hillside Capital Inc. De Corp.
David Ewing McKinney: executive secretary, mem adv board B Harriman, TN 1934. ED Vanderbilt University (1952-1953); University of Tennessee BS (1956). PRIM CORP EMPL president: IBM World Trade America/Far East Corp. CORP AFFIL director: Paxar System Group; director: Paxar Woven Label Group.
Daniel L. Moseley: member executive board
Jeanne C. Olivier: member advisory board
Stuart H. Watson: member advisory board
Thomas John Watson, III: mem adv board B 1944. ED Colby College (1969); Boston University (1972).

Grants Analysis

Disclosure Period: fiscal year ending May 31, 2003
Total Grants: $2,261,934*
Number of Grants: 151
Average Grant: $13,585*
Highest Grant: $224,160
Lowest Grant: $275
Typical Range: $1,000 to $25,000
*Note: Giving includes fellowships. Average grant figure excludes highest grant.

Recent Grants

Note: Grants derived from 2003 Form 990.
General

224,150	Social Science Research Council, New York, NY -- fellowship program
82,783	Davidson College, Davidson, NC -- fellowship program
66,000	Middlebury College, Middlebury, VT -- fellowship program
66,000	Wesleyan University, Middletown, CT -- fellowship program
53,000	Berea College, Berea, KY -- fellowship program
44,000	Amherst College, Amherst, MA -- fellowship program
44,000	Bryn Mawr College, Bryn Mawr, PA -- fellowship program
44,000	Carleton College, Northfield, MN -- fellowship program
44,000	College of Holy Cross, Worcester, MA -- fellowship program
44,000	Colorado College, Colorado Springs, CO -- fellowship program

WALTER E. AND CAROLINE H. WATSON FOUNDATION

Giving Contact

Myra Vitto
c/o National City Bank
PO Box 450
Youngstown, OH 44501
Phone: (330)742-4159

Description

Founded: 1964
EIN: 346547726

Organization Type: Private Foundation
Giving Locations: OH
Grant Types: Emergency, General Support, Project.

Donor Information

Founder: Walter E. Watson

Financial Summary

Total Giving: $357,483 (2003); $381,555 (2002)
Giving Analysis: Giving for 2003 includes: foundation grants to United Way ($124,000); 2002: foundation grants to United Way ($145,000)
Assets: $7,833,534 (2003); $6,711,759 (2002); $8,054,082 (2001)

Typical Recipients

Arts & Humanities: Arts Associations & Councils, Arts Centers, Arts Institutes, Community Arts, Arts & Humanities-General, Historic Preservation, History & Archaeology, Libraries, Music, Performing Arts, Public Broadcasting, Theater
Civic & Public Affairs: Botanical Gardens/Parks, Business/Free Enterprise, Chambers of Commerce, Economic Development, Employment/Job Training, Civic & Public Affairs-General, Hispanic Affairs, Public Policy, Urban & Community Affairs
Education: Business Education, Colleges & Universities, Education Funds, Environmental Education, Medical Education, Preschool Education, Private Education (Precollege), Public Education (Precollege), Secondary Education (Public), Special Education, Student Aid
Health: AIDS/HIV, Cancer, Children's Health/Hospitals, Emergency/Ambulance Services, Health Organizations, Heart, Hospices, Hospitals, Long-Term Care, Medical Research, Multiple Sclerosis, Nursing Services, Public Health, Single-Disease Health Associations, Speech & Hearing
International: International Relief Efforts
Religion: Churches, Jewish Causes, Ministries, Religious Welfare
Social Services: Animal Protection, Child Welfare, Community Centers, Community Service Organizations, Day Care, Domestic Violence, Family Planning, Family Services, People with Disabilities, Recreation & Athletics, Scouts, Senior Services, Social Services-General, Substance Abuse, United Funds/United Ways, YMCA/YWCA/YMHA/YWHA, Youth Organizations

Application Procedures

Initial Contact: The foundation has no formal grant application procedure or application form.
Deadlines: None.

Restrictions

Grants are limited to public institutions and hospitals in OH.

Additional Information

Trust(s): Natl City Bank

Foundation Officials

Thomas R. Hollern: trustee
John F. Zimmerman, Jr.: trustee

Grants Analysis

Disclosure Period: calendar year ending 2003
Total Grants: $257,483*
Number of Grants: 57
Average Grant: $3,191*
Highest Grant: $78,783
Lowest Grant: $1,000
Typical Range: $1,000 to $5,000
*Note: Giving excludes United Way. Average grant figure excludes highest grant.

Recent Grants

Note: Grants derived from 2001 Form 990.
General

145,500	Youngstown Mahoning Valley United Way, Youngstown, OH

62,855	Forum Health Trumbull Memorial Hospital, Youngstown, OH
13,000	Youngstown State University, Youngstown, PA
12,500	Hospice of the Valley, Youngstown, OH
10,000	PBS 45 and 49, Kent, OH
7,500	Development Potential, Inc., Youngstown, OH
7,500	Monday Musical Club, Youngstown, OH
7,500	YMCA, Youngstown, OH
6,500	Neoucom Foundation, Rootstown, OH
6,000	HELP Hotline Crisis Center, Youngstown, OH

WAUSAU-MOSINEE PAPER CORP.

Company Headquarters
1244 Kronenwetter Dr.
Mosinee, WI 54455
Web: http://www.wausaumosinee.com

Company Description
Founded: 1899
Ticker: WMO
Exchange: NYSE
Former Name: Wausau Paper Mills Co.
Revenue: US$943.8 million (2001)
Employees: 3100 (2003)
SIC(s): 2600 Paper & Allied Products.

Operating Locations
Wausau-Mosinee Paper Corp. (WI--Rhinelander, Wausau)

Wausau Paper Mills Foundation

Giving Contact
Thomas J. Howatt, Foundation Officer
1244 Kronenwetter Drive
Mosinee, WI 54455-9099
Phone: (715)962-2024

Alternate Contact
c/o Mosinee High School Principal
1000 High Street
Mosinee, WI 54455
Phone: (715)693-2550

Description
EIN: 396080502
Organization Type: Corporate Foundation
Former Name: Wausau Paper Mills Foundation, Inc..
Giving Locations: WI
Grant Types: General Support.

Donor Information
Founder: Wausau Paper Mills Co., Rhinelander Paper Mills Co.

Financial Summary
Total Giving: $317,888 (2002); $348,586 (2001)
Assets: $134,488 (2002); $122,118 (2001)
Gifts Received: $330,000 (2002); $340,000 (2001); $480,000 (1999). Note: In 2001 and 2002, contributions were received from Wausau-Mosinee Paper Corporation. In fiscal 1996, contributions were received from Wausau Paper Mills Co. ($140,000), Wausau Papers of New Hampshire ($10,000), and Rhinelander Paper Co. ($80,000). In 1997, contributions were received from Wassau Paper Mills Company, Wassau Papers of New Hampshire, and Rhinelander Paper Company.

Typical Recipients
Arts & Humanities: Arts Associations & Councils, Arts Festivals, Arts Funds, Ballet, Community Arts, Historic Preservation, History & Archaeology, Libraries, Museums/Galleries, Music, Performing Arts, Public Broadcasting, Theater, Visual Arts
Civic & Public Affairs: Botanical Gardens/Parks, Chambers of Commerce, Clubs, Community Foundations, Economic Development, Employment/Job Training, Civic & Public Affairs-General, Housing, Municipalities/Towns, Parades/Festivals, Professional & Trade Associations, Public Policy, Safety, Urban & Community Affairs, Women's Affairs
Education: Afterschool/Enrichment Programs, Arts/Humanities Education, Business Education, Colleges & Universities, Education Funds, Engineering/Technological Education, Education-General, Preschool Education, Public Education (Precollege), Science/Mathematics Education, Secondary Education (Private), Secondary Education (Public), Special Education, Student Aid, Vocational & Technical Education
Environment: Air/Water Quality, Forestry, Environment-General, Wildlife Protection
Health: Cancer, Children's Health/Hospitals, Emergency/Ambulance Services, Health Funds, Health Organizations, Heart, Hospitals, Multiple Sclerosis, Public Health, Respiratory
International: International Development, International Relief Efforts
Religion: Religious Organizations, Religious Welfare
Science: Scientific Organizations
Social Services: Animal Protection, Child Welfare, Community Service Organizations, Emergency Relief, Food/Clothing Distribution, Recreation & Athletics, Scouts, Social Services-General, Special Olympics, United Funds/United Ways, Veterans, YMCA/YWCA/YMHA/YWHA, Youth Organizations

Application Procedures
Initial Contact: Send a brief letter of inquiry.
Application Requirements: Include a description of program, courses completed, rank in class and grade point level.
Deadlines: March 10 for scholarships.
Notes: For scholarships, applications should be addressed to the principal of Mosinee High School, 1000 High St., Mosinee, WI, 54455, (715) 693-2550.

Restrictions
The Norman S. Steve Memorial Scholarship is limited to the field of study of pulp and paper technology or paper science. The Norman S. Steve Memorial Scholarship, the University of Wisconsin- Marathon Center Scholarship and the North Central Technical Institute Scholarship are limited to the graduating students of Mosinee High School only.

Additional Information
Wausau-Mosinee Paper Corp. was formerly Wausau Paper Mills Co.

Corporate Officials
Stuart R. Carlson: executive vice president administration PRIM CORP EMPL executive vice president administration: Wausau-Mosinee Paper Corp.
Scott P. Doescher: senior vice president, secretary, treasurer PRIM CORP EMPL senior vice president, secretary, treasurer: Wausau-Mosinee Paper Corp.
Thomas J. Howatt: president, chief executive officer, director PRIM CORP EMPL president, chief executive officer, director: Wausau-Mosinee Paper Corp.
San Watterson Orr, Jr.: chairman, director B Madison, WI 1941. ED University of Wisconsin BBA (1963); University of Wisconsin JD (1966). PRIM CORP EMPL chairman, director: Wausau-Mosinee Paper Corp. CORP AFFIL president, director: Woodson Fudiciary Corp.; secretary, treasurer, director: Yawkey Lumber Co.; chairman, director: Mosinee Paper Corp.; director: Marshall & Ilsley Corp.; direc-

tor: MDU Resources Group; director: M & I First America Bank; chairman, director: Marathon Electric Manufacturing Corp.; president, director: Forewood. NONPR AFFIL director: Leigh Yawkey Woodson Art Museum; vice president, director: YMCA Foundation Wausau; director: Wisconsin Taxpayers Alliance; member: Wisconsin Bar Association; director: Wisconsin Policy Research Institute; director: University Wisconsin Hospital & Clinic; member, board regents: University Wisconsin Systems; director: University Wisconsin Foundation; member: American Law Institute; director: Competitive Wisconsin. CLUB AFFIL Wausau Club.
Richard Louis Radt: vice chairman B Chicago, IL 1932. ED University of Illinois (1956). PRIM CORP EMPL vice chairman: Wausau-Mosinee Paper Corp. NONPR AFFIL director: Leigh Yawkey Woodson Art Museum.
David Byron Smith, Jr.: consultant, director B Chicago, IL 1936. ED Princeton University BSE (1958).

Foundation Officials
San Watterson Orr, Jr.: director (see above)
Richard Louis Radt: treasurer, director (see above)

Grants Analysis
Disclosure Period: calendar year ending 2002
Total Grants: $154,650*
Number of Grants: 58
Average Grant: $2,011*
Highest Grant: $40,000
Lowest Grant: $50
Typical Range: $25 to $5,000
*Note: Giving excludes United Way, scholarships, and matching gifts. Average grant figure excludes highest grant.

Recent Grants
Note: Grants derived from 2003 Form 990.
Library-Related

500	Marathon County Public Library Foundation, Wausau, WI

General

91,250	United Way of Marathon County Inc., Wausau, WI
40,000	Grand Theater Foundation Inc., Wausau, WI
19,000	Northwoods United Way Inc., Rhinelander, WI
12,500	Mosinee Fine Arts Association, Mosinee, WI
10,000	James B Haggin Memorial Hospital, Harrodsburg, KY
10,000	Weeks Hospital Association, Lancaster, NH
9,500	United Way of Mercer County Inc., Harrodsburg, KY
7,250	Leigh Yaw key Woodson Art Museum, Wausau, WI
7,000	University of Wisconsin Stevens Point Paper Science Foundation, Stevens Point, WI
6,500	United Way of the Tri-Valley Area, Farmington, ME

WAYPOINT FINANCIAL CORP.

Company Headquarters
235 N. 2nd St.
Harrisburg, PA 17101
Web: http://www.waypointbank.com

Company Description
Founded: 2000
Ticker: WYPT
Exchange: NASDAQ

Former Name: York Financial Corp.; Harris Financial.
Assets: US$5.373 billion (2001)
Employees: 890 (2003)
Parent Company: Waypoint Financial Corp., 235 N. 2nd St., Harrisburg, PA, United States

York Federal Savings & Loan Foundation

Giving Contact
Robert W. Pullo, Chairman & Chief Executive Officer
c/o York Federal Savings & Loan Foundation
101 South George Street
York, PA 17401
Phone: (717)815-4501
Fax: (717)846-5590

Description
EIN: 232111139
Organization Type: Corporate Foundation
Giving Locations: PA: York
Grant Types: Employee Matching Gifts, General Support, Scholarship.

Financial Summary
Total Giving: $315,586 (fiscal year ending June 30, 2002). Note: Contributes through foundation only.
Assets: $463,303 (fiscal 2002)
Gifts Received: $328,150 (fiscal 2002); $262,370 (fiscal 2000); $284,650 (fiscal 1998). Note: In fiscal 2002, contributions were received from Waypoint Bank ($294,000), York Container ($5,000), Susquehanna Pfalzgraff ($5,000), Wagaman Construction, Inc. ($5,000), The Wolf Foundation ($10,000), Kinsley Construction ($5,000), and miscellaneous contributions ($4,150). Substantial contributions are received from York Federal Savings & Loan Association.

Typical Recipients
Arts & Humanities: Arts Associations & Councils, Arts Centers, Arts Festivals, Arts Funds, Community Arts, Ethnic & Folk Arts, Arts & Humanities-General, Historic Preservation, History & Archaeology, Libraries, Museums/Galleries, Music, Performing Arts, Theater
Civic & Public Affairs: Business/Free Enterprise, Chambers of Commerce, Clubs, Community Foundations, Economic Development, Employment/Job Training, Civic & Public Affairs-General, Hispanic Affairs, Housing, Minority Business, Municipalities/Towns, Parades/Festivals, Urban & Community Affairs
Education: Business Education, Business-School Partnerships, Colleges & Universities, Economic Education, Education Associations, Education Funds, Education Reform, Education-General, Literacy, Preschool Education, Private Education (Precollege), Public Education (Precollege), Student Aid, Vocational & Technical Education
Environment: Environment-General, Resource Conservation
Health: Cancer, Children's Health/Hospitals, Clinics/Medical Centers, Emergency/Ambulance Services, Health-General, Health Organizations, Heart, Hospices, Hospitals, Mental Health, Multiple Sclerosis, Prenatal Health Issues, Public Health, Single-Disease Health Associations
Religion: Churches, Jewish Causes, Religious Welfare, Seminaries
Science: Science Museums
Social Services: Camps, Child Welfare, Community Centers, Community Service Organizations, Counseling, Crime Prevention, Domestic Violence, Emergency Relief, Family Services, Food/Clothing Distribution, Homes, People with Disabilities, Recreation & Athletics, Scouts, Sexual Abuse, Social Services-General, Substance Abuse, United Funds/United Ways, YMCA/YWCA/YMHA/YWHA, Youth Organizations

Application Procedures
Initial Contact: Send a written application for funding.
Deadlines: None.

Restrictions
Company does not make grants to religious organizations for sectarian purposes.

Additional Information
Special initiatives are underway to address housing and the needs of low-income communities.

Corporate Officials
Robert W. Pullo: chairman, chief executive officer, director B Cambridge, MA 1939. ED Williams College (1961-1962); Northeastern University (1960-1970). PRIM CORP EMPL chairman, chief executive officer, director: York Federal Savings & Loan Association. CORP AFFIL chairman: Y-F Service Corp.; president, chief executive officer, director: York Financial Corp. NONPR AFFIL director: York County Industrial Development Corp.; director: York Township Water Sewer Authority; member: Pennsylvania Association Savings Institute; director: York Area Enterprise Development Committee; president: Central Pennsylvania Savings Loan League; member: Mayor's Economic Advisory Council.

Foundation Officials
James H. Moss: treasurer B Lancaster, PA 1953. ED Elizabethtown College (1977). PRIM CORP EMPL executive vice president, treasurer: York Federal Savings & Loan Association. CORP AFFIL treasurer: Y-F Service Corp.; vice president: York Financial Corp. NONPR AFFIL member: Financial Executives Institute; member: Financial Managers Society; member: American Institute CPAs.
Robert W. Pullo: president, trustee (see above)

Grants Analysis
Disclosure Period: fiscal year ending June 30, 2002
Total Grants: $266,836*
Number of Grants: 73
Average Grant: $3,655
Highest Grant: $35,000
Lowest Grant: $100
Typical Range: $150 to $10,000
*Note: Giving excludes United Way.

Recent Grants
Note: Grants derived from fiscal 2004 Form 990.

Library-Related
3,333	Hanover Public Library, Hanover, PA
2,500	Mason Dixon Public Library, Stewartstown, PA

General
35,000	Strand Capitol Performing Arts Center, York, PA
30,000	Penn State York, York, PA
30,000	Penn State York, York, PA
17,500	Cultural Alliance of York County, York, PA
17,500	Cultural Alliance of York County, York, PA
16,250	United Way of York County, York, PA
16,250	United Way of York County, York, PA
16,250	United Way of York County, York, PA
16,250	United Way of York County, York, PA
15,000	York College, York, PA

WEATHERTOP FOUNDATION

Giving Contact
Weathertop Foundation
700 Capital Square
400 Locust Street
Des Moines, IA 50309-2340
Phone: (212)472-1288

Description
Founded: 1996
EIN: 421431036
Organization Type: Private Foundation
Giving Locations: CO: Granby; DC: Washington metro area; HI: Kaoaheo; IA: Des Moines metro area; MA: Boston metro area; Canada
Grant Types: General Support.

Financial Summary
Total Giving: $98,500 (fiscal year ending July 31, 2004)
Giving Analysis: Giving for fiscal 2004 includes: foundation grants to United Way ($5,000)
Assets: $4,827,626 (fiscal 2004)
Gifts Received: $13,640 (fiscal 2000). Note: In fiscal 2000, contributions were received from Thomas N. Urban, Jr. ($8,992) and Mary B. Urban ($4,648).

Typical Recipients
Arts & Humanities: Arts Centers, Historic Preservation, Libraries, Literary Arts, Public Broadcasting
Civic & Public Affairs: Botanical Gardens/Parks
Education: Colleges & Universities, Science/Mathematics Education
International: International-General
Social Services: Youth Organizations

Foundation Officials
Victoria Urban Broer: secretary
Cornelia Urban Sawczuk: director
Mary Bright Urban: vice president
Thomas N. Urban, III: director
Thomas Nelson Urban, Jr.: chairman, president
William G. Urban: treasurer

Grants Analysis
Disclosure Period: fiscal year ending July 31, 2004
Total Grants: $93,500*
Number of Grants: 34
Average Grant: $2,750
Highest Grant: $7,500
Lowest Grant: $500
Typical Range: $1,000 to $5,000
*Note: Giving excludes United Way.

Recent Grants
Note: Grants derived from 2001 Form 990.
Library-Related
5,000	Public Library of Des Moines Foundation, Des Moines, IA

General
354,125	National Tropical Botanical Gardens, Kaoaheo, HI
20,000	Carnegie Institute of Washington, Washington, DC
20,000	Youth Incentives, Inc., Des Moines, IA
10,000	Des Moines National Poetry Festival, Des Moines, IA
10,000	Ridley College, St. Catharines, ON Canada
10,000	United States Central Iowa, Des Moines, IA
5,000	Des Moines Art Center, Des Moines, IA
5,000	Thomas Jefferson Memorial Foundation, Charlottesville, VA
1,000	Drake University, Des Moines, IA
100	Iowa Public Television, Johnston, IA

WEATHERWAX FOUNDATION

Giving Contact
Maria Miceli Dotterweich, Executive Director
c/o Comerica Bank, Trust Dept.
245 W. Michigan Ave., 4th Fl.
Jackson, MI 49204
Phone: (517)787-2117
Web: http://www.lib.msu.edu/harris23/grants/wfbrochu.htm

Description
Founded: 1981
EIN: 386439807
Organization Type: Private Foundation
Giving Locations: MI: Jackson, Hillsdale, and Lenawee Counties
Grant Types: General Support.

Donor Information
Founder: the K.A. Weatherwax Trust I

Financial Summary
Total Giving: $1,300,596 (fiscal year ending September 30, 2004); $1,292,667 (fiscal 2001)
Giving Analysis: Giving for fiscal 2004 includes: foundation grants to United Way ($35,000)
Assets: $20,918,823 (fiscal 2004); $22,467,745 (fiscal 2001)
Gifts Received: $78,296 (fiscal 2000); $4,142,929 (fiscal 1999). Note: In fiscal 1999 and 2000, contributions were received from Estate of Peter Weatherwax. In fiscal 1998, contributions were received from the Estate of Peter Weatherwax. In fiscal 1991, contributions were received from the K. A. Weatherwax Trust I.

Typical Recipients
Arts & Humanities: Arts Festivals, Arts & Humanities-General, Historic Preservation, History & Archaeology, Museums/Galleries, Music, Theater
Civic & Public Affairs: Botanical Gardens/Parks, Clubs, Civic & Public Affairs-General, Housing, Legal Aid, Municipalities/Towns, Nonprofit Management, Safety
Education: Arts/Humanities Education, Colleges & Universities, Community & Junior Colleges, Education Associations, Education Funds, Elementary Education (Public), Education-General, International Exchange, Preschool Education, Private Education (Precollege), Public Education (Precollege), Science/Mathematics Education, Secondary Education (Private), Special Education
Environment: Environment-General
Health: Emergency/Ambulance Services, Health Funds, Hospices, Long-Term Care, Mental Health, Public Health, Respiratory, Speech & Hearing
International: Health Care/Hospitals
Religion: Churches, Ministries, Religious Organizations, Religious Welfare
Science: Scientific Centers & Institutes
Social Services: Animal Protection, At-Risk Youth, Child Abuse, Child Welfare, Community Centers, Community Service Organizations, Day Care, Family Services, Homes, People with Disabilities, Recreation & Athletics, Scouts, Senior Services, YMCA/YWCA/YMHA/YWHA, Youth Organizations

Application Procedures
Initial Contact: Call or write for application guidelines.
Deadlines: None.

Restrictions
Does not provide grants to individuals or religious organizations for sectarian purposes. Generally does not support the purchase of computers.

Additional Information
Trust(s): Comerica Bank
Publications: Application Guidelines

Foundation Officials
Lawrence Bullen: trustee

Grants Analysis
Disclosure Period: fiscal year ending September 30, 2004
Total Grants: $1,265,596*
Number of Grants: 47
Average Grant: $18,363*
Highest Grant: $150,000
Lowest Grant: $1,000
Typical Range: $10,000 to $40,000
*Note: Giving excludes United Way. Average grant figure excludes four highest grants ($476,000).

Recent Grants
Note: Grants derived from fiscal 2004 Form 990.
General
150,000	City of Jackson, Jackson, MI -- for new neighbor program
126,000	Artspace Projects Inc., Minneapolis, MN -- for armory park arts project
125,000	Ella Sharp Museum, Jackson, MI
100,000	Hillsdale College, Hillsdale, MI
100,000	Jackson County Intermediate School District, Jackson, MI -- for props program
53,000	Jackson Symphony Orchestra, Jackson, MI -- for concert sponsorship and programming
50,000	Albion College, Albion, MI -- funding for science building
50,000	Holy Cross Children's Services, Clinton, MI -- for technology support
50,000	Michigan Shakespeare Festival, Jackson, MI -- for 2004 festival support
40,000	Legal Services of South Central Michigan, Jackson, MI -- for legal aid for indigent clients of Jackson County

GIL AND DODY WEAVER FOUNDATION

Giving Contact
Dr. William R. Weaver, Trustee
1845 Woodall Rogers Freeway, Suite 1275
Dallas, TX 75201
Phone: (214)999-9497

Description
Founded: 1980
EIN: 751729449
Organization Type: Private Foundation
Giving Locations: KS; LA; NM; OK; PA; TX; WV
Grant Types: General Support, Multiyear/Continuing Support, Operating Expenses, Project, Research.

Donor Information
Founder: Galbraith Weaver

Financial Summary
Total Giving: $723,015 (fiscal year ending September 30, 2004); $396,100 (fiscal 2001)
Assets: $15,665,435 (fiscal 2004); $16,088,019 (fiscal 2001)
Gifts Received: $2,906,199 (fiscal 2000); $4,825,268 (fiscal 1998); $851,525 (fiscal 1996). Note: In fiscal 1998 and 2000, contributions were received from the estate of G. McF. Weaver. In fiscal 1996, contributions were received from the estate of Eudora J. Weaver.

Typical Recipients
Arts & Humanities: Libraries
Civic & Public Affairs: Economic Development, Civic & Public Affairs-General, Women's Affairs, Zoos/Aquariums
Education: Colleges & Universities, Medical Education, Private Education (Precollege), Special Education, Student Aid
Health: Alzheimer's Disease, Cancer, Children's Health/Hospitals, Clinics/Medical Centers, Diabetes, Emergency/Ambulance Services, Health Funds, Health Organizations, Hospitals, Hospitals (University Affiliated), Long-Term Care, Mental Health, Nursing Services, Public Health, Research/Studies Institutes, Trauma Treatment
Religion: Churches, Ministries, Missionary Activities (Domestic), Religious Organizations, Religious Welfare, Seminaries, Social/Policy Issues
Science: Science Museums
Social Services: At-Risk Youth, Big Brothers/Big Sisters, Camps, Child Welfare, Community Centers, Community Service Organizations, Counseling, Crime Prevention, Family Planning, Family Services, Food/Clothing Distribution, Homes, People with Disabilities, Recreation & Athletics, Scouts, Senior Services, Shelters/Homelessness, Substance Abuse, United Funds/United Ways, YMCA/YWCA/YMHA/YWHA, Youth Organizations

Application Procedures
Initial Contact: The foundation requests applications be made in writing.
Application Requirements: Include a description of organization, amount requested, purpose of funds sought, recently audited financial statement, proof of tax-exempt status, board of directors, and project budget.
Deadlines: May 31.

Restrictions
No grants to individuals or to the arts.

Foundation Officials
William R. Weaver, MD: trustee

Grants Analysis
Disclosure Period: fiscal year ending September 30, 2004
Total Grants: $723,015
Number of Grants: 93
Average Grant: $7,044*
Highest Grant: $75,000
Lowest Grant: $65
Typical Range: $5,000 to $10,000
*Note: Average grant figures excludes two highest grant.

Recent Grants
Note: Grants derived from fiscal 2004 Form 990.
General
75,000	Southwestern Medical Foundation, Dallas, TX -- to improve clinical care
59,000	Dallas Theological Seminary, Dallas, TX
50,000	Southwestern Diabetic Foundation, Gainesville, TX -- for cabin restroom renovation and campership fund
50,000	Visiting Nurse Association of Texas, Dallas, TX -- touching every life for capital campaign
45,000	Texas Scottish Rite Hospital for Children, Dallas, TX -- for spinal system and laser diffraction device
40,000	Children's Medical Center, Dallas, TX -- critical services provided by ARCH for at-risk children
28,000	Salvation Army, Dallas, TX
25,000	Genesis Women's Shelter, Dallas, TX
20,000	West Dallas Initiative, Dallas, TX -- for full sponsorship of two students

18,000   Southwestern Diabetic Foundation, Gainesville, TX -- camp scholarships to camp Sweeney based on financial need

WEBBER OIL CO.

Company Headquarters
Bangor, ME
Web: http://www.wenergy.com

Company Description
Revenue: US$30.1 million (2001)
Employees: 200 (2001)
SIC(s): 5100 Wholesale Trade--Nondurable Goods, 5172 Petroleum Products Nec, 5900 Miscellaneous Retail, 5983 Fuel Oil Dealers.

Operating Locations
Webber Oil Co. (ME--Bangor)

Webber Oil Foundation

Giving Contact
Ray Cota
700 Main St.
Bangor, ME 04401
Phone: (207)942-5501
Fax: (207)947-6522

Description
EIN: 237046575
Organization Type: Corporate Foundation
Giving Locations: ME: Bangor
Grant Types: Capital, Scholarship.

Financial Summary
Total Giving: $37,000 (fiscal year ending August 31, 2004)
Assets: $349,436 (fiscal 2004)
Gifts Received: $60,000 (fiscal 2004); $50,000 (fiscal 2000); $25,000 (fiscal 1999). Note: In 1999, contributions were received from Sargent, Tyler and West. In fiscal 1997 and 1998, contributions were received from Aroostook Petroleum Products.

Typical Recipients
Arts & Humanities: Arts Festivals, Dance, Arts & Humanities-General, History & Archaeology, Libraries, Museums/Galleries, Music, Opera, Theater
Civic & Public Affairs: Economic Development, Civic & Public Affairs-General, Municipalities/Towns, Professional & Trade Associations, Urban & Community Affairs
Education: Arts/Humanities Education, Colleges & Universities, Education Funds, Education-General, Private Education (Precollege), Public Education (Precollege), Secondary Education (Private), Student Aid, Vocational & Technical Education
Environment: Environment-General
Health: Clinics/Medical Centers, Health-General, Health Funds, Health Organizations, Hospices, Hospitals, Public Health
Religion: Churches
Social Services: Animal Protection, At-Risk Youth, Camps, Child Welfare, Community Service Organizations, Counseling, People with Disabilities, Recreation & Athletics, Scouts, Senior Services, Social Services-General, YMCA/YWCA/YMHA/YWHA, Youth Organizations

Application Procedures
Initial Contact: Request scholarship application information from high school guidance counselor. For non-scholarship grants, send a brief letter of inquiry.
Application Requirements: Include a description of organization, amount requested, and purpose of funds sought.
Deadlines: None.

Restrictions
Recipient must be a student of the high school awarding the scholarship.

Additional Information
Provides scholarships to Bangor, ME, area high school students.

Corporate Officials
Larry K. Mahaney: chairman, president, chief executive officer, director PRIM CORP EMPL chairman, president, chief executive officer, director: Webber Oil Co.
Andy Pease, Jr.: chief financial officer, vice president financial PRIM CORP EMPL chief financial officer, vice president financial: Webber Oil Co.

Foundation Officials
Linda F. Harnum: trustee

Grants Analysis
Disclosure Period: fiscal year ending August 31, 2004
Total Grants: $37,000
Number of Grants: 9
Highest Grant: $5,000
Lowest Grant: $1,000

Recent Grants
Note: Grants derived from 2004 Form 990.
General

8,000	St. Joseph's College, Standish, ME
5,000	Eastern Maine Charities, Brewer, ME
5,000	Husson College Hall of Champions, Bangor, ME
5,000	National Folk Festival, Richmond, VA
5,000	Penobscot Bay YMCA, Rockport, ME
3,000	Maine Maritime Academy, Castine, ME
3,000	United Cerebral Palsy, Washington, DC
2,000	Maine Coast Memorial Hospital, Ellsworth, ME
1,000	Foxcroft Academy, Dover-Foxcroft, ME -- to secure the traditions

FREDERICK E. WEBER CHARITIES CORP.

Giving Contact
Kerry Ann Herlihy-Sullivan, Directory, Fleet Foundation and Philanthropic Service.
PO Box 1802
Providence, RI 02901
Phone: (401)276-7316

Description
Founded: 1902
EIN: 042133244
Organization Type: Private Foundation
Giving Locations: MA: Boston metropolitan area
Grant Types: Emergency, Endowment, General Support, Scholarship.

Donor Information
Founder: the late Frederick E. Weber

Financial Summary
Total Giving: $362,500 (fiscal year ending March 31, 2004); $381,350 (fiscal 2002); $420,161 (fiscal 2001). Note: Fiscal 1997 Giving includes United Way ($12,500).
Giving Analysis: Giving for fiscal 2002 includes: foundation grants to United Way ($35,000); fiscal 2001: foundation grants to United Way ($30,000)
Assets: $8,226,600 (fiscal 2004); $8,128,632 (fiscal 2002); $8,364,592 (fiscal 2001)

Typical Recipients
Arts & Humanities: Libraries, Music, Performing Arts, Public Broadcasting
Civic & Public Affairs: Economic Development, Employment/Job Training, Ethnic Organizations, Civic & Public Affairs-General, Hispanic Affairs, Housing, Law & Justice, Municipalities/Towns, Philanthropic Organizations, Urban & Community Affairs, Women's Affairs
Education: Arts/Humanities Education, Colleges & Universities, Education-General, Minority Education, Private Education (Precollege), Secondary Education (Private), Student Aid, Vocational & Technical Education
Environment: Environment-General
Health: AIDS/HIV, Children's Health/Hospitals, Clinics/Medical Centers, Geriatric Health, Health Organizations, Hospices, Hospitals, Medical Research, Mental Health, Public Health
International: Health Care/Hospitals, International Affairs
Religion: Churches, Religious Organizations, Religious Welfare
Social Services: Camps, Child Welfare, Community Centers, Community Service Organizations, Counseling, Crime Prevention, Domestic Violence, Emergency Relief, Family Planning, Family Services, Food/Clothing Distribution, Homes, People with Disabilities, Recreation & Athletics, Shelters/Homelessness, Social Services-General, Substance Abuse, United Funds/United Ways, YMCA/YWCA/YMHA/YWHA, Youth Organizations

Application Procedures
Initial Contact: Send a brief summarizing letter setting forth the facts and need for funding.
Application Requirements: If a proposal or prospectus is available, it should accompany the letter. Also include a copy of the applicant's balance sheet, proof of tax-exempt status, and a list of board members. All requests should be approved by the president, treasurer, chief executive officer, social services director or other administrative officer of the organization.
Deadlines: None.

Restrictions
Grants are seldom awarded to national organizations or for single-disease projects. Appeals for general support are discouraged.

Additional Information
Publications: Annual Report

Grants Analysis
Disclosure Period: fiscal year ending March 31, 2004
Total Grants: $362,500
Number of Grants: 30
Average Grant: $12,083
Highest Grant: $37,500
Lowest Grant: $1,000
Typical Range: $5,000 to $25,000

Recent Grants
Note: Grants derived from 2004 Form 990.
General

40,000	United Way of Mass Bay, Boston, MA
20,000	St. Elizabeth's Hospital, Boston, MA
15,000	Boston Medical Center, Boston, MA
15,000	Bridge Over Troubled Waters, Boston, MA
15,000	Committee to End Elder Homelessness, Boston, MA
10,000	Cambridge College, Cambridge, CA
10,000	Cambridge Forum, Cambridge, MA
10,000	Family to Family Project, Somerville, MA
10,000	Family Service of Greater Boston, Boston, MA
10,000	WGBH, Boston, MA

EDWIN S. WEBSTER FOUNDATION

Giving Contact

Michelle Jenney, Foundation Administrator
Grants Management Associates
77 Summer St., Ste. 800
Boston, MA 02110-1006
Phone: (617)426-7080
Fax: (617)426-7087
E-mail: mjenney@grantsmanagement.com
Web:
http://www.grantsmanagement.com/websterguide.html
Note: Phone extension is 318.

Description

Founded: 1948
EIN: 046000647
Organization Type: General Purpose Foundation
Giving Locations: New England.
Grant Types: Capital, General Support, Operating Expenses, Project, Research.

Donor Information

Founder: Established in 1948 by the late Edwin S. Webster.

Financial Summary

Total Giving: $2,612,000 (2002); $2,957,000 (2001)
Giving Analysis: Giving for 2002 includes: foundation grants to United Way ($100,000); 2001: foundation grants to United Way ($100,000)
Assets: $30,039,383 (2002); $38,000,000 (2001)

Typical Recipients

Arts & Humanities: Arts Centers, Ethnic & Folk Arts, Arts & Humanities-General, Historic Preservation, History & Archaeology, Libraries, Museums/Galleries, Music, Performing Arts, Public Broadcasting, Theater
Civic & Public Affairs: Asian American Affairs, Botanical Gardens/Parks, Clubs, Community Foundations, Economic Development, Employment/Job Training, Civic & Public Affairs-General, Housing, Municipalities/Towns, Native American Affairs, Parades/Festivals, Urban & Community Affairs, Women's Affairs, Zoos/Aquariums
Education: Colleges & Universities, Community & Junior Colleges, Education Funds, Education Reform, Engineering/Technological Education, Faculty Development, Education-General, Leadership Training, Legal Education, Medical Education, Minority Education, Private Education (Precollege), Public Education (Precollege)
Environment: Forestry, Environment-General, Resource Conservation, Wildlife Protection
Health: Cancer, Children's Health/Hospitals, Clinics/Medical Centers, Diabetes, Emergency/Ambulance Services, Eyes/Blindness, Health Organizations, Heart, Hospitals, Hospitals (University Affiliated), Medical Rehabilitation, Medical Research, Mental Health, Public Health, Single-Disease Health Associations, Trauma Treatment
International: Foreign Educational Institutions
Religion: Churches, Jewish Causes, Religious Organizations
Science: Observatories & Planetariums, Science Museums, Scientific Centers & Institutes, Scientific Labs
Social Services: Child Welfare, Emergency Relief, Family Planning, Family Services, Food/Clothing Distribution, Homes, People with Disabilities, Recreation & Athletics, Shelters/Homelessness, Substance Abuse, United Funds/United Ways, Youth Organizations

Application Procedures

Initial Contact: Contact foundation in writing or by phone.
Application Requirements: Send a letter with evi-

dence of tax-exempt status.
Deadlines: None, but the foundation's preference months are March and September.
Review Process: The trustees meet each year in the spring and fall to review requests and make distributions. Recipients are notified usually within 15 days of the meeting date.

Restrictions

Grants are not made outside the United States. Grants are not made to individuals., or for loans, seed money, emergency funds, deficit financing, publications, or conferences.

Additional Information

Publications: Application Guidelines

Foundation Officials

Henry Upham Harris, III: trustee CORP AFFIL director: Heritage Bank & Trust.
Henry Upham Harris, Jr.: trustee B New York, NY 1926. ED Stanford University (1951). CORP AFFIL director: Tenneco Inc. NONPR AFFIL chairman emeritus, trustee: Hospital Special Surgery.
Richard Harte, Jr.: trustee PRIM CORP EMPL director: Eaton & Vance Co. PRIM NONPR EMPL chairman, director: Schepens Eye Research Institute. NONPR AFFIL chairman: Schepens Eye Research Institute. CLUB AFFIL president: Hunt Myopia Club.
Edwin W. Hiam: trustee ED California Institute of Technology MA (1948).
Michelle Jenney: foundation assistant

Grants Analysis

Disclosure Period: calendar year ending 2002
Total Grants: $2,512,000*
Number of Grants: 72
Average Grant: $32,563*
Highest Grant: $200,000
Lowest Grant: $2,000
Typical Range: $10,000 to $100,000
***Note:** Giving excludes United Way. Average grant figure excludes highest grant.

Recent Grants

Note: Grants derived from 2001 Form 990.
Library-Related
20,000	Bennington Museum, Bennington, VT	

General
200,000	Massachusetts Institute of Technology, Cambridge, MA	
120,000	Museum of Science, Boston, MA	
120,000	New England Aquarium, Boston, MA	
120,000	Woods Hole Oceanographic Institution, Woods Hole, MA	
105,000	Squam Lakes Association, Holderness, NH	
100,000	Hospital for Special Surgery, New York, NY -- capital support	
100,000	Massachusetts General Hospital, Boston, MA -- Clinical Facility Fund	
100,000	New York Botanical Garden, Bronx, NY	
100,000	United Negro College Fund, Inc., Boston, MA	
100,000	United Way of Massachusetts Bay, Boston, MA	

ELEANORE MULLEN WECKBAUGH FOUNDATION

Giving Contact

Therese A. Polakovic, President & Trustee
PO Box 3486
Englewood, CO 80155-3486
Phone: (303)337-4208

Description

Founded: 1975
EIN: 237437761
Organization Type: Private Foundation
Giving Locations: CO
Grant Types: General Support.

Donor Information

Founder: the late Eleanore Mullen Weckbaugh

Financial Summary

Total Giving: $365,290 (fiscal year ending March 31, 2004); $476,966 (fiscal 2002); $499,235 (fiscal 2001)
Assets: $9,022,224 (fiscal 2004); $9,974,673 (fiscal 2002); $10,954,787 (fiscal 2001)

Typical Recipients

Arts & Humanities: Libraries, Music, Opera, Performing Arts, Public Broadcasting
Civic & Public Affairs: Botanical Gardens/Parks, Employment/Job Training, Ethnic Organizations, Civic & Public Affairs-General, Housing, Professional & Trade Associations, Safety, Urban & Community Affairs, Zoos/Aquariums
Education: Afterschool/Enrichment Programs, Arts/Humanities Education, Business Education, Colleges & Universities, Continuing Education, Education Funds, Elementary Education (Public), Private Education (Precollege), Public Education (Precollege), Science/Mathematics Education, Secondary Education (Private), Secondary Education (Public)
Health: Alzheimer's Disease, Eyes/Blindness, Heart, Hospitals, Mental Health, Public Health
Religion: Churches, Dioceses, Ministries, Missionary Activities (Domestic), Religious Organizations, Religious Welfare
Science: Science Museums
Social Services: At-Risk Youth, Child Welfare, Community Centers, Community Service Organizations, Counseling, Domestic Violence, Family Planning, Family Services, Food/Clothing Distribution, Homes, People with Disabilities, Scouts, Senior Services, Sexual Abuse, Substance Abuse, Volunteer Services, Youth Organizations

Application Procedures

Initial Contact: Send a brief letter of inquiry.
Application Requirements: purpose of funds sought.
Deadlines: None.

Restrictions

Does not support individuals.

Foundation Officials

Michael Lascor: trustee
Edward J. Limes: treasurer, trustee
Deborah O'Dwyer: trustee
Michael J. Polakovic: vice president, trustee
Therese A. Polakovic: president, trustee

Grants Analysis

Disclosure Period: fiscal year ending March 31, 2004
Total Grants: $365,290
Number of Grants: 26
Average Grant: $11,679*
Highest Grant: $45,000
Lowest Grant: $500
Typical Range: $5,000 to $20,000
***Note:** Average grant figure excludes two highest grants ($85,000).

Recent Grants

Note: Grants derived from 2004 Form 990.
General
51,000	St. Francis Fund, Denver, CO	
45,000	Seeds of Hope, Denver, CO	
40,000	Regis High School Capital Fund, Aurora, CO	
30,000	Boys Hope Girls Hope, Aurora, CO	

25,000	Catholic University of America, Washington, DC
18,700	St. Thomas Moore Catholic School, Englewood, CO
16,259	JK Mullen High School, Denver, CO
15,000	Denver Academy, Denver, CO
15,000	Regis University, Denver, CO
12,000	Educating on the Nature and Dignity of Women, Denver, CO

WEEZIE FOUNDATION

Giving Contact
Shannon Hennessey
JP Morgan Chase Bank
345 Park Ave., 6th Fl.
New York, NY 10154
Phone: (212)464-1936

Description
Founded: 1961
EIN: 136090903
Organization Type: General Purpose Foundation
Giving Locations: Northeastern USA.
Grant Types: General Support.

Donor Information
Founder: Established in 1961 by the late Adelaide T. Corbett.

Financial Summary
Total Giving: $1,371,500 (2001)
Assets: $27,930,415 (2001)

Typical Recipients
Arts & Humanities: Arts Associations & Councils, Arts Centers, Libraries, Museums/Galleries, Public Broadcasting
Civic & Public Affairs: Botanical Gardens/Parks, Clubs, Community Foundations, Civic & Public Affairs-General, Urban & Community Affairs, Zoos/Aquariums
Education: Agricultural Education, Arts/Humanities Education, Colleges & Universities, Community & Junior Colleges, Education Associations, Education-General, Literacy, Medical Education, Private Education (Precollege), Public Education (Precollege), Religious Education, Science/Mathematics Education, Special Education, Student Aid
Environment: Environment-General
Health: Clinics/Medical Centers, Eyes/Blindness, Hospitals, Hospitals (University Affiliated), Medical Rehabilitation, Mental Health
Religion: Churches, Ministries, Religious Organizations
Science: Scientific Labs
Social Services: Community Service Organizations, Counseling, Family Services, Homes, People with Disabilities, Recreation & Athletics, Substance Abuse, YMCA/YWCA/YMHA/YWHA, Youth Organizations

Application Procedures
Initial Contact: Send a brief letter of inquiry.
Deadlines: None.

Foundation Officials
D. Nelson Adams, Esq.: member advisory committee ED Yale University AB (1932); Harvard University LLB (1935). PRIM CORP EMPL attorney: Davis, Polk & Wardwell. NONPR AFFIL member: New York County Lawyers Association; member: New York State Bar Association; member: New York City Bar Association; member: American Bar Association; member: American Law Institute.
Thomas W. Carroll: advisor
Mrs. George F. Fiske, Jr.: member advisory committee

Mrs. Kirkie T. Hall: member advisory committee
Lucille T. Hays: mem adv comm
Tyler P. Hoffman: member advisory committee
H. S. Graham McBride: adv
William Parsons, Jr.: member advisory committee

Grants Analysis
Disclosure Period: calendar year ending 2001
Total Grants: $1,371,500
Number of Grants: 28
Average Grant: $48,982
Highest Grant: $200,000
Lowest Grant: $2,500
Typical Range: $25,000 to $100,000

Recent Grants
Note: Grants derived from 2002 Form 990.
General

200,000	Massachusetts Horticultural Society, Wellesley, MA -- help with general operating fund
200,000	Nantucket New School, Nantucket, MA -- provides general operating fund
150,000	Phoenix House, New York, NY -- for general operating fund
125,000	Nantucket Antheneum, Nantucket, MA -- provides general operating fund
100,000	Fay School, Southborough, MA -- offers general operating fund
100,000	Grymes Memorial High School, Orange, VA -- for general operating fund
100,000	Nantucket Boys & Girls Club, Nantucket, MA -- for general operating fund
75,000	V.I.T.A.L Schuyler Center, New York, NY -- assists with general operating fund
75,000	Youth Counsel League, New York, NY -- provides general operating fund
50,000	WGBH, Boston, MA -- assists with general operating fund

---

WEGE FOUNDATION

Giving Contact
Peter M. Wege, President
PO Box 6388
Grand Rapids, MI 49516
Phone: (616)957-0480

Description
Founded: 1967
EIN: 386124363
Organization Type: Private Foundation
Giving Locations: MI: Greater Kent County, Grand Rapids
Grant Types: General Support.

Donor Information
Founder: Peter M. Wege

Financial Summary
Total Giving: $13,119,499 (2003); $13,719,248 (2002)
Giving Analysis: Giving for 2003 includes: foundation grants to United Way ($120,000); 2002: foundation grants to United Way ($160,000).
Assets: $161,600,025 (2003); $147,000,697 (2002)
Gifts Received: $155,000 (1997); $412,000 (1996); $100,000 (1995). Note: In 1996, contributions were received from Peter M. Wege.

Typical Recipients
Arts & Humanities: Arts Associations & Councils, Arts Centers, Ballet, Community Arts, Arts & Humanities-General, History & Archaeology, Libraries, Literary Arts, Museums/Galleries, Music, Public Broadcasting, Theater
Civic & Public Affairs: Botanical Gardens/Parks, Clubs, Community Foundations, Economic Develop-

---

ment, Employment/Job Training, Civic & Public Affairs-General, Hispanic Affairs, Housing, Inner-City Development, Municipalities/Towns, Native American Affairs, Philanthropic Organizations, Public Policy, Urban & Community Affairs, Zoos/Aquariums
Education: Arts/Humanities Education, Business Education, Colleges & Universities, Community & Junior Colleges, Education Associations, Education Funds, Environmental Education, Education-General, International Studies, Literacy, Private Education (Precollege), Public Education (Precollege), Secondary Education (Private), Special Education
Environment: Air/Water Quality, Forestry, Environment-General, Resource Conservation, Wildlife Protection
Health: Cancer, Clinics/Medical Centers, Diabetes, Emergency/Ambulance Services, Health-General, Health Organizations, Heart, Hospitals, Medical Rehabilitation, Multiple Sclerosis
International: Foreign Arts Organizations, International Environmental Issues, International Organizations
Religion: Churches, Dioceses, Religion-General, Ministries, Religious Organizations, Religious Welfare
Social Services: At-Risk Youth, Camps, Child Welfare, Community Service Organizations, Family Planning, Family Services, Homes, Refugee Assistance, Scouts, Senior Services, Substance Abuse, United Funds/United Ways, Youth Organizations

Application Procedures
Initial Contact: Submit a brief letter of inquiry.
Application Requirements: Include a a description of organization.
Deadlines: September 15 and February 15.

Restrictions
Grants are not made to individuals or political or lobbying groups.

Foundation Officials
Mary Goodwillie Nelson: director
Ellen Satterlee: treasurer, executive director
Diana Wege Sherogan: trustee
W. Michael Van Haren: secretary, trustee
Christopher Wege: trustee
Jonathan C. Wege: trustee
Peter M. Wege, II: vice president, trustee
Peter M. Wege: president, trustee B Grand Rapids, MI 1921. ED University of Michigan.

Grants Analysis
Disclosure Period: calendar year ending 2003
Total Grants: $12,999,499*
Number of Grants: 420
Average Grant: $30,951
Highest Grant: $650,384
Lowest Grant: $200
Typical Range: $5,000 to $50,000
*Note: Giving excludes United Way.

Recent Grants
Note: Grants derived from 2003 Form 990.
General

650,000	Grand Rapids Art Museum, Grand Rapids, MI
600,000	Grand Rapids Art Museum, Grand Rapids, MI
500,000	St. Mary's Health Center, Grand Rapids, MI
375,000	Grand Rapids Art Museum, Grand Rapids, MI
250,000	Catholic Secondary Schools, Grand Rapids, MI
250,000	St. Mary's Health Center, Grand Rapids, MI
250,000	St. Mary's Health Center, Grand Rapids, MI
250,000	Social Profit Network, San Rafael, CA
150,000	Aquinas College, Grand Rapids, MI
100,000	Aquinas College, Grand Rapids, MI

TODD WEHR FOUNDATION

Giving Contact
Allen E. Iding, President & Director
555 E. Wisconsin Ave., Suite 1900
Milwaukee, WI 53202
Phone: (414)273-2100

Description
Founded: 1953
EIN: 396043962
Organization Type: Private Foundation
Giving Locations: WI
Grant Types: General Support, Project.

Donor Information
Founder: the late C. Frederic Wehr

Financial Summary
Total Giving: $692,500 (2003)
Assets: $13,299,705 (2003)

Typical Recipients
Arts & Humanities: Museums/Galleries
Civic & Public Affairs: Economic Development,
Civic & Public Affairs-General
Education: Colleges & Universities, Engineering/
Technological Education, Environmental Education,
Faculty Development, Medical Education, Private Education (Precollege), Public Education (Precollege),
Science/Mathematics Education, Secondary Education (Public)
Health: Medical Research
Science: Science Museums, Scientific Centers & Institutes
Social Services: Crime Prevention, Youth Organizations

Application Procedures
Initial Contact: a brief letter of inquiry and full proposal
Deadlines: None.

Restrictions
Does not support individuals.

Foundation Officials
Allan E. Iding: director, president
M. James Termondt: vice president, treasurer, director

Grants Analysis
Disclosure Period: calendar year ending 2003
Total Grants: $692,500
Number of Grants: 12
Average Grant: $57,708
Highest Grant: $117,500
Lowest Grant: $10,000
Typical Range: $20,000 to $100,000

Recent Grants
Note: Grants derived from 2001 Form 990.
General

100,000	Carroll College, Waukesha, WI
100,000	Marian College, Fond du Lac, WI
100,000	Marquette University, Milwaukee, WI
100,000	Neighborhood Improvement Development Corporation, Milwaukee, WI
80,000	Messmer High School, Milwaukee, WI
50,000	Alverno College, Milwaukee, WI
50,000	La Causa, Inc., Greenfield, WI
40,000	Harambee School Development Corporation, Inc., Milwaukee, WI
40,000	Milwaukee Police Athletic League, Milwaukee, WI
25,000	Dominican High School, Whitefish Bay, WI

WEIL, GOTSHAL & MANGES CORP.

Company Headquarters
New York, NY
Web: http://www.weil.com

Company Description
Employees: 1,600
SIC(s): 8111 Legal Services.

Weil, Gotshal & Manges Foundation

Giving Contact
Jesse D. Wolff, Treasurer & Director
Weil, Gotshal & Manges Foundation
767 5th Ave., Suite 1270
New York, NY 10153
Phone: (212)310-8000

Description
Founded: 1983
EIN: 133158325
Organization Type: Corporate Foundation
Giving Locations: NY
Grant Types: General Support.

Donor Information
Founder: Robert Todd Lang, Ira M. Millstein, Harvey R. Miller

Financial Summary
Total Giving: $2,344,016 (2003); $2,579,705 (2001).
Note: Contributes through foundation only.
Assets: $1,280,452 (2003); $2,521,545 (2001)
Gifts Received: $2,750,000 (2003); $2,027,834 (2001); $1,500,000 (2000). Note: Contributions were received from Weil, Gotshal & Manges LLP.

Typical Recipients
Arts & Humanities: Arts Associations & Councils, Arts Centers, Arts Festivals, Arts Funds, Dance, History & Archaeology, Libraries, Museums/Galleries, Music, Opera, Performing Arts, Public Broadcasting
Civic & Public Affairs: African American Affairs, Botanical Gardens/Parks, Business/Free Enterprise, Chambers of Commerce, Civil Rights, Clubs, Community Foundations, Economic Development, Economic Policy, Employment/Job Training, Ethnic Organizations, Civic & Public Affairs-General, Law & Justice, Legal Aid, Minority Business, Municipalities/Towns, Parades/Festivals, Public Policy, Urban & Community Affairs, Women's Affairs, Zoos/Aquariums
Education: Arts/Humanities Education, Business Education, Colleges & Universities, Education Associations, Education Reform, Elementary Education (Private), Education-General, International Studies, Leadership Training, Legal Education, Medical Education, Preschool Education, Private Education (Precollege), Secondary Education (Private), Social Sciences Education, Student Aid
Environment: Environment-General
Health: AIDS/HIV, Cancer, Children's Health/Hospitals, Clinics/Medical Centers, Emergency/Ambulance Services, Health Organizations, Heart, Medical Research, Prenatal Health Issues, Public Health, Single-Disease Health Associations, Transplant Networks/Donor Banks
International: Foreign Educational Institutions, Human Rights, International Affairs, International Peace & Security Issues, International Relations, Missionary/Religious Activities
Religion: Dioceses, Religion-General, Jewish Causes, Religious Organizations, Religious Welfare
Science: Science Museums, Scientific Centers & Institutes

Social Services: At-Risk Youth, Big Brothers/Big Sisters, Camps, Child Welfare, Community Service Organizations, Crime Prevention, Emergency Relief, Family Planning, Family Services, Recreation & Athletics, Scouts, Shelters/Homelessness, United Funds/United Ways, Volunteer Services, YMCA/YWCA/YMHA/YWHA, Youth Organizations

Application Procedures
Initial Contact: Send a written proposal.
Application Requirements: Include a description of organization; statement of purpose; budget and income; and schedule of activities.
Deadlines: November 1.

Corporate Officials
Ira M. Millstein: partner B New York, NY 1926. ED Columbia University BS (1947); Columbia University LLB (1949). PRIM CORP EMPL partner: Weil, Gotshal & Manges Corp. NONPR AFFIL chairman: New York City Partnership Policy Center; member: New York State Bar Association; member: National Association Corp. Directors; professor, chairman board advisors: Columbia University Center Law Economic Studies; member: Government Cuomo's Task Force on Pension Fund Investment; chairman board trustee: Center Park Conservancy; fellow: American Academy of Arts & Sciences; member: American Bar Association; vice chairman board overseers: Albert Einstein College of Medicine. CLUB AFFIL Metro Club; Quaker Ridge Golf Club.

Foundation Officials
Robert Todd Lang: director B New York, NY 1924. ED Yale University BA (1945); Yale University LLB (1947). PRIM CORP EMPL senior partner: Weil, Gotshal & Manges Corp. NONPR AFFIL chairman: Task Force Listing Standards Self Regulatory Organizations; member: Task Force Review Federal Securities Law; chairman: Task Force Hedge Funds; member: American Bar Association; member: Committee Federal Regulation Securities.
Ira M. Millstein: director (see above)
Jesse David Wolff: director B Minneapolis, MN August 26, 1913. ED Dartmouth College BA (1935); Harvard University JD (1938). NONPR AFFIL trustee greater NY chapter: American Red Cross; member: Judge Advisory General Association; member: American Bar Association.

Grants Analysis
Disclosure Period: calendar year ending 2003
Total Grants: $2,087,516*
Number of Grants: 173
Average Grant: $6,213*
Highest Grant: $400,000
Lowest Grant: $50
Typical Range: $1,000 to $10,000
*Note: Giving excludes United Way. Average grant figure excludes six highest grants ($1,050,000).

Recent Grants
Note: Grants derived from 2003 Form 990.
General

400,000	UJA Federation of New York, New York, NY
250,000	Legal Aid Society, New York, NY
155,000	United Way of New York City, New York, NY
100,000	Central Park Conservancy, New York, NY
100,000	Greater New York Councils, Boy Scouts of America, New York, NY
100,000	Legal Aid Society, New York, NY
100,000	New York University School of Law, New York, NY
50,000	9/11 Families Giving Back, New York, NY
50,000	Vogel Alcove, Dallas, TX
30,000	V Foundation, Cary, NC

WEINGART FOUNDATION

Giving Contact

Fred J. Ali, President
1055 West 7th Street, Suite 3050
Los Angeles, CA 90017
Phone: (213)688-7799
Fax: (213)688-1515
E-mail: info@weingartfnd.org
Web: http://www.weingartfnd.org

Alternate Contact

Weingart-Price Fund
San Diego Foundation
1420 Kettner Boulevard, Suite 500
San Diego, CA 92101
Phone: (619)235-2300
Note: For agencies in San Diego and Imperial County.

Description

Founded: 1951
EIN: 956054814
Organization Type: General Purpose Foundation
Giving Locations: CA: seven counties in Southern California
Grant Types: Capital, Employee Matching Gifts, General Support, Project, Scholarship, Seed Money.

Donor Information

Founder: Ben Weingart (1888-1980) was a real estate developer in Southern California who helped create a new town, the City of Lakewood, during the 1950s. It was the first planned city in Southern California. Mr. Weingart was born in Atlanta, GA. He attended school through the eighth grade and arrived in Los Angeles when he was 18 years old.
The Weingart Foundation was established in California in 1951 as the B. W. Foundation. The name of the foundation was changed in April 1978. Funds for the foundation's incorporation were donated by the late Ben Weingart and Stella Weingart, who bequeathed their estates to the foundation.

Financial Summary

Total Giving: $36,079,626 (fiscal year ending June 30, 2003); $36,252,338 (fiscal 2002); $36,183,031 (fiscal 2001)
Assets: $678,478,745 (fiscal 2003); $675,000,000 (fiscal 2002); $779,796,365 (fiscal 2001)
Gifts Received: $50,000 (fiscal 1992 approx)

Typical Recipients

Arts & Humanities: Arts Centers, Arts Funds, Arts Institutes, Arts Outreach, Ballet, Ethnic & Folk Arts, Libraries, Museums/Galleries, Music, Performing Arts, Public Broadcasting, Theater
Civic & Public Affairs: African American Affairs, Clubs, Community Foundations, Civic & Public Affairs-General, Hispanic Affairs, Housing, Law & Justice, Philanthropic Organizations, Public Policy, Urban & Community Affairs, Zoos/Aquariums
Education: Afterschool/Enrichment Programs, Arts/Humanities Education, Business Education, Colleges & Universities, Community & Junior Colleges, Education Associations, Education Funds, Education Reform, Elementary Education (Private), Engineering/Technological Education, Faculty Development, Education-General, Leadership Training, Legal Education, Literacy, Medical Education, Minority Education, Preschool Education, Private Education (Precollege), Public Education (Precollege), Religious Education, School Volunteerism, Science/Mathematics Education, Secondary Education (Private), Secondary Education (Public), Social Sciences Education, Special Education, Student Aid, Vocational & Technical Education
Environment: Resource Conservation
Health: AIDS/HIV, Cancer, Children's Health/Hospitals, Clinics/Medical Centers, Diabetes, Emergency/Ambulance Services, Eyes/Blindness, Health-General, Health Funds, Health Organizations, Hospices, Hospitals, Long-Term Care, Medical Research, Mental Health, Nursing Services, Outpatient Health Care, Prenatal Health Issues, Preventive Medicine/Wellness Organizations, Public Health, Speech & Hearing
International: Foreign Educational Institutions, Missionary/Religious Activities
Religion: Dioceses, Jewish Causes, Religious Welfare, Synagogues/Temples
Science: Observatories & Planetariums, Science Museums, Scientific Centers & Institutes, Scientific Organizations
Social Services: Animal Protection, At-Risk Youth, Big Brothers/Big Sisters, Camps, Child Abuse, Child Welfare, Community Centers, Community Service Organizations, Counseling, Crime Prevention, Day Care, Delinquency & Criminal Rehabilitation, Domestic Violence, Emergency Relief, Family Services, Food/Clothing Distribution, Homes, People with Disabilities, Recreation & Athletics, Refugee Assistance, Scouts, Senior Services, Shelters/Homelessness, Social Services-General, Substance Abuse, Volunteer Services, YMCA/YWCA/YMHA/YWHA, Youth Organizations

Application Procedures

Initial Contact: A qualified organization that believes it meets the foundation's criteria for a grant should first submit a brief, to-the-point "test letter."
Application Requirements: The letter, not to exceed two pages, should contain a concise statement of the need for funds, amount sought, and enough factual information to enable the foundation to determine an initial response. Supporting data may be included. Three copies of the letter and one copy of supporting data are required. If the project meets the foundation's priorities, a formal application will be sent to the organization.
Deadlines: None.
Review Process: Final notification arrives three to four months after receiving the proposal.

Restrictions

The foundation does not make grants for propagandizing, influencing legislation and/or elections, promoting voter registration, for political candidates, political campaigns, or organizations engaged in political activities. The foundation does not make grants to federated appeals or to organizations that collect funds for redistribution to other nonprofit groups. It does not make grants for support of national charities, for operating budgets of agencies served by the United Way or other federated sources (except for approved special projects), for operating expenses of performing arts organizations, or for the benefit of individuals or small groups. The foundation does not consider requests for support of projects that normally would be financed from government funds. It ordinarily does not make grants for endowment funds, contingencies, or deficits. As a general rule, it does not make grants for conferences, seminars, workshops, exhibits, travel, medical research surveys, publishing activities, or films, nor does the foundation encourage applications for funding the projects of environmental, consumer, refugee, or religious programs; international organizations; or governmental or quasi-governmental agencies. The foundation does not approve grants for regular, ongoing, operating support. Applicant organizations must be tax-exempt under section 501(c)(3) of the IRS code.

Additional Information

The foundation expects applicant organizations to show project support from internal sources as well as outside sources. Grants may cover a multiyear period in some cases, but the foundation generally does not make a grant to any organization on an annual basis.
Publications: Annual Report; Guidelines; Application Procedures

Foundation Officials

Fred J. Ali: president, chief administrative officer
Andrew E. Bogen: director CORP AFFIL partner: Gibson, Dunn & Crutcher LLP. NONPR AFFIL member: California Bar Association; member: Los Angeles County Bar Association.
Steven D. Broidy: director B 1938. PRIM CORP EMPL vice chairman board, director: City National Bank. NONPR AFFIL life director: Independent Colleges of Southern California.
Rosa M. Castillo: program officer
Murray L. Galinson: director B Minneapolis, MN 1937. ED University of Minnesota (1958); United States International University (1976). PRIM CORP EMPL chairman, chief executive officer: San Diego National Bank. CORP AFFIL chairman, director: San Diego National Bank.
Deborah M. Ives: vice president, treasurer
Barbara Kaze: program officer
William D. Schulte: chairman, chief executive officer, director NONPR AFFIL director: Washington Mutual Inc..
Steven L. Soboroff: director CORP AFFIL president: Playa Vista. NONPR AFFIL chairman: Big Brothers of Greater Los Angeles.
Laurence A. Wolfe: vice president admin and real estate, secretary
Jerry C. Yu: program officer

Grants Analysis

Disclosure Period: fiscal year ending June 30, 2003
Total Grants: $36,079,626*
Number of Grants: 365
Average Grant: $98,848
Highest Grant: $2,000,000
Lowest Grant: $1,000
Typical Range: $10,000 to $200,000
*Note: Giving includes matching gifts.

Recent Grants

Note: Grants derived from fiscal 2003 Form 990.
General

2,000,000	Friends of the Observatory
1,500,000	Exposition Park Intergenerational Community Center, Los Angeles, CA
1,000,000	Accelerated School, Los Angeles, CA
1,000,000	Cedars-Sinai Medical Center, Los Angeles, CA
1,000,000	Exposition Park Intergenerational Community Center, Los Angeles, CA
1,000,000	Exposition Park Intergenerational Community Center, Los Angeles, CA
1,000,000	KCET Community Television of Southern California, Los Angeles, CA
1,000,000	Music Center, Los Angeles, CA
1,000,000	University of Southern California, Los Angeles, CA
750,000	HUC Skirball Cultural Center, Los Angeles, CA

J. WEINSTEIN FOUNDATION

Giving Contact

Salvatore Cappuzzo, Secretary & Treasurer
Rockridge Farm, Rte. 52
Carmel, NY 10512
Phone: (845)325-7647

Description

Founded: 1948
EIN: 116003595
Organization Type: Private Foundation
Giving Locations: CT; NY; TN
Grant Types: Endowment, General Support, Multiyear/Continuing Support, Research.

Donor Information

Founder: the late Joe Weinstein, J. W. Mays

Financial Summary

Total Giving: $279,525 (2003); $278,154 (2001)
Assets: $5,304,571 (2003); $4,964,419 (2001)
Gifts Received: $200,000 (2003); $50,000 (1993); $50,000 (1992). Note: In 2003, contributions were received from Weinstein Enterprises, Inc.

Typical Recipients

Arts & Humanities: Libraries, Museums/Galleries
Civic & Public Affairs: Civic & Public Affairs-General, Safety, Urban & Community Affairs, Women's Affairs
Education: Arts/Humanities Education, Colleges & Universities, Education-General, Medical Education, Private Education (Precollege), Secondary Education (Private), Special Education
Health: Cancer, Children's Health/Hospitals, Clinics/Medical Centers, Diabetes, Eyes/Blindness, Geriatric Health, Health Organizations, Hospitals, Hospitals (University Affiliated), Mental Health, Multiple Sclerosis, Research/Studies Institutes, Single-Disease Health Associations
International: Foreign Arts Organizations, Foreign Educational Institutions, International-General, Health Care/Hospitals, International Peace & Security Issues, Missionary/Religious Activities
Religion: Jewish Causes, Religious Organizations
Science: Science Museums, Scientific Centers & Institutes
Social Services: Animal Protection, At-Risk Youth, Camps, Community Service Organizations, Family Planning, People with Disabilities, Recreation & Athletics, Senior Services, Youth Organizations

Application Procedures

Initial Contact: Send a description of organization and the reason for request.
Deadlines: None.

Foundation Officials

Salvatore Cappuzzo: secretary, treasurer
Lloyd J. Shulman: president, director PRIM CORP EMPL president, chairman, director: J.W. Mays.
Sylvia W. Shulman: vice president, director B New York, NY 1918. ED Syracuse University. PRIM CORP EMPL director: J.W. Mays Inc. CORP AFFIL vice president, director: Weinstein Enterprises Inc.

Grants Analysis

Disclosure Period: calendar year ending 2003
Total Grants: $279,525
Number of Grants: 59
Average Grant: $2,664*
Highest Grant: $125,000
Lowest Grant: $100
Typical Range: $1,000 to $5,000
***Note:** Average grant figure excludes highest grant.

Recent Grants

Note: Grants derived from 2001 Form 990.
General

125,000	New York University Medical Center, New York, NY -- Department of Urology
30,000	New York Methodist Hospital, New York, NY
10,200	American Friends of the Israel Museum, New York, NY
10,000	Breast Cancer Research Foundation, New York, NY
10,000	Ethical Fieldstone Fund, New York, NY
10,000	Memorial Sloan-Kettering Cancer Center, New York, NY
10,000	Temple Beth Shalom, Mahopac, NY
5,500	Brookdale Center on Aging, New York, NY
5,000	American Committee for the Weizmann Institute, New York, NY
5,000	Lighthouse, Inc., New York, NY

CANDACE KING WEIR FOUNDATION

Giving Contact

Candace K. Weir, Trustee
c/o C. L. King & Assocs.
9 Elk St.
Albany, NY 12207
Phone: (518)431-3500

Description

Founded: 1994
EIN: 133797919
Organization Type: Private Foundation
Grant Types: General Support.

Financial Summary

Total Giving: $505,700 (2003); $512,950 (2001)
Assets: $11,786,632 (2003); $10,720,741 (2001)
Gifts Received: $999,750 (2001); $1,099,936 (1999); $1,000,000 (1998). Note: In 1998, 1999, and 2001, contributions were received from Candace K. Weir.

Typical Recipients

Arts & Humanities: Arts Institutes, Arts & Humanities-General, Historic Preservation, Libraries, Literary Arts, Museums/Galleries, Public Broadcasting, Theater
Civic & Public Affairs: Botanical Gardens/Parks, Community Foundations, Economic Development, Civic & Public Affairs-General, Urban & Community Affairs
Education: Colleges & Universities, Medical Education, Private Education (Precollege)
Environment: Environment-General, Resource Conservation
Health: Alzheimer's Disease, Clinics/Medical Centers, Hospitals, Medical Research
Religion: Churches, Dioceses, Religious Organizations, Religious Welfare
Social Services: Camps, Community Service Organizations

Application Procedures

Initial Contact: Send letter with supporting attachments to fully disclose charitable purpose of applicant.
Deadlines: None.

Foundation Officials

Meredith M. Prime: trustee
Amelia F. Weir: trustee
Candace K. Weir: trustee

Grants Analysis

Disclosure Period: calendar year ending 2003
Total Grants: $505,700
Number of Grants: 78
Average Grant: $1,886*
Highest Grant: $101,000
Lowest Grant: $100
Typical Range: $500 to $5,000
***Note:** Average grant figure excludes five highest grants ($368,000).

Recent Grants

Note: Grants derived from 2003 Form 990.
General

101,000	Albany Institute of History and Art, Albany, NY
100,000	Albany Medical Center, Albany, NY
67,000	Albany Academy for Girls, Albany, NY
50,000	Albany Catholic Diocese, Albany, NY
50,000	Nature Conservancy, Block Island, RI
10,000	National Public Radio Inc., Washington, DC
10,000	National Trust for Historic Preservation in the United States, Washington, DC
10,000	Yaddo, Saratoga Springs, NY

7,750	Greater Loudonville Association, Loudonville, NY
5,000	Block Island Conservancy, Block Island, RI

WILLIAM E. WEISS FOUNDATION

Giving Contact

Daryl Brown-Uber, President
PO Box 14270
Jackson, WY 83002
Phone: (307)739-8338

Description

Founded: 1955
EIN: 556016633
Organization Type: Private Foundation
Giving Locations: CT; DC: Washington; MT; NY; WV; WY
Grant Types: Capital, General Support, Multiyear/Continuing Support, Project, Scholarship.

Donor Information

Founder: the late William E. Weiss, Jr., the late Helene K Brown

Financial Summary

Total Giving: $409,500 (fiscal year ending March 31, 2004); $512,750 (fiscal 2002); $536,300 (fiscal 2001)
Assets: $9,461,779 (fiscal 2004); $10,761,879 (fiscal 2002); $10,562,296 (fiscal 2001)

Typical Recipients

Arts & Humanities: Arts Associations & Councils, Arts Centers, Dance, Historic Preservation, History & Archaeology, Libraries, Museums/Galleries, Music, Visual Arts
Civic & Public Affairs: Botanical Gardens/Parks, Clubs, Civic & Public Affairs-General, Philanthropic Organizations, Safety, Urban & Community Affairs, Women's Affairs, Zoos/Aquariums
Education: Colleges & Universities, Elementary Education (Public), Education-General, Literacy, Minority Education, Preschool Education, Private Education (Precollege), Public Education (Precollege), Science/Mathematics Education, Secondary Education (Private)
Environment: Air/Water Quality, Environment-General, Research, Resource Conservation
Health: Cancer, Emergency/Ambulance Services, Health Organizations, Hospitals, Mental Health
Religion: Churches, Religious Organizations, Religious Welfare
Social Services: Child Abuse, Child Welfare, Community Service Organizations, Domestic Violence, Food/Clothing Distribution, Recreation & Athletics, Shelters/Homelessness, Substance Abuse, United Funds/United Ways, Youth Organizations

Application Procedures

Initial Contact: Send a brief letter of inquiry.
Deadlines: in November.

Foundation Officials

Dwyer Brown: treasurer
Monte T. Brown: vice president
Daryl Brown Uber: president
William D. Weiss: secretary
William U. Weiss: secretary

Grants Analysis

Disclosure Period: fiscal year ending March 31, 2004
Total Grants: $409,500
Number of Grants: 23
Average Grant: $15,932*

Highest Grant: $59,000
Lowest Grant: $2,500
Typical Range: $5,000 to $25,000
*Note: Average grant figure excludes highest grant.

Recent Grants

Note: Grants derived from 2004 Form 990.
General

59,000	Miss Porter's School, Farmington, CT -- for athletic program
33,000	Delta Society, Renton, WA -- for 5 yrs capital construction
32,500	Museum of City of New York, New York, NY -- for city resilient exhibit
25,000	Ganna Walska Lotusland, Santa Barbara, CA -- for kitchen renovation
25,000	Hotchkiss School, Lakeville, CT -- for music and art initiative
25,000	Randall Museum Friends, San Francisco, CA
25,000	Santa Barbara Bowl Foundation, Santa Barbara, CA -- for safety handrails
23,000	Golden Gate National Parks Association, San Francisco, CA
20,000	Memphis Child Advocacy Center, Memphis, TN -- for forensic interview program
20,000	St. Mary's Episcopal School, Memphis, TN -- Willmott gymnasium divider at Lower

GEORGE T. WELCH TESTAMENTARY TRUST

Giving Contact

Sandra Bradley, Trust Officer
c/o Baker Boyer National Bank
PO Box 1796
Walla Walla, WA 99362
Phone: (509)525-2000

Description

Founded: 1938
EIN: 916024318
Organization Type: Private Foundation
Giving Locations: WA: Walla Walla
Grant Types: Project, Scholarship.

Financial Summary

Total Giving: $173,801 (fiscal year ending September 30, 2004); $225,198 (fiscal 2002). Note: Fiscal 1997 Giving includes scholarship ($91,832), United Way ($2,000).
Giving Analysis: Giving for fiscal 2004 includes: foundation gifts to individuals ($110,927); fiscal 2002: foundation grants to United Way ($4,000); foundation gifts to individuals ($65,971); foundation scholarships ($75,666)
Assets: $4,097,984 (fiscal 2004); $3,598,492 (fiscal 2002)
Gifts Received: $140 (fiscal 1996); $1,000 (fiscal 1993). Note: In fiscal 1993, contributions were received from Dennis K. L. Kinc.

Typical Recipients

Arts & Humanities: Arts Associations & Councils, Arts Centers, Community Arts, Dance, Arts & Humanities-General, Historic Preservation, Libraries, Museums/Galleries, Music
Civic & Public Affairs: Civic & Public Affairs-General, Housing, Parades/Festivals, Urban & Community Affairs
Education: Afterschool/Enrichment Programs, Arts/Humanities Education, Colleges & Universities, Community & Junior Colleges, Education-General, Gifted & Talented Programs, Literacy, Public Education (Precollege), Student Aid, Vocational & Technical Education

Health: AIDS/HIV, Clinics/Medical Centers, Emergency/Ambulance Services, Hospices, Hospitals, Nursing Services, Prenatal Health Issues
Religion: Religious Welfare
Science: Science Museums
Social Services: Animal Protection, At-Risk Youth, Camps, Child Abuse, Child Welfare, Community Centers, Community Service Organizations, Day Care, Domestic Violence, Family Planning, Food/Clothing Distribution, Homes, Recreation & Athletics, Senior Services, Shelters/Homelessness, YMCA/YWCA/YMHA/YWHA, Youth Organizations

Application Procedures

Initial Contact: Send an application letter stating academic plans or other need and statement of resources and expenses. Deadlines for medical requests are February 20, May 20, August 20, and November 20; for academic requests, May 1; and for community requests, July 31.

Additional Information

Provides educational grants to students in the Walla Walla, WA, area.
Publications: Application Guidelines
Trust(s): Baker Boyer Natl Bank

Grants Analysis

Disclosure Period: fiscal year ending September 30, 2004
Total Grants: $62,874*
Number of Grants: 23
Average Grant: $4,038
Highest Grant: $9,624
Lowest Grant: $1,500
Typical Range: $1,000 to $5,000
*Note: Giving excludes gifts to individuals.

Recent Grants

Note: Grants derived from fiscal 2004 Form 990.
General

10,000	Northwest Medical Teams, Portland, OR -- for dental work in community
9,624	Walla Walla Community College, Walla Walla, WA -- towards adult vocational grant
7,000	Walla Walla Family YMCA, Walla Walla, WA
4,000	Camp Fire USA - Walla Walla Council, Kansas City, MO -- after school and super summer programs
3,400	Walla Walla Court Appointed Special Advocates Association, Walla Walla, WA
3,050	St. Mary Medical Center, Walla Walla, WA -- for breast cancer screening for low income women
3,000	Friends of Children of Walla Walla, Walla Walla, WA -- support for volunteer screening
3,000	Helpline -- budget assistance and bill paying for low-income families
3,000	Mac - Hi Track Renovation Committee -- for resurface track
3,000	Walla Walla American Legion Baseball, Walla Walla, WA -- van for game travel

WELFARE FOUNDATION

Giving Contact

Peter C. Morrow, Executive Secretary
100 W. 10th Street, Suite 1109
Wilmington, DE 19801
Phone: (302)654-2477
Fax: (302)654-2323

Description

Founded: 1930
EIN: 516015916

Organization Type: General Purpose Foundation
Giving Locations: DE: Wilmington including surrounding communities; PA: Southern Chester County
Grant Types: Capital, General Support, Project, Seed Money.

Donor Information

Founder: Established in 1930 by the late Pierre Samuel du Pont(d. 1954) to support initial plans for a public secondary school system. When that project was completed, the foundation turned its support to the community at large.
Du Pont family members are the descendants of Pierre Samuel du Pont de Nemours (1739-1817), a Frenchman who emigrated to America in 1800. His son, Eleuthere Irenee, founded a gunpowder factory in 1801 which was the precursor to E. I. du Pont de Nemours & Company, a manufacturer of chemicals, plastics, fibers, and specialty products. Edward B. du Pont, a treasurer of the foundation, is a director of the company.

Financial Summary

Total Giving: $4,833,792 (2003); $4,424,665 (2002); $5,384,250 (2001)
Giving Analysis: Giving for 2003 includes: foundation grants to United Way ($170,000); 2002: foundation grants to United Way ($170,000)
Assets: $128,440,182 (2003); $107,597,802 (2002); $100,158,566 (2001)

Typical Recipients

Arts & Humanities: Arts Centers, Arts Funds, Arts Institutes, Ballet, Arts & Humanities-General, Historic Preservation, History & Archaeology, Libraries, Museums/Galleries, Music, Opera, Public Broadcasting, Theater, Visual Arts
Civic & Public Affairs: African American Affairs, Botanical Gardens/Parks, Community Foundations, Economic Development, Employment/Job Training, Civic & Public Affairs-General, Housing, Law & Justice, Municipalities/Towns, Nonprofit Management, Public Policy, Rural Affairs, Urban & Community Affairs, Zoos/Aquariums
Education: Afterschool/Enrichment Programs, Arts/Humanities Education, Colleges & Universities, Community & Junior Colleges, Economic Education, Education Funds, Environmental Education, Education-General, Legal Education, Literacy, Medical Education, Minority Education, Preschool Education, Private Education (Precollege), Public Education (Precollege), Science/Mathematics Education, Secondary Education (Private), Special Education, Student Aid
Environment: Air/Water Quality, Forestry, Environment-General, Research, Resource Conservation, Watershed, Wildlife Protection
Health: AIDS/HIV, Cancer, Children's Health/Hospitals, Clinics/Medical Centers, Emergency/Ambulance Services, Health Funds, Health Organizations, Hospices, Hospitals, Long-Term Care, Nursing Services, Prenatal Health Issues, Preventive Medicine/Wellness Organizations, Public Health, Single-Disease Health Associations
Religion: Churches, Religion-General, Ministries, Religious Organizations, Religious Welfare
Science: Science Museums, Scientific Centers & Institutes, Scientific Research
Social Services: Animal Protection, At-Risk Youth, Camps, Child Welfare, Community Centers, Community Service Organizations, Counseling, Crime Prevention, Day Care, Family Planning, Family Services, Food/Clothing Distribution, Homes, People with Disabilities, Recreation & Athletics, Scouts, Senior Services, Shelters/Homelessness, Social Services-General, Special Olympics, Substance Abuse, United Funds/United Ways, YMCA/YWCA/YMHA/YWHA, Youth Organizations

Application Procedures

Initial Contact: Applicants should send a request to the foundation.

Application Requirements: Two page letters should state the reason for the grant request, and include pertinent financial statements, an annual report, and a copy of an IRS tax-exempt status letter.
Deadlines: April 15 and October 15.

Restrictions

The foundation only makes grants to non-profit organizations in Delaware and the greater Wilmington area.

Foundation Officials

Robert H. Bolling: trustee
Robert H. Bolling, Jr.: vice president, trustee ED Princeton University (1948). CORP AFFIL director: Wilmington Trust Co.
J. Simpson Dean, Jr.: vice president, trustee
E. Bradford du Pont, Jr.: trustee
Edward Bradford du Pont: president, trustee B Wilmington, DE 1934. ED Yale University ED (1956); Harvard University MBA (1959). PRIM CORP EMPL chairman, director: Atlantic Aviation Corp. CORP AFFIL treasurer: Christiana Care Health Services. NONPR AFFIL life trustee: Pomfret School; treasurer: Wilmington Library.
Leatrice D. Ellman: secretary, trustee
Stephen A. Martinenza: assistant treasurer, assistant secretary
Peter C. Morrow: executive director PRIM CORP EMPL manager corporate contributions, executive secretary contributions committee: E.I. du Pont de Nemours & Co. NONPR AFFIL director: Delaware State Chamber of Commerce.
W. Laird Stabler, III: treasurer, trustee
Mrs. W. Laird Stabler, Jr.: trustee

Grants Analysis

Disclosure Period: calendar year ending 2003
Total Grants: $4,663,792*
Number of Grants: 69
Average Grant: $58,564*
Highest Grant: $440,000
Lowest Grant: $300
Typical Range: $25,000 to $100,000
***Note:** Giving excludes United Way. Average grant figure excludes two highest grants ($740,000).

Recent Grants

Note: Grants derived from 2003 Form 990.

General

300,000	Easter Seals Delaware and Maryland's Eastern Shore, New Castle, DE
250,000	Delaware College of Art and Design (DCAD), Wilmington, DE -- fund for building renovations
250,000	Girl Scouts of the Chesapeake Bay Council, Wilmington, DE -- fund for camp renovations
250,000	St Andrew's School, Middletown, DE -- fund for arts center construction
200,000	Bayhealth Medical Center Foundation, Dover, DE -- fund for facility renovation and construction
200,000	Wilmington Friends School, Wilmington, DE -- fund for construction/facility renovation
150,000	Innovative Schools Development Corporation, Wilmington, DE -- loan guarantee fund
145,000	United Way of Delaware, Wilmington, DE
125,000	Ronald McDonald House, Wilmington, DE
100,000	Buttonwood Civic Association, New Castle, DE -- fund for building renovations

WELLMARK BLUE CROSS AND BLUE SHIELD OF IOWA

Company Headquarters

636 Grand Ave.
Des Moines, IA 50309

Company Description

Former Name: Blue Cross & Blue Shield of Iowa.
Employees: 2,000
SIC(s): 6321 Accident & Health Insurance, 6324 Hospital & Medical Service Plans.

Wellmark Foundation

Giving Contact

Dr. Sheila Riggs, Executive Director
Wellmark Foundation
636 Grand Avenue, Station 150
Des Moines, IA 50309-2502
Phone: (515)245-4706
Fax: (515)235-4445
E-mail: wmfoundation@wellmark.com
Web: http://www.wellmark.com/community/wellmark_foundation/wellmark_foundation.htm

Alternate Contact

Helen Hoftiezer, Team Leader, Medical Management
Phone: (605)362-5497
E-mail: hoftiezer@wellmark.com
Note: Alternate information is for South Dakota.

Description

Founded: 1991
EIN: 421368650
Organization Type: Corporate Foundation
Giving Locations: IA; SD
Grant Types: General Support, Seed Money.

Donor Information

Founder: Established in 1991 by Blue Cross and Blue Shield of Iowa.

Financial Summary

Total Giving: $1,004,492 (2002); $1,177,149 (2001). Note: Contributes through foundation only.
Giving Analysis: Giving for 2001 includes: foundation grants to United Way ($245,113)
Assets: $18,604,946 (2002); $16,882,705 (2001)
Gifts Received: $4,563,328 (2002); $4,336,910 (2001); $4,204,602 (2000). Note: After 1999, contributions were received from Wellmark, Inc. In 1996, contributions were received from Blue Cross and Blue Shield of Iowa.

Typical Recipients

Arts & Humanities: Arts Centers, Libraries, Music, Opera, Theater
Civic & Public Affairs: Clubs, Civic & Public Affairs-General, Public Policy, Rural Affairs, Safety, Women's Affairs, Zoos/Aquariums
Education: Afterschool/Enrichment Programs, Agricultural Education, Business Education, Colleges & Universities, Education Funds, Education-General, Medical Education, Preschool Education, Public Education (Precollege), Student Aid
Environment: Resource Conservation
Health: Alzheimer's Disease, Arthritis, Cancer, Children's Health/Hospitals, Clinics/Medical Centers, Diabetes, Emergency/Ambulance Services, Eyes/Blindness, Health-General, Health Funds, Health Organizations, Home-Care Services, Hospices, Hospitals, Hospitals (University Affiliated), Mental Health, Multiple Sclerosis, Nursing Services, Prenatal Health Issues, Preventive Medicine/Wellness Organizations, Public Health, Respiratory

Religion: Religious Organizations, Religious Welfare
Social Services: Child Abuse, Child Welfare, Community Service Organizations, Counseling, Day Care, Domestic Violence, Family Planning, Family Services, Food/Clothing Distribution, People with Disabilities, Recreation & Athletics, Scouts, Senior Services, Social Services-General, Substance Abuse, United Funds/United Ways, YMCA/YWCA/YMHA/YWHA, Youth Organizations

Application Procedures

Initial Contact: See foundation website for detailed application information. Submit a written proposal of ten pages or less. Proposals should be one-sided, 11 point type face or larger, and unbound. The foundation requests one original and 8 copies of the proposal.
Application Requirements: Proposals should include the following information. Cover Page: Agency Information, including primary agency name, address, phone, fax number; contact name, title, and phone number; and other involved entities and contacts. Project Page (1 page): including project name, a project description paragraph (50 words or less), and project abstract (500 words or less). Problem Statement (1-2 pages): statement of need, population served and demographics, and geographic area served. Goals and Measurable Objectives (1-2 pages): including outcome measure, timeline and work plan. Evaluation: include process measures and outcome measures. Budget: include budget narrative and explanation, and sustainability plan for after Wellmark funding ceases.
Proposals must also include two appendices. Appendix 1, 501(c)(3) Organization: must include the organization's IRS letter, recent audited financial statement, and board of directors list. Appendix 2, Grant Appendix must contain letters of support, staff credentials, and any other support documents. Include both appendices in the original proposal only.
Deadlines: First cycle: February 21. Second cycle: June 26. Third cycle: and August 25.
Review Process: Proposals are evaluated by a committee of community health stakeholders and Wellmark staff using a scoring tool. Scoring is divided into sections, with some sections weighted more heavily than others. For objective criteria, Description of Need: 20 points maximum; Project Design: 25 points maximum; Feasibility: 20 points maximum; Community Involvement: 10 points maximum; Portability: 5 points maximum. For subjective criteria, Value if idea: 5 points maximum; Mix of Funded Grants: 5 points maximum; Cutting Edge/Learning Opportunity: 5 points maximum; Meets the Foundation High Priority Criteria: 5 points maximum. Total possible score is 100.
Evaluative Criteria: Proposals are evaluated based on the following criteria: Need/Relevance, with a demonstration of population's need and prevalence; Project Design, including a scientifically sound proposal, and a program that will generate results that are reproducible, valid, accurate, and can be evaluated; Feasibility, meaning that the project is "do-able," that the activities involved must be detailed in a manner that allows for evaluation, that services must be offered at a reasonable cost, and that patient confidentiality is protected; Portability, so that the program, though aimed at a specific community or population, can be replicated in other areas; Community Involvement, demonstrating broadly-based community involvement, partnerships, coalitions, and collaborations; and Staff Credentials, including education, training, and experience of project manager/coordinators and key personnel.
Decision Notification: Grants approved by the board are disbursed in June 1 for the first cycle, October 1 for the second cycle.
Notes: A postcard is sent to applicant within one week of submission deadline to confirm receipt of proposal.

Additional Information

The foundation hosts grant conferences in both Iowa and South Dakota at least 30 days prior to each submission deadline to review the foundation's guidelines and answer questions relating to the application process. Contact the foundation or visit the foundation's website for additional information.
Publications: Grant Guidelines

Foundation Officials

Rich Anderson: treasurer
John D. Forsyth: chairman ADD CORP EMPL lecturer: School Public Health; executive director, department executive, chief operating officer: University Michigan Hospital. NONPR AFFIL director: United Way; member advisory committee: University Alabama Birmingham Hospitals; director: PPO Michigan; member: Leadership Giving Committee; member: National Association State Universities & Land-Grant Colleges; Greater Detroit Area Health Council; member: Association American Universities; director: Detroit Board Federation Reserve Bank Chicago; member: Association American Medicine Colleges Council Teaching Hospitals; member: American Council Education; member: Ann Arbor Chamber of Commerce.
Janet Griffin: secretary

Grants Analysis

Disclosure Period: calendar year ending 2002
Total Grants: $754,492*
Number of Grants: 32
Average Grant: $23,578
Highest Grant: $58,000
Lowest Grant: $800
Typical Range: $7,000 to $50,000
*Note: Giving excludes United Way.

Recent Grants

Note: Grants derived from 2003 Form 990.
General

224,460	United Way of Central Iowa, Des Moines, IA -- towards agency payments in Iowa and South Dakota
58,000	St. Mary's Foundation, Pierre, SD -- towards the South Dakota frontier school health initiative
50,000	Mid Iowa Community Action, Marshalltown, IA -- towards the Searching for the Miles of Smiles project
46,533	OSACS Womens Center, Des Moines, IA -- towards the heart and hand center clinic expansion
44,630	Siouxland Human Investment Partnership, Sioux City, IA -- towards the tobacco cessation program
42,337	Washington County Public Health, Washington, IA -- towards the healthy kids dental program
38,336	Youth & Family Services, Rapid City, IA -- towards boys health advocacy program
32,705	University of Northern Iowa, Cedar Falls, IA -- towards the Meskwaki Dental PRIDE initiative
29,400	Proteus Inc., Des Moines, IA -- towards Latino diabetes promontory nutrition and health project
29,300	Iowa Department of Public Health, Des Moines, IA -- towards the Iowa covering kids project

WELLS FARGO BANK NEBRASKA, N.A.

Company Headquarters

1919 Douglas St., Ste. 1
Omaha, NE 68102

Phone: (402)536-2329
Fax: (402)536-2812

Company Description

Employees: 800
SIC(s): 6021 National Commercial Banks.
Parent Company: Wells Fargo & Co., 420 Montgomery Street, San Francisco, CA, United States

Operating Locations

Northwest Bank Nebraska, NA (NE--Omaha)

Nonmonetary Support

Type: Donated Equipment; Donated Products; Loaned Executives; Workplace Solicitation

Giving Contact

Jane Braden, Contributions Administrator
1919 Douglas Street, MAC N8000-020
Omaha, NE 68103
Phone: (402)536-2650
Fax: (402)536-2509
E-mail: Jane.Braden@wellsfargo.com

Description

Organization Type: Corporate Giving Program
Giving Locations: operating communities.
Grant Types: Capital, Employee Matching Gifts, General Support, Project, Scholarship.

Financial Summary

Total Giving: $1,000,000 (2005 approx); $1,000,000 (2004); $650,000 (2003). Note: Contributes through corporate direct giving program only.

Typical Recipients

Arts & Humanities: Arts Associations & Councils, Arts Festivals, Arts Funds, Community Arts, Dance, Libraries, Music, Performing Arts, Theater, Visual Arts
Civic & Public Affairs: Economic Development, Housing, Philanthropic Organizations, Zoos/Aquariums
Education: Agricultural Education, Colleges & Universities, Community & Junior Colleges, Education Funds, Elementary Education (Private), Public Education (Precollege), Religious Education
Health: Health Organizations, Mental Health, Public Health, Single-Disease Health Associations
Religion: Religious Welfare
Social Services: Child Welfare, Community Centers, Counseling, Family Planning, Food/Clothing Distribution, Homes, People with Disabilities, Recreation & Athletics, United Funds/United Ways, Youth Organizations

Application Procedures

Initial Contact: Send a brief letter of inquiry.
Application Requirements: Include a description of organization; proof of tax-exempt status; list of officers and board members; statement outlining the purpose, including timeline and evaluation methods; complete budget for organization or project, including breakdown of programs and administrative expenses; list of contributors and amounts received in current and past year; and a financial statement.
Deadlines: None.
Evaluative Criteria: Organization's responsiveness to community, staff capability, financial management, commitment of board members and volunteers, performance against objectives, internal evaluation process, duplication with existing programs, and stability and range of funding sources.
Decision Notification: Board meets on the last Monday of each month; checks, requests for more information, or letters of refusal are sent within seven to 10 days after proposal is reviewed.

Corporate Officials

Jane Braden: coordinator PRIM CORP EMPL coordinator: Norwest Bank of Nebraska.

FRANKLIN H. AND RUTH L. WELLS FOUNDATION

Giving Contact

Miles J. Gibbons, Jr., Executive Director
4718 Old Gettysburg Rd, Suite 209
Mechanicsburg, PA 17055-8411
Phone: (717)763-1157
Fax: (717)763-1832

Description

Founded: 1983
EIN: 222541749
Organization Type: Private Foundation
Giving Locations: PA: Cumberland County, Dauphin County, Perry County
Grant Types: Emergency, General Support, Project, Seed Money.

Donor Information

Founder: Ruth L. Wells Annuity Trust, Frank Wells Marital Trust

Financial Summary

Total Giving: $212,550 (fiscal year ending May 31, 2004); $238,550 (fiscal 2002); $210,873 (fiscal 2001)
Assets: $5,371,937 (fiscal 2004); $5,543,352 (fiscal 2002); $6,272,158 (fiscal 2001)
Gifts Received: $97,324 (fiscal 1994); $195,898 (fiscal 1992). Note: In fiscal 1994, contributions were received from Ruth L. Wells Charitable Lead Trust.

Typical Recipients

Arts & Humanities: Arts Associations & Councils, Arts Festivals, Community Arts, Arts & Humanities-General, History & Archaeology, Libraries, Museums/Galleries, Music, Opera, Theater
Civic & Public Affairs: Clubs, Community Foundations, Employment/Job Training, Civic & Public Affairs-General, Hispanic Affairs, Housing, Legal Aid, Urban & Community Affairs
Education: Arts/Humanities Education, Business Education, Colleges & Universities, Community & Junior Colleges, Education Funds, Engineering/Technological Education, Environmental Education, Education-General, Leadership Training, Literacy, Medical Education, Minority Education, Private Education (Precollege), Science/Mathematics Education, Special Education
Environment: Resource Conservation, Wildlife Protection
Health: Cancer, Children's Health/Hospitals, Clinics/Medical Centers, Emergency/Ambulance Services, Health Organizations, Hospices, Hospitals, Medical Research, Mental Health, Single-Disease Health Associations
Religion: Ministries, Religious Organizations, Religious Welfare
Science: Science Museums
Social Services: Big Brothers/Big Sisters, Child Welfare, Community Service Organizations, Delinquency & Criminal Rehabilitation, Domestic Violence, Family Planning, Family Services, Food/Clothing Distribution, People with Disabilities, Scouts, Substance Abuse, United Funds/United Ways, Volunteer Services, YMCA/YWCA/YMHA/YWHA, Youth Organizations

Application Procedures

Initial Contact: Submit a brief letter of inquiry stating purpose and goals.
Deadlines: None.

Restrictions

Does not provide support for religious activities, operating expenses, endowments, or debts.

Additional Information

Trust(s): M & T Trust Co.

Grants Analysis

Disclosure Period: fiscal year ending May 31, 2004
Total Grants: $212,550
Number of Grants: 37
Average Grant: $5,745
Highest Grant: $35,000
Lowest Grant: $250
Typical Range: $1,000 to $10,000

Recent Grants

Note: Grants derived from 2004 Form 990.
General

35,000	Messiah College, Grantham, PA
25,000	Allegheny College, Meadville, PA
25,000	Tri State University, Angola, IN
19,000	YWCA of Greater Harrisburg, Harrisburg, PA
14,550	Big Brothers/Big Sisters of Capital Region, Harrisburg, PA
10,250	Greater Harrisburg Foundation, Harrisburg, PA
10,000	Gaudenzia Inc., Norristown, PA
10,000	Mission of Mercy, Colorado Springs, CO
10,000	Penn State College of Medicine, Hershey, PA
8,500	Hawk Mountain Sanctuary Association, Kempton, PA

WELSH FAMILY FOUNDATION

Giving Contact

Patrick J. Welsh, Trustee
3 Essex Road
Summit, NJ 07901

Description

Founded: 1996
EIN: 223331136
Organization Type: Private Foundation
Giving Locations: nationally.
Grant Types: General Support.

Donor Information

Founder: Established in 1996 by Patrick J. Welsh.

Financial Summary

Total Giving: $482,000 (2003); $557,000 (2001)
Assets: $6,632,843 (2003); $7,040,807 (2001)
Gifts Received: $850,725 (2003); $3,284,299 (1996); $3,371,342 (1994). Note: In 2003, contributions were received from Patrick J. Welsh. In 1996, contributions were received from Patrick J. and Carol A. Welsh.

Typical Recipients

Arts & Humanities: Arts Associations & Councils, Arts & Humanities-General, Libraries, Music
Civic & Public Affairs: Civic & Public Affairs-General, Housing
Education: Arts/Humanities Education, Colleges & Universities, Education-General, Public Education (Precollege), Secondary Education (Public), Special Education, Student Aid
Environment: Environment-General
Health: Cancer, Children's Health/Hospitals, Heart, Hospitals, Medical Rehabilitation, Single-Disease Health Associations, Speech & Hearing
International: Missionary/Religious Activities
Religion: Religious Welfare
Social Services: Child Welfare, Community Service Organizations, Food/Clothing Distribution, United Funds/United Ways, YMCA/YWCA/YMHA/YWHA, Youth Organizations

Application Procedures

Initial Contact: Send a brief letter of inquiry.
Deadlines: None.

Foundation Officials

Carol A. Welsh: trustee
Eric A. Welsh: trustee
Patrick J. Welsh: trustee

Grants Analysis

Disclosure Period: calendar year ending 2003
Total Grants: $482,000
Number of Grants: 9
Average Grant: $15,286*
Highest Grant: $300,000
Lowest Grant: $1,000
Typical Range: $5,000 to $50,000
*****Note:** Average grant figure excludes two highest grants ($375,000).

Recent Grants

Note: Grants derived from 2003 Form 990.
General

300,000	PEP Foundation Inc., Summit, NJ -- for education & assimilation into society of disadvantaged youths
75,000	Dr. Nadler Cancercare Fund -- for furtherance of cancer research studies
50,000	Learning Circle -- for education of disadvantaged children
25,000	National Interfaith Fellowship -- for advancement of interfaith understanding
20,000	Bravo Colorado, CO -- for fine arts
5,000	House Ear Institute, Los Angeles, CA -- for the assistance of the hearing impaired
5,000	Newark Boys Choir, Newark, NJ -- for furtherance of fine arts in inner city neighborhoods
1,000	Make A Wish Foundation, Phoenix, AZ -- for the care of cancer stricken children
1,000	National Children's Cancer Foundation -- for the use of cancer care studies

MARGARET L. WENDT FOUNDATION

Giving Contact

Robert J. Kresse, Secretary & Trustee
40 Fountain Plaza, Suite 277
Buffalo, NY 14202-2220
Phone: (716)855-2146
Fax: (716)855-2149

Description

Founded: 1955
EIN: 166030037
Organization Type: General Purpose Foundation
Giving Locations: NY: Western New York state, Buffalo
Grant Types: Capital, Challenge, General Support, Operating Expenses, Project, Research, Seed Money.

Donor Information

Founder: Established in 1955, with funds donated by the late Margaret L. Wendt. The assets of the foundation more than doubled in the period between 1975 and 1980 because of the final distribution of Miss Wendt's bequest.

Financial Summary

Total Giving: $5,358,865 (fiscal year ending January 31, 2003); $6,611,610 (fiscal 2002); $6,680,696 (fiscal 2001)
Giving Analysis: Giving for fiscal 2003 includes: foundation grants to United Way ($269,245); fiscal 2002: foundation grants to United Way ($193,000); fiscal 2001: foundation grants to United Way ($163,500)
Assets: $104,703,879 (fiscal 2003); $118,168,880 (fiscal 2002); $118,203,147 (fiscal 2001)

Typical Recipients

Arts & Humanities: Arts Associations & Councils, Arts Centers, Arts Institutes, Arts Outreach, Ballet, Dance, Film & Video, Arts & Humanities-General, Historic Preservation, History & Archaeology, Libraries, Literary Arts, Museums/Galleries, Music, Opera, Performing Arts, Public Broadcasting, Theater
Civic & Public Affairs: African American Affairs, Botanical Gardens/Parks, Community Foundations, Economic Development, Employment/Job Training, Civic & Public Affairs-General, Housing, Law & Justice, Legal Aid, Municipalities/Towns, Nonprofit Management, Urban & Community Affairs, Women's Affairs, Zoos/Aquariums
Education: Arts/Humanities Education, Colleges & Universities, Education Associations, Education Funds, Education Reform, Faculty Development, Education-General, Health & Physical Education, Literacy, Medical Education, Preschool Education, Private Education (Precollege), Public Education (Precollege), Science/Mathematics Education, Special Education, Student Aid
Environment: Air/Water Quality, Forestry, Environment-General, Resource Conservation, Wildlife Protection
Health: AIDS/HIV, Alzheimer's Disease, Cancer, Children's Health/Hospitals, Clinics/Medical Centers, Emergency/Ambulance Services, Health Funds, Health Organizations, Heart, Home-Care Services, Hospices, Hospitals, Long-Term Care, Medical Research, Mental Health, Nursing Services, Outpatient Health Care, Prenatal Health Issues, Research/Studies Institutes, Single-Disease Health Associations, Speech & Hearing
International: Foreign Arts Organizations, Human Rights, International Organizations, Trade
Religion: Churches, Jewish Causes, Ministries, Religious Organizations, Religious Welfare, Seminaries
Science: Science-General, Science Museums, Scientific Centers & Institutes, Scientific Organizations
Social Services: Animal Protection, Camps, Child Welfare, Community Centers, Community Service Organizations, Counseling, Day Care, Delinquency & Criminal Rehabilitation, Family Planning, Family Services, Food/Clothing Distribution, Homes, People with Disabilities, Recreation & Athletics, Scouts, Senior Services, Shelters/Homelessness, Social Services-General, Substance Abuse, United Funds/United Ways, YMCA/YWCA/YMHA/YWHA, Youth Organizations

Application Procedures

Initial Contact: Applicants should send four copies of a letter of request.
Application Requirements: Letters should include a description of the applicant organization, need or problem to be addressed, outline of the proposed project including total budget, specific amount requested, list of the board of directors, audited financial statements for the last three years, and the most recent copy of the organization's IRS determination letter of tax-exempt status.
Deadlines: Submit applications one month prior to the foundation's quarterly meetings.

Restrictions

Grants are not made to individuals.

Foundation Officials

Janet Loew Day: trustee
Robert J. Kresse: trustee PRIM CORP EMPL partner: Hiscock & Barclay. CORP AFFIL secretary: A. Lunt Design Inc.
Thomas D. Lunt: trustee PRIM CORP EMPL vice president: E. F. Hutton. CORP AFFIL vice president: A. Lunt Design Inc.

Grants Analysis

Disclosure Period: fiscal year ending January 31, 2003
Total Grants: $5,089,620*
Number of Grants: 136
Average Grant: $23,406*
Highest Grant: $500,000
Lowest Grant: $50
Typical Range: $5,000 to $50,000
***Note:** Giving excludes United Way. Average grant figure four excludes highest grants ($2,000,000).

Recent Grants

Note: Grants derived from 2003 Form 990.
General

500,000	Hauptman-Woodward Medical Research Institute Inc. (HWI), Buffalo, NY -- To construct and equip open laboratory study center
500,000	Roswell Park Cancer Institute, Buffalo, NY -- to support the new science research building
500,000	University at Buffalo Foundation Inc., Buffalo, NY -- to support excellence in bioinformatics
500,000	YMCA, Chicago, IL -- For the construction of the new full facility branch-
250,000	Boy Scouts of America, Charlotte, NC -- to purchase building for new school service center
250,000	Niagara Lutheran Health System, Buffalo, NY -- to support the Mother house quality care project
135,000	Studio Arena Theatre, Buffalo, NY -- to support the customer relations management software
105,000	United Way of Buffalo and Erie County, Buffalo, NY -- Annual grant
83,920	Boys and Girls Clubs of Buffalo Inc., Buffalo, NY -- To support the renovations and improvements to the Babcock clubhouse
70,375	Education Fund for Greater Buffalo, Buffalo, NY -- to support the expansion and continuation of the Parent - Liaison program

WESSINGER FOUNDATION

Giving Contact

PO Box 474
Portland, OR 97207
Phone: (503)227-2995
E-mail: wessinge@gosw.org
Web: http://www.gosw.org/wessinger

Description

Founded: 1979
EIN: 930754224
Organization Type: Private Foundation
Giving Locations: Pacific Northwest, with emphasis on the Tri-County area.
Grant Types: General Support.

Donor Information

Founder: Paul Wessinger Trust

Financial Summary

Total Giving: $440,056 (fiscal year ending September 30, 2004); $525,500 (fiscal 2001)
Assets: $7,933,182 (fiscal 2004); $7,223,522 (fiscal 2001)

Typical Recipients

Arts & Humanities: Arts Associations & Councils, Arts Festivals, Arts Institutes, Ballet, Ethnic & Folk Arts, Historic Preservation, History & Archaeology, Libraries, Literary Arts, Museums/Galleries, Music, Opera, Performing Arts, Public Broadcasting, The-

ater
Civic & Public Affairs: Botanical Gardens/Parks, Clubs, Community Foundations, Economic Development, Economic Policy, Civic & Public Affairs-General, Housing, Native American Affairs, Zoos/Aquariums
Education: Arts/Humanities Education, Colleges & Universities, Continuing Education, Education Funds, Medical Education, Minority Education, Preschool Education, Private Education (Precollege), Science/Mathematics Education
Environment: Air/Water Quality, Environment-General, Resource Conservation, Wildlife Protection
Health: AIDS/HIV, Cancer, Children's Health/Hospitals, Clinics/Medical Centers, Emergency/Ambulance Services, Health Funds, Health Organizations, Medical Rehabilitation, Mental Health, Public Health, Speech & Hearing
International: International Environmental Issues
Religion: Ministries, Religious Welfare
Science: Science Museums
Social Services: Animal Protection, At-Risk Youth, Child Welfare, Community Centers, Community Service Organizations, Family Planning, Family Services, Food/Clothing Distribution, People with Disabilities, Scouts, Shelters/Homelessness, Volunteer Services, YMCA/YWCA/YMHA/YWHA, Youth Organizations

Application Procedures

Initial Contact: Send a brief letter of inquiry.
Application Requirements: proof of tax-exempt status and a list of board members.
Deadlines: None.

Restrictions

Preference is given to educational, social welfare, medical, and artistic purposes.

Foundation Officials

Gainor W. Artz: chairman
Anna W. Boggess: director
Robert D. Geddes: secretary
Thomas B. Stoel: trustee emeritus
Julie Vigeland: trustee
E. Charles Wessinger: trustee
Henry W. Wessinger: treasurer
William W. Wessinger: trustee emeritus
Kathryn W. Withers: trustee

Grants Analysis

Disclosure Period: fiscal year ending September 30, 2004
Total Grants: $440,056
Number of Grants: 51
Average Grant: $7,801*
Highest Grant: $50,000
Lowest Grant: $306
Typical Range: $1,000 to $10,000
***Note:** Average grant figure excludes highest grant.

Recent Grants

Note: Grants derived from fiscal 2004 Form 990.
General

50,000	University of California, San Francisco Foundation, San Francisco, CA
30,000	Salvation Army Cascade Division, Portland, OR
25,000	Armory Theatre Fund, Portland, OR
25,000	Boys & Girls Aid Society of Oregon, Portland, OR
25,000	St. Mary's Home for Boys, Beaverton, OR
20,000	Marylhurst University, Marylhurst, OR
20,000	Salvation Army Cascade Division, Portland, OR
15,000	Oregon Children's Foundation, Portland, OR
15,000	St. Andrew Nativity School, Portland, OR
12,500	Planned Parenthood of the Columbia-Willamette, Portland, OR

WEST BEND MUTUAL INSURANCE CO.

Company Headquarters

1900 S. 18th Ave.
West Bend, WI 53095
Web: http://www.westbendmutual.com

Company Description

Founded: 1894

West Bend Mutual Charitable Trust

Giving Contact

John R. Dedrick, Trustee
West Bend Mutual Insurance Co.
1900 S. 18th Avenue
West Bend, WI 53095-8796
Phone: (414)334-5571

Description

Founded: 1994
EIN: 396591551
Organization Type: Corporate Foundation
Giving Locations: DC: Washington; MD; WI
Grant Types: General Support, Scholarship.

Financial Summary

Total Giving: $274,200 (2002); $297,744 (2001)
Giving Analysis: Giving for 2002 includes: foundation scholarships ($3,000); foundation grants to United Way ($36,000); 2001: foundation grants to United Way ($35,000)
Assets: $4,558,037 (2002); $5,498,278 (2001)

Typical Recipients

Arts & Humanities: Historic Preservation, History & Archaeology, Libraries, Museums/Galleries, Music, Opera, Performing Arts, Public Broadcasting
Civic & Public Affairs: Botanical Gardens/Parks, Chambers of Commerce, Community Foundations, Economic Development, Civic & Public Affairs-General, Hispanic Affairs, Housing, Inner-City Development, Municipalities/Towns, Parades/Festivals, Public Policy, Zoos/Aquariums
Education: Afterschool/Enrichment Programs, Business Education, Colleges & Universities, Education Funds, Education-General, Medical Education, Student Aid
Environment: Environment-General, Protection, Resource Conservation
Health: Cancer, Clinics/Medical Centers, Diabetes, Health-General, Heart, Hospitals, Multiple Sclerosis, Public Health, Transplant Networks/Donor Banks
Social Services: Animal Protection, Big Brothers/Big Sisters, Child Abuse, Domestic Violence, People with Disabilities, Recreation & Athletics, Scouts, United Funds/United Ways, YMCA/YWCA/YMHA/YWHA, Youth Organizations

Application Procedures

Initial Contact: Submit a written application.
Application Requirements: Include proof of tax-exempt status and non-private foundation status.

Foundation Officials

John R. Dedrick: trustee
John F. Duwell: trustee
James J. Pauly: trustee
Larry G. Roth: trustee
Anthony J. Warren: trustee
Sharon S. Ziegler: trustee

Grants Analysis

Disclosure Period: calendar year ending 2002
Total Grants: $235,200*

Number of Grants: 53
Average Grant: $4,438
Highest Grant: $27,500
Lowest Grant: $500
Typical Range: $1,000 to $10,000
*Note: Giving excludes United Way, scholarships.

Recent Grants

Note: Grants derived from 2003 Form 990.
General

36,000	United Way of Washington County, Washington, DC
27,500	Kettle Moraine YMCA, West Bend, WI
22,500	Ozaukee Washington Land Trust, West Bend, WI
21,500	Washington County Campus Scholarship, West Bend, WI
20,000	Saint Josephs Hospital, Chippewa Falls, WI
10,000	Wisconsin Foundation for Independent Colleges, Milwaukee, WI
7,500	Dr James Albrecht Free Clinic, West Bend, WI
6,000	Friends of Abused Families Inc., West Bend, WI
6,000	West Bend Art Museum, West Bend, WI
5,000	Cedar Lakes Conservation Foundation, West Bend, WI

HARRY AND ETHEL WEST FOUNDATION

Giving Contact

Richard G. McBurnie, Manager
PO Box 1825
Bakersfield, CA 93303
Phone: (661)873-0360
Fax: (661)873-0362

Description

Founded: 1972
EIN: 237168492
Organization Type: Private Foundation
Giving Locations: CA: Kern County
Grant Types: Capital, General Support.

Financial Summary

Total Giving: $234,933 (2003); $305,807 (2001)
Assets: $6,409,942 (2003); $5,304,825 (2001)

Typical Recipients

Arts & Humanities: Arts Associations & Councils, History & Archaeology, Libraries, Museums/Galleries, Music, Public Broadcasting, Theater
Civic & Public Affairs: Business/Free Enterprise, Clubs, Civic & Public Affairs-General, Hispanic Affairs, Law & Justice, Legal Aid, Native American Affairs, Public Policy, Rural Affairs, Safety, Urban & Community Affairs, Women's Affairs
Education: Colleges & Universities, Education-General, Legal Education, Literacy, Private Education (Precollege), Public Education (Precollege), Secondary Education (Private), Secondary Education (Public), Special Education
Environment: Environment-General, Research, Wildlife Protection
Health: Alzheimer's Disease, Arthritis, Cancer, Health-General, Health Organizations, Heart, Hospices, Hospitals, Medical Research, Single-Disease Health Associations, Transplant Networks/Donor Banks
Religion: Churches, Religious Welfare
Social Services: Animal Protection, At-Risk Youth, Camps, Child Welfare, Community Service Organizations, Counseling, Crime Prevention, Domestic Violence, Food/Clothing Distribution, Homes, People with Disabilities, Scouts, Senior Services, Shelters/

Homelessness, Social Services-General, Substance Abuse, Volunteer Services, YMCA/YWCA/YMHA/YWHA, Youth Organizations

Application Procedures

Initial Contact: Send a brief letter of inquiry.
Deadlines: None.

Restrictions

Generally grants are limited to Kern County, CA.

Foundation Officials

Richard G. McBurnie: president, chief executive officer
Mary C. Means: secretary
Silver D. Sack: director

Grants Analysis

Disclosure Period: calendar year ending 2003
Total Grants: $234,933
Number of Grants: 46
Average Grant: $4,369*
Highest Grant: $38,320
Lowest Grant: $179
Typical Range: $1,000 to $10,000
*Note: Average grant excludes highest grant.

Recent Grants

Note: Grants derived from 2001 Form 990.
General

31,500	Bakersfield College Foundation, Bakersfield, CA -- capital improvements
27,500	C. S. U. B., Bakersfield, CA -- capital improvements
20,500	Boys & Girls Club, Bakersfield, CA -- capital improvements
20,000	Houchin Blood Bank, Bakersfield, CA -- capital improvements
18,487	Hoffman Hospice, Bakersfield, CA -- capital improvements
17,500	Friends of Mercy Cancer, Bakersfield, CA -- capital improvements
11,700	MARE, Los Angeles, CA -- capital improvements
10,362	Kern High School District Education Foundation, Bakersfield, CA -- capital improvements
9,750	Alliance Against Family Violence, Bakersfield, CA -- capital improvements
8,300	Bright Beginnings Learning Center, Bakersfield, CA -- capital improvements

NEVA AND WESLEY WEST FOUNDATION

Giving Contact

Stuart W. Stedman, Trustee
PO Box 7
Houston, TX 77001-0007
Phone: (713)520-0400
Fax: (713)520-1131

Description

Founded: 1956
EIN: 746039393
Organization Type: Family Foundation
Giving Locations: TX: Houston
Grant Types: Capital, General Support, Operating Expenses, Research.

Donor Information

Founder: Established in 1956 by the late Wesley West and Mrs. Neva Watkins West.

Financial Summary

Total Giving: $715,000 (2001)
Assets: $15,006,225 (2001)

Gifts Received: $676,438 (1992). Note: In 1992, contributions were received from Neva Watkins West.

Typical Recipients

Arts & Humanities: Ballet, Dance, Arts & Humanities-General, History & Archaeology, Libraries, Museums/Galleries, Music, Opera, Performing Arts, Theater
Civic & Public Affairs: Botanical Gardens/Parks, Clubs, Community Foundations, Civic & Public Affairs-General, Law & Justice, Municipalities/Towns, Public Policy, Zoos/Aquariums
Education: Arts/Humanities Education, Business Education, Business-School Partnerships, Colleges & Universities, Community & Junior Colleges, Education Funds, Elementary Education (Private), Engineering/Technological Education, Environmental Education, Education-General, Literacy, Medical Education, Minority Education, Private Education (Precollege), Public Education (Precollege), Religious Education, Science/Mathematics Education, Secondary Education (Private), Secondary Education (Public), Special Education, Student Aid
Environment: Forestry, Environment-General, Protection, Wildlife Protection
Health: Children's Health/Hospitals, Emergency/Ambulance Services, Eyes/Blindness, Health Funds, Health Organizations, Hospitals, Medical Research, Mental Health, Prenatal Health Issues, Public Health, Speech & Hearing
Religion: Churches, Religious Welfare
Science: Science Museums, Scientific Centers & Institutes
Social Services: At-Risk Youth, Camps, Child Welfare, Community Centers, Community Service Organizations, Family Planning, Family Services, Food/Clothing Distribution, Recreation & Athletics, Scouts, Shelters/Homelessness, Youth Organizations

Application Procedures

Initial Contact: Submit a letter or written proposal.
Application Requirements: Include a brief description of the organization's activity, purpose of funds sought, amount requested, and other data considered pertinent to the request.
Deadlines: November 30.

Restrictions

Does not support individuals. Preference is given to Texas charitable organizations.

Additional Information

Publications: Annual Report

Foundation Officials

Randolph L. Pullin: trustee
Betty Ann West Stedman: trustee
Stuart West Stedman: trustee
Neva Watkins West: don, trustee

Grants Analysis

Disclosure Period: calendar year ending 2001
Total Grants: $715,000
Number of Grants: 26
Average Grant: $20,600*
Highest Grant: $200,000
Lowest Grant: $1,000
Typical Range: $5,000 to $40,000
*Note: Average grant excludes highest grant.

Recent Grants

Note: Grants derived from 2001 Form 990.
General

200,000	Texas A & M University-Caesar Kleberg Wildlife Research Institute, Kingsville, TX
80,000	St. Luke's United Methodist Church, Houston, TX
75,000	St. John School, Houston, TX
50,000	Baylor College of Medicine-Department of Ophthalmology, Houston, TX

50,000	Houston Music Hall Foundation, Houston, TX
50,000	Lady Bird Johnson Wildflower Center, Austin, TX
50,000	Texas Children's Hospital, Houston, TX
45,000	Houston Grand Opera, Houston, TX
40,000	Museum of Fine Arts Houston, Houston, TX
10,000	Contemporary Arts Museum, Houston, TX

WEST FOUNDATION (TX)

Giving Contact
Reece A. West, President & Treasurer
PO Box 1675
Wichita Falls, TX 76307
Phone: (940)723-2177

Description
Founded: 1973
EIN: 237332105
Organization Type: Private Foundation
Giving Locations: TX: Wichita Falls
Grant Types: Award, General Support, Research, Scholarship.

Donor Information
Founder: the late Gordon T. West, the late Ellen B. West, Gordon T. West, Jr.

Financial Summary
Total Giving: $843,347 (fiscal year ending September 30, 2004); $340,575 (fiscal 2001)
Giving Analysis: Giving for fiscal 2004 includes: foundation gifts to individuals ($70,000); foundation scholarships ($83,812); fiscal 2001: foundation gifts to individuals ($50,000); foundation scholarships ($75,000)
Assets: $19,826,182 (fiscal 2004); $17,210,238 (fiscal 2001)
Gifts Received: $8,101,173 (fiscal 1992). Note: In 1992, contributions were received from Neva Watkins West.

Typical Recipients
Arts & Humanities: Arts Festivals, Libraries, Museums/Galleries
Civic & Public Affairs: Community Foundations, Safety
Education: Business Education, Colleges & Universities, Education Associations, Education Reform, Elementary Education (Private), Elementary Education (Public), Faculty Development, Health & Physical Education, Public Education (Precollege), Science/Mathematics Education, Student Aid, Vocational & Technical Education
Health: Health Funds

Application Procedures
Initial Contact: Submit a brief letter.
Application Requirements: Include name and address of applicant.
Deadlines: None.

Additional Information
Provides awards to public school teachers and teaching institutes and funds for faculty development and research.

Foundation Officials
Joseph Newton Sherrill, Jr.: vice president, trustee B Wichita Falls, TX 1929. ED Massachusetts Institute of Technology (1952); Harvard University (1955). PRIM CORP EMPL president: Sherrill, Crosnoe & Goff. CORP AFFIL general counsel, director: First National Bank Byers; president, director: Wilson Drilling Corp.

Gordon T. West, Jr.: vice president, trustee
Reece A. West: president, trustee

Grants Analysis
Disclosure Period: fiscal year ending September 30, 2004
Total Grants: $689,535*
Number of Grants: 14
Average Grant: $39,397*
Highest Grant: $116,766
Lowest Grant: $1,306
Typical Range: $10,000 to $75,000
*Note: Giving excludes gifts to individuals and scholarships. Average grant figure excludes two highest grants ($216,766).

Recent Grants
Note: Grants derived from fiscal 2004 Form 990.
General

116,768	Wichita Falls Independent School District, Wichita Falls, TX -- MSU/WFISD mentoring project
100,000	Grand Island Community Foundation, Grand Island, NE -- to establish Kim West Dinsdale endowment fund
85,164	Wichita Falls Independent School District, Wichita Falls, TX -- career and technology counselors' initiative
75,000	National Museum of Women in the Arts, Washington, DC -- for the legacy of women in the arts endowment
75,000	United Regional Healthcare Foundation, Wichita Falls, TX -- to assist in cost of constructing medical - surgical area
48,812	Wichita Falls Independent School District, Wichita Falls, TX -- for faculty scholarship program
45,914	Midwestern State University, Wichita Falls, TX -- for distance education services
26,013	Wichita Falls Independent School District, Wichita Falls, TX -- summer arts festival
23,946	Midwestern State University, Wichita Falls, TX -- for NCATE accreditation preparation
23,480	Wichita Falls Independent School District, Wichita Falls, TX -- elementary science facilities

WEST PHARMACEUTICAL SERVICES INC.

Company Headquarters
101 Gordon Dr.
Lionville, PA 19341-0645
Web: http://www.westpharma.com

Company Description
Founded: 1923
Ticker: WST
Exchange: NYSE
Former Name: West Co. Plastics Group.
Revenue: US$396.9 million (2001)
Employees: 4365 (2003)
SIC(s): 3069 Fabricated Rubber Products Nec, 3089 Plastics Products Nec, 3469 Metal Stampings Nec, 3565 Packaging Machinery.

Operating Locations
West Co. Inc. (FL--Clearwater, St. Petersburg; NE--Kearney; NC--Kinston; PA--Lionville, Lititz, Montgomery, Philadelphia; PR)

Herman O. West Foundation

Giving Contact
Maureen Goebel, Administrator
101 Gordon Drive
Exton, PA 19341
Phone: (610)594-2905
Fax: (610)594-3011
E-mail: maureen.goebel@westpharma.com

Alternate Contact
PO Box 645
Lionville, PA 19353-0645

Description
EIN: 237173901
Organization Type: Corporate Foundation
Former Name: Herman O. West Foundation (2001).
Giving Locations: FL; NE; NJ; NC; PA: headquarters and operating communities.
Grant Types: Capital, Emergency, General Support, Multiyear/Continuing Support, Scholarship.
Note: Employee matching gift ratio: 1 to 1 up to $750 per employee annually, for secondary and higher education.

Financial Summary
Total Giving: $350,000 (2004 approx); $350,000 (2003 approx); $382,554 (2002). Note: Contributes through foundation only.
Giving Analysis: Giving for 2002 includes: foundation matching gifts ($17,560); foundation scholarships ($61,403); foundation grants to United Way ($116,266); foundation ($187,325); 2001: foundation matching gifts ($9,180); foundation scholarships ($60,280); foundation grants to United Way ($110,387)
Assets: $450,000 (2004 approx); $450,000 (2003 approx); $1,112,938 (2002)
Gifts Received: $553,003 (2002); $648,518 (2001); $4,000 (2000). Note: In 2001, contributions were received from F.H. West and West Pharmaceutical Services.

Typical Recipients
Arts & Humanities: Arts Associations & Councils, Arts Centers, Arts Festivals, Community Arts, Arts & Humanities-General, Historic Preservation, History & Archaeology, Libraries, Museums/Galleries, Music, Performing Arts, Theater
Civic & Public Affairs: Business/Free Enterprise, Economic Development, Civic & Public Affairs-General, Public Policy, Safety, Urban & Community Affairs, Zoos/Aquariums
Education: Arts/Humanities Education, Business-School Partnerships, Colleges & Universities, Community & Junior Colleges, Education Associations, Education Funds, Engineering/Technological Education, Faculty Development, Education-General, Literacy, Medical Education, Minority Education, Private Education (Precollege), Public Education (Precollege), Science/Mathematics Education, Secondary Education (Private), Student Aid, Vocational & Technical Education
Environment: Environment-General, Resource Conservation, Watershed
Health: Cancer, Children's Health/Hospitals, Emergency/Ambulance Services, Health Funds, Health Organizations, Hospitals, Medical Rehabilitation, Medical Research, Nursing Services, Prenatal Health Issues, Public Health, Trauma Treatment
International: Health Care/Hospitals, International Organizations
Religion: Religious Welfare
Science: Observatories & Planetariums, Science Museums, Scientific Centers & Institutes, Scientific Organizations
Social Services: Big Brothers/Big Sisters, Community Centers, Community Service Organizations,

Counseling, Domestic Violence, Emergency Relief, Family Planning, People with Disabilities, Recreation & Athletics, Scouts, Senior Services, Shelters/Homelessness, Social Services-General, Substance Abuse, United Funds/United Ways, Veterans, Volunteer Services, YMCA/YWCA/YMHA/YWHA, Youth Organizations

Application Procedures

Initial Contact: Send a written proposal. For scholarships request an application.
Application Requirements: Include a description of organization, and extent of services provided; recently audited financial statement, indicating sources of funds and how they are disbursed; future needs and services of program; and proof of tax-exempt status.
Deadlines: February 28.

Restrictions

Foundation does not support individuals, political or lobbying groups, or organizations outside operating areas. Scholarship recipients must be dependents of west employees.

Corporate Officials

Steven A. Ellers: executive vice presidento PRIM CORP EMPL chief financial officer: West Co., Inc.
John Robert Gailey, III: vice president, general counsel, secretary B York, PA 1954. ED Haverford College (1976); Temple University (1986). PRIM CORP EMPL vice president, general counsel, secretary: West Co., Inc. CORP AFFIL secretary: Paco Pharmaceutical Services. NONPR AFFIL director: American Society of Corporate Secretaries.
William G. Little: chairman, director B 1942. ED Dunedin Teachers College. PRIM CORP EMPL chairman, president, chief executive officer, director: West Co., Inc.
Donald E. Morel, Jr.: president, chief executive officer PRIM CORP EMPL president: West Co., Inc.

Foundation Officials

Rick Luzzi: trustee

Grants Analysis

Disclosure Period: calendar year ending 2002
Total Grants: $187,325*
Number of Grants: 45
Average Grant: $4,163
Highest Grant: $40,000
Typical Range: $1,000 to $10,000
*Note: Giving excludes matching gifts, scholarships, United Way.

Recent Grants

Note: Grants derived from 2003 Form 990.

General

51,524	Fox Chase Cancer Center, Philadelphia, PA
45,000	Abington Memorial Hospital, Abington, PA
40,000	University of the Sciences in Philadelphia, Philadelphia, PA
34,640	United Way of Chester County, West Chester, PA
27,572	United Way of Tampa Bay, FL
25,762	Lycoming County United Way, Williamsport, PA
25,000	Delaware County Community College, Downingtown, PA
19,470	United Way, Lenoir, NC
16,500	Franklin Institute Science Museum, Philadelphia, PA
15,000	Phoenixville YMCA, Phoenixville, PA

KATHLEEN PATTON WESTBY FOUNDATION

Giving Contact

John Trygve-Westby, Trustee
4815 S. Harvard, Suite 395
Tulsa, OK 74135
Phone: (918)743-8321

Description

Founded: 1991
EIN: 731354412
Organization Type: Private Foundation
Giving Locations: OK: Tulsa
Grant Types: General Support.

Donor Information

Founder: Established in 1991 by Kathleen Patton Westby.

Financial Summary

Total Giving: $52,951 (fiscal year ending June 30, 2004); $122,600 (fiscal 2002); $36,950 (fiscal 2001)
Giving Analysis: Giving for fiscal 2001 includes: foundation grants to United Way ($100)
Assets: $1,878,569 (fiscal 2004); $2,005,156 (fiscal 2002); $1,903,762 (fiscal 2001)
Gifts Received: $518,538 (fiscal 2001); $100,245 (fiscal 1999); $195,088 (fiscal 1997). Note: In fiscal 2001, contributions were received from Kathleen Westby Charitable Lead Trust. In fiscal 1997, contributions were received from Kathleen Patton Westby.

Typical Recipients

Arts & Humanities: Arts Associations & Councils, Arts Centers, Arts Institutes, Ballet, Dance, Film & Video, Historic Preservation, History & Archaeology, Libraries, Museums/Galleries, Music, Opera, Performing Arts
Civic & Public Affairs: Philanthropic Organizations, Public Policy
Education: Colleges & Universities, Education Reform, Student Aid
Environment: Environment-General, Resource Conservation
Religion: Churches
Social Services: Community Service Organizations, Family Planning

Application Procedures

Initial Contact: The foundation has no formal grant application procedure or application form. Send a brief letter of inquiry.
Deadlines: None.

Foundation Officials

Kathleen Patton Westby: trustee
Gerald H. Westby: trustee
John Trygve Westby: trustee

Grants Analysis

Disclosure Period: fiscal year ending June 30, 2004
Total Grants: $52,951*
Number of Grants: 18
Average Grant: $1,678*
Highest Grant: $24,426
Lowest Grant: $100
Typical Range: $1,000 to $5,000
*Note: Average grant figure excludes highest grant.

Recent Grants

Note: Grants derived from fiscal 2004 Form 990.
General

24,426	Circle Cinema Theatre, Tulsa, OK -- towards Westby cinema furniture and fixtures
5,500	Tulsa Opera, Tulsa, OK
5,000	Oklahoma Arts Institute, Oklahoma City, OK

5,000	Philbrook Museum of Art, Tulsa, OK -- for contemporary consortium
2,500	Arts & Humanities Council, Tulsa, OK
2,500	Philbrook Museum of Art, Tulsa, OK -- towards sculpture endowment
2,500	Philbrook Museum of Art, Tulsa, OK
1,500	Mid-America Arts Alliance, Kansas City, MO
1,500	Tulsa Ballet, Tulsa, OK
1,000	Planned Parenthood, Tulsa, OK

WESTERHOFF FAMILY FOUNDATION, INC.

Giving Contact

Garret P. Westerhoff, Trustee
Care of Sax, Macy, Fromm & Co.
855 Valley Road
Clifton, NJ 07013-2441
Phone: (973)472-6250

Description

Founded: 1998
EIN: 223515621
Organization Type: Private Foundation
Grant Types: General Support.

Financial Summary

Total Giving: $16,700 (fiscal year ending April 30, 2004); $57,774 (fiscal 2001)
Assets: $174,764 (fiscal 2004); $206,857 (fiscal 2001)
Gifts Received: $7,167 (fiscal 2004); $40,208 (fiscal 2001); $23,151 (fiscal 1999). Note: In fiscal 1999, 2001, and 2004, contributions were received from Garrett and Helga Westerhoff.

Typical Recipients

Arts & Humanities: Arts & Humanities-General, Libraries, Music, Public Broadcasting
Civic & Public Affairs: Civic & Public Affairs-General
Education: Arts/Humanities Education, Education-General
Health: Public Health
Religion: Churches

Foundation Officials

Garret P. Westerhoff: trustee
Helga K. Westerhoff: trustee
Katherine Westerhoff: trustee

Grants Analysis

Disclosure Period: fiscal year ending April 30, 2004
Total Grants: $16,700
Number of Grants: 19
Average Grant: $539*
Highest Grant: $7,000
Lowest Grant: $100
Typical Range: $100 to $1,000
*Note: Average grant figure excludes highest grant.

Recent Grants

Note: Grants derived from fiscal 2001 Form 990.
Library-Related

2,075	Friends of the Kinnelon Library, Kinnelon, NJ
300	Friends of the Kinnelon Library, Kinnelon, NJ

General

10,000	Westerhoff School of Music and Art, Metuchen, NJ
10,000	Westerhoff School of Music and Art, Metuchen, NJ
10,000	Westerhoff School of Music and Art, Metuchen, NJ
5,000	Westerhoff School of Music and Art, Metuchen, NJ

5,000	Westerhoff School of Music and Art, Metuchen, NJ
3,000	Westerhoff School of Music and Art, Metuchen, NJ
2,700	Westerhoff School of Music and Art, Metuchen, NJ
2,500	Rougday Friends of Arts, Phoenix, AZ
1,000	Breckenridge Music Institute, Breckenridge, CO
1,000	KAET - TV, Tempe, AZ

WESTERN NEW YORK FOUNDATION

Giving Contact
Richard E. Moot, President
4050 Harlem Rd.
Snyder, NY 14226
Phone: (716)847-6440
Fax: (716)847-6440

Description
Founded: 1951
EIN: 160845962
Organization Type: Private Foundation
Giving Locations: NY: limited to the 8th Judicial District of NY (Erie, Niagara, Genesee, Wyoming, Allegany, Cattaraugus, and Chautauqua counties)
Grant Types: Capital, Conference/Seminar, Emergency, Endowment, General Support, Loan, Project, Seed Money.

Donor Information
Founder: the late Welles V. Moot

Financial Summary
Total Giving: $383,643 (fiscal year ending July 31, 2004); $596,362 (fiscal 2002); $650,125 (fiscal 2001)
Giving Analysis: Giving for fiscal 2004 includes: foundation grants to United Way ($50,000) fiscal 2002: foundation grants to United Way ($3,000)
Assets: $11,671,196 (fiscal 2004); $10,234,479 (fiscal 2002); $13,348,442 (fiscal 2001)

Typical Recipients
Arts & Humanities: Arts Associations & Councils, Arts Funds, Arts Institutes, Community Arts, Arts & Humanities-General, Historic Preservation, History & Archaeology, Libraries, Museums/Galleries, Music, Opera, Performing Arts, Public Broadcasting, Theater
Civic & Public Affairs: Botanical Gardens/Parks, Employment/Job Training, Civic & Public Affairs-General, Housing, Legal Aid, Municipalities/Towns, Safety, Urban & Community Affairs, Zoos/Aquariums
Education: Arts/Humanities Education, Business Education, Elementary Education (Private), Preschool Education, Private Education (Precollege), Public Education (Precollege), Science/Mathematics Education, Secondary Education (Public), Special Education, Student Aid
Environment: Environment-General
Health: Children's Health/Hospitals, Health Organizations, Hospices, Hospitals, Medical Rehabilitation, Mental Health, Public Health, Speech & Hearing
Religion: Religion-General
Science: Science Museums, Scientific Centers & Institutes
Social Services: Child Welfare, Community Centers, Community Service Organizations, Day Care, Emergency Relief, Family Planning, Family Services, Food/Clothing Distribution, Homes, People with Disabilities, Recreation & Athletics, Scouts, Substance Abuse, United Funds/United Ways, Volunteer Services, YMCA/YWCA/YMHA/YWHA, Youth Organizations

Application Procedures
Initial Contact: Call or write requesting application.
Deadlines: None.

Restrictions
Does not support individuals or organizations for religious purposes.

Additional Information
Publications: Annual Report; Application Form

Foundation Officials
Theodore V. Buerger: assistant treasurer
Anthony S. Johnson: trustee
Jennifer Johnson: trustee
Brenda W. McDuffie: trustee
Trudy A. Mollenberg: trustee
Andrew R. Moot: trustee
John R. Moot: secretary
Richard E. Moot: president
Welles V. Moot, Jr.: treasurer
John N. Walsh, III: vice president

Grants Analysis
Disclosure Period: fiscal year ending July 31, 2004
Total Grants: $333,643*
Number of Grants: 35
Average Grant: $8,342*
Highest Grant: $50,000
Lowest Grant: $300
Typical Range: $5,000 to $10,000
*Note: Giving excludes United Way. Average grant figures excludes highest grant.

Recent Grants
Note: Grants derived from 2004 Form 990.
General

50,000	United Way of Buffalo and Erie County, Buffalo, NY -- promoting financial excellence
50,000	YMCA of Greater Buffalo, Buffalo, NY -- construction of new branch
30,000	Buffalo Half-Way House Inc., Buffalo, NY -- replacement of roof
30,000	Elmwood Franklin School, Buffalo, NY -- for capital building campaign
30,000	League for the Handicapped, Springville, NY -- construction of addition
25,000	Buffalo Philharmonic Orchestra, Buffalo, NY
25,000	Summit Educational Resources, Tonawanda, NY -- construction of project
25,000	Wyoming County YMCA, Warsaw, NY -- construction project
20,000	American Red Cross, Buffalo, NY -- funds for life project
20,000	Aspire of Western New York, Buffalo, NY -- for construction facility

WESTERN & SOUTHERN LIFE INSURANCE CO.

Company Headquarters
400 Broadway St.
Cincinnati, OH 45202
Web: http://www.westernsouthernlife.com

Company Description
Revenue: US$3.795 billion (2003)
Employees: 8000 (2003)
SIC(s): 6311 Life Insurance.

Operating Locations
Western & Southern Life Insurance Co. (OH--Cincinnati)

Western-Southern Foundation, Inc.

Giving Contact
Edward J. Babbitt
Western-Southern Enterprise Fund
400 Broadway
Cincinnati, OH 45202-3341
Phone: (513)629-1464

Description
Founded: 1990
EIN: 311259670
Organization Type: Corporate Foundation
Former Name: Western-Southern Enterprise Fund, Inc..
Giving Locations: OH
Grant Types: General Support, Matching, Scholarship.

Financial Summary
Total Giving: $2,261,898 (2003); $3,069,459 (2001). Note: Contributes through foundation only.
Assets: $8,678,189 (2003); $49,154,305 (2001)
Gifts Received: $5,002 (2003); $6,985 (2001); $7,900 (2000). Note: Foundation receives contributions from Western-Southern, Columbus Life Charitable Trust, and Continental General.

Typical Recipients
Arts & Humanities: Arts Associations & Councils, Arts Centers, Arts Festivals, Arts Funds, Arts Institutes, Film & Video, Historic Preservation, Libraries, Museums/Galleries, Music, Performing Arts, Public Broadcasting, Theater, Visual Arts
Civic & Public Affairs: African American Affairs, Botanical Gardens/Parks, Business/Free Enterprise, Chambers of Commerce, Civil Rights, Clubs, Community Foundations, Economic Development, Economic Policy, Employment/Job Training, Civic & Public Affairs-General, Housing, Inner-City Development, Municipalities/Towns, Professional & Trade Associations, Public Policy, Urban & Community Affairs, Women's Affairs, Zoos/Aquariums
Education: Afterschool/Enrichment Programs, Business Education, Colleges & Universities, Economic Education, Education Funds, Education Reform, Education-General, Minority Education, Private Education (Precollege), Religious Education, Science/Mathematics Education, Secondary Education (Private), Special Education, Student Aid, Vocational & Technical Education
Environment: Environment-General
Health: Arthritis, Cancer, Children's Health/Hospitals, Clinics/Medical Centers, Diabetes, Emergency/Ambulance Services, Health Funds, Health Organizations, Home-Care Services, Hospices, Hospitals, Long-Term Care, Mental Health, Multiple Sclerosis, Prenatal Health Issues, Single-Disease Health Associations
International: International Peace & Security Issues
Religion: Churches, Dioceses, Religious Organizations, Religious Welfare, Seminaries
Social Services: Child Welfare, Community Centers, Community Service Organizations, Crime Prevention, Day Care, Family Services, Homes, People with Disabilities, Recreation & Athletics, Scouts, Senior Services, Shelters/Homelessness, Social Services-General, Substance Abuse, United Funds/United Ways, Veterans, YMCA/YWCA/YMHA/YWHA, Youth Organizations

Application Procedures
Initial Contact: Send a brief letter.
Application Requirements: Include a description of organization and project, amount requested, and purpose of funds sought.
Deadlines: None.

Foundation Officials

John E. Barrett: trustee
Thomas J. Williams: trustee
William Joseph Williams: trustee B Cincinnati, OH December 19, 1915. ED Georgetown University AB (1937); Harvard University (1938). CORP AFFIL director: Columbus Life Insurance Co. Ohio.

Grants Analysis

Disclosure Period: calendar year ending 2002
Total Grants: $2,007,547*
Number of Grants: 82
Average Grant: $16,061*
Highest Grant: $341,530
Lowest Grant: $500
Typical Range: $500 to $25,000
*Note: Giving excludes United Way. Average grant figure excludes three highest grants ($738,730).

Recent Grants

Note: Grants derived from 2003 Form 990.
General

341,530	Mount St. Mary's Seminary (stock), Cincinnati, OH
254,351	United Way, Cincinnati, OH
200,000	Cincinnati Convention Center, Cincinnati, OH
197,200	Bayley Place, Cincinnati, OH
101,318	National Underground Railroad Freedom Center, Cincinnati, OH
100,360	Taft Museum (stock), Cincinnati, OH
80,000	Dixie View Gardens
76,768	Greater Cincinnati Foundation (stock), Cincinnati, OH
66,275	Multiple Sclerosis Society, Cincinnati, OH
50,975	WCET Channel 48, Cincinnati, OH

WESTLB NEW YORK BRANCH

Company Headquarters

New York, NY
Web: http://www.westlb.de

Company Description

SIC(s): 6081 Foreign Banks--Branches & Agencies.
Parent Company: Westdeutsche Landesbank Girozentrale, Herzogstrasse 15, Dusseldorf, Germany

Operating Locations

WestLB Chicago (IL--Chicago); WestLB Los Angeles (CA--Los Angeles); WestLB New York Branch (NY--New York)

Giving Contact

Amy Budd, HR Asst.
1211 Avenue of the Americas, 24th Floor
New York, NY 10036-8701
Phone: (212)852-6000
Fax: (212)921-5494
E-mail: amy_budd@westlb.com

Description

Organization Type: Corporate Giving Program
Giving Locations: NY: New York metropolitan area
Grant Types: General Support.

Typical Recipients

Arts & Humanities: Libraries, Museums/Galleries, Music
Civic & Public Affairs: Professional & Trade Associations
Education: Private Education (Precollege)
Social Services: United Funds/United Ways

Application Procedures

Initial Contact: Send a brief letter of inquiry.
Application Requirements: Include a description of the organization, amount requested, and purpose of funds sought.
Deadlines: November.
Decision Notification: All requests are forwarded to Dusseldorf for approval at the end of the year.

Corporate Officials

John Paul Garber: head US operations PRIM CORP EMPL head US operations: WestLB NY Branch.

WEYERHAEUSER CO.

Company Headquarters

Federal Way, WA
Web: http://www.weyerhaeuser.com

Company Description

Founded: 1900
Ticker: WY
Exchange: NYSE
Acquired: Willamette Industries Inc. (2002); MacMillan Bloedel Inc..
Revenue: US$22.665 billion (2004)
Profit: US$1.283 billion (2004)
Employees: 56800 (2003)
Fortune Rank: 89, per FORTUNE Magazine's list of 500 Largest U.S. Corporations (2004).
SIC(s): 2411 Logging, 2421 Sawmills & Planing Mills--General, 2431 Millwork, 2435 Hardwood Veneer & Plywood.

Operating Locations

Weyerhaeuser Co. (AL; AR--Hot Springs; CA--Alameda, Altadena, Belmont, City of Commerce, Colton, Emeryville, Los Angeles, Modesto, Oceanside, Pleasanton, Salinas, San Francisco, San Jose, Santa Paula; FL--Miami, Tampa; GA; HI--Honolulu; IL--Belleville, Elgin, Itasca; IA--Waterloo; KY--Franklin; ME--Westbrook; MD--Dorsey, Millersville; MN--Albert Lea, Austin, White Bear Lake; MS--Columbus, Jackson; MO--Clayton, St. Joseph; NJ--Barrington, Marlton, Teaneck; NC--Charlotte, Greensboro, New Bern, Plymouth; OH--Columbus, Mount Vernon; OK--Valliant, Wright City; OR--Beaverton, Eugene, North Bend, Portland, Springfield; PA--Valley Forge; TX--Dallas, Grand Prairie, Houston, McAllen; VA--Richmond; WA--Bellevue, Centralia, Chehalis, Everett, Federal Way, Kent, Longview, Seattle, Tacoma, Union Gap, Vancouver; WI--Rothschild)

Nonmonetary Support

Type: Cause-related Marketing & Promotion; Donated Equipment; Donated Products; Loaned Employees; Loaned Executives; Workplace Solicitation
Contact: Penny Paul, Executive Assistant
Note: Nonmonetary support is contributed directly through the company. Workplace solicitation is for the United Way only.

Weyerhaeuser Co. Foundation

Giving Contact

Elizabeth A. Crossman, President
CH1 L32
PO Box 9777
Federal Way, WA 98063-9777
Phone: (253)924-3159
Fax: (253)924-3658
Web: http://www.weyerhaeuser.com/citizenship/philanthropy/

Description

EIN: 916024225
Organization Type: Corporate Foundation
Giving Locations: AL; AR; MS; NC; OK; OR; WA: nationally, with emphasis on communities, particularly remote communities, in which company has significant numbers of employees.
Grant Types: Award, Capital, Department, Employee Matching Gifts, General Support, Project.
Note: Employee matching gift ratio: 1 to 1 for higher education only.

Financial Summary

Total Giving: $7,404,264 (fiscal year ending December 29, 2002); $7,364,733 (fiscal 2001). Note: Contributes through corporate direct giving program and foundation.
Assets: $16,295,728 (fiscal 2002); $23,528,514 (fiscal 2001)
Gifts Received: $16,601,000 (fiscal 2002); $9,668,980 (fiscal 2001); $7,576,447 (fiscal 2000). Note: Foundation receives contributions from Weyerhaeuser Company.

Typical Recipients

Arts & Humanities: Arts Associations & Councils, Arts Festivals, Arts Funds, Community Arts, Dance, Arts & Humanities-General, Historic Preservation, History & Archaeology, Libraries, Museums/Galleries, Music, Opera, Performing Arts, Public Broadcasting, Theater
Civic & Public Affairs: African American Affairs, Business/Free Enterprise, Chambers of Commerce, Civil Rights, Community Foundations, Economic Development, Employment/Job Training, Civic & Public Affairs-General, Housing, Inner-City Development, Law & Justice, Legal Aid, Municipalities/Towns, Native American Affairs, Philanthropic Organizations, Professional & Trade Associations, Public Policy, Rural Affairs, Safety, Urban & Community Affairs, Zoos/Aquariums
Education: Afterschool/Enrichment Programs, Agricultural Education, Arts/Humanities Education, Business Education, Colleges & Universities, Community & Junior Colleges, Economic Education, Education Associations, Education Funds, Elementary Education (Private), Elementary Education (Public), Engineering/Technological Education, Environmental Education, Education-General, Minority Education, Private Education (Precollege), Public Education (Precollege), Science/Mathematics Education, Social Sciences Education, Student Aid, Vocational & Technical Education
Environment: Forestry, Environment-General, Resource Conservation, Wildlife Protection
Health: Cancer, Children's Health/Hospitals, Clinics/Medical Centers, Emergency/Ambulance Services, Health Funds, Hospices, Hospitals, Public Health
International: Foreign Educational Institutions, International Affairs, International Development, International Environmental Issues, International Relief Efforts
Religion: Churches
Science: Science Museums, Scientific Centers & Institutes
Social Services: Animal Protection, Child Welfare, Community Centers, Community Service Organizations, Emergency Relief, Family Services, Food/Clothing Distribution, People with Disabilities, Recreation & Athletics, Scouts, Shelters/Homelessness, Social Services-General, Substance Abuse, United Funds/United Ways, Volunteer Services, YMCA/YWCA/YMHA/YWHA, Youth Organizations

Application Procedures

Initial Contact: Call for application, then send full proposal.
Application Requirements: Completed application includes description of project and sponsoring organization; statement of why project is consistent with foundation guidelines; project cost, sources of fund-

ing, and amount requested; evidence of tax-exempt status.

Deadlines: Requests received after September may not be considered until budgets are established for the following year.

Review Process: Appropriate review committee is consulted and request is considered within budget constraints/local priorities.

Evaluative Criteria: Direct relevance to foundation's mission and geographic interests; evidence that project will address important need; innovative and cost-effective approaches; impact consistent with proposed expenditure; evidence that project does not duplicate other efforts; indication that other financial support likely will be available; demonstrated competence of administration and staff.

Decision Notification: Inquiries acknowledged as soon as possible (normally within 30 days); applicants should allow 90 to 120 days for a decision.

Notes: If further consideration is warranted, foundation may ask for additional information or formal proposal; personal meetings or site visits are normally arranged only for projects that have passed initial application.

Restrictions

Does not support religious, sacramental, or theological purposes; political campaigns; to influence legislation; for tickets or tables at fundraising events; individuals; or direct grants to organizations already receiving foundation funds through an umbrella organization.

Discourages applications seeking to cover operating deficits; for services that the public sector should reasonably be expected to provide; to establish endowments or memorials; for research or conferences outside the forest products industry; for hospital building or equipment campaigns that will result in higher costs to healthcare users; for services outside Weyerhaeuser operating area; for general administrative expenses; or for amounts that are clearly unrealistic given the foundation's total annual budget.

The foundation will not consider requests that do not meet its program and geographic criteria. If organizations are unsure about the presence of a Weyerhaeuser facility in their community, write or call the foundation for confirmation before submitting a grant request.

Additional Information

In 1998, the foundation launched a program that supports employee-initiated volunteer projects. Foundation makes cash grants only, with a $1,000 minimum. Normally, support is committed for one year at a time. Grants may be made to umbrella organizations or combined campaigns.

Publications: Biennial Report (includes Current Guidelines); Grant Application; Volunteer Employee Pamphlet

Corporate Officials

William R. Corbin: executive vice president wood products PRIM CORP EMPL executive vice president wood products: Weyerhaeuser Co. ADD CORP EMPL corporate executive: Weyerhaeuser International.

Richard C. Gozon: executive vice president pulp paper & packaging PRIM CORP EMPL executive vice president pulp paper & packaging: Weyerhaeuser Co. CORP AFFIL director: UGI Corp.; director: UGI Utilities Inc.; director: Amerisource Health Corp.

Steven Richard Hill: senior vice president human resources B Oakland, CA 1947. ED University of California at Berkeley BS (1969); University of California, Los Angeles MBA (1971). PRIM CORP EMPL senior vice president human resources: Weyerhaeuser Co. ADD CORP EMPL director: Weyerhaeuser - Canada.

Norman E. Johnson: senior vice president technology B 1933. ED Harvard University Advanced Management Program (1955); Oregon State University MS (1957); University of California at Berkeley PhD

(1961). PRIM CORP EMPL senior vice president technology: Weyerhaeuser Co.

Thomas M. Luthy: senior vice president wood products PRIM CORP EMPL senior vice president wood products: Weyerhaeuser Co.

Sandy D. McDade: secretary B Seattle, WA 1952. ED Whitman College (1974); University of Puget Sound (1979). PRIM CORP EMPL senior vice president: Weyerhaeuser Co. NONPR AFFIL member: American Society of Corporate Secretaries.

William Charles Stivers: executive vice president, chief financial officer B Modesto, CA 1938. ED Stanford University BA (1960); University of Southern California MBA (1963); Harvard University Graduate School of Business Administration (1977). PRIM CORP EMPL executive vice president, chief financial officer: Weyerhaeuser Co. CORP AFFIL vice president fin, director: Weyerhaeuser Real Estate Co.; director: Protection Mutual Insurance Co.; president, director: S&S Land & Cattle Co.; director: First Interstate Bancorp; member national advisory board: Chase Manhattan Corp.; member: Chemical Banking Corp. NONPR AFFIL director: Pacific Rim Finance Center Graduate School Business, University Washington; trustee, chairman: Saint Francis Community Hospital; trustee: Franciscan Health Systems West; member management & steering committee: American Forest & Paper Association.

George Hunt Weyerhaeuser: director B Seattle, WA 1926. ED Yale University BSIE (1949). CORP AFFIL director: Dietzgen Corp.; director: SAFECO Corp.; director: Boeing Co. NONPR AFFIL member: Business Roundtable; member: Washington State Business Roundtable; member: Business Council.

Foundation Officials

William R. Corbin: trustee (see above)

Elizabeth A. Crossman: president PRIM CORP EMPL director corporate contributions: Weyerhaeuser Co.

Richard C. Gozon: trustee (see above)

Steven Richard Hill: trustee (see above)

Mack L. Hogans: chairman, president, trustee B Abbeville, AL 1949. ED University of Michigan (1971); University of Washington (1976). PRIM CORP EMPL senior vice president corporate affairs: Weyerhaeuser Co.

Norman E. Johnson: trustee (see above)

C. Stephen Lewis: trustee B 1944. PRIM CORP EMPL director: Pacific Northwest Bancorp.

Sandy D. McDade: assistant secretary legal affairs (see above)

Susan M. Mersereau: trustee B Portland, OR 1946. ED Scripps College BA (1968); University of Chicago MA (1971); Antioch College MA (1990). PRIM CORP EMPL vice president: Weyerhaeuser Co. NONPR AFFIL director: King County United Way.

William Charles Stivers: treasurer, trustee (see above)

Linda L. Terrien: assistant treasurer

Karen L. Veitenhans: secretary

George Hunt Weyerhaeuser: trustee (see above)

Robert B. Wilson: trustee

Grants Analysis

Disclosure Period: fiscal year ending December 29, 2002

Total Grants: $5,723,733*

Number of Grants: 1106 (approx)

Average Grant: $5,175

Highest Grant: $200,000

Lowest Grant: $1,000

Typical Range: $1,000 to $10,000

*Note: Giving excludes matching gifts, scholarship, and United Way.

Recent Grants

Note: Grants derived from 2003 Form 990.

General

600,000	Boy Scouts of America Cascade Pacific Council, OR
217,082	National Merit Scholarship Corporation, Evanston, IL
200,000	International Corrugated Packaging Foundation, Alexandria, VA
200,000	World Forestry Center, Portland, OR
174,200	United Way of Pierce County, Tacoma, WA
168,802	Scholarship America, Minneapolis, MN
160,800	United Way of King County, Seattle, WA
158,682	Scholarship America, Minneapolis, MN
120,000	Corporate Council for the Arts, Seattle, WA
115,000	Corporate Council for the Arts, Seattle, WA

CHARLES A. WEYERHAEUSER MEMORIAL FOUNDATION

Giving Contact

Lucy Rosenberry Jones, President & Director
332 Minnesota St., Suite 2100
St. Paul, MN 55101-1308
Phone: (651)228-0935

Description

Founded: 1959
EIN: 416012063
Organization Type: Private Foundation
Giving Locations: MN
Grant Types: General Support, Multiyear/Continuing Support, Project.

Donor Information

Founder: Carl A. Weyerhaeuser Trusts

Financial Summary

Total Giving: $392,525 (fiscal year ending February 28, 2002); $312,900 (fiscal 2001)

Assets: $6,482,340 (fiscal 2002); $6,462,579 (fiscal 2001)

Gifts Received: $77,659 (fiscal 2002); $76,004 (fiscal 2001); $82,161 (fiscal 2000). Note: In fiscal 2002, contributions were received from 1969 IRR Trusts. In fiscal 2000 and 2001, contributions were received from 1969 IRR Trusts and Berkshire Hathaway. In fiscal 1998, contributions were received from Berkshire Hathaway and various others.

Typical Recipients

Arts & Humanities: Arts Centers, Community Arts, History & Archaeology, Libraries, Literary Arts, Museums/Galleries, Music, Opera, Performing Arts, Public Broadcasting

Civic & Public Affairs: Botanical Gardens/Parks, Nonprofit Management, Parades/Festivals, Urban & Community Affairs, Zoos/Aquariums

Education: Colleges & Universities, Elementary Education (Private), Education-General, Religious Education, Social Sciences Education, Student Aid

Environment: Environment-General, Resource Conservation

Health: Mental Health

International: Foreign Educational Institutions

Religion: Churches, Religious Welfare

Science: Science Museums

Social Services: Animal Protection, Community Service Organizations, Family Planning, Family Services, United Funds/United Ways

Application Procedures

Initial Contact: The foundation has no formal grant application procedure or application form.

Deadlines: None.

Decision Notification: Notification of Directors decision is sent as promptly as possible.

Restrictions

Does not support individuals.

Foundation Officials

Elise R. Donohue: director
Gordon E. Hed: assistant secretary, assistant treasurer
Joseph S. Micallef: secretary, treasurer, director B 1933. PRIM CORP EMPL president, chief executive officer, treasurer, director: Fiduciary Counselling Inc. PRIM NONPR EMPL sec-treas: Rock Island Co. CORP AFFIL secretary, treasurer: Rock Island Co.
Charles W. Rosenberry, II: director
Lucy Rosenberry Jones: president, director
Robert J. Sivertsen: vice president, director

Grants Analysis

Disclosure Period: fiscal year ending February 28, 2002
Total Grants: $392,525
Number of Grants: 7
Highest Grant: $300,000
Lowest Grant: $2,000
Typical Range: $6,000 to $20,000

Recent Grants

Note: Grants derived from fiscal 2002 Form 990.
General

300,000	Nature Conservancy, Minneapolis, MN -- for land purchase
35,400	Minnesota Public Radio, St. Paul, MN -- opera underwriting
25,000	Planned Parenthood of Minnesota, St. Paul, MN -- operating support
22,125	Great River Arts Association, Little Falls, MN -- for relocating charnell equipment
6,000	Minnesota Historical Society, St. Paul, MN -- operating support
2,000	Minnesota Land Trust, Minneapolis, MN -- for operating support
2,000	Minnesota Orchestral Association, Minneapolis, MN -- for operating support

WHALLEY CHARITABLE TRUST

Giving Contact

David C. Klementik, Trustee
1397 Eisenhower
Johnstown, PA 15904
Phone: (814)266-1799

Description

Founded: 1961
EIN: 237128436
Organization Type: Private Foundation
Giving Locations: IL; PA
Grant Types: General Support.

Donor Information

Founder: John J. Whalley, John Whalley, Jr., Mary Whalley

Financial Summary

Total Giving: $144,379 (2003); $301,064 (2001)
Assets: $4,603,483 (2003); $4,843,837 (2001)

Typical Recipients

Arts & Humanities: Ethnic & Folk Arts, Arts & Humanities-General, Historic Preservation, History & Archaeology, Libraries, Museums/Galleries, Music, Performing Arts, Visual Arts
Civic & Public Affairs: Botanical Gardens/Parks, Clubs, Civic & Public Affairs-General, Municipalities/Towns, Parades/Festivals, Professional & Trade Associations, Safety, Urban & Community Affairs
Education: Colleges & Universities, Education-

General, Private Education (Precollege), Secondary Education (Public), Student Aid
Health: Cancer, Children's Health/Hospitals, Clinics/Medical Centers, Emergency/Ambulance Services, Health-General, Heart, Hospitals, Public Health
Religion: Churches, Jewish Causes, Religious Organizations, Religious Welfare
Social Services: Animal Protection, Child Welfare, Community Service Organizations, Crime Prevention, Homes, People with Disabilities, Recreation & Athletics, Scouts, United Funds/United Ways, Veterans, Volunteer Services, YMCA/YWCA/YMHA/YWHA, Youth Organizations

Application Procedures

Initial Contact: The foundation has no formal grant application procedure or application form.
Deadlines: None.

Foundation Officials

David C. Klementik: trustee

Grants Analysis

Disclosure Period: calendar year ending 2003
Total Grants: $144,379
Number of Grants: 43
Average Grant: $3,358
Highest Grant: $15,000
Lowest Grant: $50
Typical Range: $1,000 to $5,000

Recent Grants

Note: Grants derived from 2001 Form 990.
Library-Related

25,000	Windber Public Library, Windber, PA

General

50,000	Windber Medical Center, Windber, PA
45,000	Mount Aloysius College, Cresson, PA
40,000	Penn State University, McKeesport, PA
15,000	Arcadia Performing Arts, Windber, PA
10,000	Windber Volunteer Fire Company 1, Windber, PA
10,000	First Presbyterian Church of Jamestown, Jamestown, NY
10,000	First Presbyterian Church of Jamestown, Jamestown, NY
10,000	St. Francis University, Chicago, IL
10,000	Windber Community, Windber, PA
6,000	Johnstown Symphony Orchestra, Johnstown, PA

WHARTON FOUNDATION

Giving Contact

Jean W. Pettitt, President & Director
1001 Arbolado Road
Santa Barbara, CA 93103
Phone: (805)884-0756
Fax: (805)884-0756
E-mail: jpettitt@homemail.com

Description

Founded: 1954
EIN: 366130748
Organization Type: Private Foundation
Giving Locations: AZ; CA; FL; IL; WA
Grant Types: General Support, Matching, Multiyear/Continuing Support.

Donor Information

Founder: Sara P. Wharton, Joseph B. and Martha W. Wharton

Financial Summary

Total Giving: $180,930 (2004); $134,843 (2001)
Giving Analysis: Giving for 2004 includes: foundation matching gifts ($8,050); 2001: foundation matching gifts ($13,295)

Assets: $3,357,750 (2004); $3,594,914 (2001)
Gifts Received: $525 (2001); $4,207 (1998); $1,947 (1996). Note: In 1994, contributions were received from Sara P. Wharton ($40,000) and Joseph B. and Martha W. Wharton ($8,500).

Typical Recipients

Arts & Humanities: Arts Funds, Historic Preservation, Libraries, Museums/Galleries, Performing Arts, Public Broadcasting
Civic & Public Affairs: Botanical Gardens/Parks, Community Foundations, Civic & Public Affairs-General, Hispanic Affairs, Housing, Native American Affairs, Parades/Festivals, Zoos/Aquariums
Education: Afterschool/Enrichment Programs, Arts/Humanities Education, Business Education, Colleges & Universities, Elementary Education (Public), Faculty Development, Education-General, Leadership Training, Literacy, Minority Education, Private Education (Precollege), Religious Education, Science/Mathematics Education, Student Aid
Environment: Resource Conservation
Health: Children's Health/Hospitals, Clinics/Medical Centers, Medical Research, Mental Health
Religion: Churches, Ministries, Religious Organizations, Religious Welfare
Science: Science Museums, Scientific Centers & Institutes
Social Services: Animal Protection, Child Welfare, Community Centers, Community Service Organizations, Domestic Violence, Family Services, Recreation & Athletics, Youth Organizations

Application Procedures

Initial Contact: Request application form and guidelines.
Deadlines: May 1 for summer programs and July 1 for all other programs.

Restrictions

Does not support individuals.

Additional Information

Publications: Application Guidelines; Application Form

Foundation Officials

Jean W. Pettitt: president, director
S. D. Pettitt: director
B. Raber: secretary
Kate Schafer: vice president

Grants Analysis

Disclosure Period: calendar year ending 2004
Total Grants: $172,880*
Number of Grants: 23
Average Grant: $4,137*
Highest Grant: $46,000
Lowest Grant: $383
Typical Range: $1,000 to $10,000
***Note:** Giving excludes matching gifts. Average grant figure excludes two highest grants ($86,000).

Recent Grants

Note: Grants derived from 2001 Form 990.
General

48,000	Future Leaders of America, Oxnard, CA -- Latino Youth Leadership Program
20,000	Cleveland Elementary School, Santa Barbara, CA -- support for professional development
10,000	East Bay Conservation Corp, Oakland, CA -- support for EBBC Charter School
10,000	Foundation for Santa Barbara City College, Santa Barbara, CA -- summer program
7,500	Endowment for Youth Committee, Santa Barbara, CA -- support for science, math engineering and technology programs
5,000	Hopi Foundation, Hoteville, AZ -- educational programs

5,000	Santa Barbara Museum of Natural History, Santa Barbara, CA -- Los Marineros
5,000	Santa Maria Valley Discovery Museum, Santa Maria, CA -- Discover After School Success Program
3,800	Future Leaders of America, Oxnard, CA
3,000	Outreach Community Ministries

WHEELER FOUNDATION

Giving Contact
Samuel C. Wheeler, President & Director
1211 SW 5th Ave., Suite 2906
Portland, OR 97204-1911
Phone: (503)228-0261

Description
Founded: 1965
EIN: 930553801
Organization Type: Private Foundation
Giving Locations: NY; OR
Grant Types: General Support, Research, Scholarship.

Donor Information
Founder: the late Coleman H. Wheeler, Cornelia T. Wheeler

Financial Summary
Total Giving: $603,500 (2003); $610,500 (2001)
Giving Analysis: Giving for 2003 includes: foundation scholarships ($7,000); 2001: foundation scholarships ($10,000)
Assets: $15,748,172 (2003); $15,484,567 (2001)
Gifts Received: $882,108 (1992). Note: In 1992, contributions were received from Cornelia T. Wheeler ($872,108) and Coleman H. Wheeler ($10,000).

Typical Recipients
Arts & Humanities: Arts Festivals, Historic Preservation, History & Archaeology, Libraries, Museums/Galleries, Music, Opera, Theater
Civic & Public Affairs: Botanical Gardens/Parks, Clubs, Community Foundations, Economic Development, Civic & Public Affairs-General, Municipalities/Towns, Public Policy
Education: Afterschool/Enrichment Programs, Arts/Humanities Education, Colleges & Universities, Continuing Education, Education Funds, Education-General, Health & Physical Education, Minority Education, Private Education (Precollege), Science/Mathematics Education, Secondary Education (Private), Student Aid
Environment: Forestry, Environment-General
Health: Cancer, Children's Health/Hospitals, Clinics/Medical Centers, Emergency/Ambulance Services, Health Funds, Health Organizations, Hospitals, Medical Research, Public Health
International: International Environmental Issues
Religion: Ministries, Religious Organizations, Religious Welfare, Seminaries
Science: Science Museums
Social Services: Child Welfare, Community Service Organizations, Crime Prevention, Day Care, Food/Clothing Distribution, Homes, People with Disabilities, Scouts, Senior Services, Substance Abuse, United Funds/United Ways, YMCA/YWCA/YMHA/YWHA, Youth Organizations

Application Procedures
Initial Contact: Send a brief letter of inquiry.
Application Requirements: Include purpose of funds sought and proof of tax-exempt status.
Deadlines: None.

Restrictions
Grants are not made to individuals.

Foundation Officials
Lil M. Hendrickson: assistant secretary
Charles B. Wheeler: vice president, director
Edward T. Wheeler: secretary, director
John C. Wheeler: vice president, director
Samuel C. Wheeler: president, director
Thomas K. Wheeler: treasurer, director

Grants Analysis
Disclosure Period: calendar year ending 2003
Total Grants: $596,500*
Number of Grants: 80
Average Grant: $7,456
Highest Grant: $30,000
Lowest Grant: $1,000
Typical Range: $1,000 to $10,000
*Note: Giving excludes scholarships.

Recent Grants
Note: Grants derived from 2001 Form 990.
General

40,000	World Forestry Center, Portland, OR
30,000	Columbia River Maritime Museum, Astoria, OR
25,000	George Fox University, Newberg, OR
25,000	Providence St. Vincent Medical Foundation, Portland, OR
25,000	YMCA of Columbia-Willamette, Portland, OR
20,000	DePaul Treatment Centers, Portland, OR
20,000	Portland Art Museum, Portland, OR
18,000	Oregon Historical Society, Portland, OR
15,000	Cascade Pacific Council Boy Scouts of America, Portland, OR
15,000	Health Data Research, Inc., Lebanon, OR

NATHANIEL WHEELER TRUST

Giving Contact
Stephen Fitch
c/o Fleet National Bank
Fleet Private Clients Group
446 Main Street
Worcester, MA 01608
Phone: (508)793-4205

Description
Founded: 1997
EIN: 046437271
Organization Type: Private Foundation
Giving Locations: MA
Grant Types: General Support.

Financial Summary
Total Giving: $52,170 (2001)
Assets: $1,428,469 (2001)

Typical Recipients
Arts & Humanities: Libraries
Civic & Public Affairs: Botanical Gardens/Parks, Civic & Public Affairs-General, Urban & Community Affairs
Religion: Churches
Social Services: Senior Services

Application Procedures
Initial Contact: Send a brief letter of inquiry.
Deadlines: None.

Restrictions
Beautification projects in and for the city of Worcester.

Additional Information
Trust(s): Fleet National Bank MA

Grants Analysis
Disclosure Period: calendar year ending 2001
Total Grants: $52,170
Number of Grants: 7
Average Grant: $7,453
Highest Grant: $14,459
Lowest Grant: $1,900

Recent Grants
Note: Grants derived from 2001 Form 990.
Library-Related

11,000	Worcester Public Library, Worcester, MA

General

14,459	Park Spirit of Worcester, Worcester, MA
10,385	Trinity Lutheran Church
6,444	Friends of Worcester Senior Center, Worcester, MA
5,260	Robert H. Goddard Association
2,722	Worcester Common Ground, Worcester, MA
1,900	Tower Hill, Worcester, MA

WHIRLPOOL CORP.

Company Headquarters
Benton Harbor, MI
Web: http://www.whirlpool.com

Company Description
Founded: 1911
Ticker: WHR
Exchange: NYSE
Revenue: US$13.22 billion (2004)
Profit: US$406 million (2004)
Employees: 68000 (2003)
Fortune Rank: 160, per FORTUNE Magazine's list of 500 Largest U.S. Corporations (2004).
SIC(s): 3582 Commercial Laundry Equipment, 3585 Refrigeration & Heating Equipment, 3631 Household Cooking Equipment, 3633 Household Laundry Equipment.

Operating Locations
Whirlpool Corp. (AR--Fort Smith; IN--Evansville, La Porte; MI--Benton Harbor; OH--Clyde, Findlay, Marion; SC--Columbia; TN--Knoxville, LaVergne)

Whirlpool Foundation

Giving Contact
Barbara Hall, Foundation Contact
Whirlpool Foundation
2000 North M-63
Benton Harbor, MI 49022
Phone: (616)923-5583
Fax: (616)923-3214
Web: http://www.whirlpoolcorp.com/whr/foundation/index.html

Description
EIN: 386077342
Organization Type: Corporate Foundation
Giving Locations: operating locations.
Grant Types: Employee Matching Gifts, Project, Scholarship.
Note: Employee matching gift ratio: 1 to 1. Scholarships are for employees' children only.

Financial Summary
Total Giving: $5,790,505 (fiscal year ending March 31, 2003); $11,800,812 (fiscal 2002); $5,397,553 (fiscal 2001). Note: Contributes through corporate direct giving program and foundation.
Giving Analysis: Giving for fiscal 2001 includes: foundation scholarships ($374,511); foundation matching gifts ($1,086,842); foundation grants to

United Way ($1,339,681); foundation ($2,596,519)
Assets: $1,034,336 (fiscal 2003); $4,109,465 (fiscal 2002); $14,194,334 (fiscal 2001)
Gifts Received: $4,000,000 (fiscal 2003); $3,000,000 (fiscal 1999); $2,000,000 (fiscal 1996). Note: Foundation receives gifts from Whirlpool Corp.

Typical Recipients

Arts & Humanities: Arts Associations & Councils, Arts Centers, Arts Funds, Arts Institutes, Ballet, Community Arts, Dance, Ethnic & Folk Arts, Arts & Humanities-General, Historic Preservation, History & Archaeology, Libraries, Literary Arts, Museums/Galleries, Music, Opera, Performing Arts, Public Broadcasting, Theater, Visual Arts
Civic & Public Affairs: Botanical Gardens/Parks, Business/Free Enterprise, Civil Rights, Clubs, Community Foundations, Economic Development, Economic Policy, Employment/Job Training, First Amendment Issues, Civic & Public Affairs-General, Hispanic Affairs, Housing, Law & Justice, Municipalities/Towns, Nonprofit Management, Philanthropic Organizations, Professional & Trade Associations, Public Policy, Safety, Urban & Community Affairs, Women's Affairs
Education: Afterschool/Enrichment Programs, Arts/Humanities Education, Business Education, Colleges & Universities, Community & Junior Colleges, Economic Education, Education Associations, Education Funds, Education Reform, Elementary Education (Private), Elementary Education (Public), Engineering/Technological Education, Education-General, International Studies, Journalism/Media Education, Literacy, Medical Education, Minority Education, Preschool Education, Private Education (Precollege), Public Education (Precollege), Science/Mathematics Education, Secondary Education (Private), Social Sciences Education, Student Aid, Vocational & Technical Education
Environment: Environment-General
Health: Cancer, Clinics/Medical Centers, Emergency/Ambulance Services, Health Funds, Health Organizations, Hospitals, Public Health
International: Foreign Educational Institutions, Health Care/Hospitals, International Development, International Organizations, International Relations
Religion: Dioceses, Ministries, Religious Welfare
Science: Science Exhibits & Fairs, Scientific Centers & Institutes, Scientific Organizations
Social Services: Animal Protection, Big Brothers/Big Sisters, Child Abuse, Child Welfare, Community Centers, Community Service Organizations, Counseling, Day Care, Delinquency & Criminal Rehabilitation, Domestic Violence, Emergency Relief, Family Planning, Family Services, Food/Clothing Distribution, Homes, People with Disabilities, Recreation & Athletics, Senior Services, Sexual Abuse, Shelters/Homelessness, Social Services-General, Substance Abuse, United Funds/United Ways, Veterans, Volunteer Services, YMCA/YWCA/YMHA/YWHA, Youth Organizations

Application Procedures

Initial Contact: Send a brief letter or telephone call for guidelines and application form.
Application Requirements: Submit a letter accompanied by the prescribed application form.
Deadlines: January 1, April 1, July 1, and October 1.

Restrictions

Does not support dinners or special events, fraternal organizations, goodwill advertising, individuals, political or lobbying groups, or religious organizations for sectarian purposes.

Corporate Officials

J. C. Anderson: vice president north americaeo, director PRIM CORP EMPL vice president north america: Whirlpool Corp.
David Ray Whitwam: chairman, president, chief executive officer, director B Madison, WI 1942. ED University of Wisconsin BS (1967). PRIM CORP EMPL

chairman, president, chief executive officer, director: Whirlpool Corp. CORP AFFIL director: Combustion Engineering Inc.; director: PP&G Industries Inc. NONPR AFFIL member: National Council Housing Industries; president: Soup Kitchen; fellow: Aspen Institute; director: Conference Board. CLUB AFFIL Point O Woods Club.

Foundation Officials

Daniel F. Hopp: president, chairman
Alan Shaw: trustee
Tom Welke: trustee
David Ray Whitwam: director (see above)

Grants Analysis

Disclosure Period: fiscal year ending March 31, 2003
Total Grants: $2,419,650*
Number of Grants: 176
Average Grant: $13,748
Highest Grant: $580,000
Lowest Grant: $100
Typical Range: $100 to $50,000
*Note: Giving excludes matching gifts, scholarship, and United Way.

Recent Grants

Note: Grants derived from 2003 Form 990.
General

662,528	United Way of Southwest Michigan, Benton Harbor, MI
580,000	Community Economic Development Corporation, Traverse City, MI
462,805	Center for World Class Communities, Benton Harbor, MI
187,196	United Way of Fort Smith Area Inc., Ft. Smith, AR
150,000	University of Notre Dame, Notre Dame, IN
143,099	United Way, Fremont, OH
130,146	United Way, Ocala, FL
124,232	United Way of Southwestern Indiana, Evansville, IN
100,000	Young Men's Christian Association of Marion Ohio, Marion, OH
91,704	Tulsa Area United Way, Tulsa, OK

WHITAKER FOUNDATION

Giving Contact

Peter G. Katona, President & Chief Executive Officer
1700 North Moore Street, Suite 2200
Arlington, VA 22209
Phone: (703)528-2430
Fax: (703)528-2431
E-mail: info@whitaker.org
Web: http://www.whitaker.org

Alternate Contact

4718 Old Gettysburg Road, Suite 405
Mechanicsburg, PA 17055-8411
Phone: (717)763-1391
Note: For Harrisburg and Naples regional programs.

Description

Founded: 1975
EIN: 222096948
Organization Type: General Purpose Foundation
Giving Locations: , Harrisburg FL: Naples for regional programs for research, special opportunity, and other grant programs.
Grant Types: Award, Conference/Seminar, Employee Matching Gifts, Fellowship, Research.

Donor Information

Founder: Established as a trust in New York in 1975 by Mr. U. A. Whitaker. Mr. Whitaker founded Aircraft-Marine Products, now known as AMP, Inc., and was

the former chairman of both the company and its operating subsidiaries abroad.

Financial Summary

Total Giving: $58,046,393 (2003); $71,187,397 (2002); $66,489,481 (2001)
Giving Analysis: Giving for 2003 includes: foundation matching gifts ($171,655); foundation fellowships ($4,669,552)
Assets: $188,295,365 (2003); $246,225,766 (2002); $370,095,910 (2001)

Typical Recipients

Arts & Humanities: Arts Associations & Councils, Arts Centers, Libraries, Museums/Galleries, Music, Opera, Theater
Civic & Public Affairs: Community Foundations, Employment/Job Training, Civic & Public Affairs-General, Housing
Education: Arts/Humanities Education, Business Education, Colleges & Universities, Community & Junior Colleges, Education Associations, Engineering/Technological Education, Education-General, Journalism/Media Education, Legal Education, Medical Education, Private Education (Precollege), Public Education (Precollege), Science/Mathematics Education, Student Aid
Environment: Environment-General
Health: Cancer, Children's Health/Hospitals, Clinics/Medical Centers, Eyes/Blindness, Geriatric Health, Heart, Hospices, Hospitals, Hospitals (University Affiliated), Medical Rehabilitation, Medical Research, Mental Health, Prenatal Health Issues, Preventive Medicine/Wellness Organizations, Public Health, Research/Studies Institutes, Respiratory, Speech & Hearing
International: Foreign Educational Institutions, Health Care/Hospitals, Missionary/Religious Activities
Religion: Churches, Ministries
Science: Science-General, Scientific Centers & Institutes, Scientific Research
Social Services: Community Service Organizations, United Funds/United Ways, YMCA/YWCA/YMHA/YWHA, Youth Organizations

Application Procedures

Initial Contact: Applicants must obtain a copy of the current program guidelines by telephone, email, or letter before submitting an application. Alternatively, program announcements and application forms are available through the Internet.
Deadlines: Varies for each of the program areas. Contact the foundation website for specific deadlines.
Review Process: In judging eligibility for research grants, the foundation looks for two factors: the project must significantly involve the use of innovative engineering techniques, and the investigators must be relative beginners in their research careers. Outside the three-county area may apply for outreach or networking grants that would benefit secondary school students residing in the three-county area.
Notes: Most programs at the foundation do not accept new applications. The foundation will close permanently in 2006.

Restrictions

To obtain a biomedical research grant, the principal investigator must be a member of the faculty or research staff of the applicant institution, and have received a doctorate less than eight years prior to submitting a preliminary proposal, or have completed all residencies less than seven years before. Grants generally will not be made to support operating expenses of established programs, nor to finance deficits.

Additional Information

The Whitaker Foundation will spend all of its assets, primarily in support of education and research programs in biomedical engineering, then go out of business at the end of 2006.

Publications: Guidelines; Annual Report; Application Form

Foundation Officials

Dr. William Ralph Brody, PhD: committee member B Stockton, CA 1944. ED Massachusetts Institute of Technology BSEE (1965); Massachusetts Institute of Technology MSEE (1966); Stanford University MD (1970); Stanford University PhDEE (1972). PRIM NONPR EMPL president: John Hopkins University School of Medicine. CORP AFFIL director: Mercantile Bankshares; directory: Medtronic Inc. NONPR AFFIL member: International Society of Magnetic Resonance in Medicine; fellow: NAS; member: Institute Sys Science; fellow: Institute Electrical & Electronic Engineers; fellow: Institute Medicine and Biomed Engineering; fellow: American Heart Association; fellow: American College Cardiology; fellow: American College Radiology; member: America Institute of Biomedical Engineering; member: America Academy of Arts and Sciences.

G. Burtt Holmes, OD: chairman

Thomas A. Holmes: committee member

Peter Geza Katona, ScD: president, chief executive officer B Budapest, Hungary 1937. ED University of Michigan BS (1960); Massachusetts Institute of Technology SM (1962); Massachusetts Institute of Technology ScD (1965). PRIM NONPR EMPL president, chief executive officer: Whitaker Foundation. NONPR AFFIL senior member: Biomedical Engineering Society; senior member: Institute Electrical & Electronics Engineers; senior member: American Society Engineering Education; fellow: American Institute Medical & Biological Engineering; senior member: American Physiological Society; fellow: American Association Advancement Science.

James E. Kielley, JD: committee member

John H. Linehan, PhD: vice president ED Marquette University BS (1960); Rensselaer Polytechnic Institute MS (1962); University of Wisconsin, Madison PhD (1968). NONPR AFFIL founding fellow: America Institute of Medical and Biological Engineers.

Harold A. McInnes: committee member B Groton, CT 1927. ED Massachusetts Institute of Technology BSME (1949). PRIM CORP EMPL chairman, chief executive officer, director: AMP Inc. NONPR AFFIL committee member: Greater Harrisburg Foundation.

Portia W. Shumaker: committee member

Grants Analysis

Disclosure Period: calendar year ending 2003
Total Grants: $53,205,186*
Number of Grants: 339
Average Grant: $126,357*
Highest Grant: $6,404,136
Lowest Grant: $2,500
Typical Range: $50,000 to $250,000
*Note: Giving excludes matching gifts; fellowships. Average grant figure excludes two highest grants ($10,623,024).

Recent Grants

Note: Grants derived from 2001 Form 990.
General

9,038,000 Regents of the University of California, Berkeley, CA -- a leadership program for bioengineering education, research and industrial corporation

4,025,167 Washington University, St. Louis, MO -- Special Grant from Leadership Application

2,708,840 Johns Hopkins University, Baltimore, MD -- Biomedical Engineering Institute at Johns Hopkins

2,390,000 University of Virginia, Charlottesville, VA -- building partnerships between engineering and medicine

2,141,471 Georgia Tech Research Corporation, Atlanta, GA -- An integrated Approach to Biomedical Engineering Education and Research

1,680,932 University of California Davis, Davis, CA -- Sensors Vectors and Systems

1,000,000 Brown University, Providence, RI -- Cellular-and SubCellular-Based Biomedical Engineering at Boston University

1,000,000 University of California Berkeley, Berkeley, CA -- A plan for the Future of Bioengineering

832,500 Greater Harrisburg Foundation, Harrisburg, PA -- March 14, 2001 Awards for 2001 Program

829,545 University of Michigan, Ann Arbor, MI -- reorganization of biomedical engineering

HELEN F. WHITAKER FUND

Giving Contact

Miles J. Gibbons, Jr., Executive Director
4718 Old Gettysburg Road, Suite 209
Mechanicsburg, PA 17055-8411
Phone: (717)763-1600
Fax: (717)763-1832

Description

Founded: 1983
EIN: 222459399
Organization Type: Specialized/Single Purpose Foundation
Giving Locations: FL: Naples; PA: Harrisburg, Philadelphia nationally.
Grant Types: Endowment, Fellowship, General Support, Matching, Multiyear/Continuing Support, Operating Expenses, Project.
Note: Program development support is also offered.

Donor Information

Founder: Established in 1983 by the late Helen F. Whitaker.

Financial Summary

Total Giving: $6,588,081 (fiscal year ending July 31, 2003); $6,494,651 (fiscal 2002); $7,763,808 (fiscal 2001)
Assets: $14,945,574 (fiscal 2003); $20,751,589 (fiscal 2002); $26,738,852 (fiscal 2001)
Gifts Received: $343,853 (fiscal 2003); $548,044 (fiscal 1993); $34,541 (fiscal 1992). Note: In 2003, contributions were received from the estate of Helen F. Whitaker.

Typical Recipients

Arts & Humanities: Arts Associations & Councils, Arts Centers, Arts Festivals, Arts Funds, Arts Outreach, Ballet, Dance, Arts & Humanities-General, Museums/Galleries, Music, Opera, Performing Arts, Public Broadcasting, Theater
Civic & Public Affairs: Community Foundations
Education: Arts/Humanities Education
International: Foreign Arts Organizations, International Organizations

Application Procedures

Initial Contact: Contact foundation for application guidelines. Preliminary proposals are required.
Application Requirements: Preliminary proposals should include the following: a brief history of the organization; a clear statement of the proposed program's objectives; a brief description of the proposed program; the proposed timetable for the program; a summary budget for each year of the program and the amount of that budget that will be requested from the Whitaker Fund; the identity and affiliation of the contact person for the program; a brief statement of the qualifications of the person who will be responsible for implementing the program; and the criteria for measuring the program's success or failure.

Deadlines: Preliminary proposal deadlines are March 1 for consideration at the June meeting, July 1 for the October meeting, November 1 for the February meeting.
Review Process: Committee meetings are held quarterly, in February, June, and October.
Evaluative Criteria: The Fund considers the following criteria when evaluating proposals: "Quality of the applicant, program participants, and musical content; integrity of program structure; relationship of program to applicant's mission; level of participants (postconservatory); scope (national in reach, reputation or impact); predominance of American or America-based participants; cost-benefit ratio per direct participant; potential for significant impact." The Fund also examines whether organizations are financially viable, have been in existence for at least five years, employ at least three full-time people, can prove reasonable support from other sources, and primary serve musicians or musical institutions in the United States. "The Helen F. Whitaker Fund: A Summary of Grant Programs"

Restrictions

Grants are made only under announced competitive grant programs that provide support for classical music in the United States. Support is not available for presenting or performing organizations.

Additional Information

The Whitaker Fund plans to spend down all of its assets by the end of 2006. Select organizations are being invited to discuss how The Fund can offer support for programs that would ensure the continued development of Western classical music. The Fund is designing such initiatives to address certain sectors of the classical music scene, rather than aiming them at single organizations. Participation in these initiatives is therefore by invitation only.
Publications: Guidelines

Foundation Officials

Carmelita Biggie: committee member
Miles J. Gibbons, Jr.: executive director, comm mem B Scranton, PA 1935. ED Dickinson College BA (1957); Georgetown University JD (1964); Harvard University (1966). NONPR AFFIL co-chairman: Foundation Executive Roundtable; member: Rotary Club Harrisburg; director, chairman: Capital Campaign Review Committee.
Ruth W. Holmes, PhD: comm mem

Grants Analysis

Disclosure Period: fiscal year ending July 31, 2003
Total Grants: $6,588,081
Number of Grants: 58
Average Grant: $67,027*
Highest Grant: $1,750,000
Lowest Grant: $750
Typical Range: $30,000 to $150,000
*Note: Average grant figure excludes two highest grants ($2,834,577).

Recent Grants

Note: Grants derived from 2002 Form 990.
General

1,500,000 Marlboro Music School and Festival -- for program endowment-matching grant

835,000 American Composers Forum, St. Paul, MN

402,087 Chamber Music America, New York, NY

311,850 Opera America, Washington, DC

275,000 Chamber Music America, New York, NY -- fund for Support Programs and Services 2002-2002

233,645 Aspen Music Festival and School, Aspen, CO -- fund for academy of conducting

200,000 Concert Artists Guild, New York, NY

200,000 Opera America, Washington, DC -- fund for National Music Leadership Coalition

175,000	American Symphony Orchestra League, Washington, DC -- fund for Orchestra Management Fellowship Program
175,000	New World Symphony, Miami Beach, FL -- fund for Musician Development Program

W. P. AND H. B. WHITE FOUNDATION

Giving Contact
M. Margaret Blanford, Executive Director
540 Frontage Rd., Suite 3240
Northfield, IL 60093
Phone: (847)446-1441

Description
Founded: 1953
EIN: 362601558
Organization Type: Private Foundation
Giving Locations: IL: Chicago metropolitan area
Grant Types: Capital, Emergency, General Support, Multiyear/Continuing Support, Operating Expenses, Professorship, Project, Research, Scholarship.

Donor Information
Founder: the late William P. White, the late Hazel B. White

Financial Summary
Total Giving: $1,297,000 (2003); $1,732,700 (2002); $2,166,750 (2001)
Giving Analysis: Giving for 2003 includes: foundation scholarships ($158,500); 2002: foundation scholarships ($325,000)
Assets: $28,616,560 (2003); $23,134,965 (2002); $33,376,812 (2001)

Typical Recipients
Arts & Humanities: Historic Preservation, Libraries, Museums/Galleries, Public Broadcasting, Theater
Civic & Public Affairs: Economic Development, Employment/Job Training, Hispanic Affairs, Housing, Public Policy, Urban & Community Affairs
Education: Afterschool/Enrichment Programs, Arts/Humanities Education, Colleges & Universities, Continuing Education, Education Associations, Education Reform, Education-General, Leadership Training, Literacy, Medical Education, Private Education (Precollege), Public Education (Precollege), Science/Mathematics Education, Secondary Education (Private), Student Aid, Vocational & Technical Education
Health: Cancer, Children's Health/Hospitals, Clinics/Medical Centers, Emergency/Ambulance Services, Heart, Hospitals, Medical Rehabilitation, Medical Research, Mental Health, Prenatal Health Issues, Public Health
Religion: Religious Welfare
Science: Science Museums, Scientific Centers & Institutes
Social Services: At-Risk Youth, Child Abuse, Child Welfare, Community Centers, Community Service Organizations, Emergency Relief, Family Services, Food/Clothing Distribution, People with Disabilities, Scouts, United Funds/United Ways, YMCA/YWCA/YMHA/YWHA, Youth Organizations

Application Procedures
Initial Contact: Send a brief letter of inquiry.
Application Requirements: Include program summary, organization history, and principals involved.
Deadlines: February 1, May 1, August 1, and November 1.

Restrictions
The foundation does not make grants to individuals or for land acquisition, building funds, endowments, publications, conferences, deficit spending, matching gifts, or loans.

Additional Information
Publications: Application Guidelines

Foundation Officials
M. Margaret Blandford: executive director
Philip O. White, Jr.: vice president, treasurer
Robert P. White: director
Roger B. White: president
Steven R. White: secretary

Grants Analysis
Disclosure Period: calendar year ending 2003
Total Grants: $1,138,500*
Number of Grants: 77
Average Grant: $14,786
Highest Grant: $30,000
Lowest Grant: $4,500
Typical Range: $10,000 to $20,000
*Note: Giving excludes scholarships.

Recent Grants
Note: Grants derived from 2001 Form 990.
General

50,000	Catholic Charities, Chicago, IL
45,000	Ada S. McKinley Community Services, Chicago, IL -- Comprehensive Educational Program
35,000	Golden Apple Foundation, Chicago, IL -- Chicago Golden Apple Scholars
35,000	Holy Trinity High School, Chicago, IL
35,000	Midtown Educational Foundation, Chicago, IL
33,000	Big Shoulders Fund, Chicago, IL -- capital funds
30,000	American Red Cross of Greater Chicago, Chicago, IL
30,000	Cristo Rey Jesuit High School, Chicago, IL
30,000	Cycle, Chicago, IL
25,000	Austin Career Education Center, Chicago, IL

G. R. WHITE TRUST

Giving Contact
Don Smith, Trust Officer
c/o Bank One
PO Box 2050
Ft. Worth, TX 76113
Phone: (817)884-4165

Description
EIN: 756094930
Organization Type: Private Foundation
Giving Locations: TX
Grant Types: Capital, General Support, Scholarship.

Donor Information
Founder: G. R. White

Financial Summary
Total Giving: $354,207 (fiscal year ending September 30, 2003); $331,534 (fiscal 2001)
Assets: $7,785,179 (fiscal 2003); $7,025,838 (fiscal 2001)

Typical Recipients
Arts & Humanities: Arts Associations & Councils, History & Archaeology, Libraries, Museums/Galleries
Civic & Public Affairs: Chambers of Commerce, Economic Development, Civic & Public Affairs-General, Municipalities/Towns, Rural Affairs, Safety, Urban & Community Affairs
Education: Agricultural Education, Colleges & Universities, Continuing Education, Engineering/Technological Education, Legal Education, Literacy, Preschool Education, Private Education (Precollege), Religious Education, Science/Mathematics Education, Secondary Education (Private), Special Education, Student Aid
Environment: Resource Conservation, Wildlife Protection
Health: Eyes/Blindness, Hospitals, Medical Rehabilitation, Public Health, Research/Studies Institutes
Religion: Churches, Religious Organizations, Religious Welfare, Seminaries
Social Services: At-Risk Youth, Child Welfare, Community Service Organizations, People with Disabilities, Senior Services, Social Services-General, United Funds/United Ways, YMCA/YWCA/YMHA/YWHA, Youth Organizations

Application Procedures
Initial Contact: Send a brief letter of inquiry.
Application Requirements: Include a description of organization, purpose of funds sought, amount requested, and list of directors.
Deadlines: September 1.

Additional Information
Trust(s): Bank One

Grants Analysis
Disclosure Period: fiscal year ending September 30, 2003
Total Grants: $354,207
Number of Grants: 39
Average Grant: $7,441*
Highest Grant: $62,457
Lowest Grant: $1,000
Typical Range: $5,000 to $10,000
*Note: Average grant figure excludes highest grant.

Recent Grants
Note: Grants derived from fiscal 2000 Form 990.
General

58,186	Texas A & M University, College Station, TX -- for student loans
50,000	Texas and Southwestern Cattle Raisers Foundation, Ft. Worth, TX -- for building fund
50,000	University of Texas Law School, Austin, TX -- funding for Fred Wulff Fund
20,000	Casa Care, Inc., Brady, TX -- charitable gift
20,000	Rochelle Volunteer Fire Department, Rochelle, TX -- for purchase of new fire truck
20,000	St. Stephens Episcopal School, Austin, TX -- for science academy
10,000	Baptist General Convention of Texas, Dallas, TX -- for boys and young men camping in Texas
10,000	City of Melvin -- for restoration of Melvin Community Center
10,000	Texas Baptist Missions Foundation, Dallas, TX -- for student center
10,000	VOCA Volunteer Fire Department, Voca, TX -- for fire fighting equipment

WHITECAP FOUNDATION

Giving Contact
800 Wilshire Blvd., Suite 1010
Los Angeles, CA 90017
Phone: (213)624-5401
E-mail: execdirector@Whitecapfdn.org
Web: http://www.whitecapfdn.org

Description
Founded: 1986
EIN: 954111120
Organization Type: Private Foundation

Giving Locations: CA
Grant Types: General Support.

Financial Summary

Total Giving: $1,623,310 (fiscal year ending November 30, 2004); $1,479,590 (fiscal 2001)
Assets: $4,359,737 (fiscal 2004); $9,034,362 (fiscal 2001)
Gifts Received: $500,000 (fiscal 2001); $500,000 (fiscal 2000); $200,000 (fiscal 1998). Note: In fiscal 2001, contributions were received from Brack and Elizabeth Duker.

Typical Recipients

Arts & Humanities: Dance, Libraries
Civic & Public Affairs: Asian American Affairs, Community Foundations, Civic & Public Affairs-General, Hispanic Affairs, Nonprofit Management, Professional & Trade Associations, Urban & Community Affairs, Women's Affairs
Education: Business Education, Colleges & Universities, Continuing Education, Education Associations, Elementary Education (Public), Education-General, Literacy, Private Education (Precollege), Public Education (Precollege), Religious Education, Special Education
Environment: Environment-General, Resource Conservation, Wildlife Protection
Health: Emergency/Ambulance Services, Mental Health
International: Foreign Educational Institutions, Health Care/Hospitals, International Relief Efforts, Missionary/Religious Activities
Religion: Churches, Religious Organizations, Religious Welfare
Social Services: Child Welfare, Community Centers, Community Service Organizations, Emergency Relief, Family Services, Recreation & Athletics, Scouts, Shelters/Homelessness, Social Services-General, YMCA/YWCA/YMHA/YWHA, Youth Organizations

Application Procedures

Initial Contact: Send a brief letter of inquiry.
Application Requirements: Include a description of organization, a description of the project, and a project budget.
Deadlines: None.

Restrictions

Preference is given to organizations involved with children and families, education, and wildlife conservation.

Foundation Officials

Brack Duker: chief financial officer, secretary
Elizabeth Duker: president

Grants Analysis

Disclosure Period: fiscal year ending November 30, 2004
Total Grants: $1,623,310
Number of Grants: 56
Average Grant: $26,842*
Highest Grant: $147,000
Lowest Grant: $3,675
Typical Range: $10,000 to $40,000
*Note: Average grant figure excludes highest grants.

Recent Grants

Note: Grants derived from fiscal 2004 Form 990.
General

147,000	Our Saviour Center, El Monte, CA
60,798	Chinatown Service Center, Los Angeles, CA
53,355	Mount St. Mary's College, Los Angeles, CA
37,500	Puente Learning Center, Los Angeles, CA
35,000	Valle Lindo School District, El Monte, CA
32,000	Angeles Girl Scout Council, Los Angeles, CA
30,741	Salvation Army Weingart Youth Center, Los Angeles, CA
30,611	Las Familias del Pueblo, Los Angeles, CA
30,210	Korean American Family Service Center, Flushing, NY
30,000	P.F. Bresee Foundation, Los Angeles, CA

JOSEPH B. WHITEHEAD FOUNDATION

Giving Contact

Charles H. McTier, President
50 Hurt Plaza, Suite 1200
Atlanta, GA 30303
Phone: (404)522-6755
Fax: (404)522-7026
E-mail: fdns@woodruff.org
Web: http://www.jbwhitehead.org

Description

Founded: 1937
EIN: 586001954
Organization Type: General Purpose Foundation
Giving Locations: GA: Atlanta including metropolitan area
Grant Types: Capital, Challenge, General Support, Matching, Multiyear/Continuing Support, Project, Seed Money.
Note: The foundation also provides grants for construction, land acquisition, and equipment.

Donor Information

Founder: Established in 1937 by the will of Joseph B. Whitehead Jr., in memory of his father, Joseph B. Whitehead, a Tennessee tax lawyer who conceived the idea of bottling Coca-Cola, (then a popular fountain beverage in the South), with friend, Benjamin Thomas, in 1899. The two men were granted an exclusive contract to bottle and sell Coca-Cola in most of the United States, by Asa Candler, president of the Coca-Cola Company. Whitehead moved to Atlanta, with partner John T. Lupton, to establish the Dixie Coca-Cola Bottling Company to serve the southeastern, southwestern and middle western states. The foundation is affiliated with the Lettie Pate Evans Foundation and the Lettie Pate Whitehead Foundation, established by Mr. Whitehead's mother and brother, respectively.

Financial Summary

Total Giving: $20,555,000 (2004); $18,925,000 (2003); $18,250,000 (2002)
Giving Analysis: Giving for 2004 includes: foundation grants to United Way ($8,000,000); 2002: foundation grants to United Way ($6,000,000)
Assets: $770,753,090 (2004); $913,278,210 (2003); $802,773,523 (2002)

Typical Recipients

Arts & Humanities: Arts Centers, Arts Festivals, Historic Preservation, History & Archaeology, Literary Arts, Performing Arts
Civic & Public Affairs: Botanical Gardens/Parks, Business/Free Enterprise, Community Foundations, Economic Development, Employment/Job Training, Civic & Public Affairs-General, Hispanic Affairs, Housing, Law & Justice, Legal Aid, Nonprofit Management, Philanthropic Organizations, Urban & Community Affairs, Zoos/Aquariums
Education: Afterschool/Enrichment Programs, Colleges & Universities, Economic Education, Education Associations, Education Reform, Elementary Education (Private), Engineering/Technological Education, Environmental Education, Faculty Development, Education-General, International Studies, Literacy, Pre-school Education, Private Education (Precollege), Public Education (Precollege), School Volunteerism, Science/Mathematics Education, Special Education, Student Aid
Environment: Energy, Environment-General
Health: Alzheimer's Disease, Arthritis, Cancer, Children's Health/Hospitals, Clinics/Medical Centers, Health-General, Health Policy/Cost Containment, Health Organizations, Home-Care Services, Hospitals, Kidney, Medical Rehabilitation, Mental Health, Nursing Services, Prenatal Health Issues, Preventive Medicine/Wellness Organizations, Public Health, Respiratory, Single-Disease Health Associations, Trauma Treatment
International: Health Care/Hospitals, International Affairs, International Organizations, International Relief Efforts
Religion: Ministries, Religious Organizations, Religious Welfare
Science: Science Museums, Scientific Organizations
Social Services: Animal Protection, At-Risk Youth, Big Brothers/Big Sisters, Camps, Child Abuse, Child Welfare, Community Centers, Community Service Organizations, Counseling, Delinquency & Criminal Rehabilitation, Domestic Violence, Family Planning, Family Services, Food/Clothing Distribution, Homes, People with Disabilities, Scouts, Senior Services, Sexual Abuse, Shelters/Homelessness, Social Services-General, Substance Abuse, United Funds/United Ways, Volunteer Services, YMCA/YWCA/YMHA/YWHA, Youth Organizations

Application Procedures

Initial Contact: Organizations seeking support should submit a letter of inquiry first. Proposals, when submitted, should be in letter form.
Application Requirements: Description of the organization, its purposes, programs, staffing, and governing board; the organization's latest financial statements, including the most recent audit report; a description of the proposed project and full justification for its funding; an itemized project budget, including other sources of support in hand or anticipated; and evidence from the IRS of the organization's tax-exempt status and that the organization is not a private foundation.
Deadlines: February 1 for the board's April meeting and September 1 for the November meeting.
Review Process: Additional information or a site visit may be requested. Applicants will receive final notification within thirty days of the trustees' meetings, which are held in April and November.

Restrictions

Grants are limited to a selected list of tax-exempt public charities and selected governmental agencies located and operating in metropolitan Atlanta, GA. Preference is given to one-time capital projects; awards for basic operating expenses usually are avoided. No grants to individuals. No loans.

Additional Information

The foundation shares offices and administrative staff with the Robert W. Woodruff Foundation, Lettie Pate Evans Foundation, Lettie Pate Whitehead Foundation, and Ichauway, Inc. Grant inquiries and proposals submitted to the Joseph B. Whitehead Foundation may also be considered by one or more of the associated foundations. It is not necessary to communicate separately with more than one of these foundations in seeking information or requesting grant support.
Publications: Guidelines; Brochure

Grants Analysis

Disclosure Period: calendar year ending 2004
Total Grants: $10,555,000*
Number of Grants: 20
Average Grant: $267,941*
Highest Grant: $2,000,000
Lowest Grant: $80,000
Typical Range: $100,000 to $500,000

*Note: Giving excludes United Way. Average grant figure excludes three highest grants ($6,000,000).

Recent Grants

Note: Grants derived from 2003 Form 990.
General

3,000,000	United Way of Metropolitan Atlanta Inc., Atlanta, GA -- continued support for Smart Start Georgia formerly the Georgia early learning initiative
3,000,000	United Way of Metropolitan Atlanta Inc., Atlanta, GA -- continued support for Smart Start Georgia
2,000,000	Sheltering Arms, Atlanta, GA -- to build and equip four new childcare centers in South Fulton county
2,000,000	YMCA of Metropolitan Atlanta Inc., Atlanta, GA
1,000,000	Boy Scouts of America, Atlanta, GA -- development of the Cub Scout Adventure Camp at Bert Adams Scout
1,000,000	Communities in Schools of Georgia, Atlanta, GA -- continued program support and statewide establishment of performance learning centers
1,000,000	Georgia Partnership for Excellence in Education, Atlanta, GA -- continued program support for the project
1,000,000	Salvation Army, Atlanta, GA -- construction of a center for worship and education adjacent to the college
1,000,000	Sheltering Arms, Atlanta, GA -- to build and equip four new childcare centers in South Fulton county
1,000,000	Sheltering Arms, Atlanta, GA -- to build and equip four new childcare centers in South Fulton county

WHITING FOUNDATION

Giving Contact

Donald E. Johnson, Jr., President & Trustee
Whiting Foundation
901 Citizens Bank Building
Flint, MI 48502
Phone: (810)767-3600

Description

Founded: 1940
EIN: 386056693
Organization Type: Private Foundation
Giving Locations: MI
Grant Types: General Support, Project, Research.

Donor Information

Founder: members of the Johnson family

Financial Summary

Total Giving: $914,500 (fiscal year ending June 30, 2004); $1,136,600 (fiscal 2001)
Giving Analysis: Giving for fiscal 2004 includes: foundation grants to United Way ($19,000); fiscal 2001: foundation grants to United Way ($17,000)
Assets: $22,510,909 (fiscal 2004); $22,374,235 (fiscal 2001)
Gifts Received: In 1990, contributions were received from the estate of Donald E. Johnson.

Typical Recipients

Arts & Humanities: Arts Associations & Councils, Arts Centers, Arts Institutes, Ballet, Libraries, Museums/Galleries, Music, Theater
Civic & Public Affairs: Community Foundations, Civic & Public Affairs-General, Housing, Parades/Festivals, Safety, Urban & Community Affairs
Education: Arts/Humanities Education, Business Education, Colleges & Universities, Education Funds, Gifted & Talented Programs, Medical Education, Minority Education, Private Education (Precollege), Public Education (Precollege), Religious Education, Secondary Education (Public), Special Education
Environment: Environment-General, Resource Conservation
Health: AIDS/HIV, Cancer, Children's Health/Hospitals, Clinics/Medical Centers, Emergency/Ambulance Services, Eyes/Blindness, Geriatric Health, Hospitals, Medical Research, Multiple Sclerosis, Public Health, Single-Disease Health Associations, Trauma Treatment
International: Health Care/Hospitals, International Relations
Religion: Churches, Ministries, Religious Welfare
Social Services: Animal Protection, Big Brothers/Big Sisters, Camps, Child Welfare, Community Service Organizations, Family Planning, Family Services, Food/Clothing Distribution, Homes, People with Disabilities, Recreation & Athletics, Scouts, Senior Services, Shelters/Homelessness, Substance Abuse, United Funds/United Ways, Volunteer Services, YMCA/YWCA/YMHA/YWHA, Youth Organizations

Application Procedures

Initial Contact: Send a brief letter of inquiry.
Application Requirements: Include a description of organization, amount requested, purpose of funds sought, recently audited financial statement, and proof of tax-exempt status.
Deadlines: April 30.

Restrictions

Emphasis is on cancer research, hospital and governmental health programs, public foundations, and educational institutions.

Foundation Officials

Mary Alice J. Heaton: trustee
Donald E. Johnson, Jr.: president, trustee CORP AFFIL president: Advertisers Press.
Marsha A. Kump: executive director
Linda J. LeMieux: trustee
John T. Lindholm: secretary, treasurer, trustee

Grants Analysis

Disclosure Period: fiscal year ending June 30, 2004
Total Grants: $895,500*
Number of Grants: 28
Average Grant: $7,820*
Highest Grant: $500,000
Lowest Grant: $1,000
Typical Range: $1,000 to $10,000
*Note: Giving excludes United Way. Average grant figure excludes three highest grants ($700,000).

Recent Grants

Note: Grants derived from fiscal 2001 Form 990.

General

800,000	Flint Cultural Center, Flint, MI -- for the Joffrey Ballet
115,000	YWCA of Greater Flint, Flint, MI
25,000	American Red Cross, Flint, MI
25,000	Genesee County Habitat for Humanity, Flint, MI
17,000	United Way of Flint and Lapeer Counties, Flint, MI
10,000	Cancer Research Institute Investigator Program, New York, NY
10,000	Cancer Research Institute Investigator Program, New York, NY -- investigator program
10,000	Humane Society of Genesee County, Burton, MI
10,000	Shelter of Flint, Inc., Flint, MI -- children's program
8,500	Genesee Area Focus Fund, Flint, MI

MACAULEY AND HELEN DOW WHITING FOUNDATION

Giving Contact

Helen Dow Whiting, Treasurer & Trustee
PO Box 1980
Sun Valley, ID 83353
Phone: (208)622-9331

Description

Founded: 1957
EIN: 237418814
Organization Type: Private Foundation
Giving Locations: FL; ID; ME; MA: nationally.
Grant Types: General Support.

Financial Summary

Total Giving: $135,000 (2003); $140,250 (2001)
Assets: $5,637,325 (2003); $5,064,283 (2001)

Typical Recipients

Arts & Humanities: Ballet, Dance, Libraries, Music, Public Broadcasting
Civic & Public Affairs: Municipalities/Towns, Zoos/Aquariums
Education: Colleges & Universities, Economic Education, Education Funds, Private Education (Precollege)
Environment: Environment-General, Resource Conservation
Health: Cancer, Clinics/Medical Centers, Hospitals, Hospitals (University Affiliated)
Social Services: Recreation & Athletics

Application Procedures

Initial Contact: Send a brief letter of inquiry describing program or project.
Deadlines: None.

Restrictions

Does not support individuals.

Foundation Officials

Macauley Whiting: president, trustee
Mary Macauley Whiting: secretary, trustee
Sara Whiting: trustee

Grants Analysis

Disclosure Period: calendar year ending 2003
Total Grants: $135,000
Number of Grants: 6
Highest Grant: $45,000
Lowest Grant: $10,000

Recent Grants

Note: Grants derived from 2001 Form 990.

General

40,000	Trinity Preparatory School, Winter Park, FL
35,000	H. Lee Moffitt Cancer Center and Research Institute Foundation, Tampa, FL
25,000	Nature Conservancy, Brunswick, MA
15,000	Hotchkiss School, Blue Hill, ME
10,000	Bay School, Blue Hill, ME
10,000	Wood River Land Trust, Ketchum, ID
5,250	Ballet Foundation, Ketchum, ID

CLAUDE R. AND ETHEL B. WHITTENBERGER FOUNDATION

Giving Contact
William J. Rankin, Chairman
PO Box 1073
Caldwell, ID 83606
Phone: (208)459-4649

Description
Founded: 1970
EIN: 237092604
Organization Type: Private Foundation
Giving Locations: ID
Grant Types: General Support, Scholarship.

Donor Information
Founder: the late Ethel B. Whittenberger

Financial Summary
Total Giving: $294,844 (2003)
Giving Analysis: Giving for 2003 includes: foundation scholarships ($58,900)
Assets: $5,465,371 (2003)

Typical Recipients
Arts & Humanities: Arts Associations & Councils, Arts Outreach, Ballet, Community Arts, Dance, Film & Video, Arts & Humanities-General, History & Archaeology, Libraries, Literary Arts, Museums/Galleries, Music, Public Broadcasting, Theater
Civic & Public Affairs: Botanical Gardens/Parks, Chambers of Commerce, Clubs, Community Foundations, Economic Development, Economic Policy, Hispanic Affairs, Housing, Law & Justice, Municipalities/Towns, Nonprofit Management, Philanthropic Organizations, Zoos/Aquariums
Education: Arts/Humanities Education, Business Education, Colleges & Universities, Economic Education, Education Funds, Education Reform, Elementary Education (Public), Faculty Development, Education-General, Gifted & Talented Programs, Literacy, Minority Education, Public Education (Precollege), Science/Mathematics Education, Secondary Education (Public), Student Aid
Environment: Resource Conservation, Wildlife Protection
Health: Public Health
International: Human Rights
Religion: Churches, Jewish Causes, Religious Welfare
Science: Science Museums, Scientific Centers & Institutes
Social Services: At-Risk Youth, Child Abuse, Child Welfare, Community Service Organizations, Day Care, Family Planning, Family Services, Food/Clothing Distribution, Homes, Recreation & Athletics, Scouts, Social Services-General, Substance Abuse, United Funds/United Ways, Youth Organizations

Application Procedures
Initial Contact: Send outline and budget of project.
Deadlines: None.

Additional Information
Publications: Application Guidelines; Informational Brochure

Foundation Officials
D. Whitman Jones: director
Joe Miller: secretary
Donald Price: director
William J. Rankin: chairman

Grants Analysis
Disclosure Period: calendar year ending 2003
Total Grants: $235,944*
Number of Grants: 41

Average Grant: $5,274*
Highest Grant: $25,000
Lowest Grant: $1,000
Typical Range: $1,000 to $10,000
*****Note:** Giving excludes scholarships. Average grant figure excludes highest grant.

Recent Grants
Note: Grants derived from 2001 Form 990.
General

25,000	Idaho Department of Education, Boise, ID -- Writing Project
14,613	New Heritage Theatre, Boise, ID -- school tours
10,212	Sacajawea Elementary, Caldwell, ID -- student intervention
10,000	Log Cabin Literary Center, Boise, ID -- writers in school
8,613	Planned Parenthood, Boise, ID -- sexuality education
8,000	Caldwell Fine Arts, Caldwell, ID -- school programs
7,113	Boise Philharmonic, Boise, ID -- recitals
6,000	Girls Athletic League, Caldwell, ID -- softball field improvements
5,726	Warhawk Air Museum, Mampa, ID -- field trips
5,000	Greenbelt Civic League, Caldwell, ID -- Rotary Pond Project

HARVEY RANDALL WICKES FOUNDATION

Giving Contact
Hugo E. Braun, Jr., President
4800 Fashion Square Boulevard
472 Plaza North
Saginaw, MI 48604
Phone: (989)799-1850
Fax: (989)799-3327
E-mail: HRWICKES@concentric.net

Description
Founded: 1945
EIN: 386061470
Organization Type: General Purpose Foundation
Giving Locations: MI: Saginaw County
Grant Types: Capital, Challenge, General Support, Scholarship.
Note: The foundation also donates equipment and buildings.

Donor Information
Founder: Established in 1945 in Michigan by the late Harvey Randall Wickes, who was president and later chairman of the Wickes Corporation, which has diversified interests including the merchandising of building supplies.

Financial Summary
Total Giving: $1,784,484 (2003); $1,939,951 (2002); $1,849,532 (2001)
Giving Analysis: Giving for 2003 includes: foundation grants to United Way ($56,500)
Assets: $38,985,619 (2003); $34,850,072 (2002); $38,931,839 (2001)

Typical Recipients
Arts & Humanities: Community Arts, Dance, Arts & Humanities-General, Historic Preservation, History & Archaeology, Libraries, Museums/Galleries, Music, Performing Arts, Theater
Civic & Public Affairs: Botanical Gardens/Parks, Business/Free Enterprise, Chambers of Commerce, Community Foundations, Economic Development, Economic Policy, Employment/Job Training, Civic & Public Affairs-General, Housing, Inner-City Develop-

ment, Municipalities/Towns, Nonprofit Management, Professional & Trade Associations, Public Policy, Safety, Urban & Community Affairs, Zoos/Aquariums
Education: Business Education, Colleges & Universities, Education Funds, Education-General, Literacy, Minority Education, Public Education (Precollege), Religious Education, Student Aid
Health: Cancer, Clinics/Medical Centers, Emergency/Ambulance Services, Eyes/Blindness, Health Funds, Health Organizations, Hospitals, Medical Rehabilitation, Public Health
Religion: Religion-General, Religious Welfare
Social Services: Big Brothers/Big Sisters, Camps, Child Abuse, Child Welfare, Community Centers, Community Service Organizations, Crime Prevention, Emergency Relief, Family Services, Food/Clothing Distribution, Homes, People with Disabilities, Recreation & Athletics, Senior Services, Shelters/Homelessness, Social Services-General, Special Olympics, Substance Abuse, United Funds/United Ways, Volunteer Services, YMCA/YWCA/YMHA/YWHA, Youth Organizations

Application Procedures
Initial Contact: Applications should be in letter form.
Application Requirements: Letters should include specific details as to the proposed use of funds. The foundation will request additional information if necessary.
Deadlines: None.
Review Process: The board of trustees meets in January, April, June, and October.

Restrictions
The foundation does not make grants to individuals, churches, or political organizations. Does not support organizations outside the Saginaw County, Michigan area.

Additional Information
Publications: Guidelines

Foundation Officials
Hugo E. Braun, Jr.: vice president, secretary, trustee B Saginaw, MI 1932. ED Yale University BA (1954); University of Michigan LLB (1957). CORP AFFIL director: Citizens Banking Corp.; director: Wolohan Lumber Co.; director: Citizens Bank Michigan.
Mary Lou Case: trustee PRIM CORP EMPL vice president: W.L. Case & Co.
Kurt Ewend: trustee PRIM CORP EMPL executive vice president, director: Saginaw Bay Underwriters Inc.
James V. Finkbeiner: president, trustee, chairman board B Green Bay, WI 1914. ED University of Michigan BA (1935); University of Michigan JD (1937). PRIM CORP EMPL attorney: Braun Kendrick Finkbeiner Schafer Murphy.
William A. Hendrick: trustee
Richard P. Heuschele, MD: trustee
Craig W. Horn: trustee
Donald E. Juenemann: trustee PRIM CORP EMPL president: Saginaw General Healthcare Corp.
Richard D. Katz: trustee B 1935. PRIM CORP EMPL president, director: Remer Plumbing & Heating Inc.
William F. Nelson, Jr.: trustee PRIM CORP EMPL president: Wm. F. Nelson Electric Inc.
Michele D. Pavlicek: assistant secretary
David F. Wallace: trustee B Brooklyn, NY 1923. ED Michigan State University BSME (1949); Michigan State University MBA (1960). PRIM CORP EMPL chairman board, director: Wolohan Lumber Co.
Lloyd J. Yeo: treasurer, trustee CORP AFFIL director: Great Lakes National Bank.

Grants Analysis
Disclosure Period: calendar year ending 2003
Total Grants: $1,727,984*
Number of Grants: 62
Average Grant: $25,049*
Highest Grant: $200,000
Lowest Grant: $250

Typical Range: $5,000 to $50,000
*Note: Giving excludes United Way. Average grant figure excludes highest grant.

Recent Grants

Note: Grants derived from 2002 Form 990.
Library-Related

25,000	Merrill District Library, Merrill, MI -- grants to purchase of new facility

General

500,000	SVSU Foundation, University Center, MI
312,500	SVSU Foundation, University Center, MI -- to support the establishment of ethics chair
250,000	Covenant Healthcare, Milwaukee, WI
225,000	Mid-Michigan Children's Museum, Saginaw, MI -- grant to renovation of children museum
200,000	Covenant Healthcare, Milwaukee, WI -- grant to construction of a building
200,000	Saginaw County Park & Recreation -- grant to phase II rail trail
200,000	SVSU Foundation, University Center, MI -- to support the college of education or regional ED center
200,000	SVSU Foundation, University Center, MI -- to support the college education
171,666	Saginaw Children's Zoo -- grant to expansion II project
166,667	Delta College, University Center, MI -- grants to digital TV

WICKSON-LINK MEMORIAL FOUNDATION

Giving Contact

Lloyd J. Yeo, President & Treasurer
PO Box 3275
3023 Davenport St.
Saginaw, MI 48602
Phone: (517)793-9830
Fax: (517)793-0186

Description

EIN: 386083931
Organization Type: Private Foundation
Giving Locations: MI: Saginaw County
Grant Types: General Support.

Donor Information

Founder: the late James Wickson, the late Meta Wickson

Financial Summary

Total Giving: $223,889 (2004); $288,133 (2001)
Giving Analysis: Giving for 2004 includes: foundation grants to United Way ($10,000); 2001: foundation grants to United Way ($6,500)
Assets: $5,434,555 (2004); $5,569,478 (2001)

Typical Recipients

Arts & Humanities: Arts Associations & Councils, Historic Preservation, History & Archaeology, Libraries, Museums/Galleries, Music, Performing Arts
Civic & Public Affairs: Business/Free Enterprise, Clubs, Community Foundations, Employment/Job Training, Civic & Public Affairs-General, Hispanic Affairs, Housing, Municipalities/Towns, Parades/Festivals, Philanthropic Organizations, Urban & Community Affairs, Zoos/Aquariums
Education: Business Education, Colleges & Universities, Education Funds, Education-General, International Studies, Preschool Education, Private Education (Precollege), Public Education (Precollege), Secondary Education (Private), Secondary Education (Public)
Health: Emergency/Ambulance Services, Geriatric

Health, Health Organizations, Hospitals, Nursing Services, Public Health, Single-Disease Health Associations
Religion: Churches, Religion-General, Religious Welfare
Science: Scientific Centers & Institutes
Social Services: At-Risk Youth, Big Brothers/Big Sisters, Child Abuse, Child Welfare, Community Centers, Community Service Organizations, Domestic Violence, Family Services, Food/Clothing Distribution, People with Disabilities, Recreation & Athletics, Scouts, Shelters/Homelessness, Social Services-General, Special Olympics, United Funds/United Ways, Volunteer Services, YMCA/YWCA/YMHA/YWHA, Youth Organizations

Application Procedures

Initial Contact: Send a brief letter of inquiry describing program or project.
Deadlines: None.

Foundation Officials

Lou Hanisko: director
B. J. Humphreys: vice president, secretary
Susan Piesko: director
Lloyd J. Yeo: president, treasurer CORP AFFIL director: Great Lakes National Bank.

Grants Analysis

Disclosure Period: calendar year ending 2004
Total Grants: $213,889*
Number of Grants: 39
Average Grant: $5,484
Highest Grant: $25,000
Lowest Grant: $500
Typical Range: $1,000 to $10,000
*Note: Giving excludes United Way.

Recent Grants

Note: Grants derived from 2004 Form 990.
General

25,000	Mid - Michigan Children's Museum, Saginaw, MI
20,000	Saginaw Children's Zoo, Saginaw, MI
16,700	St. Lorenz Lutheran Church, Saginaw, MI
15,000	Healthy Community Partners, Saginaw, MI
11,000	Boys and Girls Club, Saginaw, MI
10,750	Saginaw Art Museum, Saginaw, MI
10,000	Covenant Health Care, Saginaw, MI
10,000	Junction of Hope Restaurant, Saginaw, MI
10,000	Saginaw Valley State University Foundation, University Center, MI
10,000	Saginaw Valley State University Foundation, University Center, MI

WIDGEON FOUNDATION

Giving Contact

Elizabeth H. Robinson, President
PO Box 1084
Easton, MD 21601
Phone: (610)275-0700

Description

Founded: 1969
EIN: 136113927
Organization Type: Private Foundation
Giving Locations: MD; PA; VA
Grant Types: General Support.

Donor Information

Founder: Elizabeth H. Robinson

Financial Summary

Total Giving: $191,750 (2003); $239,100 (2001)
Assets: $4,236,893 (2003); $4,876,035 (2001)

Typical Recipients

Arts & Humanities: Arts Associations & Councils, Arts Centers, Historic Preservation, History & Archaeology, Libraries, Museums/Galleries
Civic & Public Affairs: Botanical Gardens/Parks, Community Foundations, Employment/Job Training, Civic & Public Affairs-General, Public Policy, Safety, Urban & Community Affairs, Zoos/Aquariums
Education: Agricultural Education, Colleges & Universities, Community & Junior Colleges, Education Reform, Engineering/Technological Education, Faculty Development, Education-General, Medical Education, Private Education (Precollege), Public Education (Precollege), Science/Mathematics Education, Secondary Education (Public), Student Aid, Vocational & Technical Education
Environment: Environment-General, Resource Conservation, Wildlife Protection
Health: Alzheimer's Disease, Cancer, Children's Health/Hospitals, Diabetes, Emergency/Ambulance Services, Heart, Hospices
International: Foreign Educational Institutions
Religion: Churches, Religious Organizations, Religious Welfare
Social Services: Animal Protection, Community Service Organizations, Homes, People with Disabilities, Recreation & Athletics, Scouts, United Funds/United Ways, YMCA/YWCA/YMHA/YWHA, Youth Organizations

Application Procedures

Initial Contact: Send a brief letter of inquiry.
Application Requirements: Include name, a description of organization, activities, financial statements, and purpose of funds sought.
Deadlines: None.

Restrictions

Emphasis is on medical, religious, environmental, and educational organizations.

Foundation Officials

Jennifer L. Malmberg: treasurer, secretary
Katherine P. Moyle: director
Elizabeth H. Robinson: president, director
Richard M. Robinson: vice president B 1937. ED Harvard University AB (1959). PRIM CORP EMPL chairman, president, chief executive officer, director: Scholastic. CORP AFFIL chairman, president, chief executive officer: SI Holdings.
Susan K. Stoneman: director

Grants Analysis

Disclosure Period: calendar year ending 2003
Total Grants: $191,750
Number of Grants: 42
Average Grant: $4,565
Highest Grant: $25,000
Lowest Grant: $500
Typical Range: $1,000 to $10,000

Recent Grants

Note: Grants derived from 2001 Form 990.
General

30,000	Community Systems, Bozeman, MT
30,000	Henricus Foundation, Chesterfield, VA
25,000	Lyles Baptist Church, Palmyra, VA
19,000	Salisbury State University, Salisbury, MD
15,000	Cornell Institute for Medical Research, Cherry Hill, NJ
12,500	Naval War College Foundation, Newport, RI
11,000	Dorchester County Historical Society, Cambridge, MD
10,500	Sloan Kettering Cancer Center, New York, NY
10,000	Harvard College, Cambridge, MA
7,500	Campbell University, Buies Creek, NC

E. L. WIEGAND FOUNDATION

Giving Contact

Kristen A. Avansino, President & Executive Director
Wiegand Center
165 West Liberty Street, Suite 200
Reno, NV 89501
Phone: (775)333-0310
Fax: (775)333-0314

Description

Founded: 1982
EIN: 942839372
Organization Type: General Purpose Foundation
Giving Locations: AZ; CA: Northern California; DC: Washington; ID; NV; NY: New York; OR; UT; WA
Grant Types: General Support, Project.
Note: Foundation also awards equipment grants.

Donor Information

Founder: Edwin L. Wiegand was born in Dover, OH, in 1891. He experimented with electricity as a boy and concluded that the use of electricity for heating afforded the most important growth potential for the future. In 1915, he obtained his first patent on a metal-sheathed, refractory-insulated electric heating element, and two years later founded the Edwin L. Wiegand Company in Pittsburgh. In a small room with one employee, he manufactured the first successful resistance heating units. Under the trade name "Chromalox," Mr. Wiegand developed and manufactured heating elements for home appliances and industrial uses that are still the heart of many electric appliances today. In 1968, he merged his company with Emerson Electric Company of St. Louis, MO. He moved to Reno, NV, in 1971 and became an active participant in Miami Oil Producers, especially in their development of oil and gas properties. He served on the Miami board until his death at the age of 88.
The foundation was established in 1982 for general charitable purposes. To foster the religious beliefs of E.L. Wiegand, a part of the annual grants are made to Roman Catholic charitable institutions.

Financial Summary

Total Giving: $4,727,107 (fiscal year ending October 31, 2003); $5,377,172 (fiscal 2002); $5,195,200 (fiscal 2001)
Giving Analysis: Giving for fiscal 2002 includes: foundation scholarships ($15,000)
Assets: $115,845,232 (fiscal 2003); $107,400,825 (fiscal 2002); $116,894,557 (fiscal 2001)
Gifts Received: $40,000 (fiscal 1999 approx); $199,657 (fiscal 1998); $24,998 (fiscal 1997 approx)

Typical Recipients

Arts & Humanities: Arts Associations & Councils, Arts Festivals, Ballet, Ethnic & Folk Arts, Film & Video, Arts & Humanities-General, Historic Preservation, History & Archaeology, Libraries, Museums/Galleries, Music, Opera, Performing Arts, Public Broadcasting, Theater
Civic & Public Affairs: Botanical Gardens/Parks, Civil Rights, Economic Policy, Civic & Public Affairs-General, Hispanic Affairs, Law & Justice, Legal Aid, Public Policy, Safety
Education: Agricultural Education, Arts/Humanities Education, Business Education, Colleges & Universities, Education Associations, Education Funds, Elementary Education (Private), Environmental Education, Faculty Development, Education-General, International Exchange, International Studies, Legal Education, Medical Education, Private Education (Precollege), Public Education (Precollege), Religious Education, Science/Mathematics Education, Secondary Education (Private), Secondary Education (Public), Social Sciences Education, Student Aid
Health: Alzheimer's Disease, Cancer, Children's Health/Hospitals, Clinics/Medical Centers, Diabetes,

Emergency/Ambulance Services, Health-General, Health Funds, Health Organizations, Heart, Hospitals, Long-Term Care, Medical Research, Nursing Services, Prenatal Health Issues, Public Health, Respiratory, Single-Disease Health Associations
International: Foreign Arts Organizations, Health Care/Hospitals, Human Rights, International Affairs, Missionary/Religious Activities
Religion: Churches, Dioceses, Religion-General, Religious Organizations, Religious Welfare, Seminaries
Science: Science Museums, Scientific Organizations, Scientific Research
Social Services: Camps, Child Welfare, Community Centers, Community Service Organizations, People with Disabilities, Recreation & Athletics, Scouts, Senior Services, Special Olympics, Substance Abuse, Volunteer Services, YMCA/YWCA/YMHA/YWHA, Youth Organizations

Application Procedures

Initial Contact: Submit a letter of inquiry describing the organization and the proposed request. After a review by foundation staff, a select group is invited to submit a full proposal.
Application Requirements: An original Application for Grant form, a concise description of the project, an itemized budget for the project, project starting date and schedule, qualifications of key personnel, a brief history of the institution, a list of officers and their affiliations, the name of any employee or officer of the foundation who is associated with the applicant, a copy of the IRS tax-exempt determination letter, a copy of current documentary evidence from the organization's state classifying the applicant as tax-exempt, a copy of the most recent 990, current audited financial statements, current interim financial statements, a financial budget for the current year, a statement of the applicant's major sources of support for the last five years, and an indication of how the program will be evaluated upon its completion. All proposals must be in a typewritten format.
Deadlines: Letters of inquiry are accepted throughout the year. Submission deadlines vary depending on the date of the meeting. Upon receiving the Application for Grant Form, applicants are notified of deadlines.
Review Process: Applications are reviewed by the staff and the executive advisory committee before being submitted to the board of trustees. The board meets three times a year, generally in February, June and October. The applicant will be notified if additional information, an interview, or a site inspection is required during the review process.

Restrictions

Grants will not be given for the following purposes: endowments; debt retirement or operating deficits; general, ordinary, and normal operations or their extension, including the repair and maintenance of facilities; emergency funding; general fundraising events, appeals, campaigns, dinners, or mass mailings; loans; distribution of funds to beneficiaries; the influence of legislation or elections; multi-year grants; institutions that use funds to support other institutions; production of documentaries, publications, films, or media presentations; religious institutions for the construction or restoration of buildings; or to institutions that have been in existence for less than five years; federal, state, or local government agencies or institutions; institutions supported by public tax funds; institutions served by the United Way; or individuals.

Additional Information

There are specific geographic restrictions for program areas. Education grants are considered in Nevada, Northern California, Oregon, Idaho, Utah, Washington, and Arizona. Health and medical research grants are considered in Nevada, California, Oregon, Idaho, Utah, and Arizona. Public affairs grants are made in Nevada, California, District of Columbia, and New York City. Civic and community af-

fairs grants are considered in Nevada and California. Arts and cultural affairs grants are also considered in Nevada and California.
A portion of the foundation's fund balance is held as a special fund for the benefit of Roman Catholic charitable organizations.
Publications: Informational Booklet; Application Form; Guidelines

Foundation Officials

Kristen A. Avansino: president, executive director
Raymond C. Avansino, Jr.: chairman, trustee, chief executive officer, chief operating officer B 1944. PRIM CORP EMPL president, chief operating officer, director: Conrad International Hotels Corp.
James T. Carrico: treasurer, chief financial officer
Frank Joseph Fahrenkopf, Jr.: trustee B Brooklyn, NY 1939. ED University of Nevada BA (1962); University of California at Berkeley JD (1965). PRIM CORP EMPL partner, attorney: Hogan & Hartson. NONPR AFFIL member: Washoe County Bar Association; director: Washoe County Legal Aid Society; director: Babe Ruth Baseball League; member: Northern Nevada Trial Lawyers Association; director: Reno YWCA; director: Nevada Opera Guild; member: Nevada Bar Association; director: Nevada Cancer Society; trustee: National Judicial College Council Future; co-chairman: National Commission Presidential Debates; faculty member: National Judicial College; member: Executives Association Reno; member: National Association Gaming Attorneys; member: Commercial Law League America; member: American Trial Lawyers Association; vice chairman: Center Democracy; president, chief executive officer: American Gaming Association; member: American Judicature Society; member, chairman Coalition for Justice: American Bar Association; member: Alpha Tau Omega. CLUB AFFIL Barristers NV Club.
Harvey C. Fruehauf, Jr.: vice president, trustee B Grosse Pointe Park, MI 1929. ED University of Michigan (1952). PRIM CORP EMPL president, director: HCF Enterprises Inc. CORP AFFIL president, treasurer, director: HCF Realty Inc.; chairman, president: Miami Oil Producers Inc.; director: Georgia-Pacific Corp.
Mario Joseph Gabelli: trustee B New York, NY 1942. ED Fordham University BS (1965); Columbia University MBA (1967). PRIM CORP EMPL founder, chairman: Gabelli & Co. CORP AFFIL director: Spinnaker Industries Inc.; director, principal: Lynch Michigan Tele Holding Corp.; chairman: Gamco Investors Inc.; chairman, chief executive officer, director: Lynch Corp.; president: Gabelli Funds Inc.; chairman: Gabelli Securities Inc.; chief investment officer: Gabelli Associates Fund; chairman, president, chief executive officer: Gabelli Equity Trust Inc. NONPR AFFIL director: American Stock Exchange Inc.
Michael J. Melarkey: vice president, secretary

Grants Analysis

Disclosure Period: fiscal year ending October 31, 2003
Total Grants: $4,727,107
Number of Grants: 62
Average Grant: $52,903*
Highest Grant: $1,500,000
Lowest Grant: $3,000
Typical Range: $25,000 to $100,000
*Note: Average grant figure excludes highest grant.

Recent Grants

Note: Grants derived from 2003 Form 990.
General
1,500,000 St. Mary's Health Network, Reno, NV -- for catheterization laboratory
240,187 Marylhurst University, Marylhurst, OR -- for Teaching and Learning Center
183,534 Holy Rosary Bi-Parish School, Idaho Falls, ID -- for Library and Media center
183,471 Gonzaga University, Spokane, WA -- for lab furnishings and equipment

170,006	LaSalle High School, Milwaukee, OR -- for science lab casework
169,574	Bishop Blanchett High School, Seattle, WA -- for sound and lighting equipment
169,355	St. Martin's College, Lacey, WA -- for science equipment
150,000	Boys and Girls Club, North Lake Tahoe, CA -- for Community Center furnishings and equipment
145,640	St. Mary Catholic School, Moscow, ID -- for gymnasium renovation
140,000	California Pacific Medical Center, San Francisco, CA -- for pediatric equipment

E. F. WILDERMUTH FOUNDATION

Giving Contact
Robert W. Lee, Treasurer
1014 Dublin Rd.
Columbus, OH 43215-1116
Phone: (614)487-0040

Description
Founded: 1962
EIN: 316050202
Organization Type: Private Foundation
Giving Locations: IN; KY; MI; OH; PA; WV
Grant Types: General Support.

Financial Summary
Total Giving: $253,000 (2002); $268,500 (2001)
Assets: $4,808,732 (2002); $6,015,231 (2001)
Gifts Received: $50,000 (1997)

Typical Recipients
Arts & Humanities: Ballet, Dance, History & Archaeology, Libraries, Music, Public Broadcasting
Civic & Public Affairs: Civic & Public Affairs-General
Education: Arts/Humanities Education, Business Education, Colleges & Universities, Medical Education, Minority Education, Public Education (Precollege)
Health: Children's Health/Hospitals, Clinics/Medical Centers, Eyes/Blindness, Health-General, Health Organizations, Heart, Hospitals, Mental Health, Single-Disease Health Associations
Religion: Churches, Religion-General, Religious Organizations
Social Services: Animal Protection, Big Brothers/Big Sisters, Child Welfare, Community Service Organizations, Counseling, People with Disabilities, Youth Organizations

Application Procedures
Initial Contact: The foundation has no formal grant application procedure or application form. Send a brief letter of inquiry.
Application Requirements: Include purpose of funds sought and proof of tax-exempt status.
Deadlines: August 1.

Restrictions
The foundation prefers to fund organizations in Ohio and its contiguous states.

Foundation Officials
Karl Borton: vice president
Thomas Borton: trustee
J. Patrick Campbell: chairman, president
Genevieve Connable: vice president
Bettie A. Kalb: president, secretary
Robert W. Lee: treasurer
David T. Patterson: vice president, legal counsel
Philip N. Phillipson: trustee
Harriet Slaughter: trustee

Grants Analysis
Disclosure Period: calendar year ending 2002
Total Grants: $253,000
Number of Grants: 20
Average Grant: $6,833*
Highest Grant: $75,000
Lowest Grant: $3,000
Typical Range: $5,000 to $30,000
*Note: Average grant figure excludes two highest grants ($130,000).

Recent Grants
Note: Grants derived from 2002 Form 990.
Library-Related

3,000	Ohioana Library, Columbus, OH

General

75,000	Ballet Metropolitan, Columbus, OH
55,000	Ohio State University Optometry, Columbus, OH
40,000	Wildermuth Community Church, Carroll, OH
30,000	Pennsylvania College of Optometry, Elkins Park, PA
10,000	Buckeye Ranch, Columbus, OH
10,000	Children's Hospital, Boston, MA
10,000	Illinois College of Optometry, Urbana, IL
10,000	Indiana University, Indianapolis, IN
8,000	Kalamazoo College, Kalamazoo, MI
7,500	Community of Holy Rosary St. John, Columbus, OH

JOHN WILEY & SONS INC.

Company Headquarters
Hoboken, NJ
Web: http://www.wiley.com

Company Description
Ticker: JW
Exchange: OTC
Revenue: US$854 million (2003)
Employees: 3350 (2003)
SIC(s): 2721 Periodicals, 2731 Book Publishing.

Operating Locations
John Wiley & Sons (NY--New York)

Nonmonetary Support
Type: Donated Products
Volunteer Programs: Volunteerism is promoted through the Corporate ServiceMatch Program, through which the company provides small grants to organizations where employees volunteer (for 12 to 30 hours in six months, $250; for 30 or more hours, $500). Each employee is limited to two ServiceMatch grants per year.

Giving Contact
Deborah Wiley, Senior Vice President Corp. Comm.
John Wiley & Sons, Inc.
111 River Street
Hoboken, NJ 07030
Phone: (201)748-6000
Fax: (201)748-6940

Description
Organization Type: Corporate Giving Program
Giving Locations: headquarters area only.
Grant Types: Conference/Seminar, Employee Matching Gifts, General Support, Loan, Multiyear/Continuing Support.
Note: The company sponsors a matching gifts program for employee giving.

Financial Summary
Total Giving: $200,000 (fiscal year ending April 30, 2005 approx); $230,000 (fiscal 2004); $280,000 (fiscal 2003). Note: Figures do not include matching gifts or ServiceMatch Program.
Assets: $283,844,000 (fiscal 2003); $275,259,000 (fiscal 2002)

Typical Recipients
Arts & Humanities: Ballet, Dance, Libraries, Museums/Galleries, Opera, Performing Arts, Public Broadcasting, Theater
Civic & Public Affairs: Botanical Gardens/Parks, Civil Rights, First Amendment Issues, Professional & Trade Associations, Zoos/Aquariums
Education: Arts/Humanities Education, Business Education, Colleges & Universities, Community & Junior Colleges, Continuing Education, Education Associations, Education Funds, Elementary Education (Private), Elementary Education (Public), Education-General, Legal Education, Literacy, Medical Education, Minority Education, Preschool Education, Private Education (Precollege), Public Education (Precollege), Science/Mathematics Education, Secondary Education (Private), Secondary Education (Public)
Environment: Resource Conservation, Wildlife Protection
Health: AIDS/HIV, Diabetes
Science: Science Museums, Scientific Centers & Institutes, Scientific Organizations
Social Services: Emergency Relief, Shelters/Homelessness

Application Procedures
Initial Contact: Send brief letter of inquiry. For ServiceMatch grants, employees should request application form.
Application Requirements: Include a description of organization, amount requested, purpose of funds sought, and proof of tax-exempt status.
Deadlines: None.

Restrictions
Does not support individuals, film projects, religious organizations for sectarian purposes, or political or lobbying groups. For ServiceMatch grants, support will not be made in lieu of tuition payments; in lieu of payment for tickets, subscription fees, or fundraising events; to provide benefit to the donor or a specified individual of more than a nominal value; to support political, religious, fraternal, social, or athletic organizations; to organizations for which service does not directly and in its entirety benefit the institution (e.g., United Way campaigns or community trusts); in lieu of personal tithes, pledges, or other financial commitments; to separately incorporated fundraising entities such as athletic funds, booster clubs, fraternities and sororities.

Additional Information
Contributions to education are made primarily through matching gift program.
Publications: Contributions Policy Statement

Corporate Officials
William J. Pesce: president, chief executive officer chief financial officer PRIM CORP EMPL president, chief executive officer: John Wiley & Sons.
Robert D. Wilder: executive vice president, chief financial officer PRIM CORP EMPL executive vice president, chief financial officer: John Wiley & Sons.
Bradford Wiley, II: chairman, director B Orange, NJ 1941. ED Columbia University (1965); Johns Hopkins University (1968). PRIM CORP EMPL chairman, director: John Wiley & Sons.
Deborah Wiley: chairman B 1946. ED Pine Manor College AA (1966); Boston University BA (1968); Harvard University (1983). PRIM CORP EMPL chairman: John Wiley & Sons.

Grants Analysis

Disclosure Period: fiscal year ending April 30, 2002
Total Grants: $234,300*
Number of Grants: 51
Average Grant: $4,594
Highest Grant: $20,000
Lowest Grant: $200
Typical Range: $500 to $2,500
***Note:** Grants analysis provided by company.

Recent Grants

Note: Grants derived from fiscal 1998 Form 990.
Library-RelatedNew York Public Library, New York, NY
GeneralAmerican Institute of Physics, College Park, MDAssociation of College and Research Libraries, Newton, MACentral Park Conservancy, New York, NYCouncil for Aid to Education, New York, NYJuvenile Diabetes Foundation, New York, NYLibrary of Congress Center for the Book, Washington, DCMuseum of Modern Art, New York, NYNational Association of Biology Teachers, Reston, VAMetropolitan Opera, New York, NY

WILKES, ARTIS, HEDRICK & LANE

Company Headquarters

1666 K St. NW, Ste. 1100
Washington, DC 20006

Operating Locations

Wilkes, Artis, Hedrick & Lane (DC--Washington)

Wilkes, Artis, Hedrick & Lane Foundation

Giving Contact

Stanley J. Fineman, President
1150 18th St. NW, Suite 400
Washington, DC 20036
Phone: (202)457-7804
Fax: (202)457-7814

Description

Founded: 1982
EIN: 521272246
Organization Type: Corporate Foundation
Grant Types: General Support.

Donor Information

Founder: Norman M. Glasgow, Sr., Albert L. Ledgard, Jr., Stanley J. Fineman, Whayne S. Quin, Allen Jones, Jr., Robert L. Gorham, Charles A. Camalier III, C. Francis Murphy, Maureen E. Dwyer, Joseph B. Whitebread, Jr.

Financial Summary

Total Giving: $4,300 (fiscal year ending September 30, 2004); $11,450 (fiscal 2001)
Assets: $29,332 (fiscal 2004); $38,479 (fiscal 2001)
Gifts Received: $51,434 (fiscal 1998); $60,275 (fiscal 1997); $65,364 (fiscal 1996). Note: In 1998, contributions were received from Stanley J. Fineman, Robert L. Gorham, Joseph B. Whitebread, Jr., Christopher H. Collins, Maureen E. Dwyer, Whayne S. Quin, Norman M. Glaslow, Jr., David M. Bond, and John D. Lane. In fiscal 1997, contributions were received from Stanley J. Fineman, Whayne S. Quin, and Robert L. Gorham.

Typical Recipients

Arts & Humanities: Arts Outreach, Historic Preservation, History & Archaeology, Libraries, Museums/Galleries, Opera
Civic & Public Affairs: Business/Free Enterprise, Clubs, Community Foundations, Economic Development, Employment/Job Training, Civic & Public Affairs-General, Housing, Law & Justice, Legal Aid, Parades/Festivals, Professional & Trade Associations, Public Policy, Urban & Community Affairs
Education: Colleges & Universities, International Studies, Legal Education, Secondary Education (Public), Student Aid
Environment: Environment-General
Health: Cancer, Children's Health/Hospitals, Health-General, Heart, Hospitals, Prenatal Health Issues, Single-Disease Health Associations
Religion: Churches, Jewish Causes, Religious Welfare
Science: Scientific Organizations
Social Services: Community Service Organizations, Family Services, Food/Clothing Distribution, People with Disabilities, Recreation & Athletics, Scouts, Substance Abuse, United Funds/United Ways

Application Procedures

Initial Contact: The foundation has no formal grant application procedure or application form., send a brief letter of inquiry.
Deadlines: None.

Restrictions

Supports only public charities.

Corporate Officials

Stanley J. Fineman: partner PRIM CORP EMPL partner: Wilkes Artis Hedrick & Lane.
Norman M. Glasgow, Jr.: partner PRIM CORP EMPL partner: Wilkes Artis Hedrick & Lane.
Robert L. Gorham: managing partner PRIM CORP EMPL managing partner: Wilkes Artis Hedrick & Lane.
John Salisbury: chief operating officer PRIM CORP EMPL chief officer: Wilkes Artis Hedrick & Lane.

Foundation Officials

Charles A. Camalier: vice president, director
Stanley J. Fineman: president, director (see above)
Eric S. Kassoff: secretary, treasurer, director

Grants Analysis

Disclosure Period: fiscal year ending September 30, 2004
Total Grants: $4,300
Number of Grants: 7
Highest Grant: $1,500
Lowest Grant: $100
Typical Range: $200 to $1,000

Recent Grants

Note: Grants derived from fiscal 2004 Form 990.

General

1,500	Corcoran Gallery of Arts, Washington, DC
1,000	Council for Court Excellence, Washington, DC
1,000	National Capital Area Council, Bethesda, MD
300	Kohlenstein, Ocean City, MD -- to foster scholarship
300	Recording for the Blind and Dyslexic, Washington, DC
100	Pan Massachusetts Challenge, Newton Centre, MA -- for Jimmy fund
100	Southern Arizona Race for the Cure, Green Valley, AZ

EDWARD AND RUTH WILKOF FOUNDATION

Giving Contact

Harry Mestel, President
116 Cleveland Ave. NW, Suite 525
Canton, OH 44702
Phone: (330)452-9788

Description

Founded: 1987
EIN: 341536119
Organization Type: Private Foundation
Giving Locations: FL: Sarasota; OH
Grant Types: General Support.

Donor Information

Founder: Edward and Ruth Wilkof

Financial Summary

Total Giving: $190,900 (fiscal year ending June 30, 2004); $358,450 (fiscal 2002); $219,684 (fiscal 2001)
Giving Analysis: Giving for fiscal 2004 includes: foundation grants to United Way ($2,500); fiscal 2002: foundation grants to United Way ($10,000); fiscal 2001: foundation grants to United Way ($5,000)
Assets: $1,517,728 (fiscal 2004); $1,735,368 (fiscal 2002); $1,958,975 (fiscal 2001)
Gifts Received: $25,000 (fiscal 2004); $54,750 (fiscal 2002); $28,000 (fiscal 2001). Note: In 1999, 2000, 2002, and 2004, contributions were received from Edward Wilkof. In fiscal 1990, contributions were received from Edward and Ruth Wilkof.

Typical Recipients

Arts & Humanities: Arts Centers, Arts Funds, Ballet, Libraries, Museums/Galleries, Music, Opera, Performing Arts
Civic & Public Affairs: Clubs, Economic Development, Ethnic Organizations, Civic & Public Affairs-General, Philanthropic Organizations, Urban & Community Affairs
Education: Arts/Humanities Education, Colleges & Universities, Education Associations, Education Funds, Private Education (Precollege), Religious Education, Student Aid, Vocational & Technical Education
Environment: Resource Conservation
Health: Clinics/Medical Centers, Emergency/Ambulance Services, Health Funds, Medical Research, Research/Studies Institutes
International: Foreign Educational Institutions, International Peace & Security Issues, Missionary/Religious Activities
Religion: Jewish Causes, Religious Organizations, Religious Welfare, Synagogues/Temples
Social Services: Child Welfare, Community Service Organizations, Day Care, Family Services, Food/Clothing Distribution, United Funds/United Ways, Volunteer Services, Youth Organizations

Application Procedures

Initial Contact: Send a brief letter of inquiry. Send complete information and material relating to request.
Deadlines: None.

Restrictions

Donee must have tax-exempt status by IRS determination.

Foundation Officials

Michael Sweeney: secretary
Richard Wilkof: trustee

Grants Analysis

Disclosure Period: fiscal year ending June 30, 2004
Total Grants: $188,400*
Number of Grants: 33
Average Grant: $4,465*
Highest Grant: $25,000

Lowest Grant: $300
Typical Range: $1,000 to $10,000
***Note:** Giving excludes United Way. Average grant figure excludes two highest grants ($50,000).

Recent Grants

Note: Grants derived from fiscal 2004 Form 990.
General

25,000	Canton Jewish Community Federation, Canton, OH -- facilities surveys and appraisals
25,000	Manatee Jewish Federation, Sarasota, FL -- fund raising program
22,500	Cleveland Orchestra, Cleveland, OH -- for youth chorus
15,000	Canton Jewish Community Federation, Canton, OH -- fund raising program
15,000	Florida West Coast Symphony, Sarasota, FL -- fund raising program
10,000	Cleveland Clinic Foundation, Cleveland, OH -- for medical research
10,000	Van Wezel Foundation, Sarasota, FL -- fund raising program
7,500	Sarasota Memorial Health Care Foundation, Sarasota, FL -- for medical research
5,550	Canton Symphony Orchestra, Canton, OH -- for kinder koncert
5,000	Walsh University, Canton, OH -- for education/scholarships

CECILIA YOUNG WILLARD HELPING FUND

Giving Contact

Nancy F. May, Vice President, Trust Officer
c/o Broadway National Bank, Trust Div.
PO Box 17001
San Antonio, TX 78217
Phone: (210)283-6700

Description

Founded: 1987
EIN: 746350893
Organization Type: Private Foundation
Giving Locations: NC
Grant Types: General Support, Operating Expenses, Project.

Donor Information

Founder: Celia Young Willard Trust

Financial Summary

Total Giving: $394,862 (fiscal year ending May 31, 2002); $433,468 (fiscal 2001)
Assets: $5,863,804 (fiscal 2002); $6,887,266 (fiscal 2001)

Typical Recipients

Arts & Humanities: Arts Associations & Councils, Arts Institutes, Community Arts, History & Archaeology, Libraries, Museums/Galleries, Music, Public Broadcasting, Theater
Civic & Public Affairs: Community Foundations, Civic & Public Affairs-General, Hispanic Affairs, Housing, Municipalities/Towns, Rural Affairs, Safety
Education: Colleges & Universities, Education-General, Legal Education, Literacy, Medical Education, Private Education (Precollege)
Environment: Environment-General, Resource Conservation, Wildlife Protection
Health: AIDS/HIV, Alzheimer's Disease, Arthritis, Cancer, Clinics/Medical Centers, Eyes/Blindness, Health Funds, Heart, Hospices, Hospitals, Long-Term Care, Nursing Services, Prenatal Health Issues
Religion: Churches, Religious Organizations, Religious Welfare
Science: Scientific Centers & Institutes

Social Services: Child Welfare, Community Service Organizations, Family Services, Food/Clothing Distribution, Homes, People with Disabilities, Senior Services, Shelters/Homelessness, Social Services-General, Volunteer Services, Youth Organizations

Application Procedures

Initial Contact: Send a brief letter of inquiry.
Application Requirements: Include a description of organization, amount requested, purpose of funds sought, proof of tax-exempt status
Deadlines: June 1.

Restrictions

Does not support individuals or political or lobbying groups.

Additional Information

Trust(s): Broadway Natl Bank

Grants Analysis

Disclosure Period: fiscal year ending May 31, 2002
Total Grants: $394,862
Number of Grants: 33
Average Grant: $10,152*
Highest Grant: $70,000
Lowest Grant: $1,000
Typical Range: $5,000 to $20,000
***Note:** Average grant figure excludes highest grant.

Recent Grants

Note: Grants derived from 2002 Form 990.
General

70,000	Pickersgill Retirement Community, Towson, MD
26,736	First Presbyterian Church, Greensboro, NC
25,000	Greater Baltimore Medical Center, Baltimore, MD
20,000	Any Baby Can, San Antonio, TX
20,000	Friends of Cibolo, Boerne, TX
20,000	Southwest Texas State University, San Marcos, TX
16,042	Crossnore School, Crossnore, NC
16,042	Grandfather Home for Children, Banner Elk, NC
16,042	Lees-McRae College, Banner Elk, NC
15,000	Carver Academy, San Antonio, TX

JOHN C. WILLIAMS CHARITABLE TRUST

Giving Contact

Roberta McCann, Senior Vice President
John C. Williams Charitable Trust
Care of PNC Bank NA
620 Liberty Avenue
Pittsburgh, PA 15222-2705
Phone: (412)762-3413
Fax: (412)762-5439
E-mail: roberta.mccann@pncbank.com

Description

Founded: 1936
EIN: 256024153
Organization Type: Private Foundation
Giving Locations: OH: Steubenville; WV: Weirton
Grant Types: Capital, General Support, Matching, Project, Seed Money.

Donor Information

Founder: the late John C. Williams

Financial Summary

Total Giving: $317,641 (2003); $400,000 (2002 approx); $407,561 (2001). Note: Trust donates 5% of its market value annually.

Giving Analysis: Giving for 2003 includes: foundation grants to United Way ($6,500)
Assets: $6,972,821 (2003); $7,405,098 (2001)

Typical Recipients

Arts & Humanities: Historic Preservation, History & Archaeology, Libraries, Music, Visual Arts
Civic & Public Affairs: Civic & Public Affairs-General, Housing
Education: Colleges & Universities, Community & Junior Colleges, Private Education (Precollege), Science/Mathematics Education
Health: Clinics/Medical Centers, Emergency/Ambulance Services, Health-General, Hospitals, Medical Rehabilitation, Prenatal Health Issues
Religion: Ministries, Religious Welfare
Social Services: Community Centers, Community Service Organizations, Family Planning, Family Services, Homes, People with Disabilities, Recreation & Athletics, Shelters/Homelessness, Social Services-General, Substance Abuse, United Funds/United Ways, YMCA/YWCA/YMHA/YWHA, Youth Organizations

Application Procedures

Initial Contact: Send a brief letter of inquiry and a full proposal.
Application Requirements: Include proof of tax-exempt status, latest annual operating budget, recently audited financial statement, amount requested, a description of organization, central planning agency report, history of previous William support and purpose of funds sought.
Deadlines: None.

Restrictions

Grants are not made to individuals, political or lobbying groups, or organizations outside operating areas.

Additional Information

Trust(s): PNC Advisors

Grants Analysis

Disclosure Period: calendar year ending 2003
Total Grants: $311,141*
Number of Grants: 6
Average Grant: $35,562*
Highest Grant: $133,333
Lowest Grant: $3,340
Typical Range: $5,000 to $50,000
***Note:** Giving excludes United Way. Average grant figure excludes highest grant.

Recent Grants

Note: Grants derived from 2003 Form 990.

General

133,333	Franciscan University of Steubenville, Steubenville, OH -- for J.C. Williams Center
51,428	West Virginia Northern Community College, Weirton, WV -- for furniture and equipment for learning resource
50,000	St. Paul School, Weirton, WV -- for tuition assistance and staff development
50,000	Weirton Area Civic Foundation, Weirton, WV -- for renovations-Jim Carey football stadium
23,040	Urban Mission Ministries Inc., Steubenville, OH -- towards renovations-mission center
6,500	Weirton United Way Inc., Weirton, WV -- for production and broadcasting of promotional
3,340	Neighborhood House, Columbus, OH -- for renovations-front entrance doors

MARY JO WILLIAMS CHARITABLE TRUST

Giving Contact
Michael E. Collins, Trustee
607 N. 7th
Garden City, KS 67846
Phone: (620)276-3203
Fax: (620)276-3300

Description
Founded: 1988
EIN: 486276428
Organization Type: Private Foundation
Giving Locations: KS: Garden City
Grant Types: Emergency, Endowment, General Support, Scholarship.

Financial Summary
Total Giving: $166,250 (2003)
Assets: $3,720,375 (2003)

Typical Recipients
Arts & Humanities: Libraries, Music, Public Broadcasting
Civic & Public Affairs: Housing, Professional & Trade Associations, Zoos/Aquariums
Education: Arts/Humanities Education, Community & Junior Colleges, Education Funds, Faculty Development, Education-General, Preschool Education, Public Education (Precollege), Science/Mathematics Education, Student Aid
Environment: Environment-General, Resource Conservation
Health: Emergency/Ambulance Services
Religion: Ministries, Religious Welfare
Social Services: At-Risk Youth, Community Service Organizations, Crime Prevention, Emergency Relief, Food/Clothing Distribution, Senior Services, Shelters/Homelessness, Social Services-General, United Funds/United Ways, Veterans, YMCA/YWCA/YMHA/YWHA, Youth Organizations

Application Procedures
Initial Contact: Send a brief letter of inquiry.
Deadlines: None.

Restrictions
Grants are considered for the prevention of cruelty to children and animals. The foundation does not support athletics or athletic competitions.

Foundation Officials
Michael E. Collins: trustee
Leonard Rich: trustee
Jack Williamson: trustee

Grants Analysis
Disclosure Period: calendar year ending 2003
Total Grants: $166,250
Number of Grants: 12
Average Grant: $10,568*
Highest Grant: $50,000
Lowest Grant: $2,000
Typical Range: $5,000 to $25,000
*Note: Average grant figure excludes highest grant.

Recent Grants
Note: Grants derived from 2001 Form 990.
General

51,000	Nature Conservancy, Topeka, KS
36,889	Garden City Community College, Garden City, KS -- for upgrades in CLC hardware
15,000	Emmaus House, Garden City, KS -- for food and aid to the needy
12,000	Finney County United Way, Garden City, KS -- for various charities
10,000	Mexican American Ministry, Garden City, KS -- for aid to the needy
10,000	Salvation Army, Garden City, KS -- for aid to needy and disaster victim
8,500	Spirit of the Plains CASA, Inc., Garden City, KS -- for court appointed special advocates for children
5,000	Habitat for Humanities, Garden City, KS -- for housing for needy
2,250	Garden City Civic Choral Union, Garden City, KS -- for education
2,000	Garden City Piano Teachers League, Inc., Garden City, KS -- for education

WILLIAMS COMPANIES INC.

Company Headquarters
One Williams Center
Tulsa, OK 74172
Web: http://www.williams.com

Company Description
Ticker: WMB
Exchange: NYSE
Former Name: Transco Energy Co.
Assets: US$34.988 billion (2002)
Profit: (US$504.5 million) (2003)
Employees: 4800 (2003)
SIC(s): 1221 Bituminous Coal & Lignite--Surface, 1222 Bituminous Coal--Underground, 1311 Crude Petroleum & Natural Gas, 5172 Petroleum Products Nec.

Operating Locations
Williams (MD; NJ; NY--New York; NC; OH--Lebanon; SC; TX--Houston; VA)

Nonmonetary Support
Type: In-kind Services; Loaned Executives; Workplace Solicitation

The Williams Companies Foundation

Giving Contact
Callie J. Mitchell, Director
One Williams Center
WRC-1
Tulsa, OK 74172
Phone: (918)573-4014
E-mail: communityrelationstulsa@williams.com
Web: http://www.williams.com/community/

Description
EIN: 237413843
Organization Type: Corporate Foundation
Giving Locations: areas near company headquarters and operating communities.
Grant Types: Capital, Employee Matching Gifts, Endowment, General Support.

Financial Summary
Total Giving: $5,470,694 (2003); $3,418,207 (2002); $1,293,942 (2001). Note: Contributes through corporate direct giving program and foundation.
Giving Analysis: Giving for 2002 includes: foundation scholarships ($87,667); foundation matching gifts ($374,139)
Assets: $7,963,312 (2003); $13,310,741 (2002); $16,408,829 (2001)
Gifts Received: $5,000,000 (1995). Note: Contributions were received from The Williams Companies.

Typical Recipients
Arts & Humanities: Arts Associations & Councils, Arts Centers, Arts Institutes, Dance, Historic Preservation, History & Archaeology, Libraries, Museums/Galleries, Music, Opera, Performing Arts, Public Broadcasting, Theater
Civic & Public Affairs: African American Affairs, Botanical Gardens/Parks, Business/Free Enterprise, Clubs, Economic Development, Civic & Public Affairs-General, Housing, Law & Justice, Legal Aid, Minority Business, Philanthropic Organizations, Professional & Trade Associations, Public Policy, Rural Affairs, Safety, Urban & Community Affairs, Women's Affairs, Zoos/Aquariums
Education: Afterschool/Enrichment Programs, Agricultural Education, Arts/Humanities Education, Business Education, Colleges & Universities, Community & Junior Colleges, Economic Education, Education Associations, Education Funds, Elementary Education (Private), Education-General, Medical Education, Private Education (Precollege), Public Education (Precollege), Science/Mathematics Education, Secondary Education (Private), Student Aid
Environment: Environment-General, Resource Conservation, Wildlife Protection
Health: AIDS/HIV, Children's Health/Hospitals, Clinics/Medical Centers, Health Funds, Health Organizations, Hospitals, Mental Health, Prenatal Health Issues, Preventive Medicine/Wellness Organizations, Single-Disease Health Associations
International: Foreign Arts Organizations, Health Care/Hospitals, International Organizations, International Relations
Religion: Social/Policy Issues
Science: Science Exhibits & Fairs, Scientific Organizations
Social Services: At-Risk Youth, Child Welfare, Community Service Organizations, Crime Prevention, Domestic Violence, Emergency Relief, Family Planning, Family Services, Food/Clothing Distribution, Homes, People with Disabilities, Recreation & Athletics, Scouts, Senior Services, Shelters/Homelessness, Substance Abuse, United Funds/United Ways, YMCA/YWCA/YMHA/YWHA, Youth Organizations

Application Procedures
Initial Contact: Send a brief letter and one copy of a full proposal.
Application Requirements: Include a description of organization, amount requested, purpose of funds sought, recently audited financial statement, and proof of tax-exempt status.
Deadlines: None; board meets in June and December.
Decision Notification: Usually within two weeks of receipt of request.

Restrictions
Does not support fraternal organizations, goodwill advertising, individuals, political or lobbying groups, or religious organizations for sectarian purposes.

Additional Information
Williams Companies acquired Mapco Inc. in 1998/1999.

Foundation Officials
Alan S. Armstrong: director
Gary R. Belitz: director
Robyn L. Ewing: director
Michael P. Johnson: director
Deborah B. Lawrence: director
Steven J. Malcolm: director
Callie J. Mitchell: director
Douglas J. Whisenant: director

Grants Analysis
Disclosure Period: calendar year ending 2003
Total Grants: $2,078,864*
Number of Grants: 51
Average Grant: $33,468*
Highest Grant: $405,450
Lowest Grant: $2,000
Typical Range: $10,000 to $50,000

*Note: Giving excludes matching gifts; scholarship. Average grant figure excludes highest grant.

Recent Grants

Note: Grants derived from 2003 Form 990.
Library-Related

25,000	Tulsa Library Trust, Tulsa, OK

General

766,935	Tulsa Area United Way, Tulsa, OK
405,450	University of Tulsa, Tulsa, OK
338,401	United Way of Calgary and Area, Calgary, AB Canada
296,024	United Way of the Texas Gulf Coast, Houston, TX
250,000	Achieve Inc., Washington, DC
185,350	University of Oklahoma Foundation Inc., Norman, OK
150,000	Tulsa Public Schools Foundation, Tulsa, OK
140,707	Oklahoma State University, Stillwater, OK
100,000	Teammates for Kids, Littleton, CO
95,575	United Way of the Great Salt Lake Area, Salt Lake City, UT

WILLIAMS FAMILY FOUNDATION OF GEORGIA

Giving Contact

Thomas L. Williams, III, President & Director
Williams Family Foundation of Georgia
PO Box 378
Thomasville, GA 31799
Phone: (912)226-8320

Description

Founded: 1980
EIN: 581414850
Organization Type: Private Foundation
Giving Locations: GA: Thomasville
Grant Types: General Support.

Donor Information

Founder: Diane W. Parker, Marguerite N. Williams, Thomas L. Williams III, the late Bennie G. Williams

Financial Summary

Total Giving: $2,818,128 (fiscal year ending November 30, 2002). Note: 1997 Giving includes United Way ($5,000).
Assets: $56,874,770 (fiscal 2002)
Gifts Received: $8,081,560 (fiscal 2002); $24,048,556 (fiscal 2000); $311,533 (fiscal 1997). Note: In fiscal 2000 and fiscal 2002, contributions were received from Marguerite Williams Estate. In fiscal 1996 and 1997, contributions were received from Bennie G. Williams Charitable Lead Trust.

Typical Recipients

Arts & Humanities: Arts Centers, Community Arts, Historic Preservation, History & Archaeology, Libraries, Museums/Galleries, Music, Public Broadcasting, Theater
Civic & Public Affairs: Botanical Gardens/Parks, Community Foundations, Civic & Public Affairs-General, Housing, Nonprofit Management, Philanthropic Organizations, Women's Affairs
Education: Colleges & Universities, Economic Education, Education-General, Medical Education, Private Education (Precollege), Public Education (Precollege), Science/Mathematics Education
Environment: Forestry, Environment-General, Resource Conservation, Wildlife Protection
Health: Arthritis, Cancer
International: Health Care/Hospitals

Religion: Churches, Religious Welfare
Science: Science Museums, Scientific Research
Social Services: Animal Protection, Camps, Community Centers, Community Service Organizations, Emergency Relief, Homes, People with Disabilities, Recreation & Athletics, United Funds/United Ways, YMCA/YWCA/YMHA/YWHA, Youth Organizations

Application Procedures

Initial Contact: Send a brief written letter of inquiry.
Application Requirements: Include amount requested, budget, purpose of funds sought, recently audited financial statement, and proof of tax-exempt status.
Deadlines: None.
Review Process: Board meets in May and November to review applications.

Restrictions

Preference given to education and historic preservation primarily in the Thomasville, GA, area.

Foundation Officials

Joseph E. Beverly: director
Bernard Lanigan, Jr.: treasurer, director
Diane W. Parker: vice president, director
Stephen T. Parker: director
Thomas W. Parker: director
Thomas H. Vann, Jr.: director
Alston Parker Watt: executive director
Thomas L. Williams, III: president, director

Grants Analysis

Disclosure Period: fiscal year ending November 30, 2002
Total Grants: $2,818,128
Number of Grants: 85
Average Grant: $15,888*
Highest Grant: $450,000
Lowest Grant: $100
Typical Range: $5,000 to $30,000
*Note: Average grant figure excludes seven highest grants ($1,594,740).

Recent Grants

Note: Grants derived from fiscal 2001 Form 990.
General

309,500	Brookwood School, Thomasville, GA
250,000	Bishop Hall/Thomas County Public School, Thomasville, GA
156,772	Municipal Auditorium Restoration, Thomasville, GA
113,000	City of Thomasville Auditorium, Thomasville, GA
110,000	Department of Natural Resources, Washington, DC
52,250	Ducks Unlimited, Thomasville, GA
50,000	Nacochee Valley Fund, Thomasville, GA
50,000	Odyssey School, Baltimore, MD
38,000	Habitat for Humanity, Thomasville, GA
30,000	Auburn University Foundation, Auburn University, AL

WILLIS FAMILY FOUNDATION

Giving Contact

Jennie Willis-List, President & Directory
3522 Niblick Court
Denver, NC 28037-8016
Phone: (704)483-1997

Description

Founded: 1997
EIN: 562055841
Organization Type: Private Foundation
Giving Locations: Southeastern United States.
Grant Types: General Support.

Financial Summary

Total Giving: $59,500 (2003); $81,905 (2001)
Assets: $1,005,524 (2003); $1,194,448 (2001)
Gifts Received: $994,173 (1997). Note: In 1997, contributions were received from James Richard Willis.

Typical Recipients

Arts & Humanities: Libraries
Civic & Public Affairs: Civic & Public Affairs-General
Education: Public Education (Precollege)
Religion: Ministries
Social Services: Community Service Organizations, YMCA/YWCA/YMHA/YWHA

Application Procedures

Initial Contact: Send in letter form.
Deadlines: None.

Foundation Officials

Michael Willis Good: director
Jeffery Ledward: secretary, director
Jennie Willis List: president, director
Evelyn Sayer Willis: vice president, director

Grants Analysis

Disclosure Period: calendar year ending 2003
Total Grants: $59,500
Number of Grants: 6
Highest Grant: $50,000
Lowest Grant: $500
Typical Range: $1,000 to $5,000

Recent Grants

Note: Grants derived from 2001 Form 990.
Library-Related

2,000	East Lincoln Library Fund, Denver, NC

General

66,905	New Direction Ministries, Mars Hill, NC
5,000	Echo, Ft. Myers, FL
3,000	Lee Middle School, Orlando, FL
2,500	Crown Financial Ministries, Gainesville, GA
1,500	Campus Crusade for Christ, Orlando, FL
1,000	YMCA of Greater Charlotte, Charlotte, NC

WILSEY FOUNDATION

Giving Contact

Diane B. Wilsey, Vice President
Wilsey Foundation
2351 Powell St., Suite 550
San Francisco, CA 94133
Phone: (415)956-2229

Description

EIN: 946098720
Organization Type: Private Foundation
Giving Locations: CA: San Francisco Bay Area
Grant Types: Capital, Endowment, General Support, Scholarship.

Donor Information

Founder: Alfred Wilsey, Jr.

Financial Summary

Total Giving: $161,930 (fiscal year ending March 31, 2004); $561,775 (fiscal 2001)
Assets: $1,466,066 (fiscal 2004); $4,082,981 (fiscal 2001)
Gifts Received: $167,470 (fiscal 1997); $1,076,342 (fiscal 1995); $1,069,376 (fiscal 1994). Note: In fiscal 1997, contributions were received from M. Kathleen Behrens.

Typical Recipients

Arts & Humanities: Arts Centers, Ballet, Arts & Humanities-General, Historic Preservation, Libraries, Museums/Galleries, Music, Opera, Public Broadcasting, Theater
Civic & Public Affairs: Economic Development, Ethnic Organizations, Civic & Public Affairs-General
Education: Colleges & Universities, Continuing Education, Economic Education, Elementary Education (Private), Elementary Education (Public), Education-General, Private Education (Precollege), Religious Education, Secondary Education (Private), Secondary Education (Public)
Health: AIDS/HIV, Clinics/Medical Centers, Emergency/Ambulance Services, Hospitals, Single-Disease Health Associations
International: Missionary/Religious Activities
Religion: Churches, Dioceses, Religion-General, Religious Organizations, Religious Welfare
Social Services: At-Risk Youth, Community Centers, Community Service Organizations, Food/Clothing Distribution, Sexual Abuse, Shelters/Homelessness, Social Services-General, United Funds/United Ways, Volunteer Services, Youth Organizations

Application Procedures

Initial Contact: Apply in writing.
Deadlines: None.

Restrictions

Does not support individuals or political or lobbying groups.

Foundation Officials

Alfred S. Wilsey, Jr.: secretary, treasurer
Diane B. Wilsey: vice president
Michael W. Wilsey: vice president PRIM CORP EMPL chairman, president, director: Wilsey Bennet Co.

Grants Analysis

Disclosure Period: fiscal year ending March 31, 2004
Total Grants: $161,930
Number of Grants: 55
Average Grant: $2,944
Highest Grant: $15,000
Lowest Grant: $250
Typical Range: $1,000 to $5,000

Recent Grants

Note: Grants derived from 2001 Form 990.

General

100,000	Archdiocese of San Francisco, San Francisco, CA
50,000	Archbishop Riordan High School, San Francisco, CA
50,000	University of San Francisco, San Francisco, CA
25,000	ALS Association, San Francisco, CA
25,000	American Center of Wine, Food, and the Arts, Napa, CA
25,000	Fine Arts Museums, San Francisco, CA
12,500	American Irish Fund, San Francisco, CA
10,000	Connecticut College, New London, CT
10,000	Dominican Sisters of Mission San Jose, Oakland, CA
10,000	San Francisco Planning and Urban Research Association (SPUR), San Francisco, CA

ANNE POTTER WILSON FOUNDATION

Giving Contact

Patrick Nelson, Trust Officer
Care of Bank of America
One Bank of America Plaza, M-7
Nashville, TN 37209
Phone: (615)749-3916

Alternate Contact

231 S. LaSalle Street, IL1-231-14-19
Chicago, IL 60697

Description

Founded: 1996
EIN: 626306576
Organization Type: Private Foundation
Giving Locations: DC: Washington; TN: Nashville
Grant Types: General Support.

Donor Information

Founder: Established in 1996 with funds from the Justin and Valere Potter Foundation.

Financial Summary

Total Giving: $1,415,607 (2001)
Assets: $26,401,385 (2001)

Typical Recipients

Arts & Humanities: Historic Preservation, Libraries
Civic & Public Affairs: Botanical Gardens/Parks, Zoos/Aquariums
Education: Colleges & Universities, Secondary Education (Public)
Religion: Religious Welfare
Social Services: Community Service Organizations

Application Procedures

Initial Contact: Submit brief letter with description of organization qualifications, status, and copy of 501(c)(3) determination.
Deadlines: None.

Additional Information

Trust(s): Bank of America

Grants Analysis

Disclosure Period: calendar year ending 2001
Total Grants: $1,415,607
Number of Grants: 8
Average Grant: $59,372*
Highest Grant: $1,000,000
Lowest Grant: $15,000
Typical Range: $25,000 to $100,000
*****Note:** Average grant figure excludes highest grant.

Recent Grants

Note: Grants derived from 2001 Form 990.
Library-Related
50,607	Nashville Public Library, Nashville, TN

General
1,000,000	Vanderbilt University, Nashville, TN
100,000	Nashville Zoo, Nashville, TN
100,000	National Trust for Historic Preservation, Washington, DC
100,000	University School of Nashville, Nashville, TN
25,000	Cheekwood Tennessee Botanical Gardens and Museum of Art, Nashville, TN
25,000	Nashville Rescue Mission, Nashville, TN
15,000	Renewal House, Nashville, TN

H. W. WILSON FOUNDATION

Giving Contact

W. Joyce, III, President, Treasurer
950 University Ave.
Bronx, NY 10452
Phone: (718)588-8400

Description

Founded: 1952
EIN: 237418062
Organization Type: Private Foundation
Giving Locations: CA; DC: Washington; IL; NY; PA nationally.
Grant Types: Research, Scholarship.

Donor Information

Founder: the late H. W. Wilson, the late Mrs. H. W. Wilson, the H. W. Wilson Co.

Financial Summary

Total Giving: $606,500 (fiscal year ending November 30, 2003)
Assets: $14,550,993 (fiscal 2003)

Typical Recipients

Arts & Humanities: Arts Associations & Councils, Dance, Historic Preservation, History & Archaeology, Libraries, Museums/Galleries, Public Broadcasting
Civic & Public Affairs: Botanical Gardens/Parks, Civic & Public Affairs-General, Legal Aid, Nonprofit Management, Public Policy, Urban & Community Affairs, Zoos/Aquariums
Education: Afterschool/Enrichment Programs, Colleges & Universities, Community & Junior Colleges, Literacy, Science/Mathematics Education, Student Aid
Environment: Environment-General, Resource Conservation, Wildlife Protection
Health: Eyes/Blindness, Hospitals
International: Foreign Educational Institutions, Health Care/Hospitals, International Affairs, International Organizations
Religion: Bible Study/Translation, Religious Welfare
Science: Science Museums
Social Services: Child Welfare, Community Centers, Community Service Organizations, Crime Prevention, Delinquency & Criminal Rehabilitation, People with Disabilities, Substance Abuse

Application Procedures

Initial Contact: Send a brief letter of inquiry.
Application Requirements: Including a description of organization and purpose of funds sought.
Deadlines: None.

Restrictions

Focus on is on libraries.

Grants Analysis

Disclosure Period: fiscal year ending November 30, 2003
Total Grants: $606,500
Number of Grants: 11
Average Grant: $55,136*
Highest Grant: $100,000
Lowest Grant: $2,000
Typical Range: $25,000 to $75,000
*****Note:** Average grant figure excludes highest grant.

Recent Grants

Note: Grants derived from fiscal 1999 Form 990.
Library-Related
25,000	Fund for American Libraries, Chicago, IL
25,000	New Rochelle Public Library, New Rochelle, NY
10,000	Kansas Library Association, KS
10,000	Special Libraries Association, Washington, DC

General

50,000	Iona College, New Rochelle, NY
30,000	Bronx Museum of the Arts, Bronx, NY
30,000	John Henry Newman Foundation, Dallas, TX
30,000	New York Botanical Gardens, New York, NY
25,000	French Institute Alliance Francaise, New York, NY
25,000	New York State Archives Partnership Trust, Albany, NY
25,000	University of Illinois, Chicago, IL
17,500	Rainbow After School Program
15,000	Bronx Council on the Arts, Bronx, NY
15,000	Mount Vernon Ladies Association, Mt. Vernon, VA

HUEY AND ANGELINE WILSON FOUNDATION

Giving Contact

Gregory J. Cotter, Trustee
3636 S. Sherwood Forest Blvd., Suite 650
Baton Rouge, LA 70816-2236
Phone: (225)292-1344
Fax: (225)292-1589

Description

Founded: 1987
EIN: 581714586
Organization Type: Private Foundation
Giving Locations: LA: Baton Rouge metro area
Grant Types: Capital, Emergency, General Support.

Donor Information

Founder: The foundation was established by Huey Wilson and his wife, Angelina Wilson, founders of a catalog showroom business in Baton Rouge, LA. The couple also co-founded an oilfield service business in Houma, LA.

Financial Summary

Total Giving: $302,500 (2003); $228,000 (2001)
Assets: $6,094,754 (2003); $5,175,532 (2001)
Gifts Received: $12,808 (2003); $147,785 (2001).
Note: In 2001 and 2003, contributions were received from Huey and Angelina Wilson.

Typical Recipients

Education: Education-General, Public Education (Precollege)
Health: Single-Disease Health Associations
Social Services: Child Welfare, Domestic Violence, Family Services, Food/Clothing Distribution, Volunteer Services, Youth Organizations

Application Procedures

Initial Contact: Submit a written proposal.
Application Requirements: Include a proposal summary, including the following information in the following order: organization name; chief executive officer; brief project summary of 50 words or less; project director; address; phone number; compelling reason for the project expressed in 50 words or less; amount requested; area of interest; mission statement; and service area. Also provide a narrative section including a concise history of the organization and an overview of current programs and activities; description of the challenge to be met by the project; detailed project description, including strategies, measurable objectives, and timetable; plan for continuing the project once foundation support ends; and methods for evaluating the project. Proposals should be accompanied by the following attachments: copy of the organization's IRS 501(c)(3) determination letter; a statement from the organization's board of directors authorizing the request and agreeing to imple-

ment the project if funded; list of board members, including principal occupations and a description of the term of office and rotation schedule for the board; names and qualifications of persons responsible for carrying out the program; detailed project budget and budget narrative, with income sources and expenditures and other sources of potential, pending, and approved funding; financial statements, including the organization's operating budget, balance sheet, and statements of support, revenue and expenses for the last completed and current fiscal years; and any supporting materials that the applicant wishes to include.
Deadlines: February 23, for notification by May 1; and August 24, for notification by November 1.
Notes: Proposals should be typewritten and stapled, but not bound.

Restrictions

Applicants must be 501(c)(3) tax-exempt organizations. The foundation does not provide seed funding.

Foundation Officials

Gregory J. Cotter: trustee
Angelina M. Wilson: trustee
Huey J. Wilson: trustee

Grants Analysis

Disclosure Period: calendar year ending 2003
Total Grants: $302,500
Number of Grants: 26
Average Grant: $10,180*
Highest Grant: $48,000
Lowest Grant: $2,500
Typical Range: $5,000 to $20,000
*Note: Average grant figure excludes highest grant.

Recent Grants

Note: Grants derived from 2001 Form 990.
General

41,000	National Hemophilia Foundation - Louisiana Chapter, Baton Rouge, LA
25,000	Family Road of Baton Rouge, Baton Rouge, LA -- program assistant
24,000	Society of St. Vincent de Paul, Baton Rouge, LA -- heart and blood pressure medicine
20,000	Children's Charter School, Baton Rouge, LA -- mobile computer lab
15,000	Volunteers of America Greater Baton Rouge, Inc., Baton Rouge, LA -- funding for community resource coordinator
12,000	Boys & Girls Club, Baton Rouge, LA -- the supreme program
11,000	Baton Rouge Youth, Inc, Baton Rouge, LA -- summer program
10,000	Baton Rouge Alliance for Transitional Living, Baton Rouge, LA -- emergency temporary shelter
10,000	Battered Women's Program, Baton Rouge, LA -- refurbish building
10,000	Cancer Services of Greater Baton Rouge, Baton Rouge, LA -- prescription reimbursement program

MARIE C. AND JOSEPH C. WILSON FOUNDATION

Giving Contact

Ruth H. Fleischmann-Colgan, Executive Director
Marie C. and Joseph C. Wilson Foundation
160 Allens Creek Road, Suite 206
Rochester, NY 14618
Phone: (585)461-4696
Fax: (585)473-5206
E-mail: mcjcwilsonfdn@juno.com
Web: http://www.mcjcwilsonfoundation.org

Description

Founded: 1963
EIN: 166042022
Organization Type: Private Foundation
Giving Locations: NY: Rochester
Grant Types: Capital, Conference/Seminar, Emergency, Endowment, Fellowship, General Support, Multiyear/Continuing Support, Operating Expenses, Project, Research, Scholarship, Seed Money.

Donor Information

Founder: the late Katherine M. Wilson, the late Joseph C. Wilson

Financial Summary

Total Giving: $363,565 (2003); $815,705 (2001)
Assets: $17,268,012 (2003); $16,915,144 (2001)
Gifts Received: $15,907,486 (1999); $550 (1998).
Note: In 1998 and 1999, contributions were received from United Way.

Typical Recipients

Arts & Humanities: Arts Associations & Councils, Arts Outreach, Dance, Historic Preservation, History & Archaeology, Libraries, Museums/Galleries, Performing Arts, Theater
Civic & Public Affairs: African American Affairs, Botanical Gardens/Parks, Community Foundations, Economic Development, Economic Policy, Employment/Job Training, Civic & Public Affairs-General, Housing, Legal Aid, Nonprofit Management, Urban & Community Affairs, Women's Affairs
Education: Afterschool/Enrichment Programs, Arts/Humanities Education, Colleges & Universities, Leadership Training, Minority Education, Preschool Education, Private Education (Precollege), Public Education (Precollege), Science/Mathematics Education, Special Education, Student Aid
Environment: Forestry, Environment-General
Health: Adolescent Health Issues, AIDS/HIV, Alzheimer's Disease, Children's Health/Hospitals, Clinics/Medical Centers, Diabetes, Eyes/Blindness, Health Organizations, Heart, Hospitals, Long-Term Care, Medical Research, Mental Health, Single-Disease Health Associations
International: International Relations, International Relief Efforts
Religion: Churches, Ministries, Religious Welfare
Social Services: At-Risk Youth, Big Brothers/Big Sisters, Child Welfare, Community Service Organizations, Domestic Violence, Family Planning, Family Services, Food/Clothing Distribution, People with Disabilities, Recreation & Athletics, Senior Services, Substance Abuse, United Funds/United Ways, Veterans, Volunteer Services, Youth Organizations

Application Procedures

Initial Contact: Send two copies of a succinct, one-page overview of the organization and the program for which funds are being requested.
Deadlines: None.
Notes: For immediate consideration, proposals must be submitted at least four weeks in advance of the board of managers meetings in May and October.

Restrictions

Does not support individuals.

Additional Information

Publications: Annual Report (includes Application Guidelines)
Trust(s): JP Morgan Chase Bank NA

Foundation Officials

R. Thomas Dalbey, Jr.: board of directors
Katherine Dalbey Ensign: board of directors
Ruth H. Fleischmann-Colgan: executive director
Deirdre Wilson Garton: secretary
Chris Kling: board of directors
Judith W. Martin: board of directors
Katherine W. Roby: board of directors

Mimi D. Tabah: board of directors
Janet C. Wilson: board of directors
Joseph R. Wilson: board of directors
Scott Wilson: co-chairman

Grants Analysis

Disclosure Period: calendar year ending 2003
Total Grants: $363,565
Number of Grants: 89
Average Grant: $4,085
Highest Grant: $25,000
Lowest Grant: $50
Typical Range: $1,000 to $10,000

Recent Grants

Note: Grants derived from 2003 Form 990.
Library-Related

15,000	Rundel Library Foundation, Rochester, NY -- salary support for the library youth coordinator

General

25,000	Mount Hope Family Center, Rochester, NY -- support for campaign for the children of Mt. Hope
25,000	Threshold Center for Alternative Youth Services, Rochester, NY -- support for expand hours of health care services for at - risk youth
20,000	Center for Youth Services, Rochester, NY -- support for new transitional housing program for youth
15,000	Nazareth College, Rochester, NY -- support for expansion of partners for learning program
15,000	Wilson Commencement Park, Rochester, NY
13,400	Family Resource Centers, Rochester, NY -- support for the parenting program in the Beechwood neighborhood
12,000	Monroe County Legal Assistance Corporation, Rochester, NY -- support for fair housing enforcement project
10,000	Lifetime Health - Joseph C. Wilson Center, Rochester, NY -- support to healthy steps program for young children
10,000	Ten Chimneys Foundation, Genesee Depot, WI -- donation made to the Joe Garton memorial fund

MATILDA R. WILSON FUND

Giving Contact

George D. Miller, Jr., President
100 Renaissance Center, 34th Floor
Detroit, MI 48243
Phone: (313)259-7777
Fax: (313)393-7579

Description

Founded: 1954
EIN: 386087665
Organization Type: General Purpose Foundation
Giving Locations: MI, Detroit Southeast Michigan
Grant Types: Capital, General Support, Multiyear/Continuing Support, Operating Expenses, Project, Seed Money.

Donor Information

Founder: Incorporated in 1944 in Michigan by the late Matilda R. Wilson and Alfred G. Wilson.

Financial Summary

Total Giving: $3,252,581 (2003); $4,478,137 (2002); $2,700,000 (2001)
Giving Analysis: Giving for 2002 includes: foundation grants to United Way ($7,000)

Assets: $42,055,483 (2003); $39,252,381 (2002); $56,000,000 (2001)

Typical Recipients

Arts & Humanities: Arts Associations & Councils, Arts Centers, Arts Institutes, Ethnic & Folk Arts, Arts & Humanities-General, History & Archaeology, Libraries, Literary Arts, Museums/Galleries, Music, Opera, Performing Arts, Public Broadcasting, Theater
Civic & Public Affairs: Chambers of Commerce, Clubs, Economic Development, Economic Policy, Civic & Public Affairs-General, Housing, Law & Justice, Legal Aid, Municipalities/Towns, Philanthropic Organizations, Professional & Trade Associations, Public Policy, Urban & Community Affairs, Zoos/Aquariums
Education: Arts/Humanities Education, Colleges & Universities, Community & Junior Colleges, Education Associations, Elementary Education (Private), Education-General, Leadership Training, Medical Education, Minority Education, Private Education (Precollege), Public Education (Precollege), Science/Mathematics Education, Social Sciences Education
Environment: Environment-General, Resource Conservation
Health: Children's Health/Hospitals, Clinics/Medical Centers, Emergency/Ambulance Services, Eyes/Blindness, Health Organizations, Hospices, Hospitals, Medical Rehabilitation, Public Health, Research/Studies Institutes
International: Foreign Arts Organizations, International-General
Religion: Churches, Religion-General, Religious Organizations, Religious Welfare, Social/Policy Issues
Science: Science-General, Scientific Centers & Institutes, Scientific Organizations
Social Services: At-Risk Youth, Camps, Child Welfare, Community Service Organizations, Counseling, Delinquency & Criminal Rehabilitation, Domestic Violence, Family Planning, Family Services, Food/Clothing Distribution, People with Disabilities, Recreation & Athletics, Scouts, Social Services-General, Substance Abuse, United Funds/United Ways, Volunteer Services, Youth Organizations

Application Procedures

Initial Contact: Prospective applicants should submit a letter explaining the need and use of requested funds.
Deadlines: None.
Review Process: The board meets quarterly to consider proposals, usually in March, June, September, and December.

Restrictions

The foundation does not make loans or grants to individuals.

Foundation Officials

David M. Hempstead: treasurer PRIM CORP EMPL secretary: Detroit Lions Inc. CORP AFFIL secretary: Higbie-Maxon Inc.
George Miller: president, treasurer B Detroit, MI 1928. ED Amherst College BA (1950); University of Michigan JD (1953). PRIM CORP EMPL partner: Bodman Longley & Dahling. NONPR AFFIL member: Order Coif; member: Phi Beta Kappa; member: Michigan Bar Association; trustee: Henry Ford Health Systems; trustee: Maplegrove Center/Kingswood Hospital; member: American Bar Association; member: Detroit Bar Association. CLUB AFFIL Detroit Athletic Club; Orchard Lake Country Club.
Robert McCellan Surdam: trustee B Albany, NY October 28, 1917. ED Williams College BA (1939). CLUB AFFIL Rolling Rock Club; Yondotega Club; Little Traverse Yacht Club; Jupiter Island Club; Little Harbor Club; Hobe Sound Yacht Club; Jupiter Hills Club; Country Club Detroit; Detroit Club.

Grants Analysis

Disclosure Period: calendar year ending 2003
Total Grants: $3,252,581
Number of Grants: 42
Average Grant: $58,815*
Highest Grant: $500,000
Lowest Grant: $5,000
Typical Range: $25,000 to $100,000
*__Note:__ Average grant figure excludes two highest grants ($900,000).

Recent Grants

Note: Grants derived from 2002 Form 990.
General

400,000	Michigan State University, East Lansing, MI -- capital
300,000	Michigan State University, East Lansing, MI -- capital
300,000	Michigan State University, East Lansing, MI -- capital
250,000	Detroit Symphony Orchestra Hall, Detroit, MI -- capital
250,000	Detroit Zoological Society, Royal Oak, MI -- capital
200,000	Boys and Girls Club of Auburn Hills, Auburn Hills, MI -- capital
200,000	Community Foundation of Southeastern Michigan, Detroit, MI -- capital
200,000	Community Foundation of Southeastern Michigan, Detroit, MI -- capital
200,000	Detroit Symphony Orchestra Hall, Detroit, MI -- capital
125,000	Henry Ford Museum, Dearborn, MI -- capital

THOMAS WILSON SANITARIUM FOR CHILDREN OF BALTIMORE CITY

Giving Contact

Dr. Kenneth S. Schuberth, President
PO Box 2766
250 W. Pratt St., 15th Fl.
Baltimore, MD 21225
Phone: (410)360-9510

Description

Founded: 1879
EIN: 526044885
Organization Type: Private Foundation
Giving Locations: MD: Baltimore
Grant Types: General Support, Research.

Donor Information

Founder: the late Thomas Wilson

Financial Summary

Total Giving: $622,571 (fiscal year ending January 31, 2002)
Assets: $11,917,749 (fiscal 2002)

Typical Recipients

Arts & Humanities: Arts Centers, Arts & Humanities-General, Libraries, Museums/Galleries
Civic & Public Affairs: Botanical Gardens/Parks, Zoos/Aquariums
Education: Arts/Humanities Education, Colleges & Universities, Elementary Education (Public), Education-General, Medical Education, Private Education (Precollege), Science/Mathematics Education, Special Education
Health: Adolescent Health Issues, AIDS/HIV, Children's Health/Hospitals, Clinics/Medical Centers, Eyes/Blindness, Health-General, Health Organiza-

tions, Hospitals, Medical Rehabilitation, Medical Research, Prenatal Health Issues, Public Health, Respiratory, Single-Disease Health Associations, Speech & Hearing
Science: Science Museums
Social Services: Child Abuse, Child Welfare, Day Care, Family Planning, Family Services, People with Disabilities, Social Services-General, YMCA/YWCA/YMHA/YWHA

Application Procedures

Initial Contact: Send a letter stating the entity to be benefited and services provided.
Deadlines: None.

Restrictions

Limited to grants that benefit the children of Baltimore, MD.

Foundation Officials

Dr. Kenneth S. Schuberth: president
William C. Trimble, Jr.: secretary, treasurer B Buenos Aires, Argentina 1935. ED Princeton University AB (1958); University of Maryland LLB (1964). PRIM CORP EMPL counsel: Semmes Bowen & Semmes. NONPR AFFIL member: Maryland Bar Association; honorary consul: The Netherlands; member: American Bar Association; member: Baltimore Bar Association. CLUB AFFIL Greenspring Valley Hunt Club; Society Cincinnati; Colonial Club.
Kinloch N. Yellott, III: vice president

Grants Analysis

Disclosure Period: fiscal year ending January 31, 2002
Total Grants: $622,571
Number of Grants: 36
Average Grant: $17,294
Highest Grant: $50,000
Lowest Grant: $1,500
Typical Range: $10,000 to $25,000

Recent Grants

Note: Grants derived from 2002 Form 990.
Library-Related

17,000	Johns Hopkins Children's Library and Family Resource Center, Baltimore, MD -- Family Resource Library

General

50,000	Jemicy School, Owings Mills, MD -- community outreach partnership with the Archdiocese of Baltimore
36,868	University of Maryland School of Medicine, Baltimore, MD -- physically abused children evaluating the efficacy of two treatment approaches
30,000	Families Involved Together, Inc., Baltimore, MD -- in school support and Advocacy Project
26,226	Sheppard Pratt Health System, Baltimore, MD -- conflict resolution, peer mediation and leadership program
25,000	Camp Believe, Inc., Baltimore, MD -- Camp Believe
25,000	Gilman School, Baltimore, MD -- Baltimore Independent School Learning Camp
25,000	Kennedy Krieger Institute, Baltimore, MD -- monitory sleep patterns in children with ADHD
25,000	University of Maryland Division of Pediatric Pulmonology and Allergy, Baltimore, MD -- University of Maryland Hospital for Children Breathmobile
20,000	Franciscan Youth Center, Inc., Baltimore, MD -- Summery Programs
20,000	House of Mercy, Baltimore, MD -- After-School Literacy Project

WINDHAM FOUNDATION

Giving Contact

Arthur Schubert, Vice President
PO Box 70
Grafton, VT 05146
Phone: (802)843-2211
Fax: (802)843-2205
E-mail: winfound@sover.net
Web: http://www.windham-foundation.org
Note: ALT Email:: stephan@sover.net

Description

Founded: 1963
EIN: 136142024
Organization Type: Specialized/Single Purpose Foundation
Giving Locations: VT: emphasis on Windham County
Grant Types: Capital, Challenge, General Support, Matching, Operating Expenses, Project, Scholarship, Seed Money.

Financial Summary

Total Giving: $211,770 (fiscal year ending October 31, 2001)
Giving Analysis: Giving for fiscal 2001 includes: foundation grants to United Way ($1,000); foundation scholarships ($107,375)
Assets: $53,984,679 (fiscal 2001)
Gifts Received: $60,000 (fiscal 2001); $30,000 (fiscal 1997); $30,000 (fiscal 1996). Note: Contributions were received from the Bunbury Co. and the estate of Dean Mathey.

Typical Recipients

Arts & Humanities: Arts Associations & Councils, Arts Festivals, Dance, Ethnic & Folk Arts, Film & Video, Arts & Humanities-General, Historic Preservation, History & Archaeology, Libraries, Museums/Galleries, Music, Public Broadcasting, Theater
Civic & Public Affairs: Clubs, Economic Development, Employment/Job Training, Civic & Public Affairs-General, Housing, Municipalities/Towns, Public Policy, Rural Affairs, Safety, Urban & Community Affairs, Women's Affairs
Education: Afterschool/Enrichment Programs, Arts/Humanities Education, Colleges & Universities, Elementary Education (Public), Environmental Education, Education-General, International Studies, Literacy, Minority Education, Preschool Education, Private Education (Precollege), Public Education (Precollege), Science/Mathematics Education, Secondary Education (Public), Special Education, Student Aid
Environment: Environment-General, Protection, Research, Resource Conservation
Health: Arthritis, Cancer, Diabetes, Emergency/Ambulance Services, Health-General, Health Organizations, Home-Care Services, Hospices, Hospitals, Kidney, Prenatal Health Issues, Public Health, Trauma Treatment
Religion: Churches, Dioceses, Religion-General, Religious Welfare, Seminaries
Science: Observatories & Planetariums
Social Services: Animal Protection, Camps, Community Centers, Community Service Organizations, Day Care, Domestic Violence, Family Planning, Family Services, Food/Clothing Distribution, Recreation & Athletics, Shelters/Homelessness, Social Services-General, United Funds/United Ways, Volunteer Services, Youth Organizations

Application Procedures

Initial Contact: Before submitting a grant request, organizations must first review the foundation's guidelines. Requests for a grant application and guidelines (including an annual report and application cover sheet) can be obtained either by phone or by mail.
Application Requirements: A grant request con-

sists of seven copies of the following: a completed grant application cover sheet; a cover letter, project narrative, and need for assistance, all in five pages or less; and most recent audit, or financial statement if audit is unavailable, and budget for project. Also include one copy of an IRS 501(c)(3) letter of tax free determination. Faxed or e-mailed applications are not accepted.
Deadlines: The grant application deadline changes annually; contact the foundation for further information. Grant applications must arrive at the foundation's offices before 4:00 pm the day of the designated deadline. Grants received after that time will be included in the following grant cycle.
Review Process: Organizations requesting grants will be notified by mail of the board's decision within eight to ten weeks after the deadline.

Restrictions

As of January 1, 1998, limited its giving to Vermont elementary and secondary education. Grants are not made to individuals.

Foundation Officials

Charles B. Atwater: trustee emeritus
William A. Gilbert: trustee
Samuel Waldron Lambert, III: chairman, trustee B New York, NY 1938. ED Yale University BA (1960); Harvard University LLB (1963). PRIM CORP EMPL partner: Drinker, Biddle & Reath. NONPR AFFIL member: New Jersey Bar Association; member: Princeton Bar Association; member: American Bar Association.
Stephan A. Morse: president, chief executive officer, trustee B 1947. PRIM CORP EMPL president, director: Old Tavern at Grafton Inc. ADD CORP EMPL president, administration, director: Grafton Village Cheese Co. CORP AFFIL director: United Bank; director: Vermont Finance Services.
Robert M. Olmsted: trustee
Arthur Schubert: vice president
Edward Joseph Toohey: treasurer, trustee B Jersey City, NJ 1930. ED Yale University BA (1953). CORP AFFIL vice president: Old Tavern Grafton Inc. NONPR AFFIL director emeritus: New York City Ballet; vice chairman: Peddie School. CLUB AFFIL Yale Club; Sky Club; University Club; Canoe Brook Country Club; Georgetown Club.
Charles C. Townsend, Jr.: trustee PRIM CORP EMPL secretary: The Bunbury Co. CORP AFFIL director: HTI Voice Solutions Inc.; director: Project Orbis International; director: Cary Institutional PRPTS Inc.
Edward R. Zuccaro: vice president, trustee B New York, NY 1943. PRIM CORP EMPL partner: Zuccaro, Willis & Bent. CORP AFFIL clerk, director: Phelps Enterprises; clerk, director: Phelps Real Estate; clerk, director: Music Shop; vice president, secretary, director: Old Tavern Grafton Inc.; treasurer: Grafton Village Cheese Co.; clerk, director: Movie World; clerk, director: Dana Jewelry.

Grants Analysis

Disclosure Period: fiscal year ending October 31, 2001
Total Grants: $104,395*
Number of Grants: 58
Average Grant: $1,568*
Highest Grant: $15,000
Typical Range: $500 to $3,000
***Note:** Giving excludes scholarships and United Way. Average grant figure excludes hightest grant.

Recent Grants

Note: Grants derived from 2001 Form 990.
Library-Related

1,000	St. Johnsbury Athenaeum, St. Johnsbury, VT
500	Moore Free Library, Newfane, VT

General

15,000	Vermont Symphony Orchestra, Burlington, VT

10,000	Vermont Diary Farm Sustainable Project, Burlington, VT
5,000	Artemis Wildlife Foundation, Helena, MT
5,000	Brattleboro Arts Initiative, Brattleboro, VT
5,000	Green Mountain Training Center, Brattleboro, VT
5,000	Hilltop Montessori Capital Fund, Brattleboro, VT
5,000	Youth Services, Brattleboro, VT
3,500	Snelling Center for Government, Burlington, VT
3,000	Fairbanks Museum and Planetarium, St. Johnsbury, VT
2,500	Ehtan Allen Homestead Museum, Burlington, VT

WINN-DIXIE STORES INC.

Company Headquarters

Jacksonville, FL
Web: http://www.winn-dixie.com

Company Description

Founded: 1928
Ticker: WIN
Exchange: NYSE
Revenue: US$11.732 billion (2004)
Profit: (US$100.4 million) (2004)
Employees: 113000 (2003)
Fortune Rank: 182, per FORTUNE Magazine's list of 500 Largest U.S. Corporations (2004).
SIC(s): 5411 Grocery Stores.

Operating Locations

Winn-Dixie Stores Inc. (AL--Montgomery; FL, Jacksonville, Miami, Orlando; GA, Atlanta; KY--Louisville; LA--New Orleans; NC, Charlotte; OH--Cincinnati; SC--Greenville; TX--Fort Worth; VA)

Winn-Dixie Stores Foundation

Giving Contact

D. F. Henry, President, Director
Winn-Dixie Stores Foundation
PO Box B
Jacksonville, FL 32203-0297
Phone: (904)783-5000
Fax: (904)783-5235
Web: http://www.winn-dixie.com/company/about_wd/community_commitment.asp

Alternate Contact

5050 Edgewood Court
Jacksonville, FL 32254
Phone: (904)783-5429

Description

EIN: 590995428
Organization Type: Corporate Foundation
Giving Locations: AL; FL; GA; IN; KY; LA; MS; NC; OH; OK; SC; TN; TX; VA: primarily in the company's 14-state trade area; generally within the Southern United States.
Grant Types: Award, Employee Matching Gifts, General Support, Matching, Project, Research, Scholarship.
Note: Employee matching gift ratio: 1 to 1 for educational purposes, art & health facilities, and the United Way.

Financial Summary

Total Giving: $2,533,424 (2002); $1,832,804 (2001).
Note: Contributes through corporate direct giving program and foundation.
Giving Analysis: Giving for 2002 includes: founda-

tion grants to United Way ($50,000); foundation matching gifts ($1,078,345); foundation (approx $2,000,000); 2001: foundation ($1,832,804)
Assets: $233,540 (2002); $232,494 (2001)
Gifts Received: $2,522,714 (2002); $2,000,000 (2001); $3,000,000 (2000). Note: Contributions were received from Winn-Dixie Stores, Inc.

Typical Recipients

Arts & Humanities: Arts Associations & Councils, Arts Festivals, Ballet, History & Archaeology, Libraries, Music, Public Broadcasting
Civic & Public Affairs: African American Affairs, Business/Free Enterprise, Chambers of Commerce, Clubs, Community Foundations, Economic Policy, Civic & Public Affairs-General, Housing, Law & Justice, Legal Aid, Philanthropic Organizations, Public Policy, Urban & Community Affairs, Women's Affairs, Zoos/Aquariums
Education: Business Education, Colleges & Universities, Education Associations, Education Funds, Education-General, Medical Education, Minority Education, Private Education (Precollege), Science/Mathematics Education, Secondary Education (Public), Student Aid
Health: Alzheimer's Disease, Cancer, Children's Health/Hospitals, Clinics/Medical Centers, Diabetes, Emergency/Ambulance Services, Health-General, Health Organizations, Heart, Hospices, Hospitals, Mental Health, Multiple Sclerosis, Prenatal Health Issues, Public Health, Single-Disease Health Associations
Religion: Churches, Religious Organizations, Religious Welfare
Social Services: At-Risk Youth, Big Brothers/Big Sisters, Child Welfare, Community Service Organizations, Family Services, Food/Clothing Distribution, Homes, People with Disabilities, Recreation & Athletics, Scouts, Shelters/Homelessness, Social Services-General, Special Olympics, Substance Abuse, United Funds/United Ways, YMCA/YWCA/YMHA/YWHA, Youth Organizations

Application Procedures

Initial Contact: Submit a letter.
Application Requirements: Provide a description of organization, amount requested, purpose of funds sought, recently audited financial statement, and proof of tax-exempt status.
Deadlines: None. Board meets quarterly.
Notes: Applications should be sent to the nearest division office.

Restrictions

No grants are made to individuals or religious or political organizations. No matching gifts are made to religious, political, fraternal, professional, social, or recreation groups. With the exception of matching gifts, no contributions are made outside the trade territories served by Winn-Dixie.

Additional Information

Publications: Guidelines; Annual Report

Corporate Officials

Andrew Dano Davis: chairman, chief executive officer B Henderson, AR 1945. ED Stetson University. PRIM CORP EMPL chairman: Winn-Dixie Stores Inc.
Frank Lazaran: president, chief executive officer ED California State University, Long Beach BS. PRIM CORP EMPL president, chief executive officer: Winn-Dixie Stores Inc.
Richard P. McCook: senior vice president, chief financial officer B Miami, FL 1953. ED Florida State University BS (1975); Florida State University MS (1976). PRIM CORP EMPL senior vice president, chief financial officer: Winn-Dixie Stores Inc. NONPR AFFIL member: Financial Executives Institute; member: Florida Institute CPAs; member: American Institute CPAs. CLUB AFFIL River Club.

Foundation Officials

D. D. Antonia: vice president, director
L. B. Appel: vice president, assistant secretary, director
D. M. Byrum: vice president, assistant secretary, director
Judith W. Dixon: secretary
J. R. Gage: vice president, director
D. F. Henry: president, director
R. C. Judd: vice president, director
D. G. LaFever: vice president, director
Frank Lazaran: vice president (see above)
Richard P. McCook: vice president (see above)
K. D. Ross: vice president, treasurer, director
A. R. Rowland: vice president, director
K. E. Salem: vice president, director
D. M. Sheehan: vice president, director
J. R. Sheehan: vice president, director

Grants Analysis

Disclosure Period: calendar year ending 2002
Total Grants: $1,405,079*
Number of Grants: 358
Average Grant: $3,659*
Highest Grant: $98,660
Lowest Grant: $50
Typical Range: $1,000 to $5,000
*Note: Giving excludes matching gifts and United Way. Average grant figure excludes highest grant.

Recent Grants

Note: Grants derived from 2003 Form 990.
General

175,000	Coca Cola, Jacksonville, FL
98,000	Vertis and Advo, Tampa, FL
85,000	PepsiCo, Jacksonville, FL
80,000	Flowers Bakeries, Thomasville, GA
64,000	Tyson Foods, Apopka, FL
63,000	Sanderson Farms Inc., Laurel, MS
55,000	G E Lighting, Tampa, FL
55,000	Great Dane Trailer, Savannah, GA
55,000	Kellogg's Snacks, College Park, GA
50,000	American Italian Pasta, Tampa, FL

WINNEBAGO INDUSTRIES

Company Headquarters

605 W. Crystal Lake Rd.
Forest City, IA 50436
Web: http://www.winnebagoind.com

Company Description

Founded: 1958
Ticker: WGO
Exchange: NYSE
Revenue: US$828.4 million (2002)
Employees: 3685 (2002)
SIC(s): 3355 Aluminum Rolling & Drawing Nec, 3711 Motor Vehicles & Car Bodies, 3792 Travel Trailers & Campers.

Operating Locations

Winnebago Realty Corp. (IA--Forest City)

Winnebago Industries Foundation

Giving Contact

Elsie Felland, Corporate Cashier
PO Box 152
Forest City, IA 50436-0152
Phone: (641)582-3535
Fax: (641)582-6966

Description

EIN: 237174206
Organization Type: Corporate Foundation
Giving Locations: IA
Grant Types: General Support.

Financial Summary

Total Giving: $63,675 (fiscal year ending February 28, 2004); $110,000 (fiscal 2001)
Assets: $1,666,375 (fiscal 2004); $1,565,213 (fiscal 2001)
Gifts Received: $250,000 (fiscal 2004); $250,000 (fiscal 2000)

Typical Recipients

Arts & Humanities: Arts Associations & Councils, Arts Centers, Arts Festivals, Community Arts, History & Archaeology, Libraries, Museums/Galleries, Public Broadcasting
Civic & Public Affairs: Botanical Gardens/Parks, Chambers of Commerce, Clubs, Economic Development, Civic & Public Affairs-General, Housing, Municipalities/Towns, Parades/Festivals, Rural Affairs, Safety, Urban & Community Affairs
Education: Colleges & Universities, Education-General, International Exchange, Private Education (Precollege), Public Education (Precollege), Secondary Education (Public), Student Aid
Environment: Air/Water Quality, Environment-General, Resource Conservation
Health: Cancer, Children's Health/Hospitals, Emergency/Ambulance Services, Eyes/Blindness, Health-General, Health Organizations, Heart, Hospices, Hospitals, Nursing Services
Religion: Jewish Causes, Religious Welfare
Social Services: Animal Protection, Community Centers, Community Service Organizations, Crime Prevention, Day Care, Emergency Relief, Family Planning, Family Services, Food/Clothing Distribution, Recreation & Athletics, Scouts, Special Olympics, Substance Abuse, United Funds/United Ways, YMCA/YWCA/YMHA/YWHA, Youth Organizations

Application Procedures

Initial Contact: Send a full proposal.
Deadlines: None.

Restrictions

Does not support individuals, religious organizations for sectarian purposes, political or lobbying groups, or organizations outside operating areas.

Corporate Officials

Edwin F. Barker: vice president, chief financial officer, chief operating officer B 1947. PRIM CORP EMPL vice president, chief financial officer: Winnebago Industries Inc. ADD CORP EMPL chief financial officer: Winnebago Industries Corp.
Bruce D. Hertzke: president, chief executive officer, chief operating officer PRIM CORP EMPL president, chief executive officer, chief operating officer: Winnebago Industries.

Foundation Officials

Edwin F. Barker: trustee (see above)
Bruce D. Hertzke: trustee (see above)

Grants Analysis

Disclosure Period: fiscal year ending February 28, 2004
Total Grants: $63,675
Number of Grants: 70
Average Grant: $910
Highest Grant: $10,000
Lowest Grant: $50
Typical Range: $250 to $1,500

Recent Grants

Note: Grants derived from fiscal 2001 Form 990.
Library-Related
2,000	Fertile Public Library, Fertile, IA

General
5,000	Hampton Community Christian Daycare, Inc., Hampton, IA
3,000	City of Forest City, Forest City, IA
3,000	Fertile Fire Department, Fertile, IA
3,000	Hancock County Conservation Board, Garner, IA
3,000	Mitchell County Memorial Hospital Fund, Osage, IA
2,500	Hanson Family Life Center, Forest City, IA
2,000	Forest City Ambulance Fund, Forest City, IA
2,000	Habitat for Humanity of North Central Iowa, Mason City, IA
2,000	Iowa Natural Heritage Foundation, Des Moines, IA
2,000	Iowa Natural Heritage Foundation, Des Moines, IA

NORMAN AND ROSITA WINSTON FOUNDATION

Giving Contact

John J. O'Neil, Attorney
1285 Ave. of the Americas
New York, NY 10019-6064
Phone: (212)373-3000
Fax: (212)373-2187

Description

Founded: 1954
EIN: 136161672
Organization Type: General Purpose Foundation
Grant Types: Fellowship, General Support, Professorship, Project, Research, Scholarship.

Donor Information

Founder: Established in 1954 by the late Norman K. Winston.

Financial Summary

Total Giving: $4,036,000 (fiscal year ending June 30, 2003); $5,094,000 (fiscal 2002)
Giving Analysis: Giving for fiscal 2003 includes: foundation scholarships ($15,000); fiscal 2002: foundation scholarships ($30,000)
Assets: $82,771,393 (fiscal 2003); $82,012,107 (fiscal 2002)

Typical Recipients

Arts & Humanities: Arts Associations & Councils, Arts Centers, Arts Festivals, Arts Funds, Arts Outreach, Ballet, Dance, Film & Video, Historic Preservation, Libraries, Museums/Galleries, Music, Opera, Performing Arts, Public Broadcasting, Theater, Visual Arts
Civic & Public Affairs: Botanical Gardens/Parks, Civil Rights, Civic & Public Affairs-General, Law & Justice, Philanthropic Organizations, Public Policy, Urban & Community Affairs
Education: Arts/Humanities Education, Colleges & Universities, Education Reform, Education-General, International Studies, Leadership Training, Legal Education, Medical Education, Private Education (Precollege), Science/Mathematics Education, Secondary Education (Private), Social Sciences Education, Student Aid
Environment: Air/Water Quality, Resource Conservation, Wildlife Protection
Health: Cancer, Clinics/Medical Centers, Geriatric Health, Heart, Hospitals, Hospitals (University Affiliated), Long-Term Care, Medical Research, Research/Studies Institutes
International: Foreign Arts Organizations, Foreign Educational Institutions, Human Rights, Missionary/Religious Activities

Religion: Seminaries, Synagogues/Temples
Science: Science-General, Science Museums, Scientific Centers & Institutes
Social Services: Child Welfare, Community Service Organizations, Emergency Relief, Family Services, Recreation & Athletics, Senior Services, Sexual Abuse, YMCA/YWCA/YMHA/YWHA

Application Procedures

Initial Contact: There is no prescribed form for applications.
Deadlines: None.

Foundation Officials

Laurie Levitt Friedland: secretary, director
Jan Krukowski: treasurer, director
Dr. Richard Rifkind: president, director

Grants Analysis

Disclosure Period: fiscal year ending June 30, 2003
Total Grants: $4,021,000*
Number of Grants: 136
Average Grant: $29,566
Highest Grant: $190,000
Lowest Grant: $1,500
Typical Range: $5,000 to $50,000
*****Note:** Giving excludes scholarships.

Recent Grants

Note: Grants derived from fiscal 2003 Form 990.
General
190,000	Hamilton College, Clinton, NY
150,000	Williams College, Williamstown, MA
148,000	World Music Institute Inc., New York, NY -- toward the Artistic House Foundation
125,000	Culture Project Inc., New York, NY
111,000	National Dance Institute, New York, NY
110,000	Alliance for Justice, Washington, DC
110,000	People for the American Way Foundation, Washington, DC -- toward election protection project
105,000	Hospital for Special Surgery, New York, NY
80,000	Brooklyn Academy of Music, Brooklyn, NY
80,000	Columbia University Teachers College, New York, NY

WINTER CONSTRUCTION CO.

Company Headquarters

1330 Spring St., NW
Atlanta, GA 30309

Company Description

Employees: 250
SIC(s): 1541 Industrial Buildings & Warehouses, 1542 Nonresidential Construction Nec.

Operating Locations

Winter Construction Co. (GA--Atlanta)

Nonmonetary Support

Type: In-kind Services; Loaned Employees; Loaned Executives

Giving Contact

Leslie Harris, Marketing Vice President
1330 Spring Street, NW, Suite 300
Atlanta, GA 30309-2810
Phone: (404)588-3300
Fax: (404)223-5753
E-mail: lharris@wintercompanies.com
Web: http://www.wintercompanies.com

Description

Organization Type: Corporate Giving Program
Giving Locations: headquarters and operating communities.
Grant Types: Award, General Support.

Typical Recipients

Arts & Humanities: Arts Appreciation, Arts Associations & Councils, Arts Centers, Arts Festivals, Arts Funds, Community Arts, Dance, Ethnic & Folk Arts, Historic Preservation, Libraries, Literary Arts, Museums/Galleries, Music, Opera, Performing Arts, Theater, Visual Arts
Civic & Public Affairs: Philanthropic Organizations, Safety, Urban & Community Affairs, Zoos/Aquariums
Education: Arts/Humanities Education, Business Education, Continuing Education
Environment: Environment-General
Social Services: Community Centers, Volunteer Services

Application Procedures

Initial Contact: Send a brief letter of inquiry.
Application Requirements: Include a description of organization, amount requested, and purpose of funds sought.
Deadlines: None.

Restrictions

Does not support individuals.

Corporate Officials

Sean Durkin: chief financial officer, president, chief executive officer PRIM CORP EMPL chief financial officer: Winter Construction Co.
Robert L. Silverman: chairman, president, chief executive officer PRIM CORP EMPL chairman, president, chief executive officer: Winter Construction Co.

Grants Analysis

Typical Range: $1,000 to $2,500

WINTHROP

Giving Contact

Mary D. Damas, President
12625 High Bluff Dr., Suite 215
San Diego, CA 92130
Phone: (858)793-2554

Description

Founded: 1992
EIN: 020453999
Organization Type: Private Foundation
Giving Locations: CA
Grant Types: General Support.

Donor Information

Founder: Established in 1992 by Chatam, Inc.

Financial Summary

Total Giving: $1,189,597 (fiscal year ending May 31, 2002)
Giving Analysis: Giving for fiscal 2002 includes: foundation grants to United Way ($37,611); foundation matching gifts ($242,256).
Assets: $822,588 (fiscal 2002)
Gifts Received: $1,400,000 (fiscal 2002); $5,000,000 (fiscal 1992). Note: In 2002, contributions were received from Fisher Scientific Inc.

Typical Recipients

Arts & Humanities: Ethnic & Folk Arts, History & Archaeology, Libraries, Museums/Galleries, Music, Opera, Performing Arts, Public Broadcasting, Theater
Civic & Public Affairs: Botanical Gardens/Parks, Civic & Public Affairs-General, Legal Aid, Philanthropic Organizations, Public Policy, Urban & Community Affairs, Women's Affairs
Education: Business Education, Colleges & Universities, Economic Education, Education Reform, Education-General, Health & Physical Education, Leadership Training, Private Education (Precollege), Public Education (Precollege), Secondary Education (Private), Student Aid
Environment: Resource Conservation
Health: Children's Health/Hospitals, Clinics/Medical Centers, Emergency/Ambulance Services, Eyes/Blindness, Health-General, Health Funds, Health Organizations, Heart, Hospitals, Medical Research, Mental Health, Multiple Sclerosis, Public Health, Research/Studies Institutes, Respiratory, Speech & Hearing
International: Foreign Educational Institutions, International Organizations, Missionary/Religious Activities
Religion: Churches, Jewish Causes, Religious Welfare
Science: Science Museums, Scientific Centers & Institutes, Scientific Organizations
Social Services: Big Brothers/Big Sisters, Child Abuse, Community Service Organizations, Recreation & Athletics, Social Services-General, United Funds/United Ways, Volunteer Services, YMCA/YWCA/YMHA/YWHA

Application Procedures

Initial Contact: Send a brief letter of inquiry.
Application Requirements: Include a description of organization, purpose of funds sought, and proof of tax-exempt status.
Deadlines: None.

Foundation Officials

Mary D. Damas: assistant secretary
Paul M. Meister: vice president, treasurer B Kalamazoo, MI 1952. ED University of Michigan BA (1974); Northwestern University MBA (1976). PRIM CORP EMPL chief financial officer, senior vice president finance: Fisher Science International Inc. ADD CORP EMPL managining director: Latona Associate. CORP AFFIL director: Minerals Technologies Inc.; director: Power Control Technologies; director: MF Worldwide; vice chairman: General Chemical Group Inc.; vice chairman: Gentek Inc.
Paul Michael Montrone: vice president B Scranton, PA 1941. ED University of Scranton BS (1962); Columbia University PhD (1965). PRIM CORP EMPL chief executive officer, chairman: Fisher Science International Inc. ADD CORP EMPL president: Henley Holdings Two Inc. CORP AFFIL advisory board: Zeneca Inc.; advisory board: Sintokagio Ltd.; director: Waste Management Inc.; chairman: Latona Associates; director: Prestolite Wire Corp.; director: Henley Group Inc.; advisory board: ICI Inc.; chairman: Gen Tek Inc.; chairman: General Chemical Group Inc. NONPR AFFIL member dean's advisory council: Columbia University Business School; managing director: Metropolitan Opera Association; member board overseers: Business School Columbia University; member board overseers: Business Roundtable. CLUB AFFIL Lyford Cay Club; University Club; Bald Peak Colony Club; Brook Club.
Allison G. Pellegrino: secretary
Spencer Stokes: president

Grants Analysis

Disclosure Period: fiscal year ending May 31, 2002
Total Grants: $909,730*
Number of Grants: 200
Average Grant: $4,549
Highest Grant: $50,000
Lowest Grant: $90
Typical Range: $1,000 to $10,000
*Note: Giving excludes United Way and metropolitan.

Recent Grants

Note: Grants derived from 2002 Form 990.

General

50,000	American Jewish Committee, New York, NY -- for fund raiser
50,000	Phillips Exeter Academy, Exeter, NH
50,000	Shackleton Schools, Boston, MA -- for fund raiser
25,000	Boston Medical Center, Boston, MA -- for fund raiser
25,000	Christopher Reeve Paralysis Foundation, New York, NY -- for fund raiser
25,000	Columbia Business School, New York, NY -- pledge payment
25,000	Queens College Foundation, New York, NY -- for fund raiser
25,000	World War II Memorial Fund, Washington, DC -- for pledge payment
24,000	Fidelity Investments Charitable Gift Fund, Boston, MA -- matching gift
24,000	Michael D. Dingman Foundation, Hampton, NH -- matching gift

CLARA B. WINTHROP TRUST

Giving Contact

Richard Olney, III, Trustee
c/o Welch & Forbes
45 School Street
Boston, MA 02108-3204
Phone: (617)523-1635
Fax: (617)742-6243
E-mail: ronly@welchforbes.com

Description

Founded: 1969
EIN: 046039972
Organization Type: Private Foundation
Giving Locations: MA
Grant Types: General Support.

Donor Information

Founder: the late Clara B. Winthrop

Financial Summary

Total Giving: $198,500 (2003); $275,000 (2001)
Assets: $3,344,407 (2003); $3,855,425 (2001)

Typical Recipients

Arts & Humanities: Arts Associations & Councils, Community Arts, Historic Preservation, History & Archaeology, Libraries, Museums/Galleries, Music, Public Broadcasting, Theater
Civic & Public Affairs: Civic & Public Affairs-General, Municipalities/Towns, Native American Affairs, Parades/Festivals, Public Policy, Urban & Community Affairs, Zoos/Aquariums
Education: Colleges & Universities, Education Associations, Private Education (Precollege), Secondary Education (Private)
Environment: Environment-General, Resource Conservation
Health: Hospitals, Nursing Services
International: International Organizations
Religion: Churches, Religious Welfare
Science: Science Museums
Social Services: Child Welfare, Community Service Organizations, Family Services, Youth Organizations

Application Procedures

Initial Contact: Applications may be submitted in any form.
Application Requirements: Include purpose of funds sought, the general financial situation of the organization, and proof of tax-exempt status.
Deadlines: None.

Restrictions

Does not support individuals. The Trust makes grants only to charitable organizations within Massachusetts or a state which exempts requests to Massachusetts organizations.

Foundation Officials

Arthur C. Hodges: trustee
Richard Olney, III: trustee
Oliver A. Spalding: trustee

Grants Analysis

Disclosure Period: calendar year ending 2003
Total Grants: $198,500
Number of Grants: 26
Average Grant: $7,635
Highest Grant: $25,000
Lowest Grant: $2,000
Typical Range: $5,000 to $10,000

Recent Grants

Note: Grants derived from 2001 Form 990.
Library-Related

15,000	Manchester by the Sea Conservation Trust, Manchester, MA
10,000	Boston Athenaeum, Boston, MA
7,500	New England Conservatory of Music, Boston, MA

General

22,500	Peabody Essex Museum, Salem, MA
22,000	New England Aquarium, Boston, MA
15,000	Manchester by the Sea Public Library, Manchester, MA
15,000	Trustees of Reservation, Beverly, MA
15,000	Visiting Nurse Association of the North Shore, Waltham, MA
10,000	Beverly Hospital, Beverly, MA
10,000	Friends of Manchester by the Sea, Manchester, MA
10,000	House of Seven Gables, Salem, MA
10,000	Manchester by the Sea Youth Center, Manchester, MA
10,000	Massachusetts Historical Society, Boston, MA

WIREMOLD CO.

Company Headquarters

West Hartford, CT
Web: http://www.wiremold.com

Company Description

Employees: 750 (2003)
SIC(s): 3643 Current-Carrying Wiring Devices, 3644 Noncurrent-Carrying Wiring Devices, 3646 Commercial Lighting Fixtures, 3648 Lighting Equipment Nec.

Operating Locations

Wiremold Co. (CT--West Hartford)

Wiremold Foundation

Giving Contact

Douglas Bielfeld, Treasurer
60 Woodlawn Street
West Hartford, CT 06110
Phone: (860)233-6251
Fax: (860)523-3699

Description

Founded: 1967
EIN: 066089445
Organization Type: Corporate Foundation
Giving Locations: headquarters area only.
Grant Types: Employee Matching Gifts, General Support.

Donor Information

Founder: The Wiremold Co.

Financial Summary

Total Giving: $279,720 (2002); $289,281 (2001)
Giving Analysis: Giving for 2002 includes: foundation matching gifts ($5,895); foundation grants to United Way ($80,000)
Assets: $431,357 (2002); $434,017 (2001)
Gifts Received: $273,500 (2002); $276,004 (2001); $275,104 (2000). Note: Contributions were received from The Wiremold Company.

Typical Recipients

Arts & Humanities: Arts Associations & Councils, Arts Funds, Ballet, Dance, Arts & Humanities-General, Historic Preservation, History & Archaeology, Libraries, Literary Arts, Museums/Galleries, Music, Performing Arts, Public Broadcasting
Civic & Public Affairs: African American Affairs, Botanical Gardens/Parks, Community Foundations, Employment/Job Training, Civic & Public Affairs-General, Housing, Law & Justice, Philanthropic Organizations, Public Policy, Urban & Community Affairs, Women's Affairs
Education: Afterschool/Enrichment Programs, Business Education, Colleges & Universities, Economic Education, Education Associations, Education Funds, Education-General, International Exchange, Literacy, Minority Education, Private Education (Precollege), Science/Mathematics Education, Secondary Education (Private), Special Education, Student Aid
Environment: Environment-General, Watershed
Health: AIDS/HIV, Cancer, Children's Health/Hospitals, Clinics/Medical Centers, Emergency/Ambulance Services, Health-General, Health Organizations, Hospitals, Prenatal Health Issues, Public Health
Religion: Churches, Religious Welfare
Science: Science Museums, Scientific Centers & Institutes
Social Services: Camps, Child Abuse, Child Welfare, Community Service Organizations, Domestic Violence, Emergency Relief, Family Services, Food/Clothing Distribution, Homes, People with Disabilities, Recreation & Athletics, Scouts, Senior Services, Shelters/Homelessness, Social Services-General, Special Olympics, United Funds/United Ways, YMCA/YWCA/YMHA/YWHA, Youth Organizations

Application Procedures

Initial Contact: Send a letter of inquiry. There is no formal application process.
Application Requirements: Include proof of tax-exempt status.
Deadlines: None.

Restrictions

Preference is given to written requests for capital and/or start-up campaigns over operating funds.

Corporate Officials

Arthur P. Byrne: chairman, president, chief executive officer, director PRIM CORP EMPL chairman, president, chief executive officer, director: Wiremold Co.
Orest J. Fiume: vice president finance, chief financial officer PRIM CORP EMPL vice president finance, chief financial officer: Wiremold Co.

Foundation Officials

Douglas Bielfeld: treasurer
Gary J. Brooks: vice president
John Davis Murphy: president
Michele Sitler: secretary

Grants Analysis

Disclosure Period: calendar year ending 2002
Total Grants: $193,825*
Number of Grants: 66

Average Grant: $2,314*
Highest Grant: $25,750
Lowest Grant: $500
Typical Range: $1,000 to $5,000
*Note: Giving excludes matching gifts and United Way. Average grant figure excludes two highest grants ($45,750).

Recent Grants

Note: Grants derived from 2003 Form 990.
General

80,000	United Way, Hartford, CT
20,000	Greater Hartford Arts Council, Hartford, CT
10,000	Hartford Hospital, Hartford, CT
10,000	Kamp for Kids, Brighton, MI
10,000	Saint Francis Hospital, Poughkeepsie, NY
10,000	Salvation Army, Baltimore, MD
6,000	Doc Hurley Scholarship Foundation, Hartford, CT
5,500	Greater Hartford American Red Cross, Hartford, CT
5,000	Junior Achievement of Hartford, Hartford, CT
5,000	Mark Twain House, Hartford, MI

WISCONSIN ENERGY CORP.

Company Headquarters

Milwaukee, WI
Web: http://www.wisenergy.com/

Company Description

Founded: 1981
Ticker: WEC
Exchange: NYSE
Former Name: Wicor Inc.
Revenue: US$3.912 billion (2004)
Profit: US$306.4 million (2004)
Employees: 8991 (2003)
Fortune Rank: 471, per FORTUNE Magazine's list of 500 Largest U.S. Corporations (2004).
SIC(s): 4911 Electric Services, 4923 Gas Transmission & Distribution, 6719 Holding Companies Nec.

Operating Locations

Wisconsin Energy Corp. (WI--Fox Valley, Milwaukee)
Note: Operates throughout southeastern Wisconsin and the Upper Penninsula of Michigan.

Nonmonetary Support

Type: Donated Equipment; In-kind Services; Loaned Executives
Volunteer Programs: Company actively promotes volunteerism through the Employee Volunteer Program, including mentoring programs, a speakers bureau, and other volunteer activities.

Wisconsin Energy Corp. Foundation, Inc.

Giving Contact

Carolyn Simpson, Foundation Coordinator
231 West Michigan Street
Milwaukee, WI 53203
Phone: (414)221-2106
Fax: (414)221-2412
Web: http://foundation.wisconsinenergy.com

Description

EIN: 391433726
Organization Type: Corporate Foundation
Giving Locations: headquarters and operating com-

munities.

Grant Types: Capital, Challenge, Employee Matching Gifts, General Support, Multiyear/Continuing Support.

Note: Employee matching gift ratio: 1 to 1.

Financial Summary

Total Giving: $4,807,332 (2002); $4,998,765 (2001). Note: Contributes through foundation only.

Assets: $24,983,974 (2002); $33,504,675 (2001)

Gifts Received: $20,062,500 (2001); $3,000,000 (2000); $1,250,000 (1999). Note: In 1998, contributions were received from Wisconsin Electric Power Co. ($16,000,000), Wisconsin Gas ($4,000,000), and WISPARK ($62,500).

Typical Recipients

Arts & Humanities: Arts Associations & Councils, Arts Centers, Arts Funds, Community Arts, Historic Preservation, Museums/Galleries, Music, Opera, Performing Arts, Public Broadcasting, Theater

Civic & Public Affairs: African American Affairs, Botanical Gardens/Parks, Business/Free Enterprise, Civil Rights, Community Foundations, Economic Development, Employment/Job Training, Civic & Public Affairs-General, Hispanic Affairs, Housing, Minority Business, Safety, Urban & Community Affairs, Zoos/Aquariums

Education: Arts/Humanities Education, Business Education, Colleges & Universities, Economic Education, Education Associations, Education Funds, Education Reform, Engineering/Technological Education, Education-General, Leadership Training, Medical Education, Minority Education, Private Education (Precollege), Public Education (Precollege), Science/Mathematics Education, Secondary Education (Private), Secondary Education (Public), Social Sciences Education, Student Aid, Vocational & Technical Education

Environment: Forestry, Environment-General, Protection, Resource Conservation

Health: Children's Health/Hospitals, Clinics/Medical Centers, Health Funds, Health Organizations, Hospitals, Medical Rehabilitation, Medical Research, Mental Health, Public Health, Respiratory, Single-Disease Health Associations, Trauma Treatment

Religion: Churches, Religious Organizations, Religious Welfare

Science: Science Museums, Scientific Organizations

Social Services: Child Welfare, Community Centers, Community Service Organizations, Counseling, Family Services, Food/Clothing Distribution, Homes, People with Disabilities, Recreation & Athletics, Scouts, Senior Services, Shelters/Homelessness, United Funds/United Ways, YMCA/YWCA/YMHA/YWHA, Youth Organizations

Application Procedures

Initial Contact: Send a brief letter or proposal.

Application Requirements: Include a description of organization, including the purpose and activities of the requestor, and how the funds are to be used.

Deadlines: None.

Evaluative Criteria: Supports organizations that aid large numbers of Wisconsin residents.

Decision Notification: Most large grants are awarded in June and December.

Restrictions

Preference is given to qualified recipients within the Wisconsin Electric Service Territory, however grants may be made to other states.

Additional Information

The company's subsidiaries, Wisconsin Natural Gas Co. and Wisconsin Electric Power Co., also contribute to the foundation.

Corporate Officials

Richard A. Abdoo: chairman, chief executive officer, president B Port Huron, MI 1944. ED University of Dayton BSEE (1965); University of Detroit MA

(1969). PRIM CORP EMPL chairman, president, chief executive officer: Wisconsin Energy Corp. ADD CORP EMPL chairman, chief executive officer: Wisconsin Electric Power Co.; chief executive officer, director: Badger Service Co.; chairman, president, chief executive officer: CEW Acqusition Inc.; chairman, chief executive officer: Edison Sault Electric Co.; chairman, chief executive officer: Minergy Corp.; chairman, chief executive officer: Northern Tree Service Inc.; chairman, chief executive officer: WEC International Inc.; president, chief executive officer, director: WEC Energy Capital Corp.; chairman, president, chief executive officer: WEC Nuclear Corp.; chairman, chief executive officer: WMF Corp.; chairman, chief executive officer: Wispark Corp.; chairman, chief executive officer: Wisvest Corp.; chairman, chief executive officer: Witech Corp. CORP AFFIL director: Universal Foods Corp.; director: United Wisconsin Services; director: Blue Cross & Blue Shield United Wisconsin; director: Marshall & Ilsley Corp.; director: ARI Network Services. NONPR AFFIL member: American Economic Association.

Foundation Officials

Richard A. Abdoo: president (see above)

Grants Analysis

Disclosure Period: calendar year ending 2002

Total Grants: $3,793,657*

Number of Grants: 1197

Average Grant: $3,169

Highest Grant: $553,550

Lowest Grant: $25

Typical Range: $1,000 to $5,000

*Note: Giving excludes United Way and scholarships.

Recent Grants

Note: Grants derived from 2003 Form 990.

General

500,000	Bradley Technology and Trade School Foundation Inc., Milwaukee, WI
463,200	Scholarship America, Minneapolis, MN -- towards WEC Daughters and Sons scholarship
225,000	United Way of Greater Milwaukee, Milwaukee, WI
200,000	United Way of Greater Milwaukee, Milwaukee, WI
200,000	United Way of Greater Milwaukee Inc., Milwaukee, WI
200,000	United Way of Greater Milwaukee Inc., Milwaukee, WI
60,000	Milwaukee School of Engineering, Milwaukee, WI -- towards scholarship
50,000	Bradley Technology and Trade School Foundation Inc., Milwaukee, WI
50,000	Holy Hill, National Shrine of Mary, Help of Christians, Hubertus, WI
50,000	Marquette University, Milwaukee, WI -- towards scholarship fund

WATSON W. WISE FOUNDATION

Giving Contact

110 N. College, Suite 1002
Tyler, TX 75702
Phone: (903)531-9615

Description

Founded: 1990
EIN: 756064539
Organization Type: Private Foundation
Giving Locations: TX: Tyler
Grant Types: General Support.

Donor Information

Founder: Established in 1990 with funds from the estate of Watson W. Wise.

Financial Summary

Total Giving: $477,000 (2003)

Assets: $11,061,349 (2003)

Gifts Received: $49,160 (1998); $60,932 (1996); $1,199,099 (1994). Note: In 1996 and 1998, contributions were received from the estate of Watson W. Wise.

Typical Recipients

Arts & Humanities: Libraries, Museums/Galleries, Theater

Civic & Public Affairs: Clubs, Community Foundations, Urban & Community Affairs, Women's Affairs

Education: Agricultural Education, Colleges & Universities, Community & Junior Colleges, Education Funds, Engineering/Technological Education, Education-General, Literacy, Minority Education, Private Education (Precollege), Public Education (Precollege), Science/Mathematics Education

Health: Alzheimer's Disease, Cancer, Clinics/Medical Centers, Health-General, Health Organizations, Hospices, Hospitals, Hospitals (University Affiliated), Public Health, Respiratory, Single-Disease Health Associations, Transplant Networks/Donor Banks

International: Health Care/Hospitals

Religion: Churches, Dioceses, Religious Welfare

Science: Science Museums, Scientific Centers & Institutes

Social Services: Child Welfare, Community Service Organizations, Day Care, Family Services, Food/Clothing Distribution, People with Disabilities, Scouts, Youth Organizations

Application Procedures

Initial Contact: The foundation has no formal grant application procedure or application form.

Deadlines: None.

Foundation Officials

Calvin N. Clyde, Jr.: vice president
Will A. Knight: president
Emma F. Wise: trustee

Grants Analysis

Disclosure Period: calendar year ending 2003

Total Grants: $477,000

Number of Grants: 118

Average Grant: $4,042

Highest Grant: $30,000

Lowest Grant: $1,000

Typical Range: $1,000 to $10,000

Recent Grants

Note: Grants derived from 2003 Form 990.

General

30,000	Tyler Museum of Art, Tyler, TX
25,000	Discovery Science Place, Tyler, TX -- for educational purposes
16,000	Texas Chest Foundation, Tyler, TX -- for medical purposes
15,000	Baylor University Student Foundation, Dallas, TX -- for educational purposes
15,000	Cystic Fibrosis Foundation, Tyler, TX -- for medical purposes
12,000	Grace Community School, Tyler, TX -- for educational purposes
11,500	All Saints Episcopal School, Tyler, TX -- for educational purposes
10,000	University of Arkansas, Fayetteville, AR -- for educational purposes
10,000	University of Texas, Tyler, TX -- for educational purposes
10,000	University of Texas, Tyler, TX -- for educational purposes

LIN AND ELLA WONG FOUNDATION

Giving Contact
Reuben S.F. Wong, President, Treasurer & Director
220 S. King Street, Suite 2288
Honolulu, HI 96813
Phone: (808)531-3526

Description
Founded: 1991
EIN: 990284508
Organization Type: Private Foundation
Grant Types: General Support.

Financial Summary
Total Giving: $131,650 (2003); $114,050 (2001)
Assets: $2,208,954 (2003); $1,468,874 (2001)
Gifts Received: $341,980 (2003); $45,000 (2001); $214,351 (2000). Note: In 2003, contributions were received from Dr. and Mrs. Stanley Wong ($3,000), Mr. and Mrs. Albert S.P. Wong ($206,000), Mr. and Mrs. Reuben S.F. Wong ($132,980). In 2001, contributions were received from Mr. and Mrs. Henry Chang ($500) and Reuben Wong and Vera Wong ($44,500). In 2000, contributions were received from Dr. and Mrs. Stanley Wong ($144,375), Reuben and Vera Wong ($40,442), Kenneth Huey ($100), Dr. and Mrs. William Wong ($100), and Dr. Alton S. Wong ($29,334). In 1999, contributions were received from Dr. and Mrs. Stanley Wong ($25,000), Reuben and Vera Wong ($86,188), Norwin H.G. Wong ($10,000), and Dr. Alton S. Wong ($28,576). In 1998, contributions were received from Palace Realty, Inc. ($5,500), Mr. and Mrs. Henry Chang ($1,000), Dr. and Mrs. Stanley Wong ($25,000), Dr. Alton S. Wong ($26,032) and Rueben and Vera Wong ($77,638). In 1995, contributions were received from Mr. and Mrs. Henry Chang ($2,000), Dr. and Mrs. Stanley Wong ($37,428), and Reuben and Vera Wong ($101,775).

Typical Recipients
Arts & Humanities: History & Archaeology, Libraries
Civic & Public Affairs: Asian American Affairs, Community Foundations, Civic & Public Affairs-General
Education: Colleges & Universities, Education-General, Legal Education, Minority Education, Private Education (Precollege), Secondary Education (Public), Student Aid
Health: Medical Rehabilitation, Medical Research
Religion: Bible Study/Translation, Churches, Religion-General, Religious Welfare, Synagogues/Temples
Social Services: People with Disabilities, Scouts, Social Services-General, Special Olympics, YMCA/YWCA/YMHA/YWHA, Youth Organizations

Application Procedures
Initial Contact: Send a brief letter of inquiry.
Application Requirements: a description of organization and purpose of funds sought.
Deadlines: None.

Foundation Officials
Alton S. Wong: director
Reuben S. F. Wong: president, treasurer, director
Stanley S. Wong: director
Vera H. Wong: vice president, secretary, director

Grants Analysis
Disclosure Period: calendar year ending 2003
Total Grants: $131,650
Number of Grants: 27
Average Grant: $1,172*
Highest Grant: $100,000
Lowest Grant: $100
Typical Range: $500 to $5,000
*Note: Average grant figure excludes highest grant.

Recent Grants
Note: Grants derived from 2003 Form 990.
General

100,000	Iolani School, Honolulu, HI -- for capital building campaign
6,000	Chinatown Merchants Association, Honolulu, HI -- for college scholarships
5,000	St. Louis School, Honolulu, HI -- towards scholarship fund
2,000	Sacred Hearts Academy, Honolulu, HI -- for scholarship fund
2,000	St. Andrew's Priory School, Honolulu, HI -- for scholarship fund
1,400	Organization of Chinese Americans, Honolulu, HI -- for scholarship program
1,300	Helemano Opportunities for the Retarded Inc., Wahiawa, HI -- to assist persons with special challenges
1,000	Daihonzan Chozen, Honolulu, HI
1,000	Hawaii Community Foundation, Honolulu, HI
1,000	Young Men's Christian Association of Honolulu, Honolulu, HI -- to help youth

WOOD FOUNDATION OF CHAMBERSBURG, PA

Giving Contact
Charles O. Wood, III, Trustee
One Brattle Square, 4th Fl.
Cambridge, MA 02138
Phone: (617)864-1420

Description
Founded: 1989
EIN: 251607838
Organization Type: Private Foundation
Giving Locations: CA; DE; MD; MA; PA: Chambersburg County, Franklin County
Grant Types: Capital, Emergency, Endowment, General Support, Multiyear/Continuing Support, Operating Expenses.

Donor Information
Founder: Established in 1989 by Max Zimmer.

Financial Summary
Total Giving: $677,872 (2003); $485,170 (2001)
Giving Analysis: Giving for 2001 includes: foundation grants to United Way ($15,000).
Assets: $9,309,873 (2003); $10,354,620 (2001)

Typical Recipients
Arts & Humanities: Arts Associations & Councils, Arts Festivals, Arts & Humanities-General, History & Archaeology, Libraries, Literary Arts, Museums/Galleries, Music, Theater
Civic & Public Affairs: Chambers of Commerce, Community Foundations, Economic Development, Employment/Job Training, Civic & Public Affairs-General, Housing, Legal Aid, Municipalities/Towns, Safety, Urban & Community Affairs, Women's Affairs
Education: Colleges & Universities, Continuing Education, Education Funds, Elementary Education (Public), Education-General, Private Education (Precollege), Public Education (Precollege), School Volunteerism, Secondary Education (Public)
Environment: Environment-General
Health: Cancer, Children's Health/Hospitals, Clinics/Medical Centers, Geriatric Health, Heart, Hospices/Hospitals, Long-Term Care, Mental Health, Public Health, Single-Disease Health Associations
Religion: Churches, Religious Welfare
Social Services: Animal Protection, Camps, Community Service Organizations, Counseling, Family Services, Food/Clothing Distribution, Scouts, Senior Services, Shelters/Homelessness, Social Services-General, United Funds/United Ways, YMCA/YWCA/YMHA/YWHA, Youth Organizations

Application Procedures
Initial Contact: Send a brief letter of inquiry and a full proposal.
Deadlines: None.

Restrictions
First consideration will be given to organizations serving the Chambersburg-Franklin Counties, Pennsylvania area.

Foundation Officials
Emilie W. Robinson: trustee
Charles O. Wood, III: trustee
David S. Wood: trustee
Miriam M. Wood: trustee

Grants Analysis
Disclosure Period: calendar year ending 2003
Total Grants: $677,872
Number of Grants: 42
Average Grant: $13,281*
Highest Grant: $133,333
Lowest Grant: $500
Typical Range: $5,000 to $25,000
*Note: Average grant figure excludes highest grant.

Recent Grants
Note: Grants derived from 2001 Form 990.
General

50,000	Boston Celebrity Series, Boston, MA -- annual giving
50,000	Isabella Stewart Gardner Museum, Boston, MA -- pledge
27,201	Financial Counseling Services, Chambersburg, PA -- pledge
25,000	Aurora Theatre Company, Berkeley, CA -- for capital campaign
25,000	Community Foundation of the Eastern Shore, Salisbury, MD -- for Kresge challenge grant
20,000	Community Foundation of the Eastern Shore, Salisbury, MD
18,977	Caledonia Theatre Group, Chambersburg, PA -- pledge
15,000	BOPIC, Chambersburg, PA -- for operations
15,000	Boston Celebrity Series, Boston, MA -- 2001 annual giving
15,000	Chambersburg Area United Way, Chambersburg, PA

W. A. WOODARD FOUNDATION

Giving Contact
Tod Casey Woodard, Vice President
115 W. 8th Ave., Suite 200
PO Box 10666
Eugene, OR 97440
Phone: (541)343-9402

Description
Founded: 1952
EIN: 936026550
Organization Type: Private Foundation
Giving Locations: OR
Grant Types: General Support.

Financial Summary
Total Giving: $217,640 (fiscal year ending June 30, 2004); $298,280 (fiscal 2001)
Assets: $6,490,260 (fiscal 2004); $6,137,156 (fiscal 2001)
Gifts Received: $10,000 (fiscal 1994)

Typical Recipients

Arts & Humanities: Arts Associations & Councils, Arts Funds, Ballet, Ethnic & Folk Arts, Film & Video, Arts & Humanities-General, History & Archaeology, Libraries, Museums/Galleries, Music, Opera, Performing Arts, Public Broadcasting, Theater
Civic & Public Affairs: Clubs, Community Foundations, Economic Development, Civic & Public Affairs-General, Housing, Legal Aid, Municipalities/Towns, Public Policy, Rural Affairs, Urban & Community Affairs, Women's Affairs
Education: Business Education, Colleges & Universities, Community & Junior Colleges, Continuing Education, Education Funds, Education-General, Health & Physical Education, Minority Education, Private Education (Precollege), Public Education (Precollege), Secondary Education (Private), Secondary Education (Public), Special Education, Student Aid
Environment: Forestry, Environment-General
Health: Cancer, Children's Health/Hospitals, Diabetes, Emergency/Ambulance Services, Health Organizations, Heart, Hospitals, Multiple Sclerosis, Prenatal Health Issues, Preventive Medicine/Wellness Organizations, Research/Studies Institutes, Single-Disease Health Associations
International: International Environmental Issues, International Relief Efforts
Religion: Churches, Religious Organizations, Religious Welfare
Science: Observatories & Planetariums, Science Museums, Scientific Centers & Institutes
Social Services: Animal Protection, At-Risk Youth, Big Brothers/Big Sisters, Child Welfare, Community Centers, Community Service Organizations, Counseling, Day Care, Family Services, Food/Clothing Distribution, People with Disabilities, Recreation & Athletics, Scouts, Senior Services, Special Olympics, United Funds/United Ways, Youth Organizations

Application Procedures

Initial Contact: Request application form.

Foundation Officials

Dena Woodard McCoy: director
Andrew Woodard: director
Carlton Woodard: president
Joy Woodard: director
Kim C. Woodard: director
Kristen A. Woodard: director
Tod Casey Woodard: vice president

Grants Analysis

Disclosure Period: fiscal year ending June 30, 2004
Total Grants: $217,640
Number of Grants: 81
Average Grant: $1,799*
Highest Grant: $42,000
Lowest Grant: $25
Typical Range: $500 to $3,000
***Note:** Average grant figure excludes two highest grants ($75,500).

Recent Grants

Note: Grants derived from fiscal 2001 Form 990.
General

45,000	University of Oregon Foundation, Eugene, OR
25,000	Lane Community College, Eugene, OR
20,000	McKenzie Willamette Hospital Foundation, Springfield, OR
12,500	Cottage Grove Recreation Association, Cottage Grove, OR
10,000	Aprovecho Research Center, Cottage Grove, OR
10,000	Eugene-Springfield Metro Partnership, Eugene, OR
10,000	Pacific Legal Foundation, Sacramento, CA
6,000	Melting Pot Theatre Company, New York, NY

5,500	Boy Scouts of America Oregon Trail Council, Tigard, OR
5,000	Encore Theater, Denver, CO

WOODCOCK FOUNDATION

Giving Contact

Penny Willgeroot
30 Rockefeller Plz., Rm. 5600
New York, NY 10112
Phone: (212)649-5712

Description

Founded: 1988
EIN: 341606085
Organization Type: Private Foundation
Giving Locations: NY
Grant Types: General Support, Project, Research.

Donor Information

Founder: Polly Guth

Financial Summary

Total Giving: $1,955,543 (fiscal year ending November 30, 2001)
Assets: $42,134,997 (fiscal 2001)
Gifts Received: $10,907 (fiscal 1995); $155,500 (fiscal 1993). Note: In fiscal 1993, contributions were received from John H. J. Guth ($84,000) and Polly W. Guth ($71,500).

Typical Recipients

Arts & Humanities: Arts Centers, History & Archaeology, Museums/Galleries, Music, Opera, Performing Arts
Civic & Public Affairs: Asian American Affairs, Botanical Gardens/Parks, Economic Development, Ethnic Organizations, Civic & Public Affairs-General, Municipalities/Towns, Philanthropic Organizations, Public Policy, Urban & Community Affairs, Women's Affairs
Education: Business-School Partnerships, Colleges & Universities, Community & Junior Colleges, Education Funds, Education Reform, Private Education (Precollege), School Volunteerism
Environment: Environment-General, Resource Conservation, Wildlife Protection
Health: Health Organizations
International: International-General, Health Care/Hospitals, International Environmental Issues, International Relations
Social Services: Child Welfare, Community Service Organizations, Day Care, Family Planning, Scouts, Social Services-General, Youth Organizations

Application Procedures

Initial Contact: Send a brief letter of inquiry.
Deadlines: None.

Foundation Officials

John H. J. Guth: trustee
Polly Guth: trustee
Virginia Montgomery: trustee

Grants Analysis

Disclosure Period: fiscal year ending November 30, 2001
Total Grants: $1,955,543
Number of Grants: 31
Average Grant: $54,074*
Highest Grant: $333,333
Lowest Grant: $1,000
Typical Range: $25,000 to $100,000
***Note:** Average grant figure excludes highest grant.

Recent Grants

Note: Grants derived from fiscal 2001 Form 990.

General

333,333	City Year, Boston, MA
181,000	Ashoka, Arlington, VA
110,000	Yellowstone to Yukon Conservation Initiative, Canmore, AB Canada
100,000	171 Cedar Arts Center, Corning, NY
100,000	Paraprofessional Healthcare Institute Inc., Bronx, NY
100,000	Prospect Park Alliance, Brooklyn, NY
100,000	Teach For America, New York, NY
85,000	Public Allies, New York, NY
75,000	International Women's Health Coalition, New York, NY
75,000	Public Allies, New York, NY

ROBERT W. WOODRUFF FOUNDATION

Giving Contact

Charles H. McTier, President
50 Hurt Plz., Suite 1200
Atlanta, GA 30303
Phone: (404)522-6755
Fax: (404)522-7026
E-mail: fdns@woodruff.org
Web: http://www.woodruff.org

Description

Founded: 1937
EIN: 581695425
Organization Type: General Purpose Foundation
Giving Locations: GA: Atlanta some statewide giving
Grant Types: Capital, Challenge, General Support, Matching, Multiyear/Continuing Support, Project, Seed Money.
Note: Foundation also gives grants toward land acquisition and equipment costs.

Donor Information

Founder: Established in 1937 by the late Robert W. Woodruff. Robert Woodruff assumed leadership of The Coca-Cola Company in 1923 and guided it until his death in 1985. In 1937 he incorporated the Trebor Foundation, which was renamed the Robert W. Woodruff Foundation following his death. The Foundation received funds from the estate of Mr. Woodruff's wife, Nell Hodgson Woodruff, who died in 1968, and from Mr. Woodruff's estate. The Woodruffs had no children.

Financial Summary

Total Giving: $104,139,757 (2004); $122,831,490 (2002); $113,995,585 (2001)
Assets: $2,050,719,640 (2004); $2,210,193,890 (2002)
Gifts Received: In 1990, contributions were received from the estate of Robert W. Woodruff.

Typical Recipients

Arts & Humanities: Arts Associations & Councils, Arts Centers, Community Arts, Historic Preservation, History & Archaeology, Libraries, Museums/Galleries, Music, Opera, Performing Arts, Public Broadcasting, Theater
Civic & Public Affairs: African American Affairs, Botanical Gardens/Parks, Business/Free Enterprise, Chambers of Commerce, Civil Rights, Community Foundations, Economic Development, Civic & Public Affairs-General, Hispanic Affairs, Housing, Inner-City Development, Law & Justice, Legal Aid, Municipalities/Towns, Nonprofit Management, Public Policy, Safety, Urban & Community Affairs, Zoos/Aquariums
Education: Agricultural Education, Business Education, Colleges & Universities, Education Associations, Education Funds, Education Reform, Elementary Education (Private), Engineering/Technological Educa-

tion, Education-General, Health & Physical Education, International Studies, Leadership Training, Medical Education, Minority Education, Private Education (Precollege), Science/Mathematics Education, Social Sciences Education, Special Education, Student Aid

Environment: Air/Water Quality, Environment-General, Resource Conservation, Wildlife Protection
Health: Alzheimer's Disease, Cancer, Children's Health/Hospitals, Emergency/Ambulance Services, Health-General, Geriatric Health, Health Policy/Cost Containment, Health Funds, Health Organizations, Hospices, Hospitals, Long-Term Care, Medical Rehabilitation, Medical Research, Mental Health, Nursing Services, Preventive Medicine/Wellness Organizations, Public Health, Trauma Treatment
International: Foreign Arts Organizations, Health Care/Hospitals
Religion: Jewish Causes, Religious Organizations, Religious Welfare
Science: Science Museums, Scientific Centers & Institutes, Scientific Labs, Scientific Research
Social Services: Child Welfare, Community Service Organizations, Counseling, Emergency Relief, Family Services, People with Disabilities, Recreation & Athletics, Senior Services, Social Services-General, United Funds/United Ways, YMCA/YWCA/YMHA/YWHA, Youth Organizations

Application Procedures

Initial Contact: Organizations seeking support should submit a letter of inquiry before submitting a proposal.
Application Requirements: Description of the organization, its purposes, staffing, and governing board; the organization's latest financial statements, including the most recent audited report; a description of the proposed project and full justification for its funding; an itemized project budget, including other sources of support in hand or anticipated; and evidence from the IRS of the organization's tax-exempt status and that the organization is not a private foundation.
Deadlines: For consideration at board meetings held in April and November, deadlines are February 1 and September 1, respectively.
Review Process: If the foundation is interested in the program, additional information or a site visit may be requested. Applicants will receive final notification within thirty days of the trustees' meeting.

Restrictions

The foundation does not make grants for general operating expenses or to individuals. The foundation also does not support propaganda or the influencing of legislature. Grants are generally limited to public charities located and operating in Georgia.

Additional Information

The foundation shares a common administrative arrangement with the Lettie Pate Evans Foundation, the Lettie Pate Whitehead Foundation, and the Joseph B. Whitehead Foundation. Applicants do not need to duplicate requests for information or grant funding from these other foundations.
Publications: Guidelines; Brochure; Data Sheet

Foundation Officials

Charles B. Ginden: trustee NONPR AFFIL trustee secretary: Emory University.
P. Russell Hardin: vice president, secretary PRIM NONPR EMPL vice president-secretary: Ichauway Inc. NONPR AFFIL vice president-secretary: Joseph W Jones Ecological Research Center.
Joseph W. Jones: chairman emeritus B Georgetown, DE 1912. ED Beacom College BA (1932).
Wilton D. Looney: trustee B 1919. PRIM CORP EMPL honorary chairman, director: Genuine Parts Co. NONPR AFFIL member: Automotive Hall of Fame; trustee: Joseph W Jones Ecological Research Center.
Charles Harvey McTier: president B Columbus, GA

1939. ED Emory University BBA (1961). PRIM CORP EMPL president: Ichauway Inc. NONPR AFFIL member: Management Executives Society; trustee: North Georgia United Methodist Foundation; president: Joseph W Jones Ecological Research Center; chairman board trustee: Foundation Center; pub member: Joint Commission Accreditation Health Care Organizations; member: Association Emory Alumni; vice chairman, chairman management committee: Council Foundations. CLUB AFFIL Piedmont Driving Club; director: Commerce Club; Druid Hills Golf Club.
James Malcolm Sibley: vice chairman, trustee B Atlanta, GA 1919. ED Princeton University AB (1941); Woodrow Wilson School of Law (1942); Harvard University Law School (1945-1946). CORP AFFIL director: Ichauway Inc. NONPR AFFIL trustee: AG Rhodes Home; trustee emeritus: TUFF; member: Georgia Bar Association; member: American Law Institute; member: Atlanta Bar Association; member: American College Probate Counsel; member: American Bar Association; member: American Bar Foundation. CLUB AFFIL Commerce Club; Piedmont Driving Club.
J. Lee Tribble: treasurer PRIM CORP EMPL treasurer: Ichauway Inc. NONPR AFFIL treasurer: Joseph W Jones Ecological Research Center.
James B. Williams: chairman, trustee

Grants Analysis

Disclosure Period: calendar year ending 2004
Total Grants: $104,139,757
Number of Grants: 107
Average Grant: $890,622*
Highest Grant: $10,000,004
Lowest Grant: $10,000
Typical Range: $50,000 to $1,000,000
*Note: Average grant figure excludes highest grant.

Recent Grants

Note: Grants derived from 2003 Form 990.
General

15,073,200	Children's Healthcare of Atlanta, Atlanta, GA -- for children's healthcare campaign
11,999,974	Emory University, Atlanta, GA -- towards construction of building to house the Pediatrics and children's center departments
5,000,027	Boys & Girls Clubs of America, Atlanta, GA -- for expansion and improvement programs
5,000,027	Emory University, Atlanta, GA -- towards construction of building to house the Pediatrics and children's center departments
4,000,000	Emory University, Atlanta, GA -- towards teaching and research mission at the school of medicine
4,000,000	Emory University, Atlanta, GA -- for renovation of the Henry Woodruff extension building for cancer research
3,000,041	Carter Center Inc., Atlanta, GA
3,000,041	Woodward Academy, College Park, GA -- for campus redevelopment plan
3,000,000	Emory University, Atlanta, GA -- towards construction of building to house the Pediatrics and children's center departments
2,500,000	Clark Atlanta University, Atlanta, GA -- for construction of classroom building

WOODS CHARITABLE FUND

Giving Contact

Pam Baker, Executive Director & Secretary
PO Box 81309
Lincoln, NE 68501

Phone: (402)436-5971
Fax: (402)436-4128
E-mail: pbaker@woodscharitable.org
Web: http://www.woodscharitable.org

Alternate Contact

E-mail: twoods@woodscharitable.org

Description

Founded: 1941
EIN: 476032847
Organization Type: Family Foundation
Giving Locations: NE: Lincoln
Grant Types: Award, General Support, Matching, Multiyear/Continuing Support, Operating Expenses, Project, Seed Money.

Donor Information

Founder: Established in 1941 in Nebraska by the late Frank H. Woods, his wife, the late Nelle Cochrane Woods, and their three sons. The fund received substantial support in 1952 from Frank H. Woods before his death later that year. In 1955, the fund received one-third of the net residuary estate of Nelle C. Woods. Over the years, the family-owned Sahara Coal Company has contributed to the fund's assets. Although the five founders are now deceased, other family members continue to serve as officers and trustees of the fund.
At the end of 1993, the fund underwent a major restructuring, resulting in two separate foundations: Woods Charitable Fund, giving in Lincoln, NE, and the Wood's Fund of Chicago.

Financial Summary

Total Giving: $1,600,000 (2001 approx)
Assets: $37,000,000 (2001 approx)

Typical Recipients

Arts & Humanities: Arts Associations & Councils, Arts Centers, Arts Funds, Arts Outreach, Community Arts, Dance, Arts & Humanities-General, Historic Preservation, Libraries, Literary Arts, Museums/Galleries, Music, Opera, Performing Arts, Public Broadcasting, Theater, Visual Arts
Civic & Public Affairs: African American Affairs, Asian American Affairs, Civil Rights, Community Foundations, Economic Development, Economic Policy, Employment/Job Training, Ethnic Organizations, Civic & Public Affairs-General, Hispanic Affairs, Housing, Law & Justice, Legal Aid, Municipalities/Towns, Native American Affairs, Nonprofit Management, Parades/Festivals, Public Policy, Rural Affairs, Safety, Urban & Community Affairs, Women's Affairs, Zoos/Aquariums
Education: Arts/Humanities Education, Colleges & Universities, Education Associations, Education Funds, Education Reform, Faculty Development, Education-General, International Studies, Leadership Training, Literacy, Preschool Education, Private Education (Precollege), Public Education (Precollege), Social Sciences Education, Special Education
Health: AIDS/HIV, Alzheimer's Disease, Clinics/Medical Centers, Medical Rehabilitation, Mental Health, Public Health, Single-Disease Health Associations
International: International Relief Efforts
Religion: Churches, Ministries, Religious Welfare, Social/Policy Issues
Science: Science Museums
Social Services: Animal Protection, At-Risk Youth, Big Brothers/Big Sisters, Child Abuse, Child Welfare, Community Centers, Community Service Organizations, Counseling, Crime Prevention, Day Care, Delinquency & Criminal Rehabilitation, Domestic Violence, Family Planning, Family Services, Food/Clothing Distribution, Homes, People with Disabilities, Recreation & Athletics, Scouts, Senior Services, Shelters/Homelessness, Social Services-General, Substance Abuse, United Funds/United Ways, Veterans, Volunteer Services, YMCA/YWCA/YMHA/YWHA, Youth Organizations

Application Procedures

Initial Contact: Applicants should contact the fund for a copy of guidelines, procedures, and timetables. Applicants should then send a two-page summary request and budget, or contact the fund by telephone to determine whether the project falls within funding guidelines.

Application Requirements: If the fund requests a full proposal, an organization must provide a completed application form. The fund now accepts the Lincoln/Lancaster County Grantmakers' Association common grant application form. The fund also requires a copy of the IRS determination letter of tax-exempt status; listing of board members, with addresses and phone numbers; audited financial statement for the last fiscal year; income and expense budgets for the current fiscal year and for the year for which support is sought; organization and project budgets; listing of actual commitments toward projected budget; itemization of other sources of support; and a Form 990 if annual budget exceeds $500,000.

Deadlines: Organizations must submit applications between March 1 and March 15 for the June meeting, between June 1 and June 15 for the September meeting, and between September 1 and September 15 for the December board meeting.

Review Process: Proposals arriving well before a given deadline are given more careful review. An application not clearly within the fund's priorities, but not clearly ineligible, will be reviewed by board members.

Restrictions

The fund supports work in Lincoln, NE, but occasionally reviews proposals from outside of Lincoln, if the proposed activities have statewide impact and can also demonstrate direct impact on Lincoln.

The fund does not make grants for individual needs, endowments, scholarships, fellowships, medical or scientific research, programs for individual schools, residential care and medical clinics, environment programs, recreational programs, fund-raising benefits, program advertising, or religious programs.

Additionally, the Lincoln grant program does not fund capital projects in health-care institutions, or college or university proposals that do not directly involve faculty or students in applied projects that benefit the region.

Buildings and equipment acquisition, expansion, and renovation projects are low priorities for the fund. Applicants should be organizations described in Section 501(c)(3) of the IRS code and have written ruling from the IRS that they also qualify under 509(a)(1), (2), or (3) of the code (publicly supported organizations and their affiliates). The fund occasionally considers proposals from private 501(c)(3) operating foundations; in unusual cases, it may consider fiscal agent and expenditure responsibility grants.

Additional Information

Organizations receiving grants must present written reports informing the board of the use of funds in relation to the original proposal objectives, and the results. Some grantees are asked to participate in a post-grant evaluation to compare program accomplishments with proposed objectives.

The fund offers proposal writing assistance.

Publications: Annual Report; Fund Guidelines; Application Form

Foundation Officials

Pam Baker: executive director, secretary
Joel Gajardo: vice president, director
Marilyn Johnson-Farr: director
Thomas D. Potter: director
Michael John Tavlin: assistant treasurer B Lincoln, NE 1946. ED Oklahoma City University BA (1970); University of Nebraska JD (1973); Washington University LLM (1977). PRIM CORP EMPL treasurer: Aliant Cellular Inc. ADD CORP EMPL treasurer: Aliant Communications Inc.; treasurer: Aliant System Inc.;

vice president, section, treasurer: Aliant Midwest Inc.; treasurer: Aliant Network System Inc. CORP AFFIL vice president, secretary, treasurer: Lincoln Tel & Tel Co.; vice president, secretary, treasurer: Prairie Communications Inc.

Avery L. Woods: director
Marjorie Woods: director
Thomas C. Woods, III: president, treasurer B 1945. ED Hiram Scott College (1968). PRIM CORP EMPL chairman: Aliant Communications Inc.

Grants Analysis

Disclosure Period: calendar year ending 2000
Total Grants: $1,543,205
Number of Grants: 83
Average Grant: $18,593
Highest Grant: $100,000
Lowest Grant: $475
Typical Range: $3,000 to $30,000

Recent Grants

Note: Grants derived from 2002 Form 990.
Library-Related

10,000	Lincoln City Libraries, Lincoln, NE

General

200,000	Neighborhoods, Inc, Lincoln, NE
100,000	Lincoln/Lancaster County Human Services Federation, Lincoln, NE
60,000	Cedars Youth Services, Inc, Lincoln, NE
50,000	Christian Heritage Children's Home, Hickman, NE
50,000	Lincoln Arts Council, Lincoln, NC
50,000	Lincoln Public Schools Foundation, Lincoln, NE
45,000	Hispanic Community Center, Lincoln, NE
40,000	Lincoln Lancaster County Family Resource Centers
40,000	Planned Parenthood of Lincoln Nebraska Inc
40,000	UNL-Department of Educational Psychology, Lincoln, NE

WOODWARD FUND

Giving Contact

Samuel A. Curtis, Jr., Administrator
c/o Fleet National Bank
1 East Ave.
Rochester, NY 14638
Phone: (716)435-7240

Description

Founded: 1965
EIN: 166064221
Organization Type: Private Foundation
Giving Locations: AZ; ME
Grant Types: General Support, Research.

Donor Information

Founder: Florence S. Woodward

Financial Summary

Total Giving: $140,000 (fiscal year ending November 30, 2004); $200,000 (fiscal 2001)
Assets: $3,359,934 (fiscal 2004); $3,709,339 (fiscal 2001)
Gifts Received: $1,828 (fiscal 1992)

Typical Recipients

Arts & Humanities: Art History, Arts Associations & Councils, Arts Centers, Arts Funds, History & Archaeology, Libraries, Museums/Galleries, Music, Opera
Civic & Public Affairs: Civic & Public Affairs-General, Housing, Law & Justice, Legal Aid, Municipalities/Towns, Nonprofit Management, Urban & Community Affairs, Women's Affairs, Zoos/Aquariums
Education: Colleges & Universities, Education

Funds, International Exchange, Minority Education, Preschool Education, Private Education (Precollege), Public Education (Precollege), School Volunteerism, Secondary Education (Public)
Environment: Environment-General, Protection, Resource Conservation, Wildlife Protection
Health: Emergency/Ambulance Services, Health Organizations, Hospices, Hospitals, Medical Rehabilitation, Medical Research, Multiple Sclerosis, Public Health, Single-Disease Health Associations
International: Human Rights, International Development, International Environmental Issues, International Relief Efforts
Religion: Churches, Religious Welfare
Science: Science Museums
Social Services: Animal Protection, At-Risk Youth, Child Welfare, Community Service Organizations, Day Care, Domestic Violence, Family Planning, People with Disabilities, Recreation & Athletics, Shelters/Homelessness, United Funds/United Ways, YMCA/YWCA/YMHA/YWHA, Youth Organizations

Application Procedures

Initial Contact: Foundation does not specify a particular application form.
Deadlines: None.

Restrictions

Does not support individuals.

Additional Information

Trust(s): Fleet Bank NA

Grants Analysis

Disclosure Period: fiscal year ending November 30, 2004
Total Grants: $140,000
Number of Grants: 30
Average Grant: $3,966*
Highest Grant: $25,000
Lowest Grant: $1,000
Typical Range: $1,000 to $5,000
*Note: Average grant figure excludes highest grant.

Recent Grants

Note: Grants derived from fiscal 2004 Form 990.
General

25,000	National Multiple Sclerosis Society, New York, NY
10,000	Phoenix Zoo, Phoenix, AZ
10,000	Scottsdale Cultural Council, Scottsdale, AZ
6,000	Society for the Prevention of Cruelty to Animals of Monterey County, Monterey, CA
5,000	Amnesty International, New York, NY
5,000	Mobuis Inc.
5,000	Oceana, Washington, DC
5,000	Southern Poverty Law Center, Montgomery, AL
5,000	Sponsor Kids
5,000	United Negro College Fund, Fairfax, VA

WORLD HERITAGE FOUNDATION

Giving Contact

Waltraud Prechter
2675 W. Jefferson
Trenton, MI 48183
Phone: (734)675-2200

Description

Founded: 1985
EIN: 382640416
Organization Type: Private Foundation
Giving Locations: MI
Grant Types: General Support.

Donor Information

Founder: Heinz C. Prechter, Heinz Co., Prechter Charitable Lead Trust

Financial Summary

Total Giving: $2,373,947 (2003)
Assets: $9,837,830 (2003)
Gifts Received: $26,878 (1995); $75,000 (1994); $100,000 (1993). Note: In fiscal 1995, contributions were received from the Heinz C. Prechter Charitable Lead Trust.

Typical Recipients

Arts & Humanities: Arts Associations & Councils, Arts Institutes, Community Arts, Arts & Humanities-General, History & Archaeology, Libraries, Museums/ Galleries, Music, Opera
Civic & Public Affairs: African American Affairs, Clubs, Economic Development, Civic & Public Affairs-General, Parades/Festivals, Public Policy, Urban & Community Affairs, Women's Affairs, Zoos/ Aquariums
Education: Arts/Humanities Education, Business Education, Colleges & Universities, Engineering/ Technological Education, International Studies, Literacy, Medical Education, Minority Education, Private Education (Precollege), Science/Mathematics Education, Student Aid
Health: AIDS/HIV, Alzheimer's Disease, Cancer, Children's Health/Hospitals, Emergency/Ambulance Services, Eyes/Blindness, Health Organizations, Hospitals, Long-Term Care, Public Health, Single-Disease Health Associations
International: International Affairs, International Development, International Relations, International Relief Efforts, Missionary/Religious Activities
Religion: Churches, Jewish Causes, Missionary Activities (Domestic), Religious Welfare
Science: Scientific Centers & Institutes
Social Services: Child Welfare, Community Service Organizations, Counseling, Food/Clothing Distribution, People with Disabilities, Recreation & Athletics, Scouts, United Funds/United Ways, Volunteer Services, YMCA/YWCA/YMHA/YWHA

Application Procedures

Initial Contact: Send a brief letter of inquiry.
Application Requirements: proof of tax-exempt status.
Deadlines: None.

Foundation Officials

Lori Koenig: vice president, secretary, treasurer, director
Waltraud Prechter: chairman, president, director

Grants Analysis

Disclosure Period: calendar year ending 2003
Total Grants: $2,373,947
Number of Grants: 22
Average Grant: $34,925*
Highest Grant: $1,640,514
Lowest Grant: $100
Typical Range: $10,000 to $50,000
*Note: Average grant figure excludes highest grant.

Recent Grants

Note: Grants derived from 2001 Form 990.
General

320,246	University of Michigan, Ann Arbor, MI
50,000	Detroit Symphony Orchestra, Detroit, MI
50,000	Kresge Eye Institute, Detroit, MI
50,000	University of Michigan, Ann Arbor, MI
50,000	University of Michigan Dearborn, Dearborn, MI
30,500	World of Neurology Education and Research Foundation, Winston-Salem, NC
25,000	Artrain U.S.A., Ann Arbor, MI
25,000	Michigan Opera Theater, Detroit, MI
20,000	Henry Ford Museum and Greenfield Village, Dearborn, MI
18,000	Detroit Renaissance Foundation, Detroit, MI

WORNER TRUST

Giving Contact

Jo Ann Harlan
Worner Trust
c/o National City Bank
301 SW Adams
Peoria, IL 61652
Phone: (309)655-5385

Description

Founded: 1996
EIN: 376337761
Organization Type: Private Foundation
Giving Locations: IL
Grant Types: General Support, Project.

Financial Summary

Total Giving: $111,305 (fiscal year ending March 31, 2004); $99,209 (fiscal 2001)
Assets: $2,348,089 (fiscal 2004); $2,405,602 (fiscal 2001)

Typical Recipients

Civic & Public Affairs: Urban & Community Affairs
Education: Arts/Humanities Education, Colleges & Universities, Elementary Education (Public), Public Education (Precollege), Student Aid
Health: Children's Health/Hospitals
Religion: Churches
Social Services: Child Welfare, Refugee Assistance, Youth Organizations

Application Procedures

Initial Contact: The foundation reports that it has no formal application procedure. Sent a brief letter of inquiry.
Deadlines: None.

Grants Analysis

Disclosure Period: fiscal year ending March 31, 2004
Total Grants: $111,305
Number of Grants: 38
Average Grant: $2,333*
Highest Grant: $25,000
Lowest Grant: $250
Typical Range: $500 to $5,000
*Note: Average grant figure excludes highest grant.

Recent Grants

Note: Grants derived from 2001 Form 990.
General

11,000	Peoria County Regional Office of Education, Peoria, IL -- for arts in education 2000
10,000	San Jose United Methodist Church, San Jose, IL -- for building addition
8,000	University of Illinois, Peoria, IL -- support for the Peoria Medical Care Craze
7,500	Midwest Central High School, Manito, IL
7,000	WD Boyce Council BSA, Peoria, IL -- for the Peoria Scoutreach Program
5,000	American Near East Refugee Aid, Washington, DC -- support for technology project
5,000	Bradley University, Peoria, IL
5,000	Children's Home Association, Peoria, IL -- for the Totally Integrated Electronic Records Project
5,000	Easter Seals, Peoria, IL -- for Communication Technology Camp
5,000	St. Charles Avenue Presbyterian Church, New Orleans, LA -- for Stair Program

WORONOCO SAVINGS BANK

Company Headquarters

31 Court St.
Westfield, MA 01085-0978
Web: http://www.woronoco.com

Company Description

Founded: 1871
Assets: US$642 billion (2001)
Employees: 142 (2001)
SIC(s): 6036 Savings Institutions Except Federal.
Parent Company: Woronoco Bancorp Inc., 31 Court St., Westfield, MA, United States

Nonmonetary Support

Volunteer Programs: The company encourages employee volunteerism. Woronoco Savings Bank employees contribute approximately 6,500 volunteer hours annually.

Woronoco Savings Charitable Foundation

Giving Contact

Debra L. Murphy, Senior Vice President & Chief Financial Officer
Woronoco Savings Bank
31 Court Street
Westfield, MA 01086-0978
Phone: (413)564-6241
Web:
http://www.woronoco.com/home/sponsors.php
Note: Ms. Murphy is also director and treasurer of the Woronoco Savings Charitable Foundation.

Description

Founded: 2000
EIN: 043458037
Organization Type: Corporate Foundation
Giving Locations: MA: western area
Grant Types: Capital, General Support, Operating Expenses.

Financial Summary

Total Giving: $318,203 (2002); $306,433 (2001)
Giving Analysis: Giving for 2001 includes: foundation matching gifts ($1,320); foundation scholarships ($10,500) foundation ($294,613)
Assets: $8,887,644 (2002); $7,705,347 (2001)
Gifts Received: $4,443,600 (1999). Note: In 1999, contributions were received from Woronoco Savings Bank.

Typical Recipients

Arts & Humanities: Arts Centers, Historic Preservation, History & Archaeology, Libraries, Museums/ Galleries, Music, Public Broadcasting, Theater
Civic & Public Affairs: Botanical Gardens/Parks, Clubs, Community Foundations, Civic & Public Affairs-General, Housing, Municipalities/Towns, Philanthropic Organizations, Safety, Women's Affairs
Education: Afterschool/Enrichment Programs, Business Education, Colleges & Universities, Education Funds, Private Education (Precollege), School Volunteerism, Secondary Education (Private), Secondary Education (Public), Special Education, Student Aid
Health: Cancer, Children's Health/Hospitals, Health Funds, Hospices, Hospitals, Mental Health
Religion: Ministries
Social Services: Child Welfare, Community Service Organizations, Counseling, Emergency Relief, Family Services, Food/Clothing Distribution, People with Disabilities, Recreation & Athletics, Scouts, Senior Services, Social Services-General, United Funds/ United Ways, Veterans, YMCA/YWCA/YMHA/ YWHA, Youth Organizations

Application Procedures

Initial Contact: Contact the company/foundation to request an application form.
Application Requirements: Send written request for application.

Restrictions

Awards are generally limited to western Massachusetts.

Corporate Officials

Cornelius D. Mahoney: chairman, president, chief executive officer
Debra L. Murphy: senior vice president, chief financial officer

Foundation Officials

James A. Adams: director
William G. Aiken: director
Carl J. Antonellis, Jr.: secretary
Barbara Braem: executive director
Agastino J. Calheno: president, director
Neil Mahoney: director
Debra L. Murphy: treasurer, director (see above)
Ann V. Schultz: director
D. Jeffrey Templeton: director

Grants Analysis

Disclosure Period: calendar year ending 2002
Total Grants: $311,953*
Number of Grants: 64
Average Grant: $3,687*
Highest Grant: $50,000
Lowest Grant: $500
Typical Range: $500 to $10,000
*Note: Giving excludes scholarship; United Way. Average grant figure excludes two highest grants ($83,333).

Recent Grants

Note: Grants derived from 2003 Form 990.
Library-Related

8,324	Friends of the Chicopee Public Library, Chicopee, MA

General

225,000	Boys and Girls Club, Westfield, MA
50,000	Center of Hope at Noble House, Westfield, MA
50,000	Westfield State College, Westfield, MA
25,000	Noble Hospital, Westfield, MA
25,000	Noble Hospital, Westfield, MA
21,000	Westfield United Soccer Club, Westfield, MA
15,000	YWCA of Western Massachusetts, Springfield, MA
10,000	Bs Friends of the Arts-Springfield Symphony, Springfield, MA
10,000	Discover Westfield Children's Museum, Westfield, MA
10,000	Miniature Theatre of Chester, Chester, MA

WORTHAM FOUNDATION

Giving Contact

Barbara J. Snyder, Grants Administrator
2727 Allen Parkway, Suite 1570
Wortham Tower
Houston, TX 77019
Phone: (713)526-8849
Fax: (713)526-7222

Description

Founded: 1958
EIN: 741334356
Organization Type: General Purpose Foundation
Giving Locations: TX: Houston

Grant Types: Capital, Challenge, Endowment, General Support, Operating Expenses.

Donor Information

Founder: Established in 1958 by Mr. and Mrs. Gus S. Wortham, both deceased. Mr. Wortham was a partner of John L. Wortham & Son, which organized the American General Insurance Company (now American General Corporation). Mr. Wortham was active in civic, educational, and cultural affairs. He was on the board of governors of Rice University and active in fund-raising activities for Rice Stadium, the Houston Symphony Society, Houston Grand Opera, and the Society for the Performing Arts. His wife, Lyndall Finley Wortham, was a member of the board of regents of the University of Houston, and a board member of the Houston Grand Opera Association.

Financial Summary

Total Giving: $9,393,833 (fiscal year ending September 30, 2003); $9,949,914 (fiscal 2002); $12,550,704 (fiscal 2001)
Giving Analysis: Giving for fiscal 2003 includes: foundation grants to United Way ($60,000); fiscal 2002: foundation grants to United Way ($75,000)
Assets: $221,432,396 (fiscal 2003); $178,153,116 (fiscal 2002); $2,800,000 (fiscal 2001)
Gifts Received: $816 (fiscal 1997)

Typical Recipients

Arts & Humanities: Arts Associations & Councils, Arts Centers, Arts Funds, Arts Institutes, Arts Outreach, Ballet, Community Arts, Arts & Humanities-General, Historic Preservation, History & Archaeology, Libraries, Literary Arts, Museums/Galleries, Music, Opera, Performing Arts, Public Broadcasting, Theater, Visual Arts
Civic & Public Affairs: Asian American Affairs, Botanical Gardens/Parks, Clubs, Economic Development, Employment/Job Training, Civic & Public Affairs-General, Inner-City Development, Municipalities/Towns, Parades/Festivals, Urban & Community Affairs, Zoos/Aquariums
Education: Colleges & Universities, Education Funds, Education Reform, Elementary Education (Public), Engineering/Technological Education, Environmental Education, Education-General, Medical Education, Private Education (Precollege), Science/Mathematics Education
Environment: Environment-General, Protection
Health: Cancer, Children's Health/Hospitals, Clinics/Medical Centers, Emergency/Ambulance Services, Hospitals, Public Health
International: Foreign Arts Organizations
Religion: Churches, Religious Welfare
Science: Science-General, Science Museums
Social Services: Animal Protection, Child Welfare, Community Centers, Emergency Relief, Scouts, Shelters/Homelessness, United Funds/United Ways, YMCA/YWCA/YMHA/YWHA

Application Procedures

Initial Contact: Send one unbound proposal copy. A formal application form can be requested from the foundation.
Application Requirements: The proposal should include purpose of funds sought; project budget; amount requested and date needed; proof of tax-exempt status; a list of trustees or directors and principal staff; and financial statements for the current fiscal year to date and the last complete fiscal year.
Deadlines: Applications should be received by the first week of January, April, July, or October.
Review Process: Proposals are considered at the foundation's trustee meetings held in February, May, August, and November. The staff will review and respond to requests following scheduled board meetings.

Restrictions

The foundation does not lend or give money to individuals.

Additional Information

Publications: Annual Report Guidelines; Application Form

Foundation Officials

Fred C. Burns: secretary B 1938. ED Rice University (1960). PRIM CORP EMPL managing partner: John L Wortham & Son LLP. CORP AFFIL director: American Indemnity Financial Corp.
Brady F. Carruth: chairman B 1957. ED University of Texas, Austin BA (1981); University of Texas, Austin MBA (1983). PRIM CORP EMPL vice president, director: Carruth-Doggett Inc. CORP AFFIL president: Gulf Coast Capital Corp.
James A. Elkins, III: trustee B Houston, TX 1952. ED Princeton University BA (1974); University of Texas MBA (1976). PRIM CORP EMPL chairman: Houston Trust Co. CORP AFFIL director: Central Houston Inc. NONPR AFFIL member: Texas Bankers Association; president, trustee: Texas Children's Hospital; member: Robert Morris Associates; vice chairman: Salvation Army; trustee: Menil Foundation; board governors: Rice University; trustee: Houston Zoological Society; trustee: Houston Museum Natural Science; treasurer: Houston Parks Board; member: American Bankers Association; trustee: Childrens Museum. CLUB AFFIL Houston Club; Forum Club.
E. A. Stumpf, III: trustee
R. W. Wortham, III: president

Grants Analysis

Disclosure Period: fiscal year ending September 30, 2003
Total Grants: $9,333,833*
Number of Grants: 65
Average Grant: $79,731*
Highest Grant: $1,050,000
Lowest Grant: $5,000
Typical Range: $50,000 to $100,000
*Note: Giving excludes United Way. Average grant figure excludes five highest grants ($4,550,000).

Recent Grants

Note: Grants derived from fiscal 2003 Form 990.
General

1,050,000	Houston Grand Opera, Houston, TX
1,000,000	Central Houston Civic Improvement, Houston, TX
1,000,000	Houston Livestock Show & Rodeo, Houston, TX
1,000,000	Houston Symphony Society, Houston, TX
800,000	Alley Theatre, Houston, TX
500,000	Houston Museum of Natural Science, Houston, TX
400,000	Houston Ballet, Houston, TX
375,000	Stella Link Redevelopment Association, Houston, TX
333,333	Texas Children's Hospital, Houston, TX
250,000	Buffalo Bayou Partnership, Houston, TX

WORTHINGTON FOODS

Company Headquarters

900 Proprietors Rd.
Worthington, OH 43085
Web: http://www.wfds.com

Company Description

Revenue: US$77 million (2001)
Employees: 350 (2001)
SIC(s): 2000 Food & Kindred Products.

Operating Locations

Worthington Foods (OH--Worthington)

Worthington Foods Foundation

Giving Contact
Allan R. Buller, Chairman
430 E. Dublin-Granville Rd.
Worthington, OH 43085
Phone: (614)885-4426

Alternate Contact
Dale E. Twomley, President, Chief Executive Officer & Director
Note: Contact for direct giving.

Description
EIN: 311286538
Organization Type: Corporate Foundation
Giving Locations: CA; OH: nationally.
Grant Types: Conference/Seminar, Employee Matching Gifts, General Support, Multiyear/Continuing Support, Project, Research, Scholarship.

Financial Summary
Total Giving: $14,500 (fiscal year ending June 30, 2004); $27,500 (fiscal 2002); $19,000 (fiscal 2001)
Giving Analysis: Giving for fiscal 2002 includes: foundation grants to United Way ($5,000)
Assets: $944,996 (fiscal 2004); $883,524 (fiscal 2002); $849,448 (fiscal 2001)
Gifts Received: $12,500 (fiscal 2004); $65,000 (fiscal 2002); $20,000 (fiscal 2001). Note: In fiscal 2004, contributions were received from Allan Buller ($7,500) and George T. Harding III ($5,000). In fiscal 2002, contributions were received from Allan Buller ($5,000), Dale Twomley ($30,000), and George T. Harding III ($30,000). In fiscal 2000, contributions were received from Allan R. Buller. In fiscal 1994, contributions were received from Worthington Foods.

Typical Recipients
Arts & Humanities: Arts Associations & Councils, History & Archaeology, Libraries
Civic & Public Affairs: Philanthropic Organizations
Education: Colleges & Universities, Education Funds, Faculty Development, Education-General, Health & Physical Education, International Studies, Medical Education, Minority Education, Preschool Education, Private Education (Precollege), Student Aid
Health: Adolescent Health Issues, Alzheimer's Disease, Children's Health/Hospitals, Health Organizations, Heart, Mental Health, Nutrition
Religion: Churches, Religious Organizations, Religious Welfare
Social Services: People with Disabilities

Application Procedures
Initial Contact: Send a brief letter of inquiry.
Application Requirements: appropriate support information.
Deadlines: None.

Restrictions
Preference is given to research and education in the fields of health and nutrition.

Corporate Officials
Allan R. Buller: chairman, treasurer, director PRIM CORP EMPL chairman, treasurer, director: Worthington Foods.
William T. Kirkwood: chief financial officer, vice president financial, director PRIM CORP EMPL chief financial officer, vice president financial, director: Worthington Foods.
Dale E. Twomley: president, chief executive officer, director PRIM CORP EMPL president, chief executive officer, director: Worthington Foods.

Foundation Officials
Allan R. Buller: trustee (see above)
George T. Harding, IV: trustee
Dale E. Twomley: trustee (see above)

Grants Analysis
Disclosure Period: fiscal year ending June 30, 2004
Total Grants: $14,500
Number of Grants: 4
Highest Grant: $7,500
Lowest Grant: $1,000

Recent Grants
Note: Grants derived from fiscal 2004 Form 990.
General

7,500	Alumni Achievement Awards, Greenville, TN -- support for secondary and higher education schools
5,000	Stepping Stones Learning Center, Worthington, OH -- support of pre-school children's program
1,000	Harding Evans Foundation, Washington, OH -- support for mental health programs
1,000	Loma Linda University, Loma Linda, CA -- support for scholarships in diet and nutrition

WPS RESOURCES CORP.

Company Headquarters
700 N. Adams Street
Green Bay, WI 54307-9001
Phone: (920)433-4901
Fax: (920)433-1526
Web: http://www.wpsr.com

Company Description
Founded: 1993
Ticker: WPS
Exchange: NYSE
Revenue: US$4.95 billion (2004)
Profit: US$139.7 million (2004)
Employees: 3080 (2003)
Fortune Rank: 393, per FORTUNE Magazine's list of 500 Largest U.S. Corporations (2004).
SIC(s): 4911 Electric Services, 4924 Natural Gas Distribution.

Operating Locations
Wisconsin Public Service Corp. (WI--Green Bay)

Nonmonetary Support
Type: Cause-related Marketing & Promotion; Donated Equipment; Donated Products; Loaned Employees
Volunteer Programs: The company sponsors employee volunteer programs in association with the United Way at Work Committee, Adopt-a-Classroom, and the Lyle Kingston Environmental Group.

WPS Resources Foundation, Inc.

Giving Contact
Larry Weyers, President
Wisconsin Public Service Foundation
PO Box 19001
Green Bay, WI 54307-9001
Phone: (920)433-1103
Fax: (414)433-1693
Web: http://www.wpsr.com/foundat/index.html

Alternate Contact
Wisconsin Public Service Foundation Scholarship Program
College Scholarship Service/Sponsored Scholarship Program
CN 6730
Princeton, NJ 08541
Note: Address for scholarship application form requests.

Description
EIN: 396075016
Organization Type: Corporate Foundation
Former Name: Wisconsin Public Service Foundation, Inc..
Giving Locations: MI: Northern Michigan; WI: Northeast Wisconsin
Grant Types: Capital, Matching, Operating Expenses, Scholarship.
Note: Employee matching gift ratio: 1 to 2.

Financial Summary
Total Giving: $984,006 (2002); $965,599 (2001).
Note: Contributes through corporate direct giving program and foundation.
Assets: $15,360,269 (2002); $17,718,356 (2001)
Gifts Received: $25,000 (2002); $50,000 (2001); $230,000 (1998). Note: Contributions are received from Wisconsin Public Service Corp.

Typical Recipients
Arts & Humanities: Art History, Arts Festivals, Dance, Arts & Humanities-General, History & Archaeology, Libraries, Museums/Galleries, Music, Opera, Performing Arts, Theater
Civic & Public Affairs: Botanical Gardens/Parks, Business/Free Enterprise, Chambers of Commerce, Civil Rights, Clubs, Community Foundations, Economic Development, Civic & Public Affairs-General, Housing, Municipalities/Towns, Philanthropic Organizations, Rural Affairs, Urban & Community Affairs, Women's Affairs, Zoos/Aquariums
Education: Agricultural Education, Business Education, Business-School Partnerships, Colleges & Universities, Education Associations, Education Funds, Engineering/Technological Education, Education-General, Medical Education, Minority Education, Public Education (Precollege), Science/Mathematics Education, Student Aid, Vocational & Technical Education
Environment: Environment-General, Resource Conservation, Wildlife Protection
Health: Children's Health/Hospitals, Clinics/Medical Centers, Emergency/Ambulance Services, Health-General, Health Funds, Health Organizations, Hospitals, Medical Rehabilitation, Mental Health, Prenatal Health Issues, Research/Studies Institutes, Single-Disease Health Associations
Religion: Religious Welfare
Science: Science Museums, Scientific Centers & Institutes
Social Services: Animal Protection, At-Risk Youth, Big Brothers/Big Sisters, Camps, Child Welfare, Community Centers, Community Service Organizations, Day Care, Domestic Violence, Emergency Relief, Family Services, Homes, People with Disabilities, Recreation & Athletics, Refugee Assistance, Scouts, Senior Services, Social Services-General, Special Olympics, Substance Abuse, United Funds/United Ways, Volunteer Services, YMCA/YWCA/YMHA/YWHA, Youth Organizations

Application Procedures
Initial Contact: Submit a letter of inquiry.
Application Requirements: Include organization name, a description of organization, amount requested, and reason for request.
Deadlines: None.
Notes: Scholarship applicants should write to request an application form.

Restrictions
Foundation only supports 501(c)(3) organizations.

Corporate Officials

Larry Lee Weyers: chief executive officer, chairman, director services B Tecumseh, NE 1945. ED Doane College BA (1967); Columbia University ME (1971); Harvard University MBA (1975). PRIM CORP EMPL chief executive officer, chairman, director: Wisconsin Public Service Resources Corp. ADD CORP EMPL president, director, chief executive officer, chairman: WPS Resources Corp.; vice president, director: WPS Energy Services Inc.; president, chief executive officer, director: WPS Power Development Inc.
Barth J. Wolf: secretary, manager legal services PRIM CORP EMPL secretary, manager legal services: Wisconsin Public Service Corp.

Foundation Officials

Patrick D. Schrickel: vice president B Green Bay, WI 1944. ED Illinois Institute of Technology (1966); University of Wisconsin (1974). PRIM CORP EMPL executive vice president: Wisconsin Public Service Corp. CORP AFFIL executive vice president: Wisconsin Public Service Resources Corp.
Larry Lee Weyers: president, chief executive officer (see above)
Barth J. Wolf: secretary, assistant treasurer (see above)

Grants Analysis

Disclosure Period: calendar year ending 2002
Total Grants: $632,322*
Number of Grants: 209
Average Grant: $3,025
Highest Grant: $25,000
Lowest Grant: $25
Typical Range: $500 to $20,000
***Note:** Giving excludes matching gifts, scholarship, and United Way.

Recent Grants

Note: Grants derived from 2003 Form 990.
General

90,000	United Way of Brown County Inc., Green Bay, WI
25,000	Greater Green Bay Community Foundation, Green Bay, WI
20,500	St. Norbert College, De Pere, WI
20,000	Family Services of Northeast Wisconsin Inc, Green Bay, WI
15,300	Trees for Tomorrow Inc., Eagle River, WI
15,000	Einstein Project, Green Bay, WI
15,000	Northeast Side Family Resource Center, Green Bay, WI
15,000	Northern Health Centers Inc, Lakewood, WI
12,000	Marquette University, Milwaukee, WI
10,000	Encompass Child Care Inc., Green Bay, WI

LOLA WRIGHT FOUNDATION

Giving Contact

Patrick H. O'Donnell, Jr., President
404 W. 9th Street
Suite 101-D
Georgetown, TX 78626
Phone: (512)869-2574

Description

Founded: 1954
EIN: 746054717
Organization Type: Private Foundation
Giving Locations: TX
Grant Types: Capital, Endowment, Multiyear/Continuing Support, Project, Research.

Donor Information

Founder: the late Miss Johnie E. Wright

Financial Summary

Total Giving: $741,652 (2002)
Giving Analysis: Giving for 2002 includes: foundation grants to United Way ($17,000)
Assets: $13,934,447 (2002)

Typical Recipients

Arts & Humanities: Ballet, Community Arts, Historic Preservation, History & Archaeology, Libraries, Museums/Galleries, Music, Performing Arts, Theater
Civic & Public Affairs: Botanical Gardens/Parks, Business/Free Enterprise, Community Foundations, Employment/Job Training, Civic & Public Affairs-General, Legal Aid, Nonprofit Management, Urban & Community Affairs, Women's Affairs
Education: Arts/Humanities Education, Colleges & Universities, Continuing Education, Economic Education, Education-General, Literacy, Minority Education, Preschool Education
Environment: Environment-General, Protection
Health: AIDS/HIV, Children's Health/Hospitals, Clinics/Medical Centers, Health-General, Geriatric Health, Heart, Hospices, Hospitals, Medical Rehabilitation, Mental Health, Research/Studies Institutes, Single-Disease Health Associations
Religion: Religious Welfare
Social Services: At-Risk Youth, Big Brothers/Big Sisters, Camps, Child Abuse, Child Welfare, Community Centers, Community Service Organizations, Counseling, Domestic Violence, Emergency Relief, Family Planning, Family Services, Food/Clothing Distribution, Homes, People with Disabilities, Recreation & Athletics, Scouts, Senior Services, Sexual Abuse, Shelters/Homelessness, YMCA/YWCA/YMHA/YWHA, Youth Organizations

Application Procedures

Initial Contact: Contact the foundation to request guidelines.
Deadlines: February 28 and August 31.
Review Process: The foundation board typically meets in May and November to consider grant requests.

Restrictions

Does not support individuals. Does not provide grants for operating expenses.

Additional Information

Publications: Application Guidelines; Annual Report
Trust(s): JP Morgan Chase Bank of Texas NA

Foundation Officials

Judge Wilford Flowers: director
Adrian Fowler: director
Raffy Garza-Vizcaino: director
Juan G. Gonzalez: director
Linda H. Guerrero: director
William B. Hilgers: director
Judge James Meyers: director
Patrick H. O'Donnell, Jr.: president
Sandra O'Donnell: president
Ron Oliviera: director
Carole Rylander: director
Vivian E. Todd: director

Grants Analysis

Disclosure Period: calendar year ending 2002
Total Grants: $724,652*
Number of Grants: 61
Average Grant: $11,880
Highest Grant: $30,000
Typical Range: $5,000 to $25,000
***Note:** Giving excludes United Way.

Recent Grants

Note: Grants derived from 2002 Form 990.

Library-Related

25,000	Elroy Community Library Association -- portable classroom building

General

30,000	Capital Area Food Bank, Austin, TX -- refrigerated 48 foot trailer
27,795	Hospice Austin, Austin, TX -- beds
25,000	Austin Eastside Story Foundation, Austin, TX -- van
25,000	Capitol Area Homeless Alliance, Austin, TX -- renovation of room and garden terrace
25,000	Hill Country Care
25,000	Seton Fund, Austin, TX -- renovation of patient room
23,625	Greater East Austin Youth Association, Austin, TX -- sports equipment
23,585	Extend-A-Care, Austin, TX -- child care fees
22,618	Austin Groups for the Elderly, Austin, TX -- lighting, plumbing, windows,
22,000	Helping Hand Home for Children, Austin, TX -- van

WURZBURG INC.

Company Headquarters

710 S. 4th St.
Memphis, TN 38126
Web: http://www.wurzburg.com

Company Description

Employees: 350
SIC(s): 2672 Coated & Laminated Paper Nec, 2761 Manifold Business Forms, 3536 Hoists, Cranes & Monorails, 5112 Stationery & Office Supplies.

Operating Locations

Wurzburg, Inc. (TN--Memphis)

Reginald Wurzburg Foundation

Giving Contact

Minda Wurzburg
Reginald Wurzburg Foundation
710 S. Fourth St.
PO Box 710
Memphis, TN 38101

Description

EIN: 626048546
Organization Type: Corporate Foundation
Giving Locations: TN: Memphis
Grant Types: General Support.

Financial Summary

Total Giving: $130,500 (2003)
Assets: $1,238,273 (2003)
Gifts Received: $15,000 (2003); $37,500 (2000); $50,000 (1999). Note: In 1996, 1999, 2000, and 2003, contributions were received from Wurzburg Brothers, Inc.

Typical Recipients

Arts & Humanities: Arts Associations & Councils, Ballet, Community Arts, Libraries, Museums/Galleries, Music, Performing Arts, Public Broadcasting, Theater
Civic & Public Affairs: Business/Free Enterprise, Clubs, Community Foundations, Ethnic Organizations, Civic & Public Affairs-General, Housing, Professional & Trade Associations, Public Policy, Safety, Urban & Community Affairs, Zoos/Aquariums
Education: Business Education, Colleges & Universities, Education-General, Medical Education, Minori-

ty Education, Private Education (Precollege), Religious Education

Environment: Wildlife Protection

Health: Alzheimer's Disease, Arthritis, Cancer, Children's Health/Hospitals, Clinics/Medical Centers, Diabetes, Emergency/Ambulance Services, Heart, Hospitals, Multiple Sclerosis, Nursing Services

International: Missionary/Religious Activities

Religion: Jewish Causes, Religious Organizations, Religious Welfare, Social/Policy Issues, Synagogues/Temples

Social Services: Animal Protection, Big Brothers/Big Sisters, Community Service Organizations, Crime Prevention, Family Services, Food/Clothing Distribution, Scouts, Senior Services, Youth Organizations

Application Procedures

Initial Contact: Send a brief letter of inquiry.
Deadlines: None.

Additional Information

Trust(s): National Bank Commerce

Corporate Officials

Bernard Lapides: co-chairman, co-president, director PRIM CORP EMPL co-chairman, co-president, director: Wurzburg Brothers.

Warren Seymour Wurzburg, Sr.: chairman, president, director B Memphis, TN 1926. PRIM CORP EMPL chairman, president, director: Wurzburg. CORP AFFIL co-chairman, treasurer: Feather Pak Co.; co-chairman, treasurer: Multiform; co-chairman, treasurer: Artcraft Converters; co-chairman, treasurer: Crown Office Furniture.

Grants Analysis

Disclosure Period: calendar year ending 2003
Total Grants: $130,500*
Number of Grants: 48
Average Grant: $2,245*
Highest Grant: $25,000
Lowest Grant: $200
Typical Range: $1,000 to $5,000
*Note: Average grant excludes highest grant.

Recent Grants

Note: Grants derived from 2003 Form 990.
General

25,000	Houston Jewish Community Foundation, Houston, TX
21,500	Temple Israel, Memphis, TN
15,000	Memphis Jewish Federation, Germantown, TN
10,000	Jewish Foundation of Memphis, Memphis, TN
7,000	University of Memphis, Memphis, TN
5,000	Jewish Foundation of Memphis, Memphis, TN
5,000	Memphis Jewish Foundation, Memphis, TN
4,000	Family Services of the Mid South, Memphis, TN
3,000	Christian Brothers University, Memphis, TN
3,000	Memphis Jewish Home, Cordova, TN

WYMAN-GORDON CO.

Company Headquarters

244 Worcester Street
North Grafton, MA 01536-8001
Web: http://www.wyman-gordon.com

Company Description

Revenue: US$730 million (2001)
Employees: 3400 (2001)
SIC(s): 3462 Iron & Steel Forgings, 3463 Nonferrous Forgings.

Operating Locations

Wyman-Gordon Co. (CA--Mojave, San Leandro; CT--Groton; MA--North Grafton; NV--Carson City; NH--Franklin, Tilton).

Nonmonetary Support

Type: Loaned Executives
Note: Company participates in the United Way Loaned Executive Program.

Wyman-Gordon Foundation

Giving Contact

Warner S. Fletcher, Jr., Director
370 Main Street, Suite 1100
Worcester, MA 01608
Phone: (508)798-8621
Fax: (508)791-6454

Description

EIN: 046142600
Organization Type: Corporate Foundation
Giving Locations: principally near operating locations and to national organizations.
Grant Types: Employee Matching Gifts, Fellowship, General Support, Scholarship, Seed Money.

Financial Summary

Total Giving: $299,590 (2002); $324,725 (2001).
Note: Contributes through foundation only.
Assets: $6,334,133 (2002); $7,663,870 (2001)

Typical Recipients

Arts & Humanities: Arts Appreciation, Arts Associations & Councils, Community Arts, Ethnic & Folk Arts, Arts & Humanities-General, Historic Preservation, History & Archaeology, Libraries, Museums/Galleries, Music, Public Broadcasting, Theater

Civic & Public Affairs: Botanical Gardens/Parks, Business/Free Enterprise, Chambers of Commerce, Clubs, Economic Development, Ethnic Organizations, Civic & Public Affairs-General, Housing, Law & Justice, Legal Aid, Parades/Festivals, Professional & Trade Associations, Public Policy, Safety, Urban & Community Affairs

Education: Afterschool/Enrichment Programs, Arts/Humanities Education, Business Education, Business-School Partnerships, Colleges & Universities, Community & Junior Colleges, Economic Education, Education Associations, Education Reform, Engineering/Technological Education, Education-General, Medical Education, Preschool Education, Private Education (Precollege), Science/Mathematics Education, Special Education, Student Aid, Vocational & Technical Education

Environment: Environment-General, Resource Conservation

Health: AIDS/HIV, Cancer, Children's Health/Hospitals, Diabetes, Emergency/Ambulance Services, Health-General, Health Organizations, Hospices, Hospitals, Medical Research, Mental Health, Multiple Sclerosis, Nursing Services, Public Health

International: International-General

Religion: Churches, Religious Organizations, Religious Welfare

Science: Science Exhibits & Fairs, Scientific Centers & Institutes, Scientific Research

Social Services: Child Welfare, Community Centers, Community Service Organizations, Emergency Relief, Family Services, Food/Clothing Distribution, People with Disabilities, Recreation & Athletics, Scouts, Senior Services, Social Services-General, United Funds/United Ways, YMCA/YWCA/YMHA/YWHA, Youth Organizations

Application Procedures

Initial Contact: Submit a formal proposal.
Application Requirements: Include a description of

the program, purpose of funds requested and any other pertinent information.
Deadlines: None.

Restrictions

Does not support individuals, religious organizations for sectarian purposes, or political or lobbying groups.

Foundation Officials

Warner S. Fletcher: director

David P. Gruber: president B 1941. ED Ohio State University (1965). PRIM CORP EMPL president, chief executive officer, director: Wyman-Gordon Co. CORP AFFIL chief executive officer: Wyman-Gordon Inv Castings; director: State Street Corp.; director: Wyman-Gordon Forgings Inc. NONPR AFFIL trustee: Manufacturers Alliance Productivity & Innovation.

Grants Analysis

Disclosure Period: calendar year ending 2002
Total Grants: $149,590*
Number of Grants: 28
Average Grant: $5,343
Highest Grant: $26,000
Lowest Grant: $350
Typical Range: $1,000 to $10,000
*Note: Giving excludes United Way.

Recent Grants

Note: Grants derived from 2003 Form 990.
General

150,000	United Way of Central Massachusetts, Worcester, MA
26,000	Worcester Historical Museum, Worcester, MA
15,530	Worcester Polytechnic Institute, Worcester, MA
10,000	American Red Cross, Worcester, MA
8,500	YOU Incorporated, Worcester, MA
8,000	Greater Worcester Habitat for Humanity, Worcester, MA
6,000	WICN 90.5 Public Radio, Worcester, MA
5,350	Central Massachusetts Symphony Orchestra, Worcester, MA
5,000	Dauphinais Park at Norcross, Norcross, GA
5,000	Greater Worcester 32 degrees Masonic Learning Center, Newton Ville, MA

WYMAN YOUTH TRUST

Giving Contact

D. E. Wyman, Trustee
Wyman Youth Trust
104 30th Ave. South
Seattle, WA 98144
Phone: (206)682-2255

Description

Founded: 1951
EIN: 916031590
Organization Type: Private Foundation
Giving Locations: NE: Custer County, Lancaster County, York County; WA: King County, Pierce County, Snohomish County
Grant Types: General Support.

Donor Information

Founder: members of the Wyman family

Financial Summary

Total Giving: $352,800 (2003)
Assets: $5,847,937 (2003)

Typical Recipients

Arts & Humanities: Arts Associations & Councils, Arts Centers, Arts Outreach, Ballet, Community Arts, Dance, Ethnic & Folk Arts, Historic Preservation, History & Archaeology, Libraries, Museums/Galleries, Music, Opera, Performing Arts, Theater

Civic & Public Affairs: Business/Free Enterprise, Clubs, Economic Development, Civic & Public Affairs-General, Housing, Parades/Festivals, Urban & Community Affairs, Zoos/Aquariums

Education: Arts/Humanities Education, Business Education, Colleges & Universities, Education Reform, Elementary Education (Private), Education-General, Private Education (Precollege), Public Education (Precollege), Secondary Education (Public), Social Sciences Education, Student Aid

Environment: Protection

Health: AIDS/HIV, Children's Health/Hospitals, Clinics/Medical Centers, Hospitals, Mental Health, Transplant Networks/Donor Banks

International: Foreign Arts Organizations, International Affairs

Religion: Churches, Ministries, Religious Organizations, Religious Welfare

Science: Scientific Centers & Institutes

Social Services: Child Welfare, Community Centers, Community Service Organizations, Counseling, Domestic Violence, Family Services, Food/Clothing Distribution, Recreation & Athletics, United Funds/United Ways, Volunteer Services, YMCA/YWCA/YMHA/YWHA, Youth Organizations

Application Procedures

Initial Contact: Send a letter of proposal.

Application Requirements: Include a description of organization, a description of the proposed project, a statement of financial need, a list of board members, and an annual operating budget.

Deadlines: June 15 for arts and culture grants, September 15 for civic and education, and December 1 for social and health services.

Restrictions

Grants are awarded to support the betterment of all youth and for advancement of civic and cultural development. Grants are not made to individuals.

Additional Information

Publications: Application Guidelines

Foundation Officials

David E. Wyman: trustee
Hal H. Wyman: trustee

Grants Analysis

Disclosure Period: calendar year ending 2003
Total Grants: $352,800
Number of Grants: 76
Average Grant: $3,416*
Highest Grant: $50,000
Lowest Grant: $100
Typical Range: $1,000 to $5,000
*Note: Average grant figure excludes two highest grants ($100,000).

Recent Grants

Note: Grants derived from 2001 Form 990.

General

50,000	Bush School, Seattle, WA
50,000	Museum of Flight, Seattle, WA
29,000	University of Washington, Seattle, WA
20,000	Seattle Center Foundation, Seattle, WA
20,000	YMCA, Seattle, WA
17,500	Seattle Academy of Arts and Sciences, Seattle, WA
15,000	YWCA, Seattle, WA
10,000	Planned Parenthood of Western Washington, Seattle, WA
10,000	PONCHO, Seattle, WA
10,000	Pratt Fine Arts Center, Seattle, WA

WYNN FOUNDATION

Giving Contact

Wesley E. Bellwood, President
5 Rue Deauville
Newport Beach, CA 92660
Phone: (949)644-2791

Description

Founded: 1966
EIN: 956136231
Organization Type: Private Foundation
Giving Locations: CA
Grant Types: General Support.

Donor Information

Founder: the late Bee Wynn, the late Carl Wynn

Financial Summary

Total Giving: $1,149,000 (2003); $1,450,000 (2001)
Assets: $27,366,303 (2003); $28,742,040 (2001)
Gifts Received: $34,414 (1993). Note: In 1993, contributions were received from the estate of Carl E. Wynn.

Typical Recipients

Arts & Humanities: Ballet, History & Archaeology, Libraries, Public Broadcasting

Civic & Public Affairs: Botanical Gardens/Parks, Civic & Public Affairs-General, Hispanic Affairs, Philanthropic Organizations

Education: Business Education, Colleges & Universities, Education Associations, Environmental Education, Education-General, Medical Education, Public Education (Precollege), Science/Mathematics Education, Secondary Education (Public), Special Education

Environment: Research

Health: Alzheimer's Disease, Arthritis, Cancer, Children's Health/Hospitals, Clinics/Medical Centers, Health-General, Heart, Hospitals, Hospitals (University Affiliated), Kidney, Medical Research, Mental Health, Prenatal Health Issues, Preventive Medicine/Wellness Organizations, Public Health, Research/Studies Institutes, Single-Disease Health Associations, Trauma Treatment

Religion: Religion-General, Religious Welfare

Science: Science Museums, Scientific Organizations

Social Services: Big Brothers/Big Sisters, Child Abuse, Child Welfare, Community Service Organizations, Delinquency & Criminal Rehabilitation, Domestic Violence, Family Planning, Family Services, Food/Clothing Distribution, People with Disabilities, Scouts, Shelters/Homelessness, Special Olympics, YMCA/YWCA/YMHA/YWHA, Youth Organizations

Application Procedures

Initial Contact: Application should be submitted in letter form only.
Deadlines: May 15.

Foundation Officials

Wesley E. Bellwood: president B Garfield Township, IA 1923. ED Southwestern University (1948). PRIM CORP EMPL chairman, director: Wynns International.
William Christian: assistant treasurer
Billie A. Fischer: vice president
Dorothy L. Frey: treasurer

Grants Analysis

Disclosure Period: calendar year ending 2003
Total Grants: $1,149,000
Number of Grants: 89
Average Grant: $11,828*
Highest Grant: $60,000
Lowest Grant: $5,000
Typical Range: $5,000 to $20,000
*Note: Average grant figure excludes two highest grants ($120,000).

Recent Grants

Note: Grants derived from 2001 Form 990.

General

78,000	Center for Alaskan Coastal Studies, Homer, AK -- Carl E. Wynn Nature Center
68,000	Peppermint Ridge, Corona, CA -- residential program for developmentally disabled
50,000	Citrus Valley Health Foundation, Covina, CA -- hospital programs serving local communities
50,000	City of Hope, Los Angeles, CA -- cancer research
50,000	Foothill Foundation, Glendora, CA -- Hospital Programs
50,000	Loma Linda University Medical Center, Loma Linda, CA -- hospital programs
50,000	Operation Safe House, Grand Terrace, CA -- programs for abused children
40,000	Good Shepherd Shelter, Los Angeles, CA -- serving battered women and their children
40,000	Homer Society of Natural History, Inc., Homer, AK -- Educational Program and Remote Cancer Program
38,000	St. Mary Medical Center, Applevalley, CA -- medical facilities and surgery equipment

WYOMISSING FOUNDATION

Giving Contact

Ned Diefenderfer, Secretary
12 Commerce Drive
Wyomissing, PA 19610
Phone: (610)376-7494
Fax: (610)372-7626

Description

Founded: 1929
EIN: 231980570
Organization Type: General Purpose Foundation
Giving Locations: PA: Berks County and contiguous counties
Grant Types: Capital, Emergency, Multiyear/Continuing Support, Operating Expenses, Seed Money.

Donor Information

Founder: Incorporated in 1929 by the late Ferdinand Thun and members of the Thun family.

Financial Summary

Total Giving: $1,385,676 (2001)
Assets: $33,641,811 (2001)

Typical Recipients

Arts & Humanities: Art History, Arts Funds, Arts Institutes, Ballet, Arts & Humanities-General, Historic Preservation, History & Archaeology, Libraries, Museums/Galleries, Music, Opera, Performing Arts, Public Broadcasting, Theater

Civic & Public Affairs: Community Foundations, Economic Development, Economic Policy, Ethnic Organizations, Civic & Public Affairs-General, Hispanic Affairs, Housing, Law & Justice, Legal Aid, Municipalities/Towns, Parades/Festivals, Philanthropic Organizations, Public Policy, Urban & Community Affairs, Zoos/Aquariums

Education: Arts/Humanities Education, Business Education, Business-School Partnerships, Colleges & Universities, Community & Junior Colleges, Economic Education, Education Funds, Education Reform, Environmental Education, Education-General, Literacy, Minority Education, Special Education

Environment: Air/Water Quality, Environment-

General, Protection, Resource Conservation, Watershed, Wildlife Protection
Health: AIDS/HIV, Emergency/Ambulance Services, Health Funds, Home-Care Services, Hospitals, Medical Rehabilitation, Nursing Services, Prenatal Health Issues
International: International Affairs, International Relations
Religion: Jewish Causes, Religious Organizations, Religious Welfare
Science: Science Museums, Scientific Centers & Institutes
Social Services: Animal Protection, At-Risk Youth, Child Welfare, Community Centers, Community Service Organizations, Counseling, Crime Prevention, Delinquency & Criminal Rehabilitation, Family Planning, Food/Clothing Distribution, Homes, People with Disabilities, Recreation & Athletics, Scouts, Senior Services, Shelters/Homelessness, Social Services-General, Substance Abuse, United Funds/United Ways, YMCA/YWCA/YMHA/YWHA, Youth Organizations

Application Procedures

Initial Contact: The foundation requests applications be made in writing.
Deadlines: None.

Restrictions

The foundation does not make grants to individuals, or for endowments, deficit financing, land acquisition, publications, conferences, scholarships, fellowships, or loans.

Additional Information

Publications: Application Guidelines; Annual Report; Program Policy Statement; Financial Statement

Foundation Officials

Thomas A. Beaver: treasurer PRIM CORP EMPL partner: Reinsel & Co.
Victoria F. Guthrie: trustee
Sidney Delong Kline, Jr.: trustee B West Reading, PA 1932. ED Dickinson College BA (1954); Dickinson School of Law JD (1956). PRIM CORP EMPL chairman, partner: Stevens & Lee PC. CORP AFFIL director: Reading Eagle Co. NONPR AFFIL director: Reading Center City Development Fund; campaign chairman: United Way Berks County; member: Pennsylvania Bar Association; secretary, trustee: Dickinson School Law; fellow: National Society Fund Raising Executives; member: Berks County Bar Association; chairman, trustee: Dickinson College; fellow: American College Trust & Estate Counsel. CLUB AFFIL Pelican Bay Club.
Samuel Alexander McCullough: trustee B Pittsburgh, PA 1938. ED University of Pittsburgh BBA (1960). PRIM CORP EMPL chairman, chief executive officer, president: Meridian Bancorp Inc. CORP AFFIL president: CoreStates Financial Corp.; director: MCGlinn Capital Management. NONPR AFFIL trustee: University Pittsburgh; director: University Pittsburgh Common System Education; chairman: Pennsylvania Chamber Business & Industry; president: Department Community Economic Development; member: International Financial Conference; member: American Bankers Association; member: American Institute Banking; chairman nominating committee: Albright College.
Marlin Miller, Jr.: trustee B 1932. ED Alfred University BS (1954); Harvard University MBA (1956). PRIM CORP EMPL founder, president, chief executive officer, director: Arrow International Inc. ADD CORP EMPL chairman, president, chief executive officer: Arrow Precision Products; president, chief executive officer: Kontron Instruments Inc. CORP AFFIL director: Carpenter Technology Corp.; board member: Connors Investors Services Inc.
Steffen W. Piehn: trustee
Paul Robert Roedel: trustee B Millville, NJ 1927. ED Rider College BS (1949). CORP AFFIL director: Stainless Steel Industries US; director: GPU Inc.; di-

rector: Meridian Bancorp Inc.; director: General Public Utilities Corp.; director: PH Glatfelter Co. NONPR AFFIL member: Financial Executives Institute; trustee: Gettysburg College; chairman: Berks Business Education Coalition.
Hildegarde Ryals: trustee, secretary
Lewis C. Scheffey, Jr.: trustee
Michael J. Thun: trustee

Grants Analysis

Disclosure Period: calendar year ending 2001
Total Grants: $1,254,855*
Number of Grants: 24
Average Grant: $52,286
Highest Grant: $190,000
Lowest Grant: $1,000
Typical Range: $15,000 to $100,000
*Note: Giving excludes United Way.

Recent Grants

Note: Grants derived from 2002 Form 990.
General

268,222	Hispanic Center of Reading & Berks, Reading, PA -- fund for human services - Build Organization
239,000	Berkshire Highlands, Beverly, MA -- fund for Berkshire Highland initiative
174,500	Berks County Community Foundation, Reading, PA -- fund for human services
137,540	United Way of Berks County, Reading, PA -- fund for annual campaign/Weed Seed Program
85,000	Performing Arts Campaign, Reading, PA -- to assist in arts/culture capital campaign
65,500	Schuylkill River Greenway Association, Wyomissing, PA -- fund for development expense/moving expenses
50,000	Police Athletic League, Reading, PA -- fund for development/marketing director
44,000	Children's Village, Reading, PA -- fund for restoration of exhibition barn
42,000	Children's Home of Reading & Berks County, Reading, PA -- to assist in its capital campaign
42,000	Kutztown University, Kutztown, PA -- to assist in its capital campaign

WYSS FOUNDATION

Giving Contact

Loren L. Wyss, President & Treasurer
620 SW 5th, Suite 1010
Portland, OR 97204
Phone: (503)294-4485

Description

Founded: 1989
EIN: 931010019
Organization Type: Private Foundation
Giving Locations: OR
Grant Types: Endowment, General Support.

Donor Information

Founder: Established in 1989 by Judith Wyss and Loren L. Wyss.

Financial Summary

Total Giving: $199,750 (fiscal year ending April 30, 2004); $207,200 (fiscal 2002); $210,150 (fiscal 2001)
Assets: $4,396,977 (fiscal 2004); $4,095,907 (fiscal 2002); $4,078,681 (fiscal 2001)

Typical Recipients

Arts & Humanities: Arts Associations & Councils, Arts Outreach, Film & Video, History & Archaeology, Libraries, Literary Arts, Museums/Galleries, Music, Opera, Public Broadcasting, Theater

Civic & Public Affairs: Civic & Public Affairs-General, Hispanic Affairs, Housing, Legal Aid, Women's Affairs
Education: Arts/Humanities Education, Business Education, Colleges & Universities, Education-General, Literacy, Minority Education, Public Education (Precollege), Science/Mathematics Education, Social Sciences Education
Environment: Environment-General, Protection
Health: AIDS/HIV, Alzheimer's Disease, Clinics/Medical Centers, Health Organizations
International: International Relief Efforts, Missionary/Religious Activities
Religion: Churches, Religion-General, Ministries, Religious Organizations, Religious Welfare, Seminaries
Social Services: Animal Protection, At-Risk Youth, Child Welfare, Community Service Organizations, Counseling, Delinquency & Criminal Rehabilitation, Family Planning, Family Services, Food/Clothing Distribution, Shelters/Homelessness, Substance Abuse, Volunteer Services, Youth Organizations

Application Procedures

Initial Contact: Submit a brief letter of inquiry.
Application Requirements: Include a description of organization, amount requested, purpose of funds sought, recently audited financial statement, proof of tax-exempt status, budget, list of board of directors, and organization's history.
Deadlines: None.
Review Process: The board of directors meet in December and April. Preference is given to applicants in the Portland, OR area.

Restrictions

Grants are not made to individuals. No scholarships or medical grants are provided by the foundation.

Foundation Officials

Judith Wyss: secretary, director

Grants Analysis

Disclosure Period: fiscal year ending April 30, 2004
Total Grants: $199,750
Number of Grants: 101
Average Grant: $1,978
Highest Grant: $5,000
Lowest Grant: $300
Typical Range: $1,000 to $4,000

Recent Grants

Note: Grants derived from fiscal 2004 Form 990.
General

4,500	American Field Services, New York, NY
3,000	Compassion in Dying of Oregon, Portland, OR
3,000	Deschutes Basin Land Trust, Bend, OR
2,600	Albina Youth Opportunities, Portland, OR
2,500	Dress for Success, Portland, OR
2,000	Alzheimer Association of Oregon, Portland, OR
2,000	Common Cause, Salem, OR
1,500	Christians Children's Fund, Richmond, VA
1,500	DePaul Teen Drug Treatment Program, Portland, OR
1,500	Friends of Neve Shalom, New York, NY

XCEL ENERGY

Company Headquarters

414 Nicollet Mall
Minneapolis, MN 55401-1993
Phone: 800-328-8226
Web: http://www.xcelenergy.com

Company Description
Founded: 2000
Ticker: XEL
Exchange: NYSE
Former Name: Northern States Power (2000);
Acquired: New Century Energy (2000).
Revenue: US$8.506 billion (2004)
Profit: US$356 million (2004)
Employees: 11048 (2003)
Fortune Rank: 256, per FORTUNE Magazine's list of 500 Largest U.S. Corporations (2004).
SIC(s): 4931 Electric & Other Services Combined, 4932 Gas & Other Services Combined.

Operating Locations
Northern States Power Co. (Minnesota) (DC--Washington; MN--Albany, Brainerd, Excelsior, Farmington, Granite Falls, Mankato, Maple Grove, Minneapolis, Newport, Slayton, St. Cloud, St. Paul, White Bear Lake, Winona, Winthrop; ND--Grand Forks, Mayville, Minot; SD--Sioux Falls; WI--Abbotsford, Eau Claire, Menomonee Falls)

Nonmonetary Support
Type: Donated Equipment; In-kind Services; Loaned Executives

Xcel Energy Foundation

Giving Contact
James D. Rhodes, Contribution Specialist
800 Nicollet Mall Suite 2900
Minneapolis, MN 55402
Phone: (612)330-5500
Fax: (612)330-6947
E-mail: foundation@xcelenergy.com
Web: http://www.xcelenergy.com/XLWEB/CDA/0,2914,1-1-1_4359_4842-922-0_0_0-0,00.html

Alternate Contact
Phone: (612)330-6933

Description
EIN: 412007734
Organization Type: Corporate Foundation
Giving Locations: near headquarters and service areas only.
Grant Types: Capital, Employee Matching Gifts, General Support, Project.
Note: Employee matching gift ratio: 1 to 1 to education, public broadcasting, and the Minnesota Foodshare Program.

Financial Summary
Total Giving: $6,205,165 (2003); $1,669,315 (2001). Note: Contributes through corporate direct giving program only. Giving includes corporate direct giving; domestic subsidiaries; matching gifts.
Giving Analysis: Giving for 2002 includes: foundation matching gifts ($439,892); foundation grants to United Way ($1,545,000)
Assets: $1,720,448 (2003)
Gifts Received: $6,797,000 (2003); $2,044,508 (2001); $2,000,000 (2000). Note: Contributions are received from Xcel Energy, Inc.

Typical Recipients
Arts & Humanities: Arts Centers, Arts Funds, Arts Institutes, Community Arts, Ethnic & Folk Arts, History & Archaeology, Libraries, Museums/Galleries, Music, Opera, Performing Arts, Public Broadcasting, Theater
Civic & Public Affairs: Botanical Gardens/Parks, Employment/Job Training, Hispanic Affairs, Housing, Legal Aid, Municipalities/Towns, Native American Affairs, Nonprofit Management, Parades/Festivals, Safety, Urban & Community Affairs, Women's Affairs, Zoos/Aquariums
Education: Afterschool/Enrichment Programs, Business Education, Colleges & Universities, Community & Junior Colleges, Education Reform, Elementary Education (Public), Legal Education, Minority Education, Preschool Education, Student Aid
Environment: Environment-General, Wildlife Protection
Health: AIDS/HIV, Cancer, Clinics/Medical Centers, Health Organizations, Hospitals, Mental Health, Nursing Services, Single-Disease Health Associations
Religion: Religious Welfare
Social Services: Child Welfare, Community Centers, Community Service Organizations, Counseling, Day Care, Delinquency & Criminal Rehabilitation, Domestic Violence, Emergency Relief, Family Services, Food/Clothing Distribution, Homes, People with Disabilities, Refugee Assistance, Senior Services, Shelters/Homelessness, Substance Abuse, United Funds/United Ways, Volunteer Services, Youth Organizations

Application Procedures
Initial Contact: Submit the online letter of intent, which is available on the Web site. Company states it wants online applications only.
Deadlines: Each program area has its own deadline for submitting letters of inquiry, and deadlines may vary from year to year. Contact the foundation or check its web site to obtain current deadline information.
Decision Notification: All applicants are notified of the results of its letter of inquiry within three weeks of the submission deadline. For those applicants who are requested to submit a full proposal, the foundation will provide instructions on how to proceed.

Restrictions
Company does not support endowment campaigns; athletic or scholarship competitions; religious, political, veteran or fraternal organizations except for programs these organizations sponsor for direct benefit to the community and not for themselves; benefits or fundraising activities; programs of individual organizations that receive more than 50 percent of their program budget from the United Way or other federated giving drives to which Xcel Energy contributes; disease-specific organizations; sports and athletic programs; or capital projects.

Additional Information
Within one year of receiving grant payment, recipient must submit report detailing the expenditures and results of project.
Addresses and names of the appropriate contact persons are contained in the company's funding guidelines.
First time grants are usually between $1,000 and $5,000.
Publications: Funding Guidelines; Application Form; Corporate Contributions Annual Report

Corporate Officials
Tom Micheletti: co-president, chief executive officer PRIM CORP EMPL vice president public & government affairs: Northern States Power Co.

Foundation Officials
Wayne H. Brunetti: president
Cynthia Evans: secretary
Gary Gibson: vice president
Carol Shearon: program manager
Pat Vincent: treasurer
Beth Willis: chairman

Grants Analysis
Disclosure Period: calendar year ending 2003
Total Grants: $6,205,165*
Number of Grants: 1,932
Average Grant: $3,212
Highest Grant: $420,126
Typical Range: $500 to $1,000 and $10,000 to $20,000

*Note: Giving includes matching gifts, scholarships, and United Way.

XEROX CORP.

Company Headquarters
Stamford, CT
Web: http://www.xerox.com

Company Description
Founded: 1906
Ticker: XRX
Exchange: NYSE
Revenue: US$15.722 billion (2004)
Profit: US$859 million (2004)
Employees: 61100 (2003)
Fortune Rank: 132, per FORTUNE Magazine's list of 500 Largest U.S. Corporations (2004).
SIC(s): 3577 Computer Peripheral Equipment Nec, 3578 Calculating & Accounting Equipment, 3579 Office Machines Nec, 5045 Computers, Peripherals & Software.

Operating Locations
Xerox Corp. (CA--Anaheim, El Segundo, Hayward, Los Angeles, Pasadena, Sacramento, San Francisco, Santa Clara; CT--Stamford; DC; GA--Atlanta; IL--Chicago; NY--Rochester, Webster; OK; TX--Dallas; VA--Arlington, Leesburg)

Nonmonetary Support
Value: $1,000,000 (2002 approx)
Type: Donated Equipment; Loaned Employees; Workplace Solicitation
Volunteer Programs: The company encourages employee volunteerism through the Social Service Leave and Community Involvement programs.
Contact: G. L. Watson, Vice President
Note: Nonmonetary support is provided by the company.

Xerox Foundation

Giving Contact
Joseph M. Cahalan, Vice President
The Xerox Foundation
PO Box 1600
800 Long Ridge Road
Stamford, CT 06904
Phone: (203)968-3445
Fax: (203)968-3330

Alternate Contact
800 Long Ridge Road
Stamford, CT 06904

Description
EIN: 060996443
Organization Type: Corporate Foundation
Giving Locations: nationally, with emphasis on operating locations.
Grant Types: Award, Department, Employee Matching Gifts, Fellowship, General Support, Matching, Multiyear/Continuing Support.
Note: Employee matching gift ratio: 1 to 1 for gifts from employees and/or their spouses to institutions of higher learning, up to $1,000 per institution annually.

Financial Summary
Total Giving: $398,475 (2002); $493,383 (2001). Note: Contributes through corporate direct giving program and foundation.
Assets: $8,870 (2002); $765 (2001)
Gifts Received: $405,000 (2002); $493,000 (2001); $514,830 (2000). Note: Contributions were received from Xerox Corp.

Typical Recipients

Arts & Humanities: Arts Associations & Councils, Arts Centers, Arts Funds, Arts Institutes, Dance, Historic Preservation, Libraries, Museums/Galleries, Music, Opera

Civic & Public Affairs: Civil Rights, Economic Development, Economic Policy, Employment/Job Training, Housing, Professional & Trade Associations, Public Policy, Urban & Community Affairs, Women's Affairs

Education: Business Education, Colleges & Universities, Economic Education, Education Associations, Education Funds, Engineering/Technological Education, Environmental Education, Faculty Development, Literacy, Minority Education, Science/Mathematics Education, Student Aid, Vocational & Technical Education

Environment: Environment-General

Health: Health Policy/Cost Containment

International: Foreign Educational Institutions, International-General, Health Care/Hospitals, International Organizations, International Relations

Science: Scientific Organizations

Social Services: Camps, Child Welfare, Community Service Organizations, Domestic Violence, People with Disabilities, Senior Services, Shelters/Homelessness, Substance Abuse, United Funds/United Ways, Youth Organizations

Application Procedures

Initial Contact: Call for application guidelines. Send a brief letter of inquiry no longer than two or three pages.

Application Requirements: Provide the legal name of organization, official contact person, proof of tax-exempt status, description of activities and programs, purpose of grant, benefits expected, plans for evaluation, projected budget, expected sources, amount of funds needed, and a copy of the latest annual financial statement.

Deadlines: None.

Review Process: The contributions committee reviews submissions collectively on a monthly basis and the board of trustees meets quarterly.

Evaluative Criteria: Application to Xerox focus areas of Employee/Community Affairs, Science/Technology Education, Work Force Preparation, National Affairs, or Culture.

Decision Notification: Within 30 to 60 days of receipt.

Restrictions

Foundation does not support individuals; capital grants; endowments or endowed chairs; political organizations or candidates; religious or sectarian groups; or municipal, county, state, federal, or quasi-governmental agencies.

Additional Information

All requests from organizations that have previously received support will be evaluated based on their accomplishment of the objectives included in the initial request.

Corporate Officials

Ursula M. Burns: senior vice president, chief financial officer B NY September 20, 1958. PRIM CORP EMPL senior vice president: Xerox Corp.

Emerson U. Fullwood: vice president B Supply, NC January 03, 1948. ED Columbia University MBA; North Carolina State University BA. CORP AFFIL director: SPX Corp. NONPR AFFIL member: Boy Scouts America; member: United Way.

Anne M. Mulcahy: chairman, chief executive officer B Rockville Centre, NY October 21, 1952. ED Marymount College BA (1974). PRIM CORP EMPL chairman, chief executive officer: Xerox Corp. CORP AFFIL director: Fuji Xerox Co. Ltd.; director: Target Corp.; Fannie Mae; director: Axel Johnson Inc.; director: Catalyst.

Patricia M. Nazemetz: vice president human resources B College Point, NY December 22, 1949. ED Fordham University BA (1971); Fordham University MA (1980).

Carlos Pascual: executive vice president B Malaga, Spain November 10, 1945. ED University of Madrid MEE (1968).

Lawrence A. Zimmerman: senior vice president, chief financial officer B NY December 02, 1942. ED New York University BS (1965); Adelphi University MBA (1967). PRIM CORP EMPL senior vice president, chief financial officer: Xerox Corp.

Foundation Officials

Joseph M. Cahalan: vice president

Emerson U. Fullwood: trustee (see above)

Anne M. Mulcahy: trustee (see above)

Patricia M. Nazemetz: trustee (see above)

Carlos Pascual: trustee (see above)

Martin S. Wagner: secretary, general counsel PRIM CORP EMPL assistant secretary: Xerox Corp.

Grants Analysis

Disclosure Period: calendar year ending 2002
Total Grants: $398,475
Number of Grants: 90
Average Grant: $3,915*
Highest Grant: $50,000
Lowest Grant: $500
Typical Range: $1,000 to $5,000
*Note: Average grant figure excludes highest grant.

Recent Grants

Note: Grants derived from 2003 Form 990.
General

20,000	University College Cork, Cork Ireland
20,000	University of Nottingham, Nottingham United Kingdom
20,000	University of Seville, Seville Spain
20,000	University of Toronto, Toronto, ON Canada
18,000	Simon Fraser University, BC Canada
15,000	McMaster University, ON Canada
15,000	Queen's University, ON Canada
1,000	Hole in the Wall Gang Camp, Ashford, CT
1,000	St. Mary's University, San Antonio, TX
1,000	Stanford University, Stanford, CA

YAWKEY FOUNDATION II

Giving Contact

John L. Harrington, Executive Director & Trustee
990 Washington Street
Dedham, MA 02026
Phone: (781)329-7470
Fax: (781)329-8195
Web: http://www.yawkeyfoundation.org/

Description

Founded: 1983
EIN: 042768239
Organization Type: Private Foundation
Giving Locations: MA, Boston metropolitan area
Grant Types: General Support.

Donor Information

Founder: Established in 1983 by the late Jean R. Yawkey.

Financial Summary

Total Giving: $15,466,200 (fiscal year ending June 30, 2003); $4,192,734 (fiscal 2002)
Assets: $379,203,051 (fiscal 2003); $367,849,121 (fiscal 2002)
Gifts Received: $18,000,000 (fiscal 2003); $350,000,000 (fiscal 2002); $517,846 (fiscal 2000). Note: In fiscal 2001, 2002, and 2003, contributions were received from the Jean R. Yawkey Trust. In fiscal 1998, contributions were received from the estate of Jean R. Yawkey.

Typical Recipients

Arts & Humanities: Arts Centers, Arts Institutes, Community Arts, Arts & Humanities-General, Historic Preservation, History & Archaeology, Libraries, Museums/Galleries, Music, Performing Arts, Public Broadcasting

Civic & Public Affairs: African American Affairs, Botanical Gardens/Parks, Business/Free Enterprise, Clubs, Community Foundations, Economic Development, Employment/Job Training, Civic & Public Affairs-General, Hispanic Affairs, Housing, Law & Justice, Municipalities/Towns, Philanthropic Organizations, Professional & Trade Associations, Public Policy, Urban & Community Affairs, Women's Affairs, Zoos/Aquariums

Education: Afterschool/Enrichment Programs, Arts/Humanities Education, Colleges & Universities, Education Funds, Elementary Education (Private), Education-General, International Studies, Literacy, Minority Education, Private Education (Precollege), Public Education (Precollege), Science/Mathematics Education, Secondary Education (Private), Secondary Education (Public), Special Education, Student Aid, Vocational & Technical Education

Environment: Resource Conservation, Wildlife Protection

Health: AIDS/HIV, Alzheimer's Disease, Cancer, Children's Health/Hospitals, Clinics/Medical Centers, Emergency/Ambulance Services, Eyes/Blindness, Health Organizations, Hospitals, Medical Rehabilitation, Medical Research, Mental Health, Preventive Medicine/Wellness Organizations, Single-Disease Health Associations

International: International Affairs

Religion: Religion-General, Jewish Causes, Religious Organizations, Religious Welfare, Seminaries

Social Services: At-Risk Youth, Big Brothers/Big Sisters, Camps, Child Welfare, Community Centers, Community Service Organizations, Emergency Relief, Family Services, Food/Clothing Distribution, Homes, People with Disabilities, Recreation & Athletics, Scouts, Shelters/Homelessness, Social Services-General, United Funds/United Ways, YMCA/YWCA/YMHA/YWHA, Youth Organizations

Application Procedures

Application Requirements: Check the website for updated information. Unsolicited proposals of request are not being accepted at this time.

Foundation Officials

Eleanor Armstrong: trustee
Charles I. Clough, Jr.: trustee
William B. Guttarb: trustee
Rev. Ray Hammond: trustee
John Leo Harrington: executive director, trustee B Boston, MA 1936. ED Boston College BS (1957); Boston College MBA (1966). PRIM CORP EMPL president: JRY Corp. CORP AFFIL general partner: Boston Red Sox; director: NE Sports Network Inc. NONPR AFFIL member: Massachusetts Society CPA's; director: National Baseball Hall Fame & Museum; trustee: Jimmy Fund; trustee, secretary: Dana Farber Cancer Institute; director: Hospitality Properties Trust; member: American Institute of Certified Public Accountants; member: Beta Gamma Sigma.
Edward F. Kennedy: trustee
James G. Maguire: trustee
J. Donald Monan, SJ: trustee
Judy Walden Scarafile: trustee

Grants Analysis

Disclosure Period: fiscal year ending June 30, 2003
Total Grants: $15,466,200
Number of Grants: 142
Average Grant: $46,778*
Highest Grant: $3,000,000
Lowest Grant: $400
Typical Range: $10,000 to $100,000

*Note: Average grant figure excludes five highest grants ($9,057,660).

Recent Grants

Note: Grants derived from fiscal 2003 Form 990.
General

3,000,000	Massachusetts General Hospital, Boston, MA -- for facilities and equipment
2,174,628	Fidelity Charitable Gift Fund, Boston, MA
2,000,000	Greater Worcester Community Foundation, Worcester, MA
1,382,834	Maine Community Foundation, Portland, ME
750,000	Trinity College, Hartford, CT -- fund for scholarships for needy students
500,000	Boston Foundation, Boston, MA
400,000	Nativity Preparatory School, Jamaica plain, MA -- for facilities and equipment
300,000	Egleston Square Youth Center, Roxbury, MA -- for facilities and equipment
241,791	Kennebec Valley Community College, Fairfield, ME -- fund for scholarships for needy students
200,000	Maine College of Art, Portland, ME -- for facilities and equipment

LESTER E. YEAGER CHARITABLE TRUST B

Giving Contact

Donald W. Haas, Trustee
PO Box 964
Owensboro, KY 42302-0964
Phone: (270)686-8254

Description

Founded: 1989
EIN: 611159548
Organization Type: Private Foundation
Giving Locations: IN: the Indiana counties bordering Daviess and Henderson Counties, KY; KY: Daviess and Henderson Counties
Grant Types: General Support.

Donor Information

Founder: Established in 1989 with funds from the estate of Lester E. Yeager.

Financial Summary

Total Giving: $166,480 (2003)
Giving Analysis: Giving for 2003 includes: foundation grants to United Way ($1,000)
Assets: $5,024,424 (2003)
Gifts Received: $7,500 (1999); $10,000 (1998). Note: In 1998 contributions were received from the Kellogg Foundation. In 1990, contributions the estate of Lester E. Yeager.

Typical Recipients

Arts & Humanities: Arts Associations & Councils, Arts & Humanities-General, Libraries, Museums/ Galleries, Music
Civic & Public Affairs: Botanical Gardens/Parks, Clubs, Civic & Public Affairs-General, Housing, Municipalities/Towns, Urban & Community Affairs, Zoos/ Aquariums
Education: Agricultural Education, Arts/Humanities Education, Business Education, Colleges & Universities, Community & Junior Colleges, Education Associations, Education Funds, Elementary Education (Private), Elementary Education (Public), Education-General, Literacy, Private Education (Precollege), Public Education (Precollege), Secondary Education (Public)
Environment: Environment-General
Health: Clinics/Medical Centers, Emergency/ Ambulance Services, Health-General, Hospices,

Hospitals, Medical Rehabilitation, Single-Disease Health Associations
Religion: Churches, Dioceses, Religious Welfare
Science: Science Museums
Social Services: At-Risk Youth, Child Welfare, Community Centers, Day Care, Family Services, Homes, People with Disabilities, Recreation & Athletics, Senior Services, Shelters/Homelessness, Special Olympics, United Funds/United Ways, Volunteer Services, YMCA/YWCA/YMHA/YWHA, Youth Organizations

Application Procedures

Initial Contact: Send a brief letter of inquiry requesting application form, then send a full proposal.
Application Requirements: Include a description of organization, amount requested, purpose of funds sought, recently audited financial statement, and proof of tax-exempt status.
Deadlines: October 15.

Restrictions

Grants are not made to individuals.

Additional Information

Publications: Application Form; Guidelines

Foundation Officials

Ruth F. Adkins: trustee
Donald W. Haas: trustee
Nancy C. Kennedy: trustee

Grants Analysis

Disclosure Period: calendar year ending 2003
Total Grants: $165,480*
Number of Grants: 48
Average Grant: $3,244*
Highest Grant: $13,000
Lowest Grant: $500
Typical Range: $1,000 to $5,000
*Note: Giving excludes United Way. Average grant figure excludes highest grant.

Recent Grants

Note: Grants derived from 2001 Form 990.
General

16,500	Owensboro Board of Education, Owensboro, KY -- school projects
13,000	Owensboro Area Museum of Science and History, Owensboro, KY -- exhibits
10,000	Family YMCA of Henderson County, Henderson, KY -- capital campaign
10,000	Family YMCA of Owensboro/Davies County, Inc., Owensboro, KY -- capital campaign
10,000	Pennyrile Youth Soccer Association, Henderson, KY -- lighting for soccer fields
7,500	St. Anthony's Hospice, Henderson, KY -- computer and program system
6,500	Diocese of Owensboro Educational Institute, Owensboro, KY -- school projects
5,000	Henderson Area Arts Alliance, Henderson, KY -- school programming and sponsorship of arts events
5,000	Kentucky Wesleyan College, Owensboro, KY -- scholarship fund
5,000	Volunteer Center of Owensboro, Owensboro, KY -- Reading Projects

YELLOW ROADWAY CORP.

Company Headquarters

10990 Roe Ave.
Overland Park, KS 66211
Phone: (913)696-6100
Web: http://www.yellowroadway.com

Company Description

Founded: 1924
Ticker: YELL
Exchange: NASDAQ
Formed by Merger of: Yellow Corp.; Roadway Corp..
Revenue: US$6.767 billion (2004)
Profit: US$184.3 million (2004)
Employees: 24000 (2003)
Fortune Rank: 307, per FORTUNE Magazine's list of 500 Largest U.S. Corporations (2004).
SIC(s): 4213 Trucking Except Local, 6719 Holding Companies Nec.

Operating Locations

Yellow Corp. (KS)

Nonmonetary Support

Type: In-kind Services; Workplace Solicitation
Note: Nonmonetary Support Range: $35,000 to $40,000. Workplace solicitation is only for the United Way.

Yellow Corp. Foundation

Giving Contact

Daniel J. Churay, Vice President & Trustee
10990 Roe Avenue, MS A515
Overland Park, KS 66211-1213
Phone: (913)696-6100
Fax: (913)696-6116

Description

EIN: 237004674
Organization Type: Corporate Foundation
Giving Locations: MO: Kansas City headquarters and operating communities.
Grant Types: Capital, Employee Matching Gifts, General Support, Multiyear/Continuing Support, Operating Expenses, Project.

Financial Summary

Total Giving: $151,119 (2002); $153,500 (2001). Note: Contributes through corporate direct giving program and foundation. Giving includes foundation.
Giving Analysis: Giving for 2002 includes: foundation grants to United Way ($134,453); 2001: foundation ($53,500); foundation grants to United Way ($100,000)
Assets: $124,374 (2002); $144,854 (2001)
Gifts Received: $125,000 (2002); $125,000 (2001); $60,000 (1999). Note: Contributions were received from Yellow Corporation.

Typical Recipients

Arts & Humanities: Arts Associations & Councils, Arts Centers, Arts Institutes, Ballet, Community Arts, Dance, Arts & Humanities-General, Historic Preservation, History & Archaeology, Libraries, Museums/ Galleries, Music, Opera, Performing Arts, Public Broadcasting, Theater, Visual Arts
Civic & Public Affairs: Economic Development, Civic & Public Affairs-General, Urban & Community Affairs, Women's Affairs
Education: Agricultural Education, Arts/Humanities Education, Business Education, Colleges & Universities, Community & Junior Colleges, Economic Education, Environmental Education, Minority Education
Health: Cancer, Children's Health/Hospitals, Health Organizations, Heart, Multiple Sclerosis, Public Health
Religion: Religious Welfare
Social Services: Camps, Child Welfare, Crime Prevention, Domestic Violence, Scouts, Shelters/ Homelessness, United Funds/United Ways, Youth Organizations

Application Procedures

Initial Contact: Send a letter.
Application Requirements: Include a description of organization, amount requested, purpose of funds sought, recently audited financial statement, proof of tax-exempt status.
Deadlines: None.
Review Process: Monthly review, follow-up questions, and/or site visits.
Decision Notification: Typically 30 to 60 days from receipt of proposal.

Restrictions

Foundation does not support fraternal organizations, goodwill advertising, individuals, political or lobbying groups, or religious organizations for sectarian purposes.

Additional Information

The foundation reports that they are in the process of reducing their contributions program. In the future, nearly all of the gifts will be issued to the United Way, groups in the Kansas City Area, and organizations that are current recipients of their contributions.
The Yellow Corporate Foundation was formerly known as the Yellow Freight System Foundation.

Foundation Officials

Daniel J. Churay: vice president, trustee
Bruce Gress: treasurer
Mike Kelley: president, trustee
Greg Reed: vice president, trustee

Grants Analysis

Disclosure Period: calendar year ending 2002
Total Grants: $16,666*
Number of Grants: 1
*Note: Giving excludes United Way.

Recent Grants

Note: Grants derived from 2003 Form 990.
General

100,000	Heart of America United Way, Kansas City, MO
15,000	Boys and Girls Club of Greater Kansas City, Kansas City, MO

YIH FAMILY FOUNDATION

Giving Contact

Roy Paxton Yih, President
3000 Danville Blvd., Suite 372
Alamo, CA 94507-1550
Phone: (925)855-4713

Description

Founded: 1997
EIN: 943270705
Organization Type: Private Foundation
Grant Types: General Support.

Financial Summary

Total Giving: $197,133 (fiscal year ending June 30, 2004); $143,498 (fiscal 2001)
Assets: $4,060,760 (fiscal 2004); $2,380,604 (fiscal 2001)
Gifts Received: $2,488,800 (fiscal 2004). Note: In fiscal 2004, contributions were received from Shou-Chen & Irene C.P. Yih.

Typical Recipients

Arts & Humanities: Museums/Galleries
Civic & Public Affairs: Civic & Public Affairs-General
Education: Private Education (Precollege), Science/ Mathematics Education
Environment: Wildlife Protection
Health: Cancer

Religion: Churches, Religious Organizations
Social Services: Senior Services

Foundation Officials

Cathy Yih: secretary
Irene C.P. Yih: vice president, treasurer
Roy Paxon Yih: president
Shou-Chen Yih: chairman

Grants Analysis

Disclosure Period: fiscal year ending June 30, 2004
Total Grants: $197,133
Number of Grants: 13
Average Grant: $3,928*
Highest Grant: $150,000
Lowest Grant: $500
Typical Range: $1,000 to $5,000
*Note: Average grant figure excludes highest grant.

Recent Grants

Note: Grants derived from fiscal 2001 Form 990.
General

30,000	Seven Hills School, Walnut Creek, CA -- for capital campaign and endowment fund
25,000	Seven Hills School, Walnut Creek, CA -- for capital campaign
10,000	California Alumni Association, Oakland, CA -- for library fund
10,000	Friends of the Sea Otter, Monterey, CA
10,000	Habitot Children's Museum, Berkeley, CA
10,000	Habitot Children's Museum, Berkeley, CA -- for the blast office space exhibit
10,000	St. Anthony's Foundation, San Francisco, CA
10,000	Self Help for the Elderly, San Francisco, CA
7,000	Bayside Community Church, Foster City, CA
5,000	Always Dream Foundation, Oakland, CA -- for breast cancer

J. PAUL YOST TRUST

Giving Contact

Ronald K. Fellheimer, Trustee
c/o Fellheimer Law Firm
210 N. Main Street
Pontiac, IL 61764
Phone: (815)842-3858

Description

Founded: 1991
EIN: 376274704
Organization Type: Private Foundation
Giving Locations: IL: Pontiac
Grant Types: General Support, Scholarship.

Financial Summary

Total Giving: $5,500 (2003); $31,750 (2001)
Giving Analysis: Giving for 2003 includes: foundation grants to United Way ($1,000); 2001: foundation grants to United Way ($1,000); foundation scholarships ($6,000)
Assets: $677,287 (2003); $701,646 (2001)
Gifts Received: $19,563 (1993); $543,323 (1992)

Typical Recipients

Arts & Humanities: History & Archaeology, Libraries, Performing Arts, Theater
Civic & Public Affairs: Civic & Public Affairs-General, Municipalities/Towns, Parades/Festivals
Education: Colleges & Universities, Secondary Education (Public), Student Aid
Health: Clinics/Medical Centers
Religion: Churches
Social Services: Animal Protection, Community Ser-

---

vice Organizations, Senior Services, United Funds/ United Ways, Youth Organizations

Application Procedures

Initial Contact: Send a brief letter of inquiry.
Application Requirements: Provide a description of organization, amount requested, and purpose of funds sought.
Deadlines: None.

Restrictions

Grants limited to citizens or organizations in Pontiac, IL.

Foundation Officials

Mary Catherine Dievendorf: trustee
Ronald K. Fellheimer: trustee
Dr. John C. Purnell: trustee
Robert Sear: trustee
Faraday J. Strock: trustee

Grants Analysis

Disclosure Period: calendar year ending 2003
Total Grants: $4,500*
Number of Grants: 3
Highest Grant: $1,800
Lowest Grant: $1,350
*Note: Giving excludes scholarships.

Recent Grants

Note: Grants derived from 2003 Form 990.
Library-Related

1,350	Pontiac Public library, Pontiac, IL

General

1,800	City of Pontiac, Pontiac, IL -- for Yost Museum operation
1,350	First Presbyterian Church, Pontiac, IL
1,000	Northern Illinois University, DeKalb, IL -- for scholarship

BILL B. YOUNG FOUNDATION

Giving Contact

Bill B. Young Foundation
c/o Farmers & Drovers Bank
PO Box C
Council Grove, KS 66846-0620
Phone: (316)767-5138

Description

Founded: 1995
EIN: 481161082
Organization Type: Private Foundation
Giving Locations: KS: Council Grove
Grant Types: General Support.

Financial Summary

Total Giving: $280,800 (2003); $15,613 (2001)
Assets: $1,056,362 (2003); $1,098,262 (2001)
Gifts Received: $53,899 (1996); $922,352 (1995).
Note: In 1995, contributions were received from the estate of Bill Young.

Typical Recipients

Arts & Humanities: Arts Associations & Councils
Civic & Public Affairs: Botanical Gardens/Parks, Community Foundations, Civic & Public Affairs-General, Rural Affairs, Urban & Community Affairs
Health: Hospitals, Public Health
Social Services: Community Centers, Community Service Organizations, Crime Prevention, Recreation & Athletics

Application Procedures

Initial Contact: Request an application form.
Deadlines: None.

Restrictions

Limited to recognized charitable organizations in Council Grove, KS.

Additional Information

Trust(s): Farmers & Drovers Bank

Foundation Officials

Lowell Campbell: trustee
Pat Finney: trustee
Barbara Foster: trustee
Julie Hower: trustee
Henry A. White, Jr.: trustee
John H. White: trustee

Grants Analysis

Disclosure Period: calendar year ending 2003
Total Grants: $280,800
Number of Grants: 6
Highest Grant: $233,000
Lowest Grant: $150
Typical Range: $2,000 to $15,000

Recent Grants

Note: Grants derived from 2003 Form 990.
General

233,000	Council Grove Area Foundation, Council Grove, KS -- for community building project
30,000	Council Grove Recreation Commission, Council Grove, KS -- for community baseball Diamond Park improvements
15,000	Council Grove Recreation Commission, Council Grove, KS -- for public skateboard park
2,000	Flint Hills Wind, Council Grove, KS -- for youth softball
650	Community Arts Council, Council Grove, KS -- for asbestos study of historical building
150	Fremont Park, Council Grove, KS -- for restoration of historical building

HUGO H. AND MABEL B. YOUNG FOUNDATION

Giving Contact

Michael C. Bandy
c/o Farmer's Bank
120 N. Water Street
Loudonville, OH 44842
Phone: (419)994-4115

Description

Founded: 1963
EIN: 346560664
Organization Type: Private Foundation
Giving Locations: OH: Loudonville and Holmes Counties
Grant Types: Capital, Scholarship.

Financial Summary

Total Giving: $149,143 (fiscal year ending April 30, 2004); $348,977 (fiscal 2001). Note: Fiscal 1997 Giving includes scholarship ($8,000).
Giving Analysis: Giving for fiscal 2004 includes: foundation grants to United Way ($5,000); fiscal 2001: foundation grants to United Way ($1,800); foundation scholarships ($13,000)
Assets: $5,603,254 (fiscal 2004); $5,957,479 (fiscal 2001)

Typical Recipients

Arts & Humanities: Community Arts, Libraries, Music
Civic & Public Affairs: Community Foundations, Economic Development, Civic & Public Affairs-

General, Municipalities/Towns, Philanthropic Organizations, Professional & Trade Associations, Rural Affairs, Safety, Urban & Community Affairs
Education: Education-General, Private Education (Precollege), Public Education (Precollege), Student Aid
Health: Cancer, Clinics/Medical Centers, Health Organizations, Hospices, Hospitals
Social Services: Community Service Organizations, People with Disabilities, Recreation & Athletics, Scouts, Senior Services, Youth Organizations

Application Procedures

Initial Contact: Send a brief letter of inquiry. Include a description of organization, amount requested, purpose of funds sought, recently audited financial statement, and proof of tax-exempt status.
Deadlines: None.

Restrictions

Does not support individuals or provide loans.

Foundation Officials

James J. Dudte: vice president, trustee
William B. LaPlace: trustee
James S. Lingenfelter: president, trustee
Phillip A. Ranney: counsel, trustee CORP AFFIL director: General Housewares Corp.

Grants Analysis

Disclosure Period: fiscal year ending April 30, 2004
Total Grants: $144,143*
Number of Grants: 12
Average Grant: $9,764*
Highest Grant: $26,972
Lowest Grant: $2,500
Typical Range: $5,000 to $20,000
*Note: Giving excludes United Way. Average grant excludes two highest grants ($191,520).

Recent Grants

Note: Grants derived from fiscal 2004 Form 990.
Library-Related

16,000	Loudonville Public Library, Loudonville, OH

General

26,972	Loudonville Recreation Board, Loudonville, OH
21,033	Mohican Area Growth Foundation, Mohican, OH
19,200	Loudonville Perrysville School district, Loudonville, OH
12,000	Perrysville Fire Department, Toledo, OH
11,938	Loudonville Fire Department, Loudonville, OH
10,000	Ashland Symphony Orchestra, Ashland, OH
10,000	Catholic Charities Services, Portland, OR
6,000	Loudonville Perrysville School District, Loudonville, OH
5,000	Wolf Creek, Loudonville, OH

H.B. ZACHRY CO.

Company Headquarters

527 Logwood Ave.
San Antonio, TX 78221

Company Description

Employees: 7,000
SIC(s): 1622 Bridge, Tunnel & Elevated Highway.

The Zachry Foundation

Giving Contact

Pamela W. O'Connor, Executive Director
The Zachry Foundation

310 South St. Mary's Street, Suite 2500
San Antonio, TX 78285
Phone: (210)554-4663
Fax: (210)554-4605

Description

Founded: 1960
EIN: 741485544
Organization Type: Corporate Foundation
Giving Locations: TX: higher education grants are given throughout the state, San Antonio
Grant Types: Capital, Challenge, Emergency, Multiyear/Continuing Support, Research.

Donor Information

Founder: H. B. Zachry Co. International, H. B. Zachry Co.

Financial Summary

Total Giving: $1,312,811 (2002). Note: Contributes through foundation only.
Assets: $10,088,174 (2002)
Gifts Received: $1,000,000 (2002); $1,250,000 (2000); $205,000 (1996). Note: The Zachry Construction Corporation made a contribution in 2002.

Typical Recipients

Arts & Humanities: Arts Centers, Arts Festivals, Arts Outreach, Ethnic & Folk Arts, Arts & Humanities-General, Historic Preservation, Libraries, Museums/Galleries, Music, Performing Arts, Public Broadcasting, Theater
Civic & Public Affairs: Botanical Gardens/Parks, Economic Development, Civic & Public Affairs-General, Housing, Municipalities/Towns, Nonprofit Management, Philanthropic Organizations, Public Policy, Urban & Community Affairs, Zoos/Aquariums
Education: Afterschool/Enrichment Programs, Arts/Humanities Education, Business Education, Business-School Partnerships, Colleges & Universities, Community & Junior Colleges, Continuing Education, Economic Education, Education Funds, Elementary Education (Public), Engineering/Technological Education, Faculty Development, Education-General, Leadership Training, Literacy, Medical Education, Private Education (Precollege), Public Education (Precollege), Science/Mathematics Education, Secondary Education (Public), Special Education, Student Aid, Vocational & Technical Education
Health: AIDS/HIV, Cancer, Children's Health/Hospitals, Clinics/Medical Centers, Diabetes, Emergency/Ambulance Services, Eyes/Blindness, Health-General, Health Funds, Health Organizations, Hospices, Hospitals, Hospitals (University Affiliated), Medical Rehabilitation, Medical Research, Public Health, Speech & Hearing, Transplant Networks/Donor Banks
International: Foreign Arts Organizations, International Affairs, Missionary/Religious Activities
Religion: Jewish Causes, Ministries, Religious Organizations, Religious Welfare
Science: Science-General, Observatories & Planetariums, Science Museums, Scientific Centers & Institutes, Scientific Research
Social Services: At-Risk Youth, Big Brothers/Big Sisters, Camps, Child Welfare, Community Centers, Community Service Organizations, Day Care, Delinquency & Criminal Rehabilitation, Domestic Violence, Family Planning, Family Services, Homes, People with Disabilities, Recreation & Athletics, Scouts, Senior Services, Social Services-General, Substance Abuse, United Funds/United Ways, YMCA/YWCA/YMHA/YWHA, Youth Organizations

Application Procedures

Initial Contact: a brief letter of inquiry or phone call to request application form, which is required for all proposals
Application Requirements: a description of organization, amount requested, and purpose of funds sought
Deadlines: February 15

Decision Notification: a preliminary review of agency proposals is conducted at the first board meeting held in late spring; organizations denied will be informed at this time and requests receiving interest and meriting further discussion are retained. Respective agencies are considered for funding at the second board meeting in mid-summer; majority of grants are determined and awarded at that time, and all agencies are notified in writing.
Notes: Proposals are accepted only during the first six weeks of the year.

Restrictions

Foundation does not support individuals, endowments, or organizations outside San Antonio for general grants or outside Texas for educational grants.

Corporate Officials

Bruce Benjamin Cloud, Sr.: vice chairman, director vice president B Thomas, OK February 15, 1920. ED Texas A&M University BCE (1940). PRIM CORP EMPL vice chairman, director: H.B. Zachry Co. CORP AFFIL chairman: Bruce Cloud Equipment Co. Inc.; director: Dudley R. Cloud & Son Construction. NONPR AFFIL honorary life board member: Texas State Technology College Foundation; member: Texas Transportation Institute; member: Texas Society Professional Engineers; member: Texas Good Roads-Transportation Association; member: Texas Hotmix Paving Association; member: Texas Association General Contractors; member: Texas Congress Extension Service; member: San Antonio Chamber of Commerce; member: San Antonio Livestock Association; member: National Asphalt Paving Association; member: Nocturnal Adoration Society; member: Consult Contractors Council America; member: American Institute Management; member: American Management Association; member: Alpha Epsilon Chi; member: American Concrete Paving Association.
Charles E. Ebrom: director, executive vice president B 1931. PRIM CORP EMPL director, executive vice president: H. B. Zachry Co. International.
Peter S. Van Nort: president B 1937. PRIM CORP EMPL president: H.B. Zachry Co.
Henry Bartell Zachry, Jr.: chairman, chief executive officer B College Station, TX 1933. ED Texas A&M University BScE (1954). PRIM CORP EMPL chairman, chief executive officer: Zachry Inc. CORP AFFIL chairman: H B Zachry Co. NONPR AFFIL director: Southwest Research Institute.

Foundation Officials

Charles E. Ebrom: treasurer, trustee (see above)
Murray Lloyd Johnson, Jr.: secretary, trustee B Lake Charles, LA 1940. ED Austin College (1962); University of Texas (1965). PRIM CORP EMPL vice president, general counsel, director: H.B. Zachry Co. NONPR AFFIL member: American Judicature Society; member: International Association Defense Counsel; member: American Bar Association.
Pamela O'Connor: executive director
Henry Bartell Zachry, Jr.: trustee (see above)
J. P. Zachry: president, trustee B 1937. PRIM CORP EMPL president: Tower Life Insurance Co.
Mollie Steves Zachry: trustee

Grants Analysis

Disclosure Period: calendar year ending 2002
Total Grants: $1,312,811*
Number of Grants: 48
Average Grant: $22,613*
Highest Grant: $250,000
Lowest Grant: $1,000
Typical Range: $5,000 to $30,000
*Note: Average grant figure excludes highest grant.

Recent Grants

Note: Grants derived from 2003 Form 990.
General
250,000   Cancer Therapy and Research Foundation of South Texas, San Antonio, TX

250,000   Texas A and M Foundation, College Station, TX
125,000   Centro Alameda Incorporated, San Antonio, TX
105,000   Saint Mary's University, San Antonio, TX
50,000   San Antonio Museum of Art, San Antonio, TX
25,000   Family Service Association of San Antonio, San Antonio, TX
25,000   San Antonio Metro Ministries, San Antonio, TX
25,000   San Antonio Symphony, San Antonio, TX
25,000   Santa Rosa Children's Hospital Foundation, San Antonio, TX
20,000   Hidalgo Foundation Bexar County, San Antonio, TX

ANNE AND HENRY ZARROW FOUNDATION

Giving Contact

Judith Z. Kishner, Secretary, Treasurer
401 S. Boston Suite 900
Tulsa, OK 74103
Phone: (918)295-8000

Description

Founded: 1986
EIN: 731286874
Organization Type: Private Foundation
Giving Locations: OK: Tulsa
Grant Types: Emergency, General Support, Scholarship.

Donor Information

Founder: Henry H. Zarrow

Financial Summary

Total Giving: $5,236,855 (2003); $4,786,395 (2001)
Giving Analysis: Giving for 2003 includes: foundation grants to United Way ($5,000); foundation scholarships ($336,587); 2001: foundation grants to United Way ($10,000).
Assets: $94,279,234 (2003); $89,709,323 (2001)
Gifts Received: $1,144,890 (1996); $5,000 (1995); $1,015,825 (1994)

Typical Recipients

Arts & Humanities: Arts Associations & Councils, Arts Funds, Arts Institutes, Ballet, Community Arts, Historic Preservation, History & Archaeology, Libraries, Museums/Galleries, Music, Opera, Theater
Civic & Public Affairs: Community Foundations, Civic & Public Affairs-General, Hispanic Affairs, Housing, Law & Justice, Municipalities/Towns, Native American Affairs, Urban & Community Affairs, Women's Affairs
Education: Colleges & Universities, Education Reform, Education-General, Medical Education, Minority Education, Private Education (Precollege), Public Education (Precollege), Science/Mathematics Education, Secondary Education (Public), Student Aid
Environment: Resource Conservation
Health: Alzheimer's Disease, Arthritis, Cancer, Children's Health/Hospitals, Clinics/Medical Centers, Diabetes, Heart, Hospitals, Medical Rehabilitation, Medical Research, Mental Health, Nursing Services, Prenatal Health Issues, Research/Studies Institutes, Respiratory, Single-Disease Health Associations, Speech & Hearing, Transplant Networks/Donor Banks
Religion: Churches, Jewish Causes, Religious Welfare, Synagogues/Temples
Social Services: Child Welfare, Community Service Organizations, Day Care, Domestic Violence, Family Planning, Family Services, Food/Clothing Distribution, People with Disabilities, Recreation & Athletics,

Senior Services, Sexual Abuse, Shelters/Homelessness, Substance Abuse, United Funds/United Ways, Volunteer Services, YMCA/YWCA/YMHA/YWHA, Youth Organizations

Application Procedures

Initial Contact: Send a brief letter of inquiry and a full proposal.
Application Requirements: Include a written a description of organization amount requested, purpose of funds sought, recently audited financial statement, Form 990 with schedule A and proof of tax-exempt status.
Deadlines: None.

Restrictions

Limited to organizations providing relief to the poor, distressed, or underprivileged in the Tulsa, OK, area.

Additional Information

Provides scholarships for higher education.

Foundation Officials

Steve Cochran: assistant treasurer PRIM CORP EMPL treasurer: Sooner Pipe & Supply Corp.
Julie W. Cohen: director
Judith Z. Kishner: secretary, treasurer
Henry H. Zarrow: president B 1929. PRIM CORP EMPL president, chief executive officer: Sooner Pipe & Supply Corp. CORP AFFIL president: A-Z Terminal Corp.; director: Warren Medical Research Institute.
Stuart A. Zarrow: director

Grants Analysis

Disclosure Period: calendar year ending 2003
Total Grants: $4,895,268*
Number of Grants: 280
Average Grant: $14,333*
Highest Grant: $500,000
Lowest Grant: $100
Typical Range: $5,000 to $30,000
*Note: Giving excludes United Way; scholarship. Average grant figure excludes three highest grants ($925,000).

Recent Grants

Note: Grants derived from 2001 Form 990.
General
1,548,000   Tulsa Community Foundation, Tulsa, OK -- operating
500,000   Mayo Foundation, Scottsdale, AZ -- operating
250,000   Monte Cassino School, Tulsa, OK -- operating
250,000   St. Gregory's University, Shawnee, OK -- operating
205,000   Tulsa Senior Services, Tulsa, OK -- operating
199,474   Tulsa Jewish Retirement and Health Care Center, Tulsa, OK -- operating
100,000   B'nai Emunah Congregation, Tulsa, OK -- operating
100,000   Norman Community Foundation, Norman, OK -- operating
65,500   Tulsa Day Center for the Homeless, Tulsa, OK -- operating
55,000   Community Action Project, Tulsa, OK -- operating

HENRY AND CAROL ZEITER CHARITABLE FOUNDATION

Giving Contact

Henry J. Zeiter, President
255 East Weber Avenue
Stockton, CA 95202

Phone: (209)466-5566

Description
Founded: 1996
EIN: 680369445
Organization Type: Private Foundation
Grant Types: General Support.

Financial Summary
Total Giving: $60,878 (2003); $32,527 (2001)
Giving Analysis: Giving for 2003 includes: foundation scholarships ($30,200); 2001: foundation scholarships ($10,010)
Assets: $2,572,031 (2003); $2,277,789 (2001)
Gifts Received: $110,000 (2003); $245,575 (2001); $87,883 (2000). Note: In 2003, contributions were received from John & Lynette Zeiter ($80,000) and Zeiter Eye Medical Group ($30,000). In 2001, contributions were received from Henry & Carol Zeiter ($42,400), Joe Zeiter ($40,000), Ed Kahn ($5,000), and John & Lynette ($117,839). In 2000, contributions were received from Henry & Carol Zeiter ($89,250), Joe Zeiter ($15,960), and John & Lynette ($115,917). In 1999, contributions were received from Henry & Carol Zeiter ($379,508), Joe Zeiter ($83,438), and John & Lynette ($158,190). In 1998, contributions were received from Henry and Carol Zeiter ($67,000), Joe Zeiter ($7,500), Anthony Andres ($8,000), John and Lynette Zieter ($115,000), and Buck Lewis Memorial Scholarship ($13,075).

Typical Recipients
Arts & Humanities: Libraries, Music
Civic & Public Affairs: Civic & Public Affairs-General
Education: Colleges & Universities, Education-General, Student Aid
Health: Hospitals
Religion: Religion-General, Religious Organizations, Religious Welfare, Seminaries
Social Services: Shelters/Homelessness, Social Services-General

Application Procedures
Initial Contact: Send a written request substantiating need.
Deadlines: None.

Restrictions
Contributions are currently limited to the San Joaquin Valley of CA.

Foundation Officials
Carol Zeiter: secretary
Henry J. Zeiter: president

Grants Analysis
Disclosure Period: calendar year ending 2003
Total Grants: $30,678*
Number of Grants: 33
Average Grant: $930
Highest Grant: $2,975
Lowest Grant: $40
Typical Range: $500 to $1,500
*Note: Giving excludes scholarships.

Recent Grants
Note: Grants derived from 2003 Form 990.
General

2,975	Thomas Aquinas College, Santa Paula, CA
2,950	Premier Furniture -- furniture for drug rehab clinic
2,650	Manteca Bed Quarters, Manteca, CA -- beds for homeless shelter
2,500	Catholic Charities -- help for migrant farm workers
2,500	Stockton Symphony, Stockton, CA -- tickets for poor children
2,250	University of the Pacific, Stockton, CA -- funds for piano competition prizes
1,300	SAMCO -- towards food equipment for homeless shelter
945	TC Electric -- towards repair assumption church sound system
910	Keep the Faith -- towards religious literature to encourage catholic faith
800	Stockton Shelter for the Homeless, Stockton, CA

ZELLERBACH FAMILY FUND

Giving Contact
Linda B. Howe, Program Executive
120 Montgomery Street, Suite 1550
San Francisco, CA 94104
Phone: (415)421-2629
Fax: (415)421-6713

Description
Founded: 1956
EIN: 946069482
Organization Type: Private Foundation
Giving Locations: CA: San Francisco Bay Area
Grant Types: General Support, Project.

Donor Information
Founder: Established in 1956 by the late Jennie B. Zellerbach. The Zellerbach family started a paper business in the latter part of the nineteenth century which, through mergers and acquisitions, became the Crown Zellerbach Corporation.

Financial Summary
Total Giving: $3,345,275 (2003); $3,495,966 (2002); $3,923,100 (2001)
Assets: $97,730,980 (2003); $81,636,763 (2002); $94,846,292 (2001)
Gifts Received: $206,920 (2003); $206,920 (2002); $211,920 (2001). Note: In 2003, contributions were received from The Wallace Alexander Gerbode Foundation ($100,000), Snyder Capital Management ($5,000), and William and Flora Hewlett Foundation ($100,000). In 2002, contributions were received from The Wallace Alexander Gerbode Foundation ($100,000), Levi Strauss Foundation ($5,000), and William and Flora Hewlett Foundation ($100,000). In 2001, contributions were received from Snyder Capital Management ($5,000), Wallace Alexander Gerbode Foundation ($100,000), Levi Strauss Foundation ($5,000), and William and Flora Hewlett Foundation ($100,000).

Typical Recipients
Arts & Humanities: Arts Associations & Councils, Arts Centers, Arts Funds, Arts Institutes, Ballet, Community Arts, Dance, Ethnic & Folk Arts, Film & Video, Arts & Humanities-General, History & Archaeology, Literary Arts, Museums/Galleries, Music, Opera, Performing Arts, Theater
Civic & Public Affairs: African American Affairs, Asian American Affairs, Botanical Gardens/Parks, Business/Free Enterprise, Civil Rights, Clubs, Community Foundations, Economic Development, Economic Policy, Employment/Job Training, Ethnic Organizations, Civic & Public Affairs-General, Hispanic Affairs, Housing, Law & Justice, Legal Aid, Minority Business, Nonprofit Management, Professional & Trade Associations, Public Policy, Safety, Urban & Community Affairs, Women's Affairs
Education: Afterschool/Enrichment Programs, Arts/Humanities Education, Colleges & Universities, Education Associations, Education Funds, Education Reform, Education-General, Health & Physical Education, Leadership Training, Literacy, Public Education (Precollege), Science/Mathematics Education, Secondary Education (Private), Social Sciences Education, Student Aid
Environment: Environment-General, Protection
Health: AIDS/HIV, Cancer, Children's Health/Hospitals, Clinics/Medical Centers, Health Organizations, Mental Health, Prenatal Health Issues, Public Health, Research/Studies Institutes, Trauma Treatment
Religion: Jewish Causes, Religious Organizations, Religious Welfare, Synagogues/Temples
Social Services: At-Risk Youth, Child Abuse, Child Welfare, Community Centers, Community Service Organizations, Crime Prevention, Delinquency & Criminal Rehabilitation, Domestic Violence, Emergency Relief, Family Services, Food/Clothing Distribution, Homes, People with Disabilities, Recreation & Athletics, Refugee Assistance, Shelters/Homelessness, Social Services-General, United Funds/United Ways, Volunteer Services, Youth Organizations

Application Procedures
Initial Contact: Initial approach for a grant application may be made by phone or written proposal for community art grants only. All other grants are initiated by the Foundation staff.
Application Requirements: The proposal for an arts project should include a brief summary of the purpose of the program, its goals, number of persons participating, the audience or persons to whom the efforts are directed, and information about the organization's leadership. Press clippings and a few statements from community groups or experts in the field who appreciate the program should also be sent. In addition, requests should include the most recent financial statement, detailed project budget, listing of contributions and grants as well as a list of other groups that have received or will receive a request, and proof of tax-exempt status. have received or will receive a request, and proof of tax-exempt status. have received or will receive a request, and proof of tax-exempt status.
Deadlines: Those seeking art-related grants should call the office to inquire about specific deadlines.
Review Process: Community Arts Distribution Committee meets about every two months. Other board meetings are held quarterly, in March, June, September, and December.

Restrictions
The fund discourages mail solicitation (except in the San Francisco Bay area community arts projects), and initiates most of its own projects.

Additional Information
The fund is interested in new ideas even though very few new projects can be supported. The fund generally develops its own programs with the guidance of advisory committees.
Publications: Annual Report; Guidelines; Application Form for Community Arts

Foundation Officials
Jeanette Maddux Dunckel: director
Philip S. Ehrlich, Jr.: director
Mary Ann Milias: director
Cindy Rambo: executive director ED Harvard University MA; Oklahoma State University BA. PRIM NONPR EMPL executive director: Planned Parenthood Alameda-San Francisco.
Stephen Shapiro: director
Mildred Thompson: director
Raymond H. Williams: vice president, director
Charles R. Zellerbach: director
John W. Zellerbach: vice president, treasurer, director
Thomas H. Zellerbach: president, director
William Joseph Zellerbach: chairman, director B San Francisco, CA September 15, 1920. ED University of Pennsylvania Wharton School BS (1942); Harvard University (1958). NONPR AFFIL member: National Paper Trade Association. CLUB AFFIL Villa Taverna Club; Presidio Golf Club; Pacific-Union Club;

Peninsula Country Club; Commonwealth Club.
Nancy Zellerbach-Boschwitz: secretary, director

Grants Analysis

Disclosure Period: calendar year ending 2003
Total Grants: $3,345,275
Number of Grants: 102
Average Grant: $27,676*
Highest Grant: $550,000
Lowest Grant: $1,000
Typical Range: $10,000 to $50,000
*Note: Average grant figure excludes highest grant.

Recent Grants

Note: Grants derived from 2003 Form 990.
General

102,000	Conta Costa County Service Integration Programs, Martinez, CA -- toward conflict resolution and communications skills-building program for students
83,000	California Institute for Mental Health, Sacramento, CA -- funding for mental health services for youth and families
80,000	Mission Economic Development Association, San Francisco, CA -- toward planning process for neighborhood development
70,000	American Documentary Inc., New York, NY -- toward media-based training program for administrators and teachers
65,000	University of Pennsylvania, Philadelphia, PA -- toward research training in study of distressed neighborhoods for students
60,000	Children's Hospital Medical Center of Northern California, Oakland, CA -- funding to improve at-risk families with infants
60,000	New American Foundation, Berkeley, CA -- toward promoting long-term economic self-sufficiency for immigrants
57,000	Action Alliance for Children, Oakland, CA -- toward increasing the capacity of parent leadership programs
55,000	California State University Hayward Foundation, Hayward, CA -- toward educational needs of mental health workforce
51,000	Chinese for Affirmative Action, San Francisco, CA -- toward providing access to Government services and programs

FRAN AND IRWIN ZIEGELHEIM CHARITABLE FOUNDATION

Giving Contact

Frances Ziegelheim, Trustee
28 Delaware Lane
Franklin Lakes, NJ 07417
Phone: (201)891-0183

Description

Founded: 1989
EIN: 222772946
Organization Type: Private Foundation
Grant Types: General Support, Scholarship.

Financial Summary

Total Giving: $11,818 (2003); $13,123 (2001)
Giving Analysis: Giving for 2003 includes: foundation scholarships ($250); 2001: foundation scholarships ($500)
Assets: $181,448 (2003); $201,768 (2001)

Typical Recipients

Arts & Humanities: Libraries
Civic & Public Affairs: Botanical Gardens/Parks, Clubs, Civic & Public Affairs-General, Public Policy,

Safety, Women's Affairs
Education: Education-General, Preschool Education, Private Education (Precollege), Student Aid
Health: Cancer, Diabetes, Emergency/Ambulance Services, Health-General, Health Funds, Hospitals, Long-Term Care, Medical Rehabilitation, Single-Disease Health Associations
Religion: Dioceses, Religion-General, Jewish Causes, Seminaries, Synagogues/Temples
Social Services: Community Centers, Homes, Senior Services, Social Services-General, YMCA/YWCA/YMHA/YWHA, Youth Organizations

Application Procedures

Initial Contact: Send a brief letter of inquiry.
Application Requirements: Include a description of organization, amount requested, purpose of funds sought, recently audited financial statement, and proof of tax-exempt status.
Deadlines: None.

Foundation Officials

Joel Bossom: trustee
Frances Ziegelheim: trustee

Grants Analysis

Disclosure Period: calendar year ending 2003
Total Grants: $11,568*
Number of Grants: 13
Average Grant: $890
Highest Grant: $2,956
Lowest Grant: $25
Typical Range: $100 to $1,000
*Note: Giving excludes scholarships.

Recent Grants

Note: Grants derived from 2003 Form 990.
General

2,956	J.H.R.C., Rockleigh, NJ
2,500	Temple Beth Rishon, Wyckoff, NJ
1,663	Temple Emanuel, Woodcliff Lake, NJ
1,000	Arnold B. Gold Foundation, Englewood Cliffs, NJ
1,000	Lustgarten Foundation, Bethpage, NY
813	Bergen County Y at the Jewish Community Center, Washington, NJ
500	Jewish Community Center on the Palisades, Tenefly, NJ
500	Naomi Berrie Diabetes Center, New York, NY
325	Gilda's Club, Hackensack, NJ
250	College Scholarship Fund, Tenafly, NJ

E. MATILDA ZIEGLER FOUNDATION FOR THE BLIND

Giving Contact

William Ziegler, III, President
20 Thorndal Cir.
Darien, CT 06820
Phone: (203)656-8000
Fax: (203)656-8000

Description

Founded: 1928
EIN: 136086195
Organization Type: Private Foundation
Giving Locations: Northeast USA.
Grant Types: General Support, Multiyear/Continuing Support, Research.

Donor Information

Founder: the late Mrs. William Ziegler

Financial Summary

Total Giving: $553,420 (2003); $1,333,300 (2001)
Giving Analysis: Giving for 2001 includes: foundation scholarships ($350,000)
Assets: $19,911,245 (2003); $22,802,283 (2001)
Gifts Received: $2,000 (1997)

Typical Recipients

Arts & Humanities: Arts Outreach, Museums/Galleries, Public Broadcasting, Theater
Civic & Public Affairs: Business/Free Enterprise, Economic Policy
Education: Colleges & Universities, Medical Education, Science/Mathematics Education, Special Education, Vocational & Technical Education
Environment: Environment-General
Health: Eyes/Blindness, Hospitals, Medical Research, Transplant Networks/Donor Banks
International: Health Care/Hospitals, International Relief Efforts
Religion: Religious Organizations
Social Services: Community Centers, People with Disabilities, Recreation & Athletics

Application Procedures

Initial Contact: Send a written proposal.
Application Requirements: Include needs and purpose of funds sought.
Deadlines: June 30.

Restrictions

Limited to programs for the blind.

Foundation Officials

Cynthia Z. Brighton: director
Charles B. Cook, Jr.: director
Johanna Johnson: assistant treasurer
C. Michael Mellor: director
Beatrice H. Page: treasurer, assistant secretary
Dr. Marvin L. Sears: director
Eric M. Steinkraus: director
Helen Ziegler Steinkraus: secretary, director CORP AFFIL director: America Fructose Co.
Philip C. Steinkraus: director
Karl Ziegler: director
William Ziegler, III: president, director B New York, NY 1928. ED Harvard University BA (1950); Columbia University MBA (1962). CORP AFFIL chairman, chairman executive committee: Jon H Swisher & Son; secretary, director: Matilda Ziegler Publishing Co. Blind; chairman, chief executive officer: Lloyd Lumber Division America Maize Products; chairman, chief executive officer, president, chairman executive committee, director: Park Avenue Operating Co.; president, director: GIH Corp.; chairman, chief executive officer: Helme Tobacco Co.; chairman, chief executive officer, chairman executive committee: America Fructose Co.; director: Foresight Industries, Inc. NONPR AFFIL director: Southwest Area Commerce & Industry Association; trustee, director: YMCA Darien Commun; director: Maritime Center Norwalk; director: Project Orbis; member national advisory council: Hampshire College; trustee: Lavelle School Blind. CLUB AFFIL New York Yacht Club; Noroton Yacht Club.

Grants Analysis

Disclosure Period: calendar year ending 2003
Total Grants: $553,420*
Typical Range: $10,000 to $40,000
*Note: Grants list incomplete for 2003.

Recent Grants

Note: Grants derived from 2001 Form 990.
General

415,000	Matilda Ziegler Publishing Company for the Blind, Inc., Darien, CT -- monthly magazine
250,000	Yale University School of Medicine, New Haven, CT -- basic research
70,000	Cornell University, Ithaca, NY

70,000	Princeton University, Princeton, NJ
70,000	University of Medicine and Dentistry of New Jersey, Newark, NJ
70,000	West Virginia University, Morgantown, WV
70,000	Yale University, New Haven, CT
25,000	Voluntary Services for The Blind of Fairfield County, Stamford, CT -- volunteer services
7,000	Recording for the Blind and Dyslexic, Princeton, NJ -- Library of Recording Textbooks
3,000	Ski for Light, Inc., Minneapolis, MN -- training and volunteer instructor

CHARLOTTE AND ARTHUR ZITRIN FOUNDATION

Giving Contact

Arthur Zitrin, President
32 Lockerman Sq., Suite L-100
Dover, DE 19901

Description

Founded: 1993
EIN: 510337212
Organization Type: Private Foundation
Giving Locations: NY
Grant Types: General Support, Scholarship.

Donor Information

Founder: Established in 1993 by Charlotte and Arthur Zitrin.

Financial Summary

Total Giving: $342,675 (fiscal year ending October 31, 2004)
Assets: $7,907,932 (fiscal 2004)
Gifts Received: $187,584 (fiscal 2000); $428,644 (fiscal 1999); $181,197 (fiscal 1998). Note: Contributions were received from Charlotte and Arthur Zitrin.

Typical Recipients

Arts & Humanities: Arts Outreach, Libraries, Literary Arts, Museums/Galleries, Music, Performing Arts, Public Broadcasting, Visual Arts
Civic & Public Affairs: Botanical Gardens/Parks, Civil Rights, Clubs, Employment/Job Training, Civic & Public Affairs-General, Hispanic Affairs, Legal Aid, Public Policy, Urban & Community Affairs
Education: Colleges & Universities, Education Funds, Education-General, Legal Education, Medical Education, Private Education (Precollege), Public Education (Precollege), School Volunteerism, Student Aid
Environment: Air/Water Quality, Environment-General, Protection, Resource Conservation
Health: AIDS/HIV, Cancer, Geriatric Health, Health Organizations, Hospices, Hospitals (University Affiliated), Mental Health, Public Health
International: International Relief Efforts
Religion: Jewish Causes
Science: Scientific Centers & Institutes
Social Services: Child Abuse, Child Welfare, Community Service Organizations, Counseling, Family Services, Food/Clothing Distribution

Application Procedures

Initial Contact: The foundation has no formal grant application procedure or application form. Send a brief letter of inquiry.
Deadlines: None.

Foundation Officials

Arthur Zitrin: president
Charlotte Zitrin: vice president

Grants Analysis

Disclosure Period: fiscal year ending October 31, 2004
Total Grants: $342,675
Number of Grants: 105
Average Grant: $2,718*
Highest Grant: $60,000
Lowest Grant: $250
Typical Range: $1,000 to $5,000
*Note: Average grant figure excludes highest grant.

Recent Grants

Note: Grants derived from 2004 Form 990.
General

60,000	New York University School of Medicine, New York, NY -- for CMZ scholarship
36,000	City College 21st Century Foundation, New York, NY
15,000	Bar Association of San Francisco Minority Scholarship Fund, San Francisco, CA
15,000	Oberlin College, Oberlin, OH
10,000	American Civil Liberties Union - North Carolina Foundation, San Francisco, CA
10,000	Bar Association of San Francisco, San Francisco, CA -- for USF scholarship fund
10,000	Natural Resources Defense Council, New York, NY
7,500	Environmental Defense Fund, Washington, DC
7,500	Zeum, San Francisco, CA
7,000	Nature Conservancy, Arlington, VA

ZOLLNER FOUNDATION

Giving Contact

Alice Kopfer, Administrator
c/o Wells Fargo Bank
PO Box 960
Ft. Wayne, IN 46801-6632
Phone: (219)461-6000

Description

Founded: 1983
EIN: 356381471
Organization Type: Private Foundation
Giving Locations: IN: Allen County
Grant Types: General Support.

Donor Information

Founder: the late Fred Zollner

Financial Summary

Total Giving: $583,871 (2003). Note: 1997 Giving includes United Way ($70,000).
Giving Analysis: Giving for 2003 includes: foundation grants to United Way ($70,000).
Assets: $11,290,158 (2003)
Gifts Received: $1,777 (1997); $300,500 (1995). Note: In 1995 and 1997, contributions were received from the Fred Zollner Irrevocable Trust.

Typical Recipients

Arts & Humanities: Libraries, Museums/Galleries, Public Broadcasting
Civic & Public Affairs: Botanical Gardens/Parks, Clubs, Community Foundations, Economic Development, Civic & Public Affairs-General, Philanthropic Organizations, Professional & Trade Associations, Urban & Community Affairs, Zoos/Aquariums
Education: Business Education, Colleges & Universities, Engineering/Technological Education, Education-General, Science/Mathematics Education, Secondary Education (Private), Vocational & Technical Education
Health: Health Organizations, Hospitals, Public Health
Science: Scientific Centers & Institutes
Social Services: Food/Clothing Distribution, Scouts,

Shelters/Homelessness, United Funds/United Ways, YMCA/YWCA/YMHA/YWHA, Youth Organizations

Application Procedures

Initial Contact: brief letter of inquiry
Deadlines: None.

Restrictions

Contributions are not made to organizations for retarded people; liberal arts colleges; philharmonic or other similar organizations; fine arts organizations or fine arts departments or classes at any educational organization; for the renovation of old buildings which have suffered deterioration of more than ten percent of the structure; for the renovation, reconstruction, or replacement of historic buildings, sites, or landmarks; any churches, except those having a hospital division; any minority group that directly or indirectly receives any subsidy from the U.S., state, county, or municipal government; organizations that limit their benefits to the members of particular ethnic groups; and any school that does not follow an open admissions policy.

Additional Information

Trust(s): Wells Fargo Bank

Grants Analysis

Disclosure Period: calendar year ending 2003
Total Grants: $513,871*
Number of Grants: 23
Average Grant: $19,486*
Highest Grant: $53,940
Lowest Grant: $4,335
Typical Range: $5,000 to $30,000
*Note: Giving excludes United Way. Average grant figure excludes two highest grants ($104,660).

Recent Grants

Note: Grants derived from 2001 Form 990.
General

72,700	United Way of Allen County, Ft. Wayne, IN
70,000	Junior Achievement, Ft. Wayne, IN
55,000	Indiana Institute of Technology, Ft. Wayne, IN
50,000	University of Saint Francis, Ft. Wayne, IN
45,000	Anthony Wayne Area Council Boy Scouts of America, Ft. Wayne, IN
41,000	IPFW, Ft. Wayne, IN
30,000	Indiana Vocational Technical College, Ft. Wayne, IN
30,000	Tri State University, Angola, IN
25,000	Northeast Indiana Innovation Center, Ft. Wayne, IN
25,000	YMCA, Ft. Wayne, IN

HERBERT G. AND DOROTHY ZULLIG FOUNDATION

Giving Contact

Robert W. Koester, President
Herbert G. and Dorothy Zullig Foundation
PO Box 603
Sheridan, WY 82801
Phone: (307)672-6494

Description

Founded: 1987
EIN: 830282365
Organization Type: Private Foundation
Giving Locations: WY: Sheridan County
Grant Types: General Support, Scholarship.

Financial Summary

Total Giving: $30,000 (2003); $40,000 (2001)
Giving Analysis: Giving for 2003 includes: foundation scholarships ($3,000) 2001: foundation scholarships ($4,000)
Assets: $657,948 (2003); $737,175 (2001)

Typical Recipients

Arts & Humanities: Libraries
Civic & Public Affairs: Civic & Public Affairs-General
Education: Colleges & Universities, Student Aid
Health: Health Funds, Hospitals, Mental Health, Preventive Medicine/Wellness Organizations
Religion: Religious Welfare
Social Services: Child Abuse, Child Welfare, Community Centers, Community Service Organizations, Senior Services, Social Services-General, Volunteer Services, YMCA/YWCA/YMHA/YWHA, Youth Organizations

Application Procedures

Initial Contact: Submit a letter of request.
Application Requirements: Include purpose of funds sought and financial statements.
Deadlines: None.

Foundation Officials

Robert W. Koester: president
Richard Kraft: vice president
John Pradere: secretary, treasurer

Grants Analysis

Disclosure Period: calendar year ending 2003
Total Grants: $27,000*
Number of Grants: 9
Average Grant: $3,000
Highest Grant: $5,000
Lowest Grant: $1,000
Typical Range: $1,000 to $5,000
*****Note:** Giving excludes scholarship.

Recent Grants

Note: Grants derived from 2003 Form 990.
Library-Related

2,000 Sheridan County Library Foundation, Sheridan, WY -- for purchase books and subscriptions

General

5,000 Genesis Foundation Inc., Sheridan, WY -- for Salvation Army and needy

4,000 Memorial Hospital Foundation, Sheridan, WY -- for hospital equipment and hospital construction

4,000 Wellness Council, Sheridan, WY -- for community health education and safe community program

3,000 Sheridan College Foundation, Sheridan, WY -- for Zullig scholarships

3,000 Sheridan County YMCA, Sheridan, WY -- for partnership with youth program operation

3,000 Sheridan Senior Citizen's Council, Sheridan, WY -- to develop, provide and promote needed services for the elderly

3,000 Volunteers of America, Sheridan, WY -- for Sheridan community homeless shelter

2,000 Life Link of Sheridan County, Sheridan, WY -- to provide life line monitors to the elderly

1,000 Salvation Army, Sheridan, WY

Arranges funders by the state in which their main office is located. Within each state, foundation names are listed in alphabetical order. Defunct or inactive organizations are not included in this list.

Alabama

Alabama Power Co.
Bedsole Foundation (J. L.)
Bennett Family Foundation (Claude)
Blount Educational and Charitable Foundation (Mildred Weedon)
Bruno Charitable Foundation (Joseph S.)
Comer Foundation (AL)
Compass Bank
Crampton Trust
Daniel Foundation of Alabama
Ebsco Industries Inc.
Energen Corp.
Figtree Foundation
Hill Crest Foundation
Kaul Foundation Trust (Hugh)
McGregor Foundation (Thomas and Frances)
McWane Corp.
Meyer Foundation (Robert R.)
Robert Charitable Trust 2 (John A. and Delia T.)
Shook Foundation (Barbara Ingalls)
Smith, Jr. Foundation (M. W.)
Tractor & Equipment Co.
Vulcan Materials Co.

Alaska

Nolan Charitable Trust (James and Elise)
Usibelli Coal Mine Inc.

Arizona

Dorrance Family Foundation
Fear Not Foundation
Greca Realty & Development Corporation Inc.
Kieckhefer Foundation (J. W.)
Long Foundation (John F.)
Marshall Foundation
McDonald Foundation (Armstrong)
Morris Foundation (Margaret T.)
Mulcahy Foundation
Phelps Dodge Corp.
Research Corp.
Spalding Foundation (Eliot)
Stardust Foundation

Arkansas

Altheimer Charitable Foundation (Ben J.)
Cabe Foundation (C. Louis and Mary C.)
De Queen Regional Medical Center

Frueauff Foundation (Charles A.)
McKinney Charitable Trust (Carl and Alleen)
Murphy Foundation
Ottenheimer Brothers Foundation
Rockefeller Foundation (Winthrop)
Sturgis Charitable and Educational Trust (AR) (Roy and Christine)
Tyson Foods Inc.
Walker Charitable Foundation (Willard and Pat)

California

Adobe Systems
Ahmanson Foundation
Amado Foundation (Maurice)
American Honda Motor Company Inc.
Appelbaum-Kahn Foundation
Arata Brothers Trust
Argyros Foundation
Arkelian Foundation (Ben H. and Gladys)
Arrillaga Foundation (John)
AT&T National Pro-Am Youth Fund
Atkinson Foundation
Autry Foundation
Baker Foundation (R. C.)
Bandai America Inc.
Barker Foundation (Coeta and Donald R.)
Bechtel Group Inc.
Beckman Foundation (Arnold and Mabel)
Bellamah Foundation (Dale J.)
Benbough Foundation (Legler)
Bettingen Corp. (Burton G.)
Beynon Foundation (Kathryne)
Borchard Foundation (Albert and Elaine)
The Bothin Foundation
Bourns Inc.
Bradford Foundation (George and Ruth)
Bright Family Foundation
Broderbund L.L.C.
Buck Foundation (Frank H. and Eva B.)
Burnand Medical and Educational Foundation (Alphonse A.)
California Bank & Trust
Campini Foundation (Frank A.)
Chartwell Foundation
ChevronTexaco Corp.
Cisco Systems Inc.
Clorox Co.
Colburn Fund
Columbia Foundation
Connell Foundation (Michael J.)

Copley Press Inc.
Cowell Foundation (S. H.)
Crail-Johnson Foundation
Crocker Trust (Mary A.)
Crummer Foundation (Roy E.)
Darling Foundation (Hugh and Hazel)
Day Foundation (Willametta K.)
Disney Co. (Walt)
Dr. Seuss Foundation
Doheny Foundation Trust (Carrie Estelle)
Drown Foundation (Joseph)
Ducommun Inc.
Duffield Family Foundation
Edison International
Ellis Foundation
Essick Foundation
Exchange Bank
Fireman's Fund Insurance Co.
Fleishhacker Foundation
Fluor Corp.
Friedhofer Charitable Trust (Virginia)
Friedman Family Foundation
Fujitsu America
Fuller Foundation (DE)
Furthur Foundation
Gaia Fund
Gallo Foundation (Ernest)
Gamble Foundation
Gap Inc.
Gellert Foundation (Carl Gellert and Celia Berta)
Geschke Foundation (Charles M. and Nancy A.)
Getty Trust (J. Paul)
Ghidotti Foundation
Gilmore Foundation (William G.)
Goel Foundation
Gold Foundation (David B.)
Goldman Fund (Richard and Rhoda)
Green Foundation (Robert and Susan)
Greenville Foundation
Griswold Foundation (Lillian Sherwood)
Gumbiner Foundation (Josephine)
Haas Fund (Miriam and Peter)
Haas Fund (Walter and Elise)
Haas, Jr. Fund (Evelyn and Walter)
Hafif Family Foundation
Haigh-Scatena Foundation
Hale Foundation (Crescent Porter)
Hammer Foundation (Armand)
Han Charitable Foundation (Edna and Yu-Shan)
Harden Foundation

Haynes Foundation (John Randolph and Dora)
Hedco Foundation
Heller Charitable Foundation (Clarence E.)
Hewlett Foundation (William and Flora)
Hoag Family Foundation (George)
Hodges Foundation (Bess J.)
Hoffman & Elaine S. Hoffman Foundation (H. Leslie)
Howe and Mitchell B. Howe Foundation (Lucille Horton)
Irvine Foundation (The James)
Irwin Charity Foundation (William G.)
Ishiyama Foundation
Jackson Family Foundation (Ann)
Jameson Foundation (J. W. and Ida M.)
Jewett Foundation (George Frederick)
Johnson Charitable Educational Trust (James Hervey)
Johnson Foundation (Charles and Ann)
Jones Foundation (Fletcher)
Kajima Engineering and Construction Inc.
Katz Family Foundation
Keck Foundation (W. M.)
Keck, Jr. Foundation (William M.)
Kelly Foundation
Knapp Foundation (CA)
Knight Ridder Inc.
Koret Foundation
Lane Family Charitable Trust
Langendorf Foundation (Stanley S.)
Lantz Foundation (Walter)
Latkin Charitable Foundation (Herbert and Gertrude)
Lavine Family Foundation (Richard and Ruth)
Leavey Foundation (Thomas and Dorothy)
LEF Foundation
Lesher Foundation (Dean and Margaret)
Lin Foundation (T. Y.)
Long Foundation (J. M.)
Ludwick Family Foundation
Lux Foundation (Miranda)
Lytel Foundation (Bertha Russ)
Management Compensation Group/Dulworth Inc.
Mattel Inc.
McAlister Charitable Foundation (Harold)
McBean Charitable Trust (Alletta Morris)
McBean Family Foundation
McCabe Foundation (B. C.)

McClatchy Co.
McConnell Foundation
McMahan Foundation (Catherine L. and Robert O.)
Mead Foundation (Giles W. and Elise G.)
Miller Foundation (Earl B. and Loraine H.)
Mitsubishi Electric and Electronics USA
Mitsubishi Motor Sales of America Inc.
Moldaw Family Foundation
Mosher Foundation (Samuel B. & Margaret C.)
Murphey Foundation (Lluella Morey)
Nakamichi Foundation (E.)
Newhall Foundation (Henry Mayo)
Norris Foundation (Kenneth T. and Eileen L.)
Norton Family Foundation (Peter)
Oak Tree Charitable Foundation
Odell Fund (Robert Stewart and Helen Pfeiffer)
Osher Foundation (Bernard)
Pacific Life Insurance Co.
PacifiCare Health Systems
Packard Foundation (David and Lucile)
Parsons Foundation (Ralph M.)
Parvin Foundation (Albert)
Patron Saints Foundation
Pell Family Foundation
Peppers Foundation (Ann)
Peters Foundation (Leon S.)
Pickford Foundation (Mary)
Ralph's Grocery Co.
Rosenberg Foundation
Rosenberg, Jr. Family Foundation (Louise and Claude)
Rossi Family Foundation
Ryan Foundation (David Claude)
Sandy Foundation (George H.)
Saw Island Foundation
Schermer Charitable Trust (Frances)
Schwab Corp. (Charles)
Schwab-Rosenhouse Memorial Foundation
Scott Foundation (Virginia Steele)
Sempra Energy
Setzer Foundation
Seven Springs Foundation
S.G. Foundation
Shapiro Family Charitable Foundation
Sierra Health Foundation
Sierra Pacific Industries
Skaggs Foundation (L. J. Skaggs and Mary C.)
Smith Trust (May and Stanley)

Stamps Foundation (James L.)
Stans Foundation
Stauffer Charitable Trust (John)
Stillwell Charitable Trust (Glen and Dorothy)
Stulsaft Foundation (Morris)
Swig Foundation (The)
Taper Foundation (S. Mark)
Taube Family Foundation
Teichert & Sons (A.)
Thornton Foundation
Thornton Foundation (Flora L.)
Trust Funds
Ueberroth Family Foundation
United Paramount Network
Universal Studios
Unocal Corp.
Valley Foundation
Valley Foundation (Wayne and Gladys)
Weingart Foundation
West Foundation (Harry and Ethel)
Wharton Foundation
Whitecap Foundation
Wilsey Foundation
Winthrop
Wynn Foundation
Yih Family Foundation
Zeiter Charitable Foundation (Henry and Carol)
Zellerbach Family Fund

Colorado

Ackerman Trust (Anna Keesling)
Anschutz Family Foundation
Bacon Family Foundation
BCR Foundation
Boettcher Foundation
Bonfils-Stanton Foundation
Buell Foundation (Temple Hoyne)
Castle Rock Foundation
Clark Fund (Lynn and Helen)
Coors Foundation (Adolph)
Copic Medical Foundation
Crowell Trust (Henry P. and Susan C.)
Dominic Foundation
Duncan Trust (John G.)
El Pomar Foundation
Fairchild-Meeker Charitable Trust (Freeman E.)
Fishback Foundation Trust (Harmes C.)
Forest Oil Corp.
Gates Family Foundation
Great-West Life and Annuity Insurance Co.
Hewit Family Foundation
JJJ Foundation
Johns Manville
Johnson Foundation (Helen K. and Arthur E.)
Joslin-Needham Family Foundation
King Foundation (Kenneth Kendal)
Kitzmiller/Bales Trust
Krieble Foundation (Vernon K.)
McDonald Foundation (J. M.)
McKee Charitable Trust (Thomas M.)
Monfort Family Foundation
Muchnic Foundation
Mullen Foundation (J. K.)

Petteys Memorial Foundation (Jack)
Pittsburg & Midway Coal Mining Co.
Price Foundation (Louis and Harold)
Security Life of Denver Insurance Co.
Stone Trust (H. Chase)
Storage Technology Corp.
Weckbaugh Foundation (Eleanore Mullen)

Connecticut

American Optical Corp.
Barden Precision Bearings
Barnes Foundation
Barnes Group Inc.
Brace Foundation (Donald C.)
Braitmayer Foundation
Calder Foundation (Louis)
Collis Foundation
Contempo Communications
Culpeper Memorial Foundation (Daphne Seybolt)
Dibner Fund
Dime Bank of Norwich Connecticut
Eastern S.L.A.
Educational Foundation of America
Ensign-Bickford Industries
Fischbach Foundation
Fisher Foundation
GE Capital Corp.
General Electric Co.
Goodnow Fund
Griffis Foundation
Harcourt Foundation (Ellen Knowles)
Hartford Courant Foundation
Hartford Financial Services Group Inc.
Hexcel Corp.
Hoffman Foundation (Maximilian E. and Marion O.)
Huisking Foundation
International Paper Co.
Jones and Bessie D. Phelps Foundation (Cyrus W. and Amy F.)
Kohn-Joseloff Foundation
Koopman Fund
Kreitler Foundation
Larsen Fund
Lingnan Foundation
Lydall Inc.
Masterpool Foundation
Matthies Foundation (Katharine)
Mazer Foundation (Jacob and Ruth)
Moore Charitable Foundation (Marjorie)
Muhlethaler Foundation, Inc. (Jane T.)
NEBCO Evans
NewAlliance Bancshares Inc.
Newman's Own Inc.
NewMil Bancorp
Noble Foundation, Inc. (Edward John)
Olin Corp.
Palmer Fund (Frank Loomis)
Phoenix Home Life Mutual Insurance Co.
Price Foundation (Lucien B. and Katherine E.)
Rich Foundation Inc.
Rogow Birken Foundation

Saunders Charitable Foundation Trust (Helen M.)
Smart Family Foundation
Stanley Works
Stone Foundation
Tauck Foundation (Arthur C. and Lee Anne)
Tetley U.S.A. Inc.
Valentine Foundation (Lawson)
Vance Charitable Foundation (Robert C.)
Wiremold Co.
Xerox Corp.
Ziegler Foundation for the Blind (E. Matilda)

Delaware

Arguild Foundation
Borkee-Hagley Foundation
Crestlea Foundation
Crystal Trust
CTW Foundation, Inc.
Dell Foundation (Hazel)
du Pont de Nemours & Co. (E.I.)
duPont Foundation (Chichester)
Fair Play Foundation
Glencoe Foundation
Good Samaritan
Kent-Lucas Foundation
Kutz Foundation (Milton and Hattie)
Laffey-McHugh Foundation
Longwood Foundation
Marmot Foundation
MBNA Corp.
Raskob Foundation for Catholic Activities, Inc.
Vale Foundation (Ruby R.)
Welfare Foundation
Zitrin Foundation (Charlotte and Arthur)

District of Columbia

Arca Foundation
Bender Foundation
Bloedorn Foundation (Walter A.)
Cafritz Foundation (Morris and Gwendolyn)
Cohen Foundation (Naomi and Nehemiah)
Davis Foundation (Evelyn Y.)
Fannie Mae
Fowler Memorial Foundation (John Edward)
Freed Foundation
Graham Fund (Philip L.)
Higginson Trust (Corina)
Himmelfarb Foundation (Paul and Annetta)
Kennedy, Jr. Foundation (Joseph P.)
Kiplinger Foundation
Kiplinger Washington Editors Inc.
Lea Foundation (Helen Sperry)
Loughran Foundation (Mary and Daniel)
McGowan Charitable Fund (William G.)
M.E. Foundation
Mead Family Foundation (Gilbert and Jaylee)
Meyer Foundation (Eugene and Agnes E.)

Moriah Fund, Inc.
Pepco Holdings Inc.
Public Welfare Foundation
Strong Foundation (Hattie M.)
Wallace Genetic Foundation
Wilkes, Artis, Hedrick & Lane

Florida

Appleby Trust (Scott B. and Annie P.)
BankAtlantic Bancorp
Beattie Foundation (Cordelia Lee)
Beveridge Foundation, Inc. (Frank Stanley)
Bush Charitable Foundation, Inc. (Edyth)
Carnival Corp.
Chatlos Foundation
Cobb Family Foundation
Davis Foundations (Arthur Vining)
Doyle Foundation
Dunspaugh-Dalton Foundation
duPont Foundation (Alfred I.)
Florida Rock Industries Inc.
Florida Rock & Tank Lines
Gulf Power Co.
Houck Foundation (May Kay)
Kennedy Family Foundation (Ethel and W. George)
Kennedy Foundation (Ethel)
Knight Foundation (John S. and James L.)
Koch Foundation, Inc.
Landegger Charitable Foundation
Lattner Foundation (Forrest C.)
Lowe Foundation (Joe and Emily)
Magruder Foundation (Chesley G.)
Martin Foundation
Mendel Foundation
Metal Industries Inc.
Morgan Foundation (Louie R. and Gertrude)
Peterson Charitable Foundation (Folke H.)
Publix Supermarkets
Rayonier Inc.
Royal Foundation (May Mitchell)
Scaife Family Foundation
Selby and Marie Selby Foundation (William G.)
Simon Foundation (Sidney, Milton, and Leoma)
Speer Foundation (Roy M.)
SunTrust Banks of Florida
Swisher Foundation (Carl S.)
United States Sugar Corp.
Wahlert Foundation
Winn-Dixie Stores Inc.

Georgia

Arnold Fund
BellSouth Corp.
Bowman Foundation (Wayne and Ida)
Callaway Foundation, Inc.
Camp Younts Foundation
Campbell Foundation (J. Bulow)
Citizens Union Bank
Clary Foundation, Inc. (Eugene M.)

Coca-Cola Co.
Colonial Group Inc.
Community Enterprises
Cox Enterprises Inc.
Equifax Inc.
Georgia-Pacific Corp.
Georgia Power Co.
Haley Foundation (W. B.)
Harland Charitable Foundation (John H. and Wilhelmina D.)
ING North America Insurance Corp.
Martin Charitable Trust (Margaret Lee)
Morris Communications Corp.
Petrie Trust (Lorene M.)
Porter Testamentary Trust (James Hyde)
Rich Foundation
Smith Foundation (William R. and Sara Babb)
SunTrust Bank Atlanta
SunTrust Banks Inc.
Thomaston F.S.B.
Trippe Trust (William D.)
United Parcel Service of America Inc.
Whitehead Foundation (Joseph B.)
Williams Family Foundation of Georgia
Winter Construction Co.
Woodruff Foundation (Robert W.)

Hawaii

Atherton Family Foundation
Atherton Foundation (Leburta)
Baldwin Memorial Foundation (Fred)
Castle Foundation (Harold K. L.)
Castle Foundation (Samuel N. and Mary)
Cooke Foundation
First Hawaiian Inc.
Frear Eleemosynary Trust (Mary D. and Walter F.)
McInerny Foundation
Resco Inc.
Wong Foundation (Lin and Ella)

Idaho

Albertson's Inc.
Boise Cascade Corp.
CHC Foundation
Cimino Foundation (James and Barbara)
Cunningham Foundation (Laura Moore)
Engl Family Foundation (Michael S.)
Intermountain Gas Co.
Morrison Foundation (Harry W.)
Ore-Ida Foods
Washington Group International Inc.
Whiting Foundation (Macauley and Helen Dow)
Whittenberger Foundation (Claude R. and Ethel B.)

Illinois

Abbott Laboratories

Akzo Nobel Chemicals
AMCORE Financial Inc.
Aon Corp.
Archer-Daniels-Midland Co.
Bere Foundation
Blowitz-Ridgeway Foundation
Blum-Kovler Foundation
Boothroyd Foundation (Charles H. and Bertha L.)
Brach Foundation (Helen)
Brunswick Corp.
Burnett Co. (Leo)
Caestecker Foundation (Charles and Marie)
Camp and Bennet Humiston Trust (Apollos)
Caterpillar Inc.
Cheney Foundation (Elizabeth F.)
Chicago Board of Trade
Chicago Rawhide Co.
Chicago Title Corp.
Chicago Tribune Direct Marketing
Citizens First National Bank
CLARCOR Inc.
Claypool Foundation (Silas and Ruth)
CNA Financial Corp.
Coleman Foundation (IL)
Cox Charitable Trust (A. G.)
Crown Memorial (Arie and Ida)
Cudahy Fund (Patrick and Anna M.)
Deere & Co.
Demos Foundation (N.)
Dillon Foundation
Donnelley & Sons Co. (R.R.)
Duchossois Family Foundation
Exelon
Field Foundation of Illinois
Fischer Foundation (Sonja and F. Conrad)
Fortune Brands Inc.
Fry Foundation (Lloyd A.)
Galvin Foundation (Robert)
GATX Corp.
Geifman Family Foundation
Genius Charitable Trust (Elizabeth Morse)
Graham Foundation for Advanced Studies in the Fine Arts
Hartmarx Corp.
Heath Foundation (Mary)
Hegeler II Foundation (Julius W.)
Hermann Foundation (Grover)
Ideal Industries Inc.
Illinois Tool Works Inc.
Integra Bank
Jaffee Foundation
Johnson Foundation (A.D.)
Kemper National Insurance Cos.
Kern Foundation Trust
Korte Construction Co.
Kovler Family Foundation
Lederer Foundation (Francis L.)
Lehmann Foundation (Otto W.)
MacArthur Foundation (John D. and Catherine T.)
McCormick Foundation (Chauncey and Marion Deering)

McCormick Tribune Foundation (Robert R.)
Mellinger Educational Foundation (Edward Arthur)
Meyers Charitable Family Fund
Moore and Arletta E. Moore Foundation (Kenneth S.)
Morrill Charitable Foundation
Motorola Inc.
Myers Charitable Trust
National Manufacturing Co.
Norris Foundation (Dellora A. and Lester J.)
Norton Memorial Corp. (Geraldi)
Nuveen Co. (The John)
Offield Family Foundation (The)
Ohio National Life Insurance Co.
Payne Foundation (Frank E. and Seba B.)
Peoples Energy Corp.
Pick, Jr. Fund (Albert)
Polk Brothers Foundation, Inc.
Prentice Foundation (Abra)
Quincy Newspapers
Regenstein Foundation
Retirement Research Foundation
Rice Foundation
Russell Charitable Foundation (Tom)
Saemann Foundation (Franklin I.)
Sara Lee Corp.
Scherer Foundation (Karla)
Scholl Foundation (Dr.)
Seabury Foundation
Southwest News Herald
Square D Co.
State Farm Mutual Automobile Insurance Co.
Stuart Foundation (Elbridge and Evelyn)
Tribune Co.
Tyndale House Foundation
UAL Corp.
USG Corp.
Vermilion Healthcare Foundation
White Foundation (W. P. and H. B.)
Worner Trust
Yost Trust (J. Paul)

Indiana

1st Source Corp.
American General Finance
Anderson Foundation (John W.)
Anthem Inc.
Auburn Foundry
Ayres Foundation
Ball Brothers Foundation
Ball Foundation (George and Frances)
Bowsher-Booher Foundation
Clowes Fund
Cole Foundation (Olive B.)
Conseco Inc.
Cummins Inc.
Decio Foundation (Arthur J.)
Foellinger Foundation
Ford Meter Box Co.
Glick Foundation (Eugene and Marilyn)
Griffith Foundation (W. C.)

Indiana Mills & Manufacturing
Indianapolis Newspapers Inc.
Journal-Gazette Co.
Kuhne Foundation Trust (Charles W.)
Lilly & Co. (Eli)
Lilly Endowment
McFarland Charitable Trust (H. Richard)
McMillen Foundation
Noyes, Jr. Memorial Foundation (Nicholas H.)
Oliver Memorial Trust Foundation
Ontario Corp.
Pulliam Charitable Trust (Nina Mason)
Raker Foundation (M. E.)
Reilly Industries Inc.
Rieke Corp.
Schneider Foundation (Dr. Louis A. and Anne B.)
Simon Charitable Foundation Number One (Melvin and Bren)
South Bend Tribune Corp.
Tobias Foundation (Randall L.)
Vann Family Foundation
Zollner Foundation

Iowa

Ahrens Foundation (Claude W. and Dolly)
Amerus Group Co.
Audubon State Bank
Bechtel Charitable Remainder Uni-Trust (Harold R.)
Bechtel Charitable Remainder Uni-Trust (Marie H.)
Carver Charitable Trust (Roy J.)
Employers Mutual Casualty Co.
Fiserve
Forster Charitable Trust (James W. and Ella B.)
Gazette Co.
Grinnell Mutual Reinsurance Co.
Guaranty Bank & Trust Co.
Hall-Perrine Foundation
Harper Brush Works
HON Industries Inc.
Iowa Savings Bank
Kinney-Lindstrom Foundation
Kuyper Foundation (Peter H. and E. Lucille Gaass)
Lee Endowment Foundation
Lee Enterprises Inc.
Lisle Corp.
McElroy Trust (R. J.)
Meredith Corp.
Mid-Iowa Health Foundation
Owen Industries
Pella Corp.
Principal Financial Group
Sheaffer Pen Corp.
Stebens Charitable Foundation (Bertha)
Van Buren Foundation
Weathertop Foundation
Wellmark Blue Cross and Blue Shield of Iowa
Winnebago Industries

Kansas

Baehr Foundation (Louis W. and Dolpha)

Baughman Foundation
Bryden Foundation (Blanche)
Central National Bank
Cessna Aircraft Co.
Cray Residuary Charitable Trust (Evah C.)
Davis Foundation (James A. and Juliet L.)
DeVore Foundation
Excel Corp.
Gault-Hussey Charitable Trust
Hansen Foundation (Dane G.)
Hauptli Charitable Foundation (A. John and Barbara A.)
Kansas Health Foundation
Koch Industries Inc.
Mingenback Foundation (Julia J.)
Powell Family Foundation
Ross Foundation
Security Benefit Life Insurance Co.
Smoot Charitable Foundation
Sunderland Foundation
Williams Charitable Trust (Mary Jo)
Yellow Roadway Corp.
Young Foundation (Bill B.)

Kentucky

Abercrombie Foundation
Blood-Horse Charitable Foundation
Brown Foundation, Inc. (James Graham)
Brown Foundation (W. L. Lyons)
Brown & Williamson Tobacco Corp.
C. E. and S. Foundation
Community Trust Bancorp Inc.
Cooke Foundation Corp. (V. V.)
Cralle Foundation
Duncan Trust (Louise Head)
Gheens Foundation
Houchens Foundation (Ervin G.)
Humana Inc.
LG&E Energy Corp.
Masland Trust No. 2 (Maurice H.)
Norton Foundation
Thomas Foundation (Joan and Lee)
Thomas Industries
Vogt Machine Co. (Henry)
Yeager Charitable Trust B (Lester E.)

Louisiana

Freeport-McMoRan Copper & Gold Inc.
German Protestant Orphan Asylum Association Foundation
Keller Family Foundation
Powers Foundation
RosaMary Foundation
Saia Foundation (Louis P.)
Schlieder Educational Foundation (Edward G.)
Southwestern Electric Power Co.
Wilson Foundation (Huey and Angeline)

Maine

Brook Family Foundation
Burnham Charitable Trust (Margaret E.)
Central Maine Power Co.
Davenport Trust Fund
Davies Benevolent Fund (Edward H.)
Gardiner Savings Institution
Key Bank of Maine
Mulford Trust (Clarence E.)
Oak Grove School
Orchard Foundation
Webber Oil Co.

Maryland

Abell Foundation
Alexander Edwards Trust (Margaret)
Baker, Jr. Memorial Fund (William G.)
Baker Trust (Clayton)
Baltimore Equity Society
Broomfield Charitable Foundation
Campbell Foundation (MD)
Casey Foundation (Eugene B.)
Clark-Winchcole Foundation
COMSAT International
Constellation Energy Group Inc.
Darby Foundation
Denit Trust for Charitable and Educational Purposes (Helen Pumphrey)
Fairchild Foundation, Inc. (Sherman)
France-Merrick Foundation
Giant Food Inc.
Goldseker Foundation of Maryland (Morris)
Gordon Charitable Trust (Peggy and Yale)
Gudelsky Family Foundation (Homer and Martha)
Hecht-Levi Foundation
Henson Foundation (Richard A.)
Hughes Medical Institute (Howard)
Keats Family Foundation
Kerr Fund (Grayce B.)
Knapp Foundation, Inc. (MD)
Knott Foundation (Marion I. and Henry J.)
Leidy Foundation (John J.)
Lockhart Vaughan Foundation
Marpat Foundation
McCormick & Company Inc.
Mechanic Foundation (Morris A.)
Middendorf Foundation
Morgan and Samuel Tate Morgan, Jr. Foundation (Marietta McNeill)
Perdue Farms
Price Associates (T. Rowe)
Procter & Gamble Company, Cosmetics Div.
Rollins-Luetkemeyer Foundation
Rouse Co.
Sinnisen Foundation (Albert E. and Naomi B.)
Unger Foundation (Aber D.)
Wallis Trust (Dorothy Wagner)

Warfield Memorial Fund
(Anna Emory)
Widgeon Foundation
Wilson Sanitarium for Children of Baltimore City
(Thomas)

Massachusetts

Acushnet Foundation
Alden Trust (George I.)
Alden Trust (John W.)
Allmerica Financial Corp.
Ansin Foundation (Ronald
M.)
Arakelian Foundation (Mary
Alice)
Ash Charitable Corp.
Azadoutioun Foundation
Babson Foundation (Paul
and Edith)
Balfour Foundation (L. G.)
Barrington Foundation
Bay State Bancorp Inc.
Beaucourt Foundation
Bendit Charitable Foundation
(Leo H.)
Boston Globe (The)
Building 19 Foundation
Cabot Corp.
Cabot Family Charitable
Trust
Campbell and Adah E. Hall
Charity Fund (Bushrod
H.)
Cape Cod Five Cents Savings Bank
Carroll Charitable Foundation
Childs Charitable Foundation
(Roberta M.)
Country Curtains Inc.
Cove Charitable Trust
Cox Charitable Trust (Jessie
B.)
Daniels Foundation (Fred
Harris)
Davis Foundation (Irene E.
and George A.)
Demoulas Supermarkets Inc.
Dunkin' Donuts Inc.
East Cambridge Savings
Bank
Eastern Bank
Ellsworth Foundation (Ruth
H. and Warren A.)
Erving Industries
Fidelity Investments
Fletcher Foundation
Friendship Fund
Fuller Foundation (George F.
and Sybil H.)
Gillette Co.
Goldberg Family Foundation
Grimshaw-Gudewicz Charitable Foundation
Hamilton Charitable Corp.
Hancock Financial Services
(John)
Harrington Foundation (Francis A. and Jacquelyn H.)
Henderson Foundation
Henderson Foundation
(George B.)
Hershey Family Foundation
Higgins Foundation (John W.
and Clara C.)
Hoche-Scofield Foundation
Home for Aged Men in the
City of Brockton
Hopedale Foundation
Hornblower Fund (Henry)
Hyde Manufacturing Co.

Island Foundation (MA)
Jaffe Foundation
Johnson Fund (Edward C.)
Keel Foundation
Kelley and Elza Kelley Foundation (Edward Bangs)
Kendall Foundation (Henry
P.)
Killam Trust (Constance)
Kilmartin Industries
Ladd Charitable Corp. (Helen
and George)
Levy Foundation (June Rockwell)
Massachusetts Mutual Life
Insurance Co.
McCarthy Memorial Trust
Fund (Catherine)
McEvoy Foundation (Mildred
H.)
Memorial Foundation for the
Blind
Merck Family Fund
Mifflin Memorial Fund
(George H. and Jane A.)
Millipore Corp.
Norcross Wildlife Foundation
NSTAR
Pappas Charitable Foundation (Thomas Anthony)
Parametric Technology Corp.
Pardoe Foundation (Samuel
P.)
Peabody Charitable Fund
(Amelia)
Peabody Foundation (Amelia)
Phillips Foundation (Ellis L.)
Pierce Charitable Trust (Harold Whitworth)
Poitras Charitable Trust (Dorothy W.)
Poorvu Foundation (William
J. and Lia G.)
Proctor Foundation (Mattina
R.)
Prouty Foundation (Olive
Higgins)
Provident Community Foundation
Rabb Charitable Foundation
(Sidney and Esther)
Rabb Charitable Trust (Sidney R.)
Ratshesky Foundation (A.
C.)
Riley Foundation (Mabel
Louise)
Roddy Foundation (Fred M.)
Rogers Family Foundation
Rubin Family Fund (Cele H.
and William B.)
Russell Trust (Josephine G.)
Saltonstall Charitable Foundation (Richard)
Sawyer Charitable Foundation
Shatz, Schwartz & Fentin
P.C.
Shaw's Supermarkets Inc.
Sherman Trust (Margaret E.)
Smith Family Foundation
(Richard and Susan)
State Street Corp.
Stearns Trust (Artemas W.)
Steiger Memorial Fund (Albert)
Stevens Foundation (Abbot
and Dorothy H.)
Stevens Foundation (Nathaniel and Elizabeth P.)
Stoddard Charitable Trust

Stratford Foundation
Thompson Trust (Thomas)
TJX Companies Inc.
Tupancy-Harris Foundation
of 1986
Van Buren Foundation (Elsie
Procter)
Wallace Foundation (George
R.)
Walsh Charity Trust
(Blanche)
Webster Foundation (Edwin
S.)
Wheeler Trust (Nathaniel)
Winthrop Trust (Clara B.)
Wood Foundation of Chambersburg, PA
Woronoco Savings Bank
Wyman-Gordon Co.
Yawkey Foundation II

Michigan

Abrams Foundation (Talbert
and Leota)
Ash Foundation (Stanley P.
and Blanche E.)
Barstow Foundation
Batts Foundation
Bauervic Foundation
(Charles M.)
Bauervic-Paisley Foundation
Besser Foundation
Bishop Charitable Trust (A.
G.)
Boutell Memorial Fund
Carls Foundation
Chamberlain Foundation
Comerica Inc.
Consumers Energy Co.
Delano Foundation (Mignon
Sherwood)
DeRoy Testamentary Foundation
DeVos Foundation (Richard
and Helen)
Dow Corning Corp.
Dow Foundation (Herbert H.
and Grace A.)
DTE Energy Co.
Earhart Foundation
Eddy Family Memorial Fund
(C. K.)
Ewald Foundation (H. T.)
Farmer Jack Supermarkets
Farwell Foundation (Drusilla)
Ford Fund (Walter and Josephine)
Ford Fund (William and Martha)
Ford II Fund (Edsel B.)
Ford II Fund (Henry)
Ford Motor Co.
Fruehauf Foundation
General Motors Corp.
Gerber Products Co.
Gerstacker Foundation (Rollin M.)
Gilmore Foundation (Irving
S.)
Herrick Foundation
Holnam Inc.
Hudson-Webber Foundation
Hurst Foundation
Interkal Inc.
JSJ Corp.
Kantzler Foundation
Kaufman Endowment Fund
(Louis G.)
Kaufman Foundation
Keeler Foundation
Keller Foundation

Kresge Foundation
La-Z-Boy Inc.
Lee Scholarship Fund Trust
(Whilma B.)
Loutit Foundation
Magna International of America Inc.
McGregor Fund
Merkley Charitable Trust
Miller Foundation
Mills Fund (Frances Goll)
Morley Foundation
Mott Foundation (Charles
Stewart)
National Standard Co.
Newman Family Foundation
Oleson Foundation
Plym Foundation
R&B Machine Tool Co.
Ratner Foundation (Milton
M.)
Sage Foundation
Sebastian Foundation
Skillman Foundation
Spartan Stores Inc.
Steelcase Inc.
Strosacker Foundation
(Charles J.)
Taubman Foundation (A. Alfred)
Thoman Foundation (W. B.
and Candace)
Tiscornia Foundation
Todd Co. (A.M.)
Towsley Foundation (Harry
A. and Margaret D.)
Upjohn Foundation (Harold
and Grace)
Upton Foundation (Frederick
S.)
Van Andel Foundation (Jay
and Betty)
Vicksburg Foundation
Vollbrecht Foundation (Frederick A.)
Weatherwax Foundation
Wege Foundation
Whirlpool Corp.
Whiting Foundation
Wickes Foundation (Harvey
Randall)
Wickson-Link Memorial
Foundation
Wilson Fund (Matilda R.)
World Heritage Foundation

Minnesota

ADC Telecommunications
Allianz Life Insurance Company of North America
Andersen Corp.
Andersen Foundation
Andersen Foundation (Hugh
J.)
Bemis Company Inc.
Best Buy Co.
Bigelow Foundation (F. R.)
Blandin Foundation
Bremer Foundation (Otto)
Bush Foundation
Butler Family Foundation
(Patrick and Aimee)
Cargill Inc.
Carlson Companies Inc.
Davis Foundation (Edwin W.
and Catherine M.)
Donaldson Company Inc.
Driscoll Foundation
Ecolab Inc.
Federated Mutual Insurance
Co.

Fuller Co. (H.B.)
General Mills Inc.
Graco Inc.
Griggs and Mary Griggs
Burke Foundation (Mary
Livingston)
Grotto Foundation
Hallett Charitable Trust (E.
W.)
Heilmaier Charitable Foundation (Anna M.)
Hickory Tech Corp.
Homecrest Industries Inc.
HRK Foundation
Hubbard Broadcasting Inc.
International Multifoods Corp.
Jostens Inc.
Land O'Lakes Inc.
Lilly Foundation (Richard
Coyle)
Marbrook Foundation
Mardag Foundation
McNeely Foundation
Medtronic Inc.
Metris Companies Inc.
Midcontinent Media Inc.
Minnesota Mining & Manufacturing Co.
Minnesota Mutual Life Insurance Co.
Neilson Foundation (George
W.)
Osborne Enterprises
O'Shaughnessy Foundation
(I. A.)
Phillips Family Foundation
(The Jay and Rose)
Rahr Malting Co.
Red Wing Shoe Company
Inc.
Regis Corp.
Saint Croix Foundation
St. Paul Travelers Companies Inc.
Schmoker Family Foundation
Southways Foundation
Specialty Manufacturing Co.
Stearns Foundation
Target Corp.
TCF National Bank Minnesota
Toro Co.
Tozer Foundation
U.S. Bancorp Piper Jaffray
Weyerhaeuser Memorial
Foundation (Charles A.)
Xcel Energy

Mississippi

Bryan Foods
Hardin Foundation (Phil)
Sullivan Foundation (Algernon Sydney)
Walker Foundation

Missouri

ACF Industries
Ameren Corp.
American Century Companies Inc.
Andrews McMeel Universal
Anheuser-Busch Companies
Inc.
Bakewell Corp.
Barrows Foundation (Geraldine and R. A.)
Bartlett & Co.
Bromley Residuary Trust
(Guy I.)
Burns & McDonnell

Commerce Bancshares Inc.
Cowden Foundation (Louetta M.)
Dula Educational and Charitable Foundation (Caleb C. and Julia W.)
Francis Families Foundation
Garvey Memorial Foundation (Edward Chase)
Green Foundation (Allen P. and Josephine B.)
Hall Family Foundation (The)
H&R Block Inc.
Jordan and Ettie A. Jordan Charitable Foundation (Mary Ranken)
Kansas City Southern Railway
Kauffman Foundation (Ewing Marion)
Kemper Foundation (William T.)
Loose Trust (Harry Wilson)
Lowe Family Foundation
Maritz Inc.
May Department Stores Co.
McGee Foundation (MO)
Messing Family Charitable Foundation
Miller-Mellor Association
Monsanto Co.
Morgan Charitable Residual Trust (W. and E.)
Moss Charitable Trust (Finis M.)
Nestle Purina PetCare Co.
Olin Foundation (Spencer T. and Ann W.)
Oppenstein Brothers Foundation
Pott Foundation (Herman T. and Phenie R.)
Pulitzer Inc.
Reliable Life Insurance Co.
Schutte Foundation (Victor E. and Caroline E.)
Shaw Foundation (Arch W.)
Shelter Mutual Insurance Co.
Slusher Charitable Foundation (Roy W.)
Smith Foundation (Ralph L.)
Speas Foundation (Victor E.)
Speas Memorial Trust (John W. and Effie E.)
Steadley Memorial Trust (Kent D. and Mary L.)
Stupp Foundation (Norman J.)
Sunnen Foundation
Swift Charitable Trust
Tension Envelope Corp.
Turner Charitable Trust (Courtney S.)
Van Evera Foundation (Dewitt)

Montana

Allen Foundation (Nibs and Edna)
Anderson Foundation (L. P. and Teresa)
Bair Family Trust (Charles M.)
Boe Brothers Foundation
Washington Foundation (Dennis R. and Phyllis)

Nebraska

Ameritas Life Insurance Corp.
Baright Foundation (Hollis and Helen)
Cooper Foundation
Farr Trust (Frank M. and Alice M.)
Giger Foundation (Paul and Oscar)
Heuermann Foundation (Bernard K. and Norma F.)
Hitchcock Foundation (Gilbert M. and Martha H.)
Kawasaki Motors Manufacturing Corporation U.S.A.
Kiewit Foundation (Peter)
Kiewit Sons' Inc. (Peter)
Livingston Foundation (Milton S. and Corinne N.)
Pamida Inc.
Quivey-Bay State Foundation
Reynolds Foundation (Edgar & Francis)
Scoular Co.
Union Pacific Corp.
Valmont Industries Inc.
Wells Fargo Bank Nebraska, N.A.
Woods Charitable Fund

Nevada

Bretzlaff Foundation
Buck Foundation (Carol Franc)
Cord Foundation (E. L.)
Harris Foundation (William H. and Mattie Wattis)
Hawkins Foundation (Robert Z.)
Lied Foundation Trust
Pennington Foundation (William N. and Myriam)
Ray Foundation
Redfield Foundation (Nell J.)
Reynolds Foundation (Donald W.)
Sierra Pacific Resources
Stout Foundation (Charles H.)
Wiegand Foundation (E. L.)

New Hampshire

Barker Foundation Inc.
Bean Foundation (Norwin S. and Elizabeth N.)
Benz Trust (Doris L.)
Byrne Foundation
Cogswell Benevolent Trust
Dingman Foundation (Michael D.)
Foundation for Seacoast Health
Fuller Foundation (MA)
Henney Trust (Keith)
Hunt Foundation (Samuel P.)
Jameson Trust (Oleonda)
Kingsbury Corp.
Mascoma Savings Bank
Monadnock Paper Mills Inc.
National Grange Mutual Insurance Co.
Putnam Foundation
Smyth Trust (Marion C.)
Unitrode Corp.

New Jersey

American Standard Inc.
Ballet Makers
Brady Foundation
Brundage Charitable, Scientific, and Wildlife Conservation Foundation (Charles E. and Edna T.)
Bunbury Co., Inc.
Campbell Soup Co.
Cape Branch Foundation
Carillon Importers Ltd.
Caspersen Foundation for Aid to Health and Education (O. W.)
Church & Dwight Company Inc.
CIT Group Inc.
Colt Foundation (James J.)
Conway Scholarship Foundation (Carle C.)
Cowles Charitable Trust
Crames Family Foundation (Arthur)
D&B
DBH Foundation for Law, Land, and the Felicitous Environment
Dodge Foundation (Geraldine R.)
Edison Fund (Charles)
Formosa Plastics Corporation, USA
Fund for New Jersey
Hoffmann-La Roche Inc.
Holzer Memorial Foundation (Richard H.)
Huber Foundation
Hyde and Watson Foundation
Jaqua Foundation
Jockey Hollow Foundation
Kajima International Inc.
Kalkus Foundation
Kaplen Foundation
Kirby Foundation (F. M.)
Klipstein Foundation (Ernest Christian)
Lazarus Charitable Trust
Lipton Co.
Maneely Fund
Martini Foundation (Nicholas)
New Jersey Natural Gas Co.
Newcombe Foundation (Charlotte W.)
Ohl, Jr. Trust (George A.)
Oki America Inc.
Pond Foundation (C. Northrop Pond and Alethea Marder)
Prudential Insurance Company of America
Public Service Electric & Gas Co.
Read Foundation (Charles L.)
Red Devil
Rippel Foundation (Fannie E.)
Sandy Hill Foundation
Schenck Charitable Foundation (L. P.)
Schering-Plough Corp.
Schumann Fund for New Jersey
Schwartz Foundation (Arnold A.)
Silverman Family Foundation
Simon Foundation (William E.)
Snyder Foundation (Harold B. and Dorothy A.)
Subaru of America Inc.
Terumo Medical Corp.
Tsumura International Inc.
Turrell Fund
Upton Charitable Foundation (Lucy and Eleanor S.)
Van Houten Memorial Fund (Edward W. and Stella C.)
Victoria Foundation
Welsh Family Foundation
Westerhoff Family Foundation, Inc.
Wiley & Sons Inc. (John)
Ziegelheim Charitable Foundation (Fran and Irwin)

New Mexico

Chamiza Foundation
Fab Steel Products Co.
Holt Foundation (William Knox)
Hubbard Foundation (R. D. and Joan Dale)
Maddox Foundation (J. F.)
McCune Charitable Foundation (Marshall L. and Perrine D.)
PNM Resources Inc.
Seidman Family Foundation
Stockman Family Foundation Trust

New York

ABC Inc.
Achelis Foundation
Air France
AKC Fund
Alavi Foundation
Alexander Foundation (Joseph)
Allyn Foundation
Altman Foundation
Ambrose Monell Foundation (The)
Anderson Foundation (NY)
AOL Time Warner
Archbold Charitable Trust (Adrian and Jessie)
Arkell Hall Foundation
Assurant
AT&T Corp.
Atran Foundation, Inc.
August Family Foundation (Charles J. and Burton S.)
Avery Arts Foundation (Milton and Sally)
Avon Products Inc.
Backus Foundation (Beatrice and Roy)
Badgeley Residuary Charitable Trust (Rose M.)
Baird Foundation
Baker Trust (George F.)
The Bank of Greene County
Bank of New York
Barker Foundation (J.M.R.)
Barker Welfare Foundation
Barth Foundation, Inc. (The Theodore H.)
Bat Hanadiv Foundation No. 3
Bauer Family Foundation
Bausch & Lomb Inc.
Bay Foundation
Becher Foundation (Hildegarde D.)
Benenson Foundation (Frances and Benjamin)
Benetton U.S.A. Corp.
Bernhard Foundation (Arnold)
Bingham Second Betterment Fund (William)
Birds Eye Foods Inc.
Bismarck Charitable Trust (Mona)
Bodman Foundation
Booth Ferris Foundation
Bowne Foundation (Robert)
Bristol-Myers Squibb Co.
Brookdale Foundation
Brooks Foundation (Gladys)
Burchfield Foundation (Charles E.)
Bydale Foundation
Candlesticks Inc.
Canon U.S.A. Inc.
Carnahan-Jackson Foundation
Carnegie Corp. of New York
Carvel Foundation (Thomas and Agnes)
Cary Charitable Trust (Mary Flagler)
CBS Corp.
Central Hudson Gas & Electric Corp.
Chadwick Fund (Dorothy Jordan)
Chapman Charitable Corp. (Howard and Bess)
Charitable Venture Foundation
Chazen Foundation
Cheatham Foundation (Owen)
Cheek Family Foundation (Trust for the)
Cheever Porter Foundation (Mrs.)
Children's Foundation of Erie County
Chisholm Foundation (M. A.)
Christian Dior Perfumes Inc.
CIBC World Markets
Citigroup Global Markets Holdings Inc.
Citigroup Inc.
City National Bank & Trust Co.
Claiborne and Art Ortenberg Foundation (Liz)
Claiborne Inc. (Liz)
Clark Foundation (NY)
Clark Foundation (Robert Sterling)
Commonwealth Fund (The)
ContiGroup Companies Inc.
Cook Foundation (Louella)
Cornell Trust (Peter C.)
Corning Inc.
Crary Foundation (Bruce L.)
Credit Suisse First Boston Corp.
Crosswicks Foundation
Cummings Memorial Fund (The Frances L. and Edwin L.)
Daily News L.P.
Dana Charitable Trust (Eleanor Naylor)
Dana Foundation (Charles A.)
Davenport-Hatch Foundation
de Coizart Perpetual Charitable Trust (Sarah K.)
DeCamp Foundation (Ira W.)
Decker Foundation (Dr. G. Clifford and Florence B.)
Dedalus Foundation
Delmas Foundation (Gladys Krieble)
Dewar Foundation
Dickenson Foundation (Harriet Ford)
Dickler Family Foundation

Dodge Foundation (Cleveland H.)
Doherty Charitable Foundation (Henry L. and Grace)
Donaldson Charitable Trust (Oliver S. and Jennie R.)
Dow Jones & Company Inc.
Dreyfus Corp.
Dreyfus Foundation, Inc. (Max and Victoria)
Dreyfus Foundation (Jean and Louis)
Ducommun and Gross Foundation
Duke Foundation (Doris)
Dyson Foundation
Eastman Kodak Co.
Eckman Charitable Foundation (Samuel and Rae)
Edmonds Foundation (Dean S.)
Emerson Foundation, Inc. (Fred L.)
Erpf Fund (Armand G.)
Everett Charitable Trust
Farash Charitable Foundation (Max and Marian)
Faulkner Trust (Marianne G.)
Ferkauf Foundation (Eugene and Estelle)
Ferriday Fund Charitable Trust
Fink Foundation (NY)
Ford Foundation
Foundation for Child Development
Freeman Charitable Trust (Samuel)
French Foundation (D.E.)
Frese Foundation (Arnold D.)
Fromkes Foundation (Saul)
Garfinkle-Minard Foundation, Inc.
Gebbie Foundation
Gifford Charitable Corp. (Rosamond)
Gilman Foundation (Howard)
Gleason Foundation
Goldman Foundation (Herman)
Golub Corp.
Goodman Family Foundation
Gould Foundation (The Florence)
Grant Foundation (Charles M. and Mary D.)
Greentree Foundation
Greenwall Foundation
Guardian Life Insurance Company of America
Guggenheim Foundation (Harry Frank)
Gund Foundation (Geoffrey)
Guttman Foundation (Stella and Charles)
Hagedorn Fund
Handy & Harman
Harkness Foundation for Dance
HarperCollins Publishers Inc.
Harriman Foundation (Gladys and Roland)
Harriman Foundation (Mary W.)
Hartford Foundation, Inc. (The John A.)
Hayden Foundation (Charles)
Hazen Foundation (Edward W.)
Hearst Foundation, Inc. (The)
Hearst Foundation (William Randolph)

Hebrew Technical Institute
Heckscher Foundation for Children
Heinz Trust (Drue)
Heyward Memorial Fund (DuBose and Dorothy)
Hill Foundation (Sandy)
Hilliard Corp.
Hino Diesel Trucks (U.S.A.)
Holmberg Foundation
Holtzmann Foundation (Jacob L. and Lillian)
Homeland Foundation (NY)
Hopkins Foundation (Josephine Lawrence)
Howard and Bush Foundation
Hudson River Bancorp Inc.
Hughes Foundation (Geoffrey C.)
Hugoton Foundation
Hulbert Foundation (Nila B.)
Hultquist Foundation
Icahn Foundation (Carl C.)
IF Hummingbird Foundation
International Business Machines
Ittleson Foundation
Jenjo Foundation
JM Foundation
Johnson Charitable Trust (Keith Wold)
Johnson Foundation (Howard)
Johnson Foundation (Thomas Phillips and Jane Moore)
Johnson Foundation (Willard T. C.)
Johnson Memorial Trust (John Alfred and Oscar)
Jones Foundation (Daisy Marquis)
Joy Family Foundation
Jurzykowski Foundation (Alfred)
Kahn, Lucas-Lancaster Incorporated Children's Wear
Kaplan Fund (J. M.)
Kaplun Foundation (Morris J. and Betty)
Katzenberger Foundation
KeySpan Corp.
King Family Foundation (Charles and Lucille)
Kinney Memorial Foundation
Klee Foundation (Conrad and Virginia)
Klingenstein Fund, Inc. (Esther A. and Joseph)
Klingestein Fund
Klock and Lucia Klock Kingston Foundation (Jay E.)
Klosk Fund (Rose and Louis)
Knox Foundation (Seymour H.)
Kornfeld Foundation (Emily Davie and Joseph S.)
Kovarik Foundation for Poetry (Henry P.)
Kranes Charitable Trust (Sidney and Judith)
Kress Foundation (Samuel H.)
Kurz Family Foundation
L and L Foundation
Lake Placid Education Foundation
Lang Foundation (Eugene M.)
Lasdon Foundation (William and Mildred)

Lauder Foundation
Lemberg Foundation
Lenna Foundation (Reginald A. and Elizabeth S.)
Levitt Foundation (NY)
Liberman Foundation (Bertha and Isaac)
Link, Jr. Foundation (George)
Littauer Foundation (Lucius N.)
Loews Corp.
Loewy Family Foundation
Long Island Lighting Co.
Lowenstein Foundation (Leon)
LSR Fund
Luce Foundation (Henry)
Lurcy Charitable and Educational Trust (Georges)
Macy, Jr. Foundation (Josiah)
Macy's East Inc.
Mailman Family Foundation (A. L.)
Marx Foundation (Virginia and Leonard)
Mather Fund (Richard)
Mathers Charitable Foundation (G. Harold and Leila Y.)
Mathis-Pfohl Foundation
MBIA Inc.
McCann Foundation
McGonagle Foundation (Dextra Baldwin)
McGraw-Hill Companies Inc.
Meier Foundation (Richard)
Mellon Foundation (Andrew W.)
Memton Fund
Mercury Aircraft Inc.
Merrill Lynch & Company Inc.
Metropolitan Life Insurance Co.
Mex-Am Cultural Foundation
Millbrook Tribute Garden
MONY Group Inc.
Morgan Chase & Co. (J.P.)
Morris Foundation (Norman M.)
Morris Foundation (William T.)
Moses Fund, Inc. (Henry and Lucy)
Neuberger Foundation (Roy R. and Marie S.)
New-Land Foundation
New York Foundation
New York Life Insurance Co.
New York Mercantile Exchange
New York Stock Exchange Inc.
New York Times Co.
New Yorker Magazine (The)
Newman Assistance Fund (Jerome A. and Estelle R.)
Niagara Mohawk Holdings Inc.
NLI International Inc.
Norman Foundation
Normandie Foundation
O'Connor Foundation (A. Lindsay and Olive B.)
Oishei Foundation (The John R.)
Olin Foundation (John M.)
Oneida Savings Bank
L'Oreal U.S.A.

Osborn Charitable Trust (Edward B.)
Overbrook Foundation (The)
Paley Foundation, Inc. (William S.)
Palisades Educational Foundation
Park Foundation
Parshelsky Foundation (Moses L.)
Paul and C. Michael Paul Foundation (Josephine Bay)
Pforzheimer Foundation, Inc. (The Carl and Lily)
Piankova Foundation (Tatiana)
Pinkerton Foundation
Prospect Hill Foundation
Prudential Securities Inc.
Raymond Corp.
Reader's Digest Association Inc.
Reed Foundation (NY)
Reuss Memorial Trust (Allene)
Revson Foundation (Charles H.)
Reynolds Foundation (Christopher)
Rheinstrom Hill Community Foundation
Rich Products Corp.
Richardson Fund (Ann S.)
Riedman Foundation
Robinson-Broadhurst Foundation
Robinson Fund (Maurice R.)
Rockefeller Brothers Fund, Inc.
Rockefeller Fund (David)
Rohatyn Foundation (Felix and Elizabeth)
Rose Foundation (Billy)
Rosenthal Foundation (Ida and William)
Rothschild Foundation (Judith)
Rubin Foundation (Samuel)
Rubinstein Foundation (Helena)
Rudin Foundation
Rudin Foundation (Samuel and May)
St. Giles Foundation
Samuels Foundation (Fan Fox and Leslie R.)
Sasco Foundation
Scherman Foundation
Scheuer Family Foundation Inc. (S. H. and Helen R.)
Schieffelin Residuary Trust (Sarah I.)
Schiff Foundation (Dorothy)
Schlumberger Ltd.
Schmitt Foundation (Kilian J. and Caroline F.)
Schwartz Fund for Education and Health Research (Arnold and Marie)
Seherr-Thoss Foundation
Seneca Foods Corp.
Sharp Foundation (Evelyn)
Sheldon Foundation Inc. (Ralph C.)
Shubert Foundation
Slater Trust (Lillian M.)
Snow Foundation (John Ben)
Snow Memorial Trust (John Ben)
Snyder Charitable Trust (Harrison C. and Margaret A.)

Solow Foundation
Sound Shore Foundation
Sperandio Family Foundation
Spewack Article 5th Trust (Bella)
Sprague Educational and Charitable Foundation (Seth)
Starr Foundation
Statler Foundation
Steele-Reese Foundation
Sulzberger Foundation
Summerfield Foundation, Inc. (Solon E.)
Taconic Foundation
Teagle Foundation
Thompson Co. (J. Walter)
Tinker Foundation
Trust for Mutual Understanding
Tuch Foundation (Michael)
UBS PaineWebber Inc.
Unilever United States Inc.
United Armenian Charities
United States-Japan Foundation
United States Trust Company of New York
Utica National Insurance Group
van Ameringen Foundation, Inc.
Verizon Communications Inc.
Vernon Foundation (Miles Hodsdon)
Vetlesen Foundation (G. Unger)
Viyu Foundation
Vogler Foundation (Laura B.)
The Wallace Foundation
Warhol Foundation for the Visual Arts (The Andy)
Warner Fund (Albert and Bessie)
Warren and Beatrice W. Blanding Foundation (Riley J. and Lillian N.)
Wasserstein Perella Foundation
Waterhouse Family Foundation
Weezie Foundation
Weil, Gotshal & Manges Corp.
Weinstein Foundation (J.)
Weir Foundation (Candace King)
Wendt Foundation (Margaret L.)
Western New York Foundation
WestLB New York Branch
Wilson Foundation (H. W.)
Wilson Foundation (Marie C. and Joseph C.)
Winston Foundation (Norman and Rosita)
Woodcock Foundation
Woodward Fund

North Carolina

Acme-McCrary Corp./Sapona Manufacturing Co.
Babcock Foundation (Mary Reynolds)
Bank of America Corp.
Belk Stores Services Inc.
Bergen Foundation (Frank and Lydia)
Biddle Foundation (Mary Duke)

Blue Bell Inc.
Blumenthal Foundation
Broyhill Family Foundation
Burlington Industries Inc.
Cannon Foundation, Inc. (The)
CCB Financial Corp.
Cemala Foundation
Dalton Foundation (Harry L.)
Dover Foundation
Duke Endowment
Duke Energy Corp.
Finch Foundation (Doak)
Finch Foundation (Thomas Austin)
Franklin Foundation Inc. (John and Mary)
Freas Foundation
Fredrickson Foundation (Ambrose and Ida)
Goodrich Corp.
Hanes Foundation (John Wesley and Anna Hodgin)
Harvey Foundation (C. Felix)
Hillsdale Fund
Janirve Foundation
Lowe's Cos.
McCarty Foundation (John and Margaret)
Miller Brewing Co. (Eden, NC)
Moore & Sons (B.C.)
Progress Energy Inc.
RBC Centura
Reichhold Chemicals Inc.
Rexam Inc.
Reynolds Tobacco (R.J.)
Royal & SunAlliance USA Inc.
Smith Horticultural Trust (Stanley)
SPX Corp.
Stonecutter Mills Corp.
Tanner Cos. (Rutherfordton, NC)
Thomasville Furniture Industries Inc.
Tri-County Telephone Foundation
Willis Family Foundation

North Dakota

MDU Resources Group Inc.

Ohio

AK Steel Holding Corp.
Alms Trust (Eleanora)
Amcast Industrial Corp.
Andersons Inc.
Andrews Foundation
Ashtabula Foundation
Baird Brothers Co. Foundation
Bardes Corp.
Beasley Charitable Trust (Lucy and Emily)
Beecher Foundation (Florence Simon)
Berkman Foundation (Louis and Sandra)
Berry Foundation (Loren M.)
Bicknell Fund
Bingham Foundation (William)
Britton Fund
Bruening Foundation (Eva L. and Joseph M.)
Brush Foundation

Calhoun Charitable Trust (Kenneth L.)
Cayuga Foundation
Cinergy Corp.
Cleveland-Cliffs Inc.
Codrington Charitable Foundation (George W.)
Columbus Dispatch Printing Co.
Cooper Tire & Rubber Co.
Corbett Foundation
Crandall Memorial Foundation (J. Ford)
Dana Corp.
Dater Foundation (Charles H.)
Dayton Power and Light Co.
Deuble Foundation (George H.)
Eaton Corp.
Eaton Foundation (Cyrus)
Emery Memorial (Thomas J.)
Evans Foundation (Thomas J.)
Farmer Family Foundation
Fifth Third Bancorp
Firestone, Jr. Foundation (Harvey)
Flowers Charitable Trust (Albert W. and Edith V.)
Forest City Enterprises Inc.
Fox Charitable Trust (Emma R.)
French Oil Mill Machinery Co.
Frohring Foundation (Paul and Maxine)
GAR Foundation
Grimes Foundation
Griswold Foundation (John C.)
Gund Foundation (George)
H. C. S. Foundation
Haman Family Foundation
Haskell Fund
Hershey Foundation
Honda of America Manufacturing Inc.
Hoover Foundation (The)
Hoover Foundation (Herbert W.)
Hoover Trust Fund (W. Henry)
Humphrey Fund (George M. and Pamela S.)
Huntington Bancshares Inc.
Ingalls Foundation (Louise H. and David S.)
Jarson Kaplan Foundation
Jennings Foundation (Martha Holden)
Kenridge Fund
Ketrow Foundation
Kettering Fund
Key Bank N.A.
Kilcawley Fund (William H.)
Kilworth Charitable Trust (Florence B.)
Kroger Co.
Kulas Foundation
Mandel Foundation (Jack N. and Lilyan)
Markey Charitable Fund (John C.)
Massie Trust (David Meade)
Mather Charitable Trust (S. Livingston)
Mather and William Gwinn Mather Fund (Elizabeth Ring)
Mayerson Foundation (Manuel D. and Rhoda)

McFawn-The Sisler McFawn Foundation (L. Sisler)
McMaster Foundation (Harold and Helen)
Minster Machine Co.
Morgan Foundation (Burton D.)
Musson Charitable Foundation (R. C. and Katharine M.)
National City Corp.
National Machinery Co.
Nord Family Foundation
Nordson Corp.
O'Bleness Foundation (Charles)
Peterloon Foundation
Pollock Co. Foundation (William B.)
Reeves Foundation (OH)
Reinberger Foundation
Ritter Charitable Trust (George and Mary)
Rosenberry Tuscarawas County Foundation (Harold C. and Marjorie Q.)
Rosenthal Foundation (Lois and Richard)
Ross Products Division, Abbott Laboratories
Rupp Foundation (Fran and Warren)
Russell Charitable Trust (Josephine S.)
Sapirstein-Stone-Weiss Foundation
Schlink Foundation (Albert G. and Olive H.)
Schmidlapp Trust No. 1 (Jacob G.)
Schmidlapp Trust No. 2 (Jacob G.)
Schooler Family Foundation (Ohio)
Scott Fetzer Co.
Scripps Co. (E.W.)
Semple Foundation (Louise Taft)
Sherwin-Williams Co.
Slemp Foundation
Smith Foundation (Kelvin and Eleanor)
South Waite Foundation
Stocker Foundation
Stone Foundation (France)
Straker Charitable Foundation (J. William and Mary Helen)
Stranahan Foundation
Timken Foundation of Canton
Toledo Blade Co.
Trumbull County Scholarship Foundation
Van Wert County Foundation
Watson Foundation (Walter E. and Caroline H.)
Western & Southern Life Insurance Co.
Wildermuth Foundation (E. F.)
Wilkof Foundation (Edward and Ruth)
Worthington Foods
Young Foundation (Hugo H. and Mabel B.)

Oklahoma

Aldridge Charitable and Educational Trust (Tom S. and Marye Kate)

American Fidelity Assurance Co.
Beatty Trust (Cordelia Lunceford)
Bernsen Foundation (Grace and Franklin)
Bovaird Foundation (Mervin)
Broadhurst Foundation
Chapman Charitable Trust (H. A. and Mary K.)
Collins Foundation (George and Jennie)
Collins, Jr. Foundation (George Fulton)
Goddard Foundation (Charles B.)
Harmon Foundation (Pearl M. and Julia J.)
Helmerich Foundation
Inasmuch Foundation
Kerr Foundation, Inc.
Kirkpatrick Foundation, Inc.
Lyon Foundation
Mabee Foundation, Inc. (J. E. and L. E.)
McCasland Foundation
McMahon Foundation
Meinders Foundation
Merrick Foundation
Noble Foundation (Samuel Roberts)
OG&E Electric Services
Puterbaugh Foundation
Sarkeys Foundation
Share Trust (Charles Morton)
Titus Foundation (C. W.)
Westby Foundation (Kathleen Patton)
Williams Companies Inc.
Zarrow Foundation (Anne and Henry)

Oregon

Adler Trust (Leo)
Bloch Foundation (Rene)
Braemar Charitable Trust
Carpenter Foundation
Chiles Foundation
Collins Foundation
Collins Medical Trust
Faith Foundation
Ford Family Foundation
Frank Family Foundation (A. J.)
Hunt Charitable Trust (C. Giles)
Jackson Foundation (OR)
Jeld-Wen Inc.
Johnson Foundation (Samuel S.)
Lamb Foundation
McKay Family Foundation
Meyer Memorial Trust
Mitsubishi Silicon America
Northwest Natural Gas Co.
PacifiCorp
Pioneer Trust Bank, N.A.
Templeton Foundation (Herbert A.)
Tucker Charitable Trust (Rose E.)
Wessinger Foundation
Wheeler Foundation
Woodard Foundation (W. A.)
Wyss Foundation

Pennsylvania

Air Products and Chemicals Inc.
Alcoa Inc.

Alexander Stewart MD Foundation Trust
Allegheny Foundation
AMETEK Inc.
AMP Inc.
Annenberg Foundation
Arcadia Foundation
Arronson Foundation
Asplundh Foundation
Baker Foundation (Dexter F. and Dorothy H.)
Bard Foundation (Robert)
Barra Foundation
Beneficia Foundation
Berwind Group
Betts Industries
Binney & Smith Inc.
Binswanger Cos.
Bishop Foundation (Vernon and Doris)
Bowman Proper Charitable Trust (J.)
Brossman Charitable Foundation (William and Jemima)
Bryn Mawr Bank Corp.
Buhl Foundation (PA)
Carpenter Foundation (E. Rhodes and Leona B.)
Cassett Foundation (Louis N.)
Charity Randall Foundation
Chase Trust (Alice P.)
CIGNA Corp.
Claneil Foundation
Clapp Charitable and Educational Trust (George H. and Anne L.)
Clemens Markets
Coen Family Foundation (Charles S. and Mary)
Colonial Oaks Foundation
Connelly Foundation
Crawford Estate Trust Fund A (E. R.)
Dendroica Foundation
Dentsply International Inc.
Dietrich Foundation (William B.)
Douty Foundation (Alfred and Mary)
Dynamet Inc.
Eberly Foundation
Eccles Foundation (Ralph M. and Ella M.)
Eden Hall Foundation
Elf Atochem North America Inc.
Fair Oaks Foundation
Falk Fund (Maurice)
Fels Fund (Samuel S.)
FMC Corp.
Foster Charitable Trust
Freeport Brick Co.
G/S/M Industrial Inc.
Garver Charity Fund (David B.)
Giant Eagle Inc.
Giant Food Stores
Grable Foundation
Graham Engineering Corp.
Greenfield Foundation (Albert M.)
Grundy Foundation
Hamer Foundation
Harsco Corp.
Heinz Co. (H.J.)
Heinz Endowment (Howard)
Heinz Endowment (Vira I.)
Heinz Family Foundation
Henkel Co.
Hershey Foods Corp.

High Foundation
Hillman Foundation
Hoch Foundation (Charles H.)
Holt Family Foundation
Hopwood Charitable Trust (John M.)
Hulme Charitable Foundation (Milton G.)
Hunt Corp.
Hunt Foundation (Roy A.)
Huston Charitable Trust (Stewart)
Huston Foundation
Independence Foundation
Jacobs Charitable Trust (Margaret G.)
J&L Specialty Steel Inc.
Jennings Foundation (Mary Hillman)
Jewish Healthcare Foundation
Justus Trust (Edith C.)
Kardon Foundation (Samuel and Rebecca)
Kavanagh Foundation (T. James)
Kline Foundation (Charles and Figa)
Kline Foundation (Josiah W. and Bessie H.)
Knudsen Charitable Foundation (Earl)
Kunkel Foundation (John Crain)
Lamco Communications
Laurel Foundation
Lebanon Mutual Insurance Co.
Lebovitz Fund
Lefton Co. (Al Paul)
Lehigh Cement Co.
Love Foundation (George H. and Margaret McClintic)
Ludwick Foundation (Christopher)
Mandeville Foundation
Massey Charitable Trust
McCausland Foundation
McCormick Charitable Trust (Margaret Ogilvie)
McCormick Trust (Anne)
McCune Charitable Trust (John R.)
McCune Foundation
McFeely-Rogers Foundation
McKenna Foundation (Katherine Mabis)
McKenna Foundation (Philip M.)
McLean Contributionship
Mellon Family Foundation (R. K.)
Mellon Financial Corp.
Mellon Foundation (Richard King)
Mengle Foundation (Glenn and Ruth)
Mine Safety Appliances Co.
Morris Charitable Trust (Charles M.)
Murphy Co. Foundation (G.C.)
Oxford Foundation
Patterson Charitable Fund (W. I.)
Penn Foundation (William)
Peters Charitable Trust (Edward V. and Jessie L.)
Peters Foundation (Charles F.)
Pew Charitable Trusts

Phillips Charitable Trust (Dr. and Mrs. Arthur William)
Pine Tree Foundation
Pittsburgh Child Guidance Foundation
Plankenhorn Foundation (Harry)
PNC Financial Services Group Inc.
PPG Industries Inc.
Quaker Chemical Corp.
Reidler Foundation
Rider-Pool Foundation
Robertshaw Charitable Foundation
Robinson Family Foundation (Donald and Sylvia)
S&T Bancorp Inc.
Schoonmaker J-Sewkly Valley Hospital Trust
Seton Co.
Seybert Institution for Poor Boys and Girls (Adam and Maria Sarah)
Sharon Steel Corp.
Sheary Trust for Charity (Edna M.)
Shore Fund
Smith Charitable Foundation (Arlene H.)
Smith Memorial Fund (Ethel Sergeant Clark)
Snayberger Memorial Foundation (Harry E. and Florence W.)
Snee-Reinhardt Charitable Foundation
Snyder Foundation (William I. and Patricia S.)
Sordoni Foundation
Sovereign Bank
Spang & Co.
Speyer Foundation (Alexander C. and Tillie S.)
Stabler Foundation (Donald B. and Dorothy L.)
Stackpole-Hall Foundation
Standard Steel
Staunton Farm Foundation
Steinman Foundation (James Hale)
Steinman Foundation (John Frederick)
Strauss Foundation
Strawbridge Foundation of Pennsylvania II (Margaret Dorrance)
Stuart Charitable Foundation (G. B.)
Susquehanna-Pfaltzgraff Co.
TMC Investment Co.
Trees Charitable Trust (Edith L.)
Trexler Trust (Harry C.)
U.S. Steel Corp.
Vanguard Group
Waypoint Financial Corp.
Wells Fargo (Franklin H. and Ruth L.)
West Pharmaceutical Services Inc.
Whalley Charitable Trust
Whitaker Fund (Helen F.)
Williams Charitable Trust (John C.)
Wyomissing Foundation

Rhode Island

Adams Trust (Charles E. and Caroline J.)
Adelson Trust (Diana S.)

Champlin Foundation
Chase Charity Foundation (Alfred E.)
Citizens Financial Group Inc.
Clarke Trust (John)
Cranston Print Works Co.
Dexter Charitable Trust (Henrietta)
Dimeo Construction Co.
Dorot Foundation
Feinstein Foundation
Hasbro Inc.
Hathaway Memorial Charitable Trust
Heydt Fund (Nan and Matilda)
Kimball Foundation (Horace A. Kimball and S. Ella)
Long Foundation (George A. and Grace)
North Family Trust
Providence Gas Co.
Providence Journal-Bulletin Co.
Rice Charitable Foundation (Albert W.)
Textron Inc.
Trimix Foundation
Watson Foundation (Thomas J.)
Weber Charities Corp. (Frederick E.)

South Carolina

Bell Foundation (S. Lewis and Lucia B.)
Bowater Inc.
Chapin Foundation of Myrtle Beach, South Carolina
Colonial Life & Accident Insurance Co.
Fullerton Foundation
Gregg-Graniteville Foundation
Liberty Corp.
Self Family Foundation
Smith Charities (John)
Sonoco Products Co.
Springs Foundation, Inc.
Springs Foundation, Inc.
Symmes Foundation (F. W.)

South Dakota

IBP
Vucurevich Foundation (John T.)

Tennessee

Benwood Foundation
Bridgestone Americas Holding Inc.
Christy-Houston Foundation
Davis Foundation (Joe C.)
First Tennessee National Corp.
Frist Foundation
Joyce Family Foundation
Lyndhurst Foundation
Pattee Foundation
Plough Foundation
Sedgwick Inc.
Thompson Charitable Foundation
Toms Foundation (The)
Tonya Memorial Foundation
Tucker Foundation
Wilson Foundation (Anne Potter)
Wurzburg Inc.

Texas

Abell-Hanger Foundation
Alcon Laboratories Inc.
Alexander Foundation (Robert D. and Catherine R.)
Amgen Inc.
AMR Corp.
Anderson Foundation (M. D.)
Apteckar Foundation (Marian Meaker)
Argyle Foundation
Beal Foundation
Belo Corp.
Bertha Foundation
Brackenridge Foundation (George W.)
Bragg Charitable Trust (R. B. O.)
Brown Foundation
Brown Foundation (M. K.)
Burlington Northern Santa Fe Corp.
Burlington Resources Inc.
Burnett Foundation (The)
Cain Foundation (Gordon and Mary)
Carter Foundation (Amon G.)
Cauthorn Charitable Trust (John and Mildred)
CenterPoint Energy Inc.
CH Foundation
Clayton Fund
Clements Foundation
Cockrell Foundation
Contran Corp.
Cook, Sr. Charitable Foundation (Kelly Gene)
Cooper Industries Ltd.
Coy Foundation (Dave)
Cullen Foundation (The)
Decherd Foundation
Dibrell Charitable Trust (Volney E.)
Dishman Charitable Foundation Trust (H. E. and Kate)
Doak Charitable Trust (Clifton C. and Henryetta C.)
Dodge Jones Foundation and Subsidiary
Doss Foundation, Inc. (M. S.)
Dunagan Foundation
Duncan Foundation (L. H. and C. W.)
Early Foundation
ECG Foundation
El Paso Corp.
Elkins, Jr. Foundation (Margaret and James A.)
ExxonMobil Corp.
Farish Fund (William Stamps)
Fasken Foundation
Fikes Foundation (Leland)
Fish Foundation (Ray C.)
Fleming Foundation
Fondren Foundation
Fort Worth Star-Telegram Inc.
Frost National Bank
Gage Foundation (Alfred S.)
Garvey Texas Foundation
George Foundation
Griffin Foundation (Rosa May)
Gulf Coast Medical Foundation
Halff Foundation (G. A. C.)
Hallberg Foundation (E. L. and R. F.)
Halliburton Co.

Halsell Foundation (Ewing)
Hamman Foundation (George and Mary Josephine)
Hawn Foundation
Heath Foundation (Ed and Mary)
Herd Foundation (Bob L.)
Herzstein Charitable Foundation (Albert and Ethel)
Hillcrest Foundation
Hobby Family Foundation
Hoblitzelle Foundation
Hoglund Foundation
Houston Endowment
Huthsteiner Fine Arts Trust
Jamail Foundation (Lee and Joseph D.)
Johnson Foundation (Burdine)
Johnson Foundation (M. G. and Lillie A.)
Jones Foundation (Helen)
Kayser Foundation
Kempner Fund (Harris and Eliza)
Kilroy Foundation (William S. and Lora Jean)
Kimberly-Clark Corp.
Kinder Morgan
King Foundation (Carl B. and Florence E.)
Kleberg Foundation (Robert J. Kleberg, Jr. and Helen C.)
Knox, Sr., and Pearl Wallis Knox Charitable Foundation (Robert W.)
Koehler Foundation (Marcia and Otto)
Lard Trust (Mary Potishman)
Lennox Foundation (Martha, David and Bagby)
Luse Foundation (W. P. and Bulah)
Masters Family Foundation
Mayer Foundation (James and Eva)
Mayor Foundation (Oliver Dewey)
Mays Foundation
McDermott Foundation (The Eugene)
McGovern Foundation (John P.)
McGovern Fund
McKee Foundation (Robert E. and Evelyn)
McMillan, Jr. Foundation (Bruce)
McNutt Charitable Trust (Amy Shelton)
McQueen Foundation (Adeline and George)
Meadows Foundation (The)
Meyer Foundation (Alice Kleberg Reynolds)
Meyer Foundation (Paul J.)
Moody Foundation
Munson Foundation Trust (W. B.)
Northen Foundation (Mary Moody)
O'Connor Foundation (Kathryn)
O'Donnell Foundation
O'Quinn Foundation (John M.)
Overlake Foundation
Owsley Foundation (Alvin and Lucy)
Pelz Trust (H.E. and Ruby)

Penney Company Inc. (J.C.)
Peterson Foundation (Hal and Charlie)
Pineywoods Foundation
Piper Foundation (Minnie Stevens)
Potts and Sibley Foundation
Powell Foundation
The Prairie Foundation
Priddy Foundation
Quanex Corp.
Rachal Foundation (Ed)
RGK Foundation
Richardson Foundation (Sid W.)
Roberts Foundation (Dora)
Rockwell Fund, Inc.
Rogers Fund for the Arts (Russell Hill)
Sams Foundation (Earl C.)
SBC Communications Inc.
Scott Foundation (William E.)
Scurlock Foundation
Semmes Foundation
Shell Oil Co.
Smith and W. Aubrey Smith Charitable Foundation (Clara Blackford)
South Plains Foundation
Stark Foundation (Nelda C. and H. J. Lutcher)
Steinhagen Benevolent Trust (B. A. and Elinor W.)
Stemmons Foundation
Sterling-Turner Foundation
Strake Foundation
Sturgis Charitable and Educational Trust (TX) (Roy and Christine)
Summerlee Foundation
Temple Foundation (T. L. L.)
Temple-Inland Inc.
Texas Instruments Inc.
Thornton Charitable Trust (Anna W. Thornton and Alexander P.)
Trull Foundation (The)
Vale-Asche Foundation
Vaughan Foundation (Rachael and Ben)
Vaughn Foundation (Jim M.)
Vaughn, Jr. Foundation Fund (James M.)
Waggoner Charitable Trust (Crystelle)
Walsh Foundation
Ward Heritage Foundation (Mamie McFaddin)
Weaver Foundation (Gil and Dody)
West Foundation (Neva and Wesley)
West Foundation (TX)
White Trust (G. R.)
Willard Helping Fund (Cecilia Young)
Wise Foundation (Watson W.)

Wortham Foundation
Wright Foundation (Lola)
Zachry Co. (H.B.)

Utah

Bamberger Memorial Foundation (John Ernest Bamberger and Ruth Eleanor)
Burton Private Foundation (Robert Harold)
Dee Foundation (Lawrence T. and Janet T.)
Eccles Charitable Foundation (Willard L.)
Eccles Foundation (George S. and Dolores Dore)
Eccles Foundation (Marriner S.)
Michael Foundation (Herbert I. and Elsa B.)
Novell
Stewart Educational Foundation (Donnell B. and Elizabeth Dee Shaw)
Swanson Family Foundation, Inc. (Dr. W. C.)

Vermont

Ben & Jerry's Homemade Inc.
Central Vermont Public Service Corp.
Cone-Blanchard Corp.
Fleming and Jane Howe Patrick Foundation (Robert)
Proctor Trust (Mortimer R.)
Windham Foundation

Virginia

Beazley Foundation
Bryant Foundation (The)
Burress Inc. (J.W.)
Cabell III and Maude Morgan Cabell Foundation (Robert G.)
Campbell Foundation (Ruth and Henry)
Carter Foundation (Beirne)
Chesapeake Corp.
Cole Trust (Quincy)
Dominion
Easley Trust (Andrew H. and Anne O.)
Ethyl Corp.
Evans Foundation (Edward P.)
Flagler Foundation
Gannett Company Inc.
Gray Foundation (Garland and Agnes Taylor)
Joco Foundation
Kington Foundation, Inc.
Landmark Communications Inc.

Lane Foundation (Minnie and Bernard)
Luck Stone
McDougall Charitable Trust (Ruth Camp)
Norfolk Shipbuilding & Drydock Corp.
North Shore Foundation
Old Dominion Box Co.
Olmsted Foundation (George and Carol)
Olsson Memorial Foundation (Elis)
Perry Foundation
Phipps Foundation (Columbus)
Portsmouth General Hospital Foundation
Reynolds Foundation (Richard S.)
Richardson Benevolent Foundation (C. E.)
Sale Foundation (Lucy Pannill)
Scott Foundation (William H., John G., and Emma)
Seay Memorial Trust (George and Effie)
Shenandoah Life Insurance Co.
Shenandoah Telecommunications Co.
Treakle Foundation (J. Edwin)
Vaughan Furniture Co.
Virginia Environmental Endowment
Washington Forrest Foundation
Whitaker Foundation

Washington

Archibald Charitable Foundation (Norman)
Avista Corp.
Bishop Foundation (E. K. and Lillian F.)
Bullitt Foundation
Cheney Foundation (Ben B.)
Dimmer Family Foundation
Fehsenfeld Charitable Foundation (Frank B. and Virginia V.)
Forest Foundation
Foster Foundation
Fuchs Foundation (Gottfried and Mary)
Gates Foundation (Bill and Melinda)
Glaser Foundation
Johnston-Hanson Foundation
Kawabe Memorial Fund
Kongsgaard-Goldman Foundation
Medina Foundation
Microsoft Corp.

Murdock Charitable Trust (M. J.)
Nesholm Family Foundation
Norcliffe Foundation
Russell Family Foundation
SAFECO Corp.
Shepherd Foundation (Harold and Helen)
Simpson Investment Co.
Snyder Foundation (Frost and Margaret)
Stewardship Foundation
Stubblefield (Estate of Joseph L.)
US Bank
Washington Mutual Inc.
Welch Testamentary Trust (George T.)
Weyerhaeuser Co.
Wyman Youth Trust

West Virginia

Bowen Foundation (Ethel N.)
Carter Family Foundation
Clay Foundation
Daywood Foundation
Fenton Foundation
Hunnicutt Foundation (H. P. and Anne S.)
Huntington Foundation
Jacobson Foundation (Bernard H. and Blanche E.)
McDonough Foundation (Bernard)
One Valley Bank N.A.
Shott, Jr. Foundation (Hugh I.)
Smoot Charitable Trust (Frank Litz)
Teubert Charitable Trust (James H. and Alice)

Wisconsin

Alexander Foundation (Walter)
Alliant Energy Corp.
Andres Charitable Trust (Frank G.)
Appleton Papers Inc.
Aylward Family Foundation
Badger Meter Inc.
Banta Corp.
Bemis Manufacturing Co.
Bradley Foundation (Lynde and Harry)
Brillion Iron Works
Brodbeck Enterprises
Carter Trust (Evelyn C.)
Christensen Charitable and Religious Foundation (L. C.)
Cleary Foundation
Cremer Foundation
CUNA Mutual Group
First Financial Bank
Fortis Health

Giddings & Lewis Inc.
Grede Foundries
Green Bay Packaging
Harley-Davidson Co.
Helfaer Foundation (Evan and Marion)
Johnson Controls Inc.
Johnson Foundation
Johnson & Son (S.C.)
Joy Global Inc.
Kikkoman Foods
Kohler Foundation
Lunda Charitable Trust
Marcus Corp.
Marshall & Ilsley Corp.
McBeath Foundation (Faye)
Menasha Corp.
MGE Energy Inc.
Miller Foundation (Steve J.)
National Presto Industries Inc.
Oshkosh B'Gosh Inc.
Park Bank
Peters Foundation (R. D. and Linda)
Peterson Charitable Foundation (Ellsworth and Carla)
Phillips Family Foundation (L. E.)
Rockwell Automation Inc.
Ross Memorial Foundation (Will)
Saint Francis Bank
Schoenleber Foundation
Sentry Insurance, A Mutual Co.
Siebert Lutheran Foundation
Smith Corp. (A.O.)
Stackner Family Foundation
Steigleder Charitable Trust (Bert L. and Patricia S.)
Stora Enso
Vogel Foundation
VPI Foundation
Wausau-Mosinee Paper Corp.
Wehr Foundation (Todd)
West Bend Mutual Insurance Co.
Wisconsin Energy Corp.
WPS Resources Corp.

Wyoming

Connemara Fund
Goodstein Foundation
Patterson Memorial Trust (Hazel)
Sargent Foundation (Newell B.)
Surrena Memorial Fund (Harry and Thelma)
Weiss Foundation (William E.)
Zullig Foundation (Herbert G. and Dorothy)

FUNDERS BY OPERATING LOCATIONS

Arranges corporations by the states of their major operating locations. Within each state, company names are listed in alphabetical order.

Alabama

Air Products and Chemicals Inc.
Akzo Nobel Chemicals
Alabama Power Co.
Alcoa Inc.
Amcast Industrial Corp.
American Honda Motor Company Inc.
Belk Stores Services Inc.
Blue Bell Inc.
Boise Cascade Corp.
Bowater Inc.
Caterpillar Inc.
CLARCOR Inc.
Clorox Co.
Compass Bank
Cummins Inc.
du Pont de Nemours & Co. (E.I.)
Eastman Kodak Co.
Eaton Corp.
Ecolab Inc.
Elf Atochem North America Inc.
Employers Mutual Casualty Co.
Equifax Inc.
Fannie Mae
FMC Corp.
Forest City Enterprises Inc.
Fortune Brands Inc.
Gannett Company Inc.
General Motors Corp.
Georgia Power Co.
Gerber Products Co.
Halliburton Co.
Harsco Corp.
Hartmarx Corp.
Humana Inc.
Hunt Corp.
Johnson Controls Inc.
Kimberly-Clark Corp.
Lehigh Cement Co.
Liberty Corp.
Lilly & Co. (Eli)
Minnesota Mining & Manufacturing Co.
New York Times Co.
Olin Corp.
Pittsburg & Midway Coal Mining Co.
Sara Lee Corp.
Scripps Co. (E.W.)
Square D Co.
State Farm Mutual Automobile Insurance Co.
Steelcase Inc.
Texas Instruments Inc.
Tyson Foods Inc.
United Parcel Service of America Inc.
Unocal Corp.
USG Corp.
Vulcan Materials Co.
Weyerhaeuser Co.
Winn-Dixie Stores Inc.

Alaska

AT&T Corp.
Carnival Corp.
ChevronTexaco Corp.
Eastman Kodak Co.
Fluor Corp.
FMC Corp.
General Mills Inc.
Minnesota Mining & Manufacturing Co.
PacifiCorp
Tyson Foods Inc.
United Parcel Service of America Inc.
Unocal Corp.
Usibelli Coal Mine Inc.

Arizona

Abbott Laboratories
Air Products and Chemicals Inc.
Albertson's Inc.
American General Finance
Assurant
AT&T Corp.
Badger Meter Inc.
Ben & Jerry's Homemade Inc.
Boise Cascade Corp.
Caterpillar Inc.
Cox Enterprises Inc.
Dow Jones & Company Inc.
Eastman Kodak Co.
Edison International
Equifax Inc.
Fannie Mae
Federated Mutual Insurance Co.
Fifth Third Bancorp
FMC Corp.
Fujitsu America
Gannett Company Inc.
Gerber Products Co.
Heinz Co. (H.J.)
Henkel Corp.
Hexcel Corp.
Humana Inc.
Johns Manville
Kimberly-Clark Corp.
Kroger Co.
Lee Enterprises Inc.
Lilly & Co. (Eli)
McClatchy Co.
McCormick & Company Inc.
Minnesota Mining & Manufacturing Co.
Morgan Chase & Co. (J.P.)
Olin Corp.
Phelps Dodge Corp.
Prudential Insurance Company of America
Pulitzer Inc.
Sara Lee Corp.
Scoular Co.
Scripps Co. (E.W.)
Stanley Works
State Farm Mutual Automobile Insurance Co.
Texas Instruments Inc.
Thompson Co. (J. Walter)
U.S. Bancorp Piper Jaffray

Arkansas

Air Products and Chemicals Inc.
Albertson's Inc.
Alcoa Inc.
Amcast Industrial Corp.
Anheuser-Busch Companies Inc.
Belk Stores Services Inc.
Bridgestone Americas Holding Inc.
CenterPoint Energy Inc.
Donnelley & Sons Co. (R.R.)
Dow Jones & Company Inc.
du Pont de Nemours & Co. (E.I.)
Eastman Kodak Co.
Equifax Inc.
Gannett Company Inc.
Gerber Products Co.
Hartmarx Corp.
Holnam Inc.
Illinois Tool Works Inc.
Johnson Controls Inc.
Johnson & Son (S.C.)
Kimberly-Clark Corp.
La-Z-Boy Inc.
Liberty Corp.
Magna International of America Inc.
Phelps Dodge Corp.
PPG Industries Inc.
Prudential Insurance Company of America
Quanex Corp.
Reliable Life Insurance Co.
Rouse Co.
Sara Lee Corp.
Schering-Plough Corp.
Smith Corp. (A.O.)
Southwestern Electric Power Co.
Tyson Foods Inc.
Union Pacific Corp.
United Parcel Service of America Inc.
Weyerhaeuser Co.
Whirlpool Corp.

California

Abbott Laboratories
ABC Inc.
Air France
Air Products and Chemicals Inc.
Akzo Nobel Chemicals
Albertson's Inc.
Alcoa Inc.
Allianz Life Insurance Company of North America
American General Finance
American Honda Motor Company Inc.
AMETEK Inc.
Amgen Inc.
AMP Inc.
Anheuser-Busch Companies Inc.
Assurant
AT&T Corp.
Avon Products Inc.
Banta Corp.
Barnes Group Inc.
Bausch & Lomb Inc.
Bechtel Group Inc.
Belo Corp.
Ben & Jerry's Homemade Inc.
Boise Cascade Corp.
Bourns Inc.
Bridgestone Americas Holding Inc.
Brunswick Corp.
Burlington Industries Inc.
Burnett Co. (Leo)
California Bank & Trust
Campbell Soup Co.
Canon U.S.A. Inc.
Cargill Inc.
ChevronTexaco Corp.
Church & Dwight Company Inc.
CIBC World Markets
CIT Group Inc.
Citigroup Global Markets Holdings Inc.
Citizens Financial Group Inc.
Claiborne Inc. (Liz)
CLARCOR Inc.
Clorox Co.
Comerica Inc.
Copley Press Inc.
Cox Enterprises Inc.
CUNA Mutual Group
Daily News L.P.
D&B
Disney Co. (Walt)
Donaldson Company Inc.
Donnelley & Sons Co. (R.R.)
Dow Corning Corp.
Dow Jones & Company Inc.
du Pont de Nemours & Co. (E.I.)
Ducommun Inc.
Dunkin' Donuts Inc.
Eastman Kodak Co.
Eaton Corp.
Ecolab Inc.
Edison International
Elf Atochem North America Inc.
Equifax Inc.
Exchange Bank
Fannie Mae
Fluor Corp.
FMC Corp.
Forest City Enterprises Inc.
Fujitsu America
Fuller Co. (H.B.)
Gannett Company Inc.
Gap Inc.
GATX Corp.
GE Capital Corp.
General Mills Inc.
General Motors Corp.
Gerber Products Co.
Giant Food Inc.
Gillette Co.
Graco Inc.
Halliburton Co.
HarperCollins Publishers Inc.
Harsco Corp.
Hasbro Inc.
Heinz Co. (H.J.)
Henkel Corp.
Hershey Foods Corp.
Hexcel Corp.
Hoffmann-La Roche Inc.
HON Industries Inc.
Hubbard Broadcasting Inc.
Hunt Corp.
Illinois Tool Works Inc.
International Multifoods Corp.
Johns Manville
Johnson Controls Inc.
Johnson & Son (S.C.)
Jostens Inc.
Kajima International Inc.
Kawasaki Motors Manufacturing Corporation U.S.A.
Kemper National Insurance Cos.
Kimberly-Clark Corp.
Knight Ridder Inc.
La-Z-Boy Inc.
Land O'Lakes Inc.
Lee Enterprises Inc.
Lehigh Cement Co.
Lilly & Co. (Eli)
Lipton Co.
Macy's East Inc.
Mattel Inc.
McCormick & Company Inc.
Metropolitan Life Insurance Co.
Microsoft Corp.
Minnesota Mining & Manufacturing Co.
Mitsubishi Electric and Electronics USA
Mitsubishi Motor Sales of America Inc.
Mitsubishi Silicon America
Morgan Chase & Co. (J.P.)
Nestle Purina PetCare Co.
New York Times Co.
NLI International Inc.
Nordson Corp.
Oki America Inc.
Olin Corp.
Oshkosh B'Gosh Inc.
Pacific Life Insurance Co.
Phelps Dodge Corp.
Prudential Insurance Company of America
Quaker Chemical Corp.
Ralph's Grocery Co.
Reichhold Chemicals Inc.
Reynolds Tobacco (R.J.)
Rich Products Corp.
Rockwell Automation Inc.
Rouse Co.
SAFECO Corp.
Sara Lee Corp.
Schering-Plough Corp.
Schlumberger Ltd.
Scoular Co.
Scripps Co. (E.W.)
Security Life of Denver Insurance Co.
Sempra Energy
Shell Oil Co.
Sherwin-Williams Co.
Smith Corp. (A.O.)
Square D Co.

Stanley Works
State Farm Mutual Automobile Insurance Co.
Steelcase Inc.
Subaru of America Inc.
Teichert & Sons (A.)
Tension Envelope Corp.
Texas Instruments Inc.
Thompson Co. (J. Walter)
Tyson Foods Inc.
Union Pacific Corp.
United Parcel Service of America Inc.
U.S. Bancorp Piper Jaffray
United States Trust Company of New York
Unitrode Corp.
Universal Studios
Unocal Corp.
USG Corp.
WestLB New York Branch
Weyerhaeuser Co.
Wyman-Gordon Co.
Xerox Corp.

Colorado

ABC Inc.
Air Products and Chemicals Inc.
Akzo Nobel Chemicals
Albertson's Inc.
Alcoa Inc.
AMETEK Inc.
Amgen Inc.
Anheuser-Busch Companies Inc.
Assurant
AT&T Corp.
Bemis Company Inc.
Ben & Jerry's Homemade Inc.
Boise Cascade Corp.
Caterpillar Inc.
ChevronTexaco Corp.
Church & Dwight Company Inc.
D&B
Donnelley & Sons Co. (R.R.)
Dow Jones & Company Inc.
du Pont de Nemours & Co. (E.I.)
Eastman Kodak Co.
Ecolab Inc.
Fluor Corp.
FMC Corp.
Forest Oil Corp.
Fujitsu America
General Mills Inc.
Gerber Products Co.
Graco Inc.
Great-West Life and Annuity Insurance Co.
Hoffmann-La Roche Inc.
Holnam Inc.
Illinois Tool Works Inc.
International Multifoods Corp.
Kemper National Insurance Cos.
Kimberly-Clark Corp.
Kinder Morgan
Knight Ridder Inc.
Kroger Co.
Lilly & Co. (Eli)
Microsoft Corp.
Minnesota Mining & Manufacturing Co.
Nestle Purina PetCare Co.
Rockwell Automation Inc.
Rouse Co.
SAFECO Corp.

St. Paul Travelers Companies Inc.
Scoular Co.
Scripps Co. (E.W.)
Security Life of Denver Insurance Co.
State Farm Mutual Automobile Insurance Co.
Storage Technology Corp.
Subaru of America Inc.
Texas Instruments Inc.
Union Pacific Corp.
U.S. Bancorp Piper Jaffray
Valmont Industries Inc.

Connecticut

ABC Inc.
Air Products and Chemicals Inc.
AMETEK Inc.
Barden Precision Bearings
Barnes Group Inc.
Bausch & Lomb Inc.
Ben & Jerry's Homemade Inc.
Campbell Soup Co.
CIGNA Corp.
Citigroup Global Markets Holdings Inc.
Citizens Financial Group Inc.
Country Curtains Inc.
Cox Enterprises Inc.
Donnelley & Sons Co. (R.R.)
du Pont de Nemours & Co. (E.I.)
Eaton Corp.
Ecolab Inc.
Fannie Mae
Fujitsu America
Gannett Company Inc.
General Motors Corp.
Handy & Harman
Harsco Corp.
Hershey Foods Corp.
Hunt Corp.
Illinois Tool Works Inc.
International Multifoods Corp.
Lilly & Co. (Eli)
Marcus Corp.
Massachusetts Mutual Life Insurance Co.
McClatchy Co.
McCormick & Company Inc.
Metropolitan Life Insurance Co.
Microsoft Corp.
Minnesota Mining & Manufacturing Co.
Mitsubishi Silicon America
Nestle Purina PetCare Co.
New York Life Insurance Co.
New York Times Co.
Olin Corp.
Pacific Life Insurance Co.
Phoenix Home Life Mutual Insurance Co.
Rayonier Inc.
Reader's Digest Association Inc.
St. Paul Travelers Companies Inc.
Sara Lee Corp.
Schlumberger Ltd.
Shaw's Supermarkets Inc.
Shell Oil Co.
Stanley Works
Tetley U.S.A. Inc.
Wiremold Co.
Wyman-Gordon Co.
Xerox Corp.

Delaware

Akzo Nobel Chemicals
AMETEK Inc.
Avon Products Inc.
CIBC World Markets
Country Curtains Inc.
Dentsply International Inc.
du Pont de Nemours & Co. (E.I.)
Duke Energy Corp.
Equifax Inc.
Gannett Company Inc.
GE Capital Corp.
General Motors Corp.
Johnson Controls Inc.
Kimberly-Clark Corp.
Morgan Chase & Co. (J.P.)
National Presto Industries Inc.
New York Life Insurance Co.
St. Paul Travelers Companies Inc.
Sara Lee Corp.
Schering-Plough Corp.
Sovereign Bank

District of Columbia

Air Products and Chemicals Inc.
American Honda Motor Company Inc.
Amgen Inc.
Bechtel Group Inc.
Ben & Jerry's Homemade Inc.
Burlington Industries Inc.
Caterpillar Inc.
COMSAT International
Dow Corning Corp.
Dow Jones & Company Inc.
Eastman Kodak Co.
Ecolab Inc.
Ethyl Corp.
Fluor Corp.
FMC Corp.
Gannett Company Inc.
GE Capital Corp.
General Mills Inc.
Gerber Products Co.
Giant Food Inc.
Halliburton Co.
Humana Inc.
Kimberly-Clark Corp.
Kiplinger Washington Editors Inc.
Microsoft Corp.
Minnesota Mining & Manufacturing Co.
Niagara Mohawk Holdings Inc.
Pepco Holdings Inc.
Progress Energy Inc.
Prudential Insurance Company of America
Rouse Co.
Scripps Co. (E.W.)
Shell Oil Co.
Thompson Co. (J. Walter)
TJX Companies Inc.
Wilkes, Artis, Hedrick & Lane
Xcel Energy
Xerox Corp.

Florida

Air France
Air Products and Chemicals Inc.
Alcoa Inc.

AMETEK Inc.
Anheuser-Busch Companies Inc.
Assurant
AT&T Corp.
Bausch & Lomb Inc.
Belk Stores Services Inc.
Bemis Company Inc.
Ben & Jerry's Homemade Inc.
Blue Bell Inc.
Bridgestone Americas Holding Inc.
Burnett Co. (Leo)
Canon U.S.A. Inc.
Cargill Inc.
Carnival Corp.
Caterpillar Inc.
ChevronTexaco Corp.
Chicago Tribune Direct Marketing
Church & Dwight Company Inc.
CNA Financial Corp.
Coca-Cola Co.
Comerica Inc.
Constellation Energy Group Inc.
Cox Enterprises Inc.
D&B
Disney Co. (Walt)
Donaldson Company Inc.
Donnelley & Sons Co. (R.R.)
Dow Jones & Company Inc.
du Pont de Nemours & Co. (E.I.)
Eastman Kodak Co.
Eaton Corp.
Ecolab Inc.
Equifax Inc.
Fannie Mae
Fifth Third Bancorp
Florida Rock Industries Inc.
Florida Rock & Tank Lines
FMC Corp.
Forest City Enterprises Inc.
Fuller Co. (H.B.)
Gannett Company Inc.
GATX Corp.
GE Capital Corp.
General Mills Inc.
General Motors Corp.
Gerber Products Co.
Halliburton Co.
Harsco Corp.
Heinz Co. (H.J.)
Hubbard Broadcasting Inc.
Humana Inc.
Huntington Bancshares Inc.
International Multifoods Corp.
Johnson Controls Inc.
Kimberly-Clark Corp.
Knight Ridder Inc.
Land O'Lakes Inc.
Lilly & Co. (Eli)
Lipton Co.
Macy's East Inc.
Marcus Corp.
McCormick & Company Inc.
Metropolitan Life Insurance Co.
Microsoft Corp.
Minnesota Mining & Manufacturing Co.
Mitsubishi Electric and Electronics USA
Mitsubishi Motor Sales of America Inc.
Morgan Chase & Co. (J.P.)
Morris Communications Corp.
New York Times Co.

Olin Corp.
L'Oreal U.S.A.
Pacific Life Insurance Co.
Phelps Dodge Corp.
Prudential Insurance Company of America
Publix Supermarkets
Rockwell Automation Inc.
Rouse Co.
St. Paul Travelers Companies Inc.
Sara Lee Corp.
Schering-Plough Corp.
Scoular Co.
Scripps Co. (E.W.)
Security Life of Denver Insurance Co.
Shell Oil Co.
Sherwin-Williams Co.
Smith Corp. (A.O.)
Square D Co.
Stanley Works
Storage Technology Corp.
Subaru of America Inc.
SunTrust Banks of Florida
Terumo Medical Corp.
Texas Instruments Inc.
Thompson Co. (J. Walter)
TJX Companies Inc.
Tyson Foods Inc.
United Parcel Service of America Inc.
United States Sugar Corp.
United States Trust Company of New York
Universal Studios
USG Corp.
West Pharmaceutical Services Inc.
Weyerhaeuser Co.
Winn-Dixie Stores Inc.

Georgia

Air Products and Chemicals Inc.
Akzo Nobel Chemicals
Alcoa Inc.
American Honda Motor Company Inc.
Anheuser-Busch Companies Inc.
Appleton Papers Inc.
Assurant
Barnes Group Inc.
Bausch & Lomb Inc.
Belk Stores Services Inc.
Birds Eye Foods Inc.
Bridgestone Americas Holding Inc.
Brunswick Corp.
Burlington Industries Inc.
California Bank & Trust
Campbell Soup Co.
Caterpillar Inc.
ChevronTexaco Corp.
Chicago Tribune Direct Marketing
Church & Dwight Company Inc.
CIBC World Markets
CIT Group Inc.
Citigroup Global Markets Holdings Inc.
Citizens Financial Group Inc.
Claiborne Inc. (Liz)
CLARCOR Inc.
Clorox Co.
Cox Enterprises Inc.
CUNA Mutual Group
Deere & Co.

Donnelley & Sons Co. (R.R.)
Dow Corning Corp.
Dow Jones & Company Inc.
du Pont de Nemours & Co.
(E.I.)
Eastman Kodak Co.
Ecolab Inc.
Elf Atochem North America
Inc.
Equifax Inc.
Fannie Mae
Federated Mutual Insurance
Co.
FMC Corp.
Fuller Co. (H.B.)
GE Capital Corp.
General Motors Corp.
Georgia Power Co.
Gerber Products Co.
Gillette Co.
Graco Inc.
Harsco Corp.
Hartmarx Corp.
Heinz Co. (H.J.)
Henkel Corp.
HON Industries Inc.
ING North America Insur-
ance Corp.
International Multifoods Corp.
Johnson Controls Inc.
Johnson & Son (S.C.)
Kajima International Inc.
Kawasaki Motors Manufac-
turing Corporation U.S.A.
Kimberly-Clark Corp.
Knight Ridder Inc.
Kroger Co.
Lilly & Co. (Eli)
Macy's East Inc.
Magna International of Amer-
ica Inc.
Minnesota Mining & Manu-
facturing Co.
Mitsubishi Electric and Elec-
tronics USA
New York Life Insurance Co.
Nordson Corp.
Oki America Inc.
Olin Corp.
Phelps Dodge Corp.
Prudential Insurance Compa-
ny of America
Quaker Chemical Corp.
Reader's Digest Association
Inc.
Rexam Inc.
Rich Products Corp.
Rockwell Automation Inc.
Rouse Co.
SAFECO Corp.
Sara Lee Corp.
Schering-Plough Corp.
Schlumberger Ltd.
Scripps Co. (E.W.)
Security Life of Denver Insur-
ance Co.
Shell Oil Co.
Sherwin-Williams Co.
Sonoco Products Co.
SPX Corp.
Square D Co.
Stanley Works
State Farm Mutual Automo-
bile Insurance Co.
Subaru of America Inc.
Tetley U.S.A. Inc.
Texas Instruments Inc.
Thompson Co. (J. Walter)
TJX Companies Inc.
Tyson Foods Inc.
United Parcel Service of
America Inc.

USG Corp.
Vulcan Materials Co.
Weyerhaeuser Co.
Winn-Dixie Stores Inc.
Winter Construction Co.
Xerox Corp.

Hawaii

ChevronTexaco Corp.
Eastman Kodak Co.
Ecolab Inc.
First Hawaiian Inc.
Gannett Company Inc.
General Mills Inc.
Gerber Products Co.
Kimberly-Clark Corp.
Lee Enterprises Inc.
Metropolitan Life Insurance
Co.
Minnesota Mining & Manu-
facturing Co.
Shell Oil Co.
Subaru of America Inc.
United Parcel Service of
America Inc.
Unocal Corp.
Weyerhaeuser Co.

Idaho

Albertson's Inc.
American Honda Motor Com-
pany Inc.
Anheuser-Busch Companies
Inc.
Avista Corp.
Boise Cascade Corp.
Cargill Inc.
Eastman Kodak Co.
Equifax Inc.
FMC Corp.
Gannett Company Inc.
General Mills Inc.
Gerber Products Co.
Heinz Co. (H.J.)
Intermountain Gas Co.
Kimberly-Clark Corp.
Land O'Lakes Inc.
St. Paul Travelers Compa-
nies Inc.
Union Pacific Corp.
U.S. Bancorp Piper Jaffray

Illinois

Abbott Laboratories
ABC Inc.
Air Products and Chemicals
Inc.
Akzo Nobel Chemicals
Albertson's Inc.
Alcoa Inc.
American Standard Inc.
AMETEK Inc.
AMP Inc.
Anheuser-Busch Companies
Inc.
Archer-Daniels-Midland Co.
Assurant
Avon Products Inc.
Bank of New York
Barnes Group Inc.
Bausch & Lomb Inc.
Bemis Company Inc.
Ben & Jerry's Homemade
Inc.
Birds Eye Foods Inc.
Bowater Inc.
Bridgestone Americas Hold-
ing Inc.
Brunswick Corp.

Burlington Industries Inc.
California Bank & Trust
Campbell Soup Co.
Canon U.S.A. Inc.
Cargill Inc.
Caterpillar Inc.
Chicago Rawhide Co.
Chicago Tribune Direct Mar-
keting
CIBC World Markets
CIT Group Inc.
CLARCOR Inc.
Clorox Co.
Coca-Cola Co.
Comerica Inc.
Copley Press Inc.
Cox Enterprises Inc.
D&B
Donaldson Company Inc.
Donnelley & Sons Co. (R.R.)
Dow Jones & Company Inc.
du Pont de Nemours & Co.
(E.I.)
Eastman Kodak Co.
Eaton Corp.
Ebsco Industries Inc.
Ecolab Inc.
Employers Mutual Casualty
Co.
Equifax Inc.
Fannie Mae
Fluor Corp.
FMC Corp.
Fortune Brands Inc.
Fuller Co. (H.B.)
Gannett Company Inc.
GATX Corp.
GE Capital Corp.
General Mills Inc.
General Motors Corp.
Gerber Products Co.
Gillette Co.
Graco Inc.
HarperCollins Publishers Inc.
Harsco Corp.
Hartmarx Corp.
Heinz Co. (H.J.)
Henkel Corp.
Ideal Industries Inc.
Illinois Tool Works Inc.
International Multifoods Corp.
J&L Specialty Steel Inc.
Johns Manville
Johnson Controls Inc.
Johnson & Son (S.C.)
Jostens Inc.
Kajima International Inc.
Kemper National Insurance
Cos.
Kimberly-Clark Corp.
Korte Construction Co.
Lee Enterprises Inc.
Magna International of Amer-
ica Inc.
Marcus Corp.
Maritz Inc.
Mattel Inc.
McCormick & Company Inc.
McWane Inc.
Metropolitan Life Insurance
Co.
Microsoft Corp.
Minnesota Mining & Manu-
facturing Co.
Mitsubishi Electric and Elec-
tronics USA
Mitsubishi Motor Sales of
America Inc.
Mitsubishi Silicon America
Morgan Chase & Co. (J.P.)
New York Times Co.
NLI International Inc.

Olin Corp.
Pamida Inc.
Peoples Energy Corp.
Prudential Insurance Compa-
ny of America
Prudential Securities Inc.
Quanex Corp.
Quincy Newspapers
Reichhold Chemicals Inc.
Rexam Inc.
Rockwell Automation Inc.
SAFECO Corp.
St. Paul Travelers Compa-
nies Inc.
Sara Lee Corp.
Schering-Plough Corp.
Scoular Co.
Shell Oil Co.
Sherwin-Williams Co.
Smith Corp. (A.O.)
Southwest News Herald
SPX Corp.
Square D Co.
State Farm Mutual Automo-
bile Insurance Co.
Stora Enso
Storage Technology Corp.
Subaru of America Inc.
Texas Instruments Inc.
Thompson Co. (J. Walter)
Tyson Foods Inc.
United Parcel Service of
America Inc.
Universal Studios
USG Corp.
Valmont Industries Inc.
Vulcan Materials Co.
WestLB New York Branch
Weyerhaeuser Co.
Xerox Corp.

Indiana

1st Source Corp.
Air Products and Chemicals
Inc.
Alcoa Inc.
Amcast Industrial Corp.
American Honda Motor Com-
pany Inc.
AMP Inc.
Andersons Inc.
Archer-Daniels-Midland Co.
Auburn Foundry
Ben & Jerry's Homemade
Inc.
Bridgestone Americas Hold-
ing Inc.
Campbell Soup Co.
Caterpillar Inc.
ChevronTexaco Corp.
Chicago Rawhide Co.
CLARCOR Inc.
Conseco Inc.
Cummins Inc.
Donaldson Company Inc.
Donnelley & Sons Co. (R.R.)
Dow Jones & Company Inc.
du Pont de Nemours & Co.
(E.I.)
Eaton Corp.
Ecolab Inc.
Fifth Third Bancorp
Ford Meter Box Co.
Fuller Co. (H.B.)
GATX Corp.
General Motors Corp.
Gerber Products Co.
Harsco Corp.
Hartmarx Corp.
Huntington Bancshares Inc.
Indianapolis Newspapers Inc.

International Multifoods Corp.
Johnson Controls Inc.
Knight Ridder Inc.
Kroger Co.
Lehigh Cement Co.
Liberty Corp.
Lilly & Co. (Eli)
Marcus Corp.
McCormick & Company Inc.
Microsoft Corp.
Minnesota Mining & Manu-
facturing Co.
L'Oreal U.S.A.
Phelps Dodge Corp.
Pulitzer Inc.
Rexam Inc.
St. Paul Travelers Compa-
nies Inc.
Sara Lee Corp.
Schering-Plough Corp.
Scripps Co. (E.W.)
Shell Oil Co.
Sherwin-Williams Co.
South Bend Tribune Corp.
SPX Corp.
Square D Co.
Stanley Works
State Farm Mutual Automo-
bile Insurance Co.
Subaru of America Inc.
Texas Instruments Inc.
Tyson Foods Inc.
United Parcel Service of
America Inc.
USG Corp.
Valmont Industries Inc.
Vulcan Materials Co.
Whirlpool Corp.

Iowa

Air Products and Chemicals
Inc.
Alcoa Inc.
American Honda Motor Com-
pany Inc.
Appleton Papers Inc.
Archer-Daniels-Midland Co.
Birds Eye Foods Inc.
Bridgestone Americas Hold-
ing Inc.
Chesapeake Corp.
Citizens First National Bank
Cox Enterprises Inc.
Cummins Inc.
CUNA Mutual Group
Deere & Co.
Donaldson Company Inc.
Dow Corning Corp.
Dow Jones & Company Inc.
du Pont de Nemours & Co.
(E.I.)
Eaton Corp.
Ecolab Inc.
Elf Atochem North America
Inc.
Employers Mutual Casualty
Co.
Fannie Mae
FMC Corp.
Fortune Brands Inc.
Gannett Company Inc.
Gazette Co.
General Mills Inc.
General Motors Corp.
Harsco Corp.
Heinz Co. (H.J.)
Hickory Tech Corp.
Holnam Inc.
HON Industries Inc.
Iowa Savings Bank
Land O'Lakes Inc.

Lee Enterprises Inc.
Lilly & Co. (Eli)
Lipton Co.
Lisle Corp.
Magna International of Amer-
ica Inc.
Marcus Corp.
McWane Corp.
Menasha Corp.
Minnesota Mining & Manu-
facturing Co.
Owen Industries
Pamida Inc.
Pella Corp.
Principal Financial Group
Quanex Corp.
Rockwell Automation Inc.
Rouse Co.
Sara Lee Corp.
Sheaffer Pen Corp.
Square D Co.
Tension Envelope Corp.
United Parcel Service of
America Inc.
U.S. Bancorp Piper Jaffray
USG Corp.
Vulcan Materials Co.
Weyerhaeuser Co.
Winnebago Industries

Kansas

Abbott Laboratories
Air Products and Chemicals
Inc.
Appleton Papers Inc.
Archer-Daniels-Midland Co.
Assurant
Bemis Company Inc.
Blue Bell Inc.
Burlington Industries Inc.
Chicago Rawhide Co.
Deere & Co.
Donaldson Company Inc.
du Pont de Nemours & Co.
(E.I.)
Eastman Kodak Co.
Eaton Corp.
Ecolab Inc.
Equifax Inc.
Excel Corp.
FMC Corp.
Gannett Company Inc.
General Mills Inc.
General Motors Corp.
Humana Inc.
International Multifoods Corp.
Johns Manville
Johnson Controls Inc.
Jostens Inc.
Knight Ridder Inc.
Koch Industries Inc.
Macy's East Inc.
Maritz Inc.
McCormick & Company Inc.
Metropolitan Life Insurance
Co.
Morris Communications
Corp.
Pamida Inc.
PPG Industries Inc.
Royal & SunAlliance USA
Inc.
St. Paul Travelers Compa-
nies Inc.
Sara Lee Corp.
Scoular Co.
Security Benefit Life Insur-
ance Co.
Security Life of Denver Insur-
ance Co.
Sherwin-Williams Co.

Smith Corp. (A.O.)
Stanley Works
Tension Envelope Corp.
Texas Instruments Inc.
Union Pacific Corp.
United Parcel Service of
America Inc.
U.S. Bancorp Piper Jaffray
Yellow Roadway Corp.

Kentucky

Air Products and Chemicals
Inc.
Akzo Nobel Chemicals
Alcoa Inc.
American General Finance
American Standard Inc.
Amgen Inc.
Appleton Papers Inc.
Ben & Jerry's Homemade
Inc.
Berwind Group
Chesapeake Corp.
CLARCOR Inc.
Community Trust Bancorp
Inc.
Donnelley & Sons Co. (R.R.)
Dow Corning Corp.
du Pont de Nemours & Co.
(E.I.)
Eastman Kodak Co.
Elf Atochem North America
Inc.
Fidelity Investments
Fifth Third Bancorp
Fluor Corp.
Fortune Brands Inc.
Fuller Co. (H.B.)
Gannett Company Inc.
General Motors Corp.
Harsco Corp.
Hartmarx Corp.
Hershey Foods Corp.
HON Industries Inc.
Humana Inc.
Hunt Corp.
Huntington Bancshares Inc.
International Multifoods Corp.
Johnson Controls Inc.
Knight Ridder Inc.
LG&E Energy Corp.
Liberty Corp.
Lilly & Co. (Eli)
Marcus Corp.
Minnesota Mining & Manu-
facturing Co.
National City Corp.
Nestle Purina PetCare Co.
New York Times Co.
Oshkosh B'Gosh Inc.
Phelps Dodge Corp.
Pulitzer Inc.
Rockwell Automation Inc.
Rouse Co.
Sara Lee Corp.
Shell Oil Co.
Smith Corp. (A.O.)
Square D Co.
Texas Instruments Inc.
Thomas Industries
United Parcel Service of
America Inc.
Vogt Machine Co. (Henry)
Vulcan Materials Co.
Weyerhaeuser Co.
Winn-Dixie Stores Inc.

Louisiana

Air Products and Chemicals
Inc.

Alcoa Inc.
Anheuser-Busch Companies
Inc.
Belo Corp.
Blue Bell Inc.
Boise Cascade Corp.
ChevronTexaco Corp.
Cox Enterprises Inc.
Cranston Print Works Co.
D&B
Donaldson Company Inc.
du Pont de Nemours & Co.
(E.I.)
Eastman Kodak Co.
Ecolab Inc.
FMC Corp.
Freeport-McMoRan Copper &
Gold Inc.
Gannett Company Inc.
GATX Corp.
General Motors Corp.
Harsco Corp.
Holnam Inc.
Johnson Controls Inc.
Kansas City Southern Rail-
way
Lilly & Co. (Eli)
New York Times Co.
Olin Corp.
Phelps Dodge Corp.
PPG Industries Inc.
Prudential Insurance Compa-
ny of America
Rockwell Automation Inc.
Rouse Co.
Schering-Plough Corp.
Shell Oil Co.
Southwestern Electric Power
Co.
State Farm Mutual Automo-
bile Insurance Co.
Union Pacific Corp.
Unocal Corp.
USG Corp.
Vulcan Materials Co.
Winn-Dixie Stores Inc.

Maine

Bausch & Lomb Inc.
Bowater Inc.
Central Maine Power Co.
Corning Inc.
Donnelley & Sons Co. (R.R.)
Ecolab Inc.
Johns Manville
Kimberly-Clark Corp.
New York Times Co.
Rexam Inc.
Royal & SunAlliance USA
Inc.
Shaw's Supermarkets Inc.
U.S. Bancorp Piper Jaffray
Webber Oil Co.
Weyerhaeuser Co.

Maryland

Air Products and Chemicals
Inc.
Alcon Laboratories Inc.
Aon Corp.
Assurant
Belk Stores Services Inc.
Chesapeake Corp.
ChevronTexaco Corp.
Clorox Co.
COMSAT International
Constellation Energy Group
Inc.
Country Curtains Inc.
D&B

Dow Jones & Company Inc.
Eastman Kodak Co.
Eaton Corp.
Ebsco Industries Inc.
Ecolab Inc.
Equifax Inc.
FMC Corp.
Fuller Co. (H.B.)
General Motors Corp.
Gerber Products Co.
Giant Food Inc.
Giant Food Stores
Halliburton Co.
Harsco Corp.
Johnson Controls Inc.
Johnson & Son (S.C.)
Kiewit Sons' Inc. (Peter)
Kimberly-Clark Corp.
Kiplinger Washington Editors
Inc.
Lilly & Co. (Eli)
McCormick & Company Inc.
Minnesota Mining & Manu-
facturing Co.
Morgan Chase & Co. (J.P.)
Pepco Holdings Inc.
Perdue Farms
Price Associates (T. Rowe)
Procter & Gamble Company,
Cosmetics Div.
Rexam Inc.
Rouse Co.
Royal & SunAlliance USA
Inc.
Scripps Co. (E.W.)
Shell Oil Co.
Sherwin-Williams Co.
Smith Corp. (A.O.)
Subaru of America Inc.
Terumo Medical Corp.
Texas Instruments Inc.
United Parcel Service of
America Inc.
USG Corp.
Weyerhaeuser Co.
Williams Companies Inc.

Massachusetts

Abbott Laboratories
ABC Inc.
Air Products and Chemicals
Inc.
Allmerica Financial Corp.
American Honda Motor Com-
pany Inc.
American Optical Corp.
AMP Inc.
Anheuser-Busch Companies
Inc.
Assurant
Bausch & Lomb Inc.
Ben & Jerry's Homemade
Inc.
Berwind Group
Boston Globe (The)
Bridgestone Americas Hold-
ing Inc.
Cabot Corp.
Cargill Inc.
Church & Dwight Company
Inc.
Citigroup Global Markets
Holdings Inc.
Citizens Financial Group Inc.
Corning Inc.
Country Curtains Inc.
Cox Enterprises Inc.
Cranston Print Works Co.
Demoulas Supermarkets Inc.
Donnelley & Sons Co. (R.R.)
Dow Jones & Company Inc.

du Pont de Nemours & Co.
(E.I.)
Dunkin' Donuts Inc.
Eastern Bank
Eastman Kodak Co.
Eaton Corp.
Ecolab Inc.
Elf Atochem North America
Inc.
Equifax Inc.
Erving Industries
Fannie Mae
Fidelity Investments
Fortune Brands Inc.
Fuller Co. (H.B.)
General Mills Inc.
General Motors Corp.
Gerber Products Co.
Giant Food Stores
Gillette Co.
Golub Corp.
Hancock Financial Services
(John)
HarperCollins Publishers Inc.
Heinz Co. (H.J.)
Hyde Manufacturing Co.
Illinois Tool Works Inc.
International Multifoods Corp.
Johnson Controls Inc.
Kimberly-Clark Corp.
Lilly & Co. (Eli)
Marcus Corp.
Mellon Financial Corp.
Menasha Corp.
Microsoft Corp.
Millipore Corp.
Minnesota Mining & Manu-
facturing Co.
Mitsubishi Electric and Elec-
tronics USA
New York Times Co.
NLI International Inc.
NSTAR
Pacific Life Insurance Co.
Phoenix Home Life Mutual
Insurance Co.
Providence Gas Co.
Providence Journal-Bulletin
Co.
Prudential Insurance Compa-
ny of America
Prudential Securities Inc.
Rayonier Inc.
Rexam Inc.
Rockwell Automation Inc.
Rouse Co.
Royal & SunAlliance USA
Inc.
St. Paul Travelers Compa-
nies Inc.
Security Life of Denver Insur-
ance Co.
Shaw's Supermarkets Inc.
Shell Oil Co.
Square D Co.
Stanley Works
Subaru of America Inc.
Texas Instruments Inc.
TJX Companies Inc.
United States Trust Compa-
ny of New York
USG Corp.
Wyman-Gordon Co.

Michigan

Abbott Laboratories
ABC Inc.
Air Products and Chemicals
Inc.
Akzo Nobel Chemicals
Alcoa Inc.

Amcast Industrial Corp.
American Honda Motor Company Inc.
AMETEK Inc.
AMP Inc.
Andersons Inc.
Archer-Daniels-Midland Co.
Assurant
Barnes Group Inc.
Bausch & Lomb Inc.
Bemis Company Inc.
Berwind Group
Birds Eye Foods Inc.
Bridgestone Americas Holding Inc.
Campbell Soup Co.
Cleveland-Cliffs Inc.
Comerica Inc.
Cox Enterprises Inc.
CUNA Mutual Group
Donaldson Company Inc.
Dow Corning Corp.
Dow Jones & Company Inc.
du Pont de Nemours & Co. (E.I.)
Eastman Kodak Co.
Eaton Corp.
Ecolab Inc.
Elf Atochem North America Inc.
Equifax Inc.
Ethyl Corp.
Fannie Mae
Farmer Jack Supermarkets
FMC Corp.
Fuller Co. (H.B.)
Gannett Company Inc.
General Motors Corp.
Gerber Products Co.
Graco Inc.
Handy & Harman
HarperCollins Publishers Inc.
Heinz Co. (H.J.)
Hexcel Corp.
Holnam Inc.
Huntington Bancshares Inc.
Illinois Tool Works Inc.
Interkal Inc.
International Multifoods Corp.
Johnson Controls Inc.
JSJ Corp.
Kawasaki Motors Manufacturing Corporation U.S.A.
Kimberly-Clark Corp.
Knight Ridder Inc.
Kroger Co.
La-Z-Boy Inc.
Magna International of America Inc.
Marcus Corp.
Maritz Inc.
McCormick & Company Inc.
Menasha Corp.
Metropolitan Life Insurance Co.
Minnesota Mining & Manufacturing Co.
Mitsubishi Electric and Electronics USA
Mitsubishi Motor Sales of America Inc.
Pamida Inc.
Prudential Insurance Company of America
Quaker Chemical Corp.
Quanex Corp.
R&B Machine Tool Co.
Reichhold Chemicals Inc.
Rockwell Automation Inc.
Rouse Co.
Sara Lee Corp.
Schlumberger Ltd.

Scripps Co. (E.W.)
Shell Oil Co.
Sherwin-Williams Co.
Simpson Investment Co.
Smith Corp. (A.O.)
SPX Corp.
Stanley Works
State Farm Mutual Automobile Insurance Co.
Steelcase Inc.
Texas Instruments Inc.
Thompson Co. (J. Walter)
Todd Co. (A.M.)
Universal Studios
Vulcan Materials Co.
Whirlpool Corp.

Minnesota

ABC Inc.
ADC Telecommunications
Anheuser-Busch Companies Inc.
Archer-Daniels-Midland Co.
Assurant
Banta Corp.
Bausch & Lomb Inc.
Boise Cascade Corp.
Bridgestone Americas Holding Inc.
Cargill Inc.
CenterPoint Energy Inc.
Church & Dwight Company Inc.
Clorox Co.
Cummins Inc.
Deere & Co.
Donnelley & Sons Co. (R.R.)
Eastman Kodak Co.
Ebsco Industries Inc.
Ecolab Inc.
Elf Atochem North America Inc.
Equifax Inc.
Excel Corp.
Fannie Mae
Federated Mutual Insurance Co.
FMC Corp.
Forest City Enterprises Inc.
Fuller Co. (H.B.)
General Mills Inc.
Gerber Products Co.
Gillette Co.
Graco Inc.
Harsco Corp.
Hickory Tech Corp.
Homecrest Industries Inc.
Hubbard Broadcasting Inc.
International Multifoods Corp.
Jostens Inc.
Knight Ridder Inc.
Land O'Lakes Inc.
Lee Enterprises Inc.
Lehigh Cement Co.
Lilly & Co. (Eli)
Marcus Corp.
McClatchy Co.
Menasha Corp.
Microsoft Corp.
Minnesota Mining & Manufacturing Co.
Morris Communications Corp.
National Presto Industries Inc.
Nestle Purina PetCare Co.
L'Oreal U.S.A.
Rahr Malting Co.
Regis Corp.
Rexam Inc.
Rouse Co.

St. Paul Travelers Companies Inc.
Sara Lee Corp.
Scoular Co.
Seneca Foods Corp.
Shell Oil Co.
Stanley Works
State Farm Mutual Automobile Insurance Co.
TCF National Bank Minnesota
Tension Envelope Corp.
Texas Instruments Inc.
Tyson Foods Inc.
United Parcel Service of America Inc.
U.S. Bancorp Piper Jaffray
USG Corp.
Weyerhaeuser Co.
Xcel Energy

Mississippi

Air Products and Chemicals Inc.
Akzo Nobel Chemicals
Alcoa Inc.
Barnes Group Inc.
Belk Stores Services Inc.
Blue Bell Inc.
Caterpillar Inc.
ChevronTexaco Corp.
Clorox Co.
D&B
Donnelley & Sons Co. (R.R.)
du Pont de Nemours & Co. (E.I.)
Eastman Kodak Co.
Fannie Mae
FMC Corp.
Gannett Company Inc.
General Motors Corp.
Holnam Inc.
Kansas City Southern Railway
Kimberly-Clark Corp.
Knight Ridder Inc.
La-Z-Boy Inc.
Lilly & Co. (Eli)
Magna International of America Inc.
Menasha Corp.
National Presto Industries Inc.
New York Times Co.
Prudential Insurance Company of America
Quanex Corp.
Sara Lee Corp.
Shell Oil Co.
SPX Corp.
Stanley Works
Thomasville Furniture Industries Inc.
Tyson Foods Inc.
USG Corp.
Weyerhaeuser Co.

Missouri

ABC Inc.
Air Products and Chemicals Inc.
Alcoa Inc.
Ameren Corp.
Anheuser-Busch Companies Inc.
Assurant
Bakewell Corp.
Bank of New York
Banta Corp.
Bausch & Lomb Inc.

Chicago Rawhide Co.
Church & Dwight Company Inc.
Clorox Co.
Commerce Bancshares Inc.
Cox Enterprises Inc.
Deere & Co.
Donaldson Company Inc.
Dow Jones & Company Inc.
Eastman Kodak Co.
Eaton Corp.
Ecolab Inc.
Elf Atochem North America Inc.
Fannie Mae
Fluor Corp.
Gannett Company Inc.
General Mills Inc.
General Motors Corp.
Hartmarx Corp.
Humana Inc.
International Multifoods Corp.
Johnson Controls Inc.
Kansas City Southern Railway
Kimberly-Clark Corp.
Korte Construction Co.
Lilly & Co. (Eli)
Magna International of America Inc.
Marcus Corp.
Maritz Inc.
McCormick & Company Inc.
Microsoft Corp.
Minnesota Mining & Manufacturing Co.
Morris Communications Corp.
Nestle Purina PetCare Co.
Olin Corp.
Pamida Inc.
Prudential Insurance Company of America
Pulitzer Inc.
Rexam Inc.
Rockwell Automation Inc.
Rouse Co.
SAFECO Corp.
Sara Lee Corp.
Schering-Plough Corp.
Scoular Co.
Scripps Co. (E.W.)
Shell Oil Co.
Shelter Mutual Insurance Co.
Square D Co.
Stanley Works
State Farm Mutual Automobile Insurance Co.
Tension Envelope Corp.
Tetley U.S.A. Inc.
Texas Instruments Inc.
Thompson Co. (J. Walter)
Tyson Foods Inc.
Union Pacific Corp.
United Parcel Service of America Inc.
U.S. Bancorp Piper Jaffray
USG Corp.
Weyerhaeuser Co.

Montana

American General Finance
Boise Cascade Corp.
Gannett Company Inc.
General Mills Inc.
Land O'Lakes Inc.
Lee Enterprises Inc.
PacifiCorp
Pamida Inc.
St. Paul Travelers Companies Inc.

U.S. Bancorp Piper Jaffray

Nebraska

Air Products and Chemicals Inc.
Archer-Daniels-Midland Co.
Bausch & Lomb Inc.
Bemis Company Inc.
Campbell Soup Co.
CLARCOR Inc.
Commerce Bancshares Inc.
Cox Enterprises Inc.
Eaton Corp.
Ecolab Inc.
Fannie Mae
FMC Corp.
Hershey Foods Corp.
IBP
Kinder Morgan
Land O'Lakes Inc.
Lee Enterprises Inc.
Lilly & Co. (Eli)
Magna International of America Inc.
Marcus Corp.
Minnesota Mining & Manufacturing Co.
Pamida Inc.
Principal Financial Group
Prudential Insurance Company of America
Pulitzer Inc.
Rockwell Automation Inc.
Schering-Plough Corp.
Scoular Co.
Square D Co.
State Farm Mutual Automobile Insurance Co.
Union Pacific Corp.
United Parcel Service of America Inc.
U.S. Bancorp Piper Jaffray
Valmont Industries Inc.
Wells Fargo Bank Nebraska, N.A.
West Pharmaceutical Services Inc.

Nevada

American Standard Inc.
Bechtel Group Inc.
Donnelley & Sons Co. (R.R.)
Eastman Kodak Co.
Ecolab Inc.
FMC Corp.
Gannett Company Inc.
General Mills Inc.
Landmark Communications Inc.
Sara Lee Corp.
Shell Oil Co.
Sherwin-Williams Co.
Sierra Pacific Resources
USG Corp.
Wyman-Gordon Co.

New Hampshire

Anheuser-Busch Companies Inc.
Bausch & Lomb Inc.
Clorox Co.
Demoulas Supermarkets Inc.
Ecolab Inc.
Forest City Enterprises Inc.
General Motors Corp.
J&L Specialty Steel Inc.
Johnson Controls Inc.
Kingsbury Corp.
Lydall Inc.

Millipore Corp.
Royal & SunAlliance USA Inc.
Shaw's Supermarkets Inc.
Stanley Works
United Parcel Service of America Inc.
Unitrode Corp.
Wyman-Gordon Co.

New Jersey

Abbott Laboratories
Air Products and Chemicals Inc.
Akzo Nobel Chemicals
American General Finance
American Standard Inc.
Anheuser-Busch Companies Inc.
Aon Corp.
Assurant
AT&T Corp.
Ballet Makers
Barnes Group Inc.
Bausch & Lomb Inc.
Bechtel Group Inc.
Bemis Company Inc.
Berwind Group
Birds Eye Foods Inc.
Canon U.S.A. Inc.
Chesapeake Corp.
CIT Group Inc.
Claiborne Inc. (Liz)
Country Curtains Inc.
D&B
Disney Co. (Walt)
Dow Corning Corp.
Dow Jones & Company Inc.
Dreyfus Corp.
du Pont de Nemours & Co. (E.I.)
Eastman Kodak Co.
Ebsco Industries Inc.
Equifax Inc.
Exelon
Fluor Corp.
FMC Corp.
Fujitsu America
General Motors Corp.
Gerber Products Co.
Handy & Harman
Harsco Corp.
Hasbro Inc.
Heinz Co. (H.J.)
Hoffmann-La Roche Inc.
Illinois Tool Works Inc.
International Multifoods Corp.
J&L Specialty Steel Inc.
Johns Manville
Johnson Controls Inc.
Johnson & Son (S.C.)
Kajima International Inc.
Kimberly-Clark Corp.
Knight Ridder Inc.
Lilly & Co. (Eli)
Lipton Co.
Macy's East Inc.
McCormick & Company Inc.
Menasha Corp.
Metropolitan Life Insurance Co.
Minnesota Mining & Manufacturing Co.
Mitsubishi Motor Sales of America Inc.
MONY Group Inc.
New York Life Insurance Co.
New York Times Co.
Oki America Inc.
Olin Corp.
Phelps Dodge Corp.

Prudential Insurance Company of America
Prudential Securities Inc.
Public Service Electric & Gas Co.
Rayonier Inc.
Reichhold Chemicals Inc.
Rexam Inc.
Reynolds Tobacco (R.J.)
Rich Products Corp.
Rockwell Automation Inc.
Rouse Co.
Royal & SunAlliance USA Inc.
St. Paul Travelers Companies Inc.
Sara Lee Corp.
Schering-Plough Corp.
Shaw's Supermarkets Inc.
Shell Oil Co.
Sherwin-Williams Co.
Sovereign Bank
Square D Co.
Subaru of America Inc.
Tension Envelope Corp.
Terumo Medical Corp.
Thompson Co. (J. Walter)
United Parcel Service of America Inc.
U.S. Bancorp Piper Jaffray
Universal Studios
USG Corp.
Weyerhaeuser Co.
Williams Companies Inc.

New Mexico

Air Products and Chemicals Inc.
ChevronTexaco Corp.
du Pont de Nemours & Co. (E.I.)
Ecolab Inc.
Equifax Inc.
FMC Corp.
Hershey Foods Corp.
Hubbard Broadcasting Inc.
International Multifoods Corp.
Lee Enterprises Inc.
Marcus Corp.
Phelps Dodge Corp.
Pittsburg & Midway Coal Mining Co.
PNM Resources Inc.
Pulitzer Inc.
Sara Lee Corp.
Scripps Co. (E.W.)
Unocal Corp.

New York

Abbott Laboratories
ABC Inc.
Air Products and Chemicals Inc.
Akzo Nobel Chemicals
Alcoa Inc.
American Standard Inc.
AMETEK Inc.
Anheuser-Busch Companies Inc.
Appleton Papers Inc.
Assurant
AT&T Corp.
Avon Products Inc.
Bank of New York
Barnes Group Inc.
Bausch & Lomb Inc.
Bemis Company Inc.
Ben & Jerry's Homemade Inc.
Berwind Group

Birds Eye Foods Inc.
Bridgestone Americas Holding Inc.
Burlington Industries Inc.
Burnett Co. (Leo)
California Bank & Trust
Campbell Soup Co.
Canon U.S.A. Inc.
Chesapeake Corp.
Chicago Tribune Direct Marketing
Christian Dior Perfumes Inc.
CIBC World Markets
CIT Group Inc.
Citizens Financial Group Inc.
ContiGroup Companies Inc.
Corning Inc.
Country Curtains Inc.
Cox Enterprises Inc.
Cranston Print Works Co.
Credit Suisse First Boston Corp.
Cummins Inc.
CUNA Mutual Group
D&B
Deere & Co.
Disney Co. (Walt)
Donaldson Company Inc.
Dow Jones & Company Inc.
du Pont de Nemours & Co. (E.I.)
Eastman Kodak Co.
Eaton Corp.
Ecolab Inc.
Elf Atochem North America Inc.
Equifax Inc.
Ethyl Corp.
Fannie Mae
FMC Corp.
Forest City Enterprises Inc.
Fortune Brands Inc.
Fujitsu America
Fuller Co. (H.B.)
Gannett Company Inc.
GATX Corp.
GE Capital Corp.
General Motors Corp.
Gerber Products Co.
Giant Food Stores
Golub Corp.
Handy & Harman
HarperCollins Publishers Inc.
Harsco Corp.
Hartmarx Corp.
Hasbro Inc.
Hilliard Corp.
Hino Diesel Trucks (U.S.A.)
HON Industries Inc.
Illinois Tool Works Inc.
International Multifoods Corp.
J&L Specialty Steel Inc.
Jostens Inc.
Kahn, Lucas-Lancaster Incorporated Children's Wear
Kajima International Inc.
Kawasaki Motors Manufacturing Corporation U.S.A.
Kimberly-Clark Corp.
Lilly & Co. (Eli)
Long Island Lighting Co.
Lydall Inc.
Macy's East Inc.
Maritz Inc.
Mattel Inc.
Metropolitan Life Insurance Co.
Microsoft Corp.
Minnesota Mining & Manufacturing Co.
Mitsubishi Electric and Electronics USA

Mitsubishi Motor Sales of America Inc.
Mitsubishi Silicon America
MONY Group Inc.
Morgan Chase & Co. (J.P.)
Nestle Purina PetCare Co.
Niagara Mohawk Holdings Inc.
NLI International Inc.
Oki America Inc.
Olin Corp.
L'Oreal U.S.A.
Oshkosh B'Gosh Inc.
Phelps Dodge Corp.
Phoenix Home Life Mutual Insurance Co.
Prudential Insurance Company of America
Prudential Securities Inc.
Raymond Corp.
Reader's Digest Association Inc.
Reichhold Chemicals Inc.
Reynolds Tobacco (R.J.)
Rouse Co.
Royal & SunAlliance USA Inc.
St. Paul Travelers Companies Inc.
Sara Lee Corp.
Schlumberger Ltd.
Scoular Co.
Seneca Foods Corp.
Sheaffer Pen Corp.
Shell Oil Co.
State Farm Mutual Automobile Insurance Co.
Stora Enso
Subaru of America Inc.
Sumitomo Mitsui Banking Corp.
Tetley U.S.A. Inc.
Texas Instruments Inc.
Thompson Co. (J. Walter)
TJX Companies Inc.
United Parcel Service of America Inc.
United States Trust Company of New York
Universal Studios
USG Corp.
Utica National Insurance Group
WestLB New York Branch
Wiley & Sons Inc. (John)
Williams Companies Inc.
Xerox Corp.

North Carolina

Abbott Laboratories
ABC Inc.
Air Products and Chemicals Inc.
Akzo Nobel Chemicals
American Honda Motor Company Inc.
American Standard Inc.
AMP Inc.
Archer-Daniels-Midland Co.
Assurant
Bausch & Lomb Inc.
Bechtel Group Inc.
Belk Stores Services Inc.
Benetton U.S.A. Corp.
Bridgestone Americas Holding Inc.
Brown & Williamson Tobacco Corp.
Burlington Industries Inc.
Burress Inc. (J.W.)
Campbell Soup Co.

Caterpillar Inc.
Chesapeake Corp.
Cox Enterprises Inc.
Cranston Print Works Co.
Cummins Inc.
D&B
Donaldson Company Inc.
Donnelley & Sons Co. (R.R.)
Dow Corning Corp.
Dow Jones & Company Inc.
du Pont de Nemours & Co. (E.I.)
Duke Energy Corp.
Eastman Kodak Co.
Eaton Corp.
Ecolab Inc.
Equifax Inc.
Fannie Mae
FMC Corp.
Fortune Brands Inc.
Fujitsu America
Fuller Co. (H.B.)
Gannett Company Inc.
General Motors Corp.
Gerber Products Co.
Harsco Corp.
Henkel Corp.
Hoffmann-La Roche Inc.
HON Industries Inc.
International Multifoods Corp.
Johns Manville
Kimberly-Clark Corp.
Knight Ridder Inc.
La-Z-Boy Inc.
Landmark Communications Inc.
Lilly & Co. (Eli)
Lowe's Cos.
Lydall Inc.
Marcus Corp.
Microsoft Corp.
Minnesota Mining & Manufacturing Co.
Mitsubishi Electric and Electronics USA
New York Times Co.
Pacific Life Insurance Co.
Phelps Dodge Corp.
Prudential Insurance Company of America
Pulitzer Inc.
Reichhold Chemicals Inc.
Reilly Industries Inc.
Rexam Inc.
Reynolds Tobacco (R.J.)
Rockwell Automation Inc.
Royal & SunAlliance USA Inc.
Sara Lee Corp.
Smith Corp. (A.O.)
Sonoco Products Co.
Square D Co.
Stanley Works
Steelcase Inc.
Stonecutter Mills Corp.
Tanner Cos. (Rutherfordton, NC)
Tension Envelope Corp.
Texas Instruments Inc.
Thomasville Furniture Industries Inc.
Tyson Foods Inc.
United Parcel Service of America Inc.
Unitrode Corp.
Vulcan Materials Co.
West Pharmaceutical Services Inc.
Weyerhaeuser Co.
Williams Companies Inc.
Winn-Dixie Stores Inc.

North Dakota

Employers Mutual Casualty Co.
Knight Ridder Inc.
Lee Enterprises Inc.
Pamida Inc.
St. Paul Travelers Companies Inc.
United Parcel Service of America Inc.
U.S. Bancorp Piper Jaffray
Xcel Energy

Ohio

Abbott Laboratories
ABC Inc.
Air Products and Chemicals Inc.
Akzo Nobel Chemicals
Alcoa Inc.
Amcast Industrial Corp.
American Honda Motor Company Inc.
American Standard Inc.
AMETEK Inc.
Andersons Inc.
Anheuser-Busch Companies Inc.
Appleton Papers Inc.
Assurant
Avon Products Inc.
Banta Corp.
Barnes Group Inc.
Bemis Company Inc.
Birds Eye Foods Inc.
Bridgestone Americas Holding Inc.
Broderbund L.L.C.
Campbell Soup Co.
Cessna Aircraft Co.
Chesapeake Corp.
Church & Dwight Company Inc.
CLARCOR Inc.
Clorox Co.
Coca-Cola Co.
Columbus Dispatch Printing Co.
Comerica Inc.
Cox Enterprises Inc.
Cummins Inc.
Dentsply International Inc.
Donaldson Company Inc.
Donnelley & Sons Co. (R.R.)
Dow Jones & Company Inc.
du Pont de Nemours & Co. (E.I.)
Eastman Kodak Co.
Eaton Corp.
Ecolab Inc.
Elf Atochem North America Inc.
Fannie Mae
Fidelity Investments
Fifth Third Bancorp
Fluor Corp.
Forest City Enterprises Inc.
Fortune Brands Inc.
French Oil Mill Machinery Co.
Fuller Co. (H.B.)
Gannett Company Inc.
GATX Corp.
General Mills Inc.
General Motors Corp.
Gerber Products Co.
Giant Food Stores
Gillette Co.
Handy & Harman
Harsco Corp.

Heinz Co. (H.J.)
Henkel Corp.
Hexcel Corp.
Honda of America Manufacturing Inc.
Humana Inc.
Illinois Tool Works Inc.
International Multifoods Corp.
Johns Manville
Johnson Controls Inc.
Johnson & Son (S.C.)
Kemper National Insurance Cos.
Key Bank N.A.
Kimberly-Clark Corp.
Knight Ridder Inc.
Kroger Co.
Liberty Corp.
Lilly & Co. (Eli)
Macy's East Inc.
Marcus Corp.
McWane Corp.
Menasha Corp.
Microsoft Corp.
Minnesota Mining & Manufacturing Co.
Mitsubishi Electric and Electronics USA
National City Corp.
Nestle Purina PetCare Co.
Nordson Corp.
Pacific Life Insurance Co.
Phelps Dodge Corp.
PPG Industries Inc.
Prudential Insurance Company of America
Reichhold Chemicals Inc.
Rich Products Corp.
Rockwell Automation Inc.
Rouse Co.
SAFECO Corp.
St. Paul Travelers Companies Inc.
Sara Lee Corp.
Scott Fetzer Co.
Scoular Co.
Scripps Co. (E.W.)
Shell Oil Co.
Sherwin-Williams Co.
Smith Corp. (A.O.)
Spartan Stores Inc.
SPX Corp.
Square D Co.
Stanley Works
State Farm Mutual Automobile Insurance Co.
Texas Instruments Inc.
Thompson Co. (J. Walter)
United Parcel Service of America Inc.
Unocal Corp.
USG Corp.
Western & Southern Life Insurance Co.
Weyerhaeuser Co.
Whirlpool Corp.
Williams Companies Inc.
Winn-Dixie Stores Inc.
Worthington Foods

Oklahoma

Air Products and Chemicals Inc.
Akzo Nobel Chemicals
Albertson's Inc.
Anheuser-Busch Companies Inc.
Badger Meter Inc.
Belo Corp.
Blue Bell Inc.

Bridgestone Americas Holding Inc.
Chicago Rawhide Co.
Cox Enterprises Inc.
Donaldson Company Inc.
Dow Jones & Company Inc.
du Pont de Nemours & Co. (E.I.)
Eaton Corp.
Ecolab Inc.
Elf Atochem North America Inc.
Equifax Inc.
Fluor Corp.
FMC Corp.
Fuller Co. (H.B.)
Gannett Company Inc.
General Motors Corp.
Halliburton Co.
Handy & Harman
Harsco Corp.
Johnson Controls Inc.
Kimberly-Clark Corp.
Metropolitan Life Insurance Co.
Minnesota Mining & Manufacturing Co.
Prudential Insurance Company of America
Quaker Chemical Corp.
Rockwell Automation Inc.
Scripps Co. (E.W.)
State Farm Mutual Automobile Insurance Co.
Tyson Foods Inc.
Union Pacific Corp.
United Parcel Service of America Inc.
USG Corp.
Valmont Industries Inc.
Weyerhaeuser Co.
Xerox Corp.

Oregon

ABC Inc.
Air Products and Chemicals Inc.
Albertson's Inc.
American Honda Motor Company Inc.
AMP Inc.
Appleton Papers Inc.
Assurant
Avista Corp.
Berwind Group
Boise Cascade Corp.
ChevronTexaco Corp.
D&B
Deere & Co.
Donnelley & Sons Co. (R.R.)
Eastman Kodak Co.
Equifax Inc.
Fannie Mae
Forest City Enterprises Inc.
Fujitsu America
Fuller Co. (H.B.)
GATX Corp.
General Mills Inc.
Heinz Co. (H.J.)
Johnson Controls Inc.
Land O'Lakes Inc.
Lee Enterprises Inc.
Menasha Corp.
Metropolitan Life Insurance Co.
Minnesota Mining & Manufacturing Co.
Mitsubishi Silicon America
Northwest Natural Gas Co.
Oki America Inc.
Ore-Ida Foods

Pacific Life Insurance Co.
PacifiCorp
Pioneer Trust Bank, N.A.
Rexam Inc.
St. Paul Travelers Companies Inc.
Schlumberger Ltd.
Simpson Investment Co.
Stanley Works
State Farm Mutual Automobile Insurance Co.
Subaru of America Inc.
Union Pacific Corp.
U.S. Bancorp Piper Jaffray
Unocal Corp.
Washington Mutual Inc.
Weyerhaeuser Co.

Pennsylvania

ABC Inc.
Air Products and Chemicals Inc.
Albertson's Inc.
Alcoa Inc.
Alcon Laboratories Inc.
Amcast Industrial Corp.
American General Finance
AMETEK Inc.
AMP Inc.
Anheuser-Busch Companies Inc.
Appleton Papers Inc.
Assurant
AT&T Corp.
Barnes Group Inc.
Bausch & Lomb Inc.
Bechtel Group Inc.
Bemis Company Inc.
Berwind Group
Birds Eye Foods Inc.
Brunswick Corp.
Bryn Mawr Bank Corp.
Campbell Soup Co.
Caterpillar Inc.
ChevronTexaco Corp.
CNA Financial Corp.
Coca-Cola Co.
Constellation Energy Group Inc.
Cox Enterprises Inc.
CUNA Mutual Group
D&B
Donaldson Company Inc.
Donnelley & Sons Co. (R.R.)
Dow Jones & Company Inc.
du Pont de Nemours & Co. (E.I.)
Dynamet Inc.
Eastman Kodak Co.
Eaton Corp.
Ebsco Industries Inc.
Ecolab Inc.
Elf Atochem North America Inc.
Equifax Inc.
Exelon
Fannie Mae
FMC Corp.
Forest City Enterprises Inc.
Forest Oil Corp.
Freeport Brick Co.
Gannett Company Inc.
GATX Corp.
General Motors Corp.
Giant Eagle Inc.
Giant Food Stores
Golub Corp.
Guardian Life Insurance Company of America
Halliburton Co.
Harley-Davidson Co.

Harsco Corp.
Hartmarx Corp.
Heinz Co. (H.J.)
Henkel Corp.
Hershey Foods Corp.
Hexcel Corp.
HON Industries Inc.
Hunt Corp.
Illinois Tool Works Inc.
Integra Bank
J&L Specialty Steel Inc.
Johnson Controls Inc.
Jostens Inc.
Kahn, Lucas-Lancaster Incorporated Children's Wear
Kimberly-Clark Corp.
Knight Ridder Inc.
Lamco Communications
Lebanon Mutual Insurance Co.
Lehigh Cement Co.
Lilly & Co. (Eli)
Lipton Co.
McClatchy Co.
McCormick & Company Inc.
Menasha Corp.
Metropolitan Life Insurance Co.
Millipore Corp.
Minnesota Mining & Manufacturing Co.
Mitsubishi Electric and Electronics USA
New York Times Co.
Pepco Holdings Inc.
PPG Industries Inc.
Prudential Insurance Company of America
Quaker Chemical Corp.
Rockwell Automation Inc.
Rouse Co.
Royal & SunAlliance USA Inc.
S&T Bancorp Inc.
Sara Lee Corp.
Schlumberger Ltd.
Sharon Steel Corp.
Shell Oil Co.
Sherwin-Williams Co.
Sovereign Bank
Spang & Co.
SPX Corp.
Square D Co.
Standard Steel
Stanley Works
Susquehanna-Pfaltzgraff Co.
Tetley U.S.A. Inc.
Tyson Foods Inc.
Union Pacific Corp.
United Parcel Service of America Inc.
Universal Studios
Vanguard Group
West Pharmaceutical Services Inc.
Weyerhaeuser Co.

Puerto Rico

Amgen Inc.
Credit Suisse First Boston Corp.
Ecolab Inc.
Gerber Products Co.
Millipore Corp.
Reynolds Tobacco (R.J.)
Schering-Plough Corp.
Sherwin-Williams Co.
Sonoco Products Co.
Storage Technology Corp.
West Pharmaceutical Services Inc.

Rhode Island

ABC Inc.
Ben & Jerry's Homemade Inc.
Citizens Financial Group Inc.
Country Curtains Inc.
Cox Enterprises Inc.
Cranston Print Works Co.
Dow Jones & Company Inc.
McCormick & Company Inc.
Mine Safety Appliances Co.
New York Times Co.
Providence Gas Co.
Providence Journal-Bulletin Co.
Sheaffer Pen Corp.
Stanley Works

South Carolina

Air Products and Chemicals Inc.
Alcoa Inc.
Bausch & Lomb Inc.
Bechtel Group Inc.
Belk Stores Services Inc.
Bowater Inc.
Burlington Industries Inc.
CCB Financial Corp.
Church & Dwight Company Inc.
Cox Enterprises Inc.
Cummins Inc.
Deere & Co.
Donnelley & Sons Co. (R.R.)
Dow Corning Corp.
du Pont de Nemours & Co. (E.I.)
Duke Energy Corp.
Eastman Kodak Co.
Eaton Corp.
Ecolab Inc.
Elf Atochem North America Inc.
Equifax Inc.
Fluor Corp.
FMC Corp.
Gannett Company Inc.
Giant Food Stores
Hasbro Inc.
Johnson Controls Inc.
Jostens Inc.
Kimberly-Clark Corp.
Knight Ridder Inc.
La-Z-Boy Inc.
Liberty Corp.
Marcus Corp.
Minnesota Mining & Manufacturing Co.
New York Times Co.
Progress Energy Inc.
Pulitzer Inc.
Rexam Inc.
Rockwell Automation Inc.
Sara Lee Corp.
Scoular Co.
Scripps Co. (E.W.)
Shell Oil Co.
Smith Corp. (A.O.)
Sonoco Products Co.
Square D Co.
Vulcan Materials Co.
Whirlpool Corp.
Williams Companies Inc.
Winn-Dixie Stores Inc.

South Dakota

Chicago Rawhide Co.
FMC Corp.
Gannett Company Inc.

Knight Ridder Inc.
Land O'Lakes Inc.
Midcontinent Media Inc.
Minnesota Mining & Manufacturing Co.
Morris Communications Corp.
Royal & SunAlliance USA Inc.
U.S. Bancorp Piper Jaffray
Xcel Energy

Tennessee

Air Products and Chemicals Inc.
Akzo Nobel Chemicals
Albertson's Inc.
Alcoa Inc.
American General Finance
Anheuser-Busch Companies Inc.
Aon Corp.
Archer-Daniels-Midland Co.
Banta Corp.
Barnes Group Inc.
Bechtel Group Inc.
Berwind Group
Bowater Inc.
Bridgestone Americas Holding Inc.
Burlington Industries Inc.
Cargill Inc.
CLARCOR Inc.
CNA Financial Corp.
Cummins Inc.
D&B
Donnelley & Sons Co. (R.R.)
du Pont de Nemours & Co. (E.I.)
Eastman Kodak Co.
Eaton Corp.
Ecolab Inc.
First Tennessee National Corp.
Fluor Corp.
Fuller Co. (H.B.)
Gannett Company Inc.
General Mills Inc.
General Motors Corp.
Gerber Products Co.
Harsco Corp.
Illinois Tool Works Inc.
Johns Manville
Johnson Controls Inc.
Jostens Inc.
Kimberly-Clark Corp.
Kroger Co.
La-Z-Boy Inc.
Lilly & Co. (Eli)
Magna International of America Inc.
Marcus Corp.
Minnesota Mining & Manufacturing Co.
Nestle Purina PetCare Co.
New York Times Co.
Olin Corp.
L'Oreal U.S.A.
Oshkosh B'Gosh Inc.
Pacific Life Insurance Co.
Progress Energy Inc.
Prudential Insurance Company of America
Rich Products Corp.
Rockwell Automation Inc.
SAFECO Corp.
Sara Lee Corp.
Schering-Plough Corp.
Scripps Co. (E.W.)
Sedgwick Inc.
Shell Oil Co.

Smith Corp. (A.O.)
Square D Co.
Stanley Works
State Farm Mutual Automobile Insurance Co.
Tension Envelope Corp.
Texas Instruments Inc.
Thomasville Furniture Industries Inc.
Tyson Foods Inc.
United Parcel Service of America Inc.
Vulcan Materials Co.
Whirlpool Corp.
Wurzburg Inc.

Texas

Abbott Laboratories
ABC Inc.
Air France
Air Products and Chemicals Inc.
Akzo Nobel Chemicals
Albertson's Inc.
Alcoa Inc.
Alcon Laboratories Inc.
Allianz Life Insurance Company of North America
American Standard Inc.
AMP Inc.
AMR Corp.
Anheuser-Busch Companies Inc.
Aon Corp.
Assurant
Bank of New York
Barnes Group Inc.
Bausch & Lomb Inc.
Belk Stores Services Inc.
Belo Corp.
Bemis Company Inc.
Birds Eye Foods Inc.
Blue Bell Inc.
Bridgestone Americas Holding Inc.
Broderbund L.L.C.
California Bank & Trust
Campbell Soup Co.
Caterpillar Inc.
CenterPoint Energy Inc.
ChevronTexaco Corp.
Chicago Tribune Direct Marketing
Church & Dwight Company Inc.
CIBC World Markets
CIT Group Inc.
Citigroup Global Markets Holdings Inc.
Claiborne Inc. (Liz)
CLARCOR Inc.
Cleveland-Cliffs Inc.
Clorox Co.
Comerica Inc.
Compass Bank
COMSAT International
Constellation Energy Group Inc.
Cox Enterprises Inc.
Cummins Inc.
CUNA Mutual Group
Deere & Co.
Donaldson Company Inc.
Donnelley & Sons Co. (R.R.)
Dow Jones & Company Inc.
du Pont de Nemours & Co. (E.I.)
Eastman Kodak Co.
Eaton Corp.
Ebsco Industries Inc.
Ecolab Inc.

El Paso Corp.
Elf Atochem North America Inc.
Equifax Inc.
Ethyl Corp.
Fannie Mae
Fidelity Investments
Fluor Corp.
FMC Corp.
Fort Worth Star-Telegram Inc.
Fortune Brands Inc.
Frost National Bank
Fujitsu America
Fuller Co. (H.B.)
GATX Corp.
GE Capital Corp.
General Mills Inc.
General Motors Corp.
Gerber Products Co.
Graco Inc.
Harsco Corp.
Hasbro Inc.
Heinz Co. (H.J.)
Hexcel Corp.
Holnam Inc.
HON Industries Inc.
Humana Inc.
Hunt Corp.
Illinois Tool Works Inc.
International Multifoods Corp.
Johns Manville
Johnson Controls Inc.
Johnson & Son (S.C.)
Jostens Inc.
Kajima International Inc.
Kimberly-Clark Corp.
Kroger Co.
Lilly & Co. (Eli)
Magna International of America Inc.
Management Compensation Group/Dulworth Inc.
Marcus Corp.
Maritz Inc.
Mattel Inc.
McCormick & Company Inc.
Metropolitan Life Insurance Co.
Microsoft Corp.
Minnesota Mining & Manufacturing Co.
Mitsubishi Electric and Electronics USA
Mitsubishi Motor Sales of America Inc.
Mitsubishi Silicon America
Morgan Chase & Co. (J.P.)
New York Life Insurance Co.
L'Oreal U.S.A.
Oshkosh B'Gosh Inc.
Pacific Life Insurance Co.
Penney Company Inc. (J.C.)
Pepco Holdings Inc.
Phelps Dodge Corp.
Prudential Insurance Company of America
Quaker Chemical Corp.
Quanex Corp.
Reichhold Chemicals Inc.
Reliable Life Insurance Co.
Rockwell Automation Inc.
Rouse Co.
Royal & SunAlliance USA Inc.
SAFECO Corp.
St. Paul Travelers Companies Inc.
Sara Lee Corp.
Schering-Plough Corp.
Schlumberger Ltd.
Scripps Co. (E.W.)

Security Life of Denver Insurance Co.
Shell Oil Co.
Sherwin-Williams Co.
Smith Corp. (A.O.)
Southwestern Electric Power Co.
Square D Co.
Stanley Works
State Farm Mutual Automobile Insurance Co.
Storage Technology Corp.
Subaru of America Inc.
Texas Instruments Inc.
Thompson Co. (J. Walter)
Tyson Foods Inc.
Union Pacific Corp.
United Parcel Service of America Inc.
Unocal Corp.
USG Corp.
Valmont Industries Inc.
Vulcan Materials Co.
Weyerhaeuser Co.
Williams Companies Inc.
Winn-Dixie Stores Inc.
Xerox Corp.

United States Virgin Islands

National Presto Industries Inc.
Raymond Corp.

Utah

Abbott Laboratories
Air Products and Chemicals Inc.
Albertson's Inc.
AT&T Corp.
Banta Corp.
Barnes Group Inc.
Boise Cascade Corp.
ChevronTexaco Corp.
D&B
Dow Jones & Company Inc.
Ecolab Inc.
GATX Corp.
Kimberly-Clark Corp.
La-Z-Boy Inc.
Land O'Lakes Inc.
Minnesota Mining & Manufacturing Co.
Novell
Pacific Life Insurance Co.
Quanex Corp.
Royal & SunAlliance USA Inc.
Thompson Co. (J. Walter)
U.S. Bancorp Piper Jaffray
USG Corp.
Valmont Industries Inc.
Washington Mutual Inc.

Vermont

Ben & Jerry's Homemade Inc.
Central Vermont Public Service Corp.
Gannett Company Inc.
General Motors Corp.
Golub Corp.
Johnson Controls Inc.
McCormick & Company Inc.
Stanley Works

Virginia

Abbott Laboratories

Air Products and Chemicals Inc.
Alcoa Inc.
American Honda Motor Company Inc.
American Standard Inc.
AMP Inc.
Anheuser-Busch Companies Inc.
AT&T Corp.
Banta Corp.
Bausch & Lomb Inc.
Belk Stores Services Inc.
Belo Corp.
Ben & Jerry's Homemade Inc.
Burlington Industries Inc.
Chesapeake Corp.
COMSAT International
Country Curtains Inc.
Cox Enterprises Inc.
D&B
Donnelley & Sons Co. (R.R.)
Dow Jones & Company Inc.
du Pont de Nemours & Co. (E.I.)
Eastman Kodak Co.
Ecolab Inc.
Equifax Inc.
Fluor Corp.
FMC Corp.
Fortune Brands Inc.
Gannett Company Inc.
General Motors Corp.
Giant Food Inc.
Giant Food Stores
Hershey Foods Corp.
HON Industries Inc.
Illinois Tool Works Inc.
Johns Manville
Kroger Co.
Landmark Communications Inc.
Lehigh Cement Co.
Lipton Co.
Lydall Inc.
McCormick & Company Inc.
Menasha Corp.
Old Dominion Box Co.
Prudential Insurance Company of America
Rockwell Automation Inc.
Royal & SunAlliance USA Inc.
SAFECO Corp.
Sara Lee Corp.
Scripps Co. (E.W.)
Shell Oil Co.

Shenandoah Life Insurance Co.
Stanley Works
State Farm Mutual Automobile Insurance Co.
Texas Instruments Inc.
Thomasville Furniture Industries Inc.
United Parcel Service of America Inc.
USG Corp.
Vaughan Furniture Co.
Vulcan Materials Co.
Weyerhaeuser Co.
Williams Companies Inc.
Winn-Dixie Stores Inc.
Xerox Corp.

Washington

ABC Inc.
Adobe Systems
Air Products and Chemicals Inc.
Albertson's Inc.
Alcoa Inc.
AMETEK Inc.
AT&T Corp.
Avista Corp.
Banta Corp.
Barnes Group Inc.
Belo Corp.
Birds Eye Foods Inc.
Boise Cascade Corp.
Burlington Industries Inc.
California Bank & Trust
Carnival Corp.
Caterpillar Inc.
ChevronTexaco Corp.
Church & Dwight Company Inc.
Cox Enterprises Inc.
CUNA Mutual Group
Donaldson Company Inc.
Donnelley & Sons Co. (R.R.)
Dow Corning Corp.
Dow Jones & Company Inc.
Eastman Kodak Co.
Eaton Corp.
Ecolab Inc.
Elf Atochem North America Inc.
Equifax Inc.
Fannie Mae
FMC Corp.
Fortune Brands Inc.
Fuller Co. (H.B.)
Gannett Company Inc.
GATX Corp.

GE Capital Corp.
Guardian Life Insurance Company of America
HON Industries Inc.
Hubbard Broadcasting Inc.
International Multifoods Corp.
Johnson Controls Inc.
Johnson & Son (S.C.)
Kimberly-Clark Corp.
Land O'Lakes Inc.
Lilly & Co. (Eli)
Macy's East Inc.
McCormick & Company Inc.
Menasha Corp.
Microsoft Corp.
Minnesota Mining & Manufacturing Co.
Oki America Inc.
Olin Corp.
Pacific Life Insurance Co.
PacifiCorp
Prudential Insurance Company of America
Rayonier Inc.
Rockwell Automation Inc.
Rouse Co.
St. Paul Travelers Companies Inc.
Sara Lee Corp.
Simpson Investment Co.
Smith Corp. (A.O.)
Square D Co.
Texas Instruments Inc.
Tyson Foods Inc.
Union Pacific Corp.
United Parcel Service of America Inc.
U.S. Bancorp Piper Jaffray
Unocal Corp.
US Bank
USG Corp.
Washington Mutual Inc.
Weyerhaeuser Co.

West Virginia

Air Products and Chemicals Inc.
Belk Stores Services Inc.
Berwind Group
du Pont de Nemours & Co. (E.I.)
FMC Corp.
General Motors Corp.
Giant Food Stores
Harsco Corp.
Johns Manville
Lee Enterprises Inc.
Lilly & Co. (Eli)

Metropolitan Life Insurance Co.
Minnesota Mining & Manufacturing Co.
Olin Corp.
PacifiCorp
Phelps Dodge Corp.
PPG Industries Inc.
Scripps Co. (E.W.)
United Parcel Service of America Inc.

Wisconsin

Air Products and Chemicals Inc.
Akzo Nobel Chemicals
Alliant Energy Corp.
Amcast Industrial Corp.
American Standard Inc.
Andersen Corp.
Anheuser-Busch Companies Inc.
Appleton Papers Inc.
Assurant
Bank of New York
Banta Corp.
Barnes Group Inc.
Bemis Company Inc.
Campbell Soup Co.
Cargill Inc.
Caterpillar Inc.
Chesapeake Corp.
Cox Enterprises Inc.
Donaldson Company Inc.
Dow Jones & Company Inc.
Eastman Kodak Co.
Eaton Corp.
Ecolab Inc.
Elf Atochem North America Inc.
Equifax Inc.
First Financial Bank
Fluor Corp.
FMC Corp.
Fortune Brands Inc.
Gannett Company Inc.
General Motors Corp.
Gerber Products Co.
Guardian Life Insurance Company of America
Handy & Harman
Henkel Corp.
Hunt Corp.
Johnson Controls Inc.
Joy Global Inc.
JSJ Corp.
Kemper National Insurance Cos.

Kimberly-Clark Corp.
Land O'Lakes Inc.
Lee Enterprises Inc.
Marcus Corp.
Marshall & Ilsley Corp.
Menasha Corp.
Midcontinent Media Inc.
Minnesota Mining & Manufacturing Co.
National Presto Industries Inc.
Nordson Corp.
Olin Corp.
Ore-Ida Foods
Pamida Inc.
PPG Industries Inc.
Quanex Corp.
Rexam Inc.
Reynolds Tobacco (R.J.)
Rockwell Automation Inc.
Rouse Co.
Saint Francis Bank
St. Paul Travelers Companies Inc.
Sara Lee Corp.
Sentry Insurance, A Mutual Co.
Smith Corp. (A.O.)
Square D Co.
Stora Enso
Texas Instruments Inc.
United Parcel Service of America Inc.
U.S. Bancorp Piper Jaffray
Unocal Corp.
USG Corp.
Vulcan Materials Co.
Wausau-Mosinee Paper Corp.
Weyerhaeuser Co.
Wisconsin Energy Corp.
WPS Resources Corp.
Xcel Energy

Wyoming

American General Finance
ChevronTexaco Corp.
FMC Corp.
Kinder Morgan
Land O'Lakes Inc.
Pamida Inc.
Pittsburg & Midway Coal Mining Co.
United Parcel Service of America Inc.
U.S. Bancorp Piper Jaffray
Unocal Corp.

LIBRARY RECIPIENTS BY STATE

The following index lists alphabetically grants given to libraries and other library-related projects by the state in which the library and/or project is located. Within each state, grants are listed in alphabetical order. When several grants have been given to the same organization, such as the New York Public Library, individual grants are listed in descending order by the grant amount.

Alabama

Birmingham Public Library (5,000) see John A. and Delia T. Robert Charitable Trust 2
Daleville Public Library (10,000) see Daniel Foundation of Alabama
Grove Hill Public Library (10,000) see J. L. Bedsole Foundation
Mobile Public Library (150,000) see J. L. Bedsole Foundation
Mobile Public Library (5,000) see M. W. Smith, Jr. Foundation
Mountain Brook Library Foundation -- for support of plant expansion (50,000) see Comer Foundation (AL)
Mountain Brook Library Foundation (5,000) see Tractor & Equipment Co.
Parnell Memorial Library Foundation Inc. (50,000) see Daniel Foundation of Alabama

Alaska

Friends of the Haines Borough Public Library -- towards new community facility (250,000) see M. J. Murdock Charitable Trust
Friends of the Library -- for landscaping and exterior modifications (22,264) see James and Elise Nolan Charitable Trust
Irene Ingle Public Library -- for computer purchases (5,600) see James and Elise Nolan Charitable Trust

Arizona

Desert Foothills Library (25,000) see Sarah K. de Coizart Perpetual Charitable Trust
Libraries LTD (3,000) see Eliot Spalding Foundation
Prescott Public Library (5,000) see V. V. Cooke Foundation Corp.
Prescott Public Library (1,500) see Margaret T. Morris Foundation

Arkansas

Barton Library -- operating budget (30,222) see Murphy Foundation

Central Arkansas Library System -- toward development of on-line Encyclopedia of Arkansas History and Culture (171,537) see Winthrop Rockefeller Foundation
Central Arkansas Library System (31,250) see Ottenheimer Brothers Foundation
Fayetteville Public Library (500,000) see Willard and Pat Walker Charitable Foundation
William J Clinton Presidential Fund (1,750,000) see United Paramount Network
William J. Clinton Presidential Foundation -- fund for William J. Clinton Presidential Library (1,000,000) see Annenberg Foundation

California

California State Library Foundation: Governor's Book Fund (20,000) see Motorola Inc.
David Hale Library (2,500) see Ducommun and Gross Foundation
David Hale Library (2,500) see Ducommun Inc.
Friends of the Central Library (10,000) see Niagara Mohawk Holdings Inc.
Friends of the Montecito Library (20,000) see G. Harold and Leila Y. Mathers Charitable Foundation
Henry E. Huntington Library & Art Gallery (500,000) see Ahmanson Foundation
Henry E. Huntington Library & Art Gallery (500,000) see Ahmanson Foundation
Henry E. Huntington Library & Art Gallery -- to support education and school tour programs (5,000) see Lluella Morey Murphey Foundation
Huntington Library (1,000,000) see Virginia Steele Scott Foundation
Huntington Library (175,000) see Virginia Steele Scott Foundation
Huntington Library (97,300) see Essick Foundation
Huntington Library (27,500) see Virginia Steele Scott Foundation

Huntington Library (25,000) see Fletcher Jones Foundation
Huntington Library -- offers history fellowships (22,000) see John Randolph and Dora Haynes Foundation
Huntington Library -- assists with early California population project (22,000) see John Randolph and Dora Haynes Foundation
Huntington Library (20,000) see Fletcher Jones Foundation
Huntington Library (15,000) see H. Leslie Hoffman & Elaine S. Hoffman Foundation
Huntington Library -- provides cataloging Edmund D. Edelman papers (10,000) see John Randolph and Dora Haynes Foundation
Huntington Library -- school tours (5,000) see Ann Peppers Foundation
Library Foundation (10,000) see McGraw-Hill Companies Inc.
Library Foundation (3,000) see Rene Bloch Foundation
Library Foundation of Los Angeles (35,000) see B. C. McCabe Foundation
Library Foundation of Los Angeles -- assists with electronic neighborhood (25,068) see John Randolph and Dora Haynes Foundation
Library Foundation of Los Angeles (10,000) see The Swig Foundation
Long Beach Public Library Foundation (11,700) see Josephine Gumbiner Foundation
Long Beach Public Library Foundation (10,000) see Leburta Atherton Foundation
Meiklejohn Civil Liberties Library (5,000) see Samuel Rubin Foundation
Nixon Library -- to support expenses (417,906) see Reader's Digest Association Inc.
Nixon Library -- towards partners for peace program (250,000) see Reader's Digest Association Inc.
Oakland Library (5,800) see Gardiner Savings Institution

Oakland Public Library Foundation -- to support the PASSI program (25,000) see William G. McGowan Charitable Fund
Oakland Public Library Foundation -- funds for the after school program providing assistance to children and teens (10,000) see Morris Stulsaft Foundation
Otis Library -- financial assistance for microfilming archived local newspaper (2,800) see Dime Bank of Norwich Connecticut
Richard Nixon Library & Birthplace Foundation -- towards Annenberg Court (1,500,000) see Annenberg Foundation
San Diego County Library -- charitable (5,000) see Alphonse A. Burnand Medical and Educational Foundation
San Diego Public Library (10,000) see Ellis Foundation
San Francisco Public Library -- Wallace Stegner Environmental Center (15,000) see Mary A. Crocker Trust
San Jose Public Library Partners in Reading (500) see Knight Ridder Inc.
San Mateo Public Library (10,000) see The Swig Foundation
Solano County Library Foundation (250,000) see Frank H. and Eva B. Buck Foundation
Stanford University Libraries -- towards funding present operating expenses (75,000) see Smart Family Foundation
Walnut Creek Library Foundation -- towards the Ygnacio Valley library improvement project (10,000) see Vodafone Group PLC

Colorado

Auraria Library -- for purchasing additional equipment for the computer commons area (20,000) see Kenneth Kendal King Foundation
Denver Public Library -- funding for cataloging mining collection (50,000) see El Pomar Foundation

Denver Public Library (5,000) see Harmes C. Fishback Foundation Trust
Denver Public Library see Security Life of Denver Insurance Co.
Denver Public Library Friends Foundation -- operating support of read aloud and design ongoing evaluation programs (29,000) see Temple Hoyne Buell Foundation
Dolores Public Library (100,000) see Gates Family Foundation
East Morgan County Library (43,800) see Joslin-Needham Family Foundation
Friends of the Pine River Public Library -- towards construction of community room (35,000) see Adolph Coors Foundation
Friends of the Ridgway Public Library (67,000) see Gates Family Foundation
Pikes Peak Library (20,000) see H. Chase Stone Trust
Rampart Regional Library District (100,000) see Gates Family Foundation
Rampart Regional Library District (30,000) see Adolph Coors Foundation

Connecticut

Berlin-Peck Memorial Library -- to replace books and computers (10,500) see Marjorie Moore Charitable Foundation
Berlin-Peck Memorial Library -- purchase large print books and audio taped books (1,500) see Robert C. Vance Charitable Foundation
Cornwall Library Association (3,500) see Harriet Ford Dickenson Foundation
Darien Library (10,000) see Joe and Emily Lowe Foundation
East Greenwich Free Library (500) see Trimix Foundation
Farmington Library (5,000) see Barnes Group Inc.
Ferguson Library Foundation (1,000) see Rich Foundation Inc.
Friends of Darien Library (20,000) see Goodnow Fund

Gunn Memorial Library (2,500) see Rene Bloch Foundation

Hartford Public Library (33,000) see Massachusetts Mutual Life Insurance Co.

Hartford Public Library (10,000) see Maximilian E. and Marion O. Hoffman Foundation

Mark Twain Library (5,100) see Jane T. Muhlethaler Foundation, Inc.

Norfolk Library (5,000) see AKC Fund

Simsbury Public Library (1,000) see Ensign-Bickford Industries

Southern Connecticut Library Council (2,500) see NewAlliance Bancshares Inc.

Stonington Free Library -- contribution to support organization (1,000) see Blood-Horse Charitable Foundation

Thomaston Public Library (2,500) see Thomaston F.S.B.

Voluntown Public Library -- expand and re-do youth biography section of library (1,000) see Eastern S.L.A.

Wadsworth Atheneaum (88,000) see Hartford Financial Services Group Inc.

Wadsworth Atheneaum (75,000) see The Florence Gould Foundation

Wadsworth Atheneaum -- Michael Sweerts exhibition (30,000) see Helen M. Saunders Charitable Foundation Trust

Wadsworth Atheneaum -- Sol LeWitt Cube Show (20,000) see Helen M. Saunders Charitable Foundation Trust

Wadsworth Atheneaum -- Gauguin exhibit (15,000) see Helen M. Saunders Charitable Foundation Trust

Watertown Library Association (3,000) see Thomaston F.S.B.

Wilton Library Association Inc. (100,000) see The Carl and Lily Pforzheimer Foundation, Inc.

Wilton Library Association Inc. (25,000) see Leon Lowenstein Foundation

Wilton Library Association Inc. (17,700) see Leon Lowenstein Foundation

Wilton Library Association Inc. (5,100) see Jane T. Muhlethaler Foundation, Inc.

Delaware

Friends of Concord Pike Library (35,000) see Laffey-McHugh Foundation

Georgetown Public Library (20,000) see Marmot Foundation

Intercollegiate Studies Institute, Inc. -- community service (500) see Dentsply International Inc.

Laurel Public Library (250,000) see Good Samaritan

Laurel Public Library -- renovations and expansion (150,000) see Crystal Trust

Selbyville Public Library (15,000) see Marmot Foundation

Woodlawn Library -- capital campaign (50,000) see Crystal Trust

District of Columbia

Folger Shakespeare Library -- operating support (15,000) see Memton Fund

Folger Shakespeare Library -- operating support (15,000) see Memton Fund

Laura Bush Foundation for America's Libraries (250,000) see General Motors Corp.

Laura Bush Foundation for America's Libraries (100,000) see Castle Rock Foundation

Laura Bush Foundation for America's Libraries (50,000) see Hillcrest Foundation

Laura Bush Foundation for American Libraries (10,000) see Loews Corp.

Laura Bush Foundation for Americas Libraries -- towards general operating support (10,000) see Vodafone Group PLC

Library of Congress -- towards support of acquisition and fellowship program to strengthen the Asia collection (185,000) see Henry Luce Foundation

Library of Congress -- towards an orientation seminar for new House Members of 108th congress (175,000) see Henry Luce Foundation

Library of Congress -- for Library's Fall 2001 Exhibition of Japanese Art and Literature (142,500) see United States-Japan Foundation

Library of Congress -- sponsoring 2003 national book festival (100,000) see AT&T Corp.

Library of Congress (20,000) see ContiGroup Companies Inc.

Library of Congress Trust Fund Board (9,000) see

John W. and Clara C. Higgins Foundation

Library of Congress-James Madison Council (15,000) see Liz Claiborne and Art Ortenberg Foundation

Smithsonian Institution Libraries (57,600) see Dibner Fund

Special Libraries Association (10,000) see H. W. Wilson Foundation

Florida

Bay County Library Foundation (2,500) see Gulf Power Co.

Broward Public Library Foundation (13,000) see Folke H. Peterson Charitable Foundation

Broward Public Library Foundation Inc. (3,780) see BankAtlantic Bancorp

Delray Beach Public Library (100,000) see Forrest C. Lattner Foundation

Friends of the Fruitville Public Library (20,000) see William G. Selby and Marie Selby Foundation

Friends of the LeRoy Collins Leon County Public Library -- towards support of 2003 author event (2,500) see United States Sugar Corp.

Friends of the Pensacola Library -- operations (4,000) see BCR Foundation

Harlem Community Public Library (3,000) see United States Sugar Corp.

J. Germany Public Library (16,600) see May Kay Houck Foundation

Jacksonville Public Library (50,000) see Morris Communications Corp.

Jacksonville Public Library (5,000) see Carl S. Swisher Foundation

Library Foundation of Martin County (50,000) see The Carl and Lily Pforzheimer Foundation, Inc.

Navarre Public Library (10,000) see Tom S. and Marye Kate Aldridge Charitable and Educational Trust

Georgia

Atlanta Fulton Public Library (3,000) see Whilma B. Lee Scholarship Fund Trust

Jimmy Carter Library and Museum -- for the purpose of special projects (50,000) see Cox Enterprises Inc.

Liberty County Public Library (22,241) see Margaret Lee Martin Charitable Trust

Newton County Library (64,379) see James

Hyde Porter Testamentary Trust

Idaho

Community Library Association (5,000) see James and Barbara Cimino Foundation

Eastern Idaho Library Network Consortium (28,000) see Steele-Reese Foundation

Fruitland Community Library -- maintenance and improvement (18,200) see Laura Moore Cunningham Foundation

Lewiston City Library -- capital improvements (25,000) see Laura Moore Cunningham Foundation

Priest Lake Public Library -- capital improvements (15,000) see Laura Moore Cunningham Foundation

Illinois

Abraham Lincoln Presidential Library Foundation (200,000) see State Farm Mutual Automobile Insurance Co.

American Library Association (10,000) see Scott Fetzer Co.

American Library Association -- to promote reading among young adults (7,750) see Margaret Alexander Edwards Trust

Chicago Public Library (10,000) see Elizabeth Morse Genius Charitable Trust

Chicago Public Library Foundation (15,000) see Barker Welfare Foundation

Chicago Public Library Foundation -- to provide after school homework help and guidance for children (10,000) see Dr. Scholl Foundation

Chicago Public Library Foundation (5,000) see Southwest News Herald

Chicago Public Library Foundation (1,000) see Kovler Family Foundation

Coffeen Community Library -- purchase of books (2,000) see Mary Heath Foundation

Forrest Library (2,000) see Quanex Corp.

Fund for American Libraries (25,000) see H. W. Wilson Foundation

Geneseo Public Library District -- for equipment (11,844) see Myers Charitable Trust

Gilman Area District Library -- capital support for arts and culture (59,800) see Coleman Foundation (IL)

Glencoe Public Library (500) see Jaffee Foundation

LITA (American Library Association) (10,000) see Fireman's Fund Insurance Co.

Newberry Library (20,000) see Chauncey and Marion Deering McCormick Foundation

Newberry Library (15,000) see FMC Corp.

Newberry Library -- for educational outreach (10,000) see Albert Pick, Jr. Fund

Newberry Library (10,000) see Abra Prentice Foundation

Newberry Library (2,500) see Charles H. and Bertha L. Boothroyd Foundation

PLUS (50,000) see CNA Financial Corp.

Palestine Public Library (1,970) see Silas and Ruth Claypool Foundation

Palestine Public Library District -- library lighting (400) see Mary Heath Foundation

Pontiac Public library (1,350) see J. Paul Yost Trust

Robinson Public Library District (2,000) see Silas and Ruth Claypool Foundation

Sterling Public Library (17,500) see Dillon Foundation

Sterling Public Library -- for library operation (1,500) see Donaldson Company Inc.

Stinson Memorial Library -- restoration project (50,000) see United Paramount Network

Westville Public Library (25,000) see Julius W. Hegeler II Foundation

Indiana

Allen County Public Library Foundation -- towards expansion of the foundation collection services (144,127) see Foellinger Foundation

Allen County Public Library Foundation -- towards young adult summer reading (100,000) see Foellinger Foundation

Allen County Public Library Foundation (25,000) see Dr. Louis A. and Anne B. Schneider Foundation

Eckhart Public Library (7,000) see Rieke Corp.

Indianapolis - Marion County Public Library Foundation -- renovation and expansion of the Indianapolis-Marion county central library (200,000) see Eli Lilly & Co.

Indianapolis Marion County Library -- capital fund (10,075) see Ayres Foundation

Indianapolis Marion County Public Library Foundation (25,000,000) see Lilly Endowment

Indianapolis Marion County Public Library Foundation -- towards Indianapolis special collection room (250,000) see Nina Mason Pulliam Charitable Trust

Indianapolis-Marion County Public Library Foundation Inc. -- for renovation expansion (50,000) see Nicholas H. Noyes, Jr. Memorial Foundation

Jay County Public Library (7,500) see Ball Brothers Foundation

Ligonier Public Library (5,000) see Journal-Gazette Co.

Monroe County Public Library (10,075) see Temple-Inland Inc.

Monroe County Public Library (10,000) see J. L. Bedsole Foundation

St. Joseph County Public Library (5,000) see 1st Source Corp.

Iowa

Audubon Public Library (1,375) see Audubon State Bank

Birmingham Public Library -- Ralph Shott Memorial (595) see Van Buren Foundation

Brown Memorial Library -- funding to construct new addition (60,000) see Roy J. Carver Charitable Trust

Cedar Falls Public Library -- funding to purchase security and self-checkout system (60,000) see Roy J. Carver Charitable Trust

Cedar Rapids Public Library -- toward memorial gift (250) see Hall-Perrine Foundation

Chariton Public Library (10,000) see American Optical Corp.

City of Springville -- toward the new public library see Hall-Perrine Foundation

Clarinda Foundation Inc. -- funding for library construction (190,206) see Lied Foundation Trust

Community Public Library Foundation -- funding for constructing a new library facility (60,000) see Roy J. Carver Charitable Trust

Drake Free Public Library (23,000) see Bemis Company Inc.

Ely Public Library -- toward library remodeling project (60,000) see Roy J. Carver Charitable Trust

Fertile Public Library (2,000) see Winnebago Industries

Garrett Memorial Library (1,500) see Alliant Energy Corp.

Grafton Public Library (15,000) see Bunbury Co., Inc.

Hoover Presidential Library Association -- fund towards W.R. Castle, Jr. Fellowship program (10,000) see Samuel N. and Mary Castle Foundation

Iowa City Public Library -- towards capital campaign (3,000) see Gazette Co.

Iowa City Public Library Foundation -- funding for renovation and expansion of the library (60,000) see Roy J. Carver Charitable Trust

Keosauqua Public Library -- computerize circulation system (4,125) see Van Buren Foundation

Missouri Valley Public Library -- funding for library expansion (60,000) see Roy J. Carver Charitable Trust

Mount Pleasant Library & Community Center -- toward library renovation (60,000) see Roy J. Carver Charitable Trust

Musser Public Library -- toward upgrading technology and establishing digital image archive (82,042) see Roy J. Carver Charitable Trust

Panora Public Library Foundation -- funding for purchase of technology for the new library (60,000) see Roy J. Carver Charitable Trust

Polk City Public Library Foundation -- toward construction of new library and purchase of furnishings (60,000) see Roy J. Carver Charitable Trust

Public Library of Des Moines (100,460) see Meredith Corp.

Public Library of Des Moines Foundation (300,000) see Principal Financial Group

Public Library of Des Moines Foundation (5,000) see Weathertop Foundation

Public Library of Des Moines Foundation -- towards education (1,500) see Amerus Group Co.

Rock Rapids Public Library -- serendipity club (latch-key kids) (4,000) see James W. and Ella B. Forster Charitable Trust

Southeastern Library Services -- software upgrade for county libraries (1,689) see Van Buren Foundation

Stacyville Public Library -- funding for construction of new library (60,000) see Roy J. Carver Charitable Trust

Stewart Library -- automation of library equipment (25,000) see Claude W. and Dolly Ahrens Foundation

Kansas

Atchison County Library -- audio books (3,500) see W. and E. Morgan Charitable Residual Trust

Columbus Public Library (4,000) see Commerce Bancshares Inc.

Hays Public Library Trust (5,000) see Ross Foundation

Johnson County Library Foundation (2,500) see Tension Envelope Corp.

Kansas Library Association (10,000) see H. W. Wilson Foundation

Kismet Public Library -- towards upgrades and furniture for computers (6,275) see Baughman Foundation

Liberal Memorial Library -- towards book fund (10,000) see Baughman Foundation

Topeka and Shawnee County Public Library (500) see Blanche Bryden Foundation

Kentucky

Campbell County Public Library (2,000) see Kinder Morgan

Jefferson County Law Library (300) see PPG Industries Inc.

Library Foundation (500) see PPG Industries Inc.

Louisville Free Public Library Foundation Inc. (15,000) see LG&E Energy Corp.

Louisville Free Public Library Fund (15,000) see Joan and Lee Thomas Foundation

Louisiana

St. Mary Parish Library System (7,500) see Cabot Corp.

Maine

Auburn Public Library (50,000) see Gladys and Roland Harriman Foundation

Brown Memorial Library (25,000) see William Bingham Second Betterment Fund

Brown Memorial Library (5,000) see Margaret E. Burnham Charitable Trust

Falmouth Memorial Library (5,000) see Margaret E. Burnham Charitable Trust

Library Club of Lovell -- for public library purposes (3,300) see Clarence E. Mulford Trust

Ludden Memorial Library (25,000) see William Bingham Second Betterment Fund

Maine Community Foundation (50,000) see William Bingham Second Betterment Fund

Maine Community Foundation (25,000) see William Bingham Second Betterment Fund

Northeast Harbor Library -- toward operating support (15,000) see Crestlea Foundation

Northeast Harbor Library (1,000) see Walter and Josephine Ford Fund

Norway Medical Library (25,000) see William Bingham Second Betterment Fund

Norway Memorial Library (25,000) see William Bingham Second Betterment Fund

Oakland Public Library -- educational (30,000) see Brook Family Foundation

Rockland Public Library Endowment Association -- library program (2,000) see J.C. Penney Company Inc.

Seal Harbor Library (1,000) see Walter and Josephine Ford Fund

Topsham Public Library (6,667) see Gardiner Savings Institution

William A. Farnsworth Library & Art Museum Inc. -- funding for general operating support (70,000) see The Overbrook Foundation

Maryland

Baltimore County Public Library -- capital campaign (5,000) see Campbell Foundation (MD)

Enoch Pratt Free Library (25,000) see William G. Baker, Jr. Memorial Fund

Enoch Pratt Free Library (25,000) see John J. Leidy Foundation

Enoch Pratt Free Library (22,835) see T. Rowe Price Associates

Enoch Pratt Free Library -- for youth development, After-School Program at Roland Park Public School (20,000) see Clayton Baker Trust

Enoch Pratt Free Library -- for family place program (7,500) see Baltimore Equity Society

Enoch Pratt Free Library (5,000) see Hecht-Levi Foundation

Johns Hopkins Children's Library and Family Resource Center -- Family Resource Library (17,000) see Thomas Wilson Sanitarium for Children of Baltimore City

Kennedy Krieger Institute -- capital campaign (20,000) see Constellation Energy Group Inc.

Library of American Broadcasting (5,000) see Susquehanna-Pfaltzgraff Co.

Reach, Inc. -- electric pallet jack (5,971) see Albert E. and Naomi B. Sinnisen Foundation

Roland Park Library Initiative, Inc. -- for community development (40,000) see Lockhart Vaughan Foundation

St. James School Library Fund (8,000) see Lucien B. and Katherine E. Price Foundation

Village Learning Place, Inc. -- for community development and capital campaign (50,000) see Clayton Baker Trust

Massachusetts

American Antiquarian Society -- towards capital campaign (500,000) see Mildred H. McEvoy Foundation

American Antiquarian Society (250,000) see George I. Alden Trust

American Antiquarian Society -- towards building addition and renovation (100,000) see Stoddard Charitable Trust

American Antiquarian Society (30,000) see Fred Harris Daniels Foundation

American Antiquarian Society (10,000) see Margaret E. Sherman Trust

Amesbury Public Library (27,178) see Provident Community Foundation

Boston Athenaeum -- support intern program and establish endowment fund (200,000) see Good Samaritan

Boston Athenaeum (10,000) see Constance Killam Trust

Boston Athenaeum (10,000) see Clara B. Winthrop Trust

Boston Public Library -- towards education (25,000) see Richard and Susan Smith Family Foundation

Boston Public Library Foundation (250,000) see William Randolph Hearst Foundation

Boston Public Library Foundation (100,000) see State Street Corp.

Boston Public Library Foundation (17,000) see Sidney R. Rabb Charitable Trust

Boston Public Library Foundation (8,000) see Sidney and Esther Rabb Charitable Foundation

Boston Public Library Foundation (5,000) see William J. and Lia G. Poorvu Foundation

Brockton Library (15,000) see Home for Aged Men in the City of Brockton

Brookline Library Foundation (2,500) see Bay State Bancorp Inc.

Brookline Public Library (1,000) see Hamilton Charitable Corp.

Brookline Public Library (1,000) see Hamilton Charitable Corp.

Brooks School (7,550) see Catherine McCarthy Memorial Trust Fund

Burndy Library (147,557) see Dibner Fund

Charlton Public Library (20,000) see Hyde Manufacturing Co.

Concord Free Public Library Corporation -- funds for renovation (100,000) see Fidelity Investments

French Library and Cultural Center (85,000) see Beaucourt Foundation

French Library and Cultural Center (70,000) see Beaucourt Foundation

Friends of Concord Park Library (500,000) see Longwood Foundation

Friends of the Chicopee Public Library (25,000) see Frank Stanley Beveridge Foundation, Inc.

Friends of the Chicopee Public Library (8,324) see Woronoco Savings Bank

Friends of the Worcester Public Library -- expansion and renovations to Salem Square Public Library (150,000) see Fletcher Foundation

Friends of the Worcester Public Library -- capital project for the expansion and renovation of Salem Square (30,000) see Ruth H. and Warren A. Ellsworth Foundation

Friends of the Worcester Public Library -- expansion and renovation of library (20,000) see Francis A. and Jacquelyn H. Harrington Foundation

Groton School Library (200,000) see Chauncey and Marion Deering McCormick Foundation

Hingham Public Library (1,000) see Building 19 Foundation

John Fitzgerald Kennedy Library (200,000) see Joseph P. Kennedy, Jr. Foundation

Joshua Hyde Library (5,000) see American Optical Corp.

Lenox Library (5,000) see Country Curtains Inc.

Lenox Library Association (25,000) see Country Curtains Inc.

Lenox Library Association (10,000) see Country Curtains Inc.

Manchester by the Sea Conservation Trust (15,000) see Clara B. Winthrop Trust

Mary Baker Eddy Library -- for the Betterment of Humanity (2,511) see Greca Realty & Development Corporation Inc.

Mattapoisett Library (12,000) see Olive Higgins Prouty Foundation

Mattapoisett Library (2,500) see Shaw's Supermarkets Inc.

Nantucket Athenaeum (150,000) see Tupancy-Harris Foundation of 1986

Nantucket Atheneum (10,000) see McCausland Foundation

Nantucket Atheneum (2,500) see Monadnock Paper Mills Inc.

National Yiddish Book Center (15,000) see Dibner Fund

New England Conservatory of Music (7,500) see Clara B. Winthrop Trust

Northboro Historical Society (10,000) see Margaret E. Sherman Trust

Northboro Public Library (3,000) see Margaret E. Sherman Trust

Plymouth Public Library (5,000) see Henry Hornblower Fund

Randall Library (12,500) see Joe and Emily Lowe Foundation

Somerset Public Library (1,800) see Hathaway Memorial Charitable Trust

South Dennis Library Fund (4,000) see C. Northrop Pond and Alethea Marder Pond Foundation

Stockbridge Library Association (5,000) see Country Curtains Inc.

Sturgis Library (2,500,000) see Seth Sprague Educational and Charitable Foundation

Sturgis Library (2,500,000) see Seth Sprague Educational and Charitable Foundation

Suffolk University - Mildred F. Sawyer Library (50,000) see Sawyer Charitable Foundation

Summerville Public Library (2,500) see S&T Bancorp Inc.

Wellesley Free Library (76,500) see Cele H. and

William B. Rubin Family Fund

Worcester Public Library (30,000) see Hoche-Scofield Foundation

Worcester Public Library (11,000) see Nathaniel Wheeler Trust

Michigan

Bay County Library -- towards operating expenses (166,667) see Herbert H. and Grace A. Dow Foundation

Bay County Library System (5,000) see Consumers Energy Co.

Coleman Area Library -- towards operating expenses (100,000) see Herbert H. and Grace A. Dow Foundation

Friends of the Detroit Public Library (8,000) see DeRoy Testamentary Foundation

Friends of the Detroit Public Library (100) see H. T. Ewald Foundation

Friends of the Mitchell Library (10,000) see Quivey-Bay State Foundation

Grand Rapids Public Library (12,500) see Keller Family Foundation

Grosse Pointe Library (100) see H. T. Ewald Foundation

Harbor Springs Library Association (10,000) see The Offield Family Foundation

Howard Miller Library (20,000) see Batts Foundation

Ida Township (Library) (15,000) see La-Z-Boy Inc.

Ida Township (Library) (15,000) see La-Z-Boy Inc.

Library of Michigan Foundation (179,500) see Talbert and Leota Abrams Foundation

M. Preston Palenske Library -- community welfare (25,000) see Tiscornia Foundation

Merrill District Library -- grants to purchase of new facility (25,000) see Harvey Randall Wickes Foundation

Orion Township Public Library (500) see Broomfield Charitable Foundation

Ryerson Library Foundation (255,000) see Keeler Foundation

Ryerson Library Foundation -- annual support (2,000) see Frank B. and Virginia V. Fehsenfeld Charitable Foundation

Saline Public Library (3,000) see R&B Machine Tool Co.

Spring Lake District Library (25,000) see JSJ Corp.

Vicksburg District Library (9,606) see Vicksburg Foundation

Minnesota

Bakken Library and Museum (75,000) see Medtronic Inc.

Bayport Public Library (47,500) see Andersen Corp.

City of Stillwater Public Library -- towards capital campaign (75,000) see Hugh J. Andersen Foundation

Friends of the Minneapolis Public Library (250,000) see Best Buy Co.

Friends of the Minneapolis Public Library (11,000) see Hubbard Broadcasting Inc.

Friends of the St. Paul Public Library -- for Albert J. Moorman Fund (50,000) see Edwin W. and Catherine M. Davis Foundation

Friends of the St. Paul Public Library (50,000) see Hubbard Broadcasting Inc.

Friends of the St. Paul Public Library -- system renewal (30,000) see Mary Livingston Griggs and Mary Griggs Burke Foundation

Friends of the St. Paul Public Library (10,000) see Anna M. Heilmaier Charitable Foundation

Friends of the St. Paul Public Library (10,000) see U.S. Bancorp Piper Jaffray

Friends of the St. Paul Public Library (9,000) see Tozer Foundation

Friends of the St. Paul Public Library (5,000) see Specialty Manufacturing Co.

Jessie F. Hallett Memorial Library (187,722) see E. W. Hallett Charitable Trust

Library Foundation of Hennepin County -- for read to me, daddy-read to me, mommy (5,000) see H.B. Fuller Co.

Library Foundation of Hennepin County (3,000) see Schmoker Family Foundation

Minneapolis Central Library (250,000) see McClatchy Co.

Minneapolis Central Library (3,000) see Regis Corp.

Minneapolis Public Library (100,000) see Graco Inc.

Minneapolis Public Library (20,000) see Graco Inc.

Owatonna Public Library (5,000) see Federated Mutual Insurance Co.

Pioneerland Library System (50,000) see Mardag Foundation

Mississippi

Leland Public Library (7,000) see La-Z-Boy Inc.

Missouri

Downtown Kansas City Public Library Fund (1,000,000) see William T. Kemper Foundation

Friends of the Saint Louis Public Library -- operating funds (1,000) see Bakewell Corp.

Harry S. Truman Library & Museum (6,000) see Morris Communications Corp.

Harry S. Truman Library Institute (125,000) see Francis Families Foundation

Harry S. Truman Library Institute (62,500) see William T. Kemper Foundation

Harry S. Truman Library Institute -- capital campaign (25,000) see Victor E. and Caroline E. Schutte Foundation

Harry S. Truman Library Institute (5,000) see Geraldine and R. A. Barrows Foundation

Harry S. Truman Library Institute (5,000) see Bartlett & Co.

Harry S. Truman Library Institute (3,000) see Andrews McMeel Universal

Kansas City Public Library (100,000) see Francis Families Foundation

Kansas City Public Library (5,000) see Tension Envelope Corp.

Lebanon Public Library -- library project (10,000) see Lowe Family Foundation

Linda Hall Library (6,000) see Bartlett & Co.

Missouri Development Finance Board -- classroom for democracy campaign support (20,000) see Courtney S. Turner Charitable Trust

Nelson Gallery Foundation (200,000) see Oppenstein Brothers Foundation

Nelson Gallery Foundation (200,000) see Oppenstein Brothers Foundation

St Louis Mercantile Library Association (80,000) see Herman T. and Phenie R. Pott Foundation

St. Louis Public Library (3,000) see Commerce Bancshares Inc.

Webb City Library -- for children's library (80,000) see C. W. Titus Foundation

Worth County Partnership Library (1,000) see Harper Brush Works

Nebraska

Lincoln City Libraries (10,000) see Woods Charitable Fund

Omaha Public Library (5,000) see Paul and Oscar Giger Foundation

Nevada

Smoky Valley Library District -- funding for furnishings (5,000) see Robert Z. Hawkins Foundation

Washoe County Library Foundation -- fund the young people's library (40,833) see Nell J. Redfield Foundation

Washoe County Library Foundation -- towards enhancements inline village library (10,000) see Bretzlaff Foundation

New Hampshire

Concord Public Library Foundation -- children's Room Project (20,000) see Oleonda Jameson Trust

Cook Memorial Library (10,000) see Doris L. Benz Trust

Gilmanton Year Round Library (25,000) see Doris L. Benz Trust

Howe Public Library (25,000) see Byrne Foundation

Keene Public Library -- towards expansion of reading programs (2,500) see Kingsbury Corp.

Library and Archives of New Hampshire's Political Tradition (25,000) see Citizens Financial Group Inc.

Stephenson Memorial Library -- towards building fund (5,000) see Monadnock Paper Mills Inc.

Tuck Library (25,000) see George R. Wallace Foundation

New Jersey

Arnold Schwartz Memorial Library (10,000) see Arnold A. Schwartz Foundation

Fort Lee Public Library see Oki America Inc.

Friends of the Kinnelon Library (2,075) see Westerhoff Family Foundation, Inc.

Friends of the Kinnelon Library (300) see Westerhoff Family Foundation, Inc.

Friends of the Princeton Public Library Inc. (12,500) see Dow Jones & Company Inc.

Library of the Chatham -- fund for purchase of computer & office equipment to enhance its library expansion project (100,000) see Hyde and Watson Foundation

New Brunswick Community Library -- for updated computers (8,500) see Howard and Bush Foundation

Princeton Public Library Foundation (33,333) see Bunbury Co., Inc.

Princeton Public Library Foundation Inc. (200,000) see Willard T. C. Johnson Foundation

South Brunswick Public Library Foundation Inc. (10,000) see Dow Jones & Company Inc.

New Mexico

Embudo Valley Library (5,000) see PNM Resources Inc.

Estacado Library Information Network (92,980) see J. F. Maddox Foundation

New York

Albany Public Library see Microsoft Corp.

American Friends of the Medem -- fund for Archives Project (10,000) see Lucius N. Littauer Foundation

American Library of Paris -- purchase books (3,000) see Mona Bismarck Charitable Trust

American Society for Technion Israel Institute of Technology Dibner Library (25,000) see Dibner Fund

Aurora Free Library Association (6,000) see Cayuga Foundation

Bolton Free Library (3,000) see Waterhouse Family Foundation

Brooklyn Public Library -- renewed support for children's educational programs (50,000) see Louis Calder Foundation

Brooklyn Public Library (15,000) see Henry and Lucy Moses Fund, Inc.

Brooklyn Public Library (6,000) see Michael Tuch Foundation

Brooklyn Public Library (5,000) see Daily News L.P.

Brooklyn Public Library -- for the Ready to Read Educational Program for children (2,500) see Moses L. Parshelsky Foundation

Brooklyn Public Library Foundation (10,000) see KeySpan Corp.

Buffalo 7 Erie County Public Library (1,000) see Viyu Foundation

Canajoharie Library and Art Gallery -- towards capital project (1,000,000) see Arkell Hall Foundation

Canajoharie Library and Art Gallery -- operating support (15,000) see Arkell Hall Foundation

Chautauqua Cattaraugus Library System (163,860) see Gebbie Foundation

Chautauqua Cattaraugus Library System (17,935) see Hultquist Foundation

Columbia University Rare Book and Manuscript Library (2,000) see Bella Spewack Article 5th Trust

Concord Library (250,000) see Stratford Foundation

Cuba Circulating Library (5,000) see Carnahan-Jackson Foundation

Dorot Jewish Division of the New York Public Library (10,000) see Loews Corp.

Fort Plain Free Library -- towards programs for children (2,000) see Arkell Hall Foundation

Foundation Center -- for the Philanthropic Center (1,000) see Virginia Environmental Endowment

Frick Collection -- historic archives (40,000) see Gladys Krieble Delmas Foundation

Frick Collection (5,000) see Edward B. Osborn Charitable Trust

Friends of the Shelter Island Public Library Society (10,000) see Gladys Brooks Foundation

Genesis Foundation -- library dedication (50,000) see Bender Foundation

Genesis Foundation (20,000) see Bender Foundation

Hamilton Public Library -- building fund (10,000) see Oneida Savings Bank

Hammondsport Public Library (5,000) see Mercury Aircraft Inc.

Hillsdale Public Library (2,500) see Rheinstrom Hill Community Foundation

James Prendergast Library (100,000) see Carnahan-Jackson Foundation

James Prendergast Library -- for literary program/building (41,987) see Hultquist Foundation

James Prendergast Library -- for computer resources and senior services (14,500) see John Alfred and Oscar Johnson Memorial Trust

James Prendergast Library (7,000) see Holmberg Foundation

James Prendergast Library Association -- new auto library system (80,000) see Ralph C. Sheldon Foundation Inc.

Katonah Village Library (2,500) see William S. Paley Foundation, Inc.

Kingston Area Library (8,000) see Jay E. Klock and

Lucia Klock Kingston Foundation

Lake Placid Public Library -- debt servicing (25,500) see Lake Placid Education Foundation

Lamont Memorial Free Library (40,000) see J. M. McDonald Foundation

Larchmont Public Library -- operating needs (20,000) see Huisking Foundation

Libraries for the Future -- MLF reading America program (250,000) see Metropolitan Life Insurance Co.

Libraries for the Future -- toward collaborative initiative of school districts and library (75,000) see Walter and Elise Haas Fund

Libraries for the Future -- provides initiative to help public libraries (50,000) see Helena Rubinstein Foundation

Libraries for the Future -- charitable fund (5,000) see A. L. Mailman Family Foundation

Library Foundation of Buffalo (1,000) see Tyson Foods Inc.

Library of America -- to support distribution of Reporting Civil Rights American Journalism 1941-1973 (37,500) see Charles H. Revson Foundation

Long Lake Library -- education (7,410) see Lake Placid Education Foundation

Longwood Public Library (3,950) see Henry P. Kovarik Foundation for Poetry

Louise Adelia Read Memorial Library (10,000) see Charles L. Read Foundation

Macedon Public Library (10,000) see Gleason Foundation

Manhattan College -- for library and endowment (500,000) see Starr Foundation

Miles City Public Library (10,000) see Nibs and Edna Allen Foundation

Millbrook Free Library (120,000) see Millbrook Tribute Garden

Millbrook Free Library -- toward capital campaign (2,500) see McCann Foundation

Morgan Library (100,000) see Homeland Foundation (NY)

Morgan Library (50,000) see The Carl and Lily Pforzheimer Foundation, Inc.

Morgan Library (25,000) see M. A. Chisholm Foundation

Morgan Library (10,000) see M. A. Chisholm Foundation

Morgan Library (10,000) see James J. Colt Foundation

Museum of Modern Art (20,000) see Sarah K. de Coizart Perpetual Charitable Trust

Museum of Modern Art (2,500) see Kajima Engineering and Construction Inc.

Museum of Modern Art (2,500) see Richard Meier Foundation

Mynderese Library (25,000) see J. M. McDonald Foundation

New Rochelle Public Library (25,000) see H. W. Wilson Foundation

New York Botanical Gardens (20,000) see Samuel Freeman Charitable Trust

New York Botanical Gardens (10,000) see Dendroica Foundation

New York Library Association -- library purposes and fellowships (20,000) see Lake Placid Education Foundation

New York Public Library (4,458,500) see Frances and Benjamin Benenson Foundation

New York Public Library (1,247,573) see The Carl and Lily Pforzheimer Foundation, Inc.

New York Public Library -- towards preservation of the general research collections (1,201,972) see Andrew W. Mellon Foundation

New York Public Library -- towards covering the losses the public branch library systems have incurred due to the reduction of government support after September 11 (1,185,000) see Andrew W. Mellon Foundation

New York Public Library -- for South Court Programs (500,000) see Starr Foundation

New York Public Library (250,000) see William Randolph Hearst Foundation

New York Public Library (250,000) see Esther A. and Joseph Klingenstein Fund, Inc.

New York Public Library (180,000) see Scherman Foundation

New York Public Library (150,000) see Altman Foundation

New York Public Library -- towards technology enhancement (150,000) see Booth Ferris Foundation

New York Public Library -- toward addition of a second floor dedicated to children's materials and programming at their Parkchester Branch (150,000) see Charles Hayden Foundation

New York Public Library -- provides renovation (150,000) see Helena Rubinstein Foundation

New York Public Library (100,000) see The Ambrose Monell Foundation

New York Public Library (100,000) see Felix and Elizabeth Rohatyn Foundation

New York Public Library (100,000) see Wasserstein Perella Foundation

New York Public Library (90,000) see Allene Reuss Memorial Trust

New York Public Library (75,000) see Felix and Elizabeth Rohatyn Foundation

New York Public Library -- match for city funding and purchase of books (50,000) see Louis Calder Foundation

New York Public Library (50,000) see Gladys and Roland Harriman Foundation

New York Public Library (50,000) see Pinkerton Foundation

New York Public Library -- fund for Theatre Film and Tape Archive (50,000) see Fan Fox and Leslie R. Samuels Foundation

New York Public Library (25,000) see ABC Inc.

New York Public Library -- for research (25,000) see Hagedorn Fund

New York Public Library (25,000) see McGraw-Hill Companies Inc.

New York Public Library -- towards the library's preservation program (25,000) see Prospect Hill Foundation

New York Public Library (25,000) see Sarah I. Schieffelin Residuary Trust

New York Public Library (20,000) see Barker Welfare Foundation

New York Public Library (20,000) see The Theodore H. Barth Foundation, Inc.

New York Public Library (15,310) see Liz Claiborne Inc.

New York Public Library (15,000) see Samuel and Rae Eckman Charitable Foundation

New York Public Library -- for specific programs (15,000) see Mary Livingston Griggs and Mary Griggs Burke Foundation

New York Public Library -- towards educational causes (15,000) see New

York Stock Exchange Inc.

New York Public Library (15,000) see United States Trust Company of New York

New York Public Library (12,500) see Carillon Importers Ltd.

New York Public Library (10,000) see AMETEK Inc.

New York Public Library (10,000) see Dow Jones & Company Inc.

New York Public Library (10,000) see Armand G. Erpf Fund

New York Public Library (10,000) see Mary W. Harriman Foundation

New York Public Library -- for preservation and restoration (10,000) see Hugoton Foundation

New York Public Library -- support research libraries (10,000) see Alfred Jurzykowski Foundation

New York Public Library -- for participation in the corporate partners program (10,000) see Prudential Securities Inc.

New York Public Library (7,500) see Millipore Corp.

New York Public Library (5,000) see Harriet Ford Dickenson Foundation

New York Public Library (5,000) see Cleveland H. Dodge Foundation

New York Public Library (5,000) see Eugene M. Lang Foundation

New York Public Library -- to support the Jewish Division of the library (4,000) see Moses L. Parshelsky Foundation

New York Public Library (3,500) see Atran Foundation, Inc.

New York Public Library (1,000) see Bella Spewack Article 5th Trust

New York Public Library see Dreyfus Corp.

New York Public Library see John Wiley & Sons Inc.

Patterson Library (25,000) see Carnahan-Jackson Foundation

Pencil, Inc. (500) see Richard Meier Foundation

Pierpont Morgan Library -- towards general support (250,000) see Sherman Fairchild Foundation, Inc.

Pierpont Morgan Library -- for endowment (250,000) see Rockefeller Brothers Fund, Inc.

Pierpont Morgan Library (150,000) see The Florence Gould Foundation

Pierpont Morgan Library -- towards the expansion and renovation program (125,000) see Booth Ferris Foundation

Pierpont Morgan Library -- fund for concert and lecture (105,000) see R. K. Mellon Family Foundation

Pierpont Morgan Library (100,000) see The Ambrose Monell Foundation

Pierpont Morgan Library (30,000) see Harriet Ford Dickenson Foundation

Pierpont Morgan Library -- towards conservation fellows (30,000) see Sherman Fairchild Foundation, Inc.

Pierpont Morgan Library -- towards educational causes (25,000) see New York Stock Exchange Inc.

Pierpont Morgan Library (3,500) see James M. Vaughn, Jr. Foundation Fund

Pioneer Library System -- funding for creation of online catalog and circulation system (50,000) see McLean Contributionship

Poughkeepsie Public Library -- toward capital campaign for facilities expansion (10,000) see McCann Foundation

Queens Borough Public Library (10,000) see Billy Rose Foundation

Queens Library Foundation (200,000) see Altman Foundation

Queens Library Foundation -- towards final planning and design phase of the children's discovery center (200,000) see Booth Ferris Foundation

Queens Library Foundation -- to support Cultural Program for Russian & Jewish Communities (20,000) see Lucius N. Littauer Foundation

Queens Library Foundation (15,000) see Jean and Louis Dreyfus Foundation

Queens Library Foundation (1,000) see Billy Rose Foundation

Rundel Library Foundation (25,000) see Riedman Foundation

Rundel Library Foundation -- salary support for the library youth coordinator (15,000) see Marie C. and Joseph C. Wilson Foundation

Rundel Library Foundation (10,000) see Gleason Foundation

Rundel Library Foundation (3,000) see Charles J. and Burton S. August Family Foundation

Rye Free Reading Room (15,000) see Henry L. and Grace Doherty Charitable Foundation

Rye Free Reading Room (5,000) see Scott B. and Annie P. Appleby Trust

Rye Free Reading Room (2,000) see Sound Shore Foundation

Seymour Library Foundation Inc. (25,000) see Fred L. Emerson Foundation, Inc.

Sinclairville Free Library (25,000) see Carnahan-Jackson Foundation

Skaneateles Library Association -- for operating support (28,500) see Allyn Foundation

South Salem Library Association (75,000) see Dextra Baldwin McGonagle Foundation

Standing Tall, Inc. (5,000) see Eugene and Estelle Ferkauf Foundation

Steele Memorial Library -- A. Marshall Lowman and Charles A. Winding Material Fund (20,000) see Anderson Foundation (NY)

Syracuse Children's Chorus, Inc. (2,000) see Richard Mather Fund

Tompkins County Public Library (10,000) see John Ben Snow Memorial Trust

Utica Public Library -- toward community technology center (8,500) see Utica National Insurance Group

Wadhams Free Library (450) see Bruce L. Crary Foundation

White Plains Public Library Foundation (10,000) see Virginia and Leonard Marx Foundation

North Carolina

Conservation Trust for North Carolina -- for operations (25,000) see Cemala Foundation

East Lincoln Betterment -- help build new library (50,000) see Timken Foundation of Canton

East Lincoln Library Fund (2,000) see Willis Family Foundation

Forsyth County Public Library -- establish bilingual mini-libraries (5,000) see R.J. Reynolds Tobacco

Friends of Greensboro Public Library (500) see Blue Bell Inc.

Greensboro Public Library (15,000) see Hillsdale Fund

Spindale Public Library (1,000) see Stonecutter Mills Corp.

UNC - Chapel Hill Friends of the Library (2,494) see Tanner Cos. (Rutherfordton, NC)

North Dakota

Library Foundation (10,000) see MDU Resources Group Inc.

Ohio

Bainbridge Public Library (5,000) see Paul and Maxine Frohring Foundation

Columbus Metropolitan Library System (15,000) see Giant Eagle Inc.

Columbus Metropolitan Library System (10,000) see National City Corp.

Dover Public Library -- building addition (2,500) see Haman Family Foundation

Evergreen Community Library (2,000) see Andersons Inc.

Loudonville Public Library (16,000) see Hugo H. and Mabel B. Young Foundation

Mercantile Library (15,000) see Lois and Richard Rosenthal Foundation

Minerva Public Library (25,000) see Herbert W. Hoover Foundation

National First Ladies Library -- renovate national bank building (750,000) see Timken Foundation of Canton

National First Ladies Library (75,000) see Herbert W. Hoover Foundation

National First Ladies Library (50,000) see George H. Deuble Foundation

National First Ladies Library (25,000) see Forest City Enterprises Inc.

New Madison Public Library -- for replacing the children's computer (2,100) see Ketrow Foundation

Ohioana Library (3,000) see E. F. Wildermuth Foundation.

Public Library of Cincinnati and Hamilton County -- for Westwood branch library expansion (80,000) see Charles H. Dater Foundation

Ritter Library (47,116) see George and Mary Ritter Charitable Trust

Tiffin Seneca Public Library (1,000) see National Machinery Co.

Toledo-Lucas City Public Library (20,000) see Toledo Blade Co.

Way Public Library Foundation -- operating (37,000) see Stranahan Foundation

Oklahoma

Blackwell Public Library -- children's books (1,000) see Cordelia Lunceford Beatty Trust

Cartwright Memorial Library Inc. -- towards helping a new facility to replace the current facility that is now far beyond economic repair (15,000) see Kerr Foundation, Inc.

Choctaw County Library Inc. (710,239) see Donald W. Reynolds Foundation

Choctaw Library Guild -- towards construction of a lower level sun deck (25,000) see Sarkeys Foundation

Lawton Area Reading Council -- to support special program (5,000) see McMahon Foundation

Library Endowment Trust Metropolitan Library System (2,220) see American Fidelity Assurance Co.

Nowata City County Library -- maintain grounds, Nowata library (19,380) see Pearl M. and Julia J. Harmon Foundation

Nowata City County Library -- contribution (13,743) see Pearl M. and Julia J. Harmon Foundation

Nowata City County Library -- contribution (2,000) see Pearl M. and Julia J. Harmon Foundation

Nowata City County Library -- contribution (1,500) see Pearl M. and Julia J. Harmon Foundation

Tulsa City County Library -- contribution Hardesty Library (5,000) see Pearl M. and Julia J. Harmon Foundation

Tulsa City County Library -- contribution Hardesty Library (5,000) see Pearl M. and Julia J. Harmon Foundation

Tulsa Library Trust (25,000) see Williams Companies Inc.

Oregon

Dexter Library (7,500) see Rose E. Tucker Charitable Trust

Eugene Public Library Foundation -- provides construction of library (100,000) see Collins Foundation

Friends of Jacksonville Library -- to provide enhancements for children's programs at the new library (30,000) see Ben B. Cheney Foundation

Friends of the Independence Public Library -- towards the new independence library (150,000) see Ford Family Foundation

Glendale Library Branch of the Douglas County (6,425) see C. Giles Hunt Charitable Trust

Hood River County Library Foundation -- towards library renovation project (166,000) see Ford Family Foundation

Hood River County Library Foundation -- toward ren-

ovating the community public library (120,000) see Meyer Memorial Trust

Library Foundation of Milton-Freewater -- for the construction of a new library (569,000) see Wayne and Gladys Valley Foundation

Library Foundation of Milton-Freewater -- towards campaign for the new Milton Freewater public library (325,000) see Ford Family Foundation

Library Foundation of Milton-Freewater -- for the construction of a new library (324,000) see Wayne and Gladys Valley Foundation

Library Foundation of Milton-Freewater -- for building a new library (150,000) see Meyer Memorial Trust

Reedsport Branch Library (6,000) see C. Giles Hunt Charitable Trust

Salem Public Library Foundation (1,150) see Pioneer Trust Bank, N.A.

Winston Branch Library (6,800) see C. Giles Hunt Charitable Trust

Pennsylvania

Adams Memorial Library (59,200) see McFeely-Rogers Foundation

Adams Memorial Library -- funding for community network interactive web site (25,000) see Katherine Mabis McKenna Foundation

Adams Memorial Library (25,000) see Philip M. McKenna Foundation

Allegheny County Library Association -- towards Seamless education environment (250,000) see McCune Foundation

Allegheny County Library Association -- for the expansion of e network information infrastructure (75,000) see Hillman Foundation

Allentown Public Library -- for community outreach celebrating Trexler birthday (75,000) see Harry C. Trexler Trust

Allentown Public Library -- for books, computers, software for students (65,000) see Harry C. Trexler Trust

Altoona Public Library (4,500) see Harrison C. and Margaret A. Snyder Charitable Trust

Athenaeum of Philadelphia -- towards documentation and digitization of records (264,683) see William Penn Foundation

Athenaeum of Philadelphia -- Retroconversion Project (49,000) see Barra Foundation

Athenaeum of Philadelphia -- William Birch Catalogue (10,000) see Barra Foundation

Athenaeum of Philadelphia (7,500) see Barra Foundation

Athenaeum of Philadelphia (5,000) see Vanguard Group

Bethlehem Area Public Library (143,100) see Frank E. and Seba B. Payne Foundation

Bethlehem Area Public Library -- projects (37,000) see Reidler Foundation

Bethlehem Area Public Library -- endowment fund (22,500) see Reidler Foundation

Butler Area Public Library (5,000) see Harsco Corp.

Butler Area Public Library (5,000) see Spang & Co.

CC Mellor Memorial Library & Edgewood Community House -- toward renovation project (20,000) see Laurel Foundation

Carnegie Free Library of McKeesport (30,000) see E. R. Crawford Estate Trust Fund A

Carnegie Institute -- Scientific research (10,000) see Dynamet Inc.

Carnegie Institute -- Powdermill Natural Program (1,000) see Dynamet Inc.

Carnegie Library for the Blind and Physically Handicapped (10,000) see Milton G. Hulme Charitable Foundation

Carnegie Library of McKeesport -- for additional furnishings (5,000) see Charles F. Peters Foundation

Carnegie Library of Midland (1,000) see J&L Specialty Steel Inc.

Carnegie Library of Pittsburgh -- towards capital campaign (500,000) see McCune Foundation

Carnegie Library of Pittsburgh -- for BLAST school outreach program (50,000) see Grable Foundation

Carnegie Library of Pittsburgh -- for public library system (49,969) see W. I. Patterson Charitable Fund

Carnegie Library of Pittsburgh (5,000) see Donald and Sylvia Robinson Family Foundation

Carnegie Second Century Fund (12,000) see Milton G. Hulme Charitable Foundation

Conshohocken Free Library (2,000) see Quaker Chemical Corp.

Corry Public Library (13,500) see Arlene H. Smith Charitable Foundation

Dauphin County Library System -- for construction of a new uptown branch library and partial renovation of historical downtown branch library (50,000) see Josiah W. and Bessie H. Kline Foundation

Dauphin County Library System (20,000) see Anne McCormick Trust

Eccles Lesher Memorial Library (187,333) see Ralph M. and Ella M. Eccles Foundation

Elk County Community Foundation -- toward St. Mary's library fund (2,500) see Stackpole-Hall Foundation

Ephrata Public Library (525) see G/S/M Industrial Inc.

Ester Community Library (10,000) see Sovereign Bank

Evans City Public Library (2,500) see Mine Safety Appliances Co.

Frackville Free Public Library (500) see Harry E. and Florence W. Snayberger Memorial Foundation

Franklin County Library System (10,000) see Alexander Stewart MD Foundation Trust

Franklin Library Association (25,000) see Edward V. and Jessie L. Peters Charitable Trust

Frederickson Library (10,000) see Donald B. and Dorothy L. Stabler Foundation

Fredrickson Public Library -- for building fund (50,000) see John Crain Kunkel Foundation

Free Library of Philadelphia (50,000) see Pine Tree Foundation

Free Library of Philadelphia (30,210) see Vanguard Group

Free Library of Philadelphia (25,000) see Arcadia Foundation

Free Library of Philadelphia (11,648) see GlaxoSmithKline PLC

Free Library of Philadelphia -- for cultural and educational programming (5,000) see Alfred and Mary Douty Foundation

Free Library of Philadelphia (1,000) see Binswanger Cos.

Free Library of Philadelphia Foundation (14,000) see AMETEK Inc.

Friends of Milton Public Library (100,000) see Longwood Foundation

Friends of the Free Library of Philadelphia -- towards salary of a branch group coordinator (15,000) see Samuel S. Fels Fund

Hanover Public Library (6,000) see Susquehanna-Pfaltzgraff Co.

Hanover Public Library (3,333) see Waypoint Financial Corp.

Hazelton Area Public Library -- endowment fund (20,000) see Reidler Foundation

Hazelton Area Public Library -- book fund (10,000) see Reidler Foundation

Helen Kate Furness Free Library (5,500) see Vanguard Group

Hollidaysburg Library (2,500) see Harrison C. and Margaret A. Snyder Charitable Trust

Johnsonburg Public Library -- assistance for library renovations (10,000) see Stackpole-Hall Foundation

Joseph T. Simpson Public Library (5,000) see Harsco Corp.

Kaltreider Benfer Library (10,000) see Susquehanna-Pfaltzgraff Co.

Lauri Ann West Memorial Library (12,000) see Milton G. Hulme Charitable Foundation

Lauri Ann West Memorial Library -- support programs (5,000) see Fair Oaks Foundation

Library Company of Philadelphia (50,000) see Arcadia Foundation

Library Company of Philadelphia -- dissertation fellowship (50,000) see Gladys Krieble Delmas Foundation

Library Company of Philadelphia (50,000) see Albert M. Greenfield Foundation

Library Company of Philadelphia -- funding for creation of endowment fund (50,000) see McLean Contributionship

Library Company of Philadelphia -- toward operating support (5,000) see Crestlea Foundation

Martin Library (20,000) see Susquehanna-Pfaltzgraff Co.

Martin Library (5,000) see Freas Foundation

Martin Library Building Fund -- capital campaign (10,000) see Graham Engineering Corp.

Mary S. Biesecker Library (5,000) see Dominic Foundation

Marysville Rye Library Association -- towards replacing 31 wooden bookcases with custom built new ones (52,000) see Josiah W. and Bessie H. Kline Foundation

Mason Dixon Public Library (6,000) see Susquehanna-Pfaltzgraff Co.

Mason Dixon Public Library (2,500) see Waypoint Financial Corp.

Mechanicsburg Area Public Library (10,000) see Anne McCormick Trust

Memorial Library of Nazareth and Vicinity (46,000) see Frank E. and Seba B. Payne Foundation

Mengle Memorial Library (35,000) see Glenn and Ruth Mengle Foundation

Mifflin County Library (5,000) see Standard Steel

Mifflin County Library (1,000) see Standard Steel

Minersville Public Library (500) see Harry E. and Florence W. Snayberger Memorial Foundation

Nantucket Athenaeum (75,000) see Allegheny Foundation

New Bethlehem Library (5,000) see S&T Bancorp Inc.

Oil City Library (20,000) see Edith C. Justus Trust

Orwigsburg Area Free Public Library (500) see Harry E. and Florence W. Snayberger Memorial Foundation

Oxford Library (25,000) see Oxford Foundation

Pittsburgh Technology Institute (1,000) see Trumbull County Scholarship Foundation

Plum Borough Community Library (7,500) see S&T Bancorp Inc.

Plum Borough Community Library (5,000) see S&T Bancorp Inc.

Port Carbon Public Library (500) see Harry E. and Florence W. Snayberger Memorial Foundation

Pottsville Free Public Library (500) see Harry E. and Florence W. Snayberger Memorial Foundation

Public Library Foundation (275) see Mellon Financial Corp.

Riegelsville Public Library (23,500) see Frank E. and Seba B. Payne Foundation

Schlow Library (10,000) see Hamer Foundation

Sewickley Public Library (20,000) see Mary Hillman Jennings Foundation

Sleighton School -- refurbishing library and purchase appliances (25,000) see Ethel Sergeant Clark Smith Memorial Fund

Southern Lehigh Public Library -- for new building (50,000) see Harry C. Trexler Trust

Southern York County Library (15,000) see Susquehanna-Pfaltzgraff Co.

Warren Public Library (15,000) see Betts Industries

Wilcox Public Library -- funding for computer lab (13,000) see Stackpole-Hall Foundation

William Jeanes Memorial Library (2,500) see Margaret G. Jacobs Charitable Trust

William Jeanes Memorial Library (2,500) see Quaker Chemical Corp.

Windber Public Library (25,000) see Whalley Charitable Trust

Youngsville Public Library (5,000) see Betts Industries

Rhode Island

Company of the Redwood Library and Athenaeum -- renovation and restoration of the library (500,000) see Alletta Morris McBean Charitable Trust

Company of the Redwood Library and Athenaeum -- general assistance (25,000) see George F. Baker Trust

Company of the Redwood Library and Athenaeum (15,000) see Providence Journal-Bulletin Co.

John Carter Brown Library (250,000) see CTW Foundation, Inc.

John Carter Brown Library -- scholarship fund (15,000) see Horace A. Kimball and S. Ella Kimball Foundation

Newport Public Library -- towards renovation project (200,000) see Alletta Morris McBean Charitable Trust

Providence Public Library (100,000) see Providence Journal-Bulletin Co.

Providence Public Library (83,333) see Textron Inc.

Providence Public Library -- for operating support (20,000) see June Rockwell Levy Foundation

Providence Public Library (15,000) see Textron Inc.

Providence Public Library -- program for young readers (10,000) see Collis Foundation

Providence Public Library (5,000) see John Clarke Trust

Providence Public Library -- creating readers program (2,500) see Hasbro Inc.

Ruth Woolf Adelson Medical Library Fund (1,500) see Diana S. Adelson Trust

South Carolina

Chapin Memorial Library (204,750) see Chapin Foundation of Myrtle Beach, South Carolina

Cherokee County Public Library (1,000) see Fullerton Foundation

Greenville Library Capital Fund (100,000) see John Smith Charities

Spartanburg County Public Library (10,000) see John Smith Charities

South Dakota

Rapid City Library Foundation, Inc. -- for expansion of services (50,000) see Ludwick Family Foundation

Tennessee

Blount County Public Library -- for library construction (50,000) see Thompson Charitable Foundation

Chattanooga Indigenous Resources Center and Library (21,000) see Benwood Foundation

Foundation for the Memphis Shelby County Public Library (32,200) see First Tennessee National Corp.

Lavergne Public Library -- furnishing for new library building (122,500) see Christy-Houston Foundation

Metropolitan Nashville Library (50,000) see Joyce Family Foundation

Nashville Public Library (50,607) see Anne Potter Wilson Foundation

Texas

Bryan City Library -- for educational purposes (12,500) see Clifton C. and Henryetta C. Doak Charitable Trust

Canyon Library Inc. -- towards construction of new library (33,334) see Abell-Hanger Foundation

Civil War Preservation Trust -- support for the Land and Water Conservation Fund (15,000) see Martha, David and Bagby Lennox Foundation

Denison Public Library (15,000) see Clara Blackford Smith and W. Aubrey Smith Charitable Foundation

El Paso Public Library (7,767) see Marian Meaker Apteckar Foundation

Fairfield Library Association -- for charitable purposes (5,889) see R. B. O. Bragg Charitable Trust

Fort Worth Public Library Foundation -- Provide office space for Library Foundation in new facility (175,000) see Sid W. Richardson Foundation

Fort Worth Public Library Foundation -- funding for new integrated library system gala sponsorship (25,000) see Crystelle Waggoner Charitable Trust

Fort Worth Public Library Foundation (15,000) see William E. Scott Foundation

Friends of the Dallas Public Library -- renovation of downtown library (500,000) see Hoblitzelle Foundation

Friends of the Dallas Public Library (50,000) see Hillcrest Foundation

Friends of the Dallas Public Library (1,000) see Decherd Foundation

Friends of the Dallas Public library -- for renovation (100,000) see Leland Fikes Foundation

Friends of the Public Library of Buda (2,500) see Burdine Johnson Foundation

George Bush Presidential Library Foundation -- fund for The Leonore and Walter Annenberg Presidential Conference Center (1,000,000) see Annenberg Foundation

George Bush Presidential Library Foundation -- for endowment or program support (500,000) see Starr Foundation

George Bush Presidential Library Foundation (300,000) see MBNA Corp.

George Bush Presidential Library Foundation (100,000) see Farmer Family Foundation

George Bush Presidential Library Foundation -- fund to campaign educational programs (50,000) see Fondren Foundation

George Bush Presidential Library Foundation (10,000) see Louella Cook Foundation

George Bush Presidential Library Foundation -- endowment education programs (10,000) see Strake Foundation

Harris County Public Library (10,000) see Powell Foundation

J.R. Huffman Public Library -- for furnishings (55,467) see T. L. L. Temple Foundation

Jackson County Memorial Library -- to purchase microfilm viewing equipment (11,000) see M. G. and Lillie A. Johnson Foundation

Jewish Outreach Center (5,500) see Sapirstein-Stone-Weiss Foundation

Kaufman County Library (40,000) see Edna M. Sheary Trust for Charity

Keystone School -- towards library support program (10,000) see George W. Brackenridge Foundation

Kountze Library (10,000) see Gilbert M. and Martha H. Hitchcock Foundation

Kurth Memorial Library -- construct new library facility (464,460) see T. L. L. Temple Foundation

Kurth Memorial Library (6,500) see Pineywoods Foundation

Lone Oak Area Public Library (10,000) see Tom S. and Marye Kate Aldridge Charitable and Educational Trust

Marshall Public Library -- operations (500) see H.E. and Ruby Pelz Trust

Medina Community Library -- to assist with renovations of building for new library (45,000) see Hal and Charlie Peterson Foundation

Orange Public Library -- toward purchase of reference materials (31,500) see Nelda C. and H. J. Lutcher Stark Foundation

Recording Library for the Blind (6,000) see Potts and Sibley Foundation

Rosenberg Library (5,000) see Mary Moody Northen Foundation

San Antonio Academy -- towards library support program (10,000) see George W. Brackenridge Foundation

San Antonio Public Library -- towards born to read program (20,000) see George W. Brackenridge Foundation

San Antonio Public Library Foundation -- new branch library grant (197,888) see Semmes Foundation

San Antonio Public Library Foundation -- promotion of the arts (170,000) see Russell Hill Rogers Fund for the Arts

San Antonio Public Library Foundation (5,000) see Frost National Bank

San Antonio Public Library Foundation (5,000) see Minnie Stevens Piper Foundation

St. Mary's Hall -- towards library support program (10,000) see George W. Brackenridge Foundation

T L L Temple Memorial Library (36,550) see Temple-Inland Inc.

Temple Memorial Library and Archives -- for archives budget (154,261) see T. L. L. Temple Foundation

Temple Memorial Library and Archives -- for budget deficit (117,520) see T. L. L. Temple Foundation

Tyler County Public Library -- expansion project

(25,000) see T. L. L. Temple Foundation

Vermont

Bennington Museum (20,000) see Edwin S. Webster Foundation

Brooks Memorial Library -- for Collection Improvement Program (14,200) see Thomas Thompson Trust

Fairlee Public Library -- for renovations (2,300) see Mascoma Savings Bank

Green Mountain College -- fund to establish a chaplaincy program (25,000) see Lillian M. Slater Trust

Moore Free Library (500) see Windham Foundation

Norman Williams Public Library (75,000) see LSR Fund

St. Johnsbury Athenaeum (1,000) see Windham Foundation

Virginia

Alexandria Library (2,000) see The Bryant Foundation

Alexandria Library (1,000) see Koopman Fund

Alta Vista Town of Staunton River Memorial Library -- additional space to accommodate all programs (40,000) see Timken Foundation of Canton

Blue Ridge Regional Library (20,000) see Lucy Pannill Sale Foundation

Braille Circulating Library -- Renovation Project (10,000) see Quincy Cole Trust

Charlotte County Library -- fund towards renovation

and expansion (2,500) see Beirne Carter Foundation

City of Franklin (39,000) see Ruth and Henry Campbell Foundation

Fairfax County Public Library Foundation -- to assist in the motherhood/ fatherhood program (52,627) see Gannett Company Inc.

Fairfax County Public Library Foundation -- toward endowment for early literacy program (40,000) see Clark-Winchcole Foundation

Fauquier County Library (4,000) see Luck Stone

Free Library of Northampton Township (10,000) see Hillsdale Fund

Friends of Mathews Memorial Library -- to purchase books, equipment and furnish new wing (20,000) see J. Edwin Treakle Foundation

Friends of the Waverly Public Library (75,000) see Garland and Agnes Taylor Gray Foundation

Gloucester Library Endowment Foundation -- to purchase books, equipment and bookmobile (20,000) see J. Edwin Treakle Foundation

Haysi Public Library -- grant to purchase encyclopedia, visual aids, and titles for AV collection (2,000) see Columbus Phipps Foundation

Madison County Library Inc. (50,000) see Robert G. Cabell III and Maude Morgan Cabell Foundation

Richmond Public Library Foundation -- Renovation Project (15,000) see Quincy Cole Trust

Ruth Camp Campbell Memorial Library (15,000) see Ruth and Henry Campbell Foundation

Shenandoah County Library (2,500) see Shenandoah Telecommunications Co.

Thomas Jefferson Memorial Foundation (5,000) see Trust for the Cheek Family Foundation

Wise County Friends of the Library -- funding for author's dinner (600) see Slemp Foundation

Washington

Friends of the Everett Public Library (2,500) see Sperandio Family Foundation

Pierce County Library-Foundation -- funding towards kids bookmobile (50,000) see Russell Family Foundation

Seattle Public Library Foundation (335,179) see Norcliffe Foundation

Seattle Public Library Foundation (250,000) see Bullitt Foundation

Seattle Public Library Foundation (250,000) see Foster Foundation

Sno - Isle Regional Library (5,500) see Sperandio Family Foundation

West Virginia

Bridgeport Public Library (18,199) see Evelyn C. Carter Trust

Craft Memorial Library (50,000) see Hugh I. Shott, Jr. Foundation

Greenbrier County Library -- for capital campaign (50,000) see Daywood Foundation

Kanawha County Public Library -- for new library project (7,500) see Clay Foundation

Rockbridge Regional Library (5,000) see One Valley Bank N.A.

Wisconsin

Abbotsford Library -- for 10 books on CD format and encyclopedias (5,000) see L. C. Christensen Charitable and Religious Foundation

Brillion Public Library (5,000) see R. D. and Linda Peters Foundation

Brown County Library (500,000) see Green Bay Packaging

Caestecker Public Library Foundation (25,000) see Charles and Marie Caestecker Foundation

Hawkins Area Library (121,500) see Jeld-Wen Inc.

Lakeview Community Library (1,000) see Kohler Foundation

Manitowoc Public Library (4,000) see VPI Foundation

Marathon County Public Library Foundation -- humanities challenge (10,000) see Walter Alexander Foundation

Marathon County Public Library Foundation (500) see Wausau-Mosinee Paper Corp.

Mead Library (5,000) see Kohler Foundation

Menomonee Falls Library (20,000) see Harley-Davidson Co.

Middleton Public Library (5,000) see MGE Energy Inc.

Milwaukee Public Library (25,000) see Marshall & Ilsley Corp.

Milwaukee Public Library (10,000) see Evan and Marion Helfaer Foundation

Milwaukee Public Library (5,000) see Baird Brothers Co. Foundation

Milwaukee Public Library see Microsoft Corp.

Milwaukee Public Library Foundation (50,000) see Schoenleber Foundation

Milwaukee Public Library Foundation (25,000) see Rockwell Automation Inc.

Neenah Public Library (25,000) see Aylward Family Foundation

Rosemary Garfoot Public Library (15,000) see MGE Energy Inc.

Tomah Public Library -- air conditioning for computer room (3,660) see Frank G. Andres Charitable Trust

Whitefish Bay Library Fund Inc. (25,000) see Marshall & Ilsley Corp.

Wyoming

Johnston County Library (5,000) see Harry and Thelma Surrena Memorial Fund

Sheridan County Library Foundation -- for purchase books and subscriptions (2,000) see Herbert G. and Dorothy Zullig Foundation

Arranges officers, trustees, directors, managers, and staff in alphabetical order by last name, along with the name of the funder.

A

Abbott, David T.: executive director, Gund Foundation (George)

Abbott, John L.: director, MassMutual Foundation for Hartford, Inc. (The)

Abbott, Kyle C.: director, Abrams Foundation (Talbert and Leota)

Abbs, Jan P.: secretary, Ontario Corp. Foundation

Abdoo, Richard A.: director, Marshall & Ilsley Foundation, Inc.; chairman, chief executive officer, president, Wisconsin Energy Corp.; president, Wisconsin Energy Corp. Foundation, Inc.

Abel, Alice: director, Abel Foundation

Abel, Elizabeth N.: director, Abel Foundation

Abel, James P.: president, Abel Foundation; president, director, NEBCO Evans

Abel, Jim: president, director, Ameritas Charitable Foundation

Abel, John C.: director, Abel Foundation

Abel, Mary C.: director, Abel Foundation

Abeles, Charles Calvert: trustee, Higginson Trust (Corina)

Abell, William Shepherdson, Jr.: trustee, Abell Foundation

Abercrombie, George B.: trustee, Roche Foundation

Abercrombie, Josephine E.: donor, president, trustee, Abercrombie Foundation

Abney, Cary M.: secretary, Pelz Trust (H.E. and Ruby)

Abney, Ruben K.: co-trustee, Pelz Trust (H.E. and Ruby)

Abney, William A.: co-trustee, Pelz Trust (H.E. and Ruby)

Abplanalp, Robert H.: director, Carvel Foundation (Thomas and Agnes)

Aceves, Ann N.: vice president, Neuberger Foundation (Roy R. and Marie S.)

Acker, Janet: secretary, Giger Foundation (Paul and Oscar)

Ackerman, Asche: vice president, Vale-Asche Foundation

Ackerman, F. Duane: chief executive officer, chairman, president, director, BellSouth Corp.

Ackerman, Kim: secretary, GE Foundation

Ackerman, Lisa Marilyn: vice president, Kress Foundation (Samuel H.)

Acklin, Robert G.: secretary, treasurer, Bicknell Fund

Acosta, Thomas I.: vice chairman, New York Foundation

Acton, Elizabeth S.: director, Comerica Charitable Foundation; executive vice president, chief financial officer, Comerica Inc.

Acton, Evelyn Meadows: director emeritus, Meadows Foundation (The)

Acuff, A. Marshall, Jr.: trustee, Mott Foundation (Charles Stewart)

Adam, Milton F.: director, CHC Foundation

Adamo, Pamela: director, KeySpan Foundation

Adams, Alicia: secretary, BellSouth Foundation

Adams, D. Nelson, Esq.: member advisory committee, Weezie Foundation

Adams, James A.: director, Woronoco Savings Charitable Foundation

Adams, John: director, Honda of America Foundation

Adams, Lloyd: secretary, treasurer, Tractor & Equipment Co. Foundation

Adams, Louise B.: trustee, Barnes Foundation

Adams, Melissa J.: corporate donations officer, Frost National Bank

Adams, Michael T.: senior vice president, AK Steel Holding Corp.

Adams, Peter Webster: trustee, Humphrey Fund (George M. and Pamela S.)

Adams, R. E.: vice president, Conway Scholarship Foundation (Carle C.)

Adams, Robert Merrihew: trustee, Newcombe Foundation (Charlotte W.)

Adams, Thomas B.: mem, Henderson Foundation (George B.)

Adams, Valencia: trustee, BellSouth Foundation

Adamson, Roland: executive director, George Foundation

Addison, Brian M.: secretary, trustee, Dentsply International Foundation

Adelman, Linda M.: director, Eastern Savings and Loan Foundation

Adisek, Valerie: admin secretary, Johnson Controls Foundation

Adkerson, Nancy L.: executive director, Freeport-McMoRan Foundation, Inc.

Adkerson, Richard C.: trustee, Freeport-McMoRan Foundation

Adkins, Albert G.: assistant comptroller, U.S. Steel Foundation

Adkins, Ruth F.: trustee, Yeager Charitable Trust B (Lester E.)

Adler, Arlene: board chair, Hazen Foundation (Edward W.)

Adler, Herbert S.: director, Research Corp.

Adriance, Bryan: trustee, Cranston Foundation; vice president, finance & administration, Cranston Print Works Co.

Adwan, Teresa B.: trustee, Sarkeys Foundation

Agger, David: director, Osher Foundation (Bernard)

Agnew, Dan F.: president, director, Grinnell Mutual Group Foundation; president, chief executive officer, Grinnell Mutual Reinsurance Co.

Agon, Jean-Paul: president, chief executive officer, director, L'Oreal U.S.A.

Ahlers, Linda L.: president, Target Corp.; trustee, Target Foundation

Ahmadi, Hoshang: director, Alavi Foundation

Ahmanson, Howard Fieldstead, Jr.: trustee, Ahmanson Foundation

Ahmanson, Robert H.: president, trustee, Ahmanson Foundation

Ahmanson, William H.: vice president, trustee, Ahmanson Foundation

Ahmed, Mohamed: trustee, Dow Corning Foundation

Ahnert, Edward F.: president, Exxon Mobil Foundation; corporate contribution manager, ExxonMobil Corp.

Ahonkhar, Vincent I.: director, GlaxoSmithKline Foundation

Ahrens, Chad: trustee, Ahrens Foundation (Claude W. and Dolly)

Ahrens, Claude W.: trustee, Ahrens Foundation (Claude W. and Dolly)

Ahrens, John: trustee, Ahrens Foundation (Claude W. and Dolly)

Ahrens, Richard: trustee, Ahrens Foundation (Claude W. and Dolly)

Aida, Mamoru: trustee, Subaru of America Foundation, Inc.

Aiken, J. Kirby: director, Russell Charitable Foundation (Tom)

Aiken, William G.: director, Woronoco Savings Charitable Foundation

Ainsworth, Laine: director, Hedco Foundation

Ainul, Jamal: vice president, treasurer, Schlumberger Foundation

Akel, Ferris G.: chairman, Decker Foundation (Dr. G. Clifford and Florence B.)

Akers, John Fellows: member, director, New York Times Co.

Akin, Judy S.: assistant secretary, Holt Foundation (William Knox)

Albers, C. Hugh: director, Coleman Foundation (IL)

Albert, Daniel: trustee, AT&T National Pro-Am Youth Fund

Alberts, Bruce Michael, PhD: trustee, Carnegie Corp. of New York

Albertson, Don, MD: trustee, Foundation for Seacoast Health

Alcock, Gudrun: vice president, Boothroyd Foundation (Charles H. and Bertha L.)

Alcom, W. J.: treasurer, Penney Co. Fund (J.C.)

Alcott, Kent: chief financial officer, Chicago Rawhide Co.

Alda, Alan: trustee, Jenjo Foundation

Alda, Arlene: trustee, Jenjo Foundation

Alda, Beatrice: trustee, Jenjo Foundation

Alda, Elizabeth: trustee, Jenjo Foundation

Aldax, Gary: director, Sierra Pacific Resources Charitable Foundation

Alden, Alison: senior vice president sales, service, human resources, NSTAR

Aldrich, Robert L.: trustee, Turrell Fund

Aldridge, Kimberly F.: director, Aldridge Charitable and Educational Trust (Tom S. and Marye Kate)

Aldridge, Laverne R.: director, Aldridge Charitable and Educational Trust (Tom S. and Marye Kate)

Aldridge, M. L.: director, Aldridge Charitable and Educational Trust (Tom S. and Marye Kate)

Aldridge, Robert S.: director, Aldridge Charitable and Educational Trust (Tom S. and Marye Kate)

Aldridge, Tom S., II: director, Aldridge Charitable and Educational Trust (Tom S. and Marye Kate)

Alewine, Betty L.: president, chief executive officer, COMSAT International

Alexander, Cleopatra B.: executive director, Pick, Jr. Fund (Albert)

Alexander, Helen C.: vice president, director, Kleberg Foundation (Robert J. Kleberg, Jr. and Helen C.)

Alexander, Jack H.: secretary, Peppers Foundation (Ann)

Alexander, James L.: co-trustee, Genius Charitable Trust (Elizabeth Morse)

Alexander, John D., Jr.: secretary, vice president, Kleberg Foundation (Robert J. Kleberg, Jr. and Helen C.)

Alexander, John H., Jr.: president, assistant treasurer, Johnson Foundation (Helen K. and Arthur E.)

Alexander, Norman E.: director, Gilman Foundation (Howard)

Alexander, R. Denny: trustee, Alexander Foundation (Robert D. and Catherine R.)

Alexander, Rex: director, Hammer Foundation (Armand)

Alexander, Richard G.: trustee, Douty Foundation (Alfred and Mary)

Alexander, Stephen: chief executive, Dunkin' Donuts Inc.

Alfert, Arthur S.: vice president, director, Alexander Foundation (Joseph)

Alford, L. E.: vice president, Hale Foundation (Crescent Porter)

Ali, Fred J.: president, chief administrative officer, Weingart Foundation

Allaire, Paul A.: director, Sara Lee Corp.

Allan, Karen C.: secretary, trustee, Carpenter Foundation

Allan, Richard: director, Sordoni Foundation

Allardyce, Fred A.: senior vice president chairman, chief financial officer, American Standard Inc.

Allday, Doris Fondren: board of governors, Fondren Foundation

Allday, R. Edwin: board of governors, Fondren Foundation

Allen, Alvena: director, Kennedy Family Foundation (Ethel and W. George)

Allen, Barbara Powell: secretary, Powell Family Foundation

Allen, Corinne A.: executive director, Benwood Foundation

Allen, Edna R.: president, Allen Foundation (Nibs and Edna)

Allen, Ivye L.: director, Rockefeller Foundation (Winthrop)

Allen, Leigh B., III: secretary, Walker Foundation

Allen, Leon: chairman, Tetley U.S.A. Inc.

Allen, Lew, Jr.: director, member directors grant program committee, Keck Foundation (W. M.)

Allen, Samuel R.: director, Deere Foundation (John)

Allen, Sylvia: trustee, Cisco Systems Foundation

Allen, Thomas F.: secretary, Bingham Foundation (William)

Allen, Thomas R.: vice president, chief financial officer, Dodge Jones Foundation and Subsidiary

Allen, Wells, Jr.: director, Klee Foundation (Conrad and Virginia)

Allin, William B.: treasurer, Self Family Foundation

Allison, Diane M.: executive director, Educational Foundation of America

Allison, Donn: secretary, De Queen Regional Medical Center

Allison, Ethelyn: trustee, Snyder Foundation (Harold B. and Dorothy A.)

Allison, Walter W.: vice president, assistant treasurer, Lyon Foundation

Allman, Edward Lee: trustee, Edison Fund (Charles)

Allocco, Nancy A.: vice president, Hyde and Watson Foundation

Allton, John D.: treasurer, Schlink Foundation (Albert G. and Olive H.)

Allyn, Amy: director, Allyn Foundation

Allyn, David: director, Allyn Foundation

Allyn, Dawn N.: director, Allyn Foundation

Allyn, Eric R.: director, Allyn Foundation

Allyn, Janet J.: secretary, Allyn Foundation

Allyn, Lew F.: vice president, Allyn Foundation

Allyn, Scott: director, Allyn Foundation

Allyn, William Finch: director, Emerson Foundation, Inc. (Fred L.)

Allyn, William G.: hon officer, Allyn Foundation

Alman, Larry: board of directors, Ottenheimer Brothers Foundation

Almeida, Richard: chairman, chief executive officer, GE Capital Corp.

Alpers, Ann: director, Cowell Foundation (S. H.)

Alsdorf, Marilynn Bruder: director, Rice Foundation

Alsip, John F., III: president, chief executive officer, director, Rahr Malting Co.

Altamore, Ellen: vice president, Delano Foundation (Mignon Sherwood)

Altermatt, Paul B.: president, director, Harcourt Foundation (Ellen Knowles)

Altheide, Paul D.: secretary, chief executive officer, Rachal Foundation (Ed)

Altman, Lawrence Kimball, MD: director, Macy, Jr. Foundation (Josiah)

Alton, Robert D., Jr.: trustee, Hickory Tech Corp. Foundation

Altschul, Arthur G., Jr.: director, Overbrook Foundation (The)

Altschul, Charles: director, Overbrook Foundation (The)

Altschul, Serena: director, Overbrook Foundation (The)

Altschul, Stephen Frank: vice chairman, treasurer, director, Overbrook Foundation (The)

Altschuler, Alan: trustee, New York Foundation

Altshuler, Sharman: treasurer, trustee, Merck Family Fund

Alvarez, Cesar L.: trustee, Knight Foundation (John S. and James L.)

Amado, Bernice: vice president, secretary, director, Amado Foundation (Maurice)

Amado, Ralph A.: director, Amado Foundation (Maurice)

Amado, Ralph D.: director, Amado Foundation (Maurice)

Ambach, Gordon M.: director, The Wallace Foundation

Ambach, Lucy E.: trustee, Sasco Foundation

Amboian, John P.: executive vice president, chief financial officer, Nuveen Co. (The John)

Ambrozy, Sandra McAlister: senior program officer, Kresge Foundation

Ambuel, Helen B.: director, Mead Witter Foundation, Inc.

Amemiya, Minoru: chairman, chief executive officer, Interkal Inc.

Ames, Aubin Z.: trustee, Schumann Fund for New Jersey

Ames, Edward A.: trustee, Cary Charitable Trust (Mary Flagler)

Ames, Kathleen L.F.: vice president, director, Harriman Foundation (Mary W.)

Ames, Morgan P.: treasurer, Price Foundation (Lucien B. and Katherine E.)

Amoroso, Joseph A., Jr.: director, East Cambridge Savings Charitable Foundation

Amundson, Joyce: president, chief executive officer Ross Products Division, Ross Products Division, Abbott Laboratories

Andersen, Christine E.: vice president, Andersen Foundation (Hugh J.)

Andersen, Kathy: administrator, AMR/American Airlines Foundation

Andersen, Sarah J.: president, Andersen Foundation (Hugh J.)

Anderson, Alice Childs: vice president, AKC Fund

Anderson, Amelia: assistant treasurer, Phelps Dodge Foundation

Anderson, Andrew E.: secretary, treasurer, trustee, Stone Foundation (France)

Anderson, Bradbury H.: director, Best Buy Children's Foundation; vice chairman, chief executive officer, Best Buy Co.

Anderson, Bruce C.: vice president, director, AllAmerica Financial Charitable Foundation, Inc.

Anderson, Carl T.: president, secretary, Markey Charitable Fund (John C.)

Anderson, Carmen: trustee, Pittsburgh Child Guidance Foundation

Anderson, Charles W.: trustee, Anderson Foundation

Anderson, D. Kent: chairman, director, Houston Endowment

Anderson, Deb: manager, St. Paul Travelers Companies Inc.

Anderson, Esperanza Guerrero: 1st vice chairman, director, Bush Foundation

Anderson, Eugene Karl: vice president, Contran Corp.; treasurer, Simmons Foundation, Inc. (Harold)

Anderson, Fred C.: director, Norcross Wildlife Foundation

Anderson, Gary E.: chairman, president, chief executive officer, Dow Corning Corp.

Anderson, J. C.: vice president north america, Whirlpool Corp.

Anderson, Jeffrey W.: trustee, Anderson Foundation

Anderson, John: chairman, Florida Rock & Tank Lines

Anderson, John Firth: chairman, Pineywoods Foundation

Anderson, Judy M.: senior vice president charitable giving, Georgia Power Co.; president, Georgia Power Foundation

Anderson, Kenneth G.: president, trustee, Swisher Foundation (Carl S.)

Anderson, Kristin: vice president, director community affairs, Burnett Co. (Leo)

Anderson, Lisa: trustee, Norcliffe Foundation

Anderson, Mary A.: vice president, Stearns Foundation

Anderson, Matthew C.: trustee, Anderson Foundation

Anderson, Michael Scott: director, Overlake Foundation

Anderson, Paul M.: chairman, chief executive officer, Duke Energy Corp.; trustee, Duke Energy Foundation

Anderson, Peter A.: treasurer, Trust Foundation

Anderson, Rich: treasurer, Wellmark Foundation

Anderson, Richard M.: trustee, Anderson Foundation

Anderson, Richard P.: trustee, Anderson Foundation

Anderson, Robert P., PhD: director, South Plains Foundation

Anderson, Sandra K.: president, Anderson Foundation (L. P. and Teresa)

Anderson, Stefan Stolen: director, Ball Foundation (George and Frances)

Anderson, Steven Craig: director, Overlake Foundation

Anderson, Steven L.: president, Reynolds Foundation (Donald W.)

Anderson, Thomas Harold: chairman, trustee, Anderson Foundation; chair-

man, director, Andersons Inc.

Anderson, Wilbur L.: trustee, Ashtabula Foundation

Anderson, William J.: treasurer, Kuyper Foundation (Peter H. and E. Lucille Gaass)

Andreas, G. Allen: chairman, chief executive officer, Archer-Daniels-Midland Co.; director, Archer-Daniels-Midland Foundation

Andrews, Christie F.: vice president, director, Hewit Family Foundation

Andrews, Hugh T.: director, Andrews McMeel Universal Foundation

Andrews, James C.: director, Andrews McMeel Universal Foundation

Andrews, Joseph, Jr.: vice president corporate relations, Luck Stone; secretary, Luck Stone Foundation

Andrews, Kathleen W.: vice president, secretary, Andrews McMeel Universal Foundation

Andrews, Richard J.: director, Hewit Family Foundation

Andriessen, Frans H.J.J.: director, Sara Lee Corp.

Angelastro, Linda W.: director corporate communications, Ensign-Bickford Industries

Angell, Christopher C.: president, director, Kornfeld Foundation (Emily Davie and Joseph S.)

Anglin, Patricia: secretary, director, Vodaphone-US Foundation

Angood, Arthur W.: president, chief executive officer, trustee, Miller Foundation

Anik, Ruby: director, Best Buy Children's Foundation

Anlyan, William George, MD: trustee, Duke Endowment

Anneberg, A. Lee, MD: director, Copic Medical Foundation

Annenberg, Leonore A.: president, chairman, director, Annenberg Foundation

Annenberg, Wallis: vice president, Annenberg Foundation

Annexstad, A. T.: president, Federated Mutual Insurance Foundation

Anschutz-Rodgers, Sue: donor, president, trustee, Anschutz Family Foundation

Ansin, Ronald M.: trustee, Ansin Foundation (Ronald M.)

Anthony, Barbara Cox: president, trustee, Cox Foundation (James M.)

Augustine, Avery: director, Noyes, Jr. Memorial Foundation (Nicholas H.)

Auletta, Patrick V.: trustee, Key Foundation

Aull, William E.: director, Castle Foundation (Harold K. L.)

Aumiller, Wendy: treasurer, Cinergy Foundation

Aupperle, Tammy B.: program director, Heinz Co. Foundation (H.J.)

Austen, W. Gerald, MD: chairman, trustee, Knight Foundation (John S. and James L.)

Austin, Ann W.: member, Staunton Farm Foundation

Austin, Carlos: secretary, director, Tribune New York Foundation

Austin, Edward H., Jr.: trustee, Halsell Foundation (Ewing)

Austin, H. Brent: president, chief operating officer, director, El Paso Corp.

Austin, Leroy: corporator, Oak Grove School

Autry, Jacqueline: vice president, director, Autry Foundation

Autry, Rebecca: secretary, treasurer, Bardes Fund

Auw, Pierre E.: trustee, Hodges Foundation (Bess J.)

Avampato, Charles M.: president, Clay Foundation

Avansino, Kristen A.: president, executive director, Wiegand Foundation (E. L.)

Avansino, Raymond C., Jr.: chairman, trustee, chief executive officer, chief operating officer, Wiegand Foundation (E. L.)

Avanzino, Richard: president, director, Duffield Family Foundation

Avedisian, James R.: director, Atkinson Foundation

Avery, William Joseph: trustee, Connelly Foundation

Avis, Greg: director, Irvine Foundation (The James)

Axelrod, Margaret G.: treasurer, director, mem, Katzenberger Foundation

Axtell, Clayton M., III: director, Klee Foundation (Conrad and Virginia)

Axtell, Clayton M., Jr.: president, Klee Foundation (Conrad and Virginia)

Axworthy, Lloyd: director, MacArthur Foundation (John D. and Catherine T.)

Ayaub, John J.: vice president, secretary, trustee, Sage Foundation

Ayer, Everett L.: mem, Gardiner Savings Institution Charitable Foundation

Ayer, Ramani: chairman, president, chief executive officer, Hartford Financial Services Group Inc.

Ayers, Margaret C.: executive director, Clark Foundation (Robert Sterling)

Aylmer, John F.: director, Kelley and Elza Kelley Foundation (Edward Bangs)

Aylward, A. A.: vice president, Aylward Family Foundation

Aylward, E. W.: president, Aylward Family Foundation

Aylward, R. J.: director, Aylward Family Foundation

Aylward, Rayna: executive director, Mitsubishi Electric America Foundation

Ayres, Nancy: president, director, Noyes, Jr. Memorial Foundation (Nicholas H.)

Azoulay, Bernard: president, chief executive officer, Elf Atochem North America Inc.

B

Baack, Margaret: vice president, Ideal Industries Foundation

Babbio, Lawrence T., Jr.: vice chairman, president, Verizon Communications Inc.

Babcock, Bruce M.: director, Babcock Foundation (Mary Reynolds)

Babicka, Jerry: director, Educational Foundation of America

Babicka, Laren: adjunct director, Educational Foundation of America

Babicka, Lynn P.: director, Educational Foundation of America

Babington, Catherine V.: president, director, Abbott Laboratories Fund

Babson, James A.: trustee, Babson Foundation (Paul and Edith)

Babson, Katherine L.: trustee, Babson Foundation (Paul and Edith)

Bacal, Michael: treasurer, Hexcel Foundation

Bach, Neil C.: chairman, trustee, Camp and Bennet Humiston Trust (Apollos)

Bachman, C. William: director, Utica National Foundation

Bachman, Dale: trustee, Cooke Foundation

Bachmann, Bruce R.: director, Polk Brothers Foundation, Inc.

Bachmann, Tom: director, Grinnell Mutual Group Foundation

Bacigalupi, Jean: president, Haigh-Scatena Foundation

Bacon, Carolyn R.: chief executive director, O'Donnell Foundation

Bacon, Herbert L.: director, Bacon Family Foundation

Bacon, Kenneth J.: senior vice president, Fannie Mae; vice chairman, Fannie Mae Foundation

Bacon, Laura May: director, Bacon Family Foundation

Bacot, John Carter: director, Macy, Jr. Foundation (Josiah)

Baden, Helen T.: director, Fullerton Foundation

Baer, Timothy R.: senior vice president, secretary, Target Corp.; secretary, Target Foundation

Bagley, Nancy R.: vice president, director, Arca Foundation

Bagley, Nicole: director, Arca Foundation

Bagley, Smith: president, Arca Foundation

Bailey, Andrew C., Esq.: trustee, Riley Foundation (Mabel Louise)

Bailey, Anita Lamb: director, Lamb Foundation

Bailey, Ben: director, Lamb Foundation

Bailey, Hoyt Q.: president, Dover Foundation

Bailey, James D.: director, Cudahy Fund (Patrick and Anna M.)

Bailey, Joanne S.: assistant secretary, Claneil Foundation

Bailey, Liza: trustee, Credit Suisse First Boston Foundation Trust

Bailey, Toff: director, Lamb Foundation

Bailin, Michael: director, Penn Foundation (William)

Baillon, Austin J.: director emeritus, Grotto Foundation

Bains, Harrison MacKellar, Jr.: vice president, Bristol-Myers Squibb Co.; treasurer, Bristol-Myers Squibb Foundation Inc.

Baiocchi, Christina K.: director, van Ameringen Foundation, Inc.

Baird, Dugald Euan: chairman, president, chief executive officer, Schlumberger Ltd.

Baird, Joni E.: vice president, fund administrator, Johns Manville Fund

Baird, Laura Trammell: board of governors, Fondren Foundation

Baird, Philip F., Jr.: trustee, McKay Family Foundation

Baird, Richard A.: president, Giant Food Foundation

Bakalis, Desi: director, Demos Foundation (N.)

Baker, Anne: manager corporate contributions

Baker, Anthony K.: trustee, Baker Trust (George F.)

Baker, Benjamin M., III: director, Lockhart Vaughan Foundation

Baker, C. Allen: executive vice president, Alcon Laboratories Inc.

Baker, David S.: trustee, Rich Foundation

Baker, Dexter Farrington: chairman, Baker Foundation (Dexter F. and Dorothy H.); trustee, Trexler Trust (Harry C.)

Baker, Dorothy H.: trustee, Baker Foundation (Dexter F. and Dorothy H.)

Baker, Douglas, Jr.: president, chief operating officer, Ecolab Inc.

Baker, Edward L.: president, Florida Rock Industries Foundation; chairman, director, Florida Rock Industries Inc.; president, Florida Rock & Tank Lines Foundation

Baker, George F., III: trustee, Baker Trust (George F.)

Baker, Gwendolyn C.: director, Gilman Foundation (Howard)

Baker, James Addison, III: trustee, Hughes Medical Institute (Howard)

Baker, Joeseph, Jr.: committee member, Smith, Jr. Foundation (M. W.)

Baker, John Daniel, II: vice president, Florida Rock Industries Foundation

Baker, Kane K.: trustee, Baker Trust (George F.)

Baker, Larry: vice president employee relations, National Machinery Co.; secretary, treasurer, trustee, National Machinery Foundation, Inc.

Baker, Leslie Mayo, Jr.: trustee, Knight Foundation (John S. and James L.)

Baker, Norman D., Jr.: secretary, treasurer, trustee, Kimball Foundation (Horace A. Kimball and S. Ella)

Baker, Pam: executive director, secretary, Woods Charitable Fund

Baker, Paula W.: vice president, IBM International Foundation; director corporate community relations, International Business Machines

Baker, Richard W.: trustee, Speer Foundation (Roy M.)

Baker, Robert W.: senior vice president, general counsel, director, El Paso Corporate Foundation

Baker, Thomas E.: president, director, Oishei Foundation (The John R.)

Baker, Tracy A.: trustee, Gerber Foundation

Baker, W. A., Jr.: vice president, Colonial Foundation

Baker, William C.: trustee, Baker Trust (Clayton)

Baker, William O.: chairman emeritus, Mellon Foundation (Andrew W.)

Baker, William Oliver: director, Guggenheim Foundation (Harry Frank)

Bakewell, Edward L., III: chairman, chief executive officer, Bakewell Corp.; president, director, Bakewell, Jr. Family Foundation (Edward L.)

Bakken, Douglas Adair: executive director, Ball Brothers Foundation

Balaban, Donald: director, Kirkpatrick Foundation, Inc.

Balderston, Frederick Emery: director, Osher Foundation (Bernard)

Baldree, Edwin M.: president, Tri-County Telephone Foundation

Baldwin, Christopher W.: assistant treasurer, Gannett Company Inc.

Baldwin, John C.: treasurer, trustee, Baldwin Memorial Foundation (Fred); vice president, trustee, Castle Foundation (Samuel N. and Mary)

Baldwin, Robert Hayes Burns: chairman emeritus, Dodge Foundation (Geraldine R.)

Baledge, Les: director, IBP Foundation

Bales, Carol: secretary, treasurer, trustee, Hansen Foundation (Dane G.)

Balgooyen, Warren: director, Norcross Wildlife Foundation

Ball, Anne F.: trustee, Firestone, Jr. Foundation (Harvey)

Ball, Frank E.: vice president, director, Ball Brothers Foundation

Ballard, A. L.: director, Hale Foundation (Crescent Porter)

Ballentine, George W., Jr.: trustee, Self Family Foundation

Ballmer, Steven Anthony: chief executive officer, president, director, Microsoft Corp.

Bamberger, Clarence, Jr.: mem, Bamberger Memorial Foundation (John Ernest Bamberger and Ruth Eleanor)

Banach, Joan: secretary, Dedalus Foundation

Banbury, Hunter: president, chief executive officer, treasurer, Cone-Blanchard Corp.

Bane, Richard C.: trustee, Eastern Bank Charitable Foundation

Banfield, Dick: president, Magna International of America Inc.

Banis, Richard P.: treasurer, Pennington Foundation (William N. and Myriam)

Bankowski, Elizabeth: secretary, Ben & Jerry's Foundation

Banner, Matthew R., III: director, King Foundation (Kenneth Kendal)

Bannerman, Douglas: member distribution committee, Bruening Foundation (Eva L. and Joseph M.)

Bannister, Thomas J., Jr.: president, Bakewell Corp.

Banno, Tetsuji: president, Oki America Inc.

Bannon, Kevin J.: treasurer, director, Link, Jr. Foundation (George)

Bannon, Mel B.: trustee, Beynon Foundation (Kathryne)

Bannon, Robert D.: trustee, Beynon Foundation (Kathryne)

Baptie, Tilly J.: executive director, Disney Co. Foundation (Walt)

Barbato, Randall: trustee, Nord Family Foundation

Barber, John: director, GlaxoSmithKline Foundation

Barber, Walter: trustee, Thomaston Savings Bank Foundation

Barcus, Marian: trustee, Blandin Foundation

Bardes, Judith L.: executive director, trustee, Douty Foundation (Alfred and Mary); executive director, Seybert Institution for Poor Boys and Girls (Adam and Maria Sarah)

Bardes, Merrilyn B.: president, Bardes Corp.

Bardige, Betty S.: chairman, director, Mailman Family Foundation (A. L.)

Bardin, Mary Beth: executive vice president public affairs & communications, Verizon Communications Inc.

Bardoff, Ralph: vice president, director, Ishiyama Foundation

Bardusch, William E., Jr.: trustee, Sullivan Foundation (Algernon Sydney)

Barhoum, Ann F.: director, executive committee, Francis Families Foundation

Bark, Dennis L.: chairman, trustee, Earhart Foundation

Barkeley, Norman A.: chairman emeritus, Ducommun Inc.

Barker, Allan M.: treasurer, trustee, Barker Foundation Inc.

Barker, Coeta: trustee, Barker Foundation (Coeta and Donald R.)

Barker, Dorothy A.: trustee, Barker Foundation Inc.

Barker, Douglas M.: secretary, Barker Foundation Inc.

Barker, Edwin F.: vice president, chief financial officer, Winnebago Industries; trustee, Winnebago Industries Foundation

Barker, James R.: vice president, director, Barker Foundation (J.M.R.)

Barker, Mary L.: trustee, Stewart Educational Foundation (Donnell B. and Elizabeth Dee Shaw)

Barker, Norman, Jr.: director, member audit committee, member grant committee, Keck Foundation (W. M.)

Barker, Peter Keefe: vice president, trustee, Jones Foundation (Fletcher); treasurer, director, member executive committee, member grant, Keck Foundation (W. M.)

Barker, William P.: trustee, McFeely-Rogers Foundation

Barkow, Richard C.: director, Siebert Lutheran Foundation

Barksdale, Mary F.: director, Foellinger Foundation

Barletta, Robert J.: treasurer, Prospect Hill Foundation

Barnes, Carlyle Fuller: president, Barnes Foundation

Barnes, Corbin: treasurer, Cook, Sr. Charitable Foundation (Kelly Gene)

Barnes, Judith A.: director, Howard and Bush Foundation

Barnes, Ronald R.: executive director, trustee, Norris Foundation (Kenneth T. and Eileen L.)

Barnes, Thomas O.: secretary, director, Barnes Group Foundation Inc.; board chairman, Barnes Group Inc.

Barnes, W. Michael: senior vice president finance & planning, chief financial officer, Rockwell Automation Inc.; member trust committee, Rockwell International Corp. Trust

Barnett, Carol J.: director, Publix Supermarkets; chairman, chief executive officer, Publix Supermarkets Charities

Barnett, Hoyt R.: vice president, director, Publix Supermarkets Charities

Barney, Marlene S.: director, Exchange Bank Foundation

Barnhart, Lorraine: director, Freed Foundation; vice president, trustee, Huber Foundation

Baron, Blue: secretary, Mechanic Foundation (Morris A.)

Baron, Jules M.: director, Goldman Foundation (Herman)

Baron, Richard K.: executive director, Goldman Foundation (Herman)

Baronner, Robert Francis: director, One Valley Bank Foundation

Barr, John H.: vice president, Oak Tree Charitable Foundation

Barrak, Marion L.: president, director, Hoffman Foundation (Maximilian E. and Marion O.)

Barrett, Allen M., Jr.: vice president corporate communications, McCormick & Company Inc.

Barrett, John E.: trustee, Western-Southern Foundation, Inc.

Barrett, John F.: treasurer, Emery Memorial (Thomas J.)

Barrett, Julie: member, Bamberger Memorial Foundation (John Ernest Bamberger and Ruth Eleanor)

Barris, Marty: trustee, Donaldson Foundation

Barron, John H. C., Jr.: secretary, Cafritz Foundation (Morris and Gwendolyn)

Barrow, Steve: program officer, Sierra Health Foundation

Barry, Elizabeth T.: director, Gazette Foundation

Barry, Tina S.: senior vice president corporate communications, Kimberly-Clark Corp.; president, Kimberly-Clark Foundation

Barsky, Barbara: trustee, PNM Foundation; vice president, PNM Resources Inc.

Barsness, W. E. Bye: vice chairman, trustee, McNeely Foundation

Barstow, David O.: trustee, Barstow Foundation

Barstow, John C.: trustee, Barstow Foundation

Barstow, Richard G.: co-chairman, trustee, Barstow Foundation

Barstow, Robert G.: trustee, Barstow Foundation

Barstow, Robert O.: trustee, Barstow Foundation

Barth, John M.: member advisory board, Johnson Controls Foundation; president, chief executive officer, Johnson Controls Inc.

Bartha, Louis A.: secretary, director, The Prairie Foundation

Bartl, James F.: secretary, director, Phillips Family Foundation (L. E.)

Bartlett, Paul Dana, Jr.: chairman, director, Bartlett & Co.; trustee, Bartlett & Co. Grain Charitable Foundation

Bartlett, Thomas Alva: chairman, United States-Japan Foundation

Bartley, Charles R., Sr.: vchairman, Exchange Bank Foundation

Barton, Shannon: program officer, Davis Foundation (Joe C.)

Barton, Willis H., Jr.: vice president, New Milford Savings Bank Foundation

Bartos, John N.: trustee, Strosacker Foundation (Charles J.)

Bartwink, Theodore S.: treasurer, secretary, Harkness Foundation for Dance

Bartz, Carol: director, New York Stock Exchange Foundation, Inc.

Barwick, Kent L.: director, Clark Foundation (NY)

Basner, Ruth H.: mem, Hoover Foundation (Herbert W.)

Bass, Edward Perry: vice president, director, Richardson Foundation (Sid W.)

Bass, F. W.: trustee, Exxon Mobil Foundation

Bass, John T.: vice chairman, treasurer, Crowell Trust (Henry P. and Susan C.)

Bass, Lee M.: vice president, director, Richardson Foundation (Sid W.)

Bass, Nancy Lee: vice president, director, Richardson Foundation (Sid W.)

Bass, Perry Richardson: president, director, Richardson Foundation (Sid W.)

Bass, Sid Richardson: vice president, director, Richardson Foundation (Sid W.)

Bassett, Bonnie: executive director, Land O'Lakes Foundation

Bastian, Frank W.: secretary, director, Schoenleber Foundation

Bateman, Janey F.: secretary, director, Hawn Foundation

Bateman, Mary Michael: chairman, Vermilion Healthcare Foundation

Bates, Arthur: trustee, Charitable Venture Foundation

Bates, James C.: vice president, chief financial officer, ACF Industries

Bates, Jeanne M.: vice president, program officer, Hall Family Foundation (The)

Bates, R. K.: director, Hegeler II Foundation (Julius W.)

Bates, Ronnie L.: senior vice president, planning,

sales, service, Georgia Power Co.; director, Georgia Power Foundation

Batkin, Jonathan: director, Chamiza Foundation

Batten, Frank, Jr.: president, director, Landmark Communications Foundation; executive vice president, Landmark Communications Inc.

Batten, Frank, Sr.: chairman, director, Landmark Communications Foundation; chairman, Landmark Communications Inc.

Batts, James L.: director, Batts Foundation

Batts, John H.: president, director, Batts Foundation

Batts, John T.: director, Batts Foundation

Batts, Julie: secretary, Gilmore Foundation (Irving S.)

Batts, Michael A.: director, Batts Foundation

Batts, Robert H.: director, Batts Foundation

Bauder, Lillian: chairman, trustee, Skillman Foundation

Bauer, Chris Michael: vice chairman, director, Siebert Lutheran Foundation

Bauer, David P.: trustee, Bauer Family Foundation

Bauer, Lisa M.: trustee, Bauer Family Foundation

Bauer, M. J.: director, Jostens Foundation Inc. (The)

Bauer, Mary Grace: trustee, Bauer Family Foundation

Bauer, Paul D.: trustee, Bauer Family Foundation

Bauernfeind, George G.: vice president, Humana Foundation

Baum, Alexio R.: trustee, Gerstacker Foundation (Rollin M.)

Bauman, Steve: secretary, Ottenheimer Brothers Foundation

Baumann, Marvin J.: secretary, trustee, La-Z-Boy Foundation

Bawa, Rookaya, PhD: program officer international development, Carnegie Corp. of New York

Baxter, Joe E.: secretary, treasurer, director, Meyer Foundation (Paul J.)

Bay, Frederick: executive director, Bay Foundation; chairman, executive director, Paul and C. Michael Paul Foundation (Josephine Bay)

Bay, Mogens C.: trustee, Kiewit Foundation (Peter); chairman, chief executive officer, Valmont Industries Inc.

Bayardelle, Eddy: secretary, Merrill Lynch & Co. Foundation Inc.

Bayless, Mary C.: director, Connell Foundation (Michael J.)

Beach, Clarence E.: director, Broyhill Family Foundation

Beach, E. D.: secretary, treasurer, director, Broyhill Family Foundation

Beach, Ross: trustee, Hansen Foundation (Dane G.)

Beal, Barry A.: trustee, Beal Foundation

Beal, Carlton E., Jr.: chairman, Beal Foundation

Beal, Keleen H.: trustee, Beal Foundation

Beal, Kelly S.: trustee, Beal Foundation

Beal, Richard M.: treasurer, Gallo Foundation (Ernest)

Beal, Spencer E.: trustee, Beal Foundation

Beale, Susan M.: vice president, secretary, DTE Energy Co.; director, DTE Energy Foundation

Beall, Carolyn C.: secretary, Campbell Foundation (MD)

Beall, Donald Ray: director, executive committee, Rockwell Automation Inc.; president, Rockwell International Corp. Trust

Beall, Kenneth S., Esq.: secretary, Fuller Foundation (DE)

Bean, Roy H.: trustee, Ashtabula Foundation

Bear, Stephen E.: senior vice president, human resources, Bristol-Myers Squibb Co.; director, Bristol-Myers Squibb Foundation Inc.

Beard, Anson McC., Jr.: trustee, Hartford Foundation, Inc. (The John A.)

Beard, Ellanor Allday: board of governors, Fondren Foundation

Beard, Peter: senior vice president, Fannie Mae Foundation

Beardsley, George B.: trustee, Gates Family Foundation

Beardsley, Pamela D.: trustee, Boettcher Foundation

Bearse, Stacy V.: treasurer, Blood-Horse Charitable Foundation

Beason, Jeffrey I.: senior vice president, controller, El Paso Corporate Foundation

Beattie, Art P.: vice president, secretary, treasurer, Alabama Power Co.; treasurer, director, Alabama Power Foundation

Beattie, Catherine Hamrick: director, Fullerton Foundation

Beatty, Sean A.: treasurer, director, Royal & SunAlliance Insurance Foundation, Inc.

Beauchamp, Gary: director, Ambrose Monell Foundation (The)

Beaulieu, Rita H.: treasurer, director, Vance Charitable Foundation (Robert C.)

Beaver, Thomas A.: treasurer, Wyomissing Foundation

Beaz, Marianne: vice president client service & pension investments, Pacific Life Insurance Co.

Becalli, Nani: director, GE Foundation

Becht, James H.: secretary, Deere Foundation (John)

Becht, Loretta J.: assistant secretary, Hyde and Watson Foundation

Bechtel, Riley Peart: chairman, director, Bechtel Foundation; chairman, chief executive officer, director, Bechtel Group Inc.

Bechtel, Robert W.: co-trustee, mgr, director, Potts and Sibley Foundation

Bechthold, Ned W.: chairman, director, Siebert Lutheran Foundation

Beck, Joyce M.: administrative assistant, Ball Foundation (George and Frances)

Beck, Nancy: trustee, The MBNA Foundation

Beck, Phyllis Whitman: chairman, director, Independence Foundation

Beck, Susan K.: member distribution committee, trustee, Kettering Fund

Becker, Don: trustee, The Kroger Co. Foundation

Becker, Harold M.: chairman, chief executive officer, Guaranty Bank & Trust Co.; director, Guaranty Bank and Trust Co. Charitable Trust

Becker, Howard C.: trustee, Ohio National Foundation; vice president, Ohio National Life Insurance Co.

Becker, Katrina H.: vice president, secretary, director, Barker Welfare Foundation

Becker, Richard K.A.: assistant secretary, Loughran Foundation (Mary and Daniel)

Becker, Robert A.: president, director, Provident Community Foundation

Becker, Robert D.: director, Guaranty Bank and Trust Co. Charitable Trust

Becker, Steve: chief executive officer, chief financial officer, Kawasaki Motors Manufacturing Corporation U.S.A.

Beckman, Arnold Orville, PhD: founder, chairman emeritus, Beckman Foundation (Arnold and Mabel)

Beckman, Arnold W.: director, Beckman Foundation (Arnold and Mabel)

Beckman, G. Patricia: director, Beckman Foundation (Arnold and Mabel)

Beckner, Lou: assistant secretary, Houchens Foundation (Ervin G.)

Beckworth, Laura H.: vice president, Hobby Family Foundation

Bedsole, M. Palmer: member distribution committee, Bedsole Foundation (J. L.)

Bedsole, T. Massey: chairman distribution committee, trustee, Bedsole Foundation (J. L.)

Bedsole, Travis M., Jr.: member distribution committee, Bedsole Foundation (J. L.)

Beebe, Lydia I.: corporate secretary, ChevronTexaco Corp.

Beeby, Thomas H.: trustee, Graham Foundation for Advanced Studies in the Fine Arts

Beech, Thomas Foster: executive vice president, Burnett Foundation (The)

Beer, James: chief financial officer, AMR Corp.

Beer, Robert A.: trustee, Brace Foundation (Donald C.)

Beers, Julius H.: treasurer, Oleson Foundation

Beetle, Vivian: director community affairs, Hoffmann-La Roche Inc.; executive director, Roche Foundation

Begemann, Brett D.: director, Monsanto Fund

Behrend, Catherine H.: director, Hebrew Technical Institute

Behrenhausen, Richard A.: president, chief executive officer, McCormick Tribune Foundation (Robert R.)

Behrens, Roger: director, HON Industries Charitable Foundation

Beinecke, Elizabeth G.: vice president, director, Prospect Hill Foundation

Beinecke, Frederick William: secretary, treasurer, trustee, Kress Foundation (Samuel H.)

Beinecke, John B.: president, director, Prospect Hill Foundation

Beinecke, William Sperry: chairman, director, Prospect Hill Foundation

Beisler, Ralph: secretary, trustee, Robinson-Broadhurst Foundation

Beland, Elizabeth A.: administrator, Stevens Foundation (Abbot and Dorothy H.)

Belcher, Donald David: chairman, president, chief executive officer, director, Banta Corp.

Belda, Ricardo E.: director, Alcoa Foundation

Belden, Frederick H., Jr.: mem, trustee, One Valley Bank Foundation; executive vice president, One Valley Bank N.A.

Beling, Betty: assoc director, Borchard Foundation (Albert and Elaine)

Beling, Willard A.: chairman, director, Borchard Foundation (Albert and Elaine)

Belinkie, Julie Bender: president, Bender Foundation

Belitz, Gary R.: director, Williams Companies Foundation (The)

Belk, Claudia W.: member board advisors, Belk Foundation

Belk, John Montgomery: chairman, member board advisors, Belk Foundation; chairman, chief executive officer, Belk Stores Services Inc.

Bell, David L.: trustee, Self Family Foundation

Bell, Diane Fisher: vice president, Fisher Foundation

Bell, Jane A.: clerk, Cabot Corp. Foundation

Bell, Judy: trustee, El Pomar Foundation

Bell, Larry: trustee, Beal Foundation

Bell, Lawrence T.: vice president, director, Ecolab Foundation; vice president law, general counsel, Ecolab Inc.

Bell, R. Terry: president, trustee, Rockwell Fund, Inc.

Bell, Richard A.: trustee, vice president, Sarkeys Foundation

Bell, Robert Morrall: president, director, Gregg-Graniteville Foundation

Bell, Samuel P.: vice president, trustee, Jones Foundation (Fletcher)

Bell, Susan M.: senior supervisor-corporate communications, Ameren Corp.

Bellairs, Robert J.: co-trustee, Bishop Charitable Trust (A. G.)

Bellamy, George E.: director, Morgan Foundation (Louie R. and Gertrude)

Belles, Lawrence L.: president, director, Cheney Foundation (Elizabeth F.)

Belloff, Frederick: director, Bush Charitable Foundation, Inc. (Edyth)

Belloff, Mary Gretchen: vice chairman, director, Bush Charitable Foundation, Inc. (Edyth)

Bellor, Mary: secretary, secretary, Graham Fund (Philip L.)

Bellwood, Wesley E.: president, Wynn Foundation

Belt, John L.: director, Kirkpatrick Foundation, Inc.

Beltz, Susan W.: director, Pine Tree Foundation

Bemis, Peter F.: vice president, Bemis Family Foundation (F.K.)

Bemis, Richard A.: president, Bemis Family Foundation (F.K.); president, chief executive officer, director, Bemis Manufacturing Co.

Benard, Michael P.: vice president, director communications & public affairs, Eastman Kodak Co.

Benckenstein, Eunice R.: vice chairman, trustee, Stark Foundation (Nelda C. and H. J. Lutcher)

Bender, Barbara A.: vice president, Bender Foundation

Bender, Christine: secretary, treasurer, director, Cimino Foundation (James and Barbara)

Bender, David S.: vice president, Bender Foundation

Bender, Howard Marvin: executive vice president, Bender Foundation

Bender, Sondra D.: chairman, Bender Foundation

Bender, Stanley Seymour: secretary, Bender Foundation

Bendheim, Andrew: director, Lowenstein Foundation (Leon)

Bendheim, John M.: vice president, director, Lowenstein Foundation (Leon)

Bendheim, John M., Jr.: director, Lowenstein Foundation (Leon)

Bendheim, Kim: director, Lowenstein Foundation (Leon)

Bendheim, Robert Austin: president, director, Lowenstein Foundation (Leon)

Bendheim, Thomas L.: director, Lowenstein Foundation (Leon)

Bendheim-Thoman, Lynn: director, Lowenstein Foundation (Leon)

Benenson, Bruce W.: vice president, Benenson Foundation (Frances and Benjamin)

Benenson, Charles B.: president, Benenson Foundation (Frances and Benjamin)

Benenson, Lawrence A.: director, Hebrew Technical Institute

Benetton, Luciano: chairman, president, chief executive officer, director, Benetton U.S.A. Corp.

Benjamin, Adelaide Wisdom: trustee, RosaMary Foundation

Benjamin, Andrew: trustee, RosaMary Foundation

Benjamin, Michael: vice president, controller, Schlumberger Foundation

Bennack, Frank Anthony, Jr.: vice president, director, Hearst Foundation (William Randolph)

Bennett, Clark: trustee, Bennett Family Foundation (Claude)

Bennett, Franklin: trustee, Pollock Co. Foundation (William B.)

Bennett, Joann: treasurer, Argyle Foundation

Bennett, John J., Jr.: secretary, St. Giles Foundation

Bennett, Robert B.: trustee, Statler Foundation

Bennett O'Leary, Katherine: trustee, Bennett Family Foundation (Claude)

Bennington, Ronald Kent: committee member, Hoover Foundation (The)

Bensen, M. James: trustee, Blandin Foundation

Bensley, Bruce N.: trustee, member, Rippel Foundation (Fannie E.)

Benson, Donald: trustee, Share Trust (Charles Morton)

Benson, Gregory L.: director, treasurer, Andersen Foundation

Benson, John W.: director, Minnesota Mining & Manufacturing Co.

Benson, Keith W., III: president, chief executive officer, National Manufacturing Co.

Benson, Keith W., Jr.: chairman, director, National Manufacturing Co.

Benson, Lee-Hoon: program officer, Bush Foundation

Benson, Peter M.: director, NMC Foundation

Benten, R. Anthony: assistant treasurer, New York Times Co. Foundation

Bentley, Greg: director, Trust Foundation

Bentley, Maria C.: treasurer, director, Gellert Foundation (Carl Gellert and Celia Berta)

Bentson, Larry: assistant secretary, director, Midcontinent Media Foundation

Bentson, Nathan L.: chairman, chief executive officer, director, Midcontinent Media Inc.

Bentzen, Michael P.: secretary, trustee, Fowler Memorial Foundation (John Edward)

Benz, Wanda: assistant secretary, MDU Resources Foundation

Beran, R. D.: treasurer, Caterpillar Foundation

Bere, Barbara Van Dellen: president, director, Bere Foundation

Bere, David L.: secretary, treasurer, director, Bere Foundation

Bere, James Frederick, Jr.: vice president, director, Bere Foundation

Bere, Robert P.: vice president, director, Bere Foundation

Berelson, Ellen S.: vice president, director, Barth Foundation, Inc. (The Theodore H.)

Berelson, Thelma D.: secretary, director, Barth Foundation, Inc. (The Theodore H.)

Berenato, Joseph C.: president, chief executive officer, Ducommun Inc.

Berey, Mark H.: senior vice president, chief financial officer, treasurer, Giant Food Inc.

Berg, Alan: vice president, Becher Foundation (Hildegarde D.)

Berg, Anne P.: grant consultant, Rich Foundation

Berg, Don: director, Land O'Lakes Foundation

Berg, Lois: secretary, Johnson Foundation

Berg, Susan M.: secretary, CLARCOR Foundation

Bergenfield, Burt: trustee, Simon Foundation (Sidney, Milton, and Leoma)

Bergent, Nancy W.: trustee, Kunkel Foundation (John Crain)

Berger, Claudia: secretary, Lin Foundation (T. Y.)

Berger, Gretchen: director, Patron Saints Foundation

Berger, Miles Lee: director, Graham Foundation for Advanced Studies in the Fine Arts

Bergeron, Peter L.: trustee, Foundation for Seacoast Health

Bergethon, K. Roald: trustee, Newcombe Foundation (Charlotte W.)

Bergin, Suzanne M.: director, MassMutual Foundation for Hartford, Inc. (The)

Bergquist, Renee: vice president investor relations, Albertson's Inc.

Bergreen, Bernard D.: director, Gilman Foundation (Howard)

Bergtold, Susanna: secretary, director, Scherman Foundation

Berilgen, Bulent A.: vice president, chief operating officer, director, Forest Oil Corp.

Berk, Samuel: trustee, Nord Family Foundation

Berk, Tony B.: trustee, Parshelsky Foundation (Moses L.)

Berkeley, Alice D.: director, Dodge Foundation (Cleveland H.)

Berkenstadt, James A.: director, Cremer Foundation

Berkery, Rosemary T.: executive vice president, general counsel, Merrill Lynch & Company Inc.

Berkley, Eliot S.: secretary, Tension Envelope Foundation

Berkley, Eugene Bertram: chairman, director, Tension Envelope Corp.; treasurer, Tension Envelope Foundation

Berkley, Richard L.: treasurer, secretary, director, Tension Envelope Corp.; president, Tension Envelope Foundation

Berkley, William S.: president, chief executive officer, director, Tension Envelope Corp.; director, Tension Envelope Foundation

Berkman, Andrew: director, Hebrew Technical Institute

Berkman, Louis: president, trustee, Berkman Foundation (Louis and Sandra); chairman, trustee, Fair Oaks Foundation

Berlamino, Betty Ellen: president, director, Tribune New York Foundation

Berlanti, Merryl A.: vice president, Dominic Foundation

Berlanti, Richard A.: president, Dominic Foundation

Berlanti, Todd A.: secretary, treasurer, Dominic Foundation

Berliant, Jennie D.: trustee, Rosenthal Foundation (Lois and Richard)

Berliantt, Mark H.: trustee, Rosenthal Foundation (Lois and Richard)

Berlin, Charles, PhD: director, Littauer Foundation (Lucius N.)

Berman, Cheryl: vice president, Burnett Co. Charitable Foundation (Leo)

Bermas, Stephen: president, Conway Scholarship Foundation (Carle C.)

Bernadotte, Christian C.: vice president, Nordson Corp.

Bernard, Carolyn K.: trustee, Hawkins Foundation (Robert Z.)

Bernard, Lewis W.: trustee, Mellon Foundation (Andrew W.)

Bernard, Robert: senior vice president international sales, Claiborne Inc. (Liz)

Berndt, Richard O.: director, Baltimore Equitable Insurance Foundation

Bernhardson, Ivy S.: 2nd vice chairman, director, Bush Foundation

Bernhardt, Stephen J.: president, treasurer, Baltimore Equitable Insurance Foundation; chairman, president, chief executive officer, chief financial officer, Baltimore Equity Society

Bernstein, Alan S.: trustee, Lurcy Charitable and Educational Trust (Georges)

Bernstein, Alison R.: vice president knowledge creativity and freedom, Ford Foundation

Bernstein, Daniel Lewis: trustee, Lurcy Charitable and Educational Trust (Georges)

Bernstein, Erik P.: trustee, Phillips Family Foundation (The Jay and Rose)

Bernstein, George Lurcy: trustee, Lurcy Charitable and Educational Trust (Georges)

Bernstein, Henry B.: director finance, Pew Charitable Trusts

Bernstein, Jay S.: trustee, Lawrence Foundation

Bernstein, Lawrence: trustee, Lawrence Foundation

Bernstein, Leonard S.: chairman, president, chief executive officer, Candlesticks Inc.; trustee, Lawrence Foundation

Bernstein, Loraine: assistant director, Gordon Charitable Trust (Peggy and Yale)

Bernstein, Morton J.: director, Samuels Foundation (Fan Fox and Leslie R.)

Bernstein, Paula P.: trustee, Phillips Family Foundation (The Jay and Rose)

Bernstein, William E.: trustee, Phillips Family Foundation (The Jay and Rose)

Berresford, Susan Vail: president, trustee, Ford Foundation

Berrier, Ronald G.: vice president, treasurer, assistant secretary, Thomasville Furniture Industries Inc.

Berry, Archie: corporator, Oak Grove School

Berry, Charles D.: trustee, Berry Foundation (Loren M.)

Berry, David L.: trustee, Berry Foundation (Loren M.)

Berry, Donald C., Jr.: treasurer, trustee, McDonald Foundation (J. M.)

Berry, Drew: trustee, Scripps Howard Foundation

Berry, George W.: trustee, Berry Foundation (Loren M.)

Berry, John William, Jr.: president, trustee, Berry Foundation (Loren M.)

Berry, Karen R.: secretary, Kornfeld Foundation

Berry, Sharon: director, M.E. Foundation

Berry, Thomas Eugene: assistant secretary, trustee, Sterling-Turner Foundation

Berry, Thomas W.: director, treasurer, Hyde and Watson Foundation

Berry, William S.: director, Rayonier Foundation; executive vice president forest resources & wood products, Rayonier Inc.

Berryhill, John: co-trustee, Latkin Charitable Foundation (Herbert and Gertrude)

Berryman, Kevin: trustee, Ralston Purina Trust Fund

Bersoff, Edward H., PhD: vice chairman, Meyer Foundation (Eugene and Agnes E.)

Bertolini, Robert: board of trustees, Schering-Plough Foundation

Bertrand, Frederic Howard: chairman, Central Vermont Public Service Corp.

Berwald, John J.: director, Crail-Johnson Foundation

Berylson, Amy S.: trustee, Smith Family Foundation (Richard and Susan)

Berylson, John G.: trustee, Smith Family Foundation (Richard and Susan)

Bescherer, Edwin A., Jr.: trustee, Dun & Bradstreet Corp. Foundation, Inc.

Beschloss, Afsaneh M.: trustee, Ford Foundation

Beshkov, Lisa: trustee, Price Foundation (Louis and Harold)

Bessant, Catherine P.: trustee, Bank of America Foundation

Bessemer, Mary T.: director emeritus, Holmberg Foundation

Besser, John Edward: senior vice president finance & law, Barnes Group Inc.

Bessette, Andy: executive vice president, chief administrative officer, St. Paul Travelers Companies Inc.; director, vice chairman, St. Paul Travelers Foundation

Best, Barbara D.: director, member relations, Dana Foundation (Charles A.)

Betten, Michael G.: director, Dime Savings Bank of Norwich Foundation

Bettis, Bernice A.: secretary, director, King Foundation (Kenneth Kendal)

Bettis, Harry Little: president, director, Cunningham Foundation (Laura Moore)

Bettis, Laura: secretary, treasurer, Cunningham

Foundation (Laura Moore)

Betts, C. R.: trustee, Betts Foundation

Betts, R. E.: trustee, Betts Foundation

Betts, Richard T.: trustee, Betts Foundation; chairman, president, director, Betts Industries

Betz, Bill B.: secretary, director, Jameson Foundation (J. W. and Ida M.)

Beukema, Henry S.: executive director, McCune Foundation

Beverly, Joseph E.: director, Williams Family Foundation of Georgia

Bewley, Peter D.: senior vice president, general counsel, secretary, Clorox Co.; vice president, secretary, Clorox Co. Foundation

Bezahler, Lori: president, board secretary, Hazen Foundation (Edward W.)

Bezik, Cynthia B.: senior vice president finance, Cleveland-Cliffs Inc.

Bhojwani, Sayu: trustee, New York Foundation

Bianchini, Thomas J.: secretary, treasurer, Kirby Foundation (F. M.)

Bibb, Thomas F.: vice president, treasurer, trustee, Halff Foundation (G. A. C.)

Biber, David D.: secretary, treasurer, Lilly Endowment

Bicknell, Warren, III: vice president, trustee, Bicknell Fund

Bicknell, Wendy H.: trustee, Bicknell Fund

Bielfeld, Douglas: treasurer, Wiremold Foundation

Biemer, Linda: director, Klee Foundation (Conrad and Virginia)

Bienz, Walt: trustee, Auburn Foundry Foundation

Biever, John P.: treasurer, Badger Meter Foundation

Biggers, Covella H.: treasurer, Houchens Foundation (Ervin G.)

Biggers, Erin: director, Houchens Foundation (Ervin G.)

Biggers, Gil E.: director, Houchens Foundation (Ervin G.)

Biggers, Gil M.: president, Houchens Foundation (Ervin G.)

Biggie, Carmelita: committee member, Whitaker Fund (Helen F.)

Biggins, Edward J., Jr.: secretary, Public Service Electric & Gas Foundation

Biggs, John Herron: chairman, trustee, Getty Trust (J. Paul)

Biggs, Victor: assistant vice president, Brookdale Foundation

Bigham, James John: executive vice president, chief financial officer, director, ContiGroup Companies Inc.

Bigue, Christa Palmer: director, Beveridge Foundation, Inc. (Frank Stanley)

Bihary, Kristen: vice president corporate communications, Eaton Corp.

Bilezikian, Doreen: director, Kelley and Elza Kelley Foundation (Edward Bangs)

Billegsly, James R.: director, Doherty Charitable Foundation (Henry L. and Grace)

Billings, Clyde A., Jr.: secretary, First Tennessee Foundation

Billingsley, Helen Lee: director, Doherty Charitable Foundation (Henry L. and Grace)

Billingsley, James Ray: vice president, treasurer, director, Doherty Charitable Foundation (Henry L. and Grace)

Bilski, Berthold: director, Littauer Foundation (Lucius N.)

Bilton, Stuart Douglas: president, chief executive officer, Chicago Title Corp.; trustee, Chicago Title and Trust Co. Foundation

Bing, Dave: trustee, McGregor Fund

Binswanger, David R.: president, chief executive officer, Binswanger Cos.; treasurer, Binswanger Foundation

Binswanger, Frank G., III: secretary, Binswanger Foundation

Binswanger, Frank G., Jr.: co-chairman, director, Binswanger Cos.

Binswanger, John K.: co-chairman, director, Binswanger Cos.; president, Binswanger Foundation

Binswanger, Robert B.: vice chairman, Binswanger Foundation

Birch, Edward E.: president, Mosher Foundation (Samuel B. & Margaret C.)

Birchenough, David: vice president, Klee Foundation (Conrad and Virginia)

Birckhead, Toni: trustee, Rosenthal Foundation (Lois and Richard)

Bircumshaw, Colin: vice president, Price Foundation (Lucien B. and Katherine E.)

Bircumshow, Colin: director, Price Foundation (Lucien B. and Katherine E.)

Bird, Hobart M.: trustee, Braemar Charitable Trust

Bird, Marian A.: trustee, Braemar Charitable Trust

Bird, Peter F., Jr.: president, chief executive officer, Frist Foundation

Birdsall, C. L.: assistant secretary, Exxon Mobil Foundation

Bischoff, Manfred: aerospace and industrial businesses, DaimlerChrysler AG

Bisesi, James T.: director, Glick Foundation (Eugene and Marilyn)

Bisgrove, Debra: secretary, vice president, director, Stardust Foundation

Bisgrove, Gerald: president, director, Stardust Foundation

Bishop, Donald F., II: president, executive director, O'Connor Foundation (A. Lindsay and Olive B.)

Bishop, John L.: treasurer, director, Russell Charitable Foundation (Tom)

Bishop, Margaret: gov, Munson Foundation Trust (W. B.)

Bishop, Robert L., II: chairman, member advisory committee, O'Connor Foundation (A. Lindsay and Olive B.)

Bishop, Timothy R.: treasurer, Collins Foundation

Bishop, Vernon: trustee, Bishop Foundation (Vernon and Doris)

Bittner, R. Richard: trustee, Bechtel Charitable Remainder Uni-Trust (Harold R.); director, Bechtel Charitable Remainder Uni-Trust (Marie H.)

Bittorf, Joseph L.: chairperson, NMC Foundation

Bjornson, Donald R., MD: vice president, CHC Foundation

Black, Creed Carter: trustee, Knight Foundation (John S. and James L.)

Black, Gary, Jr.: chairman, trustee, Abell Foundation

Black, Gary E.: president claims division, director, Fireman's Fund Insurance Co.

Black, Isabelle E.: vice president, Miller Foundation (Steve J.)

Black, Louis E.: secretary, director, Dodge Foundation (Cleveland H.)

Black, Natalie A.: vice president, director, Kohler Foundation

Black, Thomas F., III: president, trustee, Kimball Foundation (Horace A. Kimball and S. Ella)

Blackford, Robert N.: trustee, Magruder Foundation (Chesley G.)

Blackwell, Anna Derby: trustee, Cooke Foundation

Blackwell, Jean: secretary, treasurer, Cummins Foundation; vice president, human resources, Cummins Inc.

Blair, Gary J.: treasurer, trustee, Blade Foundation

Blair, Ian D.: trustee, Todd Co. Foundation (A.M.)

Blake, Benjamin L.: director, The Prairie Foundation

Blake, Jonathan D.: director, Daniels Foundation (Fred Harris)

Blamey, Richard L.: secretary, treasurer, director, VPI Foundation

Blanchard, Cayce: director, Mitsubishi Electric America Foundation; director corporate communications, Mitsubishi Electric and Electronics USA

Blanchard, J. A., III: chairman, ADC Telecommunications

Blanchard, Larry H.: assistant secretary, assistant treasurer, CUNA Mutual Group Foundation, Inc.

Blandford, M. Margaret: executive director, White Foundation (W. P. and H. B.)

Blaney, Carolyn E.: president, director, Eberly Foundation

Blankenship, Robert P.: chairman, director, McConnell Foundation

Blanton, Ben W.: director, Clowes Fund

Blanton, Eddy S.: vice president, director, Scurlock Foundation

Blanton, Jack S., Jr.: vice president, director, Scurlock Foundation

Blanton, Laura L.: president, director, Scurlock Foundation

Blasdale, William: trustee, Acushnet Foundation

Blass, Gus, III: board of directors, Ottenheimer Brothers Foundation

Blass, Noland, Jr.: board director, Ottenheimer Brothers Foundation

Blaxter, H. Vaughan, III: director, secretary, Hillman Foundation

Blaylock, Marcia: trustee, CLARCOR Foundation

Blazedale, Bill: trustee, Acushnet Foundation

Blazek, Frank A.: president, Giger Foundation (Paul and Oscar)

Bleck, Eugene Edmund, MD: director, Hale Foundation (Crescent Porter)

Bleier, Edward: director, Dana Foundation (Charles A.)

Bleier, Michael E.: trustee, Mellon Financial Corp. Foundation

Bleustein, Jeffrey L.: chief executive officer, chairman, Harley-Davidson

Co.; director, Harley-Davidson Foundation

Blevins, Kerrie: foundation director, Butler Family Foundation (Patrick and Aimee)

Bliss, Paul: secretary, adv comm mem, Moore and Arletta E. Moore Foundation (Kenneth S.)

Bliumis, Sarah W.: trustee, Bydale Foundation

Bloch, Donald B.: trustee, Bendit Charitable Foundation (Leo H.)

Bloch, Ernest, II: executive director, PacifiCorp Foundation

Bloch, Henry Wollman: chairman, treasurer, director, H&R Block Foundation

Bloch, Kenneth D.: trustee, Bendit Charitable Foundation (Leo H.)

Bloch, Kurt Julius: trustee, Bendit Charitable Foundation (Leo H.)

Bloch, Mary: member disbursement committee, Oppenstein Brothers Foundation

Bloch, Robert L.: secretary, program officer, H&R Block Foundation

Block, Allan James: vice president, trustee, Blade Foundation; director, Toledo Blade Co.

Block, John Robinson: vice president, trustee, Blade Foundation; co-publisher, editor-in-chief, european corresp, Toledo Blade Co.

Block, L. Thomas: trustee, J.P. Morgan Chase Foundation

Block, William: vice president, trustee, Blade Foundation; chairman, director, Toledo Blade Co.

Block, William, Jr.: president, trustee, Blade Foundation; president, director, Toledo Blade Co.

Bloem, James H.: senior vice president, Humana Foundation

Blohm, Donald E.: administrator, La-Z-Boy Foundation

Bloodworth, Carolyn A.: secretary-trs, Consumers Energy Co.; secretary, treasurer, Consumers Energy Foundation

Bloom, Aimee Simon: vice president, treasurer, director, Simon Foundation (William E.)

Bloom, Larry L.: chief financial officer, Lee Enterprises Inc.

Bloomquist, Keith: controller, Sheaffer Pen Corp.

Blossom, C. Bingham: trustee, president, chairman investment committee, Bingham Foundation (William)

Blossom, C. Perry: trustee, treasurer, Bingham Foundation (William)

Blossom, Laurel: trustee, chairman grant eval committee, Bingham Foundation (William)

Blossom, Robin Dunn: trustee, chairman education committee, Bingham Foundation (William)

Blount, William Houston: director, Kaul Foundation Trust (Hugh)

Blow, Timothy: chief financial officer, Hudson River Bancorp Inc.

Blue, Suzanne: director, Red Wing Shoe Co. Foundation

Bluemle, Lewis William, Jr.: senior vice president, trustee, Connelly Foundation

Blum, Eva T.: chairman, PNC Bank Foundation

Blum, Felicia H.: director, Clark Foundation (NY)

Blumenthal, Alan: trustee, Blumenthal Foundation

Blumenthal, Anita: trustee, Blumenthal Foundation

Blumenthal, Philip: trustee, Blumenthal Foundation

Blumenthal, Samuel, PhD: trustee, Blumenthal Foundation

Blumenthal, Yvonne: vice president & manager, community investment, US Bank

Blummer, William E.: secretary, treasurer, Vale-Asche Foundation

Blurton, J. R.: treasurer, Halliburton Foundation, Inc.

Blystone, John B.: chairman, president, chief executive officer, director, SPX Corp.; trustee, SPX Foundation

Boatman, Dennis L.: director, Hall-Perrine Foundation

Bobilya, David A.: director, Foellinger Foundation

Bobins, Norman: trustee, Chicago Title and Trust Co. Foundation

Bocko, Mindy: trustee, Fuller Foundation (MA)

Bodager, Brian: president, Associated Banc-Corp Foundation

Bodie, Carroll A.: vice president, secretary, treasurer, Procter & Gamble Cosmetics Foundation

Bodine, Jean G.: trustee, McLean Contributionship

Boeckman, Duncan Eugene: director, O'Donnell Foundation

Boeckmann, Alan L.: chairman, chief executive officer, Fluor Corp.; trustee, Fluor Foundation

Boehl, Kenneth F.: treasurer, trustee, The MBNA Foundation

Boehne, Dean: trustee, Presto Foundation

Boer, William: vice president, assistant secretary, DeVos Foundation (Richard and Helen)

Boesel, Stephen W.: vice president, secretary, treasurer, trustee, Price Associates Foundation (T. Rowe)

Boesen, James M.: secretary, director, Dillon Foundation

Boettiger, John R.: director, Reynolds Foundation (Christopher)

Bogart, Jane Olds: vice president, trustee, Irwin Charity Foundation (William G.)

Bogen, Andrew E.: director, Weingart Foundation

Bogert, Jeremiah Milbank: member, JM Foundation

Bogert, Margaret Milbank: vice president, director, JM Foundation

Boggess, Anna W.: director, Wessinger Foundation

Bogle, John C.: senior chairman, Vanguard Group; chairman, Vanguard Group Foundation

Bohart, James, Jr.: adjunct director, Educational Foundation of America

Bohling, John A.: senior vice president, PacifiCorp; board member, PacifiCorp Foundation

Bohne, Phillip W.: trustee, German Protestant Orphan Asylum Association Foundation

Boisi, Geoffrey T.: trustee, Carnegie Corp. of New York

Boklund, Thomas B.: trustee, Gilmore Foundation (William G.)

Bokor, Peter: director, Kornfeld Foundation (Emily Davie and Joseph S.)

Bolger, Thomas: director, Marshall & Ilsley Foundation, Inc.

Bolliger, Ralph: vice president, trustee, Collins Foundation

Bolling, Carol: 2nd vice president, community relations, Hancock Financial Services (John)

Bolling, Robert H.: trustee, Welfare Foundation

Bolling, Robert H., Jr.: vice president, trustee, Welfare Foundation

Bollinger, Lee C.: trustee, Kresge Foundation

Bolt, John F.: secretary, Landegger Charitable Foundation

Bolton, Archer L., Jr.: trustee, Russell Trust (Josephine G.)

Bolton, Charles L.: trustee, Smith Foundation (Kelvin and Eleanor)

Boltz, Gerald E.: director, Hoag Family Foundation (George)

Boman, Keith G., MD: trustee, Reynolds Foundation (Donald W.)

Bomberger, Carolyn L.: president, Koch Foundation, Inc.

Bomberger, Dorothy C.: assistant treasurer, director, Koch Foundation, Inc.

Bomberger, Matthew A.: director, Koch Foundation, Inc.

Bomberger, Michelle H.: director, Koch Foundation, Inc.

Bomberger, Rachel A.: secretary, director, Koch Foundation, Inc.

Bomberger, William A.: assistant secretary, director, Koch Foundation, Inc.

Bon, Lauren: trustee, Annenberg Foundation

Bonachi, Edward J.: senior vice president, treasurer, chief financial officer, Allianz Life Insurance Company of North America

Bonanno-Regelski, Dana: associate IR manager, AT&T Foundation

Bonansinga, Joseph: director, Oakley-Lindsay Foundation of Quincy Newspapers and Its Subsidiaries

Bond, Arthur D., III: president, director, Green Foundation (Allen P. and Josephine B.)

Bond, Christopher Samuel: director, Green Foundation (Allen P. and Josephine B.)

Bond, Ina B. Hamilton: president, trustee, Brown Foundation (W. L. Lyons)

Bond, Richard: director, IBP Foundation

Boney, Sion A., III: trustee, Hillsdale Fund

Boney, Sion A., Jr.: manager, Hillsdale Fund

Bonner, Charles J.: associate director, Fullerton Foundation

Bonner, Henry M.: director, Lake Placid Education Foundation

Bonner, Marsha: trustee, Hazen Foundation (Edward W.)

Bonner, Sarah H.: vice president, trustee, Dunspaugh-Dalton Foundation

Bonner, Tim, MD: trustee, Blandin Foundation

Bonno, Anthony J.: senior vice president human resources, Pacific Life Insurance Co.

Bonvino, Frank W.: vice president, secretary, general counsel, International Multifoods Corp.

Bonzani, A.: secretary, IBM International Foundation

Booker, W. Wayne: vice chairman, Ford Motor Co.

Booker, William W.: secretary, treasurer, Daywood Foundation

Boone, D. William: trustee, Seabury Foundation

Boone, Rick: trustee, Priddy Foundation

Boone, Robert S.: trustee, Seabury Foundation

Booth, Margaret Ann: trustee, New York Foundation

Borchers, Judith: executive director, Cudahy Fund (Patrick and Anna M.)

Borden, Ann R.: trustee, Raskob Foundation for Catholic Activities

Borden, Noel M.: vice chairman, director, Shenandoah Telecommunications Co.; director, ShenTel Foundation

Borek, Jo Anne: executive director, trustee, Peabody Charitable Fund (Amelia)

Borer, Jeffrey: vice president, director, Gilman Foundation (Howard)

Borin, James L.: trustee, Strosacker Foundation (Charles J.)

Borman, Eric: assistant secretary, Borman's Inc. Fund

Borman, Gilbert: secretary, treasurer, Borman's Inc. Fund

Borman, Marlene: vice president, Borman's Inc. Fund

Borman, Paul: president, Borman's Inc. Fund; chief executive officer, Farmer Jack Supermarkets

Borman, Stuart: assistant secretary, Borman's Inc. Fund

Borseth, J. Mark: treasurer, 3M Foundation

Borton, Karl: vice president, Wildermuth Foundation (E. F.)

Borton, Thomas: trustee, Wildermuth Foundation (E. F.)

Bosacker, Lyle T.: director, Hickory Tech Corp.; trustee, Hickory Tech Corp. Foundation

Boskin, Michael J.: director, Koret Foundation

Boss, W. Andrew: president, director, Boss Foundation

Bossom, Joel: trustee, Ziegelheim Charitable Foundation (Fran and Irwin)

Boswell, Robert S.: president, chief executive officer, director, Forest Oil Corp.

Bosworth, Arthur H., II: trustee, Buell Foundation (Temple Hoyne)

Botham, Lydia: treasurer, Land O'Lakes Founda-

tion; director test kitchens, Land O'Lakes Inc.

Bothwell, Henry J.: fund comm mem, Kaufman Endowment Fund (Louis G.)

Bott, Thomas: director, Vermilion Healthcare Foundation

Bottemiller, Donald L.: trustee, Homecrest Foundation; president, Homecrest Industries Inc.

Bottemiller, Mark: secretary, treasurer, Homecrest Foundation

Bottomley, George T.: honorary trustee, Fuller Foundation (MA)

Bottomley, John T.: executive director, trustee, Fuller Foundation (MA)

Bouchard, Mike: secretary, treasurer, McDonald Foundation (Armstrong)

Bouchard, Ryan: vice president, McDonald Foundation (Armstrong)

Boucher, Mark: trustee, Golub Foundation

Boudouris, William: chief financial officer, Korte Construction Co.

Bouldin, Granville S. R.: director, Christy-Houston Foundation

Bouligny, James A.: trustee, Johnson Foundation (M. G. and Lillie A.)

Bouma, Mary: trustee, Ghidotti Foundation

Bouque, Roy L.: director, Stulsaft Foundation (Morris)

Bourchard, Laurie: president, McDonald Foundation (Armstrong)

Bourdeau, Paul: secretary, Rogow Birken Foundation

Bourns, Gordon L.: president, director, Bourns Foundation; chairman, Bourns Inc.

Bouscaren, Helen Hunt: trustee, Hunt Foundation (Roy A.)

Boutault, Delores J.: manager, Stamps Foundation (James L.)

Boutault, E. C.: president, trustee, Stamps Foundation (James L.)

Boven, Thomas: vice president, Loutit Foundation

Bowden, Travis J.: chairman, president, chief executive officer, director, Gulf Power Co.

Bowen, Arthur H., Jr.: trustee, Cowden Foundation (Louetta M.)

Bowen, Henry: director, Bowen Foundation (Ethel N.)

Bowen, Otis R., MD: director, Lilly Endowment

Bowen, William G.: president, trustee, Mellon Foundation (Andrew W.)

Bowen, William H.: vice president, assistant secretary, Altheimer Charitable Foundation (Ben J.)

Bower, Charles W.: treasurer, director, CTW Foundation, Inc.

Bowes, Donald C.: director, Howard and Bush Foundation

Bowles, Beatrice: secretary, treasurer, Lux Foundation (Miranda)

Bowles, Crandall C.: director, Springs Foundation, Inc.

Bowles, Margaret C.: secretary, Clowes Fund

Bowlus, Bradford A.: president, chief executive officer, PacifiCare Health System Foundation; executive vice president, PacifiCare Health Systems

Bowman, Bob: secretary, Pineywoods Foundation

Bowman, David S.: director, Bowman Foundation (Wayne and Ida)

Bowman, Dick D.: treasurer, ShenTel Foundation

Bowman, Donald W.: president, director, Bowman Foundation (Wayne and Ida)

Bowman, George A., Jr.: vice president community affairs, State Street Corp.; foundation manager, vice president, State Street Foundation

Bowman, Jocelyn: director, Kelley and Elza Kelley Foundation (Edward Bangs)

Bowman, Mayne J.: vice president, Bowman Foundation (Wayne and Ida)

Bowman, Roberta B.: president, Duke Energy Foundation

Bowman, Susan D.: secretary, director, Ralph and Donna Korte Family Charitable Foundation

Bowman, William H.: secretary, director, Bowman Foundation (Wayne and Ida)

Boxx, Linda McKenna: chairman, director, McKenna Foundation (Katherine Mabis)

Boxx, T. William: treasurer, McKenna Foundation (Katherine Mabis); secretary, treasurer, officer, McKenna Foundation (Philip M.)

Boyce, Ann Allston: vice president, trustee, Price Associates Foundation (T. Rowe)

Boyce, Doreen Elizabeth: president, Buhl Foundation (PA)

Boyce, Phillip R.: chairman, Valley Foundation

Boyd, David E.: member, Campbell Foundation (J. Bulow)

Boyd, Dennis W.: vice president, secretary, MDU Resources Foundation

Boyd, Morton: trustee, Gheens Foundation

Boyette, John G.: treasurer, Cox Foundation (James M.)

Boylan, Elizabeth J.: vice president, Maneely Fund

Boyle, Beverly: executive director, Fisher Foundation

Boyle, Donald C.: director, IMMI Word and Deed Foundation

Bozman, William H.: vice president, director, Marpat Foundation

Bozzelli, Andrew J.: trustee, Connelly Foundation

Brace, Frederic F.: treasurer, director, United Airlines Foundation

Bracht, Chuck: president, Management Compensation Group/Dulworth Inc.

Bracken, Frank A.: president, director, Ball Foundation (George and Frances)

Bracken, William M.: director, Ball Brothers Foundation

Brackett, Norman E.: trustee, National Grange Mutual Charitable Trust

Bradburn, Thomas J.: chief executive officer, president, Norfolk Shipbuilding & Drydock Corp.

Brademas, John: trustee, United States-Japan Foundation

Braden, Jane: coordinator, Wells Fargo Bank Nebraska, N.A.

Bradford, Hilary P.: trustee, Children's Foundation of Erie County

Bradford, Pamela: executive director, PacifiCorp Foundation

Bradford, Robert: director, Bradford Foundation (George and Ruth)

Bradlee, Dudley H., II: director, Hornblower Fund (Henry)

Bradley, Bill: trustee, Cord Foundation (E. L.)

Bradley, Darby: trustee, Friendship Fund

Bradley, Ernestine Schlant: trustee, Fund for New Jersey

Bradley, James: director, Springs Foundation, Inc.

Bradley, Jane C.: trustee, Cabot Family Charitable Trust

Bradley, John F.: trustee, Stillwell Charitable Trust (Glen and Dorothy)

Bradley, Joseph S.: trustee, Cord Foundation (E. L.)

Bradley, William O.: trustee, Cord Foundation (E. L.)

Bradshaw, James H.: trustee, Bigelow Foundation (F. R.)

Brady, James C., Jr.: president, treasurer, trustee, Brady Foundation

Brady, Katherine D.: trustee, Darby Foundation

Brady, Nicholas Frederick: trustee, Brady Foundation

Braem, Barbara: executive director, Woronoco Savings Charitable Foundation

Braitmayer, Eric A.: trustee, Braitmayer Foundation

Braitmayer, John W.: trustee, Braitmayer Foundation

Braitmayer, Karen L.: trustee, Braitmayer Foundation

Bramante, Christina: director, Cabot Corp. Foundation

Bramble, Forrest F., Jr.: vice president, trustee, Middendorf Foundation

Branch, J. Read: president, treasurer, Cabell III and Maude Morgan Cabell Foundation (Robert G.)

Branch, J. Read, Jr.: director, Cabell III and Maude Morgan Cabell Foundation (Robert G.)

Branch, Patteson, Jr.: director, Cabell III and Maude Morgan Cabell Foundation (Robert G.)

Brand, Elizabeth D.: president, treasurer, director, Dalton Foundation (Harry L.)

Brand, Michael M.: trustee, Morley Foundation

Brand, R. Alfred, III: vice president, director, Dalton Foundation (Harry L.)

Brandenburg, R. N.: president, Glaser Foundation

Brandman, Etta: vice president, assistant treasurer, secretary, Harkness Foundation for Dance

Brandt, E. N.: vice president, assistant secretary, trustee, Gerstacker Foundation (Rollin M.)

Brant, Theresa: assistant executive secretary, Raymond Foundation

Brantley, Overtis Hicks: director, Rockefeller Foundation (Winthrop)

Brantley, Rena: secretary, director, Hedco Foundation

Brasel, Susan S.: director, Sunnen Foundation

Bratton, Dennis: vice president finance, treasurer, French Oil Mill Machinery Co.

Brauer, Rhonda L.: secretary, New York Times Co. Foundation

Braught, Barbara: executive director, McCasland Foundation

Braun, Hugo E., Jr.: vice president, secretary, trustee, Wickes Foundation (Harvey Randall)

Braun, Mary Connolly: president, Arguild Foundation

Brauner, David A.: vice president, director, Goldman Foundation (Herman)

Braverman, Alan N.: vice president, ABC Broadcasting Foundation, Inc.

Brawer, Catherine Coleman: president, director, Rosenthal Foundation (Ida and William)

Brawer, Robert A.: vice president, director, Rosenthal Foundation (Ida and William)

Bray, Thomas Joseph: trustee, Earhart Foundation

Brecher, Howard A.: vice president, director, Bernhard Foundation (Arnold)

Breckenridge, Charles: vice president, director, Murphy Co. Foundation (G.C.)

Breckenridge, Isabella: president, director, Marpat Foundation

Breene, William E.: trustee, Phillips Charitable Trust (Dr. and Mrs. Arthur William)

Bregar, Hymen H.: secretary, director, Kovler Family Foundation

Breitmeyer, Julie F.: trustee, Keller Family Foundation

Brennan, Anthony L.: director, Baltimore Equitable Insurance Foundation

Brennan, John D.: trustee, Barker Foundation (Coeta and Donald R.)

Brennan, John Joseph: director, president, Vanguard Group; president, Vanguard Group Foundation

Brennan, Michael J.: chief financial officer, executive vice president, Binswanger Cos.

Brennan, Robert: president, Burnett Co. Charitable Foundation (Leo)

Brennan, Troyen A., MD: director, Greenwall Foundation

Brennan, Virginia S.: trustee, chairman, Self Family Foundation

Brenner, Charles S.: director, Guttman Foundation (Stella and Charles)

Brenner, Edgar H.: vice president, director, Guttman Foundation (Stella and Charles)

Brenner, Paul R.: trustee, Calder Foundation (Louis)

Bresko, Andrew G.: trustee, Crandall Memorial Foundation (J. Ford)

Brest, Paul: president, director, Hewlett Foundation (William and Flora)

Brett, Thomas R.: assistant secretary, trustee, Mabee Foundation, Inc. (J. E. and L. E.)

Brevig, Yasue: mem allocations comm, Kawabe Memorial Fund

Brewer, Herman: program director, MacArthur Foundation (John D. and Catherine T.)

Brewer, Sebert, Jr.: president, Benwood Foundation

Brewerton, Iris G.: director, Redfield Foundation (Nell J.)

Bridgeford, Gregory M.: trustee, Lowe's Charitable and Educational Foundation

Bridgeland, James Ralph, Jr.: secretary, trustee, Semple Foundation (Louise Taft)

Bridgeman, Gary: director, American Optical Foundation

Bridgeman, Jeannette C.: treasurer, assistant secretary, Beazley Foundation

Bridgers, Wilbur Y.: president, Smith Charities (John)

Bridges, Kenneth: trustee, McMahon Foundation

Briggs, Eleanor: director, Griggs and Mary Griggs Burke Foundation (Mary Livingston)

Briggs, Robert: co-trustee, executive director, GAR Foundation; trustee, Knight Foundation (John S. and James L.)

Bright, Calvin E.: president, Bright Family Foundation

Bright, James R.: assistant secretary, Ingalls Foundation (Louise H. and David S.)

Bright, Lyn: director, Bright Family Foundation

Bright, Marjorie H.: director, Bright Family Foundation

Brighton, Cynthia Z.: director, Ziegler Foundation for the Blind (E. Matilda)

Briloff, Abraham Jacob: assistant secretary, assistant treasurer, Eckman Charitable Foundation (Samuel and Rae)

Brimner, David: chairman, Shaw's Supermarkets Inc.

Brind, Ira: trustee, Connelly Foundation

Brinkman, Robert J.: director, Davenport-Hatch Foundation

Brinn, Mildred Cunningham: president, treasurer, director, L and L Foundation

Brinton, S. Jervis, Jr.: trustee emeritus, Rippel Foundation (Fannie E.)

Brinzo, John S.: president, trustee, Cleveland-Cliffs Foundation (The); president, chief executive officer, Cleveland-Cliffs Inc.

Brisbane, Paul: trustee, Fairchild-Meeker Charitable Trust (Freeman E.)

Briscoe, D. Daniel: director, Stonecutter Foundation

Briselli, Iso: board member, Fels Fund (Samuel S.)

Bristol, Barbara F.: vice president, Fruehauf Foundation

Bristow, Elliott B.: treasurer, Barnes Foundation

Britton, John E., Esq.: assistant secretary, director, Smith Charitable Foundation (Arlene H.)

Britton, Lynda R.: president, trustee, Britton Fund

Britton, Terence B.: vice president, trustee, Britton Fund

Britton, Timothy C.: vice president, trustee, Britton Fund

Broadfoot, John W., Jr.: director, Meadows Foundation (The)

Brock, M. H.: chairman, trustee, Johnson Foundation (M. G. and Lillie A.)

Brock, Marissa J.: trustee, Johnson Foundation (Howard)

Brock, Paul K., Jr.: trustee, Benwood Foundation

Brock, Rodney G.: trustee, Foundation for Seacoast Health

Brockington, Randolph W.: trustee, Pittsburgh Child Guidance Foundation

Brockman, Carla: secretary, treasurer, Oklahoma Gas & Electric Co. Foundation

Brockmeyer, Alison: director, Stuart Charitable Foundation (G. B.)

Brockway, Eleanor: director, Memorial Foundation for the Blind

Brockway, Jerome R.: trustee, Ashtabula Foundation

Brodbeck, Barry J.: president, treasurer, Brodbeck Foundation

Brodbeck, Helen S.: director, Brodbeck Foundation

Brodbeck, Robert J.: president, chief executive officer, director, Brodbeck Enterprises; vice president, secretary, Brodbeck Foundation

Broder, Hans: president, Smith Foundation (William R. and Sara Babb)

Brodhead, Richard H.: trustee, Carnegie Corp. of New York

Brodhead, William McNulty: trustee, Skillman Foundation

Brodsky, William: director, Washington Foundation (Dennis R. and Phyllis)

Brody, William R., MD: director, Commonwealth Fund (The)

Brody, William Ralph, PhD: committee member, Whitaker Foundation

Broeker, Richard C.: director, Mardag Foundation

Broer, Victoria Urban: secretary, Weathertop Foundation

Broidy, Steven D.: director, Weingart Foundation

Broman, Susan K.: executive director, trustee, Steelcase Foundation

Bronson, Edgerton: treasurer, Saint Croix Foundation

Bronson-Hodge, Eleanor D.: director, Daniels Foundation (Fred Harris)

Bronstein, Lenore: trustee, Ferkauf Foundation (Eugene and Estelle)

Bronstein, Robert: trustee, Ferkauf Foundation (Eugene and Estelle)

Brook, Jacqueline C.: director, Brook Family Foundation

Brook, Paul F.: secretary, treasurer, Brook Family Foundation

Brook, Robert L.: director, Brook Family Foundation

Brook, Shirley W.: director, Brook Family Foundation

Brooking, Garland M.: founder, Trull Foundation (The)

Brooking, Gladys Trull: founder, Trull Foundation (The)

Brooks, Balbi A.: treasurer, director, Atherton Foundation (Leburta)

Brooks, Conley, Jr.: trustee, Marbrook Foundation

Brooks, Conley, Sr.: trustee, Marbrook Foundation

Brooks, E. R.: chairman, Southwestern Electric Power Co.

Brooks, Gary J.: vice president, Wiremold Foundation

Brooks, John G., Esq.: trustee, Mifflin Memorial Fund (George H. and Jane A.)

Brooks, Julie B. A.: grants coordinator, Sara Lee Foundation

Brooks, Lynn A.: president, chief executive officer, Rieke Corp.

Brooks, Markell: trustee, Marbrook Foundation

Brooks, Roger Kay: president, director, AmerUs Group Charitable Foundation; chairman, Amerus Group Co.

Brooks, William C.: trustee, Hudson-Webber Foundation

Broomfield, Jane: vice president, secretary, treasurer, Broomfield Charitable Foundation

Broomfield, William S.: president, Broomfield Charitable Foundation

Broomfield Aiken, Nancy: director, Broomfield Charitable Foundation

Broomfield Shaffer, Barbara: director, Broomfield Charitable Foundation

Broomhead, Paul: trustee, Thomaston Savings Bank Foundation

Brostowitz, James M.: vice president, assistant secretary, treasurer, director, Harley-Davidson Foundation

Brovitz, Cortland L.: trustee, August Family Foundation (Charles J. and Burton S.)

Brower, Sam R.: secretary, treasurer, Owen Foundation

Browman, Brett: assistant vice president, American Fidelity Assurance Co.

Brown, Ann B.: trustee, Cacioppo Foundation (Joseph and Mary)

Brown, Ann Noble: trustee, Noble Foundation (Samuel Roberts)

Brown, Barbara: president, Ingalls Foundation (Louise H. and David S.)

Brown, Barbara J.: president, director, Abrams Foundation (Talbert and Leota)

Brown, Bertram S., MD: trustee, Falk Fund (Maurice)

Brown, Bruce E.: vice president, Boothroyd Foundation (Charles H. and Bertha L.)

Brown, Carol R.: director, Heinz Endowment (Howard)

Brown, Catherine: director communities programs, McCormick Tribune Foundation (Robert R.)

Brown, Charles: director, Fuller Co. Foundation (H.B.)

Brown, Christine James: director, Penn Foundation (William)

Brown, Clarence J., Jr.: trustee, Grimes Foundation

Brown, Craig C.: treasurer, director, Abrams Foundation (Talbert and Leota)

Brown, David Lloyd: director, Phillips Foundation (Ellis L.)

Brown, David R., MD: trustee emeritus, Noble Foundation (Samuel Roberts)

Brown, Diane Solomon: secretary, Cohen Foundation (Naomi and Nehemiah)

Brown, Doug J.: assistant treasurer, DaimlerChrysler Corp. Fund

Brown, Dwyer: treasurer, Weiss Foundation (William E.)

Brown, Elizabeth Anschutz: trustee, Anschutz Family Foundation

Brown, Forrest C., MD: trustee, Lattner Foundation (Forrest C.)

Brown, Frances Carroll: vice president, treasurer, director, M.E. Foundation

Brown, Francis A.: vice president, treasurer, Colonial Foundation; chief financial officer, director, Colonial Group Inc.

Brown, Frank C.: president, Rexam Foundation

Brown, Fred E.: director, Lake Placid Education Foundation

Brown, Gifford E.: global vice president, chief financial officer, Dow Corning Corp.

Brown, Harold: president, treasurer, director, Hamilton Charitable Corp.

Brown, Harold, PhD: chairman, director, Mattel Foundation

Brown, Hillary: director, Scherman Foundation

Brown, James Knight: secretary, Clay Foundation

Brown, Jeanette Grasselli: trustee, Jennings Foundation (Martha Holden)

Brown, JoAnn Fitzpatrick: director, High Meadow Foundation

Brown, JoBeth Goode: director, Anheuser-Busch Foundation

Brown, John Seely: director, MacArthur Foundation (John D. and Catherine T.)

Brown, Joseph Warner, Jr.: chairman, chief executive officer, MBIA Inc.

Brown, Keith A.: trustee, Morgan Foundation (Burton D.)

Brown, Kiyoko O.: director, Doherty Charitable Foundation (Henry L. and Grace)

Brown, Margarite: secretary, treasurer, trustee, Crummer Foundation (Roy E.)

Brown, Martin S.: trustee, Brown Foundation (W. L. Lyons)

Brown, Mary M.: trustee, Hamman Foundation (George and Mary Josephine)

Brown, Mickey A.: senior vice president distribution, Georgia Power Co.; director, Georgia Power Foundation

Brown, Monte T.: vice president, Weiss Foundation (William E.)

Brown, Nancy Juckett: trustee, Hill Foundation (Sandy)

Brown, Owsley, II: treasurer, trustee, Brown Foundation (W. L. Lyons)

Brown, Patricia: assistant secretary, McDermott Foundation (The Eugene)

Brown, Patricia A.: secretary, treasurer, executive director, director, Bettingen Corp. (Burton G.)

Brown, Philip: co-trustee, Jacobs Charitable Trust (Margaret G.)

Brown, Prudence: trustee, Levitt Foundation (NY)

Brown, Robert C.: director, Valley Foundation (Wayne and Gladys)

Brown, Robert S.: director, Hewit Family Foundation

Brown, Robert William, MD: vice president, director, Carter Foundation (Amon G.)

Brown, Stuart: treasurer, Cohen Foundation (Naomi and Nehemiah)

Brown, Tammy S.: secretary, Progress Energy Foundation; manager community relations, Progress Energy Inc.

Brown, Theodore Lawrence: director, Beckman Foundation (Arnold and Mabel)

Brown, Timothy Charles: president, chief executive officer, Thomas Foundation; chairman, president, chief executive officer, director, Thomas Industries

Brown, W. D.: chairman, trustee, Air Products Foundation

Brown, W. L. Lyons: secretary, trustee, Brown Foundation (W. L. Lyons)

Brown, Walter R.: president, director, Doherty Charitable Foundation (Henry L. and Grace)

Brown, Wanda W.: secretary, Bovaird Foundation (Mervin)

Brown, William Hill, III: director, Flagler Foundation; trustee, Scott Foundation (William H., John G., and Emma)

Brown, William J.: president, director, Mex-Am Cultural Foundation

Brown, William Lee Lyons, Jr.: trustee, Brown Foundation (W. L. Lyons)

Brown, Willie: vice president, State Farm Companies Foundation

Browne, Rodney M.: mgr, Porter Testamentary Trust (James Hyde)

Brownell, John R.: secretary, Reynolds Foundation (Edgar & Francis)

Brownfield, Roberta F.: trustee, Perry Foundation

Brownhart, Stacy: director, Red Wing Shoe Co. Foundation

Browning, Peter C.: chief executive officer, president, director, Sonoco Products Co.

Brownlee, Susan H.: executive director, Grable Foundation

Brownlie, Edward Carter: assistant secretary, assistant treasurer, duPont Foundation (Alfred I.)

Broyhill, Faye A.: director, Broyhill Family Foundation

Broyhill, M. Hunt: president, director, Broyhill Family Foundation

Broyhill, Paul Hunt: chairman, director, Broyhill Family Foundation

Brozyna, Jeffry H.: vice president, general counsel, Lehigh Cement Co.

Bruce, Carole W.: director, Cemala Foundation

Bruce, Donald: director, Gilman Foundation (Howard)

Bruce, Gerald E.: director, Ford Family Foundation

Bruce, Peter Wayne: director, Badger Meter Foundation

Brucia, Charles J.: vice president, treasurer, director, King Family Foundation (Charles and Lucille)

Bruehler, Carol: secretary, McNutt Charitable Trust (Amy Shelton)

Bruen, William D., Jr.: trustee, Sullivan Foundation (Algernon Sydney)

Brumback, Charles T.: director, McCormick Tribune Foundation (Robert R.)

Brumback, D. L., Jr.: trustee, Van Wert County Foundation

Brumberg, Pamela Ween: program officer, Littauer Foundation (Lucius N.)

Brumm, Paul Michael: executive vice president, chief financial officer, Fifth Third Bancorp

Brunetti, Wayne H.: president, Xcel Energy Foundation

Brusati, Peter J.: president, director, Gellert Foundation (Carl Gellert and Celia Berta)

Brush Wright, Barbara: president, Brush Foundation

Brusseau, Carolyn J.: vice chairman, trustee, Bigelow Foundation (F. R.)

Bryan, John, III: chairman, president, chief executive officer, Bryan Foods

Bryant, Arthur H., Jr.: secretary, Bryant Foundation (The)

Bryant, Arthur Herbert, II: president, treasurer, Bryant Foundation (The)

Bryant, Candice: president, Graham Fund (Philip L.)

Bryant, Douglas E.: secretary, treasurer, Cockrell Foundation

Bryson, Jane T.: vice president, trustee, Templeton Foundation (Herbert A.)

Bryson, John D., Jr.: president, Ross Memorial Foundation (Will)

Bryson, John E.: director, Keck Foundation (W. M.); member, Templeton Foundation (Herbert A.)

Bryson, Louise Henry: vice chairman, trustee, Getty Trust (J. Paul)

Buch, Robert H.: president, trustee, Barden Foundation, Inc.

Buchanan, Carol P.: trustee, Phipps Foundation (Columbus)

Buchanan, D.: vice president, director, Square D Foundation

Buchanan, Valda M.: secretary, Merrick Foundation

Buck, Carol: president, Buck Foundation (Frank H. and Eva B.)

Buck, Carol F.: trustee, Buck Foundation (Carol Franc)

Buck, Paul: director, Buck Foundation (Frank H. and Eva B.)

Buck, Walter: secretary, Buck Foundation (Frank H. and Eva B.)

Buck, Winthrop Lawrence: trustee, Children's Foundation of Erie County

Buckler, Robert J.: chief operating officer, president, DTE Energy Co.; director, DTE Energy Foundation

Buckless, Shawn P.: clerk, Roddy Foundation (Fred M.)

Buckley, Francis J., Jr.: director, Dime Savings Bank of Norwich Foundation

Buckley, George W.: director, Brunswick Foundation

Buckley, Jerry S.: senior vice president public affairs, Campbell Soup Co.; chairman, trustee, Campbell Soup Foundation

Buckley, Michael: president, director, Allmerica Financial Charitable Foundation, Inc.

Buckley, Tim: director, Vanguard Group Foundation

Buckmaster, Raleigh D.: trustee, McElroy Trust (R. J.)

Bucknam, Elizabeth M.: president, trustee, Barker Foundation Inc.

Buckner, Bill: president, chief executive officer, Excel Corp.

Buckner, Elizabeth B.: member advisory board, Watson Foundation (Thomas J.)

Buckner, Linda: secretary, treasurer, Dodge Jones Foundation and Subsidiary

Buckner, Walker G., Jr.: member advisory board, Watson Foundation (Thomas J.)

Buda, J. B.: secretary, Caterpillar Foundation

Budd, MacDonald: secretary, director, Cheatham Foundation (Owen)

Budd, Wayne A.: executive vice president, general counsel, Hancock Financial Services (John)

Budney, Albert J., Jr.: president, director, Niagara Mohawk Holdings Inc.

Buechel, Kathleen W.: president, treasurer, director, Alcoa Foundation

Buechner, Thomas S.: trustee, Corning Inc. Foundation

Buerger, Theodore V.: assistant treasurer, Western New York Foundation

Buford, Georgia L.: secretary, Copic Medical Foundation

Buhler, Amy: secretary, treasurer, Old Dominion Box Co. Foundation

Buhler, Frank H.: chairman, Old Dominion Box Co.; president, Old Dominion Box Co. Foundation

Buhler, Michael O.: president, director, Old Dominion Box Co.; vice president, Old Dominion Box Co. Foundation

Buhlman, Karla: vice president music and film, Autry Foundation

Buhrmaster, Robert C.: president, chief executive officer, chairman, Jostens Inc.

Buice, William T., III: co-trustee, Steele-Reese Foundation

Buker, Robert H., Jr.: co-trustee, United States Sugar Corp. Charitable Trust

Bukowski, Gerard T., Jr.: vice president, counsel, Burns & McDonnell; secretary, Burns & McDonnell Foundation

Bulkley, Maureen: foundation administrator, Kinder Morgan Foundation

Bullen, Lawrence: trustee, Weatherwax Foundation

Buller, Allan R.: chairman, treasurer, director, Worthington Foods; trustee, Worthington Foods Foundation

Bullis, Eugene: chief financial officer, Parametric Technology Corp.

Bullitt, Harriett Stimson: trustee, Bullitt Foundation

Bullitt, Katharine M.: vice president, trustee, Bullitt Foundation

Bullitt, William C.: president, trustee, Seybert Institution for Poor Boys and Girls (Adam and Maria Sarah)

Bulloch, Steven N.: assistant secretary, Key Foundation

Bullock, Ellis F.: secretary, executive director, Grotto Foundation

Bullock, Herbert E.: director, New Milford Savings Bank Foundation

Bullock, Maurice Randolph: co-trustee, director, Potts and Sibley Foundation

Bultena, John: secretary, treasurer, O'Shaughnessy Foundation (I. A.)

Bumsted, William J.: director, Lake Placid Education Foundation

Bunch, Charles E.: director, PPG Industries Foundation

Bundy, Charles Alan: director, Springs Foundation, Inc.

Bunnen, Melissa: director, treasurer, Norman Foundation

Bunnen, Robert L., Jr.: director, Norman Foundation

Bunting, George L.: director, Baltimore Equitable Insurance Foundation

Bunting, George Lloyd, Jr.: trustee, Abell Foundation

Bunting, Susan R., EdD: president, Foundation for Seacoast Health

Bunton, Mary Anne: vice president, Liberty Corp.

Burch, Ken L.: director, ShenTel Foundation

Burchfield, Albert H., III: member, Staunton Farm Foundation

Burchfield, C. Arthur: president, director, Burchfield Foundation (Charles E.)

Burchfield, Violet P.: vice president, director, Burchfield Foundation (Charles E.)

Burd, Loretta M.: chairman, CUNA Mutual Group; president, director, CUNA Mutual Group Foundation, Inc.

Burdette, H. Speer, III: president, general manager, Callaway Foundation, Inc.

Burdiss, Paul: treasurer, Comerica Charitable Foundation

Burenga, Kenneth L.: president, chief operating officer, chief executive officer, Dow Jones & Company Inc.

Buresh, Ernest J.: director, Hall-Perrine Foundation

Burger, Edward A.: secretary, treasurer, director, Hubbard Foundation (R. D. and Joan Dale)

Burger, Jane C.: trustee, Pittsburgh Child Guidance Foundation

Burgess, Christopher R.: assistant vice president, Chesapeake Corp.

Burke, Charles R.: chairman emeritus, director, Grable Foundation

Burke, Charles R., Jr.: chairman, director, Grable Foundation

Burke, Daniel Barnett: director, ABC Inc.

Burke, Daniel W.: board member, Fels Fund (Samuel S.)

Burke, F. William: director, secretary, Loughran Foundation (Mary and Daniel)

Burke, James M.: trustee, Altman Foundation

Burke, Judith A.: trustee, Gordon Charitable Trust (Peggy and Yale)

Burke, Mary Griggs: honorary president, director, Griggs and Mary Griggs Burke Foundation (Mary Livingston)

Burke, Patricia G.: director, Grable Foundation

Burke, Patrick M.: assistant secretary, Public Service Electric & Gas Foundation

Burke, Steven E.: treasurer, Grable Foundation

Burke, Thomas C.: trustee emeritus, Altman Foundation

Burke, Thomas R.: secretary, Hitchcock Foundation (Gilbert M. and Martha H.)

Burke, Vincent C., III: president, trustee, Clark-Winchcole Foundation

Burke, Vincent C., Jr.: trustee, Clark-Winchcole Foundation

Burke, Walter: treasurer, director, Fairchild Foundation, Inc. (Sherman)

Burke, Walter F., III: director, chairman, Fairchild Foundation, Inc. (Sherman)

Burke, Ward R.: trustee, Temple Foundation (T. L. L.)

Burke, William L.: trustee, Merrill Lynch & Co. Foundation Inc.

Burkett, Radford: adv board comm mem, Heath Foundation (Mary)

Burkhart, Megan: director, Comerica Charitable Foundation

Burkholder, Robert E.: secretary, treasurer, Gooding Group Foundation

Burkle, Ron: chairman, Ralph's-Food 4 Less Foundation

Burkle, Ronald W.: trustee, Getty Trust (J. Paul)

Burks, Lawrence E.: assistant treasurer, trustee, Strosacker Foundation (Charles J.)

Burleigh, William Robert: chairman, Scripps Co. (E.W.); member, Scripps Howard Foundation

Burlingame, Harold W.: executive vice president wireless group, AT&T Corp.

Burlinson, R. F.: treasurer, trust, Handy & Harman Foundation

Burmaster, John M.: treasurer, Key Foundation

Burnand, Audrey Steele: president, Burnand Medical and Educational Foundation (Alphonse A.)

Burner, David L.: chairman, Goodrich Corp.

Burnes, Kennett F.: chairman, chief executive officer, president, Cabot Corp.; president, director, Cabot Corp. Foundation

Burnett, James F.: vice president, trustee, Fair Play Foundation

Burnett, Nancy Ann Packard: trustee, vice chairman, Packard Foundation (David and Lucile)

Burnett, Rebecca: director, Delano Foundation (Mignon Sherwood)

Burnett, Stephanie S.: treasurer, Memorial Foundation for the Blind

Burnham, Alice B.: trustee, Humphrey Fund (George M. and Pamela S.)

Burnham, Duane L.: director, Sara Lee Corp.

Burnham, Patricia R.: trustee, Plough Foundation

Burns, Angie: secretary, Menasha Corp. Foundation

Burns, Edward W.: director, Morris Foundation (William T.)

Burns, Fred C.: secretary, Wortham Foundation

Burns, Red: director, Revson Foundation (Charles H.)

Burns, Rex: vice chairman, Mid-Iowa Health Foundation

Burns, Ruth Ann: secretary, director, Foundation for Child Development

Burns, Ruthelen Griffith: adv, Griffith Foundation (W. C.)

Burns, Sara J.: president, director, Central Maine Power Co.

Burns, Ursula M.: senior vice president, Xerox Corp.

Burns, Valerie: secretary board designators, Henderson Foundation (George B.)

Burns, William L., Jr.: board membership, CCB Foundation

Burr, Robert B., Jr.: treasurer, trustee, Mellon Foundation (Richard King)

Burrell, Jack L., Jr.: co-trustee, Luse Foundation (W. P. and Bulah)

Burress, John W., III: president, treasurer, Burress Foundation (J.W.); chairman, president, chief executive officer, Burress Inc. (J.W.)

Burress Wall, Sue: secretary, Burress Foundation (J.W.)

Burrill, W. Gregory: secretary, director, Hopedale Foundation

Burris, Berlean M.: director, Field Foundation of Illinois

Burrows, Jim: director, Donaldson Foundation

Burrows, Robert Lee, Jr.: vice president, Harvey Foundation (C. Felix)

Burrows, Sunny Harvey: secretary, treasurer, Harvey Foundation (C. Felix)

Burson, Glenda: vice president, treasurer, McWane Corp.

Burt, Barbara A.: chairman, director, Foellinger Foundation

Burt, R. M.: senior vice president, director, Bechtel Foundation

Burton, Edson: trustee, Chicago Title and Trust Co. Foundation

Burton, Richard R.: member, Burton Private Foundation (Robert Harold)

Bury, Anita: assistant secretary, Regenstein Foundation

Burza, Eileen F.: secretary, treasurer, Perdue Foundation (Arthur W.)

Buscarino, Carolyn M.: director, New York Life Foundation

Busch, August Adolphus, III: chairman, Anheuser-Busch Companies Inc.; director, Anheuser-Busch Foundation

Busch, Lawrence S.: trustee, assistant treasurer, Mellon Foundation (Richard King)

Busch, Paul: trustee, Dibner Fund

Bush, Antoinette Cook: partner, CNA Financial Corp.

Bush, Bonnie: assistant trustee, BellSouth Foundation

Bush, Michael J.: vice president real estate, Giant Food Inc.

Bush, William L.: trustee, Gerber Foundation

Bushkin, Katherine: president, director, Time Warner Foundation, Inc.

Bushyeager, Peter J.: president, director, chief executive officer, New York Life Foundation

Butcher, Gary: president, chief executive officer, Chicago Rawhide Co.

Buthman, Mark A.: senior vice president, chief financial officer, Kimberly-Clark Corp.; vice president, Kimberly-Clark Foundation

Butler, Brigid M.: trustee, Butler Family Foundation (Patrick and Aimee)

Butler, Carol H.: president, trustee, Humphrey Fund (George M. and Pamela S.)

Butler, Cecelia M.: trustee, Butler Family Foundation (Patrick and Aimee)

Butler, Dixon M.: president, director, Virginia Environmental Endowment

Butler, Eugene W.: treasurer, Norris Foundation (Dellora A. and Lester J.)

Butler, Henry King, MD: director, Christy-Houston Foundation

Butler, Herbert Johnston: director, Johnston-Hanson Foundation

Butler, John D.: executive vice president, chief human resources officer, Textron Inc.

Butler, John K.: treasurer, trustee, Butler Family Foundation (Patrick and Aimee)

Butler, John R.: chairman, JJJ Foundation

Butler, Katharine: trustee, Brace Foundation (Donald C.)

Butler, Patricia M.: trustee, Butler Family Foundation (Patrick and Aimee)

Butler, Patrick, Jr.: vice president, trustee, Butler Family Foundation (Patrick and Aimee)

Butler, Peter M.: president, trustee, Butler Family Foundation (Patrick and Aimee)

Buttner, Jean Bernhard: president, director, Bernhard Foundation (Arnold)

Butzel, Laura E.: assistant secretary, Greentree Foundation

Butzer, Bart: executive vice president, Target Stores, Target Corp.; executive vice president, Target Foundation

Byers, Fritz: assistant secretary, Blade Foundation

Byom, John E.: vice president, director, International Multifoods Charitable Foundation; chief financial officer, International Multifoods Corp.

Byrd, Benjamin F., Jr.: director, Joyce Family Foundation

Byrd, Edward R.: chief financial officer, Pacific Life Foundation

Byrd, Harold, Jr.: trustee, Hillcrest Foundation

Byrne, Arthur P.: chairman, president, chief executive officer, director, Wiremold Co.

Byrne, Brendan: director, Carvel Foundation (Thomas and Agnes)

Byrne, Dana W.: vice president, assistant treasurer,

Cleveland-Cliffs Foundation (The)

Byrne, Dorothy M.: president, Byrne Foundation

Byrne, John J., III: director, Byrne Foundation

Byrne, Mark J.: director, Byrne Foundation

Byrne, Patricia: vice president, Citigroup Foundation

Byrne, Patrick M.: director, Byrne Foundation

Byrne, Stephen J.: director, Haley Foundation (W. B.)

Byrnes, Maureen K.: director health human services program, Pew Charitable Trusts

Byrnes, William H., Jr.: director, Kirby Foundation (F. M.)

Byrns, Priscilla U.: trustee, Upton Foundation (Frederick S.)

Byrum, D. M.: vice president, assistant secretary, director, Winn-Dixie Stores Foundation

C

Caamano, Rafael F.: trustee, Homeland Foundation (NY)

Cabe, Anita B.: secretary, treasurer, director, Cabe Foundation (C. Louis and Mary C.)

Cabe, Charles L., Jr.: president, director, Cabe Foundation (C. Louis and Mary C.)

Cabe Long, Marianne: vice president, director, Cabe Foundation (C. Louis and Mary C.)

Cabell, Charles L.: secretary, Cabell III and Maude Morgan Cabell Foundation (Robert G.)

Cabell, John Branch: director, Cabell III and Maude Morgan Cabell Foundation (Robert G.)

Cabell, Susan M.: trustee, Perry Foundation

Cable, Howard W., Jr.: trustee, Beasley Charitable Trust (Lucy and Emily)

Cabot, John Godfrey Lowell: trustee, Cabot Family Charitable Trust

Cabot, Louis Wellington: trustee, Cabot Family Charitable Trust

Cachine, Michael N., Sr.: director, McGowan Charitable Fund (William G.)

Cacioppo, Joseph F., Jr.: chairman, president, chief executive officer, Greca Realty & Development Corporation Inc.

Caestecker, Thomas E.: trustee, Caestecker Foundation (Charles and Marie)

Caffrey, Thomas F., Esq.: co-trustee, McCarthy

Memorial Trust Fund (Catherine)

Cafritz, Calvin: chairman, president, chief executive officer, Cafritz Foundation (Morris and Gwendolyn)

Caggiano, Ida: clerk, Home for Aged Men in the City of Brockton

Cagle, Ronald E., MD: trustee, McMahon Foundation

Cahalan, Joseph M.: vice president, Xerox Foundation

Cahill, Robert V.: vice president, Chartwell Foundation

Cahn, Becky: trustee, Donaldson Foundation

Cahners, Nancy L.: trustee, Rabb Charitable Trust (Sidney R.)

Cahners-Kaplan, Helene R.: trustee, Rabb Charitable Foundation (Sidney and Esther)

Cahouet, Frank Vondell: director, Heinz Endowment (Howard)

Caimi, Gina: secretary, Erpf Fund (Armand G.)

Cain, Gordon R.: trustee, Cain Foundation (Gordon and Mary)

Cain, Mary H.: vice president, Cain Foundation (Gordon and Mary)

Calaway, Tonit M.: assistant secretary, Harley-Davidson Foundation

Calder, Frederick C.: vice president, Lake Placid Education Foundation

Calder, Peter D.: executive director, trustee, Calder Foundation (Louis)

Caldwell-Johnson, Terry: director, Mid-Iowa Health Foundation

Calfee, William Rushton: trustee, Cleveland-Cliffs Foundation (The); executive vice president, commercial, Cleveland-Cliffs Inc.

Calheno, Agastino J.: president, director, Woronoco Savings Charitable Foundation

Calhoun, Essie L.: vice president, Eastman Kodak Charitable Trust

Calhoun, Lawrence E.: secretary, treasurer, vice president finance, Homecrest Industries Inc.

Caligiuri, Mark: trustee, Jenjo Foundation

Calil, Cassio A.: treasurer, IBM International Foundation

Calise, William Joseph, Jr.: senior vice president, secretary, general counsel, Rockwell Automation Inc.

Call, Curtis: treasurer, Central Maine Power Co.

Callahan, Daniel J., III: director, vice chairman, treasurer, Cafritz Foundation (Morris and Gwendolyn)

Callahan, Eugene J., Esq.: trustee, Plough Foundation

Callanan, Laura: executive director, secretary, Prospect Hill Foundation; director, Public Welfare Foundation

Callanan, Meredith: trustee, Price Associates Foundation (T. Rowe)

Callard, David Jacobus: trustee, Rockefeller Brothers Fund, Inc.

Callaway, Mark Clayton: trustee, Callaway Foundation, Inc.

Calligaris, Alfred E.: director, Utica National Foundation

Callow, Elisa Crystal: program director, Irvine Foundation (The James)

Callum, Brian: director, Building 19 Foundation

Calpeter, Lynn A.: executive vice president, Universal Studios Foundation

Calvert, Lloyd P.: member, trustee, One Valley Bank Foundation; senior vice president corporate committee, One Valley Bank N.A.

Camalier, Charles A.: vice president, director, Wilkes, Artis, Hedrick & Lane Foundation

Cambell, Colin G.: director, Rockefeller Fund (David)

Cambrom, William M.: president, American Fidelity Corp. Founders Fund

Cameron, John J.: director, Provident Community Foundation

Cameron, Paul E.: assistant secretary, assistant treasurer, Gamble Foundation

Cammarata, Bernard: chairman, TJX Companies Inc.

Camp, John M., Jr.: trustee, Camp Younts Foundation; director, Campbell Foundation (Ruth and Henry)

Camp, Paul D., III: director, Campbell Foundation (Ruth and Henry)

Campbell, Benjamin K.: vice president, treasurer, Knox Foundation (Seymour H.)

Campbell, Bert Louis: trustee, Cullen Foundation (The)

Campbell, Beth: director, Gumbiner Foundation (Josephine)

Campbell, Brenda: treasurer, Sovereign Bank Foundation

Campbell, Bruce S., III: treasurer, Campbell Foundation (MD)

Campbell, C. David: president, assistant secretary, trustee, McGregor Fund

Campbell, Carol: director, Argyros Foundation

Campbell, Cole C.: director, Pulitzer Foundation; editor, Pulitzer Inc.

Campbell, Dennis M., PhD: trustee, Duke Endowment

Campbell, Donald G.: executive vice president, chief financial officer, TJX Companies Inc.; treasurer, director, TJX Foundation, Inc.

Campbell, Douglas: vice president, Erpf Fund (Armand G.)

Campbell, George: director, Gebbie Foundation

Campbell, Hazard K.: chairman, treasurer, Knox Foundation (Seymour H.)

Campbell, J. D.: director, Gilman Foundation (Howard)

Campbell, J. Patrick: chairman, president, Wildermuth Foundation (E. F.)

Campbell, J. Tyler: director, Campbell Foundation (MD)

Campbell, Jack D.: trustee, Cooper Foundation

Campbell, John D.: trustee, member, Rippel Foundation (Fannie E.)

Campbell, John L.: trustee, Peterloon Foundation

Campbell, Keith M.: vice president, director, Minnesota Mutual Foundation

Campbell, King: chairman, Smith and W. Aubrey Smith Charitable Foundation (Clara Blackford)

Campbell, Kleber A., III: director, Memorial Foundation for the Blind

Campbell, Lowell: trustee, Young Foundation (Bill B.)

Campbell, Lynette E.: trustee, Douty Foundation (Alfred and Mary)

Campbell, Martha S.: vice president program, Irvine Foundation (The James)

Campbell, Mary Jo: director, Campbell Foundation (MD)

Campbell, Nelson D.: trustee, Lyndhurst Foundation

Campbell, Robert Henderson: director, Pew Charitable Trusts

Campbell, Sallie G.: associate director, Newcombe Foundation (Charlotte W.)

Campbell, Sarah P.: vice president, Plym Foundation

Campbell, William B.: president, Campbell Foundation (MD)

Campion, Ashley C.: treasurer, trustee, Johnson Foundation (Helen K. and Arthur E.)

Campion, Berit K.: secretary, trustee, Johnson Foundation (Helen K. and Arthur E.)

Campion, Lynn H.: vice chairman, trustee, Johnson Foundation (Helen K. and Arthur E.)

Campion, Thomas B., Jr.: trustee, Johnson Foundation (Helen K. and Arthur E.)

Canales, James E.: president, chief executive officer, director, Irvine Foundation (The James)

Candler, Peter M.: member, Campbell Foundation (J. Bulow)

Cann, Samuel A.: trustee, Huston Charitable Trust (Stewart)

Canning, John Beckman: secretary, Rayonier Foundation

Cannon, Charles G.: president, trustee, Gates Family Foundation

Cannon, Ted: secretary, treasurer, Quivey-Bay State Foundation

Cannon, William C., Jr.: director, president, Cannon Foundation, Inc. (The)

Canoles, Leroy T., Jr.: trustee, Beazley Foundation

Canon, Joseph E.: executive vice president, executive director, Dodge Jones Foundation and Subsidiary

Canter, Lisa: board member, Roberts Foundation (Dora)

Canter, Roger: board member, Roberts Foundation (Dora)

Cantrell, Barbara B.: director, Strong Foundation (Hattie M.)

Capehart, Thomas R.: vice president, Oak Tree Charitable Foundation

Cappelloni, Robert: trustee, Lux Foundation (Miranda)

Cappuzzo, Salvatore: secretary, treasurer, Weinstein Foundation (J.)

Capranica, Ruth M.: vice president, Knapp Foundation, Inc. (MD)

Capranica, Steven F.: treasurer, Knapp Foundation, Inc. (MD)

Capron, Jeffery P.: treasurer, trustee, Fowler Memorial Foundation (John Edward)

Cara, Phillip C.: director, Monsanto Fund

Carano, Donald L.: trustee, Pennington Foundation (William N. and Myriam)

Caraway, R. B., MD: director, Gulf Coast Medical Foundation

Cardinale, Ruth A.: secretary, Sunnen Foundation

Cardinali, Albert J.: trustee, Heyward Memorial Fund (DuBose and Dorothy)

Cardman, Thomas: executive director, Gebbie Foundation

Cardwell, Bickerton W., Jr.: member, Campbell Foundation (J. Bulow)

Carey, C. M.: director, Frank Family Foundation (A. J.)

Carey, Charles P.: chairman, Chicago Board of Trade Foundation

Carey, Claire Z., PhD: trustee, The MBNA Foundation

Carey, Kathryn Ann: foundation manager, American Honda Foundation

Carlisle, Ann C.: secretary, vice president, Stemmons Foundation

Carlson, Cheryl C.: secretary, director, Vance Charitable Foundation (Robert C.)

Carlson, Christopher A.: trustee, Ohio National Foundation

Carlson, David: treasurer, Thomaston Savings Bank Foundation

Carlson, Herbert E., Jr.: chairman, president, director, Vance Charitable Foundation (Robert C.)

Carlson, Herbert E., Sr.: treasurer, trustee, Vance Charitable Foundation (Robert C.)

Carlson, Joseph, II: director, New Milford Savings Bank Foundation

Carlson, Marjorie M.: trustee, Gund Foundation (George)

Carlson, Rod: vice president, director, Midcontinent Media Foundation

Carlson, Ronald P.: trustee, Hyde Charitable Foundation

Carlson, Stuart R.: executive vice president administration, Wausau-Mosinee Paper Corp.

Carlson, T. A.: assistant treasurer, Bechtel Foundation

Carlston, Douglas G.: chairman, Broderbund L.L.C.; president, director, Carlston Family Foundation

Carlston, Erin G.: director, Carlston Family Foundation

Carlstrom, R. William: secretary, Glaser Foundation

Carmichael, Daniel P.: director, Lilly Endowment

Carmichael, David R.: senior vice president, general counsel, director, Pacific Life Insurance Co.

Carney, Victoria Butler: director, Johnston-Hanson Foundation

Carothers, Andre: director, Furthur Foundation

Carothers, Suzanne C.: vice president, Bowne Foundation (Robert)

Carp, Daniel A.: chairman, chief executive officer, director, Eastman Kodak Co.

Carpenter, Carroll M.: vice president, Good Samaritan

Carpenter, Dale: treasurer, Duke Energy Foundation

Carpenter, Dunbar: treasurer, trustee, Carpenter Foundation

Carpenter, Edmund Mogford: president, director, Barnes Group Foundation Inc.; president, chief executive officer, Barnes Group Inc.

Carpenter, Edmund Nelson, II: secretary, treasurer, Good Samaritan

Carpenter, Jane H.: president, trustee, Carpenter Foundation

Carpin, John: director, Illinois Tool Works Foundation

Carr, Elliot: chairman, Cape Cod Five Cents Savings Bank Charitable Trust

Carr, James H.: senior vice president, Fannie Mae Foundation

Carr, Robert, MD: president, director, GlaxoSmithKline Foundation

Carr, Robert F., III: director, Prentice Foundation (Abra)

Carrico, James T.: treasurer, chief financial officer, Wiegand Foundation (E. L.)

Carriere, Margaret E.: trustee, Halliburton Foundation, Inc.

Carrigg, James A.: trustee, Decker Foundation (Dr. G. Clifford and Florence B.)

Carrington, Lisa: director, Noyes, Jr. Memorial Foundation (Nicholas H.)

Carrion, Gladys: trustee, New York Foundation

Carroll, Daniel B.: trustee, Massey Charitable Trust

Carroll, Francis R.: president, director; trustee, Carroll Charitable Foundation

Carroll, Mary M.: trustee, Carroll Charitable Foundation

Carroll, R. J.: controller, IBM International Foundation

Carroll, Thomas W.: advisor, Weezie Foundation

Carroll, Walter J.: managing trustee, Massey Charitable Trust

Carroll-Pankhurst, Cindie: secretary, Brush Foundation

Carruth, Brady F.: chairman, Wortham Foundation

Carsky, Katherine: vice president, Robinson Fund (Maurice R.)

Carswell, Robert: treasurer, Greentree Foundation

Carter, Hodding, III: president, chief executive officer, trustee, Knight Foundation (John S. and James L.)

Carter, James J., Jr.: director, Trippe Trust (William D.)

Carter, John Boyd, Jr.: director, Kleberg Foundation (Robert J. Kleberg, Jr. and Helen C.)

Carter, Larry R.: chief financial officer, secretary, Cisco Systems Foundation

Carter, Lee A.: president, trustee, Emery Memorial (Thomas J.)

Carter, M. H.: director, Archer-Daniels-Midland Foundation

Carter, Richard J., Jr.: trustee, Ferriday Fund Charitable Trust

Carter, Ruth Ann: director, Eberly Foundation

Carter, S. E.: trustee, Exxon Mobil Foundation

Carter, Susan M.: secretary, assistant treasurer, Georgia Power Foundation

Carter, Virginia P.: treasurer, Brush Foundation

Cartmill, Molly: chairman, president, Sempra Energy

Cartwright, Cheri D.: executive director, assistant secretary-treasurer, Sarkeys Foundation

Cartwright, Herbert L., III: secretary, treasurer, comptroller, Abell-Hanger Foundation

Caruso, Anthony: director, Bay State Federal Savings Charitable Foundation

Caruth, W. W., II: trustee, Hillcrest Foundation

Carver, John A.: trustee, Carver Charitable Trust (Roy J.)

Carver, Roy James, Jr.: chairman, trustee, Carver Charitable Trust (Roy J.)

Casady, Simon: director, Mid-Iowa Health Foundation

Casale, Carl M.: chairman, director, Monsanto Fund

Casale, Cynthia L.: assistant treasurer, Utica National Foundation

Case, Mary Lou: trustee, Wickes Foundation (Harvey Randall)

Case, Richard G.: assistant secretary, Gifford Charitable Corp. (Rosamond)

Case, Stephen M.: chairman, AOL Time Warner; director, Time Warner Foundation, Inc.

Casey, A. Michael: vice president, treasurer, The Bothin Foundation

Casey, Betty Brown: chairman, president, director, trustee, Casey Foundation (Eugene B.)

Casey, Coleman H.: trustee, Saunders Charitable Foundation Trust (Helen M.)

Casey, John P.: treasurer, Altman Foundation

Casey, Lyman H.: executive director, The Bothin Foundation

Casey, Michele: treasurer, Burnett Co. Charitable Foundation (Leo)

Casey, Thomas W.: vice president, Washington Mutual Foundation

Casper, Bonnie B.: director, Staunton Farm Foundation

Caspersen, Barbara M.: vice president, treasurer, Caspersen Foundation for Aid to Health and Education (O. W.)

Caspersen, Erik Michael Westby: vice president, director, Caspersen Foundation for Aid to Health and Education (O. W.)

Caspersen, Finn M. W., Jr.: vice president, director, Caspersen Foundation for Aid to Health and Education (O. W.); director, CTW Foundation, Inc.

Caspersen, Finn M. W., Sr.: president, Caspersen Foundation for Aid to Health and Education (O. W.); vice president, director, CTW Foundation, Inc.

Caspersen, Samuel Michael Westby: vice president, director, Caspersen Foundation for Aid to Health and Education (O. W.)

Cassel, Christine Karen, MD: director, Greenwall Foundation

Casselman, Elizabeth A.: executive director, Clowes Fund

Cassidy, Ann S.: chairman, Broadhurst Foundation

Cassidy, Frank: trustee, Public Service Electric & Gas Foundation

Cassidy, John, Jr.: trustee, Broadhurst Foundation

Cassidy, M. Sharon: assistant secretary, U.S. Steel Foundation

Cassutt, Mark: director, Jostens Foundation Inc. (The)

Castagna, V. J.: director, Penney Co. Fund (J.C.)

Castaing, Philippe: director, Monsanto Fund

Castelyn, Neil: adv comm mem, Moore and Arletta E. Moore Foundation (Kenneth S.)

Castillo, Rosa M.: program officer, Weingart Foundation

Castle, Alfred L.: executive director, treasurer, trustee, Castle Foundation (Samuel N. and Mary)

Castleberry, John K.: director, MDU Resources Foundation

Castles, John W.: trustee, Murdock Charitable Trust (M. J.)

Castro, Donald: mem allocations comm, Kawabe Memorial Fund

Castruccio, Louis M.: trustee, Leavey Foundation (Thomas and Dorothy)

Caswell, Philip: president, director, Beveridge Foundation, Inc. (Frank Stanley)

Caswell, Ward S.: director, clerk, Beveridge Foundation, Inc. (Frank Stanley)

Catalano, Joseph A.: secretary, director, Norcross Wildlife Foundation

Catanzaro, Michael J.: vice president, director, Link, Jr. Foundation (George)

Catell, Robert Barry: chairman, chief executive officer, KeySpan Corp.

Cater, Charles B.: vice president, treasurer, trustee, Brundage Charitable, Scientific, and Wildlife Conservation Foundation (Charles E. and Edna T.)

Cater, June B.: vice president, trustee, Brundage Charitable, Scientific, and Wildlife Conservation Foundation (Charles E. and Edna T.)

Cater, Kerry: vice president, trustee, Brundage Charitable, Scientific, and Wildlife Conservation Foundation (Charles E. and Edna T.)

Cater, William B.: vice president, trustee, Brundage Charitable, Scientific, and Wildlife Conservation Foundation (Charles E. and Edna T.); trustee, Upton Charitable Foundation (Lucy and Eleanor S.)

Cater, William B., Jr.: president, trustee, Brundage Charitable, Scientific, and Wildlife Conservation Foundation (Charles E. and Edna T.)

Cates, Margaret: corporator, Oak Grove School

Cates, Paul: corporator, Oak Grove School

Catherwood, Susan Williams: vice president, mgr, Ludwick Foundation (Christopher); director, Pew Charitable Trusts

Catlin, Sarah H.: president, Howard and Bush Foundation

Causey, John Paul, Jr.: senior vice president, secretary, general counsel, Chesapeake Corp.; president, trustee, secretary, Chesapeake Corp. Foundation

Cavanagh, Daniel: director, MetLife Foundation

Cavanaugh, March A.: trustee, Avery Arts Foundation (Milton and Sally)

Cavanaugh, Philip: trustee, Avery Arts Foundation (Milton and Sally)

Cavanaugh, R. B.: director, Penney Co. Fund (J.C.)

Cavanaugh, Sarah R.: secretary, director, Russell Family Foundation

Cavanaugh, Sean Avery: trustee, Avery Arts Foundation (Milton and Sally)

Cavanaugh, William, III: president, director, Progress Energy Foundation; chairman, president, chief executive officer, Progress Energy Inc.

Cavataio, Michele M.: executive director, Time Warner Foundation, Inc.

Cavell, Walter E.: executive director, Fullerton Foundation

Cawley, C. Michael: trustee, The MBNA Foundation

Cawley, Charles M.: chief executive officer, president, director, MBNA Corp.; trustee, The MBNA Foundation

Cawley, Michael A.: trustee, Merrick Foundation; president, Noble Foundation (Samuel Roberts)

Ceccarelli, Jeff: chairman, Sierra Pacific Resources Charitable Foundation

Cecil, Joe D.: trustee, Unocal Foundation

Ceppos, Jerome: director, Knight Ridder Fund

Cerino, Harry E.: director, Barra Foundation

Cerrone, Pamela: trustee, Golub Foundation

Cerwick, Joel A.: director, Burns & McDonnell Foundation

Cescau, Patrick: president, chief executive officer, Lipton Co.

Chace, Roger: assistant treasurer, Harcourt Foundation (Ellen Knowles)

Chadwick, John: director, Oakley-Lindsay Foundation of Quincy Newspapers and Its Subsidiaries

Chadwick, Laura Farish: trustee, Farish Fund (William Stamps)

Chafin, James T., III: secretary, treasurer, Smith Foundation (William R. and Sara Babb)

Chaho, Doris C.: director, Hoffman Foundation (Maximilian E. and Marion O.)

Chaho, Joseph B.: vice president, secretary, Hoffman Foundation (Maximilian E. and Marion O.)

Chaho, Michael B.: treasurer, Hoffman Foundation (Maximilian E. and Marion O.)

Chain, John T., Jr.: trustee, Kemper Foundation (James S.); president, Kemper National Insurance Cos.

Chait, Gerald: trustee, Giant Eagle Foundation

Chalfant, William Y.: secretary, treasurer, Davis Foundation (James A. and Juliet L.)

Chalsty, John Steele: chairman, Teagle Foundation

Chamberlain, Calvin M.: president, director, Chamberlain Foundation

Chamberlin, Nat: trustee, Merck Family Fund

Chamberlin, Patience: trustee, Merck Family Fund

Chambers, Anne Cox: chairman, trustee, Cox Foundation (James M.)

Chambers, Caroline Solomon: vice president, assistant secretary, director, Comerica Charitable Foundation

Chambers, John T.: president, trustee, Cisco Systems Foundation

Chambers, Karla S.: director, Ford Family Foundation

Chambers, Merle Catherine: vice president, trustee, Buell Foundation (Temple Hoyne)

Chameli, Kathy: director, Wahlert Foundation

Champagne, Robert E.: vice president, director, Porter Paint Foundation, Inc.

Champion, Don E.: trustee, Peterson Charitable Foundation (Folke H.)

Chan, Paul H.: trustee, Boettcher Foundation

Chandler, John T.: corporate vice president, chief administrative officer, Equifax Inc.

Chandler, Stephen M.: president, director, Valley Foundation (Wayne and Gladys)

Chandler, William Everett: senior vice president finance, secretary, chief financial officer, Hunt Corp.

Chandler-Hauge, Jennifer: director, Hyde and Watson Foundation

Chaney, William R.: director, Tinker Foundation

Chang, David: assistant treasurer, Mitsubishi Electric America Foundation

Chang, Kathy: treasurer, director, Dana Corp. Foundation

Chapin, Charles M., III: trustee, Victoria Foundation

Chapin, E. Y., III: vice president, Benwood Foundation

Chapin, Richard Earl: trustee, Thoman Foundation (W. B. and Candace)

Chapin, Terry D.: secretary, Thornton Foundation

Chapin, William: trustee, Benwood Foundation

Chaplin, C. Edward: treasurer, Prudential Foundation; senior vice president, treasurer, Prudential Insurance Company of America

Chapman, Craig J.: director, Washington Mutual Foundation; chief mortgage div., Washington Mutual Inc.

Chapman, Daniel H.: director, trustee, Meadows Foundation (The)

Chapman, Fay L.: board of directors, Washington Mutual Foundation

Chapman, Hugh McMaster: vice chairman, trustee, Duke Endowment

Chapman, Steve: director, Cummins Foundation

Chapman, Thomas F.: trustee, Equifax Foundation

Chapman, Thomas W.: secretary, treasurer, Meyer Foundation (Eugene and Agnes E.)

Chappell, Charles A., Jr.: trustee, Gifford Charitable Corp. (Rosamond)

Chappell, M. E.: treasurer, director, Richardson Foundation (Sid W.)

Chappell, Sally A. Kitt: trustee, Graham Foundation for Advanced Studies in the Fine Arts

Chapple, Thomas Leslie: senior vice president, general counsel, chief administrative officer, Gannett Company Inc.; president, director, Gannett Foundation

Chappuis, Barbara: secretary, director, Harcourt Foundation (Ellen Knowles)

Charbonnet, Carolyn H.: secretary, trustee, Swisher Foundation (Carl S.)

Charles, Patricia A.: assistant treasurer, Ford Motor Co. Fund

Charlestein, Gary: secretary, treasurer, PacifiCorp Foundation

Charmichael, Jay: trustee, Andres Charitable Trust (Frank G.)

Charron, Paul: trustee, Claiborne Foundation (Liz)

Chase, Stephen E.: trustee, Mather Fund (Richard)

Chase-Lansdale, P. Lindsay: chairman, director, Foundation for Child Development

Chasin, Richard M.: trustee, Rockefeller Brothers Fund, Inc.

Chatlos, Carol J.: vice chairman, secretary, trustee, Chatlos Foundation

Chatlos, William J.: president, chief executive officer, chief investment officer, trustee, Chatlos Foundation

Chavez, Sandra J.: secretary, trustee, Blade Foundation

Chazen, Simona A.: trustee, Chazen Foundation

Cheatham, Celeste Wickliffe: president, director, Cheatham Foundation (Owen)

Chee, William: chairman, president, director, Resco Inc.

Cheeley, C. Ron: board of trustees, Schering-Plough Foundation

Chen, Ida K.: board member, treasurer, Fels Fund (Samuel S.)

Cheney, Bradbury B.: president, executive director, director, Cheney Foundation (Ben B.)

Cheney, Carolyn: director, Cheney Foundation (Ben B.)

Cheney, Eleanor M.: secretary, McCarty Foundation (John and Margaret)

Cheney, Jeffrey P.: vice president, treasurer, Kohler Foundation

Cheney, Piper: treasurer, director, Cheney Foundation (Ben B.)

Cheney, William H., Sr.: president, McCarty Foundation (John and Margaret)

Chenoweth, Richard A.: trustee, Morgan Foundation (Burton D.)

Cherry, James R.: chairman, treasurer, director, Rose Foundation (Billy)

Cherry, James R., Jr.: vice president, assistant treasurer, director, Rose Foundation (Billy)

Cherry, Lavina J.: trustee, Tucker Foundation

Chesebrough, Robert, Jr.: director, Newhall Foundation (Henry Mayo)

Chessum, Darrell D.: treasurer, Unocal Corp.

Chieger, Kathryn J.: vice president, Brunswick Foundation

Child, Orville Rex: trustee, Stewart Educational Foundation (Donnell B. and Elizabeth Dee Shaw)

Childs, Hope S.: director, AKC Fund

Childs, John D.: treasurer, AKC Fund

Chiles, Earle M.: president, trustee, Chiles Foundation

Chillingworth, Sherwood C.: executive vice president, Oak Tree Charitable Foundation

Chilton, Nelle Ratrie: member, trustee, One Valley Bank Foundation

Chisholm, Donald Herbert: trustee, Loose Trust (Harry Wilson)

Chizauskas, Cathleen: director, ethnic marketing, Gillette Co.

Chizen, Bruce: president, chief executive officer, director, Adobe Systems

Chokey, James A.: vice president, Joy Global Foundation, Inc.

Chomeau, David: chairman, president, chief operating officer, director, Reliable Life Insurance Co.

Chomeau, David D.: trustee, Reliable Life Insurance Co. Foundation

Chomeau, Stuart: vice chairman, director, Reliable Life Insurance Co.

Chong, Michael: director, MassMutual Foundation for Hartford, Inc. (The)

Chow, Philip: director, Lin Foundation (T. Y.)

Christ, Donald: secretary, trustee, McBean Charitable Trust (Alletta Morris)

Christ, William F.: executive vice president, chief operating officer, Hershey Foods Corp.

Christensen, Carol: director, Christensen Charitable and Religious Foundation (L. C.)

Christensen, Gary M.: president, chief executive officer, Pella Corp.; president, director, Pella Rolscreen Foundation

Christensen, Harold K., Jr.: president, Christensen Charitable and Religious Foundation (L. C.)

Christensen, Marc: trustee, PNM Foundation

Christensen, Ross D.: trustee, McElroy Trust (R. J.)

Christian, Frances R.: chairman, Rupp Foundation (Fran and Warren)

Christian, Frank P.: mng trustee, Rogers Fund for the Arts (Russell Hill)

Christian, Miles W.: trustee, Rupp Foundation (Fran and Warren)

Christian, William: assistant treasurer, Wynn Foundation

Christiansen, Kim B.: trustee, J.P. Morgan Chase Foundation

Christie, Elizabeth W.: trustee, Turrell Fund

Christman, Anne K.: trustee, Kilcawley Fund (William H.)

Christman, Eileen H.: president, Pittsburgh Child Guidance Foundation

Christman, Thomas H.: executive director, Trexler Trust (Harry C.)

Christopher, Stephen: president, chief operating officer, chief executive officer, Security Life of Denver Insurance Co.

Christy, Ralph D.: director, Rockefeller Foundation (Winthrop)

Christy, Stephen: president, chief executive officer, Mascoma Savings Bank

Chrystal, John: chairman, Iowa Savings Bank

Chrystal, Tom: vice president, director, Iowa Savings Bank Charitable Foundation

Chu, Benjamin K., MD: director, Commonwealth Fund (The)

Chu, Jack W.: treasurer, director, Cowell Foundation (S. H.)

Chubb, Percy, III: president, trustee, Victoria Foundation

Chubb, Sally: trustee, Victoria Foundation

Chung, H. Young: trustee, Donaldson Foundation

Churay, Daniel J.: vice president, trustee, Yellow Corp. Foundation

Church, Roy: trustee, Jennings Foundation (Martha Holden)

Chute, Kenneth L.: chairman, trustee, Foundation for Seacoast Health

Cieslukowski, Carol A.: secretary, Eastern Savings and Loan Foundation

Cimbalik, Marian L.: assistant secretary, trustee, Strosacker Foundation (Charles J.)

Cimino, Barbara: vice president, director, Cimino Foundation (James and Barbara)

Cimino, David: director, Cimino Foundation (James and Barbara)

Cimino, James A.: director, Cimino Foundation (James and Barbara)

Cimino, James N.: president, director, Cimino Foundation (James and Barbara)

Cimino, Robert: director, Cimino Foundation (James and Barbara)

Cioffi, Meghan Walsh: vice president, Sandy Hill Foundation

Cioffi, Robert F.: vice president, Sandy Hill Foundation

Cipriani, Donald A.: president, Eastern Savings and Loan Foundation

Ciraulo, Jerry: treasurer, director, Grand Marnier Foundation

Cirigliano, Gale A.: director eSolutions & technology programs, Verizon Foundation

Cischke, Susan M.: trustee, Ford Motor Co. Fund

Cisco, Thomas E.: vice president, secretary, treasurer, director, Benbough Foundation (Legler)

Citrone, Neil: director, New York Mercantile Exchange Charitable Foundation

Civil, Patricia T.: treasurer, Gifford Charitable Corp. (Rosamond)

Clabaugh, Gavin T.: vice president information services, Mott Foundation (Charles Stewart)

Clabes, Judy G.: president, chief executive officer, member, Scripps Howard Foundation

Clapp, Jacqueline: trustee, Medina Foundation

Clapp, James N., II: trustee, Medina Foundation

Clapp, Matthew N., Jr.: trustee, Medina Foundation

Clapp, Tamsin O.: trustee, Medina Foundation

Clardy, Harold D.: chairman emeritus, Chapin Foundation of Myrtle Beach, South Carolina

Clareman, Jack: treasurer, Reynolds Foundation (Christopher)

Clark, Benic M., III: vice president, secretary, treasurer, Lyndhurst Foundation

Clark, Eugene V.: vice president, secretary, trustee, Homeland Foundation (NY)

Clark, Gregory F.: trustee, Johnson Fund (S.C.)

Clark, Jane Forbes: president, donor daughter, director, Clark Foundation (NY)

Clark, Kim N.: vice president, Island Foundation (MA)

Clark, M. A.: assistant secretary, USG Foundation

Clark, Margaret Barker: director, president, Barker Foundation (J.M.R.)

Clark, Mary W.: director, Lennox Foundation (Martha, David and Bagby)

Clark, Priscilla G.: member, Staunton Farm Foundation

Clark, Robert W.: president, chief executive officer, director, Shenandoah Life Insurance Co.

Clark, Roy Thomas, Esq.: co-trustee, Knudsen Charitable Foundation (Earl)

Clark, Shirley M.: director, Bush Foundation

Clark, Stephen H.: president, director, Island Foundation (MA)

Clark, Susan R.: executive director, Columbia Foundation

Clark Austin, Joann, Esq.: president, Oak Grove School

Clary, Eugene M.: chairman, treasurer, Clary Foundation, Inc. (Eugene M.)

Clay, Buckner W.: chairman, Clay Foundation

Clay, David: trustee, Ahrens Foundation (Claude W. and Dolly)

Clay, Garland: trustee, Goddard Foundation (Charles B.)

Clay, Hamilton G.: vice president, Clay Foundation

Clay, John W., Jr.: member, SunTrust Bank Atlanta Foundation

Clay, Laura: trustee, Merrick Foundation

Clay, Lyell Buffington: chairman, Clay Foundation

Clay, Richard H. C.: director, Norton Foundation

Claybourn, Colleen: secretary, treasurer, trustee, member contributions committee, Trull Foundation (The)

Clayton, Constance: president, director, MassMutual Foundation for Hartford, Inc. (The)

Clayton, G. Dwight: director, Hammer Foundation (Armand)

Clayton, Jon Kerry: president, chief executive officer, Assurant; trustee, Fortis Foundation

Clayton, Trip: director, Tanner Foundation

Cleary, Gail K.: president, director, Cleary Foundation

Cleary, Kristine H.: vice president, secretary, director, Cleary Foundation

Cleary, Sandra G.: vice president, treasurer, director, Cleary Foundation

Clemence, Richard R.: trustee, Hyde Charitable Foundation

Clemens, James S., Jr.: chairman, president, chief executive officer, director, Clemens Markets

Clement, Dale E.: adv board, Vucurevich Foundation (John T.)

Clement, Ronald W.: executive director, Haigh-Scatena Foundation

Clements, B. Gill: vice president, Clements Foundation

Clements, Rita C.: vice president, O'Donnell Foundation

Clements, William P., Jr.: president, Clements Foundation

Cleveland, Cotton Mather: trustee, National Grange Mutual Charitable Trust

Cliff, Ursula: director, Hughes Foundation (Geoffrey C.)

Cliff, Walter Conway: assistant treasurer, secretary, director, Gould Foundation (The Florence)

Clifford, Charles H.: treasurer, Langendorf Foundation (Stanley S.)

Clifford, Charles H., Jr.: director, Langendorf Foundation (Stanley S.)

Clifford, Ed: trustee, McKinney Charitable Trust (Carl and Alleen)

Clifford, Patrick A.: program assistant, Portsmouth General Hospital Foundation

Cline, Micah: assistant secretary, Duke Energy Foundation

Cloonan, Brian: assistant comptroller, Prudential Foundation

Close, Anne Springs: chairman, president, director, Springs Foundation, Inc.

Close, Derick Springsteen: director, Springs Foundation, Inc.

Close, Elliott Springs: director, Springs Foundation, Inc.

Close, Frances A.: director, Springs Foundation, Inc.

Close, Hugh William, Jr.: president, director, Springs Foundation, Inc.

Close, Katherine Anne, MD: director, Springs Foundation, Inc.

Close, Leroy Springs: director, Springs Foundation, Inc.

Close, Pat: director, Springs Foundation, Inc.

Cloud, Bruce Benjamin, Sr.: vice chairman, director, Zachry Co. (H.B.)

Clough, Charles I., Jr.: trustee, Yawkey Foundation II

Clough, William P., III: trustee, Bingham Second Betterment Fund (William)

Clowes, Alexander W.: president, Clowes Fund

Clowes, Edith W.: director, Clowes Fund

Clowes, Jonathan J.: director, Clowes Fund

Clowes, Margaret J.: vice president, Clowes Fund

Clowes, Thomas J.: director, Clowes Fund

Clyde, Calvin N., Jr.: vice president, Wise Foundation (Watson W.)

Cobb, Charles E., Jr.: president, Cobb Family Foundation

Cobb, Christian M.: vice president, Cobb Family Foundation

Cobb, Kevin W.: chief tax officer, General Motors Foundation

Cobb, Sara B.: vice president education, Lilly Endowment

Cobb, Sue M.: vice president, Cobb Family Foundation

Cobb, Tobin T.: vice president, Cobb Family Foundation

Cobbe, Joseph R.: president, director, Sale Foundation (Lucy Pannill)

Coblentz, William Kraemer: director, Koret Foundation

Coburn, Clayton D.: trustee, Glendorn Foundation

Cochran, John R., III: president; chief executive officer MBNA America Bank, MBNA Corp.; trustee, The MBNA Foundation

Cochran, Peyton S., Jr.: director, Guggenheim Foundation (Harry Frank)

Cochran, Steve: assistant treasurer, Zarrow Foundation (Anne and Henry)

Cochrane, Eugene W., Jr.: president, Duke Endowment

Cocke, Dudley: secretary, director, Bush Foundation

Cockerham, Haven E.: senior vice president human resources, Donnelley & Sons Co. (R.R.)

Cockrell, Ernest Harris: president, director, Cockrell Foundation

Cockrell, Janet S.: director, Cockrell Foundation

Cody, Katherine P.: treasurer, Phoenix Foundation

Coen, Charles R.: trustee, Coen Family Foundation (Charles S. and Mary)

Coen, Kent: trustee, Reynolds Foundation (Edgar & Francis)

Coffey, Deeda: secretary, director, Dalton Foundation (Harry L.)

Coffey, Eve Alda: trustee, Jenjo Foundation

Coffey, James: trustee, Jenjo Foundation

Coffin, Dwight C.: vice president human resources, ContiGroup Companies Inc.

Cogan, James Richard: treasurer, director, Bunbury Co., Inc.

Cogger, William: executive trustee, Kingsbury Fund

Cohen, Bluma D.: vice president, executive director, foundation manager, trustee, Jurzykowski Foundation (Alfred)

Cohen, Charlotte McKee: vice president, trustee, McKee Foundation (Robert E. and Evelyn)

Cohen, Eileen Phillips: trustee, Presto Foundation

Cohen, Jordan J., MD: director, Macy, Jr. Foundation (Josiah)

Cohen, Julie W.: director, Zarrow Foundation (Anne and Henry)

Cohen, Ken P.: chairman, trustee, Exxon Mobil Foundation; vice president, public affairs, ExxonMobil Corp.

Cohen, Kenneth P.: director, Teagle Foundation

Cohen, Martin: trustee, treasurer, Graham Fund (Philip L.)

Cohen, Maryjo Rose: president, chief executive officer, director, National Presto Industries Inc.; vice president, treasurer, director, Phillips Family Foundation (L. E.); vice president, treasurer, trustee, Presto Foundation

Cohen, Melvin Samuel: chairman, National Presto Industries Inc.; chairman, president, trustee, Presto Foundation

Cohen, Michael: trustee, Dibner Fund

Cohen, Michael I.: vice chairman, director, Foundation for Child Development

Cohen, Stephen M.: vice president, chief financial officer, Hughes Medical Institute (Howard)

Cohl, Claudia: vice president, Robinson Fund (Maurice R.)

Cohn, Richard: director, Bruno Charitable Foundation (Joseph S.)

Coit, Barbara E.: committee member, Eccles Charitable Foundation (Willard L.)

Coit, Susan E.: committee member, Eccles Charitable Foundation (Willard L.)

Coit, William E.: committee member, Eccles Charitable Foundation (Willard L.)

Coker, Charles W.: director, Sara Lee Corp.

Coker, Charles Westfield: trustee, Sonoco Foundation; vice president, Sonoco Products Co.

Coker, Robert E.: co-trustee, United States Sugar Corp. Charitable Trust

Colage, Vera L.: vice president, director, Hopkins Foundation (Josephine Lawrence)

Colburn, Richard Dunton: director, Colburn Fund

Colby, Benjamin N.: trustee, Appleby Trust (Scott B. and Annie P.)

Colby, F. Jordan: trustee, Appleby Trust (Scott B. and Annie P.)

Colby Pierce, Sarah Rob: trustee, Appleby Trust (Scott B. and Annie P.)

Cole, Elizabeth: corporator, Oak Grove School

Cole, Kathleen: president, chief executive officer, Parametric Technology Corp.

Cole, Margaret Ann: trustee, Seidman Family Foundation

Colello, Joan: secretary, executive director, trustee, Pinkerton Foundation

Coleman, Burlin: chairman, president, chief executive officer, Community Trust Bancorp Inc.

Coleman, J. Reed: trustee, Kemper Foundation (James S.)

Coleman, John A.: assistant secretary, Rockwell International Corp. Trust

Coleman, Leonard S., Jr.: trustee, Schumann Fund for New Jersey

Coleman, Mary Sue: trustee, Knight Foundation (John S. and James L.)

Coleman, Reed: vice chairman, director, Bradley Foundation (Lynde and Harry)

Coles, T. T.: director, Shell Oil Co. Foundation

Coletti, Brynne F.: trustee, Farmer Family Foundation

Coletti, Robert E.: trustee, secretary, Farmer Family Foundation

Collesano, Marguerite: trustee, Statler Foundation

Collette, Gay: secretary, McGovern Foundation (John P.)

Collier, Jean: controller, GE Foundation

Collins, Arthur D., Jr.: director, Medtronic Foundation; chairman, chief executive officer, Medtronic Inc.

Collins, Frances R.: trustee, Collins Foundation (George and Jennie)

Collins, Fulton: trustee, Collins Foundation (George and Jennie); chairman, Collins, Jr. Foundation (George Fulton)

Collins, James: executive director, member advisory committee, Pott Foundation (Herman T. and Phenie R.)

Collins, James E.: treasurer, trustee, Alden Trust (George I.)

Collins, James H.: president, director, Deere Foundation (John)

Collins, James W.: director, Oakley-Lindsay Foundation of Quincy Newspapers and Its Subsidiaries

Collins, Joann N.: president, Norris Foundation (Dellora A. and Lester J.)

Collins, John P., Jr.: trustee, Smith Horticultural Trust (Stanley)

Collins, Leland: manager, Porter Testamentary Trust (James Hyde)

Collins, Maribeth Wilson: president, trustee, Collins

Foundation; trustee, Collins Medical Trust

Collins, Michael E.: trustee, Williams Charitable Trust (Mary Jo)

Collins, R. M.: trustee, Smith Horticultural Trust (Stanley)

Collins, Robert R.: director, Green Foundation (Allen P. and Josephine B.)

Collins, Roger B.: chairman, Collins Foundation (George and Jennie); treasurer, Collins, Jr. Foundation (George Fulton)

Collins, Suzanne M.: secretary, Collins, Jr. Foundation (George Fulton)

Collins, Truman W., Jr.: vice president, trustee, Collins Foundation

Collins, William F., Jr.: trustee, Eastern Bank Charitable Foundation

Collins, William R., Jr.: trustee, Snyder Charitable Trust (Harrison C. and Margaret A.)

Collis, Charles A.: director, Collis Foundation

Collis, Elfried A.: director, Collis Foundation

Collision, Arthur R.: trustee, Blowitz-Ridgeway Foundation

Collyer, Michael, Esq.: director, King Family Foundation (Charles and Lucille)

Colodny, Edwin I.: chairman, COMSAT International

Colon, Sandy: executive secretary, AT&T Foundation

Colson, Charles Wendell: acting president, M.E. Foundation

Colten, M.: vice president, secretary, treasurer, Conway Scholarship Foundation (Carle C.)

Colton, S. David: vice president, general counsel, Phelps Dodge Corp.; director, Phelps Dodge Foundation

Colvard, Karen: senior program officer, Guggenheim Foundation (Harry Frank)

Comai, Barbara L.: trustee, Miller Foundation

Comay, Estelle: secretary, treasurer, Falk Fund (Maurice)

Combs, W. G.: vice president, trustee, Long Foundation (J. M.)

Comer, Richard J., Jr.: trustee, Comer Foundation (AL)

Comfort, William T., Jr.: trustee, Hartford Foundation, Inc. (The John A.)

Commes, Thomas Allen: president, chief operating officer, director, Sherwin-Williams Co.

Compton, Gary: board, McKinney Charitable Trust (Carl and Alleen)

Compton, Kelly Hoglund: secretary, treasurer, Hoglund Foundation

Compton, Michael S.: president, Pioneer Trust Bank, N.A.

Compton, Robert A.: trustee, Plough Foundation

Comstock, Henry W., Jr.: secretary, director, Beaucourt Foundation

Conant, Colleen Christner: branch manager, Scripps Co. (E.W.)

Conant, John A.: secretary, Harland Charitable Foundation (John H. and Wilhelmina D.)

Conant, Miriam Harland: president, Harland Charitable Foundation (John H. and Wilhelmina D.)

Conaty, William J.: chairman, director, GE Foundation; senior vice president, human resources, General Electric Co.

Concino, Frank, Jr.: president, chief executive officer, Lamco Communications

Condit, David P.: trustee, AT&T Foundation

Condos, Barbara S.: mng trustee, Rogers Fund for the Arts (Russell Hill)

Condron, Christopher M.: president, chief executive officer, Dreyfus Corp.

Cone, Ceasar, III: vice chairman, director, Cemala Foundation

Cone, Janet G.: director, Cemala Foundation

Cone, Walter C.: treasurer, Cemala Foundation

Coniglio, Peter J.: trustee, AT&T National Pro-Am Youth Fund

Conkling, Phillip W.: trustee, The MBNA Foundation

Conn, James P.: trustee, Odell Fund (Robert Stewart and Helen Pfeiffer)

Conn, Michael K.: vice president, secretary, National Standard Foundation

Connable, Genevieve: vice president, Wildermuth Foundation (E. F.)

Connell, Michael J.: president, director, Connell Foundation (Michael J.)

Connell, Richard: vice president, treasurer, chief information officer, Skillman Foundation

Connell, Tara J.: executive director, Gannett Foundation

Connelly, Christine C.: trustee, Connelly Foundation

Connelly, Daniele M.: trustee, Connelly Foundation

Connelly, James F.: director, DTE Energy Foundation

Connelly, Thomas M., Jr.: senior vice president, chief science & technology officer, du Pont de Nemours & Co. (E.I.)

Connelly, Thomas S.: trustee, donor son, Connelly Foundation

Conner, Robert P.: treasurer, assistant secretary, director, Barker Foundation (J.M.R.)

Conners, Joseph C.: trustee, Schering-Plough Foundation

Connery, Crispin H.: director, Harriman Foundation (Gladys and Roland)

Connolly, Arthur G., Jr.: secretary, Arguild Foundation

Connolly, Arthur Gould, Jr.: president, Laffey-McHugh Foundation

Connolly, Brian: vice president, director, Avon Products Foundation, Inc.

Connolly, Francis H.: director taxes, Perdue Farms; secretary, treasurer, Perdue Foundation (Arthur W.)

Connolly, John J.: director corporate relations, NSTAR

Connolly, Robert M.: trustee, Massey Charitable Trust

Connolly, Sherry S.: secretary, treasurer, director, Vann Family Foundation

Connolly, Thomas A., Esq.: treasurer, Arguild Foundation

Connolly, William M.: director, member, Cannon Foundation, Inc. (The)

Connor, C. M.: president, trustee, Sherwin-Williams Foundation

Connor, James W.: president, Lyon Foundation

Connor, Richard L.: president, publisher, Fort Worth Star-Telegram Inc.

Connor, Walter Robert: president, Teagle Foundation

Connors, John G.: senior vice president, chief financial officer, Microsoft Corp.

Connors, Mary Jean: director, Knight Ridder Fund

Conomikes, John G.: trustee, Hearst Foundation, Inc. (The); vice president, director, Hearst Foundation (William Randolph)

Conover, Charles W.: trustee, Anderson Foundation (John W.)

Conover, Joseph I.: director, Oakley-Lindsay Foundation of Quincy Newspapers and Its Subsidiaries

Conover, Robert V.: director, Kikkoman Foundation

Conrad, William C.: executive secretary, Stackpole-Hall Foundation

Conroy, Patrick F.: vice president, New York Mercantile Exchange

Considine, Terry: director, Bradley Foundation (Lynde and Harry)

Contino, Francis A.: executive vice president, chief financial officer, McCormick & Company Inc.

Conway, E. Virgil: director, Macy, Jr. Foundation (Josiah)

Conway, Jill Kathryn Ker: vice chairman, trustee, Knight Foundation (John S. and James L.)

Conway, John H., Jr.: vice chairman, trustee, Mabee Foundation, Inc. (J. E. and L. E.)

Conway, John K.: secretary, Kemper Foundation (James S.)

Conway, Maribeth: vice president, trustee, Nolan Charitable Trust (James and Elise)

Conway, William G.: director, Noble Foundation, Inc. (Edward John)

Cook, B. J.: vice president, USG Foundation

Cook, Charles B., Jr.: director, Ziegler Foundation for the Blind (E. Matilda)

Cook, Floyd P., Jr.: chief financial officer, Shapiro Family Charitable Foundation

Cook, Kim: trustee, Fairchild-Meeker Charitable Trust (Freeman E.)

Cook, Mary McDermott: president, trustee, McDermott Foundation (The Eugene)

Cook, Melvin: trustee, Snyder Foundation (Harold B. and Dorothy A.)

Cook, Mildred: chief financial officer, treasurer, secretary, Freeport Brick Co.

Cook, Phyllis: director, Osher Foundation (Bernard)

Cook, Wallace L.: director, Dana Foundation (Charles A.)

Cooke, John Warren: president, mgr, Treakle Foundation (J. Edwin)

Cooke, Kevann M.: corp secretary, Aon Foundation

Cooke, Richard A., Jr.: trustee, Cooke Foundation

Cooke, Samuel A.: president, trustee, Cooke Foundation

Cooke, V. V., Jr.: director, Cooke Foundation Corp. (V. V.)

Coolidge, Lawrence: trustee, Mifflin Memorial Fund (George H. and Jane A.)

Coombs, Frederick A.: trustee, Fredrickson Foundation (Ambrose and Ida)

Coon, Marcia M.: trustee, Mercury Aircraft Foundation

Cooney, Sandra: treasurer, Meredith Corp. Foundation

Cooper, Barry: trustee, Klosk Fund (Rose and Louis)

Cooper, Deborah: administrator assistant, Scripps Howard Foundation

Cooper, Douglas C.: chairman, Gardiner Savings Institution

Cooper, Evern: president, UPS Foundation

Cooper, Frank G., Esq.: secretary, assistant treasurer, Dietrich Foundation (William B.)

Cooper, Marsh Alexander: vice president, director, member grant program committee, Keck Foundation (W. M.)

Cooper, Nathan: trustee, Klosk Fund (Rose and Louis)

Cooper, Richard Casey: president, trustee, Bovaird Foundation (Mervin)

Cooper, William Allen: chairman, director, TCF Foundation

Coors, Holland H.: trustee, Castle Rock Foundation

Coors, Jeffrey H.: treasurer, Castle Rock Foundation

Coors, Peter: trustee, Castle Rock Foundation

Coors, Peter Hanson: president, chief executive officer, director; vice president, trustee, Coors Foundation (Adolph)

Coors, William K.: trustee, Castle Rock Foundation; president, Coors Foundation (Adolph)

Cope, Andrew G.: trustee, Tucker Foundation

Copeland, Charles T.L.: trustee, Longwood Foundation

Copeland, Gerret van Sweringen: trustee, Longwood Foundation

Copeland, Lisa W.: director, Andersen Foundation (Hugh J.)

Copeland, Margot J.: trustee, Key Foundation

Copeland, Peter: trustee, Scripps Howard Foundation

Copeland, Roxanne Givens: director, Bush Foundation

Copes, Ronald Adrian: second vice president, Massachusetts Mutual Life Insurance Co.; executive director, director, MassMutual Foundation for Hartford, Inc. (The)

Copley, David C.: president, trustee, Copley Foundation (James S.); president, chief executive officer, director, senior management board, Copley Press Inc.

Copley, Edward Alvin: director, Hawn Foundation

Copley, Helen K.: chairman, Copley Foundation (James S.)

Coppock, P. C.: trustee, Harsco Corp. Fund

Coppola, Joseph R.: chairman, president, chief executive officer, director, Giddings & Lewis Inc.

Corbally, Richard V.: secretary, director, McCann Foundation

Corbett, Cornelia Gerry: trustee, Farish Fund (William Stamps)

Corbett, Patricia A.: chairman, president, Corbett Foundation

Corbett, Thomas R.: trustee, Corbett Foundation

Corbin, Hunter W.: director, president, Hyde and Watson Foundation

Corbin, Lee Harrison: assistant secretary, assistant treasurer, director, Hopkins Foundation (Josephine Lawrence)

Corbin, William R.: executive vice president wood products, Weyerhaeuser Co.; trustee, Weyerhaeuser Co. Foundation

Corcoran, Robert: president, director, GE Foundation

Corcoran, William W., Esq.: co-trustee, Clarke Trust (John)

Cordaro, Nancy Anne: director, Alexander Foundation (Walter)

Corey, William G., MD: medical advisor, trustee, Norris Foundation (Kenneth T. and Eileen L.)

Corken, Wilton C., Jr.: trustee, Higginson Trust (Corina)

Corkery, Nancy W.: trustee, Braitmayer Foundation

Corley, A. Wayne: executive director, Temple Foundation (T. L. L.)

Cormier, Robert: ex-officio member, Henderson Foundation (George B.)

Cornell, Ann D.: vice president, secretary, director, Wallace Genetic Foundation

Cornell, Jennifer: secretary, Charitable Venture Foundation

Cornog, Robert: member advisory board, Johnson Controls Foundation

Cornwall, John W.: trustee, Fund for New Jersey

Cornwall, Joseph C.: chairman emeritus, Fund for New Jersey

Cornwall, Mary: secretary, treasurer, Ray Foundation

Cornwell, Diane: administrative director, Haynes Foundation (John Randolph and Dora)

Cornwell, W. Don: director, The Wallace Foundation

Corpus, Janet: trustee, Azadoutioun Foundation

Corrigan, Ann G.: trustee, Goddard Foundation (Charles B.)

Cortese, Arline Snyder: trustee, Snyder Foundation (Harold B. and Dorothy A.)

Corti, Robert: treasurer, director, Avon Products Foundation, Inc.

Cortines, Ramon C.: trustee, Getty Trust (J. Paul)

Corvin, Adele: president, Stulsaft Foundation (Morris)

Corvin, Dana: director, Stulsaft Foundation (Morris)

Corvin, Dorothy S.: director, Stulsaft Foundation (Morris)

Corvino, Robert: vice chairman, Chicago Board of Trade Foundation

Corwin, Laura J.: secretary, New York Times Co. Foundation

Cory, William F.: secretary, trustee, Carver Charitable Trust (Roy J.)

Cosgrove, Michael J.: treasurer, GE Foundation

Cosper, Judith McBean: vice president, director, McBean Family Foundation; director, Newhall Foundation (Henry Mayo)

Costas, Elizabeth: administration director, Cummings Memorial Fund (The Frances L. and Edwin L.)

Costello, James P.: director, French Foundation (D.E.)

Costello, Lawrence B.: vice president, director, American Standard Foundation

Costello, Michael J.: director, Patron Saints Foundation

Costley, Gary E.: chief executive officer, director, International Multifoods Charitable Foundation; chairman, president, chief executive officer, director, International Multifoods Corp.

Costley, Gary Edward: trustee, Miller Foundation

Costley, Lew: trustee, Swanson Family Foundation, Inc. (Dr. W. C.)

Cotsen, Lloyd E.: trustee, Ahmanson Foundation

Cotsen, Lloyd Edward: trustee, Ahmanson Foundation

Cotter, Gregory J.: trustee, Wilson Foundation (Huey and Angeline)

Cotter, Patrick William: assistant secretary, Stackner Family Foundation

Cottingham, Patty: executive director, secretary, Scripps Howard Foundation

Cottle, John I., III: secretary, Blount Educational and Charitable Foundation (Mildred Weedon)

Cotton, Richard: executive vice president, Universal Studios Foundation

Cotton, Rose M.: chairman, Mellon Financial Corp. Foundation

Couchman, John G.: assistant secretary, Bigelow Foundation (F. R.); assistant secretary, director, Mardag Foundation

Coughenour, Katherine N.: trustee, Quaker Chemical Foundation

Coughlin, Barring: trustee, Eaton Foundation (Cyrus)

Coughlin, Brian T.: corporate manager government affairs, AK Steel Holding Corp.

Coulter, David A.: vice chairman, J.P. Morgan Chase Foundation

Coulthard, Diana S.: trustee, Smoot Charitable Trust (Frank Litz)

Courts, R. W., II: chairman, Campbell Foundation (J. Bulow)

Courts, Richard Winn, II: trustee, Franklin Foundation Inc. (John and Mary)

Coury, Maxime: director, Grand Marnier Foundation

Couzens, Melinda A. Rodgers: trustee, Anschutz Family Foundation

Covert, Geoff: trustee, The Kroger Co. Foundation

Covington, Joe S., MD: director, Hardin Foundation (Phil)

Covitt, Regina: assistant treasurer, Bettingen Corp. (Burton G.)

Cowal, Sally Grooms: director, Tinker Foundation

Cowan, G. M.: director, Shell Oil Co. Foundation

Cowan, James R.: vice president, director, Stonecutter Foundation; chairman, president, chief executive officer, director, Stonecutter Mills Corp.

Cowan, Keith O.: vice president corporate development, BellSouth Corp.

Cowan, Kim: program officer, Bruening Foundation (Eva L. and Joseph M.)

Coward, Ira E., II: director, Gregg-Graniteville Foundation

Cowden, W. H., Jr.: vice president, Peterson Foundation (Hal and Charlie)

Cowen, Robert J.: trustee, Beal Foundation

Cowin, Peter G.: trustee, Hill Crest Foundation

Cowles, Charles: trustee, Cowles Charitable Trust

Cowles, Gardner, III: president, trustee, Cowles Charitable Trust

Cowles, Jan S.: trustee, Cowles Charitable Trust

Cox, Clint V.: trustee, Broadhurst Foundation

Cox, Daniel T.: chairman, Aon Corp.

Cox, Kenneth: director, McGowan Charitable Fund (William G.)

Cox, M. F.: vice president, director, Square D Foundation

Cox, Martha B.: trustee, Braemar Charitable Trust

Cox, Phillip R.: director, Cinergy Foundation

Cox, Robert T.: director, Shelter Insurance Foundation

Cox, Stephanie: vice president, secretary, Schlumberger Foundation

Cox, William Coburn, Jr.: trustee, Cox Charitable Trust (Jessie B.)

Coy, Oona: trustee, Merck Family Fund

Coyle, Martin: director, Gebbie Foundation

Coyne, Ava: secretary, Shapiro Family Charitable Foundation

Coyte, Julia D.: director, Hubbard Foundation

Cradick, Susan J.: secretary, treasurer, HON Industries Charitable Foundation

Craig, Albert, III: director, Staunton Farm Foundation

Craig, Debbie F.: trustee, Meyer Memorial Trust

Craig, Gregory L.: member, Staunton Farm Foundation

Craig, James P.: trustee, Boettcher Foundation

Craig, Jane Alice: trustee, Callaway Foundation, Inc.

Craig, John Edwin, Jr.: director, Greenwall Foundation

Craig, Lee C.: director, East Cambridge Savings Charitable Foundation

Craig, Myrita P.: trustee, Hickory Tech Corp. Foundation

Crain, James T., Jr.: executive director, Cralle Foundation

Crain, John W.: program director, vice president, Summerlee Foundation

Cramb, Charles W.: senior vice president finance, chief financial officer, Gillette Co.

Cramer, Theiline: trustee, Norcliffe Foundation

Crames, Arthur: director, Crames Family Foundation (Arthur)

Crames, Dale: director, Crames Family Foundation (Arthur)

Crampton, Stuart Jessup Bigelow: director, Research Corp.

Crane, Charles M.: trustee, Friendship Fund

Crane, Diane: trustee, Friendship Fund

Crane, Marjorie Knight: trustee, Knight Foundation (John S. and James L.)

Crane, Sylvia E.: trustee, Friendship Fund

Crane, Thomas S.: treasurer, Friendship Fund

Crank, Celia Whitfield: board of governors, Fondren Foundation

Cranston, H. Stephen: secretary, Knapp Foundation (CA)

Crary, Horace I., Jr.: treasurer, Achelis Foundation; treasurer, trustee, Bodman Foundation

Crary, Miner D., Jr.: secretary, Clark Foundation (Robert Sterling)

Craven, David Leigh: trustee, Longwood Foundation

Crawford, Alan, Jr.: mgr, Ludwick Foundation (Christopher)

Crawford, Amy K.: executive director, Phillips Family Foundation (The Jay and Rose)

Crawford, Donald D., Jr.: treasurer, director, Skaggs Foundation (L. J. Skaggs and Mary C.)

Crawford, Helen: director, Huisking Foundation

Crawford, James C., Jr.: chairman, president, chief executive officer, director, Moore & Sons (B.C.)

Crawford, John: vice president, director, VPI Foundation

Crawford, Kirk: chief financial officer, Moore & Sons (B.C.)

Crawford, Lucy: executive director, Norton Foundation

Crawford, Patricia Bates: trustee, Johnson Foundation (Howard)

Cray, Cloud L.: co-trustee, Cray Residuary Charitable Trust (Evah C.)

Creason, Karen K.: director, Johnson Foundation (Samuel S.)

Creason, Kennard: trustee, Loutit Foundation

Credle, Gary: director, Time Warner Foundation, Inc.

Creed, Victoria: director, Babcock Foundation (Mary Reynolds)

Creedon, John F.: president, Home for Aged Men in the City of Brockton

Cremer, Frances H.: president, Cremer Foundation

Cremer, Holly L.: treasurer, Cremer Foundation

Cresci, Andrew A.: vice president, director, Gellert Foundation (Carl Gellert and Celia Berta)

Crew, Donald W.: treasurer, director, Greenville Foundation

Crew, Herb: director, chairman, Greenville Foundation

Crew, John: director, treasurer, Greenville Foundation

Crew, Richard A.: chairman, director, Greenville Foundation

Criscuoli, Phyllis M.: executive director, treasurer, Dodge Foundation (Cleveland H.)

Critchlow, Paul W.: chairman, Merrill Lynch & Co. Foundation Inc.; counselor to chairman, vice chairman, public markets, Merrill Lynch & Company Inc.

Crockard, Francis H.: trustee, Comer Foundation (AL)

Crocker, Charles: trustee, Crocker Trust (Mary A.)

Croft, Mary: secretary, treasurer, Cowles Charitable Trust

Cromwell, M. Jenkins, Jr.: director, Baltimore Equitable Insurance Foundation

Cronin, James P.: director, Dime Savings Bank of Norwich Foundation

Cronson, Mary: president, trustee, Sharp Foundation (Evelyn)

Cronson, Paul: secretary, trustee, Sharp Foundation (Evelyn)

Crooke, Edward A.: director, Baltimore Equitable Insurance Foundation

Croom, Marshall A.: trustee, Lowe's Charitable and Educational Foundation

Cropper, Stephen W.: vice president, director, Gilman Foundation (Howard)

Crory, Elizabeth L.: trustee, Mascoma Savings Bank Foundation

Cross, Jane C.: director, Cooke Foundation Corp. (V. V.)

Cross, Joe D., Jr.: vice president, Cooke Foundation Corp. (V. V.)

Cross, Michael R.: vice president finance, treasurer, Bush Charitable Foundation, Inc. (Edyth)

Cross, Michael T.: trustee, Van Wert County Foundation

Crossett, Susan M.: secretary, Niagara Mohawk Foundation

Crossman, Elizabeth A.: president, Weyerhaeuser Co. Foundation

Crouch, Robert F.: vice president, trustee, Copley Foundation (James S.)

Crouse, Jackie: director, Amgen Foundation

Crouter, Henry E.: mgr, Ludwick Foundation (Christopher)

Crow, Jon K.: vice president, Southways Foundation

Crowe, Timothy J.: vice president, chief financial officer, Knight Foundation (John S. and James L.)

Crowley, Caroline M.: trustee, Connelly Foundation

Crowley, Samantha K.: trustee, Bicknell Fund

Crown, Arie Steven: vice president, director, Crown Memorial (Arie and Ida)

Crown, James S.: director, Sara Lee Corp.

Crown, James Schine: vice president, director, Crown Memorial (Arie and Ida)

Crown, Lester: treasurer, director, Crown Memorial (Arie and Ida)

Crown, Rebecca: vice president, director, Crown Memorial (Arie and Ida)

Crown, Susan: president, director, Crown Memorial (Arie and Ida)

Crown, William: director, vice president, Crown Memorial (Arie and Ida)

Crown Star, Sara: director, vice president, Crown Memorial (Arie and Ida)

Crozier, Daniel G., Jr.: trustee, McFeely-Rogers Foundation

Crozier, James Brooks: trustee, McFeely-Rogers Foundation

Crozier, Nancy R.: vice president, trustee, McFeely-Rogers Foundation

Cruikshank, Robert J.: vice president, assistant secretary, trustee, Fish Foundation (Ray C.)

Crump, Susanne B.: trustee, Scott Foundation (William H., John G., and Emma)

Cruz, Frank H.: director, Irvine Foundation (The James)

Cruz, Patricia: director, Warhol Foundation for the Visual Arts (The Andy)

Cryer, Arthur W.: trustee, Baird Foundation

Cryor, Allison W.: president, Kington Foundation, Inc.

Csaszar, Bernice: administrator, Bridgestone/Firestone Trust Fund (The)

Cudahy, Janet S., MD: president, director, donor daughter-in-law, Cudahy Fund (Patrick and Anna M.)

Cudahy, Michaela: director, Cudahy Fund (Patrick and Anna M.)

Cudahy, Molly: director, Cudahy Fund (Patrick and Anna M.)

Cudahy, Richard D.: chairman, director, donor son, Cudahy Fund (Patrick and Anna M.)

Cudlip, Brittain B.: chairman, Bardes Corp.

Culbertson, Judy B.: director, trustee, Meadows Foundation (The)

Cullen, James D., Esq.: secretary, director, Smith Charitable Foundation (Arlene H.)

Cullen, Matthew P.: trustee, Hudson-Webber Foundation

Cullen, Roy Henry: president, trustee, Cullen Foundation (The)

Cullum, Charles E.: vice president, trustee, McDermott Foundation (The Eugene)

Cullum, William Bennett: secretary, treasurer, Decherd Foundation

Culman, Ann LaFarge: vice president, Abell Foundation

Culpepper, Jerry: advisor, director, Smith and W. Aubrey Smith Charitable Foundation (Clara Blackford)

Culver, Ellsworth: director, Arca Foundation

Culver, Margaret S.: secretary, treasurer, Vogt Foundation (Henry)

Cumming, Marilee J.: president, women's apparel, Penney Company Inc. (J.C.)

Cummings, Douglas R.: honorary director, Kirkpatrick Foundation, Inc.

Cummings, Patricia A.: executive director, Phillips Family Foundation (The Jay and Rose)

Cummings, Robert: trustee, North Family Trust

Cummings, Susan Hurd: trustee, Payne Foundation (Frank E. and Seba B.)

Cundiff, Richard M.: treasurer, Ford Fund (Walter and Josephine); treasurer,, Ford II Fund (Henry)

Cunin, Marilyn A.: chairman distribution committee, Bruening Foundation (Eva L. and Joseph M.)

Cunningham, Betty: adv board comm mem, Heath Foundation (Mary)

Cunningham, Helen: executive director, secretary, Fels Fund (Samuel S.)

Cunningham, John W.: vice president, director, Gregg-Graniteville Foundation

Cunningham, Michael W.: chief financial officer, ING North America Insurance Corp.

Cunningham, Richard: vice president, director, Fleming and Jane Howe Patrick Foundation (Robert)

Cunningham, Thomas P.: director, Chicago Board of Trade Foundation

Cunningham, William J., Jr.: trustee, Statler Foundation

Cunnisse, Maurice: chairman, president, American Optical Corp.

Cuny, Lynn: director, Summerlee Foundation

Curci, John L.: director, Hoag Family Foundation (George)

Curl, Paul T.: director, Piper Foundation (Minnie Stevens)

Curley, Walter Joseph Patrick, Jr.: trustee, Bodman Foundation

Curley, Walter W.: president, Lake Placid Education Foundation

Curnes, Thomas J.: treasurer, trustee, Buell Foundation (Temple Hoyne)

Curran, Carol Cockrell: director, Cockrell Foundation

Curran, Charles E.: director, H&R Block Foundation

Curran, Richard B.: director, Cockrell Foundation

Currault, Douglas N., II: secretary, Freeport-McMoRan Foundation

Currie, Dan: member, Giant Food Foundation

Currie, John Thornton "Jack": vice chairman, trustee, Kempner Fund (Harris and Eliza)

Curry, Anna A.: trustee, Alexander Edwards Trust (Margaret)

Curry, Elizabeth R.: director, Hyde and Watson Foundation

Curry, Jennifer: trustee, Huber Foundation

Curry, Nancy E.: trustee, Pittsburgh Child Guidance Foundation

Curry, Natalie H.: trustee, Hulme Charitable Foundation (Milton G.)

Curry, R. Boykin, Jr.: trustee emeritus, Self Family Foundation

Curtin, Michael: vice president, trustee, Wolfe Associates, Inc.

Curtis, C.: vice president, director, Square D Foundation

Curtis, Carlton L.: vice president, Coca-Cola Co.

Curtis, Diane: director, Barker Welfare Foundation

Curtis, Elizabeth H.: director, admin, Atkinson Foundation

Curtis, Gerald L.: trustee, United States-Japan Foundation

Curvin, Robert, PhD: trustee, Victoria Foundation

Cushman, John C.: secretary, Howe and Mitchell B. Howe Foundation (Lucille Horton)

Cuthrie, Sarah Walker: trustee, Metal Industries Foundation

Cutino, Peter: trustee, AT&T National Pro-Am Youth Fund

Cutler, Alexander MacDonald: chairman, president, chief executive officer, Eaton Corp.

Cutlip, Randall Brower: trustee, McNutt Charitable Trust (Amy Shelton)

Cutter, Nancy L.: admin assistant, Foundation for Seacoast Health

Cuzzort, Pamela K.: treasurer, Tucker Foundation

Cyphers, Judith B.: secretary, director grants, office, Strong Foundation (Hattie M.)

Cyrus, Michael J.: director, Cinergy Foundation

D

D'Agnes, Glenn: chief financial officer, HarperCollins Publishers Inc.

D'Alessandro, David F.: president, chief operating officer, Hancock Financial Services (John)

D'Aloia, G. Peter: president, director, American Standard Foundation

D'Amato, Lawrence L.: president, director, Vogler Foundation (Laura B.)

D'Arcy, Stephen R.: trustee, Hudson-Webber Foundation

D'Elia, Lorraine: director, Gellert Foundation (Carl Gellert and Celia Berta)

d'Harnoncourt, Anne: director, administration committee, Luce Foundation (Henry)

D'Olier, Henry Mitchell: president, chief executive officer, director, Castle Foundation (Harold K. L.)

Daberko, David A.: officer, National City Corp. Charitable Foundation II

Dabney, Fred E., II: executive director, vice president, Royal & SunAlliance Insurance Foundation, Inc.; vice president corporate communications, Royal & SunAlliance USA Inc.

Daddario, Richard M.: chief financial officer, MONY Foundation

Dadourian, Alexander: vice president, United Armenian Charities

Dadourian, Haig: president, United Armenian Charities

Dadourian, Peter: treasurer, United Armenian Charities

Daggett, Christopher J.: chairman, Schumann Fund for New Jersey

Dahlin, Peter: president, trustee, Thomaston Savings Bank Foundation

Dahlstrom, Donald F.: senior communications officer, Mott Foundation (Charles Stewart)

Daigneau, Susan L.: director, Grede Foundation

Dalbey, R. Thomas, Jr.: board of directors, Wilson Foundation (Marie C. and Joseph C.)

Dale, Kenneth: trustee, Baker Foundation (R. C.)

Daley, Michael: director, Chicago Board of Trade Foundation

Daley, Pamela: director, GE Foundation

Daley, Victor: executive vice president, director, AmerUs Group Charitable Foundation

Daley, William: chairman, SBC Foundation

Dalhouse, Warner Norris: director, Shenandoah Life Insurance Co.

Dallis, Flinn: fund mgr., Burnett Co. Charitable Foundation (Leo)

Dalneoff, Stanley: treasurer, Fink Foundation (NY)

Dalrymple, Elizabeth T.: trustee, Anderson Foundation (NY)

Daly, Denis G.: secretary, Amcast Industrial Corp.

Daly, James J.: member board governors, Brooks Foundation (Gladys)

Daly, Robert P.: director, Huisking Foundation

Damas, Mary D.: assistant secretary, Winthrop

Dame, W. Page, Jr.: trustee, Warfield Memorial Fund (Anna Emory)

Dammerman, Dennis Dean: vice chairman, director, General Electric Co.

Damonti, John L.: director, Bristol-Myers Squibb Foundation Inc.

Dana, Alden P.: trustee, Cone Automatic Machine Co. Charitable Foundation

Dana, Charles A., III: director, Dana Foundation (Charles A.)

Danenhauer, Edwin H.: assistant secretary, Dingman Foundation (Michael D.)

Daniel, Barbara Fish: president, trustee, Fish Foundation (Ray C.)

Daniel, Bill: trustee, Priddy Foundation

Daniel, Charles W.: president, Daniel Foundation of Alabama

Daniel, Christopher J.: vice president, treasurer, trustee, Fish Foundation (Ray C.)

Daniel, Frank, MD: director, De Queen Regional Medical Center

Daniel, James L., Jr.: vice president, trustee, Fish Foundation (Ray C.)

Daniel, Martha Cobb: chairman, Daniel Foundation of Alabama

Daniel, Robert A.: assistant treasurer, Kemper Foundation (James S.)

Daniels, Fred H., II: director, Daniels Foundation (Fred Harris)

Daniels, Janet B.: director, Daniels Foundation (Fred Harris)

Daniels, Karen: director, Amgen Foundation

Daniels, Lillian I.: secretary, treasurer, Memton Fund

Danielson, John G.: vice president, treasurer, Albertson's Inc.

Danis, Ross: program director, education, Dodge Foundation (Geraldine R.)

Dann, Jesse: trustee, Viyu Foundation

Dann, Marion: trustee, Viyu Foundation

Dann, William: trustee, Viyu Foundation

Dann, William R., Jr.: trustee, Viyu Foundation

Danner, Douglas: trustee, Riley Foundation (Mabel Louise)

Danser, Gordon O.: trustee, Cape Branch Foundation

Dantzscher, Adam B.: executive director, Fleming and Jane Howe Patrick Foundation (Robert)

Darden, Joshua P., Jr.: president, director, North Shore Foundation

Dardess, Margaret B.: director, GlaxoSmithKline Foundation

Darland, Tye: secretary, Koch Foundation, Inc. (Fred C. and Mary R.)

Darling, Robert Edward, Jr.: chairman, Ensign-Bickford Foundation

Darnieder, Gregory M.: secretary, Pick, Jr. Fund (Albert)

Darrell, John S.: director, Ray Foundation

Dascoli, D. Paul: chief financial officer, vice president, Thomasville Furniture Industries Inc.

Dass, Ram: director, Furthur Foundation

Daughdrill, James M., III: president, Walker Foundation

Daugherty, David M.: treasurer, Kiplinger Foundation

Daugherty, Robert B.: director, Valmont Industries Inc.

Dauska, Walter J.: treasurer, Green Bay Packaging

Davenport, David M.: director, Royal & SunAlliance

Insurance Foundation, Inc.

Davenport, Judith: director, Heinz Endowment (Howard)

Davenport, Judith M.: trustee, Pittsburgh Child Guidance Foundation

Davenport, Palmer: director, Kelley and Elza Kelley Foundation (Edward Bangs)

David, Daryl: director, Washington Mutual Foundation; executive vice president, human resources, Washington Mutual Inc.

Davidson, Brad: trustee, Kaplan Fund (J. M.)

Davidson, Denise S.: secretary, Jamail Foundation (Lee and Joseph D.)

Davidson, Endicott P.: trustee, Ingalls Foundation (Louise H. and David S.)

Davidson, Gretchen D.: director, Mardag Foundation

Davidson, Hilary: vice president, Duke Energy Foundation

Davidson, John B.: member admin committee, Selby and Marie Selby Foundation (William G.)

Davidson, Park R.: trustee, Burlington Industries Foundation

Davidson, Peter W.: chairman, trustee, Kaplan Fund (J. M.)

Davidson, R. K.: chairman, trustee, Union Pacific Foundation

Davidson, Sheila C.: director, Chicago Tribune Foundation

Davidson, William M., IV: treasurer, mgr, Ludwick Foundation (Christopher)

Davies, Robert N.: director, Goldman Foundation (Herman)

Davies, Trevor C.: chief financial officer treasurer, assistant secretary, director, Coleman Foundation (IL)

Davis, Andrew: assistant vice president, Fredrickson Foundation (Ambrose and Ida)

Davis, Andrew Dano: chairman, Winn-Dixie Stores Inc.

Davis, Betty G.: director, Grede Foundation

Davis, Brad Bradley: director, Washington Mutual Foundation; executive vice president, chief marketing officer, Washington Mutual Inc.

Davis, Brenda S.: trustee, Dodge Foundation (Geraldine R.)

Davis, Brigit Ann: vice president, assistant secretary, Johnson Foundation (Helen K. and Arthur E.)

Davis, Caleb N.: trustee, Davis Foundations (Arthur Vining)

Davis, Catherine: treasurer, assistant secretary, director, Tribune New York Foundation

Davis, Charles, Jr.: treasurer, Gulf Coast Medical Foundation

Davis, Craig: vice president, Washington Mutual Foundation; president, home loans, Washington Mutual Inc.

Davis, Dana Michelle: trustee, New York Foundation

Davis, Donald H., Jr.: president, chief executive officer, chairman, Rockwell Automation Inc.; chairman trust committee, Rockwell International Corp. Trust

Davis, Eddie L.: trustee, Hartford Courant Foundation

Davis, Edward: secretary, director, mem, Katzenberger Foundation

Davis, Edwin W.: secretary, administrator, director, Murphy Co. Foundation (G.C.)

Davis, Eleanor L.: trustee, Connelly Foundation

Davis, Elizabeth K.: trustee, Kunkel Foundation (John Crain)

Davis, Erroll Brown, Jr.: chairman, president, chief executive officer, Alliant Energy Corp.

Davis, Evelyn Y.: trustee, Davis Foundation (Evelyn Y.)

Davis, F. Elwood: chairman, director, Bloedorn Foundation (Walter A.)

Davis, Florence A.: president, director, Starr Foundation

Davis, Frederick W., II: secretary, director, Davis Foundation (Edwin W. and Catherine M.)

Davis, G. L.: director, Penney Co. Fund (J.C.)

Davis, Gale Lansing: vice president, director, Griggs and Mary Griggs Burke Foundation (Mary Livingston)

Davis, Gilbert S.: director, Memorial Foundation for the Blind

Davis, Holbrook R.: trustee, Davis Foundations (Arthur Vining)

Davis, J. H. Dow: chairman, Davis Foundations (Arthur Vining)

Davis, James N.: executive director, Gheens Foundation

Davis, Jane C.: vice president, director, Skaggs Foundation (L. J. Skaggs and Mary C.)

Davis, Joel P.: trustee, Davis Foundations (Arthur Vining)

Davis, John H.: trustee, Davis Foundation (Irene E. and George A.)

Davis, Jonathan: fund mgr., Burnett Co. Charitable Foundation (Leo)

Davis, Karen: director, Hasbro Charitable Trust Inc.

Davis, Karen Padgett: president, director, Commonwealth Fund (The)

Davis, Karyll A.: trustee, Heinz Co. Foundation (H.J.)

Davis, Laurianne T.: president, executive director, Tiscornia Foundation

Davis, Marjorie Alexandre: contact, Palmer Fund (Frank Loomis)

Davis, Mary E.: vice president, director, Davis Foundation (Edwin W. and Catherine M.)

Davis, Mike: trustee, Paine Webber Foundation

Davis, Milton Austin: director, Field Foundation of Illinois

Davis, Nathanael V.: chairman emeritus, Davis Foundations (Arthur Vining)

Davis, Robert Edwin: president, treasurer, director, Bloedorn Foundation (Walter A.)

Davis, Robert M.: trustee, Barden Foundation, Inc.

Davis, Robert S.: president, director, Saint Croix Foundation; chairman, Tozer Foundation

Davis, Scott Scott: treasurer, trustee, UPS Foundation

Davis, Stephen A.: trustee, Davis Foundation (Irene E. and George A.)

Davis, Ted C.: trustee, Gerber Foundation

Davis, Todd R.: vice president, Universal Studios Foundation

Davis, Ulla Z.: executive director, Hale Foundation (Crescent Porter)

Davis, W. Stewart: secretary, treasurer, Grede Foundation

Davis, William E.: chairman, chief executive officer, Niagara Mohawk Holdings Inc.

Davis, William L.: chairman, president, chief executive officer, Donnelley & Sons Co. (R.R.)

Davis, Willie D.: director, Sara Lee Corp.

Davis, Winifred S.: trustee, Harland Charitable Foundation (John H. and Wilhelmina J.)

Davison, Daniel Pomeroy: vice president, treasurer, ast secretary, director, Gould Foundation (The Florence)

Dawley, Gary: trustee, Besser Foundation

Dawson, Brennan: vice president external affairs, Brown & Williamson Tobacco Corp.

Dawson, Judith: vice president, secretary, director, Atherton Family Foundation

Day, Ann B.: president, director, Carpenter Foundation (E. Rhodes and Leona B.)

Day, Antonia Scott: vice president, director, secretary, Powell Foundation

Day, Betty T.: assistant secretary, assistant treasurer, Cemala Foundation

Day, Dorothy W.: trustee, Day Foundation (Willametta K.)

Day, Elizabeth: trustee, Cacioppo Foundation (Joseph and Mary)

Day, Fred N., IV: vice president, director, Progress Energy Foundation

Day, H. Corbin: director, Hyde and Watson Foundation

Day, Howard M.: president, trustee, Day Foundation (Willametta K.); vice president, director, member director grant program committee, Keck Foundation (W. M.)

Day, Janet Loew: trustee, Wendt Foundation (Margaret L.)

Day, Paul B., Jr.: vice president, secretary, treasurer, director, Carpenter Foundation (E. Rhodes and Leona B.)

Day, Robert A., Jr.: chairman, trustee, Day Foundation (Willametta K.); chairman, president, chief executive officer, director, Keck Foundation (W. M.)

Day, Susan C., MD: vice president, trustee, Seybert Institution for Poor Boys and Girls (Adam and Maria Sarah)

Day, Tammis M.: vice president, trustee, Day Foundation (Willametta K.); director, Keck Foundation (W. M.)

Day, Theodore J.: vice president, trustee, Day Foundation (Willametta K.); director, member audit committee, Keck Foundation (W. M.)

Day, Walter R., III: trustee, Mellon Financial Corp. Foundation

Days, Drew Saunders, III: director, MacArthur Foundation (John D. and Catherine T.)

Dayton, Pat: vice president, treasurer, trustee, Rouse Co. Foundation

De Gaetano, Peter F.: secretary, director, Piankova Foundation (Tatiana)

de Garne, Lilo Navales: foundation officer, State Street Foundation

De La Vega, Ralph: trustee, BellSouth Foundation

de Lone, Madeline: trustee, Hazen Foundation (Edward W.)

De Raismes, Ann D.: member, Hartford Financial Services Group Inc.

de Rham, Casimir, Jr.: trustee, Campbell and Adah E. Hall Charity Fund (Bushrod H.)

De Witt, William: trustee, Semple Foundation (Louise Taft)

Deacy, Jean: trustee emeritus, Halsell Foundation (Ewing)

Deal-Koestner, Janet J.: president, Upjohn Foundation (Harold and Grace)

Dean, Anthony M.: treasurer, trustee, Blowitz-Ridgeway Foundation

Dean, Anthony Taylor: president, chief operating officer, Nuveen Co. (The John)

Dean, J. Simpson, Jr.: vice president, trustee, Welfare Foundation

Dean, Roger W.: controller, chief administrative officer, Fifth Third Bancorp

DeAramas, Frank: director, Comerica Charitable Foundation

Deas, Tom: treasurer, FMC Foundation

Deatherage, Marie: program officer, Meyer Memorial Trust

DeBacker, Lois R.: program director, environment, Mott Foundation (Charles Stewart)

Debevoise, Dickinson Richards: trustee, Fund for New Jersey

DeBoer, Anne M.: executive director, Dow Corning Foundation

Debs, Barbara Knowles: trustee, Dodge Foundation (Geraldine R.)

Decherd, Maureen H.: president, Decherd Foundation

Decherd, Robert William: chairman, president, chief executive officer, director, Belo Corp.; trustee, Belo Foundation; chairman, Decherd Foundation

Decio, Arthur J.: trustee, Decio Foundation (Arthur J.)

Decio, Patricia C.: trustee, Decio Foundation (Arthur J.)

Decio, Terrence M.: trustee, Decio Foundation (Arthur J.)

Decker, A. Dean: adv comm mem, trustee, Moore and Arletta E. Moore Foundation (Kenneth S.)

Decker, Don M.: vice president corporate services, Dana Corp.

Decker, Janet: gov, Crary Foundation (Bruce L.)

Decker, Robert W.: president, treasurer, director, Scott Foundation (William E.)

DeCotis, Deborah: director, Rubinstein Foundation (Helena)

DeCrona, Bruce: chief financial officer, controller, vice president finance, Exchange Bank

Decyk, R. J.: director, Shell Oil Co. Foundation

Dedrick, John R.: trustee, West Bend Mutual Charitable Trust

Dee, Shelly Louise Hoglund: director, Hoglund Foundation

Deegan-Day, Thomas Joseph: trustee, Day Foundation (Willametta K.); director, Keck Foundation (W. M.)

Deems, Richard Emmet: vice president, director, Hearst Foundation (William Randolph)

Deen, R. B., Jr.: secretary, director, Hardin Foundation (Phil)

Deeney, Gerald D.: secretary, Hubbard Foundation

Deering, Anthony W.: chairman, chief executive officer, Rouse Co.; chairman, president, trustee, Rouse Co. Foundation

DeGaetano, Peter F.: secretary, director, L and L Foundation

DeGive, Josephine: trustee, Friendship Fund

DeGraan, Edward F.: vice chairman, director, Gillette Co.

DeGroot, Dana Riley: director, Engl Family Foundation (Michael S.)

Deitrick, Scott R.: vice president, Hammer Foundation (Armand)

DeKruif, Robert M.: trustee, Ahmanson Foundation

del Sol, Carlos: vice chairman, trustee, Campbell Soup Foundation

Delahaye, Michael T.: director, New York Life Foundation

Deland, Emme Levin: director, Kornfeld Foundation (Emily Davie and Joseph S.)

Delaney, Gene: vice president, Motorola Foundation

Delaney, Wayne E.: director, advisor, Smith and W. Aubrey Smith Charitable Foundation (Clara Blackford)

Delattre, Edwin J.: trustee, Quaker Chemical Foundation

DeLauder, William B.: trustee, The MBNA Foundation

DeLauro, Debra G.: secretary, Greenfield Foundation (Albert M.)

Delbridge, Ed: chairman, president, director, Christy-Houston Foundation

Delgado, Gloria: vice president, SBC Pioneers, SBC Communications Inc.

Delgado, Jane L.: trustee, Kresge Foundation

DeLissio, Janet: secretary, treasurer, director, Ensign-Bickford Foundation

Dellinger, Kent: director, American Honda Foundation

DeLoach, Harris E., Jr.: president, chief executive officer, Sonoco Products Co.

DeLoache, Bond D.: co-trustee, Davis Foundation (Joe C.)

DeLoache, William R.: co-trustee, Davis Foundation (Joe C.)

DeLoache, William R., Jr.: co-trustee, Davis Foundation (Joe C.)

Delori, Rosamond P.: trustee, secretary, Putnam Foundation

DeMaio, Susan M.: assistant secretary, assistant director, Barker Welfare Foundation

DeMajistre, Robert: trustee, Seton Co. Foundation

Demarest, Daniel Anthony: secretary, treasurer, Paul and C. Michael Paul Foundation (Josephine Bay)

Demere, Robert H.: president, Colonial Foundation; chairman, Colonial Group Inc.

Demere, Robert H., Jr.: vice president, secretary, Colonial Foundation; president, chief executive officer, Colonial Group Inc.

Demeritt, Stephen R.: trustee, General Mills Foundation; vice chairman, director, General Mills Inc.

Demorest, Byron, MD: director, Sierra Health Foundation

DeMott, Alfred E.: director, Hoch Foundation (Charles H.)

Demoulas, Arthur T.: trustee, Demoulas Foundation

Dempsey, James Howard, Jr.: secretary, trustee, Andrews Foundation

Denham, Robert E.: director, MacArthur Foundation (John D. and Catherine T.)

Denigan, Susan: trustee, Ralston Purina Trust Fund

Denison, Harriet S.: trustee, Smith Foundation (Ralph L.)

Denk, Fred: secretary, PPG Industries Foundation

Denkers, Julie: committee member, Eccles Charitable Foundation (Willard L.)

Denkers, Stephen G.: committee member, Eccles Charitable Foundation (Willard L.)

Denkers, Susan E.: committee member, Eccles Charitable Foundation (Willard L.)

Denlea, Leo E., Jr.: trustee, Leavey Foundation (Thomas and Dorothy)

Denman, Leroy G., Jr.: trustee, Brackenridge Foundation (George W.)

Dennery, Linda: trustee, Fund for New Jersey

Denninger, William C.: vice president, Barnes Group Foundation Inc.

Dennis, Andre L., Esq.: director, Independence Foundation

Dent, Abrahm: director, American Honda Foundation

DePopolo, Margaret: mem, Henderson Foundation (George B.)

Derisley, Arthur B.: trustee, Carls Foundation

Derrer, Suzanne: director, Reynolds Foundation (Christopher)

Derrickson, Lloyd J.: secretary, director, Freed Foundation

Derry, William S.: trustee, Van Wert County Foundation

Des Marais Vought, Anne: co-president, director, Menasha Corp. Foundation

Desai, Vishakha N.: director, Warhol Foundation for the Visual Arts (The Andy)

DeSanti, Frederick D.: trustee, Public Service Electric & Gas Foundation

Deschamps, Bruno: president, chief operating officer, Ecolab Inc.

Deschepper, James L.: director, Oakley-Lindsay Foundation of Quincy Newspapers and Its Subsidiaries

Deshotel, Adrian B.: vice president human resources, American Standard Inc.

DeSoto, Pete: trustee, Metal Industries Foundation; chairman, president, chief executive officer, Metal Industries Inc.

Dessingue, William: executive director, Charitable Venture Foundation

Destruel, Jean E.: director, Exchange Bank Foundation

Detlefs, Suzanne H.: trustee, vice president, Bell-South Foundation

Deubel, George: director, Sierra Health Foundation

Deuble, Andrew H.: secretary, trustee, Deuble Foundation (George H.)

Deuble, Steven G.: president, trustee, Deuble Foundation (George H.)

Deuble, Walter C.: trustee, Deuble Foundation (George H.)

Deuble, Walter J.: trustee, Deuble Foundation (George H.)

Devaney, Phyllis: director, Building 19 Foundation

Devine, John M.: vice chairman, chief financial officer, General Motors Corp.

DeVita, M. Christine: president, director, The Wallace Foundation

DeVore, Richard A.: president, secretary, DeVore Foundation

DeVore, Ronald: chairman, president, chief executive officer, Terumo Medical Corp.

DeVore, William O.: vice president, treasurer, DeVore Foundation

DeVos, Helen June (Van Wesep): president, DeVos Foundation (Richard and Helen)

Dewar, Robert: director, Claiborne and Art Ortenberg Foundation (Liz)

Dewey, Henry Bowen, Esq.: co-trustee, Hoche-Scofield Foundation

DeWoody, Beth Rudin: president, director, Rudin Foundation

Di Re, Cheryl: secretary, Washington Mutual Foundation; senior vice president, community relations, Washington Mutual Inc.

di San Faustino, Genevieve Bothin Lyman: president, director, donor granddaughter, The Bothin Foundation

Diamond, Lorraine: secretary, Vogler Foundation (Laura B.)

Diaz, Francisco: director, Monsanto Fund

Dibner, Brent: trustee, Dibner Fund

Dibner, Daniel: trustee, Dibner Fund

Dibner, David: president, treasurer, trustee, Dibner Fund

Dibner, Frances K.: vice president, treasurer, trustee, Dibner Fund

Dick, Rollin M.: executive vice president, chief financial officer, Conseco Inc.

Dicke, Richard M., Esq.: trustee, Ferkauf Foundation (Eugene and Estelle)

Dickenson, Gwen: administrative assistant, Self Family Foundation

Dickes, Don D.: secretary, treasurer, trustee, Timken Foundation of Canton

Dickey, Eileen D.: secretary, CTW Foundation, Inc.

Dickler, Ruth: president, Dickler Family Foundation

Dickler, Susan: executive vice president, Dickler Family Foundation

Dickman, J. Jerry: trustee, Chapman Charitable Trust (H. A. and Mary K.)

Dickman, Norbert J.: vice president, director, The Prairie Foundation

Dickson, Alan T.: director, Royal & SunAlliance Insurance Foundation, Inc.

Dickson, Margaret C.: vice president, treasurer, Harland Charitable Foundation (John H. and Wilhelmina D.)

Dickson, Michael M.: trustee, Harland Charitable Foundation (John H. and Wilhelmina D.)

Dickson, Robert T.: president, director, The Prairie Foundation

Dickson, Stanley S.: trustee, Brown Foundation, Inc. (James Graham)

Dicus, John: trustee, Security Benefit Life Insurance Co. Charitable Trust

Diehl, Betty: vice president, Lytel Foundation (Bertha Russ)

Dietl, Wally: secretary, Holzer Memorial Foundation (Richard H.)

Dietler, Cortland S.: trustee, El Pomar Foundation

Dietrich, G. Phillip: secretary, Delano Foundation (Mignon Sherwood)

Dietrich, William B.: president, treasurer, Dietrich Foundation (William B.)

Dietz, Carolyn Emmerson: chairman, president, Sierra Pacific Foundation

Dietzel, Lois Fisher: vice president, Fisher Foundation

Dievendorf, Mary Catherine: trustee, Yost Trust (J. Paul)

Diez-Morales, Luis: trustee, Hartford Courant Foundation

Diggs, James C.: vice president, PPG Industries Foundation

Dikeou, George D., Esq.: director, Copic Medical Foundation

DiLeo, Victor: trustee, Schwartz Foundation (Arnold A.)

Dill, Agnes M.: director, Chamiza Foundation

Dill, Tern C.: director, Metris Companies Foundation

Diller, Whitney Clay: treasurer, Clay Foundation

Dillon, David Brian: chief executive officer, Kroger Co.; trustee, The Kroger Co. Foundation

Dillon, Francis B.: trustee, Arata Brothers Trust

Dillon, John T.: chairman, chief executive officer, director, International Paper Co.

Dillon, Margo: assistant treasurer, director, Dillon Foundation

Dillon, Patrick: director, Dillon Foundation

Dillon, Peter W.: president, director, Dillon Foundation

Dillon, Ray E., III: trustee, Davis Foundation (James A. and Juliet L.)

Dillon, Tanya: honorary director, Allyn Foundation

Dills, Joan Nelson: administrator, Stulsaft Foundation (Morris)

Dills, Max J.: director, Shelter Mutual Insurance Co.

Dimeo, Bradford S.: vice president, Dimeo Construction Co.

Dimeo, Thomas P.: chairman, president, chief executive officer, director, Dimeo Construction Co.

Dimmer, Carolyn J.: vice president, Dimmer Family Foundation

Dimmer, Diane C.: secretary, Dimmer Family Foundation

Dimmer, John B.: treasurer, Dimmer Family Foundation

Dimmer, John C.: president, Dimmer Family Foundation

Dimmer, Marilyn J.: vice president, Dimmer Family Foundation

DiNardo, Joseph: trustee, Statler Foundation

Dinerstein, Martha L.: managing director, head marketing & corporate communications, United States Trust Company of New York

Dingell, Deborah I.: vice chairman, trustee, General Motors Foundation

Dingman, Elizabeth T.: vice president, Dingman Foundation (Michael D.)

Dingman, Michael David: president, chief financial officer, Dingman Foundation (Michael D.)

Dinner, Joan Withers: director, Hale Foundation (Crescent Porter)

Dinner, Richard S.: trustee, Swig Foundation (The)

Dinse, Ann G.: trustee, Turrell Fund

DiPilla, Betty: secretary, Maneely Fund

Disney, Anthea: president, chief executive officer, HarperCollins Publishers Inc.

Ditz, Nancy J.: secretary, treasurer, Saw Island Foundation

Diver, Karen: trustee, Blandin Foundation

Divers-White, Beverly: trustee, Hazen Foundation (Edward W.)

Dix, Lawrence: treasurer, Becher Foundation (Hildegarde D.)

Dix, Ronald H.: vice president, director, Badger Meter Foundation; vice president administration & human resources, Badger Meter Inc.

Dixon, Ashley M.: director, Fear Not Foundation

Dixon, Judith W.: secretary, Winn-Dixie Stores Foundation

Dixon, Paul Edward: secretary, trustee, Handy & Harman Foundation

Dixon, Ruth B.: co-chairman, trustee, Barstow Foundation

Dixon, Thomas F.: vice president, director, Harriman Foundation (Gladys and Roland)

Dixon, Thomas H.: director, Oneida Savings Bank Charitable Foundation

Dixon, William R.: trustee, Barstow Foundation

Doan, Herbert Dow: chairman, trustee, Dow Foundation (Herbert H. and Grace A.)

Doane, Ken: program officer, Cowell Foundation (S. H.)

Dobbins, Allen L., EdD: director, Hedco Foundation

Dobbins, Z. E., Jr.: president, director, Stonecutter Foundation

Dobbs, David L.: trustee, Nolan Charitable Trust (James and Elise)

Dobbs, W. L.: mgr, Porter Testamentary Trust (James Hyde)

Doberstein, Stephen C.: director, Crystal Trust

Dobkin, Kendal Kennedy: director, Kennedy Family Foundation (Ethel and W. George)

Dobras, Mary Ann: trustee, Stocker Foundation

Dobrof, David J.: trustee, New York Foundation

Dobrof, Rose: secretary, New York Foundation

Dobson, Douglas R.: trustee, vice chairman, Stackpole-Hall Foundation

Dockson, Robert Ray: trustee, Haynes Foundation (John Randolph and Dora)

Dodd, Ruth E.: secretary, Connell Foundation (Michael J.)

Dodge, Bayard: vice president, director, Dodge Foundation (Cleveland H.)

Dodge, Cleveland Earl, Jr.: director, member executive committee, member finance committee, Dodge Foundation (Cleveland H.)

Dodge, David S.: mem executive comm, director, Dodge Foundation (Cleveland H.)

Dodge, James H.: chairman, chief executive officer, president, director, Providence Gas Co.

Dodson, Betty Jo: mem, Phipps Foundation (Columbus)

Dodson, David: secretary, director, Babcock Foundation (Mary Reynolds)

Dodson, Paulette: secretary, Chicago Tribune Foundation

Doerfler, Ronald J.: senior vice president, chief financial officer, ABC Inc.

Doescher, Scott P.: senior vice president, secretary, treasurer, Wausau-Mosinee Paper Corp.

Doherty, Janice L.: secretary, Smoot Charitable Foundation

Doherty, Philip B.: treasurer, Chicago Tribune Foundation

Dolan, James F.: trustee, Heinz Trust (Drue)

Dolan, Joseph S.: executive director, secretary, Bodman Foundation

Dolan, Peter R.: chairman, chief executive officer, Bristol-Myers Squibb Co.; chairman, Bristol-Myers Squibb Foundation Inc.

Dolan, Regina A.: trustee, Paine Webber Foundation; chief financial officer, vice president, UBS PaineWebber Inc.

Dolan, Ronald J.: trustee, Ohio National Foundation; senior vice president, chief financial officer, director, Ohio National Life Insurance Co.

Dolden, Roger: chief financial officer, L'Oreal U.S.A.

Doll, Thomas J.: trustee, Subaru of America Foundation, Inc.; vice president, chief financial officer, Subaru of America Inc.

Dolle, Guy: chairman, J&L Specialty Steel Inc.

Dolvin, Neal: director, Citizens Union Bank Foundation

Domke, Doreta J.: treasurer, director, McConnell Foundation

Donahue, Frank R., Jr.: secretary, director, Barra Foundation

Donahue, Jeffrey H.: senior vice president, chief

financial officer, Rouse Co.

Donahue, Josephine C.: director administration, Dana Foundation (Charles A.)

Donaldson, Don: vice president, assistant secretary, Lyon Foundation

Donaly, Joyce: treasurer, CNA Foundation

Donati, John: director, S.G. Foundation

Donley, Edward J.: trustee, Rider-Pool Foundation

Donnelley, James R.: director, Donnelley & Sons Co. (R.R.); vice president, treasurer, Griswold Foundation (John C.)

Donofrio, Nicholas M.: senior vice president technology & manufacturing, International Business Machines

Donoghue, Norman E., II: trustee, Bard Foundation (Robert)

Donohoe, John C.: trustee, Walsh Charity Trust (Blanche)

Donohue, Elise R.: director, Weyerhaeuser Memorial Foundation (Charles A.)

Donovan, Thomas F.: trustee, Connelly Foundation

Donovan, Thomas J.: senior trustee, Bean Foundation (Norwin S. and Elizabeth N.)

Donovan, Thomas Roy: president, chief executive officer, Chicago Board of Trade

Dooley, Eugene: director, Kovarik Foundation for Poetry (Henry P.)

Dooner, Marie E.: secretary, Maneely Fund

Doordan, Helen R.: president, trustee, Raskob Foundation for Catholic Activities, Inc.

Dopson, Arnold B.: chairman, Blount Educational and Charitable Foundation (Mildred Weedon)

Dor, Barbara: trustee, Ferkauf Foundation (Eugene and Estelle)

Dor, Benny: trustee, Ferkauf Foundation (Eugene and Estelle)

Doramus, Mark C.: director, Rockefeller Foundation (Winthrop)

Dorman, David W.: chairman, chief executive officer, AT&T Corp.

Dorn, David F.: trustee, Glendorn Foundation

Dorn, Gail J.: trustee, vice president, Target Foundation

Dorn, John C.: trustee, Glendorn Foundation

Dorn, William L.: chairman, chief executive officer, director, Forest Oil Corp.

Dornsife, David H.: vice president, director, Hedco Foundation

Dornsife, Ester M.: president, director, Hedco Foundation

Dornsife, Harold W.: cfo, director, Hedco Foundation

Dorrance, Bennett: president, director, Dorrance Family Foundation

Dorrance, Bennett, Jr.: vice president, director, Dorrance Family Foundation

Dorrance, Jackie: executive director, Beckman Foundation (Arnold and Mabel)

Dorrance, Jacquelynn W.: secretary, treasurer, director, Dorrance Family Foundation

Dorrance, Roy G.: trustee, U.S. Steel Foundation

Dorsey, Lynne L.: trustee, duPont Foundation (Chichester)

Dossman, Curley M., Jr.: president, Georgia-Pacific Foundation

Double, Richard W.: director, St. Francis Bank Foundation

Double, William F.: director, St. Francis Bank Foundation

Dougherty, Robert J., Jr.: trustee, Public Service Electric & Gas Foundation

Douglas, David: vice president, director, Wallace Genetic Foundation

Douglas, Jean Wallace: president, director, Wallace Genetic Foundation

Douglas, Laurinda L.: trustee, Hillsdale Fund

Douglas, Walter E.: trustee, Skillman Foundation

Douglass, William Birch, III: secretary, Gray Foundation (Garland and Agnes Taylor)

Douthat, E. M., III: director, Smith Foundation (Ralph L.)

Douthat, Neil T.: director, Smith Foundation (Ralph L.)

Douthat, Paul N.: trustee, Smith Foundation (Ralph L.)

Dow, Michael Lloyd: vice president, treasurer, trustee, Dow Foundation (Herbert H. and Grace A.)

Dowd, Hector G.: secretary, Frese Foundation (Arnold D.)

Dowdle, James C.: director, McCormick Tribune Foundation (Robert R.)

Dowling, Edward C.: trustee, Cleveland-Cliffs Foundation (The); senior vice president, operations, Cleveland-Cliffs Inc.

Downer, Edwin E.: director, Hardin Foundation (Phil)

Downes, Laurence M.: president, chief executive officer, director, chairman, New Jersey Natural Gas Co.; trustee, New Jersey Natural Gas Foundation

Downey, Thelma L.: executive director, Olsson Memorial Foundation (Elis)

Downing, Danna M.: director, Vicksburg Foundation

Downing, Kathryn M.: vice chairman, Times Mirror Foundation; executive vice president, Tribune Co.

Downs, John H., Jr.: secretary, director, Coca-Cola Foundation

Doyle, Allen: trustee, Valentine Foundation (Lawson)

Doyle, Daniel M.: president, director, Doyle Foundation

Doyle, Daniel M., Jr.: director, Doyle Foundation

Doyle, Donald W.: vice president, trustee, Gheens Foundation

Doyle, Janice C.: assistant secretary, CUNA Mutual Group Foundation, Inc.

Doyle, L. F. Boker: trustee, Taconic Foundation

Doyle, Michael P., PhD: vice president, secretary, Research Corp.

Doyle, Robert A.: director, AMCORE Foundation

Doyle, Rosaleen J.: vice president, director, Doyle Foundation

Doyle, Terence N.: co-trustee, Heilmaier Charitable Foundation (Anna M.)

Doyle, Valentine: trustee, Valentine Foundation (Lawson)

Dozal, Kathy: director, employee representative, Mitsubishi Electric America Foundation; administrative assistant, Mitsubishi Electric and Electronics USA

Dragon, Robert E., MD: director, Vance Charitable Foundation (Robert C.)

Dramis, Fran: trustee, BellSouth Foundation

Drasner, Fred: co-founder, president, chief executive officer, co-publisher, director, Daily News L.P.

Dray, James R.: director, Schmitt Foundation (Kilian J. and Caroline F.)

Drebin, Allan I.: treasurer, director, Cheney Foundation (Elizabeth F.)

Drees, Charles F.: director, Gulf Coast Medical Foundation

Dresler, Michael D.: executive director, Valley Foundation (Wayne and Gladys)

Dresner, Bruce: director, Fairchild Foundation, Inc. (Sherman)

Dresser, Joyce G.: trustee, Arkell Hall Foundation

Drew, Helen Hall: trustee, Stackpole-Hall Foundation

Drexel, Noreen: president, trustee, McBean Charitable Trust (Alletta Morris)

Drexler, Millard S.: president, chief executive officer, director, Gap Inc.

Drinkwater, Clover M.: assistant secretary, trustee, Anderson Foundation (NY)

Driscoll, Elizabeth S.: director, Driscoll Foundation

Driscoll, Rudolph Weyerhaeuser: vice president, director, Driscoll Foundation

Driscoll, Walter John: president, director, Driscoll Foundation

Droege, Mark E.: trustee, BellSouth Foundation

Drost, Carolyn Jill: director, Eberly Foundation

Drowota, Frank F., III: director, Frist Foundation

Druckenmiller, Fiona: trustee, Carnegie Corp. of New York

Druliner, Kathryn: trustee, Cooper Foundation

Drumwright, Elenita M.: president, Memton Fund

Drumwright, Elizabeth: director, Memton Fund

Drury, David J.: director, St. Francis Bank Foundation

Drushel, William H., Jr.: trustee, Cullen Foundation (The)

Dryfoos, Jacqueline H.: chairman, director, New York Times Co. Foundation

Drymalski, Raymond Hibner: treasurer, Offield Family Foundation (The)

du Pont, Christopher T.: treasurer, trustee, duPont Foundation (Chichester)

du Pont, E. Bradford, Jr.: trustee, Welfare Foundation

du Pont, Edward Bradford: president, trustee, Welfare Foundation

du Pont, Irenee, Jr.: trustee, Crystal Trust

du Pont, Lammot Joseph: trustee, Marmot Foundation

du Pont, Miren de Amezola: trustee, Marmot Foundation

du Pont, Willis Harrington: president, trustee, Marmot Foundation

Dubiel, Robert S.: trustee, Acushnet Foundation

Dubin, Seth Harris: director, Hebrew Technical Institute

Dubinsky, Sheila K.: assistant treasurer, Phoenix Foundation

DuBose, Vivian Noble: trustee, Noble Foundation (Samuel Roberts)

Duchossois, Craig J.: chief executive officer,

Duchossois, Dayle Paige: director, Duchossois Family Foundation

Duchossois, Kimberly: president, Duchossois Family Foundation

Duchossois, Richard Louis: chairman, chief executive officer, director; secretary, Duchossois Family Foundation

Ducommun, Robert E.: president, Ducommun and Gross Foundation

Ducommun Depeyster, Electra: vice president, treasurer, Ducommun and Gross Foundation

Dudgeon, Clair: trustee, Van Wert County Foundation

Dudley, Joan R.: treasurer, Brown Foundation, Inc. (James Graham)

Dudte, James J.: vice president, trustee, Young Foundation (Hugo H. and Mabel B.)

Duello, J. Donald: president, treasurer, director, Shelter Insurance Foundation

Duff, Charles F.: vice president, trustee, Gray Foundation (Garland and Agnes Taylor)

Duff-Bloom, Gale: president co. communications & marketing, Penney Company Inc. (J.C.)

Duffell, Carol: secretary, treasurer, Semmes Foundation

Duffield, Cheryl D.: director, Duffield Family Foundation

Duffield, David A.: director, Duffield Family Foundation

Duffield, Michael D.: director, Duffield Family Foundation

Duffy, Vivien Stiles: executive director, Rohatyn Foundation (Felix and Elizabeth)

Duggan, Robert D.: chairman, S&T Bancorp Charitable Foundation; chairman, chief executive officer, S&T Bancorp Inc.

Dugger, Albia: director, Norcross Wildlife Foundation

Duke, Anthony Drexel, Sr.: trustee, Achelis Foundation

Duke, Robin Chandler Tippett: trustee, United States-Japan Foundation

Duker, Brack: chief financial officer, secretary, Whitecap Foundation

Duker, Elizabeth: president, Whitecap Foundation

Dukess, A. Carleton: chairman, trustee, New York Foundation

Dulaney, Robert W.: vice president, Norton Foundation

Dulle, Mary: co-chairman, Alcon Foundation

Duman, Louis J., MD: trustee, Bonfils-Stanton Foundation

Dumas, Kevin L.: director, New Milford Savings Bank Foundation

Dunagan, John C.: vice president, Dunagan Foundation

Dunagan, Kathleen: secretary, Dunagan Foundation

Dunagan, Kathlyn C.: president, Dunagan Foundation

Dunbar, C. Wendell: treasurer, trustee, Towsley Foundation (Harry A. and Margaret D.)

Duncan, C. W., III: vice president, director, Duncan Foundation (L. H. and C. W.)

Duncan, Charles William, Jr.: chairman, director, Duncan Foundation (L. H. and C. W.)

Duncan, Deana: director, Beneficia Foundation

Duncan, George T.: trustee, Franklin Foundation Inc. (John and Mary)

Duncan, John D., Esq.: trustee, Davies Benevolent Fund (Edward H.)

Duncan, John H., Jr.: vice president, director, Duncan Foundation (L. H. and C. W.)

Duncan, John H., Sr.: president, director, Duncan Foundation (L. H. and C. W.)

Duncan, Sam: president, Ralph's-Food 4 Less Foundation; president, chief executive officer, Ralph's Grocery Co.

Duncan, William G., Jr.: trustee, Gheens Foundation

Dunckel, Jeanette Maddux: director, Haigh-Scatena Foundation

Dunford, Betty P.: vice president, trustee, Cooke Foundation

Dunlap, Nancy E.: director, Kaul Foundation Trust (Hugh)

Dunlap, Richard Lowell: program director, information systems, Kresge Foundation

Dunlop, Joy S.: president, director, Dell Foundation (Hazel)

Dunmire, Cyril C., Jr.: director, Stabler Foundation (Donald B. and Dorothy L.)

Dunn, Edward K., Jr.: director, Baltimore Equitable Insurance Foundation; treasurer, trustee, Warfield Memorial Fund (Anna Emory)

Dunn, Harry E.: vice president, Treakle Foundation (J. Edwin)

Dunn, Norma F.: senior vice president investor & public relations, El Paso Corp.

Dunn, Peter M., Esq.: secretary, general counsel, Chapman Charitable Corp. (Howard and Bess)

Dunnington, Patricia: trustee, Sprague Educational and Charitable Foundation (Seth)

Dunstan, Christopher T.: director, Oishei Foundation (The John R.)

Dunton, Gary C.: president, chief operating officer, MBIA Inc.

Dunworth, Gerald J.: treasurer, director, Palisades Educational Foundation

Duplessie, David: corporator, Oak Grove School

duPont, Allaire: trustee, duPont Foundation (Chichester)

DuPont, Eleuthere I.: trustee, Longwood Foundation

DuPont, Elizabeth Lee: vice president, Good Samaritan

DuPont, Lea C.: vice president, Good Samaritan

DuPont, Pierre S., IV: director, Bradley Foundation (Lynde and Harry); trustee, Longwood Foundation

Durand, Carolyn Thrune: trustee, Strosacker Foundation (Charles J.)

Durand, H. Whitney: treasurer, trustee, Tonya Memorial Foundation

Durbin, Vaughn: secretary, Colt Foundation (James J.)

Durden, J. C.: vice president, director, Tractor & Equipment Co. Foundation

Durein, Nancy: trustee, AT&T National Pro-Am Youth Fund

Durham, Earl: vice chair, trustee, Hazen Foundation (Edward W.)

Durkin, Marian M.: director, United Airlines Foundation

Durkin, Sean: chief financial officer, Winter Construction Co.

Duronio, Carolyn D.: secretary, Pittsburgh Child Guidance Foundation

Durrett, Joseph P.: chief executive officer, Broderbund L.L.C.

Durrett, William E.: senior chairman, American Fidelity Assurance Co.

Dury, Joseph D., Jr.: director, Staunton Farm Foundation

Dutcher, Judi: president Minnesota community, Bigelow Foundation (F. R.)

Dutton, Uriel E.: trustee, Anderson Foundation (M. D.)

Duvick, Dave F.: secretary, Ecolab Foundation

Duwell, John F.: trustee, West Bend Mutual Charitable Trust

Dworetzky, Joseph A.: director, Penn Foundation (William)

Dworsky, Alan J.: trustee, Taconic Foundation

Dwyer, Dean P.: vice president finance, treasurer, senior management board, Copley Press Inc.

Dwyer, John J.: mem supervisory board, Codrington Charitable Foundation (George W.)

Dyer, Leila Gordon: advisory trustee, McLean Contributionship

Dyer, Sara R.: trustee, Reinberger Foundation

Dykstra, Craig Richard: vice president rel, Lilly Endowment

Dykstra, Timothy P.: vice president, treasurer, DaimlerChrysler Corp. Fund

Dyson, E. Charles: director, Janirve Foundation

Dyson, Robert R.: president, director, Dyson Foundation

E

Eagan, J. Murray: trustee, contact, Trees Charitable Trust (Edith L.)

Eardley, Vernon: president, chief executive officer, Korte Construction Co.

Earhart, Steve: vice president, Motorola Foundation

Earl, J. Benjamin: director, Patron Saints Foundation

Earley, Anthony Francis, Jr.: chairman, president, chief executive officer, chief operating officer, DTE Energy Co.

Earls, Jeffrey W.: vice president, Griswold Foundation (John C.)

Earls, Julian M.: trustee, Jennings Foundation (Martha Holden)

Earls, Lynda: secretary, Griswold Foundation (John C.)

Early, Jeannette B.: president, Early Foundation

Early, Julie A.: executive director, Island Foundation (MA)

Early, William Bernard: trustee, Jeld-wen Foundation; senior vice president, assistant secretary, director, Jeld-Wen Inc.

Eason, J. Rodney: chairman, director, Sierra Health Foundation

Eason, Richard: director, mem, Katzenberger Foundation

Easter, Bill: trustee, Duke Energy Foundation

Easterly, David E.: president, chief operating officer, Cox Enterprises Inc.

Eastham, Thomas: western director, Hearst Foundation, Inc. (The); vice president, executive director, Hearst Foundation (William Randolph)

Easton, Kenneth: trustee, McMahon Foundation

Eastwood, Susan: trustee, August Family Foundation (Charles J. and Burton S.)

Eaton, Geraldine: secretary, trustee, Presto Foundation

Eaton, Mary Stephens: vice president, trustee, Eaton Foundation (Cyrus)

Eber, Andrew J.: director, Haigh-Scatena Foundation

Eberhardt, Joachim W.: trustee, DaimlerChrysler Corp. Fund

Eberhardt, Thomas J.: assistant treasurer, Fidelity Foundation

Eberhart, Cornelia: director, Mardag Foundation

Eberle, William: controller, Reichhold Chemicals Inc.

Eberly, Paul O.: director, Eberly Foundation

Eberly, Robert E., Jr.: director, Eberly Foundation

Eberly, Robert E., Sr.: director, Eberly Foundation

Ebert, Michael G.: secretary, trustee, Gerber Foundation

Ebrahimi, Alireza: secretary, Alavi Foundation

Ebrom, Charles E.: director, executive vice president, Zachry Co. (H.B.); treasurer, trustee, Zachry Foundation (The)

Eccles, C. Hope: committee member, Eccles Foundation (Marriner S.)

Eccles, Lisa: executive director, Eccles Foundation (George S. and Dolores Dore)

Eccles, Spencer Fox: committee member, Eccles Foundation (Marriner S.)

Echols, Peggy: vice president, State Farm Companies Foundation

Eckert, Constance L.: assistant secretary, Hubbard Foundation

Eckert, Robert A.: chairman, chief executive officer, Mattel Inc.

Eckstein, Marie N.: vice president, trustee, Dow Corning Foundation

Eddy, Jane Lee: trustee, Taconic Foundation

Eddy, Jeanne: trustee, National Grange Mutual Charitable Trust

Eddy, Latimer B.: director, Beveridge Foundation, Inc. (Frank Stanley)

Edelman, Peter Benjamin: director, Public Welfare Foundation

Edelman, Sandra A.: executive director, Chamiza Foundation

Edelson, Lanny, MD: trustee, The MBNA Foundation

Eden, Thomas: adv board committee member, Heath Foundation (Mary)

Eden, Tom: trustee, Claypool Foundation (Silas and Ruth)

Edgar, Arlen L.: trustee, Abell-Hanger Foundation

Edgar, James M.: director, Rosenberg Foundation

Edgar, James R.: trustee, Kemper Foundation (James S.)

Edgar, Robert V.: director, Memton Fund

Edge, Kenneth: director, AMCORE Foundation

Edmiston, W. Allan: president, director, Patron Saints Foundation

Edmonds, Dean S., III: trustee, Edmonds Foundation (Dean S.)

Edmonds, Mary Virginia: trustee, Slemp Foundation

Edmonds, Pamela S.: trustee, Slemp Foundation

Edmonds, David: trustee, Children's Foundation of Erie County

Edson, Catherine H.: trustee, Halff Foundation (G. A. C.)

Edson, Thomas H.: trustee, Halff Foundation (G. A. C.)

Edwards, Claudia L.: executive director, Reader's Digest Foundation

Edwards, David M.: president, GATX Corp.

Edwards, Donna F.: executive director, Arca Foundation

Edwards, Frank G.: trustee, Puterbaugh Foundation

Edwards, Jack Kenneth: executive president, group president power generation, Cummins Inc.

Edwards, James K.: trustee, Levy Foundation (June Rockwell)

Edwards, James M.: member, McCune Charitable Foundation (Marshall L. and Perrine D.); executive director, McCune Charitable Trust (John R.); chairman, McCune Foundation

Edwards, R. A.: trustee, Davis Foundation (James A. and Juliet L.)

Edwards, Scott: secretary, treasurer, CCB Foundation

Edwards, T. Ashley: assistant treasurer, Memorial Foundation for the Blind

Edwards, William F.: trustee, Niagara Mohawk Foundation

Effren, Garry: vice president, treasurer, director, Knight Ridder Fund

Egan, Karin P.: program officer education, Carnegie Corp. of New York

Egan, Thomas P., Jr.: officer, Valmont Foundation

Egbert, Brad: chief financial officer, Bryan Foods

Egbert, Marcia: senior program officer, Gund Foundation (George)

Ege, Hans A.: vice president, Bay Foundation

Egger, Bruce P.: secretary, Bank of Greene County Charitable Foundation

Egger, Terrance C.Z.: director, Pulitzer Foundation

Eggers, William D.: trustee, Corning Inc. Foundation

Egner, David O.: president, trustee, Hudson-Webber Foundation

Ehrenkranz, Sanford B.: trustee, Meier Foundation (Richard)

Ehrhardt, Anke A.: trustee, Ford Foundation

Ehrlich, Bill: director, Washington Mutual Foundation; executive vice president, corporate relations, Washington Mutual Inc.

Ehrlich, Delia Fleishhacker: director, Fleishhacker Foundation

Ehrlich, Jodi: director, Fleishhacker Foundation

Ehrlich, John Stephen, Jr.: vice president, Fleishhacker Foundation

Ehrlich, Linda: administrative director, Scheuer Family Foundation Inc. (S. H. and Helen R.)

Ehrlich, M. Gordon, Esq.: trustee, Rabb Charitable Trust (Sidney R.)

Ehrlich, Philip S., Jr.: director, Zellerbach Family Fund

Ehrlich, Thomas: director, Goldman Fund (Richard and Rhoda)

Ehrman, Daniel S.: vice president, Gannett Foundation

Eichenbaum, E. C.: chairman, Ottenheimer Brothers Foundation

Eichleay, John W., Jr.: director, Staunton Farm Foundation

Eichman, Thelma L.: director, Strong Foundation (Hattie M.)

Eielson, Rodney S.: president, Culpeper Memorial Foundation (Daphne Seybolt)

Eilert, Norman E.: chief financial officer, Teichert Foundation; senior vice president, chief financial officer, Teichert & Sons (A.)

Einhorn, Jessica P.: trustee, Rockefeller Brothers Fund, Inc.

Eisenberg, Richard: vice president, Read Foundation (Charles L.)

Eisenberg, Saul: treasurer, Read Foundation (Charles L.)

Eisenberg, Sharon R.: trustee, Plough Foundation

Eisenhans, L. L.: director, president, Shell Oil Co. Foundation

Eisenhardt, Elizabeth Haas: trustee, Haas Fund (Walter and Elise)

Eisner, Erica: program officer, Crown Memorial (Arie and Ida)

Eisner, Michael Dammann: president, trustee, Disney Co. Foundation (Walt); chairman, chief executive officer, director, Disney Co. (Walt)

Eklund, Christopher S.: treasurer, Norton Memorial Corp. (Geraldi)

Eklund, Dariel Ann: vice president, Norton Memorial Corp. (Geraldi)

Eklund, Peter H.: member, Norton Memorial Corp. (Geraldi)

Eklund, Sally S.: secretary, Norton Memorial Corp. (Geraldi)

Elam, Ed: director, Christy-Houston Foundation

Elbel, Christine: executive director, Fleishhacker Foundation

Elbert, Paul A.: president, chief executive officer natural gas, Consumers Energy Co.

Elbling, Paul U.: director, treasurer, Virginia Environmental Endowment

Elder, T. L.: director, vice president, Caterpillar Foundation

Elderfield, John: director, Dedalus Foundation

Eldridge, Elizabeth: corporator, Oak Grove School

Eletz, Bonnie: trustee, Lasdon Foundation (William and Mildred)

Elias, Arthur: trustee, Spewack Article 5th Trust (Bella)

Elias, Clifford E., Esq.: managing trustee, Russell Trust (Josephine G.); trustee, Stearns Trust (Artemas W.)

Elias, Lois: trustee, Spewack Article 5th Trust (Bella)

Elias, Norma: trustee, Douty Foundation (Alfred and Mary)

Elicker, Elizabeth M.: trustee, Muchnic Foundation

Elkins, James A., III: trustee, Wortham Foundation

Elkins, James Anderson, Jr.: president, Elkins, Jr. Foundation (Margaret and James A.)

Ellenson, Patricia: assistant secretary-treasurer, Phillips Family Foundation (L. E.)

Ellers, Steven A.: executive vice president, West Pharmaceutical Services Inc.

Elliman, Christopher J.: president, trustee, Dodge Foundation (Geraldine R.)

Elliot, C. Bill: vice president, Harden Foundation

Elliot, Steven G.: executive management, Mellon Financial Corp.; trustee, Mellon Financial Corp. Foundation

Elliott, Andrew C., Jr.: director, Fasken Foundation

Elliott, Donald H.: vice chairman, KeySpan Foundation

Elliott, Edward: director, Tyndale House Foundation

Ellis, Bernie: member, Giant Food Foundation

Ellis, Elayne J.: assistant secretary, trustee, Earhart Foundation

Ellis, Jack: manager, Porter Testamentary Trust (James Hyde)

Ellis, James D.: senior vice president, general counsel, SBC Communications Inc.; director, SBC Foundation

Ellis, John B.: trustee, Franklin Foundation Inc. (John and Mary)

Ellis, Michael, II: director, Ellis Foundation

Ellis, Monica: director, Ellis Foundation

Ellis, Peter S.: vice chairman, director, Hopedale Foundation

Ellis, William B.: director, MassMutual Foundation for Hartford, Inc. (The)

Ellison, Jody: trustee, Morgan Charitable Residual Trust (W. and E.)

Ellman, Leatrice D.: secretary, trustee, Welfare Foundation

Ellsworth, David H.: trustee, Ellsworth Foundation (Ruth H. and Warren A.)

Ellsworth, Peter Kennedy: president, director, Benbough Foundation (Legler)

Ellyn, Lynne: director, DTE Energy Foundation

Elovitz, Debra: director, Building 19 Foundation

Elovitz, Elaine: director, Building 19 Foundation

Elovitz, Gerald: director, Building 19 Foundation

Else, Robert K.: director, Hickory Tech Corp.; trustee, Hickory Tech Corp. Foundation

Elston, Frances Beinecke: director, Prospect Hill Foundation

Ely, Gary G.: chairman, president, chief executive officer, Avista Corp.

Ely, William L.: director, Davenport-Hatch Foundation

Elzufon, John A., Esq.: director, Kutz Foundation (Milton and Hattie)

Embry, Robert C., Jr.: president, trustee, Abell Foundation

Emerling, Carol G.: co trustee, Appelbaum-Kahn Foundation

Emerling, Keith S.: co trustee, Appelbaum-Kahn Foundation

Emerling, Susan C.: co trustee, Appelbaum-Kahn Foundation

Emerson, C. Lee: vice president, treasurer, Gilmore Foundation (William G.)

Emerson, Christopher S.: director, Emerson Foundation, Inc. (Fred L.)

Emerson, David L.: president, director, Emerson Foundation, Inc. (Fred L.)

Emerson, Frances: senior vice president, Corporate Communications Mass-Mutual, Massachusetts Mutual Life Insurance Co.; director, MassMutual Foundation for Hartford, Inc. (The)

Emerson, Heather A.: director, Emerson Foundation, Inc. (Fred L.)

Emerson, Peter J.: director, Emerson Foundation, Inc. (Fred L.)

Emerson, W. Gary: director, Emerson Foundation, Inc. (Fred L.)

Emery, Ethan: trustee, Peterloon Foundation

Emfinger, Lloyd F., Jr.: trustee, Blount Educational and Charitable Foundation (Mildred Weedon)

Emling, John: vice president, Barden Precision Bearings

Emmerson, A. A.: president, Sierra Pacific Industries

Emmerson, George: director, Sierra Pacific Foundation; vice president, Sierra Pacific Industries

Emmet, Robert: vice president financial planning, treasurer, Cleveland-Cliffs Inc.

Emmett, Denis L.: chief financial officer, Erving Industries; treasurer, assistant clerk, Housen Foundation

Emory, Benjamin: trustee, Sasco Foundation

Emrick, John: trustee, Meyer Memorial Trust

Ench, Alberta: secretary, Edison Fund (Charles)

Endries, Kari H.: assistant secretary, Unocal Foundation

Engel, Alan: vice president, secretary, Figtree Foundation

Engel, William V., Esq.: director, secretary, Hyde and Watson Foundation

Engelhardt, Rebecca A.: secretary, treasurer, trustee, Miller Foundation

Engelman, Ephraim P., MD: director, Hale Foundation (Crescent Porter)

Engibous, Thomas James: director, Texas Instruments Foundation; chairman, Texas Instruments Inc.

Engl, Leslie: director, Engl Family Foundation (Michael S.)

Engl, Michael S.: director, Engl Family Foundation (Michael S.)

Engle, Allan: secretary, Van Andel Foundation (Jay and Betty)

Englert, Laurie O.: director, Graco Foundation

English, Edmond J.: president, chief executive officer, TJX Companies Inc.; president, director, chairman, TJX Foundation, Inc.

English, Natalie: secretary, Goodrich Foundation, Inc. (B.F.)

Eno, Kathy E.: director, Hall-Perrine Foundation

Enright, Michael: trustee, Leavey Foundation (Thomas and Dorothy)

Enright, William Gerald: director, Lilly Endowment

Ensign, Katherine Dalbey: board of directors, Wilson Foundation (Marie C. and Joseph C.)

Ensor, Carl, Jr.: director, Thompson Charitable Foundation

Epp, Phyllis: executive director, International Paper Co. Foundation

Eppig, Michael D., MD: trustee, Smith Foundation (Kelvin and Eleanor)

Epps, Claude M., Jr.: chairman, Chapin Foundation of Myrtle Beach, South Carolina

Epstein, Bennett N.: secretary, Kutz Foundation (Milton and Hattie)

Epstein, Deena M.: senior program officer, Gund Foundation (George)

Epstein, Lisa K. Simmons: president, director, Simmons Foundation, Inc. (Harold)

Epstein, Sidney: treasurer, Polk Brothers Foundation, Inc.

Erbaugh, J. Martin: trustee, Morgan Foundation (Burton D.)

Erburu, Robert F.: trustee, Ahmanson Foundation; director, Doheny Foundation Trust (Carrie Estelle); vice president, trustee, Jones Foundation (Fletcher); chairman, director, Parsons Foundation (Ralph M.)

Erdle, Allison A.: trustee, Washington Forrest Foundation

Erdman, Christian P.: trustee, Buck Foundation (Carol Franc); treasurer, Buck Foundation (Frank H. and Eva B.)

Erhard, Helmut: president, chief executive officer, Lehigh Cement Co.

Erichson, John W.: director, Janirve Foundation

Erickson, Erica: trustee, Ghidotti Foundation

Erickson, Greg: director, Thompson Charitable Foundation

Ericson, Lois G.: off, Griswold Foundation (Lillian Sherwood)

Eriksen, Rolf F.: treasurer, Kutz Foundation (Milton and Hattie)

Ernst, Mark A.: director, H&R Block Foundation

Erpf, Armand B.: director, Erpf Fund (Armand G.)

Erpf, Cornelia A.: director, Erpf Fund (Armand G.)

Erskine, John E., Jr.: director, Christensen Charitable and Religious Foundation (L. C.)

Erskine, Linwood M., Jr.: trustee, Sherman Trust (Margaret E.)

Ertel, Barbara: trustee, Plankenhorn Foundation (Harry)

Esber, Suzanne Huffmon: manager, community relationss, Fluor Foundation

Eshleman, Jon W.: president, Loutit Foundation

Eskew, Michael L.: trustee, UPS Foundation

Eskridge, T. Hillis: trustee, assistant to president, Bovaird Foundation (Mervin)

Esposito, Anthony G.: trustee, Ohio National Foundation

Esposito, Louis J.: trustee, Kavanagh Foundation (T. James)

Essex, Kathleen: vice president human resources, Hunt Corp.

Essick, Robert N.: president, treasurer, Essick Foundation

Esteban, Manuel A., PhD: director, Sierra Health Foundation

Esterline, Bruce H.: vice president grants, Meadows Foundation (The)

Estes, Jane M.: chief financial officer, Davis Foundations (Arthur Vining)

Estess, Sandra: trustee, Hillcrest Foundation

Estess, Sandra Street: director, Bertha Foundation

Etheridge, Anne: secretary, treasurer, Norton Family Foundation (Peter)

Ettinger, Barbara P.: director, Educational Foundation of America

Ettinger, Christian P.: adjunct director, Educational Foundation of America

Ettinger, Heidi P.: director, Educational Foundation of America

Ettinger, Leland P.: adjunct director, Educational Foundation of America

Ettinger, Matthew: adjunct director, Educational Foundation of America

Ettinger, Wendy W. P.: director, Educational Foundation of America

Etzwiler, David: director, Medtronic Foundation

Eurich, Juliet: director, Baltimore Equitable Insurance Foundation

Euwer, Paul, Jr.: executive director, Jennings Foundation (Mary Hillman)

Evans, Akosua Barthwell: director, Babcock Foundation (Mary Reynolds)

Evans, Barbara Richardson: trustee, Hillsdale Fund

Evans, Bobby: trustee, Duke Energy Foundation

Evans, Cynthia: secretary, Xcel Energy Foundation

Evans, David S.: director, Ayres Foundation

Evans, Edward Parker: off, Evans Foundation (Edward P.)

Evans, Eli N.: president emeritus, Revson Foundation (Charles H.)

Evans, Gorton M., Jr.: president, chief executive officer, director, Stora Enso

Evans, I. J.: trustee, Union Pacific Foundation

Evans, Jack B.: president, director, Hall-Perrine Foundation

Evans, John C.: vice president, treasurer, director, Luce Foundation (Henry)

Evans, Linda Perryman: president, chief executive officer, trustee, director, Meadows Foundation (The)

Evans, Nancy H.: director, Guaranty Bank and Trust Co. Charitable Trust

Evans, Richard G.: secretary, Metris Companies Foundation

Evans, Richard W., Jr.: chairman, chief executive officer, Frost National Bank

Evans, Robert: member, Giant Food Foundation

Evans, Robert E.: director, McDonough Foundation (Bernard)

Evans, Thomas H.: trustee, Henson Foundation (Richard A.)

Evarts, William Maxwell, Jr.: director, Clark Foundation (NY)

Everett, C. Taylor: trustee, Gray Foundation (Garland and Agnes Taylor)

Everett, Timothy C.: secretary, director, Kimberly-Clark Foundation

Everett, Wendy: director, Sierra Health Foundation

Ewald, Holly: vice president, Ewald Foundation (H. T.)

Ewald, John Clifford: treasurer, Ewald Foundation (H. T.)

Ewald, Kristi: president, Ewald Foundation (H. T.)

Ewald Kratzet, Carolyn T.: vice president emeritus, Ewald Foundation (H. T.)

Ewasyshyn, Frank J.: trustee, DaimlerChrysler Corp. Fund

Ewend, Kurt: trustee, Wickes Foundation (Harvey Randall)

Ewing, Robyn L.: director, Williams Companies Foundation (The)

Ewing, Stephen E.: director, DTE Energy Foundation; vice chairman, trustee, Skillman Foundation

Eychaner, Barbara: director, WPWR-TV Channel 50 Foundation

Eychaner, Fred: president, WPWR-TV Channel 50 Foundation

F

Fabens, Andrew Lawrie, III: secretary, Smith Foundation (Kelvin and Eleanor)

Faber, Herbert: trustee, DeCamp Foundation (Ira W.)

Facer, Thomas: trustee, Birds Eye Foods Foundation

Facini, Deborah L.: trustee, Kunkel Foundation (John Crain)

Fad, Otto C.: vice president, Crestlea Foundation

Fadim, Melissa Sage Booth: chairwoman, president, treasurer, trustee, Sage Foundation

Faechner, Allen D.: trustee, Boe Brothers Foundation

Fagin, Claire M.: director, van Ameringen Foundation, Inc.

Fahey, Christine: assistant secretary, Schering-Plough Foundation

Fahrenkopf, Frank Joseph, Jr.: trustee, Wiegand Foundation (E. L.)

Fair, F. Doyle: president, trustee, Hansen Foundation (Dane G.)

Fair, Jewell L.: secretary, Landegger Charitable Foundation

Fair, Russell B.: vice president pharmacy operations, Giant Food Inc.

Fairbanks, J. Nelson: president, chief executive officer, United States Sugar Corp.

Faison, Helen S.: trustee, director, Buhl Foundation (PA)

Faith, Marshall E.: chairman, director, Scoular Co.; trustee, Scoular Foundation

Faith, Richard G.: president, director, Faith Foundation

Falahee, William: controller, Kaplan Fund (J. M.)

Falberg, Kathryn E.: senior vice president finance, chief financial officer, Amgen Inc.

Falco, Mathea: director, Goldman Fund (Richard and Rhoda)

Falconer, Barbara E.: president, Stuart Charitable Foundation (G. B.)

Falconer, Keith D.: director, Stuart Charitable Foundation (G. B.)

Falencki, Karin: trustee, Jurzykowski Foundation (Alfred)

Fales, Nancy C.: trustee, Laurel Foundation

Falgoust, Dean T.: vice president, trustee, Freeport-McMoRan Foundation

Falk, Harvey L.: president, vice chairman, Claiborne Inc. (Liz)

Falk, Sigo: chairman, Falk Fund (Maurice)

Falk, Thomas J.: chairman, president, chief executive officer, Kimberly-Clark Corp.; director, Kimberly-Clark Foundation

Fallat, Dale W.: trustee, Anderson Foundation

Fallon, Elena: director, Andrews McMeel Universal Foundation

Fallon, James P.: chief financial officer, trustee, Frueauff Foundation (Charles A.)

Falsgraf, William Wendell: secretary, trustee, Frohring Foundation (Paul and Maxine)

Famer, Terri L.: assistant secretary, Bradley Foundation (Lynde and Harry)

Fannan, Phyllis: trustee, Heckscher Foundation for Children

Fanning, Karl P.: trustee, Frueauff Foundation (Charles A.)

Fanton, Jonathan Foster: president, director, MacArthur Foundation (John D. and Catherine T.)

Farabee, Mary Margaret: secretary, ECG Foundation

Faraci, John V.: director, International Paper Co. Foundation

Farash, Max M.: trustee, Farash Charitable Foundation (Max and Marian)

Farkouh, Fred C.: treasurer, Dickler Family Foundation

Farley, James Duncan: chairman emeritus, trustee, Hartford Foundation, Inc. (The John A.)

Farley, Michele U.: director, Phoenix Foundation

Farley, Terrence Michael: director, Harriman Foundation (Gladys and Roland)

Farmer, Charles Albert: trustee, National Grange Mutual Charitable Trust

Farnsworth, Philip Richeson: secretary, ABC Inc.

Farrar, Elizabeth S.: director, Memton Fund

Farrar, Marjorie M.: vice president, Memton Fund

Farrar-Wellman, Olivia: director, Memton Fund

Farrell, Bruce C.: member, Seherr-Thoss Foundation

Farrell, John: trustee, J.P. Morgan Chase Foundation

Farrell, W. James: chairman, chief executive officer, Illinois Tool Works Inc.

Farrington, Jerry S.: director, Hoblitzelle Foundation

Farver, Charles: vice president, Kuyper Foundation (Peter H. and E. Lucille Gaass); chairman, Pella Corp.; treasurer, director, Pella Rolscreen Foundation

Farver, Joan Kuyper: president, director, Kuyper Foundation (Peter H. and E. Lucille Gaass); chairman emeritus, director, Pella Corp.; director, Pella Rolscreen Foundation

Fasenmyer, Janet: controller, Metal Industries Inc.

Fasken, F. Andrew: vice president, Fasken Foundation

Fasken, Steven P.: president, Fasken Foundation

Fatone, Joseph A.: director, Eastern Savings and Loan Foundation

Fatzinger, Walter Robert, Jr.: director, Loughran Foundation (Mary and Daniel)

Fauliso, Joseph J.: director, Hoffman Foundation (Maximilian E. and Marion O.)

Fauquher, Ronald K.: vice president, Ontario Corp. Foundation

Faust, Drew G.: trustee, Mellon Foundation (Andrew W.)

Faust, Mary Lou: secretary, Decker Foundation (Dr. G. Clifford and Florence B.)

Faust, Michael L.: administrator, Kiewit Companies Foundation

Faust, Robert J.: secretary, treasurer, Duncan Foundation (L. H. and C. W.)

Favret, John A.: member distribution committee, Bruening Foundation (Eva L. and Joseph M.)

Fawcett, Daniel W.: trustee, Thompson Trust (Thomas)

Fawley, Dan: assistant treasurer, Reynolds Foundation (R. J.)

Fay, Paul B., Jr.: trustee, Odell Fund (Robert Stewart and Helen Pfeiffer)

Fayard, Gary P.: chief financial officer, executive vice president, Coca-Cola Co.; treasurer, director, Coca-Cola Foundation

Fazendeiro, Anne: trustee, Grimshaw-Gudewicz Charitable Foundation

Fazzolari, Salvatore D.: treasurer, secretary, trustee, Harsco Corp. Fund

Fearon, Janet A.: executive director, trustee, Newcombe Foundation (Charlotte W.)

Fearon, Robert H., Jr.: vice president, Chapman Charitable Corp. (Howard and Bess)

Feather-Francis, Carol: vice president, trustee, Baughman Foundation

Featherman, Sandra, PhD: vice president, director, Fels Fund (Samuel S.)

Federal, Joseph L.: director, Price Foundation (Lucien B. and Katherine E.)

Fee, Allen K.: trustee, Davis Foundation (James A. and Juliet L.)

Feenan, John: senior vice president, chief financial officer, Fuller Co. (H.B.)

Feeney, Thomas J., Esq.: trustee, Sandy Foundation (George H.)

Fegan, Ann B.: president, Reidler Foundation

Fegan, Howard D.: trustee, Reidler Foundation

Fegan, John H.: trustee, Reidler Foundation

Fehsenfeld, Frank B.: president, treasurer, Fehsenfeld Charitable Foundation (Frank B. and Virginia V.)

Fehsenfeld, John A.: trustee, Fehsenfeld Charitable Foundation (Frank B. and Virginia V.)

Fehsenfeld, Thomas V.: trustee, Fehsenfeld Charitable Foundation (Frank B. and Virginia V.)

Fehsenfeld, William S.: trustee, Fehsenfeld Charitable Foundation (Frank B. and Virginia V.)

Fehsenfeld Smith, Nancy: secretary, Fehsenfeld Charitable Foundation (Frank B. and Virginia V.)

Feinblatt, John A.: president, Unger Foundation (Aber D.)

Feinstein, Alan Shawn: president, director, Feinstein Foundation

Feinstein, Karen Wolk, PhD: president, Jewish Healthcare Foundation

Feith, Susan A.: president, Mead Witter Foundation, Inc.

Fejes, Frank S.: director, Hugoton Foundation

Felderstein, Sandra: distribution trustee, Schwab-Rosenhouse Memorial Foundation

Feldman, Justin N.: director, Gilman Foundation (Howard)

Feldman, Marc: treasurer, Dyson Foundation

Feldman, Roberta: trustee, Graham Foundation for Advanced Studies in the Fine Arts

Fella, Leon: director, Schmitt Foundation (Kilian J. and Caroline F.)

Fella, Robert H.: president, Schmitt Foundation (Kilian J. and Caroline F.)

Feller, James R.: secretary, director, Hoch Foundation (Charles H.)

Feller, Mimi A.: senior vice president public affairs & government relations, Gannett Company Inc.

Feller, Nancy P.: assistant secretary, associate general counsel, Ford Foundation

Feller, Robert J.: vice president, Shelter Mutual Insurance Co.

Fellheimer, Ronald K.: trustee, Yost Trust (J. Paul)

Felsinger, Donald E.: president, chief operating officer, director, Sempra Energy

Felts, Thomas J.: director, Foellinger Foundation

Fenlon, Thomas B., Esq.: trustee, Schieffelin Residuary Trust (Sarah I.)

Fennessy, Anne: trustee, Bullitt Foundation

Fennessy, Jacquie: executive director, Patron Saints Foundation

Fentin, Gary S.: trustee, Shatz, Schwartz & Fentin Charitable Foundation; senior partner, Shatz, Schwartz & Fentin P.C.

Fenton, Frank M.: treasurer, director, Fenton Foundation

Fenton, Thomas K.: president, director, Fenton Foundation

Feole, Ron: president, director, Fuller Co. Foundation (H.B.)

Ferguson, James M., III: trustee, Trees Charitable Trust (Edith L.)

Ferkauf, Estelle: trustee, Ferkauf Foundation (Eugene and Estelle)

Ferkauf, Eugene: trustee, Ferkauf Foundation (Eugene and Estelle)

Ferland, E. James: chairman, president, chief executive officer, Public Service Electric & Gas Co.

Fernandes, Alvin C., Jr.: secretary, director, Ayres Foundation

Fernandez-Palmer, Lydia: director, Patron Saints Foundation

Ferranti, Anthony L.: comptroller, Pforzheimer Foundation, Inc. (The Carl and Lily)

Ferrara, Al: trustee, AK Steel Foundation

Ferraro, Jim: chief financial officer, Giant Food Stores

Ferrasci, Frank E.: treasurer, Harden Foundation

Ferruccio, Anthony: director, Washington Group Foundation, Inc.

Fesenmyer, Bob: general manager, vice president, Dana Corp.; director, Dana Corp. Foundation

Festo, Charles F.: assistant secretary, Simon Foundation (William E.)

Fey, Eugene C.: treasurer, trustee, Pinkerton Foundation

Fick, Jeffrey D.: director, HON Industries Charitable Foundation

Ficke, Gregory C.: director, Cinergy Foundation

Fidel, Arthur: dist committee member, Morris Charitable Trust (Charles M.)

Fiedl, Arthur: dist committee member, Morris Charitable Trust (Charles M.)

Field, Arthur Norman: director, Brookdale Foundation

Field, Benjamin R., III: senior vice president, chief financial officer, treasurer, Bemis Company Inc.

Field, Marshall, IV: director, Field Foundation of Illinois

Fields, Candice: Distribution trustee, Schwab-Rosenhouse Memorial Foundation

Fields, Carmen: director, KeySpan Foundation

Fields, Curtland E.: executive director, trustee, Turrell Fund

Fields, Gregory F.: secretary, trustee, duPont Foundation (Chichester)

Fields, Kenneth H.: assistant treasurer, Klingenstein Fund, Inc. (Esther A. and Joseph)

Fields, Laura Kemper: mem disbursement comm, Oppenstein Brothers Foundation

Fields, Michael D.: president, director, Commerce Bancshares Foundation

Fields, Randolph: president, Farwell Foundation (Drusilla)

Fields, Sara A.: director, United Airlines Foundation

Fiery, Michael A.: mem, Teubert Charitable Trust (James H. and Alice)

Fiez, Terri: manager community relations, CUNA Mutual Group

Fife, Francis: vice president, trustee, Perry Foundation

Fife, Jesse, Jr.: trustee, Pittsburgh Child Guidance Foundation

Fifield, Helen D.: director, Memorial Foundation for the Blind

Fike, Marilyn: director of admin, Bullitt Foundation

Fikes, Amy L.: vice president, trustee, Fikes Foundation (Leland)

Fikes, Lee: president, treasurer, trustee, chairman, Fikes Foundation (Leland)

Finch, Edward Ridley, Jr.: general counsel, trustee, St. Giles Foundation

Finch, Thomas Austin, Jr.: manager, Finch Foundation (Thomas Austin)

Findlay, Marjorie M.: vice chairman, vice president, director, Claneil Foundation

Findley, Barry B.: trustee, Sturgis Charitable and Educational Trust (AR) (Roy and Christine)

Fineberg, Harvey V., MD: director, Hewlett Foundation (William and Flora)

Finelli, Michael A., Jr.: treasurer, Kemper Foundation (James S.)

Fineman, Stanley J.: partner, Wilkes, Artis, Hedrick & Lane; president, director, Wilkes, Artis, Hedrick & Lane Foundation

Fink, David: president, Auburn Foundry

Fink, Harold: secretary, Fink Foundation (NY)

Fink, Richard H.: director, Koch Foundation, Inc. (Fred C. and Mary R.)

Fink, William E.: chairman, Auburn Foundry; trustee, Auburn Foundry Foundation

Finkbeiner, James V.: president, trustee, chairman board, Wickes Foundation (Harvey Randall)

Finkelstein, Bernard: trustee, Altman Foundation

Finkelstein, Michael: assistant treasurer, Fisher Foundation

Finkelstein, Paul: director, Regis Foundation

Finkle, H. Michael: director, Vermilion Healthcare Foundation

Finlay, Louis M., Jr.: comm mem, Smith, Jr. Foundation (M. W.)

Finlayson, John L.: vice president finance & administration, Susquehanna-Pfaltzgraff Co.

Finley, Warren: trustee, Argyros Foundation

Finneran, Laurey: trustee, LEF Foundation

Finney, Graham Stanley: trustee, Seybert Institution for Poor Boys and Girls (Adam and Maria Sarah)

Finney, Jon: vice chairman, secretary, Van Buren Foundation

Finney, Pat: trustee, Young Foundation (Bill B.)

Finney, Redmond C.S.: director, France-Merrick Foundation

Fiola, Janet S.: director, Medtronic Foundation; senior vice president human resources, Medtronic Inc.

Fiorani, R. P.: vice president, director, Square D Foundation

Fiorella, Peter J., Jr.: trustee, Statler Foundation

Firestine, Larry: adv, Ritter Charitable Trust (George and Mary)

Firth, Edmee de Montmollin: executive director, Dreyfus Foundation (Jean and Louis)

Firth, Katherine V.: vice president, Dreyfus Foundation (Jean and Louis)

Firth, Nicholas L. D.: president, Dreyfus Foundation (Jean and Louis)

Fischbach, Nancy: president, Fischbach Foundation

Fischer, Billie A.: vice president, Wynn Foundation

Fischer, Diane: corporate secretary, Atran Foundation, Inc.

Fischer, Duane A.: president, chief executive officer, director, Scoular Co.

Fischer, F. Conrad: trustee, Fischer Foundation (Sonja and F. Conrad)

Fischer, Patrick: trustee, Donaldson Foundation

Fischer, Richard Lawrence: executive vice president, chairman counsel, Alcoa Inc.

Fischer, Sonja: trustee, Fischer Foundation (Sonja and F. Conrad)

Fish, Brian: director, Greenville Foundation

Fish, Eugene C., Esq.: vice president, director, Independence Foundation; trustee, Reidler Foundation

Fish, John: trustee, Stauffer Communications Foundation

Fish, Lawrence K.: trustee, Citizens Charitable Foundation; chairman, chief executive officer, president, Citizens Financial Group Inc.

Fish-Sadin, Susanne: director, secretary, Greenville Foundation

Fisher, David I.: chairman,

Fisher, Donald G.: chairman, director, Gap Foundation

Fisher, Doris F.: director, Gap Foundation

Fisher, Francis M., Jr.: trustee, Gulf Power Foundation

Fisher, Frederick E.: secretary, director, Doyle Foundation

Fisher, Grace Pond: trustee, Pond Foundation (C. Northrop Pond and Alethea Marder)

Fisher, Hinda N.: president, treasurer, Fisher Foundation

Fisher, John Wesley: chairman, president, Ball Brothers Foundation

Fisher, Kenneth: secretary, treasurer, director, Scurlock Foundation

Fisher, L. N.: secretary, Fluor Foundation

Fisher, William S.: vice president, director, member, Cannon Foundation, Inc. (The)

Fishman, Jay: chairman, chief executive officer, St. Paul Travelers Companies Inc.; director, chairman, St. Paul Travelers Foundation

Fishman, Joseph L.: vice president, director, treasurer, secretary, Moses Fund, Inc. (Henry and Lucy)

Fishman, Steven S.: chairman, president, chief executive officer, Pamida Inc.

Fisk, Robert D.: trustee, Seabury Foundation

Fiske, George F., Jr.: member advisory committee, Weezie Foundation

Fitzgerald, Dennis M.: vice president, secretary, director, Vernon Foundation (Miles Hodsdon)

Fitzgerald, J. T.: vice president, Price Foundation (Lucien B. and Katherine E.)

FitzGerald, John R.: director, Eastern Savings and Loan Foundation

Fitzgerald, Margaret Boles: chairperson, director, Luce Foundation (Henry)

Fitzgerald, Michele C.: director, Vernon Foundation (Miles Hodsdon)

FitzGibbon, David J.: president, chief executive officer, Bardes Corp.

Fitzpatrick, Jane P.: chairman, chief executive officer, treasurer, Country Curtains Inc.; treasurer, High Meadow Foundation

Fitzpatrick, John H.: president, High Meadow Foundation

Fitzpatrick, John J.: executive director, secretary, Gellert Foundation (Carl Gellert and Celia Berta)

Fitzpatrick, Nancy J.: director, High Meadow Foundation

Fitzsimmons, Hugh A., Jr.: trustee, Halsell Foundation (Ewing)

Fitzsimmons, Mark D.: associate director fellows program, MacArthur Foundation (John D. and Catherine T.)

FitzSimons, Dennis J.: director, McCormick Tribune Foundation (Robert R.)

FitzSimons, John S.: secretary, director, Dyson Foundation

Fiume, Orest J.: vice president finance, chief financial officer, Wiremold Co.

Fix, Duard: trustee, Kitzmiller/Bales Trust

Fizdale, Richard B.: chairman, chief executive officer, director, Burnett Co. (Leo)

Fizer, Don: secretary, director, Mathers Charitable Foundation (G. Harold and Leila Y.)

Flack, David: trustee, Priddy Foundation

Flad, Eleanor Beecher: chairman, Beecher Foundation (Florence Simon)

Flad, Erle L.: director, Beecher Foundation (Florence Simon)

Flad, Ward Beecher: director, Beecher Foundation (Florence Simon)

Flake, Floyd Harold: director, Fannie Mae Foundation

Flam, Jack: president, treasurer, Dedalus Foundation

Flanagan, Edward P.: secretary, Price Foundation (Lucien B. and Katherine E.)

Flanagan, Sheila: treasurer, Price Foundation (Lucien B. and Katherine E.)

Flanders, Grame L.: trustee, Acushnet Foundation

Flanigan, Peter Magnus: trustee, Olin Foundation (John M.)

Flaville, Victoria K.: vice president, Connelly Foundation

Flaws, James B.: executive vice president, chief financial officer, director, Corning Inc.; trustee, Corning Inc. Foundation

Fleischer, Henry: trustee, Carls Foundation

Fleischman, Barbara G.: trustee, Getty Trust (J. Paul)

Fleischmann-Colgan, Ruth H.: executive director, Wilson Foundation (Marie C. and Joseph C.)

Fleishhacker, David: president, Fleishhacker Foundation

Fleishhacker, Mortimer, III: treasurer, Fleishhacker Foundation

Fleishhacker, William: director, Fleishhacker Foundation

Fleishman, Ernest B.: first vice president, Robinson Fund (Maurice R.)

Fleishman, Susan N.: senior vice president, director, Universal Studios Foundation

Fleitman, Sandra K.: secretary, director, Star Tribune Foundation

Fleming, David D.: president, Mellinger Educational Foundation (Edward Arthur)

Fleming, Richard Harrison: executive vice president, chief financial officer, USG Corp.

Fleming, Samuel C.: director, Commonwealth Fund (The)

Fleming-McGrath, Lucy: trustee, Homeland Foundation (NY)

Fletcher, Allen W.: chairman, trustee, Fletcher Foundation; trustee, Stoddard Charitable Trust

Fletcher, Ernest P., Jr.: treasurer, trustee, Robinson-Broadhurst Foundation

Fletcher, Mary F.: trustee, Fletcher Foundation

Fletcher, Maureen T.: grants administrator, assistant secretary, Hayden Foundation (Charles)

Fletcher, Patricia A.: trustee, Fletcher Foundation

Fletcher, Warner S.: secretary, trustee, Alden Trust (George I.); secretary, treasurer, trustee, Fletcher Foundation; chairman, trustee, Stoddard Charitable Trust; director, Wyman-Gordon Foundation

Flippin, Doreen A.: vice president administrator, Davis Foundations (Arthur Vining)

Flood, Al: chairman, chief executive officer, CIBC World Markets

Flores-New, Fernando: trustee, vice president, Gerber Foundation

Florie, Walter M., Jr.: president, chief executive officer, Miller Foundation (Earl B. and Loraine H.)

Florino, Joanne V.: executive director, Park Foundation

Florio, Carl A.: president, chief executive officer, Hudson River Bancorp Inc.; director, Hudson River Bancorp Inc. Foundation

Florio, Thomas: chairman, president, chief executive officer, director, New Yorker Magazine (The)

Flournoy, Houston I.: vice president, Jones Foundation (Fletcher)

Flower, Allen E.: chief financial officer, vice president, COMSAT International

Flower, Walter C., III: secretary, German Protestant Orphan Asylum Association Foundation

Flowers, Robert: director, Washington Mutual Foundation

Flowers, Thomas J.: president, Hultquist Foundation

Flowers, Wilford: director, Wright Foundation (Lola)

Floyd, James M., Sr.: trustee, Martin Charitable Trust (Margaret Lee)

Floyd, Joseph H.: vice president, director, Midcontinent Media Foundation; president, director, Midcontinent Media Inc.

Fluor, John Robert, II: vice president corporate & public affairs, Fluor Corp.; president, trustee, Fluor Foundation

Flynn, Edward M.: trustee, Statler Foundation

Flynn, James T.: executive vice president, chief operating officer, Long Island Lighting Co.

Flynn, Joan B.: secretary, Barnes Foundation

Flynt, Wayne: director, Babcock Foundation (Mary Reynolds)

Foege, William H., MD: director, MacArthur Foundation (John D. and Catherine T.)

Foerster, Barbara: director, Aldridge Charitable and Educational Trust (Tom S. and Marye Kate)

Foley, Eileen D.: trustee, Foundation for Seacoast Health

Foley, Janet B.: director, Memorial Foundation for the Blind

Foley, William: vice chairman, Chicago Title and Trust Co. Foundation

Folger, Peter: director, McBean Family Foundation

Folta, Carl: president, Viacom Foundation

Fondren, Bentley B.: board of governors, Fondren Foundation

Fondren, Leland T.: board of governors, Fondren Foundation

Fondren, Robert E.: board of governors, Fondren Foundation

Fondren, Walter W., III: board of governors, Fondren Foundation

Fondren, Walter W., IV: board of governors, Fondren Foundation

Fonseca, Alicia: executive secretary, AT&T Foundation

Fonseca, Caio: trustee, Kaplan Fund (J. M.)

Fonseca, Elizabeth K.: trustee, Kaplan Fund (J. M.)

Fonseca, Isabel: trustee, Kaplan Fund (J. M.)

Fonseca, Quina: trustee, Kaplan Fund (J. M.)

Fonstad, Eric B.: secretary, Joy Global Foundation, Inc.

Fontaine, George R.: trustee, Lyndhurst Foundation

Fontaine, John C.: chairman, trustee, Kress Foundation (Samuel H.)

Fonteyne, Herman J.: president, chief executive officer, director, Ensign-Bickford Industries

Fooks, Thomas H., V: trustee, Fair Play Foundation

Foord, Deborah C.: member, Seherr-Thoss Foundation

Foot, Silas B., III: director, Red Wing Shoe Co. Foundation

Foran, James T.: general counsel, Public Service Electric & Gas Foundation

Forbes, Orcilia Zuniga: trustee, Meyer Memorial Trust

Ford, Alfred B.: trustee, Ford Motor Co. Fund

Ford, Allyn C.: director, Ford Family Foundation

Ford, Cynthia N.: trustee, McGregor Fund

Ford, Daniel H.: vice chairman, Ford Meter Box Foundation

Ford, David: executive director, Smith Family Foundation (Richard and Susan)

Ford, Edsel B., II: president, director, member, Ford II Fund (Edsel B.); president, trustee, mem, Ford II Fund (Henry); trustee, Skillman Foundation

Ford, Josephine Clay: president, trustee, mem, Ford Fund (Walter and Josephine)

Ford, Martha F.: trustee, Firestone, Jr. Foundation (Harvey); trustee, mem, Ford Fund (William and Martha)

Ford, Michael C., Esq.: senior executive vice president, MBNA American Bank, MBNA Corp.; trustee, The MBNA Foundation

Ford, Richard: secretary, Oleson Foundation

Ford, Richard Edmond: vice president, Daywood Foundation

Ford, Steven R.: treasurer, Ford Meter Box Foundation

Ford, Virginia: trustee, Birds Eye Foods Foundation

Ford, William Clay, Jr.: chairman, chief executive officer, Ford Motor Co.

Ford, William Clay, Sr.: president, trustee, mem, Ford Fund (William and Martha)

Fordyce, Michael J.: director, Grinnell Mutual Group Foundation; chairman, director, Grinnell Mutual Reinsurance Co.

Foreman, Robert B.: vice president, trustee, SPX Foundation

Forgason, Caroline A.: director, Kleberg Foundation (Robert J. Kleberg, Jr. and Helen C.)

Forlini, Rina: secretary, Macy, Jr. Foundation (Josiah)

Forman, Leonard P.: senior vice president, New York Times Co. Foundation

Formica, Mark J.: vice president, director, Citizens Financial Group Inc.

Forrester, Margaretta: co-trustee, Van Evera Foundation (Dewitt)

Fors, Richard D.: director, Oishei Foundation (The John R.)

Forster, Peter Hans: director, Dayton Power and Light Co. Foundation

Forsyte, Carol: assistant secretary, Motorola Foundation

Forsyth, John D.: chairman, Wellmark Foundation

Forsyth, Stephen C.: senior vice president finance & administration, chief financial officer, Hexcel Corp.; president, Hexcel Foundation

Forsythe, Carl S., III: trustee, de Coizart Perpetual Charitable Trust (Sarah K.)

Forsythe, John G.: vice president, Ecolab Foundation; vice president tax and public affairs, Ecolab Inc.

Fort, John F., III: secretary, trustee, Brown Foundation

Forte, D. A.: vice president, Johns Manville Fund

Forte, Linda D.: director, Comerica Charitable Foundation

Fortier, Albert M., Jr.: trustee, Thompson Trust (Thomas)

Fortson, Benjamin J.: trustee, Burnett Foundation (The)

Foshee, Douglas L.: president, chief executive officer, director, El Paso Corp.

Foskett, Nettie: admin, Prospect Hill Foundation

Foster, Barbara: trustee, Young Foundation (Bill B.)

Foster, D. S.: secretary, Eden Hall Foundation

Foster, Diana: trustee, Stranahan Foundation

Foster, F. Jay: acct, Hegeler II Foundation (Julius W.)

Foster, Howard K., MD: member, Staunton Farm Foundation

Foster, J. R.: trustee, Foster Charitable Trust

Foster, Jay L.: trustee, Foster Charitable Trust

Foster, Joe C., Jr.: secretary, director, Abrams Foundation (Talbert and Leota)

Foster, Karen C.: secretary, treasurer, Sierra Pacific Resources Charitable Foundation

Foster, Lee B.: trustee, Foster Charitable Trust

Foster, Louise Lewis: president, director, Flagler Foundation

Foster, Louise M.: chief financial officer, Penn Foundation (William)

Foster, Michael G., Jr.: director, Foster Foundation

Foster, Richard N.: director, Keck Foundation (W. M.)

Foster, Stephen A.: president, chief executive officer, Overbrook Foundation (The)

Foster, Tyler H.: director, East Cambridge Savings Charitable Foundation

Foti, Samuel J.: director, MONY Foundation; president, chief operating officer, director, MONY Group Inc.

Foulkrod, Fred A.: treasurer, Plankenhorn Foundation (Harry)

Fountain, W. Frank: trustee, Hudson-Webber Foundation

Fountain, W. Frank, Jr.: senior vice president government affairs, Daimler-Chrysler AG; president, DaimlerChrysler Corp. Fund

Fournier, Lucinda: trustee, Day Foundation (Willametta K.); director, Keck Foundation (W. M.)

Fowler, Adrian: director, Wright Foundation (Lola)

Fowler, Elizabeth P.: treasurer, Park Foundation

Fowler, Fred J.: president, chief operating officer, Duke Energy Corp.; trustee, Duke Energy Foundation

Fowler, Robert F., III: trustee, Arnold Fund

Fox, Bernard Michael: trustee, Hartford Courant Foundation

Fox, Jerry D.: secretary, treasurer, director, Journal-Gazette Foundation, Inc.

Fox, Joseph Carter: chairman, president, chief executive officer, Chesapeake Corp.; vice president, trustee, Chesapeake Corp. Foundation

Fox, Lewis M.: director, Piper Foundation (Minnie Stevens)

Foxley, Griffith W.: president, ABC Broadcasting Foundation, Inc.

Foy, Douglas J.: treasurer, assistant secretary, director, Ball Brothers Foundation; treasurer, director, Ball Foundation (George and Frances)

Fraedrich, David S.: director, Baird Brothers Co. Foundation

Fraenkel, Fabian I.: director, Kline Foundation (Charles and Figa)

Fraenkel, George Kessler: treasurer, Atran Foundation, Inc.

Fraher, Paula J.: vice chairman, secretary, Bank of America Foundation

Fraim, Martha B.: trustee, Berry Foundation (Loren M.)

Fraim, William L.: trustee, Berry Foundation (Loren M.)

France, Donald R.: trustee, Lee Scholarship Fund Trust (Whilma B.)

Franceschelli, Anthony D.: vice president, Emerson Foundation, Inc. (Fred L.)

Franchi, Daniel A.: assistant treasurer, Unocal Foundation

Francis, Cheryl A.: executive vice president, chief financial officer, Donnelley & Sons Co. (R.R.)

Francis, David V.: director, executive committee, Francis Families Foundation

Francis, Frank: trustee, Ghidotti Foundation

Francis, J. Scott: director, president, Francis Families Foundation

Francis, Mary Harris: director, Francis Families Foundation

Francis, R. Lewis: vice president, chief financial officer, Old Dominion Box Co.; secretary, treasurer, Old Dominion Box Co. Foundation

Franciscovich, Linda R.: vice president, Freeman Charitable Trust (Samuel)

Frank, Dennis D.: director, Frank Family Foundation (A. J.)

Frank, J. T.: director, Frank Family Foundation (A. J.)

Frank, John: vice president, trustee, Presto Foundation

Frank, John V.: president, trustee, Morgan Foundation (Burton D.)

Frank, Michael J.: committee partner, vice president, City National Bank & Trust Co.

Frank, Paul C.: president, director, Chamiza Foundation

Frank, Seth E.: trustee, Lurcy Charitable and Educational Trust (Georges)

Frank, Stanley J., Jr.: treasurer, director, Dater Foundation (Charles H.)

Frank, Stephen E.: president, chief operating officer, director, Edison International

Frankel, Joan Murtagh: assistant secretary, assistant treasurer, Hughes Foundation (Geoffrey C.)

Franklin, Alice: director, vice president, Norman Foundation

Franklin, Andrew D.: director, Norman Foundation

Franklin, Carl M.: chairman, Stauffer Charitable Trust (John)

Franklin, Marc Scott: senior vice president strategic planning, Pacific Life Insurance Co.

Franklin, Nick: senior vice president, PacifiCare Health System Foundation

Franklin, Robert N.: senior vice president public affairs, PacifiCare Health Systems

Franklin, William P.: trustee, Fasken Foundation

Franks, Martin: vice president, Viacom Foundation

Frantz, Susan C.: program officer, Sarkeys Foundation

Fraser, Russell: director, S.G. Foundation

Frazier, Mell Meredith: chairman, director, Meredith Corp. Foundation

Freas, Arthur K.: mgr, Freas Foundation

Freas, Margery H.: mgr, Freas Foundation

Frederick, Catherine H.: trustee, Harmon Foundation (Pearl M. and Julia J.)

Frederick, David C.: member, Staunton Farm Foundation

Frederick, Richard, III: member, Staunton Farm Foundation

Fredericksen, Jay A.: vice president, director, Rayonier Foundation

Fredrickson, Robert R.: director, Mosher Foundation (Samuel B. & Margaret C.)

Freed, Elizabeth Ann: president, director, Freed Foundation

Freeman, Annette Stoddard: director, Cudahy Fund (Patrick and Anna M.)

Freeman, Geoffrey T.: director, Claneil Foundation

Freeman, James D.: secretary, Schurz Communications Foundation

Freeman, Nancy S.: secretary, Fisher Foundation

Freeman, Robert: director, Virginia Environmental Endowment

Frehse, Robert M., Jr.: executive director, Hearst Foundation, Inc. (The); vice president, executive director, Hearst Foundation (William Randolph)

Freimuth, Steve: director, Washington Mutual Foundation; senior vice president, corporate services, Washington Mutual Inc.

Frelinghuysen, George L. K.: assistant treasurer, director, Pforzheimer Foundation, Inc. (The Carl and Lily)

Frelinghuysen, Peter: vice president, trustee, Achelis Foundation

French, Christopher E.: president, director, Shenandoah Telecommunications Co.; president, ShenTel Foundation

French, Daniel P.: chairman, president, chief executive officer, director, French Oil Mill Machinery Co.

French, Fuller: treasurer, Fuller Foundation (DE)

French, Janel: treasurer, Graco Foundation

French, Jerry: director, Shelter Insurance Foundation

French, Warren B., Jr.: chairman, director, Shenandoah Telecommunications Co.

Frenzel, William: trustee, United States-Japan Foundation

Frerichs, Ernest S.: president, Dorot Foundation

Frese, Ines: chairman, Frese Foundation (Arnold D.)

Freund, Frederick W.: executive director, trustee, Gilmore Foundation (Irving S.)

Frey, Dorothy L.: treasurer, Wynn Foundation

Frey, James: director, Pacifi-Care Health System Foundation

Friauf, Cynthia K.: vice president finance, treasurer, assistant secretary, Bradley Foundation (Lynde and Harry)

Fribourg, Paul J.: vice president, ContiGroup Companies Foundation; chairman, president, chief executive officer, ContiGroup Companies Inc.

Frick, David R.: president, director, Anthem Foundation, Inc.

Fricke, Howard R.: chairman, Security Benefit Life Insurance Co.; trustee, Security Benefit Life Insurance Co. Charitable Trust

Fricks, William Peavy: chairman, chief executive officer, Norfolk Shipbuilding & Drydock Corp.

Friedberg, Bruce: director, Fireman's Fund Foundation

Friedlaender, Helmut N.: director, AMETEK Foundation

Friedland, Laurie Levitt: secretary, director, Winston Foundation (Norman and Rosita)

Friedlander, Linda M.: vice president, Key Foundation

Friedlander, W. John: director, Lake Placid Education Foundation

Friedman, Alan D.: co-trustee, Lard Trust (Mary Potishman)

Friedman, David A.: secretary, Friedman Family Foundation

Friedman, Eleanor: vice president, Friedman Family Foundation

Friedman, Harold Edward: secretary, Fox Charitable Trust (Emma R.)

Friedman, Marjorie N.: director, Harriman Foundation (Mary W.)

Friedman, Nancy: trustee, Fox Charitable Trust (Emma R.)

Friedman, Phyllis C.: trustee, Gordon Charitable Trust (Peggy and Yale)

Friedman, Phyllis K.: president, Friedman Family Foundation

Friedman, Robert E.: treasurer, Friedman Family Foundation; director, Rosenberg Foundation

Friedman, Robert S.: secretary, treasurer, Rubinstein Foundation (Helena)

Friedman, Saul: co-trustee, Schermer Charitable Trust (Frances)

Friedman, Walker C.: co-trustee, Lard Trust (Mary Potishman)

Friedrich, Richard A., Sr.: vice president, Eastern Savings and Loan Foundation

Friend, Eugene L.: vice chairman, director, Koret Foundation

Friend, Robert: director, Osher Foundation (Bernard)

Friess, Polly J.: trustee, Connemara Fund

Frink, Jeannine: trustee, Barden Foundation, Inc.

Frist, Thomas Fearn, Jr.: chairman, director, Frist Foundation

Fritch, Sandra: adv, Cayuga Foundation

Fritsche, E. Alan: executive director, Hamman Foundation (George and Mary Josephine)

Fritze, Steven L.: vice president, controller, Ecolab Inc.

Frizen, Edwin L., Jr.: chairman, trustee, Crowell Trust (Henry P. and Susan C.); director, Tyndale House Foundation

Froelich, Georgia A.: treasurer, Hershey Foundation

Frohring, Paul Robert: president, trustee, Frohring Foundation (Paul and Maxine)

Fromkes, Otto: director, Fromkes Foundation (Saul)

Fronterhouse, Gerald W.: chairman, director, Hoblitzelle Foundation

Frost, Robert D.: director, Littauer Foundation (Lucius N.)

Frost, William Lee: president, treasurer, director, Littauer Foundation (Lucius N.)

Frueauff, Anna Kay: trustee, Frueauff Foundation (Charles A.)

Frueauff, David A.: president, chief executive officer, trustee, Frueauff Foundation (Charles A.)

Frueauff, Sue M.: chief administrative officer, trustee, Frueauff Foundation (Charles A.)

Fruehauf, Harvey C., Jr.: president, Fruehauf Foundation; vice president, trustee, Wiegand Foundation (E. L.)

Fry, Lloyd A., III: vice chairman, director, Fry Foundation (Lloyd A.)

Fry, Ray M.: trustee, Alexander Edwards Trust (Margaret)

Frye, Clayton Wesley, Jr.: trustee, LSR Fund

Frymoyer, John W., MD: director, Macy, Jr. Foundation (Josiah)

Fuemmeler, Carl D.: vice president, director, Green Foundation (Allen P. and Josephine B.)

Fuhrman, Susan H.: trustee, Fund for New Jersey

Fujiki, Yasuo: chairman, chief executive officer, director, Subaru of America Inc.

Fukukawa, Shinji: trustee, United States-Japan Foundation

Fuller, Charles A., Jr.: fdn mgr, Slusher Charitable Foundation (Roy W.)

Fuller, Geraldine: president, Fuller Foundation (DE)

Fuller, Gillian: vice president, Fuller Foundation (DE)

Fuller, Jack W.: director, McCormick Tribune Foundation (Robert R.)

Fuller, Jan: trustee, Fuller Foundation (George F. and Sybil H.)

Fuller, Joyce I.: assistant treasurer, trustee, Fuller Foundation (George F. and Sybil H.)

Fuller, Kathryn Scott: chairman, trustee, Ford Foundation

Fuller, Lincoln E.: trustee, Fuller Foundation (George F. and Sybil H.)

Fuller, Mark W.: chairman, treasurer, trustee, Fuller Foundation (George F. and Sybil H.)

Fuller, Peter, Jr.: trustee, Fuller Foundation (MA)

Fuller, Peter D., Sr.: trustee, Fuller Foundation (MA)

Fuller, Russell E.: chairman, trustee, Fuller Foundation (George F. and Sybil H.)

Fullinwider, Jerome M.: trustee, Abell-Hanger Foundation

Fullwood, Emerson U.: vice president, Xerox Corp.; trustee, Xerox Foundation

Fulstone, Georgia: vice president, director, Skaggs Foundation (L. J. Skaggs and Mary C.)

Fulton, Mike: director, Comerica Charitable Foundation

Fulton, Richard: chief financial officer, Iowa Savings Bank

Fulton, V. Neil: assistant secretary, Gilmore Foundation (William G.)

Funaro, Patricia P.: program manager, U.S. Steel Foundation

Funderburk, Charles B.: trustee, Blount Educational and Charitable Foundation (Mildred Weedon)

Funnell, James D., Jr.: secretary, Muhlethaler Foundation, Inc. (Jane T.)

Fuqua, Doylene: board, McKinney Charitable Trust (Carl and Alleen)

Furichi, Takeshi: president, chief executive officer, NLI International Inc.

Furlong, R. Michael: director, Coleman Foundation (IL)

Furman, Jeffrey: treasurer, Ben & Jerry's Foundation

Furmansky, Stewart: director, Kline Foundation (Charles and Figa)

Furr, Richard: board membership, CCB Foundation

Furth, John L.: treasurer, director, Foundation for Child Development

Fuson, Scott: trustee, Dow Corning Foundation

Fusscas, Amanda C.: secretary, Krieble Foundation (Vernon K.)

Fusscas, Christopher P.: treasurer, Krieble Foundation (Vernon K.)

Fusscas, Frederick B.: director, Krieble Foundation (Vernon K.)

Futamura, Hiroshi: director, Kikkoman Foundation

Futo, Kyle Monfort: vice president, Monfort Family Foundation

Fynboe, Carl T.: board member, Stewardship Foundation

G

Gabelli, Mario Joseph: trustee, Wiegand Foundation (E. L.)

Gaberman, Barry D.: senior vice president, Ford Foundation

Gabier, Russell L.: secretary, trustee, Gilmore Foundation (Irving S.)

Gable, Robert L.: chairman, director, Unitrode Corp.

Gabriel, Nicholas M.: treasurer, director financial services, Ford Foundation

Gackle, George D.: treasurer, director, Rahr Foundation

Gadosik, Barbara: director corporate contributions, Sherwin-Williams Foundation

Gaffney, Joseph M.: director, Nesholm Family Foundation

Gage, Barbara C.: director, Carlson Companies Inc.; president, Carlson Family Foundation (Curtis L.)

Gage, J. R.: vice president, director, Winn-Dixie Stores Foundation

Gage, Jack D.: director, Rahr Foundation

Gage, Kelly K.: trustee, Carlson Family Foundation (Curtis L.)

Gage, Richard C.: trustee, Carlson Family Foundation (Curtis L.)

Gage, Scott C.: trustee, Carlson Family Foundation (Curtis L.)

Gagnier, Charles E.: chairman, AMCORE Financial Inc.

Gagnon, Pierre: chief operating officer, president, Mitsubishi Motor Sales of America Inc.

Gahagan, Alexis duPont: trustee, duPont Foundation (Chichester)

Gahagan, Katharine G.: president, trustee, duPont Foundation (Chichester)

Gailey, John Robert, III: vice president, general counsel, secretary, West Pharmaceutical Services Inc.

Gaines, Sharon: trust, Morgan Charitable Residual Trust (W. and E.)

Gaines, Thomas W., Jr.: adv comm, Duncan Trust (Louise Head)

Gaines, Tyler B.: trustee, Hitchcock Foundation (Gilbert M. and Martha H.)

Gainey, W. W., Jr.: treasurer, Dover Foundation

Gaither, James C.: director, Hewlett Foundation (William and Flora)

Gajardo, Joel: vice president, director, Woods Charitable Fund

Galante, Edward G.: senior vice president, ExxonMobil Corp.

Galbraith, Margaret R.: director, Scott Foundation (Virginia Steele)

Galik, Jeffrey: assistant treasurer, Bristol-Myers Squibb Foundation Inc.

Galinson, Murray L.: director, Weingart Foundation

Gallagher, Daniel J.: member, Knott Foundation (Marion I. and Henry J.)

Gallagher, Donald J.: vice president, treasurer, trustee, Cleveland-Cliffs Foundation (The); vice president, sales, Cleveland-Cliffs Inc.

Gallagher, Edward: director, Norcross Wildlife Foundation

Gallagher, James J.: director, Haigh-Scatena Foundation

Gallagher, John Peter: trustee, Hillsdale Fund

Gallagher, Lindsay R.: member, Knott Foundation (Marion I. and Henry J.)

Gallagher, Margaret W.: trustee, Hillsdale Fund

Gallagher, Michael L.: vice chairman, trustee, Kiewit Foundation (Peter)

Gallagher, Patrick S.: executive director, Paley Foundation, Inc. (William S.)

Gallagher, Richard S.: director, Badger Meter Foundation

Gallo, Ernest: president, Gallo Foundation (Ernest)

Gallo, Joseph E.: vice president, Gallo Foundation (Ernest)

Gallo, Martha J.: trustee, J.P. Morgan Chase Foundation

Gallo, Mary I.: vice president, Gallo Foundation (Ernest)

Galloway, T. Eric: director, van Ameringen Foundation, Inc.

Gallucci-David, Sheila: trustee, Subaru of America Foundation, Inc.

Gallwas, Gerald E.: director, Beckman Foundation (Arnold and Mabel)

Galvin, Mary G.: secretary, treasurer, Galvin Foundation (Robert)

Galvin, Robert William: president, Galvin Foundation (Robert)

Gambet, Daniel George: trustee, Trexler Trust (Harry C.)

Gamble, George F.: vice president, Gamble Foundation

Gamble, Launce E.: president, Gamble Foundation

Gamble, Mark D.: vice president, treasurer, Gamble Foundation

Gamble Price, Aimee: vice president, secretary, Gamble Foundation

Gammon, Donald A.: secretary, director, Thompson Co. Fund (J. Walter)

Gamper, Albert R., Jr.: president, chief executive officer, director, CIT Group Foundation; president, chief executive officer, chairman, CIT Group Inc.

Gamron, W. Anthony: vice president, Kimberly-Clark Corp.

Gancer, Donald Charles: president, Boothroyd Foundation (Charles H. and Bertha L.)

Ganci, Paul J.: president, chief operating officer, Central Hudson Gas & Electric Corp.

Gann, P.: vice president, Square D Foundation

Gannett, William B.: chairman, director, Hopedale Foundation

Gannon, William S.: trustee, Turrell Fund

Gansner, Katherine Gosin: director, Menasha Corp. Foundation

Ganzi, Victor F.: vice president, secretary, director, Hearst Foundation (William Randolph)

Garavaglia, Jim: director, Comerica Charitable Foundation

Garber, John Paul: head US operations, WestLB New York Branch

Garber, Karlene Beal: trustee, Beal Foundation

Garcia, Juliet V.: trustee, Ford Foundation

Garcia, Juliet Villarreal: director, Public Welfare Foundation

Garcia, Pedro: trustee, Chiles Foundation

Garcia, Sharon S.: assistant secretary, Universal Studios Foundation

Gardner, Barbara Vanderkolk: president, chief executive officer, Rippel Foundation (Fannie E.)

Gardner, Dorsey: trustee, Evans Foundation (Edward P.)

Gardner, Frank: director, Washington Foundation (Dennis R. and Phyllis)

Gardner, Joan L.: trustee, Bigelow Foundation (F. R.)

Gardner, Patricia: trustee, Besser Foundation

Gardner, Roger L.: president, director, Jones Foundation (Daisy Marquis)

Gareau, Joseph H.: executive vice president, chief investment officer, Hartford Financial Services Group Inc.

Garfinkle, Gillian: director, Garfinkle-Minard Foundation, Inc.

Garfinkle, Nicholas: director, Garfinkle-Minard Foundation, Inc.

Garfinkle, Norton: chairman, director, Garfinkle-Minard Foundation, Inc.

Gargano, Marilyn: assistant treasurer, American Standard Foundation

Garland, T. J.: secretary, Shell Oil Co. Foundation

Garofalo, D. L.: director, Bayport Foundation of Andersen Corporation

Garrett, Joseph H., Jr.: vice president government & international operations, Rockwell Automation Inc.

Garrett, Judith M.: president, executive director, Belo Foundation

Garrett, Ken: president, director, FMC Foundation

Garrett, Robert: trustee, Abell Foundation; director, Dodge Foundation (Cleveland H.)

Garrett, Wendy: trustee, Owsley Foundation (Alvin and Lucy)

Garrison, Milton: director, Lebanon Mutual Foundation

Garrity, Carlene E.: secretary, Mellon Financial Corp. Foundation

Garst, Mary: director, Audubon State Bank Charitable Foundation

Gartland, John J., Jr.: president, director, McCann Foundation

Gartland, Michael G.: assistant secretary, director, McCann Foundation

Gartner, Peggy: admin, Blumenthal Foundation

Garton, Deirdre Wilson: secretary, Wilson Foundation (Marie C. and Joseph C.)

Garvey, Richard F.: secretary, Garvey Texas Foundation

Garvey, Shirley F.: president, Garvey Texas Foundation

Garwood, William L., Jr.: vice president, Clayton Fund; vice president, director, ECG Foundation

Garza-Roberts, Cyndy: president, Reliant Resources Foundation

Garza-Vizcaino, Raffy: director, Wright Foundation (Lola)

Gassaway, James M.: trustee, Grundy Foundation

Gassman, Robert S.: treasurer, director, Guttman Foundation (Stella and Charles)

Gast, Aaron E.: trustee, Newcombe Foundation (Charlotte W.)

Gaston, Karen H.: trustee, Equifax Foundation; chief executive officer, Equifax Inc.

Gaston, Patrick: president, Verizon Foundation

Gates, Carol Ware: vice president, treasurer, Oxford Foundation

Gates, Charles Cassius, Jr.: trustee emeritus, Gates Family Foundation

Gates, Henry Louis, Jr.: director, Revson Foundation (Charles H.)

Gates, Melinda French: co-founder, Gates Foundation (Bill and Melinda)

Gates, Signe S.: director, Barnes Group Foundation Inc.

Gates, Valerie: vice president, trustee, Gates Family Foundation

Gates, William H., Sr.: co-chairman, chief executive officer, Gates Foundation (Bill and Melinda)

Gates, William Henry, III: co-founder, Gates Foundation (Bill and Melinda)

Gaudiani, Claire L.: director, Luce Foundation (Henry)

Gault, Stanley Carleton: trustee, Morgan Foundation (Burton D.)

Gaus, William Thomas: treasurer, Miller Foundation (Steve J.)

Gavin, Austin F.: director, Doheny Foundation Trust (Carrie Estelle)

Gavin, Robert Michael, Jr.: director, Research Corp.

Gay, Frank William: trustee, Hughes Medical Institute (Howard)

Gayle, Gibson, Jr.: president, trustee, Anderson Foundation (M. D.)

Gayle, Helene, MPH: director HIV, TB and reprod health program, Gates Foundation (Bill and Melinda)

Gayle, Karla: vice president, trust officer, Kaul Foundation Trust (Hugh)

Gaynor, George N.: vice president, Norris Foundation (Dellora A. and Lester J.)

Gebel, Riva: director, PacifiCare Health System Foundation

Gebert, J. J.: vice president, treasurer, trustee, Johns Manville Fund

Gebhard, Elizabeth R.: director, Demos Foundation (N.)

Geddes, Robert D.: secretary, Wessinger Foundation

Gehrke, Patrice: trustee, Gilmore Foundation (William G.)

Geifman, Geraldine: secretary, director, Geifman Family Foundation

Geifman, Stephen L.: president, Geifman Family Foundation

Geifman, Terri: assistant treasurer, director, Geifman Family Foundation

Geillser, Thomas: director, Fireman's Fund Foundation

Geisel, Audrey S.: president, assistant secretary, Dr. Seuss Foundation

Geisel, Jean F.: secretary, Bausch & Lomb Foundation, Inc.

Geissinger, Frederick Wallace: president, vice chairman, chief executive officer, American General Finance; president, American General Finance Foundation

Geist, Carol Berg: trustee, Bingham Second Betterment Fund (William)

Geist, D. L.: assistant secretary, Air Products Foundation

Geldin, Sherri: director, Warhol Foundation for the Visual Arts (The Andy)

Gell, Carl L.: director, Loughran Foundation (Mary and Daniel)

Gellert, Michael E.: director, Humana Foundation

Gelston, Steven: secretary, treasurer, J.P. Morgan Chase Foundation

Genter, Beth H.: vice president, trustee, Scaife Family Foundation

Gentile, James M.: president, Research Corp.

Gentle, William J.: trustee, treasurer, Retirement Research Foundation

Gentry, Nolden: director, Mid-Iowa Health Foundation

Geogheghan, Jack: secretary, Becher Foundation (Hildegarde D.)

George, A. Fred: trustee, Campbell Soup Foundation

George, Donald A.: clerk, trustee, Ash Charitable Corp.

George, Helen A.: secretary, Cremer Foundation

George, Henrietta A.: director, Kleberg Foundation (Robert J. Kleberg, Jr. and Helen C.)

George, Pamela L.: secretary, Hobby Family Foundation

Gerace, Frank: trustee, Gerstacker Foundation (Rollin M.)

Geramian, Mohammad: president, Alavi Foundation

Gerard, Jamie K.: secretary, Newman's Own Foundation

Gerard, Karen N.: director, Foundation for Child Development

Gerber, Harry: director, First Source Foundation

Gerber, Margaret L.: trustee, Lyndhurst Foundation

Gerken, Walter Bland: vice president, director, chairman audit comm, Keck Foundation (W. M.)

Geronime, Karen: trustee, Donaldson Foundation

Gerry, Elbridge Thomas, Jr.: president, director, Harriman Foundation (Gladys and Roland)

Gerry, Martha Farish: president, trustee, Farish Fund (William Stamps)

Gerst, Christopher: assistant corporate secretary, St. Paul Travelers Foundation

Gerstle, Mark R.: vice president, cummins business services, Cummins Inc.

Gerstley, Carol: trustee, Cassett Foundation (Louis N.)

Gerstung, Sandra L.: president, director, Hecht-Levi Foundation

Gerth, Robert L.: adv, Archibald Charitable Foundation (Norman)

Geschke, Charles Matthew: co-chairman, Adobe Systems; president, Geschke Foundation (Charles M. and Nancy A.)

Geschke, Kathleen A.: director, Geschke Foundation (Charles M. and Nancy A.)

Geschke, Nancy A.: secretary, treasurer, Geschke Foundation (Charles M. and Nancy A.)

Getman, Michael F.: treasurer, secretary, Dewar Foundation

Co. (Eli); director, Lilly Foundation (Eli)

Golden, Gail: secretary, ACF Foundation

Golden, Michael: senior vice president, director, New York Times Co. Foundation

Golden, Robert C.: trustee, Prudential Foundation; executive vice president, Prudential Insurance Company of America

Golden, Terence C.: director, Cafritz Foundation (Morris and Gwendolyn)

Golden-Icahn, Gail: vice president, Icahn Foundation (Carl C.)

Goldman, Douglas E.: director, vice president, Goldman Fund (Richard and Rhoda)

Goldman, John D.: trustee, Haas Fund (Walter and Elise)

Goldman, Peter: vice president, Kongsgaard-Goldman Foundation

Goldman, Richard Nathaniel: president, director, member executive committee, Goldman Fund (Richard and Rhoda)

Goldschmid, Harvey J.: director, Greenwall Foundation

Goldseker, Ana: trustee, Goldseker Foundation of Maryland (Morris)

Goldseker, Deby: trustee, Goldseker Foundation of Maryland (Morris)

Goldseker, Sharna: trustee, Goldseker Foundation of Maryland (Morris)

Goldseker, Sheldon: chairman, trustee, Goldseker Foundation of Maryland (Morris)

Goldseker, Simon: vice chairman, trustee, Goldseker Foundation of Maryland (Morris)

Goldsmith, Stephen: director, Fannie Mae Foundation

Goldstein, Bruce D.: secretary, Haigh-Scatena Foundation

Goldstein, Joseph L., MD: trustee, Hughes Medical Institute (Howard)

Goldstein, Michael L.: director, Goldman Foundation (Herman)

Goldstein, Robert H.: president, trustee, Ash Charitable Corp.

Goldstein, Steve: director, Bush Foundation

Goldstein, Steven: chief financial officer, RBC Centura

Golieb, Abner J.: president, director, mem, Katzenberger Foundation

Gollihue, Alan E.: executive director, Portsmouth General Hospital Foundation

Golston, Allan C., CPA: chief financial officer, chief administrative officer, Gates Foundation (Bill and Melinda)

Golub, David: trustee, Golub Foundation

Golub, Lewis: chairman, chief executive officer, director, Golub Corp.

Gomer, Adelaide P.: vice president, secretary, Park Foundation

Gomer, Alicia P.: jr. advisory, Park Foundation

Gomez, Ernesto: tax officer, Burlington Resources Foundation

Gonthier, Laurie G.: director, New Milford Savings Bank Foundation

Gonthier, Robert A., Jr.: director, Provident Community Foundation

Gonzalez, Bethaida C.: vice president, trustee, Gifford Charitable Corp. (Rosamond)

Gonzalez, Jose: program officer health, Bush Foundation

Gonzalez, Juan G.: director, Wright Foundation (Lola)

Gonzelez, Ramon: secretary, treasurer, PNM Foundation

Gonzelez, Rosa: trustee, Children's Foundation of Erie County

Good, Michael Willis: director, Willis Family Foundation

Good, Robert Alan, MD: trustee, Dana Charitable Trust (Eleanor Naylor)

Goodale, Irene E.: trustee, Peterloon Foundation

Gooding, John S.: chairman, director, G/S/M Industrial Inc.; president, Gooding Group Foundation

Goodman, Barbara F.: trustee, Goodman Family Foundation

Goodman, Carroll R.: assistant secretary, trustee, Sterling-Turner Foundation

Goodman, Charles: vice president, director, Crown Memorial (Arie and Ida)

Goodman, Harold S.: trustee, Messing Family Charitable Foundation

Goodman, Helen G.: senior vice president, Hartford Financial Services Group Inc.

Goodman, Roy Matz: trustee, Goodman Family Foundation

Goodmanson, Richard R.: executive vice president, chief operating officer, du Pont de Nemours & Co. (E.I.)

Goodnow, Edward B.: trustee, Goodnow Fund

Goodrich, Bernard: executive director, McGowan Charitable Fund (William G.)

Goodrich, Gillian C.: chairman, Comer Foundation (AL)

Goodsell, Jill: admin, trustee, Foster Foundation

Goodspeed, Lisa: trustee, Huber Foundation

Goodstein, Les: president, Daily News L.P.

Goodstein, Lucy M.: vice president, Goodstein Foundation

Goodwillie Nelson, Mary: director, Wege Foundation

Goodwin, Catherine R.: trustee, Foundation for Seacoast Health

Goodwin, David P.: trustee, Cogswell Benevolent Trust

Goodwin, Neva R.: vice chairman, trustee, Rockefeller Brothers Fund, Inc.

Goodwin, Richard L.: vice chairman, Gardiner Savings Institution Charitable Foundation

Goodwin, William Maxwell: vice president commun devel, Lilly Endowment

Gordan, Mary Elizabeth: director, IMMI Word and Deed Foundation

Gordon, Ellen Rubin: president, director, Rubin Family Fund (Cele H. and William B.)

Gordon, H. Stephen: vice president, Universal Studios Foundation

Gordon, Hunter R.: advisory trustee, McLean Contributionship

Gordon, Jonathan R.: director, Mailman Family Foundation (A. L.)

Gordon, Joseph K.: trustee, McLean Contributionship

Gordon, Lois: director, Fleishhacker Foundation

Gordon, Melvin Jay: vice president, director, Rubin Family Fund (Cele H. and William B.)

Gordon, Raymond J.: trustee, Gordon Charitable Trust (Peggy and Yale)

Gordon, Susan: assistant treasurer, Icahn Foundation (Carl C.)

Gordon, Thomas Christian, Jr.: assistant secretary, trustee, Gray Foundation (Garland and Agnes Taylor)

Gore, Ruth T.: vice chairman, Chapin Foundation of Myrtle Beach, South Carolina

Gorelick, Jamie Shona: director, MacArthur Foundation (John D. and Catherine T.)

Gorham, John: chairman distribution comm, mem investigating comm, Champlin Foundation

Gorham, Robert L.: managing partner, Wilkes, Artis, Hedrick & Lane

Goriup, Mary A.: mgr, Hedco Foundation

Gorman, Mary V.: chief financial officer, Newhall Foundation (Henry Mayo)

Gorman, Michael R.: executive director, Irwin Charity Foundation (William G.)

Gormley, Patrick A.: director, Bacon Family Foundation

Gorski, Cheryl: assistant treasurer, Earhart Foundation

Gorsuch, Joan: secretary, Regenstein Foundation

Gosney, Timothy J.: trustee, Stillwell Charitable Trust (Glen and Dorothy)

Goss, Carol: president, chief executive officer, Skillman Foundation

Gottlieb, Art: secretary, Gumbiner Foundation (Josephine)

Gottschalk, Thomas A.: director, General Motors Foundation

Gottwald, Thomas E.: president, chief executive officer, Ethyl Corp.

Gougeon, Meade A.: trustee, Kantzler Foundation

Gould, Brian: controller, treasurer, Interkal Inc.

Gould, Jay E.: director, Provident Community Foundation

Gourneau, Dwight: director, Bush Foundation

Gow, Ian F.: trustee, Crummer Foundation (Roy E.)

Gozon, Richard C.: executive vice president pulp paper & packaging, Weyerhaeuser Co.; trustee, Weyerhaeuser Co. Foundation

Gozonsky, Edwin S.: trustee, Adelson Trust (Diana S.)

Graber, Samuel W.: gov, Mayor Foundation (Oliver Dewey)

Graber, Thomas H., II: trustee, Ketrow Foundation

Grabois, Neil R.: vice president & director strategic planning, Carnegie Corp. of New York

Graceffa, Al C.: member, Gardiner Savings Institution Charitable Foundation

Graddick-Weir, Mirian: trustee, AT&T Foundation

Grado, John, Jr.: trustee, Wallace Foundation (George R.)

Grady, Thomas M.: member, director, Cannon Foundation, Inc. (The)

Graf, Don: executive director, secretary, CH Foundation

Grafer, W. D.: vice president finance, National Standard Co.; treasurer, National Standard Foundation

Graff, David: chief financial officer, controller, Quincy Newspapers

Graham, Barbara L.: assistant secretary, Burns & McDonnell Foundation

Graham, Colleen: secretary, Rich Foundation Inc.

Graham, Donald C.: trustee, Graham Foundation

Graham, Donald Edward: trustee, Graham Fund (Philip L.)

Graham, Ingrid A.: trustee, Graham Foundation

Graham, Julie: director, Overbrook Foundation (The)

Graham, Kathryn C.: director, Overbrook Foundation (The)

Graham, Kathryn G.: director, Overbrook Foundation (The)

Graham, Marilyn F.: assistant vice president, assistant secretary, Daimler-Chrysler Corp. Fund

Graham, Mary: director, MacArthur Foundation (John D. and Catherine T.)

Graham, Patricia Albjerg: director, Macy, Jr. Foundation (Josiah)

Graham, Patricia Albjerg, PhD: vice president, Johnson Foundation

Graham, Robert C., Jr.: chairman, director, Overbrook Foundation (The)

Graham, Robert M.: treasurer, Eccles Foundation (George S. and Dolores Dore)

Graham, Stanley E.: trustee, Hill Crest Foundation

Grainger, Joseph C.: executive director, Harden Foundation

Gralnek, Ann D.: senior advisor, Jewett Foundation (George Frederick)

Granadillo, Pedro P.: senior vice president, Lilly & Co. (Eli); director, Lilly Foundation (Eli)

Grandon, Carleen M.: director, Hall-Perrine Foundation

Graner, James: vice president, controller, Graco Inc.

Grangaard, Paul: director, U.S. Bancorp Piper Jaffray Foundation

Grange, David L.: secretary, chief operating officer, McCormick Tribune Foundation (Robert R.)

Grano, Joseph J., Jr.: chairman, chief executive officer, UBS PaineWebber Inc.

Grant, David: executive director, Dodge Foundation (Geraldine R.)

Grant, Hugh: president, chief executive officer, Monsanto Co.

Grant, Maria O.: president, director, Scott Foundation (Virginia Steele)

Grant, R. Gene: director, Cheney Foundation (Ben B.)

Grant, Richard A.: vice president, director, Connell Foundation (Michael J.)

Grasley, Michael Howard: senior vice president, Shell Oil Co.

Grasmere, Robert H.: president, trustee, Turrell Fund

Grassilli, Robert J.: vice president, director, Gellert Foundation (Carl Gellert and Celia Berta)

Graunke, James W.: secretary, director, Patron Saints Foundation

Graven, Dennis L.: chief financial officer, vice president finance, Brillion Iron Works

Graves, Gregory M.: chairman, president, director, Burns & McDonnell Foundation

Graves, Herbert C.: chairman, Standard Steel

Graves, Howard: director, Guggenheim Foundation (Harry Frank)

Graves, Milton T.: vice president, director, Cockrell Foundation

Gravett, Benjamin C.: trustee, Washington Forrest Foundation

Gray, Bruce B.: assistant treasurer, trustee, Gray Foundation (Garland and Agnes Taylor)

Gray, Charles Agustus: director, Cabot Corp. Foundation

Gray, Charles M.: president, Demos Foundation (N.)

Gray, Clyde: trustee, Scripps Howard Foundation

Gray, Constance F.: trustee, Duke Endowment

Gray, Dan L.: secretary, treasurer, director, member, Cannon Foundation, Inc. (The)

Gray, Elizabeth B.: trustee, Berry Foundation (Loren M.)

Gray, Elmon T.: president, treasurer, trustee, Gray Foundation (Garland and Agnes Taylor)

Gray, Garland, II: assistant secretary, trustee, Gray Foundation (Garland and Agnes Taylor)

Gray, Harry Barkus: director, Beckman Foundation (Arnold and Mabel)

Gray, James E.: president, chief operating officer, Macy's East Inc.

Gray, John D.: director, Rice Foundation

Gray, Lloyd H., Jr.: director, Trippe Trust (William D.)

Graybill, Charles S., MD: chairman, trustee, McMahon Foundation

Grealis, William J.: vice president, Cinergy Corp.

Grebe, Michael W.: president, chief executive officer, director, Bradley Foundation (Lynde and Harry)

Green, Bennie: treasurer, trustee, Rockwell Fund, Inc.

Green, Bill: trustee, Taconic Foundation

Green, D. H.: vice president, Air Products Foundation

Green, Don C.: secretary, treasurer, Mid-Iowa Health Foundation

Green, Edward S.: president, trustee, Gifford Charitable Corp. (Rosamond)

Green, Ernestine R.: chairwoman, trustee, Statler Foundation

Green, Lois B.: co-trustee, Hoche-Scofield Foundation

Green, Margaret H: trustee, chairman, BellSouth Foundation

Green, Michael: vice president, director, Loewy Family Foundation

Green, Richard C.: director, Hall Family Foundation (The)

Green, Robert L.: president, Green Foundation (Robert and Susan)

Green, Stephen W.: trustee, Unocal Foundation

Greenawalt, W. Eileen: secretary, trustee, Bonfils-Stanton Foundation

Greenbaum, Maurice Coleman: secretary, director, Mandeville Foundation

Greenberg, Eileen Bender: vice president, Bender Foundation

Greenberg, Gary: vice president, Rogow Birken Foundation

Greenberg, Maurice Raymond: chairman, director, Starr Foundation

Greenberg, Michael: treasurer, director, Newman Assistance Fund (Jerome A. and Estelle R.)

Greenberg, Sidney: president, Rogow Birken Foundation

Greene, John K.: director, Kaul Foundation Trust (Hugh)

Greene, Marion E.: president, LEF Foundation

Greene, Paul F.: trustee, Levy Foundation (June Rockwell)

Greene, Richard L.: director, Koret Foundation

Greene, Roger W.: director, Memorial Foundation for the Blind

Greener, Chuck: director, Fannie Mae Foundation

Greenfield, Albert M., III: trustee, Greenfield Foundation (Albert M.)

Greenfield, Bruce Harold: trustee, Greenfield Foundation (Albert M.)

Greenfield, Jerry: president, Ben & Jerry's Foundation; co-founder, vice chairman, Ben & Jerry's Homemade Inc.

Greenfield, Stewart: trustee, Dibner Fund

Greenlaw, Patricia A.: trustee, Carroll Charitable Foundation

Greenleaf, Arline Ripley: trustee, Sprague Educational and Charitable Foundation (Seth)

Greenlee, Paul, Jr.: vice president, trustee, Anderson Foundation (NY)

Greenstein, Andrew M.: trustee, August Family Foundation (Charles J. and Burton S.)

Greenway, Lumina V.: trustee, Verney Foundation (Gilbert)

Greenwood, Donald F.: director, Burns & McDonnell Foundation

Greer, David S.: trustee, Jaffe Foundation

Greer, George C.: chairman, Eden Hall Foundation

Greer, Margaret Weyerhaeuser Jewett: trustee, Jewett Foundation (George Frederick)

Greer, William Hershey, Jr.: trustee, Jewett Foundation (George Frederick)

Greevy, Charles F., III: president, Plankenhorn Foundation (Harry)

Grefenstette, Carl G.: director, vice president, Hillman Foundation

Gregg, Ingrid A.: secretary, trustee, Earhart Foundation

Gregg, Kirk P.: trustee, Corning Inc. Foundation

Gregorian, Vartan: president, Carnegie Corp. of New York

Gregory, Peter S.: managing director, director, Cabot Corp. Foundation

Gregory, Theophilus: associate vice president, El Pomar Foundation

Greiner, Amelia: trustee, Gifford Charitable Corp. (Rosamond)

Greiner, David C.: assistant treasurer, U.S. Steel Foundation

Greisman, Stuart L., D.O.: director, Copic Medical Foundation

Grenz, M. Kay: senior vice president human resources, Minnesota Mining & Manufacturing Co.

Gresham, James Thomas: president, general manager, treasurer, Callaway Foundation, Inc.

Gresham, Mary: secretary, director, Rahr Foundation

Gress, Bruce: treasurer, Yellow Corp. Foundation

Gretta, John W.: assistant treasurer, Scott & Fetzer Foundation

Greve, John H.: trustee, Kinney-Lindstrom Foundation

Griffin, Diane P.: trustee, Beazley Foundation

Griffin, Donald Wayne: chairman, president, chief executive officer, director, Olin Corp.; trustee, Olin Corp. Charitable Trust

Griffin, Janet: secretary, Wellmark Foundation

Griffin, Leslie: director, Boston Globe Foundation

Griffin, Sandra L.: admin, Bernsen Foundation (Grace and Franklin)

Griffin, Sandy: scholarship administration, Moody Foundation

Griffin, William E.: president, director, Carvel Foundation (Thomas and Agnes)

Griffis, Hughes: president, director, Griffis Foundation

Griffith, Alan Richard: vice chairman, Bank of New York

Griffith, Charles P., Jr.: adv, Griffith Foundation (W. C.)

Griffith, Chip: vice president, Kuyper Foundation (Peter H. and E. Lucille Gaass)

Griffith, J. Larry: vice chairman, trustee, Carver Charitable Trust (Roy J.)

Griffith, Mary: vice president, Kuyper Foundation (Peter H. and E. Lucille Gaass)

Griffith, Walter S.: adv, Griffith Foundation (W. C.)

Griffith, William C., III: adv, Griffith Foundation (W. C.)

Griffiths, Andrea Q.: vice president, Staunton Farm Foundation

Griffiths, Clark A.: chairman, Mascoma Savings Bank

Griffiths, Mary Elizabeth: member, Staunton Farm Foundation

Grigal, Dennis: trustee, Donaldson Foundation

Griggs, Alfred L.: director, assistant clerk, Beveridge Foundation, Inc. (Frank Stanley)

Griggs, C. E. Bayliss: president, director, Griggs and Mary Griggs Burke Foundation (Mary Livingston)

Grimes, Anne Windfohr: trustee, Burnett Foundation (The)

Grimes, L. E.: treasurer, trustee, Fair Play Foundation

Grimes, Steve: chief financial officer, Bandai America Inc.

Grimm, Janet L.: trustee, Toms Foundation (The)

Grimm, R. Brett: trustee, Toms Foundation (The)

Grimm, Ronald L.: chairman, Toms Foundation (The)

Grisanti, Eugene P.: director, Ambrose Monell Foundation (The)

Grisham, Don: fund committee member, Kaufman Endowment Fund (Louis G.)

Griswold, D. Ross, Jr.: vice president, Griswold Foundation (John C.)

Griswold, David E.: off, Griswold Foundation (Lillian Sherwood)

Grogan, Paul S.: trustee, Knight Foundation (John S. and James L.)

Grolf, Keralyn: director, Fuller Co. Foundation (H.B.)

Groom, Bruce M.: secretary, trustee, Barstow Foundation

Gross, Bert M.: secretary, Regis Foundation

Gross, Charles: assistant secretary, WPWR-TV Channel 50 Foundation

Gross, Cornelia B.: secretary, treasurer, McCausland Foundation

Gross, Courtlandt D.: adv director, Ducommun and Gross Foundation

Gross, Malcolm J.: trustee, Trexler Trust (Harry C.)

Grosser, Steven E.: director, vice president, Mid-continent Media Foundation

Grossman, Roberta: vice president, Badgeley Residuary Charitable Trust (Rose M.)

Groth, Frederick H.: director, Siebert Lutheran Foundation

Groth, Terri L.: treasurer, Giddings & Lewis Foundation

Grotjohn, Mo: executive director, treasurer, Meinders Foundation

Grover, Carol: president, director, VPI Foundation

Grover, R. Bruce: vice president, director, VPI Foundation

Grover Scott, Karen: director, VPI Foundation

Groves, Helen K.: president, director, Kleberg Foundation (Robert J. Kleberg, Jr. and Helen C.)

Grubb, Dale B.: trustee, Glendorn Foundation

Gruber, David P.: president, Wyman-Gordon Foundation

Gruenberg, Jennifer: director, Marx Foundation (Virginia and Leonard)

Grumman, Cornelia: director, Phillips Foundation (Ellis L.)

Grumman, David L.: director, mem, Phillips Foundation (Ellis L.)

Grundfest, Judy: board director, Ottenheimer Brothers Foundation

Grundfest, Julianne D.: board of directors, Ottenheimer Brothers Foundation

Grune, George Vincent: chairman, director, The Wallace Foundation

Gudelsky, John: secretary, director, Gudelsky Family Foundation (Homer and Martha)

Gudelsky, Martha: president, director, Gudelsky Family Foundation (Homer and Martha)

Gudelsky, Medda: secretary, director, Gudelsky Family Foundation (Homer and Martha)

Guennewig, Victoria B.: president, trustee, Cooper Industries Foundation

Guenther, Jack Egon: trustee, McNutt Charitable Trust (Amy Shelton)

Guenther, Paul Bernard: trustee, Cary Charitable Trust (Mary Flagler)

Guerrero, Anthony R., Jr.: director, First Hawaiian Foundation

Guerrero, Linda H.: director, Wright Foundation (Lola)

Guggenhime, Richard Johnson: president, trustee, Langendorf Foundation (Stanley S.)

Guggimio, Kathleen: director, Bellamah Foundation (Dale J.)

Guidone, Rosemary: executive vice president, secretary, treasurer, trustee, Price Foundation (Louis and Harold)

Guild, Henry Rice, Jr.: trustee, Henderson Foundation (George B.)

Guin, James M.: vice president human resources & public relations, Burlington Industries Inc.

Gula, Richard: president, director, Boston Globe Foundation

Gulick, Alice J.: trustee, secretary, Eaton Foundation (Cyrus)

Gulick, Henry W.: treasurer, trustee, Eaton Foundation (Cyrus)

Gulley, Joan L.: director, PNC Bank Foundation

Gully, Philip G.: member, Staunton Farm Foundation

Gumbiner, Alis: cfo, vp, Gumbiner Foundation (Josephine)

Gumbiner, Burke F.: chief financial officer, Gumbiner Foundation (Josephine)

Gumbiner, Lee: vice president, Gumbiner Foundation (Josephine)

Gumprecht, Pamela (Howard): trustee, Scripps Howard Foundation

Guna, Edward F.: vice president, treasurer, U.S. Steel Foundation

Gund, Agnes: trustee, Getty Trust (J. Paul)

Gund, Ann Landreth: secretary, trustee, Gund Foundation (George)

Gund, Catherine: trustee, Gund Foundation (George)

Gund, Geoffrey de Conde: trustee, Gund Foundation (Geoffrey); president, treasurer, trustee, Gund Foundation (George)

Gund, George, III: trustee, Gund Foundation (George)

Gund, Llura A.: vice president, trustee, Gund Foundation (George)

Gund, Zachary: trustee, Gund Foundation (George)

Gunn, Barbara: director, Glick Foundation (Eugene and Marilyn)

Gunn, Colin: director, Palisades Educational Foundation

Gunning, Gary J.: vice president, Prudential Securities Foundation

Gunter, Margaret C.: trustee, Dula Educational and Charitable Foundation (Caleb C. and Julia W.)

Gunther, Donald J.: director, Bechtel Group Inc.

Gupta, Geeta Rao: director, Moriah Fund, Inc.

Guren, Debra S.: president, Hershey Foundation

Gurieva, Diana M.: executive vice president, Dyson Foundation

Gust, Anne B.: secretary, treasurer, Gap Foundation; executive vice president human resources, legal, administration, Gap Inc.

Gustafson, Karl W.: treasurer, Stockman Family Foundation Trust

Guster, Timothy S.: vice president, secretary, Scott & Fetzer Foundation

Gustin, Marie: director, Hoffman Foundation (Maximilian E. and Marion O.)

Guth, Bernard M.: trustee, Greenfield Foundation (Albert M.)

Guth, Janet: trustee, Greenfield Foundation (Albert M.)

Guth, John E., Jr.: chairman, director, National Standard Co.

Guth, John H. J.: trustee, Woodcock Foundation

Guth, Polly: trustee, Woodcock Foundation

Guthman, Sandra P.: president, chief executive officer, Polk Brothers Foundation, Inc.

Guthridge, Charles M.: trustee, Scott Foundation (William H., John G., and Emma)

Guthrie, Victoria F.: trustee, Wyomissing Foundation

Gutierrez, Ernest B., Jr.: senior program officer, Kresge Foundation

Gutschewski, B. R.: vice president taxes, Union Pacific Foundation

Guttarb, William B.: trustee, Yawkey Foundation II

Guttmacher, Richard: vice president, Oak Grove School

Guttowsky, Lois K.: secretary, Morley Foundation

Guy, Catherine B.: vice president, Reliant Resources Foundation

Guyaux, Joseph C.: director, PNC Bank Foundation

Gvozdjak, John M.: secretary, treasurer, NMC Foundation

Gwyn, John E.: director, Klee Foundation (Conrad and Virginia)

H

Haar, Charles M.: director, DBH Foundation for Law, Land, and the Felicitous Environment

Haar, Susan E.: director, DBH Foundation for Law, Land, and the Felicitous Environment

Haas, David W.: chairman, Penn Foundation (William)

Haas, Donald W.: trustee, Yeager Charitable Trust B (Lester E.)

Haas, Duncan A.: director, Penn Foundation (William)

Haas, Evelyn Danzig: don, co-chairman, trustee, Haas, Jr. Fund (Evelyn and Walter)

Haas, Frederick R.: vice chairman, secretary, Penn Foundation (William)

Haas, Jean Hamrick: director, Fullerton Foundation

Haas, Miriam Lurie: don, president, trustee, Haas Fund (Miriam and Peter)

Haas, Peter Edgar, Jr.: president, Haas Fund (Walter and Elise)

Haas, Peter Edgar, Sr.: honorary president, Haas Fund (Walter and Elise)

Haas, Robert Douglas: chairman,

Haas, Walter J.: trustee, Haas Fund (Walter and Elise); co-chairman, trustee, Haas, Jr. Fund (Evelyn and Walter)

Haas, William D.: director, Penn Foundation (William)

Haas-Dehejia, Jennifer: trustee, Haas Fund (Walter and Elise)

Haase, Herman A.: admin, Peters Foundation (Charles F.)

Haasen, Adolf: director, Backus Foundation (Beatrice and Roy)

Habegger, Gary L.: vice president human resources, Goodrich Corp.

Habermeier, Juergen: vice chairman, Hexcel Corp.

Habermeyer, H. William, Jr.: vice president, director, Progress Energy Foundation

Hack, Gary: director, Penn Foundation (William)

Hackett, James P.: trustee, Steelcase Foundation; president, chief executive officer, Steelcase Inc.

Haefling, Karen R.: trustee, Key Foundation

Haensel, Peter C.: president, director, Schoenleber Foundation

Haffenreffer, T. C., Jr.: vice chairman, director, Rahr Malting Co.

Hafif, Herbert: director, Hafif Family Foundation

Hagan, David I.: trustee, Seybert Institution for Poor Boys and Girls (Adam and Maria Sarah)

Hageman, Andrew F.: manager, corporate philanthropy, Schering-Plough Corp.; secretary, Schering-Plough Foundation

Hagenbuch, Diane: trustee, Ohio National Foundation

Haggerty, Gretchen R.: vice president, treasurer, U.S. Steel Corp.

Haggerty, John: director, Comerica Charitable Foundation

Hahl, Elizabeth G.: director, Staunton Farm Foundation

Hahn, Charles J.: secretary, Children's Foundation of Erie County

Hahn, James K.: assistant secretary, Sara Lee Foundation

Haibloom, George: director, member, Katzenberger Foundation

Haigney, John E.: president, director, Huisking Foundation

Haines, Jordan L.: trustee, Cessna Foundation, Inc.

Haines, Robert H.: secretary, director, Newman Assistance Fund (Jerome A. and Estelle R.)

Hajduk, Alice J.: vice president, director, Murphy Co. Foundation (G.C.)

Hajtman, L. Michael: president, Herzstein Charitable Foundation (Albert and Ethel)

Hale, J. Joseph, Jr.: president, director, Cinergy Foundation

Hale, James Thomas: executive vice president, general counsel, secretary, Target Corp.

Hale, Michael V.: trustee, Cauthorn Charitable Trust (John and Mildred)

Hale, Roger W.: chairman, chief executive officer, director, LG&E Energy Corp.

Halepeska, Robert L.: executive vice president, Johnson Foundation (M. G. and Lillie A.)

Hales, Tony: chairman, Dunkin' Donuts Inc.

Haley, Eloise T.: president, Haley Foundation (W. B.)

Haley, Jane: director, Dayton Power and Light Co. Foundation

Halff, Hugh, Jr.: chairman, Halff Foundation (G. A. C.)

Halff, Marie M.: trustee, Halff Foundation (G. A. C.)

Halfon, Ellen E.: assistant secretary, Kulas Foundation

Hall, Anthony W., Jr.: director, Houston Endowment

Hall, Charles T.: director, Gebbie Foundation

Hall, Charles W.: trustee, Anderson Foundation (M. D.)

Hall, Donald Joyce: chairman, director, Hall Family Foundation (The)

Hall, Euphemia V.: president, trustee, Crary Foundation (Bruce L.)

Hall, J. W., Jr.: adv comm, Duncan Trust (Louise Head)

Hall, Joy W.: trustee, Ellsworth Foundation (Ruth H. and Warren A.)

Hall, Karla: administrator corporate contributions, DTE Energy Co.; secretary, director, DTE Energy Foundation

Hall, Kirkie T.: member advisory committee, Weezie Foundation

Hall, Linda M.: trustee, Gifford Charitable Corp. (Rosamond)

Hall, Lowell K.: secretary, Kinney-Lindstrom Foundation

Hall, Lyle G.: chairman, trustee, Stackpole-Hall Foundation

Hall, Marie Fondren: vice chairman, board of governors, Fondren Foundation

Hall, Megan: trustee, Stackpole-Hall Foundation

Hall, Mortimer W.: treasurer, Schiff Foundation (Dorothy)

Hall, Neil F.: director, PNC Bank Foundation

Hall, Raymond L., Jr.: secretary, director, Vaughan Foundation

Hall, Rose Ethel: adv comm, Duncan Trust (Louise Head)

Hall, William A.: president, Hall Family Foundation (The)

Hall Rossi, Craig: trustee, Rossi Family Foundation

Hallenbeck, Alfred: director, Schmitt Foundation (Kilian J. and Caroline F.)

Haller, Calvin J.: trustee, Children's Foundation of Erie County

Haller, J. Gary: president, German Protestant Orphan Asylum Association Foundation

Hallinan, Cornelia I.: secretary, Mather and William Gwinn Mather Fund (Elizabeth Ring)

Hallock, David P.: trustee, Fuller Foundation (George F. and Sybil H.)

Halpern, Stephen: treasurer, Jewish Healthcare Foundation

Halvorsen, Andrew Christian: treasurer, trustee, Schumann Fund for New Jersey

Halvorson, Newman T., Jr.: assistant secretary, assistant treasurer, Meyer Foundation (Eugene and Agnes E.)

Hamer, Donald W.: trustee, Hamer Foundation

Hamill, John: director, Sovereign Bank Foundation

Hamilton, Betsy: grants director, Campbell Foundation (J. Bulow)

Hamilton, Charles H.: secretary, Clark Foundation (NY)

Hamilton, David Ley, Esq.: trustee, The MBNA Foundation

Hamilton, Emory A.: vice president, treasurer, Kleberg Foundation (Robert J. Kleberg, Jr. and Helen C.)

Hamilton, James: trustee, Blandin Foundation

Hamilton, Jean D.: trustee, Prudential Foundation

Hamilton, M. Hayne: president, Tucker Foundation

Hamilton, Peter Bannerman: trustee, Kemper Foundation (James S.)

Hammack, John A.: trustee, director, Meadows Foundation (The)

Hamman, Henry R.: president, director, Hamman Foundation (George and Mary Josephine)

Hamman, Russell R.: trustee, Hamman Foundation (George and Mary Josephine)

Hammatt, R. Bruce, Jr.: clerk, director, Kelley and Elza Kelley Foundation (Edward Bangs)

Hammer, Carolyn S.: secretary, Staunton Farm Foundation

Hammer, Dru: cfo, secretary, director, Hammer Foundation (Armand)

Hammer, Michael A.: president, chief executive officer, director, Hammer Foundation (Armand)

Hammer, Roy A.: trustee, Cox Charitable Trust (Jessie B.)

Hammer, Thomas J.: director, Teichert Foundation

Hammerschmidt, John A.: assistant secretary, U.S. Steel Foundation

Hammond, J. David: treasurer, Emerson Foundation, Inc. (Fred L.)

Hammond, Lynn A.: trustee, McKee Charitable Trust (Thomas M.)

Hammond, Ray: trustee, Yawkey Foundation II

Hammons, Royce Mitchell: treasurer, Kerr Foundation, Inc.

Hamp, Sheila F.: trustee, Ford Motor Co. Fund

Hamp, Steve K.: trustee, Kresge Foundation

Hampton, Louis R.: mem distribution comm, Champlin Foundation

Hampton, Mark I.: vice president, Sheldon Foundation Inc. (Ralph C.)

Hamrick, A. Wardlaw: director, Fullerton Foundation

Hamrick, Charles F.: director, Fullerton Foundation

Hamrick, Charles F., II: vice chairman, director, Fullerton Foundation

Hamrick, Harvey B.: secretary, Dover Foundation

Hamrick, John M.: director, Fullerton Foundation

Hamrick, Kathleen D.: vice president, Dover Foundation

Hamrick, Lyman W.: secretary, director, Fullerton Foundation

Hamrick, W. Carlisle: treasurer, Fullerton Foundation

Hamrick, Wylie L.: chairman, director, Fullerton Foundation

Hanafin, V. M.: director, Shell Oil Co. Foundation

Hanavan, Claire F.: director, Huisking Foundation

Hanavan, Taylor W.: director, Huisking Foundation

Hance, Charles E.: trustee, Victoria Foundation

Hancock, John W.: chairman, trustee, Kiewit Foundation (Peter)

Hand, Elbert O.: chairman, chief executive officer, director, Hartmarx Corp.

Hand, Marion: trustee, Medina Foundation

Handelman, Donald E.: president, director, Math-

ers Charitable Foundation (G. Harold and Leila Y.)

Handelman, James H.: executive director, Mathers Charitable Foundation (G. Harold and Leila Y.)

Handelman, Joseph W.: treasurer, assistant secretary, director, Mathers Charitable Foundation (G. Harold and Leila Y.)

Handelman, William R.: vice president, director, Mathers Charitable Foundation (G. Harold and Leila Y.)

Handler, Cherie: assistant secretary, director, Geifman Family Foundation

Handley, Leon Hunter: trustee, Magruder Foundation (Chesley G.)

Hanes, Frank Borden, Jr.: trustee, Hanes Foundation (John Wesley and Anna Hodgin)

Hanes, Ralph Philip, Jr.: trustee, Hanes Foundation (John Wesley and Anna Hodgin)

Hanford, James: assistant treasurer, ABC Broadcasting Foundation, Inc.

Hangs, George L., Jr.: secretary, treasurer, trustee, directory, Harmon Foundation (Pearl M. and Julia J.)

Hanisko, Lou: director, Wickson-Link Memorial Foundation

Hanks, Stephen G.: president, Washington Group Foundation, Inc.

Hanley, John E.: chief financial officer, vice president finance, treasurer, Lydall Inc.

Hanley, William Lee, Jr.: treasurer, director, JM Foundation

Hanna, Barbara H.: trustee, Reynolds Foundation (Donald W.)

Hanonik, Francoise: director, Reader's Digest Foundation

Hanower, L. David: senior vice president, Burlington Resources Foundation

Hanrahan, Robert E., Jr.: director, Penn Foundation (William)

Hansen, Alice G.: secretary, Burnand Medical and Educational Foundation (Alphonse A.)

Hansen, Lisa D.: chairman, trustee, Norris Foundation (Kenneth T. and Eileen L.)

Hansen, Marka: director, Gap Foundation

Hansen, Maxine: director, Autry Foundation

Hansen, Nancy Huston: vice president evangelical relations, Huston Foundation

Hansen, Robert: director, Petteys Memorial Foundation (Jack)

Hansen, Robert U.: trustee, Kitzmiller/Bales Trust

Hansen, Robert V.: director, Joslin-Needham Family Foundation

Hanshaw, Frank E., Jr.: vice president, Huntington Foundation

Hansler, John F.: secretary, director, Cheney Foundation (Ben B.)

Hanson, Elizabeth J.: chp, secretary, treasurer, Johnston-Hanson Foundation

Hanson, Eric: director, Johnston-Hanson Foundation

Hanson, Erik A.: vice president, director, Loewy Family Foundation

Hanson, Fred L.: vice president, Johnston-Hanson Foundation

Hanson, John Nils: president, Joy Global Foundation, Inc.; chairman, president, chief executive officer, Joy Global Inc.

Hanson, Jon F.: trustee, Prudential Foundation; director, Prudential Insurance Company of America

Hanson, Stan: vice president, Kawasaki Motors Manufacturing Corporation U.S.A.

Hanson, Terry A.: secretary, treasurer, Madison Gas & Electric Foundation; chief financial officer, MGE Energy Inc.

Hanson, Virginia Wilson: trustee, director, Meadows Foundation (The)

Hanssen, Marty Voelkel: vice president, Knott Foundation (Marion I. and Henry J.)

Hanway, H. Edward: chairman, chief executive officer, CIGNA Corp.; director, CIGNA Corp.

Hapgood, Barbara: director, Educational Foundation of America

Hapgood, Elaine P.: president, Educational Foundation of America

Haqq, Constance T.: executive director, Nordson Corp. Foundation

Harckham, Peter B.: vice president, trustee, Heller Charitable Foundation (Clarence E.)

Harden, Glen: executive vice president, chief financial officer, Progress Energy Inc.

Harden, Oleta J.: secretary, New Jersey Natural Gas Foundation

Hardin, Jacob C., Jr.: director, Doherty Charitable Foundation (Henry L. and Grace)

Hardin, P. Russell: vice president, secretary, Woodruff Foundation (Robert W.)

Hardin, Vaughn C.: trustee, The MBNA Foundation

Harding, David R.: trustee, Camp and Bennet Humiston Trust (Apollos)

Harding, George T., IV: trustee, Worthington Foods Foundation

Harding, Leslie: director, Portsmouth General Hospital Foundation

Harding, Louis: secretary, Schwartz Foundation (Arnold A.)

Hardy, Gene M.: director, La-Z-Boy Foundation

Hardy, Richard B.: trustee, Hyde Charitable Foundation; chairman, chief executive officer, director, Hyde Manufacturing Co.

Hargrave, Karen: trustee, Houck Foundation (May Kay)

Hargrave, Louis W.: vice president, trustee, Warfield Memorial Fund (Anna Emory)

Hargreaves, David: senior vice president, chief financial officer, Hasbro Charitable Trust Inc.

Hargrow, Ralph: senior vice president Human Resources, International Multifoods Corp.

Harl, Sidney W.: vice president, director, Paley Foundation, Inc. (William S.)

Harlem, Robert A.: trustee, Warren and Beatrice W. Blanding Foundation (Riley J. and Lillian N.)

Harless, Katherine J.: director, Verizon Foundation

Harleston, Bernard W.: director, Macy, Jr. Foundation (Josiah)

Harley, Jill A.: treasurer, Chicago Board of Trade Foundation

Harley, Patricia R.: secretary, Johnson Fund (Edward C.)

Harmon, Brenda S.: vice president human resources, AK Steel Holding Corp.

Harmony, Jane E.: director, Baird Brothers Co. Foundation

Harnett, Ralph: director, Ensign-Bickford Foundation

Harnum, Linda F.: trustee, Webber Oil Foundation

Harper, Barry: president, chief executive officer, Harper Brush Works

Harper, Billy: trustee, Gifford Charitable Corp. (Rosamond)

Harper, Fletcher: director, Educational Foundation of America

Harper, Ralph E.: secretary, treasurer, director, Gleason Foundation

Harper, Valerie: admin, Dana Charitable Trust (Eleanor Naylor)

Harrell, Dorothy: executive director, Bonfils-Stanton Foundation

Harrell, Pauline Chase: mem, Henderson Foundation (George B.)

Harrer, Donald G.: president, Lee Endowment Foundation

Harrigan, Wendy T.: director, Royal & SunAlliance Insurance Foundation, Inc.; information technology executive, Royal & SunAlliance USA Inc.

Harrington, Charles M.: trustee, Mascoma Savings Bank Foundation

Harrington, Deborah Weil: director, Norman Foundation

Harrington, Earl W., Jr.: mem distribution comm, Champlin Foundation

Harrington, Francis A., Jr.: trustee, Harrington Foundation (Francis A. and Jacquelyn H.)

Harrington, George S.: trustee, Marmot Foundation

Harrington, James H.: trustee, Harrington Foundation (Francis A. and Jacquelyn H.)

Harrington, John Leo: executive director, trustee, Yawkey Foundation II

Harrington, Phyllis: trustee, Harrington Foundation (Francis A. and Jacquelyn H.)

Harris, E. Lee, Jr.: executive vice president human resources, Compass Bank

Harris, E. S.: controller, DaimlerChrysler Corp. Fund

Harris, Ellen H.: trustee, Callaway Foundation, Inc.

Harris, Franco: director, Heinz Endowment (Vira I.)

Harris, Fred: vice president, 3M Foundation

Harris, George: assistant secretary, assistant treasurer, director, Littauer Foundation (Lucius N.)

Harris, George R.: trustee, Schumann Fund for New Jersey

Harris, Henry Upham, III: trustee, Webster Foundation (Edwin S.)

Harris, Henry Upham, Jr.: trustee, Webster Foundation (Edwin S.)

Harris, Isaiah: trustee, BellSouth Foundation

Harris, J. Ira: vice president, Polk Brothers Foundation, Inc.

Harris, Kelly L.: secretary, Knott Foundation (Marion I. and Henry J.)

Harris, Lindsay: member, Knott Foundation (Marion I. and Henry J.)

Harris, Lisa: administrator, Sierra Pacific Resources Charitable Foundation

Harris, Marilyn A.: trustee, U.S. Steel Foundation

Harris, Martin R.: treasurer, Piper Foundation (Minnie Stevens)

Harris, O. Ben: director, assistant secretary, Georgia Power Foundation

Harris, Paul N.: trustee, Key Foundation

Harris, Paul W.: executive vice president, Hoblitzelle Foundation

Harris, Richard M.: trustee, Lattner Foundation (Forrest C.)

Harris, Robert C.: president, Gilmore Foundation (William G.)

Harris, Roland J.: director, Dime Savings Bank of Norwich Foundation

Harris, Suzanne C.: assistant treasurer, Clemens Foundation

Harris, Thomas K.: member, Knott Foundation (Marion I. and Henry J.)

Harris, W. Patrick: executive vice president investments, Carter Foundation (Amon G.)

Harris, William C.: trustee, Camp and Bennet Humiston Trust (Apollos)

Harrison, Carl: vice president finance, chief financial officer, Owen Industries

Harrison, Lois Cowles: trustee, Cowles Charitable Trust

Harrison, Lois Eleanor: trustee, Cowles Charitable Trust

Harrison, Marian P.: director, assistant treasurer, Powell Foundation

Harrison, R. Reed, III: trustee, AT&T Foundation

Harrison, William B., Jr.: vice chairman, J.P. Morgan Chase Foundation; director, New York Stock Exchange Foundation, Inc.

Harrold, Mike: director, Georgia Power Foundation

Hart, Dehler: director, Springs Foundation, Inc.

Hart, George G.: secretary, Lake Placid Education Foundation

Hart, Joseph T. C.: treasurer, Ambrose Monell Foundation (The)

Hart, Marilie: grants manager, program officer, Buell Foundation (Temple Hoyne)

Hart, Michael A.: treasurer, Gannett Foundation

Hart, William D., Jr.: secretary, trustee, Heckscher Foundation for Children

Harte, Richard, Jr.: trustee, Webster Foundation (Edwin S.)

Hartl, Charles R.: director, Graco Foundation

Hartley, Barbara: chairperson, trustee, Johnson Foundation (Helen K. and Arthur E.)

Hartley, Richard O.: chairman grant comm, Royal Foundation (May Mitchell)

Hartley, Susan J.: grant committee, Royal Foundation (May Mitchell)

Hartman, Andrea R.: assistant secretary, Universal Studios Foundation

Hartman, Betty Regenstein: vice president, director, Regenstein Foundation

Hartman, Jerry J.: director, Utica National Foundation

Hartmann, David B.: trustee, Pittsburgh Child Guidance Foundation

Hartshorn, Terry O'Dell: chairman, PacifiCare Health System Foundation

Hartshorne, Harold, Jr.: director, Chapin Foundation of Myrtle Beach, South Carolina

Hartung, Suzanne R.: president, co-chairperson, Rupp Foundation (Fran and Warren)

Hartz, Greg: director, Rockefeller Foundation (Winthrop)

Harvey, A. Mosby, Jr.: vice president, secretary, general counsel, HON Industries Inc.

Harvey, Ann: director, Harvey Foundation (C. Felix)

Harvey, C. Felix: vice president, Harvey Foundation (C. Felix)

Harvey, James D.: adv, Ritter Charitable Trust (George and Mary)

Harvey, Joan: director, New-Land Foundation

Harvey, Margaret B.: president, Harvey Foundation (C. Felix)

Harvey, Ralph, III: trustee, Priddy Foundation

Harvey, Robert W.: vice chairman, CenterPoint Energy Inc.

Harvey, Thomas B., Esq.: trustee, Douty Foundation (Alfred and Mary)

Harvey, Tom: assistant treasurer, BellSouth Foundation

Hasbrouck, Jerry: director, Midcontinent Media Foundation

Hashim, Carlisle V.: member, Knott Foundation (Marion I. and Henry J.)

Hashorva, Tanya: vice president, Arcadia Foundation

Haskell, Antoinette M.: director emeritus, Public Welfare Foundation

Haskell, Coburn: president, trustee, Haskell Fund

Haskell, Eric T.: trustee, Haskell Fund

Haskell, John G.: president, Chapman Charitable Corp. (Howard and Bess)

Haskell, Mark: trustee, Haskell Fund

Haskell, Mary E.: trustee, Haskell Fund

Haskell, Melville H., Jr.: trustee, Haskell Fund

Haskell, Robert G.: president, director, Pacific Life Foundation; senior vice president public affairs, Pacific Life Insurance Co.

Haskell, Robert H.: vice chairman, Public Welfare Foundation

Haskell, Schuyler A.: vice president, trustee, Haskell Fund

Haskell-Green, Sarah: trustee, Haskell Fund

Haslam, Anne S.: secretary, Teichert Foundation

Hasler, James A.: trustee, Clorox Co. Foundation

Hassan, Fred: chairman, chief executive officer, president, director, Schering-Plough Corp.

Hassenfeld, Alan Geoffrey: president, director, Hasbro Charitable Trust Inc.

Hasting, Carl D.: vice president, secretary, treasurer, director, Keck, Jr. Foundation (William M.)

Hastings, Alfred B., Jr.: trustee, Murphey Foundation (Lluella Morey)

Hastings, David R., II: trustee, Mulford Trust (Clarence E.)

Hastings, Peter G.: trustee, Mulford Trust (Clarence E.)

Hatayama, Kuniki: chief financial officer, Kikkoman Foods; director, Kikkoman Foundation

Hathaway, Catherine Gray: director, Flagler Foundation

Hathaway, D. C.: trustee, Harsco Corp. Fund

Hathaway, Derek C.: director, Kline Foundation (Josiah W. and Bessie H.)

Hattler, Robert L.: treasurer, German Protestant Orphan Asylum Association Foundation

Hauben, David: vice president, treasurer, Lowe Foundation (Joe and Emily)

Hauck, Edward C.: vice president, S&T Bancorp Charitable Foundation

Haught, M. R.: president, director, Pella Rolscreen Foundation

Hauptfuhrer, Robert Paul: director, Barra Foundation

Hauptli, Barbara A.: trustee, Hauptli Charitable Foundation (A. John and Barbara A.)

Hauselt, Denise A.: secretary, Corning Inc. Foundation

Hauser, David: trustee, Duke Energy Foundation

Hauswirth, Lisa G.: director, Langendorf Foundation (Stanley S.)

Hauswirth, Lynda: assistant vice president, Knight Ridder Fund

Haviland, David Sands: director, Howard and Bush Foundation

Hawk, Daniel D.: vice president, treasurer, Burlington Resources Foundation

Hawkins, Chaille W.: assistant secretary, trustee, Sterling-Turner Foundation

Hawkins, Prince A.: trustee, Hawkins Foundation (Robert Z.)

Hawley, Philip Metschan: trustee, Haynes Foundation (John Randolph and Dora)

Hawn, Bruce Sams: president, chief executive officer, director, Sams Foundation (Earl C.)

Hawn, Gates: trustee, Credit Suisse First Boston Foundation Trust

Hawn, Gates Helms: director, Clark Foundation (NY)

Hawn, Joe Verne, Jr.: director, Hawn Foundation

Hawn, Nancy: director, Sams Foundation (Earl C.)

Hawn, W. A., Jr.: president, Hawn Foundation

Hawn, William Russell, Jr.: director, Hawn Foundation

Haworth, Joanne: assistant treasurer, Hasbro Charitable Trust Inc.

Hay, Susan: manager, National Grange Mutual Charitable Trust

Hayakawa, Y.: chairman, president, chief executive officer, Hino Diesel Trucks (U.S.A.)

Hayes, Arthur H., Jr.: director, Macy, Jr. Foundation (Josiah)

Hayes, Denis Allen: president, Bullitt Foundation

Hayes, John: director, secretary, Hermann Foundation (Grover)

Hayes, Mariam C.: director, member, Cannon Foundation, Inc. (The)

Hayes, Patricia Ann: trustee, RGK Foundation

Hayes, Rob: director, Mid-Iowa Health Foundation

Hayes, Robert C.: director, member, Cannon Foundation, Inc. (The)

Hayes, Stephen L.: vice president, Unocal Foundation

Hayes, Synnova Bay: president, treasurer, Bay Foundation

Hayes, Thomas F.: trustee, New Jersey Natural Gas Foundation

Haygood, Paul: trustee, German Protestant Orphan Asylum Association Foundation

Haylon, Michael E.: director, chairman, Phoenix Foundation

Hayne, Roxana Catto: vice president, secretary, Gage Foundation (Alfred S.)

Hayner, Herman Henry: trustee, Shepherd Foundation (Harold and Helen)

Hayner, James K.: trustee, Stubblefield (Estate of Joseph L.)

Haynes, Larry N.: director, Christy-Houston Foundation

Hays, Frances McKee: senior vice president, McKee Foundation (Robert E. and Evelyn)

Hays, Lucille T.: mem adv comm, Weezie Foundation

Hays, Thomas Chandler: chairman, chief executive officer, director, Fortune Brands Inc.

Hazard, Susan J.: trustee, Lantz Foundation (Walter)

Hazel, John T., Jr.: director, Loughran Foundation (Mary and Daniel)

Hazel, Lewis F.: trustee emeritus, Children's Foundation of Erie County

Hazelett, Susie: executive director, Tobias Foundation (Randall L.)

Hazelrigg, Charles R.: trustee emeritus, Johnson Foundation (Helen K. and Arthur E.)

Hazelton, Richard A.: president, chief executive officer, trustee, Strosacker Foundation (Charles J.)

Hazelton, Robert L.: senior vice president, McKee Foundation (Robert E. and Evelyn)

Hazen, Kathy: executive director, Buck Foundation (Frank H. and Eva B.)

Head, Beverly P., III: director, Kaul Foundation Trust (Hugh)

Head, Deidra: director, McBean Family Foundation

Head, Hillery: director, Kaul Foundation Trust (Hugh)

Head, Marion Daniel: vice president, Daniel Foundation of Alabama

Head, Sheila McBean: director, McBean Family Foundation

Head, Susan: trust associate, Van Houten Memorial Fund (Edward W. and Stella C.)

Healey, Louis: chief financial officer

Healy, James T.: president, Trust Funds

Healy, Jo Ann: administrator, Alliant Energy Foundation, Inc.

Heard, Drew R.: chairman, McMillan, Jr. Foundation (Bruce)

Heard, Jane: director, Colt Foundation (James J.)

Heard, Karen: director, Colt Foundation (James J.)

Heard, Thomas H.: vice president, director, Colt Foundation (James J.)

Hearn, Thomas A.: president, director, Russell Charitable Foundation (Tom)

Hearst, George Randolph, Jr.: vice president, director, Hearst Foundation (William Randolph)

Hearst, John Randolph, Jr.: vice president, director, Hearst Foundation (William Randolph)

Hearst, William R., III: president, director, Hearst Foundation (William Randolph)

Heath, Ruth: assistant secretary, Harvey Foundation (C. Felix)

Heaton, Mary Alice J.: trustee, Whiting Foundation

Hebenstreit, James B.: president, Bartlett & Co.; trustee, Bartlett & Co. Grain Charitable Foundation

Hecht, John: chief financial officer, AMCORE Financial Inc.

Hed, Gordon E.: assistant secretary, assistant treasurer, Weyerhaeuser Memorial Foundation (Charles A.)

Heddens, B. Spencer: director, Francis Families Foundation

Hedemark, N. Charles: executive vice president, chief operating officer, director, Intermountain Gas Co.; director, Intermountain Gas Industries Foundation

Hedges, James R., III: chairman, trustee, Tonya Memorial Foundation

Hedges, M. D.: trustee, Betts Foundation

Heeg, Peggy A.: executive vice president, general counsel, El Paso Corp.

Heegaard, Peter A.: trustee, Blandin Foundation

Heemstra, Linda R.: trustee, Kantzler Foundation

Heenan, Earl I., III: trustee, Earhart Foundation

Hefferline, Arline: secretary, Norcliffe Foundation

Heffernan, E. Mary: treasurer, Noble Foundation, Inc. (Edward John)

Heffernan, Elizabeth Blossom: vice president, trustee, chairman public information committee, Bingham Foundation (William)

Heffner, Jane E.: vice president, Citigroup Global Markets Holdings Inc.

Hefty, Noel M.: trustee, Messing Family Charitable Foundation

Hefty, Terrance: trustee, Messing Family Charitable Foundation

Hegarty, Neal R.: program officer, Mott Foundation (Charles Stewart)

Hegel, Garrett R.: chief financial officer, Compass Bank; president, Compass Bank Foundation

Hegeler, Alix S.: director, Hegeler II Foundation (Julius W.)

Hegeler, Julius W., II: director, Hegeler II Foundation (Julius W.)

Hegeler, Madelle G.: mgr, Hegeler II Foundation (Julius W.)

Hehl, David K.: director, La-Z-Boy Inc.

Heidt, Julia Scripps: trustee, Scripps Howard Foundation

Heil, Mark: committee member, Haman Family Foundation

Heilala, John A.: trustee, Vulcan Materials Co. Foundation

Heiland, Donna, PhD: vice president programs, Teagle Foundation

Heill, Mark: committee member, Haman Family Foundation

Heimerman, Quentin O.: vice president, Saint Croix Foundation

Heineman, Benjamin Walter, Jr.: director, GE Foundation; senior vice president, law and public affairs, General Electric Co.

Heinemen, Melvin L.: secretary, treasurer, director, Rohatyn Foundation (Felix and Elizabeth)

Heinen, Stacy: director, Grinnell Mutual Group Foundation

Heinrich, Daniel: vice president, treasurer, Clorox Co. Foundation

Heintz, Stephen B.: president, Rockefeller Brothers Fund, Inc.

Heinz, Andre: director, Heinz Family Foundation

Heinz, Andre T.: director, Heinz Endowment (Vira I.)

Heinz, Drue: director emeritus, Heinz Endowment (Howard); trustee, Heinz Trust (Drue)

Heinz, H. John, IV: director, Heinz Endowment (Howard)

Heinz, Teresa: chairwoman, Heinz Endowment (Howard); director, Heinz Endowment (Vira I.)

Heiser, James S.: chief financial officer, Ducommun Inc.

Heiskell, Marian Sulzberger: president, director, Sulzberger Foundation

Heisler, Robert B., Jr.: president, trustee, Key Foundation

Heldman, Paul: secretary, The Kroger Co. Foundation

Helfrich, Thomas E.: trustee, Key Foundation

Heller, Helen H.: secretary, treasurer, director, Davenport-Hatch Foundation

Heller, Katherine: trustee, Heller Charitable Foundation (Clarence E.)

Heller, Miranda: president, trustee, Heller Charitable Foundation (Clarence E.)

Hellie, Thomas L.: executive director, Kemper Foundation (James S.)

Hellman, Daryl A.: trustee, Eastern Bank Charitable Foundation

Helm, George T.: trustee, Levy Foundation (June Rockwell)

Helm, John: director, Johnson Foundation (Samuel S.)

Helmerich, Walter Hugo, III: trustee, Helmerich Foundation

Helmick, Walter E.: vice president, assistant treasurer, Stans Foundation

Helmig, Albert: director, New York Mercantile Exchange Charitable Foundation

Helms, Ann Marie: program officer, assistant secretary, Mellon Foundation (Richard King)

Helsby, Keith R.: treasurer, New York Stock Exchange Foundation, Inc.

Helseth, Nancy L.: admin, Collins Medical Trust

Helzner, Judith F.: director population & reprod health, MacArthur Foundation (John D. and Catherine T.)

Hemme, Dennis: vice president, CNA Foundation

Hemphill, Caroline M.: director special programs, assistant secretary-treasurer, Olin Foundation (John M.)

Hempstead, David M.: secretary, trustee, Ford Fund (Walter and Josephine); secretary, trustee, member, Ford Fund (William and Martha); secretary, trustee, Ford II Fund (Henry); treasurer, Wilson Fund (Matilda R.)

Henderson, Barclay G. S.: trustee, Henderson Foundation

Henderson, Darryl K.: trustee, Lowe's Charitable and Educational Foundation

Henderson, Ernest, III: trustee, Henderson Foundation

Henderson, George, III: treasurer, Pineywoods Foundation

Henderson, George W., III: trustee, Burlington Industries Foundation; chief executive officer, chairman, Burlington Industries Inc.

Henderson, Gerald C.: trustee, Henderson Foundation (George B.)

Henderson, James D.: trustee, Fuller Foundation (MA)

Henderson, Rhoe B., III: president, director, Gebbie Foundation

Henderson, Robert P.: director, Fairchild Foundation, Inc. (Sherman)

Henderson, Scott: treasurer, The Kroger Co. Foundation

Henderson, Thomas J.: vice president, director, Atkinson Foundation

Henderson, William: director, U.S. Bancorp Piper Jaffray Foundation

Henderson, William M.: trustee, Edison Fund (Charles)

Hendrick, William A.: trustee, Wickes Foundation (Harvey Randall)

Hendricks, Ben F.: mgr, Porter Testamentary Trust (James Hyde)

Hendrickson, Lil M.: assistant secretary, Wheeler Foundation

Hendrickson, Nancy: assistant secretary, assistant clerk, assistant treasurer, TJX Foundation, Inc.

Hendrix, C. E., Jr.: president, De Queen Regional Medical Center

Heningburg, Gustav: trustee, Fund for New Jersey

Henkels, Alexander Ardley, Jr.: president, Staunton Farm Foundation

Henley, Arlene S.: co-trustee, Robert Charitable Trust 2 (John A. and Delia T.)

Hennessey, Frank Martin: trustee, Hudson-Webber Foundation

Hennessy, Marilyn: president, Retirement Research Foundation

Hennessy, Michael W.: president, chief executive officer, director, Coleman Foundation (IL)

Hennessy, S. P.: secretary, treasurer, trustee, Sherwin-Williams Foundation

Henney, Jane E., MD: director, Commonwealth Fund (The)

Henning, Leo T.: director, Oakley-Lindsay Foundation of Quincy Newspapers and Its Subsidiaries

Henrikson, C. Robert: director, MetLife Foundation; president, chief operating officer, Metropolitan Life Insurance Co.

Henry, Brent L.: director, Public Welfare Foundation

Henry, C. L.: chairman, president, chief executive officer, Johns Manville

Henry, Carl F.H.: director, M.E. Foundation

Henry, D. F.: president, director, Winn-Dixie Stores Foundation

Henry, Dorothy J.: trustee, Johnson Foundation (Howard)

Henry, Douglas: director, Joyce Family Foundation

Henry, John: director, employee representative, Mitsubishi Electric America Foundation; production engineer, Mitsubishi Electric and Electronics USA

Henry, Kim: trustee, Sarkeys Foundation

Henry, Leland W.: trustee, Berry Foundation (Loren M.)

Henry, Patricia: plant manager, Miller Brewing Co. (Eden, NC)

Henry, Patricia M.: secretary, trustee, Medina Foundation

Henry Wood, Margaret: chairperson, Joyce Family Foundation

Henseler, Gerald A.: executive vice president, chief financial officer, director, Banta Corp.

Henson, Jackson W.: director, secretary, Reynolds Foundation (R. J.)

Henson, Richard A.: chairman, trustee, Henson Foundation (Richard A.)

Henson, William C.: treasurer, trustee, Foundation for Seacoast Health

Herald, James E.: vice president finance, Mine Safety Appliances Co.; secretary, Mine Safety Appliances Co. Charitable Foundation

Herbert, Gavin, Sr.: director, Beckman Foundation (Arnold and Mabel)

Herbert, Gavin Shearer, Jr.: co-founder, chairman emeritus,

Herbert, John K., III: trustee, Henderson Foundation (George B.)

Herbert, Peter A.: president, director, Guttman Foundation (Stella and Charles)

Herbst, Linda Vitti: trustee, Price Foundation (Louis and Harold)

Herd, Bob L.: president, Herd Foundation (Bob L.)

Herd, Patsy L.: vice president, Herd Foundation (Bob L.)

Herd, Tevis: president, trustee, Abell-Hanger Foundation

Herder, Charles: trustee, George Foundation

Hereford, J.: vice president, Conway Scholarship Foundation (Carle C.)

Heresaty, Robert M., MD: director, Hoffman Foundation (Maximilian E. and Marion O.)

Herlich, Harold N., Jr.: secretary, Kaufman Endowment Fund (Louis G.)

Herlin, Cara: advisory trustee, Trull Foundation (The)

Herlin, Jean Trull: founder, trustee emeritus, Trull Foundation (The)

Herman, Iving, PhD: Distribution trustee, Schwab-Rosenhouse Memorial Foundation

Herman, Ronald D.: treasurer, Employers Mutual Charitable Foundation

Herman, Tom: director, Hedco Foundation

Herman, William A., III: secretary, treasurer, director, Morris Communications Corp.

Hermance, Frank S.: president, director, AMETEK Foundation; chairman, chief executive officer, director, AMETEK Inc.

Hermanson, Everett J.: trustee, Kinney-Lindstrom Foundation

Hernandez, Colleen: director, Fannie Mae Foundation

Hernandez, Robert M.: vice chairman, chief financial officer, director, U.S. Steel Corp.; chief financial officer, U.S. Steel Foundation

Herndon, Herschel: director, Global Communication, Stanley Works

Herr, Earl Binkley, Jr.: director, Lilly Endowment

Herrell, John E.: treasurer, assistant secretary, Atkinson Foundation

Herrera, Julia: director, Chamiza Foundation

Herrera, Sharon Hays: vice president, trustee, McKee

Foundation (Robert E. and Evelyn)

Herrick, Kenneth G.: chairman, trustee, president, treasurer, Herrick Foundation

Herrick, Martie S. H.: assistant secretary, assistant treasurer, board of governors, Fondren Foundation

Herrick, Todd W.: vice president, trustee, Herrick Foundation

Herrigel, Fred, III: president, Read Foundation (Charles L.)

Herrigel, Rodger K.: secretary, Read Foundation (Charles L.)

Herriman, M. Davis, Jr.: vice president, grocery operations, Giant Food Inc.

Herrington, Ed: vice president, Rheinstrom Hill Community Foundation

Herrington, Marilyn A.: president, Hudson River Bancorp Inc. Foundation

Hershey, Loren W.: chairman, Hershey Foundation

Herterich, Karen Kennedy: director, Kennedy Family Foundation (Ethel and W. George)

Hertzke, Bruce D.: president, chief executive officer, chief operating officer, Winnebago Industries; trustee, Winnebago Industries Foundation

Herweg, D. F.: assistant secretary, Union Pacific Foundation

Herweg, Darlynn: director, Union Pacific Corp.; assistant secretary, Union Pacific Foundation

Herzan, Alexandra: director, van Ameringen Foundation, Inc.

Herzstein, Stanley: director, Koret Foundation

Hesdorffer, Lisa S.: vice president, director, Schmoker Family Foundation

Heselton, George W.: chairman, Gardiner Savings Institution Charitable Foundation

Heske, Douglas: director, U.S. Bancorp Piper Jaffray Foundation

Hess, Bev: secretary, treasurer, Mingenback Foundation (Julia J.)

Hess, Donald E.: secretary-treasurer, Figtree Foundation

Hess, Donald Marc: president, treasurer, Figtree Foundation

Hess, George B., Jr.: director, Baltimore Equitable Insurance Foundation

Hess, William C.: vice president, director, Audubon State Bank Charitable Foundation; chief execu-

tive officer, Iowa Savings Bank; president, secretary, treasurer, director, Iowa Savings Bank Charitable Foundation

Hessler, Deborah: secretary, Bush Charitable Foundation, Inc. (Edyth)

Hesson, Jeffrey L.: director, Ray Foundation

Heston, W. Craig: director, Utica National Foundation; chairman, chief executive officer, director, Utica National Insurance Group

Heuer, Laura Baxter: president, trustee, Andrews Foundation

Heuermann, Bernard K.: president, director, Heuermann Foundation (Bernard K. and Norma F.)

Heuermann, Norma F.: vice president, director, Heuermann Foundation (Bernard K. and Norma F.)

Heuschele, Richard P., MD: trustee, Wickes Foundation (Harvey Randall)

Heuser, Henry V.: director, Vogt Foundation (Henry); chairman, director, Vogt Machine Co. (Henry)

Heuser, Henry V., Jr.: president, director, Vogt Foundation (Henry)

Hewey, Kristina B.: trustee, Braitmayer Foundation

Hewit, Betty Ruth: vice president, director, Hewit Family Foundation

Hewit, William D.: president, treasurer, director, Hewit Family Foundation

Hewitt, Henry: director, PacifiCorp Foundation

Hewitt, James Watt: vice president, treasurer, Abel Foundation

Hewlett, Walter B.: chairman, Hewlett Foundation (William and Flora)

Heyler, David B., Jr.: trustee, McAlister Charitable Foundation (Harold)

Heyman, Joseph S.: president, trustee, Stone Foundation (France)

Heyman, Stephen: trustee, New York Foundation

Hiam, Edwin W.: trustee, Webster Foundation (Edwin S.)

Hibara, Shoji: treasurer, Mitsubishi Electric America Foundation

Hibben, Seabury J.: trustee, Seabury Foundation

Hibberd, William F.: secretary, Harriman Foundation (Gladys and Roland)

Hickey, James H.: trustee, Baker Foundation (R. C.)

Hickey, M.: director, Vodaphone-US Foundation

Hickox, Danielle A.: director, Barker Welfare Foundation

Hickox, John B.: director, Barker Welfare Foundation

Hiddeman, J.: trustee, Alcon Foundation

Hieber, Carl O.: trustee, Plankenhorn Foundation (Harry)

Hiersteiner, Walter L.: vice chairman, Tension Envelope Corp.; vice president, Tension Envelope Foundation

Higashi, Shuntaro: director, SMBC Global Foundation, Inc.

Higgins, Barbara: director, Memorial Foundation for the Blind

Higgins, Eunice O.: secretary, trustee, Olin Foundation (Spencer T. and Ann W.)

Higgins, Michael R.: treasurer, Amcast Industrial Foundation

Higgins, Paul M., Jr.: director, Dime Savings Bank of Norwich Foundation

Higgins, Ralph P.: assistant treasurer, trustee, Eaton Foundation (Cyrus)

Higgins, Richard: trustee, Higgins Foundation (John W. and Clara C.)

Higgins, William W.: board member, trustee, Olin Foundation (Spencer T. and Ann W.)

High, Calvin G.: trustee, High Foundation

High, Gregory A.: trustee, High Foundation

High, Janet C.: trustee, High Foundation

High, Richard L.: trustee, High Foundation

High, S. Dale: trustee, High Foundation

High, Sadie H.: trustee, High Foundation

High, Steven D.: trustee, High Foundation

High, Suzanne M.: trustee, High Foundation

Hightower, George H., Jr.: vice president, trustee, Community Enterprises

Hightower, Neil Hamilton: trustee, Community Enterprises

Higie, William F.: secretary, mgr, Glendorn Foundation

Higley, Robert A.: secretary, treasurer, O'Quinn Foundation (John M.)

Hilbert, Robert J.: secretary, treasurer, senior vice president admin, trustee, El Pomar Foundation

Hilbert, Stephen C.: founder, chairman, president, chief executive officer, Conseco Inc.

Hilbrich, Gerald F.: director, Bush Charitable Foundation, Inc. (Edyth)

Hildebrandt, A. Thomas: director, Davenport-Hatch Foundation

Hildebrandt, Austin E.: president, director, Davenport-Hatch Foundation

Hildebrandt, Mary: director, Davenport-Hatch Foundation

Hildestad, Terry Dean: director, MDU Resources Foundation

Hilgers, William B.: director, Wright Foundation (Lola)

Hill, Allen M.: president, chief executive officer, Dayton Power and Light Co.; director, Dayton Power and Light Co. Foundation

Hill, Bill J.: secretary, treasurer, Beal Foundation

Hill, Bonnie Guiton: president, chief executive officer, Times Mirror Foundation; vice president, Tribune Co.

Hill, C. Dennis: director, Fleming and Jane Howe Patrick Foundation (Robert)

Hill, Charlotte Bishop: vchairwoman, mem adv comm, O'Connor Foundation (A. Lindsay and Olive B.)

Hill, David N.: president, Newhall Foundation (Henry Mayo)

Hill, Frederick W.: vice chairman, J.P. Morgan Chase Foundation

Hill, James: senior vice president corporate affairs, GlaxoSmithKline PLC

Hill, John P., Jr.: administrator, Dominic Foundation

Hill, Karra Mays: director, Mays Foundation

Hill, Kent: president, Gulf Coast Medical Foundation

Hill, Linda A.: vice president, director, Bourns Foundation

Hill, Louis Shea: director, Grotto Foundation

Hill, Marion: vice president, Newhall Foundation (Henry Mayo)

Hill, Michael: executive vice president, Dorot Foundation

Hill, Pamela: executive secretary, treasurer, O'Connor Foundation (A. Lindsay and Olive B.)

Hill, Steven Richard: senior vice president human resources, Weyerhaeuser Co.; trustee, Weyerhaeuser Co. Foundation

Hill, Suzanne: director, O'Connor Foundation (A. Lindsay and Olive B.)

Hill, Thomas J.: treasurer, Ecolab Foundation

Hill Johnson, Elizabeth: president, director, Johnson Foundation (Samuel S.)

Hill-Edgar, W. Keyes: general counsel, secretary, Viacom Foundation

Hiller, William T.: executive director, Jennings Foundation (Martha Holden)

Hilliard, Frank P.: secretary, treasurer, Cooke Foundation Corp. (V. V.)

Hilliard, Robert Glenn: chairman, ING North America Insurance Corp.

Hilliker, Don: secretary, WPWR-TV Channel 50 Foundation

Hillman, Elsie Hilliard: director, Hillman Foundation

Hillman, Henry Lea, Jr.: chairman, director, Hillman Foundation

Hillmer, M. Patricia: trustee, National Machinery Foundation, Inc.

Hillyard, Gerald R., Jr.: trustee, Johnson Foundation (Helen K. and Arthur E.)

Hiltz, Francie S.: trustee, H. C. S. Foundation

Hiltz, L. Thomas: trustee, H. C. S. Foundation

Himmelfarb, Paul: secretary, director, Himmelfarb Foundation (Paul and Annetta)

Himmelman, Bonnie: president, director, Fairchild Foundation, Inc. (Sherman)

Hines, Rodney: program manager, Microsoft Corp.

Hines, William H.: assistant secretary, Freeport-McMoRan Foundation

Hing, Bill Ong: director, Rosenberg Foundation

Hinrichs, Horst: vice chairman, director, American Standard Inc.

Hintz, Gregory J.: mgr, Mercury Aircraft Foundation; treasurer, Mercury Aircraft Inc.

Hipp, William Hayne: president, chief executive officer, director, Liberty Corp.; chairman, president, director, Liberty Corp. Foundation

Hipwell, Arthur J.: senior vice president, Humana Foundation

Hiraki, Phyllis: trustee, Priddy Foundation

Hirano, Irene Y.: chairman, trustee, Kresge Foundation

Hirose, Masaaki: director, Kikkoman Foundation

Hirsch, Bruce A.: executive director, Heller Charitable Foundation (Clarence E.)

Hirsch, Clement L.: president, Oak Tree Charitable Foundation

Hirsch, Jillian: chief financial officer, Christian Dior Perfumes Inc.

Hirschfield, Ira S.: president, trustee, Haas, Jr. Fund (Evelyn and Walter)

Hirschman, Robert B.: director, Kelley and Elza Kelley Foundation (Edward Bangs)

Hitchcock, Meacham: vice president, Brush Foundation

Hite, Henry: president, Harris Foundation (William H. and Mattie Wattis)

Hite, James W.: vice president, Harris Foundation (William H. and Mattie Wattis)

Hite, Marilyn Harris: secretary, Harris Foundation (William H. and Mattie Wattis)

Hixson, Christina M.: trustee, Lied Foundation Trust

Hladky, Joseph F., III: president, chief executive officer, publisher, editor, Gazette Co.; president, director, Gazette Foundation

Ho, Robert P. H.: chief financial officer, Formosa Plastics Corporation, USA

Hoag, George Grant, III: vice president, chief financial officer, director, Hoag Family Foundation (George)

Hobbie, Lynn K.: vice president, Madison Gas & Electric Foundation

Hobby, Diana P.: vice president, Hobby Family Foundation

Hobby, Paul W.: vice president, Hobby Family Foundation

Hobby, William Pettus: president, Hobby Family Foundation

Hoberman, Gerald A.: trustee, Livingston Foundation (Milton S. and Corinne N.)

Hochberg, Alvin S.: trustee, Proctor Foundation (Mattina R.)

Hochman, Kenneth G.: vice president, Kenridge Fund

Hock, W. Fletcher, Jr.: secretary, Jaqua Foundation

Hockaday, Irvine O.: director, Hall Family Foundation (The)

Hockberger, John J.: director, Morrison Foundation (Harry W.)

Hocker, Mark: controller, South Bend Tribune Corp.

Hocker, Sam L.: director, Lennox Foundation (Martha, David and Bagby)

Hodge, Katherine K.: treasurer, Kreitler Foundation

Hodges, Arthur C.: trustee, Winthrop Trust (Clara B.)

Hodges, James H.: secretary, treasurer, director, Springs Foundation, Inc.

Hodges, John E., Jr.: chairman, Gulf Power Foundation

Hodges, Thomas: secretary, Chicago Title and Trust Co. Foundation

Hodgkin, Krista L.: trustee, Knapp Foundation, Inc. (MD)

Hodjat, Mehdi: director, Alavi Foundation

Hodson, Thomas W.: president, drc, Ford Meter Box Co.

Hoefler, Karen E.: secretary, Bemis Family Foundation (F.K.)

Hoekstra, Douglas: treasurer, Medtronic Foundation

Hoel, George O.: director, Andersen Foundation

Hoenemeyer, Frank Joseph: trustee, Cape Branch Foundation

Hoenig, Thomas M.: trustee, Kauffman Foundation (Ewing Marion)

Hofer, Annabel: director, Swanson Family Foundation, Inc. (Dr. W. C.)

Hoff, Susan S.: president, Best Buy Children's Foundation; senior vice president public affairs, Best Buy Co.

Hoffman, Eli: chairman, Jaqua Foundation

Hoffman, James E.: director, Alliant Energy Foundation, Inc.

Hoffman, Karen A.: secretary, Ahmanson Foundation

Hoffman, Lee R.: assistant secretary, CIGNA Foundation

Hoffman, Tyler P.: member advisory committee, Weezie Foundation

Hoffmann, Richard W.: general counsel, Employers Mutual Casualty Co.; secretary, Employers Mutual Charitable Foundation

Hogan, Dan: director, Kirkpatrick Foundation, Inc.

Hogan, David O.: director, Inasmuch Foundation

Hogan, Edward T.: trustee, North Family Trust

Hogan, John E.: executive vice president, treasurer, Cole Foundation (Olive B.); president, Raker Foundation (M. E.)

Hogan, Lee W.: vice chairman, executive vice president, CenterPoint Energy Inc.

Hogans, Mack L.: chairman, president, trustee, Weyerhaeuser Co. Foundation

Hogg, Christopher Anthony: chairman, Dunkin' Donuts Inc.

Hogle, Lucinda S.: assistant secretary, Hall Family Foundation (The)

Hoglund, Forrest Eugene: don, president, Hoglund Foundation

Hoglund, Sally Sue Roney: vice president, Hoglund Foundation

Hoke, Peter: director, King Foundation (Kenneth Kendal)

Hokin, Richard: chairman, director, Intermountain Gas Co.; director, Intermountain Gas Industries Foundation

Holcomb, Allen R.: trustee, Magruder Foundation (Chesley G.)

Holcombe, Robert, Jr.: director, Springs Foundation, Inc.

Holcombe, Robert L., Jr.: director, Springs Foundation, Inc.

Holden, Arthur S., Jr.: chairman emeritus, trustee, Jennings Foundation (Martha Holden)

Holder, Idalia: director human resources, Carnegie Corp. of New York

Holder, J. R.: trustee, Share Trust (Charles Morton)

Holder, Vickie: general manager, administrator operations, Thomasville Furniture Industries Foundation

Holdrege, James H.: director, Hickory Tech Corp.; trustee, Hickory Tech Corp. Foundation

Holdren, John Paul: director, MacArthur Foundation (John D. and Catherine T.)

Holland, Beverly J.: public affairs manager, Simpson Investment Co.

Holland, Hudson, Jr.: secretary, trustee, Hudson-Webber Foundation

Holland, Robert, Jr.: director, Research Corp.

Hollander, Clara: director, Kutz Foundation (Milton and Hattie)

Hollenbeck, Douglas W.: trustee, Lattner Foundation (Forrest C.)

Holler, Grover M., Jr.: director, ShenTel Foundation

Hollern, Thomas R.: trustee, Watson Foundation (Walter E. and Caroline H.)

Holliday, Charles O., Jr.: chairman, chief executive officer, director, du Pont de Nemours & Co. (E.I.)

Holliday, Steve: adv board committee member, Heath Foundation (Mary)

Holliman, Vonda: treasurer, Koch Foundation, Inc. (Fred C. and Mary R.)

Holling, Henry W.: vice president, Caterpillar Foundation

Hollingsworth, John Mark: assistant secretary, Simmons Foundation, Inc. (Harold)

Hollingsworth, Susan Hunt: trustee, Hunt Foundation (Roy A.)

Hollis, Meredith H.: director, Mandeville Foundation

Holloway, Edward, Jr.: trustee, Kinney Memorial Foundation

Holloway, Janet: director, Monsanto Fund

Holloway, Wesley, Jr.: trustee, Golub Foundation

Holm, Richard T.: assistant treasurer, Davis Foundation (Edwin W. and Catherine M.)

Holman, John W., III: director, Hyde and Watson Foundation

Holman, John W., Jr.: director, Barker Foundation (J.M.R.); chairman, director, Hyde and Watson Foundation

Holmes, Beverly: director, MassMutual Foundation for Hartford, Inc. (The)

Holmes, G. Burtt, OD: chairman, Whitaker Foundation

Holmes, Richard: director, Georgia Power Foundation

Holmes, Robert, Jr.: chairman, Alabama Power Foundation

Holmes, Robert W., Jr.: trustee, Riley Foundation (Mabel Louise)

Holmes, Ruth W., PhD: comm mem, Whitaker Fund (Helen F.)

Holmes, Thomas A.: committee member, Whitaker Foundation

Holmquist, Carl: trustee, Lunda Charitable Trust

Holt, Jack: trustee, AT&T National Pro-Am Youth Fund

Holt, June W.: trustee, Holt Family Foundation

Holt, Lawrence J.: director, Kovarik Foundation for Poetry (Henry P.)

Holt, Leon Conrad, Jr.: trustee, Holt Family Foundation; treasurer, Rider-Pool Foundation

Holt, Richard B.: senior vice president, Hasbro Charitable Trust Inc.

Holt, Richard W., Jr.: trustee, Holt Family Foundation

Holt, Timothy J.: president, Air Products Foundation

Holton, A. Linwood, Jr.: director, Loughran Foundation (Mary and Daniel)

Holton, Earl: trustee, Steelcase Foundation

Holton, Richard D., Esq.: director, Joyce Family Foundation

Holtz, Jean: director, Cudahy Fund (Patrick and Anna M.)

Holtzmann, Howard Marshall, Esq.: trustee, Holtzmann Foundation (Jacob L. and Lillian)

Holzer, Alan: controller, New York Stock Exchange Foundation, Inc.

Holzer, Robert: vice president, treasurer, Holzer Memorial Foundation (Richard H.)

Holzer, Vivian: president, Holzer Memorial Foundation (Richard H.)

Holzman, Katharine: director, Menasha Corp. Foundation

Hom, Gloria S.: director, Haigh-Scatena Foundation

Homberger, Rosmarie E.: corporate secretary, Greenwall Foundation

Homer, Constance J.: trustee, Prudential Foundation

Hong, Beverly: secretary, Taube Family Foundation

Hong, Chung Wha: trustee, New York Foundation

Hood, Donald Charles: director, Guggenheim Foundation (Harry Frank)

Hood, Jane Renner: trustee, Cooper Foundation

Hood, R. K.: secretary, Penney Co. Fund (J.C.)

Hook, June C.: director, Cooke Foundation Corp. (V. V.)

Hook, Robert L., Jr.: president, Cooke Foundation Corp. (V. V.)

Hooks, Lawrence: director, Land O'Lakes Foundation

Hoolihan, James: president, trustee, Blandin Foundation

Hoops, Alan R.: director, PacifiCare Health System Foundation

Hooser, Karen R.: trustee, Reinberger Foundation

Hooton, Paula: executive administrator, Fish Foundation (Ray C.)

Hoover, Carl Good: member, Hoover Foundation (Herbert W.)

Hoover, Elizabeth Lacy: chairman, Hoover Foundation (Herbert W.)

Hoover, Lawrence Richard: chairman, trustee, Hoover Foundation (The)

Hoover, Roderick P., Jr.: director, Royal & SunAlliance Insurance Foundation, Inc.

Hoover, Rose: vice president, secretary, Fair Oaks Foundation

Hoover, Thomas H.: committee member, Hoover Foundation (The)

Hopkins, J. L.: trustee, Fluor Foundation

Hopkins, Maureen A.: secretary, admin, Barker Foundation (J.M.R.)

Hopkins, S. B.: vice president, Shell Oil Co. Foundation

Hopkins, Thomas E.: vice president human resources, Sherwin-Williams Co.; assistant secretary, trustee, Sherwin-Williams Foundation

Hopkinson, Sealy H.: trustee, Middendorf Foundation

Hopp, Daniel F.: president, chairman, Whirlpool Foundation

Hoppe, Rudolph T.: director, St. Francis Bank Foundation

Hopper, John J.: vice president, treasurer, El Paso Corporate Foundation

Hopwood, William J.: trustee, Hopwood Charitable Trust (John M.)

Horak, Ron: controller, Bakewell Corp.

Horan, Douglas S.: senior vice president, general counsel, secretary, NSTAR; trustee, NSTAR Foundation

Horan, William: vice president, Prudential Securities Foundation

Hord, Tom: director, Christy-Houston Foundation

Horike, Tsuyoshi: mem allocations comm, Kawabe Memorial Fund

Horn, Craig W.: trustee, Wickes Foundation (Harvey Randall)

Horn, David: trustee, AK Steel Foundation

Horner, Matina Souretis: chairman, director, Greenwall Foundation

Horning, Jackie A.: secretary, treasurer, Humphrey Fund (George M. and Pamela S.); assistant secretary, Kenridge Fund

Hornor, Townsend: director, Kelley and Elza Kelley Foundation (Edward Bangs)

Horowitz, Steven G.: director, DBH Foundation for Law, Land, and the Felicitous Environment

Horsley, Cynthia B.: grants admin, Treakle Foundation (J. Edwin)

Horton, Alan M.: senior vice president newspapers, Scripps Co. (E.W.)

Horton, Alice Kirby: director, Kirby Foundation (F. M.)

Horton, K. H.: director, Tractor & Equipment Co. Foundation

Horwitz, Joy A.: director legal affairs, Pew Charitable Trusts

Hoshino, Hiroaki: treasurer, trustee, Kajima Foundation; president, chief executive officer, Kajima International Inc.

Hosler, Darrell M.: executive vice president, secretary, director, Burns & McDonnell

Hossack, Erroll C.: treasurer, Copic Medical Foundation

Hotchner, Aaron Edward: vice president, treasurer, Newman's Own Inc.

Hotz, Willaim: vice president, St. Francis Bank Foundation

Houchens, George Suel: director, Houchens Foundation (Ervin G.)

Houghton, James L.: assistant secretary, trustee, Mabee Foundation, Inc. (J. E. and L. E.)

Houghton, James Richardson: chairman emeritus, Corning Inc.; trustee, Corning Inc. Foundation

Hougland, W. G.: assistant secretary, Shell Oil Co. Foundation

Housen, Charles B.: chairman, president, chief executive officer, director, Erving Industries; president, director, Housen Foundation

Housen, Marjorie G.: director, Housen Foundation

Housen, Morris: director, vice president, assistant treasurer, clerk, Housen Foundation

Houser, Gary: trustee, Shepherd Foundation (Harold and Helen)

Houston, John D., II: trustee, Pittsburgh Child Guidance Foundation

Houstoun, Feather: president, director, Penn Foundation (William)

Howard, David M.: director, Tyndale House Foundation

Howard, Derek G.: trustee, Greenfield Foundation (Albert M.)

Howard, Ernestine Broadhurst: vchairman, Broadhurst Foundation

Howard, Frances L.: assistant secretary, trustee, Arkell Hall Foundation

Howard, Glen S.: secretary, senior vice president, general counsel, Fannie Mae Foundation

Howard, Jerry: trustee, U.S. Steel Foundation

Howard, John T.: director, Andrews McMeel Universal Foundation

Howard, K. Mason, MD: president, director, Copic Medical Foundation

Howard, Pamela: trustee, Scripps Howard Foundation

Howatt, Thomas J.: president, chief executive officer, director, Wausau-Mosinee Paper Corp.

Howe, Calvin E.: director, M.E. Foundation

Howe, J. Franklin: trustee, Davenport Trust Fund

Howe, James Everett: trustee, Edison Fund (Charles)

Howe, James J.: director, Howe and Mitchell B. Howe Foundation (Lucille Horton)

Howe, Jonathan T.: executive director, Davis Foundations (Arthur Vining)

Howe, Mitchell B., Jr.: president, treasurer, Howe and Mitchell B. Howe Foundation (Lucille Horton)

Howe, Stanley M.: director, HON Industries Charitable Foundation

Howe Lossi, Jean: secretary, Rheinstrom Hill Community Foundation

Howell, Alfred H., Jr.: director, Dodge Foundation (Cleveland H.)

Howell, George L.: trustee, Hilliard Foundation

Howell, Joe: director, Kirkpatrick Foundation, Inc.

Hower, Frank B., Jr.: trustee, Brown Foundation, Inc. (James Graham)

Hower, Julie: trustee, Young Foundation (Bill B.)

Howitt, Robert: treasurer, trustee, Hayden Foundation (Charles)

Hoyes, Louis W.: vice president, Fannie Mae; director, Fannie Mae Foundation

Hoyt, Jonathon, MD: director, De Queen Regional Medical Center

Hoyt, Lawrence C., Jr.: director, Provident Community Foundation

Hrabowski, Freeman: director, France-Merrick Foundation

Hrabowski, Jaqueline: trustee, Abell Foundation

Hsu, Ta Chun: director, Starr Foundation

Hubbard, Albert C., Jr.: president, Price Associates Foundation (T. Rowe)

Hubbard, Ann: advisory committee member, Dickenson Foundation (Harriet Ford)

Hubbard, David: advisory committee member, Dickenson Foundation (Harriet Ford)

Hubbard, G. Morrison, Jr.: director emeritus, Hyde and Watson Foundation

Hubbard, Joan Dale: vice president, director, Hubbard Foundation (R. D. and Joan Dale)

Hubbard, Randall Dee: president, director, Hubbard Foundation (R. D. and Joan Dale)

Hubbard, Robert W.: director, Hubbard Foundation

Hubbard, Stanley E.: director, Hubbard Foundation

Hubbard, Stanley S.: chairman, president, chief executive officer, Hubbard Broadcasting Inc.; president, director, Hubbard Foundation

Hubbard, Thomas J.: secretary, Dreyfus Foundation (Jean and Louis)

Hutchinson, Herman R.:
vice president, director,
Barra Foundation

Hutchison, S. L.: chief
financial officer, director,
Crail-Johnson Foundation

Hutta, Jane: secretary,
SMBC Global Founda-
tion, Inc.; general coun-
sel, assistant treasurer,
staff attorney, Sumitomo
Mitsui Banking Corp.

Hutterly, Jane M.: executive
vice president, Johnson
Fund (S.C.); vice presi-
dent, Johnson & Son
(S.C.)

Hutton, Patricia E.: executive vice president, Uni-
versal Studios Founda-
tion

Hyatt, Linda S.: vice president, executive director,
Landmark Communica-
tions Foundation

Hyatt, Richard: trustee,
National Grange Mutual
Charitable Trust

Hybl, William J.: chairman,
chief executive officer,
trustee, El Pomar Foun-
dation

Hyde, Douglas W.: chairman, president, chief
executive officer, Osh-
kosh B'Gosh Inc.

Hyde, Henry B.: director,
Erpf Fund (Armand G.)

Hynes, Mary Ann: director,
Scholl Foundation (Dr.)

Hynnek, Julia L.: director,
HRK Foundation

I

l'Anson, Lawrence W., Jr.:
president, executive
director, Beazley Founda-
tion

Iakovos, Metropolitan:
director, Demos Founda-
tion (N.)

Icahn, Carl Celian: president, ACF Foundation;
owner, chairman, direc-
tor, ACF Industries; president, director, Icahn
Foundation (Carl C.)

Ice, Carl R.: executive vice
president, chief operating
officer, Burlington Northern Santa Fe Corp.;
director, Burlington Northern Santa Fe Foundation

Iding, Allan E.: director,
president, Wehr Founda-
tion (Todd)

Iger, Robert A.: treasurer,
trustee, Disney Co. Foun-
dation (Walt)

Ignat, Pam: trustee, Nord
Family Foundation

Iijima, Hirao: chairman, Mitsubishi Motor Sales of
America Inc.

Imboden, Connie: governor,
Baker, Jr. Memorial Fund
(William G.)

Imeson, Tom: chairman,
director, PacifiCorp Foundation

Immelt, Jeffrey R.: chairman, chief executive officer, General Electric Co.

Ince, Max L.: secretary, treasurer, South Plains Foun-
dation

Indenbaum, Michael A.:
secretary, trustee, Herrick
Foundation

Ine, Hiroshi: treasurer,
SMBC Global Founda-
tion, Inc.

Ingalls, Rebekah: secretary,
trustee, Ingalls Foundation
(Louise H. and David
S.)

Ingalls, Walter H.: director,
Bank of Greene County
Charitable Foundation

Ingato, Robert J.: vice president, CIT Group Founda-
tion

Inglee, Douglas: director,
Dillon Foundation

Inglee, Gale D.: assistant
secretary, director, Dillon
Foundation

Inglis, Timothy M.: vice
president, treasurer, Laurel Foundation

Inglish, David Winston:
trustee, Towsley Founda-
tion (Harry A. and Marga-
ret D.)

Ingram, Beverly: vice president, Giger Foundation
(Paul and Oscar)

Ingstad, D. Scott: trustee,
Carver Charitable Trust
(Roy J.)

Ingwersen, James C.: secretary, assistant treasurer, director, Atkinson
Foundation

Inouye, Minoru: vchairman,
trustee, United States-
Japan Foundation

Inskeep, Harriet J.: director,
Journal-Gazette Founda-
tion, Inc.

Inskeep, Richard G.: owner,
president, public, Journal-
Gazette Co.; president,
director, Journal-Gazette
Foundation, Inc.

Inskeep, Thomas R.: director, Journal-Gazette
Foundation, Inc.

Inskip, Gregory A.: director,
Glencoe Foundation

Ireland, Cornelia W.: trustee, Mather and William
Gwinn Mather Fund (Eliz-
abeth Ring)

Ireland, George R.: treasurer, Mather and William
Gwinn Mather Fund (Eliz-
abeth Ring)

Ireland, Gregg A.: trustee,
Stauffer Communications
Foundation

Ireland, James D., III: president, Mather and William
Gwinn Mather Fund (Eliz-
abeth Ring)

Irish, Ann K.: trustee, Earhart Foundation

Irvin, Nathaniel, II: president, director, Babcock
Foundation (Mary Rey-
nolds)

Irvin, Patricia L.: vice president, operations and
planning, Mellon Founda-
tion (Andrew W.)

Irwin, John N., III: chairman,
chief executive officer,
treasurer, trustee, Bod-
man Foundation; mem
adv board, Watson Foun-
dation (Thomas J.)

**Irwin, Robert James Arm-
strong:** trustee, Baird
Foundation

Irwin, William Baird: trustee, Baird Foundation

Isakower, Glorie: vice president, Kaplun Foundation
(Morris J. and Betty)

Iscol, Jill: president, treasurer, director, IF Humming-
bird Foundation

Iscol, Kenneth H.: vice
president, secretary,
director, IF Hummingbird
Foundation

Isdaner, Scott Rosen: trustee, Strauss Foundation

Iselin, John Jay, PhD:
director, Macy, Jr. Foun-
dation (Josiah)

Ishiyama, George I.: president, director, Ishiyama
Foundation

Ishiyama, Jean: assistant
secretary, Ishiyama
Foundation

Ishiyama, Setsuko: secretary, treasurer, director,
Ishiyama Foundation

Isom, Ralph: director, CHC
Foundation

Ittleson, Henry Anthony:
chairman, president,
director, Ittleson Foundation

Ivens, Barbara J.: president,
trustee, Gerber Founda-
tion

Iversen, Robert C.: chief
operating officer, Air
France

Iverson, Kenneth A.: vice
president, corporate sec-
retary, Ecolab Inc.

Ives, Deborah M.: vice president, treasurer, Weingart
Foundation

Ivey, Harriet M.: president,
chief executive officer,
Pulliam Charitable Trust
(Nina Mason)

Ivey, Susan: president, chief
executive officer, Brown
& Williamson Tobacco
Corp.

Iwata, Ruth S.: mem allocations comm, Kawabe
Memorial Fund

Izzo, Ralph: trustee, Public
Service Electric & Gas
Foundation

Izzo, Scott D.: associate
director, secretary, Mel-
lon Foundation (Richard
King)

J

Jaber, Paul N.: director,
New Milford Savings
Bank Foundation

Jackman, J. Warren: trustee, Bernsen Foundation
(Grace and Franklin)

Jackson, Basil L., Jr.: vice
president, Bowen Founda-
tion (Ethel N.)

Jackson, Blaine: trustee,
McKinney Charitable
Trust (Carl and Alleen)

Jackson, Charles: president, Marshall Founda-
tion

Jackson, Charles A.: vice
president, director, Jackson Family Foundation
(Ann)

Jackson, David D.: president, Summerlee Founda-
tion

Jackson, Deborah C.: trustee, Eastern Bank Chari-
table Foundation

Jackson, Edgar R.: director,
Parsons Foundation
(Ralph M.)

Jackson, Herrick: trustee,
Connemara Fund

Jackson, Jack: vice chairman, secretary, treasurer,
Heath Foundation (Ed
and Mary)

Jackson, James H.: vice
president, director, Jackson Family Foundation
(Ann)

Jackson, James W.: secretary, trustee, Blowitz-
Ridgeway Foundation

Jackson, Kenneth T.: director, Luce Foundation
(Henry)

Jackson, Lucy: support,
AT&T Foundation

Jackson, Palmer G.: president, director, Jackson
Family Foundation (Ann)

Jackson, Palmer G., Jr.:
secretary, director, Jackson Family Foundation
(Ann)

Jackson, Peggy E.: trustee,
Lantz Foundation (Wal-
ter)

Jackson, Richard E.: trustee, Davenport Trust Fund

Jackson, Robert T.: treasur-
er, director, American
Century Companies
Foundation

Jackson, William L.: chief
financial officer, director,
Jackson Family Founda-
tion (Ann)

Jacob, John E.: director,
Anheuser-Busch Founda-
tion

Jacob, P. Bernard: chairman, Gulf Power Founda-
tion

Jacobs, Bruce E.: vice president, director, Grede
Foundation; president,
chief executive officer,
Grede Foundries; direc-
tor, Marshall & Ilsley
Foundation, Inc.

Jacobs, Burleigh Edmund:
president, director, Grede
Foundation

Jacobs, Debra M.: administration agent, Beattie
Foundation (Cordelia

Lee); president, secre-
tary, chief executive officer, Selby and Marie
Selby Foundation (Wil-
liam G.)

Jacobs, Frank D.: assistant
secretary, McMaster
Foundation (Harold and
Helen)

Jacobs, Terry S.: trustee,
National Grange Mutual
Charitable Trust

Jacobson, Knute: director,
Siebert Lutheran Founda-
tion

Jacobson, Lyle Gordon:
trustee, Hickory Tech
Corp. Foundation

Jacobson, Malcolm B.:
trustee, Cassett Founda-
tion (Louis N.)

Jacobson, Nelson C.: trustee, JSJ Foundation

Jacobson, Richard J.: vice
president, treasurer, Cox
Enterprises Inc.

Jacobson, Sibyl C.: president, chief executive officer, director, MetLife
Foundation

Jacoby, Jennifer: vice president, secretary, director,
Crown Memorial (Arie
and Ida)

Jaeger, Sylvia Watson:
trustee, Brown Founda-
tion, Inc. (James Gra-
ham)

Jaenke, Norma: executive
director, Presto Founda-
tion

Jaffe, Edwin A.: chairman,
Jaffe Foundation

Jaffe, Ira J.: trustee, McGregor Fund

Jaffe, Lola: vchairman, Jaffe
Foundation

Jaffe, Mary Hewlett: director, Hewlett Foundation
(William and Flora)

Jaffe, Robert: trustee, Jaffe
Foundation

Jaffe, Ruth M.: trustee, Kantzler Foundation

Jaffe, Suzanne Denbo: treasurer, Research Corp.

Jaffrey, Jonathan D.: vice
president, secretary, Day
Foundation (Willametta
K.); vice president, chief
admin officer, Keck Foun-
dation (W. M.)

Jagow, Elmer: trustee, Frohring Foundation (Paul
and Maxine)

Jalkut, Thomas P.: trustee,
Killam Trust (Constance)

Jamail, Joseph D., III: vice
president, Jamail Foun-
dation (Lee and Joseph
D.)

Jamail, Lee H.: president,
Jamail Foundation (Lee
and Joseph D.)

Jamail, Randall Hage: vice
president, Jamail Foun-
dation (Lee and Joseph
D.)

Jamail, Robert Lee: secre-
tary, treasurer, Jamail
Foundation (Lee and
Joseph D.)

Officers and Directors by Name

James, Diana L.: secretary, treasurer, Reidler Foundation

James, Don: director, Kaul Foundation Trust (Hugh)

James, Donald M.: chairman, Vulcan Materials Co. Foundation

James, John J.: trustee, Gerber Foundation

James, Lynda: secretary, The Prairie Foundation

James, Wilmot G.: trustee, Ford Foundation

Jameson, Kelly J.: assistant secretary, El Paso Corporate Foundation

Jammal, Eleanor A.: secretary, treasurer, Ashtabula Foundation

Jander, Steve M.: trustee, Campbell Soup Foundation

Janke, Lucinda P.: trustee, Kiplinger Foundation

Janney, Mary D.: director, Strong Foundation (Hattie M.)

Jansen, Larry: director, Grinnell Mutual Group Foundation

Jansing, Caroline C.: trustee, Cook Foundation (Louella)

Jansing, Christopher C.: trustee, Cook Foundation (Louella)

Jansing, John Cook: trustee, Cook Foundation (Louella)

Janson, Julia S.: secretary, Cinergy Foundation

Japlon, H.: president, director, Square D Foundation

Jaquay, Robert B.: associate director, Gund Foundation (George)

Jarcho, Fredrica: vice president, program, Greenwall Foundation

Jarrells, Judy: director, Joco Foundation

Jarrow, Sidney F.: trustee, Jaffee Foundation

Jaskol, Leonard R.: chairman, president, chief executive officer, director, Lydall Inc.

Jasse, Andre C., Jr.: trustee, Eastern Bank Charitable Foundation

Jastrow, Kenneth M., II: director, Temple-Inland Foundation

Javitch, Jonathan: director, Lebovitz Fund

Jay Rossi, Safford: trustee, Rossi Family Foundation

Jean, Raymond A.: chairman, president, chief executive officer, director, Quanex Corp.

Jeannero, Jane M.: trustee, Gerber Foundation

Jelinek, Don: trustee, Reynolds Foundation (Edgar & Francis)

Jelley, Philip M.: secretary, director, Skaggs Foundation (L. J. Skaggs and Mary C.)

Jenkins, David H., DVM: director, Bank of Greene County Charitable Foundation

Jenkins, Greg G.: director, El Paso Corporate Foundation

Jenkins, James R.: director, Deere Foundation (John)

Jenkins, John E., Jr.: director, Huntington Foundation

Jenkins, John S.: director, Walker Foundation

Jenkins, Scott M.: trustee, Connelly Foundation

Jenks, John R.: treasurer, chief information officer, Irvine Foundation (The James)

Jenks, Rodney P., Jr.: secretary, Hexcel Foundation

Jenney, Michelle: foundation assistant, Webster Foundation (Edwin S.)

Jennings, Elizabeth Cabell: director, Cabell III and Maude Morgan Cabell Foundation (Robert G.)

Jennings, Evan D., II: president, Jennings Foundation (Mary Hillman)

Jennings, J. Webb, III: director, Cockrell Foundation

Jennings, Karen E.: executive vice president, SBC Communications Inc.; director, SBC Foundation

Jennings, Lenore: assistant secretary, Dingman Foundation (Michael D.)

Jennings, Perry G.: trustee, Lowe's Charitable and Educational Foundation

Jenrette, Richard Hampton: trustee, Duke Endowment

Jensen, A. C.: co-trustee, Hallett Charitable Trust (E. W.)

Jensen, Ed: assistant treasurer, Sams Foundation (Earl C.)

Jensen, Jon Mark: senior program officer, Gund Foundation (George)

Jensen, Kenneth L.: chief financial officer, Johns Manville

Jensen, Kent: chief financial officer, treasurer, Holnam Inc.

Jenson, Ole C.: director, Andrews McMeel Universal Foundation

Jenson, Thor J.: trustee, Kinney-Lindstrom Foundation

Jeppson, Nancy: director, Memorial Foundation for the Blind

Jernstedt, Derek: director, Hedco Foundation

Jernstedt, Dorothy: secretary, director, Hedco Foundation

Jeschke, Thomas: director, Mid-Iowa Health Foundation

Jesmain, Gary R.: president, Niagara Mohawk Foundation

Jester, Cindy: administrative assistant, Lane Foundation (Minnie and Bernard)

Jeter, Mark: director, TCF Foundation

Jeter, Norman W.: president, Ross Foundation

Jewell, Robert: vice president communications, Goodrich Corp.

Jewett, George Frederick, Jr.: chairman, Jewett Foundation (George Frederick)

Jewett, Lucille Winifred McIntyre: trustee, Jewett Foundation (George Frederick)

Jines, Michael L.: secretary, Reliant Resources Foundation

Joblow, Wendy: director, Ideal Industries Foundation

Joffe, Harvey G.: cfo, director, Parvin Foundation (Albert)

Johansen, Judi: director, PacifiCorp Foundation

John, Winfield C.: director, Huntington Foundation

Johns, Lisa R.: assistant treasurer, Hillman Foundation

Johns, Sheryl Lightfoot: vice president, treasurer, chief financial officer, Houston Endowment

Johns, William M.: trustee, Goddard Foundation (Charles B.)

Johnson, Abigail P.: director, Fidelity Foundation

Johnson, Alan C.: director, Crail-Johnson Foundation

Johnson, Alan H.: director, vice president, Andersen Foundation

Johnson, Ann L.: director, Crail-Johnson Foundation; trustee, Johnson Foundation (Charles and Ann)

Johnson, Anna M.: administrative assistant, Altman Foundation

Johnson, Anthony S.: trustee, Western New York Foundation

Johnson, B. Gerald: trustee, Bullitt Foundation

Johnson, B. Larry: president, Guaranty Bank & Trust Co.

Johnson, Bari: trustee, Loutit Foundation

Johnson, Berkley D., Jr.: trustee, Chadwick Fund (Dorothy Jordan)

Johnson, Betty Wold: chairman, director, Johnson Foundation (Willard T. C.)

Johnson, Burdine C.: president, Clayton Fund

Johnson, Carol A.: chairman, Henderson Foundation (George B.)

Johnson, Carolyn E.: president, director, Crail-Johnson Foundation

Johnson, Charleen: executive director, Millipore Foundation (The)

Johnson, Charles B.: president, Cessna Aircraft Co.

Johnson, Charles Bartlett: trustee, Johnson Foundation (Charles and Ann)

Johnson, Charlotte S.: trustee, Bremer Foundation (Otto)

Johnson, Christopher W.: trustee, Johnson Charitable Trust (Keith Wold)

Johnson, Craig C.: director, Crail-Johnson Foundation

Johnson, Dale D.: director, Graco Foundation

Johnson, Diane T.: vice president, secretary, Johnson Foundation (A.D.)

Johnson, Donald A.: chairman, trustee, JSJ Foundation

Johnson, Donald E., Jr.: president, trustee, Whiting Foundation

Johnson, Douglas: treasurer, Decker Foundation (Dr. G. Clifford and Florence B.)

Johnson, Edward C., III: director, president, Fidelity Foundation

Johnson, Edward Crosby, III: chairman, president, chief executive officer, director; president, director, Johnson Fund (Edward C.)

Johnson, Edward Crosby, IV: director, Johnson Fund (Edward C.)

Johnson, Elizabeth L.: director, Johnson Fund (Edward C.)

Johnson, Elizabeth Ross: trustee, Johnson Charitable Trust (Keith Wold)

Johnson, Eric C.: chairman, director, Crail-Johnson Foundation

Johnson, F. Martin: chairman, director, JSJ Corp.; trustee, JSJ Foundation

Johnson, Forde: president, CHC Foundation

Johnson, Glenn: trustee, Acushnet Foundation

Johnson, Gretchen W.: trustee, director, Cape Branch Foundation

Johnson, H. Fisk: trustee, Johnson Fund (S.C.); chairman, Johnson & Son (S.C.)

Johnson, Harold B.: director, Noble Foundation, Inc. (Edward John)

Johnson, Harry A., III: chairman, First Tennessee Foundation

Johnson, Howard Bates: trustee, Johnson Foundation (Howard)

Johnson, Howard Brennan: trustee, Johnson Foundation (Howard)

Johnson, Ivan: chairman, Mid-Iowa Health Foundation

Johnson, J. M. Hamlin: trustee, Stackpole-Hall Foundation

Johnson, James Lawrence: director, Cape Branch Foundation

Johnson, James M.: president, trustee, Johnson Foundation (Thomas Phillips and Jane Moore)

Johnson, Jane T.: trustee, Johnson Foundation (Thomas Phillips and Jane Moore)

Johnson, Jennifer: trustee, Western New York Foundation

Johnson, Jerry Ray: director, Gregg-Graniteville Foundation

Johnson, Jesse D.: treasurer, Johnson Foundation (Thomas Phillips and Jane Moore)

Johnson, Johanna: assistant treasurer, Ziegler Foundation for the Blind (E. Matilda)

Johnson, John C.: member, Crampton Trust

Johnson, Judy: vice president, director, Midcontinent Media Foundation

Johnson, Kate L.: director, Carter Foundation (Amon G.)

Johnson, Keith A.: controller, Simmons Foundation, Inc. (Harold)

Johnson, Leslie A.: secretary, Holmberg Foundation

Johnson, Lynne: secretary, Cooke Foundation

Johnson, M. O.: director, Bayport Foundation of Andersen Corporation

Johnson, Madeleine Rudin: vice president, director, Rudin Foundation (Samuel and May)

Johnson, Mark L.: treasurer, director, Carter Foundation (Amon G.); vice president, Carter Star Telegram Employees Fund (Amon G.)

Johnson, Michael: second vice president, Grotto Foundation

Johnson, Michael O.: director, assistant secretary, Reynolds Foundation (R. J.)

Johnson, Michael P.: director, Williams Companies Foundation (The)

Johnson, Mike: trustee, Blandin Foundation

Johnson, Murray Lloyd, Jr.: secretary, trustee, Zachry Foundation (The)

Johnson, Nan: assistant trustee, BellSouth Foundation

Johnson, Norman E.: trustee, CLARCOR Foundation; senior vice president technology,

Weyerhaeuser Co.; trustee, Weyerhaeuser Co. Foundation

Johnson, Patricia C.: cfo, director, Johnson Foundation (Samuel S.)

Johnson, Paula: director, Jostens Foundation Inc. (The)

Johnson, Phillip M.: treasurer, Georgia-Pacific Foundation

Johnson, Robbin S.: vice president, Cargill Foundation; corporate vice president public affairs, Cargill Inc.

Johnson, Robert Wood, IV: trustee, Johnson Charitable Trust (Keith Wold); president, director, Johnson Foundation (Willard T. C.)

Johnson, Roland H.: executive director, Grundy Foundation

Johnson, Samuel Curtis: chairman emeritus, Johnson Foundation; chairman, president, trustee, Johnson Fund (S.C.); chairman emeritus, Johnson & Son (S.C.)

Johnson, Sandra: secretary, Donaldson Foundation

Johnson, Sheila B.: secretary, director, Carter Foundation (Amon G.)

Johnson, Thomas P., Jr.: chairman, trustee, Johnson Foundation (Thomas Phillips and Jane Moore)

Johnson, Thomas Stephen: trustee, United States-Japan Foundation

Johnson, Tina P.: senior vice president, director, Publix Supermarkets; treasurer, Publix Supermarkets Charities

Johnson, Tom: trustee, secretary, Mellinger Educational Foundation (Edward Arthur)

Johnson, Wayne J.: president, treasurer, Johnson Foundation (A.D.)

Johnson, Wendy S.: director, Babcock Foundation (Mary Reynolds)

Johnson, William B.: president, director, Alabama Power Foundation

Johnson, William D.: vice president, director, Progress Energy Foundation

Johnson, William R.: chairman, president, chief executive officer, Heinz Co. (H.J.)

Johnson, William T.: trustee, Johnson Foundation (Burdine)

Johnson, Wyatt Thomas, Jr.: secretary, trustee, Mellinger Educational Foundation (Edward Arthur)

Johnson-Farr, Marilyn: director, Woods Charitable Fund

Johnson-Helm, Elizabeth K.: vice president, director, Johnson Foundation (Samuel S.)

Johnson-Leipold, Helen P.: trustee, Johnson Foundation; chairman, chief executive officer, Johnson Outdoors Inc., Johnson & Son (S.C.)

Johnston, Chapman: president, chief executive officer, Tanner Cos. (Rutherfordton, NC); vice president, Tanner Foundation

Johnston, Charles H.: director, Peterson Foundation (Hal and Charlie)

Johnston, Gerald E.: president, chief executive officer, Clorox Co.; chairman, Clorox Co. Foundation

Johnston, James W.: director, La-Z-Boy Inc.

Johnston, Lawrence R.: chairman, chief executive officer, director, Albertson's Inc.

Johnston, S. K., Jr.: trustee, Tucker Foundation

Jokiel, Peter E.: senior vice president, chief financial officer, CNA Financial Corp.

Jones, B. L.: trustee, Fasken Foundation

Jones, Betty Alyce: director, Redfield Foundation (Nell J.)

Jones, Boisfeuillet, Jr.: director, Meyer Foundation (Eugene and Agnes E.)

Jones, Charles N., MD: vice president, De Queen Regional Medical Center

Jones, Christopher: chief executive officer, Thompson Co. (J. Walter)

Jones, D. Paul, Jr.: chairman, chief executive officer, Compass Bank; trustee, Compass Bank Foundation

Jones, D. Whitman: director, Whittenberger Foundation (Claude R. and Ethel B.)

Jones, David A., Jr.: director, Humana Foundation

Jones, David Allen: president, director, Humana Foundation; co-founder, chairman, director, Humana Inc.

Jones, David R.: director, Scherman Foundation

Jones, Edward A.: director, Crosswicks Foundation

Jones, Emily J.: assistant vice president, corporate secretary, Meadows Foundation (The)

Jones, Farrell: president, trustee, Levitt Foundation (NY)

Jones, Helen DeVitt: director, Jones Foundation (Helen)

Jones, Helen Jeane: director, Redfield Foundation (Nell J.)

Jones, Howard D., III: secretary, Baltimore Equitable Insurance Foundation

Jones, Ingrid Saunders: senior vice president, Coca-Cola Co.; chairman, director, Coca-Cola Foundation

Jones, J. Michael: director, Rockefeller Foundation (Winthrop)

Jones, James E.: trustee, Mabee Foundation, Inc. (J. E. and L. E.)

Jones, James H.: secretary, assistant treasurer, director, Coleman Foundation (IL)

Jones, James W.: chairman, Meyer Foundation (Eugene and Agnes E.)

Jones, JoAnn: trustee, Cauthorn Charitable Trust (John and Mildred)

Jones, John M.: adv, O'Bleness Foundation (Charles)

Jones, John P., III: chairman, president, chief executive officer, Air Products and Chemicals Inc.; trustee, Rider-Pool Foundation

Jones, Johnny C.: trustee, Share Trust (Charles Morton)

Jones, Joseph W.: chairman emeritus, Woodruff Foundation (Robert W.)

Jones, Josephine: executive vice president, Crosswicks Foundation

Jones, Kenneth W.: controller, Liberty Corp.

Jones, Leslie A.: chairman, Dentsply International Inc.

Jones, Louise G.: trustee, Bigelow Foundation (F. R.)

Jones, Martha: trustee, New York Foundation

Jones, Mary Duke Trent: second vice chairman, assistant secretary, assistant treasurer, trustee, Biddle Foundation (Mary Duke); trustee, Duke Endowment

Jones, Melissa A.: director, Houston Endowment

Jones, Nathan J.: director, Deere Foundation (John)

Jones, O. D.: trustee, Long Foundation (J. M.)

Jones, Owen: chief executive officer, chief operating officer, director, Sheaffer Pen Corp.

Jones, Patrick A.: chief financial officer, vice president, treasurer, Noble Foundation (Samuel Roberts)

Jones, Raymond E.: secretary, director, Shelter Insurance Foundation; executive vice president, secretary, Shelter Mutual Insurance Co.

Jones, Robert G.: trustee, Key Foundation

Jones, Robert J.: director, Bush Foundation

Jones, Ronald D.: president, director, Siebert Lutheran Foundation

Jones, Steve: gov, Munson Foundation Trust (W. B.)

Jones, Sumner: executive vice president, Eastern Bank

Jones, Timothy: president, trustee, Price Foundation (Louis and Harold)

Jones, Tony: chairman, Hudson River Bancorp Inc.

Jones, William H.: vice president, Hudson River Bancorp Inc. Foundation

Jones Joyce, Alexis: director, Joyce Family Foundation

Jonklaas, Anthony: trustee, Kenridge Fund

Jonklaas, Clair Hanna B.: president, trustee, Kenridge Fund

Jonsen, Albert R.: director, Sierra Health Foundation

Joos, David W.: president, chief executive officer electric, executive vice president, Consumers Energy Co.; director, Consumers Energy Foundation

Jope, Alan C.: director, Unilever United States Foundation

Joralemon, Jane G.: president, trustee, Anderson Foundation (NY)

Jordan, Ann K.: fund comm mem, Kaufman Endowment Fund (Louis G.)

Jordan, Barbara M.: secretary, director, Claneil Foundation

Jordan, Grady: director, Hawn Foundation

Jordan, Gretchen M.: director, Claneil Foundation

Jordan, Henry A.: president, chairman, , director, Claneil Foundation

Jordan, Vernon E., Jr.: director, Sara Lee Corp.

Jordan, William Chester: director, Teagle Foundation

Jorstad, Laurin: director, Oakley-Lindsay Foundation of Quincy Newspapers and Its Subsidiaries

Jose, Katharine P.: president, trustee, Southways Foundation

Joseph, Amy F.: trustee, Farmer Family Foundation

Joseph, J. Gonzalez: program director, Campbell Soup Foundation

Joslin, David C.: trustee, Gerber Foundation

Joslyn, Robert B.: trustee, Fruehauf Foundation

Joy, Joan H.: trustee, Joy Family Foundation

Joy, Paul W.: don, trustee, Joy Family Foundation

Joy, Stephen T.: trustee, Joy Family Foundation

Joy Reinhold, Paula: trustee, Joy Family Foundation

Joy Sullivan, Marsha: trustee, Joy Family Foundation

Joyce, Bernard F.: vice president, director, Link, Jr. Foundation (George)

Joyce, Joseph M.: senior vice president, general counsel, assistant secretary, Best Buy Co.

Joyce, Michael Stewart: trustee, Pinkerton Foundation

Juday, David W.: president, Ideal Industries Foundation; chairman, director, Ideal Industries Inc.

Judd, R. C.: vice president, director, Winn-Dixie Stores Foundation

Judge, James J.: senior vice president corporate service business unit, treasurer, NSTAR; trustee, NSTAR Foundation

Juenemann, Donald E.: trustee, Wickes Foundation (Harvey Randall)

Juett, Katherine Crosland: trustee, Lyndhurst Foundation

Juhl, Randy: trustee, Ahrens Foundation (Claude W. and Dolly)

Juilfs, George C.: director, Cinergy Foundation

Jukosky, James A.: vice president, trustee, Brundage Charitable, Scientific, and Wildlife Conservation Foundation (Charles E. and Edna T.)

Jukosky, Susan: vice president, trustee, Brundage Charitable, Scientific, and Wildlife Conservation Foundation (Charles E. and Edna T.)

Juliano, Marie: executive secretary, AT&T Foundation

Junck, Mary: president, Lee Foundation

Junck, Mary E.: trustee, Hartford Courant Foundation

Juneman, Lou: director, American Honda Foundation

Jung, Andrea: chairman, chief executive officer, Avon Products Inc.

Jurzykowski, M. Christine: secretary, treasurer, trustee, Jurzykowski Foundation (Alfred)

Jurzykowski, Yolande L.: executive vice president, trustee, Jurzykowski Foundation (Alfred)

Justice, Larry: mgr, Porter Testamentary Trust (James Hyde)

Justice, Rita F.: mem, Phipps Foundation (Columbus)

Jutte, Larry: director, Honda of America Foundation

K

Kaden, Ellen O.: senior vice president, Campbell Soup Co.

Kaemmer, Arthur W., MD: chairman, treasurer, HRK Foundation

Kaemmer, Frederick C.: director, HRK Foundation

Kaemmer, Martha H.: vice president, director, HRK Foundation

Kaesemeyer, C. Thomas: executive director, secretary, Gates Family Foundation

Kahn, Andrew: director, Kahn Foundation; chief executive officer, Kahn, Lucas-Lancaster Incorporated Children's Wear

Kahn, Michael: president, director, Reynolds Foundation (Christopher)

Kahn, Peggy Anne: director, Kahn Foundation

Kahn, Richard D.: director, Barker Foundation (J.M.R.)

Kahrer, Mark G.: assistant treasurer, Public Service Electric & Gas Foundation

Kailbourne, Erland E.: director, board chairman, Oishei Foundation (The John R.)

Kain, Herbert, MD: director, Valley Foundation

Kaiser, Ferdinand C.: vice president, secretary, trustee, Arkell Hall Foundation

Kakabadse, Yolanda: trustee, Ford Foundation

Kalaher, Richard A.: vice president, secretary, general counsel, American Standard Inc.

Kalainov, Sam Charles: chairman, president, chief executive officer, Amerus Group Co.

Kalb, Bettie A.: president, secretary, Wildermuth Foundation (E. F.)

Kalish, Katherine M.: mgr, Porter Testamentary Trust (James Hyde)

Kalisman, Gayle T.: president, Taubman Foundation (A. Alfred)

Kalkus, June: vice president, Kalkus Foundation

Kalkus, Mark: secretary, Kalkus Foundation

Kalkus, Peter: president, Kalkus Foundation

Kallaus, Kurt J.: president, Sunnen Foundation

Kallet, Michael R.: president, Oneida Savings Bank Charitable Foundation

Kaloski, John: trustee, AK Steel Foundation

Kaltenbacher, Philip K.: chairman, president, chief executive officer, director, Seton Co.; trustee, Seton Co. Foundation

Kaminski, Francis: chairman, trustee, Thomaston Savings Bank Foundation

Kaminsky, Kenneth P.: president, director, NewAlliance Foundation

Kaminsky, Marcia S.: vice president, USG Foundation

Kamras, Marvin: distribution trustee, Schwab-Rosenhouse Memorial Foundation

Kane, Douglas C.: executive vice president, chief operating officer, director, MDU Resources Group Inc.

Kane, John F.: treasurer, Lyon Foundation

Kaney, Thomas K.: director, GlaxoSmithKline Foundation

Kangisser, Dianne: trustee, Bowne Foundation (Robert)

Kaniewski, James: trustee, Thomaston Savings Bank Foundation

Kanin-Lovers, Jill: vice president, director, Avon Products Foundation, Inc.

Kann, Peter Robert: chairman, chief executive officer, director, Dow Jones & Company Inc.

Kanner, Abraham Pascal: vice president, Rosenthal Foundation (Ida and William)

Kantor, Gregg: vice president, Northwest Natural Gas Co.

Kaplan, Burton B.: treasurer, vice president, Pick, Jr. Fund (Albert)

Kaplan, Helene L.: director, vice chairman, Commonwealth Fund (The)

Kaplan, Mary E.: trustee, Kaplan Fund (J. M.)

Kaplan, Myran J.: trustee, Jarson Kaplan Foundation

Kaplan, Renee T.: director, Amado Foundation (Maurice)

Kaplan, Richard D.: trustee, Kaplan Fund (J. M.)

Kaplan, Richard J.: assistant vice president institutional research & grants management, MacArthur Foundation (John D. and Catherine T.)

Kaplan, Stanley Meisel, MD: trustee, Jarson Kaplan Foundation

Kaplen, Alexander: trustee, Kaplen Foundation

Kaplen, Lawrence: trustee, Kaplen Foundation

Kaplen, Margaret: fdn mgr, trustee, Kaplen Foundation

Kaplen, Wilson R.: trustee, Kaplen Foundation

Kapusta, Susan M.: trustee, U.S. Steel Foundation

Karaba, Frank Andrew: trustee, Caestecker Foundation (Charles and Marie)

Karatsu, Jeanne: secretary, trustee, Miller Foundation (Earl B. and Loraine H.)

Karbowiak, Christine: chairman, Bridgestone/Firestone Trust Fund (The)

Karkut, K. A.: treasurer, Fluor Foundation

Karl, Rosemary M.: trustee, Fredrickson Foundation (Ambrose and Ida)

Karlstrom, Paul Johnson: secretary, director, Scott Foundation (Virginia Steele)

Karmel, Robert S.: trustee, Kemper Foundation (James S.)

Karvellas, Steven: director, New York Mercantile Exchange Charitable Foundation

Kass, Roberta E.: secretary, Unocal Foundation

Kassel, Sylvia: director, Schwartz Fund for Education and Health Research (Arnold and Marie)

Kassel, Terry: trustee, Merrill Lynch & Co. Foundation Inc.

Kassoff, Eric S.: secretary, treasurer, director, Wilkes, Artis, Hedrick & Lane Foundation

Kastelic, Kathleen A.: assistant secretary, Mabee Foundation, Inc. (J. E. and L. E.)

Kastner, Richard: treasurer, Fuller Co. Foundation (H.B.)

Katayama, Akira: chairman, chief executive officer, Mitsubishi Electric and Electronics USA

Katayama, Ayao: president, trustee, Kajima Foundation

Katch, Kim: secretary, Trust Foundation

Katchadourian, Herant, MD: director, Hewlett Foundation (William and Flora)

Kathman, Daniel E.: secretary, director, Gebbie Foundation

Katona, Peter Geza, ScD: president, chief executive officer, Whitaker Foundation

Katz, Bruce: trustee, Katz Family Foundation

Katz, Richard D.: trustee, Wickes Foundation (Harvey Randall)

Katz, Roger: trustee, Katz Family Foundation

Katz, Saul: trustee, Katz Family Foundation

Katzowitz, Lauren: secretary, Dickler Family Foundation

Kaufman, Clementine: officer, Hecht-Levi Foundation

Kaufman, Marvin A.: chairman, director, Samuels Foundation (Fan Fox and Leslie R.)

Kaufman, Michael: fund committee member, Kaufman Endowment Fund (Louis G.)

Kaufman, Peter: chairman, fund comm mem, Kaufman Endowment Fund (Louis G.)

Kaufman, Richard F.: trustee, Kaufman Foundation

Kaufman, Ron: director, Osher Foundation (Bernard)

Kaufman, Sylvia C.: trustee, Kaufman Foundation

Kaufmann, Thomas C.: vice president, Boothroyd Foundation (Charles H. and Bertha L.)

Kavanagh, Thomas E.: trustee, Kavanagh Foundation (T. James)

Kawakami, Kiyoshi: president, director, Mitsubishi Electric America Foundation; president, chief executive officer, Mitsubishi Electric and Electronics USA

Kawamoto, Naoyuki: president, director, SMBC Global Foundation, Inc.

Kay, David R.: treasurer, director, Goldman Foundation (Herman)

Kay, Herma Hill: director, Rosenberg Foundation

Kayajan, John M.: director, Kelley and Elza Kelley Foundation (Edward Bangs)

Kayden, Jerold: director, DBH Foundation for Law, Land, and the Felicitous Environment

Kaye, Brian T.: secretary, St. Francis Bank Foundation

Kaylor, Howard S.: trustee, Sinnisen Foundation (Albert E. and Naomi B.)

Kaylor, Omer T.: contact person, Sinnisen Foundation (Albert E. and Naomi B.)

Kayne, Barry: director, Kutz Foundation (Milton and Hattie)

Kayser, Kraig H.: president, chief executive officer, director, Seneca Foods Corp.

Kaze, Barbara: program officer, Weingart Foundation

Kazlauskas, Deborah: secretary, Trimix Foundation

Keane, Thomas M.: vice chairman, trustee, Foundation for Seacoast Health

Kear, Joseph G.: trustee, Massie Trust (David Meade)

Kearney, Christopher J.: trustee, SPX Foundation

Kearney, Lynn: director, Dedalus Foundation

Kearney, R. Wynn, Jr.: director, Hickory Tech Corp.; president, Hickory Tech Corp. Foundation

Kearns, Fred M., Jr.: president, Acme-McCrary and Sapona Foundation

Kearns, Joseph P.: director, Ford Family Foundation

Keating, Phillip: chairman, Rieke Corp.

Keator, William C.: program director, Davis Foundations (Arthur Vining)

Keats, Gregory A.: director, Keats Family Foundation

Keats, Karen H.: vice president, secretary, Keats Family Foundation

Keats, Robert M.: president, treasurer, Keats Family Foundation

Keck, Howard B., Jr.: director, member audit & executive committees, Keck Foundation (W. M.)

Keck, William M., II: vice president, director, membership audit & executive committee, Keck Foundation (W. M.)

Keck, William M., III: director, Keck Foundation (W. M.)

Keckher, Kelly J.: trustee, Pittsburgh Child Guidance Foundation

Kedash, David B.: chief financial officer, The MBNA Foundation

Kee, Dorothy Davis: trustee, Davis Foundations (Arthur Vining)

Kee, John L., Jr.: trustee, Davis Foundations (Arthur Vining)

Keefe, Catherine G.: assistant secretary, treasurer, McFeely-Rogers Foundation

Keefe, Pamela B.: trustee, Humphrey Fund (George M. and Pamela S.)

Keegan, John Phillip: president, chairman, trustee, Edison Fund (Charles)

Keegan, Peter: senior vice president, Loews Foundation

Keeler, Issac S.: vice president, Keeler Foundation

Keeler, John: advisory committee member, Dickenson Foundation (Harriet Ford)

Keeler, Mary Ann: president, Keeler Foundation

Keeler, Shirley: advisory committee member, Dickenson Foundation (Harriet Ford)

Keeling, Rudolph W.: vice president, LG&E Energy Foundation

Keen, Gordon L., Jr.: director, McCausland Foundation

Keenan, Frances Murray: vice president finance, Abell Foundation

Keenan, James F.: secretary, Plym Foundation

Keesee, Christian Kirkpatrick: vice president, director, Kirkpatrick Foundation, Inc.

Keeth, M. F.: director, Shell Oil Co. Foundation

Keever, William: director, Vodaphone-US Foundation

Kefauver, Horace D.: trustee, Sinnisen Foundation (Albert E. and Naomi B.)

Keibaum, Jack: general manager, Cone-Blanchard Corp.

Keilty, Nancy: director, Ball Brothers Foundation

Keir, Gerald J.: director, First Hawaiian Foundation

Keith, Garnett L.: trustee, Hughes Medical Institute (Howard)

Keith, M. Langhorne: assistant secretary, Loughran Foundation (Mary and Daniel)

Kelleher, Joan N.: president, treasurer, Gage Foundation (Alfred S.)

Keller, Bernedine J.: vice president, Keller Foundation

Keller, Betsy: trustee, Lux Foundation (Miranda)

Keller, Fred M.: president, Keller Foundation

Keller, Frederick P.: treasurer, Keller Foundation

Keller, Linn Maxwell: director, Keller Foundation

Keller, Lorissa K.: director, Keller Foundation

Keller, Rayford L.: president, assistant treasurer, Overlake Foundation

Keller, Robert G.: executive director, KeySpan Foundation

Keller, Susan: director, Keller Foundation

Keller, Suzanne: chairman, DBH Foundation for Law, Land, and the Felicitous Environment

Keller, Thomas L.: vice president, treasurer, assistant secretary, Overlake Foundation

Kelley, Barbara M.: vice president, director, Bausch & Lomb Foundation, Inc.

Kelley, Bruce Gunn: president, chief executive officer, Employers Mutual Charitable Foundation

Kelley, Donald E.: trustee, Rieke Corp. Foundation

Kelley, Mike: president, trustee, Yellow Corp. Foundation

Kelley, Natalie R.: director, Robertshaw Charitable Foundation

Kelley, Ruth B.: hon director, Kelley and Elza Kelley Foundation (Edward Bangs)

Kelley, Thomas J.: director, Trust Funds

Kelling, Robert S., Jr.: director, Hale Foundation (Crescent Porter)

Kelly, A. William: director, Sordoni Foundation

Kelly, D. C.: treasurer, trustee, Handy & Harman Foundation

Kelly, Edward J.: chairman, trustee, Retirement Research Foundation

Kelly, Ernest M.: trustee, Magruder Foundation (Chesley G.)

Kelly, Flaminia Odescalchi: trustee, Bonfils-Stanton Foundation

Kelly, Jack: director, Pacifi-Corp Foundation

Kelly, Jim A.: trustee, UPS Foundation

Kelly, Jon S.: director, Kelly Foundation

Kelly, Joseph: director, King Foundation (Kenneth Kendal)

Kelly, Lorraine A.: vice president, director, Park Bank Foundation

Kelly, Michael J.: vice president, director, Park Bank Foundation

Kelly, Raymond B., III: vice president, secretary, director, Scott Foundation (William E.)

Kelly, Thomas E.: trustee, Fasken Foundation

Kelly, William M.: trustee, New York Foundation

Kelly-Judd, Virginia: executive director, Humana Foundation

Kelmer, Steven B.: director, Medtronic Foundation

Kelson, Richard B.: director, Alcoa Foundation

Kemper, David W.: director, Commerce Bancshares Foundation

Kemper, David Woods: chairman, president, chief executive officer, director, Commerce Bancshares Inc.

Kemper, Jonathan M.: vice president, assistant secretary, director, Commerce Bancshares Foundation

Kemper, Talfourd H.: secretary, treasurer, Carter Foundation (Beirne)

Kempner, Carl L.: treasurer, Erpf Fund (Armand G.)

Kempner, Hetta Ellen Towler: trustee, Kempner Fund (Harris and Eliza)

Kempner, Isaac Herbert, III: trustee, Kempner Fund (Harris and Eliza)

Kenan, James G., III: trustee, Hartford Foundation, Inc. (The John A.)

Kenan, Thomas Stephen, III: trustee, Duke Endowment

Kendall, John P.: trustee, Kendall Foundation (Henry P.)

Kendall, Rebecca O.: director, Lilly Foundation (Eli)

Kennan, Christopher J.: director, Rockefeller Fund (David)

Kennedy, Bruce C.: trustee, Van Wert County Foundation

Kennedy, Caroline: trustee, Kennedy, Jr. Foundation (Joseph P.)

Kennedy, David Boyd: president, trustee, Earhart Foundation

Kennedy, Derek: chief financial officer, Excel Corp.

Kennedy, Donald: trustee, Packard Foundation (David and Lucile)

Kennedy, Edward F.: trustee, Yawkey Foundation II

Kennedy, Edward Moore: president, trustee, Kennedy, Jr. Foundation (Joseph P.)

Kennedy, Jack E.: director, Hewit Family Foundation

Kennedy, James Cox: chairman, chief executive officer, director, Cox Enterprises Inc.

Kennedy, Janice W.: program director, Murdock Charitable Trust (M. J.)

Kennedy, Kimberly: director, Kennedy Family Foundation (Ethel and W. George)

Kennedy, Marie: chief executive officer, president, Amgen Foundation

Kennedy, Nancy C.: trustee, Yeager Charitable Trust B (Lester E.)

Kennedy, Parker S.: vice president, trustee, Jones Foundation (Fletcher)

Kennedy, Rory: trustee, Kennedy, Jr. Foundation (Joseph P.)

Kennedy, Thomas: vice president, Sovereign Bank Foundation

Kennedy, Thomas J.: vice president, Smoot Charitable Foundation

Kennedy, Wayne G.: president, director, Kennedy Family Foundation (Ethel and W. George)

Kennedy, William: director, Kennedy Family Foundation (Ethel and W. George)

Kennedy Olsen, Kathleen P.: director, Kennedy Family Foundation (Ethel and W. George)

Kennerly, Kenneth: director, Cheatham Foundation (Owen)

Kennerly, Michael: grant committee, Royal Foundation (May Mitchell)

Kenny, John J.: treasurer, Loews Corp.; secretary, treasurer, trustee, Loews Foundation

Kent, Katherine G.: trustee, Bryden Foundation (Blanche)

Kentz, Frederick C., III: vice president, secretary, general counsel, Hoffmann-La Roche Inc.; secretary, trustee, Roche Foundation

Kenyon, Robert W.: mem distribution comm, Champlin Foundation

Kerlin, William H., Jr.: chairman, Graham Engineering Corp.; trustee, Graham Foundation

Kerly, Diane M.: trustee, Hamer Foundation

Kern, John C.: trustee, Kern Foundation Trust

Kerr, Breene M.: chairman, treasurer, life trustee, Kerr Fund (Grayce B.)

Kerr, Cody T.: trustee, Kerr Foundation, Inc.

Kerr, Daniel L.: secretary, treasurer, Faith Foundation

Kerr, Robert Samuel, Jr.: president, chairman, trustee, Kerr Foundation, Inc.

Kerr, Sharon: assistant secretary, trustee, Kerr Foundation, Inc.

Kerr, Sheryl V.: president, secretary, Kerr Fund (Grayce B.)

Kerr, Steven: vice president corporate leadership development, General Electric Co.; assistant secretary, trustee, Kerr Foundation, Inc.

Kerr, William T.: chairman, chief executive officer, director, Meredith Corp.; president, director, Meredith Corp. Foundation

Kerr Yuknat, Marcy S.: trustee, Kerr Fund (Grayce B.)

Kersey, Pamela W.: trustee, J.P. Morgan Chase Foundation

Kerstein, Ruth: secretary, director, Schwartz Fund for Education and Health Research (Arnold and Marie)

Kersten, Katherine: director, treasurer, Cargill Foundation

Kesler, Robert: director, Vermilion Healthcare Foundation

Kessler, Gary: vice president, American Honda Foundation

Kessler, James Lee: trustee, Kempner Fund (Harris and Eliza)

Kessler, Richard: secretary, Benenson Foundation (Frances and Benjamin)

Ketcham, Geoff C.: executive vice president, treasurer, chief financial officer, Energen Corp.

Ketcherside, James Lee: director, Mingenback Foundation (Julia J.)

Ketelsen, James L.: director, Sara Lee Corp.

Kettering, Virginia W.: trustee, Kettering Fund

Keune, Donald J.: adv, Cayuga Foundation

Key, Amy Bronson: director, Daniels Foundation (Fred Harris)

Key, Martha: co-trustee, Pelz Trust (H.E. and Ruby)

Keydel, Frederick R.: trustee, Fruehauf Foundation

Keyes, James Henry: member advisory board, Johnson Controls Foundation

Keys, Brian S.: secretary, Time Warner Foundation, Inc.

Keyser, Alan J.: trustee, Quaker Chemical Foundation

Keyser, F. Ray, Jr.: chairman, director, Central Vermont Public Service Corp.

Keyser, Jenny, PhD: vice president, director, Fuller Co. Foundation (H.B.)

Keyte, David H.: vice president, chief financial officer, Forest Oil Corp.

Khouri, Naif A.: treasurer, director, DTE Energy Foundation

Khoury, Eileen M.: trustee, Russell Trust (Josephine G.)

Khoury, Kenneth F.: vice president, Georgia-Pacific Foundation

Kibbe, Sharon: director, Glick Foundation (Eugene and Marilyn)

Kick, Frank J.: treasurer, Bydale Foundation

Kidder, Rushworth Moulton: trustee, Mott Foundation (Charles Stewart)

Kieckhefer, John I.: trustee, Kieckhefer Foundation (J. W.)

Kieckhefer, Robert H.: trustee, Kieckhefer Foundation (J. W.)

Kieding, Richard: president, S.G. Foundation

Kiefer, Gerald A., Esq.: director, St. Francis Bank Foundation

Kielley, James E., JD: committee member, Whitaker Foundation

Kienker, James W.: senior vice president, chief financial officer, Maritz Inc.

Kiernat, Elizabeth M.: treasurer, trustee, Bigelow Foundation (F. R.)

Kiker, John D.: vice president corporate communications, UAL Corp.

Kilen, C. Bruce: trustee, McKay Family Foundation

Kilgus, Amy C.: trustee, Saemann Foundation (Franklin I.)

Kilgus, Joann A.: trustee, Saemann Foundation (Franklin I.)

Killen, John V.: president, director, Sovereign Bank Foundation

Killinger, Kerry Kent: president, Washington Mutual Foundation; chairman, president, chief executive officer, director, Washington Mutual Inc.

Killinger, William: director, Joco Foundation

Kilmartin, David F.: chairman, president, chief executive officer, director, Kilmartin Industries; president, director, Kilmartin Industries Charitable Foundation

Kilroy, Lora Jean: trustee, Kilroy Foundation (William S. and Lora Jean)

Kilroy, Mari Angela: trustee, Kilroy Foundation (William S. and Lora Jean)

Kilroy, William S.: trustee, Kilroy Foundation (William S. and Lora Jean)

Kilts, James M.: chairman, chief executive officer, director, Gillette Co.

Kim, Ho-il: director, Cabot Corp. Foundation

Kimball, David: board membership, CCB Foundation

Kimball, Ray: director, De Queen Regional Medical Center

Kime, Jack E.: chief financial officer, Heinz Family Foundation

Kimelman, Donald: director information initiatives, Pew Charitable Trusts

Kimmet, Gary J.: director, Gleason Foundation

Kin, Donna J.: executive secretary, National Machinery Foundation, Inc.

Kind, Kenneth A.: director, van Ameringen Foundation, Inc.

Kind, Patricia: director, van Ameringen Foundation, Inc.

Kind-Rubin, Valerie: director, van Ameringen Foundation, Inc.

Kindfuller, Andrew: director, van Ameringen Foundation, Inc.

Kindred, John J., III: trustee, Hagedorn Fund

King, Betty S.: secretary, Richardson Benevolent Foundation (C. E.)

King, David A.: member distribution committee, Champlin Foundation

King, Diana: president, director, King Family Foundation (Charles and Lucille)

King, Gregory L.: secretary, assistant treasurer, J.P. Morgan Chase Foundation

King, Judith S.: trustee, treasurer, Stoddard Charitable Trust

King, Mary E.: secretary, director, Arca Foundation

King, Raymond B.: secretary, SunTrust Bank Atlanta Foundation

King, Richard S.: assistant treasurer, Alabama Power Foundation

King, Sharon B.: trustee, assistant secretary, Altman Foundation

King, Susan Robinson: vice president public affairs, Carnegie Corp. of New York

King, Thomas A.: president, Lilly Foundation (Eli)

King, Wendall: director, Harper Brush Works Foundation

King, William Joseph: vice president, treasurer, director, Kline Foundation (Josiah W. and Bessie H.); chairman, Stabler Foundation (Donald B. and Dorothy L.)

Kingsbury, Sherilyn: director, McGowan Charitable Fund (William G.)

Kingsland, Richard M.: chief financial officer, secretary, vice president, Valley Foundation (Wayne and Gladys)

Kingsley, Alfred D.: vice president, ACF Foundation

Kington, Ann A.: director, Kington Foundation, Inc.

Kington, Helen: director, Kington Foundation, Inc.

Kington, Mark J.: secretary, director, Kington Foundation, Inc.

Kinnamon, David Lucas: secretary, director, Ross Memorial Foundation (Will)

Kinney, George R.: trustee, Kinney Memorial Foundation

Kinney, Josephine J.: trustee, Kinney Memorial Foundation

Kintzel, Lee: co-trustee, Roddy Foundation (Fred M.)

Kiplinger, Austin Huntington: president, trustee, Kiplinger Foundation; chairman, director, Kiplinger Washington Editors Inc.

Kiplinger, Knight Austin: trustee, Kiplinger Foundation; president, publisher, director, Kiplinger Washington Editors Inc.

Kiplinger, Todd Lawrence: trustee, Kiplinger Foundation; vice chairman, director, Kiplinger Washington Editors Inc.

Kipp, Robert Almy: director, Hall Family Foundation (The)

Kirby, Fred Morgan: president, director, Kirby Foundation (F. M.)

Kirby, James: local grants manager, AT&T Foundation

Kirby, Jefferson Walker: director, Kirby Foundation (F. M.)

Kirby, John L.: chief administrative officer, executive vice president, United States Trust Company of New York

Kirby, Nancy J.: trustee, Douty Foundation (Alfred and Mary)

Kirby, S. Dillard: executive vice president, executive director, director, Kirby Foundation (F. M.)

Kirby, Walker D.: vice president, director, Kirby Foundation (F. M.)

Kirker, James M.: director, Dime Savings Bank of Norwich Foundation

Kirklin, Starr J.: director, Hickory Tech Corp.; trustee, Hickory Tech Corp. Foundation

Kirkpatrick, Joan E.: chairman, Kirkpatrick Foundation, Inc.

Kirkpatrick, John Elson: honorary chairman, director, Kirkpatrick Foundation, Inc.

Kirkpatrick, Ken: president, US Bank

Kirkwood, Gloria: secretary, Britton Fund

Kirkwood, William T.: chief financial officer, vice president financial, director, Worthington Foods

Kiser, Gerald L.: president, chief executive officer, director, La-Z-Boy Inc.

Kishner, Judith Z.: secretary, treasurer, Zarrow Foundation (Anne and Henry)

Kissam, Kathryn S.: director, Monsanto Fund

Kissinger, Henry A.: chairman, director, Paley Foundation, Inc. (William S.)

Kissinger, Thomas F.: secretary, director, Marcus Corp. Foundation

Kita, John J.: vice president, treasurer, controller, Smith Corp. (A.O.); treasurer, Smith Foundation, Inc. (A.O.)

Kitabjian, Mary: assistant secretary, Pforzheimer Foundation, Inc. (The Carl and Lily)

Kitchen, Michael B.: president, chief executive officer, director, CUNA Mutual Group; secretary, treasurer, director, CUNA Mutual Group Foundation, Inc.

Kitko, Paulette F.: secretary, treasurer, Haskell Fund

Kittner, David: president, trustee, Kardon Foundation (Samuel and Rebecca)

Kittner, Marc: director, Washington Mutual Foundation; chief legal counsel, Washington Mutual Inc.

Kizer, John Oscar: secretary, treasurer, Daywood Foundation

Klassen, Helen: trustee, Blandin Foundation

Klatman, Michael: president, StorageTek Foundation

Klausner, Richard D., MD: executive director, global health, Gates Foundation (Bill and Melinda)

Klebba, Kenneth J.: president, treasurer, Vollbrecht Foundation (Frederick A.)

Klebe, Terry: treasurer, trustee, Cooper Industries Foundation

Kleeman, R. Henry: assistant secretary, Sara Lee Foundation

Kleh, Jack: assistant secretary, director, Bloedorn Foundation (Walter A.)

Klein, Bruce: trustee, CLARCOR Foundation

Klein, Bruce A.: trustee, CLARCOR Foundation; chief financial officer, vice president, CLARCOR Inc.

Klein, Charles T.: vice president, trustee, Frueauff Foundation (Charles A.)

Klein, David M.: vice president, Hartford Financial Services Group Inc.

Klein, Edith Miller: director, Morrison Foundation (Harry W.)

Klein, Jeffrey: president, Liberman Foundation (Bertha and Isaac)

Klein, Raphael: president, Bank of Greene County Charitable Foundation

Klein, Ray: trustee, Kerr Foundation, Inc.

Kleiner, Charlene: secretary, McBean Family Foundation

Kleinkramer, Jane: director, Land O'Lakes Foundation

Klementik, David C.: trustee, Whalley Charitable Trust

Klepfer, Kathleen L.: director, Monsanto Fund

Kleven, Cynthia F.: secretary, 3M Foundation

Klimek, Mary: director, Jostens Foundation Inc. (The)

Kline, Cheryl: director, Dana Corp. Foundation

Kline, Daniel L.: vice president, trustee, Blowitz-Ridgeway Foundation

Kline, Darrell: trustee, Share Trust (Charles Morton)

Kline, Gary H.: secretary, Field Foundation of Illinois

Kline, Lowell L.: co-trustee, treasurer, Crowell Trust (Henry P. and Susan C.)

Kline, Sidney Delong, Jr.: trustee, Wyomissing Foundation

Kling, Chris: board of directors, Wilson Foundation (Marie C. and Joseph C.)

Klingenstein, Frederick A.: vice president, Klingenstein Fund, Inc. (Esther A. and Joseph)

Klingenstein, John: president, treasurer, director, Klingenstein Fund, Inc. (Esther A. and Joseph)

Klingenstein, Patricia: director, Klingenstein Fund, Inc. (Esther A. and Joseph)

Klingenstein, Sharon: director, Klingenstein Fund, Inc. (Esther A. and Joseph)

Klinger, Andrew M.: trustee, Mex-Am Cultural Foundation

Klinger, Linda L.: executive director, McElroy Trust (R. J.)

Klingestein, Alan L.: treasurer, Klingestein Fund

Klingestein, Lee P.: president, Klingestein Fund

Klingestein, Paul H.: vice president, Klingestein Fund

Klingner, Linda: secretary, treasurer, Morrison Foundation (Harry W.)

Klipstein, David C.: vice president, Klipstein Foundation (Ernest Christian)

Klipstein, David H.: president, Klipstein Foundation (Ernest Christian)

Klipstein, Pamela: treasurer, Klipstein Foundation (Ernest Christian)

Kloenhammer, Janet S.: chairman, director, Fireman's Fund Foundation

Kloska, Ronald Frank: trustee, Decio Foundation (Arthur J.)

Kluge, John Werner: director, Shubert Foundation

Kluge, Patricia: vice president, director, Virginia Environmental Endowment

Klugman, Craig: editor, Journal-Gazette Co.

Klumpp, H. William: treasurer, S&T Bancorp Charitable Foundation

Knabusch-Taylor, June E.: president, trustee, La-Z-Boy Foundation

Knapp, Anthony: vice president, Motorola Foundation

Knapp, Cleon Talboys: president, Knapp Foundation (CA)

Knapp, Elizabeth W.: vice president, Knapp Foundation (CA)

Knapp, George R.: executive director, trustee, Tippins Foundation

Knapp, Laurie H.: director, Provident Community Foundation

Kneezel, Ronald D.: treasurer, Banta Corp. Foundation

Knell, Theresa N.: secretary, trustee, Middendorf Foundation

Kneppler, Robert B., Jr.: director, Cook, Sr. Charitable Foundation (Kelly Gene)

Knese, William F.: vice president, treasurer, CLARCOR Inc.

Knez, Brian J.: trustee, Smith Family Foundation (Richard and Susan)

Knez, Debra S.: trustee, Smith Family Foundation (Richard and Susan)

Kniffen, Jan Rogers: senior vice president, treasurer, May Department Stores Co.; vice president, secretary, treasurer, director, May Department Stores Co. Foundation (The)

Knight, Charles Field: trustee, Olin Foundation (John M.)

Knight, Dale: director, McDonough Foundation (Bernard)

Knight, Kathleen C.: member, Staunton Farm Foundation

Knight, Lester B.: chairman, director, Aon Foundation

Knight, Patricia H.: secretary, director, director, Gregg-Graniteville Foundation

Knight, Timothy: director, Tribune New York Foundation

Knight, W. H., Jr.: director, State Farm Companies Foundation

Knight, Will A.: president, Wise Foundation (Watson W.)

Knoble, Lindsey: director, Davenport-Hatch Foundation

Knoell, John: trustee, Grundy Foundation

Knorr, Eric T.: director, Kansas Health Foundation

Knott, Marion I.: chairman, Knott Foundation (Marion I. and Henry J.)

Knott, Martin G., Jr.: member, Knott Foundation (Marion I. and Henry J.)

Knott, Patty L.: member, Knott Foundation (Marion I. and Henry J.)

Knott, Teresa A.: member, Knott Foundation (Marion I. and Henry J.)

Knowles, Jeremy R., PhD: trustee, Hughes Medical Institute (Howard)

Knowles, Rachel Hunt: trustee, Hunt Foundation (Roy A.)

Knox, M. S.: vice president, treasurer, Bechtel Foundation

Knox, Northrup Rand, Jr.: president, Knox Foundation (Seymour H.)

Knox, Seymour Horace, IV: vice president, secretary, Knox Foundation (Seymour H.)

Knox, Wendell J.: trustee, Eastern Bank Charitable Foundation

Knudsen, Nancy: secretary, treasurer, Timken Foundation of Canton

Knudson, John E., Jr.: vice president, chief financial officer, Henkel Corp.

Kobusch, Margaret W.: trustee, Dula Educational and Charitable Foundation (Caleb C. and Julia W.)

Koch, Charles G.: director, Koch Foundation, Inc. (Fred C. and Mary R.)

Koch, Curtis J.: vice president, Schlink Foundation (Albert G. and Olive H.)

Koch, David Hamilton: director, Koch Foundation, Inc. (Fred C. and Mary R.)

Koch, Elizabeth B.: president, director, Koch Foundation, Inc. (Fred C. and Mary R.)

Koch, Justine: accountant, Altman Foundation

Kochheiser, George W.: vice president, Employers Mutual Charitable Foundation

Kochis, Paul M.: trustee, Mellon Financial Corp. Foundation

Kodama, Ryuzo: director, head Americas Division, Sumitomo Mitsui Banking Corp.

Koenig, Lori: vice president, secretary, treasurer, director, World Heritage Foundation

Koenigsberger, Joseph A.: treasurer, Guggenheim Foundation (Harry Frank)

Koepke, James E.: trustee, Farr Trust (Frank M. and Alice M.)

Koeppe, Alfred C.: trustee, Public Service Electric & Gas Foundation

Koerner, Philip D.: trustee, National Grange Mutual Charitable Trust; chairman, president, chief executive officer, National Grange Mutual Insurance Co.

Koester, Robert W.: president, Zullig Foundation (Herbert G. and Dorothy)

Kohler, Ruth DeYoung, II: president, chief operating officer, director, Kohler Foundation

Kohn, Bernhard L., Jr.: president, Kohn-Joseloff Foundation

Kohn, Edith: vice president, secretary, Arronson Foundation

Kohn, Ellen: vice president, Arronson Foundation

Kohn, Joan J.: secretary, treasurer, Kohn-Joseloff Foundation

Kohn, Joseph C.: president, treasurer, Arronson Foundation

Kohn, Lisa G.: assistant secretary, Unilever United States Foundation

Kohnen, Theodore J.: treasurer, New York Life Foundation

Kohnstamm, Abby V.: vice chairman, director, IBM International Foundation; senior vice president, marketing, International Business Machines

Koike, Wayne: treasurer, Haigh-Scatena Foundation

Kojima, K.: chairman, chief executive officer, Fujitsu America

Kokjer, Ralph L., Jr.: president, director, Harden Foundation

Kokot, Eugene V.: secretary, director, King Family Foundation (Charles and Lucille)

Kolb, John E.: director, mem executive committee, chairman legal committee, Keck Foundation (W. M.)

Komstadius, Lori: director, CNA Foundation

Kondo, Koichi: chief executive officer, director, American Honda Motor Company Inc.

Kongsgaard, Martha: president, Kongsgaard-Goldman Foundation

Kononowitz, Thomas J.: vice president, New Jersey Natural Gas Foundation

Koo, Grace: trustee, Credit Suisse First Boston Foundation Trust

Kooijman, C.: director, Overbrook Foundation (The)

Koop, Dick W.: trustee, Johnson Foundation (M. G. and Lillie A.)

Koopman, Beatrice F.: trustee, Koopman Fund

Koopman, Dorothy B.: trustee, Koopman Fund

Koopman, Georgette A.: president, trustee, Koopman Fund

Koopman, Rena B.: secretary, trustee, Koopman Fund

Koopman, Richard, Jr.: trustee, Koopman Fund

Kopnisky, Jack L.: trustee, Key Foundation

Koraleski, J. J.: vice president finance, trustee, Union Pacific Foundation

Korell, Brad: trustee, Cooper Foundation

Koren, John: secretary, trustee, Berkman Foundation (Louis and Sandra)

Koret, Susan: chairman, director, Koret Foundation

Korniczky, Anna T.: treasurer, Harriman Foundation (Gladys and Roland)

Kornmeier, Richard K.: trustee, Peterson Charitable Foundation (Folke H.)

Korstange, Jason E.: president, TCF Foundation

Korte, Greg O.: director, Ralph and Donna Korte Family Charitable Foundation

Korte, Ralph F.: chairman, Korte Construction Co.; president, director, Ralph and Donna Korte Family Charitable Foundation

Korte, Todd J.: vice president, director, Ralph and Donna Korte Family Charitable Foundation

Korte Solheim, Vicki: director, Ralph and Donna Korte Family Charitable Foundation

Kortendick, Russel L., Sr.: vice president, Christensen Charitable and Religious Foundation (L. C.)

Kortepeter, Wendy Griffith: adv, Griffith Foundation (W. C.)

Kosai, Aizo: mem allocations comm, Kawabe Memorial Fund

Kosak, Stephen P.: consultant, Bowman Proper Charitable Trust (J.)

Kosche, Peter C.: senior vice president corporate affairs, Olin Corp.; trustee, Olin Corp. Charitable Trust

Koskey, Richard P.: secretary, Rheinstrom Hill Community Foundation

Koskinas, Helen: director, Memorial Foundation for the Blind

Koskinen, Jean A.: director, Alexander Foundation (Walter)

Koskinen, Walter: vice president, director, Alexander Foundation (Walter)

Kostishack, John: executive director, Bremer Foundation (Otto)

Kountze, Charles Denman: trustee, Hitchcock Foundation (Gilbert M. and Martha H.)

Kountze, Denman: president, trustee, Hitchcock Foundation (Gilbert M. and Martha H.)

Kountze, Edward H.: trustee, Hitchcock Foundation (Gilbert M. and Martha H.)

Kountze, Mary: trustee, Hitchcock Foundation (Gilbert M. and Martha H.)

Kountze, Neely: trustee, Hitchcock Foundation (Gilbert M. and Martha H.)

Koupal, Raymond: vice president, chief financial officer,

Koutsky, Lori J.: foundation manager, Minnesota Mutual Foundation

Koven, Joan Follin: secretary, treasurer, director, Marpat Foundation

Kovler, H. Jonathan: president, Kovler Family Foundation

Kovler, Peter: assistant secretary, Kovler Family Foundation

Kowalke, Stephen C.: vice president, treasurer, Target Foundation

Koziar, Stephen F., Jr.: president, director, Dayton Power and Light Co. Foundation

Kozmetsky, Cynthia: trustee, treasurer, vice president, secretary, RGK Foundation

Kozmetsky, Gregory Allen: president, chairman, trustee, RGK Foundation

Kozmetsky, Ronya: don, trustee, RGK Foundation

Kozusko, Donald: trustee, Gund Foundation (Geoffrey)

Kraen, Donald P.: trustee, Patterson Memorial Trust (Hazel)

Kraft, Richard: vice president, Zullig Foundation (Herbert G. and Dorothy)

Kramarsky, Sara Ann: secretary, Schiff Foundation (Dorothy)

Kramarsky, Werner: director, Warhol Foundation for the Visual Arts (The Andy)

Kramer, Terry: director, Vodaphone-US Foundation

Krantez, Leo: president, chief executive officer, Integra Bank

Krantz, David: trustee, AT&T Foundation

Kraus, Claire: director, Jostens Foundation Inc. (The)

Kraus, John P.: trustee, Anderson Foundation

Krause, Charles A.: vice chairman, trustee, McBeath Foundation (Faye)

Krause, Jimmy L.: director grants administration, assistant treasurer, Mott Foundation (Charles Stewart)

Krause, Sandra S.: trustee, Strauss Foundation

Krauter, Donald W.: trustee, Slater Trust (Lillian M.)

Krave, Helmuth: trustee, Farwell Foundation (Drusilla)

Kreamer, Janice C.: trustee, Johnson Foundation

Kredel, Richard S.: secretary, treasurer, trustee, Stamps Foundation (James L.)

Kreh, Susan M.: treasurer, PPG Industries Foundation

Kreitler, Hobart C.: president, Kreitler Foundation

Kreitler, James S.: director, Kreitler Foundation

Kreitler, John M.: director, Kreitler Foundation

Kreitler, Karen R.: director, Kreitler Foundation

Kreitler, Sally S.: secretary, Kreitler Foundation

Kreitler, Thomas S.: vice president, Kreitler Foundation

Kresa, Kent: trustee, Haynes Foundation (John Randolph and Dora); director, Keck Foundation (W. M.)

Kress, Ingrid: director, Kress Foundation (George)

Kress, James F.: chairman, director, Green Bay Packaging; director, Kress Foundation (George)

Kress, John F.: president, director, Kress Foundation (George)

Kress, William F.: president, director, Green Bay Packaging; director, Kress Foundation (George)

Kresse, Robert J.: trustee, Wendt Foundation (Margaret L.)

Kressley, Larry: executive director, Public Welfare Foundation

Krieble, Frederick K.: vice president, Krieble Foundation (Vernon K.)

Krieble, Helen E.: president, Krieble Foundation (Vernon K.)

Krieger, Theresa R.: trustee, Carls Foundation

Krinsky, Josephine B.: trustee, Parshelsky Foundation (Moses L.)

Krinsky, Robert Daniel: trustee, Parshelsky Foundation (Moses L.)

Krishok, Edward: assistant secretary, Harley-Davidson Foundation

Krone, Bruce A.: secretary, director, Dater Foundation (Charles H.)

Krone, Dorothy G.: director emeritus, Dater Foundation (Charles H.)

Kroner, Herbert: president, Becher Foundation (Hildegarde D.)

Kronstadt, Annette: director, Himmelfarb Foundation (Paul and Annetta)

Kronstadt, Lillian: executive director, Himmelfarb Foundation (Paul and Annetta)

Kropf, Susan J.: director, The Wallace Foundation

Krsulich, Lorraine: assistant treasurer, J.P. Morgan Chase Foundation

Kruger, Barbara: director, Warhol Foundation for the Visual Arts (The Andy)

Krukowski, Francis V.: president, Price Foundation (Lucien B. and Katherine E.)

Krukowski, Jan: treasurer, director, Winston Foundation (Norman and Rosita)

Krulak, Allan C.: vice president corporate & public affairs, director, Forest City Enterprises Inc.

Krull, Thomas R.: vice president, Madison Gas & Electric Foundation

Kryor, Allison W.: president, Kington Foundation, Inc.

Kubasak, Thomas F.: chief financial officer, Trust Funds

Kuechle, Scott E.: vice president, treasurer, Goodrich Corp.; treasurer, Goodrich Foundation, Inc. (B.F.)

Kuehn, Henry: trustee, Graham Foundation for Advanced Studies in the Fine Arts

Kuehn, Ronald L., Jr.: chairman, chief executive officer, director, El Paso Corporate Foundation; chairman, chief executive officer, El Paso Corp.

Kuester, Dennis J.: president, director, Marshall & Ilsley Corp.; vice president, director, Marshall & Ilsley Foundation, Inc.

Kully, Robert I.: president, trust, Livingston Foundation (Milton S. and Corinne N.)

Kummer, Robert W., Jr.: vice president, trustee, Jones Foundation (Fletcher)

Kump, Marsha A.: executive director, Whiting Foundation

Kunce, Marquita L.: assistant treasurer, Olin Foundation (Spencer T. and Ann W.)

Kunin, Constance B.: trustee, Bigelow Foundation (F. R.)

Kunin, David B.: vice president, Regis Foundation

Kunin, Myron: chairman, director, Regis Corp.; president, Regis Foundation

Kunkel, John C., II: trustee, Kunkel Foundation (John Crain)

Kunkel, Paul A.: trustee, Kunkel Foundation (John Crain)

Kunkel, W. Minster, MD: trustee, Kunkel Foundation (John Crain)

Kunkle, Gary K.: chairman, trustee, Dentsply International Foundation; president, chief operating officer, Dentsply International Inc.

Kuntz, Jean M.: trustee, Harmon Foundation (Pearl M. and Julia J.)

Kunzman, Edward D.: president, Schwartz Foundation (Arnold A.)

Kunzman, Steven: vice president, Schwartz Foundation (Arnold A.)

Kupferberg, Max: director, Vogler Foundation (Laura B.)

Kuprenski, Shelagh: secretary, Ewald Foundation (H. T.)

Kurczewski, Walter W.: vice president, secretary, general counsel, Square D Co.; president, director, Square D Foundation

Kurisaki, Mickey: director, Mitsubishi Electric America Foundation; group president automotive, Mitsubishi Electric and Electronics USA

Kurth, Jeri: co-trustee, Cray Residuary Charitable Trust (Evah C.)

Kurtz, Samuel B.: director, Lebanon Mutual Foundation

Kurtz, Samuel G.: chairman, director, Lebanon Mutual Insurance Co.

Kurtzahn, Rebecca: secretary, U.S. Bancorp Piper Jaffray Foundation

Kury, Mark C.: president, director, McDonough Foundation (Bernard)

Kurz, Ellen: director, Kurz Family Foundation

Kurz, Herbert: president, Kurz Family Foundation

Kurz, Leonard: director, Kurz Family Foundation

Kurzig, Carol: vice president, director, Avon Products Foundation, Inc.

Kushlan, James: director, Frohring Foundation (Paul and Maxine)

Kushlan, Paula Frohring: trustee, Frohring Foundation (Paul and Maxine)

Kusic, Joseph: chairman, administrator, J&L Specialty Steel Charitable Foundation

Kustosz, Susan N.: director, Harcourt Foundation (Ellen Knowles)

Kutella, Ronald J.: president, Sedgwick Inc.

Kuth, Byron: vice president, LEF Foundation

Kuth, Lyda Ebert: cfo, secretary, LEF Foundation

Kuzma, Greg: treasurer, AK Steel Foundation

Kwoh, Stewart: director, Fannie Mae Foundation

Kwong, Peter: trustee, New York Foundation

L

L'Engle Franklin, Madeleine: president, Crosswicks Foundation

La Boon, Robert Bruce: vice president, Kayser Foundation

La Faye, John B.: director, Sale Foundation (Lucy Pannill)

La Valley, Frederick J. M.: trustee, Grundy Foundation

LaBahn, Mary Ann: vice president, treasurer, Ross Memorial Foundation (Will)

Labaree, Frances: vice chairman, secretary, director, Overbrook Foundation (The)

LaBelle, Jenijoy: vice president, secretary, Essick Foundation

Labik, Nancy: foundation coord, Chicago Title and Trust Co. Foundation

Laboutin Bannon, Alexandra: trustee, Beynon Foundation (Kathryne)

Labrato, Ronnie R.: trustee, Gulf Power Foundation

Labutka, Carolyn E.: vice president, executive director, Aon Foundation

Lacasse, Robert P.: member, Gardiner Savings Institution Charitable Foundation

Lachman, Marguerite Leanne: trustee, Chicago Title and Trust Co. Foundation

Lackland, David: trustee, Schwartz Foundation (Arnold A.)

LaCounte, Maage E.: director, Johnston-Hanson Foundation

Lacourse, Julien: executive vice president, Demoulas Supermarkets Inc.

Lacy, Stephen: vice president, director, Meredith Corp. Foundation

Ladd, George E., III: director, Ladd Charitable Corp. (Helen and George)

Ladd, Lincoln F.: director, Ladd Charitable Corp. (Helen and George)

Ladd, Robert M.: director, Ladd Charitable Corp. (Helen and George)

Ladds, Herbert P., Jr.: director, Utica National Foundation

LaFever, D. G.: vice president, director, Winn-Dixie Stores Foundation

Laffoon, Polk, IV: secretary, Knight Ridder Fund; vice president corporate relations, corporate secretary, Knight Ridder Inc.

Lafleur, Richard B.: treasurer, Roddy Foundation (Fred M.)

Lafond, Colette: advisory board, Van Evera Foundation (Dewitt)

LaFreniere, Norma B.: member distribution comm, Champlin Foundation

Lagasse, Raymond A.: chairman, Mascoma Savings Bank Foundation

Lagomasino, Maria Elena: trustee, J.P. Morgan Chase Foundation

Laird, Fiona C.: director, Unilever United States Foundation

Laird, Walter Jones, Jr.: director, Glencoe Foundation

Laisure, Mike: president, director, Dana Corp. Foundation

Laitman, Nanette L.: trustee, Lasdon Foundation (William and Mildred)

Lakin, Charles: director, Lytel Foundation (Bertha Russ)

Lally, Joachim: trustee, Russell Trust (Josephine G.)

Lamb, Barbara: director, Lamb Foundation

Lamb, Carl: director, Lamb Foundation

Lamb, Dorothy: director, Lamb Foundation

Lamb, Frank: chairman, Lamb Foundation

Lamb, Greg: director, Lamb Foundation

Lamb, Helen: director, Lamb Foundation

Lamb, Isabelle Smith: director, Bishop Foundation (E. K. and Lillian F.)

Lamb, John R.: trustee, Barker Foundation (Coeta and Donald R.)

Lamb, Maryann: treasurer, Lamb Foundation

Lamb, Paula L.: vchairman, Lamb Foundation

Lamb, Peter: director, Lamb Foundation

Lambert, Greg: director, Sierra Pacific Resources Charitable Foundation

Lambert, Joseph: treasurer, S.G. Foundation

Lambert, Samuel Waldron, III: president, trustee, Bunbury Co., Inc.; chairman, trustee, Windham Foundation

Lamboley, C. A.: director, Shell Oil Co. Foundation

Lammel, Bruce E.: assistant secretary, U.S. Steel Foundation

Lammers, Bruce: director, AMCORE Foundation

Lamontagne, Raymond A.: director, Dyson Foundation

Lampros, Jack D.: chairman, Stewart Educational Foundation (Donnell B. and Elizabeth Dee Shaw)

Lancaster, Rose C.: trustee, member contributions committee, Trull Foundation (The)

Lancaster, Sally Rhodus, PhD: director emeritus,

Meadows Foundation (The)

Land, Lillie S.: secretary, director, duPont Foundation (Alfred I.)

Landegger, Carl Clement: treasurer, director, Landegger Charitable Foundation

Landegger, George Francis: president, director, Landegger Charitable Foundation

Landels, William: director, PacifiCorp Foundation

Landman, Carole: trustee, Heckscher Foundation for Children

Landry, Edward A.: trustee, Lantz Foundation (Walter)

Landry, Margaret: adv, Patron Saints Foundation

Landvater, Carrie: secretary, treasurer, Ray Foundation

Landy, Laura K.: trustee, member, Rippel Foundation (Fannie E.)

Lane, Bernard Bell: director, Lane Foundation (Minnie and Bernard)

Lane, Joan: trustee, Lane Family Charitable Trust

Lane, Lynn L.: director, treasurer, Reynolds Foundation (R. J.)

Lane, Minnie B.: director, Lane Foundation (Minnie and Bernard)

Lane, Nancy Wolfe: vice president, Wolfe Associates, Inc.

Lane, Ralph: trustee, Lane Family Charitable Trust

Lane, Robert: president, Ideal Industries Inc.

Lane, Robert W.: vice president, director, Deere Foundation (John)

Lane, Thomas H.: trustee, Dow Corning Foundation

Lane, William A., Jr.: president, trustee, Dunspaugh-Dalton Foundation

Laney, James Thomas: director, Luce Foundation (Henry)

Laney, John: vice president, Hall Family Foundation (The)

Lang, David: trustee, Lang Foundation (Eugene M.)

Lang, Eugene Michael: donor, trustee, Lang Foundation (Eugene M.)

Lang, Isaiah: director, Overbrook Foundation (The)

Lang, Jane: trustee, Lang Foundation (Eugene M.)

Lang, Keith H.: executive director, Champlin Foundation

Lang, LeeAnne M.: assistant secretary, Bechtel Foundation

Lang, Robert Todd: director, Weil, Gotshal & Manges Foundation

Lang, Sherry: vice president & director investor rela-

tions, TJX Companies Inc.

Lang, Stephen: trustee, Lang Foundation (Eugene M.)

Lang, Theresa: trustee, Lang Foundation (Eugene M.)

Langfitt, Thomas W., MD: director, Pew Charitable Trusts

Langland, R. Marc: director, Usibelli Foundation

Langner, Jay B.: director, Mailman Family Foundation (A. L.)

Langstaff, Carol: director, Guggenheim Foundation (Harry Frank)

Lanier, John E.: trustee, Peterloon Foundation

Lanier, Linda L.: director, Atkinson Foundation

Lanier, Melissa Emery: vice president, trustee, Peterloon Foundation

Lanier, Richard S.: director, Trust for Mutual Understanding

Lanigan, Bernard, Jr.: treasurer, director, Williams Family Foundation of Georgia

Lansing, John F.: trustee, Scripps Howard Foundation

Lansing, John S.: executive director, Lake Placid Education Foundation

Lansky, Gregg I.: president, treasurer, First Tennessee Foundation

Lant, Steven V.: chief financial officer, Central Hudson Gas & Electric Corp.

Lanterman, A. Kirk: secretary, treasurer, Usibelli Foundation

Lantz, Joanne Baldwin: director, Foellinger Foundation

Lapeyre, Pierre S.: executive consult, assistant secretary, Schlieder Educational Foundation (Edward G.)

Lapham, Lewis H.: director, Guggenheim Foundation (Harry Frank)

Lapides, Bernard: cochairman, co-president, director, Wurzburg Inc.

LaPierre, Susan: vice president community relations, East Cambridge Savings Charitable Foundation

LaPlace, William B.: trustee, Young Foundation (Hugo H. and Mabel B.)

LaPlace, William G.: treasurer, Smith Foundation (Kelvin and Eleanor)

LaRich, Jeffrey: trustee, Frohring Foundation (Paul and Maxine)

Lark, Carolyn: vice president, Donaldson Charitable Trust (Oliver S. and Jennie R.)

Lark, J. Andrew: co-trustee, Cummings Memorial

Fund (The Frances L. and Edwin L.)

Larkin, Al: president, Boston Globe Foundation

Larkin, Frank Y.: vice chairman, director, Noble Foundation, Inc. (Edward John)

Larkin, June Noble: chairwoman, director, Noble Foundation, Inc. (Edward John)

Larkins, Michealle: program officer, Ratshesky Foundation (A. C.)

Larouche, Carol A.: assistant treasurer, Barker Foundation Inc.

Larsen, Brent: director, Grinnell Mutual Group Foundation

Larsen, Christopher: president, Larsen Fund

Larsen, John O.: director, Alliant Energy Foundation, Inc.

Larsen, Jonathan Zerbe: vice president, Larsen Fund

Larsen, Marshall O.: president, chief executive officer, director, Goodrich Corp.; vice president, Goodrich Foundation, Inc. (B.F.)

Larsen, Nancy D.: secretary, treasurer, Allen Foundation (Nibs and Edna)

Larson, Carol S.: president, chief executive officer, trustee, Packard Foundation (David and Lucile)

Larson, Marie: secretary, Offield Family Foundation (The)

Larson, Peter N.: chairman, chief executive officer, director, Brunswick Corp.

Larson, Robert C.: trustee, Kresge Foundation

Larson, Tim: director, Jostens Foundation Inc. (The)

LaRussa, Anne: director, Bruno Charitable Foundation (Joseph S.)

LaRussa, Benny M., Jr.: vice president, treasurer, Bruno Charitable Foundation (Joseph S.)

LaScala, Fanny: executive secretary, AT&T Foundation

Lascor, Michael: trustee, Weckbaugh Foundation (Eleanore Mullen)

Lashley, Elinor Huston: vice president ed and cultural rels, Huston Foundation

Laske, Arthur Charles, Jr.: treasurer, director, Morris Foundation (William T.)

Lasley, Robert: co-trustee, Moss Charitable Trust (Finis M.)

Lasota, Kathleen: secretary, Quaker Chemical Foundation

Laspa, J. P.: president, director, Bechtel Foundation

Lassalle, Honor: president, Norman Foundation

Lassalle, Nancy Norman: vice president, secretary, Normandie Foundation

Lassalle, Philip E.: director, Norman Foundation

Lasser, Miles L.: executive director, secretary, Sheldon Foundation Inc. (Ralph C.)

Lasurdo, I. Jerry: director, Vogler Foundation (Laura B.)

Latham, John Brace: trustee, Brace Foundation (Donald C.)

Latham, Robert C.: second vice chairman, director, Grinnell Mutual Reinsurance Co.

Lathem, Edward: director, Dr. Seuss Foundation

Latta, Courtney E.: senior program officer, Reynolds Foundation (Donald W.)

Laub, Mindy: assistant secretary, State Farm Companies Foundation

Laub, Russell K.: first vice president, Hoch Foundation (Charles H.)

Laube, F. H., III: chairman, chief executive officer, president, Freeport Brick Co.; secretary, Freeport Brick Co. Charitable Trust

Laube, Harry R.: assistant secretary, assistant treasurer, Freeport Brick Co. Charitable Trust

Lauchert, F. H.: trustee, Atofina Chemicals Foundation

Lauck, Joseph: director, Lebanon Mutual Foundation

Lauder, Estee: president, director, Lauder Foundation

Lauder, Leonard Alan: secretary-treasurer, director, Lauder Foundation

Lauder, Ronald Stephen: vice president, director, Lauder Foundation

Laughon, Kenneth C.: vice president, director, Carter Foundation (Beirne)

Launius, Leigh Ann (Korns): assistant secretary, Cox Foundation (James M.)

Lauren, Charles B.: trustee, Hagedorn Fund

Lautz, Terrill E.: vice president, secretary, program director Asia, Luce Foundation (Henry)

LaVeque, Edgar G., MD: director, Valley Foundation

Lavezzo, Janette: trustee, Arata Brothers Trust

LaVigne, Gregory P.: trustee, Reliable Life Insurance Co. Foundation

Lavin, R. P.: vice president, Caterpillar Foundation

Lavine, Ruth J.: president, director, Lavine Family Foundation (Richard and Ruth)

Lavis, Stella Amado: director, Amado Foundation (Maurice)

Law, D. Brian: trustee, Kantzler Foundation

Lawford, Patricia Kennedy: trustee, Kennedy, Jr. Foundation (Joseph P.)

Lawin, Bruce A.: president, chief executive officer, Specialty Manufacturing Co.

Lawler, John J.: director, treasurer, Cabot Corp. Foundation

Lawler, Kathleen A.: director, Harley-Davidson Foundation

Lawless, Robert J.: chairman, president, chief executive officer, chief operating officer, director, McCormick & Company Inc.

Lawrence, Anne I.: vice president, Ingalls Foundation (Louise H. and David S.)

Lawrence, Anne T.: trustee, Semple Foundation (Louise Taft)

Lawrence, Belinda Turner: vice president, chief administrative officer, Knight Foundation (John S. and James L.)

Lawrence, Charles M.: president, Lytel Foundation (Bertha Russ)

Lawrence, Christopher: trustee, Credit Suisse First Boston Foundation Trust

Lawrence, Deborah B.: director, Williams Companies Foundation (The)

Lawrence, Elizabeth Atwood: trustee, Donaldson Charitable Trust (Oliver S. and Jennie R.)

Lawrence, James A.: chief financial officer, executive vice president, General Mills Inc.

Lawrence, John T., Jr.: vice president, trustee, Emery Memorial (Thomas J.); treasurer, Ingalls Foundation (Louise H. and David S.); treasurer, trustee, Semple Foundation (Louise Taft)

Lawrence, Keith: chief financial officer, director, Pickford Foundation (Mary)

Lawrence, Laura S.: director, Royal & SunAlliance Insurance Foundation, Inc.

Lawrence, Ralph: president, chief operating officer, Hyde Manufacturing Co.

Lawrence, Robert Ashton: trustee, Saltonstall Charitable Foundation (Richard)

Lawrence, Warren: secretary, Vicksburg Foundation

Laws, Donald P.: member advisory committee, Blue Bell Foundation

Lawson, A. Peter: secretary, Motorola Foundation

Lawson, Arleen E.: executive director, Exxon Mobil Foundation

Lawson, Floyd: director, Klee Foundation (Conrad and Virginia)

Lawson, John K.: senior vice president, Deere & Co.

Lawson-Johnston, Peter Orman, II: director, Guggenheim Foundation (Harry Frank)

Lay, Kenneth R.: trustee, J.P. Morgan Chase Foundation

Laybourne, Everett Broadstone: director, Parsons Foundation (Ralph M.)

Layman, Sandy: secretary, trustee, Blandin Foundation

Layton, Donald H.: chairman, J.P. Morgan Chase Foundation

Lazaran, Frank: vice president, Winn-Dixie Stores Foundation; president, chief executive officer, Winn-Dixie Stores Inc.

Lazarof, Janice Anne: president, director, Taper Foundation (S. Mark)

Lazarus, Charles P.: president, Lazarus Charitable Trust

Lazarus, Leonard: secretary, Solow Foundation

Lea, Anna L.: vice president, treasurer, director, Lea Foundation (Helen Sperry)

Lea, Helena A.: vice president, director, Lea Foundation (Helen Sperry)

Lea, R. Brooke, II: vice president, director, Lea Foundation (Helen Sperry)

Lea, Sperry: president, director, Lea Foundation (Helen Sperry)

Leach, Willis R.: trustee, Stamps Foundation (James L.)

Leaders, Rance: secretary, treasurer, trustee, Miller Foundation

Leahey, William E., Jr.: director, Alcoa Foundation

Leahy, Charles F.: trustee, Jameson Trust (Oleonda)

Leahy, Edwin D., OSB: trustee, The MBNA Foundation

Leahy, Richard A.: trustee, Peabody Charitable Fund (Amelia)

Leaman, Dean: trustee, George Foundation

Leary, Carol A., PhD: director, Beveridge Foundation, Inc. (Frank Stanley)

Leary, Hugh K.: executive director, treasurer, Scott Foundation (William H., John G., and Emma)

Leath, Berneice R.: secretary, treasurer, Priddy Foundation

Leavey, Joseph James: trustee, Leavey Foundation (Thomas and Dorothy)

Lebedoff, Randy Miller: vice president, general counsel, McClatchy Co.

Lebens, Jeffrey Kent: senior vice president financial & administration, treasurer, Intermountain Gas Co.

LeBlanc, Robert: president, chief operating officer, Handy & Harman

LeBoeuf, Raymond W.: director, PPG Industries Foundation; director, chairman, chief executive officer, PPG Industries Inc.

Lebovitz, Herbert C.: president, treasurer, director, Lebovitz Fund

Lebovitz, James: director, Lebovitz Fund

Lebow, Jane: vice president, Dickler Family Foundation

LeBreton, Pierre R., PhD: trustee, Blowitz-Ridgeway Foundation

LeBuhn, Robert: chairman, chief executive officer, trustee, Dodge Foundation (Geraldine R.)

Lechleiter, John C.: executive vice president, Lilly & Co. (Eli); director, Lilly Foundation (Eli)

LeClerc, Paul: trustee, Mellon Foundation (Andrew W.)

Leder, Philip: director, chairman, Revson Foundation (Charles H.)

Lederer, Adrienne: president, director, Lederer Foundation (Francis L.)

Ledes, John G.: assistant treasurer, assistant secretary, director, Hopkins Foundation (Josephine Lawrence)

Ledgett, Ronald A.: senior vice president, NSTAR

Ledward, Jeffery: secretary, director, Willis Family Foundation

Lee, C. T.: president, Formosa Plastics Corporation, USA

Lee, Donna: trustee, Bell-South Foundation

Lee, Greg: director, IBP Foundation

Lee, H. Clifford: chairman, director, Bush Charitable Foundation, Inc. (Edyth)

Lee, James R.: director, Patron Saints Foundation

Lee, Jane T.: chairman, director, Red Devil; trustee, Red Devil Foundation

Lee, John J.: chairman, president, chief executive officer, director, Hexcel Corp.

Lee, Mary: trustee, Red Devil Foundation

Lee, Pat: co-executive director, Wallace Genetic Foundation

Lee, Richard H.: president, trustee, Fowler Memorial Foundation (John Edward)

Lee, Robert W.: treasurer, Wildermuth Foundation (E. F.)

Lee, Sarah M.: assistant secretary, United Airlines Foundation

Lee, Wanda A.: senior vice president corporate human resources, PacifiCare Health Systems

Leemputte, Peter: trustee, Chicago Title and Trust Co. Foundation

Leeson, Cathy: treasurer, Hobby Family Foundation

LeFeber, Marilyn Stein: vice president communications, Mott Foundation (Charles Stewart)

Leffall, LaSalle D., Jr.: director, Dana Foundation (Charles A.)

Lefton, Al Paul, Jr.: president, chief executive officer, director, Lefton Co. (Al Paul); trustee, Lefton Co. Foundation (Al Paul)

Legare, Richard J.: director, Dime Savings Bank of Norwich Foundation

Legg, Louis E.: vice president, Thoman Foundation (W. B. and Candace)

Leggat, John E., Esq.: trustee, Walsh Charity Trust (Blanche)

Lehner, Carl P.: president, chief executive officer; trustee, Orchard Foundation

Lehner, Philip: chairman,

Lehr, Gustav J.: vice president, director, Shelter Insurance Foundation; chairman, director, Shelter Mutual Insurance Co.

Lehr, Ronald L.: trustee, Johnson Foundation (Helen K. and Arthur E.)

Leiberman, Patricia S.: vice chair, Mailman Family Foundation (A. L.)

Leibowitz, Martin L.: vice chairman, Carnegie Corp. of New York

Leibrock, Robert C.: trustee, Abell-Hanger Foundation

Leininger, Jeffrey L.: vice chairman, Mellon Financial Corp.; trustee, Mellon Financial Corp. Foundation

Lelaurin, Christine: trustee, Unocal Foundation

LeMieux, Linda J.: trustee, Whiting Foundation

Lemle, Stuart: director, JJJ Foundation

Lemons, Mark C.: trustee, Leavey Foundation (Thomas and Dorothy)

Lemons, Thomas: trustee, Leavey Foundation (Thomas and Dorothy)

Lemons, Wishard: trustee, Broadhurst Foundation

Lempke, R. Michael: vice president inventor, Bradley Foundation (Lynde and Harry)

Lenahan, Joan O.: secretary, Humana Foundation

Lenhard, John E.: secretary, Cleveland-Cliffs Foundation (The); secretary, associate general counsel, Cleveland-Cliffs Inc.

Lenhart, Carole S.: vice president, treasurer, Beveridge Foundation, Inc. (Frank Stanley)

Lenihan, F. Thomas, Esq.: trustee, Kimball Foundation (Horace A. Kimball and S. Ella)

Lenkowsky, Leslie, PhD: trustee, Bodman Foundation

Lenna, Elizabeth S.: president, director, Lenna Foundation (Reginald A. and Elizabeth S.)

Lennartz, Ann: vice president, Kuyper Foundation (Peter H. and E. Lucille Gaass)

Lenny, Richard H.: president, chief executive officer, Hershey Foods Corp.

Lenox, John W.: director, Shelter Insurance Foundation

Lenzmeier, Allen U.: director, Best Buy Children's Foundation; president, chief operating officer, Best Buy Co.

Leonard, Anna B.: 2nd vice president, Vale-Asche Foundation

Leonard, Joan S., Esq.: vice president, general counsel, Hughes Medical Institute (Howard)

Leonard, Kathryn: director, Bauervic Foundation (Charles M.)

Leonard, Patricia A.: president, secretary, Bauervic Foundation (Charles M.)

Leonard, Theodore J.: treasurer, Bauervic Foundation (Charles M.)

Leonard, Timothy J.: director, Bauervic Foundation (Charles M.)

Leone, Daniel A.: director, East Cambridge Savings Charitable Foundation

Leone, Joseph M.: vice president, treasurer, controller, CIT Group Foundation; executive vice president, CIT Group Inc.

Leopold, Estella: trustee, Bullitt Foundation

Lerer, Kenneth B.: director, Time Warner Foundation, Inc.

Lerner, Ralph E.: secretary, Lingnan Foundation

Lerner, Randolph D., Esq.: chairman, director, MBNA Corp.

Leroux, Robert J.: vice president, controller, Cleveland-Cliffs Inc.

Lesar, David J.: chairman, president, chief executive officer, Halliburton Co.; president, trustee, Halliburton Foundation, Inc.

Lesher, Cynthia: director, Lesher Foundation (Dean and Margaret)

Lesher, Melinda: director, Lesher Foundation (Dean and Margaret)

Lesher, Stephen: director, Lesher Foundation (Dean and Margaret)

Lesser, Richard G.: executive vice president, chief operating officer, director, TJX Companies Inc.

Lessersohn, James C.: vice president, treasurer, New York Times Co. Foundation

Lester, Jack: treasurer, Vodaphone-US Foundation

Letbetter, R. Steve: chairman, president, chief executive officer, CenterPoint Energy Inc.

Letcher, Edith Gilmore: trustee, Phillips Charitable Trust (Dr. and Mrs. Arthur William)

Letrillart, Thierry: president, chief executive officer, Christian Dior Perfumes Inc.

Leung, Sandra: vice president, secretary, Bristol-Myers Squibb Co.; secretary, Bristol-Myers Squibb Foundation Inc.

Levan, Alan: chairman, president, chief executive officer, BankAtlantic Bancorp; president, trustee, BankAtlantic Foundation

Levan Margolis, Shelley: secretary, trustee, BankAtlantic Foundation

Leveille, Raymond G., Jr.: trustee, Levy Foundation (June Rockwell)

Leven, Ann R.: director, Warhol Foundation for the Visual Arts (The Andy)

Leven, Steve: director, Texas Instruments Foundation

Levenson, Beatrice: secretary, Fischbach Foundation

Leverenz, Robert H.: director, VPI Foundation

Levett, Edith: secretary emeritus, Greenwall Foundation

Levi, Alexander H.: vice president, director, Hecht-Levi Foundation

Levi, Richard H.: vice president, treasurer, director, Hecht-Levi Foundation

Levi, Ryda H.: vice president, director, Hecht-Levi Foundation

Levin, Gail C.: executive director, Annenberg Foundation

Levin, Jack I.: trustee, Phillips Family Foundation (The Jay and Rose)

Levin, John P.: trustee, Phillips Family Foundation (The Jay and Rose)

Levin, John P., Jr.: director, Rosenberg, Jr. Family Foundation (Louise and Claude)

Levin, Richard C.: director, Hewlett Foundation (William and Flora)

Levin, Robert J.: executive vice president, Fannie Mae

Levin, Suzan: trustee, Phillips Family Foundation (The Jay and Rose)

Levine, Kenneth M.: director, MONY Foundation; executive vice president, chief investment officer, director, MONY Group Inc.

Levine, Richard E.: secretary, Rollins-Luetkemeyer Foundation

Levine, Sidney: president, Dewar Foundation

Levine, Victoria M.: director, Barra Foundation

Levinson, Donald M.: director, CIGNA Foundation

Levitan, David Maurice: vice president, Fink Foundation (NY)

Levitan, Matthew: trustee, Paine Webber Foundation

Levy, Andrew H.: director, Newman Assistance Fund (Jerome A. and Estelle R.)

Levy, David B.: treasurer, director, Rudin Foundation

Levy, H. George: director, La-Z-Boy Inc.

Levy, Richard: chief financial officer, Community Trust Bancorp Inc.

Levy, Roberta Morse: secretary, Ratshesky Foundation (A. C.)

Levy, Susan M.: director community relations, Donnelley & Sons Co. (R.R.)

Levy, William R.: co-trustee, Jacobs Charitable Trust (Margaret G.)

Lewin, John: vice president, director, Rudin Foundation

Lewis, A. D.: secretary, Federated Mutual Insurance Foundation

Lewis, Art: director, Mitsubishi Electric America

Foundation; senior vice president automotive, Mitsubishi Electric and Electronics USA

Lewis, C. Stephen: trustee, Weyerhaeuser Co. Foundation

Lewis, Craig: treasurer, trustee, Middendorf Foundation

Lewis, Diana D.: vice president, Ecolab Foundation; vice president human resources, Ecolab Inc.

Lewis, Emily S.: trustee, Saltonstall Charitable Foundation (Richard)

Lewis, George Ralph: trustee, Kemper Foundation (James S.)

Lewis, Jeffrey R.: executive director, chief operating officer, Heinz Family Foundation

Lewis, Jim: director, CNA Foundation

Lewis, Joanna M.: director, Barra Foundation

Lewis, John: Distribution trustee, Schwab-Rosenhouse Memorial Foundation

Lewis, John D.: chairman, director, Comerica Charitable Foundation; vice chairman, Comerica Inc.

Lewis, K.: trustee, Campbell Soup Foundation

Lewis, Kenneth D.: chairman, president, chief executive officer, Bank of America Corp.

Lewis, Marilyn Ware: vice president, secretary, Oxford Foundation

Lewis, Merry S.: secretary, trustee, Cacioppo Foundation (Joseph and Mary)

Lewis, Priscilla: program officer, peace and security, Rockefeller Brothers Fund, Inc.

Lewis, Russell T.: president, chief executive officer, New York Times Co.

Lewis, Sharon: trustee, Harris Foundation (William H. and Mattie Wattis)

Lewis, Sherry L.: secretary, trustee, Wolfe Associates, Inc.

Lewis, W. Ashton: secretary, trustee, Beazley Foundation

Lewis, Warren: director, Lebanon Mutual Foundation

Lewis Sauer, Janet P.: director, Flagler Foundation

Lewy, Ralph I.: treasurer, Pick, Jr. Fund (Albert)

Lexvold, Tom: director, Dillon Foundation

Ley, Watson: trustee, Van Wert County Foundation

Leydorf, Frederick Leroy: vice president, director, Jameson Foundation (J. W. and Ida M.)

Liberatore, Robert G.: trustee, DaimlerChrysler Corp. Fund

Libin, Jerome B.: director, Park Foundation

Lichtenstein, Harvey: director, Gilman Foundation (Howard)

Lichtman, Judith: 1st vice president, treasurer, Moriah Fund, Inc.

Lidvall, John Gabrielson: treasurer, director, Hall-Perrine Foundation

Lieberman, Leonard: chairman, trustee, Fund for New Jersey

Liebich, Richard C.: trustee, Charitable Venture Foundation

Liebler, Arthur C.: vice president communications, DaimlerChrysler AG

Liebman, Kate: program officer, Altman Foundation

Liebman, Seymour: executive vice president finance, chief financial officer, Canon U.S.A. Inc.

Lien, Tracy K.: assistant secretary, CUNA Mutual Group Foundation, Inc.

Lieser, W. E.: secretary, treasurer, trustee, Reeves Foundation (OH)

Lifton, Robert B.: director, chairman, Pick, Jr. Fund (Albert)

Lightfoot, Sara Lawrence: chairman, director, MacArthur Foundation (John D. and Catherine T.)

Ligon, Bill A., Jr.: trustee, Hawkins Foundation (Robert Z.)

Liles, George W., Jr.: director, member, Cannon Foundation, Inc. (The)

Lilienthal, Steve: chairman, director, CNA Foundation

Lilley, Jack: director, Smith and W. Aubrey Smith Charitable Foundation (Clara Blackford)

Lillios, Paul C.: director, Demos Foundation (N.)

Lilly, Adrienne: assistant secretary, Knight Ridder Fund

Lilly, Bruce A.: director, Lilly Foundation (Richard Coyle)

Lilly, David M.: president, Lilly Foundation (Richard Coyle)

Lilly, David M., Jr.: president, Lilly Foundation (Richard Coyle)

Lilly, Eli, II: director, Lilly Endowment

Lilly, Elizabeth M.: vice president, Lilly Foundation (Richard Coyle)

Lim, Jean: vice president, Amgen Foundation

Liman, Ellen: president, Lowe Foundation (Joe and Emily)

Limbert, G. Christian, Jr.: chief financial officer,

treasurer, Clemens Markets

Limes, Edward J.: treasurer, trustee, Weckbaugh Foundation (Eleanore Mullen)

Lin, Feifei: trustee, Dow Corning Foundation

Lin, Kun: director, Texas Instruments Foundation

Lincoln, William T.: treasurer, trustee, Berry Foundation (Loren M.)

Lindberg, Mark: senior program officer, Bremer Foundation (Otto)

Linde, Robert R.: mng trustee, Rogers Fund for the Arts (Russell Hill)

Lindenauer, Arthur: executive vice president, chief financial officer, Schlumberger Ltd.

Linder, M.: trustee, Campbell Soup Foundation

Lindheim, Elaine L.: president, Amado Foundation (Maurice)

Lindholm, John T.: secretary, treasurer, trustee, Whiting Foundation

Lindley, F. Haynes, Jr.: trustee, Haynes Foundation (John Randolph and Dora)

Lindquist, David S.: vice president, director, Russell Charitable Foundation (Tom)

Lindsay, David J.: trustee, CLARCOR Foundation; vice president, CLARCOR Inc.

Lindsay, F. M., Jr.: director, Oakley-Lindsay Foundation of Quincy Newspapers and Its Subsidiaries

Lindsay, Gary J.: secretary, treasurer, Schmitt Foundation (Kilian J. and Caroline F.)

Lindsay, Martin M.: director, Oakley-Lindsay Foundation of Quincy Newspapers and Its Subsidiaries

Lindsay, Nancy D.: trustee emeritus, Dodge Foundation (Geraldine R.)

Lindsay Smith, Lucy: director, Oakley-Lindsay Foundation of Quincy Newspapers and Its Subsidiaries

Lindsey, Handy L., Jr.: president, Field Foundation of Illinois

Lindsey, John H.: vice president, trustee, Swisher Foundation (Carl S.)

Lindt, Gillian: director, Guggenheim Foundation (Harry Frank)

Linebarger, Thomas: director, Cummins Foundation; vice president, chief financial officer, Cummins Inc.

Linehan, John H., PhD: vice president, Whitaker Foundation

Lingenfelter, James S.: president, trustee, Young

Foundation (Hugo H. and Mabel B.)

Link, Robert Emmett: vchairman, director, Link, Jr. Foundation (George)

Linnell, Norman C.: vice president, general counsel, Donaldson Company Inc.; president, trustee, Donaldson Foundation

Linnen, Mary Lou: director, Barker Welfare Foundation

Linnert, Terrence G.: president, Goodrich Foundation, Inc. (B.F.)

Linowes, R. Robert: director, Loughran Foundation (Mary and Daniel)

Lione, Gail A.: vice president, secretary, director, Harley-Davidson Foundation

Lipetz, Marcia: executive director, WPWR-TV Channel 50 Foundation

Lipkowitz, Irving: director, Hebrew Technical Institute

Lipnick, Dale K.: director, Keats Family Foundation

Lippe, Gary M.: trustee, Sapirstein-Stone-Weiss Foundation

Lipschultz, William H.: trustee, Bremer Foundation (Otto)

Lipscomb, James L.: director, MetLife Foundation

Lipton, Harvey L.: vice president, director, Hearst Foundation (William Randolph)

Lisher, Mary K.: director, Lilly Endowment

Lishman, Ruth C.: grant comm, Royal Foundation (May Mitchell)

Lisle, Edwin: chairman, Lisle Corp.

Lisle, John C.: president, chief executive officer, Lisle Corp.; trustee, Lisle Foundation

Lisle, Larry D.: trustee, Markey Charitable Fund (John C.)

Lisle, Lorance W.: vice president, Markey Charitable Fund (John C.)

List, Jennie Willis: president, director, Willis Family Foundation

List, Thomas E.: trustee, Saemann Foundation (Franklin I.)

Lister, William H.: trustee, Robinson-Broadhurst Foundation

Litow, Stanley S.: president, director, IBM International Foundation; vice president, International Business Machines

Littejohn, Myrl: advisory board, committee member, Heath Foundation (Mary)

Litteken, Martin: trustee, Priddy Foundation

Little, Dan: trustee, Sarkeys Foundation

Little, James S.: director, Hedco Foundation

Little, Lew: treasurer, ECG Foundation

Little, William A.: chairman, trustee, George Foundation

Little, William G.: chairman, director, West Pharmaceutical Services Inc.

Litvack, Sanford M.: member, director, Disney Co. (Walt)

Litwin, Gordon N.: director, Scherman Foundation

Liveris, Andrew N.: trustee, Dow Foundation (Herbert H. and Grace A.)

Livingston, John H.: vice president, St. Giles Foundation

Livingston, Johnston R.: chairman emeritus, trustee, Bonfils-Stanton Foundation

Llosa, Patricia: director, Kornfeld Foundation (Emily Davie and Joseph S.)

Lloyd, John: director, Gebbie Foundation

Lloyd, Susan L.: president, trustee, Lattner Foundation (Forrest C.)

Lobbia, John E.: trustee, Hudson-Webber Foundation

Loble, Lester H., II: director, MDU Resources Foundation

Locher, John J.: vice president, treasurer, Barnes Group Inc.

Locke, Hubert Gaylord: trustee, Bullitt Foundation

Lockridge, B. Russell: president, director, Brunswick Foundation

Lockwood, Glenn C.: senior vice president, chief financial officer, New Jersey Natural Gas Co.; treasurer, New Jersey Natural Gas Foundation

Lockwood, Theodore Davidge: director, Guggenheim Foundation (Harry Frank)

Loehr, Sarita: trustee, PNM Foundation

Loers, Lloyd: vice president, Lee Endowment Foundation

Loewenstern, Richard J.: chairman, director, Herzstein Charitable Foundation (Albert and Ethel)

Lofrese, Anke: assistant secretary, Hyde and Watson Foundation

Lofton, Thomas M.: chairman, director, Lilly Endowment

Lohr, David H.: trustee, U.S. Steel Foundation

Lohse, Ashby I.: secretary, Mulcahy Foundation

Lohse, Florence: vice president, Mulcahy Foundation

Lohse, Kathy: treasurer, Mulcahy Foundation

Lohse, Linda: secretary, treasurer, Mulcahy Foundation

Lohse, Robert D.: president, Mulcahy Foundation

Lomb, Chris: director, Ideal Industries Foundation

Lombard, Jane K.: mem distribution comm, trustee, Kettering Fund

Lombardi, Thomas J.: treasurer, Merrill Lynch & Co. Foundation Inc.

Lonergan, Becky: assistant secretary, Marshall & Ilsley Foundation, Inc.

Long, Jacob F.: trustee, Long Foundation (John F.)

Long, John F.: director, Long Foundation (John F.)

Long, Mary P.: director, Long Foundation (John F.)

Long, Michael Thomas: director, Ensign-Bickford Foundation

Long, Milton: trustee, Long Foundation (J. M.)

Long, Robert A.: director, McGee Foundation (MO)

Long, Robert Merrill: president, trustee, Long Foundation (J. M.)

Long, Robert R.: chairman, SunTrust Bank Atlanta

Longacre, Joseph M.: trustee, Mascoma Savings Bank Foundation

Longenecker, Kent: vice president, Davis Foundation (James A. and Juliet L.)

Longford, Bernadette Williams: manager corporate giving, ABC Broadcasting Foundation, Inc.

Longley, Elizabeth A.: vice president corporate affairs, Prudential Securities Foundation; 1st vice president, Prudential Securities Inc.

Longstreet, Al: director, Fuller Co. Foundation (H.B.)

Longwell, Harry J.: executive vice president, director, ExxonMobil Corp.

Loomis, Worth: president, trustee,

Looney, Wilton D.: trustee, Woodruff Foundation (Robert W.)

Loos, Henry J.: trustee, Steigleder Charitable Trust (Bert L. and Patricia S.)

Lopdrup, Kim: board member, Dunkin' Donuts Inc.

Loper, Graham B.: vice president, trustee, Brown Foundation, Inc. (James Graham)

Lopez, Al: director, Rockefeller Foundation (Winthrop)

Lopez, Owen M.: executive director, McCune Charita-

ble Foundation (Marshall L. and Perrine D.)

Lord, G. S.: controller, Campbell Soup Foundation

Lord, John S.: director, Bush Charitable Foundation, Inc. (Edyth)

Loren, Allan Z.: chairman, chief executive officer, director, D&B

Loring, Jonathan B.: president, trustee, Levy Foundation (June Rockwell)

Loring, Karl H., CPA: chief financial officer, Knapp Foundation (CA)

Loring, Peter B.: trustee, Mifflin Memorial Fund (George H. and Jane A.)

Loring, Valerie S.: secretary, trustee, Stoddard Charitable Trust

Losinger, Sarah McCune: chairman, McCune Charitable Foundation (Marshall L. and Perrine D.)

Lotter, C. R.: director, Penney Co. Fund (J.C.)

Louden, G. Malcolm: assistant treasurer, assistant secretary, director, Fleming Foundation

Loughlin, Caroline: trustee, RosaMary Foundation

Loughlin, Caroline K.: treasurer, trustee, Keller Family Foundation

Loughlin, Elizabeth M.: director, Keller Family Foundation

Loughman, Thomas F.: secretary, treasurer, trustee, Barden Foundation, Inc.

Loughrey, F. Joseph: director, Cummins Foundation

Loughry, Ed C., Jr.: secretary, treasurer, director, Christy-Houston Foundation

Louis, Kenneth C.: president, chief operating officer, director, Ameritas Life Insurance Corp.

Love, Howard McClintic: director, Heinz Endowment (Howard)

Love, Jeff: vice president, Kayser Foundation

Lovejoy, Joseph Ensign: chairman, director, Ensign-Bickford Industries

Lovelace, John G.: trustee, Pittsburgh Child Guidance Foundation

Lovett, Tiffany W.: trustee, Mott Foundation (Charles Stewart)

Lowe, Albert: director, Patron Saints Foundation

Lowe, David M.: vice president lubrication equip division, Graco Inc.

Lowe, Derrick C.: vice president, Lowe Family Foundation

Lowe, Elizabeth H.: director, Parsons Foundation (Ralph M.)

Lowe, Kenneth W.: president, chief executive officer, director, Scripps Co. (E.W.)

Lowe, Walter M.: manager, director, French Foundation (D.E.)

Lowell, William A.: trustee, Peabody Charitable Fund (Amelia)

Lower, James Paul: director, mem legal comm, Keck Foundation (W. M.)

Lower, Judith A.: secretary, Keck Foundation (W. M.)

Lowet, Henry A.: vice president, secretary, director, Littauer Foundation (Lucius N.)

Lowry, Robert L.: chief financial officer, Pulliam Charitable Trust (Nina Mason)

Loyd, Mary Jo: corp secretary, trustee, Rockwell Fund, Inc.

Lubin, Arline J.: president, Morris Foundation (Norman M.)

Lubin, Kenneth A.: trustee, Morris Foundation (Norman M.)

Lubin, Marvin: vice president, Morris Foundation (Norman M.)

Lubow, Mary Ellen: trustee, Beynon Foundation (Kathryne)

Lucas, Charles C., III: trustee, Duke Endowment

Lucas, Colin: trustee, Mellon Foundation (Andrew W.)

Lucas, Robert C.: vice president, Allen Foundation (Nibs and Edna)

Lucckese, Deborah G.: vice president, Washington Forrest Foundation

Luce, H. Christopher: director, program director public policy & environment, Luce Foundation (Henry)

Luce, Henry, III: chairman emeritus, director, Luce Foundation (Henry)

Luce, Priscilla: president, Greenfield Foundation (Albert M.)

Luck, C. S., III: chairman, chief executive officer, Luck Stone; president, Luck Stone Foundation

Ludington, Cassandra V. A.: trustee, Kent-Lucas Foundation

Ludington, John Samuel: trustee, Strosacker Foundation (Charles J.)

Ludington, Thomas L.: trustee, Gerstacker Foundation (Rollin M.)

Ludwick, Arthur J.: cfo, director, Ludwick Family Foundation

Ludwick, Erik Arthur: director, Ludwick Family Foundation

Ludwick, Heidi Ann: director, Ludwick Family Foundation

Ludwick, Sarah Lynne: president, director, Ludwick Family Foundation

Ludwick Warner, Sharon Lynne: secretary, director, Ludwick Family Foundation

Luers, William Henry: director, Gilman Foundation (Howard); advisory trustee, Rockefeller Brothers Fund, Inc.

Luetkemeyer, Anne A.: secretary, director, Rollins-Luetkemeyer Foundation

Luetkemeyer, John A., Jr.: president, Rollins-Luetkemeyer Foundation

Lukas, John: director, Gilman Foundation (Howard)

Lukaszewicz, Peter: treasurer, director, Bemis Manufacturing Co.

Luke, David Lincoln, III: honorary director, Macy, Jr. Foundation (Josiah)

Luke, John A., Jr.: chairman, president, chief executive officer, director,

Luke, Monica: manager, Thompson Charitable Foundation

Lukins, Scott: assistant treasurer, assistant secretary, Johnston-Hanson Foundation

Lukowski, Stanley J.: chairman, chief executive officer, Eastern Bank; trustee, Eastern Bank Charitable Foundation

Luli Heras-De Leon, M. L.: trustee, Unocal Foundation

Lummis, Isabel S.: trustee, Brown Foundation

Lummis, William R., Esq.: trustee, Hughes Medical Institute (Howard)

Lund, Margaret McKee: senior vice president, McKee Foundation (Robert E. and Evelyn)

Lunda, Larry: trustee, Lunda Charitable Trust

Lunda, Lydia: trustee, Lunda Charitable Trust

Lunda, Milton: trustee, Lunda Charitable Trust

Lundback, Lee C.: director, Staunton Farm Foundation

Lundberg, Minnie P.: treasurer, director, King Foundation (Kenneth Kendal)

Lundgren, Dan: vice president, trustee, Jones Foundation (Fletcher)

Lundgren, H. David: director, Fireman's Fund Foundation

Lundgren, Kenneth: trustee, chairman, Blandin Foundation

Lunger, Francis: chief financial officer, corporate vice president, Millipore Corp.

Lunsford, David H.: mem, Teubert Charitable Trust (James H. and Alice)

Lunt, Thomas D.: trustee, Wendt Foundation (Margaret L.)

Lupton, T. Cartter, II: trustee, Lyndhurst Foundation

Lurcott, Robert: president, chief executive officer, Henkel Corp.

Lustberg, Lawrence S.: trustee, Fund for New Jersey

Luthy, Thomas M.: senior vice president wood products, Weyerhaeuser Co.

Luttgens, Leslie L.: director, Rosenberg Foundation

Lutz, Theodore M.: trustee, Graham Fund (Philip L.)

Lux, Mike: director, Arca Foundation

Luzius, Kate B.: president, trustee, Bicknell Fund

Luzzi, Rick: trustee, West Foundation (Herman O.)

Lyall, Katharine Culbert: trustee, Kemper Foundation (James S.)

Lyddon, Grant: vice president, Seven Springs Foundation

Lyddon, John Knight: secretary, Seven Springs Foundation

Lyddon, Martha D.: president, Seven Springs Foundation

Lyle, Paul: trustee, Mayer Foundation (James and Eva)

Lyman, Carol L.: vice president, director, O'Shaughnessy Foundation (I. A.)

Lynch, Daniel: assistant treasurer, Graham Fund (Philip L.)

Lynch, Harry H.: director, Maddox Foundation (J. F.)

Lynch, James M.: treasurer, MassMutual Foundation for Hartford, Inc. (The)

Lynch, Judith: treasurer, secretary, GlaxoSmithKline Foundation

Lynch, Luba H.: executive director, secretary, Mailman Family Foundation (A. L.)

Lynch, Michael: director, Illinois Tool Works Foundation

Lynch, Robert L. K.: chairman, Kempner Fund (Harris and Eliza)

Lynch, Thomas P.: chairman, trustee, Stamps Foundation (James L.)

Lynham, John Marmaduke, Jr.: director, Strong Foundation (Hattie M.)

Lynn, June: co-trustee, Cray Residuary Charitable Trust (Evah C.)

Lyon, Marina: director public affairs, U.S. Bancorp Piper Jaffray

Lyons, Bernard E.: director, Colburn Fund

Lyons, Louis: trustee, Camp and Bennet Humiston Trust (Apollos)

Lyons, Shaun L.: vice president, assistant secretary, trustee, Baldwin Memorial Foundation (Fred)

Lyons, Tony J.: gov, Mayor Foundation (Oliver Dewey)

Lyons, William M.: president, director, American Century Companies Foundation

M

Maas, Suzanne W.: executive director, Boston Globe Foundation

Mabbett, John R., III: president, chief executive officer, Florida Rock & Tank Lines

Mabee, Joseph G.: chairman, trustee, Mabee Foundation, Inc. (J. E. and L. E.)

Mabee, Joseph Guy, Jr.: trustee, Mabee Foundation, Inc. (J. E. and L. E.)

Mabry, Rhett N.: director child care division, Duke Endowment

Mac Kimm, Margaret (Pontius) "Mardie": trustee, Chicago Title and Trust Co. Foundation

MacAffer, Kenneth S., Jr.: director, Kelley and Elza Kelley Foundation (Edward Bangs)

MacAlister, Patricia A.: trustee, Blowitz-Ridgeway Foundation

MacAllaster, Archie F.: director, Clark Foundation (NY)

Macauley, Victoria J.: vice president, Stuart Charitable Foundation (G. B.)

MacBeth, Anita L.: director, Bourns Foundation

MacColl, John A.: vice chairman, general counsel, St. Paul Travelers Companies Inc.; director, St. Paul Travelers Foundation

MacColl, Stephanie: director, The Bothin Foundation

MacConnell, Diane: director, Memorial Foundation for the Blind

MacConnell, Gary: director, Memorial Foundation for the Blind

MacConnell, Jocelyn H.: trustee, Hulme Charitable Foundation (Milton G.)

MacDonald, Harold C.: comptroller, Moody Foundation

MacDonald, John A.: vice president, treasurer, Hall Family Foundation (The)

MacDonald, Susanne Fuller: trustee, Fuller Foundation (MA)

MacDougall, Joseph W., Jr.: director, clerk, Allmerica Financial Charitable Foundation, Inc.

MacElree, Jane Cox: trustee, Cox Charitable Trust (Jessie B.)

Macfie, Valerie A.: board member, Snow Foundation (John Ben)

MacGregor, David Lee: assistant secretary, director, Stackner Family Foundation

Machado, Edward J.: senior vice president, chief financial officer, Shenandoah Life Insurance Co.

Machold, Roland M.: director, Teagle Foundation

Maciel, Manuel, Jr.: chairman, Land O'Lakes Foundation

Mack, John E., III: chairman, chief executive officer, Central Hudson Gas & Electric Corp.

Mack, John J.: chief executive officer, Credit Suisse First Boston Corp.

Mackay, Clader M.: president, Mead Foundation (Giles W. and Elise G.)

Mackay, Richard N.: secretary, treasurer, Mead Foundation (Giles W. and Elise G.)

Mackay, Robert Battin: trustee, St. Giles Foundation

Mackell, John: trustee, Pennington Foundation (William N. and Myriam)

Mackell, Thomas, Jr.: trustee, New York Foundation

Mackenzie, Wendy Jacobus: secretary, Heinz Family Foundation

Mackey, Mary Ann: foundation accountant, PPG Industries Foundation

Mackey, William R.: trustee, Gilmore Foundation (William G.)

Mackler, Harvey A.: director, Alexander Foundation (Joseph)

Mackler, Helen: secretary, director, Alexander Foundation (Joseph)

Macklin, B. G.: trustee, Exxon Mobil Foundation

MacLeod, Gary: treasurer, Medina Foundation

Macleod, Ivor: trustee, Roche Foundation

Maclin, Samuel Todd: trustee, J.P. Morgan Chase Foundation

MacPhee, Chester R., Jr.: trustee, Sandy Foundation (George H.)

MacPherson, D. R.: president, chief executive officer, director, Red Devil

Maddox, Don: vice president, Maddox Foundation (J. F.)

Maddox, James M.: president, Maddox Foundation (J. F.)

Maddox, Thomas M.: director, Maddox Foundation (J. F.)

Maddux, Thomas H.: trustee, Warfield Memorial Fund (Anna Emory)

Madhavpeddi, Kalidas: member, Phelps Dodge Foundation

Madiera, Anthony G.: treasurer, Eastern Savings and Loan Foundation

Madigan, John W.: chairman, director, McCormick Tribune Foundation (Robert R.)

Madison, Michael H.: president, chief executive officer, chief financial officer, Southwestern Electric Power Co.

Maerki, Max H.: senior vice president, PNM Resources Inc.

Maffucci, David G.: executive vice president, chief financial officer, Bowater Inc.

Mafreci, August: trustee, August Family Foundation (Charles J. and Burton S.)

Magaram, Philip S.: director, Drown Foundation (Joseph)

Magee, Wayne E.: grants analyst, Moody Foundation

Magill, William H.: treasurer, Reader's Digest Foundation

Magliochetti, Joseph M.: president, chief executive officer, director, Dana Corp.

Magruder, G. Brock: trustee, Magruder Foundation (Chesley G.)

Maguire, James G.: trustee, Yawkey Foundation II

Mahaney, Larry K.: chairman, president, chief executive officer, director, Webber Oil Co.

Maher, Colleen: program officer, Mitsubishi Electric America Foundation

Maher, Francesca M.: senior vice president, general counsel, secretary, UAL Corp.

Mahle, Steve: director, Medtronic Foundation

Mahn, Thomas E.: director, Perdue Foundation (Arthur W.)

Mahon, Arthur Joseph: trustee, Archbold Charitable Trust (Adrian and Jessie)

Mahone, Andrea Torres: member, Staunton Farm Foundation

Mahoney, Cornelius D.: chairman, president, chief executive officer, Woronoco Savings Bank

Mahoney, Elaine: director, Drown Foundation (Joseph)

Mahoney, Hildegarde E.: director, Dana Foundation (Charles A.)

Mahoney, Joseph A.: director, New York Stock Exchange Foundation, Inc.

Mahoney, Mary Jane: assistant secretary, American Standard Foundation

Mahoney, Neil: director, Woronoco Savings Charitable Foundation

Mahoney, P. Michael: chairman, president, chief executive officer, director, Park Bank; president, director, Park Bank Foundation

Mahoney, Stephen J.: president, director, Smith Charitable Foundation (Arlene H.)

Mahowald, Douglass A.: assistant treasurer, MDU Resources Foundation

Maiden, Margaret Davis: trustee, Davis Foundations (Arthur Vining)

Maisano, Lise Einfeld: senior program officer, Cowell Foundation (S. H.)

Maitland, Peter K.: president, director, USG Foundation

Makowski, Bob: chief financial officer, Park Bank

Makupson, Amyre: trustee, Skillman Foundation

Malaquias, Stephen W., MD: director, Kelley and Elza Kelley Foundation (Edward Bangs)

Malcolm, Allen R.: board member, Snow Foundation (John Ben); trustee, Snow Memorial Trust (John Ben)

Malcolm, Bruce L.: board member, Snow Foundation (John Ben)

Malcolm, Steven J.: director, Williams Companies Foundation (The)

Malcom, Shirley M.: director, Heinz Endowment (Howard)

Mallahan, Mary Ann: secretary, Illinois Tool Works Foundation

Mallardi, Michael Patrick: senior vice president, ABC Inc.

Malley, Bonnie J.: director, Phoenix Foundation

Mallick, Craig D.: general manager, U.S. Steel Foundation

Malloy, Mary T.: secretary, Sara Lee Foundation

Malmberg, Jennifer L.: treasurer, secretary, Widgeon Foundation

Malmloff, Cheryl: community relations administrator, Donnelley & Sons Co. (R.R.)

Malo, J. Kenneth, Jr.: director, Mullen Foundation (J. K.)

Malo, John F.: president, director, Mullen Foundation (J. K.)

Malo, Kathleen: director, Mullen Foundation (J. K.)

Malone, Donna: assistant trustee, BellSouth Foundation

Malone, Frank M., Jr.: trustee, Franklin Foundation Inc. (John and Mary)

Maloni, William R.: senior vice president policy & affairs, Fannie Mae

Malouf, Donald J.: vice president, secretary, Overlake Foundation

Malquist, Malyn K.: senior vice president, chief financial officer, Avista Corp.

Malti, George M.: director, Holt Foundation (William Knox)

Malvaso, James J.: president, chief executive officer, director, Raymond Corp.

Manapat, Christine: assistant secretary, treasurer, United States-Japan Foundation

Mancasola, John A.: executive vice president, secretary, director, McConnell Foundation

Mandel, Deborah: assistant treasurer, MetLife Foundation

Mandel, Jack N.: trustee, Mandel Foundation (Jack N. and Lilyan)

Mandel, Ruth: director, Revson Foundation (Charles H.)

Mandelbaum, Eric S.: vice president, secretary, CIT Group Foundation

Mandelstam, Charles L.: secretary, Rubin Foundation (Samuel)

Mandeville, Hubert T.: president, treasurer, director, Mandeville Foundation

Mandeville, Josephine C.: chairman, chief executive officer, president, donor daughter, Connelly Foundation

Mandeville, Matthew T.: director, Mandeville Foundation

Mandeville, P. Kempton: vice president, director, Mandeville Foundation

Mangan, Lawrence T.: vice president, Connelly Foundation

Mangino, Terri C.: executive director, assistant secretary, Rose Foundation (Billy)

Manilow, Barbara Goodman: vice president, director, Crown Memorial (Arie and Ida)

Mankiller, Wilma Pearl: trustee, Ford Foundation

Manley, Joan D.: director, Sara Lee Corp.

Manly, Marc E.: director, Cinergy Foundation

Manne, Larry R.: director, Oakley-Lindsay Foundation of Quincy Newspapers and Its Subsidiaries

Manning, Lori: assistant secretary, State Farm Companies Foundation

Manning, Victor P.: president, executive director, trustee, The MBNA Foundation

Mannion, Geraldine P.: program chair U.S. democracy, Carnegie Corp. of New York

Mannion, Patrick A.: trustee, Gifford Charitable Corp. (Rosamond)

Manns, Andrew: vice president financial, treasurer, Monadnock Paper Mills Inc.

Manny, Carter Hugh, Jr.: director emeritus, Graham Foundation for Advanced Studies in the Fine Arts

Mansell, Edmona Lyman: vice president, director, The Bothin Foundation

Manske, Susan E.: vice president, chief investment officer, MacArthur Foundation (John D. and Catherine T.)

Manton, Edwin Alfred Grenville: director, Starr Foundation

Manuel, Mary: director, Grotto Foundation

Maples, Roger C.: director, Christy-Houston Foundation

Marangi, Leonard M.: trustee, Murphey Foundation (Lluella Morey)

Marbut, Margo: president, Argyle Foundation

Marbut, Mike: director, Argyle Foundation

Marbut, Robert: chairman, Argyle Foundation

Marcantonio, Richard L.: vice president, chairman, Ecolab Inc.

Marcela, Paul A.: secretary, trustee, Dow Corning Foundation

March, Kevin P.: treasurer, director, Texas Instruments Foundation

Marcinelli, Ron: director, Comerica Charitable Foundation

Marciniak, Jere D.: president, trustee, Dow Corning Foundation

Marconi, Michael A.: executive director, Koch Foundation, Inc.

Marcotte, Brian W. G.: trustee, Unocal Foundation

Marcus, Gregory S.: director, Marcus Corp. Foundation

Marcus, Lorraine: secretary, Boothroyd Foundation (Charles H. and Bertha L.)

Marcus, Stephen Howard: chairman, chief executive officer, Marcus Corp.;

president, treasurer, director, Marcus Corp. Foundation

Marcuse, Edgar K., MD: director, Nesholm Family Foundation

Margenthaler, Donald R.: president, director, Deere & Co.

Margolin, Abraham E.: director, Tension Envelope Foundation

Margotta, Gisela L.: treasurer, East Cambridge Savings Charitable Foundation

Marin, Lawrence: vice president, Kaplun Foundation (Morris J. and Betty)

Marion, Anne W.: president, trustee, Burnett Foundation (The)

Marion, John Louis: trustee, Burnett Foundation (The)

Maritz, W. Stephen: president, chief executive officer, Maritz Inc.

Mark, Sarah E.: trustee, Greenfield Foundation (Albert M.)

Markel, Charles A., III: vice president finance, treasurer, LG&E Energy Corp.

Markel, Larry G., MD: assistant secretary, Lyon Foundation

Markey, John Clifton, II: treasurer, Markey Charitable Fund (John C.)

Markham, Marianna: director, Jones Foundation (Helen)

Markham, Sharon F.: associate vice president, Retirement Research Foundation

Markins, Jane A.: secretary, treasurer, Suntrust Foundation - Agency

Markman, Joanne W.: director, Pine Tree Foundation

Markos, Arthur C.: president, chief executive officer, Gardiner Savings Institution; president, director, Gardiner Savings Institution Charitable Foundation

Marks, Dennis A.: vice president, Boothroyd Foundation (Charles H. and Bertha L.)

Marks, Nancy: trustee, Priddy Foundation

Marks, Paul C.: trustee, Camp Younts Foundation

Marks, Paul Camp: director, Campbell Foundation (Ruth and Henry)

Marks, Randolph A.: director, Knox Foundation (Seymour H.)

Marks, Raymond: secretary, treasurer, Stulsaft Foundation (Morris)

Marlar, Donald F.: trustee, Bernsen Foundation (Grace and Franklin)

Marley, James Earl: director, Kline Foundation

(Josiah W. and Bessie H.)

Marmer, Lynn: president, The Kroger Co. Foundation

Marmion, William H.: trustee, Miller Foundation (Earl B. and Loraine H.)

Maroney, Eleanor Silliman: secretary, Borkee-Hagley Foundation; adv trustee, Crystal Trust

Marosek, Edwin P.: trustee, Anderson Foundation (NY)

Marram, Ellen R.: director, New York Times Co. Foundation

Marran, Elizabeth: vice president, Kennedy Foundation (Ethel)

Marran, Ethel K.: president, treasurer, Kennedy Foundation (Ethel)

Marran, Laura: secretary, Kennedy Foundation (Ethel)

Marron, Brian H.: assistant treasurer, Harley-Davidson Foundation

Marron, Donald Baird: director, Dana Foundation (Charles A.)

Marrone, Lynda: grants mgr, Bremer Foundation (Otto)

Mars, Bernard S.: trustee, Foster Charitable Trust

Mars, Peter F.: trustee, Foster Charitable Trust

Marsh, Edward W.: secretary, treasurer, Murphy Foundation

Marsh, Helsel R., Jr.: member, Staunton Farm Foundation

Marsh, Larry R.: director, president, chief executive officer, Olmsted Foundation (George and Carol)

Marsh, Richard S. T.: director, Strong Foundation (Hattie M.)

Marshall, Collin S., Esq.: trustee, Van Buren Foundation (Elsie Procter)

Marshall, David B.: president, director, Contempo Communications Foundation for the Arts, Inc.

Marshall, David L.: secretary, treasurer, director, Contempo Communications Foundation for the Arts, Inc.

Marshall, Jim: manager, Porter Testamentary Trust (James Hyde)

Marshall, Joan F.: president, Contempo Communications; vice president, director, Contempo Communications Foundation for the Arts, Inc.

Marshall, John Elbert, III: president, chief executive officer, trustee, Kresge Foundation

Marshall, Rose M.: co-trustee, Arakelian Foundation (Mary Alice)

Marshall, Shauna I.: vice chairman, director, Rosenberg Foundation

Marshall, Siri S.: senior vice president, general counsel, secretary, General Mills Inc.

Marshall, Stephanie Pace, PhD: vice president, director, Fry Foundation (Lloyd A.)

Marshall, Thomas C.: director, Drown Foundation (Joseph)

Marshall, William H.: treasurer, Clowes Fund

Martin, C. Alan: director, Alabama Power Foundation

Martin, C. Cecil: director, Houchens Foundation (Ervin G.)

Martin, Carmel C., Jr.: secretary, treasurer, AT&T National Pro-Am Youth Fund

Martin, Casper: treasurer, secretary, director, Martin Foundation

Martin, Don: manager, Porter Testamentary Trust (James Hyde)

Martin, Elizabeth: director, Martin Foundation

Martin, George: treasurer, Anthem Foundation, Inc.

Martin, Geraldine F.: president, director, Martin Foundation

Martin, Glenn R.: vice president, director, Reynolds Foundation (Richard S.)

Martin, J. Landis: chairman, trustee, Bonfils-Stanton Foundation

Martin, James R.: trustee, Norris Foundation (Kenneth T. and Eileen L.)

Martin, Jennifer: director, Martin Foundation

Martin, JoAnn M.: controller, Ameritas Charitable Foundation; senior vice president, partner, chief financial officer, Ameritas Life Insurance Corp.

Martin, John: comm mem, Smith, Jr. Foundation (M. W.)

Martin, John W.: chief financial officer, Ontario Corp.; treasurer, Ontario Corp. Foundation

Martin, Joseph W., Jr.: treasurer, director, Skaggs Foundation (L. J. Skaggs and Mary C.)

Martin, Judith W.: board of directors, Wilson Foundation (Marie C. and Joseph C.)

Martin, Karen C.: associate director, Corning Inc. Foundation

Martin, Lauralee: chief financial officer, GE Capital Corp.

Martin, Lois Lynne: secretary, Houchens Foundation (Ervin G.)

Martin, Mary Ann: trustee, New Jersey Natural Gas Foundation

Martin, Maurice H.: president, trustee, Tonya Memorial Foundation

Martin, N. E.: trustee, National Machinery Foundation, Inc.

Martin, Patricia: trustee, Clorox Co. Foundation

Martin, R. Eden: chairman, director, Aon Foundation

Martin, Richard J.: executive vice president public relations employee communications, AT&T Corp.

Martin, Susan Fasken: trustee, Fasken Foundation

Martin, Webb Franklin: trustee, Mott Foundation (Charles Stewart)

Martinenza, Stephen A.: treasurer, Crestlea Foundation; assistant treasurer, assistant secretary, Welfare Foundation

Martinez, Eric: director, Burnett Co. Charitable Foundation (Leo)

Martinez, Jorge: director information, Knight Foundation (John S. and James L.)

Martini, Gloria: vice president, Martini Foundation (Nicholas)

Martini, William J.: trustee, Martini Foundation (Nicholas)

Martiny, Mary Anne: assistant secretary, Harley-Davidson Foundation

Martore, Gracia C.: senior vice president, chief financial officer, Gannett Company Inc.; vice president, Gannett Foundation

Marty, Mary: assistant treasurer, Boston Globe Foundation

Marx, Leonard: vice president, Marx Foundation (Virginia and Leonard)

Marx, Leonard, Jr.: treasurer, Marx Foundation (Virginia and Leonard)

Marx, Robert: director, vice president, Samuels Foundation (Fan Fox and Leslie R.)

Marx, Virginia: president, Marx Foundation (Virginia and Leonard)

Marzio, Peter C.: director, The Wallace Foundation

Masaoka, Jan: treasurer, Haigh-Scatena Foundation

Mascotte, John P.: director, Hall Family Foundation (The)

Masi, Wendy S.: vice president, Mailman Family Foundation (A. L.)

Masket, Steven N.: assistant secretary, Rosenthal Foundation (Ida and William)

Mason, Emma Newby: trustee, Nord Family Foundation

Mason, Frederick T.: assistant secretary, assistant treasurer, Sulzberger Foundation

Mason, Jack Arliss: 2nd vice president, Tri-County Telephone Foundation

Mason, James C.: director, Bishop Foundation (E. K. and Lillian F.)

Mason, James L.: vice president community initiatives, Eaton Corp.

Mason, Kathleen B.: treasurer, Earhart Foundation

Mason, Kimberly B.: trustee, Earhart Foundation

Massar, Mike: director, Heath Foundation (Ed and Mary)

Massaro, George E.: trustee, Eastern Bank Charitable Foundation

Massengil, R. Scott: vice president, director, American Standard Foundation

Massey, Joe B.: trustee, Massey Charitable Trust

Massey, Morris: president, Goodstein Foundation

Massey, Walter Eugene: director, Commonwealth Fund (The); trustee, Mellon Foundation (Andrew W.)

Massie, Timmian C.: director, Dyson Foundation

Masson, Rick C.: executive director, trustee, Plough Foundation

Masters, James L., IV: president, Masters Family Foundation

Masters, Jane J.: assistant secretary, assistant treasurer, Mather and William Gwinn Mather Fund (Elizabeth Ring)

Masters, Mickey Jo: chairman, Masters Family Foundation

Mastream, Michele: vice president, corp. secretary, Halliburton Foundation, Inc.

Masuda, Shigeru: chairman, director, Mitsubishi Silicon America

Masumoto, Davis Mas: director, Irvine Foundation (The James)

Mates, David E.: assistant treasurer, assistant secretary, McCormick Foundation (Chauncey and Marion Deering)

Matheny, Edward Taylor, Jr.: director, H&R Block Foundation

Matheny, N. D.: trustee, Smith Horticultural Trust (Stanley)

Mather, Karen W.: grants manager, program officer, Gates Family Foundation

Matherne, Louis K.: treasurer, Chesapeake Corp.

Mathes, Stephen Jon, Esq.: secretary, trustee, Levitt Foundation (NY)

Matheson, Alline: director, Barker Welfare Foundation

Matheson, Bonnie B.: trustee, Dow Foundation (Herbert H. and Grace A.)

Mathews, Odonna: vice president consumer affairs, Giant Food Inc.

Mathews, Sharron D.: assistant secretary, Chiles Foundation

Mathews, Sylvia M.: chief operating officer, executive director, libraries, pac northwest, Gates Foundation (Bill and Melinda)

Mathias, Charles McC.: director, Tinker Foundation

Mathias, Charles McCurdy, Jr.: director, Tinker Foundation

Mathiasen, Karl: secretary, Moriah Fund, Inc.

Mathieson, Peter F.: trustee, director, Buhl Foundation (PA)

Mathis, David B.: trustee, chairman, Kemper Foundation (James S.)

Mathis, Travis A.: trustee, Brown Foundation

Mathison, William A.: member corporate contributions committee, Ecolab Inc.

Matosziuk, Edward J.: trustee, Hamer Foundation

Matsui, Takashi: mem allocations comm, Kawabe Memorial Fund

Matsuzaki, Motoyasu: executive vice president, chief financial officer, Fujitsu America

Matt, Nicolas O.: director, Utica National Foundation

Matteo, Donna: treasurer, Thompson Co. Fund (J. Walter)

Matteson, William B.: secretary, trustee, Hartford Foundation, Inc. (The John A.)

Matthews, Allan: program officer, Moody Foundation

Matthews, B. Frank, II: member board advisors, Belk Foundation

Matthews, David: adv comm mem, Moore and Arletta E. Moore Foundation (Kenneth S.)

Matthews, E. E.: director, Starr Foundation

Matthews, Janice C.: director, CHC Foundation

Matthews, Joseph B.: director, Dodge Jones Foundation and Subsidiary

Matthews, Julia Jones: president, director, Dodge Jones Foundation and Subsidiary

Matthews, Kade L.: director, Dodge Jones Foundation and Subsidiary

Matthews, Robert: member advisory committee, Blue Bell Foundation

Matthews, William: director, Oneida Savings Bank Charitable Foundation

Matthews Shatteen, Westina Lomax: trustee, Merrill Lynch & Co. Foundation Inc.; senior director, first vice president corporate respons, Merrill Lynch & Company Inc.

Mattison, Robert Mayer: president, Graco Foundation

Mattox, Martha L.: trustee, Johnson Foundation (Burdine)

Mattson, David C.: director, Shelter Mutual Insurance Co.

Mattson, Ellwood: fund comm mem, Kaufman Endowment Fund (Louis G.)

Matz, Dorothy A.: director, Kleberg Foundation (Robert J. Kleberg, Jr. and Helen C.)

Maughan, Deryck C.: director, New York Stock Exchange Foundation, Inc.

Maurer, Eleanor Johnson: treasurer, director, Kirkpatrick Foundation, Inc.

Maurer, Gilbert Charles: vice president, director, Hearst Foundation (William Randolph)

Maurer, Jeffrey Stuart: president, chief operating officer, director, United States Trust Company of New York

Maurer, Kathleen C.: treasurer, chief financial officer, director, Warhol Foundation for the Visual Arts (The Andy)

Mauro, Margaret: executive director, secretary, trustee, Rouse Co. Foundation

Maus, Blair Collins: trustee, McCormick Foundation (Chauncey and Marion Deering)

Mavec, Ellen S.: president, Smith Foundation (Kelvin and Eleanor)

Maxwell, Kenneth: director, Tinker Foundation

May, Carolyn A.: director, Niagara Mohawk Foundation

May, Cordelia Scaife: chairman, trustee, donor, Laurel Foundation

May, Ernest N., Jr.: adv trustee, Crystal Trust

May, Irenee du Pont, Jr.: secretary, trustee, Longwood Foundation

May, Jeff: trustee, Donaldson Foundation

May, T. L.: vice president, Caterpillar Foundation

May, William H.: director, Beckman Foundation (Arnold and Mabel)

Maybee, Terri R.: assistant treasurer, Hall Family Foundation (The)

Mayer, Charles B.: vice president, German Protestant Orphan Asylum Association Foundation

Mayer, Deedee Gale: trustee, Buell Foundation (Temple Hoyne)

Mayer, John A. "Tony", Jr.: chairman, trustee, Kauffman Foundation (Ewing Marion)

Mayerson, Arlene B.: vice president, Mayerson Foundation (Manuel D. and Rhoda)

Mayerson, Donna: secretary, Mayerson Foundation (Manuel D. and Rhoda)

Mayerson, Fred: trustee, Mayerson Foundation (Manuel D. and Rhoda)

Mayerson, Manuel D.: trustee, Mayerson Foundation (Manuel D. and Rhoda)

Mayerson, Neal H.: president, treasurer, Mayerson Foundation (Manuel D. and Rhoda)

Mayerson, Rhoda: trustee, Mayerson Foundation (Manuel D. and Rhoda)

Mayfield, Nelda: trustee, Cauthorn Charitable Trust (John and Mildred)

Mayhew, Eva: assistant trustee, BellSouth Foundation

Mayman, Todd A.: secretary, Gannett Foundation

Maynard, Olivia P.: trustee, Mott Foundation (Charles Stewart)

Mayo, James Otis: vice chairman, secretary, director, Kiplinger Washington Editors Inc.

Mayo, Joanna M.: director, Peters Foundation (Charles F.)

Mayr, Gerhard N.: director, Lilly Foundation (Eli)

Mays, Troy M.: director, Mays Foundation

Maza, Bruce A.: executive director, C. E. and S. Foundation

Mazer, David: vice president, treasurer, Mazer Foundation (Jacob and Ruth)

Mazer, Richard: vice president, secretary, Mazer Foundation (Jacob and Ruth)

Mazmanian, Daniel A.: trustee, Haynes Foundation (John Randolph and Dora)

Mazur, John M.: treasurer, Eden Hall Foundation

Mazzilli, Philip J.: trustee, Equifax Foundation

McAfee, Emily Jean H.: director, Haley Foundation (W. B.)

McAlister, James P.: president, trustee, McAlister Charitable Foundation (Harold)

McAllister, Leo: secretary, director, Sierra Health Foundation

Mcaulay, Carl D.: vice president, trustee, Unocal Foundation

McBean, Nancy H.: director, McBean Family Foundation

McBride, H. S. Graham: adv, Weezie Foundation

McBryde, Nowlin: director, Peterson Foundation (Hal and Charlie)

McBurnie, Richard G.: president, director, Arkelian Foundation (Ben H. and Gladys); president, chief executive officer, West Foundation (Harry and Ethel)

McCabe, Barry E.: executive vice president, chief operating officer, Mascoma Savings Bank Foundation

McCall, John R.: vice president, secretary, director, LG&E Energy Foundation

McCallie, Allen L.: chairman, trustee, Lyndhurst Foundation

McCallister, Beth M.: secretary, Badger Meter Foundation

McCallum, James: director, Washington Group Foundation, Inc.

McCallum, William T.: president, chief executive officer, Great-West Life and Annuity Insurance Co.

McCalmont, Susan: executive director, Kirkpatrick Foundation, Inc.

McCalpin, William F.: executive vice president, chief operating officer, Rockefeller Brothers Fund, Inc.

McCandless, June: director, Hughes Foundation (Geoffrey C.)

McCandless, O. Carlysle: executive vice president, assistant secretary, treasurer, director, Hughes Foundation (Geoffrey C.)

McCandliss, Len: president, director, Sierra Health Foundation

McCann, Linda: assistant trustee, BellSouth Foundation

McCann, Nancy W.: president, Kulas Foundation

McCartan, Patrick F., Esq.: trustee, vice president, Kulas Foundation

McCarthy, Charles: president, chief executive officer, Tetley U.S.A. Inc.

McCarthy, Gerald Patrick: executive director, secretary, Virginia Environmental Endowment

McCarthy, John: trustee, Leavey Foundation (Thomas and Dorothy)

McCarthy, Kathleen Leavey: chairman, Leavey Foundation (Thomas and Dorothy)

McCarthy, Peter John: trustee, Atofina Chemicals Foundation; vice president public affairs, Elf Atochem North America Inc.

McCarthy, Robert J.: director, New Milford Savings Bank Foundation

McCarthy, Thomas F.: chairman, trustee, Henson Foundation (Richard A.)

McCarty, Marilu H.: executive secretary, Franklin Foundation Inc. (John and Mary)

McCasland, Thomas H., Jr.: trustee, McCasland Foundation

McCauley, Ann: assistant secretary, assistant clerk, TJX Foundation, Inc.

McCauley, Joan D.: director, Heinz Family Foundation

McCausland, Bonnie: president, McCausland Foundation

McCausland, Peter: vice president, McCausland Foundation

McClain, David H.: assistant secretary, PPG Industries Foundation

McClain, John David: president, chief executive officer, Brillion Iron Works

McClain, Terry James: director, Valmont Foundation; senior vice president, chief financial officer, Valmont Industries Inc.

McClay, Paul F.: mem, Gardiner Savings Institution Charitable Foundation

McCleery, Tania L-J.: director, Guggenheim Foundation (Harry Frank)

McClenahan, Carol T.: member, Staunton Farm Foundation

McClintock, John R. D.: trustee, Childs Charitable Foundation (Roberta M.)

McCloskey, Geoffrey: assistant treasurer, CUNA Mutual Group Foundation, Inc.

McCloskey, Shaun: treasurer, Honda of America Foundation

McCluskey, Lynn A.: assistant secretary, assistant treasurer, Dyson Foundation

McCluski, Stephen C.: president, director, Bausch & Lomb Foundation, Inc.

McConn, Christiana R.: secretary, trustee, Sterling-Turner Foundation

McConnell, Doug C.: president, Tyndale House Foundation

McCook, Richard P.: vice president, Winn-Dixie Stores Foundation; senior vice president, chief financial officer, Winn-Dixie Stores Inc.

McCord, Kathy: secretary, Kirkpatrick Foundation, Inc.

McCorkindale, Douglas H.: chairman, president, chief executive officer, Gannett Company Inc.; director, Gannett Foundation

McCormack, Elizabeth J.: trustee, Trust for Mutual Understanding

McCormack, Kristen J.: vice president, trustee, Hayden Foundation (Charles)

McCormick, Brooks: chairman, director, McCormick Foundation (Chauncey and Marion Deering)

McCormick, Charlotte Deering: vice president, trustee, McCormick Foundation (Chauncey and Marion Deering)

McCormick, Nancy V.T.: trustee, McCormick Foundation (Chauncey and Marion Deering)

McCormick, Thomas P.: treasurer, director, Barker Welfare Foundation

McCormick, William Thomas, Jr.: chairman, chief executive officer, director, Consumers Energy Co.

McCown, J. Ross: vice president, secretary, Abel Foundation

McCoy, Alan H.: executive director, AK Steel Foundation; vice president public affairs, AK Steel Holding Corp.

McCoy, Dena Woodard: director, Woodard Foundation (W. A.)

McCoy, Joseph P.: vice president, controller, Burlington Resources Foundation

McCoy, Louise Boney: trustee, Hillsdale Fund

McCrae, Angela: executive director, Springs Foundation, Inc.

McCrary, C. W., III: director, Acme-McCrary and Sapona Foundation

McCrary, Charles D.: director, Alabama Power Foundation

McCrary, Charles W., Jr.: chairman, chief executive officer, director, Acme-McCrary Corp./Sapona Manufacturing Co.; vice president, Acme-McCrary and Sapona Foundation

McCraven, Paul A.: vice president, secretary, treasurer, NewAlliance Foundation

McCray, Ronald D.: vice president, Kimberly-Clark Corp.

McCrodden, Bruce: senior vice president, corp. public affairs, National City Corp.

McCubbin, Don A.: director, Shelter Insurance Foundation

McCue, Howard McDowell, III: secretary, director, Cheney Foundation (Elizabeth F.)

McCullouch, John: trustee, BellSouth Foundation

McCullough, F. E.: mem distribution comm, Flowers Charitable Trust (Albert W. and Edith V.)

McCullough, Hubert L., Jr.: director, Christy-Houston Foundation

McCullough, P. Michael: director, trustee, Meadows Foundation (The)

McCullough, Samuel Alexander: trustee, Wyomissing Foundation

McCullough, W. R.: trustee, Cone Automatic Machine Co. Charitable Foundation

McCully, A. C., MD: president emeritus, trustee, Frueauff Foundation (Charles A.)

McCully, George E.: director, Phillips Foundation (Ellis L.)

McCune, John R., VI: director, McCune Charitable Foundation (Marshall L. and Perrine D.); member distribution committee, McCune Foundation

McCusker, Francis C.: treasurer, McDonough Foundation (Bernard)

McCutcheon, Hilary H.: trustee, McCormick Foundation (Chauncey and Marion Deering)

McDade, Sandy D.: secretary, Weyerhaeuser Co.; assistant secretary legal affairs, Weyerhaeuser Co. Foundation

McDaniel, Glen P.: trustee, Thornton Foundation (Flora L.)

McDermott, Margaret M.: trustee, McDermott Foundation (The Eugene)

McDonagh, William M.: president, chief operating officer, Broderbund L.L.C.; director, Carlston Family Foundation

McDonald, Anne E.: trustee, Stout Foundation (Charles H.)

McDonald, Charles R.: vice president, trustee, Ratner Foundation (Milton M.)

McDonald, Charline: program officer, Meyer Memorial Trust

McDonald, Douglas B.: secretary, Stout Foundation (Charles H.)

McDonald, Ellice, Jr.: president, director, Glencoe Foundation

McDonald, Frank J.: vice president, quality, Cummins Inc.

McDonald, James, IV: vice president, McDonald Foundation (Armstrong)

McDonald, James M., III: trustee, McDonald Foundation (Armstrong)

McDonald, James P.: president, Mellon Financial Corp. Foundation

McDonald, Katherine: trustee, McDonald Foundation (Armstrong)

McDonald, Malcolm S.: trustee, treasurer, Ford Motor Co. Fund

McDonald, Malcolm W.: treasurer, director, Grotto Foundation; secretary, treasurer, trustee, McNeely Foundation

McDonald, Nellie Jane: director, Schwartz Fund for Education and Health Research (Arnold and Marie)

McDonald, Peter D.: vice president, director, United Airlines Foundation

McDonald, Rosa H.: vice president, director, Glencoe Foundation

McDonald, William E.: mem supervisory board, Codrington Charitable Foundation (George W.)

McDonnell, Archie R., Sr.: treasurer, director, Hardin Foundation (Phil)

McDonnell, Brian: vice president, director, CUNA Mutual Group Foundation, Inc.

McDonnell, Thomas A.: trustee, Kauffman Foundation (Ewing Marion)

McDonough, M. E.: director, Bayport Foundation of Andersen Corporation

McDonough, Marie: trustee, Leavey Foundation (Thomas and Dorothy)

McDougal, Ted: director, vice president, Caterpillar Foundation; secretary, treasurer, director, Illinois Tool Works Foundation; director, Sara Lee Foundation

McDowell, Deborah E.: trustee, Kresge Foundation

McDuffie, Brenda W.: trustee, Western New York Foundation

McEachran, Angus: trustee, Scripps Howard Foundation

McElhinny, C.A.: vice president, director, Murphy Co. Foundation (G.C.)

McElroy, Dee: executive vice president, foundation manager, Gulf Coast Medical Foundation

McEvoy, George H.: trustee, McEvoy Foundation (Mildred H.)

McFadden, R. Bruce: director, Mosher Foundation (Samuel B. & Margaret C.)

McFaddin, Eugene H. B.: trustee, Ward Heritage Foundation (Mamie McFaddin)

McFaddin, James L. C., Jr.: trustee, Ward Heritage Foundation (Mamie McFaddin)

McFadyen, Barbara N.: director, Grable Foundation

McFarland, Catherine M.: executive off, secretary, Victoria Foundation

McFarland, Duncan: director, Claneil Foundation

McFarland, H. Richard: trustee, McFarland Charitable Trust (H. Richard)

McFarland, Sarah F.: trustee, McFarland Charitable Trust (H. Richard)

McFate, William J.: trustee, Phillips Charitable Trust (Dr. and Mrs. Arthur William)

McGee, Gary C.: secretary, trustee, Perry Foundation

McGee, Henry: director, Time Warner Foundation, Inc.

McGee, Thomas R., Jr.: vice president, McGee Foundation (MO)

McGee, Vincent: director, Overbrook Foundation (The)

McGeehan, Tim: director, Best Buy Children's Foundation

McGehee, Robert B.: vice president, director, Progress Energy Foundation; executive vice president, general counsel, Progress Energy Inc.

McGill, Joe K.: president, chairman, trustee, Doss Foundation, Inc. (M. S.)

McGilvreay, William F.: president, director, East Cambridge Savings Charitable Foundation

McGinnis, Kermit E.: secretary, treasurer, Huntington Foundation

McGinnis, W. Patrick: chief executive officer, Nestle Purina PetCare Co.

McGlinn, Barbara T.: assistant secretary, Colonial Oaks Foundation

McGlinn, John F., II: assistant treasurer, Colonial Oaks Foundation

McGlinn, Terrence J.: president, Colonial Oaks Foundation

McGlinn, Terrence J., Jr.: trustee, Colonial Oaks Foundation

McGlinn Auman, Christine R.: secretary, Colonial Oaks Foundation

McGoldrick, John L.: director, Bristol-Myers Squibb Foundation Inc.

McGougan, Joseph: director, AMCORE Foundation

McGough, W. Thomas, Jr.: secretary, Pittsburgh

Child Guidance Foundation

McGovern, John Phillip, MD: president, McGovern Fund

McGovern, Kathrine G.: vice president, treasurer, McGovern Foundation (John P.)

McGowan, Andrew J.: chairman, director, McGowan Charitable Fund (William G.)

McGowan, Gertrude: director, McGowan Charitable Fund (William G.)

McGowan, Leo: director, McGowan Charitable Fund (William G.)

McGowan, Tim: director, McGowan Charitable Fund (William G.)

McGrath, Barry G.: chairman, president, Pittsburg & Midway Coal Mining Co.

McGrath, J. Paul: vice president, director, American Standard Foundation

McGrath, Joan S.: contributions administrator, Fortune Brands Inc.

McGraw, Dave: trustee, Fairchild-Meeker Charitable Trust (Freeman E.)

McGraw, Michael J.: senior vice president law & human resources, Brown & Williamson Tobacco Corp.

McGregor, Douglas A.: trustee, Rouse Co. Foundation

McGregor, Mark: vice president, treasurer, Storage Technology Corp.

McGrew, Margery: director, Meyers Charitable Family Fund

McGrory, Patrick W.: trustee, Raskob Foundation for Catholic Activities, Inc.

McGuigan, William: assistant treasurer, Bunbury Co., Inc.

McGuinn, Martin Gregory: chairman, chief executive officer, Mellon Financial Corp.; trustee, Mellon Financial Corp. Foundation

McGuire, Allen G.: director, co-trustee, Potts and Sibley Foundation

McGuire, Grant: chairman, Teubert Charitable Trust (James H. and Alice)

McGuire, Patricia A.: director, Meyer Foundation (Eugene and Agnes E.)

McGuire, Raymond J.: director, Gilman Foundation (Howard)

McHale, Patrick J.: director, Graco Foundation

McHenry, James F.: director, Green Foundation (Allen P. and Josephine B.)

McHugh, Ann: vice president, treasurer, director,

Carvel Foundation (Thomas and Agnes)

McHugh, Katherine S.: director, Cox Charitable Trust (Jessie B.)

McIninch, Douglas A.: co-trustee, Hunt Foundation (Samuel P.)

McInnes, Harold A.: committee member, Whitaker Foundation

McIntosh, James C.: vice president, trustee, Castle Foundation (Samuel N. and Mary)

McIntosh, Robert E.: assistant secretary, assistant treasurer, director, Green Foundation (Allen P. and Josephine B.)

McIntyre, David I.: director, Roddy Foundation (Fred M.)

McJunkin, Donald R.: president, trustee, McDonald Foundation (J. M.)

McJunkin, Eleanor F.: vice president, trustee, McDonald Foundation (J. M.)

McJunkin, Reed L.: secretary, trustee, McDonald Foundation (J. M.)

McKasy, Bert J.: trustee, Bigelow Foundation (F. R.)

McKay, Emily B.: director, Mead Witter Foundation, Inc.

McKay, Shawn: director, Grinnell Mutual Group Foundation

McKean, Robert: trustee, Claiborne Foundation (Liz)

McKee, C. Steven: trustee, McKee Foundation (Robert E. and Evelyn)

McKee, David C.: secretary, assistant treasurer, trustee, McKee Foundation (Robert E. and Evelyn)

McKee, E. Marie: senior vice president, Corning Inc.; chairman, trustee, Corning Inc. Foundation

McKee, Joan: secretary, director, Ball Foundation (George and Frances)

McKee, John S.: senior vice president, McKee Foundation (Robert E. and Evelyn)

McKee, Louis B.: president-treasurer, trustee, McKee Foundation (Robert E. and Evelyn)

McKee, Michael D.: vice president, director, Jones Foundation (Fletcher)

McKee, Nelson D.: vice president, trustee, McKee Foundation (Robert E. and Evelyn)

McKee, Philip Russell: vice president, trustee, McKee Foundation (Robert E. and Evelyn)

McKee, R. Brian: trustee, McKee Foundation (Robert E. and Evelyn)

McKee, Robert E., III: trustee, treasurer, McKee Foundation (Robert E. and Evelyn)

McKee, Susan J.: vice president, trustee, McKee Foundation (Robert E. and Evelyn)

McKee, Timothy E.: director, Kansas Health Foundation

McKenna, Andrew James: director, Aon Foundation

McKenna, Laura K.: director, van Ameringen Foundation, Inc.

McKenna, Thomas M.: director, Penn Foundation (William)

McKenna, William P.: vice president finance, chief financial officer, treasurer, Bourns Inc.

McKenna, Wilma F.: vchairman, director, McKenna Foundation (Katherine Mabis)

McKenzie, Charles K.: executive director, president, Robinson-Broadhurst Foundation

McKenzie, D. Ray, Jr.: vice president, Callaway Foundation, Inc.

McKenzie, Dorma J.: program officer, Brown Foundation, Inc. (James Graham)

McKenzie, Floretta Dukes: trustee, Higginson Trust (Corina)

McKenzie, Wendy Jacobus: director, Heinz Endowment (Vira I.)

McKeown, Dan: treasurer, Boss Foundation

McKeown, Heidi: vice president, secretary, director, Boss Foundation

McKim, Karen P.: secretary, executive director, Corbett Foundation

McKinney, David B.: vice president, treasurer, trustee, Bovaird Foundation (Mervin)

McKinney, David Ewing: executive secretary, mem adv board, Watson Foundation (Thomas J.)

McKonly, Donald E.: director, Kahn Foundation; chief financial officer, Kahn, Lucas-Lancaster Incorporated Children's Wear

McKown, C. H.: director, Huntington Foundation

McLain, Sandy: vice president, Van Buren Foundation

McLane, Derek: director, Educational Foundation of America

McLane, John P.: director, French Foundation (D.E.)

McLane, Malcolm: trustee, Jameson Trust (Oleonda)

McLane-Bradley, Elizabeth: trustee, Friendship Fund

McLaren, Ross: chief executive officer, Shaw's Supermarkets Inc.

McLaughlin, Elizabeth: president, director, Royal & SunAlliance Insurance Foundation, Inc.; chairman, Royal & SunAlliance USA Inc.

McLaughlin, Loretta: director, Boston Globe Foundation

Mclaughlin, Marcie: trustee, Blandin Foundation

McLaughlin, Michael T.: general counsel, Pacific Life Foundation

McLaughlin, Sandra J.: member corporate review commission, Mellon Financial Corp.

McLaughlin, Wendy A., MD: trustee, Foundation for Seacoast Health

McLaughlin Korologos, Ann: director, Dana Foundation (Charles A.)

McLean, Sandra L.: executive drc, advisory trustee, McLean Contributionship

McLean, William L., III: chairman, trustee, McLean Contributionship

McLean, William L., IV: vice chairman, trustee, McLean Contributionship

Mcleish, Sally: director, Amgen Foundation

McLendon, Charles A.: trustee, Burlington Industries Foundation

McLeod, E. Douglas: director/development, Moody Foundation

McMahan, John J., Jr.: director, Kaul Foundation Trust (Hugh)

McMahan, Michael L.: chief financial officer, McMahan Foundation (Catherine L. and Robert O.)

McMahan, Neal W.: executive director, McMahan Foundation (Catherine L. and Robert O.)

McMahan, Nicki Wilson: director, McMahan Foundation (Catherine L. and Robert O.)

McMahon, Ian: treasurer, New Milford Savings Bank Foundation; chief financial officer, treasurer, NewMil Bancorp

McMahon, John J., Jr.: chairman, president, chief executive officer, treasurer, McWane Corp.; trustee, McWane Foundation

McMahon, Kevin G.: treasurer, CH Foundation

McMahon, Paul: treasurer, Unilever United States Foundation

McManus, Joseph, Esq.: secretary, treasurer, Olmsted Foundation (George and Carol)

McManus, Patrick J.: treasurer, Raymond Foundation

McMaster, Helen E.: vice president, secretary, McMaster Foundation (Harold and Helen)

McMaster, Ronald A.: trustee, McMaster Foundation (Harold and Helen)

McMeel, Bridget J.: director, Andrews McMeel Universal Foundation

McMeel, John Paul: president, treasurer, Andrews McMeel Universal Foundation

McMeel, Susan S.: director, Andrews McMeel Universal Foundation

McMeel Glynn, Suzanne E.: director, Andrews McMeel Universal Foundation

McMeel Jackoboice, Maureen: director, Andrews McMeel Universal Foundation

McMenamin, Joan B. S.: director, Clark Foundation (NY)

McMillan, C. Steven: president, chief executive officer, Sara Lee Corp.; director, Sara Lee Foundation

McMillan, Cary D.: executive vice president, chief financial officer, chief administrative officer, Sara Lee Corp.

McMillan, Douglas D.: trustee, Bigelow Foundation (F. R.)

McMillan, S. Sterling, PhD: trustee, Mather Fund (Richard)

McMillen, Dale W., III: director, McMillen Foundation

McMillen, John F.: president, director, McMillen Foundation

McMillion, R. D.: vice president, secretary, National Standard Foundation

McMinn, William A.: vice president, Cain Foundation (Gordon and Mary)

McMurray, Sharon: director, Comerica Charitable Foundation

McNabb, F. William: director, Vanguard Group Foundation

McNamara, Julia: director, NewAlliance Foundation

McNamara, Michael William: chairman, president, chief executive officer, director, Key Bank of Maine

McNamee, George C.: chairman, director, New York Stock Exchange Foundation, Inc.

McNeeley, Robert D.: president, director, Reilly Industries Inc.

McNeely, Gregory: trustee, McNeely Foundation

McNeely, Harry G., III: trustee, McNeely Foundation

McNeely, Harry G., Jr.: chairman, trustee, McNeely Foundation

McNeer, Charles Selden: treasurer, Johnson Foundation

McNeil, Collin F.: director, Barra Foundation

McNeil, Jennifer C.: secretary, director, Claneil Foundation

McNeil, Robert D.: director, Claneil Foundation

McNeil, Robert L., Jr.: president, treasurer, director, Barra Foundation

McNeill, Corbin Asahel, Jr.: president, chief executive officer, director, chairman, Exelon

McNellis, Gregory T.: director, U.S. Bancorp Piper Jaffray Foundation

McNerney, W. James, Jr.: chairman, chief executive officer, director, Minnesota Mining & Manufacturing Co.

McParland, Nathaniel P., MD: trustee, Retirement Research Foundation

McPhail, Gary: president emeritus, Amerus Group Co.

McPhee, Rod: president, trustee, Castle Foundation (Samuel N. and Mary)

McPherson, Mary Patterson: director, Teagle Foundation

McPherson, Mary Patterson, PhD: director, Macy, Jr. Foundation (Josiah)

McQuiston, W. James: chairman, trustee, Miller Foundation

McTier, Charles Harvey: president, Woodruff Foundation (Robert W.)

McWane, C. Phillip: trustee, McWane Foundation

McWilliams, D. Bradley: chief financial officer, senior vice president finance, Cooper Industries Ltd.

Meachum, Bruce: director, Vermilion Healthcare Foundation

Mead, Elizabeth: president, treasurer, director, Mead Family Foundation (Gilbert and Jaylee)

Mead, George Wilson, II: chairman, treasurer, Mead Witter Foundation, Inc.; chairman, director, Stora Enso

Mead, Gilbert Dunbar: chairman, director, Mead Family Foundation (Gilbert and Jaylee)

Mead, Jane W.: vice president, Mead Foundation (Giles W. and Elise G.)

Mead, Jaylee M.: vice president, director, Mead Family Foundation (Gilbert and Jaylee)

Mead, Marilyn K.: director, Mead Family Foundation (Gilbert and Jaylee)

Mead, Parry W.: vice president, Mead Foundation (Giles W. and Elise G.)

Mead-Siohan, Diana: secretary, director, Mead Family Foundation (Gilbert and Jaylee)

Meade, Joseph F., III: trustee, Mercury Aircraft Foundation; president, Mercury Aircraft Inc.

Meade, Joseph F., Jr.: trustee, Mercury Aircraft Foundation; chairman, director, Mercury Aircraft Inc.

Meader, Mary U.: trustee, Upjohn Foundation (Harold and Grace)

Meador, David E.: senior vice president, chief financial officer, DTE Energy Co.

Meadows, Amy Mettlen: executive director, Belo Foundation

Meadows, Curtis W., Jr.: director emeritus, Meadows Foundation (The)

Meadows, Eric R.: director, Meadows Foundation (The)

Meadows, John M.: trustee, director, Meadows Foundation (The)

Meadows, Mark A.: trustee, director, Meadows Foundation (The)

Meadows, Robert A.: chairman, trustee, vice president, director, Meadows Foundation (The)

Meaney, Lisa Collins: trustee, McCormick Foundation (Chauncey and Marion Deering)

Means, Mary C.: bookkeeper, Arkelian Foundation (Ben H. and Gladys); secretary, West Foundation (Harry and Ethel)

Means, Rick L.: director, Shelter Insurance Foundation

Mebane, David Cummins: chairman, president, chief executive officer, director, MGE Energy Inc.

Mebane, John G., Jr.: trustee, mem investments comm, Biddle Foundation (Mary Duke)

Mecca, Robert A.: vice president, director, treasurer, Regenstein Foundation

Mechanic, Clarisse B.: president, Mechanic Foundation (Morris A.)

Medlin, John Grimes, Jr.: trustee, Duke Endowment

Medovitch, J. Terry: treasurer, Freeport Brick Co. Charitable Trust

Medvin, Harvey Norman: executive vice president, treasurer, chief financial officer, Aon Corp.; treasurer, Aon Foundation

Meehan, Dorothy A.: vice president, Sierra Health Foundation

Meenan, Julie: executive director, Gumbiner Foundation (Josephine)

Meeusen, Richard A.: vice president, chief financial officer, treasurer, Badger Meter Inc.

Meggers, Steph: manager, Grinnell Mutual Group Foundation

Meier, Richard: trustee, Meier Foundation (Richard)

Meier, Richard W.: director, secretary, Bakewell, Jr. Family Foundation (Edward L.)

Meier, Stephen Charles: vice chairman, Tribune Co.

Meinders, Herman: president, trustee, Meinders Foundation

Meinders, LaDonna: vice president, trustee, Meinders Foundation

Meinders, Robert: secretary, trustee, Meinders Foundation

Meister, Paul M.: vice president, treasurer, Winthrop

Melarkey, Michael J.: vice president, secretary, Wiegand Foundation (E. L.)

Melican, James Patrick, Jr.: executive vice president, International Paper Co.

Melley, Maura L.: trustee, Hartford Courant Foundation

Mellon, Richard Prosser: chairman, trustee, Mellon Foundation (Richard King)

Mellon, Seward Prosser: don, director, trustee, Mellon Family Foundation (R. K.); president, chairman executive comm, trustee, Mellon Foundation (Richard King)

Mellon, Thomas J., Jr.: president, Hale Foundation (Crescent Porter)

Mellor, C. Michael: director, Ziegler Foundation for the Blind (E. Matilda)

Melnicoff, David C.: board member, Fels Fund (Samuel S.)

Melrose, Kendrick B.: chairman, co-president, chief executive officer, director, Toro Co.; director, Toro Foundation

Melton, Rollan D.: trustee, Snow Memorial Trust (John Ben)

Melton-Williams, Emelie: secretary, Snow Foundation (John Ben)

Meltzer, Jay: secretary, clerk, TJX Foundation, Inc.

Meltzer, Jay J.: director, Hebrew Technical Institute

Memmen, Ava-Lisa: trustee, Stratford Foundation

Menapace, John J.: director, Sordoni Foundation

Menard, Raymond N.: trustee, Levy Foundation (June Rockwell)

Mendel, Audre D.: vice president, Mendel Foundation

Mendel, Herbert D.: president, Mendel Foundation

Mendel, Julie: director, Mendel Foundation

Mengebier, David G.: president, Consumers Energy Foundation

Mengel, Andre, PhD: director, Independence Foundation

Menke, John R.: director, Hebrew Technical Institute

Menschel, Richard L.: trustee, Morris Foundation (Margaret T.)

Mentesana, Carolyn A.: vice president, Kimberly-Clark Foundation

Menton-Nightlinger, Deborah A.: executive director, secretary, Noble Foundation, Inc. (Edward John)

Mentzer, Edward W.: director, St. Francis Bank Foundation

Menzies, Julia Baker: director, Lockhart Vaughan Foundation

Merced, Victor: program officer, Meyer Memorial Trust

Mercer, Henry D., Jr.: trustee, Frese Foundation (Arnold D.)

Merchant, David: trustee, Thomaston Savings Bank Foundation

Merck, Adele Shook: trustee, Shook Foundation (Barbara Ingalls)

Merck, Antony M.: secretary, trustee, Merck Family Fund

Merck, Josephine A.: trustee, Merck Family Fund

Merck, Wilhelm M.: president, trustee, Merck Family Fund

Merdek, Andrew Austin: vice president legal affairs, secretary, Cox Enterprises Inc.; secretary, Cox Foundation (James M.)

Merin, Kenneth D.: president, chief executive officer, trustee, Hayden Foundation (Charles)

Merkle, Karen A.: secretary, General Motors Foundation

Merlotti, Frank Henry: trustee, Steelcase Foundation

Merrick, Robert B.: trustee, Merrick Foundation

Merrick, Robert G., III: vice president, director, France-Merrick Foundation

Merrick, Ward S., Jr.: trustee, Merrick Foundation

Merrill, Thomas M.: vice president, director, Harden Foundation

Merritt, Pamela M.: secretary, McMillan, Jr. Foundation (Bruce)

Mersereau, Susan M.: trustee, Weyerhaeuser Co. Foundation

Merthan, Claudia Boettcher: chairman, trustee, Boettcher Foundation

Merva, John: secretary, Sovereign Bank Foundation

Meserow, J. Tod: secretary, director, Russell Charitable Foundation (Tom)

Messier, Andre J., Jr.: director, Eastern Savings and Loan Foundation

Messing, Roswell, III: trustee, Messing Family Charitable Foundation

Messing, Wilma E.: trustee, Messing Family Charitable Foundation

Messman, Jack L.: president, chief executive officer, Novell

Messner, Robert T.: vice president, director, Murphy Co. Foundation (G.C.)

Metcalf, J. S.: vice president, USG Foundation

Metts, Harold: director, Houston Endowment

Metz, Mary Seawell: president, director, Cowell Foundation (S. H.)

Metzger, Michael D.: vice president, chief financial officer, JSJ Corp.

Metzger, William L.: vice president, treasurer, Brunswick Foundation

Meyer, Alex Alfred: director, Hall-Perrine Foundation

Meyer, Alice Jane: vice president, director, Meyer Foundation (Paul J.)

Meyer, Henry L., III: trustee, Bicknell Fund

Meyer, Karen: director, Toro Foundation

Meyer, Lawrence H. (Bud): vice president commun, Knight Foundation (John S. and James L.)

Meyer, Patricia: secretary, Argyle Foundation

Meyer, Paul J., Sr.: president, director, Meyer Foundation (Paul J.)

Meyer, Roger F.: president, trustee, Laurel Foundation

Meyer, Ronald: president, chief operating officer, director, Universal Studios; president, director, Universal Studios Foundation

Meyer, Russell William, Jr.: president, Cessna Foundation, Inc.

Meyers, David H.: vice president, assistant controller, Universal Studios Foundation

Meyers, David R.: president, director, Meyers Charitable Family Fund

Meyers, Frederick C.: secretary, treasurer, Meyers Charitable Family Fund

Meyers, Gail: trustee, Heckscher Foundation for Children

Meyers, James: director, Wright Foundation (Lola)

Meyerson, Marvin: trustee, Retirement Research Foundation

Meysman, Frank L.: director, Sara Lee Corp.

Micallef, Joseph S.: secretary, Driscoll Foundation; secretary, treasurer, director, Weyerhaeuser Memorial Foundation (Charles A.)

Michaelis, Mary F.: trustee, McCasland Foundation

Michaels, Jack D.: chairman, director, HON Industries Charitable Foundation; chairman, chief executive officer, director, HON Industries Inc.

Michalis, Clarence F.: chairman, director, Macy, Jr. Foundation (Josiah)

Michel, Betsy S.: trustee, Dodge Foundation (Geraldine R.)

Michel, Clifford Lloyd: treasurer, Jockey Hollow Foundation

Michel, Robert T.: secretary, Banta Corp. Foundation

Michel, Sally J.: trustee, Abell Foundation

Micheletti, Tom: co-president, chief executive officer, Xcel Energy

Micheletti, Carla: secretary, Burnett Co. Charitable Foundation (Leo)

Mickelson, P. Gregory: director, VPI Foundation

Mida, Richard E.: vice president, secretary, Vollbrecht Foundation (Frederick A.)

Middeleer, William P.: vice president, Muhlethaler Foundation, Inc. (Jane T.)

Middleton, Reginald: vice president, Strauss Foundation

Midkif, Robin: director, First Hawaiian Foundation

Midkiff, Robert Richards: president, director, Atherton Family Foundation

Mifflan, Robert B.: executive director, Christy-Houston Foundation

Mihori, James S.: trustee, Grimes Foundation

Mikell, Jo Ann: secretary, Cook, Sr. Charitable Foundation (Kelly Gene)

Mikush, Sandra H.: assistant director, Babcock Foundation (Mary Reynolds)

Milanese, W.: secretary, Campbell Soup Foundation

Milbank, David L.: director, Memton Fund

Milbank, Jeremiah, III: director, Guggenheim Foundation (Harry Frank); mem, JM Foundation

Milbank, Jeremiah, Jr.: president, director, JM Foundation

Milbank, Michelle: director, Memton Fund

Milbank, Samuel L.: director, Memton Fund

Milbank, Thomas L.: director, Memton Fund

Milbourn, George B.: chairman, president, Jennings Foundation (Martha Holden)

Milby, Charles D., Jr.: treasurer, Hamman Foundation (George and Mary Josephine)

Miles, David P.: president, H&R Block Foundation

Miles, David W.: director, AMCORE Foundation

Miles, John C., II: president, chief executive officer, director, Dentsply International Inc.

Miles, Pat: secretary, director, Greenville Foundation

Miles, Robert H.: treasurer, Washington Mutual Foundation; senior vice president, controller, Washington Mutual Inc.

Miles, William: director, Greenville Foundation

Milfs, Audrey L.: secretary, Pacific Life Foundation; vice president, corporate secretary, director, Pacific Life Insurance Co.

Milias, Mary Ann: director, Zellerbach Family Fund

Millard, Elisabeth: trustee, Credit Suisse First Boston Foundation Trust

Millender, Edith Morse: assistant secretary, Ratshesky Foundation (A. C.)

Miller, Allen L.: trustee, Miller Foundation

Miller, Carl: director, Brillion Foundation

Miller, Diana: trustee, Valentine Foundation (Lawson)

Miller, Ed: secretary, Honda of America Foundation

Miller, Edward A.: director, Stulsaft Foundation (Morris)

Miller, Edward E., Jr.: director emeritus, Christy-Houston Foundation

Miller, Eugene A.: chairman, trustee, McGregor Fund

Miller, George: president, treasurer, Wilson Fund (Matilda R.)

Miller, Gerald W.: trustee, Stranahan Foundation

Miller, Gordon E.: director, The Bothin Foundation

Miller, Harlan: treasurer, trustee, Miller Foundation (Earl B. and Loraine H.)

Miller, Harvey S. Shipley: treasurer, Arcadia Foundation

Miller, Harvey Shipley: trustee, Avery Arts Foundation (Milton and Sally)

Miller, James C.: president, S&T Bancorp Charitable Foundation; president, director, S&T Bancorp Inc.

Miller, James D.: trustee, Richardson Benevolent Foundation (C. E.)

Miller, James E.: director, MassMutual Foundation for Hartford, Inc. (The)

Miller, James H., III: senior vice president, Alabama Power Co.

Miller, James Ludlow: secretary, treasurer, Miller-Mellor Association

Miller, Jeffrey W.: trustee, Glendorn Foundation

Miller, JoZach, IV: vice president, Miller-Mellor Association

Miller, Joe: secretary, Whittenberger Foundation (Claude R. and Ethel B.)

Miller, Joseph A., Jr.: trustee, Corning Inc. Foundation

Miller, Joyce G.: executive director, Amado Foundation (Maurice)

Miller, Julia A.: trustee, Turrell Fund

Miller, Kay: director, Honda of America Foundation

Miller, Lucy: trustee, Valentine Foundation (Lawson)

Miller, Mark F.: vice president, director, Hearst Foundation (William Randolph)

Miller, Marlin, Jr.: trustee, Wyomissing Foundation

Miller, Mary Frances: trustee, Mellinger Educational Foundation (Edward Arthur)

Miller, Mary J.: vice president, trustee, Price Associates Foundation (T. Rowe)

Miller, Nancy A.: director, Harcourt Foundation (Ellen Knowles)

Miller, Norman C.: president, Miller Foundation (Steve J.)

Miller, Patricia Hillman: vice president, secretary, director, Eberly Foundation

Miller, Robert Branson, Jr.: trustee, Miller Foundation

Miller, Robert Branson, Sr.: trustee emeritus, Miller Foundation

Miller, Robert E.: director, Oakley-Lindsay Foundation of Quincy Newspapers and Its Subsidiaries

Miller, Roy D.: trustee, McCabe Foundation (B. C.)

Miller, Sally C.: director emeritus, Meadows Foundation (The)

Miller, Theodore W.: trustee, Miller Foundation (Steve J.)

Miller, Wilford: committee member, Haman Family Foundation

Miller, Will: director, Cummins Foundation

Miller, William: vice president, director, South Plains Foundation

Millhouse, Barbara B.: vice president, director, Babcock Foundation (Mary Reynolds)

Mills, Armon: treasurer, Valley Foundation

Mills, John T.: trustee, U.S. Steel Foundation

Mills, Kelly L.: assistant secretary, Noyes, Jr. Memorial Foundation (Nicholas H.)

Mills, Phyllis J.: trustee, Cary Charitable Trust (Mary Flagler)

Mills, Rick J.: director, Cummins Foundation; president, fleetguard, Cummins Inc.

Mills, Sophie: trustee, duPont Foundation (Chichester)

Millspaugh, Gordon A., Jr.: assistant treasurer, trustee, Victoria Foundation

Millstein, Ira M.: partner, Weil, Gotshal & Manges Corp.; director, Weil, Gotshal & Manges Foundation

Milne, Garth Leroy: president, treasurer, Motorola Foundation

Milner, John C.: secretary, treasurer, Glencoe Foundation

Milski, Mark: director, Littauer Foundation (Lucius N.)

Milstein, Richard Sherman: clerk, Steiger Memorial Fund (Albert)

Milton, John D., Jr.: secretary, treasurer, Florida Rock Industries Foundation

Minard, Sally: president, director, Garfinkle-Minard Foundation, Inc.

Minella, L. C.: trustee, Air Products Foundation

Miner, Joshua L., IV: trustee, Stevens Foundation (Nathaniel and Elizabeth P.)

Miner, Phebe S.: trustee, Stevens Foundation (Abbot and Dorothy H.)

Minnis, Ann: grants administrator, director, Texas Instruments Foundation

Minow, Martha Louise: director, Revson Foundation (Charles H.)

Minter-Dowd, Christine: vice president, director, Marpat Foundation

Minton, Dwight Church: chairman, director, Church & Dwight Company Inc.

Miori, Sylvan: director, Gulf Coast Medical Foundation

Mirakhor, Abbas: director, treasurer, Alavi Foundation

Mire, Weldon: trustee, Halliburton Foundation, Inc.

Miro, Jeffrey H.: secretary, Taubman Foundation (A. Alfred)

Mirsky, Burton M.: vice president finance, Dana Foundation (Charles A.)

Mirsky, Susan: vice president, director, Thompson Co. Fund (J. Walter)

Mister, Melvin: trustee, Taconic Foundation

Mitchell, Betsy: president, trustee, Children's Foundation of Erie County

Mitchell, Braxton D.: vice president, trustee, Warfield Memorial Fund (Anna Emory)

Mitchell, Callie J.: director, Williams Companies Foundation (The)

Mitchell, Charlotte: assistant trustee, BellSouth Foundation

Mitchell, David: trustee, August Family Foundation (Charles J. and Burton S.)

Mitchell, Donald D.: co-trustee, Arakelian Foundation (Mary Alice)

Mitchell, Duncan: trustee, Cisco Systems Foundation

Mitchell, John A.: trustee, Cornell Trust (Peter C.)

Mitchell, John Daniel: vice president, director, Beneficia Foundation

Mitchell, Joseph C.: trustee, Delmas Foundation (Gladys Krieble); president, director, Samuels Foundation (Fan Fox and Leslie R.)

Mitchell, Judith M.: trustee, Peterloon Foundation

Mitchell, Kim S.: assistant secretary, Van Andel Foundation (Jay and Betty)

Mitchell, Lucy C.: assistant treasurer, trustee, Southways Foundation

Mitchell, M.: vice president, trustee, Johns Manville Fund

Mitchell, Miriam Pitcairn: director, Beneficia Foundation

Mitchell, Robert J.: treasurer, ACF Industries

Mitchell, Susan: vice president, director, CIT Group Foundation

Mitchinson, Geoffrey C.: director, GlaxoSmithKline Foundation

Mixer, David P.: treasurer, Trimix Foundation

Mixer, Gail S.: president, Trimix Foundation

Mixon, Bobby C.: president, Morgan Foundation (Louie R. and Gertrude)

Mize, Ann: director, Muchnic Foundation

Mize, David C.: secretary, Muchnic Foundation

Mobley, E. B.: president, Griffin Foundation (Rosa May)

Mobley, Ebb: vice president, Griffin Foundation (Rosa May)

Mobley, Ernestine L.: manager, Finch Foundation (Thomas Austin)

Mobley, Margreta D.: treasurer, General Motors Foundation

Mobley, Stacey J.: senior vice president, chief administrative officer, general counsel, du Pont de Nemours & Co. (E.I.)

Mochon, Margaret: director, Howard and Bush Foundation

Moe, James D.: corporate vice president, general counsel, secretary, Cargill Inc.

Moe, Thomas O.: secretary, Cargill Foundation

Moeller, Joseph W.: president, chief operating officer, Koch Industries Inc.

Moeller, Lisa Robertshaw: director, Robertshaw Charitable Foundation

Moench, Pamela S.: assistant treasurer, Monsanto Fund

Moffat, William R.: trustee, Carpenter Foundation

Moffett, F. Wesley, Jr.: trustee, Houck Foundation (May Kay)

Moffitt, James F.: vice president, trustee, Kerr Fund (Grayce B.)

Mogg, Jim: trustee, Duke Energy Foundation

Mogi, Yuzaburo: chairman, president, chief executive officer, Kikkoman Foods; director, Kikkoman Foundation

Mogilnik, Nina B.: senior program officer, Altman Foundation

Mogren, Scott: trustee, Subaru of America Foundation, Inc.

Mohn, Richard E.: chairman, director, Sovereign Bank; director, Sovereign Bank Foundation

Mohraz, Judy J.: director, Baltimore Equitable Insurance Foundation

Moldaw, Carol A.: director, Moldaw Family Foundation

Moldaw, Phyllis: vice president, treasurer, Moldaw Family Foundation

Moldaw, Stuart G.: president, Moldaw Family Foundation

Moldaw, Susan J.: director, Moldaw Family Foundation

Mole, Sally Dodge: director, Dodge Foundation (Cleveland H.)

Molella, Salvador: vice president, director, Carvel Foundation (Thomas and Agnes)

Molina, Mario J.: director, MacArthur Foundation (John D. and Catherine T.)

Moline, Carmen: treasurer, Mulcahy Foundation

Moll, John H.: director, Ball Foundation (George and Frances)

Mollenberg, Trudy A.: trustee, Western New York Foundation

Moltz, James E.: trustee, Rockefeller Brothers Fund, Inc.

Molyneux, Cynthia M.: president, trustee, Freeport-McMoRan Foundation

Molyneux, Richard A.: chairman, director, Key Bank of Maine

Monahan, Michael J.: president, director, Ecolab Foundation; vice president external affairs, Ecolab Inc.

Monan, J. Donald, SJ: trustee, Yawkey Foundation II

Monastiere, Dominic: president, Kantzler Foundation

Moncla, Jean: vice president, trust officer, Ward Heritage Foundation (Mamie McFaddin)

Monell, Ambrose K.: director, Ambrose Monell Foundation (The)

Monello, Joseph D.: vice president finance, Kansas City Southern Railway

Monfort Runyan, Myra: secretary, Monfort Family Foundation

Monroe, Michael J.: trustee, Key Foundation

Monsted, Charles, III: trustee, German Protestant Orphan Asylum Association Foundation

Monte, Jeffery P.: secretary, Burlington Resources Foundation

Montelro-Tribble, Velma: secretary, Alcoa Foundation

Montgomery, J. R.: secretary, treasurer, Bertha Foundation

Montgomery, Mary Louise: clerk, director, Kelley and Elza Kelley Foundation (Edward Bangs)

Montgomery, Philip O'Bryan, Jr.: director, O'Donnell Foundation

Montgomery, Virginia: trustee, Woodcock Foundation

Montoya, Robert: treasurer, director, Chamiza Foundation

Montrone, Paul Michael: vice president, Winthrop

Moody, Frances A.: executive director, Moody Foundation

Moody, Natalie P.: director, Gilman Foundation (Howard)

Moody, Robert Lee: secretary, director, Northen Foundation (Mary Moody)

Moody, Ross R.: trustee, Moody Foundation

Moore, Albert W.: director, Gleason Foundation

Moore, Bob: board mem, Roberts Foundation (Dora)

Moore, Charles R., Jr.: trustee, Long Foundation (George A. and Grace)

Moore, E. Kevin: vice president, treasurer, Schering-Plough Corp.; treasurer, Schering-Plough Foundation

Moore, Gregory: trustee, Grimes Foundation

Moore, Hannah T. C.: treasurer, Island Foundation (MA)

Moore, Hardy: president, Lennox Foundation (Martha, David and Bagby)

Moore, Harvin, IV: director, Powell Foundation

Moore, Irving, Jr.: secretary, Gulf Coast Medical Foundation

Moore, Jack: vice president, Gulf Coast Medical Foundation

Moore, Jacqueline G.: president, Griswold Foundation (John C.)

Moore, Jim S., PhD: director, South Plains Foundation

Moore, John E.: executive vice president human resources, Cessna Aircraft Co.

Moore, John H.: trustee, Earhart Foundation

Moore, Joseph A.: trustee, Barker Foundation (Coeta and Donald R.)

Moore, Kevin S.: treasurer, director, Clark Foundation (NY)

Moore, Lewis B.: trustee, Grimes Foundation

Moore, Mary: vice president & manager community relations, US Bank

Moore, Michael J.: director, Island Foundation (MA)

Moore, Nancy Powell: foundation manager, director, president, treasurer, Powell Foundation

Moore, Peter M.: grants director, Moody Foundation

Moore, Randolph G.: director, Castle Foundation (Harold K. L.)

Moore, Robert P.: trustee, Barden Foundation, Inc.

Moore, Rosemary: president, director, United Airlines Foundation

Moore, Royanna L.: president, trustee, Cacioppo Foundation (Joseph and Mary)

Moore, Stephen O.: director, vice president, Hardin Foundation (Phil)

Moore, Steven: president, Oklahoma Gas & Electric Co. Foundation

Moore, Terence F.: trustee, Dow Foundation (Herbert H. and Grace A.)

Mooremasunas, Anna Lisa: trustee, Cacioppo Foundation (Joseph and Mary)

Moorman, Bette D.: president, director, Davis Foundation (Edwin W. and Catherine M.)

Moot, Andrew R.: trustee, Western New York Foundation

Moot, John R.: secretary, Western New York Foundation

Moot, Richard E.: president, Western New York Foundation

Moot, Welles V., Jr.: treasurer, Western New York Foundation

Mora, Susan: assistant administration, Stulsaft Foundation (Morris)

Moran, Edward P., Jr.: trustee, Barker Foundation Inc.

Moran, Elizabeth A.: trustee, The MBNA Foundation

Moran, Harry J.: executive vice president, Sonoco Products Co.

Moran, Susan B.: vice president, trustee, Barker Foundation Inc.

Moravitz, Edward: trustee, Giant Eagle Foundation

Morby, Carolyn R.: trustee, Gerber Foundation

Morehead, Carolyn R.: director, Metris Companies Foundation

Morel, Donald E., Jr.: president, chief executive officer, West Pharmaceutical Services Inc.

Moreland, Jeffrey: director, Burlington Northern Santa Fe Foundation

Morello, Maurizio J.: secretary, assistant treasurer, director, Ambrose Monell Foundation (The); secretary, assistant treasurer, Vetlesen Foundation (G. Unger)

Moreno, Albert F.: chairman, director, Rosenberg Foundation

Moret, H. J.: vice president, Federated Mutual Insurance Foundation

Moreton, Fred A., Jr.: vice chairman, Burton Private Foundation (Robert Harold)

Morf, Darrel Arle: vice president, director, Hall-Perrine Foundation

Morgan, Alethia, MD: director, Copic Medical Foundation

Morgan, Anne Hodges: trustee, Kauffman Foundation (Ewing Marion)

Morgan, Charles O., Jr.: trustee, Chatlos Foundation

Morgan, Davis: mgr, Porter Testamentary Trust (James Hyde)

Morgan, Edward L.: group senior vice president, Hartford Financial Services Group Inc.

Morgan, Gayle: program director music, Cary Charitable Trust (Mary Flagler)

Morgan, George A.: trustee, City National Bank Foundation; executive vice president, City National Bank & Trust Co.

Morgan, Glenn R.: vice president, director, Hartmarx Charitable Foundation; executive vice president, chief financial officer, treasurer, member, Hartmarx Corp.

Morgan, John A.: chairman disbursement comm, Oppenstein Brothers Foundation

Morgan, Michael: director, Koch Foundation, Inc. (Fred C. and Mary R.)

Morgan, Paul F.: vice president, director, Atherton Family Foundation

Morgridge, John P.: chairman, trustee, Cisco Systems Foundation

Morian, Wilhelmina Cullen Robertson: secretary-treasurer, trustee, Cullen Foundation (The)

Moriarty, Brunilda: vice president, Hyde and Watson Foundation

Moriguchi-Matsuno, Tomoko: trustee, Bullitt Foundation

Morley, Burrows, Jr.: trustee, Morley Foundation

Morley, Christopher: trustee, Morley Foundation

Morley, David H.: trustee, Morley Foundation

Morley, Edward B., Jr.: past president, trustee, Morley Foundation

Morley, George B., Jr.: trustee, Morley Foundation

Morley, Katharyn M.: trustee, Morley Foundation

Morley, Mark B.: treasurer, Morley Foundation

Morley, Peter B., Jr.: trustee, Morley Foundation

Morley, Robert S.: president, Morley Foundation

Morley Beck, Carol: trustee, Morley Foundation

Morning, John: trustee, Mott Foundation (Charles Stewart)

Moroney, James McQueen, Jr.: trustee, Belo Foundation

Morrell, Michael W.: vice president, controller, Verizon Foundation

Morressey, Karen M.: vice president, director, Cabot Corp. Foundation

Morrill, Amy B.: trustee, Morrill Charitable Foundation

Morrill, Richard L.: director, Teagle Foundation

Morris, Benjamin H.: trustee, Brown Foundation (W. L. Lyons)

Morris, Donna T.: secretary, trustee, Strosacker Foundation (Charles J.)

Morris, Gabriella: president, Prudential Foundation

Morris, Joseph W.: trustee, Sarkeys Foundation

Morris, Katherine B.: member board advisors, Belk Foundation

Morris, Leah, RN: program officer managed care and health grants, Sierra Health Foundation

Morris, Leland M.: trustee, Morris Foundation (Norman M.)

Morris, Louise Fisk: trustee, Seabury Foundation

Morris, Max King: trustee, Davis Foundations (Arthur Vining)

Morris, Robert E.: secretary, treasurer, Morris Foundation (Norman M.)

Morris, Stacey: director, Buck Foundation (Frank H. and Eva B.)

Morris, Thelma Lovette: trustee, Pittsburgh Child Guidance Foundation

Morris, Thomas Q.: director, Clark Foundation (NY)

Morris, Thomas Q., MD: member board governors, Brooks Foundation (Gladys)

Morris, Virginia H.: director, Hubbard Foundation

Morris, William Shivers, III: founder, chairman, chief executive officer, director, Morris Communications Corp.; trustee, Stauffer Communications Foundation

Morris, William Shivers, IV: president, director, Morris Communications Corp.; trustee, Stauffer Communications Foundation

Morrisette, Karl S.: director, Portsmouth General Hospital Foundation

Morrison, Harold, Jr.: director, ShenTel Foundation

Morrison, J. Holmes: mem, trustee, One Valley Bank Foundation; chairman, director, One Valley Bank N.A.

Morrison, Jack, Jr.: assistant secretary, Johnson Foundation (M. G. and Lillie A.)

Morrison, James K.: secretary, Lytel Foundation (Bertha Russ)

Morrison, Lucian L., Jr.: director, Semmes Foundation

Morrison, Velma V.: president, Morrison Foundation (Harry W.)

Morrissey, Thomas L.: vice president, trustee, Brundage Charitable, Scientific, and Wildlife Conservation Foundation (Charles E. and Edna T.)

Morrow, Dillard: director, Stonecutter Foundation

Morrow, Peter C.: executive director, Welfare Foundation

Morse, Alan: vice president, Ratshesky Foundation (A. C.)

Morse, Alan R., Jr.: trustee, Ratshesky Foundation (A. C.)

Morse, Cecily: director, Ratshesky Foundation (A. C.)

Morse, Eric Robert: president, Ratshesky Foundation (A. C.)

Morse, John, Jr.: treasurer, Ratshesky Foundation (A. C.)

Morse, Peter C.: director, JM Foundation

Morse, Sarah D.: director, Daniels Foundation (Fred Harris)

Morse, Stephan A.: director, Bunbury Co., Inc.; president, chief executive officer, trustee, Windham Foundation

Morse, Timothy: assistant treasurer, Ratshesky Foundation (A. C.)

Morse Steinfield, Rebecca: trustee, Ratshesky Foundation (A. C.)

Mortimer, David H.: president, director, Harriman Foundation (Mary W.)

Mortimer, Kathleen H.: director, Harriman Foundation (Mary W.)

Mortimer, Robert J.: vice president, secretary, treasurer, director, Johnson Foundation (Willard T. C.)

Mosbacher, Emil, Jr.: trustee, Frese Foundation (Arnold D.)

Mosbacher, Patricia R.: vice president, Saw Island Foundation

Mosbacher, R. Bruce: president, Saw Island Foundation

Moseley, Carlos: trustee, Dana Charitable Trust (Eleanor Naylor)

Moseley, Carlos Dupre: director, Samuels Foundation (Fan Fox and Leslie R.)

Moseley, Colin: director, Matlock Foundation; chairman, chief executive officer, Simpson Investment Co.

Moseley, Daniel L.: director, Noble Foundation, Inc. (Edward John); member executive board, Watson Foundation (Thomas J.)

Moseley, Joe: director, Shelter Insurance Foundation

Moser, Eyvonne: executive director, Sterling-Turner Foundation

Moses, William F. L.: senior program officer, Kresge Foundation

Moses, Yolanda T.: trustee, Ford Foundation

Mosley, Daniel: director, Simon Foundation (William E.)

Mosley, Daniel L.: director, secretary, treasurer, Paley Foundation, Inc. (William S.); trustee, Pinkerton Foundation

Moss, Diane: president, chief executive officer, Rubinstein Foundation (Helena)

Moss, James H.: treasurer, York Federal Savings & Loan Foundation

Moss, Roger, Jr.: secretary, mgr, Ludwick Foundation (Christopher)

Mostrom, Joel K.: treasurer, Chesapeake Corp. Foundation

Mostue, Brian: trustee, Carpenter Foundation

Mostue, Emily C.: vice president, trustee, Carpenter Foundation

Mosty, John: secretary, treasurer, Peterson Foundation (Hal and Charlie)

Moteberg, Butch: vice president, director, Midcontinent Media Foundation

Motono, Moriyuki: trustee, United States-Japan Foundation

Motoshige, Eiichi: chairman, president, chief executive officer, Kajima Engineering and Construction Inc.

Mott, Kerry K.: director, Keck Foundation (W. M.)

Mott, Maryanne T.: trustee, Mott Foundation (Charles Stewart)

Mott, Ruth Rawlings: trustee, Rockefeller Brothers Fund, Inc.

Mottaz, Rolla: board member, trustee, Olin Foundation (Spencer T. and Ann W.)

Mottola, Maria: executive director, New York Foundation

Mountcastle, Katharine Reynolds: director, Babcock Foundation (Mary Reynolds)

Mountcastle, Kenneth F., III: director, Babcock Foundation (Mary Reynolds)

Mountcastle, Laura Lewis: treasurer, director, Babcock Foundation (Mary Reynolds)

Mountcastle, Mary: director, Babcock Foundation (Mary Reynolds)

Mountjoy, Michael B.: trustee, secretary, treasurer, Gheens Foundation

Mouzakas, Karen: director, Kovarik Foundation for Poetry (Henry P.)

Mowat, Donald W.: board member, Stewardship Foundation

Mower, Judith: trustee, Gifford Charitable Corp. (Rosamond)

Mox, Gregory C.: vice president human resources, Sentry Insurance, A Mutual Co.; president, chairman, director, Sentry Insurance Foundation Inc.

Moyer, Charles I.: vice president, trustee, Hansen Foundation (Dane G.)

Moyer, Keith: director, Star Tribune Foundation

Moyle, Judith Burton: chairman, Burton Private Foundation (Robert Harold)

Moyle, Katherine P.: director, Widgeon Foundation

Moyles, Denise L.: director, Bourns Foundation

Mrstik, Doug: vice chairman, Selby and Marie Selby Foundation (William G.)

Muchmore, Iris: director, secretary, Hall-Perrine Foundation

Muchnic, Daphne Nan: director, Muchnic Foundation

Muckler, Dick: trustee, Ahrens Foundation (Claude W. and Dolly)

Mudd, Daniel H.: vice chairman, chief operating officer, Fannie Mae; chairman, Fannie Mae Foundation

Muehlhauser, Regina L.: director, Irvine Foundation (The James)

Mueller, Greg: director, Fuller Co. Foundation (H.B.)

Mugar, Carolyn G.: trustee, Azadoutioun Foundation

Muhammad, Mark D.: trustee, Gifford Charitable Corp. (Rosamond)

Muhlenkamp, Caroline E.: group vice president, chief financial officer, Dayton Power and Light Co.; treasurer, trustee, Dayton Power and Light Co. Foundation

Muhlethaler, Jane T.: president, Muhlethaler Foundation, Inc. (Jane T.)

Muir, David F.: director, Keller Foundation

Muir, Edward D.: trustee, McNutt Charitable Trust (Amy Shelton)

Muir, Elizabeth M.: director, Keller Foundation

Muir, Kathleen K.: secretary, Keller Foundation

Muir, William M.: director, Keller Foundation

Muir, William W., Jr.: director, Keller Foundation

Muire, Annie S.: trustee, Richardson Benevolent Foundation (C. E.)

Mukai, N.: executive vice president, secretary, treasurer, Hino Diesel Trucks (U.S.A.)

Mulcahey, Forrest I.: director, Kennedy Family Foundation (Ethel and W. George)

Mulcahy, Anne M.: chairman, chief executive officer, Xerox Corp.; trustee, Xerox Foundation

Mulcahy, Betty Jane: trustee, H. C. S. Foundation

Mulderrig, Steve: director, Tribune New York Foundation

Mulhern, Timothy P.: trustee, Shatz, Schwartz & Fentin Charitable Foundation; partner, Shatz, Schwartz & Fentin P.C.

Mulkey, Kim: director, Technology program, BellSouth Foundation

Mullaney, John: executive director, Nord Family Foundation

Mullen, Dennis M.: trustee, Birds Eye Foods Foundation; president, chief executive officer, director, Birds Eye Foods Inc.

Mullen, Judith: vice president, State Street Foundation

Mullendore, Stuart L.: trustee, Sinnisen Foundation (Albert E. and Naomi B.)

Muller, George T.: president, chief operating officer, director, Subaru of America Inc.

Muller, Karen P.: executive director, secretary, Fuller Co. Foundation (H.B.)

Mullin, Shan J.: adv, Archibald Charitable Foundation (Norman)

Mullinax, A. R.: trustee, Duke Energy Foundation

Mullins, Terrell: trustee, Johnson Foundation (M. G. and Lillie A.)

Mulready, Stephen M.: director, Royal & SunAlliance Insurance Foundation, Inc.

Munder, Barbara A.: senior vice president new initiatives, McGraw-Hill Companies Inc.

Mundy, George E.: director, Trippe Trust (William D.)

Mundy, Rodney O.: director, Alabama Power Foundation

Munger, Molly: director, Irvine Foundation (The James)

Munitz, Barry: president, chief executive officer,

trustee, Getty Trust (J. Paul)

Munro, Julie Simon: director, Simon Foundation (William E.)

Munson, Ben, IV: gov, Munson Foundation Trust (W. B.)

Munson, David, Jr.: gov, Munson Foundation Trust (W. B.)

Munson, David M., Sr.: gov, Munson Foundation Trust (W. B.)

Munson, Edwin Palmer: secretary, Scott Foundation (William H., John G., and Emma)

Munson, John K.: gov, Munson Foundation Trust (W. B.)

Munson, Peter: gov, Munson Foundation Trust (W. B.)

Munyan, Winthrop R.: president, Clark Foundation (Robert Sterling)

Munyon, Wendy Nelson: secretary, Grinnell Mutual Group Foundation

Murase, Haruo: chairman, president, chief executive officer, Canon U.S.A. Inc.

Murchison, George M.: trustee, Hodges Foundation (Bess J.)

Murfree, Matt B., III: director, Christy-Houston Foundation

Murguia, Ramon: director, Francis Families Foundation

Murphy, Arthur: director, Eckman Charitable Foundation (Samuel and Rae)

Murphy, Bart T.: trustee, Retirement Research Foundation

Murphy, Bruce D.: trustee, Key Foundation

Murphy, Charles H., Jr.: director, Murphy Foundation

Murphy, Christopher J., III: president, chief executive officer, director, 1st Source Corp.; director, First Source Foundation

Murphy, D. P., Jr.: president trustee, Handy & Harman Foundation

Murphy, Debra L.: senior vice president, chief financial officer, Woronoco Savings Bank; treasurer, director, Woronoco Savings Charitable Foundation

Murphy, Diana E.: director, Bush Foundation

Murphy, Frank H.: executive vice president, MBNA Corp.; trustee, The MBNA Foundation

Murphy, Heather: trustee, Reilly Foundation

Murphy, Henry L., Jr.: vice president, admin mgr, director, Kelley and Elza Kelley Foundation (Edward Bangs)

Murphy, John: trustee, Self Family Foundation

Murphy, John Davis: president, Wiremold Foundation

Murphy, John E.: chairman, president, chief executive officer, Bay State Federal Savings Charitable Foundation

Murphy, Johnie W.: president, director, Murphy Foundation

Murphy, Mark M.: secretary, executive director, Fund for New Jersey

Murphy, Michael P.: director, Dyson Foundation

Murphy, R. Madison: president, director, Murphy Foundation

Murphy, Robert F., Jr.: trustee, Walsh Charity Trust (Blanche)

Murphy, Robert M.: director, New York Stock Exchange Foundation, Inc.

Murphy, Tern C.: trustee, The MBNA Foundation

Murphy, Terry M.: vice president finance, chief financial officer, Quanex Corp.; vice president, director, Quanex Foundation

Murphy, William J.: director, mem adv comm, O'Connor Foundation (A. Lindsay and Olive B.)

Murrah, Jack: president, trustee, Lyndhurst Foundation

Murray, Arthur W.: trustee, Mellinger Educational Foundation (Edward Arthur)

Murray, Catherine Fondren Underwood: board of governors, Fondren Foundation

Murray, Daniel T.: secretary, Gallo Foundation (Ernest)

Murray, Elizabeth: director, Warhol Foundation for the Visual Arts (The Andy)

Murray, Joan D.: vice president, treasurer, director, Wallace Genetic Foundation

Murray, Linda T.: assistant secretary, director, Vernon Foundation (Miles Hodsdon)

Murray, Robert E.: vice president, trustee, Edison Fund (Charles)

Murray, William E.: trustee, Donaldson Charitable Trust (Oliver S. and Jennie R.)

Murrin, Evelyn L.: trustee, Pittsburgh Child Guidance Foundation

Murtaugh, James: program director, Claiborne and Art Ortenberg Foundation (Liz)

Musarra, Arthur F.: trustee, Statler Foundation

Muse, Martha Twitchell: chairman, Tinker Foundation

Musgrave, Todd: adv board committee member, Heath Foundation (Mary)

Musson, Irvin J., III: trustee, Musson Charitable Foundation (R. C. and Katharine M.)

Musson, Irvin J., Jr.: trustee, Musson Charitable Foundation (R. C. and Katharine M.)

Myers, Lynn Howe: chairman, vice president, Howe and Mitchell B. Howe Foundation (Lucille Horton)

Myers, Marilyn B.: adv, Kirkpatrick Foundation, Inc.

Myers, Michele Tolela: director, Fairchild Foundation, Inc. (Sherman)

Myers, Mitchell C.: director, Howe and Mitchell B. Howe Foundation (Lucille Horton)

Myers, Stanley Thomas: president, chief executive officer, director, Mitsubishi Silicon America

Myers, Toni: admin, RosaMary Foundation

Myhers, Richard: trustee, Presto Foundation

Myszka, Michele: vice president, director, Pacific Life Foundation; community relations director, public affairs, Pacific Life Insurance Co.

N

Nabers, Hugh C., Jr.: trustee, Comer Foundation (AL)

Nadel, Susan Bryson: member, Templeton Foundation (Herbert A.)

Nadler, Charles, PhD: Distribution trustee, SchwabRosenhouse Memorial Foundation

Naeve, Stephen W.: vice chairman, executive vice president, chief financial officer, CenterPoint Energy Inc.

Nagel, Robert D.: director investments, The Wallace Foundation

Nagle, James: trustee, Graham Foundation for Advanced Studies in the Fine Arts

Nagler, Barry: senior vice president, general counsel, secretary, director, Hasbro Charitable Trust Inc.

Nagy, Julia Ann: treasurer, Huber Foundation

Naiman, Norma Lee: director, Himmelfarb Foundation (Paul and Annetta)

Najarian, Richard: trustee, Raymond Foundation

Nakano, Tsuyoshi: mem allocations comm, Kawabe Memorial Fund

Nakfoor, Emil: advisory director, Herzstein Charitable Foundation (Albert and Ethel)

Nalbach, Kay C.: president, director, Hartmarx Charitable Foundation

Nally, Joseph: director, Doheny Foundation Trust (Carrie Estelle)

Nalty, Donald J.: chairman, director, Schlieder Educational Foundation (Edward G.)

Nalty, Elizabeth S.: president, director, Schlieder Educational Foundation (Edward G.)

Nalty, Jill: treasurer, director, Schlieder Educational Foundation (Edward G.)

Nanon, Patricia: vice president, director, Newman Assistance Fund (Jerome A. and Estelle R.)

Nanula, Richard D.: director, Amgen Foundation

Napier, William Sammie: director, GreggGraniteville Foundation

Naples, Ronald James: president, chief executive officer, director, Quaker Chemical Corp.

Napoli, F. N.: assistant treasurer, Penney Co. Fund (J.C.)

Nardi, Nicholas J.: secretary, treasurer, Culpeper Memorial Foundation (Daphne Seybolt)

Narten, Janet E.: executive director, Bruening Foundation (Eva L. and Joseph M.)

Narvarte, Rebecca S.: trustee emeritus, Doss Foundation, Inc. (M. S.)

Narvarte Romanow, Julia: assistant treasurer, trustee, Doss Foundation, Inc. (M. S.)

Naschke, Arlene M.: trustee, Messing Family Charitable Foundation

Nascimento, Renata Camargo: director, Alcoa Foundation

Nash, Bob J.: director, Rockefeller Foundation (Winthrop)

Nash, Lucia S.: cochairman, Smith Foundation (Kelvin and Eleanor)

Nash, Martin: director, Kennedy Family Foundation (Ethel and W. George)

Nash, Regina F.: administrative assistant, Frist Foundation

Nash, Robert: director, Klee Foundation (Conrad and Virginia)

Nathan, David G., MD: director, Dyson Foundation

Nation, Robert F.: president, director, Kline Foundation

(Josiah W. and Bessie H.)

Naus, Laura: secretary, Ambrose Monell Foundation (The)

Navick, Jerald I.: director, Eastern Savings and Loan Foundation

Nazemetz, Patricia M.: vice president human resources, Xerox Corp.; trustee, Xerox Foundation

Neal, Alexander W., Jr.: trustee, Bryant Foundation (The)

Neal, Diane L.: president, Mervyns, Target Corp.; president, trustee, Target Foundation

Neal, Monica: contact,

Nedley, Robert E.: president, duPont Foundation (Alfred I.)

Neeleman, Stanley Duane: trustee, Johnson Foundation (Helen K. and Arthur E.)

Neff, Zane: director, ShenTel Foundation

Nefsky, Robert: trustee, Cooper Foundation

Negley, Nancy B.: trustee, first vice president, Brown Foundation

Negley, W. Walter: trustee, Brown Foundation

Neiger, John: vice president financial, Auburn Foundry

Neill, Rolfe: trustee, Knight Foundation (John S. and James L.)

Nelson, Anne: secretary, treasurer, Marshall Foundation

Nelson, Betsy: director, Baltimore Equitable Insurance Foundation

Nelson, Charles E.: chairman, director, Kirkpatrick Foundation, Inc.

Nelson, Charley: director, Jostens Foundation Inc. (The)

Nelson, Clark: treasurer, McBean Family Foundation

Nelson, David L.: vice president, grant director, Houston Endowment

Nelson, Diana L.: trustee, Carlson Family Foundation (Curtis L.)

Nelson, Donald: advisory, Allyn Foundation

Nelson, Fredric C.: secretary, director, Cowell Foundation (S. H.)

Nelson, H. Joe, III: president, director, Houston Endowment

Nelson, Marilyn Carlson: chairman, chief executive officer, Carlson Companies Inc.; trustee, Carlson Family Foundation (Curtis L.)

Nelson, Marjorie A.: trustee, Carlson Family Foundation (Curtis L.)

Nelson, Virginia: corporate communications manager, TJX Companies Inc.

Nelson, Wendy M.: trustee, Carlson Family Foundation (Curtis L.)

Nelson, William E.: vice president, Kikkoman Foods; director, Kikkoman Foundation

Nelson, William F., Jr.: trustee, Wickes Foundation (Harvey Randall)

Nemirow, Arnold M.: chairman, president, chief executive officer, Bowater Inc.

Neppl, Walter J.: trustee emeritus, Dodge Foundation (Geraldine R.)

Neptune, Lionel: trustee, Graham Fund (Philip L.)

Nesbeda, Peter J.: corporator, Island Foundation (MA)

Nesbitt, Robert: director, Patron Saints Foundation

Nesbitt, William A.: trustee, director, Meadows Foundation (The)

Neshek, Milton E.: director, Kikkoman Foundation

Nesholm, John F.: director, Nesholm Family Foundation

Nesholm, Laurel: executive director, Nesholm Family Foundation

Nestor, Alexander R.: vice president, trustee, Jones and Bessie D. Phelps Foundation (Cyrus W. and Amy F.)

Nestor, Karen R.: member distribution committee, Bruening Foundation (Eva L. and Joseph M.); trustee, Jennings Foundation (Martha Holden)

Netzer, Leon L.: trustee, Jewish Healthcare Foundation

Neubauer, Nickalas: director, Chicago Board of Trade Foundation

Neuberger, James A.: vice president, Neuberger Foundation (Roy R. and Marie S.)

Neuberger, Roy R.: president, treasurer, director, Neuberger Foundation (Roy R. and Marie S.)

Neuberger, Roy S.: vice president, Neuberger Foundation (Roy R. and Marie S.)

Neuenfeldt, Bonnie: executive director, Land O'Lakes Foundation

Nevers, Thomas J.: grant mgr, Bishop Foundation (E. K. and Lillian F.)

Nevin-Folino, Nancy: trustee, Gerber Foundation

Nevins, Jane: vice president, Dana Press editor, Dana Foundation (Charles A.)

Newberry, Edith McBean: president, director,

McBean Family Foundation

Newburger, May W.: trustee, Levitt Foundation (NY)

Newcom, Jennings Jay: assistant secretary, director, Hubbard Foundation (R. D. and Joan Dale)

Newcombe, Margaret P.: trustee, Knapp Foundation, Inc. (MD)

Newell, Elizabeth A.: assistant secretary, Universal Studios Foundation

Newell, Marjory A.: vice president, director, Atherton Foundation (Leburta)

Newell, Wanda Y.: director education programs, McCormick Tribune Foundation (Robert R.)

Newhall, Anthony: secretary, Newhall Foundation (Henry Mayo)

Newhall, David S.: president, Newhall Foundation (Henry Mayo)

Newhall, George A.: director, Newhall Foundation (Henry Mayo)

Newhall, Henry K.: director, McBean Family Foundation

Newhall, Jane: director, Newhall Foundation (Henry Mayo)

Newhall, John Breed: trustee, Killam Trust (Constance)

Newhall, Jon: director, Newhall Foundation (Henry Mayo)

Newhall, Roger: director, Newhall Foundation (Henry Mayo)

Newhall Woods, Edwin: director, Newhall Foundation (Henry Mayo)

Newman, David A.: trustee, Arnold Fund

Newman, Donald L.: vice president, Newman Family Foundation

Newman, Frances Moody: chairman, trustee, Moody Foundation

Newman, Howard A.: chairman, director, Newman Assistance Fund (Jerome A. and Estelle R.)

Newman, K. Sidney: secretary, Snyder Foundation (William I. and Patricia S.)

Newman, Martha: executive director, Fisher Foundation

Newman, Michael: vice president, St. Paul Travelers Foundation

Newman, Murray H.: vice president, trust, Livingston Foundation (Milton S. and Corinne N.)

Newman, Patricia: trustee, Livingston Foundation (Milton S. and Corinne N.)

Newman, Paul L.: president, director, Newman's Own

Foundation; president, Newman's Own Inc.

Newman, Steven E.: president, Newman Family Foundation

Newman, William C.: president, director, Newman Assistance Fund (Jerome A. and Estelle R.)

Newnham, Dennis: president, chief executive officer, Tsumura International Inc.

Newquist, Dana: trustee, Barker Foundation (Coeta and Donald R.)

Newton, Frederick J., III: director, Cinergy Foundation

Newton, Jane Norton: vice president, Norton Foundation

Ney, Lillian V.: vice president, director, Gebbie Foundation

Neys, Hendrika C.: director, Campini Foundation (Frank A.)

Neys, Patricia: secretary, treasurer, Campini Foundation (Frank A.)

Ng, Ho Yan J.: supervisor administration and budget, Sara Lee Foundation

Niblock, W. Robert: president, director, Porter Paint Foundation, Inc.

Nichols, James R.: trustee, Babson Foundation (Paul and Edith)

Nichols, Kate Cowles: trustee, Cowles Charitable Trust

Nichols, Scott G.: treasurer, Kelly Foundation

Nichols, W. Barrett: trustee, Brown Foundation, Inc. (James Graham)

Nicholson, David A.: director, Daniels Foundation (Fred Harris)

Nicholson, James B.: trustee, McGregor Fund

Nicholson, Jan: president, Grable Foundation

Nicholson, Mamie W.: program officer, Self Family Foundation

Nicholson, Marion G.: director, Grable Foundation

Nicholson, William B.: director, Grable Foundation

Nicholson, William S.: director, Daniels Foundation (Fred Harris)

Nickelson, Donald E.: vice president, trustee, Jones Foundation (Fletcher)

Nickerson, E. Carlton: hon director, Kelley and Elza Kelley Foundation (Edward Bangs)

Nickerson, Frank L.: hon director, Kelley and Elza Kelley Foundation (Edward Bangs)

Nickerson, Joshua A., Jr.: director, Kelley and Elza Kelley Foundation (Edward Bangs)

Nicol, James: secretary, Thomaston Savings Bank Foundation

Nicolau, Siobhan: trustee, Kauffman Foundation (Ewing Marion)

Nides, Thomas: trustee, Credit Suisse First Boston Foundation Trust

Nielsen, Anne B.: assistant secretary, Universal Studios Foundation

Nielsen, Jeffrey M.: secretary, treasurer, Good Samaritan

Niemeyer, Ken: trustee, Bedsole Foundation (J. L.)

Niffenegger, Joyce U.: committee member, Hoover Foundation (The)

Niles, Clayton E.: director, Spalding Foundation (Eliot)

Niles, Clayton N.: president, Spalding Foundation (Eliot)

Nimick, Francis B., Jr.: trustee, director, Buhl Foundation (PA)

Nisita, Maurizio: senior vice president global operations, Ecolab Inc.

Nisselson, Allan: director, Goldman Foundation (Herman)

Nitschke, John A.: treasurer, director, Scholl Foundation (Dr.)

Noble, Edward E.: trustee, Noble Foundation (Samuel Roberts)

Noble, Maria: trustee, Noble Foundation (Samuel Roberts)

Noble, Mary Jane: trustee emeritus, Noble Foundation (Samuel Roberts)

Noble, Ted: director, Tyndale House Foundation

Noble Smith, E. J.: president, director, Noble Foundation, Inc. (Edward John)

Nobles, G. Edmund: director, Haley Foundation (W. B.)

Noel, Brenda: director, Kurz Family Foundation

Nogales, Luis Guerrero: trustee, Getty Trust (J. Paul)

Nogi, Yoshiyuki: director, Kikkoman Foundation

Noguchi, Ted: director, Honda of America Foundation

Nogueira, Gilda M.: clerk, East Cambridge Savings Charitable Foundation

Nojima, Paul: chairman, president, chief executive officer, Bandai America Inc.

Nolan, Cori: vice president, secretary, director, Rice Foundation

Nolan, Peter G.: president, director, Rice Foundation

Nolan, Robin: vice president, director, Rice Foundation

Noland, Mariam C.: trustee, Knight Foundation (John S. and James L.)

Nolte, A. M.: assistant treasurer, Shell Oil Co. Foundation

Nomakuchi, Tamotsu: director, Mitsubishi Electric America Foundation

Noojin, A. Y.: director, Shell Oil Co. Foundation

Noon, Prudence J.: president, Newhall Foundation (Henry Mayo)

Noonan, James W.: secretary, trustee, Levy Foundation (June Rockwell)

Noonan, John: trustee, Schumann Fund for New Jersey

Norcross, Arthur D., Jr.: director, Norcross Wildlife Foundation

Norcross, Elizabeth: trustee, Baldwin Memorial Foundation (Fred)

Nord, Shannon: trustee, Nord Family Foundation

Norden, William Benjamin, Esq.: secretary, treasurer, director, Eckman Charitable Foundation (Samuel and Rae)

Nordhoff, Carroll D.: executive vice president, McCormick & Company Inc.

Nordolf, Richard D.: director, AMCORE Foundation

Nored, Anita M.: treasurer, Gardiner Savings Institution Charitable Foundation

Norfleet, Robert Fillmore, Jr.: president, Scott Foundation (William H., John G., and Emma)

Norman, Abigail: director, Norman Foundation

Norman, Andrew E.: president, treasurer, Normandie Foundation

Norman, Margaret: director, secretary, Norman Foundation

Norman, Rebecca: director, Norman Foundation

Norman, Sarah E.: director, Norman Foundation

Normile, Robert John: secretary, Mattel Foundation

Norquist, Helena Miller: president, Miller-Mellor Association

Norris, Bradley K.: trustee, Norris Foundation (Kenneth T. and Eileen L.)

Norris, Edward: director, Menasha Corp. Foundation

Norris, Harlyne J.: trustee, Norris Foundation (Kenneth T. and Eileen L.)

Norris, Kenneth T., Jr.: trustee emeritus, Norris Foundation (Kenneth T. and Eileen L.)

Norris, Pamela: director, Norris Foundation (Dellora A. and Lester J.)

Norris, Robert C.: chairman, Norris Foundation (Dellora A. and Lester J.)

Norris-Szanto, Gillian: senior program officer, Annenberg Foundation

Northcutt, G. R.: president, National Standard Foundation

Northridge, Mark: trustee, Cogswell Benevolent Trust

Northrup, Sharon C.: trustee, Gifford Charitable Corp. (Rosamond)

Northrup, Wilhem E.: director, Harriman Foundation (Gladys and Roland)

Norton, Benjamin P.: trustee, Stocker Foundation

Norton, Eileen: vice president, Norton Family Foundation (Peter)

Norton, Patrick H.: chairman, director, La-Z-Boy Inc.

Norton, Peter: president, Norton Family Foundation (Peter)

Norton, Sara Jane: trustee, Stocker Foundation

Nosbush, Mark: chief financial officer, Specialty Manufacturing Co.

Noss, Stanley: trustee, Barden Foundation, Inc.

Novack, Kenneth J.: director, Time Warner Foundation, Inc.

Novak, Lance: director, Jostens Foundation Inc. (The)

Novak, Richard F.: vice president human resources, Cleveland-Cliffs Inc.

Nowicki, Douglas R.: trustee, McFeely-Rogers Foundation

Nowicki, Sandra G.: president, director, Bettingen Corp. (Burton G.)

Noyes, Elizabeth H.: director, Noyes, Jr. Memorial Foundation (Nicholas H.)

Noyes, Evan L., Jr.: director, Noyes, Jr. Memorial Foundation (Nicholas H.)

Noyes, Henry S.: director, Noyes, Jr. Memorial Foundation (Nicholas H.)

Noyes, Nicholas S.: vice president, secretary, director, Noyes, Jr. Memorial Foundation (Nicholas H.)

Nozaki, Roger: executive director, GE Foundation

Nozari, Mohamed S.: executive vice president, Minnesota Mining & Manufacturing Co.

Nozzolillo, Anthony: senior vice president financial, chief financial officer, Long Island Lighting Co.

Nuce, Michael: member, Teubert Charitable Trust (James H. and Alice)

Nunan, Caroline S.: chairman, Steinman Foundation (James Hale)

Nuness, Al: director, Jostens Foundation Inc. (The)

Nunn, Sam: trustee, Carnegie Corp. of New York

Nunn, Warne Harry: trustee, Meyer Memorial Trust

Nussbaum, Samuel R., MD: executive vice president, chief medical officer, Anthem Inc.

Nutter, Wallace L.: director, Rayonier Foundation; president, chief executive officer, director, Rayonier Inc.

Nye, Elizabeth: vice president, director, Griffis Foundation

Nylander, Jane C.: ex-officio mem, Henderson Foundation (George B.)

Nystrom, William B.: director emeritus, McConnell Foundation

O

O'Brien, Donal Clare, Jr.: trustee, LSR Fund

O'Brien, Francis X.: vice president, trustee, Brundage Charitable, Scientific, and Wildlife Conservation Foundation (Charles E. and Edna T.); trustee, Upton Charitable Foundation (Lucy and Eleanor S.)

O'Brien, John Francis, Jr.: president, chief executive officer, Allmerica Financial Corp.

O'Brien, John M.: senior vice president, New York Times Co. Foundation

O'Brien, Julia P.: trustee, Lockhart Vaughan Foundation

O'Brien, Richard T.: senior executive vice president, chief financial officer, PacifiCorp; member, PacifiCorp Foundation

O'Brien, Robert C.: trustee, Credit Suisse First Boston Foundation Trust

O'Brien, Robert S.: mem, Hoover Foundation (Herbert W.)

O'Brien, Timothy J.: trustee, Ford Motor Co. Fund

O'Callaghan, Debbie: trustee, PNM Foundation

O'Connell, Jane B.: president, trustee, Altman Foundation

O'Connell, Margaret Mary: executive director, Allyn Foundation

O'Connor, Edward J.: secretary, director, Smith Foundation, Inc. (A.O.)

O'Connor, George R.: trustee, Brown Foundation

O'Connor, James John: director, Brach Foundation (Helen)

O'Connor, Kristen K.: chief financial officer, treasurer, Ahmanson Foundation

O'Connor, Maconda Brown: chairman, trustee, Brown Foundation

O'Connor, Pamela: executive director, Zachry Foundation (The)

O'Connor, Roxana: trustee, treasurer, Andres Charitable Trust (Frank G.)

O'Connor, Sally A.: vice president, executive director, Barnes Foundation

O'Connor, Sarane R.: director, Barker Welfare Foundation

O'Connor, Timothy M.: secretary, director, Mullen Foundation (J. K.)

O'Connor, Tom: trustee, Duke Energy Foundation

O'Donnell, Doris: trustee, Allegheny Foundation

O'Donnell, Edith Jones: secretary, treasurer, O'Donnell Foundation

O'Donnell, James E.: president, treasurer, Maneely Fund

O'Donnell, Kerry J.: president, Falk Fund (Maurice)

O'Donnell, Patrick H., Jr.: president, Wright Foundation (Lola)

O'Donnell, Paul J.: trustee emeritus, Dodge Foundation (Geraldine R.)

O'Donnell, Peter, Jr.: president, O'Donnell Foundation

O'Donnell, Sandra: president, Wright Foundation (Lola)

O'Dwyer, Deborah: trustee, Weckbaugh Foundation (Eleanore Mullen)

O'Flynn, Thomas M.: executive vice president, chief financial officer, Public Service Electric & Gas Co.; trustee, Public Service Electric & Gas Foundation

O'Grady, Dennis R.: director, Bank of Greene County Charitable Foundation

O'Hanlon, Helen J.: trustee, Buck Foundation (Carol Franc)

O'Hara, Bonnie: admin, Long Foundation (John F.)

O'Hara, James: trustee, Gund Foundation (Geoffrey)

O'Healy, Quill: chairman, chief executive officer, director, Sedgwick Inc.

O'Leary, Brian J., Jr.: vice president, Universal Studios Foundation

O'Leary, David C.: deputy chairman, trustee, Credit Suisse First Boston Foundation Trust

O'Leary, Patrick J.: vice president finance, treasurer, chief financial officer, SPX Corp.; secretary, treasurer, trustee, SPX Foundation

O'Maley, David B.: trustee, Ohio National Foundation; chairman, president, chief executive officer, director, Ohio National Life Insurance Co.

O'Malley, Mary P.: president, director, Prudential Securities Foundation

O'Neal, E. Stanley: trustee, Merrill Lynch & Co. Foundation Inc.; chairman, chief executive officer, president, chief operating officer, Merrill Lynch & Company Inc.

O'Neil, Abby McCormick: trustee, McCormick Foundation (Chauncey and Marion Deering)

O'Neil, James E.: vice president technology, Kingsbury Corp.; executive trustee, Kingsbury Fund

O'Neil, John J., Esq.: director, Scherman Foundation

O'Neil, Thomas J.: president, chief operating officer, Cleveland-Cliffs Inc.

O'Neill, Abby Milton Rockefeller: advisory trustee, Rockefeller Brothers Fund, Inc.

O'Neill, William G., Jr.: trustee, Smith Foundation (Kelvin and Eleanor)

O'Quinn, John M.: president, O'Quinn Foundation (John M.)

O'Reilly, David J.: chairman, chief executive officer, director, Chevron-Texaco Corp.

O'Reilly, William M.: secretary, Sentry Insurance Foundation Inc.

O'Rourke, Eileen: treasurer, Abell Foundation

O'Rourke, Joan C.: secretary, Trust Funds

O'Shanna, Dick: treasurer, vice president, director, Square D Foundation

O'Shaughnessy, Eileen: secretary, director, O'Shaughnessy Foundation (I. A.)

O'Shaughnessy, John F., Jr.: vice president, director, O'Shaughnessy Foundation (I. A.)

O'Shaughnessy, Mary K.: vice president, director, O'Shaughnessy Foundation (I. A.)

O'Shea, W. J.: treasurer, Campbell Soup Foundation

O'Sullivan, Benjamin C., Esq.: trustee, Holtzmann Foundation (Jacob L. and Lillian)

O'Toole, Robert Joseph: chairman, president, chief executive officer, director, Smith Corp. (A.O.); director, Smith Foundation, Inc. (A.O.)

Oakley, Allen M.: director, Oakley-Lindsay Foundation of Quincy Newspapers and Its Subsidiaries

Oakley, David R.: director, Oakley-Lindsay Foundation of Quincy Newspapers and Its Subsidiaries

Oakley, Donald M.: director, Oakley-Lindsay Foundation of Quincy Newspapers and Its Subsidiaries

Oakley, Peter Anthony: secretary, Oakley-Lindsay Foundation of Quincy Newspapers and Its Subsidiaries; committee relations director, Quincy Newspapers

Oakley, R. W.: trustee, Fluor Foundation

Oakley, Ralph M.: director, Oakley-Lindsay Foundation of Quincy Newspapers and Its Subsidiaries

Oakley, Thomas A.: president, treasurer, Oakley-Lindsay Foundation of Quincy Newspapers and Its Subsidiaries; president, chief executive officer, publisher, editor, Quincy Newspapers

Oakley Day, Susan: director, Oakley-Lindsay Foundation of Quincy Newspapers and Its Subsidiaries

Ober, Gayle M.: vice president, director, Mardag Foundation

Ober, Richard B.: treasurer, director, Mardag Foundation

Ober, Timothy M.: president, director, Mardag Foundation

Oberbeck, Christian L.: trustee, Sharon Steel Foundation

Obolensky, Ivan: president, treasurer, director, Hopkins Foundation (Josephine Lawrence)

Obrow, Norman C.: chairman, president, director, Drown Foundation (Joseph)

Obser, Fred: trustee, Heckscher Foundation for Children

Ochsner, Ronald C., MD: director, Copic Medical Foundation

Odahowski, David A.: president, director, Bush Charitable Foundation, Inc. (Edyth)

Oddo, Nancy E.: vice president, director, Dreyfus Foundation, Inc. (Max and Victoria)

Odlozil, Becky W.: executive director, Belo Foundation

Odom, Roderick: trustee, BellSouth Foundation

Oechsle, Vernon E.: chairman, director, Quanex Corp.

Oehmig, Margaret W.: vice president, Cain Foundation (Gordon and Mary)

Oehmig, William C.: secretary, treasurer, Cain Foundation (Gordon and Mary)

Oelman, Robert S.: trustee, Grimes Foundation

Oesterle, Steve: director, Medtronic Foundation

Oetinger, Judith F.: director, Ball Brothers Foundation

Offield, Chase: director, Offield Family Foundation (The)

Offield, James S.: vice president, director, Offield Family Foundation (The)

Offield, Meighan: director, Offield Family Foundation (The)

Offield, Paxson H.: president, director, Offield Family Foundation (The)

Offutt, James A.: director, Shelter Insurance Foundation

Ogawa, Diane: trustee, PNM Foundation

Ogilvie, Donna Brace: trustee, Brace Foundation (Donald C.)

Ogle, Laura Kerr: trustee, Kerr Foundation, Inc.

Ogletree, Sandy: director, South Plains Foundation

Ohm, Paul: trustee, Miller Foundation

Ohnmacht, Susan: secretary, Sams Foundation (Earl C.)

Oiness, S. A.: treasurer, Union Pacific Foundation

Okada, Alan: vice president, treasurer, Citigroup Foundation

Okada, Natsuo: president, Sumitomo Mitsui Banking Corp.

Oken, Loretta M.: program director, Heinz Co. Foundation (H.J.)

Okonak, James R.: executive director, secretary, trustee, McFeely-Rogers Foundation

Olander, Chris K.: executive director, assistant treasurer, JM Foundation

Olds, William Lee, III: trustee, Irwin Charity Foundation (William G.)

Olds, William Lee, Jr.: president, trustee, Irwin Charity Foundation (William G.)

Oleson, Donald W.: vice president, Oleson Foundation

Oleson, Gerald W.: president, Oleson Foundation

Olfers, Sarah: advisory trustee, Trull Foundation (The)

Olin, Kent Oliver: trustee, El Pomar Foundation

Oliveri, Michael: assistant treasurer, Simon Foundation (William E.)

Olivett, John M.: treasurer, Bank of Greene County Charitable Foundation

Olivier, Jeanne C.: member advisory board, Watson Foundation (Thomas J.)

Oliviera, Ron: director, Wright Foundation (Lola)

Olmstead, Tommy: manager, Porter Testamentary Trust (James Hyde)

Olmsted, Dodge: director, Dodge Foundation (Cleveland H.)

Olmsted, Robert M.: director, Bunbury Co., Inc.; trustee, Windham Foundation

Olney, Richard, III: trustee, Winthrop Trust (Clara B.)

Olofson, Elizabeth: executive director, Guttman Foundation (Stella and Charles)

Olrogg, Elgin E.: vice president, director, Cheney Foundation (Ben B.)

Olschwang, Alan P., Esq.: executive vice president, Mitsubishi Electric America Foundation

Olsen, Eeva-Liisa Aulikki: trustee, Stratford Foundation

Olsen, Kenneth Harry: trustee, Keel Foundation; don, trustee, Stratford Foundation

Olsen, Thomas S.: treasurer, director, Kelley and Elza Kelley Foundation (Edward Bangs)

Olson, Beverly Knight: trustee, Knight Foundation (John S. and James L.)

Olson, Jim: chief financial officer, controller, vice president financial, Rahr Malting Co.

Olson, Keith D.: secretary, treasurer, Bayport Foundation of Andersen Corporation

Olson, Neil D.: vice president, treasurer, Verizon Foundation

Olson, R. Thomas: mem, Glaser Foundation

Olsson, Shirley C.: vice president, trustee, Olsson Memorial Foundation (Elis)

Olsson, Sture Gordon: chairman, director, Olsson Memorial Foundation (Elis)

Olvany, Karen L.: contact, Guardian Life Insurance Company of America

Olwell, Carol: member, Bamberger Memorial Foundation (John Ernest Bamberger and Ruth Eleanor)

Omachinski, David L.: chief financial officer, treasurer, vice president, Oshkosh B'Gosh Inc.

Oman, Richard Heer: secretary, trustee, Reinberger Foundation

Omohundro, William D.: trustee, Patterson Memorial Trust (Hazel)

Ono, Masatoshi: chairman, chief executive officer, Bridgestone Americas Holding Inc.

Oppenheimer, Deanna W.: group president, Washington Mutual Foundation

Oppenheimer, James Richard: director, Tozer Foundation

Oreffice, Paul Fausto: trustee, Gerstacker Foundation (Rollin M.)

Oresman, Donald: treasurer, Colt Foundation (James J.)

Orlando, Sharon: assistant secretary, Knight Ridder Fund

Orlikoff, Richard: secretary, Herald Newspapers Foundation, Inc.; vice president, Southwest News Herald

Ormseth, Milo E.: co-trustee, Jackson Foundation (OR); trustee, Tucker Charitable Trust (Rose E.)

Orosz, Florence U.: trustee, Upjohn Foundation (Harold and Grace)

Orr, Franklin M., Jr.: trustee, Packard Foundation (David and Lucile)

Orr, San Watterson, Jr.: chairman, director, Wausau-Mosinee Paper Corp.; director, Wausau Paper Mills Foundation

Orr, Susan Packard: chairman, trustee, Packard Foundation (David and Lucile)

Orser, William Stanley: vice president, director, Progress Energy Foundation; executive vice president energy supply, Progress Energy Inc.

Ortenberg, Arthur: don, trustee, director, Claiborne and Art Ortenberg Foundation (Liz)

Ortenberg, Elisabeth Claiborne: donor, director, trustee, Claiborne and Art Ortenberg Foundation (Liz)

Ortiz, Emanuel: board member, Fels Fund (Samuel S.)

Ortiz, Pat: trustee, PNM Foundation

Ortwein, Linda G.: trustee, Ratshesky Foundation (A. C.)

Osborn, June Elaine, MD: president, director, Macy, Jr. Foundation (Josiah)

Osborne, Burl: president publishing division, director, Belo Corp.; chairman, trustee, Belo Foundation

Osborne, Katherine: director, Powell Foundation

Osborne, Richard J.: group vice president, Duke Energy Corp.; chairman, trustee, Duke Energy Foundation

Osborne, Richard de J.: secretary, director, Tinker Foundation

Osgood, Edward H.: trustee, Levy Foundation (June Rockwell)

Osher, Barbro: president, Osher Foundation (Bernard)

Oswald, Ellen: director, member, Smart Family Foundation

Oswalt, William: president, treasurer, Vicksburg Foundation

Otani, Tim: vice president community relations department, Washington Mutual Inc.

Otero, Carlos: executive director, assistant secretary-treasurer, Piper Foundation (Minnie Stevens)

Ottaway, James Haller, Jr.: senior vice president, director, Dow Jones & Company Inc.

Otteman, Merlin G., MD: director, Copic Medical Foundation

Otunnu, Olara A.: trustee, Carnegie Corp. of New York

Ouichi, Sadamori: mem allocations comm, Kawabe Memorial Fund

Outcalt, Jon: trustee, Jennings Foundation (Martha Holden)

Outlaw, Karen: director, Norcross Wildlife Foundation

Overholt, J. C.: vchairman, Freeport Brick Co. Charitable Trust

Overstreet, Jane: co-trustee, secretary, Crowell Trust (Henry P. and Susan C.)

Ovrom, Arthur P.: chairman, Van Buren Foundation

Owen, Dolores C.: trustee, Owen Foundation

Owen, Gene V.: trustee, Mayer Foundation (James and Eva)

Owen, Richard F.: vice president, trustee, Owen Foundation

Owen, Robert E.: president, trustee, Owen Foundation; chairman, president, chief executive officer, Owen Industries

Owen-Jones, Lindsay: chairman, director, L'Oreal U.S.A.

Owens, Barry C.: director, Alcoa Foundation

Owens, Charlotte Kay: trustee, officer mgr, Harmon Foundation (Pearl M. and Julia J.)

Owens, J. W.: director, vice president, Caterpillar Foundation

Owens, Samuel H.: treasurer, St. Giles Foundation

Owens, William A.: trustee, Carnegie Corp. of New York

Owings, John R.: vice president, chief financial officer, Air Products and Chemicals Inc.

Owsley, Alvin Mansfield, Jr.: trustee, Owsley Foundation (Alvin and Lucy)

Owsley, David Thomas: trustee, Owsley Foundation (Alvin and Lucy)

Oxnam, Robert B.: director, Erpf Fund (Armand G.); trustee, Rockefeller Brothers Fund, Inc.

Oyler, Gregory: secretary, trustee, Clark-Winchcole Foundation

Ozark, Edward L.: vice president administration, assistant secretary, JSJ Corp.

P

Pacheco, Albert M.: director, East Cambridge Savings Charitable Foundation

Pachon, Harry P.: trustee, Haynes Foundation (John Randolph and Dora)

Packard, Charles E.: trustee, Argyros Foundation

Packard, George R.: trustee, United States-Japan Foundation

Packard, Julie Elizabeth: vice chairman, trustee, Packard Foundation (David and Lucile)

Packard, Ralph K.: director, chief financial officer, Vanguard Group; treasurer, Vanguard Group Foundation

Packard, Susan: trustee, Scripps Howard Foundation

Pacocha, Betty F.: secretary, director, New Milford Savings Bank Foundation

Padgett, Melissa A. Rodgers: trustee, Anschutz Family Foundation

Padilla, Eddie: vice president, PNM Foundation

Page, Arthur B.: trustee, Campbell and Adah E. Hall Charity Fund (Bushrod H.)

Page, Beatrice H.: treasurer, assistant secretary, Ziegler Foundation for the Blind (E. Matilda)

Page, David Keith: vice chairman, trustee, Kresge Foundation

Paine, Walter C.: director, Phillips Foundation (Ellis L.)

Paisley, Beverly: president, director, Bauervic-Paisley Foundation

Paisley, Bonnie: director, Bauervic-Paisley Foundation

Paisley, Charles: director, Bauervic-Paisley Foundation

Paisley, Martha: vice president, director, Bauervic-Paisley Foundation

Paisley, Peter, Jr.: director, Bauervic-Paisley Foundation

Paisley, Peter W.: director, Bauervic-Paisley Foundation

Palantoni, Frank: chief executive officer, Gerber Products Co.

Palenchar, David J.: senior vice president operations, trustee, El Pomar Foundation

Palermo, James P.: trustee, Mellon Financial Corp. Foundation

Paley, Robert A.: treasurer, Monsanto Fund

Paley, William Cushing: vice president, director, Paley Foundation, Inc. (William S.)

Palmer, Denise: vice president, strategy & finance, Chicago Tribune Direct Marketing

Palmer, George C., II: president, trustee, Perry Foundation

Palmer, Ian Campbell: director, Beveridge Foundation, Inc. (Frank Stanley)

Palmer, Joseph Beveridge: director, Beveridge Foundation, Inc. (Frank Stanley)

Palmer, L. Guy, II: director, Dana Foundation (Charles A.)

Palmer, Patricia S.: grants admin, Larsen Fund

Palmer, Ralph W.: co-trustee, Baright Foundation (Hollis and Helen)

Palmisano, Samuel J.: director, chairman, IBM International Foundation; chairman, president, chief operating officer, director, International Business Machines

Palmore, Roderick A.: vice president, secretary, Sara Lee Foundation

Palotay, Marc: vice president, Universal Studios Foundation

Palumbo, Lillian, PhD: trustee, Snyder Foundation (Harold B. and Dorothy A.)

Pampusch, Anita Marie, PhD: president, Bush Foundation

Panagulias, Robert G.: assistant treasurer, Charity Randall Foundation

Panaritis, Andrea: executive director, secretary, Reynolds Foundation (Christopher)

Panazzi, Donna M.: vice president, secretary, Laurel Foundation

Pancoast, Terrence Russell: secretary, treasurer, trustee, Templeton Foundation (Herbert A.)

Pang, Sarah: executive director, CNA Foundation

Pannetta, Leon: 2004, New York Stock Exchange Foundation, Inc.

Paolozzi, Anthony C.: treasurer, Utica National Foundation

Paparelli, Ellen: administrator, Chicago Board of Trade Foundation

Papasan, Larry: trustee, Plough Foundation

Pappas, Helen K.: director, Pappas Charitable Foundation (Thomas Anthony)

Pappas, John C.: director, Pappas Charitable Foundation (Thomas Anthony)

Pappas, Sophia H.: director, Pappas Charitable Foundation (Thomas Anthony)

Pappous, Perry: director, Mitsubishi Electric America Foundation

Paras, Philip G.: treasurer, assistant secretary, Seneca Foods Foundation

Pardoe, Charles E.: treasurer, Pardoe Foundation (Samuel P.)

Pardoe, Charles H., II: president, Pardoe Foundation (Samuel P.)

Pardoe, Prescott Bruce: vice president, Pardoe Foundation (Samuel P.)

Pardoe Ballou, E. Spencer: secretary, Pardoe Foundation (Samuel P.)

Parenti, Renato R.: trustee, Arata Brothers Trust

Parisi, Joseph: director, Valley Foundation

Park, Bernard G.: director, Eastern Savings and Loan Foundation

Park, Dorothy D.: president, chairman, Park Foundation

Park, James Charles: vice president, secretary, Besser Foundation

Park, Roy H., III: jr. advisory, Park Foundation

Park, Roy H., Jr.: vice president, Park Foundation

Parke, Jennifer H.: vice chairman, trustee, Hudson-Webber Foundation

Parker, Arthur: trustee, Grimshaw-Gudewicz Charitable Foundation

Parker, Bertram B.: director, Gebbie Foundation

Parker, Carol Himmelfarb: director, Himmelfarb Foundation (Paul and Annetta)

Parker, Diane W.: vice president, director, Williams Family Foundation of Georgia

Parker, Franklin E., IV: trustee, Victoria Foundation

Parker, J. H., III: treasurer, Luck Stone Foundation

Parker, John F.: trustee, Victoria Foundation

Parker, Maclyn T., Esq.: president, director, Cole Foundation (Olive B.)

Parker, Margaret H.: vice president, trustee, Victoria Foundation

Parker, Renee: advisory board, Vucurevich Foundation (John T.)

Parker, Ronald C.: director, Ford Family Foundation

Parker, Scott: president, Peterson Foundation (Hal and Charlie)

Parker, Stephen T.: director, Williams Family Foundation of Georgia

Parker, Tara Biggers: director, Houchens Foundation (Ervin G.)

Parker, Thomas W.: director, Williams Family Foundation of Georgia

Parks, Carol S.: mgr, trustee, Sawyer Charitable Foundation

Parks, Floyd L.: vice president, treasurer, trustee, Gilmore Foundation (Irving S.)

Parks, Martin A.: vice president, trustee, Robinson-Broadhurst Foundation

Parmelee, David W.: trustee, Howard and Bush Foundation

Parr, Helen Frye: trustee, Victoria Foundation

Parrott, John C., Jr.: director, Audubon State Bank Charitable Foundation

Parrs, Marianne: director, International Paper Co. Foundation

Parrs, Marianne M.: executive vice president, International Paper Co.

Parry, Frances: trustee, Stranahan Foundation

Parry, Gwyn P.: director, Hoag Family Foundation (George)

Parsons, Donald: director, Kutz Foundation (Milton and Hattie)

Parsons, Donald, Esq.: director, Kaufman Endowment Fund (Louis G.)

Parsons, Myers B.: director emeritus, Christy-Houston Foundation

Parsons, Richard D.: advisory trustee, Rockefeller Brothers Fund, Inc.; chairman, president, Time Warner Foundation, Inc.

Parsons, Robert W., Jr.: director, assistant treasurer, assistant section, Hyde and Watson Foundation

Parsons, Roger B.: director, Hyde and Watson Foundation

Parsons, William, Jr.: member advisory committee, Weezie Foundation

Partee, Sue Garrett: board mem, Roberts Foundation (Dora)

Partridge, George F., Jr.: director, McDonough Foundation (Bernard)

Parvin, Phyllis: president, Parvin Foundation (Albert)

Parvin, Stanley: director, Parvin Foundation (Albert)

Pascoe, William T., III: vice president, treasurer, Oak Tree Charitable Foundation

Pascual, Carlos: executive vice president, Xerox Corp.; trustee, Xerox Foundation

Pashos, Kay E.: director, Cinergy Foundation

Pasqual, Leandro: director, Harcourt Foundation (Ellen Knowles)

Pastin, Max: president, trustee, Blowitz-Ridgeway Foundation

Pate, Galen T.: trustee, Bigelow Foundation (F. R.)

Pate, William C.: chairman, BellSouth Foundation

Patel, Homi Burjor: president, chief operating officer, director, Hartmarx Corp.

Paterson, Allan G., Jr.: mng trustee, Rogers Fund for the Arts (Russell Hill)

Paterson, Basil A.: chairman, KeySpan Foundation

Paton, Leland B.: president capital marketings, director, member executive committee, Prudential Securities Inc.

Patram, Bruce T.: chief financial officer, Acme-McCrary Corp./Sapona Manufacturing Co.; secretary, treasurer, Acme-McCrary and Sapona Foundation

Patrick, Charles F.: treasurer, trustee, Copley Foundation (James S.); executive vice president, chief operating officer, senior management board, Copley Press Inc.

Patrick, Deval Laurdine: trustee, Ford Foundation

Patrick, Harriet S.: president, director, Fleming and Jane Howe Patrick Foundation (Robert)

Patrick, Michael: director, Norcross Wildlife Foundation

Patrick, Michael E.: vice president, chief investment officer, Meadows Foundation (The); director, RGK Foundation

Patrone, Mary Jane: director, clerk, Boston Globe Foundation

Pattee, Anne L.: secretary, director, Pattee Foundation

Foundation (Ellsworth and Carla)

Peterson, Ellsworth Lorin: trustee, Peterson Charitable Foundation (Ellsworth and Carla)

Peterson, Jeffrey T.: secretary, treasurer, Lilly Foundation (Richard Coyle); secretary, director, Saint Croix Foundation

Peterson, John S.: general counsel, director, Crail-Johnson Foundation

Peterson, Mary E.: trustee, Lehmann Foundation (Otto W.)

Peterson, Nills P.: trustee, Eastern Bank Charitable Foundation

Peterson, Pam L.: secretary, Swig Foundation (The)

Peterson, Richard J.: trustee, Lehmann Foundation (Otto W.)

Peterson, Robert L.: chairman, chief executive officer, director, IBP

Peterson, Sally D.: trustee, Bigelow Foundation (F. R.)

Peterson, Stephen M.: president, Giddings & Lewis Foundation

Peterson, Wendy Rice: trustee, Baldwin Memorial Foundation (Fred)

Peterson, William E.: general counsel, Sierra Pacific Resources

Petracca, Kim: trustee, Foster Charitable Trust

Petrites, Mary E.: grant administrator, MacArthur Foundation (John D. and Catherine T.)

Petrizzo, John: vice president, chief financial officer, Tetley U.S.A. Inc.

Petrone, Joseph Carlton, Jr.: trustee, Henderson Foundation

Petrone, Victor: director, Patron Saints Foundation

Petteys, Robert: director, Joslin-Needham Family Foundation

Petteys, Robert A.: director, Petteys Memorial Foundation (Jack)

Pettigrew, Linda Y.: secretary, Royal & SunAlliance Insurance Foundation, Inc.

Pettinato, Fred: trustee, Alcon Foundation

Pettit, William O., Jr.: director, Daniels Foundation (Fred Harris)

Pettitt, Jean W.: president, director, Wharton Foundation

Pettitt, S. D.: director, Wharton Foundation

Pettker, Jack: director, Scott Foundation (Virginia Steele)

Petty, Marty: trustee, Hartford Courant Foundation

Petzoad, Arthur: vice president, trustee, Presto Foundation

Pew, Arthur E., III: director, Pew Charitable Trusts

Pew, J. Howard, II: chairman, director, Pew Charitable Trusts

Pew, Joseph N., IV, MD: director, Pew Charitable Trusts

Pew, Mary Catharine, MD: director, Pew Charitable Trusts

Pew, Robert Anderson: director, Pew Charitable Trusts

Pew, Robert Cunningham, II: trustee, Steelcase Foundation

Pew, Sandy: director, Pew Charitable Trusts

Pfaff, Christian J.: president, chief executive officer, Thomasville Furniture Industries Inc.

Pfaltz, Hugo M.: trustee, Fredrickson Foundation (Ambrose and Ida)

Pfeifer, Shirley E.: vice president emeritus, Ewald Foundation (H. T.)

Pfenning, Wayne E.: trustee, Cone Automatic Machine Co. Charitable Foundation

Pfenninger, Elizabeth M.: adv, Cayuga Foundation

Pfohl, James M.: president, Mathis-Pfohl Foundation

Pforzheimer, Carl A.: director, Pforzheimer Foundation, Inc. (The Carl and Lily)

Pforzheimer, Carl Howard, III: president, treasurer, director, Pforzheimer Foundation, Inc. (The Carl and Lily)

Pforzheimer, Carol K.: director, Pforzheimer Foundation, Inc. (The Carl and Lily)

Pforzheimer, Elizabeth S.: director, Pforzheimer Foundation, Inc. (The Carl and Lily)

Pfotenhauer, James: treasurer, Ideal Industries Foundation; chief financial officer, Ideal Industries Inc.

Phanstiel, Howard G.: president, chief executive officer, PacifiCare Health System Foundation; president, chief executive officer, director, PacifiCare Health Systems

Phelps, Don C.: mng trustee, Puterbaugh Foundation

Phelps, W. H.: trustee, McCasland Foundation

Phibbs, Joan F.: director, Gregg-Graniteville Foundation

Philbin, Ann: director, Warhol Foundation for the Visual Arts (The Andy)

Phillippe, Gilbert: adv board comm mem, Heath Foundation (Mary)

Phillips, Blaine T.: president, trustee, Fair Play Foundation

Phillips, Carmen R.: director, Ford Family Foundation

Phillips, Charles R.: vice president finance, National Manufacturing Co.

Phillips, Dan: secretary, treasurer, Griffin Foundation (Rosa May)

Phillips, Edith: vice president, director, Phillips Family Foundation (L. E.)

Phillips, Edward Jay: trustee, Phillips Family Foundation (The Jay and Rose)

Phillips, Ellis Laurimore, III: president, director, mem, Phillips Foundation (Ellis L.)

Phillips, Ellis Laurimore, Jr.: vice president, director, mem, Phillips Foundation (Ellis L.)

Phillips, Gifford: director, Chamiza Foundation

Phillips, J. B.: assistant treasurer, Union Pacific Foundation

Phillips, James: chief executive officer, Management Compensation Group/Dulworth Inc.

Phillips, James L.: chairman, Chamiza Foundation

Phillips, Jeanne: trustee, Phillips Family Foundation (The Jay and Rose)

Phillips, Joann K.: secretary, assistant treasurer, director, Chamiza Foundation

Phillips, Morton B.: trustee, Phillips Family Foundation (The Jay and Rose)

Phillips, Pauline: trustee emeritus, Phillips Family Foundation (The Jay and Rose)

Phillips, Robert G.: director, El Paso Corporate Foundation; president, El Paso Field Services, El Paso Corp.

Phillips, Rose: trustee, Phillips Family Foundation (The Jay and Rose)

Phillips, Susan: director, State Farm Companies Foundation

Phillips, T. Ward: director, Mid-Iowa Health Foundation

Phillipson, Philip N.: trustee, Wildermuth Foundation (E. F.)

Phipps, Mary Stone: vice president, trustee, Bodman Foundation

Piacentini, Carmella V.: administrator, Olin Corp. Charitable Trust

Picard, William: director, Hedco Foundation

Pichler, Joseph A.: chairman, Kroger Co.

Pichon, Emily E.: secretary, Cole Foundation (Olive B.)

Pichon, John N.: director, Raker Foundation (M. E.)

Pichon, John N., Jr.: chairman, Cole Foundation (Olive B.)

Pick, Albert, III: vice president, director, Pick, Jr. Fund (Albert)

Pickard, Mary: vice president committee affairs, St. Paul Travelers Companies Inc.; director, president, St. Paul Travelers Foundation

Pickering, Thomas R.: trustee, Carnegie Corp. of New York

Pidherny, Dennis N.: assistant treasurer, Dun & Bradstreet Corp. Foundation, Inc.

Piehn, Steffen W.: trustee, Wyomissing Foundation

Piepel, J. D.: director, Bayport Foundation of Andersen Corporation

Pierce, A. Kenneth, Jr.: vice president, chief financial officer, director, Columbus Dispatch Printing Co.

Pierce, C. Fenning: secretary, Schooler Family Foundation (Ohio)

Pierce, Charles: director, Fairchild Foundation, Inc. (Sherman)

Pierce, Larry S.: director, Kinder Morgan Foundation

Pierce, Richard B.: director, Foellinger Foundation

Pierce, Thomas M.: trustee, Burnham Charitable Trust (Margaret E.)

Piereson, James, PhD: director, Simon Foundation (William E.)

Piersall, Rick: sr vice president, Roberts Foundation (Dora)

Pierskalla, William Peter: chairman, director, Bush Foundation

Piersol, Catherine V.: director, Bush Foundation

Pierson, Robert L.: secretary, Leidy Foundation (John J.)

Pierson, W. Michel: president, Leidy Foundation (John J.)

Pierson, Wayne George: chief financial officer, treasurer, Meyer Memorial Trust

Pierz, Ann K.: director, Oneida Savings Bank Charitable Foundation

Piesko, Susan: director, Wickson-Link Memorial Foundation

Piggott, J. Miller: trustee, Bennett Family Foundation (Claude)

Pigott, Dana: trustee, Norcliffe Foundation

Pigott, James C.: trustee, Norcliffe Foundation

Pigott, Mary P.: trust, Norcliffe Foundation

Pildner, Henry, Jr.: trustee, Steinman Foundation (John Frederick)

Piletic, William: director, Doheny Foundation Trust (Carrie Estelle)

Pillsbury, George Sturgis, Jr.: trustee, Southways Foundation

Pillsbury, John S., III: trustee, Southways Foundation

Pillsbury, Marnie S.: executive director, Rockefeller Fund (David)

Pinckney, C. Cotesworth: vice president, Scott Foundation (William H., John G., and Emma)

Pincus, Lionel Irwin: director, Ittleson Foundation

Pindroh, Corene L.: trustee, Murphey Foundation (Lluella Morey)

Pineda, Patricia S.: director, Irvine Foundation (The James)

Pinkard, Anne M.: chairman emeritus, France-Merrick Foundation

Pinkard, Gregory C.: treasurer, France-Merrick Foundation

Pinkard, Robert M.: secretary, France-Merrick Foundation

Pinkard, Walter D., Jr.: president, director, France-Merrick Foundation

Pinkerton, Mark: vice president, treasurer, Universal Studios Foundation

Pinkett, Preston D., III: trustee, Dodge Foundation (Geraldine R.)

Pinover, Bruce M.: trustee, Chesapeake Corp. Foundation

Piper, Tad: president, U.S. Bancorp Piper Jaffray Foundation

Piper, William H.: vice chairman, trustee, Mott Foundation (Charles Stewart)

Pirayandeh, Mohammad: director, Alavi Foundation

Pirkle, Linda: assistant secretary, Berkman Foundation (Louis and Sandra)

Pisano, Jane G.: chairman comm res & grants, trustee, Haynes Foundation (John Randolph and Dora)

Pissocra, Ronald L.: trustee, Reeves Foundation (OH)

Piszel, Anthony: comptroller, Prudential Foundation; senior vice president, Prudential Insurance Company of America

Pitcairn, Feodor Urban: executive secretary, director, Beneficia Foundation

Pitcairn, Kirstin Odhner: director, Beneficia Foundation

Pitcairn, Laren: president, director, Beneficia Foundation

Pitcairn, Mary Eleanor: director, Beneficia Foundation

Pitcairn, Sharon R.: director, Beneficia Foundation

Piteleski, Dan N.: director, Metris Companies Foundation; executive vice president, chief information officer, Metris Companies Inc.

Pitluk, Marvin J., PhD: trustee, Blowitz-Ridgeway Foundation

Pitman, Donne W.: trustee, Chapman Charitable Trust (H. A. and Mary K.)

Pittman, Michael: chairman, PacifiCorp Foundation

Pittman, Nancy: executive director, Brown Foundation

Pittman, W. Dayton: director, Hammer Foundation (Armand)

Pitts, C. L.: secretary, Callaway Foundation, Inc.

Pivnick, Isadore: vice president, director, Stulsaft Foundation (Morris)

Pizzey, G. John: director, Alcoa Foundation

Plaeger, Frederick J., II: senior vice president, assistant secretary, general counsel, Burlington Resources Foundation

Planitzer, Russell E.: chairman, Parametric Technology Corp.

Platt, Lewis Emmett: trustee, Packard Foundation (David and Lucile)

Plawner, Morton A.: vice president, treasurer, Public Service Electric & Gas Foundation

Pledger, Pauline: secretary, Trippe Trust (William D.)

Plemenos, T.: secretary, Exxon Mobil Foundation

Plummer, Michelle M.: chief financial officer, Bank of Greene County Charitable Foundation

Plummer, Roberta S.: director, Holt Foundation (William Knox)

Plye, Joe: secretary, AK Steel Foundation

Plym, Andrew J.: vice president, Plym Foundation

Plym, J. Eric: president, Plym Foundation

Poff, W. Herbert, III: trustee, Plankenhorn Foundation (Harry)

Pogue, Richard Welch: chairman, vice president, trustee, Kulas Foundation

Pohl, Jack H.: assistant treasurer, Bigelow Foundation (F. R.); assistant treasurer, director, Mardag Foundation

Pohl, Rachel L.: program officer, Cox Charitable Trust (Jessie B.)

Pohl, Susan Wyckoff: trustee, Norcliffe Foundation

Poindexter, Christian Herndon: chairman, president

Poissant, Gerald R.: assistant treasurer, Taubman Foundation (A. Alfred)

Poitras, Edward: trustee, Poitras Charitable Trust (Dorothy W.)

Poitras, James: trustee, Poitras Charitable Trust (Dorothy W.)

Poitras, Kay: trustee, Poitras Charitable Trust (Dorothy W.)

Poitras, Patricia: trustee, Poitras Charitable Trust (Dorothy W.)

Polakovic, Michael J.: vice president, trustee, Weckbaugh Foundation (Eleanore Mullen)

Polakovic, Therese A.: president, trustee, Weckbaugh Foundation (Eleanore Mullen)

Polisi, Joseph W.: director, Noble Foundation, Inc. (Edward John)

Politeo, Janet L.: vice president, Glaser Foundation

Polk, Cheryl: executive director, Haas Fund (Miriam and Peter)

Polk, Eugene P.: trustee, Morris Foundation (Margaret T.)

Polk, Howard J.: director, Polk Brothers Foundation, Inc.

Polk, Thomas E.: trustee, Morris Foundation (Margaret T.)

Pollano, John T., Esq.: treasurer, trustee, Ash Charitable Corp.

Pollard, David R.: officer, Fireman's Fund Insurance Co.

Pollard, Lewis B., Jr.: vice president, director, Flagler Foundation

Pollay, Richard L.: vice chairman emeritus, director, Chicago Title Corp.; trustee, Chicago Title and Trust Co. Foundation

Pollock, John Phleger: president, Jones Foundation (Fletcher)

Pollock, Robert B.: trustee, Fortis Foundation

Pomeroy, Ellen R.C.: trustee, LSR Fund

Pomeroy, Gay M.: trustee, Mather Fund (Richard)

Pond, Byron O., Jr.: president, Amcast Industrial Foundation

Pond, Charles N., Jr.: trustee, Pond Foundation (C. Northrop Pond and Alethea Marder)

Pond, Dale C.: trustee, Lowe's Charitable and Educational Foundation

Pontarelli, Tom: president, director, CNA Foundation

Pool, Peggy Cook: president, Cook, Sr. Charitable Foundation (Kelly Gene)

Poole, Steven W.: trustee, Gerber Foundation

Poorvu, Lia G.: trustee, Poorvu Foundation (William J. and Lia G.)

Poorvu, William J.: trustee, Poorvu Foundation (William J. and Lia G.)

Pope, John Rogers: vice chairman, McMillan, Jr. Foundation (Bruce)

Popoff, Jean U.: trustee, Gerstacker Foundation (Rollin M.)

Popovich, J. Kristoffer: trustee, Hoffman & Elaine S. Hoffman Foundation (H. Leslie)

Popovich, Jane H.: trustee, Hoffman & Elaine S. Hoffman Foundation (H. Leslie)

Poppleton, Jay K.: trustee, Metal Industries Foundation

Porges, Leigh Simon: vice president, secretary, director, Simon Foundation (William E.)

Portenoy, Norman S.: vice president, director, Dreyfus Foundation, Inc. (Max and Victoria)

Portenoy, Winifred Riggs: president, director, Dreyfus Foundation, Inc. (Max and Victoria)

Porter, J. Benson: director, Washington Mutual Foundation; senior vice president, Washington Mutual Inc.

Porter, Joann O.: member, Knott Foundation (Marion I. and Henry J.)

Porter, John E.: trustee, Kemper Foundation (James S.)

Porter, John W.: trustee, Mott Foundation (Charles Stewart)

Porter, Martin F.: member, Knott Foundation (Marion I. and Henry J.)

Porter, Michael C.: director, DTE Energy Foundation

Porter, Russell M.: trustee, Bismarck Charitable Trust (Mona)

Posley, Steven: trustee, Grimes Foundation

Posoff, Mindy M.: board member, Fels Fund (Samuel S.)

Post, David A.: corporate vice president, chief financial officer, Equifax Inc.

Post, Jeffery H.: director, Fireman's Fund Foundation; executive vice president, chief financial officer, chief actuary, Fireman's Fund Insurance Co.

Poston, Met R.: chairman, director, Janirve Foundation

Poteat-Flores, Jennifer: trustee, Towsley Foundation (Harry A. and Margaret D.)

Potenziani, A. F.: president, director, manager, Bellamah Foundation (Dale J.)

Potenziani, Frank A.: vice president, director, Bellamah Foundation (Dale J.)

Potenziani, Martha M.: director, Bellamah Foundation (Dale J.)

Potenziani, William: director, Bellamah Foundation (Dale J.)

Potter, Thomas D.: director, Woods Charitable Fund

Pottruck, David Steven: president, co-chief executive officer, director, Schwab Corp. (Charles)

Pouliot, Raymond E.: director, Provident Community Foundation

Powell, Ben H., V: director, vice president, Powell Foundation

Powell, Brentnall M.: trustee, Lockhart Vaughan Foundation

Powell, David: president, 3M Foundation

Powell, E. Bryson: trustee, Scott Foundation (William H., John G., and Emma)

Powell, Jerry W.: chief financial officer, Compass Bank; trustee, Compass Bank Foundation

Powell, John B., Jr.: trustee, Baker Trust (Clayton)

Powell, John Brentnall, Jr.: director, Lockhart Vaughan Foundation

Powell, Kitty King: director, Powell Foundation

Powell, Myrtis H.: director, Public Welfare Foundation

Powell, Nancy: administrative assistant, Treakle Foundation (J. Edwin)

Powell, Nicholas K.: vice president, Powell Family Foundation

Powell, Paul: director, Intermountain Gas Industries Foundation

Powell, Susan Baker: director, Lockhart Vaughan Foundation

Power, Jill W.: corporate secretary, Bay State Federal Savings Charitable Foundation

Powers, Edward: foundation managing, trustee, Acushnet Foundation

Powers, John P.: director, Educational Foundation of America

Powers, Suzanne L.: director, New Milford Savings Bank Foundation

Pozen, Robert C.: director, Commonwealth Fund (The)

Pradere, John: secretary, treasurer, Zullig Foundation (Herbert G. and Dorothy)

Prager, William W., Jr.: vice president, Summerfield Foundation, Inc. (Solon E.)

Pramberg, John H., Jr.: co-trustee, Arakelian Foundation (Mary Alice)

Pratt, Abby: vice president, Dickler Family Foundation

Pratt, G. Gerald: trustee, Meyer Memorial Trust

Pratt, Harold I.: trustee, Pierce Charitable Trust (Harold Whitworth)

Pratt, Mitchell C.: treasurer, program officer, Scherman Foundation

Pray, Donald E.: trustee, Bernsen Foundation (Grace and Franklin)

Prechter, Waltraud: chairman, president, director, World Heritage Foundation

Prendergast, S. Larry: trustee, chairman, Turrell Fund

Prescott, Ann: treasurer, Brown Foundation

Prescott, Claudia: chief financial officer, Dr. Seuss Foundation

Presley, Kimberley: trustee, Norris Foundation (Kenneth T. and Eileen L.)

Pressler, Paul: president, director, Gap Foundation

Preston, Carole: director, Himmelfarb Foundation (Paul and Annetta)

Preston, Seymour S., III: director, Barra Foundation

Prestrud, Stuart H.: adv, Archibald Charitable Foundation (Norman)

Price, Allen R.: trustee, Claypool Foundation (Silas and Ruth)

Price, Ann Sage: trustee, Sage Foundation

Price, Carry: director public relations, Liberty Corp.

Price, Charles F.: vice president, Hultquist Foundation

Price, Clement A.: trustee, Fund for New Jersey

Price, Donald: director, Whittenberger Foundation (Claude R. and Ethel B.)

Price, Helen Smith: director, Coca-Cola Foundation

Price, Morton L.: secretary, Crosswicks Foundation

Price, Pauline: chairman, trustee, Price Foundation (Louis and Harold)

Price, Steven F.: assistant treasurer, Alliant Energy Foundation, Inc.

Price, William James, IV: trustee, Casey Foundation (Eugene B.)

Price, William W.: trustee, Slater Trust (Lillian M.)

Prickett, Caroline J. du Pont: vice president, trustee, duPont Foundation (Chichester)

Priddy, Betsy: adv director, Priddy Foundation

Priddy, Randy: adv director, Priddy Foundation

Priddy, Robert T.: trustee emeritus, Priddy Foundation

Priddy, Ruby N.: advisory trustee, Priddy Foundation

Priest Rose, Sandra: director, Hebrew Technical Institute

Prime, Meredith: director, Lake Placid Education Foundation

Prime, Meredith M.: gov, Crary Foundation (Bruce L.); trustee, Weir Foundation (Candace King)

Prince, Larry L.: vice chairman, trustee, Campbell Foundation (J. Bulow)

Prince, Robert: treasurer, Home for Aged Men in the City of Brockton

Principi, Amy: director, Wahlert Foundation

Printz, Albert: mem distribution comm, Flowers Charitable Trust (Albert W. and Edith V.)

Pritchard, Lee E.: assistant secretary, assistant treasurer, Broyhill Family Foundation

Pritchard, Marc S.: president, Procter & Gamble Cosmetics Foundation

Pritzlaff, John C., Jr.: board member, trustee, Olin Foundation (Spencer T. and Ann W.)

Pritzlaff, Mary O.: vice president, trustee, Olin Foundation (Spencer T. and Ann W.)

Privette, Ray: secretary, treasurer, director, Nakamichi Foundation (E.)

Probert, Edward W.: chairman, trustee, member, Rippel Foundation (Fannie E.)

Proctor, Mattina R.: trustee, Proctor Foundation (Mattina R.)

Proctor, Venable B.: secretary, O'Connor Foundation (Kathryn)

Proczko, Taras R.: secretary, director, Hartmarx Charitable Foundation

Prohofsky, Dennis E.: secretary, Minnesota Mutual Foundation; senior vice president, general counsel, secretary, Minnesota Mutual Life Insurance Co.

Prosser, Cynthia Phillips: secretary, director, Phillips Foundation (Ellis L.)

Prosser, Thomas J.: director, Menasha Corp. Foundation

Prothro, Caren H.: treasurer, director, Hoblitzelle Foundation

Protsch, Eliot G.: director, Alliant Energy Foundation, Inc.

Protz, Edward L.: president, director, Northen Foundation (Mary Moody)

Prout, Curtis, MD: trustee, Campbell and Adah E. Hall Charity Fund (Bushrod H.)

Prouty, Hillary: trustee, Prouty Foundation (Olive Higgins)

Prouty, Lewis I.: treasurer, Prouty Foundation (Olive Higgins)

Prouty, Richard: trustee, Prouty Foundation (Olive Higgins)

Pruis, John J.: executive vice president, director, Ball Foundation (George and Frances)

Pruitt, Gary B.: vice chairman, director, Irvine Foundation (The James)

Prussian, Gordon S.: secretary, Polk Brothers Foundation, Inc.

Pryor, Jeff W.: assistant executive director, Anschutz Family Foundation

Pryor, Millard H., Jr.: managing director,

Puck, P. E.: vice president, treasurer, trustee, Air Products Foundation

Puerto, Mariella: project director, Boston Globe Foundation

Puff, Randy A.: trustee, Gerber Foundation

Pugnetti, Wendy: assistant secretary, Rayonier Foundation

Puhala, James P., III: secretary, director, MassMutual Foundation for Hartford, Inc. (The)

Pulatie, David L.: senior vice president human resources, Phelps Dodge Corp.; president, Phelps Dodge Foundation

Pulick, Kenneth: assistant treasurer, SMBC Global Foundation, Inc.

Pullen, Dave E.: president, Johns Manville Fund

Pulles, Gregory J.: secretary, director, TCF Foundation; vice chairman, general counsel, secretary, TCF National Bank Minnesota

Pulley, Cassandra M.: director, Sara Lee Foundation

Pulliam, Eugene S.: senior vice president, publisher, Indianapolis Newspapers Inc.

Pulliam, Larry A.: executive vice president, secretary, Noble Foundation (Samuel Roberts)

Pullin, Randolph L.: trustee, West Foundation (Neva and Wesley)

Pulling, Thomas Leffingwell: director, Luce Foundation (Henry)

Pullo, Robert W.: chairman, chief executive officer,

director, Waypoint Financial Corp.; president, trustee, York Federal Savings & Loan Foundation

Purcell, Cindy: director, Swanson Family Foundation, Inc. (Dr. W. C.)

Purcell, Nancy L.: secretary, Anthem Foundation, Inc.

Purchase, Lara: vice president, Kalkus Foundation

Purkey, Sheila L.: secretary, treasurer, Goldseker Foundation of Maryland (Morris)

Purmort, Francis W., III: director, Van Wert County Foundation

Purmort, Paul W., Jr.: trustee, Van Wert County Foundation

Purnell, John C.: trustee, Yost Trust (J. Paul)

Putman, Gerald: executive director, Decker Foundation (Dr. G. Clifford and Florence B.)

Putnam, David F.: trustee, Putnam Foundation

Putnam, James A.: trustee, Putnam Foundation

Putnam, Rosamond: trustee, Putnam Foundation

Putz, R. J.: controller, Union Pacific Foundation

Pyle, Edwin T.: director, Mingenback Foundation (Julia J.)

Pyle, Ida M.: trustee, Ward Heritage Foundation (Mamie McFaddin)

Pyne, Joe: trustee, UPS Foundation

Pytte, Agnar: director, Fairchild Foundation, Inc. (Sherman)

Q

Quackenbush, Karen: director, Memton Fund

Quammen, David: director, Claiborne and Art Ortenberg Foundation (Liz)

Queenan, Charles J., Jr.: trustee, Evans Foundation (Edward P.)

Queller, Robert L.: trustee, Earhart Foundation

Questrom, Allen I.: chairman, chief executive officer, Penney Company Inc. (J.C.)

Quick, Elizabeth L.: director, member, Cannon Foundation, Inc. (The)

Quinn, John: treasurer, Robinson Fund (Maurice R.)

Quinn, Mary: assistant secretary, director, Avon Products Foundation, Inc.

Quinn, Mary S.: mgr, Sawyer Charitable Foundation

Quintal, Janet: assistant treasurer, Reynolds Foundation (R. J.)

Quirk, Gloria: assistant secretary, PacifiCorp Foundation

Quirk, Kathleen L.: vice president, treasurer, Freeport-McMoRan Foundation

Quiroz, Lisa: director, Time Warner Foundation, Inc.

Quisenberry, Cynthia: secretary, trustee, Castle Foundation (Samuel N. and Mary)

R

Rabbino, Robert A., Jr.: director, SMBC Global Foundation, Inc.; joint general manager, Sumitomo Mitsui Banking Corp.

Raber, B.: secretary, Wharton Foundation

Raber, Chester A.: trustee, High Foundation

Rabinovich, N. Regina, MPH: director, infectious disease program, Gates Foundation (Bill and Melinda)

Radcliffe, Sandra: trustee, Providence Journal Charitable Foundation

Radecki, Gene: trustee, Blandin Foundation

Radeske, Joanne P.: director, Associated BancCorp Foundation

Radia, Suku V.: vice president, chief financial officer, Meredith Corp.; director, Meredith Corp. Foundation

Rado, Patricia A.: trustee, Public Service Electric & Gas Foundation

Radosevich, Carol: president, PNM Foundation

Radt, Richard Louis: vice chairman, Wausau-Mosinee Paper Corp.; treasurer, director, Wausau Paper Mills Foundation

Rae, Nancy A.: trustee, DaimlerChrysler Corp. Fund

Raffin, Margaret: director, Ishiyama Foundation

Ragin, Shirley: trustee, PNM Foundation

Rahjes, Doyle Dean: trustee, Hansen Foundation (Dane G.)

Rahr, Frederick W.: president, director, Rahr Foundation

Rahr, Guido R., Jr.: vice president, director, Rahr Foundation; chairman, director, Rahr Malting Co.

Raibley, Lewis A., III: chief financial officer, New York Mercantile Exchange Charitable Foundation

Rainbolt, Harold E.: vice president, secretary, SBC Foundation

Rainey, Daniel V.: director, Rockefeller Foundation (Winthrop)

Rainey, Esther S.: treasurer, Callaway Foundation, Inc.

Raish, S. F.: director, Penney Co. Fund (J.C.)

Raisler, Herbert A.: director, Hebrew Technical Institute

Raley, J. Gary: trustee, Johnson Fund (S.C.); president, North American Professional, Johnson & Son (S.C.)

Rambo, Cindy: executive director, Zellerbach Family Fund

Ramsay, Scott W.: executive vice president administration, treasurer, director, Shaw's Supermarkets Inc.

Ramsey, Diane H.: vice president, Alliant Energy Foundation, Inc.

Ramsey, JoElla: secretary, American Fidelity Corp. Founders Fund

Ramsey, John D.: president, CCB Foundation

Ramsey, Sam: manager, Porter Testamentary Trust (James Hyde)

Ramsey, Thomas R.: secretary, Toms Foundation (The)

Ramseyer, Roger: vice president, Koch Foundation, Inc. (Fred C. and Mary R.); director community relations, Koch Industries Inc.

Ramsland, Jane B.: trustee, Beal Foundation

Ranck, Richard G.: trustee, Fredrickson Foundation (Ambrose and Ida)

Randall, Brett R.: treasurer, Charity Randall Foundation

Randall, James A.: director, Gregg-Graniteville Foundation

Randall, Karen: executive vice president, secretary, director, Universal Studios Foundation

Randall, Robert P.: president, Charity Randall Foundation

Randall, Robin S.: secretary, Charity Randall Foundation

Randall, Sandra Fleishhacker: director, Fleishhacker Foundation

Randall, William B.: president emeritus, Grotto Foundation

Randall-Dana, Nancy: director, Grotto Foundation

Randazzo, Margaret: assistant treasurer, Knight Ridder Fund

Randle, Kathryn A.: chairman, executive vice president, trustee, Chatlos Foundation

Randolph, Susan R.: chairman, Benwood Foundation

Random, Cindee: trustee, Chatlos Foundation

Randt, Virginia H.: director, Hearst Foundation, Inc. (The); vice president, director, Hearst Foundation (William Randolph)

Rankin, Alex: trustee, Brown Foundation, Inc. (James Graham)

Rankin, William J.: chairman, Whittenberger Foundation (Claude R. and Ethel B.)

Ranney, George A., Jr.: director, Field Foundation of Illinois

Ranney, Phillip A.: counsel, trustee, Young Foundation (Hugo H. and Mabel B.)

Rapaport, Bernard R.: secretary, treasurer, Lowenstein Foundation (Leon)

Rapoport, Leonard: director, Kline Foundation (Charles and Figa)

Rappaport, Daniel: chairman, director, New York Mercantile Exchange; president, director, New York Mercantile Exchange Charitable Foundation

Rappleyea, Holly: secretary, treasurer, Hudson River Bancorp Inc. Foundation

Rapport, Carmi: vice president, Rheinstrom Hill Community Foundation

Raskob, Anthony W., Jr.: first vice president, trustee, Raskob Foundation for Catholic Activities, Inc.

Raskob, B. Russell: treasurer, trustee, Raskob Foundation for Catholic Activities, Inc.

Raskob, Christopher R.: second vice president, trustee, Raskob Foundation for Catholic Activities, Inc.

Raskob, Richard G.: trustee, Raskob Foundation for Catholic Activities, Inc.

Raskob, Timothy T.: assistant treasurer, trustee, Raskob Foundation for Catholic Activities, Inc.

Raskob, William F., III: chairman, trustee, Raskob Foundation for Catholic Activities, Inc.

Raspberry, William J.: trustee, Johnson Foundation

Raspe, Phillip A., Jr.: assistant treasurer, Paley Foundation, Inc. (William S.)

Rast, L. Edmund: trustee, member executive committee, chairman, Franklin Foundation Inc. (John and Mary)

Ratchford, Daniel J.: trustee, Snyder Charitable Trust (Harrison C. and Margaret A.)

Ratcliffe, David M.: director, Georgia Power Co.

Rath, D. F.: trustee, Spang & Co. Charitable Trust

Rath, Frank E., Jr.: chairman, president, chief executive officer, director, Spang & Co.; trustee, Spang & Co. Charitable Trust

Rath, R. A., Jr.: trustee, Spang & Co. Charitable Trust

Ratliff, Eugene F.: director, Lilly Endowment

Rau, John: secretary, treasurer, trustee, McCormick Foundation (Chauncey and Marion Deering)

Rau, John E.: trustee, Chicago Title and Trust Co. Foundation

Raub, Philip J.: director, Baltimore Equitable Insurance Foundation

Rawls, John P.: trustee, Hyde Charitable Foundation

Ray, David C.: vice president, Schurz Communications Foundation

Ray, Gilbert T.: trustee, Haynes Foundation (John Randolph and Dora)

Ray, James C.: president, Ray Foundation

Ray, John L.: trustee, Jacobson Foundation (Bernard H. and Blanche E.)

Ray, June M.: director, Ray Foundation

Raymond, Carolyn M.: trustee, McLean Contributionship

Raymond, Charles V.: president, Citigroup Foundation

Raymond, George G., III: executive secretary, Raymond Foundation

Raymond, Larry: vice president, Memorial Foundation for the Blind

Raymond, Lee R., PhD: chairman, chief executive officer, ExxonMobil Corp.

Raymond, Louise: director corporate contributions, McGraw-Hill Companies Inc.

Rayport, Jeffrey F.: director, Andrews McMeel Universal Foundation

Rea, Bayard D.: director, Dodge Foundation (Cleveland H.)

Rea, William H.: director, Heinz Endowment (Howard)

Read, Deborah Z.: secretary, trustee, Jennings Foundation (Martha Holden)

Reagan, Richard: president, treasurer, director, Norcross Wildlife Foundation

Reagan, Terry A.: vice president, Universal Studios Foundation

Reali, Joseph A.: secretary, counsel, MetLife Foundation

Reardon, Daniel C.: trustee, Bremer Foundation (Otto)

Reardon, Edward J., II: vice president, treasurer, director, Commerce Bancshares Foundation

Reardon, John E.: director, GlaxoSmithKline Foundation

Reber, Brett: director, Mingenback Foundation (Julia J.)

Rebl, Joseph W.: senior vice president finance, Bryn Mawr Bank Corp.

Rebmann, David: director, Mitsubishi Electric America Foundation

Reckling, Isla C.: treasurer, trustee, Sterling-Turner Foundation

Reckling, James S.: assistant secretary, trustee, Sterling-Turner Foundation

Reckling, John B.: assistant secretary, trustee, Sterling-Turner Foundation

Reckling, Stephen M.: assistant secretary, trustee, Sterling-Turner Foundation

Reckling, T. R., III: president, trustee, Sterling-Turner Foundation

Reckling, T. R., IV: assistant secretary, trustee, Sterling-Turner Foundation

Reckling, Thomas K.: assistant secretary, trustee, Sterling-Turner Foundation

Records, George Jeffrey: director, Kirkpatrick Foundation, Inc.

Reddick, Joanne: trustee, Gifford Charitable Corp. (Rosamond)

Redding, S. Steele: vice president, Acme-McCrary and Sapona Foundation

Redding, William H., Jr.: president, director, Acme-McCrary Corp./Sapona Manufacturing Co.; vice president, Acme-McCrary and Sapona Foundation

Reddy, Jack: director, Royal & SunAlliance Insurance Foundation, Inc.

Reddy, Lata N.: secretary, Prudential Foundation

Redgrave, Martyn R.: executive vice president, chief financial officer, Carlson Companies Inc.

Redies, Karen: treasurer, secretary, Redies Foundation (Edward F.)

Redman, Manville: vchairman, McMahon Foundation

Reece, Matt: treasurer, Washington Group Foundation, Inc.

Reece Tacha, Deanell: vice chairman, director, Kansas Health Foundation

Reed, Barbara, MD: director, Copic Medical Foundation

Reed, Cynthia: senior vice president, general counsel, Hasbro Inc.

Reed, Gene: trustee, George Foundation

Reed, Greg: vice president, trustee, Yellow Corp. Foundation

Reed, Hariett: trustee, McBean Charitable Trust (Alletta Morris)

Reed, Marsha: secretary, ABC Broadcasting Foundation, Inc.

Reed, Marsha L.: secretary, Disney Co. Foundation (Walt)

Reed, Richard W., Jr.: director, Staunton Farm Foundation

Reed, Ronald: treasurer, Cape Cod Five Cents Savings Bank Charitable Trust

Reed, Vincent Emory: director emeritus, Strong Foundation (Hattie M.)

Reed, William Garrard, Jr.: director, Simpson Investment Co.

Reeder, Robert M.: assistant secretary, Plankenhorn Foundation (Harry)

Reekie, Robert: director, Tyndale House Foundation

Reese, J. Gilbert: chairman, chief executive officer, Evans Foundation (Thomas J.)

Reese, Louella H.: vice president, treasurer, Evans Foundation (Thomas J.)

Reese, Lowell O.: vice president, director, Brillion Foundation; director, Peters Foundation (R. D. and Linda)

Reeves, Charles B., Jr.: president, trustee, Warfield Memorial Fund (Anna Emory)

Reeves, J. Paul: vice president, director, Gregg-Graniteville Foundation

Reeves, Ken: vice president, administrator, director, International Paper Co. Foundation

Reeves, Margaret H.: president, trustee, Reeves Foundation (OH)

Regan, Lois M.: consultant, Cary Charitable Trust (Mary Flagler)

Regan, Timothy J.: chief financial officer, Scoular Co.

Regenstein, Joseph, Jr.: president, director, Regenstein Foundation

Regenstreif, Isaac: executive director, PacifiCorp Foundation

Regino, Rita: vice president, director, Gudelsky Family Foundation (Homer and Martha)

Reich, Charles: executive vice president, Minnesota Mining & Manufacturing Co.

Reich, Laurence: assistant vice president, Brundage Charitable, Scientific, and Wildlife Conservation Foundation (Charles E. and Edna T.)

Reich, Victoria J.: director, Brunswick Foundation

Reichert, Joshua S.: director environment program, Pew Charitable Trusts

Reichl, Alexander: president, director, Alexander Foundation (Walter)

Reid, J. Marshall: governor, chair, Baker, Jr. Memorial Fund (William G.)

Reid, John A.: trustee, Slemp Foundation

Reid, Robert J.: executive director, Maddox Foundation (J. F.)

Reid, Vernon: trustee, Price Associates Foundation (T. Rowe)

Reidler, Carl J.: trustee, Reidler Foundation

Reidler, Paul G.: president emeritus, Reidler Foundation

Reidy, Janet: director, Memorial Foundation for the Blind

Reidy, Joseph: director, Memorial Foundation for the Blind

Reigle, Jeffrey A.: director, St. Francis Bank Foundation

Reigle, Thomas J.: vice president, executive director, secretary, Johnson Fund (S.C.)

Reilly, Edward Arthur: vice president, treasurer, Cheatham Foundation (Owen)

Reilly, Elizabeth C.: trustee, Reilly Foundation

Reilly, Theresa A.: assistant secretary, CTW Foundation, Inc.

Reilly, Thomas E., Jr.: chairman, chief executive officer, director, Reilly Industries Inc.

Reilly, William Kane: trustee, Packard Foundation (David and Lucile)

Reimer, Gary: director, Mid-continent Media Foundation

Rein, Catherine Amelia: director, chairman, MetLife Foundation; senior executive vice president, Metropolitan Life Insurance Co.

Reinberg, Jeffrey D.: senior vice president, Maritz Inc.

Reinberger, Robert N.: co-director, trustee, Reinberger Foundation

Reinberger, William C.: co-director, trustee, Reinberger Foundation

Reinders, Dave: vice chairman, secretary, Land O'Lakes Foundation

Reiner, John P.: treasurer, director, Loewy Family Foundation

Reinhart, M. H.: director, Carpenter Foundation (E. Rhodes and Leona B.)

Reinking, C. William: president, chief executive officer, director, Exchange Bank; chairman, Exchange Bank Foundation

Reis, Jean S.: vice president, treasurer, trustee, Corbett Foundation

Reising, Richard P.: senior vice president, general counsel, secretary, Archer-Daniels-Midland Co.

Reiss, Vicki: executive director, Shubert Foundation

Reister, Raymond A.: director, Saint Croix Foundation

Reiten, Richard G.: president, chief executive officer, chairman, Northwest Natural Gas Co.

Reitz, Carl F.: treasurer, Besser Foundation

Renaghan, Denise M.: executive vice president, director, Bay State Federal Savings Charitable Foundation

Reneker, Emily: director, Harper Brush Works Foundation

Renken, Susan K.: trustee, Cooper Foundation

Renner, Tom: director, Lytel Foundation (Bertha Russ)

Renner, Trevor: director, Educational Foundation of America

Rennie, Renate: president, Tinker Foundation

Rennolds, Edmund A., Jr.: vice president, Cabell III and Maude Morgan Cabell Foundation (Robert G.)

Reno, Robert H.: trustee, Jameson Trust (Oleonda)

Renyi, Thomas A.: chairman, chief executive officer, director, Bank of New York

Renzi, Elaine: secretary, Hornblower Fund (Henry)

Repine, John E., MD: trustee, Bonfils-Stanton Foundation

Rescorla, Charles L.: director, Graco Foundation

Resnick, Alan H.: treasurer, director, Bausch & Lomb Foundation, Inc.; vice president, treasurer, Bausch & Lomb Inc.

Resnik, Jeffrey P.: treasurer, Fidelity Foundation

Respess, Gary: director, Tri-County Telephone Foundation

Restucci, R. M.: director, Shell Oil Co. Foundation

Reuben, Don Harold: secretary, Prentice Foundation (Abra)

Reusch, Belinda Bunnen: director, Norman Foundation

Reusche, Robert F.: chairman, Demos Foundation (N.)

Reuter, Carol Joan: vice president, New York Life Insurance Co.

Reutter, James L.: treasurer, Thoman Foundation (W. B. and Candace)

Reveley, Walter Taylor, III: trustee, Mellon Foundation (Andrew W.)

Revere, Elspeth: director general program, MacArthur Foundation (John D. and Catherine T.)

Revson, Charles H., Jr.: secretary, treasurer, Revson Foundation (Charles H.)

Rex, John: president, American Fidelity Assurance Co.; treasurer, American Fidelity Corp. Founders Fund

Reyna, Diane: vice president, director, Chamiza Foundation

Reynolds, David Parham: president, director, Reynolds Foundation (Richard S.)

Reynolds, Harold: chairman, chief executive officer, Citizens Union Bank

Reynolds, Heather C.: director, Beneficia Foundation

Reynolds, Karen M.: manager, McNeely Foundation

Reynolds, Mary: vice president, TJX Foundation, Inc.

Reynolds, Richard M.: finance vice president, treasurer, trustee, Strosacker Foundation (Charles J.)

Reynolds, Richard Samuel, III: secretary, director, Reynolds Foundation (Richard S.)

Reynolds, Robert Hugh: president, director, Noyes, Jr. Memorial Foundation (Nicholas H.)

Reynolds, Sigrid S.: director, Strong Foundation (Hattie M.)

Reynolds, Thomas A., Jr.: trustee, Hartford Foundation, Inc. (The John A.)

Reynolds, Timothy T.: trustee, Titus Foundation (C. W.)

Reynolds, William Gray, Jr.: treasurer, director, Reynolds Foundation (Richard S.)

Reznick, Marilyn: executive director, AT&T Foundation

Rheinstrom, Carrol: president, Rheinstrom Hill Community Foundation

Rheinstrom, Majorie: vice president, Rheinstrom Hill Community Foundation

Rhinehart, M. K.: treasurer, Johns Manville Fund

Rhoads, Katheryn V.: executive director, Hermann Foundation (Grover)

Rhoads, Paul Kelly: president, director, Hermann Foundation (Grover)

Rhodes, Carleen: secretary, director, Mardag Foundation

Rhodes, Carleen K.: secretary, Bigelow Foundation (F. R.)

Rhodes, Skip: manager corporate contributions, ChevronTexaco Corp.

Rhodes, Thomas L.: chairman, director, Bradley Foundation (Lynde and Harry)

Rhodes, William Reginald: senior vice chairman, Citigroup Inc.

Rhodus, G. Tomas: director, trustee, Meadows Foundation (The)

Rhone, Sylvia: director, Time Warner Foundation, Inc.

Rhone, Thomas J.: trustee, Kauffman Foundation (Ewing Marion)

Ribeiro, Carl: trustee, Acushnet Foundation

Riccobene, Mary: vice president, director, McDonough Foundation (Bernard)

Rice, Charles M.: treasurer, CHC Foundation

Rice, J. Elisabeth: trustee, Peabody Charitable Fund (Amelia)

Rice, John W.: president, director, Unilever United States Foundation

Rice, Katherine D.: director, HRK Foundation

Rice, Liston Michael, Jr.: president, director, Texas Instruments Foundation

Rice, Lois Dickson: director, Guggenheim Foundation (Harry Frank)

Rice, Mary E.: director, HRK Foundation

Rice, Mary H.: vice president, director, HRK Foundation

Rice, Patricia E.: trustee, Peabody Charitable Fund (Amelia)

Rice, Robert V.: director, St. Francis Bank Foundation

Rice, Sheila K.: program officer, Oppenstein Brothers Foundation

Rice, William D.: trustee, Birds Eye Foods Foundation

Rich, Frank D., Jr.: president, Rich Foundation Inc.

Rich, Gary S.: director, Reader's Digest Foundation

Rich, Leonard: trustee, Williams Charitable Trust (Mary Jo)

Rich, Marsha E.: trustee, Russell Trust (Josephine G.)

Rich, Robert E., Jr.: secretary, Rich Family Foundation; president, director, Rich Products Corp.

Rich, Robert N.: vice president, Rich Foundation Inc.

Rich, Robert S., Esq.: vice president, secretary, assistant treasurer, trustee, Anschutz Family Foundation

Rich, Thomas L.: vice president, Rich Foundation Inc.

Rich, Zan McKenna: director, McKenna Foundation (Katherine Mabis)

Richards, Bruce C., MD: director, Copic Medical Foundation

Richards, J. Stephen: grant department administrator, MacArthur Foundation (John D. and Catherine T.)

Richards, Jim: trustee, Barker Foundation (Coeta and Donald R.)

Richards, Thomas W.: vice president, director emeritus, Marpat Foundation

Richards, Yale: asst secy, Livingston Foundation (Milton S. and Corinne N.)

Richardson, Alan: executive director, PacifiCorp Foundation

Richardson, Beatrix W.: trustee, Hillsdale Fund

Richardson, C.: vice president, Square D Foundation

Richardson, Eudora L.: trustee, Hillsdale Fund

Richardson, George E., Jr.: chairman contributions, Northwest Natural Gas Co.

Richardson, John P., Jr.: trustee, JSJ Foundation

Richardson, Lunsford, Jr.: chairman, trustee, Hillsdale Fund

Richardson, Robert: president, chief executive officer, director, Unitrode Corp.

Richardson, Sarah Beinecke: director, Prospect Hill Foundation

Richardson, Susan H.: trustee, Holtzmann Foundation (Jacob L. and Lillian)

Richenthal, Arthur: director, Fromkes Foundation (Saul)

Richman, John M.: trustee, Johnson Foundation

Richman, Martin Franklin: secretary, Pforzheimer Foundation, Inc. (The Carl and Lily)

Richmand, Frederick Alexander: secretary, Ducommun and Gross Foundation

Richmond, Charles P.: co-trustee, Arakelian Foundation (Mary Alice)

Richmond, Henry R.: assistant scr, trustee, member, Templeton Foundation (Herbert A.)

Richmond, John: treasurer, Cemala Foundation

Richmond, Julius Benjamin: director, Foundation for Child Development

Richmond, Katherine K.: director, Cemala Foundation

Richmond, Merritt: secretary, Cemala Foundation

Richmond, Ruth B.: president, trustee, member, Templeton Foundation (Herbert A.)

Richwine, Marilyn: secretary, treasurer, trustee, Cessna Foundation, Inc.

Ridder, Bernard J.: vice president, Oak Tree Charitable Foundation

Ridder, Paul Anthony: president, director, Knight Ridder Fund; chairman, chief executive officer, director, Knight Ridder Inc.

Ridenour, Eric R.: trustee, DaimlerChrysler Corp. Fund

Rider, G. William: vice president, treasurer, director, Northen Foundation (Mary Moody)

Ridgway, Ronald H.: secretary, treasurer, director, Pulitzer Foundation; senior vice president, Pulitzer Inc.

Ridgway, Rozanne L.: director, Sara Lee Corp.

Ridler, Gregory L.: director, Beecher Foundation (Florence Simon)

Riecker, John E.: secretary, Towsley Foundation (Harry A. and Margaret D.)

Riecker, Margaret Ann: chairman, trustee, Towsley Foundation (Harry A. and Margaret D.)

Riecker, Steven: trustee, Towsley Foundation (Harry A. and Margaret D.)

Riedel, Walter G., III: secretary, treasurer, Stark Foundation (Nelda C. and H. J. Lutcher)

Rieder, Corrine H., EdD: executive director, treasurer, Hartford Foundation, Inc. (The John A.)

Riedman, John R.: manager, Riedman Foundation

Rieger, Kathryn K.: vice president, Kohn-Joseloff Foundation

Riehl, Margaret K.: member, Knott Foundation (Marion I. and Henry J.)

Roe, Paul: chairman, trustee, Birds Eye Foods Foundation

Roedel, Paul Robert: president, Wyomissing Foundation

Roeder, R. Kent: director, Oakley-Lindsay Foundation of Quincy Newspapers and Its Subsidiaries

Roff, John Hugh, Jr.: director, Inasmuch Foundation

Rogers, Christopher W.: trustee, Stevens Foundation (Abbot and Dorothy H.)

Rogers, Desiree Glapion: senior vice president, Peoples Energy Corp.

Rogers, Fred McFeely: president, trustee, McFeely-Rogers Foundation

Rogers, Irving E., III: trustee, Rogers Family Foundation

Rogers, Irving E., Jr.: trustee, Rogers Family Foundation

Rogers, Jacqueline H.: trustee, Rogers Family Foundation

Rogers, James B.: trustee, McFeely-Rogers Foundation

Rogers, James E., Jr.: vice chairman, president, chief executive officer, director, Cinergy Corp.; chairman, director, Cinergy Foundation

Rogers, Jeffrey B.: chief financial officer, Indianapolis Newspapers Inc.

Rogers, John F.: trustee, McFeely-Rogers Foundation

Rogers, John W., Jr.: trustee, Knight Foundation (John S. and James L.)

Rogers, Samuel S.: mng trustee, Stevens Foundation (Abbot and Dorothy H.); trustee, Stevens Foundation (Nathaniel and Elizabeth P.)

Rogers, Stephen Hitchcock: trustee, Rogers Family Foundation

Rogers, William R.: director, Cemala Foundation

Rogers-Rice, Gail: gov, Crary Foundation (Bruce L.)

Rogow, Bruce: executive vice president, Rogow Birken Foundation

Rogus, Mark S.: treasurer, Corning Inc. Foundation

Rohatyn, Elizabeth: vice president, director, Rohatyn Foundation (Felix and Elizabeth)

Rohatyn, Felix George: president, director, Rohatyn Foundation (Felix and Elizabeth)

Rohatyn, Nicholas: secretary, treasurer, director, Rohatyn Foundation (Felix and Elizabeth)

Rohlfing, Joan H.: vice president, director, Atherton Family Foundation

Rohm, Robert F., Jr.: secretary, treasurer, Hultquist Foundation

Rohr, James Edward: chairman, chief executive officer, president, director, PNC Financial Services Group Inc.

Rohrbach, Matthew A.: mem, Teubert Charitable Trust (James H. and Alice)

Rohrback, William: trustee, Harris Foundation (William H. and Mattie Wattis)

Roland, Peter F.: director, Lake Placid Education Foundation

Rolfe, Lee W.: trustee, Norcliffe Foundation

Rolfs, Edward C.: chairman, president, chief executive officer, director, Central National Bank

Rolfs, Edward J.: mem, Central Charities Foundation

Rolfsen, Carl D.: treasurer, director, Foellinger Foundation

Romano, Linda E.: director, Utica National Foundation

Romoser, W. David: assistant treasurer, director, Siebert Lutheran Foundation

Roof, Donald C.: vice president, Joy Global Foundation, Inc.; executive vice president, chief financial officer, treasurer, Joy Global Inc.

Rooks, Cynthia A.: assistant treasurer, Harley-Davidson Foundation

Rooney, J. M.: assistant secretary, Caterpillar Foundation

Rooney, Maria R.: vice president, Crosswicks Foundation

Rooney, Patrick T.: advisory committee member, Inasmuch Foundation

Root, Kimberly Lowe: secretary, Lowe Family Foundation

Roper, John L., IV: executive vice president, chief operating officer, secretary, director, Norfolk Shipbuilding & Drydock Corp.

Roper, John Lonsdale, III: president, chief executive officer, director, Norfolk Shipbuilding & Drydock Corp.

Roque, Marcia: member, Staunton Farm Foundation

Rosa, Karen L.: vice president, executive director, Altman Foundation

Rosacker, Jo Helen: secretary, associate director,

Richardson Foundation (Sid W.)

Rosand, David: director, Dedalus Foundation

Rose, Gary D.: treasurer, trustee, Fund for New Jersey

Rose, Karen M.: group vice president, chief financial officer, Clorox Co.

Rose, Matthew K.: president, chief executive officer, director, Burlington Northern Santa Fe Corp.; director, Burlington Northern Santa Fe Foundation

Rose, Thomas F.: vice president, chief financial officer, Todd Co. (A.M.)

Rosebrock, Charles A.: director, Ladd Charitable Corp. (Helen and George)

Roselle, David P., PhD: trustee, The MBNA Foundation

Rosen, Louis: board director, Ottenheimer Brothers Foundation

Rosenbaum, Howard: assistant treasurer, trustee, Heckscher Foundation for Children

Rosenberg, Claude Newman, Jr.: secretary, Rosenberg, Jr. Family Foundation (Louise and Claude)

Rosenberg, Louise J.: president, Rosenberg, Jr. Family Foundation (Louise and Claude)

Rosenberg, Sonia: director, Guttman Foundation (Stella and Charles)

Rosenberry, Charles W., II: director, Weyerhaeuser Memorial Foundation (Charles A.)

Rosenberry Jones, Lucy: president, director, Weyerhaeuser Memorial Foundation (Charles A.)

Rosenblatt, Roger: director, Greenwall Foundation

Rosenblatt, Toby: director, Irvine Foundation (The James)

Rosenfield, Allan, MD: trustee, Packard Foundation (David and Lucile)

Rosenfield, Patricia L.: chairman Carnegie Scholars program, Carnegie Corp. of New York

Rosenthal, Alan: trustee, Schumann Fund for New Jersey

Rosenthal, David S.: trustee, Rosenthal Foundation (Lois and Richard)

Rosenthal, Jonathan: treasurer, director, MetLife Foundation

Rosenthal, Lois R.: trustee, Rosenthal Foundation (Lois and Richard)

Rosenthal, Richard H.: trustee, Rosenthal Foundation (Lois and Richard)

Rosenthal, Robert, Esq.: director, Hebrew Technical Institute

Rosenwasser, Helena: assistant treasurer, controller, Teagle Foundation

Rosenzweig, Elias: director, Goldman Foundation (Herman)

Roser, Eleanor: chairman, member, Bamberger Memorial Foundation (John Ernest Bamberger and Ruth Eleanor)

Rosica, A. Joseph: director, McGowan Charitable Fund (William G.)

Rosica, Daniel: director, McGowan Charitable Fund (William G.)

Rosica, Kathryn: director, McGowan Charitable Fund (William G.)

Rosica, Lenore M.: director, McGowan Charitable Fund (William G.)

Rosica, Mark: director, McGowan Charitable Fund (William G.)

Rosin, Axel G.: director, chairman emeritus, Scherman Foundation

Rosin, Katharine S.: secretary, director, Scherman Foundation

Rosloniec, James J.: treasurer, trustee, Van Andel Foundation (Jay and Betty)

Ross, Alexander B.: director, Barker Welfare Foundation

Ross, D. P., Jr.: trustee, Fair Play Foundation

Ross, David P.: bank rep, contact, Speas Foundation (Victor E.); trust officer, Turner Charitable Trust (Courtney S.)

Ross, Dickinson C.: vice president, trustee, Jones Foundation (Fletcher)

Ross, Eleanor: assistant secretary, assistant treasurer, Oxford Foundation

Ross, Frances Reaves: director, Fullerton Foundation

Ross, Hal: vice president, Ross Foundation

Ross, John: director, Davenport-Hatch Foundation

Ross, K. D.: vice president, treasurer, director, Winn-Dixie Stores Foundation

Ross, Ralph: vchairman, Valley Foundation

Ross, Robert D.: vice president, Lee Endowment Foundation

Ross, Robert J.: director, Inasmuch Foundation

Ross, Samuel D., Jr.: director, Kline Foundation (Josiah W. and Bessie H.)

Ross, Sarane H.: president, director, Barker Welfare Foundation

Ross, Sharryn: trustee, Azadoutioun Foundation

Ross, Tom: secretary, treasurer, American Honda Foundation

Ross, William Jarboe: director, Inasmuch Foundation

Rossellini, Isabella: president, director, Gilman Foundation (Howard)

Rossi, Janeen: director, Rossi Family Foundation

Rossi, L. Jay: president, Rossi Family Foundation

Rossi, Marjorie Nye: vice president, secretary, treasurer, Rossi Family Foundation

Rossi, Merilee: director, Rossi Family Foundation

Rossi, Steve: director, Knight Ridder Fund

Rossi Buckley, Merilee: trustee, Rossi Family Foundation

Rossi Kouzi, Janeen: trustee, Rossi Family Foundation

Rossi Schuetz, Lizabeth: trustee, Rossi Family Foundation

Rossin, Alan: materials director, Dynamet Inc.

Rossley, Paul Robert: trustee, McEvoy Foundation (Mildred H.)

Rosson, Mary Jo Ratner: president, trustee, Ratner Foundation (Milton M.)

Rossway, Melvin: fund comm mem, Kaufman Endowment Fund (Louis G.)

Rosta, Fannie: trustee, Martini Foundation (Nicholas)

Rostami, Ardeshir: assistant treasurer, Public Service Electric & Gas Foundation

Rotan, Caroline P.: secretary, Farish Fund (William Stamps)

Roth, Charles: director, Oakley-Lindsay Foundation of Quincy Newspapers and Its Subsidiaries

Roth, Larry G.: trustee, West Bend Mutual Charitable Trust

Roth, Michael I.: director, MONY Foundation; chairman, chief executive officer, director, MONY Group Inc.

Rothenberg, Laraine S.: director, The Wallace Foundation

Rothhammer, Amilu S., MD: director, Copic Medical Foundation

Rotholz, Max: director, Gulf Coast Medical Foundation

Rounsavall, Robert, III: trustee, Brown Foundation, Inc. (James Graham)

Rourke, Floyd H.: trustee, Hill Foundation (Sandy)

Rouse, Eloise Meadows: director emeritus, Meadows Foundation (The)

Rout, Robert E.: senior vice president, chief financial officer, S&T Bancorp Inc.

Routt, J. Robert: vice president, controller, Scripps Co. (E.W.); trustee, Scripps Howard Foundation

Roux, Michel: president, chief executive officer, director, Carillon Importers Ltd.; president, director, Grand Marnier Foundation

Rover, Edward F.: president, director, Dana Foundation (Charles A.)

Rovira, Luis Dario: trustee, secretary, Buell Foundation (Temple Hoyne)

Rowe, George, Jr.: vice president, secretary, director, van Ameringen Foundation, Inc.; president, director, Vetlesen Foundation (G. Unger)

Rowland, A. R.: vice president, director, Winn-Dixie Stores Foundation

Rowland, Jennifer: vice president, Faith Foundation

Rowland, Landon Hill: president, chief executive officer, director, Kansas City Southern Railway

Roy, Madeleine J.: treasurer, Crosswicks Foundation

Royalty, David L.: director, Scholl Foundation (Dr.)

Royer, David L.: vice president, treasurer, chief financial officer, director, National Grange Mutual Insurance Co.

Royer, Robert Lewis: trustee, Brown Foundation, Inc. (James Graham)

Rozett, Martha: president, Tuch Foundation (Michael)

Rubacka, Kristen E.: director, Emerson Foundation, Inc. (Fred L.)

Rubenstein, Ernest: secretary, director, Guttman Foundation (Stella and Charles)

Rubenstein, Michael: director, Valley Foundation

Rubenstein, William H.: secretary, treasurer, Andersen Foundation (Hugh J.)

Rubin, Donald S.: senior vice president investor relations, McGraw-Hill Companies Inc.

Rubin, Jane Gregory: secretary, director, Reed Foundation (NY)

Rubin, Lara R.: director, Reed Foundation (NY)

Rubin, Maia R.: treasurer, Reed Foundation (NY)

Rubin, Pearl W.: trustee, Jones Foundation (Daisy Marquis)

Rubin, Peter L.: director, Reed Foundation (NY)

Rubin, Reed: president, director, Reed Foundation (NY)

Rubin, Richard: chairman, Dedalus Foundation

Rubin, Steve: treasurer, Copic Medical Foundation

Rubin, Steven M.: member, trustee, One Valley Bank Foundation

Ruby, Paul J.: director, Campini Foundation (Frank A.)

Rude, N. Jean: co-trustee, Hallett Charitable Trust (E. W.)

Rudin, Jack: chairman, director, Rudin Foundation (Samuel and May)

Rudin, Jeffrey: vice president, general counsel, Millipore Corp.; trustee, Millipore Foundation (The)

Rudin, Katherine L.: vice president, director, Rudin Foundation (Samuel and May)

Rudin, Mary C.: director, Parvin Foundation (Albert)

Rudner, Diane: trustee, Plough Foundation

Rudner, Jocelyn P.: trustee, Plough Foundation

Rudolph, Frank W.: president, Banta Corp. Foundation

Rudy, Dale: corporate trustee rep, Kern Foundation Trust

Rueckert, William Dodge: president, chairman fin committee, chairman executive committee, Dodge Foundation (Cleveland H.)

Ruelle, Mark A.: senior vice president, chief financial officer, treasurer, Sierra Pacific Resources

Ruemenapp, Harold A.: trustee, Besser Foundation

Ruf, Dave G., Jr.: chairman, president, chief executive officer, director, Burns & McDonnell

Ruff, Scott T.: director, Oakley-Lindsay Foundation of Quincy Newspapers and Its Subsidiaries

Ruggiero, Anthony W.: executive vice president, chief financial officer, Olin Corp.

Ruh, Ronald R.: trustee, Hitchcock Foundation (Gilbert M. and Martha H.)

Rumelhart, Judith D.: vice president, trustee, Towsley Foundation (Harry A. and Margaret D.)

Rummel, Mason B.: executive director, secretary, Brown Foundation, Inc. (James Graham)

Rumsey, Julie: director, Donaldson Foundation

Runnells, Clive: director, Gulf Coast Medical Foundation

Runnells, Clive, III: director, Gulf Coast Medical Foundation

Runser, C. Allan: trustee, Van Wert County Foundation

Rupp, Sheron Adeline: chairperson, Rupp Foundation (Fran and Warren)

Ruppert, Barbara L.: assistant secretary, Bunbury Co., Inc.

Rurik, Dion R.: director, Russell Family Foundation

Russ, Jack: director, Lytel Foundation (Bertha Russ)

Russ, Susan Warren: vice president, Children's Foundation of Erie County

Russack, Richard A.: president, director, Burlington Northern Santa Fe Foundation

Russell, Charles P.: president, director, Columbia Foundation

Russell, Christine Haas: treasurer, director, donor, Columbia Foundation; chief executive officer, director, Gaia Fund

Russell, Cristine: vice chairman, director, Commonwealth Fund (The)

Russell, Donald B.: co-trustee, Moss Charitable Trust (Finis M.)

Russell, Eric A.: director, Russell Family Foundation

Russell, Frank Eli: trustee, Pulliam Charitable Trust (Nina Mason)

Russell, G. Richard: trustee, Kiewit Foundation (Peter)

Russell, George F., Jr.: vice president, director, Russell Family Foundation

Russell, Grover B.: vice president, trustee, Clark-Winchcole Foundation

Russell, Ida H.: trustee, Callaway Foundation, Inc.

Russell, Jane T.: president, treasurer, director, Russell Family Foundation

Russell, Jenny D.: executive director, Merck Family Fund

Russell, John A.: director, Kline Foundation (Josiah W. and Bessie H.)

Russell, John G.: director, Consumers Energy Foundation

Russell, Nancy M.: trustee, Pulliam Charitable Trust (Nina Mason)

Russell, Richard: director, Russell Family Foundation

Russell, Timothy M.: manager community initiatives program, Sara Lee Foundation

Russell-Shapiro, Alice: secretary, director, Columbia Foundation

Russo, Steven: director, Fear Not Foundation

Russom, Mary S.: secretary, treasurer, Vulcan Materials Co.

Rust, Edward Barry, Jr.: chairman, State Farm Companies Foundation; chairman, president, chief executive officer, director, State Farm Mutual Automobile Insurance Co.

Rust, Judge Lloyd: vice chairman, trustee, Johnson Foundation (M. G. and Lillie A.)

Ruszin, Thomas E., Jr.: treasurer

Rutherfurd, Guy G.: chairman emeritus, trustee, Bodman Foundation

Rutledge, Jessica L.: administrative assistant, Brooks Foundation (Gladys)

Rutledge, Thomas M.: director, Time Warner Foundation, Inc.

Rutstein, David W.: senior vice president, general counsel, chief administrative officer, Giant Food Inc.

Ryals, Hildegarde: trustee, secretary, Wyomissing Foundation

Ryan, Arthur Frederick: trustee, Prudential Foundation; chairman, president, chief executive officer, director, Prudential Insurance Company of America

Ryan, Gladys B.: vice president, secretary, treasurer, Ryan Foundation (David Claude)

Ryan, James: trustee, Ralston Purina Trust Fund

Ryan, James M.: director, Exchange Bank Foundation

Ryan, Jerome D.: president, Ryan Foundation (David Claude)

Ryan, John Thomas, III: chairman, chief executive officer, Mine Safety Appliances Co.

Ryan, Mark: trustee, Providence Journal Charitable Foundation

Ryan, Nancy L.: secretary, Rippel Foundation (Fannie E.)

Ryan, Patrick G.: chairman, president, chief executive officer, Aon Corp.; president, director, Aon Foundation

Ryan, Patrick G., Jr.: director, Aon Foundation

Ryan, Stephen J.: director, member executive committee, member grant committee, Keck Foundation (W. M.)

Ryan, Stephen M.: vice president, secretary, trea-surer, Ryan Foundation (David Claude)

Ryder, Thomas O.: chairman, Reader's Digest Foundation

Rylander, Carole: director, Wright Foundation (Lola)

S

Saal, William Dunne: trustee, H. C. S. Foundation

Sabatino, Thomas: board of trustees, Schering-Plough Foundation

Sabia, Arthur V.: trustee, Statler Foundation

Sacconaghi, Michel C.: treasurer, Time Warner Foundation, Inc.

Sack, Kelly: community affairs officer, TCF National Bank Minnesota

Sack, Silver D.: director, West Foundation (Harry and Ethel)

Sackett, John I.: director, CHC Foundation

Sadler, Gale: secretary, treasurer, McMahon Foundation

Sadusky, Gaylord A.: trustee, Citizens First National Bank Foundation

Saeki, Takehiko: president, Kawasaki Motors Manufacturing Corporation U.S.A.

Safire, William L.: chairman, director, Dana Foundation (Charles A.)

Sagan, Bruce: president, Herald Newspapers Foundation, Inc.

Saia, Ann M.: trustee, Saia Foundation (Louis P.)

Saia, John S.: trustee, Casey Foundation (Eugene B.)

Saia, Louis P.: trustee, Saia Foundation (Louis P.)

Saia, Lyndon: trustee, Saia Foundation (Louis P.)

Saint-Amand, Cynthia C.: trustee, Chisholm Foundation (M. A.)

Saito, Takao: president, trustee, Subaru of America Foundation, Inc.

Sakahara, Toru: mem allocations comm, Kawabe Memorial Fund

Sakrison, James M.: director, Spalding Foundation (Eliot)

Salanitri, Marie: trustee, Martini Foundation (Nicholas)

Salavantis, Peter: assistant secretary-treasurer, Mitsubishi Electric America Foundation

Salazar, Marguerite: trustee, Buell Foundation (Temple Hoyne)

Sale, Lucy P.: director, Sale Foundation (Lucy Pannill)

Salem, K. E.: vice president, director, Winn-Dixie Stores Foundation

Salisbury, John: chief operating officer, Wilkes, Artis, Hedrick & Lane

Salizzoni, Frank L.: vice chairman, director, H&R Block Foundation; chairman, director, H&R Block Inc.

Salomon, Richard E.: secretary, treasurer, director, Rockefeller Fund (David)

Salstrom, Heidi: program manager, Microsoft Corp.

Salter, Lee W.: president, chief executive officer, director, McConnell Foundation

Salvadore, Eugene Anthony: president, chief executive officer, J&L Specialty Steel Inc.

Salyer, Richard: vice president, Stamps Foundation (James L.)

Salzer, Richard L., Jr.: director, Greenwall Foundation

Sama, Doriann: administrative assistant, Altman Foundation

Sample, Steven B.: trustee, Getty Trust (J. Paul)

Sampson, Glenda: adv comm mem, Moore and Arletta E. Moore Foundation (Kenneth S.)

Samson, D. H.: assistant treasurer, Exxon Mobil Foundation

Samuels, Victoria Woolner: director, Newman Assistance Fund (Jerome A. and Estelle R.)

Sanborn, J. Gregg: trustee, Foundation for Seacoast Health

Sanborn, Lorraine E.: director, Provident Community Foundation

Sanchez, Mary: director, Rockefeller Foundation (Winthrop)

Sand, Carolyn: co-executive director, Wallace Genetic Foundation

Sandalls, William Thomas, Jr.: senior vice president, chief financial officer, Dreyfus Corp.

Sandberg, Nancy B.: chairman, director, Boss Foundation

Sanders, John W.: senior vice president, international development, Cleveland-Cliffs Inc.

Sandler, David P.: secretary, Arcadia Foundation

Sandler, Malvin Gustav: trustee, Sharon Steel Foundation

Sandman, Dan D.: senior vice president human resources, secretary, general counsel, U.S. Steel Corp.; trustee, U.S. Steel Foundation

Sandman, John B.: executive vice president, chief operating officer, Teichert & Sons (A.)

Sando, Joe: director, Chamiza Foundation

Sanford, Claire C.: trustee, Baldwin Memorial Foundation (Fred)

Sanford, Kay: president, CH Foundation

Sanford, Laura P.: president, SBC Foundation

Sanford, Mary Cameron: trustee, Baldwin Memorial Foundation (Fred)

Sanger, Michael: director, JM Foundation

Sanger, Stephen W.: chairman, trustee, General Mills Foundation; chairman, chief executive officer, director, General Mills Inc.

Sanobe, Takashi: senior chief executive officer, chairman, Mitsubishi Motor Sales of America Inc.

Santangelo, Joseph A.: vice president, treasurer, Arkell Hall Foundation

Santomero, Anthony: board member, Fels Fund (Samuel S.)

Santos, John F., PhD: trustee, Retirement Research Foundation

Saperstein, Marc: director, GE Foundation

Sapp, Charles: vice president, Kayser Foundation

Sarakatsannis, Thomas: secretary, legal counsel, director, Avon Products Foundation, Inc.

Saraya, Yusuke: trustee, board secretary, United States-Japan Foundation

Sargent, Alison: senior program manager, Calder Foundation (Louis)

Sargent, Hugh A. A., Esq.: president, mgr, Ludwick Foundation (Christopher)

Sargent, John A.: director, Bloedorn Foundation (Walter A.)

Sargent, Joseph Dudley: president, chief executive officer, director, Guardian Life Insurance Company of America

Sargent, Kevin J.: director, Oakley-Lindsay Foundation of Quincy Newspapers and Its Subsidiaries

Saricea, Lewis: treasurer, trustee, BankAtlantic Foundation

Sarin, Arun: director, Vodaphone-US Foundation

Sarofim, Christopher B.: trustee, Brown Foundation

Sarofim, Louisa Stude: president, trustee, Brown Foundation

Sarosiek, James J.: director, Menasha Corp. Foundation

Sarrow, Robert D.: secretary, Kantzler Foundation

Sarver, James H.: vice president, Hunnicutt Foundation (H. P. and Anne S.)

Sarver, James H., II: treasurer, Hunnicutt Foundation (H. P. and Anne S.)

Sasakawa, Yohei: trustee, United States-Japan Foundation

Sasiela, Joseph: vice president, Kantzler Foundation

Sasser, Barbara Weston: secretary, Kempner Fund (Harris and Eliza)

Satterfield, Byron K.: treasurer, Bowen Foundation (Ethel N.)

Satterlee, Ellen: treasurer, executive director, Wege Foundation

Sauer, Bradford B.: vice president, treasurer, director, Flagler Foundation

Sauer, William: vice president, S.G. Foundation

Sauvayre, Sara Chubb: trustee, Victoria Foundation

Sauve, Brad: treasurer, trustee, Dow Corning Foundation

Savage, Arthur V., Esq.: vice president, trustee, Crary Foundation (Bruce L.)

Savage, Horace S., Jr.: chairman, Portsmouth General Hospital Foundation

Savage, Toy D., Jr.: secretary, treasurer, director, North Shore Foundation

Savageau, Judy: director, Memorial Foundation for the Blind

Saville, Kay: secretary, Duke Energy Foundation

Savitske, Michael B.: president, chief executive officer, director, National Standard Co.; president, National Standard Foundation

Sawczuk, Cornelia Urban: director, Weathertop Foundation

Sawyer, Alden, Jr.: trustee, Davies Benevolent Fund (Edward H.)

Sawyer, John C.: executive director, Arnold Fund

Sawyer, Raymond Terry: chairman, Codrington Charitable Foundation (George W.)

Scagliotti, Sandra: program administrator, Fuller Foundation (MA)

Scaife, Curtis S.: trustee, Laurel Foundation

Scaife, Jennie K.: chairman, trustee, Scaife Family Foundation

Scaife, Margaret R.: trustee, Allegheny Foundation

Scaife, Richard Mellon: chairman, trustee, Allegheny Foundation

Scanlan, Donna: trustee, McKinney Charitable Trust (Carl and Alleen)

Scanlan, John M.: trustee, Bigelow Foundation (F. R.)

Scanlon, Ann M.: program director, Snow Memorial Trust (John Ben)

Scanlon, Patricia M.: secretary, Scott & Fetzer Foundation

Scanlon, Raymond D.: vice president, chief financial officer, director, Lefton Co. (Al Paul); trustee, Lefton Co. Foundation (Al Paul)

Scanlon, Thomas J.: chairman, Public Welfare Foundation

Scarafile, Judy Walden: trustee, Yawkey Foundation II

Scarborough, Ann Hanson: director, Johnston-Hanson Foundation

Scarborough, Collin Wesley: vice chairman, Kerr Fund (Grayce B.)

Scarbrough, Arlan Earl: vice president financial, Gulf Power Co.

Scarlati, Frank S., Jr.: assistant secretary, director, Russell Charitable Foundation (Tom)

Scarpa, Michael: trustee, Claiborne Foundation (Liz)

Scavo, Al: trustee, Rouse Co. Foundation

Schadler, William: director, Lebanon Mutual Foundation

Schaefer, Donald A.: vice president, director, Palisades Educational Foundation

Schaefer, Elizabeth H.: trustee, Mather Fund (Richard)

Schaefer, George A., Jr.: president, Fifth Third Bancorp

Schaefer, Judy E.: assistant vice president, Sara Lee Foundation

Schaefer, Robert: executive director, France-Merrick Foundation

Schaeffer, Richard: director, New York Mercantile Exchange Charitable Foundation

Schaeffers, Charlotte: program director, trustee, Heath Foundation (Ed and Mary)

Schafer, Glenn Stanley: president, director, Pacific Life Insurance Co.

Schafer, Kate: vice president, Wharton Foundation

Schafer, Thomas M.: vice president, director, Abrams Foundation (Talbert and Leota)

Schaffer, Archie: director, IBP Foundation

Schaffer, Richard: president, Greentree Foundation

Schaller, George H.: president, chief executive officer, Citizens First National Bank; trustee, Citizens First National Bank Foundation

Schaller, Harry P.: chairman, Citizens First National Bank; trustee, Citizens First National Bank Foundation

Schamberger, John P.: president, chairman jeanswear coalition, Blue Bell Inc.

Schaper, David H.: director, Stabler Foundation (Donald B. and Dorothy L.)

Schapiro, Mary: director, Cinergy Foundation

Scharbauer, Clarence, III: trustee, Abell-Hanger Foundation

Scharff, Joseph T.: secretary, treasurer, trustee, Subaru of America Foundation, Inc.

Schatt, Carol P.: trustee, Pulliam Charitable Trust (Nina Mason)

Schauer, Bob: trustee, AT&T Foundation

Scheele, Nicholas V.: president, director, Ford Motor Co.

Scheer, Ruth C.: executive director, Cabot Family Charitable Trust

Scheffer, Thomas R.: vice president, trustee, Reeves Foundation (OH)

Scheffey, Lewis C., Jr.: trustee, Wyomissing Foundation

Scheflen, John W.: senior vice chairman, secretary, MBNA Corp.; secretary, The MBNA Foundation

Schehr, Barry: chief financial officer, Amgen Foundation

Scheid, Karen: trustee, Brace Foundation (Donald C.)

Schelling, Dennis C.: treasurer, Christensen Charitable and Religious Foundation (L. C.)

Schendel, Richard: treasurer, Rachal Foundation (Ed)

Scher, Barry F.: vice president, Giant Food Foundation; vice president public affairs, Giant Food Inc.

Scherer, Karla: chairman, chief executive officer, trustee, Scherer Foundation (Karla)

Schermer, Greg: director, Lee Foundation

Scheuer, Elizabeth H.: secretary, Scheuer Family Foundation Inc. (S. H. and Helen R.)

Scheuer, Laura L.: vice president, Scheuer Family Foundation Inc. (S. H. and Helen R.)

Scheuer, Richard Jonas: president, Scheuer Family Foundation Inc. (S. H. and Helen R.)

Scheumann, Theiline P.: treasurer, Norcliffe Foundation

Schey, Ralph Edward: chairman, chief executive officer, director, Scott Fetzer Co.; chairman, Scott & Fetzer Foundation

Schiano, Anthony: president, chief executive officer, Giant Food Stores

Schichtel, Gerald F.: president, chief operating officer, director, Hilliard Corp.; trustee, Hilliard Foundation

Schiek, Fredrick A.: executive vice president, chief operating officer, Employers Mutual Casualty Co.

Schierbeek, Robert H.: treasurer, DeVos Foundation (Richard and Helen)

Schiltz, Timothy D.: committee member, Hoover Foundation (The)

Schindler, Andrew J.: director, chairman, Reynolds Foundation (R. J.)

Schirmeyer, Paul: director, Cole Foundation (Olive B.)

Schlecht, Rebecca: director, Vermilion Healthcare Foundation

Schlechter, Bruce D.: director, Hebrew Technical Institute

Schlegel, Leland D., Jr.: vice president, director, Vogt Foundation (Henry)

Schlereth, John V.: trustee, Reynolds Foundation (Donald W.)

Schlesinger, Mark L.: cfo, secretary, director, Gaia Fund

Schliesman, Paul D.: co-trustee, Hallett Charitable Trust (E. W.)

Schlosser, John C.: chairman, director, Saint Francis Bank; president, director, St. Francis Bank Foundation

Schlossman, John I.: trustee, Graham Foundation for Advanced Studies in the Fine Arts

Schmalz, D. J.: president, Archer-Daniels-Midland Foundation

Schmertz, Ida F.: trustee, Prudential Foundation

Schmidt, Anthony O.: director, St. Francis Bank Foundation

Schmidt, Carl: secretary, Lee Foundation

Schmidt, Daniel P.: vice president program, Bradley Foundation (Lynde and Harry)

Schmidt, Dessie: assistant secretary, S.G. Foundation

Schmidt, Eric: chairman, Novell

Schmidt, Jill W.: vice president communications, International Multifoods Corp.

Schmidt, Paul W.: chief financial officer, General Motors Foundation

Schmidt, Rick: vice president, Goodrich Foundation, Inc. (B.F.)

Schmidt, Thomas Mellon: trustee, Laurel Foundation

Schmitt, Carl: trustee, Homeland Foundation (NY)

Schmitt, Jennifer Rea: director, Dodge Foundation (Cleveland H.)

Schmitt, Jonathan: vice president, Marshall Foundation

Schmoker, Catherine M.: president, director, Schmoker Family Foundation

Schmoker, Richard C.: treasurer, director, Schmoker Family Foundation

Schmoker, William C.: secretary, director, Schmoker Family Foundation

Schmoll, William: treasurer, 3M Foundation

Schnack, Thomas W.: vice president, Ecolab Foundation

Schneeweiss, Steven: treasurer, Chapman Charitable Corp. (Howard and Bess)

Schneider, Gail: director, Goldman Foundation (Herman)

Schneider, Hilary A.: director, Knight Ridder Fund

Schneider, Jacqueline: vice president, director, Moses Fund, Inc. (Henry and Lucy)

Schneider, Pamela C.: trustee, Corning Inc. Foundation

Schneider, Sieglinde: secretary, director, Rice Foundation

Schneider, Stanley: treasurer, director, Autry Foundation

Schnupp, Julia B.: trustee, Lockhart Vaughan Foundation

Schnupp, Kevin A.: trustee, Lockhart Vaughan Foundation

Schnurr, Andrew V., Jr.: trustee, Kaplen Foundation

Schoch, Steven J.: treasurer, chief financial officer, Times Mirror Foundation; vice president, treasurer, Tribune Co.

Schoenberg, Barbara H.: director, Kutz Foundation (Milton and Hattie)

Schoenfeld, Gerald: chairman, director, Shubert Foundation

Scholl, Daniel: director, Scholl Foundation (Dr.)

Scholl, Jack E.: secretary, director, Scholl Foundation (Dr.)

Scholl, Jeanne M.: director, Scholl Foundation (Dr.)

Scholl, Michael W.: director, Scholl Foundation (Dr.)

Scholl, Pamela: president, director, chairperson, Scholl Foundation (Dr.)

Scholl, Susan: director, Scholl Foundation (Dr.)

Scholten, Maarten: chairman, president, Schlumberger Foundation

Schooler, David R.: vice president, Schooler Family Foundation (Ohio)

Schooler, Heather L.: trustee, Schooler Family Foundation (Ohio)

Schooler, S. Dean: president, treasurer, Schooler Family Foundation (Ohio)

Schorgl, James: assistant treasurer, Burns & McDonnell Foundation

Schornack, John James: trustee, Graham Foundation for Advanced Studies in the Fine Arts

Schorr, Donna: assistant secretary, 3M Foundation

Schorrak, Walter: director, Schoenleber Foundation

Schott, Milton B., Jr.: trustee, H. C. S. Foundation

Schramm, Carl J.: president, chief executive officer, trustee, Kauffman Foundation (Ewing Marion)

Schrempp, Jurgen E.: chairman, DaimlerChrysler AG

Schrickel, Patrick D.: vice president, WPS Resources Foundation, Inc.

Schroeder, Charles Edgar: president, director, McCormick Foundation (Chauncey and Marion Deering)

Schroeder, Richard T.: treasurer, director, Rice Foundation

Schroeder, W. Craig: trustee, The MBNA Foundation

Schroth, Virginia Cowles: trustee, Cowles Charitable Trust

Schubert, Arthur: vice president, Windham Foundation

Schubert, James, MD: director, Sierra Health Foundation

Schuberth, Kenneth S.: president, Wilson Sanitarium for Children of Baltimore City (Thomas)

Schueler, John R.: publisher, president, McClatchy Co.

Schuh, Dale R.: president, chief executive officer, chairman, Sentry Insurance, A Mutual Co.

Schuh, Kevin: treasurer, Menasha Corp. Foundation

Schullinger, John N., MD: trustee, Edison Fund (Charles)

Schulman, Joanna: director, Lowenstein Foundation (Leon)

Schulte, Anthony M.: director, Scherman Foundation

Schulte, William D.: chairman, chief executive officer, director, Weingart Foundation

Schulten, Warren R.: vice president, trustee, Miller Foundation (Earl B. and Loraine H.)

Schultz, Ann V.: director, Woronoco Savings Charitable Foundation

Schultz, Larry G.: vice president, comptroller, U.S. Steel Foundation

Schultz, Rhoda: director, The Bothin Foundation

Schulze, Richard M.: chairman, director, Best Buy Children's Foundation; founder, chairman, Best Buy Co.

Schumacher, Diane K.: trustee, Cooper Industries Foundation

Schuman, Allan L.: chairman, Ecolab Foundation; chairman, chief executive officer, director, Ecolab Inc.

Schundler, Eloise T.: assistant secretary, director, Vernon Foundation (Miles Hodsdon)

Schupp, Joseph E.: vice president, Sovereign Bank Foundation

Schurz, James Montgomery: treasurer, Schurz Communications Foundation

Schurz, Todd F.: president, Schurz Communications Foundation; president, publisher, editor, director, South Bend Tribune Corp.

Schwab, Charles R.: chairman, co-chief executive officer, director, Schwab Corp. (Charles); chairman, Schwab Corp. Foundation (Charles)

Schwab, Cindy A.: vice president, Abbott Laboratories Fund

Schwab, Roger: director, Hedco Foundation

Schwabacher, Christopher C.: director, Goldman Foundation (Herman)

Schwander, Stephen S.: director, Vogler Foundation (Laura B.)

Schwanke, Jodie: vice president, Faith Foundation

Schwartz, Arthur L.: vice president, Landegger Charitable Foundation

Schwartz, Carol Levitt: director, Strong Foundation (Hattie M.)

Schwartz, Dennis R.: assistant treasurer, Deere Foundation (John)

Schwartz, Glenn A.: trustee, Jaffee Foundation

Schwartz, Marie D.: trustee, Schwartz Fund for Education and Health Research (Arnold and Marie)

Schwartz, Renee Gerstler: secretary-treasurer, director, New-Land Foundation

Schwartz, Stephen L.: president, director, Brookdale Foundation

Schwartz, Steven J.: trustee, Shatz, Schwartz & Fentin Charitable Foundation; senior partner, Shatz, Schwartz & Fentin P.C.

Schwarz, H. Marshall: chairman, chief executive officer, United States Trust Company of New York

Schwarzkopf, Kurt: corporate secretary, St. Paul Travelers Foundation

Schweid, Edward: chairman, Fox Charitable Trust (Emma R.)

Schweitzer, Catherine F.: foundation manager, Baird Foundation

Schweitzer, Peter A.: vice president, director, Thompson Co. Fund (J. Walter); president, Thompson Co. (J. Walter)

Schweizer, Paul A.: trustee, Hilliard Foundation

Schwendener, Benjamin O., Jr.: president, secretary, Thoman Foundation (W. B. and Candace)

Schwertfeger, Timothy R.: chairman, chief executive officer, Nuveen Co. (The John)

Scirica, Anthony J.: director, Penn Foundation (William)

Scott, Bruce K.: director, Olmsted Foundation (George and Carol)

Scott, Cornell: chairman, director, NewAlliance Foundation

Scott, D. Dwight: executive vice president, chief financial officer, director, El Paso Corporate Foundation; executive vice president, chief financial officer, El Paso Corp.

Scott, Edgar, Jr.: director, Cheever Porter Foundation (Mrs.)

Scott, Frank L.: chairman board trustees, Baker Foundation (R. C.)

Scott, George A.: president, **Scott, Harold A.:** director, Harley-Davidson Foundation

Scott, Michael D.: director, Alabama Power Foundation

Scott, Nadya Ann Kozmetsky: vice president, trustee, RGK Foundation

Scott, Peter M., III: treasurer, director, Progress Energy Foundation

Scott, Tom: director, Potts and Sibley Foundation

Scott, Walter, Jr.: chairman emeritus, Kiewit Companies Foundation

Scott, Wesley L.: director, Cudahy Fund (Patrick and Anna M.)

Scott, William C.: director, Newman Assistance Fund (Jerome A. and Estelle R.)

Scotten, Daniel: director, Shelter Insurance Foundation

Scoville, Roger D.: trustee, Eastern Bank Charitable Foundation

Scoville, Thomas W.: director, Public Welfare Foundation

Scribner, Charles, III: trustee, Homeland Foundation (NY)

Scripps, Charles Edward: chairman executive committee, director, Scripps Co. (E.W.); member, Scripps Howard Foundation

Scripps, Edward W., Jr.: trustee, Scripps Howard Foundation

Scripps, Edward Wyllis, II: member, Scripps Howard Foundation

Scripps, Maggie: trustee, Scripps Howard Foundation

Scripps, Paul K.: director, Scripps Co. (E.W.); trustee, Scripps Howard Foundation

Seabourne, George: trustee, Thomaston Savings Bank Foundation

Seabury, Charlene Brown: executive secretary, trustee, Seabury Foundation

Seabury, David D.: trustee, Seabury Foundation

Seale, Pete: treasurer, Elkins, Jr. Foundation (Margaret and James A.)

Sealvino, Pauline C.: secretary, Vanguard Group Foundation

Seaman, Elizabeth D.: consult, Morgan and Samuel Tate Morgan, Jr. Foundation (Marietta McNeill)

Seaman, Richard N.: trustee, Morgan Foundation (Burton D.)

Sear, Robert: trustee, Yost Trust (J. Paul)

Sear, Timothy R. G.: trustee, Alcon Foundation; president, chief executive officer, Alcon Laboratories Inc.

Sears, Marvin L.: director, Ziegler Foundation for the Blind (E. Matilda)

Sebastian, Audrey M.: trustee, Sebastian Foundation

Sebastian, David S.: executive director, Sebastian Foundation

Sebastian, John O.: trustee, Sebastian Foundation

Sebastiano, Patrick A.: director, Beecher Foundation (Florence Simon)

Sebesta, Carol A.: treasurer, Abbott Laboratories Fund

Sebree, Michael M.K.: assistant secretary, director, Skaggs Foundation (L. J. Skaggs and Mary C.)

Secosky, Phyllis: secretary, Fireman's Fund Foundation

Sedgwick, Michael B.: treasurer, Hoag Family Foundation (George)

Seelbach, William Robert: mem supervisory board, Codrington Charitable Foundation (George W.)

Seely, Christopher W.: trustee, Huber Foundation

Segal, Beth Ann: vice president, secretary, director, Lebovitz Fund

Segal, Marilyn Mailman: chairman emeritus, Mailman Family Foundation (A. L.)

Segal, Richard D.: president, director, Mailman Family Foundation (A. L.)

Segal, Susan L.: director, Tinker Foundation

Segel, Kenneth T.: director, Staunton Farm Foundation

Segers, Ben: trustee, Musson Charitable Foundation (R. C. and Katharine M.)

Segers, Robert S.: trustee, Musson Charitable Foundation (R. C. and Katharine M.)

Seherr-Thoss, Henry W.: vice president, Seherr-Thoss Foundation

Seherr-Thoss, Sonia P.: president, Seherr-Thoss Foundation

Seidel, Arnold: trustee, Friedhofer Charitable Trust (Virginia)

Seidenberg, Ivan G.: chairman, chief executive officer, director, Verizon Communications Inc.; chairman, director, Verizon Foundation

Seidler, James F.: trustee, Reliable Life Insurance Co. Foundation

Seidler, Lee J.: treasurer, director, Shubert Foundation

Seidler, Terry: director, Doheny Foundation Trust (Carrie Estelle)

Seidman, D. Thomas: chairman, Seidman Family Foundation

Seidman, Jane R.: vice chairman, Seidman Family Foundation

Seidman, Lewis William: trustee, Seidman Family Foundation

Seidman, Nancy Caroline: treasurer, Seidman Family Foundation

Seidman, Sarah B.: trustee, Seidman Family Foundation

Seidman, Sarah L.: secretary, Seidman Family Foundation

Seidman, Tracy H.: trustee, Seidman Family Foundation

Seifert, Carolyn: trustee, Plankenhorn Foundation (Harry)

Seiler, Donald H.: director, member executive committee, Goldman Fund (Richard and Rhoda)

Sekerak, James C.: treasurer, Haskell Fund

Selby, Charles W.: secretary, director, Lyon Foundation

Self, James Cuthbert, III: trustee, Self Family Foundation

Self, Sally E.: secretary, trustee, Self Family Foundation

Self, William Matthews: vice chairman, trustee, Self Family Foundation

Selfe, Jane B.: trustee, Comer Foundation (AL)

Selig, John S.: president, secretary, treasurer, Altheimer Charitable Foundation (Ben J.)

Selig, Michael J.: vice president, Altheimer Charitable Foundation (Ben J.)

Selig, Stephen F., Esq.: president, director, Eckman Charitable Foundation (Samuel and Rae)

Seligman, Cathy Sorkin: trustee, Lasdon Foundation (William and Mildred)

Seligson, Aaron: president, Kaplun Foundation (Morris J. and Betty)

Selinger, Maurice A., Jr.: trustee, Altman Foundation

Sell, Ed S., Jr.: mgr, Porter Testamentary Trust (James Hyde)

Sellers, Merl F.: president, Davis Foundation (James A. and Juliet L.)

Sellstrom, John L.: co-trustee, Johnson Memorial Trust (John Alfred and Oscar)

Selover, R. Edwin: trustee, Public Service Electric & Gas Foundation

Seltzer, Louis N.: trustee, Huston Charitable Trust (Stewart)

Selz, Fred: board director, Ottenheimer Brothers Foundation

Seman, Robert J.: finance director, Carnegie Corp. of New York

Semans, James Duke Biddle Trent: trustee, Biddle Foundation (Mary Duke)

Semans, James H.: chairman, trustee, secretary

grants comm, Biddle Foundation (Mary Duke)

Semans, Mary Duke Biddle Trent: vice chairman, chairman grants comm, donor daughter, Biddle Foundation (Mary Duke); trustee, Duke Endowment

Semelsberger, Kenneth J.: president, chief executive officer, chief operating officer, director, Scott Fetzer Co.; president, Scott & Fetzer Foundation

Semler, Matthew D.: trustee, Johnson Foundation (Helen K. and Arthur E.)

Semmes, D. R., Jr.: director, Semmes Foundation

Semmes, Patricia A.: director, Semmes Foundation

Semmes, Thomas R.: president, director, Semmes Foundation

Senecal, H. Jess: co-trustee, Stauffer Charitable Trust (John); trustee, Stillwell Charitable Trust (Glen and Dorothy)

Senhauser, Rebecca: director, Fannie Mae Foundation

Senkler, Robert L.: president, director, Minnesota Mutual Foundation; chairman, president, chief executive officer, Minnesota Mutual Life Insurance Co.

Senko, Jere Scott: director, Prentice Foundation (Abra)

Sensebrenner, Nancy B.: director, Menasha Corp. Foundation

Seramur, John C.: president, chief executive officer, director, First Financial Bank

Sermier, Edward M.: vice president, chief administrative officer, corp. secretary, Carnegie Corp. of New York

Setzer, G. Cal: trustee, Setzer Foundation

Setzer, Hardie C.: trustee, Setzer Foundation

Setzer, Mark: trustee, Setzer Foundation

Severson, Bonnie: director, Jostens Foundation Inc. (The)

Sevier, Sheila: director, Mullen Foundation (J. K.)

Sewell, Cecil W., Jr.: chairman, president, RBC Centura

Sewell, David: director, Hammer Foundation (Armand)

Sewell, Mark: trustee, Arata Brothers Trust

Shabshelowitz, Andrew: trustee, Grimshaw-Gudewicz Charitable Foundation

Shabshelowitz, Harold: trustee, Grimshaw-

Gudewicz Charitable Foundation

Shafer, George A.: president, chief executive officer, director, Hoblitzelle Foundation

Shafer, Jack: board member, Dunkin' Donuts Inc.

Shafer, John (Jack) D.: president, Dunkin' Donuts Inc.

Shaftman, Fred: trustee, BellSouth Foundation

Shands, Bliss Lewis: trustee, Garvey Memorial Foundation (Edward Chase)

Shane, W. John: director, Vermilion Healthcare Foundation

Shaner, John: vice president corporate relations, Dana Corp.

Shanks, Christopher: vice president, director, Ford Meter Box Co.

Shanley, Kevin: treasurer, trustee, Victoria Foundation

Shanok, Charles: director, Fink Foundation (NY)

Shaper, C. Park: director, Kinder Morgan Foundation

Shapira, Amy: trustee, Ferkauf Foundation (Eugene and Estelle)

Shapira, David S.: trustee, Giant Eagle Foundation; chairman, chief executive officer, director, Giant Eagle Inc.

Shapira, Israel: trustee, Ferkauf Foundation (Eugene and Estelle)

Shapiro, Alison D.: vice president, Shapiro Family Charitable Foundation

Shapiro, Peter W.: vice president, Shapiro Family Charitable Foundation

Shapiro, Ralph J.: chairman, Shapiro Family Charitable Foundation

Shapiro, Robert: trustee, Schwartz Foundation (Arnold A.)

Shapiro, Romie: president, Fink Foundation (NY)

Shapiro, Shirley: president, Shapiro Family Charitable Foundation

Shapiro, Stephen: trustee, Dibner Fund; director, Zellerbach Family Fund

Shapiro, Steven J.: senior vice president, chief financial officer, Burlington Resources Foundation

Shapleigh, Warren M.: president, trustee, Olin Foundation (Spencer T. and Ann W.)

Sharer, Kevin W.: president, chief executive officer, Amgen Inc.

Sharp, Hugh Rodney, III: president, trustee, Longwood Foundation

Sharp, Paul F.: trustee, Sarkeys Foundation

Sharp, Peggy: secretary, CHC Foundation

Sharp, Philip R.: director, Cinergy Foundation

Sharpe, Henry D., Jr.: trustee, Providence Journal Charitable Foundation

Shattuck, Mayo A., III: president, chief executive officer, chairman, Constellation Energy Group Inc.

Shatz, Stephen A.: trustee, Shatz, Schwartz & Fentin Charitable Foundation; counsel, Shatz, Schwartz & Fentin P.C.

Shaver, Craig, III: president, U.S. Bancorp Piper Jaffray Foundation

Shaw, Alan: trustee, Whirlpool Foundation

Shaw, Arch W., II: trustee, Shaw Foundation (Arch W.)

Shaw, Bill: director, Tribune New York Foundation

Shaw, Bruce P.: trustee, Shaw Foundation (Arch W.)

Shaw, George T.: trustee, Cox Charitable Trust (Jessie B.)

Shaw, Greg: director foundation library & pac northwest advocacy, Gates Foundation (Bill and Melinda)

Shaw, Minor Mickel: trustee, Duke Endowment

Shaw, Roger D., Jr.: trustee, Shaw Foundation (Arch W.)

Shaw, Ruth G.: president, Duke Energy Corp.; trustee, Duke Energy Foundation

Shaw, William W.: trustee, Shaw Foundation (Arch W.)

Shea, Dorothy B.: president, director, Patron Saints Foundation

Shea, Jeremiah Patrick: vice president, Kutz Foundation (Milton and Hattie)

Shea, Julia V.: secretary, trustee, Altman Foundation

Sheaffer, Barbara H.: director, Kelley and Elza Kelley Foundation (Edward Bangs)

Sheahan, Mark: vice president, Graco Inc.

Sheahan, Patrick M.: deputy director, assistant vice president, Sara Lee Foundation

Sheahan, William: secretary, Jostens Foundation Inc. (The)

Shearon, Carol: program manager, Xcel Energy Foundation

Sheble-Hall, Alexander: trustee, Stackpole-Hall Foundation

Shed, Nathaniel: treasurer, Oak Grove School

Sheehan, D. M.: vice president, director, Winn-Dixie Stores Foundation

Sheehan, Daria: secretary, Citigroup Foundation

Sheehan, J. R.: vice president, director, Winn-Dixie Stores Foundation

Sheesley, DeVere L.: trustee, Mengle Foundation (Glenn and Ruth)

Sheets, Susan Ross: secretary, treasurer, Ross Foundation

Sheils, James Bernard: trustee, Shatz, Schwartz & Fentin Charitable Foundation; partner, vice president, Shatz, Schwartz & Fentin P.C.

Sheinbaum, Moshe: vice president, Kaplun Foundation (Morris J. and Betty)

Shelbourn, Tony: vice president, director, Dana Corp. Foundation

Shelden, William W., Jr.: trustee, McGregor Fund

Sheldon, J. Elizabeth: president, Sheldon Foundation Inc. (Ralph C.)

Shell, Frederick E.: vice president corporate & governmental affairs, DTE Energy Co.; president, director, DTE Energy Foundation

Shelton, James J.: trustee, Baker Foundation (R. C.)

Shelton, Rena: assistant secretary, Dunagan Foundation

Shenefelt, Jamie: director, Stewart Educational Foundation (Donnell B. and Elizabeth Dee Shaw)

Shenk, Janet: director, Arca Foundation

Shenk, Willis Weidman: treasurer, Steinman Foundation (James Hale)

Shenker, Joseph: director, The Wallace Foundation

Shepard, Andrew J.: chairman, director, Exchange Bank; director, Exchange Bank Foundation

Shepard, Charles E.: director, Menasha Corp. Foundation

Shepard, James D.: trustee, McCabe Foundation (B. C.)

Shepherd, Ann H.: secretary, Hamman Foundation (George and Mary Josephine)

Shepherd, J. Michael: secretary, director, Link, Jr. Foundation (George)

Shepley, Hamilton N.: director, Kelley and Elza Kelley Foundation (Edward Bangs)

Shepley, Lewis Baker: executive vice president, chief financial officer, director, Reliable Life Insurance Co.

Sherbrooke, Ross E.: director, Fidelity Foundation

Sherburne, Philip S.: assistant treasurer, director, Star Tribune Foundation

Sheridan, Brian: director, Washington Foundation (Dennis R. and Phyllis)

Sheridan, John J.: director, Brach Foundation (Helen)

Sherin, Keith S.: director, GE Foundation; senior vice president finance, chief financial officer, General Electric Co.

Sherman, Bruce: co-trustee, Schermer Charitable Trust (Frances)

Sherman, Bruce R.: treasurer, St. Francis Bank Foundation

Sherman, Harris D.: trustee, Boettcher Foundation

Sherman, Michael B.: trustee, Eastern Bank Charitable Foundation

Sherman, Susan Elizabeth: president, chief executive officer, Independence Foundation

Sherogan, Diana Wege: trustee, Wege Foundation

Sherr, Sidney S.: director, Gordon Charitable Trust (Peggy and Yale)

Sherrill, Edmund K., II: director, Good Samaritan

Sherrill, H. Sinclair: director, Good Samaritan

Sherrill, Henry W.: president, Good Samaritan

Sherrill, Hugh Virgil: director, Kleberg Foundation (Robert J. Kleberg, Jr. and Helen C.)

Sherrill, Joseph Newton, Jr.: vice president, trustee, West Foundation (TX)

Sherry, Judith K.: director, Staunton Farm Foundation

Sherry, Peter J., Jr.: secretary, Ford Motor Co. Fund

Sherwell, Jon: trustee, Henson Foundation (Richard A.)

Sherwin, Brian: president, South Waite Foundation

Sherwin, Dennis: mem, South Waite Foundation

Sherwin, Douglas F.: vice president, Lee Endowment Foundation

Sherwin, Peter: mem, South Waite Foundation

Sherwood, Lynne: corporate secretary, JSJ Corp.; secretary, treasurer, trustee, JSJ Foundation

Shields, Margaret M.: treasurer, Colonial Oaks Foundation

Shifler, E. H.: director, Eden Hall Foundation

Shiflett, B. B.: founder, Trull Foundation (The)

Shiflett, Laura Trull: founder, Trull Foundation (The)

Shine, Fredrick J., III: director, First Hawaiian Foundation

Shine, Warren: trustee, Dibner Fund

Shineman, Edward W., Jr.: president, trustee, Arkell Hall Foundation

Shinoda, Shunji: director, Nakamichi Foundation (E.)

Shipley, Larry: chief financial officer, IBP

Shipley, Walter Vincent: mem, director, The Wallace Foundation

Shipley Miller, Harvey S.: trustee, Rothschild Foundation (Judith)

Shippee, Patricia Morel: director, Griffis Foundation

Shirk, Susan: trustee, United States-Japan Foundation

Shirley, Betsy B.: vice president, Jockey Hollow Foundation

Shirley, Paul V., Jr.: trustee, Hitchcock Foundation (Gilbert M. and Martha H.)

Shoaff, Thomas Mitchell: director, vice president, McMillen Foundation

Shoffner, Gary E.: secretary, director, Pickford Foundation (Mary)

Shojai, Tracie M.: trustee, McKay Family Foundation

Shook, Barbara Ingalls: chairman, treasurer, Shook Foundation (Barbara Ingalls)

Shook, Elesabeth Ridgely: trustee, Shook Foundation (Barbara Ingalls)

Shook, Robert P.: president, secretary, Shook Foundation (Barbara Ingalls)

Shore, Alastair: president, director, Fireman's Fund Foundation

Short, Harry: director, Portsmouth General Hospital Foundation

Short, Randall K.: assistant treasurer, Boston Globe Foundation

Shostek, Rick: president, director, Honda of America Foundation

Shott, Scott: vice president, Shott, Jr. Foundation (Hugh I.)

Shoup, Helen H.: trustee, Hulme Charitable Foundation (Milton G.)

Shriver, Eunice Kennedy: executive vice president, trustee, Kennedy, Jr. Foundation (Joseph P.)

Shuey, John Henry: chairman, president, chief executive officer, director, Amcast Industrial Corp.

Shuler, Gloria: financial grants manager, AT&T Foundation

Shulman, Becky S.: assistant treasurer, H&R Block Foundation

Shulman, Lloyd J.: president, director, Weinstein Foundation (J.)

Shulman, Sylvia W.: vice president, director, Weinstein Foundation (J.)

Shultz, Kevin: director, Ensign-Bickford Foundation

Shumaker, Portia W.: committee member, Whitaker Foundation

Shuman, D. Ellen: vice president, chief investment officer, Carnegie Corp. of New York

Shust, Robert B.: trustee, Patterson Charitable Fund (W. I.)

Shuster, George Whitcomb: trustee, Cranston Foundation; president, chief executive officer, director, Cranston Print Works Co.

Shute, Benjamin R., Jr.: secretary, Rockefeller Brothers Fund, Inc.

Shutis, Larry: trustee, Fairchild-Meeker Charitable Trust (Freeman E.)

Shyer, Marlene: trustee, Heckscher Foundation for Children

Sibbison, Virginia Hayes: director, Clark Foundation (Robert Sterling)

Sibert, Leslie R.: vice president transmission, Georgia Power Co.

Sibley, D. J.: director, Potts and Sibley Foundation

Sibley, Hiram: chairman, Potts and Sibley Foundation

Sibley, James Malcolm: trustee, Harland Charitable Foundation (John H. and Wilhelmina D.); vice chairman, trustee, Woodruff Foundation (Robert W.)

Sibol, Mike: director, Susquehanna-Pfaltzgraff Co.

Siddall, David L.: vice president, associate general counsel, corporate section, El Paso Corporate Foundation

Sides, Dolores C.: executive director, Burlington Industries Foundation

Sidhu, Jay S.: president, chief executive officer, chairman, Sovereign Bank; director, Sovereign Bank Foundation

Siebert, Sara: trustee emeritus, Alexander Edwards Trust (Margaret)

Siegel, Bernard L.: president, Kutz Foundation (Milton and Hattie)

Siegel, Herbert: chairman, Statler Foundation

Siegel, Herbert Jay: director, Dana Foundation (Charles A.)

Siegel, Jeannette: committee relations, manager, Penney Company Inc. (J.C.)

Sieve, Richard, MD: secretary, Valley Foundation

Siewert, Richard L. (Jake): director, Alcoa Foundation

Sigfusson, Becky B.: vice president, director, Bere Foundation

Signorile, A. J.: trustee, Dana Charitable Trust (Eleanor Naylor)

Signorile, Stephen A.: trustee, Dana Charitable Trust (Eleanor Naylor)

Silas, Cecil Jesse: director, The Wallace Foundation

Silberblatt, Steven: president, Clorox Co. Foundation

Silberman, Sidney J., Esq.: treasurer, Scheuer Family Foundation Inc. (S. H. and Helen R.)

Silbersack, Donna C.: assistant secretary, assistant treasurer, France-Merrick Foundation

Silbert, Bernard: director, Parvin Foundation (Albert)

Silbert, Steven: director, Parvin Foundation (Albert)

Silk, Dorothy: trustee, Thoman Foundation (W. B. and Candace)

Silliman, Henry Harper, Jr.: president, treasurer, Borkee-Hagley Foundation; treasurer, trustee, Longwood Foundation

Silliman, John E.: vice president, Borkee-Hagley Foundation

Silliman, Perry: secretary-treasurer, Murphy Foundation

Silliman, Robert M.: director, Borkee-Hagley Foundation

Sills, John Leland: director, Rudin Foundation

Silvati, John Donald: vice president, director, Dater Foundation (Charles H.)

Silver, Bob: trustee, Paine Webber Foundation

Silver, Stanley: president, Kahn, Lucas-Lancaster Incorporated Children's Wear

Silverglat, Alan G.: secretary, treasurer, director, Pulitzer Foundation

Silverman, Barry S.: chairman, director,

Silverman, Jeffrey: trustee, Silverman Family Foundation

Silverman, Lawrence D.: treasurer, director, Lederer Foundation (Francis L.)

Silverman, Michael David: president, chief executive officer, director; trustee, Silverman Family Foundation

Silverman, Robert L.: chairman, president, chief

executive officer, Winter Construction Co.

Silverman, Sandra: president, executive director, Scherman Foundation

Simi, Jean: executive assistant, corporate assistant secretary, Mott Foundation (Charles Stewart)

Simmons, Glenn Reuben: vice chairman, Contran Corp.

Simmons, Hardwick: chairman, chief executive officer, Prudential Securities Inc.

Simmons, Harold Clark: chairman, director, Simmons Foundation, Inc. (Harold)

Simmons, Laurence E.: director, Houston Endowment

Simock, Debbie: manager community relations, Avista Corp.

Simon, Allison S.: president, Stemmons Foundation

Simon, Heinz K.: vice president, Stemmons Foundation

Simon, J. Peter: co-chairman, director, Simon Foundation (William E.)

Simon, John Gerald: trustee, Taconic Foundation

Simon, Kenneth: secretary, treasurer, Kayser Foundation

Simon, R. Matthew: vice chairman, director, Brach Foundation (Helen)

Simon, Raymond F.: president, director, Brach Foundation (Helen); vice president, Polk Brothers Foundation, Inc.

Simon, William Edward, Jr.: co-chairman, director, Simon Foundation (William E.)

Simon-Morris, Johanna K.: director, Simon Foundation (William E.)

Simonet, John Thomas: vice president, Tozer Foundation

Simons, Bren: trustee, Simon Charitable Foundation Number One (Melvin and Bren)

Simons, Melvin J.: trustee, Simon Charitable Foundation Number One (Melvin and Bren)

Simonson, Anne Larsen: vice president, Larsen Fund

Simpkins, Jacqueline DeNeuflize: trustee, Sprague Educational and Charitable Foundation (Seth)

Simpson, Betty: clerk, Memorial Foundation for the Blind

Simpson, Irma E.: manager, Gannett Foundation

Simpson, Julie Inskeep: director, Journal-Gazette Foundation, Inc.

Simpson, William H.: president, chief executive officer, Susquehanna-Pfaltzgraff Co.; secretary, Susquehanna-Pfaltzgraff Foundation

Sims, Don: director, Sierra Pacific Resources Charitable Foundation

Sims, Frank L.: director, vice president, Cargill Foundation

Sims, Robert L.: trustee, Cord Foundation (E. L.)

Sims, Sally: director, Patron Saints Foundation

Sinclair, John P., Esq.: director, Glencoe Foundation

Sinclair, K. Richard C.: mem, trustee, One Valley Bank Foundation

Singer, Suzanne: secretary, trust, Livingston Foundation (Milton S. and Corinne N.)

Singleton, Matt: vice president, chief executive officer, director, CIBC World Markets

Singley Koontz, Frederick: trustee, Wallis Trust (Dorothy Wagner)

Sinnett, Clifford H.: trustee, Burnham Charitable Trust (Margaret E.)

Sircy, Melissa Smith: trustee, Slemp Foundation

Sirek, John: director citizenship programs, McCormick Tribune Foundation (Robert R.)

Siriporn, Chaiyasuta: trustee, Unocal Foundation

Sirota, Wilbert H., Esq.: secretary, treasurer, Hecht-Levi Foundation

Sisco, Robbie D.: director, Cabot Corp. Foundation

Sisk, John F.: trustee, Donaldson Charitable Trust (Oliver S. and Jennie R.)

Siska, Nancy P.: corp. vice president human resources, Cargill Inc.

Sitler, Michele: secretary, Wiremold Foundation

Sitnick, Irving: president, director, Moses Fund, Inc. (Henry and Lucy)

Sittenfeld, Paul George: secretary, trustee, Peterloon Foundation

Sittinger, Tammy: coord, Square D Foundation

Sivertsen, Robert J.: vice president, director, Weyerhaeuser Memorial Foundation (Charles A.)

Six, Julie G.: treasurer, Greenfield Foundation (Albert M.)

Skaalrud, Nancy: secretary, Graco Foundation

Skaggs, Mary C.: president, director, Skaggs Foundation (L. J. Skaggs and Mary C.)

Skelton, Anne: trustee, Reliable Life Insurance Co. Foundation

Skena, Robert: treasurer, Mellon Financial Corp. Foundation

Skidmore, Brenda L.: trustee, Chesapeake Corp. Foundation; president, Suntrust Foundation - Agency

Skilling, Raymond Inwood: executive vice president, chief counsel, director, Aon Corp.; director, Aon Foundation

Skinner, Frank: director, vice president, Reynolds Foundation (R. J.)

Skinner, William L.: secretary, director, Ball Brothers Foundation

Skirvin, Michael: vice president, TJX Foundation, Inc.

Sklar, Eric: treasurer, director, Arca Foundation

Skott, Allen: director, American Optical Foundation

Skule, John L., III: senior vice president environment affairs, Bristol-Myers Squibb Co.; director, Bristol-Myers Squibb Foundation Inc.

Skulsky, Craig S.: treasurer, Newman Family Foundation

Slamar, Charles, Jr.: trustee, Mellinger Educational Foundation (Edward Arthur)

Slater, Robert E.: trustee, Reynolds Foundation (Donald W.)

Slaughter, Harriet: trustee, Wildermuth Foundation (E. F.)

Slaughter, Ken: chief financial officer, Gazette Co.; vice president, secretary, treasurer, director, Gazette Foundation

Slaymaker, Eugene W.: president, trustee, Baughman Foundation

Slesh, Cristin: program officer, Bruening Foundation (Eva L. and Joseph M.)

Slesin, Louis E.: director, Rubinstein Foundation (Helena)

Slesin, Suzanne: director, Rubinstein Foundation (Helena)

Slifka, Marlee: trustee, Lunda Charitable Trust

Sligar, James S.: trustee, LSR Fund

Slizewski, Beatrice B.: vice president corporate communications, Birds Eye Foods Inc.

Sloan, Barbara: president, secretary, treasurer, trustee, Scaife Family Foundation

Sloan, Sue: senior program officer, PPG Industries Foundation

Sloane, Ann Brownell: assistant treasurer, Rosenthal Foundation (Ida and William)

Sloane, Howard Grant: chairman, trustee, Heckscher Foundation for Children

Sloane, Virginia: president, trustee, Heckscher Foundation for Children

Slomka, Stella Louise: trustee, Retirement Research Foundation

Slosburg, Stanley J.: trust, Livingston Foundation (Milton S. and Corinne N.)

Sloss, Deborah: secretary, Fleishhacker Foundation

Sloss, Hillary: director, Fleishhacker Foundation

Sloss, Laura: director, Fleishhacker Foundation

Slusark, Arthur J.: secretary, foundation manager, Meredith Corp. Foundation

Slutzky, Paul: director, Bank of Greene County Charitable Foundation

Sly, Helen S.: director, Sunnen Foundation

Smadbeck, Arthur J.: trustee, Heckscher Foundation for Children

Smadbeck, Louis, Jr.: trustee, Heckscher Foundation for Children

Smadbeck, Mina: trustee, Heckscher Foundation for Children

Smadbeck, Paul: vice president, trustee, Heckscher Foundation for Children

Smaldone, Laurie, MD: director, Bristol-Myers Squibb Foundation Inc.

Small, Malinda B.: director national-state affairs & corporate contributions, Constellation Energy Group Inc.

Smallenberger, James: secretary, AmerUs Group Charitable Foundation

Smallwood, Thomas L.: secretary, director, Bradley Foundation (Lynde and Harry); trustee, Helfaer Foundation (Evan and Marion)

Smarr, Karen J.: secretary, treasurer, director, Bourns Foundation

Smart, Mary: secretary, Smart Family Foundation

Smith, Alexander Wyly, Jr.: trustee, member executive committee, Franklin Foundation Inc. (John and Mary)

Smith, Alice: trustee, Lyndhurst Foundation

Smith, Allen C.: trustee, Hilliard Foundation

Smith, Alson H., Jr.: sr vice president, director, Virginia Environmental Endowment

Smith, Arthur O.: president, Smith Foundation, Inc. (A.O.)

Smith, Benjamin M., Jr.: treasurer, Washington Forrest Foundation

Smith, Bill: chief executive officer, City National Bank & Trust Co.

Smith, Bob: director, Bradley Foundation (Lynde and Harry)

Smith, Bradford K.: vice president peace & social justice, Ford Foundation; director, Noble Foundation, Inc. (Edward John)

Smith, Brenda J.: trustee, El Pomar Foundation

Smith, Brian J.: secretary, Abbott Laboratories Fund

Smith, Cecil O.: director, Tri-County Telephone Foundation

Smith, Charles W.: secretary, executive director, director, Hoag Family Foundation (George); trustee, Sargent Foundation (Newell B.)

Smith, Cherida C.: vice president, trustee, Collins Foundation

Smith, Clark C.: director, El Paso Corporate Foundation

Smith, D. Gates: trustee, Ohio National Foundation

Smith, D. J.: vice president, secretary, Archer-Daniels-Midland Foundation

Smith, D. Scarborough, III: director, SMBC Global Foundation, Inc.; joint general manager, Sumitomo Mitsui Banking Corp.

Smith, David A.: director, Kline Foundation (Josiah W. and Bessie H.)

Smith, David Byron, Jr.: consultant, director, Wausau-Mosinee Paper Corp.

Smith, David L.: executive director, trustee, Abell-Hanger Foundation

Smith, David S., Jr.: director, Noble Foundation, Inc. (Edward John)

Smith, Donald E.: president, Rupp Foundation (Fran and Warren)

Smith, Eaton: director, King Foundation (Kenneth Kendal)

Smith, Ervie L.: executive director, Valley Foundation

Smith, Frank K.: vice president, director, Smith Charitable Foundation (Arlene H.)

Smith, Fred W.: chairman, trustee, Reynolds Foundation (Donald W.)

Smith, Gavin H.: president, director, Burlington Resources Foundation

Smith, Gerald C.: manager, director, Redfield Foundation (Nell J.)

Smith, Gerald J.: program officer, Moody Foundation

Smith, H. I.: treasurer, director, Starr Foundation

Smith, H. Warren: vice president, Fehsenfeld Charitable Foundation (Frank B. and Virginia V.)

Smith, Harold Byron, Jr.: president, Illinois Tool Works Foundation

Smith, J. Burleson: director, Piper Foundation (Minnie Stevens)

Smith, J. Kay: vice president, Corp. Communications/Public Policy, Ameren Corp.

Smith, Jack: director, Lytel Foundation (Bertha Russ)

Smith, Jack A.: senior vice president, Reader's Digest Association Inc.

Smith, James Allen: director, Clark Foundation (Robert Sterling)

Smith, James C.: trustee, Slemp Foundation

Smith, James S.: president, treasurer, Frese Foundation (Arnold D.)

Smith, Jeanne H.: adv comm mem, Inasmuch Foundation

Smith, Jefferson V., III: director, secretary, Smith Charities (John)

Smith, Jeremy T.: director, Noble Foundation, Inc. (Edward John)

Smith, Jonathan, OD: trustee, Reynolds Foundation (Donald W.)

Smith, Joseph A.: manager, executive director, Employers Mutual Charitable Foundation

Smith, Julious P., Jr.: counsel, Flagler Foundation

Smith, Kim: director, Menasha Corp. Foundation

Smith, L. Edwin: treasurer, director, Jones Foundation (Helen)

Smith, Langhorne B.: treasurer, director, Claneil Foundation

Smith, Laura: trustee, Frese Foundation (Arnold D.)

Smith, Lee M.: director, MONY Foundation

Smith, Lewis W.: director, Morgan Foundation (Louie R. and Gertrude)

Smith, Lunsford Richardson: trustee, Hillsdale Fund

Smith, Lydia B.: director, Menasha Corp. Foundation

Smith, M. Munson: trustee, secretary, Johnson Foundation (M. G. and Lillie A.)

Smith, Margaret: director, Heath Foundation (Ed and Mary)

Smith, Maria Emma: executive assistant, Crown Memorial (Arie and Ida)

Smith, Maribeth: director, Noble Foundation, Inc. (Edward John)

Smith, Mark C.: president, Ontario Corp. Foundation

Smith, Marschall I.: vice president, secretary, director, Brunswick Foundation

Smith, Martin C.: director, Bank of Greene County Charitable Foundation

Smith, Mary Mills Abel: trustee, duPont Foundation (Chichester)

Smith, Mary Welles Mooers: vice president, trustee, Hilliard Foundation

Smith, Melinda Hoag: president, chief executive officer, director, Hoag Family Foundation (George)

Smith, Michael J.: assistant vice president investments, Mott Foundation (Charles Stewart)

Smith, Michael L.: director, Anthem Foundation, Inc.; executive vice president, chief financial officer, Anthem Inc.

Smith, Mickie Beth: director, Aldridge Charitable and Educational Trust (Tom S. and Marye Kate)

Smith, Molly R.: trustee, Hillsdale Fund

Smith, Nancey E.: trustee, Slemp Foundation

Smith, Nancy DuVergne: treasurer, trustee, Levy Foundation (June Rockwell)

Smith, Nancy R.: vice president, Smith Foundation (William R. and Sara Babb)

Smith, Nancy Z.: vice president, Sumitomo Mitsui Banking Corp.

Smith, Neil T.: trustee, Smith Foundation (Ralph L.)

Smith, Norman J.: president, Ford Family Foundation

Smith, Olcott D.: hon trustee, Hartford Courant Foundation

Smith, Oliver C.: chairman, director, Menasha Corp. Foundation

Smith, Orville D.: trustee, McMahon Foundation

Smith, Pamela Klipstein: vice president, Klipstein Foundation (Ernest Christian)

Smith, Philip J.: director, Shubert Foundation

Smith, Phyllis W.: trustee, Masland Trust No. 2 (Maurice H.)

Smith, Ralph L., Jr.: director, Smith Foundation (Ralph L.)

Smith, Raymond W.: trustee, Carnegie Corp. of New York

Smith, Richard G., III: trustee, Hillsdale Fund

Smith, Richard M.: trustee, Pinkerton Foundation

Smith, Robert A.: trustee, Smith Family Foundation (Richard and Susan)

Smith, Robert A., III: director, Doheny Foundation Trust (Carrie Estelle)

Smith, S. Garry: executive director, Daniel Foundation of Alabama

Smith, S. Kennard: director, Intermountain Gas Industries Foundation

Smith, S. Kinnie, Jr.: director, Consumers Energy Foundation

Smith, Scott C.: chairman, director, Chicago Tribune Foundation

Smith, Stephen Byron: director, Illinois Tool Works Foundation

Smith, Stephen J.: secretary, Christensen Charitable and Religious Foundation (L. C.)

Smith, Steve C.: trustee, McBeath Foundation (Faye)

Smith, Susan F.: trustee, Smith Family Foundation (Richard and Susan)

Smith, Theodore M.: executive director, Kendall Foundation (Henry P.)

Smith, Timothy S.: secretary, treasurer, Rupp Foundation (Fran and Warren)

Smith, Tracy D.: trustee, Michael Foundation (Herbert I. and Elsa B.)

Smith, Van P.: chairman, Ontario Corp.

Smith, W. Keith: chairman, Dreyfus Corp.

Smith, W. R.: director, Heath Foundation (Ed and Mary)

Smith, W. Thomas: vice president, treasurer, Smith Charities (John)

Smith, Walt: treasurer, Glaser Foundation

Smith, Wes: trustee, Reynolds Foundation (Donald W.)

Smith, William Kennedy: trustee, Kennedy, Jr. Foundation (Joseph P.)

Smith, William Mason, III: president, Prouty Foundation (Olive Higgins)

Smith, William N.: president, trustee, City National Bank Foundation; president, chief executive officer, director, City National Bank & Trust Co.

Smith, William R.: chairman, Smith Foundation (William R. and Sara Babb)

Smith Campbell, Barbara: trustee, Reynolds Foundation (Donald W.)

Smith Magness, Debby: trustee, Reynolds Foundation (Donald W.)

Smitson, Robert M.: director, Ball Foundation (George and Frances)

Smoley, Sandra R., RN: director, Sierra Health Foundation

Smoot, J. Thomas, Jr.: trustee, Edison Fund (Charles)

Smyth, Geralynn D.: member, Knott Foundation (Marion I. and Henry J.)

Smyth, John C.: president, Knott Foundation (Marion I. and Henry J.)

Smyth, Maureen H.: vice president programs, Mott Foundation (Charles Stewart)

Smyth, Patricia K.: member, Knott Foundation (Marion I. and Henry J.)

Snider, Richard C.: secretary, director, Rudin Foundation

Snider, Timothy R.: senior vice president, Phelps Dodge Corp.; member, Phelps Dodge Foundation

Snow, David H.: president, Snow Foundation (John Ben)

Snow, Jonathan L.: vice president, treasurer, Snow Foundation (John Ben); trustee, Snow Memorial Trust (John Ben)

Snow, Ronald: trustee, Jameson Trust (Oleonda)

Snyder, Abram M.: vice president, Plankenhorn Foundation (Harry)

Snyder, Audrey: executive director, trustee, Snyder Foundation (Harold B. and Dorothy A.)

Snyder, Donna D.: secretary, Carlson Family Foundation (Curtis L.)

Snyder, Leonard N.: trustee, Grundy Foundation

Snyder, Molly Sue: trustee, Braemar Charitable Trust

Snyder, Patricia: admin, Graham Foundation for Advanced Studies in the Fine Arts

Snyder, Patricia S.: vice president, Snyder Foundation (William I. and Patricia S.)

Snyder, Phyllis Johnson: trustee, Snyder Foundation (Harold B. and Dorothy A.)

Snyder, Robert E.: secretary, treasurer, Byrne Foundation

Snyder, William I.: president, Snyder Foundation (William I. and Patricia S.)

Sobol, Thomas: director, Pforzheimer Foundation, Inc. (The Carl and Lily)

Soboroff, Steven L.: director, Weingart Foundation

Socolow, Daniel J.: director fellows program, MacArthur Foundation (John D. and Catherine T.)

Soda, Hiroshi: president, American Honda Foundation

Soderberg, Elsa A.: treasurer, Allyn Foundation

Soderberg, Jon: director, Allyn Foundation

Soderberg, Libby: director, Allyn Foundation

Soderberg, Peer: director, Allyn Foundation

Soderberg, Peter: director, Allyn Foundation

Sohn, Catherine A.: director, GlaxoSmithKline Foundation

Soiefer, Ronald M.: secretary, director, Unilever United States Foundation

Solana, Nancy J.: vice president, secretary, Fikes Foundation (Leland)

Solano, Patrick J.: director, Sordoni Foundation

Sollins, Karen R.: chairman, director, Scherman Foundation

Solomon, Daniel: president, Cohen Foundation (Naomi and Nehemiah)

Solomon, David: director, Cohen Foundation (Naomi and Nehemiah)

Solomon, Milton D.: vice president, secretary, trustee, Bydale Foundation

Solomon, Peter J.: director, Littauer Foundation (Lucius N.)

Solomon, Richard: director, Graham Foundation for Advanced Studies in the Fine Arts

Solomon, William Tarver: director, Hoblitzelle Foundation

Solow, Sheldon Henry: don, president, Solow Foundation

Solso, Theodore Matthew: chairman, chief executive officer, director, Cummins Inc.

Solso, Tim: chairman, Cummins Foundation

Soltz, Judith: executive vice president, CIGNA Corp.; chairman, director, CIGNA Foundation

Somerhalder, John W., II: director, El Paso Corporate Foundation; president, El Paso Pipeline Group, El Paso Corp.

Somerville, Ron: treasurer, Jostens Foundation Inc. (The)

Someya, Mitsuo: director, Kikkoman Foundation

Sommer, Melanie S.: assistant secretary, Fidelity Foundation

Somnolet, Michel: chief operating officer, director, executive, vice president, L'Oreal U.S.A.

Sondheim, Walter, Jr.: trustee, Abell Foundation; governor, Baker, Jr. Memorial Fund (William G.)

Sordoni, Andrew John, III: chairman, secretary, Sordoni Foundation

Sordoni, Margaret: director, Sordoni Foundation

Sordoni, Susan F.: director, Sordoni Foundation

Sordoni, William B.: president, treasurer, Sordoni Foundation

Sorensen, J. William: trustee, Boettcher Foundation

Sorenson, John: chief financial officer, Saint Francis Bank

Sosland, Morton Irvin: director, Hall Family Foundation (The)

Soulliere, Anne-Marie: director, Fidelity Foundation; foundation director, Johnson Fund (Edward C.)

Soupata, Lea: chairman, trustee, UPS Foundation

Southworth, Louis Sweetland, II: assistant secretary-treasurer, Clay Foundation

Souyoultzis, M. J.: trustee, Long Foundation (J. M.)

Souza, Tracy H.: president, Cummins Foundation

Sovern, Michael Ira: director, president, Shubert Foundation

Sowell, Sam C.: board of directors, Ottenheimer Brothers Foundation

Sowell, Shaunna: director, Texas Instruments Foundation

Sowers, Frances: associate director, McCune Charitable Foundation (Marshall L. and Perrine D.)

Spacinsky, Charlotte: director, Koch Foundation, Inc.

Spaeth, Karl Henry: chairman, trustee, Quaker Chemical Foundation

Spalding, Charles C.: vice president, trustee, Cooke Foundation

Spalding, Oliver A.: trustee, Winthrop Trust (Clara B.)

Spalding, Philip F.: vice president, Lux Foundation (Miranda)

Spanier, David B.: president, McGonagle Foundation (Dextra Baldwin)

Spanier, Helen G.: vice president, McGonagle Foundation (Dextra Baldwin)

Spanier, Jonathan: president, chief executive officer, McGonagle Foundation (Dextra Baldwin)

Spanier, Maury L.: chairman, McGonagle Foundation (Dextra Baldwin)

Sparber, Norman H.: director, Goldman Foundation (Herman)

Sparber, Roy M.: director, Goldman Foundation (Herman)

Sparling, Alfred H., Jr.: director, Hopedale Foundation

Spartin, David W.: vice chairman, MBNA Corp.; trustee, The MBNA Foundation

Spaulding, Jean G., MD: trustee, Duke Endowment

Spears, Arthur C.: executive vice president, East Cambridge Savings Charitable Foundation

Speedie, David C., III: director Islam Project, Carnegie Corp. of New York

Speer, Katie: trustee, Sturgis Charitable and Educational Trust (AR) (Roy and Christine)

Spence, Joseph T.: member, Campbell Foundation (J. Bulow)

Spencer, Clayton B.: director, Seherr-Thoss Foundation

Spencer, John R., MD: director, Oleson Foundation

Spencer, Steve R.: director, Alabama Power Foundation

Spencer, William M., III: member advisory committee, Meyer Foundation (Robert R.)

Spendiff, James A.: president, chief operating officer, director, Standard Steel

Sperandio, Elizabeth F.: trustee, Sperandio Family Foundation

Sperandio, Jacqueline: vice president, Sperandio Family Foundation

Sperandio, Mark C.: trustee, Sperandio Family Foundation

Sperandio, Robert B.: president, secretary, Sperandio Family Foundation

Spetnagel, Thomas M.: trustee, Massie Trust (David Meade)

Speyer, Darthea: trustee, Speyer Foundation (Alexander C. and Tillie S.)

Speyer, Jerry I.: director, Newman Assistance Fund (Jerome A. and Estelle R.)

Spiegel, Debra J.: adv, Patron Saints Foundation

Spika, Nicholas C.: secretary, Forest Foundation

Spina, David Anthony: chairman, chief executive officer, State Street Corp.

Spindler, Susan A.: treasurer, Anschutz Family Foundation

Spink, William G.: secretary, Johns Manville Fund

Spraberry, Richard: vice president, trustee, Doss Foundation, Inc. (M. S.)

Sprague, Laurie Morse: assistant treasurer, Ratshesky Foundation (A. C.)

Sprain, Robert H., Jr.: vice president, secretary, Bruno Charitable Foundation (Joseph S.)

Sprain, Theresa: director, Bruno Charitable Foundation (Joseph S.)

Spratt, Anne D.: secretary, director, Bloedorn Foundation (Walter A.)

Sprenger, Paul: member, Lang Foundation (Eugene M.)

Spreyer, Kurt: trustee, Miller Foundation (Steve J.)

Spriggs, Ray: director, Grinnell Mutual Group Foundation

Springer, Anne B.: member distribution committee, Bruening Foundation (Eva L. and Joseph M.)

Springer, Eric W.: trustee, Falk Fund (Maurice)

Springer, Michael W.: board of governors, Fondren Foundation

Springfield, James Francis: trustee, Plough Foundation

Sproule, Michael E.: chief financial officer, director, Amerus Group Co.

Sprow, F. B.: trustee, Exxon Mobil Foundation; vice president, safety, health & environment, ExxonMobil Corp.

Spurgeon, Carol: assoc director, Borchard Foundation (Albert and Elaine)

Spurgeon, Edward Dutcher: president, director, Borchard Foundation (Albert and Elaine)

Squillace, Scott E.: director, Cabot Corp. Foundation

St. Clair, Margaret N.: co-managing trustee, Peabody Foundation (Amelia)

Staats, Elmer Boyd: trustee, Kerr Foundation, Inc.

Stabler, Andrew: adv comm, Lamco Foundation

Stabler, Lem C., Jr.: trustee, Shook Foundation (Barbara Ingalls)

Stabler, W. Laird, III: treasurer, trustee, Welfare Foundation

Stabler, W. Laird, Jr.: trustee, Welfare Foundation

Stack, Edward William: director, Clark Foundation (NY)

Stack, Richard L.: trustee, Darling Foundation (Hugh and Hazel)

Stackpole, Harrison Clinton: honorary trustee, Stackpole-Hall Foundation

Stackpole, R. Dauer: trustee, Stackpole-Hall Foundation

Stackpole, Sara-Jane: trustee, Stackpole-Hall Foundation

Stackpole, Scott: trustee, Stackpole-Hall Foundation

Staehle, William L.: trustee, Anderson Foundation (John W.)

Staff, Joel V.: chairman, Reliant Resources Foundation

Staffieri, Victor A.: president, director, LG&E Energy Foundation

Stafford, William, II: secretary, Hunnicutt Foundation (H. P. and Anne S.)

Stafford, William P.: president, Hunnicutt Foundation (H. P. and Anne S.)

Staheli, Donald L.: chairman, director, ContiGroup Companies Inc.

Stahr, Don: trustee, Hansen Foundation (Dane G.)

Stajduhar, Michael W.: mem, One Valley Bank Foundation; senior vice president, One Valley Bank N.A.

Staley, Robert A.: director, Dime Savings Bank of Norwich Foundation

Staley, Walter G., Jr.: secretary, treasurer, director, Green Foundation (Allen P. and Josephine B.)

Staley, Warren R.: president, Cargill Foundation; chairman, chief executive officer, Cargill Inc.

Stam, David Harry: trustee, Delmas Foundation (Gladys Krieble)

Stamm, Doug: executive director, Meyer Memorial Trust

Stamy, Lloyd F., Jr.: treasurer, Pittsburgh Child Guidance Foundation

Stamy, Mary Margaret: trustee, Pittsburgh Child Guidance Foundation

Stancaxi, Joe: secretary, director, Dana Corp. Foundation

Standish, William L.: member, Staunton Farm Foundation

Stanger, James: chief financial officer, Essick Foundation

Stanley, Brian C.: officer, Valmont Foundation

Stanley, Edmund Allport, Jr.: trustee, Bowne Foundation (Robert)

Stanley, Jennifer: chairman, president, trustee, Bowne Foundation (Robert)

Stanley, Kelly N.: president, chief executive officer, Ontario Corp.; vice president, Ontario Corp. Foundation

Stanley, Larry W.: treasurer, Lowe's Charitable and Educational Foundation

Stans, Steven H.: president, Stans Foundation

Stans, Theodore M.: executive vice president, treasurer, Stans Foundation

Stanton, Anne B.: program director youth, Irvine Foundation (The James)

Stapleton, Katharine H.: trustee, Fishback Foundation Trust (Harmes C.)

Stark, Jay V.: trustee, Kunkel Foundation (John Crain)

Stark, John K.: trustee, Kunkel Foundation (John Crain)

Stark, K. R.: trustee, Kunkel Foundation (John Crain)

Stark, Kenneth J.: treasurer, Joy Global Foundation, Inc.

Stark, Nelda Childers: chairman, Stark Foundation (Nelda C. and H. J. Lutcher)

Starkey, Cathy A.: administration assistant, Bruening Foundation (Eva L. and Joseph M.)

Starkey, Joseph P.: president, Schering-Plough Foundation

Starkins, Clifford E.: director, Cheever Porter Foundation (Mrs.)

Starner, Lloyd: treasurer, Benenson Foundation (Frances and Benjamin)

Starr, Karen: senior program officer, Bremer Foundation (Otto)

Starr, Sally: clerk, Hamilton Charitable Corp.

Staszak, Thomas A.: contr, assistant treasurer, Regenstein Foundation

Stauffer, John H.: trustee, Stauffer Communications Foundation

Stavro, William: treasurer, Mattel Foundation

Stavropoulos, William S.: trustee, Gerstacker Foundation (Rollin M.)

Stawarz, Raymond R.: chief financial officer, Federated Mutual Insurance Co.; treasurer, Federated Mutual Insurance Foundation

Steadman, Michael W.: assistant vice president, Kilworth Charitable Trust (Florence B.)

Stearns, Kathy: trustee, Millipore Foundation (The)

Stearns, Nancy: secretary, Plankenhorn Foundation (Harry)

Stearns, Roger R.: president, secretary, Stearns Foundation

Stecher, Frederick William: director, Beveridge Foundation, Inc. (Frank Stanley)

Stecher, Patsy Palmer: director, Beveridge Foundation, Inc. (Frank Stanley)

Stedman, Betty Ann West: trustee, West Foundation (Neva and Wesley)

Stedman, Stuart West: trustee, West Foundation (Neva and Wesley)

Steeger, Dean H.: secretary, trustee, Hayden Foundation (Charles)

Steel, Corrine: secretary, Bay Foundation; director, Paul and C. Michael Paul Foundation (Josephine Bay)

Steel, John: trustee, Warner Fund (Albert and Bessie)

Steel, Kitty: trustee, Warner Fund (Albert and Bessie)

Steel, Lewis M.: trustee, Warner Fund (Albert and Bessie)

Steel, Ruth M.: trustee, Warner Fund (Albert and Bessie)

Steele, Finley M.: trustee, Hilliard Foundation

Steele, George: vice president, Marshall Foundation

Steele, James M.: committee member, Eccles Foundation (Marriner S.)

Steele, Lela Emery: president, treasurer, trustee, Peterloon Foundation

Steele, Susan J.: executive director, Buell Foundation (Temple Hoyne)

Steele, William G., Jr.: senior trustee, Bean Foundation (Norwin S. and Elizabeth N.)

Steele Hoyt, Elizabeth: trustee, Peterloon Foundation

Stefano, Steven: director, GlaxoSmithKline Foundation

Steffen, Phyllis: director, Grinnell Mutual Group Foundation

Steffens, Marian I.: secretary, Robinson Fund (Maurice R.)

Steffens, Roger S., Jr.: treasurer, Georgia Power Foundation

Steffes, Don C.: president, Mingenback Foundation (Julia J.)

Stehling, James: director, Peterson Foundation (Hal and Charlie)

Steiger, Albert E., III: director, Steiger Memorial Fund (Albert)

Steiger, Albert E., Jr.: president, Steiger Memorial Fund (Albert)

Steiger, Allen: treasurer, Steiger Memorial Fund (Albert)

Steiger, Philip C., II: director, Steiger Memorial Fund (Albert)

Steiger, Ralph A., II: director, Steiger Memorial Fund (Albert)

Stein, Christine D.: program director, Price Associates Foundation (T. Rowe)

Stein, Malcolm L.: director, Noble Foundation, Inc. (Edward John)

Stein, Mary Ann Efroymson: president, Moriah Fund, Inc.

Steinberg, Robert A.: trustee, Gordon Charitable Trust (Peggy and Yale)

Steinbright, Marilyn L.: president, Arcadia Foundation

Steiner, Gerald A.: director, Monsanto Fund

Steinhafel, Gregg W.: president, Target Stores, Target Corp.; president, trustee, Target Foundation

Steinhauer, Bruce W., MD: trustee, vice chairman, McGregor Fund

Steinhause, Mitchell: vice president, director, New York Mercantile Exchange Charitable Foundation

Steinkraus, Eric M.: director, Ziegler Foundation for the Blind (E. Matilda)

Steinkraus, Helen Ziegler: secretary, director, Ziegler Foundation for the Blind (E. Matilda)

Steinkraus, Philip C.: director, Ziegler Foundation for the Blind (E. Matilda)

Steinman, Beverly R.: vchairman, Steinman Foundation (James Hale)

Steinman, Jeffrey: executive vice president, director, Rudin Foundation

Steinschneider, Jean M.: director, Huisking Foundation

Stekas, Lynn: president, MONY Foundation

Stemmons, Jean H.: vice president, Stemmons Foundation

Stemple, Ernest Edward: director, Starr Foundation

Stender, Bruce W.: trustee, Blandin Foundation

Stepanian, Tania W.: chairperson, Crocker Trust (Mary A.)

Stephanoff, Kathryn A.: chairwoman, Trexler Trust (Harry C.)

Stephans, William W. T.: chief financial officer, Scott Fetzer Co.; vice president, treasurer, Scott & Fetzer Foundation

Stephens, Alice: trustee, McKinney Charitable Trust (Carl and Alleen)

Stephens, Christopher H.: secretary, director, Backus Foundation (Beatrice and Roy)

Stephens, Elton Bryson: founder, chairman, Ebsco Industries Inc.

Stephens, Gene: member, Bridgestone/Firestone Trust Fund (The)

Stephens, Inge T.: treasurer, president, Backus Foundation (Beatrice and Roy)

Stephens, James T.: president, director, Ebsco Industries Inc.

Stephens, Robert: trustee, Packard Foundation (David and Lucile)

Stephenson, John W.: executive director, Campbell Foundation (J. Bulow)

Stephenson, Randall: director, SBC Foundation

Sterba, Jeffry: chairman, president, chief executive officer, PNM Resources Inc.

Sterling, Helen N.: trustee emerita, Rockwell Fund, Inc.

Stern, Henry: vice president, secretary, Lowe Foundation (Joe and Emily)

Stern, William: vice president, director, Atran Foundation, Inc.

Sternberg, Sy: chairman, director, New York Life Foundation; chairman, president, chief executive officer, New York Life Insurance Co.

Sternheim, Marci B.: executive director, Dibner Fund

Stettinius, Wallace: vice president, trustee, Gray Foundation (Garland and Agnes Taylor)

Steuart, Guy T., II: director, Cafritz Foundation (Morris and Gwendolyn)

Steuert, D. Michael: senior vice president, chief financial officer, Fluor Corp.; trustee, Fluor Foundation

Stevens, E. W. Dann: trustee, Viyu Foundation

Stevens, Gregory W.: vice president, treasurer, Phelps Dodge Corp.; treasurer, vice president, Phelps Dodge Foundation

Stevens, James P.: treasurer, trustee, Swisher Foundation (Carl S.)

Stevens, James W.: treasurer, trustee, Dodge Foundation (Geraldine R.)

Stevens, Lorne G.: director, La-Z-Boy Inc.

Stevens, M. A.: trustee, Fluor Foundation

Stevens, Robert L.: chairman, president, chief executive officer, Bryn Mawr Bank Corp.

Stevens, Rowland: trustee, Chapman Charitable Corp. (Howard and Bess)

Stevens, Tamara T.: director, High Meadow Foundation

Stevenson, Ruth Carter: president, director, donor daughter, Carter Foundation (Amon G.)

Steward, Larry E.: director, DTE Energy Foundation

Stewart, Alan M.: executive director, Cullen Foundation (The)

Stewart, Cynthia: secretary, Texas Instruments Foundation

Stewart, Donald M.: director, New York Times Co. Foundation

Stewart, Jerry L.: director, Alabama Power Foundation

Stewart, Marise M.M.: trustee, Mott Foundation (Charles Stewart)

Stewart, Stacey Davis: president, chief executive officer, director, Fannie Mae Foundation

Steyer, Hume R.: trustee, Sharon Steel Foundation

Stickels, Eric E.: treasurer, secretary, Oneida Savings Bank Charitable Foundation

Stieg, Elizabeth A.: executive director, Carls Foundation

Stieg, Harold E.: trustee, Carls Foundation

Stiles, Robert: director, Bausch & Lomb Foundation, Inc.

Stimpel, Richard J.: director, McConnell Foundation

Stine, Lynn B.: vice president, director, Bere Foundation

Stinnett, J. Daniel: secretary, Commerce Bancshares Foundation

Stinson, Kenneth E.: member contributions committee, Kiewit Companies Foundation; chairman, chief executive officer, director, Kiewit Sons' Inc. (Peter)

Stirn, Cara S.: co-chairman, trustee, Smith Foundation (Kelvin and Eleanor)

Stivers, William Charles: executive vice president, chief financial officer, Weyerhaeuser Co.; treasurer, trustee, Weyerhaeuser Co. Foundation

Stock, John P.: director, Valley Foundation (Wayne and Gladys)

Stocker, Beth K.: president, Stocker Foundation

Stockly, Doris Silliman: director, Borkee-Hagley Foundation

Stockman, Hervey S.: president, Stockman Family Foundation Trust

Stockman, Hervey S., Jr.: vice president, Stockman Family Foundation Trust

Stockman, Sarah A.: chairman, secretary, Stockman Family Foundation Trust

Stockwell, Lance: trustee, Bovaird Foundation (Mervin)

Stoddard, James A.: executive director, Hubbard Foundation (R. D. and Joan Dale)

Stoel, Thomas B.: trustee, Tucker Charitable Trust (Rose E.); trustee emeritus, Wessinger Foundation

Stoga, Alan: director, Tinker Foundation

Stokes, Jerome W. D.: director, Public Welfare Foundation

Stokes, Patrick T.: president, chief executive officer, director, Anheuser-Busch Companies Inc.

Stokes, Samuel N.: vice president, director, Marpat Foundation

Stokes, Spencer: president, Winthrop

Stokes, Thomas C.: trustee, treasurer, Gates Family Foundation

Stokesbary, Terry: program director, Murdock Charitable Trust (M. J.)

Stone, Anne L.: vice president, Rollins-Luetkemeyer Foundation

Stone, Charles Lynn, Jr.: president, trustee, Stone Foundation

Stone, Edward Carroll, Jr.: director, chairman science engineering liberal arts committee, Keck Foundation (W. M.)

Stone, Edward Eldredge: vice president, trustee, Stone Foundation

Stone, Holly: vice president, director, Gudelsky Family Foundation (Homer and Martha)

Stone, James D.: director, Rollins-Luetkemeyer Foundation

Stone, Larry D.: chairman, Lowe's Charitable and Educational Foundation

Stone, Robert A.: admin, Peters Foundation (Charles F.)

Stone, Robert G.: director, Exchange Bank Foundation

Stone, Roger David: director, Erpf Fund (Armand G.)

Stoneman, Susan K.: director, Widgeon Foundation

Stonesifer, Patty: co-chairman, president, Gates Foundation (Bill and Melinda)

Stookey, John Hoyt: director, Clark Foundation (NY)

Stookey, Katherine Emory: trustee, Sasco Foundation

Stopher, Joseph E.: president, trustee, Gheens Foundation

Storch, Gerald L.: vice chairman, Target Corp.; trustee, Target Foundation

Storey, Charles Porter: trustee, Hillcrest Foundation

Storey, Robert Davis: trustee, Gund Foundation (George)

Storr, Robert: director, Warhol Foundation for the Visual Arts (The Andy)

Stotsenberg, Henry: president, director, Pickford Foundation (Mary)

Stottlemyer, Charles E.: chairman, mem admin comm, Selby and Marie Selby Foundation (William G.)

Stout, David M.: chairman, director, GlaxoSmithKline Foundation

Stout, Jean C.: treasurer, director, Hugoton Foundation

Stout, Joan K.: president, managing director, Hugoton Foundation

Stout, Joan M.: secretary, director, Hugoton Foundation

Stout, John K.: director, Hugoton Foundation

Stout, Ray E., III: vice president, director, Hugoton Foundation

Stout, Richard M.: president, trustee, Stout Foundation (Charles H.)

Stout, William J.: assistant secretary, treasurer, Ayres Foundation

Stout Gilweit, Martha: trustee, vice president, Stout Foundation (Charles H.)

Stovall, David: director, Gulf Coast Medical Foundation

Stovall, Guy F., III: director, Gulf Coast Medical Foundation

Stracener, J. O.: director, Tractor & Equipment Co. Foundation

Strachan, Camille: trustee, German Protestant Orphan Asylum Association Foundation

Strait, Rex: director, Van Buren Foundation

Straitor, George A.: assistant treasurer, Ford Fund (Walter and Josephine)

Strake, George W., Jr.: director, Herzstein Charitable Foundation (Albert and Ethel)

Straker, John W., Jr.: secretary, Straker Charitable Foundation (J. William and Mary Helen)

Straker Henderson, Susan: president, treasurer, Straker Charitable Foundation (J. William and Mary Helen)

Stranahan, Duane, Jr.: trustee, Stranahan Foundation

Stranahan, Julie: trustee, Fruehauf Foundation

Stranahan, Mark: trustee, Stranahan Foundation

Stranahan, Stephen: trustee, Stranahan Foundation

Strand, Allan E.: president, Sullivan Foundation (Algernon Sydney)

Strassler, David H.: president, Barrington Foundation

Strassler, Robert B.: secretary, treasurer, Barrington Foundation

Straton, Suzanne J.: trustee, Perry Foundation

Strausburg, Virginia M.: executive director, Dayton Power and Light Co. Foundation

Strauss, Benjamin: trustee, Strauss Foundation

Strauss, Robert Perry: trustee, Strauss Foundation

Strauss, Sam B., Jr.: board director, Ottenheimer Brothers Foundation

Strecker, A. M.: executive vice president, chief operating officer, Oklahoma Gas & Electric Co. Foundation

Strecker, J. R.: vice president, director, Oklahoma Gas & Electric Co. Foundation

Streep, Mary B. Simon: director, Simon Foundation (William E.)

Street, Alice Ann: president, director, Bertha Foundation

Street, E. Bruce: director, Bertha Foundation

Street, James E.: director, Kinder Morgan Foundation

Street, Jerry O.: trustee, Halff Foundation (G. A. C.)

Street, Malcolm Boyd, Jr.: director, Bertha Foundation

Street, Stephanie H.: trustee, Halff Foundation (G. A. C.)

Streeter, Margaret B.: trustee, Anderson Foundation (NY)

Streeter, Stephanie A.: vice president, Banta Corp. Foundation

Streng, William Paul: secretary, treasurer, Lennox Foundation (Martha, David and Bagby)

Stresser, Chris: director, Norcross Wildlife Foundation

Stribling, Jera G.: executive director, Bruno Charitable Foundation (Joseph S.)

Strickland, Carol A.: chairman corporate contributions committee, U.S. Trust Corp. Foundation

Strickland, David J.: assistant secretary, Unilever United States Foundation

Strickland, Frances: director, Citizens Union Bank Foundation

Strickland, James T.: director, Stonecutter Foundation

Stringfellow, Ladson F.: trustee, Bell Foundation (S. Lewis and Lucia B.)

Strock, Faraday J.: trustee, Yost Trust (J. Paul)

Stroik, G. J.: assistant secretary, assistant treasurer, Federated Mutual Insurance Foundation

Strom, Lee D.: trustee, Crummer Foundation (Roy E.)

Stromberg, Burle U.: director, Portsmouth General Hospital Foundation

Stromberg, C. William: co-vice chairman, Stewart Educational Foundation (Donnell B. and Elizabeth Dee Shaw)

Stromberg, Jean G.: director, Hewlett Foundation (William and Flora)

Stromberg, Richard: director, Stewart Educational Foundation (Donnell B. and Elizabeth Dee Shaw)

Strong, Bente: director, Strong Foundation (Hattie M.)

Strong, Gregory S.: treasurer, Minnesota Mutual Foundation; vice president actuary, Minnesota Mutual Life Insurance Co.

Strong, Henry: chairman, president, officer, Strong Foundation (Hattie M.)

Strong, Henry L.: vice president, officer, Strong Foundation (Hattie M.)

Strong, John D., Jr.: trustee, Bernsen Foundation (Grace and Franklin)

Strother, Jack W., Jr.: co-trustee, Commercial Bank Foundation

Stroucken, Albert P. L.: director, Fuller Co. Foundation (H.B.); chairman, president, chief executive, Fuller Co. (H.B.)

Stroud, Robert R.: vice president, Cremer Foundation

Stroup, Colleen D.: director, Strake Foundation

Strovers, Clifford L.: vice president, director, Grinnell Mutual Group Foundation; director, Grinnell Mutual Reinsurance Co.

Strudwick, Barry: trustee, Warfield Memorial Fund (Anna Emory)

Strudwick, Lewis C.: trustee, Warfield Memorial Fund (Anna Emory)

Strum, Jeff D.: director, GlaxoSmithKline Foundation

Strumpf, Linda B.: vice president, chief investment officer, Ford Foundation

Strunk, Albert L., MD: trustee, member, Rippel Foundation (Fannie E.)

Stryker, Jon L.: trustee, Upjohn Foundation (Harold and Grace)

Stuart, Susan W.: director, Seneca Foods Foundation

Stubblefield, Joel R.: trustee, Reynolds Foundation (Donald W.)

Stubing, William C.: president, director, Greenwall Foundation

Stude, Herman L.: assistant secretary, Brown Foundation

Stude, Mike S.: vice president, trustee, Brown Foundation

Stuecker, Phillip James: vice president, chief financial officer, secretary, Thomas Foundation

Stuker, Robert: trustee, Chicago Title and Trust Co. Foundation

Stumpf, E. A., III: trustee, Wortham Foundation

Sturgeon, Barry M.: trustee, Davenport Trust Fund

Sturges, Caren: trustee, Ingalls Foundation (Louise H. and David S.)

Sturges, Carrie Trammell: board of governors, Fondren Foundation

Suarez, Rocio: executive director, Baker Trust (George F.)

Subotnick, Stuart: director, Shubert Foundation

Subourne, Mary Lee: trustee, Red Devil Foundation

Sudhoff, Robert J.: vice president financial, chief financial officer, Minster Machine Co.; vice president, secretary, Minster Machine Co. Foundation

Sugasawa, Kiyoshi: chief financial officer, Kajima International Inc.

Sugges, Elizabeth: student board mem, Marshall Foundation

Sullivan, Ann B.: executive secretary, AT&T Foundation

Sullivan, Austin Padraic, Jr.: secretary, General Mills Foundation

Sullivan, Barbara D., Esq.: president, Robinson Fund (Maurice R.)

Sullivan, D. Harold: fiscal officer, Demoulas Foundation

Sullivan, Dennis: assistant comptroller, Prudential Foundation

Sullivan, Elizabeth C.: vice president, program, Kresge Foundation

Sullivan, Frank P.: vice president sales & marketing, Square D Co.; vice president, director, Square D Foundation

Sullivan, G. Craig: chairman, Clorox Co.

Sullivan, John M.: assistant secretary, assistant treasurer, Cain Foundation (Gordon and Mary)

Sullivan, Kerry H.: trustee officer, director grant making, Balfour Foundation (L. G.); director grant making, Chase Charity Foundation (Alfred E.)

Sullivan, Kevin F.: vice president, PPG Industries Foundation

Sullivan, Laura P.: vice president, secretary, State Farm Companies Foundation; vice president, secretary, counsel, State Farm Mutual Automobile Insurance Co.

Sullivan, Peter B.: director, Sheldon Foundation Inc. (Ralph C.)

Sullivan, Richard J.: trustee, Fund for New Jersey

Sullivan, Susan A.: director strategic planning, Verizon Foundation

Sullivan, T. Dennis: treasurer, director, Greenwall Foundation

Sullivan, Timothy B.: chairperson, NMC Foundation

Sullivan, William J.: treasurer, director, Dell Foundation (Hazel)

Sullivan, Wilma J.: secretary, Dime Savings Bank of Norwich Foundation

Sulzberger, Arthur Ochs, Jr.: director, chairman, publisher, New York Times Co.

Sulzberger, Arthur Ochs, Sr.: vice president, secretary, Sulzberger Foundation

Sulzberger, Judith P., MD: vice president, director, Sulzberger Foundation

Sulzer, Joseph P.: trustee, Massie Trust (David Meade)

Sumida, Sheila M.: director, First Hawaiian Foundation

Summerall, Robert, Jr.: director, Morgan Foundation (Louie R. and Gertrude)

Summerfield, Esthel: secretary, Abell Foundation

Summers, Von: Manager of Philanthropy, Northwest Natural Gas Co.

Summerville, Frances M.: trustee, Slater Trust (Lillian M.)

Summey, Mark L.: director, Stonecutter Foundation

Sundberg, Greg: director, U.S. Bancorp Piper Jaffray Foundation

Sunderland, Charles T.: vice president, trustee, Sunderland Foundation

Sunderland, James P.: secretary, trustee, Sunderland Foundation

Sunderland, Kenton W.: president, trustee, Sunderland Foundation

Sunderland, Robert: vice president, trustee, Sunderland Foundation

Sunderland, W.: trustee, Sunderland Foundation

Sundram, Clarence J.: director, van Ameringen Foundation, Inc.

Sung, Patsy: co-trustee, Han Charitable Foundation (Edna and Yu-Shan)

Sung, Robert: co-trustee, Han Charitable Foundation (Edna and Yu-Shan)

Suomi, Marvin J.: secretary, Kajima Foundation

Surdam, Robert McCellan: trustee, Wilson Fund (Matilda R.)

Surma, John P., Jr.: trustee, U.S. Steel Foundation

Surrey, Mary P.: secretary, treasurer, director, Dreyfus Foundation, Inc. (Max and Victoria)

Surrey, Sara R.: vice president, director, Dreyfus Foundation, Inc. (Max and Victoria)

Suttles, William Maurrelle: trustee, Franklin Foundation Inc. (John and Mary)

Sutton, Donald C.: trustee, Van Wert County Foundation

Sutton, Howard: president, chief executive officer, Providence Journal Charitable Foundation; trustee, Steelcase Foundation

Sutton, Mark: trustee, Paine Webber Foundation

Sutton, Thomas C.: chairman, director, Pacific Life Foundation; chairman, chief executive officer, director, Pacific Life Insurance Co.

Swain, Kristin A.: president, Corning Inc. Foundation

Swan, Barbara J.: director, Alliant Energy Foundation, Inc.

Swan, Philip V.: vice president, treasurer, Peppers Foundation (Ann)

Swan, Richard W.: trustee, Hilliard Foundation

Swan, Robert C.: vice president, secretary, Phelps Dodge Corp.

Swander, Dan C.: president, director, International Multifoods Charitable Foundation; president, chief operating officer, International Multifoods Corp.

Swaney, Robert E., Jr.: vice president, chief investment officer, Mott Foundation (Charles Stewart)

Swann, Roy W.: trustee, Smith Foundation (William R. and Sara Babb)

Swanson, E. William: secretary, treasurer, director, Hale Foundation (Crescent Porter)

Swanson, Earl: director, member, Katzenberger Foundation

Swanson, Linda: treasurer, director, Gebbie Foundation

Swanson, Lynwood W.: trustee, Murdock Charitable Trust (M. J.)

Swanson, Marilyn: director, Kress Foundation (George)

Swanson, Terry: director, Kress Foundation (George)

Swanson, W. Charles: chief financial officer, Swanson Family Foundation, Inc. (Dr. W. C.)

Swartz, Mary Pat: director, McGowan Charitable Fund (William G.)

Swasey, Frederick W.: honorary trustee, Fuller Foundation (MA)

Sweasy, William J.: chief executive officer, Red Wing Shoe Co. Foundation

Sweat, Carol G.: vice president, Garvey Texas Foundation

Sweeney, G. T.: chairman, trustee, Credit Suisse First Boston Foundation Trust

Sweeney, Kevin M.: director, MassMutual Foundation for Hartford, Inc. (The)

Sweeney, Michael: secretary, Wilkof Foundation (Edward and Ruth)

Sweeney, Robert: president, director, King Foundation (Kenneth Kendal)

Sweeney, Thomas Joseph, Jr.: co-trustee, Kranes Charitable Trust (Sidney and Judith); trustee, Pinkerton Foundation

Sweet, Adele Hall: president, Schiff Foundation (Dorothy)

Swenson, Susan: executive director, Kennedy, Jr. Foundation (Joseph P.)

Swift, Bryan M.: president,

Swift, E. Clinton: director, Phillips Foundation (Ellis L.)

Swift, Hampden M.: co-trustee, Swift Charitable Trust

Swig, Kent: trustee, Swig Foundation (The)

Swig, Richard L.: trustee, Swig Foundation (The)

Swig, Robert: trustee, Swig Foundation (The)

Swig, Steven L.: trustee, Swig Foundation (The)

Swindle, Jack E.: chairman, director, Texas Instruments Foundation

Swindoll, B. Carver: director, Mingenback Foundation (Julia J.)

Swinney, Caroline T.: assistant secretary, foundation manager, Motorola Foundation

Switz, Robert E.: president, chief executive officer, ADC Telecommunications; trustee, Hickory Tech Corp. Foundation

Sykes, James T.: director, Cremer Foundation

Syrmis, Pamela L.: vice president, director, Ittleson Foundation

Syrmis, Victor P., MD: director, Ittleson Foundation

Szabad, George Michael: secretary, treasurer, trustee, Dibner Fund

Szabo, Raymond: president, trustee, Eaton Foundation (Cyrus)

Szapary, Gladys V.: trustee, McBean Charitable Trust (Alletta Morris)

T

Tabah, Mimi D.: board of directors, Wilson Foundation (Marie C. and Joseph C.)

Tabankin, Margery: director, Arca Foundation

Taft, Dudley S.: chairman, trustee, Semple Foundation (Louise Taft)

Taft, Robert A., II: trustee, Semple Foundation (Louise Taft)

Taggart, Richard: vice president financial, chief financial officer, Brodbeck Enterprises

Tail, Norbert: secretary, director, McKenna Foundation (Philip M.)

Takahara, Sumiko: trustee, United States-Japan Foundation

Takanishi, Ruby: director, Rockefeller Foundation (Winthrop)

Takeuchi, Seiichi: secretary, treasurer, Bandai Foundation

Talamantes, Pat: treasurer, director, Star Tribune Foundation

Taleff, Lynne: director, Hardin Foundation (Phil)

Tallent, Charles J.: trustee, Arkell Hall Foundation

Tallon, James J., Jr.: director, Commonwealth Fund (The)

Taniguchi, Ichiro: director, Mitsubishi Electric America Foundation; chairman, Mitsubishi Electric and Electronics USA

Tanner, Harold: president, Revson Foundation (Charles H.)

Tanner, Henry J.: vice president, treasurer, director, Scott Foundation (Virginia Steele)

Tanner, James T.: chairman, Tanner Cos. (Rutherfordton, NC); president, Tanner Foundation

Tanner, K. S., Jr.: director, Stonecutter Foundation

Tanner, L. Gene: treasurer, director, Noyes, Jr. Memorial Foundation (Nicholas H.)

Tanner, Michael S.: secretary, Tanner Foundation

Tanner, Pell: director, Tanner Foundation

Tanner, Robin C.: treasurer, director loans, office, Strong Foundation (Hattie M.)

Tansey, Andrew L.: trustee, Bingham Second Betterment Fund (William)

Taper Bolker, Cynthia: vice president, Taper Foundation (S. Mark)

Taper Ringel, Deborah: treasurer, Taper Foundation (S. Mark)

Taper Stabler, Amelia: secretary, Taper Foundation (S. Mark)

Taradash, Bernard A. G.: trustee, Grimshaw-Gudewicz Charitable Foundation

Tarica, Regina Amado: vice president, cfo, director, Amado Foundation (Maurice)

Tarica, Samuel R.: vice president, director, Amado Foundation (Maurice)

Tarnok, Robert C.: controller, MetLife Foundation

Tasaki, Akira: director, president, Mitsubishi Electric America Foundation

Tasker, Steven W.: treasurer, Niagara Mohawk Foundation

Tata, Ratan Naval: trustee, Ford Foundation

Tatar, Steven: trustee, Sapirstein-Stone-Weiss Foundation

Tate, Linda Crowe: director, McMillen Foundation

Tate, Warren E.: treasurer, Gulf Power Foundation

Tatlock, Anne M.: chairman, trustee, Mellon Foundation (Andrew W.); director, Teagle Foundation

Tatro, Wayne S.: director, Provident Community Foundation

Tatum, Jacquelyn: assistant trustee, BellSouth Foundation

Tatum, Nenetta Carter: president, Carter Star Telegram Employees Fund (Amon G.)

Taube, Thaddeus N.: president, director, Koret Foundation; chairman, president, Taube Family Foundation

Taubman, A. Alfred: chairman, treasurer, trustee, Taubman Foundation (A. Alfred)

Taubman, Judith M.: trustee, Taubman Foundation (A. Alfred)

Taubman, Robert S.: trustee, Skillman Foundation

Taubman, William S.: trustee, Taubman Foundation (A. Alfred)

Tauck, Arthur C., Jr.: trustee, Tauck Foundation (Arthur C. and Lee Anne)

Tauke, Thomas J.: executive vice president, Verizon Communications Inc.; vice chairman, secretary, director, Verizon Foundation

Taunton, Michael J.: treasurer, KeySpan Foundation

Taurel, Sidney: chairman, president, chief executive officer, Lilly & Co. (Eli); director, Lilly Foundation (Eli)

Tavlin, Michael John: assistant treasurer, Woods Charitable Fund

Taxter, M. W.: director, Penney Co. Fund (J.C.)

Taylor, Albert P.: director, Comerica Charitable Foundation

Taylor, Alexander S., II: trustee, Bicknell Fund

Taylor, Alice: director, Memorial Foundation for the Blind

Taylor, Barbara Olin: board member, trustee, Olin Foundation (Spencer T. and Ann W.)

Taylor, Benjamin: chairman, director, Star Tribune Foundation

Taylor, Benjamin B.: director, Boston Globe Foundation

Taylor, Brett M., Jr.: director, Hickory Tech Corp.

Taylor, Cheryl K.: president, chief executive officer, director, Foellinger Foundation

Taylor, David H.: vice president, director, Davenport-Hatch Foundation

Taylor, Douglas F.: director, Davenport-Hatch Foundation

Taylor, F. Morgan, Jr.: board member, trustee, Olin Foundation (Spencer T. and Ann W.)

Taylor, Frederick B.: vice chairman, chief investment officer, United States Trust Company of New York

Taylor, J. P.: board mem, Roberts Foundation (Dora)

Taylor, Jacqueline: director, Samuels Foundation (Fan Fox and Leslie R.)

Taylor, John R.: investment officer, Heinz Family Foundation

Taylor, Julia H.: director, St. Francis Bank Foundation

Taylor, Kenneth Nathaniel: director, Tyndale House Foundation

Taylor, Kris J.: vice president, Ecolab Foundation

Taylor, Margaret L.: treasurer, chief financial officer, Duffield Family Foundation

Taylor, Margaret W.: secretary, Tyndale House Foundation

Taylor, Mark Douglas: vice president, treasurer, Tyndale House Foundation

Taylor, Mark H.: vice president, Burns & McDonnell; treasurer, director, Burns & McDonnell Foundation

Taylor, Nick R.: co-trustee, Baright Foundation (Hollis and Helen)

Taylor, Penelope J.: trustee, The MBNA Foundation

Taylor, Peter J.: director, Irvine Foundation (The James)

Taylor, Peter W.: director, Tyndale House Foundation

Taylor, Philip E.: president, chief executive officer, JSJ Corp.

Taylor, Priscilla P.: executive director, Cemala Foundation

Taylor, S. Martin: senior vice president human resources & corporate affairs, DTE Energy Co.; vice president, director, DTE Energy Foundation

Taylor, Sharon C.: chairman, trustee, Prudential Foundation

Taylor, Steven W.: trustee, Puterbaugh Foundation

Taylor, Teddy O.: trustee, Blount Educational and Charitable Foundation (Mildred Weedon)

Taylor, William G.: director, Springs Foundation, Inc.

Tchen, Tina: director, Field Foundation of Illinois

Teagle, Walter C., III: director, Teagle Foundation

Teague, Barry L.: member, Campbell Foundation (J. Bulow)

Teichert, Frederick A.: executive director, director, Teichert Foundation

Teichert, Melita M.: director, Teichert Foundation

Teitz, Jeffrey J.: trustee, Adelson Trust (Diana S.)

Telg, Ken: trustee, Priddy Foundation

Tellalian, Aram H., Jr.: president, treasurer, trustee, Jones and Bessie D. Phelps Foundation (Cyrus W. and Amy F.)

Tellalian, Robert S.: vice president, secretary, trustee, Jones and Bessie D. Phelps Foundation (Cyrus W. and Amy F.)

Tellez, Cora M.: vice president, director, Cowell Foundation (S. H.)

Tempas, Jeffrey J.: director, Ray Foundation

Temple, Arthur, III: director, Temple-Inland Foundation

Temple, Arthur, Jr.: chairman, trustee, Temple Foundation (T. L. L.)

Templeton, D. Jeffrey: director, Woronoco Savings Charitable Foundation

Templeton, Edward O.: director, St. Francis Bank Foundation

Templeton, Richard: president, chief executive officer, Texas Instruments Inc.

Templeton, Robert: member, Templeton Foundation (Herbert A.)

Templin, Gary A.: director, Haigh-Scatena Foundation

Ten Pas, Paul H.: secretary, director, Kohler Foundation

Tenney, Daniel Gleason, Jr.: secretary, director, JM Foundation

Tenny, Barron M.: executive vice president, secretary, general counsel, Ford Foundation

Tepner, Ronald: member, Bridgestone/Firestone Trust Fund (The)

Terlizzi, Donald: treasurer, Capezio/Ballet Makers Dance Foundation

Terlizzi, Nick, Jr.: chairman, director, Ballet Makers; vice president, Capezio/Ballet Makers Dance Foundation

Termondt, M. James: president, treasurer, director, Fry Foundation (Lloyd A.); vice president, treasurer, director, Wehr Foundation (Todd)

Terrien, Linda L.: assistant treasurer, Weyerhaeuser Co. Foundation

Terry, Charles R., Sr.: chairman, Hill Crest Foundation

Terry, Mary: secretary, Reader's Digest Foundation

Terry, Thomas T.: trustee, Mascoma Savings Bank Foundation

Terry, Wade: director, American Honda Foundation

Tessler, C.: secretary, Long Foundation (J. M.)

Testa, Linda: program manager, Microsoft Corp.

Testa, Richard J.: trustee, Keel Foundation

TeStrake, Harvey D.: mgr, secretary, Miller Foundation (Steve J.)

Tetterton, Clarence E.: secretary, treasurer, Tri-County Telephone Foundation

Thacher, Michael: general manager public relations & communications, Unocal Corp.

Thacker, Frank: chairman, AT&T National Pro-Am Youth Fund

Thacker, Michael J.: secretary, Key Foundation

Thain, John A.: chief executive officer, New York Stock Exchange Inc.

Thakkar, Kelly L.: trustee, McKay Family Foundation

Thatcher, Gerald D.: trustee, Van Wert County Foundation

Thaxter, Sidney F.: clerk, Barker Foundation Inc.

Thayer, Tyrone K.: corp. vice president, Cargill Inc.

Theisen, Herbert J.: assistant secretary, general counsel, Johnson Foundation (A.D.)

Theobald, Jon A.: chairman, trustee, Bigelow Foundation (F. R.)

Theobald, Thomas Charles: director, MacArthur Foundation (John D. and Catherine T.)

Thieman, Frederick W.: director, Heinz Endowment (Howard)

Thier, Samuel O., MD: chairman, director, Commonwealth Fund (The)

Thomas, Bart: director, Texas Instruments Foundation

Thomas, David A.: director, member legal committee, Keck Foundation (W. M.)

Thomas, Dennis: director, International Paper Co. Foundation

Thomas, Franklin A.: trustee, Greentree Foundation

Thomas, Gladys R.: vice president, secretary, Starr Foundation

Thomas, Glenn E.: director, Thomas Foundation (Joan and Lee)

Thomas, James A.: director, Parsons Foundation (Ralph M.)

Thomas, Jane R.: trustee, Skillman Foundation

Thomas, Joan E.: director, Thomas Foundation (Joan and Lee)

Thomas, L. Newton, Jr.: president, Daywood Foundation; trustee, Jacobson Foundation (Bernard H. and Blanche E.)

Thomas, Lee B.: director, Thomas Foundation (Joan and Lee)

Thomas, Lowell S., Jr.: director, Barra Foundation

Thomas, Lyda Ann Quinn: trustee, Kempner Fund (Harris and Eliza)

Thomas, M. Antoinette: secretary, director, Warhol Foundation for the Visual Arts (The Andy)

Thomas, Michael E.: director, Morrison Foundation (Harry W.)

Thomas, Richard L.: director, Sara Lee Corp.

Thompson, Billie: secretary, trustee, Doss Foundation, Inc. (M. S.)

Thompson, Christine: secretary, Marshall Foundation

Thompson, Donald L.: chairman, chief executive officer, Hunt Corp.

Thompson, E. Arthur: president, trustee, Cooper Foundation

Thompson, Frederic: trustee, Davies Benevolent Fund (Edward H.)

Thompson, George: trustee, Blandin Foundation

Thompson, Janice: secretary, treasurer, Herd Foundation (Bob L.)

Thompson, Jim: president, chief executive officer, ING North America Insurance Corp.

Thompson, John R.: director, Best Buy Children's Foundation

Thompson, Kirby A.: trustee, Equifax Foundation

Thompson, Kris: director, Jostens Foundation Inc. (The)

Thompson, Leonora Kempner: chairman emeritus, Kempner Fund (Harris and Eliza)

Thompson, Marcia T.: director, Scherman Foundation

Thompson, Margaret E.: trustee, Dow Foundation (Herbert H. and Grace A.)

Thompson, Margaret E., MD: trustee, Towsley Foundation (Harry A. and Margaret D.)

Thompson, Melinda: treasurer, director, Patron Saints Foundation

Thompson, Mildred: director, Zellerbach Family Fund

Thompson, Mona: trustee, Coen Family Foundation (Charles S. and Mary)

Thompson, Nelda: trustee, CH Foundation

Thompson, Peter K., MD: treasurer, Kempner Fund (Harris and Eliza)

Thompson, Ralph LaSalle: treasurer, Grinnell Mutual Group Foundation

Thompson, Richard L.: director, Bristol-Myers Squibb Foundation Inc.

Thompson, Roger K.: trustee, Van Wert County Foundation

Thompson, Sylvia M.: director, Thompson Charitable Foundation

Thompson, Thomas C., Jr.: vice president, trustee, Clark-Winchcole Foundation

Thompson, W. Craig: treasurer, trustee, Clark-Winchcole Foundation

Thomsen, C. J.: trustee, McDermott Foundation (The Eugene)

Thomson, Lucy M.: vice president, trustee, Morley Foundation

Thomson, R. Patrick: president, director, New York Mercantile Exchange

Thomson, Richard B., Jr.: trustee, Morley Foundation

Thomson, Robert C., Jr.: president, treasurer, director, Vernon Foundation (Miles Hodsdon)

Thoreen, John F.: director, Tozer Foundation

Thorn, Therese M.: treasurer, Ratner Foundation (Milton M.)

Thorne, Daniel Kempner: trustee, Kempner Fund (Harris and Eliza)

Thorne, Felicitas Selter: vice president, Millbrook Tribute Garden

Thorne, Jane W.: trustee emeritus, Fund for New Jersey

Thorne, Oakleigh: trustee, Millbrook Tribute Garden

Thorne, Oakleigh Blakeman: president, trustee, Millbrook Tribute Garden

Thornton, Charles B., Jr.: president, Thornton Foundation

Thornton, Flora L.: trustee, Thornton Foundation (Flora L.)

Thornton, Thomas N.: director, Andrews McMeel Universal Foundation

Thornton, William Laney: vice president, Thornton Foundation; trustee, Thornton Foundation (Flora L.)

Thorpe, Neal O.: executive director, trustee, Murdock Charitable Trust (M. J.)

Thorson, Steven J., MD: director, Copic Medical Foundation

Thralls, Sharon: director, Patron Saints Foundation

Throop, William M., Jr.: trustee, Bingham Second Betterment Fund (William)

Thrower, Larry W.: vice president, director, Copic Medical Foundation

Thrune, Charles J.: trustee, Strosacker Foundation (Charles J.)

Thrune, Charlie C.: trustee, Strosacker Foundation (Charles J.)

Thun, Michael J.: trustee, Wyomissing Foundation

Thurber, Peter Palms: trustee emeritus, McGregor Fund

Thurston, Samuel E.: senior vice president distribution, Giant Food Inc.

Thuss, Emily D.: trustee, Brackenridge Foundation (George W.)

Thye, Pamela M.: chairman, Steinman Foundation (John Frederick)

Tibitts, Daniel: trustee, AT&T National Pro-Am Youth Fund

Tice, Mark Randolph: director, Lebanon Mutual Foundation

Tilleman, Paul J.: treasurer, director, Stackner Family Foundation

Tillman, Krista: trustee, BellSouth Foundation

Tillman, Robert L.: chairman, president, chief executive officer, Lowe's Cos.

Tilton, Sumner B., Jr.: trustee, Ellsworth Foundation (Ruth H. and Warren A.)

Timken, W. R., Jr.: vice president, trustee, Timken Foundation of Canton

Timken, Ward J.: president, trustee, Timken Foundation of Canton

Timmerman, Robert P.: director, Gregg-Graniteville Foundation

Tippett, Henry H.: treasurer, Tiscornia Foundation

Tippins, Carolyn H.: trustee, Tippins Foundation

Tippins, George W.: trustee, Tippins Foundation

Tippins, John H.: trustee, Tippins Foundation

Tippitt, Anna: vice president, Vale-Asche Foundation

Tipsord, Michael: treasurer, State Farm Companies Foundation

Tipton, Gwendlyn I.: scholarship admin, director, Cole Foundation (Olive B.)

Tipton, Ronald D.: director, MDU Resources Foundation

Tisch, Andrew H.: trustee, Loews Foundation

Tisch, James S.: president, chief executive officer, director, Loews Corp.

Tisch, Preston R.: trustee, Loews Foundation

Tisch, Preston Robert: co-chairman, co-chief executive officer, director, CBS Corp.

Tiscornia, Bernice: vice president, Tiscornia Foundation

Tiscornia, James: vice president, Tiscornia Foundation

Toben, Doreen A.: director, Verizon Foundation

Tobias, Barry: treasurer, trustee, Sharp Foundation (Evelyn)

Tobias, Randall L.: president, treasurer, Tobias Foundation (Randall L.)

Tobias, Todd C.: vice president, Tobias Foundation (Randall L.)

Tobias-Button, Paige N.: vice president, secretary, Tobias Foundation (Randall L.)

Tobin, Gerald C.: assistant treasurer, assistant secretary, director, Hopkins Foundation (Josephine Lawrence)

Tobisman, Stuart B.: vice president, director, counsel, Bettingen Corp. (Burton G.)

Todd, A. J., III: chairman, president, chief executive officer, Todd Co. (A.M.); trustee, Todd Co. Foundation (A.M.)

Todd, Sandra: trustee, Patterson Memorial Trust (Hazel)

Todd, Vivian E.: director, Wright Foundation (Lola)

Toft, Richard Paul: chairman, Chicago Title Corp.; trustee, Chicago Title and Trust Co. Foundation

Toledano, John O. H.: vice chairman, secretary, director, Acme-McCrary Corp./Sapona Manufacturing Co.; vice president, Acme-McCrary and Sapona Foundation

Toledano, John O.H., Jr.: director, Acme-McCrary and Sapona Foundation

Tomas, Kay: secretary, Gilmore Foundation (Irving S.)

Tomikawa, Jeanette: director, American Honda Foundation

Tomlinson, Bruce R.: director, Oakley-Lindsay Foundation of Quincy Newspapers and Its Subsidiaries

Toms, William: trustee, Ghidotti Foundation

Toohey, Edward Joseph: president, director, Bunbury Co., Inc.; treasurer, trustee, Windham Foundation

Tookmanian, Donna: treasurer, Mailman Family Foundation (A. L.)

Topek, Nathan H., MD: director, Herzstein Charitable Foundation (Albert and Ethel)

Toppeta, William J.: director, MetLife Foundation; president, international, Metropolitan Life Insurance Co.

Torcivia, Carolyn A.: secretary, Park Bank Foundation

Torgerson, William T.: vice president, cfo, Pepco Holdings Inc.

Torkildsen, John: assistant controller, IBM International Foundation

Toronto, Shannon K.: executive director, Eccles Foundation (Marriner S.)

Torray, Robert E.: director, Kirkpatrick Foundation, Inc.

Torregrossa, Bernice C.: grants analyst, Moody Foundation

Totten, H. W., Jr.: director, Smith and W. Aubrey Smith Charitable Foundation (Clara Blackford)

Toussaint, Carol: Interim executive director, Alliant Energy Foundation, Inc.

Tower, Caroline: director, Haigh-Scatena Foundation

Towers, James K., III: vice president, Gooding Group Foundation

Townsend, Charles C., Jr.: secretary, director, Bunbury Co., Inc.; trustee, Windham Foundation

Townsend, John W., IV: vice president, trustee, Altman Foundation

Townsend, Wilbur L.: director, Allyn Foundation

Trachtenberg, Bruce: director commun, The Wallace Foundation

Tracy, Charles S.: director, Allyn Foundation

Tracy-Nagle, Patricia: senior vice president, Osher Foundation (Bernard)

Traeger, Michelle O'Shaughnessy: vice president, director, O'Shaughnessy Foundation (I. A.)

Traina, Richard P.: vice chairman, trustee, Alden Trust (George I.)

Trammell, Ann Gordon: secretary, treasurer, board of governors, Fondren Foundation

Trammell, Harper B.: board of governors, Fondren Foundation

Tran, Khanh T.: executive vice president, chief financial officer, director, Pacific Life Insurance Co.

Tranquada, Robert E.: director, Parsons Foundation (Ralph M.)

Trapani, Cosmo S.: executive vice president, chief financial officer, Unitrode Corp.

Trapp, George J.: secretary, director, New York Life Foundation

Trask, Robert B.: president, chief operating officer, director, Country Curtains Inc.; clerk, High Meadow Foundation

Traylor, Fasaha M.: senior program officer, Foundation for Child Development

Treadwell, Alexander F.: vice president, director, Clark Foundation (NY)

Treat, Charles O.: vice president, Dime Savings Bank of Norwich Foundation

Treckelo, Richard M.: trustee, Decio Foundation (Arthur J.)

Treeger, Clarence R.: president, trustee, Summerfield Foundation, Inc. (Solon E.)

Treeger, Thomas C.: treasurer, secretary, Summerfield Foundation, Inc. (Solon E.)

Treiber, John A.: vice president, secretary, executive director, Stackner Family Foundation

Treiber, Patricia S.: president, director, Stackner Family Foundation

Tremblay, Wade: trustee, Perry Foundation

Trencher, Lewis J.: chairman, director, Thompson Co. Fund (J. Walter); chief operating officer, director, Thompson Co. (J. Walter)

Trethewey, James A.: senior vice president, operations services, Cleveland-Cliffs Inc.

Tribble, J. Lee: treasurer, Woodruff Foundation (Robert W.)

Trice, Thomas L., IV: treasurer, trustee, Henson Foundation (Richard A.)

Trimble, William C., Jr.: secretary, treasurer, Wilson Sanitarium for Children of Baltimore City (Thomas)

Trobster, Glenn: trustee, Fairchild-Meeker Charitable Trust (Freeman E.)

Trochu, Cynthia: secretary, Texas Instruments Foundation

Trosino, Vincent Joseph, Sr.: assistant secretary, State Farm Companies Foundation; vice chairman, chief operating officer, director, State Farm Mutual Automobile Insurance Co.

Trost, Carlisle Albert H.: director, chairman, Olmsted Foundation (George and Carol)

Trott, James I.: trustee, Abell-Hanger Foundation

Trotter, Ann: secretary-treasurer, Anderson Foundation (M. D.)

Trotter, Jack T.: vice president, trustee, Anderson Foundation (M. D.)

Trotter, Lloyd G.: director, GE Foundation; senior vice president, GE Industrial Systems, General Electric Co.

Trout, David M., Jr.: mgr, Freas Foundation

Trout, Rebecca F.: mgr, Freas Foundation

Trower, Thomas H.: trustee, Bovaird Foundation (Mervin)

True, Lawrence Y.: trustee, Johnson Charitable Educational Trust (James Hervey)

Trueb, Martin R.: senior vice president, treasurer, Hasbro Charitable Trust Inc.

Trull, R. Scott: trustee, Trull Foundation (The)

Trull, Robert B.: founder, trustee emeritus, Trull Foundation (The)

Trussell, Philip A.: director, East Cambridge Savings Charitable Foundation

Tryloff, Robin: executive director community relations, Sara Lee Corp.; president, executive director, director, Sara Lee Foundation

Tse, E. S.: director, Starr Foundation

Tsui, John K.: vice president, director, First Hawaiian Foundation

Tsuji, Masaaki: chairman, president, Bandai Foundation

Tsumura, Monty: chairman, Tsumura International Inc.

Tubergen, Jerry L.: vice president, secretary, chief operating officer, DeVos Foundation (Richard and Helen)

Tuchler, John E.: president, Marx Foundation (Virginia and Leonard)

Tuck, Daniel H.: director, Tuch Foundation (Michael)

Tuck, Jonathan S.: secretary, treasurer, Tuch Foundation (Michael)

Tucker, Elmer D.: comm mem, Eccles Foundation (Marriner S.)

Tucker, Robert A.: president, director, CTW Foundation, Inc.

Tulley, Michael: director, AMCORE Foundation

Tullidge, Thomas H.: vice president, trustee, Gray Foundation (Garland and Agnes Taylor)

Tullius, Raymond L., Jr.: assistant secretary, trustee, Mabee Foundation, Inc. (J. E. and L. E.)

Tully, Ellen D. B. F.: president, Friendship Fund

Tulsky, James A.: director, Greenwall Foundation

Tunheim, Kathryn H.: treasurer, director, Bush Foundation

Tunioli, Carlo: vice president, general manager, Benetton U.S.A. Corp.

Tupper, Christopher N.: corporator, Island Foundation (MA)

Turcik, John J.: controller, Mellon Foundation (Richard King)

Turissini, Christina H.: comptroller, Gates Family Foundation

Turk, James C.: trustee, Richardson Benevolent Foundation (C. E.)

Turletes, Vincent N.: secretary, Millbrook Tribute Garden

Turley, Bob: president, chief operating officer, director, Perdue Farms

Turnbull, Kenneth W.: treasurer, Schwartz Foundation (Arnold A.)

Turner, Diana Lassalle: director, Norman Foundation

Turner, Frank B.: trustee, Arnold Fund

Turner, James L.: director, Cinergy Foundation

Turner, Laura Jennings: director, Cockrell Foundation

Turner, R. F.: trustee, Jeldwen Foundation

Turner, R. W.: president, trustee, Union Pacific Foundation

Turner, Reginald M.: trustee, Hudson-Webber Foundation

Turner, Richard: manager corporate contributions, Peoples Energy Corp.

Turner, Ronald G.: vice chairman board trustees, Baker Foundation (R. C.)

Turner, Vivian L.: chairman, Reynolds Foundation (R. J.)

Turtell, Dan: chief financial officer, Harper Brush Works

Tusch, Carol: treasurer, International Paper Co. Foundation

Tuthill, Howard S., III: secretary, Norris Foundation (Dellora A. and Lester J.)

Tutt, Russell Thayer, Jr.: president, chief investment officer, trustee, El Pomar Foundation

Tuttle, Thomas N., Jr.: treasurer, secretary, Miller Foundation (Steve J.)

Twomley, Dale E.: president, chief executive officer, director, Worthington Foods; trustee, Worthington Foods Foundation

Tyburski, Charles: member distribution committee, Flowers Charitable Trust (Albert W. and Edith V.)

Tyler, Ronnie Curtis: director, Summerlee Foundation

Tyler, William B.: trustee, Alden Trust (John W.)

Tynan, Ronald B.: chairman, Flowers Charitable Trust (Albert W. and Edith V.)

Tynan-Chapman, Patricia: secretary, director, Harden Foundation

Tyrie, James C.: co-trustee, Hunt Foundation (Samuel P.)

Tyson, Janice C.: assistant secretary, Clemens Foundation

Tyson, John: director, IBP Foundation

Tytus, John: trustee, Semple Foundation (Louise Taft)

U

Uber, Daryl Brown: president, Weiss Foundation (William E.)

Uchida, Hisashi: senior executive vice president administration, Mitsubishi Silicon America

Ueberroth, Joseph: treas, Ueberroth Family Foundation

Ueberroth, Virginia: president, Ueberroth Family Foundation

Ueberroth Booth, Vicki: secretary, Ueberroth Family Foundation

Uihlein, David V., Jr.: director, Bradley Foundation (Lynde and Harry)

Ukropina, James R.: director, member legal com-

mittee, Keck Foundation (W. M.)

Ulf, Franklin E.: director, Parsons Foundation (Ralph M.)

Ulrich, Don A.: executive director, Reeves Foundation (OH)

Ulrich, Robert J.: chairman, chief executive officer, director, Target Corp.; chairman, trustee, Target Foundation

Ulsh, Sandy E.: president, Ford Motor Co. Fund

Underwood, Cecil H.: president, Huntington Foundation

Underwood, David M.: board of governors, Fondren Foundation

Underwood, David M., Jr.: board of governors, Fondren Foundation

Underwood, Duncan K.: chairman, board of governors, Fondren Foundation

Underwood, Frank D.: executive director, director, Forest Foundation

Underwood, Joanna Dehaven: director, Clark Foundation (Robert Sterling)

Underwood, Lynda Knapp: board of governors, Fondren Foundation

Unger, James J.: vice chairman, chief executive officer, ACF Industries

Unger, Leonard: secretary, treasurer, director, Lavine Family Foundation (Richard and Ruth)

Unger, Ruth Halls: trustee, Ghidotti Foundation

Ungerland, Thomas J.: trustee, Edison Fund (Charles)

Upton, David F.: trustee, Upton Foundation (Frederick S.)

Upton, Stephen E., LHD: chairman board trustees, Upton Foundation (Frederick S.)

Urahn, Susan K.: director, policy initiatives, education program, Pew Charitable Trusts

Urban, Henry Zellar: director, Knox Foundation (Seymour H.)

Urban, Mary Bright: vice president, Weathertop Foundation

Urban, Thomas N., III: director, Weathertop Foundation

Urban, Thomas Nelson, Jr.: chairman, president, Weathertop Foundation

Urban, William G.: treasurer, Weathertop Foundation

Urdan, James A.: director, Marshall & Ilsley Foundation, Inc.

Uribe de Mena, Joanna: vice president, Haigh-Scatena Foundation

Urion, Melinda: treasurer, AmerUs Group Charitable Foundation

Ury, Robert I.: vice president, secretary, director, Lederer Foundation (Francis L.)

Usdan, Adam: vice president, Lemberg Foundation

Usdan, John: treasurer, Lemberg Foundation

Usdan, Suzanne: president, Lemberg Foundation

Usher, Thomas J.: chairman, chief executive officer, U.S. Steel Corp.; chairman board trustees, U.S. Steel Foundation

Ushijima, Shigeomi: director, Kikkoman Foundation

Ushio, Jiro: vchairman board trustee, United States-Japan Foundation

Usibelli, Joseph E., Jr.: president, chief executive officer, director, Usibelli Coal Mine Inc.; president, Usibelli Foundation

Usibelli, Joseph E., Sr.: chairman, Usibelli Coal Mine Inc.

Ussery, Gene L.: trustee, Gulf Power Foundation

Utecht, Andrea: vice president, secretary, FMC Foundation

Utley, David M.: trustee, Carver Charitable Trust (Roy J.)

Utley, Lorna G.: president, General Motors Foundation

Utterback, Ann M.: director, Maddox Foundation (J. F.)

V

Vaccaro, Marc: director, Menasha Corp. Foundation

Vagelos, Pindaros Roy: trustee, Prudential Foundation

Vahlberg, Vivian: journalism program director, McCormick Tribune Foundation (Robert R.)

Vaimberg, Mitzi: secretary, AT&T Foundation

Valade, Gary C.: executive vice president, chief financial officer, Daimler-Chrysler AG; trustee, DaimlerChrysler Corp. Fund

Valentine, E. Massey, Sr.: trustee, Chesapeake Corp. Foundation

Valentine, J. E.: chief financial officer, Bardes Corp.

Valentine, Joan Selverstone: director, Research Corp.

Valentine, Joseph: director, Stulsaft Foundation (Morris)

Valentine, Katrina A.: secretary, McDonough Foundation (Bernard)

Valentine, Volina Cline: director, Fullerton Foundation

Valentino, Nick: treasurer, Britton Fund

Vallene, Joseph A., III: trustee, Snyder Foundation (Harold B. and Dorothy A.)

Valley, Tamara A.: chairman, Valley Foundation (Wayne and Gladys)

Valliant, John R.: trustee, Kerr Fund (Grayce B.)

Van Alen, Elizabeth K.: president, treasurer, trustee, Kent-Lucas Foundation

Van Alen, James L., II: trustee, Kent-Lucas Foundation

Van Alen, William L.: vice president, trustee, Kent-Lucas Foundation

Van Allen, William G.: treasurer, Bretzlaff Foundation

van Ameringen, Henry P.: president, director, treasurer, van Ameringen Foundation, Inc.

Van Andel, David: vice president, trustee, Van Andel Foundation (Jay and Betty)

Van Andel, Jay: president, trustee, Van Andel Foundation (Jay and Betty)

Van Atten, Carol: assistant secretary, Hayden Foundation (Charles)

Van Benschoten, David: treasurer, General Mills Foundation; vice president, treasurer, General Mills Inc.

Van Berkel, Thomas M.: trustee, National Grange Mutual Charitable Trust

van Beuren, John A.: trustee, McBean Charitable Trust (Alletta Morris)

Van Bronkhorst, Edwin E.: emeritus trustee, Packard Foundation (David and Lucile)

Van Buren, Elsie Proctor: trustee, Van Buren Foundation (Elsie Procter)

Van Cleave, Julie: director, Siebert Lutheran Foundation

Van Clief, Mary Ann: vice president, director, Brookdale Foundation

Van de Bovenkamp, Sue Erpf: president, director, Erpf Fund (Armand G.)

van den Blink, Jan: trustee, Hilliard Foundation

van den Blink, Nelson Mooers: chairman, chief executive officer, treasurer, director, Hilliard Corp.; president, trustee, Hilliard Foundation

Van Doren, James E.: trustee, Sage Foundation

Van Dusen, Albert Clarence: trustee, director, Buhl Foundation (PA)

Van Dyk, Alison Jackson: trustee, Connemara Fund

Van Dyke, Clifford D.: vice president, Kantzler Foundation

Van Dyke, John W.: senior vice president, chief financial officer, director, American Optical Corp.; director, American Optical Foundation

Van Dyke, William Grant: chairman, president, chief executive officer, director, Donaldson Company Inc.

Van Gorden, Mary: trustee, Lunda Charitable Trust

Van Gorder, John Frederic: executive director, Lowenstein Foundation (Leon)

Van Haren, W. Michael: secretary, trustee, Wege Foundation

Van Liemt, Hans B.: director, Sara Lee Corp.

Van Ness, Stanley C.: trustee, Prudential Foundation

Van Nort, Peter S.: president, Zachry Co. (H.B.)

Van Pelt, Lester, Jr.: vice president, trustee, Abell-Hanger Foundation

Van Rees, Linda: financial trustee, Schwab-Rosenhouse Memorial Foundation

Van Riper, Jeffrey L.: secretary, Seneca Foods Foundation

Van Vliet, Emily: trustee, Peterson Charitable Foundation (Folke H.)

Van Zante, Mary: secretary, Pella Rolscreen Foundation

Van Zyl, Jane: director, Bettingen Corp. (Burton G.)

Van Zytveld, John: senior program director, Murdock Charitable Trust (M. J.)

Vandagriff, Judy A.: senior vice president, El Paso Corporate Foundation

vanden Henvel, Melinda F.: trustee, Fuller Foundation (MA)

Vander Ark, Tom: executive director education, Gates Foundation (Bill and Melinda)

VanderRoest, Stan M.: treasurer, trustee, Gerber Foundation

Vandiver, Susan T.: vice president grant programs, Cowell Foundation (S. H.)

Vandusen, Amanda: trustee, Hudson-Webber Foundation

Vanison, Richard C.: assistant treasurer, Clark Foundation (NY)

VanLoenen, Barbara: director, treasurer, Best Buy Children's Foundation

Vann, James M.: chairman, director, Vann Family Foundation

Vann, Marjorie Lee: president, director, Vann Family Foundation

Vann, Thomas H., Jr.: director, Williams Family Foundation of Georgia

Vanosdol, Thomas G.: chairman, Ford Meter Box Foundation

Vanz, Robert: trustee, Acushnet Foundation

Vargas, Arturo: trustee, Hazen Foundation (Edward W.)

Varney, Jolene L.: treasurer, Kimberly-Clark Foundation

Vaughan, Anne V.: assistant secretary, Burlington Resources Foundation

Vaughan, Ben F., III: president, trustee, Vaughan Foundation (Rachael and Ben)

Vaughan, Ben F., IV: vice president, trustee, Vaughan Foundation (Rachael and Ben)

Vaughan, Daphne duPont: secretary, treasurer, trustee, Vaughan Foundation (Rachael and Ben)

Vaughan, Genevieve: vice president, trustee, Vaughan Foundation (Rachael and Ben)

Vaughan, John B.: chairman, chief executive officer, Vaughan Furniture Co.

Vaughan, William B.: executive vice president, director, Vaughan Foundation; president, Vaughan Furniture Co.

Vaughn, James M.: director, Vaughn Foundation (Jim M.)

Vaughn, James M., Jr.: director, Vaughn Foundation (Jim M.); president, Vaughn, Jr. Foundation Fund (James M.)

Vaughn, R. C.: assistant secretary, Burress Foundation (J.W.)

Vaughn, Salle: vice president, Vaughn, Jr. Foundation Fund (James M.)

Vawnnek, J. J.: assistant secretary, Penney Co. Fund (J.C.)

Vawter, Paul E.: trustee, Valentine Foundation (Lawson)

Veitenhans, Karen L.: secretary, Weyerhaeuser Co. Foundation

Venteicher, Louis: chairman, president, chief executive officer, Audubon State Bank

Veon, Greg: director, Lee Foundation

Vera, George: vice president, chief financial officer, Packard Foundation (David and Lucile)

Verenes, George: treasurer, director, Harcourt Foundation (Ellen Knowles)

Vergas, Sophia G.: secretary, administrator, Liberty Corp. Foundation

Verity, C. William, Jr.: director emeritus, Keck Foundation (W. M.)

Verney, E. Geoffrey: trustee, Verney Foundation (Gilbert)

Verney, Richard Greville: chairman, chief executive officer, director, Monadnock Paper Mills Inc.; president, Verney Foundation (Gilbert)

Vernon, Russell O.: director, Hebrew Technical Institute

Verrecchia, Alfred J.: executive vice president, director, Hasbro Charitable Trust Inc.; executive, director, Hasbro Inc.

Vetrovec, Pauline: treasurer, Jameson Foundation (J. W. and Ida M.)

Vett, Thomas W.: secretary, treasurer, King Foundation (Carl B. and Florence F.)

Viault, Raymond G.: trustee, General Mills Foundation; vice chairman, director, General Mills Inc.

Vierk, Richard J.: trustee, Cooper Foundation

Vigeland, Julie: co-trustee, Jackson Foundation (OR); trustee, Wessinger Foundation

Vill, Robert: trustee, Claiborne Foundation (Liz)

Villani, Edmond D.: trustee, Rockefeller Brothers Fund, Inc.

Villarosa, Lori: director, Rockefeller Foundation (Winthrop)

Vincent, Kirk F.: executive vice president, J&L Specialty Steel Inc.

Vincent, Luci Daley: director, Hamilton Charitable Corp.

Vincent, Pat: treasurer, Xcel Energy Foundation

Vinney, Les C.: senior vice president, chief financial officer, Goodrich Corp.

Vinolus, Peter: vice chairman, trustee, Statler Foundation

Vinovich, William N.: vice chairman, trustee, Anderson Foundation (John W.)

Viola, Mike: vice president, treasurer, SBC Foundation

Viola, Vincent: chairman, director, New York Mercantile Exchange Charitable Foundation

Virch, Claus: trustee, Sharp Foundation (Evelyn)

Virkler, Laura H.: director, Kirby Foundation (F. M.)

Visbal, J. Malcolm: director, Gellert Foundation (Carl Gellert and Celia Berta)

Visci, Joseph: director, Knight Ridder Fund

Vitarelli, Robert: program officer, Reynolds Foundation (Christopher)

Vitti, Bonnie: trustee, Price Foundation (Louis and Harold)

Vliet, Marni: president, chief executive officer, director, Kansas Health Foundation

Voelkel, Alice K.: member, Knott Foundation (Marion I. and Henry J.)

Vogel, Daniel C.: vice president, Vogel Foundation

Vogel, David L.: president, Vogel Foundation

Vogel, Judith: director, Mid-Iowa Health Foundation

Vogel, Peter C.: secretary, Vogel Foundation

Vogt, David: adv, O'Bleness Foundation (Charles)

Voilleque, Anne S.: director, CHC Foundation

Vojvoda, Antoinette P.: president, Knapp Foundation, Inc. (MD)

Volanakis, Peter F.: president Corning technologies, Corning Inc.; trustee, Corning Inc. Foundation

Volden, Mary Ellen: director global philanthropy, Binney & Smith Inc.

Volk, Norman Hans: chairman, trustee, Hartford Foundation, Inc. (The John A.)

Volk, Stephen R.: chairman, Credit Suisse First Boston Corp.

Volland, Patricia J.: trustee, Altman Foundation

von Bernuth, C. W.: general counsel, secretary, trustee, Union Pacific Foundation

von Habsburg-Lothringen, Inmaculada: trustee, Kress Foundation (Samuel H.)

von Kalinowski, Julian Onesime: director, member legal committee, Keck Foundation (W. M.)

von Ziegesar, Franz: trustee, Bowne Foundation (Robert)

Vonderhaar, Douglas B.: vice president, Giddings & Lewis Foundation

Vora, Sonia: assistant secretary, Bristol-Myers Squibb Foundation Inc.

Vorhees, Charles A.: director, Brach Foundation (Helen)

Vorous, Steve: chief financial officer, Sierra Health Foundation

Votek, Glenn A.: assistant secretary, CIT Group Foundation

Vought, Lucas: director, Menasha Corp. Foundation

Vout, Murray C.: trustee, AT&T National Pro-Am Youth Fund

Voyles, Bobby L.: president, Citizens Union Bank; chairman, director, Citizens Union Bank Foundation

Vradenburg, George, III: director, Time Warner Foundation, Inc.

Vraney, Inge: vice president, director, Koch Foundation, Inc.

Vraney, Lawrence: treasurer, Koch Foundation, Inc.

Vraney, Maura J.: director, Koch Foundation, Inc.

Vucurevich, Alex: adv board, Vucurevich Foundation (John T.)

Vucurevich, Thomas J.: adv board, Vucurevich Foundation (John T.)

Vujovich, Christina M.: vice president environmental policy, Cummins Inc.

W

Wabich, James A.: assistant secretary, Sara Lee Foundation

Wacaster, C. Thompson: vice president, Hardin Foundation (Phil)

Wachenfeld, Howard G.: trustee, Hayden Foundation (Charles)

Wachs, James S.: secretary, trustee, Emery Memorial (Thomas J.)

Wachs, Joel: president, director, Warhol Foundation for the Visual Arts (The Andy)

Wachtel, Michael D.: president, Oshkosh B'Gosh Foundation Inc.; chief operating officer, Oshkosh B'Gosh Inc.

Wachtell, Wendy: vice president, director, program director, Drown Foundation (Joseph)

Waddell, James S.: president, director, AMCORE Foundation

Wade, Malcolm S., Jr.: co-trustee, United States Sugar Corp. Charitable Trust

Wade, William: manager, Porter Testamentary Trust (James Hyde)

Wade, Wyatt R.: president, Memorial Foundation for the Blind

Wadleigh, Theodore: trustee, Cogswell Benevolent Trust

Wages, Robin A.: secretary, IBP Foundation

Waggoner, Robert E.: director, Bush Charitable Foundation, Inc. (Edyth)

Wagman, Sandy: vice president, secretary, CNA Foundation

Ware, Marian S.: chairman, president, Oxford Foundation

Ware, Paul W.: vice president, Oxford Foundation

Wareing, Elizabeth B.: president, Scurlock Foundation

Warfield, Guy: trustee, Warfield Memorial Fund (Anna Emory)

Wargo, Bruce W.: secretary, treasurer, Anderson Foundation (John W.)

Warhola, John: vice president, director, Warhol Foundation for the Visual Arts (The Andy)

Waring, Bayard D.: co-managing trustee, Peabody Foundation (Amelia)

Waring, Philip B.: vice president grant making, Peabody Foundation (Amelia)

Wark, Robert Rodgers: president emeritus, Scott Foundation (Virginia Steele)

Warlick, Rick: program director, UPS Foundation

Warman, Michele S.: secretary, general counsel, Mellon Foundation (Andrew W.)

Warner, C. Elizabeth: secretary, treasurer, Public Welfare Foundation

Warner, Carolyn D.: trustee, Glendorn Foundation

Warner, Glen W.: trustee, Ashtabula Foundation

Warner, Joseph C.: trustee, Simon Foundation (Sidney, Milton, and Leoma)

Warner, Meryll: trustee, Simon Foundation (Sidney, Milton, and Leoma)

Warner, Norton E.: trustee, Cooper Foundation

Warner, Theodore Kugler, Jr.: secretary, treasurer, Independence Foundation

Warnock, John E.: co-chairman, chief technology officer, Adobe Systems

Warren, Anthony J.: trustee, West Bend Mutual Charitable Trust

Warren, Ingrid R.: director, Dodge Foundation (Cleveland H.)

Warren, Shirley: director, Davenport-Hatch Foundation

Warren, Wilbert W., Jr.: director, Baird Brothers Co. Foundation

Warren, William Michael, Jr.: chairman, president, chief executive officer, chief operating officer, director, Energen Corp.

Warsaw, James: president, chief executive officer, director, AMCORE Financial Inc.

Warwin, Jason: trustee, New York Foundation

Wascoe, Thomas M.: director, Abbott Laboratories Fund

Washington, Nancy D.: president, Pittsburgh Child Guidance Foundation

Washington, Phyllis: chairman, Washington Foundation (Dennis R. and Phyllis)

Wasserstein, Wendy: director, Educational Foundation of America

Watanabe, August M., MD: director, Lilly Foundation (Eli)

Waterbury, James B.: trustee, chairman, McElroy Trust (R. J.)

Waterhouse, Christine A.: director, Waterhouse Family Foundation

Waterhouse, Jennifer A.: director, Waterhouse Family Foundation

Waterhouse, Kevin C.: director, Waterhouse Family Foundation

Waterhouse, Lawrence M., III: director, Waterhouse Family Foundation

Waterhouse, Lawrence M., Jr.: president, Waterhouse Family Foundation

Waterhouse, Patrick R.: director, Waterhouse Family Foundation

Waters, Frank: director, Tri-County Telephone Foundation

Waters, John: chief financial officer, Guaranty Bank & Trust Co.; director, Warhol Foundation for the Visual Arts (The Andy)

Waters, Richard: director, Mitsubishi Electric America Foundation

Watkins, Gregory W.: vice president, El Paso Corporate Foundation

Watkins, Ruth Ann: secretary, trustee, Retirement Research Foundation

Watkins, W. C.: director, Penney Co. Fund (J.C.)

Watrous, Helen C.: director, Petteys Memorial Foundation (Jack)

Watson, Alonzo Wallace, Jr.: secretary, director, Eccles Foundation (George S. and Dolores Dore); committee member, Eccles Foundation (Marriner S.)

Watson, Colin P.: vice chairman, KeySpan Foundation

Watson, Daniel E.: director, Kinder Morgan Foundation

Watson, Jane W.: assistant secretary, assistant treasurer, Ingalls Foundation (Louise H. and David S.)

Watson, Jerome P.: director, Oakley-Lindsay Foundation of Quincy Newspapers and Its Subsidiaries

Watson, JoAnn: corporator, Island Foundation (MA)

Watson, Michael: trustee, BellSouth Foundation

Watson, Michael B.: vice president, director, Mellon Family Foundation (R. K.); vice president, trustee, Mellon Foundation (Richard King)

Watson, Raymond L.: vice chairman, Pacific Life Insurance Co.

Watson, Solomon Brown, IV: senior vice president, general counsel, New York Times Co. Foundation

Watson, Steven L.: president, director, Contran Corp.; vice president, secretary, director, Simmons Foundation, Inc. (Harold)

Watson, Stuart H.: member advisory board, Watson Foundation (Thomas J.)

Watson, Thomas John, III: mem adv board, Watson Foundation (Thomas J.)

Watt, Alston Parker: executive director, Williams Family Foundation of Georgia

Watts, Douglas D.: vice president financial, chief financial officer, Amcast Industrial Corp.

Waughtal, Bill: trustee, Lunda Charitable Trust

Way, Ann M.: senior program officer, Sarkeys Foundation

Weakley, Samuel D., MD: trustee, Gheens Foundation

Weary, Daniel C.: trustee, Turner Charitable Trust (Courtney S.)

Weatherford, T. L.: member advisory committee, Blue Bell Foundation

Weaver, Andrew P.: assistant treasurer, Reliant Resources Foundation

Weaver, Connie: president, AT&T Foundation

Weaver, Henry V.: president, Kayser Foundation

Weaver, James D.: president, Cain Foundation (Gordon and Mary)

Weaver, James R.: secretary, Kent-Lucas Foundation

Weaver, John F.: director, La-Z-Boy Inc.

Weaver, Lance L.: executive vice chairman, chief administrative officer, MBNA Corp.; chairman, trustee, The MBNA Foundation

Weaver, Philip G.: executive vice president, chief financial officer, trustee, Cooper Tire & Rubber Co.; trustee, Cooper Tire & Rubber Foundation

Weaver, R. H.: board mem, Roberts Foundation (Dora)

Weaver, Sharyn A.: vice president, Cain Foundation (Gordon and Mary)

Weaver, Thomas C.: trustee, Acushnet Foundation

Weaver, William R., MD: trustee, Weaver Foundation (Gil and Dody)

Webb, Anne B.: trustee, Braitmayer Foundation

Webb, Charles E.: director, Oakley-Lindsay Foundation of Quincy Newspapers and Its Subsidiaries

Webb, G.: director, Archer-Daniels-Midland Foundation

Webb, Jack H.: trustee, Gifford Charitable Corp. (Rosamond)

Webb, R. Davis, Jr.: trustee, Braitmayer Foundation

Webb, Thomas J.: director, Consumers Energy Foundation

Webber, W. Temple, Jr.: trustee, Temple Foundation (T. L. L.)

Weber, A. I.: partner, Shatz, Schwartz & Fentin P.C.

Weber, Arnold R.: director, vice president, Crown Memorial (Arie and Ida)

Weber, Irene B.: treasurer, Rippel Foundation (Fannie E.)

Weber, Lisa M.: director, MetLife Foundation; president, individual business, Metropolitan Life Insurance Co.

Weber, Robert W.: president, Smoot Charitable Foundation

Weberpal, Mike: counsel, Halliburton Foundation, Inc.

Webster, Gordon: chief financial officer, Hilliard Corp.; treasurer, trustee, Hilliard Foundation

Webster, Kate: director, Bishop Foundation (E. K. and Lillian F.)

Wechsler, Irving A.: treasurer, Jennings Foundation (Mary Hillman)

Wechsley, Lewis: director, Kurz Family Foundation

Weckbaugh, Heather: director, Mullen Foundation (J. K.)

Weckbaugh, John K.: vice president, director, Mullen Foundation (J. K.)

Weckbaugh, Walter S.: treasurer, director, Mullen Foundation (J. K.)

Wedel, Kermit, MD: chairman, director, Kansas Health Foundation

Weeks, Joshua J.: trustee, Johnson Foundation (Howard)

Weeks, Wendell P.: president, chief operating officer, director, Corning Inc.; trustee, Corning Inc. Foundation

Weeks, William H.: trustee, Johnson Foundation (Howard)

Weese, Benjamin Horace: president, trustee, Graham Foundation for Advanced Studies in the Fine Arts

Wege, Christopher: trustee, Wege Foundation

Wege, Jonathan C.: trustee, Wege Foundation

Wege, Peter M.: president, trustee, Wege Foundation

Wege, Peter M., II: vice president, Steelcase Foundation; director, Steelcase Inc.; vice president, trustee, Wege Foundation

Wegen, Jennifer A.: vice president, secretary, director, JJJ Foundation

Wegen, Keith W.: president, director, JJJ Foundation

Wehr, James D.: director, Phoenix Foundation

Weidemeyer, Thomas H.: secretary, trustee, UPS Foundation

Weigel, David V.: treasurer, MONY Foundation

Weigel, Judy: treasurer, director, Best Buy Children's Foundation

Weigell, Bonnie R.: trustee, McBeath Foundation (Faye)

Weil, Amanda E.: director, vice president, Norman Foundation

Weil, Andrew L.: secretary, Jennings Foundation (Mary Hillman)

Weil, Andrey: director, Time Warner Foundation, Inc.

Weil, Deborah Holt: trustee, Holt Family Foundation

Weil, Robert J.: vice president operations, McClatchy Co.; director, Star Tribune Foundation

Weil, Sandison E.: director, Norman Foundation

Weil, William B., Jr.: trustee, Gerber Foundation

Weil, William S.: director, Norman Foundation

Weill, Sanford I.: chairman, Citigroup Inc.

Weiller, Margaret S.: treasurer, trustee, Rich Foundation

Weilman, Charles: director, Hebrew Technical Institute

Weinberg, Eli: treasurer, secretary, Teagle Foundation

Weiner, Susan E.: assistant secretary, Universal Studios Foundation

Weinfeld, Sonya: director, Allyn Foundation

Weingarten, Charles Annenberg: trustee, Annenberg Foundation

Weingarten, Gregory Annenberg: trustee, Annenberg Foundation

Weinstein, Elaine: director, KeySpan Foundation

Weintraub, Robert M.: president, director, Alexander Foundation (Joseph)

Weir, Amelia F.: trustee, Weir Foundation (Candace King)

Weir, Candace K.: trustee, Weir Foundation (Candace King)

Weir, Robert H.: director, Furthur Foundation

Weis, Konrad M.: chairman, director,

Weisbrod, Carl B.: trustee, Ford Foundation

Weiser, Ann: member, Giant Food Foundation

Weisman, Walter L.: trustee, Kress Foundation (Samuel H.)

Weiss, Catherine: trustee, Huber Foundation

Weiss, Cathy M.: executive director, Claneil Foundation

Weiss, Cora: president, Rubin Foundation (Samuel)

Weiss, Dana A.: trustee, Smith Family Foundation (Richard and Susan)

Weiss, Daniel: director, Rubin Foundation (Samuel)

Weiss, David E.: chairman, president, chief executive officer, director, Storage Technology Corp.

Weiss, Elie: trustee, Sapirstein-Stone-Weiss Foundation

Weiss, Gary: vice president, secretary, trustee, Sapirstein-Stone-Weiss Foundation

Weiss, Howard M.: corporate co-trustee, member investment committee, Goldseker Foundation of Maryland (Morris)

Weiss, Jeffrey: trustee, Sapirstein-Stone-Weiss Foundation

Weiss, Judith: trustee, Sapirstein-Stone-Weiss Foundation

Weiss, Judy: vice president, Rubin Foundation (Samuel)

Weiss, Margie: director, Menasha Corp. Foundation

Weiss, Morry: president, trustee, Sapirstein-Stone-Weiss Foundation

Weiss, Peter: treasurer, Rubin Foundation (Samuel)

Weiss, Robert E.: vice president admin, Meadows Foundation (The)

Weiss, Stephen H.: director, Teagle Foundation

Weiss, Tamara: director, Rubin Foundation (Samuel)

Weiss, William D.: secretary, Weiss Foundation (William E.)

Weiss, William U.: secretary, Weiss Foundation (William E.)

Weiss, Zev: treasurer, trustee, Sapirstein-Stone-Weiss Foundation

Weitzenhoser, Max: director, Kirkpatrick Foundation, Inc.

Weizenbaum, Norman: trustee, Giant Eagle Foundation

Welch, Edwin H.: member, trustee, One Valley Bank Foundation

Welch, James S.: director, Cralle Foundation

Welch, Mark: co-trustee, Arakelian Foundation (Mary Alice)

Welch, William J.: vice president, director, Kornfeld Foundation (Emily Davie and Joseph S.)

Welder, Paul E.: trustee, Self Family Foundation

Welke, Tom: trustee, Whirlpool Foundation

Welker, Norris J.: trustee, Puterbaugh Foundation

Welker, T. E.: director, King Foundation (Kenneth Kendal)

Wellen, Dennis: director, Washington Group Foundation, Inc.

Weller, Lucy I.: vice president, Mather and William Gwinn Mather Fund (Elizabeth Ring)

Welling, Eleanor: trustee, Symmes Foundation (F. W.)

Welling, F. K.: treasurer, National Standard Foundation

Wellman, Barclay O.: treasurer, Sheldon Foundation Inc. (Ralph C.)

Wells, Mike: trustee, George Foundation

Wells, Nina M.: president, Schering-Plough Foundation

Wells, Nina Mitchell: trustee, Victoria Foundation

Wells, T. Diane: trustee, McKinney Charitable Trust (Carl and Alleen)

Wells, W. David: mem adv comm, Jordan and Ettie A. Jordan Charitable Foundation (Mary Ranken)

Welsh, Carol A.: trustee, Welsh Family Foundation

Welsh, Eric A.: trustee, Welsh Family Foundation

Welsh, Patrick J.: trustee, Welsh Family Foundation

Welte, Wendy B.: secretary, American Century Companies Foundation

Wendel, Larry L.: executive secretary, Van Wert County Foundation

Wendell, James F.: assistant secretary, assistant treasurer, Knox Foundation (Seymour H.)

Wendler, William F., II: vice president, trustee, Price Associates Foundation (T. Rowe)

Wendt, Greg: director, Cowell Foundation (S. H.)

Wendt, Nancy: trustee, Jeld-wen Foundation

Wendt, Richard L.: trustee, Jeld-wen Foundation; chief executive officer, chairman, Jeld-Wen Inc.

Wendt, Roderick C.: trustee, Jeld-wen Foundation; president, director, Jeld-Wen Inc.

Wente, Deborah: director, VPI Foundation

Wentling, Thomas L., Jr.: member, Staunton Farm Foundation

Wentworth, Elizabeth B.: co-trustee, Bishop Charitable Trust (A. G.)

Werderman, Del V.: treasurer, Hoag Family Foundation (George)

Werner, Jan: secretary, treasurer, Vaughn, Jr. Foundation Fund (James M.)

Werner, John B.: executive director, Cabell III and Maude Morgan Cabell Foundation (Robert G.)

Wertich, Richard: secretary, Morgan Foundation (Louie R. and Gertrude)

Wertz, Ronald W.: president, Hillman Foundation

Wesby, Meridith D.: director, Daniels Foundation (Fred Harris)

Wescombe, Gary T.: treasurer, chief financial officer, Beckman Foundation (Arnold and Mabel)

Wesley, Norman H.: president, chief operating officer, Fortune Brands Inc.

Wesselink, David D.: president, director, Metris Companies Foundation; chairman, chief executive officer, Metris Companies Inc.

Wessely, Boris A.: treasurer, Rockefeller Brothers Fund, Inc.

Wessinger, E. Charles: trustee, Wessinger Foundation

Wessinger, Henry W.: treasurer, Wessinger Foundation

Wessinger, William W.: trustee emeritus, Wessinger Foundation

Wesson, Mark D.: treasurer, controller, Liberty Corp. Foundation

West, A. Stanley: senior vice president, sales & commercial planning, Cleveland-Cliffs Inc.

West, David M., MD: director, Copic Medical Foundation

West, Doreen: director, Midcontinent Media Foundation

West, Gordon T., Jr.: vice president, trustee, West Foundation (TX)

West, Neva Watkins: don, trustee, West Foundation (Neva and Wesley)

West, Reece A.: president, trustee, West Foundation (TX)

West, Ronald D.: executive director, secretary, Emerson Foundation, Inc. (Fred L.); president, director, French Foundation (D.E.)

West, Tem: vice president, director, Texas Instruments Foundation

West, Terry W.: president, trustee, Sarkeys Foundation

West, W. Richard, Jr.: trustee, Ford Foundation

Westby, Gerald H.: trustee, Westby Foundation (Kathleen Patton)

Westby, John Trygve: trustee, Westby Foundation (Kathleen Patton)

Westerhoff, Garret P.: trustee, Westerhoff Family Foundation, Inc.

Westerhoff, Helga K.: trustee, Westerhoff Family Foundation, Inc.

Westerhoff, Katherine: trustee, Westerhoff Family Foundation, Inc.

Western, David: director, Claiborne and Art Ortenberg Foundation (Liz)

Westfeldt, Thomas D.: director, vice president, Schlieder Educational Foundation (Edward G.)

Westman, Steve: vice president, CNA Foundation

Wetter, Larry V.: vice chairman, director, Jeld-Wen Inc.

Wettingfeld, Robert F., MD: president, Holmberg Foundation

Wetz, P. A.: trustee, Exxon Mobil Foundation

Wetzel, Mark R.: trustee, Ellsworth Foundation (Ruth H. and Warren A.)

Wetzel, Todd H.: trustee, Ellsworth Foundation (Ruth H. and Warren A.)

Weyerhaeuser, Annette B.: vice president, director, Forest Foundation

Weyerhaeuser, Annette Thayer Black: board member, Stewardship Foundation

Weyerhaeuser, Gail T.: president, treasurer, director, Forest Foundation

Weyerhaeuser, George Hunt: director, Weyerhaeuser Co.; trustee, Weyerhaeuser Co. Foundation

Weyerhaeuser, William T.: director, Forest Foundation

Weyerhaeuser, William Toycen: chairman, Stewardship Foundation

Weyers, Larry Lee: chief executive officer, chairman, director, WPS Resources Corp.; president, chief executive officer, WPS Resources Foundation, Inc.

Weyland, Wendell P.: trustee, Benz Trust (Doris L.)

Weymouth, George A.: trustee, Allegheny Foundation

Whalen, George T., Jr.: treasurer, Millbrook Tribute Garden

Whalen, Michael S.: co-trustee, Stauffer Charitable Trust (John)

Whalen, Robert W.: trustee, Millbrook Tribute Garden

Wharton, Clifton R., Jr.: director, Clark Foundation (NY)

Wheeler, Arnold: chief financial officer, Bartlett & Co.

Wheeler, Charles B.: vice president, director, Wheeler Foundation

Wheeler, Edward T.: secretary, director, Wheeler Foundation

Wheeler, John C.: vice president, director, Wheeler Foundation

Wheeler, Joyce W.: director, Royal & SunAlliance Insurance Foundation, Inc.; vice president, corporate secretary, Royal & SunAlliance USA Inc.

Wheeler, Margaret S.: senior program officer, Bruening Foundation (Eva L. and Joseph M.)

Wheeler, Ruth B.: trustee, Dow Foundation (Herbert H. and Grace A.)

Wheeler, Samuel C.: president, director, Wheeler Foundation

Wheeler, Thomas K.: treasurer, director, Wheeler Foundation

Wheeler, Wilmot Fitch, Jr.: vice president, director, Morris Foundation (William T.)

Whelan, Tim: trustee, Morgan Charitable Residual Trust (W. and E.)

Whetzel, William: director, Staunton Farm Foundation

Whipple, Kenneth: chairman, Consumers Energy Foundation

Whipple, William Perry: chairman, director, Hall-Perrine Foundation

Whisenant, Douglas J.: director, Williams Companies Foundation (The)

Whisler, J. Steven: chairman, president, chief executive officer, Phelps Dodge Corp.; member, Phelps Dodge Foundation

Whitacre, Edward E., Jr.: chairman, director, chief executive officer, SBC Communications Inc.

Whitaker, Lisa A.: assistant treasurer, Deere Foundation (John)

Whitaker, Shannon McNeely: trustee, McNeely Foundation

Whitaker, T. E.: assistant secretary, Union Pacific Foundation

White, A. Dennis: vice president, MetLife Foundation

White, B. Briscoe, III: director, Flagler Foundation

White, C. Cody, Jr.: president, treasurer, Powers Foundation

White, Charles H., Jr.: director, Heath Foundation (Ed and Mary)

White, Claire Mott: trustee, Mott Foundation (Charles Stewart)

White, Edward D., III: trustee, Boettcher Foundation

White, Eileen B.: trustee, Cooper Tire & Rubber Foundation

White, Henry A., Jr.: trustee, Young Foundation (Bill B.)

White, J. Randall: director, Sara Lee Foundation

White, James: trustee, Dow Corning Foundation

White, James M., Jr.: trustee, Levy Foundation (June Rockwell)

White, James R.: secretary, director, Square D Foundation

White, John D.: chairman, Rachal Foundation (Ed)

White, John H.: trustee, Young Foundation (Bill B.)

White, John P.: chairman, director, Kornfeld Foundation (Emily Davie and Joseph S.)

White, John W., Jr.: trustee, Cooper Foundation

White, Kenan Lewis: secretary, director, Flagler Foundation

White, Lynn T.: president, trustee, Towsley Foundation (Harry A. and Margaret D.)

White, Margaret R.: trustee, Hillsdale Fund

White, Marion C.: secretary, Klipstein Foundation (Ernest Christian)

White, Miles D.: chairman, chief executive officer, Abbott Laboratories; director, Abbott Laboratories Fund

White, Nancy G.: director, Green Foundation (Allen P. and Josephine B.)

White, Pamela: director, Memton Fund

White, Philip O., Jr.: vice president, treasurer, White Foundation (W. P. and H. B.)

White, Robert P.: director, White Foundation (W. P. and H. B.)

White, Roger B.: president, White Foundation (W. P. and H. B.)

White, Sara Margaret: vice president, secretary, Powers Foundation

White, Stephen C.: vice president, Powers Foundation

White, Steven R.: secretary, White Foundation (W. P. and H. B.)

White, William Bew, Jr.: trustee, Shook Foundation (Barbara Ingalls)

White, William Samuel: chairman, president, chief executive officer, trustee, Mott Foundation (Charles Stewart)

Whitehead, John C.: chairman emeritus, Mellon Foundation (Andrew W.)

Whitfield, Sue Trammell: board of governors, Fondren Foundation

Whitfield, Susan T.: board of governors, Fondren Foundation

Whitfield, W. Trammell: board of governors, Fondren Foundation

Whitfield, William F., Jr.: board of governors, Fondren Foundation

Whitfield, William F., Sr.: board of governors, Fondren Foundation

Whiting, Eleanor W.: assistant treasurer, Plankenhorn Foundation (Harry)

Whiting, Helen Dow: trustee, Dow Foundation (Herbert H. and Grace A.)

Whiting, Macauley: president, trustee, Whiting Foundation (Macauley and Helen Dow)

Whiting, Macauley, Jr.: secretary, trustee, Dow Foundation (Herbert H. and Grace A.)

Whiting, Mary Macauley: secretary, trustee, Whiting Foundation (Macauley and Helen Dow)

Whiting, Sara: trustee, Whiting Foundation (Macauley and Helen Dow)

Whitmire, Julia: trustee, Priddy Foundation

Whitney, Charles L.: atty, secretary, director, Heuermann Foundation (Bernard K. and Norma F.)

Whitney, Donald W.: chairman, trustee, Jones Foundation (Daisy Marquis)

Whitney, Kate R.: vice president, trustee, Greentree Foundation

Whitney, Steven C.: program officer, Bullitt Foundation

Whitridge, Fredrick W.: trustee, Crocker Trust (Mary A.)

Whitridge, Serena H.: vice president, trustee, Merck Family Fund

Whittaker, E. William: treasurer, trustee, Anderson Foundation (NY)

Whittaker, J. Bruce: president, Bank of Greene County Charitable Foundation

Whittelsey, Lucia: clerk, Oak Grove School

Whittemore, Clark M., Jr.: director, Dana Foundation (Charles A.)

Whittenburg, James V.: trustee, Snyder Foundation (Harold B. and Dorothy A.)

Whitton, Roger: controller, Thomas Foundation

Whitwam, David Ray: chairman, president, chief executive officer, director, Whirlpool Corp.; director, Whirlpool Foundation

Whyel, Rosalie A.: vice president, Usibelli Foundation

Whyte, Joseph L.: director, Loughran Foundation (Mary and Daniel)

Wiatr, Francis J.: president, director, New Milford Savings Bank Foundation; president, chief executive officer, director, NewMil Bancorp

Wice, David Herschel: board member, president, Fels Fund (Samuel S.)

Wideman, Frank J., III: president, Self Family Foundation

Widener, Mary Lee: director, Cowell Foundation (S. H.)

Wiedemann, Dorothy E.: trustee, Schlink Foundation (Albert G. and Olive H.)

Wiedemann, Robert A.: president, Schlink Foundation (Albert G. and Olive H.)

Wiegley, Allan R.: treasurer, director, Oishei Foundation (The John R.)

Wiens, Harold J.: executive vice president, Minnesota Mining & Manufacturing Co.

Wierichs, James R.: secretary, Morgan Foundation (Louie R. and Gertrude)

Wiertelak, James B.: senior vice president, chief financial officer, director, Sedgwick Inc.

Wierzba, Thomas M.: trustee, Johnson Fund (S.C.)

Wiese, Barbara P.: trustee, Ashtabula Foundation

Wigchers, Nancy: secretary, director, Best Buy Children's Foundation

Wigdale, James B.: chairman, director, Marshall & Ilsley Corp.; president, director, Marshall & Ilsley Foundation, Inc.

Wightman, Orrin S., III: trustee, Dula Educational and Charitable Founda-

tion (Caleb C. and Julia W.)

Wilband, Laura: trustee, Cacioppo Foundation (Joseph and Mary)

Wilbanks, Daniel P.: vchairman, Blount Educational and Charitable Foundation (Mildred Weedon)

Wilboith, Bert M.: director, Ayres Foundation

Wilbur, Colburn S.: trustee, Packard Foundation (David and Lucile)

Wilcox, Diane E. H., Esq.: director, Joco Foundation

Wildenstein, Daniel Leopold: vice president, director, Gould Foundation (The Florence)

Wilder, David: trustee, Mayer Foundation (James and Eva)

Wilder, Robert D.: executive vice president, chief financial officer, Wiley & Sons Inc. (John)

Wilding White, Mary Louise: trustee, Higgins Foundation (John W. and Clara C.)

Wilding White, Philip Q.: trustee, Higgins Foundation (John W. and Clara C.)

Wile, Sarah W.: director, Hardin Foundation (Phil)

Wiley, Barbara M.: director, Badger Meter Foundation

Wiley, Bradford, II: chairman, director, Wiley & Sons Inc. (John)

Wiley, Deborah: chairman, Wiley & Sons Inc. (John)

Wiley, Donna L.: director, Clowes Fund

Wiley, S. Donald: director, Heinz Co. (H.J.); trustee, Heinz Endowment (Vira I.)

Wilfley, Mike: trustee, Gates Family Foundation

Wilfong, Scott: member, SunTrust Bank Atlanta Foundation

Wilford, Ronald A.: trustee, Greentree Foundation

Wilford, Sara R.: vice president, trustee, Greentree Foundation

Wilhelm, Kevin: trustee, Reilly Foundation

Wilhelm, Suzanne Anthony: director, IMMI Word and Deed Foundation

Wilkening, Laurel Lynn: director, Research Corp.

Wilkerson, Thomas D.: mem, trustee, One Valley Bank Foundation

Wilkes, Andrea: secretary, trustee, Kiplinger Foundation

Wilkes, Corbin M.: vice president finance, Kiplinger Washington Editors Inc.

Wilkes, Susan Cornell: trustee, Cornell Trust (Peter C.)

Wilkie, Valleau, Jr.: executive vice president, exec-

utive director, The Wallace Foundation

Wilkin, Abra Prentice: president, Prentice Foundation (Abra)

Wilkin, George: co-trustee, Luse Foundation (W. P. and Bulah)

Wilkins, Rayford, Jr.: director, SBC Foundation

Wilkins, Wilfred G.: chairman, trustee, Anderson Foundation (John W.)

Wilkinson, Darla J.: trustee, Sullivan Foundation (Algernon Sydney)

Wilkinson, F. McKinnon: trustee, Symmes Foundation (F. W.)

Wilkinson, Frank W.: secretary, Bowen Foundation (Ethel N.)

Wilkinson, Jill Matthews: director, Dodge Jones Foundation and Subsidiary

Wilkinson, Richard W.: president, Bowen Foundation (Ethel N.)

Wilkof, Richard: trustee, Wilkof Foundation (Edward and Ruth)

Wille, Robert H.: vice president, trustee, Arkell Hall Foundation

Willemetz, J. Lester: board member, treasurer, Olin Foundation (Spencer T. and Ann W.)

Willes, Mark Hinckley: chairman, Times Mirror Foundation

Willhardt, Gary, PhD: trustee, Mellinger Educational Foundation (Edward Arthur)

Williams, A. Morris, Jr.: president, director, Pine Tree Foundation

Williams, Allison F.: trustee, Harland Charitable Foundation (John H. and Wilhelmina D.)

Williams, Dale: trustee, McKay Family Foundation

Williams, David R.: trustee, Heinz Co. Foundation (H.J.); executive vice president, director, Heinz Co. (H.J.)

Williams, Dennis: director, Oakley-Lindsay Foundation of Quincy Newspapers and Its Subsidiaries

Williams, E. Belvin: secretary, trustee, Turrell Fund

Williams, E. Grainger: board director, Ottenheimer Brothers Foundation

Williams, Elynor Alberta: director, Sara Lee Foundation

Williams, Eugene Flewellyn, Jr.: chairman, trustee, Olin Foundation (John M.)

Williams, Gary S.: treasurer, director, Bank of America Foundation

Williams, Gayle: executive director, Babcock Foundation (Mary Reynolds)

Williams, Gray, Jr.: trustee, Sullivan Foundation (Algernon Sydney)

Williams, James B.: chairman, trustee, Woodruff Foundation (Robert W.)

Williams, Jane: trustee, Quaker Chemical Foundation

Williams, John: member, trustee, One Valley Bank Foundation

Williams, John O.: director, CTW Foundation, Inc.

Williams, Karen Hastie: director, Fannie Mae Foundation

Williams, M. Nancy: executive vice president, Cockrell Foundation

Williams, Marty: chief financial officer, Lisle Corp.

Williams, Mary C.: vice president, director, New Milford Savings Bank Foundation

Williams, Neil: trustee, Duke Endowment

Williams, Raymond H.: vice president, director, Zellerbach Family Fund

Williams, Robert: member distribution committee, Bedsole Foundation (J. L.)

Williams, Robert G.: director, Pew Charitable Trusts

Williams, Robert M.: assistant secretary, Progress Energy Foundation

Williams, Ruth W.: secretary, treasurer, director, Pine Tree Foundation

Williams, Stella R.: assistant secretary, Kent-Lucas Foundation

Williams, Stephen J.: director, Raker Foundation (M. E.)

Williams, Thomas: trustee, Boettcher Foundation

Williams, Thomas J.: trustee, Western-Southern Foundation, Inc.

Williams, Thomas L.: trustee, Emery Memorial (Thomas J.)

Williams, Thomas L., III: president, director, Williams Family Foundation of Georgia

Williams, William Joseph: trustee, Western-Southern Foundation, Inc.

Williamson, Anne: executive director, Keller Foundation

Williamson, Charles R.: chief executive officer, chairman, director, Unocal Corp.

Williamson, Harold: director, Copic Medical Foundation

Williamson, Jack: trustee, Williams Charitable Trust (Mary Jo)

Williamson, Richard: trustee, Chicago Title and Trust Co. Foundation

Williamson, Susan K.: mem distribution comm, trustee, Kettering Fund

Williamson, W. Bland: secretary, trustee, Bernsen Foundation (Grace and Franklin)

Williard, David: secretary, Cape Cod Five Cents Savings Bank Charitable Trust

Willis, Beth: chairman, Xcel Energy Foundation

Willis, Dudley H.: trustee, Saltonstall Charitable Foundation (Richard)

Willis, Evelyn Sayer: vice president, director, Willis Family Foundation

Willis, Jo Ellyn: vice president, director, Square D Foundation

Willis, Mark A.: trustee, J.P. Morgan Chase Foundation

Willis, Sally S.: trustee, Saltonstall Charitable Foundation (Richard)

Willis, Steve: director, Trust Foundation

Willner, Robin: director, IBM International Foundation; member, International Business Machines

Willock, Norman A.: director, Fear Not Foundation

Willock, Scott: director, Fear Not Foundation

Willrich, Mason: director, Goldman Fund (Richard and Rhoda)

Wills, Rosemary C.: assistant secretary, assistant treasurer, duPont Foundation (Alfred I.)

Willson, George C., III: president, director, Green Foundation (Allen P. and Josephine B.)

Willson, Harry: director, Haley Foundation (W. B.)

Willumstad, Robert B.: president, chief operating officer, director, Citigroup Inc.

Wilmers, Robert G.: director, Warhol Foundation for the Visual Arts (The Andy)

Wilsey, Alfred S., Jr.: secretary, treasurer, Wilsey Foundation

Wilsey, Diane B.: vice president, Wilsey Foundation

Wilsey, Michael W.: vice president, Wilsey Foundation

Wilson, Angelina M.: trustee, Wilson Foundation (Huey and Angeline)

Wilson, Blenda Jacqueline: trustee, Getty Trust (J. Paul)

Wilson, Bret G.: assistant secretary, H&R Block Foundation

Wilson, D. W.: trustee, Fluor Foundation

Wilson, Don M.: trustee, J.P. Morgan Chase Foundation

Wilson, Dorothy B.: vice chairman, Toms Foundation (The)

Wilson, Dorothy Cheney: director emeritus, Meadows Foundation (The)

Wilson, Eric: director, U.S. Bancorp Piper Jaffray Foundation

Wilson, Faye C.: executive director, Gilmore Foundation (William G.)

Wilson, Frances Fondren: board of governors, Fondren Foundation

Wilson, Gayle: director, Parsons Foundation (Ralph M.)

Wilson, George E.: director, East Cambridge Savings Charitable Foundation

Wilson, H.: secretary, treasurer, Square D Foundation

Wilson, Harold S.: president, executive director, Osborne Foundation (Weldon F.)

Wilson, Howard O.: treasurer, Peppers Foundation (Ann)

Wilson, Huey J.: trustee, Wilson Foundation (Huey and Angeline)

Wilson, Isabel Brown: vice president, trustee, Brown Foundation

Wilson, J. Richard: president, Besser Foundation

Wilson, Janet C.: board of directors, Wilson Foundation (Marie C. and Joseph C.)

Wilson, John H., II: president, Piper Foundation (Minnie Stevens)

Wilson, Joseph R.: board of directors, Wilson Foundation (Marie C. and Joseph C.)

Wilson, Kirke P.: president, secretary, Rosenberg Foundation

Wilson, Peter: director, CNA Foundation

Wilson, Peter A.: trustee, Keel Foundation

Wilson, Richard A.: treasurer, director, Connell Foundation (Michael J.)

Wilson, Robert B.: trustee, Weyerhaeuser Co. Foundation

Wilson, Robert F.: treasurer, Rollins-Luetkemeyer Foundation

Wilson, Rosine M.: trustee, Ward Heritage Foundation (Mamie McFaddin)

Wilson, Sandra C.: vice president administration, director, International Paper Co. Foundation

Wilson, Scott: co-chairman, Wilson Foundation (Marie C. and Joseph C.)

Wilson, Ted: director, Norcross Wildlife Foundation

Wilson Arnold, Louise: vice president, CH Foundation

Winawer, Gail T.: director, Crames Family Foundation (Arthur)

Winch, David C.: treasurer, Minster Machine Co. Foundation

Winch, Harold S.: president, Minster Machine Co. Foundation

Winch, Heather E.: secretary, Minster Machine Co. Foundation

Winch, John: president, chief operating officer, director, Minster Machine Co.; vice president, Minster Machine Co. Foundation

Winch, Nancy E.: president, Minster Machine Co. Foundation

Winchell, Jean Rogers: mng trustee, Rogers Fund for the Arts (Russell Hill)

Winchester, David P.: director, Rice Foundation

Windsor, Robert G.: trustee, Castle Rock Foundation

Winford, Benny F.: secretary, treasurer, director, Tractor & Equipment Co. Foundation

Winkel, John: director, Bloedorn Foundation (Walter A.)

Winkelman, Edie C.: chairman, Trust Foundation

Winkhaus, Hans Dietrich: chairman, director, Henkel Corp.

Winkleman, Dennis R.: vice president, Joy Global Foundation, Inc.

Winkler, Virginia: co-trustee, Hallberg Foundation (E. L. and R. F.)

Winkley, V. Carol: assistant secretary, assistant treasurer, Davis Foundation (James A. and Juliet L.)

Winner, Bob: director, Land O'Lakes Foundation

Winship, William B.: trustee, Bingham Second Betterment Fund (William)

Winsor, Frank: director, Morrison Foundation (Harry W.)

Winston, Bert F., III: assistant secretary, trustee, Sterling-Turner Foundation

Winston, Bert F., Jr.: vice president, trustee, Sterling-Turner Foundation

Winston, Blake W.: assistant secretary, trustee, Sterling-Turner Foundation

Winston, Eleanor C.: secretary, trustee, Southways Foundation

Winston, Harold R., Sr.: director, Stebens Charitable Foundation (Bertha)

Winston, L. David: assistant secretary, trustee, Sterling-Turner Foundation

Winston, Melinda: hon director, Patron Saints Foundation

Winston, Samuel G.: trustee, Blowitz-Ridgeway Foundation

Wintrob, Jay S.: trustee, Getty Trust (J. Paul)

Wisdom, Betty: trustee, RosaMary Foundation

Wise, Emma F.: trustee, Wise Foundation (Watson W.)

Wise, Janelle Bettis: vice president, Cunningham Foundation (Laura Moore)

Wise, Kathryn E.: secretary, Norton Memorial Corp. (Geraldi)

Wise, Leslie: secretary, treasurer, Farwell Foundation (Drusilla)

Wise, Robert Edward, MD: trustee, Dana Charitable Trust (Eleanor Naylor)

Wise, Tami: foundation manager, Vanguard Group Foundation

Wiseman, Ronald D.: treasurer, Thomas Foundation

Wishnia, Steven: trustee, Plough Foundation

Wiskowski, Carol A.: assistant vice president administration, MGE Energy Inc.

Wislow, Robert A.: trustee, Graham Foundation for Advanced Studies in the Fine Arts

Wisner, Frank G.: trustee, Rockefeller Brothers Fund, Inc.

Wisnom, David, Jr.: president, Lux Foundation (Miranda)

Wisnosky, Karen: secretary, assistant treasurer, Brady Foundation

Wister, Diana S.: president, director, Strawbridge Foundation of Pennsylvania II (Margaret Dorrance)

Witham, John A.: executive vice president, chief financial officer, Metris Companies Inc.

Withers, Kathryn W.: trustee, Wessinger Foundation

Witherspoon, Douglas C.: director, Scholl Foundation (Dr.)

Withington, Nathan N.: president, Hornblower Fund (Henry)

Withum, Lawrence A., Jr.: trustee, Coen Family Foundation (Charles S. and Mary)

Wittmann, Lin: director, Brillion Foundation

Wlahofsky, Jeffrey A.: trustee, Pittsburgh Child Guidance Foundation

Wobst, Frank: chairman, director, Huntington Bancshares Inc.

Wohlgenant, Richard G.: trustee, Johnson Foundation (Helen K. and Arthur E.)

Wohlstetter, John: vice president, director, Rose Foundation (Billy)

Wolcott, Arthur S.: chairman, director, Seneca Foods Corp.

Wolf, Barth J.: secretary, manager legal services, WPS Resources Corp.; secretary, assistant treasurer, WPS Resources Foundation, Inc.

Wolf, Harold: director, Peters Foundation (R. D. and Linda)

Wolf, Harold J.: treasurer, director, Brillion Foundation

Wolf, Linda: director, Burnett Co. Charitable Foundation (Leo)

Wolf, Robert B.: trustee, Patterson Charitable Fund (W. I.)

Wolfe, John F.: chairman, president, trustee, Wolfe Associates, Inc.

Wolfe, Kenneth L.: chairman, director, Hershey Foods Corp.

Wolfe, Laurence A.: vice president admin and real estate, secretary, Weingart Foundation

Wolfe, Merle D.: president, director, Thompson Charitable Foundation

Wolfe, Rita: vice president, trustee, Wolfe Associates, Inc.

Wolfe, Tim: director, Jostens Foundation Inc. (The)

Wolfert, Rick: president, chief operating officer, GE Capital Corp.

Wolff, Jesse David: director, Weil, Gotshal & Manges Foundation

Wolff, Paula: trustee, Johnson Foundation

Wolff, Rosalie S.: vice president, Solow Foundation

Wolfgang, Martha: vice president, treasurer, Macy, Jr. Foundation (Josiah)

Wolford, Donna P.: assistant secretary, Ford Family Foundation

Wolfson, Stephen S.: director, Andersen Foundation (Hugh J.)

Wolfzom, E. John: trustee, treasurer, Scripps Howard Foundation

Wollen, Carolyn S.: trustee, Bingham Second Betterment Fund (William)

Woller, Basil R.: senior vice president, general auditor, El Paso Corporate Foundation

Wollseiffen, Shelley: trustee, Cranston Foundation

Wolman, J. Martin: vice president, treasurer, Lee Endowment Foundation

Wolman, Paul C., III: director, Unger Foundation (Aber D.)

Woloshyn, Sonyia: treasurer, Turrell Fund

Wolter, Gary J.: president, Madison Gas & Electric Foundation; senior vice president administration, MGE Energy Inc.

Wolter, Robert: director, U.S. Bancorp Piper Jaffray Foundation

Wolters, Kate Pew: chairperson, Steelcase Foundation

Wolverton, David: president, Priddy Foundation

Womack, Chris: senior vice president, fossil & hydro power, Georgia Power Co.; director, Georgia Power Foundation

Womble, Astrid C.: president, director, Collis Foundation

Womble, Ralph H.: trustee, Hanes Foundation (John Wesley and Anna Hodgin)

Wondergem, Casey: contact, Van Andel Foundation (Jay and Betty)

Wong, Alton S.: director, Wong Foundation (Lin and Ella)

Wong, Reuben S. F.: president, treasurer, director, Wong Foundation (Lin and Ella)

Wong, Stanley S.: director, Wong Foundation (Lin and Ella)

Wong, Vera H.: vice president, secretary, director, Wong Foundation (Lin and Ella)

Wood, Anthony C.: executive director, secretary, Ittleson Foundation

Wood, C. William: president, PacifiCare Health System Foundation

Wood, Charles O., III: trustee, Wood Foundation of Chambersburg, PA

Wood, David S.: trustee, Wood Foundation of Chambersburg, PA

Wood, Edward Jenner, III: chairman, member, SunTrust Bank Atlanta

Wood, James F.: director, McMahon Foundation

Wood, Kate B.: director, Hyde and Watson Foundation

Wood, Miriam M.: trustee, Wood Foundation of Chambersburg, PA

Wood, Paul W.: vice president, director, Unilever United States Foundation

Wood, Robert A.: director, Green Foundation (Allen P. and Josephine B.)

Wood, Robert C.: trustee, Trexler Trust (Harry C.)

Wood, Robert Elkington, II: president, director, MDU Resources Foundation

Wood, Stephen R.: president, LG&E Energy Corp.

Wood, Sylvia Upton: secretary, trustee, Upton Foundation (Frederick S.)

Wood, Willis B., Jr.: trustee, Haynes Foundation (John Randolph and Dora)

Wood Knight, Elizabeth: director, Green Foundation (Allen P. and Josephine B.)

Woodard, Andrew: director, Woodard Foundation (W. A.)

Woodard, Carlton: president, Woodard Foundation (W. A.)

Woodard, Joy: director, Woodard Foundation (W. A.)

Woodard, Kim C.: director, Woodard Foundation (W. A.)

Woodard, Kristen A.: director, Woodard Foundation (W. A.)

Woodard, Tod Casey: vice president, Woodard Foundation (W. A.)

Woodbury, Susan B.: chairman, trustee, Alden Trust (George I.)

Wooden, Douglas: senior vice president, chief financial officer, Great-West Life and Annuity Insurance Co.

Woodling, Anne: trustee, Stocker Foundation

Woodling, Nancy Elizabeth: trustee, Stocker Foundation

Woodruff, Fred M., Jr.: trustee, Miller Foundation

Woods, Avery L.: director, Woods Charitable Fund

Woods, H. A. (Al): trustee, McKee Foundation (Robert E. and Evelyn)

Woods, Jerry Dean: treasurer, Grinnell Mutual Group Foundation; vice president financial, Grinnell Mutual Reinsurance Co.

Woods, Marjorie: director, Woods Charitable Fund

Woods, Robert F.: director, IBM International Foundation; vice president, controller, International Business Machines

Woods, Thomas C., III: president, treasurer, Woods Charitable Fund

Woodside, Blair C., Jr.: member, Hoover Foundation (Herbert W.)

Woodson, C. E., MD: director, Gulf Coast Medical Foundation

Woodward, Joanne Gignilliat: director, Newman's Own Foundation

Woodward, Sharon V.: president, treasurer, Baltimore Equitable Insurance Foundation

Woodward, Susan: vice president, trustee, Earhart Foundation

Woodworth, Robert C.: president, director, Pulitzer Foundation

Woollcott, James: director, Janirve Foundation

Wooster, Mark A.: assistant secretary, Universal Studios Foundation

Word, Jeanne Whittaker: trustee, Anderson Foundation (NY)

Worley, Kay I.: assistant secretary, Alabama Power Foundation

Worth, Carolyn A.: assistant vice president, Valley Foundation (Wayne and Gladys)

Wortham, R. W., III: president, Wortham Foundation

Worthington, Dave: chief financial officer, Rieke Corp.

Wortman, Judy B.: executive secretary, Kutz Foundation (Milton and Hattie)

Wraase, Dennis: president, chief executive officer, Pepco Holdings Inc.

Wren, Nancy G.: vice chairman, Portsmouth General Hospital Foundation

Wright, Arnold W., Jr.: vice president, executive director, CIGNA Foundation

Wright, Barbara: secretary, Packard Foundation (David and Lucile)

Wright, Charles E.: trustee, Arkell Hall Foundation

Wright, Donald Franklin: director, Times Mirror Foundation

Wright, G. James: trustee, Cacioppo Foundation (Joseph and Mary)

Wright, Gay: trust officer, trustee, Cray Residuary Charitable Trust (Evah C.)

Wright, Glen A.: director, Fleming and Jane Howe Patrick Foundation (Robert)

Wright, Hasbrouck S.: executive trustee, Kunkel Foundation (John Crain)

Wright, James: director, Fairchild Foundation, Inc. (Sherman)

Wright, James O.: president, director, Badger Meter Foundation; chairman, director, Badger Meter Inc.

Wright, James W.: treasurer, director, Park Bank Foundation

Wright, K. G.: secretary, Air Products Foundation

Wright, Lawrence A.: director, Atkinson Foundation

Wright, Linda: treasurer, Fireman's Fund Foundation

Wright, Martha C.: chairman, director, Cemala Foundation

Wright, Randell: director, De Queen Regional Medical Center

Wright, Randy L.: treasurer, Jones Foundation (Helen)

Wright, Richard L.: trustee, Fund for New Jersey

Wright, Soraya: trustee, Clorox Co. Foundation

Wright, Thomas H.: director, Lowenstein Foundation (Leon)

Wright, Vernon H.C.: executive vice chairman, chief financial officer, director, MBNA Corp.

Wright, Wilhelmina M.: director, Mardag Foundation

Wright, William Bigelow: director, Bunbury Co., Inc.

Wright, William L.: vice president, Hultquist Foundation

Wright, William R.: trustee emeritus, Davis Foundations (Arthur Vining)

Wright, William T., II: trustee, Kunkel Foundation (John Crain)

Wriston, Kathryn Dineen: president, trustee, Hartford Foundation, Inc. (The John A.)

Wroclawski, John: director, Scherman Foundation

Wulf, Gene C.: trustee, Bemis Co. Foundation

Wulf, Jerold W.: director, president, Andersen Foundation

Wurzburg, Warren Seymour, Sr.: chairman, president, director, Wurzburg Inc.

Wyatt, Jane C.: director, Trippe Trust (William D.)

Wyatt, Judy: secretary, trustee, Dayton Power and Light Co. Foundation

Wyckoff, Ann Pigott: president, Norcliffe Foundation

Wyckoff, Ed Lisk, Jr.: president, treasurer, trustee, Homeland Foundation (NY)

Wycliff, Don: director, Chicago Tribune Foundation

Wyeth, Phyllis Mills: trustee, duPont Foundation (Chichester)

Wylie, D. C., Jr.: trustee, Bell Foundation (S. Lewis and Lucia B.)

Wylie, Jean: regional grants director, Moody Foundation

Wyman, David E.: trustee, Wyman Youth Trust

Wyman, Hal H.: trustee, Wyman Youth Trust

Wynia, Ann: director, Bush Foundation

Wynkoop, Roger D.: president, ACF Industries

Wynne, Richard B.: director, Janirve Foundation

Wyrsch, Martha: trustee, Duke Energy Foundation

Wysong, Kathryn: vice president, director, O'Shaughnessy Foundation (I. A.)

Wyss, Judith: secretary, director, Wyss Foundation

Wyss, Loren L.: trustee, Templeton Foundation (Herbert A.)

Wyszomierski, Jack L.: trustee, member, Schering-Plough Foundation

Y

Yalich, Barbara L.: advisory committee member, Inasmuch Foundation

Yamada, Albert M.: director, First Hawaiian Foundation

Yamada, Tadataka, MD: trustee, Rockefeller Brothers Fund, Inc.

Yamasaki, Ken: director, Nakamichi Foundation (E.)

Yamate, Gordon: director, Knight Ridder Fund

Yamazaki, Yashiro: president, director, Nakamichi Foundation (E.)

Yamba, A. Zachary: trustee, Victoria Foundation

Yancey, Helen Lund: vice president, trustee, McKee Foundation (Robert E. and Evelyn)

Yanchura, Marc P.: treasurer, MacArthur Foundation (John D. and Catherine T.)

Yancy, Howard: president, director, ECG Foundation

Yang, Y. C.: chairman, Lin Foundation (T. Y.)

Yantek, Dawn: director, Washington Group Foundation, Inc.

Yantz, Jerome: treasurer, Kantzler Foundation

Yao, Lily K.: president, director, First Hawaiian Foundation; director, First Hawaiian Inc.

Yarnevich, George W.: vice president, Smoot Charitable Foundation

Yastine, Barbara: chief financial officer, Credit Suisse First Boston Corp.

Yasui, Lise: director, Penn Foundation (William)

Yasutake, Chiyoko: member allocations committee, Kawabe Memorial Fund

Yasutake, Webster T.: member allocations committee, Kawabe Memorial Fund

Yates, Edward D.: senior vice president, chief financial officer, Dentsply International Inc.

Yates, Mary-Alice: secretary, Guggenheim Foundation (Harry Frank)

Yates, Samuel E.: director, Kaul Foundation Trust (Hugh)

Yeager, Charles G.: trustee, Stranahan Foundation

Yeager, Jane Meseck: program manager, community affairs, Microsoft Corp.

Yeatman, C. Perry: director, Unilever United States Foundation

Yeckel, Carl L.: president, director, King Foundation (Carl B. and Florence E.)

Yedlin, Joseph: treasurer, director, Gudelsky Family Foundation (Homer and Martha)

Yee, Robert B.: treasurer, Lin Foundation (T. Y.)

Yehle, Eugene C.: trustee, Strosacker Foundation (Charles J.)

Yehling, Mary Kleine: executive director, Tyndale House Foundation

Yellott, Kinloch N., III: vice president, Wilson Sanitarium for Children of Baltimore City (Thomas)

Yeo, Lloyd J.: treasurer, trustee, Wickes Foundation (Harvey Randall); president, treasurer, Wickson-Link Memorial Foundation

Yhouse, Paul A.: president, chief executive officer, director, Holnam Inc.

Yih, Cathy: secretary, Yih Family Foundation

Yih, Irene C.P.: vice president, treasurer, Yih Family Foundation

Yih, Roy Paxon: president, Yih Family Foundation

Yih, Shou-Chen: chairman, Yih Family Foundation

Yingling, John Edward, Jr.: chief administrative and financial officer, Dodge Foundation (Geraldine R.)

Yocum, Robert G.: chairman, trustee, Harsco Corp. Fund

Yonkman, Mark: vice president, secretary, director, Comerica Charitable Foundation

Yontz, Merle R.: vice president, trustee, Mellinger Educational Foundation (Edward Arthur)

Yoo, Tae: trustee, Cisco Systems Foundation

York, Glen T.: president, Trippe Trust (William D.)

York, Mary J.: director, Grede Foundation

York, Michael H., Sr.: director, Trippe Trust (William D.)

Yost, Karen M.: director, Vogler Foundation (Laura B.)

Young, Chad: director, Masters Family Foundation

Young, Charles R.: first vice president, trustee, Cacioppo Foundation (Joseph and Mary)

Young, Charles R., II: treasurer, trustee, Cacioppo Foundation (Joseph and Mary)

Young, Dona D.: director, Phoenix Foundation

Young, Donald J.: director, Pappas Charitable Foundation (Thomas Anthony)

Young, Emily B.: trustee, Baldwin Memorial Foundation (Fred)

Young, George F., Jr.: trustee, Crawford Estate Trust Fund A (E. R.)

Young, Gerald T.: director, Bourns Foundation

Young, John R.: president, Gould Foundation (The Florence); president, director, Hughes Foundation (Geoffrey C.); director, Mathers Charitable Foundation (G. Harold and Leila Y.)

Young, Leslie D.: trustee, Glendorn Foundation

Young, Lindsay: director, Thompson Charitable Foundation

Young, Mary K.: director, Hughes Foundation (Geoffrey C.)

Young, Merrilynn: comptroller, Grable Foundation

Young, Michael-Anne: executive director, Cacioppo Foundation (Joseph and Mary)

Young, Richard B.: trustee, Acushnet Foundation

Young, Richard C.: trustee, McElroy Trust (R. J.)

Young, Robert C.: trustee, Van Wert County Foundation

Young, Robert Harris: president, chief executive officer, Central Vermont Public Service Corp.

Young, Toni P.: director, Kutz Foundation (Milton and Hattie)

Young, William: trustee, Acushnet Foundation

Youngberg, Francey Lim: director, Meyer Foundation (Eugene and Agnes E.)

Younger, Charles M., MD: trustee, Abell-Hanger Foundation

Younger, Laurie: vice president, ABC Broadcasting Foundation, Inc.

Younglove, Eileen M.: contributions manager, UAL Corp.

Youngman, Owen: director, Chicago Tribune Foundation

Youngren, James: trustee, Bullitt Foundation

Yovan, Gregory: assistant treasurer, Comerica Charitable Foundation

Yoxall, James R.: secretary, treasurer, trustee, Baughman Foundation

Yu, Jerry C.: program officer, Weingart Foundation

Yu, Pauline: director, Teagle Foundation

Yuen, Cheryl L.: consultant - cultural program, Sara Lee Foundation

Yun, William Y.: director, Commonwealth Fund (The)

Yuras, Susan Hawn: chairman, vice president, director, Sams Foundation (Earl C.)

Yutrzenka, Mike: executive director, Cisco Systems Foundation

Z

Zabel, William D.: trustee, Valentine Foundation (Lawson)

Zabotin, Mischa A.: vice president, director, Loewy Family Foundation

Zabrodsky, Kristy: director, Gebbie Foundation

Zaccaria, Adrian: director, Bechtel Foundation; vice chairman, president, director, Bechtel Group Inc.

Zachry, Henry Bartell, Jr.: chairman, chief executive officer, Zachry Co. (H.B.); trustee, Zachry Foundation (The)

Zachry, J. P.: president, trustee, Zachry Foundation (The)

Zachry, Mollie Steves: trustee, Zachry Foundation (The)

Zahr, Andrew A.: treasurer, Hartmarx Charitable Foundation

Zahumensky, Marsha: secretary, treasurer, Buhl Foundation (PA)

Zales, William E., Jr.: secretary, Alabama Power Foundation

Zambie, Allan John: vice president, secretary, Kulas Foundation

Zamora, Rosie: director, Houston Endowment

Zander, Edward J.: chairman, chief executive officer, Motorola Inc.

Zanino, Walter J.: controller, trustee, Norris Foundation (Kenneth T. and Eileen L.)

Zante, Mary Van: secretary, treasurer, Kuyper Foundation (Peter H. and E. Lucille Gaass)

Zanze, Anthony Olds: trustee, Irwin Charity Foundation (William G.)

Zanze, James F.: trustee, Irwin Charity Foundation (William G.)

Zapall, Marianne T.: secretary, St. Francis Bank Foundation

Zapisek, John R.: director, Utica National Foundation; senior vice president financial, chief financial officer, treasurer, director, Utica National Insurance Group

Zarrow, Henry H.: president, Zarrow Foundation (Anne and Henry)

Zarrow, Stuart A.: director, Zarrow Foundation (Anne and Henry)

Zatorski, Karen O.: vice president, treasurer, Viacom Foundation

Zeagler, M. F.: assistant executive director, Temple Foundation (T. L. L.)

Zech, Ronald H.: chairman, president, chief executive officer, chief operating officer, GATX Corp.

Zedaker, Michael R.: trustee, Van Wert County Foundation

Zeftel, Leo: director, Kutz Foundation (Milton and Hattie)

Zeglis, John D.: chairman and chief executive officer wireless group, AT&T Corp.; director, Sara Lee Corp.

Zeifang, Amy D.: chairman, director, Duffield Family Foundation

Zeifang, Kathleen H.: acting executive director, Cafritz Foundation (Morris and Gwendolyn)

Zeigon, James W.: executive vice president, Morgan Chase & Co. (J.P.)

Zeiter, Carol: secretary, Zeiter Charitable Foundation (Henry and Carol)

Zeiter, Henry J.: president, Zeiter Charitable Foundation (Henry and Carol)

Zellerbach, Charles R.: director, Zellerbach Family Fund

Zellerbach, John W.: vice president, treasurer, director, Zellerbach Family Fund

Zellerbach, Thomas H.: president, director, Zellerbach Family Fund

Zellerbach, William Joseph: chairman, director, Zellerbach Family Fund

Zellerbach-Boschwitz, Nancy: secretary, director, Zellerbach Family Fund

Zelus, Marsha: director, McMahan Foundation (Catherine L. and Robert O.)

Zemsky, Howard: president, Tyson Foods Inc.; trustee, Zemsky Family Trust

Zemsky, Sam: chairman, director, Tyson Foods Inc.; trustee, Zemsky Family Trust

Zemsky, Shirley: trustee, Zemsky Family Trust

Zenner, Patrick J.: president, chief executive officer, director, Hoffmann-La Roche Inc.

Zerhusen, David E.: senior vice president, director, El Paso Corporate Foundation

MASTER INDEX

Arranges in alphabetical order the foundations profiled in this directory and includes the page number on which the profile appears. Also listed are former names of funders. These citations also include the page number of the profile in which this information is located.

H

Master Index